Weights and Measures

Imperial, with Metric Equivalents

Linear Measure
1 inch (in)	= 25.4 millimetres
1 foot (ft) = 12 inches	= 0.3048 metre
1 yard (yd) = 3 feet	= 0.9144 metre
1 (statute) mile = 1,760 yards	= 1.609 kilometres

Square Measure
1 square inch (in^2 or sq in)	= 6.45 sq centimetres
1 square foot (ft^2) = 144 sq in	= 9.29 sq decimetres
1 square yard (yd^2) = 9 sq ft	= 0.836 sq metre
1 acre = 4,840 sq yd	= 0.405 hectare
1 square mile (mile^2) = 640 acres	= 259 hectares

Cubic Measure
1 cubic inch (in^3 or cu in)	= 16.4 cu centimetres
1 cubic foot (ft^3) = 1,728 cu in	= 0.0283 cu metre
1 cubic yard (yd^3) = 27 cu ft	= 0.765 cu metre

Capacity Measure
British
1 pint (pt) = 20 fluid oz	
= 34.68 cu in	= 0.568 litre
1 quart = 2 pints	= 1.136 litres
1 gallon (gal) = 4 quarts	= 4.546 litres
1 peck = 2 gallons	= 9.092 litres
1 bushel = 4 pecks	= 36.4 litres
1 quarter = 8 bushels	= 2.91 hectolitres

American dry
1 pint = 33.60 cu in	= 0.550 litre
1 quart = 2 pints	= 1.101 litres
1 peck = 8 quarts	= 8.81 litres
1 bushel = 4 pecks	= 35.3 litres

American liquid
1 pint = 16 fluid oz	
= 28.88 cu in	= 0.473 litre
1 quart = 2 pints	= 0.946 litre
1 gallon = 4 quarts	= 3.785 litres

Avoirdupois Weight
1 grain	= 0.065 gram
1 dram	= 1.772 grams
1 ounce (oz) = 16 drams	= 28.35 grams
1 pound (lb) = 16 ounces	
= 7,000 grains	= 0.4536 kilogram
1 stone (st) = 14 pounds	= 6.35 kilograms
1 quarter = 2 stones	= 12.70 kilograms
1 hundredweight (cwt) = 4 quarters	= 50.80 kilograms
1 (long) ton = 20 hundredweight	= 1.016 tonnes
1 short ton = 2,000 pounds	= 0.907 tonne

Metric, with Imperial (British) Equivalents

Linear Measure
1 millimetre (mm)	= 0.039 inch
1 centimetre (cm) = 10 mm	= 0.394 inch
1 decimetre (dm) = 10 cm	= 3.94 inches
1 metre (m) = 10 dm	= 1.094 yards
1 decametre (dam) = 10 m	= 10.94 yards
1 hectometre (hm) = 100 m	= 109.4 yards
1 kilometre (km) = 1,000 m	= 0.6214 mile

Square Measure
1 square centimetre (cm^2 or sq cm)	= 0.155 sq in
1 square metre (m^2)	= 1.196 sq yards
1 are = 100 sq metres	= 119.6 sq yards
1 hectare (ha) = 100 ares	= 2.471 acres
1 square kilometre (km^2)	= 0.386 sq mile

Cubic Measure
1 cubic centimetre (cm^3 or cu cm)	= 0.061 cu inch
1 cubic metre (m^3)	= 1.308 cu yards

Capacity Measure
1 millilitre (ml)	= 0.002 pint (British)
1 centilitre (cl) = 10 ml	= 0.018 pint
1 decilitre (dl) = 10 cl	= 0.176 pint
1 litre (l) = 10 dl	= 1.76 pints
1 decalitre (dal) = 10 l	= 2.20 gallons
1 hectolitre (hl) = 100 l	= 2.75 bushels
1 kilolitre (kl) = 1,000 l	= 3.44 quarters

Weight
1 milligram (mg)	= 0.015 grain
1 centigram (cg) = 10 mg	= 0.154 grain
1 decigram (dg) = 10 cg	= 1.543 grain
1 gram (g) = 10 dg	= 15.43 grain
1 decagram (dag) = 10 g	= 5.64 drams
1 hectogram (hg) = 100 g	= 3.527 ounces
1 kilogram (kg) = 1,000g	= 2.205 pounds
1 tonne (metric ton) = 1,000 kg	= 0.984 (long) ton

Temperature

Fahrenheit: water boils (under standard conditions) at 212° and freezes at 32°.

Celsius or Centigrade: water boils at 100° and freezes at 0°.

Kelvin: water boils at 373.15 and freezes at 273.15.

$$C° = \tfrac{5}{9}(°F - 32)$$
$$F° = (\tfrac{9}{5}°C) + 32$$
$$K = C° + 273.15$$

The New World Encyclopedia

The
New World Encyclopedia

COLOUR LIBRARY BOOKS

CLB 2304

This edition published 1988 by
Colour Library Books
Godalming Business Centre
Catteshall Lane
Godalming, Surrey GU7 1XW

ISBN 0 86283 677 8

First published by
Century Hutchinson Ltd
Brookmount House
62-65 Chandos Place
London WC2N 4NW

Phototypset in Autologic Times 7.5/9pt

Computer typesetting and make-up by Unwin Brothers Ltd,
Old Woking, Surrey

Printed and bound in United States of America
by R.R. Donnelley & Sons Co.

Introduction

The New World Encyclopedia is designed to serve as a single-volume companion to world events, history, arts, and sciences, for home, school, or library use. The aim throughout has been to provide up-to-date, readable entries, using clear and non-technical language. It is hoped that the Encyclopedia will also be useful in providing background details for particular subject areas such as current affairs and major historical events, as well as giving specific facts and dates.

Arrangement of entries

Entries are ordered alphabetically, as if there were no spaces between words. Thus, entries for words beginning "federal" follow the order:

> **Federal Bureau of Investigation**
> **Federalism**
> **Federal Reserve System**

However, we have avoided a purely mechanical alphabetization in cases where a different order corresponds more with human logic. For example, sovereigns with the same name are grouped according to country before number, so that King George II of England is placed before George III of England, and not next to King George II of Greece. Words beginning "Mc" and "Mac" are treated as if they begin "Mac"; and "St" and "Saint" are both treated as if they were spelt "Saint".

Foreign names and titles

Names of foreign sovereigns and places are usually shown in their English form, except where the foreign name is more familiar; thus, there are entries for **Charles V of Spain**, but **Juan Carlos** (not **John Charles**), and for **Florence,** not **Firenze.** Entries for titled people are under the name by which they are best known to the general reader: thus, **Anthony Eden,** not **Lord Avon.** Cross-references have been provided in cases where confusion is possible.

Cross-references

are shown by a ⚪ symbol immediately preceding the reference. Cross-referencing is selective; a cross-reference is shown when another entry contains material directly relevant to the subject matter of an entry, and where the reader may not otherwise think of looking. To assist the reader, we have avoided as far as possible entries which consist only of a cross-reference; even the shortest cross-reference gives some indication of the subject involved. Common alternative spellings, where there is no agreed consistent form, are also shown; thus there is a cross-reference to **Muhammad** at **Mohammed.**

Units

SI (metric) units are used throughout for scientific entries. Measurements of distances, temperatures, sizes, and so on, usually include an approximate imperial equivalent. Entries are also included for a wide variety of measurements no longer in common use.

Science and technology

An up-to-date encyclopedia has a dual function with regard to science and technology. Technical terms and current terminology must of course be included. However, many of these terms are not in common use. Entries are generally placed under the better-known name (thus, **acetylene** is placed under A and not under its technically correct name **ethyne**), but the technical term is also given. To aid comprehension, particularly for the non-specialist, technical terms are frequently explained when used within the text of an entry, even though they may have their own entry elsewhere.

Chinese names

Pinyin, the preferred system for transcribing Chinese names of people and places, is generally used: thus, there is an entry at **Mao Zedong,** not **Mao Tse-tung**; an exception is made for a few names which are more familiar in their former (Wade-Giles) form, such as **Peking,** rather than **Beijing.** Where confusion is likely, Wade-Giles forms are given as cross-references.

Pronunciations

Pronunciations are given for the names of people and places, using a transcription which conforms to the International Phonetic Alphabet (IPA). If the name is from a foreign language, the pronunciation given is the nearest English equivalent; this provides the English speaker with at least an intelligible pronunciation of the name. A key to the pronunciation symbols is shown on the back endpapers.

The headings at the beginning of each new letter are from a typeface designed in 1660 by Johann Neudörffer.

Contributors

Editors

Editor
Michael Upshall

Project Editor
Bonnie Falconer

Consultant Editors
John Ayto MA
Lionel Bender BSc, ChBiol, MIBiol
Steve Parker BSc

Pronunciation Editor
J C Wells MA, PhD

Text Editors
Jane Anson
Genevieve Clarke
Jane Crippen
Ingrid von Essen
Jane Farron
Ruth Graham-Pole
Edith Harkness
Susannah Hickling
Alison Kepple
Sharon Lucas
Mike March
Bodie Mauger
Barbara Morris
Jane Oxenford
Jo Russian
Carole Varley

Research
June Averill ALA

Editorial Assistant
Penny Hext

Picture Research
Gabrielle Allan
Barbara Bagnall

Typography
Gwyn Lewis

Illustrations
Taurus Graphics
Marlborough Design
Swanston Graphics
Rodney Paull
Ian Sandom

Contributors

David Armstrong MSc, PhD
John Ayto MA
Brendan P Bradley MA, MSc, PhD
Mark Bridge BA
Hans Brill MA
Suzanne Brill MA
Gertrude Buckman
John O E Clark BSc
Anne Cordwent BA, Cert Ed
David Cotton BA, PhD
Nigel Davis MSc
Alan J Day MA
Ian D Derbyshire MA, PhD
J Denis Derbyshire BSc, PhD, FBIM
Peter Dews PhD
Norman Thomas di Giovanni
Dougal Dixon BSc, MSc
Robin Dunbar BA, PhD
Graham Fawcett
Elizabeth Fenwick MA
Linda Gamlin BSc, MSc
Hildi Hawkins BSc
Tim Homfray ARCM
Jane Insley MSc
Roz Kaveney BA
Robin Kerrod FRAS

Chris Lawn BA
Miren Lopategui BA
Tom McArthur MA, MLitt, PhD
Karin L A Mogg BSc, MSc
Bob Moore BA, PhD
Ian Morrison
Gerald Norris
Maureen O'Connor
Elizabeth Porges Watson MA, BLitt
Ian Ridpath
Kate Salway BA, DFA
Marian Short
Tim Shreeve BSc, MSc, PhD, FRES
Martin Slattery BA, MSc
Angela Smith BA
Michael Sproule LLB
John Stidworthy MA
Graham Storrs BA, MBCS
Stephen Webster BSc, MPhil
Elizabeth L Whitelegg BSc

with special thanks to E M Horsley

A the first letter in nearly all the alphabets. The English *a* is derived from the Etruscan *a* through the Latin alphabet, which is the parent of the West-European alphabets. The Greeks called the first letter *alpha*; the Semites *aleph* or *alph*, which meant 'ox', but more probably because the word began with this letter – a simple mnemonic device – than because the letter was formed as the rough outline of an ox-head, as some scholars have claimed.

Aachen /ˈɑːxən/ German cathedral city and spa in the *Land* of North Rhine-Westphalia, 72 km/45 mi SW of Cologne. It has thriving electronics, glass, and rubber industries, and is one of Germany's principal railway junctions.
history Aachen was the Roman Aquisgranum, and from the time of Charlemagne until 1531 the German emperors were crowned there. Charlemagne was born and buried in Aachen, and founded the cathedral in 796. The 14th century town hall, containing the hall of the emperors, is built on the site of Charlemagne's palace. In World War II Aachen was the first major German town captured by the Allies (20 Oct 1944). Leading citizens established the annual *Charlemagne prize* (1949) for service to European cooperation. Population (1980) 250,000.

Aalborg /ˈɔːlbɔːg/ Danish port 32 km/20 mi inland from the Kattegat, on the south shore of the Limfjord. One of the oldest towns in Denmark, it has a castle and the fine Budolfi church. Population (1980) 154,400.

Aalst /ɑːlst/ Flemish name for the Belgian town of ◊Alost.

Aalto /ˈɑːltəu/ Alvar 1898–1976. Finnish architect and designer. One of Finland's first modernists, he evolved an architectural style entirely his own, characterized by asymmetry, curved walls, and contrast of natural materials, including the Hall of Residence, Massachusetts Institute of Technology, Cambridge, Massachusetts 1947–49; Village Hall at Säynätsalo 1951; Technical High School, Otaniemi 1962–65; Finlandia Hall, Helsinki 1972. He also invented a new form of laminated bent plywood furniture in 1932.

Aaltonen /ˈɑːltənen/ Wäinö 1894–1966. Finnish artist. At first a painter, he later turned to sculpture, and was a pioneer in the revival of carving directly from the stone, his favourite medium being granite. His works include portrait busts, notably one of Sibelius, and statues for the Finnish Parliament House and the University of Helsinki.

aardvark Afrikaans name, 'earth-pig', for the nocturnal mammal *Orycteropus afer* found in central and southern Africa. A timid defenceless animal about the size of a pig, it has a long head, pig-like snout, and large asinine ears. It feeds on termites which it licks up with its long sticky tongue.

aardwolf nocturnal mammal *Proteles cristatus* of the ◊hyena family. It is found in E and S Africa, usually in the burrows of the aardvark, and feeds on termites.

Aarhus /ˈɔːhuːs/ second city of Denmark, on the East coast overlooking the Kattegat; population (1981) 245,600. It is the capital of Aarhus county in Jutland, and a shipping and commercial centre with a university.

Aaron /ˈeərən/ in the Bible, the elder brother of Moses and leader with him of the Israelites in their march from Egypt to the Promised Land of Canaan.

Aasen /ˈɔːsən/ Ivar Andreas 1813–1896. Norwegian philologist, poet and playwright. Through a study of rural dialects he evolved by 1853 a native 'country language', which he called *Landsmaal*, to take the place of literary Dano-Norwegian.

abacus method of calculating with a handful of stones on 'a flat surface' (Latin *abacus*), familiar to the Greeks and Romans, and used by earlier peoples, possibly even in ancient Babylon; it still survives in the more sophisticated beadframe form of the Russian *schoty* and the Japanese *soroban*. In the West arithmetic with written Arabic figures, the so-called 'pen-reckoning', replaced 'counter-casting' for some 200 years, but has now been replaced by electronic calculators, themselves based on the principle of the abacus.

Abadan /ˌæbəˈdɑːn/ Iranian island on the east side of the Shatt-al-Arab. Abadan is the chief

Aarhus The 'Old Town' is an open-air museum of old buildings gathered together from all over Denmark, and re-erected in part of the botanical gardens. There are shops and workshops where crafts are continued, as in the watchmaker's house on the right.

refinery and shipping centre for Iran's oil industry, nationalized 1951. This measure was the beginning of the worldwide movement by oil-producing countries to assume control of profits from their own resources. It was besieged 1980–81 by Iraq in the Iran–Iraq War. Population (1976) 296,000.

Abakan /ˌæbəˈkæn/ coalmining city in South USSR; population (1981) 136,000.

abalone snail-like marine mollusc, genus *Haliotis* (also known from its shape as the ear shell), with a bluish mother-of-pearl used in ornamental work. Various species are eaten in America, China and Japan.

Abbado /əˈbɑːdəu/ Claudio 1933– . Italian conductor, long associated with ◊La Scala, Milan. Principal conductor of London Symphony Orchestra from 1979, he also worked with the European Community Youth Orchestra from 1977.

abacus The ancient counting method of the abacus shares many mathematical principles with today's electronic calculator. Still widely used in the eastern world, the abacus is used here at work in Red China's Logan commune.

Abbas I Called the Great, Abbas I was Shah of Persia from 1588–1629. He fought a long war against the Ottoman Turks, regaining lost territory, including Baghdad. He introduced reforms, and encouraged European trade and the flowering of Persian arts. This is an engraving from Herbett's *Travels* 1638.

Abbasids /'æbəsɪdz/ dynasty of the Islamic empire who reigned as caliphs in Baghdad 750–1258. They were descended from Abbas, Mohammed's uncle, and some of them, such as Harun-al-Rashid (786–809) and Mamun (813–33), were outstanding patrons of cultural development. Later their power dwindled, and in 1258 Baghdad was burnt by the Tartars. From then until 1517 they retained limited power as caliphs of Egypt.

Abbas I /'æbəs/ the Great c. 1557–1629. Shah of Persia from 1588, he defeated the Uzbegs near Herat in 1597 and also the Turks. Bandar-Abbas is named after him. At his death his empire reached from the Tigris to the Indus.

Abbas II /'æbəs/ Hilmi 1874–1944. Last khedive of Egypt, 1892–1914. On the outbreak of war between Britain and Turkey in 1914, he sided with Turkey and was deposed following the establishment of a British protectorate over Egypt.

Abbeville /'æbvɪl/ town in N France in the Somme *département*, 19 km/12 mi inland from the mouth of the Somme. During World War I it was an important base for the British armies. Population (1982) 26,000.

abbey in the Christian church, a monastery (of monks) or a nunnery or convent (of nuns), all vowed to a life of celibacy and religious seclusion, governed by an abbot or abbess respectively. Sometimes the word is applied to a religious edifice which was once the church of an abbey, for example Westminster Abbey, or to a building or society that has long since been secularized, for example Battle Abbey. The first abbeys as established in Syria or Egypt were mere collections of huts, but in course of time massive and extensive buildings were constructed. St Benedict's Abbey at Monte Cassino in Italy – so strongly built that for weeks in 1944 it defied blasting by bomb and shell – set the pattern, and soon every country of Christendom could boast a number of noble abbeys. England, especially the north, is rich in abbey ruins.

Abbey Theatre playhouse in Dublin associated with the Irish literary revival of the early 1900s that owed its origin to the cooperation of the theatre manager and patron, Miss Horniman, the writers George ◊Russell (AE) and W B◊Yeats, with the actors W G and Frank Fay. The theatre was opened in 1904, and provided a stage for the works of a number of brilliant dramatists, including Lady Gregory, Yeats, J M ◊Synge, Lennox Robinson, Padraic Colum, Conal O'Riordan, St John Ervine, Seumas O'Kelly, and Sean O'Casey. Burned out in 1951, the Abbey Theatre was rebuilt 1966.

Abbotsford /'æbətsfəd/ home of Sir Walter ◊Scott from 1811, on the right bank of the Tweed, Borders region. Originally a farmhouse, it was rebuilt 1817–25 as a Gothic baronial hall, and is still in the possession of his descendants.

Abd el-Kader /'æbd el 'kɑːdə/ c. 1807–1883. Algerian nationalist. Emir of Mascara from 1832, he led a tribal struggle against the French until his surrender in 1847.

Abd el-Krim /'æbd el 'krɪm/ el-Khettabi 1881–1963. Moroccan Arab chief known as the 'Wolf of the Rif'. With his brother Mohammed, he led the Rif revolt, inflicting disastrous defeat on the Spanish at Anual in 1921, but surrendering to a large French army under Pétain in 1926. Banished to the island of Réunion, he was released in 1947 and died in voluntary exile in Cairo.

abdication renunciation of an office or dignity, usually the throne, by a ruler or sovereign.

abdomen the part of the vertebrate body containing the digestive organs; the hind part of the body in insects and other arthropods. In mammals, the abdomen is separated from the chest (◊thorax) by the diaphragm, a sheet of muscular tissue. In arthropods it is commonly separated from the thorax by a narrow constriction, and in insects and spiders is characterized by the absence of limbs.

Abdul-Hamid II /'æbdul 'hæmɪd/ 1842–1918. Last sultan of Turkey 1876–1909. In 1908 the Young Turks under Enver Bey forced Abdul Hamid to restore the constitution of 1876, and in 1909 insisted on his deposition. He died in confinement. For his part in the brutal suppression of the ◊Armenian revolt of 1894–96 he was known as the Great Assassin and still motivates Armenian terrorism against the Turks.

Abdullah /æb'dʌlə/ ibn Hussein 1882–1951. Arab leader who worked with T E ◊Lawrence in the Arab revolt of World War I; he became king of independent ◊Transjordan 1946; and following the incorporation of Arab Palestine (after 1948–49 Arab-Israeli War), he renamed the country the Hashemite Kingdom of Jordan. He was assassinated by an Arab fanatic.

Abdullah /æb'dʌlə/ Sheikh Mohammed 1905– . Kashmiri leader, known as the 'Lion of Kashmir'. He headed the struggle for constitutional government against the Maharajah of Kashmir, and in 1947 became prime minister. He agreed to the accession of the state to India to halt tribal infiltration, but was imprisoned from 1953 (with brief intervals) until 1968, when he reaffirmed the right of the people of Kashmir 'to decide the future of the State'. He became prime minister 1975, accepting the sovereignty of India.

Abdul Mejid I /'æbdul 'medʒɪd/ 1823–1861. Sultan of Turkey from 1839 until his death. During his reign the ◊Ottoman Empire was increasingly weakened by internal nationalist movements and the incursions of the other great powers.

Abdul Rahman /'æbdul 'rɑːmən/ Tunku 'Prince' 1903– . Malaysian negotiator of the formation of the Federation of Malaysia 1961–62; he was its first prime minister 1963–70.

Abel /'eɪbəl/ in the Old Testament, second son of ◊Adam and ◊Eve; as a shepherd, he made burnt offerings of meat to God which were more acceptable than the fruits offered by his brother Cain; he was killed by the jealous Cain.

Abel /'eɪbəl/ Frederick Augustus 1827–1902. British scientist and inventor, who developed new explosives. As a chemist to the War Department, he introduced a new method of making gun-cotton and was joint inventor with ◊Dewar of cordite. He also invented the Abel close-test instrument for determining the ◊flash point of petroleum.

Abelard /'æbəlɑːd/ Peter 1079–1142. French scholastic philosopher. Born near Nantes, he became canon of Notre Dame in Paris, and master of the cathedral school in 1115. When his seduction of, and secret marriage to, his pupil Héloïse became known, she entered a convent and he was castrated at the instigation of her uncle, Canon Fulbert, and became a monk. Resuming teaching a year later, he was cited for heresy and became a hermit at Nogent, where he built the oratory of the Paraclete, and later abbot of a monastery in Brittany. His autobiographical *Historia Calamitatum* drew from Héloïse the famous love letters. He died at Châlon-sur-Saône, on his way to defend himself against a new charge of heresy. Héloïse was buried beside him at the Paraclete in 1164, their remains being taken to Père Lachaise, Paris, in 1817. Abelard has a great place in medieval thought as a 'conceptualist', for whom 'universals' have only a mental existence. See also ◊logic and ◊scholasticism.

Abeokuta /ˌæbiəʊˈkuːtə/ agricultural trade centre in Nigeria, West Africa, on the Ogun river, 103 km/64 mi N of Lagos; population (1975) 253,000.

Aberbrothock /ˌæbəˈbrɒθək/ another name for ◊Arbroath.

Abercrombie /ˈæbəkrʌmbi/ Leslie Patrick 1879–1957. Pioneer of British town planning. He is best known for his work of replanning British cities after damage in World War II (such as the Greater London Plan, 1944) and for the ◊New Towns policy. See also ◊garden city.

Abercromby /ˈæbəkrʌmbi/ Ralph 1734–1801. Scots soldier who in 1801 commanded an expedition to the Mediterranean, charged with the liquidation of the French forces left behind by Napoleon in Egypt. He decisively defeated the French at Aboukir Bay, but was mortally wounded in the action.

Aberdare /ˌæbəˈdeə/ town in Mid Glamorgan, Wales, formerly producing high-grade coal, and now with electrical and light engineering industries; population (1981) 36,621.

Aberdeen /ˌæbəˈdiːn/ city, seaport, and holiday resort on the E coast of Scotland, administrative headquarters of Grampian region; population (1986) 214,082. It is Scotland's third largest city, and is rich in historical interest and fine buildings, including the Municipal Buildings (1867); King's College (1494) and Marischal College (founded 1593; housed in one of the largest granite buildings in the world, 1836) which together form Aberdeen University; St Machar Cathedral (1378), and the Auld Brig o'Balgownie (1320). Industries include the manufacture of agricultural machinery, paper and textiles; fishing, ship-building, granite-quarrying, and engineering. However, oil discoveries in the North Sea in the 1960s–70s transformed Aberdeen to the European 'offshore capital', with an airport and heliport linking the mainland to the rigs, and new sources of employment in the shore-based maintenance and service depots.

Aberdeen /ˌæbəˈdiːn/ George Hamilton Gordon, 4th Earl of Aberdeen 1784–1860. British statesman. Born in Edinburgh, he succeeded his grandfather as earl in 1801, and was a prominent diplomat. In 1828, and again in 1841, he was Foreign Secretary under Wellington. Although a Tory, he supported Catholic emancipation and followed Peel in his conversion to Free Trade. In 1852 he became prime minister in a government of Peelites and Whigs (Liberals), but resigned in 1855 because of the hostile criticism aroused by the miseries and mismanagement of the Crimean War.

Aberdeen George Hamilton Gordon, 4th Earl of Aberdeen, painted by John Partridge c. 1847. Although the coalition ministry over which he presided as prime minister from 1852 was extremely popular for a time, within three years he was forced to resign over his poor handling of the Crimean War.

Aberdeenshire /ˌæbəˈdiːnʃə/ former county in E Scotland, merged in 1975 in Grampian region.

Aberfan /ˌæbəˈvæn/ mining village in Mid Glamorgan, Wales. Coal waste overwhelmed a school and houses in 1966; of 144 dead, 116 were children.

aberration of starlight the apparent displacement of a star from its true position, due to the combined effects of the speed of light and the speed of the Earth in orbit around the ◊Sun (about 30 km/18.5 mi per sec). Aberration was discovered in 1728 by James ◊Bradley, and was the first observational proof that the Earth orbits the Sun.

aberration of starlight

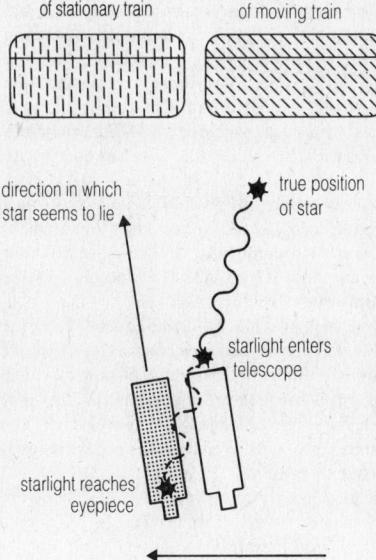

rain falling past window of stationary train

rain falling past window of moving train

direction in which star seems to lie

true position of star

starlight enters telescope

starlight reaches eyepiece

movement of earth

aberration, optical any of a number of defects that impair the image in an optical instrument. In *chromatic aberration* the image is surrounded by coloured fringes, because light of

different colours is brought to different focal points by a ◊lens. In *spherical aberration* the image is blurred because different parts of the lens or mirror have different focal lengths. In *astigmatism* the image appears elliptical or cross-shaped. In *coma*, the images appear progressively elongated towards the edge of the field of view. Optical aberration occurs because of minute variations in the glass and because different parts of the light ◊spectrum are reflected or refracted by varying amounts.

aberration, optical

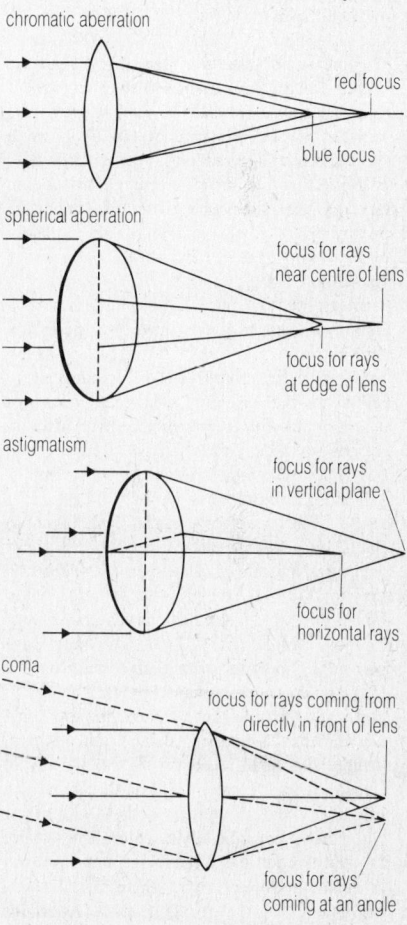

chromatic aberration

red focus

blue focus

spherical aberration

focus for rays near centre of lens

focus for rays at edge of lens

astigmatism

focus for rays in vertical plane

focus for horizontal rays

coma

focus for rays coming from directly in front of lens

focus for rays coming at an angle

Aberystwyth /ˌæbəˈrɪstwɪθ/ town in Wales; population (1981) 8,666. It is the unofficial capital of the Welsh-speaking area of Wales; the University College of Wales 1872, Welsh Plant Breeding Station, and National Library of Wales are here.

Abidja'n /ˌæbiːˈdʒɑːn/ capital of the Republic of Ivory Coast, W Africa; population (1982) 1,850,000. It is an important port with a trade in coffee, palm oil, cocoa and timber (mahogany); is linked by rail with Ougadougou, and has an airport. There is a university.

Abilene /ˈæbɪliːn/ town in Kansas, USA, on the Smoky Hill river; population (1980) 98,315. A western railway terminus, Abilene was a shipping point for cattle in the 1860s. President

Eisenhower lived here as a boy and is buried here, and there is an Eisenhower Memorial Museum.

Abingdon /'æbɪŋdən/ town in Oxfordshire, England, on the Thames 10 km/6 mi S of Oxford; population (1981) 22,686. The remains of the 7th century abbey include Checker Hall, restored as an Elizabethan-type theatre. The 15th century bridge was reconstructed in 1929. There are light industries.

Abomey /ə'bəumi/ town and port of ◊Benin, W Africa; population (1982) 54,418. It was once the capital of the kingdom of Dahomey, which flourished in the 17th–19th centuries, and had a mud-built defence-wall 10 km/6 mi in circumference.

abominable snowman legendary creature, said to resemble a human, with long arms and a thick-set body covered with reddish-grey hair. Reports of the existence of the abominable snowman in the Himalayas, where it is locally known as the 'yeti', have been current since 1832, but gained substance from a published photograph of a huge footprint in the snow taken by Eric Shipton of the Everest Reconnaissance Expedition in 1951.

aborigine any one of the inhabitants of a country who are believed to have been there from time immemorial (Latin *ab origine*, from the beginning). The word now more particularly refers to the original peoples of countries colonized by Europeans, especially Australia. *Australian Aborigines* arrived from Asia 13–38,000 years ago and developed a complex and enduring culture as a hunting and gathering people. They numbered about 300,000 when British settlers first arrived in 1788: the largest concentration is now in Queensland (34,000) and they total (1984) 160,000, with some 20,000 of mixed ancestry. They have a rich tradition of legends, songs, rituals, and bark and cave paintings concerned with their 'dreamtime', a long-ago era when humans were first on Earth, and when the tribal totem ancestors (the spirit eaglehawk, kangaroo, snake, and others) wandered abroad. About 40% live tribally in remote desert areas, but are threatened by mineral discoveries on their lands, to which their rights have been officially disputed. The rest live in squalid conditions as casual labour on the town fringes. In recent years there has been a movement for the recognition of Aborigine rights; there is still unofficial segregation in housing, education, and wages, and medical facilities are inadequate in both the slums and the outback.

abortion medically, expulsion of the foetus from the womb before it is capable of independent life. It is controversial as a means of birth control (methods include the use of drugs and vacuum aspiration), but was legalized within certain guidelines in the UK in 1967 if carried out during the first 28 weeks of pregnancy. When it happens naturally (spontaneous abortion) it is normally called a miscarriage. If induced intentionally it is often called a termination of pregnancy.

Aboukir Bay /,æbuː'kɪə/ **Battle of** also known as the Battle of the Nile: Nelson defeated Napoleon's fleet at the Egyptian seaport of Aboukir on 1 Aug 1798.

Abraham /'eɪbrəhæm/ c. 2300 BC. Founder of the Jewish nation. Born at Ur, Abram (as he was then called) was the son of Terah, and migrated to Haran, North Mesopotamia, with his father, his wife Sarah, and his nephew Lot. Proceeding to Canaan, he received Jehovah's promise of the land to his descendants, and after sojourning in Egypt during a famine, separated from Lot at Bethel before settling in Hebron. On renaming him Abraham 'father of many nations', Jehovah promised him a legitimate heir, and then tested him by a command to slay the boy Isaac in sacrifice. By his second wife, Keturah, Abraham had six sons. He was buried in Machpelah cave, Hebron.

Abraham, Plains/Heights of /'eɪbrəhæm/ plateau near Quebec, Canada, where ◊Wolfe defeated the French, under ◊Montcalm, 13 Sept 1759.

Abraham /'eɪbrəhæm/ Edward Penly 1913– . British biochemist, who isolated the antibiotic cephalosporin, capable of destroying penicillin-resistant bacteria.

abrasive substance used for cutting and polishing or for removing small amounts of the surface of hard materials. They are divided into *natural* abrasives, quartz, sandstone, pumice, diamond, corundum, and emery among them; and *artificial*, such as bath brick, rouge, whiting, and Carborundum. They are usually referred to ◊Mohs scale of hardness.

Abruzzi /ə'brutsi/ mountainous area of S central Italy; Gran Sasso d'Italia 2,914 m/9,560 ft, is the highest point of the ◊Apennines.

Absalom /'æbsələm/ in the Old Testament, favourite son of King David; when defeated in a revolt against his father, he fled on a mule, but was caught up by his hair in a tree branch, and killed by Joab, one of David's officers.

abscissa in ◊coordinate geometry the horizontal or *x* coordinate, that is, the distance of a point from the vertical or *y*-axis. For example, a point with the coordinates (3,4) has an abscissa of 3.

abscission in botany, the controlled separation of part of a plant from the main plant body – most commonly, the falling of leaves or the dropping of fruit. Abscission occurs after the formation of an abscission zone at the point of separation. Within this a thin layer of cells, the abscission layer, becomes weakened and breaks down through the conversion of pectic acid to pectin. Consequently the leaf, fruit or other part can easily be dislodged by wind or rain. The process is thought to be controlled by the amount of ◊auxin present.

In ◊deciduous plants the leaves are shed before the winter or dry season, whereas ◊evergreen plants drop their leaves continually throughout the year. Fruit-drop, the abscission of fruit while still immature, is a naturally ocurring process. It is particularly common in fruit trees such as apple, and orchards are often sprayed with artificial auxin to prevent excessive fruit-drop.

absinth drink containing 60–80% alcohol, which was originally flavoured with oil of wormwood; the latter attacks the nervous system, and is widely banned, so that substitutes are used,

absolute zero the lowest temperature that could possibly exist, equivalent to – 273.16°C at which molecules would have no energy. Near this temperature the physical properties of materials change substantially, for example some metals will lose their electrical resistance (superconductivity).

absolutism a system of government in which the ruler or rulers have unlimited power. The principle of an absolute monarch, given a divine right to rule by God, was extensively used in Europe during the 17th and 18th centuries.

absorption term with several meanings in science. It most commonly describes the taking up of one substance by another, such as liquid into a solid (like ink into blotting-paper) or a gas into a liquid (like ammonia into water). With pure single substances, the result of such absorption is a uniform solution. In optics, absorption is the phenomenon by which a substance retains radiation of particular wavelengths; for example, a piece of blue glass absorbs all visible light except the wavelengths in the blue part of the spectrum. In nuclear physics, the capture by elements such as boron of neutrons produced by fission in a reactor is also called absorption.

abstract art non-representational art; that is, art which does not depict the real world. Abstract art is found in many cultures, but the concept was triggered into a movement in the West at the turn of the 20th century, partly because the invention of photography had made it unnecessary to use painting as a method of depicting reality. The pioneer 20th-century work was a ◊Kandinsky watercolour of 1910. Abstract works of art may be classified as *semi-abstract* – that is, those works which are based on nature, though they bear little resemblance to natural forms; and *pure abstract* – that is, those works which have no relation to nature, but consist of shapes and colours of the artist's own invention. Semi-abstract art includes ◊Cubism, ◊Futurism, ◊Vorticism, and the work of certain artists, such as Henry ◊Moore and ◊Archipenko, who have evolved their own individualistic styles. Pure abstract art includes ◊Constructivism, ◊Suprematism, and ◊Neo-Plasticism. Other movements include ◊Expressionism, and ◊Surrealism, although in the latter, subject-matter is more important than expression.

abstract expressionism term used in 20th century (especially American) painting to describe non-figurative canvases painted with large brushstrokes and many colours, often forming an intricate pattern. Generally the method of creation is seen as as important as the final work itself. It is similar to ◊action painting; exponents include Jackson ◊Pollock and Mark ◊Rothko.

Absurd, Theatre of the term applied to the works of a group of playwrights in the 1950s, including ◊Beckett, ◊Ionesco, ◊Genet, and ◊Pinter. They expressed through drama the belief that in a godless universe human existence has no meaning or purpose and therefore all communication breaks down. This concern was shown in the form as well as the content of their plays, so that logical construction and argument gives way to irrational and illogical speech and to its ultimate conclusion, silence, as in Beckett's play *Breath* 1970.

Abu Bakr /ˌæbuːˈbekə/ or Abu-Bekr name meaning 'father of the virgin', used by Abd-el-Ka'aba (573–634), from about 618 when ◊Muhammad married his daughter Ayesha (c. 618). On Muhammad's death, he became the first ◊caliph and proved a vigorous ruler, adding Mesopotamia to the Muslim world.

Abu Dhabi /ˌæbuːˈdɑːbi/ sheikhdom in SW Asia, on the Arabian Gulf, one of the ◊United Arab Emirates. Formerly under British protection, it has been ruled since 1971 by Sheikh Zayed Bin Al-Nahayan, who is also president of the Supreme Council of Rulers of the United Arab Emirates.

Abu Dhabi Sheikh Zayed leaves his royal palace followed by his bodyguard. Sheikh Zayed is president of the Supreme Council of the seven rulers of the federation of United Arab Emirates, of which Abu Dhabi is the capital.

Abuja /əˈbuːdʒə/ newly built city in Nigeria which is planned to replace Lagos as capital. Shaped like a crescent, it was designed by Kenzo ◊Tange.

Abú Nuwás /ˈæbuː ˈnuːwɑːs/ Hasan ibn Háni 762–c. 815. Arab poet. His work was based on old forms, but the new freedom with which he used them, his eroticism, and his ironic humour, have contributed to his reputation as perhaps the greatest of Arab poets.

Abu Simbel site of ancient temple in Egypt, built during the reign of ◊Rameses II.

Abydos /əˈbaɪdɒs/ ancient city in Upper Egypt; the Great Temple of ◊Seti I dates from about 1300 BC.

abyssal zone dark ocean area 2–6,000 m/6,500–19,500 ft deep; temperature 4°C/39°F. Some fish and crustaceans living there may be blind, or have their own light sources.

Abyssinia /ˌæbɪˈsɪniə/ former name of ◊Ethiopia.

acacia one of a large group of shrubs and trees, genus *Acacia*, belonging to the pea family, found in warm regions of the Old World and, especially, Australia. Most have leaves subdivided into many leaflets. Acacias include: the 'thorn trees' of the African savannah, the *gum arabic tree Acacia senegal* of N Africa, used in manufacturing jellies and sweets (90 per cent of world supplies come from Sudan); a number of wattle species with fluffy golden flowers, adapted to warm, dry regions, such as Australia where the wattle is the national floral emblem. The Australian *silver wattle Acacia dealbata* is the 'mimosa' of florists.

Academy school of philosophy founded by ◊Plato in the gardens of Academe, north west of Athens; it was closed by the Byzantine Emperor ◊Justinian, with the other pagan schools, in 529. First of the academies, in the modern sense of a recognized society established for the promotion of one or more of the arts and sciences, was the Museum of Alexandria, founded by Ptolemy Soter in the 3rd century BC.

Academy Award annual cinema award given from 1927 onwards by the American Academy of Motion Pictures, nicknamed 'Oscar' (1931), allegedly because a new secretary exclaimed (of the bronze statuette presented to winners) 'That's like my uncle Oscar!'

Academy, French or *Académie Française*. Literary society founded by ◊Richelieu in 1635; it is especially concerned with maintaining the purity of the French language; membership is limited to 40 'immortals' at a time.

Academy of Sciences, Soviet society founded in 1725 by Catherine the Great in Leningrad; it has been responsible for such achievements as ◊Sputnik, and has branches in the Ukraine (welding, cybernetics), Armenia (astrophysics), and Georgia (mechanical engineering).

Acadia /əˈkeɪdiə/ or Acadie. Name given to ◊Nova Scotia by French settlers in 1604, from which the term ◊Cajun derives.

acanthus herbaceous plant with handsome leaves. Some 20 species are found in the Mediterranean region and the Old World tropics, including *bear's breech Acanthus mollis*, whose leaves were used as a motif in classical architecture.

Acapulco /ˌækəˈpʊlkəʊ/ port and holiday resort in Mexico; population (1985) 638,000.

Accad /ˈækæd/ alternative form of ◊Akkad, ancient city of Mesopotamia.

accelerated freeze drying see ◊AFD.

acceleration the rate of increase in the velocity of a moving body, expressed in metres per second squared/feet per second squared. The acceleration due to gravity is the acceleration shown by a body falling freely under the influence of gravity, either in a vacuum or after allowing for the retardation due to air resistance; it varies slightly at different latitudes and altitudes. Retardation (deceleration) is actually negative acceleration, for example, a rising rocket as it slows down is being negatively accelerated towards the centre of the Earth.

accelerator device to bring charged particles (such as protons) up to high kinetic ◊energies, at which they have uses in industry, medicine and in pure physics: when high energy particles collide with other particles the products formed give insights into the fundamental forces of nature. To give particles the energies needed requires many successive applications of a high voltage to electrodes placed in the path of the particles. To save space the particles can be confined to a circular track using a magnetic field. The first *accelerator* to work on this principle was the *cyclotron* built in the early 1930s. Whereas the first cyclotrons were some 30 cm/12 in in diameter, the Super Proton Synchrotron at ◊CERN near Geneva, which came into operation in 1976, has an unravelled length of some 2.2 km/1.4 mi; the Large Electron Proton Machine due to start up in 1987 will have a total length of 30 km/18.6 mi.

accelerometer apparatus for measuring ◊acceleration or deceleration – that is, the rate of increase or decrease in the ◊velocity of a moving object. Accelerometers are used to measure the efficiency of the braking systems on road and rail vehicles; those employed in aircraft and spacecraft can determine accelerations in several directions simultaneously.

accent a way of speaking that identifies a person with a particular country ('a New Zealand accent'), region ('a Northern Irish accent'), language ('a French accent'), social class ('an upper-class accent'), linguistic style ('a Country and Western accent'), or some mixture of these ('a French-Canadian accent'; 'a working-class Glasgow accent'; 'a middle-class South-East of England accent'). People often describe only those who belong to groups other than their own as having accents ('She spoke with a funny accent'; 'He had a harsh foreign accent'), and may give them special names; for example, an Irish brogue, a Northumbrian burr.

accessory in law, an *accessory before the fact* is one who instigates another person to commit a crime which that person then commits. If he or she is present when the crime is committed, he is not an accessory but an *abettor*. An *accessory after the fact* is one who assists a person whom he knows to have committed a crime. In English law these distinctions are no longer made, for by the Criminal Law Act 1967 a person who aids, abets, counsels or procures the commission of an offence is punishable as if he or she committed the crime.

access time in computing, the 'reaction time': the time taken after being given an instruction before the computer reads from, or writes to, ◊memory.

acclimation (*acclimatization*) the physiological changes induced in an organism by exposure to new environmental conditions. When humans move to higher altitudes, for example, the number of red blood cells rises to increase the oxygen-carrying capacity of the blood, in order to compensate for the lower levels of oxygen in the air.

accolade symbolic blow on the shoulders with the flat of the sword, given by the sovereign, or a representative, in conferring a knighthood.

ACADEMY AWARD WINNERS (OSCARS)

Year

1970 Best Picture: Patton
Best Director: Franklin J Schaffer *Patton*
Best Actor: George C Scott *Patton*
Best Actress: Glenda Jackson *Women in Love*

1971 Best Picture: *The French Connection*
Best Director: William Friedkin *The French Connection*
Best Actor: Gene Hackman *The French Connection*
Best Actress: Jane Fonda *Klute*

1972 Best Picture: *The Godfather*
Best Director: Bob Fosse *Cabaret*
Best Actor: Marlon Brando *The Godfather*
Best Actress: Liza Minnelli *Cabaret*

1973 Best Picture: *The Sting*
Best Director: George Roy Hill *The Sting*
Best Actor: Jack Lemmon *Save the Tiger*
Best Actress: Glenda Jackson *A Touch of Class*

1974 Best Picture: *The Godfather II*
Best Director: Francis Ford Coppola *The Godather II*
Best Actor: Art Carney *Harry and Tonto*
Best Actress: Ellen Burstyn *Alice Doesn't Live Here Anymore*

1975 Best Picture: *One Flew Over the Cuckoo's Nest*
Best Director: Milos Forman *One Flew Over the Cuckoo's Nest*
Best Actor: Jack Nicholson *One Flew Over the Cuckoo's Nest*
Best Actress: Louise Fletcher *One Flew Over the Cuckoo's Nest*

1976 Best Picture: *Rocky*
Best Director: John G Avildsen *Rocky*
Best Actor: Peter Finch *Network*
Best Actress: Faye Dunaway *Network*

1977 Best Picture: *Annie Hall*
Best Director: Woody Allen *Annie Hall*
Best Actor: Richard Dreyfuss *The Goodbye Girl*
Best Actress: Diane Keaton *Annie Hall*

1978 Best Picture: *The Deer Hunter*
Best Director: Michael Cimino *The Deer Hunter*
Best Actor: Jon Voight *Coming Home*
Best Actress: Jane Fonda *Coming Home*

Year

1979 Best Picture: *Kramer vs Kramer*
Best Director: Robert Beaton *Kramer vs Kramer*
Best Actor: Dustin Hoffman *Kramer vs Kramer*
Best Actress: Sally Field *Norma Rae*

1980 Best Picture: *Ordinary People*
Best Director: Robert Redford *Ordinary People*
Best Actor: Robert de Niro *Raging Bull*
Best Actress: Sissy Spacek *Coalminer's Daughter*

1981 Best Picture: *Chariots of Fire*
Best Director: Warren Beaty *Reds*
Best Actor: Henry Fonda *On Golden Pond*
Best Actress: Katharine Hepburn *On Golden Pond*

1982 Best Picture: *Gandhi*
Best Director: Richard Attenborough *Gandhi*
Best Actor: Ben Kingsley *Gandhi*
Best Actress: Meryl Streep *Sophie's Choice*

1983 Best Picture: *Terms of Endearment*
Best Director: James L Brooks *Terms of Endearment*
Best Actor: Robert Duvall *Tender Mercies*
Best Actress: Shirley MacLaine *Terms of Endearment*

1984 Best Picture: *Amadeus*
Best Director: Milos Forman *Amadeus*
Best Actor: F Murray Abraham *Amadeus*
Best Actress: Sally Field *Places in the Heart*

1985 Best Picture: *Out of Africa*
Best Director: Sidney Pollack *Out of Africa*
Best Actor: William Hurt *Kiss of the Spider Woman*
Best Actress: Geraldine Page *The Trip to Bountiful*

1986 Best Picture: *Platoon*
Best Director: Oliver Stone *Platoon*
Best Actor: Paul Newman *The Color of Money*
Best Actress: Marlee Matlin *Children of a Lesser God*

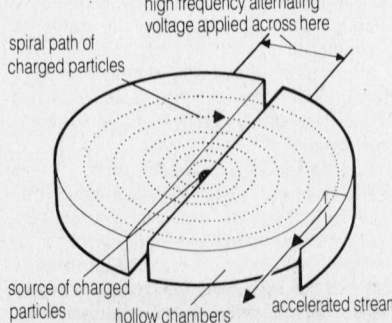

accelerator
high frequency alternating voltage applied across here
spiral path of charged particles
source of charged particles
hollow chambers
accelerated stream

accomplice in popular usage, one who is associated with another in the commission of a crime. In English law, the word is applied not only to persons who played a minor part in the crime, but also to the principal offenders.

accordion a musical instrument, invented by Buschmann in Berlin in 1822. Box-like in form, and small enough to be portable, it comprises a pair of bellows with many folds and a keyboard of up to 50 keys. On these being pressed and the bellows worked, wind is admitted to metal reeds, whose length and thickness determine the notes emitted.

accountancy financial management of business, from balance sheets to policy decisions. Forms of ◊inflation accounting, such as CCA (current cost accounting) and CPP (current purchasing power) are aimed at providing valid financial comparisons over a period in which money values change. See also ◊audit.

Accra /ə'krɑː/ capital and port of Ghana; population (1984) 1,420,000. Christiansborg Castle is the presidential residence, and the University of Ghana is at nearby Legon.

Accrington /'ækrɪŋtən/ industrial town (textiles, engineering) in Lancashire, England; population (1981) 35,890.

accumulator in electricity, a storage battery – that is, a group of rechargeable secondary cells. An ordinary 12-volt car battery is an accumulator consisting of six lead-acid cells which are continually recharged by the car's alternator or dynamo. It has electrodes of lead and lead oxide in an electrolyte of sulphuric acid. Another common type is the 'nife' or Ni-Fe cell, which has electrodes of nickel and iron in a potassium hydroxide electrolyte.

Acer genus of trees and shrubs of N temperate regions with over 115 species. *Acer* includes the sycamores and maples.

acetaldehyde *ethanal* in chemistry, one of the

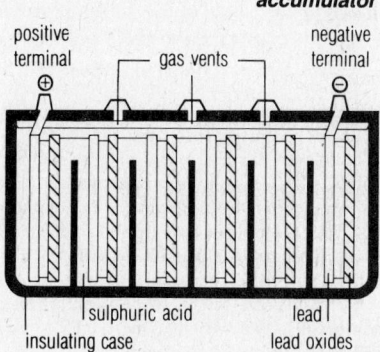

accumulator

positive terminal — gas vents — negative terminal

sulphuric acid — lead
insulating case — lead oxides

chief members of the group of organic compounds known as ◊aldehydes. It is a colourless inflammable liquid boiling at 20.8°C (69.6°F). Acetaldehyde is used to make many other organic chemical compounds.

acetate in chemistry, salt of acetic (ethanoic) acid. In textiles, acetate rayon is a synthetic fabric made from modified cellulose (wood pulp) treated with acetic acid; in photography, acetate film is a non-flammable film made of cellulose acetate.

acetic acid *ethanoic acid* one of the simplest members of a series of organic acids called ◊fatty acids. In the pure state it is a colourless liquid with an unpleasant pungent odour; it solidifies to an ice-like mass of crystals at 16.7°C, and hence is often called glacial acetic acid. Vinegar is 3–6% acetic acid. Cellulose (derived from wood, etc.) is treated with acetic acid to produce a cellulose acetate solution, which can be used to make plastic items by injection moulding, or extruded to form synthetic textile fibres.

acetone *propanone* a colourless inflammable liquid used extensively as a solvent, as in nail-varnish remover. It boils at 56.5°C, mixes with water in all proportions, and has a pleasant and characteristic odour.

acetylene *ethyne* a colourless inflammable gas, originally produced by the action of water on calcium carbide. It was discovered by Edmund Davy in 1836 by the action of water on impure by-products of the preparation of potassium. One important modern development in its use is conversion into the synthetic rubber, neoprene. Since the combustion of acetylene provides more heat, relatively, than almost any other fuels known – its calorific value is five times that of hydrogen – the gas is of great value in obtaining an intensely hot flame, for example in oxyacetylene welding and cutting.

acetylsalicylic acid chemical name for the painkilling drug ◊asprin.

Achaea /ə'kiːə/ in ancient Greece, and also today, an area of the N Peloponnese; the *Achaeans* were the predominant group in the Mycenaean period, and are said by Homer to have taken part in the siege of Troy.

Achaean League union in 275 BC of most of the cities of the N Peloponnese, which managed to defeat Sparta, but was itself defeated by the Romans 146 BC.

Achaemenids /ə'kiːmənɪdz/ dynasty ruling the Persian Empire 550–330 BC, and named after Achaemenes, ancestor of Cyrus the Great, founder of the Empire. His successors included Cambyses, Darius I, Xerxes I and Darius III, who, as the last Achaemenid ruler, was killed after defeat in battle against Alexander the Great in 330 BC.

Achebe /ə'tʃeɪbi/ Chinua 1930– . Nigerian novelist, whose themes include the social and political impact of European colonialism on African people, and the problems of newly-independent African nations. His first novel, *Things Fall Apart* 1958, was widely acclaimed; *Anthills of the Savannah* 1987 is also set in a fictional African country.

achene a dry, one-seeded ◊fruit that develops from a single ◊ovary and which does not split open to disperse the seed. Achenes commonly occur in groups, for example the fruiting heads of buttercup (*Ranunculus*) and clematis. The outer surface may be smooth, spiny, ribbed or tuberculate, depending on the species. An achene with part of the fruit wall extended to form a membranous wing is called a ◊samara; an example is the pendulous fruit of the ash (*Fraxinus*). During the development of a ◊caryopsis, the ◊carpel wall becomes fused to the seed coat; this type of fruit is typical of grasses and cereals. A cypsela is derived from an inferior ovary and is characteristic of the daisy family (Compositae). It often has a pappus of hairs attached, which aids its dispersal by the wind, as in the dandelion.

Acheron /'ækərən/ in Greek mythology, one of the rivers of the lower world. The name was taken from a river in S Epirus which flowed through a deep gorge into the Ionian Sea.

Acheson /'ætʃɪsən/ Dean (Gooderham) 1893–1971. American statesman; as Under-Secretary of State 1945–47, he was associated with George C Marshall in preparing the ◊Marshall Plan, and succeeded him as Secretary of State 1949–53. He helped establish NATO and criticized Britain for having 'lost an empire and not yet found a role'.

Achill /'ækɪl/ largest of the Irish islands, off County Mayo; area 148 sq km/57 sq mi.

Achilles /ə'kɪliːz/ Greek hero of the *Iliad* attributed to Homer. He was the son of Peleus, king of the Myrmidons in Thessaly. His mother, the sea nymph Thetis, rendered him invulnerable, except for the heel by which she held him, by dipping him in the River ◊Styx. He killed Hector in the ◊Trojan War, and was himself killed by Paris with a poisoned arrow in the heel.

Achilles tendon the tendon pinning the calf muscle to the heelbone. It is one of the largest in the human body.

achromatic lens combination of lenses made from glasses of different refractive index, constructed in such a way as to minimize chromatic aberration (which in a single lens causes coloured fringes round images because the lens diffracts the different wavelengths in white light to slightly different extents).

acid a substance which in solution in an ionizing solvent (usually water) gives rise to hydrogen ions (H^+ or protons). Acids react with ◊alkalis to form salts, and they act as solvents. Strong acids are corrosive; dilute acids have a sour or sharp taste. Acids can be detected using coloured indicators such as litmus and methyl orange. The strength of an acid is measured by its hydrogen ◊ion concentration, indicated by the pH value, and expressed on a scale of numbers from 0 (extremely acid) through 7 (neutral) to 14 (extremely alkaline). The first known acid was vinegar (acetic acid). Inorganic acids include boric, carbonic, hydrochloric, hydrofluoric, nitric, phosphoric, sulphuric. Organic acids include acetic, benzoic, citric, formic, lactic, oxalic and salicylic.

acid rain acidic rainfall linked with the death of forests and lake organisms in Scandinavia, Europe, North America and other places. Increased acidity is thought to be caused principally by release into the atmosphere of sulphur dioxide (SO_2) from coal-burning power stations. Acid gases, especially those of nitrogen oxides, are also contributed from other industrial activities and automobile exhaust fumes.

aclinic line the magnetic equator, an imaginary line near the equator, where the compass needle has no 'dip' or magnetic inclination.

aclinic line

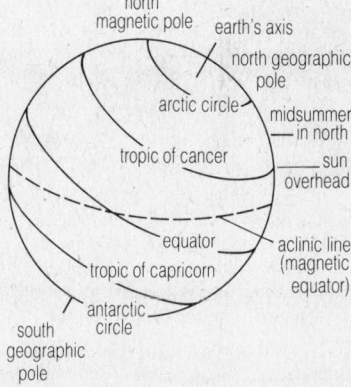

north magnetic pole
earth's axis
north geographic pole
arctic circle
midsummer in north
tropic of cancer
sun overhead
equator
aclinic line (magnetic equator)
tropic of capricorn
antarctic circle
south geographic pole

acne skin eruption caused by inflammation of the sebaceous glands which secrete an oily substance (sebum), the natural lubricant of the skin. Sometimes their openings become stopped and they swell; the contents decompose and pimples form.

Aconcagua /ˌækən'kægwə/ an extinct volcano in the Argentine Andes, the highest peak in the Americas. Height 6960 m/22,834 ft. It was first climbed by Vines and Zeebruggen in 1897.

aconite herbaceous plant *Aconitum napellus* of the buttercup family, with hooded blue-mauve flowers, known commonly as **monkshood**, that produces aconitine, a powerful alkaloid with narcotic and analgesic properties. All other species of the genus *Aconitum*, 100 or so throughout the N temperate region, also contain poisons. *Winter aconite Eranthus hyemalis* also belongs to the buttercup family and is poisonous, but has yellow buttercup-like flowers with six petals and a ruff of leaves below. It flowers from Jan to Mar.

acorn fruit of the oak tree, a nut growing in a shallow cup.

acoustics in general, the experimental and theoretical science of sound; in particular, that branch of the science that has to do with the phenomena of sound in space, for example, public buildings, concert halls, cinemas. Acoustical engineering is concerned with the technical control of sound, and the subject also enters into architecture and building, with the necessity for the control of vibration, for soundproofing, and the elimination of noise; it also includes all forms of sound recording and reinforcement, the hearing and perception of sounds, and hearing aids.

acoustics The anechoic room at the Building Research Centre of the UK Department of the Environment at Watford. Lined with sponge wedges to absorb echoes, it is used for the study of sound transmission and general acoustic research.

Acquaviva /ˌækwə'viːvə/ Claudius 1543–1615. Neapolitan General of the Jesuits from 1581 and one of their most able organizers and educators.

acquired character a feature of the body that develops during the lifetime of an individual, usually as a result of repeated use or disuse, such as the enlarged muscles of a weightlifter. ◊Lamarck's theory of evolution assumed that acquired characters were passed from parent to offspring. Modern evolutionary theory does not recognize the inheritance of acquired characters because there is no reliable evidence that it occurs, and because no mechanism is known whereby bodily changes can influence the ◊genetic material. See also ◊central dogma.

acquired immune deficiency syndrome full name for the disease ◊AIDS.

acquittal in law, the setting free of someone charged with a crime after a trial. In English courts it follows a verdict of 'not guilty', but in

Scotland the verdict may be either 'not guilty' or 'non-proven'. Acquittal by the jury must be confirmed by the judge.

acre /'eɪkə/ traditional English land measure (4,047 sq m/4,840 sq yd/0.405 ha). Originally meaning a field, it was the size that a yoke of oxen could plough in a day, but as early as Edward I's reign it was standardized by statute for official use, although local variation in Ireland, Scotland and some English counties continued.

Acre /'eɪkə/ seaport in Israel; population (1983) 37,000. Taken by the ◊Crusaders in 1104, it was captured by ◊Saladin in 1187 and retaken by ◊Richard I (the Lionheart) in 1191. ◊Napoleon failed in a siege in 1799; ◊Allenby captured it in 1918; and it became part of Israel in 1948.

acre-foot unit sometimes used to measure large volumes of water, such as the capacity of a reservoir (equal to its area in ◊acres multiplied by its average depth in feet). 1 acre-foot equals 1,233.5 m³.

acridine an organic compound which occurs in crude anthracene oil, extracted by dilute acids. It is also obtained synthetically. It is used to make many dye-stuffs and some valuable drugs.

acromegaly the unsightly enlargement of prominent parts of the body, for example hands, feet, and – more conspicuously – the eyebrow ridges and lower jaw, caused by excessive output of growth hormone in adult life by the ◊pituitary gland.

acronym a word formed from the initial letters and/or syllables of other words, intended as a pronounceable abbreviation, for example *NATO* (*N*orth *A*tlantic *T*reaty *O*rganization), *radar* (*ra*dio *d*etecting *a*nd *r*anging), and *Asda* (*A*ssociated *D*airies). Many acronyms are so successfully incorporated into everyday language that their original significance is widely overlooked.

acrophobia a ◊phobia involving fear of heights.

acropolis citadel of an ancient Greek town. Best known is the Acropolis at Athens, famous for the ruins of the Parthenon, built there during the great days of the Athenian empire. The term is also used for analogous structures, as in the massive granite-built ruins of Great ◊Zimbabwe.

acrostic a number of lines of writing, especially verse, whose initial letters (read downwards) form a word, phrase or sentence. A *single acrostic* is formed by the initial letters of lines only, while a *double acrostic* is formed by both initial and final letters. In the original Greek, Acrostic means 'at the extremity of a line or row'.

acrylic acid *propenoic acid* obtained from the ◊aldehyde acrolein (propenal) derived from glycerol or fats. Glass-like thermoplastic resins are made by polymerizing esters of acrylic acid or methacrylic acid, and used for transparent components, lenses, dentures. Other acrylic compounds are used for adhesives, artificial fibres and artists' acrylic paint.

Actaeon /æk'tiːən/ in Greek mythology, a hunter, son of Aristaeus and Autonöe. He surprised ◊Artemis bathing; she changed him

into a stag and he was torn to pieces by his own hounds.

ACTH (adreno-cortico-tropic hormone) a ◊hormone, secreted by the ◊pituitary gland, which controls the production of corticosteroid hormones by the ◊adrenal gland. It is commonly produced as a response to stress.

actinides chemical elements with ◊atomic numbers 89–105. All are radioactive, and they are synthetic above uranium (atomic number 92). They are grouped because of their chemical similarities, and also by analogy with the rare-earth elements (◊lanthanides).

actinium rare radioactive element, atomic number 89, atomic weight of most stable isotope 227; the first of the ◊actinides and a weak emitter of high-energy alpha-rays. Made by bombarding radium with neutrons.

actinium K original name given in 1939 by its discoverer (the French scientist Marguerite Perey) to the radioactive element later (1947) called ◊francium.

action in law, one of the proceedings whereby a person enforces his or her rights in a court of justice. Actions fall into three principal categories, namely civil (such as the enforcement of a debt), penal (where a punishment is sought for the person sued), and criminal (where in Britain the Crown prosecutes a person accused of an offence).

action and reaction in physical mechanics, equal and opposite effects produced by a force acting on an object. This is one way of stating Newton's third law of motion. For example, the pressure of expanding gases from the burning of fuel in a rocket motor (a force) produces an equal and opposite reaction which causes the rocket to move.

Action Française French political movement founded 1899, first led by Charles Maurras 1868–1952. It began by espousing nationalist and republican aims, combined with strong anticapitalism and antiparliamentarism. From 1914 nationalism became the main element, and the movement stressed the essential unity of all French people in contrast to the socialist doctrines of class warfare. In the 1920s the movement obtained a degree of respectability through an alliance with ◊Clemenceau and seats in the chamber of deputies. By the 1930s, Action Française had been superseded by more radical right wing movements such as the Jeunesses Patriotes and the Croix de Feu.

action painting ◊abstract expressionist style developed in New York in the 1950s, named by art critic Harold Rosenberg, who wrote that the painter's canvas seemed to these artists 'an arena in which to act'. The paint was often violently applied, for example by bicycling over the canvas. Jackson ◊Pollock was the originator of this school, which includes Franz Kline and Mark ◊Rothko.

action potential in biology, a change in the potential difference (voltage) across the membrane of a nerve cell when an impulse passes along it. The potential change (from about – 60 to +45 millivolts) accompanies the passage of sodium and potassium ions across the membrane.

Acropolis The Parthenon (5th century BC), which stands on the Acropolis at Athens, was originally the temple of the goddess Athena Parthenos. It was later used as a Christian church and a Turkish mosque.

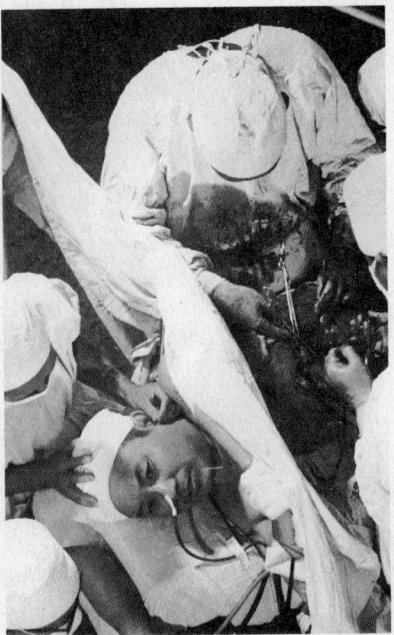

acupuncture Although the patient is fully conscious, the three needles piercing him in the body, the left ear, and the left forearm make him unaware of pain. The operation, at the Peking Medical Colledge, is for the removal of a tumour of the oesophagus.

Actium, Battle of /æktɪəm/ naval battle in which ◊Octavian defeated the combined fleets of ◊Antony and ◊Cleopatra in 31 BC. The site is modern Akri, a promontory in western Greece.

Act of Congress in the USA, a bill or resolution passed by both houses of Congress, the Senate and the House of Representatives, which then becomes law unless it is vetoed by the President. If the president vetoes it, it may still become a law if it is returned to Congress again and passed by a majority of two-thirds in each house.

act of God legal term meaning some sudden and irresistible act of nature which could not reasonably have been foreseen, such as extraordinary storms, snow, frost, or sudden death.

Act of Indemnity in Britain, an Act of Parliament relieving someone from the consequences of some action or omission which, at the time it took place, was illegal or of doubtful legality.

Act of Parliament in Britain, a change in the law originating in Parliament and called a statute. Such acts may be either public (of general effect), local, or private. Before an act receives the royal assent and becomes law it is a 'bill'. The body of English statute law comprises all the Acts passed by Parliament: the existing list opens with the Statute of Merton, passed in 1235. An Act (unless it is stated to be for a definite period and then to come to an end) remains on the statute book until it is repealed. See also ◊Act of Congress.

Acton /'æktən/ Eliza 1799–1859. English cookery writer and poet. Famous for her *Modern Cookery for Private Families* 1845, one of the most influential cookery books ever written in England. She influenced Mrs Beeton.

Acton /'æktən/ John Emerich Edward Dalberg-Acton, 1st Baron Acton 1834–1902. British historian. Elected a Liberal Member of Parliament in 1859, he was a friend and admirer of Gladstone. As leader of the Liberal Roman Catholics, he opposed the declaration of the doctrine of papal infallibility in 1870. Appointed professor of modern history at Cambridge in 1895, he planned and edited the *Cambridge Modern History*, but died after completing the first two volumes.

Actors Studio theatre workshop in New York City, established 1947 by Cheryl Crawford, Elia Kazan, and Lee Strasberg for the study of Stanislavsky's ◊method of acting.

actuary an official of a government department, insurance company, or friendly society, whose task it is to make the calculations concerning human life expectancy, and other risks, on which the tables of mortality, sickness, accident, and hence the premiums or charges, are based. Professional bodies are the Institute of Actuaries (England, 1848), Faculty of Actuaries (Scotland, 1856), and Society of Actuaries (US, 1949, by a merger of two earlier bodies).

acupuncture system developed in ancient China of inserting needles into the body at predetermined points to relieve pain and assist healing. The method, increasingly popular in the West, is thought to work partly by stimulating the brain's own painkillers, or endorphins.

ACV abbreviation of air-cushion vehicle. See ◊hovercraft.

Ada computer-programming language developed in the early 1980s to meet the need of reacting to events in the world as they happen. Incorporates a number of advanced features and several different styles of programming. The US Department of Defence has been closely involved in its development and it is widely used for military purposes. Named after Ada Augusta Byron, an assistant of Charles Babbage.

Adam /'ædəm/ family of Scottish architects and interior designers, including William and his three sons, Robert, James, and John.
William Adam 1689–1748 was the leading Scottish architect of his day. He trained his three sons in his Edinburgh office.
Robert Adam 1728–92, the most distinguished member of the family, is considered the greatest architect of the late 18th century, and leader of the neo-classical revival. He was born at Kirkcaldy, travelled in Italy and Dalmatia, and was appointed architect to King George in 1762. In interiors including Harewood House, ◊Luton Hoo, Syon House, and Osterley Park, he employed delicate stucco decoration with neo-classical motifs. With the assistance of his brothers *James Adam* 1732–94 and *John Adam* 1721–92 he designed and speculatively developed the district of London between Charing Cross and the Thames, which was named after them the Adelphi (Greek for 'brothers'). The area was largely rebuilt in 1936. He also earned a considerable reputation as a furniture designer.

Adam /'ædəm/ in the Old Testament, founder of the human race (Hebrew *adham* 'man'). Formed by God from the dust, and given the breath of life, Adam was placed in the Garden

Adam Influenced by Roman and Greek models, Robert Adam based his style on the principle that exterior, interior, and furnishings should blend into a harmonious whole. This portrait is attributed to G Willison, and dates from 1770–75.

of Eden, where ◊Eve was given to him as a companion. With her, he tasted the forbidden fruit of the Tree of Knowledge of Good and Evil, and was expelled with her from the Garden.

Adam /æ'dɒŋ/ Adolphe Charles 1803–1856. French composer of light operas. Some 50 of his works were staged; he is best remembered for the classic ballet *Giselle*.

Adam de la Halle /æ'dɒm də lɑː 'æl/ c. 1240–c. 1290. French poet-composer. His *Jeu de Robin et Marion*, written in Italy c. 1282, was a theatrical work with dialogue and songs set to what were apparently popular tunes of the day. It is sometimes called the forerunner of comic opera.

Adams /'ædəmz/ Ansel 1902–1984. American photographer, particularly known for his superbly-printed images of dramatic landscapes and organic forms of the American West. He was associated with the ◊Zone System of exposure estimation.

Adams /'ædəmz/ Henry Brooks 1838–1918. American historian, the grandson of John Quincy ◊Adams; he wrote *Mont-Saint-Michel and Chartres* 1904, and a classic autobiography *The Education of Henry Adams* 1907.

Adams /'ædəmz/ John 1735–1826. 2nd president of the USA 1797–1801, and vice-president 1789–97. Born at Quincy, Massachusetts, he was a member of the Continental Congress, 1774–78, and signed the ◊Declaration of Independence. In 1779 he went to France and negotiated the treaties that ended the War of ◊American Independence. In 1785 he became the first US ambassador in London.

Adams /'ædəmz/ John Couch 1819–1892. British astronomer, who deduced the existence of the planet ◊Neptune in 1845, and in 1858 became professor of astronomy at Cambridge.

Adams /'ædəmz/ John Quincy 1767–1848. 6th president of the USA 1825–29. Eldest son of President John Adams, he was born at Quincy, and became US minister in turn at The Hague,

Adams American photographer Ansel Adams is particularly remembered for his superb images of dramatic landscapes in the American West. For many years he published and taught in his subject, and was instrumental in establishing the department of photography at the Museum of Modern Art in New York.

Berlin, St Petersburg, and/1815 London. In 1817 he became Monroe's secretary of state, and succeeded him in the presidency.

Adams John Quincy Adams, 6th president of the USA, painted by Chapel. He travelled widely as a diplomat before a term as Monroe's secretary of state, during which he formulated the Monroe Doctrine (1823). He succeeded Monroe as president in 1825.

Adams /'ædəmz/ Neil 1958– . English judo champion. The most sucessful British international judo competitor of modern times, he won two junior and five senior European titles

1974–85, eight senior national titles, and two Olympic silver medals 1980, 1984. In 1981 he was world champion in the 78 kg class.

Adams /'ædəmz/ Richard 1920– . British novelist. A civil servant 1948–72, he achieved fame with *Watership Down* 1972, a tale of a rabbit community, which was popular with adults and children. Later novels include *The Plague Dogs* 1977, and *Girl on a Swing* 1980.

Adams /'ædəmz/ Roger 1889–1971. American organic chemist, best known for his painstaking analytical work to determine the composition of naturally occuring substances such as complex vegetable oils and plant ◊alkaloids.

Adams /'ædəmz/ Samuel 1722–1803. American statesman, second cousin of President John ◊Adams. He was the chief prompter of the ◊Boston Tea Party. He was also a signatory of the ◊Declaration of Independence, and anticipated Napoleon in calling the British a 'nation of shopkeepers'.

Adamson /'ædəmsən/ Joy 1910–1985. German-born author-painter, who with her third husband, British game warden *George Adamson*, was famous for work with wildlife in Kenya, especially the lioness Elsa described in *Born Free* 1960. She was murdered at her home in Kenya.

Adamson /'ædəmsən/ Robert R 1821–1848. Scottish photographer who, with David Octavius ◊Hill, turned out 2,500 ◊calotypes (mostly portraits) in five years from 1843.

Adana /'ædənə/ major cotton-growing centre in Turkey-in-Asia; population (1980) 574,515.

adaptation in biology, any change in the structure or function of an organism that allows it to survive better in its environment. In ◊evolution, adaptation occurs as a result of random variation in the genetic make-up of organisms, (produced by ◊mutation and ◊recombination) coupled with natural selection. This produces individuals whose genetically determined characteristics allow them to survive and reproduce more effectively. Thus, the webbed feet of ducks or otters are adaptations to living in water, enabling them to swim more efficiently. In physiology, adaptation is said to occur in sense organs, when the sensitivity of an organ alters in response to changes in environmental conditions. Examples include an increase in the size of the eye's pupil to admit more light as night falls.

adaptive radiation in evolution, the production of several new ◊species, with ◊adaptations to different ways of life, from a single parent stock. An example is provided by the finches on the Galapagos Island which are probably descended from a few finches of a single species that flew there from the South American mainland. This parent stock has evolved into 13 species that now occupy a range of diverse lifestyles. On the mainland comparable niches are filled by other groups of birds, including woodpeckers and warblers, as well as seed-eating finches. Adaptive radiation is likely to occur whenever a species enters a new habitat that contains few, if any, similar species. The first invasion of land by creatures from the sea provides an early example.

adaptation

hummingbird

toucan

eagle

nightjar

spoonbill

skimmer

oystercatcher

the Organization of African Unity.

Addison /'ædɪsən/ Joseph 1672–1719. British writer. In 1704 he celebrated ◊Marlborough's victory at Blenheim in a poem, 'The Campaign', and subsequently held political appointments, including under-secretary of state, secretary to the Lord-Lieutenant of Ireland 1708 and member of parliament. In 1709 he contributed to the *Tatler*, begun by Richard ◊Steele, with whom he was co-founder in 1711 of the *Spectator*. His essays set a new standard of easy elegance in English prose; especially notable were the Coverley papers concerning an idealized country squire, Sir Roger de Coverley. As a literary critic, he was satirized by Alexander ◊Pope as willing to 'damn with faint praise' any rival.

Addison Kneller's portrait of the British essayist and poet Joseph Addison was done for the dining-room of the Kit-Cat Club, to which Congreve, Steele and Vanbrugh also belonged. The pictures were less than half-length because the room was so low, hence portraits to the waist are still called 'kit-cat'.

Addison /'ædɪsən/ Thomas 1793–1863. British physician; he first recognized the condition known as ◊Addison's disease.

Addison's disease disease affecting the suprarenal capsules or ◊adrenal glands.

additive in food, a chemical added to prolong shelf life (such as salt), alter colour, or improve food value (such as vitamins or minerals). Many chemical additives are used in the manufacture of food. They have a variety of properties, as outlined below. They are subject to regulation since individuals may be affected by constant exposure to even small concentrations of certain additives and suffer side-effects such as hyperactivity. See ◊E-number.

flavours may be natural or artificial. They are said to increase the appeal of the food. Enhancers may also be used, such as monosodium glutamate. Artificial sweeteners are the most common, especially in beverages.

Addams /'ædəmz/ Jane 1860–1935. American sociologist and feminist. She founded and led the social settlement of Hull House, Chicago, one of the earliest community centres, in 1889 and was Vice-President of the National American Woman Suffrage Association from 1911 to 1914. In 1915 she led the Woman's Peace Party and the first Women's Peace Congress. Her publications include *Newer Ideals of Peace* 1907 and *Twenty Years at Hull House* 1910. She was a co-winner of the Nobel prize 1931.

addax light-coloured ◊antelope *Addax nasomaculatus* of the Sahara desert, where it exists on the scanty vegetation without drinking. It is about 1.1 m/3.5ft at the shoulder and both sexes have spirally twisted horns.

adder venomous European ◊snake *Vipera berus*, belonging to the ◊viper family. Growing to about 60 cm/2 ft long, it has a thick body

and triangular head, and often zig-zag markings along the back. A shy animal, it feeds on small mammals and lizards. The *puff adder Bitis arietans* is a large yellowish thick-bodied viper up to 1.6 m/5 ft long living in Africa and Arabia.

adding machine device for adding numbers, usually operated mechanically or electro-mechanically; now largely superseded by electronic ◊calculators.

Addington /'ædɪŋtən/ Henry 1757–1844. British Tory prime minister 1801–04, later Viscount Sidmouth.

Addis Ababa /'ædɪs 'æbəbə/ capital of Ethiopia; population (1982) 1,408,000. It was founded in 1887 by Menelik, chief of Shoa, who ascended the throne of Ethiopia in 1889. His former residence, Menelik Palace, is now occupied by the chairman of the Provisional Military Council; the city is the headquarters of

nutrients may be added to replace or enhance food value. Minerals and vitamins are the most common, especially where the diet would otherwise be deficient, leading to diseases such as beri-beri and pellagra.

preservatives are primarily anti-oxidants and anti-microbials that control natural oxidation and the action of micro-organisms. See ◊food technology.

emulsifiers and *surfactants* are used to regulate the consistency of fats in the food and the surface of the food where it is in contact with the air.

thickeners, primarily vegetable gums, regulate the consistency of the product. Pectin acts in this way on fruit products.

leavening agents act to lighten the texture of baked goods without the use of yeasts. Sodium bicarbonate is the best known of these.

acidulants give the product a sharper taste, but may also perform a buffering function in the control of acidity.

bleaching agents assist in the ageing of flours and so improve the quality of baked goods.

anti-caking agents prevent powdered products coagulating into solid lumps.

humectants control the humidity of the product by absorbing and retaining moisture.

clarifying agents are used in fruit juices, vinegars and other fermented liquids. Gelatin is the most common.

firming agents act to replace the texture of vegetables that may be damaged during processing.

foam regulators are used in beer to provide a controlled 'head' on top of the poured product.

address in a computer memory, a number indicating a specific location. At each address, a single piece of data can be stored. For microcomputers, this normally amounts to one byte (enough to represent a single character such as a letter or number). The maximum capacity of a computer memory depends on how many memory addresses it can have. This is normally measured in units of 1,024 bytes (known as kilobytes, or K).

Adelaide /'ædɪleɪd/ 1792–1849. Queen consort of ◊William IV of England. Daughter of the Duke of Saxe-Meiningen, she married William, then Duke of Clarence, in 1818. No children of the marriage survived infancy.

Adelaide /'ædɪleɪd/ capital and industrial city of South Australia; population (1985) 987,080. It is a fine example of town planning, with residential districts separated from the commercial area by the river Torrens, dammed to form a lake. Founded in 1834, Adelaide was named after William IV's queen. Impressive streets include King William Street and North Terrace, and fine buildings include Parliament House, Government House, the Anglican cathedral of St Peter, the Roman Catholic cathedral, two universities, the State observatory, and the museum and art gallery.

Aden /'eɪdn/ capital of the People's Democratic Republic of Yemen, on a rocky peninsula at the SW corner of Arabia, commanding the entrance to the Red Sea. It comprises the new administrative centre Madinet al-Sha'ab; the commercial and business quarters of Crater and Tawahi, and the harbour area of Ma'alla. There is an international airport. Population (1981) 264,300.

history Aden and its immediately surrounding area (121 sq km/75 sq mi) were annexed by Britain in 1839 and developed as a ship refuelling station after the opening of the Suez Canal. It was a colony 1937–63, and then, after a period of transitional violence between rival nationalist groups and British forces, was combined with the former Aden protectorate (290,000 sq km/112,000 sq mi) to create in 1967 the Southern Yemen People's Republic, later renamed the People's Democratic Republic of ◊Yemen.

Adenauer /'ædənaʊə/ Konrad 1876–1967. German statesman. He was Lord Mayor of his native city of Cologne from 1917 until his imprisonment in 1933 by Hitler for opposition to the Nazi regime. After the war he headed the Christian Democratic Union, and was Chancellor of the Federal Republic 1949–63; he was known as the 'Old Fox'. With ◊de Gaulle he achieved the postwar reconciliation of France and Germany and strongly supported all measures designed to strengthen the Western bloc in Europe, for example his support of Britain's entry into the Common Market.

Adenauer German politician Konrad Adenauer was forced out of public life and imprisoned by the Nazis. After the war he emerged as chairman of the Christian Democratic Union and became the first chancellor of the Federal Republic of Germany. He helped to restore the prestige of post-war Germany in the West.

adenoids masses of lymphoid tissue, similar to ◊tonsils, located in the upper part of the throat. They are part of a child's natural defences against the entry of germs but usually shrink and disappear by the age of ten years. Adenoids may, however, swell and grow – particularly if infected – and block the breathing passages through the nose. If they become repeatedly infected they may be removed surgically (adenoidectomy).

Ader /æ'deə/ Clement 1841–1925. French aviator-pioneer whose first steam-driven aeroplane, the *Éole*, made the first powered take-off in history (1890), but it could not fly. In 1897, with his *Avion III*, he failed completely, despite his false claims made later.

adhesive substance that sticks two surfaces together. Natural adhesives include gelatine in its crude industrial form (made from bones, hide fragments and fish offal), and vegetable gums. Synthetic adhesives include thermoplastic and thermosetting resins, which are often stronger than the substances they join; mixtures of epoxy resin and hardener that set by chemical reaction; and elastomeric (stretching) adhesives for flexible joins.

adiabatic the adiabatic expansion or contraction of a gas is one in which a change takes place in the pressure or volume of the gas, although no heat is allowed to enter or leave.

Adige /'ɑːdɪdʒeɪ/ after the Po, the longest river in Italy, 410 km/254 mi in length. It crosses the Lombardy Plain and enters the Adriatic just north of the Po delta.

Adi Granth /'ɑːdi 'grɑːnθ/ or Granth Sahib. The holy book of ◊Sikhism.

adipose tissue a type of ◊connective tissue of ◊vertebrates, commonly called fat tissue and consisting of large spherical cells filled with ◊fat. In mammals, major layers of adipose tissue are in the inner layer of skin and around the ◊kidneys and ◊heart. It is the main energy store of the body and material is transported to and from it via the blood system.

Adirondacks /,ædɪ'rɒndæks/ mountainous area in the NE of ◊New York State, USA, noted for its scenery and sports facilities.

adjective the grammatical ◊part of speech for words that describe nouns (for example, *new* and *enormous*, as in 'a new hat' and 'an enormous dog'). Adjectives generally have three degrees (grades or levels for the description of relationships): the positive degree (*new*; *enormous*, the comparative degree (*newer*; *more enormous*), and the superlative degree (*newest*; *most enormous*). Some adjectives, however, because of their meanings, do not normally need comparative and superlative forms; one person is not normally ◊'more asleep' than someone else, a lone action is unlikely to be ◊'the most single-handed action ever seen', and many people dislike the expression 'most unique', because something unique is supposed to be the only one that there is. However, for purposes of emphasis or style these conventions are often set aside ('I don't know who is more unique; they are both remarkable people'). Double comparatives such as 'more bigger' are unnecessary and not grammatical in Standard English, but Shakespeare is on record as using a double superlative ('the most unkindest cut of all'). Some adjectives may have both of the comparative and superlative forms (*commoner* and *more common*; *commonest* and *most common*), while occasionally shorter words may be given the forms for longer words ('Which of them are the *most clear*?') for emphasis or other reasons. When an adjective comes before a noun it is attributive; if it comes after noun and verb (for example, 'It looks *good*'), it is predicative. Some adjectives can only be used predicatively ('The child was asleep', but not ◊'the asleep child'). The participles of verbs are regularly used adjectivally ('a *sleeping* child', 'boiled milk') and often in compound forms ('a *quick-acting* medicine', 'a *glass-making* factory'; 'a *hard-boiled* egg', '*well-trained* teachers'). Adjectives are often formed by adding suffixes to nouns (sand: sand*y*; nation: nation*al*).

Adler /'ɑːdlə/ Alfred 1870–1937. Austrian psychologist. Born in Vienna, he was a general practitioner and nerve specialist there 1897–1927, serving as an army doctor in World War I He joined the circle of Freudian doctors in Vienna about 1900. Adler saw the 'will to power' as more influential in accounting for human behaviour than the underlying sexual drive theory of ◊Freud, and parted company with Freud after a ten-year collaboration. His books include *Organic Inferiority and Psychic Compensation* 1907 and *Understanding Human Nature* 1927.

Adler /'ædlə/ Larry 1914– . American musician, best known as a virtuoso performer on the ◊harmonica.

administrative law the body of laws made and the judicial decisions arrived at by the executive branch of government under powers delegated to it by the legislature; such legislative powers have been vastly extended in the 20th century in many countries and have been attacked by lawyers. In the US the Administrative Procedure Act (1946) was an attempt to cope with the problem.

In the UK the very many new powers delegated to ministers of the Crown are so wide that they may enable the ministers to make regulations which amend or override Acts of Parliament, and in some cases they further take away from the courts of law the power they have hitherto exercised of confining the legislative activities of the Executive within the limits of the authority delegated to them by Parliament by declaring any regulation that exceeds these limits to be *ultra vires*, and so of no effect.

admiral highest ranking naval officer; in the Royal Navy (in descending order) Admiral of the Fleet, Admiral, Vice-Admiral, Rear-Admiral; in the US Navy, Fleet Admiral, Admiral, Vice-Admiral, Rear-Admiral.

admiral name for several species of butterfly related to the tortoiseshells. The red admiral *Vanessa atalanta*, wingspan 6 cm/2 in migrates each year from the Mediterranean to N Europe, where it cannot survive the winter.

Admiral's Cup sailing series first held in 1957 and since held biennially for three-boat national teams which compete in three inshore and two offshore courses; the series culminates in the Fastnet race; similar series are the Southern Cross, Rio Circuit and the Onion Patch.

Admiralty, Board of the in Britain, the controlling department of state for the Royal Navy from the reign of Henry VIII until 1964, when most of its functions – apart from that of management – passed to the Ministry of Defence. The 600-year-old office of Lord High Admiral reverted to the sovereign.

Admiralty Islands group of small islands in the SW Pacific, part of ◊Papua New Guinea.

Adonis /ə'dəʊnɪs/ in Greek mythology, a beautiful youth beloved by ◊Aphrodite. He was killed while boar-hunting, but from his blood sprang the anemone. He was allowed to return from the lower world for six months every year to rejoin her. Worshipped as a god of vegetation, he was known as *Tammuz* in Babylonia, Assyria, and Phoenicia (where it was his sister, ◊Ishtar, who brought him from the lower world). He seems also to have been identified with ◊Osiris.

adoption the legal acquisition of a child not one's own by birth. It was first legalized in England in 1926; in 1958 an adopted child was enabled to inherit on parental intestacy; and from 1975 in the Childrens' Act provision was made for ◊custodianship by foster-parents, step-parents etc., and an adopted child was enabled at the age of 18 to know its original name.

Adowa /'ædəʊɑː/ alternative form of ◊Aduwa.

adrenal gland a ◊gland situated on top of the ◊kidney, also known as the suprarenal gland. The adrenals are soft and yellow, and consist of two parts. The cortex (outer part) secretes various steroid ◊hormones, and controls salt and water metabolism and other processes. The medulla (inner part) secretes the hormones epinephrine and norepinephrine (adrenalin and noradrenalin) which constrict the blood vessels of the belly and skin so that more blood is available for the ◊heart, ◊lungs and voluntary ◊muscles, an emergency preparation for the stress reaction 'fight or flight'.

adrenaline hormone, also called epinephrine, secreted by the medulla of the ◊adrenal glands.

Adrian /'eɪdrɪən/ Edgar, 1st Baron Adrian 1889–1977. British physiologist. He received the Nobel prize for medicine in 1932, for his work with Sherrington in the field of nerve impulses, and was professor and Master of Trinity College 1951–65. Awarded the Order of Merit in 1942, he was created a baron in 1955.

Adrianople /,eɪdrɪən'əʊpəl/ older name of ◊Edirne, after the Emperor Hadrian, who rebuilt it c. 125 AD.

Adrian IV Nicholas Breakspear, pope 1154–59, the only British pope. He was born at Abbots Langley, became a monk in France, and in 1137 abbot of St Rufus, near Arles. As pope, he secured the execution of ◊Arnold of Brescia; crowned ◊Frederick I Barbarossa as German Emperor; refused ◊Henry II's request that Ireland should be granted to the English crown in absolute ownership; and was at the height of a quarrel with the Emperor when he died.

Adriatic Sea /,eɪdri'ætɪk/ large arm of the Mediterranean Sea, lying north west to south east between the Italian and the Balkan peninsulas. The western shore is Italian; the eastern Yugoslav and Albanian. The sea is about 805 km/500 mi long, and its area is 135,250 sq km/52,220 sq mi.

adsorption the taking up of a gas or liquid by the surface of a solid (as activated charcoal, for example, adsorbs gases). It is a surface phenomenon involving molecular attraction at the surface and should be distinguished from ◊absorption (in which a uniform solution results from a gas or liquid being incorporated into the bulk structure of a liquid or solid).

adultery voluntary sexual intercourse by a married person with someone other than his or her legal partner. It is one factor which may prove 'irretrievable breakdown' of marriage in suits for judicial separation or divorce in Britain. It is almost universally recognized as grounds for divorce in the USA, and is theoretically a punishable offence in some states.

Aduwa /'ædʊɑː/ former capital of Ethiopia, about 180 km/110 mi south west of Massawa at an altitude of 1,910 m/6,270 ft. It was the site of the Battle of Aduwa. Population (1971) 16,400.

Aduwa, Battle of /'ædʊɑː/ defeat of the Italians by the Ethiopians at ◊Aduwa in 1896. See ◊Menelik II.

advanced gas-cooled reactor see ◊AGR.

Advent in the Christian calendar, the preparatory season for Christmas, including the four Sundays preceding it, beginning with the Sunday which falls nearest (before or after) to St Andrew's Day (30 Nov).

Adventists those who hold the view that Christ will return to make a second appearance on the earth. Expectation of the Second Coming of Christ is found in New Testament writings generally. Adventist views are held in particular by the Seventh Day Adventists, Christadelphians, Jehovah's Witnesses, and the Four Square Gospel Alliance.

adverb the grammatical ◊part of speech for words that modify or describe verbs ('She ran *quickly*'), adjectives ('a *beautifully* clear day'), and adverbs ('They did it *really* well'). Most adverbs are formed from adjectives or past participles by adding -*ly* (quick: quickly; hurried: hurriedly), or -*ally* (automatic: automatically). Sometimes they are formed by adding -*wise* (like: likewise , and clockwise, as in 'moving clockwise'; in 'a clockwise direction', *clockwise* is an adjective). Some adjectives have a distinct form from their partnering adjective, as with good/well ('It was *good* work; they did it *well*'). Others do not derive from adjectives (*very* in 'very nice'; *tomorrow* in 'I'll do it tomorrow'), and some are unadapted adjectives (*pretty*, as in, 'It's pretty good'). Sentence adverbs modify whole sentences or phrases: '*Generally*, it rains a lot here'; '*Usually*, the town is busy at this time of year'. Sometimes there is controversy in such matters. *Hopefully* is universally accepted in sentences like 'He looked at them hopefully' (= in a hopeful way), but some people dislike it in 'Hopefully, we'll see you again next year' (= We hope that we'll see you again next year).

advocate (Latin *advocatus*, one summoned to one's aid, especially in a court of justice). A professional pleader in a court of justice. The English term is ◊barrister or counsel, but advocate is retained in Scotland and in other countries, such as France, where the Roman law is still retained. The term advocate has no special significance in the US.

Advocate Judge manager of the prosecution in British courts martial.

Advocates, faculty of Scottish legal body, incorporated in 1532 under James V. In their powers, members closely resemble English ◊barristers.

advowson the right of selecting a person to a church living or benefice; a form of ◊patronage.

Aegean Sea /iːˈdʒiːən/ branch of the Mediterranean between Greece and Turkey. The Dardanelles connect it with the Sea of Marmara. The numerous islands in the Aegean Sea include Crete, the Cyclades, the Sporades and the Dodecanese. There is political tension between Greece and Turkey over sea limits claimed by Greece around such islands as Lesbos, Chios, Samos and Kos.

Aegina /iːˈdʒaɪnə/ Greek island in the Gulf of Aegina about 32 km/20 mi south west of Piraeus. In 1811 remarkable sculptures were recovered from a Doric temple in the north east (restored by Thorwaldsen) and taken to Munich.

Aegir /ˈægə/ in Scandinavian mythology, the god of the sea.

Aegis in Greek mythology, the shield of Zeus, symbolic of the storm cloud associated with him. In representations of deities it is commonly shown as a protective animal skin.

Aehrenthal /ˈeərəntɑːl/ Count Aloys von 1854–1912. Foreign Minister of Austria-Hungary during the Bosnian Crisis of 1908.

Aelfric /ˈælfrɪk/ c. 955–1020. Old-English prose writer. He became a priest and taught at Cernel monastery (now Cerne Abbas) in Dorset, and was abbot of Eynsham from 1005. He is celebrated for his writings in the vernacular, particularly for his two collections of homilies and the *Lives of the Saints*.

Aeneas /iːˈniːəs/ in classical legend, a Trojan prince who became the ancestral hero of the Romans. According to Homer, he was the son of Anchises and the goddess Aphrodite. During the Trojan war he owed his life several times to the intervention of the gods. The legend on which Virgil's *Aeneid* is based describes his escape from Troy and eventual settlement in Latium. The Latins accorded him divine honours, and Julius ◊Caesar and ◊Augustus claimed to be descended from him.

Aeolian harp a wooden sound box, rectangular and fitted with loose gut strings which vibrate in the wind to produce a chordal impression. It became popular in parts of Europe in the 19th century.

Aeolian Islands /iːˈəʊliən/ another name for the ◊Lipari Islands.

Aeolus /ˈiːələs/ in Greek mythology, the god of the winds, who kept them imprisoned in a cave on the ◊Lipari Islands.

aepyornis type of huge extinct flightless bird living in Madagascar until a few thousand years ago. Some stood 3 m/10ft high and laid eggs with a volume of 9 litres/2 gallons.

aerenchyma a plant tissue with numerous air-filled spaces between the cells. It occurs in the stems and roots of many aquatic plants where it aids buoyancy and facilitates transport of oxygen around the plant.

aerial in radio broadcasting, a conducting device that radiates or receives radio waves. The design of an aerial (also known as an antenna)

depends principally on the wavelength of the radio signal. Long waves (in the order of hundreds of metres) may employ long wire aerials; short waves (of several centimetres wavelength) may employ rods and dipoles; and microwaves may also use dipoles – often with reflectors arranged like a toast rack – or highly directional parabolic dish aerials. Because microwaves travel in straight lines, giving line-of-sight communication, microwave aerials are usually located at the tops of tall masts or towers.

aerobic in biology, a description of those living organisms which use molecular oxygen (usually dissolved in water) for the efficient release of energy: this includes almost all living organisms. Oxygen is used to convert glucose to carbon dioxide and water, thereby releasing energy. Most aerobic organisms die in the absence of oxygen but certain organisms and cells, such as muscle cells, can function for short periods without oxygen. See also ◊anaerobic.

aerobics (Greek 'air' and 'life') strenuous combination of dance, stretch exercises, and running that became a health fashion in the 1980s.

aerodynamics the branch of fluid physics that studies the flow of gases, particularly as it applies to solid objects (such as land vehicles, bullets, rockets and aircraft) moving at speed through air. For maximum efficiency and ease of control, the aim is usually to design the shape of the object to produce streamlined flow, with a minimum of turbulence in the moving air.

aeronautics the science of travel through the earth's atmosphere, including aerodynamics, aircraft structures, jet and rocket propulsion, and also aerial navigation. It should not be confused with *astronautics*, which is the science of travel through space; *astronavigation* is, however, used in aircraft as in ships and is a part of aeronautics. ◊*Aerodynamics* comprises the study of the airflow around bodies moving through the atmosphere. In *subsonic aeronautics* (below the speed of sound) aerodynamic forces increase as the square of the speed, and are thus simply calculated. *Transsonic aeronautics* covers the speed range from just below to just above the speed of sound. Ordinary sound waves move at about 1,225 kph/760 mph at sea level, and air in front of an aircraft moving slower than this is 'warned' by the waves so that it can move aside. But, as the flying speed approaches that of the sound waves, the warning is too late for the air to escape and the aircraft pushes the air aside, creating shock waves which absorb much power and create design problems. On the ground the shock waves give rise to a ◊sonic boom. It was once thought that the speed of sound was a speed limit to aircraft, and the term ◊sound barrier came into use. *Supersonic aeronautics* concerns speeds above that of sound and in one sense may be considered a much older study than aeronautics itself, since the study of the flight of bullets, known as ◊ballistics, was undertaken soon after the introduction of firearms. *Hypersonics* is the study of airflows and forces at speeds above five times that of sound (Mach 5), for example for guided missiles, space rockets and advanced concepts such as ◊HOTOL. For all

flight speeds streamlining is necessary to reduced the effects of air resistance.

aeroplane a powered heavier-than-air craft supported in flight by fixed wings, often abbreviated to *plane*. The wings have the cross-sectional shape of an aerofoil ('airfoil' in the USA.) An aerofoil is broad and curved at the front, flat underneath, curved on top, and tapers to a sharp point at the rear. It is so shaped that air passing above it is speeded up, reducing pressure below atmospheric. This follows from ◊Bernoulli's effect and results in a force acting vertically upwards, called lift, which counters the planes weight. In level flight lift equals weight. The wings develop sufficient lift to support the plane when they move quickly through the air. The plane is propelled by the thrust of an airscrew, or ◊propeller, or by the thrust of a ◊jet engine.

The thrust comes from the reaction to the air stream accelerated backwards by the propeller or the gases shooting backwards from the jet exhaust. In flight the engine thrust must overcome the air resistance, or ◊drag. Drag depends on frontal area (for example, large, airliner; small, fighter) and shape (drag coefficient); in level flight drag equals thrust. The drag is reduced by streamlining the plane, resulting in higher speed and reduced fuel consumption for a given power. Less fuel need be carried for a given distance of travel, so a larger payload (cargo or passengers) can be carried.

design and construction planes are constructed using light but strong aluminium alloys such as duralumin (with copper, magnesium and so on). For supersonic planes special stainless steel and titanium may be used in areas subjected to high heat loads. The structure of the plane, or the airframe (wings, fuselage, and so on). consists of a surface skin of alloy sheets supported at intervals by struts known as ribs and stringers. The structure is bonded together by riveting or by powerful adhesives such as ◊epoxy resins. In certain critical areas, which have to withstand particularly high stresses (such as the wing roots), body panels are machined from solid metal for extra strength.

The shape of a plane is dictated very much by the speed at which it will operate. A low-speed plane operating at well below the speed of sound (c. 965 kph/600 mph) need not be particularly well streamlined, and it can have its wings broad and projecting at right-angles from the fuselage. An aircraft operating close to the speed of sound must be well streamlined and have swept-back wings. This prevents the formation of shock waves over the body surface and particularly the wings, whcih would result in instability and high power loss. ◊Supersonic planes need to be more severely streamlined still, and require a needle nose, highly swept-back wings, and what is often termed a 'Coke-bottle' fuselage. Then they can pass through the sound barrier without suffering undue disturbance. To give great flexibility of operation at low as well as high speeds, some supersonic planes are designed with variable-geometry, or ◊swing wings. For low-speed flight the wings are outstretched; for high-speed flight they are swung close to the fuselage to form an efficient ◊delta-wing configuration. Aircraft designers experiment with different designs in a ◊wind tunnel before they make up their minds. The wind-tunnel tests indicate how their designs will behave in practice.

On the ground a plane rests on wheels, usually in a tricycle arrangement, with a nose wheel and two wheels behind, one under each wing. For all except some light planes the landing gear, or undercarriage, is retracted in flight to reduce drag. Seaplanes which take off and land on water are fitted with non-retractable hydrofoils.

flight control wings by themselves are unstable in flight, and a plane requires a tail to provide stability. It comprises a horizontal tailplane and vertical tail-fin, also called the horizontal and vertical stabilizer respectively. The tailplane has hinged flaps at the rear called elevators to control pitch (attitude). Raising the elevators depresses the tail and inclines the wings upwards (increases the angle of attack). This speeds the airflow above the wings until lift exceeds weight and the plane climbs. But the steeper attitude increases drag, amd more power is needed to maintain speed. So the engine throttle must be opened up. Moving the elevators in the opposite direction produces the reverse effect. The angle of attack is reduced, and the plane descends. Speed builds up rapidly if the engine is not throttled back. Turning (changing direction) is effected by moving the rudder hinged to the rear of the tail-fin, and by backing (rolling) the plane. It is banked by moving the ailerons, which are interconnected flaps at the rear of the wings which move in opposite directions, one up, the other down. In planes with a delta wing, such as ◊Concorde, the ailerons and elevators are combined. Other moveable control surfaces called flaps are fitted at the rear of the wings closer to the fuselage. They are extended to increase the width and camber (curve) of the wings during take-off and landing, thereby creating extra lift. Moveable sections at the front, or leading edge of the wing called slats also extend at these times, to improve the airflow.

To land, the nose of the plane is brought up so that the angle of attack of the wings exceeds a critical point, and the airflow around them breaks down. Lift is lost (a condition known as stalling) and the plane drops to the runway. A few planes, (for example, the Harrier) have a novel method of take-off and landing, rising and dropping vertically by swivelling nozzles to direct the exhaust of their jet engines downwards.

The control surfaces of a plane are operated by the pilot on the flight deck, by means of a control stick, or wheel, and by foot pedals (for the rudder). The controls are brought into action by hydraulic power systems. Advanced experimental high-speed craft known as control-configured vehicles (CCV) use a sophisticated computer-controlled system. The pilot instructs the computer which manoeuvre the plane must perform and the computer, informed by a series of sensors around the craft about the attitude, speed and turning rate of the plane, sends signals to the control surface and throttle to enable the manoeuvre to be executed. See also ◊flight.

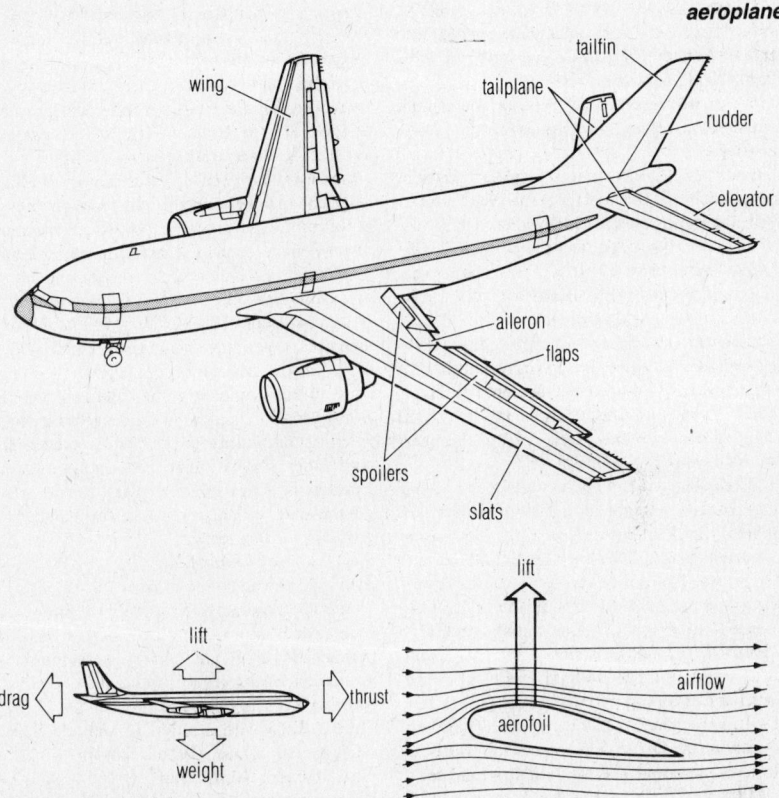

aeroplane

aerosol colloidal system, for example mist or fog, in which air is the dispersion medium; and popularly a form of packaging in which gas under pressure, or a liquefied gas with a pressure greater than atmospheric at ordinary temperatures, is used to spray a very fine mist of liquid droplets from a nozzle; it is generally actuated by a press-button device. Aerosol cans are used for insecticides, paints, hair lacquers, perfumes, and so on. There is some evidence that the fluorocarbon propellants (such as Freon) used in aerosols break down the ◊ozone layer, protecting earth against ultra-violet rays from the sun. This has led to a call to restrict their use.

Aeschines /ˈiːskɪniːz/ 4th century BC orator of ancient Athens, a rival of ◊Demosthenes.

Aeschylus /ˈiːskɪləs/ c. 525–c. 456 BC. Greek dramatist. Born near Athens, he came of a noble family; fought against the Persians at Marathon (490 BC), and wrote nearly 90 plays between 499 and 458BC. He twice visited the court of Hiero, king of Syracuse, and died at Gela in Sicily.

The earliest of his seven surviving plays is *The Suppliant Women* performed about 490. There followed *The Persians* (472), *Seven against Thebes* (467) and *Prometheus Bound* (about 460). Then came the trilogy of the *Oresteia* which won the first prize at the festival of Dionysus in 458; the three plays – *Agamemnon*, *Choephori*, and *Eumenides* – deal with the curse on the house of Agamemnon which was eventually resolved by the action and suffering of Orestes.

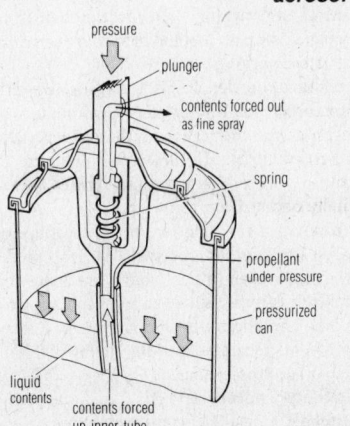

aerosol

Aeschylus became famous for the majesty of his language, the boldness of his speculation upon problems of religion and human destiny, and the grandeur and simplicity of his plots and characters.

Aesculapius /ˌiːskjʊˈleɪpɪəs/ in Greek and Roman mythology, the god of medicine; his emblem was a staff with a snake coiled round it, since snakes seemed to renew life by sloughing their skin. Sacred snakes were kept in the sanctuaries of Aesculapius at Epidaurus and elsewhere. The customary offering to Aesculapius was a cock.

Aesop /ˈiːsɒp/ ancient Egyptian writer of fables. According to Herodotus he lived in the reign of Amasis of Egypt (mid-6th century BC). Born a slave, he was represented in later art as deformed. He received his freedom and visited Lydia and Greece. No writings by him have survived.

Aesthetic Movement English artistic movement of the last quarter of the 19th century. With the motto 'Art for art's sake', it reached its apogee with ◊Wilde, and the periodical *The Yellow Book* 1894–97. It was exemplified by such figures as ◊Pater, ◊Beardsley, ◊Whistler, ◊Dowson, and J A ◊Symonds.

aesthetics the branch of philosophy which deals with the nature of beauty, especially in art. Aesthetics only emerged as a distinct branch of enquiry in the mid-18th century, the term first being used by the German philosopher Baumgarten (1714–62).

aestivation in zoology, a state of inactivity and reduced metabolic activity, similar to ◊hibernation, that occurs during the dry season in species like lungfish and snails. In botany, the term is used to describe the way in which flower petals and sepals are folded in the buds. This feature is important in ◊plant classification.

Aetolia /iːˈtəʊliə/ district of ancient Greece on the north west of the gulf of Corinth. The *Aetolian League* was a confederation of the cities of Aetolia which, following the death of Alexander the Great, was the chief rival of the Macedonian power and the Achaean League.

Afars and the Issas /ˈæfɑːz, ˈɪsəz/ French Territory of the former French territory which became known as the Republic of ◊Djibouti in 1977.

AFD abbreviation for accelerated freeze drying, a common method of food preservation. See ◊freeze drying.

affiliation order English magistrate's order for maintenance, usually of an illegitimate child, made against the father at the instance of an unmarried mother. In 1969 blood tests were first used to prove 'non-paternity'; they are not equally conclusive of paternity.

affinity in law, relationship by marriage not blood, for example between stepparent and stepchild, which may legally preclude their marriage. It is distinguished from consanguinity or blood relationship. A Church of England report 1984 recommended the ending of this and some other prohibitions.

affinity in chemistry, the force of attraction between chemical elements, which thus helps to keep them in combination in a ◊molecule. A given element may have a greater affinity for one particular element than for another (for example, hydrogen has a great affinity for chlorine, with which it easily and rapidly combines to form hydrochloric acid, but has little or no affinity for argon).

affirmation a solemn declaration made instead of taking the oath by a person who has no religious belief or objects to taking an oath on religious grounds.

Afghan hound dog resembling the saluki, though less thickly coated, first introduced to Britain by army officers serving on the North-West Frontier in the late 19th century. It has an aloof, aristocratic expression, and in the 1970s became increasingly fashionable.

Afghanistan /æfˈɡænɪstɑːn/ mountainous, landlocked country in S central Asia, bounded by the USSR to the north, Iran to the west, and Pakistan to the south and east.

government the 1977 constitution was abolished after a coup in 1978 and legislative and executive authority was assumed by a 57-member revolutionary council, controlled by a smaller presidium of leaders from the only political party, the communist People's Democratic Party of Afghanistan (PDPA). In 1985 a national assembly *Loya Jirgah* of indirectly elected elders from various ethnic groups approved a new constitution, upholding the right to practise Islam and promising a directly elected national assembly in the future. Meanwhile, power rests with the Revolutionary Council and its permanent presidium, with day-to-day government administration in the hands of a council of ministers appointed by the Revolutionary Council.

history in the ancient world part of the Persian Empire, Afghanistan first became an independent emirate in 1747. During the 19th century three ◊Afghan Wars were fought to secure British interests in India and counter the growing Russian influence.

During the 1950s, Lieutenant-General Sardar Mohammad Daud Khan, cousin of King Mohammad Zahir Shah (ruled 1933–73), governed as prime minister and introduced a programme of social and economic modernization, with Soviet aid. Opposition to his authoritarian rule forced Daud's resignation in 1963; the king was made a constitutional monarch but political parties were outlawed.

After a famine in 1972, General Daud Khan overthrew the monarchy in a Soviet-backed military coup in 1973. The King fled to exile and a republic was declared. Daud introduced more moderate policies, built up support among minority ethnic groups and reduced Afghanistan's dependence on Russia by drawing closer to the ◊Non-Aligned and Middle East oil states (where many Afghans were employed). A new presidential constitution was adopted in 1977, although undermined by fundamentalist Muslim insurgents funded by Libya, Iran, and Pakistan.

In 1978 President Daud was assassinated in a military coup and Nur Mohammad Taraki, the imprisoned leader of the radical Khalq (masses) faction of the banned PDPA, took charge as president of a revolutionary council. A one-party constitution was adopted, a Treaty of Friendship and Mutual Defence signed with the USSR, and major reforms introduced. Conservative Muslims opposed these initiatives, thousands of refugees fled to Iran and Pakistan and there was an uprising in the Herat region. Taraki was replaced in 1979 by foreign minister Hafizullah Amin.

Internal unrest continued, and the USSR organized a further coup in Dec 1979. Hafizullah Amin was executed and Babrak Karmal (1929–), the exiled leader of the gradualist Parcham (banner) faction of the PDPA, was installed in power, an action condemned by many UN members and resulting in US sanctions against the USSR. The numbers of Soviet forces in Afghanistan grew to over 120,000 in 1985 as Muslim guerrilla resistance by the 'mujahadeen' ('holy warriors') continued. A war of attrition developed with the USSR launching regular land and air offensives, but failing to gain control of rural areas.

Faced with high troop casualties and a drain of economic resources, the new Soviet administration of ◊Gorbachev moved towards a compromise settlement in 1986. In May 1986 Karmal was replaced as PDPA leader by the Pushtun (Pathan) former secret police chief Dr Najibullah Ahmadzai (1947–), and several non-communist politicians joined the new government. Greater toleration towards Muslims was also seen and in Oct 1986, 8,000 Soviet troops were withdrawn as a goodwill gesture, followed in Jan 1987 by the Afghan government's announcement of a six-month unilateral cease-fire to facilitate the formation of a pro-Soviet 'coalition government of national unity'. The Afghan guerrillas rejected this initiative, however, insisting on a full Soviet withdrawal and replacement of the communist government. Since 1980 more than 5,000,000 Afghan refugees have settled in Iran and the NW Pakistan border region, while some 500,000 have died in the civil war.

Afghan Wars wars waged between Britain and Afghanistan to counter the threat to British India from expanding Russian influence in Afghanistan.

First Afghan War 1838–42, when the British garrison at Kabul was wiped out.

Second Afghan War 1878–80, when General Roberts captured Kabul and relieved Kandahar.

Third Afghan War 1919, when peace followed the despatch by Britain of the first aeroplane ever seen in Kabul.

Africa, Horn of /ˈæfrɪkə/ the projection constituted by Somalia and adjacent territories.

Africa /ˈæfrɪkə/ second largest of the continents, and three times the area of Europe.

area 30,097,000 sq km/11,617,000 sq mi

largest cities Cairo, Algiers, Lagos, Kinshasa, Abidjan, Tunis, Cape Town, Nairobi

physical dominated by a central plateau, which includes the world's largest desert (◊Sahara); Nile and Zaïre rivers, but generally there is a lack of rivers, and also of other inlets, so that Africa has proportionately the shortest coastline of all the continents; comparatively few offshore islands; 75% is within the tropics; Great Rift ◊Valley; immensely rich fauna and flora

exports has 30% of the world's minerals; crops include coffee (Kenya), cocoa (Ghana, Nigeria), cotton (Egypt, Uganda)

population (1984) 537,000,000; annual growth rate 3%

language Hamito-Semitic in the north; Bantu below the Sahara; Khoisian languages with 'click' consonants in the far south

religion Islam in the north; Animism below the Sahara, which survives alongside Christianity

Afghanistan

DEMOCRATIC REPUBLIC OF (*De Afghanistan Democrateek Jamhuriat*)

AREA 636,000 sq km/246,000 sq mi
CAPITAL Kabul
TOWNS Kandahár, Herát
PHYSICAL mountainous, with rivers and desert areas
FEATURES Hindu Kush mountain range (Khyber and Salang passes and Panjshir Valley)
HEAD OF STATE Najibullah Ahmadzai from 1986
HEAD OF GOVERNMENT Ali Keshtmand from 1981
GOVERNMENT one-party communist
EXPORTS dried fruit, rare minerals, natural gas (piped to USSR), karakul lamb skins, Afghan coats
CURRENCY afgháni (99.25 = £1 Sept 1987)
POPULATION (1985) 15,065,000 (more than 3 million have become refugees since 1979); annual growth rate 2.6%
LANGUAGE Pushtu
RELIGION Muslim: 80% Sunni, 20% Shi'ite
LITERACY 33% male/6% female (1980)
GDP $3.5 bn (1982); $168 per head of population
CHRONOLOGY
1747 Afghanistan became an independent emirate.
1838–1919 Afghan Wars waged between Afghanistan and Britain to counter the threat to British India from expanding Russian influence in Afghanistan.
1919 Afghanistan recovered full independence following Third Afghan War.
1953 Lt-Gen Daud Khan became prime minister and introduced reform programme.

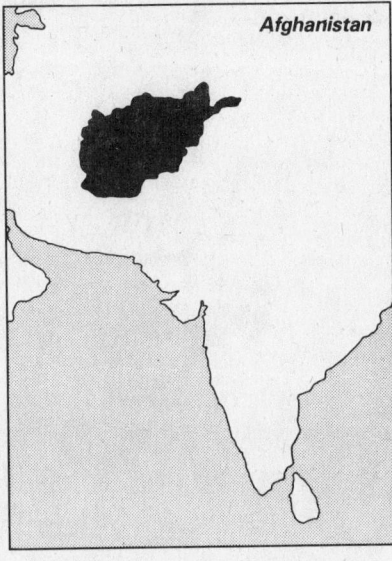

Afghanistan

1963 Daud Khan forced to resign and constitutional monarchy established.
1973 Monarchy overthrown in coup by Daud Khan.
1978 Daud Khan ousted by Taraki and the People's Democratic Party (PDP) of Afghanistan.
1979 Soviet invasion installed Babrak Karmal in power.
1986 Replacement of Karmal as leader by Dr Najibullah Ahmadzai. Partial Soviet troop withdrawal.
1987 Afghan government ceasefire offer.

(both Catholic and Protestant) in many central and southern areas.

African art the chief centres of art are in Nigeria, Zaïre, Ghana, the Ivory Coast, and the Republic of Cameroon. In S Nigeria the most notable works were produced by the people of Benin and of ancient Ife. The Beni used the *cire-perdue* process – as used in Italy during the Renaissance – in executing their bronze relief work. In Zaïre the Bakuba and Baluba peoples are famous for their decorative works such as ornamental spoons, bobbins, and head rests. The artists of the Bushango kingdom/15th–16th centuries produced beautiful wood-carvings, and also practised the art of portraiture, and the wooden statues of their early kings are notable. Among the most interesting products of Ghana are the brass weights from Ashanti. These are used for measuring gold-dust, and are made in the form of tiny figures which are said to illustrate local legends. The most skilful artists of the Ivory Coast are the people of Baoulé, who are closely related to the Ashanti peoples. Wood-carvings, drinking cups, basketry, statues, and masks are among the artefacts of the people of the

Cameroons. The masks of the Cross River are particularly famous for their realism.
The indigenous art of W Africa, remarkable for its beauty of form and intense vitality, has had a profound influence on the work of many European artists in the 20th century, such as ◊Picasso, ◊Matisse, ◊Brancusi, ◊Modigliani, and ◊Epstein.

African National Congress (ANC) multiracial nationalist organization formed in South Africa 1912 to extend the franchise to the whole population and end all racial discrimination there. Although nonviolent, it was banned by the government in 1960, and in exile in Mozambique developed a military wing, *Umkhonto we Sizwe*, which has engaged in sabotage and guerrilla training. The ANC is now based in Lusaka, Zambia, and its leader in exile is Oliver ◊Tambo; former ANC leaders include Albert ◊Luthuli, Nelson ◊Mandela, and Solomon Plaatje (1877–1932). It is supported by the Organization of African Unity as a movement aimed at introducing majority rule in South Africa.

African violet herbaceous plant *Saintpaulia ionantha* from tropical central and E Africa, with

velvety green leaves and scentless purple flowers. A popular house plant, other colours and 'double' varieties have been bred.

Afrikaans language along with English, an official language of the Republic of South Africa. Spoken mainly by the Afrikaners, descendants of Dutch and other 17th century colonists, it is a variety of the Dutch language, modified by circumstance and the influence of German, French, and other immigrant and local languages. It became a standardized written language c. 1875.

Afrika Korps the German army in the Western Desert of North Africa in World War II 1941–43. They first came into contact with British troops at El Agheila on 24 March 1941, but were driven out of North Africa by May 1943.

Afrikaner white, Afrikaans-speaking citizen of S Africa; usually of ◊Boer descent.

after-burning method of increasing the thrust of a gas turbine (jet) aero engine by spraying additional fuel between the turbojet and the tail pipe. Used for short-term increase of power during take-off or combat in military aircraft.

after-image persistence of an image on the retina of the ◊eye after the object producing it has been removed, which leads to persistence of vision, a necessary phenomenon for the illusion of continuous movement in films (cinema) and television. The colours of an after-image are often complementary ('opposite') to those producing it.

after-ripening the process undergone by seeds of some plants before germination can occur. The length of the after-ripening period may vary from a few weeks to many months, depending on the species, and helps to ensure that seeds germinate at a time when conditions are most favourable for growth. In some cases the embryo is not fully mature at the time of dispersal and must develop further before germination can take place. However, other seeds do not germinate even when the embryo is mature, probably owing to growth-inhibitors within the seed which must be leached out or broken down before germination can begin.

Aga title of nobility, probably of ◊Tatar derivation. The Turks applied it to military commanders and, in general, to men of high station.

Agadir /ˌægəˈdɪə/ most southern seaport in Morocco; near the mouth of the river Sus. Population (1984) 62,300. It was destroyed by an earthquake in 1960, but was rebuilt.

Agadir Incident demand in 1911 by William II of Germany, expressed by sending the gunboat *Panther*, for territorial concessions in Morocco from France – hence 'gunboat diplomacy'.

Aga Khan IV /ˈɑːɡə ˈkɑːn/ 1936– . Spiritual head of the ◊Ismaili Muslim sect. He succeeded his grandfather in 1957.

agama type of ◊lizard. There are about 280 varied species in the agama family, living in Africa, Asia, and Australia. The typical *Agama stellio* in the Near East is 30 cm/1 ft long, can change colour, and feeds on insects.

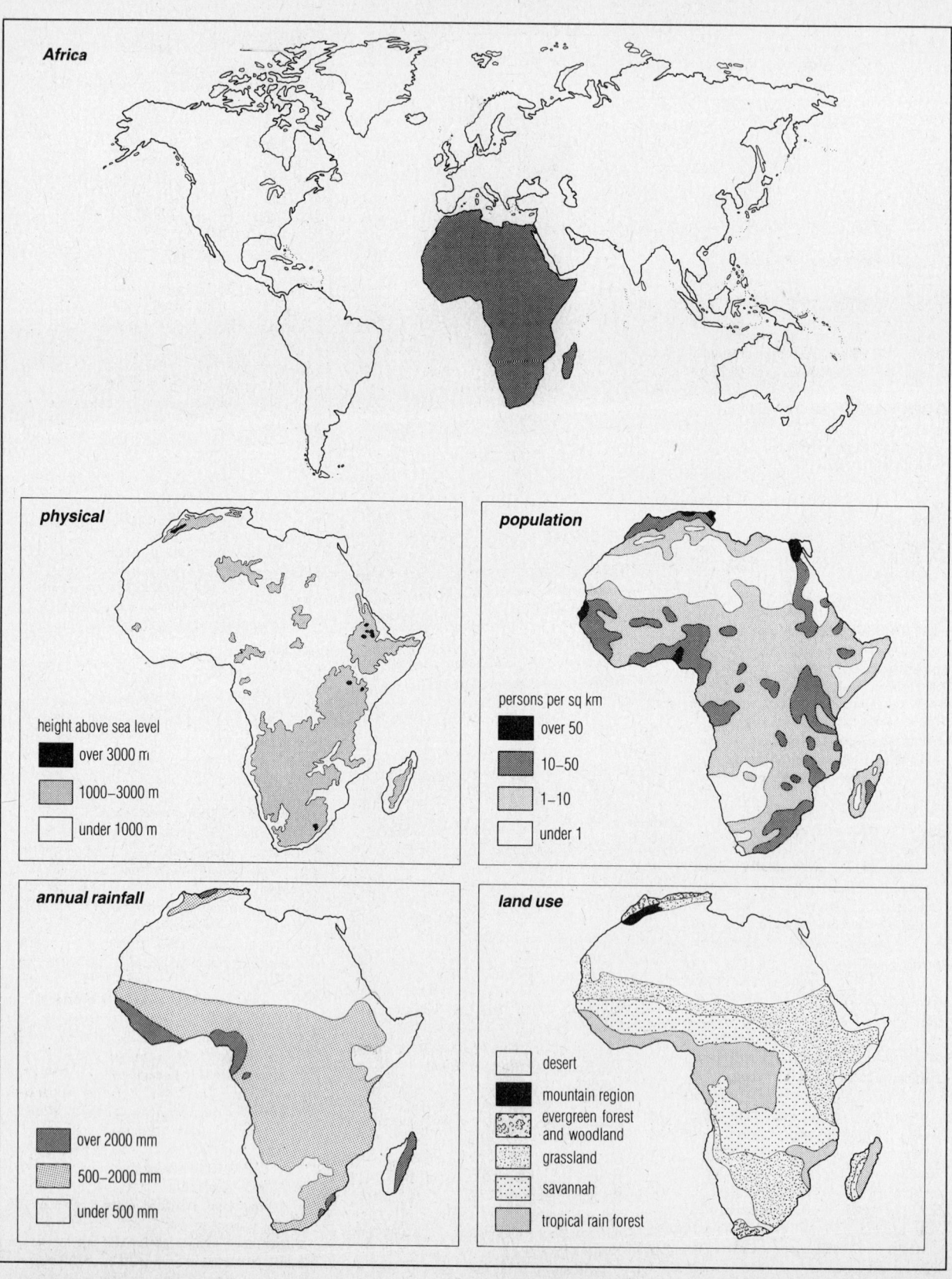

Africa

physical

height above sea level

■ over 3000 m

▨ 1000–3000 m

☐ under 1000 m

population

persons per sq km

■ over 50

▨ 10–50

☐ 1–10

☐ under 1

annual rainfall

▨ over 2000 mm

▨ 500–2000 mm

☐ under 500 mm

land use

☐ desert

■ mountain region

▨ evergreen forest and woodland

☐ grassland

☐ savannah

▨ tropical rain forest

AFRICA: HISTORY

BC

14 million	Africa, which is considered the 'cradle-continent', probably produced the first human-like creatures.
3–5 million	Direct line of descent of modern humans was established in East Africa.
15,000	Agriculture first practised in Egypt.
10,000–2000	The originally fertile Sahara became a barrier desert between north and south.
5450–2500	Era of Saharan rock and cave paintings.
7th cent. BC *6th cent. AD*	Assyria, Persia, Greece, Rome, and Byzantium in turn made conquests in North Africa. Meroe: the Egyptian and Negro tradition met in the Nubian kingdom of Kush.
320–50	The kingdom of Axum flourished in Ethiopia, and gave rise to the later legend of Prester John.
640	Islamic expansion began in North, East and Central Africa.
300–1500	Period of the great medieval states: Ghana, Mali, Songhai, Benin, Ife, and the culture of Great Zimbabwe.
12–15th cent.	Era of the Arab travellers: Ibn Batuta; and of trade, Kilwa.
1488	Diaz rounded the Cape of Good Hope.
15–16th cent.	European sea trade in gold, ivory, timber, and pepper.
17–19th cent.	Height of the Atlantic and Indian Ocean slave trade.
18–19th cent.	European travellers in Africa: Park, Livingstone, Stanley, Speke, Mary Kingsley.
19th cent.	Colonial wars against organized native states: Ashanti, Dahomey, Zululand.
1880–90	Peak of European colonization in the 'scramble for Africa'.
1899–1902	South African War, the first large-scale war between whites in Africa.
1920	League of Nations mandate system introduced the idea of European trusteeship.
1936	Italy's conquest of Ethiopia.
1942	World War II reached its turning point in the Battles of Alamein.
1951	Libya became the first independent state to be declared by the United Nations.
1954–62	Civil war in Algeria precipitated end of French Fourth Republic in 1958.
1957	Ghana became independent, the first of the revived black nation states.
1952–60	Mau-Mau movement in Kenya began the ousting of white settlers south of the Sahara.
1963	Organization of African Unity founded.
1967–70	Revolt of Biafra within the federation of Nigeria constituted the first civil war in a modern black state.
1975	Mozambique's independence led to the end of dictatorship in Portugal.
1979	Zimbabwe's achievement of independence left S Africa as the last white-ruled state in Africa.
1980	Future of the OAU doubtful due to division over Western Sahara and Libyan aggression towards Chad. Extensive food shortages in many parts of Central and East Africa.
1984	Increasing internal disaster in South Africa leading to violence between black population and minority white groups.

Agamemnon /ˌægəˈmemnən/ in Greek mythology, a Greek hero, son of Atreus, King of Mycenae. He married Clytemnestra, and their children included Electra, Iphigenia, and Orestes. Setting out from Aulis to the Trojan War, he would have sacrificed Iphigenia to Artemis to secure fair winds (she was saved by the godess and made a priestess). He led the capture of Troy, received Priam's daughter Cassandra as a prize, and was murdered by Clytemnestra and her lover, Aegisthus, on his return home. Orestes and Electra later killed the guilty couple. Aeschylus, Euripides, T S Eliot, O'Neill and Sartre all based plays on the theme.

Agaña /əˈgɑːnjə/ capital of Guam, island in the West Pacific; population (1981) 110,000.

agar jelly-like substance obtained from seaweed and used mainly as a culture medium in biology and medicine for growing bacteria and other micro-organisms.

agaric type of ◊fungus, the typical 'mushroom', with a rounded cap with radially arranged gills and central stalk. Agarics include the *field mushroom Agaricus campestris* and the **horse mushroom Agaricus arvensis.** The *fly agaric Amanita muscaria* is a familiar poisonous toadstool, with a white-spotted red cap, growing under birch or pine.

agate a banded or cloudy type of silica, SiO_2, used to form ornamental stones and objects of art. Agate stones are used to burnish and polish gold deposited on glass and ceramics.

agave plant with stiff sword-shaped spiny leaves arranged in a rosette. All species of the genus Agave come from the warmer parts of the New World. They include ◊sisal, and the Mexican *century plant Agave americana* which may take many years to mature, then throws up a tall flowering stalk before dying. Alcoholic drinks such as ◊tequila and pulque are made from agave sap.

ageing in common usage, the period of deterioration of the physical condition of a living organism that leads to death; but in biological terms, the entire life-process, beginning at the moment when an egg is fertilized and starts to develop into a new individual, and continuing to its eventual death. Three current theories attempt to account for ageing. The first suggests that the process is genetically determined, to remove individuals that can no longer reproduce by causing their death. The second suggests that it is due to the accumulation of mistakes during the replication of ◊DNA at cell division. The third suggests that it is actively induced by pieces of DNA which move between cells, or cancer-causing viruses; these may become abundant in old cells and induce them to produce unwanted ◊proteins or interfere with the control functions of their DNA.

agglutination in medicine, the clumping together of ◊antigens, such as blood cells or bacteria, to form larger, visible masses, under the influence of ◊antibodies. As each antigen clumps only in response to its particular antibody, agglutination provides a way of determining ◊blood groups and the identity of unknown bacteria.

ageing A photograph of Shigechyo Izumi at 115 years of age, when he was the oldest of Japan's centenarians and possibly the world's oldest man. There are theories to explain ageing, but no evidence yet that it can be prevented.

Agincourt, Battle of Scene of the Battle of Agincourt, taken from the *St Albans Chronicle*. At this famous battle, in 1415, the English under Henry V routed the superior French forces.

aggression in biology, behaviour used to intimidate or injure another organism (of the same or of a different species), usually for the purposes of gaining a territory, a mate or food. Aggression often involves an escalating series of threats aimed at intimidating an opponent, without having to engage in physical contact that might cause itself injury. Examples include roaring in red deer, snarling by dogs, fluffing up the feathers in birds and of raising the fins in some species of fish. Such signals allow the individual to assess the strength of an opponent and so decide whether to risk a fight. Many species use specialized structures during aggression, such as antlers in deer, or display plumage such as crests in birds. Most interactions end with one individual submitting or withdrawing before physical battle occurs: 'fights to the death' are rare in nature.

Agincourt, Battle of /'ædʒɪnkɔː/ battle in which ◊Henry V of England defeated the French on 24 Oct 1415, St Crispin's Day. The village of Agincourt is south of Calais, in northern France.

Agnew /'ægnju:/ Spiro 1918– . American vice-president 1969–73. A Republican, he was governor of Maryland 1966–69, and vice-president under Nixon. He resigned in 1973, shortly before pleading 'no contest' to a charge of income tax evasion.

Agni /'ʌgni/ in Hindu mythology, the god of fire, the guardian of homes, and the protector of humans against the powers of darkness.

Agnon /'ægnɒn/ Shmuel Yosef 1888–1970. Israeli novelist. Born in Buczacz, Galicia (now in the USSR), the setting of his most famous book *A Guest for the Night*, he shared a Nobel prize 1966.

agnostic word coined by T H Huxley in 1869 for a person believing that we cannot know anything beyond the world of natural phenomena. It would seem he had in mind the Greek words *Agnosto theo* (To an unknown God) found inscribed on an altar in Athens. An ◊atheist denies the existence of gods or God; an agnostic asserts that God or a First Cause is one of those concepts – others include the Absolute, Infinity, Eternity, and Immortality – which lie beyond the reach of human intelligence.

agoraphobia a ◊phobia involving fear of open spaces and crowded places.

Agostini /ˌɑːgəˈstiːni/ Giacomo 1943– . Italian motor cycle road race rider. He made his reputation during the 1960s and went on to win a record 15 world titles 1966–75. He was 500cc champion seven times in succession 1966–72 and won a record 122 world championship races.

agouti type of small rodent, genus *Dasyprocta*, found in the forests of Central and South America. They are herbivorous, swift-running, and about the size of a rabbit.

AGR abbreviation for advanced gas-cooled reactor, a type of ◊nuclear reactor widely used in Britain. The first two AGR stations became operational at Hinkley Point and Hunterston in 1976. They each have a power output of 1320 megawatts from twin reactors.
The AGR uses a fuel of enriched uranium dioxide in stainless steel cladding and a moderator of graphite. Carbon dioxide gas is pumped through the reactor core to extract the heat produced by the ◊fission of the uranium. The heat is transferred to water in a steam generator, and the steam drives a turbogenerator to produce electricity.

Agra /'ɑːgrə/ city of Uttar Pradesh, republic of India, on the river Jumna, 160 km/100 mi south east of Delhi. It is a commercial and university centre. Population (1981) 747,318.
history ◊Baber, the first great Mogul ruler, made Agra his capital in 1527. His grandson Akbar rebuilt the Red Fort of Salim Shah (1566), and is buried outside the city in the splendid tomb at Sigandra. In the 17th century the buildings of ◊Shah Jehan made Agra one of the most beautiful cities in the world. The Taj Mahal, erected as a tomb for the emperor's wife Mumtaz Mahal, took more than 20 years to build, and was completed in 1650. Agra's political importance dwindled from 1658, when Aurangzeb moved the capital back to Delhi. It was taken from the Mahrattas by Lord Lake in 1803.

Agricola /əˈgrɪkələ/ Gnaeus Julius 37–93 AD. Roman general and statesman. Born in Provence, he became Consul in 77 AD, and then governor of Britain 78–85 AD. He extended Roman rule to the Firth of Forth in Scotland, and won the battle of Mons Graupius (site uncertain, but in the ◊Grampian mountains), before being recalled by ◊Domitian, who had grown jealous. His fleet sailed round the north of Scotland and proved Britain an island. His daughter married the historian ◊Tacitus in 78 AD.

agriculture cultivation of land by people, developed in Egypt at least 7,000 years ago. Its

advanced gas-cooled (AGR) reactor

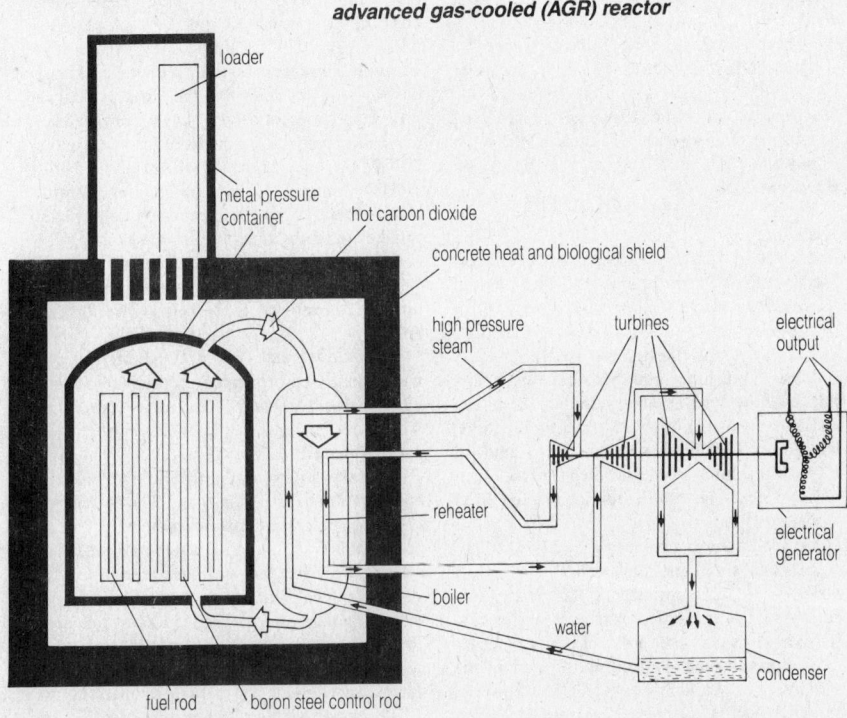

loader

metal pressure container

hot carbon dioxide

concrete heat and biological shield

high pressure steam

turbines

electrical output

reheater

electrical generator

boiler

water

condenser

fuel rod   boron steel control rod

modernization began in 18th-century Britain, and its mechanization in 19th-century USA.

There are two main categories – raising ◊crops and raising animals. Crops are for human nourishment, animal fodder, or commodity crops such as cotton and sisal. Animals are raised for wool, milk, leather, dung (as fuel) or meat.

For plant products, the land must be prepared (ploughing, cultivating, harrowing and rolling). Seed must be planted and the growing plant nurtured. This may involve fertilizers, irrigation, pest control (pesticides, fungicides, herbicides and insecticides), and monitoring of acidity or nutrients. When the crop has grown, it must be harvested, the grain separated from the rest of the plant, and sent for further processing or to market.

Greenhouses allow plants to be cultivated that would otherwise find the climate too harsh. Hydroponics allows commercial cultivation of crops using nutrient-enriched solutions and not soil. Special methods may be adopted to allow cultivation in hostile terrain, such as terracing, to retain topsoil in mountainous areas with heavy rainfall, and paddy fields, for growing rice.

Animals may be semi-domesticated, such as reindeer, domesticated but nomadic (particularly where food supplies are sparse), or static. Animal farming involves accommodation (buildings or pasture), feeding, breeding, gathering the produce (eggs, milk, or wool), slaughtering, and further processing (such as butchery or tanning).

The units for managing agricultural production vary from crofting, small holdings and farms to

collective farms run by entire communities. Scientific knowledge of soil mechanics and plant and animal breeding must be combined with awareness of markets, and can be critically affected by government subsidies.

Following World War II, there was an explosive growth in agricultural chemicals – herbicides, insecticides, fungicides, and fertilizers, in the 1960s there was development of high-yielding species for special conditions, especially in the *green revolution* in the Third World, and in the industrialized countries cattle and poultry production on 'production lines' and battery systems. In the 1970s there was a movement towards more sophisticated natural methods and a reversion to *organic farming* without chemical sprays and fertilizers whose continued use become essential as fertility declines. In the 1980s hybridization by genetic engineering methods was developed, and pest control by the use of chemicals plus ◊pheromones.

The greatest efficiencies in agriculture thus achieved, coupled with postwar government subsidies for domestic production, especially in US and EEC, has led to overpriced overproduction and the development of high stocks, nicknamed 'lakes' (wine, milk) or 'mountains' (butter, beef, grain). The solution to this problem is intractable, as any large-scale dumping displaces regular merchandise. In the EEC, a quota system for milk production coupled with price controls has driven small uneconomic producers out of business, but the slaughter of dairy cattle affects the price of beef, which is also subsidized. Increasing public outrage at the cost

of storage has led the EEC to discuss measures, including the possibility of letting arable land lie fallow to reduce the grain mountain (Dec 1986), but environmental outcry may be expected if the land is turned over to building development or conifer plantations that rapidly denutrify the soil. The US has had some success at selling wheat to the USSR when its crop is poor, but the cost of bulk transport acts against the producers exporting excess production on a regular basis.

Agrigento /ˌægrɪˈdʒentəʊ/ town in Sicily, noted for Greek temples; population 55,000. The Roman Agrigentum, it was long called Girgenti until renamed Agrigento in 1927 under the Fascist regime.

agrimony herbaceous plant *Agrimonia eupatoria* of the rose family, with small yellow flowers in a slender spike, growing in hedgebanks and fields.

Agrippa /əˈgrɪpə/ Marcus Vipsanius 63–12 BC. Roman general. He commanded the victorious fleet at ◊Actium and married Julia, daughter of ◊Augustus.

agronomy study of crops and soils, a branch of agricultural science. It includes such topics as selective breeding (of plants and animals), irrigation, pest control, and soil analysis and its modification -always with a view to improving the health and yields of crops and farm animals.

Aguascalientes /ˌægwəskælɪˈenteɪs/ city in central Mexico, with hot springs; population (1980) 359,454.

Agulhas /əˈgʌləs/ southernmost cape in Africa, South Africa.

Ahab /ˈeɪhæb/ King of Israel c. 875–854 BC. His empire included the suzerainty of Moab, and Judah was his subordinate ally; but his kingdom was weakened by constant wars with Syria. By his marriage with Jezebel, princess of Sidon, Ahab was led to introduce into Israel the worship of the Phoenician god Baal, thus provoking the hostility of Elija and the prophets. Ahab died in battle against the Syrians at Ramoth Gilead.

Ahaggar /əˈhægə/ mountainous plateau of the central Sahara, Algeria, whose highest point, Tahat, about 3,000 m/9,850 ft, lies between Algiers and the mouth of the Niger. It is the home of the formerly nomadic Tuaregs.

Ahasuerus /əˌhæzjuˈɪərəs/ Latinized Hebrew form of the Persian Khshayarsha (Greek *Xerxes*). Name given to several Persian kings in the Bible, notably to the husband of Esther. Traditionally it was also the name of the ◊Wandering Jew.

ahimsa in ◊Hinduism, ◊Buddhism, and especially ◊Jainism, rule of respect for all life, and consequently non-violence. It arises in part from the concept of ◊reincarnation .

Ahmadabad /ˈɑːmədəbɑːd/ or *Ahmedabad* capital of Gujerat, India; population (1981) 2,515,195. It has many edifices of the Hindu, Muslim, and Jain faiths.

history Ahmadabad was founded in the reign of Ahmad Shah in 1412, and came under the control of the East India Company in 1818. ◊Gandhi marched to the sea from here in 1930 to protest against the government salt monopoly.

Ahmadiyya /ˌɑːməˈdiːə/ Islamic religious movement founded by Mirza Ghulam Ahmad

(1839–1908). His followers reject the doctrine that Muhammad was the last of the prophets and accept Ahmad's claim to be the Mahdi and Promised Messiah. In 1974 the Ahmadis were denounced by their coreligionists as non-Muslims.

Ahmadnagar /ˌɑːməd'nʌɡə/ city in Maharashtra, India, 195 km/120 mi east of Bombay, on the left bank of the river Sina. It is a centre of cotton trade and manufacture. Population (1981) 181,210.

Ahmad Shah /'ɑːmæd 'ʃɑː/ 1724–1773. first ruler of Afghanistan. Elected king in 1747, he had made himself master of the Punjab◊ by 1751. He defeated the Mahrattas at Panipat in 1761, and then the Sikhs.

Ahriman /'ɑːrɪmən/ in ◊Zoroastrianism, the supreme evil spirit, Lord of the darkness and death, waging eternal war with ◊Ahura Mazda (Ormuzd).

Ahura Mazda (Ormuzd) /ə'huərə 'mæzdə, 'ɔːməzd/ in ◊Zoroastrianism, the spirit of supreme good. As god of life and light, he will finally prevail over his enemy, Ahriman.

Ahvenanmaa Island /'ɑːvənənmɑː/ island in the Gulf of Bothnia, Finland. See ◊Aland Islands.

Ahwaz /ɑː'wɑːz/ capital of the Arab province of Khuzestan, Iran; population 329,000.

Aidan, Saint /'eɪdn/ c. 600–651. Irish monk from Iona who converted Northumbria to Christianity and founded Lindisfarne monastery on Holy Island. He died at Bamburgh. His feast day is 31 August.

AIDS *A*cquired *I*mmune *D*eficiency *S*yndrome, a disease marked by weight loss, diarrhoea, swollen glands, and resulting in the destruction of the body's immune system, leaving it vulnerable to infection by viruses and bacteria. It is as yet incurable. Identified 1980, it is caused by a blood-borne virus (HIV, Human Immuno-deficiency Virus). It is transmitted by sexual contact; by shared syringes among drug users; and by infected blood products. In Britain, AIDS patients in a condition dangerous to others, for example bleeding badly, may be legally detained in hospital under a Public Health Act of 1984.

Aigun, Treaty of /'aɪɡuːn/ treaty between Russia and China signed in 1858 at the port of Aigun in China on the Amur river. It ceded the left bank to Russia, but has since been repudiated by China.

Aiken /'eɪkən/ Conrad Potter 1899–1973. American poet and novelist; associated with the ◊Imagist movement; his novel *Great Circle* 1933 reflects his own life (when he was a boy, his father committed suicide after killing Aiken's mother).

Aiken /'eɪkən/ Howard 1900– . US mathematician. He began work in 1937 on the first electro-mechanical computer, which incorporated many features retained in modern models, and initiated the concept of 'time-sharing'. He became director of Harvard Computation Laboratory in 1946.

aikido one of the ◊martial arts.

Ailsacraig /'eɪlsə 'kreɪɡ/ rocky islet in the Firth of Clyde, Scotland, about 16 km/10 mi off the coast of Strathclyde, opposite Girvan. It is famous as a breeding ground for birds.

Ain /æn/ French river giving its name to a *département* (administrative region); it is a right-bank tributary of the Rhône.

Ainsworth /'eɪnzwɜːθ/ William Harrison 1805–1882. British historical novelist. He produced in all some 40 novels and helped popularize the legends of Dick ◊Turpin in *Rookwood* 1834 and ◊Herne the Hunter in *Windsor Castle* 1834.

Aintab /aɪn'tɑːb/ Syrian name of ◊Gaziantep.

Aintree /'eɪntriː/ racecourse, Liverpool, Merseyside; its most famous race is the *Grand National* steeplechase (established in 1839) in Mar/Apr, over 7 km 242 m/4 mi 880 yd, with 30 formidable jumps. See ◊horse-racing.

Ainu /'aɪnu/ aboriginal people of Japan; fair-skinned, blue-eyed, and hairy. In the 4th century AD they were driven out by the modern Japanese, but some 16,000 survive on the island of Hokkaido. Ainu women are noted for their blue-tattooed lips. The Ainu language has few links with any other.

air see under ◊atmosphere.

airbrush small fine spray gun used by artists and photographic retouchers. Driven by air-pressure from a compressor or pressurized can, it can apply a very even layer of ink or paint.

air conditioning controlling the state of the air inside a building or vehicle. American inventor W H Carrier developed the first effective air-conditioning unit in 1902 for a New York printing plant.
A complete air-conditioning unit controls the temperature and ◊humidity of the air, removes dust and odours from it and circulates it by means of a fan. The air in an air conditioner is cooled by a kind of ◊refrigeration unit comprising a compressor and a condenser. It is heated by electrically heated wires, or in large systems, pipes heated by hot water or steam. The air is cleaned by means of filters and activated charcoal. The air may be humidified by circulating it over pans of water or through a water spray. Moisture can be extracted by condensation on cool metal plates.
A specialized air-conditioning system is installed in spacecraft as part of the life-support system. This includes the provision of oxygen to breathe and the removal of exhaled carbon dioxide.

aircraft aeronautical vehicle, which may be lighter than air (supported by buoyancy) or heavier than air (supported by the dynamic action of air on its surfaces). Balloons and airships are lighter-than-air craft. Heavier-than-air craft include the ◊aeroplane, glider and helicopter.

aircraft carrier sea-going base for aircraft. Although ships were used to carry aircraft in World War I, the first purpose-designed aircraft carrier was HMS *Hermes*, completed 1913. In World War II the most famous was HMS *Ark Royal* completed 1938; repeatedly falsely claimed as sunk by the Axis powers, it was eventually torpedoed off Gibraltar, foundering in tow Nov 1941. After World War II the cost and vulnerability of such large vessels was considered to outweigh their advantages, and they were built only by the USSR (such as

Komsomolec 1979, 40,000 tonnes, 15 fixed-wing aircraft, 20 helicopters) and the USA (such as *Eisenhower* 1979, 81,600 tonnes, 95 aircraft). By 1980, however, the need to have a means of destroying aircraft beyond the range of a ship's own weapons, especially on convoy duty, had led to a widespread revival of aircraft carriers in the 20–30,000 tonne range (HMS *Invincible* 1980, 19,500 tonnes). They are equipped with combinations of fixed-wing aircraft, helicopters, missile launchers and anti-aircraft guns.

air cushion vehicle (ACV) a craft that is supported by a layer, or cushion of high-pressure air. The ◊hovercraft is the best-known form of ACV.

Airedale terrier /'eədeɪl/ large ◊terrier dog with a rough red-brown coat. It originated about 1850 in the Aire and Wharfedale districts of Yorkshire, England, as a cross of the otter hound and Irish and Welsh terriers.

air force a nation's fighting aircraft, and the organization to maintain them. The emergence of the aeroplane at first brought only limited recognition of its potential value as a means of waging war; like the balloon, used from the American Civil War, it was considered a way of extending the vision of surface forces. The need for a unified Air Force – foreseen in the United Kingdom in 1911–was realized with the formation of the RAF in 1918 by merging the Royal Naval Air Service and the Royal Flying Corps. During the inter-war period, unity of air control was achieved by Italy (1923), France (1928), Germany (1935, after repudiating the arms limitations of the Versailles treaty), and by the USA in 1947. While the main specialized groupings formed during World War I – such as combat, bombing, reconnaissance, and transport – were adapted and modified in World War II, activity was extended, with self-contained tactical Air Forces to meet the needs of surface commanders in the main theatres of land operations; and for the attack and defence of shipping over narrow seas. In 1945–60 the piston engine was superseded by the jet engine which propelled its craft at supersonic speeds; extremely precise electronic guidance systems lessened the difference between missile and aircraft; and flights of unlimited duration became a reality by means of air-to-air refuelling. Together with Polaris-armed submarines, the 24 hour-a-day patrol of the United States strategic air command's bombers armed with thermonuclear weapons, constitute the West's main ultimate deterrents. It was fomerly anticipated that even the pilot might become obsolete, but the continuation of conventional warfare, and the evolution of tactical nuclear weapons, has led in the 1960s and 1970s to the development of advanced combat aircraft able to fly supersonically beneath an enemy's radar on strike and reconnaissance missions, for example, the Phantom FGR2 and Jaguar.

airglow a faint and variable light in the earth's ◊atmosphere produced by chemical reactions in the ionosphere.

air lock airtight chamber that allows people to pass to and from air at ordinary pressure and

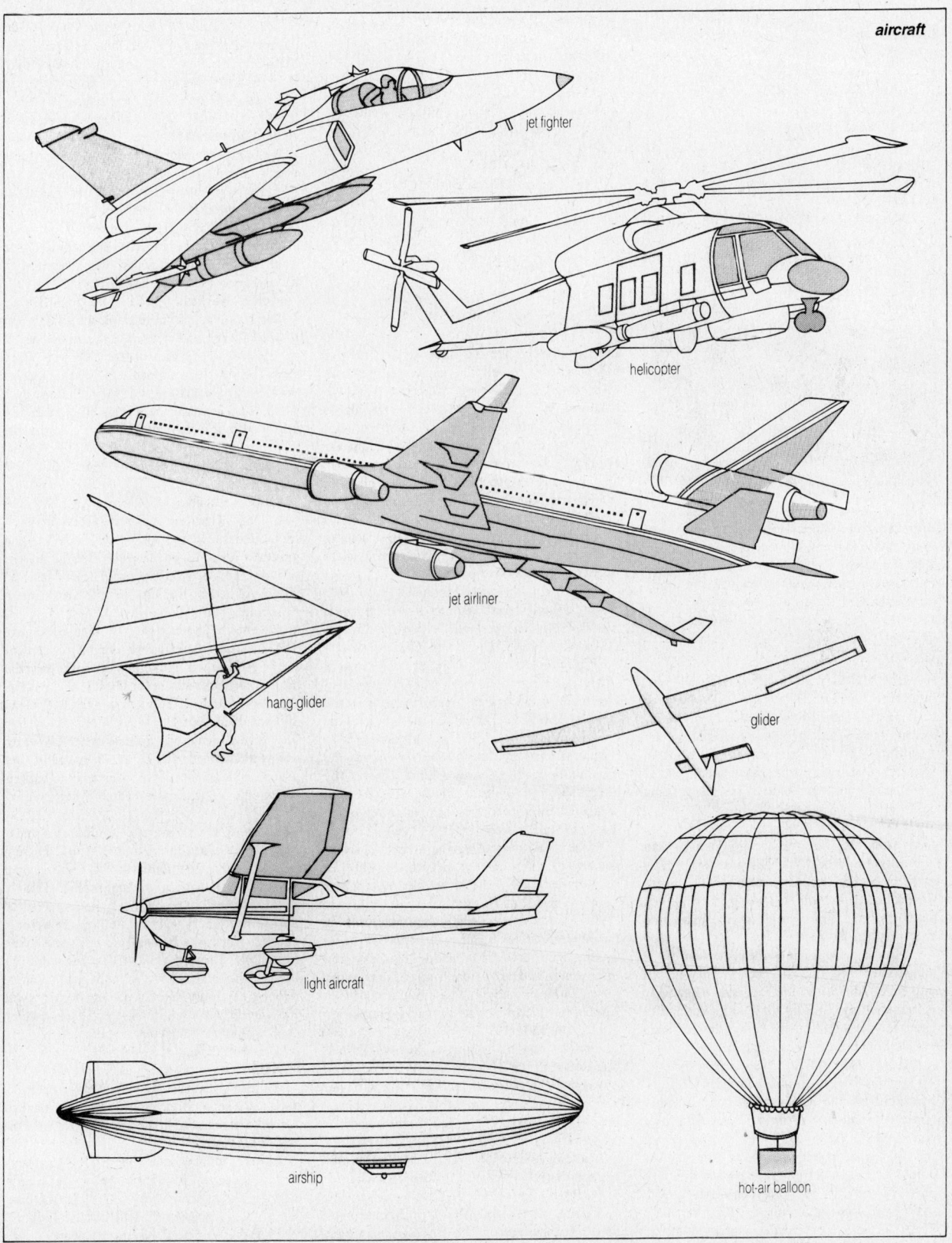

jet fighter

helicopter

jet airliner

hang-glider

glider

light aircraft

airship

hot-air balloon

aircraft carrier HMS Invincible, 1980, was used by the British in the war in the Falkland Islands in 1982. Carriers of this class, about 20,000 tonnes, have a speed of 28 knots and are designed to carry eight Sea Harrier aircraft and ten Sea King helicopters. They are armed with Sea Dart missiles.

an area that has high air pressure (such as a submerged caisson used for tunnelling or building dams and bridge foundations). An air lock may also permit someone wearing breathing apparatus to pass into an area with no air at all (as into water from a submerged submarine or into the vacuum of space from an orbiting spacecraft).

air pollution see ◊pollution.

air raid aerial attack, usually on a civilian population. In World War II, raids were usually made by bomber aircraft, but many thousands were killed in London in 1944 by German V1 and V2 rockets. The air raids on Britain became known as 'the Blitz'.

air sac in birds, a thin-walled extension of the lungs. There are nine of these and they extend into the abdomen and bones, effectively increasing lung capacity. In mammals, another name for the alveoli in the ◊lungs and, in some insects, widenings of the ◊tracheae.

airship essentially a power-driven ◊balloon. All airships have streamlined envelopes or hulls, which contain the inflation gas, and are either non-rigid, semi-rigid or rigid. Count Ferdinand von Zeppelin (1838–1917) was the pioneer of the rigid type, named after him, and used for bombing raids on Britain in World War I. The destruction by fire of the British R101 in 1930 led to a cessation of airship building in Britain. The Germans continued building airships, including the 248 m/812 ft long *Hindenburg*. In 1937, however, this airship exploded at

air sac

Lakehurst, New Jersey, marking the effective end of airship travel. The early airships were vulnerable because they used hydrogen for inflation. It is the lightest gas, but highly flammable. Since World War II, now that large supplies of the non-flammable gas helium are available, there has been renewed interest in airships which cause minimum noise pollution, can lift enormous loads, and are economical on fuel. The products of Britain's Airship Industries have been among the most successful, with large orders in 1987 from the US Navy for airships to be used for coastguard patrols.

Airy /'eəri/ George Biddell 1801–1892. Seventh English Astronomer Royal. Born in Alnwick, Northumberland, he became director of the Cambridge University Observatory in 1828, and took the post of Astronomer Royal in 1835. At Greenwich he installed a transit ◊telescope for accurately measuring time by the stars. The position of this instrument defines the Greenwich meridian, internationally accepted as the line of zero longitude in 1884. Airy began the distribution of Greenwich time signals by telegraph, and ◊Greenwich Mean Time as measured by Airy's telescope was adopted as legal time in Britain in 1880.

Aisne /eɪn/ river of northern France, giving its name to a *département*. Length: 282 km/175 mi. For the Battle of the Aisne, see ◊World War I and ◊World War II.

Aix-en-Provence /'eɪks ɒm prə'vɒns/ town in the *département* of Bouches-du-Rhône, France, 29 km/18 mi north of Marseilles. It is the capital of Provence, and dates from Roman times. It has a fine Gothic cathedral and a university (1409). The painter ◊Cézanne was born here. Population (1982) 124,550.

Aix-la-Chapelle /'eɪks læ ʃæ'pel/ French name of ◊Aachen.

Aix-les-Bains /'eɪks leɪ 'bæn/ spa with hot springs in the *département* of Savoie, France, near Lake Bourget, 13 km/8 mi north of Chambéry. Population (1982) 22,534.

Ajaccio /æ'ʒæksɪəʊ/ capital of Corsica and birthplace of ◊Napoleon; it has been French since 1768. Population (1982) 55,279.

Ajanta /ə'dʒʌntə/ village in Maharashtra state, India, famous for its Buddhist cave temples, dating from 200 BC to 7th century AD, first described by J Ferguson in 1843.

Ajax /'eɪdʒæks/ Greek hero in ◊Homer. Son of Telamon, king of Salamis, he was second only to Achilles among the Greek heroes in the Trojan War. When Agamemnon awarded the armour of the dead Achilles to Odysseus, Ajax is said to have gone mad with jealousy, and then committed suicide in shame.

Ajman /'ædʒmɑːn/ one of the seven states which make up the ◊United Arab Emirates.

Ajmer /ɑːdʒ'mɪə/ town of Rajasthan state, India. Situated in a deep valley in the Aravalli mountains. It has many ancient remains, notably a Jain temple. It was formerly the capital of the small state of Ajmer, which was merged with Rajasthan in 1956. Population (1981) 375,593.

ajolote Mexican reptile of the genus *Bipes*. Like other members of the amphisbaenian group it lives underground, but unlike the others, which have no legs, has a pair of front legs which are short but well-developed. In line with its burrowing habits the skull is very solid, the eyes small, and external ears absent. The scales are arranged in rings, giving the body a worm-like appearance.

Akaba /'ækəbə/ alternative transliteration of ◊Aqaba.

Akbar /'ækbɑː/ Jellaladin Mohammed 1542–1605. Greatest of the Mogul emperors of India. He succeeded his father in 1556, and gradually established his rule throughout the whole of India N of the Deccan. The firmness and wisdom of his rule won him the title 'Guardian of Mankind'.

A Kempis, Thomas see ◊Thomas á Kempis.

Akhetaton /ˌækɪ'tɑːtɒn/ capital of ancient Egypt established by the monotheistic pharaoh ◊Ikhnaton as the centre for his cult of the Aten, the sun's disc; it is the modern Tell el Amarna 300 km/190 mi south of Cairo. His palace had fine, formal enclosed gardens. After his death it was abandoned, and the *Amarna tablets* are probably the contents of the 'wastepaper' baskets of his officials, such as outdated 'foreign office' letters.

Akhmatova /æk'mætəvə/ Anna, pen name of Anna Andreevna Gorenko 1889–1966. Russian poet. She achieved fame in the 1920s with several collections of poetry in the realist style of ◊Mandelstam, but her lack of sympathy with the post-revolutionary regimes inhibited her writing, and her work was banned 1922–40 and again from 1946. From the mid-1950s her work has been gradually rehabilitated in the Soviet Union. Among her most notable poems are the cycle *Requiem* 1963 (written in the 1930s), which deals with the Stalinist terror, and *Poem without a hero* 1962 (begun in 1940).

Akhnaton another name for ◊Ikhnaton.

Akihito /ˌækɪ'hiːtəʊ/ 1933–. Crown prince of Japan, the son of ◊Hirohito; in 1959 he married Michiko Shoda, the first commoner to enter the Imperial family.

Akins /'eɪkɪnz/ Zoe 1886–1958. American writer. Born in Missouri, she wrote poems, literary criticism, and plays, of which the best-known is *The Greeks Had a Word for It* 1930.

Akkad northern semitic people who conquered the Sumerians in 2350 BC and ruled Mesopotamia. The ancient city of Akkad in central Mesopotamia, founded by ◊Sargon, was an imperial centre in the 3rd millennium BC; the site is unidentified, but it was on the Euphrates.

Akkaia alternative form of ◊Achaea.

Akko /'ækəʊ/ Israeli name for ◊Acre.

Akola /ə'kəʊlə/ town in Maharashtra state, India, near the Purnar. It is an important centre for the cotton and grain trade. Population (1981) 176,385.

Akron /'ækrən/ city of Ohio, USA, on the Cuyahoga river. Almost half the world supply of rubber is processed here. A university was founded 1870. Population (1980) 237,000.
history Akron was first settled in 1807. Dr B F Goodrich established a rubber factory there in 1870, and the industry grew immensely with the rising demand for car tyres from about 1910.

Akrotiri /,ækrəʊ'tɪəri/ peninsula on the south coast of Cyprus; it has a British military base.

Aksakov /'æk'sɑːkɒv/ Sergei Timofeyevich 1791–1859. Russian writer. Born at Ufa, in the Urals, he became a civil servant, entered the censorship department, and, under the influence of ◊Gogol, wrote autobiographical novels, including *Chronicles of a Russian Family* 1856, and *Years of Childhood* 1858.

Aksum /'ɑːksʊm/ ancient Greek-influenced Semitic kingdom which flourished 1st–6th centuries AD and covered a large part of modern Ethiopia as well as the Sudan. The ruins of its capital, also called Aksum, lie north west of Aduwa, but the site has been developed as a modern city.

Aksum The tallest of the obelisks still standing at Aksum. Some 18 m/60 ft high, it represents a many-storeyed castle and has an altar at its base. These monoliths were probably raised in the 1st-3rd centuries AD and are thought to be linked to sun-worship.

Aktyubinsk /æk'tjuːbɪnsk/ industrial city in Republic of Kazakh, USSR; population (1985) 231,000.

Alabama /,ælə'bæmə/ state of southern USA; Heart of Dixie/Cotton State

area 133,665 sq km/51,609 sq mi
capital Montgomery
towns Birmingham, Mobile
physical the state comprises the Cumberland Plateau in the north; the Black Belt, or Canebrake, which is excellent cotton-growing country, in the centre; and south of this, the coastal plain of Piny Woods. The main river is the river Alabama.
features Alabama and Tennessee rivers; Appalachian mountains; George Washington ◊Carver Museum at the Tuskegee Institute (a college founded for blacks by Booker T ◊Washington) and Helen ◊Keller's birthplace at Tuscumbia.
products cotton no longer prime crop, though still important; soybeans, peanuts; wood products; coal, iron
population (1980) 3,893,888
famous people Nat King Cole, Helen Keller, Joe Louis, Jesse Owens, Booker T Washington
history first settled by the French in the early 18th century, it was ceded to Britain in 1763, passed to the USA in 1783, and became a state in 1819. It was one of the ◊Confederate States in the American Civil War.

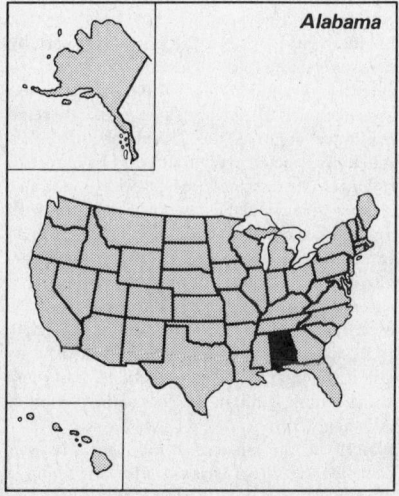

Alabama

Alabama /,ælə'bæmə/ Confederate warship cruiser (1,040 tonnes) in the American ◊Civil War. Built in Britain, it was allowed to leave port by the British, and sank many US merchantmen, until itself sunk by a US warship in 1864. The international court in 1871 awarded damages of $15,500,000 from Britain to the USA, an important legal precedent.

alabaster a naturally occurring five-grained translucent form of gypsum which, chemically, is hydrated calcium sulphate, $CaSO_4.2H_2O$. It is a soft material, used for carvings.

Alain-Fournier /æ'læ̃ 'fʊənieɪ/ pen name of Henri-Alban Fournier 1886–1914. French novelist, who was killed in action on the Meuse in World War I His haunting semi-autobiographical fantasy *Le Grand Meaulnes/The Lost Domain* 1913 was a cult novel of the 1920s and 1930s. His life is intimately recorded in his correspondence with his brother-in-law Jacques Rivière.

Alamagordo /,æləmə'gɔːdəʊ/ town in New Mexico, USA, near which the first atom bomb was exploded at Trinity Site Jul 16,1945. There is now a test site for guided missiles.

Alamein, El /'æləmeɪn/ site in the Western Desert, North Egypt, of the *First Battle of El Alamein* 1–27 Jul 1942, when the British 8th Army under Auchinleck held the German and Italian forces under ◊Rommel; and *Second Battle of El Alamein* 23 Oct–4 Nov 1942, when ◊Montgomery defeated Rommel; these battles were a turning point of World War II.

Alamo /'æləməʊ/ The mission-fortress in San Antonio, Texas, USA; besieged 23 Feb–6 Mar 1836 by Santa ◊Anna and 4,000 Mexicans; they killed the garrison of about 150, including Davy ◊Crockett and Jim ◊Bowie.

Alanbrooke /'ælənbrʊk/ Alan Francis Brooke, 1st Viscount Alanbrooke 1883–1963. British soldier, born in Ireland. He served in the artillery in World War I, and in World War II, as commander of the 2nd Corps 1939–40, did much to aid the extrication of the British Expeditionary Force from Dunkirk. He was commander in chief of the Home Forces 1940–41, and while chief of the Imperial General Staff 1941–46 was largely responsible for the strategy that led to the German defeat. He became a field marshal in 1944, was created a baron 1945 and viscount 1946. His published war diaries were controversial in their depiction of ◊Churchill.

Åland Islands /'ɔːlənd/ group of some 300 islands in the Baltic Sea, at the southern extremity of the Gulf of Bothnia. Only 80 are inhabited; the island of Ahvenanmaa is the largest and has a small town, Marienhamn. Area 1,481 sq km/572 sq mi; population (1983) 23,435. The islands became Finnish as a result of agitation by the Swedish-speaking population for the island to be made an autonomous province of Finland.

Alarcón /,ælɑː'kɒn/ Pedro Antonio de 1833–1891. Spanish journalist and writer, born at Guadix. Out of his experiences as a soldier in Morocco he produced a *Diario/Diary* which was acclaimed as a masterpiece. His *El Sombrero de tres picos/The Three-Cornered Hat* 1874 was the basis of Manuel de ◊Falla's ballet.

Alaric /'ælərɪk/ c. 370–410. King of the Visigoths. In 396 he invaded Greece and retired with much booty to Illyria. In 400 and 408 he invaded Italy, and in 410 captured and sacked Rome, but died the same year on his way to invade Sicily. The River Busento was diverted by his soldiers so that he could be buried in its course with his treasures; the labourers were killed to keep the secret.

Alaska /ə'læskə/ Pacific state of the USA
area 1,500,000 sq km/586,400 sq mi; largest state of USA
capital Juneau
towns Anchorage, Fairbanks, Fort Yukon, Holy Cross
physical much of Alaska is mountainous and includes Mount McKinley, 6,194 m/20,320 ft, the highest peak in North America, surrounded

by a national park. Reindeer thrive in the Arctic tundra and elsewhere there are extensive forests.

features Yukon river; Rocky mountains, including Mount McKinley, Mount Katmai, a volcano which erupted 1912 and formed the Valley of Ten Thousand Smokes (the smoke and steam still escaping from fissures in the floor) now a national monument; Arctic Wild Life Range, with the only large herd of North American caribou; Little Diomede Island, which is only 3.9 km/2.4 mi from Big Diomede/Ratmanov Island in the USSR; reindeer herds on the tundra; an Act of 1980 gave environmental protection to 42 million ha/104 million acres. The chief railway line runs from Seward to Fairbanks, which is linked by motor road (via Canada) with Seattle. Air services are frequent. Near Fairbanks is the University of Alaska.

products oil and natural gas, exploited from 1968 especially in the Prudhoe Bay area to the south east of Point Barrow, are the most valuable mineral resources. An oil pipeline (1977) runs from Prudhoe Bay to the Port of Valdez, and an underground natural gas pipeline is under construction to Chicago and San Francisco. Other minerals include coal, copper, iron, gold and tin. There is an important fur trade. Salmon fisheries and canneries, and lumbering are thriving industries.

population (1980) 401,851, including about 50,000 American Indians, Aleuts and Inuits.

history the first European to visit Alaska was Vitus ◊Bering in 1741. Alaska was a Russian colony from 1744 until purchased by the USA in 1867 for $7,200,000; it became a state in 1959.

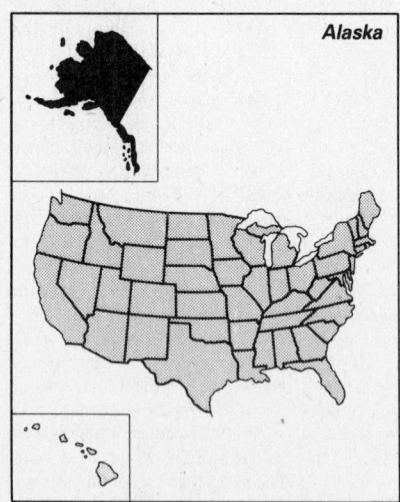

Alaska

Alaska Highway road which runs from Fort St John, British Columbia, to Fairbanks, Alaska (2,450 km/1,523 mi).

Alba /'ælbə/ Celtic name for ◊Scotland.

Albacete /ˌælbə'θeɪtɪ/ market town in the province of Murcia, south east Spain; population 117,125. Famous for cutlery.

Albacore name loosely applied to several sorts of fish found in the Atlantic, in particular to a large ◊tunny and to several species of mackerel.

Alaska The Trans-Alaska Pipeline runs above ground for half its 1,300 km/800 mi length. It is subject to an enormous range of temperature and the trapezoidal zig-zag sections allow for contraction and expansion. When pumping oil at full rate, it gets hot enough to melt the permafrost, which would have disastrous environmental results. The candle-like devices lower the soil temperature as soon as it rises above that of the air.

Albania /æl'beɪnɪə/ country in SE Europe, bounded to the west and southwest by the Mediterranean sea, to the north and east by Yugoslavia, and to the southeast by Greece.

government under the 1946 constitution (amended 1950), Albania's sole and supreme legislative organ is the 250-member People's Assembly, elected every four years by universal suffrage. This assembly meets twice a year and elects a permanent 15-member presidium, with a chair who acts as state president, to take over its functions in its absence. The People's Assembly also elects a council of ministers, headed by a chair or prime minister, to act as the day-to-day executive government. The Communist Party (Albanian Party of Labour), controlled by its political bureau, is the only political party and is the leading force in the Democratic Front of Albania.

history in the ancient world the area was occupied by the Illyrians, later becoming a Roman province until the end of the 4th century AD. Albania then came under Byzantine rule, which lasted until 1347. There followed about 100 years of invasions by Bulgarians, Serbs, Venetians, and finally Turks, who arrived in 1385 and, after the death of the nationalist leader Skanderberg (George Castriota) (1403–68), eventually made Albania part of the ◊Ottoman empire in 1468.

Albania became independent in 1912, and a republic in 1925. In 1928 President Ahmed Beg Zogu was proclaimed King Zog. Overrun by Italy and Germany 1939–44, Albania became a republic with a communist government in 1946, after a guerrilla struggle led by Enver ◊Hoxha. At first closely allied with Yugoslavia, Albania backed ◊Stalin in his 1948 dispute with ◊Tito and developed close links with the USSR 1949–55, entering ◊Comecon in 1949. Hoxha remained a committed Stalinist and, rejecting ◊Khrushchev's denunciations of the Stalin era,

broke off diplomatic relations with the USSR in 1961 and withdrew from Comecon. Albania also severed diplomatic relations with China in 1978, after the post-Mao accommodation with the US. Albania has chosen instead a neutral position and isolation from outside contact.

Hoxha imposed a Stalinist system with rural collectivization, industrial nationalization, central planning and one-party control. In 1967 mosques and churches were closed in an effort to create the 'first atheist state'. The 'Hoxha experiment' left Albania with the lowest per capita income in Europe. Since his death in 1985, there have been policy adjustments and a widening of external economic contacts.

Alban, Saint /'ɔːlbən/ first Christian martyr in England (died 303 AD). According to tradition, he was born at Verulamium, served in the Roman army, became a convert to Christianity after giving shelter to a priest, and on openly professing his belief, was beheaded. In 793 King Offa founded a monastery on the site of Alban's martyrdom, and round this the city of St Albans grew up.

Albany /'ɔːlbənɪ/ capital of New York State, USA, Situated on the river Hudson, about 225 km/140 mi north of New York City. With Schenectady and Troy it forms a metropolitan area: population (1980) 794,298.

Albany /'ɔːlbənɪ/ port in Western Australia, which suffered from the initial development of ◊Fremantle, but has grown with the greater exploitation of the surrounding area. The Albany Doctor is a cooling breeze from the sea, rising in the afternoon. Population (1984) 13,990.

albatross large seabird, genus *Diomedea*, with narrow wings up to 3 m/10 ft long adapted for gliding, mainly found in the S hemisphere. It belongs to the ◊petrel group.

albedo the fraction of the incoming light that a surface or object reflects (see ◊reflection). A body with a high albedo, near 1, is very bright, while a body with a low albedo, near 0, is dark. The ◊Moon has an average albedo of 0.07; the albedo of ◊Venus is 0.65; the Earth's albedo is 0.37.

Albee /'ælbiː/ Edward 1928– . American playwright. Born in Washington, D.C., he was adopted as an infant into a New York family with theatrical links, but did not begin writing until he was 30. His plays belong to the drama of the absurd and include *The Zoo Story* (1961), *The American Dream*, and *Who's Afraid of Virginia Woolf?* (1962) (later filmed with Elizabeth Taylor and Richard Burton as the quarrelling, alcoholic couple), and *Little Alice* (1966).

Albéniz /æl'beɪnɪθ/ Isaac 1860–1909. Spanish composer and pianist, born in Catalonia. He composed the suite *Iberia* and other piano pieces, making use of traditional Spanish tunes.

Alberoni /ˌælbə'rəʊnɪ/ Giulio 1664–1752. Spanish-Italian cardinal and politician. Born in Parma, he became a priest. Philip V made him prime minister of Spain in 1715. In 1717 he became a cardinal. He introduced many reforms, but was forced to flee to Italy in 1719.

Albert /'ælbət/ Albert, Prince Consort 1819–1861. Second son of the Duke of Saxe-Coburg-Gotha; he married Queen ◊Victoria of

Albania
SOCIALIST PEOPLE'S REPUBLIC OF (*Republika Popullore Socialiste e Shqipërisë*)

AREA 28,748 sq km/11,100 sq mi
CAPITAL Tirana
TOWNS Shkodër, Vlorë, chief port Durrës
PHYSICAL mainly mountainous, with rivers flowing E–W, and a small coastal plain
FEATURES Dinaric Alps, with wild boar and wolves
HEAD OF STATE Ramiz Alia from 1982
HEAD OF GOVERNMENT Adil Carcani from 1982
GOVERNMENT one-party communist
EXPORTS crude oil, bitumen, chrome, iron ore, nickel, coal, copper wire, tobacco, fruit
CURRENCY lek (10.11 = £1 Sept 1987)
POPULATION (1985) 3,046,000; annual growth rate 2.1%
LANGUAGE Albanian
RELIGION Muslim 70%, although since 1967 Albania is officially a secular state
LITERACY 75% (1983)
GDP $2.3 bn (1981 est); $830 per head of population
CHRONOLOGY
1912 Albania achieved independence from Turkey.
1925 Republic proclaimed.
1928–39 Monarchy of King Zog.
1939–44 Under first Italian and then German rule.

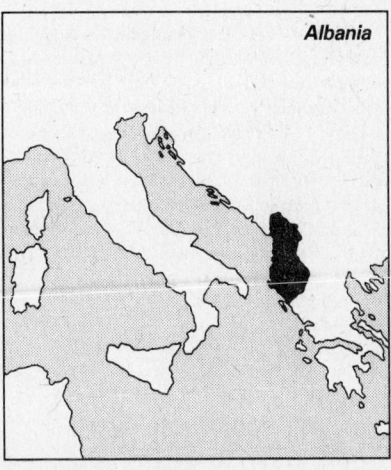

Albania

1946 Communist republic proclaimed under the leadership of Enver Hoxha.
1949 Admitted into Comecon.
1961 Break with Khrushchev's USSR.
1978 Break with 'revisionist' China.
1985 Death of Hoxha.
1987 Normal diplomatic relations restored with Canada, Greece, and West Germany.

England, his first cousin, in 1840. He planned the Great Exhibition of 1851, which made a handsome profit (£186,000); this was used to buy the sites of all the South Kensington museums and colleges, and the Royal Albert Hall, built 1871. The Albert Memorial 1872, designed by Sir Gilbert ◊Scott, in Kensington Gardens, typifies Victorian decorative art. Albert popularized the Christmas tree in England. He was regarded by the British people with groundless suspicion because of his German connections. He died at Windsor of typhoid, and was buried at Frogmore.

Albert /'ælbət/ Victor Christian Edward 1864–1892. Duke of Clarence and Avondale and Earl of Athlone. Born at Frogmore Lodge, Windsor, he was the eldest son of Edward, Prince of Wales, afterwards Edward VII, and his consort Alexandra. In 1891 he was betrothed to Princess Victoria May of Teck, afterwards Queen Mary, but before the marriage could take place he died at Sandringham after a short illness.

Alberta /æl'bɜːtə/ province of north western Canada.
area 661,187 sq km/255,285 sq mi
capital Edmonton
towns Calgary, Lethbridge, Medicine Hat, Wetaskiwin, Red Deer, Drumheller
physical Alberta lies between Saskatchewan and

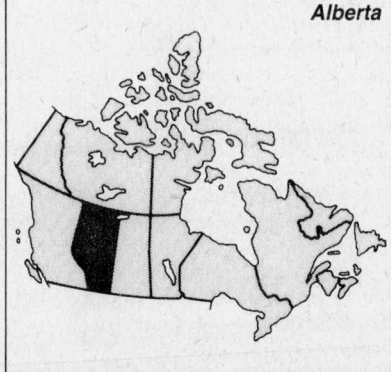

Alberta

the Rocky mountains, many of whose highest peaks it includes; and most of it is arable. In the centre and south is the dry, treeless prairie; towards the north this merges into a zone of poplar, then mixed forest. The valley of the Peace River is the most northerly farming land in Canada (except for Inuit pastures), and there are good grazing lands in the foothills of the Rockies.
features Banff, Jasper, and Waterton Lake national parks; annual Calgary stampede
products Alberta is pre-eminently agricultural, producing wheat, barley and oats on a vast scale.

Sugar-beet is grown in the south. More than a million head of cattle graze on the natural pastures east of the Rockies. Alberta has the largest coal resources in Canada, the principal mines being near Edmonton and at Anthracite, Mountain Park, Lethbridge and Canmore. Alberta also produces oil and natural gas; an oil pipeline extends from Edmonton to Lake Superior. The McMurray district has deposits of bituminous sands to the south west of Lake Athabasca, which become economic to work at times of high world fuel prices. Lumbering is important.
population (1984) 2,361,300
history in the 17th century much of its area was part of a grant to the ◊Hudson's Bay Company for the fur trade. It became a province in 1905.

Albert Canal /'ælbət/ designed as part of Belgium's frontier defences; it also links the industrial basin of Liège with the port of Antwerp. Built 1930–39, it was named after King ◊Albert I.

Alberti /æl'beəti/ Leon Battista 1404–1472. Italian ◊Renaissance architect and theorist, noted for his recognition of the principles of classical architecture and their modification for Renaissance practice in *On Architecture* 1452/85.

Albert, Lake /'ælbət/ former name of Lake ◊Mobutu.

Albertus Magnus /æl'bɜːtəs 'mægnəs/ St 1206–1280. Scholastic philosopher; known as 'doctor universalis' because of the breadth of his knowledge, he gained a reputation as a wizard. He studied at Bologna and Padua, and entered the Dominican order in 1223. He taught at Cologne and lectured from 1245 in Paris University. St Thomas ◊Aquinas was his pupil there, and followed him to Cologne in 1248. In 1254 he became provincial of the Dominicans in Germany, and was made bishop of Ratisbon in 1260. Two years later he resigned and eventually retired to his convent at Cologne. He was a man of vast learning on a variety of subjects – theology and philosophy (especially Aristotle), but also the natural sciences, chemistry, and physics. He wrote numerous works and was canonized in 1932.

Albert I /'ælbət/ 1875–1934. King of the Belgians. The younger son of Philip, Count of Flanders – the brother of Leopold II – in 1900 he married the Duchess Elisabeth of Bavaria. He became king in 1909, and in World War I commanded the Allied army that conquered the Belgian coast in 1918, re-entering Brussels in triumph on 22 Nov. He was killed while mountaineering.

Albi /æl'biː/ chief town in the region of Tarn, south west France, on the river Tarn, 72 km/45 mi north east of Toulouse. It was the centre of the Albigensian heresy (see ◊Albigenses) and the birthplace of ◊Toulouse-Lautrec. It has a 13th century cathedral. Population (1983) 45,291.

Albigenses /ˌælbɪ'dʒensiːz/ heretical sect of Christians (associated with the ◊Cathars) who flourished in Southern France near Albi and Toulouse during the 11th–13th centuries. They adopted the Manichean belief in the duality of good and evil and pictured Jesus as being a rebel against the cruelty of an omnipotent God. They showed a consistently anti-Catholic attitude with distinctive sacraments, especially the *consolamentum*, or baptism of the spirit. In the 11th–12th centuries the Pope declared a crusade against them under the elder Simon de ◊Montfort, and thousands were killed before the movement was crushed in 1229.

albinism absence or great deficiency in the body of the dark pigment melanin. As a result the hair is very light or white, the skin is white, and the eyes pink, yellow, or pale blue. It occurs rarely among most ethnic groups of people; it has been observed in most domestic and many wild animals. Poor daylight vision in albino people, formerly compensated only by dark glasses, may now be overcome by fitting coloured contact lenses.

Albinoni /ˌælbɪˈnəuni/ Tomaso 1671–1751. Italian Baroque composer and violinist, whose work was studied and adapted by Bach. He composed over 40 operas.

Albion /ˈælbiən/ ancient name for Britain used by the Greeks and Romans. It was mentioned by Pytheas of Massilia (4th century BC), and is probably of Celtic origin, but the Romans, having in mind the white cliffs of Dover, assumed it to be derived from *albus* (white). The kindred name of Albany was given to the Scottish highlands in the 10th century.

Alboin /ˈælbɔɪn/ ruled c. 561–73. King of the ◊Lombards, at that time settled north of the Alps. Early in his reign he attacked the Gepidae in Rumania, killing their king and taking his daughter Rosamund to be his wife. About 568 he invaded Italy, conquering the country as far as Rome. He was murdered at the instigation of his wife, whom he had forced to drink from a wine-cup made from her father's skull.

albumin sulphur-containing ◊protein substance, best known in the form of egg white (when it is often spelled *albumen*). It also occurs in milk and as a major component of blood serum. The presence of albumin in the ◊urine, termed albuminuria or proteinuria, may be a symptom of a ◊kidney disorder.

Albuquerque /ˈælbəkɜːki/ largest city of New Mexico, USA, situated east of the Rio Grande, in the Pueblo district. Population (1982) 342,000. Founded in 1706, it was named after Alfonso de ◊Albuquerque. A resort and industrial centre, it specializes in electronics. The University of New Mexico was founded here in 1889.

Albuquerque /ˈælbəkɜːki/ Alfonso de 1453–1515. Viceroy and founder of the Portuguese East Indies 1508–15, when the King of Portugal replaced him by his worst enemy and he died at sea on the way home; his ship *Flor del Mar* was lost between Malaya and India with all his treasure.

Albury-Wodonga /ˈɔːbəri wəˈdɒŋgə/ twin town on the New South Wales/Victoria border, Australia; population (1981) 54,214. Planned to relieve overspill from Melbourne and Sydney, it produces car components.

Alcaeus /ælˈsiːəs/ c. 611–c. 580 BC. Greek lyric poet. Born at Mytilene in Lesbos, he was a member of the aristocratic party and went into exile when the popular party triumphed. He

wrote odes, and the Alcaic stanza is named after him.

Alcatraz /ˈælkətræz/ small island in San Francisco Bay, California, USA. Its fortress was a military prison 1886–1934, and then a famous federal penitentiary until closed in 1963. The dangerous currents meant few successful escapes. Famous inmates included Al ◊Capone and the 'Birdman of Alcatraz', a prisoner who used his time in solitary confinement to become an authority on cage birds. American Indian 'nationalists' took over the island in 1970 as a symbol of their lost heritage.

alcázar /ælˈkæθɑː/ Moorish palace (Arabic 'fortress') in Spain; one of five in Toledo was defended by the Nationalists against the Republicans for 71 days in 1936 during the Spanish ◊Civil War.

Alcazarquivir, Battle of battle on 4 Aug 1578 between the forces of Sebastian, king of Portugal, and those of the Berber kingdom of Fez. Sebastian's death on the field of battle paved the way for the incorporation of Portugal into the Spanish kingdom of Philip II.

alchemy the supposed art of transmuting base metals, such as lead and mercury, into silver and gold by 'the philosopher's stone' which also gave eternal life. It originated in Egypt. This aspect of alchemy constituted much of the chemistry of the Middle Ages. More broadly, however, alchemy was a system of philosophy which dealt alike with the mystery of life and formation of inanimate substances. Alchemy was a complex and indefinite conglomeration of chemistry, astrology, occultism, and magic, blended with obscure and abstruse ideas derived from various religious systems and other sources.

Alcibiades /ˌælsɪˈbaɪədiːz/ 450–404 BC. Athenian general. Handsome and dissolute, he became the archetype of capricious treachery for his military intrigues against his native state with the ◊Spartans and ◊Persians; the Persians eventually had him assassinated. He had been brought up by ◊Pericles and was a friend of ◊Socrates, whose reputation as a teacher suffered from the association.

Alcmaeonidae /ˌælkmiˈɒnidiː/ a noble family of ancient Athens; its members include ◊Pericles and ◊Alcibiades.

Alcock /ˈælkɒk/ John William 1892–1919. British airman, on 14 Jun 1919 in a Vickers-Vimy biplane, he and Lieutenant Whitten-Brown made the first nonstop trans-Atlantic flight. He died after an aeroplane accident in the same year.

Alcoforado /ˌælkəufəˈrɑːdəu/ Marianna 1640–1723. Portuguese nun. The *Letters of a Portuguese Nun* 1699, supposed to have been written by her to a young French nobleman who abandoned her when their relations became known, are no longer accepted as authentic.
In 1972 three writers, the three Marias (Maria Isabel Barreno, Maria Teresa Horta, and Maria Velho da Costa), published *New Portuguese Letters*, a feminist plea in a male-dominated Portugal which led to their trial. They were acquitted after the 1974 coup.

alcoholic liquor intoxicating drink; ethyl alcohol, a colourless liquid, C_2H_5OH, is the basis of all common intoxicants:
wines, ciders, sherry and other drinks in which alcohol is produced by direct fermentation using yeasts of the sugar content in the relevant fruit.
malt liquors beers, and stouts in which the starch of the grain is converted to sugar by malting, and the sugar is then fermented into alcohol by yeasts.
spirits distilled from malted liquors or wines. A concentration of 0.15 per cent alcohol in the blood causes mild intoxication; 0.3 per cent definite drunkenness and partial loss of consciousness; 0.6 per cent endangers life.

Alcoholics Anonymous voluntary self-help organization established in 1934 in the USA to combat alcoholism; organizations now exist in many other countries.

alcoholism dependence on alcoholic liquor. It is characterized as an illness when consumption of alcohol interferes with normal physical or emotional health or behaviour, and may produce physical and psychological addiction. Treatment may include drugs, counselling, or support groups such as ◊Alcoholics Anonymous.

alcohols group of organic chemical compounds characterized by the presence of one or more OH-(hydroxyl) groups in the ◊molecule. They may be liquids or solids, according to the size and complexity of the molecule. The five best-known alcohols form a series in which the number of carbon and hydrogen atoms increases progressively, each one having an extra CH_2–(methylene) group in the molecule, viz. methyl alcohol or wood spirit (CH_3OH); ethyl alcohol or ethanol (the alcohol of beer, wine and sprits) (C_2H_5OH), propyl alcohol (C_3H_7OH); butyl alcohol (C_4H_9OH); and amyl alcohol($C_5H_{11}OH$). The lower alcohols are liquids that mix with water. The higher alcohols such as amyl alcohol are oily liquids not miscible with water, and the highest are waxy solids, for example cetyl alcohol ($C_{16}H_{33}OH$) and melissyl alcohol ($C_{30}H_{61}OH$) which occur in sperm whale spermaceti and beeswax respectively. The main uses of alcohols are in alcoholic drinks, as solvents for gums and resins, in lacquers and varnishes, in the making of dyes, for essential oils in perfumery and for medical substances in pharmacy. Ethanol is used as a raw material in the manufacture of ether, chloral, and iodoform. It can also be added to petrol, where it improves the performance of the engine, or used as a fuel in its own right. Crops such as sugar cane may be grown to provide ethanol (by fermentation) for this purpose.

Alcott /ˈɔːlkət/ Louisa May 1832–1888. US author of the children's classic *Little Women* 1869, which drew on her own home circumstances, the heroine Jo being a partial self-portrait. *Good Wives* 1869 was among its sequels. She was born near Philadelphia, daughter of Amos B Alcott (1799–1888), a poet and transcendentalist philosopher.

Alcuin /ˈælkwɪn/ 735–804. English scholar. Born at York, he went to Rome in 780, and in 782 took up his residence at Charlemagne's court in Aachen. From 796 he was abbot of Tours.

Though not a profound scholar like ◊Bede, he disseminated Anglo-Saxon scholarship, organized education and learning in the Frankish empire, gave a strong impulse to the Carolingian Renaissance, and was a prominent member of Charlemagne's academy.

Aldabra /æl'dæbrə/ high limestone island group in the ◊Seychelles, some 400 km/260 mi NW of Madagascar. Renowned for its plants and animals, including the giant tortoise.

Aldebaran /æl'debərən/ brightest ◊star in the constellation ◊Taurus, marking the eye of the 'bull', and the 13th brightest star in the entire sky. It is a red giant 68 light years away.

Aldeburgh /'ɔːldbərə/ small town in Suffolk, England, famous for its annual music festival founded by Benjamin ◊Britten. Also the home of the Britten-Pears School for Advanced Studies.

aldehydes group of organic chemical compounds prepared by oxidation of primary alcohols, so that the hydroxyl group (-OH) loses its hydrogen to give an oxygen joined by a double bond to a carbon atom (the aldehyde group having the formula -CHO). The name is made up from *al*cohol *dehyd*rogenatum, that is, alcohol from which hydrogen has been removed. Aldehydes are usually liquids and include acetaldehyde, formaldehyde, benzaldehyde, and citral.

alder tree *Alnus glutinosa* allied to the birch and found in wet places and by water. Growing to 20 m/65 ft it lives in Europe and N Asia. About 30 other species of alder occur in the northern hemisphere and South America.

alderman the title of the senior members of the borough or county councils in England and Wales until its abolition in the 1970s (Old English 'older man'); it is still used in the City of ◊London, and for members of a municipal corporation in certain towns in the USA.

Aldermaston /'ɔːldəmɑːstən/ village in Berkshire, England; site of an atomic and biological weapons research establishment. In 1958 the ◊Campaign for Nuclear Disarmament made it the goal of an annual Easter protest march from London.

Alderney /'ɔːldəni/ third largest of the ◊Channel Islands, with its capital at St Anne's; population (1980) 2,000; area 8 sq km/3 sq mi. It gives its name to a breed of cattle, better known as the Guernsey.

Aldershot /'ɔːldəʃɒt/ town in Hampshire, south west of London, England, with a military camp and barracks dating from 1854. Population (1981) 32,650.

Aldhelm /'ɔːldhelm/ c. 640–709. English saint, prelate, and scholar. He was abbot of Malmesbury from 673 AD and bishop of Sherborne from 705 AD. Of his poems and treatises in Latin, some survive, notably his Riddles in hexameters, but his English verse has been lost. He was also known as a skilled architect.

Aldington /'ɔːldɪŋtən/ Richard 1892–1962. British ◊Imagist poet, novelist and critic, who was married to Hilda ◊Doolittle from 1913 to 1937. He wrote biographies of D H Lawrence and T E Lawrence. His novels include *Death of a Hero* 1929 and *All Men are Enemies* 1933.

Aldiss /'ɔːldɪs/ Brian 1925– . British science-fiction writer, anthologist, and critic. His novels include *Non-Stop* 1958, *Helliconia Summer* 1983, and *Trillion Year Spree* 1986.

aleatory music method of composition (pioneered by John ◊Cage) from about 1945 in which the elements are assembled by chance, for example by using dice (Latin *alea*) or by computer.

Aleixandre /ˌæleɪk'sɑːndreɪ/ Vicente 1898–1984. Spanish lyric poet, born in Seville. His verse, which was influential with younger Spanish writers, had ◊Republican sympathies, and his work was for a time banned by ◊Franco's government. Nobel Prize for Literature 1977.

Alembert /ˌæləm'beə/ Jean le Rond d' 1717–1783. French mathematician and encyclopedist. He was a foundling, born in Paris and educated by the Jansenist Catholic sect, and studied law and medicine before devoting himself to mathematics. He was associated with ◊Diderot in planning the great *Dictionnaire Encyclopédique*.

Alençon /ˌælɒn'sɒŋ/ capital of the Orne département of France, situated in a rich agricultural plain to the SE of Caen. Alençon is famed for its lace, now a declining industry. Population (1983) 32,939.
Fourth son of Henry II of France and Catherine de Medici. At one time considered as a suitor to Elizabeth I of England.

Aleppo /ə'lepəʊ/ former name of ◊Haleb, a town in Syria.

Alessandria /ˌæli'sændriə/ town in N Italy on the river Tanaro; population (1981) 100,500. There is an annual motorcyclists' rally at the shrine of their patroness, the Madonna of the Centaurs.

Aletsch /'ɑːletʃ/ most extensive glacier in Europe, 16 km/10 mi long, beginning on the southern slopes of the Jungfrau in the Bernese Alps.

Aleutian Islands volcanic island chain in the N Pacific, stretching 1900 km/1200 mi SW of Alaska, of which it forms part. There are 14 large and over 100 small islands, running along the ◊Aleutian Trench. The islands are mountainous, barren, and treeless; they are ice-free all the year round, but are often foggy.
Population 6,000 ◊Inuit, most of whom belong to the Greek Orthodox Church, plus a large US defence establishment.

A Level (Advanced Level) in the UK, examinations usually taken in no more than four subjects at the age of 18 after two years' study. Two A Level passes are required for entry to a degree course.

alewife edible fish *Pandopus pseudoharengus* of the ◊herring group, up to 30 cm/1 ft long, found off the coast and in the Great Lakes of North America.

Alexander /ˌælɪg'zɑːndə/ Frederick Matthias 1869–1955. Australian founder and teacher of the psycho-physical method named after him. At one time a professional reciter, he developed throat and voice trouble, and his experiments in curing himself led him to work out the system of mental and bodily control described in his *Use of the Self*.

Alexander /ˌælɪg'zɑːndə/ Harold Rupert Leofric George, 1st earl Alexander of Tunis 1891–1969. British soldier. Third son of the fourth earl of Caledon, he was educated at Harrow and Sandhurst and commissioned in the Irish Guards. After distinguished service during World War I, he held various staff appointments until 1938 when he commanded the 1st Division in France 1939. As lieutenant-general he commanded the 1st Corps, organized the last phases of defence and was the last man to leave ◊Dunkirk. He was then General Officer Commander-in-Chief, Southern Command until he became General Officer Commander-in-Chief in Burma in Mar 1942, where he fought a delaying action for 5 months against vastly superior Japanese forces. In Aug 1942 he went to N Africa, and in 1943 became deputy to Eisenhower in charge of the Allied forces in Tunisia. When the Axis forces in N Africa surrendered, Alexander became deputy Commander-in-Chief of the Mediterranean Combined Operations and was promoted General Officer Commanding, then Supreme Allied Commander in the Mediterranean and, in 1944, field marshal. Appointed governor-general of Canada in 1946, he was created earl Alexander of Tunis in 1952, and was minister of defence 1952–54. In 1959 he was awarded the Order of Merit.

Alexander /ˌælɪg'zɑːndə/ Samuel 1859–1938. Australian philosopher, professor at Manchester University 1893–1924. He originated the theory of emergent evolution: that the space-time matrix evolved matter; matter evolved life; life evolved mind; and finally God emerged from mind. His books include *Space, Time and Deity* 1920. He received the Order of Merit in 1930.

Alexander /ˌælɪg'zɑːndə/ **the Great** 356–323 BC. king of Macedonia and conqueror of the Persian empire. The son of Philip, king of Macedonia, and Olympias, he was educated by the philosopher Aristotle. He first saw fighting in 340, and at the battle of Chaeronea 338 contributed to the victory by a cavalry charge. When his father was murdered in 336, the Macedonian throne and army passed into his hands. He first secured his northern frontier, suppressed an attempted rising in Greece by his capture of Thebes, and in 334 crossed the Dardanelles for the campaign against the vast Persian empire. Alexander marched with 20,000 foot and 5,000 horse, and at the river Granicus near the Dardanelles won his first success. In 333 he routed the Persian king Darius at Issus, and then set out for Egypt, where he was greeted as Pharaoh, son of the god Ra, and hailed as son of Zeus. He founded Alexandria, the future centre of Hellenistic civilization. Meanwhile, Darius collected half a million men, with scythed chariots and elephants, for a final battle, but at Arbela on the Tigris in 331 Alexander with 47,000 men drove the Persians into headlong retreat.
After the victory he stayed a month in Babylon, then marched to Susa and Persepolis, and in 330 to Ecbatana. Soon after he learned that Darius was dead. In Afghanistan he founded colonies at

Herat and Kandahar, and in 328 reached the plains of Sogdiana, where he married Roxana, daughter of King Oxyartes. India now lay before him, and he pressed on to the Indus. Near the Hydaspes he fought one of his fiercest battles against the rajah Porus. At the river Hyphasis his men refused to go farther, and reluctantly he turned back down the Indus and along the coast. They reached Susa in 324, where Alexander took Darius' daughter for his second wife. He died at Babylon of a malarial fever.

Alexander left no successor, and his empire broke up into independent kingdoms. But his personality left deep impressions on East and West; peoples of the East all had their traditions of him, while medieval romances made him a hero of the type of Arthur and Charlemagne.

way to the papacy, where he furthered the advancement of his illegitimate children, who included Cesare and Lucrezia ◊Borgia. He secured the execution of ◊Savonarola when he preached against his corrupt practices, and is said to have died of poison he had prepared for his cardinals. He was a great patron of the arts during the time of ◊Raphael, and ◊Michelangelo.

Alexander /ˌælɪgˈzɑndə/ three tsars of Russia:

Alexander I /ˌælɪgˈzɑndə/ 1777–1825. Tsar of Russia from 1801. Defeated by ◊Napoleon at Austerlitz, he made peace at Tilsit 1807, but later broke with Napoleon's economic policy and opened Russian ports to British trade; this led to Napoleon's ill-fated invasion of Russia. He gave a constitution to Poland.

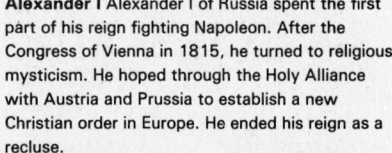

Alexander I Alexander I of Russia spent the first part of his reign fighting Napoleon. After the Congress of Vienna in 1815, he turned to religious mysticism. He hoped through the Holy Alliance with Austria and Prussia to establish a new Christian order in Europe. He ended his reign as a recluse.

Empire of Alexander the Great 323 BC

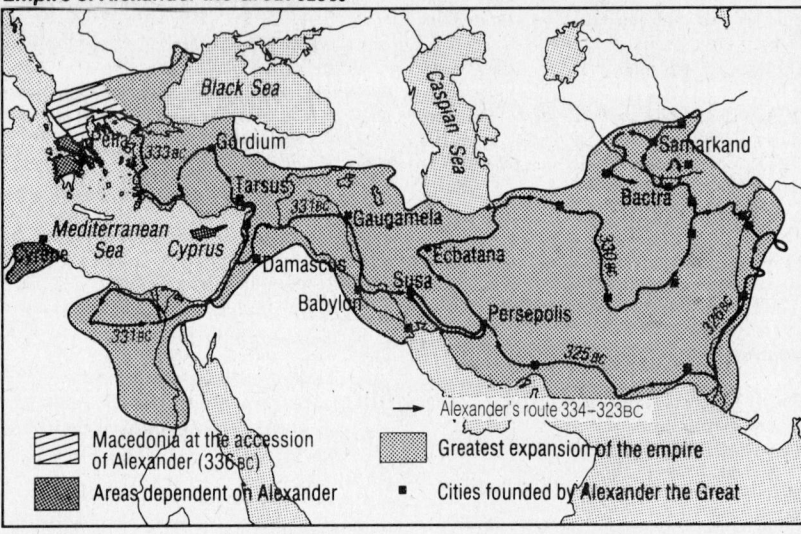

Macedonia at the accession of Alexander (336 BC)

Areas dependent on Alexander

Greatest expansion of the empire

■ Cities founded by Alexander the Great

→ Alexander's route 334–323 BC

Alexander Nevski, St /ˈnevski/ 1220–1263. Russian hero, son of the Grand Duke of Novgorod; in 1240 he defeated the Swedes on the banks of the Neva (hence Nevski), and in 1242 defeated the ◊Teutonic knights on frozen Lake Peipus.

alexanders stong-smelling tall herbaceous plant *Smyrnium olusatrum* of the carrot family. Found in hedgebanks and on cliffs, the yellow flowers appear in spring and early summer.

Alexander Severus /sɪˈvɪərəs/ 208–235 AD. Roman emperor. Born in Palestine. He succeeded his cousin Heliogabalus in 222. His campaign against the Persians in 232 achieved some success, but in 235 when proceeding to defend Gaul against German invaders he was killed in a mutiny.

Alexander III /ˌælɪgˈzɑndə/ Pope 1159–81; his authority was opposed by ◊Frederick Barbarossa, but Alexander eventually compelled him to render homage in 1178. He supported ◊Henry II of England in his invasion of Ireland, but subjugated him after the murder of Thomas à Becket.

Alexander VI /ˌælɪgˈzɑndə/ Pope 1492–1503, known as the 'infamous Borgia pope'. He was of Spanish origin, and bribed his

Alexander II /ˌælɪgˈzɑndə/ 1818–1881. Tsar of Russia from 1855. He is remembered as 'the Liberator' for his freeing of the serfs in 1861, but the revolutionary element remained unsatisfied, and Alexander became increasingly autocratic and reactionary. He was assassinated by ◊Nihilists.

Alexander III /ˌælɪgˈzɑndə/ 1845–1894. Tsar of Russia from 1881, when he succeeded his father, ◊Alexander II. He pursued a reactionary policy, persecuting the Jews. He married Dagmar 1847–1928, daughter of Christian IX of Denmark and sister of Queen Alexandra of the UK, in 1866.

Alexander /ˌælɪgˈzɑndə/ **Obrenovich** 1876–1903. King of Serbia from 1889 while still a minor, upon the abdication of his father King Milan. He took power into his own hands in 1893, and in 1900 married a widow, Madame Draga Mashin. In 1903 Alexander and his queen were murdered, and Peter Karageorgevich was placed on the throne.

Alexander /ˌælɪgˈzɑndə/ name of three kings of Scotland:

Alexander I /ˌælɪgˈzɑndə/ c. 1078–1124. King of Scotland from 1107, known as 'the Fierce'.

Alexander II Alexander II of Russia embarked on reforms of the army, the government, and education and in 1861 emancipated the serfs. The latter part of his reign was notable for conflict between the tsar and his government. Repressive measures led to several assassination attempts until he was killed by a bomb thrown into his coach in 1881.

Alexander II /ˌælɪgˈzɑndə/ 1198–1249. King of Scotland from 1214, when he succeeded his father William the Lion. He supported the English barons in their struggle with King John after Magna Carta. By the treaty of Newcastle in 1244 Alexander acknowledged Henry III of England as his liege lord.

Alexander III /ˌælɪgˈzɑːndə/ 1241–1285. King of Scotland from 1249, son of Alexander II. In 1263 he extended his authority over the Western Isles, which had been dependent on Norway, and strengthened the power of the central Scottish government. He died as the result of a fall from his horse, leaving his granddaughter ◊Margaret, the Maid of Norway, to become queen of Scotland.

Alexander I /ˌælɪgˈzɑːndə/ Karageorgevich 1888–1934. King of Yugoslavia 1921–34. Second son of Peter Karageorgevich, king of Serbia, he was declared regent for his father in 1912, and in 1921, on his father's death, became king of the state of South Slavs – Yugoslavia – which had come into being in 1918. Rivalries of neighbouring powers and of the Croats, Serbs, and Slovenes within the country led Alexander to establish a personal dictatorship in 1929. He was assassinated on a state visit to France, and Mussolini's government was later declared to have instigated the crime.

Alexandra /ˌælɪgˈzɑːndrə/ 1844–1925. Queen consort of ◊Edward VII of the UK, whom she married in 1863 (she was the daughter of Christian IX of Denmark). An annual Alexandra Rose Day in aid of hospitals commemorates her charitable work.

Alexandra /ˌælɪgˈzɑːndrə/ 1872–1918. Last tsarina of ◊Russia; granddaughter of Queen ◊Victoria, she married ◊Nicholas II in 1894. From 1907 she fell under the spell of ◊Rasputin, brought to the palace to try and cure her son of haemophilia, though there are no grounds for an alleged more intimate relationship between them. She was shot with the rest of her family by the Bolsheviks.

Alexandretta /ˌælɪgzɑːnˈdretə/ former name of ◊Iskenderun, a port in S Turkey.

Alexandria /ˌælɪgˈzɑːndriə/ city and chief port of Egypt, situated between the Mediterranean and Lake Maryut; population (1986) 5,000,000. It is linked by canal with the Nile and is an industrial city with oil refineries. The Egyptian cotton trade passes through the port. A university was founded in 1942.

history Alexandria was founded in 331 BC by Alexander the Great, and for over 1,000 years was the capital of Egypt and the principal centre of Hellenistic culture. Since the 4th century AD it has been the seat of a Christian patriarch. In 641 it was captured by the Muslim Arabs, and after the opening of the Cape route its trade rapidly declined. Early in the 19th century it began to recover its prosperity, and its growth was encouraged by its being the main British naval base in the Mediterranean during both world wars; the Egyptian cotton trade passes through the port and there is an oil refinery. Few relics of antiquity remain. The Pharos, the first lighthouse and one of the seven wonders of the ancient world, has long since disappeared. The world-famous Alexandrian library was finally destroyed by the Arabs in 641. Pompey's Pillar is a column erected, as a landmark from the sea, by the emperor Diocletian. Two obelisks that once stood before the Caesarum temple are

now in London (Cleopatra's Needle) and New York respectively.

Alexandria, School of /ˌælɪgˈzɑːndriə/ name given to the writers and scholars of Alexandria who from about 331 BC to 642 AD made the city the chief centre of culture in the Western world. They include the poets ◊Callimachus, ◊Apollonius ◊Rhodius, and ◊Theocritus; ◊Euclid, pioneer of geometry; ◊Eratosthenes, the geographer; ◊Hipparchus, who developed a system of trigonometry; ◊Ptolemy, who gave his name to the Ptolemaic system of astronomy that endured for over 1,000 years; and ◊Philo, the Jewish philosopher. The ◊Gnostics and ◊Neo-Platonists also flourished in Alexandria.

alexandrite rare gemstone of the mineral chrysoberyl which is green in daylight but appears red in artificial light.

Alexandrovsk /ˌælɪkˈsɑːndrɒfsk/ older name of ◊Zaporozhe, city in the USSR.

Alexeev /ælɪkˈseɪef/ Vasily 1942– . Russian weightlifter. Reputedly the strongest man in the world, he was world champion 1970–77, and broke 80 world records, a new record in itself in any sport. He was Olympic super-heavyweight champion 1972 and 1976 and European champion 1970–78. At one time the most decorated man in the Soviet Union, he carried the flag at the opening ceremony for the 1980 Moscow Olympics, but he performed disappointingly in the competition and retired soon afterwards.

Alexius I Comnenus /əˈleksiəs, kɒmˈniːnəs/ 1048–1118. Byzantine emperor 1081–1118. The Latin Crusaders helped him repel Norman and Turkish invasions, and he devoted great skill to buttressing the threatened empire. His daughter ◊Anna Comnena (1083–c. 1148) wrote the *Alexiad* descriptive of the Byzantine world.

alfalfa tall herbaceous plant *Medicago sativa* of the pea family, having spikes of small purple flowers in late summer. Native to Eurasia, it is now an important fodder crop.

al-Fatah (Arabic 'the victory') a Palestinian organization founded in 1956 to bring about an independent state of Palestine. Also called the Palestian National Liberation Movement, it is the main component of the ◊Palestine Liberation Organization. Its leader is Yassir ◊Arafat.

Alfieri /ˌælfiˈeəri/ Vittorio, count Alfieri 1749–1803. Italian dramatist. Born at Asti in Piedmont, the best of his 28 plays, most of them tragedies, are *Saul* 1782 and *Mirra* 1786. From 1789 he lived in Florence with the Countess of Albany, the separated wife of Charles Edward Stuart, the 'Young Pretender'.

Alfonsin Foulkes /ˌælfɒnˈsiːn/ Raul 1926– . Argentine politician, member of the Radical Union Party (UCR), president from 1983.

Alfonsin, a lawyer, was imprisoned for his political activities in 1953 under ◊Peron. He was a member of the Chamber of Deputies 1963–66

and 1973–76 and was elected president of Argentina in 1983.

Alfonso X /ælˈfɒnsəʊ/ called *el Sabio*/the Wise 1252–1284.. King of Castile, whose reign was politically unsuccessful but who is remembered for his contribution to learning: he made Castilian the official language of the country, and commissioned a history of Spain and an encyclopedia, as well as several translations from Arabic.

Alfonso XII son of Isabella, Queen of Spain, who assumed the throne in 1875 after a period of Republican government following his mother's flight and abdication in 1868.

Alfonso XIII /ælˈfɒnsəʊ/ 1886–1931. King of Spain 1886–1931. Assumed power 1906 and married Princess Ena, grand-daughter of Queen ◊Victoria of the UK in the same year. He abdicated soon after the fall of the Primo de Rivera dictatorship and Spain became a Republic.

Alfred the Great /ˈælfrɪd/ c. 848–c. 900. English king. Born at Wantage, Berkshire, the youngest son of Ethelwulf (died 858), king of the West Saxons; he gained a brilliant victory over the Danes at Ashdown in 871, and succeeded his brother Ethelred after a series of defeats later in the same year. Five years of uneasy peace followed until the Danes attacked once more in 876, and in 878 Alfred was forced to retire to the stronghold of ◊Athelney, from where he finally emerged to win the victory of Edington, Wiltshire. By the Peace of Wedmore in 878 the Danish leader Guthrum (died 890) agreed to withdraw from Wessex and from Mercia west of Watling Street. A new landing in Kent encouraged a revolt of the East Anglian Danes, which was suppressed (884–86), and after the final foreign invasion was defeated (892–96), Alfred strengthened the navy to prevent fresh incursions.

Alfred the Great The profile of Alfred the Great featured on a coin of about 887. He defended England against the Danish invasions.

algae diverse group of plants formerly included within the division Thallophyta together with fungi and bacteria, but increased awareness of the important differences existing between the algae and these other organisms, and also between the groups of algae themselves, has resulted in many botanists placing each algal group in a separate class or division of its own. Algae include the plants commonly called seaweeds and they show great variety of form, the lowest types consisting of only a single cell, while some of the higher seaweeds attain to considerable size and complexity of structure. They can be divided into 12 divisions, largely to be distinguished by their pigmentation, including the *Chlorophyta* green algae, freshwater or terrestrial; *Charophyta* stoneworts; *Chrysophyta* golden-brown algae; *Phaeophyta* brown algae, mainly marine and including the kelps, *Laminaria* and allies, the largest of all algae; *Rhodophyta* red algae, mainly marine and often living parasitically or as epiphytes on other algae; *Bacillariophyta* diatoms; *Xanthophyta* yellow-green algae, mostly freshwater and terrestrial and *Cyanophyta*, blue-green of simple cell structure, in which reproduction is never sexual, mostly freshwater or terrestrial.

Algardi /æl'gɑːdi/ Alessandro c. 1595–1654. Italian Baroque sculptor, a contemporary and rival of ◊Bernini in Rome. Born in Bologna, Algardi was a pupil at the famous Academy run by the ◊Carracci family. His work, more restrained and classical than Bernini's, gained favour under the pontificate of Innocent X (1644–55), during which period Bernini was out of favour. His greatest work, on which he was intermittently occupied from 1634 to 1652, is the tomb of Pope Leo XI (Medici), in St Peter's, Rome.

Algarve /æl'gɑːv/ ancient kingdom in S Portugal, the modern district of Faro, which began to be wrested from the ◊Moors in the 12th century and was united with Portugal as a kingdom in 1253. It incudes the SW extremity of Europe, Cape St Vincent, where the British fleet defeated the Spanish in 1797. Today it is a popular holiday region.

algebra method of solving mathematical problems by the use of symbols (letters and signs) when figures are inadequate (the numbers involved may be very large or not known exactly). The basics of algebra were familiar in Babylon 2000 BC, and were practised by the Arabs in the Middle Ages. The Arab mathematician Mohammed ibn-Musa al-Khwarizmi in the 9th century first used the word *al-jabr* in the title of a book. More advanced algebra is used to work out general problems, for example the equations derived by Einstein from his general theory of relativity, and the method of algebraic reasoning first devised in the 19th century by the British mathematician George Boole and used in working out the construction of computers.

Algeciras /ˌældʒɪ'sɪərəs/ port in S Spain, to the W of Gibraltar across the Bay of Algeciras; population (1981) 86,042. Founded by the ◊Moors in 713, Algeciras was taken from them by Alfonso XI of Castile in 1344. Virtually destroyed in a fresh attack by the Moors, it was re-founded 1704 by Spanish refugees from

Gibraltar after that place was captured by the British.

Algeciras Conference a conference held in Jan 1906 when the Great Powers together with the United States, Spain, the Low Countries, Portugal and Sweden met to settle the question of Morocco. The conference was prompted by increased German demands in what had, traditionally, been seen as a French area of influence.

Algeria /æl'dʒɪərɪə/ country in N Africa, bounded to the E by Tunisia and Libya, to the SE by Niger, to the SW by Mali, to the NW by Morocco, and to the N by the Mediterranean Sea.

government the 1976 constitution, amended in 1979, created a socialist republic with Islam as the state religion and Arabic the official language. Algeria is a one-party state with ultimate power held by the National Liberation Front (FLN). FLN nominates the president, who is elected by universal suffrage for a five-year term. The president chooses the prime minister and the council of ministers and is the effective head of government. There is a single-chamber national people's assembly of 281 deputies, all nominees of FLN, elected for a five-year term.

history from the 9th century BC the area now known as Algeria was ruled by ◊Carthage, and subsequently by Rome (2nd century BC–5th century AD). St ◊Augustine was bishop of Hippo (now called Annaba) 396–430.

The area was invaded by the ◊Vandals after the decline of Roman rule, and was ruled by ◊Byzantium from the 6th–8th century, after which the ◊Arabs invaded the region, introducing ◊Islam and ◊Arabic. Islamic influence continued to dominate, despite Spain's attempts to take control in the 15th–16th centuries, and from the 16th century Algeria was under ◊Ottoman rule and flourished as a centre for the slave trade. However, the Sultan's rule was often nominal, and in the 18th century Algeria became a pirate state, preying on Mediterranean shipping. European intervention became inevitable, and in 1816 an Anglo-Dutch force bombarded Algiers. In 1830 a French army landed and siezed Algiers; by 1847 the N had been brought under French control, and in 1848 waas formed into the *départements* of Algiers, Oran, and Constantine. Many French colonists settled in these *départements*, which in 1881 were made part of Metropolitan France. The mountainous region inland, inhabited by the Kabyles, occupied 1850–70, and the Sahara region, subdued 1900–09, remained under military rule.

After the defeat of France in 1940, Algeria came under the control of the Vichy government until the Allies landed in N Africa in 1942. post-war hopes of integrating Algeria more closely with France were frustrated by opposition in Algeria from those of both French and non-French origin. An embittered struggle for independence from France continued 1954–62, when referenda in both Algeria and France resulted in 1963 in the recognition of Algeria as an independent one-party republic with Ben Bella as its first

president. In 1965 Colonel Houari Boumédienne deposed Ben Bella in a military coup, suspended the constitution and ruled through a revolutionary council.

In 1976 a new constitution confirmed Algeria as an Islamic, socialist, one-party state. Boumédienne died in 1978 and power was transferred to Bendjedid Chadli, secretary-general of FLN. In 1979 Chadli released Ben Bella from the house arrest imposed on him in the 1965 coup. In the same year FLN adopted a new structure, with a central committee nominating a party leader who automatically becomes president. Chadli was re-elected under this system in 1983.

During Chadli's presidency, relations with France and the US have improved and there has been some progress in achieving greater co-operation with neighbouring states, particularly Tunisia. In 1981 Algeria acted as an intermediary in securing the release of the American hostages in ◊Iran. In 1987 a proposal by Colonel ◊Khaddhafi for political union with Libya received a cool response.

Algiers /æl'dʒɪəz/ capital of Algeria, N Africa, situated on the narrow coastal plain between the Atlas mountains and the Mediterranean; population (1980) 2,200,000. Founded by the Arabs 935 AD, Algiers was taken by the Turks in 1518, and by the French in 1830. The old town is dominated by the Kasbah, the palace and prison of the Turkish rulers. The new town, constructed under French rule, is in European style.

Algiers, Battle of /æl'dʒɪəz/ the bitter conflict in Algiers 1954–62 between the Algerian nationalist population and the French army and French settlers. The conflict ended with Algerian independence in 1962.

alginate salt of alginic acid, obtained from brown seaweeds, and used in textiles, paper, food products and pharmaceuticals.

Algoa Bay /æl'gəʊə/ broad and shallow inlet in Cape Province, South Africa, where Diaz landed after rounding the Cape in 1488.

Algol in computing, an early high-level programming language, developed in the 1950s and 1960s, for scientific applications. Although a general-purpose language, Algol (short for algorithmic language) is best suited for mathematical work and has an algebraic style. It is no longer in common use.

Algol in astronomy, a ◊star of variable brightness in the constellation ◊Perseus. Also known as Beta Persei, Algol is actually a pair of rotating stars (see ◊binary star, ◊double star), one of which eclipses the other every 69 hours, causing its brightness to drop by two-thirds. The brightness changes were first explained in 1782 by amateur astronomer John Goodricke.

Algonquin /æl'gɒŋkwɪn/ N American Indians of the sub-Arctic; noted for their porcupine-quill ornamental work and the accurate prophecies of their ◊shamans. Languages of an Algonquian type are spoken by many other American peoples. Akin to the Algonquins are the Mohicans and Mohegans (two related peoples confused by Fenimore

Algeria
DEMOCRATIC AND POPULAR REPUBLIC OF (*al-Jumhuriya al-Jazairiya ad-Dimuqratiya ash-Shabiya*)

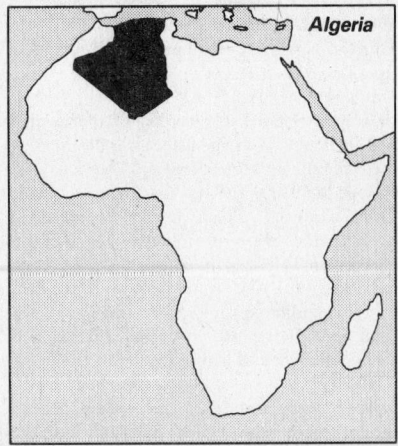

Algeria

AREA 2,381,745 sq km/919,590 sq mi
CAPITAL al-Jazair/Algiers
TOWNS Qacentina/Constantine; ports are Ouahran/Oran, Annaba
PHYSICAL coastal plains, mountain plateau, desert
FEATURES Atlas mountains, Barbary Coast
HEAD OF STATE Benjedid Chadli
GOVERNMENT one-party socialist
EXPORTS oil, natural gas, iron, wine, olive oil
CURRENCY dinar (7.72 = £1 Sept 1987)
POPULATION (1985) 22,107,000 (75% Arab, 25% Berber); annual growth rate 3.3%
LANGUAGE Arabic (official); Berber, French
RELIGION Sunni Muslim
LITERACY 57% male/32% female (1984)
GDP $51.7 bn (1984); $2,085 per head of population
CHRONOLOGY
1954 War for independence from France led by the National Liberation Front (FLN).
1963 Independence achieved. Ben Bella elected president.
1965 Ben Bella deposed by military, led by Col Houari Boumédienne.
1976 New constitution approved.
1978 Death of Boumédienne.
1979 Bendjedid Chadli elected president. Ben Bella released from house arrest. FLN adopted new party structure.
1981 Algeria helped in securing release of US prisoners in Iran.
1983 Chadli re-elected president.

▷Cooper) who formerly occupied Connecticut and the Hudson Valley: about 3,000 survive.

algorithm a ▷procedure or series of steps by which a problem can be solved. In computer science, where the term is most often used, algorithm describes the logical sequence of operations to be performed by a computer program. See also ▷flowchart. An algorithmic programming language is ▷Algol.

Alhambra /æl'hæmbrə/ fortified palace at Granada, Spain, built by Moorish kings mainly between 1248 and 1354. The finest example of Moorish architecture, it stands on a rocky hill.

Ali /'ɑːli/ (Ali Pasha) 1741–1822. Turkish statesman, known as Arslan (the lion). An Albanian, he was appointed pasha of Janina in 1788, and there he maintained a semibarbarous court, visited by Byron. He was murdered by the Sultan's order.

Ali /ɑː'liː/ Muhammad 1942– . Name adopted by American boxer Cassius Clay on joining the Black Muslim Movement; he was world heavyweight champion 1964–67 (losing the title for refusing military service), 1974–Feb 1978, Sept 1978–Jun 1979.

Ali /'ɑːli/ 4th Caliph c. 600–661. Born at Mecca, he was the son of Abu Talib, uncle to ▷Muhammad, who gave him his daughter Fatima in marriage. On Muhammad's death in 632, Ali had a claim to succeed him, but this was not conceded until 656. After a stormy reign, he was assassinated. Around Ali's name has raged the controversy of the Sunnites and the Shiites, the former denying his right to the caliphate and the latter supporting it.

alibi the legal defence that the accused was at some other place when the crime was committed (from Latin 'elsewhere').

Alicante /ˌælɪ'kænti/ seaport and tourist resort in Valencia, Spain; population (1981) 251,390.

alien in law, a person who is not a ▷citizen of a particular state. In the UK, under the British Nationality Act 1981, an alien is anyone who is neither a British Overseas citizen (for example ▷Commonwealth) nor a member of certain other categories; citizens of the Republic of Ireland are not regarded as aliens. Aliens may not vote or hold public office in the UK.

alienation a sense of frustration, isolation, and powerlessness; a feeling of loss of control over one's life; a sense of estrangement either from society or from oneself. As a sociological concept it was developed by ▷Hegel and ▷Marx, who used it as a description and criticism of the condition of workers in capitalist society. The term has also been used by non-Marxist writers to explain industrial unrest in modern factories, and to describe the sense of powerlessness felt by groups such as young people, black people, and women in western industrial society.

Aligarh /ˌɑːlɪ'gɑː/ city in Uttar Pradesh, India; population (1981) 20,861.

alimentary canal long tube extending from the mouth to the anus, about 9 m/33 ft long in a human adult. Its function is to convey and digest food, and it consists of the ▷oesophagus (gullet), ▷stomach, duodenum, small intestine and large intestine (▷colon and ▷rectum).

alimony in the US and formerly in the UK, money allowance given by court order to a former

wife or husband after separation or divorce; in the UK the legal term is maintenance. In some legal systems the right has been extended outside marriage and is colloquially termed 'palimony'.

aliphatic compound any organic chemical compound that is made up of chains of carbon atoms, rather than rings (as in cyclic compounds). The chains may be linear, as in hexane C_6H_{14}, or branched as in isopropanol (2-propanol) $(CH_3)_2CHOH$.

alkali chemical compound classed as a ▷base which is soluble in water. Alkalis neutralize acids and are soapy to the touch. The word comes from the Arabic *al-qualīy*, 'ashes', since soda and potash were derived from the ashes of plants. The hydroxides of metals are alkalis, those of sodium (caustic soda NaOH) and of potassium (caustic potash KOH) being chemically powerful.

alkali metals group of elements in the ▷periodic table of the elements – group I or group Ia: lithium (Li), sodium (Na), potassium (K), rubidium (Rb), caesium (Cs) and francium (Fr). In general, the elements of this group are reactive, soft, low-melting-point metals. Because of their reactivity they are only found as ▷compounds in nature and are not used as structural metals, but as chemical reactants.

alkaline earth elements a group of elements in the ▷periodic table of the elements – group II or IIa: beryllium (Be), magnesium (Mg), calcium (Ca), strontium (Sr), barium (Ba), and radium (Ra). All the elements are metallic but none occurs free in nature. They have closely-related properties and they and their compounds are used to make alloys, oxidizers and drying agents.

alkaloids physiologically active and frequently poisonous substances contained in certain plants. They are usually bases, forming salts with acids and, when soluble, giving alkaline solutions. But substances are included in the group rather by custom than by scientific rules. Examples include morphine, cocaine, quinine, caffeine, strychnine, nicotine, and atropine.

Alken /'ælkən/ Henry Thomas 1784–1851. British sporting artist. Fox-hunting and steeplechasing were the subjects that most frequently occupied him, but the whole range of field sports was covered in his *National Sports of Great Britain* 1821.

al-Khwarizmi /ˌælkwɑː'rizmi/ Muhammad ibn-Musa 780–c. 850. Arab mathematician who lived and worked in Baghdad and is best known for introducing ▷algorithms (a word based on his name) and for introducing the word ▷algebra (*al-jabr*) in an adaptation of an earlier Indian text. He compiled astronomical tables, put forward Arabic numerals, and pioneered calculation using decimal numbers.

Allah /'ælə/ Islamic name for God, Arabic *al-Ilah* 'the God'.

Allan /'ælən/ David 1744–1796. Scottish historical painter. He studied in Rome and, after a period in London, became director of the Academy of Arts in Edinburgh in 1786. Noted for portrait and genre paintings such as *Scotch Wedding*.

Allan /'ælən/ Sir William 1782–1850. Scottish historical painter, born in Edinburgh, who spent several years in Russia and neighbouring countries, and returned to Edinburgh in 1814. He was elected Royal Academician in 1835, president of the Royal Scottish Academy in 1838, and was knighted in 1842. His paintings include scenes from ◊Scott's *Waverley* novels.

Allegheny Mountains /ˌælɪˈɡeɪnɪ/ range over 800 km/500 mi long extending from Pennsylvania to Virginia, USA, rising to more than 1,500 m/4,800 ft and averaging 750 m/2,500 ft. They initially hindered western migration, the first settlement to the west being Marietta in 1788.

allegory in literature, the description or illustration of one thing in terms of another; a work of poetry or prose in the form of an extended metaphor or parable which makes use of symbolic fictional characters, as in the allegorical romantic epic *The Faerie Queene* 1590–96 by Edmund Spenser in homage to Queen Elizabeth I. Allegory is often used for moral purposes, as in John Bunyan's *Pilgrim's Progress* 1678. Medieval allegory often used animals as characters; this tradition survives today in such works as *Animal Farm* 1945 by George Orwell.

Allegri /əˈleɪɡriː/ Gregorio 1582–1652. Italian Baroque composer, born at Rome, he became a priest, and entered the Sistine chapel choir in 1629. His *Miserere* for nine voices was reserved for performance by the chapel choir until ◊Mozart (at 14) was able to write out the music from memory.

allele an alternative form of a given ◊gene. Thus, blue and brown eyes are determined by different alleles of the gene for eye colour. See also ◊dominance, ◊recessivity.

Allen, Lough /ˈælən/ lake in county Leitrim, Republic of Ireland, on the upper course of the river Shannon. It is 11 km/7 mi long and 5 km/3 mi broad.

Allen, Bog of /ˈælən/ morasses east of the river Shannon in the Republic of Ireland, comprising some 96,000 ha/240,000 acres of the counties of Offaly, Leix, and Kildare, the country's main source of peat fuel.

Allen /ˈælən/ Hervey 1889–1949. American novelist, best known for his historical novel *Anthony Adverse* 1933 set in the Napoleonic era.

Allen /ˈælən/ Woody, pseudonym of Allen Stewart Konigsberg 1935– . American comedian-philosopher, writer, film director and clarinettist. Allen is best known for his cynical, witty, often self-deprecating parody and special brand of off-beat humour. His films include *Play It Again Sam* 1972, *Annie Hall* 1977 (for which he won three Academy Awards), and *Hannah and her Sisters* 1986 – all of which he also directed.

Allenby /ˈælənbi/ Henry Hynman, 1st viscount Allenby 1861–1936. British field marshal. In World War I he was with the BEF in France before taking command in 1917–1919 of the British Forces in the Near East. He proceeded to crush the Turks in Palestine, the crowning victory being at Megiddo in Spain in Sept 1918, which was followed almost at once by the capitulation of Turkey.

Allende (Gossens) /aɪˈendi/ Salvador 1908–1973. Chilean politician. Born in Valparaiso, Allende became a Marxist activist in the 1930s and rose to prominence as a left-wing presidential candidate in 1952, 1958 and 1964. In each election he had the support of the socialist and communist movements but was defeated by the Christian Democrats and Nationalists. Elected in 1970 as the candidate of the Popular Front alliance, Allende never succeeded in keeping the electoral alliance together in government. His failure to solve the country's economic problems or to deal with political subversion allowed the army to stage the 1973 coup which brought about Allende's death, and those of many of his supporters.

allergy special sensitivity of the body which makes it react, with an exaggerated response of the natural immune defence mechanism, to the introduction of a harmless foreign substance termed an allergen. The person subject to hayfever in summer is allergic to one or more kinds of pollen. Many asthmatics are allergic to certain kinds of dust or to microorganisms in animal fur or feathers. Others come out in nettle-rash, or are violently sick if they eat shellfish or egg. Drugs may be used to reduce sensitivity or produce tolerance, but there is no universal remedy.

All Fools' Day another name for ◊April Fools' Day.

Alliance arrangement by which the British ◊Liberal Party and ◊Social Democratic Party formed a loose union for electoral purposes, 1981–87. It was set up soon after the formation of the SDP, and involved a joint manifesto at national elections and the apportionment of constituencies in equal numbers to Liberal and SDP candidates. The difficulties of presenting two separate parties to the electorate as if they were one proved insurmountable, and after the Alliance's poor showing in the 1987 general election the SDP voted to merge with the Liberals.

Allied Mobile Force permanent multinational military force established 1960 to move immediately to any NATO country under threat of attack; see ◊North Atlantic Treaty Organization.

Allier /ˌæliˈeɪ/ river in central France, a tributary of the Loire; it is 565 km/350 mi long, and gives its name to a *département*. Vichy is the chief town on it.

Allies term used for the 23 countries allied against Germany in World War I, notably Britain, France, Italy, Russia, and the United States; and for the 49 countries allied against the ◊Axis (Germany, Italy and Japan) in World War II, including Britain, the USA and the USSR.

alligator type of reptile resembling crocodiles. There are two species *Alligator mississipiensis* of the southern states of the USA, and *Alligator sinensis* from the swamps of the lower Chang Jiang river in China. The former grows to about 4 m/12 ft, but the latter only to 1.5 m/5 ft. Closely related are the caimans of South America. Alligators swim well with lashing movements of the tail and feed on fish and mammals but seldom attack people. The eggs are laid in sand. The skin is of value for fancy leather and alligator farms have been established in the USA.

Allingham /ˈælɪŋəm/ Margery Louise 1904–1966. British detective novelist, creator of detective Albert Campion, as in *More Work for the Undertaker* 1949.

alliteration in poetry and prose, the use within a line or phrase of words beginning with the same sound. It was a common device in Old English poetry, and its use survives in many traditional English phrases such as 'kith and kin', 'hearth and home', and so on.

allium genus of plants belonging to the Lily family. They are usually acrid in their properties, but form bulbs in which sugar is stored. Cultivated species include onion, garlic, chives, and leek.

allometry in biology, a regular relationship between a given feature (for example, the size of an organ) and the size of the body as a whole, when this relationship is not a simple proportion of body size. Thus, an organ may increase in size proportionately faster, or slower, than body size does. The best known allometric relationship is the surface area law: the ratio of body surface to total body volume decreases as body size gets larger. Large animals therefore lose less heat than small ones because they have proportionately less skin surface from which to radiate heat.

allopathy the treatment of disease of one kind by exciting a disease process of another kind or in another part; sometimes incorrectly used as a name for orthodox medicine, in distinction from ◊homoeopathy, which means treatment with minute doses of drugs that induce the same ailment.

allotrope different forms of the same element, for example the two forms of oxygen: 'normal' oxygen (O_2) and ozone (O_3), which have different molecular configurations. More commonly, allotropes of an element have different crystal structures when solid, e.g. the two forms of tin – white and grey. The allotropes of carbon are diamond and graphite.

alloy metal blended with some other metallic or non-metallic substance in order to give it special qualities, such as resistance to ◊corrosion, greater hardness and tensile strength. Among the oldest alloys is ◊bronze, whose widespread use ushered in a historical period known as the Bronze Age. Among other useful alloys are brass, cupronickel, duralumin, German silver, gunmetal, pewter, solder, steel and stainless steel. Among the most recent alloys are the superplastic alloys which may stretch 100% at specific temperatures. For example, at 450°C, an alloy of aluminium and zirconium stretches so easily that it can be injected into moulds as easily as plastic. Today, complex alloys are widespread, for example a cheaper alternative to gold in dentistry is made of chromium, cobalt, molybdenum, and titanium.

All Saints' Day festival on 1 Nov for all Christian saints and martyrs who have no special day of their own. Also known as All-Hallows or Hallowmas.

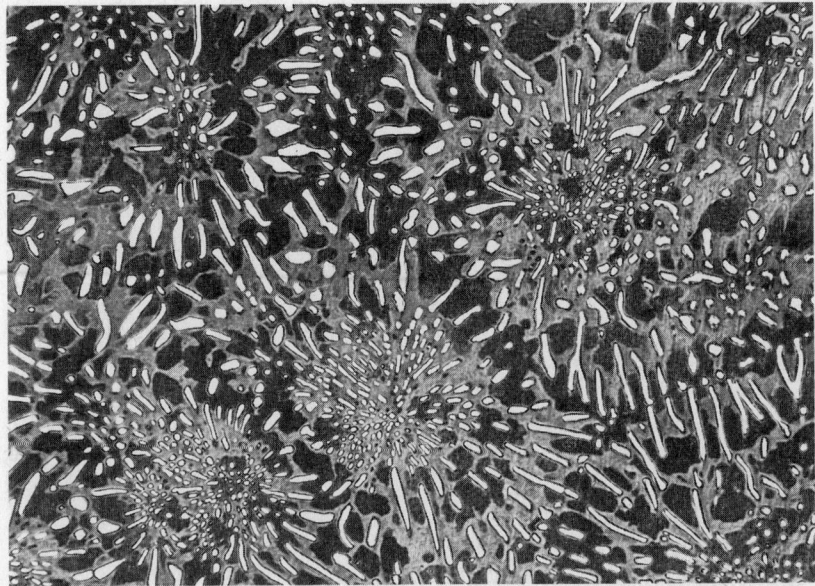

alloy Ternary eutectic microstructure of a silver-copper-cadmium alloy, magnified 600 times. An alloy is prepared by adding other substances to a basic metal to secure desirable properties. Eutectic alloys consist of solid solutions having the lowest melting point. They are used in fuses and safety mechanisms.

All Souls' Day festival in the Catholic Church, held on 2 Nov, following ◊All Saints' Day in the conviction that the faithful, by prayer and self-denial can hasten the deliverance of souls expiating their sins in ◊Purgatory.

allspice spice prepared from dried berries of the tree or pimento *Pimenta dioica*, cultivated chiefly in Jamaica.

Allston /ˈɔːlstən/ Washington 1779–1843. US artist and writer; a ◊Romantic painter, chiefly of religious subjects.

alluvial deposit a layer of broken rocky matter, formed from material that has been washed along by a river or stream and dropped as the current changed. River plains and deltas are made entirely of alluvial deposits, but smaller pockets can be found in the beds of upland torrents. They can consist of a whole range of particle sizes, from boulders down through cobbles, pebbles, gravel, sand, silt and clay. The raw materials are the rocks and soils of upland areas that are broken by erosion and washed away by mountain streams. Much of the world's richest farmland lies on alluvial deposits, and they can also provide an economic source of minerals. River currents produce a winnowing action, with particles of heavy material deposited first while lighter materials are washed onwards. Hence heavy minerals such as gold and tin, present in the original rocks in small amounts, can be concentrated and deposited on stream beds in commercial quantities. Such deposits are called 'placer ores'.

Alma, Battle of the battle in 1854 between Russian forces and those of Britain, France and Turkey which formed part of the Crimean war of 1854–56.

Alma Ata /ælˈmɑː əˈtɑː/ capital of the Republic of Kazakh, USSR; population 871,000.

Kazakh nationalist riots here in Dec 1986 resulted in some 20 deaths.

alma mater Latin 'bounteous mother', the title given by the Romans to the goddess Ceres; it is applied to universities and schools as 'foster-mothers' of their students.

Almansa /ælˈmænsə/ Spanish town in Albacete, about 80 km/50 mi NW of Alicante, where on 25 Apr 1707 British and allied forces were defeated by the French under the duke of Berwick.

Alma-Tadema /ˈælmə ˈtædɪmə/ Laurence 1836–1912. Anglo-Dutch painter. Born at Dronrijp, Holland, he settled in England in 1873. Some of his best-known paintings, which enjoyed a revival in the 1980s, are pseudo genre scenes from ancient Greek and Roman daily life. He was knighted in 1899.

Almeida /ælˈmeɪdə/ Francisco de c. 1450–1510. First viceroy of Portuguese India 1505–08. He was killed in a skirmish with the Hottentots at Table Bay, S Africa, and was buried where Cape Town now stands.

Almería /ˌælmeˈriːə/ Spanish city, chief town of a province of the same name on the Mediterranean; population (1981) 140,750. The province is famous for its white grapes and in the Sierra Nevada are rich mineral deposits.

Almohad a Berber dynasty 1130–1269 founded by the Berber prophet Mohammed ibn Tumart (c. 1080–1130), which ruled much of Morocco and Spain, which they took by defeating the ◊Almoravids; they later took the area which today forms Algeria and Tunis. They were themselves defeated by the Christian kings of Spain in 1212, and in Morocco in 1269.

almond seed of the almond tree *Prunus dulcis*, which is closely related to the peach and the apricot. Originally a native of N Africa and

the near East, it has for a long time been introduced into Europe, and its fruit will ripen in southern England.

Almoravid a Berber dynasty 1056–1147 founded by the prophet Abdullah ibn Tashfin, ruling much of Morocco and Spain in the 11th–12th centuries. They came from the Sahara and in the 11th century began laying the foundations of an empire covering the whole of Morocco and parts of Algeria; their capital was the newly founded Marrakesh. In 1086 they defeated Alfonso VI of Castile to gain much of Spain. They were later overthrown by the ◊Almohads.

aloe genus of African plants of the family Liliaceae, distinguished by their long fleshy leaves. From the juice of the leaves of several species is prepared the drug aloes, a powerful cathartic.

Alost /ɑːˈlɒst/ (Flemish *Aalst*) industrial town (brewing, textiles) in East Flanders, Belgium, on the river Dender; population (1980) 78,700.

Aloysius, St /ˌæləʊˈɪsɪəs/ 1568–1591. Italian Jesuit who died while nursing plague victims. He is the patron saint of youth. Feast day: 21 Jun.

alpaca domesticated South American member of the camel family found in Chile, Peru, and Bolivia, and herded at high elevations in the Andes. About 1 m/3 ft tall, it is mainly bred for its long fine wool, and like the llama was probably bred from the wild ◊guanaco.

alpha and omega first (α) and last (o) letters of the Greek alphabet, hence the beginning and end, or sum total, of anything.

alphabet a set of conventional symbols for the purpose of writing, so-called from *alpha* and *beta*, the names of the first two letters of the classical Greek alphabet. Alphabetic writing began in W Asia during the second millennium BC among the N semitic peoples, and now takes many forms, for example the Arabic script, written from right to left, the Devanagari script of the Hindus, in which the symbols 'hang' from a line common to all the symbols, and the Greek alphabet, with the first clearly delineated vowel symbols. Each letter of the alphabets descended from Greek represents a particular sound or sounds, usually described as *vowels* (*a, e, i, o, u,* in the English version of the Roman alphabet), *consonants* (*b, p, d, t*) and *semi-vowels* (*w, y*). Letters may operate in special arrangements to produce distinct sounds (for example *a* and *e* together in words like *tale* and *take*, or *o* and *i* together to produce a 'wa' sound in the French *loi*), or may have no sound whatsoever (for example the silent letter *gh* in 'high' and 'through').

Alpha Centauri closest ◊star to the Sun, 4.3 light years away. It is the brightest star in the constellation of ◊Centaurus, and the third-brightest in the sky. Telescopes show that Alpha Centauri is actually a triple star (see ◊binary star); the two brighter stars orbit each other every 80 years while the third, ◊Proxima Centauri, is slightly closer to us.

alpha particle positively charged particle ejected with very great velocity from the nucleus of an ◊atom. It is one of the products of the spontaneous disintegration of radioactive substances such as radium and thorium and is identical with the nucleus of a helium atom, that is, it consists of two protons and two neutrons.

Alphege, St /ˈælfɪdʒ/ 954–1012. Anglo-Saxon priest, bishop of Winchester from 984, archbishop of Canterbury from 1006. When the Danes attacked Canterbury he tried to protect the city, was thrown into prison, and, refusing to deliver the treasures of his cathedral, was stoned and beheaded at Greenwich on 19 Apr, his feast day.

Alps /ælps/ mountain chain, the barrier between N Italy and France, Germany and Austria.

famous peaks include *Mont Blanc* the highest at 4,807 m/15,772 ft, first climbed by Jacques Balmat and Michel Paccard 1786;

Matterhorn in the Pennine Alps 4,477 m/14,688 ft, first climbed by Edward Whymper 1865 (four of the party of seven were killed when the rope broke during their descent);

Eiger in the Bernese Alps/Oberland, 3,970 m/13,101 ft, with a near-vertical rock wall on the north face;

Jungfrau 4,166 m/13,668 ft, of exceptional beauty, and *Finsteraarhorn* 4,274 m/14,014 ft.

famous passes include *Brenner* the lowest, Austria/Italy;

Great St Bernard the highest, 2,472 m/8,110 ft, Italy/Switzerland (by which ◊Napoleon marched into Italy 1800);

Little St Bernard Italy/France (which ◊Hannibal is thought to have used), and *St Gotthard* S Switzerland, which ◊Suvorov used when ordered by the tsar to withdraw his troops from Italy. All have been superseded by all-weather road/rail tunnels. The Alps extend into Yugoslavia with the Julian and Dinaric Alps.

Alps, Australian /ælps/ highest area of the E Highlands in Victoria/New South Wales, Australia, noted for winter sports. They include the *Snowy mountains* and *Mt Kosciusko*, Australia's highest mountain, 2,229 m/7,316 ft, (first noted by Polish-born Sir Paul Strzelecki 1829, and named after a Polish hero).

Alps, Lunar /ælps/ a mountain range on the moon, north east of the Sea of Showers, cut by a valley 150 km/93 mi long.

Alps, Southern /ælps/ range of mountains running the entire length of South Island, New Zealand. They are forested to the W, with scanty scrub to the E The highest point is Mount Cook 3,764 m/12,349 ft. Scenic features include gorges, glaciers, lakes and waterfalls. Among its most famous lakes are those at the southern end of the range: Manapouri, Te Anau, and the largest, Wakatipu, 83 km/52 mi long, which lies about 300 m/1,000 ft above sea level and has a depth of 378 m/1,242 ft.

Alsace-Lorraine /ælˈsæs lɒˈreɪn/ area of NE France. Forming part of Celtic Gaul in Caesar's time, the area was invaded by the Alemanni and other Germanic tribes in the 4th century, and remained part of the German Empire till the 17th century. In 1648 part of the territory was ceded to France; in 1681 Louis XIV seized Strasbourg. The few remaining districts were seized by France after the Revolution. Conquered by Germany in 1870–71 (chiefly for its iron ores),

it was regained by France in 1919, then again annexed by Germany 1940–44, when it was liberated by the ◊Allies. It now forms the modern French regions of *Alsace* capital Strasbourg; population (1982) 1,566,000 and *Lorraine* capital Nancy; population (1982) 2,320,000. The German dialect spoken does not have equal rights with French, and there is autonomist sentiment.

Outdated iron and steel industries are being replaced by electronics, chemicals, and precision engineering. The *Cross of Lorraine* with double cross bars, emblem of ◊Joan of Arc, was adopted by the Free French forces in World War II.

Alsatia /ælˈseɪʃə/ the old name for ◊Alsace. In 17th-century London this name was given to the district of Whitefriars between Fleet Street and the Thames. It afforded sanctuary to debtors and other lawless characters, a privilege derived from the convent of Carmelites, established there in 1241. In 1697 this privilege was withdrawn.

alsatian breed of dog introduced from Germany into Britain after World War I and known officially from 1977 as the German shepherd. It has a wolflike appearance, a beautiful coat with many varieties of colouring, and distinctive gait. Alsatians are used as war and police dogs.

Altai Mountains /ælˈtaɪ/ mountain system of W Siberia and Mongolia. It is divided into two parts, the Russian Altai, which includes the highest peak, Mount Belukha, 4,540 m/15,157 ft, and the Mongolian or Great Altai.

Altair brightest ◊star in the constellation of ◊Aquila, the eagle, and the twelfth-brightest star in the sky. It is a white star 16 light years away and forms the so-called Summer Triangle with the stars Deneb (in ◊Cygnus) and ◊Vega (in Lyra).

Altamira /ˌæltəˈmɪərə/ cave near the Spanish village of Santillana del Mar in ◊Santander province where in 1879 remarkable palaeolithic wall-paintings were discovered.

Altdorf /ˈæltdɔːf/ capital of the Swiss canton Uri at the head of Lake Lucerne, Switzerland; population 9,000. It was the scene of the legendary exploits of William ◊Tell.

Altdorfer /ˈæltdɔːfə/ Albrecht 1480–1538. German artist, born at Regensburg, where he worked as an architect. One of the first European painters of landscapes in which human figures are reduced to insignificance by the immensity of nature; his work breaks with the medieval tradition of 'story-telling'. Few of his pictures survive.

alternate angles in geometry one of a pair of angles that lie on opposite sides of a transversal (a line cutting two other lines). If the two other lines are parallel, the alternate angles are equal.

alternating current (AC) electric current that flows for an interval of time in one direction and then in the opposite direction, that is, a current that flows in alternately reversed directions through or round a circuit. Alternating current power is the usual form in which electric energy is generated in a power station, and alternating currents may be used for both power and lighting. The virtue of alternating current over direct current (DC) (as

from a battery) is that its voltage can be raised or lowered economically by a transformer, high voltage for generation and transmission, and low voltage for utilization and safety, for example, railways, factories, and domestic appliances.

alternation of generations the typical lifecycle of terrestrial plants and some seaweeds, in which there are two distinct forms occurring alternately. One is ◊diploid and produces ◊haploid spores by ◊meiosis; this is called the sporophyte (spore-producer). The other is haploid and produces ◊gametes (sex cells); this is called the gametophyte (gamete-producer). The gametes fuse to form a diploid ◊zygote which develops into a new sporophyte, and so the sporophyte and gametophyte alternate. In mosses, the familiar green moss plant is gametophyte, while the long-stalked spore capsules growing from it are sporophyte. In ferns the familiar plant is the sporophyte and the gametophyte, which grows separately from it, is very small and inconspicuous. All higher plants are sporophytes, and the gametophyte is not seen because it completes its life within the body of the sporophyte. The life cycles of certain animals (such as the jellyfish) are sometimes said to show alternation of generations, but this is rarely as regular and clearly-defined as in plants.

alternative energy sources of energy that are renewable, as opposed to sources that are expendable, such as coal, oil or gas (fossil fuels) and ◊uranium (for nuclear power).

Hydroelectric power (HEP) is the most important of the alternative energy sources already being exploited. This harnesses the energy in flowing water. HEP schemes are feasible only in certain locations where the terrain is suitable, but many sites worldwide remain to be developed.

Tidal power is a specialized form of HEP, harnessing the twice daily surge of the tides to generate electricity. This has been done successfully at the Rance estuary in Brittany since 1966. Other potential sites include the Severn estuary in Britain and the Bay of Fundy in Canada, where the tidal rise and fall are large enough (over 10 m/33 ft).

Windmills have been used for centuries to harness the energy blowing in the wind.

Wind turbines of advanced aerodynamic design are used in modern wind power installations. Some consist of large propellers mounted on tall towers, such as that at Tvind in Denmark. It has an output of some 2 megawatts. Other machines use novel rotors, such as the 'egg-beater' design developed at Sandia Laboratories in New Mexico.

Solar power is a renewable source also being exploited successfully in many parts of the world. Domestic hot-water systems and swimming pools can be heated by means of flat-plate collectors. Solar 'power tower' schemes use hundreds of mirrors to concentrate the sun's heat on a central tower, where the heat is made to raise steam in a boiler. Advanced schemes have been proposed that will use giant solar reflectors in space that would harness ◊solar energy and beam it down to Earth in the form of ◊microwaves.

Other alternative energy schemes seek to harness the heat trapped in rocks in the earth's crust (geothermal energy) and in the waves.

alternator an electricity ◊generator, which produces an alternating current.

Altgeld /'ɔːltgeld/ John Peter 1847–1902. US political and social reformer. Born in Prussia, he was taken in infancy to the USA. During the Civil War he served in the Union Army. He was a judge of the supreme court in Chicago 1886–91, and as governor of Illinois 1893–97 was champion of the worker against the government-backed power of big business.

Althing /'ælθɪŋ/ the parliament of Iceland, established about 930 and the oldest in the world.

Althusser /ˌæltuˈseə/ Louis 1918– . French philosopher and Marxist, born in Algeria, who had a major impact on Marxist thought after 1968, arguing that the idea that the economic system determines everything about such elements as the family and political systems is too simple. He divides each mode of production into four key elements – the economic, political, ideological, and theoretical, all of which interact. His structuralist analysis of capitalism sees individuals and groups as agents or bearers of the structures of social relations rather than as independent influences on history. In particular he attempted to show how the ruling class ideology of a particular era is a crucial form of class control. A controversial figure, he dismisses mainstream sociology as bourgeois and has influenced thinkers in fields as diverse as social anthropology, literature, and history. Works include *For Marx* 1965, *Lenin and Philosophy* 1969, and *Essays in Self-Criticism* 1976.

altimeter an instrument that measures the altitude, or height above sea level, commonly used in aircraft. The common type is a form of aneroid ◊barometer, which works by sensing the differences in air pressure at different altitudes. This type must continually be recalibrated because of the change in air pressure with changing weather conditions. The radar altimeter measures the height of the aircraft above the ground. It works on the principle of ◊radar, measuring the time it takes for radio pulses emitted by the aircraft to be reflected. Radar altimeters are essential features of automatic and blind-landing systems.

altitude in geometry, the perpendicular distance from a vertex (corner) of a triangle to the base (the side opposite the vertex). In ordinary terms, the altitude is the height of the triangle.

Altmark incident /'æltmɑːk/ the *Altmark*, a German auxiliary cruiser, was intercepted on 15 Feb 1940, by HM destroyer *Intrepid* off the coast of Norway. It was carrying the captured crews of Allied merchantmen sunk by the German battleship *Admiral Graf Spee* in the S Atlantic, and took refuge in Jösing fjord. There it was cornered by HMS *Cossack*, under Captain Vian, and ran aground. Vian's men released 299 British sailors.

alto (Italian 'high') (1) low-register female voice also called *contralto*; (2) high adult male voice, also known as a counter tenor; (3) (French) viola.

altruism the giving of help or charity without expectation of return. In biology, altruism often means helping another individual to reproduce more effectively, as a direct result of which the altruist may leave fewer offspring itself. Female honey bees behave altruistically by rearing sisters in order to help their mother, the queen bee, reproduce. In doing so they forego any possibility of reproducing themselves. Explaining altruistic behaviour has taxed evolutionary theorists, but the concepts of ◊kin selection and ◊inclusive fitness allow it to be reconciled with ◊neo-Darwinism.

ALU (arithmetic and logic unit) in a computer, the part of the ◊CPU (central processing unit) that performs simple arithmetic or logical operations on data.

alum a white crystalline powder readily soluble in water; a double sulphate of potassium and aluminium. Its chemical formula is K_2SO_4. $Al_2(SO_4)_3$. $24H_2O$, and it is the commonest member of a group of double sulphates called alums, all of which have similar formulae and the same crystalline form. Used in paper making, and to help colour 'take' in dyeing textiles.

alumina oxide of aluminium, AC_2O_3, sometimes called corundum, which is widely distributed in clays, slates and shales. It is formed by the decomposition of the feldspars in granite. Typically it is a white powder, soluble in most strong acids or caustic alkalis, but not in water. Alumina is used as an abrasive; impure alumina is called 'emery'.

aluminium the most abundant metal, valuable for its light weight, having atomic number 13, atomic weight 26.98, and chemical symbol Al. Nearly one-twelfth of the substance of the earth's crust is composed of aluminium compounds, but aluminium in its pure state was not readily obtained until the middle of the 19th century, for it oxidizes rapidly, and much energy is needed to separate the metal from its ores. Pure aluminium is a soft white metal. It is one of the lightest of metals, its specific gravity being 2.70, and for this reason is widely used in shipbuilding and aircraft. In the pure state it is a weak metal, but if combined with other elements such as copper, silicon, or magnesium, it forms alloys of great strength. Commercially, aluminium is obtained from bauxite, a mineral composed of hydrated aluminium oxides. Aluminium is much used in steel-cored aluminium overhead cables and for canning uranium slugs for nuclear reactors. It is an essential constituent in some magnetic materials; and, as a good conductor of electricity, is used as foil in electrical capacitors. A plastic form of aluminium, developed in 1976, which moulds to any shape and extends to several times its original length, has uses in electronics, cars, building construction, etc. In the USA the original name suggested by Sir Humphry Davy *aluminium* is retained.

Alva, or Alba /'ælvə/ Ferdinand Alvarez de Toledo, Duke of 1508–1582. Spanish politician and general. He commanded the Spanish armies of Charles V and Philip II, and in 1567 was appointed governor of the Netherlands, where he set up a reign of terror to suppress the revolt against the Spanish tyranny of the Inquisition. In 1573 he retired, and returned to Spain.

Alvarado /ˌælvəˈrɑːdəʊ/ Pedro de c. 1485–1541. Spanish conquistador. In 1519 he accompanied Hernando Cortez, and distinguished himself in the conquest of Mexico. In 1523–24, he conquered Guatemala.

Alvarez /'ælvərez/ Luis Walter 1911– . US physicist. Professor of physics at the University of California from 1945 as well as associate director of the Lawrence Radiation Laboratory 1954–59; he headed the research team which in 1959 discovered the Xi-zero atomic particle. He was awarded a Nobel Prize in 1968.

alveolus one of the many thousands of tiny air sacs in the ◊lung in which exchange of oxygen and carbon dioxide takes place between air and blood. See also ◊respiration.

Alwar /'ʌlwɑː/ city in Rajasthan, India, chief town of the district (formerly princely state) of the same name. It has fine palaces, temples and tombs. Population (1971) 100,791.

Alzheimer's Disease /'æltshaɪməz/ a degenerative disease of the brain cells causing loss of memory and intellectual impairment. Its cause is as yet unknown, and there is no known treatment. It is named after Alois Alzheimer, who first described the condition in 1906.

AM abbreviation for amplitude ◊modulation, one way in which radio waves are modulated, or altered, for the transmission of broadcasting signals.

Amelekites /əˈmæləkaɪts/ in the Old Testament, ancient Semitic tribe of south west Palestine and the Sinai peninsula. According to Exodus xvii they harried the rear of the Israelites after their crossing of the Red Sea, were defeated by Saul and David, and finally crushed in the reign of Hezekiah.

Amalfi /əˈmælfi/ port 39 km/24 mi south east of Naples, Italy. Situated at the foot of Monte Cerrato, on the Gulf of Salerno. For 700 years it was an independent republic. It is an ancient archiepiscopal see, (seat of archbishop) and has a fine Romanesque cathedral. Population 7,000.

amalgam an alloy of ◊mercury with other metals. Most metals will form amalgams, the notable exceptions being iron and platinum. The most familiar form of amalgam is used in dentistry for filling teeth. It usually contains copper, silver and zinc as the main alloying ingredients. The amalgam is pliable when first mixed and then sets hard.
Amalgamation, the process of forming an amalgam, is a technique sometimes used to extract gold and silver from their ores. The ores are treated with mercury which combines with the precious metals.

Amalia /əˈmɑːliə/ Anna 1739–1807. Duchess of Saxe-Weimar-Eisenach. As widow of Duke Ernest, she reigned from 1758 until her son Karl August succeeded her in 1775 with prudence and skill, making the court of Weimar a literary centre of Germany. She was a friend of Wieland, Goethe, and Herder.

Amanita genus of fungi, closely allied to ◊*Agaricus*. It is distinguished by having a ring, or *volva*, round the stem, and warty patches on the cap, and by the clear white colour of the gills.

Amalfi Set at the mouth of a deep ravine, Amalfi has spectacular cliff scenery. It was Italy's most ancient maritime republic, and its law of the sea, *Tabula Amalfitana* was recognized throughout the Mediterranean until the mid-18th century.

Many of the species are brightly coloured and highly poisonous. Fly agaric (*Amanita muscaria*), with bright red cap and white warty patches, is dangerous, and the Death's Cap (*Amanita phalloides*) is deadly: both are found in Britain.

Amanullah Khan /ˌæməˈnʊlə ˈkɑːn/ 1892–1960. Emir of Afghanistan, 3rd son of Habibullah Khan. On his father's assassination in 1919 he seized the throne and concluded a treaty with the British, but his policy of westernization led to rebellion in 1928. Amanullah had to flee, abdicated in 1929, and settled in Rome.

Amarna tablets /əˈmɑːnə/ collection of clay tablets with cuneiform inscriptions, found in the ruins at Tell-el Amarna (the ancient ◊Akhetaton), about 300 km/190 m south of Cairo on the east bank of the Nile. The majority of the tablets, which comprise royal archives and letters of 1411–1375 BC, are in the British Museum. They possibly represent the 'waste-paper basket' of officials who discarded inessential documents when the city was abandoned.

Amaterasu /əˌmɑːtəˈrɑːsuː/ in Japanese mythology, the sun-goddess, grandmother of Jimmu Tenno, first ruler of Japan, from whom the emperors claimed to be descended.

Amati /əˈmɑːti/ Italian family of violin-makers, working in Cremona, c. 1550–1700.

amatol an explosive consisting of ammonium nitrate and ◊TNT (trinitrotoluene) in almost any proportions.

Amazon /ˈæməzən/ South American river. The largest river in the world as regards volume, and the second longest, 6,518 km/4,050 mi. Its main headstreams, the Marañón and the Ucayali, rise in central Peru and unite to flow

Amazon Most famous of the peoples of the Amazon basin are the Xingu of the Mato Grosso. The warrior chief Kamaiura and his men are being threatened by the encroaching settlers whose farms and roads are destroying their hunting grounds.

eastwards across Brazil for about 4,000 km/2,500 mi. The total network is 48,280 km/30,000 mi of navigable waterways, draining 7,000,000 sq km/2,750,000 sq mi, nearly half the South American land mass. The Amazon reaches the Atlantic on the Equator, its estuary is 80 km/50 mi wide and discharges a volume of water so immense that 64 km/40 mi out to sea fresh water remains at the surface. The name Amazon probably derives from Indian *Amossona* 'destroyer of boats', navigation being hindered by floods, rapids and tidal waves.

River Amazon

Amazon /ˈæməzən/ in Greek mythology, a member of a group of legendary female warriors living near the Black Sea, who cut off their right breasts to use the bow more easily; their queen, Penthesilea, was killed by ◊Achilles at the siege of Troy. The term has come to mean a strong, fierce woman.

ambassador officer of the highest rank in the diplomatic service, who represents the head of one state at the court or capital of another.

amber fossilized gum from coniferous trees of the Middle Tertiary period, often washed ashore on the Baltic coast with plant and animal specimens preserved in it. When rubbed, it attracts light objects, such as feathers, as the ancient Greeks noticed. The effect is due to acquisition of negative electric charge, hence the adaptation of the Greek word for amber, *elektron*, for the negatively charged particle, the electron, and the derived term 'electricity'.

ambergris fatty substance, resembling wax, found in the stomach and intestines of the sperm ◊whale, which was used in perfumery as a fixative. Basically intestinal matter, ambergris is not the result of disease, but probably the pathological product of an otherwise normal intestine. The name derives from the French *ambre gris* (grey amber).

Ambler /ˈæmblə/ Eric 1909–1986. British novelist. Born in London, he used Balkan/Levant settings in the thrillers *The Mask of Dimitrios* 1939 and *Journey into Fear* 1940.

Amboina /æmˈbɔɪnə/ small island in the Moluccas, republic of Indonesia. The town of Amboina, formerly an historic centre of Dutch influence, has shipyards. Population (1980) c. 208,898.

Ambrose, Saint /ˈæmbrəʊz/ c. 340–397. A Father of the Christian Church. Born at Trèves, in Southern Gaul, the son of a Roman prefect, Ambrose became governor of Northern Italy. In 374 he was chosen bishop of Milan, although he was not yet a member of the Christian Church. He was then baptized, and was consecrated as bishop eight days later, on 7 Dec (St Ambrose's day). His writings on theological subjects earned him a prominent place among the Latin Fathers of the Church; he also wrote many hymns, and devised the arrangement of church music known as the *Ambrosian Chant*, which is still used in Milan.

ambrosia Greek 'immortal', the food of the gods, supposed to confer eternal life upon all who ate it.

amen Hebrew word signifying affirmation ('so be it'), commonly used at the close of a Jewish or Christian prayer or hymn. As used by Jesus Christ in the New Testament it was traditionally translated 'verily'.

Amenhotep /ˌæmenˈhaʊtep/ four Egyptian pharaohs, including: *Amenhotep III* 1400 BC, who built great monuments at Thebes, including the temples at Luxor; two portrait statues at his tomb were known to the Greeks as the Colossi of Memnon – one was cracked, and when the temperature changed at dawn gave out a weird sound, then thought supernatural. His son *Amenhotep IV* changed his name to ◊Ikhnaton.

America /əˈmerɪkə/ the western hemisphere of the earth, containing the continents of ◊North America and ◊South America, with Central America in between. This great land mass extends from the Arctic to the Antarctic, from beyond 75° north to past 55° south. The area is about 42,000,000 sq km/16,000,000 sq mi, and the estimated population is over 500,000,000. It is usually divided into the continents of North America and South America.

The name America is derived from Amerigo Vespucci, the Florentine navigator who was falsely supposed to have been the first European to reach the American mainland in 1497. The name is also popularly used to refer to the ◊United States of America (USA), a usage which many Canadians, South Americans and other non-US Americans dislike.

American Civil War see ◊Civil War, American.

American Federation of Labor and Congress of Industrial Organizations (AFL-CIO) federation of trade unions in the USA. The AFL was founded in 1881, and the CIO in 1935 as a breakaway union opposed to the AFL policy of including only skilled workers. A merger reunited them in 1955.

American football see ◊football, American.

American Independence, War of the revolt 1775–83 of the British North American colonies which resulted in the establishment of the USA. It was caused by colonial resentment at the contemporary attitude that commercial or industrial interests of any colony should be subordinate to those of the mother country; and the unwillingness of the colonists to pay for a standing army. It was preceded by:

1773 a government tax on tea led citizens disguised as N American Indians to board the ships carrying the tea and throw it into the harbour, the 'Boston Tea Party'.

1774–75 the *First Continental Congress* held in Philadelphia to call for civil disobedience in reply to British measures.

The War:

1775 19 Apr hostilities began at Lexington and Concord Massachusetts, the first shots being fired when British troops, sent to seize illegal military stores, were attacked by the local militia (Paul ◊Revere). The first battle was *Bunker Hill* Massachusetts, 17 Jun 1775, in which the colonists were defeated; George ◊Washington was appointed colonial commander soon afterwards.

1775–76 the *Second Continental Congress* on 4 Jul 1776 issued the Declaration of ◊Independence. See also ◊Ticonderoga.

1776 27 Aug at *Long Island* Washington was defeated, forced to evacuate New York and retire to Pennsylvania but re-crossed the Delaware to win successes at *Trenton* (26 Dec) and *Princeton* (3 Jan 1777).

1777 a British plan, for Sir William Howe (advancing from New York) and General Burgoyne (from Canada) to link up, miscarried. Burgoyne surrendered at *Saratoga* (17,0ctober), but Howe invaded Pennsylvania, defeating Washington at *Brandywine* (11 Sept) and *Germantown* (4 Oct), and occupying Philadelphia; Washington wintered at Valley Forge 1777–78.

1778 France and Spain entered the war on the American side (see John Paul ◊Jones).

1780 12 May capture of *Charleston* the most notable of a series of British victories in the

American south, but they alienated support by attempting to enforce conscription.

1781 19 Oct Cornwallis, besieged in *Yorktown* by Washington and the French fleet, surrendered.

1782 peace negotiations opened.

1783 3 Sept *Treaty of Paris* American independence recognized.

American Indian an aboriginal of the Americas. They were called Indians by Columbus because he believed he had found, not the New World, but a new route to India. They entered N America from Asia via the former land-bridge, Beringia, from 35,000 BC or even 60,000 BC. Their languages and cultures developed in great variety and intermingled. They were the first cultivators of maize, potatoes, sweet potatoes, manioc, peanuts, peppers, tomatoes, pumpkins, cacao, and chicle and were the first users of the drugs ◊tobacco, coco (◊cocaine), peyote (◊mescalin), cinchona (◊quinine), and ◊tequila.

Canada 300,000, including the Inuits; the largest group are the Six Nations (Iroquois), with a reserve near Brantford, Ontario, for 7,000. They are organized in the National Indian Brotherhood of Canada.

United States 1 million, more than half living on reservations, mainly in Arizona, where the Navajo have the largest of all reservations, Oklahoma, New Mexico, California, N Carolina, S Dakota. The population level is thought now to be the same as at the time of Columbus, but now includes many people who are of mixed ancestry. There is an organized American Indian Movement (AIM).

Latin America comparatively few pure Indians, the majority being mestizo (mixed Indian-Spanish descent), among them half the 12 million in Bolivia and Peru. Since the 1960s there has been an increasing stress on the Indian half of their inheritance in terms of their language and culture. The few 'wild tribes' formerly beyond white contact are being transported or killed in the clearing of ◊Amazonia. See also the countries of the Americas and cross-referenced items in the list below.

North America: Arctic ◊Inuit-Aleut;
Sub-Arctic ◊Algonquin, Cree, Ottawa;
NE Woodlands Huron, ◊Iroquois, ◊Mohican, Shawnee (◊Tecumseh);
Great ◊*Plains* Blackfoot, Cheyenne, Comanche, Pawnee, ◊Sioux;
NW Coast Chinook, ◊Tlingit, Tsimshian;
Desert West ◊Apache, ◊Navajo, ◊Pueblo, Hopi, Mojave, Shoshone;
SE Woodlands Cherokee, Choctaw, Creek, ◊Hopewell, ◊Natchez, Seminole.
Central America: ◊Maya, ◊Toltec, ◊Aztec, Mexican.
South America: Eastern ◊Carib, ◊Xingu;
Central ◊Guarani, ◊Miskito;
Western ◊Araucanian, ◊Aymara, ◊Chimu, ◊Inca, ◊Jivaro, ◊Quechua.

American Legion community organization in USA, originally for ex-servicemen of World War I, founded in 1919.

American literature see ◊United States literature.

American Samoa see ◊Samoa, American.

America's Cup international yacht-racing trophy. Won from the Royal Yacht Squadron in 1851 by the schooner-yacht *America*, owned by J C Stevens, in a race round the Isle of Wight, the silver cup was presented to the New York Yacht Club in 1857 to be held and competed for every three years internationally: USA held it until Australia won it in 1984. The original J-class sloops were 39.6 m/130 ft long, but even the modern 12-metre (design formula) yachts which average 19.8 m/65 ft are too expensive for any but syndicates to finance. The seven-race series over a course c. 39.1 km/24.3 m long, had been sailed since 1857 at Newport, Rhode Island, until the 1987 race in Perth, Western Australia, when the USA regained the trophy.

Americium artificial element, produced by bombarding plutonium with neutrons; atomic number 95 (see actinides). Its isotope of mass 243 has a ◊half-life of 7650 years.

Amersfoort /'ɑːməzfɔːt/ town in the Netherlands, 19 km/12 mi north east of Utrecht. Population (1984) 86,896.

Amery /'eɪməri/ Leopold Stennett 1873–1955. British ◊Conservative politician. Secretary of state for India and Burma 1940–45; famous for his exhortation to Neville ◊Chamberlain in May 1940, in words adapted from ◊Cromwell: 'In the name of God, go!' His books include *India and Freedom* (1942) and *My Political Life* (1953–55). Father of Julian ◊Amery.

Ames /eɪmz/ Adelbert 1880–1955. American scientist best known for his research into optics and the psychology of visual perception. He concluded that much of what a person sees depends on what he or she expects to see, based (consciously or unconsciously) on previous experience.

amethyst a variety of quartz, SiO_2, coloured violet by the presence of small quantities of manganese, and used as a semi-precious stone. Amethysts are found chiefly in the USSR, India, the USA, Uruguay, and Brazil.

Amethyst Incident on 20 Apr 1949 a British frigate, HMS Amethyst, sailing on the Yangtse-Kiang River was fired on by communist Chinese forces. The ship was trapped for a total of 14 weeks before breaking free and completing the journey to the sea. The temporary detention of this British vessel has been interpreted as an attempt by the Chinese to assert their sovereignty over what had been considered an international waterway.

Amiel /ˌæmiˈel/ Henri Frédéric 1821–1881. Swiss philosopher and writer. Born at Geneva, he became professor of philosophy at the university there. His fame rests on his *Journal Intime*, 1882–84.

Amiens /'æmiæn/ ancient city of north east France at the confluence of the rivers Somme and Avre; capital of Somme administrative region. Population (1982) 136,358. It has a magnificent Gothic cathedral with a spire 113 m/370 ft high, and gave its name to the battles of Aug 1918, when ◊Haig launched his victorious offensive in World War I.

Amies /'eɪmiz/ Hardy 1909– . British couturier, one of Queen Elizabeth II's dressmakers. Noted from 1934 for his tailored clothes for women, he also designed successfully for men from 1959.

Amin Dada /æ'miːn 'dɑːdɑː/ Idi 1925– . Ugandan politician, president of ◊Uganda 1971–79. He led the coup that deposed ◊Obote in 1971, expelled the Asian community in 1972, and exercised a reign of terror over his own people. He fled when 'rebel' Ugandan and Tanzanian troops invaded his country in 1979.

Amin Dada Idi Amin, Ugandan president from 1971 until his overthrow in 1979, surrounded by his bodyguard. He is being asked to explain to reporters how the Archbishop of Uganda and two cabinet ministers met a violent death while they were in custody in 1977.

amines class of organic chemical compounds which can be considered to be derived from ammonia, one or more of the hydrogen atoms of ammonia being replaced by other groups of atoms. The *simple amines* are divided into primary, secondary, or tertiary according to whether one, two or three hydrogen atoms of ammonia are replaced. The *methyl amines* have unpleasant ammonia odours and occur in decomposing fish. They are all gases at ordinary temperature. Amino acids are compounds of which the basic and acidic groups exist in the same molecule (the amine group is -NH₂). Of the *aromatic amine compounds* the most important is aniline, used in dyeing.

amino acid a water-soluble ◊molecule mainly composed of carbon, oxygen, hydrogen and nitrogen. When joined in chains, amino acids form ◊peptides and ◊proteins. The proteins of living organisms are largely made up of combinations of 20 kinds of amino acids, although there are others that occur infrequently in nature. Eight of these, the *essential amino acids*, cannot be synthesized by humans and

must be obtained from the diet. Children need another two amino acids that are not 'essential' for adults. Other animals also need some amino acids pre-formed in the diet, but plants can make all the amino acids they need, from simpler molecules.

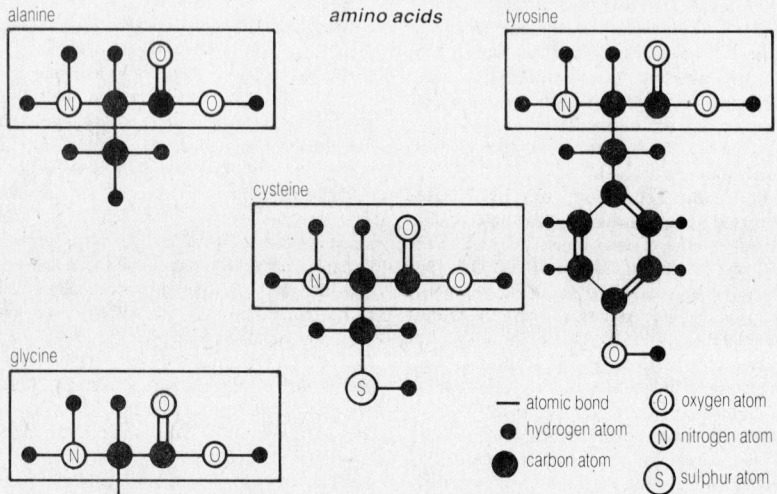

alanine   *amino acids*   tyrosine

cysteine

glycine

— atomic bond   Ⓞ oxygen atom
● hydrogen atom   Ⓝ nitrogen atom
● carbon atom   Ⓢ sulphur atom

Amis /'eɪmɪs/ Kingsley 1922– . British novelist and poet. His works include *Lucky Jim* 1954, a comic portrayal of life in a provincial university, and *Take a Girl Like You* 1960. He won the Booker Prize in 1986 for *The Old Devils*. Father of Martin ◊Amis.

Amis /'eɪmɪs/ Martin 1949– . British novelist, son of Kingsley ◊Amis. His works include *The Rachel Papers* 1974 and *Money* 1984.

Amman /ə'mɑːn/ capital and chief industrial centre of Jordan; population (1980) 1,232,600, it is built on on the site of the Old Testament Rabbath-Ammon (Philadelphia), capital of the ◊Ammonites, Israel's enemies, who made human sacrifices to their god, Moloch. There is a fine Roman amphitheatre. The university of Jordan was established here in 1962, and Amman is the centre of a road network and is on the Cairo-Baghdad air route. Many of the population are Palestinian refugees.

ammeter an instrument that measures electric current. See ◊ampere.

Ammon in Egyptian mythology, the king of the gods, the equivalent of ◊Zeus/◊Jupiter; the name is also spelt Amen/Amun, as in the name of the pharaoh Tutankh*amen*. In art, he is represented as a ram, as a man with a ram's head, or as a man crowned with feathers. He had famous temples at Siwa oasis, Libya and ◊Thebes, Greece.

ammonia a colourless pungent-smelling gas (chemical formula NH₃) about two-thirds as dense as air, and soluble in water forming ammonium hydroxide, NH₄OH. The solution is strongly alkaline, and forms crystalline salts on neutralization with acids. Ammonia is produced by the Haber and Cyanamide processes. It is used mainly to produce nitrogenous fertilizers. In aquatic organisms, and some insects, nitrogenous waste (from breakdown of ◊amino

acids and so on) is excreted in the form of ammonia, rather than urea as in mammals.

Ammonite ancient Semitic people who lived to the northwest of the Dead Sea on the edge of the Syrian desert. Worshippers of Moloch, to whom they offered human sacrifices, they were frequently at war with the Israelites. See also ◊Amman.

ammonite extinct ◊cephalopod mollusc akin to the modern nautilus. The shell was curled in a plane spiral and made up of numerous gas-filled chambers, the outermost containing the body of the animal. Many species flourished between 200 million and 65 million years ago, ranging in size from that of a small coin to 2 m/6 ft across.

Amnesty International human rights organization established in the UK 1961 to campaign for the release of political prisoners worldwide; politically unaligned, it was awarded a Nobel prize in 1977.

amnion innermost of three membranes that enclose the embryo within the egg (reptiles and birds) or within the uterus (mammals). It contains the amniotic fluid which helps to cushion the embryo. See also ◊chorion.

amoeba one of the simplest living animals, consisting of a single cell and belonging to the group ◊Protozoa. The body, which may be just visible to the naked eye, consists of colourless protoplasms. Its activities are controlled by its nucleus, and it feeds on organic debris by flowing round and engulfing it. It reproduces by splitting, not sexually. Some of its relatives are harmful parasites. See also ◊amoebiasis.

amoebiasis infection of the intestines, caused by the ◊amoeba *Entamoeba histolytica*, resulting in chronic dysentery and consequent weakness and dehydration. Endemic in the Third World, it is now occurring in Europe and North America.

Amorites ancient people of ◊Semitic or ◊Indo-European origin, who were among the inhabitants of ◊Canaan at the time of the Israelite invasion. They provided a number of Babylonian kings. See also ◊Hammurabi.

Amos /'eɪmɒs/ lived c. 760 BC. first ◊prophet of the Old Testament.

Amoy /ə'mɔɪ/ ancient name for ◊Xiamen, a port in south east China.

ampere unit (symbol A) of electrical current producing a force between long, straight parallel conductors, one metre apart in a vacuum, of 2×10^7 ◊newtons per metre length.

Ampère /ɒm'peə/ André Marie 1775–1836. French physicist and mathematician. The ◊ammeter and ◊ampere are named after him.

amphetamine synthetic drug ($C_6H_5CH_2CHNH_2CH_3$, or its sulphate or phosphate), which stimulates the central nervous system. It relieves depression, increases alertness, and counteracts fatigue. After World War II it was used by teenagers for 'kicks', notably as benzedrine, or in the ◊barbiturate-amphetamine combination known as 'purple hearts'.

amphibian member of the class of vertebrates (Greek 'double life') which generally spend their larval ('tadpole') stage in fresh water, transferring to land at maturity. However, they generally return to water to breed. Like fish and reptiles they continue to grow throughout life, and cannot maintain a temperature greatly differing from that of their environment. The class includes ◊caecilians, worm-like in appearance; ◊salamanders; and ◊frogs and ◊toads.

amphibian life cycle

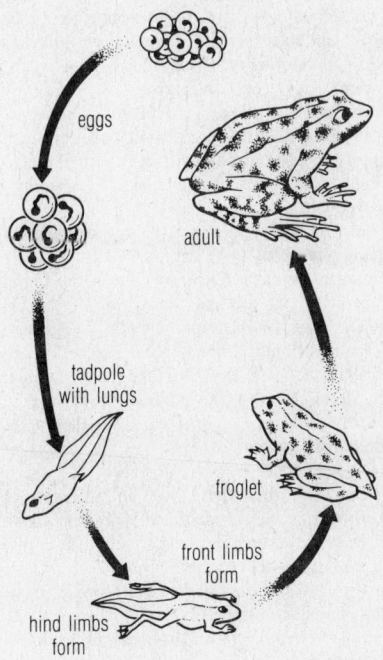

eggs

adult

tadpole with lungs

froglet

front limbs form

hind limbs form

amphibole any one of a large group of rock-forming silicate minerals, closely related to ◊pyroxene. The general formula is $X2\text{-}8(Si_4)_{11})_2$ where X includes Ca, Na, Mg, Fe and Al. Amphiboles form orthorhombic, monoclinic and triclinic ◊crystals. They occur in a wide range of ◊igneous and ◊metamorphic rocks. Common examples are hornblende and cummingtonite.

amphioxus filter-feeding animal about 6 cm/2 in long with a fish-like shape and a ◊notochord running down the body. A primitive relative of vertebrates, it lacks organs such as heart or eye, and lives half-buried in the sea floor.

amphitheatre large oval or circular building used by the Romans for the exhibition of gladiatorial contests, fights of wild beasts, and other similar spectacles; the arena of an amphitheatre is completely surrounded by the seats of the spectators, hence the name (Greek *amphi*, around). The Romans built many amphitheatres, the best known being the ◊Colosseum at Rome, completed in 80 AD, and holding 87,000 spectators.

amphora large pottery storage jar in the Graeco-Roman world used for wine, oil, and dry goods.

amplitude maximum displacement of an oscillation from the equilibrium position. For a wave motion, it is the height of a wave (or the depth of a trough). With a sound wave, for example, amplitude corresponds to the intensity (loudness) of the sound. In AM (amplitude modulation) radio broadcasting, the required audiofrequency signal is made to modulate (slightly vary) the amplitude of a continuously transmitted radio carrier wave.

ampulla small vessel with a round body and narrow neck, used for holding oil, perfumes, and so on, used by the Greeks and Romans for toilet purposes. At British coronations the oil is contained in an eagle-shaped ampulla.

Amritsar /æm'rɪtsə/ industrial city in the Punjab, India; population (1981) 594,844. It is the holy city of ◊Sikhism, with the Guru Nanak University, named after the first Sikh guru, and the Golden Temple from which armed demonstrators were evicted by the Indian Army under General Dayal in 1984, 325 being killed. It is the headquarters of the Akali Dal Sikh (moderate) political party, and of the extremist All-India Sikh Students' Federation. In 1919 it was the scene of the ◊Amritsar massacre.

Amritsar Massacre the killing of 379 Indians (and wounding of 1,200) in Amritsar in 1919, when British troops under General Edward Dyer opened fire without warning on an angry crowd of some 10,000, assembled to protest against the arrest of two ◊India National Congress leaders. Dyer was subsequently censured and resigned his commission, but gained popular support in Britain for his action, both by mention in the House of Lords and by private subscriptions totalling δ26,000. The favourable treatment Dyer received spurred Mahatma ◊Gandhi to a policy of active non-cooperation with the British.

Amsterdam /'æmstədæm/ capital of the Netherlands; population (1985) 998,130. Canals cut through the city link it with the North Sea and the Rhine, and as a port it is second only to Rotterdam. There is shipbuilding, printing, food processing, banking, and insurance. Schipol international airport is to the south-west. Art galleries include Rijksmuseum, Stedelijk, Vincent Van Gogh Museum, and Rembrandt house. Notable also are the Royal Palace (1655), and the Anne ◊Frank house.

Amsterdam The Magere Bridge over the Amstel river, and in the background the high, narrow houses favoured by the city burghers who made maximum use of land which sold at a premium in this wealthy port.

Amu Darya /'æmuː ˌdɑːri'ɑː/ river formerly called Oxus in Soviet central Asia, flowing 2,540 km/1,490 mi from the ◊Pamirs to the ◊Aral Sea.

Amundsen /'æməndsən/ Roald 1872–1928. Norwegian explorer. Born in Borge, he was the first person to navigate the ◊North West Passage in 1906. In 1910 he set sail in the *Fram* to discover the North Pole, but on hearing that he had been forestalled by Peary, he raced Scott to the South Pole instead 1911. In 1918 he made an unsuccessful attempt to drift across the North Pole in the *Maud*, and in 1925 tried to fly from Spitzbergen to the Pole by aeroplane. This too failed, but the following year he and Ellsworth joined the Italian General Nobile in his airship the *Norge*, which circled the pole twice and landed in Alaska. Amundsen died when searching by plane for Nobile and his airship *Italia*.

Amur /ə'mʊə/ river in E Asia. Formed by the Argun and the Shilka, the Amur enters the sea of Okhotsk. At its mouth at Nikolaevsk it is 16 km/10 mi wide. For much of its course of over 4,345 km/2,700 mi it forms, together with its tributary, the ◊Ussuri, the boundary between the USSR and China. Under the treaties of Aigun (1858) and Peking (1860), 984,200 sq km/380,000 sq mi of territory N and E of the two rivers were ceded by China to the tsarist government. From 1963 China raised the question of its return and there have been border clashes.

amyl alcohol a clear colourless oily liquid, usually having a characteristic choking odour.

amylase one of a group of ◊enzymes that break down ◊starches into their component molecules (sugars) for use in the body. It occurs widely in both plants and animals. In humans, it is found in pancreatic juices and saliva.

anabolic steroid one of the synthetic ◊steroid ◊hormones which stimulate constructive chemical processes in living creatures. They are illegally used – the 'bulk bomb' – to give athletes phenomenal size and strength, and are difficult to detect. A single dose, in combination with a high protein diet, is effective in increasing mass over several months, so that anabolic steroids were at first used chiefly by weight-lifters and javelin throwers. Later, sprinters found that, taken shortly before racing, they improved muscular performance by immediately increasing aggressiveness and competitiveness. In women they tend to produce unwanted tendencies to male characteristics.

anabranch stream (Greek *ana* 'again') which branches from a main river, then reunites with it. For example, the Great Anabranch in New South Wales, Australia, leaves the Darling near Menindee, and joins the Murray below the Darling-Murray confluence.

Anaconda /ˌænə'kɒndə/ town in Montana, USA, which has the world's largest copper plant. The city was founded as Copperopolis 1883, by the Anaconda Copper Mining Company, and was incorporated as Anaconda in 1888. The town is 1,615 m/5,300 ft above sea level, and 42 km/26 mi north west of Butte. Population (1980) 12,518.

anaconda /ˌænə'kɒndə/ South American ◊snake *Eunectes murinus* allied to the boa-constrictor. One of the largest snakes, growing to 9 m/30 ft or more, it is found in and near water.

anaemia medical condition characterized by too few red blood cells or too little ◊haemoglobin (the red oxygen-carrying substance in red blood cells), so that the sufferer becomes quickly tired, faint and breathless. It may result from iron deficiency (as in pregnant women), be linked with ◊rheumatoid arthritis, be the result of nuclear radiation, or inherited. Genetic anaemic diseases include *sickle cell anaemia*, and *pernicious anaemia*, a failure of the stomach to secrete the substances necessary to produce blood from food. This is cured by doses of vitamin B12.

anaerobic in biology, a description of those living organisms that do not require oxygen for the release of energy food. Anaerobic organisms include many bacteria, yeasts and internal parasites. *Obligate anaerobes* such as ◊archaebacteria cannot function in the presence of oxygen, but *facultative anaerobes* like the fermenting yeasts and some bacteria can function with or without oxygen. Anaerobic organisms release less of the available energy from their food than ◊aerobic organisms.

anaesthesia a state of insensibility to pain. Anaesthesia of a part of the skin, so that the patient is insensitive to a pin-prick or other stimulus, is a sign of nerve disorder, but the more common meaning of anaesthesia is a loss of sensation or consciousness produced by an anaesthetic drug.
The beginning of modern anaesthesia was the discovery by Thomas Beddoes in 1776 of nitrous oxide (laughing gas). Sir Humphry Davy, inventor of the miner's lamp, did much of the experimental work and first suggested its application to surgery. Horace Wells, a dentist from New England, USA, had a tooth extracted under nitrous oxide for the first time in 1844. Ether was successfully used by Dr Crawford Long of Georgia in 1842 for the removal of a tumour of the neck. The credit for the discovery

of anaesthesia is, however, given to W T G Morton, another dentist, of Boston, Massachusetts, who in 1846 anaesthetized a patient with ether for the removal of a skin tumour at the Massachusetts General Hospital. Professor James Simpson of Edinburgh used it soon afterwards on women in childbirth, and met great opposition from religious people. Meanwhile chloroform had been known in France since 1831, and Simpson began to use it in preference to ether. Its use by Queen Victoria at the birth of Prince Leopold in 1853 settled the religious controversy. Local anaesthesia came into use about the beginning of the 20th century. Cocaine was used as long ago as 1847, but is too poisonous and too likely to lead to addiction to be generally useful. The relatively harmless synthetic substance novocaine, invented about 1905, marked the beginning of the general use of local anaesthetic. Large areas of the body can be anaesthetized by injecting anaesthetic into nerve junctions. Varied anaesthetics are now given, both general and local, and there have been experiments in modern times in the use of ◊acupuncture and ◊hypnosis, which are less easily controlled, but have no side-effects. *Epidural anaesthesia* (injection into the space outside the outermost membrane covering the spinal cord) is used in childbirth, and increasingly for major abdominal operations; the patient remains conscious, and there is reduced risk of complication, with quicker recovery.

analgesic drug reducing sensitivity to pain, for example ◊cocaine and ◊novocaine for local application; opium and its derivatives morphine and heroin, antipyrine, aspirin, and ◊paracetamol; certain barbiturate drugs. Dangers of increasing dosage and addiction may arise.

analogue computer early computing device which performs calculations through the interaction of continuously varying physical quantities such as voltages. Such a computer is said to operate in 'real time', and can therefore be used to monitor and control other things, or events, as they are happening. Although popular in engineering since the 1920s, analogue computers are not general-purpose computers (as are digital computers) and are best confined to solving ◊differential equations and similar mathematical problems.

analysis branch of mathematics concerned with continuous variation (as opposed to ◊algebra, which deals with discrete variation); ◊calculus is thus a type of analysis. In chemistry, analysis is the determination of the composition or properties of substances (see ◊analytical chemistry).

analytic in philosophy, a term derived from ◊Kant: the converse of ◊synthetic. In an analytic judgement the subject is contained in the predicate, and the judgement therefore provides no new knowledge. For example: 'All bachelors are unmarried'.

analytical chemistry branch of chemistry that deals with the determination of the chemical composition of substances. Quantitative analysis determines exact composition in terms of concentration, using such techniques as titration (volumetric analysis) and weighing (gravimetric

analysis). Qualitative analysis determines the elements or compounds in a given sample, without necessarily finding their concentrations. Traditional methods of 'wet' chemistry, using a scheme of consecutive chemical reactions, have been largely superseded by physical methods such as ◊chromatography and ◊spectroscopy.

analytical engine a mechanical computer, designed but never built by Charles ◊Babbage, a 19th-century mathematician. Using a program on punched cards to determine the exact type of calculation to be performed, it would have been the first true computer. It was inspired by the Jacquard loom, which used punched cards to determine the pattern to be woven on a piece of cloth or carpet.

analytical geometry another name for ◊coordinate geometry.

Ananda /ə'nændə/ 5th century BC–. favourite disciple of the ◊Buddha. At his plea, a separate order was established for women.

Anand Marg Indian religious sect, 'the pathway to bliss'; their leader *Prabhat Ranjan Sarkar* (1921–) claims to be god incarnate. Imprisoned for alleged murder of defectors from the sect, he was released after acquittal in 1978.

anarchism the political belief that society should have no government, laws, police, or other authority, but should be a free association of all its members (Greek *anarkhos*, 'without ruler'). It does not mean 'without order'; most theories of anarchism imply an order of a very strict and symmetrical kind, but they maintain that such order can be achieved by cooperation, and they claim that other methods of achieving order, which rely on authority, are morally reprehensible and politically unstable. Anarchism must not be confused with nihilism, a purely negative and destructive activity directed against society as such: it is essentially a ◊pacifist movement.
The religious type of anarchism, claimed by many anarchists to be exemplified in the early organization of the Christian church, has found expression in modern times in the social philosophy of ◊Tolstoy and ◊Gandhi. The growth of political anarchism may be traced through William ◊Godwin, ◊Shelley, and P J ◊Proudhon to ◊Bakunin who had a strong following in Europe, especially France. The theory of anarchism is best expressed in the works of ◊Kropotkin.
From the 1960s there was an outbreak of terrorism popularly identified with anarchism; in Britain the bombing and shooting incidents carried out by the 'Angry Brigade' 1968–71 and in the 1980s, incidents directed towards peace and animal-rights issues, and to demonstrate against huge financial and business corporations.

Anastasia /ˌænə'steɪzɪə/ 1901–1918. Russian Grand Duchess, youngest daughter of ◊Nicholas II. She was murdered with her parents, but it has been alleged that Anastasia escaped, and of those who claimed her identity the most famous was Anna Anderson (1902–1980). Alleged by some to be a Pole, Franziska Schanzkowski, she was rescued from a Berlin canal in 1920: the German Federal Supreme Court rejected her claim in 1970.

Anatolia /ˌænəˈtəuliə/ alternative name for Turkey-in-Asia (Turkish Anadolu).

anatomy the study of the structure of the body, as distinguished from physiology, which is the study of its functions.

Herophilus of Chalcedon (about 300 BC) and Erasistratus of Chios are regarded as the founders respectively of anatomy and physiology. In the 2nd century AD Galen produced an account of anatomy which was the only source of anatomical knowledge until the appearance in 1543 of *On the Working of the Human Body* by Andreas Vesalius (1514–64). In 1628 William ◊Harvey published his demonstration of the circulation of the blood. Anatomy was immensely advanced by the invention of the microscope, and ◊Malpighi (1628–94) and ◊Leeuwenhoek (1632–1723) laid the foundations of the study of a minute anatomy, or ◊histology. In 1747 Albinus (1697–1770), with the help of the artist Wandelaar (1691–1759), produced the most beautiful and exact account of the bones and muscles, and in 1757–65 Albrecht von Haller (1708–77) gave the most complete and exact description of the organs that had yet appeared. The anatomy of the nervous system was advanced by the Frenchman Vicq d'Azyr (1748–94), comparative anatomy G ◊Cuvier (1769–1832), while in England J. Hunter (1728–93) developed an anatomical museum.

Among the most notable anatomical writers of the early 19th century are the surgeon Sir Charles Bell (1774–1842), Jonas Quain (1796–1865), and Henry Gray (1825–1861). Later in the century came the inventions of techniques to stain tissues by dyes for microscopic examination, and the method of mechanically cutting very thin sections of stained tissues. Radiographic anatomy has been one of the triumphs of the 20th century, which has also been marked by immense activity in embryological investigation. See also ◊human body.

Anaximander /æˌnæksɪˈmændə/ 610–c. 547 BC. Greek astronomer and philosopher. Born in Miletus, in what is now Turkey, he was a pupil of ◊Thales. Anaximander is thought to have been the first to determine solstices and equinoxes, to have invented the sundial, and to have produced the first geographical map. In philosophy, he believed that the universe originated as a formless mass (*apeiron*, 'indefinite') containing within itself all contraries such as hot and cold, wet and dry, from which land, sea, and air were formed out of the union and separation of these opposites.

ANC abbreviation for ◊African National Congress.

ancestor worship religious attitude to deceased members of a group or family, prevalent in many societies. Adherents believe that the souls of the dead remain involved in this world, and may influence it if appealed to. Thus the Zulus used to invoke the spirits of the great warriors of their race before engaging in battle. The Greeks deified their early heroes, and the ancient Romans held in reverential honour the *manes* or departed spirits of their forebears. It was also particularly prevalent in old China.

Anchorage /ˈæŋkərɪdʒ/ port and largest town of Alaska, USA, at the head of Cook Inlet. Population (1984) 244,030. There is a salmon canning industry, and coal and gold are mined. Alaska's international airport is here.

anchovy small fish *Engraulis encrasicholus* of the ◊herring family. It is abundant in the Mediterranean, and is also found on the Atlantic coast of Europe and in the Black Sea. It grows to 20 cm/8 in and is fished extensively. Pungently flavoured, it is processed into fish pastes and essences rather than eaten fresh.

Ancien Régime see under ◊French Revolution.

ancient art *prehistoric art* 25,000–1000 BC. The history of the fine arts, painting and sculpture, begins about 21,000 BC in the Paleolithic, or Old Stone Age. Vivid, lifelike images of animals and humans have been found incised, painted or sculptured on the walls deep inside the caves where our ancestors sheltered, mostly in Spain and in SW France, but also in Portugal, Sicily, and Russia. cave paintings also formed part of Indian art as recent discoveries at ◊Bophal indicate, and Aboriginal art in Australia. The images of reindeer, mammoth, horses and bison are most common, varying from very small to almost lifesize. It is thought that they served as part of a 'magic' ritual to ensure a successful hunt. Paintings such as those at the cave of Lascaux in France show great skill in draughtsmanship, with vigorous and sweepingly graceful outlines. Stone Age people also used flint tools to carve small figurines in bone, horn, or stone. The most famous of these is the so-called Venus of Willendorf, a limestone statuette 11.5 cm/4.5 in high, found in lower Austria and dating from about 21,000 BC. Her exaggeratedly bulbous form makes clear her magic significance as a fertility figure.

art of early civilizations 14,000–300 BC. Architecture became the new art form when people began to settle in communities as farmers rather than hunters. They decorated their buildings with sculpture, imposing a sense of pattern and order on them, although Stonehenge in Britain 1800–1400 BC had not achieved this sophistication. In Europe, ◊Celtic art ornamented tombs, crosses, metalwork and pottery with stylized animal and plant forms in swirling curvilinear patterns. Pottery had reached Europe from the Near East where it began as early 5500 BC in Melsopotamia, where sign pictures also grew into cuneiform (wedge-shaped) writing. The Near and Middle East Produced many highly developed urban civilizations, including the *Sumerian* 4000 BC, and the *Persian* 550 BC. In these cultures, sculptures and reliefs of people, gods, and animals decorated palaces (for example the palaces of Darius and Xerxes), temples, and tombs telling stories or praising their gods and rulers. A fine example is the grand stairway of the Persian royal palace, Persepolis, from 518–516 BC. Outstanding examples of precious metalwork, glassware, and pottery (particularly the pottery ware made at Rhages c. 12th century)

also survive, of which there are splendid collections in the British Museum and the Louvre.

Egyptian art 3000–200 BC. The Great Sphinx at Giza 2680–2565 BC, a gigantic human-headed lion carved from an outcropping of natural rock, is the supreme example of Egyptian sculpture, 56.4 m/185 ft long and 19.2 m/63 ft high, it was meant to guard for eternity the god-king's pyramid tomb nearby. Most Egyptian art is funerary, largely consisting of sculptured relief panels painted in bright, lifelike colours covering the walls of tombs and temples. They depend on strong, simple outlines, the main aim being clarity: to picture in their idealized prime the dead, their servants and families, and the objects, animals, foods and activities they enjoyed so that they could be magically transported into the afterworld to be enjoyed forever. Human forms are recomposed almost diagrammatically to show the whole of a person, face and legs in profile, upper torso in front view, hips three-quarters and with the eye magnified. If anything needed further description a hieroglyphic label would be added. Statues, whether of wood or stone, were also generally painted. They retain a strong cubic sense of the block from which they were hewn, with the figures facing straight ahead, the arms in a single unit with the body. The serene vision of eternity found in all Egyptian art is epitomized in the portrait head of Queen Nefertiti in the Staatlich Museum, Berlin, dating from about 1360 BC.

art of Aegean civilizations 2800–100 BC. The Minoan and Mycenean civilizations flourished in the area of the Aegean Sea from about 2800 major monument, the new palace at Knossos 1700 BC, was decorated with cheerful frescoes of scenes from daily life, plants, birds and leaping fish and slphins. Their pottery was painted in the same fresh, spontaneous style with plant and animal motifs curving to suit the form of the vases. In 1400 they were conquered by the Myceneans from the Peloponnese, whose art reflected its more warlike society. Instead of airy palaces, they constructed fortified citadels such as Myceanae itself, which was entered through the Lion Gate 1330, named for the remarkable monumental sculpture that adorns it. In the nearby Cyclades Islands a unique art form emerged about 2800: the small marble Cycladic figures much admired today, which represent the Great Mother Goddess in such streamlined simplicity that her faced is simple an elongated oval with a triangular nose. Many of the ideas and art forms of these early sea-faring civilizations were to be adapted by the Greeks who came from Central Asia between 2000–1000 BC to establish their own splendid culture that was to dominate Western taste and thought for many centuries.

ancient lights in Britain, the right of an owner of a building, arising through long use, to receive an uninterrupted flow of light at one or more of the windows of the building. The right may be acquired in various ways, but usually under the Prescription Act, 1832, by the enjoyment of the right for 20 years without interruption.

Ancona /ænˈkəunə/ Italian town and naval base on the Adriatic Sea, capital of the Marches province. It has a Romanesque cathedral and a former palace of the popes. Population (1981) 106,498.

Andalusia /ˌændə'luːsiə/ fertile autonomous region (Spanish Andalucía) of S Spain. It includes ◊Almería, ◊Cádiz, ◊Córdoba, ◊Granada, ◊Málaga, and ◊Seville; population 6,442,000. It is noted for its Moorish architecture, having been under Muslim rule between the 8th and 15th centuries.

Andamans /'ændəmənz/ group of islands in the Bay of Bengal, between India and Burma. There are five principal islands (forming the Great Andaman), the Little Andaman, and about 204 islets. The Andamans were formerly used as a penal settlement, abolished in 1945, and were occupied by Japan 1942–45. Area 6,500 sq km/2,500 sq mi; With the ◊Nicobars, they form a territory of the Republic of India; population (1981) 188,254.

Andean Group (Spanish *Grupo Andino*) South American organization aimed at economic and social cooperation between member states. It was established under the Treaty of Cartagena 1969, by Bolivia, Chile, Colombia, Ecuador and Peru; Venezuela joined 1973, but Chile withdrew in 1977. The organization is based in Peru.

Andersen /'ændəsən/ Hans Christian 1805–1875. Danish writer. He was born, the son of a shoemaker, at Odense in Fünen. His first book was published when he was only 17, but it was not until 1829 that he attracted notice. In 1835 his novel *The Improvisatore* brought him popularity, and he began to write the fairy tales, such as 'The Ugly Duckling', 'The Emperor's New Clothes', and 'The Snow Queen', which, though Andersen himself did not value them highly, gained him international fame and have been translated into many languages. His other works include romances and an autobiography.

Anderson /'ændəsən/ Carl David 1905– . American physicist, who discovered the positive electron or positron in 1932; he shared a Nobel prize 1936.

Anderson /'ændəsən/ Elizabeth Garrett 1836–1917. First English woman doctor, born Garrett. She qualified in 1865 as a medical practitioner, despite prejudiced opposition, and established a dispensary for women in 1866, which survives as the Elizabeth Garrett Anderson Hospital (diagnostic). She was the sister of Millicent Fawcett and the first (and only) female member of the BMA (1873–92). In 1908 she became mayor of her native Aldeburgh, Suffolk, England's first woman mayor.

Anderson /'ændəsən/ Marian 1902– . US contralto singer, born in Philadelphia. She toured Europe in 1930, but in 1939 she was barred from singing at Constitution Hall, Washington, because she was black. In 1955 she sang at the Metropolitan Opera, the first black singer to appear there. Her voice was noted for its range and richness.

Anderson /'ændəsən/ Maxwell 1888–1959. US playwright, noted for *What Price Glory?* 1924, written in collaboration with Laurence Stallings, a realistic portrayal of the American soldier in action during World War I.

Andersen The Danish writer Hans Christian Andersen achieved worldwide fame with his fairy stories such as *The Snow Queen, The Ugly Duckling* and *The Emperor's New Clothes*. He was much admired by Charles Dickens, whom he visited in 1857.

Anderson /'ændəsən/ Sherwood 1876–1941. US writer, noted for his short stories of a midwestern small town – *Winesburg, Ohio* 1919.

Andes /'ændiːz/ the great mountain system or cordillera that forms the western fringe of South America, extending through some 67° of latitude and the republics of Colombia, Venezuela, Ecuador, Peru, Bolivia, Chile, and Argentina. The mountains exceed 3,600 m/12,000 ft for half their length of 6,500 km/4,000 mi. Geologically speaking, they are new mountains, having attained their present height by vertical upheaval of the entire strip of the earth's crust as recently as the latter part of the Tertiary era and the Quaternary. But they have been greatly affected by weathering. Rivers have cut profound gorges, and glaciers have produced characteristic valleys. The majority of the individual mountains are volcanic, some are still active.

The whole system may be divided into two almost parallel ranges. The southernmost extremity is Cape Horn, but the range extends into the sea and forms islands. Among the highest peaks are Cotopaxi and Chimborazo in Ecuador, Cerro de Pasco and Misti in Peru, Illampu and Illimani in Bolivia, Aconcagua in Argentina (the highest mountain in the New World), and Ojos del Salado in Chile.

Andean mineral resources include gold, silver, tin, tungsten, bismuth, vanadium, copper, and lead. Difficult communications make mining expensive. Transport was for a long time chiefly by pack animals, but air transport has greatly reduced difficulties of communications. Three railways cross the Andes from Valparaiso to Buenos Aires, Antofagastato Salta, and Antofagasta via Uyuni to Asunción. New roads are being built, including the Pan-American Highway from Alaska to Cape Horn.

The majority of the sparse population are dependent on agriculture, the nature and products of which vary with the natural environment. Newcomers to the Andean plateau, which includes Lake ◊Titicaca, suffer from *puna*, mountain sickness, but indigenous peoples have hearts and lungs adapted to altitude.

andesite a volcanic ◊igneous rock, intermediate in composition (containing less silica than ◊rhyolite but more than ◊basalt). It is characterized by a large quantity of the mineral ◊feldspar, giving it a light colour. Andesite erupts from volcanoes at destructive plate margins (where one plate of the earth's surface is being drawn down beneath another), particularly in the Andes, from which it gets its name. See◊plate tectonics.

Andhra Pradesh /'ændrə prə'deʃ/ state in E central India
area 276,814 sq km/106,285 sq mi
capital Hyderabad
towns Secunderabad
population (1971) 47,900,000
language Telugu
history formed in 1953 from the Telegu-speaking areas of ◊Madras, and enlarged in 1956 from the former Hyderabad state.

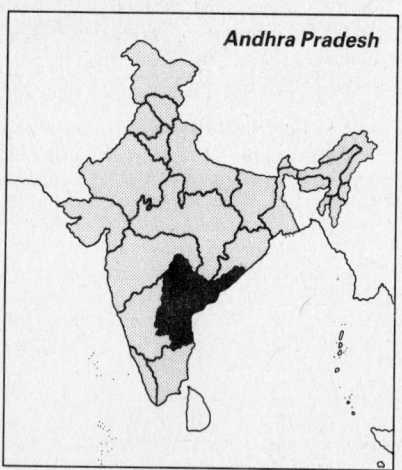

Andhra Pradesh

Andorra /æn'dɔːrə/ landlocked country in the E Pyrenees, bounded to the north by France and to the south by Spain.
government Andorra has no formal constitution and the government is based on its feudal origins. Although administratively independent, it has no individual international status, its joint heads of state being the bishop of Urgel, in Spain, and the president of France. They are represented by permanent delegates, the vicar general of the Urgel diocese, and the prefect of the French department of Pyrénées-Orientales. There is a general council of the villages, consisting of four people from each of the seven parishes, elected by Andorran citizens for a four-year term. The council submits motions and proposals to the permanent delegates for approval.
Until 1982 the general council elected someone called the First Syndic to act as its chief

executive, but there is now an executive council, headed by a prime minister. This has resulted in some separation of the legislative and executive powers and is an important step towards a more constitutional form of government. For the time being, reforms are dependent on the two co-princes, through their representatives.

history co-princes have ruled Andorra since 1278. Until 1970 only third-generation Andorran males had the vote. Now the franchise extends to all first-generation Andorrans of foreign parentage aged 28 or over. The electorate is small in relation to the total population, up to 70% of which consists of foreign residents, who are demanding political and nationality rights. Immigration, controlled by a quota system, is restricted to French and Spanish nationals intending to work in Andorra. Since 1980 there have been signs of a fragile, but growing, democracy. There are loose political groupings but no direct party representation on the General Council. There is a technically illegal political organisation, the Democratic Party of Andorra, which may well provide the basis for a future democratic system.

Andorra
PRINCIPALITY OF (*Principat D'Andorra*)

AREA 465 sq km/190 sq mi
CAPITAL Andorre-la-Vella
PHYSICAL mountainous, with narrow valleys
FEATURES the E Pyrenees
HEAD OF STATE Joan Marti y Alanis (bishop of Seo de Urgel, Spain) and François Mitterrand (president of France)
GOVERNMENT feudal
EXPORTS main industries tourism and smuggling
CURRENCY French franc and Spanish peseta
POPULATION (1985) 43,000 (25% Andorrans, 75% immigrant Spanish workers)
LANGUAGE Catalan (official); French, Spanish
RELIGION Roman Catholic
LITERACY 100% (1984)
CHRONOLOGY
1970 Extension of franchise to third-generation women and second-generation men.
1976 First political party formed.

Andorra

1977 Franchise extended to first-generation Andorrans.
1981 First prime minister appointed by General Council.

and Piero de Cosimo, but he owed more to his study of ◊Masaccio, ◊Michelangelo, and others. He is noted for fresco and portrait work, and painted his wife in various roles. In 1518, he went to work for ◊Francis I in France, but returned to Italy in 1519 with funds to enlarge the royal French art collection; he spent it on a house for himself and never went back. His frescoes in Florence (especially the *Birth of the Virgin* and *The Madonna del Sacco*) rank among the greatest of the Renaissance. His work shows the origins of the ◊Mannerist style developed by his pupils ◊Pontormo, ◊Rosso, and ◊Vasari.

Andrew /'ændruː/ **Saint** New Testament ◊apostle. A native of Bethsaida, he was Simon Peter's brother. With Peter, James, and John, who worked with him as fishermen at Capernaum, he formed the inner circle of the 12 disciples. According to tradition he went with John to Ephesus, preached in Scythia, and was crucified at Patras on an X-shaped cross (St Andrew's cross). His feast is held on 30 Nov. He is the patron saint of Scotland.

Andrewes /'ændruːz/ Lancelot 1555–1626. Church of England cleric. Born in London, he

went to Cambridge, and took holy orders in 1580, becoming bishop successively of Chichester (1605), Ely (1609), and Winchester (1618). He took part in preparing the text of the Authorized Version of the Bible, and was known for his fine preaching.

Andrews /'ændruːz/ Julie 1935– . British singer and actress. Formerly a child performer with her mother and father in a music-hall act, she was the original *My Fair Lady* 1956 on stage. Her films include *Mary Poppins* 1963, *The Sound of Music* 1964, *10* 1980, and *Victor/Victoria* 1982.

Andreyev /æn'dreɪev/ Leonid Nicolaievich 1871–1919. Russian author. Most of his works show his obsession with death and madness including the symbolic drama *Life of Man* 1907,

the melodrama *He Who Gets Slapped* 1915; and the novels *Red Laugh* 1904, *Seven that were Hanged* 1908, and *S.O.S* 1919 published in Finland, where he fled after the Russian Revolution.

Andrić /'ændrɪtʃ/ Ivo 1892–1974. Yugoslavian novelist. An ardent nationalist, he was a member of the Young Bosnia organization, another member of which shot Francis Ferdinand in 1914, and spent World War I in an internment camp because of his politics. He later became a diplomat, and was Yugoslav ambassador to Berlin in 1940. While in prison, he began writing; his best work is *Na Drini čuprija/The Bridge on the Drina* 1945, an epic history of a small Bosnian town. He won a Nobel prize in 1961.

Androcles /'ændrəkliːz/ 1st century AD. Roman slave. Traditionally, he fled from a cruel master to the African desert, where he drew a thorn from the paw of a crippled lion. Recaptured, and sentenced to combat a lion in the arena, he found his adversary was his old friend. ◊Tiberius was said to have freed them both. The story was used in a play by G B ◊Shaw.

androecium the male part of a flower, comprising a number of ◊stamens.

androgen a general name for any male sex hormone, of which ◊testosterone is the most important. They are all ◊steroids and are principally involved in the production of male ◊secondary sexual characters (such as facial hair).

Andromache /æn'drɒməki/ heroine of Homer's *Iliad*; the wife of Hector, who was killed in combat with Achilles, and mother of the boy Astyanax, who was flung from the battlements by the conquerors. After the fall of Troy she was awarded to Neoptolemus, Achilles' son.

Andromeda /æn'drɒmɪdə/ in Greek mythology, a princess chained to a rock as a sacrifice to a sea monster. She was rescued by ◊Perseus.

Andromeda /æn'drɒmɪdə/ in astronomy, a major star ◊constellation of the northern hemisphere, representing the princess of Greek mythology; it is best placed for viewing in autumn. Its main feature is the ◊Andromeda galaxy. The star Alpha Andromedae forms one corner of the Square of ◊Pegasus.

Andromeda Galaxy a spiral ◊galaxy 2 million light years away in the constellation of ◊Andromeda, and the most distant object visible to the naked eye. It is similar in nature to our own ◊Milky Way but contains about twice as many stars. It is the largest member of the ◊Local Group of galaxies.

Andropov /æn'drɒpɒf/ Yuri 1914–1984. Soviet communist politician, KGB chief 1967–82, president 1983–84.

Andropov was politically active from the 1930s. His part in quelling the Hungarian national rising 1956, when he was Soviet ambassador, brought him into the Communist Party secretariat in 1962 as a specialist on East European affairs. As chief of the ◊KGB 1967–82, he established a reputation for efficiently suppressing dissent. Andropov was brought into the Politburo in 1973 and succeeded ◊Brezhnev

Andrássy /æn'dræsi/ Count Gyula 1823–1890. Prime minister and foreign minister of the Austro-Hungarian Empire (1871–79).

André /'ændreɪ/ John 1751–1880. British soldier, born in London, the son of a merchant from Geneva. He served with the British army in America from 1774, and when ◊Arnold offered to betray West Point to the British, Major André was chosen to negotiate the surrender. Captured by the Americans, he was hanged as a spy. A monument to André was set up in Westminster Abbey.

Andrea del Sarto /'ændreɪə del 'saːtəʊ/ 1486–1531. Italian Renaissance painter, born d'Agnola, but called del Sarto because he was the son of a Florentine tailor. He was apprenticed to a goldsmith, later studied under Giovanni, Barile,

Andrea del Sarto Draped kneeling figure in red chalk, attributed to Andrea del Sarto. The accuracy of his drawings in this medium inspired Vasari to name him 'the faultless painter'.

as party general secretary in 1982. Elected president 1983, he introduced economic reforms, but died in Feb 1984. The city of Rybinsk was renamed Andropov in 1984.

anemone plant of the buttercup family Ranunculaceae. The **wood anemone** *Anemone nemorosa*, or wind-flower, grows in shady woods, flowering in spring. *Pulsatilla vulgaris*, the Pasque flower, and *Pulsatilla pratensis*, now placed in a separate genus, are powerful emetics. *Hepatica nobilis*, also once included within *Anemone*, is common in the Alps. The **garden anemone** is *Anemone coronaria*.

anemophily a type of ◊pollination in which the pollen is carried on the wind (also known as wind-pollination). Anemophilous flowers are usually unscented, have very reduced petals and sepals, or lack them altogether, and do not produce nectar. In some species they are borne in ◊catkins. Male and famale reproductive structures are commonly found in separate flowers. The male flowers have numerous exposed stamens, often on long filaments; the female flowers have long, often branched, feathery stigmas. Many wind-pollinated plants, such as hazel (*Corylus avellana*), bear their flowers before the leaves to facilitate the free transport of pollen. Since air movements are random, vast amounts of pollen are needed: a single birch catkin, for example, may produce over five million pollen grains.

aneroid a kind of ◊barometer.

angel in Christian, Jewish, and Muslim belief, supernatural being (Greek *angelos*, messenger) intermediate between God and humans. The Christian hierarchy has nine orders; Seraphim, Cherubim, Thrones (who contemplate God and reflect his glory); Dominations, Virtues, Powers (who regulate the stars and the Universe); Principalities, Archangels, and Angels (who minister to humanity). In traditional Catholic belief, every human being has a guardian angel.

angelfish name for a number of unrelated fishes. The freshwater *angelfish*, genus *Pterophyllum* of South America is popular in aquaria. A tall flattened fish with a striped body it can be up to 26 cm/10 in tall, but is seldom this large in captivity. The *angelfish* or *monkfish Squatina* is a bottom-living shark up to 1.8 m/6 ft long with a body flattened from top to bottom. The *marine angelfish, Pomacanthus* and others, are tall narrow-bodied fish, often brilliantly coloured, up to 65 cm/2 ft long, living around coral reefs in the tropics.

angelica type of umbelliferous plant. *Angelica sylvestris*, the species found in Britain, is a tall perennial herb, with wedge-shaped leaves and clusters of white, pale violet, or pinkish flowers. *Angelica archangelica* is a culinary herb, the stems preserved in sugar.

Angelico /æn'dʒelɪkəʊ/ Fra c. 1400–1455. Nickname of Italian Renaissance painter and Dominican friar Guido di Pietro, so called on account of his 'angelic' nature. The monastery of San Marco, Florence, where he lived from 1436 and where he produced some 50 devotional frescoes, is now a museum of his work. In 1446 he was summoned to Rome by the Pope to decorate a chapel – the Vatican. Among his outstanding pictures are *The Coronation of the Virgin* in the Louvre, Paris, and a Christ with 265 saints, in the National Gallery, London. He was a mystic, and the intensity of his religious feeling is expressed in sweet colours and a delicately simple style.

Angell /'eɪndʒəl/ Norman 1872–1967. British writer on politics and economics. In 1910 he acquired an international reputation with his book *The Great Illusion*, which maintained that any war must prove ruinous to both winners and losers. Nobel Peace Prize 1933.

Angelou /'æˌndʒəluː/ Maya 1928– . US novelist, poet, playwright, and short story writer, born Marguerite Johnson. She is best known for her powerful autobiographical work *I Know Why the Caged Bird Sings* 1970 and its sequels, telling of the struggles towards physical and spiritual liberation of a black woman growing up in the American South.

Angers /,ɒn'ʒeɪ/ ancient French town, capital of Maine-et-Loire département, on the river Maine. It has a 12th–13th century cathedral and castle, and was formerly the capital of the duchy and province of Anjou, whose people are called Angevins – a name also applied by the English to the ◊Plantagenet kings. Population (1983) 136,855.

angina or **angina pectoris**, Latin 'tightness of the chest', may be a sign of a heart disease caused by restricted blood supply to the heart because a coronary artery is narrowed; the pain seems to shoot across the chest and arm, rather than appearing to come from the heart.

angiosperm flowering plant in which the seeds are enclosed within an ovary, which ripens to a fruit. Angiosperms are divided into monocotyledons and dicotyledons, and include the vast majority of flowers, herbs, grasses, bushes and trees (except conifers).

Angkor /'æŋkɔː/ name applied to the ruins in and around the ancient ruined capital of the

Andromeda Galaxy The Andromeda galaxy (M31), observed through the 200 inch optical telescope at Palomar. Like the Milky Way, it is a spiral galaxy orbited by two companion galaxies, seen as bright spots above and below the Andromeda. It is about 20,000 light years across and about 2 million light years away.

Angelou American writer Maya Angelou. The first volume of her autobiography, *I Know Why the Caged Bird Sings* 1970, gained her a wide and devoted readership. She has increased her reputation with plays, poetry and short stories. Her work has a universal quality which expresses the spirit of oppressed women everywhere.

Khmers in Cambodia. The remains date mainly from the 10–12th century AD, and comprise temples originally dedicated to the Hindu gods, shrines associated with Hinayana Buddhism, and royal palaces. Many are grouped within the great enclosure called Angkor Thom, but the great temple of Angkor Vat (early 12th century), one of the most imposing edifices in the world, lies some little distance outside. Angkor was abandoned in the 15th century, and the ruins were not adequately described until 1863. Buildings on the site suffered damage during the civil war 1970–75.

angle in geometry, the inclination between a pair of lines. Angles are measured in ◊degrees or ◊radians. An angle of 90° (90 degrees) is a right angle. Angles of less than 90° are called *acute angles*; angles of more than 90° but less than 180° are *obtuse angles*. A *reflex angle* is an angle of more than 180° but less than 360°. Angles can be measured using a protractor.

angler fish *Lophius piscatorius* living in the N Atlantic and Mediterranean. It grows to 2 m/6.5 ft and has a flattened body and broad head and jaws. It waits camouflaged on the sea bottom and twitches the enlarged tip of the thread-like first ray of the dorsal fin. This entices prey to be snapped up. Also known as frogfish or monkfish. The many species of anglerfishes form the order Lophiiformes and include deep-sea forms.

Anglesey /'æŋgəlsi/ island off the N coast of Wales, separated from the mainland by the Menai Straits, which are crossed by the Britannia tubular railway bridge and Telford's suspension bridge, built 1819–26 but since rebuilt. Nature-lovers visit Anglesey for its fauna (especially bird life) and flora, and antiquarians for its many buildings and relics of historic interest; it is also a popular holiday resort. The ancient granary of Wales, Anglesey now has growing industries, such as toy-making, electrical goods, and bromine extraction from the sea. Holyhead is the principal town and port; but Beaumaris was the county town until the county of Anglesey was merged in Gwynedd 1974. Area 715 sq km/276 sq mi; population (1981) 67,340.

Anglesey /'æŋgəlsi/ Henry William Paget, 1st Marquess of 1768–1854. British cavalry leader during the Napoleonic wars. He led a great charge at Waterloo, in which he lost a leg, and was made a marquess for his conspicuous services. He was twice lord-lieutenant of Ireland, and succeeded his father as earl of Uxbridge in 1812.

Anglican Communion family of churches including the Church of England and those holding the same essential doctrines, that is the Lambeth Quadrilateral 1888 Holy Scripture as the basis of all doctrine, the Nicene and Apostles' Creeds, Holy Baptism and Holy Communion, and the historic episcopate.

The Church of England originated during the Roman occupation during the 2nd century, and, after a period of decline, was established as part of the Catholic Church by the mission of St Augustine who became first archbishop of Canterbury in 597. At the Reformation the chief change was political; the sovereign (Henry VIII) replaced the Pope as head of the church and assumed the right to appoint archbishops and bishops. The Book of Common Prayer, the basis of worship throughout the Anglican Church, dates from Edward VI's reign; the Thirty-Nine Articles, the Church's doctrinal basis, were drawn up under Elizabeth I; and the canons of ecclesiastical discipline are essentially those framed under James I.

The Church was early carried by colonizers and explorers to North America (where three American bishops were consecrated after the War of Independence, whose successors still lead the Episcopal Church in the USA), Australia and New Zealand, and by traders to India. The main missionary effort, however, came in the 19th century, especially in Africa, and in the 20th century work has been extended to South America.

In England the two archbishops head the provinces of Canterbury and ◊York, which are subdivided into bishoprics. The Church Assembly of 1919 was replaced in 1970 by a General Synod with three houses (bishops, other clergy, and laity) to regulate Church matters, subject to Parliament and the royal assent. A decennial Lambeth Conference (first held 1867) attended by bishops from all parts of the Anglican Communion is presided over in London by the archbishop of Canterbury: it is not legislative but its decisions are often put into practice. The Church Commissioners for England 1948 manage the estates of the Church and endowment of livings.

The main parties, all products of the 19th century, are: the *Evangelical* or *Low Church*, which maintains the Church's Protestant character; the *Anglo-Catholic* or *High Church*, which stresses continuity with the pre-Reformation Church (see ◊Keble, ◊Froude, ◊Newman, ◊Pusey) and is marked by ritualistic practices, the use of confession, maintenance of religious communities of both sexes; the *Liberal* or *Modernist*, concerned with the reconciliation of the Church with modern thought (see J A T ◊Robinson, M ◊Stockwood). There is also the *Pentecostal Charismatic* movement, emphasizing spontaneity, and speaking with tongues.

In the 20th century there have been moves towards reunion with the Methodist and Roman Catholic Churches. The ordination of women has been accepted by some overseas churches, for example the American Episcopalian Church in 1976, but the General Synod in Britain, although voting in 1976 that there were no fundamental objections, was reluctant to proceed further, and, indeed, voted in 1979 against allowing women ordained overseas to officiate in Britain. Despite further debate on the matter, particularly from 1984 on, the General Synod has not yet given any indication that the ordination of women is imminent. See also ◊Movement for the Ordination of Women.

angling fishing with rod and line; the most popular sport in the UK. *Freshwater* coarse fishing includes members of the carp family and pike (not usually eaten but thrown back); freshwater game fish are salmon and trout. *Seafishing* the catch includes flatfish, bass, mackerel; big-game fish (again usually not eaten) include shark, tuna or tunny, marlin, and swordfish, usually caught from specially equipped motor-boats. Competition angling is very popular and world championships exist for most branches of the sport. The oldest is the World Freshwater Championship, inaugurated in 1957, four years after the staging of the first European championship.

World Freshwater Championship
individual
1982 Kevin Ashurst *(England)*
1983 Rudiger Kremkus *(West Germany)*
1984 Bobby Smithers *(England)*
1985 Dave Roper *(England)*
1986 Lud Wever *(Holland)*
team
1982 Holland
1983 Belgium
1984 Luxembourg
1985 England
1986 Italy

Anglo a combining form with several related meanings. In 'Anglo-Saxon' it refers to the Angles, a Germanic people who invaded Britain in the 5th to 7th centuries. In 'Anglo-Welsh' it refers to England or the English. In 'Anglo-American' it may refer either to England and the English, or commonly but less accurately to Britain and the British; it may also refer to the English language and to the Anglo-Saxon element in American society (often in contrast to 'Hispano-American'). In many parts of the world 'an Anglo' is a person of Anglo-Saxon background or type and/or someone who speaks English.

Anglo-Saxon the Teutonic invaders who conquered Britain between the 5th and 7th centuries. According to the chronicler Bede they consisted of the Angles, who settled in East

Angola

PEOPLE'S REPUBLIC OF (*República Popular de Angola*)

AREA 1,246,700 sq km/481,350 sq mi
CAPITAL and chief port Luanda
TOWNS Lobito and Benguela, also ports
PHYSICAL elevated plateau, desert in the S
FEATURES Kwanza river and Cabinda rain forest
HEAD OF STATE AND OF GOVERNMENT José Eduardo dos Santos from 1979
GOVERNMENT one-party Marxist
EXPORTS oil, coffee, diamonds, palm oil, sisal, iron ore, fish
CURRENCY kwanza (49.92 = £1 Sept 1987)
POPULATION (1985) 7,948,000 (largest ethnic group Ovimbundu); annual growth rate 2.5%
LANGUAGE Portuguese (official); Umbundu, Kimbundu
RELIGION Roman Catholic 46%, Protestant 12%, animist 42%
LITERACY 36% male/19% female (1980)
GDP $7.6 bn (1982); $500 per head of population
CHRONOLOGY
1951 Angola became an overseas territory of Portugal.
1956 First independence movement formed, the People's Movement for the Liberation of Angola (MPLA).
1961 Unsuccessful independence rebellion.
1962 Second nationalist movement formed, the National Front for the Liberation of Angola (FNLA).
1966 Third nationalist movement formed, the National Union for the Total Independence of Angola (UNITA).
1975 Transitional government of independence formed from representatives of MPLA, FNLA, UNITA, and Portuguese government. MPLA supported by USSR and Cuba, FNLA by 'non-left' power groups of southern Africa, and UNITA by Western

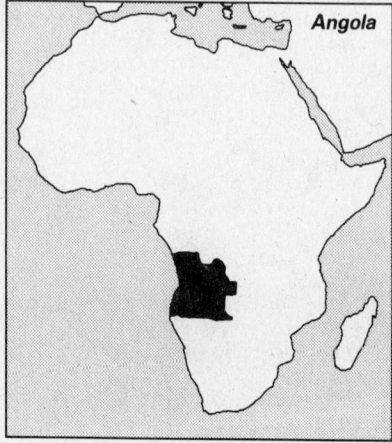

Angola

powers. Angola declared independent. MPLA proclaimed People's Republic under the presidency of Dr Agostinho Neto. FNA and UNITA proclaimed People's Democratic Republic of Angola.
1976 MPLA gained control of most of the country. South African troops withdrawn but Cuban units remained.
1977 MPLA restructured to become the People's Movement for the Liberation of Angola–Workers' Party (MPLA-PT).
1979 Death of Neto, succeeded by José Eduardo dos Santos.
1980 Constitution amended to provide for an elected people's assembly. UNITA guerrillas, aided by South Africa, continued to operate South African raids on the South West Africa People's Organization's bases in Angola.
1984 The Lusaka agreement.
1985 South African forces officially withdrawn.
1986 Further South African raids into Angola. UNITA continuing to receive South African support.

Anglia, Mercia, and Northumbria; the Saxons, in Essex, Sussex, and Wessex; and the Jutes, in Kent and S Hampshire. The Jutes probably came from the Rhineland and not, as was formerly believed, from Jutland. The Angles and Saxons came from Schleswig-Holstein, and may have united before the invasion. There must have been a good deal of intermarriage with the Romanized Celts, although the latter's language and civilization almost disappeared. After the conquest a number of kingdoms were set up, commonly referred to as the *Heptarchy*; these were united in the early 9th century under the overlordship of Wessex. The English-speaking peoples of Britain, the Commonwealth, and the USA are often referred to today as Anglo-Saxons, but the term is completely unscientific, as the Welsh, Scots, and Irish are mainly of Celtic descent, and by the 1980s fewer than 15 per cent of Americans were of British descent.

Anglo-Saxon language the group of dialects

spoken by the Anglo-Saxon peoples who in the 5th to 7th centuries invaded and settled in Britain (in what became England and Lowland Scotland). Anglo-Saxon is traditionally known as Old English. See ◊English Language.

Angola /æŋ'gəʊlə/ country in SW Africa, bounded to the west by the Atlantic ocean, to the north and northeast by Zaïre, to the east by Zambia, and to the south by Namibia.
government the 1975 constitution, amended 1976 and 1980, created a one-party 'People's Republic', with political power held by the People's Movement for the Liberation of Angola -Workers' Party (MPLA-PT). The president, elected by the congress of MPLA-PT, chooses and chairs the council of ministers and is commander-in-chief of the armed forces. There is a 223-member people's assembly, 20 of whom are nominated by MPLA-PT and the rest elected by electoral colleges of 'loyal' citizens.
history Angola became a Portuguese colony in

1491 and an Overseas Territory of Portugal in 1951. In 1956 a movement for complete independence was established, the MPLA, based originally in the Congo. This was followed by the formation of two other nationalist movements, the National Front for the Liberation of Angola (FNLA) and the National Union for the Total Independence of Angola (UNITA). Civil war broke out in 1961, with MPLA supported by socialist and communist states, UNITA helped by the Western powers and FNLA backed by the 'non-left' power groups of southern Africa.

Three months of civil war followed the granting of full independence in 1975, with MPLA and UNITA the main contestants and foreign mercenaries and South African forces helping FNLA. By 1975 MPLA, with the help of mainly Cuban forces, controlled most of the country and had established the People's Republic of Angola in Luanda. Dr Agostinho Neto, the MPLA leader, became its first president. FNLA and UNITA had, in the meantime, proclaimed their own People's Democratic Republic of Angola, based in Nova Lisboa, renamed Huambo.

President Neto died in 1979 and was succeeded by José Eduardo dos Santos, who maintained Neto's links with the Soviet bloc. UNITA guerrillas, supported by South Africa, continued to operate and in 1980–81 South African forces raided Angola to attack bases of the South West Africa People's Organisation (SWAPO), who were fighting for Namibia's independence. Angola supported Namibia's claim but South Africa and the US called for the withdrawal of Cuban troops from Angola before South Africa's departure from Namibia.

In 1983 South Africa proposed a complete withdrawal of its forces if Angola could guarantee that the areas vacated would not be filled by Cuban or SWAPO units. In 1984 Angola accepted South Africa's proposals and a settlement was made, (the Lusaka Agreement), whereby a Joint Monitoring Commission (JMC) was set up to oversee South Africa's withdrawal. In 1985 South Africa announced that this was complete and JMC was wound up. In 1986 relations between the two countries deteriorated when further South African raids into Angola occurred. UNITA also continued to receive South African support.

Angora /æŋ'gɔːrə/ earlier form of ◊Ankara, which gave its name to the Angora goat (see ◊mohair), and hence to other species of long-haired animal, such as the Angora rabbit, source of Angora 'wool', and the Angora cat.

Angostura /ˌæŋgə'stjʊərə/ former name of ◊Ciudad Bolivar.

Angoulême /ˌɒŋguː'leɪm/ French town, capital of the département of Charente, on the Charente, with a fine cathedral and a castle and papermills dating from the 16th century. Population (1975) 98,000.

Angry Young Men name given to a group of British writers who emerged about 1950 after the creative hiatus which followed World War II. They included Kingsley ◊Amis, John ◊Wain, John ◊Osborne, and Colin ◊Wilson. Also linked to the group were Iris ◊Murdoch and Kenneth ◊Tynan.

Angström /'ɒŋstrɜːm/ Anders Jonas 1814–1874. Swedish physicist, who did notable work in spectroscopy and solar physics. He gave his name to the *angstrom unit*, used to express the wavelength of electromagnetic radiation (light, radiant heat, X-rays). One angstrom or angstrom unit is one ten-millionth of a millimetre (10^{-7} mm).

Anguilla /æŋ'gwɪlə/ *area* 90 sq km/35 sq mi
capital The Valley
features white coral sand beaches
exports lobster, salt
currency Eastern Caribbean dollar
population 7,000
language English and Creole
government from 1982, governor, executive council, and legislative house of assembly (chief minister Emile Gumbs from 1984)
recent history a British colony from 1650, Anguilla was long associated with St ◊Kitts, but revolted against alleged domination by the larger island, and in 1969 declared itself a republic. A small British force restored order, and Anguilla retained a special position at its own request, since 1980 a separate dependency of the UK.

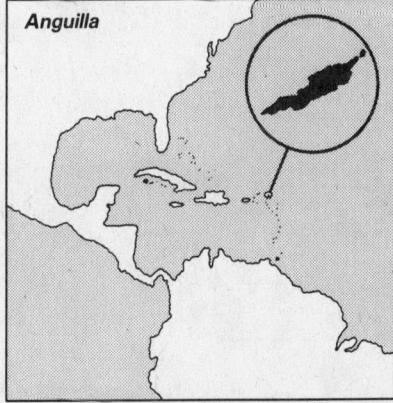

Anguilla

Angus /'æŋgəs/ former county on the E coast of Scotland, merged in 1975 in Tayside region.

Anhui /ˌæn'hweɪ/ province of E China (formerly Anhwei), watered by the Jinsha Jiang, and producing cereals in the north and cotton, rice and tea in the south. There are coal mines, and iron and steel works. The capital is Hofei. Area 139,900 sq km/54,000 sq mi; population (1978) 45,000.

Anhwei /ˌæn'hweɪ/ former name of ◊Anhui.

aniline the simplest aromatic, basic chemical known, originally prepared by the dry distillation of indigo, hence its name (Portugese *anil*, indigo). When pure it is a colourless oily liquid; it has a characteristic odour, and turns brown in contact with air. It occurs in coal tar, and was discovered in 1826. Aniline is used in the rubber industry and to make drugs and dyes. It is highly poisonous.

animal behaviour the scientific study of the behaviour of animals, either by comparative psychologists (with an interest mainly in the mental processes involved in the control of behaviour) or by ethologists (with an interest in the biological context and relevance of behaviour). See also ◊ethology, ◊social behaviour.

animal kingdom one of the major ◊kingdoms of living things, the science of which is zoology. Animals are all ◊heterotrophs (that is they obtain their energy from organic substances produced by other organisms); they have ◊eukaryotic cells (the genetic material is contained within a distinct nucleus) bounded by a thin cell membrane rather than a thick cell wall. In the past, it was common to include the single-celled ◊protozoa with the animals, but these are now classified as protists. Thus all animals are multicellular. Most are capable of moving around but some, such as sponges and corals, are stationary. Their cells may bear the surface features ◊flagella and ◊cilia, unlike plant cells.

animism in psychology and physiology, the view of human personality which rejects materialistic mechanism as a valid explanation of human behaviour. In religious theory, the conception of a spiritual reality behind the material one: for example, beliefs in the soul as a shadowy duplicate of the body capable of independent activity, both in life and death. Linked with this is the worship of natural objects such as stones and trees, thought to harbour spirits (naturism), fetishism, and ancestor worship.

anion ion carrying a negative charge. An electrolyte, such as the salt zinc chloride, is dissociated in aqueous solution or in the molten state into doubly-charged Zn^{2+} zinc cations and singly-charged Cl^- anions. During electrolysis, the zinc cations flow to the cathode (to become discharged and liberate zinc metal) and the chloride anions flow to the anode (to liberate chlorine gas). See also ◊cation.

anise umbelliferous plant *Pimpinella anisum* whose fruits, 'aniseeds', are used to flavour foods. Oil from them is used in cough medicines.

Anjou /ˌɒŋ'ʒuː/ an old countship and former province in northern France: capital Angers. In 1154 the count of Anjou became King of England as Henry II, but the territory was lost by King John in 1204. In 1480 the countship was annexed to the French crown. The départements of Maine-et-Loire and part of Indre-et-Loire, Mayenne, and Sarthe cover the area.

Ankara /'æŋkərə/ (formerly Angora) capital of Turkey; population (1980) 1,877,755. It replaced ◊Istanbul (then in Allied occupation) as capital in 1923. It has the presidential palace and Grand National Assembly buildings; three universities, including a technical university to serve the whole Middle East; ◊Atatürk's mausoleum on a nearby hilltop, and the largest mosque in Turkey at Kocatepe.

ankh Ancient Egyptian symbol (derived from the simplest form of sandal), meaning 'eternal life', as in Tut*ankh*amun. It consists of a 'T' shape surmounted by an oval, and is now used as a good luck charm.

Annaba /'ænəbə/ seaport in Algeria (formerly Bône), the name meaning 'city of jujube trees'. There are metallurgical industries, and iron ore and phosphates are exported. Population (1974) 313,174.

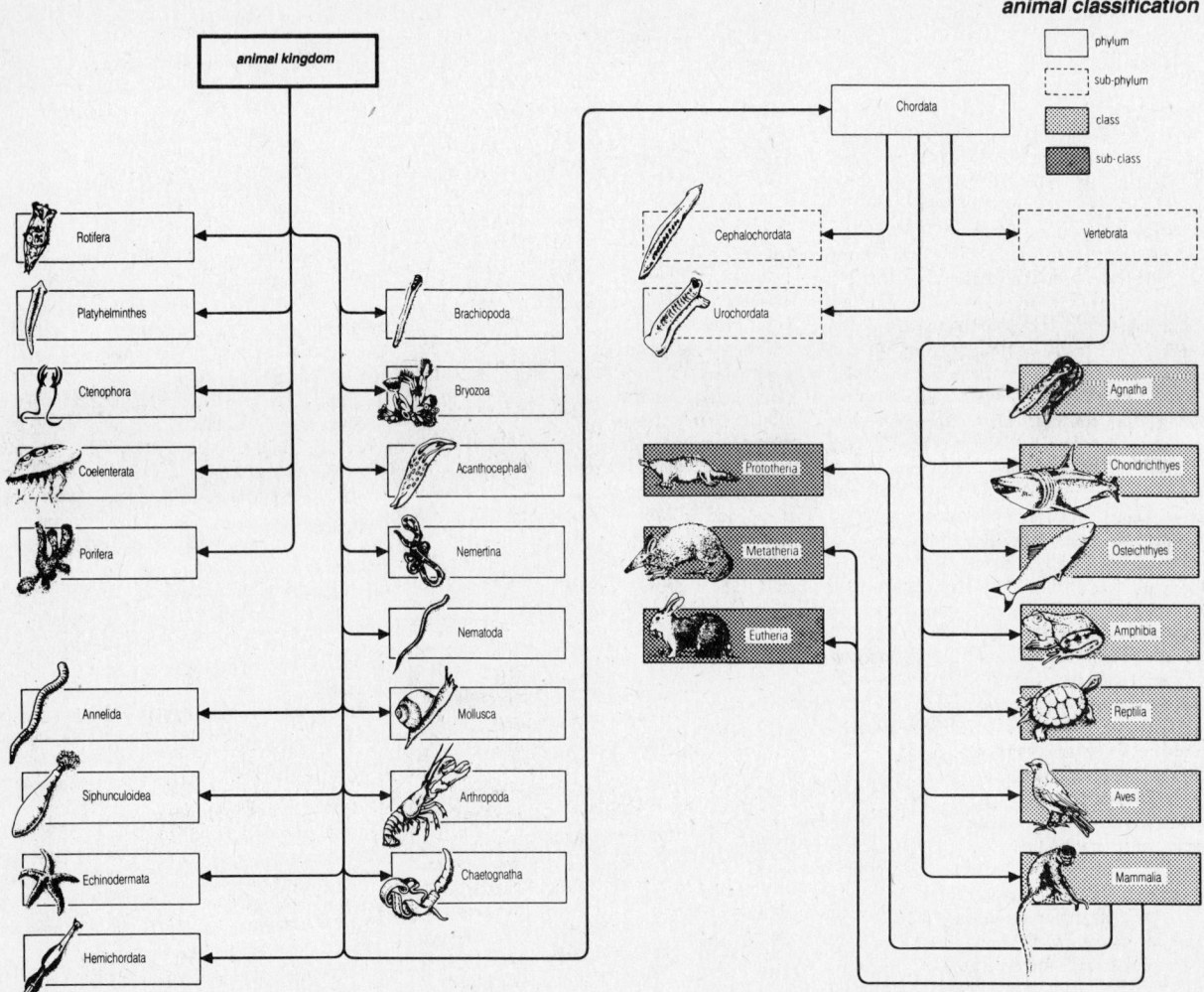

animal classification

	phylum
	sub-phylum
	class
	sub-class

animal kingdom

Rotifera
Platyhelminthes
Ctenophora
Coelenterata
Porifera
Annelida
Siphunculoidea
Echinodermata
Hemichordata

Brachiopoda
Bryozoa
Acanthocephala
Nemertina
Nematoda
Mollusca
Arthropoda
Chaetognatha

Chordata
Cephalochordata
Urochordata
Vertebrata

Prototheria
Metatheria
Eutheria

Agnatha
Chondrichthyes
Osteichthyes
Amphibia
Reptilia
Aves
Mammalia

Anna Comnena /'ænə kɒm'niːnə/ 1083–after 1148. Byzantine historian, daughter of the emperor ◊Alexius I, and chiefly remembered as the historian of her father's reign. After a number of abortive attempts to alter the imperial succession in favour of her husband, Nicephorus Bryennius (c. 1062–1137), she retired to a convent to write her major work, the *Alexiad*. This dealt with the period 1069–1118 and followed on from the writings of her husband. It describes the Byzantine view of public office, as well as religious and intellectual life of the period.

Annam /æn'æm/ former country of SE Asia, incorporated in ◊Vietnam in 1946 as Central Vietnam. A Bronze Age civilization was flourishing in the area when China conquered in c. 214 BC. The Chinese named their conquest An-Nam, 'peaceful south'. Independent from 1428, Annam signed a treaty with France in 1787, and in 1884 became a French protectorate, part of Indochina. During World War II Annam was occupied by Japan.

Annapolis /ə'næpəlɪs/ seaport and capital of Maryland, USA; population (1980) 31,740. It was in session here Nov 1783–Jun 1784 that ◊Congress received George ◊Washington's resignation as Commander-in-Chief in 1783, and ratified the peace treaty of the War of American Independence. The US Naval Academy is here, and John Paul ◊Jones is buried in the chapel crypt.

Annapurna /ˌænə'pɜːnə/ mountain 8,075 m/26,502 ft in the Himalayas, Nepal. The north face was climbed by a French expedition (Maurice Herzog) in 1950 and the south by a British one in 1970.

Anne of Cleves /kliːvz/ 1515–1557. Fourth wife of ◊Henry VIII of England, she was the daughter of the Duke of Cleves, and was recommended to Henry as a wife by Thomas ◊Cromwell, who wanted an alliance with German Protestantism against the Holy Roman Emperor. Henry did not like her looks, had the marriage declared void and pensioned her.

Anne /æn/ Princess of the UK 1950– . Second child of Queen ◊Elizabeth II, she was created Princess Royal in 1986. She gained a European reputation as a horsewoman, and in 1973 married *Lieutenant Mark Phillips* (1949–), of the Queen's Dragoon Guards, himself a gold medallist in equestrian events at the 1972 Olympics. Their son Peter (1977–) was the first direct descendant of the Queen not to receive a title.

Anne /æn/ Queen of Great Britain and Ireland 1665–1714. Second daughter of James, Duke of York, who became James II, and Anne Hyde, she received a Protestant upbringing, and in 1683 married Prince George of Denmark. Of their 17 children only one survived infancy, William, Duke of Gloucester, who died at the age of 12. For the greater part of her life Anne was a close friend of Sarah Churchill, wife of John Churchill, afterwards Duke of Marlborough; the Churchills' influence helped lead her to desert her father for her brother-in-law, William of Orange, during the revolution of 1688, and later to engage in Jacobite intrigues. She succeeded William on the throne in 1702. She aimed at national unity under the Crown, and recent research shows that her replacement of the Tories by a Whig government 1703–04 was her own act, not due to Churchillian influence. The outstanding events of her reign were the War of the Spanish Succession (1702–13),

Marlborough's victories at Blenheim, Ramillies, Oudenarde, and Malplaquet, and the union of the English and Scottish parliaments in 1707. Anne finally broke with the Marlboroughs in 1710, when Mrs Masham succeeded the duchess as her favourite, and supported the Tory government of the same year.

annealing process of heating a material (usually glass or metal) for a given time at a given temperature, followed by slow cooling, to increase ductility and strength. It is a common form of ◊heat treatment.

Annecy /æn'siː/ capital of the *département* of Haute-Savoie, France, at the northern end of Lake Annecy. A beautiful town, it has some light industry, including precision instruments. Population (1975) 53,000.

annelid general name for a segmented worm of the phylum Annelida. Annelids include earthworms, leeches and marine worms such as lugworms. There is a distinct head and the soft body is divided into a number of similar segments shut off from one another internally by membranous partitions, but there are no jointed appendages.

Anne of Austria /æn/ 1601–1666. Queen of France. Daughter of Philip III of Spain, she married Louis XIII of France in 1615, and on his death in 1643 became regent for her son, Louis XIV. She was much under the influence of Mazarin, to whom she was supposed to be secretly married. She is one of the major characters in ◊Dumas' novel *The Three Musketeers* 1844.

Anne of Denmark /æn/ 1574–1619. Queen consort of Great Britain. Daughter of Frederick II of Denmark and Norway, she married in 1589 James VI of Scotland, who became James I of Great Britain in 1603. Anne was suspected of Catholic leanings, and was notably extravagant.

Annigoni /ˌænɪˈɡəʊni/ Pietro 1910– . Italian artist. He is noted for the etherealized Renaissance style of his portraits, for example Elizabeth II in 1955: other sitters include the Duke of Edinburgh and Princess Margaret.

anno domini (Latin 'in the year of our Lord') in the Christian chronological system, dates since the birth of Christ, denoted by the letters AD. Earlier years are denoted by the letters BC (Before Christ). There is no year 0, so 1 AD follows immediately after the year 1 BC. The system is based on the calculations made in 525 by Dionysius Exiguus, a Scythian monk, but the birth of Christ should more correctly be placed in 3 BC or 4 BC. The system became standard in the West when adopted by Bede in the 8th century.

annual plant a plant that completes its life-cycle within one year, during which time it germinates, grows to maturity, bears flowers, produces seed and then dies. Examples include the common poppy (*Papaver rhoeas*) and groundsel (*Senecio vulgaris*). Among garden plants, some that are described as "annuals" are actually perennials, although usually cultivated as annuals because they cannot survive winter frosts. See also ◊ephemeral, ◊biennial, ◊perennial.

annual rings or *growth rings* the concentric rings visible on a cut tree trunk or other woody stem. They represent the growth of secondary ◊xylem during the year and are caused by the seasonal size variation in the elements making up the xylem, especially the vessels. In spring and early summer spring wood is formed which has larger and more numerous vessels than the autumn wood produced when growth is slowing down. The result is a clear boundary between the paler spring wood and the dark, dense autumn wood. The annual rings may be used to estimate the age of the plant (see ◊dendrochronology), but occasionally more than one growth ring is produced in a given year, giving rise to a false annual ring.

Annunciation in the New Testament, the announcement to Mary by the angel ◊Gabriel that she was to be the mother of Christ; the feast of the Annunciation is 25 Mar, also known as Lady Day.

anode the electrode towards which negative particles (anions, electrons) move within a device, such as the cells of a battery, electrolytic cells, and diodes.

anodizing a process that increases the resistance to ◊corrosion of a metal such as aluminium by building up a protective oxide layer on the surface. The natural corrosion resistance of aluminium is provided by a thin film of aluminium oxide. Anodizing increases the thickness of this film and thus the corrosion protection. It is so called because the metal is made the ◊anode in an electrolytic bath. The bath contains a solution of, for example, sulphuric or chromic acid as the ◊electrolyte. During ◊electrolysis oxygen is produced at the anode, where it combines with the metal to form an oxide film.

anomie in the social sciences, term used to describe a state of normlessness created by the breakdown of commonly agreed standards of behaviour and morality; the term is often used to refer to situations where the social order appears to have collapsed. It was developed as a sociological concept by ◊Durkheim to describe societies in transition, particularly during industrialization, and adapted by the American sociologist Robert Merton to explain deviancy and crime in the US in terms of the disparity between high goals and limited opportunities.

Anouilh /ˌænuːˈiː/ Jean 1910–1987. French playwright, whose plays dramatize the contrasts between innocence and experience, poverty in a world of riches, and the role of memory. His plays include *Antigone* 1942, *L'Invitation au château/Ring Round the Moon* 1947, *Colombe* 1950, and *Becket* 1959, about Thomas à Becket and Henry II.

Anschluss term used for the union of Austria with Germany, accomplished by Hitler on 12 Mar 1938.

Anselm, Saint /ˈænselm/ 1033 ?–1109. Medieval churchman, born near Aosta, in Piedmont. Educated at the abbey of Bec in Normandy, which as an abbot (from 1078) he made the greatest centre of scholarship in Europe, he was appointed archbishop of Canterbury by William II in 1093, but was later forced into exile. He was recalled by Henry I, with whom he bitterly disagreed on the investiture of the clergy; a final agreement gave the king the right of temporal investiture and the clergy that of spiritual investiture. Anselm was canonized in 1494. He holds an important place in the development of ◊scholasticism. In his *Proslogion* he developed the ontological proof of theism, which infers God's existence from our capacity to conceive of a perfect Being. His most important work, *Cur deus homo*, deals with the Atonement.

Anshan /ˌænˈʃæn/ Chinese city and iron and steel centre, in Liaoning province, 89 km/55 mi SE of Shenyang (Mukden). Started here in 1918, expanded by the Japanese, dismantled by the Russians, the iron works were restored by the Communist government of China: production 6,000,000 tonnes of steel annually. Population (1982) 1,210,000.

Anson /ˈænsən/ George, 1st Baron Anson 1697–1762. British admiral. In 1740 he commanded the squadron attacking the Spanish colonies and shipping in South America; he returned home, by circumnavigating the world, with £500,000 of Spanish treasure; his chaplain's *Voyage Round the World* 1748 is a classic. He carried out invaluable reforms at the ◊Admiralty.

GEORGE ANSON ESQ. COMMANDER IN CHIEF OF THE LATE EXPEDITION TO THE SOUTH SEAS.

Anson When war broke out with Spain in 1740, the English admiral George Anson set out for the Pacific with six vessels. This engraving done four years later, celebrated his return with only one ship, laden with half a million pounds of Spanish treasure, having circumnavigated the world.

ant insect with a conspicuous 'waist' and elbowed antennae belonging to the family Formicidae and belonging to the same order of insects (Hymenoptera) as the bees and wasps. About 10,000 different species are known, all social in habit, and construct nests of various kinds. 'White ants' or ◊termites are also social but belong to a very different group. *Communities* include: *workers* sterile wingless females, often all alike but in some species large-headed 'soldiers' are differentiated; *fertile females* fewer in number and usually winged; and *males* also winged and smaller than their consorts, with whom they leave the nest on a nuptial flight at certain times of the year. After aerial mating, the males die, and the fertilized queens lose their wings when they settle, laying eggs to found their own new colonies. The eggs hatch into worm-like larvae, which then pupate in silk cocoons before emerging as adults. *Remarkable species* include: army (New World) and driver (African) ants which march nomadically in huge columns, devouring even tethered animals in their path; leaf-cutter ants, genus *Atta*, which use pieces of leaf to grow edible fungus in underground 'gardens'; weaver ants, genus *Oecophylla*, which use their silk-producing larvae as living shuttles to bind the edges of leaves together to form the nest; robber ants, *Formica sanguinea*, which raid nests of another ant *Formica fusca* for pupae then use the adults as 'slaves' when they hatch; and honey ants, in which some workers serve as distended honey stores. Ant behaviour is complex, but serves the colony rather than the individual. Ants find their way by light patterns, gravity (special sense organs are found in the joints of their legs), and chemical trails between food areas and the nest. In some species, 'warfare' is conducted. Others are 'pastoralists', tending herds of ◊aphids and collecting a sweet secretion ('honeydew') from them.

antacid a substance that neutralizes stomach acid. It may be taken between meals to relieve indigestion and 'heartburn'. Excessive or prolonged need for antacids should be medically investigated.

Antananarivo /ˌæntəˌnænəˈriːvəʊ/ capital (formerly Tananarive) of Madagascar, on the interior plateau, with a rail link to ◊Tamatave; population (1979) 551,000.

Antarctica /æntˈɑːktɪkə/ the Antarctic continent
area 13,727,000 sq km/5,300,000 sq mi
features there is less than 50 mm/2 in of rainfall a year (less than the Sahara). Little more than 1 per cent is ice-free, the temperature falling to -70°C/-100°F and below, and in places the ice is 5,000 m/16,000 ft deep, comprising over two-thirds of the world's fresh water. Each annual layer of snow preserves a record of global conditions, and where no melting at the surface of the bedrock has occurred the ice can be a million years old. It covers extensive mineral resources, including iron, coal, and with indications of uranium and other strategic metals, as well as oil (see also ◊meteorite). There are only two species of flowering plants, plus a number of mosses, algae, and fungi; see under ◊lichen. Animal life is restricted to visiting whales, seals, penguins, and other seabirds. There is no permanent human population, only research stations. The continent, once part of ◊Gondwanaland, is a vast plateau, of which the highest point is the Vinson

Massif in the Ellsworth mountains, 5,139 m/16,860 ft high. The Ross Ice Shelf is formed by several glaciers coalescing in the Ross Sea, and Mount Erebus on Ross Island is the world's southernmost active volcano. Fossils of apes resembling humans have been found. The territorial claims of the nations are in cold storage, and Britain's is overlapped by later claims of Argentina and Chile. The Soviet Union and USA have made no claim, but recognize no one else's.
population settlement is limited to scientific research stations with changing personnel.

the sun never sets, and at least one day during the southern winter during which the sun never rises. The line encompasses the continent of Antarctica and the Antarctic Ocean.

Antarctic Ocean /æntˈɑːktɪk/ popular name for the reaches of the Atlantic, Indian and Pacific Oceans extending south of the Antarctic Circle (66°,32' S). The term is not used by the International Hydrographic Bureau.

Antares brightest ◊star in the constellation of ◊Scorpius. It is a red supergiant several hundred times larger than the ◊Sun, lies about 400 light years away, and fluctuates slightly in brightness.

Antarctica Sir Ernest Shackleton's ship *The Endurance* has floundered in pack ice on its transantarctic expedition in 1915. F Hurley's photograph shows the dogs 'housed' on the ice. With sledges and boats the men managed to reach Elephant Island, and dug themselves in, while Shackleton's party made a desperate journey back to South Georgia to organize a rescue.

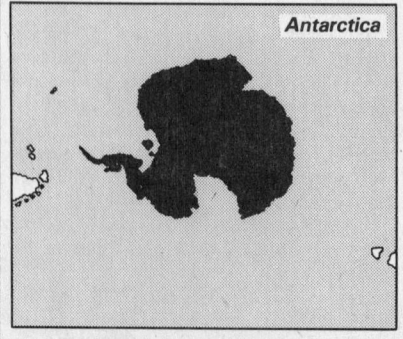

Antarctica

Antarctic Circle an imaginary line that runs round the South Pole at latitude 66°33 ' S. The region south of this line experiences at least one night during the southern summer during which

anteater name given to several mammals of various genera that live almost entirely on ants of termites. All share toothless jaws, extensile tongue and claws for breaking into nests of their prey. The true anteaters are South American animals such as the great anteater *Myrmecophaga tridactyla*, about 50 cm/2 ft high and common in Brazil. The name is also applied to the ◊aardvark, ◊echidna and ◊pangolin.

antelope name for a number of distinct kinds of even-toed hoofed wild mammals belonging to the cow family. Most are lightly built and good runners. They are grazers or browsers and chew the cud. They range in size from the dik-diks and duikers, only 30 cm/1 ft high, to the eland up to 1.8 m/6 ft at the shoulder. Some live in Asia, such as the ◊saiga, blackbuck and ◊nilgai; and various ◊gazelles inhabit the deserts of Arabia and the

ANTARCTIC EXPLORATION

1773–74   James Cook first sailed in Antarctic seas, but exploration was difficult until the development of iron ships able to withstand ice pressure.

1819–21   Antarctica circumnavigated by Bellingshausen.

1823   James Weddell sailed into the sea named after him.

1841–42   James Ross sighted the Great Ice Barrier named after him.

1895   Borchgrevink was one of the first landing party on the continent.

1898   Borchgrevink's British expedition first wintered in Antarctica.

1901–04   Scott first penetrated the interior of the continent.

1907–08   Shackleton came within 182 km/113 mi of the Pole.

1911   Amundsen reached the Pole, 14 Dec, overland with dogs.

1912   Scott reached the Pole, 18 Jan, initially aided by ponies.

1928–29   Byrd made the first flight to the Pole.

1935   Ellsworth first flew across Antarctica.

1957–58   Fuchs made the first overland crossing.

1959   Soviet expedition from the West Ice Shelf to the Pole.

1959   International Antarctic Treaty suspended all territorial claims, reserving an area south of 60° S latitude for peaceful purposes.

1961–62   Bentley Trench discovered, which suggested that there may be an Atlantic-Pacific link beneath the continent.

1966–67   Specially Protected Areas established internationally for animals and plants.

1979   Fossils of apemen resembling E Africa's Proconsul found 500 km/300 mi from the Pole.

1980   International Convention on the exploitation of resources — oil, gas, fish, krill.

1982   First circumnavigation of Earth (2 Sept 1979–29 Aug 1982) via the Poles by Sir Ranulph Fiennes and Charles Burton (UK).

Middle East. The majority of antelopes, however, are African, including such types as the ◊eland, ◊gnu, ◊kudu, ◊springbok, and ◊waterbuck.

antenna in zoology, an appendage ('feeler') on the head. Insects, centipedes and millipedes each have one pair of antennae, but there are two pairs in crustaceans, such as shrimps. In insects, the antennae are usually involved with the senses of smell and touch. They are frequently complex structures with large surface areas which increase the ability to detect scents.

antenna in radio, another name for ◊aerial.

Antheil /'ɑːntaɪl/ George 1900–1959. US composer, the son of a Polish political exile. He was at one time a concert pianist, but was best known for his *Ballet mécanique* 1926, scored for anvils, aeroplane propeller, electric bells, automobile horns, and pianos.

anthelion antisun; a kind of solar halo, sometimes appearing at the same altitude as the Sun, but opposite to it.

anthem in music, a short, usually elaborate, religious choral composition, sometimes accompanied by the organ.

anther in a flower, the terminal part of a stamen in which the ◊pollen grains are produced. It is usually borne on a slender stalk, or filament, and has two lobes, each containing two chambers or pollen sacs within which the pollen is formed.

antheridium an organ producing the male gametes (◊antherozoids) in algae, bryophytes (mosses and lichens), and pteridophytes (ferns and horsetails). It may be either single-celled, as in most algae, or multicellular, as in bryophytes and pteridophytes.

antherozoid a motile male gamete produced by algae, bryophytes (mosses and liverworts), pteridophytes (ferns and horsetails), and some gymosperms (notably the cycads). Antherozoids are formed in an ◊antheridium and, after being released, swim by means of one or more ◊flagella, to the female gametes. Higher plants have non-motile male gametes contained within ◊pollen grains.

Anthony /'ænθənɪ/ Susan B 1820–1906. American pioneering feminist, who also worked for the anti-slavery and temperance movements. Her campaigns included demands for equality of pay for female teachers, the married women's property act and women's suffrage. In 1869 with Elizabeth Cady Stanton she founded the National Woman Suffrage Association. From 1868 to 1870 she edited and published a radical women's newspaper *The Revolution* and from 1881 to 1886 she worked on the *History of Woman Suffrage*. She was intrumental in setting up the International Council of Women and founded the International Woman Suffrage Alliance in 1904 in Berlin.

Anthony of Padua, Saint /'æntənɪ/ 1195–1231. Born in Lisbon, the son of a nobleman, he became an Augustinian monk, but in 1220 joined the Franciscans. He opposed the relaxations introduced into the Order. Like St Francis, he is said to have preached to animals. He died at Padua and was canonized in 1232.

Anthony, Saint /'æntənɪ/ c. 250–350. Founder of Christian monasticism. Born in Egypt, he renounced at the age of 20 all his possessions and lived in a tomb, and at 35 sought further solitude on a mountain in the desert. In 305 he founded the first cenobitic order, or community of Christians following a rule of life under a superior. When he was about 100, Anthony went to Alexandria and preached against the Arians. Anthony's temptations in the desert were a popular subject in art.

anthracene white glistening crystalline hydrocarbon with a faint blue fluorescence when pure. Its melting-point is about 216°C and its boiling point 351°C. It occurs in the high boiling fractions of coal tar, where it was discovered in 1832 by Laurent and Dumas.

anthracite a hard, dense glossy variety of coal, containing over 90 per cent of fixed carbon, and a low percentage of ash and of volatile matter, which causes it to burn without flame, smoke, or smell. It gives an intense heat, but is slow-burning and slow to catch alight, and is therefore unsuitable for use in open fires. Its characteristic composition is thought to be due to the action of bacteria in disintegrating the coal-forming material when it was laid down in the ◊Carboniferous period. Among the chief sources of anthracite coal are S Wales, Pennsylvania, the ◊Donbas, and the Shanxi province of China. The word is derived from the Greek *anthrakos*, coal.

anthrax cattle and sheep disease communicable to humans, usually via infected hides and fleeces; a black lesion and fever is caused by *Bacillus anthracis*, and treatment is by penicillin.

anthropoid ape a synonym for ◊ape, now rarely used.

anthropology scientific study of humankind. The term comes from the Greek *anthropos* + *logos*, 'man' + 'discourse', coined by Otto Casman in 1594, but the study was only developed following 19th-century evolutionary theory to deal with the human species physically, socially, and culturally. Anthropology overlaps with ◊sociology, ◊linguistics, and ◊psychology.

anthropometry science dealing with the measurement of the human body, particularly stature, body-weight, cranial capacity, length of limb, and so on, in the two sexes and across the different living and extinct peoples of the human species.

anthropomorphism attribution of human characteristics to gods (as in Greek and Scandinavian mythology), plants, animals, or inanimate objects (the wind, stones, and so on).

anthroposophy system of mystical philosophy developed by Rudolf ◊Steiner, who claimed to possess a power of intuition giving him access to knowledge not attainable by scientific means.

Antibes /ɒn'tiːb/ resort, which includes Juan les Pins, on the French Riviera, in the *département* of Alpes Maritimes; population (1982) 63,248. There is a Picasso collection in the 17th-century castle museum.

antibiotic chemical produced by moulds and bacteria which can destroy or prevent the growth of other micro-organisms, mainly bacteria. The older penicillins have in some cases been replaced by cephalosporins; they are used against bacterial diseases, including forms of pneumonia and venereal disease, and TB. Most viruses are not affected by antibiotics.

antibody a protein molecule produced by certain white blood cells (◊lymphocytes) in response to the presence of invading substances, or ◊antigens, including the proteins carried on the surface of bacteria and viruses. Each antibody is specific for its particular antigen, and combines with it to form a 'complex', thus rendering the antigen harmless and inactive. Antibody production is just one aspect of ◊immunity in vertebrates.

Antichrist the great opponent of Christ, by whom he is finally to be conquered. Although the term first occurs in Christian writings, the idea of conflict between Light and Darkness is present in Persian, Babylonian, and Jewish literature, and influenced early Christian thought. The Antichrist may be a false Messiah, or be connected with false teaching, or be identified with an individual, for example Nero at the time of the persecution of Christians, and the Pope and Napoleon in later Christian history.

anticline geological term for a fold in the rocks of the earth's crust in which the layers or beds bulge upwards forming a sort of arch, which, however, is seldom preserved intact. The fold may be undulating or sharply curved. Should one side of an anticlinal fold be compressed until it is nearly vertical, it forms a monocline. The opposite of an anticline is a syncline.

anticoagulant a substance which suppresses the formation of ◊blood clots. Most anticoagulants prevent the production of thrombin; in normal clotting thrombin induces the formation from blood ◊plasma of fibrin, to which blood platelets adhere. Common anticoagulants are heparin, produced by the liver and lungs, and derivatives of coumarin. Anticoagulants are used medically, in treating heart attacks, for example. They are also produced by blood-feeding animals such as mosquitoes, leeches and vampire bats, to keep the victim's blood flowing.

Anti-Comintern Pact (Anti-Communist Pact) agreement signed between Germany and Japan on 25 Nov 1936, opposing Communism as a menace to peace and order. The pact received the adhesion of Italy in 1937 and of Hungary, Spain, and Manchukuo in 1939.

anticonvulsant drug used to prevent epileptic fits (convulsions or seizures). Although most have some side-effects, in many cases seizures can be completely controlled, after a trial-and-error period, by the right drug.

anticyclone an area of high atmospheric pressure caused by descending air, which becomes warm and dry. Winds radiate from a calm centre, taking a clockwise direction in the northern hemisphere, and an anticlockwise direction in the southern hemisphere. Anticyclones are associated with clear weather and distinguished by the absence of rain and violent winds. In summer they bring hot, sunny days and in winter they bring fine, frosty spells, although fog and low cloud are not uncommon. Blocking anticyclones, which prevent the normal air circulation of an area, caused the summer drought in Britain in 1976, and the severe winters of 1947 and 1963.

antidepressant drug prescribed to lift depression. The two main groups of antidepressants are tricyclics and the monoamine-oxidase inhibitors (MAOIs). Both groups take about three to four weeks to show any beneficial effects and both have side-effects. The MAOIs tend to react with other drugs and some foods, and are less often prescribed. Long-term reliance on antidepressants is discouraged. They are a short-term treatment.

anti-emetic drug that reduces or removes the feeling of nausea or vomiting.

Antietam, Battle of /æn'tiːtəm/ decisive engagement of the American ◊Civil War (sometimes called Battle of Sharpsburg) on 17 Sept 1862 at Antietam Creek, off the Potomac river. General McClellan blocked the advance of Lee on Washington.

antifreeze a substance added to a car's water-cooling system, for example, to prevent it freezing in cold weather. The most common types of antifreeze contain the chemical ◊ethylene glycol, or $(CH_2OH.CH_2OH)$, an organic alcohol with a freezing point of about -15°C. The addition of this chemical depresses the freezing point of water significantly. A solution containing 33.5 per cent by volume of ethylene glycol will not freeze until about minus 20°C. A 50 per cent solution will not freeze until minus 35°C.

antifungal drug that acts against fungi, the cause of many skin disorders such as ringworm and athlete's foot.

antigen any substance which causes certain white blood cells (◊lymphocytes) to produce ◊antibodies. Common antigens include the proteins carried on the surface of ◊bacteria, ◊viruses and pollen grains. The protein of incompatible types of blood or tissue also act as antigens, a factor that has to be taken into account in medical procedures such as blood transfusion and organ transplants. See ◊blood group.

Antigone /æn'tɪgəni/ in Greek legend, a daughter of Jocasta, by her son ◊Oedipus.

Antigonus /æn'tɪgənəs/ 382–301 BC. a general of Alexander the Great, after whose death in 323 he made himself master of Asia Minor. He was defeated and slain by Seleucus at the battle of Ipsus.

Antigua and Barbuda /æn'tiːgə, bɑː'bjuːdə/ three islands (Antigua, Barbuda, and uninhabited Redonda) in the eastern Caribbean. *government* Antigua and Barbuda constitute an independent sovereign nation within the Commonwealth, with the British monarch as head of state. The constitution came into effect with independence in 1981. The governor-general, representing the British monarch, is appointed on the advice of the Antiguan prime minister, who is chosen by the governor-general as the person most likely to have the support of the legislature. The parliament is similar to Britain's, with a prime minister and cabinet answerable to it. It consists of a senate and a house of representatives, each having 17 members. Senators are appointed for a five-year term by the governor-general, 11 on the advice of the prime minister, four on the advice of the leader of the opposition, one at the governor-general's own discretion, and one on the advice of the Barbuda Council, the main instrument for local government. Members of the House of Representatives are elected by universal suffrage for a similar term. There are several political parties, the most significant being the Antigua Labour Party (ALP).

history the first European to visit Antigua was Christopher ◊Columbus in 1493. It was first colonized by Britain in 1632 and Barbuda was annexed in 1860. Between 1860 and 1959 it was administered by Britain within a federal system known as the Leeward Islands.

In 1967 it was made an associated state and given full internal independence, with Britain retaining responsibility for defence and foreign affairs. In the 1971 general election, the Progressive Labour Movement (PLM) won a decisive vistory and its leader, George Walter, replaced Vere Bird, leader of the ALP, as prime minister.

The PLM fought the 1976 election on a call for early independence while the ALP urged caution until a firm economic foundation had been laid. The ALP won and in 1978 declared that the country was ready for independence. Opposition from the inhabitants of Barbuda delayed the start of constitutional talks and the territory eventually became independent as Antigua and Barbuda in 1981. Despite its policy of ◊non-alignment, the ALP government actively assisted the US invasion of ◊Grenada in 1983, and went on to win 16 of the 17 seats in the 1984 general election.

antihypertensive drug used to lower raised blood pressure. The most widely used are ◊beta blockers and ◊diuretics.

anti-inflammatory substance that reduces the redness, swelling and locally increased temperature of inflammation. The body makes its own anti-inflammatory agents as a part of its natural defence and repair processes. In disease, such drugs as steroids help to suppress unwanted inflammation.

Antilles /æn'tɪliːz/ the whole group of West Indian islands, divided north-south into the Greater Antilles (◊Cuba, ◊Jamaica, Haiti-Dominican◊Republic, Puerto◊Rico) and Lesser Antilles, sub-divided into the Leeward Islands (◊Virgin Islands, ◊St Kitts-Nevis, ◊Antigua and Barbuda, ◊Anguilla, ◊Montserrat and ◊Guadeloupe) and the Windward Islands (◊Dominica, ◊Martinique, ◊St Lucia, ◊St Vincent and the Grenadines, ◊Barbados, and ◊Grenada).

Antigua and Barbuda
STATE OF

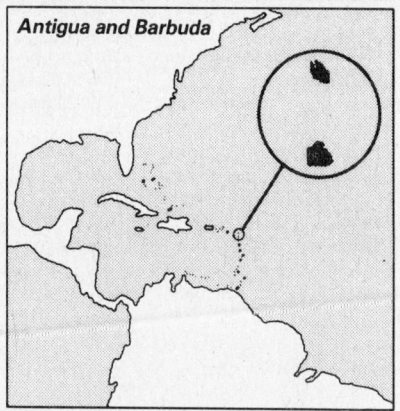

Antigua and Barbuda

AREA Antigua 280 sq km/108 sq mi, Barbuda 160 sq km/62 sq mi, plus Redonda 1 sq km/0.6 sq mi
CAPITAL and chief port St John's
PHYSICAL tropical island country
FEATURES Antigua is the largest of the Leeward Islands; Redonda is uninhabited
HEAD OF STATE Elizabeth II from 1981 represented by Wilfred Ebenezer Jacobs
HEAD OF GOVERNMENT Vere C Bird from 1981
GOVERNMENT constitutional monarchy
EXPORTS sea-island cotton, rum
CURRENCY East Caribbean dollar (4.46 = £1 Sept 1987)
POPULATION (1985) 80,000; annual growth rate 1.3%
LANGUAGE English
RELIGION Christian
LITERACY 90% (1985)
GDP $130 million (1983)
CHRONOLOGY
1967 Antigua and Barbuda became an associated state within the Commonwealth, with full internal independence.
1971 Progressive Labour Movement (PLM)

won the general election by defeating the Antigua Labour Party (ALP).
1976 PLM called for early independence but ALP urged caution. ALP won the general election.
1981 Full independence.
1983 Assisted US invasion of Grenada.
1984 ALP won a decisive victory in the general election.

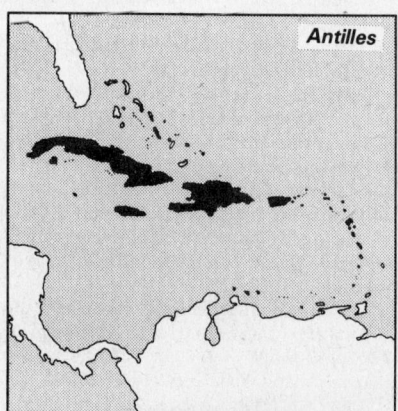

Antilles

antimatter in physics, a form of matter in which all the attributes of an ordinary atomic particle, such as electrical charge and spin, are reversed. Such antiparticles can be created in particle accelerators, such as those at ◊CERN and America's Fermilab, and are of vital potential importance. For example, nuclear fusion of two ordinary protons would result in a fraction of their mass being converted to energy (about 1 per cent), whereas fusion of a proton and an antiproton would result in the complete destruction of both, with all their mass (100 per cent) being converted into energy.

antimony in chemistry, a metallic element, symbol Sb, atomic number 51, atomic weight 121.76. It is a silver-white metal, brittle, and readily powdered. It occurs chiefly as stibnite, and is used in a number of alloys and in photosensitive substances in colour photography

and optical electronics, with a response in the blue and blue-green areas of the spectrum.

Antioch /'æntiɒk/ ancient capital of the Greek kingdom of Syria, founded 300 BC by Seleucus Nicator in memory of his father Antiochus, and for long famed for its splendour and luxury. Under the Romans it was an early centre of Christianity. The site is now occupied by the Turkish town of Antakiyah; population (1970) 57,600.

Antiochus /æn'taɪəkəs/ name of 13 kings of Syria of the Seleucid dynasty. *Antiochus I* (born 324; reigned 281–261 BC), son of Seleucus, one of the generals of Alexander the Great, earned the title of Antiochus Soter or Saviour by his defeat of the Gauls in Galatia (278 BC). His son *Antiochus II* (born 286; reigned 261–246 BC), was known as Antiochus Theos, the Divine. During his reign the eastern provinces broke away from the Graeco-Macedonian rule, and set up native princes. *Antiochus III* the Great (born about 241; king 223–187 BC), grandson of Antiochus II, secured a loose suzerainty over Armenia and Parthia (209), overcame Bactria, received the homage of the Indian king of the Kabul valley, and returned by way of the Persian Gulf (204 BC). He took possession of Palestine, entering Jerusalem in 198 BC. He crossed into NW Greece, but was decisively defeated by the Romans at Thermopylae in 191 and at Magnesia in 190 BC. He had to abandon his domains in Asia Minor,and perished at the hands of the people of Elymais. *Antiochus IV* (king 175–164 BC), second son of Antiochus III, was known as Antiochus Epiphanes, the Illus trious; he occupied Jerusalem about 170 BC, seizing much of the Temple treasure, and instituted worship of the Greek type in the Temple. This produced the

revolt of the Jewish people under the Macabees, and Antiochus died before he could suppress it. *Antiochus VII* Sidetes (king 138–129 BC), the last strong ruler of the dynasty, took Jerusalem in 134 BC, reducing the Maccabees to subjection, and fought successfully against the Parthians. Under *Antiochus XIII* Asiaticus (reigned 69–65 BC), the last of the dynasty, Syria was converted into a province by Pompeii.

antiparticle in nuclear physics, a particle that differs from another fundamental particle in having the opposite charge or magnetic moment. For example, an electron carries a negative charge whereas its antiparticle, the positron, carries a positive one. In all other respects, such as mass, the particles are identical. Other antiparticles include the negatively-charged antiproton and the antineutron. Antiparticles anihilate each other, with the production of energy, when they collide. A (hypothetical) substance consisting entirely of antiparticles is known as ◊antimatter.

antipodes places exactly opposite on the globe (Greek 'opposite feet'). In Britain, Australia and New Zealand are called the Antipodes.

antipsychotic (sometimes called major tranquillizer) drug used to treat the symptoms of severe mental disorder.

antipyretic drug, such as aspirin, used to lower a raised temperature (fever).

anti-racism and anti-sexism active opposition to ◊racism and ◊sexism; positive action or a set of policies designed to counteract racism and sexism, often on the part of an official body or an institution, such as a school, a business, or a government agency. The growth of anti-racist and anti-sexist policies in the UK in the 1980s, for example in the ILEA (Inner London Education Authority), reflects the belief that to ensure equality of opportunity, conscious efforts must be made to counteract the effects of unconscious racism and sexism as well as the effects of previous systematic ◊discrimination against members of minority ethnic groups and women.

antirrhinum or *snapdragon* plant belonging to the same family as the foxglove and toadflax (Scrophulariaceae). *Antirrhinum majus*, a native of the Mediterranean region, is a familiar garden flower.

antisemitism literally, prejudice against semitic people (see ◊Semite), but in practice it has meant prejudice or discrimination against, and persecution of, the Jews as an ethnic group. The fall of Jerusalem in 70 AD led many Jews to settle in Europe. The adoption of Christianity as the official religion of the Roman Empire in the 4th century then led to a reinforcing of existing prejudice against a distinctive group, since Jews were considered the murderers of Christ. Antisemitism was increased in the Middle Ages by the ◊Crusades, and by legislation forbidding Jews to own land or be members of a craft guild, so that to earn a living they were forced to become money lenders and middlemen (thus adding to prejudice against them). By the 16th century they were forced by law in many cities to live in a ◊ghetto. Late 18th-and early 19th-century liberal thought improved the position of Jews in

European society – for example, after the French Revolution the 'rights of man' were extended to the Jews in 1790 – until 19th-century nationalism and the rise of unscientific theories of race. Antisemitism became strong in Austria, France (see ◊Dreyfus), and Germany, and from 1881 ◊pogroms in Poland and Russia led to the flight of refugees to Britain and, particularly, the USA, where freedom of religion was enshrined in the constitution. In the 20th century, Hitler's application of racial theories led to the ◊Holocaust of 1933–45, when about six million Jews died in concentration camps (Auschwitz, Belsen, Buchenwald, Dachau, Maidanek). After World War II the creation of Israel (1948) led to Palestinian anti-Zionism, backed by the Arab world, and antisemitism has also occurred in the USSR and the eastern bloc, and in European neo-fascist groups such as the ◊National Front in England.

antiseptic substance killing or hindering the growth of germs. The use of antiseptics was pioneered by Joseph ◊Lister.

anti-theatre a theory advanced by Peter ◊Handke in *Insulting the Audience*, 1966.

antiviral drug that kills viruses or stops them multiplying. Most viral diseases are not affected by antibiotics; traditionally antivirals have been some of the most difficult drugs to develop.

anti-vivisection opposition to vivisection. Vivisection, that is, experiments on living animals, is practised on the grounds that it results, or may result, in discoveries of great importance to medical science. Anti-vivisectionists argue that it is immoral to inflict pain on helpless creatures, even for the best of motives, that it is unjust that animals should suffer in order that people may benefit, that it is unscientific in that results achieved with animals may not be paralleled with human beings, and that vivisection has not added to people's power over disease. Anti-vivisectionist groups, such as the Animal Liberation Front, sometimes take illegal action to draw attention to their cause.

antler the 'horn' of a deer, often branched, and made of bone rather than horn. Antlers are shed and regrown each year, and only borne by males except in ◊caribou where both sexes have them.

ant lion larva of one of the insects of the family Myrmeleontidae, mainly tropical but occurring in Europe, which traps insects by waiting at the bottom of a pit it digs in sandy soil.

Antofagasta /ˌæntəfəˈɡæstə/ port of N Chile, capital of a province of the same name. Nitrates from the ◊Atacama desert are exported. Population (1982) 166,964.

Antonello da Messina /ˌæntəˈneləu/ c. 1430–1477. Italian painter, who in 1475 brought to Venice the new Flemish technique of oil painting perfected by ◊van Eyck.

Antonine's Wall /ˈæntənaɪn/ Roman line of fortification 142–200 AD, the Roman Empire's north west frontier, between the Clyde and Forth, Scotland.

Antoninus Pius /ˌæntəˈnaɪnəs/ 86–161 AD. Roman emperor, who had been adopted in 138 as Hadrian's heir, and succeeded him later that year; he enjoyed a prosperous reign. His daughter married ◊Marcus Aurelius, and the *Age of the Antonines* (especially the reigns of himself and his son-in-law) became a focus of nostalgic regret.

Antonioni /ænˌtəuniˈəuni/ Michelangelo 1912– . Italian film director, famous for his subtle analysis of neuroses and personal relationships of the leisured classes. His work includes *L'Avventura* 1960, *Blow Up* 1967, and *The Passenger* 1975.

antonymy near or precise oppositeness between or among words. 'Good' and 'evil' are antonyms, 'good' and 'bad' are also antonyms, and therefore 'evil' and 'bad' are synonyms in this context. Antonymy may vary with context and situation; in discussing the weather, 'dull' and 'bright' are antonymous, but when talking about knives and blades the opposite of 'dull' is 'sharp'.

Antrim /ˈæntrɪm/ county of Northern Ireland
area 2906 sq km/1122 sq mi
towns Belfast (county town), port of Larne
features Giant's Causeway of natural hexagonal basalt columns which, in legend, was built to enable the giants to cross between Ireland and Scotland; Antrim borders Lough Neagh, and is separated from Scotland by the 32 km/20 mi wide North Channel.
products potatoes, oats; linen, and synthetic textiles
population (1971) 352,549.

Antwerp /ˈæntwɜːp/ port (Flemish Antwerpen, French Anvers) in Belgium on the ◊Scheldt; population (1984) 490,000. One of the world's busiest ports, it has shipbuilding, oil-refining, petrochemical, textile, and diamond-cutting industries. Historic treasures include the home of Rubens (many of his works are in the Gothic cathedral), and an art gallery with a collection of the Flemish school.
history it was not until the 15th century that Antwerp rose to prosperity; from 1500 to 1560 it was the richest port in N Europe. After this Antwerp was distracted by religious troubles and the Netherlands revolt against Spain. In 1648 the treaty of Westphalia gave both shores of the Scheldt estuary to the United Provinces, which closed it to Antwerp trade. The treaty of Paris, 1814, opened the estuary to all nations on payment of a small toll to the Dutch, abandoned in 1863. During World War I Antwerp was occupied by Germany from Oct 1914 to Nov 1918; during World War II from May 1940 to Sept 1944.

Anubis /əˈnjuːbɪs/ in Egyptian mythology, the jackal-headed god of the dead.

Anuradhapura /əˈnuərədəpuərə/ site of the ruins of the capital of the Sinhalese kings of Sri Lanka 5th century BC–8th century AD; rediscovered in the mid-19th century, it has a ◊Bo tree descended from the original.

Anvers /ɒŋˈveə/ French form of ◊Antwerp.

anxiety an emotional state of fear or apprehension. Normal anxiety is a response to dangerous situations. Abnormal anxiety can either be free-floating, when the person may feel anxious much of the time in a wide range of situations, or it may be phobic, when the person is excessively afraid of an object or situation.

Anyang /ˌænˈjæŋ/ city in Henan province, China, the capital of the Shang dynasty (13th–12th centuries BC). Rich archaeological remains have been uncovered since the 1930s. Population (1970) 225,000.

ANZAC acronym (1915) from the initials of the Australia and New Zealand Army Corps, but applied in general to all troops of both countries serving in World War I and to some extent those in World War II. Most famous of their campaigns was that in Gallipoli: the date of their landing, 25 Apr 1915, is marked by a public holiday, Anzac Day, in both Australia and New Zealand.

Anzhero-Sudzhensk /ænˈʒeərəu ˈsuːdʒənsk/ coal mining town in W Siberia, USSR, 80 km/50 mi N of Kemerovo. Population (1977) 105,000.

Anzio /ˈæntsɪəu/ seaport on the W coast of Italy, 53 km/33 mi SE of Rome, the site of the Roman town of Antium. Population (1971) 22,927.

Anzio, Battle of the beach-head invasion of Italy 22 Jan–23 May 1944, by Allied troops; failure to use ◊Ultra intelligence information led to Allied troops being stranded for a period after German attacks.

ANZUS collective security organization established 1951 by Australia, New Zealand and the US. It was replaced by ◊SEATO. The acronym is from the initials of its members.

Aomori /ˈauməri/ port at the head of Mutsu Bay, on the N coast of Honshu Island, Japan, 40 km/25 mi NE of Hirosaki. The port handles a large local trade. Population (1977) 273,000.

aorta the chief ◊artery; the dorsal blood vessel carrying oxygenated blood from the left ventricle of the heart of birds and mammals. It branches to form smaller arteries which in turn supply all body organs except ◊lungs. In fish the ventral aorta carries deoxygenated blood from the heart to the ◊gills and the dorsal aorta carries oxygenated blood from the gills to other parts of the body.

Aosta /ɑːˈɒstə/ Italian city, capital of Valle d'Aosta (French-speaking) autonomous region, 79 km/49 mi NW of Turin. It has extensive Roman remains. Population (1971) 35,000.

Apache /əˈpætʃɪ/ one of the North ◊American Indian peoples, related to the Navajo, who now number about 10,000. The surviving Apaches live in reservations in Arizona (the Apache state), SW Oklahoma, and New Mexico. Formerly known as great warriors (the name means 'enemy'), their greatest leader was ◊Geronimo.

apartheid (Afrikaans 'apartness') the policy of racial segregation of the government of ◊South Africa. The practice of segregation had always been widespread, but the term 'apartheid' was coined by the South African Bureau for Racial Affairs (Sabra) in the late 1930s. Apartheid was legally first formulated in 1948, when the Afrikaner National Party gained power.
It has two main facets: internally, non-whites do not share full rights of citizenship with the 4.5 million whites (for example, the 23 million blacks cannot vote in parliamentary elections), and many public facilities and institutions are restricted to the use of one race only; and in the

long term a group of ◊Black National States (formerly known as Bantustans) is being introduced, which theoretically give self-government to blacks, although these states are within the borders of, and economically dependent on, South Africa.

Opposition to apartheid has always been considerable, both externally and within the country. In 1961 South Africa was forced to withdraw from the Commonwealth because of it; during the 1960s. and 1970s calls for international sanctions grew, centring especially on sporting and cultural links; and in the 1980s advocates of sanctions have sought to extend them into trade and finance. Internally the banned ◊African National Congress under ◊Luthuli and ◊Tambo, with the help of leading figures such as Nelson and Winnie ◊Mandela, ◊Biko, and Archbishop ◊Tutu, has campaigned for the abolition of apartheid. Anger at the policy has sparked off many uprisings, from ◊Sharpeville 1960 and ◊Soweto 1976 to the Crossroads squatter camps 1986. The South African government's reaction to internal and international pressure has been twofold: it has abolished some of the more hated apartheid laws (the ban on interracial marriages was lifted in 1985 and the pass laws, which restricted the movement of non-whites, were repealed in 1986); and it has sought to replace the term apartheid with the term 'plural democracy'. Under states of emergency in 1985 and 1986 it has used severe measures to quell internal opposition, and since 1986 there has been an embargo on the reporting of it in the media. Outside South Africa there are anti-apartheid movements in many countries (see also ◊boycott, ◊protest, ◊sanctions).

ape name given to those ◊primates most closely related to humans, including ◊gibbon, ◊orang-utan, ◊chimpanzees and ◊gorilla.

Ape City Yerkes Regional Primate Center, Atlanta, Georgia, USA, where large numbers of primates are kept for physiological and psychological experiment.

Apennines /'æpənaɪnz/ chain of mountains stretching the length of the Italian peninsula. A continuation of the Maritime Alps, from Genoa it swings across the peninsula to Ancona on the E coast, and then back to the W coast and into the 'toe' of Italy. The system is continued over the Strait of Messina along the N Sicilian coast, then across the Mediterranean sea in a series of islands to the Atlas mountains of North Africa.

Apennines mountain range on the ◊Moon, SE of the Sea of Showers.

aperture in photography, an opening through which light passing through the lens to strike the film can be controlled by shutter speed and iris diaphragm, set mechanically or electronically at various diameters.

aphasia difficulty in speaking, writing, and reading, caused by damage to the brain.

aphid small insect also known as plant-louse, greenfly or blackfly, living by sucking sap from plants. There are many species, often adapted to particular plants and in many cases with complicated life histories. In some stages wingless females rapidly produce large numbers of live young by ◊parthenogenesis, leading to

Ape City A major area of research at Ape City is language. By pushing the buttons on the machine the young chimpanzee can convey the meaning of words, and develop the rudiments of grammar.

enormous infestations. Numbers can approach 2,000 million per hectare/2 acres. As well as feeding they can cause damage by transmitting virus diseases. Some research suggests, however, that they may help promote fertility in the soil through the waste they secrete, termed 'honeydew'.

aphid Scanning electron micrograph (SEM) of the bird cherry aphid, *Rhopalosiphum padi*, known also as *Aphis avenae*, feeding on barley. Next to it is the exoskelton, made of inelastic chilin shed to allow growth. This pest transmits the viral diseases yellow dwarf virus and maize leaf fleck virus, infecting such crops as barley, oat, wheat and maize.

aphrodisiac anything arousing or increasing sexual desire (from Aphrodite, the Greek goddess of love). Sexual activity can be stimulated in humans and animals by drugs affecting the pituitary gland. Preparations commonly sold for the purpose can be dangerous (cantharidin) or useless (rhinoceros horn), and alcohol and cannabis, popularly thought to be effective, because they lessen inhibition, may even have the opposite effect.

Aphrodite /ˌæfrə'daɪtɪ/ in Greek mythology, the goddess of love (Roman ◊Venus, ◊Phoenician Astarte, Babylonian ◊Ishtar); said to be either a daughter of ◊Zeus (in Homer) or sprung from the foam of the sea (in Hesiod). She was the unfaithful wife of ◊Hephaestus, the mother of ◊Eros, and was awarded the prize for beauty by ◊Paris; centres of her worship were Cyprus (◊Paphos) and Cythera.

Aphrodite The Greek goddess of beauty and sexual love whose statue in Naples Museum bears the epithet Kallipygos, 'of the beautiful buttocks'. Swans and pomegranates are two of her emblems. Her lovers included Anchises, father of Aeneas, and Adonis.

Apia /'ɑːpɪə/ capital and port of Western Samoa, on the north coast of Upolu island, in the West Pacific. It was the home of Robert Louis ◊Stevenson 1889–94. Population (1981) 33,170.

Apis /'ɑːpɪs/ ancient Egyptian god with a bull's head, linked with ◊Osiris (hence the name for the Ptolemaic god ◊Serapis); his cult centres were Memphis and Heliopolis, where sacred bulls were mummified.

Apocalypse in literature, a movement which developed from Surrealism in 1938, and included G S Fraser, Henry Treece, J F Hendry, Nicholas Moore, and Tom Scott. Largely influenced by the work of Dylan ◊Thomas, it favoured Biblical symbolism.

Apollinaire /əˌpɒlɪ'neə/ Guillaume. Pen name of Guillaume Apollinaire de Kostrowitsky 1880–1918. French poet of aristocratic Polish descent. He was born in Rome and educated in

Monaco, but in 1898 went to Paris. There he was a leader of the *avant garde* in literary and artistic circles. His lyrics (*Alcools/Alcohols* 1913 and *Calligrammes/Word Pictures* 1918, his novel *Le Poète assassiné/The Poet Assassinated* 1916, and play *Les Mamelles de Tirésias/The Breasts of Tiresias*1917, show him as a representative of the cubist and futurist manner, and his work greatly influenced younger French writers, such as ◊Aragon.

Apollo /ə'pɒləʊ/ in Greek mythology, the god of sun, music, poetry, and prophecy, agriculture and pastoral life, and leader of the Muses. He was the twin child (with ◊Artemis), of ◊Zeus and Leto. His chief cult centres were his supposed birthplace on the island of ◊Delos, and ◊Delphi. Ancient statues show Apollo as the embodiment of the Greek ideal of male beauty.

Apollo In Greek mythology, the god Apollo is identified with the beauty of the male form and with the sun. A highly moral god, he was associated with philosophy and reason, poetry and the law, and pilgrims went to his shrine at Delphi for purification and to hear truth from his oracle. This representation of him is on an amphora in Wurzburg.

Apollo asteroid a member of a group of ◊asteroids whose orbits cross that of the Earth. They are named after the first of their kind, Apollo itself discovered in 1932, and then lost until 1973. Apollo asteroids are so small and faint that they are difficult to see except when close to Earth (Apollo itself is about 2 km across) . A closely related group, the Amor asteroids, come close to Earth but do not cross its orbit. Apollo asteroids are important because they can collide with the Earth from time to time. In 1937 the Apollo asteroid Hermes passed 800,000 km from Earth, the closest observed approach of any asteroid. A collision with an Apollo asteroid 65 million years ago may have been responsible for the death of the dinosaurs.

Apollonius of Rhodes /ˌæpə'ləʊnɪəs/ c. 220–180 BC. Greek poet, author of the epic *Argonautica*.

Apollonius of Tyana /'taɪənə/ fl. 50 AD—. Greek ascetic philosopher of the Neo-

Pythagorean school. He travelled in Babylonia and India, where he acquired a wide knowledge of oriental religions and philosophies, and taught at Ephesus. He was credited with many miraculous powers.

Apollo of Rhodes the Greek statue of Apollo generally known as the ◊Colossus of Rhodes.

Apollo project the US space project to land a person on the ◊Moon, as authorized in 1961 by President John F Kennedy. To achieve Moon landing the world's most powerful rocket, Saturn V, was built to launch the Apollo spacecraft, containing three astronauts, towards the Moon. When the Apollo spacecraft was in orbit around the Moon, two astronauts entered the Lunar Module in which they descended to the lunar surface. The first Apollo mission carrying a crew, Apollo 7 in October 1968, was a test flight in orbit around the Earth. After three other preparatory flights, Apollo 11 commanded by Neil ◊Armstrong made the first lunar landing by human beings, in July 1969.

apologetics philosphical writings which attempt to refute attacks on the Christian faith. Famous apologists include ◊Justin Martyr, ◊Origen, St ◊Augustine, Thomas ◊Aquinas, Blaise Pascal, and Joseph Butler. The questions raised by modern scientific and historical discoveries have widened the field of apologetics.

aposematic colouration or *warning colouration*; markings that make a dangerous, poisonous or foul-tasting animal particularly conspicuous and recognizable to a predator. Examples include the yellow and black stripes of bees and wasps, and the bright red or yellow colours of many poisonous frogs. See also ◊mimicry.

a posteriori a Latin term meaning 'from what comes after'. In philosphy, a posteriori propositions are true or false in relation to known and established facts of experience. the converse of ◊a priori.

apostle (Greek 'messenger') in the Christian New Testament, missionaries sent out to preach by Jesus, especially the Twelve ◊Disciples. In the earliest days of Christianity the term was extended to include some who had never known Jesus in the flesh, notably St Paul.

Apostles discussion group founded 1820 at University of Cambridge, England; members have included ◊Tennyson, G E ◊Moore, Bertrand ◊Russell, Lytton ◊Strachey, Maynard ◊Keynes, Guy ◊Burgess and Anthony ◊Blunt.

Apostolic Age early period in the Christian Church dominated by those personally known to Jesus or his disciples.

apostolic succession the doctrine in the Christian Church that certain spiritual powers

Apollo project Extravehicular activity (facing page) while Apollo 9 modules docked. The Apollo 9 mission testing the lunar module in earth orbit was successfully completed in March 1969. Four months later Apollo 11 made the first moon landing. The recovery of Apollo 17 (above) included a scientist-astronaut for the first time and was the final moon landing in the programme. Remaining hardware was used in Skylab project.

were received by the first Apostles direct from Christ, and have been handed down in the ceremony of 'laying on of hands' from generation to generation of bishops.

apostrophe a mark used in the written presentation of English ('). It serves primarily to indicate a missing letter or number (as in *don't* for 'do not' and *'47* for '1947'). It also often precedes the plural *s* used with numbers and abbreviations (for example, *the 1970's* and *a group of P.O.W's*); it is possible, however, to do without the apostrophe in such usages (for example, *the 1970s, a group of POWs*). The use of an apostrophe to help indicate a plural (as in a shopkeeper's *Apple's* and *Tomato's*, followed by their prices) is nonstandard and regarded by many as semi-literate. Grammatically, the apostrophe indicates possession (as in *the gentleman's hat, the gentlemen's hats, the lady's hat, the ladies' hats*). In the case of certain words ending with *s*, usage is split, as between *James's book* and *James' book*. In current English, the possessive apostrophe is often omitted from such usages as *in ten months' time/in ten months time* and such titles as *Barclays Bank*. Many people otherwise competent in writing have great difficulty with the apostrophe, which has never been stable at any point in its history, and some authorities argue that its use will decline over the next few decades, especially as a marker of possession.

apothecary an early name for a person who mixed and dispensed medicines, a pharmacist. The word retains its original meaning in the USA and other countries, but in England apothecary came to mean a licensed medical practitioner. The Society of Apothecaries (1815) was given the right to grant licences to practise medicine in England and Wales.

Appalachians /ˌæpəˈleɪtʃənz/ mountain system of eastern North America, stretching about 2,400 km/1,500 mi from Alabama in the south west to Quebec province in the north east, composed of very ancient eroded rocks. The chain includes the ◊Allegheny, ◊Catskill and ◊Blue Ridge mountains, the later having the highest peak, Mount Mitchell, 2,045 m/6,684 ft. The eastern edge has a fall line to the coastal plain where Philadelphia, Baltimore and Washington stand.

appeasement term for the generally conciliatory policy adopted by the British government, particularly under Neville Chamberlain, towards the Nazi-Fascist dictators in the 1930s. It was strongly opposed by Winston Churchill, but the ◊Munich Agreement of 1938 was almost universally hailed as its justification. Appeasement ended when Germany occupied Bohemia-Moravia in March 1939.

appendicitis inflammation of the small blind extension of the bowel in the lower right abdomen, the *appendix*, which is about the size of a little finger and which is not essential to healthy life. In *acute appendicitis* the infection spreads to the peritoneum (see ◊peritonitis), for example, by the bursting of the appendix. The attack often comes suddenly in the night with a sharp pain in the lower right abdomen, accompanied by vomiting, high temperature, quick breathing and rapid pulse. Removal of the appendix became fashionable after Edward VII of England had the operation. It is less common today, partly because the condition is more easily controlled by antibiotics.

Appert /æˈpeə/ Nicolas 1750–1841. French pioneer of food preservation by canning; author of *L'art de conserver les substances animales et végétales*.

apple fruit of *Malus pumila*, a tree of the family Rosaceae. It has been an important food-plant in Europe from the earliest times, the cultivated varieties being derived from the wild crab-apple. There are several thousand varieties of cultivated apples, which may be divided into eating, cooking, and cider apples. They grow best in temperate countries with a cool climate and plenty of rain during the winter. The continent of Europe and North America (both the USA and Canada) are the main sources of supply, but apples are also produced in Australia, New Zealand, South Africa and some parts of Asia.

Appleton /ˈæpəltən/ Edward Victor 1892–1965. British physicist, who worked at Cambridge under ◊Rutherford from 1920. He proved the existence of the ◊Kennelly-Heaviside layer in the atmosphere, and the ◊Appleton layer beyond it, and was involved in the initial work on the atomic bomb. Nobel prize 1947.

Appleton layer a band containing ionized gases in the Earth's upper atmosphere, above the Heaviside layer. It can act as a reflector of radio signals, although its ionic composition varies with the sunspot cycle. It was named after the British physicist Edward Victor ◊Appleton (1892–1965), who was awarded the 1974 Nobel Prize in Physics for its discovery.

application in computing, a job that can be performed by a specialist program designed for the non-expert user. The term is also used to describe such a program. Typical applications include stock control, payroll, and word processing. Application programs differ from systems programs, which perform functions within the machine that are normally invisible to the user (the computer's internal 'housekeeping').

Appomatox Court House /ˌæpəˈmætəks/ village in Virginia, USA, 5 km/3 mi from the modern village of Appomatox and scene of the surrender on 9 Apr 1865 of the Confederate Army under Robert E Lee to the Federals under Ulysses S Grant, which ended the Civil War. In 1954 a National Historical Park was established and the court house restored as a museum.

apricot tree *Prunus armeniaca*, closely related to the almond, peach, plum, and cherry with a yellow fleshed fruit. A native of the Far East, it has long been cultivated in Armenia, whence it has been introduced into Europe and USA.

April Fools' Day the first day of April, when it is customary in Western Europe and the USA to expose people to ridicule by causing them to believe some falsehood or to go on a fruitless errand. The victim is known in England as an April Fool; in Scotland as a gowk (cuckoo or fool); and in France as a *poisson d'avril* (April fish). There is a similar Indian custom on the last day of the Huli festival in late March.

Apsley House /ˈæpsli/ home of the Dukes of ◊Wellington at Hyde Park Corner, London, from 1820; now the Wellington Museum.

Apuleius /ˌæpjuːˈliːəs/ Lucius fl. c. 160 AD– . Roman lawyer, ◊philosopher and author, whose picaresque adventure tale *Metamorphoses, or The Golden Ass*, is sometimes called the world's first novel. The work preserved several ancient legends, notably the story of Cupid and ◊Psyche.

Apulia /əˈpjuːliə/ or *Puglia* region of Italy, the south eastern 'heel'; capital Bari, chief industrial centre Taranto; population (1981) 3,871,617.

Aqaba, Gulf of /ˈækəbə/ gulf extending for 160 km/100 mi between the Negev and the Red Sea; its coastline is uninhabited except at its head, where the frontiers of Israel, Egypt, Jordan, and Saudi Arabia converge. Here are the two ports Eilat (Israeli Elath) and Aqaba, Jordan's only port.

Aquae Sulis /ˈækwaɪ ˈsuːlɪs/ Roman name of the city of ◊Bath in Western England.

aqualung self-contained underwater breathing apparatus (scuba) worn by divers. It was developed in the early 1940s by the French diver Jacques Cousteau, now renowned for his underwater explorations. The main feature of the aqualung is that it provides air to the diver at the same pressure as that of the surrounding water (which increases with increasing depth). The vital component is the demand-regulator, a two-stage valve in the diver's mouthpiece. When the diver breathes in, air passes from compressed-air cylinders on the diver's back, through a valve to the inner chamber of the mouthpiece. Water enters the outer chamber and pressurizes the air in the inner chamber to the same pressure, which the diver breathes.

aquamarine a blue variety of the mineral ◊beryl $Be_3Al_2Si_6O_{18}$.

aquaplaning phenomenon in which the tyres of a road vehicle cease to make direct contact with the surface of the road, caused by the presence of a thin film of water. As a result, the vehicle can go out of control (particularly if the steered wheels are involved). Aquaplaning can be prevented by fitting tyres with a good tread pattern at the correct pressure and by avoiding excessive speed in wet road conditions.

aquarium tank or similar container used for the study and display of living aquatic plants and animals. The same name is used for institutions that exhibit aquatic life. These have been common since Roman times, but the first modern public aquarium was opened in Regent's Park, London, in 1853. A recent development is the oceanarium, a large display of marine life forms. See also ◊terrarium.

Aquarius in astronomy, a constellation of the ◊zodiac. It represents a man pouring water from a jar. The Sun passes through Aquarius from late February to early March.

aquatint a process of ◊etching in tone. It deals with broad masses in various gradations of tone, and thus differs from the usual type of etching, in which lines are bitten into a metal plate. J B le Prince (1734–81) is credited with its invention, and Goya is its most famous exponent.

Aquaviva /ˌækwəˈviːvə/ Claudius (Claudio) 1543–1615. Fifth general of the ◊Jesuits. Born in Naples, of noble family, he entered the order in 1567 and became its head in 1581. Under his rule the Society greatly increased in numbers, and the revolt of the Spanish Jesuits was put down. He published a treatise on education.

aqueduct artificial channel or conduit for water, commonly an elevated structure of stone, wood, or iron built for conducting water across a valley. Greek were marvels at engineering skill, and many of those built by the Romans are still standing, for example the aqueduct at Nimes in S France, built about 18 AD. The first modern aqueduct in Britain was that carrying the ◊Bridgewater Canal over the Irwell at Barton, built 1959–72. An outstanding recent aqueduct is the California State Water Project taking water from Lake Oroville in the N., through two power plants and across the Tehachapi mountains, more than 177 km/110 mi to Southern California.

aqueous humour watery fluid found in the space between the cornea and lens of the vertebrate eye. Similar to blood serum in composition, it is renewed every four hours.

aquifer any ◊bed of rock containing water that can be extracted by a well. The rock of an aquifer must be porous and permeable (full of interconnected holes) so that it can absorb water. It may overlie an impermeable layer so that water percolating down from the surface or laterally gathers there. Sandstones and porous limestones make the best aquifers. They are actively sought in arid areas as sources of drinking and irrigation water.

Aquila a ◊constellation of the equatorial region of the sky, representing an eagle. Its

aqueduct The Pont du Gard at Nîmes in southern France is a magnificent example of a Roman aqueduct, dating from about 18 AD. Water still flows along the top, and the bridge is still used by motor traffic.

brightest ◊star is the first-magnitude Altair, flanked by the stars Beta and Gamma Aquilae.

Aquinas /əˈkwaɪnəs/ St Thomas c. 1226–1274. Italian Dominican scholastic philosopher, monk and theologian, known as the 'Angelic Doctor'; canonized in 1323. His *Summa Contra Gentiles* (1259–64), argues that reason and faith are compatible. His unfinished *Summa Theologica*, begun 1265, deals with the nature of God, morality and the work of Christ. His works embodied the world view taught in universities up till the mid-17th century, and include scientific ideas derived from ◊Aristotle; in 1879 they were recognized as the basis of Catholic theology by Pope Leo XIII, who had launched a modern edition of his works. See also ◊scholasticism.

Aquino /əˈkiːnəʊ/ Maria Corazón (born Cojuangco) 1933– . Populist president of the Philippines from 1986.
The daughter of a sugar baron, she studied in the USA and married the politician Benigno Aquino in 1956. The chief political opponent of President ◊Marcos, he was assassinated by a military guard at Manila airport in 1983. Corazón Aquino was drafted by the opposition to contest the Feb 1986 presidential election and claimed victory over Marcos, accusing the government of ballot-rigging. She led a non-violent 'people's power' campaign which overthrew Marcos on 25 Feb. A devout Roman Catholic, Aquino enjoyed strong church backing in her 1986 campaign and, as president, has sought to rule in a conciliatory manner.

Aquitaine /ˌækwɪˈteɪn/ region of SW France, capital Bordeaux; population 2,584,400, comprising the *départements* of Dordogne, Gironde, Landes, Lot-et-Garonne, and Pyréenées-Atlantiques. It coincides roughly with the Roman province of Aquitania, and the ancient French province of Aquitaine. Eleanor of Aquitaine married the future Henry II of England in 1152, and brought it to him as her dowry; it remained an English possession until 1452. Red wines, for example Margaux and St Julien, are produced in the district of Médoc, north of Bordeaux and bordering the Gironde.

Aquino Angeles City, Philippines, Jan 1987. Nearly a year after she came to power after the overthrow of the Marcos regime, President Corazón Aquino of the Philippines campaigns to win approval of the draft constitution in a bid to stabilize her government.

There are early human remains in the ◊Dordogne.

Arab Emirates see ◊United Arab Emirates.

arabesque a pose in which the dancer stands on one leg, straight or bent, with the other leg raised behind, fully extended. The arms are held in a harmonious position to give the longest possible line from fingertips to toes.

Arabian Gulf a large inlet of the Arabian Sea dividing the Arabian peninsula from Iran. See ◊Gulf.

Arabian Nights oriental tales in oral circulation among Arab storytellers from the 10th century, and probably having roots in India. They are also known as *The Thousand Nights and One Night* and include *Ali Baba*, *Aladdin*, and *Sindbad*. They were supposed to have been told to the sultan by his bride Scheherazade to avoid her predecessors' fate – they were all executed following the wedding night to prevent their infidelity. She began a new tale each evening, which she would only agree to finish on the following night. Eventually the 'sentence' was rescinded.

Arabian sea the north west branch of the ◊Indian Ocean.

Arabic language a Hamito-Semitic language of W Asia and North Africa, originating among the Arabs of the Arabian peninsula. Arabic script is written from right to left. A feature of the language is its consonantal roots; for example, *s-l-m* is the root for *salaam*, a greeting that implies peace, *Islam*, the creed of submission to God and calm acceptance of His will, and *Muslim*, one who submits to that will (a believer in Islam). The *Quran*, the sacred book of Islam, is 'for reading' by a *qari* ('reader') who is engaged in *qaraat* ('reading'). The 7th century style of the Quran is the basis of Classical Arabic. The language has spread as far west as Morocco and as far east as Malaysia, Indonesia and the Philippines. Forms of Colloquial Arabic vary in the countries where it is the dominant language: Algeria, Bahrain, Egypt, Iraq, Jordan, Kuwait,

Lebanon, Libya, Mali, Mauretania, Morocco, Oman, Sudan, Syria, Tunisia, the United Arab Emirates, and the two Yemens. It is also a language of religious and cultural significance in such other countries as Bangladesh, India, Indonesia, Iran, Malaysia, Pakistan, the Philippines and Somalia.

arabic numerals the signs 0,1,2,3,4,5,6,7,8,9, which were in use among the Arabs before being adapted by the peoples of Europe during the Middle Ages in place of Roman numerals. They appear to have originated in India, and reached Europe by way of Spain.

Arab-Israeli Wars a series of wars between Israel and various Arab states in the Middle East since the founding of the state of Israel in 1948. Arab opposition to such a state began after the ◊Balfour Declaration 1917, which supported the idea of a Jewish national homeland. In the 1920s there were anti-Zionist riots in Palestine, then governed by Britain under a League of Nations mandate. In 1936 an Arab revolt led to a British Royal Commission which recommended partition (approved by the United Nations in 1947, but rejected by the Arabs).

First Arab-Israeli War 14 Oct 1948–13 Jan/24 Mar 1949. As soon as the independent state of Israel had been proclaimed it was invaded by combined Arab forces. However, the Israelis defeated them and went on to annexe more territory, so that they controlled 75 per cent of Palestine.

Second Arab-Israeli War 29 Oct–4 Nov 1956. After Egypt had taken control of the Suez Canal, Israel invaded and captured Sinai and the Gaza Strip, from which it withdrew after the entry of a UN force.

Third Arab-Israeli War 5–10 Jun 1967, the 'Six Day War'. It resulted in the Israeli capture of the Golan Heights from Syria; Old Jerusalem and the West Bank from Jordan; and, in the south, occupation of the Gaza Strip and Sinai Peninsula as far as the Suez Canal.

Fourth Arab-Israeli War 2–22/24 Oct 1973, the 'October War' or 'Yom Kippur War'. So-called because the Israeli forces were taken by surprise on the Day of ◊Atonement. It resulted in the recrossing of the Suez Canal by Egyptian forces and initial gains, though there was some later loss of ground by the Syrians in the north. Tension in the Middle East remained high after the war, and confrontation was fuelled by Soviet adoption of the Arab cause and US support for Israel, although actual hostilities were limited to the activities of Palestinian guerrilla organizations such as the PLO, and frequent Israeli reprisals. Particularly in view of the area's strategic sensitivity as an oil producer, pressure grew for a settlement, and in 1978 the ◊Camp David Agreements brought Egypt–Israeli peace, but this was denounced by other Arab countries. Israel withdrew from Sinai 1979–82, but no final agreement on Jerusalem and the establishment of a Palestinian state on the West Bank was reached.

Fifth Arab-Israeli War from 1978 the presence of Palestinian guerrillas in Lebanon led to alternate Arab raids on Israel and Israeli retaliatory incursions, but on 6 Jun 1982 Israel launched a full-scale invasion. By 14 Jun Beirut was encircled, and ◊PLO and Syrian forces were evacuated (mainly to Syria) 21–31 Aug, but in Feb 1985 there was a unilateral Israeli withdrawal from the country without any gain for losses incurred. Despite this, Israeli incursions into Lebanon have continued.

Arab-Israeli Wars 22 October, 1973. Having crossed the Suez Canal, Israeli troops enter Egypt. Part of the occupied area was within 72 km/45 mi of Cairo.

Arabistan /ˌærəbɪˈstɑːn/ former name of the Iranian province of ◊Khuzestan, which was revived in the 1980s by the 2 million Sunni Arab inhabitants who demand autonomy. Unrest and sabotage 1979–80 led to a pledge of a degree of autonomy by Ayatollah Khomeni.

Arab League an organization of Arab states established in Cairo in 1945 to promote Arab unity, especially in opposition to Israel. The original members were Egypt, Syria, Iraq, Lebanon, Transjordan (Jordan 1949), Saudi Arabia, and Yemen. In 1979 Egypt was suspended and the League's headquarters transferred to Tunis in protest against the Egypt-Israeli peace.

Arachne /əˈrækni/ in Greek mythology, a Lydian girl who was so skilful a weaver that she challenged the goddess Athena to a contest. Athena tore Arachne's beautiful tapestries to pieces, whereupon Arachne hanged herself. She was transformed into a spider, and her weaving became a cobweb. Arachne in Greek means spider.

Arad /ˈæræd/ Romanian town on the river Mures, 160 km/100 mi NE of Belgrade; an important route centre with many industries. Population (1983) 171,198.

Arafat /ˈærəfæt/ Yassir 1929– . Palestinian politician, co-founder of ◊al-Fatah in 1956 and president of the ◊Palestine Liberation Organization (PLO) from 1969. In the 1970s his activities in pursuit of an independent homeland for Palestinians made him a prominent figure in world politics, but in the 1980s the growth of factions within the PLO effectively reduced his power. He was forced to evacuate Lebanon 1983, but remained leader of the majority of the PLO. In 1985 he agreed with Hussein of Jordan to recognize the existence of Israel if territory seized since 1967 was restored, but the peace initiative foundered in 1986.

Arafat Palestinian leader Yassir Arafat photographed in Abu Dhabi in in 1987. Educated at Cairo University, he worked as an engineer in Egypt and Kuwait. He was the leader of the Palestinian Liberation Organization from 1969 despite being forced out of Beirut in 1983 and the opposition of the more radical elements in the party.

Arafura Sea /ˌærəˈfʊərə/ the area of the Pacific Ocean between N Australia and Indonesia, bounded by the Timor Sea in the west and the Coral Sea in the east, is 1,290 km/800 mi long and 560 km/350 mi wide.

Aragón /ˈærəgən/ autonomous region of NE Spain (capital Saragossa); population (1981) 1,213,099. A Roman province until taken by the Visigoths, who lost it to the Moors in the 8th century, it became a kingdom in 1035. It was united with Castile after the marriage of ◊Ferdinand and ◊Isabella in 1469.

Aragon /ˌærəˈgɒn/ Louis 1897–1982. French poet and novelist. Beginning as a Dadaist, he became one of the leaders of ◊Surrealism, published volumes of verse and in 1930 joined the Communist party. Taken prisoner in World War II he escaped to join the Resistance, experiences reflected in the poetry of *Le Crève-Coeur* (1942) and *Les Yeux d'Elsa* (1944).

Arakan /ˌærəˈkɑːn/ province of Burma on the Bay of Bengal coast, some 645 km/400 mi long and strewn with islands. It is bounded along its eastern side by the Arakan Yoma, a mountain range rising to 3,000 m/1,000 ft. The ancient kingdom of Arakan was conquered by Burma in 1782.

Aral Sea /ˈɑːrəl/ inland sea in the USSR; the world's fourth largest lake; divided between Kazakhstan and Uzbekistan; former area 62,000 sq km/24,000 sq mi, but decreasing. Water from its tributaries, the Amu Darya and Syr Darya, has been diverted for irrigation and city use, and the sea is disappearing, with long-term consequences for the climate.

Aram /'ærəm/ Eugene 1704–1759. British murderer remembered as the subject of works by Lytton, Hood, and others. He was a schoolmaster at Knaresborough, and in 1745 was tried and acquitted on a charge concerned with the disappearance of a local shoemaker. After achieving some distinction as a philologist, he was arrested at Lynn in Norfolk, following the discovery of a skeleton in a cave at Knaresborough. He was tried at York, confessed to the murder after his conviction, and was hanged.

Aramaic language a Hamito Semitic language of W Asia, the everyday language of Palestine in the time of Christ. In the 13th century BC Aramaean nomads set up states in Mesopotamia, and over the next 200 years spread into N Syria, where Damascus, Aleppo, and Carchemish were among their chief centres. Araimic spread throughout Syria and Mesopotamia, becoming one of the official languages of the Persian empire under the Achaemenids and serving as a lingua franca of the day. Aramaic dialects survive among small Christian communities in various parts of W Asia.

Aran Islands /'ærən/ three rocky islands (Inishmore, Inishmaan, Inisheer) in the mouth of Galway Bay, Republic of Ireland. Population approximately 4,600. The capital is Kilronan. J M ◊Synge used the language of the islands in his plays.

Aranjuez /,ærən'xweθ/ Spanish town on the river Tagus, 40 km/25 mi SE of Madrid. The palace was a royal residence for centuries. Population approximately 29,000.

Arany /'ɒrəni/ János 1817–1882. Hungarian writer, born at Nagyszalonta (now in Romania). His comic epic *The Lost Constitution* 1846 was followed in 1847 by *Toldi*, a product of the popular nationalist school. In 1864 his epic masterpiece *The Death of King Buda* appeared. During his last years Arany produced the rest of the *Toldi* trilogy, and his most personal lyrics.

Ararat /'ærəræt/ double-peaked mountain on the Turkish-Iranian border; the higher, Great Ararat, 5,156 m/17,000 ft, was the reputed resting place of ◊Noah's Ark after the Flood.

Ararat /'ærəræt/ wheat and wool centre in NW Victoria, Australia. Population (1981) 8,336.

Araucanian Indian /,ærɔː'keɪnɪən/ any member of the original inhabitants of central Chile. An agricultural and hunting people, they lived in small villages, and were excellent warriors, defeating the Incas and resisting the Spanish for 200 years. Some 200,000 still survive in reserves.

araucaria coniferous tree allied to the firs, native to the southern hemisphere, and often attaining a gigantic size. Araucarias include the *monkey-puzzle tree Araucaria araucana*, the *bunya-bunya pine Araucaria bidwillii* of Australia, and the Norfolk Island pine *Araucaria heterophylla*.

Arawak native American civilization of the Caribbean and Amazon basin, dating from approximately 1000–1550 AD. A peaceful people, they lived mainly by tropical forest agriculture, based on cassava and manioc. They were driven out of the Lesser Antilles by ◊Caribs shortly before the arrival of the Spanish in the 16th century.

Arbenz Guzmán /ɑː'bens gʊθ'mæn/ Jacobo 1876–1933. Leader of Guatemala from 1951 until his overthrow by rebels operating with CIA help in 1954.

arbitrageur in international finance, a person who buys securities (such as ◊currency or commodities) in one country or market for immediate resale in another market, so as to take advantage of different prices in different markets. The practice became widespread during the 1970s and 1980s with the increasing ◊deregulation of financial markets.

arbitration submission of a dispute to a third, unbiased party for settlement. It may be personal litigation, trade union issues, or international disputes (as the case of the warship ◊*Alabama*). The first permanent international court was established at The Hague in 1900, and the League of Nations set up an additional Permanent Court of International Justice in 1921 to deal with frontier disputes and the like. The latter was replaced with the formation of the ◊United Nations. Another arbiter is the European Court of Justice of the ◊European Community, which rules on disputes arising out of the ◊Rome treaties.

Arbroath /ɑː'brəʊθ/ fishing town in Tayside, Scotland; population (1981) 24,100. In 1320 the Scottish Parliament asserted Scotland's independence here in a letter to the Pope. The town was celebrated by Walter ◊Scott as 'Fairport' in *The Antiquary*.

Arbuthnot /ɑː'bʌθnət/ John 1667–1735. Scottish physician, attendant on Queen Anne 1705–14. He was a friend of Pope, Gray, and Swift, and was the chief author of the satiric *Memoirs of Martinus Scriblerus*. He created the national character of John Bull, a prosperous farmer, in his *The History of John Bull* 1712, pamphlets advocating peace with France.

arbutus genus of evergreen shrubs, family Ericaceae, especially the strawberry tree *Arbutus unedo*, grown for its ornamental strawberry-like fruit.

arc in geometry, a section of a curve. A circle has two kinds of arcs. An arc that is less than a semicircle is called a *minor arc*; an arc that is greater than a semicircle is a *major arc*.

Arcadia /ɑː'keɪdɪə/ central plateau of S Greece; later writers, such as Sir Philip ◊Sidney idealized the life of shepherds here in antiquity.

Arc de Triomphe /'ɑːk də 'triːɒmf/ triumphal arch in the Place de l'Etoile, Paris, France, begun by Napoleon in 1806 and completed in 1836. It was intended to commemorate the French victories of 1805–06. Beneath it rests France's 'Unknown Soldier'.

Arc de Triomphe, Prix de l' /'ɑːk də 'triːɒmf/ French horse race, the most important 'open-age' race in Europe outside Britain, run at Longchamp.

arch a curved structure consisting of several wedge-shaped stones or other hard blocks which are supported by their mutual pressure. The term is also applied to any curved structure which is an arch in form only.

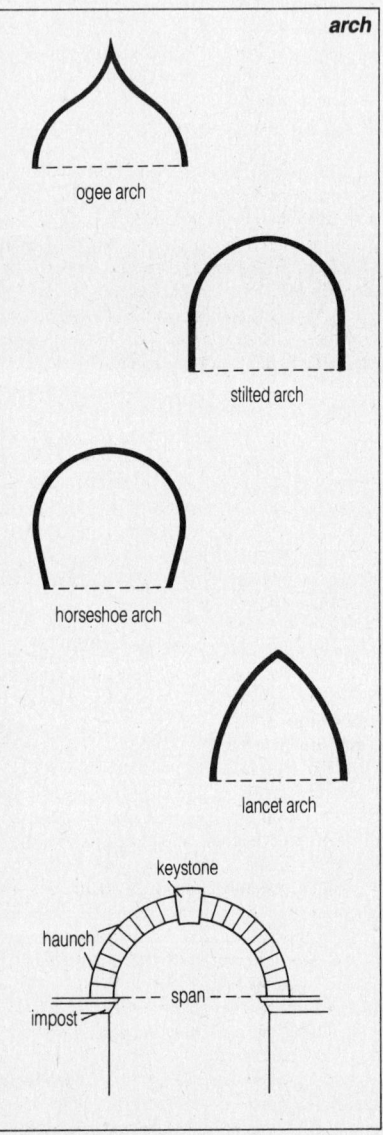

arch

ogee arch

stilted arch

horseshoe arch

lancet arch

keystone

haunch

impost

span

Arch /ɑːtʃ/ Joseph 1826–1919. British Radical politician and trade unionist. Born at Barford, Warwickshire, the son of an agricultural labourer, he worked in the fields from boyhood. Entirely self-taught, he became a Methodist preacher, founded the National Agricultural Union (the first of its kind) in 1872, and was Liberal-Labour MP for north west Norfolk.

Archaean an early eon of geological time, usually regarded as the earliest part of the ◊Precambrian era, from the formation of the Earth up to about 2,500 million years ago. Traces

Arch Joseph Arch started work at nine, and travelled all over England for 40 years as an agricultural labourer. Appalled at the miserable conditions, he grew to hate the rural elite; his 'call' came in 1872 and he started the National Agriculural Labourers' Union. In later life he became one of the first working class members of Parliament.

of life have recently been found in Archaean rocks. See also ◊Proterozoic.

archaebacteria a name given to three groups of bacteria whose DNA differs significantly from that of other bacteria (called the 'eubacteria'). All are strict anaerobes, that is, they are killed by oxygen. This is a primitive condition, and shows that the archaebacteria are related to the earliest life forms, which appeared about 4,000 million years ago, when there was little oxygen in the Earth's atmosphere. The ◊methanogens represent one group of archaebacteria.

archaeology the study of prehistory and ancient periods of history, based on the examination of their physical remains.

Archaeopteryx fossil from the limestone of Bavaria about 160 million years old, and popularly known as 'the first bird'. *Archaeopteryx* was about the size of a crow and had feathers and wings, but in many respects its skeleton is reptilian (long bony tail, teeth) and very like some small dinosaurs of the time.

Archangel /'ɑːkeɪndʒəl/ port in the northern USSR (Russian Archangelsk), blocked by ice during half the year. It was made an open port by Boris Godunov and was of prime importance wntil Peter the Great built St Petersburg. It was used 1918–20 by the Allied interventionist armies in collaboration with the ◊White Army in their effort to overthrow the newly established Soviet State. In World War II it was the receiving station for Anglo-American supplies. An open city in a closed area, it can be visited by foreigners only by air, and is a centre for ◊IBM computers. It is the chief timber-exporting port of the USSR.

ARCHAEOLOGY

14–16th cent.	Renaissance interest in classical art, for example, Cellini.
1748	Pompeii rediscovered, and aroused the interest of connoisseurs.
1790	John Frere identified Old Stone Age tools and large extinct animals.
1822	Champollion deciphered Egyptian hieroglyphics.
1832	Charles and John Deane pioneered the recording of underwater finds, such as *Mary Rose*.
1836	C J Thomsen devised the Stone, Bronze, and Iron Age classification.
1840s	Layard excavated the Assyrian capital, Nineveh.
1868	Great Zimbabwe ruins first seen by Europeans.
1871	Schliemann began work at Troy.
1879	Stone Age paintings were first discovered at Altamira.
1880s	Pitt-Rivers developed the technique of stratification (identification of successive layers of soil with different archaeological periods).
1891	Petrie began excavating Tell el Amarna (Akhetaton).
1899–1935	A J Evans excavated Minoan Knossos in Crete.
1911	Hiram Bingham discovered the Inca city of Machu Picchu.
1911–12	Piltdown skull 'discovered'; proved a fake in 1949.
1914–18	Osbert Crawford developed the technique of aerial survey of sites.
1922	Tutankhamen's tomb opened by Howard Carter.
1935	A E Douglas developed dendrochronology (dating events in the distant past by counting tree rings).
1939	Anglo-Saxon ship-burial treasure found at Sutton Hoo.
1947	First of the Dead Sea Scrolls discovered.
1948	Proconsul apeman discovered by Mary Leakey in Kenya.
1953	Ventris deciphered Minoan 'Linear B'.
1960s	Radiocarbon dating and thermoluminescence developed.
1961	Swedish warship *Wasa* raised at Stockholm.
1963	W B Emery pioneered 'rescue archaeology' at Abu Simbel.
1974	Tomb of Shi Huangdi discovered in China.
1978	Tomb of Philip of Macedon (Alexander's father) discovered.
1979	Aztec capital Tenochtitlán excavated beneath Mexico city.
1982	Henry VIII's warship *Mary Rose* raised.
1985	Major work on wreck of the Dutch East Indiaman *Amsterdam* near Hastings begun, and tomb of Maya, Tutankhamen's treasurer, discovered at Saqqara.

Population (1985) 408,000. Plesetsk, to the south, is a launch site for manned space flight.

archbishop in the Christian Church, a bishop of superior rank, who has authority over other bishops in his jurisdiction and often over an ecclesiastical province. In the Church of England there are two archbishops, both of them metropolitans – the Archbishop of Canterbury ('Primate of All England') and the Archbishop of York ('Primate of England').

archdeacon originally an ordained dignitary of the Christian Church charged with the supervision of the deacons attached to a cathedral. Today in the Roman Catholic Church the office is purely titular; in the Church of England an archdeacon still has many business duties, such as the periodic inspection of the churches.

archegonium the female sex organ found in bryophytes (mosses and liverworts),

pteridophytes (ferns and horsetails), and some gymnosperms. It is a multicellular, flask-shaped structure consisting of two parts, the swollen base or venter containing the egg cell, and the long, narrow neck. When the egg cell is mature the cells of the neck dissolve, allowing the passage of the male gametes, or ◊antherozoids.

Archer /'ɑːtʃə/ Frederick James 1857–1886. British jockey. He had 2,748 wins in 8,084 races including five Derbys 1877, 1880, 1881, 1885, 1886, four Oaks, six St Legers, five Two Thousand Guineas and two One Thousand Guineas. His record of 246 winners in one season was not beaten till 1933 (see Gordon ◊Richards). He shot himself while ill with typhoid fever in 1886.

Archer /'ɑːtʃə/ Jeffrey 1940– . British author and politician. A Conservative member of parliament 1969–74, he lost a fortune in a disastrous investment, but recouped it as a best-selling novelist. Works include *Not a Penny More, Not a Penny Less* 1975 and *First Among Equals* 1984. In 1985 he became deputy chairman of the Conservative party but in Nov 1986 resigned after a scandal involving a payoff to a prostitute.

archerfish surface-living fish, genus *Toxotes*, of brackish mangrove swamps of SE Asia and Australia, growing to about 25 cm/10 in and able to shoot down insects up to 1.5 m/5 ft above the water by spitting a water-jet from the mouth.

archery the use of the bow and arrow in war and hunting. Flint arrowheads have been found in very ancient archaeological deposits, and bowmen are depicted in the sculptures of Assyria and Egypt and indeed all the nations of antiquity. Until the introduction of gunpowder in the 14th century, bands of archers were to be found in every European army. The English archers distinguished themselves in the French wars of the later Middle Ages; and to this day the Queen's bodyguard in Scotland is known as the Royal Company of Archers. The Honourable Artillery Company was originally a body of archers. Up to the time of Charles II the practice of archery was fostered and encouraged by English rulers. Henry VIII in particular loved the sport, and it was in his reign that Roger Ascham wrote his *Toxophilus*. By the mid-17th century archery was no longer important in warfare and interest waned until the 1780s, although in the north of England shooting for the Scorton Arrow has been carried on, with few breaks, from 1673. Organizations include the world governing body Fédération Internationale de Tir à l'Arc 1931; the British Grand National Archery Society 1861; and in the USA the National Archery Association 1879 and, for actual hunting with the bow, the National Field Archery Association 1940. In competitions, results are based on double FITA rounds, that is 72 arrows at each of four targets at 90, 70, 50, and 30 metres (70, 60, 50, and 30 for women). The best possible score is 2,880.

World Championships first held 1931 and formerly an annual event, now biennial

men – individual
1977 Richard McKinney *(United States)*
1979 Darrell Pace *(United States)*
1981 Kyosti Laasonen *(Finland)*
1983 Richard McKinney *(United States)*
1985 Richard McKinney *(United States)*
1987 Vladimir Asheyer *(USSR)*

men – team
1977 United States
1979 United States
1981 United States
1983 United States
1985 South Korea
1987 South Korea

women – individual
1977 Luann Ryon *(United States)*
1979 Jin-Ho Kim *(South Korea)*
1981 Natalia Butuzova *(USSR)*
1983 Jin-Ho Kim *(South Korea)*
1985 Irina Soldatova *(USSR)*
1987 Ma Xiagjuan *(China)* women – team
1977 United States
1979 South Korea

1981 USSR
1983 South Korea
1985 USSR
1987 China

Archimedes /ˌɑːkɪˈmiːdiːz/ c. 287–212 BC. Greek mathematician, who made important discoveries in geometry, hydrostatics, and mechanics. Born at Syracuse in Sicily. He proved that the goldsmith of the king of Syracuse had adulterated a gold crown with silver by a fluid-displacement method, formulated when he stepped into the public bath and saw it overflow (see ◊Archimedes' principle). He was so delighted that he rushed home naked, crying 'Eureka! Eureka!' ('I've got it! I've got it!'). He is also credited with the invention of the ◊Archimedes screw, a cylindrical device for raising water, still in use in the Nile delta. He designed engines of war for the defence of Syracuse and was killed by a Roman soldier while working on a problem.

Archimedes' principle or law, states that an object totally or partly submerged in a fluid displaces a volume of fluid which weighs the same as the apparent loss in weight of the object (which equals the upthrust on it). The principle was named after ◊Archimedes.

Archimedes screw one of the earliest kinds of pump, thought to have been invented by ◊Archimedes. It consists of a spiral screw revolving inside a close-fitting cylinder. It is used, for example, to raise water for irrigation.

archimedes screw

archipelago a group of islands, or an area of sea containing a group of islands. The islands of an archipelago are often volcanic in origin, formed either when a hot spot within the Earth's mantle produces a chain of volcanoes on the surface, such as the Hawaiian Archipelago, or at a destructive plate margin (see ◊plate tectonics) where the subduction of one plate beneath another produces an arc-shaped island group, such as the Aleutian Archipelago. Alternatively an archipelago may be caused by a rise in sea level flooding a hilly landscape, leaving hills as islands, as in Novaya Zemlya in the Arctic Ocean, the northern extension of the Ural Mountains.

Archipenko /ˌɑːkɪˈpeŋkəu/ Alexander 1887–1964. Russo-American sculptor, pioneer of ◊Cubism. Born in Kiev, he moved to Paris in

1908, produced his first Cubist structure in 1911 under the influence of ◊Léger, and moved to New York in 1923. In his later years he experimented with carved plastic.

architecture the art of building structures. The term covers the design of any structure for living or working in: houses, churches, temples, palaces, castles; and, as such, the style of building of any particular country at any period of history. Some theorists include under the term architecture only structures designed by a particular architect; others include so-called vernacular architecture: traditional buildings such as the cottages and farms of particular areas that have evolved slowly through the centuries but can claim no particular designer.

Ancient architecture the earliest buildings were shelter structures, more or less permanent, which began to appear during the Bronze Age: circular bases constructed of dry-stone walling, with thatched roofs. All over Europe, the same societies began to erect megaliths for religious reasons we can only guess at; *Stonehenge* (dating from about 2000 BC) is a fairly late example. But it was in the Middle East, between 3000 and 1200 BC, that the first civilization arose, the Babylonian, and with it the first examples of what we should call architecture. Ur was a walled city dominated by a *ziggurat*, a huge structure topped by a temple. The civilization of ancient Egypt provided the *pyramids*, massive monuments of exact symmetry with decorative sculptures and wall painting and the first use of the decorated column and lintel to form colonnades. Examples include Karnak, Akhenaton, Abu Simbel, tombs of the Valley of the Kings, temple of Isis at Philae.

Classical with the Greeks, between about the 16th and the 2nd centuries BC, architecture as an art form really came into being. Their codification and use of the Classical orders – Doric, Ionic and Corinthian – provided a legacy which, refined and modified by the Romans, has influenced all subsequent Western architecture. The great example of Greek architecture is the *Parthenon*. The Romans were the first to use bricks and cement to produce the vault, arch and dome; they added the Tuscan and Composite orders to the Greek system. The emphasis in Roman architecture was on impressive public buildings: (*Colosseum*), basilicas (*Pantheon*), triumphal arches and monuments (*Trajan's Column*) and aqueducts (*Nîmes*).

Byzantine in Byzantium a wholly Christian architecture was developing, from the 4th century onwards, with churches based on the Greek cross plan (*Hagia Sophia*, Istanbul; *St Mark's*, Venice); they used formalized, symbolic painted and mosaic decoration.

Romanesque the architecture of the Christianity of the West developed first as *Romanesque*, 8th to 12th century, marked by rounded arches, solid volumes and emphasis on perpendicular elements. In England, this was the period of Norman architecture (*Durham Cathedral*). Experiments in vaulting led towards the Gothic.

Gothic architecture developed in France in the 12th century and lasted until the 16th. It is marked out by the use of the rib vault, pointed arch and flying buttress, particularly in religious buildings; there is an emphasis on the vertical, with galleries and arcades replacing internal walls. It is divided into *Early Gothic* (*Sens Cathedral*), *High Gothic*(*Chartres Cathedral*) and *Late Gothic* or *Flamboyant*. In England the corresponding divisions are *Early English* (*Salisbury Cathedral*), *Decorated* (*Wells Cathedral*) and *Perpendicular* (*Kings College Chapel*, Cambridge).

Islamic in Spain, from the 7th century onwards, the Moorish occupation was also having a profound influence on Christian architecture, introducing the dome and the pointed arch (later incorporated into Gothic). Examples of influential *Islamic* buildings are the *Great Mosque*, Cordoba, and the *Alhambra*, Granada.

Renaissance the 15th and 16th centuries saw the rebirth of Classical architecture in the *Neo-Classical movement*, largely through the work of ◊Vitruvius. Major Italian architects were ◊Alberti, ◊Brunelleschi, ◊Bramante, ◊Michelangelo and ◊Palladio; in England *Palladianism* was represented by Inigo Jones. A 16th-century offshoot was *Mannerism*, in which motifs were used in deliberate opposition to their original significance, that is, for their manner rather than their meaning.

Baroque architecture of the 17th and 18th centuries was exuberantly extravagant, and seen at its best in large-scale public buildings in the work of ◊Bernini, ◊Borromini, ◊Vanbrugh, ◊Hawksmoor, and ◊Wren. Its last stage is the *Rococo*, characterized by still greater extravagance, a new lightness in style, and the use of naturalistic motifs such as shells, flowers and trees.

Neo-Classical the 18th and 19th centuries saw a return to classical principles, for example in the large-scale rebuilding of London and Paris by ◊Adam, ◊Nash and ◊Haussmann.

Neo-Gothic the later 19th century saw a renewed enthusiasm for the Gothic style in the *Gothic revival*, particularly evident in churches and public buildings (*Houses of Parliament*, C ◊Barry).

Art Nouveau was a new movement which surfaced at the end of the 19th century, characterized by sinuous, flowing shapes, informal room plans and attention not only to architectural design but to every last detail of the interior. The style is best seen in England in the work of Charles Rennie ◊Mackintosh (*Glasgow Art School*) and in Spain by that of Antonio ◊Gaudí.

Modernism an increasing emphasis on rationalism and reduction of ornament led to Modernism, also known as *Functionalism* or *International Style*, which sought to exclude everything that did not have a purpose, and used the latest technological advances in glass, steel and concrete to full advantage. Major architects include Frank Lloyd ◊Wright, ◊Mies van der Rohe, ◊Le Corbusier, and Alvar ◊Aalto.

town planning also emerged as a discipline in its own right and whole new cities were planned, Le Corbusier's Chandigarh in India and Brasilia in Brazil being particularly striking examples.

neo-vernacular by the 1970s a reversion from the modern movement's box-like structure and synthetic materials began to be felt in a renewed enthusiasm for *vernacular* architecture (traditional local styles), to be seen in the work of, for instance, the British firm Darbourne and Darke.

Post-Modernism in the 1980s a *post-modernist* movement has emerged, split into two camps: *high tech*, represented in Britain by architects such as Norman ◊Foster, Richard ◊Rogers and James ◊Stirling (*Hong Kong and Shanghai Bank, Lloyd's, Staatsgalerie Stuttgart* respectively), and architects using elements from the architecture of previous times, whether consciously obeying the tenets of the Classical orders – *Neo-Classicism* yet again – like Quinlan ◊Terry, or using such elements at whim, like Michael Graves.

archives a collection of historically valuable records, ranging from papers and documents to films, videotapes and sound recordings.

United Kingdom: the *National Register of Archives* (founded 1945) is in London; the *Public Record Office* (London and Kew) has documents of law and government departments from the Norman Conquest, including ◊Domesday Book and ◊Magna Carta; the *National Portrait Gallery* has photographs, paintings and sculptures; the *British Broadcasting Corporation Archives* have sound recordings, films and videotapes, which form one of the world's largest collections; there is also a British National Film Archive.

United States: *National Archives Hall*, Washington, contains the Declaration of Independence, the United States US Constitution, Bill of Rights; the *National Archives and Records Service* is responsible for preserving federal records and administration of the presidential libraries, usually established in the incumbent's birthplace.

archon (Greek 'ruler') in Ancient Greece, the title of the chief magistrate in many cities. In Athens, there were originally three: the King Archon, the Eponymous Archon (who gave his name to the year, hence the modern use of the word), and the polemarch. Their numbers were later increased to nine, with the extra six keeping a record of judgements.

arc lamp an electric light that uses the illumination of an electric arc. Humphry ◊Davy developed an arc lamp in 1808, but it did not become practical until much later. Its major use in recent years has been for the lamp in cinema projectors. The lamp consists essentially of two carbon electrodes, between which a very high voltage is maintained. Electric current arcs (jumps) between the two, creating a brilliant light. The lamp incorporates a mechanism for automatically advancing the electrodes as they gradually burn away. Modern lamps have the electrodes enclosed in an inert gas such as ◊xenon.

Units for measuring small angles, used in geometry, surveying and map-making, and astronomy. An arc minute is one-sixtieth of a ◊degree. An arc second is one-sixtieth of an arc minute. Distances in the sky, as between two close stars or the apparent width of a planet's disc, are expressed in minutes and seconds of arc.

Arctic, the /'ɑktɪk/ region north of the ◊Arctic Circle. There is no Arctic continent, merely pack ice (which breaks into ice floes in summer) surrounding the Pole and floating on the ◊Arctic Ocean. Pack ice is carried by the south-flowing current into the Atlantic Ocean as ◊icebergs. In winter the Sun disappears below the horizon for a time (and in summer, which only lasts up to two months, remains above it), but the cold is less severe than in parts of E Siberia or the Antarctic. Land areas in the Arctic have mainly stunted tundra vegetation, with an outburst of summer flowers. Animals include reindeer, caribou, musk ox, fox, hare, lemming, and wolf, polar bear, seal, and walrus. There are few birds, except in summer, when insects, especially mosquitoes, are plentiful. The aboriginal people are the ◊Inuit of the American/Canadian Arctic and Greenland. The most valuable resource is oil.

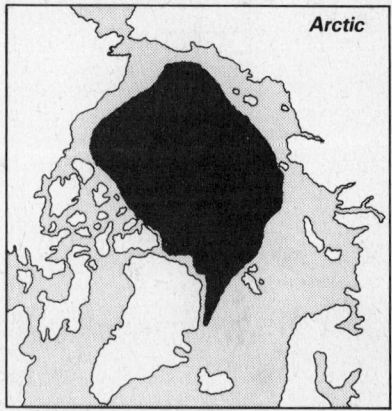

Arctic

Arctic Circle an arbitrary line drawn round the North Pole at 66°,33' N.

Arctic Ocean ocean surrounding the North Pole; area 14,090,000 sq km/5,440,000 sq mi. Because of the Siberian rivers flowing into it, it has comparatively low salinity and freezes readily. It is divided into various seas:

Beaufort Sea off Canada/Alaska coast, named after Sir Francis ◊Beaufort; oil drilling is allowed only in winter because the sea is the breeding and migration route of the bowhead whales, staple diet of the local Inuit.

Greenland Sea between Greenland and Svalbard, and *Norwegian Sea* between Greenland and Norway. West to east along the north coast of the USSR:

Barents Sea named after Willem ◊Barents, which has oil and gas reserves and is strategically important as the meeting point of the North Atlantic Treaty Organization (NATO) and Warsaw Pact forces.

Kara Sea renowned for bad weather, and known as the 'great ice cellar'.

Laptev Sea between Taimyr Peninsula and New Siberian Island.

East Siberian Sea and *Chukchi Sea* between the USSR and the USA; the semi-nomadic Chukchi people of NE Siberia finally accepted Soviet rule only in the 1930s. See also ◊White Sea.

Arcturus brightest ◊star in the constellation

architecture

Gothic arch

mouldings

corbel   spandrel

spring of arch

capital

column

base

Tuscan

the orders of
classical architecture

Doric

Corinthian

classical temple

cornice

tympanum

cornice

frieze

architrave   triglyph   metope

capital

abacus

shaft

entablature pediment

column

Ionic

entablature

capital

shaft

base

Composite

ARCTIC EXPLORATION

35000BC   Ancestors of the Inuit and American Indians began migration from Siberia to N America by the 'lost' landbridge of Beringia.

320BC   Pytheas, Greek sailor contemporary with Alexander the Great, possibly reached Iceland.

9–10th cent.   Vikings colonized Iceland and Greenland, which then had a much warmer climate.

c. 1000   Leif Ericsson reached Baffin Island (NE of modern Canada) and Labrador.

1497   John Cabot first sought the NW Passage as a trade route round N America for Henry VII of England.

1553   Richard Chancellor tried to find the NE Passage round Siberia and first established direct English trade with Russia.

1576   Martin Frobisher reached Frobisher Bay, but found only 'fools' gold' (iron pyrites) for Elizabeth I of England.

1594–97   Willem Barents made three expeditions in search of the NE Passage.

1607   Henry Hudson failed to cross the Arctic Ocean, but his reports of whales started the northern whaling industry.

1670   Hudson's Bay Company started the fur trade in Canada.

1728   Vitus Bering passed Bering Strait.

1773   Nelson, as a midshipman, accompanied the naval expedition of Constantine Phipps.

1829–33   John Ross discovered the N Magnetic Pole.

1845   Mysterious disappearance of Sir John Franklin's expedition to the NW Passage stimulated further exploration.

1878–79   Nils Nordensköld the first European to discover the NE Passage.

1893–96   Fridtjof Nansen's ship *Fram* drifted across the Arctic, locked in the ice, proving that no Arctic continent existed.

1903–06   Roald Amundsen sailed through the NW Passage.

1909   Robert Peary, Matt Henson, and four Inuits, reached the N Pole on 2 Apr.

1926   Richard Byrd and Floyd Bennett flew to the Pole on 9 May.

1926   Umberto Nobile and Amundsen crossed the Pole (Spitzbergen–Alaska) in the airship *Norge* on 12 May.

1954   First regular commercial flights over the short-cut polar route by Scandinavian Airlines.

1958   The American submarine *Nautilus* crossed the Pole beneath the ice.

1960   From this date a Soviet nuclear-powered icebreaker has kept open a 4,000 km/2,500 mi Asia-Europe passage along the north coast of Siberia 150 days a year.

1969   First surface crossing, by dog sled, of the Arctic Ocean (Alaska–Spitzbergen) by Wally Herbert, British Transarctic Expedition, Feb–May.

1977   The Soviet ice-breaker *Arktika* made the first surface voyage to the Pole.

1982   First circumnavigation of Earth (2 Sept 1979–29 Aug 1982) via the Poles by Sir Ranulph Fiennes and Charles Burton.

◊Bootes, and the fourth-brightest star in the sky. It is a red giant, 36 light years away.

Ardebil /ˌɑːdəˈbiːl/ Iranian town, near the Russian frontier. An important road centre, it also has an airport. Ardebil exports dried fruits, carpets, and rugs. Population (1976) 148,000.

Ardèche /ɑːˈdeʃ/ river in SE France, a tributary of the Rhône. Near Vallon it flows under the Pont d'Arc, a natural bridge. It gives its name to a *département*.

Arden /ˈɑːdn/ John 1930– . British playwright. His plays *Serjeant Musgrave's Dance* 1959 (an attack on war and military values) and *The Workhouse Donkey* 1963 (on corruption in local government) show the influence of ◊Brecht. Subsequent works, often written in collaboration with his wife, Margaretta D'Arcy, show increasing concern with the political situation in Northern Ireland and a dissatisfaction with the professional and subsidized theatre world.

Arden, Forest of /ˈɑːdn/ former forest region of N Warwickshire, the setting for Shakespeare's *As You Like It*.

Ardennes /ɑːˈden/ wooded plateau in NE France, SE Belgium and N Luxembourg, cut through by the River Meuse; there was heavy fighting here in both world wars. See ◊Champagne-Ardenne.

Ardennes offensive Hitler's concept, code 'Watch on the Rhine', of a breakthrough by ◊Rundstedt aimed at the American line here 16 Dec 1944–31 Jan 1945; also known as the *Battle of the Bulge*. There were 77,000 American casualties; 130,000 German, including Hitler's last powerful reserve, his Panzer elite.

area in geometry, the size of a surface, measured in square units (such as cm^2 or km^2). The area A of a square is the length of side l squared: $A = l \times l = l^2$. For a rectangle, the area is given by $A = l \times b$ where b is the breadth (the shorter side). The area of a triangle is half the length of the base l times the perpendicular height h (altitude): $A = 1/2l \times h$; of a ◊parallelogram (a quadrilateral with opposite sides equal and parallel) is the length times the height (the perpendicular distance between the longer pair of sides): $A = l \times h$; of a circle is π times the square of the radius, r: $A = \pi r^2$. The areas of more complex shapes can often be found by dividing them into simpler shapes whose areas can be calculated or estimated.

areca a type of palm; see ◊betel-nut.

Arecibo /ˌærɛɪˈsiːbəʊ/ site in Puerto Rico of the world's largest single ◊radio-telescope dish, 305 m/1,000 ft in diameter. Suspended between towers in a hollow in the hills, it uses the rotation of the Earth to scan the sky. It is operated by the Cornell University, USA.

Arequipa /ˌærɛɪˈkiːpə/ city of Peru at the base of the volcano El Misti. Founded by ◊Pizarro in 1540, it is the cultural focus of South Peru. Population (1981) 447,400.

Ares /ˈeəriːz/ in Greek mythology, the god of war (Roman ◊Mars). The son of Zeus and Hera, he was worshipped chiefly in Thrace.

arête a sharp narrow ridge separating two glaciated valleys (a French term; in the USA often called a combe-ridge; in German a grat).

See ◊glacier. Arêtes are common in glaciated mountain regions such as the Alps, the Himalayas, and the Rockies. The typical U-shaped cross-sections of glacier valleys give arêtes very steep sides.

Arethusa /ˌærɪˈθjuːzə/ in Greek mythology, a nymph of the fountain and spring of Arethusa in the island of Ortygia near Syracuse.

Aretino /ˌærəˈtiːnəʊ/ Pietro 1492–1556. Italian writer, born at Arezzo. He earned his living, both in Rome and Venice, by publishing satirical pamphlets while under the protection of a highly placed family. His *Letters* 1537–57 are a unique record of the cultural and political events of his time, and illustrate his vivacious, exuberant character. He also wrote poems and comedies.

Aretino Italian poet Pietro Aretino, painted by his great friend, Titian. Aretino began as a protégé of Pope Leo X, but left Rome after the publication of his lewd verses. He settled in Venice, and quickly became known as the 'Scourge of Princes' with his vicious satires on powerful contemporaries; he was also well paid for not taking up his pen.

Arezzo /əˈretsəʊ/ town in Italy; population (1981) 92,105. ◊Petrarch was born here.

argali wild sheep *Ovis ammon* of Central Asia. The male may stand 1.2 m/4 ft at the shoulder, and has massive spiral horns.

Argenteuil /ˌɑːʒɒnˈtɜːi/ NW suburb of Paris, France, on the Seine. Population (1982) 96,045.

Argentina /ˌɑːdʒənˈtiːnə/ country in South America, bounded by Chile to the south and west, Bolivia to the northwest, and Paraguay, Brazil, Uruguay, and the Atlantic Ocean to the east.
government the return to civilian rule in 1983 brought a return to the 1853 constitution, with some changes in the electoral system. The constitution created a federal system with a president elected by popular vote through an electoral college, serving a six-year term. The president is head of both state and government, and chooses the cabinet.
Argentina is a federal union of 22 provinces, one national territory and the Federal District. The

two-chamber Congress consists of a 46-member senate chosen by provincial legislatures for a nine-year term, and a directly elected chamber of deputies serving a four-year term. Each province has its own elected governor and legislature, dealing with matters not assigned to the federal government. The two most significant parties are the Radical Union Party (UCR), and the Justice Party.
history originally inhabited by various South American Indian peoples, Argentina was first visited by Europeans in the early 16th century. Buenos Aires was founded first in 1536 and again in 1580 after being abandoned because of Indian attacks. Made a Spanish viceroyalty in 1776, Argentina achieved full independence in 1816, and developed as a democracy with active political parties. Since 1930 it has been subject to alternate civilian and military rule. The UCR held power from 1916 until the first military coup in 1930.
Civilian government returned in 1932 and a second military coup in 1943 paved the way for the rise of Lieutenant-General Juan Domingo Perón. Strengthened by the popularity of his wife, Eva Duarte Perón, the legendary 'Evita', Perón created the Peronista party, based on extreme nationalism and social improvement. Evita Perón died in 1952 and in 1955 her husband was overthrown and civilian rule restored. Perón continued to direct the Peronista movement from exile in Spain.
A coup in 1966 restored military rule and in 1973 the success of the Peronist party, Frente Justicialista de Liberación, brought Dr Héctor Campora to the presidency. After three months he resigned to make way for Perón, with his third wife, Maria Estela Martinez de Perón, 'Isabelita', as vice-president. Perón died in 1974 and was succeeded by his widow. Two years later, because of concern about the economy, a military coup ousted her and installed a three-man junta, led by Lieutenant-General Jorge Videla. The constitution was amended, political and trade union activity banned and several hundred people arrested.
The years 1976–83 witnessed a ferocious campaign by the junta against left-wing elements, the 'dirty war', during which it is believed that between 6,000 and 15,000 people 'disappeared'. Political activity was banned 1976–80. Although confirmed in office until 1981, in 1978 Videla retired, to be succeeded by General Roberto Viola, who promised a return to democracy. In 1981 Viola died and was replaced by General Leopoldo Galtieri.
In 1982 Galtieri, seeking popular support and wishing to distract attention from the deteriorating economy, ordered the invasion of the Islas Malvinas, the ◊Falkland Islands, over which Britain's claim to sovereignty had long been disputed. After a short war, during which 750 Argentinians were killed, the islands were reoccupied by Britain. US support for Britain pushed Argentina closer to Cuba, Nicaragua and the ◊non-aligned states.
With the failure of the Falklands invasion, Galtieri was replaced in a bloodless coup by General Reynaldo Bignone. A military inquiry

reported in 1983 that Galtieri's junta was to blame for the defeat. Several officers were tried and some, including Galtieri, given prison sentences. It was announced that the 1853 constitution would be revived and an amnesty was granted to all convicted of political crimes over the past ten years. The ban on political and trade union activity was lifted and general elections were held in Oct 1983. The main parties were the UCR, led by Dr Raul Alfonsín, and the Peronist Justice Party, led by Dr Italo Luder. Having won the election, Alfonsín announced radical reforms in the armed forces, leading to the retirement of more than half the senior officers, and the trial of the first three military juntas which had ruled Argentina since 1976. He set up the National Commission on the Disappearance of Persons (CONADEP) to investigate the 'dirty war' between 1976 and 1983. A report by CONADEP in 1984 listed over 8,000 people who had disappeared and 1,300 army officers who had been involved in the campaign of repression.
Alfonsín's government was soon faced with huge economic problems, resulting in recourse to help from the ◊IMF and an austerity programme, described by the president as an 'economy of war'. In 1986 he survived an assassination attempt and undertook a six-nation tour to re-establish Argentina's external relations. In 1987 Congress approved the establishment of a new capital,

argon a chemically inert gaseous element, symbol Ar, atomic weight. 39.944, atomic number 18. It was discvered in air by Rayleigh and Ramsay after all oxygen and nitrogen had been removed chemically. It is used in electric discharge lamps (see discharge tube) and in argon ◊lasers.

argonaut type of pelagic octopus, genus *Argonauta*, in which the 20 cm/8 in female secretes a papery shell from the web of the first pair of arms, hence the alternative name 'paper nautilus'. The male is 1 cm/0.4 in shell-less dwarf. 'Argonaut' is sometimes used to refer to the ◊nautilus.

Argonauts in Greek legend, the band of heroes who accompanied ◊Jason when he set out in the ship *Argo* to fetch the Golden Fleece.

Argonne /ɑːˈgɒn/ wooded plateau in north east France, separating Lorraine and Champagne. It was the scene of much fighting in both world wars.

Argos /ˈɑːgɒs/ city in ancient Greece, at the head of the Gulf of Nauplia. In the Homeric age the name Argives was sometimes used instead of Greeks. It was once a cult centre of the goddess ◊Hera.

argument in mathematics, independent variable of a ◊function; for example in the function $2y = 3x + 4$, x is the argument. Argument is also the name given to the angle between the position vector of a ◊complex number and the limb of the real axis.

argument from design a line of reasoning, argued most influentially by Bishop William Paley in 1794, that the Universe is so complex that it can only have been designed by a superhuman power; and that we can learn

Argentina
REPUBLIC OF (*República Argentina*)

AREA 2,780,000 sq km/1,073,000 sq mi
CAPITAL Buenos Aires
TOWNS Rosario, Córdoba, Tucumán,
Mendoza, Santa Fé; ports are La Plata and
Bahía Blanca
PHYSICAL mountains in the W, forest in the N
and E, pampas (treeless plains) in the central
area; rivers Colorado, Paraná, Uruguay, Rio
de la Plata estuary
TERRITORIES Tierra del Fuego; disputed claims
to S Atlantic islands; part of Antarctica
FEATURES Andes, with Aconcagua the highest
peak in the W hemisphere
HEAD OF STATE AND OF GOVERNMENT Raúl
Alfonsín from 1983
GOVERNMENT republic
EXPORTS beef, livestock, cereals, wool, tannin,
groundnuts, linseed oil, minerals (coal, copper,
molybdenum, gold, silver, lead, zinc, barium,
uranium), and the country has huge resources
of oil, natural gas, and hydroelectric power
CURRENCY austral (4.1 = £1 Sept 1987)
POPULATION (1985) 7,451,000 (mainly of
Spanish or Italian origin, only about 30,000
American Indians surviving); annual growth
rate 1.6%
LANGUAGE Spanish
RELIGION Roman Catholic (state-supported)
LITERACY 95% male/94% female (1980)
GDP $58 bn (1983); $2,331 per head of
population
CHRONOLOGY
1816 Achieved independence from Spain.
1946 Juan Perón elected president, supported
by his wife 'Evita'.
1952 'Evita' Perón died.
1955 Perón overthrown and civilian
administration restored.
1966 Coup brought back military rule.
1973 The Perónist party won the presidential
and congressional elections. Perón returned
from exile in Spain as president, with his third
wife, 'Isabelita', as vice-president.
1974 Perón died. Succeeded by 'Isabelita'.
1976 Coup resulted in rule by a military junta
led by Lt-Gen Jorge Videla. Congress
dissolved and hundreds of people, including
'Isabelita' Perón, detained.

Argentina

1976–78 Ferocious campaign against left-
wing elements. The start of the 'dirty war'.
1978 Videla retired. Succeeded by Gen
Roberto Viola, who promised a return to
democracy.
1981 Viola died suddenly. Replaced by Gen
Leopoldo Galtieri.
1982 With a deteriorating economy, Galtieri
sought popular support by ordering an
invasion of the British-held Falkland Islands.
After losing the short war, Galtieri was
removed and replaced by Gen Reynaldo
Bignone.
1983 Amnesty law passed and 1853
democratic constitution revived. General
elections won by Dr Raúl Alfonsín and his
party. Armed forces under scrutiny.
1984 Commission on the Disappearance of
Persons (CONADEP) reported on over 8,000
people who had disappeared during the 'dirty
war' of 1976–83.
1985 A deteriorating economy forced Alfonsín
to seek help from the IMF and introduce a
harsh austerity programme.
1986 Unsuccessful attempt on Alfonsín's life.

John, 2nd Duke 1678–1743, became a peer of
the United Kingdom for helping to promote the
Union of England and Scotland.
George Douglas, 8th Duke 1823–1900, was
secretary for India 1868–74, and opposed Irish
home rule. In his writings he attempted to
reconcile Christianity with the logic of scientific
discovery.
John Douglas Sutherland, 9th Duke 1845–1914,
married Princess Louise, daughter of Queen
Victoria, in 1871, and was governor general of
Canada, 1878–83.

Argyllshire /ɑːˈɡaɪlʃə/ former county on the
west coast of Scotland, including many of the
Western Isles, which was for the most part
merged in Strathclyde region in 1975, although
a small area to the north west including
Ballachulish, Ardgour and Kingairloch went to
the Highland region.

aria (Italian 'air') solo vocal piece in opera or
oratorio, often in three sections, the third
repeating the first, after a contrasting central
section.

Ariadne /ˌæriˈædni/ in Greek mythology, the
daughter of Minos, king of Crete. When Theseus
came from Athens as one of the victims offered
to the Minotaur, she fell in love with him and
gave him the ball of thread which enabled him to
find his way out of the labyrinth.

Ariane /ˌæriˈæn/ a rocket built by the
◊European Space Agency to launch satellites,
particularly ◊communications satellites, into
geostationary orbit (first flight 1979). Ariane is
a three-stage rocket using liquid fuels, but small
solid-fuel boosters can be attached to its first
stage to increase carrying power. Its launch site
is at Kouru in French Guiana and since 1984 it
has been operated commercially by Arianespace,
a private company financed by European banks
and aerospace industries. Future versions of
Ariane may carry astronauts.

Arianism a system of Christian theology
which denied the complete divinity of Christ. It
was founded c. 310 AD by ◊Arius, and condemned
as heretical at the Council of ◊Nicaea in 325 AD.
Some 17th-and 18th-century theologians held
Arian views akin to those of modern
◊Unitarianism (that God is a single being, and
that there is no such thing as the ◊Trinity). In
1979 the heresy again caused concern to the
Vatican in the writings of such theologians as
Edouard Schillebeeckx of Nijmegen University,
the Netherlands.

Arica /əˈriːkə/ port in Chile; population
(1982) 120,046. It is much used by land-locked
Bolivia, which is negotiating a land corridor at
this point.

arid zone infertile area with a small,
infrequent rainfall that rapidly evaporates
because of high temperatures. There are arid
zones in Morocco, Pakistan, Australia, USA,
and elsewhere. The scarcity of water is a problem
for the inhabitants, and constant research goes
into discovering, for example, cheaper methods
of distilling sea water, conserving existing
sources by avoiding evaporation (for example,
artificially recharging natural groundwater
reservoirs), and the eradication of salt in

something of that superhuman power (God) by
examining how the world is. The argument from
design became popular with Protestant
theologians in the 18th century as a means of
accommodating Newtonian science. It was
attacked by David ◊Hume, among other
Enlightenment thinkers.

Argus /ˈɑːɡəs/ in Greek mythology, a giant
with 100 eyes, sent by the jealous Hera to watch
over Io, the beloved of Zeus, who had been turned
into a cow. Hermes charmed Argus to sleep with
his flute and cut off his head, and Hera
transplanted his eyes to the tail of her favourite
bird, the peacock.

Argyll /ɑːˈɡaɪl/ **earls and dukes of** line of
Scottish peers who trace their descent to the
Campbells of Lochow. The earldom dates from
1457.
Archibald, 8th Earl 1607–61, led the
Covenanting party during the Civil Wars,
crowned Charles II in 1651, submitted to
Cromwell in 1652, and was beheaded after the
Restoration.
Archibald, 9th Earl 1629–85, was executed for
leading a rebellion in cooperation with
Monmouth's rising.
Archibald, 10th Earl 1651–1703, received a
dukedom in 1701.

Arica Set on a rainless coastline, Arica has a dramatic history. Several times devastated by earthquake, it was razed in 1880 when captured by Chile from Peru.

irrigation supplies from underground sources or where it forms a surface soil deposit in poorly drained areas.

Ariège /ˌæriˈeɪʒ/ river in southern France, a tributary of the Garonne. It gives its name to a *département*.

Aries constellation of the ◊zodiac, representing the legendary ram whose golden fleece was sought by Jason and the Argonauts. Its most distinctive feature is a curve of three stars of decreasing brightness. The spring ◊equinox once lay in Aries, but has now moved into ◊Pisces through the effect of the Earth's ◊precession (wobble). The Sun passes through Aries from late Apr to mid-May.

aril an accessory seed-cover other than a ◊fruit; it may be fleshy and sometimes brightly coloured, woody or hairy. In flowering plants (◊angiosperms) it is often derived from the stalk which originally attached the ovule to the ovary wall. Examples of arils include the bright red, fleshy layer surrounding the yew seed (yews are ◊gymnosperms, so they lack true fruits), and the network of hard filaments which partially cover the nutmeg seed; it is the latter which yields the spice known as mace. A horny outgrowth found towards one end of the seed of the castor oil plant (*Ricinus communis*) is called a caruncle. It is formed from the integuments (protective layers enclosing the ovule) and develops after fertilization.

Ariosto /ˌæriˈɒstəʊ/ Ludovico 1474–1533. Italian poet, born at Reggio. He wrote Latin poems and comedies on Classical lines, joined the household of Cardinal Ippolito d'Este in 1503, was frequently engaged in embassies and diplomacy, and published the *Orlando Furioso* at Ferrara in 1516. This is a romantic epic, dealing with the wars of Charlemagne against the Saracens, and the love of Orlando (Roland) for Angelica, a princess of Cathay. The perfection of its style and its unflagging narrative interest place Ariosto among the great Italian poets. In 1521 he became governor of a province in the Apennines, and after three years retired to Ferrara, where he died.

Aristarchus of Samos /ˌærɪˈstɑːkəs/ c. 310–264 BC. Greek astronomer. The first to argue

Ariosto Italian poet Ludovico Ariosto, engraved by Eneo Vico. While in the diplomatic service of the Duke of Ferrar, he wrote his poem *Orlando Furioso*, an epic treatment of the *Roland* story. The poem influenced Shakespeare, Byron, and Milton, and is considered to be the perfect poetic expression of the Italian Renaissance.

that the earth moves round the sun, he was rdiculed for his beliefs.

Aristides /ˌærɪˈstaɪdiːz/ c. 530–468 BC. Athenian statesman. He was one of the ten Athenian generals at the battle of ◊Marathon in 490 BC and was elected chief archon, or magistrate. Later he came into conflict with the democratic leader Themistocles, and was exiled c. 483 BC. He returned to fight against the Persians at Salamis in 480 BC, and next year commanded the Athenians at Plataea. He was sent into political exile in 482 BC because the citizens tired of hearing him praised as 'Aristides the Just', probably derived from his just assessment of the contribution to be paid by the Greek states who entered the Delian league against the Persians. He later fought at ◊Salamis and ◊Plataea.

Aristippus /ˌærɪˈstɪpəs/ c. 435–356 BC. Greek philosopher, founder of the ◊Cyrenaic or ◊Hedonist school. A pupil of Socrates, he developed the doctrine that pleasure is the only good in life. He lived at the court of ◊Dionysius of Syracuse, and then with his mistress Laïs, the courtesan, at Corinth.

Aristophanes /ˌærɪˈstɒfəniːz/ c. 448–380 BC. Greek comic dramatist. Of his 11 extant plays, the early comedies are remarkable for the violence of the satire with which he ridiculed the democratic war leaders. In 425 he produced the *Acharnians*, a plea for peace with Sparta. The *Knights* 424 shows the figure of the 'Demos' or 'democracy' beguiled by Cleon. The *Clouds* 423 pours ridicule on the new learning of Socrates. The *Wasps* 422 is a satire on the Athenian love of litigation. The *Peace* 421 was written when negotiations for peace with Sparta were far

advanced. In the *Birds* 414, written after the renewed outbreak of the Peloponnesian War, Aristophanes tells how two Athenians persuade the birds to build a kingdom in the air known as 'Cloud-cuckoo-land'. In the *Lysistrata* 411 the women, tired of the war, deny conjugal relations to their husbands until they have made peace with Sparta. The *Thesmophoriazusae* (Priestesses of Demeter) 411 satirizes Euripides and the women of Athens. The *Frogs* 405 tells how the god Dionysus was sent to the lower world to bring back Aeschylus to Athens. The *Ecclesiazusae* or *Women in Parliament* 393 describes what happened when the women seized the Athenian parliament. In *Plutus* or *Wealth* 388 the abolition of poverty results in a series of comic episodes. Besides the extant plays, Aristophanes is known to have written about 40 comedies, which are now lost.

Aristotle /ˈærɪstɒtl/ 384–322 BC. Greek philosopher. Born at Stagira in Thrace, he studied at Athens under ◊Plato, became tutor to ◊Alexander the Great, and in 335 opened a school in the Lyceum (grove sacred to Apollo) at Athens. He walked up and down as he talked, hence 'peripatetic school', and his works are a collection of his lecture notes. When Alexander died he was forced to flee to Chalcis, where he died. He is sometimes referred to as 'the Stagirite'.

Of Aristotle's works some 22 treatises survive, dealing with logic; metaphysics; physics; astronomy and meteorology; biology; psychology; ethics; politics; and literary criticism.

Aristotle maintained that sense-experience is our only source of knowledge, and that by reasoning we can discover the essences of things, that is, their distinguishing qualities. The essence of a thing he regarded as real, but not as capable of existing apart from it. He conceived of all being as potentiality and actuality, in the physical order represented by matter and form; God alone is all actuality. Change consists in bringing the potentiality of a substance into actuality. All change is caused, the Supreme Cause being God, the Unmoved Mover.

Aristotle held that all matter consisted of a single 'prime matter', which was always determined by some form. The simplest kinds of matter were the four elements, earth, water, air and fire, which in varying proportions constituted all the things we know. Aristotle saw nature as always striving to perfect itself, and first classified organisms into species and genera to show how they subserve this purpose.

The principle of life he termed a soul, which he regarded as the form of the living creature, not as a substance separable from it. The intellect, he believed, can discover in sense-impressions the universal, and since the soul thus transcends matter, it must be immortal. In his works on ethics and politics Aristotle suggested that man's happiness consists in living in conformity with nature, according to reason and moderation. He derived his political theory from the recognition that mutual aid is natural to humankind, and refused to set up any one constitution as univerally ideal. Art embodies nature, but in a more perfect fashion, its end being the purifying and ennobling of the affections. The essence of beauty is order and symmetry.

In the Middle Ages Aristotle's philosophy first became the foundation of Islamic philosophy, and was then incorporated into Christian theology; medieval scholars tended to accept his vast output without question. See ◊logic, ◊scholasticism.

arithmetic branch of mathematics that concerns all questions involving numbers, as in counting, measuring, or weighing.

Simple arithmetic existed in prehistoric times. In China, Egypt, Babylon, and early civilizations generally, arithmetic was used for commercial purposes, for records of taxation, and for astronomy. During the Dark Ages in Europe, knowledge of arithmetic was preserved in India and later among the Arabs. European mathematics revived with the development of trade and overseas exploration. Arabic numerals replaced Roman numerals, allowing calculations to be made on paper, instead of by the ◊abacus. With the invention of logarithms in 1614, and of the slide rule in 1620–30, arithmetic acquired its modern form. The chief development since then has been the growing use of ready reckoners, calculating machines, and computers.

The basic operation of arithmetic is counting. Most arithmetical questions could be answered by counting alone, though with great labour and expenditure of time. Formal calculations allow the same result to be achieved more quickly. The fundamental operations are addition and subtraction, and multiplication and division. Fractions arise naturally in the process of measurement. Decimals are a form of fractions. Powers, that is repeated multiplication of the same number, are represented by an ◊index, for example 2^5 = '2 to the 5th' = $2\times2\times2\times2\times2$. Roots are the reverse of powers. For example, 2 is the 5th root of 32, because $2\times2\times2\times2\times2 = 32$. ◊Logarithms form a convenient means of carrying out complicated fundamental arithmetic operations.

The essential feature of modern arithmetic is the *place-value* system. The decimal numeral system employs ten numerals (0123456789) and therefore operates in 'base ten'. In a base-ten number, each position has a value ten times that of the position to its immediate right: for example, in the number 23 the numeral 3 represents the number 3, but moved one place to the left it would equal three tens. The Babylonians, however, used a complex base-sixty system; the Mayas a base-twenty system. Modern computers operate in base two, using only two numerals (0,1), known as a binary system. In binary, each position has a value twice as great as the position to its immediate right, so that for example binary 111 is equal to 7 in the decimal system, and 1111 is equal to 15. Because the main operations of subtraction, multiplication, and division can be reduced mathematically to addition, digital computers carry out calculations by adding, usually in binary numbers in which the numerals 0 and 1 can be represented by off and on pulses of electric current.

Modular arithmetic deals with events recurring in regular cycles, and is used in describing the functioning of petrol engines, electrical generators, and so on. For example, in the modulo-twelve system, the answer to a question as to what time it will be in five hours if it is now ten o'clock, can be expressed 10+5=3.

arithmetic sequence sequence of numbers or terms that have a common difference between any one term and the next in the sequence. For example, 2, 7, 12, 17, 22, 27... is an arithmetic progression with a common difference of 5. In the progression $3x$, $6x$, $9x$, $12x$, $15x$... the common difference is $3x$. The general formula for the nth term is $a + (n-1)d$, where a is the first term and d is the common difference. The sum of n terms of the progression is $1/2n\ [2a + (n-1)d]$. See also ◊geometric progression.

Arius /'eəriəs/ c. 256–336. Egyptian priest whose ideas gave rise to ◊Arianism, a Christian belief which denied the complete divinity of Christ. Born in Libya, he became a priest of Alexandria in 311. In 318 he was excommunicated and fled to Palestine, but his theology spread to such an extent that the emperor Constantine called a council at ◊Nicaea to resolve the question. Arius was condemned and he and his adherents were banished, though later he was allowed to return.

Arizona /ˌærɪ'zəʊnə/ mountain state in SW USA; Grand Canyon State.
area 295,023 sq km/113,909 sq mi
capital Phoenix
towns Tucson
features Grand Canyon National Park (the multi-coloured gorge through which the Colorado flows, 6–29 km/4–18 mi wide, up to 1.5 km/1 mi deep and 350 km/217 mi long), the Painted Desert (including the Petrified Forest, of fossil trees), Organ Pipe Cactus National Monument Park, Gila Desert, and Sonoran Desert; Colorado river; Roosevelt and Hoover dams; old London Bridge was transported 1971 to the tourist resort of Lake Havasu City
products cotton under irrigation; livestock; copper, molybdenum, silver; electronics, aircraft
population (1980) 2,717,866 including over 100,000 American Indians (Navajo, Hopi, Apache), who still own a quarter of the state
famous people ◊Geronimo, Barry ◊Goldwater, Zane ◊Grey, Percival ◊Lowell, Frank Lloyd ◊Wright
history Arizona is believed to derive its name from the Spanish *arida-zona* (dry belt). The first Spaniard to visit Arizona was the Franciscan Marcos de Niza in 1539. By 1715 Arizona was part of the New Spain; in 1824 it became part of the united Mexican States. After the Mexican war it passed to the USA in 1848, became a territory in 1863, and developed rapidly as a result of the gold-rush in neighbouring California. In 1912 it was admitted as a state of the Union. Irrigation has been carried out since the 1920s on a colossal scale. The Roosevelt dam on Salt river, and Hoover Dam on the Colorado between Arizona and Nevada, provide the state with both hydro-electric power and irrigation water. At the end of the 19th century rich copper

deposits were found in Arizona and subsequently deposits of many other minerals.

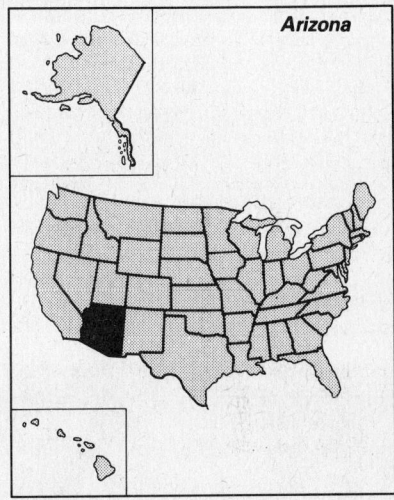
Arizona

Arkansas /'ɑːkənsɔː/ border state in S central USA; Wonder State/Land of Opportunity.
area 137,533 sq km/53,102 sq mi
capital Little Rock
towns Fort Smith
features Ozark mountains; Mississippi river; Hot Springs National Park
products cotton, soya beans, rice; oil, natural gas, bauxite; timber, processed foods
population (1980) 2,285,500

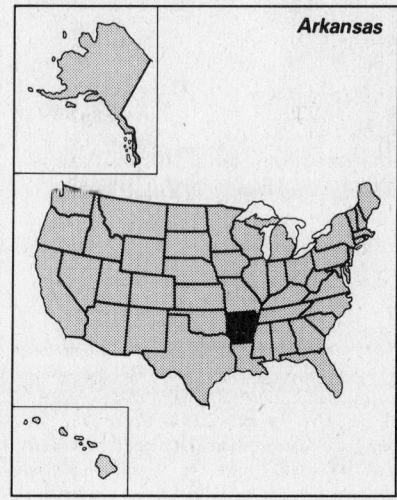
Arkansas

famous people Douglas MacArthur.
history The Spaniard Hernando de Soto explored the area in 1541. The first European settlement, Arkansas Post, was founded by some of the companions of the French explorer La Salle in 1648, who began trading with the local Indians. It formed part of the Louisiana Purchase in 1803 and became a state in 1836. After seceding from the Union in 1861 (see ◊Confederacy), it was readmitted in 1886.

Arkwright /'ɑːkraɪt/ Richard 1732–1792. British inventor and manufacturing pioneer, who is best known for his 'spinning frame'. Born in Preston, Lancashire, he experimented in machine-designing with a watchmaker, John Kay of Warrington, and in 1768, with Kay and John Smalley, he set up his celebrated 'spinning frame' at Preston. He moved to Nottingham shortly after to escape the fury of the spinners, who feared that their handicraft skills would become redundant. In 1771 he went into partnership with Jedediah Strutt, a Derby man who had improved the stocking frame, and Samuel Need, and built a water-powered factory at Cromford in Derbyshire. In 1790 he installed steam power in his Nottingham works. His business prospered and he was knighted in 1786.

Arkwright The inventor Sir Richard Arkwright, painted at the studio of Joseph Wright in 1790. He invented the spinning frame, which was first used in Preston in 1768.

Arlen /'ɑːlən/ Michael 1895–1956. British novelist. Born in Ruschuk, Bulgaria, of Armenian parents, he changed his name from Dikran Kuyumjian when he became a naturalized British subject in 1922. His greatest success was the cynical *The Green Hat* 1924, story of a *femme fatale*. He died in New York.

Arles /ɑːl/ town in Bouches-du-Rhône *département*, south east France, on the left bank of the Rhône, in a great fruit-and vine-growing district; population (1982) 50,772. Roman relics include an amphitheatre for 25,000 spectators. The cathedral of St Trophime is the finest Romanesque structure in Provence. The artist Van Gogh lived here during the last years of his life.

Arlington /'ɑːlɪŋtən/ town in Virginia, USA, and suburb of Washington DC. It is the site of the National Cemetery for the dead of the United States wars. The grounds were first used as a military cemetery in 1864 during the American Civil War. By 1975, 165,142 military, naval, and civilian persons had been buried there, including the ◊Unknown Soldier of both world wars, President J F ◊Kennedy and his brother Robert ◊Kennedy.

Armada term for fleet sent by Philip II of Spain against England in 1588. See ◊Spanish Armada.

armadillo mammal with an armour of bony plates on its back. Some 20 species live from Texas to Patagonia and range in size from the fairy armadillo at 13 cm/5 in to the giant armadillo, 1.5 m/4.5 ft long. They feed on insects, fruit and carrion. Some can roll into an armoured ball if attacked; others rely on burrowing for protection. They belong, with sloths and anteaters, to a group termed edentates (without teeth); nevertheless, armadillos can have up to 90 peg-like teeth.

Armageddon in New Testament (Revelation 16), the site of the final battle between the nations which will end the world; it has been identified with ◊Megiddo.

Armagh /ɑːˈmɑː/ county of Northern Ireland
area 1,266 sq km/489 sq mi
population (1971) 133,969
towns county town ◊Armagh; Lurgan, Portadown, Keady
features smallest county of N Ireland. The N is flat, and there are extensive bogs. The better drained parts are under crops, especially flax. The chief rivers are the Bann and Blackwater, flowing into Lough Neagh, and the Callan tributary of the Blackwater
products chiefly agricultural: apples, potatoes, flax

Armagh /ɑːˈmɑː/ county town of Armagh, Northern Ireland; population 12,300. It is the seat of the Protestant Archbishop of Armagh, nominally 'Primate of All Ireland'.

Armagnac /'ɑːmənjæk/ former French province in southern France (capital Auch), which now survives chiefly as the name of a deep-coloured brandy.

armature in an electrical machine such as a motor or dynamo, the wire-wound coil which carries the current and rotates in a magnetic field. It is also the name given to the pole-piece of a permanent magnet or electromagnet. The moving, iron part of a solenoid, especially if it acts as a switch, may also be referred to as an armature.

Armenia /ɑːˈmiːnɪə/ constituent republic of the Soviet Union from 1936
area 29,800 sq km/11,500 sq mi
capital Yerevan
towns Leninakan
features mainly mountainous and wooded
products copper, molybdenum; cereals, cotton, silk
population 3,000,000, 89% Armenian
language ◊Armenian
religion traditionally ◊Armenian Christian
history Armenia became an independent republic in 1918, was occupied by the Red Army in 1920, and became a constituent republic of the USSR in 1936.

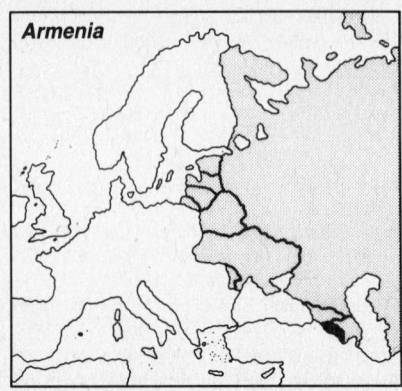

Armenia

Armenian church the form of Christianity adopted in Armenia in the 3rd century. About 295 Gregory the Illuminator (c. 257–332) was made exarch of the Armenian church, which has developed along national lines. The Seven Sacraments, or Mysteries, are administered, baptism being immediately followed by confirmation. The Catholicos or exarch is the supreme head, and Echmiadzin, near Yerevan, is his traditional seat.

Armenian language one of the main divisions of the Indo-European language family. Old Armenian, the classic literary language, is still used in the liturgy of the Armenian church. Armenian was not written down until the fifth century AD, when an alphabet of 36 (now 38) letters was evolved. Literature flourished in the 4th–14th centuries, revived in the 18th; contemporary Armenian, with modified grammar and enriched with words from other languages, is used by a group of 20th century writers.

Armenian massacres series of massacres of Armenians by Turkish soldiers between 1895 and 1915. Reforms promised to Armenian Christians by Turkish rulers never materialized; unrest broke out and there were massacres by Turkish troops in 1895. Again in 1909 and 1915, the Turks massacred altogether more than a million Armenians, and deported others into the N Syrian desert, where they died of starvation; those who could fled to Russia or Persia, and only some 100,000 were left.

Armentières /ˌɑːmɒntiˈeə/ town in N France; population (1982) 25,992. The song 'Mademoiselle from Armentières' originated during World War I, when the town was held by the British. It was flattened by German bombardment in 1918 and rebuilt.

Armidale /'ɑːmɪdeɪl/ town in New South Wales, Australia; population (1985) 21,500. The University of New England is here, and mansions of the ◊squatters survive.

Arminius /ɑːˈmɪnɪəs/ 17 BC–21 AD. German chieftain. An ex-soldier of the Roman army, he annihilated a Roman force led by Varus in the Teutoburger Wald area in 9AD, and saved Germany from becoming a Roman province. He thus ensured that the Empire's frontier did not extend beyond the Rhine.

Arminius /ɑːˈmɪnɪəs/ Jacobus. Latinized name of Jakob Harmensen 1560–1609. Dutch Protestant divine who founded ◊Arminianism, a school of theology opposed to ◊Calvinism. Born in southern Holland, he was ordained at Amsterdam in 1588, and from 1603 lived as professor of theology at Leyden. Arminius opposed Calvin's doctrine of predestination, and asserted that forgiveness and eternal life are bestowed on all who repent of their sins and unfeignedly believe in Jesus Christ. His views were developed by Episcopius, his follower. Arminianism is the basis of Wesleyan ◊Methodist theology in England.

Arminius Dutch Reformed Theologian Jacobus Arminius turned against the Calvinist doctrine of predestination and formulated his ideas about conditional election, which depended on God's grace but allowed humankind free will. He was drawn into many controversies, and his followers were expelled from the church and persecuted.

Armory show art exhibition Feb 1913 in the armory of the 69th Cavalry Regiment, New York, which marked the arrival of modern non-realistic art in the USA. The rioting crowd threatened to destroy the Cubist work by Marcel ◊Duchamp *Nude Descending a Staircase* 1912.

armour personal body protection worn in battle. Body armour is depicted in Greek and Roman art; chain mail was developed in the Middle Ages but the craftsmanship of the armourer reached its height in design in the 15th century, when knights were completely encased in plate armour which still allowed freedom of movement. The invention of gunpowder led, though only by degrees, to the virtual abandonment of armour until in World War I the helmet reappeared as a defence against shrapnel. Suits of armour in the Tower of London were studied by American designers of astronaut

wear. Modern armour, used not only by the army, but by police and security guards and assassination-prone statesmen, uses nylon and fibre-glass, and is often worn beneath other clothing.

Armstrong /ˈɑːmstrɒŋ/ Edwin Howard 1890–1954. American radio engineer, who developed superheterodyne tuning for reception over a very wide spectrum of radio frequencies and frequency ◊modulation for static-free reception.

Armstrong /ˈɑːmstrɒŋ/ Louis ('Satchmo') 1900–1971. US jazz trumpet player and singer. He was born in New Orleans and joined Kid Ory's band in 1918. He first came to prominence in the 1920s with the Creole Jazz Band, and from 1925 had his own Hot Five and Hot Seven. He was legendary for his trumpet technique and improvisation, and for his gravelly voice.

Armstrong American jazz trumpet player, singer and bandleader Louis Armstrong, or 'Satchmo', led his own Hot Five and Seven bands in the 1920s. He was the first solo jazz virtuoso, and invented the 'scat' singing style.

Armstrong /ˈɑːmstrɒŋ/ Neil 1930– . American astronaut, first person to set foot on the Moon. Born in Ohio, he gained his pilot's licence at 16, and served as a naval aviator in Korea 1949–52 before joining NASA as a test pilot. Selected as an astronaut in 1962, he stepped on to the Moon from Apollo 11 in 1969, saying 'That's one small step for a man, one giant leap for mankind'. See also ◊Apollo project.

Armstrong /ˈɑːmstrɒŋ/ William George 1810–1900. British engineer, who developed a revolutionary method of making gun barrels. A former lawyer, he set up a factory near Newcastle-upon-Tyne and in 1855 made a breech-loading artillery piece with a steel and wrought iron barrel (previous guns were muzzle loaded and had cast bronze barrels). By 1880 the 150 mm/16 in Armstrong gun was the standard for all British ordnance.

army an organized military force. Armies were common to all ancient civilizations: Sumeria, Babylonia, Egypt, Assyria, China, India, Persia, Greece, Carthage and – above all – Rome. In Britain the Anglo-Saxon *fyrd*, or local militia, saved the country from being wholly overrun by the Danes, but the first body of standing troops was raised by Canute. After the Norman Conquest military organization was based on the feudal system common to all Europe, whereby vassals supplied their overlords with a certain number of men for so many days a year, which had obvious drawbacks for continuous campaigning, though mercenaries were also employed. The superiority of the mounted knight was ended by the longbow (Crécy, Poitiers, Agincourt), and firearms and cannon favoured centralization in the hands of professionals and the development of sustained campaigns and strategy. In Tudor England small standing bodies of troops were employed for external and internal defence, but the defects of raw levies, noble amateurs and mercenaries led to Cromwell's creation of the New Model Army for the larger campaigns of the Civil War. After the Restoration Charles II established a small standing army, the beginning of the modern British army, which was expanded under James II and William III. Under George III it failed to subdue the American colonists. The success of citizen, or people's, armies was also dramatically illustrated in Europe by the forces of the French Revolution. Conscription was first adopted in Prussia to counter Napoleon's imperial ambitions. The British army under Wellington, which eventually broke Napoleon, was one of the best ever put into the field, but it afterwards decreased in numbers and efficiency. Its

Armstrong Seen here with fellow Apollo 11 crew-members Michael Collins and Edwin Aldrin, Neil Armstrong was the first man to set foot on the moon, on 20 Jul 1969.

weaknesses were patent in the Crimean War and, despite reforms by Cardwell and Wolseley, in the South African war. R B Haldane (on the advice of Roberts) organized an expeditionary force, and for home defence a territorial force, though these were still inadequate. In the 19th century there had been immense development of rapidly produced missile weapons, use of railways (the American Civil War has been called the 'railway war'). World War I was one of trench warfare employing enormous armies; the British army, for instance, expanded from 750,000 to 5½ million men. In the inter-war period armies were greatly reduced until the rise of the Italo-German forces led to reluctant increases: Britain was in many respects less prepared in 1939 than 1914. The armies of World War II were remarkable for their mobility, notably the Allied forces in the Pacific area, and also for close coordination of land, sea and air forces.

On the assumption that the nuclear age – especially the perfection of the H-bomb (1952) – meant the virtual end of conventional warfare, the USA 1955 and USSR 1960 announced reductions in their armies, but this theory was disproved by the Vietnam and Arab-Israeli campaigns. Not only were there sophisticated developments in tanks and anti-tank missiles, low-level and very-low-level air defence guided weapons, and mortar locating radar, but tactical nuclear weapons capable of use for strategic purposes without endangering the attacker were evolved. The modern army, however, tends to be smaller than those of the early post-World War II period, and is specialized and professional.

Arnauld /ɑːˈnəʊ/ French family closely associated with ◊Jansenism, a church movement in the 17th century. *Antoine Arnauld* (1560–1619) was a Paris advocate, strongly

critical of the Jesuits. Many of his 20 children were associated with the abbey of ◊Port Royal, a convent of Cistercian nuns near Versailles, that became the centre of Jansenism: the second daughter, *Angélique* (1591–1661), became abbess through her father's instrumentality at the age of eight. Later she served as prioress under her sister *Agnes* (1593–1671), and her niece, *La Mère Angélique* (1624–84), succeeded to both positions. Arnauld's youngest child, *Antoine* (1612–94), the 'great Arnauld', was religious director of the nuns at Port Royal. With Pascal, Nicole, and others, he produced not only Jansenist pamphlets, but works on logic, grammar, and geometry. For years he had to live in hiding, and the last 16 years of his life were spent in Brussels.

Arne /ɑːn/ Thomas Augustus 1710–1778. British composer, whose musical drama *Alfred* includes the song 'Rule Britannia!'.

Arnhem /ˈɑːnəm/ town in the Netherlands, on the Rhine SE of ◊Utrecht. The English poet Sir Philip ◊Sidney died here in 1586.

Arnhem, Battle of /ˈɑːnəm/ airborne operation, 17–27 Sept 1944, to secure a bridgehead over the Rhine for an Allied drive to the heart of Germany. It failed, with 7,600 casualties, owing to miscalculations.

Arnhem Land /ˈɑːnəm/ plateau of the central peninsula in Northern Territory, Australia. It is the largest of the Aboriginal reserves, and a traditional way of life is maintained, now threatened by mineral exploitation.

Arnim /ˈɑːnɪm/ Ludwig Achim von 1781–1831. German Romantic poet and novelist. Born in Berlin, he wrote short stories, a romance, *Gräfin Dolores/Countess Dolores* 1810, and plays, but left his finest work, the historical novel *Die Kronenwächter* 1817,

unfinished. With Clemens Brentano he collected the German folk-songs in *Des Knaben Wunderhorn/The Boy's Magic Horn* 1805–08. In 1811 he married Brentano's sister, Bettina 1785–1859, who when she was younger had an intimate friendship with Goethe. In 1835 she published her correspondence with the poet, largely spurious.

Arno /ˈɑːnəʊ/ Italian river 240 km/150 mi long, rising in the Apennines, and flowing westward to the Mediterranean. Florence and Pisa stand on its banks.

Arnold /ˈɑːnld/ Benedict 1741–1801. American soldier, chiefly remembered as a traitor to the American side in the War of American Independence. A merchant in Newhaven, Connecticut, he joined the Colonial forces, but in 1780 plotted to betray the strategic post at West Point to the British. Major André was sent by the British to discuss terms with him, but was caught and hanged as a spy. Arnold escaped to the British, who gave him an army command.

Arnold /ˈɑːnld/ Edwin 1832–1904. British scholar and poet. He wrote the *Light of Asia* 1879, a rendering of the life and teaching of the Buddha in blank verse. *The Light of the World* 1891 retells the life of Christ.

Arnold /ˈɑːnld/ Malcolm (Henry) 1921– . British composer. Born in Northampton, he began his career as a trumpeter, becoming principal trumpet in the London Philharmonic Orchestra. His music is tonal, and includes a large amount of orchestral, chamber, and vocal music. His operas include *The Dancing Master* 1951, and he has written music for more than 80 films, including *The Bridge on the River Kwai* 1957, for which he won an Academy Award.

Arnold /ˈɑːnld/ Matthew 1822–1888. British poet and critic, son of Thomas ◊Arnold. After a short spell as an assistant master at Rugby, he became a school inspector 1851–86. He published two unsuccessful volumes of poetry, anonymously, but two further publications under his own name in 1853 and 1855 led to his appointment of professor of poetry at Oxford. His best-known poems are 'The Forsaken Merman' 1849, 'Thyrsis' 1867 – commemorating his friend A H Clough – 'Dover Beach' 1867, and 'The Scholar Gypsy' 1853. His *Essays in Criticism* 1865 and 1888 demand 'high seriousness' and 'a criticism of life' in the poet; *Culture and Anarchy* 1869 attacks 19th-century philistinism.

Arnold /ˈɑːnld/ of Brescia 1100–1155. Italian Augustinian monk, who attacked the holding of property by the Church; he was hanged and burnt, and his ashes were thrown into the Tiber.

Arnold /ˈɑːnld/ Thomas 1795–1842. British schoolmaster, father of Matthew ◊Arnold. Ordained in the Church of England in 1818, he was headmaster of Rugby School 1828–42. His regime at Rugby has been graphically described in Thomas ◊Hughes's *Tom Brown's Schooldays* 1857. His emphasis was on training of character, and his influence on public school education was profound.

aromatic compounds organic chemical compounds derived from benzene. They have

Arnold The poet and critic Matthew Arnold, painted by G F Watts. In *Culture and Anarchy*, Arnold first used the word 'philistine' in its modern sense in his attack on the cultural values of the middle classes.

special properties and undergo chemical substitution reactions. See also cyclic compounds.

Arras /'ærəs/ French town, capital of Pas-de-Calais département, on the Scarpe, north east of Paris. It was formerly famed for its tapestry. Population (1975) 50,400.

Arras /'ærəs/ Battles of five battles of World War I; the fiercest was in 1917. The town was also captured in 1940 by the Germans in the advance on Dunkirk.

Arrau /əˈrau/ Claudio 1903– . Chilean pianist. A concert performer since the age of five, he excels in 19th-century music.

arrest deprivation of personal liberty with a view to detention. In Britain an arrest in civil proceedings now takes place only on a court order, usually for contempt of court. In criminal proceedings an arrest may be made on a magistrate's warrant, but a police constable is empowered to arrest without warrant in all cases where he or she has reasonable ground for thinking a serious offence has been committed. Private persons may, and are indeed bound to, arrest anyone committing a serious offence or breach of the peace in their presence. In the USA police officers and private persons have similar rights and duties.

Arrhenius /əˈreɪniəs/ Svante August 1859-1927. Swedish scientist, the founder of physical chemistry. Born near Uppsala, he became a professor at Stockholm in 1895, and made a special study of ◊electrolysis. He wrote *Worlds in the Making* and *Destinies of the Stars*, and in 1903 received the Nobel Prize for Chemistry.

product from metallurgical processes. As it is a cumulative poison, its presence in food and drugs is very dangerous. The symptoms of arsenic poisoning are vomiting, diarrhoea, tingling and possibly numbness in the limbs, and collapse.

arson the malicious and wilful setting fire to property, crops, possessions, in Britain covered by the Criminal Damage Act (1971).

art in the broadest sense, all the processes and products of human skill, imagination, and invention; the opposite of nature. In the Middle Ages the term was used, chiefly in the plural, to signify a branch of learning which was regarded as an instrument of knowledge. The seven *Liberal Arts* consisted of the *trivium*, that is grammar, logic, and rhetoric, and the *quadrivium*, that is arithmetic, music, geometry, and astronomy.

In Western culture, aesthetic criteria introduced by the ancient Greeks still influence our perceptions and judgements of art, notably the belief that art should represent or reflect reality, and that it should give pleasure and exaltation. In contemporary usage, definitions of art usually reflect aesthetic criteria, and the term may encompass ◊literature, ◊music, ◊drama, ◊painting, ◊sculpture, and so on. Popularly, the term is most commonly used to refer to the visual arts.

Two currents of thought run through our ideas about art. In one, derived from Aristotle, art is concerned with *mimesis* ('imitation'), the representation of appearances, and gives pleasure through the accuracy and skill with which it depicts the real world. The other view, derived from Plato, holds that the artist is inspired by the Muses (or by God, or by the inner impulses, or by the collective unconscious) to express that which is beyond appearances – inner feelings, eternal truths, or the essence of the age. In the visual arts of Western civilizations, painting and sculpture have been the dominant forms for many centuries. This has not always been the case in other cultures. Islamic art, for example, is one of ornament, for under the Muslim religion artists were forbidden to usurp the divine right of creation by portraying living creatures. In some cultures masks, tattoos, pottery, and metalwork have been the main forms of visual art. In the recent past technology has made new art forms possible, such as ◊photography and ◊cinema, and today electronic media have led to entirely new ways of creating and presenting visual images.

See also under historical periods such as ◊ancient art, ◊medieval art, and under the arts of individual countries, such as ◊French art, ◊French literature, and so on, and under individual movements, such as ◊Classicism, ◊Romanticism, ◊Cubism, ◊Impressionism.

Artaud /aːˈtəu/ Antonin 1896–1948. French theatre director. His play, *Les Cenci/The Cenci* 1935, was a failure, but his concept of the 'Theatre of Cruelty', intended to release feelings usually repressed in the unconscious, has been an important influence on modern drama, notably in the plays of ◊Camus, ◊Genet, and in the productions of Peter ◊Brook. He became insane in 1936, and was confined in an asylum.

aromatic compounds

— atomic bond
● carbon atom
• hydrogen atom
Ⓞ oxygen atom
Ⓝ nitrogen atom

benzene

a hexose (glucose)

a pyridine (nicotinic acid, vitamin B₃)

pyrimidine   pyridine   +   imidazole   =   purine

Arp /aːp/ Jean (Hans) 1887–1966. French painter and sculptor. Born in Strasbourg, he was one of the founders of ◊Dadaism in Zurich c. 1917, and was later a member of the ◊Surrealist and Abstract-Creation groups. His early painting is fluid, and when he turned to sculpture it was notable for its boneless curves; also remarkable are his *papiers déchirês*, torn paper designs pasted on a white ground.

Arran /'ærən/ large mountainous island in the Firth of Clyde, Scotland, in Strathclyde: 32 km/20 mi by 16 km/10 mi. Area 427 sq km/165 sq mi; Population (1981) 4,726. Popular as a holiday resort.

arrowroot starchy substance derived from the roots and tubers of various plants. The true arrowroot *Maranta arundinacea* was used by the Indians of South America as an antidote against the effects of poisoned arrows. The West Indian island of St Vincent is the main source of supply today. The edible starch is easily digested and is good for invalids.

arsenic a greyish-white semi-metallic crystalline element, symbol As, atomic weight 74.91, atomic number 33. It occurs in many ores, and is widely distributed, being present in minute quantities in the soil, the sea and the human body. The chief source of arsenic compounds is as a by-

Art Deco style, in art and architecture, originating in France in 1925, and continuing through the 1930s, using rather heavy, geometric simplification of form, for example Radio City Music Hall, New York.

Artemis /'ɑːtəmɪs/ in Greek mythology, the goddess (Roman ◊Diana) of chastity, childbirth, and the young; she was envisaged as a virgin huntress; her cult centre was at ◊Ephesus. She was later also identified with ◊Selene, goddess of the Moon.

arteriography a method of examining the interior of an artery by injecting into it a radio-opaque solution which is visible on an x-ray photograph. Used for the heart's coronary arteries (coronary arteriogram), for example.

arteriosclerosis hardening of the arteries, the thickening and loss of elasticity of the circulatory system. It is associated with ageing and a diet high in saturated fats.

artery a vessel which conveys blood from the ◊heart of ◊vertebrates to the body tissues. The largest of the arteries is the ◊aorta, which in mammals leads from the left ventricle of the heart, up over the heart and down through the diaphragm into the belly. Arteries are flexible, elastic tubes consisting of three layers, the middle of which is muscular; by its rhythmic contraction this aids the pumping of blood around the body. Not all arteries carry oxygen-rich blood – the pulmonary arteries convey oxygen-poor blood from heart to lungs. The cutting of an artery of any size is a dangerous injury. With middle and old age the arteries normally lose their elasticity; the walls degenerate, and often become impregnated with fatty deposits, resulting in arteriosclerosis, hardening of the arteries.

artesian well a well in which water rises from its ◊aquifer under natural pressure. Such a well may be drilled into an aquifer that is confined by impermeable beds both above and below. If the water table (the top of the region of water saturation) in that aquifer is above the level of the well head, hydrostatic pressure will force the water to the surface. Much use is made of artesian wells in E Australia, where aquifers filled by water in the Great Dividing Range run beneath the arid surface of the Simpson Desert. It is named after Artois, a French province, where the phenomenon was first observed.

arthritis inflammation of the joints, of which the most widespread form is *rheumatoid arthritis*, which usually begins in middle age in the small joints of the hands and feet, causing a greater or lesser degree of deformity and painfully restricted movement. Aspirin is still the most commonly used alleviating drug. *Osteoarthritis* tends to affect larger joints, such as the knee and hip, so that artificial joints may be used to restore mobility. It appears in later life, especially in those whose joints may have been subject to earlier stress or damage. The disease seems influenced by heredity and may be triggered by a virus infection.

arthropod invertebrate animal with jointed legs and a segmented body with a horny or chitinous casing, the latter being shed periodically and replaced as the animal grows. This definition includes arachnids such as spiders

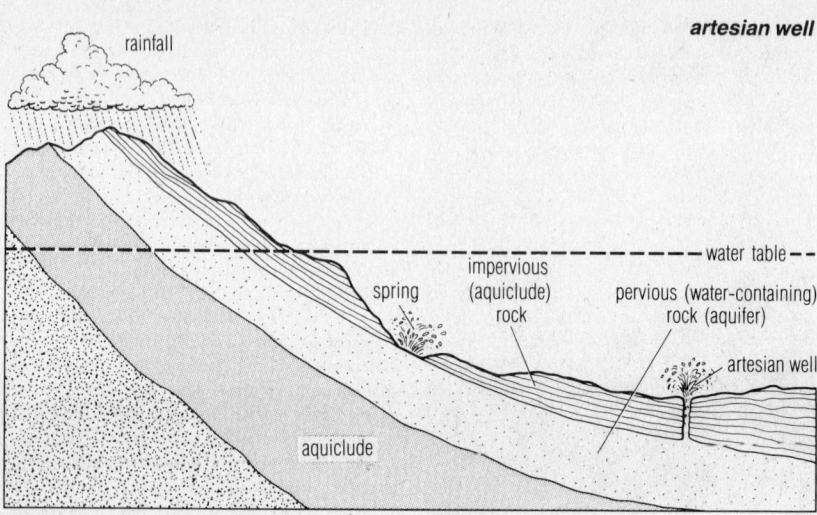

rainfall

water table
impervious (aquiclude) rock
spring
pervious (water-containing) rock (aquifer)
artesian well
aquiclude

and mites, as well as crustaceans, millipedes, centipedes and insects. All formerly placed in the same phylum, Arthropoda, it is now believed that some groups had a separate origin.

Arthur /'ɑːθə/ legendary English 'king' and hero, 6th century AD. He may have been a Romano-British leader against pagan Saxon invaders. The story of the Round Table (so shaped to avoid strife over precedence among the knights of his court at ◊Camelot), and the quest for the Holy ◊Grail, was developed in the 12th century by Geoffrey of Monmouth. Later writers on the theme include the anonymous author of *Sir Gawayne and the Greene Knight* 1346, Sir Thomas ◊Malory, ◊Tennyson, T H ◊White, J C ◊Powys, and John ◊Steinbeck. Arthur is said to have been born at ◊Tintagel and be buried at ◊Glastonbury. Arthur's seat, a hill 251 m/822ft of volcanic origin in King's Park, east of Edinburgh, is linked with the hero only by name.

Arthur /'ɑːθə/ Chester Alan 1830–1886. 21st president of the USA. Son of a Baptist minister, he was born in Vermont, and became a lawyer and Republican spokesman. In 1880 he was elected vice-president to ◊Garfield, who was assassinated the following year. Arthur succeeded him as president, and held office until 1885.

Arthur /'ɑːθə/ Duke of Brittany 1187–1203. Grandson of Henry II of England and nephew of King ◊John, who is supposed to have had him murdered, 13 Apr 1203, as a rival for the crown.

Arthur /'ɑːθə/ Prince of Wales 1486–1502. Eldest son of Henry VII of England. He married ◊Catherine of Aragon in 1501, when he was 16 and she was 15. The marriage was allegedly unconsummated, and he died the next year.

Arthur's Pass /'ɑːθə/ road-rail link across the Southern Alps, New Zealand, at 926 m/3,038 ft, linking Christchurch with Greymouth.

Arthur's Seat /'ɑːθə/ hill of volcanic origin, Edinburgh, Scotland, only fancifully linked with King Arthur.

artichoke two plants of the family Compositae, both familiar as table-vegetables. The **common** or **globe artichoke Cynara**

scolymus is tall, with purplish blue flowers; the bracts of the unopened flower are eaten. The *Jerusalem artichoke Helianthus tuberosus* has edible tubers; it is a native of North America, and its name is a corruption of the Italian *girasole*, sunflower.

article a grammatical ◊part of speech, of which there are two in English: the *definite article* 'the', which serves to specify or identify a noun (as in 'This is the book I need'), and the *indefinite article* 'a' or "an') (before vowels), which indicates a single unidentified noun ('They gave me a piece of paper and an envelope'). Some people use the form 'an' before *h* ('an historic building'); this practice dates from the 17th century, when an initial *h* was often not pronounced (as in '*h*onour'), and is nowadays considered rather grandiose and unnecessary.

artificial intelligence (AI) a branch of cognitive science concerned with creating computer programs that can perform actions comparable with those of an intelligent human. Early AI programs, developed in the 1960s, attempted simulations of human intelligence or were aimed at general problem-solving techniques. It is now thought that intelligent behaviour depends as much on the knowledge a system possesses as on its reasoning power. Present emphasis is on ◊knowledge-based systems such as ◊expert systems. Current AI research covers areas such as planning (for robot behaviour), language understanding, pattern recognition, and knowledge representation.

artificial limb a device to replace a limb that has been removed by surgery or one that is malformed because of genetic defects. It is one form of ◊prosthesis. See ◊surgery.

artificial respiration the maintenance of breathing when the natural process is suspended, if it is permanently suspended, as in paralysis, an *iron lung* is used; in cases of electric shock or apparent drowning, for example, the first choice is the expired air method, the *'kiss of life'* by mouth-to-mouth breathing until natural breathing is resumed.

artificial selection in biology, selective breeding of individuals that exhibit particular characters which a plant or animal breeder wishes to develop in a strain. The development of particular breeds of cattle for improved meat production (such as the Aberdeen-Angus) or milk production (such as Jerseys) are examples. See also ◊breed.

artillery collective term for large military ◊firearms. Cannons were in general use from the 14th century, but were most effective in siege warfare until, in the Napoleonic period (early 19th century), field artillery became smaller and more mobile. The howitzer, halfway between a gun and a mortar (muzzle-loading cannon), was used from the 16th century in sieges, and in World War I to demolish trench systems. Giant cannons were also favourite weapons in World War I, not only in the entrenched conditions of the Western Front, but at sea against the lumbering, heavily armoured battleships. However, the fire accuracy on small or moving targets was poor, even by World War II. The breakthrough came in the 1970s (see ◊weapons list) with electronically-operated target devices and remote control firing; on modern battleships gun turrets are also unmanned. Today even howitzers are self-mobile, computer-controlled, and can fire a 43 kg/95 lb shell 32 km/20 mi in five seconds, or a nuclear warhead. Shells may be made to home in automatically on an unseen target, such as a tank, but so far cannot distinguish tanks already disabled.

artillery On exercise in Germany, members of the 5th Regiment Royal Artillery and 3rd Royal Tank Regiment, with an M107 gun.

Art Nouveau art style developed in France in the 1890s, marked by sinuous lines and stylized flowers and foliage. Also known as Jugendstil (Germany); Stile Liberty (Italy). Exponents included ◊Beardsley, ◊Gaudí, ◊Gilbert, C R ◊Mackintosh, René ◊Lalique.

Artois /ɑːˈtwɑː/ former province of northern France, bounded by Flanders and Picardy, and almost corresponding with the modern *département* of Pas-de-Calais. Its capital was Arras.

Arts and Crafts movement a social movement based in design and architecture, founded by William ◊Morris in the latter half of the 19th century and supported by A W ◊Pugin

and John ◊Ruskin, stressing the importance of manual processes and largely anti-machine in spirit.

Arts Council of Great Britain UK arts organization, incorporated in 1945, which aids music, drama, and visual arts from government funds. It originated in 1940 as a committee of the Pilgrim Trust to encourage the arts in wartime and was known as the Council for the Encouragement of Music and the Arts (CEMA).

Aruba /əˈruːbə/ island in the Caribbean, the westernmost of the Lesser Antilles; an overseas part of the Netherlands
area 193 sq km/74.5 sq mi
population (1983) 67,000
history Aruba obtained separate status from the other Netherlands Antilles in 1986 and has full internal autonomy.

arum plant of the family Araceae. The typical species *Arum maculatum*, known as cuckoo-pint or lords-and-ladies, is a common British hedgerow plant. The arum or trumpet lily *Zantedeschia aethiopica*, a well-known ornamental plant, is a native of South Africa.

Arunachal Pradesh /ˌɑːrəˈnɑːtʃəl prəˈdeʃ/ union territory of the republic of India, in the Himalayas on the borders of China (Tibet) and Burma. Formerly nominally part of Assam, and known as the north east frontier agency, it became a union territory in 1972, and was renamed Arunachal Pradesh 'Hills of the Rising Sun'. Its peoples speak 50 different dialects. The capital is Itanagar. Area 81,426 sq km/31,438 sq mi; population (1981) 628,050.

Arundel /ˈærəndl/ town in Sussex, England, on the river Arun. It has a magnificent castle (much restored and rebuilt), the seat for centuries of the earls of Arundel and dukes of ◊Norfolk. The parish church of St Nicolas dates from the 14th century; the Roman Catholic church of St Philip Neri was built by the 15th duke in 1873. Population (1981) 2,200.

Arundel /ˈærəndl/ Thomas Howard, 2nd Earl of Arundel 1586–1646. English politician and patron of the arts. The Arundel Marbles, part of his collection of Italian sculptures, were given to Oxford University in 1667 by his grandson.

Arval Brethren (Latin *Fratres Arvales*, brothers of the field) body of priests in ancient Rome who offered annual sacrifices to the Lares or divinities of the fields in order to ensure a good harvest. They formed a college of 12 priests, and their chief festival fell in May.

Aryan name given to an ancient people who were believed to have lived between Central Asia and Eastern Europe, and to have reached India in about 1500 BC, lighter in colour than the aboriginal ◊Dravidians. In the ◊Nazi period Hitler and other German theorists erroneously propagated the idea of the Aryans as a white-skinned master-race of which the blue-eyed, fair-haired 'Nordic' was the finest expression, and used it as justification for ◊antisemitism.

Aryana /ˌeəriˈɑːnə/ ancient name of Afghanistan.

Aryan language name of either one of the languages of the Aryan peoples of India, or a 19th-century name for the ◊Indo-European languages.

Arya Samaj /ˈɑːriə səˈmɑːdʒ/ ◊Hindu religious sect founded by Dayanand Saraswati (1825–88), about 1875. He renounced idol-worship, and urged a return to the purer principles of the Rig Veda (Hindu scriptures).

ASA in photography, a numbering system for rating the speed of films, devised by the American Standards Association. It has now been superseded by *ISO*, the International Standards Organization.

asbestos any of several related minerals of fibrous structure which offer great heat resistance because of their non-flammability and poor conductivity. Commercial asbestos is generally made from chrysolite, a kind of ◊serpentine mineral found in Quebec, the USSR, and Zimbabwe. It has been used for brake linings, suits for firemen and astronauts, insulation of electric wires in furnaces, cement sheets and pressure pipes for the building industry. Exposure to asbestos is a recognized cause of industrial cancer (mesothelioma), especially in the 'blue' form (from South Africa), rather than the more common 'white', and usage is now subject to stringent regulation. *Asbestosis* is a chronic lung inflammation caused by asbestos dust.

ascariasis infection by **roundworm** *Ascaris lumbricoides*, an intestinal parasite in humans.

Ascension /əˈsenʃən/ British island of volcanic origin in the S Atlantic, a dependency of ◊St Helena since 1922. A Portuguese navigator landed there on Ascension Day 1501, but it remained uninhabited, until occupied by Britain in 1815. The chief settlement is Georgetown. Population (1982) 1,625. It is famous for sea turtles and sooty terns, and its role as a staging post to the Falkland Islands.

Ascension Day or *Holy Thursday* in the Christian calendar, the feast day commemorating Christ's ascension into heaven. It is the 40th day after Easter.

asceticism the renunciation of physical pleasure, for example, in eating, drinking, exercizing sexual instincts; and seeking discomfort or pain, often for religious reasons.

Ascham /ˈæskəm/ Roger c. 1515–1568. English scholar. After writing a treatise on archery, King Henry VIII's favourite sport, he was appointed tutor to Princess Elizabeth in 1548. He retained favour under Edward VI and Queen Mary (despite his Protestant views), and returned to Elizabeth's service as her secretary after she became queen. He wrote *The Scholemaster* 1570 on the art of education.

ASCII (American Standard Code for Information Interchange) in computing, a seven or eight-digit binary code for communicating alphabetic, numeric and other characters. For example, the ASCII code for A is 01000001, for B 01000010, and for C 01000011. The eighth bit (binary digit) is not needed for the code, but is sometimes used to check for errors or allow special characters to be included. See also ◊binary number system.

ascorbic acid or *vitamin C*. A relatively simple organic acid found in fresh fruits and vegetables. It is soluble in water and destroyed by prolonged boiling, so soaking or overcooking of vegetables reduces their vitamin C content. Ascorbic acid plays an important role in the synthesis of collagen, and lack of it results in skin sores or ulcers, tooth and gum problems, and burst capillaries ('scurvy').

Ascot /'æskət/ village in Berkshire, 9.5 km/6 mi SW of Windsor. Queen Anne established the racecourse on Ascot Heath in 1711, and the Royal Ascot meeting is a social, as well as a sporting event. Races include the Gold Cup, Ascot Stakes, Coventry Stakes, and King George VI and Queen Elizabeth Stakes.

Asean acronym of ◊Association of South East Asian Nations.

asepsis freedom from bacteria, particularly in surgery, distinguished from antisepsis, or killing bacteria. Modern surgery rests on a meticulously careful technique of asepsis, by which 'germs' are not ever allowed to reach a surgical wound, and are removed from an accidental wound by cutting out damaged tissues and careful cleansing. Similar precautions are used in childbirth and accidents.

asexual reproduction a biological term applied to reproductive processes which are not ◊sexual and so which do not involve fusion of ◊gametes. They include ◊binary fission, in which the parent organism splits into two or more 'daughter' organisms, or ◊budding, in which a new organism is formed initially as an outgrowth of the parent organism. The asexual production of spores, as in ferns and mosses, is another common process, and many plants reproduce asexually by means of runners, rhizomes, bulbs and corms; see ◊vegetative reproduction. Unlike sexual reproduction, these processes do not involve the fusion of two gametes. See also ◊parthenogenesis.

ash tree of the genus *Fraxinus*, belonging to the family Oleaceae. *Fraxinus excelsior* is the European species. The timber is of importance. The *mountain ash* or *rowan Sorbus aucuparia* belongs to the Rosaceae.

Ashanti (or Asante) /ə'ʃænti/ region of Ghana, West Africa; area 25,100 sq km/9,700 sq mi. Population (1984) 2,089,683. Kumasi is the capital. The main crop is cocoa, and the region is noted for its metalwork and textiles. For more than 200 years forming an independent kingdom, during the 19th century the Ashanti (more correctly Asante) lost their independence to the British who sent four expeditions against them, and who in 1901 formally annexed their country. Otomfuo Sir Osei Agyeman, nephew of the then deposed king, Prempeh I, was made head of the re-established Ashanti confederation in 1935 as Prempeh II, and the Golden Stool (actually a chair), symbol of the Ashanti peoples since the 17th century, was returned to Kumasi. (The rest of the Ashanti treasure is in the British Museum.) The Asantahene (King of the Ashanti) still holds ceremonies in which this stool is ceremonially paraded.

Ashbee /'æʃbi/ C(harles) R(obert) 1863–1942. British designer, architect, and writer, one of the major figures of the ◊Arts and Crafts movement. Basing his ideas on the social function of art from the writings of William ◊Morris and John ◊Ruskin, Ashbee founded a

Ashanti (or Asante) Bearing the king's stool in procession. An Ashanti king is always 'enstooled', not crowned.

'Guild of Handicraft' in the East End of London in 1888 (later moved to Gloucestershire). At its peak, the guild employed over 100 craftworkers. The guild satisfied Ashbee's philanthropic aims in promoting handmade articles in an environment where emotional fulfilment was more important than profit. The Guild finally collapsed for lack of demand in 1908.

Ashbery /'æʃbəri/ John 1927– . US poet and art critic. His collections of poetry, including *Self-Portrait in a Convex Mirror* 1975, which won a Pulitzer prize, are distinguished by their strong visual element and narrative power.

Ashby-de-la-Zouch /'æʃbi də lə 'zuːʃ/ town in Leicestershire, England; population (1985) 11,906. It was named from the La Zouche family who built the castle, which was later used to imprison Mary Queen of Scots in 1569. The 15th-century castle features in Sir Walter Scott's novel *Ivanhoe*.

Ashcan school name given to a group of American painters of 1900–10, who included John Sloan and George ◊Bellows, because of their realistic squalid cityscapes.

Ashcroft /'æʃkrɒft/ Peggy 1907– . British actress. She was born in Croydon, Surrey, where a theatre is now named after her. She was created Dame of the British Empire in 1956. Her many roles include Desdemona, in Shakespeare's *Othello* (with Paul Robeson), and appearances in the TV series *The Jewel in the Crown* 1984 and the film *A Passage to India* 1985.

Ashdod /'æʃdɒd/ deepwater port of Israel, on the Mediterranean 32 km/20 mi south of Tel-Aviv, which it superseded in 1965. It stands on the site of the ancient Philistine stronghold of Askalon. Population (1982) 66,000.

Ashes, the cricket trophy theoretically held by the winning team in England-Australia Test Match series (it actually remains at ◊Lord's). The urn contains the ashes of stumps and bails

Ashcroft British actress Dame Peggy Ashcroft photographed by Cecil Beaton in the 1930s. She had her first success in London as Naomi in *Jew Süss* (1929). She played Desdemona to Paul Robeson's Othello, and Juliet in Sir John Gielgud's production of *Romeo and Juliet* (1935).

used in the match in 1883, and was presented by a group of Melbourne ladies to the victorious British captain, Ivo Bligh.

Asheville /'æʃvɪl/ textile town in N Carolina, USA. Population (1980) 53,583. Showplaces include the 19th-century Biltmore mansion, home of millionaire George W Vanderbilt, and the home of the writer Thomas Wolfe.

Ashford /'æʃfəd/ town of Kent, England, on the river Stour, SW of Canterbury. It has expanded in the 1980s as a new commercial and industrial centre for SE England. Population (1985) 47,000.

Ashford /'æʃfəd/ Daisy 1881–1972. British author of *The Young Visiters* 1919, a classic of unconscious humour written at the age of nine.

Ashkenazim /ˌæʃkə'nɑːzɪm/ Jews of German or East European descent, as opposed to the Sephardim, of Spanish and Portuguese descent.

Ashkenazy /ˌæʃkə'nɑːzi/ Vladimir 1937– . Russian pianist and conductor. He has a keyboard technique rather differing from standard Western practice and in 1962 was joint winner of the Tchaikovsky competition with John Ogdon. He excels in Rachmaninov, Prokofiev, and Liszt.

Ashkhabad /ˌæʃkə'bæd/ capital and business and cultural centre of Republic of Turkmen, USSR. Population (1985) 356,000. 'Bukhara' carpets are made here, and it is the hottest place in the USSR.

Ashley /'æʃli/ Laura 1925–1985. Welsh designer, born Mountney. Born in Merthyr Tydfil, she established and gave her name to a neo-Victorian country style in clothes and furnishings from 1953 and an international chain of shops.

Ashmole /'æʃməʊl/ Elias 1617–1692. British antiquary. Born at Lichfield, he became a lawyer, served with the Royal forces during the Civil War, and after the Restoration held posts in the excise and other offices. He wrote books on alchemy and on antiquarian subjects, amassed a fine library and a collection of curiosities, both of which he presented to Oxford University. His collection was housed in the 'Old Ashmolean' (built 1679–83), and forms the basis of the present Ashmolean Museum, erected in 1897.

Ashmole Portrait of the English antiquarian Elias Ashmole after J Riley. Rare items from America, Africa, and the South Seas bequeathed to him from his friend John Tradescant formed the basis of the Ashmolean Collection presented to Oxford University in 1682.

Ashmore and Cartier Islands /'æʃmɔː, 'kɑːtieɪ/ group of islands comprising Middle, East and West Island (the Ashmores), and Cartier Island, in the Indian Ocean about 320 km/200 mi off the NW coast of Australia, transferred to the authority of the Commonwealth of Australia by Britain in 1931. They are administered as part of the Northern Territory and are uninhabited, although West Ashmore has an automatic weather station.

ashram an Indian community, the members of which lead a simple life of discipline and self-denial, and devote themselves to social service. Noted ashrams are that of Mahatma Gandhi at Wardha, and the poet Sir Rabindranath Tagore at Santiniketan.

Ashridge /'æʃrɪdʒ/ the former seat of the earls Brownlow near Berkhamsted, Hertfordshire, England. In 1928 it was bought and endowed as a college on conservative and constitutional lines as a memorial to British statesman Bonar Law. In 1959 it was converted into a management training centre backed by major British industries.

Ashton /'æʃtən/ Frederick 1904– . British dancer and choreographer. Born in Ecuador, he studied with ◊Massine and ◊Rambert before joining the Vic-Wells in 1935 as chief choreographer during which time he created several roles for Margot ◊Fonteyn. He succeeded ◊De Valois as director of the ◊Royal Ballet in 1963, a post he held until 1970. His works include *Façade* 1931, *Cinderella* 1948, *La Fille mal gardée* 1960, *Marguerite and Armand* – for Fonteyn and Nureyev – 1963 and *A Month in the Country* 1976. Knighted 1962, Order of Merit 1977.

Ashton The distinguished British choreographer and co-founder of the Royal Ballet, Sir Frederick Ashton. He contributed much to the popularity of ballet in the mid-20th century.

Ashton under Lyne /'æʃtən ʌndə 'laɪn/ industrial town in Greater Manchester, England; there are light industries, coal and cotton. Population (1981) 44,476.

Ash Wednesday first day of Lent, the period in the Christian calendar leading up to Easter; in the Catholic Church the foreheads of the congregation are marked with a cross in ash, as a sign of penitence.

Asia largest of the continents, forming the eastern part of Eurasia to the east of the Ural mountains, one third of the total land surface of the world.

area 44,000,000 sq km/17,000,000 sq mi

largest cities (over 5 million) Tokyo, Peking, Seoul, Jakarta, Tehran, Bangkok

physical five main divisions: (1) central triangular mountain mass, including the Himalayas; to the N the great Tibetan plateau, bounded by the Kunlun mountains, to the N of which lie further ranges, as well as the Gobi desert. (2) The SW plateaux and ranges, forming Afghanistan, Baluchistan, Iran. (3) The northern lowlands, from the central mountains to the Arctic Ocean, much of which is frozen for several months each year. (4) The eastern margin and islands, where much of the population is concentrated. (5) The southern plateau and river plains, including Arabia, the Deccan, and the alluvial plains of the Euphrates, Tigris, Indus, Ganges, and Irrawaddy. The climate shows great extremes and contrasts, the heart of the continent becoming bitterly cold in winter and very hot in summer. This, with the resulting pressure and

wind systems, accounts for the Asiatic monsoons, bringing heavy rain to all SE Asia, China, and Japan, between May and October.

features rivers (over 2000 miles) Ob-Irtysh, Yangtze, Huang, Amur, Lena, Mekong, Yenisei, Euphrates; lakes (over 7000 sq mi) Caspian and Aral seas, Baikal, Balkhash.

population (1984) 2,778,000, the most densely populated of the continents; annual growth rate 1.7%

language predominantly tonal languages (Chinese, Japanese) in the east, Indo-Iranian languages in central India and Pakistan (Hindi/Urdu), and Semitic (Arabic) in the south-west

religion Hinduism, Islam, Buddhism, Christianity, Confucianism, Shintoism.

Asia Minor /'eɪʃə/ historical name for Anatolia, the Asian part of Turkey.

Asia, Soviet Central /'eɪʃə/ see ◊Soviet Central Asia.

Asiento treaty of 1713, whereby British traders were permitted by Spain to introduce 144,000 black slaves into the Spanish-American colonies in the course of the next 30 years. In 1750 the right was bought out by the Spanish government for $100,000.

Asimov /'æzɪmɒf/ Isaac 1920– . American science-fiction writer and writer on science, born in the USSR. He has published about 200 books, and is possibly best known for his *I, Robot* 1950, and the 'Foundation' trilogy 1951–53, continued in *Foundation's Edge* 1983.

AS Level (Advanced Supplementary) examinations introduced in the UK in 1988 as the equivalent to 'half an ◊A Level' as a means of broadening the sixth form curriculum.

Asmara /æs'mɑːrə/ capital of Eritrea, Ethiopia; 64 km/40 mi SW of Massawa on the Red Sea. Population (1984) 275,385. There is a naval school. In 1974 unrest here precipitated the end of the Ethiopian Empire.

Asnières /ˌɑːni'eə/ NW suburb of Paris, France, on the left bank of the Seine; a boating centre and pleasure resort. Population (1982) 71,220.

Asoka /ə'səʊkə/ reigned 264–228 BC. Indian emperor, who was a Buddhist convert. He had edicts enjoining the adoption of his new faith carved on pillars and rock faces, throughout his dominions, and many survive. In ◊Patna, there are the remains of a hall built by him.

asp name applied to several venomous snakes, including *Vipera aspis* of S Europe allied to the ◊adder, and the Egyptian cobra *Naja haje*, reputed to have been used by Cleopatra for her suicide.

asparagus plant of the lily family Liliaceae. *Asparagus officinalis* is cultivated, and the young shoots are eaten as a vegetable.

Aspasia /ə'speɪzɪə/ lived c. 440 BC–. Greek courtesan, the mistress of the Athenian statesman ◊Pericles. As a 'foreigner' from Miletus, she could not be recognized as his wife, but their son was later legitimized. ◊Socrates visited her salon, a famous meeting place for the celebrities of Athens. Her free thinking led to a charge of impiety from which Pericles had to defend her.

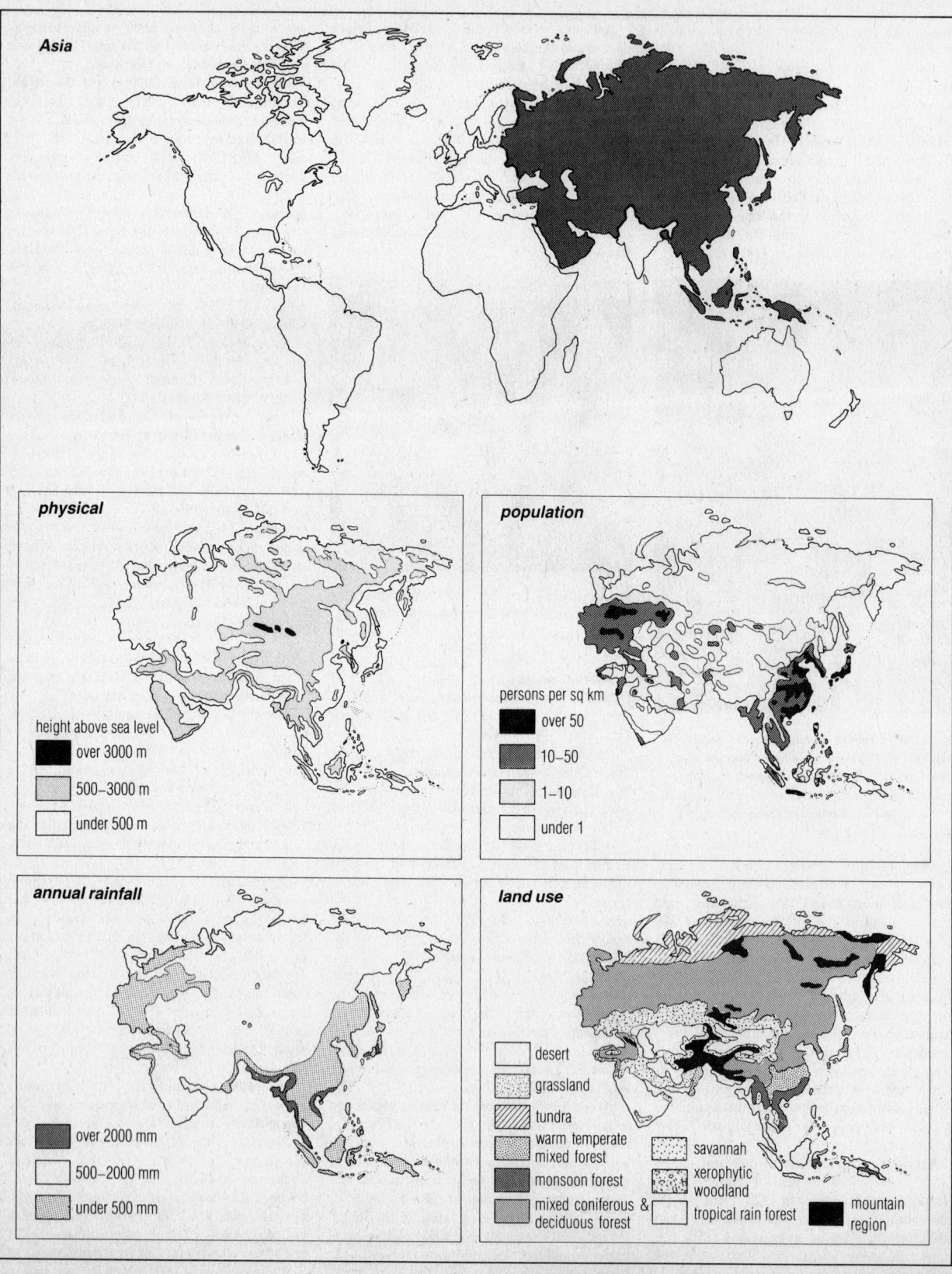

Asia

physical

height above sea level
- over 3000 m
- 500–3000 m
- under 500 m

population

persons per sq km
- over 50
- 10–50
- 1–10
- under 1

annual rainfall

- over 2000 mm
- 500–2000 mm
- under 500 mm

land use

- desert
- grassland
- tundra
- warm temperate mixed forest
- monsoon forest
- mixed coniferous & deciduous forest
- savannah
- xerophytic woodland
- tropical rain forest
- mountain region

ASIA: HISTORY

c. 3000 BC	First dynasties of Mesopotamia; king Gilgamesh.
2800–2205	Sage Kings in China, earliest Chinese dynasty; civilization spread to all of China.
2500–1500	Indus Valley civilization.
1950–1282	First Babylonian Empire.
625	Chaldeans established second Babylonian Empire.
560	Birth of Buddha.
551	Birth of Confucius.
538	Cyrus the Great defeated last Babylonian ruler and founded Persian Empire.
334–326	Alexander the Great conquered the Persian Empire.
246	Great Wall of China.
166	Tartar invasion of China.
93 AD	Mesopotamia became part of Roman Empire.
320–550	Gupta dynasty in India.
570	Birth of Muhammad.
1192	First Muslim kingdom of India established.
1280	Kublai Khan became emperor of China.
1395	Tamerlanc defeated the Golden Horde.
1398	Tamerlane captured Delhi.
1526	Babur established Mogul empire (which lasted until 1857).
1600	British East India Company chartered.
1757	Clive defeated the Nawal of Bengal at Plassey.
1840–02	Opium War between Britain and China ended with ceding of Hong Kong to Britain.
1854	US Commodore Perry forced Japanese shogun to grant commercial treaty.
1857–08	Indian Mutiny.
1904–05	Russo–Japanese War.
1931	Japan invades China.
1941	Japan attacked US fleet at Pearl Harbor.
1947	India and Pakistan gained independence.
1949	Chiang Kai-Shek forced by Chinese Communists to flee to Formosa.
1950	Korean War.
1954	End of French war in Indo-China.
1965	US troops sent to fight North Vietnamese in large numbers.
1971	E Pakistan declared independence as Bangladesh.
1976	Death of Mao Zedong.
1980	Trial of Jiang Qing.
1986	Agreement on future sovereignty of Hong Kong between British and Chinese governments.

aspen a variety of ◊poplar tree.

Aspen Lodge /'æspən/ US presidential residence at the country retreat of ◊Camp David.

asphalt a mixture of different hydrocarbons forming a kind of semi-solid, brown or black bitumen. Considerable natural deposits occur round the Dead Sea and in the Philippines, Cuba, Venezuela and the Pitch Lake of Trinidad. Bituminous limestone occurs at Neufchâtel. Asphalt is mixed with rock chips to form paving material, and the purer kinds are used for insulating material and for waterproofing masonry. Asphalt can be produced artificially by the distillation of petroleum.

asphodel plant, genus *Asphodelus* belonging to the Liliaceae. *Asphodel albus*, the white asphodel or king's spear, is found in Italy and Greece, sometimes covering large areas, and providing grazing for sheep. *Asphodeline lutea* is the yellow asphodel. These beautiful plants were connected by the Greeks with the dead, and were supposed to grow in the Elysian fields.

aspidistra Asiatic plant of the family Liliaceae. The broad-leaved Chinese aspidistra *Aspidistra lurida* survives much ill-treatment as an indoor plant, and was popular in Britain in the Victorian parlour.

aspirin acetylsalicylic acid, a popular pain reliever invented by the firm Bayer, Meister & Lucius in the early 20th century, for headaches, arthritis and so on; in the long term, even moderate use may involve side effects including kidney damage and hearing defects, and it is no longer considered suitable for children under 12. However, recent medical research suggests that aspirin may be of value in preventing heart attack (myocardial infarction) and stroke.

asplenium fern of the family Aspleniaceae, and generally known as spleenwort.

Asquith /'æskwɪθ/ Herbert Henry, 1st Earl of Oxford and Asquith 1852–1928. British Liberal politician. Born in Yorkshire. Elected Member of Parliament in 1886, he was home secretary in Gladstone's 1892–95 government. He was chancellor of the Exchequer 1905–08 (when he introduced old-age pensions), and succeeded Campbell-Bannerman as prime minister in 1908. Forcing through the radical budget of his chancellor (◊Lloyd George) led him into two elections in 1910, which resulted in the Parliament Act of 1911, limiting the right of the Lords to veto legislation. His endeavours to pass the Home Rule for Ireland Bill led to the ◊Curragh Incident and incipient civil war. Unity was re-established by the outbreak of World War I, and a coalition government was formed in May 1915. However, his attitude of 'wait and see' was not adapted to all-out war, and in Dec 1916 he was replaced by Lloyd George. In 1918 the Liberal election defeat led to the eclipse of the party.

Asquith Herbert Asquith introduced old age pensions, and became British prime minister in 1908, but following criticisms within the country and the Cabinet on his war policy, a coalition government was formed. His caricature is by 'Spy', Leslie Ward.

Asquith /'æskwɪθ/ Lady Cynthia 1887–1960. British author, born Charteris. She married Herbert, second son of H H ◊Asquith, and wrote a diary of the World War I years.

ass domesticated donkey, or the wild form from which it was derived, the African wild ass *Equus asinus*; also the Asian wild ass *Equus hemionus*. They differ from horses in their smaller size, larger ears, tufted tail, dorsal stripes and characteristic bray.

Assad /'æsæd/ Hafez al 1930– . Syrian statesman, Baathist and Shia (Alawite) Muslim; he became Prime Minister after the bloodless military coup in 1970, and in 1971 was the first president to be elected by popular vote; re-elected 1978.

Assam /æ'sæm/ state of NE India.
area 78,523 sq km/30,310 sq mi
capital Dispur
towns Shilling
features half India's tea is grown here, and half its oil produced
population (1981) 19,900,000, including 12,000,000 Assamese (Hindus), 5,000,000 Bengalis (chiefly Muslim immigrants from Bangladesh), and Nepalis; and 2,000,000 native people (Christian and traditional religions); in 1983 there were massacres of Muslim Bengalis by Hindus
language Assamese
history part of British India from 1826, Assam was made a separate province in 1874, and in 1947 was included in the Dominion of India, except for most of Silhet district, which went to Pakistan. The Gara, Khasi and Jaintia tribal hill districts became the state of ◊Meghalaya in 1970. In 1972 the Mizo hill district became the union territory of ◊Mizoram.

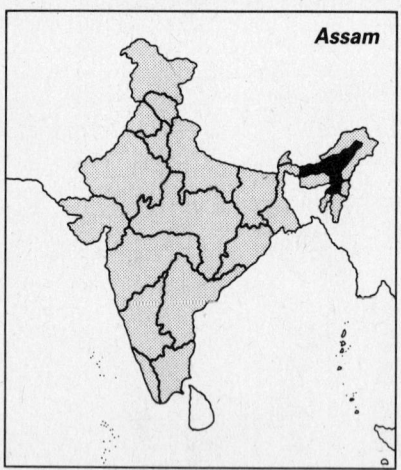

Assam

assassination murder, especially of a political, royal, or public person. The term derives from a sect of Muslim fanatics in the 11th and 12th centuries, who were reputed to take cannabis (Arabic *hashshash* 'taker of hashish') before their expeditions.

Famous Assassinations
BC
  681 Sennacherib of Assyria
  514 Hipparchus, tyrant of Athens
  336 Philip II of Macedon
  44 Julius Caesar
AD
  14 Caligula, Roman emperor
  96 Domitian
1170 Thomas à Becket
1437 James I of Scotland
1488 James III of Scotland
1584 William the Silent
1589 Henry III of France
1610 Henry IV of France
1628 Duke of Buckingham
1634 Prince Wallenstein
1793 J P Marat
1801 Paul I of Russia
1812 Spencer Perceval
1865 Abraham Lincoln
1881 J A Garfield
1881 Alexander II of Russia
1882 Lord F Cavendish
1894 M F Carnot
1900 Humbert I of Italy
1901 W McKinley
1903 Alexander and Draga of Serbia
1908 Carlos of Portugal
1913 George I of Greece
1914 Archduke Francis Ferdinand
1934 Dr Dollfuss
1934 Alexander of Yugoslavia
1940 Leon Trotsky
1942 Reinhard Heydrich
1948 Mahatma Gandhi
1948 Count Bernadotte
1951 Abdullah of Jordan
1951 Liaquat Ali Khan
1958 Feisal II (Iraq)
1963 J F Kennedy
1966 H F Verwoerd
1968 M Luther King
1968 R F Kennedy
1974 L Carrero Blanco
1975 Faisal (Saudi Arabia)
1979 Lord Mountbatten
1980 John Lennon
1984 Anwar Sadat
1984 Indira Gandhi
1986 Olof Palme

---

assault ship naval vessel with a platform for helicopters, a dock for large landing craft, tank decks, troop accommodation, and defended by missiles, machine guns and anti-aircraft guns. The Royal Navy's *Fearless* and *Intrepid* took part in the ◊Falklands landings.

assaying the determination of the quantity of a given chemical substance present in a sample. Usually it refers to determining the purity of precious metals. The assay may be carried out by 'wet' methods, when the sample is wholly or partially dissolved in some reagent (often an acid), or by 'dry' or 'fire' methods, in which fusion techniques are used.

assembly code computer-programming language closely related to the internal codes of the machine itself. It consists chiefly of a set of short mnemonics which are translated, by a program called an assembler, into ◊machine code for the computer's CPU (central processing unit)

to follow directly. In assembly language, for example, JMP means 'jump' and LDA is 'load accumulator'. Used by programmers who need to write very fast or efficient programs.

assembly line a method of mass production in which a product is built up step-by-step by successive workers adding one part at a time. American inventor Eli ◊Whitney pioneered the modern concept of industrial assembly in the 1790s, when he employed unskilled labour to assemble muskets from sets of identical precision-made parts. In 1901 Ransome Olds in the USA began mass-producing motor cars on an assembly-line principle. The method was further refined in 1913 by Henry Ford in the USA, who introduced the moving conveyor to carry the workpiece past the assembly workers. On the modern assembly line human workers now stand side by side with ◊robots.

Assent, Royal in the UK, formal consent given by a British sovereign to the passage of a bill through Parliament, after which it becomes an Act of Parliament. Usually given by Letters Patent (official document), the Lord Chancellor in the Lords and Speaker in the House of Commons merely make an announcement that consent has been given. The last instance of a royal refusal was the rejection of the Scottish Militia Bill of 1702 by Queen Anne.

asset generally, something valuable or useful. In economics, the land or property of a company or individual, payments due from bills, and anything owned that has a money value.

Assisi /ə'siːzi/ town in Umbria, Italy, 19 km/12 mi south east of Perugia. ◊St Francis was born here and is buried in the Franciscan monastery, completed in 253. The churches of St Francis are adorned with frescoes by Giotto, Cimabue, and others. Population (1971) 25,000.

Assisted Places Scheme in UK education, a scheme established in 1980 by which the government assists parents with the cost of fees at ◊independent schools, on a means-tested basis.

Assiut /æ'sjuːt/ alternative transliteration of ◊Asyut.

assizes in Britain, the courts formerly held by judges of the High Court in each county: they were abolished under the Courts Act (1971).

Associated State of the UK status with full internal government, within the ◊Commonwealth, under which Britain is responsible for external relations and defence. It is designed for countries with too few resources for full independence: the first created was ◊Antigua in 1966.

association football soccer, or ◊football played under the rules of the Football Association 1863.

Association of South East Asian Nations (ASEAN) a regional alliance formed in Bangkok in 1967; it took over the non-military role of ◊SEATO in 1975. Its members are Indonesia, Malaysia, the Philippines, Singapore, Thailand, and (from 1984) Brunei; headquarters Jakarta, Indonesia.

associative law in mathematics, the law that states that the result of performing certain consecutive operations is independent of the order in which they are performed. Thus addition

assassination Lee Harvey Oswald did not live to answer the charge of assassinating President Kennedy. Here he begins to collapse as a bullet from the gun of Jack Ruby fired at point blank range enters his abdomen at Dallas City Jail, 24 November, 1963. He died several hours later. Ruby, a 50-year-old club-owner, was then charged with Oswald's murder.

is associative because, for example 3 + (4 + 5) gives the same sum as (3 + 4) + 5. Multiplication is also associative, for example 2 × (3 × 4) gives the same product as (2 × 3) × 4; division, however, is not associative.

assortative mating in ◊population genetics, selective mating between individuals that are genetically related, or that have similar characteristics. If sufficiently consistent, assortative mating can eventually result in the evolution of two or more new ◊species.

Assuan /æ'swɑːn/ alternative transliteration of ◊Aswan.

Assy /'æsi/ village and sanatorium in Haute-Savoie, France, 994 m/3,280 ft above sea level, where the church of Nôtre Dame de Toute Grâce, begun in 1937, consecrated in 1950, is adorned with works by Braque, Chagall, Matisse, Derain, Rouault, and other artists. Population (1973) 1,400.

Assyria /ə'sɪrɪə/ empire of antiquity in the Near East. The land of Assyria originally consisted of a narrow strip of alluvial soil on each side of the Tigris, starting where the Lower Zab joins the river, and reaching to the foothills beyond Dur-Sharrukin, the old city of Sargon. The area was settled about 3500 BC, and the empire collapsed in 612 BC.

Sumerian civilization in Mesopotamia came to an end about 2500 BC, with the rise to power of Sargon of Akkad; for nearly 200 years Assyria was subject first to the dynasty of Akkad and then to the Gutians, barbarians from the north. The first Assyrian kings are mentioned during the wars following the decline of the 3rd dynasty of Ur. For many centuries yet, however, Assyria

was under Babylonian and subsequently Egyptian suzerainty. About 1450 BC a fresh resurgence of Assyria began. Under King Ashur-uballit (reigned about 1380–1340 BC) the future greatness of Assyria as a military power was laid. His work was continued by Adad-nirari I, Shalmaneser I, and Tukulti-enurta I, who conquered Babylonia and assumed the title of king of Sumer and Akkad. During the reign of Nebuchadnezzar I (1150–1110 BC), Assyria was subject to Babylonia, but Tiglath-pileser I threw off the yoke. In the Aramaean invasions, most of the ground gained was lost. From the accession of Adad-nirari II in 911 BC Assyria pursued a triumphant course of expansion and conquest, culminating in the mastery of Elam, Mesopotamia, Syria, Palestine, the Arabian marches, and finally of Egypt. Of this period the Old Testament records and many 'documents' such as the Black Obelisk celebrating the conquest of Shalmaneser III in the 9th century BC survive.

The reign of Ashur-nazir-pal II (885–860 BC) was spent in unceasing warfare, in which he is said to have introduced 'frightfulness' as evidenced by many bas-reliefs. Shalmaneser III warred against the Syrian states. At the battle of Qarqar (854 BC) the Assyrian advance received a setback, and there followed a period of decline. The final period of Assyrian ascendancy began with the accession of Tiglath-pileser III (746–728 BC). Sargon, Sennacherib, Esarhaddon, and Ashurbanipal raised Assyria to the highest peak of its glory, culminating in the conquest of Egypt by Esarhaddon in 671 BC. From this time the empire seems to have fallen

into decay, and a union of Nabopolassar of Babylonia and Cyaxares of Media led to its destruction. Nineveh was destroyed, and Assyria became a Median province and subsequently a principality of the Persian empire.

Much of Assyrian religion, law, social structure and artistic achievement was based on, or derived from, neighbouring sources. The Assyrians adopted the cuneiform script invented by the Sumerians, and took over the Sumerian pantheon, although their national god, Ashur (Assur), assumed the chief place in the cult. They adopted in the main the Sumerian structure of society. The famous library of Ashurbanipal excavated at Nineveh witnesses to the thoroughness with which Babylonian culture was being assimilated. See also ◊Babylonia.

Astaire /ə'steə/ Fred 1899–1987. American dancer. Born in Omaha, Nebraska, he danced in partnership with his sister Adele (1898–81) from 1916 until her marriage in 1932. Entering films in 1933, he appeared in *Roberta* and *Top Hat* 1935, *Follow the Fleet* 1936, *Easter Parade* 1948, *Funny Face* 1957, and others which contained many sequences he designed himself. Most famous of his partners was Ginger Rogers.

Astaire Stylish American dancer Fred Astaire and his favourite partner, Ginger Rogers. Astaire was a virtuoso dancer and perfectionist. He choreographed many of his films, which were hugely successful in the 1930s and have since become treasured classics.

Astarte /ə'stɑːti/ alternative name for the Babylonian and Assyrian goddess ◊Ishtar.

astatine a ◊halogen-like and highly radioactive element, symbol At, atomic number 85, atomic weight 210. It is made by bombarding bismuth in a ◊cyclotron (particle accelerator).

aster plant of the family Compositae, belonging to the same subfamily as the daisy. The sea aster *Aster tripolium* grows wild on sea cliffs in the south of England, but many more species are familiar as cultivated garden flowers. These include the Michaelmas daisy *Aster novi-belgii*. The China aster *Callistephus chinensis* belongs to a closely allied genus; it was introduced to Europe from China and Japan in the early 18th century.

asterisk a star-like punctuation mark (*) used to link the asterisked word with a note at the bottom of a page; to mark that certain letters are missing from a word (especially a taboo word such as f**k); or to indicate that a word or usage is nonexistent, for example, 'In English we say three boys and not *three boy'.

asteroid any of many thousands of small bodies, composed of rocks and iron, that orbit the Sun. They are also known as minor planets. Most asteroids lie in a belt between the orbits of ◊Mars and ◊Jupiter, though some are on orbits that bring them close to the Earth, and some, such as the ◊Apollo asteroids, even cross the Earth's orbit. One group, the Trojans, moves along the same orbit as Jupiter, 60° ahead and behind the planet. One unusual asteroid, Chiron, orbits beyond ◊Saturn. Asteroids are thought to be fragments left over from the formation of the ◊solar system. As many as 100,000 may exist, but their total mass is only a few hundredths the mass of the Moon. The largest is ◊Ceres, 1,000 km/621 mi in diameter. The brightest as seen from Earth is Vesta, which has a light-coloured surface. See also ◊Eros and ◊Icarus.

asthenosphere a division of the earth's structure lying beneath the ◊lithosphere, at a depth of approximately 70 km/45 mi to 250 km/160 mi. It is thought to be the soft, relatively mobile layer of the ◊mantle on which the rigid plates of the earth's surface move to produce the motions of ◊plate tectonics.

asthma recurrent difficulty in breathing in (inhaling) due to the contraction of muscles in the walls of the lungs' breathing passages. It is either allergic in origin, for example a reaction to dust, eggs, milk, the hair or scurf of an animal, or caused by a form of heart disease (cardiac asthma) and can be brought on by anxiety.

Asti /'æsti/ town in Piedmont, SE of Turin, Italy. Population (1983) 76,439. Asti province is famed for its sparkling wine.

Aston /'æstən/ Francis William 1877–1945. British physicist, who developed the ◊mass spectrometer, which can separate ◊isotopes by projecting their ◊ions (charged atoms) through a magnetic field. From 1910 he worked in the Cavendish Laboratory, Cambridge. He published his *Isotopes* and received the Nobel Prize for Chemistry in 1922. His researches were of the utmost value in the development of atomic theory.

Astor /'æstə/ prominent American and English family. *John Jacob Astor* (1763–1848) was an American millionaire. His son *William Backhouse Astor* (1792–1875), was known as the 'landlord of New York'. John Jacob's grandson *William Waldorf Astor* 1848–1919, an American diplomat and writer, became naturalized British in 1899. In 1917 he was made 1st Viscount Astor. His son *Waldorf Astor*, 2nd Viscount Astor (1879–1952), was Conservative member of parliament for Plymouth 1910–19,

when he succeeded to the peerage. He was chief proprietor of the British *Observer* newspaper. His wife was Nancy Witcher Langhorne (1879–1964) *Lady Astor*, the first woman member of parliament to take her seat in the House of Commons in 1919, when she succeeded her husband as member of parliament for Plymouth. She was also a temperance fanatic and great political hostess. Government policy was said to be decided at Cliveden, their country home.

Astrakhan /ˌæstrəˈkɑːn/ city in the USSR, on the delta of the Volga, capital of Astrakhan region. In ancient times a Tatar capital, it became Russian in 1556. It is the chief port for the Caspian fisheries. Population (1981) 493,000.

astrolabe ancient time-measuring instrument, forerunner of the sextant, used by astronomers and navigators. Astrolabes usually consisted of a flat disc with a sighting rod which could be pivoted to point at the Sun or bright stars. From the altitude of the Sun or star above the horizon, the local time could be estimated.

astrology (Greek *astron*, star; *legein*, speak) study of the relative position of the planets and stars in the belief that they influence events on earth. A strongly held belief in ancient Babylon, it spread to the Mediterranean world, and was widely held among the Greeks and Romans. In Europe during the Middle Ages astrology had a powerful influence, as kings and other public figures had their own astrologers, and astrological beliefs are reflected in Elizabethan and Jacobean literature. Astrology has no scientific basis, but has remained popular. The first edition of *Old Moore's Almanac* which gives a forecast of the year ahead, appeared in 1700, and there have been annual editions since. Astrological forecasts are also prominent in newspapers and magazines.

The astrologer 'casts a ◊horoscope' based on the date and hour of his subject's birth, that is, draws a diagram showing the position at that moment of the sun and moon, the planets, and the 12 signs of the ◊Zodiac. These heavenly bodies are supposed to represent different character traits and influences, and by observing their positions and inter-relations the astrologer professes to assess the person's character and to foretell the main outlines of his or her career.

astron large-scale cosmic impact features on the surface of the Earth, Moon, etc., caused by meteorites. The Moon has more than 300,000 craters over 1 km in diameter easily visible; those on Earth are more obscure because they have been more rapidly eroded.

astronaut term used in the West for a person making flights into space; the Russian term is ◊cosmonaut.

astronautics the science of space travel. See ◊rocket; ◊satellite; ◊space probe.

Astronomer Royal honorary post in British astronomy. Originally it was held by the Director of the Royal Greenwich Observatory; since 1972 the title of Astronomer Royal has been awarded separately. A separate post of Astronomer Royal for Scotland is attached to the directorship of the Royal Observatory, Edinburgh.

astronometry the measurement of the precise positions of stars, planets and other bodies in space. Such information is needed for practical purposes including accurate timekeeping, surveying and navigation, as well as calculating orbits and measuring distances in space. Astronometry is not concerned with the surface features or the physical nature of the body under study. Before telescopes, astronomical observations were simple astronometry. Precise astronometry has shown that stars are not fixed in position, but have a proper motion caused as they and the Sun orbit the ◊Galaxy. The nearest stars also show ◊parallax (apparent change in position), from which their distances can be calculated. The ◊European Space Agency has an astronometry satellite, Hipparcos, planned for launch in 1988. Above the distorting effects of the atmosphere, this should make even more precise measurements than ground telescopes, so refining the distance scale of space.

astronomical unit the average distance of the Earth from the Sun. 149,597,870 km/92,955,800 mi.

astronomy the science that deals with the celestial bodies – the Sun; the Moon; the planets and other members of the solar system; the stars, and the galaxies. It is concerned with the positions and motions of these bodies; with the explanation of their motions; with their distances, sizes, masses, temperatures and physical conditions.

There can be little doubt that astronomy is the oldest science in the world, since there are observational records from Babylonia, China and Ancient Egypt. The first true astronomers, however, were the Greeks such as ◊Thales, ◊Pythagoras, and ◊Hipparchus. The Greeks knew that the Earth is a sphere, and not flat as earlier peoples had believed; ◊Eratosthenes of Cyrene measured the size of the Earth with considerable accuracy. Star catalogues were drawn up, the most celebrated being that of Hipparchus. The work of the Greek philosophers was summarized by Ptolemy of Alexandria in a great book which has survived in its Arab translation, the *Almagest*. However the Greeks still regarded the Earth as the centre of the universe – though this was doubted by some philosophers, notably ◊Aristarchus of Samos, who maintained that the Earth moves round the Sun.

Ptolemy, the last famous astronomer of the Greek school, died in or about the year 180 AD, and little progress was made for some centuries. The Arabs revived the science, carrying out theoretical researches from the 8th and 9th centuries, and producing good star catalogues. Unfortunately there was a general belief in the pseudo-science of astrology, and this continued until the end of the Middle Ages.

The dawn of a new era came in 1543, when a Polish canon, ◊Copernicus, published a work entitled *De Revolutionibus Orbium Coelestium*, in which he demonstrated that the Sun, not the Earth, is the centre of our planetary system. Copernicus was wrong in many respects – for instance, he still believed that all celestial orbits must be perfectly circular – but he had taken the

ASTRONOMY – CHRONOLOGY

2300 BC Chinese astronomers made their earliest observations.

2000 BC Babylonian priests made their first observational records.

1900 BC Stonehenge was constructed: first phase.

365 BC The Chinese observed the satellites of Jupiter with the naked eye.

3rd cent. BC Aristarchus argued that the Sun is the centre of the solar system.

2nd cent. AD Ptolemy's Earth-centred system was promulgated.

1543 AD Copernicus revived the ideas of Aristarchus in *De Revolutionibus*.

1608 Lippershey invented the telescope, which was first used by Galileo in 1609.

1609 Kepler's first two laws of planetary motion were published (the third in 1619).

1632 Leiden established the world's first official observatory.

1633 Galileo's theories were condemned by the Inquisition.

1675 The Royal Greenwich Observatory was founded in England.

1687 Newton's *Principia* was published, including his law of universal gravitation.

1704 Halley predicted the return of the comet now named after him, which duly reappeared in 1758: it was last seen in 1985-86.

1781 Herschel discovered Uranus and recognised stellar systems beyond our galaxy.

1796 Laplace elaborated his theory of the origin of the solar system.

1801 Piazzi discovered the first asteroid, Ceres.

1814 Fraunhofer first studied absorption lines in the solar spectrum.

1846 Neptune was discovered by Galle and D'Arrest.

1859 Kirchhoff explained dark lines in the Sun's spectrum.

1887 The earliest photographic star charts were produced.

1889 E E Barnard took the first photographs of the Milky Way.

1890 The first photograph of the spectrum was taken.

1908 The Tunguska comet fell in Siberia.

1920 Eddington began the study of interstellar matter.

1923 Hubble proved that the galaxies are systems independent of the Milky Way, and by 1930 had confirmed that the universe is expanding.

1930 Pluto was discovered by Clyde Tombaugh at the Lowell Observatory, Arizona.

1931 Jansky founded radioastronomy.

1945 Radar contact with the Moon was established.

1948 The 200-inch Hale reflector telescope was installed at Mount Palomar, California.

1955 The Jodrell Bank radioastronomy dish in England was completed.

1957 The first Sputnik satellite (USSR) opened the age of space observation.

1962 The first X-ray source was discovered in Scorpio.

1963 The first quasar was discovered by Mount Palomar Observatory.

1967 The first pulsar was identified by Jocelyn Bell and Antony Hewish, in England.

1969 The first manned Moon landing was made by US astronauts.

1970 The black hole theory was confirmed for the first time.

1976 A 236-inch reflector telescope was installed at Mount Semirodniki (USSR); Viking probes (USA) soft-landed on Mars; experiments indicated no signs of life.

1977 Uranus was discovered to have rings; the spacecraft Voyager 1 and 2 were launched, the latter passing Jupiter and Saturn 1979-81, and Uranus 1986; due Neptune 1989.

1978 The spacecraft Pioneer Venus 1 and 2 reached Venus; a satellite of Pluto, Charon, was discovered by James Christie of the US Naval Observatory; Herculina was discovered to be the first asteroid with a satellite.

1979 The UK infra-red telescope (UKIRT) was established on Hawaii.

1985 Halley's comet returned.

1986 Voyager 2 discovered six new moons around Uranus.

fundamental step. ◊Brahe, of Denmark, increased the accuracy of observations by means of improved instruments, allied to his own personal skill, and his observations were used by the German mathematician ◊Kepler to prove the validity of the Copernican system. However, there was considerable opposition to the idea of removing the Earth from its central position in the universe; the Christian Church was openly hostile, and ironically Brahe never accepted the idea that the Earth could move round the Sun. Yet before the end of the 17th century the theoretical work of Sir Isaac Newton had placed ◊celestial mechanics on a firm footing.

The telescope was invented in or about 1608, by ◊Lippershey in Holland, and was first applied to astronomy by the Italian scientist ◊Galileo in the winter of 1609–10. Immediately Galileo made a series of spectacular discoveries. He found the four satellites of Jupiter, which gave strong support to the Copernican theory; he saw the craters of the Moon, the phases of Venus, and the myriad faint stars of the ◊Milky Way. His telescope magnified only 30 times, but before long larger telescopes were built, and official ◊observatories were established.

Galileo's telescope was a *refractor*; that is to say, it collected its light by means of a glass ◊lens or object-glass. Difficulties with this design led Newton, in 1671, to construct a *reflecting telescope*, in which the light is collected by means of a curved mirror.

Theoretical researches continued, and astronomy made rapid progress in many directions. New planets were discovered – Uranus in 1781, by ◊Herschel and Neptune in 1846, by ◊Galle. Also significant was the first measurement of the distance of a star, in 1838, when the German astronomer ◊Bessel established that the star 61 Cygni lies at a distance of about 11 light years. Astronomical spectroscopy was developed, first by Fraunhofer in Germany and then by people such as Secchi and Huggins, while Kirchhoff successfully interpreted the spectra of the Sun and stars. By the 1860s good photographs of the Moon had been obtained, and by the end of the century photographic methods had started to play a leading role in research.

Herschel, probably the greatest observer in the history of astronomy, investigated the shape of the star-system or ◊Galaxy during the latter part of the 18th century, and concluded that the stars are arranged roughly in the form of a double-convex lens. Basically Herschel was correct, though he placed our Sun near the centre of the system; in fact, it is well out toward the edge, and lies some 25,000 light-years from the galactic nucleus. Herschel also studied the luminous 'clouds' or nebulae, and made the tentative suggestion that those nebulae capable of resolution into stars might be separate galaxies, far outside our own Galaxy. It was not until 1923 that ◊Hubble, using the 2.5 m/100 in reflector at the Mount Wilson Observatory, was able to verify this suggestion. It is now known that the 'starry nebulae' are galaxies in their own right, and that they lie at immense distances. The most distant galaxy visible to the naked eye, the Great

Spiral in ◊Andromeda, is 2,000,000 light-years away; the most remote galaxy so far measured lies over 10,000 million light-years away. It was also found that galaxies tended to form groups, and that the groups were apparently receding from each other at speeds proportional to their distance.

This concept of an expanding and evolving ◊Universe at first rested largely on ◊Hubble's law, relating the distance of objects to the amount their spectra shift towards red – the 'red shift' (see ◊Doppler). Subsequent evidence derived from objects studied in other parts of the ◊electromagnetic spectrum, at radio and X-ray wavelengths, has provided confirmation. Radio astronomy had established its place in probing the structure of the Universe by demonstrating in 1954 that an optically visible distant galaxy was identical with a powerful radio source known as Cygnus A. Later analysis of the comparative number, strength and distance of radio sources suggested that in the distant past these, including the ◊quasars discovered in 1964, had been much more powerful and numerous than today. This fact suggested that the Universe has been evolving from an origin, and is not of infinite age as expected under a 'steady state' theory. The discovery in 1965 of microwave background radiation suggested that a residue survived the tremendous thermal power of the giant explosion or ◊Big Bang which brought the Universe into existence. See also ◊black hole, ◊cosmology, ◊infra-red radiation, ◊pulsar, and ◊radio astronomy.

Although the practical limit in size and efficiency of optical telescopes has apparently been reached, the siting of these and other types of telescope at new observatories in the previously neglected southern hemisphere has opened fresh areas of the sky to search. Australia has been especially to the fore in these developments. The most remarkable recent extension of the powers of astronomy to explore the Universe is in the use of rockets, satellites, space stations and space probes. Even the range and accuracy of the conventional telescope may be greatly improved free from the Earth's atmosphere. Costs have so far prevented the establishment of a large optical telescope permanently in space.

astrophysics the study of the physical nature of ◊stars, ◊galaxies and the ◊Universe. It began with the development of spectroscopy in the 19th century, which allowed astronomers to analyse the composition of stars from their light. Astrophysicists view the Universe as a vast natural laboratory in which they can study matter under conditions of temperature, pressure and density that are unattainable on Earth.

Asturias /æ'stʊəriəs/ autonomous region of N Spain (including Oviedo); population 1,127,000. It was once a separate kingdom and the eldest son of a king of Spain is still called Prince of Asturias.

Asturias /æ'stʊəriəs/ Miguel Angel 1899–1974. Guatemalan author and diplomat. He published poetry, Guatemalan legends, and novels, such as *El Presidente/The President*

astronomy

astrophysics
planetary
science
cosmology   astronomy   celestial
mechanics

1946, attacking Latin-American dictatorships and 'Yankee imperialism'. Nobel prize 1967.

Asunción /æ,suːnθi'ɒn/ capital and port of Paraguay, on the Paraguay river, founded in 1537. It is a commercial centre with docks. There are two universities. Population (1983) 708,000.

Aswan /æs'wɑːn/ town in Upper Egypt, near the High Dam 1960–70, which keeps the level of the Nile constant throughout the year without flooding; see Lake ◊Nasser. Population (1971) 144,654.

asymptote in ◊coordinate geometry, a straight line towards which a curve approaches more and more closely but never reaches. Among ◊conic sections (curves obtained by the intersection of a plane and a cone), a ◊hyperbola has two asymptotes, which in the case of a rectangular hyperbola are at right angles to each other.

Asyut /æs'juːt/ commercial centre in Upper Egypt, near the Nile, 322 km/200 mi S of Cairo. An ancient Graeco-Egyptian city, it has many tombs of 11th and 12th dynasty nobles. Population (1976) 214,000.

Atacama /,ætə'kɑːmə/ desert in N Chile; area about 80,000 sq km/31,000 sq mi. Inland are mountains, and the coastal area is rainless and barren. There are silver and copper mines and extensive nitrate deposits.

Atahualpa /,ætə'wɑːlpə/ c. 1502–1533. last of the Incas of Peru. He was taken prisoner in 1532 when the Spaniards arrived, and agreed to pay a huge ransom, but was accused of plotting against Pizarro and sentenced to be burnt. On his consenting to Christian baptism, the sentence was commuted to strangulation.

Atalanta /,ætə'læntə/ in Greek mythology, a huntress who challenged all her suitors to a foot

race; if they lost they were killed. Milanion was given three golden apples to drop by Aphrodite; this ensured that when Atalanta stopped to pick them up, she lost the race.

Atatürk /'ætətɜːk/ Kemal 1881–1938. name assumed in 1934 by Mustafa Kemal Pasha, Turkish statesman and soldier; it means 'Father of the Turks'. Born at Salonika, he was banished in 1904 for joining a revolutionary society. Later he was pardoned and promoted, and was largely responsible for the successful defence of the Dardanelles against the British in 1915. In 1918 after Turkey had been defeated he was sent into Anatolia to carry through the demobilization of the Turkish forces in accordance with the armistice terms, but instead established a provisional government opposed to that of Constantinople (under Allied control), and in 1921 led the Turkish armies against the Greeks who had occupied a large part of Asia Minor. He checked them at the 21-day battle of the Sakaria, 23 Aug to 13 Sept 1921, for which he was granted the title of Ghazi (the Victorious) and within a year had expelled the Greeks from Turkish soil. War with the British was averted by his diplomacy and Turkey in Europe passed under Kemal's control. On 29 Oct 1923, Turkey was proclaimed a republic with Kemal as first president. He ruled as virtual dictator, embarking upon a policy of consistent and radical westernization.

Atatürk The maker of modern Turkey, Kemal Atatürk, was a dictator who introduced many social and administrative reforms which affected Turkish religion, justice, education, language, and the status of women.

atavism (Latin *atavus* 'ancestor') in ◊genetics, the reappearance of a characteristic not apparent in the immediately preceding generations; in psychology, the manifestation of primitive forms of behaviour.

ataxia medical term meaning lack of muscular coordination, caused by brain disease.

Atget /æ'dʒeɪ/ Eugène 1857–1927. French photographer. He took up photography at the age of 40, and for 30 years documented urban Paris, leaving a huge body of work.

Athabasca /,æθə'bæskə/ lake and river in Alberta and Saskatchewan, Canada, with huge tar sand deposits (source of the hydrocarbon mixture 'heavy oil') to the SW of the lake.

Athanasian creed one of the three ancient creeds of the Christian Church. Mainly a definition of the Trinity and Incarnation, it was written many years after the death of ◊Athanasius, but was attributed to him as the chief upholder of Trinitarian doctrine.

Athanasius, Saint /ˌæθəˈneɪʃəs/ 298–373. Christian bishop of Alexandria, supporter of the doctrines of the Trinity and Incarnation. He was a disciple of St Anthony the hermit, and an opponent of ◊Arianism in the great Arian controversy. Arianism was officially condemned at the council of ◊Nicaea in 325, and in 328 Athanasius was appointed bishop of Alexandria. Banished in 335 by the emperor Constantine because of his intransigence towards the defeated Arians, in 346 he was recalled but suffered three more banishments before his final reinstatement about 366. The ◊Athanasian creed was not actually written by him, although it reflects his views.

atheism non-belief in, or the positive denial of, the existence of a god or gods. In Western philosophy, atheism takes many forms and expressions. *Dogmatic atheism* asserts that there is no God. *Sceptical atheism* maintains that the finite human mind is so constituted as to be incapable of discovering that there is or is not a God. *Critical atheism* holds that the evidence for theism is inadequate. This is akin to *philosophical atheism*, which fails to find evidence of a God manifest in the universe. *Speculative atheism* comprises the belief of those who, like ◊Kant, find it impossible to demonstrate the existence of God. A related concept is agnosticism, the assertion that knowledge of a God is impossible, or that the answer cannot be known with certainty.
◊Buddhism has been called an atheistic religion since it does not postulate any Supreme Being. The ◊Jains are similarly atheistic; and so are those who adopt the Sankhya system of philosophy in ◊Hinduism. Following the revolution of 1917 Soviet Russia and later Communist states, for example, Albania, adopted an atheist outlook.

Athelney, Isle of /ˈæθəlni/ area of firm ground in marshland near Taunton in Devon, England. In 878 the headquarters of King ◊Alfred when he was in hiding from the Danes, it was here that the legend of his burning the cakes is set.

Athelstan /ˈæθəlstən/ c. 895–939. King of the Mercians and West Saxons. Son of Edward the Elder and grandson of Alfred the Great, he was crowned king in 925 at Kingston-upon-Thames. He subdued parts of Cornwall and Wales, and in 937 defeated the Welsh, Scots, and Danes at Brunanburh.

Athena /əˈθiːnə/ in Greek mythology, the goddess (Roman ◊Minerva) of war, wisdom, and the arts and crafts, who was supposed to have sprung fully-armed from the head of ◊Zeus. Her chief cult centre was Athens, where the Parthenon was dedicated to her. In Rome a statue of her (the 'Palladium'), allegedly brought by ◊Aeneas from Troy, was kept in the temple of ◊Vesta.

Athens /ˈæθɪnz/ capital city of modern Greece and of ancient Attica. Situated 8 km/5 mi inland NE of its port of Piraeus on the Gulf of Aegina, it is built around the rocky hills of the Acropolis 169 m/412 ft and the Areopagus 112 m/370 ft, and is overlooked from the NE by the hill of Lycabettus 277 m/909 ft. It lies in the south of the central plain of Attica, watered by the mountain streams of Cephissus and Ilissus. The ◊Acropolis dominates the city. Here stand architectural remains of the great days of ancient Greece, for example, the Parthenon, the Erechtheum, and the temple of Athena Nike. Near the site of the ancient Agora (market place) stands the Theseum, and south of the Acropolis is the theatre of Dionysus. To the SE stand the gate of Hadrian and the columns of the temple of Olympian Zeus. Nearby is the marble stadium built about 330 BC and restored in 1896.
The site was first inhabited about 3000 BC and Athens became the capital of a united Attica before 700 BC. Captured and sacked by the Persians in 480 BC, subsequently under Pericles it was the first city of Greece in power and culture. After the death of Alexander the Great the city fell into comparative decline, but it flourished as an intellectual centre until 529 AD, when the philosophical schools were closed by Justinian. In 1458 it was captured by the Turks who held it until 1833; it was chosen as the capital of modern Greece in 1834. Among the modern buildings are the Royal Palace and several museums. There is an international airport at Hellenikon. Population (1981) 885,150.

atherosclerosis medical term meaning thickening of the lining of the arteries, thus hindering blood flow and increasing the risk of heart attack or stroke by the formation of a blood clot. It is associated with a high ◊cholesterol diet.

athletics competitive track and field events, especially forms of running, jumping, walking, ◊throwing. Among the Greeks, vase paintings show that competitive athletics were established at least by 1600 BC (◊Olympic Games). However, the concept of the unpaid amateur is a recent innovation, ancient athletes having been well paid and sponsored. ◊Aristotle paid the expenses of a boxer contestant at Olympia, and chariot races were sponsored by the Greek city states. Athletics have recently been dominated by the 'world record'; development of computer selection of the best potential competitors and analysis of motion for greatest speed, and so on; specialization of equipment for maximum performance (for example, glass fibre vaulting poles, foam landing pads, aerodynamically designed javelins, composition running tracks), and the unlawful use of drugs, such as ◊anabolic steroids and growth hormones.
1984 *Olympic Champions* The 23rd Olympics were held in Los Angeles 1984, from 28 Jul to 12 Aug. Track and field champions:
men/women
100 metres Carl Lewis *(USA)*/Evelyn Ashford *(USA)*
200 metres Carl Lewis *(USA)*/Valerie Brisco-Hooks *(USA)*

400 metres Alonzo Babers *(USA)*/Valerie Brisco-Hooks *(USA)*
800 metres Joachim Cruz *(Brazil)*/Doina Melinte *(Romania)*
1,500 metres Sebastian Coe *(UK)*/Gabriella Dorio *(Italy)*
3,000 metres Maricica Puica *(Romania)*
5,000 metres Said Aouita *(Morocco)*
10,000 metres Alberto Cova *(Italy)*
marathon Carlos Lopes *(Portugal)*/Joan Benoit *(USA)*
100 metres hurdles Benita Fitzgerald-Brown *(USA)*
110 metres hurdles Roger Kingdom *(USA)*
400 metres hurdles Edwin Moses *(USA)*/Nawal El Moutawakel *(Morocco)*
3,000 metres steeplechase Julius Korir *(Kenya)*
4 × 100 metres relay USA/USA
4 × 400 metres relay USA/USA
20,000 metres walk Ernesto Canto *(Mexico)*
50,000 metres walk Raul Gonzalez *(Mexico)*
high jump Dietmar Moegenburg *(West Germany)*/Ulrike Meyfarth *(West Germany)*)
pole vault Pierre Quinon *(France)*
long jump Carl Lewis (USA)/Anisoara Cusmir-Stanciu *(Romania)*
triple jump Al Joyner *(USA)*
shot put Alessandro Andrei *(Italy)*/Claudia Losch *(West Germany)*
discus Rolf Danneberg *(West Germany)*/Ria Stalman *(Holland)*
hammer Juha Tiainen *(Finland)*
javelin Arto Haerkoenen *(Finland)*/Tessa Sanderson *(UK)*
decathlon Daley Thompson *(UK)*
heptathlon Glynnis Nunn *(Australia)*
World Cross Country Championship first held in 1903 as the International Championships, it came under the auspices of the International Amateur Athletic Federation in 1973.
men -individual/women -individual
1977 Leon Schotts *(Belgium)*/Carmen Valero *(Spain)*
1978 John Treacy *(Ireland)*/Grete Waitz *(Norway)*
1979 John Treacy *(Ireland)*/Grete Waitz *(Norway)*
1980 Craig Virgin *(USA)*/Grete Waitz *(Norway)*
1981 Craig Virgin *(USA)*/Grete Waitz *(Norway)*
1982 Mohamad Kedir *(Ethiopia)*/Maricica Puica *(Romania)*
1983 Bekele Debele *(Ethiopia)*/Grete Waitz *(Norway)*
1984 Carlos Lopes *(Portugal)*/Maricica Puica *(Romania)*
1985 Carlos Lopes *(Portugal)*/Zola Budd *(England)*
1986 John Ngugi *(Kenya)*/Zola Budd *(England)*
1987 John Ngugi *(Kenya)*/Annette Sergent *(France)*
men -team/women -team
1977 Belgium/USSR
1978 France/Romania
1979 England/USA
1980 England/USSR
1981 Ethiopia/USSR
1982 Ethiopia/USSR

1983 Ethiopia/USA
1984 Ethiopia/USA
1985 Ethiopia/USA
1986 Kenya/UK
1987 Kenya/USA
World Records some of the principal world records as at 1 August 1987
men
100 metres 9.93 Calvin Smith *(USA)*
200 metres 19.72 Pietro Mennea *(Italy)*
400 metres 43.86 Lee Evans *(USA)*
800 metres 1:41.73 Sebastian Coe *(UK)*
1,500 metres 3:29.46 Said Aouita *(Morocco)*
one mile 3:46.32 Steve Cram *(UK)*
5,000 metres 12:58.39 Said Aouita *(Morocco)*
10,000 metres 27:13.81 Fernando Mamede *(Portugal)*
110 metres hurdles 12.93 Renaldo Nehemiah *(USA)*
400 metres hurdles 47.02 Edwin Moses *(USA)*
high jump 2.42 Patrick Sjoberg *(Sweden)*
long jump 8.90 Bob Beamon *(USA)*
triple jump 17.97 Willie Banks *(USA)*
pole vault 6.03 Sergei Bubka *(USSR)*
decathlon 8,847 Daley Thompson *(UK)*
women
100 metres 10.76 Evelyn Ashford *(USA)*
200 metres 21.71 Marita Koch *(East Germany)*
400 metres 47.60 Marita Koch *(East Germany)*
800 metres 1:53.28 Jarmila Kratochvilova *(Czechoslovakia)*
1,500 metres 3:52.47 Tatyana Kazankina *(USSR)*
one mile 4:16.71 Mary Decker *(USA)*
3,000 metres 8:22.62 Tatyana Kazankina *(USSR)*
10,000 metres 30:13.74 Ingrid Kristiansen *(Norway)*
100 metres hurdles 12.26 Yordanka Donkova *(Bulgaria)*
400 metres hurdles 52.94 Marina Stepanova *(USSR)*
high jump 2.08 Stefka Kostadinova *(Bulgaria)*
long jump 7.45 Heike Dreschler *(East Germany)*
javelin 78.90 Petra Felke *(East Germany)*
heptathlon 7,161 Jackie Joyner *(USA)*.

Athos /'eɪθɒs/ a mountainous peninsula on the Macedonian coast of Greece. Its peak is 2,033 m/6,670 ft high. The promontory is occupied by a community of 20 Basilian monasteries inhabited by some 3,000 monks and lay brothers.

Atkins /'ætkɪnz/ Tommy. Popular name for the British soldier. The earliest discoverable use of the name is in a specimen in an official handbook circulated at the end of the Napoleonic War. A story that Tommy Atkins was a British soldier mortally wounded under Wellington in 1794, and that the Duke chose his name some 50 years later, seems to have first appeared in an article by Colonel Newnham-Davis in *Printer's Pie*.

Atlanta /ət'læntə/ capital and largest city of Georgia, USA. Originally named Terminus in 1837, and renamed in 1845, it was burned by General Sherman during the American Civil War in 1864. It has two universities and a college founded in 1885 for black students. There are Ford and Lockheed assembly plants, and it is the headquarters of Coca-Cola. Nearby Stone Mountain Memorial shows the Confederate heroes Jefferson Davis, Robert E Lee, and Stonewall Jackson on horseback. Population (1980) 425,000.

Atlantic, Battle of the the continuous battle fought in the Atlantic Ocean throughout World War II (1939–45) by the sea and air forces of Britain and Germany. The battle opened on the first night of the war, when on 4 Sept 1939 the Donaldson liner, *Athenia*, sailing from Glasgow to New York, was torpedoed by a German submarine off the Irish coast. Germany tried U-boats, surface-raiders, indiscriminate mine-laying, and aircraft, but every method was successfully countered by, for example, the convoy system and degaussing. Outstanding incidents were the engagements in which the armed merchantmen *Rawalpindi* (23 Nov 1939) and *Jervis Bay* (5 Nov 1940) were sunk by German warships, and the destruction of the great German battleship *Bismarck* on 27 May 1941. The total number of U-boats destroyed by the Allies during the whole war was nearly 800. At least 2,200 convoys of 75,000 merchant ships crossed the Atlantic.

Atlantic Charter declaration issued by British Prime Minister Churchill and US President Roosevelt during World War II following meetings in Aug 1941. It stated that Britain and the USA sought no territorial gains; desired no territorial changes not acceptable to the peoples concerned; respected the rights of all peoples to choose their own form of government; wished to see self-government restored to the occupied countries; would promote access by all states to trade and raw materials; desired international collaboration for the raising of economic standards; hoped to see a peace affording security to all nations and enabling them to cross the seas without hindrance; and proposed the disarmament of the aggressor states as a preliminary to general disarmament. The Charter was largely a propaganda exercise to demonstrate public solidarity between the Allies.

Atlantic City /ət'læntɪk 'sɪti/ seaside resort in New Jersey, USA. It is noted for its 'boardwalk'; and the Miss America contest has been held here since 1921. Formerly a family resort, it has become a centre for casino gambling, which was legalized in New Jersey in the 1970s. Population (1980) 48,000.

Atlantic College international educational experiment conceived by Kurt ◊Hahn and Air Marshal Sir Lawrence Darvell. The first Atlantic College (for boys of 17–18 drawn from N America and Europe) was opened in 1962 in St Donat's castle (once owned by W R ◊Hearst), near Cardiff in Wales; there are others in Singapore and Vancouver Island, Canada.

Atlantic Ocean sea lying between Europe and Africa to the east and the Americas to the west, probably named after ◊Atlantis. Area of Atlantic Ocean basin 81,500,000 sq km/31,500,000 sq mi; including Arctic Ocean, and Antarctic seas, 106,200,000 sq km/41,000,000 sq mi. The average depth is 3 km/2 mi; greatest depth the Puerto Rico Trench 9,219 m/27,498 ft. The Mid-Atlantic Ridge, of which the Azores, Ascension, St Helena and Tristan da Cunha form part, divides it from N to S Lava welling up from this central area annually increases the distance between South America and Africa. The North Atlantic is the saltiest of the main oceans, and it has the largest tidal range.

Atlantis /ət'læntɪs/ legendary island continent, said to have sunk c. 9600 BC, following underwater convulsions. Although the Atlantic Ocean is probably named after it, the structure of the sea bottom rules out its ever having existed there. The story told by ◊Plato (derived from an account by Egyptian priests) may refer to the volcanic eruption which destroyed Santorini in the ◊Cyclades north of Crete, c. 1500 BC. The ensuing earthquakes and tidal waves brought about the collapse of the empire of Minoan Crete.

Atlas /'ætləs/ in Greek mythology, one of the ◊Titans who revolted against the gods; as a punishment Atlas was compelled to support the heavens upon his head and shoulders. Growing weary, he asked Perseus to turn him into stone, and he was transformed into Mount ◊Atlas.

atlas the use of the word to denote a book of maps was introduced in the 16th century by ◊Mercator; such books had a frontispiece showing ◊Atlas supporting the globe. The first modern atlas was the *Theatrum orbis terrarum* 1570; the first English atlas has a collection of the counties of England and Wales by Christopher Saaxon 1579.

Atlas Mountains mountain system of NW Africa, stretching 2,400 km/1,500 mi from the Atlantic coast of Morocco to the Gulf of Gabes, Tunisia, and lying between the Mediterranean on the north and the Sahara on the south. The highest peak is Mount Toubkal 4,165 m/13,664 ft. Geologically the Atlas Mountains compare with the ◊Alps in age, but their structure is much less complex. They are recognized as the continuation of the great Tertiary fold mountain systems of Europe.

Atlas rocket US rocket, originally designed and built as an intercontinental missile, but subsequently adapted for space use. Atlas rockets launched astronauts in the Mercury series into orbit, as well as numerous other satellites and space probes.

atman in ◊Hinduism, the individual soul or the eternal essential self.

atmosphere the mixture of gases that surrounds the earth, prevented from escaping by the pull of the earth's gravity. As we go higher in the atmosphere, a smaller and smaller fraction of it is 'resting' above us, so atmospheric pressure decreases. In its lowest layer, the *troposphere*, the atmospheric pressure consists of nitrogen (78 per cent) and oxygen (21 per cent), both in molecular form (two atoms bounded together). The other 1 per cent is largely argon, but there are very small quantities of other gases, as well as water vapour. The troposphere is heated by the earth, which is warmed by infrared and visible radiation from the sun. Warm air rises in the troposphere, cooling as it does so. This is the primary cause of rain and most other weather phenomena.
Infrared and visible radiations form only that part of the sun's output of electromagnetic radiation. Almost all the shorter- wavelength

ultraviolet radiation is filtered out by the upper
layers of the atmosphere. The filtering process is
an active one: at heights above about 50 km/31
mi ultraviolet photons collide with atoms,
knocking out electrons to create a ◊plasma of
electrons and positively charged ions. The
resulting *ionosphere* acts as a reflector of radio
waves, enabling radio transmissions to 'hop'
between widely separated points on the earth's
surface. As shown on the diagram, waves of
different wavelengths are reflected best at
different heights. The collisions between
ultraviolet photons and atoms lead to a heating
of the upper atmosphere, though as we descend
from a great height through the *thermosphere* the
temperature drops as the high-energy photons
have progressively been absorbed in collisions.
Between the thermosphere and the tropopause
(at which the warming effect of the earth starts
to be felt) there is a 'warm bulge' in the
temperature vs. height graph, at a level called
the *stratopause*. This is due to longer-wavelength
ultraviolet photons that have survived their
journey through the upper layers; now they
encounter molecules and split them apart into
atoms. These atoms eventually bond together
again, but often in different combinations. In
particular, many ozone molecules (oxygen atom
triplets) are formed. Ozone is a better absorber
of ultraviolet than even ordinary (two-atom)
oxygen, and it is the *ozone layer* that prevents
lethal amounts of ultraviolet from reaching the
earth's surface.

Far above the atmosphere, as so far described, lie
the *Van Allen radiation belts*. These are regions
in which high-energy charged particles
travelling outwards from the sun (as the so-called
solar wind) have been captured by the earth's
magnetic field. The outer belt (at about 1,600
km/1,000 mi) contains mainly protons, the inner
belt (at about 2,000 km/1,250 mi) contains
mainly electrons. Sometimes electrons spiral
down towards the earth, especially at polar
latitudes, where the magnetic field is strongest.
When such particles collide with atoms and ions
in the thermosphere, light is emitted. This is the
origin of the glows visible in the sky as the *aurora
borealis* (northern lights) and the *aurora
australis* (southern lights). A fainter, more
widespread, *airglow* is caused by a similar
mechanism.

atmosphere a unit of pressure (atm) equal to
15 lb/in², 101,325 pascals or 760 mmHg; the
actual pressure exerted by the atmosphere
fluctuates around this value, which is the
standard at sea level and 0°C used with reference
to very high pressures.

atmospheric pollution see ◊pollution.

atoll a ◊coral reef surrounding a lagoon.

atom name given to the very small, discrete
particles of which all matter is composed. There
are 92 kinds of atom occurring naturally, which
correspond to the 92 elements. They differ in
chemical behaviour and cannot be broken up by
chemical means to anything simpler. Belief in
the existence of atoms dates back to the ancient
Greek natural philosophers. Atoms are much too
small to be seen even by the microscope – the
largest (caesium) is 0.000,000,5 mm in diameter

atmosphere

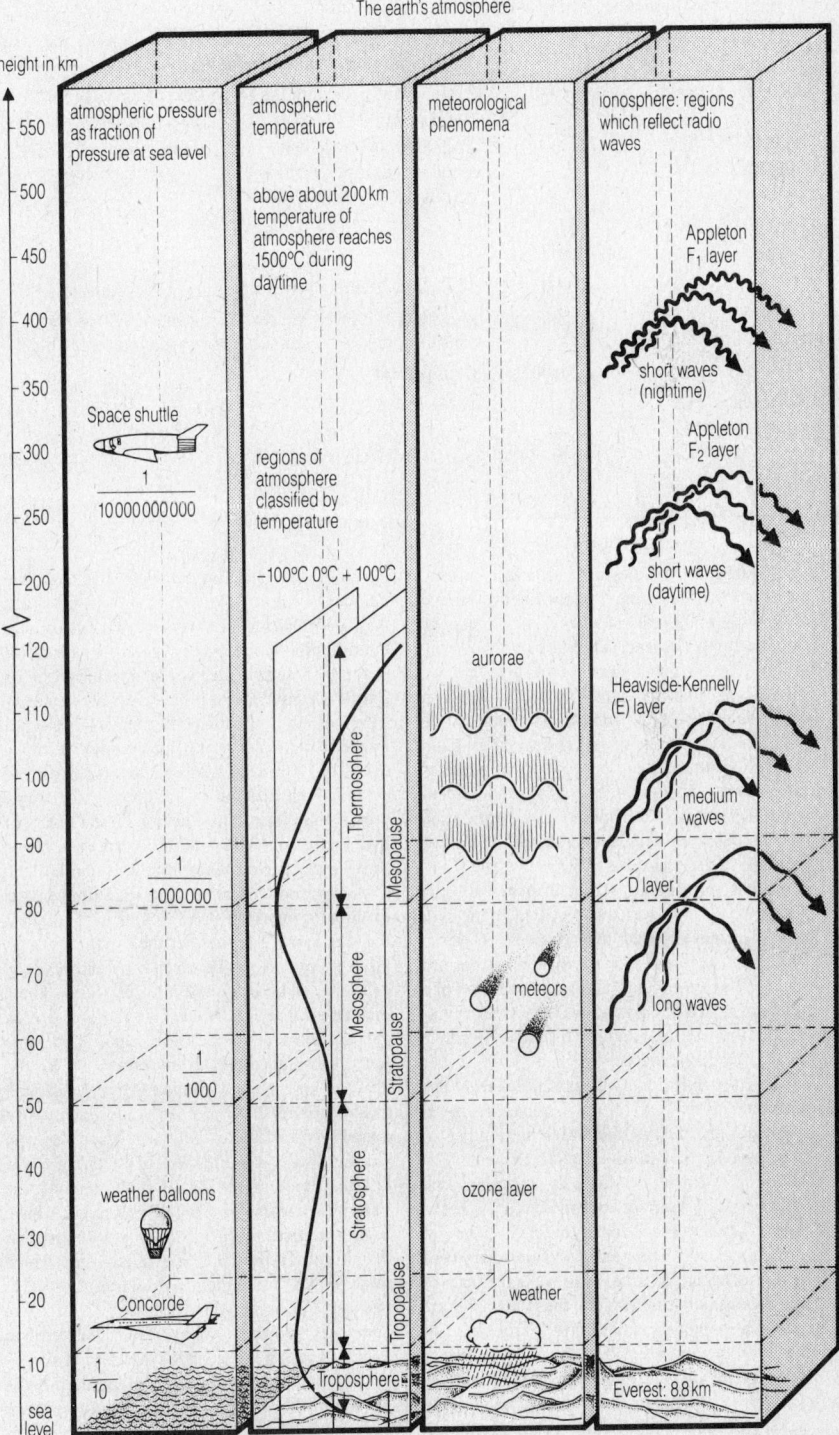

The earth's atmosphere

COMPOSITION OF THE ATMOSPHERE

Air is primarily a mixture of nitrogen, oxygen, and carbon dioxide, but with minute traces of other gases.

Gas	Symbol	% Volume	Role
Nitrogen	N	78.08	Cycled through human activities and through the action of micro-organisms on animal and plant waste
Oxygen	O_2	20.94	Cycled mainly through the respiration of animals and plants and through the action of photosynthesis
Carbon dioxide	CO_2	0.03	Cycled through respiration and photosynthesis in exchange reactions with oxygen. It is also a product of burning fossil fuels
Argon	Ar	0.093	
Neon	Ne	0.0018	
Helium	He	0.0005	Chemically inert and with only a few industrial uses
Ozone	O_3	0.00006	A product of oxygen molecules split into single atoms by the sun's radiation and unaltered oxygen molecules
Hydrogen	H_2	0.00005	Unimportant
Krypton	Kr	Trace	
Xenon	Xe	Trace	

(0.000,01 in) – and they are in constant motion. Methods for detecting the presence of single atoms all make use of effects which can be produced by the energy of a rapidly-moving atom. ▷Rutherford showed that atoms of certain radioactive elements spontaneously emit alpha rays (single atoms of helium) at about 16,000 km/10,000 mi a second. At this speed an atom has sufficient energy to produce a tiny speck of light when it hits a thin layer of phosphorescent zinc sulphide, and this momentary scintillation can be observed with a microscope. It is then possible to determine its path.

The first scientist to gather evidence for the existence of atoms was John ▷Dalton, in the 19th century, who believed that every atom was a complete unbreakable entity. Rutherford showed by experiment that an atom consists of a nucleus, a particle only one 10,000th as big across as the atom itself, surrounded by units of negative charge called *electrons*.

All electrons have identical mass and charge. The different properties of the various chemical elements are due to the different number of electrons in the atom of each element. The simplest element, hydrogen, contains one electron; each atom of carbon contains six; the most complex atom found naturally, that of uranium, has 92. The mass of an atom of any kind is several thousand times as great as the mass of the electrons it contains. In their normal state atoms have no excess of electric charge. Except for hydrogen, the atomic nucleus is composed of two kinds of particle, the *proton* and the *neutron*. Each proton has a positive electric charge, equal in magnitude to that of the negative electron; a neutron has no charge. Proton and neutron have nearly equal mass, about 1,839 times as great as the mass of the electron. The number of protons within the atomic nucleus equals the number of electrons surrounding it. See also ▷atomic number.

Atoms which have the same number of protons but differ in their number of neutrons are called isotopes; these have identical chemical properties since they have the same number of electrons. Most of the chemical elements consist of mixtures of two or more isotopes; for example, about one atom in 4,000 of natural hydrogen contains one neutron in addition to the single proton that forms the nucleus of the ordinary hydrogen atom. This kind of hydrogen is called heavy hydrogen or deuterium. At the other end of the ▷periodic table, natural uranium consists of three isotopes, U^{234}, U^{235}, and U^{238}, the last forming over 99 per cent of the mixture.

High-energy physics research has discovered the existence of other sub-atomic particles. These include anti-particles (such as the anti-proton and anti-neutron) which are opposite in some properties but identical in others to known charged and neutral particles; hyperons, with masses greater than protons; and mesons, with masses intermediate between electrons and protons. More than 300 kinds of particle are now known. Experiments by ▷CERN and at the Fermi laboratory (▷Fermilab) in the USA have suggested that these particles are themselves made up of sub-particles, known as quarks, which may be the fundamental building blocks of matter. However, some sub-atomic particles have been shown to change from one form to another and to behave in a way that is not always predictable (see ▷uncertainty priciple). This is something that Einstein himself was unwilling to accept – that chance rather than exact physical law is at the heart of the Universe. See also ▷determinism.

Atoms as a whole are held together by the electrical forces of attraction between each negative electron and the positive protons within the nucleus. The latter *repel* one another with relatively enormous forces; a nucleus holds together only because other forces, not of a simple electrical character, attract the protons and neutrons to one another. These additional forces act only so long as the protons and neutrons are virtually in contact with one another. If, therefore, a fragment of a complex nucleus, containing some protons becomes only slightly loosened from the main agglomeration of neutrons and protons, the strong natural repulsion between the protons will cause this fragment to fly apart from the rest of the nucleus at high speed. As it does so, it carries with it energy that is very much greater than the energy released in chemical reactions between atoms – reactions which involve only the weak forces existing between the outer electrons of the atoms. It is by such fragmentation of atomic nuclei (*nuclear fission*) that 'atomic energy' (more strictly nuclear energy) is released.

Energy is also released by the process of *nuclear fusion*, as in the sun. This involves the building up of more complex nuclei by the combination, or fusion, of simpler ones, such as deuterium and lithium, as has been attempted in the JET (Joint European Torus) experiment. Plasma would be held in a strong magnetic field at 50– 100 million °C and if a method could be found to maintain the correct temperature and densities for the requisite time, tritium, an isotope of hydrogen produced from the deuterium and lithium, would fuse to form heavier elements. The method involves no radioactive waste disposal problems, only a small quantity of commonly available 'fuel' is consumed and the amount of energy released in such a controlled thermonuclear reaction is greater than with nuclear fission.

Some of the most complex natural nuclei, for example those of uranium and radium, are ▷radioactive, that is, they spontaneously disintegrate with the emission of a fragment containing 2 neutrons and 2 protons, an ▷alpha particle. Out of a large number of atoms of U^{238}, for example, about half of them will have disintegrated after about 4,000 million years; so the ▷half-life of U^{238} is 4,000 million. See also ▷molecule.

atom bomb bomb deriving its explosive force from ▷nuclear energy. The possibility was explored in Britain from 1940, but work was transferred to the USA after its entry into World War II. As the Manhattan Project, it was under the direction of ▷Oppenheimer at ▷Los Alamos. See also ▷bomb.

atomic energy alternative name for ▷nuclear energy.

atomic number the number of protons in the nucleus of an ▷atom of an element; it is given the symbol Z. The atomic number is equivalent to the number of electrons in an electrically neutral atom of that element. The 105 elements are numbered 1 (hydrogen) to 105 (hahnium) in the ▷periodic table. See ▷chemistry and ▷inorganic chemistry.

atomic physics the study of the properties of the ▷atom.

atom bomb Giant waterspout at Bikini Island after the explosion of the atom bomb in underwater tests. The dark streak in the column (left) was the approximate position of the battleship sunk by the blast.

atomic time the time derived from integrating seconds intervals as realized by caesium beam atomic clocks. In 1967 a new definition of the second was adopted in the international system of units as the duration of 9,192,631,770 periods of the radiation corresponding to the transition between two hyperfine levels of the ground state of the caesium-133 atom. The International Atomic Time Scale is based on clock data from a number of countries; it is a continuous scale in days, hours, minutes, and seconds from the origin on 1 Jan 1958, when the Atomic Time Scale was made 0h 0m 0s when Greenwich Mean Time was 0h 0m 0s.

atomic weight in chemistry, the weight of a single atom of an element, measured on a scale on which the weight of an oxygen atom is 16. The more correct term is atomic mass, although it is not commonly used. Atomic weights are relative numbers, not absolute weights.

atomizer a device that produces a spray of fine droplets of liquid. A scent spray is a common kind of atomizer. It consists of a bottle containing the scent, into which dips a vertical tube connected at the top with a horizontal tube. At one end of the horizontal tube is a nozzle, at the other a rubber bulb. When the bulb is squeezed, air rushes over the top of the vertical tube and out through the nozzle. Following ◊Bernoulli's effect, the pressure at the top of the vertical tube is reduced, allowing the scent to rise. The air stream picks up the scent, breaks it up into tiny drops and carries it out of the nozzle as a spray. Paint spray guns and carburettors also use the principle of the atomizer.

Aton in ancient Egypt, the sun's disc as an emblem of the single deity whose worship was enforced by ◊Ikhnaton.

atonality in music, name given to a modern system of composition, in which there is an absence of ◊key. Towards the end of the 19th century, the chromaticism of such composers as ◊Liszt and ◊Wagner, and later ◊Debussy, had the effect of leading the music away from the original key. The first completely atonal music was composed by ◊Schoenberg from 1909 onwards, and by 1923 systematized by him in works employing the 12-note row; however, Schoenberg and his followers reject the term atonality as meaningless. Their system, though totally different from that which underlies diatonic harmony, is by no means arbitrary but is bound by strict rules. Exponents of atonality include Schoenberg, ◊Berg, ◊Webern, ◊Stockhausen, ◊Boulez, and many other modern composers.

Atonement, Day of Jewish holy day (Yom Kippur) held on the tenth day of Tishri (Sept-Oct), the seventh month of the Jewish year. It is a day of fasting, penitence, and cleansing from sin.

atonement in Christian theology, the doctrine (a 'bringing to be at one') that Christ suffered on the cross to bring about reconciliation and forgiveness between God and humans.

ATP (adenosine triphosphate) ◊nucleotide molecule found in all ◊cells. It can yield large amounts of energy, used to drive many biological processes, including muscle contraction and the synthesis of complex molecules needed by the cell. ATP is formed during photosynthesis in plants, or by the breakdown of food molecules during ◊metabolism in animals. In metabolism the food's energy is 'captured' in the form of ATP, to be used later when needed. Thus ATP is often called the 'energy currency' of the cell.

atrium in architecture, an inner, open courtyard.

atropine an ◊alkaloid, the active principle of deadly nightshade, or belladonna, named from the Greek *Atropos*, one of the three Fates who cut people's lives short. As atropine sulphate, it is administered as a mild anti-spasmodic drug.

Attainder, Bill of a legislative device which allowed the English parliament to declare guilt and impose a punishment on an individual without bringing the matter before the courts. Such bills were used during the Wars of the Roses, and under Henry VIII, before being revived by James I and Charles I, whose most famous bill of attainder involved the Earl of ◊Strafford in 1641. The last bill of attainder was passed against Lord Edward Fitzgerald for leading the rebellion in Ireland in 1798. The use of the device has generally been deplored as it did not require the accusers to prove their case and was usually employed to punish 'new' crimes of treason which were detrimental to those in power. Some acts of attainder were also passed by American colonial legislators during the wars of independence to deal with 'loyalists' who continued to support the English Crown.

attar of roses Perfume derived from the essential oil of roses, obtained by crushing and distilling the petals of the flowers.

attempt criminal offence in the UK under the Criminal Attempts Act 1981, which repealed the 'suspected person offence', commonly known as the 'sus' law. The offence must involve 'more than a mere preparatory act'; that is, it must include at least a partial performance of the crime.

Attenborough /'ætnbərə/ David 1926– . British traveller and zoologist, brother of Richard ◊Attenborough. He was director of programmes for BBC television 1969–72, and commentator in the television series *Life on Earth* 1979 and *The Living Planet* 1983. Knighted 1985.

Attenborough /'ætnbərə/ Richard 1923– . British actor, film producer, and director. An influential figure in the British cinema, he was outstanding in the film roles of Pinkie in *Brighton Rock* 1947, and the murderer Christie in *10 Rillington Place* 1970; films directed include *Oh! What a Lovely War* 1968, *A Bridge Too Far* 1967, dealing with Arnhem, and *Gandhi* 1982, which won six Academy Awards. He was knighted in 1976.

died on the night of his marriage with Ildico, poison being suspected as the cause.

Attila Line line dividing Greek and Turkish ◊Cyprus, so called because of a fanciful identification of the Turks with the Huns.

Attis /'ætɪs/ in Classical mythology, a Phrygian god, whose death and resurrection symbolized the end of winter and the arrival of spring. Beloved by the goddess Cybele, he was driven mad by her as a punishment for his infidelity, and castrated himself and bled to death. His worshippers sought identification with the god by castrating themselves.

government was returned to power with a much reduced majority in 1950 and was defeated in 1951. On his resignation as prime minister, he was awarded the Order of Merit and in 1955 accepted an earldom on his retirement as leader of the opposition. His books include *The Labour Party in Perspective* 1937 and *As it Happened* 1954, an autobiography.

attorney a person appointed to act for another in legal matters . In Britain the term is largely obsolete, but the head of the English Bar and principal law officer of the Crown is still known as the ◊Attorney General. In the USA attorney is the formal title for a lawyer, who combines the functions performed in the UK by a barrister and a solicitor.

Attorney General in England, principal law officer of the Crown and head of the English Bar; the post is one of great political importance. In the USA, the chief law officer of the government and head of the Department of Justice.

Attwell /'ætwel/ Mabel Lucie 1879–1964. British artist, illustrator of many books for children, including her own stories and verse.

Atwood /'ætwʊd/ Margaret (Eleanor) 1939– . Canadian novelist, short story writer, and poet. Her novels, which often treat feminist themes with wit and irony, include *The Edible Woman* 1969, *Life Before Man* 1979, *Bodily Harm* 1981 , and *The Handmaid's Tale* 1986, a chilling vision of a future society in which the ability to breed belongs to a select few. Collections of poetry include *Power Politics* 1971 and *You are Happy* 1974.

Attenborough Sir Richard Attenborough, British director and actor, and Sir Ralph Richardson working on the script of *Oh! What a Lovely War* in 1968. The film won 16 international awards.

Atterbury /'ætəbəri/ Francis 1662–1732. English cleric and politician. Taking holy orders in 1687, he was appointed a royal chaplain by William III. Under Queen Anne he received rapid promotion, becoming bishop of Rochester in 1713. His Jacobite sympathies prevented his attaining to the primacy, and in 1722 he was sent to the Tower and subsequently banished. He was a friend of ◊Pope and ◊Swift.

Attica /'ætɪkə/ region of Greece comprising Athens and the district around it, noted for its language, art and philosophical thought in Classical times. It is a prefecture of modern Greece with Athens as its capital. Population (1981) 342,100.

Attila /ə'tɪlə/ c. 406–453. King of the Huns, called the 'Scourge of God'. Becoming king in 434 of hordes of Huns roaming the area from the Caspian to the Danube, he embarked on a career of vast conquests ranging from the Rhine to Persia. In 451 he invaded Gaul, but was defeated near Châlons-sur-Marne by the Roman and Visigothic armies under Aëtius and Theodoric. In 452 he led his Huns into Italy and only the personal intervention of Pope Leo I prevented the sacking of Rome. He returned to Pannonia and

Attlee /'ætli/ Clement Richard, 1st Earl 1883–1967. British Labour politician. He was educated at Oxford and practised at the Bar 1906–09. Social work in London's East End and cooperation in Poor Law reform led him to become a socialist: he joined the ◊Fabian Society and the ◊Independent Labour Party in 1908. He became secretary to ◊Toynbee Hall in 1910 and lecturer in social science at the London School of Economics in 1913. After service in World War I he was mayor of Stepney 1919–20; Labour Member of Parliament for Limehouse 1922–50 and for W Walthamstow 1950–55.

In the first and second Labour governments he was under-secretary for war 1924 and chancellor of the Duchy of Lancaster and postmaster general 1929–31. In 1935 he became leader of the opposition. In the wartime coalition government he was Lord Privy Seal 1940–42, dominions secretary 1942–43 and Lord President of the Council 1943–45, as well as deputy prime minister from 1942. In July 1945 he became prime minister after a Labour landslide in the general election, and introduced a sweeping programme of nationalization and a whole new system of social services. The

Atwood Canadian novelist Margaret Atwood first made her reputation as a poet, but she is now best known for her feminist novels. She has travelled and taught in Europe and America and has a wide and devoted readership.

Aube /əub/ river of NE France, a tributary of the Seine, giving its name to a *département*.

Auber /əʊ'beə/ Daniel François Esprit 1782–1871. French operatic composer. Born at Caen, he studied under Cherubini. He wrote about 50 operas, the best known being *La Muette de Portici/The Mute Girl of Portici* 1828 and the comic opera *Fra Diavolo* 1830.

aubergine the eggplant, *Solanum melongena*, family ◊Solanaceae, native to tropical Asia but widely grown in the tropics. The purple-skinned (sometimes white) fruits are eaten as a vegetable.

Aubrey /'ɔːbri/ John 1626–1697. British antiquary. Born in Wiltshire, he studied law, but became dependent on patrons including Ashmole and Hobbes. He published *Miscellanies* 1696 of folklore and ghost-stories, and the material he collected for surveys of Surrey and Wiltshire appeared posthumously in 1719 and 1862 respectively. His *Brief Lives* 1898 contain gossip and anecdotes on celebrities of his time. Aubrey was the first to claim Stonehenge as a Druid temple.

aubrietia spring-flowering dwarf perennial plant of the family Cruciferae, trailing in habit and bearing purple flowers. It was named in 1763 after Claude Aubriet, (c. 1665–1742), painter for the French Royal Garden.

Aubusson /ˌəʊbjuːˈsɒŋ/ town in the *département* of Creuse, France, famous for its carpets and tapestries, the industry dating from the 15th century.

Auchinleck /'ɔːkɪnlek/ Sir Claude John Eyre 1884–1981. British soldier, nicknamed 'the Auk'. He succeeded Wavell in the Middle East Jul 1941, and in the summer of 1942 was forced back to the Egyptian frontier by Rommel, but his victory at the First Battle of El ◊Alamein is regarded by some as more important to the outcome of World War II than the Second Battle. In 1943 he became commander-in-chief India, founded the modern Indian and Pakistani armies, and gave background support to the Burma campaign. In 1946 he was promoted to field marshal; he retired in 1947.

Auckland /'ɔːklənd/ largest city in New Zealand, situated in the N of North Island. It fills the isthmus that separates its two harbours (Waitemata and Manukau), and its suburbs spread N across the Harbour Bridge. There was a small whaling settlement on the site in the 1830s, but Auckland was officially founded as New Zealand's capital in 1840, remaining so until 1865. It is the country's chief port and leading industrial centre, having iron and steel plants, engineering, car assembly, textiles, food-processing, sugar-refining and brewing. The university was founded in 1882, and there are Anglican and Roman Catholic cathedrals. The international airport is at Mangere. Population (1983) 800,000.

Auckland /'ɔːklənd/ George Eden, 1st Earl of Auckland 1784–1849. British politician. He became Tory Member of Parliament in 1810, and 1835–41 was governor general of India. Auckland, New Zealand, is named after him.

Auckland Islands six volcanic islands 480 km/300 mi south of South Island, New Zealand.

auction the sale of goods or property in public to the highest bidder. There are usually conditions of sale by which all bidders are bound. A bid may be withdrawn at any time before the auctioneer brings down the hammer, and the seller is likewise entitled to withdraw any lot before the hammer falls. It is illegal for the seller or anyone on his behalf to make a bid for his own goods unless his right to do so has been reserved and notified before the sale. 'Rings' of dealers agreeing to keep prices down are illegal. A reserve price is kept secret, but an upset price (the minimum price fixed for the property offered) is made public before the sale. An auction where property is first offered at a high price and gradually reduced until a bid is received is known as a *Dutch auction*.

auction bridge card game played by two pairs of players. A development of ◊bridge, it originated in India among members of the Indian Civil Service, reached England in 1903, and was first played at the Portland Club in 1908. Its chief characteristic is that trumps are decided by preliminary bid or auction. It has now largely been supplanted by contract bridge.

Aude /əʊd/ river in SE France, 210 km/130 mi long, which gives its name to a *département*. Carcassonne is the chief town through which it passes.

Auden /'ɔːdn/ W(ystan) H(ugh) 1907–1973. American poet of British origin. Educated at Oxford, he was (with C ◊Day Lewis and ◊Spender) one of the 'committed' poets of the 1930s, espousing left-wing politics and the Spanish Republican cause. His first volume of poems was published in 1930 and by 1936 (*Look Stranger*) he had achieved a mature poetic style. By the time of the long poem *The Age of Anxiety* 1947, he had moved to a more conventional Christian viewpoint. He collaborated with ◊Isherwood in verse dramas, *The Dog Beneath the Skin* 1935 and *The Ascent of F6* 1936; collaborated in the libretti for Stravinsky's *The Rake's Progress* 1951 and Henze's *The Bassarids* 1966. In 1939 he became associate professor of English literature at the University of Michigan. A naturalized American from 1946, he was professor of poetry at Oxford 1956–61. His daring technique, influenced by Hopkins and Eliot, opened the way for younger writers.

Audenarde /əʊd'nɑːd/ French form of ◊Oudenaarde, a town in Belgium.

audiometer electrical instrument testing pitch and loudness of sounds heard by a patient.

Audit Commission independent body in the UK established by the Local Government Finance Act 1982. It administers the District Audit Service (established 1844) and appoints auditors for the accounts of all UK local authorities. The Audit Commission consists of 15 members: its aims include finding ways of saving costs, and controlling illegal local-authority spending.

auditor person appointed to examine accounts, in particular a specialist accountant who gives annual independent checking of a company's accounts as required by law, to ensure the company balance sheet reflects the true state of its affairs.

Audubon /'ɔːdəbɒn/ John James 1785–1851. American naturalist, born in Santo Domingo and educated in Paris. In 1827 he published the first part of his *Birds of North America*, with a remarkable series of colour plates. Later he produced a similar work on American quadrupeds. The National Audubon Society (originating 1886) has branches throughout the USA and Canada for the study and protection of birds.

Auerbach /'aʊəbæk/ Frank Helmuth 1931– . British artist, whose portraits and landscapes blend figurative and abstract work.

Augier /ˌəʊʒi'eɪ/ É mile 1820–1889. French dramatist. He is remembered for *Le Gendre de M Poirier* 1854, written in prose in collaboration with Jules Sandeau, a realistic delineation of bourgeois society.

Augsburg /'aʊgzbʊəg/ industrial city in Bavaria, W Germany; at the confluence of the Wertach and Lech rivers, 52 km/32 mi NW of Munich. Population (1980) 246,200. A major industrial centre, it is named after the Roman emperor Augustus who founded it in 15 BC. Noted for its great medieval merchant families, the Fuggers and the Welsers; as the birthplace of ◊Holbein; and as the site of the Messerschmitt works in World War II.

Augsburg, Confession of /'aʊgzbʊəg/ statement of the Protestant faith as held by the German Reformers composed by Philipp ◊Melanchthon. Presented to Charles V, Holy Roman Emperor, at the conference known as the Diet of Augsburg in 1530, it is the creed of the modern Lutheran Church.

augur member of a college of Roman priests who interpreted the will of the gods from signs or 'auspices' such as the flight of birds, the condition of entrails of sacrificed animals, and the direction of thunder and lightning. Their advice was sought before battle and on other important occasions. Consuls and other high officials had the right to consult the auspices themselves, and a campaign was said to be conducted 'under the auspices' of the general who had consulted the gods.

Augustan age the golden age of the Roman emperor ◊Augustus 63 BC–14 AD, noted for its art, particularly literature. The name was also given to later periods which used Classical ideals, such as that of Queen Anne in England.

Augustin /ˌəʊguˈstæn/ Eugène 1791–1861. French dramatist, who wrote *Une Nuit de la Garde Nationale* 1815, and the originator and exponent of the 'well-made' plays which achieved contemporary success but were subsequently forgotten.

Augustine of Hippo /ɔː'gʌstɪn/ St 354–430. Christian saint, theologian, and a father of the Church. Born at Tagaste, Numidia, of Roman descent, he studied rhetoric in Carthage where he became the father of a natural son, Adeodatus. He lectured at Tagaste and Carthage and for ten years was attached to the ◊Manichaean heresy. In 383 he went to Rome, and on moving to Milan came under the influence of Ambrose. After prolonged study of ◊Neo-Platonism Augustine was converted to Christianity and was baptized by Ambrose together with his son. Resigning his chair in rhetoric, he returned to Africa, his mother St Monica dying at Ostia on the journey, and settled at Tagaste. His son died at 17. In 391, while visiting Hippo, Augustine was ordained priest. In 395 he was given the right of succession to the bishopric of Hippo (modern ◊Annaba), and in 396 succeeded to the office. He died at Hippo during its siege by the Vandals.

Many of Augustine's books resulted from his share in three great controversies: he refuted Manichaeism; attacked and did much to eliminate ◊Donatism (conference of Carthage, 411); and devoted the last 20 years of his life to the ◊Pelagian controversy, in which he maintained the doctrine of original sin and the necessity of divine grace. He estimated the number of his works at 230, and also wrote many sermons, as well as pastoral letters. Augustine's most famous writings are his 'Confessions', his spiritual autobiography, and the influential *De Civitate Dei* (City of God) vindicating the Christian Church and Divine Providence in 22 books.

Augustine, Saint /ɔː'ɡʌstɪn/ d. 604. First archbishop of Canterbury. Originally prior of the Benedictine monastery of St Andrew, Rome, he was sent to convert England to Christianity by Pope Gregory I Landing at Ebbsfleet, Thanet, in 597, he soon baptized Ethelbert, King of Kent. He was consecrated bishop of the English at Arles 597 and appointed archbishop in 601. In 603 he attempted unsuccessfully to unite the Roman and native Celtic churches at a conference on the Severn. Augustine was the founder of Christ Church, Canterbury, in 603, and the abbey of Saints Peter and Paul, now the site of Saint Augustine's Missionary College. His festival is celebrated on 26 May.

Augustinian name applied to all religious communities which follow the Rule of St ◊Augustine of Hippo. It includes the Canons of St Augustine, Augustinian Friars and Hermits, Premonstratensians, Gilbertines, and Trinitarians.

Augustus /ɔː'ɡʌstəs/ 63 BC–14 AD. Title of Octavian (Caius Julius Caesar Octavianus), first of the Roman emperors. He was the son of a senator who married a niece of Julius Caesar, and he became his great-uncle's adopted son and principal heir. Following Caesar's murder, Octavian formed with Mark Antony and Lepidus the triumvirate which divided the Roman world between them, and proceeded to eliminate the opposition. Antony's victory in 42 BC over Brutus and Cassius brought the Republic to an end. Soon after Antony became enamoured of Cleopatra and spent most of his time at Alexandria, while Octavian consolidated his hold on the western part of the Roman dominion. War was declared against Cleopatra, and the naval victory at Actium in 31 BC left Octavian in unchallenged supremacy, since Lepidus had been forced to retire. After his return to Rome in 29 BC, Octavian was created *princeps senatus*, and in 27 BC he was given the title of Augustus (venerable). He then resigned his extraordinary powers, and received from the Senate in return the proconsular command, which gave him control of the army, and the tribunician power, whereby

he could initiate or veto legislation. In his programme of reforms Augustus received the support of three loyal and capable helpers, Agrippa, Maecenas, and his wife, Livia, while Virgil and Horace acted as the poets laureate of the new regime. A firm frontier for the empire was established: on the north, the friendly Batavians held the Rhine delta, and then the line followed the course of the Rhine and Danube; on the east, the Parthians were friendly, and the Euphrates gave the next line; on the south, Africa was protected by the desert, on the west were Spain and Gaul. The provinces were governed either by imperial legates responsible to the *princeps*, or by proconsuls appointed by the Senate. The army was made a profession, with fixed pay and length of service, and a permanent fleet was established. Finally, Rome itself received an adequate water supply, a fire brigade, a police force, and a large number of public buildings. The years after 12 BC were marked by private and public calamities; the marriage of Augustus's daughter Julia to his stepson Tiberius proved disastrous, while a serious revolt occurred in Pannonia in 6 AD, and in Germany three legions under Varus were annihilated in the Teutoburg Forest in 9 AD. Augustus died a broken man, but his work remained secure. He was an enlightened and generous patron of literature and the arts, and the period of his rule is known as the Augustan Age.

Augustus Great-nephew of Julius Caesar, the 'venerable' Augustus was the first Roman emperor. He was a ruler of great administrative ability and initative , and his reign marks the golden age of Latin literature.

auk any member of the family of marine diving birds that includes ◊razorbills, ◊puffins, and ◊guillemots. Confined to the N hemisphere they feed on fish, and use their wings to 'fly' underwater in pursuit. In air the short wings beat fast in flight. The smallest, at 20 cm/8 in is the little auk *Alle alle*, an arctic bird that winters as

far S as Britain. The largest was the great auk *Pinguinis impennis*, 75 cm/2.5 ft and flightless, the last recorded individual being killed in 1844.

Auld Lang Syne song written by Robert Burns about 1789, based on lines attributed to Sir Robert Aytoun, and particularly associated with New Year gatherings; the title means 'old long since' or 'long ago'.

Auld Reekie former nickname of Edinburgh (Scottish dialect -'old smoky').

Aung San /'auŋ 'sæn/ 1914–1947. Burmese politician. Imprisoned for his nationalist activities while a student in Rangoon, he escaped in 1940 to Japan, returned to lead the Burma Independence Army, which assisted the Japanese invasion of 1942, and became defence minister in the puppet government set up. Before long, however, he secretly contacted the resistance movement, and from March 1945 openly co-operated with the British in the expulsion of the Japanese. As leader of the Anti-Fascist People's Freedom League he became vice-president of the executive council in Sept 1946. He was assassinated by political opponents in July 1947.

Aurangzeb /'ɔːrənzeb/ or Aurungzebe 1618–1707. Mogul emperor of Hindustan (N India). Third son of Shah Jahan, he made himself master of the court by a palace revolution, and ruled as emperor from 1658. His reign was the most brilliant period of the Mogul dynasty, but by despotic tendencies and Muslim fanaticism aroused much opposition. His latter years were spent in war with the princes of Rajputana and Mahrattas.

Aurelian /ɔː'riːliən/ (Lucius Domitius Aurelianus) c. 214–275. Roman emperor from 270. A successful soldier, he was chosen emperor by his troops on the death of Claudius II. He defeated the Goths and Vandals, defeated and captured ◊Zenobia of Palmyra, and was planning a campaign against Parthia when he was murdered. The *Aurelian Wall*, a fortification surrounding Rome, was built by Aurelian in 271. It was made of concrete, and substantial ruins exist. The *Aurelian Way* ran from Rome through Pisa and Genoa to Antipolis (Antibes) in Gaul.

Aurelius /ɔː'riːliəs/ (Antoninus), Marcus Roman emperor; see ◊Marcus Aurelius.

Auric /ɔː'riːk/ Georges 1899–1983. French composer. He was one of the musical group known as ◊*Les Six*, who were influenced by Erik ◊Satie. Auric composed a comic opera, several ballets, and incidental music.

auricula primrose *Primula auricula*, well known as a garden flower. It is a native of the Alps, but has been grown in English gardens for three centuries, and there are many colour varieties.

Auriga ◊constellation of the northern hemisphere star, representing a man driving a chariot. The charioteer is usually identified as Erichthonius, legendary king of Athens, who invented the four-horse chariot. Its brightest star is first-magnitude Capella; Epsilon Aurigae is a peculiar eclipsing ◊binary star with a period of 27 years, the longest of its kind (last eclipse 1983).

Aurignacian in archaeology, name given to an Old Stone Age culture which came between the Mousterian and the Solutrian in the Upper Palaeolithic. It is derived from a cave at Aurignac in the Pyrenees.

Auriol /ˌɔːriˈəʊl/ Vincent 1884–1966. French socialist politician. He was president of the two Constituent Assemblies of 1946 and first president of the Fourth Republic 1947–54.

auroch extinct species of wild cattle *Box primigenius* that formerly roamed Europe. Depicted in cave paintings, it may have survived in Poland until the end of the 16th century. Black to reddish or grey, it was up to 1.8 m/6 ft at the shoulder.

Aurora /ɔːˈrɔːrə/ coloured light in the night sky, *Aurora Borealis*, 'northern dawn' (a name given by Gassendi in 1621) in the northern hemisphere, and *Aurora Australis* in the southern. Auroras are usually in the form of a luminous arch with its apex towards the magnetic pole followed by arcs, bands, rays, curtains and coronas, ranging in colour from smoky black to flaming red. Auroras are caused at a height of 100 km/60 mi by a fast stream of charged particles, originating in the sun. These enter the upper ◊atmosphere and, by bombarding the gases in the atmosphere, cause them to emit visible light. The ◊magnetic field of the earth divides the concentration into two zones.

auscultation medical investigation by listening to sounds inside the body. Auscultation is used to examine the heart, lungs, bowels, arteries, joints, liver, spleen, thyroid gland, and the state of the child within the womb. It was introduced by the French physician Laënnec, who in 1819 invented the stethoscope, originally a trumpet-shaped wooden tube.

Ausgleich name given to the compromise between Austria and Hungary of 8 Feb 1867, which established the Austro-Hungarian Dual Monarchy, under Habsburg rule. It endured until the collapse of ◊Austria-Hungary in 1918.

Austen /ˈɒstɪn/ Jane 1775–1817. British novelist, noted for her domestic novels of manners. All her novels are set within the confines of middle-class provincial society, and show her skill at drawing characters and situations with delicate irony.
Born at Steventon, Hampshire, where her father was rector, she began writing early; the burlesque *Love and Freindship* (sic), published 1922, was written in 1790. In 1801 the family moved to Bath, and after the death of her father in 1805, to Southampton, finally settling in Chawton, with her brother Edward.
Between 1795 and 1798 she worked on three novels. The first to be published (like its successors, anonymously), was *Sense and Sensibility* 1811 (drafted in letter form about 1797). *Pride and Prejudice* 1813 followed, but *Northanger Abbey*, a skit on the contemporary Gothic novel (sold to a London publisher in 1803 and bought back in 1816), did not appear till 1818. The fragmentary *Watsons* and *Lady Susan* written about 1803–05 remained unfinished. The success of her published works, however, stimulated Jane Austen to write in rapid succession *Mansfield Park* 1814, *Emma*

1816, *Persuasion* 1818, and the final fragment *Sanditon* written 1817. She died at Winchester, and is buried in the cathedral.

Austen Jane Austen, in a drawing by her sister Cassandra. Her work appeared anonymously in her lifetime, and she received very little recognition or payment for it, but she has since become one of the most popular English novelists.

Austerlitz /ˈaʊstəlɪts/ small town in Czechoslavakia, formerly in Austria, 19 km/12 mi E of Brno, where on 2 Dec 1805 Napoleon defeated Alexander I of Russia and Francis II of Austria. Its Czech name is Slavkov.

Austin /ˈɒstɪn/ capital of Texas, USA, on the Colorado river. Population (1980) 345,500.

Austin /ˈɒstɪn/ Alfred 1835–1913. British poet. He made his name with the satirical poem *The Season* 1861, which was followed by plays and volumes of poetry little read today; from 1896 he was Poet Laureate.

Austin /ˈɒstɪn/ Herbert, 1st Baron Austin 1866–1941. British pioneer motor-car manufacturer. Born at Little Missenden, Buckinghamshire, he went to Australia and was a works manager in Melbourne. Returning to England, he began manufacturing cars in 1905 at Northfield, Birmingham, notably the 'Austin Seven' in 1921.

Austin /ˈɒstɪn/ J(ohn) L(angshaw) 1911–1960. British philosopher. Influential in later work on the philosophy of language, Austin was a pioneer in the investigation of the way words are used in everyday speech. His lectures *Sense and Sensibilia* and *How to do Things with Words* were published posthumously in 1962.

Australasia /ˌɒstrəˈleɪziə/ loosely applied geographical term, usually meaning Australia, New Zealand, and such Pacific islands as either are or were their dependencies.

Australia /ɒsˈtreɪliə/ the smallest continent and largest island in the world, situated south of Indonesia, between the Pacific and Indian oceans.

government Australia is an independent sovereign nation within the Commonwealth, retaining the British monarch as head of state, represented by a governor-general. The

AUSTRALIA, COMMONWEALTH OF

State (Capital)	Area sq km
New South Wales *(Sydney)*	801,396
Victoria *(Melbourne)*	227,620
Queensland *(Brisbane)*	1,736,524
South Australia *(Adelaide)*	984,341
Western Australia *(Perth)*	2,527,632
Tasmania *(Hobart)*	68,331
Territories	
Northern Territory *(Darwin)*	1,356,165
Capital Territory *(Canberra)*	2,432
	7,704,441
Dependencies	
Ashmore and Cartier Islands	1
Australian Antarctic Territory	5,402,480
Cocos (Keeling) Island	14
Christmas Island	135
Heard and McDonald Islands	412
Norfolk Island	34

constitution came into effect on 1 Jan 1901. As in the British system, the executive, in the shape of the prime minister and cabinet, is drawn from the federal parliament and is answerable to it. It consists of two chambers, an elected senate of 76, (12 for each of the six states, two for the Australian Capital Territory and two for the Northern Territory); and a house of representatives of 148, elected by universal adult suffrage. Senators serve for six years and members of the house for three years. Voting is compulsory and both chambers are elected by proportional representation.
The federal system is modelled on that of the USA, each state having its own governor and executive, legislative and judicial system. There are some ten political parties, the major three being the Australian Labour Party, the Liberal Party of Australia, and the National Party of Australia. In 1986 the UK removed the last relics of its legislative control over Australia.
history Australia was first settled 30,000–10,000 BC by immigrants from S India, Sri Lanka, and SE Asia. The first recorded sightings of Australia by Europeans were in 1606, when the Dutch ship *Duyfken* sighted the W shore of Cape York, and the Spaniard Luis Vaez de Torres sailed along the coast S of Cape York, and through Torres Strait. Later voyagers include Dirk Hartog in 1616, who left an inscribed pewter plate (Australia's most famous early European relic, now in Amsterdam) in W Australia; François ◊Pelsaert, Abel ◊Tasman, and William ◊Dampier. A second wave of immigration began in 1770, when Capt James ◊Cook claimed New South Wales as a British colony.
Exploration of the interior began with thhe crossing of the barrier of the ◊Blue Mountains in 1813. Famous explorers include Hamilton Hume (1797–1873) and William Hovel (1786–1875) who in 1824 reached Port Phillip Bay and were the first Europeans to see the river Murray; George ◊Sturt; Thomas Mitchell (1792–1855), surveyor-general for New South Wales 1828–55,

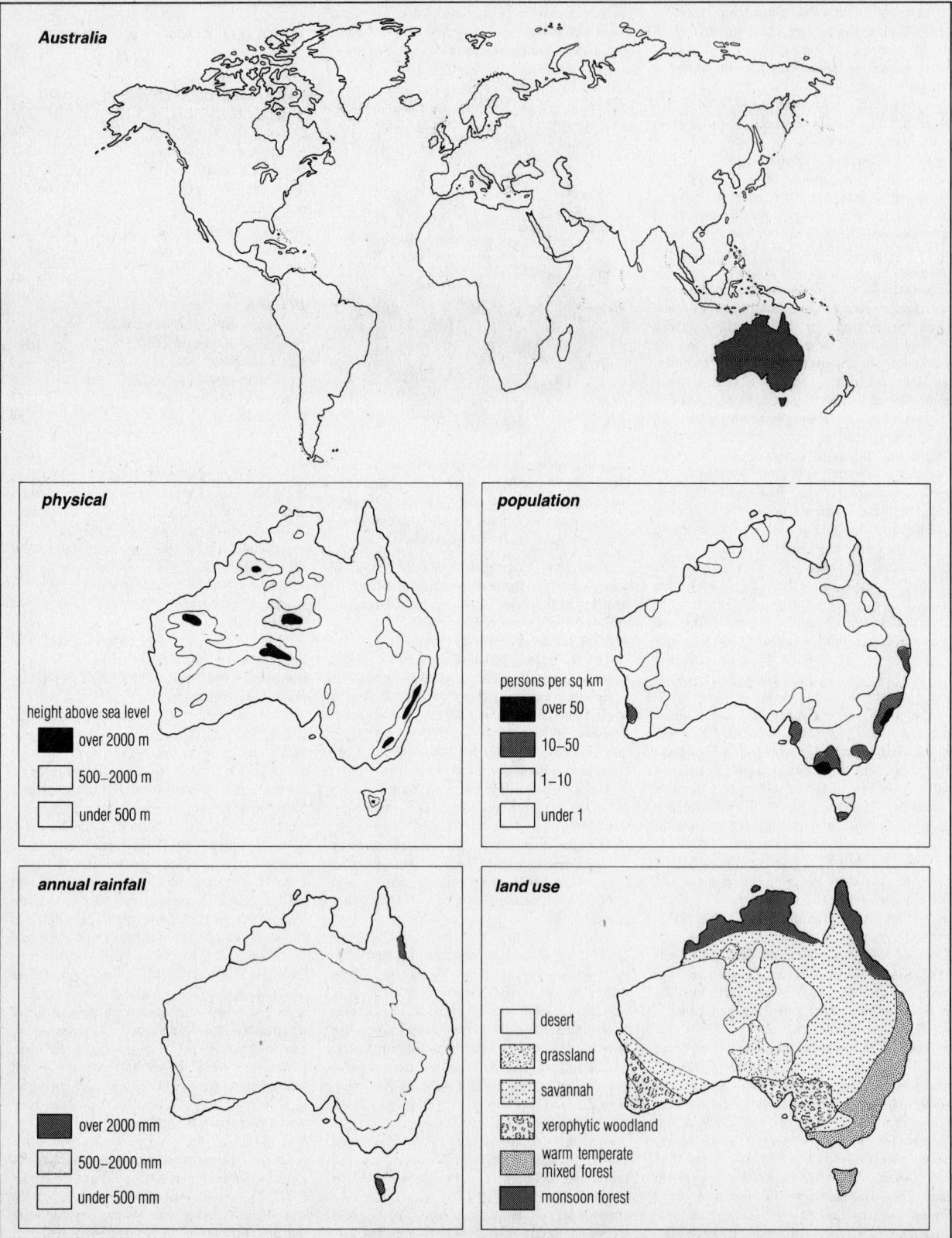

Australia

physical

height above sea level

over 2000 m

500–2000 m

under 500 m

population

persons per sq km

over 50

10–50

1–10

under 1

annual rainfall

over 2000 mm

500–2000 mm

under 500 mm

land use

desert

grassland

savannah

xerophytic woodland

warm temperate mixed forest

monsoon forest

who opened up the fertile W area of Victoria; Edward ◊Eyre, Friedrich ◊Leichardt, Robert ◊Burke and William Wills (1834–61), and John ◊Stuart. In the 1870s the last gaps were filled in by the famous crossings of W Australia, which made the names of John ◊Forrest, William Giles (1835–97) in 1875–76, and Peter Warburton (1813–89) in 1873.

The gold rushes 1851–61, and sporadically to the early 1890s, contributed to the exploration as well as to the economic and constitutional growth of Australia, as did the pioneer work of the ◊overlanders. The creation of other separate colonies followed the first settlement in New South Wales at Sydney in 1788: Tasmania 1825; Western Australia 1829; South Australia 1836; Victoria 1851; and Queensland 1859. The system of transportation of convicts from Britain was never introduced in South Australia and Victoria, and ended in New South Wales 1840, Queensland 1849, Tasmania 1853, and Western Australia 1868. Their contribution to the economic foundation of the country was considerable, and many would not have been convicted under a less harsh and capricious penal system than that operating in Britain at this period.

In the 1890s there was a halt in the rapid expansion that Australia had enjoyed, and the resulting depression produced the Labour Party and an increase in trade union activity, which has proved such a feature of Australian politics ever since. State powers waned following the creation of the ◊Commonwealth in 1901. Australia played an important role in both World Wars, and after World War II it embarked on a fresh period of expansion, with new mineral finds playing an important part in economic growth. Since 1945 Australia has strengthened its ties with India and other SE Asian countries, especially since Britain's entry into the EEC in 1973, and under the Labour government which came to power in 1973 there was a growth of nationalism.

After heading a Liberal government for 17 years, Robert Menzies resigned in 1966 and was succeeded by Harold Holt, who died in a swimming accident in 1967. In 1968 John Gorton became prime minister but lost a vote of confidence in the House and was succeeded in 1971 by a Liberal-Country Party coalition under William McMahon. At the end of 1972, the Australian Labour Party took office, led by Gough Whitlam.

The 1974 general election gave the Labour Party a fresh mandate to govern despite having a reduced majority in the House and losing control of the Senate. In 1975 the Senate blocked the government's financial legislation and, with Whitlam unwilling to resign, the Governor-General took the unprecedented step of dismissing him and his cabinet and inviting Malcolm Fraser to form a Liberal-Country party coalition caretaker admimistration. The wisdom of this action was widely questioned and eventually, in 1977, Governor-General Sir John Kerr himself resigned. In the 1977 general election the coalition was returned with a reduced majority which became even smaller in 1980.

In the 1983 general election the coalition was eventually defeated and the Australian Labour Party under Bob Hawke again took office. Hawke called together employers and unions to agree a prices and incomes policy and to deal with unemployment. In 1984 he called a general election 15 months early, and was returned with a reduced majority. Hawke has placed even greater emphasis than his predecessors on links with SE Asia, and has imposed trading sanctions against South Africa as a means of influencing the dismantling of apartheid. In the 1987 general election, Labour marginally increased its majority in the House but did not have an overall majority in the Senate, where the balance is held by the Australian Democrats.

Australian Prime Ministers
Sir Edmund Barton (*Liberal*) 1901
Alfred Deakin (*Liberal*) 1903
John Watson (*Labour*) 1904
Sir G Reid (*Free Trade*) 1904
Alfred Deakin (*Liberal*) 1905
Andrew Fisher (*Labour*) 1908
Alfred Deakin (*Liberal*) 1909
Andrew Fisher (*Labour*) 1910
Sir J Cook (*Free Trade*) 1913
Andrew Fisher (*Labour*) 1914
W M Hughes (*Labour*) 1915
W M Hughes (*National*) 1917
S M Bruce (*National*) 1923
J H Scullin (*Labour*) 1929
J A Lyons (*United Australia Party*) 1932
Sir Earle Page (*Country Party*) 1939
R G Menzies (*United Australia Party*) 1939
A W Fadden (*Country Party*) 1941
John Curtin (*Labour*) 1941
F M Forde (*Labour*) 1945
J B Chifley (*Labour*) 1945
R G Menzies (*Liberal*) 1949
Harold Holt (*Liberal*) 1966
John McEwen (*Liberal*) 1967
J G Gorton (*Liberal*) 1968
William McMahon (*Liberal*) 1971
Gough Whitlam (*Labour*) 1972
Malcolm Fraser (*Liberal*) 1975
Robert Hawke (*Labour*) 1983

Australia Day public holiday in Australia, the anniversary of Captain Phillip's arrival in Sydney 26 Jan 1788 to found the first colony.

Australian Antarctic Territory from 1933, when established by a British Order in Council, the islands and territories south of 60° S, between 160° E and 45° E longitude, excluding Adélie Land, and including the ◊Cocos Islands and ◊Christmas Island. Area 5,402,480 sq km/2,472,000 sq mi. The population on the Antarctic continent is limited to research personnel. There are scientific bases at Mawson (1954) in MacRobertson Land, named after the explorer; at Davis (1957) on the coast of Princess Elizabeth Land, named in honour of Mawson's second-in-command; at Casey (1969) in Wilkes Land, named after Lord Casey, and at Macquarie Island (1948).

Australian architecture Aboriginal settlements tended to be based around caves, or a construction of bark huts, arranged in a circular group; there was some variation in different areas.

Architecture of the early settlers includes Vaucluse House, and the Sydney home of William Charles Wentworth. Queensland has old-style homes with screened areas for coolness beneath their floors. Outstanding examples of modern architecture are the the the layout of the town of Canberra, by Walter Burley Griffin (1876–1937); Victoria Arts Centre, Melbourne, by Roy Grounds (1905–), who also designed the Academy of Science, Canberra; and the Sydney Opera House, by Joern Utzon (begun 1957).

Australian Capital Territory territory ceded to the Commonwealth of Australia by New South Wales in 1911 to provide the site of ◊Canberra, with its port at Jervis Bay, which was ceded in 1915; area 2,432 sq km/939 sq mi. Population (1981) 227,250.

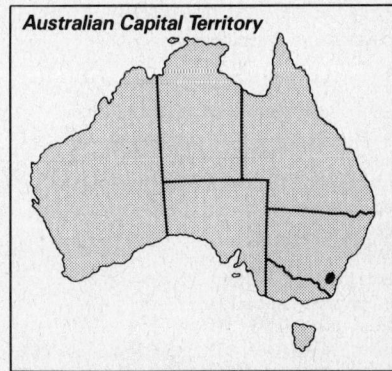

Australian Capital Territory

Australian literature Australian literature begins with the letters, journals, and memoirs of early settlers and explorers. The first poet of note was Charles Harpur (1813–68), and idioms and rhythms typical of the country were developed by, among others, Henry Kendall (1841–82) and Andrew Barton (Banjo) ◊Paterson (1864–1941). More recent poets include Christopher ◊Brennan and Judith ◊Wright, Kenneth Sleesor (1901–71), R D (Robert David) Fitzgerald (1902–), A D (Alec Derwent) Hope (1907–), and James McAuley (1917–76). Among early Australian novelists are Marcus ◊Clarke, Rolfe ◊Boldrewood, and Henry Handel Richardson (1870–1946). Contemporary writers include the dramatist Ray ◊Lawler and novelist Patrick ◊White. Thomas ◊Keneally is a recent Booker prize winner.

Australian painting art in Australia began with Aboriginal paintings and crafts some 15,000 years ago. Aboriginal art is closely linked with religion and ceremony; decoration was applied to the human body, headdresses, and armbands, as well as on walls, using brightly coloured natural pigments.

The first paintings by European settlers were topographical scenes of Sidney and the surrounding region. Painting developed with the

Australia
COMMONWEALTH OF

AREA 7,704,441 sq km/2,974,693 sq mi
CAPITAL Canberra
TOWNS Adelaide, Alice Springs, Brisbane,
Darwin, Melbourne, Perth, Sydney
PHYSICAL the world's driest continent, arid in
N and W, Great Dividing Range in the E; NE
peninsula has rainforest; rivers N–S and
Darling River and Murray system E–S; Lake
Eyre basin and fertile Nullarbor Plain in S
TERRITORIES Norfolk Island, Christmas Island,
Cocos Islands; part of Antarctica
FEATURES Great Australian Desert, Great
Barrier Reef; unique animals include
kangaroo, koala, numbat, platypus, wombat,
Tasmanian devil and 'tiger'; budgerigar,
cassowary, emu, kookaburra, lyre bird, black
swan; and such deadly insects as the bulldog
ant and funnel-web spider
HEAD OF STATE Elizabeth II from 1952
represented by Ninian Stephen
HEAD OF GOVERNMENT Robert Hawke from
1983
GOVERNMENT federal democracy
EXPORTS cereals, meat and dairy products;
wool (30% of world production); fruit, wine,
nuts, sugar, and honey; minerals include
bauxite (world's largest producer), coal, iron,
copper, lead, tin, zinc, opal, mineral sands,
and uranium; machinery and transport
equipment
CURRENCY Australian dollar (2.24 = £1 Sept
1987)
POPULATION (1985) 15,345,000 (1.5%
Aborigines); annual growth rate 1.4%
LANGUAGE English
RELIGION Anglican 36%, other Protestant 25%,
Roman Catholic 33%
LITERACY 100% (1984)
GDP $170.2 bn (1984); $9,960 per head of
population
CHRONOLOGY
1901 Creation of Commonwealth of Australia.
1911 Site for capital at Canberra acquired.

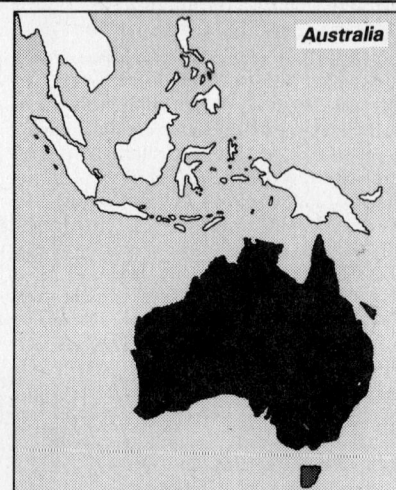

1944 Liberal Party founded by Sir Robert
Menzies.
1966 Menzies resigned after being Liberal
prime minister for 17 years, and was succeeded
by Harold Holt.
1968 John Gorton became prime minister
after Holt's death.
1971 Gorton succeeded by William
McMahon, heading a Liberal–Country Party
coalition.
1972 Gough Whitlam became prime minister,
leading a Labour government.
1975 Senate blocked the government's
financial legislation; Whitlam declined to
resign but was dismissed by the governor
general, who invited Malcom Fraser to form
a Liberal–Country Party caretaker
government. The action of the governor
general, Sir John Kerr, was widely criticized.
1977 Kerr resigned.
1983 Australian Labour Party, returned to
power under Bob Hawke, convened a meeting
of employers and unions to seek a consensus
on economic policy to deal with growing
unemployment.

miniatures of John Webber (1752–93), and the
drawings and watercolours of Thomas Watling
and Thomas Wainewright (1794–1847). Conrad
Martens, who reached Australia in the 1830s,
was the first notable landscape painter; S T Gill
made sketches of life in the goldfields of Victoria;
the Swiss artist Louis Buvelot (1814–88)
represented the Australian scene with an
objective eye. Tom ◊Roberts, Arthur Streeton
(1867–1943), and Julian Ashton (1851–1942)
are others who became known outside Australia.
20th-century artists include William Dobell,
Russell Drysdale, Sidney Nolan, Albert
Namatjira (1902–59). Phil May (1864–1903)
and Will Dyson (1883–1938) were famous
cartoonists.

Austral Islands /'ɒstrəl/ part of ◊French
Polynesia.

Austria /'ɒstriə/ landlocked country in
central Europe, bounded by Hungary to the east,
Yugoslavia to the southeast, Italy to the
southwest, Switzerland to the west, West
Germany to the northwest, and Czechoslovakia
to the northeast.

government Austria is a federal republic,
consisting of nine provinces (*Länder*), each with
its own provincial assembly (*Landtag*),
provincial governor, and councillors. The 1920
constitution was amended in 1929, suspended
during ◊Hitler's regime, and reinstated in 1945.
The two-chamber federal assembly consists of
a national council (*Nationalrat*), and a federal
council (*Bundesrat*). The *Nationalrat* has 183
members, elected by universal suffrage through
proportional representation, for a four-year
term.
The *Bundesrat* has 63 members elected by the
Provincial Assemblies for varying terms. Each
province provides a chair for the *Bundesrat* for a
six-month term. The federal president, elected
by popular vote for a six-year term, is formal
head of state, and chooses the federal chancellor
on the basis of support in the *Nationalrat*. The
federal chancellor is head of government and
chooses the cabinet. Most significant of several
political parties, are the Socialist Party of
Austria (SPO), the Austrian People's Party
(OVP), and the Freedom Party of Austria
(FPO).

history Austria was inhabited in prehistoric
times by Celtic tribes; the country south of the
Danube was conquered by the Romans in 14 BC,
and became part of the Roman Empire. After the
fall of the empire in the 5th century, the region
was occupied by Vandals, Goths, Huns,
Lombards, and Avars. Having conquered the
Avars in 791, ◊Charlemagne established the
East Mark, nucleus of the Austrian empire. In
973 Otto II granted the Mark to the House of
Babenburg, which ruled until 1246. Rudolf of
◊Hapsburg, who became king of the Romans and
Holy Roman Emperor in 1273, siezed Austria
and invested his son as duke in 1282. Until the
empire ceased to exist in 1806, most of the dukes
(from 1453 archdukes) of Austria were elected
Holy Roman Emperor.
Austria, which in 1526 acquired control of
◊Bohemia, was throughout the 16th century a
bulwark of resistance against the Turks, who
besieged Vienna in vain 1529. The ◊Thirty
Years' War (1618–48) did not touch Austria, but
it weakened its rulers. A second Turkish siege of
Vienna failed in 1683, and by 1697 Hungary was
liberated from the ◊Ottoman empire and
incorporated in the Austrian dominion. As a
result of their struggle with ◊Louis XIV the
Hapsburgs in 1713 secured the Spanish
Netherlands and Milan. When Charles VI, last
male Hapsburg in the direct line, died 1740, his
daughter Maria Theresa became Archduchess
of Austria and Queen of Hungary, but the
Elector of Bavaria was elected emperor as
Charles VII. Frederick II of Prussia siezed
Silesia, and the War of the Austrian Succession
(1740–48) followed. Charles VII died in 1745,
and Maria Theresa secured the election of her
husband as Francis I, but she did not recover
Silesia from Frederick.

AUSTRIA: PROVINCES

Province	Capital	Area sq km
Vienna		415
Lower Austria	Wiener Neustadt	19,170
Burgenland	Eisenstadt	3,965
Upper Austria	Linz	11,979
Salzburg	Salzburg	7,153
Styria	Graz	16,385
Carinthia	Klagenfurt	9,533
Tirol	Innsbruck	12,648
Vorarlberg	Bregenz	2,602
		83,850

The archduke Francis who succeeded in 1792 was also elected emperor as Francis II; sometimes opposing, sometimes allied with ◊Napoleon, in 1804 he proclaimed himself emperor of Austria as Francis I, and in 1806 even the name ◊Holy Roman Empire fell out of use. Under the Treaty of Vienna 1815, Francis failed to recover the Austrian Netherlands (annexed by France 1797), but received Lombardy and Venetia.

In 1848 the mixed nationalities within the Austrian empire flared into a rebellion, which was soon crushed. As a result of the Seven Weeks' War of 1866 with Prussia, Austria lost Venetia to Italy. In the following year Francis-Joseph established the dual monarchy of ◊Austria-Hungary. The treaty of Berlin 1878 gave Austria the administration of Bosnia-Hercegovina in the Balkans, though they remained nominally Turkish until Austria annexed them 1908. World War I began 1914 with an Austrian attack on Serbia, Austria-Hungary collapsed 1918, after which Austria comprised only Vienna and its immediately surrounding provinces. A precarious republic was proclaimed, and in 1938 Austria was incorporated into the German Reich under Hitler.

Austria returned to its 1920 constitution in 1945, with a provisional government led by Dr Karl Renner. The Allies divided the country into four zones, occupied by the USSR, the US, Britain, and France. The first post-war elections resulted in an SPO-OVP coalition government. The country was occupied until independence was formally recognized in 1955.

The first post-war non-coalition government was formed in 1966 when the OVP came to power with Josef Klaus as chancellor. In 1970 the SPO formed a minority government under Dr Bruno Kreisky and increased its majority in the 1971 and 1975 general elections. In 1978 the government was nearly defeated over proposals to install the first nuclear power plant. The plan was abandoned, but nuclear energy remained a controversial issue.

In 1983 the SPO lost its majority. Kreisky resigned, refusing to join a coalition. The SPO decline was partly attributed to the emergence of two environmentalist groups, the United Green Party (VGO), and the Austrian Alternative List (ALO). Dr Fred Sinowatz, the new SPO chairman, formed an SPO-FPO coalition government.

In 1985 a controversy arose with the announcement that Dr Kurt Waldheim, former UN secretary-general, was to be a presidential candidate. Despite allegations of his having been a Nazi officer in Yugoslavia, Waldheim eventually became president in 1986. Later that year Sinowatz resigned as chancellor for what he described as personal reasons and was succeeded by Franz Vranitzky. The SPO-FPO coalition broke up when an extreme right-winger, Jorg Haider, became FPO leader. In the Nov elections the SPO's *Nationalrat* seats fell from 90 to 80, the OVP's from 81 to 77, while the FPO's increased from 12 to 18. For the first time the VGO was represented, winning eight seats. Vranitzky offered his resignation but was persuaded by the president to try to form a 'grand coalition' of the SPO and the OVP. Agreement was reached and Vranitzky remained as chancellor with the OVP leader, Dr Alois Mock, as vice-chancellor. Sinowatz denounced the coalition as a betrayal of socialist principles and resigned as chairman of the SPO.

Austria
REPUBLIC OF (*Republik Österreich*)

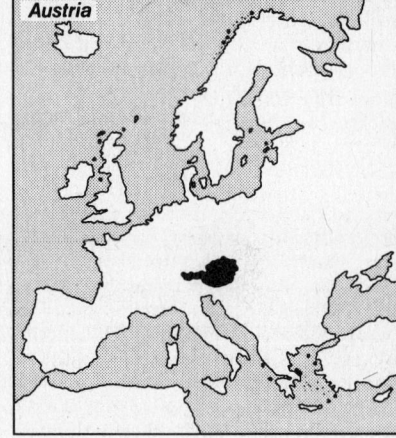

Austria

AREA 83,850 sq km/32,375 sq mi
CAPITAL Vienna
TOWNS Graz, Linz, Salzburg, Innsbruck
PHYSICAL mountainous, with the Danube river basin in the E
FEATURES Austrian Alps (including Zugspitze and Brenner and Semmering passes); river Danube; Hainburg, the largest primeval rain forest left in Europe, now under threat from a dam
HEAD OF STATE Kurt Waldheim from 1986
HEAD OF GOVERNMENT Franz Vranitzky from 1986
GOVERNMENT parliamentary democracy
EXPORTS minerals, manufactured goods
CURRENCY Schilling (21.01 = £1 Sept 1987)
POPULATION (1985) 7,451,000; annual growth rate 0%
LANGUAGE German
RELIGION Roman Catholic 90%
LITERACY 98% (1983)
GDP $66.7 bn (1983); $8,280 per head of population
CHRONOLOGY
1918 Hapsburg rule ended, republic proclaimed.
1938 Incorporated into German Third Reich by Hitler.
1945 1920 constitution reinstated and coalition government formed by the Socialist Party of Austria (SPÖ) and the Austrian People's Party (ÖVP).
1955 Allied occupation ended and the independence of Austria formally recognized.
1966 ÖVP in power with Josef Klaus as chancellor.
1970 SPÖ formed a minority government, with Dr Bruno Kreisky as chancellor.
1983 Kreisky resigned and was replaced by Dr Fred Sinowatz, leading an coalition.
1986 Dr Kurt Waldheim elected president. Sinowatz resigned and was succeeded by Franz Vranitzky. In the Nov general election no party won an overall majority and Vranitzky formed a coalition of the SPÖ and the ÖVP, with the ÖVP leader, Dr Alois Mock, as vice-chancellor. Sinowatz denounced the coalition as a betrayal of socialist principles and resigned his SPÖ chair.

Austria-Hungary /ˈɒstrɪə ˈhʌŋɡəri/ name given to the 'Dual Monarchy' established by Francis Joseph in 1867 between his Empire of Austria and his Kingdom of Hungary. In 1910 it had an area of 100,864 sq km/261,239 sq mi with a population of 51 million. It collapsed in the autumn of 1918. There were only two king-emperors: Francis Joseph 1867–1916 and Charles 1916–18.

Austrian Succession, War of war fought 1740–48 between Austria, supported by England and Holland, and Prussia, France, and Spain. It began when a number of European powers disputed the succession of Maria Theresa, daughter of the Emperor Charles VI, when the latter died in 1740. Frederick the Great of Prussia seized Silesia from the Austrians. At Dettingen in 1743 an army of British, Austrians, and Hanoverians under the command of George II – the last action in which an English sovereign was personally engaged – was victorious over the French, but at Fontenoy in 1745 an Austro-English army was defeated. British naval superiority was confirmed, and there were gains in America and India. The war was ended by the Treaty of Aix-la-Chapelle in 1748.

authoritarianism rule of a country by a dominant elite, who ruthlessly repress opponents and the free press to maintain their own wealth and power. They are frequently indifferent to activities not affecting their security. See also ◊totalitarianism.

autism, infantile a rare syndrome, generally present from birth, characterized by a withdrawn state and a failure to develop normally in language or social behaviour, although the autistic child may show signs of high intelligence in other areas, such as music. Its cause is unknown.

autobiography a person's own biography, or written account of his or her life, distinguished from the journal or diary by being a connected narrative, and from memoirs by dealing less with contemporary events and personalities. A form of autobiography is the confession, concerned with the inner spiritual life, for example, the Confessions of St Augustine and Margery Kempe. *The Boke of Margery Kempe* c. 1432–36 is the oldest autobiography in English; in modern times *Apology* by Colley Cibber is the earliest widely-known autobiography.

autochrome in photography, a single-plate additive colour process devised by the ◊Lumière brothers in 1903. It was the first commercially available process, in use from 1907 to 1935.

autoclave pressurized vessel that uses superheated steam to sterilize materials and equipment such as surgical instruments, similar in principle to a pressure cooker.

auto-da-fé (Portuguese 'act of faith') religious ceremony, including a procession, solemn mass, and sermon, which accompanied the sentencing of heretics by the ◊Spanish Inquisition before they were handed over to the secular authorities for punishment, usually burning.

autogiro or *autogyro* a heavier-than-air craft that supports itself in the air with a rotary wing, or rotor. The Spanish aviator Juan de la ◊Cierva designed the first successful autogiro in 1923. The autogiro was the forerunner of the ◊helicopter but the rotor provides only the lift not the propulsion. In a helicopter the rotor provides both the lift and the propulsion. The autogiro is propelled by an orthodox ◊propeller, like an aeroplane. The three-or four-bladed rotor spins in a horizontal plane on top of the craft. It is not driven by the engine. The blades have an aerofoil cross-section like a plane's wings do. When the autogiro moves forward, the rotor starts to rotate by itself, a state known as autorotation. When travelling fast enough, the rotor develops enough lift from its aerofoil blades to support the craft.

auto-immune disease disease in which the body's defence system is turned against itself, as in rheumatoid ◊arthritis, some types of ◊diabetes, ◊multiple sclerosis, ◊AIDS.

Autolycus /ɔː'tɒlɪkəs/ in Greek mythology, an accomplished thief and trickster, son of the god Hermes, who gave him the power of invisibility.

autolysis in biology, the destruction of a ◊cell after its death by the action of its own ◊enzymes, which break down its structural molecules.

automatic pilot a control device that keeps a plane flying automatically on a given course at a given height and speed. Most airliners cruise on automatic pilot, also called autopilot and gyropilot, for much of the time. American businessman Lawrence Sperry flight-tested a successful autopilot in 1912. The automatic pilot contains a set of ◊gyroscopes that provide reference for the plane's desired course through the air. Sensors detect when the plane deviates from this course and send signals to the control surfaces – the ailerons, elevators and rudder – to take the appropriate corrective action.

automation term coined by American business consultant John Diebold. It refers to the widespread use of self-regulating machines in industry. It builds upon the process of ◊mechanization to further improve manufacturing efficiency. Automation involves the addition of control devices, using electronic sensing and computing techniques which often follow the pattern of human nervous and brain functions, to already mechanized physical processes of production and distribution, for example, steel processing, mining, chemical production, and road, rail and air control. See also ◊cybernetics.

automaton a mechanical figure imitating human or animal performance. The earliest recorded automaton is an Egyptian wooden pigeon of 400 BC. Automatons are usually designed for decorative appeal rather than being purely functional, like robots. The charm of the automaton has been exploited in ballet, for example, *Coppélia* and *La Boutique Fantasque*.

autonomic nervous system in mammals, the part of the ◊nervous system which controls the involuntary activities of the smooth ◊muscles (of the digestive tract, blood vessels, etc.), the heart and the glands. It is made up of two systems, the *sympathetic* and the *parasympathetic*. Most major body organs are controlled by both these systems, working together to coordinate bodily functions. The sympathetic system is involved in response to stress, when it speeds the heart rate, increases ◊blood pressure and generally prepares the body for action. The parasympathetic system is more important when the body is at rest, since it slows the heart rate, decreases blood pressure and stimulates the ◊digestive system.

Autonomisti semi-clandestine amalgam of Marxist student organizations, linked with ◊guerrilla groups and such acts as the kidnapping and murder of Italian premier Aldo Moro by the Red Brigade in 1978.

autosome any ◊chromosome in the cell other than a sex chromosome.

auto-suggestion conscious or unconscious acceptance of an idea as true, without demanding rational proof, but with potential subsequent effect for good or ill. Pioneered by ◊Coué in healing, it is used in modern psychotherapy to conquer nervous habits, dependence on tobacco, alcohol, and so on.

autotroph any living organism which synthesizes ◊organic substances from inorganic molecules using light or chemical energy. All green plants and many ◊planktonic organisms are autotrophs, using sunlight to convert carbon dioxide and water into sugars by ◊photosynthesis. A few bacteria use chemical energy; for example, some bacteria use the chemical energy of sulphur compounds to synthesize organic substances. Materials synthesized and stored by autotrophs provide the energy sources of all other organisms: they are the *primary producers* in all ◊food chains. See also ◊heterotrophs.

autumn crocus the mauve meadow saffron *Colchicum autumnale*, family Liliaceae. It yields *colchicine*, used in treating gout, and is used in in plant breeding (it causes plants to double the numbers of their chromosomes).

Auvergne /əu'veən/ ancient province of central France and a modern region (*départements* Allier, Cantal, Haute-Loire and Puy-de-Dôme). Mountainous, it lies in the heart of the Central Plateau, composed chiefly of volcanic rocks in several masses.

Auxerre /əu'seə/ capital of Yonne *département* France, 170 km/106 mi SE of Paris, on the river Yonne. The Gothic cathedral, founded in 1215, has fine sculptures and stained glass. Population (1973) 40,000.

auxin a ◊plant hormone that promotes stem and root growth in plants. Auxins influence many aspects of plant growth and development, including cell enlargement, inhibition of development of axillary buds, ◊tropisms and the initiation of roots. The most common, naturally occuring auxin is known as indoleacetic acid, or IAA, which is synthesized in the shoot apex and transported to other parts of the plant. Synthetic auxins are used in rooting powders for cuttings, and in some weedkillers, where the high concentrations cause such rapid growth that the plants die.

Ava /'ɑːvə/ ancient capital of Burma. Situated on the Irrawaddy, 30 kings reigned in Ava from 1364 to 1783. Ava was also formerly famous for its Buddhist temples.

avalanche (French *avaler*, to swallow) a fall of a mass of snow and ice down a steep slope. Avalanches occur because of the unstable nature of snow masses in mountain areas. Changes of temperature or sudden sound or earth-borne vibrations can cause a snowfield to start moving, particularly on slopes of more than 35°. The snow compacts into ice as it moves, and rocks may be carried along, both important factors in the damage caused by an avalanche.

Avalon /'ævəlon/ in Celtic legend, the island of the blest or paradise, and in the Arthurian legend the land of heroes, to which the dead king was conveyed. It has been associated with Glastonbury.

Avar member of a ◊Tatar nomadic people who in the 6th century invaded the area of Russia N of the Black Sea previously held by the Huns.

Avatar in Hindu mythology, the descent of a deity to earth in a visible form. Most famous are the ten Avatars of ◊Vishnu.

Avebury /'eɪvbəri/ Europe's largest stone circle (diameter 412 m/450 yd), Wiltshire, England; probably constructed in the Neolithic period 3500 years ago; it is linked with nearby ◊Silbury Hill. The village of Avebury was built within the circle, and many of the stones were used for building material.

Avebury /'eɪvbəri/ John Lubbock, 1st Baron Avebury 1834–1913. British banker. Liberal (from 1886 Liberal Unionist) Member of Parliament 1870–1900, he was largely responsible for the Bank Holidays Act 1871.

Avedon /'eɪvdən/ Richard 1923– . American photographer. A successful fashion photographer with *Harper's Bazaar* magazine in New York in the mid 1940s, he has become one of the highest-paid commercial photographers.

Ave Maria (Latin 'Hail, Mary'); Christian prayer to the Virgin Mary, which takes its name from the Archangel Gabriel's salutation of the Virgin Mary (Luke 11:28), when announcing that she would be the mother of the Messiah.

avens name given to several low-growing plants of the rose family. *Wood avens* or *herb bennet Geum urbanum* grows through most of Europe, N Asia and North Africa, in woods and shady places on damp soils. It has yellow five-petalled flowers and pinnate leaves and grows up to 60 cm/2 ft. *Water avens Geum rivale* has nodding pink flowers and is found in marshes and other damp places. *Mountain avens Dryas octopetala* is found in mountain and arctic areas of Europe, Asia and North America. A creeping perennial, it has, as its name suggests, eight petals, sometimes more on its white flowers with yellow stamens.

average number that represents the typical member of a group of numbers. The simplest include the arithmetic and geometric ◊mean; a ◊median or root-mean square is a more complex average.

Avernus /ə'vɜːnəs/ circular lake, near Naples, Italy. Because it formerly gave off fumes that killed birds, it was thought by the Romans to be the entrance to the lower world.

Averroes /,ævə'rəuiːz/ 1126–1198. Arabian philosopher; in Arabic, Ibn Roshd. Born at Córdova in Spain, he became judge of Seville and of Córdova, but was accused of heresy and banished 1195. Later he was recalled, and died at Marrakesh. His philosophical writings, including the important commentaries on Aristotle, became known to the West through Latin translations, and exercised a great influence on Christian thinkers. 'Averroism' was taught at Paris and elsewhere in the 13th century by the 'Averroists', who distinguished philosophical truth from revealed religion.

Avicenna /,ævi'senə/ 979–1037. (in Arabic, Ibn Sina). Arabian philosopher and physician. Born near Bokhara, he made a profound study of the Koran, philosophy, and the science of his day, and won a high reputation as physician. He died at Hamadan, where he had been vizier. His *Canon Medicinae* was a standard work for centuries. His philosophical writings were influenced by Al-Farabi and by Aristotle and the Neoplatonists, and influenced the scholastics of the 13th century.

Aviemore /,ævi'mɔː/ winter sports centre, in the Highlands, Scotland, SE of Inverness among the Cairngorms Mountains.

Avignon /'æviːnjɒn/ city in Provence, France, capital of Vaucluse *département*, on the river Rhône NW of Marseilles. An important Gallic and Roman city, it has its 14th-century walls, the famous 12th-century bridge (only half still standing), a 13th-century cathedral, and the palace built 1334–42 during the residence here of the popes. Avignon was papal property 1348–1791. Population (1983) 88,650.

Avila /'ævilə/ town in Spain, capital of province of the same name, 90 km/56 mi NW of Madrid. It has the remains of the Moorish castle, a Gothic cathedral, and the convent and church of ◊Saint Teresa, who was born here. Population (1981) 40,200.

avocado tree of the laurel family *Persea americana*, native to Central America. Its dark green pear-shaped 'fruit', with a flesh of buttery texture, is used in salads.

avocet wading bird, genus *Recurvirostra*, with characteristic long narrow upturned bill used in sifting water as it feeds. About 45 cm/1.5 ft long, it has long legs and partly-webbed feet to wade in the shallows, and black and white plumage. Four species occur around the world.

Avogadro /,ævə'gɑːdrəu/ Amedeo Conte di Quaregna 1776–1856. Italian physicist. His work on gases still has relevance for modern atomic studies.

Avogadro's hypothesis in chemistry, the law which states that equal volumes of all gases, when at the same temperature and pressure, have the same numbers of molecules. This law was first propounded by Count Amadeo ◊Avogadro.

avoirdupois system of weights based on the pound (equal to 0.45 kg), which consists of 16 ounces (each of 16 drams) or 7,000 grains (each equal to 65 mg). The Troy pound, used for precious metals, has only 12 ounces or 5,250 grains; one Troy pound = 0.37kg.

Avon /'eivən/ Celtic word for 'river', name of several rivers in England and Scotland. The chief are: the Upper, or Warwickshire, Avon, rising in the Northampton uplands near Naseby and joining the Severn at Tewkesbury; 154 km/96 mi. The Lower, or Bristol, Avon, 121 km/75 mi rises in the Cotswolds, and flows into the Bristol Channel at Avonmouth. The East, or Salisbury, Avon rises S of the Marlborough Downs, and flows into the English Channel at Christchurch, length, 104 km/65 mi.

Avon /'eivən/ county of SW England, created in 1974. It includes Bristol, the southern part of Gloucestershire, and a large part of Somerset, including Bath, Weston-super-Mare, Radstock and Clevedon. Area 1,336 sq km/516 sq mi; population (1981) 909,400.

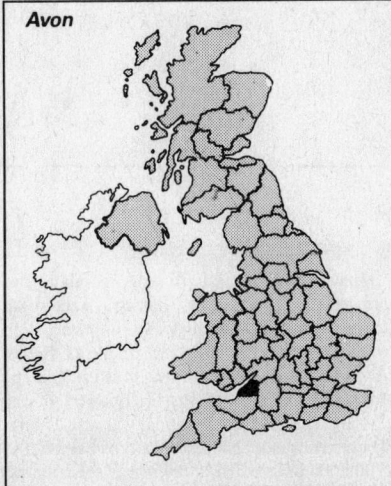

Avon

Awe /ɔː/ longest (37 km/23 mi) of the Scottish freshwater lochs, in Strathclyde, SE of Oban. It is drained by the river Awe into Loch Etive. The hydroelectric installations are a tourist attraction.

Axholme, Isle of /'ækshəum/ area of 2,000 ha/5,000 acres in Humberside, England, bounded by the Trent, Don, Idle, and Torne rivers, where 'medieval type' open field strip farming is still practised. The largest village, Epworth, is the birthplace of John ◊Wesley.

axil the upper angle between a leaf (or bract) and the stem from which it grows. Organs developing in the axil, such as flowers, shoots and buds, are termed axillary, or lateral.

Axis name given to the alliance of Nazi Germany and Fascist Italy before and during World War II. The Rome-Berlin Axis was formed in 1936, when Italy was being threatened with sanctions because of its invasion of Abyssinia, and became a full military and political alliance in May 1939. A 10-year alliance between Germany, Italy and Japan (Rome-Berlin-Tokyo Axis) was signed in Sept 1940, and was subsequently joined by Hungary, Bulgaria, Romania, and the puppet states of Slovakia and Croatia. The Axis collapsed with the fall of Mussolini and the surrender of Italy in 1943.

Axminster /'æksminstə/ carpet type of cut-pile, patterned carpet originally made in Axminster, a small town in Devon, England, near Exeter. Slightly coarser than Wilton, it is produced by a method that permits up to 240 colours.

axolotl aquatic larval form ('tadpole') of the Mexican salamander *Ambystoma mexicanum* which may reach 30 cm/1 ft long and breed without changing to the adult form.

axon the long thread-like extension of a ◊nerve cell that conducts electro-chemical impulses received by the cell body towards other nerve cells, or towards an effector organ such as a muscle. At the tip of the axon are ◊synapses which transmit the nerve impulse.

Axum alternative transliteration of ◊Aksum, an ancient town in Ethiopia.

ayatollah honorific title, meaning 'sign of God', awarded to Shi'ite Muslims in Iran by popular consent, as, for example, to the Ayatollah Ruhollah ◊Khomeini.

Ayckbourn /'eikbɔːn/ Alan 1939– . British playwright, and director of the Theatre-in-the-Round, Scarborough, from 1959. His prolific output, characterized by his acute ear for comic dialogue, includes the trilogy *The Norman Conquests* 1974, *A Woman in Mind* 1986, and *A Small Family Business* 1987.

Aycliffe /'eiklif/ town in Durham, England, on the river Skerne, developed from 1947 as a new town. Population (1981) 36,825.

aye-aye nocturnal tree-climbing ◊lemur *Daubentonia madagascariensis* of Madagascar. It has gnawing, rodent-like teeth and a long middle finger with which it probes for insects. Just over 1 m/3 ft long, it is now very rare through loss of its forest habitat.

Ayer /eə/ A(lfred) J(ules) 1910– . British philosopher, Wykeham professor of logic at Oxford from 1959. He established his reputation with *Language, Truth and Logic* 1936, an exposition of the theory of 'logical positivism', presenting a criterion by which meaningful statements (essentially truths of logic and mathematics, as well as statements deriving from observation and experience) could be distinguished from metaphysical utterances (for example, claims that there is a God, or that the world external to our own minds is illusory), which the logical positivists considered to be meaningless. Later works included *Probability and Evidence* 1972. He was knighted in 1970.

Ayers Rock /ˈeəz/ vast ovate mass of pinkish rock in Northern Territory, Australia; 335 m/1,100 ft high and 9 km/6 mi round, named after Sir Henry Ayers, a premier of South Australia. For the Aboriginals, whose paintings decorate its caves, it has magical significance.

Ayesha /ˈaɪʃə/ 611–678. third and favourite wife of ◊Muhammad, whom he married when she was nine. Her father, Abu Bakr, became ◊caliph on Muhammad's death in 632, and she bitterly opposed the later succession to the caliphate of ◊Ali, who had once accused her of infidelity.

Aymara /ˌaɪməˈrɑː/ member of an ◊American Indian people of Bolivia and Peru, who were conquered first by the Incas and then by the Spaniards. Their language survives and their modern Roman Catholicism incorporates elements of their old beliefs.

Ayot St Lawrence /ˈeɪət sənt ˈlɒrəns/ village in Hertfordshire, England, where Shaw's Corner (home of G B ◊Shaw) is preserved.

Ayr /eə/ town in Strathclyde, Scotland, at the mouth of the river Ayr. The 'Auld Brig' was built in the 15th century, the 'New Brig' in 1788 (rebuilt 1879). Ayr is famous for its associations with Robert Burns. Prestwick airport is to the north. Population (1981) 49,500.

Ayrshire /ˈeəʃə/ former county of SW Scotland, with a 113 km/70 mi coastline on the Firth of Clyde. In 1975 the major part was merged in the region of Strathclyde, the remaining sector, approximately S of the Water of Girvan and including Girvan itself, became part of Dumfries and Galloway.

Ayrton /ˈeətn/ Michael 1921–1975. British painter, sculptor, and illustrator. Ayrton developed an obsession with the Daedalus myth from 1961, producing bronzes of Icarus and a fictional autobiography of Daedalus, *The Maze Maker* 1967. He designed and built a maze with 2 m/6 ft walls of stone and brick and 1,000 m/3,300 ft long, in the Catskill Mountains, New York State, USA.

Aytoun /ˈeɪtn/ Robert 1570–1638. Scottish poet employed and knighted by James I; noted for his love poems. Aytoun is the reputed author of the lines on which Robert Burns based 'Auld Lang Syne'.

Aytoun /ˈeɪtn/ William Edmonstoune 1813–1865. Scottish poet, born in Edinburgh, chiefly remembered for his *Lays of the Scottish Cavaliers* 1848, and for the *Bon Gaultier Ballads* 1855, which he wrote in collaboration with Sir T Martin.

Ayurveda ancient Hindu system of medicine, the main principles of which are derived from the Vedas, and still practised in India in Ayurvedic hospitals and dispensaries.

azalea plant of the family Ericaceae, closely related to *Rhododendron*, in which genus they are now generally included. There are several species, natives of Asia and North America, and from these many cultivated varieties have been derived which make fine ornamental shrubs – particularly the Japanese azaleas. Several species are highly poisonous.

Azaña /əˈθænjə/ Manuel 1880–1940. Spanish politician and first prime minister (1931–33) of the second Spanish Republic. He was last president of the Republic during the Civil War (1936–39), before the establishment of a dictatorship under Francisco Franco.

Azerbaijan /ˌæzəbaɪˈdʒɑːn/ constituent republic of the Soviet Union from 1936.
area 86,600 sq km/33,400 sq mi
capital Baku
towns Kirovabad
features Caspian Sea; the country ranges from semi-desert to the Caucasus mountains
products oil, iron, copper; fruit, vines; cotton, silk; carpets
population 6,100,000, 74% Azerbaijani, 10% Russian, 9% Armenian
language Turkic
religion traditionally Shi'ite Muslim
recent history A member of the Transcaucasian Federation in 1917, it became an independent republic in 1918, but was occupied by the Red Army in 1920. (See ◊Georgia).

Azerbaijan

Azerbaijan /ˌæzəbaɪˈdʒɑːn/ Iranian two provinces of NW Iran, Eastern Azerbaijan (capital Tabriz) and Western Azerbaijan (capital Rezayeh). Like the people of Soviet Azerbaijan, the people are Muslim (Shiah) ethnic Turks, descendants of followers of the ◊Mongol Khans, whose capital was also Tabriz. There are about 5,000,000 in Azerbaijan, and 3,000,000 distributed in the rest of the country, where they form a strong middle class. In 1946, with Soviet backing, they briefly established their own republic. Denied autonomy under the Shah, they rose 1979–80 against the supremacy of Ayatollah ◊Khomeini, and were forcibly repressed, although a degree of autonomy was promised.

Azhar /əˈzɑː/ El. Muslim university and mosque at Cairo. Founded by Jawhar, commander in chief of the army of the Fatimid caliph, in 970, it is claimed to be the oldest university in the world. It became the centre of Islamic learning, with several subsidiary foundations, and is now primarily a school of Koranic teaching.

Azilian name given to an archaeological period following the close of the Old Stone (Palaeolithic) Age, and regarded as one of the cultures of the Mesolithic Age. It was first recognized by Piette at Mas d'Azil, a village in Ariège, France.

Azincourt /ˌæzæŋˈkʊə/ French form of ◊Agincourt.

Azores /əˈzɔːz/ group of nine islands in the N Atlantic; area 2,335 sq km/922 sq mi; population (1981) 251,350. They are outlying peaks of the Mid-Atlantic Ridge, and are volcanic in origin. The capital is Ponta Delgada on the main island, San Miguel. Portuguese from 1430, they were granted partial autonomy in 1976, but remain a Portuguese overseas territory. They command the Western shipping lanes, and a separatist movement is backed by USSR and Libya.

Azorín /ˌæθɔːˈriːn/ pseudonym of José Martínez Ruiz 1873–1967. Spanish writer, born in Alicante province. His works include volumes of critical essays and short stories, plays and novels, such as the autobiographical *La voluntad/The Choice* 1902 and *Antonio Azorín* 1903 – the author adopted the name of the eponymous hero of the latter as his pseudonym.

Azov /ˈeɪzɒv/ inland sea of the USSR forming a gulf in the NE of the Black Sea.

Aztec /ˈæzteks/ member of a Mexican ◊American Indian people who migrated from further north in the 12th century, and in 1325 began reclaiming lake marshland to build their capital, Tenochtitlán, on the site of modern Mexico City. Under Montezuma I (reigned from 1440), they created a great empire in central and southern Mexico. Aztec rule was resented as oppressive, and Montezuma II (reigned from 1502) was able to put up only slight resistance when the conquistador Cortes landed in 1519. Montezuma was killed and Tenochtitlán was subsequently destroyed.
Aztec architecture, jewellery (gold, jade, and turquoise), and textiles were magnificent. Their form of writing combined the hieroglyph and pictograph, and they used a complex calendar, which combined a sacred period of 260 days with the solar year of 365 days. Propitiatory rites were performed at the 'dangerous' period, once in every 52 years, when the beginning of the two coincided, and all temples were rebuilt (useful as a date mark for archaeologists). Their own god was Huitzilopochtli (Humming-bird Wizard), but they also worshipped the feathered serpent ◊Quetzalcoatl, inherited from the conquered Toltecs, and others. They practised human sacrifice on a large scale, tearing the heart from the living body or flaying people alive. War captives were obtained for this purpose, but their own people may also have been used. Pictures show that they played a type of football, in which legs rather than feet were used to propel a solid rubber ball. Some of the players were killed after the game, but it is not certain whether the losers were sacrificed for having lost, or the winners promoted to the next world for having won.

B second letter of the alphabet. It corresponds to the Greek *beta* and the Semitic *beth*; and as written in the modern W European alphabet is derived from the classical Latin.

Baade /'bɑːdə/ Walter 1893–1960. US astronomer, who made observations that doubled the distance scale of the Universe. Born in Germany, Baade worked at Mount Wilson observatory during World War II, where he discovered that ◊stars come in two distinct populations according to their age, known as Population I (the youngest) and Population II (the oldest). Later, he found that Cepheid variable stars of Population I are brighter than had been supposed, and that distances calculated from them were wrong. Baade's figures showed that the ◊Universe was twice as large as previously thought, and twice as old.

Baader-Meinhof gang /'bɑːdə 'maɪnhɒf/ name by which the West German guerrilla group the *Rote Armee Fraktion*/Red Army Faction, formed in the 1970s, was known. The name derives from its two leaders Andreas Baader 1943–77 and Ulrike Meinhof 1934–76.

Baal /beɪl/ Semitic word meaning 'lord' or 'owner', used as a divine title of their chief male gods by the Phoenicians and Canaanites. Their worship, often orgiastic and of a phallic character, deities of fertility, was strongly denounced by the Hebrew prophets.

Baalbek /'bɑːlbek/ city of ancient Syria, in modern Lebanon, 60 km/36 mi NE of Beirut. Originally a centre of Baal worship. Its ruins, including Roman temples, survive. The Greeks identified Baal with Helios, the sun, and renamed Baalbek Heliopolis. The Temple of Bacchus, built in the second century AD, is still almost intact. At 1,150 m/3,000 ft above sea level, it lies today among orchards of the Bekaa region.

Ba'ath Party socialist party aiming at the extended union of all Arab countries, active in Iraq and Syria.

Babbage /'bæbɪdʒ/ Charles 1801–1871. British mathematician credited with being the inventor of the computer. As a young man he assisted John Herschel with his astronomical calculations but became involved with calculating machines when he worked on his

Baalbek The Temple of Bacchus, built in the 2nd century AD, is still almost intact. At 1,150 m/3,000 ft above sea level, it lies today among orchards of the Bekaa region.

◊difference engine for the British Admiralty, though this was never completed. He designed an ◊analytical engine, a general-purpose computing device for performing different calculations according to a program input on punched cards (an idea borrowed from the Jacquard loom). This device too was never built, but it embodied many of the principles on which modern digital computers are based.

Babbit metal an ◊alloy of tin, copper and antimony used to make bearings. American inventor Isaac Babbit developed the alloy in 1839.

babbler bird of the thrush family Muscicapidae with a loud babbling cry. Babblers, subfamily Timaliinae, are found in the Old World, and there are some 250 species in the group.

Babel /'beɪbl/ Hebrew name for ◊Babylon, chiefly associated with the ◊Tower of Babel which, in the Genesis story, was erected in the plain of Shinar by the descendants of Noah. The site has been identified with the temple of E-sagila in Babylon and the mound of Birs Nimrud (Borsippa) near the city.

Babbage English mathematician Charles Babbage was grandfather to the modern computer. He spent most of his resources and much of his life wrestling with this prototype of a complex analytical machine, which would use punched cards to store answers for future operations and print results.

Babel /'bɑːbl/ Isaak Emmanuilovich 1894–1939/40. Russian writer. Born in Odessa, he was an ardent supporter of the Revolution and fought with Budyenny's cavalry in the Polish campaign of 1921–22, an experience which inspired *Konarmiya*/*Red Cavalry* 1926. Best known of his other works is *Odesskie rasskazy*/*Stories from Odessa* 1924, which portrays the life of the Odessa Jews.

Bab-el-Mandeb /'bæb el 'mændeb/ strait that joins the Red Sea and the Gulf of Aden, and separates Arabia and Africa. The name, meaning 'gate of tears', refers to its currents.

Babeuf /bɑː'bɜːf/ François Noël 1760–1797. French revolutionary journalist, a pioneer of practical socialism. In 1794 he founded a newspaper in Paris, later known as the *Tribune of the People*, in which he demanded the equality of all people. He was guillotined for conspiring against the Directory.

Babi faith alternative name for ◊Baha'i faith.

Babington /'bæbɪŋtən/ Anthony 1561–1586. English traitor who hatched a plot to assassinate ◊Elizabeth I and replace her by ◊Mary, Queen of Scots; its discovery led to Mary's execution and his own.

babirusa a wild pig *Babirousa babyrussa* found in Sulawesi, Buru and nearby Indonesian islands. The male has large upper tusks which grow upwards through the skin of the snout and curve back towards the forehead. Nocturnal, and becoming rare, the babirusa is up to 80 cm/2.5 ft at the shoulder, lives in moist forests and by water, and swims well.

Babi Yar /'baːbi 'jaː/ site of a massacre of Jews by the Germans in 1941, near Kiev, USSR. It is also the title of a poem by Yevgeni ◊Yevtushenko 1961, condemning Soviet anti-semitism.

baboon type of large monkey, genus *Papio*, with a long dog-like muzzle and large canine teeth, spending much of its time on the ground in open country. Various species inhabit Africa and SW Arabia, including the *olive baboon Papio anubis* from W Africa to Kenya, the *chacma Papio ursinus* from S Africa, and the *sacred baboon Papio hamadryas* from NE Africa and SW Arabia, in which the male has a 'cape' of long hair. Males, with head and body up to 1.1 m/3.5 ft long, are larger than females and dominant males rule the 'troops' in which baboons live.

Babur title (Arabic 'lion') given to ◊Zahir ud-din Mohammed.

Babylon /'bæbɪlən/ capital of ancient Babylonia, on the left bank of the Euphrates. The site is in modern Iraq, 88 km/55 mi S of Baghdad and 8 km/5 mi N of Hilla, which is built chiefly of bricks from the ruins of Babylon. Babylon first rose to importance under Hammurabi, and under Nebuchadnezzar I it was a magnificent city. The site of the famous hanging gardens, probably built by Nebuchadnezzar II, has not been determined.

Babylonian captivity originally, the exile of Jewish deportees to Babylon after ◊Nebuchadnezzar's capture of Jerusalem in 586 BC; traditionally, it lasted 70 years, but ◊Cyrus actually allowed them home in 536 BC. By analogy, the name was also applied to the Papal exile to ◊Avignon 1309–77.

Bacău /baː'kəu/ industrial city (oil refining) in Romania, 250 km/155 mi NNE of Bucharest, on the Bistrita; population (1983) 700,300.

Baccalauréat the French school-leaving certificate and qualification for university entrance, also available on an international basis as an alternative to English ◊A Levels.

baccarat casino card game with two forms: *chemin de fer* and *banque*. The cards are dealt from a shoe-like box.

Bacchus /'bækəs/ Greek and Roman god of wine, also known in Greece as ◊Dionysus. In Greek legend Bacchus was the son of Zeus and

Semele. He toured the cities of Greece, bringing the gift of the vine to those who welcomed him, and overwhelming those who opposed him with madness and intoxication. The worship of Bacchus took the form of wild and licentious revels, called *Bacchanalia*.

Bach /baːx/ Carl Philip Emmanuel 1714–1788. German composer. The most gifted of the children of Johann Sebastian ◊Bach, he was in the service of Frederick the Great 1740–67. He wrote over 200 pieces for the clavier, and published an important critical textbook on its technique. From 1768 he was Kapellmeister at Hamburg. His church music includes the oratorio *The Israelites in the Wilderness*. He is important as a pioneer of the new 'harmonic' (as opposed to 'polyphonic') music, and Mozart, Haydn and Beethoven all owed a considerable debt to him. He preferred the clavier to the old-fashioned harpsichord, was a brilliant concert performer, and developed a style of composition better suited to the modern piano.

Bach /baːx/ Johann Christian 1735–1782. German composer, the eleventh son of Johann Sebastian ◊Bach. Born in Leipzig, he became well known in Italy as a composer of operas. In 1762 he was invited to London, where he became music master to the royal family. He remained in England until his death, enjoying great popularity both as a composer and performer.

Bach /baːx/ Johann Sebastian 1685–1750. German composer. Born at Eisenach, in Thuringia, he came of a distinguished musical family. At 15 he became a chorister at Lüneburg, and at 19 organist at Arnstadt. Subsequent appointments included positions at the courts of Weimar and Anhalt-Köther, and finally, in 1723, that of musical director at St Thomas's choir school in Leipzig, where, apart from his brief visit to the court of Frederick the Great of Prussia in 1747, he remained until his death. Bach married twice, and had numerous children, several of whom died in infancy. His second wife, Anna Magdalena Wülkens, was a soprano singer; she also acted as his amanuensis, when in later years his sight failed. Bach was a master of contrapuntal technique, and his music marks the culmination of the Baroque polyphonic style. His sacred music includes 200 church cantatas, the Easter and Christmas oratorios, the two great Passions, of St Matthew and St John, and the Mass in B minor. His orchestral music includes the six *Brandenburg concertos*, other concertos for clavier and for violin, and four orchestral suites. Bach's keyboard music, for clavier and for organ, is of equal importance and includes the collection of 48 preludes and fugues known as *The Well-tempered Clavier*, the *Goldberg Variations*, the *Italian Concerto*, and the *French* and *English Suite*. Of his organ music the most important examples are the chorale preludes. He also wrote chamber music and songs. Two important works written in his later years illustrate the principles and potential of his polyphonic art – the *Musical Offering* and *The Art of Fugue*.

Bach /baːx/ Wilhelm Friedemann 1710–1784. German composer, and famous as an organist, improviser, and master of counterpoint, he was the eldest son of Johann Sebastian ◊Bach.

bacillus a group of rod-like ◊bacteria that occur everywhere in the soil and air, and are responsible for diseases such as anthrax as well as causing food spoilage. See ◊bacteria.

backgammon board game (Old English 'back game'), of which the children's version is ludo. The board is marked out in 24 triangular points of alternating colours, 12 to each side. Throwing two dice, the players move their 15 flat, circular pieces round the board to the six points which form their own 'inner table'; the first player to move all his pieces off the board is the winner. Players have included Tutankhamen, Chaucer, Henry VIII, and Pepys. In the 1920s it became a casino game when a group was allowed to play a single opponent, and the American innovation of a 'doubling cube' made it more exciting by repeatedly doubling the stakes. Its popularity revived in the 1970s.

Bacon /'beɪkən/ Francis 1561–1626. English statesman, philosopher, and essayist. The nephew of Queen Elizabeth's adviser, Lord ◊Burghley, he was a follower of the Earl of ◊Essex, but when his patron lost favour, he helped secure his conviction as a traitor (in 1601). Knighted on the accession of James I (in 1603), he became Lord Chancellor in 1618 and a peer, first as Baron Verulam, then in 1621 as Viscount St Albans. Later that year he was accused of bribe-taking, and, having confessed, was fined £40,000 and spent four days in the Tower of London. Although he had admitted taking the money, he claimed that he had not always given the verdict to his paymasters. His works include *Essays* 1597, notable for proverbial brevity; *The Advancement of Learning* 1605, a seminal work discussing scientific method; and *The New Atlantis* 1626 describing a Utopian state in which scientific knowledge is systematically sought and exploited. These works were in large measure the inspiration behind the founding of the ◊Royal Society. The *Baconian Theory*, originated by James Willmot in 1785, suggests that the works of Shakespeare were written by Bacon.

Bacon /'beɪkən/ Francis 1909– . British artist. Born in Dublin, he was largely self-taught, beginning to paint c. 1930 and holding his first show in London in 1949. A realist who maintains an interest in figurative painting in an era dominated by abstraction, Bacon distorts and mutilates his human figures to express the complexity of their emotions, for example *Study after Velazquez* 1953, a series of variations on that artist's portrait of Pope Innocent X.

Bacon /'beɪkən/ Roger 1214–1292. English philospher and scientist, one of the boldest thinkers of the Middle Ages. Born in Somerset, and educated at Oxford and Paris, he became a Franciscan friar and until c.1251 was in Paris lecturing on Aristotle. Then he wrote a number of works in Latin, eg *On Mirrors, Metaphysical Questions, On the Multiplication of Species*, and in 1266, at the invitation of his friend Pope

Bacon English philosopher and statesman Sir Francis Bacon was a long-serving adviser to Elizabeth I and James I, and writer on scientific thought and method.

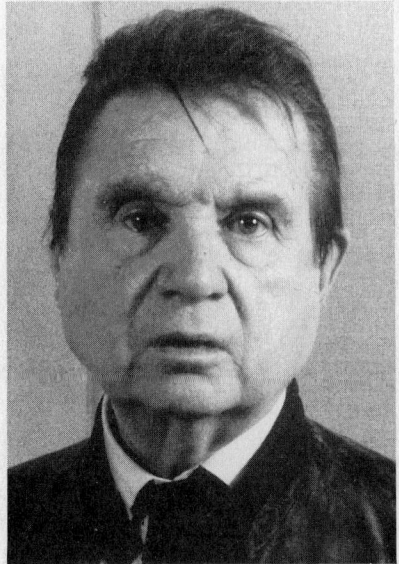

Bacon British artist Francis Bacon, photographed in 1958. In an era dominated by abstract art, Bacon is the leading figurative painter. A large collection of his work is housed at the Tate Gallery, London.

Clement IV, he began his *Opus Majus*, a compendium of all branches of knowledge. In 1268 he sent this with his *Opus Minus* and other writings to the Pope. In 1277 he was condemned and imprisoned by the Church for 'certain novelties' and not released till 1292. He followed the maxim 'Cease to be ruled by dogmas and authorities; look at the world!' He foresaw the magnifying properties of convex lenses, the extensive use of gunpowder, and the possibility of mechanical cars, boats, and flying machines.

bacteria microscopic unicellular organisms with ◊prokaryotic cells. They are now classified biochemically, but their varying shapes provide a rough classification, for example, *cocci* are round or oval, *rods* are cylindrical, and *spirillae* are spiral. They reproduce by ◊binary fission, and since this may occur approximately every 20 minutes, a single bacterium is potentially capable of producing 16 million copies of itself in a day. Bacteria mutate readily, a characteristic which accounts for the rapid emergence of strains which are resistant to antibiotics. Unlike ◊viruses, bacteria do not necessarily need contact with a live cell to become active. Bacteria are generally thought of as harmful, and certain types do cause such diseases as anthrax, cholera, diphtheria, pneumonia, scarlet fever and tuberculosis. However, many other types perform useful functions in the healthy human body, break down waste products or improve soil fertility. Bacteria are essential in many food and industrial processes, for example, making butter, cheese and yoghurt, as well as curing tobacco, tanning leather, sewage disposal, and (by virtue of the ability of bacteria to attack metal) in cleaning a ship's hull and de-rusting its tanks, and even extracting minerals from a mine. Bacteria cannot normally survive temperatures above 100°C/212°F (see ◊pasteurization), but those in deep sea hot vents in the eastern Pacific are believed to withstand temperatures of 350°C/662°F. See also ◊archaebacteria, ◊cyanobacteria, ◊biosynthesis.

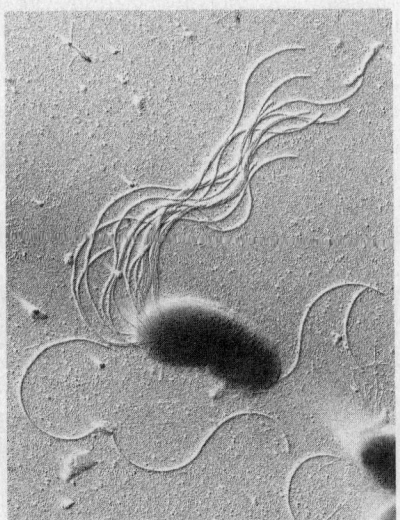

bacteria Transmission electron micrograph (TEM) shadowed technique of *Pseudomonas fluorescens*, a rod-shaped, motile bacterium, magnified 37,500 times. Pseudomonas species are found in the soil, the most active spoilage organisms, decomposing organic matter and recycling nitrogen.

bacteriology the study of ◊bacteria.

bacteriophage a ◊virus that attacks ◊bacteria.

Bactria /'bæktrɪə/ former region of central Asia (modern Afghanistan, Pakistan and Soviet Central Asia) which was partly conquered by ◊Alexander the Great; in the 3rd–6th centuries BC it was a great centre of E–W trade and cultural exchange.

Bactrian species of camel *Camelus bactrianus* found wild in the Gobi Desert in Central Asia. Body fat is stored in two humps on the back. It has very long winter fur, which is shed in ragged lumps. The head and body length is about 3 m/10 ft, and the camel is up to 2.1 m/6.8 ft tall at the shoulder. Most Bactrian camels are domesticated and are used as beasts of burden in W Asia.

Badajoz /ˌbædəˈxəʊθ/ city in Extremadura, Spain, on the Portuguese frontier; population (1981) 111,500. It has a 13th-century cathedral and ruins of a Moorish castle. Badajoz has often been besieged, and was stormed by ◊Wellington in 1812, with the loss of 59,000 British troops.

Baden /'baːdn/ former state of SW Germany, which had Karlsruhe as its capital. Baden was captured from the Romans in 282 by the Alemanni, later it became a margravate, and in 1806 a grand duchy. A state of the German empire 1871–1918, then a republic, and under Hitler a *Gau* (province), it was divided between the *Länder* of Württemberg-Baden and Baden in 1945, and in 1952 made part of ◊Baden-Württemberg.

Baden /'baːdn/ town in Aargau canton, Switzerland, near Zurich, whose radioactive mineral waters have been visited since Roman times.

Baden-Baden /'baːdn 'baːdn/ Black Forest spa in Baden-Württemberg, West Germany; population (1984) 49,000. Fashionable in the 19th century, it is now a conference centre.

Baden-Powell /'beɪdn 'pəʊəl/ Agnes 1854–1945. sister of Robert ◊Baden-Powell, she helped him found the Girl ◊Guides.

Baden-Powell /'beɪdn 'pəʊəl/ Lady Olave 1889–1977. Wife of Robert ◊Baden-Powell from 1912, she was the first and only World Chief Guide 1918–1977.

Baden-Powell /'beɪdn 'pəʊəl/ Robert Stephenson Smyth, 1st Baron Baden-Powell 1857–1941. British soldier, and World Chief Scout from 1920. Born in London, he was educated at Charterhouse and commissioned in the Hussars in 1876. Worldwide fame came to him after his defence of Mafeking during the South African War. Invalided home, he was knighted in 1910 with the rank of lieutenant general.

In 1907 he had held a camp for Boy Scouts on Brownsea Island, Poole Harbour, and in 1908 he wrote *Scouting for Boys*. He devoted his retirement to developing the ◊Scout movement, which rapidly spread throughout the world. In 1929 he was created a peer, and received the Order of Merit in 1937.

Baden-Württemberg /'baːdn 'vʊətəmbɜːg/ administrative region (German *Land*) of West Germany

area 35,750 sq km/13,805 sq mi

capital Stuttgart

towns Karlsruhe, Mannheim, Freiburg, Heidelberg

features Black Forest; Rhine boundary S and W; source of the Danube; see also ◊Swabia
products wine; jewellery, watches, clocks; musical instruments; textiles, chemicals, iron and steel, electrical equipment, surgical instruments
population (1985) 9,241,000
religion Roman Catholic 47 per cent, Protestant 44 per cent
history formed in 1952 (following a plebiscite) by the merger of the *Länder* Baden, Württemberg-Baden, and Württemberg-Hohenzollern.

Bader /'bɑːdə/ Douglas 1910–82. British air ace. He lost both legs in a stunt accident in 1931, but won 227 victories as a fighter pilot in World War II. Knighted 1976 for his work for disabled people.

badger large mammal of the weasel family with molar teeth of a crushing type adapted to a partly vegetable diet, and short strong legs with long claws suitable for digging. The Eurasian *common badger Meles meles* is about 1 m/3 ft long, with long coarse greyish hair on the back, and a white face with a broad black stripe along each side. Mainly a woodland animal, it is harmless and nocturnal, and spends the day in a system of burrows called a 'sett'. It feeds on worms, roots and a variety of fruits and nuts, and also on insects, mice and young rabbits. The *American badger Taxidea taxus* is a little smaller and lives in open country in N America. Various species of hog badger, ferret badger and stink badger occur in S and E Asia, the last having the anal scent glands characteristic of the weasel family especially well developed.

badger The badger's sett has tunnels that may run long distances in many directions, and when left undisturbed, colonies persist through many generations.

Bad Godesburg /'bæd 'gəʊdəsbɜːg/ SE suburb of ◊Bonn, West Germany, formerly a spa, and the meeting place of Chamberlain and Hitler before the Munich Agreement 1938.

badlands the name given to a barren landscape cut by erosion into a maze of ravines, pinnacles, gullies and sharp-edged ridges. The best-known badland region is in South Dakota and Nebraska, USA. Badlands, which can be created by overgrazing, are so called because of their total lack of value for agriculture and their inaccessibility.

Badoglio /bɑːˈdəʊljəu/ Pietro 1871–1956. Italian soldier. A veteran of campaigns against

the peoples of Tripoli and Cyrenaica, he replaced de Bono in 1935 as Commander-in-Chief in Ethiopia, adopting ruthless measures to break patriot resistance, and being created Viceroy of Ethiopia and Duke of Addis Ababa in 1936. He succeeded Mussolini as prime minister of Italy from July 1943 to June 1944.

Baedeker /'beɪdɪkə/ Karl 1801–1859. German publisher of foreign travel guides; these are now based in Hamburg (before World War II Leipzig).

Baedeker raids German air raids in World War II on British cities, so called because they accurately pinpointed architectural treasures.

Baekeland /'beɪklənd/ Leo Hendrik 1863–1944. American chemist, the inventor of ◊bakelite, the first commercial ◊plastic. He later made a photographic paper, Velox, which could be developed in artificial light.

Baer /beə/ Karl Ernst von 1792–1876. German zoologist. Born in Estonia, he held scientific posts at Königsberg and St Petersburg, and was the founder of comparative ◊embryology.

Baez /baɪˈez/ Joan 1941– . US folk singer who came to prominence in the early 1960s with her versions of traditional English and American folk songs such as 'Silver Dagger'. She introduced Bob Dylan to a wide audience and later became a leading pacifist and anti-war campaigner.

Baffin /'bæfɪn/ William 1584–1622. English navigator and explorer, a Londoner by birth. In 1612 he was chief pilot of an expedition in search of the N W passage, and in 1613–14 commanded a whaling fleet near Spitzbergen . In 1615 he became pilot for Robert Bylot of the *Discovery* examining Hudson Strait. In 1616 they discovered Baffin Bay and reached Latitude 77° 45' which for 236 years remained the 'furthest north'. After 1617 Baffin transferred his services to the East India Company and made surveys of the Red Sea and Persian Gulf. In 1622 he was killed in an Anglo-Persian attack on Ormuz.

Baffin Island /'bæfɪn/ island in the Northwest Territories, Canada
area 507,450 sq km/195,930 sq mi
features largest island in the Canadian Arctic; mountains rise above 2,000 m/6,000 ft and there are several large lakes. The northernmost part of the strait separating Baffin Island from Greenland forms Baffin Bay, the southern end is Davis Strait.

bagatelle /ˌbægəˈtel/ a game resembling billiards, played on a board with numbered cups instead of pockets. The object is to drive the nine balls into the cups. In *ordinary bagatelle* each player sends all the balls up in turn. In *French bagatelle* two or four players, playing alternately, take part.

bagatelle /ˌbægəˈtel/ (French 'trifle') in music, a short character piece, often for piano.

Bagehot /'bædʒət/ Walter 1826–1877. British economist. Manager of the London office of his family banking house, he published an analysis of the London money market, *Lombard Street* 1873. Other books include *The English Constitution* 1867, a classic explanation of the political system at the end of the Palmerstonian

era, and *Physics and Politics* 1869, applying the laws of natural selection to the development of human communities. He edited *The Economist* from 1860.

Baggara /'bægərə/ a Bedouin people of the Nile Basin, principally in Kordofan, Sudan, W of the White Nile. They are Muslims, formerly chiefly occupied in cattle-breeding and big-game hunting.

Baghdad /ˌbægˈdæd/ historic city and capital of Iraq, on the Tigris; population (1977) 3,205,500.
features To the SE, on the Tigris, are the ruins of *Ctesiphon*, capital of ◊Parthia from about 250 BC to about 226 AD and of the ◊Sassanian Empire about 226–641; the remains of the Great Palace include the world's largest single-span brick arch 26 m/85 ft wide and 29 m/95 ft high.
history The present city was founded 762. A route centre from the earliest times, it was developed by the 8th-century caliph ◊Harun-al-Rashid, though little of the Arabian Nights city remains. It was overrun in 1258 by the Mongols, who destroyed the irrigation system. In 1639 it was taken by the Turks. During World War I Baghdad was captured by Gen. Maude in 1917, and in 1921 was made capital of the new country of Iraq.

Baghdad Pact defence treaty of 1955 concluded by Britain, Iran, Iraq, Pakistan and Turkey, with the USA co-operating; it was replaced by the Central Treaty Organization (CENTO) when Iraq withdrew in 1958.

Bagnold /'bægnəʊld/ Enid 1889–1981. British author; her works include a novel and play about horse racing, *National Velvet* 1935, which was also successful as a play and a film, and the play *The Chalk Garden* 1954.

bagpipe ancient musical instrument of many countries, known to the Romans and ancient Egyptians and found in different forms in various parts of Europe. It consists of a chanter (melody) pipe and drones (which emit invariable notes to supply a ground bass). All are supplied from a windbag inflated by the performer. The most famous variety is that of the Highlands, the Scottish national instrument: others are the Irish and Greek.

Bagritsky /bəˈɡrɪtski/ Eduard, pseudonym of the Soviet poet Eduard Dzyubin 1895–1934. One of the Constructivist group, he published a volume of verse, *South-West*, the heroic poem *Lay About Opanas* 1926, and collections of verse called *The Victors* 1932 and *The Last Night* 1932.

Baguio /bæˈɡwiːəʊ/ summer resort on Luzon island in the Philippines, 200 km/125 mi N of Manila, 1,370 m/4,500 ft above sea level; population (1970) 84,500.

Bahadur Shah II /bəˈhɑːdə ˈʃɑː/ 1775–1862. last of the Mogul emperors of India. He reigned, though in name only, and under the British, as king of Delhi 1837–57, when he was hailed by the mutineers (see ◊Indian mutiny) as an independent emperor at Delhi. After the mutiny he was deported to Rangoon, Burma.

Baha'i religion foreshadowed by the teachings of Iranian Mirza Ali Muhammad 1819–50 known as the Bab, 'the Gate'. His claim that Islam was not God's final revelation ended in his being shot on government orders at Tabriz. Another of his countrymen, Husayn Ali, known as Baha'u'llah, 'God's Glory', proclaimed himself as the prophet the Bab had foretold. The most important principle of his message was that all great religious leaders, including the Bab and Baha'u'ullah, are manifestations of the unknowable God; therefore all founders of religions are to be honoured and all scriptures are sacred. Baha'is are expected to work towards world unification, and great stress is laid on equality regardless of religion, race or gender. Drugs and alcohol are forbidden, as is monastic celibacy. Marriage is strongly encouraged; there is no arranged marriage, but parental approval must be given. Baha'is are expected to pray daily, but there is no set prayer. From 2 to 20 Mar, adults under 70 fast from sunrise to sunset. There is no priesthood: all Baha'is are expected to teach, and administration is carried out by an elected body, the Universal House of Justice.

Bahamas /bə'hɑːməz/ group of islands in the Caribbean, off the SE coast of Florida.
government The Bahamas are an independent sovereign nation within the Commonwealth, with the British monarch as head of state, represented by an appointed, resident governor-general. The constitution, effective since independence in 1973, provides for a two-chamber parliament with a senate and house of assembly. The governor-general appoints a prime minister and cabinet drawn from and responsible to the legislature. The governor-general appoints 16 senate members, nine on the advice of the prime minister, four on the advice of the leader of the opposition, and three after consultation with the prime minister. The house of assembly has 43 members, elected by universal suffrage. Parliament has a maximum life of five years and may be dissolved within that period. The major political parties are the Progressive Liberal Party (PLP), and the Free National Movement (FNM)
history Becoming a British colony in 1783, the Bahamas were given internal self-government in 1964 and the first elections for the national assembly on a full voting register were held in 1967. The PLP, drawing its support mainly from voters of African origin, won the same number of seats as the European-dominated United Bahamian Party (UBP). Pindling became prime minister with support from outside his party. In the 1968 elections the PLP scored a resounding victory and this was repeated in 1972, enabling Pindling to lead his country to full independence within the Commonwealth in 1973, and increase his majority in 1977.
The main contestants in the 1982 elections were the FNM, which consisted of a number of factions which had split and reunited, and the PLP. Despite allegations of government complicity in drug trafficking, the PLP was again successful and Pindling was unanimously endorsed as leader at a Party convention in 1984. The 1987 general election was won by the PLP, led by Pindling, but with a reduced majority.

Bahawalpur /bə,hɑːwəl'puə/ industrial town (textiles, rice mills) in the Punjab, Pakistan, once

Bahamas
COMMONWEALTH OF THE

AREA 13,935 sq km/5,380 sq mi
CAPITAL Nassau on New Providence
PHYSICAL comprises 700 tropical coral islands and about 1,000 cays
FEATURES desert islands: only 30 are inhabited; Blue Holes of Andros, the world's longest and deepest submarine caves
HEAD OF STATE Elizabeth II from 1973 represented by Gerald C Cash from 1979
HEAD OF GOVERNMENT Lynden Oscar Pindling from 1967
GOVERNMENT parliamentary democracy
EXPORTS cement, pharmaceuticals, petroleum products, crawfish, rum, pulpwood; over half the islands' employment comes from tourism
CURRENCY Bahamian dollar (1.65 = £1 Sept 1987)
POPULATION 230,000 (1985); annual growth rate 1.8%
LANGUAGE English
RELIGION Christian
LITERACY 93% (1985)
GDP $780 million (1981); $5,756 per head of population
CHRONOLOGY
1964 Internal self-government attained.

Bahamas

1967 First national assembly elections.
1972 Constitutional conference to discuss full independence.
1973 Full independence achieved.
1983 Allegations of drug trafficking by government ministers.
1984 Deputy prime minister and two cabinet ministers resigned. Pindling denied any personal involvement and was endorsed as party leader.

capital of a former state of Bahawalpur; population (1981) 134,000.

Bahia /bə'iːə/ state of E Brazil
area 562,000 sq km/217,000 sq mi
capital Salvador
population (1980) 9,474,500.

Bahía Blanca /bə'iːə 'blæŋkə/ industrial port (meat packing) in S Argentina, on the Naposta, 5 km/3 mi from its mouth; population (1980) 233,126.

Bahrain /,bɑː'reɪn/ group of islands in the Arabian Gulf, between Saudi Arabia and Iran.
government The 1973 constitution provided for an elected national assembly of 30 members but it was dissolved in 1975 after the prime minister said he could not work with it. The Emir now governs Bahrain by decree, through a cabinet chosen by him. There are no recognizable political parties.
history Traditionally an Arab monarchy, Bahrain was under Portuguese rule during the 16th century, and from 1602 was dominated by Persia. Since 1783 it has been a sheikhdom under the Khalifa dynasty. It became a British Protected State in 1816, with government shared between the ruling sheikh and a British adviser. In 1928 Iran (then Persia) claimed sovereignty but in 1970 accepted a UN report showing that the inhabitants of Bahrain preferred independence.
In 1968 Britain announced the withdrawal of its forces and Bahrain joined two other territories under British protection, Qatar and the Trucial States (now the United Arab Emirates), to form a Federation of Arab Emirates. In 1971 Qatar and the Trucial States left the Federation and

Bahrain became an independent state, signing a new treaty of friendship with Britain.
In 1973 a new constitution provided for an elected national assembly but two years later the prime minister, Sheikh Khalifa, complained of obstruction by the assembly which was then dissolved. Since then the Emir and his family have ruled with virtually absolute power.
Since the Iranian revolution of 1979, relations between the two countries have been uncertain, with fears of Iranian attempts to disturb Bahrain's stability. Bahrain has now become a focal point in the Gulf, being the site of the new Gulf University and its international airport the centre of Gulf aviation. A causeway linking Bahrain with Saudi Arabia has also been constructed.

Baikal /baɪ'kæl/ largest freshwater lake in Asia 31,500 sq km/12,150 sq mi and deepest in the world (up to 1,740 m/5,710 ft), in S Siberia, USSR. Fed by more than 300 rivers, it is drained only by the Lower Angara. It has sturgeon fisheries, and a rich fauna largely unique to it, including its own breed of seals, but it is threatened by pollution.

Baikonur /,baɪkə'nʊə/ the name given in the Soviet Union to the rocket launching site at ◊Tyuratam.

bail the setting at liberty of a person in the custody of the law on an undertaking, usually backed by some security, given either by that person or by someone else, that he or she will attend at a court at a stated time and place. If the person does not attend, the bail is 'estreated', that is, forfeited. The Bail Act of 1976 presumes that a suspect will be granted bail, unless the police can

Bahrain

AREA 600 sq km/400 sq mi
CAPITAL Manama on the largest island (also called Bahrain)
TOWNS oil port Mina Sulman
PHYSICAL 33 islands, flat and hot
FEATURES a causeway 25 km/15 mi long (1985) links Bahrain to the mainland of Saudi Arabia; Sitra island is a communications centre for the lower Persian Gulf, and has a satellite-tracking station; there is a wildlife park featuring the oryx on Bahrain, and most of the S of the island is preserved for the ruling family's falconry
HEAD OF STATE AND OF GOVERNMENT Sheikh Isa bin Sulman Al-Khalifa (1933–) from 1961
GOVERNMENT the emir is absolute ruler
EXPORTS oil and natural gas
CURRENCY Bahrain dinar (0.62 = £1 Sept 1987)
POPULATION (1985) 431,000 (two thirds are nationals); annual growth rate 3.6%
LANGUAGE Arabic, Farsi
RELIGION Muslim (Shi'ite 60%, Sunni 40%)
LITERACY 60.8% (1981); 75% male/52% female
GDP $4.1 bn (1984); $6,315 per head of population
CHRONOLOGY
1816 Under British protection.
1968 Britain announced its intention to

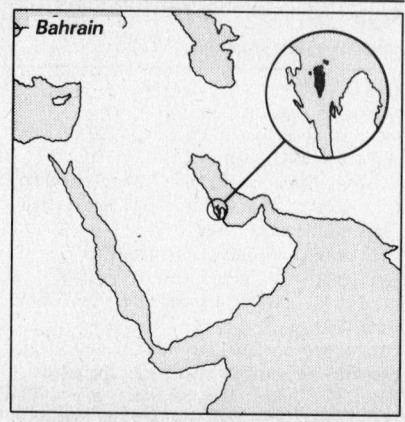
Bahrain

withdraw its forces. Bahrain formed, with Qatar and the Trucial States, the Federation of Arab Emirates.
1971 Qatar and the Trucial States left the federation and Bahrain became an independent state.
1973 New constitution adopted, with an elected national assembly.
1975 Prime minister resigned and national assembly dissolved. Emir and his family assumed virtually absolute power.
1986 Gulf University established in Bahrain. Causeway built linking Bahrain to Saudi Arabia.

prove clearly that the suspect should remain in custody: for example, by showing evidence that a further offence may take place, such as interfering with a witness.

Baile Atha Cliath /ˈblɑː ˈkliə/ official Gaelic name of ◊Dublin, capital of the Republic of Ireland, from 1922.

Bailey /ˈbeɪli/ Donald Coleman 1901–1985. British engineer, inventor of the portable *Bailey bridge* in World War II, made of interlocking, interchangeable, adjustable and easily transportable units. He was knighted in 1946.

Baillie /ˈbeɪli/ Isobel 1895–1983. British soprano. Born in Hawick, Scotland, she became celebrated for her work in oratorio. She was professor of singing at Cornell University in New York 1960–61.

Bailly /bɑːˈjiː/ Jean Sylvain 1736–1793. French astronomer, who wrote on the satellites of Jupiter and the history of astronomy. Early in the French Revolution he was president of the National Assembly and mayor of Paris, but resigned in 1791, and was guillotined during the Terror.

Baily's beads bright spots of sunlight seen around the edge of the Moon for a few seconds immediately before and after a total ◊eclipse of the Sun, caused by sunlight shining between the mountains at the Moon's edge. Sometimes one bead is much brighter than the others, producing the so-called *diamond ring* effect. The effect was discovered in 1836 by the English astronomer Francis Baily (1774–1844), a wealthy stockbroker who retired in 1825 to devote himself to astronomy.

Bainbridge /ˈbeɪnbrɪdʒ/ Beryl 1933– . British novelist, Liverpool-born and originally an actress, whose works have the drama and economy of a stage-play. They include *The Dressmaker* 1973, *The Bottle Factory Outing* 1974, and the collected short stories in *Mum and Mr Armitage* 1985.

Bainbridge /ˈbeɪnbrɪdʒ/ Kenneth Tompkins 1904– . American physicist, who worked at the Cavendish Laboratory, Cambridge, England, in the 1930s and was director of the first atomic bomb test at ◊Alamagordo, USA, in 1945.
He also carried out research in radar, and from 1961 was George Vasmer Everett professor of physics at Harvard and from 1975 professor emeritus.

Baird /beəd/ John Logie 1888–1946. British electrical engineer, who pioneered television. Born at Helensburgh, Scotland, he studied electrical engineering in Glasgow at what is now the University of Strathclyde, at the same time serving several practical apprenticeships. He was working on television possibly as early as 1912, and took out his first provisional patent in 1923. The first public demonstration was given at Selfridges London store in 1925. In 1926 he pioneered fibre optics, radar (in advance of Sir Robert Watson-Watt) and, also for the long-distance detection of objects, infra-red television. He also developed video recording on both wax records and magnetic steel discs (1926–27), colour television (1925–28), 3D-colour television (1925–46), transatlantic television (1928), and facsimile television (1944), the forerunner of ◊Ceefax. In 1936 his

mechanically scanned 240-line system competed with EMI-Marconi's 405-line, but the latter was preferred for the BBC service from 1937, partly because it used electronic scanning and partly because it handled live indoor scenes with smaller, more manoeuvrable cameras. In 1944 Baird demonstrated the world's first all-electronic colour and 3D-colour receiver (500 lines).

Bairnsfather /ˈbeənzfɑːðə/ Bruce 1888–1959. British artist, celebrated for his 'Old Bill' cartoons of World War I. In World War II he was official cartoonist to the US Army in Europe, 1942–44.

Baja California /ˈbɑːhɑː/ the mountainous peninsula that forms the twin NW states of Lower (Spanish *baja*) California, Mexico. The northern state, Baja California Norte, includes the busy towns of Mexicali and Tijuana, but the southern, Baja California Sur, is sparsely populated.

Bakelite the first synthetic ◊plastic. It was discovered by the Belgian-born American chemist Leo ◊Baekeland in 1909 while working to find a substitute for shellac, a resinous substance used in lacquers and varnishes.
Bakelite is made by reacting together two substances, phenol and formaldehyde. It is first made in the form of a powdery ◊resin which sets solid when heated. Objects are made by subjecting the resin to simultaneous heat and pressure in a mould, a method known as compression moulding. Bakelite is hard, tough and heatproof. It is one of the thermosetting plastics, which do not remelt when heated. It is an excellent electrical insulator, much used for electrical fittings.

Baker /ˈbeɪkə/ Benjamin 1840–1907. British engineer, who designed (with Sir John Fowler) London's first underground railway (the Metropolitan and District) in 1869, the ◊Forth Bridge 1890, and the original Aswan Dam on the River Nile.

Baker /ˈbeɪkə/ Janet 1933– . British mezzo-soprano. Born in Hatfield, S Yorkshire, she excels in lieder, oratorio, and opera. Her great performances include Dido in both *Dido and Aeneas* and *The Trojans*, Marguerite in *Faust*, and *The Dream of Gerontius* and *The Song of the Earth*. She was made a Dame of the British Empire in 1976.

Baker /ˈbeɪkə/ Kenneth (Wilfrid) 1934– . British Conservative politician, Education Secretary from 1986.
Undergoing national service in North Africa Baker was, for a time, a gunnery instructor to the Libyan army. He then read history at Oxford, and was elected to the House of Commons in 1968. From 1983 he represented Mole Valley. Despite a reputation of being on the liberal wing of the Conservative Party, he became a minister of state in Margaret ◊Thatcher's 1979 administration, and rose to Education Secretary in 1986.

Baker /ˈbeɪkə/ Richard St Barbe 1889–1982. British forestry expert, founder of the Men of the Trees Society, which in 1932 became worldwide. In 1959 he settled in New Zealand.

Baker /'beɪkə/ Samuel White 1821–1893. British explorer, born in London. He founded an agricultural colony in Ceylon (now Sri Lanka), built a railway across the Dobruja, and in 1861 set out to discover the source of the Nile. In 1863 he met Irish explorers Speke and Grant, who had anticipated him, but he pushed on into Central Africa to be the first European to sight the lake Albert Nyanza and to find that the Nile flowed through it. His wife, Florence von Sass, accompanied him. From 1869–73 he was Governor-General of the Nile equatorial regions.

Bakke /'bækə/ Allan 1940– . American student who, in 1978, gave his name to a test case claiming 'reverse discrimination' when appealing against his exclusion from medical school, since less well-qualified blacks were to be admitted as part of a special programme for ethnic minorities. He won his case against quotas before the Supreme Court, although other affirmative action for minority groups was still endorsed.

Bakst /bækst/ Leon. Stage name of Russian artist Leon Rosenberg 1866–1924. Born in St Petersburg, he displayed remarkable gifts as a theatrical designer, and from 1900 was scenic artist to the Imperial theatres. From 1909 he painted the scenery and designed the exotic costumes for ◊Diaghilev's ballets. During the latter part of his life, when living in Paris, he exercised worldwide influence on the decorative arts of the theatre.

Baku /bə'kuː/ capital city of the Azerbaijan Republic, USSR, and industrial port (oil refining) on the Caspian Sea; population (1985) 1,693,000. Baku is the centre of the Russian oil industry, which began here in the 1870s, and is linked by pipelines with Batumi on the Black Sea.

Bakunin /bə'kuːnɪn/ Mikhail 1814–1876. Russian anarchist. Born of a noble family, he served in the Imperial Guard but, disgusted with tsarist methods in Poland, resigned his commission and travelled abroad. In 1848 he was expelled from France as a revolutionary agitator. For his share in a brief revolt at Dresden in 1849 he was sentenced to death. The sentence was commuted to imprisonment, and he was handed over to the Tsar's government and sent to Siberia in 1855. In 1861 he managed to escape to Switzerland, where he became recognized as the leader of the anarchist movement. In 1869 he joined the 'First International' but, after stormy conflicts with ◊Marx, was expelled in 1872. He had a large following, particularly in the Latin American countries. He wrote books and pamphlets, including *God and the State*.

Bala /'bælə/ (Welsh *Llyn Tegid*) lake in Gwynedd, N Wales, about 6.4 km/4 mi long and 1.6 km/1 mi wide.

Balaclava /,bælə'klɑːvə/ town in Ukraine Soviet Socialist Republic, in the Crimea, 10 km/6 mi SE of Sevastopol, which gives its name to a battle fought on 25 Oct 1854, during the ◊Crimean War, rendered famous by an ill-timed but gallant charge of the British Light Brigade of cavalry against the Russian entrenched artillery. About 700 soldiers took part, but only 195 returned. *Balaclava helmets* were knitted hoods

Bakunin Russian anarchist Mikhail Bakunin was expelled from France and Germany in his youth for political agitation. The Tsar sent him to Siberia in 1855, but he escaped to Switzerland and led the European anarchists.

worn here by soldiers in the bitter weather of the Crimean War.

Balakirev /bə'lɑːkɪref/ Mily Alexeyevich 1837–1910. Russian composer, born at Nijni-Novgorod. At St Petersburg he won fame as a pianist, worked with ◊Glinka, established the Free School of Music 1862, which stressed the national element, and was director of the Imperial Chapel 1883–95. He wrote orchestral and piano music, songs, and a symphonic poem 'Tamara', all imbued with the Russian national character and spirit. He was leader of the group known as The Five or The Mighty Handful and taught its members, ◊Mussorgsky, ◊Rimsky-Korsakov, and ◊Borodin.

balalaika Russian musical instrument, resembling a guitar. It has a triangular sound box and two, three, or four strings played by plucking with the fingers.

balance an apparatus for weighing – that is, for measuring mass. There are various types, from a beam balance, consisting of a centrally-pivoted lever with pans hanging from each end, to a spring balance in which the object to be weighed stretches (or compresses) a vertical coil spring fitted with a pointer that indicates the weight on a scale. Kitchen scales and bathroom scales are examples of balances.

balance of nature in ecology, the idea that there is an inherent stability in most ◊ecosystems; and that human interference can disrupt this stability. Organisms in the ecosystem are adapted to each other, waste products produced by one species are used by another, resources used by some are replenished by others, and so on. This stability is not seen in all natural ecosystems: in ◊succession, for example, there is

progressive change, while some ecosystems are characterized by ◊population cycles with an explosion of numbers being followed by catastrophic decline.

balance of payments in economics, the difference between debits and credits in the buying and selling of goods (visible trade) and services (invisible trade, including such things as tourism and banking) between one country and other countries, and including differences in capital ◊investment. A balance of payments crisis usually means that more is leaving the country (in paying for ◊imports) than is coming in (in payments for ◊exports).

balance of power in politics, the theory that the best way of ensuring international order is to have power so distributed among states that no single state is able to achieve a preponderant position. The term, which may also refer more simply to the actual distribution of power, is one of the most enduring concepts in international relations. Since the development of nuclear weapons, it has been asserted that the balance of power has been replaced by a balance of terror.

balance sheet a statement of the financial position of a company or individual on a specific date, showing both ◊assets and ◊liabilities.

Balanchine /,bælən'tʃiːn/ George 1904–1983. Russian-American choreographer. After leaving the USSR in 1924, he worked with Diaghilev in France. He moved to the USA in 1933, where he became a major influence on modern dance, starting the New York City Ballet in 1948. His works include *Apollon Musagète* 1928 and *The Prodigal Son* 1929 for Diaghilev, several works for music by Stravinsky such as *Agon* 1957 and *Duo Concertante* 1972 (for the Stravinsky Festival that year) and musicals such as *On Your Toes* 1936 and *The Boys from Syracuse* 1938.

Balaton /'bɒlətɒn/ lake in W Hungary; area 600 sq km/230 sq mi.

Balboa /bæl'bəʊə/ Vasco Núñez de 1475–1517. Spanish ◊conquistador, the first European to see the Pacific Ocean on 29 Sept 1513, from the island of Darien (now Panama). He was made Admiral of the Pacific and Governor of Panama, but was removed by Spanish court intrigue, imprisoned and executed.

Balchin /'bɔːltʃɪn/ Nigel Marlin 1908–1970. British author. During World War II he was engaged on scientific work for the army with the rank of brigadier, and established his reputation as a novelist with *The Small Back Room* 1943, dealing with the psychology of the 'back room boys' of wartime research.

Balcon /'bɔːlkən/ Michael 1896–1977. British film producer, responsible for the 'Ealing Comedies' of the 1940s and early 1950s, *Kind Hearts and Coronets* 1949, and *The Lavender Hill Mob* 1951.

Balder /'bɔːldə/ in Norse mythology, the son of Odin and Frigga and husband of Nanna, and the best, wisest, and most loved of all the gods. He was killed, at Loki's instigation, by a twig of mistletoe shot by the blind god Hodur.

baldness loss of hair from the upper scalp, especially common in older men. Its onset and extent is influenced by genetic make-up and male sex ◊hormones. There is no cure and expedients such as hair implants from elsewhere on the head may not have lasting effect. Hair loss in both sexes may also occur as a result of various forms of ill-health or following radiation treatment, such as for cancer. Alopecia, a condition in which the hair falls out, is different from the 'male pattern baldness' described above.

Baldwin /'bɔːldwɪn/ James 1924–1987. American writer, born in Harlem, who portrayed the condition of black Americans in contemporary society. His works include the novels *Go Tell It on the Mountain* 1953, *Another Country* 1962, and *Just Above My Head* 1979; the play *The Amen Corner* 1955; and the autobiographical essays *Notes of a Native Son* 1955 and *The Fire Next Time* 1963.

Baldwin Brought up in a background of domestic strife, bigotry and religious fanaticism in Harlem, the author James Baldwin started preaching at the Fireside Pentecostal Church at the age of 14.

Baldwin /'bɔːldwɪn/ Stanley, 1st Earl Baldwin of Bewdley 1867–1947. British Conservative politician. Born in Bewdley, Worcestershire, the son of an iron and steel magnate, in 1908 he was elected Unionist Member of Parliament for Bewdley, and in 1916 he became parliamentary private secretary to Bonar ◊Law. He was financial secretary to the Treasury 1917–21, and then appointed to the presidency of the Board of Trade. In 1919 he gave the Treasury £150,000 of War Loan for cancellation, representing about 20 per cent of his fortune. He was a leader in the disruption of the ◊Lloyd George coalition of 1922, and, as chancellor under Bonar ◊Law, achieved a settlement of war debts with the USA.

Baldwin became prime minister 1923–24 and again 1924–29. This period was marked by the General Strike of 1926, the Trades Disputes Act of 1927, the grant of widows' and orphans' pensions, and the securing of complete adult suffrage in 1928. He joined the National

Government of ◊MacDonald in 1931 as Lord President of the Council. During his third premiership 1935–37, he handled the abdication crisis of ◊Edward VIII, but was later much criticized for his failure to resist popular desire for an accommodation with ◊Hitler and ◊Mussolini, and failure to rearm more effectively.

Baldwin Prime Minister Stanley Baldwin on the steps of No 10 Downing Street after the notice of the termination of the Great Strike has been handed in by the Trades Union Congress, 1926. Baldwin's government then passed the severe Trades Disputes Act 1927.

Baldwin I /'bɔːldwɪn/ 1058–1118. King of Jerusalem. A French nobleman, who joined his brother Godfrey on the First ◊Crusade in 1096, he established the kingdom in 1100, which was destroyed by Islamic conquest in 1187.

Bâle /bɑːl/ French form of Basle or ◊Basel, town in Switzerland.

Balearic Islands /ˌbæliˈærɪk/ (Spanish *Baleares*) Mediterranean group of islands forming an autonomous region of Spain
area 5,014 sq km/1,935 sq mi
capital Palma on Majorca
features the largest island is ◊Majorca; others are ◊Minorca, ◊Ibiza, Cabrera, and Formentera
products figs, olives, oranges; wine, brandy; coal, iron, slate; tourism is important
population (1981) 685,088
history a Roman colony from 123 BC, the Balearic Islands were an independent Moorish

kingdom 1009–1232; the islands were conquered by Aragon in 1343.

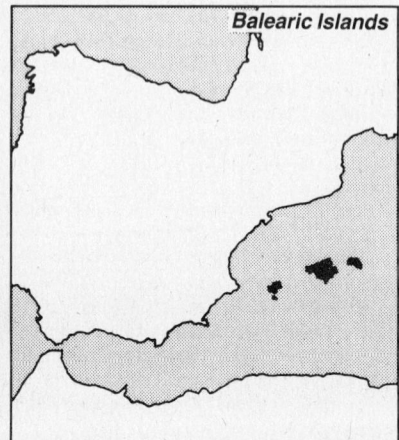

Balearic Islands

Balewa alternative title of Nigerian politician ◊Tafawa Balewa.

Balfe /bælf/ Michael William 1808–1870. Irish composer. Born in Dublin, he was a violinist and baritone at Drury Lane, London, when only 16. In 1825 he went to Italy, where he sang in Palermo and at La Scala, and in 1846 he was appointed conductor at Her Majesty's Theatre. He composed operas, including *The Bohemian Girl* 1843.

Balfour /'bælfə/ Arthur James, 1st Earl of Balfour 1848–1930. British Conservative politician. Son of a Scottish landowner, he was elected a Conservative Member of Parliament in 1874. In Lord ◊Salisbury's ministry he was secretary for Ireland 1887, and for his ruthless vigour was called 'Bloody Balfour' by Irish nationalists. In 1891, and again in 1895, he became First Lord of the Treasury and leader of the Commons, and in 1902 he succeeded Salisbury as prime minister. His cabinet was divided over Joseph ◊Chamberlain's Tariff Reform proposals, and in the 1905 elections suffered a crushing defeat.

Balfour retired from the party leadership in 1911. In 1915 he joined the ◊Asquith coalition as 1st Lord of the Admiralty, and was foreign secretary 1916–19; as such he issued the ◊Balfour Declaration of 1917 in favour of a national home in Palestine for the Jews and signed the Treaty of ◊Versailles. He was Lord President of the Council 1919–22 and 1925–29, and received the Order of Merit in 1916 and an earldom in 1922. He was also a philosopher, and wrote *A Defence of Philosophic Doubt* 1879, *Foundations of Belief*, and *Theism and Humanism* 1914.

Balfour Declaration a letter, dated 2 Nov 1917, from British foreign secretary A J ◊Balfour to Lord Rothschild (chair, British Zionist Federation) stating: 'HM government view with favour the establishment in Palestine of a national home for the Jewish people'; it led to the foundation of Israel in 1948.

Bali /'bɑːli/ island of Indonesia, E of Java, one of the Sunda Islands

area 5,800 sq km/2,240 sq mi
capital Singaradja
physical volcanic mountains
features Balinese dancing, music, drama
products gold and silver work, woodcarving, weaving
population (1980) 2,470,000
history the Hindu culture of Bali goes back to the 7th century.

Balikesir /ˌbɑːlɪkeˈsɪə/ town in NW Turkey; population (1980) 124,051. There are silver mines nearby.

Balikpapan /ˌbɑːlɪkˈpɑːpən/ port and oil centre in Indonesia, on the E coast of Borneo; population (1971) 137,500.

Bali Strait a narrow strait between the two islands of Bali and Java, Indonesia. It was the scene on 19–20 Feb 1942 of a naval action between Japanese and US and Dutch forces which served to delay slightly the Japanese invasion of Java.

Balkans /'bɔːlkənz/ peninsula of SE Europe, stretching into the Mediterranean between the Adriatic and Aegean Seas. It comprises Albania, Bulgaria, Greece, Romania, Turkey-in-Europe, and Yugoslavia. It is joined in the rest of Europe by an isthmus 1,200 km/750 m wide between Rijeka on the W and the mouth of the Danube on the Black Sea to the E. A byword for political dissension historically, a tendencey fostered by the great ethnic diversity resulting from successive waves of invasion, the Balkans developed comparatively slowly economically until after World War II, largely because of the predominantly mountainous terrain, apart from the plains of the Save-Danube basin in the N. Political differences have remained strong, for example the confrontation of Greece and Turkey over Cyprus, and the differing types of Communism prevailing in the rest, but in the later years of the 20th century, a tendency to regional union emerged both economically and politically. To *Balkanize* is to divide into small warring states.The name is Turkish for 'mountains'.

Balkan Wars two wars which resulted in the expulsion of Turkey from Europe except for a small area round Istanbul. The *First Balkan War*, in 1912, of Bulgaria, Serbia, Greece, and Montenegro against Turkey, forced the Turks to ask for an armistice, but the peace negotiations, in London, broke down when the Turks, while agreeing to surrender all Turkey-in-Europe W of the city of Edirne (formerly Adrianople) refused to give up the city itself. In Feb 1913 hostilities were resumed, Edirne fell on 26 Mar and on 30 May by the Treaty of London Turkey retained in Europe only a small piece of eastern Thrace and the Gallipoli peninsula.
In the *Second Balkan War*, Jun–Jul 1913 – among the victors – Bulgaria attacked Greece and ◊Serbia which were joined by Romaina. Bulgaria was defeated, and Turkey secured from that country the cession of Edirne.

Balkhash /bæl'xɑːʃ/ salt lake in Kazakhstan, USSR; area 17,300 sq km/668 sq mi. It is 600 km/375 mi long, receives several rivers, but has no outlet. Very shallow, it is frozen throughout the winter.

Balkhash /bæl'xɑːʃ/ copper-mining town on the N shore of Lake Balkhash in Kazhakstan, USSR, founded 1928; population 90,000.

Ball /bɔːl/ John 1381. English priest who led the ◊Peasants' Revolt of 1381. In Blackheath, London, he preached from the text 'When Adam delved and Eve span, who was then the gentleman?' When the revolt collapsed he was taken prisoner and executed.

ballad type of popular poem which tells a story. Derived from late Latin *ballare*, 'to dance', the ballad was primarily intended for singing at the communal ring-dance, the refrains representing the chorus.
Of simple metrical form and dealing with some strongly emotional event, the ballad is half-way between the lyric and the epic. The majority of English ballads date from the 15th century but were not collected until modern times, the most famous collections being Bishop Percy's *Reliques of Ancient Poetry* 1765, Scotts's *Minstrelsy of the Scottish Border* 1802–03, and Professor F J Child's *English and Scottish Popular Ballads* 1857–59. Opinion is divided as to whether the authorship of the ballads may be attributed to individual poets or to the community. Later ballads tend to centre round a popular folk-hero, as in the case of the *Gest of Robyn Hode* and in the American cycles concerning Jesse James and Yankee Doodle. Other later forms are the 'broadsheets' with a satirical or political motive, and the testamentary 'hanging' ballads of the condemned criminal. Poets of the Romantic movement both in England and in Germany were largely influenced by the ballad revival, for example, the *Lyrical Ballads* 1798 of Wordsworth and Coleridge. Other writers of modern ballads include Keats, Southey, Rossetti, S Dobell, Tennyson, Morris and Kipling.
In 19th century music the refined drawing-room ballad had a vogue, but a more robust tradition survived in the music hall, and folk-song played its part in the growth of pop music.

ballade in music, an instrumental piece based on a story; a form used in piano works by ◊Chopin and ◊Liszt. In literature, a poetic form developed in France in the later Middle Ages from popular ◊ballad, generally consisting of one or more groups of three stanzas of seven or eight lines each, followed by a shorter stanza or envoy, the last line being repeated as a chorus.

Ballance /'bæləns/ John 1839–1893. New Zealand statesman. Born in Ulster, he emigrated to New Zealand, founded and edited the *Wanganui Herald*, held many cabinet posts, and was Prime Minister 1891–93.

Ballantyne /'bæləntaɪn/ R(obert) M(ichael) 1825–1894. Scottish writer of children's books. Childhood visits to Canada and six years as a trapper for the Hudson's Bay company provided material for his adventure stories, which include *The Young Fur Traders* 1856, *Coral Island* 1857, and *Martin Rattler* 1858.

Ballarat /'bæləræt/ industrial town in Victoria, Australia; population (1981) 62,641. It was founded in the 1851 gold rush, and the mining village and workings have been restored for tourists. The ◊*Eureka Stockade* miners' revolt took place here in 1854.

Ballard /'bælɑːd/ J(ames) G(raham) 1930– . British novelist, whose works include science fiction on the theme of disaster, such as *The Drowned World* 1962, and *High-Rise* 1975, and the partly autobiographical *Empire of the Sun* 1984, dealing with his internment in China during World War II.

ballet (Italian *balletto* a little dance) a theatrical representation in dance form where music also plays a major part in telling a story or conveying a mood. Some such form of entertainment existed in ancient Greece, but ballet as we know it today first appeared in a recognizable form in Italy, from where it was brought by Catherine de ◊Medici to France in the form of a spectacle combining singing, dancing, and declamation.
The first important dramatic ballet, the *Ballet comique de la reine*, was mounted in 1581 by the Italian Balthasar de Beaujoyeux at the French court and was performed by male courtiers, with ladies of the court forming the *corps de ballet*. In 1661 Louis XIV founded *L'Acadê mie royale de danse*, from which all subsequent ballet activities throughout the world can be traced. Long flowing court dress was worn by the dancers. In the 1720s Marie-Anne ◊Camargo, the first great ballerina, shortened her skirt to reveal her feet, thus allowing greater movement *à terre* and the development of dancing *en l'air*. In the early 19th century a Paris costumier, Maillot, invented tights, thus completing muscular freedom. The first of the great ballet masters was J-G ◊Noverre, and great contemporary dancers were Vestris, Heinel, Dauberval, and Gardel. Carlo ◊Blasis is regarded as the father of Classical ballet, defining the standard conventional steps and accompanying gestures.
Romantic ballet the great Romantic era of ◊Taglioni, Elssler, Grisi, Grahn, and Cerrito began about 1830, but survives today only in *Giselle* 1841 and *La Sylphide* 1832. Characteristics of this era were the new calf-length classical white dress and the introduction of dancing on the toes, *sur les pointes*. The technique of the female dancer was developed, but the role of the man was reduced to that of the partner to the woman.
Russian ballet was introduced to the West by ◊Diaghilev, who set out for Paris in 1909, at about the same time that the American Isadora ◊Duncan, a rigid opponent of Classical ballet, was touring the Continent. Associated with Diaghilev were ◊Fokine, ◊Nijinsky, ◊Pavlova, ◊Massine, ◊Balanchine, and ◊Lifar, and ballets presented by his company before its break-up on his death in 1929 included *Les Sylphides*, *Schêhêrazade*, *Petrouchka*, and *Blue Train*. Diaghilev and Fokine pioneered a new and exciting combination of the perfect technique of imperial Russian dancers and the appealing naturalism favoured by Isadora Duncan. In Russia ballet continues to flourish, the two chief companies being the Kirov and the Bolshoi. Best-known ballerinas are◊Ulanova and◊Plisetskaya, and among the men Rudolf ◊Nureyev and Alexander Godunov, both now dancing in the

West, and husband-and-wife team Vyacheslav Gordeyev and Nadezhda Pavlova, now also dancing in the West.

American ballet was firmly established by the founding of Balanchine's School of American Ballet 1934, and by de Basil's Ballets Russes de Monte Carlo and ◊Massine's Ballet Russe de Monte Carlo, which also carried on the Diaghilev tradition. Since 1948 the New York City Ballet with Maria Tallchief, Nora Kaye, and choreographer Jerome ◊Robbins, under the guiding influence of Balanchine, has developed a genuine American classic style. See also Martha ◊Graham.

British ballet Marie ◊Rambert initiated in 1926 the company which developed into the Ballet Rambert, and in 1930 Arnold Haskell and Philip Richardson formed the Camargo Society, but the modern national company, the ◊Royal Ballet (so named 1956), grew from foundations laid by Ninette ◊de Valois and Frederick ◊Ashton in 1928. British dancers include Margot ◊Fonteyn, Beryl ◊Grey, Alicia ◊Markova, Anton Dolin, Antoinette ◊Sibley, and Anthony ◊Dowell; choreographers include Sir Frederick Ashton, and Sir Kenneth ◊MacMillan.

For other forms of dance see under ◊dance.

Portrait of the 18th-century ballet dancer Marie-Anne de Cupis de Camargo, by Nicholas Lancret.

ballet blanc /'bæleɪ 'blɒŋ/ (French 'white ballet') a ballet in which the female dancers wear calf-length white dresses, such as *Giselle* . The costume was introduced by Marie ◊Taglioni in *La Sylphide* 1832.

ballet d'action /'bæleɪ dæk'sjɒŋ/ a ballet with a plot, developed by ◊Noverre in the 18th century.

Ballinasloe /ˌbælɪnəˈsləʊ/ town in Galway Bay, Republic of Ireland, whose livestock fair every Oct is the largest in Ireland.

ballistics study of the motion of projectiles, both while still inside the weapon and after launching. In the case of a gun, relevant exterior factors include temperature, barometric pressure, and wind strength; and in the case of nuclear missiles extend to such factors as the speed at which the Earth turns.

balloon impermeable fabric bag which rises when filled with gas lighter than the surrounding

THE BALLET REPERTORY

DATE	BALLET	COMPOSER	CHOREOGRAPHER	PLACE
1670	Le Bourgeois Gentilhomme	Lully	Beauchamp	Chambord
1735	Les Indes Galantes	Rameau	Blondy	Paris
1761	Don Juan	Gluck	Angiolini	Vienna
1778	Les Petits Riens	Mozart	Noverre	Paris
1801	The Creatures of Prometheus	Beethoven	Viganò	Vienna
1828	La Fille Mal Gardée	Hérold	Aumer	Paris
1832	La Sylphide	Schneitzhoffer	F. Taglioni	Paris
1841	Giselle	Adam	Coralli/Perrot	Paris
1844	La Esmeralda	Pugni	Perrot	London
1869	Don Quixote	Minkus	M Petipa	Moscow
1870	Coppélia	Delibes	Saint-Léon	Paris
1876	Sylvia	Delibes	Mérante	Paris
1877	La Bayadère	Minkus	M Petipa	St Petersburg
1877	Swan Lake	Tchaikovsky	Reisinger	Moscow
1890	The Sleeping Beauty	Tchaikovsky	M Petipa	St Petersburg
1892	Nutcracker	Tchaikovsky	M Petipa/Ivanov	St Petersburg
1905	The Dying Swan	Saint-Saëns	Fokine	St Petersburg
1907	Les Sylphides	Chopin	Fokine	St Petersburg
1910	Carnival	Schumann	Fokine	St Petersburg
1910	The Firebird	Stravinsky	Fokine	Paris
1911	Petrushka	Stravinsky	Fokine	Paris
1911	Le Spectre de la Rose	Weber	Fokine	Monte Carlo
1912	L'Après-midi d'un Faune	Debussy	Nijinsky	Paris
1912	Daphnis et Chloë	Ravel	Fokine	Paris
1913	Jeux	Debussy	Nijinsky	Paris
1913	Le Sacre du Printemps	Stravinsky	Nijinsky	Paris
1915	El Amor Brujo	Falla	Imperio	Madrid
1917	Parade	Satie	Massine	Paris
1919	La Boutique Fantasque	Rossini/Respighi	Massine	London
1919	The Three-Cornered Hat	Falla	Massini	London
1923	Le Creation du Monde	Milhaud	Börlin	Paris
1923	Les Noces	Stravinsky	Nijinska	Paris
1923	Les Biches	Poulenc	Nijinska	Monte Carlo
1928	Apollon Musagète	Stravinsky	Balanchine	Paris
1928	La Baiser de la Fée	Tchaikovsky	Nijinska	Paris
1928	Bolero	Ravel	Nijinska	Paris
1929	The Prodigal Son	Prokofiev	Balanchine	Paris
1929	La Valse	Ravel	Nijinska	Monte Carlo
1931	Façade	Walton	Ashton	London
1931	Job	Vaughan Williams	de Valois	London
1937	Checkmate	Bliss	de Valois	Paris
1938	Billy the Kid	Copland	Loring	Chicago
1938	Gaîté Parisienne	Offenbach/Rosenthal	Massine	Monte Carlo
1938	Romeo and Juliet	Prokofiev	Psota	Brno, Moravia
1942	Gayaneh	Khachaturian	Anisimova	Molotov-Perm
1942	The Miraculous Mandarin	Bartók	Milloss	Milan
1942	Rodeo	Copland	de Mille	New York
1944	Appalachian Spring	Copland	Graham	Washington
1944	Fancy Free	Bernstein	Robbins	New York
1945	Cinderella	Prokofiev	Zakharov	Moscow
1951	Pineapple Poll	Sullivan/Mackerras	Cranko	London
1956	Spartacus	Khachaturian	Jacobson	Leningrad
1957	Agon	Stravinsky	Balanchine	New York
1962	A Midsummer Night's Dream	Mendelssohn	Balanchine	New York
1962	Pierrot Lunaire	Schoenberg	Tetley	New York
1965	Lied von der Erde	Mahler	MacMillan	Stuttgart
1967	Anastasia	Martinu	MacMillan	New York
1968	Enigma Variations	Elgar	Ashton	London
1972	Duo Concertante	Stravinsky	Balanchine	New York
1974	Elite Syncopations	Joplin, etc	MacMillan	London
1980	Gloria	Poulenc	MacMillan	London
1980	Rhapsody	Rachmaninov	Ashton	London

air. The first successful human ascent was piloted by Pilâtre de Rozier, Paris 1783, in a hot-air balloon designed by the ◊Montgolfier brothers. Balloons were first used in war for observation during the French revolutionary period. They are now used for sport, and as an economical means of meteorological, infra-red, gamma ray, ultra-violet, and other types of observation. The first transatlantic crossing was made 11–17 Aug 1978 by a US team.

balloon A stratospheric research balloon ready for launch at the National Scientific Balloon Faculty, Texas. To the left is a helium truck.

ballroom dancing collective term for social dances such as the ◊foxtrot, quickstep, ◊tango, and ◊waltz.

ball valve a valve used in lavatory cisterns to cut off the water supply when it has reached the correct level. It consists of a flat rubber washer at one end of a pivoting arm and a hollow ball at the other. The ball floats on the water surface, rising as the cistern fills. At the correct level, the rubber washer is pushed against the water-inlet pipe, cutting off the flow.

balm herb *Melissa officinalis*, family Labiatae, with lemon-scented leaves. It is used in herb teas.

Balmoral Castle /bæl'mɒrəl/ royal residence in Scotland on the river Dee, 10.5 km/6½ mi NE of Braemar, Grampian region. The castle, built of granite in the Scottish baronial style, is dominated by a square tower and circular turret rising 30 m/100 ft. It was rebuilt 1853–55.

balometer sensitive ◊thermometer, devised in 1880 by the American astronomer Samuel ◊Langley, for measuring radiation from stars. It works by measuring the change in electrical resistance of a fine wire when it is exposed to heat or light.

balsam in medicine and perfumery, plant oils and resins such as Balsam of Peru from the tree *Myroxylon balsamum*, and ◊Friar's Balsam. Also garden plants of the genus *Impatiens*, usually annuals with red or white flowers.

Baltic, Battle of the /'bɔːltɪk/ British victory, 2 Apr 1801, when ◊Nelson secured the surrender of the entire Danish fleet off Copenhagen after putting his telescope to his blind eye when his commander, Admiral Sir Hyde Parker, signalled 'disengage'.

Baltic Sea /'bɔːltɪk/ large shallow arm of the North Sea, extending NE from the narrow Skagerrak and Kattegat, between Sweden and Denmark, to the Gulf of Bothnia between Sweden and Finland. Its coastline is 8,000 km /5,000 mi long, and its area, including the gulfs of Riga, Finland and Bothnia, is 422,300 sq km/163,000 sq mi. Its shoreline is shared by Denmark, Germany, Poland, USSR, Finland, and Sweden. Many large rivers flow into it, including the Oder, Vistula, Niemen, W Dvina, Narva, and Neva. Tides are hardly perceptible, salt content is low; weather is often stormy and navigation dangerous. Most ports are closed by ice from Dec until May. The Kiel canal links the Baltic and the North Sea, the Göta canal connects the two seas by way of the S Swedish lakes, and since 1975 it has been linked by the Leningrad–Belomorsk seaway with the White Sea.

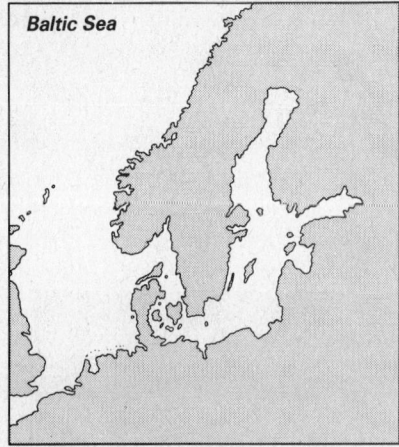

Baltic Sea

Baltic States collective name for the former independent states of ◊Estonia, ◊Latvia, and ◊Lithuania, from 1940 republics within the USSR.

Baltimore /'bɔːltɪmɔː/ industrial port and largest city in Maryland, USA, on the W shore of Chesapeake Bay, NE of Washington DC; population (1980) 787,000.
history Named after the founder of Maryland, Lord Baltimore (1606–75), the city of Baltimore dates from 1729 and was incorporated in 1797. At Fort McHenry Francis Scott Key wrote 'The Star Spangled Banner'. The writer Edgar Allan Poe and the baseball player Babe Ruth lived here.

Baluchistan /bə,luːtʃɪ'stɑːn/ mountainous desert area, comprising a province of Iran (capital Zahedan), population 1,000,000, a province of Pakistan of the same name, population 2,500,000, and a small area of Afghanistan, population 300,000. The port of Gwadar in Pakistan is strategically important, on the Indian Ocean and the Strait of Hormuz.

Baluchistan /bə,luːtʃɪ'stɑːn/ province of SW Pakistan, capital Quetta. It was a territory of British India until 1947.

Balzac /bæl'zæk/ Honoré de 1799–1850. French novelist. Born in Tours, he studied law and worked as a notary's clerk in Paris, before turning to literature. His first attempts included tragedies such as *Cromwell* and novels published pseudonymously with no great success. A venture in printing and publishing 1825–28 involved him in a lifelong web of debt, but in 1829 he achieved his first success with *Les Chouans/The Chouans* and *La Physiologie du mariage/The Physiology of Marriage* 1829, inspired by Scott. This was the beginning of the long series of novels, the *La Comédie humaine/The Human Comedy*, which, according to the complete plan of 1842 was to consist of 143 volumes depicting 19th-century French life in every conceivable aspect, but of which only some 80 were completed. They include studies of human folly and vice such as the miser in *Eugénie Grandet* 1833, the monomaniac of *La Recherche de l'absolu/The Search for the Absolute* 1834, the doting father of *Le Père Goriot* 1834, the jealous *Cousine Bette* 1846, and the acquisitive *Cousin Pons* 1847; and analyses of professions or ranks such as the commercial traveller of *L'Illustre Gaudissart/The Famous Gaudissart* 1833, the doctor of *Le Médicin de la campagne/The Country Doctor* 1833, the great business man of *La Maison de Nucingen/The House of Nucingen* 1838, and the cleric of *Le Curé de village/The Village Parson* 1839. Apart from the novels stand the collection of Rabelaisian *Contes drôlatiques/Ribald Tales* 1833.

In 1833, before the death of his patroness, Madame de Berny, who figures in *Le Lys dans la vallée/The Lily in the Valley* 1836, Balzac met the Polish countess Evelina Hanska; they corresponded constantly, but married only four months before his death in Paris. He was buried in Père Lachaise cemetery.

Balzac French novelist Honoré de Balzac planned to depict every aspect of French life in *La Comédie Humaine*, but only managed to complete about 80 of the planned 143 volumes.

Bamako /,bæmə'kəʊ/ capital and port of Mali; population (1976) 404,022.

Bamberg /'bæmbɜːg/ town in Bavaria, West Germany; population (1985) 70,400.

bamboo plant of the group Bambuseae, belonging to the grass family Gramineae, mainly found in tropical and sub-tropical countries, and remarkable for the gigantic size which some species can attain. The stems are hollow and jointed, and can be used in furniture, house and boat construction. The young shoots are eaten in China; paper is made from the stem.

Banaba /'bɑːnəbə/ formerly Ocean Island in the Republic of ◊Kiribati.

banana tree-like tropical plants 8 m/25 ft high, family Musaceae, which include the *commercial banana*, sterile hybrid forms of the genus *Musa*. The curved yellow fruits, arranged in rows of 'hands', form cylindrical masses of a hundred or more, and are exported green (often after being grown in plastic bags to avoid damage), and ripened aboard refrigerated ships. The plant is destroyed after cropping. The *plantain*, a larger, coarser subspecies which is used green, as a cooked vegetable, is a staple of the diet in many countries.

Banaras /bə'nɑːrəs/ another transliteration of ◊Varanesi, holy Hindu city in Uttar Pradesh, India.

Banbury /'bænbəri/ town in Oxfordshire, England; population (1981) 35,796. The *Banbury Cross* of the nursery rhyme was destroyed by the ◊Puritans in 1602, but replaced in 1858; *Banbury cakes* are criss-cross pastry cases with a mince-pie style filling.

Banca alternative form of the Indonesian island ◊Banka.

band music group, usually falling into a specialist category, for example, *military* developed in the 18th century, comprising woodwind, brass, percussion, for which the British Royal Military School of Music (Kneller Hall, Twickenham) is a training centre; *brass*, solely brass and percussion, which are especially typical of the north of England, many sponsored by collieries or industrial firms; *marching*, a variant of the brass, which developed as an adjunct of American football and has been introduced to Britain; ◊*dance*; ◊*jazz*; rock and pop (see ◊pop music), generally electric guitar, bass, and drums (or drum machine), variously augmented; and *steel* popular in the West Indies, especially Trinidad, using percussion instruments made from oildrums.

Banda /'bændə/ Hastings Kamuzu 1905– . Malawi politician. Once a student and medical practitioner in Britain, he led his country's independence movement, and was prime minister of Nyasaland from 1963, and first president of Malawi from 1966.

Bandar Abbas /'bændər 'æbəs/ port and winter resort in Iran on the Persian Gulf. Formerly called Gombroon, it was renamed and made prosperous by Shah Abbas I (1587–1629).

Bandaranaike /ˌbændərə'naɪkə/ Sirimavo (born Ratwatte) 1916– . Sri Lankan politician, who succeeded her husband Solomon ◊Bandaranaike to become the world's first woman prime minister 1960–65, 1970–77, but was expelled from parliament in 1980 for abuse of her powers while in office.

Banda Once a student at Edinburgh university and a practising doctor in the USA and Britain, Hastings Banda was the first president of Malawi.

Bandaranaike Sri Lankan politician Sirimavo Bandaranaike became the world's first woman prime minister in 1960, less than a year after her husband's assassination. She was largely responsible for the new constitution in 1972, but in 1980 was expelled from Parliament for abuse of her powers.

Bandaranaike /ˌbændərə'naɪkə/ Solomon West Ridgeway Dias 1899–1959. Sri Lankan politician. An ardent nationalist, he founded in 1951 the Sri Lanka Freedom Party and in 1956 became prime minister, pledged to a socialist programme and a neutral foreign policy. He failed to satisfy extremists and was assassinated by a Buddhist monk.

Bandar Seri Begawan /'bændə 'seri bə'gɑːwən/ capital of Brunei; population (1983) 57,558.

Bandar Shah /'bændə 'ʃɑː/ port in Iran on the Caspian Sea, and northern terminus of the Trans-Iranian railway.

bandicoot type of small marsupial mammal inhabiting Australia and New Guinea. There are about 11 species, family Peramelidae, rat or rabbit-sized and living in burrows. Nocturnal, they have long snouts and eat insects.

banding term used in UK education for the division of school pupils into broad streams by ability. Banding is used by some local authorities to ensure that comprehensive schools receive an intake of children spread right across the ability range. Banding is used internally by some schools as a means of avoiding groups of very wide mixed ability.

Bandung /'bændʊŋ/ commercial city in Java, Indonesia; population (1980) 1,462,637.

Bandung Conference the first conference 1955 of the Afro-Asian nations, proclaiming anti-colonialism and neutrality between East and West.

bandy-bandy venomous Australian snake *Vermicella annulata* growing to about 75 cm/2.5 ft. It is banded in black and white, and belongs to the cobra family, but is not aggressive towards humans.

Banff /bænf/ holiday resort in Alberta, Canada; population (1984) 4,246. It is a centre for Banff National Park (Canada's first, founded in 1885) in the Rocky Mountains.

Banffshire /'bænfʃə/ former county of NE Scotland, now in Grampian region.

Bangalore /ˌbæŋgə'lɔː/ capital of Karnataka state, S India; population (1981) 2,482,500.

Bangkok /ˌbæŋ'kɒk/ capital and port of Thailand, on the river Chao Phraya; population (1983) 4,030,000.
features Temple of the Emerald Buddha and the vast palace complex.
history Bangkok was established as the capital by Phra Chao Tak in 1769, after the Burmese had burned down the former capital Avuthia about 65 km/40 mi to the N.

Bangladesh /ˌbæŋglə'deʃ/ country in S Asia, surrounded by India to the E, N, and W, and bounded to the S by the bay of Bengal.
government Bangladesh's political system is in a transitional state. The 1972 constitution was suspended in 1982 after a military coup by Lieutenant-General Ershad, who governed first as chief martial law administrator and then, from 1983, as president with an appointed council of ministers. A move back to civilian rule began 1983–85 with local elections, and in 1986 the constitution was revived, with martial law lifted in Nov.
At the head of the present system is an executive president, popularly elected for five-year terms by universal suffrage, who serves as head of state, head of the armed forces and head of government, appointing cabinet ministers and judicial officers. There is also a single-chamber legislative parliament *Jatiya Sangsad*, composed of 300 members directly elected for five-year terms from single-member constituencies and 30 women elected by the legislature itself.
history For history before 1947 see ◊India; for history 1947–1971 see◊Pakistan. Contemporary Bangladesh formerly comprised E Bengal province and Sylhet district of Assam in British

Bangladesh
PEOPLE'S REPUBLIC OF

AREA 143,000 sq km/55,000 sq mi
CAPITAL Dhaka
TOWNS ports Chittagong, Khulna
PHYSICAL flat delta of rivers Ganges and
Brahmaputra; annual rainfall of 2,540
mm/100 in; some 75% of the land is less than
3 m/10 ft above sea level and vulnerable to
flooding and cyclones
HEAD OF STATE AND OF GOVERNMENT Hussain
Mohammad Ershad from 1983
GOVERNMENT military
EXPORTS jute (50% of world production), tea
CURRENCY taka (50.3 = £1 Sept 1987)
POPULATION 101,408,000 (1985); annual
growth rate 2.2%
LANGUAGE Bangla (Bengali)
RELIGION Sunni Muslim 85%, Hindu 14%
LITERACY 43% male/20% female (1980)
GDP $11.2 bn (1983); $119 per head of
population
CHRONOLOGY
1947 Formed into E province of Pakistan on
partition of British India.
1970 Half a million killed in flood.
1971 Independent Bangladesh emerged under
leadership of Sheikh Mujib ur-Rahman after
civil war.
1975 Assassination of Sheikh Mujib. Martial
law imposed.

Bangladesh

1976–77 Maj-Gen Zia ur-Rahman assumed
power.
1978–79 Elections held and civilian rule
restored.
1981 Assassination of Maj-Gen Zia.
1982 Lt-Gen Ershad assumed power in army
coup. Martial law imposed.
1986 Elections held but disputed. Martial law
ended.
1987 State of emergency declared in response
to opposition demonstrations.

India. Predominantly Muslim, it was formed into the E province of Pakistan when India was partitioned in 1947. Substantially different in culture, language and geography from the W provinces of Pakistan 1,000 miles away and, with a larger population, it resented the political and military dominance exerted by W Pakistan during the 1950s and 60s. A movement for political autonomy grew after 1954 under the Awami League headed by Sheikh ◊Mujib ur-Rahman. This gained strength as a result of W Pakistan's indifference in 1970 when cyclones killed 500,000 in floods in E Pakistan.

In Pakistan's first general elections in 1970 the Awami League gained an overwhelming victory in the E and an overall majority in the all-Pakistan National Assembly. Talks on redrawing the constitution broke down, leading to E Pakistan's secession and the establishment of a Bangladesh ('Bengal Nation') government in exile in Calcutta (India) in 1971. Civil war resulted in the flight of 10,000,000 E Pakistani refugees to India, administrative breakdown, famine, and cholera. The W Pakistani forces in E Pakistan surrendered in 1971 after India intervened on the secessionists' side. A republic of Bangladesh was proclaimed and rapidly gained international recognition in 1972.

Sheikh Mujib ur-Rahman became prime minister in 1972 under a secular, parliamentary constitution. He introduced a socialist economic programme of nationalisation, but became intolerant of opposition, establishing an emergency one-party, presidential system in Jan 1975. In Aug 1975 Sheikh Mujib ur-Rahman, his wife and close relatives were assassinated in a military coup. The Awami League held power for three months under Khandakar Mushtaq Ahmed before a further military coup in Nov 1975 established as president and chief martial law administrator the non-political chief justice Abu Sadat Mohammed Sayem.

In 1976, Major-General Zia ur-Rahman (1936–81) became chief martial law administrator. Becoming president in 1977, he adopted an Islamic constitution, approved by a national referendum in May. In Jun he won a 4:1 majority in a direct presidential election. Major-General Zia's newly formed Bangladeshi Nationalist Party won a parliamentary majority. A civilian government was installed and martial law and the state of emergency were lifted in 1979. The administration was undermined, however, by charges of corruption and by a guerrilla movement in Chittagong in 1980. On 30 May 1981 Major-General Zia was assassinated in an attempted coup, and interim power was assumed by Vice-President Justice Abdus Sattar.

With disorder increasing, the civilian administration was overthrown in Mar 1982 by a coup led by Lieutenant-General Mohammad Hussain Ershad (1930–). Martial law was re-imposed and political activity banned. With a more market-orientated approach and a 'food for work' rural programme, the economy improved.

Agitation for a return to democracy grew in 1983 when a broad opposition coalition, the Movement for the Restoration of Democracy, was formed. Lieutenant-General Ershad promised presidential and parliamentary elections in 1984, but both were cancelled after an opposition threat of a boycott and campaign of civil disobedience if martial law was not first lifted.

In Jan 1986 the ban on political activity was removed and parliamentary elections were held in May. The Awami League agreed to participate in these elections, but the Bangladesh National Party and many other opposition parties boycotted them. With a campaign marked by violence, widespread abstentions and claims of ballot-rigging, and the re-running of 37 constituency contests, Lieutenant-General Ershad and his Jatiya Front party gained the two-thirds majority required to pass a law granting retrospective immunity. In Oct 1986 Lieutenant-General Ershad was re-elected president in a direct election and in Nov 1986 martial law was lifted. The principal parliamentary opposition party is the Awami League, led by Sheikha Hasina Wazed (the daughter of Sheikh Mujib ur-Rahman), heading an eight-party alliance. Outside parliament is the Bangladesh National Party, led by Begum Khalida Zia (the widow of Major-General Zia ur-Rahman), heading a seven-party alliance.

In foreign affairs, Bangladesh has remained a member of the Commonwealth since 1972. It has been heavily dependent on foreign economic aid, but has pursued a broader policy of ◊Non-Alignment. Relations with India have deteriorated since 1975 as a result of disputes over the sharing of Ganges water and the annual influx of 200,000 Bangladeshi refugees to Assam and W Bengal which has prompted India to threaten to construct a frontier fence.

Bangor /'bæŋgə/ cathedral city in Gwynedd, N Wales; population (1981) 46,585. University College, of the University of Wales, is here. The cathedral was begun in 1495.

Bangui /bɒŋ'giː/ capital and river port of the Central African Republic; population (1975) 302,000.

Banjermasin /ˌbɑːnjəˈmɑːsɪn/ river port in Indonesia, on Borneo; population (1971) 281,700.

banjo stringed musical instrument of tinny quality, with a long neck and circular drum-type sound box; it is played with a plectrum. It originated in the USA with black slaves, and, introduced to Britain in 1846, became a popular amateur instrument.

Banjul /bænˈdʒuːl/ capital and chief port of Gambia, on an island at the mouth of the river Gambia; population (1983) 44,536. It was known as Bathurst until 1973.

bank generally, a financial institution which uses funds deposited with it to extend loans to companies or individuals, and also provides financial services to its customers. A central bank issues currency for the government, in order to provide cash for circulation and exchange.

Banka /'bæŋkə/ island in Indonesia off the E coast of Sumatra

area 12,000 sq km/4,600 sq mi
capital Pangkalpinang
towns port Mintok
products Banka is one of the world's largest producers of tin
population (1970) 300,000.

Bank for International Settlements a bank established 1930 to handle German reparations settlements from World War I, which today assists cooperation of central banks; its London agent is the Bank of England. Its headquarters is in Basel, Switzerland.

Bankhead /'bæŋkhed/ Tallulah 1903–1968. American actress, noted for her wit and flamboyant lifestyle; she starred in *The Little Foxes* 1939.

Bank of England UK central bank originally founded by Act of Parliament in 1694. It was entrusted with note issue in 1844, and nationalized in 1946. Known by its London site as the 'Old Lady of Threadneedle Street', it is banker to the UK government and assists in implementing financial and monetary policies.

bank rate ◊interest rate fixed by the Bank of England as a guide to mortgage, hire purchase rates, and so on, which was replaced in 1972 by the *minimum lending rate* (lowest rate at which the Bank acts as lender of last resort to the money market), which from 1978 was again a 'bank rate' set by the Bank.

bankruptcy the process by which the property of a person unable to pay debts is taken away and divided rateably among his or her creditors, after preferential payments such as taxes and wages. Proceedings may be instituted either by the debtor (voluntary bankruptcy), or by any creditor for a substantial sum (involuntary bankruptcy). Until 'discharged', a bankrupt is severely restricted in financial activities. When 'discharged' he or she becomes free of most debts dating from the time of bankruptcy.

Banks /bæŋks/ Joseph 1743–1820. British naturalist-explorer. He accompanied Captain ◊Cook on his voyage round the world 1768–71, and was a founder of the Botanical Gardens, Kew, and was President of the Royal Society from 1778. The ◊banksia genus of shrubs is named after him.

banksia Australian genus of shrubs and trees, family Proteaceae, including the 'honeysuckle tree'; they are named after Sir Joseph ◊Banks.

Bannister /'bænɪstə/ Roger 1929– . British doctor athlete. On 6 May 1954, at Oxford, he became the first man in the history of athletics to run the mile in under four minutes, his time being 3 min 59.4 sec.

Bannockburn, Battle of /'bænəkbɜːn/ battle in central Scotland, near Stirling, on 24 Jun 1314, when ◊Robert the Bruce defeated the English under ◊Edward II.

bantam small variety of domestic chicken. This can either be a small version of one of the large breeds, or a separate type. Some are prolific layers, and bantam cocks have a reputation as spirited fighters.

banteng wild species of cattle *Bos banteng*, now scarce, but formerly ranging from Burma through Indo-China to Malaya and Java. Inhabiting hilly forests, its colour varies from

Bannister British athlete Roger Bannister ran races while a student at Oxford and in the 1952 Olympics. In 1954 he became the first man to run a mile in under four minutes.

pale brown to blue-black, usually with white stockings and rump patch, and it is up to 1.5 m/5 ft at the shoulder.

Banting /'bæntɪŋ/ Frederick Grant 1891–1941. Canadian discoverer, with ◊Best and others, of insulin treatment for diabetes in 1922; he shared a Nobel prize in 1923.

Bantock /'bæntək/ Granville 1868–1946. British composer. Born in London, he became known as a conductor of musical comedy and modern English music, and was professor of music at the University of Birmingham 1908–34. He was knighted in 1930. His works include the choral symphony *Atalanta in Calydon*, *Hebridean Symphony*, and a setting of *Omar Khayyám*.

Bantu languages a group of related languages spoken widely over the greater part of Africa S of the Sahara, including Swahili, Xhosa and Zulu. Meaning 'people' in Zulu, the word Bantu itself illustrates a characteristic use of prefixes: *mu-ntu*, 'man', *ba-ntu*, 'people'. The Bantu-speaking peoples probably originated in N Central Africa. Until 1978, the black people of the Republic of South Africa were officially designated *Bantu(s)*.

Bantustan name until 1978 for the ◊Black National ◊States in the Republic of South Africa.

banyan tree *Ficus benghalensis* of the family Moraceae. It produces aerial roots which grow down from its spreading branches, forming supporting pillars which have the appearance of separate trunks.

baobab tree *Adansonia digitata*, family Bombacaceae, with root-like branches (hence its nickname 'upside-down tree'); the edible fruit are known as monkey bread. It may live 1000 years and is found in Africa and Australia, a relic of the time when both were part of ◊Gondwanaland.

baptism (Greek 'to dip') immersion in or sprinkling with water as a religious rite of initiation. It was practised long before the beginning of Christianity, and was universal in the Christian Church from the first days, being administered to adults by immersion. The baptism of infants was not practised until the 2nd century, but became general in the 6th. Baptism by sprinkling (christening) when the child is named is now general among Western Christians except for some sects, notably the ◊Baptists, where complete immersion of adults is the rule. The Eastern Orthodox Church also practises immersion. In the baptism ceremony, sponsors or godparents make vows on behalf of the child which are renewed by the child at confirmation.

Baptist member of a world-wide Christian community, practising baptism by immersion of believers only on profession of faith. Baptists stand in the Protestant and evangelical tradition, seek their authority in the Bible, emphasize the right of the soul to an immediate relation to God, and conceive the Church as a fellowship of the spiritually regenerate.

Baptists originated among the English Separatists who took refuge in Holland in the early 17th century, the first English Baptist being Reverend John Smyth, a Cambridge scholar and an ordained minister of the Church of England. The first Baptist Church in the USA was organized in Rhode Island in 1639 by Roger Williams. In the 19th century there was considerable Baptist development on the continent of Europe. There are flourishing Baptist communities in the Commonwealth. Of the world total of approximately 31,000,000, some 26,500,000 are in the USA, and 265,000 in the UK.

The Baptist Missionary Society, formed in 1792 under the inspiration of William Carey, pioneered in the modern missionary movement. In 1905 the Baptist World Alliance was formed.

bar a ◊CGS unit of pressure (b) equal to 10^5 pascals or 10^6 dynes/cm^2, approximately 750 mmHg or 0.987 atm. Its diminutive, the *millibar* is commonly used by meteorologists.

Barabbas /bə'ræbəs/ in the New Testament, the robber released at ◊Passover instead of Jesus.

barb general name for fish of the genus *Barbus* and some related genera of the family Cyprinidae. As well as the ◊barbel, barbs include many small tropical Old World species, some of which are familiar aquarium species. They are active egglaying species, usually of 'typical' fish shape and with barbels at the corner of the mouth.

Barbados /bɑː'beɪdɒs/ island in the Caribbean, one of the Lesser Antilles.
government The constitution dates from 1966 and provides for a system of parliamentary government on the British model, with a prime minister and cabinet drawn from and responsible

to the legislature, consisting of a senate and a house of assembly. The senate has 21 members appointed by the governor-general, 12 on the advice of the prime minister, two on the advice of the leader of the opposition and the rest on the basis of wider consultations. The house of assembly has 27 members elected by universal suffrage. The legislature has a maximum life of five years and may be dissolved within this period. The governor-general appoints both the prime minister (on the basis of support in the house of assembly) and the leader of the opposition. The two main political parties are the Barbados Labour Party (BLP), and the Democratic Labour Party (DLP).

history Originally inhabited by Arawak indians, all of whom were wiped out soon after the arrival of the first Europeans. Barbados became a British colony in 1627 and remained so until independence in 1966. Universal adult suffrage was introduced in 1951 and the BLP won the first general election. Ministerial government was established in 1954 and the BLP leader, Sir Grantley Adams, became the first prime minister. In 1955 a group broke away from the BLP and formed the DLP. Six years later full internal self-government was achieved and in the 1961 general election the DLP was victorious under its leader, Errol Barrow.

When Barbados attained full independence in 1966, Barrow became its first prime minister. The DLP was re-elected in 1971 but in the 1976 general election the BLP, led now by Sir Grantley Adams' son 'Tom', ended Barrow's 15-year rule. Both parties were committed to maintaining free enterprise and alignment with the USA although, the DLP government established diplomatic relations with Cuba in 1972 and the BLP administration supported the US invasion of ◊Grenada in 1983.

In 1981 the BLP was re-elected. After Adams' sudden death in 1985 he was succeeded by his deputy, Bernard St John, a former BLP leader. In the 1986 general election the DLP, led by Barrow, was returned to power with 24 of the 27 seats in the House of Assembly. Errol Barrow died in 1987, and was succeeded by Erskine Lloyd Sandiford .

Barbarossa /ˌbɑːbəˈrɒsə/ nickname 'red beard' given to the German emperor ◊Frederick I, and also to two brothers who were Barbary pirates: Horuk was killed by the Spaniards in 1518, Khair-ed-Din took Tunis in 1534, and died at Constantinople in 1546.

Barbarossa, operation name given to the plans for the German invasion of the Soviet Union 1941.

Barbary ape tailless yellowish-brown macaque monkey *Macaca sylvanus*, found in mountains and wilds of Algeria and Morocco, and introduced to the Rock of Gibraltar, where legend has it that the British will leave if the colony dies out.

barbastelle medium-sized insect-eating bat *Barbastella barbastellus* with 'frosted' black fur and a wingspan of about 25 cm/10 in. It is found in Britain, where it is uncommon, and Europe.

barbed wire a cheap fencing material made of strands of ◊galvanized wire with sharp barbs

Barbados

AREA 430 sq km/166 sq mi
CAPITAL Bridgetown
PHYSICAL most easterly island of the West Indies; surrounded by coral reefs
FEATURES subject to hurricanes
HEAD OF STATE Elizabeth II from 1966 represented by Hugh Springer from 1984
HEAD OF GOVERNMENT Erskine Lloyd Sandiford from 1987
GOVERNMENT parliamentary democracy
EXPORTS sugar, rum; oil
CURRENCY Barbados dollar (3.31 = £1 Sept 1987)
POPULATION 252,000 (1985); annual growth rate 0.3%
LANGUAGE English
RELIGION Christian
LITERACY 99% (1984)
GDP $1 bn (1984); $3,040 per head of population
CHRONOLOGY
1951 Universal adult suffrage introduced. The Barbados Labour Party (BLP) won the general election.
1954 Ministerial government established.
1961 Full internal self-government. Democratic Labour Party (DLP), led by Errol Barrow, in power.
1966 Barbados achieved full independence within the Commonwealth. Barrow became the new nation's first prime minister.

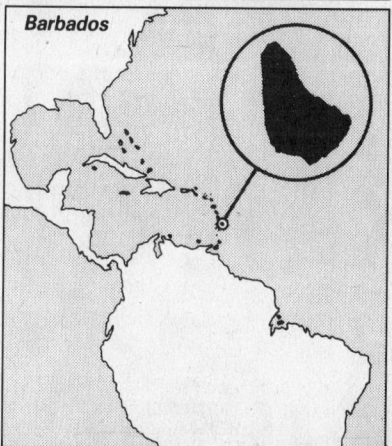

Barbados

1972 Diplomatic relations with Cuba established.
1976 BLP, led by Tom Adams, returned to power.
1983 Barbados supported US invasion of Grenada.
1985 Adams died suddenly. Bernard St John became prime minister.
1986 DLP, led by Barrow, returned to power.
1987 Barrow died, succeeded by Erskine Lloyd Sandiford.

wound upon them at intervals. In 1873 Joseph Glidden in the USA devised a machine to mass produce barbed wire. Its use on the American prairies led to range warfare between farmers and cattle ranchers, used to driving their herds cross country.

barbel freshwater fish *Barbus barbus* found in fast-flowing rivers with sand or gravel bottoms in Britain and Europe. Long-bodied, and up to 1 m/3 ft long, the barbel has four *barbels* ('little beards' – sensory fleshy filaments) near the mouth.

Barbellion /bɑːˈbelɪən/ W N P, pseudonym of Bruce Frederick Cummings 1889–1919. English diarist, author of *The Journal of a Disappointed Man* 1919, an account of his struggle with the illness multiple sclerosis.

Barber /ˈbɑːbə/ Samuel 1910– . American composer, with an increasingly dissonant style, whose works include *Adagio for Strings* 1936 and the opera *Vanessa* 1958.

barber's shop unaccompanied close-harmony singing, which originated among waiting customers in such shops in 19th-century USA. Temporarily superseded by radio, it was taken up in the 1970s as a hobby, and large touring choirs were formed.

barbet type of small fruit and insect eating bird found in forests throughout the tropics. There are some 78 species of barbet in the family Capitonidae, about half living in Africa. Distant relations of woodpeckers, barbets drill nest holes with their beaks. Many are brightly coloured.

The name comes from the 'little beard' of bristles at the base of the beak.

Barbie /ˈbɑːbi/ Klaus 1913– . German member of the Nazi party and a member of the SS from 1936. He was transferred to the occupied Netherlands in 1940 where he was involved in the deportation of Jews. In 1942 he was transferred to France where he was involved in tracking down Jews and resistance workers. Based in Lyon, his work included the rounding up of Jewish children from an orphanage at Iziev and the torture of the resistance leader Jean Moulin. During this time, his ruthlessness earned him the epithet 'Butcher of Lyon'.

Having escaped capture in 1945, Barbie was eventually employed by the US intelligence services in Germany before moving to Bolivia in 1951. Expelled from there in 1983, Barbie was returned to France where he was convicted by a court in Lyon in 1987.

Barbirolli /ˌbɑːbɪˈrɒli/ John 1899–1970. British conductor. Born in London, of French and Italian descent, he made a name as a cellist, and was permanent conductor to the Hallé Orchestra, Manchester, from 1943 until his death. He was knighted in 1949.

barbiturate salt or ◊ester of barbituric acid, which is derived from malic acid (found in unripe apples and urea). It is used as a sleeping aid, and as an anaesthetic in the control of epilepsy. It is addictive in indiscriminate prescription, and in the UK from 1979 there were legal penalties for misuse.

Barbie Nazi SS commander in Lyon, France, during World War II, Klaus Barbie. The 'Butcher of Lyon' lived for many years in Bolivia, enjoying the protection of military régimes. He was handed over to the French authorities in 1983 and convicted of crimes against humanity.

Barbirolli Meticulous in preparation as in performance, Barbirolli working on the score of Vaughan Williams' Fifth Symphony in the recording studio.

Barbizon /ˌbɑːbɪˈzɒn/ French village near the Forest of ◊Fontainebleau, Paris; the *Barbizon School* of landscape artists – inspired by ◊Constable – include ◊Corot, ◊Courbet, ◊Daubigny, ◊Millet, and ◊Rousseau.

Barbour /ˈbɑːbə/ John c. 1316–1395. Scottish poet whose chronicle-poem *The Brus* is amongst the earliest Scottish poetry.

Barcelona /ˌbɑːsɪˈləʊnə/ capital, industrial city (textiles, engineering, chemicals), and port of Catalonia; second city of Spain.
features The Ramblas, tree-lined promenades which lead from the Plaza de Cataluña, the largest square in Spain; ◊Gaudi's unfinished church of the Holy Family 1883; the Pueblo Espagñol 1929, with specimens of Spanish architecture of all periods; a replica of Columbus's ship, the *Santa Maria*, in the Maritime Museum; a large collection of art by Picasso.
population (1981) 1,752,500.

Bardeen /bɑːˈdiːn/ John 1908– . American physicist, who won a Nobel prize, with Brattain and Shockley, in 1956, for the development of the transistor in 1948. In 1972 he was the first double winner of a Nobel prize in the same subject (with Cooper and Schrieffer) for his work on superconductivity.

Bardot /bɑːˈdəʊ/ Brigitte 1934– . French film actress, whose appeal as a 'sex kitten' did much to popularize French cinema internationally. Her films include *And God Created Woman* 1950.

Bardsey Island /ˈbɑːdsi/ former pilgrimage centre in Gwynedd, Wales, with a 6th-century ruined abbey.

Bareilly /bəˈreɪli/ city in Uttar Pradesh, India; population (1981) 394,938.

Barenboim /ˈbærənbɔɪm/ Daniel 1942– . Israeli pianist and conductor, born in Argentina. He made his debut as a pianist in his native Buenos Aires at the age of seven, and as a conductor is a celebrated interpreter of Beethoven. He married the cellist Jacqueline ◊du Pré in 1967, and became musical director of the Orchestre de Paris in 1975.

Barents /ˈbærənts/ Willem 1550–1597. Dutch explorer, who made three expeditions to seek the ◊North-East Passage; he died on the last. The Barents Sea is named after him.

Barents Sea /ˈbærənts/ section of the E ◊Arctic Ocean. It has oil and gas reserves and is strategically important.

Barham /ˈbɑːrəm/ Richard Harris 1788–1845. British writer and clergyman, author of verse tales of the supernatural, and *The Ingoldsby Legends*, published under his pen name Thomas Ingoldsby.

Bari /ˈbɑːri/ industrial port in S Italy on the Adriatic; university 1924; population (1981) 371,022. The part of the town known as Tecnopolis is the Italian Silicon Valley.

Baring-Gould /ˈbeərɪŋ ˈguːld/ Sabine 1834–1924. British writer, rector of Lew Trenchard in N Devon from 1881. He was a prolific writer of novels, books of travel, mythology and folklore, and wrote the words of 'Onward, Christian Soldiers'.

baritone lower-range male voice midway between bass and tenor.

barium a metallic chemical element, symbol Ba, atomic number 56, atomic weight 137.36. The name comes from the Greek word for 'heavy', since barium was first discovered in barytes or heavy spar. It is silver-white in colour, oxidizes very easily, and is a little harder than lead. Barium is used in medicine, in the form of barium sulphate, which is taken in solution (a 'barium meal') and its progress followed using x-rays, to reveal abnormalities of the digestive tract. Barium, with ◊strontium, forms the emissive surface in ◊cathode-ray tubes.

bark the protective, outer layer on the stems and roots of woody plants, composed mainly of dead cells. Bark technically includes all the tissues external to the vascular ◊cambium (the ◊phloem, cortex, and periderm), and its thickness may vary from a few millimetres to 30 cm or more, as in the giant redwood (*Sequoia*) where it forms a thick, spongy layer. To allow for expansion of the stem, the bark is continually added to from within, and the outer surface often becomes fissured or is shed as scales. The bark from the cork oak (*Quercus ruber*) is economically important and harvested commercially, usually about every ten years. The spice ◊cinnamon, and the drugs cascara and ◊quinine all come from bark.

Barker /ˈbɑːkə/ George 1913– . British poet noted for his vivid imagery, as in *Calamiterror* 1937, *The True Confessions of George Barker* 1950, and *Collected Poems, 1930–50*.

Barker /ˈbɑːkə/ Herbert 1869–1950. British manipulative surgeon, whose work established the popular standing of ◊orthopaedics, but who was never recognized by the world of orthodox medicine.

Barking and Dagenham /ˈbɑːkɪŋ, ˈdægənəm/ borough of E Greater London
products Ford motor industry at Dagenham
population 152,600.

Barkly Tableland /ˈbɑːkli/ large-scale open-range cattle-raising area in Northern Territory and Queensland, Australia.

bark painting painting on the inner side of strips of tree bark produced by Australian aborigines of Arnhem Land, etc. In red, yellow, white, brown and black pigments, they were often painted with the fingers as the artist lay inside the low bark-roofed shelters.

bark painting The traditional designs of Australian aboriginals include both abstract and animal forms, such as the turtle in the foreground.

Barletta /bɑːˈletə/ industrial port on the Adriatic, Italy; population (1972) 80,000. There is a Romanesque cathedral.

barley cereal genus *Hordeum* belonging to the family Gramineae. The cultivated barley *Hordeum vulgare* comprises three distinct races – six-rowed barley, four-rowed barley or Scotch Bigg, and two-rowed barley.

Barley was one of the earliest cereals to be cultivated, and no other cereal can thrive in so wide a range of climate. Polar barley is sown and reaped well within the Arctic circle in Europe. Barley is no longer much used in bread-making, but finds a wide use for pig, horse, and cattle foods. Its main importance, however, is in brewing and distilling.

bar mitzvah (Hebrew 'son of the commandment') in ◊Judaism, initiation of a boy, which takes place at the age of 13, into the adult Jewish community; less common is the bat or bas mitzvah for girls. The boy reads a passage from the Torah in the synagogue on the Sabbath. After this he is regarded as a full member of the congregation.

Barnabas, St /'bɑːnəbəs/ Christian saint, mentioned in the New Testament as a 'fellow-labourer' with St Paul; he went with St Mark on a missionary journey to Cyprus, his birthplace.

barnacle marine crustacean of the subclass Cirripedia. The larval form is free-swimming, but after a time it settles down, and fixes itself by the head to rock or floating wood. The animal then remains attached, enclosed in a shell through which the cirri (modified legs) protrude to sweep food into the mouth. Barnacles include the stalked *goose barnacle Lepas anatifera* found on ships' bottoms and the *acorn barnacles*, such as *Balanus balanoides* common on rocks.

Barnardo /bəˈnɑːdəʊ/ Thomas John 1845–1905. British philanthropist, who was known as Dr Barnardo, though not medically qualified. He opened the first of a series of homes for destitute children in 1867 in Stepney, London.

Barnard's star /'bɑːnɑːd/ second-closest ◊star to the Sun, 6 light years away in the constellation ◊Ophiuchus. It is a faint red dwarf of 9th magnitude, visible only through a telescope. It is named after the US astronomer Edward E Barnard, who discovered in 1916 that it has the fastest proper motion of any star, crossing 1 degree of sky every 350 years. Some observations suggest that Barnard's star may be accompanied by planets.

Barnaul /ˌbɑːnɑːˈuːl/ industrial city in S Siberia, USSR; population (1981) 549,000.

Barnes /bɑːnz/ Ernest William 1874–1953. British cleric. A lecturer in mathematics at Cambridge 1902–15, he was an ardent advocate of the significance of scientific thought on modern religion. In 1924 he became bishop of Birmingham and published the controversial work *The Rise of Christianity* 1947.

Barnes /bɑːnz/ Thomas 1785–1841. British journalist, editor of *The Times* from 1817, during which time it became known as the 'Thunderer'.

Barnes /bɑːnz/ William 1800–1886. English poet and cleric who published volumes of poems in the Dorset dialect.

Barnet /'bɑːnɪt/ borough of NW Greater London

features site of the Battle of ◊Barnet; Hadley Woods; Hampstead Garden Suburb; part of Brent reservoir ('the Welsh Harp'); department for newspapers and periodicals of the British Library at Colindale; residential district of *Hendon*, which includes Metropolitan Police Detective Training and Motor Driving schools, and the Royal Air Force Battle of Britain and Bomber Command museums

population (1981) 292,500.

Barnsley /'bɑːnzli/ industrial town (iron and steel, glass, paper, carpet, and clothing) in S Yorkshire, England, on one of Britain's richest coalfields; population (1981) 73,500.

Barnum /'bɑːnəm/ Phineas T(aylor) 1810–1891. American showman, who after an adventurous career exhibited the midget 'Tom Thumb', toured USA with the singer Jenny Lind, and in 1871 established the 'Greatest Show on Earth', comprising circus, menagerie, and exhibition of 'freaks', conveyed in 100 rail cars.

Barocci /bəˈrɒtʃi/ Federico 1535–1612. Italian painter. Born in Urbino, he remained there for most of his working life, despite achieving international fame. His paintings defy easy classification, falling between Renaissance and Baroque. The *Descent from the Cross* 1567 shows his soft, emotional style and the influence of ◊Correggio on his art.

Baroda /bəˈrəʊdə/ former name of ◊Vadodara, in Gujarat, India.

barograph device for recording variations in atmospheric pressure in which a pen, governed by the movements of an aneroid ◊barometer, makes a continuous line on a paper strip on a cylinder which rotates over a day or week to create a *barogram*, or permanent record of variations in atmospheric pressure.

Baroja /bæˈrəʊxə/ Pio 1872–1956. Spanish novelist of Basque extraction whose works include a trilogy dealing with the Madrid underworld, *La lucha por la vida/The Struggle for Life* 1904–05, and the multi-volume *Memorias de un hombre de acción/Memoirs of a Man of Action* 1913–28.

barometer measure of atmospheric pressure as an indication of weather. In a *mercury barometer* a column of mercury in a glass tube roughly 0.75 m/2 ft high (closed at one end, curved upward at the other) is balanced by the pressure of the atmosphere on the open end; any change in the height of the column reflects a change in pressure. An *aneroid barometer* achieves a similar result by changes in the distance between the faces of a shallow cylindrical metal box which is partly exhausted of air.

baron lowest rank in the ◊peerage of the UK, above a baronet and below a viscount. The first English barony was created in 1387, but barons by 'writ' existed earlier. Life peers, created under the Act of 1958, are always of this rank.

baronet hereditary title in the UK below the rank of baron, but above that of knight; the first creations were in 1611 by James I, who needed funds from their sale to finance an army in Ulster.

Barons' Wars civil wars in England:
1215–17 between King ◊John and his barons, over his failure to honour ◊Magna Carta;

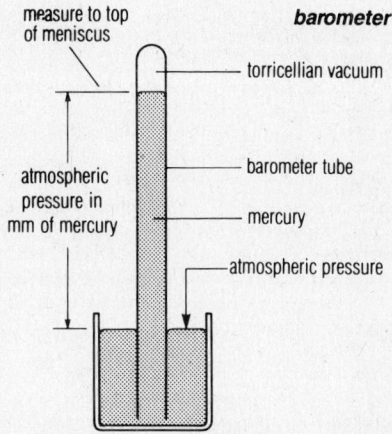

barometer

measure to top of meniscus — torricellian vacuum

barometer tube

atmospheric pressure in mm of mercury

mercury

atmospheric pressure

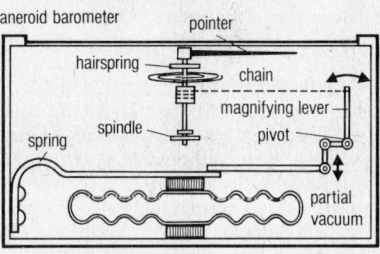

aneroid barometer   pointer

hairspring   chain

magnifying lever

spindle   pivot

spring

partial vacuum

1264–67 between ◊Henry III (and the future Edward I) and his barons (led by Simon de ◊Montfort);
1264 14 May *Battle of Lewes* at which Henry III was defeated and captured;
1265 4 Aug Simon de Montfort was defeated by Edward at Evesham and killed.

Baroque exuberant and extravagant style developed in 17th and early 18th century Europe in art (◊Caravaggio, ◊Rubens) and architecture, when it often involved large-scale building, for example, ◊Versailles and ◊Wren's plan for London: also ◊Bernini, ◊Borromini, ◊Vanbrugh, ◊Hawksmoor, Le ◊Vau, ◊Hardouin-Mansart.

In music the Baroque era lasted from about 1600 to 1750, and its major composers included ◊Monteverdi, ◊Vivaldi, J S ◊Bach, and ◊Handel. The term may possibly derive from the Spanish 'barrucco', an irregular pearl.

Barossa Valley /bəˈrɒsə/ wine-growing area in the Lofty mountain ranges, South Australia.

Barotseland /bəˈrɒtsɪlænd/ former kingdom in Western Province of ◊Zambia.

Barquisimeto /bɑːˌkiːsɪˈmeɪtəʊ/ city in NW Venezuela; population (1979) 474,000.

Barra /'bærə/ most southerly of the larger Outer ◊Hebrides islands, Scotland.

barracuda large predatory fish *Sphyraena barracuda* found in the warmer seas of the world, which can grow over 2 m/6 ft long and has a superficial resemblance to a pike. Young fish shoal but the older ones are solitary. Esteemed for food, the barracuda has very sharp shearing teeth, and sometimes attacks people.

Barragán /ˌbærəˈgɑːn/ Luis 1902– . Mexican architect, noted for his use of rough wooden beams, cobbles, lava, and adobe; his simple houses with walled gardens, and his fountains. Pritzker Award 1980.

Barranquilla /ˌbærən'kiːljə/ seaport in N Colombia, on the river Magdalena; population (1979) 855,000.

Barras /bæ'rɑːs/ Paul François Jean Nicolas, Count 1755–1829. French revolutionary. He fought against the English in India, was elected to the National Convention in 1792, and helped to overthrow Robespierre (1794). In 1795 he became a member of the Directoire. In 1796 he brought about the marriage of his former mistress, Joséphine de Beauharnais, with Napoleon, and assumed dictatorial powers. After Napoleon's *coup d'état* of 19 Nov 1799, Barras fell into disgrace.

Barrault /bæ'rəʊ/ Jean Louis 1910– . French actor and director. He was producer and director to the ◊Comédie-Française 1940–46, and was director of the Théâtre de France (formerly Odéon) from 1959 until dismissed 1968 because of statements made during the occupation of the theatre by student rebels. His films include *La Symphonie fantastique*, *Les Enfants du Paradis* 1944, and *La Ronde* 1950.

barre the wooden bar running along the walls of a ballet studio at waist height, designed to help dancers find their balance while going through the initial daily exercises.

Barre /bɑː/ Raymond 1924– . Prime minister of France 1976–81, member of the centre-right Union pour la Démocratie Française.
Barre, born on the French dependency of Réunion, made his reputation as a neo-liberal economist at the Sorbonne and as vice president of the ◊European Commission (1967–72). He served as minister of foreign trade to President ◊Giscard d'Estaing and became prime minister on the resignation of ◊Chirac in 1976. Barre, who was at the same time given the Finance Ministry portfolio, gained a reputation as a tough and determined budget-cutter (nicknamed Monsieur Economy), but unemployment increased during his term. He built up a strong political base in the Lyon region during the early 1980s.

barrel a unit of liquid capacity, used particularly for measuring petroleum. A barrel of petroleum contains 159 litres/35 gallons.

barrel organ portable cylindrical musical instrument. When a handle is turned, it produces tunes mechanically, since an arrangement of pins is thus successively released to open the pipe valves. Later the name was also given to a type of piano with a similar barrel mechanism, which was used by street buskers.

Barren Lands/Grounds the ◊tundra region of Canada, W of Hudson Bay.

Barrie /'bæri/ James Matthew 1860–1937. Scottish novelist and playwright. Born in Kirriemuir, Angus, he entered journalism in Nottingham in 1883, and settled in London in 1885. He became known by his studies of Scottish rural life in *Auld Licht Idylls* 1888, and *A Window in Thrums* 1889 which began the vogue of the Kailyard school. His first novel, *The Little Minister*, was dramatized in 1897 and, together with *The Professor's Love Story* 1894, established his reputation as a playwright. The most important of his later plays are: *Quality Street* 1901, *The Admirable Crichton* 1902, *What Every Woman Knows* 1908, *Dear Brutus* 1917, and *Mary Rose* 1920. The perennial children's play, *Peter Pan* 1904, was drawn from an idea in the *Little White Bird* 1902. Other works include a biography of his mother, *Margaret Ogilvie* 1896. He was made a baronet in 1913 and received the Order of Merit in 1922.

barrier reef a ◊coral reef that lies offshore, separated from the mainland by a shallow lagoon.

barrister in the UK, a lawyer qualified by study at the ◊Inns of Court to plead for a client at the Bar (the railed division separating off the judges and officers of the court); barristers remain outside the Bar till they become King's/Queen's Counsel, when they 'take silk' – wear a silk instead of a stuff gown – and are called 'within the Bar'. Barristers are grouped in 'chambers' and act for clients only on the instructions of a solicitor (the actual arrangements being made by their shared 'clerk'), and in the highest courts only they can be heard on behalf of a litigant. Britain is almost alone in the English-speaking world in maintaining the distinction between barrister and ◊solicitor; in Scotland a barrister is an 'advocate', and in the USA an attorney (lawyer) may serve both functions.

barrow a burial mound, usually composed of earth, but sometimes of stones, examples of which are found in many parts of the world. There are two main types, long and round.
The *long barrow* is held to be the earlier, dating from the New Stone Age. Sometimes it may be a mere mound, but usually it contained a chamber of wood or stone slabs in which were placed the bodies of the deceased. Such are especially common in the southern counties of England from Sussex to Dorset. They seem to have been communal burial-places of the long-headed Mediterranean race. *Round barrows* were the work of the round-headed or 'beaker' people of the early Bronze Age. The commonest type is the bell barrow, consisting of a circular mound, enclosed by a ditch and an outside bank of earth. Many dot the Wiltshire downs. In historic times certain of the Saxon and most of the Danish invaders were barrow-builders.

Barrow /'bærəʊ/ most northerly town in the USA, at Point Barrow, Alaska; the world's largest Inuit settlement. There is oil at nearby Prudhoe Bay.

Barrow-in-Furness /'bærəʊ ɪn 'fɜːnɪs/ industrial port (building nuclear submarines) in Cumbria, England; population (1981) 69,500.

Barry /'bæri/ port in S Glamorgan, Wales; population (1981) 44,000. With *Barry Island*, it is a holiday resort.

Barry /'bæri/ Charles 1795–1860. British architect of the neo-Gothic Houses of Parliament at Westminster, London, 1840–60, in collaboration with ◊Pugin.

Barry /'bæri/ Comtesse du see ◊Du Barry.

Barrymore /'bærɪmɔː/ US family of actors, the children of British-born Maurice Barrymore and Georgie Drew, both stage personalities.
Lionel Barrymore (1878–1954) first appeared on the stage with his grandmother, Mrs John Drew, in 1893. After studying art in Paris, he returned to the stage, and from 1909 made numerous films.
Ethel Barrymore (1879–1959) played with the British actor Henry Irving in London in 1898 and in 1928 opened the Ethel Barrymore Theatre in New York; she also appeared in many films from 1914.
John Barrymore (1882–1942), a flamboyant personality, appeared on stage and screen, often with his brother and sister.

Barrymore US actor John Barrymore was the youngest of the three talented Barrymores, whose parents were also actors. He made his name in the early years of the 20th century in Shakespearean roles.

Barstow /'bɑːstəʊ/ Stan 1928– . British novelist. Born in W Yorkshire, he wrote novels about northern working-class life including *A Kind of Loving* 1960.

Bart /bɑː/ Jean 1651–1702. French naval hero. Born at Dunkirk, the son of a fisherman, he served in the French navy, and harassed the British fleet in many daring exploits.

Bart /bɑːt/ Lionel 1930– . British composer, born in London, author of both words and music for the musicals *Fings Ain't Wot They Us'd T'Be* 1959 and *Oliver!* 1960.

barter trade by the exchange of goods (or services), which preceded the introduction of money.

Barth /bɑːt/ Karl 1886–1968. Swiss Protestant theologian; socialist in his political views, he attacked the ◊Nazis. His *Church Dogmatics* 1932–62 makes the resurrection of Jesus the focal point of Christianity.

Barthes /bɑːt/ Roland 1915–1980. French critic, born in Cherbourg. He was an influential theorist of ◊semiology, the science of signs and symbols. One of the French 'new critics', he attacked traditional literary criticism in his early works, including *Sur Racine/On Racine* 1963, and set out his own theories in *Eléments de sémiologie* 1964. He also wrote an autobiographical novel, *Roland Barthes sur Roland Barthes* 1975. He was killed in a car accident.

Barthes French critic Roland Barthes, a fresh, individual, and often provocative writer. He developed his own methods of literary criticism, which caused great controversy in the academic world.

Bartholdi /bɑːˈtɒldi/ Auguste 1834–1904. French sculptor. He completed the Statue of Liberty overlooking New York harbour in 1884.

Bartholomew, St /bɑːˈθɒləmjuː/ Christian saint and ◊apostle. Legends relate that after the Crucifixion he took Christianity to India, or that he was a missionary in Asia Minor and Armenia, where he suffered martyrdom by being flayed alive. His feast day is 24 Aug.

Bartholomew, Massacre of St start of French religious persecution 1572; see under ◊Huguenots.

Bartók /ˈbɑːtɒk/ Béla 1881–1945. Hungarian composer, born in Transylvania. He was regarded as a child prodigy, studied music at Budapest, and collaborated with ◊Kodály in research into Hungarian folk music, which coloured his later compositions and led him to develop a new musical language making tonal use of the 12 notes of the chromatic scale. His large output includes string quartets, violin and piano concertos, orchestral suites, and operas. When Hungary joined Germany in World War II, Bartók went to the USA. He died in New York.

Bartolommeo /bɑːˌtɒləˈmeɪəʊ/ Fra c. 1475–c. 1517. Florentine artist, also called Baccio della Porta, whose painting of the *Last Judgment* in Santa Maria Nuova greatly influenced ◊Raphael. Deeply moved by ◊Savonarola's death, he entered a Dominican monastery, but turned again to painting in 1504. His works, influenced by ◊Leonardo da Vinci and

Bartók Hungarian composer Béla Bartok turned from 19th century romantic music to an interest in Balkan folk music. Driven from Budapest by the Nazi occupation, he went to the USA. His works combine tradition with modernism.

◊Giorgione, are the best Florentine examples of High Renaissance classicism.

Barton /ˈbɑːtn/ Edmund 1849–1920. Australian politician. He was leader of the Federation movement from 1896, and first prime minister of the Commonwealth of Australia 1901–03. On his retirement, 1903, he became a high-court judge.

Bart's Short for St Bartholomew's Hospital, in Smithfield, one of the great teaching hospitals of London, England. It was founded by Henry VIII at the Reformation.

Baruch /bəˈruːk/ Bernard Mannes 1870–1965. US stock-market wizard. He was a friend of the British premier Churchill and a self-appointed, unpaid adviser to US presidents Wilson, F D Roosevelt, and Truman. He strongly advocated international control of atomic energy.

baryon see ◊fundamental particle.

Baryshnikov /bəˈrɪʃnɪkɒf/ Mikhail 1948– . Russian dancer. He joined the Kirov Ballet in 1967 and soon became acclaimed worldwide as a soloist. After defecting 'on artistic, not political grounds' while in Toronto in 1974, he worked with various companies, becoming director of the American Ballet Theatre in 1980. He has created many roles, notably in *Push Comes to Shove* 1976 (music by Haydn/J Lamb) and Jerome Robbins' *Opus 19* 1979 (Prokofiev). He made his film debut in *Turning Point* 1978.

basalt the commonest volcanic ◊igneous rock, and the principal rock type on the ocean floor, basic in composition, that is, containing relatively little silica: 45–50%. It is usually dark grey, but sometimes green, brown or black. The ground mass may be glassy or finely crystalline, sometimes with large crystals embedded. Bosalite lava tends to be runny and flows for great distances before solidifying and successive eruptions have formed the great plateaux of

Colorado and the Indian Deccan. In some places, such as Fingal's Cave in the Inner Hebrides of Scotland and the Giant's Causeway in Antrim, N Ireland, shrinkage during the solidification of the molten lava caused the formation of hexagonal columns.

bascule bridge a kind of movable bridge in which one or two counterweighted deck members pivot upwards to allow shipping to pass underneath. One of the best-known examples is the double bascule bridge Tower Bridge, near the Tower of London.

base in mathematics, the number of different single-digit symbols used in a particular number system. Thus our usual (decimal) counting system of numbers has the base 10 (using the symbols 0,1,2,3,4,5,6,7,8,9). In the ◊binary number system, which has only the numbers 1 and 0, the base is 2. A base is also a number which, when raised to a particular power (that is, when multiplied by itself a particular number of times as in $10^2 = 10 \times 10 = 100$), has a ◊logarithm equal to the power. For example, the logarithm of 100 to the base 10 is 2.

The value of any position in an octal (base 8) number increases by a factor of 8 with each move from right to left (1,8,64,512,...); for a hexadecimal (base 16) number, the factor is 16 (1,16,256,4096,...). In base 16, all numbers up to 16 must be represented by single-digit 'numbers', since 10 in hexadecimal would mean 16 in decimal. Hence decimal 10,11,12,13,14,15, are represented in hexadecimal by letters A,B,C,D,E,F.

BASE

binary (base 2)	octal (base 8)	decimal (base 10)	hexadecimal (base 16)
0	0	0	0
1	1	1	1
10	2	2	2
11	3	3	3
100	4	4	4
101	5	5	5
110	6	6	6
111	7	7	7
1000	10	8	8
1001	11	9	9
1010	12	10	A
1011	13	11	B
1100	14	12	C
1101	15	13	D
1110	16	14	E
1111	17	15	F
10000	20	16	10
1111111	377	255	FF
11111010001	3721	2001	7D1

baseball national summer game of USA, possibly derived from the English game of rounders. According to tradition it was invented in Cooperstown, New York, by Abner Doubleday in 1839.

Baseball is played with a bat and ball between two teams, each of nine players, on a pitch ('field') marked out in the form of a diamond, with a base at each corner. The ball is struck with a cylindrical bat, and the players try to make a run ('score') by circuiting the bases round the diamond before the ball can be retrieved. A 'home run' is a circuit on one hit.

The game is divided into nine innings (inning is the singular form), each with two halves, with each team taking turns to bat while the other team takes the field, pitching, catching, and on the bases.

The pitcher throws the ball, and the batter tries to make a 'hit'. If he hits the ball the batter tries to make a 'run', either in stages from home base to first, second, and third base and back to home base, or in a 'home run'.

He is declared out if, (1) he fails to hit the ball after 3 'strikes', (2) he hits the ball into the air and it is caught by a fielder, (3) he is touched by the ball in the hand of one of his opponents while he is between bases, and (4) a fielder standing on one of the bases catches the ball before he reaches the base.

The first batter is followed by the other members of his team in rotation until three members of the batting side are put out: the opposing team then take their turn to bat. After nine innings, the team scoring the most runs wins the game. The game is controlled by umpires.

Cooperstown contains the Baseball Hall of Fame (1939) and the National Museum of Baseball. The National Association of Baseball Players was formed in 1858 and the first professional team was Cincinnati's Red Stockings (1869).

The *World Series* was first held as an end-of-season game between the winners of the two professional leagues, the National League and the American League, in 1903, and was established as a series of seven games in 1905. Recent winners have been:

1977 New York Yankees
1978 New York Yankees
1979 Pittsburgh Pirates
1980 Philadelphia Phillies
1981 Los Angeles Dodgers
1982 St Louis Cardinals
1983 Baltimore Orioles
1984 Detroit Tigers
1985 Kansas City Royals
1986 New York Mets
1987 Minnesota Twins

Basel /'bɑːzəl/ (also known as *Basle*; the French form is *Bâle*) financial, commercial, and industrial centre in Switzerland; population (1980) 182,000. It has the chemical firms Hoffman–La Roche, Sandoz, Ciba-Geigy (dyes, vitamins, agro-chemicals, dietary products, genetic products). There are trade fairs, and it is the headquarters of the Bank for International Settlements. There is an 11th-century cathedral (rebuilt after an earthquake 1356), a 16th-century town hall and a university dating from the 15th century.

history Basel was a strong military station under the Romans. In 1501 it joined the Swiss confederation, and later developed as a centre for the Reformation.

basenji breed of dog originating in Central Africa, where it is used as a hunter. It has no true

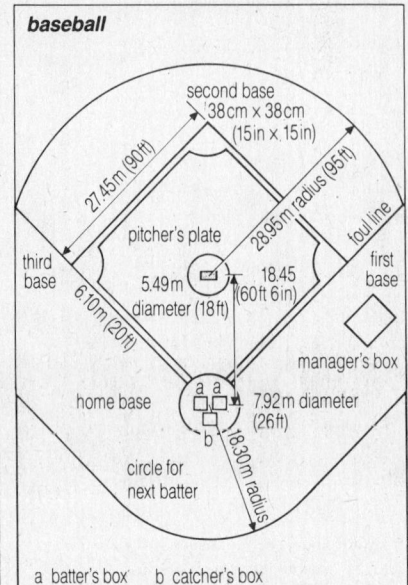

baseball

second base
38cm × 38cm
(15in × 15in)
27.45m (90ft)
28.95m radius (95ft)
foul line
pitcher's plate
third base
5.49m diameter (18ft)
6.10m (20ft)
18.45 (60ft 6in)
first base
manager's box
home base
a a
b
7.92m diameter (26ft)
18.30m radius
circle for next batter

a batter's box   b catcher's box

bark. About 41 cm/1.3 ft tall, it has a wrinkled forehead, curled tail, and short glossy coat.

base pair the linkage of two base (purine or pyrimidine) molecules in ◊DNA. One base of each pair lies on one of the two strands of the DNA double helix, and one on the other strand, so the base pairs link the two strands, rather like the rungs of a ladder. In DNA, there are four bases: adenine and guanine (purines) and cytosine and thymine (pyrimidines). Adenine always pairs with thymine and cytosine with guanine. Because the pairs are so specific, DNA can replicate itself precisely, by separating the two strands of the helix and forming new strands using the original ones as templates. This is the basis of ◊heredity. When ◊RNA is formed from DNA, base pairs are again used to copy the genetic message, but in RNA another base, uracil, substitutes for thymine. See also ◊nucleic acid.

Bashkir /bæʃ'kɪə/ a republic of the USSR, with the Ural Mountains on the E
area 143,600 sq km/55,430 sq mi
capital Ufa
products minerals, oil
population (1982) 3,876,000
history Bashkir was annexed by Russia 1557, and became the first Soviet Autonomous Republic 1919.

Bashkirstsev /bæʃ'kɪəstsef/ Mary 1860–1884. Russian diarist whose journals, written in French, were cited by Simone de Beauvoir as the archetypal example of 'self-centred female narcissism', but also as the discovery by the female of her independent existence. She died of tuberculosis.

Bashō /'bɑːʃəu/ pseudonym of Japanese poet Matsuo Munefusa 1644–1694. He was master of the *haiku*, a 17-syllable poetic form with lines of 5, 7, and 5 syllables, which he infused with subtle allusiveness and made the accepted form of poetic expression in Japan. His most famous work is *Oku-no-hosomichi/The Narrow Road to*

the Deep North 1694, an account of a visit to northern Japan, which consists of haikus interspersed with prose passages.

BASIC a computer-◊programming language, developed in 1971 from ◊Fortran and designed for ease of use. BASIC uses an ◊interpreter (enabling programs to be entered and run line by line with no preparation) rather than a ◊compiler (which involves having to write complete programs before they can be tested). Most home computers (micros) operate using BASIC.

Basic English a simplified form of English devised and promoted by C K ◊Ogden in the 1920s and 30s as (1) an international auxiliary language, (2) a route into Standard English for foreign learners, and (3) a reminder to the English-speaking world of the virtues of plain language. Its name derives from the letters of *B*ritish, *A*merican, *S*cientific, *I*nternational, *C*ommercial. Basic has a vocabulary of 850 words (plus names, technical terms, and so on), only 18 of which are verbs or 'operators'. *Get* therefore replaces 'receive', 'obtain' and 'become', while *buy* is replaced by the phrase 'give money for'.

basic-oxygen process the most widely used method of steel-making which involves the blasting of oxygen into molten pig iron. The basic-oxygen process was developed in 1948 at a steelworks near the towns of Linz and Donawitz. It is a modern version of the ◊Bessemer process. Pig iron from the blast furnace, together with steel scrap, is poured into a vessel called a converter, shaped rather like a concrete mixer. A jet of oxygen is then projected into the mixture at supersonic speed. The excess carbon in the mix and other impurities quickly burn out or form a slag. The converter is emptied by tilting. It takes only about 45 minutes to refine 350 tonnes of steel.

basic oxygen process

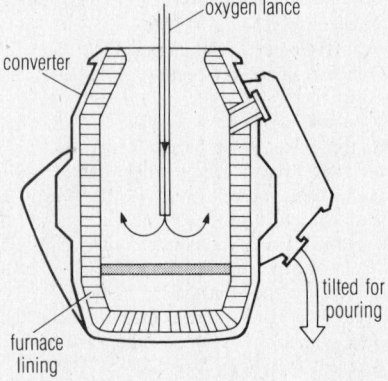

oxygen lance
converter
tilted for pouring
furnace lining

basidiocarp the spore-bearing body or 'fruiting body' of all basidiomycete fungi, except the rusts and smuts. A well-known example is the edible mushroom. Other types include globular basidiocarps (puffballs) or flat ones that project from tree trunks (brackets). They are made up of a mass of tightly packed, intermeshed ◊hyphae. The tips of these hyphae develop into the reproductive cells, or basidia, which form a fertile layer known as the hymenium or the *gills*

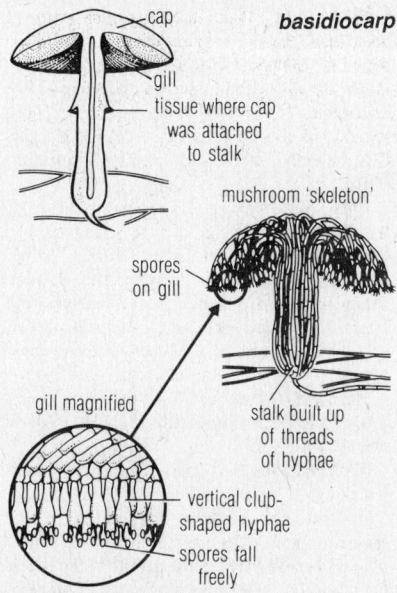

basidiocarp

cap

gill

tissue where cap
was attached
to stalk

mushroom 'skeleton'

spores
on gill

gill magnified

stalk built up
of threads
of hyphae

vertical club-
shaped hyphae

spores fall
freely

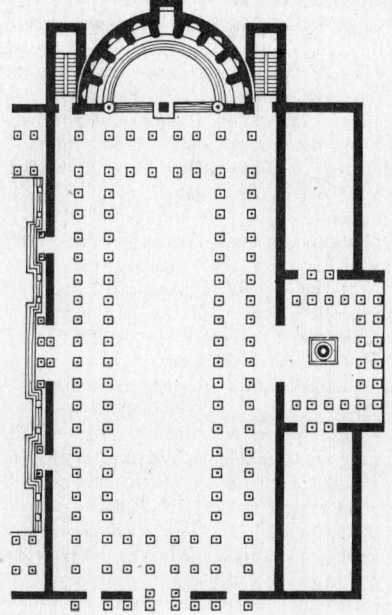

basketball

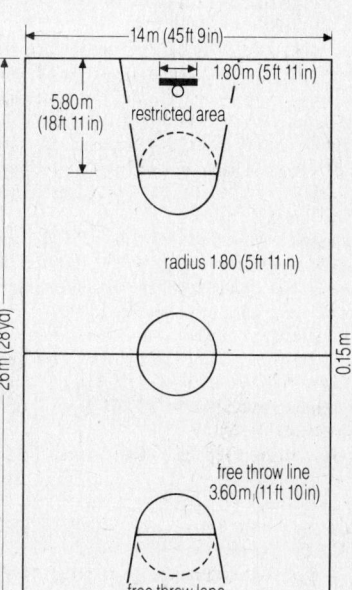

basilica Plan of the Basilica Ulpia in Rome.

of the basidiocarp. Four spores are budded off from the surface of each basidium.

Basie /'beisi/ 'Count' (William) 1904–1984. US band leader, pianist, and organist, who won great popularity for his simplified, swinging style of music. He developed the big-band sound and led impressive groups of musicians in a career spanning more than 50 years.

basil plant *Ocimum basilicum* of the family Labiatae. A native of the tropics, it is cultivated in Europe as a potherb and for seasoning.

Basil II /'bæzl/ c. 958–1025. Byzantine emperor. His achievement as emperor from 976 was to contain, and later decisively defeat, the Bulgarians, earning for himself the title 'Bulgar-slayer' after a victory in 1014. After the battle he blinded almost all 15,000 of the defeated, leaving only a few men with one eye to lead their fellows home. At the time of his death the Byzantine empire reached its greatest extent.

Basil, St /'bæzl/ c. 330–379. Christian saint, founder of the Basilian monks, and known as 'the Great'. He entered a monastery in Asia Minor about 358, and developed a monastic rule based on community life, work, and prayer. These ideas form the basis of monasticism in the Greek Orthodox church.

Basildon /'bæzldən/ industrial ◊new town (chemicals, clothing, printing, engineering) in Essex, England; population (1981) 152,500.

basilica type of Roman public building; a large roofed hall flanked by columns, generally with an aisle on each side, used for judicial or other public business. The earliest known basilica, at Pompeii, dates from the 2nd century BC. The type was adopted by the early Christians for their churches.

Basilicata /bə,zılı'kɑːtə/ region of S Italy.
area 9,985 sq km/3,855 sq mi
capital Potenza
features mountainous, mainly agricultural (vines, olives, sheep)
population (1981) 610,000
history it was the Roman province of Lucania.

basilisk S American lizard genus *Basiliscus* in which the male has a well-developed crest on the head, body, and tail.

Basingstoke /'beizıŋstəuk/ industrial town in Hampshire, England, 72 km/45 mi WSW of London; population (1981) 67,500.

Baskerville /'bæskəvıl/ John 1706–1775. British printer. In 1756 he published a quarto edition of the classical poet Virgil, which was followed by 54 books remarkable for their craft.

basketball ball game invented by a YMCA instructor, James Naismith, in Springfield, Massachusetts, in 1891. There are two teams of five, plus seven substitutes, and a large inflated ball is thrown through a circular net goal 3.05 m/10 ft above the ground at each end of a rectangular court.

Basle /bɑːl/ alternative form of ◊Basel, city in Switzerland.

Basov /'bɑːsɒf/ Nikolai Gennadievich 1912– . Soviet physicist who in 1953, with his compatriot Alexander Prokhorov, developed the microwave amplifier called a ◊maser (*microwave amplification by simulated emission of radiation*). Their work was recognized by the award of the Nobel Prize in Physics, which they shared with the American Charles ◊Townes.

Basque /bæsk/ a member of a people who occupy the autonomous Basque region (created 1980) of N Spain and the French department of Pyrénées-Atlantiques (see ◊Bayonne). They are directly descended from the Stone Age hunters of ◊Altamira. In 778 they annihilated the rearguard of the emperor Charlemagne's army at Roncesvalles. During the Spanish Civil War of 1936–39, they were on the Republican side, and were vindictively crushed by the dictator Franco. Guerrilla activity from 1968 by ETA (*Euskadi ta Azkatasuna* Basque Nation and Liberty) and the French organization *Enbata*

(Ocean Wind), aimed at securing a united Basque state, was not ended by autonomy.

Basque Country (Basque *Euskadi*) autonomous region of NW Spain
area 7,250 sq km/2,800 sq mi
towns Bilbao, ◊Guernica, San Sebastián, Vitoria
population (1981) 2,142,000, mostly ◊Basques.

Basque language a language of W Europe known to its speakers, the Basques, as *Euskara*, and apparently unrelated to any other language on earth. It is spoken by some half a million people in N Spain and SW France, around the Bay of Biscay ('the Basque bay'), as well as by emigrants in both Europe and the Americas. Although officially discouraged in the past, Basque is now accepted as a regional language in both France and Spain, and is of central importance to the Basque nationalist movement.

Basra /'bæzrə/ only port in Iraq, in the Shatt-al-Arab delta, 97 km/60 mi from the Persian Gulf; population (1970) 450,000.

bass /bæs/ long-bodied scaly sea fish *Morone labrax* found in N Atlantic and Mediterranean, growing to 1 m/3 ft, often seen in shoals, and penetrating to brackish water. Other fish of the same family (Serranidae) are also called bass, as are N American freshwater fishes of the family Centrarchidae such as black bass and small-mouthed bass.

bass /beis/ 1) lowest range of male voice; 2) lower regions of musical pitch; 3) a double bass (see ◊violin family).

basset type of hound with a long low body, wrinkled forehead, and long pendulous ears, originally bred in France for hunting hares.

Basseterre /ˈbæs ˈteə/ capital and port of St Kitts–Nevis, in the Leeward Islands; population (1980) 15,000.

Basse-Terre /ˈbæs ˈteə/ port on the Leeward Island Basse-Terre, capital of the French overseas *département* of Guadeloupe; population (1980) 16,000.

Basse-Terre /ˈbæs ˈteə/ main island of the French West Indian island group of Guadeloupe.

basset horn a musical ◊wind instrument resembling a clarinet.

bassoon woodwind instrument of the oboe family, of which it is the bass. It is descended from the bass pommer, which was approximately 2 m/6 ft in length and perfectly straight, whereas the bassoon is doubled back on itself in a tube about 2.5 m/7.5 ft long. Its tone is rich and deep.

Bass Rock /bæs/ islet in the Firth of Forth, Scotland, about 107 m/350 ft high, with a lighthouse.

Bass Strait /bæs/ channel between Australia and Tasmania, named after the British explorer George Bass (1760–1912), where oil was discovered in the 1960s.

Bastia /ˈbæstiə/ port and commercial centre in NE Corsica, France; population (1983) 50,500.

Bastille /bæsˈtiːl/ name given to the castle of St Antoine, part of the fortifications of Paris, which was used for centuries as a state prison; it was singled out for the initial attack by the revolutionary mob that set the French Revolution in motion on 14 Jul 1789. Only seven prisoners were found in the castle when it was stormed; the governor and most of the garrison were killed, and the Bastille was razed.

Basutoland /bəˈsuːtəʊlænd/ former name for ◊Lesotho.

bat flying mammal in which the forelimbs are developed as wings capable of rapid and sustained flight. These wings consist of a thin hairless skin stretched between the four fingers of the hand, and from the last finger down to the hindlimb. The thumb is free and furnished with a sharp claw to help in climbing. The hind feet have five toes with sharp hooked claws which suspend the animal head downwards when resting. Bats are nocturnal, and those native to temperate countries hibernate in winter. Bats are widely distributed, their powers of flight taking them to oceanic islands which other mammals cannot reach.

There are about 1000 species of bats forming the order Chiroptera, making this the second-largest mammal order. There are two main groups. The Megachiroptera are fruit-eating bats living in the tropical regions of the Old World, Australia, and the Pacific. Relatively large, up to 900 gm/2 lb and 1.5 m/5 ft wingspan, they have large eyes and a long face earning them the name 'flying fox'. The Microchiroptera are the majority of bats, mainly small and insect-eating, though some species specialize in blood (◊vampire bats), frogs or fish. With small eyes, although by no means blind, many of these bats rely largely on echolocation for navigation and finding prey, sending out pulses of high pitched sound and listening for the echo. Roosting in caves, crevices, and hollow trees, many bats have become rarer in parts of the world with dense human populations, such as Britain, where since 1981 they have been protected by law.

Bataan /bəˈtɑːn/ peninsula in Luzon, the Philippines, which was defended against the Japanese by US and Filipino troops, under ◊MacArthur, 1 Jan-9 Apr 1942. MacArthur was evacuated, but some 70,000 Allied prisoners died on the *Bataan Death March* to camps in the interior.

Batavia /bəˈteɪviə/ former name until 1949 for ◊Jakarta, capital of Indonesia on Java.

Batavian Republic /bəˈteɪvɪən/ name given to the Netherlands after the overthrow of the Stadholderate by French arms in 1795 which lasted until the establishment of the kingdom of the Netherlands at the end of the Napoleonic Wars.

batch system in computing, a system for processing large volumes of data. Quantities of data are collected into a 'batch' and processed during regular 'runs' (each night, say, or at weekends). This enables efficient use of the computer and is well suited to ◊applications of a repetitive nature, such as a company payroll.

Bateman /ˈbeɪtmən/ H(enry) M(ayo) 1887–1970. British cartoonist. Born in Australia, he was brought to England when only 18 months old. During the 1920s and 1930s he had enormous success with cartoons based on themes of social embarrassment and confusion, in such series as *The Man who. . .* (as in *The Guardsman who dropped his rifle*).

Bates /beɪts/ H(enry) W(alter) 1825–1892. British naturalist and explorer, born in Leicester. He spent 11 years collecting animals and plants in South America, during which time he discovered 8,000 species of insects new to science. He made a special study of ◊camouflage in animals, and his observation of insect imitation of the appearance of species unpleasant to predators is known as 'Batesian mimicry'.

Bath /bɑːθ/ historic city in Avon, England; population (1981) 75,000.

features Bath has hot springs 37°C/93°F, and the ruins of the baths for which it is named, as well as a great temple, are the finest Roman remains in Britain. Excavations in 1979 revealed thousands of coins and 'curses', offered at a place which was thought to be the link between the upper and lower worlds. The Gothic Bath Abbey has an unusually decorated W front and fan vaulting. There is much 18th-century architecture, notably the Royal Crescent by John ◊Wood. The Assembly Rooms 1771 were destroyed in an air raid in 1942 but reconstructed in 1963. The University of Technology was established 1966.

history The Roman city of Aquae Sulis ('waters of Sul' – the British goddess of wisdom) was built in the first 20 years after the Roman invasion. In medieval times the hot springs were crown property, administered by the church, but the city was transformed in the 18th century to a fashionable spa, presided over by 'Beau' ◊Nash. At his home here the astronomer Herschel discovered Uranus 1781. Visitors included the novelists Smollett, Fielding, and Jane ◊Austen.

Bath /bɑːθ/ Order of the British order of knighthood, believed to have been founded in the reign of Henry IV (1399–1413). Formally instituted 1815, it included civilians from 1847 and women from 1970. There are three grades: Knights of the Grand Cross (GCB), Knights Commanders (KCB), and Knights Companions (CB).

Báthory /ˈbɑːtəri/ Stephen 1533–1586. Elected King of Poland by a diet convened in 1575 and crowned in 1576. Báthory proved extremely sucessful in driving the Russian Troops of Ivan the Terrible out of his country. His military successes brought potential conflicts with Sweden, but he died before these could develop.

Bathurst /ˈbæθɜːst/ town in New South Wales, Australia; population 19,600. It dates from the 1851 gold rush.

Bathurst /ˈbæθɜːst/ zinc-mining port in New Brunswick, Canada; population (1981) 19,500.

bathyscaphe and bathysphere types of deep sea-diving apparatus used to investigate animal life and conditions at great depths in the ocean. One of the most famous descents was made by the bathyscaphe *Trieste*, which descended nearly 11,000 m/6.8 mi into Challenger Deep in the Pacific Ocean in 1960.

batik Javanese technique of hand-applied colour design for fabric; areas undyed in any colour are successively sealed with wax. Practised throughout Indonesia, the craft was introduced into Europe by the Dutch.

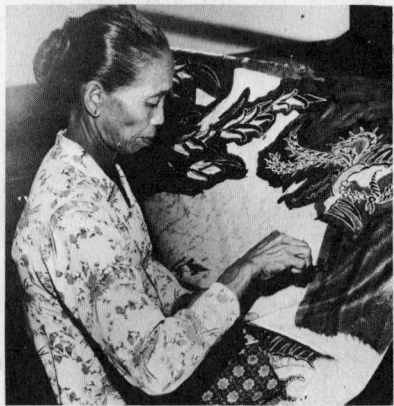

batik To apply the wax to the cloth preparatory to dyeing, the material is hung on a rack, contrary to the European practice, when a table is used.

Batista /bəˈtiːstə/ Fulgencio 1901–1973. Cuban dictator 1933–59; he was overthrown by ◊Castro.

Batoni /bəˈtəʊni/ Pompeo 1707–1787. Italian artist, celebrated in his lifetime as a portraitist, particularly by British visitors to Rome, portraits of whom form the majority of his surviving works. Most of his portraits are painted with a famous Roman antiquity in the background (the precursor of the modern holiday snapshot).

Baton Rouge /ˈbætn ˈruːʒ/ port on the Mississippi and capital of Louisiana, USA; population (1980) 219,500. The bronze and marble state capitol was built by Governor Huey ◊Long.

Batten /'bætn/ Jean 1909–1982. New Zealand aviator, who made the first return solo flight by a woman Australia–Britain 1935, and established speed records.

Battenberg /'bætnbɜːg/ German noble family which included three sons of Prince Alexander of Hesse.

Battersea /'bætəsi/ district of the Inner London borough of Wandsworth on the S bank of the Thames, noted for its park (including a funfair 1951–74), a classically styled power station, and Battersea Dogs' Home (1860) for strays.

battery energy storage device allowing release of electricity on demand. A battery is made up of one or more cells, each containing two conducting ◊electrodes (one positive, one negative) immersed in a liquid ◊electrolyte, in a container. When an outside connection (say, through a light bulb) is made between the electrodes, a current flows through the circuit, and chemical reactions releasing energy take place within the cells. Primary cells are disposable, secondary cells are rechargeable. The common **dry cell** is a primary cell battery based on the ◊Leclanché cell and consists of a central carbon electrode immersed in a paste of manganese dioxide and ammonium chloride as the electrolyte. The zinc casing forms the other electrode. The lead-acid **car battery** is a secondary cell battery, or accumulator. It consists of sets of lead (positive) and lead peroxide (negative) plates in an electrolyte of sulphuric acid.

battery

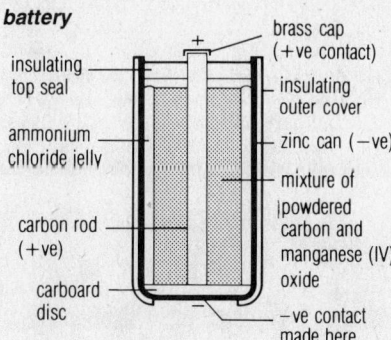

insulating top seal
ammonium chloride jelly
carbon rod (+ve)
carboard disc

brass cap (+ve contact)
insulating outer cover
zinc can (−ve)
mixture of powdered carbon and manganese (IV) oxide
−ve contact made here

Battle /'bætl/ town in Sussex, England, named for the Battle of ◊Hastings, which actually took place here.

battle cruiser warship with the size and armament of a battleship, plus the speed and lighter armour of a cruiser, largely obsolete since World War II.

battleship warship, formerly predominating over all others in armour and firepower, but obsolete from World War II.

Batumi /bə'tuːmi/ industrial port (oil refining) and capital of the Republic of Adzhar, USSR; population (1981) 126,000.

baud unit measuring the rate at which electrical signals are sent between electronic devices such as telegraphs and computers.

Named after French inventor J M Baudot (1845–1903).

Baudelaire /,bəʊdə'leə/ Charles Pierre 1821–1867. French poet, whose work combined rhythmical and musical perfection with a morbid romanticism and eroticism, often using oriental imagery and finding beauty in decadence and evil. His first book of verse, *Les Fleurs du mal/Flowers of Evil* 1857, caused a scandal, and was condemned by the censor as endangering public morals, but paved the way for Rimbaud, Verlaine, and the symbolist school.

Baudelaire Perhaps the first great poet of the modern city, celebrating its contrasts of rich and poor, beauty and ugliness, Baudelaire spent almost all his adult life in Paris.

Baudouin /,bəʊdu'æn/ 1930–. King of the Belgians. In 1950 his father, ◊Leopold III, relinquished to him his constitutional powers, and Baudouin was known until his succession in July 1951 as *Le Prince Royal*. In 1960 he married Fabiola de Mora y Aragón (1928–), member of a Spanish noble family and author of fairy tales for children.

Bauhaus /'bauhaus/ a German school founded in 1919 in an attempt to fuse all the arts and crafts in a unified whole, by the architect Walter ◊Gropius at Weimar. Moved to Dessau under political pressure in 1925, it was closed by the Nazis in 1933. Associated with the Bauhaus were ◊Klee, ◊Kandinsky, and Ludwig ◊Mies van der Rohe. The tradition never died, and in 1972 the *Bauhaus Archive* was installed in new premises in W Berlin.

Baum /bɔːm/ Lyman Frank 1856–1919. American writer, best known for the children's fantasy *The Wonderful Wizard of Oz* (1900).

bauxite the most widely known ore of aluminium, providing the major part of the world's supplies of that metal; it is named after

the district of Les Baux, near Arles, in S France, where it was first discovered. Bauxite, $Al_2O_3.2H_2O$, contains aluminium oxide, generally contaminated with compounds of iron, which give it a red colour. Chief producers of bauxite are Australia, Guinea, Jamaica, the USSR, Suriname, and Brazil

Bavaria /bə'veəriə/ (German **Bayern**) administrative region (German *Land*) of West Germany
area 70,550 sq km/27,230 sq mi
capital Munich
towns Augsburg, Nuremberg, Regensburg
features largest of the German *Länder*; forms the Danube basin; festivals at Bayreuth and Oberammergau
products beer; electronics, electrical engineering, optics, cars, aerospace, chemicals, plastics, oil-refining, textiles, glass, toys
population (1981) 10,940,000
famous people Lucas Cranach, Hitler, Franz Josef Strauss, Richard Strauss
religion 70 per cent Roman Catholic, 26 per cent Protestant
history the original Bavarians were Teutonic invaders from Bohemia who occupied the country at the end of the 5th century AD. They were later ruled by dukes who recognized the supremacy of the emperor. The house of Wittelsbach ruled parts or all of Bavaria from 1181 to 1918; Napoleon made the ruler a king in 1806. In 1871 Bavaria became a state of the German Empire. The last king, ◊Ludwig III, abdicated in 1918, and Bavaria declared itself a republic. Prince Albert (1905–), the present claimant to the throne, is also the inheritor of the Stuart claim to the British throne.

Bax /bæks/ Arnold Edward Trevor 1883–1953. British composer, born in Streatham. His works were often based on Celtic legends, and include seven symphonies, *The Garden of Fand* (a symphonic poem), *Tintagel* (an orchestral tone poem), and 'Coronation March', played in Westminster Abbey for the Coronation of Queen Elizabeth II. He was Master of the King's Musick 1942–53.

Baxter /'bækstə/ George 1804–1867. British inventor in 1834 of a special process for printing in oil colours, which he applied successfully in book illustrations.

Baxter /'bækstə/ Richard 1615–1691. English cleric. During the Civil War he was a chaplain in the Parliamentary army. Ill-health caused his retirement to Rouse-Lench, Worcestershire, where he composed the Puritan classic *The Saints' Everlasting Rest* 1650. After the Restoration he lived in London and was a royal chaplain. In 1662 the Act of Uniformity drove him out of the Church. In 1685 he was tried before Judge Jeffreys for alleged sedition, and imprisoned for nearly 18 months.

bay name applied to various species of laurel *Laurus* and some other plants. The victor's laurel of the ancients was the sweet bay *L. nobilis*, a native of S Europe. Its aromatic evergreen leaves are used in cookery, for flavouring.

Bayard /'beɪɑːd/ Pierre du Terrail (Chevalier) 1473–1524. French soldier. He served under Charles VIII, Louis XII, and Francis I, and was killed in action at the crossing of the Sesia in Italy. His heroic exploits in battle and in tournaments, his chivalry and magnanimity, won him the name of 'knight without fear and reproach'.

Bay City /'beɪ 'sɪti/ industrial city in Michigan, USA; population (1970) 50,000.

Bayern /'baɪən/ German name for ◊Bavaria, region of West Germany.

Bayeux /baɪ'ɜː/ town in N France where the ◊Bayeux Tapestry is housed; it has a 13th-century Gothic cathedral. Bayeux was the first town in W Europe to be liberated by the Allies in World War II, 8 Jun 1944.

Bayeux Tapestry a linen hanging 70 m/231 ft long, and 50 cm/20 in wide, made about 1067–70, which gives a vivid pictorial record of the invasion of England by ◊William the Conqueror in 1066. It is an embroidery rather than a true tapestry, sewn with woollen threads in blue, green, red, and yellow, and contains 72 separate scenes with descriptive wording in Latin.

Bayle /beɪl/ Pierre 1647–1706. French critic and philosopher. Son of a Calvinist pastor, he held chairs of philosophy at Sedan and Rotterdam. Suspected of ◊rationalist views, he was suspended in 1693. Three years later his *Dictionnaire historique et critique* appeared, which had a wide influence, particularly on the French Encyclopedists.

Bay of Pigs inlet on the S coast of Cuba, site of an unsuccessful invasion attempt by Cuban exiles against ◊Castro 17–20 Apr 1961; instigated by the CIA and sanctioned by the US president Eisenhower, it was executed by his successor Kennedy.

Bayonne /baɪ'ɒn/ river port in SW France; population (1983) 42,500. It is a centre of ◊Basque life. The bayonet was invented here.

bayou (corruption of French *boyau*, gut): in southern USA an oxbow lake or marshy offshoot of a river. Bayous may be formed, as in the lower Mississippi, by a river flowing in exaggeratedly wide curves in flat country, and then cutting a straight course across them in time of flood, so leaving loops of dead water behind.

Bayreuth /baɪ'rɔɪt/ town in Bavaria, West Germany, famous for its associations with the composer ◊Wagner; population (1970) 64,000. The Wagner theatre was established 1876, and opera festivals are held.

Bazaine /bæ'zeɪn/ Achille François 1811–1888. Marshal of France. From being a private soldier in 1831 he rose to command the French troops in Mexico in 1862–67, and was made a marshal in 1864. In the Franco-Prussian War Bazaine commanded the Third Corps of the Army of the Rhine, allowed himself to be taken in the fortress of Metz, and surrendered on 27 Oct 1870, with nearly 180,000 men. For this in 1873 he was court-martialled and sentenced to death; the sentence was at once commuted to 20 years' imprisonment. In 1874 he escaped to Spain.

BBC abbreviation for ◊British Broadcasting Corporation.

BBC English see ◊English language.

Beachy Head /'biːtʃi/ the loftiest headland 162 m/531 ft on the S coast of England, between Seaford and Eastbourne in Sussex, the E termination of the South Downs. The lighthouse off the shore is 38 m/125 ft high. The French name for the promontory is *Béveziers*.

Beaconsfield /'bekənzfiːld/ English town in Buckinghamshire 37 km/23 mi WNW of London where Benjamin Disraeli is commemorated. The poet Edmund Waller and the political theorist Burke lived in Beaconsfield, and Disraeli, whose parliamentary seat was Hughenden Manor in the neighbourhood, took his title from it.

Beaconsfield /'biːkənzfiːld/ title taken by Benjamin ◊Disraeli, prime minister of Britain 1868 and 1874–80.

Beadle /'biːdl/ George Wells 1903– . US biologist. Born in Wahoo, Nebraska, he was professor of biology at the California Institute of Technology 1946–61, and in 1958 shared a Nobel prize for his work with Edward L Tatum in biochemical genetics.

beagle short-haired hound with pendant ears, sickle tail, and bell-like voice for hunting hares on foot ('beagling').

Beagle Channel /'biːgl/ channel to the S of Tierra del Fuego, S America, named after the ship of ◊Darwin's voyage. Three islands at its E end are disputed between Argentina and Chile, but what is really at issue is the krill and oil in the sea within the 200-mi territorial waters, and the dependent sector of the Antarctic with its resources.

beak the horn-covered projecting jaws of a bird, or other horny jaws such as those of tortoise or octopus. The beaks of birds are adapted by shape and size to the diet of their owner.

beaker people people of Iberian origin who spread out over Europe in the second millenium BC, and who began Stonehenge. Their remains include earthenware beakers.

Beale /biːl/ Dorothea 1831–1906. British pioneer in women's education. She became a teacher at the Queen's College for Ladies in London, and as headmistress of the Ladies' College at Cheltenham from 1858 and founder of St Hilda's Hall, Oxford, 1892 was influential in raising the standard of women's education and the status of women teachers.

beam weapon a weapon capable of destroying a target by means of a high-energy beam. Beam weapons similar to the 'death ray' of science fiction are currently under development by the major powers, particularly the USA under its 'Star Wars' programme. Most frequently discussed are the following two types. The *high-energy laser* (HEL) produces a beam of high accuracy which burns through the surface of its target. The USSR is thought to have an HEL able to put orbiting spacecraft out of action. The *charged particle beam* (CPB) uses either electrons or protons, which have been accelerated almost to the speed of light, to slice through its target.

bean name given to the seeds of various leguminous plants, which are rich in nitrogenous or proteid matter, and are grown both for human consumption and as food for cattle and horses.

The broad bean *Vicia faba* has been cultivated in Europe since prehistoric times. The French bean, kidney bean, or haricot *Phaseolus vulgaris* is probably of S American origin; the runner bean *P. coccineus* is closely allied to it, but differs in its climbing habit. Among beans of warmer countries are the Lima or butter bean *P. lunatus* of S America, the soya, much used in China and Japan *Glycine max*, and the winged bean *Psophocarpus tetragonolobus* of SE Asia, of which the tuberous root has great potential as a main crop in tropical areas where protein deficiency is common. The tiny Asiatic mung bean *Phaseolus mungo* forms the bean sprouts of China. Canned baked beans are a variety of *Phaseolus vulgaris* which grows well in the USA.

bear large mammal with a heavily built body, large head, short powerful limbs and very short tail. Bears walk on the sole of the foot and have long non-retractile claws. The lips are mobile. Although related to carnivores such as dogs and weasels, the bear family, Ursidae, contains species that are omnivorous or largely vegetarian, but all are capable of killing prey from time to time. Bears breed once a year, producing one to four cubs. In northern regions bears hibernate and the tiny young are born in the winter den.

There are seven species of bear, including the *brown bear Ursus arctos*, formerly ranging across most of Europe, N Asia and N America, but now reduced in number in many places. It varies in size from under 2 m/7 ft long in parts of the Old World to 2.8 m/9 ft long and 780 kg/1700 lb in Alaska. The grizzly bear is a N American variety of this species. The white *polar bear Thalarctos maritimus* is up to 2.5 m/8 ft long, is circumpolar in distribution, has furry undersides to the feet, and feeds mainly on seals. The American *black bear Euarctos americanus* and the *Asiatic black bear Selenarctos thibetanus* are smaller, only about 1.6 m/5 ft long. The latter has a white V-mark on its chest, and a reputation for bad temper. The *spectacled*

bear The Syrian brown bear seen here at Whipsnade Zoo, near London.

bear Tremarctos ornatus of the Andes is similarly sized, as is the *sloth bear Melursus ursinus* of India and Sri Lanka, which has a shaggy coat and uses its claws and protrusible lips to obtain termites, one of its favourite foods. The smallest bear is the Malayan *sun bear Helarctos malayanus*, rarely more than 1.2 m/4 ft long, a good climber fond of honey.

Bear, Great and Little. Common names of the stars constellation, ◊Ursa Major and ◊Ursa Minor.

bear baiting baiting by dogs of a chained bear; a 'sport' once popular in Europe but illegal in Britain from 1835.

bearberry evergreen prostrate-growing shrub *Arctostaphylos uva-ursi* of the heather family found on moorland and rocky places. Most bearberries arc American but this species is found also in Asia and Europe in mountain and northern regions, such as the Scottish Highlands. It bears small pink flowers in spring, followed by red berries 0.8 cm/0.3 in across, edible but dry.

Beardsley /'bɪədzli/ Aubrey (Vincent) 1872–1898. British illustrator. He was associated with the ◊*Yellow Book*, for which he produced delicate unorthodox work which was attacked as decadent. He became a Roman Catholic in 1897. He died of tuberculosis.

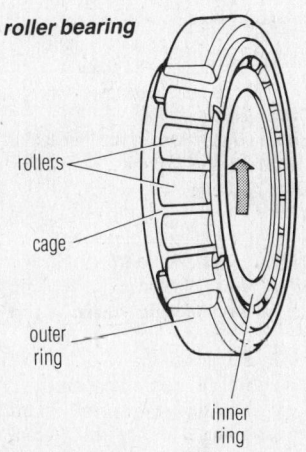

Beardsley One of the founders of the Art Nouveau style in Europe, Aubrey Beardsley worked almost entirely in black and white. His drawings were often charged with being grotesque and decadent.

bearing a device used in a machine to allow free movement between two parts, typically the rotation of a shaft in a housing.
The *sleeve* or *journal bearing* is the simplest bearing. This is a hollow cylinder, may be split into two halves. This type is used for the big-end bearings and main bearings on a car ◊crankshaft. They are lubricated by oil under pressure by the car's lubrication system.
Ball-bearings are widely used to support shafts, such as the spindle in the hub of a bicycle wheel. The bearing consists of two rings, one fixed to a housing, one to the rotating shaft. Between them

is a set, or race of steel balls. In other machinery the balls are replaced by cylindrical rollers or thinner, *needle bearings*.
Jewel bearings In precision equipment such as watches and aircraft instruments, bearings may be made from material such as ruby. They are known as jewel bearings.
For some applications bearings made from nylon and other plastics are used. They need no lubrication because their surface is naturally waxy.

roller bearing

rollers

cage

outer ring

inner ring

journal bearing

journal

ball bearing

outer ring

cage

steel balls

inner ring

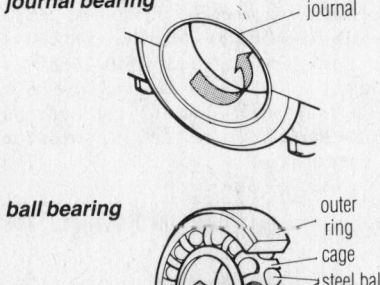

bears and bulls in economics, bears are speculators on the ◊stock exchange who anticipate a fall in share prices, and bulls are those who anticipate a rise.

Beas /'biːəs/ river in Himachal Pradesh, N India, an upper tributary of the Sutlej, which in turn joins the Indus. It is one of the five rivers that give the Punjab its name. The ancient Hyphasis, it marked the limit of the invasion of India by Alexander the Great.

beat generation name given by the writer Jack ◊Kerouac to the beatniks of the 1950s, characterized by dropping out of conventional life styles and opting for life on the road, drugs, and anti-materialist values.

beatification in the Catholic Church, the first step towards ◊canonization.

Beatitudes in the New Testament, the sayings of Jesus reported in Matthew v, 1–12; Luke vi, 20–38, depicting the spiritual qualities which characterize members of the Kingdom of God.

Beatles, the /'biːtlz/ English pop group, formed 1960, the first UK group to achieve international stardom and challenge the dominance of American rock and roll in the early 1960s. The members, all born in Liverpool, were George Harrison (1943–); John (Winston) Lennon (1940–80); Paul McCartney (1942–); and Ringo Starr (formerly Richard Starkey, 1940–). They made their name in Hamburg, Germany, and the Cavern Club in Liverpool (later razed, but restored in 1982). Using songs written by Lennon and McCartney, they took the pop world by storm 1963–65 with the ◊Mersey beat; they influenced the dress, life style, and thought of young people even beyond the break-up of the group in 1971, when they developed as individual performers, especially John Lennon (with his wife, Yoko Ono, 1933–) until he was shot dead in 1980, and Paul McCartney with the group Wings (formed 1971). The Beatles' hits included 'She Loves You' 1963, 'A Hard Day's Night' 1964, 'Can't Buy Me Love' 1964, 'Yesterday' 1965, and 'Yellow Submarine' 1966. The album *Sergeant Pepper's Lonely Hearts Club Band* 1967, recorded on two four-track machines, anticipated subsequent technological developments.

Beaton /'biːtn/ Cecil 1904–1980. British portrait and fashion photographer, designer, illustrator, diarist, and conversationalist. He produced notable portrait studies and designed sets for plays and films, for example the London and New York production of *My Fair Lady*; and scenery and costumes for ballets.

Beaton /'biːtn/ David 1494–1546. Scottish cardinal and politician, adviser to ◊James V Under ◊Mary Queen of Scots, he was opposed to the alliance with England and persecuted reformers, such as George Wishart, who was condemned to the stake; he was assassinated by Wishart's friends.

Beatrix /'biːtrɪks/ 1936–. Queen of the Netherlands. The eldest daughter of Queen ◊Juliana, she succeeded to the throne on her mother's abdication in 1980. She married in 1966 W German diplomat, Claus von Amsberg (1926–), who was created duke of the Netherlands: her heir is Prince Alexander (1967–).

Beatty /'biːti/ David, 1st earl 1871–1936. British admiral. Entering the navy in 1888, he commanded the cruiser squadron 1912–16, and bore the brunt of the Battle of Jutland. In 1916 he succeeded Jellicoe in command of the Grand Fleet, and in 1918 received the surrender of the German Fleet, being subsequently made admiral of the Fleet and receiving an earldom and the Order of Merit.

Beaufort /'bəʊfət/ Francis 1774–1857. British admiral, hydrographer to the Royal Navy from 1829; the ◊Beaufort scale and the Beaufort Sea in the ◊Arctic Ocean are named after him.

Beaton British photographer and designer Cecil Beaton in 1951.

Beaufort scale system of recording wind velocity, devised in 1806 by Francis ◊Beaufort. It is a numerical scale ranging from 0 to 17, calm being indicated by 0 and a hurricane by 12; 13–17 indicate degrees of hurricane force. In 1874 it received international recognition; it was modified in 1926. Measurements are made at 10 m/33 ft above ground level.

and migration route of bowhead whales, the staple diet of local Inuit.

Beauharnais /ˌbəʊɑːˈneɪ/ Alexandre, Vicomte de Beauharnais 1760–1794. French liberal aristocrat, who served in the American War of Independence, and joined the popular party in the early days of the Revolution.

Beaujolais /ˈbəʊʒəleɪ/ red wine produced in the area S of Burgundy in E France. Ordinary Beaujolais is best drunk while young; the broaching date is the third Thursday in Nov, when the new vintage is taken to London in 'the Beaujolais *nouveau*/ new Beaujolais race'.

Beaulieu /ˈbjuːlɪ/ village in Hampshire, England; the former abbey is the home of Lord Montagu of Beaulieu and has the Montagu Museum of vintage cars.

Beauly Firth /ˈbjuːlɪ/ arm of the North Sea cutting into Scotland N of Inverness, spanned by Kessock Bridge 1982.

Beaumarchais /ˌbəʊmɑːˈʃeɪ/ Pierre Augustin Caron de 1732–1799. French dramatist. His great comedies *Le barbier de Seville* (1775) and *Le Mariage de Figaro* (1778, but prohibited until 1784 because of revolutionary tendencies) in which he ridicules the aristocracy, form the basis of operas by ◊Rossini and ◊Mozart. Louis XVI entrusted Beaumarchais with secret missions, and he was responsible for the shipment of arms to the American colonies during the War of Independence, conducting a private traffic with great profit.

Beaumont /ˈbəʊmɒnt/ Francis 1584–1616. English dramatist and poet. From about 1608 he collaborated with John ◊Fletcher. The best of their joint plays are: *Philaster* 1610, *The Maid's Tragedy* c. 1611, and *A King and No King* c. 1611. *The Woman Hater* c. 1606 and *The Knight of the Burning Pestle* c. 1607 are ascribed to Beaumont alone.

Beaumarchais French comic dramatist Pierre Augustin Caron de Beaumarchais. He twice married wealthy widows and was able to devote his time to his satirical plays which were enormously popular. He was forced to flee France during the Revolution.

American ◊Confederate general whose opening fire on Fort Sumter started the ◊Civil War.

Beauvais /bəʊˈveɪ/ town NW of Paris; population (1982) 54,150. It has a fine Gothic cathedral and is famous for tapestries (◊Gobelin), now made in Paris.

Beauvoir /bəʊˈvwɑː/ Simone de 1908–1986. French socialist, feminist and writer, who taught philosophy at the Sorbonne 1931–43. Her book *Le Deuxième sexe/The Second Sex* 1949 is a classic text which became a seminal work for many feminists. Her novel of postwar Paris, *Les Mandarins/The Mandarins* 1954, has characters resembling the writers Camus, Koestler, and ◊Sartre (she was long associated with the last-named); she also published autobiographical volumes.

beaver aquatic rodent *Castor fiber* with webbed hind feet, broad flat scaly tail and thick waterproof fur. It has very large incisor teeth and fells trees to feed on the bark and to use the logs to construct the 'lodge', in which the young are reared and much of the winter is spent. Beavers store twigs and shoots underwater for winter feeding. They may also construct dams on streams and regulate water levels. Their activities can modify the environment considerably. Beavers once ranged across Europe, N Asia and N America, but in Europe now only survive where they are protected, and are reduced elsewhere, partly through trapping for the valuable fur.

Beaverbrook /ˈbiːvəbrʊk/ William Maxwell Aitken, 1st baron Beaverbrook 1879–1964. Canadian newspaper proprietor. Having made a fortune in cement in Canada, he entered British politics, first in support of Bonar ◊Law, then of ◊Lloyd George, becoming minister of information 1918–19. In the inter-war years, he used his newspapers, especially the *Daily Express*, to campaign for Empire free trade and against ◊Baldwin; in World War II, he was a

BEAUFORT SCALE

Number and Description	Features	Air speed mi per hr	m per sec
0 calm	smoke rises vertically; water smooth	less than 1	less than 0.3
1 light air	smoke shows wind direction; water ruffled	1-3	0.3-1.5
2 slight breeze	leaves rustle; wind felt on face	4-7	1.6-3.3
3 gentle breeze	loose paper blows around	8-12	3.4-5.4
4 moderate	branches sway	13-18	5.5-7.9
5 fresh breeze	small trees sway, leaves blown off	19-24	8.0-10.7
6 strong breeze	whistling in telephone wires; sea spray	25-31	10.8-13.8
7 moderate gale	large trees sway	32-38	13.9-17.1
8 fresh gale	twigs break from trees	39-46	17.2-20.7
9 strong gale	branches break from trees	47-54	20.8-24.4
10 whole gale	trees uprooted, weak buildings collapse	55-63	14.5-28.4
11 storm	widespread damage	64-72	28.5-32.6
12 hurricane	widespread structural damage	Above 73	Above 32.7

Beaufort Sea /ˈbəʊfət/ section of the Arctic Ocean off the N Alaskan coast, named after Sir Francis Beaufort. Oil drilling is allowed only in the winter months because the sea is the breeding

Beaune /bəʊn/ town SW of Dijon, France; centre of the Burgundian wine trade; population (1982) 21,100.

Beauregard /ˌbəʊrəˈgɑː/ Pierre 1818–1893.

Beauvoir Simone de Beauvoir, the distinguished French literary figure and philosopher of the feminist movement, in a 1952 photograph. She died on 14 Apr 1986. Her volumes of autobiography are major 20th century works.

successful minister of aircraft production 1940–41.

Bebel /'beɪbəl/ August 1840–1913. German socialist and founding member of the Verband deutsche Arbeitervereine (League of Workers' Clubs), together with Wilhelm Liebknecht. Also known as the Eiserach Party, it was based in Saxony and SW Germany before being incorporated into the SPD in 1875. Bebel remained one of the leading lights in this new party until his death.

beaver Branches are painstakingly ferried to dam a stream. In this way the water is kept at the right depth, so that it does not freeze to the bottom and beavers can still swim under water to their lodges in mid-stream.

Bebington /'bebɪŋtən/ industrial town (soap, margarine, oil) on Merseyside, England; population 64,150 (1981). There is a model housing estate originally built for Unilever workers, Port Sunlight.

Beccaria /ˌbekəˈriːə/ Cesare, Marese di Beccaria 1738–1794. Italian philanthropist, born in Milan. He opposed capital punishment and torture; advocated education as a crime preventative; influenced ◊Bentham; and coined the phrase 'the greatest happiness of the greatest number', the tenet of ◊Utilitarianism.

Bechet /'beʃeɪ/ Sidney Joseph 1897–1959. US virtuoso soprano saxophonist, the first jazz artist to achieve fame with this instrument. He joined Noble Sissle's band in Paris in 1928 and later became a major entertainer in France.

Bechuanaland /ˌbetʃuˈɑːnəlænd/ former name until 1966 of ◊Botswana.

Becker /'bekə/ Lydia 1827–1890. English botanist and campaigner for women's rights. Born in Manchester, she gave lectures to girls' schools and corresponded with Darwin. Her first publication was *Botany for Novices* in 1864. In 1865 she established the Manchester Ladies Literary Society as a forum for women to study scientific subjects. She campaigned for women's suffrage and in 1867 she co-founded and became secretary of the National Society for Women's Suffrage.

In 1870 she founded a monthly newsletter 'The Women's Suffrage Journal' and edited it over the next 20 years. She became secretary of the London Central Committee for Women's Suffrage and eventually its parliamentary candidate.

Becket /'bekɪt/ St Thomas 1118–1170. English cleric. A personal friend of ◊Henry II, he was his chancellor 1155–62, but on becoming archbishop of Canterbury transferred his allegiance to the church. In 1164 he opposed Henry's attempt to regulate the relations between church and state, and had to flee the country, returning in 1170, but the reconciliation soon broke down. Encouraged by a hasty outburst of the king's, four knights murdered Becket before the altar of Canterbury cathedral. He was canonized in 1172, and his shrine became the most revered centre of pilgrimage in England until the Reformation.

Beckett /'bekɪt/ Samuel 1906– . Irish novelist and dramatist, who writes in French and English. His most famous play, *En attendant Godot/Waiting for Godot* 1952, in which two tramps wait endlessly for the enigmatic 'Godot', is possibly the best-known example of Theatre of the ◊Absurd. This predicament is explored to further extremes in *Fin de Partie/Endgame* 1957, and *Happy Days* 1961. He won the Nobel Prize for Literature in 1969.

Beckford /'bekfəd/ William 1760–1844. British eccentric and author. Forced out of England by scandals about his private life, he published *Vathek* 1787 in Paris, a fantastic Arabian Nights tale, and on returning to England in 1796, rebuilt his home, Fonthill Abbey in Wiltshire, as a Gothic fantasy.

Beckmann /'bekmən/ Max 1884–1950. German ◊Expressionist painter. Born in Leipzig,

he fought in World War I, and was discharged following a breakdown, reflected in the agony of his work; pictures include *Carnival* and *The Titanic*.

becquerel /ˌbekəˈrel/ the SI unit of radioactivity, equivalent to the number of atoms of a radioactive substance that disintegrate per second. Named after Antoine ◊Becquerel. It is much smaller than the previous standard unit, the ◊curie, and can be used for measuring smaller quantities of radioactivity.

Becquerel /ˌbekəˈrel/ Antoine Henri 1852–1908. French physicist, who discovered penetrating, invisible radiation coming from uranium salts, the first indication of ◊radioactivity, and shared a Nobel prize with the ◊Curies in 1903.

bed in geology, the unitary 'building block' of ◊sedimentary rock. A bed consists of a simple layer of rock, often separated above and below from other beds by well-defined partings called bedding planes. It can be from a millimetre to many metres thick, and can extend over any area. Also used to indicate the floor beneath a body of water (lake bed) and a layer formed by a fall of particles (lava bed).

bedbug flattened wingless red-brown insect *Cimex lectularius* with piercing mouthparts that hides by day in crevices or bedclothes and emerges at night to suck human blood.

Beddoes /'bedəuz/ Thomas Lovell 1803–1849. British poet and dramatist. He started his most famous play, *Death's Jest Book*, in 1825, but it was not published until 1850, much revised.

Bede /biːd/ c. 673–735. English theologian and historian, known as the Venerable Bede. Born at Monkwearmouth, Durham, he entered the local monastery at the age of seven, later

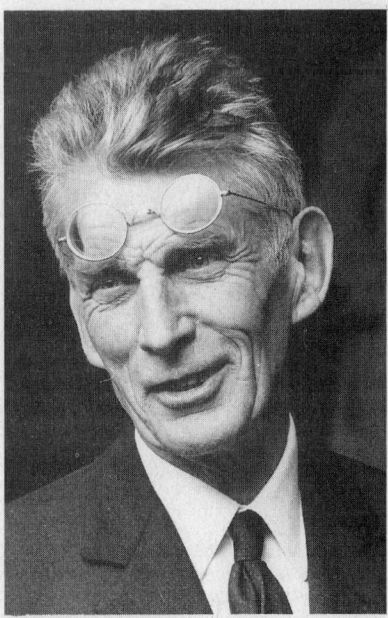

Irish novelist and dramatist Samuel Beckett, winner of the Nobel Prize for Literature in 1969.

Becket Thomas Becket unexpectedly turned to oppose King Henry II when he was made archbishop of Canterbury. In this scene from a French manuscript from about 70 years after his murder, Thomas excommunicates his enemies and argues with Henry and Louis VII of France.

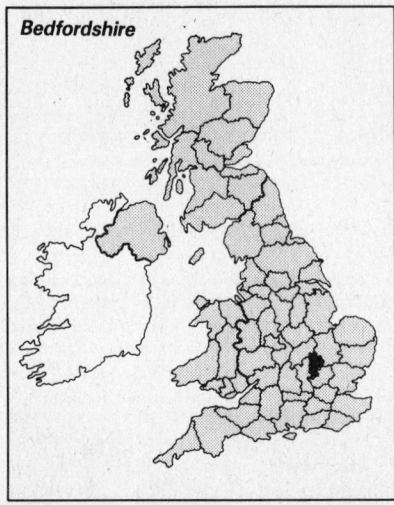

Bedfordshire

transferring to Jarrow, where he became a priest in about 703. He devoted his life to writing and teaching, the most famous of his pupils being Egbert, archbishop of York. He wrote many scientific, theological, and historical works, the most celebrated being his *Historia Ecclesiastica Gentis Anglorum/Ecclesiastical History of the English People*, an important source for early English history, which he finished in 731.

Bedford /'bedfəd/ industrial town (agricultural machinery and airships) and administrative headquarters of Bedfordshire, England; population 89,200 (1983).

Bedford /'bedfəd/ John Robert Russell, 13th Duke of Bedford 1917– . English peer. Succeeding to the title 1953, he restored the family seat Woburn Abbey, Bedfordshire, now a tourist attraction.

Bedfordshire /'bedfədʃə/ county in central S England
area 1,235 sq km/477 sq mi
towns administrative headquarters Bedford; Luton, Dunstable
features Whipsnade Zoo 1931, near Dunstable,

a zoological park belonging to the London Zoological Society (2 sq km/500 acres); Woburn Abbey, seat of the duke of Bedford
products cereals, vegetables; agricultural machinery, electrical goods
population (1986) 521,000
famous people John Bunyan.

Bedlam /'bedləm/ popular abbreviation of the name, Bethlehem, of the earliest mental hospital in Europe; it was opened in the 14th century in a former priory in Bishopsgate, London, and the hospital is now in Surrey.

Bedlington breed of ◊terrier with short body, long legs, and curly hair, usually grey, named after a district of Northumberland.

Bedouin member of a nomadic people (Arabic 'desert-dweller') of Arabia and N Africa, now becoming increasingly settled.

bee four-winged insect of the super-family Apoidea in the order Hymenoptera, usually with a sting. There are over 12,000 species, of which less than 1 in 20 are social in habit.

Bedouin Although many Bedouins are now urbanized, traditions survive in remote areas. The little girls will adopt the heavy veiling worn by their mothers as soon as they are old enough.

solitary bees include species useful in pollinating orchards in spring, and may make their nests in tunnels under the ground, in hollow plant stems, etc; the 'cuckoo' bees lay their eggs in the nests of bumblebees, which they closely resemble.
social bees include the stingless S American *vulture bee Trigona hypogea*, discovered in 1982, which is solely carnivorous. More familiar is the *bumblebee* genus *Bombus*, which is larger and stronger than the hive bee and so is adapted to fertilize plants in which the pollen and nectar lie deep, as in red clover; they can work in colder weather than the hive bee. The *hive* or *honey bee Apis mellifera* establishes perennial colonies of about 80,000, the majority being infertile females or workers, with a few larger fertile males or drones, and a single very large fertile female or queen. Bees transmit information to each other about food sources by a 'dance', each movement giving rise to sound impulses which are picked up by tiny hairs on the back of the bee's head, the orientation of the dance also having significance. They use the sun in navigation (see also under ◊migration). Besides their use in crop pollination and production of honey and wax, these bees (by a measure of contaminants brought back to their hives) provide an inexpensive and effective monitor of industrial and other pollution of the atmosphere and soil. Most bees are pacific unless disturbed, but some species of S America are aggressive. In people who are allergic, bee stings may be fatal, and a vaccine treatment with concentrated venom has been developed; see ◊melitin.

beech genus of trees *Fagus*, family ◊Fagaceae. *Common beech Fagus sylvaticus* is one of the handsomest of European forest trees, with a smooth grey trunk and edible nuts or 'mast' which are used as animal feed or processed for oil. The timber is used in furniture.

Beecham /'biːtʃəm/ Thomas 1879–1961. English conductor, the grandson of the founder of the Beecham pharmaceutical firm. He established the Royal Philharmonic Orchestra in 1946, and made recordings of Haydn, Mozart, and Delius. He established the musical reputation of the last-named. Knighted in 1916, he was renowned for his wit, as in the autobiographical *A Mingled Chime*.

Beecher /'biːtʃə/ Harriet maiden name of Harriet Beecher ◊Stowe.

Beecher /'biːtʃə/ Henry Ward 1813–1887. US Congregational minister and opponent of slavery, son of the pulpit orator Lyman ◊Beecher and brother of the writer Harriet Beecher ◊Stowe.

Beecher /'biːtʃə/ Lyman 1775–1863. US Presbyterian minister, one of the most influential pulpit orators of his time. He was the father of Harriet Beecher ◊Stowe and Henry Ward Beecher. As pastor of Plymouth church, Brooklyn, New York, from 1847, he was a leader in the movement for the abolition of slavery, and an eloquent preacher.

Beeching /'biːtʃɪŋ/ Richard, Baron Beeching 1913–1985. British scientist and administrator. A director of ICI 1957–61 and 1965–68, he was chair of British Railways Board 1963–65, when the *Beeching Report* (1963) planning concentration on inter-city passenger traffic and a freight system was controversial. He became a life peer in 1965.

bee-eater bird *Merops apiaster* found in Africa, S Europe, and Asia. It feeds on a variety of insects, including bees, which it catches in its long narrow bill. Chestnut, yellow and blue-green, it is gregarious and generally nests colonially in river banks and sandpits. Some 23 other species are spread through the Old World and Australasia.

beer alcoholic drink made from malt (fermented barley or other grain), flavoured with hops; stronger types are often referred to as ale. Like beer, *stout* is top fermented, but is sweet and strongly flavoured with roasted grain; *lager* is a light beer, bottom fermented and matured over a longer period (German *Lager*, store).

Beerbohm /'bɪəbəum/ Max 1872–1956. British caricaturist and author, the half-brother of the actor and manager Sir Herbert Beerbohm Tree (1853–1917). A perfectionist in style, he contributed to *The Yellow Book*; wrote the novel of Oxford undergraduate life *Zuleika Dobson* 1911; and published volumes of caricature, including *Rossetti and his Circle* 1922. He succeeded G B Shaw as critic to the *Saturday Review* 1898. He was knighted in 1939.

Beersheba /bɪə'ʃiːbə/ industrial town in Israel; population (1983) 110,800. It is the chief centre of the Negev desert, and has been a settlement from the Stone Age.

beet genus *Beta* family Chenapodiaceae, of plants including **common beet** *Beta vulgaris*, of which one variety is used to produce sugar, and another, the mangelwurzel, grown as cattle fodder; the *beetroot* or *red beet Beta rubra* is a salad plant.
The family also includes the Asian *spinach Spinacia oleracea* of which the leaves are used as a vegetable, though its nutritional value (as claimed by ◊Popeye) has been much exaggerated; *spinach beet* used as a spinach substitute is *Beta vulgaris cicle*; (see ◊Goosefoot).

Beethoven /'beɪthəuvən/ Ludwig van 1770–1827. German composer. Born in Bonn, the son and grandson of musicians, he became deputy organist at the court of the Elector of Cologne at Bonn before he was 12; later he had lessons from ◊Haydn and possibly ◊Mozart, whose influence dominated his early work. From 1801 deafness overtook him, becoming total by 1824, but he continued composition, and from 1809 had a small allowance from aristocratic patrons. Often in love, frequently with his noble pupils, he never married.
In a career which spanned the transition from Classicism to Romanticism, his mastery of musical expression in every genre made him the dominant influence in 19th-century music. He was influential in the development of all musical forms, but especially the symphony. His works include the *Egmont* overture; the opera *Fidelio*; five piano concertos and one for violin; 32 piano sonatas, including the *Appassionata;* 17 string quartets; the *Mass in D* (*Missa solemnis*); and nine symphonies, notably the Third (*Eroica,* originally intended to be dedicated to Napoleon,

with whom Beethoven became disillusioned), the Fifth, the Sixth (*Pastoral*) and Ninth (*Choral*), which includes the passage from Schiller's 'Ode to Joy' chosen as the national anthem of Europe.

beetle common name of insects in the order Coleoptera (Greek 'sheath-winged') with leathery forewings folding down in a protective sheath over the membranous hindwings which are those used for flight. They pass through a complete metamorphosis, the young larval forms being very varied, and include some of the largest and smallest of all insects; the largest is the **Hercules beetle** *Dynastes hercules* of the S American rainforests, 15 cm/6 in long, the smallest only 0.05 cm/0.02 in. The largest order in the animal kingdom, beetles number some 370,000 named species, with many more to be described.
Many beetles are useful to humans, others are extremely destructive. Weevils, ladybirds, scarabs, and glowworms belong to this order, and beetles are found in virtually every land and freshwater habitat, and feeding on virtually everything edible. Examples include: *click beetle* or *skipjack* species of the family Elateridae, so called because if they fall on their backs they right themselves with a jump and a loud click; the larvae, known as *wireworms*, feed on the roots of crops. In some tropical species of Elateridae the beetles have luminous organs between the head and abdomen and are known as *fireflies*. The *Colorado beetle Leptinotarsa decemlineata* is striped in black and yellow and an important pest of potatoes. The *blister beetle Lytta vesicatoria*, a shiny green species from S Europe, was once sold pulverized as an aphrodisiac and contains the toxin cantharidin. The *furniture beetle Anobium punctatum* and its relatives are serious pests of timber buildings and furniture through their *'woodworm'* larvae.

Beeton, Mrs /'biːtn/ (Isabella Mary Mayson) 1836–1865. British writer on cookery and domestic management. Wife of a publisher, she produced *Beeton's Household Management* 1859, the first really comprehensive work on domestic science.

Begin /'beɪgɪn/ Menachem 1913– . Israeli politician, born in Poland. He was a leader of the extremist Irgun Zvai Leumi organization in Palestine from 1942; he was prime minister of Israel 1977–83, as head of the right-wing Likud party, and in 1978 shared a Nobel Peace Prize with President ◊Sadat of Egypt for work on the ◊Camp David peace agreement.

begonia genus of the tropical and subtropical plant family Begoniaceae. They have fleshy and succulent leaves, and often large, brilliant flowers. There are numerous species, natives of the tropics, especially South America and India.

Behan /'biːən/ Brendan 1923–1964. Irish dramatist. His early experience of prison and knowledge of the workings of the ◊IRA (recounted in his autobiography *Borstal Boy* 1958) provided him with two recurrent themes in his plays. *The Quare Fellow* 1954 was followed by the tragicomedy *The Hostage* 1958, first written in Gaelic, which recounts the accidental shooting of an English soldier taken hostage in a seedy brothel which is a centre for the IRA.

Beeton, Mrs Isabella Beeton became a household name in England with her comprehensive book *Household Management* 1859. Her high standards included keeping servants and children in order, chimneys swept, linen crisp and silver gleaming.

Begin Jerusalem 1983. Israeli prime minister Menachem Begin announces his resignation. A man of hard-line views on the Arab-Israeli conflict, in the late 1970s he seemed to be working towards a peaceful settlement, and was jointly awarded the Nobel Prize for Peace with President Sadat of Egypt.

behaviourism school of psychology originating in the USA, of which the leading exponent was John Broadus ◊Watson. Behaviourists maintain that all human activity can ultimately be explained in terms of conditioned reactions or reflexes and habits formed in consequence. Leading behaviourists include ◊Pavlov.

behaviour therapy in psychology, the application of behavioural principles, derived from learning theories, to the treatment of clinical conditions such as ◊phobias, ◊obsessions, sexual and interpersonal problems. For example, in treating a phobia the person is taken into the situation that he or she is afraid of, in gradual steps. Over time, the fear typically reduces, and the problem becomes less acute.

Behn /ben/ Aphra 1640–1689. English novelist and playwright, the first English woman to earn her living as a writer. Celebrated in her day, she was also often criticized for her sexual explicitness. She was also unusual in often presenting her novels and plays from a woman's point of view. She had the patronage of James I and was employed as a government spy in Holland in 1666. In 1688 her novel *Oronooko*, an attack on slavery, was published. Between 1670 and 1687 fifteen of her plays were produced to great acclaim. Her best play was *The Rover*, which attacked forced and mercenary marriages.

Behrens /'beərənz/ Peter 1868–1940. German architect. He pioneered the adaptation of architecture to modern industry, and designed the AEG turbine factory in Berlin 1909, a landmark in industrial design. He influenced ◊Le Corbusier and ◊Gropius.

Behring /'beərɪŋ/ Emil von 1854–1917. German bacteriologist, founder of immunology. Nobel prize 1901.

Beiderbecke /'baɪdəbek/ Bix (Leon Bismarck) 1903–1931. US jazz cornettist, composer, and pianist. He was greatly inspired by the classical composers Debussy, Ravel, and Stravinsky. A romantic soloist with Paul ◊Whiteman's orchestra, he became legendary after his early death.

Beijing /,beɪ'dʒɪŋ/ pinyin form of ◊Peking, capital of China.

Beira /'baɪrə/ port and railway terminal at the mouth of the river Pungwe, Mozambique; population (1970) 114,000.

Beirut /,beɪ'ruːt/ capital and port of Lebanon; population 702,000 (1980). Destroyed as an international financial and educational centre by the civil war 1975–76, it also formerly had a reputation as a centre of espionage (see ◊Philby). It was beseiged and virtually destroyed by the Israeli army Jul–Sept 1982 to enforce the withdrawal of the forces of the Palestinian Liberation Organization. After the ceasefire, 500 Palestinians were massacred in the Sabra–Chatila camps 16–18 Sept by dissident ◊Phalangist and ◊Maronite troops, with alleged Israeli complicity. Civil disturbances continue, characterized by sporadic street fighting and hostage taking. In 1986, President Gemayel was assassinated.

Bejaia /bɪ'dʒaɪə/ seaport in Algeria, 193 km/120 mi E of Algiers, linked by pipeline with oil wells at Hassi Messaoud; population (1974) 104,000. Called Bougie until 1962.

bel a unit used in comparing levels of power in electrical communication, equal to ten decibels.

Belasco /bə'læskəʊ/ David 1859–1931. American playwright. His works include *Madame Butterfly* 1900, and *The Girl of the Golden West* 1905, both of which Puccini used as libretti for operas.

Belau /bə'laʊ/ Republic of. Island of the ◊Carolines, formerly known as Palau, which became internally self-governing in 1980; a free association agreement with the USA signed 1982 has not yet been ratified. Three referendums have shown that Belau wishes to remain 'non-nuclear', although the USA is exerting strong pressure to secure military facilities for itself on the island.

bel canto /'bel 'kæntəʊ/ (Italian 'beautiful song') term which usually refers to the 18th-century Italian style of singing with great emphasis on perfect technique and beautiful tone which reached its peak in the operas of ◊Rossini, ◊Donizetti, and ◊Bellini.

Belém /bə'lem/ port and naval base in N Brazil; population (1980) 758,000. The chief trade centre of the Amazon Basin, it is also known as Pará, the name of the branch of the Amazon on which it stands. It was founded about 1615 as Santa Maria de Belém do Grãs Pará.

belemnite extinct relative of the squid with rows of little hooks rather than suckers on the arms. The most frequent parts of belemnites to be found as fossils are the bullet-shaped shells which were within the body. Like modern squid these animals had an ink sac, so could produce a smokescreen when attacked.

Belfast /,bel'fɑːst/ industrial port (shipbuilding, engineering, electronics, textiles, tobacco) and capital of Northern Ireland; Queen's University; population (1985) 300,000. The former parliament buildings are to the S at Stormont. Aldergrove airport is a free port.

history Belfast grew up around a castle built in 1177 by John de Courcy, and was created a city in 1888, with a lord mayor from 1892. From 1968 it has been heavily damaged by guerrilla activities.

Belfort /bel'fɔː/ capital of the *département* of Territoire de Belfort, France; population (1983) 54,500. It is in the strategic **Belfort Gap** between the Vosges and Jura mountains.

Belgaum /bel'gɔːm/ industrial city (textiles) in Karnataka, India; population (1981) 300,000.

Belgian Congo former name 1908–60 of ◊Zaïre.

Belgian literature writers in French have included Georges Eekhoud (1854–1927), who wrote of Flemish peasant life; Emile Verhaeren (1855–1916) and Maurice ◊Maeterlinck. For writers in Flemish, see ◊Flemish literature.

Belgium /'beldʒəm/ country in northern Europe, bounded to the northwest by the North Sea, to the southwest by France, to the east by Luxembourg and West Germany, and to the northeast by the Netherlands.

government the constitution dates from 1831 and was most recently revised in 1971. The prime minister and cabinet are drawn from and answerable to the legislature, which exercises considerable control over the executive. The legislature consists of a senate and a chamber of representatives. The senate has 182 members, 106 nationally elected, 50 representing the provinces, 25 co-opted and, by right, the heir to the throne. It has a life of four years. The chamber of representatives has 212 members elected by universal suffrage, through a system of proportional representation, for a four-year term. On the basis of parliamentary support, the monarch appoints the prime minister, who chooses the cabinet.

The multiplicity of political parties reflects the linguistic and social divisions. The main parties are the Dutch-speaking Social Christian Party (CVP), the French-speaking Social Christian Party (PSC), the Dutch-speaking Socialist Party (SP), the French-speaking Socialist Party (PS), the Dutch-speaking Liberal Party (PVV), the French-speaking Liberal Party (PRL), and the Flemish People's Party (VU).

history known from 15 BC as the Roman province of Belgica, the area was overrun by the Franks from the 3rd century AD onwards. Under ◊Charlemagne Belgium became the centre of the Carolingian dynasty, and the peace and order during this period fostered the growth of such towns as Ghent, Bruges, and Brussels; following the division of his empire in 843 the area became part of Lotharingia. By the 11th century seven feudal states had emerged: the counties of Flanders, Hainault, and Namur, the duchies of Brabant, Limburg, and Luxembourg, and the bishopric of Liège, all nominally subject to the French kings or the German emperor, but in practice independent. From the 12th century the economy flourished; Bruges, Ghent, and Ypres became centres of the cloth industry, while the artisans of Dinant and Liège exploited the copper and tin of the Meuse valley. During the 15th century the states came one by one under the rule of the dukes of Burgundy, and in 1477, by the marriage of Mary, heir of Charles the Bold, duke of Burgundy, to Maximilian, Archduke of Austria, passed into the ◊Hapsburg dominions. Other dynastic marriages brought all the Low Countries under Spain, and in the 16th century the religious and secular tyranny of Philip II led to revolt in the Netherlands; the independence of the Netherlands as the Dutch Republic was recognized 1648; the south, reconquered by Spain, remained Spanish until the Treaty of ◊Utrecht, 1713, transferred it to Austria. In 1719 the Austrian Netherlands was annexed by revolutionary France. The Congress of Vienna reunited North and South Netherlands as one kingdom under William, King of Orange-Nassau; but historical differences, and the fact that the language of the wealthy and influential in the south was (as it remains) French, made the union uneasy. A rising in 1830 of the largely French-speaking people in the south, and continuing disturbances, led in 1839 to the Great Powers' recognition of the South Netherlands as the independent and permanently neutral kingdom of Belgium, with Leopold of Saxe-Coburg (widower of Charlotte, daughter of George IV of England) as king, and a parliamentary constitution.

Although Prussia had been a party to the treaty of 1839 recognizing Belgium's permanent neutrality, Germany invaded belgium in 1914 and occupied a large part of it until 1918. Again in 1940 Belgium was overrun by Germany, to whom Leopold III surrendered. His government escaped to London, and Belgium had a strong

Belgium

KINGDOM OF (French *Royaume de Belgique*,
Flemish *Koninkrijk België*)

AREA 30,513 sq km/11,779 sq mi
CAPITAL Brussels
TOWNS Ghent, Liège, Charleroi, Bruges,
Mons, Blankenburghe, Knokke; ports are
Antwerp, Ostend, Zeebrugge
PHYSICAL mostly flat, with hills and forest in
SE
FEATURES Ardennes; rivers Scheldt and Meuse
HEAD OF STATE King Baudouin from 1951
HEAD OF GOVERNMENT Wilfried Martens from
1981
GOVERNMENT constitutional monarchy
EXPORTS iron and steel, textiles, manufactured
goods, petrochemicals
CURRENCY Belgian franc (62 = £1 Sept 1987)
POPULATION (1985) 9,858,000 (comprising
Flemings and Walloons); annual growth rate
0.1%
LANGUAGE in the N (Flanders) Flemish (a
Dutch dialect, known as *Vlaams*) 55%, in the
S (Wallonia) Walloon (a French dialect which
is almost a separate language) 44%, with 11%
bilingual, and German (E border); all are
official
RELIGION Roman Catholic
LITERACY 98% (1984)
GDP $77 bn (1984); $3,040 per head of
population
CHRONOLOGY
1830 Belgium became an independent
kingdom.
1914 Invaded by Germany.
1940 Again invaded by Germany.
1948 Belgium became founder member of
Benelux Customs Union.
1949 Belgium became founder member of
Council of Europe.
1951 Leopold III abdicated in favour of his
son Baudouin.
1952 Belgium became founder member of
European Coal and Steel Community
(ECSC).

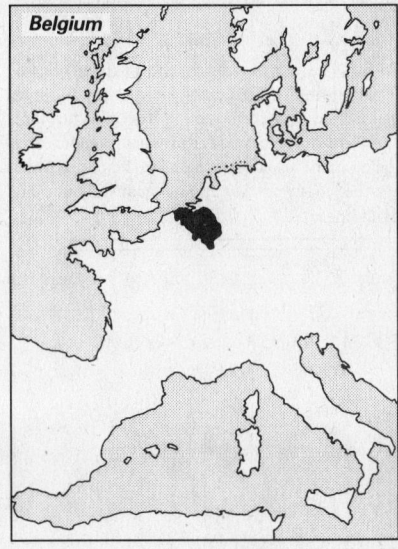

Belgium

1957 Belgium became founder member of the
European Community (EEC).
1971 Steps towards regional autonomy taken.
1972 German-speaking members of the
cabinet included for the first time.
1973 Linguistic parity achieved in government
appointments.
1974 Separate regional councils and
ministerial committees established.
1978 Wilfred Martens succeeds Leo
Tindemans as prime minister.
1980 Open violence over language divisions.
Regional assemblies for Flanders and
Wallonia and a three-member executive for
Brussels created.
1981 Short-lived coalition led by Mark
Eyskens was followed by the return of
Martens.
1987 Martens head of caretaker government
after breakup of coalition.

less than four coalition governments. In 1981 a
new coalition, led by Mark Eyskens (CVP),
lasted less than a year and Martens again
returned to power.
Between 1981 and 1982 economic difficulties
resulted in a series of public sector strikes and
in 1983 linguistic divisions again threatened the
government. Between 1983 and 1985 there was
much debate about the siting of US cruise
missiles in Belgium before a majority vote in
parliament allowed their installation. The 1985
elections led to Martens forming another
coalition, which broke up in Sept 1987, when the
King asked Martens to form a new caretaker
government pending a general election and the
adoption of a new constitution, devolving more
power to the regions.

Belgrade /ˌbelˈgreɪd/ (Serbo-Croat
Beograd) capital of Yugoslavia and Serbia;
population (1981) 1,470,000. It is a Danube river
port and is linked with the port of Bar on the
Adriatic.

Belgravia /belˈgreɪvɪə/ district of London,
laid out in squares by Thomas ◊Cubitt 1825–30,
and bounded to the N by Knightsbridge.

Belisarius /ˌbelɪˈsɑːrɪəs/ c. 505–565. Roman
general under the Emperor ◊Justinian.

Belitung /bɪˈliːtʊŋ/ alternative name for the
Indonesian island of ◊Billiton.

Belize /bəˈliːz/ country in Central America,
bounded to the north by Mexico, to the west and
south by Guatemala, and to the east by the
Caribbean Sea.

government the 1981 constitution provides for a
parliamentary government on the British model
with a prime minister and cabinet drawn from the
legislature and accountable to it. The national
assembly consists of a senate and a house of
representatives. The senate has eight members
appointed by the governor-general for a five-year
term, five on the advice of the prime minister, two
on the advice of the leader of the opposition and
one after wider consultations. The house of
representatives has 28 members elected by
universal suffrage. The governor-general
appoints both the prime minister and the leader
of the opposition.

history once part of the ◊Maya civilization, and
colonized in the 17th century, British Honduras,
as it was called until 1973, became a recognized
British colony in 1862. A 1954 constitution
provided for internal self-government, with
Britain responsible for defence, external affairs
and internal security.
The first general election under the the new
constitution, and all subsequent elections until
1984, were won by the People's United Party
(PUP), led by George Price. In 1964 full internal
self-government was granted and Price became
prime minister. In 1970 the capital was moved
from Belize City to the new town of Belmopan.
In 1975 British troops were sent to defend the
long-disputed frontier with Guatemala.
Negotiations begun in 1977 were inconclusive.
In 1980 the UN called for full independence for
Belize. A constitutional conference in 1981 broke
up over Guatemala's demand for territory rather
than just access to the Caribbean. In 1981, full
independence was achieved with George Price as

resistance movement. After Belgium's liberation
by the Allies, 1944–45, the king's surrender
caused acute controversy, ended only by his
abdication 1951 in favour of his son Baudouin.
Since 1945 Belgium has been a major force for
international co-operation in Europe, being a
founder member of the ◊Benelux Economic
Union, the Council of Europe and the EEC.
Belgium's main problems stem from the division
between French-and Dutch-speaking members
of the population, aggravated by the polarization
between the predominantly Conservative
Flanders in the north, and the mainly Socialist
French-speaking Wallonia in the south. About
55 per cent of the population speak Dutch, 44 per
cent French, and the remainder German.
Belgium has an hereditary monarchy. In 1951
King Leopold III, who had reigned since 1934,
abdicated in favour of his son, Baudouin.
Between 1971 and 1973, attempts to close the
linguistic and social divisions included the

transfer of greater power to the regions, the
inclusion of German-speaking members in the
cabinet and linguistic parity in the government.
In 1974 separate regional councils and
ministerial committees were established.
In 1977 a coalition government, headed by Leo
Tindemans (CVP) proposed the creation of a
federal Belgium, based on Flanders, Wallonia
and Brussels, but the proposals were not adopted
and in 1978 Tindemans resigned. He was
succeeded by Wilfried Martens, heading another
coalition.
In 1980 the language conflict developed into open
violence and it was eventually agreed that
Flanders and Wallonia should be administered
by separate regional assemblies, with powers to
spend up to 10 per cent of the national budget on
cultural facilities, health, roads and urban
projects. Brussels was to be governed by a three-
member executive. Such was the political
instability that by 1980 Martens had formed no

the first prime minister. Britain agreed to protect the frontier and to assist in the training of Belizean forces. In 1984 PUP's uninterrupted 30-year rule ended when the United Democratic Party (UDP) leader, Manuel Esquivel, became prime minister. Britain reaffirmed its undertaking to protect Belize's frontier which, despite more talks with Guatemala in 1985, is still disputed.

Belize

AREA 22,965 sq km/8,867 sq mi
CAPITAL Belmopan
TOWNS port Belize City
PHYSICAL half the country is forested, much of it high rain forest
HEAD OF STATE Elizabeth II from 1981 represented by Elmira Minita Gordon
HEAD OF GOVERNMENT Manuel Esquivel from 1984
GOVERNMENT parliamentary democracy
EXPORTS sugar, citrus, rice, lobster
CURRENCY Belize dollar (3.23 = £1 Sept 1987)
POPULATION (1985) 166,400 (including Maya minority in the interior); annual growth rate 1.8%
LANGUAGE English (official), but Spanish is widely spoken
RELIGION Roman Catholic 60%, Protestant 35%, Hindu and Muslim minorities
LITERACY 80% (1985)
GDP $176 million (1983); $1,000 per head of population
CHRONOLOGY
1862 Belize became a British colony.
1954 Constitution adopted, providing for limited internal self-government. General election won by George Price.
1964 Full internal self-government granted.
1965 Two-chamber national assembly introduced, with Price as prime minister.

Belize

1970 Capital moved from Belize City to Belmopan.
1975 British troops sent to defend the frontier with Guatemala.
1977 Negotiations undertaken with Guatemala but no agreement reached.
1980 United Nations called for full independence.
1981 Full independence achieved. Price became prime minister.
1984 Price defeated in general election. Manuel Esquivel formed the government. Britain reaffirmed its undertaking to defend the frontier.

Belize City /bɪˈliːz/ chief port of Belize, and capital until 1973; population (1981) 40,000. It was destroyed by a hurricane 1961 and it was decided to move the capital inland, to Belmopan.

bell instrument of hollowed metal (usually four parts bronze to one of tin) struck to produce a musical sound. The world's largest is the *Tsar Kolokol* or *King of Bells*, 220 tonnes, cast 1734, which still stands on the ground in the Kremlin, Moscow, where it fell when being hung.

Bell /bel/ Alexander Graham 1847–1922. British scientist, who invented the telephone. Born in Edinburgh, he was educated at the universities of Edinburgh and London, and in 1870 went first to Canada and then to the US where he opened a school for teachers of the deaf in Boston in 1872, and in 1873 became professor of vocal physiology at the university. In 1876 he patented his invention of the telephone.

Bell /bel/ Patrick 1799–1869. Scottish inventor of a reaping machine, which he developed in 1829 while studying for the ministry. The reaper was pushed by two horses and used a rotating cylinder of horizontal bars to bend the standing corn on to a reciprocating

cutter which was driven off the machine's wheels (much as on a modern combine harvester).

belladonna deadly nightshade *Atropa belladonna*. The leaves, which contain the alkaloids hyoscyamine, atropine, hyoscine, and belladonnine, are dried and powdered. The plant and all its preparations are highly poisonous, and the cosmetic use of it to enlarge the pupil of the eye (hence the name meaning 'beautiful lady') is dangerous.

Bellarmine /ˈbelɑːmɪn/ Roberto Francesco Romolo 1542–1621. Italian theologian, cardinal, and controversialist. He taught at the Jesuit College in Rome, and became archbishop of Capua in 1602. *Disputationes de controversersiis fidei christianae* 1581–93 is his chief work. He was canonized in 1930.

Bellay /beˈleɪ/ Joaquim du 1522?–1560. French poet and prose-writer, who published the great manifesto of the new school of French poetry, the Pléiade: *Défense et illustration de la langue française* 1549.

bellflower general name for many plants of the family Campanulaceae, especially those of the genus *Campanula*. The *clustered bellflower* *C. glomerata* is characteristic of chalk grassland, and found in Europe and N Asia. Erect and downy, it has violet bell-shaped flowers in late summer in tight clusters at the top of a stalk, which is often short. The *Canterbury bell* of gardens is *C. medium*, originally from S Europe, and the ◊harebell is also a *Campanula*.

Bellingshausen /ˈbelɪŋzhaʊzən/ Fabian Gottlieb von 1779–1852. Russian Antarctic

explorer, the first to sight the Antarctic continent, though without realizing what it was.

Bellingshausen Sea /ˈbelɪŋzhaʊzən/ the section of the S Pacific off the Antarctic coast.

Bellini /beˈliːni/ family of Venetian artists. *Jacopo Bellini* c. 1400–70 was founder of the Venetian School. Only five of his paintings – a Crucifixion and four Madonnas – have survived. There are, however, two books containing his drawings – one in the British Museum, the other in the Louvre. His elder son, *Gentile Bellini* c. 1429–1507, was a painter of great achievement and versatility. In 1474 he was commissioned to assist in the decoration of the Great Hall of Council in the Ducal Palace, and later he worked in the court of Muhammad II at Constantinople. A portrait of the Sultan is in the National Gallery, London. His other important works include paintings of processional groups in the Academy at Venice, the *Adoration of the Magi* in the National Gallery, London, and *St Mark Preaching at Alexandria* 1505, in the Brera, Milan. His younger brother, *Giovanni Bellini* c. 1430–1516, studied under his father, and specialized in devotional pictures of the Madonna. His sensitive appreciation of light and colour introduced a sensuality to Venetian art that was to be fully expressed in the work of his pupil ◊Titian. Giovanni Bellini's early works show the influence of the Paduan School, particularly of his brother-in-law, ◊Mantegna. He worked in oil rather than tempera.

Bellini /beˈliːni/ Vincenzo 1801–1835. Italian composer, born in Catania, Sicily. His best-known operas include *La sonnambula* 1831, *Norma* 1831, and *I puritani* 1835.

Bellinzona /ˌbelɪntˈsəʊnə/ capital of Ticino canton, Switzerland, 16 km/10 m from Lake Maggiore, a traffic centre for the St Gotthard Pass. Population (1980) 17,000.

Belloc /ˈbelɒk/ (Joseph) Hilaire Pierre 1870–1953. British author, best remembered for his nonsense verse for children, *The Bad Child's Book of Beasts* 1896 and *Cautionary Tales* 1907. Son of a French father and an English mother, he was naturalized in 1902. With G K ◊Chesterton, he advocated a return to the ◊Distributist theories of the late Middle Ages in place of modern capitalism or socialism. He also wrote *The Path to Rome*, a walker's classic.

Bellot /beˈləʊ/ Joseph René 1826–1853. French arctic explorer, who discovered Bellot Strait, and lost his life while searching for Franklin.

Bellow /ˈbeləʊ/ Saul 1915– . American novelist. Canadian-born of Russian descent, he settled in Chicago with his family at the age of nine, assisting his father in bootlegging; his works include the picaresque *The Adventures of Augie March* 1953, the philosophically speculative *Herzog* 1964, *Humboldt's Gift* 1975, *The Dean's December* 1982, and *More Die of Heartbreak* 1987. He won the Nobel prize for literature in 1975.

bell ringing the art of ringing church bells. *Change ringing* by hand (by means of a rope fastened to the wheel of the bell mechanism) is an English art perfected by Fabian Stedman, a Cambridge printer, in the 17th century.

Bellow American novelist Saul Bellow. In 1975 the Nobel Committee awarded him a prize for his 'human understanding and subtle analysis of contemporary culture'.

area 207,600 sq km/80,134 sq mi
capital Minsk
features more than 25 per cent forested; rivers W Dvina, Dnieper and its tributaries, including the Pripet and Beresina; the Pripet Marshes in the E. The climate is mild and damp
products peat (used as fuel in power stations)
history the republic suffered severely under German invasion and occupation during World War II.

Bellini The Doge Leonardo Loredan painted by Venetian artist Giovanni Bellini about 1459. Bellini studied under his father and worked with older brother Gentile who decorated the Great Hall at the Ducal Palace. He was one of the first Italian painters to work in oil.

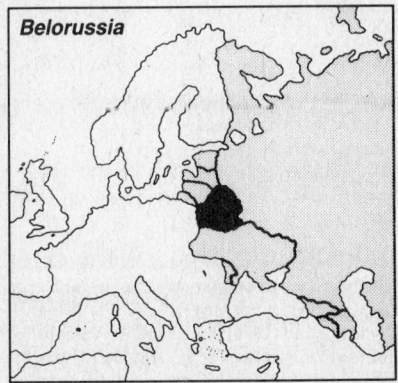

Belorussia

Mathematical permutations are rung on 5–12 bells, and ringers are organized in guilds. The *carillon* method, popular in Europe and in the USA, involves a single executant using a 'keyboard' linked only to the clapper of the bells.

bells nautical term applied to half-hours of watch. A day is divided into seven watches, five of four hours each and two of two hours. Each half-hour of each watch is indicated by the striking of a bell, 'eight bells' being the end of the watch.

Bell's theorem hypothesis of Swiss physicist John S Bell, that an unknown force, of which space, time and motion are all aspects, continues to link separate parts of the universe which were once united, and that this force travels faster than the speed of light.

Belmopan /ˌbelmə'pæn/ capital of Belize from 1973, in the foothills of the mountains; population (1980) 3,000.

Beloff /'belɒf/ Max 1913– . British historian. From 1974 to 1980 he was principal of the University College at Buckingham, Britain's first independent institution at university level.

Belo Horizonte /'beləʊ ˌhɒrɪ'zɒnteɪ/ industrial city (steel, engineering, textiles) in Brazil, capital of the fast-developing state of Minas Gerais; population (1980) 1,442,500.

Belorussia /bɪˌeləʊ'rʌʃə/ republic of western USSR

Belsen /'belsən/ site of a Nazi concentration camp in Lower Saxony, West Germany.

Beltane Celtic name for the 1st day of May, formerly one of the Scottish quarter days. The ancient feasts held on this day were marked by the kindling of Beltane fires on the hillsides.

Benares /bɪ'nɑːrɪz/ another transliteration of ◊Varanasi, holy city in India.

Ben Barka /ben 'bɑːkə/ Mehdi 1920–1965. Moroccan politician. Tutor to King Hassan, he became president of the National Consultative

Assembly in 1956 on the country's independence from France. Increasingly leftist in his views, he was in 1963 twice sentenced to death in his absence (for alleged involvement in an attempt on the king's life and for supporting Algeria in Algerian-Moroccan border disputes). After being lured to Paris to discuss an anti-colonial film, he was kidnapped and shot by Moroccan agents with the aid of French foreign service men. His body was not found. The case disturbed Franco-Moroccan relations, and led to de Gaulle's reorganisation of the secret service.

Ben Bella /ben 'belə/ Ahmed 1916– . Algerian leader of the National Liberation Front (FLN) from 1952; he was prime minister of independent Algeria 1962–65, when he was overthrown by ◊Boumédienne and detained till 1980. He founded a new party, Mouvement pour la Démocratie en Algerie, 1985.

Ben Bella Algerian leader Ahmed Ben Bella worked for independence and was imprisoned in France before becoming prime minister of independent Algeria in 1962. In 1965 he was overthrown by Boumédienne and imprisoned until 1980.

Benbow /'benbəʊ/ John 1653–1702. English admiral. He ran away to sea as a boy, and from 1689 served in the Royal Navy. He fought at Beachy Head (1690), La Hogue (1692), and died of wounds received in a great fight with the French off Jamaica. He was a popular hero.

Benchley /'bentʃli/ Robert 1889–1945. American humorist, born in Massachusetts. His books include *Of All Things* 1921 and *Benchley Beside Himself* 1943, and his film skit *How to Sleep* illustrates his ability to extract humour from daily living.

Benda /bæn'dɑ:/ Julien 1867–1956. French writer and philosopher. Born in Paris, he was an outspoken opponent of the philosophy of ◊Bergson, and in 1927 published a manifesto on the necessity of devotion to the absolute truth which he felt his contemporaries had betrayed,

La Trahison des clercs/The Treason of the Intellectuals.

Bendigo /'bendɪgəʊ/ industrial town in Victoria, Australia, about 120 km/75 mi NNW of Melbourne; population (1981) 53,000. Founded 1851 at the start of a gold rush, the town takes its name from the pugilist William Thompson (1811–89), known as 'Bendigo'.

bends popular name for paralytic affliction of divers, arising from too rapid release of nitrogen after solution in the blood under pressure. Immediate treatment is compression and slow decompression in a special chamber.

Benedict XV /'benɪdɪkt/ 1854–1922. Pope from 1914. During World War I he endeavoured to remain neutral, and his papacy is noted for the renewal of British official relations with the Vatican, suspended since the 17th century.

Benedict, St /'benɪdɪkt/ c. AD 480–c. 547. founder of Christian monasticism in the West, and of the order of the ◊Benedictine monks. Born of wealthy parents at Nursia, he was sent to be educated in Rome, but fled from that city and spent three years in ascetic solitude. He founded 12 monasteries near Subiaco, and later migrated to Cassino, and founded the monastery of Monte Cassino. Here he wrote out his rule for monastic life, and was visited shortly before his death by the Ostrogothic king Totila, whom he converted to the Christian faith. In 1964 he was proclaimed patron saint of Europe.

Benedict, St Italian St Benedict, whose *Rule* was an important influence in the development of Western medieval monasticism and learning. In addition to spiritual exercises and meditation, he directed that monks should engage in manual labour and teaching.

Benedictine order religious monastic order of monks and nuns in the Roman Catholic Church, founded by St ◊Benedict at Subiaco, in Italy, in the 6th century. St Augustine brought the order to England. At the beginning of the 14th century it was at the height of its prosperity, and had a strong influence on medieval learning. A number

of Oxford and Cambridge colleges have a Benedictine origin. At the Reformation there were nearly 300 Benedictine monasteries and nunneries in England, all of which were suppressed. The English novice house survived in France, and in the 19th century monks expelled from France moved to England and built abbeys at Downside, Ampleforth, and Woolhampton. The monks from Pierre-qui-vive, who went over in 1882, rebuilt Buckfast Abbey in Devon on the ruins of a Cistercian monastery. Celebrated Benedictine monasteries in the USA are at Latrobe, Pennsylvania, and St Meinrad, Indiana.

Benelux /'benɪlʌks/ customs union of *Be*lgium, *Ne*therlands and *Lux*embourg (agreed 1944, fully effective 1960); precursor of the ◊European Economic Community.

Benes /'beneʃ/ Eduard 1884–1948. Czech politician. President of the republic from 1935 until forced to resign by the Germans, he headed a government in exile in London during World War II. Returning home as president in 1945, he resigned again in 1948.

Benes Czech politician Eduard Beneš was president of the Republic from 1935 until forced to resign by the Nazis. He headed a government in exile in London in World War II and returned home as president in 1945. He resigned after the Communist coup of 1948.

Benét /bə'neɪ/ Stephen Vincent 1898–1943. American poet, noted for his narrative poem of the ◊Civil War *John Brown's Body* 1928.

Benevento /,benɪ'ventəʊ/ historic town in Campania, S Italy; population (1981) 62,500.

Bengal /,ben'gɔːl/ former province of British India, divided 1947 into ◊West Bengal, a state of India, and East Bengal, from 1972 ◊Bangladesh. The famine in 1943, caused by a slump in demand for jute and a bad harvest, resulted in over 3 million deaths.

Bengali language a member of the Indo-Iranian branch of the Indo-European language family, the official language of Bangladesh and of the state of Bengal in India.

Benghazi /ben'gɑːzi/ historic city and industrial port in Libya on the Gulf of Sirte; population (1977) 282,200. Its ancient names are *Hesperides* and *Berenice*.

Benguela /ben'gweɪlə/ port and railway terminal in Angola; population (1970) 41,000. Founded 1617.

Benguela current the cold ocean current in the S Atlantic Ocean, moving northwards along the west coast of southern Africa and merging with the south equatorial current at a latitude of 15° S. Its rich plankton supports large, commercially exploited fish populations.

Ben Gurion /ben 'guəriən/ David 1886–1973. Israeli politician, the country's first prime minister 1948–53, 1955–63.

Ben Gurion Born in Poland, David Ben Gurion became the first prime minister of his adopted country Israel. He held this post twice from 1948, when he proclaimed Israel's independence.

Benin /be'niːn/ former black African kingdom 1200–1897, now part of Nigeria; its capital was ◊Benin City.

Benin /be'niːn/ country in W Africa, sandwiched between Nigeria on the east and Togo on the west, with Burkina Faso to the northwest, Niger to the northeast, and the Atlantic Ocean to the south.

government the constitution is based on a Fundamental Law *Loi Fondamentale* of 1977, which established a national revolutionary assembly, representing socioprofessional classes, rather than geographical constituencies, elected for a five-year term by universal suffrage. The assembly elects the president, as head of state, to serve a similar five-year term. Since 1975 Benin has been a one-party state, committed to 'scientific socialism'. The party is the Party of the People's Revolution of Benin (PRPB) and is chaired by the president.

history known until 1975 as Dahomey, in the 12th–13th centuries the country was settled by the Aja, whose kingdom reached its peak in the 16th century. Later known as the Dahomey, in the 17th–19th centuries they captured and sold their neighbours as slaves to Europeans.

Under French influence from the 1850s, Benin formed part of French West Africa from 1899, and in 1958 became a self-governing dominion within the French Community. In 1960 it became fully independent.

Benin went through a period of political instability 1960–72, with swings from civilian to military rule and disputes between regions. In 1972 the deputy chief of the army, Mathieu Kerekou, established a military regime pledged to give fair representation to each region. His initial instrument of government was the National Council of the Revolution (CNR). In 1974 Kerekou announced that the country would follow 'scientific socialism', based on Marxist-Leninist principles.

In 1977 CNR was dissolved and a civilian government formed. A fundamental law established a national revolutionary assembly which in 1980 elected Kerekou as president and head of state. He was re-elected in 1984 and after initial economic and social difficulties, his government grew more stable and relations with France, Benin's biggest trading partner, improved considerably. In 1983 President Mitterrand became the first French head of state to visit Benin.

Benin

PEOPLE'S REPUBLIC OF (*République Populaire du Benin*)

AREA 112,600 sq km/43,480 sq mi
CAPITAL Porto Novo
TOWNS Abomey, Natitingou; chief port Cotonou
PHYSICAL flat, humid, with dense vegetation
FEATURES coastal fishing villages on stilts
HEAD OF STATE AND OF GOVERNMENT Mathieu Kerekou from 1972
GOVERNMENT one-party socialist
EXPORTS cocoa, groundnuts, cotton, palm oil
CURRENCY CFA franc (498.38 = £1 Sept 1987)
POPULATION 4,005,000 (1984); annual growth rate 2.8%
LANGUAGE French (official); Fan 47%
RELIGION animist 65%, Christian 17%, Muslim 13%
LITERACY 40% male/17% female (1980 est)
GDP $1.1 bn (1983); $290 per head of population
CHRONOLOGY
1851 Under French control.
1958 Became self-governing dominion within the French Community.
1960–72 Acute political instability, with switches from civilian to military rule.

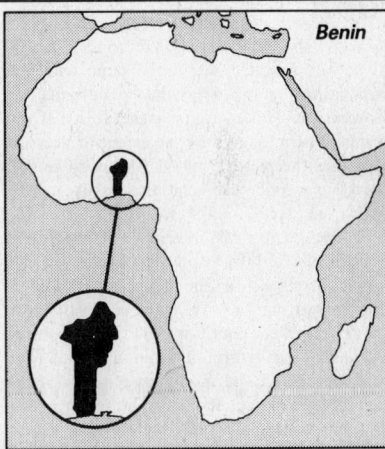

1972 Military regime established by Gen Mathieu Kerekou.
1974 Kerekou announced that the country would follow a path of 'scientific socialism'.
1975 Name of country changed from Dahomey to Benin.
1977 Return to civilian rule under a new constitution.
1980 Kerekou formally elected president by the National Revolutionary Assembly.

Benn /ben/ Tony (Anthony Wedgwood) 1925– . British◊Labour politician. Son of Lord Stansgate, a Labour peer, he succeeded his father in 1960, though he never used his title and in 1963 was the first person to disclaim it under the Peerage Act. He was minister of technology 1966–70 and of industry 1974–75, but his campaign against entry to the Common Market led to his transfer to the Department of Energy 1975–79. In 1981 he challenged ◊Healey for the deputy leadership of the party and was so narrowly defeated that he established himself as the acknowledged leader of the Left.

Bennett /'benɪt/ (Enoch) Arnold 1867–1931. British novelist. Born in Hanley, Staffordshire, one of the 'five towns' of the Potteries which formed the setting of his major books, he became a London journalist in 1893, and editor of *Woman* in 1896. His books include *Anna of the Five Towns* 1904, *Sacred and Profane Love* 1905, *The Old Wives' Tale* 1908, and the trilogy *Clayhanger*, *Hilda Lessways*, and *These Twain* 1910–15.

Bennett /'benɪt/ Alan 1934– . British playwright, whose settings are usually his native north of England, and subjects senility, illness and death, treated with macabre comedy. His

Benjamin /'bendʒəmɪn/ Arthur 1893–1960. Australian pianist and composer. Born in Sydney, he taught composition at the Royal College of Music in London from 1925, where ◊Britten was one of his pupils. His works include *Jamaican Rumba*, inspired by a visit to the West Indies in 1937, and a harmonica concerto for Larry ◊Adler.

work includes TV films, for example, *An Englishman Abroad* 1982, the cinema film, *A Private Function* 1984, and plays *Forty Years On* 1968 and *Getting On* 1971.

Bennett /'benɪt/ Richard Rodney 1936– . British composer of jazz, film music – *Far from the Madding Crowd* 1967, *Nicholas and Alexandra* 1971, *Murder on the Orient Express*

1974 (all three scores receiving Oscar nominations) – symphonies, and operas, including *The Mines of Sulphur* 1963 and *Victory* 1970.

Ben Nevis /ben 'nevɪs/ highest mountain in the British Isles (1,340 m/4,406 ft), in the Grampians, Scotland.

Benoni /bɪ'nəʊni/ gold-mining city in the Transvaal, South Africa; population (1980) 207,000.

Benson /'bensən/ E(dward) F(rederic) 1867–1940. British writer, son of Edward White ◊Benson. He specialized in novels gently satirizing the foibles of upper middle class society, and is best known for his series of books featuring the formidable female antagonists Mapp and Lucia, including *Queen Lucia* 1920.

Benson /'bensən/ Edward White 1829–1896. British cleric, first headmaster of Wellington College 1859–68, and, as archbishop of Canterbury from 1883, responsible for the 'Lincoln Judgment' on questions of ritual in 1887.

bent name for grasses of the genus *Agrostris*. *Creeping bent* or *fiorin A. stolonifera* is common in lowland Britain and across Europe, N Asia and N America. It spreads by stolons. Thin flowering stalks bear a large attractive panicle of yellowish or purplish flowers.

Bentham /'benθəm/ Jeremy 1748–1832. British philosopher and legal reformer, founder of ◊utilitarianism. He rose to fame with the publication in 1776 of his *Fragments on Government*. He declared that the 'utility' of any law is to be measured by the extent to which it promotes the pleasure, good, and happiness of the people concerned, and the essence of his utilitarian philosophy is found in the pronouncement in his *Principles of Morals and Legislation* (1789), that the object of all legislation should be 'the greatest happiness of the greatest number'. He made suggestions for the reform of the poor law 1798 , which formed the basis of the reforms enacted in 1834, and in his *Catechism of Parliamentary Reform* (1817) he proposed annual elections, the secret ballot, and universal male suffrage. He was also a pioneer of prison reform. In economics Bentham was an apostle of *laissez-faire*, and in his *Defence of Usury* (1787) and *Manual of Political Economy* 1798 he contended that his principle of 'utility' was best served by allowing every man to pursue his own interests unhindered by restrictive legislation. He was made a citizen of the French Republic in 1792.

Bentinck /'bentɪŋk/ Lord William Cavendish 1774–1839. British soldier. First governor-general of India 1828–35, he acted against thuggee and ◊suttee, and established English as the medium of instruction.

Bentley /'bentli/ Edmund Clerihew 1875–1956. British author. He invented the four-line humorous verse form known as the ◊clerihew, first used in *Biography for Beginners* 1905 and in *Baseless Biography* 1939. He was also the author of the classic detective story *Trent's Last Case* 1912.

bentonite type of clay, consisting mainly of montmorillonite and resembling ◊fuller's earth,

Bentham English philosopher Jeremy Bentham, founder of utilitarianism, wrote on jurisprudence and moral philosophy. He was a friend of James Mill, whose son John Stuart was later to modify Bentham's theories. He also founded University College, London.

which swells when wet. It is used in papermaking, moulding sands, drilling muds for oil wells and as a decolourant in food processing.

Benue /'benuei/ river in Nigeria, largest affluent of the Niger; it is navigable for most of its length of 1,400 km/870 mi.

Benz /bents/ Karl 1844–1929. German automobile engineer, who produced the world's first petrol driven motor car. Born in Karlsruhe, he built his first model engine in 1878 and in 1885 the petrol driven car.

benzaldehyde a clear colourless liquid with the characteristic odour of almonds. It occurs in certain leaves, such as the cherry, laurel and peach, and in a combined form in certain nuts and kernels. It can be extracted from such natural sources, but is usually made from toluene. It is used as a solvent, and to make perfumes and dyes.

Benzedrine trade name for a stimulant of the central nervous system, a 'pep pill' or amphetamine.

benzene a clear liquid hydrocarbon chemical of characteristic odour, occurring in coal tar. It is used as a solvent in the synthesis of many important chemicals. The benzene molecule consists of a ring of six carbon atoms, and it is one of the simplest ◊cyclic compounds. Benzene and its derivatives are collectively known as aromatic compounds. Some are considered carcinogenic (cancer-inducing).

benzodiazepine mood-altering drug (tranquillizer), for example, Librium and Valium. It interferes with the process by which information is transmitted from one brain cell to another, and various ill effects arise from continued use.

benzoic acid a white crystalline solid, sparingly soluble in water, and used as a preservative for certain foods. It is obtained chemically by the direct oxidation of benzaldehyde, and occurs in certain natural resins, some essential oils, and, in the compound state, as hippuric acid.

benzoin or **gum** a resin obtained by making incisions in the bark of *Styrax benzoin*, a tree native to the E Indies. It is used in the preparation of cosmetics, perfumes, and incense.

Ben Zvi /ben 'zviː/ Izhak 1884–1963. Israeli politician. Born in Atpoltava, he was active in the Zionist movement in the Ukraine. In 1907 he went to Palestine and was deported together with Ben Gurion in 1915 and, with him, served in the Jewish Legion under General Allenby. He succeeded Ben Gurion as president of Israel 1952–63.

Beograd /'beɪəʊgræd/ the Serbo-Croatian form of ◊Belgrade, capital of Yugoslavia.

Beowulf /'beɪəʊwʊlf/ Old English poem (composed c. 700), the only complete surviving example of Germanic folk-epic. It is extant in a single manuscript copied c. 1000 in the Cottonian collection of the British Museum. The hero Beowulf delivers the Danish king Hrothgar from the water-demon Grendel and his monstrous mother, and, returning home, succeeds his cousin Heardred as king of the Geats. After 50 years' prosperity, he is killed in slaying a dragon.

Béranger /ˌbeɪrɒn'ʒeɪ/ Pierre Jean de 1780–1857. French poet, famous for his light satirical lyrics, dealing with love, wine, popular philosophy, and politics.

Berber member of a people of North Africa, who since prehistoric times have inhabited Barbary, the Mediterranean coastlands from Egypt to the Atlantic. Their language is Berber, and about one-third of the Algerians and nearly two-thirds of the Moroccans speak it. Berber customs survive in the mountain communities, such as the Kabyles of Algeria and the ◊Riffs of the Atlas ranges in Morocco. Berbers are noted equestrians.

Berbera /'bɑːbərə/ seaport in Somalia, with the only sheltered harbour on the S side of the Gulf of Aden, and in a strategic position on the oil route; population (1980) 65,000. Under British control 1884–1960.

Berchtesgaden /ˌbeəxtɪs'gɑːdn/ village in SE Bavaria, West Germany, site of ◊Hitler's country residence, the Berghof, which was captured by US troops 4 May 1945 and destroyed.

Berchtold /'beəxtəʊlt/ Count Leopold von 1863–1942. Prime minister and foreign minister of Austria-Hungary in the crucial years before and during World War I.

Berdichev /bɪə'diːtʃef/ town in the Ukraine, USSR, 48 km/30 mi S of Zhitomir; population (1972) 90,000.

Berdyaev /bɪə'djaɪef/ Nikolai Alexandrovich 1874–1948. Russian philosopher. Born in Kiev, he often challenged official viewpoints and although appointed professor of philosophy in 1919 at the university of Moscow, his defence of religion caused his exile in 1922. He based his ideas on Russian Orthodox Christian thought. His books include *The Meaning of History* 1923 and *The Destiny of Man* 1935.

Berdyansk /bɪə'djænsk/ Black Sea port in the Ukraine, USSR; population (1980) 124,000.

Berezniki /bɪˌreznɪ'kiː/ industrial city (chemicals) in the USSR, on the Kama river N of Perm, formed 1932 by the amalgamation of several older towns; population (1981) 188,000.

Berg /beəg/ Alban 1885–1935. Austrian composer. Born in Vienna, he studied under ◊Schoenberg, and was associated with him as one of the leaders of the serial, or 12-tone, school of composition. His music is emotionally expressive, and sometimes anguished, but can also be lyrical, as in the *Violin Concerto* 1935. His output is not large, but includes orchestral, chamber, and vocal music, and operas, notably *Wozzeck*, a grim story of working-class life, first produced in 1925, and an unfinished opera, *Lulu*.

Berg Austrian composer Alban Berg was taught by Schoenberg, and did much to popularize his master's 12-tone system by combining it with a lyrical style. His opera *Wozzeck* 1925 is widely acclaimed, as is his unfinished *Lulu* 1937.

Bergama /'beəgəmə/ modern form of ◊Pergamum, ancient city in Turkey.

Bergamo /'beəgəməʊ/ city in Lombardy, Italy, 48 km/30 mi NE of Milan, with industries (silk, metal) and a noted collection of paintings (Academia Carrara); population (1981) 122,000.

bergamot tree of the genus citrus *Citrus bergamia*; from the rind of its fruit a fragrant orange-scented essence used as a perfume is obtained. The sole source of supply is southern Calabria, but the name comes from the town of Bergamo, in Lombardy.

Bergen /'beəgən/ industrial port (shipbuilding, engineering, fishing) in SW Norway; population (1980) 207,500.

Bergen-op-Zoom /'beəxən ɒp 'zəʊm/ fishing port in SW Netherlands; population (1972) 40,000.

Bergius /'beəgiəs/ Friedrich Karl Rudolph 1884–1949. German research chemist, who received the Nobel Prize for chemistry in 1931. He invented processes for converting coal into oil, and wood into sugar.

Bergman /'beəgmən/ Ingmar 1918– . Swedish film producer and director, regarded by many as one of the greatest film artists. His work

Bergius German chemist and Nobel prizewinner for chemistry in 1931, Friedrich Bergius was forced to flee Germany by the Nazis. He researched processes for converting coal into oil and the hydrolysis of wood to sugar.

deals with complex moral, psychological, and metaphysical problems and is often heavily tinged with pessimism. His films include *Wild Strawberries* 1957, *The Seventh Seal* 1957, *Persona* 1966, *Cries and Whispers* 1972, *The Serpent's Egg* 1978, *Autumn Sonata* 1978, and *Fanny and Alexander* 1982.

Bergman /'beəgmən/ Ingrid 1917–1982. Swedish actress. Born in Stockholm, she was trained there at the school of the Royal Dramatic Theatre. Her films include *Casablanca* 1943, and *For Whom the Bell Tolls* 1943. By leaving her husband for film producer Roberto Rossellini, whom she married in 1950, she broke an unofficial moral code of Hollywood 'star' behaviour and was ostracized for many years. She was re-admitted to make *Anastasia* 1956, for which she won an Academy Award. Her later films include *Murder on the Orient Express* 1974.

Bergson /beək'sɒn/ Henri 1859–1941. French philosopher. He was professor of philosophy at the Collège de France (1900–21), and in 1928 was awarded the Nobel Prize for literature. For Bergson time, change, and development were the essence of reality; and he considered that time was not a succession of distinct and separate instants, but a continuous process in which one period merged imperceptibly into the next.

Beria /'beəriə/ Lavrenti 1899–1953. Soviet politician. Born in Georgia, of peasant parentage, he became head of the Soviet police force and Minister of the Interior. On Stalin's death he, with Malenkov and Molotov, formed a

virtual triumvirate, but later he was shot after a secret trial.

beri-beri endemic polyneuritis, an inflammation of the nerve endings, mostly occurring in the tropics and resulting from deficiency of vitamin B.

Bering /'beərɪŋ/ Vitus 1681–1741. Danish explorer, the first European to sight Alaska. He died on Bering Island in Bering Sea, both named after him, as are Bering Strait and Beringia.

Beringia /be'rɪndʒiə/ former land bridge 1,600 km/1,000 mi wide between Asia and America before 35000 BC and 2400–9000 BC; now covered by Bering Strait and Chukchi Sea.

Bering Sea /'beərɪŋ/ section of the N Pacific between Alaska and Siberia, from the Aleutian Islands N to Bering Strait.

Bering Strait /'beərɪŋ/ strait between Alaska and Siberia, linking the N Pacific and Arctic oceans.

Berio /'beəriəʊ/ Luciano 1925– . Italian composer. His style has been described as graceful ◊serialism, and he has frequently experimented with electronic music and taped sound. His works include nine *Sequenzas/Sequences* for various solo instruments or voice, *Sinfonia* for voices and orchestra 1969, *Points on the curve to find...* 1974, and a number of dramatic works.

Beriosova /ˌberi'ɒsəvə/ Svetlana 1932– . British ballerina. Born in Lithuania, she was brought up partly in the USA and danced with the ◊Royal Ballet from 1952. Her style had a lyrical dignity and she excelled in *The Lady and the Fool*, *Ondine*, and *Giselle*.

Berkeley /'bɜːkli/ town on San Francisco Bay in California, USA, a seat of the University of California, noted for its nuclear research; population (1980) 103,500.

Berkeley /'bɜːkli/ Busby 1895–1976. American film director, who used female dancers to create large-scale pattern effects in ingeniously extravagant sets, as in *Gold Diggers of 1933*.

Berkeley /'bɑːkli/ George 1685–1753. Irish philosopher, who became Bishop of Cloyne. He is best known for his immaterialism, the belief that there is no such thing as material substance. This is not a denial that things exist, merely that they lack substantiality. For Berkeley, everyday objects are collections of ideas or sensations, hence the dictum 'esse est percipi' ('to exist is to be perceived').

Berkeley /'bɑːkli/ Lennox (Randal Francis) 1903– . British composer. He is noted for works for the voice, as in 'The Hill of the Graces' (1975), verses from Spenser's *Faerie Queene* set for eight-part unaccompanied chorus; and his operas *Nelson* and *Ruth*. Other works include symphonies. He was knighted in 1974.

berkelium an artificially-made radioactive element, symbol Bk, atomic number 97. It was discovered at Berkeley, USA, in 1949 by Seaborg and others.

Berkshire /'bɑːkʃə/ county in S central England
area 1,259 sq km/486 sq mi

towns administrative headquarters Reading; Eton, Slough, Maidenhead, Ascot, Bracknell, Newbury, Windsor

features rivers Thames and Kennet; Inkpen Beacon 297 m/975 ft; Bagshot Heath; Ridgeway Path, walkers' path (partly prehistoric) running from Wiltshire across the Berkshire Downs into Hertfordshire; Windsor Forest and Windsor Castle; Eton College; Royal Military Academy at Sandhurst; atomic-weapons research establishment at ◊Aldermaston, and the main UK base for US cruise missiles at ◊Greenham Common, Newbury

products general agricultural and horticultural, electronics

population (1986) 716,811

famous people King Alfred, Stanley Spencer.

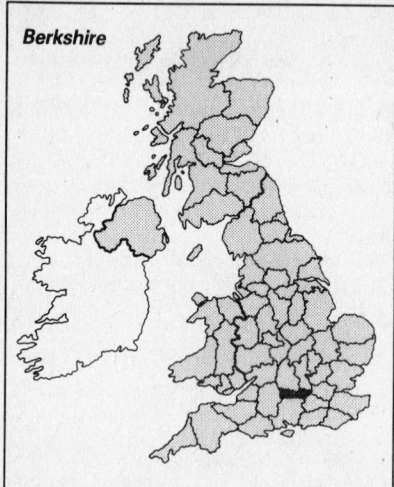

Berkshire

Berlin /bɜː'lɪn/ industrial city (machine tools, electrical goods, paper and printing) within East Germany, with a Western sector; population (1984) East Berlin 1,197,000, West Berlin 1,848,500.

features In World War II air raids and conquest by the Soviet army 23 Apr–2 May 1945 destroyed much of Berlin, but Unter den Linden, the tree-lined avenue once the whole city's focal point, has been restored on the East side of the wall. In West Berlin the fashionable shopping area includes the Kurfürstendamm and Europa-Center; the Alexander-platz complex has a giant hotel and television tower; and the Hansa quarter is a striking residential district. Notable buildings include the Kaiser-Wilhelm Gedächtniskirche (rebuilt 1959–61, but with ruined 19th century tower); Reichstag (former parliament building); Schloss Bellevue (Berlin resident of the president); Schloss Charlottenburg (housing several museums); Congress Hall; restored 18th century State Opera, new Komische Oper, and Philharmonic concert hall; 20th century art gallery and Dahlem picture gallery. The attractive environs of Berlin include the Grünewald forest and Wannsee lake. The international airport is at Tegel.

history First mentioned about 1230, the city grew out of a fishing village, joined the Hanseatic League in the 15th century, became the permanent seat of the Hohenzollerns, and was capital of the Brandenburg electorate 1486–1701, of the kingdom of Prussia 1701–1871. From the middle of the 18th century it developed into an important commercial and cultural centre, capital of united Germany 1871–1945.

After World War II, Berlin was divided into four sectors – British, US, French, and Soviet – and until 1948 was under quadripartite government by the Allies; in that year the USSR withdrew from the combined board and created a separate municipal government in their sector. The other three sectors (West Berlin) were made a *Land* of the Federal Republic in May 1949, and in Oct 1949 East Berlin was proclaimed capital of East Germany. The◊Berlin Wall dividing the city was built in 1961.

Berlin, Congress of /bɜː'lɪn/ congress of the European Powers held at Berlin in 1878 under ◊Bismarck, to determine the boundaries of the Balkan states after the Russo-Turkish war. ◊Disraeli attended as Britain's chief envoy, and declared on his return to England that he had brought back 'peace with honour'.

The Balkans after the Congress of Berlin 1878-1913

1889 Year of independence

Berlin /bɜː'lɪn/ Irving 1888– . Adopted name of Israel Baline, Russian-born American composer, whose hits include 'Alexander's Ragtime Band', 'Always', 'God Bless America', and 'White Christmas', and the musicals *Top Hat* 1935, *Annie Get Your Gun* 1950, and *Call Me Madam* 1953. He also wrote the scores of films such as *Blue Skies* and *Easter Parade*.

Berlin /bɜː'lɪn/ Isaiah 1909– . British philosopher. The son of a refugee from the Russian revolution, he was professor of Social and Political Theory, Oxford, 1957–67. His books include *Historical Inevitability* 1954 and

Four Essays on Liberty 1969. He was awarded the Order of Merit in 1971.

Berlinguer /ˌbeəlɪŋ'gweə/ Enrico 1922–1984. Italian Communist, who freed the party from Soviet influence, and by 1976 was near to the premiership, but the Red Brigade murder of Aldo ◊Moro revived the Socialist vote.

Berlin Wall the dividing line between East and West Berlin which, from 13 Aug 1961, was reinforced by the Russians with armed guards and barbed wire to prevent the escape of unwilling inhabitants of East Berlin to the greater freedom of West Berlin. The interconnecting link between East and West Berlin is Checkpoint Charlie, where both sides exchange captured spies. Escapers from east to west are shot on sight.

Berlioz /'beəliəuz/ (Louis) Hector 1803–1869. French composer. He studied music at the Paris Conservatoire. He gained the *Grand Prix de Rome* in 1830, and spent two years in Italy. In 1833 he married Harriet Smithson, an Irish actress playing Shakespearian parts in Paris, but they separated in 1842. After some years of poverty and public neglect, Berlioz went to Germany in 1842, and there conducted his own works with triumphant success. Subsequently he

made successful visits to Russia and England. In 1854 he married Marie Recio, a singer.

Berlioz was the only great French Romantic composer, and the founder of modern orchestration. Much of his music has a theatrical quality and was inspired by drama and literature. He wrote symphonic works such as *Symphonie fantastique* and *Roméo et Juliette*, based on literary or dramatic programmes. His dramatic cantatas include *La Damnation de Faust* and *L'Enfance du Christ*, and his sacred music, a *Te Deum* and a *Requiem*. He wrote three operas, *Béatrice et Bénédict*, *Benvenuto Cellini*, and *Les Troyens*.

Berlioz French Romantic composer Hector Berlioz expanded the language of the symphony orchestra in works for concert hall and stage. He admired Shakespeare, and fell in love with Irish actress Harriet Smithson when she came to Paris to play Shakespearean roles.

Bermuda /bə'mjuːdə/ British colony in NW Atlantic
area 54 sq km/21 sq mi
capital and chief port Hamilton
features consists of about 150 small islands, of which 20 are inhabited, linked by bridges and causeways; Britain's oldest colony; the USA has a naval air base and there is a NASA tracking station
products Easter lilies, pharmaceuticals; tourism and banking are important
currency Bermuda dollar
population (1980) 54,893
language English
religion Christian
government under the constitution of 1968, Bermuda is a fully self-governing British colony, with a Governor, Senate and elected House of Assembly (premier from 1982 John Swan, United Bermuda Party).
recent history the islands were named after Juan de Bermudez, who visited them in 1515, and were settled by British colonists in 1609. Racial violence in 1977 led to intervention, at the request of the government, by British troops.
   Bermuda Triangle the sea area bounded by Bermuda, Florida and Puerto Rico, which gained the nickname Deadly Bermuda Triangle in 1964 when it was suggested that unexplained disappearances of ships and aircraft were exceptionally frequent there: analysis of the data did not eventually confirm the idea.
   Bernadette, St /ˌbɜːnə'det/ 1844–1879. French saint, born at Lourdes in the French Pyrenees. In Feb 1858 she had a vision of the Virgin Mary in the grotto of Massabielle, which was later opened to the public by command of Napoleon III. Many sick people who were dipped

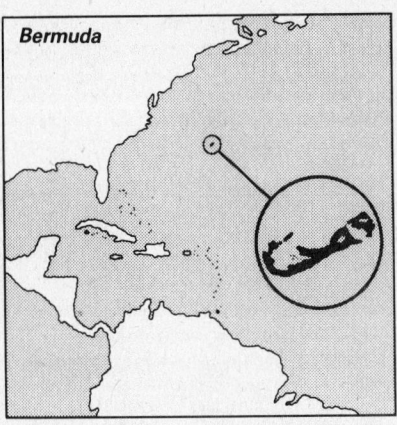

Bermuda

in the water of a spring there were said to have been cured. A church built on the rock above the grotto became a shrine. At the age of 20 Bernadette became a nun at Nevers, and nursed the wounded of the Franco-Prussian War. She died of tuberculosis.
   Bernadotte /ˌbɜːnə'dɒt/ Count Folke 1895–1948. Nephew of the King of Sweden and president of the Swedish Red Cross. In 1945 he conveyed Himmler's offer of capitulation to the British and US governments, and in 1948 was UN mediator in Palestine. He was assassinated by Stern Gang guerrillas.
   Bernadotte /ˌbɜːnə'dɒt/ Jean–Baptiste Jules 1764–1844. Marshal in Napoleon's army, who in 1818 became Charles XIV of Sweden. Hence, Bernadotte is the family name of the present royal house of Sweden.
   Bernanos /ˌbeənə'nəʊs/ Georges 1888–1948. French author. Born in Paris, he achieved fame in 1926 with *Sous le soleil de Satan/The Star of Satan*. His strongly Catholic viewpoint emerged equally in his *Journal d'un curê de campagne/The Diary of a Country Priest* 1936.
   Bernard /beə'nɑː/ Claude 1813–1878. French physiologist. He made many valuable discoveries, particularly in connection with the ◊liver, the ◊blood, and the ◊nervous system, and wrote a *Physiologie expérimentale* 1865.
   Bernardin de Saint-Pierre /'bɜːnardaŋ/ Jacques Henri 1737–1814. French writer and naturalist, whose works include *Etudes de la nature* (3 vols) 1784–88, which showed the influence of ◊Rousseau, and the pastoral romance *Paul et Virginie* 1788, set on the island of Mauritius.
   Bernard of Clairvaux, St /kleə'vəʊ/ 1090–1153. Founder in 1115 of Clairvaux monastery in Champagne, France, he reinvigorated the ◊Cistercian order; he preached the Second ◊Crusade in 1146, and had ◊Abelard condemned for heresy. He was canonized in 1174.
   Bernard of Menthon /mɒn'tɒŋ/ 923–1008. Christian saint, founder of the hospices for travellers on the Alpine passes that bear his name. The large, heavily-built St Bernard dogs formerly used to find travellers lost in the snow were also called after him.
   Berne /beən/ (German *Bern*) capital of Switzerland and of Berne canton, in W

Switzerland on the Aar; industries (textiles, chocolate, light metal goods); university 1834; population (1980) 154,000.
features Minster begun in 1421, town hall 1406; Berne is the seat of the Universal Postal Union.
history Founded in 1191, and made a free imperial city by Frederick II in 1218. It joined the Swiss confederation in 1353 and became the capital 1848. Its name is derived from the bear in its coat of arms, and there has been a bear pit in the city since the 16th century.
   Bernese Oberland /'bɜːniːz 'əʊbəlænd/ or **Bernese Alps** the mountainous area in the S of Berne canton which include some of the most famous peaks, such as the Jungfrau, Eiger, and Finsteraarhorn. Interlaken is the chief town.
   Bernhard /'beənɑːt/ Prince of the Netherlands 1911– . Formerly Prince Bernhard of Lippe-Biesterfeld, he married Princess ◊Juliana in 1937. When the Germans attacked Holland in 1940, he led the defence of the royal palace at The Hague. He escaped to England in 1940, and next year became liaison officer for the Netherlands and British forces, playing a part in the organization of the Dutch underground. In 1976 he was censured for his conduct in connection with the purchase of Lockheed aircraft by the Dutch.
   Bernhardt /'bɜːnhɑːt/ Sarah. Stage name of French actress Rosine Bernard. 1845–1923. She dominated the stage of her day, frequently performing at the Comédie-Française. Her most famous roles were as Cordelia in *King Lear*, ◊Racine's *Phèdre*, Dona Sol in ◊Hugo's *Hernani*, and in the male roles of Hamlet, and of Napoleon's son in ◊Rostand's *L'Aiglon*.
   Bernini /beə'niːni/ Giovanni Lorenzo 1598–1680. Italian architect, sculptor, and painter; one of the great masters of the Baroque style. His most famous piece of sculpture is his *Apollo and Daphne*; his architectural masterpiece is the colonnade surrounding the piazza outside St Peter's in Rome.
   Bernoulli /bɜː'nuːli/ family of mathematicians. *Jacques* (or *Jakob*), 1654–1705, and *Jean* (or *Johann*), 1667–1748, sons of the Swiss Daniel Bernoulli, helped to develop the ◊calculus as conceived by the German philosopher Leibnitz. Jacques' best-known work was on transcendental curves (1696) and the so-called Bernoulli numbers and probability theory (published posthumously in *Ars Conjectandi* 1713). Bernouilli numbers are a series of complex fractions used in higher mathematics. Jean Bernoulli found the equation to the ◊catenary (1690) and developed exponential calculus (1691), concentrating more on applied mathematics. His son *Daniel Bernoulli* (1700–82) was a Dutch mathematical physicist who made important contributions to ◊trigonometry and differential equations (◊differentiation), and in physics proposed Bernoulli's principle, which states that the pressure of a moving fluid decreases the faster it flows (which explains the origin of lift on the aerofoil of an aircraft's wing). This and other work on hydrodynamics was published in *Hydrodynamica* 1738.

Bernhardt French tragic actress Sarah Bernhardt, called by Oscar Wilde 'the divine Sarah', in her role as Marguérite in *La Dame aux Camélias*, 1881. She was a huge success at the Comédie-Française and played to rapt audiences in England and America.

Bernoulli effect a drop in hydraulic pressure, such as that in a fluid flowing through a constriction in a pipe. It is also responsible for the pressure differences on each surface of an aerofoil, which gives lift to the wing of an aircraft. The effect was named after the Swiss physicist Daniel ◊Bernoulli.

Bernouilli effect

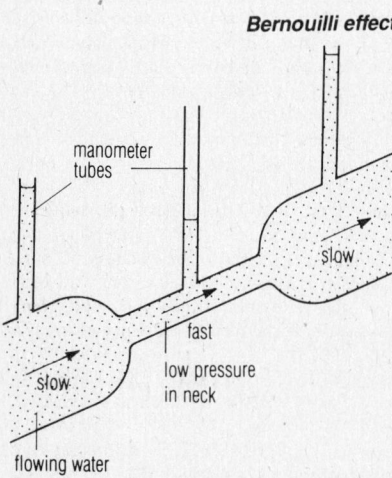

Bernstein /'bɜːnstaɪn/ Edouard 1850–1932. German socialist thinker, proponent of reformist rather than revolutionary socialism, whereby a socialist society could be achieved within an existing parliamentary structure, merely by workers' parties obtaining a majority.

Bernstein /'bɜːnstaɪn/ Leonard 1918– . American composer, conductor and pianist. His works, which established a vogue for contemporary themes, include symphonies – *Jeremiah* 1944, *The Age of Anxiety* 1949; ballets – *Fancy Free* 1944 and *Facsimile* 1946; scores for musicals – *Wonderful Town* 1953, *Candide* 1956, *West Side Story* 1957; the *Chichester Psalms* 1965; and a *Mass* 1971 in memory of J F Kennedy.

Berrigan /'berɪgən/ Daniel 1921– and Philip 1924– American Roman Catholic priests. The brothers, opponents of the Vietnam War, broke into the draft records offices at Catonsville to burn the files with napalm, and were sentenced in 1968 to three and six years' imprisonment, but went underground.

berry in botany, a fleshy, many-seeded ◊fruit that does not split open to release the seeds. The outer layer of tissue, the exocarp, forms an outer skin which is often brightly coloured to attract birds; these eat the fruit and thus disperse the seeds. Examples of berries are the tomato and the grape. A pepo is a type of berry that has developed a hard exterior, such as the cucumber fruit. Another type of berry is the hesperidium, which has a thick, leathery outer layer, such as that found in the citrus fruits, and fluid-containing vesicles within, which form the characteristic segments.

Berry /'beri/ Chuck (Charles Edward) 1931– . US rock-and-roll singer, songwriter, and guitarist. Influenced by rhythm and blues, he was one of the pioneers of rock and roll from the mid-1950s with a string of hits including 'Maybellene' 1955 and 'Roll Over Beethoven' 1956.

Berryman /'berimən/ John 1914–1972. US poet, whose complex and personal works include *Homage to Mistress Bradstreet* 1956, *77 Dream Songs* 1964 (Pulitzer prize), and *His Toy, His Dream, His Rest* 1968.

berserker member of a legendary Scandinavian warrior cult, who went into battle in a frenzy of destructive energy – hence 'to go berserk' – and who were rendered immune to sword and flame.

Berthelot /ˌbeətə'ləu/ Pierre Eugene Marcelin 1827–1907. French chemist and politician, who carried out research into dyes and explosives, and proved that hydrocarbons and other organic compounds can be synthesized from inorganic materials.

Bertholet /ˌbeətə'leɪ/ Claude Louis 1748–1822. French chemist, who carried out research on dyes and bleaches (introducing the use of ◊chlorine as a bleach) and determined the composition of ◊ammonia. Modern chemical nomenclature is based on a system worked out by Bertholet and Antoine ◊Lavoisier.

Bertolucci /ˌbeətəu'luːtʃi/ Bernardo 1940– . Italian director, regarded as one of the most talented of the younger generation of Italian film directors. His work combines political and historical satire with an elegant visual appeal. His films include *The Spider's Stratagem* 1970, *The Conformist* 1970, *Novecento/1900* 1976, and *The Last Emperor* 1987, but he is probably best known for his controversial *Last Tango in Paris* 1972.

Bertrand de Born /beə'trɒn də 'bɔːn/ c. 1140–c. 1215. Provençal ◊troubadour. He was viscount of Hautefort in Périgord, accompanied Richard Cœur de Lion to the Holy Land, and died a monk.

Berwick /'berɪk/ James Fitzjames, Duke of Berwick 1670–1734. French marshal. Illegitimate son of the Duke of York (afterwards James II of England) and Arabella Churchill (1648–1730). He was made duke of Berwick in 1687.

Berwickshire /'berɪkʃə/ former county of SE Scotland, a district of Borders region from 1975.

Berwick-upon-Tweed /'berɪk əpɒn 'twiːd/ industrial fishing port (iron foundries, shipbuilding) in NE England, at the mouth of the Tweed, Northumberland, 5 km/3 mi SE of the Scottish border.

features Three bridges cross the Tweed: the Old Bridge 1611–34 with 15 arches, the Royal Border railway bridge 1850 constructed by Robert Stephenson, and the Royal Tweed Bridge 1928.

history Held alternately by England and Scotland for centuries, Berwick was in 1551 made a neutral town; it was attached to Northumberland in 1885.

beryl a mineral, beryllium aluminium sillicate, $Be_3Al_2Si_6O_{18}$, which forms crystals chiefly in granite. It is the chief ore of ◊beryllium. Two of its gem forms are aquamarine (light blue crystals) and emerald (dark green crystals).

beryllium a light silvery hard metallic element, symbol Be, atomic weight 9.013, atomic number 4. It is used as a source of neutrons when bombarded, to make windows for x-ray tubes, to toughen copper for high-grade gear-wheels and spark-free tools and as a neutron reflector, ◊moderator, and uranium sheathing in nuclear reactors.

Berzelius /bə'ziːliəs/ Jöns Jakob 1779–1848. Swedish chemist, who specialized in the determination of atomic and molecular weights.

Berzelius A contemporary engraving of Swedish chemist J J Berzelius, whose accurate determination of atomic and molecular weights helped to establish the laws of combination and the atomic theory. He also introduced the chemical symbols which we now use.

He invented (1813–14) the system of chemical symbols now in use.

Besançon /bə'zɒnsɒn/ industrial town, capital of Franche-Comté, France; population (1983) 120,000. It has fortifications by ◊Vauban, Roman remains, a Gothic cathedral, and the writer Victor Hugo was born here.

Besant /'besənt/ Annie 1847–1933. British socialist and feminist activist. She was associated with the radical atheist Charles Bradlaugh and the ◊Fabians, and became a disciple of Mme ◊Blavatsky in 1889. She thereafter preached theosophy and, as a supporter of Indian independence, became president of the Hindu National Congress in 1917.

Besant /'besənt/ Walter 1836–1901. British writer. He wrote novels in partnership with James Rice (1844–82), and produced an attack on the social evils of the East End, *All Sorts and Conditions of Men* 1882.

Bessarabia /ˌbesə'reɪbɪə/ territory in SE Europe, annexed by Russia in 1812, which broke away at the Russian Revolution to join Romania. The cession was confirmed by the Allies, but not by Russia, in a Paris treaty of 1920; Russia reoccupied it in 1940 and divided it between the Moldavian and Ukrainian republics. Romania recognized the position in the 1947 peace treaty.

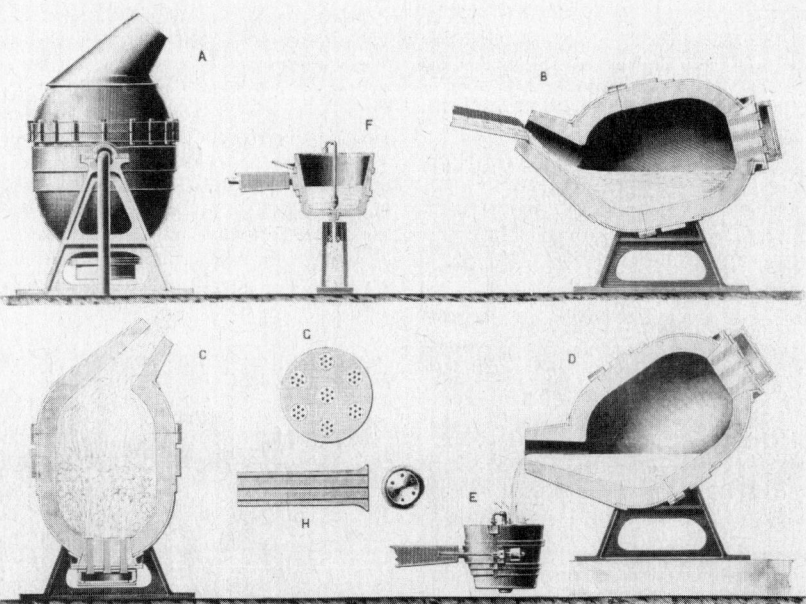

Bessemer The British metallurgist Henry Bessemer needed a form of iron which would be strong enough for use in his high-power cannons, but steel was far too expensive at that time. He patented an economical process by which pig iron blasted by a current of air is turned directly into steel. This is a diagram of the first movable form of his converter and ladle, taken from his autobiography.

Besant British feminist Annie Besant in 1868. After a brief marriage to a clergyman, she was associated with Charles Bradlaugh, the social reformer. They published a treatise advocating birth control and were prosecuted. As a result she lost custody of her daughter.

Bessel /'besl/ Friedrich Wilhelm 1784–1846. German astronomer, the first person to find the distance to a star by direct methods when he measured the ◊parallax of 61 Cygni in 1838.

Bessemer /'besɪmə/ Henry 1813–1898. British civil engineer, who invented a method of converting molten pig-iron into steel (the Bessemer process).

Bessemer process the first cheap method of making ◊steel, invented by Henry ◊Bessemer in England in 1856. It has since been superseded by more efficient steelmaking processes, particularly the ◊basic-oxygen process. In the Bessemer process compressed air is blown into the bottom of a converter, a furnace shaped rather like a cement mixer, containing molten pig iron. The excess carbon in the iron burns out, and other impurities form a slag. The furnace is emptied by tilting.

Best /best/ Charles Herbert 1899–1978. Canadian physiologist, one of the team of Canadian scientists including Sir Frederick ◊Banting, whose researches resulted in 1922 in the discovery of insulin as a treatment for diabetes. A Banting-Best Department of Medical Research was founded in Toronto, and Best was its director from 1941 to 1967.

beta blocker drug used to block nerve impulses to special sites (beta receptors) in heart nerves and other body tissues; they reduce the rate of heartbeat and the force of its contractions, and are used to lower raised blood pressure and in post-heart attack treatment.

beta particle an electron or positron emitted from a radioactive substance whilst undergoing spontaneous disintegration. Beta particles do not exist in the nucleus, but are created on disintegration when a neutron converts to a proton to emit an electron, or a proton converts to a neutron to emit a positron. See ◊particle physics, ◊radioactivity.

Betelgeuse /'biːtldʒɜːz/ a red supergiant ◊star in the constellation of ◊Orion and the tenth-brightest star in the sky, although its brightness varies. Betelgeuse is over 300 times the diameter of the Sun, about the same size as the orbit of Mars. It lies 350 light years away.

betel nut fruit of the areca palm (*Areca catechu*), used as a masticatory by peoples of the East: chewing it results in blackened teeth and the mouth is stained deep red.

Bethe /'beɪtə/ Hans Albrecht 1906– . German-American physicist. A refugee from Hitler in 1933, he taught first in Britain, then in the USA, where he became professor of theoretical physics at Cornell in 1937. He worked on the first atomic bomb, and was in 1967 awarded a Nobel prize, especially for his discoveries on energy production in stars.

Bethlehem /'beθlɪhem/ industrial city (steel) in E Pennsylvania, USA; population (1970) 72,500.

Bethlehem /'beθlɪhem/ (*Beit-Lahm*) town on the W bank of the river Jordan, S of Jerusalem, occupied by Israel in 1967; population (1980) 14,000. In the New Testament it was the birthplace of Jesus Christ and associated with King David.

Bethmann Hollweg /'beɪtmæn 'hɒlveg/ Theobald von 1856–1921. German politician who succeeded Prince Bülow as Imperial Chancellor in 1909. At the outbreak of World War I he defended Germany's invasion of Belgium and Luxemburg. He was dismissed in 1917.

Béthune /beɪ'tjuːn/ industrial city (machinery, tyres) in N France, W of Lille; population (1975) 145,000.

Betjeman /'betʃɪmən/ John 1906–1984. English poet and essayist, originator of a peculiarly English light verse, nostalgic and delighting in Victorian and Edwardian architecture. His *Collected Poems* appeared in 1968 and a verse autobiography *Summoned by Bells* in 1960. He was knighted in 1969 and became Poet Laureate in 1972.

Betjeman The poet Betjeman was regarded with much affection for his ability to capture the popular mood and his care for England's architectural heritage.

betony plant *Betonica officinalis* of the family Labiatae, a hedgerow weed in Britain. It has a hairy stem and leaves and reddish-purple flowers, and was formerly supposed to have curative properties.

Betterton /'betətən/ Thomas c. 1635–1710. British actor. A member of the Duke of York's company after the Restoration, he attracted the attention of Charles II, and was particularly famous in such parts as Hamlet and Othello.

Betti /'beti/ Ugo 1892–1953. Italian poet and dramatist. His best-known plays are *Delitto all'isola delle capre/Crime on Goat Island* 1948 and *La regina e gli insorte/The Queen and the Rebels* 1949.

betting wagering money on the outcome of a game, race, or other event. In the UK on-course betting on *horses* and *dogs* may be through individual bookmakers at given odds, or on the tote (totalizator), when the total amount (with fixed deductions) staked is divided among those making the correct forecast. Off-course betting is mainly through betting 'shops' (legalized 1960) which, like bookmakers, must have a licence. *Football* betting is in the hands of 'pools' promoters who must be registered with a local authority to which annual accounts are submitted. The size of the money prizes is determined by the number of successful forecasts of the results of matches received; the maximum first dividend on football pools is fixed at £1 million.

Betty /'beti/ William Henry West 1791–1874. British boy actor, called the 'Young Roscius', after the greatest comic actor of ancient Rome. First appearing in Belfast aged 11, he was enthusiastically received for six years, especially in Shakespeare. As an adult actor he was not remarkable.

Betws-y-coed /'betʊs ə 'kɔɪd/ village tourist centre, noted for its waterfalls, in Gwynned, Wales.

Bevan /'bevən/ Aneurin 1897–1960. British ◊Labour politician. Son of a Welsh miner, and himself a miner at 13, he became Member of Parliament for Ebbw Vale 1929–60. As minister of health 1945–51, he inaugurated the National Health Service (NHS); he was minister of labour Jan–Apr 1951, when he resigned (with Harold ◊Wilson) on the introduction of NHS charges and led a Bevanite faction against the government. He was noted as an orator.

Bevan British Labour politician Aneurin Bevan led the Welsh miners in the 1926 strike. A man of radical socialist fervour and acute intellect, he established a reputation in Parliament in World War II as Churchill's 'one-man opposition'.

Beveridge /'bevərɪdʒ/ William Henry, 1st Baron Beveridge 1879–1963. British economist. A civil servant, he acted as ◊Lloyd George's lieutenant in the social legislation of the ◊Liberal government before World War I, and the Beveridge Report 1942 formed the basis of the welfare state in Britain.

Beverly Hills /'bevəli/ residential part of greater Los Angeles, California, USA, known as the home of Hollywood film stars.

Bevin /'bevɪn/ Ernest 1881–1951. British ◊Labour politician. Chief creator of the Transport and General Workers' Union, he was its general secretary 1921–40, when he entered the war cabinet as minister of labour and National Service. He organized the 'Bevin boys', chosen by ballot to work in the coal mines as war service, and was foreign secretary in the Labour government 1945–51.

Bewick /'bjuːɪk/ Thomas 1753–1828. British wood engraver, excelling in animal subjects, for example *British Birds* 1797–1804. His birthplace, Cherryburn, Mickley, Northamptonshire, is a museum of wood engraving, with many of his original blocks.

Bewick Although English illustrator Thomas Bewick was trained in metal engraving, he revived the art of wood engraving and made many improvements in its techniques. He did a celebrated series of *Quadrupeds*; this one is the Old English Hound.

Bexhill /ˌbeks'hɪl/ seaside resort in E Sussex, England; population (1981) 35,500.

Beza (properly *De Bèsze*) /beɪ'zɑː/ Théodore 1519–1605. French church reformer. He settled at Geneva, where he worked with ◊Calvin, and succeeded him in 1564 as head of the reformed church at Geneva, a post he resigned in 1600. He wrote in defence of the burning of Servetus (1554), translated the New Testament into Latin, and presented in 1581 a 5th-century Graeco-Latin manuscript of the Gospels and the Acts, the *Codex Bezae*, to Cambridge university.

Béziers /bez'jeɪ/ city in S France, a centre of the wine trade; population (1983) 84,000. It was once a Roman station, and was the site of a massacre 1209 in the Albigensian Crusade.

bézique /bɪ'ziːk/ (French *Bésigue*) card game, supposed to have originated in Spain, and introduced into England in 1861. About 1869 it became very popular in the London clubs. *Rubicon bézique* has a code of laws promulgated by the Portland Club in 1887.

Bhagalpur /'bɑːglpʊə/ town in N India, on the Ganges, with Jain temples and silk manufacture; population (1971) 172,700.

Bhagavad-gita /'bʌɡəvəd 'giːtə/ (the Song of the Blessed). Religious and philosophical Sanskrit poem forming an episode in the sixth book of the Mahabharata, one of the two great Hindu epics. It is the supreme religious work of ◊Hinduism.

Bhamo /bə'məʊ/ town in Burma, near the Chinese frontier, at the head of navigation of the Irrawaddy river.

bhang another name for ◊cannabis.

Bharat /'bʌrət/ Hindi name for ◊India.

Bharata Natyam /'bʌrətə 'nɑːtjəm/ type of Indian classical dancing, supposed to have been described by the ancient expert Bharata.

Bhatgaon /bɑːt'ɡɑːɒn/ town in Nepal, 11 km/7 mi SE of Katmandu; a religious centre from the 9th century, with a palace; population (1973) 82,250.

Bhavnagar /bau'nʌɡə/ industrial port (textiles) in Gujarat, NW India, in the Kathiawar peninsula; population (1981) 308,000. It was capital of the former Rajput princely state of Bhavnagar.

Bhopal /bəʊ'pɑːl/ industrial city (textiles, chemicals), capital of Madhya Pradesh, central India; population (1981) 672,500. It was capital of the former princely state of Bhopal. In 1984 some 2,000 people died after an escape of poisonous gas from a factory owned by the US company Union Carbide; the long-term effects are yet to be discovered.

Bhubaneswar /ˌbuvə'neɪʃwə/ historic city and capital of Orissa, NE India; Utkal University 1843; population (1971) 105,500. A place of pilgrimage and centre of Siva worship, it has temples of the 6th–12th centuries; it was capital of the Kesaris (Lion) dynasty of Orissa 474–950.

Bhumibol Adulyadej /'puːmɪpəʊn ə'dunlədeɪt/ King of Thailand 1927– . Educated in Bangkok and Switzerland, he succeeded on the assassination of his brother in 1946, formally taking the throne in 1950. In 1973, the king was active, with popular support in overthrowing the military govt of Field-Marshal Kittachorn, and ending a sequence of army dominated regimes in power from 1932.

Bhutan /buː'tɑːn/ mountainous, landlocked country in SE Asia, bordered to the N by China and to the S by India.

government Bhutan is an hereditary monarchy and although since 1953 there has been an elected national assembly (*Tsogdu*) and since 1965 a partially elected royal advisory council with whom the monarch shares power, in the absence of a written constitution, it is in effect an absolute monarchy. There are, however, certain written rules governing the methods of electing members of the Royal Advisory Council and Tsogdu. There are no political parties, though there is a gradual trend towards greater democracy.

history ruled by Tibet from the 16th century and by China from 1720, Bhutan was invaded by Britain in 1865 and a trade agreement signed, under which an annual subsidy was paid to Bhutan. In 1907 the first hereditary monarch was installed and three years later, under the Anglo-Bhutanese Treaty, foreign relations were placed under the control of the British government in India.

When India became independent in 1945, an Indo-Bhutan treaty of friendship was signed, under which Bhutan agreed to seek Indian advice on foreign relations but not necessarily to accept it. There is no formal defence treaty, but India would regard an attack on Bhutan as an act of aggression against itself. In 1952 King Jigme Dorji Wangchuk came to power and in 1953 a national assembly was established.

In 1959, after the Chinese annexation of Tibet, Bhutan gave asylum to some 4,000 Tibetan refugees who in 1979 were given the choice of taking up Bhutanese citizenship or returning to Tibet. Most became citizens and the rest went to India. In 1968, as part of a move towards greater democracy, the king appointed his first cabinet. He died in 1972 and was succeeded by his Western-educated son Jigme Singye Wangchuk. In 1983 Bhutan became a founder member of the South Asia Regional Co-operation organization (SARC) and in 1985 the first meeting of SARC foreign ministers was held in Bhutan.

Bhutan
KINGDOM OF (*Druk-yul*)

AREA 46,600 sq km/18,000 sq mi
CAPITAL Thimphu
PHYSICAL occupies S slopes of the Himalayas, and is cut by valleys of tributaries of the Brahmaputra
HEAD OF STATE AND OF GOVERNMENT Jigme Singye Wangchuk from 1972
GOVERNMENT absolute monarchy
EXPORTS timber, minerals
CURRENCY ngultrum (21.30 = £1 Sept 1987); also Indian currency
POPULATION 1,286,000 (1985); annual growth rate 2%
LANGUAGE Dzongkha (a Tibetan dialect), Nepali, and English (all official)
RELIGION Mahayana Buddhist
LITERACY 10%
GDP $150 million (1983); $120 per head of population
CHRONOLOGY
1865 Trade treaty with Britain signed.
1907 First hereditary monarch installed.
1910 Anglo-Bhutanese Treaty signed.
1945 Indo-Bhutan Treaty of Friendship signed.
1952 King Jigme Dorji Wangchuk installed.
1953 National assembly established.
1959 4,000 Tibetan refugees given asylum.
1968 King established first cabinet.
1972 King died and was succeeded by his son Jigme Singye Wangchuk.
1979 Tibetan refugees told to take up Bhutanese citizenship or leave. Most stayed.
1983 Bhutan became a founder member of the South Asian Regional Cooperation organization (SARC).

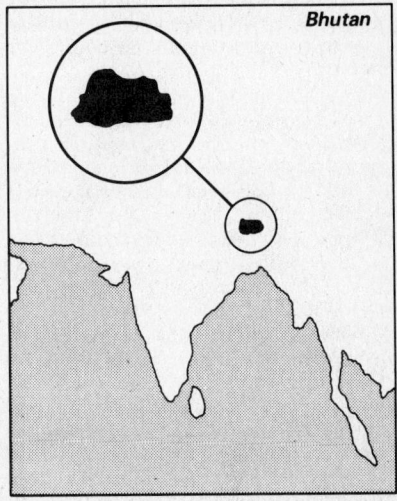

Bhutan

Bhutto /'buːtəʊ/ Benazir 1953– . Pakistani politician, leader of the Pakistan People's Party (PPP).
The daughter of the former prime minister of Pakistan, Zulfiqar Ali ◊Bhutto, Benazir Bhutto was educated at Harvard and Oxford universities. She returned to Pakistan in 1977 and was placed under house arrest 1977–84, after the military coup led by General ◊Zia ul Haq. She then moved to Britain and became, with her mother Nusrat (1934–), the joint leader in exile of the opposition PPP. When martial law had been lifted, she returned to Pakistan in Apr 1986 to launch a campaign for open elections.

Bhutto /'buːtəʊ/ Zulficar Ali 1928–1979. Pakistani politician, who was president 1971–73, and then prime minister until the 1977 military coup. In 1978 he was sentenced to death for conspiracy to murder a political opponent, and was hanged. His followers, led by his daughter Benazir ◊Bhutto, continue in opposition to the new regime.

Biafra, Republic of /bi'æfrə/ state proclaimed in 1967 when the predominantly Ibo Eastern Region of Nigeria seceded under Lieutenant-Colonel Odumegwu Ojukwu, an Oxford-educated Ibo. On the proclamation of Biafra civil war ensued with the rest of the Federation, but in a bitterly fought campaign Federal forces had confined the Biafrans to a shrinking area of the interior by 1968, and by 1970 Biafra ceased to exist.

Biafra, Bight of name until 1975 of the Bight of ◊Bonny, W Africa.

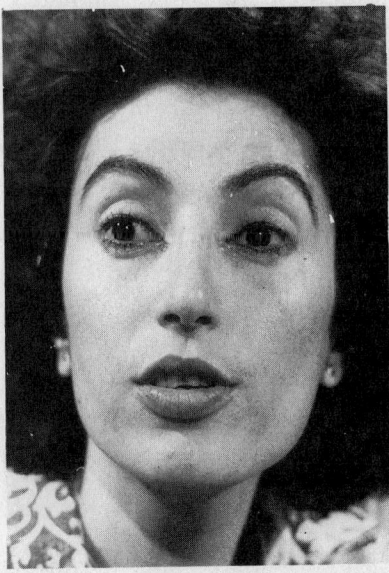

Bhutto Pakistani opposition leader Benazir Bhutto is the daughter of former prime minister Zulfikar Ali Bhutto, who was hanged in 1979. She spent seven years under house arrest and returned from exile in 1986, urging an end to military dictatorship.

Bialystok /bjæ'wɪstɒk/ industrial city (textiles, chemicals, tools) in E Poland, capital of Bialystok region; population (1979) 218,000.

Founded 1310, belonged to Prussia 1795–1807 and to Russia 1807–1919.

Biarritz /bɪəˈrɪts/ seaside resort and spa on the Bay of Biscay, France, near the Spanish border; population (1975) 27,000. It was popularized by Queen Victoria and Edward VII.

biathlon cross-country race on skis, contestants also shooting at targets with rifles on the way: it is used as a military training exercise.

Biber /ˈbiːbə/ Heinrich von 1644–1704. Bohemian composer, Kapellmeister at the Archbishop of Salzburg's court. A virtuoso violinist, he composed a wide variety of music, notably the *Nightwatchman Serenade*.

Bible (Greek *ta biblia* 'the books') the authorized documentation of the Jewish and Christian religions. The Hebrew Bible, recognized by both Jews and Christians, is called the *Old Testament* by Christians. Its first five books are traditionally ascribed to Moses and known as the Pentateuch (by Christians) or the Torah (by Jews). The Christian Bible also includes the *Apocryrypha*, books not included in the final Hebrew canon, but recognized by Roman Catholics, though segregated or omitted in Protestant bibles, and the *New Testament*, books recognized by the Christian Church from the 4th century as canonical. The latter include the Gospels, which tell of the life and teachings of Jesus, the history of the early church, teachings of St Paul, and mystical writings.

Bible society society founded for the promotion of the translation and distribution of the Scriptures. The largest is the British and Foreign Bible Society, founded in 1804.

bicarbonate of soda a white crystalline solid (NaHCO$_3$) more properly called sodium hydrogen carbonate. It neutralizes acids and is used in medicine to treat acid indigestion. It is also used in baking powders and effervescent drinks.

bichir African fish, genus *Polypterus*, found in tropical swamps and rivers, and showing many 'primitive' features, such as breathing air using the swimbladder, having a spiral valve in the intestine, having heavy bony scales, and having a larva with external gills. These, and the fleshy fins, lead some scientists to think they are related to lungfish and coelacanths. Cylindrical in shape, some species grow to 70 cm/2.3 ft or more.

bicycle a pedal-driven two wheeled vehicle; see ◊cycling.

Bidault /biːˈdəu/ Georges 1899– . French politician. Before World War II he made a reputation as a journalist, fought in the 1940 campaign and also in the resistance movement. As a leader of the *Movement Républicaine Populaire*, he held office as prime minister and foreign minister in a number of unstable administrations of 1944–54.

Biedermeier German style of art (naturalistic) and furniture (conventional) in the first half of the 19th century, so named from Gottlieb Biedermeier, a fictional character created 1855 by Swabian comic writer Ludwig Eichrodt (1827–92), embodying bourgeois taste.

Biel /biːl/ (French *Bienne*) industrial town (watchmaking) in NW Switzerland; population (1980) 54,000.

Bielefeld /ˈbiːləfeld/ manufacturing city in North Rhine–Westphalia, West Germany, 55 km/34 mi E of Münster; population (1980) 312,500.

Bielostok /ˌbjeləˈstɒk/ Russian form of ◊Bialystok, city in Poland.

THE BIBLE

The Books of the Old Testament

Name of book	Chapters	Date written	
Genesis	50	mid 8th century BC	⎫
Exodus	40	950–586 BC	the Pentateuch
Leviticus	27	mid 7th century BC	or Five Books of
Numbers	36	850–650 BC	Moses
Deuteronomy	34	mid 7th century BC	⎭
Joshua	24	c. 550 BC	
Judges	21	c. 550 BC	
Ruth	4	end 3rd century BC	
1 Samuel	31	c. 900 BC	
2 Samuel	24	c. 900 BC	
1 Kings	22	550–600 BC	
2 Kings	25	550–600 BC	
1 Chronicles	29	c. 300 BC	
2 Chronicles	36	c. 300 BC	
Ezra	10	c. 450 BC	
Nehemiah	13	c. 450 BC	
Esther	10	c. 200 BC	
Job	42	600–400 BC	
Psalms	150	6th–2nd century BC	
Proverbs	31	350–150 BC	
Ecclesiastes	12	c. 200 BC	
Song of Solomon	8	3rd century BC	
Isaiah	66	end 3rd century BC	
Jeremiah	52	604 BC	
Lamentations	5	586–536 BC	
Ezekiel	48	6th century BC	
Daniel	12	c. 166 BC	
Hosea	14	c. 732 BC	
Joel	3	c. 500 BC	
Amos	9	775–750 BC	
Obadiah	1	6th–3rd century BC	
Jonah	4	600–200 BC	
Micah	7	end 3rd century BC	
Nahum	3	c. 626 BC	
Habakkuk	3	c. 600 BC	
Zephaniah	3	3rd century BC	
Haggai	2	c. 520 BC	
Zechariah	14	c. 520 BC	
Malachi	4	c. 430 BC	

The Books of the New Testament

Name of book	Chapters	Date written	
Matthew	28	before AD 70	⎫
Mark	16	before AD 70	the Gospels
Luke	24	AD 70–80	
John	21	AD 90–100	⎭
The Acts	28	AD 70–80	
Romans	16	AD 120	
1 Corinthians	16	AD 57	
2 Corinthians	13	AD 57	
Galatians	6	AD 53	
Ephesians	6	AD 140	
Philippians	4	AD 63	
Colossians	4	AD 140	
1 Thessalonians	5	AD 50–54	
2 Thessalonians	3	AD 50–54	
1 Timothy	6	before AD 64	
2 Timothy	4	before AD 64	
Titus	3	before AD 64	
Philemon	1	AD 60–62	
Hebrews	13	AD 80–90	
James	5	before AD 52	
1 Peter	5	before AD 64	
2 Peter	3	before AD 64	
1 John	5	AD 90–100	
2 John	1	AD 90–100	
3 John	1	AD 90–100	
Jude	1	AD 75–80	
Revelation	22	AD 81–96	

Bible Two plates from the Bible Pauperum c. 1470. The left-hand page shows Joseph in the pit, the burial of Christ, and Jonah. The right-hand plate shows David slaying Goliath, the resurrection of Christ, and Samson and the lion.

Bienne /bjen/ French form of ◊Biel, town in Switzerland.

biennial plant a plant that completes its life cycle in two years. During the first year it grows vegetatively and the surplus food produced is stored in its ◊perennating organ, usually the root. In the following year these food reserves are used for the production of leaves, flowers and seeds, after which the plant dies. Many root vegetables are biennials, including carrots (*Daucus carota*) and parsnips (*Pastinaca sativa*). Among garden plants, some that are grown as biennials are actually perennials, for example the wallflower (*Cheiranthus cheiri*).

Bierce /bɪəs/ Ambrose (Gwinett) 1842–1914?. American author. Born in Ohio, he spent most of his life as a journalist in San Francisco. He established his reputation as a master of supernatural and psychological horror with his *Tales of Soldiers and Civilians* 1891, and *Can Such Things Be?* 1893. He also wrote *The Devil's Dictionary* 1906, a collection of ironic definitions. He disappeared on a secret mission to Mexico.

Biffen /ˈbɪfɪn/ (William) John 1930– . British Conservative politician, leader of the House of Commons from 1982. In 1971 Biffen was elected to Parliament for a Shropshire seat. Despite being to the left of Margaret ◊Thatcher, he held key positions in government from 1979 and became leader of the House of Commons in 1982.

bigamy in law, the offence of marrying another person when one's husband or wife is still alive, and the marriage has neither been dissolved nor annulled.

big band description of jazz sound created in the late 1930s and 1940s by bands of 15 or more players, such as those of Duke ◊Ellington and Benny ◊Goodman, when there is more than one instrument to some of the parts.

Big Bang in economics, popular term for the major changes instituted in late 1986 to the organization and practices of the City of London as Britain's financial centre, with the aim of ensuring that London retained its place as one of the leading world financial centres. Facilitated in part by computerization and on-line communications, the changes included the liberalization of the London ◊Stock Exchange. This involved merging the functions of jobber (dealer in stocks and shares) and broker (who mediates between the jobber and the public), introducing negotiated commission rates, and allowing foreign banks and financial companies to own British brokers/jobbers, or themselves to join the London Stock Exchange.

Big Bang in astronomy, the hypothetical event which marked the origin of the ◊Universe as we know it. At the time of the Big Bang, the entire Universe – all space and matter – were squeezed into a hot, super-dense state. The Big Bang explosion threw this material outwards, producing the ◊expanding Universe. The cause of the Big Bang is unknown; observations of the current rate of expansion of the Universe suggest that it took place between 10,000 million and 20,000 million years ago. See also ◊cosmology.

Big Ben popular name for the bell in the clock tower of the Houses of Parliament in London, cast at the Whitechapel Bell Foundry in 1858, and popularly known as 'Big Ben' after Sir Benjamin Hall, First Commissioner of Works at the time. It weighs 13,700 kg (13½ tons).

bight a coastal indentation, such as the Bight of ◊Bonny and Great Australian Bight.

Bihar /bɪˈhɑː/ state of NE India
area 173,876 sq km/67,132 sq mi
capital Patna
features river Ganges in the N, Rajmahal Hills in the S
products iron, coal, rice
population (1981) 70,000,000
language Hindi, Bihari
famous people Chandragupta, Asoka
history the ancient kingdom of Magadha roughly corresponded to central and S Bihar (see ◊Maurya dynasty and ◊Patna), and many incidents in ◊Buddha's life took place here.

Bijapur /ˌbɪdʒəˈpʊə/ ancient city of

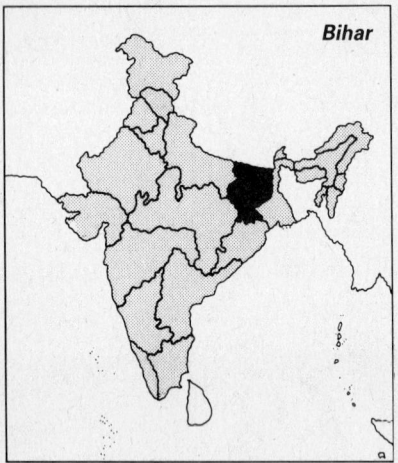
Bihar

Karnataka, Republic of India. Capital of Muslim kingdom of Biafra, 15th–17th centuries, it has splendid remains.

Bikaner /ˌbɪkəˈnɪə/ city in Rajasthan, N India, once capital of the Rajput state of Bikaner; noted for carpets; population (1971) 188,500.

Bikini /bɪˈkiːni/ atoll in the ◊Marshall Islands, N Pacific, where in 1946–63 atom-bomb tests were carried out by the USA.

Biko /ˈbiːkəʊ/ Steve (Stephan) 1946–1977. Black civil rights leader in South Africa, who since his death in the custody of South African police has been a symbol of the anti-apartheid movement. He founded the South African Students Organization (SASO) in 1968 and was co-founder in 1972 of the Black People's Convention, also called the Black Consciousness movement, a radical association of South African students which aimed to develop black pride. An active opponent of ◊apartheid, he was arrested in Sep 1977 and died in detention six days later.

Bilbao /bɪlˈbaʊ/ industrial port (iron and steel, chemicals, cement, food) in N Spain, capital of Biscay province; population (1981) 433,000.

bilberry plant *Vaccinium myrtillus* of the family Ericaceae closely resembling the cranberry, but distinguished by its bluish berries.

bilby name for the rabbit-eared bandicoot *Macrotis lagotis*, a lightly-built marsupial with big ears and long nose. The pouch opens backwards, and these burrowing animals are mainly carnivorous.

Bildungsroman (German 'education novel') novel that deals with the psychological development of its central character, tracing his or her life from inexperienced youth to maturity. The first example of the type is generally considered to be ◊Wieland's *Agathon* 1765–66, but it was ◊Goethe's *Wilhelm Meisters Lehrjahr/Wilhelm Meister's Apprenticeship* 1795–96 which established the genre. Although taken up by writers in other languages, it remained chiefly a German form, and later notable examples have included ◊Mann's *Der Zauberberg/The Magic Mountain* 1924.

bile a brownish fluid produced by the ◊liver.

In most vertebrates it is stored in the ◊gall bladder and emptied into the small intestine as food passes through. The fluid consists of *bile salts*, which assist the digestion of fats, and *bile pigments* which are the breakdown products of old red blood cells and are passed into the gut to be eliminated with the ◊faeces.

bilharzia see ◊schistosomiasis.

billiards game played with cues and composition balls (one red, two white) on a rectangular table covered with a green cloth, and with six pockets, one at each corner and in each of the long sides at the middle. The world's greatest player was Walter Lindrum, whose phenomenal skill helped to kill the game in favour of pool, in which there is a greater element of chance; the most popular form of the latter is ◊snooker.

World Professional Championship instituted in 1870, organized on a challenge basis; restored as an annual tournament in 1980

1980 Fred Davis (*England*)
1981 not held
1982 Rex Williams (*England*)
1983 Rex Williams (*England*)
1984 Mark Wildman (*England*)
1985 Ray Edmonds (*England*)
1986 Robert Foldvari (*Australia*)
1987 Norman Dagley (*England*)

Billingsgate /ˈbɪlɪŋzgeɪt/ chief London fish market, from 1981 on the Isle of Dogs; formerly (from the 9th century) near London Bridge.

billion in British usage, a million million (1,000,000,000,000); but in the USA and France, a thousand million (1,000,000,000), which in Britain is a milliard.

Billiton /ˈbɪlɪtən/ Indonesian island in the Java Sea, between Borneo and Sumatra, one of the Sunda Islands; area 4,830 sq km/1,860 sq mi.

Bill of Exchange a form of commercial credit instrument, or IOU, used in international trade. In Britain it is defined by the Bills of Exchange Act, 1882, as an unconditional order in writing addressed by one person to another, signed by the person giving it, requiring the person to whom it is addressed to pay on demand or at a fixed or determinate future time a certain sum in money to or to the order of a specified person, or to the bearer. A ◊cheque is a Bill of Exchange drawn on a bank payable on demand. US practice is governed by the Uniform Negotiable Instruments Law, drafted on the same lines as the British, and accepted by all states by 1927.

Bill of Rights in Britain, Act of 1689 embodying the Declaration of Rights presented by the House of Commons to ◊William and Mary before they replaced ◊James II on the throne. It made illegal the suspension of laws by royal authority without Parliament's consent; the power to dispense with laws; the establishment of special courts of law; levying money by royal prerogative without Parliament's consent; a standing army in peacetime without Parliament's consent. It also asserted a right to petition the sovereign, freedom of parliamentary elections, freedom of speech in parliamentary debates, and the necessity of frequent parliaments. See ◊Constitution.

Bill of Rights in the USA, the first ten amendments (1791) to the American

◊constitution:
1 freedom of worship, of speech, of the press, of assembly, and to petition the government;
2 the right to keep and bear arms (which has hindered modern attempts to control illicit use of arms);
3 prohibits billeting of soldiers in private homes in peacetime;
4 forbids unreasonable search and seizure;
5 none to be 'deprived of life, liberty or property without due process of law' or be compelled in any criminal case to be a witness against himself (frequently quoted in the ◊McCarthy era);
6 the right to speedy trial, to call witnesses, and have defence counsel;
7 the right to trial by jury;
8 excessive bail or fines, or 'cruel and unusual punishment', not to be inflicted (used in recent times to oppose the death penalty);
9 and 10 safeguard to the states and people all rights not given to the central government.

Billy the Kid /ˈbɪli/ nickname of William H Bonney 1859–1881. American Wild West 'hero', a leader in the Lincoln County cattle war in New Mexico. He was sentenced to death for murdering a sheriff, but escaped (killing two guards), and was finally shot trying to escape being retaken.

Biloxi /bɪˈlɒksi/ industrial seaport (seafood canning) in Mississippi, USA; population (1970) 48,500. Named after a local Indian people.

bimetallic strip strip made from two metals each having a different coefficient of thermal expansion which therefore bends when subjected to a change in temperature. Used widely for temperature measurement and control.

bimetallism monetary system in which gold and silver both circulate together at a ratio fixed by the state, are coined by the ◊mint on equal terms, and are legal tender to any amount. Advocates of bimetallism have argued that the 'compensatory action of the double standard' makes for a currency more stable than one based only on gold, since the changes in the value of the two metals taken together may be expected to be less than the changes in one of them.

binary fission in biology, a form of asexual reproduction, whereby a single-celled organism divides into two smaller 'daughter' cells. It can also occur in a few simple multicellular organisms, such as sea anemones, producing two smaller sea anemones of equal size.

binary number system or *binary number code* a system of numbers to base 2 using combinations of the two digits 1 and 0. The value of any position in a binary number increases by powers of 2 (doubles) with each move from right to left (1,2,4,8,16, etc). For example, 1011 in the binary number system means $(1 \times 8) + (0 \times 4) + (1 \times 2) + (1 \times 1)$, which adds up to 11 in the everyday, ◊decimal system (which uses successive powers of 10). Binary numbers play a key role in modern digital ◊computers, where they form the basis of the internal coding of information, the values of bits (short for 'binary digits') being represented as on/off (1 and 0) states of switches and high/low voltages in circuits.

binary star a pair of stars moving in orbit around their common ◊centre of mass.

Billy the Kid Historic photograph of American outlaw William Bonney, Billy the Kid, who allegedly killed his first man at 12, and went on to commit 21 murders before he was shot by Sheriff Pat Garrett in 1881.

Observations show that most stars are binary, or even multiple, for example the nearest star to the Sun, ◊Alpha Centauri. A *spectroscopic binary* is a binary in which two stars are so close together that they cannot be seen separately, but their separate light spectra can be distinguished by a spectroscope.

binary weapon chemical weapon consisting of two substances which in isolation are harmless but when mixed together form a poisonous nerve gas. They are loaded into the delivery system independently, and combined after launch.

binding energy in physics, the amount of energy needed to break a ◊nucleus into the ◊neutrons and ◊protons that make it up. See ◊bond, chemical.

bingo game played with cards divided into randomly numbered squares. As numbers are called, the players mark off the appropriate squares until one has a complete line or 'full house' (hence the alternative name 'housey-housey'), and receives a prize.

binoculars an optical instrument for viewing an object with both eyes, for example, field-glasses and opera-glasses. The first binocular telescope was constructed by a Dutchman, H Lippershey, in 1608, but interest then lapsed until 1823, when the Dutch binocular telescope was reinvented by a Viennese optician, J Voigtlaender. Later development was largely due to E Abbé, of Jena, who at the end of the last century designed prism binoculars that foreshadowed the instruments of today, in which not only magnification but stereoscopic effect is

obtained. Use of prisms has the effect of 'folding' the light path, allowing for a compact design.

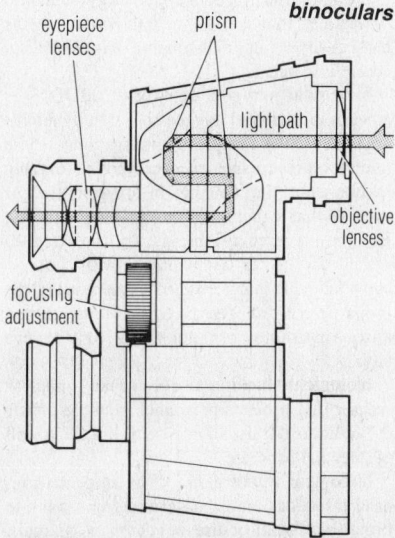

binoculars

binomial in algebra, an expression consisting of two terms, such as $a + b$, $a - b$. The *binomial theorem*, discovered by Isaac ◊Newton and first published in 1676, is a formula whereby any power of a binomial quantity may be found without performing the progressive multiplications.

binomial system of nomenclature in biology, the system in which all organisms are identified by a two-part Latinized name. Devised by the biologist ◊Linnaeus, it is also known as the Linnean System. The first name identifies the ◊genus, the second the ◊species within that genus. Usually the names are descriptive. Thus, the name of the dog, *Canis familiaris*, means the 'familiar species of the dog genus', *Canis* being Latin for 'dog'. Each species is defined by an officially designated *type specimen* housed at a particular museum. The rules for naming organisms in this way are specified in a number of International Codes of Taxonomic Nomenclature administered by two International Commissions on Nomenclature, one zoological and one botanical. See also ◊classification and ◊taxonomy.

binturong shaggy-coated mammal *Arctitis binturong*, the largest member of the mongoose family, nearly 1 m/3 ft long plus a long muscular tail with a prehensile tip. Mainly nocturnal and tree-living, the binturong is found in the forests of South East Asia, feeding on fruit, eggs and small animals.

Binyon /ˈbɪnjən/ Laurence 1869–1943. British poet. His verse volumes include *Lyric Poems* 1894 and *London Visions*, but he is best remembered for his ode *For the Fallen* 1914.

Bío-Bío /ˈbiːəʊ ˈbiːəʊ/ longest river in Chile; length 370 km/230 mi from its source in the Andes to its mouth on the Pacific. The name is an Araucanian-language term 'much water'.

biochemistry science concerned with the chemistry of living organisms: the structure and reactions of proteins (especially enzymes), nucleic acids, carbohydrates, lipids and so on.

The study of biochemistry has increased our knowledge of how animals and plants react with their environment, for example in creating and storing energy by photosynthesis, taking in food and releasing waste products, and passing on their characteristics through their genes. It is important in many areas of research, including medicine and agriculture.

biodegradable capable of being decomposed by living organisms, principally bacteria and fungi.

bioeconomics theory put forward in 1979 by Chicago economist Gary Becker that the concepts of sociobiology apply also in economics. The competitiveness and self-interest built into human genes are said to make capitalism an effective economic system, whereas the selflessness and collectivism proclaimed as the socialist ideal are held to be contrary to human genetic make-up and to produce an ineffective system.

bioengineering the application of engineering to biology and medicine. Common applications include the design and use of artificial limbs, joints and organs, including hip joints and heart valves.

biogenesis biological term coined in 1870 by T H Huxley to express the hypothesis that living matter always arises out of other similar forms of living matter. The now discredited opposite idea, that of ◊spontaneous generation or abiogenesis (that is, that living things may arise out of non-living matter) was generally held until then. Presumably there was abiogenesis in the original formation of primitive organic matter (for example, amino acids) from chemicals in the atmosphere during the earliest stages of the evolution of ◊life on earth.

biogeography the study of how plants and animals are distributed around the world, and the reasons for their distribution. More specifically, a theory describing the geographical distribution of ◊species developed by Robert MacArthur and E O ◊Wilson. The theory argues that for many species, ecological specializations mean that suitable habitats are patchy in their occurrence. Thus, for a dragonfly, ponds in which to breed are separated by large tracts of land, for eidelweiss adapted to alpine peaks, the deep valleys between cannot be colonized. Preferred habitats are thus like 'islands'. The theory also holds that the number of species that can coexist in a given 'island' is determined by its size. Biogeography also provides evidence for ◊continental drift.

biography an account of a person's life. When it is written by that person, it is an ◊autobiography. Biography can be simply a factual narrative, but it was also established as a literary form in the 18th–19th centuries.
Among ancient biographers are Xenophon, Plutarch, Tacitus, Suetonius, and the authors of the Gospels of the New Testament. Medieval biography was mostly devoted to religious edification and produced chronicles of saints and martyrs; among the biographies of laymen are Einhard's *Charlemagne* and Asser's *Alfred*. In England modern biography begins with the early Tudor period and such works as Roper's *Sir*

Thomas More. By the 18th century it became a literary form in its own right through Johnson's *Lives of the Most Eminent English Poets* 1779–81 and Boswell's biography of Johnson 1791. 19th-century biographers include Southey, Lockhart, Moore, Elizabeth Gaskell, J Forster, G H Lewes, Morley, and Carlyle, but the general tendency was to provide irrelevant detail and suppression of the more 'human' facts. Lytton Strachey's *Eminent Victorians* opened the modern era of frankness. 20th-century biographers include Churchill, Stefan Zweig, Richard Ellman (James Joyce and Oscar Wilde), Michael Holroyd (Lytton Strachey and Shaw), Martin Gilbert (Churchill), and Elizabeth Longford (Queen Victoria and Wellington).

The earliest biographical dictionary in the modern sense was that of Pierre Bayle 1696, followed during the 19th century by the development of national biographies in Europe, and the foundation of the *English Dictionary of National Biography* in 1882 and the *Dictionary of American Biography* in 1928.

Bioko /bɪˈəʊkəʊ/ island in the Bight of Bonny, West Africa, part of Equatorial Guinea. Formerly a Spanish possession, as Fernando Po, it was known 1973–7 as Macías Nguema.

biological clock a regular internal rhythm of activity, produced by mechanisms unknown, and not dependent on external time-signals. Such clocks are known to exist in almost all animals, and also in many plants, fungi and unicellular organisms. Some clocks may control several activities, but in higher organisms, there appears to be a series of clocks of graded importance. For example, although body temperature and activity cycles in human beings are normally 'set' to 24 hours, the two cycles may vary independently, showing that two clock mechanisms are involved. Research into the exact nature of these clocks is being directed into enzyme systems and membrane activity. Some biological clocks produce cycles of 28 days (lunar rhythms) or 365 days (annual rhythms). See also ◊biorhythms and ◊circadian rhythm.

biological computer proposed technology for ◊computing devices based on growing complex organic molecules (biomolecules) as components. Its theoretical basis is that cells, the building blocks of all living things, have chemical systems that can store and exchange electrons and therefore function as electrical components. It is currently the subject of long-term research.

biological control the control of pests such as insects and fungi through biological means, rather than the use of chemicals. This can include breeding resistant crop strains (for example, wheat varieties resistant to the fungi that cause 'rust'), inducing infertility in the pest (for example, by sterilizing male insects, or spraying with a juvenile hormone that prevents insect larvae maturing into adults), breeding viruses that attack the pest species, or introducing the pest's natural predator (for example, the release of a cactus-eating moth caterpillar to control the spread of prickly pear cactus in Australia). Biological control is preferable to chemical control of pests because it tends to be naturally self-regulating (for example, the predators of a

pest will die off when there are few pests left to eat), and it does not involve using ◊pesticides that affect human health. However, living systems are so complex that it is difficult to predict all the consequences of introducing a biological controlling agent.

biological oxygen demand (BOD) the amount of dissolved oxygen taken up by micro-organisms in a sample of water. Since these micro-organisms live by decomposing organic matter, and the amount of oxygen used is proportional to their number and metabolic rate, BOD can be used as a measure of the extent to which the water is polluted with organic compounds. It is determined by measuring the proportion of oxygen converted into carbon dioxide in a sample of water kept at 20°C for five days.

biological shield a shield around a nuclear reactor that protects personnel from the effects of ◊radiation. It usually consists of a thick wall of steel and concrete.

biological warfare use of living organisms, or of infectious material derived from them, to bring about death or disease in humans, animals, or plants. It was condemned by the Geneva Convention 1925, to which the United Nations has urged all states to adhere. See also ◊chemical warfare.

biology the science of life. The word was first used by the German physician Treviranus in 1802, and was popularized by Lamarck. Strictly speaking, biology includes all the life sciences, for example, anatomy and physiology, cytology, zoology and botany, ecology, genetics, biochemistry and biophysics, animal behaviour, embryology, and plant breeding. Although medical students such as Hippocrates, in the fifth century BC, made the first accurate biological observations, describing medicinally useful plants and their properties, attempts at a scientific physiology were bound to fail in the absence of scientific instruments, a tradition of experiment, and a body of organized knowledge with its own terminology. Only with the Renaissance did free enquiry come into its own. The 16th century saw the production of encyclopedias of natural history, such as that of Gesner (1516–65), and the beginnings of modern anatomy, notably at Padua under Vesalius (1514–64), who was succeeded by Fabricius. William Harvey laid the foundation of modern physiology by his work on the circulation of the blood – the first time any basic function of the body had been scientifically explained. ◊Linnaeus introduced a ◊binomial system of classification. During the 19th century, attempts to understand the origins of the great diversity of life forms gave rise to several theories of biological evolution, culminating in ◊Darwin's theory of evolution by natural selection. The ensuing debates over the processes of evolution then stimulated an interest in the new fields of ◊embryology and ◊genetics towards the end of the century. More recently still, the application of the principles of ◊chemistry to organic substances led to developments in ◊biochemistry and ◊molecular biology.

bioluminescence the production of light by living organisms. It is a feature of many fish, crustaceans, and other marine animals, especially deep-sea organisms. On land, bioluminescence is seen in some nocturnal insects such as glowworms and fireflies, and in certain bacteria and fungi. Light is usually produced by the oxidation of luciferin, a reaction catalysed by the ◊enzyme luciferase. This reaction is unique, being the only known biological oxidation which does not produce heat. Animal luminescence is involved in communication, camouflage, or luring prey, but its function in other organisms is unclear.

biomass the gross weight of organisms present in a given area. It may be specified for one particular species (for example, earthworm biomass), for a category of species (for example, herbivore biomass) or for all species (total biomass).

biome a large-scale natural assemblage of plants and animals living in a particular type of environment. Examples include the tundra biome and the desert biome.

biometry literally, the measurement of living things, but generally used to mean the application of mathematics to biology. The term is obsolete now, since mathematical or statistical work is an integral part of most biological disciplines.

bionics a word coined from 'biological electronics'. It refers to the design and development of artificial systems that imitate those of living things. The artificial bionic arm is an example. It uses electronics to amplify minute electrical signals generated in body muscles to work electric motors, which operate the joints of artificial fingers and wrist.

biophysics the application of physical laws to the properties of living organisms. Examples include using the principles of ◊mechanics to calculate the strength of bones and muscles, and ◊thermodynamics to study plant and animal energetics.

biopsy removal of tissue from a living body for the purpose of diagnostic examination.

biorhythms rhythmic changes in the physical state and activity patterns of animals. Biorhythms, mediated by ◊hormones, are seen in plants and animals which have seasonal activities, such as winter hibernation, spring flowering or breeding, or periodic migration. The hormonal changes themselves are often a response to changes in day length (◊photoperiodism); these changes signal the time of year to the animal or plant. Other biorhythms are innate, and continue even if external stimuli such as day length are removed. These include a 24-hour or ◊circadian rhythm, a 28-day or circalunar rhythm (corresponding to the phases of the moon) and even a year-long rhythm in some organisms. Such innate biorhythms are linked to an internal or ◊biological clock, whose mechanism is still poorly understood. Often both types of rhythm operate; thus many birds have a circalunar rhythm that prepares them for the breeding season, backed up by a photoperiodic response. There is also a theory that human activity is governed by three biorhythms: the *intellectual* (33 days), the *emotional* (28 days), and the *physical* (23 days). Certain days in each cycle are regarded as 'critical', especially if one coincides with that of another cycle. In the USA and Japan commercial firms have allegedly used the theory successfully in reducing accident rates by taking special precautions on critical days.

biosphere or *ecosphere* that region of the earth's surface (land and water), and the atmosphere above it, which can be occupied by living organisms.

biosynthesis the synthesis of ◊organic compounds from simple inorganic ones by living cells. One important biosynthetic reaction is the conversion of carbon dioxide and water to glucose by plants, during ◊photosynthesis. Other biosynthetic reactions produce cell constituents including ◊proteins and ◊fats. Biosynthesis requires energy, and in photosynthesis this is obtained from sunlight, but in most biosynthetic reactions it is supplied by ◊ATP. The term is also used in connection with ◊biotechnology processes.

biotechnology the industrial use of living organisms, to produce food, drugs or other products. Historically biotechnology has been largely restricted to the brewing and and baking industries, using ◊fermentation by yeast. Modern processes include fermentation to produce methane and alcohol for fuel from sugar or waste food products; the use of bacteria to remove heavy metals from polluted areas; and the production of protein from oil residues. The most recent advances in biotechnology involve ◊genetic engineering, in which single-celled organisms with modified ◊DNA are used to produce useful substances such as insulin.

biotin a ◊vitamin of the B-complex; it is found in many different kinds of food, with egg-yolk, liver and yeast containing large amounts.

birch tree of the genus *Betula*, including about 40 species, found in the cool temperate parts of the northern hemisphere, of which the white or silver birch *Betula pendula*, is the best-known. It is of great importance to man, as its timber is quick-growing and very durable. The bark is used for tanning and dyeing leather, and an oil is obtained from it.

Birch /bɜːtʃ/ John M 1918–1945. American Baptist missionary, commissioned by the US Air Force to carry out intelligence work behind the Chinese lines, where he was killed by the Communists; the US ultranationalist John Birch Society 1958 is named after him.

bird backboned animal of the class Aves, characterized by a combination of warm-blood, lung-breathing egg-laying, and the body covering of feathers. Birds are bipedal, the front limb modified to form a wing and retaining only three digits. The heart has four chambers, and the body is maintained at a high temperature (about 41°C, 106°F). Most birds fly, but some groups (such as ostriches) are flightless and others include flightless members. Birds have highly developed patterns of instinctive behaviour. Many communicate by sounds, or by visual displays, in connection with which many species are brightly coloured, particularly the males. Hearing and, especially, eyesight are well

BIRD CLASSIFICATION

The following simple classification of orders ranges approximately from the most 'primitive' to the most 'advanced', with a 'typical' bird or birds in bold letters. An estimate of the number of living species in each order is given for comparison.

Struthioformes	**ostrich** *1*
Rheiformes	**rhea** *2*
Casuariformes	**cassowary**, emu *4*
Apterygiformes	**kiwi** *3*
Tinamiformes	**tinamou** *46*
Podicipediformes	**grebe** *19*
Gaviiformes	**diver** *4*
Procellariiformes	**petrel**, albatross, shearwater *90*
Sphenisciformes	**penguin** *16*
Pelicaniformes	**pelican**, booby, cormorant
Ciconiiformes	**stork**, heron, ibis *116*
Anseriformes	**goose**, duck, swan *149*
Falconiformes	**falcon**, eagle, vulture *281*
Galliformes	**pheasant**, grouse, hoatzin *266*
Gruiformes	**crane**, bustard, rail *190*
Charadriiformes	**plover**, auk, gull *314*
Columbiformes	**pigeon**, sandgrouse *296*
Psittaciformes	**parrot**, cockatoo *328*
Cuculiformes	**cuckoo**, turaco *149*
Strigiformes	**owl** *136*
Caprimulgiformes	**nightjar**, frogmouth *97*
Apodiformes	**swift**, hummingbird *389*
Coliiformes	**mousebird** *6*
Trogoniformes	**trogon** *36*
Coraciiformes	**roller**, kingfisher, hornbill *196*
Piciformes	**woodpecker**, barbet, toucan *383*
Passeriforms	**sparrow**, bird of paradise, crow, jay, honeyeater, lark, lyrebird, shrike, starling, swallow, thrush, tit, warbler, wren. These 'perching birds' form the largest and most varied of all the orders *5159*.

developed, but the sense of smell is usually poor. Typically the eggs are brooded in a nest, and, on hatching, the young receive a period of parental care. There are nearly 8,500 species of birds, the biggest group of land vertebrates.

bird of paradise one of 40 species of crow-like birds, family *Paradiseidae*, native to New Guinea and neighbouring islands. Females are drably coloured, but the males have bright and elaborate plumage used in courtship display. Hunted almost to extinction for their plumage, they are now being actively conserved.

Birkenhead /'bɜːkənhed/ industrial seaport (shipbuilding) in Merseyside, England, on the Mersey estuary opposite Liverpool; population (1981) 123,884. The rail Mersey Tunnel 1886 and road Queensway Tunnel 1934 link Birkenhead with Liverpool.

history The first settlement grew up round a Benedictine priory, and Birkenhead was still a small village when William Laird established a small shipbuilding yard, the forerunner of the huge Cammell Laird yards. In 1829 the first iron vessel in England was built at Birkenhead. Wallasey dock, first of the series, was opened in 1847.

Birkenhead /'bɜːkənhed/ Frederick Edwin Smith, 1st Earl of Birkenhead 1872–1930. British Conservative politician. A flamboyant character, known as FE, he joined with ◊Carson in organizing armed resistance in Ulster to Irish Home Rule; he was Lord Chancellor 1919–22,

Birkenhead 'FE', the flamboyant Conservative politician and lawyer, Frederick Edwin Smith, 1st Earl of Birkenhead, organized armed resistance in Ulster to Irish Home Rule, and was a much criticized secretary for India 1924–28.

Tinamiformes tinamidae

Casuariformes cassowary

Apterygiformes kiwi

Rheiformes rhea

Struthioniformes ostrich

Spheniciforme penguin

Anseriformes goose

Procellariiformes petrel

Podicipediformes grebe

Pelecaniformes pelican

Galliformes pheasant

Ciconiiformes stork

Gruiformes crane

Charadriiformes plover

Falconiformes falcon

Strigiformes owl

Columbiformes pigeon

Cuculiformes cuckoo

Gaviiformes diver

Psittaciformes parrot

Caprimulgiformes nightjar

Apodidae swift

Coliiformes mousebird

Trogoniformes trogon

Coraciiformes kingfisher

Piciformes woodpecker

Passeriformes starling

Passeriformes thrush

and a much criticized secretary for India 1924–28.

Birmingham /'bɜːmɪŋəm/ industrial city (motor vehicles – British Leyland – machine tools, aerospace control systems, plastics, chemicals, food) in the West Midlands, second largest city of the UK; two universities; population (1981) 920,500.

features National Exhibition Centre at Bickenhill 1976; Aston University is linked with a ◊science park; a school of music and symphony orchestra; the art gallery has a Pre-Raphaelite collection; the repertory theatre was founded 1913 by Sir Barry Jackson (1897–1961). Lawn tennis was invented here. Sutton Park, in the residential suburb of Sutton Coldfield, has been a public country recreational area since the 16th century.

history As mayor, Joseph ◊Chamberlain carried out reforms in the 1870s.

Birmingham /'bɜːmɪŋhæm/ industrial city (iron, steel, chemicals, building materials, cotton textiles) and commercial centre in Alabama, USA; University of Alabama; population (1984) 280,000.

Biro /'bɪrəʊ/ Lazlo 1900–1985. Hungarian-born Argentinian who invented a ballpoint pen in 1944. His name became generic for ballpoint pens in the UK.

Birobijan /ˌbɪrəbɪ'dʒɑːn/ industrial town (sawmills, clothing) in Kharabovsk Territory, E USSR, near the Chinese border, capital of the Jewish Autonomous Region 1928–51 (sometimes also called Birobijan); population (1981) 72,000.

birth the act of producing young individuals from within the body of female animals. Both ◊viviparous and ◊ovoviviparous animals give birth to young. See also ◊pregnancy.

Birtwistle /'bɜːtwɪsl/ Harrison 1934– . British avant-garde composer. He has specialized in chamber music, for example, his chamber opera *Punch and Judy* 1967, and *Down by the Greenwood Side* 1969; orchestral works include *The Triumph of Time* 1972 and *Silbury Air* 1977; he has also written one large-scale opera *The Mask of Orpheus* 1986 and has experimented with electronic music. His *Chronometer* 1972 is based on clock sounds.

Biscay, Bay of /'bɪskeɪ/ bay of the Atlantic between N Spain and W, known for rough seas and exceptionally high tides.

biscuit a crisp, flat cake, consisting of flour, sometimes sugar, and fat. Other ingredients are used to give variety of flavour – such as eggs, milk, coconut, almonds, and spices. In the USA the word biscuit refers to something resembling a scone, and the British biscuit is referred to as a cracker or cookie. *Biscuitware* is pottery that has not been glazed.

bishop /'bɪʃəp/ clergyman (Greek 'overseer') next in rank to an ◊archbishop in the Roman Catholic, Greek Orthodox and Anglican Churches. Originally, they were chosen by the congregation, but in the Roman Catholic Church are appointed by the Pope, although in some countries, such as Spain, the political authority nominates appointees. In the Greek Orthodox Church bishops must be unmarried, and so are always monks. In the Church of England the Prime Minister selects bishops on the advice of the Archbishop of Canterbury; when a diocese is very large, assistant (suffragan) bishops are appointed.

Biskra /'bɪskrɑː/ oasis town in Algeria on the edge of the Sahara; population (1968) 60,000.

Bismarck /'bɪzmɑːk/ Otto Eduard Leopold, Prince von Bismarck 1815–1898. German politician. Ambitious to establish Prussia's hegemony inside Germany and eliminate the influence of Austria, he became foreign minister in 1862. He secured Austria's support for his successful war of 1863–64 against Denmark, then in 1866 went to war against Austria and its allies, his victory forcing Austria out of the German Bund, and unifying the North German states in the North German Confederation under his own chancellorship in 1867. He then defeated France, under Napoleon III, in the Franco-Prussian War of 1870, proclaimed the German Empire in 1871, and annexed ◊Alsace-Lorraine. He tried to secure his work by a Triple Alliance (1881) with Austria and Italy, but ran into difficulties at home with the Roman Catholic Church and the Socialist movement, and was dismissed by William II in 1890.

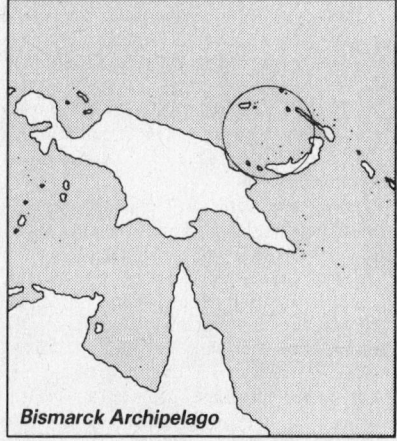

Bismarck Archipelago

Bismarck Archipelago /'bɪzmɑːk/ group of over 200 islands in SW Pacific Ocean, part of ◊Papua New Guinea; area 49,660 sq km/19,200 sq. mi. Largest island New Britain.

bismuth a pinkish-white metallic element, symbol BI, atomic weight 208.98, atomic number 83. It is a poor conductor of heat and electricity and is used in alloys of low melting point, and in medical compounds to soothe gastric ulcers.

bison type of wild cattle, of which there are two species. The *European bison* or *wisent Bison bonasus* is about 2 m/7 ft high and weighs a tonne. Mainly a woodland animal, only a few protected herds survive. The *American bison* (often known as 'buffalo') *Bison bison* is slightly smaller, has a heavier mane and more sloping hindquarters, but is the same brown colour. Formerly roaming the prairies in vast numbers, it was almost exterminated in the 19th century, but survives in protected areas.

Bissau /bɪ'sau/ capital and chief port of Guinea-Bissau; population (1979) 109,500.

bit in computing, a unit of information; a *bi*nary dig*it* or place in a binary number. See also ◊byte.

Bithynia /bɪ'θɪnɪə/ district of north west Asia which became a Roman province in 74 BC.

bittern name given to several small herons, in particular the common bittern *Botaurus stellaris* of Europe and Asia. It is shy, stoutly built, has a streaked camouflage pattern and a loud booming call. An inhabitant of marshy country, it is less abundant in Britain than it was, but remains in fen country where it is protected.

bittersweet alternative name for the woody ◊nightshade plant.

bitumen an impure mixture of hydrocarbons, including such deposits as petroleum, ◊asphalt and natural gas, although sometimes the term is restricted to a soft kind of pitch resembling asphalt. Solid bitumen may have arisen as a residue from the evaporation of petroleum. If evaporation took place from a pool or lake of petroleum, the residue may form a pitch or asphalt lake, such as the asphalt lake in Trinidad. Bitumen was used by the ancients as a mortar, and by the Egyptians for embalming.

bivalent in biology, a name given to the pair of homologous chromosomes during reduction division (◊meiosis). In chemistry the term is sometimes used to describe an element or group with a ◊valency of two, although the term 'divalent' is more common.

bivalve marine or freshwater mollusc in which the body is enclosed between two shells hinged together by a ligament on the dorsal side of the body. The shell is closed by strong 'adductor' muscles. Ventrally, a retractile 'foot' can be put out to assist movement in mud or sand. Two large plate-like gills are used for breathing and also, with the ◊cilia present on them, make a mechanism for collecting the small particles of food on which bivalves depend. The bivalves form one of the five classes of molluscs, the Lamellibranchiata, otherwise known as Bivalvia or Pelycypoda, containing about 8,000 species.

Bizerta /bɪ'zɜːtə/ industrial port (metal, oil) in Tunisia.

Bizet /'biːzeɪ/ Georges (Alexandre César Léopold) 1838–1875. French composer. Born near Paris, he studied at the Paris Conservatoire and won the Grand Prix de Rome in 1857. On his return from Italy he became known as a pianist, and began to compose operas, among them *Les Pêcheurs de perles/The Pearl Fishers* 1863, and *La Jolie Fille de Perth/The Fair Maid of Perth* 1866. He also wrote the concert overture *Patrie*, and incidental music to Daudet's *L'Arlésienne*. The latter forms the material of two well-known orchestral suites. His operatic masterpiece *Carmen* was produced a few months before his death in 1875.

Bismarck Prusso-German politician Prince Otto von Bismarck established his popularity in Germany by whipping up nationalist fervour and advocating military power to achieve prosperity, as in his famous 'blood and iron' exhortation to parliament, 1886.

Bizet French composer Georges Bizet's best known work is the opera *Carmen* 1845. It proved too robust at first for French society and achieved its reputation in England, where it was admired for its delicate orchestration and remarkable operatic intensity.

Bizonia name given to the unified British and US occupied zones of Germany after l Jan 1947. This unification was brought about largely by increasing East-West tensions and the need for integrated economic planning. Bizonia became a Tri-zone in Apr 1948 with the inclusion of the French zone.

Björneborg /ˌbjɜːnəˈbɔːri/ Swedish name of the town of ◊Pori, Finland.

Björnson /ˈbjɜːnsɒn/ Björnstjerne 1832–1910. Norwegian novelist, playwright, poet, and journalist. His plays, in the realist school, and dealing with politics and sexual morality amongst other themes, include *The Newly Married Couple* 1865 and *Beyond Human Power* 1883. Amongst his novels is *In God's Way* 1889. In 1903 he received the Nobel Prize for Literature.

black term used to describe a member of the indigenous people of Africa south of the Sahara, today distributed around the world. In the UK and some other countries (but not the US) the term is sometimes also used for people originally from the Indian sub-continent. The term black, at one time considered offensive by many people, was first adopted by black militants in the US in the mid-1960s to emphasize ethnic pride; they rejected the terms 'colored' and Negro as euphemistic. It has since become the preferred term in the US and largely in the UK.

history the history of most black people outside ◊Africa begins with ◊slavery, and is largely one of oppression and survival. Black people were first brought to the West Indies from Africa in large numbers as slaves by Spaniards in the early 16th century, and to the North American mainland in the early 17th century as indentured servants and subsequently as slaves to work on southern plantations. Although blacks fought beside whites in the American Revolutionary War, the US Constitution ratified 1788 protected the slave trade, and slaves had no ◊civil rights. Slavery was gradually abolished in the northern US states during the early 19th century, but as the foundation of the southern economy it was one of the issues that led to the secession of the southern states, which provoked the American ◊Civil War 1861–65. During the Civil War about 200,000 blacks fought in the Union (Northern) Army, but in segregated units led by white officers.

The Emancipation Proclamation 1863 of President Abraham Lincoln officially freed the slaves (about four million); it could not be enforced until the Union victory 1865 and the period after the war known as ◊Reconstruction. Freed slaves were often resented by poor whites as economic competitors, particularly in the South, and vigilante groups such as the ◊Ku Klux Klan were formed to intimidate them. In addition, although freed slaves had full US citizenship under the 14th Amendment to the Constitution, and were thus entitled to vote, they were often disenfranchised in practice by literacy tests and poll taxes.

A 'separate but equal' policy was established when the US Supreme Court ruled 1896 that segregation was legal if equal facilities were provided for blacks and whites. This ruling was overturned in 1954, with the Supreme Court decision outlawing segregation in state schools, which led to a historic confrontation in Little Rock, Arkansas, in 1957 when Governor Orval Faubus attempted to prevent black pupils from entering Central High School and President Eisenhower sent federal troops to enforce their right to attend.

Another landmark in the struggle for civil rights was the ◊Montgomery bus boycott in Alabama 1955; it also first brought Martin Luther ◊King to national attention.

By the early 1960s the civil rights movement had gained impetus, largely under the leadership of King, who in 1957 had founded the ◊Southern Christian Leadership Conference, a coalition group advocating non-violence. Moderate groups such as the ◊National Association for the Advancement of Colored People had been active since early in the century; for the first time they were joined in large numbers by whites, particularly students, as in the historic march converging on Washington DC 1963 from all over the US. At about this time, impatient with the lack of results gained through moderation, the militant ◊Black Power movement began to emerge, as in the Black Panther Party founded 1966, and black separatist groups such as the ◊Black Muslims gained support.

Increasing pressure led to the passage of civil rights acts 1964 and 1968 and the voting rights act 1965 under President Johnson, which guaranteed equal rights under the law and prohibited discrimination in public facilities, schools, employment, and voting. However, in the 1980s, despite legislation and affirmative action (positive discrimination), in practice blacks, who comprise some 12 per cent of the US population, continued to suffer discrimination and inequality of opportunities, particularly in education, employment, and housing. Nevertheless, the positive contributions of individual blacks in most fields, including the arts, the sciences, and politics, have played an important part in US history.

Unlike the US, England did not have a history of slavery at home; Britain outlawed the slave trade 1807 and abolished slavery in the British Empire 1833. In the UK only a tiny proportion of the population was black until after World War II, when immigration from Commonwealth countries increased. Legislation such as the Race Relations Act 1976 specifically outlawed discrimination on grounds of race and emphasized the official policy of equality of opportunity in all areas, and the Commission for Racial Equality was established 1977 to work towards eliminating discrimination; nevertheless, there is still considerable evidence of ◊racism in British society as a whole. The Swann Report on education 1985 emphasized that Britain was a multicultural society, and suggested various ways in which teachers could ensure that black children were able to reach their full potential. Black people are now beginning to take their place in public life in the UK; the election of Diane Abbott as Britain's first black woman member of parliament 1987 was a notable example.

Black /blæk/ Davidson 1884–1934. Canadian anatomist. In 1927, when professor of anatomy at the Union Medical College, Peking, he unearthed the remains of ◊Peking man, a very early human.

Black /blæk/ Joseph 1728–1799. Scottish physicist and chemist, who in 1754 discovered carbon dioxide (which he called fixed air). Born at Bordeaux, of Scottish descent, he qualified as a doctor in Edinburgh. In chemistry he prepared the way for ◊Cavendish, ◊Priestley, and ◊Lavoisier – and in physics, by his investigations (1761) of latent heat and specific heat, he laid the foundation for the work of his pupil James ◊Watt.

Black Scottish chemist and physicist Joseph Black, by Tassie in 1788. Black trained and practised as a doctor, and his investigations into latent and specific heat inspired his pupil James Watt.

Black /blæk/ James 1924– . British physiologist, director of therapeutic research at Wellcome Laboratories (near London) from 1978. He was active in the development of ◊beta-blockers and anti-ulcer drugs. Knighted 1981.

Black and Tans nickname of a specially raised force of military police employed by the British in 1920–21 to combat the Sinn Feiners (Irish nationalists) in Ireland; the name was derived from the colours of the uniforms.

black-beetle name given to a ◊cockroach, although cockroaches belong to an entirely different order of insects (Dictyoptera) from the beetles (Coleoptera).

blackberry fruit of the bramble *Rubus fruticosus*, a prickly shrub, closely allied to the raspberry. It is native to the northern parts of the Old World, is exceedingly abundant in Britain, and produces pink or white blossoms and edible, black, compound fruits. There are 400 or so types of bramble found in Britain. In the past some have been regarded as distinct species.

blackbird bird *Turdus merula* of the thrush family in which the male is black with yellow bill and eyelids, the female dark brown with a dark beak. Found across Europe to East Asia, the blackbird adapts well to human presence and gardens, and is one of the commonest British birds. About 25 cm/10 in long, it lays three to five blue-green eggs with brown spots. lts song is rich and flute-like. American 'blackbirds' belong to a different family of birds, the Icteridae.

black body a hypothetical object in physics that completely absorbs all radiation falling on it. It is also a perfect emitter of temperature-dependent radiation. For a perfect black body, the radiation E emitted at all wavelengths is proportional to the fourth power of its absolute temperature T; that is, $E = KT^4$, where K is the Stefan-Boltzmann constant (and the equation represents the Stefan-Boltzmann law).

black box popular name for the robust box, usually orange-painted for easy recovery, containing an aeroplane's flight and voice recorders, monitoring the plane's behaviour and the crew's conversation, thus providing valuable clues as to the cause of a disaster.

blackbuck an antelope (*Antilope cervicapra*) found in central and north west India. It is related to the gazelles, from which it differs in having the horns spirally twisted. The males are black above and white beneath, whereas the females and young are fawn-coloured above. It is about 76 cm/2.5 ft in height.

Blackburn /'blækbɜːn/ industrial town (engineering) in Lancashire, England, 32 km/20 mi NW of Manchester; population (1981) 88,000. It was pre-eminently a cotton-weaving town until World War II.

blackcap ◊warbler *Sylvia atricapilla* in which the male has a black cap, the female a reddish-brown one. About 14 cm/5.5 in long, the blackcap likes wooded areas , and is a summer visitor to Northern Europe.

blackcock type of large grouse *Lyrurus tetrix* found on moors and in open woods in N Europe and Asia. The male is mainly black with a lyre-shaped tail, and up to 54 cm/1.7 ft. The female is speckled brown and only 40 cm/1.3 ft.

Black Country /blæk/ central area of England, around and to the N of Birmingham, which in 1974 became the new county of West Midlands. Heavily industrialized, it gained its name in the 19th century from its belching chimneys, but pollution laws have given it a changed aspect.

Black Death modern name (first used in England in the early 19th century) for the great epidemic of bubonic ◊plague, which spread from China to devastate Europe in the 14th century It completely demoralized society, and it is estimated that one-third to one-half of the population of England succumbed in 1348–49. The disease remained endemic in London for the next three centuries, the last great outbreak being that of 1665, when about 100,000 of the 400,000 inhabitants died.

black earth name applied to the exceedingly fertile soil which covers a belt of land in Europe and Asia, extending from Bohemia through Hungary, Rumania, South Russia, and Siberia, as far as Manchuria. It is a kind of ◊loess, and was laid down when the great Eurasian inland ice sheet melted at the close of the last ice age.

black economy the hidden economy of a country, which includes undeclared earnings from a second job ('moonlighting'), and

enjoyment of undervalued goods and services (such as company 'perks'), designed for tax evasion purposes. In industrialized countries, it is reckoned to equal, on average, about 10 per cent of ◊gross domestic product.

Blackett /'blækɪt/ Patrick Maynard Stuart, Baron Blackett 1897–1974. British physicist. He was awarded a Nobel prize in 1948 for work in cosmic radiation and his perfection of the Wilson cloudchamber. He was president of the Royal Society 1965–70, was awarded the Order of Merit in 1967 and became a life peer 1969.

blackfly plant-sucking insect, a type of ◊aphid.

Blackfoot /'blækfʊt/ member of a ◊Plains Indian people who now live in Saskatchewan, Canada. They are so called because of their black moccasins.

Black Forest /blæk/ mountainous region of coniferous forest in Baden-Württemberg, West Germany. Bounded W and S by the Rhine, which separates it from the Vosges, it has an area of 4,660 sq km/1,800 sq mi and rises to 1,493 m/4,905 ft in the Feldberg.

Blackheath /,blæk'hiːθ/ English common which gives its name to a residential suburb of London partly in Greenwich, partly in Lewisham. Wat Tyler encamped on Blackheath in the 1381 Peasants' Revolt.

Black Hills /blæk/ mountains in Dakota and Wyoming, USA.

black hole a hypothetical object whose ◊gravity would be so great that nothing could escape from it, not even light. Anything that fell into a black hole would not be seen again. Black holes are thought to form when massive stars, much heavier than our Sun, shrink at the ends of their lives. A black hole can grow by sucking in more matter, including other stars, from the space around it. Matter that falls into a black hole is squeezed to infinite density at the centre of the hole. Black holes can be detected because gas falling towards them becomes so hot that it emits ◊X-rays. Satellites above the Earth's atmosphere have detected X-rays from a number of objects in our Galaxy that might be black holes. Massive black holes containing the mass of millions of stars are thought to lie at the centres of ◊quasars. Microscopic black holes may have been formed in the chaotic conditions of the ◊Big Bang. The English physicist Stephen ◊Hawking has shown that such tiny black holes could 'evaporate' and explode in a flash of energy.

blackmail the criminal offence of the unwarranted demanding of money with menaces of violence and other injury, or of exposure of some misconduct on the part of the victim (from French *maille* rent, paid in labour or base coin); punishable in the UK with 14 years' imprisonment.

black market illegal trade in food or other rationed goods, for example, petrol and clothing, during World War II and after.

Blackmore /'blækmɔː/ R(ichard) D(oddridge) 1825–1900. British novelist, author of *Lorna Doone* 1869, a romance set in Exmoor in the late 17th century.

Black Mountain Poets group of experimental US poets of the 1950s who were

linked with the Black Mountain liberal arts college, North Carolina. They rejected the formalistic constraints of rhyme and metre. Leading members included Charles Olsen (1910–70) and Robert Creeley (1926–   ).

Black Mountains /blæk/ group of hills in S Powys, Wales, overlooking the Wye Valley and honeycombed with caves discovered in 1966.

Black Muslims member of a religious group founded 1929 in the USA and led from 1934 by Elijah Muhammad (1897–1975) (then Elijah Poole) after a vision of Allah. Its growth from 1946 as a black separatist organization was due to Malcolm X (1926–65), son of a Baptist minister, who in 1964 broke away and founded his own Organization for Afro-American Unity, preaching 'active self-defence'.

Black National State an area set aside in the Republic of South Africa for development to full self-government by black Africans in accordance with the theory of plural democracy (see ◊apartheid): before 1980 these states were known as black homelands or bantustans. They comprise less than 14% of the country; tend to be in arid areas, though some have mineral wealth; and may be in scattered blocks. Those that have so far reached nominal independence are Transkei 1976, Bophuthatswana 1977, Venda 1979, Ciskei 1981. They are not recognized outside South Africa because of their racial basis, and 11 million blacks live permanently in the country's white-designated areas.

Blackpool /'blækpuːl/ seaside resort in Lancashire, England, 45 km/28 mi N of Liverpool; population (1981) 148,000. Amusement facilities include 11 km/7 mi of promenades, known for their 'illuminations' of coloured lights, fun fairs, and a tower 152 m/500 ft high. Political party conferences are often held here.

black power general term for a concept which arose in the USA during the 1960s, when existing ◊civil-rights organizations such as the National Association for Advancement of Colored People and the Southern Christian Leadership Conference were seen to be ineffective in producing major change in the status of black people. Stokely Carmichael then advocated the exploitation of political and economic power and abandonment of nonviolence, with a move towards the type of separatism first developed by the ◊Black Muslims. Leaders such as Martin Luther King rejected this approach, but the Black Panther Party adopted it fully and achieved nationwide influence. So named because the panther, though not generally aggressive, will fight to the death under attack, it was founded in 1966 by Huey Newton and Bobby Seale, and put forward as the ultimate aim establishment of a separate black state in the USA established by a black plebiscite under the aegis of the UN. Following a National Black Political Convention in 1972 a National Black Assembly was established to exercise pressure on the Democratic and Republican parties.

Black Prince name given to ◊Edward, Prince of Wales, eldest son of Edward III of England.

Black Sea inland sea in SE Europe, linked with the seas of Azov and Marmara, and via the

Dardanelles with the Mediterranean. Uranium deposits beneath it are among the world's largest.

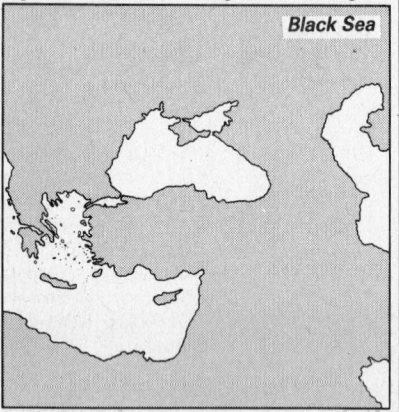

Black Sea

blacksnake name given to several secies of snake. The Australian **blacksnake** *Pseudechis porphyriacus* is a venomous snake of the cobra family found in damp forests and swamps in East Australia. The American **blacksnake** *Coluber constrictor* from the east of the USA is a relative of the grass snake about 1.2 m/4 ft long, and without venom.

blackthorn densely branched spiny bush, *Prunus spinosa*, family Rosaceae, with white blossom on black and as yet leafless branches in early spring. The sour blue-black fruit sloe is used to flavour sloe gin.

Black Thursday the name given to the day of a Wall Street stock market crash, 29 Oct 1929, followed by the worst depression in American history.

Blackwell /'blækwel/ Elizabeth 1821–1910. First British woman doctor, and first woman to gain a medical degree anywhere. Taken to the USA at 11, she qualified there in 1849, and was admitted to the English medical register in 1859.

black widow North American spider *Latrodectus mactans*. The male is small and harmless, but the female is 1.3 cm/0.5 in long with a red patch below the abdomen and a powerful venomous bite. The bite causes pain and fever in human victims, but they usually recover.

bladder hollow elastic-walled organ of amphibians, mammals and some reptiles in which urine accumulates. Urine enters the bladder through two ureters, one leading from each kidney, and leaves it through the urethra. See also ◊urinary system.

bladderwort carnivorous aquatic plant genus *Utricularia* of the family Lentibulariaceae, which feeds on small crustacea.

Blagonravov /ˌblægənrəˈvɒf/ Anatoly Arkadievich 1894–1975. Russian specialist in rocketry and instrumentation. He directed the earth satellite programme leading to the launching of Sputnik I and II.

Blake /bleɪk/ Robert 1599–1657. British admiral. In 1652 he won several engagements against the Dutch before being defeated by Tromp off Dungeness, and revenged himself in 1653 by defeating the Dutchman off Portsmouth and the northern Foreland. In 1654 he bombarded Tunis, the stronghold of the Barbary corsairs, and in 1657 captured the Spanish

treasure fleet in Santa Cruz.
bombarded Tunis, the stronghold of the Barbary corsairs, and in 1657 captured the Spanish treasure fleet in Santa Cruz.

Blake /bleɪk/ William 1757–1827. British poet and artist. Born in Soho, London, he was apprenticed to an engraver 1771–78, and studied at the Royal Academy under ◊Reynolds, of whom he formed a very low opinion. His works, for which he engraved both text and illustrations himself, embody his own mystic mythology, and include *Songs of Innocence* 1789, *The Marriage of Heaven and Hell* 1793, *Songs of Experience* 1794, and *Milton* 1804 (his most famous lines 'And did those feet in ancient time', set to music by ◊Parry, are taken from the preface). He also produced illustrations for *Paradise Lost*, *The Book of Job*, and ◊Dante's *Divine Comedy*.

drummer, famous for his rolls and explosions. He formed and led the Jazz Messengers from 1955 onwards, and widely explored and expanded percussion possibilities, including the assimilation of African rhythms.

Blanc /blɒŋ/ Louis 1811–1882. French socialist. In 1839 he founded the *Revue du progrès*, in which he published his *Organisation du travail*, advocating the establishment of cooperative workshops and other socialist schemes. He was a member of the provisional government of 1848 (see ◊revolutions of 1848) and from its fall lived in England until 1871.

Blanchard /blɒnˈʃɑː/ Jean Pierre 1753–1809. French balloonist, who made the first balloon flight across the Channel with Dr John Jeffries in 1785. He also made the first balloon flight in the USA in 1793.

Blake English poet and artist William Blake was a mystic and visionary. His paintings and engravings include illustrations to Dante's *Divine Comedy* and Milton's *Paradise Lost*: in this example from Book One of *Paradise Lost*, Satan arouses the rebel angels after the fall.

Blakey /'bleɪki/ Art 1919– . (Muslim name: Abdullah Ibn Buhaina). Dynamic US jazz

blank verse in literature, the unrhymed iambic pentameter or ten syllable line of five stresses. Originated by the Italian Gian Giorgio Trissino, in his tragedy *Sofonisba* 1514–15, it was introduced to England by the Earl of Surrey, about 1540, and developed by Marlowe. Blank verse was used with increasing freedom by Shakespeare, Fletcher, Webster, and Middleton. It was remodelled by Milton, who was imitated in the 18th century by Thomson, Young, and Cowper, and revived in the early 19th century by Wordsworth, Shelley, and Keats, and later by Tennyson, Browning, and Swinburne. More recent exponents of blank verse in English include Hardy, T S Eliot, and Robert Frost.

Blanqui /blɒŋˈkiː/ Louis Auguste 1805–1881. French revolutionary politician. He formulated the theory of the 'dictatorship of the proletariat', used by ◊Marx, and spent a total of 33 years in prison for insurrection. He became a martyr figure for the French workers' movement.

Blantyre-Limbe /ˈblæntaɪə ˈlɪmbeɪ/ the chief industrial and commercial centre of Malawi, in the Shire highlands; university 1965; population (1985) 355,000. It was formed by the union of the towns of Blantyre (named after the explorer Livingstone's birthplace) and Limbe in 1959.

Blarney /ˈblɑːni/ small town in County Cork, Republic of Ireland, possessing, inset in the wall of the 15th-century castle, the *Blarney Stone*, reputed to give those kissing it persuasive speech.

Blashford-Snell /ˈblæʃfəd ˈsnel/ John 1936– . British soldier-explorer. From 1963 he organized Adventure Training at Sandhurst. His expeditions have included the first descent and exploration of the Blue Nile 1968; the trans-Americas journey from Alaska to Cape Horn, crossing the ◊Darien Gap for the first time 1971–72; and the first complete navigation of the Zaire river 1974–75.

Blasis /blæˈsiː/ Carlo 1797–1878. Italian ballet teacher of French extraction. He had a successful career as a dancer in Paris and in Milan, where he established a famous dancing school 1837. His famous treatise on the art of dancing, *Traité élémentaire, théoretique et pratique de l'art de la danse* 1820, forms the basis of classical dance training.

blasphemy (Greek 'evil-speaking') written or spoken insult directed against religious belief or sacred things with deliberate intent to outrage believers. Blasphemy against the Christian church is still an offence in English common law, despite several recommendations (for example by the Law Commission in 1985) that it should be abolished, or widened to apply to all religious faiths. The most recent case was in 1977, when the magazine *Gay News* and its editor Denis Lemon were successfully prosecuted for publishing a poem that suggested Christ was a homosexual.

blast furnace furnace in which the temperature is raised by the injection of an air blast. It is employed in the extraction of metals from their ores, particularly pig-iron from iron ore. The principle has been known for thousands of years, but the modern blast furnace is a heavy engineering development combining a number of special techniques.

blastocyst in mammals, a stage in the development of the ◊embryo that is roughly equivalent to the ◊blastula of other animal groups.

blastomere in biology, a cell formed in the early stages as a fertilised ovum splits. See also ◊blastocyst.

blastula an early stage in the development of a fertilized egg, when the egg changes from a solid mass of cells to a hollow ball of cells (the blastula), containing a fluid-filled cavity (the *blastocoel*). See also ◊embryology.

Blaue Reiter, Der /ˈblaʊə ˈraɪtə/ German expressionist art movement 1911–14, named from the painting *Der blaue Reiter/The Blue Rider* by ◊Kandinsky, averse to academic rule and proclaiming the artist's 'inner necessity' for expression. The movement also included members of Die ◊Brücke.

Blavatsky /bləˈvætski/ Helena Petrovna (born Hahn) 1831–1891. Russian spiritualist and mystic, co-founder of the Theosophical Society (see ◊Theosophy) 1875, which has its headquarters near Madras. In Tibet she underwent spiritual training, and later became a Buddhist. Her books include *Isis Unveiled* 1877 and *The Secret Doctrine* 1888. She was declared a fraud by the London Society for Psychical Research 1885.

Blavatsky Russian 19th century theosophist Helena Blavatsky travelled widely in the East. She convinced a large following that she had intuitive insight into the divine nature, but her powers did not pass investigation by the Society for Psychical Research.

bleaching decolorization of coloured materials. Bleaching processes have been known from antiquity, especially those acting through sunlight. Both natural and synthetic pigments usually possess highly complex ◊molecules, the colour property often being due only to a part of the molecule. Bleaches usually attack only that small part, giving another substance similar in chemical structure but colourless. The two main types of bleaching agent are the *oxidizing bleaches*, which add oxygen and remove hydrogen, and include the ultraviolet rays in sunshine, hydrogen peroxide, and chlorine in household bleaches, and the *reducing bleaches* which add hydrogen or remove oxygen, for example sulphur dioxide.

bleak freshwater fish *Alburnus alburnus* of the carp family. Up to 20 cm/8 in long, usually less, it lives in still or slow-running clear water in Britain and Europe. In Eastern Europe its scales are used in preparing artificial pearls.

bleeding loss of blood from the circulation; see haemorrhage.

blending inheritance see ◊inheritance.

Blenheim /ˈblenɪm/ centre of a sheep-grazing area in the NE of South Island, New Zealand; population (1983) 18,300.

Blenheim, Battle of /ˈblenɪm/ battle on 13 Aug 1704 in which English troops under ◊Marlborough defeated the French and Bavarians near the Bavarian village of Blenheim (now in West Germany) on the left bank of the Danube.

blenny any fish of the family Blenniidae, mostly small fishes found on or near rocky shores, with elongated bodies tapering from head to tail, no scales, and long pelvic fins set far forward. The commonest British species is the *shanny Blennius pholis*.

Bleriot /ˈbleriəʊ/ Louis 1872–1936. French aviator who, in a monoplane of his own construction, made the first flight across the English Channel on 25 Jul 1909.

blesbok African antelope *Damaliscus albifrons* with curved horns, brownish body and a white blaze on the face. About 1 m/3ft high, it was seriously depleted in the wild at the end of the 19th century. A few protected herds survive in South Africa. It is farmed for meat.

Blessington /ˈblesɪŋtən/ Marguerite, Countess of Blessington 1789–1849. Irish writer. A doyenne of literary society, she published *Conversations with Lord Byron* 1834, travel sketches, and novels.

Bligh /blaɪ/ William 1754–1817. British admiral. He accompanied Captain ◊Cook on his second voyage 1772–74, and in 1787 commanded HMS *Bounty* on an expedition to the Pacific. On the return voyage the crew mutinied 1789, and cast Bligh adrift with 18 men in a boat. The mutineers settled in Tahiti and on Pitcairn Island, while Bligh brought his boat to Timor Island, near Java. He was appointed governor of New South Wales in 1805, where his discipline again provoked a mutiny 1808, but on returning to England he was made an admiral in 1811.

blight number of plant diseases caused mainly by parasitic species of ◊fungi, which produce a whitish appearance on leaf and stem surfaces, for instance *potato blight Phytophthora infestans*. General damage caused by aphids, pollution and so on to plants is also sometimes known as blight.

Blighty popular name for England among British troops in World War I, possibly from Hindi *bitayati* 'foreign' land.

Bleriot The pilot's licence of French aviator Louis Bleriot. He made the first flight across the English Channel on 25 Jul 1909 from Baraques to Dover in a small 24 horsepower monoplane.

Bligh The dreaded British sailor William 'Breadfruit' Bligh, 1792. He went to Tahiti with the *Bounty* to collect breadfruit. On the return journey in 1789 his men mutinied, leaving Captain Bligh and 18 men in a small craft, with no map and few provisions. They survived after drifting 5,822 km/3618 miles.

blimp term for an airship or barrage balloon. British lighter than air aircraft were divided in World War I into A-rigid, and B-limp (that is without rigid internal framework), a barrage balloon therefore becoming known as a blimp. ◊Low, the cartoonist, adopted the name for his stuffy character Colonel Blimp.

blindness complete absence or impairment of sight. It may be caused by heredity, accident, disease, or deterioration with age. Education of the blind was begun by Valentin Haüy, who published a book with raised lettering 1784, and founded a school. Aids to the blind include the use of the ◊Braille or ◊Moon alphabet in reading and writing, or of electronic devices now under development which convert print to recognizable mechanical speech; guide dogs; and sonic torches.

blind spot the area where the optic nerve and blood vessels pass through the retina of the ◊eye. Because there are no light-sensitive cells in this part of the retina, no visual image can be formed. Thus the organism is blind to objects that fall in this part of the visual field.

Bliss /blɪs/ Arthur (Drummond) 1891–1975. British composer, born in London. He became Master of the Queen's Musick in 1953. Works include *A Colour Symphony* 1922, music for ballets *Checkmate* 1937, *Miracle in the Gorbals* 1944, and *Adam Zero* 1946; an opera *The Olympians* 1949; and dramatic film music, including *Things to Come* 1935.

Blitzkrieg (German 'lightning war') a swift military campaign, as in 1939–41, when Hitler's Germany conquered Poland, France, Yugoslavia, and Greece, and advanced to Moscow. The abbreviation 'blitz' was applied to the German air raids on London 1940.

Blitzstein /'blɪtsstiːn/ Marc 1905–1964. US composer. Born in Philadelphia, he was a child prodigy as a pianist at the age of six. He served with the US Army 8th Air Force 1942–45, for which he wrote *The Airborne* 1946, a choral symphony. His operas include *The Cradle Will Rock* 1937.

Blixen /'blɪksən/ Karen, born Karen Dinesen 1885–1962. Danish writer. Much of her early adulthood was spent in Kenya running a coffee plantation, which provided the material for her autobiography *Out of Africa* 1937. In 1931 she returned to Denmark and began to write fiction, mainly in English, under the pen name Isak Dinesen. She is admired for her short stories, Gothic fantasies with a haunting, often mythic quality, published in such collections as *Seven Gothic Tales* 1934 and *Winters' Tales* 1942.

Bloch /blɒk/ Ernest 1880–1959. US composer, born in Geneva, Switzerland. He went to the USA in 1916 and became founder-director of the Cleveland Institute of Music 1920–25. He later taught at the San Francisco Conservatoire and at the University of California at Berkeley. His works include the lyrical drama *Macbeth* 1910, *Schelomo* for cello and orchestra 1916, five string quartets, and *Suite Hébraïque*, for viola and orchestra, 1953. He often used themes based on Jewish liturgical music and folk song.

Bloch /blɒk/ Felix 1905–1983. US physicist. Born in Zürich, he was professor of physics at Stanford University, USA, 1934–71, receiving a Nobel prize jointly with E M Purcell in 1952, for his work on nuclear magnetic resonance (NMR) spectroscopy.

block and tackle a type of ◊pulley.

Bloemfontein /'bluːmfɒnteɪn/ capital of the Orange Free State and judicial capital of the Republic of South Africa; population (1985) 204,000. Founded 1846.

Blois /blwɑː/ town on the river Loire in central France, with a château partly dating from the 13th century; population (1983) 49,500.

Blok /blɒk/ Alexander Alexandrovich 1880–1921. Russian poet of the Symbolist school, who backed the 1917 Revolution, as in his most famous poems *The Twelve* 1918, and *The Scythians* 1918, the latter appealing to the West to join in the revolution.

Blomberg /'blɒmbeak/ Werner von 1878–1946. German soldier and politician, minister of defence 1933–35, and minister of war and head of the *Wehrmacht* 1935–38 under Hitler's chancellorship. He was discredited by his marriage to a prostitute and dismissed in Jan 1938, enabling Hitler to exercise more direct control over the armed forces. In spite of his removal from office, Blomberg was put on trial in 1946 at Nuremberg.

Blondin /'blɒndɪn/ Charles 1824–1897. Assumed name of the French tightrope-walker Jean François Gravelet. He became world famous when he crossed Niagara Falls on a rope at a height of 49 m/160 ft in 1859, a feat which he repeated blindfolded and wheeling a barrow. He later performed in England.

blood liquid circulating in the arteries, veins, and capillaries of vertebrate animals, and the corresponding fluid in those invertebrates which possess a closed ◊circulatory system. In humans it makes up 5% of the body weight, occupying a volume of 5.5 litres/10 pints. It consists of a colourless, transparent liquid called *plasma*, containing microscopic cells of three main varieties: red cells, white cells and platelets. *Red cells* form nearly half the volume of the blood, with 5,000 billion cells per litre. Their red colour is caused by ◊haemoglobin, which takes oxygen from the air in the lungs, and yields it to the body tissues. *White cells* or ◊leucocytes are an important part of the body's immune system; some have the power to ingest invading bacteria and so protect the body from disease

Blondin The French rope-dancer Charles Blondin crossed the Niagara Falls on a tightrope in 1859, and later repeated his stunt with variations: blindfolded, with a wheelbarrow, with a man on his back, and on stilts.

(◊phagocytes); these also help to repair injured tissues. Others (◊lymphocytes) produce antibodies, which help provide ◊immunity. Blood *platelets* assist in the clotting of blood. Blood cells constantly wear out and die, and are replaced from the bone marrow. Dissolved in the plasma are salts, proteins, sugars, fats, hormones and fibrinogen, which are transported around the body, the last having a role in clotting. See also ◊blood group, ◊haemolymph.

Blood /blʌd/ Thomas 1618–1680. Irish adventurer, known as Colonel Blood. His most daring exploit was an attempt to steal the Crown Jewels from the Tower of London 1671.

blood group the classification of ◊blood types according to antigenic activity. Red blood cells of one individual may carry molecules on their surface which act as ◊antigens in another individual whose red blood cells lack these molecules. The two main antigens are designated A and B. These give rise to four blood groups; having A only (A), having B only (B), having both (AB), and having neither (O). These ABO blood groups were the first to be described, by Karl ◊Landsteiner, in 1902. Subsequent research revealed at least 14 main types of blood groupings, 11 of which are involved with induced ◊antibody production. Correct typing of blood groups is vital in transfusion since incompatible types of donor and recipient blood will result in blood clotting, with possible death of the recipient. Blood typing is also of importance in forensic science, cases of disputed paternity, and in anthropological studies, because different peoples or geographical populations have different distributions of blood group types. See also ◊rhesus factor.

bloodhound ancient breed of dog. Black and tan in colour, it has long, pendulous ears and distinctive wrinkles on the head. Its excellent

blood circulation

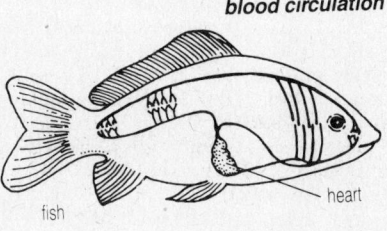

fish / heart

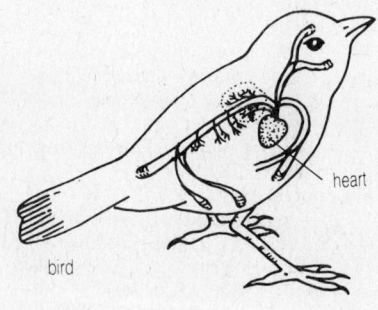

bird / heart

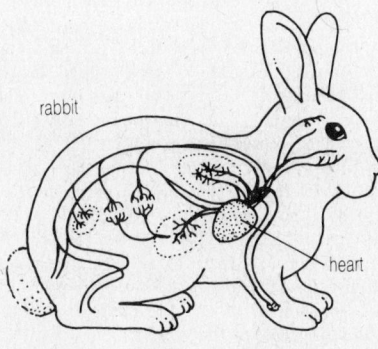

rabbit / heart

powers of scent have been employed in tracking and criminal work from very early times.

blood poisoning infection caused by bacteria or bacterial toxins present in the blood (septicaemia); treatment is by antibiotics.

blood pressure the pressure, or tension, of the blood in the arteries and veins of the ◊circulatory system due to the muscular activity of the heart. In mammals, the left ventricle of the ◊heart pumps blood into the arterial system. This pumping is assisted by waves of muscular contraction by the ◊arteries themselves, but resisted by the elasticity of the inner and outer walls of the same arteries. Pressure is greatest when the heart ventricle contracts (*systolic pressure*) and least when the ventricle is filling up with blood and pressure is solely maintained by the elasticity of the arteries (*diastolic pressure*). Blood pressure is measured in millimetres of mercury, with an instrument called a sphygmomanometer. Normal human blood pressure is around 120/80 mm Hg; the first number represents the systolic pressure and the second the diastolic. Large deviations from this figure usually indicate ill-health, and persistently

high blood pressure (hypertension) can contribute to a heart attack or kidney failure.

blood test any of a variety of tests made to detect levels of body chemicals, disease or foreign substances such as poisons or alcohol in the blood. Blood tests in commonest use are cell counts, determination of the time taken to coagulate (clot), and the chemical measurement of the major constituents of blood.

blood transfusion injection of blood into the circulation to treat conditions resulting from loss or impairment of blood, such as haemophilia, shock due to injury, or poisoning by carbon monoxide. The first human-to-human blood transfusion was made in 1818. Practically all blood transfusions are now made, not as formerly directly from donor to patient, but with blood stored at refrigerated temperature (treated with sodium citrate to prevent clotting). Unless used within 3 or 4 weeks, the stored blood has its red cells removed, and the remaining liquid is reduced to powder. This dried plasma is kept for emergency use. During World War II Birmingham University developed a blood plasma substitute, prepared by the large-scale fermentation of sugar. See also ◊plasmapheresis.

bloom whitish powdery or wax-like coating over the surface of certain fruits that easily rubs off with handling. It often contains ◊yeasts which live on the sugars in the fruit. The term bloom is also used to describe a rapid increase in number of certain species of algae found in lakes and ponds.

Bloom /bluːm/ Claire 1931– . British actress. Born in London, she first made her reputation in Shakespearian roles. Her films include *Richard III* and *The Brothers Karamazov*, and television appearances include *Brideshead Revisited* 1980.

Bloomer /'bluːmə/ Amelia Jenks 1818–1894. American advocate of women's rights. She introduced in 1849 a knee-length skirt combined with loose trousers gathered at the ankles, hence the name 'bloomers'. She published the magazine *The Lily* 1849–54, which campaigned for women's rights and dress reform, and lectured with Susan B ◊Anthony in New York.

Bloomsbury /'bluːmzbəri/ area in Camden, London, England, between Gower Street and High Holborn. It contains London University headquarters, the British Museum and the Royal Acadamy of Dramatic Arts. It was the home of the ◊Bloomsbury Group.

Bloomsbury Group name given to a group of writers and artists based in ◊Bloomsbury, London, between the world wars. The group included the artists Duncan Grant and Vanessa Bell, and the writers Lytton ◊Strachey and Leonard and Virginia ◊Woolf.

Blow /bləʊ/ John 1648–1708. English composer. He influenced ◊Purcell, his pupil, and wrote church music, for example the anthem 'I Was Glad when They Said unto Me' 1697. His masque *Venus and Adonis* 1685 is sometimes called the first English opera.

blowfly fly, genus *Calliphora*, also known as *bluebottle*, or one of the related genus *Lucilia*, *greenbottle*, which lays its eggs on dead flesh, on which the maggots feed.

Bloy /blwɑ:/ Léon-Marie 1846–1917. French author. He achieved a considerable reputation with his literary lampoons in the 1880s.

blubber the thick layer of ◊fat under the skin of marine mammals, which provides an energy store and an effective insulating layer, preventing the loss of body heat to the sea. Blubber has been used (when boiled down) in engineering, food processing, cosmetics and printing.

Blücher /'blu:kə/ Gebhard Leberecht von 1742–1819. Prussian general and field marshal, popular as 'Marshal Forward'. He took an active part in the patriotic movement, and in the War of Liberation defeated the French as commander-in-chief at Leipzig 1813, crossed the Rhine to Paris 1814, and was made prince of Wahlstadt (Silesia). In 1815 he was defeated by Napoleon at Ligny, but played a crucial role in Wellington's triumph at Waterloo.

blue UK sporting honour, awarded to Oxford and Cambridge students representing their university in games or forms of athletics. It consists of a strip of light or dark blue ribbon, and is said to have originated with the second Oxford and Cambridge Boat Race in 1836.

Bluebeard /'blu:brəd/ folktale character, popularized by the writer Charles Perrault in France about 1697, and historically identified with Gilles de ◊Rais. He murdered six wives for disobeying his command not to enter a locked room, but was himself killed before he could murder the seventh.

bluebell name given in Scotland to the harebell *Campanula rotundifolia*, and in England to the wild hyacinth *Endymion nonscriptus*, belonging to the family Liliaceae.

bluebird North American bird, genus *Sialia*, belonging to the thrush family. The *eastern bluebird Sialia sialis* is affectionately regarded as the herald of spring. Slightly larger than a robin, it has a similar reddish breast, the upper plumage being sky-blue, and its song is sweet.

bluebird A male bluebird alights at its nesting hole, carrying food. A North American member of the thrush family, it is traditionally regarded as the herald of spring.

bluebuck name used for several antelopes, including the *blue* ◊*duiker Cephalophus monticola* of South Africa, about 33 cm/13 in high. The bluebuck or *blaubok Hippotragus leucophaeus* was a large blue-grey South African antelope. Once abundant, it was hunted to extinction, the last being shot in 1800. The male of the Indian ◊*nilgai* antelope is also known as the bluebuck.

Blue division name given to the Spanish volunteers who fought with the German army against the Soviet Union during World War II.

bluegrass dense, spreading grass which grows in clumps. The blue-tinted *Poa compressa* provides fine pasture for horses, and Kentucky, where it is abundant, is known as the bluegrass state.

blue gum Australian tree *Eucalyptus globulus* with bluish bark, a chief source of eucalyptus oil.

Blue Mountains part of the ◊Great Dividing Range, New South Wales, Australia, ranging 600–1,100 m/2,000–3,600 ft and blocking Sydney from the interior until the crossing in 1813 by surveyor William Lawson, Gregory Blaxland, and William Wentworth.

blueprint process widely used for copying engineering drawings and architectural plans. It is so called because it produces a white copy of the original against a blue background. The plan to be copied is made on transparent tracing paper, which is placed in contact with paper sensitized with a mixture of iron (III) ammonium citrate and potassium hexacyanoferrate (III). The paper is exposed to ◊ultraviolet light, and then washed in water. Where the light reaches the paper, it turns blue (Prussian blue). The paper underneath the lines of the drawing is unaffected, so remains white.

blue riband or *blue ribbon* the highest distinction in any sphere; for example, the blue riband of horse racing in the UK is held by the winner of the Derby. The term derives from the blue riband of the Order of the Garter (see under ◊knighthood). The term *cordon bleu* in French has the same meaning. The *Blue Riband of the Atlantic* is held by the vessel making the fastest crossing in both east and west directions. Holders have included the *Great Western* 1838, *Queen Mary 1938–52*, and *United States* from 1952 (3 days, 10 hours 40 minutes). A trophy, originally presented 1935 by Harold K Hales 1868–1942, was in abeyance until accepted by the United States Lines 1952. The *Virgin Atlantic Challenger*, a British twin-hulled speedboat, broke the record at its second attempt in 1986.

Blue Ridge Mountains range extending from West Virginia to Georgia, USA, and including Mount Mitchell 2,045 m/6,684 ft; part of the ◊Appalachians.

blues 12-bar folk song in which, typically, the second line of the three-line verse is a repetition of the first, with variations, so giving the singer time to improvise the third line. It originated among American blacks in the rural South in the late 19th century, and the words are often melancholy. The *rural* or *delta blues* was usually performed solo with guitar or harmonica, for example by Robert Johnson (1911–38) and Bukka White (1906–77), but the earliest recorded style, *classic blues*, by musicians such as W C Handy (1873–1958) and Bessie Smith, was sung with a small band. In the 1940s *urban blues*, using electric amplification, emerged in the cities of the North, especially Chicago. As exemplified by Howlin' Wolf (real name Chester Burnett, 1910–76), Muddy Waters (real name McKinley Morganfield, 1915–83), and John Lee Hooker (1917–), urban blues became ◊rhythm and blues. The jazz-influenced guitar style of B B King (1925–) inspired many later musicians, including Eric Clapton (1945–) and Robert Cray (1953–).

blue shift in astronomy, a manifestation of the ◊Doppler effect in which an object appears bluer when it is moving towards the observer (or the observer is moving towards it (blue light is of a higher frequency than other colours in the spectrum). The blue shift is the opposite of the ◊red shift.

bluestocking term, often disparaging, for a learned woman. It originated in 1750 in England with the literary gatherings of Mrs Vesey in Bath and Mrs Elizabeth Montagu in London. According to Fanny Burney, the diarist, the term arose when the poet Benjamin Stillingfleet was invited to a party by Mrs Vesey; when he protested that he had nothing formal to wear she told him to come in his 'blue stockings' – that is, ordinary clothes. Most famous of later bluestockings is Hannah ◊More, author of the poem *The Bas Bleu, or Conversation*.

Blum /blu:m/ Léon 1872–1950. French politician. He was converted to socialism by the ◊Dreyfus affair (1899), and in 1936 he became the first socialist prime minister of France. He was again premier for a few weeks in 1938. After the German defeat of France he was imprisoned in 1942 under the Vichy government as a danger to French security, but released by the Allies in 1945. He was again premier for a few weeks in 1946.

Blunden /'blʌndən/ Edmund 1896–1974. English poet. Born in Kent, and educated at Oxford, he served in France and Belgium in World War I, and published the prose work *Undertones of War* 1928. He was professor of poetry at Oxford 1966–68. His poetry is mainly about rural life. Among his scholarly contributions was the discovery and publication of some poems by the 19th-century poet John Clare.

Blunt /blʌnt/ Anthony 1907–1983. British art historian. As a Cambridge don, he recruited for the Soviet secret service, and, as a member of the British Secret Service 1940–45, passed information to the Russians. In 1951 he assisted the defection of Guy ◊Burgess and Donald ◊Maclean. Unmasked in 1964, he was given immunity after his confession, but was stripped of his knighthood in 1979 when the affair became public.

Blunt /blʌnt/ Wilfrid Scawen 1840–1922. British poet. He married Lady Anne Noel, Byron's grand-daughter, and travelled with her in the Middle East, becoming a supporter of Arab nationalism. He also supported Irish Home Rule (imprisoned 1887–88), and wrote anti-imperialist books, poetry and diaries.

Blyton /'blaɪtn/ Enid 1897–1968. British writer of children's books. Originally a teacher, she created the little boy Noddy, with a gnome-like hat, and the adventures of the 'Famous Five' and 'Secret Seven', but has been criticized by educationalists for social, racial, and sexual stereotyping.

boa type of non-venomous snake that kills its prey by constriction. Some small burrowing boas live in North Africa and Western Asia, and other species live on Madagascar and some Pacific islands, but the majority of boas live in South and Central America. The true **boa constrictor**, *Constrictor constrictor*, can be up to 5.5 m/18.5 ft long, but is rarely more than 4 m/12 ft. It feeds mainly on small mammals and birds. Other boas include the ◊**anaconda** and the **emerald tree boa**, *Boa canina*, about 2 m/6 ft long and bright green. The name boa is sometimes used loosely to include the pythons of the Old World, also of the family Boidae, which share with boas vestiges of hind limbs and constricting habits.

Boadicea /ˌbəʊədɪˈsiːə/ alternative form of ancient British queen ◊Boudicca.

boar name used for some wild members of the pig family, such as the Eurasian **wild boar** *Sus scrofa*, from which domestic breeds derive. The wild boar is sturdily built, being 1.5 m/4.5 ft long and 1 m/3 ft high, and possesses formidable tusks. The dark coat is made up of coarse bristles with varying amounts of underfur. The young are striped. Mainly woodland-dwelling, these gregarious animals feed on roots, nuts and other plantstuffs, with some carrion and insects. The male is known as a boar, the female as a sow.

boarding school school offering board and lodging as well as tuition. Most boarding education in the UK is provided in the private, fee-paying sector, but there are a number of state schools with boarding facilities.

Boat Race in the UK, the annual rowing race between Oxford and Cambridge University crews, first held at Henley 1829, and since 1845 usually on the Thames (Putney–Mortlake, 6.8 km/4.25 mi), during the Easter vacation.

bobcat cat *Felis rufa* living from South Canada to South Mexico in a variety of habitats. It is similar to the lynx but only 75 cm/2.5 ft long, and with reddish fur and less well-developed ear-tufts.

bobolink North American songbird *Dolichonyx oryzivorus*, so named from its call.

Bobruisk /bəˈbruːɪsk/ timber centre in Byelorussia, USSR, on the Beresina river; population (1985) 223,000.

bobsledding the sport of racing steel-bodied, steerable toboggans down a mountain ice-chute, manned by two or four people at speeds up to 130 kmph/80 mph. World championships have been held every year since 1931.

Olympic Champions four-man event introduced at the 1924 Winter Olympics, two-man in 1932
two-man/four-man
1948 Switzerland/USA
1952 West Germany/West Germany
1956 Italy/Switzerland
1960 not held
1964 Great Britain/Canada
1968 Italy/Italy
1972 West Germany/Switzerland
1976 East Germany/East Germany
1980 Switzerland/East Germany
1984 East Germany/East Germany

World Championship four-man championship introduced 1924, two-man 1931; in Olympic years winners automatically become world champions
two-man/four-man
1977 Switzerland/East Germany
1978 Switzerland/East Germany
1979 Switzerland/West Germany
1980 Switzerland/East Germany
1981 East Germany/East Germany
1982 Switzerland/Switzerland
1983 Switzerland/Switzerland
1984 East Germany/East Germany
1985 East Germany/East Germany
1986 East Germany/Switzerland
1987 Switzerland/Switzerland

Boccaccio /bɒˈkɑːtʃɪəʊ/ Giovanni 1313–1375. Italian poet. Son of a Florentine merchant, he lived in Naples 1328–41, where he fell in love with the unfaithful 'Fiametta', who inspired his early poetry. Before returning to Florence in 1341 he had written *Filostrato* and *Teseide* (used by Chaucer in his *Troilus and Criseyde* and *Knight's Tale*). His great work is the *Decameron* 1348–53, a hundred tales told by ten young people seeking refuge in the country from the plague. Its bawdiness and exuberance as well as narrative skill and characterization made the work enormously popular and influential, inspiring Chaucer, Shakespeare, Dryden, and Keats, among many others.

Boccaccio The Italian poet Giovanni Boccaccio (1313–75), author of the *Decameron*, in a portrait by Andrea de Castagno from the Covent of Sant'Apollonia in Florence.

Boccherini /ˌbɒkəˈriːni/ (Ridolfo) Luigi 1743–1805. Italian composer and cellist. He studied in Rome, made his mark in Paris 1768, and was court composer in Prussia and Spain.

Boccherini composed some 350 instrumental works, an opera, and oratorios.

Bochum /ˈbəʊxʊm/ industrial town (metallurgy, vehicles, chemicals) in the Ruhr district, West Germany; university; population (1985) 412,000.

Bode /ˈbəʊdə/ Johann Elert 1747–1826. German astronomer, director of the Berlin observatory where, in 1801, he published the first atlas of all stars visible to the naked eye, *Uranographia*. He popularized **Bode's law**, which states a numerical sequence that gives the approximate distances, in astronomical units (distance between Earth and Sun = one astronomical unit) of the planets from the Sun by adding 4 to each term of the series 0, 3, 6, 12, 24 etc. and then dividing by 10. Bode's law predicted the existence of a planet between ◊Mars and ◊Jupiter, which led to the discovery of the asteroids. The 'law' breaks down for ◊Neptune and ◊Pluto. The relationship was first noted by the German mathematician Johann Titius in 1772 (it is also known as the **Titius-Bode law**).

Bodensee /ˈbəʊdnzeɪ/ German name for Lake ◊Constance, N of the Alps.

Bodhidharma /ˌbəʊdɪˈdɑːmə/ born 6th century. Indian ◊Buddhist. He entered China from South India c. 520, and was the founder of Zen (Japanese 'religious meditation', derived from Chinese *cha'an*), the school of Mahayana Buddhism in which intuitive meditation, prompted by contemplation of the beautiful, leads to enlightenment. It passed to Japan in the 12th century, where it is the best-known school.

Bodichon /ˈbəʊdɪʃɒn/ Barbara (born Leigh-Smith) 1827–1891. English feminist, campaigner for women's education and suffrage. Born into a radical family which believed in female equality, she attended Bedford College, London. In 1852 she opened a primary school in London. She wrote *Women and Work* 1857, and was a founder of the feminist magazine *The Englishwoman's Journal* in 1858. She also helped to found the college for women which became Girton College, Cambridge.

Bodin /bəʊˈdæn/ Jean 1530–1596. French political philosopher. An attorney in Paris, in 1574 he published a tract explaining that prevalent high prices were due to the influx of precious metals from the New World. His six-volume *De la République* 1576 is considered the first work on political economy.

Bodley /ˈbɒdli/ Thomas 1545–1613. English diplomat and scholar. After retiring from Queen Elizabeth I's service in 1597, he began to restore the library at Oxford which had originally been founded in the 15th century by Humphrey, Duke of Gloucester (1391–1447). Named after Bodley, the Bodleian Library was opened in 1602. He was knighted in 1604.

Bodmin /ˈbɒdmɪn/ administrative headquarters of Cornwall, England, 48 km/30 m from Plymouth; population (1984) 15,000. *Bodmin Moor* to the NE is a granite upland, culminating in Brown Willy 419 m/1,375 ft.

Bodoni /bəˈdəʊni/ Giambattista 1740–1813. Italian printer, who managed the printing-press of the Duke of Parma and produced high-quality

Bodichon English feminist Barbara Bodichon was first cousin to Florence Nightingale. Beautiful and determined, she was probably the model for George Eliot's *Romola*. She used her resources to fight for women's suffrage, and founded and endowed Girton College in 1873.

editions of the classics. He designed several typefaces, including one bearing his name, which is still in use today.

Boehme /ˈbɜːmə/ Jakob 1575–1624. German mystic. A shoemaker, he claimed divine revelation of the unity of everything and nothing, and found in God's eternal nature a principle to reconcile good and evil. He was the author of the treatise *Aurora* 1612.

Boeotia /biˈəʊʃə/ ancient district of central Greece, of which ◊Thebes was the chief city; the *Boeotian League* (formed by ten city states in the 6th century BC) superseded ◊Sparta in the leadership of Greece in the 4th century.

Boer (Dutch 'farmer') name formerly applied to the Dutch settlers and their descendants in South ◊Africa; see ◊Afrikaner.

Boer War war between the Dutch settlers in South Africa and the British; see ◊South African Wars.

Boethius /bəʊˈiːθɪəs/ Anicius Manilus Severinus 480–524. Roman philosopher. While imprisoned on suspicion of treason by ◊Theodoric, he wrote treatises on music and mathematics, and *De Consolatione Philosophiae*/*The Consolation of Philosophy*. A vastly influential book in the Middle Ages, it was translated into English by ◊Alfred the Great and by Chaucer.

bog an area of soft, wet, spongy ground consisting of decaying vegetable matter (◊peat). Bogs occur on cold uplands where drainage is poor. The typical bog plant is sphagnum moss; rushes, cranberry, cotton grass, and sundew also grow under these conditions. Unlike marshes, bogs usually have little open water, and the water is acidic and devoid of oxygen.

Bogarde /ˈbəʊɡɑːd/ Dirk. Stage-name of Derek van den Bogaerde 1921– . Dutch-born British actor. He acquired an international reputation for complex roles in films such as

Death in Venice 1971, and *A Bridge Too Far* 1977. He has also written autobiographical books, for example *A Postillion Struck by Lightning* 1977, *Snakes and Ladders* 1978, *Orderly Man* 1983, *Backcloth* 1986.

Bogarde British actor and author Dirk Bogarde distinguished himself in several films made in the 1960s with director Joseph Losey, such as *Accident* 1967, and with Luchino Visconti in *Death in Venice* 1971. He has also written autobiographical works and best-selling novels.

Bogart /ˈbəʊɡɑːt/ Humphrey 1899–1957. American film actor, born in New York. In *The Petrified Forest* 1936 he achieved fame with his portrayal of a gangster. Later films include *The Maltese Falcon* 1941, *Casablanca* 1943 (with Ingrid Bergman), *To Have and Have Not* (with Lauren Bacall, who became his fourth wife in 1945), and *The Caine Mutiny* 1954. He became a cult figure as the romantic, tough 'loner'.

Bogazköy /bɔːˈɑːzkɔɪ/ village in Turkey 145 km/90 mi E of Ankara on the site of *Hattusas*, the ancient ◊Hittite capital established about 1640 BC. Thousands of tablets discovered by excavations here over a number of years by the German Oriental Society revealed, when their cuneiform writing was deciphered by Bedrich Hrozny (1879–1952), a great deal about the customs, religion, and history of the Hittite people.

bogbean aquatic or bog plant *Menyanthes trifoliata* with a creeping rhizome and leaves and flower held above water. The leaves have three lobes, and the flowers are pink with white hairs, ten to twenty on a spike. Flowering in midsummer, it is found over much of the northern hemisphere.

Bognor Regis /ˈbɒɡnə ˈriːdʒɪs/ seaside resort in West Sussex, England, 105 km/66 mi SW of London, which owes the Regis in its name to the convalescent visit by King George V in 1929.

Bogotá /ˌbɒɡəˈtɑː/ capital of Colombia, South America; 2,640 m/8,660 ft above sea level

on the edge of the plateau of the E Cordillera; population (1985) 3,967,988. Founded 1538.

Bogart The celebrated husband-and-wife acting team, Humphrey Bogart and Lauren Bacall, in a scene from the film *Key Largo*, 1948. Bogart usually portrayed a 'wised-up' gangster-hero, the tough guy with the soft inside.

Bohemia /bəʊˈhiːmɪə/ kingdom of central Europe from the 9th century, under Hapsburg rule 1526–1918, when it was included in ◊Czechoslovakia. The name Bohemia derives from the Celtic Boii, its earliest known inhabitants.

Bohlen /ˈbəʊlən/ Charles 'Chip' 1904–1974. American diplomat. Educated at Harvard, he entered the foreign service in 1929. Interpreter and adviser to Roosevelt at Tehran and Yalta, and to Truman at Potsdam, he served as ambassador to the USSR 1953–57.

Böhm /bɜːm/ Karl 1894–1981. Austrian conductor, noted for his interpretation of Beethoven, and of the Mozart and Strauss operas.

Bohr /bɔː/ Niels Henrik David 1885–1962. Danish physicist. Nobel prize winner 1922. After work with ◊Rutherford at Manchester, he became professor at Copenhagen in 1916 and founded the Institute of Theoretical Physics there, of which he became director in 1920. He fled from the Nazis in World War II and took part in work on the atomic bomb in the USA. In 1952 he helped to set up ◊CERN in Geneva. His son, *Aage Bohr* (1922–), also a physicist, shared a Nobel Prize in 1975 for work on the theory of the atomic nucleus.

Boiardo /bɔɪˈɑːdəʊ/ Matteo Maria, Count 1434–1494. Italian poet, famed for his *Orlando Innamorato*/*Roland in Love* 1486.

boil abscess originating at a hair root or in a sweat gland, usually caused by a ◊staphylococcus.

Boileau /bwæˈləʊ/ Nicolas 1636–1711. French poet and critic. Called to the bar in 1656, he turned to literature on receiving a legacy.

After a series of contemporary satires, his *Epîtres/Epistles* 1669–77 led to his joint appointment with Racine as historiographer royal in 1677. Later works include *L'Art poétique/The Art of Poetry* 1674, the mock-heroic *Le Lutrin/The Lectern* 1674–83, and a translation of Longinus *On the Sublime* 1674. A close friend of Racine, Molière, and La Fontaine, he was elected to the French Academy in 1684.

boiler a vessel designed to convert water into steam. Boilers are used in conventional power stations to generate steam to feed to steam ◊turbines, which drive the electricity generators. They are also used in steam ships, which are propelled by steam turbines. ◊Steam locomotives have boilers to generate steam to drive pistons in cylinders.

Every boiler has a furnace in which fuel (coal, oil or gas) is burned to produce hot gases. It has a system of tubes in which heat is transferred from the gases to the water. The most common kind of boiler used in ships and power stations is the water-tube type. In this type the water circulates in tubes surrounded by the hot furnace gases. The water-tube boilers at power stations produce steam at a pressure of up to 300 atmospheres and at a temperature of up to 600° C to feed to the steam turbines. The water-tube boiler is more efficient than the type used in steam locomotives, the fire-tube type. In this boiler the hot furnace gases are drawn through tubes surrounded by water.

boiling point for any given liquid, the temperature at which the application of heat raises the temperature of the liquid no further, but converts it to vapour. The boiling point of water under normal pressure is 100°C or 212°F. The lower the pressure, the lower the boiling point and vice versa.

Bois-le-Duc /'bwaː lə 'djuːk/ French form of ◊Hertogenbosch, a town in N Brabant, Netherlands.

Bokassa /bɒ'kæsə/ Jean Bedel 1921– . President and later self-proclaimed emperor of the Central African Republic. Born at Bobangui, he joined the French army in 1939 and was awarded the Croix de Guerre for his service with the French colonial forces in Indo-China. When the Central African Republic achieved independence in 1960, Bokassa was invited to establish an army, becoming commander-in-chief in 1963. In 1966 he led a military coup which gave him the presidency, and on 4 Dec 1977 he proclaimed the Central African Empire with himself as emperor for life. His regime was characterized by arbitrary state violence and cruelty before his overthrow in 1979. In exile until 1986, Bokassa then returned to the Central African Republic to face the charges against him and received a death sentence on 12 June 1987.

Bokhara /bɒ'kɑːrə/ another form of ◊Bukhara, city in the USSR.

Boldrewood /'bəʊldəwʊd/ Rolf. Pseudonym of Thomas Alexander Browne 1826–1915. Australian writer, born in London, he was taken to Australia as a child in 1830; became a pioneer squatter, and a police magistrate in the goldfields. His best known book is *Robbery Under Arms* 1888.

Bokassa Marshal Jean Bokassa changed his country's name to the Central African Empire, and crowned himself emperor in 1977 in an extravagant ceremony. He is in front of the two-ton gilded throne crafted in the shape of a giant eagle.

bolero /bɒ'leərəʊ/ a Spanish dance in triple time for a solo dancer or a couple, usually with castanet accompaniment. Also the title of a one-act ballet score by ◊Ravel, choreographed by ◊Nijinsky for Ida Rubinstein in 1928.

boletus European fungus, resembling mushrooms, and belonging to the Basidiomycetes. *Boletus edulis* is edible, but some species are poisonous.

Boleyn /bə'lɪn, 'bʊlɪn/ Anne 1507–1536. Queen of England. Second wife of King ◊Henry VIII, she was married to him in 1533 and gave birth to the future Queen ◊Elizabeth I in the same year. Accused of adultery and incest with her half-brother, she was beheaded.

Bolingbroke /'bʊlɪŋbrʊk/ Henry of. Title of ◊Henry IV of England.

Bolingbroke /'bʊlɪŋbrʊk/ Henry John, Viscount Bolingbroke 1678–1751. British ◊Tory politician and philosopher. He was secretary of war 1704–08, became foreign secretary in ◊Harley's ministry in 1710, and in 1713 negotiated the Treaty of ◊Utrecht. His plans to restore the 'Old ◊Pretender' were ruined by Queen ◊Anne's death only five days after he had secured the dismissal of Harley in 1714. He fled abroad, returning in 1723, when he worked to overthrow ◊Walpole.

Bolívar /bɒ'liːvɑː/ Simón 1783–1830. South American revolutionary leader, known as the Liberator. Born in Venezuela, he joined the

Boleyn English queen Anne Boleyn had Henry VIII among her suitors. He married her after divorcing Catherine of Aragon in Jan 1533, and Anne was crowned with splendour. Her triumph was brief: before the birth of Elizabeth in September, Henry's ardour had cooled.

patriots working for Venezuelan independence, and was sent to Britain in 1810 as the representative of their government. Forced to flee to Colombia in 1812, he joined the revolutionists there, and invaded Venezuela in 1813. A bloody civil war followed and in 1814 Bolívar had to withdraw to Colombia, and eventually to the West Indies, from where he raided the Spanish-American coasts. In 1817 he returned to Venezuela to set up a provisional government, crossed into Colombia 1819, where he defeated the Spaniards, and returning to Angostura proclaimed the republic of Colombia, comprising Venezuela, New Granada, and Quito (Ecuador), with himself as president. The independence of Venezuela was finally secured in 1821, and 1822 Bolívar liberated Ecuador. He was invited to lead the Peruvian struggle in 1823; and final victory having been won by Sucre at Ayacucho in 1824, he turned his attention to framing a constitution. In 1825 the independence of Upper Peru was proclaimed, which adopted the name Bolivia in Bolívar's honour.

Bolivia /bə'lɪvɪə/ landlocked country in South America, bordered to the north and east by Brazil, to the southeast by Paraguay, to the south by Argentina, and to the west by Chile and Peru.
government becoming independent in 1825 after nearly 300 years of Spanish rule, Bolivia adopted its first constitution in 1826 and since then a number of variations have been produced. The present one provides for a congress consisting of a 27-member senate and a 130-member chamber of deputies, both elected for four years by universal suffrage. The president, directly elected for a four-year term, is head of both state and government, and chooses the cabinet. For administrative purposes, the country is divided into nine departments, each governed by a

Bolívar A portrait of Simón Bolívar, the Liberator, by an unknown artist.

prefect appointed by the president. Most significant among the many political parties are the National Revolutionary Movement (MNR), and the Nationalist Democratic Action Party (ADN).

history once part of the ◊Inca civilization, and conquered by Spain in 1538, Bolivia took its name from Simón ◊Bolívar, who liberated it in 1825. Between 1836–39 Bolivia formed a Peruvian-Bolivian Confederation under Bolivian President Andrés Santa Cruz, a former president of Peru. Chile declared war on the confederation, Santa Cruz was defeated, and the confederation was dissolved. Bolivia was again at war with Chile 1879–84, when it lost its coastal territory and land containing valuable mineral deposits, and with Paraguay (the Chaco War) 1932–35, again losing valuable territory.

In the 1951 election, Dr Victor Paz Estenssoro, the MNR candidate exiled in Argentina since 1946, failed to win an absolute majority and an army junta took over. A popular uprising, supported by MNR and a section of the army, demanded the return of Paz, who became president and began a programme of social reform. He lost the 1956 election, but returned to power in 1960. In 1964 a coup, led by Vice-President General René Barrientos, overthrew Paz and installed a military junta. Two years later Barrientos won the presidency. He was opposed by left-wing groups and in 1967 a guerrilla uprising led by Dr Ernesto 'Che' ◊Guevara was only put down with US help.

In 1969 President Barrientos died in an air crash and was replaced by the vice-president. He was later replaced by General Alfredo Ovando, who was ousted by General Juan Torres, who in turn was ousted by Colonel Hugo Banzer in 1971. Banzer announced a return to constitutional government but another attempted coup in 1974

Bolivia
REPUBLIC OF (*República de Bolivia*)

AREA 1,098,000 sq km/424,000 sq mi
CAPITAL La Paz (seat of government), Sucre (legal capital and seat of judiciary)
TOWNS Santa Cruz, Cochabamba
PHYSICAL high plateau between mountain ridges; forest and lowlands in the E
FEATURES Andes, and lakes Titicaca and Poopó
HEAD OF STATE AND OF GOVERNMENT Víctor Paz Estenssoro from 1985
GOVERNMENT republic
EXPORTS tin (second largest world producer), other non-ferrous metals, oil, gas (piped to Argentina), agricultural products
CURRENCY boliviano (3.45 = £1 Sept 1987)
POPULATION (1985) 6,195,000; (Quechua 25%, Aymara 17%, Mestizo 30%, European 14%); annual growth rate 2.8%
LANGUAGE Spanish (official); Aymara, Quechua
RELIGION Roman Catholic (state-recognized)
LITERACY 79% male/58% female (1980 est)
GDP $3 bn (1983); $570 per head of population
CHRONOLOGY
1825 Independence achieved.
1952 Dr Víctor Paz Estenssoro elected president.
1956 Dr Hernan Siles Zuazo became president.
1960 Estenssoro returned to power.
1964 Army coup led by vice-president.
1966 Gen René Barrientos became president.
1967 Uprising, led by 'Che' Guevara, put down with US help.
1969 Barrientos killed in air crash, replaced by vice-president Siles Salinas. Army coup deposed him.
1970 Army coup put Gen Juan Torres Gonzalez in power.
1971 Torres replaced by Col Hugo Banzer Suarez.
1973 Banzer promised a return to democratic government.
1974 An attempted coup prompted Banzer to

postpone elections and ban political and trade-union activity.
1978 Elections declared invalid after allegations of fraud.
1980 More inconclusive elections followed by another coup, led by Gen Garcia. Allegations of corruption and drug trafficking led to cancellation of US and EEC aid.
1981 Garcia forced to resign. Replaced by Gen Celso Torrelio Villa.
1982 Torrelio resigned. Replaced by military junta led by Gen Vildoso. Because of worsening economy, Vildoso asked congress to install a civilian administration. Dr Siles Zuazo chosen as president.
1983 Economic aid from US and Europe resumed.
1984 New coalition government formed by Siles. Attempted abduction of president by right-wing officers. The president undertook a five-day hunger strike as an example to the nation.
1985 President Siles resigned. Election result inconclusive. Dr Paz Estenssoro, at the age of 77, chosen by congress.

prompted him to postpone elections, ban all trade union and political activity and proclaim that military government would last until at least 1980. Banzer agreed to elections in 1978 but there were allegations of fraud and, in that year, two more military coups.

In the 1979 elections Dr Siles and Dr Paz received virtually equal votes and an interim administration was installed. An election in 1980 proved equally inconclusive and was followed by the 189th military coup in Bolivia's 154 years of independence. General Luis García became president but resigned the following year after allegations of drug trafficking. He was replaced by General Celso Torrelio who promised to fight corruption and return the country to democracy within three years. In 1982 a mainly civilian cabinet was appointed but rumours of an impending coup resulted in Torrelio's resignation. A military junta led by the hard-line General Guido Vildoso was installed.

With the economy deteriorating, the junta asked congress to elect a president and Dr Siles Zuazo was chosen to head a coalition cabinet. Economic aid from Europe and the US, cut off in 1980, was resumed but the economy continued to deteriorate. The government's austerity measures proved unpopular and in Jun the president was temporarily abducted by a group of right-wing army officers. In an attempt to secure national unity, President Siles embarked on a five-day hunger strike.

Following a general strike and another abortive army coup in 1985, President Siles resigned and an election was held. No candidate won an absolute majority and Dr Victor Paz Estenssoro, aged 77, was chosen by congress. Despite austerity measures, including a wage freeze, inflation continues and the currency has weakened.

Böll /bɜːl/ Heinrich 1917–1985. West German novelist. A radical Catholic and anti-

Nazi, he attacked Germany's political past and the materialism of its contemporary society. His books include *Billard um Halbzehn/Billiards at Half-Past Nine* 1959 and *Gruppenbild mit Dame/Group Portrait with Lady* 1971. He was awarded the Nobel Prize for Literature in 1972.

Böll West German writer Heinrich Böll speaking at a peace rally in Bonn in 1983. Böll was awarded the Nobel Prize for literature in 1972. His many publications include poems, short stories, and novels which satirize modern German society.

Bollandists body of Belgian Jesuits who edit and publish the *Acta Sanctorum*, the standard collection of saints' lives and other scholarly publications. They are named after John Bolland (1596–1665), who published the first two volumes in 1643.

boll-weevil small American beetle *Anthonomus grandis* of the weevil family. The female lays eggs in the unripe pods or 'bolls' of the cotton plant, and on these the larva feeds, causing great destruction.

Bologna /bə'lɒnjə/ historic and industrial city (food), capital of Emilia-Romagna, Italy, 80 km/50 mi N of Florence; university from 11th century; population (1984) 442,307. The city has a cathedral and medieval towers.

history Bologna was the site of an Etruscan town, later of a Roman colony, and became a republic in the 12th century. The university laid the foundations of the study of anatomy and was attended by the poets Dante, Petrarch, and Tasso, and the astronomer Copernicus. The city came under papal rule in 1506, and in 1860 was united with Italy.

Bolshevism (from Russian *bolshinstvo*, 'a majority') doctrines of the extreme socialists or communists who effected the Russian Revolution of 1917. The word came into use following a conference of European and British socialists held in London in 1903, at which there was a split between the Russian Social Democratic Party led by Lenin, and the moderate delegates. The former, being in the majority, were called *Bolsheviki*, and their opponents the *Mensheviki* (from Russian *menshinstvo*, a minority). The Bolsheviks advocated the destruction of capitalist political and economic institutions and the setting up of a socialist state with power in the hands of the workers.

Bolt /bəʊlt/ Robert (Oxton) 1924– . British dramatist, noted for his historical plays *A Man for All Seasons* 1960, about Thomas More, which was filmed 1967, and *Vivat! Vivat Regina!* 1970, about Queen Elizabeth I and Mary Queen of Scots, and for his screenplays including *Lawrence of Arabia* 1962, *Dr Zhivago* 1965.

Bolton /'bəʊltən/ industrial city (chemicals, textile machinery) in Greater Manchester, England, 18 km/11 mi NW of Manchester; population (1985) 261,000.

Boltzmann /'bɒltsmæn/ Ludwig 1844–1906. Austrian physicist and authority on the kinetic theory of gases. Boltzmann's constant ($k = 1.381 \times 10^{-23}$ joule per kelvin) is the ratio of the mean total energy of a molecule to its absolute temperature, and the principle of the equipartition of energy is known as *Boltzmann's law*.

Bolzano /bɒlt'saːnəʊ/ town in Italy, in Trentino–Alto Adige region (alternate capital with Trento), on the Isarco in the Alps; population (1981) 105,000. Bolzano belonged to Austria until 1919; its German name is *Bozen*.

Boma /'bəʊmə/ port in Zaïre, on the estuary of the river Zaïre 88 km/55 mi from the Atlantic; population (1976) 93,965. The oldest European settlement in Zaïre, it was a centre of the slave trade, and capital of the Belgian Congo until 1927.

bomb an explosive projectile used in warfare. Aerial bombing started in World War I when the German air force carried out 103 raids on Britain, dropping 269 tonnes of bombs. In World War II nearly twice this tonnage was dropped on London in a single night, and at the peak of the Allied air offensive against Germany more than ten times this tonnage was regularly dropped in successive nights, on one target. Raids in which nearly 1,000 heavy bombers participated were frequent. They were delivered either in 'precision' or 'area' attacks and great advances were made in 'blind' bombing, in which the target is located solely by instruments and is not visible through a bomb-sight. In 1939 bombs were commonly about 115kg (250lb) and 230kg (500lb) but by the end of the war the ten-tonner was being produced, though even the power of these paled in significance beside the atom bomb. This derives its explosive force from nuclear fission as a result of a neutron chain reaction; three were exploded during World War II: first a test explosion on 16 Jul 1945, at Alamogordo, New Mexico, USA. Then on 6 Aug the first to be used in actual warfare was dropped over ◊Hiroshima and three days later another over Nagasaki. These were 'nominal', that is, nominally equal in destructive power to 20,000 tonnes of TNT. Russia first detonated an atom bomb in 1949 and Britain in 1952 (in the Monte Bello Islands off Australia). Later developments have included the fusion or ◊hydrogen bomb, and by the 1960s intercontinental 100-megatonne nuclear warheads could be produced (5,000 times more powerful than those of World War II) and the USA and USSR between them possessed a stockpile sufficient to destroy all of humankind. (See ◊fallout.) Methods of delivery have also changed since Germany pioneered the V1 flying bomb and V2 rocket bomb, so that in the 1960s it was recognized that the era of bombers with free-falling bombs was over, and that future development would lie with missiles launched from aircraft, land sites or submarines. The danger of such nuclear weapons increases with the number of nations possessing the ability to produce them (France and China became nuclear powers in 1960 and 1964 respectively), and the possibility of 'policing' states to check on their testing of bombs has been complicated by the development of underground testing. It was agreed under the Outer Space Treaty (1966) that nuclear warheads may not be sent into orbit, but this measure has been circumvented by more sophisticated weapons. The Fractional Orbital Bombardment System (FOBS) sends a warhead into a low partial orbit, followed by a rapid descent to Earth. This renders it both less vulnerable to ballistic missile defence systems and cuts the warning time to three minutes. More recent bombs also tend to produce less fall-out, a 'dirty' bomb being one which produces large quantities of radioactive debris from a U-238 casing. Testing grounds include Lop Nor (China); Mururoa Atoll in the South Pacific (France); Nevada Desert, Amchitka Islands in the Aleutians (USA); Semipalatinsk in Central Asia, Novaya Zemlya Islands in the Arctic (USSR).

The rapid development of laser guidance systems in the 1970s meant that precise destruction of small but vital targets could be more effectively achieved with standard 450 kg/1,000 lb high explosive bombs. The laser beam may be directed at the target by the army from the ground, but additional flexibility is gained by coupling ground directed beams with those of guidance carried in high performance aircraft accompanying the bombers, for example, the Laser Ranging Marler Target System (LRMPS).

Bombay /ˌbɒm'beɪ/ former province of British India. Together with a number of interspersed princely states, it was included in the Domain of India in 1947, and the major part became in 1960 the two new states of Gujarat and ◊Maharashtra. The capital was the city of ◊Bombay.

Bombay /ˌbɒm'beɪ/ industrial port (textiles, engineering, pharmaceuticals, diamonds) and capital of Maharashtra, W India, centre of commerce and the Hindi film industry; population (1981) 8,203,000.

features World Trade Centre 1975, National Centre for the Performing Arts 1969.

history Bombay was founded in the 13th century, came under Mogul rule, was occupied by Portugal in 1530, and passed to Britain in 1662 as part of Catherine of Braganza's dowry.

bombay duck small fish (*Harpodon nehereus*), found off the Bombay coast and in other Eastern waters. Salted and dried, it is eaten with dishes such as curry.

bona fide (Latin 'in good faith'). Legal phrase signifying that a contract is undertaken without intentional misrepresentation.

Bonaparte /'bəʊnəpɑːt/ Corsican family of Italian origin, which gave rise to the Napoleonic dynasty: see ◊Napoleon I, ◊Napoleon II, and ◊Napoleon III. Other well-known members were the brothers and sister of Napoleon 1:

Joseph 1768–1844, whom Napoleon made king of Naples 1806 and Spain 1808.

Lucien 1775–1840, whose handling of the Council of Five Hundred on 10 Nov 1799 ensured Napoleon's future.

Louis 1778–1846, made king of Holland 1806–10, and who was the father of Napoleon III.

Caroline 1782–1839, who married Joachim ◊Murat in 1800.

Jerome 1784–1860, made king of Westphalia in 1807. A descendant of the last-named, *Louis Jerome* 1914– , is the present Bonaparte 'pretender'.

or lose electrons to become ◊ions; for example, sodium (Na) loses an electron to form a sodium ion (Na+) while chlorine(Cl) gains an electron to form a chloride ion (Cl-) in the ionic bond of sodium chloride (NaCl). In a covalent bond, the atomic ◊orbitals of two atoms overlap to form a molecular orbital containing two electrons, which are thus effectively shared between the two atoms. Covalent bonds are common in organic compounds, such as the four carbonhydrogen bonds in methane (CH_4). In a dative covalent or coordinate bond, one of the combining atoms supplies both of the valence electrons in the bond.

Bond /bɒnd/ Edward 1935– . British dramatist, whose work has aroused controversy because of the savagery of some of his themes, for example the brutal killing of a baby, symbol of a society producing unwanted children, in *Saved* 1965. His later works include *Black Mass* 1970 about apartheid, *Bingo* 1973, and *The Sea* 1973.

Bondfield /'bɒndfiːld/ Margaret Grace 1873–1953. British socialist. Originally a shop assistant, she became a trade-union organizer to improve working conditions for women. She was a Labour member of Parliament 1923–24 and

may be 80 cm/2.6 ft or more long, with a spiral twist. The body is rich chestnut with a black belly, and has a series of narrow white stripes vertically down the sides. Up to 1.4 m/4.5 ft at the shoulder, bongos live in dense humid forests, where they browse on the vegetation.

Bonham-Carter /'bɒnəm 'kɑːtə/ Violet, Lady Asquith of Yarnbury 1887–1969. British peeress, an active Liberal and president of the party organization 1945–47.

Bonheur /bɒ'nɜː/ Rosa (Marie Rosalie) 1822–1899. French artist, noted for her paintings of animals. She exhibited at the Paris Salon every year from 1841, and received international awards and became the first woman Officer of the Légion d'Honneur in 1894. Her best known work is *Horse Fair* 1853.

Bonhoeffer /'bɒnhɜːfə/ Dietrich 1906–1945. German Lutheran theologian and opponent of Nazism. Involved in an anti-Hitler plot, he was executed by the Nazis in Flossenburg concentration camp. His *Letters and Papers from Prison*, published 1953, became the textbook of modern radical theology, anticipating the prospect of a secular 'religionless' Christianity.

BONAPARTE, HOUSE OF

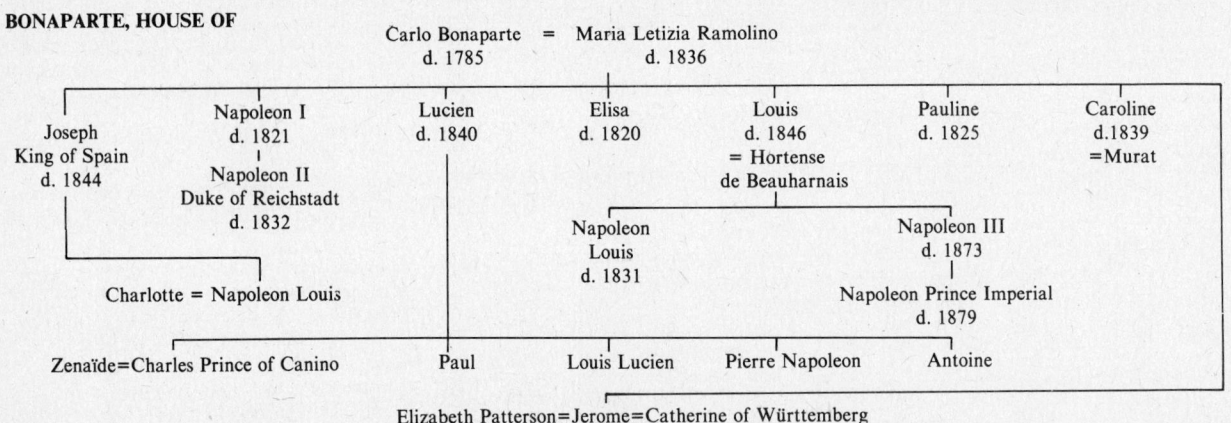

Bonar /'bəʊnə/ Horatius 1808–1889. Scottish (Free Church) clergyman, and author of many hymns.

Bonar Law Andrew. See ◊Law, Andrew Bonar.

Bonaventura /ˌbɒnəven'tʊərə/ St (John of Fidanza) 1221–1274. Italian Roman Catholic theologian, canonized in 1482. He entered the Franciscan order in 1243, became professor of theology at Paris, and in 1256 general of his order. In 1273 he was created cardinal and bishop of Albano. He died at the Second Council of Lyons. His eloquent writings earned him the title of the 'Seraphic Doctor'.

bond chemical result of the forces of attraction that hold together ◊atoms of an element or elements to form a ◊molecule. The type of bond formed depends on the elements concerned and their electronic structure. In an ionic or electrovalent bond, common among inorganic compounds, the combining atoms gain

1926–31, and was the first woman to enter the cabinet – as minister of labour, 1929–31.

bondservant another term for a slave or serf; as used in the Caribbean in the 18th and 19th centuries, a person who was offered a few acres of land in return for some years of compulsory service. The system was used as a means of obtaining labour from Europe.

bone hard connective tissue of most vertebrate animals consisting of a network of collagen fibres impregnated with calcium phospate. In strength, the toughest bone is comparable with reinforced concrete. Bones develop initially from ◊cartilage. Humans have about 206 distinct bones in the ◊skeleton. The interior of long bones comprises a spongy matrix filled with marrow which produces ◊blood cells.

Bône /bəʊn/ (or Bohn) former name of ◊Annaba, Algerian port.

bongo Central African antelope *Boocercus eurycerus* in which both sexes have horns. These

Boniface /'bɒnɪfeɪs/ name of nine popes. The most notable was *Boniface VIII* (born Benedict Caetani) (c. 1228–1303). Succeeding to the office in 1294, he clashed unsuccessfully with secular rulers. He exempted the clergy from taxation by the secular government in a bull (edict) of 1296, but Philippe IV of France and Henry III of England forced him to give way by excluding the clergy from certain lay privileges. His bull of 1302 asserting the complete temporal and spiritual power of the papacy was equally ineffective.

Boniface, St /'bɒnɪfeɪs/ 680–754. English monk, known as the 'Apostle of Germany'. Originally named Wynfrith, he was born in Devon and became a Benedictine monk. After a missionary journey to Frisia in 1716, he was given the task of bringing Christianity to Germany by Pope Gregory II in 718, and was appointed archbishop of Mainz in 746. He returned to Frisia 754 and was martyred near Dockum.

Bonin and Volcano islands /'bəʊnɪn/ small Japanese groups of islands in the Pacific, N of the Marianas and 1,300 km/800 mi E of the Ryukyu islands. They were under US control 1945–68. The *Bonin Islands* (Japanese *Ogasawara Gunto*) number 27 (in three groups), the largest being Chichijima: area 104 sq km/40 sq mi, population (1970) 300.
The *Volcano Islands* (Japanese *Kazan Retto*) number three, including Iwo Jima, scene of some of the fiercest fighting of World War II; total area 28 sq km/11 sq mi.

Bonington /'bɒnɪŋtən/ Chris(tian) 1934–   . British mountaineer. He took part in the first British ascent of the north face of the Eiger 1962, climbed the central Tower of Paine in Patagonia in 1963, and was the leader of an Everest expedition 1975 and again in 1985, reaching the summit.

Bonington /'bɒnɪŋtən/ Richard Parkes 1801–1828. British artist, noted for seascapes and landscapes in oil and watercolour. The Wallace Collection in London has a selection of his work.

bonito name for various species of small tuna, predatory fish of the mackerel family. The ocean bonito *Katsuwonus pelamis* grows to 1 m/3 ft and is common in tropical seas. The bonito *Sarda sarda* is found in the Mediterranean and tropical Atlantic and grows to the same length but has a narrow body.

Bonn /bɒn/ industrial city (chemicals, textiles), capital of West Germany, 18 km/15 mi SSE of Cologne, on the left bank of the Rhine; population (1985) 289,900.
history Bonn was an important Roman outpost. It was captured by the French in 1794, annexed by them in 1801, and was allotted to Prussia in 1815. Beethoven was born here. It became the West German capital 1949.

Bonnard /bɒ'nɑː/ Pierre 1867–1947. French painter, influenced by the ◊Impressionists. His subjects include Paris street scenes, landscapes and interiors with figures, noted for their light and colour.

Bonneville Salt Flats /'bɒnəvɪl/ bed of a prehistoric lake in Utah, USA, of which the Great Salt Lake is the surviving remnant. It has been used for motor speed records.

Bonny, Bight of /'bɒni/ name since 1975 of the former Bight of Biafra, an area of sea off the coasts of Nigeria and Cameroon.

bonsai the cultivation of dwarf trees and shrubs by using small pots to restrict their growth, and periodically pruning stems and roots to stunt development. The art of bonsai originated in China many centuries ago, and then later spread to Japan. Some specimens in the Imperial Japanese collection are over 300 years old.

boobook owl *Ninox novaeseelandiae* found in Australia, so called because of its call.

booby tropical seabird, genus *Sula*, closely related to the northern ◊gannet. There are six species, including the circumtropical brown booby *Sula leucogaster*. They fly above the sea and plunge for food. They got their name because their tameness was seen as stupidity by sailors.

book a portable written record. Early substances used in making books include leaves, bark, linen, silk, clay, leather, and papyrus. Early in the Christian era (c. 100–150), the codex or paged book, as against the roll, began to be adopted. Vellum was generally used for book production by the beginning of the 4th century and its use lasted until the 15th, when it was superseded by paper. Printed text is also reproduced in ◊microform.

bookbinding the art or craft of securing the pages of a book between protective covers. (Bookbinding only emerged as a distinct art when ◊printing was introduced to Europe in the 15th century.) Gold tooling, the principal ornament of leather bookbinding, was probably introduced to Europe from the East by the Venetian Aldus Manutius, and adopted in England by Thomas Berthelet, binder to King Henry VIII. Famous binders include Nicholas and Clovis Eve 16th century; Le Gascon, Samuel Mearne 17th century; A M Padeloup, N D Derome, Roger Paynes 18th century; Francis Bedford 19th century; and T J Cobden-Sanderson, and C Ricketts 20th century. Modern cloth binding common to England and the USA was first introduced by Leighton in 1822, but since World War II synthetic bindings have been increasingly employed, and most hardback books are bound by machine (paperbacks and some hardbacks are glued rather than sewn).

Booker Prize British literary prize of £15,000 awarded annually (from 1969) by the Booker company (formerly Booker McConnell) to a novel published in the United Kingdom during the previous year.

Booker Prize for fiction
1969 P H Newby *Something to Answer For*
1970 Bernice Rubens *The Elected Member*
1971 V S Naipaul *In a Free State*
1972 John Berger *G*
1973 J G Farrell *The Siege of Krishnapur*
1974 Nadine Gordimer *The Conservationist*; Stanley Middleton *Holiday* (joint winners)
1975 Ruth Prawer Jhabvala *Heat and Dust*
1976 David Storey *Saville*
1977 Paul Scott *Staying On*
1978 Iris Murdoch *The Sea, The Sea*
1979 Penelope Fitzgerald *Offshore*
1980 William Golding *Rites of Passage*
1981 Salman Rushdie *Midnight's Children*
1982 Thomas Keneally *Schindler's Ark*
1983 J M Coetzee *Life and Times of Michael K*
1984 Anita Brookner *Hotel du Lac*
1985 Keri Hulme *The Bone People*
1986 Kingsley Amis *The Old Devils*
1987 Penelope Lively *Moon Tiger*.

bookkeeping process of keeping books of account, that is, records of commercial transactions, in a systematic and accurate manner (see also ◊accountancy). The earliest-known work on double entry bookkeeping, a system in which each item of a business transaction is entered twice – as debit and as credit – was by Luca Pacioli, published in Venice in 1494. The method which he advocated had, however, been practised by Italian merchants for several hundred years before that date. The first English work on the subject, by the schoolmaster Hugh Oldcastle, appeared in 1543.

booklouse tiny wingless insect *Atropus pulsatoria* which lives in books and papers, feeding on starches and moulds. There are many species of 'booklice' in the order Psocoptera, but most live in bark, leaves and lichens. They thrive in dark and damp conditions.

Book of the Dead ancient Egyptian book, known to them as the *Book of Coming Forth by Day*, buried with the dead as a guide to reach the kingdom of ◊Osiris.

Book Trust British association of authors, publishers, booksellers, librarians, and readers, to encourage the reading and production of books. Founded as the National Book Council in 1925, it was renamed the National Book League in 1944 and renamed Book Trust in 1986.

Boole /buːl/ George 1814–1864. British mathematician, whose work *The Mathematical Analysis of Logic* 1847 established the basis of modern mathematical logic, and whose *Boolean algebra* can be used in designing computers.

boomerang hand-thrown wooden missile shaped in a curved angle, which returns to the thrower if it does not hit its target. It was developed by the Australian Aborigines.

boomslang venomous African snake *Dispholidus typus*, often green, but sometimes brown or blackish. It lives in trees and feeds on tree-dwelling lizards such as chameleons. Its fangs are at the rear of the mouth, and it rarely strikes at people, but the venom is so powerful it can be fatal to a human if the snake manages to get a good grip.

Boone /buːn/ Daniel 1734–1820. American frontiersman, who explored the Wilderness Road (East Virginia/Kentucky) in 1775 and paved the way for the first westward migration of settlers.

booster the first-stage rockets of a space launching vehicle, or additional rockets strapped on to the main rocket to assist take-off. The American *Delta* rocket, for example, has a cluster of nine strap-on boosters that fire on lift-off. Europe's *Ariane 3* rocket uses twin strap-on boosters, as does the American Space Shuttle.

Bootes ◊constellation of the northern hemisphere representing a herdsman driving a bear (Ursa Major) around the pole. Its brightest star is first-magnitude ◊Arcturus.

Booth /buːð/ Charles 1840–1916. British sociologist, author of the study *Life and Labour of the People in London* 1891–1903, and pioneer of an old-age pension scheme.

Booth /buːθ/ John Wilkes 1839–1865. American actor, who assassinated President ◊Lincoln 14 Apr 1865; he escaped with a broken leg and was later shot in a barn in Virginia when he refused to surrender.

Booth /buːð/ William 1829–1912. British founder of the ◊Salvation Army in 1878, and its first 'General'. Born in Nottingham, the son of a builder, he experienced religious conversion at the age of 15. In 1865 he founded in Whitechapel

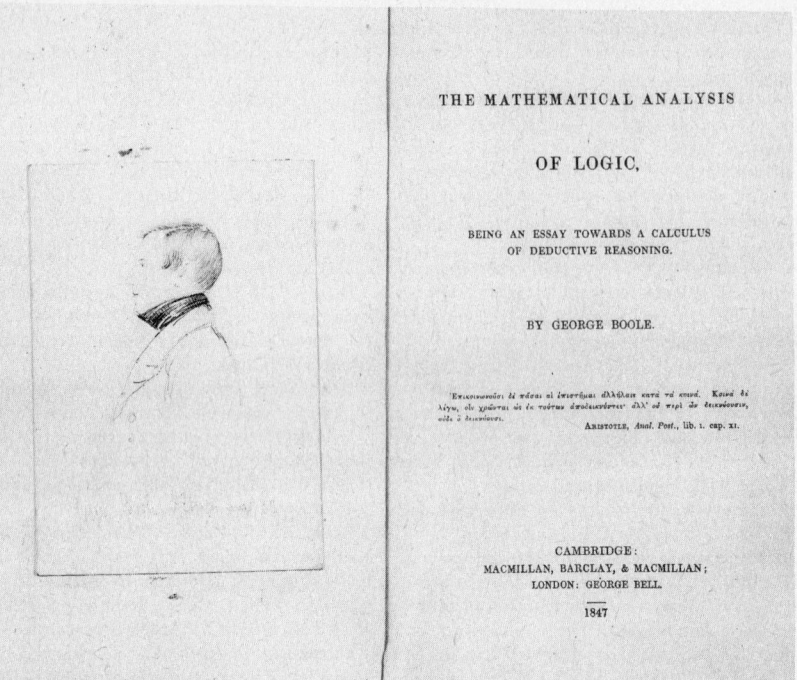

THE MATHEMATICAL ANALYSIS

OF LOGIC,

BEING AN ESSAY TOWARDS A CALCULUS
OF DEDUCTIVE REASONING.

BY GEORGE BOOLE.

CAMBRIDGE:
MACMILLAN, BARCLAY, & MACMILLAN;
LONDON: GEORGE BELL.

1847

Boole The son of a shoemaker, George Boole established the basis of modern mathematical logic in his work, *The Mathematical Analysis of Logic*. His work is the foundation of computer logic.

the Christian Mission which in 1878 became the Salvation Army. *In Darkest England, and the Way Out* 1890 contained proposals for the physical and spiritual redemption of the great mass of 'down-and-outs'. His wife Catherine 1829–90 (born Mumford), whom he married in 1855, became a public preacher in about 1860, initiating the ministry of women. Their eldest son, *William Bramwell Booth* (1856–1929) became chief of staff of the Salvation Army in 1880 and was General from 1912 until his deposition 1929. *Evangeline Booth* (1865–1950), 7th child of General William Booth, was a prominent Salvation Army officer, and 1934–39 was General. She became a US citizen. *Catherine Bramwell Booth* (1884–1987), a granddaughter of William Booth, was a commissioner in the Salvation Army.

Boothby /'buːðbi/ Robert John Graham, Baron Boothby 1900–1986. Scottish politician. He became a Unionist Member of Parliament in 1924 and was parliamentary private secretary to Churchill 1926–29. An ardent advocate of Britain's entry into Europe, a noted speaker and a powerful personality in British politics, he published *Recollections of a Rebel* 1978.

Boothe /buːθ/ Clare 1903–1987. American journalist, playwright, and politician. Born in New York, she was managing editor of the magazine *Vanity Fair* (1933–34), and wrote several successful plays, including *The Women* 1936 and *Margin for Error* 1939. She was a Republican member of Congress 1943–47 and ambassador to Italy 1953–57. She was married to Henry Robinson Luce 1898–1967, founder of the magazines *Time* 1923 and *Life* 1936.

William Booth STEPHEN REID 1906

Booth William Booth was a British evangelist and itinerant preacher. He established a mission among the poor in Whitechapel, London, but the churches were reluctant to accept his converts and in 1878 he founded the Salvation Army and became its first General.

Bootle /'buːtl/ port in Merseyside, England, adjoining Liverpool; population (1981) 62,463. The National Girobank headquarters is here.

bootlegging colloquial term for the illegal selling or smuggling of alcoholic liquor. It is said to have originated in the USA, when the sale

of alcohol to American Indians was illegal and bottles were hidden for sale in the legs of the jackboots of unscrupulous traders. The term was later used for all illegal liquor sales in the period of ◊Prohibition 1920–33.

Bophuthatswana /bəʊ,puːtət'swɑːnə/ Republic of
area 40,330 sq km/15,571 sq mi
capital Mmbatho or Sun City, a casino resort frequented by many white South Africans
features divided into six 'blocks'
exports platinum, chrome, vanadium, asbestos, manganese
currency South African rand
population (1980) 1,328,637
language Setswana, English
religion Christian
government executive president elected by the Assembly: Chief Lucas Mangope.
recent history first 'independent' Black National State from 1977, but not recognized by any country other than South Africa.

borage salad plant *Borago officinalis* cultivated in Britain and occasionally naturalized. It has small blue flowers and hairy leaves.

Borah /'bɔːrə/ William Edgar 1865–1940. American Republican politician. Born in Illinois, he was a Senator for Idaho from 1906. He is remembered as an arch-isolationist, one of those chiefly responsible for America's repudiation of the League of Nations.

Borås /buː'rɔːs/ industrial town (textiles, engineering) in SW Sweden; population (1982) 211,197.

borax hydrated sodium borate, $Na_2B_4O_7$, found as soft, whitish crystals or incrustations on the shores of hot springs and lakes associated with recent volcanoes. A major industrial source is Borax Lake, California. It provides a starting material for ◊perborates (used in bleaches and washing powders), and is also used in glazing pottery, soldering, as a mild antiseptic and as a metallurgical flux.

Bordeaux /bɔː'dəu/ port on the Garonne, capital of Aquitaine, SW France, a centre for the wine trade, aeronautics and space industries; population (1983) 221,500.
history Bordeaux was under the English crown for three centuries until 1453. In 1870, 1914, and 1940 the French government was moved here in the face of German invasion.

Borders /'bɔːdəz/ region of Scotland
area 4,670 sq km/1,803 sq mi
towns administrative headquarters Newtown St Boswells; Hawick, Jedburgh
features river Tweed; Lammermuir, Moorfoot, and Pentland hills; home of the novelist ◊Scott at Abbotsford; Dryburgh Abbey, burial place of Field Marshal Haig and Sir Walter Scott; ruins of 12th-century Melrose Abbey
products knitted goods, tweed
population (1983) 101,202
famous people Duns Scotus, Mungo Park.

bore a surge of tidal water up an estuary or a river, caused by the funnelling of the rising tide by a narrowing river mouth. A particularly high tide, possibly fanned by wind, may build up when it is held back by a river current in the river

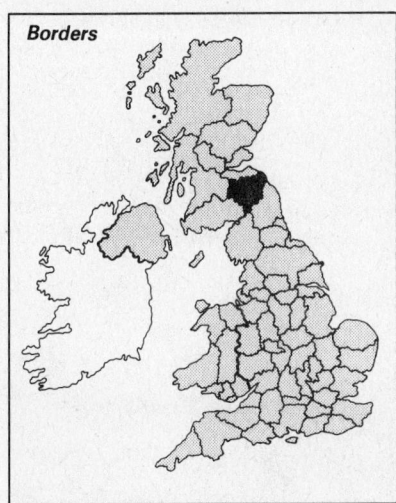

Borders

Borges The Argentinian author and former university professor is seen here after receiving an honorary degree at the University of Oxford in 1970.

mouth. The result is a broken wave, a metre or so high, that rushes upstream. Famous bores are found in the rivers Severn (England), Seine (France), Hooghly (India), and Yangtze-kiang (China), where bores of over 4 m/13 ft have been reported.

Borg /bɔːg/ Björn 1956– . Swedish lawn-tennis player, winner of the Wimbledon singles championship 1976–80.

Borges /'bɔːxes/ Jorge Luis 1899–1986. Argentinian poet and short-story writer. In 1961 he became director of the National Library, Buenos Aires, and was professor of English literature at the university there. He is best known for his *Ficciones/Fictions* 1944. He was almost blind.

Borgia /'bɔːdʒə/ Cesare 1476–1507. Italian soldier, illegitimate son of Pope ◊Alexander VI. Made a cardinal at 17 by his father, he resigned the honour to become captain-general of the Papacy, campaigning successfully against the city republics of Italy. Ruthless and treacherous in war, he was an able ruler (the model of ◊Machiavelli's *The Prince*) of conquered territory, but his power crumbled on the death of his father. He was a patron of artists, including Leonardo da Vinci.

Borgia /'bɔːdʒə/ Lucrezia 1480–1519. Illegitimate daughter of Pope ◊Alexander VI, and sister of Cesare ◊Borgia. She was married at 12 and again at 13 to further her father's ambitions, both marriages being annulled by him. At 18 she was again married, her husband being murdered in 1500 on the order of her brother, with whom (as well as with her father) she was said to have committed incest. Her final marriage in 1501 was to the son and heir of the Duke of Ferrara. She encouraged authors and artists such as Ariosto and Titian, and she made the court a centre of culture.

Borglum /'bɔːgləm/ Gutzon 1871–1941. American sculptor, born in Idaho. He is best known for monumental works, for example, a six-tonne marble head of Lincoln at Washington DC and a series of giant heads of Washington,

Jefferson, Lincoln and T Roosevelt carved on Mount Rushmore, South Dakota.

boric acid an acid formed by the combination of hydrogen and oxygen with non-metallic ◊boron; also called boracic acid. It is a weak antiseptic.

Boris Godunov /'bɒrɪs/ 1552–1605. Tsar of Russia from 1598, when he was elected after the death of Fyodor, son of ◊Ivan the Terrible. He died during a revolt led by one who professed to be Dmitri, a brother of Fyodor and the rightful tsar. The true Dmitri, however, had died in 1591 by cutting his own throat during an epileptic fit. The apocryphal legend of Boris Godunov killing the true Dmitri to gain the throne was fostered by Russian historians anxious to discredit Boris, who was not descended from any of the main ruling families, as being outside the true line of Russian tsars. This legend forms the basis of ◊Pushkin's play *Boris Godunov* 1831 and ◊Mussorgsky's opera of the same name 1874. Godunov's rule was marked by a strengthening of the Russian church, but also the beginning of the 'Time of Troubles', a period of instability.

Boris III /'bɒrɪs/ 1894–1943. Tsar of Bulgaria from 1918, when he succeeded his father, Ferdinand I. From 1934 he was virtual dictator until his sudden and mysterious death following a visit to Hitler. His son Simeon II was tsar until deposed in 1946.

Borlaug /'bɔːlɔːg/ Norman Ernest 1914– . US microbiologist, breeder of high-yielding wheat and other crops for Third World countries. Nobel peace prize 1970.

Bormann /'bɔːmæn/ Martin 1900–? 1945. German Nazi leader, born in Halberstadt. He took part in the abortive Munich Putsch of 1923, and rose to high positions in the National Socialist Party. After Hess's flight to England he

became 'party chancellor' in May 1941. Believed to have escaped the fall of Berlin in May 1945, he was tried in absence and sentenced to death at Nuremberg 1945–46, but a skeleton uncovered by a mechanical excavator in Berlin in 1972 was officially recognized as his by forensic experts in 1973.

Born /bɔːn/ Max 1882–1970. British physicist, of German origin, who received a Nobel Prize in 1954 for fundamental work on ◊quantum mechanics.

Born German physicist Max Born seated surrounded by his colleagues at Göttingen in 1922, left to right, William Osler, Niels Bohr, James Franck and Oscar Klein. Like many others he left Germany for Britain during the Nazi era.

Borneo /'bɔːnɪəʊ/ third largest island in the world, one of the Sunda Islands in the W Pacific; area 750,000 sq km/290,000 sq mi. It comprises the Malaysian territories of ◊Sabah and ◊Sarawak; ◊Brunei; and, occupying by far the largest part, the Indonesian territory of ◊Kalimantan. It is mountainous and densely forested. In coastal areas the people of Borneo are mainly of Malaysian origin, with a few Chinese, and the interior is inhabited by the indigenous Dayaks.

Bornholm /,bɔːn'həʊm/ Danish island in the Baltic Sea, 35 km/22 mi SE of the nearest point of the Swedish coast
area 587 sq km/227 sq mi
capital Roønne
population (1985) 47,164.

Bornu /bɔː'nuː/ kingdom of the 9th–19th centuries to the west and south of Lake Chad. Converted to Islam in the 11th century, it reached its greatest strength in the 15th–18th centuries. From 1901 it was absorbed in the British, French and German colonies in this area, which are now the Republics of Niger and Cameroon, and the Federation of Nigeria. The largest section of ancient Bornu falls in the modern state of Bornu in Nigeria, of which the capital is Maiduguri.

Borobudur /ˌbɒrəʊˈbuːdə/ site of Buddhist shrine near ◊Yogyakarta, Indonesia.

Borodin /ˈbɒrədɪn/ Alexander Porfir'yevich 1833–1887. Russian composer. Born in St Petersburg, the illegitimate son of a Russian prince, he became by profession an expert in medical chemistry, but in his spare time devoted himself to music. His principal work is the opera *Prince Igor*; left unfinished, this was completed by ◊Rimsky-Korsakov and Glazunov, and includes the Polovtsian Dances. Borodin's works include symphonies, songs, and chamber music, and use traditional Russian themes.

Borodino, Battle of /ˌbɒrəˈdiːnəʊ/ battle NW of Moscow in which French troops under Napoleon defeated the Russians under Kutusov 7 Sept 1812.

boron a chemical element, symbol B, atomic weight 10.81, atomic number 5. It is found in two forms, brown (non-metallic) and black (metallic). It is used to harden steel and, because it absorbs slow neutrons, to make control rods for nuclear reactors.

borough unit of local government in the UK from the 8th century until 1974, when it continued as an honorary status granted by royal charter to a district council, entitling its leader to the title of mayor.

Borromeo /ˌbɒrəʊˈmeɪəʊ/ Carlo 1538–1584. Roman Catholic saint and cardinal. Born at Arona of noble Italian family, he was created a cardinal and archbishop of Milan by his uncle Pope Pius IV in 1560. Borromeo wound up the affairs of the Council of Trent, and largely drew up the catechism that contained its findings. He lived the life of an ascetic, and in 1578 founded the community later called the Oblate Fathers of St Charles. He was canonized 1610. His feast day is 4 Nov.

Borromini /ˌbɒrəʊˈmiːni/ Francesco 1599–1667. Italian ◊Baroque architect. He worked under ◊Bernini, later his rival, on St Peter's, Rome, and created the oval-shaped San Carlo alle Quattro Fontane, Rome.

Borstal prison near Rochester, Kent, England, where the Borstal system of reformatories (from 1983 known as Youth Custody Centres) was first introduced in 1908 for young offenders.

borzoi large breed of dog originating in Russia, 75 cm/2.5 ft or more at the shoulder, of the greyhound type with a thick silky coat, white with darker markings. Its name is Russian for swift.

Bosch /bɒs/ Hieronymus (Jerome) 1460–1516. Dutch painter named from his birthplace, 's Hertogenbosch. His works, of a bizarre and grotesque style, foreshadowed surrealism and were greatly admired by Philip II of Spain.

Bose /bəʊs/ Jagadis Chunder 1858–1937. Indian physicist. Born near Dacca, he was professor of physical science at Calcutta 1885–1915, and studied plant-life, especially the growth and minute movements of plants, and their reaction to electrical stimuli. He founded the Bose Research Institute, Calcutta.

Bose /bəʊs/ Satyendra Nath 1894–1974. Indian physicist. With ◊Einstein, he formulated the Bose-Einstein law of quantum mechanics, and was professor of physics at the University of Calcutta 1945–58.

Bosnia and Herzegovina /ˈbɒznɪə, ˌhɜːitsɪɡəˈviːnə/ constituent republic of Yugoslavia
area 51,129 sq km/19,745 sq mi
capital Sarajevo
features barren, mountainous country
population (1981) 4,116,500, including 1,321,000 Serbs and 758,000 Croats
language Serbian variant of Serbo-Croat
religion Sunni Muslim, Serbian Orthodox, and Roman Catholic
history once the Roman province of ◊Illyria, it enjoyed brief periods of independence in medieval times, then was ruled by the Ottoman Empire 1463–1878 and Austria 1878–1918, when it was incorporated in the future Yugoslavia. It was a Bosnian student who murdered the Austrian archduke Ferdinand at ◊Sarajevo in 1914.

Bosporus /ˈbɒspərəs/ strait 27 km/17 mi long joining the Black Sea with the Sea of Marmara and forming part of the water division between Europe and Asia. Istanbul stands on its W side. The *Bosporus Bridge* 1973 links Istanbul and Turkey-in-Asia (1,621 m/5,320 ft).

Bossuet /ˌbɒsjuˈeɪ/ Jacques Bénigne 1627–1704. French Roman Catholic divine, pulpit orator, and theologian. Appointed bishop of Meaux in 1681, Bossuet became involved in the Gallican controversy between Louis XIV and the pope.

Boston /ˈbɒstən/ seaport in Lincolnshire, England, on the Witham river; population (1981) 26,500. St Botolph's is England's largest parish church, and its tower 'Boston stump' is a landmark for sailors.

Boston /ˈbɒstən/ industrial and commercial centre, capital of Massachusetts, USA; population (1980) 563,000; met area 2,800,000. It is a publishing centre, and Harvard University and Massachusetts Institute of Technology are nearby. Among historic buildings is the Paul ◊Revere House. Residents have included the writers Poe, Emerson, Hawthorne, Thoreau, and Longfellow.

Boswell /ˈbɒzwəl/ James 1740–1795. Scottish biographer and man-of-letters, noted for his biography of Samuel ◊Johnson. He first met Johnson in 1763 before setting out on the European tour during which he met Rousseau, Voltaire, and General Paoli, whom he commemorated in his popular *Account of Corsica* 1768. In 1766 he became a lawyer, and in 1772 renewed his acquaintance with Johnson in London. Establishing a place in his intimate circle, he became a member of the Literary Club in 1773, and in the same year accompanied Johnson on the journey later recorded in the *Journal of the Tour to the Hebrides* 1785. On his succession to his father's estate in 1782, he made further attempts to enter Parliament, was called to the English bar in 1786, and was Recorder of Carlisle 1788–90. In 1789 he settled in London, and in 1791 produced the classic English biography, the *Life of Samuel Johnson*. His long-lost personal papers were acquired for publication by Yale University in 1949, and the *Journals* are of exceptional interest.

Boswell Scottish lawyer James Boswell met Dr Johnson in 1763 and travelled with him in England and in Europe, meeting many of the notable people of their day, and writing down their conversations. The sketch is by George Dance 1793.

Bosworth, Battle of /ˈbɒzwəθ/ last battle of the Wars of the Roses, fought on 22 Aug 1485 near the village of Market Bosworth, 19 km /12 m west of Leicester. Richard III, the Yorkist king, was defeated and slain by Henry of Richmond, who became Henry VII.

botanic garden a place where a wide range of plants are grown, providing the opportunity to see a botanical diversity not likely to be encountered elsewhere. Among the earliest forms of botanic garden was the physic garden, devoted to the study and growth of medicinal plants, for example, the Chelsea Physic Garden in London, established in 1673 and still in existence today. Following increased botanical exploration, the botanical gardens were used as testing grounds for potentially important new economic plants being sent back from all parts of the world. A modern botanic garden serves many purposes: education, science, and conservation. Many are associated with universities and also maintain large collections of preserved specimens (see ◊herbarium), libraries, research laboratories, and gene banks.

botany the study of plants. It is subdivided into a number of specialized studies, such as the identification and classification of plants (termed taxonomy), their external formation (plant morphology), their internal arrangement (plant anatomy), their microscopic examination (histology), their life history (plant physiology), and their distribution over the earth's surface in relation to their surroundings (plant ecology). Palaeobotany concerns the study of fossil plants, while economic botany deals with the utility of plants. Horticulture, agriculture, and forestry are specialized branches of botany. The most ancient botanical record is carved on the walls of the temple at Karnak, about 1500 BC. The Greeks in the fifth and fourth centuries BC used many plants for medicinal purposes, the first Greek Herbal being drawn up about 350 BC by Diocles of Carystus. Botanical information was collected into the works of Theophrastus of Eresus (380–287 BC), a pupil of Aristotle, who founded the technical plant nomenclature. Cesalpino in the 16th century sketched out a system of classification based on flowers, fruits, and seeds, while Jung (1587–1658) used flowers only as his criterion. John Ray (1627–1705) arranged plants systematically, based on his findings on fruit, leaf and flower, and described about 18,600 plants. Swedish Carl von Linné or ◊Linnaeus (1707–78), who founded systematics, included in his classification all known plants and animals, giving each a binomial descriptive label. Banks, Solander, Brown, Bauer, and others travelled throughout the world studying plants, and found that all could be fitted into a systematic classification based on Linnaeus' work. Linnaeus was also the first to recognize the sexual nature of flowers, this work being followed up later by Sprengel, Amici, Robert Brown, and Charles ◊Darwin. Later work revealed the detailed cellular structure of plant tissues, and the exact nature of ◊photosynthesis. Julius von Sachs (1832–97) defined the function of ◊chlorophyll, and the significance of plant ◊stomata. In the period since World War II much has been achieved towards the clarification of cell function, repair and growth by the hybridization of plant cells: the combination of the nucleus of one cell with the protoplasm of another.

Botany Bay /'botəni/ inlet on the E coast of Australia, 8 km/5 mi S of Sydney, New South Wales. So named by Captain Cook in 1770 on account of the variety of plants found on its shores by Joseph Banks, the expedition's botanist. Chosen in 1787 as the site for a penal colony, it proved unsuitable, and the settlement was made where Sydney stands. But the name Botany Bay continued to be popularly used for any convict settlement in Australia.

botfly type of fly, family Oestridae, in which the larvae are parasites feeding in the skin (warblefly of cattle) or in the nasal cavity (nostril-flies of sheep, deer). The horse botfly, family Gasterophilidae, has a parasitic larva feeding in the horse's stomach.

Botha /'bəʊtə/ Louis 1862–1919. South African soldier and politician, born at Greytown, Natal, of Boer parents. Elected a member of the Volksraad in 1897, he supported the more moderate Joubert against Kruger. On the outbreak of the Boer War he commanded the Boers besieging Ladysmith, and in 1900 succeeded Joubert in command of the Transvaal forces. In 1907 Botha became premier of the Transvaal and in 1910 of the first Union government. On the outbreak of war in 1914 he rallied South Africa to the Commonwealth, suppressed the Boer revolt under de Wet, and conquered German South West Africa. At Versailles in 1919 he represented South Africa.

Botha /'bəʊtə/ P(ieter) W(illem) 1916– . South African politician. Prime minister from 1978, he initiated a modification of ◊apartheid

which later slowed owing to the force of ◊Afrikaner opposition. In 1984 he became first executive state president. He has been widely criticized in the rest of the world for the harsh enforcement of fundamentally racist policies.

Botham /'bəʊθəm/ Ian Terrence 1955– . English all-round cricketer. He made his debut for Somerset 1974, and played his first test match against Australia in 1977. He has since broken the record for the most wickets in a test career (357 wickets, 96 catches, and 4,636 runs by the end of the 1986 English season). Generally acknowledged to be a brilliant cricketer, he is a controversial figure and has been disciplined by the Cricket Council. He started playing for Worcestershire in 1987. He has also played Football League soccer for Scunthorpe United.

Botham English cricketer Ian Botham batting for England at the Benson and Hedges challenge at Perth, 1986. One of the best all-rounders of the modern game, he has also been a controversial figure.

Bothwell /'bɒθwəl/ James Hepburn, 4th Earl of Bothwell c. 1536–1578. Scottish nobleman, who is alleged to have arranged the explosion that killed Darnley, husband of ◊Mary Queen of Scots, in 1567. Tried and acquitted a few weeks later, he abducted Mary, and (having divorced his wife) married her on 15 May. A revolt ensued, and Bothwell was forced to flee to Norway and on to Sweden. In 1570 Mary obtained a divorce on the ground that she had been ravished by Bothwell before marriage. Later, Bothwell was confined in a castle in Zeeland, the Netherlands, where he died insane.

bo tree another name for the ◊peepul. See also under ◊fig.

Botswana /bɒt'swɑːnə/ landlocked country in central southern Africa, bounded to the south and east by South Africa, to the west and north by Namibia, and to the northeast by Zimbabwe.
government the 1966 constitution blends the British system of parliamentary accountability with representation for each of Botswana's major

ethnic groups. It provides for a national assembly of 40 members, 34 elected by universal suffrage, four by the assembly itself, plus the speaker and the attorney-general, and has a life of five years. The president is elected by the assembly for its duration and is an ex-officio member of it and answerable to it. There is also a 15-member house of chiefs, consisting of the chiefs of Botswana's eight principal ethnic groups, plus four members elected by the chiefs themselves and three elected by the house in general. The president may delay a bill for up to six months and then either sign it or dissolve the assembly and call a general election. The house of chiefs is consulted by the president and the assembly in matters affecting them. The president appoints a cabinet which is answerable to the assembly. Most significant of the seven political groupings are the Botswana Democratic Party (BDP), and the Botswana National Front (BNF).
history inhabited by the Tswana from the 18th century, Botswana occupies a delicate position geographically and politically. It was originally Bechuanaland which, at the request of local rulers, became a British protectorate in 1885. On passing the Union of South Africa Act in 1910, making South Africa independent, the British Parliament provided for the possibility of Bechuanaland becoming part of South Africa, but said that this would not happen without popular consent. Successive South African governments requested the transfer but Botswana preferred full independence.
The 1960 constitution provided for a legislative council, though remaining under British High Commission control. In 1963 High Commission rule ended and in the legislative assembly elections the newly formed Bechuanaland Democratic Party (BDP) won a majority. Its leader, Seretse Khama, had been deposed as chief of the Bangangwato Tribe in 1950, and had since lived in exile, after marrying an Englishwoman two years before.
In 1966 the country, renamed Botswana, became an independent state within the Commonwealth with Sir Seretse Khama, as he had now become, as president. He continued to be re-elected until his death in 1980 when he was succeeded by the vice-president, Dr Quett Masire, who was re-elected in 1984.
Since independence Botswana has earned a reputation for stability and has followed a path of ◊non-alignment. South Africa has accused it of providing bases for the African National Congress (ANC). This has always been denied by both Botswana and the ANC itself. South Africa has persistently pressed Botswana to sign a non-aggression pact, similar to the ◊Nkomati Accord between South Africa and Mozambique.

Botticelli /ˌbɒtɪ'tʃeli/ Sandro 1445–1510. Florentine artist, real name Filipepi, but his elder brother's nickname Botticelli 'little barrel' was passed on to him. He was patronized by the ◊Medici, with whom he broke after their execution of ◊Savonarola, and became more sombre and religious in his later style. His best-known works are *Primavera* and *The Birth of Venus*, both in the Uffizi, Florence.

Botswana
REPUBLIC OF

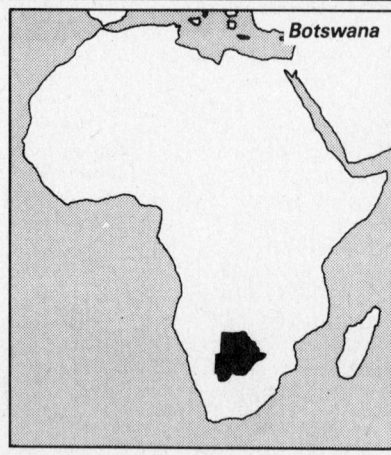

AREA 575,000 sq km/222,000 sq mi
CAPITAL Gaborone
PHYSICAL desert in SW, plains in E, fertile lands and swamp in N
FEATURES larger part of Kalahari Desert, including Okovango Swamp, remarkable for its wildlife
HEAD OF STATE AND OF GOVERNMENT Quett Ketamile Joni Masire from 1980
GOVERNMENT democracy
EXPORTS diamonds, copper-nickel and meat
CURRENCY pula (2.78 = £1 Sept 1987)
POPULATION (1985) 1,068,000 (80% Bamangwato, 20% Bangwaketse); annual growth rate 3.1%
LANGUAGE English (official); Setswana (national)
RELIGION Christian (majority)
LITERACY 61% male/61% female (1980 est)
GDP $810 million (1984); $544 per head of population
CHRONOLOGY
1885 Became a British protectorate.
1960 New constitution created a legislative council.
1963 End of high-commission rule.
1965 Capital transferred fron Mafeking to

Gaborone. Internal self-government granted. Seretse Khama elected head of government.
1966 Full independence achieved. New constitution came into effect. Name changed from Bechuanaland to Botswana. Sir Seretse Khama elected president.
1980 Sir Seretse Khama died and was succeeded by Vice-President Quett Masire.
1984 Masire re-elected.
1985 South African raid on Gaborone.

Latin form Boadicea. Her husband, King Prasutagus, had been a tributary of the Romans, but on his death 61 AD, the territory of the Iceni was violently annexed, Boudicca was scourged and her daughters raped. Boudicca raised the whole of SE England in revolt, and before the main Roman armies could return from campaigning in Wales she burned London and Colchester. Later the British were annihilated somewhere between London and Chester, and Boudicca poisoned herself.

Boudin /buːˈdæŋ/ Eugène 1824–1898. French painter, a forerunner of Impressionism, noted for his seascapes.

Bougainville /ˈbuːɡənvɪl/ island province of Papua New Guinea; largest of the Solomon Islands archipelago
area 10,620 sq km/4,100 sq mi
capital Kieta
products copper
population (1975) 90,000
history named for the French navigator ◊Bougainville who arrived in 1768. In 1976 Bougainville became a province (with substantial autonomy) of Papua New Guinea.

Bougainville /ˈbuːɡənvɪl/ Louis Antoine de 1729–1811. French navigator. After service with the French in Canada during the Seven Years' War he sailed round the world, 1766–69. Several islands are named after him, and also the climbing plant ◊bougainvillea.

bougainvillea genus of South American climbing plants, family Nyctaginaceae, now

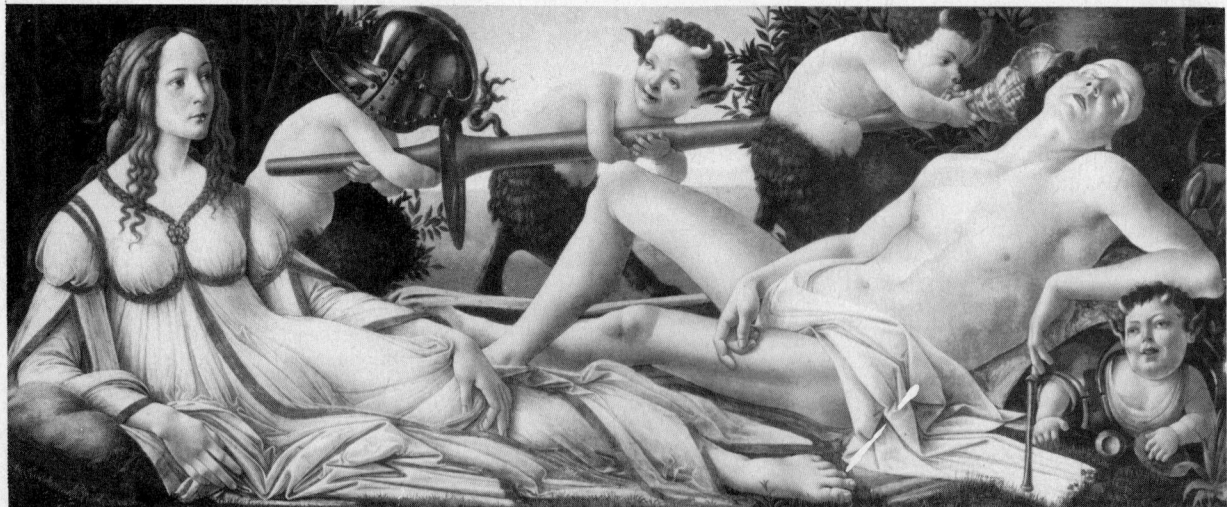

Botticelli *Venus and Mars* by Italian artist Sandro Botticelli. Apprenticed to Fra Filippo Lippi, according to tradition, and patronized by the Medici, he decorated many churches and chapels, including the Sistine.

bottlebrush trees and shrubs common in Australia, belonging to the genera *Melaleuca* and *Callistemon*, with characteristic cylindrical, composite flowerheads, often brightly coloured.

botulism often fatal type of food poisoning, caused by the anaerobic bacterium *Clostridium botulinum*, sometimes found in canned food.

Boucher /buːˈʃeɪ/ François 1703–1770. French painter. Born in Paris, he became director of the ◊Gobelin tapestry works in 1755,

and ten years later court painter. He is famous for his paintings of maidens, shepherds, and cupids.

Boucher de Crèvecoeur de Perthes /buːˈʃeɪ dəkrevˈkɜː də ˈpeət/ Jacques 1788–1868. French geologist, whose discovery of Palaeolithic hand-axes in 1837 led him to promote the controversial recognition of human history as antedating the popularly accepted limit of 4000 BC.

Boudicca /ˈbuːdɪkə/ died 60 AD. Queen of the Iceni (native Britons), often referred to by the

cultivated in warm countries throughout the world for the red and purple bracts, which cover the flowers. They are named after ◊Bougainville.

Bougie /buːˈʒiː/ name until 1962 of ◊Bejaia, port in Algeria.

Bouguer anomaly in geophysics, an increase in the earth's gravity observed near a mountain or a particularly dense rock mass. This is due to the gravitational force exerted by the rock itself. It is named after its discoverer, the French mathematician Pierre Bouguer (1698–1758), who observed it in 1735.

Boulanger /ˌbuːlɒn'ʒeɪ/ George Ernest Jean Marie 1837–1891. French general. After service in Indo-China and North Africa, he became minister of war in 1886. He won immense popularity because of his anti-German speeches, and nearly provoked a war with Germany in 1887. In 1889 he was suspected of aspiring to dictatorial powers by a coup d'état, fled to London, and was tried in his absence for treason. He committed suicide in Brussels on the grave of his mistress.

Boulanger /ˌbuːlɒn'ʒeɪ/ Nadia (Juliette) 1887–1979. French music teacher. A pupil of ◊Fauré, and admirer of ◊Stravinsky, she included among her pupils at the Conservatoire Américain de Fontainebleau in Paris (from 1921) Aaron ◊Copland, Roy ◊Harris, Walter ◊Piston and Lennox ◊Berkeley.

boules (French 'balls') French game (also *boccie*) between two players or teams, each of which try to place their boules which are 11 cm/8 in in diameter, nearer to the target jack than their opponent, and improve the position of their own. Standard length of the pitch is 27.5 metres.

Boulestin /ˌbuːle'stæn/ Marcel 1878–1943. French cookery writer and restaurateur. He was influential in spreading the principles of simple but high-quality French cooking in Britain in the first half of the 20th century, with a succession of popular books such as *What Shall We Have Today?* (1931).

Boulez /'buːlez/ Pierre 1925– . French composer and conductor. He studied with ◊Messiaen, and is a pioneer of electronic music. His works include *Le Visage nuptial* 1946–52 for two solo voices, female choir and orchestra; *Le Marteau sans maître* 1955, a cantata; *Pli selon pli* 1962 for soprano and orchestra; and *Répons* 1981 for chamber orchestra and electronics.

Boulogne-sur-Mer /buː'lɔɪn sjuə 'meə/ industrial (oil refining, food processing), fishing and ferry port and seaside resort on the English Channel, Pas-de-Calais *département*, France; population (1983) 48,500.
history Boulogne was a medieval countship, but became part of France in 1477. Napoleon assembled his invading force for England here. In World War II it was evacuated by the British 23 May 1940 and recaptured by the Canadians 22 Sept 1944.

Boult /bəult/ Adrian (Cedric) 1889–1983. British conductor. He was conductor of the BBC Symphony Orchestra 1930–50 and the London Philharmonic 1950–57. He promoted the work of ◊Holst and ◊Vaughan Williams, and was a noted interpreter of ◊Elgar. He was knighted in 1937.

Boulting /'bəultɪŋ/ John 1913–85 and Roy 1913– . British twin-brother director-producer team that was particularly influential in the years following World War II. Their films include *Brighton Rock* 1947, *Lucky Jim* 1957, and *I'm All Right Jack* 1959.

Boulton /'bəultən/ Matthew 1728–1809. British factory-owner, who helped to finance James ◊Watt's development of the steam engine. Boulton had an engineering works at Soho near Birmingham, and in 1775 he went into partnership with Watt to develop engines to power factory machines that had previously been driven by water.

Boumédienne /ˌbuːmeɪd'jen/ Houari. Adopted name of Algerian politician Mohammed Boukharouba 1925–78, who brought ◊Ben Bella to power by a revolt in 1962, and superseded him as president 1965–78 by a further coup.

Bounty, Mutiny on the Pacific mutiny in 1789 against British admiral William ◊Bligh.

Bourbon /'buəbən/ name 1649–1815 of the French island of Réunion in the Indian Ocean.

Bourbon /'buəbən/ French royal house (succeeding that of ◊Valois) beginning with ◊Henry IV, and ending with ◊Louis XVI, with a brief revival under ◊Louis Philippe; the present pretender is *Henri d'Orléans* Count of Paris 1908– , who served in the French Foreign Legion 1939–40. The Bourbons also ruled Spain almost uninterruptedly from ◊Philip V to ◊Alfonso XIII, and were restored in 1975 (◊Juan Carlos); as well as Naples and several Italian duchies.

Bourbon /'buəbən/ Charles, Duke of Bourbon 1490–1527. He was made Constable of France for his courage at the Battle of Marignano, 1515. Later he served the emperor Charles V, and helped to drive the French from Italy. In 1526 he was made duke of Milan, and in 1527 allowed his troops to sack Rome. He was killed by a shot Cellini claimed to have fired.

Bourdon /buə'dɒn/ Eugène 1808–1884. French engineer and instrument maker, who invented the pressure gauge which bears his name. The key to a Bourdon gauge is a tapering, C-shaped tube closed at its narrow end which changes circumference slightly when a gas or liquid under pressure flows into it. Levers and gears make the movement of the end of the tube work a pointer, which indicates pressure on a circular scale.

Bourgeois /buə'ʒwɑː/ Léon Victor Auguste 1851–1925. French politician. Entering politics as a Radical, he defeated General Boulanger in 1888, was prime minister in 1895, and later served in many cabinets. He was one of the pioneer advocates of the League of Nations. In 1920 he received the Nobel peace prize.

bourgeoisie the middle classes. The French word originally meant the freemen of a borough. Hence it came to mean the whole class above the workers and peasants, and below the nobility. Bourgeoisie has also acquired a contemptuous sense, as implying commonplace, philistine respectability. By socialists it is applied to the whole propertied class, as distinct from the proletariat.

Bourges /buəʒ/ historic and industrial city (aircraft, engineering, tyres) in central France, 200 km/125 mi S of Paris, with a 13th-century Gothic cathedral and notable art collections; population (1983) 76,500.

Bourgogne /buə'gɔɪn/ region of France, capital Dijon. A former independent kingdom and duchy (see ◊Burgundy), it was incorporated into France in 1477, on the death of the duke Charles the Bold. It is famous for its wines, such as Chablis and Nuits-Saint-Georges, and for its cattle (the Charolais herdbook is maintained at Nevers). Population (1982) 1,596,054.

Bourguiba /buə'giːbə/ Habib ben Ali 1903– . Tunisian politician. Educated at the University of Paris. He was frequently imprisoned by the French for his nationalist aims as leader of the Néo-Destour party. He became prime minister in 1956, president (for life from 1974) and prime minister of the Tunisian Republic in 1957; overthrown in a coup 1987.

Bournemouth /'bɔːnməθ/ seaside resort in Dorset, England; population (1981) 145,000.

Bournonville /ˌbuənɒŋ'viːl/ August 1805–1879. Danish dancer and choreographer. He worked with the Royal Danish Ballet for most of his life, giving Danish ballet a worldwide importance. His ballets, many of which have been revived in the last 50 years, include *La Sylphide* 1836 (music by Lövenskjold) and *Napoli* 1842.

Bouts /bauts/ Dierick c. 1400–1475. Dutch painter. Born at Haarlem, he settled in Louvain sometime before 1448, where he executed his finest works such as the *Last Supper* and the *Martyrdom of St Erasmus*. He is also known for his portraits and landscapes.

Bouvet Island /'buːveɪ/ uninhabited island in the S Atlantic Ocean, area 48 sq km/19 sq mi, a dependency of Norway since 1930. Discovered by the Frenchman Jacques Bouvet in 1738, it was made the subject of a claim by Britain in 1825, but this was waived in Norway's favour in 1928.

Bovet /bəu'veɪ/ Daniel 1907– . Swiss physiologist. He pioneered research into anti-histamine drugs used in the treatment of nettle rash and hay fever, and won a Nobel prize 1957 for his production of a synthetic form of curare, used as a muscle relaxant in anaesthesia.

Bow /bəu/ Clara 1905–1965. American silent film actress, known as the 'It' girl from the sex appeal of her appearance in *It* 1927.

Bow bells /bəu/ the bells of St Mary-le-Bow church, Cheapside, London; a person born within their sound is traditionally considered a true Cockney. The church was nearly destroyed by bombs in 1941. The bells, recast from the old metal, were restored in 1961.

Bowdler /'baudlə/ Thomas 1754–1825. British editor, whose prudishly expurgated versions of Shakespeare and other authors gave rise to the verb 'bowdlerize'.

Bowen /'bəuɪn/ Elizabeth 1899–1973. Irish novelist. Born in Dublin, she followed her first volume of short stories, *Encounters* 1923, with *Look at all those Roses* 1941, *The Demon Lover* 1945 and others. Her novels include *Friends and Relations* 1931, *The Death of the Heart* 1938, *The Heat of the Day* 1949, and *The Little Girls* 1964.

bower-bird Australian bird allied to the ◊birds of paradise. The males are dully-coloured but build elaborate bowers of sticks and grass, decorated with shells, feathers or flowers, to attract the females. There are 17 species in the family Ptilonorhynchidae.

bowfin North American fish *Amia calva* with a swimbladder highly developed as an air sac, enabling it to breathe air.

BOURBON AND BOURBON-ORLEANS, HOUSES OF

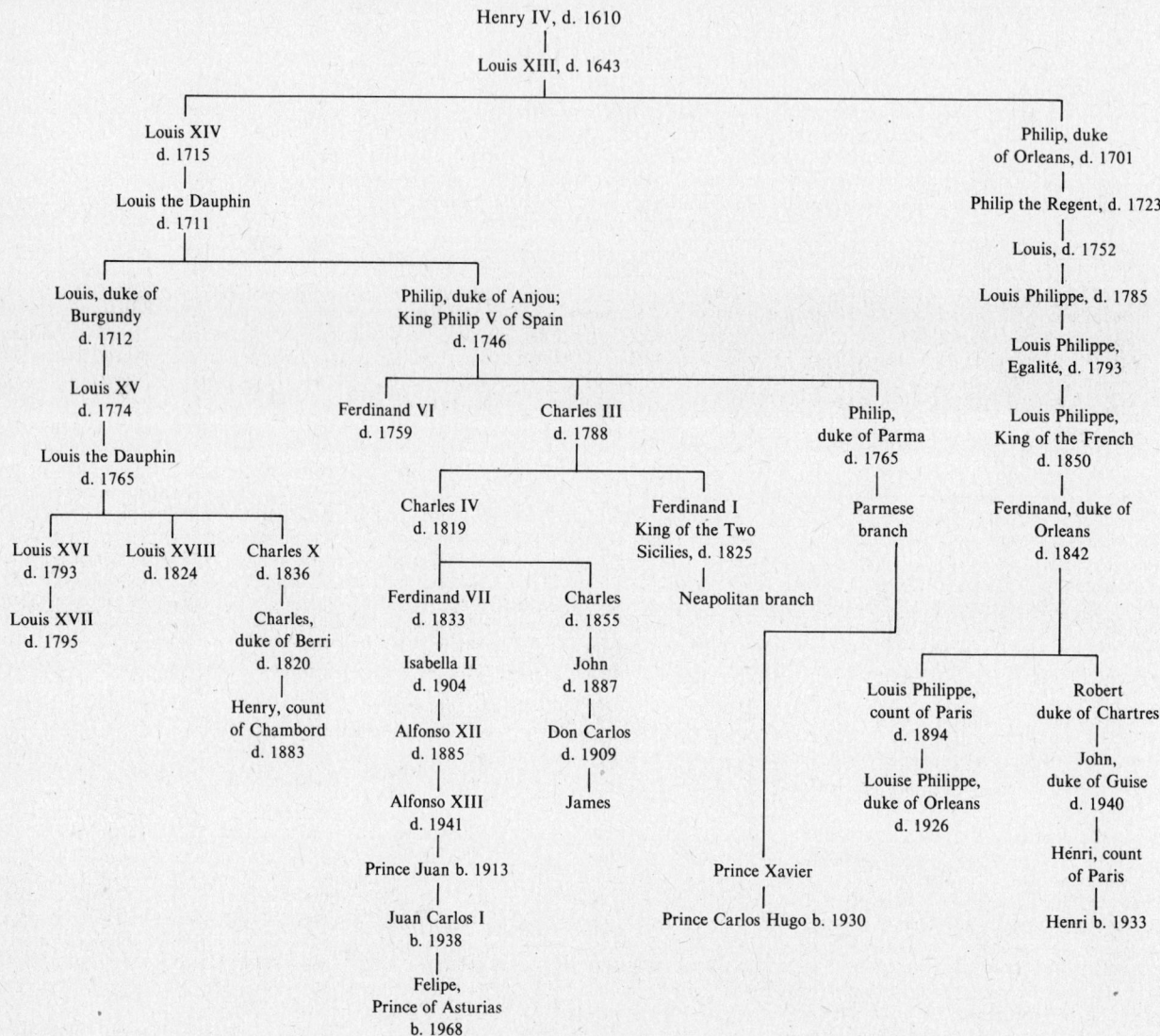

Henry IV, d. 1610

Louis XIII, d. 1643

Louis XIV
d. 1715

Louis the Dauphin
d. 1711

Louis, duke of
Burgundy
d. 1712

Louis XV
d. 1774

Louis the Dauphin
d. 1765

Louis XVI
d. 1793

Louis XVII
d. 1795

Louis XVIII
d. 1824

Charles X
d. 1836

Charles,
duke of Berri
d. 1820

Henry, count
of Chambord
d. 1883

Philip, duke of Anjou;
King Philip V of Spain
d. 1746

Ferdinand VI
d. 1759

Charles III
d. 1788

Charles IV
d. 1819

Ferdinand VII
d. 1833

Charles
d. 1855

Isabella II
d. 1904

John
d. 1887

Alfonso XII
d. 1885

Don Carlos
d. 1909

Alfonso XIII
d. 1941

James

Prince Juan b. 1913

Juan Carlos I
b. 1938

Felipe,
Prince of Asturias
b. 1968

Ferdinand I
King of the Two
Sicilies, d. 1825

Neapolitan branch

Philip,
duke of Parma
d. 1765

Parmese
branch

Prince Xavier

Prince Carlos Hugo b. 1930

Philip, duke
of Orleans, d. 1701

Philip the Regent, d. 1723

Louis, d. 1752

Louis Philippe, d. 1785

Louis Philippe,
Egalité, d. 1793

Louis Philippe,
King of the French
d. 1850

Ferdinand, duke of
Orleans
d. 1842

Louis Philippe,
count of Paris
d. 1894

Louise Philippe,
duke of Orleans
d. 1926

Robert
duke of Chartres

John,
duke of Guise
d. 1940

Henri, count
of Paris

Henri b. 1933

bowhead Arctic whale *Balaena mysticetus* with huge curving upper jaw bones supporting the plates of baleen which it uses to sift the water for planktonic crustaceans. Averaging 15 m/50 ft long and 90 tonnes in weight, these slow-moving placid whales were once extremely common, but by the 17th century were already becoming scarce through hunting. Now only an estimated 3,000 remain.

Bowie /'bəʊi/ David. Stage name of David Jones 1947– . British pop singer and songwriter, born in Brixton, London. He became a glitter-rock star with the album *The Rise and Fall of Ziggy Stardust and the Spiders from Mars* 1972, and collaborated in the mid-1970s with the electronic virtuoso Brian Eno (1948–) and the lyricist Iggy Pop (1947–). He has also

acted in plays and films, including Nicolas Roeg's *The Man Who Fell to Earth* 1976.

Bowie /'bəʊi/ James 'Jim' 1796–1836. American folk hero. A colonel in the Texan forces during the Mexican War, he is said to have invented the single-edge, guarded, hunting and throwing knife which is still known as a Bowie knife.

bowls outdoor game played in England at least since the 13th century. It is played on flat or crown greens with biased bowls of lignum vitae (c. 13 cm/5 in diameter), and the object of the game is to draw each bowl as near as possible to the small white jack. The game can be played as singles, pairs, triples, or rinks (four people a side). The indoor game is becoming increasingly popular.

World Championship first held 1966 for men, 1969 for women
men: singles/pairs
1966 David Bryant *(England)*/Australia
1972 Malwyn Evans *(Wales)*/Hong Kong
1976 Doug Watson *(South Africa)*/South Africa
1980 David Bryant *(England)*/Australia
1984 Peter Bellis *(New Zealand)*/United States
triples/fours
1972 United States/England
1976 South Africa/South Africa
1980 England/Hong Kong
1984 Ireland/England
women: singles/pairs
1969 Gladys Doyle *(Papua New Guinea)*/South Africa

1973 Elsie Wilke *(New Zealand)*/Australia
1977 Elsie Wilke *(New Zealand)*/Hong Kong
1981 Norma Shaw *(England)*/Ireland
1985 Merle Richardson *(Australia)*/Australia
triples/fours
1969 South Africa/South Africa
1973 New Zealand/New Zealand
1977 Wales/Australia
1981 Hong Kong/England
1985 Australia/Scotland
Crown Green Bowls the **Waterloo Handicap** first held 1907 at The Waterloo Hotel, Blackpool, is Crown Green bowling's principal tournament
1977 Len Barrett
1978 Arthur Murray
1979 Brian Duncan
1980 Vernon Lee
1981 Roy Nicholson
1982 Dennis Mercer
1983 Stan Frith
1984 Steve Ellis
1985 Tommy Johnstone
1986 Brian Duncan.

box genus *Buxus* of small evergreen trees and shrubs, family Buxaceae; **common box**, *B sempervirens*, is slow growing, and ideal for hedging.

boxer active breed of dog of bulldog type with a smooth coat, set-back nose and docked tail. About 60 cm/2 ft tall, it is usually brown but may be brindled or white.

boxers name given to bands of fanatical Chinese nationalists who in 1900 at the instigation of the Empress Dowager besieged the foreign legations in Peking, and murdered European missionaries and thousands of Chinese converts. An international punitive force was dispatched, Peking was captured on 14 Aug 1900, and China agreed to pay a large indemnity. Mao Zedong claimed them as national heroes, but his successors refer to them as 'blind xenophobes'.

boxfish type of fish in which the scales are hexagonal bony plates fused to form a box covering the body, only the mouth and fins being free of the armour. Boxfishes, also known as *trunkfishes*, family Ostraciodontidae, swim slowly. The *cowfish*, genus *Lactophrys*, with two 'horns' above the eyes, is a member of this group.

boxing fighting with the fists. The modern sport dates from the 18th century when fights were bare-knuckle and without timed rounds; Jack Broughton 1704–89, who was champion 1729–50, laid down the first 'rules' in 1743, and introduced gloves for his pupils; Queensberry Rules (drawn up by the 8th Marquess in 1866) still prevail in modified form; the ring is 6.10 m/20 ft square maximum and 4.3 m/14 ft square minimum. In professional boxing, a round lasts three minutes, with a one-minute interval between rounds. A world championship bout recognized by the WBA and IBF lasts 15 rounds whereas those recognized by the WBC last only 12, as do European and British title fights. Amateur contests last only three rounds. Professional boxers are classified from light-flyweight 49 kg/108 lb to heavyweight 88 kg/195 lb, with no upward limit. Amateurs do, however, go up to super-heavyweights.

World Champions
WBC = World Boxing Council
WBA = World Boxing Association
IBF = International Boxing Federation
heavyweight (since 1978)
1978 Leon Spinks *USA* (Undisputed)
1978 Ken Norton *USA (WBC)*
1978 Muhammad Ali *USA (WBA)*
1978 Larry Holmes *USA (WBC)*
1979 John Tate *USA (WBA)*
1980 Mike Weaver *USA (WBA)*
1982 Mike Dokes *USA (WBA)*
1983 Gerry Coetzee *South Africa (WBA)*
1984 Larry Holmes *USA (IBF)*
1984 Tim Witherspoon *USA (WBC)*
1984 Pinklon Thomas *USA (WBC)*
1984 Greg Page *USA (WBA)*
1985 Michael Spinks *USA (IBF)*
1985 Tony Tubbs *USA (WBA)*
1986 Tim Witherspoon *USA (WBA)*
1986 Trevor Berbick *Canada (WBC)*
1986 Mike Tyson *USA (WBC/WBA)*
1986 James Smith *USA (WBA)*
1987 Mike Tyson *USA (WBC)*
1987 Tony Tucker *USA (IBF)*
World champions at three different weights:
Bob Fitzsimmons *(Great Britain)* middleweight 1891, heavyweight 1897, light-heavyweight 1903
Tony Canzoneri *USA* featherweight 1928, lightweight 1930, junior-welterweight 1931
Barney Ross *USA* lightweight 1933, junior-welterweight 1933, welterweight 1934
Henry Armstrong *USA* featherweight 1937, welterweight 1938, lightweight 1938
Wilfred Benitez *USA* junior-welterweight 1976, welterweight 1979, WBC junior-middleweight 1981
Alexis Arguello *(Nicaragua)* WBA featherweight 1974, WBC junior-lightweight 1978, WBC lightweight 1981
Roberto Duran *(Panama)* lightweight 1972, welterweight 1980, WBA junior-middleweight 1983
Wilfredo Gomez *(Puerto Rico)* WBC junior-featherweight 1977, WBC featherweight 1984, WBA junior-lightweight 1985
Sugar Ray Leonard *USA* WBC welterweight 1979, WBA junior-middleweight 1981, WBC middleweight 1987
Thomas Hearns *USA* WBA welterweight 1980, WBC junior-middleweight 1982, WBC light-heavyweight 1987

Great heavyweights include: John L Sullivan (bare-knuckle champion) 1882–92; Jim Corbett (first Marquess of Queensberry champion) 1892–97; Jack Dempsey 1919–26; Joe Louis 1937–49; Floyd Patterson 1956–59, 1960–62, Muhammad ◊Ali 1964–67, 1974–78, 1978–79, and Larry Holmes 1978–85.

boyar (Russian *boyarin*) a landed proprietor in the Russian aristocracy. During the 16th century boyars formed a powerful interest group threatening the tsar's power, until their influence was decisively broken by ◊Ivan the Terrible in 1565 when he confiscated much of the boyars' land.

Boycott /ˈbɔɪkɒt/ Charles Cunningham 1832–1897. Land agent in County Mayo, Ireland, who strongly opposed the demands for agrarian reform by the Irish Land League 1879–81, with the result that the peasants refused to work for him; hence the word 'boycott'.

Boyer /bwɑːˈjeɪ/ Charles 1899–1977. French film actor, who made his name in Hollywood in the 1930s as the 'great lover' in films such as *Mayerling* 1937, and *The Garden of Allah* 1936.

Boyle /bɔɪl/ Charles, 4th Earl of Orrery 1676–1731. Irish soldier and diplomat. The orrery, a device for studying the solar system, is named after him.

Boyle /bɔɪl/ Robert 1627–1691. Irish physicist and chemist. He published the seminal *The Skeptical Chymist* 1661; enunciated *Boyle's law* in 1662; was one of the founders of the ◊Royal Society; and endowed the Boyle Lectures for the defence of Christianity.

Boyle The fourteenth child of the Earl of Cork, Robert Boyle was the first chemist to collect a gas, and enunciated the law of the compressibility of gases in 1662 (Boyle's law).

Boyle's law in physics, law stating that the volume (V) of a given mass of gas at a constant temperature is inversely proportional to its pressure (p). It was discovered in 1662 by Robert ◊Boyle.

Boyne, Battle of the /bɔɪn/ battle fought on 11 Jul 1690 in E Ireland, in which James II was defeated by William III. Named after the river Boyne in the Republic of Ireland 113 km/70 mi long, flowing past Drogheda into the Irish Sea.

Boyoma Falls /bɔɪˈəʊmə/ series of seven cataracts in under 100 km/60 mi in the Lualaba (upper Zaïre river) above Kisangani, central

Africa. They have a total drop of over 60 m/200 ft.

boy scout see ◊scout.

Bozen /ˈbəʊtsən/ German form of ◊Bolzano, town in Italy.

Bo Zhu Yi /ˈbəʊ ˌdʒuː ˈjiː/ 772–846. Chinese poet (formerly known as Po Chü-i). President from 841 of the imperial war department, he criticized government policy. He is said to have checked his work with an old peasant woman for clarity of expression.

Brabançonne, La /ˌbræbænˈsɒn/ national anthem of Belgium, written and composed during the revolution of 1830.

Brabant /brəˈbænt/ district of W Europe, comprising the Belgian provinces of Brabant and Antwerp and the Dutch province of North Brabant. During the Middle Ages it was an independent duchy, and after passing to Burgundy, and thence to the Spanish crown, was divided during the Dutch War of Independence. The S portion was Spanish until 1713, then Austrian until 1815, when the whole area was included in the Netherlands. In 1830 the influential French-speaking part of the population in the S Netherlands rebelled and when Belgium was recognized in 1839, S Brabant was included in it.

Bracegirdle /ˈbreɪsɡɜːdl/ Anne c. 1663–1748. British actress, the mistress of ◊Congreve, and possibly his wife; she played Millamant in his *The Way of the World*.

brachiopod phylum of marine clamlike creatures (c. 300 species). They are suspension feeders, ingesting minute food particles from water. A single internal organ, the iophophore, handles feeding, aspiration, and excretion.

bracken species of fern *Pteridium aquilinum*, abundant in most parts of Europe. It has a perennial root-stock, which throws up large fronds.

bracket fungus a ◊fungus, class ◊Basidiomycetes, with bracket-shaped fruiting body, often seen on tree trunks.

Bracknell /ˈbræknəl/ ◊new town in Berkshire, England, founded 1949; population (1981) 49,000. The headquarters of the Meterological Office is here, and (with Washington DC) is one of the only two global area forecasting centres (of upper-level winds and temperatures) for the world's airlines.

bract a leaf-life structure, in whose ◊axil a flower or inflorescence develops. They are generally green and smaller than the true leaves. However, in some plants the bracts may be brightly coloured and conspicuous, taking over the role of attracting pollinating insects to the flowers, whose own petals are small; examples include poinsettia (*Euphorbia pulcherrima*) and *Bougainvillea*. A whorl of bracts surrounding an inflorescence is termed an involucre. A bracteole is a leaf-like organ which arises on an individual flower stalk, between the true bract and the calyx.

Bracton /ˈbræktən/ Henry de died 1268. English judge, writer on English law, and chancellor of Exeter cathedral from 1264. He compiled an account of the laws and customs of the English, the first of its kind.

Bradbury /ˈbrædbəri/ Malcolm 1932– . British novelist and critic, particularly noted for his comic and satiric portrayals of academic life. His best-known work is *The History Man* 1975, set in a provincial English university, which was adapted as a television series. Other works include the novels *Eating People is Wrong* 1959 and *Rates of Exchange* 1983.

Bradbury /ˈbrædbəri/ Ray 1920– . American writer. Born in Waukegan, Illinois, he was one of the first science fiction writers to make the genre 'respectable' to a wider readership. His work had its basis in developments of existing inventions and mental attitudes: *The Martian Chronicles* 1950, *Something Wicked This Way Comes* 1962 and *Fahrenheit 451*.

Bradford /ˈbrædfəd/ industrial city (engineering, machine tools, electronics, printing) in West Yorkshire, England, 14 km/9 mi W of Leeds; university 1965; population (1981) 280,500.

features A 15th-century cathedral; Cartwright Hall art gallery; the National Museum of Photography, Film, and Television 1983 (with Britain's largest cinema screen 14 x 20 m); and the Alhambra, built as a music hall and restored for ballet, plays, and pantomime.

history From the time its first markets were granted in the 13th century, Bradford developed as a great wool-and, later, cloth-manufacturing centre, but the industry has declined from the 1970s with Third World and Common Market competition. The city has received a succession of immigrants, Irish in the 1840s, German merchants in the mid-19th century, then Poles and Ukrainians, and more recently West Indians and Asians.

Bradlaugh /ˈbrædlɔː/ Charles 1833–1891. British freethinker and radical politician. He served in the army, was a lawyer's clerk, became well known as a speaker and journalist under the name of Iconoclast, and from 1860 ran the *National Reformer*. In 1880 he was elected Liberal Member of Parliament for Northampton, but was not allowed to take his seat until 1886 because, as an atheist, he had expressed his unbelief in the efficacy of the oath and claimed to affirm instead. He was associated with the feminist Annie ◊Besant.

Bradley /ˈbrædli/ Francis Herbert 1846–1924. British philosopher. He became a fellow of Merton College, Oxon, in 1870. In *Ethical Studies* 1876 and *Principles of Logic* 1883 he attacked the utilitarianism of J S Mill, and in *Appearance and Reality* 1893 and *Truth and Reality* 1914 he outlined his Neo-Hegelian doctrine of the universe as a single ultimate reality. His brother, *Andrew Cecil Bradley* (1851–1935), was professor of poetry at Oxford (1901–06).

Bradley /ˈbrædli/ James 1693–1762. English astronomer, who in 1728 discovered the ◊aberration of starlight. From the amount of aberration in star positions, he was able to calculate the speed of light. In 1742 he became Astronomer Royal, and in 1748 announced the discovery of ◊nutation (variation in the Earth's axial tilt).

Bradley /ˈbrædli/ Omar Nelson 1893–1981. American general. In 1943 he commanded the 2nd US Corps in Tunisia and Sicily, and in 1944 led the US troops in the invasion of France. He was chief of staff of the US Army 1948–49 and chairman of the joint chiefs of staff 1949–53. He was appointed general of the army in 1950.

Bradman /ˈbrædmən/ Donald George 1908– . Australian cricketer. Born in New South Wales, he played for Australia 1928–48 and was captain 1936–48. He has the highest aggregate score and greatest number of centuries in England v Australia Test Matches.

Braemar /ˌbreɪˈmɑː/ village in Grampian, Scotland, where Highland games are held annually in Aug.

Braga /ˈbrɑːɡə/ historic city in N Portugal 48 km/30 mi NNE of Oporto; population (1970) 48,500. It has a 12th-century cathedral, and the archbishop is primate of the Iberian peninsula. As *Bracara Augusta* it was capital of the Roman province Lusitania.

Bragança /brəˈɡænsə/ name of the royal house of Portugal, whose members reigned 1640–1853; another branch were emperors of Brazil 1822–89.

Bragg /bræɡ/ William Henry 1862–1942. British physicist. In 1915 he shared with his son *(William) Lawrence Bragg* (1890–1971) a Nobel prize for physics for their research work on X-rays and crystals.

Brahe /ˈbrɑːhə/ Tycho 1546–1601. Danish astronomer, who made the observations from which Johannes ◊Kepler proved that planets orbit the Sun in ellipses. In 1576 Frederick II of Denmark gave him the island of Hven, where he set up an observatory. Brahe was the greatest observer in the days before telescopes, making the most accurate measurements of the positions of stars and planets. His observations of the ◊comet of 1577 proved that it moved on an orbit among the planets, overthrowing the Greek view that comets were in the Earth's atmosphere. He moved to Prague as Imperial Mathematician in 1599, where he was joined by Kepler who inherited his observations when he died.

Brahma /ˈbrɑːmə/ in ◊Hinduism, the Supreme Being, or Universal Soul, the Absolute, self-existing and eternal. When referred to in the masculine he is the creator who forms with Vishnu and Siva the 'Trimurti'.

Brahmanism the earliest stage in the development of ◊Hinduism. Its sacred scriptures are the Vedas, with their accompanying literature of comment and explanation known as Brahmanas, Aranyakas, and Upanishads.

Brahmaputra /ˌbrɑːməˈpuːtrə/ river in Asia 2,900 km/1,800 mi long, a tributary of the Ganges. It rises in the Himalayan glaciers as Zangbo and runs E through Tibet, to the mountain mass of Namcha Barwa. Turning S, as the Dihang, it enters India and flows into the Assam valley near Sadiya. Now known as the Brahmaputra, it flows generally W until, shortly after reaching Bangladesh, it turns S and divides into the Brahmaputra proper, without much water, and the main stream, the Yamuna, which joins the Padma arm of the Ganges. The river is navigable for 1,285 km/800 mi from the sea.

Brahe The Danish astronomer Tycho Brahe, who had to wear a metal nose after his own was cut off in a duel, dabbled in alchemy, retained a lifelong interest in astrology, and is remembered as one of the greatest naked-eye astronomers.

Brahms The composer in his study. Brahms' work has many romantic qualities, but represents in essence a continuation of the classical tradition.

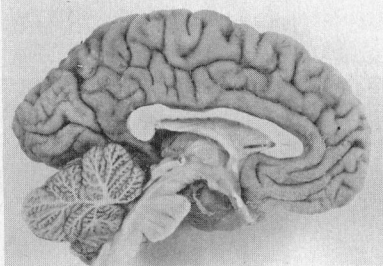

brain The human brain still holds a wealth of secrets from science. It is thought that verbal and analytical tasks are controlled by the left side of the brain and that the right side is used for intuitive and artistic skills.

Brahma Samaj /'braːmə səˈmaːdʒ/ Indian monotheistic religious movement, founded in 1830 in Calcutta by Ram Mohun Roy, who attempted to recover the primitive simple worship of the Vedas and purify Hinduism.

Brahms /braːmz/ Johannes 1833–1897. German composer, pianist, and conductor. Born in Hamburg, he attracted the attention of the great violinist ◊Joachim in 1853 and was introduced by him to ◊Liszt and ◊Schumann. From 1863 Brahms made his home in Vienna. Though his music has many romantic qualities, it represents in essence a continuation of the classical tradition from the point to which ◊Beethoven had brought it. As a composer of symphonic music and of songs, he is ranked with the greatest. His works include four symphonies; *lieder*; concertos for piano and for violin; chamber music; works for piano; and the choral *A German Requiem* 1868. He was famed as a performer and conductor of his own works.

Brăila /brəˈiːlə/ industrial port (artificial fibres, iron and steel, machinery, paper) and naval base in Romania on the Danube, 170 km/106 mi from its mouth; population (1979) 204,000. Controlled by the Ottoman Empire 1544–1828.

Braille /breɪl/ a system of writing for the blind. Letters are represented by a combination of raised dots on paper or other materials, which are then read by touch. It was invented in 1929 by *Louis Braille* (1809–52), who was blind from the age of three.

brain in higher animals, a mass of interconnected ◊nerve cells, forming the anterior part of the ◊central nervous system, whose activities it coordinates and controls. In ◊vertebrates, the brain is contained by the skull and consists of several different parts. An enlarged portion of the upper spinal cord, called the medulla oblongata, contains centres for the control of respiration, heartbeat rate and strength, and ◊blood pressure. Overlying the medulla is the *cerebellum* which is particularly well developed in higher vertebrates and is concerned with coordinating complex muscular processes such as maintaining posture and moving limbs. The cerebral hemispheres (*cerebrum*) are paired outgrowths of the front end of the forebrain, in early vertebrates mainly concerned with sense and smell, but in higher vertebrates greatly developed and involved in intelligent behaviour. In mammals the cerebrum is the largest part of the brain, forming the *cerebral cortex*. This consists of a thick surface layer of cell bodies (grey matter) below which fibre tracts (white matter) connect various parts of the cortex to each other and to other points in the central nervous system. As cerebral complexity grows the surface of the brain becomes convoluted into deep folds. Areas of this surface can be assigned some sensory motor function, but in higher mammals there are large unassigned areas of the brain which seem to be connected with intelligence, personality and higher mental faculties. Certain functions are localized to one side of the brain; language is controlled in two special regions usually in the left side of the brain; *Broca's area* governs the ability to talk, and *Wernicke's area* is responsible for the comprehension of spoken and written words. It has been suggested that the left side of the brain is specialized for verbal and analytical tasks and the right is more important for spatial perception, musical abilities and other artistic or intuitive skills.

brain damage impairment which can be caused by trauma (for example, accidents) or disease (such as encephalitis), or which may be present at birth. Depending on the area of the brain which is affected, language, movement, sensation, judgement, or other abilities may be impaired.

Braine /breɪn/ John 1922–1986. English novelist. His novel *Room at the Top* 1957, created the character of Joe Lampton, one of the first of the northern working-class anti-heroes.

Brains Trust nickname applied to a group of experts who advised President F D Roosevelt on his New Deal Policy.

Braithwaite /'breɪθweɪt/ Eustace Adolph 1912– . Guyanese author. His experiences as a teacher in London prompted *To Sir With Love* 1959. His *Reluctant Neighbours* (1972) deals with black/white relations.

Braithwaite /'breɪθweɪt/ Richard Bevan 1900– . British philosopher. Originally a physicist and mathematician, he was Knightbridge professor of moral philosophy at Cambridge 1953–67 and has experimented in the provision of a rational basis for religion and moral choice.

brake a device used to slow down or stop the movement of a moving body or vehicle. One familiar kind of brake is the caliper brake used on bicycles. It uses a scissor action to press hard rubber blocks against the wheel rim. The brakes are applied mechanically by means of levers or cables. The main braking system of a car works hydraulically, or by means of liquid pressure. When the driver depresses the brake pedal, liquid pressure forces pistons to apply brakes on each wheel.
Disc brakes are used on the front wheels of most cars. Braking pressure forces brake pads against both sides of a steel disc that rotates with the wheel. *Drum brakes* are fitted on rear wheels of most cars. Braking pressure forces brake shoes to expand outwards into contact with a drum rotating with the wheels. The brake pads and shoes have a tough ◊friction lining that grips well and withstands wear. Disc brakes are the more efficient and less prone to fading (losing their braking power) when they get hot. Many trucks and trains have *air brakes* which work by compressed air. On landing, jet planes reverse the thrust of their engines to reduce their speed quickly. Space vehicles use retrorockets for braking in space. They use the air resistance, or drag of the atmosphere to slow down when they return to Earth.

Bramah /'braːmə/ Joseph 1748–1814. British inventor of a flushing water closet (1778), an 'unpickable' lock (1784), and the hydraulic press (1795). The press made use of ◊Pascal's

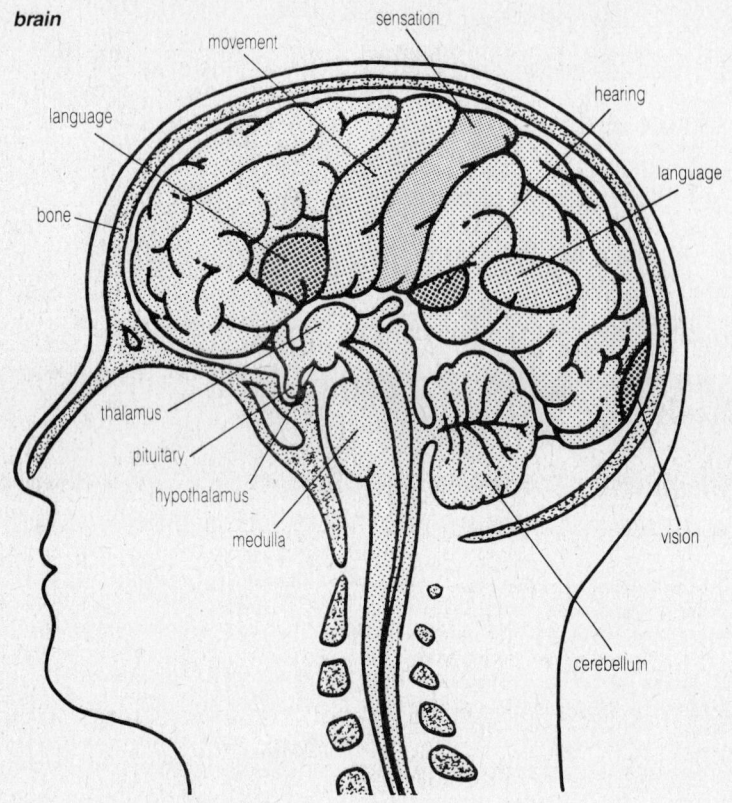

brain

language · movement · sensation · hearing · language · bone · thalamus · pituitary · hypothalamus · medulla · cerebellum · vision

principle (that pressure in fluid contained in a vessel is evenly distributed) and employed water as the hydraulic fluid; it enabled the 19th-century bridge-builders to lift massive girders.

Bramante /brə'mæntɪ/ Donato c. 1444–1514. Italian Renaissance architect and artist. Inspired by Classical designs, he was employed by Pope Julius II in rebuilding part of the Vatican and St Peter's in Rome.

bramble bush that produces the ◊blackberry.

brambling bird *Fringilla montifringilla* about 15 cm/6 in long belonging to the finch family. It breeds in Northern Europe and Asia and visits Britain in winter.

Brancusi /bræŋ'kuːzi/ Constantin 1876–1957. Romanian sculptor. Born in South Romania, he studied at Bucharest before going to Paris in 1904. Important in his work are the abstractions of animal and bird form, such as his bronze *Bird in Space* 1919. In 1927 this was assessed by the American Customs as a piece of metal, not a work of art, and therefore dutiable: the claim caused controversy and was overruled in 1928. ◊Rodin had an important influence on his work.

Brand /brænd/ 'Dollar' (Adolf Johannes) 1934– . (Muslim name: Abdullah Ibrahim). South African pianist and composer. He first performed in the USA in 1965, and has had a great influence on the fusion of African rhythms with American jazz. His compositions range from songs to large works for orchestra.

Brandenburg /'brændənbɜːɡ/ former Prussian and German province. The area, then inhabited by Slavonic tribes, was conquered in the 12th century by Albert the Bear. Frederick of Hohenzollern became margrave in 1415, and an elector of the Holy Roman Empire; the Elector Frederick III achieved the crown of Prussia in 1701. Potsdam was the capital. When Germany was united in 1871, Brandenburg became one of its provinces. That part of it east of the Oder came under Polish administration, in accordance with the Potsdam agreement, in 1945; the remainder became a *Land* of (East) Germany, abolished in 1952 when its boundaries were obliterated in the newly created administrative districts of Neubrandenburg, Potsdam, Frankfurt-an-der-Oder, and Kottbus.

Brandenburg /'brændənbɜːɡ/ town in (East) Germany, on the river Havel, 60 km/36m west of Berlin. There is a 12th-century cathedral, and textile, automotive, and aircraft industries. Population (1978) 95,000.

Brando /'brændəʊ/ Marlon 1924– . American actor, whose casual mumbling speech and use of ◊method acting earned him a place as one of the most distinctive actors of all time. His films include *A Streetcar Named Desire* 1951, *Julius Caesar* 1953, *On the Waterfront* 1954, *The Godfather* and *Last Tango in Paris* both 1972, and *Apocalypse Now* 1979.

Brandt /brænt/ Bill 1905–1983. British photographer, who produced a large body of richly-printed and romantic black and white studies of people, London, and nudes. He also published many photographic books.

Brandt /brænt/ Willy 1913– . West German socialist politician. Born Karl Herbert Frahm in Lübeck, Brandt changed his name when he fled to Norway in 1933 and became active in the anti-Nazi resistance. He returned in 1945 and entered the Bundestag (federal parliament) in 1949 and played a key role in the remoulding of the Social Democratic Party as a more moderate socialist force (chair 1964–87). As mayor of West Berlin 1957–66, Brandt became internationally known during the Berlin Wall crisis of 1961. In the 'grand coalition' of 1966–69 he served as foreign minister and introduced ◊Ostpolitik, a policy of reconciliation between East and West Europe, which was continued when Brandt became federal chancellor (prime minister) in 1969. He won the Nobel Peace Prize in 1971, and his Ostpolitik policy culminated in the 1972 signing of the Basic Treaty with East Germany.

Brandt resigned from the chancellorship in 1974 following the discovery that a close aide, Günther Guillaume, had been an East German spy. He continued to wield considerable influence in the SPD, especially over the party's new radical left wing. From 1977 he chaired the ◊Brandt Commission, and was a member of the European Parliament 1979–83.

Brandt Commission officially the Independent Commission on International Development Issues, established in 1977 and

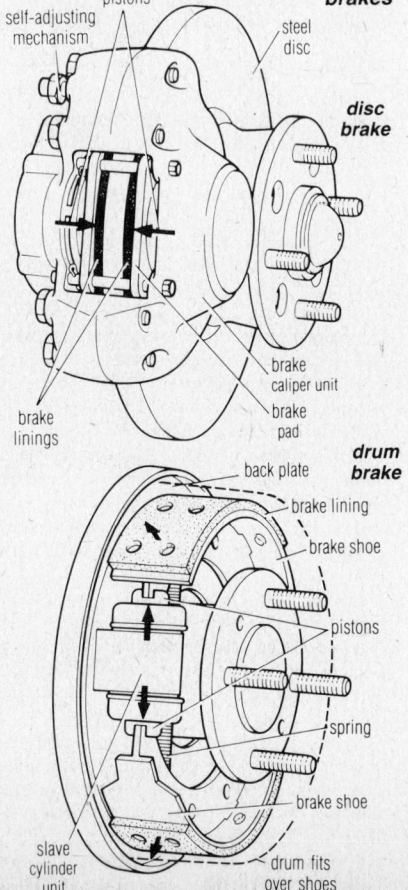

brakes

self-adjusting mechanism · pistons · steel disc · **disc brake** · brake caliper unit · brake pad · brake linings

drum brake · back plate · brake lining · brake shoe · pistons · spring · brake shoe · slave cylinder unit · drum fits over shoes

chaired by the former West German chancellor Willy ◊Brandt. Consisting of 18 eminent persons acting independently of governments, the Commission examined the problems of developing countries in the world economic system and sought to identify corrective measures that would command international support. Its main report, published in 1980 under the title *North-South: A Programme for Survival*, made detailed recommendations for accelerating the development of poorer countries (involving the transfer of resources to the latter from the rich countries). Little government action was taken on the report, however, and the Commission was disbanded in 1983, after producing a second report called *Common Crisis.*

brandy spirit distilled from fermented grape juice (notably that of France, for example Armagnac and Cognac), or that of other fruits.

Brangwyn /'bræŋgwɪn/ Frank 1867–1956. British artist. Of Welsh extraction, he was born at Bruges, where his father was working as an ecclesiastical architect. He worked for William ◊Morris as a textile designer, then travelled widely, developing a sense of colour and power of large-scale decorative concepts. In 1925 he completed five of a series of panels for the Royal Gallery of the House of Lords, but these were rejected after much controversy and now hang in the Brangwyn Hall, Swansea. In 1932 he was commissioned to work on panels for Radio City, New York. He produced furniture, pottery, carpets, schemes for interior decoration and architectural designs, as well as book illustrations, lithographs and etchings. There is a Brangwyn Museum (1936) at Bruges, Belgium, and at Orange, France (1947). He was knighted in 1941.

Brando Marlon Brando as the rebellious biker Johnny in *The Wild One* 1954.

Braque /brɑːk/ Georges 1882–1963. French artist, associated with Picasso in introducing the

◊Cubist movement in 1908, and the main initiator of *papiers collés,* paper, wood, and other materials, being glued to his canvases.

Brasília /brə'zɪlɪə/ capital of Brazil from 1960, some 1,000 m/3,000 ft above sea level; population (1980) 411,500. It was designed by Lucio Costa (1902–63), with Oscar Niemeyer as chief architect, as a completely new city to bring life to the interior.

Braşov /brɑː'sɒv/ industrial city (machine tools, industrial equipment, cement, woollens) in central Romania at the foot of the Transylvanian Alps; population (1979) 299,000. It belonged to Hungary until 1920; its Hungarian name is *Brassó* and its German name *Kronstadt*; it was called Urasul Stalin (Stalintown) 1948–56.

brass an ◊alloy of copper and zinc, with not more than 5 or 6% of other metals. The zinc content ranges from 20 to 45%, and the colour of brass varies accordingly from coppery to whitish yellow. Brasses are characterized by the ease with which they may be shaped and machined. They are strong and ductile, and resist many forms of ◊corrosion. Usually they are classed into those that can be worked cold (up to 25% zinc) and those which are better worked hot (about 40% zinc). Brass has widespread applications, being used for such things as electrical fittings, ammunition cases, screws, household fittings and ornaments.

brass in music, instruments made of brass, which are directly blown through a 'cup' or 'funnel' mouthpiece. They comprise:
symphony orchestra: *French horn* a descendant of the natural hunting horn, valved and curved into a circular loop, with a wide bell; *trumpet* a cylindrical tube curved into an oblong, with a narrow bell and three valves (the state *fanfare trumpet* has no valves); *trombone* instrument with a 'slide' to vary the effective length of the tube (the *sackbut* common from the 14th century, was its forerunner); *tuba* normally the lowest toned instrument of the orchestra; valved and with a very wide bore to give sonority, its bell points upward.
brass band: *cornet* three-valved instrument, looking like a shorter, broader trumpet, and with a wider bore; and then in descending order of tone: *flugelhorn* valved instrument, rather similar in range to the cornet; *tenor horn*; *B-flat baritone*; *euphonium*; *trombone*; *bombardon* (bass tuba). A brass band also normally includes bass and side drums, triangle, and cymbals.

Brassaï /,bræsɑː'iː/ pseudonym of Gyula Halesz 1899–1986. French photographer of Hungarian origin. From the early 1930s on he documented, mainly by flash, the nightlife of Paris, before turning to more abstract work.

brassica genus of plants of the family Cruciferae. The best-known species is the common cabbage (*Brassica oleracea*) with its varieties broccoli, cauliflower, kale, brussels sprouts.

Bratby /'brætbɪ/ John 1928– . British artist, popularly regarded as the leader of the 'kitchen-sink' school because of a preoccupation in early work with working-class domestic interiors. He has also published books illustrated

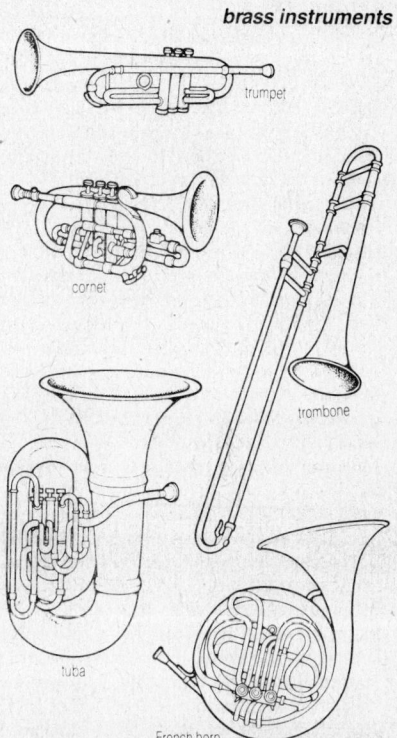

brass instruments

by himself which have a similar bold energy of style, including *Breakdown* 1960.

Bratislava /'brætɪslɑːvə/ (German *Pressburg*) industrial port (engineering, chemicals, oil refining) in Czechoslovakia, on the Danube; population (1981) 381,000. It was the capital of Hungary 1526–1784.

Brattain /'brætn/ Walter Houser 1902– . American physicist. Born in Amoy, China, son of a teacher, he joined 1929–67 the staff of Bell Telephone Laboratories. In 1956 he was awarded a Nobel prize jointly with William Shockley and John Bardeen for their work on the development of the transistor, which replaced the comparatively costly and clumsy vacuum tube in electronics.

Brauchitsch /'braʊxɪtʃ/ Walther von 1881–1948. German field marshal. A staff officer in World War I, he replaced in 1938 von Fritsch as commander-in-chief of the army and became a member of Hitler's secret cabinet council. He was dismissed after the failure before Moscow in 1941. Captured in 1945, he died before being tried.

Braun /braʊn/ Eva 1910–1945. German Nazi. Born at Munich, she became secretary to Hitler's photographer and personal friend, Hoffmann. She was Hitler's mistress for years, and she married him in the air-raid shelter of the Chancellory at Berlin on 29 Apr 1945. They then committed suicide together.

Brazil /brə'zɪl/ country in South America, bounded to the southwest by Uruguay, Argentina, Paraguay and Bolivia, to the west by Peru and Colombia, to the north by Venezuela, Guyana, Suriname and French Guiana, and to the west by the Atlantic Ocean.

government Brazil is a federal republic of 23 states, three territories and a federal district (Brasilia). There is a two-chamber national congress consisting of a senate of 69 members, on the basis of one senator per state, elected for an eight-year term, and a 479-member chamber of deputies elected for a four-year term. The number of deputies is determined by the population of each state and each territory is represented by one deputy. Elections to both chambers are by universal suffrage. The cabinet is chosen by the president, who is elected by universal adult suffrage for a five-year term and is not eligible for re-election. The states and the federal district each have an elected governor. The two main political parties are the Social Democratic Party (PDS) and the Brazilian Democratic Movement Party (PMDB).

history inhabited from about 5000 BC by American Indians, Brazil was a Portuguese colony from 1500. In 1808, after ◊Napoleon invaded Portugal, King João moved his capital from Lisbon to Brazil. In 1821 he returned to Lisbon and his son, Crown Prince Pedro, remained as regent. In 1822 Pedro declared Brazil an independent kingdom and took the title Emperor Pedro I. His son, Pedro II, persuaded large numbers of Portuguese to emigrate and the centre of Brazil developed quickly, largely on the basis of slavery, which was abolished in 1888, despite right-wing opposition. In 1889 a republic was founded and in 1891 a constitution for a federal state adopted.

After social unrest in the 1920s, the world economic crisis of 1930 produced a revolt which brought Dr Getúlio Vargas to the presidency. He held office, as a benevolent dictator, until the army forced him to resign in 1945 and General Eurico Dutra became president. In 1950 Vargas returned to power but committed suicide in 1954 and was succeeded by Dr Juscelino Kubitschek. In 1961 Dr Jânio Quadros became president but resigned after seven months, to be succeeded by Vice-President João Goulart. Suspecting him of having left-wing leanings, the army forced a restriction of presidential powers and created the office of prime minister. A referendum in 1963 brought back the presidential system, with Goulart choosing his own cabinet.

In a bloodless coup in 1964, General Castelo Branco assumed dictatorial powers and banned all political groupings except for two artificially created parties, the pro-government National Renewal Alliance (ARENA) and the opposition PMBD. In 1967 Branco named Marshal da Costa e Silva as his successor and a new constitution was adopted. In 1969 da Costa e Silva resigned because of ill health and a military junta took over. In 1974 General Ernesto Geisel became president until succeeded by General Baptista de Figueiredo in 1978. In 1979 the ban on opposition parties was lifted.

President Figueiredo held office until 1985; his last few years as president witnessing economic decline, strikes, and calls for the return of democracy. In 1985 Tancredo Neves became the first civilian president for 21 years, but died within months of taking office. He was succeeded by Vice-President José Sarney, who continued

to work with Neves' cabinet and policies. The constitution was again amended to allow direct presidental elections. In Sept 1987 the moderate members of PMDB and PDS, the Liberal Party Front (PFL), pulled out of their coalition with PMDB, forcing President Sarney to reconstruct the government.

Brazil nut seed, rich in oil and highly

Brazil

FEDERAL REPUBLIC OF (*República Federativa do Brasil*)

AREA 8,512,000 sq km/3,286,000 sq mi
CAPITAL Brasília
TOWNS Sao Paulo; ports are Rio de Janeiro, Belo Horizonte, Recife, Porto Alegre, Salvador
PHYSICAL the densely forested Amazon basin covers the N half of the country with a network of rivers; the S is fertile; enormous energy resources, both hydroelectric (Itaipú dam on the Paraná, and Tucurui on the Tocantins) and nuclear (uranium ores)
FEATURES Mount Roraima, Xingu National Park
HEAD OF STATE AND OF GOVERNMENT José Sarney from 1985
GOVERNMENT federal republic
EXPORTS coffee, sugar, cotton; textiles and motor vehicles; iron, chrome, manganese, tungsten and other ores, as well as quartz crystals, industrial diamonds
CURRENCY cruzado (introduced 1986; value = 100 cruzeiros, the former unit) (82.51 = £1 Sept 1987)
POPULATION (1985) 135,000,000 (including 200,000 Indians, survivors of 5 million, especially in Rondonia and Mato Grosso, mostly living on reserves); annual growth rate 2.3%
LANGUAGE Portuguese; 120 Indian languages
RELIGION Roman Catholic 89%, Indian faiths
LITERACY 78% male/74% female (1978)
GDP $218 bn (1984); $1,523 per head of population
CHRONOLOGY
1822 Brazil became an independent empire, ruled by Dom Pedro, son of the refugee King João VI of Portugal.
1889 Monarchy abolished and republic established.
1891 Constitution for a federal state adopted.
1930 Dr Getulio Vargas became president.

Brazil

1945 Vargas deposed by the military.
1946 New constitution adopted.
1950 Vargas returned to office.
1954 Vargas committed suicide.
1956 Juscelino Kubitschek became president.
1960 Capital moved to Brasília.
1961 João Goulart became president.
1964 Bloodless coup made Gen Castelo Branco president. He assumed dictatorial powers, abolishing free political parties.
1967 New constitution adopted. Branco succeeded by Marshal da Costa e Silva.
1969 Da Costa e Silva resigned and a military junta took over.
1974 Gen Ernesto Geisel became president.
1978 Gen Baptista de Figueiredo became president.
1979 Political parties legalized again.
1984 Mass calls for a return to fully democratic government.
1985 Tancredo Neves became first civilian president for 21 years. Neves died and was succeeded by the vice-president, José Sarney.

---

nutritious, of the S American tree *Bertholletia excelsa*. The seeds are enclosed in a hard outer casing, each fruit containing 10–20 arranged like the segments of an orange. The timber of the tree is also valuable.

brazing a method of joining two metals by melting an ◊alloy into the joint. It is akin to ◊soldering but takes place at a much higher temperature. Copper and silver alloys are widely used for brazing, at temperatures up to about 900°C.

Brazzaville /ˈbræzəvɪl/ capital of the Congo, industrial port (foundries, railway repairs, shipbuilding, shoes, soap, furniture, bricks) on the river Zaïre, opposite Kinshasa; population (1980) 422,500.
features There is a cathedral 1892 and the Pasteur Institute 1908. It stands on Pool Malebo (Stanley Pool).

history Brazzaville was founded by the Italian Count Pierre Savorgnan de Brazza (1852–1905), employed in African expeditions by the French government. It was the African headquarters of the Free (later Fighting) French during World War II.

bread food made with ground cereals, usually wheat, and water, though with many other variants of the contents. The dough may be unleavened, or raised (usually with yeast) and then baked.

breadfruit fruit of a tree *Artocarpus communis* of the mulberry family Moraceae. When toasted, it is said to taste like bread, and is an important article of food among the people of the South Sea Islands to which it is native.

Breakspear /ˈbreɪkspɪə/ Nicholas original name of Pope ◊Adrian IV, the only Englishman to become pope.

bream deep-bodied flattened fish *Abramis brama* of the carp family, growing to about 50 cm/1.6 ft, typically found in lowland rivers across Europe. The sea-breams are also deep-bodied flattened fish, but unrelated, belonging to the family Sparidae. The *red sea-bream Pagellus bogaraveo*, up to 45 cm/1.5 ft is heavily exploited as a food fish in the Mediterranean.

Bream /briːm/ Julian (Alexander) 1933– . British virtuoso of the guitar and lute. He has revived much Elizabethan lute music, and encouraged composition by contemporaries for both instruments. ◊Britten and ◊Henze have written for him.

breathalyzer instrument for on-the-spot checking by the police of the amount of alcohol in the blood of a suspect driver, who breathes into a plastic bag connected to a tube containing a chemical (such as a diluted solution of potassium dichromate in 50% sulphuric acid) which changes colour. Another method is to use a gas chromatograph, again from a breath sample. This instrument is usually kept in a police station.

breathing in terrestrial animals, the process of taking air into the lungs for ◊gas exchange. It is sometimes referred to as external respiration, for true respiration is a cellular (internal) process.

breccia a coarse ◊sedimentary rock, made up of broken fragments of pre-existing rocks (a clastic sedimentary rock). The fragments in breccia are large and jagged and the rock can be regarded as a fossilized scree slope. A particular type, explosion breccia, is formed from fragments blasted out of a volcano. The term 'breccia' is an Italian word, derived from the French, in turn from the Germanic for 'break'.

Brecht /brext/ Bertolt 1898–1955. German dramatist and poet, who aimed to destroy the 'suspension of disbelief' usual in the theatre, and express Marxist ideas. He first made a name with his adaptation of John Gay's *Beggar's Opera* as *Die Dreigroschenoper/The Threepenny Opera* 1928, set to music by Kurt Weill. As an anti-Nazi, he left Germany in 1933. Later plays are *Galileo* 1938, *Mutter Courage/Mother Courage* 1941, set in the ◊Thirty Years' War, which attacks all war, and *Der kaukasische Kreidekreis/The Caucasian Chalk Circle* 1949. He became an Austrian citizen after World War II, and from 1949 established in East Germany the theatre group, the Berliner Ensemble.

Brecknockshire /ˈbreknɒkʃə/ former county of Wales, merged in ◊Powys in 1974.

Breda, Treaty of /breɪˈdɑː/ 1667 treaty that ended the Second Anglo-Dutch War (1664–67). By the terms of the treaty, England gained New Amsterdam, which was renamed New York.

Breda /breɪˈdɑː/ historic town in N Brabant, Netherlands, where Charles II made the

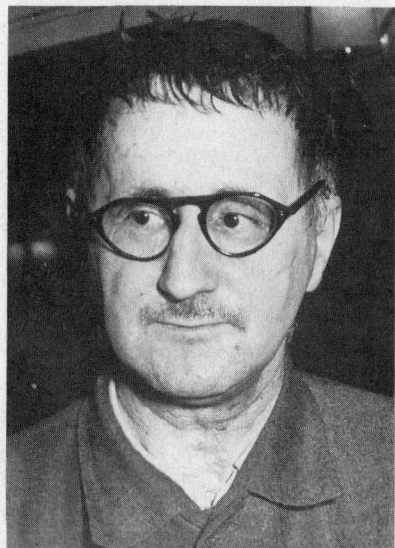

Brecht German dramatist and poet Bertolt Brecht was a committed Marxist. He made important reforms in the theatre, and sought to control the powerful illusion it creates so that he could confront the audience with political issues.

declaration that paved the way for his restoration in 1660; population (1981) 117,000.

breed a recognizable group of domestic animals, within a species, with distinctive characteristics that have been produced by ◊artificial selection. The Saint Bernard is a breed of dog, the Merino a breed of sheep. The corresponding term for plants is usually *variety* (or *cultivar*).

breeder reactor a ◊nuclear reactor which produces more fuel than it consumes. Breeder reactor is an alternative name for the fast reactor.

breeding in biology, the rearing of animals or the cultivation of plants, using planned crossing and selection to change the characteristics of an existing ◊breed or ◊cultivar (variety), or to produce a new one. Cattle may be bred for increased meat or milk yield, sheep for thicker or finer wool, and horses for speed or stamina. Plants, such as wheat or maize, may be bred for disease resistance, heavier and more rapid cropping, and hardiness to adverse weather.

breeding in nuclear physics, process in a reactor in which more fissionable material is produced than is consumed in running the reactor. For example, plutonium-239 can be made from the relatively plentiful (but non-fissile) uranium-238, or uranium-233 can be produced from thorium. The Pu-239 or U-233 can then be used to fuel other reactors. The French breeder reactor *Phênix*, one of the most successful, generates 250 megawatts of electrical power.

Breizh /breɪz/ Celtic name for ◊Brittany, region of France.

Bremen /ˈbreɪmən/ industrial port (iron and steel, oil refining, chemicals, aircraft, shipbuilding, cars) in West Germany, on the

Weser 69 km/43 mi from the open sea; population (1980) 555,000.

history Bremen was a member of the ◊Hanseatic League, and a free imperial city from 1646. It became a member of the N German Confederation in 1867, and of the German Empire in 1871.

Bremen /ˈbreɪmən/ administrative region (German *Land*) of West Germany, consisting of the cities of Bremen and Bremerhaven
area 404 sq km/156 sq mi
population (1978) 703,200.

Bremerhaven /ˌbreɪməˈhɑːfən/ port at the mouth of the Weser, Germany, serving as outport for Bremen; population (1980) 138,500. Named Wesermünde until 1947.

Brenner Pass /ˈbrenə/ lowest of the Alpine passes, 1,370 m/4,495 ft; it leads from Trentino–Alto Adige, Italy, to the Austrian Tirol, and is 19 km/12 mi long.

Brentano /brenˈtɑːnəʊ/ Franz 1838–1916. German-Austrian philosopher, whose *Psychology from the Empirical Standpoint* 1874 developed the concept of 'intensionality', the directing of the mind to an object, for example in perception.

Brentano /brenˈtɑːnəʊ/ Klemens 1778–1842. German writer, leader of the ◊Young Romantics. He published a seminal collection of folktale and song with Ludwig von ◊Arnim (*Des Knaben Wunderhorn*) 1805–08, and popularized the legend of the Lorelei (see under ◊Rhine). He also wrote mystic religious verse *Romanzen vom Rosenkranz* 1852.

Brenton /ˈbrentən/ Howard 1942– . British dramatist, noted for *The Romans in Britain* 1980, and a translation of Brecht's *The Life of Galileo.*

Brescia /ˈbreʃə/ historic and industrial city (textiles, engineering) in N Italy, 84 km/52 mi E of Milan; population (1981) 206,500. It has medieval walls and two cathedrals (12th and 17th century). Ancient name *Brixia.*

Breslau /ˈbreslaʊ/ German name of ◊Wrocław, town in Poland.

Brest /brest/ naval base and industrial port (electronics, engineering, chemicals) on *Rade de Brest* (Brest Roads), a great bay at the W extremity of Brittany, France; population (1983) 166,500. Occupied as a U-boat base by the Germans 1940–44, the town was destroyed by Allied bombing and rebuilt.

Brest /brest/ town in Byelorussia, USSR, on the river Bug and the Polish frontier; population (1981) 194,000. It was in Poland (*Brześć nad Bugiem*) until 1795 and 1921–39. The *Treaty of* ◊*Brest-Litovsk* (an older Russian name of the town) was signed here.

Brest-Litovsk, Treaty of treaty signed 3 Mar 1918 between Russia and the Central Powers. Under it Russia agreed to recognize the independence of the Baltic states, Georgia, the Ukraine and Poland, and pay heavy 'compensation'. Under the Nov Armistice between the Central Powers and the Allies it was annulled.

Bretagne /brəˈtænj/ French name for ◊Brittany, region of W France.

Brétigny, Treaty of /ˌbretɪnˈjiː/ treaty made between Edward III of England and John II of France in 1360 at the end of the first phase of the Hundred Years' War, under which Edward received Aquitaine and its dependencies in exchange for renunciation of his claim to the French throne.

Breton /ˈbretɒn/ André 1896–1966. French author. Among the leaders of ◊Dada – *Les Champs magnétiques/Magnetic Fields* 1921, an experiment in automatic writing, was one of the most notable products of the movement – he was also a founder of ◊Surrealism, publishing *Le Manifeste de surréalisme/Surrealist Manifesto* 1924. Of his other works, *Najda* 1928, the story of his love affair with a medium, is the most striking.

Breton language a member of the Celtic branch of the Indo-European language family; the language of Brittany in France, related to Welsh and Cornish, and descended from the speech of Celts who left Britain as a consequence of the Anglo-Saxon invasions of the 5th and 6th centuries. Although subject to official neglect for centuries, Breton is now a recognized language of France and has since 1985 received some encouragement from the central government. The Breton Liberation Movement claims equal status in Brittany for Breton and French.

Bretton Woods /ˈbretn/ township in New Hampshire, USA, where an International Monetary Conference was held 1–22 Jul 1944, under Henry Morgenthau, US Secretary to the Treasury. At the conclusion of the Conference a Draft of a United Nations' Monetary Agreement was published, providing for the creation of the ◊International Monetary Fund.

Breuer /ˈbrɔɪə/ Josef 1842–1925. Viennese physician, one of the pioneers of psychoanalysis. He applied it successfully to cases of hysteria, and collaborated with Freud in *Studien über Hysterie* 1895.

Breuer /ˈbrɔɪə/ Marcel 1902– . Hungarian-born architect and designer, who studied and taught at the ◊Bauhaus. He is best known for his tubular steel chair, 1925, the first of its kind. He moved to England, then to the USA, where he was in partnership with Gropius 1937–40. His buildings show an affinity with natural materials; best known among them is the Bijenkorf, Rotterdam (with Elzas) 1953.

Breuil /ˈbrɔɪ/ Henri 1877–1961. French prehistorian. Born at Mortain, the Abbé Breuil became professor of historic ethnography and director of research at the Institute of Human Palaeontology, Paris, in 1919. He established the genuine antiquity of Palaeolithic cave art and stressed the anthropological approach to the early human history.

breviary (Latin, 'a summary or abridgement') the book of the canonical office in use in the Roman Catholic church. It is usually in four volumes, one for each season.

brewing the alcoholic fermentation of an aqueous extract of cereal grains with the addition of hops. The medieval distinction between ◊beer (containing hops) and ale (without hops) has now fallen into disuse and in modern terminology beer is strictly a generic term including ale, stout and lager. However, it is usual in Britain to refer to ale as beer and to regard stout and lager as products different from beer.

Brewster /ˈbruːstə/ David 1781–1868. Scottish physicist, who made discoveries regarding the diffraction and polarization of light, and invented the kaleidoscope. He was knighted in 1832.

Brezhnev /ˈbreʒnef/ Leonid Ilyich 1906–1982. Soviet leader. A protégé of Stalin and Khrushchev, he came into power as general secretary of the Soviet Communist Party (CPSU) 1964–82 and was president 1977–82. Domestically he was conservative, abroad imperialist.

Brezhnev, born in the Ukraine, joined the CPSU in the 1920s. In 1938 he was made head of propaganda by the new Ukrainian party chief ◊Khrushchev, and ascended in the local party hierarchy. After World War II he caught the attention of the CPSU leader ◊Stalin, who inducted Brezhnev into the secretariat and Politburo in 1952. Brezhnev was removed from these posts after Stalin's death in 1953, but returned in 1956 with Khrushchev's patronage. In 1960, as criticism of Khrushchev mounted, he was moved to the ceremonial post of state president and began to criticize Khrushchev's policies.

Brezhnev stepped down as president in 1963 and returned to the Politburo and secretariat. He was elected CPSU general secretary in 1964, when Khrushchev was ousted, and gradually came to dominate the conservative and consensual coalition. In 1977 he regained the additional title of state president. As his health deteriorated, policy making became paralysed and economic difficulties mounted. The Brezhnev era saw the USSR establish itself as a military and political superpower, extending its influence in Africa and Asia. At home, however, it was period of caution and stagnation.

Brezhnev Doctrine Soviet doctrine (1968) designed to justify the invasion of Czechoslovakia. It laid down for the USSR as a duty the direct maintenance of 'correct' socialism in countries within the Soviet sphere of influence. In 1979 it was extended, by the invasion of Afghanistan, to the direct establishment of 'correct' socialism in countries not already within its sphere.

Briand /briˈɒn/ Aristide 1862–1932. French politician. Born at Nantes, he became a journalist in Paris. An ardent socialist, he helped Jaurès to found *L'humanité* and in 1902 was elected to the French Chamber. In 1906, as minister of public instruction and worship, he carried through the law separating church and state. Henceforth he was one of the Radical Socialists. Briand was several times prime minister: 1909–11, when he broke the railway strike of 1910 by mobilizing the strikers for army service; 1913, when he extended the period of military service from two to three years; 1915–17; 1921–22; 1925–26; and 1929. Subsequently he was often foreign minister. In 1925 he concluded the Locarno Pact, and in 1928 the Kellogg Pact; in 1930 he outlined his a scheme for the United States of Europe.

brick a common building material, rectangular in shape and made of clay that has been fired in a kiln. Sun-dried bricks of mud reinforced with straw were first used in Mesopotamia some 8,000 years ago. Similar mud bricks, called adobe, are still used today in Mexico and other parts of the world where the climate is warm. Bricks are made by kneading a mixture of crushed clay and other materials into a stiff mud and ◊extruding it into a ribbon. The ribbon is cut into individual bricks which are fired at a temperature up to about 1,000°C. Bricks may alternatively be pressed into shape in moulds. Refractory bricks used to line furnaces are made from heat-resistant materials such as silica and dolomite. They must withstand operating temperatures of 1,500°C or more.

bridge a construction which provides a continuous path or road over water, valleys, ravines, or above other roads.

Bridges may be classified into four main groups: *Arch*, for example, Sydney Harbour bridge (steel arch) with a span of 503 m/1,650 ft. *Beam or girder*, for example, Rio-Niteroi (1974) Guanabara Bay, Brazil, the world's longest continuous box and plate girder bridge: centre span 300 m/984 ft; length 13,900 m/8 mi 3,363 ft. *Cantilever*, for example, Forth rail bridge which is 1,658 m/5,440 ft long and has two main spans, each consisting of two cantilevers, one from each tower. *Suspension*, for example, Humber bridge, the world's longest-span suspension bridge with a centre span of 1,410 m/4,626 ft. Steel is pre-eminent in the construction of long-span bridges because of its high strength-to-weight ratio, but in other circumstances reinforced concrete has the advantage of lower maintenance costs. The Newport Transporter Bridge (built 1906) is a high-level suspension bridge which carries a car suspended a few feet above the water. It was used in preference to a conventional bridge where expensive high approach roads would have to be built.

bridge card game, derived from ◊whist and introduced to Britain about 1880, of which the most popular form is *contract bridge*, developed in USA from 1925 and made popular by the American expert Ely Culbertson 1891–1955. Played by two teams of two, who 'contract' to win a stated number of 'tricks' and who can name their own trumps. One partner's cards are exposed (the 'dummy') and played by the other partner.

Bridge /brɪdʒ/ Frank 1879–1941. British composer, the teacher of Benjamin ◊Britten. His works include the orchestral *The Sea* 1912, and *Oration* 1930 for cello and orchestra.

Bridgeport /ˈbrɪdʒpɔːt/ industrial city (metal goods, electrical appliances, aircraft) in Connecticut, USA, on Long Island Sound; universities; population (1980) 142,500. The nearby town of Stratford has the American Shakespeare Festival Theater.

Bridges /ˈbrɪdʒɪz/ Robert (Seymour) 1844–1930. British poet. In 1913 he was appointed Poet Laureate and became a founder of the Society for Pure English. He is remembered for his lyrics, and *The Testament of*

bridge The Golden Gate Bridge across San Francisco Bay, USA. Completed in 1937, this suspension bridge is 1.3 km/0.8 mi long, and was when finished the longest single-span bridge in the world.

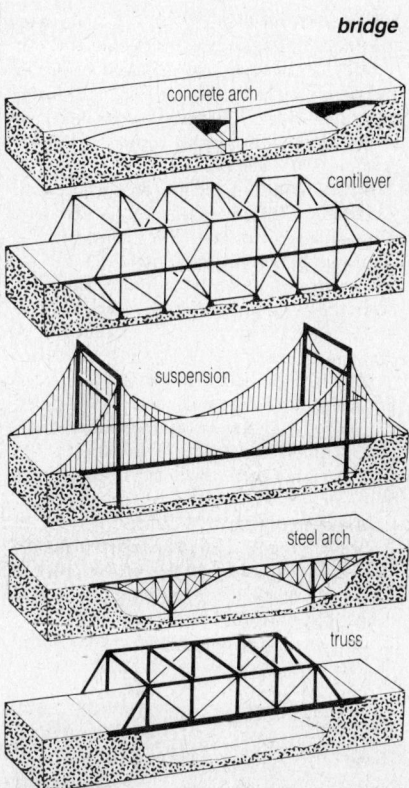

bridge

concrete arch

cantilever

suspension

steel arch

truss

Beauty 1929, a long philosophical poem which won immediate acclaim.

Bridgetown /'brɪdʒtaʊn/ port and capital of Barbados; population (1980) 7,500. Founded 1628.

Bridget, St /'brɪdʒɪt/ 453–523. A patron saint of Ireland, also known as St Brigit or St Bride. She founded a church and monastery at Kildare, and is said to have been the daughter of a prince of Ulster.

Bridgewater /'brɪdʒwɔːtə/ Francis Egerton, 3rd Duke of Bridgewater 1736–1803. Pioneer of British inland navigation. With James ◊Brindley as his engineer, he constructed 1762–72 the Bridgewater ◊canal from Worsley to Manchester, and thence to the Mersey, a distance of 67.5 km/42 mi.

Bridgman /'brɪdʒmən/ Percy Williams 1882–1961. American physicist. Born in Cambridge, Massachusetts, he was educated at Harvard where he was Hollis professor of mathematics and natural philosophy 1926–50 and Higgins university professor 1950–54. His

research in machinery producing high pressure led in 1955 to the creation of synthetic diamonds by General Electric.

Bridgwater /'brɪdʒwɔːtə/ industrial port (plastics, electrical goods) in Somerset, England, on the Parret; population (1981) 26,000.

Bridie /'braɪdi/ James. Pseudonym of Scottish dramatist Osborne Henry Mavor. 1888–1951. professor of medicine, and a founder of Glasgow Citizens' Theatre. His plays include *Tobias and the Angel* 1930, and *The Anatomist* 1931, dealing with Burke and Hare.

Brieux /bri'ɜː/ Eugène 1858–1932. French dramatist, an exponent of the naturalistic problem play attacking social evils. His most powerful plays are *Les trois filles de M Dupont* 1897; *Les Avariés/Damaged Goods* 1901, long banned for its outspoken treatment of syphilis; and *Maternité*.

Brighouse /'brɪghaʊs/ Harold 1882–1958. British playwright. Born and bred in Lancashire, in his most famous play *Hobson's Choice* 1916 he dealt with a Salford bootmaker's courtship.

Bright /braɪt/ John 1811–1889. British Liberal politician. Bright, a Quaker millowner, was among the founders of the Anti-Corn Law League in 1839, and after entering parliament in 1843 led the struggle there for free trade, together with ◊Cobden, which achieved success in 1846. His ◊*laissez-faire* principles also made him a prominent opponent of factory reform. His influence was constantly exerted on behalf of peace, as when he opposed the Crimean War, Palmerston's aggressive policy in China, Disraeli's anti-Russian policy, and the bombardment of Alexandria. During the American Civil War he was outspoken in support of the North, and he was largely instrumental in securing the passage of the Reform Bill of 1867. He sat in Gladstone's cabinets as president of the Board of Trade 1868–70 and chancellor of the Duchy of Lancaster 1873–74 and 1880–82, but broke with him over the Irish Home Rule Bill. Bright owed much of his influence to his oratorical powers.

Bright /braɪt/ Richard 1789–1858. British physician. He was for many years on the staff of Guy's Hospital, London; *Bright's disease*, an inflammation of the kidneys, is named after him.

Brighton /'braɪtn/ resort on the E Sussex coast, England; University of Sussex 1963; population (1981) 146,000. It has Regency architecture and Brighton Pavilion 1782 in oriental style. There are two piers and an aquarium.

history Originally a fishing village called Brighthelmstone, it became known as Brighton at the beginning of the 19th century, when it was already a fashionable health resort patronized by the Prince Regent, afterwards George IV.

brill flatfish *Scophthalmus laevis* similar to the turbot, but less prized for food. Growing to 60 cm/2 ft it is a freckled sandy brown, and lives in shallow water over sandy bottoms in the NE Atlantic and Mediterranean.

Brillat-Savarin /bri'ja: ˌsævə'ræŋ/ Jean Anthelme 1755–1826. French gastronome. Most of his professional life was spent as a politician, but in his spare time he wrote *La Physiologie du Goût* 1825, a compilation of observations on food and drink which has come to be regarded as the first great classic of gastronomic literature.

Brindisi /'brɪndɪzi/ industrial port (food processing, petrochemicals) and naval base on the Adriatic, in Apulia, on the heel of Italy; population (1981) 90,000. It is one of the oldest Mediterranean ports, at the end of the Appian Way from Rome; ancient name *Brundisium*.

Brindley /'brɪndli/ James 1716–1772. British canal builder, who was the first to employ tunnels and aqueducts extensively in order to reduce the number of locks on a direct-route canal. His 580 km/360 mi of canals included the Bridgewater (Manchester-Liverpool) and Grand Union (Manchester-Potteries) canals.

Brindley A portrait of James Brindley, the first canal builder to use tunnels and aqueducts extensively.

Brinell /brɪ'nel/ Johann Auguste 1849–1925. Swedish engineer, who devised the Brinell hardness test in 1900.

Brinell hardness test test for the hardness of a substance according to the area of indentation made by a 10-mm/0.4-in hardened steel or sintered tungsten carbide ball under standard loading conditions in a test machine; it is equal to the load (kg) divided by the surface area (mm²). Named after its inventor Johann ◊Brinell.

Brisbane /'brɪzbən/ industrial port (brewing, tanning, tobacco, shoes; oil pipeline from Moonie), capital of Queensland, E Australia, near the mouth of Brisbane river, dredged to carry ocean-going ships; Queensland University 1909; population (1981) 943,000.

history Sir Thomas ◊Brisbane took over the site as a penal colony 1824–39, opened to free settlers 1842.

Brisbane /'brɪzbən/ Thomas Makdougall 1773–1860. Scottish soldier and astronomer. After serving under Wellington, he was Governor of New South Wales 1821–25, and Brisbane in Queensland is named after him.

brisling edible fish; the processed form of sprat *Sprattus sprattus* fished in Norwegian fjords, then seasoned and canned.

Brissot /briː'sɔʊ/ Jacques Pierre 1754–1793. French revolutionary leader. Born at Chartres, he became a member of the Legislative Assembly and the National Convention, but his party of moderate republicans – the Girondins, or Brissotins – fell foul of Robespierre and Brissot was guillotined.

bristlecone pine see ◊pine.

bristletail primitive wingless insect, order Thysanura. Up to 2 cm/0.8 in long, bristletails have a body tapering from front to back, two long antennae and three 'tails' at the rear end. They include the *silverfish Lepisma saccharina* which feeds on glue, flour, and other items in food cupboards, and the *firebrat Thermobia domestica*, a pest of kitchens and bakeries. The two-tailed bristletails, order Diplura, live under stones and fallen branches feeding on decaying material.

Bristol /'brɪstəl/ industrial port (aircraft engines, engineering, microelectronics, tobacco, chemicals, paper, printing), administrative headquarters of Avon, SW England; university 1909; population (1981) 388,000. Includes Avonmouth, Portishead, and Portbury docks.

features 12th-century cathedral; 14th-century St Mary Redcliffe; 16th-century Acton Court, built by Sir Nicholas Poynz, a courtier of Henry VIII; the Georgian residential area of Clifton; the Clifton Suspension Bridge designed by Brunel and his SS *Great Britain*.

history John Cabot sailed from here 1497 to Newfoundland, and there was a great trade with the American colonies and the West Indies in the 17th–18th centuries, including slaves. The poet Chatterton was born here.

Bristow /'brɪstəʊ/ Eric 1957– . English darts player, nicknamed 'the Crafty Cockney'. He was world professional champion 1980–81 and 1983–86, and has also won World Masters, World Cup, British Open, Nations' Cup, and News of the World titles.

Britain, Ancient /'brɪtn/ the name Britain, indicating present-day England, Scotland and Wales, is derived from the Roman name Britannia, which is in its turn derived from the ancient Celtic. Britain was inhabited for thousands of years by people who kept livestock and grew corn; they had built ◊Stonehenge, and they buried their chiefs in ◊barrow mounds. After 1000 BC Britain was conquered by the ◊Celts, tall, fair-haired people who migrated in two waves from the Continent. First came the Goidelic Celts, of whom traces may still be seen in the Gaels of Ireland and the Highlands; there followed the Brythonic Celts or Bretons, who were closely allied in blood and culture to the Gauls of France. The early British craftsmen

were highly skilled in pottery and metalwork. Tin mines in Cornwall attracted merchant seamen from Carthage.

Britain, Battle of /'brɪtn/ World War II air battle between German and British air forces over Britain which lasted from 10 Jul to 31 Oct 1940. It has been divided into five phases: (1) 10 July–7 Aug, the preliminary phase; (2) 8–23 Aug, attack on coastal targets; (3) 24 Aug–6 Sept, attack on Fighter Command airfields; (4) 7–30 Sept, daylight attack on London, chiefly by heavy bombers; and (5) 1–31 Oct, daylight attack on London chiefly by fighter-bombers.

At the outset the Germans had the advantage of airfields almost completely free from attack in the Netherlands, Belgium and France, dominating SE England. On 1 Aug 1940 the Luftwaffe had c. 4,500 aircraft of all kinds, as against c. 3,000 for the RAF, but the main battle was between some 600 Hurricanes and Spitfires and the Luftwaffe's 800 Messerschmidt 109s and 1,000 bombers (Dornier 17s, Heinkel 111s and Junkers 88s). Losses Aug–Sept were for the RAF: 832 fighters totally destroyed, and for the Luftwaffe 668 fighters and some 700 bombers and other aircraft. The Battle of Britain had been intended as a preliminary to the German invasion plan *Seeloewe* (Sea Lion), which Hitler indefinitely postponed 17 Sept and abandoned 10 Oct.

Britannicus /brɪ'tænɪkəs/ Tiberius Claudius c. 41–55 AD. Roman prince, son of the Emperor Claudius and Messalina, so-called from his father's expedition to Britain. He was poisoned by Nero.

British Antarctic Territory colony created in 1962 and comprising all British territories S of latitude 60°S: the British sector of the Antarctic continent (Graham Land and areas round the Weddell Sea) approximately 388,500 sq km/150,000 sq mi; the South Orkneys, 722 sq km/240 sq mi, and South Shetlands, 337 sq km/130 sq mi. Scientific personnel are the only population: about 250.

British Broadcasting Corporation (BBC) in the UK, the state-owned broadcasting network. It was converted from a private company (established 1922) to a public body under royal charter (1927), it operates television, and national and local radio stations, financed solely by the sale of television viewing licences, and is not allowed to carry advertisements, but overseas radio broadcasts (World Service) have a government subsidy. See also ◊Independent Broadcasting Authority.

British Columbia /kə'lʌmbiə/ province of W Canada on the Pacific
area 948,599 sq km/366,255 sq mi
capital Victoria
towns Vancouver, Prince George, Kamloops, Kelowna
features Rocky Mountains and Coast Range; the coast is deeply indented; rivers include the Fraser and Columbia; there are more than 80 lakes; more than half the land is forested
products fruit and vegetables; timber and wood products; fish; coal, copper, iron, lead; oil and natural gas, and hydroelectricity
population (1981) 2,744,467

history Captain Cook explored the coast in 1778; a British colony was founded on Vancouver Island in 1849, and the gold rush of 1858 extended settlement to the mainland; it became a province in 1871.

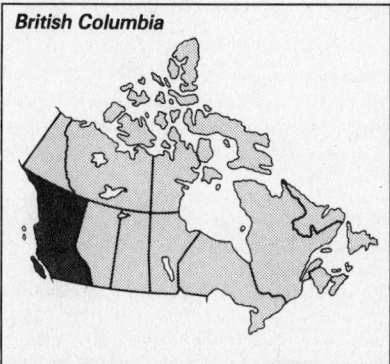

British Columbia

(British) Commonwealth (of Nations) see ◊Commonwealth.

British Council semi-official organization set up 1935 (royal charter 1940) to promote a wider knowledge of the United Kingdom, excluding politics and commerce, and to develop cultural relations with other countries.

British Empire, Order of the British order of chivalry, instituted by George V in 1917. There are military and civil divisions, and the ranks are GBE, Knight Grand Cross or Dame Grand Cross; KBE, Knight Commander; DBE, Dame Commander; CBE, Commander; OBE, Officer; MBE, Member. In 1974 awards for civilian gallantry previously made within the order were replaced by the Queen's Gallantry Medal (QGM), which ranks after the George Cross and George Medal

British Empire the first successful English colony was founded at Jamestown, Virginia, in 1607. British settlement spread up and down the east coast of North America and by 1664, when the British secured New Amsterdam (New York) from the Dutch, there was a continuous fringe of colonies. The attempt of George III to coerce the colonists into paying taxes to England roused them to resistance, which came to a head in the War of American Independence 1775–81 and led to the creation of the United States of America from the 13 English colonies then lost. But before this, the British had set up colonies and trading posts in other parts of the world, and conquered territories from other European empire builders. Settlements were made in Gambia and on the Gold Coast 1618; in Bermuda 1609 and others of the West Indian islands; Jamaica was taken from Spain in 1655; Acadia (Nova Scotia) was secured from France by the Treaty of Utrecht 1713, which recognized Newfoundland and Hudson Bay (as well as Gibraltar in Europe) as British. New France (Quebec), Cape Breton Island, and Prince Edward Island became British as a result of the Seven Years' War 1756–63.

In the Far East, the East India Company, chartered 1600, set up trading posts on the W coast of India at Surat, 1612; on the E coast at Madras, 1639; and on the Hooghli, one of the mouths of the Ganges, 1640. Bombay came to the British crown in 1662, and was granted to the East India Company for £10 a year. The company steadily increased its possessions and the territories over which it held treaty rights up to the eve of the Indian Mutiny 1857. Although this rising was put down, it resulted in the taking over of the government of British India by the crown 1858; Queen Victoria was proclaimed Empress of India on 1 Jan 1877. Ceylon had also been annexed to the East India Company in 1796, and Burma, after a series of Anglo-Burmese Wars from 1824, became a province of British India in 1886.

Constitutional development in Canada started with an act of 1791 which set up Lower Canada (Quebec), and Upper Canada (Ontario). But there was sufficient discontent there to lead in 1837 to rebellion in both Canadas. After the suppression of these risings, Lord Durham was sent out to advise on the affairs of British North America; his report, published in 1839, became the basis for the future structure of the Empire. In accordance with its recommendations, the two Canadas were united in 1840 and given a representative legislative council: the beginning of colonial self-government. With the British North America Act 1867, the self-governing dominion of Canada came into existence, to the original union of Ontario, Quebec, New Brunswick, and Nova Scotia were later added further territories until the federal government of Canada controlled all the northern part of the continent except Alaska.

In the antipodes, colonization began with the desire to find a place for penal settlement after the loss of the original American colonies. The first shipload of convicts landed in Australia in 1788; New South Wales was opened to free settlers in 1819; and in 1853 transportation of convicts was abolished. Before the end of the century five Australian colonies – New South Wales, Western Australia, South Australia, Victoria, Queensland – and the island colony of Tasmania had each achieved responsible government; an act of the Imperial Parliament at Westminster created the federal commonwealth of Australia, an independent dominion, 1901. New Zealand, annexed in 1840, was at first a dependency of New South Wales; made a separate colony in 1853, it was created a dominion 1907.

The Cape of Good Hope in South Africa was occupied by two English captains in 1620. The Dutch occupied it in 1650, and Cape Town remained a port of call for their East India Company until 1795 when the British bought it from the new kingdom of the Netherlands for $6,000,000. British settlement began in 1824 on the coast of Natal, proclaimed a British colony in 1843.

Resentment over the abolition of slavery 1833 in all British possessions led a body of Boers (Dutch for farmers) from the Cape to make the great trek north east 1836, to found Transvaal and Orange

Free State. Conflict between the British government, which claimed sovereignty over those areas and the Boers culminated in the South African War of 1899–1902. Given self-government in 1907, they were in 1910, with Cape Colony (self-governing 1872) and Natal (self-governing 1893), formed into the Union of South Africa, fourth dominion of the Empire. The British South Africa Company, chartered 1889, extended British influence over south Rhodesia (a colony in 1923) and north Rhodesia (a protectorate in 1924); with Nyasaland, taken under British protection in 1891, the Rhodesias were in 1953 formed into a federation 1953–63 with representative government. Uganda was made a British protectorate in 1894, and became a colony in 1920. Kenya, formerly a protectorate, became a colony in 1920; certain districts on the coast forming part of the sultan of Zanzibar's dominions remaining a protectorate.

In West Africa, British control was extended from time to time in Gambia and the Gold Coast. Sierra Leone colony started in 1788 with the cession of strip of land to provide a home for liberated slaves; a protectorate was established over the hinterland in 1806. British influence in Nigeria began through the activities of the National Africa Company which bought Lagos from an African chief in 1861 and steadily extended its hold over the Niger Valley until it surrendered its charter in 1899; in 1900 the two protectorates of N and S Nigeria were proclaimed. World War I ousted Germany from the African continent, and in 1921–22, under League of Nations mandate, Tanganyika was transferred to British administration, SW Africa to South Africa; Cameroons and Togoland, in West Africa, were divided between Britain and France.

The establishment of the greater part of Ireland as the Irish Free State, with dominion status, came in 1922. A new constitution adopted by the Free State in 1937 dropped the name and declared Ireland (Eíre) to be a 'sovereign independent state'; 12 years later Southern Ireland became a republic outside the Commonwealth, though remaining in a special relationship with Britain.

British India was given independence in 1947 as the two dominions of India and Pakistan. India decided to become a republic in 1950 but, with the full consent of the other members, to remain within the ◊Commonwealth.

British Expeditionary Force (BEF) a British army which served in France in World War I 1914–18 (see Earl of ◊Ypres and ◊Haig); also the army of World War II 1939–40, which was evacuated from ◊Dunkirk; commander General ◊Gort.

British Honduras /hɒnˈdjuərəs/ former name of ◊Belize, a country in Central America.

British Indian Ocean Territory British colony in the Indian Ocean directly administered by the Foreign and Commonwealth Office. It consists of the Chagos Archipelago some 1,900 km/1,200 mi NE of Mauritius
area 186 sq km/72 sq mi
features lagoons; US naval and air base on Diego Garcia

BRITISH EMPIRE

Current name	Colonial Names and History	Colonized	Independent
India	British E India Co. 18th cent.–1858	18th cent.	1947
Pakistan	British E India Co. 18th cent.–1858	18th cent.	1947
Sri Lanka	Portuguese, Dutch 1602-1796; Ceylon 1802–1972	16th cent.	1948
Ghana	Gold Coast	1618	1957
Nigeria		1861	1960
Cyprus	Turkish to 1878, then British rule	1878	1960
Sierra Leone	British protectorate	1788	1961
Tanzania	German E Africa to 1921; British mandate from League of Nations/UN as Tanganyika	19th cent.	1961
Jamaica	Spanish to 1655	16th cent.	1962
Trinidad & Tobago	Spanish 1532–1797; British 1797–1962	1532	1962
Uganda	British protectorate	1894	1962
Kenya	British colony from 1920	1895	1963
Malaysia	British interests from 1786; Federation of Malaya 1957–63	1874	1963
Malawi	British protectorate of Nyasaland 1907–53; Federation of Rhodesia & Nyasaland 1953–64	1891	1964
Malta	French 1798–1814	1798	1964
Zambia	N Rhodesia – British protectorate; Federation of Rhodesia & Nyasaland 1953–64	1924	1964
The Gambia		1888	1965
Singapore	Federation of Malaya 1963–65	1858	1965
Guyana	Dutch to 1796; British Guiana 1796–1966	1620	1966
Botswana	Bechuanaland – British protectorate	1885	1966
Lesotho	Basutoland	1868	1966
Bangladesh	British E India Co. 18th cent.–1858; British India 1858-1947; E Pakistan 1947–71	18th cent.	1971
Zimbabwe	S Rhodesia from 1923; UDI 1965–79 under Ian Smith	1895	1980

products copra, salt fish, tortoiseshell
population (1982) 3,000
history established in 1965 to provide certain military facilities for the governments of the UK and USA. The Chagos Archipelago was previously administered by Mauritius. The island of Aldabra, Farquhar, and Desroches, some 485 km/300 mi N of Madagascar, originally formed part of the British Indian Ocean Territory, but were returned to the administration of the Seychelles in 1976.

British Isles group of islands off the NW coast of Europe, consisting of Great Britain (England, Wales, and Scotland), Ireland, the Channel Islands, Orkney and Shetlands, Isle of Man, and many others which are included in various counties, such as the Isle of Wight, Scilly Isles, Lundy Island, and the Inner and Outer Hebrides. The islands are divided from Europe by the North Sea, Strait of Dover, and English Channel, and face the Atlantic to the W.

British Legion organization to promote the welfare of British veterans of war service and their dependants. Established under the leadership of Haig in 1921 (royal charter 1925) it became the *Royal British Legion* 1971; it is non-political. The sale on Remembrance Sunday of Flanders poppies made by disabled members raises much of its funds.

British Library the national library of the UK. Created 1973, it comprises the *reference division* (the former library departments of the British Museum, being rehoused at the Euston Road, London, site); *lending division* at Boston Spa, Yorkshire, from which full text documents and graphics can be sent, using a satellite link, to other countries; and *bibliographic services division* (incorporating the British National Bibliography).

British Museum largest and most important museum of the UK. Founded in 1753 with the purchase of Sir Hans Sloane's library and art collection, and the subsequent acquisition of the Cottonian, Harleian, and other libraries, the British Museum was opened at Montagu House, Bloomsbury, in 1759. Rapid additions led to the construction of the present buildings (designed by Sir Robert Smirke) by 1852, with later extensions in the circular reading room 1857, and the N wing or Edward VII galleries (1914). In 1881 the Natural History Museum was transferred to S Kensington.

British Telecom a British company that formed part of the Post Office until 1980, and was privatized in 1984. It is responsible for ◊telecommunications, including the telephone network, and radio and television broadcasting. Previously a monopoly, it now faces commercial competition for some of its services. It operates Britain's ◊viewdata network called ◊Prestel.

British thermal unit (Btu) imperial unit of heat. Defined as the amount of heat required to raise the temperature of 0.45 kg/1 lb of water by 1°F. Now replaced by its equivalent in the ◊SI system of 1,055.06 joules, but still used by public utilities.

British Volunteer Programme name by which the various schemes under which volunteers from the UK are sent to work in overseas developing countries have been known since 1966. Voluntary Service Overseas (VSO)

(1958) is the best-known of these organizations, which inspired the American ◊Peace Corps.

Brittain /'brɪtɪn/ Vera 1894–1970. British socialist writer, a nurse to the troops overseas 1915–19, as told in her *Testament of Youth* 1933; *Testament of Friendship* 1950 commemorated Winifred ◊Holtby. She married political scientist Sir George Catlin (1896–1979); their daughter is Shirley ◊Williams.

Brittan /'brɪtn/ Leon 1939– . British Conservative politician, and lawyer. Chief secretary to the Treasury 1981–83, he was Home Secretary 1983–85, and Secretary for Trade and Industry 1985–86, but resigned over his part in the ◊Westland affair.

Brittany /'brɪtəni/ (French *Bretagne*) region of NW France in the Breton peninsula between the Bay of Biscay and the English Channel
capital Rennes
features a dam 1967 on the river Rance uses the 13 m/44 ft tides to feed the world's first successful tidal power station. The military college founded by Napoleon at St Cyr, near Versailles, was destroyed in an air raid in World War II and transferred to Coëtquidan, SE of Rennes
population (1982) 2,707,886
history as Armorica, it was conquered by Julius Caesar in 56 BC, and was devastated by the Northmen after the Roman withdrawal. During the Anglo-Saxon invasion of Britain so many Celts migrated across the Channel that it gained the name of Brittany. By 1547 it had been formally annexed by France, and the ◊Breton language was banned in education. A separatist movement developed after World War II, and there has been guerrilla activity.

Britten /'brɪtn/ (Edward) Benjamin, Baron Britten 1913–1976. British composer. Born in Lowestoft, he was educated at Gresham's School, Holt, and the Royal College of Music. In America when World War II broke out, he returned in 1942 and devoted himself to composing at his home in ◊Aldeburgh, Suffolk, where he established an annual music festival. He wrote for the individual voice, for example Peter ◊Pears and Janet ◊Baker, and is also known for his operas, *Peter Grimes* 1945 based on a tale by Crabbe, the chamber opera *The Rape of Lucretia* 1946, *Billy Budd* 1951, *A Midsummer Night's Dream* 1960, and *Death in Venice* 1973. His oratorio *War Requiem* 1962 was written for the dedication of Coventry Cathedral. He was awarded the Order of Merit in 1965, and a life peerage in 1976.

brittle star type of ◊starfish, with a small central rounded body and long flexible spiny arms used for walking. About 2,000 species of brittle star and basket star are known, comprising the ◊echinoderm class Ophiuroidea. The *small brittle-star Amphipholis squamata* is greyish, about 4.5 cm/2 in across, and found on shores almost worldwide. It broods its young, and its arms can be luminous.

Brno /'bɜːnəʊ/ industrial city in Czechoslovakia, capital of Moravia; population (1981) 371,500. Gregor Mendel devised the theory of inheritance here, and the Bren gun was first manufactured here.

Britten British composer and pianist Benjamin Britten wrote tenor songs and many successful operas, inspired by the talent of his life–long friend Peter Pears. A keen and often amused observer of human nature, he portrayed realistic people in everyday life.

Broad /brɔːd/ Charles Dunbar 1887–1971. British philosopher. Born in London, he was educated at Trinity College, Cambridge, and was Knightbridge professor of moral philosophy at the university 1933–53. His books include *Perception, Physics and Reality* and *Lectures on Psychic Research* 1962, discussing modern scientific evidence for survival after death.

broad arrow the mark resembling an arrow-head on British government stores. Of doubtful origin, the broad arrow came into general use in the 17th century and is still used to mark government property, such as military supplies, but it has long been abolished on prison dress.

broadbill bird of the family Eurylaimidae found in Africa and S Asia. Broadbills are forest birds and are often found near water. They have brilliant coloration and wide bills, and feed largely on insects.

broadcasting the transmission of sound and vision programmes by radio and television. Broadcasting may be organized under complete state control, for example, as in the USSR; or private enterprise, for example, as in the USA, where it is only limited by the issue of licences from the Federal Communications Commission to competing commercial companies; or operate under a compromise system, for example, Australia (where a government corporation also sells time to advertisers) and Britain, where there is a television and radio service controlled by the ◊British Broadcasting Corporation (a centralized body appointed by the state and responsible to parliament, but with policy and programme content not controlled by the state), and also a commercial ◊Independent Broadcasting Authority (television from 1955, radio from 1973). In Japan, which ranks next to the USA in the number of television sets owned,

there is a semi-governmental radio and television broadcasting corporation (NHK) and numerous private television companies.

broad-leaved tree another name for a tree belonging to the ◊angiosperms, such as ash, beech, oak, maple or birch. Their leaves are generally broad and flat, in contrast to the needle-like leaves of most ◊conifers. See also ◊deciduous tree.

Broadmoor /'brɔːdmɔː/ site of special hospital (established 1863) at Crowthorne, Berkshire, England, for those formerly described as 'criminally insane'.

Broads, the Norfolk /brɔːdz/ area of some 12 interlinked fresh-water lakes in E England created about 600 years ago by the digging out of peat deposits; they are noted for wildlife and boating facilities.

Broadway /'brɔːdweɪ/ major street of ◊Manhattan, New York, famous for its ◊theatres.

broccoli a variety of ◊cabbage.

Broch /brɒx/ Hermann 1880–1951. Austrian novelist, later an American citizen, best known for his *Der Tod des Vergil/The Death of Virgil* 1945.

Brocken /'brɒkən/ highest peak of the Harz Mountains (1,142 m/3,746 ft) in East Germany. On 1 May (Walpurgis night) witches were said to gather here.
The *Brocken Spectre* is a phenomenon of mountainous areas, so named because first scientifically observed at Brocken in 1780. The greatly enlarged shadow of the observer, accompanied by coloured rings, is cast by a low sun upon a cloud bank.

brocket name for a deer stag in its second year, when it has short straight pointed antlers. *Brocket deer* genus *Mazama* include a number of species of small shy solitary deer, up to 1.3 m/4 ft body length and 65 cm/2 ft at the shoulder, found in Central and S America which have similar small straight antlers even when adult.

Brodsky /'brɒdski/ Joseph 1940– . Russian poet, who emigrated to the USA in 1972. His work, often dealing with themes of exile, is admired for its wit and economy of language, particularly in its use of understatement. Many of his poems, written in Russian, have been translated into English (*A Part of Speech* 1980). More recently he has also written in English. He was awarded a Nobel prize in 1987.

Broglie, de see ◊de Broglie.

Broken Hill /'brəʊkən/ mining town in New South Wales, Australia; population (1981) 27,000.

Broken Hill /'brəʊkən/ former name of ◊Kabwe, town in Zambia.

brolga Australian crane *Grus rubicunda*, about 1.5 m/5 ft tall, mainly grey with a red patch on the head.

Bromberg /'brɒmbɜːg/ German name of ◊Bydgoszcz, port in Poland.

brome general name for annual grasses of the genus *Bromus* and some related grasses.

bromeliad plant of the family Bromeliaceae, to which the pineapple belongs. Bromeliads all originate in tropical America, where there are some 1,400 species. Some are terrestrial, in

habitats from scrub desert to tropical forest floor. Many, however, are epiphytes and grow on trees. They are supported by the tree but do not take nourishment from it, instead using rain and decayed plant and animal remains for sustenance. Some species, such as '*Spanish moss*' *Tillandsia usneoides*, can even grow on telegraph wires. In many bromeliads the leaves are arranged in rosettes, and in some the leaf bases trap water to form little pools, in which organisms from microscopic to frog may pass the whole life cycle. Many bromeliads have attractive flowers. Often, too, the leaves are coloured and patterned. They are therefore popular greenhouse plants.

bromine an element that exists as a red, volatile liquid at room temperature; symbol Br, atomic weight 79.909, atomic number 35. Bromine is poisonous and a member of the halogen series of elements. It is found in small quantities in sea water and is used as an anti-knock petrol additive. Its compounds are used in photography, and in the chemical and pharmaceutical industries. Salts of bromine are known as bromides.

bronchitis inflammation of the bronchi (the tubes admitting air to the lungs), usually caused initially by a viral infection (a cold or flu); chronic bronchitis may develop in those exposed to atmospheric pollutants (for example sulphur dioxide SO_2) or cigarette smoke.

bronchodilator drug that causes the airways (bronchi and bronchioles) of the lungs to relax and widen, useful in disorders such as asthma.

Brontë /'brɒnti/ family of English writers, including the three sisters *Charlotte* (1816–55), *Emily Jane* (1818–48) and *Anne* (1820–49), and their brother *Patrick Branwell* (1817–48). They were brought up by an aunt at Haworth rectory (now a museum) in Yorkshire. In 1846 the sisters published a volume of poems under the pseudonyms Currer (Charlotte), Ellis (Emily) and Acton (Anne) Bell. In 1847 (using the same names), they published the novels *Jane Eyre* (in which Charlotte reflected her experiences at boarding school), *Wuthering Heights* (a tale of destructive passions set on the Yorkshire moors), and *Agnes Grey*, Anne's much weaker work. During 1848–49 Branwell, Emily, and Anne all died of tuberculosis, aided in Branwell's case by alcohol and opium addiction: he is remembered for his portrait of the sisters. Charlotte subsequently published *Shirley* 1849, in which the heroine resembles Emily, and *Villette* 1853 which recalls her years teaching in Brussels. Charlotte married her father's curate, A B Nicholls, in 1854, and died during pregnancy.

brontosaurus large plant-eating dinosaur, now called *Apatosaurus*, which flourished about 145 million years ago. Up to 21 m/69 ft long and 30 tonnes in weight, it stood on four elephant-like legs and had a long tail, long neck and small head. It probably snipped off low-growing vegetation with peg-like front teeth and swallowed it whole to be ground by pebbles in the stomach.

Bronx, the /brɒŋks/ borough of New York City, USA, NE of Harlem river; largely residential.

Brontë Emily, Anne, and Charlotte, painted by their brother, Patrick Branwell, c. 1835.

bronze ◊alloy of copper and tin, yellow or brown in colour; one of the first metallic alloys known to man and used widely by early peoples during the period of history known as the ◊Bronze Age. It is harder than pure copper and more suitable for ◊casting. It also resists ◊corrosion well. Bronze may contain as much as 25 per cent tin, together with small amounts of other metals, particularly lead.

Bell-metal the bronze used for casting bells, contains 15 per cent or more tin. *Phosphor bronze* is hardened by the addition of a small percentage of phosphorus. *Silicon bronze* (for telegraph wires) and *aluminium bronze* are similar alloys of copper with silicon or aluminium and small amounts of iron, nickel or manganese, but usually no tin.

Bronze Age period of early history and pre-history when bronze was the chief material used for tools and weapons. It lies between the Stone Age and the Iron Age and may be dated 5000–1200 BC in the Near East, and about 2000–500 BC in Britain. Mining and metalworking were the first specialized industries, and the invention of the wheel revolutionized transport. Agricultural productivity, and hence the size of the population which could be supported, was transformed by the ox-drawn plough.

Recent discoveries in ◊Thailand suggest that the Far East, rather than the Near East, was the cradle of the Bronze Age.

Bronzino /brɒndˈziːnəʊ/ pseudonym of Italian artist Agnolo di Cosimo 1503–1572. Court painter to Cosimo I, Duke of Tuscany, he was influenced by Michelangelo, and was noted for his impressive, elegant, ◊Mannerist portraits, including many of the Medici family.

Brook /brʊk/ Peter 1925– . British theatrical producer and director. He is best known for his work with the Royal Shakespeare Company in England, and the Paris-based Le Centre International de Créations Théâtrales. Films he has directed include *Lord of the Flies* 1962 and *Meetings with Remarkable Men* 1979.

Brooke /brʊk/ James 1803–1868. British administrator, known as the 'the white rajah'. Born near Benares, he served in the army of the East India Company. In 1838 he headed a private expedition to Borneo, where he helped to suppress a revolt, and in 1841, the sultan gave him the title of Rajah of Sarawak. He was succeeded as rajah by his nephew, Sir Charles Johnson (1829–1917), whose son Sir Charles Vyner (1874–1963) in 1946 arranged for the transfer of Sarawak to the British crown.

Brooke /brʊk/ Rupert Chawner 1887–1915. English poet, symbol of the World War I 'lost generation'. Born in Rugby, where he was educated, he travelled abroad after a nervous breakdown in 1911, but in 1913 won a fellowship at King's College Cambridge. Later that year he toured America (*Letters from America* 1916), New Zealand and the South Seas, and in 1914 became an officer in the Royal Naval Division. After fighting at Antwerp, he sailed for the Dardanelles, but died of blood-poisoning on the Greek Island of Skyros, where he is buried. The five war sonnets published immediately after his death, including 'Grantchester' and 'The Great Lover', have become classics.

Brookeborough /ˈbrʊkbərə/ Basil Brooke, Viscount Brookeborough 1888–1973. Politician of Northern Ireland. He entered parliament as a Unionist in 1929, held ministerial posts 1933–45, and was prime minister of Northern Ireland 1943–63. He was a staunch advocate of strong links with Britain.

Brook Farm farm in W Roxbury, near Boston, Massachusetts, USA, which in 1841–47 was the scene of an idealistic experiment in communal living, led by George Ripley (1802–80), a former Unitarian minister. Financial difficulties and a fire led to the community's dissolution.

Brooklands /ˈbrʊkləndz/ motor racing track, near Weybridge, Surrey, England, opened in 1907 as a testing-ground for early motor-cars. The site was sold to aircraft builders Vickers in 1946.

Brooklyn /ˈbrʊklɪn/ borough of New York City, USA, occupying the SW end of Long Island. It is linked to Manhattan Island by Brooklyn Bridge 1883 and others, and by the Verrazano-Narrows Bridge (see ◊bridge) 1964 to Staten Island. Brooklyn US Navy Yard is here. Of the more than 60 parks, Prospect is the most important. There is also a botanic garden, and a beach and funfair at Coney Island.

Brookner /ˈbrʊknə/ Anita 1938– . British novelist and art historian, whose novels include *Hotel du Lac* 1984, winner of the ◊Booker prize, and *A Misalliance* 1986.

Brooks /brʊks/ Louise 1906–1985. US actress, famous for her impassive expression and bobbed hair. Her best roles were when she was directed by G W ◊Pabst, in the films *Die Büchse der Pandora/Pandora's Box* 1928 and *Das Tagebuch einer Verlorenen/Diary of a Lost Girl* 1929. She retired from the screen in 1931.

Brooks /brʊks/ Mel 1926– . American film director, whose comic films include *Blazing Saddles* 1974, and *History of the World Part I* 1981.

Brooks One of the greatest stars of the silent screen in her portrayal of Lulu in *Pandora's Box*, Louise Brooks never achieved such a powerful screen presence in her talking roles.

Brooks /brʊks/ Van Wyck 1886–1963. American literary critic. His study *The Flowering of New England* 1936 was the first of an influential series of critical works on American literature 1800–1915.

broom shrub of the family Leguminosae, especially species of *Cytisus*, such as the *common broom Cytisus scoparius*, with yellow flowers, of Britain.

Brougham /bruːm/ Henry Peter, 1st Baron Brougham and Vaux 1778–1868. British ◊Whig politician. Born in Edinburgh, he was a founder of the *Edinburgh Review*. From 1811 he was chief adviser of the Princess of Wales (afterwards Queen Caroline), and in 1820 he defeated the attempt of George IV to divorce her. He sat in parliament 1810–12 and from 1816, and supported the causes of public education and law reform. He was one of the founders of University College, London (1828). When the Whigs returned to power in 1830, Brougham was returned as member of parliament for York, but accepted the Chancellorship and a peerage a few weeks later. His speeches in support of the Reform Bill were notable, but his allegedly dictatorial and eccentric ways led to his exclusion from office when the Whigs next assumed power in 1835. After 1837 he was active in the House of Lords.

Brouwer /ˈbraʊə/ Adriaen 1605–1638. Flemish artist, influenced by ◊Hals, who excelled in scenes of peasant revelry.

Brown /braʊn/ Ford Madox 1821–93. British painter. Born in Calais, he studied in Belgium, and later moved to England, where he was associated with the ◊Pre-Raphaelite Brotherhood. His best-known pictures include *The Last of England* (Birmingham), and *Christ Washing St Peter's Feet* (Tate Gallery, London), and two versions of *Work* 1863 (Birmingham Art

Gallery), and 1868 (City Art Gallery, Manchester).

Brown /braʊn/ George, Baron George-Brown 1914–1985. British Labour politician. He entered parliament in 1945, was briefly minister of works in 1951 and contested the leadership of the party on the death of Gaitskell, but was defeated by Harold Wilson. He was secretary for economic affairs 1964–66, and foreign secretary 1966–68. He was created a life peer in 1970.

Brown /braʊn/ John 1800–1859. American anti-slavery leader. Born in Connecticut, he settled as a farmer in Kansas in 1855. In 1856 he was responsible for the 'Pottawatomie massacre' when five pro-slavery farmers were killed. In 1858 he formed a plan for a refuge for runaway slaves in the mountains of Virginia. With 18 men, he seized, on the night of 16 Oct 1859, the government arsenal at Harper's Ferry in W Virginia. On 18 Oct the arsenal was stormed by Robert E ◊Lee, and Brown was tried and hanged on 2 Dec, becoming a martyr, and the hero of the popular song 'John Brown's Body' c. 1860.

Brown /braʊn/ John 1825–1883. Scottish servant and confidant of Queen Victoria from 1858.

Brown /braʊn/ Lancelot 1716–1783. English landscape gardener, known as 'Capability Brown' because he said sites had 'capability'; his works include the gardens at Blenheim Palace (Oxfordshire), Highclere (Hampshire) and Bowood (Wiltshire). His style is characterized by a contrived informality, with artificial lakes, mounds, and paths made to imitate and rival nature.

Browne /braʊn/ Hablot Knight 1815–1882. British illustrator, pseudonym Phiz, best known for his illustrations of Dickens's works.

Browne /braʊn/ Robert 1550–1633. English Puritan leader, founder of the Brownists. Born near Stamford, he preached in Norwich, and was imprisoned several times in 1581 82 for attacking Episcopalianism. He retired to Middelburg in Holland, but returned after making his peace with the Church and became master of Stamford Grammar School. From 1591 he was a rector in Northamptonshire.

The community which Browne founded in Norwich and Holland continued on ◊Nonconformist lines, developing into modern ◊Congregationalism. In a work published in 1582 Browne advocated congregationalist doctrine.

Browne /braʊn/ Thomas 1605–1682. English author and physician. Born in London, he travelled widely in Europe before settling in Norwich in 1637. He is noted for his personal richness of style in *Religio Medici/The Religion of a Doctor* 1643, a justification of his profession; *Vulgar Errors* 1646, an examination of popular legend and superstition; *Urn Burial* and *The Garden of Cyrus* 1658; and *Christian Morals* 1717. He was knighted in 1671.

Brownian movement continuous random motion of particles in a fluid medium (gas or liquid) as they are subject to impact from the molecules of the medium, observed in 1827 by the Scottish botanist Robert Brown

(1773–1858) but not convincingly explained until ◊Einstein in 1905.

Browning /'braʊnɪŋ/ Elizabeth Barrett 1806–1861. British poet. Born near Durham, as a child she fell from her pony and injured her spine, and was treated by her father as a confirmed invalid. In 1844 she published *Poems* (including 'The Cry of the Children'), which led to her friendship and secret marriage with Robert ◊Browning in 1846. The *Sonnets from the Portuguese* 1847 were written during their courtship. Freed from her father's oppressive influence, Elizabeth Browning's health improved, and during the years in Italy she wrote *Casa Guidi Windows* 1851, the poetic novel *Aurora Leigh* 1857, and other verse.

Browning Lyric poet Elizabeth Barrett Browning was one of 11 children of a tyrannical father. She wrote strong verse about social injustice and oppression in Victorian England. Robert Browning admired her work; they married in 1846.

Browning /'braʊnɪŋ/ Robert 1812–1889. British poet. Born in Camberwell, he wrote his first poem 'Pauline' 1833 under the influence of Shelley; it was followed by 'Paracelsus' 1835 and 'Sordello' 1840, which marked the development of his use of psychological analysis and interest in obscure characters of literature and history. In 1837 he achieved moderate success with his play *Strafford*, and in the pamphlet series of *Bells and Pomegranates* 1841–46, which contained *Pippa Passes* 1841, *Dramatic Lyrics* 1842 and *Dramatic Romances* 1845, he included the dramas *King Victor and King Charles*, *Return of the Druses* and *Colombe's Birthday*. In 1846 he met Elizabeth Barrett, whom he married the same year and took to Italy. Here he wrote *Christmas Eve and Easter Day* 1850; and *Men and Women* 1855, containing some of his finest love-poems and dramatic monologues, which were followed later by *Dramatis Personae* 1864, and *The Ring and the Book* 1868–69, based on an Italian murder story. After his wife's death in 1861 Browning settled in England and

enjoyed an established reputation, although his latest works such as *Red-Cotton Night-Cap Country* 1873, *Dramatic Idylls* 1879–80, and *Asolando* 1889, still prompted opposition by their rugged obscurity of style. His best known work includes 'The Pied Piper of Hamelin', 'Home Thoughts from Abroad', and 'Rabbi ben Ezra'.

Browning Admired for his innovative works incorporating psychological analysis and obscure historical characters, Robert Browning (husband of Elizabeth Barrett Browning) was one of the most popular Victorian poets.

Brownshirts the SA (*Sturm-Abteilung*), or Storm Troops, the private army of the German Nazi Party; so called from the colour of their uniform.

Brubeck /'bruːbek/ David Warren 1920– . US jazz musician of the intellectual tradition, a student of Milhaud. The Dave Brubeck Quartet (formed 1951) combines improvisation with modern classical discipline.

Bruce /bruːs/ James 1730–1794. Scottish explorer, British consul at Algiers 1763–65, known as the first European to reach the source of the Blue Nile in 1770, and to follow the river downstream to Cairo by 1773.

Bruce /bruːs/ Robert 1274–1329. Scottish hero. He was the grandson of Robert de Bruce 1210–95, who unsuccessfully claimed the Scottish throne in 1290. Bruce shared in the national rising led by ◊Wallace, and soon after the latter's execution in 1305 he rose again against Edward I of England, and was crowned king of Scotland in 1306. He defeated Edward II at Bannockburn in 1314, and in 1328 the treaty of Northampton recognized Scottish independence, and Bruce as king. See also ◊Robert, kings of Scotland.

Bruce /bruːs/ Stanley Melbourne, 1st Viscount Bruce of Melbourne 1883–1967. Australian politician. Called to the Bar in 1906, he practised in England until 1914. After serving in World War I, he returned to Australia, where he was elected to the Commonwealth parliament in 1918 as a member of the National Party,

Bruce Robert Bruce was crowned king of Scotland in 1306. A military genius, he was also a strong character who inspired devotion, and he remains a Scottish hero. He died of leprosy in 1329, contracted during his campaigns.

Bruckner Austrian composer Anton Bruckner was influenced by Wagner. He wrote ten symphonies, the last of which is unfinished. He was often persuaded to abridge and modify the orchestration of his lengthy works, so that are some problems in establishing authentic versions.

becoming Prime Minister and Minister for External Affairs in a National-Country Party coalition (1923–29). He was noted for his unemployment insurance scheme, and other social and welfare measures; he was a member of the British war cabinet 1942–5

brucellosis disease of cattle, goats and pigs, also known when transmitted to humans as *undulant fever* since it remains in the body and recurs. It was named after Australian doctor Sir David Bruce 1855–1931, and is caused by bacteria present in the milk of infected cattle. It has largely been eradicated in Britain through vaccination of the animals and pasteurization of milk.

Bruch /brux/ Max 1838–1920. German composer and conductor, best known for his Violin Concerto in G minor.

Brucke, die /'bruka/ (German 'the bridge') ◊Expressionist art movement, which flourished 1905–13. Ernst Ludwig ◊Kirchner was one of its founders and Emil ◊Nolde a member 1906–07. Strongly influenced by black art, they sought to charge everything with spiritual significance using raw colours to express different emotions. The movement shared characteristics with ◊Blaue Reiter.

Bruckner /'brukna/ (Joseph) Anton 1824–1896. Austrian Romantic composer. As cathedral organist at Linz 1856–68, he composed in his leisure time and was much influenced by ◊Wagner, and from 1868 was at Vienna, where he became professor at the Conservatoire. His works include many choral pieces, and ten symphonies, the last unfinished.

Bruderhof (German 'Society of Brothers') Christian sect with beliefs similar to the ◊Mennonites.

Brueghel /'brɜːxəl/ Pieter c. 1525–1569. Flemish artist, nicknamed 'Peasant' Brueghel, noted for his satirical and humorous pictures of peasant life, and for his landscapes such as the five paintings of the *Months* (or *Seasons*) 1565 in which he evokes both the cold silence of winter and the warmth of summer. His son *Pieter Brueghel the Younger* (1564–1637), called 'Hell' Brueghel, specialized in religious subjects, and another son *Jan Brueghel* (1568–1625), called 'Velvet' Brueghel, painted flowers and land and seascapes, and collaborated with ◊Rubens.

Bruges /bruːʒ/ (Flemish *Brugge*) historic city in NW Belgium; capital of W Flanders province, 16 km/10 mi from the North Sea, with which it is connected by canal; population (1982) 118,048.

features Among many notable buildings are the 14th-century cathedral, the church of Nôtre Dame with a Michelangelo statue of the Virgin and Child, the Gothic town hall and market hall; there are remarkable art collections. It was named for its many bridges. The College of Europe is the oldest centre of European studies.

history Bruges was the capital of medieval ◊Flanders, and was the chief European wool manufacturing town as well as its chief market.

Brugge /'bruxə/ Flemish form of ◊Bruges, town in Belgium.

Brummell /'brʌməl/ George Bryan 1778–1840. British dandy and leader of fashion, known as Beau Brummell. A friend of the Prince of Wales, the future George IV, he later quarrelled with him, and was driven by gambling losses to exile in France in 1816.

Brundtland /'bruntlænd/ Gro Harlem 1939– . Norwegian politician. Educated at Oslo and Harvard universities, she entered politics with the Norwegian Labour party and became its leader (and, briefly, prime minister) in 1981. She was again elected prime minister in 1985.

Brunei /'bruːnaɪ/ country on the N coast of Borneo, surrounded to the landward side by Sarawak, and bounded to the N by the South China Sea.

government the 1959 constitution gives supreme authority to the sultan, advised by various councils. Since the constitution was suspended after a revolution in 1962, the sultan rules by decree. One political party, the Brunei National Democratic Party (BNDP), consisting of businessmen loyal to the sultan, is allowed. Others have been banned or have closed down.

history an Islamic monarchy from the 15th century, Brunei became a British protected state in 1888. Under an agreement of 1906, a British Resident was appointed as adviser to the sultan, Sir Muda Omar Ali Saiffuddin Saadul Khairi Waddien, known as Sir Omar(1916–86). Japan occupied Brunei 1941–45.

In 1959 Britain was made responsible for defence and external affairs until independence, and a proposal that Brunei should join the Federation of Malysia was opposed by a revolution which was put down with British help. As a result the Sultan decided to rule by decree. In 1967 he abdicated in favour of his son, Hassanal Bolkiah, but continued to be his chief adviser. Four years later Brunei was given full internal self-government. In 1975 the UN called for Britain's withdrawal and in 1984 full independence was achieved, the sultan becoming prime minister, minister of finance and home affairs, and presiding over a cabinet of six, three of whom were close relatives. Britain agreed to maintain a small force to protect the oil and gas fields which make Brunei the wealthiest nation, per capita, in Asia. In 1985 the sultan cautiously allowed the formation of the loyal and reliable Brunei National Democratic Party. In Sep 1986 the sultan's father, Sir Omar, died at the age of 71.

Brunel /bruː'nel/ Isambard Kingdom 1806–1859. British engineer and inventor (son of Marc ◊Brunel), who made major contributions in ship-building and bridge construction. After assisting his father in the Thames tunnel project, in 1833 he became engineer to the Great Western Railway, which adopted the 2.1 m/7 ft gauge on his advice. He also built the Clifton Suspension Bridge over the river Severn at Bristol and the Saltash Bridge over the river Tamar near Plymouth. In 1838 he designed the *Great Western*, which was the first steamship to cross the Atlantic regularly, and sailed from Bristol to New York. His next ship was the *Great Britain* 1845, the first large ship to be constructed of iron and to have a screw propeller. Larger still was the *Great Eastern* 1858, which later laid the first transatlantic telegraph cable. Brunel University, in Uxbridge, London, is named after both father and son.

Brunel /bruː'nel/ Marc Isambard 1769–1849. French-born British engineer and inventor, who built the Rotherhithe tunnel. Coming to England in 1799, he did engineering work for the Admiralty, improved the port of Liverpool, and planned a tunnel under the Thames from Wapping to Rotherhithe which was constructed between 1825 and 1843. He was knighted in 1841.

Brunei

AREA 5,800 sq km/2,226 sq mi
CAPITAL and chief port Bandar Seri Begawan
PHYSICAL 75% of the area is forested; the Limbang valley splits Brunei in two, and its cession to Sarawak in 1890 is disputed by Brunei
HEAD OF STATE AND OF GOVERNMENT Sir Muda Hassanal Bolkiah Mu'izzaddin Waddaulah from 1968
GOVERNMENT absolute monarchy
EXPORTS liquefied natural gas (world's largest producer) and oil, both expected to be exhausted by 2000 AD
CURRENCY Brunei dollar (3.45 = £1 Sept 1987)
POPULATION (1985) 232,000 (of Malaysian origin); 50,000 Chinese (few granted citizenship); annual growth rate 12%
LANGUAGE Malay (official), English
RELIGION Muslim
LITERACY 75% male/50% female (1971)
GDP $3.8 bn (1983); $20,000 per head of population
CHRONOLOGY
1888 Brunei became a British protectorate.
1941–45 Occupied by Japan.
1959 Written constitution made Britain responsible for defence and external affairs.
1962 Sultan began rule by decree.

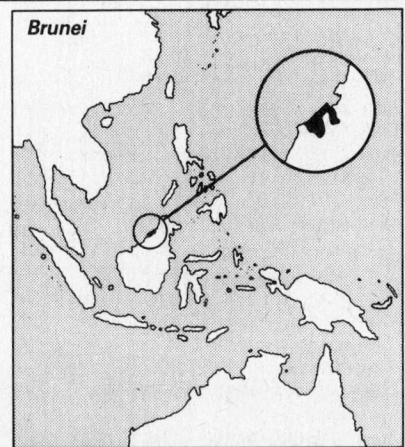
Brunei

1963 Proposal to join Malaysia abandoned.
1967 Sultan abdicated in favour of his son Sir Hassanal Bolkiah.
1971 Brunei given internal self-government.
1975 UN resolution called for independence for Brunei.
1984 Full independence achieved, with Britain maintaining a small force to protect the oil and gas fields.
1985 A 'loyal and reliable' political party legalized.

Brunelleschi /ˌbruːnəˈleski/ Filippo 1377–1446. Italian Renaissance architect. One of the earliest and greatest Renaissance architects, he was a pioneer in the scientific use of perspective. He was responsible for the construction of the dome of Florence Cathedral (completed 1438), a feat deemed impossible by many of his contemporaries.

Bruning /ˈbruːnɪŋ/ Heinrich 1885–1970. German politician. Elected to the Reichstag in 1924, he led the Catholic Centre Party from 1929 and was Reich Chancellor 1930–32, when political and economic crisis forced his resignation.

Brünn /brʊn/ German form of ◊Brno, a town in Czechoslovakia.

Bruno /ˈbruːnəʊ/ Giordano 1548–1600. Italian philosopher. He became a ◊Dominican in 1563, but his sceptical attitude to Catholic doctrines forced him to flee Italy in 1577. After visiting Geneva and Paris, he lived in England 1583–85, where he wrote some of his finest works. After returning to Europe, he was arrested by the ◊Inquisition in 1593 in Venice, and burned at the stake for his adoption of ◊Copernican astronomy and his heretical religious views.

Bruno, St /ˈbruːnəʊ/ 1030–1101. Founder of the ◊Carthusian order. Born in Cologne, he became a priest, and controlled the cathedral school of Rheims 1057–76. Withdrawing to the mountains near Grenoble, as a result of an ecclesiastical controversy, he founded the monastery at Chartreuse in 1084. Feast day 6 Oct.

Brunswick /ˈbrʌnzwɪk/ former independent duchy, a republic from 1918, which is now part of Lower ◊Saxony, West Germany.

Brunswick /ˈbrʌnzwɪk/ (German *Braunschweig*) city in Lower Saxony, West Germany; population (1985) 253,478.
history It was one of the chief cities of N Germany in the Middle Ages, and a member of the ◊Hanseatic League. It was capital of the duchy of Brunswick from 1671.

Brusa /ˈbruːsə/ alternative form of ◊Bursa, a town in Turkey.

Brussels /ˈbrʌsəlz/ (Flemish *Brussel*/French *Bruxelles*) capital of Belgium, industrial city (lace, textiles, machinery, chemicals); population (1985) 952,434 (80 per cent French-speaking, the suburbs Flemish-speaking).
features Notable buildings include the 13th-century church of Sainte Gudule; the Hôtel de Ville, Maison du Roi, and others in the Grand Place; and the royal palace; the Musées Royaux des Beaux-Arts de Belgique hold a large art collection. It is the headquarters of the European Economic Community and since 1967 of the international secretariat of NATO.
history First settled in the 6th century AD, and a city from 1312, Brussels became the capital of the Spanish Netherlands 1530 and of Belgium 1830.

Brussels, Treaty of /ˈbrʌsəlz/ pact of economic, political, cultural, and military alliance established 17 Mar 1948 for 50 years by Britain, France, and the ◊Benelux countries, joined by W Germany and Italy in 1955. It was the forerunner of the ◊North Atlantic Treaty Organization and the ◊European Community.

brussels sprout a type of small ◊cabbage.

Brussilov /bruːˈsiːlɒf/ Aleksei Alekseevich 1853–1926. Russian general, military leader of World War I, who achieved major sucesses against the Austro-Hungarian forces in 1916. Later he was commander of the Red Army (1920) which drove the Poles to within a few miles of Warsaw before being repulsed.

Brutus /ˈbruːtəs/ Marcus Junius c. 78–42 BC. Roman soldier, a supporter of ◊Pompey (against Caesar) in the Civil War. Pardoned by ◊Caesar, and raised to high office by him, he nevertheless plotted Caesar's assassination to restore the purity of the Republic. When Brutus was defeated (with ◊Cassius) by ◊Mark Antony, Caesar's lieutenant, at Philippi in 42 BC, he committed suicide.

Bruxelles /bruːˈsel/ French form of ◊Brussels, capital of Belgium.

Bryansk /briˈænsk/ industrial city (foundries, sawmills, cement, bricks) in W central USSR, SW of Moscow on the Desna; population (1981) 407,000.

Bryant /ˈbraɪənt/ David 1931– . English flat green bowls player, who has won every major honour in the game: three world titles (two singles, one triples), three world indoor titles and record five Commonwealth Games titles. He is known as a great sportsman who is generous in defeat, and his trademark is a pipe held between his teeth, often unlit.

Bryce /braɪs/ James, 1st Viscount Bryce 1838–1922. British politician. Author of *The American Commonwealth* 1888, he was ambassador to Washington 1907–13, and improved US–Canadian relations.

bryony either of two hedgerow climbing plants found in Britain; *white bryony Bryonia cretica* belonging to the gourd family Cucurbitaceae, and *black bryony Tamus communis* of the yam family Dioscoreaceae.

bryophytes members of the Bryophyta, a division of the plant kingdom containing three classes, the Hepaticae (liverworts), Musci (mosses), and Anthocerotae (hornworts). Bryophytes are generally small, low-growing, terrestrial plants with no ◊vascular (water-conducting) system in higher plants. Their lifecycle shows a marked ◊alternation of generations and the sporophyte, consisting only of a spore-bearing capsule upon a slender stalk, is wholly or partially dependent on the gametophyte (the familiar moss or liverwort 'plant') for water and nutrients. In some liverworts the plant body is a simple ◊thallus, but in the majority of bryophytes it is differentiated into stem, leaves and rhizoids. Bryophytes chiefly occur in damp habitats and require water for the dispersal of the male gametes (◊antherozoids).

Bryusov /briˈuːsɒf/ Valery 1873–1924. Russian ◊Symbolist poet and critic.

Brześć nad Bugiem /ˈbʒeʃtʃ nad ˈbuːgjem/ Polish name of ◊Brest, a town in the USSR.

Brzezinski /brəˈʒɪnski/ Zbigniew 1928– . US Democrat politician. Born in Warsaw; he taught at Harvard and became a US citizen in 1949. He is best known for his role as national security adviser to President Carter from 1977 and as chief architect of Carter's human-rights policy.

bubble chamber a vessel filled with a transparent highly superheated liquid. When an ionizing particle moves through a bubble chamber, it may start violent boiling along its path shown by a string of tiny bubbles. Photographic study of these tracks gives much information about the nature and movement of atomic particles and the interaction of particles and radiations. See also ◊Glaser, Donald and ◊spark chamber.

bubble memory in computing, a ◊memory device based on the creation of small magnetic 'bubbles' on a ◊chip. The bubbles are magnetically moved across the chip to a reading head, which records the presence of a bubble as 1 and its absence as 0. Bubble-memory chips typically store up to four megabits (4 million ◊bits) of information. They are not sensitive to shock and vibration, unlike other memory devices such as disk drives, yet, like magnetic ◊disks, they do not lose their information when the computer is switched off.

Buber /'buːbə/ Martin 1878–1965. Israeli philosopher, a ◊Zionist and advocate of the reappraisal of ancient Jewish thought in modern terms. Born in Vienna, he was forced to abandon a professorship in comparative religion at Frankfurt by the Nazis, and taught social philosophy at the Hebrew University, Jerusalem, 1937–51.

Bucaramanga /buˌkɑːrəˈmæŋgə/ industrial and commercial city in N central Colombia; population (1980) 441,000.

buccaneer name given to a member of the band of pirates off the Spanish American coast in the 17th century, who plundered Spanish ships and colonies. Though mainly British, some were French, Dutch, and Portuguese. Among the most famous buccaneers was Henry ◊Morgan. The ranks of the buccaneers were divided by the outbreak of war between England and France in 1689, and the growth of naval power in the 18th century put an end to their activities.

Bucer /'butsə/ Martin 1491–1551. German ◊Protestant reformer, regius professor of divinity at Cambridge university from 1549, who tried to reconcile the views of ◊Luther and ◊Zwingli.

Buchan /'bʌxən, 'bʌkən/ John, Baron Tweedsmuir 1875–1940. Scottish politician and author. He published adventure stories which won wide popularity and included *Prester John* 1910, *The Thirty-Nine Steps* 1915, *Greenmantle* 1916, *Huntingtower* 1922, *The Three Hostages* 1924, and *The House of the Four Winds* 1935.

Buchanan /bəˈkænən/ George 1506–1582. Scottish humanist. Forced to flee to France in 1539 owing to some satirical verses on the Franciscans, he returned to Scotland *c.* 1562 as tutor to Mary Queen of Scots. He became principal of St Leonard's College, St Andrews, in 1566, and wrote *Rerum Scoticarum Historia/A History of Scotland* 1582 biased against ◊Mary Queen of Scots.

Buchanan /bəˈkænən/ Jack 1891–1957. British musical comedy actor. Born in Helensburgh, Scotland, he played in London and New York in *Charlot's Revue*, and his songs such as 'Good-Night Vienna' epitomized the period between World Wars I and II.

Bucharest /ˌbuːkəˈrest/ (Romanian *Bucureşti*) capital of Romania; population (1983) 1,834,377.
features 18th-century Mogosoaia Palace.
history Originally a citadel built by Vlad the Impaler (see ◊Dracula) to stop the advance of the Ottoman invasion in the 14th century. It became the capital of the princes of Wallachia 1698 and of Romania 1861.

Buchenwald /'buːxənvælt/ village NE of Weimar, E Germany, site of a Nazi concentration camp 1937–45.

Buck /bʌk/ Pearl S 1892–1973. American novelist. Daughter of missionaries to China, she wrote novels about Chinese life, such as *East Wind–West Wind* 1930 and *The Good Earth* 1931. She won the Nobel Prize for Literature in 1938.

Buckingham /'bʌkɪŋəm/ town in Buckinghamshire, England, seat of University College 1974.

Buckingham /'bʌkɪŋəm/ George Villiers, 1st Duke of Buckingham 1592–1628. English courtier. Introduced to the court of James I in 1614, he soon became his favourite and was made Earl of Buckingham in 1617 and a duke in 1623. He failed to arrange the marriage of Prince Charles and the Infanta of Spain 1623, and on returning to England negotiated Charles's alliance with Henrietta Maria, sister to the French king. Following Charles's accession, Buckingham attempted to form a Protestant coalition in Europe which led to war with France, but he failed to relieve the Protestants besieged in La Rochelle (1627). His policy was attacked in parliament, and when about to sail again for La Rochelle he was assassinated at Portsmouth.

Buckingham /'bʌkɪŋəm/ George Villiers, 2nd Duke of Buckingham 1628–1687. English politician. A dissolute son of the 1st duke, he was brought up with the royal children, and was a member of the ◊Cabal under Charles II. His play *The Rehearsal* satirized the style of ◊Dryden, who portrayed him as Zimri in *Absalom and Achitophel*.

Buckingham Palace London home of the British sovereign, built 1703 for the duke of Buckingham, but bought by George III in 1762 and reconstructed by ◊Nash 1821–36; a new front was added in 1913.

Buckinghamshire /'bʌkɪŋəmʃə/ county in SE central England
area 1,883 sq km/727 sq mi
towns administrative headquarters Aylesbury; Buckingham, High Wycombe, Beaconsfield, ◊Olney
features ◊Chequers (country seat of the prime minister); Burnham Beeches and the church of the poet Gray's 'Elegy' at Stoke Poges; Cliveden, a country house designed by Charles Barry (now a hotel, it was used by the newspaper-owning Astors for house parties); Bletchley Park, home of World War II code-breaking activities, now used as a training post for GCHQ (Britain's communications spy centre); homes of the poets William Cowper at Olney and John Milton at

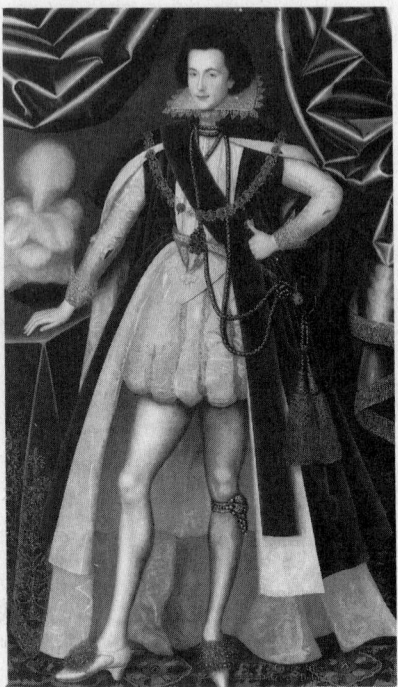

Buckingham Four times imprisoned in the Tower of London, dissolute courtier George Villiers, 2nd Duke of Buckingham, was satirically portrayed as Zimri in Dryden's *Absalom and Achitophel*.

Chalfont St Giles, and of the Tory prime minister Disraeli at Hughenden
products furniture, especially beech; agricultural
population (1986) 617,900.

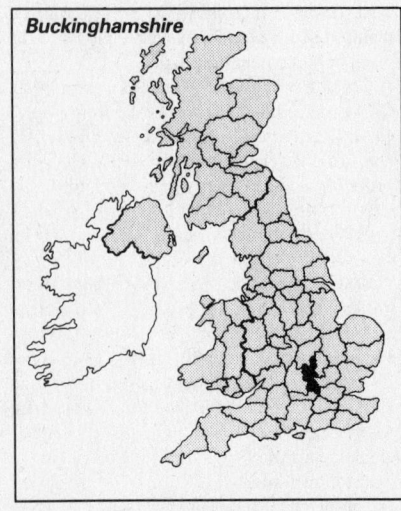

Buckinghamshire

Buckley /'bʌkli/ William 1780–1856. Australian convict, who escaped from Port Phillip and lived 1803–35 among the Aborigines before giving himself up, hence *Buckley's chance* meaning an 'outside chance'.

Buckley /'bʌkli/ William Frank 1925– . American conservative political writer, founder-editor of the *National Review* 1955. In such books as *Up from Liberalism* 1959, and a weekly television debate 'Firing Line', he represented the 'intellectual' right wing, anti-liberal stance in American political thought.

buckthorn thorny shrubs of the family Rhamnaceae, of which two species, the buckthorn *Rhamnus catharticus* and the alder buckthorn *Frangula alnus*, are native to Britain.

buckwheat high nutritive value grain plant *Fagopyrum esculentum*, family Polygonaceae. It can grow on poor soil in a short summer. Consumed by humans and animals.

bud an undeveloped shoot usually enclosed by protective scales; inside is a very short stem and numerous undeveloped leaves, or flower parts, or both. Terminal buds are found at the tips of shoots, while axillary buds develop in the ◊axils of the leaves, often remaining dormant unless the terminal bud is removed or damaged. Adventitious buds may be produced anywhere on the plant, their formation sometimes stimulated by an injury, such as that caused by pruning.

Budaeus /bu:'di:əs/ Latin form of the name of Guillaume Budé 1467–1540. French scholar. He persuaded Francis I to found the Collège de France, and also the library that formed the nucleus of the French national library, the Bibliothèque Nationale.

Budapest /,bju:də'pest/ capital of Hungary, industrial city (chemicals, textiles) on the Danube; population (1983) 2,064,000.
history Buda, on the right bank of the Danube, became the Hungarian capital in 1867 and was joined with Pest, on the left bank, in 1872. Budapest saw fighting between German and Soviet troops in World War II 1944–45, and between the Hungarians and Soviet troops in the rising of 1956.

Buddha /'budə/ c. 563–483 BC. Title of prince Gautama Siddhartha, born at ◊Lumbini in Nepal. At the age of 29, he left a life of luxury, and his wife and son, to seek a way of escape from the burdens of existence. After six years of austerity he became enlightened (Buddha means 'enlightened one') under a banyan or bo tree near ◊Buddh Gaya. He acquired the Four Truths: the fact of pain or evil; that pain has a cause; that pain can be ended; and that it can be ended by following the Eightfold Way of right views, right intention, right speech, right action, right livelihood, right effort, right mindfulness, and right concentration, and so arriving at Nirvana, the extinction of all craving for things of the senses. He began teaching at Varanasi, and founded the Sangha, or order of monks. He spent the rest of his life moving around N India and died at Kusinagara in Uttar Pradesh.

Buddh Gaya /'bud gə'ja:/ village in Bihar, India, where Gautama became ◊Buddha while sitting beneath a Bo (Bodhi) tree; a descendant of the original bo (banyan) tree is preserved.

Buddhism one of the great world religions, which originated in India. It derived from the teaching of ◊Buddha, who is regarded as one of a series of such enlightened beings, the next incarnation being due c. 3000 AD.
scriptures the only complete canon of the Buddhist scriptures is that of the Sinhalese (Sri

Buddha The 13 metre high sacred bronze Buddha at Kamakura, Japan. Buddha, the 'enlightened one', was a prince who left a life of luxury to teach the Eightfold Way of attaining Nirvana. His teachings are the basis of Buddhism, one of the great world religions.

Lanka) Buddhists, in Pali, but other schools have essentially the same canon in Sanskrit. The scriptures are known as Pitakas or 'baskets'. They are three divisions: *Vinaya* or Discipline, listing offences and rules of life; 'Sutta' or Discourse or *Dhamma* or Doctrine, the exposition of Buddhism by Buddha and his disciples; *Abhidhamma* or Further Doctrine, later discussions on doctrine. The most important doctrine is that of *karma*, good or evil deeds meeting an appropriate reward or punishment either in this life or (through transmigration or rebirth) in a long succession of lives. The self is not regarded as permanent, and the aim of the Noble Eightfold Way is to break the chain of karma, and achieve dissociation from the body by attaining *Nirvana* 'blowing out', the eradication of all desires, either in annihilation, or by absorption of the self in the infinite. There are no gods, but great reverence is accorded to Buddha, and other such advanced incarnations.
divisions: Theravāda Buddhism, the School of the Elders, which is also known as *Hinayana* or Base Career, prevails in southern Asia (Sri Lanka, Thailand, and Burma), and its scriptures are written in *Pali*, an Indo-Aryan language with its roots in N India;
Mahayana or Great Career, which arose at the beginning of the Christian era, exhorts the individual not merely to attain Nirvana as an individual, but to become a trainee Buddha (or Boddhisattva), and so save others. This prevails in northern Asia (China, Korea, Japan, and Tibet). The form established in ◊Tibet, *Lamaism*, dates from 750 AD when the ◊Dalai Lama became both spiritual and temporal ruler; its outward forms include prayer wheels and it had strong magical elements. In India itself Buddhism was replaced by ◊Hinduism, but still

has five million devotees, and is growing. *Zen* originated with a Mahayana monk, Bodhidharma, c. 520 AD, in China, and from the 12th century was adopted in Japan; it is characterized by anecdotes giving rise to exchanges between master and pupil which result in sudden enlightenment. Japan is also noted for such lay organizations as *Soka Gakkai* (Value Creation Society), founded 1937, which equates absolute faith with immediate material benefit, and by the 1980s was followed by more than seven million households.

budding a type of ◊asexual reproduction in which a bubble-like outgrowth develops from a cell, enlarges, and eventually becomes detached to form a new individual. The majority of yeasts reproduce in this way, and in a suitable environment they may grow rapidly, forming long chains of cells as the buds themselves produce further buds before being separated from the parent. Simple invertebrates, such as hydra, can also reproduce by budding.
In horticulture, the term is used for a technique of plant propagation whereby a bud (or scion) and a slither of bark from one plant are transferred to an incision made in the bark of another plant (the stock). This method of ◊grafting is often used for roses.

buddleia genus of shrubs and trees, family Buddlejaceae, of which the best-known is the *butterfly bush Buddleja davidii*, of which the purple or white flower heads attract the insects.

budgerigar small Australian parakeet *Melopsittacus undulatus*. Feeding mainly on grass seeds, it breeds freely in captivity. Normally it is bright green, but varieties with yellow, white, blue and mauve have been produced.

budget an estimate of income and expenditure for some future period. In the UK the national budget, which generally includeds changes in ◊taxation, is presented in Apr of each year by the chancellor of the exchequer.

Budějovice see ◊České Budějovice, town in Czechoslovakia.

Budweis /'budvais/ German form of České Budějovice, a town in Czechoslovakia.

Buenos Aires /'bweinɒs 'airiz/ capital and industrial city of Argentina, largest city in S America; university 1821; population (1980) 9,677,000.
features The Palace of Congress, and, on the Plaza de Mayo, the cathedral and presidential palace (known as the Pink House).
history Buenos Aires was founded in 1536. It became the capital in 1853, and was developed on a modern gridiron plan.

Buffalo /'bʌfələu/ industrial port in New York State, USA, at the E end of Lake Erie, linked with New York City by the New York State Barge Canal; population (1980) 357,870.

buffalo name given to two species of wild cattle. The Asiatic *water buffalo Bubalis bubalis* is found domesticated all across S Asia and wild in parts of Bengal, Assam and Nepal. It likes moist conditions. Usually grey or black, up to 1.8 m/6 ft high, both sexes carry large horns. The *African buffalo Syncerus caffer* is found in Africa S of the Sahara where there is grass, water and cover in which to retreat. There are various races, the biggest up to 1.6 m/5 ft high, black, and with massive horns set close together over the head. A small reddish-brown form lives in the Congo forest. The American ◊bison is sometimes called buffalo.

buffalo In the wild, water buffalo inhabit marshland and this domestic herd in Thailand still favours moist conditions. They are kept as draught animals as well as for their rich milk supply.

Buffet /buːˈfeɪ/ Bernard 1928– . French artist, born in Paris. A prolific artist, he has used oils and water colours, but is best known for his lithographs, book illustrations and murals.

Buffon /buˈfɒn/ George Louis Leclerc, comte de Buffon 1707–1788. French naturalist. In 1739 he became keeper of the Jardin du Roi, and was elected to the French Academy in 1753, when he delivered his *Discours sur le style*. He encouraged the popular study of natural history, and published a Natural History in 44 volumes 1749–1804.

Bug /buːg/ two rivers in E Europe: the *West Bug* rises in the SW Ukraine and flows to the Vistula, and the *South Bug* rises in the W Ukraine and flows to the Black Sea.

bug in computing, an error in a program. It can be an error in the logical structure of a program or a syntactic error such as a spelling mistake. Either can cause serious problems in major ◊applications such as controlling a power station. ◊Debugging is the process of finding bugs and eliminating them from a program.

bug in entomology, name sometimes applied indiscriminately to insects, but strictly only those belonging to the order Hemiptera. All these have piercing mouthparts adapted for sucking the juices of plants or animals, the 'beak' being tucked under the body when not in use. They include the ◊bedbug which sucks human blood, the *shieldbugs* or stinkbugs which have a strong odour and feed on plants, the ◊pondskaters, ◊waterboatmen and other water bugs, ◊aphids and ◊cicadas.

Buganda /buːˈgændə/ two provinces (North and South Buganda) of Uganda, home of the Baganda people, and formerly a kingdom from the 17th century. The *kabaka* or king, Sir Edward Mutesa II (1924–69), was the first president of independent Uganda 1962–66, and

his son Ronald Mutebi (1955–) is *sabataka* (head of the Baganda clans).

bugle in music, a wind instrument of the brass family, with a shorter tube and less expanded bell than the trumpet. Constructed of copper plate with brass, it has long been in wide use as a military instrument.

bugle in botany, a low-growing perennial plant *Ajuga reptans* of the family Labiatae, with two-lipped blue flowers in a purplish spike. The leaves may be whole or faintly toothed, the lower ones with a long stalk. Bugle is found across Europe and N Africa, usually in damp woods or pastures.

bugloss name of several plants of the family Boraginaceae, distinguished by their rough bristly leaves and small blue flowers.

buhl process of inlaying various metals, particularly brass and silver, into tortoise-shell or occasionally wood, which was invented by the Frenchman C A Boulle (1642–1732).

building society financial institution originating in Britain, in Birmingham, 1781, which attracts ◊investment, in order to lend money, repayable at interest, for the purchase or building of a house on security of a ◊mortgage. In Britain the Building Societies Act 1986 enabled societies to raise up to 20% of their funds on the international capital market. Among other changes, the act also provided that building societies could grant unsecured loans of up to £5,000; they were also able to offer interest-bearing cheque accounts, a challenge to the clearing banks' traditional role in this area. The USA has from 1840 had savings and loan associations, similar institutions with money deposited on both instant withdrawal and term share basis.

Bujumbura /ˌbuːdʒʊmˈbuərə/ capital of Burundi; university 1960; population (1979) 141,000. Formerly called Usumbura.

Bukavu /buːˈkɑːvuː/ port in E Zaïre, on Lake Kivu; population (1976) 209,050. Called Costermansville until 1966.

Bukhara /buˈxɑːrə/ city in Uzbekistan, USSR, capital of Bukhara region which has given its name to carpets (made in Ashkhabad); Islamic centre; population (1985) 209,000.
history An ancient city in central Asia, it was formerly the capital of the independent emirate of Bukhara, annexed to Russia in 1868. It was included in Bukhara region 1924.

Bukharest /ˌbuːkəˈrest/ alternative form of ◊Bucharest, capital of Romania.

Bukharin /buˈxɑːrɪn/ Nikolai Ivanovich 1888–1938. Russian politician and theorist. A moderate, he was the most influential Bolshevik thinker after ◊Lenin. He wrote the major defence of war communism in his *Economics of the Transition Period* 1920, and was one of the chief supporters of the ◊New Economic Policy, which in turn led to the doctrine of ◊Socialism in One Country. He drafted the Soviet Constitution of 1936, but in 1938 was imprisoned and tried for treason in the most famous of ◊Stalin's 'show trials'. He pleaded guilty to treason, but defended his moderate policies and denied criminal charges. He was nonetheless executed, as were

all other former members of Lenin's Politburo except Stalin and ◊Trotsky.

Bukovina /ˌbukəˈviːnə/ region in SE Europe, divided between the USSR and Romania. It covers some 10,500 sq km/over 4,000 sq mi.
history Part of Moldavia during the Turkish regime, it was ceded by the Ottoman Empire to Austria in 1777, becoming a duchy of the ◊Dual Monarchy, 1867–1918; then it was included in Romania. N Bukovina was ceded to the USSR 1940 and included in the Ukraine as the region of Chernovtsy; the cession was confirmed by the peace treaty of 1947, but the question of its return has been raised by Romania. The part of Bukovina remaining in Romania became the district of Suceava.

Bulawayo /ˌbuləˈweɪəʊ/ industrial city and railway junction in Zimbabwe at an altitude of 1,355 m/4,450 ft on the river Matsheumlope, a tributary of the Zambezi; population (1980) 373,000.
features Government House, once belonging to colonial politician Cecil Rhodes, who is buried in the Matopo hills above Bulawayo.
history The former capital of Matabeleland, founded on the site of the kraal (enclosed village), burned down 1893, of the Matabele chief Lobenguela, Bulawayo developed with the exploitation of goldmines in the neighbourhood.

bulb instrument of vegetative reproduction consisting of a modified leaf bud with fleshy leaves containing a reserve food supply; roots form from its base. Characteristic of many monocotyledenous plants such as daffodil, snowdrop, and onion. Bulbs are grown on a commercial scale in temperate countries, especially England and Holland.

bulbil a small bulb that develops above ground from a bud. Bulbils may be formed on the stem from axillary buds, as in *Saxifraga hypnoides*, or in the place of flowers, as seen in many species of onion (*Allium*). They drop off the parent plant and develop into new individuals, providing a means of ◊vegetative reproduction and dispersal.

bulbul small fruit-eating bird of the family Pycnonotidae. There are about 120 species, mainly in the forests of the Old World tropics.

Bulganin /bʊlˈgɑːnɪn/ Nikolai 1895–1975. Russian soldier. He helped to organize Moscow's defence in World War II, became a Marshal of the Soviet Union in 1947, and was Minister of defence 1947–49 and 1953–55. On the fall of Malenkov in 1955 he became 'prime minister' (chair of Council of Ministers) 1955–58 until ousted by Krushchev.

Bulgaria /bʌlˈgeərɪə/ country in SE Europe, bounded to the N by Romania, to the W by Yugoslavia, to the S by Greece, to the SW by Turkey, and to the E by the Black Sea.
government Under the 1971 constitution the supreme legislative and executive organ of power in Bulgaria is the 400-member national assembly, elected every five years by universal adult suffrage. It meets at least three times a year, but elects a permanent 28-member state council, headed by a president who acts as head of state, to take over its functions in its absence. The national assembly also elects a council of ministers,

headed by a prime minister, which forms the executive government. The controlling force is the Bulgarian Communist Party (BCP), which heads the broader Fatherland Front.

history In the ancient world Bulgaria comprised ◊Thrace and Moesia, and was the Roman province of Moesia Inferior. It was later occupied by the Slavs who, conquered in the 7th century by the Bulgars from Asia, eventually absorbed the invaders. In 865 Khan Boris adopted Easern Orthodox Christianity, and under his son Simeon (193–927), who assumed the title Tsar, Bulgaria became a leading power. It was ruled by ◊Byzantium from the 11th century, and although a second Bulgarian empire was founded after the revolt of 1185, the last independent tsar died c. 1393, and from the 14th century Bulgaria formed part of the ◊Ottoman empire for almost 500 years, becoming an independent kingdom in 1908.

Bulgaria allied itself with Germany in both World Wars, being occupied in 1944 by the USSR. In 1946 the monarchy was abolished and a republic was proclaimed under a communist-leaning alliance, the Fatherland Front, led by Georgi ◊Dimitrov (1882–1949). Bulgaria reverted largely to its 1919 frontiers.

The new republic adopted a Soviet-style constitution in 1947, with nationalized industries and co-operative farming introduced. Vulko Chervenkov, Dimitrov's brother-in-law, became the dominant political figure 1950–56, introducing a Stalinist regime. He was succeeded by the more moderate Todor ◊Zhivkov, who pursued a programme of industrialization and introduced a new presidential constitution in 1971. Under Zhivkov, who enjoyed close relations with Leonid ◊Brezhnev, Bulgaria became one of the Soviet Union's most loyal satellites.

In recent years the country has faced mounting economic problems caused by the rising cost of energy imports. Since 1985, with pressure from Soviet leader Mikhail ◊Gorbachev, administration, economy, and leadership have been subject to reform, though Zhivkov was re-elected as state president and BCP leader in 1986. These reforms include proposals to replace the state council and council of ministers by a new 'national co-ordinating body'; introduce competition into legislature elections, and introduce greater factory 'self-management'.

bulimia (Greek 'ox hunger') counteraction of stress or depression by uncontrollable overeating, compensated for by forced vomiting or an overdose of laxatives.

Bull /bul/ John typical Englishman, especially as represented in cartoons. The name came into popular use after the publication of Dr John Arbuthnot's *History of John Bull* 1712 advocating the ◊Tory policy of peace with France.

Bull /bul/ John c. 1562–1628. English composer, organist, and virginalist, one of the finest keyboard players of his time. Most of his output is for keyboard, and includes ◊'God Save the King'. He also wrote sacred vocal music.

Bull /bul/ Olaf 1883–1933. Norwegian lyric poet, son of humourist and fiction writer Jacob

Bulgaria

PEOPLE'S REPUBLIC OF (*Narodna Republika Bulgaria*)

AREA 110,840 sq km/42,796 sq mi
CAPITAL Sofia
TOWNS Plovdiv, Rusé; Burgas and Varna are Black Sea ports
PHYSICAL Balkan and Rhodope mountains; Danube river in the N
FEATURES Black Sea coast
HEAD OF STATE Todor Zhivkov from 1971 (also head of Politburo)
HEAD OF GOVERNMENT Georgi Atanasov from 1986
GOVERNMENT communist
EXPORTS textiles, chemicals, non-ferrous metals, timber, minerals, machinery
CURRENCY lev 1.39 = £1 Sept 1987)
POPULATION (1985) 8,947,000 (including 800,000 ethnic Turks now subjected to compulsory assimilation); annual growth rate 0.3%
LANGUAGE Bulgarian, Turkish
RELIGION Eastern Orthodox Christian 90%, Sunni Muslim 10%, but the latter faith is discouraged
LITERACY 96% male/93% female (1980 est)
GNP $26 bn (1983); $2,625 per head of population
CHRONOLOGY
1908 Bulgaria became a kingdom independent of Turkish rule.

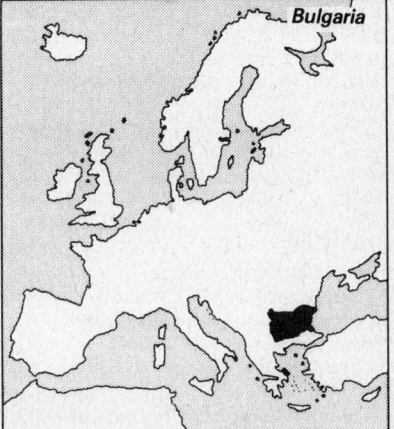

1944 Soviet invasion of German-occupied Bulgaria.
1946 Monarchy abolished and communist-dominated people's republic proclaimed.
1947 Soviet-style constitution adopted.
1949 Death of Georgi Dimitrov.
1954 Election of Todor Zhivkov as Communist Party general secretary.
1971 Constitution modified. Zhivkov elected president.
1985–86 Large-scale administrative and personnel changes effected under Soviet stimulus.

Breda Bull (1853–1930), who often celebrated his birthplace Christiania (now Oslo) in his poetry.

bull papal document or edict issued by the pope; so called from the circular seals (medieval Latin *bulla*) attached to them. Famous papal bulls include Leo X's condemnation of Luther in 1520; and Pius IX's proclamation of papal infallibility in 1870.

bull-baiting 'sport', illegal in UK from 1835, of setting dogs to attack a chained bull.

bulldog British dog of ancient but uncertain origin. Coming into prominence in the days of bull-baiting, it developed the characteristic underjaw which left the nostrils free for breathing while the dog retained its grip on the bull's throat. The head is broad and square, with a deeply wrinkled skull, small folded ears, and nose laid back between the eyes.

bulldozer an earth-moving machine widely used in construction work for clearing rocks and tree stumps and generally levelling a site. The bulldozer is a kind of ◊tractor with a powerful engine and a curved blade at the front, which can be lifted and forced down by hydraulic rams. It usually has crawler, or ◊caterpillar tracks so that it can move easily over rough grounds.

Buller /'bulə/ Redvers Henry 1839–1908. British commander against the ◊Boers in the South African War 1899–1902, who was defeated at Colenso and Spion Kop, but relieved ◊Ladysmith.

Bulletin, The weekly Sydney magazine established in 1880 which, until the 1920s, was the chief Australian periodical. It has done much to foster Australian literature and cinema.

bullfighting 'sport' popular in Spain (common in Greece and Rome, it was introduced by the Moors in the 11th century), and Spanish America. *Picadores* on horseback first wound the bull with lances; *banderillos* then plunge darts into its neck; and finally a *matador* with sword and *muleta* (a red cloth attached to a stick) attempts to subdue the bull and then deal a death blow by plunging a sword between the bull's left shoulder and the shoulder blade.

bullfinch bird *Pyrrhula pyrrhula* of the finch family, with a chunky silhouette with little neck, and a short heavy bill. Strikingly coloured, both sexes have a black capital. The male is grey above, pink below, the female browner. 14.5 cm/6 in long and usually seen in pairs, bullfinches feed on tree buds as well as seeds and berries, and are unpopular in orchards. They are found from Britain across N Europe and Asia.

bullhead small fish *Cottus gobio* also called *miller's thumb*, with a large head and a spine on the gill cover, found in fresh water in the N hemisphere, often under stones. It grows to 10 cm/4 in. Related bullheads live in coastal waters, such as the *father lasher Myxocephalus scorpius*, up to 30 cm/1 ft long, whose male guards the eggs and fans them with his tail.

Bullock Report the report of a committee of inquiry headed by Lord Bullock, published in 1975, on the teaching of English in the UK. The report, *A Language for Life*, recommended major reforms in both primary and secondary schools.

bullroarer aboriginal musical instrument given magical significance; it consists of a piece of wood fastened by one of its pointed ends to a cord, by which it is whirled round the head to make a whirring noise.

Bull Run /'bʊl rʌn/ **Battles of** two engagements of the American ◊Civil War.

bull-terrier heavily built smooth-coated breed of dog, usually white, originating as a cross between terrier and bulldog and formerly used in bullbaiting.

Bülow /'bjuːləʊ/ Hans (Guido) von 1830–1894. German conductor and pianist. He studied with ◊Wagner and ◊Liszt, and in 1857 married Cosima, daughter of Liszt. From 1864 he served ◊Ludwig II of Bavaria, conducting first performances of Wagner's *Tristan und Isolde* and *Die Meistersinger*. His wife left him to live with Wagner, whom she married in 1870.

Bülow /'bjuːləʊ/ Prince Bernhard von 1849–1929. German diplomat and politician. He was chancellor of the German empire 1900–09 under Kaiser Wilhelm II and, holding that self-interest was the only rule for any state, adopted attitudes to France and Russia which unintentionally precipitated Europe into the opposing power groups of the ◊Triple Entente (Britain, France, Russia) and ◊Triple Alliance (Germany, Austria-Hungary, Italy).

bulrush type of sedge *Scirpus lacustris* found by the waterside with tufts of reddish-brown flowers at the top of the stem, which is rounded, soft and rush-like. Also, and perhaps more commonly, used as a name for the **great reed-mace** or **cattail** *Typha latifolia*, which grows in large patches in reed swamps and has a chocolate-brown tight-packed flowering spike up to 15 cm/6 in long. Both are distributed over much of the N hemisphere and part of the S.

Bulwer-Lytton /'bʊlwə 'lɪtn/ Edward George Earle Lytton, First Baron Lytton 1803–1873. See ◊Lytton.

bumble-bee large hairy ◊bee, usually dark coloured but banded with yellow, orange or white, belonging to the genus *Bombus*. Most species live in small colonies, usually underground, often in an old mousehole. The queen lays her eggs in a hollow nest of moss or grass at the beginning of the season. The larvae are fed on pollen and honey and develop into workers. In the summer males and perfect females are produced. All die at the end of the season except fertilized females, which hibernate and produce fresh colonies in the spring.

Bunche /bʌntʃ/ Ralph 1904–1971. American statesman, specializing in African and colonial affairs. Grandson of a slave, he was principal director of the UN Department of Trusteeship 1947–54, and then UN under-secretary acting as mediator in Palestine 1948–49 and as special representative in the Congo 1960. In 1950 he was awarded the Nobel Peace Prize.

bumble-bee A bumble-bee extracts pollen from a flower. Bumble-bees are found naturally all over the world, with the exception of Australia, where they have been introduced to facilitate the pollination of some cultivated varieties of clover.

Bunin /'buːnɪn/ Ivan Alexeyevich 1870–1953. Russian writer, born in Voronezh, known for *Derevnya/The Village* 1910 which tells of the passing of peasant life; and *Gospodin iz San Frantsisko/The Gentleman from San Francisco* 1916, about the death of a millionaire on Capri, which won him a Nobel prize in 1933. He was also a poet and translated Byron into Russian.

Bunker Hill small hill in Charlestown (now part of Boston), Massachusetts, USA near which on 17 June 1775 the first considerable engagement was fought in the War of ◊American Independence; although the colonists were defeated they were able to retreat to Boston and suffered far fewer casualties than the British.

Bunsen /'bʊnzən/ Robert Wilhelm von 1811–1899. German chemist, credited with the invention of the **Bunsen burner**. His name is also given to the carbon–zinc electric cell, which he invented in 1841 for use in arc-lamps. In 1859 he discovered two new elements, ◊caesium and ◊rubidium.

bunting name given to a number of sturdy finch-like birds with short thick bills, of the family Emberizidae. Most live in the New World, but some live in the Old World, such as the ◊ortolan, the ◊yellowhammer, and the **snow bunting** *Plectrophenax nivalis* of the far north, with much white in the plumage, which migrates to temperate Europe in the winter.

Buñuel /'buːnjuel/ Luis 1900–1983. Spanish film director, who made controversial and often anti-clerical ◊surrealist films, running from the early *L'Age d'Or/The Golden Age* 1930, through *Los Olvidados/The Young and the Damned* 1950, to *Le Charme discret de la bourgeoisie/The Discreet Charm of the Bourgeoisie* 1972 and his last film, a fitting epitaph, *Cet obscur objet de désir/That Obscure Object of Desire* 1977.

Bunyan /'bʌnjən/ John 1628–1688. English author, best known for *The Pilgrim's Progress*. Born near Bedford, the son of a tinker, he at first followed his father's trade, but at 16, during the civil war, was conscripted into the Parliamentary

army. Released in 1646, he passed through a period of religious doubt before joining the fellowship of the ◊Baptists in 1653. In 1660 he was committed to Bedford county gaol for preaching, where he remained for 12 years, refusing all offers of release conditional on his not preaching again. During his confinement he wrote *Grace Abounding* 1666 describing his early spiritual struggles. Set free in 1672, he was elected pastor of the Bedford congregation, but in 1675 was again arrested and imprisoned for six months in the gaol on Bedford Bridge, where he began *The Pilgrim's Progress* 1678. The book achieved instant success, and a second part followed in 1684. Later publications include *The Life and Death of Mr Badman* 1680 and *The Holy War* 1682.

Bunyan Imprisoned for the second time in his life in 1675, for preaching, John Bunyan, the English religious author, began writing his literary classic *The Pilgrim's Progress*.

bunyip mythical animal of the Australian Aborigines: it is a river creature, rather like a slender, long-necked hippopotamus. The word has been adopted in Australian English to mean 'fake' or 'impostor'.

buoy a floating object used to mark channels for shipping or warn of hazards to navigation. Buoys come in many different shapes, such as a pole (spar buoy), cylinder (car buoy), cone (nun buoy). Light buoys carry a small tower surmounted by a flashing lantern. Bell buoys house a bell, which rings as the buoy moves up and down with the waves.

buoyancy the lifting effect of a fluid on a body wholly or partly immersed in it. This was studied by ◊Archimedes in the 3rd century BC.

bur or **burr** in botany, a type of 'false fruit' or ◊pseudocarp, surrounded by numerous hooks; for instance, that of burdock (*Arctium*) where the hooks are formed from bracts surrounding the flower-head. The term is also used more generally to include any type of fruit or seed bearing hooks, such as that of goosegrass (*Galium aparine*) and wood avens (*Geum urbanum*). Burs catch in the feathers or fur of passing animals, and thus may be dispersed over considerable distances.

Burbage /'bɜːbɪdʒ/ Richard c. 1567–1619. English actor, thought to have been the original Hamlet, Othello, and Lear. He also appeared in first productions of works by Ben ◊Jonson, ◊Kyd, and ◊Webster. His father *James Burbage* (c. 1530–97) built the first English playhouse, known as 'The Theatre'; his brother *Cuthbert Burbage* (c. 1566–1636) built the original ◊Globe Theatre 1599 on Bankside, Southwark, London.

burbot long, rounded fish *Lota lota* of the cod family, the only one living entirely in fresh water. Up to 1 m/3 ft, usually less, it lives on the bottom of clear lakes and rivers, often in holes or under rocks. Found in Europe, Asia and N America, it is now very rare, if not extinct, in the rivers of E England, in which it used to occur.

Burckhardt /'buəkhɑːt/ Jacob 1818–1897. Swiss art historian, born in Basel, professor of history at Basel University 1858–93. *The Civilization of the Renaissance in Italy* 1860, intended as part of a study of world cultural history, is one of the most influential works on the Italian Renaissance. Burckhardt also wrote on Greek cultural history.

Burckhardt /'buəkhɑːt/ Johann 1784–1817. Swiss traveller, whose knowledge of Arabic enabled him to travel throughout the Middle East, visiting Mecca disguised as a Muslim pilgrim in 1814.

burdock a plant *Arctium lappa*, of the family Compositae, a frequent roadside weed in Britain. It is a bushy herb, with hairy leaves, and the ripe fruit is enclosed in burs with strong hooks.

bureaucracy an organization whose structure and operations are governed to a high degree by written rules and a hierarchy of offices: in its broadest sense, all forms of administration; in its narrowest, rule by officials. Max ◊Weber saw the growth of bureaucracy in industrial societies as an inevitable reflection of the underlying shift from traditional authority to a rational and legal system of organization and control. Contemporary writers have highlighted the problems of bureaucracy, such as its inflexibility and rigid adherence to rules, and the term today is often used critically rather than in its original neutral sense.

Burgas /'buəgəs/ Black Sea port in Bulgaria; population (1983) 183,477.

Burgenland /'buəgənlænd/ province of SE Austria, extending from the Danube S along the W border of the Hungarian plain
area 3,965 sq km/1,531 sq mi
capital Eisenstadt
features forested
products timber; lignite, antimony, limestone
population (1981) 269,771.

Bürger /'bjuəgə/ Gottfried 1747–1794. German ◊Romantic poet, remembered for his ballad 'Lenore' 1773.

Burges /'bɜːdʒɪz/ William 1827–1881. British Gothic revivalist architect. Main works are Cork Cathedral 1862–76, additions to and remodelling of Cardiff Castle 1865 and Castle Coch near Cardiff c. 1875. His work is characterized by sumptuous interiors with carving, painting, and gilding.

Burgess /'bɜːdʒɪs/ Anthony, pen name of Anthony John Burgess Wilson 1917– . British novelist, critic, and composer. Born in Manchester, he became a teacher, but following a diagnosis of a brain tumour in 1959 which gave him only one year to live he decided to concentrate on writing. His prolific work since then has included *A Clockwork Orange* 1962, set in a future London terrorized by teenage gangs, and the panoramic *Earthly Powers* 1980. His vision has been described as bleak and pessimistic, but his work is also comic and satiric, as in his novels featuring the poet Enderby. He is particularly noted for his fascination with language and word-play.

Burgess /'bɜːdʒɪs/ Guy (Francis de Moncy) 1910–1963. British spy, a diplomat recruited by USSR as agent; linked with Kim ◊Philby, Donald ◊Maclean (1913–83), and Anthony ◊Blunt (1907–83).

burgh former unit of Scottish local government, abolished in 1975; the terms burgh and royal burgh once gave mercantile privilege but are now only an honorary distinction.

Burgh Hubert de /də 'bɜːg/ died 1243. English justiciar (chief political and legal official) 1215–32. He was a supporter of King John against the barons; ended French intervention in England by his defeat of the French fleet in the Straits of Dover in 1217.

Burghley /'bɜːli/ William Cecil, Baron Burghley 1520–1598. English politician. One of Edward VI's secretaries, he lost office under Queen Mary, but on Queen Elizabeth's succession became one of her most trusted ministers. He was largely responsible for the religious settlement of 1559, and took a leading role in the events preceding the execution of ◊Mary, Queen of Scots, in 1587. He carefully avoided a premature breach with Spain in the difficult period leading up to the attack by the Spanish Armada in 1588, did a great deal towards abolishing monopolies and opening up trade, and was created Baron Burghley 1571, and Lord High Treasurer 1572.

burglary in UK law, the offence of entering a building with the intent to commit theft or other serious crime; the maximum sentence is 14 years, though aggravated burglary (involving the use of firearms or other weapons) can mean life imprisonment.

Burgos /'buəgɒs/ city in Castilla-León, 217 km/135 mi N of Madrid, Spain; population (1981) 156,500. It was capital of the old kingdom of Castile and the national hero El Cid is buried in the Gothic cathedral, built 1221–1567.

Burgoyne /bɜː'gɔɪn/ John 1722–1792. British general and dramatist. He served in the Seven Years' War 1756–63, and on the outbreak of the American War of Independence 1775–83 was given command of a force intended to invade the colonies from Canada, but was surrounded and surrendered at Saratoga in 1777. He wrote comedies, among them *The Maid of the Oaks* 1775 and *The Heiress* 1786. He figures in George Bernard Shaw's play *The Devil's Disciple*.

Burgundy /'bɜːgəndi/ ancient kingdom and duchy in the valleys of the Saône and Rhône, France. The Burgundi were a Teutonic tribe and overran the country about 400. From the 9th century to the death of the duke Charles the Bold in 1477, it was the nucleus of a powerful principality. On Charles's death the duchy was incorporated into France. The capital of Burgundy was Dijon. The modern region to which it corresponds is ◊Bourgogne.

Burke /bɜːk/ Edmund 1729–97. British ◊Whig politician and political theorist. Born in Dublin, he achieved literary fame with his *Philosophical Inquiry into the Origin of our Ideas on the Sublime and Beautiful* 1756, on aesthetics, and opposed the government's attempts to coerce the American colonists, for example in *Thoughts on the Present Discontents* 1770. He was paymaster of the forces in Rockingham's government of 1782 and in the Fox-North coalition of 1783, and after the collapse of the latter spent the rest of his career in opposition. He attacked ◊Hastings's misgovernment in India and promoted his impeachment; and, as a resolute opponent of direct democracy, denounced the French Revolution in *Reflections on the Revolution in France* 1790. He defended his conduct in his *Appeal from the New to the Old Whigs* 1791 and *Letter to a Noble Lord* 1796, and attacked the suggestion of peace with France in *Letters on a Regicide Peace* 1795–97. He retired in 1794. He is regarded by modern ◊Conservatives as the greatest of their political theorists.

Burke Born in Dublin, the British Whig politician and theorist Edmund Burke achieved literary fame with his *Philosophical Inquiry into the Origin of our Ideas of the Sublime and Beautiful*. The picture is after the Irish painter James Barry.

Burke /bɜːk/ John 1787–1848. First publisher, in 1826, of ◊*Burke's Peerage*.

Burke /bɜːk/ Martha Jane c. 1852–1903. Real name of American heroine ◊Calamity Jane.

Burke /bɜːk/ Robert O'Hara 1820–1861. Australian explorer. Born in Galway, Ireland, he became a police inspector on the goldfields of Victoria. Made the South–North crossing of Australia (Victoria–Gulf of Carpentaria), with William Wills 1834–61. Both died on the return journey, only one man of their party surviving.

Burke /bɜːk/ William 1792–1829. Irishman, who with his partner *William Hare*, living in Edinburgh, dug up the dead to sell for dissection. They increased their supplies by murdering at least 15 people. Burke was hanged on the evidence of Hare. Hare is said to have died a beggar in London in the 1860s.

Burke's Peerage Popular name of the regularly updated *Genealogical and Heraldic History of the Peerage, Baronetage, and Knightage of the United Kingdom*, first issued by John ◊Burke in 1826.

Burkina Faso /bɜːˈkiːnə ˈfæsəʊ/ landlocked country in W Africa, bounded to the E by Niger, to the NW and W by Mali, to the S by Ivory Coast, Ghana, Togo and Benin.
government A military coup in 1980 suspended the 1977 constitution and after two further coups in 1982 and 1983, power was taken by a national revolutionary council, comprising the only political factions: the Patriotic League for Development (LIPAD), the Union of the Communist Struggle (ULC) and the Communist Officers' Regrouping (ROC).
history The area now known as Burkina Faso was conquered in the 12th century by the Mossi, whose powerful warrior kingdoms lasted for over 500 years. In the 1890s it became a province of French West Africa, known as Upper Volta.
In 1958 it became a self-governing republic and in 1960 achieved full independence with Maurice Yameogo as president. A military coup in 1966 removed Yameogo and installed Col Sangoulé Lamizana as president and prime minister. He suspended the constitution, dissolved the national assembly, banned political activity and set up a supreme council of the armed forces as the instrument of government.
In 1969 the ban on political activity was lifted and in 1970 a referendum approved a new constitution, based on civilian rule, which was to come into effect after four years of combined military and civilian government. After disagreements between military and civilian members of the government, Gen Lamizana announced in 1974 a return to army rule and dissolved the national assembly.
In 1977 political activity was allowed again and a referendum approved a constitution which would create a civilian goverment. In the 1978 elections the Volta Democratic Union (UDV) won a majority in the national assembly and Lamizana became president, but a deteriorating economy led to strikes and a bloodless coup led by Col Zerbo overthrew him in 1980. Zerbo formed a government of national recovery, suspended the constitution and dissolved the national assembly. In 1982 Zerbo was ousted and Maj Jean-Baptiste Ouédraogo emerged as leader of a military regime, with Capt Thomas Sankara as prime minister. In 1983 Sankara seized power in another coup, becoming president and ruling

through a council of ministers. Opposition members were arrested, the national assembly was dissolved, and a National Revolutionary Council (CNR) set up. In 1984 Sankara announced that the country would be known as Burkina Faso ('land of the incorruptible'), symbolizing a break with its colonial past; his government strengthened ties with Ghana and established links with Benin and Libya. Sankara was killed in Oct 1987 in a military coup led former close colleague, Capt Blaise Compaore (1951–), who claimed that the president's death was not intended.

Burkina Faso
'LAND OF UPRIGHT MEN'

AREA 274,000 sq km/106,000 sq mi
CAPITAL Ouagadougou
TOWNS Bobo-Doiulasso
PHYSICAL landlocked plateau, savannah country; headwaters of the river Volta
HEAD OF STATE AND OF GOVERNMENT Blaise Compaore from 1987
GOVERNMENT communist
EXPORTS cotton, groundnuts, livestock, hides and skins
CURRENCY CFA franc (498.38 = £1 Sept 1987)
POPULATION 6,773,931 (1985); annual growth rate 2.4%
LANGUAGE French (official); about 50 native languages
RELIGION animist 53%, Sunni Muslim 36%, Roman Catholic 11%
LITERACY 18% male/5% female (1980 est)
GDP $1.2 bn (1983); $180 per head of population
CHRONOLOGY
1958 Became a self-governing republic within the French Community.
1960 Full independence achieved, with Maurice Yameogo as the first president.
1966 Military coup led by Col Lamizana. Constitution suspended, political activities banned, and a supreme council of the armed forces established.
1969 Ban on political activities lifted.
1970 Referendum approved a new constitution leading to a return to civilian rule.

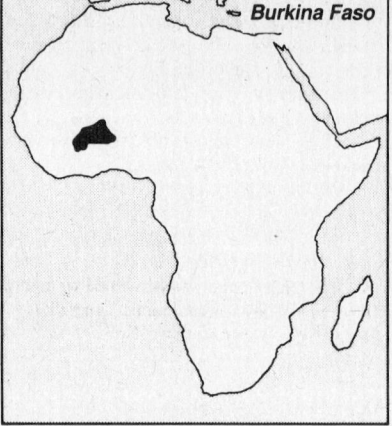
Burkina Faso

1974 After experimenting with a mixture of military and civilian rule, Lamizana reassumed full power.
1977 Ban on political activities removed. Referendum approved a new constitution based on civilian rule.
1978 Lamizana elected president.
1980 Lamizana overthrown in a bloodless coup led by Col Zerbo.
1982 Zerbo ousted in a coup by junior officers. Maj Ouédraogo became president and Thomas Sankara prime minister.
1983 Sankara seized complete power.
1984 Upper Volta renamed Burkina Faso.
1987 Sankara killed in coup led by Blaise Compaore.

burlesque in the 17th and 18th centuries, a form of satirical comedy parodying a particular play or dramatic genre. For example, ◊Gay's *The Beggar's Opera* 1728 is a burlesque of 18th-century opera, and ◊Sheridan's *The Critic* 1777 satirizes the sentimentality in the drama of this time. In the US the term burlesque was used for a sex and comedy show invented by Michael Bennett Leavitt in 1866 consisting of a variety of acts including acrobats, chorus and comedy numbers. During the 1920s the striptease was introduced to counteract the growing popularity of the cinema, and Gypsy Rose Lee became its most famous artiste. Burlesque was banned in New York in 1942.

Burlington /ˈbɜːlɪŋtən/ Richard Boyle, 3rd Earl of 1694–1753. British architectural patron and architect; one of the premier exponents of Palladianism in Britain. His major protégé was William Kent. His buildings – best known among them is Chiswick House in London 1725–29 – are characterized by absolute adherence to the Classical rules and are consequently somewhat dry and fastidious.

Burma /ˈbɜːmə/ country in SE Asia, bordered by India to the NW, China to the NE, Laos and Thailand to the SE, and the Bay of Bengal to the SW.
government Under the 1973 constitution, Burma is a unitary republic. The highest organ of state power is the 475-member people's assembly (*Pyithu Hluttaw*), elected by universal suffrage every four years. The people's assembly elects the nation's executive, the 30-member state council, which has a representative from each of Burma's 14 states and divisions and is headed by a chairman who acts as president. It also functions as the sole legislature and elects a council of ministers, headed by a prime minister, in charge of day-to-day administration. The controlling force and sole party in Burma is the Burma Socialist Programme Party.
history The Burmese date their era from 638 AD, when they had arrived from the region where China meets Tibet. By 850 they had organized a state in the centre of the plain at Pagan, and 1044–1287 maintained a hegemony over most of

the area now known as Burma. In 1287 Kublai Khan's grandson Ye-su Timur occupied Burma after destroying the Pagan dynasty. After he withdrew, anarchy supervened. From c. 1490–1750 the Toungoo dynasty maintained itself, with increasing difficulty; and in 1752 Alaungpaya reunited the country and founded Rangoon as his capital. In a struggle with Britain 1824–26, his descendants lost the coastal strip from Chittagong to Cape Negrais. The second Burmese War, 1852, resulted in the British annexation of Lower Burma, including Rangoon. Thibaw, the last Burmese king, precipitated the third Burmese War, 1885, and the British siezed Upper Burma in 1886. The country was united as a province of India until 1937, when it was made a Crown Colony with a degree of self-government.

Burma was occupied 1942–45 by Japan, under a government of anti-British nationalists. The nationalists, led by Aung San and U Nu, later founded the Anti-Fascist People's Freedom League (AFPFL). Burma was liberated in 1945 and achieved full independence outside the Commonwealth in 1948.

A parliamentary democracy was established under the socialist AFPFL led by Prime Minister U Nu. The republic was weakened by civil war between ◊Karens, communist guerrillas and ethnic group separatists. Splits within the AFPFL forced the formation of an emergency caretaker government by Gen Ne Win (1911–) between 1958–60, leading to a military coup in 1962 and abolition of the parliamentary system. Gen Ne Win became head of a revolutionary council and established a strong one-party state.

In 1973 a new presidential-style constitution was adopted and in 1974 the revolutionary council was dissolved. The military leaders became civilian rulers. Ne Win became president and was re-elected in 1978, before stepping down to be replaced by U San Yu (1918–) in 1981.

Internal opposition by armed separatist groups has continued since 1962, causing the economy to deteriorate. The Burmese Communist Party, which received Chinese funding during the 1960s, remains powerful in the N; the Karen National Liberation Army operates in the SE; and the Kachin Independence Army in the NE. The non-communist ethnic separatist groups joined together to form the broad National Democratic Front in 1975 with the aim of creating a new federal union. The post-1962 government has adopted a foreign policy of ◊non-alignment, while pursuing at home its own 'Burmese Way' towards socialism.

burn tissue damage (*first degree* turning the skin red, as in sunburn; *second degree* causing blistering; and *third degree* resulting in damage to deeper tissue) caused by heat, light, other radiation, or corrosive substances; similar damage by hot liquid or vapour is a scald. Treatment is directed against shock and infection (by use of antibiotics); wet 'soaks' to cover the wound; air cushion 'hoverbeds' to support the badly burned; and artificial skin grafts (animal cartilage + silicon + a derivative

Burma
SOCIALIST REPUBLIC OF THE UNION OF
(*Pyidaungsu Socialist Thammada Myanma Naingngandaw*)

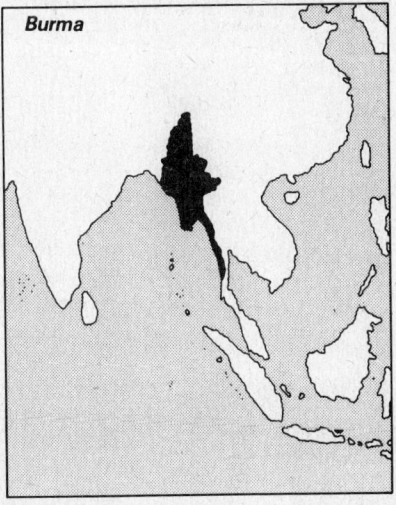

Burma

AREA 678,000 sq km/261,789 sq mi
CAPITAL and chief port Rangoon
TOWNS Mandalay, Karbe
PHYSICAL over half is forested; rivers Irrawaddy and Chindwin; mountains in N, W, and E
HEAD OF STATE U San Yu
HEAD OF GOVERNMENT U Maung Maung Kha
GOVERNMENT one-party socialist
EXPORTS rice, rubber, jute, teak; varied minerals; jade, rubies, sapphires
CURRENCY kyat (10.89 = £1 Sept 1987)
POPULATION 36,919,000 (1985); annual growth rate 2.8%
LANGUAGE Burmese
RELIGION Hinayana Buddhist; religious centre Pagan
LITERACY 76% male/66% female (1980 est)
GDP $6.5 bn (1983); $174 per head of population
CHRONOLOGY
1886 United as province of British India.
1937 Became crown colony in the British Commonwealth.
1942–45 Occupied by Japan.
1948 Granted independence from Britain. Left the Commonwealth.
1962 Gen Ne Win assumed power following army coup.
1973–74 Adoption of presidential-style 'civilian' constitution.
1975 Formation of opposition National Democratic Front.

of cowhide) to avoid problems of rejection of the new tissue.

Burne-Jones /'bɜːn 'dʒəʊnz/ Edward Coley 1833–98. British ◊Pre-Raphaelite painter and designer, influenced by ◊Rossetti. He drew inspiration from legend and myth, believing that a painting should be 'a beautiful romantic dream of something that never was, never will be', as in *King Cophetua and the Beggar Maid* 1880–84 now in the Tate Gallery, London; *The Beguiling of Merlin* 1874; and *The Mirror of Venus* 1877. He also designed tapestries and stained glass for William ◊Morris. He received a baronetcy in 1894.

burnet or *salad burnet*, *Sanguisorba minor*, a herb of the rose family which can be used in salads. It smells of cucumber.

Burnet /'bɜːnɪt/ Gilbert 1643–1715. British historian, author of *History of His Own Time* 1723–24. His Whig views having brought him into disfavour, he retired to The Hague on the accession of James II, and became the confidential adviser of ◊William of Orange, with whom he sailed to England in 1688. He was appointed Bishop of Salisbury in 1689.

Burnet /'bɜːnɪt/ Macfarlane 1899–1985. Australian physician, authority on immunology and viral diseases. He was awarded the Order of Merit in 1958 in recognition of his work on such diseases as influenza, polio and cholera. In 1944–65 he was director of the Walter and Eliza Hall Institute for Medical Research and professor of experimental medicine at Melbourne. Knighted in 1951.

Burnett /bə'net/ Frances Eliza Hodgson 1849–1924. British writer, living in the USA from 1865, who wrote children's stories inclusing the rags-to-riches tale *Little Lord Fauntleroy* 1886, and the sentimental *The Secret Garden* 1909.

Burney /'bɜːni/ Frances (Fanny) 1752–1840. British novelist and diarist, daughter of the musician Dr Charles Burney (1726–1814). She achieved success with *Evelina*, published anonymously 1778, became a member of Dr ◊Johnson's circle, received a post at court from Queen Charlotte, and in 1793 married the émigré General D'Arblay. She published two further novels, *Cecilia* 1782, and *Camilla* 1796, and her diaries and letters appeared in 1842.

Burnham /'bɜːnəm/ Forbes 1923–1985. Guyanese politician. A Marxist-Leninist; he was prime minister 1964–80, leading the country to independence 1966, and declaring it the world's first cooperative republic 1970. He was executive president 1980–85. Resistance to the US landing in ◊Grenada in 1983 was said to be due to his forewarning the revolutionaries of the attack.

Burnham /'bɜːnəm/ James 1905– . American philosopher. Born in Chicago, he was a Rhodes scholar at Oxford. Professor of philosophy at New York university 1932–54, he argued in *The Managerial Revolution* 1941 that world control is passing from politicians and capitalists to the new class of business executives, the managers.

Burnley /'bɜːnli/ industrial town in Lancashire, England, 19 km/12 mi NE of

Burne-Jones The Burne-Jones and Morris families, photographed by Frederick Hollyer in 1874. Burne-Jones (rear, left) and William Morris (standing) became close friends at Oxford and relinquished their idea of going into the Church to paint and to found the Pre-Raphaelite brotherhood.

Blackburn; population (1983) 92,000. Formerly a cotton-manufacturing town.

Burns /bɜːnz/ John 1858–1943. British labour leader, sentenced to six weeks' imprisonment for his part in the Trafalgar Square demonstration on 'Bloody Sunday' 13 Nov 1887, and leader of the strike in 1889 securing the dockers' tanner (wage of 6d per hour). An Independent Labour member of parliament 1892–1918, he was the first person from the labouring classes to be a member of the Cabinet, as president of the Local Government Board 1906–14.

Burns /bɜːnz/ Robert 1759–1796. Scottish poet, notable for his use of the Scots dialect at a time when it was not considered suitably 'elevated' for literature. Born at Alloway near Ayr, he became joint tenant with his brother of his late father's farm at Mossgiel in 1784, but was unsuccessful, as well as being crossed in his love for Jean Armour. His emigration to Jamaica was only prevented by the success of his *Poems, Chiefly in the Scottish Dialect* 1786, which enabled him to marry Jean Armour in 1788 and settle to farming at Ellisland, near Dumfries. From 1789 he was a part-time district excise-officer, becoming full-time on the failure of his farm in 1791. His fame rests equally on his poems (such as 'Holy Willie's Prayer', 'Tam o'Shanter', 'The Jolly Beggars', and 'To a Mouse') and his songs – sometimes wholly original, sometimes adaptations – of which he contributed some 300 to Johnson's *Scots Musical Museum* 1787–1803, and Thomson's *Scottish Airs with Poetry* 1793–1811.

Burns /bɜːnz/ Terence 1944– . British economist. A ◊monetarist, he was director of the London Business School for Economic Forecasting 1976–79, and became chief economic adviser to the ◊Thatcher government 1980. Knighted 1983.

Burr /bɜː/ Aaron 1756–1836. American politician. Born in New Jersey, he was on Washington's staff during the War of Independence. He tied with ◊Jefferson in the presidential election of 1800, but Alexander ◊Hamilton influenced the House of Representatives to vote Jefferson in, Burr becoming vice-president. Burr believed Hamilton also prevented him becoming Governor of New York state and he killed him in a duel in 1804. He became a social outcast, and had to leave the USA for some years following his attempt to raise a force to invade Mexico.

Burra /ˈbʌrə/ Edward 1905–1976. British artist. Born in Kensington, his work (which remained remarkably consistent in style over a long working life) included genre watercolours with a humorous touch, as well as more dramatic works influenced by El ◊Greco and ◊Goya. Notable are *Mexican Church* 1938 and *Soldiers* 1942, both in the Tate Gallery.

Burroughs /ˈbʌrəʊz/ Edgar Rice 1875–1950. American novelist, born in Chicago. He wrote *Tarzan of the Apes* 1914, the story of an aristocratic child lost in the jungle and reared by chimpanzees. Many more Tarzan books followed.

Burroughs /ˈbʌrəʊz/ William 1914– . American novelist, born in St Louis, Missouri. He 'dropped out', and produced the 'beat' novels *Junkie* 1953, *The Naked Lunch* 1959, *The Soft Machine* 1961, *Dead Fingers Talk* 1963, and *Queer* 1986.

Burroughs /ˈbʌrəʊz/ William Steward 1857–1898. American industrialist, who invented the first hand-operated adding machine to give printed results.

Bursa /ˈbɜːsə/ city in NW Turkey, with a port at Mudania; population (1980) 445,113. It was the capital of the Ottoman Empire 1326–1423.

Burt Cyril Lodowic 1883–1971. British psychologist. A specialist in child and mental development, he argued in *The Young Delinquent* 1925 the importance of social and environmental factors in delinquency. Since his death it was discovered that he falsified some of his experimental results in an attempt to prove his theory that intelligence is largely inherited.

Burton /ˈbɜːtn/ Richard Francis 1821–1890. British traveller, master of 35 oriental languages, and translator of the *Arabian Nights* 1885–88. In 1853 he made the pilgrimage to Mecca in disguise, and in 1856 was commissioned by the Foreign Office to explore the sources of the Nile, and (with ◊Speke) reached Lake Tanganyika 1858.

Burton /ˈbɜːtn/ Richard. Stage name of Welsh actor Richard Jenkins 1925–1984. British actor, remarkable for his voice, as in the radio adaptation of Dylan ◊Thomas's *Under Milk Wood*, and for his marital and acting partnership with Elizabeth ◊Taylor, with whom he appeared in the films *Cleopatra* 1962, and *Who's Afraid of Virginia Woolf?* 1966. He also appeared in the film *The Spy Who Came in from the Cold* 1966. His later portrayals include Wagner in Tony Palmer's 1982 film *Richard Wagner*.

Burton /ˈbɜːtn/ Robert 1577–1640. English philosopher. Born in Leicester, he was educated at Oxford, and remained there for the rest of his life as a fellow of Christ Church. His fame rests on his analysis of depression, *Anatomy of Melancholy* 1621, a remarkable compendium of information on the medical and religious opinions of the time, much used by later authors.

Burton upon Trent /ˈbɜːtn əpɒn ˈtrent/ industrial town (brewing, engineering) in Staffordshire, England, NE of Birmingham; population (1983) 57,725.

Burundi /buˈrʊndi/ country in E central Africa, bounded to the north by Rwanda, to the west by Zaïre, to the south by Lake Tanganyika, and to the southeast and east by Tanzania.

government under its 1981 constitution, Burundi's only political party is the Union for National Progress (UPRONA). The president is elected by universal suffrage for a five-year term and a 65-member national assembly has the same period of tenure, 52 of its members being elected by suffrage and 13 appointed by the president. Ultimate power lies with UPRONA.

history originally inhabited by the Twa, but taken over by the Hutu in the 13th century, Burundi was overrun in the 15th century by the Tutsi. In 1890, ruled by a Tutsi king and known as Urundi, it became part of German East Africa and during World War I was occupied by Belgium. Later, as part of Ruanda-Urundi, it was administered by Belgium as a League of Nations, and then UN, trust territory.

The 1961 elections, supervized by the UN, were won by UPRONA, a party formed by Louis, one of the sons of the reigning king, Mwambutsa IV. Louis was assassinated after only two weeks as prime minister, and was succeeded by his brother-in-law, André Muhirwa. In 1962 Urundi separated from Ruanda, and, as Burundi, was given internal self-government and then full independence.

In 1966 King Mwambutsa IV, after a 50-year reign, was deposed by another son, Charles, with army help, and the constitution was suspended. Later that year Charles, now Ntare V, was deposed by his prime minister, Captain Michel Micombero, who declared Burundi a republic. Micombero was a Tutsi, whose main rivals were the numerically superior Hutu. In 1972 the deposed Ntare V was killed, allegedly by the Hutu, giving the Tutsi an excuse to massacre large numbers of Hutu.

In 1973 amendments to the constitution made Micombero president and prime minister and in the following year UPRONA was declared the only political party. In 1976 Micombero was deposed in an army coup led by Colonel Jean-Baptiste Bagaza, who became president, with a prime minister and a new council of ministers. In 1977 the prime minister announced a return to civilian rule and a five-year plan to eliminate corruption and secure social justice, including promoting some Hutu to government positions. In 1978 the post of prime minister was abolished and in 1981 a new constitution, providing for a national assembly, was adopted after a referendum. Bagaza was re-elected in 1984 (he was the only presidential candidate) but was deposed in a military coup in Sept 1987, his government being replaced by a 'Military Council for National Redemption' headed by Major Pierre Buyoya, believed to be a Tutsi.

Bury /'beri/ industrial town (cotton, chemicals, engineering) in Greater Manchester, England, on the river Irwell, 16 km/10 mi N of central Manchester; population (1986) 173,650.

Buryat /ˌbʊri'ɑːt/ republic of the USSR, in Soviet central Asia
area 351,300 sq km/135,650 sq mi
capital Ulan-Ude
features Lake Baikal; mountainous and forested
population (1984) 850,000
history annexed from China 1689–1727.

Bury St Edmunds /'beri/ market town in Suffolk, England, on the river Lark; population (1985) 29,500. It was named after St Edmund, and there are remains of a Benedictine abbey founded in 1020.

bus a vehicle that carries fare-paying passengers on a fixed route, with frequent stops where passengers can get on and off. The word 'bus' is an abbreviation for Latin *omnibus*, a conveyance 'for all'.

An omnibus appeared briefly on the streets of Paris in the 1660s, when Blaise Pascal introduced the first public horse-drawn vehicles for public use. But a successful service, again in Paris, was not established until 1827. Two years later George Shillibeer introduced a horse-drawn bus in London. Many bus companies sprang up, the most successful being the London General Omnibus Company, which operated from 1856 until 1911, by which time petrol-driven buses had taken over.

Busby /'bʌzbi/ Richard 1606–1695. English headmaster of Westminster school from 1640. Among his pupils were Dryden, Locke,

Burundi
REPUBLIC OF

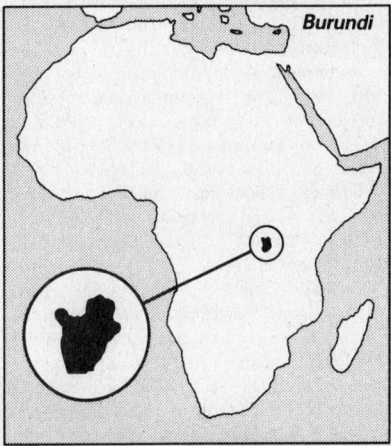

Burundi

AREA 27,834 sq km/10,747 sq mi
CAPITAL Bujumbura
TOWNS Kitega
PHYSICAL grassy highland
FEATURES Lake Tanganyika, Great Rift Valley; source of the White Nile
HEAD OF STATE AND GOVERNMENT Jean Baptiste Bagaza from 1976
GOVERNMENT one-party military
EXPORTS coffee, cotton, tea; nickel; hides, livestock; there are also 500 million tonnes of peat reserves in the basin of the Akanyaru river
CURRENCY Burundi franc (204.75 = £1 Sept 1987)
POPULATION (1985) 4,673,000 (of whom 15% are the Nilotic Tutsi, still holding most of the land and political power, and the remainder the Bantu Hutu); annual growth rate 2.4%
LANGUAGE Kirundi (a Bantu language) and French (official); Kiswahili
RELIGION Roman Catholic over 50%, with a Sunni Muslim minority
LITERACY 39% male/15% female (1980 est)
GDP $1 bn (1983); $273 per head of population
CHRONOLOGY
1962 Separated from Ruanda-Urundi, as Burundi, and given independence as a monarchy under King Mwambutsa IV.
1966 King deposed by his son Charles, who became Ntare V and was in turn deposed by his prime minister, Capt Michel Micombero, who declared Burundi a republic.
1972 Ntare V killed, allegedly by the Hutu ethnic group. Massacres of 150,000 Hutus by the rival Tutsi ethnic group, of which Micombero was a member.
1973 Micombero made president and prime minister.
1974 Union for National Progress (UPRONA) declared the only legal political party, with the president as its secretary general.
1976 Army coup deposed Micombero. Col Jean-Baptiste Bagaza appointed president by Supreme Revolutionary Council.
1981 New constitution adopted, providing for a national assembly.
1984 Bagaza elected president as sole candidate.
1987 Bagaza deposed in coup in Sept. Maj Pierre Buyoya headed new Military Council for National Redemption.

Atterbury, and Prior; he was renowned for his floggings.

Bush /bʊʃ/ Alan (Dudley) 1900– . British composer. A student of ◊Ireland, he later adopted a didactic simplicity in his compositions in line with his Marxist beliefs. He has written a large number of works for orchestra, voice, and chamber groups; his operas include *Wat Tyler* 1952, and *Men of Blackmoor* 1956. Peter ◊Pears recorded his cantata, *Voices for the Prophets* 1952.

Bush /bʊʃ/ George 1924– . US Republican politician, director of the ◊Central Intelligence Agency (CIA) 1976–81, and US vice president from 1981.

Bush, son of a Connecticut senator, moved to Texas in 1948 to build up his own oil-drilling company. A Republican congressman 1967–70, he was appointed US ambassador to the United Nations (1971–73) and Republican National Chairman (1973–74) by President ◊Nixon. During the ◊Ford administration, Bush was a special envoy to China 1974–75 and became director of the CIA 1976. He was ◊Reagan's vice president from 1981. During 1987 his standing was damaged by the scandal over arms secretly supplied to Iran and the Nicaraguan Contra guerrillas.

bushbuck antelope *Tragelaphus scriptus* found over most of Africa S of the Sahara. Up to 1 m/3 ft high, the males have keeled horns twisted into spirals, and are brown to blackish. The females are generally hornless, lighter and redder. All have white markings, including stripes or vertical rows of dots down the sides. Rarely far from water, bushbuck live in woods and thick brush.

bushel a British imperial dry or liquid measure of 8 gallons (2219.36 cu in): some US states have different standards according to the goods measured.

bushido chivalric code of honour of the Japanese military caste, the ◊Samurai.

bushman former term for ◊Kung, aboriginal people of southern Africa, still living to some extent nomadically, especially in the Kalahari Desert. Formerly numerous, only some 26,000 remain. Of small stature and with dark yellow skins, they are traditionally hunters and gatherers, and have a language marked by the same 'clicks' as that of the ◊Hottentots. Both are described as Khoisan languages. Their early art, surviving in cave paintings, is remarkable.

bushmaster large snake *Lachesis muta* related to the rattlesnakes. Up to 4 m/12 ft long, found in wooded areas of S and Central America, it has a powerful venomous bite. Although without a rattle, it produces a noise when alarmed by vibrating its tail amongst dry leaves.

bushranger Australian armed robber of the 19th century. The first bushrangers were escaped convicts. The last gang was led by Ned Kelly and his brother Dan in 1878–80. They form the subject of many Australian ballads.

business school institution for training in management and marketing, such as London Business School (LBS) 1965; Harvard in the USA, Insead in France.

Busoni /buːˈsəuni/ Ferruccio (Dante Michelangiolo Benvenuto) 1866–1924. Italian pianist, composer, and music critic. Born near Florence, he made his first public appearance at the age of seven. In 1891–93 he was at the Conservatoire of Boston, USA, and later lived in Berlin, Bologna, and Zürich. Much of his music was for the piano, but he also composed several operas including *Doktor Faust*, completed by a pupil after his death. As a critic he was also influential.

Buss /bʌs/ Frances Mary 1827–1894. British pioneer in education for women. She first taught in a school run by her mother, and at 18 she founded her own school for girls in London, which became the North London Collegiate School in 1850. She also founded the Camden School for Girls in 1871. As a founder-member of the Council for Teacher Training and the first president of the Association of Headmistresses, she was influential in raising the status of women teachers and the academic standard of women's education in the UK.

Bustamante /ˌbʌstəˈmænti/ (William) Alexander 1884–1977. Jamaican politician, born William Alexander Clarke. He was adopted at 15 by a Spanish seaman called Bustamante. As leader of the Labour Party, he was first prime minister of independent Jamaica 1962–67.

bustard type of bird, family Otididae, related to cranes but with rounder bodies, thicker necks and relatively short beaks, found on the ground on open plains and fields. The *great bustard Otis tarda* is one of the heaviest flying birds at 18 kg/40 lb, and the larger males may have a length up to 1 m/3 ft and wingspan of 2.3 m/7.5 ft. It is found in Europe and N Asia, but is extinct in some parts of its former range such as Britain, although attempts are being made by the Great Bustard Trust (1970) to naturalize it again on Salisbury Plain. The *little bustard Otis tetrax* is less than half the size of the great bustard, and is also found in continental Europe.

butadiene an inflammable gas, $CH_2{:}CHCH{:}CH_2$, derived from petroleum, and used in making synthetic rubber.

butane an alkane (paraffin hydrocarbon) gas, C_4H_{10}, a by-product of petroleum manufacture or from natural gas. Liquefied under pressure, it is used as a fuel for industrial and domestic purposes, for example in portable cookers.

Bute /bjuːt/ island and resort in the Firth of Clyde, Scotland; area 122 sq km/47 sq mi. The chief town is Rothesay. It is separated from the mainland in the N by a winding channel, the *Kyles of Bute*. With Arran and the adjacent

islands it comprised the former county of Bute, merged 1975 in the region of Strathclyde.

Bute /bjuːt/ John Stuart, 3rd Earl of Bute 1713–1792. British ◊Tory politician. He succeeded his father in 1723, and in 1737 was elected a representative peer for Scotland. On the accession of George III in 1760, he became the chief instrument in the king's policy for breaking the power of the ◊Whigs and establishing the personal rule of the monarch through Parliament, and became prime minister in 1762. His position as the king's favourite and the supplanter of the popular ◊Pitt made him hated in the country. After the ◊Seven Years' War in 1763 he resigned.

Buthelezi /ˌbuːtəˈleɪzi/ Chief Gatsha 1928– . Zulu leader and politician, chief minister of KwaZulu, a black 'homeland' in Republic of South Africa from 1970. Great-grandson of ◊Cetewayo, he is strongly opposed to KwaZulu becoming a ◊Black National State, but envisages a confederation of the black areas, with eventual black majority rule over all South Africa under a one-party socialist system. He is founder-president of *Inkatha* (from the grass coil worn by Zulu women for carrying head loads; its many strands give it strength) 1975, a para-military organization for attaining a non-racial democratic political system.

Butler /ˈbʌtlə/ Joseph 1692–1752. British churchman, who became Dean of St Paul's in 1740 and Bishop of Durham in 1750; his *Analogy of Religion* 1736 argued that it is no more rational to accept ◊Deism, arguing for God as the first cause, than revealed religion.

Butler /ˈbʌtlə/ Josephine 1828–1906. British social reformer, born Grey. She promoted women's education and the Married Women's Property Act, and campaigned against the Contagious Diseases Acts of 1862–70, which made women in garrison towns liable to compulsory examination for venereal disease. As a result of her campaigns the acts were repealed in 1883.

Butler /ˈbʌtlə/ Reg 1913–1981. British sculptor. Born in Hertfordshire, he was originally an architect and also worked as a blacksmith – hence many of his pieces are in cast or forged iron. He held his first one-man show in 1949, and caused a sensation by winning the international competition for a monument to The Unknown Political Prisoner 1953. He is primarily concerned with the human figure, using distortion to achieve striking effects.

Butler /ˈbʌtlə/ Richard Austen, Baron Butler 1902–1982. British ◊Conservative politician, known from his initials as Rab. As minister of education 1941–45, he was responsible for the Education Act 1944; he was chancellor of the Exchequer 1951–55 and Lord Privy Seal 1955–59. As a candidate for the premiership, he was defeated by ◊Macmillan in 1957 (under whom he was home secretary 1957–62), and by ◊Douglas-Home in 1963, but was foreign minister 1963–64. He was master of Trinity College, Cambridge, 1965–78. His attitude to politics was summed up in his autobiographical *The Art of the Possible* 1971.

Butler /ˈbʌtlə/ Samuel 1612–1680. English satirist. The son of a farmer, he served in the household of the countess of Kent, and then of Sir Samuel Luke, a colonel in the Parliamentary army. After the Restoration he became secretary to the earl of Carberry. His poem *Hudibras*, published in three parts in 1663, 1664 and 1678, became immediately popular for its biting satire against the Puritans.

Butler /ˈbʌtlə/ Samuel 1835–1902. British author, who made his name in 1872 with his satiric attack on contemporary utopianism, *Erewhon* ('nowhere' reversed), but is now best remembered for his autobiographical *The Way of All Flesh* written 1872–85 and published 1903. *The Fair Haven* examined the miraculous element in Christianity. *Life and Habit* 1877 and other works were devoted to a criticism of the theory of natural selection. In *The Authoress of the Odyssey* he maintained that the *Odyssey* was the work of a woman.

Butlin /ˈbʌtlɪn/ William 'Billy' 1899–1980. British pioneer of holiday camps. Born in South Africa, he went in early life to Canada, but later entered the fair business in England. His chain of camps provide 'all-in' holidays with amusements, meals and sleeping chalets at an inclusive price. He was knighted in 1964.

Butor /bjuːˈtɔː/ Michel 1926– . French writer, a practitioner of the 'anti-novel'. These include *Passage de Milan/Passage from Milan* 1954, *Dêgrès/Degrees* 1960, and *L'Emploi du temps/Passing Time* 1963: *Mobile* 1962 is a volume of essays.

Butskellism UK term for political policies tending towards the middle ground in an effort to gain popular support. Named after R A ◊Butler (moderate Conservative) and Hugh ◊Gaitskell (moderate Labour politician).

butte /bjuːt/ a steep-sided hill, possibly with a flat top, formed in horizontal sedimentary rocks, particularly in arid areas. A large butte with a pronounced tablelike flat-topped profile is a ◊mesa. Buttes and mesas are characteristic of semi-arid areas where the surface is capped by a resistant layer of rock, as in the plateau region of the western USA.

Butte /bjuːt/ mining town in Montana, USA, in the Rocky Mountains; population (1970) 23,500. Butte was founded in 1864 during a rush for gold, soon exhausted; copper was found some 20 years later.

buttercup species of *Ranunculus* with divided leaves and yellow flowers, family Ranunculaceae, for example, *common buttercup Ranunculus acris* and *creeping buttercup Ranunculus repens*. One of Britain's rarest plants is the *adderstongue crowfoot Ranunculus ophioglossifolius* in the Cotswolds. See also ◊celandine.

butterfly insect belonging, like moths, to the order Lepidoptera, in which the wings are covered with tiny scales, often brightly coloured. Butterfly is an everyday rather than exact scientific term, but butterflies usually differ from moths in having the antennae club-shaped rather than plumed or feathery, no 'lock' between the fore and hindwing, and resting with the wings in the vertical position rather than flat or sloping.

There are some 15,000 species of butterfly (about 70 in Britain, out of 165,000 Lepidoptera. Butterflies have a tubular proboscis through which they suck up nectar, or, in some species, carrion, dung or urine. Metamorphosis is complete, the caterpillars being very varied, and the pupa or chrysalis usually being without the protection of a cocoon. Adult lifespan may be only a few weeks, but some species hibernate and lay eggs in the spring.

The largest family, Nymphalidae, has some 6,000 species: it includes the Peacock, Tortoiseshells, and Fritillaries. The family Pieridae includes the *cabbage white*, one of the few butterflies injurious to crops. The Lycaenidae are chiefly small, often with metallic coloration, for example the Blues, Coppers, and Hairstreaks. The *large blue Lycaena arion*, extinct in Britain from 1979, but being re-established 1984, has a complex life history, in that it lays its eggs on wild thyme, and the caterpillars are then taken by Myrmica ants to their nests, where they milk their honey glands, while the caterpillars feed on the ant larvae; in the spring the caterpillars finally pupate and emerge as butterflies. The mainly tropical Papilionidae, or Swallowtails, are large and very beautiful, especially the South American species. The world's largest butterfly is *Queen Alexandra's birdwing Ornithoptera alexandrae* of Papua New Guinea, with a body 7.5 cm/3 in long and a wingspan of 25 cm/10 in. The most spectacular migrant is the orange and black *monarch butterfly Danaus plexippus*, which may fly from Alaska to Mexico to overwinter. Some individuals find their way from America to Europe.

butterfly fish name applied to several fishes, not all related. The freshwater *butterfly fish Pantodon buchholzi* of W Africa can leap from the water and glide for a short distance on its large wing-like pectoral fins. Up to 10 cm/4 in long, it lives in stagnant water. The tropical marine *butterfly fishes*, family Chaetodontidae, are brightly coloured with laterally flattened bodies, often with long snouts which they poke into crevices in rocks and coral when feeding.

butterwort insectivorous plant, genus *Pinguicula*, with purplish flowers, and a rosette of leaves which can inroll their margins to trap insects.

Buxtehude /ˌbukstəˈhuːdə/ Dieterik 1637–1707. Danish composer and organist at Lübeck, Germany, who influenced ◊Bach and ◊Handel. He is remembered for his organ works and cantatas written for his evening concerts or *Abendmusiken*.

Buxton /ˈbʌkstən/ spa town in Derbyshire, England; population (1981) 21,000. Known from Roman times for its hot springs. It has a restored Edwardian opera house.

buzzard name given to a number of species of medium-sized hawks with broad wings, often seen soaring. The *common buzzard Buteo buteo* of Europe and Asia is about 55 cm/1.8 ft long with a wingspan of over 1.2 m/4 ft. In Britain it lives mostly in the W and N. It preys on a variety of small animals up to the size of a rabbit. The *rough-legged buzzard Buzzard lagopus* lives in

butterfly A painted lady (*Vanessa cardui*) – a species widely found in Africa – just emerged from its pupa.

the northern tundra and specializes in lemmings. The *honey buzzard Pernis apivora* feeds largely, as its name suggests, on honey and insect larvae. It summers in Europe and W Asia and winters in Africa.

Byblos /ˈbɪblɒs/ ancient Phoenician city (modern Jebeil), 32 km/20 mi N of Beirut, Lebanon. Known to the Assyrians and Babylonians as Gubla it had a thriving export of cedar and pinewood to Egypt as early as 1500 BC. In Roman times called Byblus, it boasted an amphitheatre, baths and a temple dedicated to an unknown male god, and was noted for its celebration of the resurrection of ◊Adonis.

Bydgoszcz /ˈbɪdgɒʃtʃ/ industrial river port in N Poland, 105 km/65 mi NE of Poznan on the Warta; population (1981) 352,500. As *Bromberg* it was under Prussian control 1772–1919.

Byng /bɪŋ/ George, Viscount Torrington 1663–1733. British admiral. He captured Gibraltar in 1704; commanded the fleet which prevented an invasion of England by the Old ◊Pretender in 1708; and destroyed the Spanish fleet at Messina in 1718. John ◊Byng was his fourth son.

Byng /bɪŋ/ John 1704–1757. British admiral. When in 1756 the island of Minorca was invaded by France, Byng was ordered to sail to the relief of Fort St Philip which was still resisting, but failed in the attempt. After the fort's fall he was court-martialled and condemned to death, and shot at Portsmouth. As Voltaire commented, it was done 'to encourage the others'.

Byng /bɪŋ/ Julian, 1st Viscount of Vimy 1862–1935. British general. A son of the second earl of Strafford, he commanded the third

Cavalry Division in 1914, the Cavalry Corps in 1915, the ninth Army Corps at the ◊Dardanelles, and the Canadian Army Corps in 1916–17 in France. After his victory at ◊Vimy Ridge he took command of the Third Army, and in Nov 1917 made a succesful tank attack on Cambrai. He was governor-general of Canada 1921–26, and was made a viscount in 1926, and a field marshal in 1932.

Byrd /bɜːd/ Richard Evelyn 1888–1957. American explorer. Born in Virginia, he flew to the North (1926) and South Pole (1929), and led five overland expeditions in Antarctica. See ◊Arctic and ◊Antarctic tables.

Byrd /bɜːd/ William 1543–1623. English composer, born probably at Lincoln, where he became organist in 1563. He shared with ◊Tallis the honorary post of organist in Queen Elizabeth's Chapel Royal, and in 1575 he and Tallis were granted a monopoly in the printing and selling of music. Byrd composed secular vocal and instrumental music, but his church choral music (set to Latin words, as he was a firm Catholic) represents his most important work.

Byrd English composer William Byrd, often regarded as the greatest Tudor composer. He was a firm Catholic and several times prosecuted as a recusant but wrote for both Catholic and Anglican churches.

Byrds, the /bɜːdz/ US pioneering folk rock group, formed 1964. Original group included Roger McGuinn, David Crosby, Gene Clark, Chris Hillman, and Michael Clarke. Best remembered for their hits 'Mr Tambourine Man' 1965 (a version of Bob Dylan's song) and 'Eight Miles High' 1966, they moved towards country rock in the late 1960s, and dissolved 1973 after many changes of line-up.

Byron /ˈbaɪrən/ Ada Augusta 1815–1851. British mathematician, daughter of Lord ◊Byron. She was the world's first computer programmer, working with ◊Babbage's mechanical invention, and in 1983 a new high-level computer language, ADA, was named after her.

Byron /ˈbaɪrən/ George Gordon, 6th Baron Byron 1788–1824. British poet, who became the symbol of ◊Romanticism and political liberalism throughout Europe in the 19th century. Born in London, he succeeded his great-uncle to the title in 1798. Educated at Harrow and Cambridge, he published his first volume *Hours of Idleness* 1807, and attacked its harsh critics in *English Bards and Scotch Reviewers* 1809. Overnight fame came with the first two cantos of *Childe Harold* 1812, romantically describing his tours in Portugal, Spain, and the Balkans (third canto 1816, fourth 1818). In 1815 he married the mathematician Anne Milbanke, (by whom he had a daughter, Augusta Ada ◊Byron), separating from her a year later amid much scandal. During his resultant 'exile' he produced *The Prisoner of Chillon* 1816, under the influence of ◊Shelley; *Beppo* 1818, *Mazeppa* 1819, and his masterpiece *Don Juan* 1819–24. He dabbled in Italian revolutionary politics, and sailed for Greece in 1823 to further the Greek struggle for independence, but died of fever at Missolonghi. He is remembered for his lyrics, his colloquially easy *Letters*, and, particularly in Europe, as the patron saint of romantic liberalism. His friend Thomas ◊Moore wrote one of the first biographies of Byron.

Byron A portrait of Lord Byron by Richard Westall, painted in 1813 at the height of the poet's early fame.

Byron /ˈbaɪrən/ Robert 1904–1941. British writer on travel and architecture, including *The Byzantine Achievement* 1929 and *The Road to Oxiana* 1937, an account of a journey Iran–Afghanistan in 1933–34.

byte in computing, a sequence or string of usually eight bits (binary digits) constituting a unit of memory or a character (a letter, number or symbol). Strictly it is a subdivision of a 'word' (the number of bits of information that a computer can process in a single operation, perhaps 32 bits in a minicomputer and 64 in a mainframe). A byte is the number of bits needed to represent a single character (eight bits in extended ASCII). Byte also now refers to a single memory location; large computer memory size is measured in thousands of bytes (kilobytes or Kb) or millions of bytes (megabytes or Mb).

Byzantine art see ◊medieval art.

Byzantine Empire the Eastern Roman Empire, with its capital at Constantinople (Byzantium). The Emperor Constantine removed his capital to Constantinople in 330 AD, but it was not until 395 that the Empire was finally divided into eastern and western halves. When the Western Empire was overrun by barbarian invaders, the Byzantine Empire stood firm, and Justinian I (527–565) temporarily recovered Italy, North Africa, and parts of Spain. During the 7th century Syria, Egypt and North Africa were lost to the Arabs,who twice besieged Constantinople (673–77, 718), but the Byzantines maintained their hold on Asia Minor. The ◊Iconoclastic controversy of the eighth and ninth centuries brought the emperors into conflict with the papacy, and in 867 the Greek Church broke with the Roman. Under the Macedonian dynasty (867–1056) the Byzantine Empire reached the height of its prosperity; the Bulgars proved a formidable danger, but after a long struggle were finally crushed in 1018 by ◊Basil II ('the Bulgar-Slayer'). After Basil's death the Byzantine Empire declined, and in 1071–73 the ◊Seljuk Turks conquered most of Asia Minor. In 1204 the western crusaders sacked Constantinople and set Baldwin of

Flanders on the throne. The Latin Empire was overthrown in 1261, and the Byzantine Empire maintained a precarious existence, until in 1453 the Turks captured Constantinople.

Byzantine literature written mainly in the Greek *koinē*, a form of Greek accepted as the literary language of the 1st century AD and increasingly separate from the spoken tongue of the people, it is chiefly concerned with theology, history, and commentaries on the Greek classics. Its chief authors are the theologians St Basil, Gregory of Nyssa, Gregory of Nazianzus, Chrysostom (4th century AD), and John of Damascus (8th century); the historians Zosimus (about 500), Procopius (6th century), Bryennius and his wife ◊Annacomnena (about 1100), and Georgius Acropolita (1220–82); and the encyclopaedist Suidas (about 975). Drama was non-existent and poetry, save for the hymns of the 6th–8th centuries, scanty and stilted, but there were many popular saints' lives.

Byzantine style a style in the visual arts and architecture, which originated in Byzantium (fourth–fifth centuries) and the Eastern Orthodox Church, and spread to Italy, throughout the Balkans, and to Russia, where it survived until modern times. It is a mixture of Greek and Oriental elements, and is characterized by the use of rich colours, particularly gold, geometrical designs on a flat surface, distorted figures, and (in architecture) the use of the dome supported on pendentives. Classical examples of Byzantine architecture are St Sophia, Constantinople, and St Mark's, Venice. A modern example is Westminster Cathedral. The first great Italian painters to break away from the formalism of the Byzantine style were Cimabue and Giotto, who painted religious subjects in a naturalistic style. See also ◊medieval art.

Byzantium /baɪˈzæntiəm/ ancient Greek city on the Bosphorus, founded by the Megarians about 660 BC. In 330 AD the capital of the Roman Empire was transferred there by Constantine the Great, who renamed it ◊Constantinople, modern ◊Istanbul.

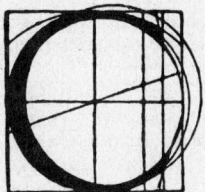

C third letter of the alphabet. It corresponds to Hebrew *gimel* and Greek *gamma*, both derived from the Semitic word for 'camel'. Originally representing a hard *g*, it was used by the Romans for *k* also. In the Roman system the numeral C stands for a hundred.

C a general-purpose computer-programming language popular on minicomputers. Developed in the early 1970s from an earlier language called BCPL, C is closely associated with the development of the operating system ◊Unix. It is especially good for writing fast and efficient ◊systems programs, such as ◊operating systems (which control the operations of the computer).

cabal a clique of scheming politicians; applied particularly to Charles II's ministry (1667–73) whose initials made up the word by coincidence – C(lifford), A(shley), B(uckingham), A(rlington), and L(auderdale).

cabbage plant *Brassica oleracea* of the family Cruciferae, allied to the turnip and wild charlock. It is an important table vegetable, and the numerous cultivated varieties – all probably descended from the wild cabbage – include kale, Brussels sprouts, common cabbage, savoy, cauliflower, sprouting broccoli, and kohlrabi.

cabbala alternative spelling of ◊kabbala.

caber, tossing the (Gaelic *cabar*, a pole). Scottish athletic sport. The caber is a tapering tree-trunk, 6.1 m/20 ft long. The tosser rests the caber on his shoulder, holding the thin end which he raises till it is about level with his elbow, runs forward as the caber begins to topple over, and hurls it into the air. A champion may achieve throws of over 12 m/40 ft.

Cabinda /kə'bɪndə/ or Kabinda African coastal enclave, a province of ◊Angola. The capital is also called Cabinda. There are oil reserves. Cabinda has made claims to separate independence. Area 7,770 sq km/3,000 sq mi; population (1980) 81,300.

cabinet in Britain the committee of ministers holding the most important executive offices who decide the government's policy.
The cabinet system originated under the Stuarts; the 'cabinet councils' (cabinet meaning a small room, implying secrecy) or subcommittees of the ◊Privy Council undertook special tasks. Under William III it became customary for the king to select his ministers from the party with a parliamentary majority. When George I ceased to attend cabinet meetings, the office of prime minister, not officially recognized until 1905, came into existence to provide a chair (◊Walpole was the first). Cabinet policy is collective and the meetings are secret, minutes being taken by the secretary of the cabinet, a high civil servant; secrecy has been infringed in recent years by 'leaks' or unauthorised disclosures to the press. Members are chosen by the prime minister.
In the USA a cabinet system developed early and the term was used from 1793, although the US cabinet, unlike the British, does not initiate legislation. Members are selected by the president and, again contrary to British practice, may neither be members of Congress nor speak there, being responsible to the president alone.

The UK Cabinet
Prime Minister
Lord President of the Council and Leader of the House of Lords
Lord Chancellor
Secretary of State for Foreign and Commonwealth Affairs
Chancellor of the Exchequer
Home Secretary
Secretary of State for Trade and Industry
Secretary of State for Defence
Secretary of State for Wales
Lord Privy Seal and Leader of the House of Commons
Secretary of State for Social Services
Secretary of State for Northern Ireland
Minister of Agriculture, Fisheries and Food
Secretary of State for the Environment
Secretary of State for Employment
Secretary of State for Education and Science
Chief Secretary to the Treasury
Secretary of State for Scotland
Secretary of State for Energy
Chancellor of the Duchy of Lancaster
Secretary of State for Transport.

---

cable car a method of transporting passengers up steep slopes by cable. The oldest type of cable car is the *cable railway*, in which passenger cars are hauled along rails by a cable wound by a powerful winch. A pair of cars usually operates together on the ◊funicular principle, one going up as the other goes down. The *aerial cable car*, is the other main type, properly called a téléphérique. The passenger car is suspended from a trolley that runs along an aerial cableway. A unique form of cable-car system operates in San Francisco, where it has been working since 1873. The street cars travel along rails and are hauled by means of moving cables under the ground.

Cabot /'kæbət/ John 1450–1498. Italian navigator, who made many voyages to the Levant. In 1484 he moved to London. Commissioned with his three sons by Henry VII to discover unknown lands, he arrived at Cape Breton Island on 24 Jun 1497, thus, according to tradition, discovering the North American mainland (he thought he was in north east Asia). In 1498 he sailed again, touched Greenland, and probably died on the voyage.

Cabot /'kæbət/ Sebastián 1474–1557. English navigator and cartographer, the second son of John ◊Cabot. In 1526–30 he explored the Brazilian coast and the River Plate for Charles V and was also employed by Henry VIII, Edward VI and Ferdinand of Spain. He planned a voyage to China by way of the ◊North-East Passage, encouraged the formation of the Company of Merchant Adventurers of London in 1551, and in 1553 and 1556 directed the Company's expeditions to Russia, where he opened British trade.

Cabral /kə'brɑːl/ Pedro Alvarez 1460–1526. Portuguese explorer who claimed Brazil for Portugal in 1500. Setting sail from Lisbon March 1500 for the East Indies, he accidentally reached Brazil by taking a course too far west. He claimed the country for Portugal 25 Apr, as Spain had not followed up Vicente Pinzón's landing there earlier in the year. Sailing on round Africa, he lost seven of his fleet of 13 ships (◊Diaz being one of those drowned), and landed in Mozambique. Proceeding to India, he negotiated the first Indo-Portuguese treaties for trade, and returned to Lisbon July 1501.

Cabrini /kə'briːni/ Frances or Francesca 1850–1917. First Roman Catholic saint in the USA. Born in Lombardy, Italy, she founded the Missionary Sisters of the Sacred Heart in America, and established many schools and hospitals in the care of her nuns. She was canonized in 1946.

cachalot name for the sperm whale. See ◊whale.

cactus in botany, a plant of the family Cactaceae, but in common speech applied to many different succulent and prickly plants. True cacti are recognized by their woody axis being overlaid with an enlarged fleshy stem, which assumes various forms and is usually covered with spines. The leaves are usually very much reduced, and frequently are absent. The flowers are often large and brightly coloured. The fruit is fleshy and often edible, as in the case of the prickly pear.

The Cactaceae are a New World family, though some species have been introduced from the New to the Old, for example, in the Mediterranean area, and have become a pest. They grow in the driest and rockiest situations.

CAD (Computer Aided Design) the use of computer facilities for creating and editing design drawings. CAD also allows such things as automatic testing of designs and multiple or animated three-dimensional views of designs. CAD systems are widely used in architecture, electronics, and engineering, especially in the motor-vehicle industry where cars designed by computer are now commonplace. See also ◊CAM (computer-assisted manufacture).

computer aided design

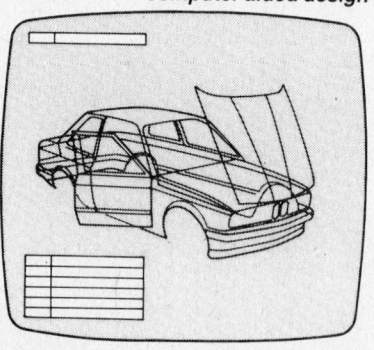

Cadarache /ˌkædə'rɑːʃ/ French nuclear research site, NE of Aix-en-Provence.

caddis fly insect of the order Trichoptera. Adults are generally dull brown, rather moth like, with wings covered with tiny hairs. Mouthparts are poorly developed and many do not feed as adults. They are usually near water, and the larvae are aquatic. Many larvae make cases, open at both ends, out of sand or plant remains, in which to live. Some caddis make silk nets among aquatic vegetation to help trap food. About 190 species are found in Britain.

Cade /keɪd/ Jack d. 1450. English rebel. A prosperous landowner, he led a revolt in Kent against the misgovernment of Henry VI in 1450. He defeated the royal forces at Sevenoaks and

occupied London, whereupon under promise of reforms and pardon the rebels dispersed. But Cade was then hunted down and killed near Heathfield, Sussex.

cadenza /kə'denzə/ in music, usually a bravura passage for the soloist in a concerto.

Cadiz /kə'dɪz/ Spanish city and naval base, capital and seaport of the province of Cadiz, standing on Cadiz Bay, an inlet of the Atlantic, 103 km/64 mi S of Seville. Probably founded by the Phoenicians about 1100 BC, it was a centre for the tin trade with Cornwall, England. It was recaptured from the ◊Moors by the king of Castile in 1262, and rose to great importance after the discovery of America in 1492. Drake burnt a Spanish fleet here in 1587 to prevent the sailing of the ◊Armada. Modern development was restricted by its peninsular location until a bridge to the further shore of Cadiz Bay was completed in 1969. Population (1981) 157,766.

cadmium a metallic element, symbol Cd, atomic weight 112.41, atomic number 48. Cadmium is a soft, silver-white, highly toxic metal. It is used in electroplating, as a constituent of one of the lowest-melting alloys, and in bearing alloys with low coefficients of friction. Cadmium sulphide is used in photovoltaic cells. Cadmium is also used as control rods in nuclear reactors owing to its high absorption of neutrons. Its industrial importance has greatly increased in recent years.

Cadwalader /kæd'wɒlədə/ Welsh hero. The son of ◊Cadwallon, King of Gwynedd, North Wales, he defeated and slew Eadwine of Northumbria in 633. About a year later he was killed in battle.

Cadwallon king of Gwynedd, North Wales, in the 6th century AD, father of ◊Cadwalader.

caecilian type of amphibian of rather worm-like appearance. Caecilians have a grooved skin giving a 'segmented' appearance, no trace of limbs, and mostly live below ground. Some species bear live young, others lay eggs. There are about 170 species known, living in the tropical parts of the world, forming the amphibian order Apoda (also known as Caecilia or Gymnophiona).

Caedmon /'kædmən/ born in the 7th century AD. First known English Christian poet. According to ◊Bede, when he was a cowherd at the monastery of Whitby, he was commanded to sing by a stranger in a dream, and on waking produced a hymn on the Creation. Bede appends a Latin translation of this but the original Old English poem is preserved in some manuscripts. He became a monk and composed religious poems.

Caen /kɒŋ/ capital of Calvados *département*, France, on the river Orne, linked by canal with the English Channel 14.5 km/9 mi to the north east. The church of St Étienne was founded by William the Conqueror, and the university by Henry VI of England in 1432. Caen was captured by the British in World War II, after five weeks' fighting, on 9 Jul 1944, during which the town was badly damaged. It is a business centre, with ironworks, and electric and electronic industries. Caen building stone is famous. Population (1982) 183,526.

Caernarvon /kə'nɑːvən/ town in Gwynedd, North Wales, the administrative headquarters of the region, situated on the south west shore of the Menai Strait. Formerly a Roman station, it is now a market town and port. The first Prince of Wales (later ◊Edward II) was born in Caernarvon Castle; ◊Edward VIII was invested here in 1911 and Prince ◊Charles in 1969. The Earl of Snowdon became Constable of the castle in 1963. Population (1981) 9,506.

Caernarvonshire /kə'nɑːvənʃə/ former county of North Wales, merged in ◊Gwynedd in 1974.

Caerphilly /kə'fɪli/ market town in Mid Glamorgan, Wales, 11 km/7 mi N of Cardiff. The castle was built by Edward I The town is noted for its mild Caerphilly cheese. Population (1981) 42,736.

Caesar /'siːzə/ powerful family of ancient Rome which included Gaius Julius ◊Caesar, whose grand-nephew and adopted son ◊Augustus assumed the name of Caesar, and in turn passed it on to his adopted son ◊Tiberius. Henceforth, it was borne by the successive emperors, becoming a title of the Roman rulers. The title Tsar in Russia and Kaiser in Germany are both derived from the name Caesar.

Caesar /'siːzə/ Gaius Julius c. 102–44 BC. Roman statesman and general. A patrician, he allied himself with the popular party, and when elected Aedile in 65 BC nearly ruined himself with lavish amusements for the Roman populace. Although a free thinker, he was elected chief pontiff in 63 BC, and in 61 BC was appointed governor of Spain. Returning to Rome in 60 BC, he formed with ◊Pompey and ◊Crassus the first triumvirate, but as governor of Gaul was engaged in its subjugation 58–50 BC, defeating the Germans under Ariovistus, and selling thousands of the Belgic tribes into slavery. In 55 BC he crossed into Britain, with a further campaigning visit in 54 BC. A revolt by the Gauls in 52 BC, under ◊Vercingetorix, was crushed in 51 BC. His own commentaries on the campaigns have a mastery worthy of fiction, as does his account of the ensuing Civil War. His governorship of Spain was to end in 49 BC, and, Crassus being dead, Pompey was now a rival. Declaring 'the die is cast', Caesar crossed the Rubicon (the small river separating Gaul from Italy) to meet the army raised against him. In the ensuing Civil War, he followed Pompey to Epirus in 48 BC, defeated him at Pharsalus, and chased him to Egypt, where he was murdered. Caesar stayed some months in Egypt, where he had a son (Caesarion) by ◊Cleopatra, then executed a lightning campaign in 47 BC against King Pharnaces in Asia Minor, which he summarized: *Veni vidi vici* 'I came, I saw, I conquered'. By his final victory in Spain at Munda in 45 BC over the sons of Pompey, he established his position, having been awarded a ten-year dictatorship in 46 BC. On 15 Mar 44 BC, however, he was stabbed to death at the foot of Pompey's statue (see ◊Brutus, ◊Cassius) in the Senate house.

Caesarea /ˌsiːzə'rɪə/ alternative form of ◊Qisaraya, port in Israel.

Caesarean section the removal of a child from the womb through an incision in the

Caesar One of the world's greatest military commanders, Julius Caesar was considered to possess an unhealthy quantity of personal ambition. He was assassinated in the senate house on the Ides of March.

abdominal wall. Julius ◊Caesar is said to have entered the world in this way: hence the name.

caesium a chemical element, symbol Cs, atomic weight 132.91, atomic number 55. It is used in the manufacture of photoelectric cells. A highly radioactive isotope, caesium 137 (◊half-life 30 years), is a waste product from nuclear power stations and is used for mass radiation and sterilization of foodstuffs, medically for irradiation of surface tumours, and as the basis of atomic clocks.

Caetano /kaɪˈtɑːnəʊ/ Marcello 1906–1980. Portuguese statesman. Professor of administrative law at Lisbon from 1940, he was assistant prime minister 1955–58, and succeeded ◊Salazar as prime minster from 1968 until his exile after the revolution of 1974. He was granted political asylum in Brazil.

caffeine one of a group of organic substances called ◊alkaloids. Caffeine is found in tea and coffee, and is partly responsible for their stimulant effect. Too much caffeine can be detrimental to health (more than six average cups of tea or coffee per day).

Cage /keɪdʒ/ John 1912– . American composer. A pupil of ◊Schoenberg, he has re-assessed musical aesthetics and defines the role of music as 'purposeless play'. All sounds that can be heard are to be available for musical purposes, for example electrical buzzers and tin cans as used in *Imaginary Landscape No 3*. See also ◊aleatory music.

Cagliari /kælˈjɑːri/ capital and port of Sardinia, Italy, on the Gulf of Cagliari. The cathedral, completed 1312, was later modernized; the university was founded in 1626. Population (1981) 233,848.

Cagliostro /kælˈjɒstrəʊ/ Alessandro di, Count Cagliostro 1743–1795. assumed name of Giuseppe Balsamo. Born at Palermo, Italy, he travelled widely, married and was an Italian specialist in the 'occult'. In Paris, France, in 1785 he was involved in the affair of the 'diamond necklace' – supposed to have been ordered by Marie Antoinette, but in fact by a band of swindlers – and was imprisoned in the Bastille. Later arrested by the Inquisition in Rome, he died in the fortress of San Leone.

Cagnes-sur-Mer /ˈkæn sjuə ˈmeə/ capital of the *département* of Alpes-Maritimes, to the south west of ʿNice, France. The château (13th–17th century) contains mementoes of Renoir, who lived and died here 1900–19. Population (1986) 35,214.

Cain /keɪn/ in the Old Testament, the first-born son of Adam and Eve. He murdered his brother Abel from motives of jealousy, as Abel's sacrifice was more acceptable to the Lord than his own.

Cain /keɪn/ James M(allahan) 1892–1977. American novelist, born at Annapolis. He was the author of thrillers, including *The Postman Always Rings Twice* 1934, *Double Indemnity*, and *Mildred Pierce* 1941.

Caine /keɪn/ Michael. Stage-name of Maurice Micklewhite 1933– . British actor born in South London, he has appeared in many films, including *The Ipcress File* 1965, *Alfie* 1966, and *Hannah and her Sisters* 1986. He is noted for his dry, laconic Cockney style.

Ça Ira /ˈsɑː ɪəˈr ɑː/ song of the French Revolution, written by a street singer, Ladré, and set to an existing tune by Bécourt, a drummer of the Paris opera.

cairn Scottish breed of ◊terrier, once used in digging out foxes and badgers. Shaggy, short-legged and compact, it can be sandy, greyish brindle or red.

Cairngorms /ˈkeəngɔːmz/ mountain group in Scotland, north part of the ◊Grampians, the highest peak being Ben Macdhui 1,309 m/4,296 ft. Aviemore (Britain's first complete holiday and sports centre) was opened in 1966, and 11 km/7 mi to the south is the Highland Wildlife Park at Kincraig.

Cairo /ˈkaɪrəʊ/ (Arabic *El Qahira*) capital of the Arab Republic of Egypt, on the east bank of the Nile 13 km/8 mi above the apex of the Delta and 160 km/100 mi from the Mediterranean. Population (1979) 8,540,000.
The modern government and business quarters reflect Cairo's importance as an administrative and commercial centre, and the semi-official newspaper *al Ahram* is an influential voice in the Arab world. At Helwan, 24 km/15 mi to the south, an industrial centre is developing, with iron and steel works powered by electricity from the Aswan High Dam. There are two secular universities: Cairo University (1908) and Ein Shams (1950).
history El Fustat (Old Cairo) was founded by the Arabs about 64 AD, Cairo itself about 1000 by the ◊Fatimite ruler Gowhar. The city is 32 km/20 mi north of the site of the ancient Egyptian centre

of ◊Memphis, and the Great Pyramids and the Sphinx are at nearby Giza. The Mosque of Amr dates from 643 AD; the Citadel, built by ◊Saladin in the 12th century, contains the impressive 19th century Mohammed Ali mosque; and the mosque which houses the El Azhar university (founded 970 AD) is the heart of traditional Islam.

caisson a cylindrical or box-like structure, usually of reinforced ◊concrete, that is sunk into the river bed to form the foundations of a bridge. An open caisson is open at the top and bottom. At the bottom is a wedge-shaped cutting edge. Material is excavated from inside, allowing the caisson to sink. A pneumatic caisson has a pressurized chamber at the bottom, in which workers carry out the excavation. The air pressure prevents the surrounding water entering. The workers enter the chamber through an air lock. They can leave through the airlock only after a suitable ◊decompression period, in order to prevent caisson disease, or the ◊bends.

Cajun member of a French-speaking community of Louisiana, USA, descended from French-Canadians who in the 18th century were driven there from Nova Scotia (then known as Acadia, from which the name Cajun comes). Their popular music, which enjoyed a vogue in the mid-1980s, has a lively beat and features steel guitar, fiddle, and accordion.

Calabar /ˈkæləbɑː/ port and capital of Cross River State, south east Nigeria, on the Cross River, 64 km/40 mi from the Atlantic. It was a centre of the 18th–19th-century slave trade. Rubber, timber, and vegetable oils are exported. Population (1975) 103,000.

calabash evergreen tree, *Crescentia cujete*, family Bignoniaceae, found in South America, India, and Africa, producing gourds 50 cm/1.5 ft across, used as pots.

Calabria /kəˈlæbriə/ mountainous earthquake region occupying the 'toe' of Italy, comprising the provinces of Catanzaro, Cosenza and Reggio; the capital is Catanzaro, Reggio is the industrial centre. Area 15,080 sq km/5,820 sq mi. Population (1981) 2,061,182.

Calais /ˈkæleɪ/ port in northern France; population (1982) 76,935. Taken by Edward III in 1347, it was saved from destruction by the personal surrender of the Burghers of Calais commemorated in Rodin's sculpture; the French retook it in the reign of Mary in 1558. In German occupation May 1940–Oct 1944, it surrendered to the Canadians.

Calais, Pas de /ˈkæleɪ/ French name for the Strait of ◊Dover.

calamine a zinc mineral. In Britain it refers to zinc carbonate ($ZnCO_3$), in the USA it refers to zinc silicate ($Zn_4Si_2O_7(OH)_2$). When referring to skin-soothing lotions and ointments calamine means a pink powder of zinc oxide and 0.5% iron (II) oxide, used, for example, in treating eczema, measles rash and insect bites or stings.

Calamity Jane nickname of American heroine, Martha Jane Burke c. 1852–1903, of Deadwood, South Dakota, mining camps. She adopted male dress and, as an excellent shot, promised 'calamity' to any aggressor.

calcite the common rock-forming mineral, calcium carbonate, $CaCO_3$. It forms in hexagonal and rhombohedral ◊crystals. Calcite is the major constituent of ◊limestone and ◊marble. It is also found deposited in veins through many rocks because of the ease with which it is dissolved and transported by groundwater. A colourless or white substance, it rates 3 on Mohs' Scale of Hardness and often forms stalactites and stalagmites in caves.

calcium a silvery-white metallic element, one of the alkaline earth metals; symbol Ca, atomic weight 40.07, atomic number 20. It was discovered by Sir Humphry ◊Davy in 1808 and is very widely distributed, mainly in the form of its carbonate $CaCO_3$ which occurs in a fairly pure condition as chalk and limestone; see calcite. Calcium is an essential component of bones, teeth, shells, milk and leaves, and it forms 1.5% of the human body. Calcium compounds are very important to the chemical industry and include slaked lime (calcium hydroxide $Ca(OH)_2$), plaster of Paris (calcium sulphate $CaSO_4 2H_2O$), calcium hypochlorite $(CaOCl_2)$ a bleaching agent, calcium nitrate $(Ca(NO_3)_2 4H_2O)$ a nitrogenous fertilizer, calcium carbide (CaC_2) which reacts with water to give acetylene, calcium cyanamide $(CaCN_2)$ the basis of pharmaceuticals, fertilizers and plastics including melamine, and calcium cyanide $(Ca(CN)_2)$ used in the extraction of gold and silver and in electroplating, and others used in baking powders, and fillers for paints.

calculator an electronic computing device for performing numerical calculations. It generally has at least four arithmetic functions (add, subtract, multiply, and divide); many also have squares, roots, and advanced trigonometric and statistical functions. Input is by a small keyboard and results are shown on a one-line screen (VDU) which is typically a ◊liquid-crystal display (LCD). Some calculators can print out results on a small roll of paper. The first electronic calculator was manufactured by the Bell Punch Company, USA, in 1963.

calculus branch of mathematics that permits the manipulation of continuously varying quantities, applicable to practical problems involving such matters as changing speeds, problems of flight, varying stresses in the framework of a bridge, electrical circuits with varying currents and voltages, and so on. The term is the Latin word for pebble, used in calculations on the ◊abacus.

Integral calculus deals with the method of summation or adding together the effects of continuously varying quantities. *Differential calculus* deals in a similar way with rates of change. Many of its applications arose from the study of speed. Each of these branches of calculus deals with small quantities which during manipulation are made smaller and smaller, hence both comprise the *infinitesimal calculus*. Differential equations represent complex rates of change and integrals are their empirical solutions. If no known mathematical processes are available, integration can be performed graphically or by a machine, increasingly by computers.

Calculator The first electronic calculator was made in 1963. Today, this device is widely used in the office and at home. This Hewlett-Packard HP-28C is capable of vector and matrix mathematics.

Calculus originated with Archimedes in the 3rd century BC in the means he devised for finding the areas of curved shapes and for drawing tangents to curves. These ideas were not expanded on until the 17th century, when the French philosopher Descartes introduced ◊coordinate geometry, showing how geometrical curves can be described and manipulated by means of algebraic expressions. Then the French mathematician Fermat and later the German philosopher Leibnitz and the British scientist Isaac Newton immensely advanced the study.

Calcutta /kæl'kʌtə/ city of India, on the Hooghli, the most westerly mouth of the Ganges, some 130 km/80 mi north of the Bay of Bengal. It is the capital of West Bengal.

history Calcutta was founded 1686–90 by Job Charnock, head of Hooghli factory of the East India Company. Captured by Suraj-ud-Dowlah in 1756, during the Anglo-French wars in India, in 1757 it was retaken by Robert Clive. Calcutta was the seat of government of British India 1773–1912. Buildings include a magnificent Jain temple, the palaces of former Indian princes; and the Law Courts and Government House, survivals of the British Raj.

Calcutta is chiefly a commercial and industrial centre. Industries include engineering, shipbuilding, jute, and other textiles. Across the river is ◊Howrah, and between Calcutta and the sea there is a new bulk cargo port, Haldia, which is the focus of oil refineries, petrochemical plants, and fertilizer factories.

Educational institutions include the University of Calcutta (1857), oldest of several universities; the Visva Bharati at Santiniketan, founded by Tagore; the Bose Research Institute; and a fine museum; population (1981) 9,194,018

Calcutta, Black Hole of /kæl'kʌtə/ according to tradition Suraj-ud-Dowlah confined 146 British prisoners on the night of 20 Jun 1756 in one small room, of whom only 23 allegedly survived; later research reduced the deaths to 43, a result of negligence rather than intention.

Caldecott /'kɔːldɪkət/ Randolph 1846–1886. British book illustrator, best known for illustrations to books by Washington ◊Irving and his work for children: *John Gilpin* and *The House that Jack Built.*

Calder /'kɔːldə/ Alexander 1898–1976. American artist, born in Philadelphia, Pennsylvania. He studied as an engineer, but in 1923 turned to art and invented 'stabiles' in 1931, and in 1932 'mobiles', suspended sculptures, with their parts moved by air currents, with which his name is usually associated.

caldera in geology, a very large basin-shaped ◊crater. Calderas are found at the tops of volcanoes, where the original peak has collapsed into an empty chamber beneath. The basin, many times larger than the original volcanic vent, may be flooded, producing a crater lake, or the flat floor may contain a number of small volcanic cones, showing where the volcanic activity continued after the collapse. Typical calderas are Kilauea, Hawaii; Crater Lake, Oregon, USA; and the summit of Olympus Mons, on Mars; some calderas are wrongly referred to as craters, such as Ngorongoro, Tanzania.

Calderón de la Barca /ˌkældə'rɒn deɪ lɑː 'bɑːkə/ Pedro 1600–1681. Spanish dramatist and poet. Born in Madrid, he studied law at Salamanca (1613–19). In 1620 and 1622 he was successful in the poetical contests at Madrid; and while still writing dramas served in the army in Milan and the Netherlands (1625–35). By 1636 his first volume of plays was published and he had been made master of the revels at the court of Philip IV, receiving a knighthood in 1637. In 1640 he assisted in the suppression of the Catalan rebellion. After the death of his mistress he became a Franciscan in 1650, was ordained in 1651, and appointed to a prebend of Toledo in 1653. As honorary chaplain to the king in 1663, he produced outdoor religious plays for the festival of the Holy Eucharist. Most famous of some 118 plays are the tragedies *El pintor de su deshonra/The Painter of his own Dishonour* 1645, *El Alcalde de Zalamea/The Mayor of Zalamea* 1640, and *El Médico de su honra/The Surgeon of his Honour* 1635; the historical *El Principe constante/The Constant Prince* 1629; the dashing intrigue *La Dama duende/The Phantom Lady* 1629; the philosophical *La Vida es sueño/Life is a Dream* 1635. He died in poverty.

Caldey Island /'kɔːldi/ island off the coast of ◊Dyfed, Wales, near Tenby.

Caldwell /'kɔːldwel/ Erskine (Preston) 1903– . American novelist, born in Georgia. He worked among poor whites in the South as a journalist, cotton picker and stage assistant and achieved success with *Tobacco Road* 1932, and *God's Little Acre* 1933, earthy and vivid presentations of the poverty-stricken southern sharecroppers.

Caledonian Canal /ˌkælɪ'dəʊnɪən/ a waterway in north west Scotland, 98 km/61 mi long, linking the Atlantic and the North Sea. Of its 98 km/61 mi length only a 37 km/23 mi stretch is artificial, the rest being composed of lochs Lochy, Oich, and Ness. The canal was built by Thomas ◊Telford, 1803–23.

Calderón de la Barca Don Pedro Calderón de la Barca produced his first play at the age of 13. A prolific poet and dramatist, he combined raw emotion with detailed examinations of intellectual themes in over 100 plays.

calendar the divisions of the ◊year, and the method of ordering the years. The word comes from the Latin *kalendae* or *calendae*, the first day of each month on which solemn proclamation was made of the appearance of the new moon. All early calendars except the ancient Egyptian were lunar. The original *lunar month* (period between one new moon and the next) averages naturally 29.5 days, but the Western calendar uses for convenience a *calendar month* with a complete number of days, 30/31, except that Feb has 28. Since there are still slightly fewer than six extra hours a year left over, they are added to Feb as a 29th day every 4th (or 'leap') year. The English month names have the probable derivation: Jan from ◊Janus, Feb from *februar*, Roman festival of purification, Mar from ◊Mars, Apr from Latin *aperire* to open, May from Maia, a Roman goddess, Jun perhaps from ◊Juno, Jul from Julius ◊Caesar, Aug from ◊Augustus, Sept, Oct, Nov, Dec (originally the 7th–10th months, named from the Latin words meaning 7th, 8th, 9th, and 10th respectively. The days of the week are Monday (which in Britain officially replaced Sunday as the first day of the week 1971) named after the moon, Tuesday from Tiu/Tyr, Anglo-Saxon and Norse god of war, Wednesday from ◊Woden, Thursday from ◊Thor, Friday from ◊Freya, Saturday from ◊Saturn, and Sunday named after the sun. The *Western* calendar derives from that of Rome, as revised by Julius Caesar and Augustus in 46BC and adjusted in 1582 by Pope Gregory XIII, who eliminated the accumulated error, and avoided its recurrence by restricting century leap years (those with an extra day) to those divisible by 400. Other states only gradually changed from 'Old Style' to 'New Style'; Britain adopted it in 1751, when the error amounted to 11 days and 3 Sept 1752 became 14 Sept (at the same time the beginning of the year

was put back from 25 Mar to 1 Jan). Russia did not adopt it till the Oct Revolution of 1917, so that the event (25 Oct) is currently celebrated on 7 Nov. The assumed date of the birth of Christ is taken as a mark; events before that date being reckoned backwards from it (BC), and subsequent events forward from it (AD, Latin *anno domini*, in the year of the Lord). The *Jewish* calendar is a complex combination of lunar and solar cycles, varied by considerations of religious observance. A year may have 12 or 13 months, which normally alternate between 30 and 29 days; New Year (Rosh Hashanah) falls between 5 Sept and 5 Oct. Its beginning is dated from the Creation (taken as 7 Oct 3761BC). In *China* both the Western (from 1911) and the local calendar are in use; the latter is lunar, with a cycle of 60 years. The *Muslim* calendar is purely lunar, with 12 months of alternately 30 and 29 days, and a year of 354 days. This results in the calendar rotating round the seasons in a 30-year cycle, so that when the 9th month of Ramadan (when Muslims fast without eating or drinking in the day) occurs in summer, hardship is incurred. The era is counted as beginning on the day Muhammad fled from Mecca in 622AD.

Calgary /'kælgəri/ city in Alberta, Canada, on the Bow, in the foothills of the Rockies. At 1,048 m/3,440 ft it is one of the highest Canadian towns. Founded as Fort Calgary by the North West Mounted Police in 1875, it was reached by the Canadian Pacific Railway in 1885, and developed rapidly after the discovery of oil in 1914. Calgary is now the oil and financial centre of Alberta and West Canada, and its commercial centre, bounded on the north by the Bow, is known as the 'Golden Crescent'. It has oil-linked and agricultural industries, such as fertilizer factories and flour mills, and is also a tourist centre; the annual Calgary Exhibition and Stampede is held in Jul. The University of Calgary became independent of Alberta University in 1966. Population (1984) 619,814.

calibration preparing the scale of a measuring instrument for use. A mercury ◊thermometer, for example, can be calibrated with a Celsius scale by noting the heights of the mercury column at two standard temperatures – the freezing point (0°C) and boiling point of water (100°C) – and dividing up the distance between them into 100 equal parts and continuing these divisions above and below.

calico in the UK, a plain woven cotton material; in the USA, a printed cotton, the name derives from Calicut, India, an original source of India calicos.

California /,kælɪ'fɔːniə/ Pacific state of the USA; called the Golden State, originally because of its gold mines, but more recently because of its sunshine
area 411,013 sq km/158,693 sq mi
capital Sacramento
towns Los Angeles, San Diego, San Francisco
features Sierra Nevada (including Yosemite and Sequoia National Parks, Lake Tahoe and Mount Whitney, 4,418 m/14,494 ft, the highest mountain in the continental USA excluding Alaska); and the Coast Range; Death Valley 86 m/282 ft below sea level; Colorado and Mojave

deserts (Edwards Air Force base is in the latter); Monterey Peninsula; Salton Sea; offshore in the Pacific there are huge underwater volcanoes with tops 8 km/5 mi across; California Institute of Technology (Caltech); Lawrence Livermore Laboratory (named after Ernest ◊Lawrence), which shares nuclear weapons research with Los Alamos; Stanford University, which has both the Hoover Institute and the Reagan presidential library, and is the powerhouse of ◊Silicon Valley; Paul Getty art museum at Malibu, built in the style of a Roman villa.
products leading agricultural state with fruit (peaches, citrus, grapes), nuts (pistachios, almonds), wheat, vegetables, cotton, rice, all mostly grown by irrigation, the water being carried by immense concrete-lined canals to the Central Valley (valley of the San Joaquin and Sacramento rivers) and Imperial Valley; beef cattle; timber; fish; oil and natural gas; aerospace, electronics (see ◊Silicon Valley), food-processing; films and television programmes. There are also great reserves of energy (geothermal) in the hot water which lies beneath much of the state.
population (1980) 23,667,902, largest of the USA, 66% non-Hispanic white; 20% Hispanic; 7.5% Black; 7% Asian (including many Vietnamese)
famous people Bret Harte, W R Hearst, Jack London, Marilyn Monroe, Richard Nixon, William Saroyan, John Steinbeck
history colonized by Spain in 1769, it was ceded to the USA after the Mexican War of 1848, and became a state in 1850. Gold had been discovered in the Sierra Nevada in Jan 1848, and was followed by the gold rush 1849–56 (the 'Forty-niners'), using the California Trail overland and the California clippers (for example, *Flying Cloud*) by sea.

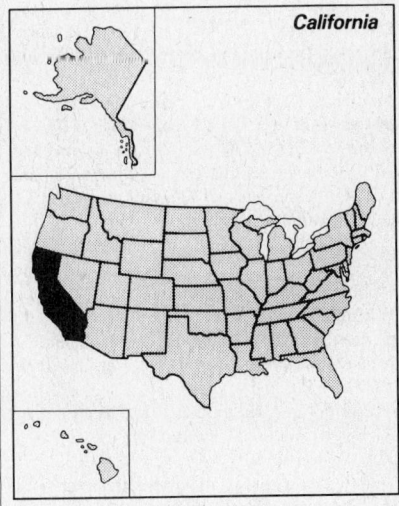

California

California, Lower /,kælɪ'fɔːniə/ English name for ◊Baja California.

California current the cold ocean ◊current in the East Pacific Ocean flowing southwards down the west coast of North America. It is part of the

North Pacific ◊gyre (a vast, circular movement of ocean water).

californium an artificially made element, atomic number 98. It is a radioactive metal produced in very small quantities and used in nuclear reactors as a neutron source. See also ◊transuranic elements.

Caligula /kə'lɪgjulə/ Gaius Caesar 12–41 AD. Roman emperor, son of Germanicus, and successor to Tiberius in 37 AD; a tyrant and alleged to be mad, he was assassinated by an officer of his guard.

calima dust cloud (Spanish 'haze') in Europe, coming from the Sahara Desert, which sometimes causes heatwaves and eye irritation.

caliph title adopted by Muhammad's successors as civic and religious heads of the world of Islam. The first Caliph was Abu ◊Bekr (d. 634). Nominally elective, the office became hereditary, being held by the Ummayyad dynasty 661–750, and then by the Abbasids. During the 10th century the political and military power passed to the leader of the Caliph's Turkish bodyguard; about the same time an independent Fatimite caliphate sprang up in Egypt. After the death of the last Abbasid (1258) the title was claimed by a number of Muslim chieftains in Egypt, Turkey, and India. The most powerful of these were the Turkish sultans of the Ottoman Empire, (the last was deposed by Kemal Atatürk in 1924)

calla another name for ◊arum lily.

Callaghan /'kæləhæn/ (Leonard) James 1912– . British Labour politician. As chancellor of the Exchequer 1964–67, he introduced corporation and capital gains tax and resigned in 1967 following devaluation. He was home secretary 1967–70, and as foreign secretary 1974 renegotiated Britain's EEC membership. In 1976 he succeeded Harold Wilson as prime minister in a period of increasing economic stress, and in 1977 entered into a pact with the Liberals to maintain his government in office. Strikes in the winter of 1978–79 led to his being the first prime minister since Ramsay MacDonald in 1924 to be forced into an election by the will of the Commons, and he was defeated at the polls in May 1979. In 1980 he resigned the party leadership under left-wing pressure, and in 1985 announced that he would not stand for parliament in the next election.

Callas /'kæləs/ Maria. Stage name of Maria Kalogeropoulou 1923–1977. American lyric soprano, born in New York of Greek parents. With a voice of fine range and a gift for dramatic expression, she excelled in operas including *Norma*, *Madame Butterfly*, *Aïda*, *Lucia di Lammermoor* and *Medea*.

Callicrates /kə'lɪkrəti:z/ 5th century BC. Athenian architect (with Ictinus) of the ◊Parthenon.

calligraphy the art of handwriting, regarded in China and Japan as the greatest of the visual arts, and playing a large part in Islamic art because the depiction of the human and animal form is forbidden owing to the risk of idolatry (see ◊Chinese, ◊Japanese, and ◊Islamic art). Modern letter forms have gradually evolved from originals which were shaped by the tools used to make them – the flat brush and chisel on stone, the stylus on wax and clay, and the reed and quill on papyrus and skin.

The principal formal hands used in early books were written in capital letters or majuscules. In the 4th and 5th centuries books were written in square capitals derived from classical Roman inscriptions. The cursive forms developed differently in different countries and in particular in Italy the beautiful italic script was evolved which became the model for italic type faces. Printing and the typewriter destroyed the art in the West until the 20th century revival by Edward Johnston 1872–1944.

Callimachus /kə'lɪməkəs/ 310–240 BC. Greek poet and critic known for his epigrams. Born in Cyrene, he taught in Alexandria where he was head of the great library.

Calliope /kə'laɪəpi/ in Greek mythology, the ◊Muse of epic poetry, and chief of the Muses.

callipers a measuring instrument used, for example, to measure the internal and external diameter of pipes. Some callipers are made like a pair of compasses, having two legs, often curved, pivoting about a screw at one end. The ends of the legs are placed in contact with the object to be measured. The gap between the ends is then measured against a rule. The slide calliper looks rather like an adjustable spanner. It carries a scale for direct measuring, usually with a ◊vernier scale for accuracy.

callipers

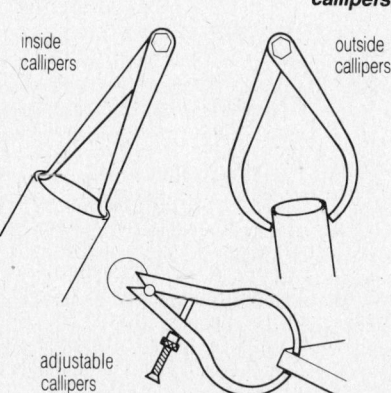

inside callipers

outside callipers

adjustable callipers

Callisto /kə'lɪstəʊ/ in Greek mythology, the ◊nymph beloved by Zeus (Jupiter).

Callisto /kə'lɪstəʊ/ in astronomy, second-largest moon of ◊Jupiter, 4,800 km/3,000 miles in diameter, orbiting every 16.7 days at a distance of 1.9 million km/1.2 million miles from the planet. Its surface is covered with large craters.

Callot /kæ'ləʊ/ Jacques 1592–1635. French engraver and painter. He engraved about 1,600 pieces, of which the best known are his *Miseries of War* 1632–33, prompted by the Thirty Years War, *Sieges, Fairs, Temptation of St. Anthony*, and *Conversion of St. Paul*.

callus in botany, a tissue that forms at a damaged plant surface. Composed of large, thin-walled ◊parenchyma cells, it grows over and around the wound, eventually covering the exposed area. In animals, a callus is a thickened pad of skin, formed where there is repeated rubbing against a hard surface. In humans, calluses often develop on the feet, and on the hands of those involved in heavy manual work.

Calmette /kæl'met/ Albert 1863–1933. French bacteriologist. A student of Pasteur, who developed (with Camille Guérin 1872–1961) the BCG vaccine against tuberculosis in 1921.

calomel mercurous chloride, Hg_2Cl_2, a white, heavy powder formerly used as a laxative, now used as a pesticide and fungicide.

calorie a unit of heat (that is, the quantity of heat required to raise the temperature of 1 gram of water by 1°C), which has now been replaced by the ◊joule, equivalent to 0.24 calories. In dietetics, a calorie (more accurately kilocalorie) is 1,000 of the units defined above. It measures the energy value of food in terms of its heat output. 28 grams/1 oz of protein yields 120 kilocalories, carbohydrate 110, fat 270, and alcohol 200.

calorimeter an instrument used in physics to measure heat. A simple calorimeter consists of a heavy copper vessel which is polished (to reduce heat losses by radiation) and lagged with insulating material (to reduce losses by convection and conduction). In a typical experiment – say to measure the heat capacity of a piece of metal – the calorimeter is filled with water, whose temperature rise is measured using a thermometer when a known mass of the heated metal is immersed in it. Chemists use a bomb calorimeter to measure the heat produced by burning a fuel completely in oxygen.

calotype a paper-based photograph using a wax paper negative, the first example of the ◊negative/positive process invented by Fox ◊Talbot around 1834.

Calpe /'kælpi/ former name of ◊Gibraltar.

Calvados departement in Bas-Normandie region of France, which has given its name to an apple brandy distilled from cider in Normandy.

Calvary /'kælvəri/ in the New Testament, the site (Aramaic *Golgotha* 'skull'), of Christ's crucifixion at Jerusalem. Two chief sites are suggested. One is where the Church of the Sepulchre now stands; the other, first suggested by General ◊Gordon, is the skull-like hill beyond the Damascus gate. The name Calvary is also applied to any monument commemorating the Crucifixion.

Calvin /'kælvɪn/ John 1509–1564. French-born Swiss church reformer and theologian. Born at Noyon, Picardy, he studied theology and then law, and about 1533 became prominent as an evangelical preacher. In 1534 he was obliged to leave Paris and retired to Basle, where he studied Hebrew and wrote his *Institutes of the Christian Religion*, published in 1536. In the same year he accepted an invitation to go to Geneva, Switzerland, and assist in the Reformation. In 1538 he was expelled because of public resentment at the many and too-drastic changes he introduced. At Strasbourg he married a widow, and devoted himself to translating the New Testament. In 1541 he returned to Geneva and established in the face of strong opposition a strict theocracy. In 1553 he had Servetus burnt for heresy. He supported the Huguenots in their struggle in France, and the English Protestants persecuted by Queen Mary

I His theological system is known as ◊Calvinism, and his Church government as ◊Presbyterian.

Calvin One of the leading reformers of the 16th century, John Calvin preached the doctrine of predestination which was central to his Protestant philosophy, known as Calvinism.

Calvin /'kælvɪn/ Melvin 1911– . American chemist who, using radioactive carbon-14 as a tracer, determined the biochemical processes of ◊photosynthesis, in which green plants use ◊chlorophyll to convert carbon dioxide and water into sugar and oxygen. He was awarded the 1961 Nobel Prize in chemistry for this work.

Calvinism Christian doctrine as interpreted by John ◊Calvin and adopted in Scotland, parts of Switzerland and Holland. Its central doctrine is predestination, under which certain souls (the elect) are predestined by God through the sacrifice of Christ to salvation, and the rest to damnation. Although Calvinism is rarely accepted today in its strictest interpretation, the 20th century has seen a Neo-Calvinist revival through the work of Karl ◊Barth.

Calypso /kə'lɪpsəʊ/ in Greek mythology, a sea ◊nymph who waylaid the homeward-bound Odysseus for seven years.

calypso /kə'lɪpsəʊ/ in music, a type of West Indian satirical ballad with a syncopated beat.

calyptra a layer of cells that encloses and protects the young sporophyte (spore capsule) in mosses and liverworts, forming a sheath-like hood around the capsule. Also used to describe the root cap, a layer of ◊parenchyma cells covering the end of a root that gives protection to the root tip as it grows through the soil. This is constantly being worn away and replaced by new cells from a special meristem, the calyptrogen.

calyx the collective term for the ◊sepals of a flower, forming the outermost whorl of the ◊perianth. It surrounds the other flower parts, and protects them while in bud. In some flowers, for example, the campions (*Silene*), the sepals are fused along their sides, forming a calyx-tube.

cam a part of a machine that transmits a regular movement to another part when it rotates. The most common type of cam, often called an *edge cam*, is to be found in a car engine. It takes the form of a rounded projection on a shaft, the camshaft. When the camshaft turns, the cams press against linkages (followers) that open the valves in the cylinders. A *face cam* is a disc with a groove in its face, in which the follower travels. A *cylindrical cam* carries angled parallel grooves which impart a to-and-fro motion to the follower when it rotates.

CAM (Computer Aided Manufacture) the use of computers to control production processes; in particular, the control of machine tools and ◊robots in factories. In some experimental factories, the whole design and production system has been automated by linking ◊CAD (computer-aided design) to CAM. Very flexible manufacturing with CAD/CAM can be utilized by computer-based sales and distribution methods to mass-produce semi-customized products.

Camagüey /ˌkæmə'gweɪ/ city in Cuba, capital of Camaguey province in the centre of the island, founded about 1514. It has a 17th century cathedral. Population (1981) 480,620.

Camargo /ˌkæmɑː'gəʊ/ Marie-Anne de Cupis de 1710–1770. French ballet dancer of Spanish descent. She was the first ballerina to adopt a shortened skirt, which allowed *danse en l'air*, and the first to obtain the ◊*entrechat quatre*.

Camargue /kæ'mɑːg/ the marshy area of the ◊Rhône delta, south of Arles, France: area about 780 sq km/300 sq mi. Bulls and horses are bred there, and the nature reserve, which is rich in bird life, forms the southern part.

cambium a layer of actively dividing cells (lateral ◊meristem), found within stems and roots, which gives rise to ◊secondary growth in perennial plants, causing an increase in girth. There are two main types of cambium: vascular cambium which gives rise to secondary xylem and phloem tissues, and the cork cambium or phellogen which gives rise to secondary cortex and cork tissues (see ◊bark).

Cambodia /kæm'bəʊdiə/ former name of ◊Kampuchea.

Cambrai /kɒm'breɪ/ chief town of Nord *département*, France, on the Escaut (Scheldt). Industries include light textiles (cambric is named after the town), and confectionery; population (1982) 36,618. The Peace of Cambrai or Ladies' Peace (1529) was concluded on behalf of Francis I of France by his mother Louise of Savoy and on behalf of Charles V by his aunt Margaret of Austria. Cambrai was severely damaged During World War I.

Cambrai, Battles of /kɒm'breɪ/ battles in World War I; in the *First Battle* Nov–Dec 1917 ◊Cambrai was almost captured by the British when large numbers of tanks were used for the first time; in the *Second* 26 Aug–5 Oct 1918 the town was taken during the final British offensive.

Cambrian the period of geological time between 570 and 500 million years ago. It is the first period of the ◊Palaeozoic era, and is characterized by the earliest appearance of fossils with hard shells, such as trilobites. The

name comes from Cambria, an old name for Wales, where Cambrian rocks are typically exposed.

Cambridge /'keɪmbrɪdʒ/ English city, the administrative headquarters of Cambridgeshire, on the river Cam (a river sometimes called by its earlier name, Granta), 82 km/51 mi north of London.

history as early as 100 BC, a Roman settlement grew up on a slight rise in the low-lying plain, commanding a ford over the river. Apart from those of ◊Cambridge University, notable buildings include St Benet's church, the oldest building in Cambridge; the round church of the Holy Sepulchre; and the Guildhall (1939). The Cambridge ◊science park, started by Trinity College in 1973, is the most successful in Europe. Industries include the manufacture of scientific instruments, radio and electronics, paper, flour milling, and fertilizers; population (1983) 100,500.

Cambridge /'keɪmbrɪdʒ/ city in Massachusetts, USA; population (1980) 95,322. Harvard University 1636 (the oldest educational institution in the USA, named after John Harvard 1607–38, who bequeathed it his library and half his estate), Massachusetts Institute of Technology 1861, and the John F Kennedy School of Government and Memorial Library are here, as well as a park named after him. Industries include paper and publishing.

Cambridgeshire /'keɪmbrɪdʒʃə/ county in East England,

area 3,409 sq km/1,316 sq mi

towns administrative headquarters Cambridge; Ely, Huntingdon, Peterborough

features rivers Ouse, Cam, and Nene, Isle of Ely; Cambridge University, RAF Molesworth, near Huntingdon, Britain's second ◊cruise missile base

products mainly agricultural

population (1987) 627,900

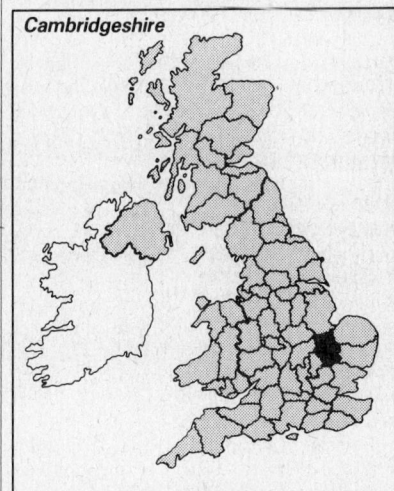

Cambridgeshire

Cambridge University one of the oldest of European universities, founded probably in the 12th century, though the earliest of the existing colleges, Peterhouse, was not founded until about

1284. The chancellor is the titular head, and the vice-chancellor the active head. The Regent House is the legislative and executive body, with the Senate as the court of appeal. Each college has its own corporation, and is largely independent. The head of each college (in the case of men's college usually called the master), assisted by a council of fellows, manages its affairs.

The most famous colleges of the university back on to the gardens and lawns through which the river Cam flows (known as the Backs) and are the chief architectural glory of the city of Cambridge. Among the most beautiful buildings is King's College Chapel, noted for its choir. Famous students of the university include: Rupert Brooke, S T Coleridge, Thomas Gray, Christopher Marlowe, John Milton, Samuel Pepys, and William Wordsworth. In 1987, there were 9,000 undergraduates and 3,000 graduates. The Cambridge ◊science park, started by Trinity College 1973, is the most successful in Europe.

Cambyses /kæm'baɪsiːz/ (reigned 529–522 BC.) Emperor of Persia. Succeeding his father Cyrus, he assassinated his brother Smerdis and conquered Egypt in 525. Here he outraged many of the native religious customs, and was said to have become mad. He died on his journey home in Syria by suicide or accident.

Camden /'kæmdən/ industrial city of New Jersey, USA, on the Delaware river, linked with Philadelphia, Pennsylvania, by the Benjamin Franklin suspension bridge (1926). The Walt ◊Whitman House, where the poet lived 1884–92, is now a museum; population (1980) 84,910.

Camden /'kæmdən/ inner borough of NW Greater London
features the ◊Camden Town Group of artists; includes the districts of
Bloomsbury with London University, Royal Academy of Dramatic Art (RADA), and the British Museum; and home between World War I and II of 'intellectual' writers and artists including Leonard and Virginia Woolf, and Lytton Strachey;
Fitzrovia W of Tottenham Court Road with the Telecom Tower and Fitzroy Square as its focus;
Hampstead, with Primrose Hill, Hampstead Heath, and nearby Kenwood House; Keats's home, now a museum; the churchyard where the painter ◊Constable is buried; and Hampstead Garden Suburb;
Highgate, with a cemetery which has the graves of George ◊Eliot, Michael ◊Faraday, and Karl ◊Marx;
Holborn, with the Inns of Court (Lincoln's Inn and Gray's Inn), Hatton Garden (diamond dealers), the London Silver Vaults;
Somers Town between Euston and King's Cross railway stations.
population (1981) 171,563.

Camden /'kæmdən/ William 1551–1623. English antiquary, author of topographical survey. Born in London. He published his *Britannia* in 1586, and was headmaster of Westminster School from 1593. The *Camden Society* (1838) commemorates his work.

Camden Town Group British art group 1911–13; based in Camden Town, London, it

included ◊Sickert, Duncan ◊Grant, Spencer Gore 1878–1914 and Harold Gilman 1876–1919. The group is usually said to be responsible for introducing ◊Post-Impressionism into English art.

camel large cud-chewing mammal of the even-toed hoofed order Artiodactyla. It differs from typical ruminants by having a three-chambered stomach, and by the two toes having broad soft soles for walking on sand, and hoofs resembling nails. Camels carry a food reserve of fatty tissue in the hump. They are also able to go without drinking for long periods, and can feed on salty vegetation. They are good at conserving body water and can withstand extremes of heat and cold. All these characteristics adapt them well to desert conditions. There are two species of camel. The *Arabian camel* (*Camelus dromedarius*) has a single hump and has long been domesticated, so that its original range is not known. It is used throughout Arabia and North Africa and has been taken to other places such as North America and Australia, in the latter country playing an important part in the development of the interior. The dromedary is strictly speaking, a lightly built fast riding variety of the Arabian camel, but often the name is applied to all one-humped camels. Arabian camels can be used as pack animals, for riding, racing, milk production and for meat. The *Bactrian camel* (*C. bactrianus*) is native to the central Asian deserts, where a small number still live wild, but most are domestic animals. With a head and body length of 3 m/10 ft and shoulder height of about 2 m/6 ft the Bactrian camel is a large animal, but not so long in the leg as the Arabian. It has a shaggy winter coat and has two fatty humps.

camellia oriental evergreen shrub of the family Theaceae, closely allied to the tea plant. Numerous species, such as *Camellia japonica* and *Camellia reticulata* have been introduced into Europe.

Camelot /'kæmələt/ legendary capital of King ◊Arthur. A possible site is the Iron Age hill fort of South Cadbury Castle, near Yeovil in Somerset, England, where excavations in 1967 have revealed relics dating from 3000 BC to AD 1100, including remains of a large 6th-century settlement.
Because of its combination of idealism and sophistication the name was also given to the 'court' of US president J F Kennedy 1960–63.

Camembert /'kæməmbeə/ village in Normandy, France, where Camembert cheese originated.

cameo small relief carving, usually on a semi-precious stone, popular in Rome, Greece, during the Renaissance, and in the Victorian era. They were used for decorating goblets, vases, and are worn as jewellery.

camera apparatus used in ◊photography or ◊cinema.

camera obscura a darkened box with a tiny hole for projecting the inverted image of the scene outside on a screen inside. For its development as a device for producing photographs, see ◊photography.

Cameron /'kæmərən/ Julia Margaret 1815–1879. British photographer. She made lively, revealing portraits of the Victorian intelligentsia using a large camera, five minute exposures and wet plates. Her sitters included Darwin and Tennyson.

Cameroon /,kæmə'ruːn/ country in W Africa, bounded northwest by Nigeria, northeast by Chad, east by the Central African Republic, south by Congo, Gabon, and Equatorial Guinea, and west by the Atlantic.
government Cameroon was a federal state until 1972 when a new constitution, revised in 1975, made it unitary. The constitution provides for a president and a single-chamber national assembly of 120, each elected for a five-year term. The president has the power to choose the cabinet, to lengthen or shorten the life of the assembly, and may stand for re-election. The only political party is the Democratic Assembly of the Cameroon People (RDPC), formed in 1966 by a merger of the governing party of each state of the original federation and the four opposition parties. The state president is also president of the party.
history first visited by Europeans in 1472, when the Portuguese began slave-trading in the area, in 1884 Cameroon became a German Protectorate. After World War I, France governed about 80 per cent of the area under a League of Nations mandate, with Britain administering the remainder. In 1946 both became UN trust territories.
In 1957 French Cameroons became a state within the French Community and three years later achieved full independence as the Republic of Cameroon. After a plebiscite in 1961, the northern part of British Cameroons merged with Nigeria, and the southern part joined the Republic of Cameroon to form the Federal Republic of Cameroon. The French zone became East Cameroon and the British part West Cameroon.
Ahmadou Ahidjo, who had been the first president of the republic in 1960, became president of the federal republic and was re-elected in 1965. In 1966 Cameroon was made a one-party state when the two government parties and most of the opposition parties merged into the Cameroon National Union (UNC). Extreme left-wing opposition to the UNC was crushed in 1971. In 1972 the federal system was abolished and in 1973 a new national assembly was elected. In 1982 Ahidjo resigned, nominating Paul Biya as his successor. In 1983 Biya began to remove Ahidjo's supporters and in protest Ahidjo resigned the presidency of UNC. Biya was re-elected in 1984 while Ahidjo went into exile in France. Biya strengthened his position by abolishing the post of prime minister and reshuffling his cabinet. He also changed the nation's name from the United Republic of Cameroon to the Republic of Cameroon. Many of Ahidjo's supporters were executed after a failed attempt to overthrow Biya. In 1985 UNC changed its name to RPDC and Biya tightened his control by more cabinet changes.
In Aug 1986 a volcanic vent under Lake Nyos released a vast quantity of carbon dioxide and

hydrogen sulphide, which suffocated large numbers of people and animals.

Cameroon
UNITED REPUBLIC OF (*République du Cameroun*)

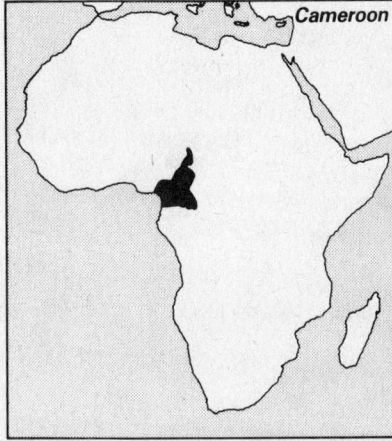

AREA 474,000 sq km/183,580 sq mi
CAPITAL Yaoundé
TOWNS chief port Douala
PHYSICAL desert in the far N in the Lake Chad basin, dry savanna plateau in the intermediate area, and in the S dense tropical rain forest
FEATURES Mount Cameroon 4,070 m/13,352 ft, an active volcano on the coast, W of the Adamawa Mountains
HEAD OF STATE AND OF GOVERNMENT Paul Biya from 1982
GOVERNMENT one-party republic
EXPORTS cocoa, coffee, bananas, cotton, timber, rubber, groundnuts; gold, aluminium
CURRENCY CFA franc (498.38 = £1 Sept 1987)
POPULATION 9,737,000 (1985); annual growth rate 2.7%
LANGUAGE French and English in pidgin variations (official), but there has been some discontent with the emphasis on French; there are 163 indigenous peoples with many African languages
RELIGION Roman Catholic 35%, animist 25%, Muslim 22%, Protestant 18%
LITERACY 62% male/36% female (1980 est)
GDP $7.3 bn (1984); $802 per head of population
CHRONOLOGY
1884 Under German rule.
1916 Captured by Allied forces in World War I.
1922 Divided between Britain and France.
1946 French and British Cameroons made UN trust territories.
1960 French Cameroon became the independent Republic of Cameroon.
Ahmadou Ahidjo elected president.
1961 N part of British Cameroon merged with Nigeria and S part joined the Republic of Cameroon to become the Federal Republic of Cameroon.
1966 A one-party regime was introduced.
1972 New constitution made Cameroon a unitary state, the United Republic of Cameroon.
1973 New national assembly elected.
1982 Ahidjo resigned and was succeeded by Paul Biya.
1983 Biya began to remove his predecessor's supporters and was accused by Ahidjo of trying to create a police state. Ahidjo went into exile in France.
1984 Biya re-elected and defeated a plot to overthrow him. Country's name changed to Republic of Cameroon.

Camoëns /'kæməuenz/ or *Camões*, Luís Vaz de 1524–1580. Portuguese poet. A soldier, he lost an eye fighting in North Africa, and, having wounded an equerry of the king in 1552, was banished to India. He went on various military expeditions, and was shipwrecked in 1558, but the manuscript of his poem, *Os Lusiades/The Lusiads*, was saved with him. It was published in 1572, telling the story of the explorer Vasco da Gama, and incorporating much Portuguese history, and is therefore the country's national epic. He received a small pension, but died in poverty of plague. His posthumously published lyric poetry is also now valued.

Camorra Italian secret society formed about 1820 by criminals in the dungeons of Naples, and continued once they were 'outside'. It dominated politics from 1848, was suppressed in 1911, but many members eventually surfaced in the US ◊Mafia. It still flourishes in the Naples area.

camouflage colours or structures that allow an animal to blend with its surroundings, so as to avoid detection by other animals. These may be animals that prey on it or, in the case of predators, those it preys upon. Camouflage can take the form of matching the background colour, of counter-shading (darker on top, lighter below, to counteract natural shadows) or of irregular patterns that break up the outline of the animal's body. More elaborate camouflage, as seen in many insects, involves closely resembling some feature of the natural environment. Such camouflage is closely akin to ◊mimicry. Some animals, such as chameleons, are able to change their colour to match that of the background.

Campagna Romana /kæm'pænjə rəu'mɑːnə/ lowland stretch of the Italian peninsula, including and surrounding the city of Rome. Lying between the Tyrrhenian Sea and the Sabine Hills to the NE, and the Alban Hills to the SE, it is drained by the lower course of the Tiber and a number of small streams, most of which dry up in the summer. Prosperous in Roman times, it later became virtually derelict through over-grazing, lack of water, and the arrival in the area of the malaria-carrying Anopheles mosquito. Extensive land reclamation and drainage in the 19th and 20th centuries restored its usefulness.

Campaign for Nuclear Disarmament (CND) nonpolitical British organization advocating the abolition of nuclear weapons worldwide: CND seeks unilateral British initiatives to help start the multilateral process and end the ◊arms race. It has held annual marches to Aldermaston, Berkshire (site of the government's Atomic Weapons Research Establishment) from its foundation 1958. From 1970 CND has also opposed nuclear power.

Campania /kæm'peɪnɪə/ region of southern Italy, including the volcano, ◊Vesuvius; capital Naples, industrial centres Benevento, Caserta and Salerno; population (1981) 5,463,825.

campanile bell-tower erected near, or attached to, churches or town halls in Italy. The leaning tower of Pisa is a famous example; another is the great campanile of Florence, 90 m/275 ft high.

Campbell /'kæmbəl/ Colin. See ◊Clyde, Colin Campbell, 1st Baron Clyde.

Campbell /'kæmbəl/ Donald Malcolm 1921–1966. British car and speedboat enthusiast, who simultaneously held the land speed and water speed records. He was invalided out of the RAF in World War II and took up the interests of his father, Malcolm ◊Campbell; in 1964 he set up the world water speed record of 444.7 kph/276.3 mph on Lake Dumbleyung, Australia, with the turbo-jet hydroplane *Bluebird*. He achieved the land speed record of 648.7 kph/403.1 mph at Lake Eyre salt flats, Australia, in a car of the same name on 17 Jul 1964. He was killed in an attempt to raise his water speed record on Coniston Water, England.

Campbell /'kæmbəl/ Malcolm 1885–1949. British speed record holder, including the world land speed record in 1935 with his *Bluebird* at 484.5 kph/301.1 mph and the water speed record with his boat of the same name in 1939 at 228.1 kph/141.74 mph.

Campbell /'kæmbəl/ Mrs Patrick 1865–1940. British actress, born Beatrice Stella Tanner, whose great roles included Paula in Pinero's *The Second Mrs Tanqueray* 1893, and Eliza in *Pygmalion*, specially written for her by Shaw, with whom she had a witty correspondence.

Campbell /'kæmbəl/ Roy 1901–1957. South African poet. Born at Durban, he became a professional jouster and bull-fighter in Spain and Provence, France. He fought for Franco in the Spanish Civil War, and was with the Commonwealth forces in World War II. He established his poetic reputation with the *The Flaming Terrapin* 1924.

Campbell-Bannerman /'kæmbəl 'bænəmən/ Henry 1836–1908. British Liberal politician, born in Glasgow. He was Liberal member of Parliament for Stirling, Scotland, from 1868, chief secretary for Ireland in 1884–85, war minister in 1886 and again in 1892–95, and leader of the Liberals in the House of Commons from 1899. In 1905 he became prime minister, and led the Liberals to an overwhelming electoral victory in 1906. He granted self-government to

Campbell Donald Campbell preparing for his fatal attempt at the water-speed record on 5th Jan 1967. His jet-boat *Bluebird* went out of control on Coniston Water, somersaulted 50 feet into the air, then crashed and sank.

the South African colonies, passed the Trades Disputes Act 1906, and began the conflict between Commons and Lords that led to the Parliament Act of 1911. He resigned in 1908 and died shortly afterwards.

Camp David /'kæmp 'deɪvɪd/ official country home of US presidents in the Appalachian mountains, Maryland, USA; it was originally named Shangri-la by F D Roosevelt; was renamed Camp David by Eisenhower (after his grandson), and was briefly known (for security reasons) as Camp Number Four after the Kennedy assassination. It is guarded by Marines, and consists of a series of lodges, Aspen Lodge being the presidential residence. (See also ▷Camp David Agreements.)

Camp David Agreements two framework agreements signed at ▷Camp David in 1978 by ▷Begin and ▷Sadat at the instance of Carter, covering an Egypt–Israel peace treaty and phased withdrawal of Egypt from Sinai, which was completed in 1982, and an overall Middle East settlement including the election by the Palestinians of the West Bank and Gaza Strip of a 'self-governing authority'. The latter remained unsettled in 1987.

camphor a volatile, aromatic ▷ketone substance ($C_{10}H_{16}O$) obtained from the camphor tree (*Cinnamonum camphora*), a member of the Lauraceae, native to South China, Taiwan and Japan. Camphor is distilled from chips of the wood of the root, trunk, and branches. It is used in insect repellents and in the manufacture of ▷celluloid.

campion /'kæmpɪən/ name given to several plants, belonging to the genera *Lychnis* and *Silene*, of the family Caryophyllaceae, for example the garden campion *Lychnis coronaria*, the wild white and red campions *Silene alba* and *Silene dioica*, and bladder campion *Silene vulgaris*.

Campion /'kæmpɪən/ Edmund 1540–1581. English Jesuit and Roman Catholic martyr. Born in London, he took deacon's orders in the English church, but fled to Douai, where in 1571 he recanted Protestantism. In 1573 he became a Jesuit in Rome, and in 1580 was sent to England as a missionary. He was betrayed as a spy in 1581, committed to the Tower, and hanged, drawn and quartered as a traitor. He was canonized in 1970.

Campion /'kæmpɪən/ Thomas 1567–1620. English poet and musician. He entered Gray's Inn in 1586 and later qualified as a doctor and practised in London. He was the author of the critical *Art of English Poesie* 1602, and four *Bookes of Ayres*, for which he composed both words and music.

Campobasso /ˌkæmpəʊ'bæsəʊ/ capital of Molise region, Italy, about 190 km/120 mi south east of Rome; it is noted for cutlery; population (1980) 40,000.

Campo-Formio, Treaty of /'kæmpəʊ 'fɔːmɪəʊ/ peace settlement in 1797 between Napoleon and Austria, by which France gained the region of modern Belgium and Austria was compensated with Venice, and part of modern Yugoslavia.

Cam Ranh /'kæm 'ræn/ port in South Vietnam. In the Vietnam War it was a US base, and is now a major staging complex for the Soviet Pacific fleet.

Camus /kæ'mjuː/ Albert 1913–1960. Algerian-born French writer, of Breton and Spanish parentage. A journalist in France, he was active in the Resistance during World War II. His novels include *L'Étranger/The Outsider* 1942, *La Peste/The Plague* 1948, and *L'Homme Révolté/The Rebel* 1952, a study of revolutionary ideals corrupted by murder and oppression, which ended his association with Sartre. Nobel prize winner in 1957.

Camus French novelist and dramatist Albert Camus, awarded the Nobel Prize for literature, 1957. He had a deprived childhood in Algeria, where much of his work is set. His respect for the individual set him against Communism and led to a fierce dispute with Sartre.

Canaan /'keɪnən/ an ancient region between the Mediterranean and the Dead Sea, in the Bible the 'Promised Land' of the Israelites. Occupied as early as the 3rd millennium BC by the Canaanites, a Semitic-speaking people who were known to the Greeks of the 1st millennium BC as Phoenicians.

The Canaanite Empire included Syria, Palestine, and part of Mesopotamia, and had its capital at Ebla, excavated 1976–77 in Tell Mardikh, Syria, where an archive of inscribed tablets includes place-names such as Gaza and Jerusalem (no excavations at the latter had suggested occupation at so early a date) and to Semitic personal names including Abraham, Ishmael, David, and Saul, though these cannot be identified individually with the heroes of the Old Testament.

Canada /'kænədə/ country occupying almost all of the North American continent, bounded to the south and west by the USA, to the north by the Arctic, to the east by the Atlantic Ocean, and to the southwest by the Pacific Ocean.

government the Canada Act of 1982 gave Canada power to amend its constitution and added a charter of rights and freeedoms. This represented Canada's complete independence, though it remains a member of the Commonwealth.

Canada is a federation of ten provinces, Alberta, British Columbia, Manitoba, New Brunswick, Newfoundland, Nova Scotia, Ontario, Prince Edward Island, Quebec, and Saskatchewan, and two territories, Northwest Territories and Yukon. Each province has a single-chamber assembly, popularly elected, and a prime minister appointed by a lieutenant-governor representing the Crown. The provincial prime minister, chosen on the basis of support in the assembly, chooses the cabinet. The two-chamber federal parliament consists of the senate, whose 104 members are appointed for life, or until the age of 75, and who must be resident in the provinces they represent, and the house of commons, which has 282 members, elected by universal suffrage.

The federal prime minister is chosen by the governor-general from the best-supported party in the house of commons and is accountable, with the cabinet, to it. Parliament has a maximum life of five years. Legislation must be passed by both chambers and signed by the governor-general.

history Canada was reached by an English expedition led by John Cabot in 1497 and a French expedition under Jacques Cartier in 1534. Both countries developed colonies from the 17th century, with hostility between them culminating in the ◊French and Indian Wars (1689–1763), in which France was defeated. Antagonism continued and in 1791 Canada was divided into English-speaking Upper and French-speaking Lower Canada (Ontario and Quebec). The two were united as Canada Province 1841–67, when the self-governing Dominion of Canada was founded.

The Progressive Conservatives returned to power in 1957, after 36 years of Liberal Party rule. In 1963 the Liberals were reinstated in office under Lester Pearson, until he was succeeded by Pierre Trudeau in 1968. Trudeau maintained Canada's defensive alliance with the US but sought to widen its world influence. Faced with the problem of Quebec's separatist movement he set about creating the 'just society'. His success was such that he won both the 1972 and 1974 elections.

In 1979, with no party having an overall majority in the commons, the Progressive Conservatives formed a government under Joe Clark. Later that year Trudeau announced his retirement from politics but when, in 1980, Clark was defeated on his budget proposals, Trudeau reconsidered his decision and won the general election with a large majority.

Trudeau's third administration was concerned with 'patriation', or the extent to which the British parliament should determine Canada's constitution. The position was resolved with the passing of the Canada Act 1982, the last piece of UK legislation to have force in Canada.

In 1983 Clark was replaced as leader of the Progressive Conservatives by Brian Mulroney, a businessman with no previous political experience, and in 1984 Trudeau retired to be replaced as Liberal leader and prime minister by John Turner, a former minister of finance. Within nine days of taking office, Turner called a general election and the Progressive Conservatives, under Mulroney, won 211 seats, the largest majority in Canadian history, with the Liberal Party and the New Democratic Party winning 40 and 30 seats respectively.

Soon after taking office, Mulroney began an international realignment, placing less emphasis on links established by Trudeau with Asia, Africa and Latin America, and more on cooperation with Europe and a closer relationship with the US. One outcome of this cooperation was discussion about greater freedom of trade between the two countries.

Canadian Prime Ministers
1867 John A Macdonald (*Conservative*)
1873 Alexander Mackenzie (*Liberal*)
1878 John A Macdonald (*Conservative*)
1891 John J Abbott (*Conservative*)
1892 John S D Thompson (*Conservative*)
1894 Mackenzie Bowell (*Conservative*)
1896 Charles Tupper (*Conservative*)
1896 Wilfred Laurier (*Liberal*)
1911 Robert L Bordern (*Conservative*)
1920 Arthur Meighen (*Conservative*)
1921 William Lyon Mackenzie King (*Liberal*)
1926 Arthur Meighen (*Conservative*)
1926 William Lyon Mackenzie King (*Liberal*)
1930 Richard Bedford Bennett (*Conservative*)
1935 William Lyon Mackenzie King (*Liberal*)
1948 Louis Stephen St Laurent (*Liberal*)
1957 John G Diefenbaker (*Conservative*)
1963 Lester Bowles Pearson (*Liberal*)
1968 Pierre Elliot Trudeau (*Liberal*)
1979 Joseph Clark (*Progressive Conservative*)
1980 Pierre Elliot Trudeau (*Liberal*)
1984 John Turner (*Liberal*)
1984 Brian Mulroney (*Progressive Conservative*)

Canadian literature Canadian literature in English began early in the 19th century in the Maritime Provinces with the humorous tales of T C Haliburton (1796–1865). The later 19th century brought the lyrical output of Charles G D Roberts (1860–1943), Bliss Carman (1861–1929), Archibald Lampman (1861–99), and Duncan Campbell Scott (1862–1944).

Realism in fiction developed with Frederick P Grove (1871–1948), Mazo de la Roche (1885–1961), creator of the 'Jalna' series, and Hugh MacLennan (1907–). Humour of worldwide appeal emerged in Stephen Leacock (1869–1944), Brian Moore (1921–), author of *The Luck of Ginger Coffey* (1960), and Mordecai ◊Richler. Also popular outside Canada was Lucy Montgomery (1874–1942), whose *Anne of Green Gables* 1908, became a children's classic. Saul Bellow and Marshall McLuhan were both Canadian-born, and contemporary novelists include Robertson ◊Davies and Margaret ◊Atwood.

See also ◊French Canadian literature.

canal artificial waterway constructed for drainage, irrigation, or navigation.

Irrigation Canals carry water for ◊irrigation from rivers, reservoirs, or wells, and are carefully designed to maintain an even flow of water over the whole length. Irrigation canals fed from the Nile have maintained life in Egypt since the earliest times; the division of the waters of the Upper Indus and its tributaries for the extensive system in Pakistan and Punjab, India, was for more than ten years a major cause of dispute between India and Pakistan, settled by a treaty in 1960; the Murray basin, Victoria, Australia, and of the Great Valley of California, USA, are examples of 19th and 20th century irrigation canal development.

Navigation and Ship Canals constructed at one level between ◊locks, canals frequently link with other forms of waterway – natural rivers, modified river channels, and sea links – to form a waterway system. The world's two major international ship canals are the ◊Suez canal and the ◊Panama canal which provide invaluable short cuts for shipping respectively between Europe and the East and between the east and west coasts of the Americas. Probably the oldest to be still in use is the Grand Canal waterway in China, which links Tianjin and Hangzhou, and interconnects the Huang He (Yellow River) and Chang Jiang. It was originally built in three stages 485 BC–AD 283, reaching a total length of 1,780 km/1,107 mi. Large sections silted up in later years, but the entire system was dredged, widened and rebuilt 1958–72 in combination with work on flood protection, irrigation and hydroelectric schemes.

The first major British canal was the Manchester-Bridgewater Canal 1761–76, constructed for the 3rd Duke of Bridgewater to carry coal from his collieries to Manchester. The engineer, ◊Brindley, overcame great difficulties in the route. Today many of Britain's canals form part of an inter-connecting system of waterways some 4,000 km/2,500 mi long. Many which have become disused commercially have been restored for recreation and the use of pleasure craft.

The economy of energy for transporting in such a means of goods transport, where speed is not a prime factor, has encouraged a modern revival and Belgium, France, Germany, and the USSR are among countries which have extended and modernized their canal facilities. Baltic-White Sea (USSR 1933), the Baltic–Volga Waterway begun in the USSR in 1964 will link the northern port of Klaipeda with Kahovka, at the mouth of the Dnieper on the Black Sea, a distance of 2,430 km/1,510 mi. A further canal cuts across the north Crimea, thus shortening the onward voyage of ships from the Dnieper through the Black Sea to the Sea of Azov. See also ◊Rhine. In North America, the great modern example is the St Lawrence Seaway and the Great Lakes Waterway in which the St Lawrence Seaway 1954–59 extends from Montreal to Lake Ontario (290 km/180 mi) and, with the deepening of the Welland Canal and some of the river channels, provides a waterway that enables ocean-going vessels to travel during the ice-free months between the Atlantic and Duluth, Minnesota, USA, at the western end of Lake Superior.

Canaletto /ˌkænəˈletəʊ/ Antonio 1697–1768. Nickname of Venetian painter Giovanni Antonio Canale. He painted many scenes of Venice; his works are particularly notable for their handling of perspective and control of colour.

Canada
DOMINION OF

AREA 9,975,223 sq km/3,851,809 sq mi
CAPITAL Ottawa
TOWNS Toronto, Montreal, Vancouver, Winnipeg, Edmonton, Quebec, Hamilton, Calgary
PHYSICAL St Lawrence Seaway, Mackenzie river; Great Lakes; Arctic Archipelago; Rocky Mountains; Great Plains or Prairies; Canadian Shield
TERRITORIES Arctic sector N of mainland
HEAD OF STATE(F14) ELIZABETH II FROM 1952
REPRESENTED BY JEANNE SAUVE£1
(F14)HEAD OF GOVERNMENT Brian Mulroney from 1984
GOVERNMENT parliamentary democracy
EXPORTS wheat; timber, pulp and newsprint; fish, especially salmon; furs (ranched fox and mink exceed the value of wild furs); oil and natural gas; aluminium, asbestos, coal, copper, iron, nickel; motor vehicles and parts, industrial and agricultural machinery, fertilizers
CURRENCY Canadian dollar (2.17 = £1 Sept 1987)
POPULATION (1985) 25,399,000 (including 300,000 American Indians, of whom 75% live on over 2,000 reserves in Ontario and the four W provinces; some 300,000 Métis (people of mixed race) and 19,000 Inuit (or Eskimo), of whom 75% live in the NW Territories). Over half Canada's population lives in Ontario and Quebec. Annual growth rate 1.1%
LANGUAGE English, French (both official) (about 70% speak English, 20% French, and the rest are bilingual); there are also N American Indian languages and the Inuit Inuktitut
RELIGION Roman Catholic 40%, Protestant 35%

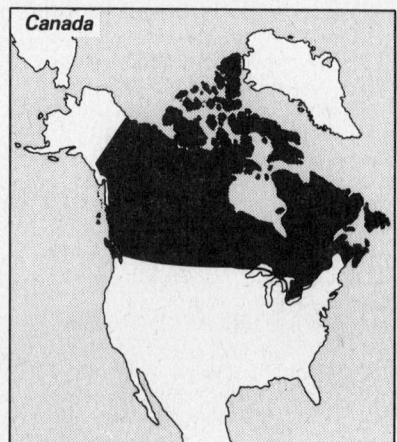

Canada

LITERACY 99%
GDP $317 bn (1984); $13,000 per head of population
CHRONOLOGY
1957 Progressive Conservatives returned to power after 36 years in opposition.
1963 Liberals elected under Lester Pearson.
1968 Pearson suceeded by Pierre Trudeau.
1979 Joe Clark, leader of the Progressive Conservatives, formed a minority government.
1980 Clark defeated on budget proposals. Liberals under Trudeau returned with a large majority.
1982 Canada Act removed Britain's last legal control over Canadian affairs.
1983 Clark replaced as leader of the Progressive Conservatives by Brian Mulroney.
1984 Trudeau retired and was succeeded as Liberal leader and prime minister by John Turner. Progressive Conservatives won the general election and Brian Mulroney became prime minister.

CANADA: PROVINCES

Province (Capital)	Area sq km
Alberta *(Edmonton)*	661,187
British Columbia *(Victoria)*	948,599
Manitoba *(Winnipeg)*	650,088
New Brunswick *(Fredericton)*	73,437
Newfoundland *(St John's)*	404,517
Nova Scotia *(Halifax)*	54,558
Ontario *(Toronto)*	1,068,587
Prince Edward Island *(Charlottetown)*	5,657
Québec *(Québec)*	1,540,676
Saskatchewan *(Regina)*	651,901
Territories	
Northwest Territories *(Yellowknife)*	3,379,689
Yukon Territory *(Whitehorse)*	536,327
	9,975,223

Canaries current the cold ocean current in the North Atlantic Ocean flowing south west from Spain along the north west coast of Africa. It meets the northern equatorial current at a latitute of 20° N.

canary bird *Serinus canaria* of the finch family found wild in the Canary Islands and Madeira. The wild bird is greenish with a yellower underside, but canaries have been bred as cage-birds in Europe since the 15th century, and many domestic varieties are yellow or orange. The canary is bred mainly for its song, but some are used in mines as detectors of bad air.

Canary Islands /kəˈneəri/ group of volcanic islands 100 km/60 mi off the north west coast of Africa, which forms an autonomous region of Spain.
area 7273 sq km/2808 sq mi
population (1981) 1,444,626
features tThe chief centres are Santa Cruz on Tenerife (which also has the highest peak in extra-continental Spain, Pico de Teyde 3713 m/12,182 ft), and Las Palmas on Gran Canaria. The province of Santa Cruz comprises Tenerife, Palma, Gomera and Hierro, and the province of Las Palmas comprises Gran Canaria, Lanzarote, and Fuerteventura. There are also six uninhabited islets. The Northern Hemisphere Observatory (1981) is on the island of La Palma, the first in the world to be remotely controlled. Observation conditions are among the best in the world, since there is no moisture, no artificial light pollution, and little natural ◊airglow. The Organization of African Unity (OAU) supports an independent Guanch Republic (so-called from the indigenous islanders, a branch of the North African Berbers) and revival of the Guanch language.

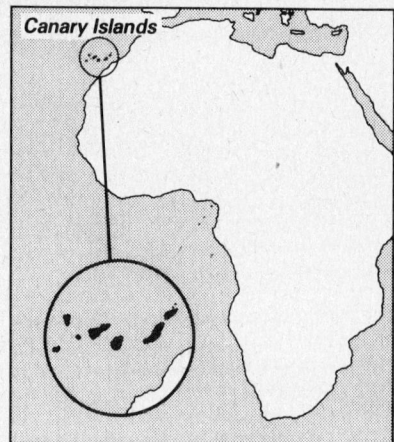

Canary Islands

Canberra /ˈkænbərə/ capital of Australia, situated in the Australian Capital Territory enclosed within New South Wales, on a tributary of the Murrumbidgee; it was selected as capital in 1908. Population (1981) 238,387. It contains the Parliament House, first used by the Commonwealth Parliament in 1927, the Australian National University (1946), the Canberra School of Music (1965), and the National War Memorial. Area (Australian Capital Territory including the port at Jervis Bay) 2,432 sq km/939 sq mi.

cancan /ˈkænkæn/ high-kicking stage dance for women (solo or line of dancers) originating in Paris about 1830, which came to symbolize Parisian naughtiness. The music usually associated with the cancan is the *galop* from Offenbach's *Orpheus in the Underworld*.

cancer group of diseases resulting in malignant growths or tumours classified as carcinomas, growing from the skin or mucous membrane, and sarcomas, which affect bone, cartilage, and muscle (connective tissue), also including leukaemia (a 'cancer' of the blood).
Production of cancer cells may be triggered by the activation of genes which are present in normal cells, but which are either dormant or make themselves known at very low levels. Such cells then grow and divide without restriction, forming 'lumps' and sometimes spreading to other parts of the body (metastasizing).

CANALS AND WATERWAYS

Name	Country	Opened	Length km	mi
Amsterdam	Netherlands	1876	26.6	16.5
Baltic-Volga	USSR	1964-	2,430	1,510
Baltic-White Sea	USSR	1933	235	146
Corinth	Greece	1893	6.4	4
Elbe and Trave	Germany	1900	66	41
Göta	Sweden	1832	185	115
Grand Canal	China	485BC–AD1972	1,050	650
Kiel	West Germany	1895	98	61
Manchester	England	1894	57	35.5
Panama	Panama	1914	81	50.5
Princess Juliana	Netherlands	1935	32	20
St Lawrence	Canada	1959	3,770	2,342
Saulte Ste Marie	USA	1855	2.6	1.6
Saulte Ste Marie	Canada	1895	1.8	1.1
Welland	Canada	1929	45	28
Suez	Egypt	1869	166	103

Triggering agents include chemical carcinogens, for example asbestos dust, benzpyrene, household chemicals, cigarette-smoking; viruses; radiation, for example X-rays; and possibly psychological stress. Many experts believe that avoiding such factors would avert more than half of cancers. *Treatment* of cancer includes surgery, radiotherapy, and chemotherapy using cytotoxic drugs which slow or halt cell division. Cancer cells are immortal, so that tumour cells can be grown for ever in culture.

The most common cancer sites in men:
1. Lung
2. Prostate
3. Large intestine
4. Urinary tract
5. Blood (leukaemias) and lymph (lymphomas)

The most common cancer sites in women:
1. Breast
2. Large intestine
3. Uterus
4. Lung
5. Blood (leukaemias) and lymph (lymphomas).

Cancer constellation of the ◊zodiac representing a crab, through which the Sun passes during late July and early August. It is the faintest of the zodiacal constellations and its main feature is the star cluster Praesepe, popularly known as the Beehive.

Cancún /kæn'kuːn/ Caribbean resort in Mexico, site in 1981 of a north-south summit to discuss the widening gap between the developed countries and the Third World.

candela /kæn'deɪlə/ the ◊SI unit of luminous intensity (cd). Defined as the intensity in a perpendicular direction of a surface of 1/6,000,000 m² of a black body at the temperature of freezing platinum, under a pressure of 101,325 pascals. Formerly called the candle or standard candle.

Candia /'kændiə/ Italian name for the Greek island of ◊Crete, also formerly the name of the largest city, ◊Iraklion, founded about 824. It has many Venetian remains.

candle means of producing light consisting typically of a vertical cylinder of wax (such as tallow or paraffin wax) with a central wick of string. A flame applied to the end of the wick melts the wax, and it is the burning wax that produces a luminous flame. The wick is treated with a substance such as alum so that it carbonizes but does not rapidly burn out. Formerly candles and oil lamps were the chief form of artificial lighting. Accurately made candles – which burned at a steady rate – were calibrated along their length and used as a type of clock. The candle was also the name of a unit of luminous intensity, now replaced by the candela (Cd), equal to 1/60 of the luminance of 1 cm2 of a black body radiator at a temperature of 2042K.

Candlemas in the Christian Church, the feast of the Purification of the Blessed Virgin Mary, and the Presentation of the Infant Christ in the Temple, celebrated on 2 Feb.

cane name applied to the reed-like stem of various plants such as the sugar-cane and bamboo, but more particularly to the group of palms called rattans, consisting of the genus *Calamus* and its allies; their slender stems are dried and used for making walking sticks, baskets, and furniture.

Canea /'kɑːniə/ (Greek *Khania*) capital and principal port of Crete, roughly midway along the north coast. It was founded in 1252 by the Venetians, and is still surrounded by a wall. Vegetable oils, soap, and leather are exported. Heavy fighting took place here during World War II, after the landing of German parachutists in May 1941. Population (1981) 47,338.

Canes Venatici constellation of the northern hemisphere, representing the hunting dogs of ◊Bootes, the herdsman. Its stars are faint, but it contains the celebrated spiral galaxy M51, known popularly as the Whirlpool on account of its shape.

Canetti /kə'neti/ Elias 1905– . Bulgarian-born writer. He was exiled from Austria as a Jew in 1938, and settled in England in 1939. His books, written in German, include the novel *Auto*

da Fé/Die Blendung; and an autobiography. Concerned with crowd behaviour and the psychology of power, he received a Nobel prize in 1981.

Canetti The first Bulgarian to win the Nobel Prize for literature was Elias Canetti in 1981. The award recognized his masterful writings on the psychology of power.

Canis Major brilliant ◊constellation of the southern hemisphere representing one of the two dogs following at the heel of ◊Orion. Its main star is ◊Sirius the 'dog star' and the brightest star in the sky.

Canis Minor small ◊constellation of the equatorial region, representing the second of the two dogs of ◊Orion (the other dog is represented by ◊Canis Major). Its brightest star is ◊Procyon.

cannabis tall annual herb, *Cannabis sativa*, family Urticaceae, originally Asian. Some strains are cultivated for fibre, birdseed, and oil; others for the dried leaf female flowers, and resin, known as bhang (India), dagga (South Africa), hashish (Arabia), kif (North Africa), and pot or marijuana, which are hallucinogens when smoked or eaten and have an intoxicating and stimulating effect. Cannabis is a 'soft' drug in that any dependence is psychological rather than physical. It has medicinal use in countering depression and the side effects of cancer therapy (pain and nausea). Its cultivation is illegal in the UK and USA except under licence.

Cannae /'kæniː/ village in Apulia, Italy, site of Hannibal's defeat of the Romans in 216 BC.

Cannes /kæn/ resort in Alpes-Maritimes *département*, southern France; population (1980) 72,787. The world's most important film festival is held here annually. Formerly only a small seaport, in 1834 it attracted the patronage of Lord ◊Brougham (who died here) and other distinguished visitors, and became a fashionable and popular holiday resort. A new town (La Bocca) grew up facing the Mediterranean.

cannibalism the practice of eating human flesh, also called anthropophagy. The name is derived from the Caribs, a South American and West Indian people, alleged by the conquering Spaniards to eat their captives.

Canning /'kænɪŋ/ Charles John, 1st Earl 1812–62. British administrator, son of George ◊Canning. As governor-general of India from 1856, he suppressed the Indian Mutiny with an unvindictive firmness which earned him the nickname 'Clemency Canning', and was the first viceroy of India from 1858.

canning /'kænɪŋ/ food preservation in hermetically sealed containers by the application of heat. Originated by Nicolas Appert in France in 1809 with glass containers, it was developed by Peter Durand in England in 1810 with tin cans, which are actually made of sheet steel with a thin coating of tin to postpone corrosion.

Canning /'kænɪŋ/ George 1770–1827. British Tory politician. He entered Parliament in 1793. His verse, satires, and parodies for the *Anti-Jacobin* 1797–98 led to his advancement by Pitt. As foreign secretary 1807–10, he was largely responsible during the Napoleonic Wars for the seizure of the Danish fleet and British intervention in the Spanish peninsula, but his disapproval of the ◊Walcheren expedition involved him in a duel with ◊Castlereagh and led to his resignation. He was president of the Board of Control (1816–20). On Castlereagh's death in 1822, he again became foreign secretary, supported the national movements in Greece and South America, and was made prime minister in 1827. When Wellington, Peel, and other Tories refused to serve under him, he formed a coalition with the Whigs. He died in office.

Cannizzaro /ˌkæni'zɑːrəʊ/ Stanislao 1826–1910. Italian chemist who revived interest in the work of ◊Avogadro (1811) which had revealed the difference between ◊atoms and ◊molecules, and so established atomic and molecular weights as the basis of chemical calculations. Cannizzaro also worked in aromatic organic chemistry, and a reaction he discovered in 1853 for making benzyl alcohol and benzoic acid from benzaldehyde is named after him.

Cano /'kɑːnəʊ/ Juan Sebastian del c. 1476–1526. Spanish voyager. It is claimed that he was the first person to sail round the world. He sailed with a Magellan, the explorer, in 1519, and after the latter's death in the Philippines, brought the *Victoria* safe home to Spain.

canoeing sport of propelling a lightweight, shallow boat, pointed at both ends, by paddles or sails. The construction of early canoes varied from the hollowed tree-trunk of African tribes to the framework covered with bark or skin used by the American Indians, the latter design being the basis of modern plastic and fibre-glass versions. Canoeing became a sport in the 19th century and the Royal Canoe Club in Britain was founded 1866. Two types of canoe are used, the *kayak* derived from the Eskimo model, has a keel and the canoeist sits, and the *Canadian style canoe*, which has no keel and the canoeist kneels. In addition to straightforward racing, there are slalom courses, with up to 30 'gates' to be negotiated through rapids and round artificial rock formations. Penalty seconds are added to

Canning A bust in the National Portrait Gallery, London, of George Canning, the British politician. His advancement came through his writing ability, much appreciated by the then prime minister William Pitt. Canning was himself twice foreign secretary, and prime minister for a short time. He died in office.

course time for touching suspended gate poles or missing a gate. One to four canoeists are carried.

canon a type of priest in the Roman Catholic and Anglican churches. Originally, in the Catholic Church, a canon was a clergyman holding a prebend in a cathedral or collegiate church. Canons lived within its precinct, and their lives were ordered by ecclesiastical rules (termed ◊canon law). About the 11th century a distinction was drawn between *regular* or Augustinian canons who observed the rules, and *secular* canons who lived outside the precinct, and were in effect the administrative officers of a cathedral, but in holy orders. Following the Reformation, all canons in England became secular canons. Canons, headed by the dean, are the resident ecclesiastical dignitaries attached to a cathedral and constitute the chapter.

canon in theology, the collection or list of books of the ◊Bible that are accepted by the Christian Church as divinely inspired and authoritative, that is, the Old and New Testaments. The canon of the Old Testament was drawn up at the assembly of Rabbis held at Jamnia in Palestine between AD 90 and 100; certain excluded books were included in the ◊Apocrypha. The earliest list of New Testament books is known as the Muratorian Canon (c. AD 160–70). ◊Athanasius promulgated c. 365 a list which corresponds with that in modern Bibles.

canon in music, a form for a number of 'voices' or parts in which each enters successively, at fixed time intervals, in exact imitation of each other. The parts may then end together or continue their repetition as in a round.

canonical hours in the Catholic Church, set periods of devotion: matins and lauds, prime, terce, sext, nones, evensong or vespers, compline. In the Anglican Church, the period 8 am–6 pm within which marriage can be legally performed in a parish church, without a special licence.

canonization in the Catholic Church, the admission of one of its members to the Calendar of ◊Saints. Under a system laid down mainly in the 17th century, the process of investigation was seldom completed in under 50 years, although in the case of a martyr it took less time. However, since 1969 the gathering of the proof of the candidate's virtues has been left to the bishop of the birthplace, and, miracles being difficult to substantiate, stress is placed on extraordinary 'favours' or 'graces' that can be proved or attested by serious investigation. The findings are contested before the Congregation for the Causes of Saints by the Promotor Fidei, popularly known as the devil's advocate. Papal ratification of a favourable verdict results in 'beatification' (the candidate can be venerated in the neighbourhood), and full sainthood (conferred in the Vatican basilica) follows after proof of further 'favours'. Many modern saints have come from the Third World where the expansion of the Catholic Church is most rapid, for example the American Mohawk Indian Kateri Tekakwitha (died 1680), beatified in 1980. In the revised Calendar of Saints (1970) only 58 saints were recognized as of worldwide importance, and some, such as Christopher and Valentine, were removed as probably non-existent.

canon law the rules and regulations of the Christian Church, especially the Greek Orthodox, Roman Catholic, and Anglican churches. Its origin is sought in the declarations of Christ and the Apostles, and it has been extended under the guidance of the papacy. The earliest compilations were in the East, and the Canon Law of the Eastern Orthodox Church is comparatively small. Through the centuries, a great mass of Canon Law was accumulated in the Western Church, which in 1918 was condensed in the *Corpus juris canonici* under Benedict XV. Even so, however, this is supplemented by many papal decrees. The Canon Law of the Anglican Church remained almost unchanged from 1603 until it was completely revised in 1969, and is kept under constant review by the Canon Law Commission of the General Synod. In 1983 Pope John Paul II issued a new canon law code reducing offences carrying automatic excommunication, extending the grounds for annulment of marriage, removing the ban on marriage with non-Catholics, and banning trade union and political activity by priests.

Canopus second-brightest ◊star in the sky, magnitude – 0.7. It lies in the constellation ◊Carina. Canopus is a yellow-white supergiant about 300 light years away, thousands of times more luminous than our own Sun.

Canossa /kə'nɒsə/ ruined castle 19 km/12 mi south west of Reggio, Italy. Emperor ◊Henry IV did penance here before Pope Gregory VII in 1077 for having opposed him in the question of investitures.

Canova /kə'nəʊvə/ Antonio 1757–1822. Italian ◊Neoclassical sculptor, born near Treviso. He exalted Napoleon and members of his family in several classicizing portraits. He also executed the tombs of Popes Clement XIII, Pius VII, and Clement XIV, but is best remembered for his marble sculptures *Cupid and Psyche* in the Louvre, and *The Three Graces* at the Hermitage, Leningrad.

Cantabria /kæn'tæbriə/ autonomous region of northern Spain (including ◊Santander and ◊Altamira); population (1981) 511,000.

Cantabrian Mountains /kæn'tæbriən/ mountains running along the north coast of Spain, reaching 2,400 m/8,000 ft in height, and containing coal and iron.

Cantal /kɒn'tɑːl/ volcanic mountain range in central France, which gives its name to Cantal *département*. The highest point is the Plomb du Cantal, 1,858 m/6,096 ft.

cantaloupe name of several small varieties of the melon *Cucumis melo*, distinguished by their small and round ribbed fruits.

cantata in music, an extended work for voices, from Italian, meaning 'sung', as opposed to ◊sonata ('sounded') for instruments. A cantata can be sacred or secular, sometimes with solo voices, and usually with orchestral accompaniment.

Canterbury /'kæntəbəri/ city in Kent, England, on the Stour, 100 km/62m south east of London; population (1984) 39,000.
history the Roman Durovernum, it was the Saxon capital of Kent. The modern name derives from *Cantwarabyrig* (Old English fortress of the men of Kent). In 597 King ◊Ethelbert welcomed Augustine's mission to England here, and the city has since been the metropolis of the Anglican Communion and seat of the Archbishop of ◊Canterbury. The foundations of the present cathedral were laid by ◊Lanfranc, Archbishop 1070–89, but subsequent additions range from Norman to Perpendicular. In the Middle Ages it was a centre of pilgrimage to the tomb of St Thomas à Becket, murdered in the cathedral in 1170, but the shrine was destroyed by Henry VIII. The Black Prince and Henry IV are buried there. The city has links with Geoffrey ◊Chaucer, Christopher ◊Marlowe, and Somerset ◊Maugham, who was educated at the King's School (refounded by Henry VIII in 1541) on the site of the Benedictine Abbey of St Augustine, of which only fragments remain. The first college of the University of Kent, established in 1965, was named after T S Eliot.

Canterbury, archbishop of /'kæntəbəri/ primate of all England, metropolitan of the Church of England, and first peer of the realm, ranking next to royalty. He crowns the sovereign, has a seat in the House of Lords, and is a member of the Privy Council. He appoints many livings, and Lambeth degrees in divinity, law and medicine. His seat is Lambeth Palace, with a second residence at the Old Palace, Canterbury. He is appointed by the prime minister, formerly by political consultation, but from 1980 on the suggestion of the church group, the Crown Appointments Commission (formed 1977). The first holder of the office was ◊Augustine; his 20th-century successors have been: Randal T Davidson 1903, C G Lang 1928, William Temple 1942, G F Fisher 1945, A M Ramsey 1961, D Coggan 1974, and R A A Runcie 1980.

Canterbury Plains /'kæntəbəri/ area of rich grassland between the mountains and the sea on the east coast of South Island, New Zealand, source of Canterbury lamb. Area 10,000 sq km/4,000 sq mi.

Canterbury Plain Merino sheep on a station in New Zealand's Canterbury Plains, an area noted for its lamb.

cantilever a beam or structure that is fixed at one end only, though it may be supported part way along its length. A diving board is a common example of a simple cantilever. The cantilever principle is widely used in construction engineering. Eliminating the need for a second main support at the free end of the beam allows for more elegant structures and reduces the amount of materials required. Many large-span ◊bridges have been built on the cantilever principle. A typical cantilever bridge consists of two beams cantilevered out from either bank, each supported part way along, with their free ends meeting in the middle. Most notable of the world's cantilever bridges is the multiple-cantilever Forth Rail Bridge (completed 1890) across the Firth of Forth in Scotland. It has twin main spans of 521 m/1,710 ft. See also ◊bridge.

canton /ˌkæn'tɒn/ in France, an administrative district, a subdivision of the *arrondissement*; in Switzerland, one of the 23 subdivisions forming the Confederation.

Canton /ˌkæn'tɒn/ former name of Kwangchow or ◊Guangzhou in China.

Canton and Enderbury /'kæntən, 'endəbəri/ two atolls in the Phoenix group which forms part of the Republic of ◊Kiribati. They were a UK–USA condominium 1939–80, and there are US aviation, radar and tracking stations.

Canute /kə'njuːt/ c. 995–1035. King of England, Denmark, and Norway. Son of Sweyn, king of Denmark. Accompanying his father on his invasion of England in 1013 (see ◊Vikings), Canute was acclaimed king by the army on his father's death in 1014. In 1016 he defeated ◊Edmund Ironside at Assandun in Essex, and ruled Mercia and Northumbria until he inherited the whole kingdom on Edmund's death. He compelled King Malcolm to pay homage by invading Scotland about 1027; succeeded his brother Harold as king of Denmark in 1018; and conquered Norway in 1028. His empire collapsed on his death. He was buried at Winchester. According to legend, he deflated his flattering courtiers by showing that the sea would not retreat at his command.

canyon a deep narrow hollow running through mountains. There are many canyons in the western USA and in Mexico, for example the Grand Canyon of the Colorado River, the canyon in Yellowstone National Park, and the Black Canyon in Colorado. The word is an anglicized spelling of the Spanish *cañon*. Canyons are cut by river action, usually in areas of low rainfall, where the river receives water from outside the area.

capacitance, electrical ratio of the electric charge on a body to the resultant change of potential. See ◊capacitor.

capacitor device for storing electric charge, used in electronic circuits; it consists of two metal plates separated by an insulating 'dielectric'. Its capacitance is the ratio of the charge stored on either plate to the potential difference between the plates. 1 farad is a capacitance of 1 coulomb stored per volt, but most capacitors have much smaller capacitances, and the microfarad (a millionth of a farad) is more commonly used as a practical unit.

Cape Canaveral /kə'nævərəl/ promontory on the Atlantic coast of Florida, USA, 367 km/228 mi north of Miami. First mentioned in 1513, it was known 1963–73 as Cape Kennedy. The John F Kennedy Space Center, from which all US manned space flights have been launched, is here.

Cape Coast /'keɪp 'kəʊst/ port of Ghana, West Africa, 130 km/80 mi west of Accra, superseded as the main port since 1962 by Tema. The town, first established by the Portuguese in the 16th century, is built on a natural breakwater, adjoining the castle; population (1970) 71,600.

Cape Cod /'keɪp 'kɒd/ peninsula in SE Massachusetts, USA, where in 1620 the English Pilgrims landed at Provincetown.

Cape Coloured term used in South Africa for people of mixed African and European descent, mainly living in Cape Province.

Cape gooseberry plant *Physalis peruviana* of the potato family, originating in South America, but grown elsewhere, including South Africa, from which it is named. It is cultivated for its fruit, a yellow berry surrounded by a papery ◊calyx.

Cape Horn /'keɪp hɔːn/ most southerly point of South America, in the Chilean part of the archipelago of ◊Tierra del Fuego. It was named in 1616 by its Dutch discoverer Willem Schouten 1580–1625 after his birthplace (Hoorn).

Čapek /'tʃæpek/ Karel Matej 1890–1938. Czech playwright, best-remembered for *R.U.R.* (Rossum's Universal Robots) 1921, in which robots (a term he coined) rebel against their masters, and for *The Insect Play* 1921.

Capella brightest ◊star in the constellation ◊Auriga, and the sixth-brightest star in the sky. It consists of a pair of yellow giant stars 42 light years away orbiting each other every 104 days.

Cape of Good Hope /ˈkeɪp əv gʊd ˈhəʊp/ South African headland forming a peninsula between Table Bay and False Bay, Cape Town. The first European to sail round it was Bartholomew ◊Diaz in 1488. Formerly named Cape of Storms, it was given its present name by King John II of Portugal.

Cape Province /ˈkeɪp ˈprɒvɪns/ (Afrikaans *Kaapprovinsie*) largest province of the Republic of South Africa, named after the famous promontory.

area 721,00 sq km/278,400 sq mi, excluding Walvis Bay

capital Cape Town

towns Port Elizabeth, East London, Kimberley, Grahamstown, Stellenbosch

features Orange river, Drakensberg, Table Mountain (highest point Maclear's Beacon 1087 m/3567 ft); Great Karoo Plateau, Walvis ◊Bay

products fruit (citrus, peaches, etc.), vegetables, wine; meat, ostrich feathers; diamonds, copper, asbestos, manganese

population (1980) 5,091,360, officially including 2,226,200 Coloured; 1,569,000 Black; 1,264,000 White; 32,120 Asian

history the Dutch occupied the Cape in 1652, but it was taken by the British in 1795 after the French Revolutionary armies had occupied the Netherlands, and was sold to Britain for £6 million in 1814. The Orange river was proclaimed the northern boundary in 1825. Griqualand western (1880) and the southern part of Bechuanaland (1895) were later incorporated, and Walvis Bay, although administered with SW Africa, is legally an integral part of Cape Province. The Cape was given self-government in 1872. It was an original province of the Union in 1910.

caper shrub *Capparis spinosa*, family Capparidaceae, native to the Mediterranean; the flower buds are preserved in vinegar as a condiment.

capercaillie large bird *Tetrao uroqallus* of the grouse type found in coniferous woodland in Europe and N Asia. At nearly 1 m/3 ft long the male is the biggest gamebird in Europe, with a largely black plumage and rounded tail which is fanned out in courtship. The female is speckled brown and about 60 cm/2 ft. Hunted to extinction in Britain in the 18th century the capercaillie was reintroduced from Sweden in the 1830's and has re-established itself in Scotland.

Capet /ˈkæˈpet/ Hugh 938–996. King of France. Claiming the throne on the death of ◊Louis V in 987, he founded the Capetian dynasty, of which various branches continued to reign until the French Revolution, for example, ◊Valois and ◊Bourbon.

Cape Town /ˈkeɪptaʊn/ (Afrikaans *Kaapstad*) port and oldest town in South Africa; population (1980) 213,830. It is the legislative capital of the Republic of South Africa, and

capital of Cape Province, and was founded in 1652 by Johan van Riebeeck of the Dutch East India Company. It includes the Houses of Parliament, City Hall, Cape Town Castle (1666), and Groote Schuur, 'great barn', the estate of Cecil Rhodes (he designated the house as the home of the premier, and a university and the National Botanical Gardens occupy part of the grounds). The naval base of *Simonstown* is to the SE; in 1975 Britain's use of its facilities was ended by the Labour government in disapproval of South Africa's racial policies. Industries include shipping and horticulture.

Cape Verde /vɜːd/ group of islands in the Atlantic, off the coast of Senegal.

government the 1980 constitution provides for a national people's assembly of 56, elected by universal suffrage for a five-year term, and a president, elected for a similar term by the assembly. The constitution had also provided for union with Guinea-Bissau but this was deleted in 1981 and an amendment inserted replacing the African Party for the Independence of Portuguese Guinea and Cape Verde (PAIGC) with the African Party for the Independence of Cape Verde (PAICV) as the only political party. As well as combining the roles of head of state and head of government, the president is secretary-general of PAICV. There is an opposition party, the Independent Democratic Union of Cape Verde (UCID), but it operates from Lisbon.

history the Cape Verde islands were first settled in the 15th century by Portugal, the first black inhabitants being slaves imported from W Africa.

A liberation movement developed in the 1950s. The mainland territory to which Cape Verde is linked, Guinea, now Guinea-Bissau, was granted independence in 1974, and a process began for their eventual union. A transitional government was set up, composed of Portuguese and PAIGC members. In 1975 a national people's assembly was elected and Aristides Pereira, PAIGC secretary-general, became president of Cape Verde. The 1980 constitution provided for the union of the two states but in 1981 this aspect was deleted because of insufficient support and the PAIGC became the PAICV. Pereira was re-elected and relations with Guinea-Bissau improved. Under President Pereira, Cape Verde has adopted a policy of non-alignment and achieved considerable respect within the region.

Cape Wrath /rɑːθ/ headland at the NW extremity of Scotland.

Cape York /jɔːk/ peninsula, the most northerly point (10°,41'S) of the Australian mainland, so named by Capt James ◊Cook in 1770. The peninsula is about 800 km/500 mi long and 640 km/400 mi wide at its junction with the mainland. Its barrenness deterred early Dutch explorers, although the south is being developed for cattle (Brahmin type) and in the north there are large bauxite deposits.

capillary in anatomy, a fine blood vessel that connects the ◊arteries and ◊veins of vertebrates. Capillaries are between 8 and 20 thousandths of a millimetre in diameter and the capillary wall consists of a single layer of cells. Water, proteins,

soluble food substances, gases and white blood cells pass through this wall between the fluid (◊lymph) bathing the body tissue outside the capillary and the ◊blood within the capillary.

capillary in physics, a very narrow, thick-walled tube, usually made of glass – as in a thermometer. Properties of fluids such as surface tension and viscosity can be studied using capillary tubes. The movement of liquids through tubes and pores, such as the upward flow of liquid in filter paper (used in a form of chromatography) is known as capillarity.

capital in architecture, a stone placed on the top of a column, pier, or pilaster, and usually wider on the upper surface than the diameter of the supporting shaft. It consists of three parts: the top member called the *abacus*, a block which acts as the supporting surface to the superstructure; the middle portion known as the bell or *echinus*; and the lower part called the necking or *astragal*. See also ◊order.

capital in economics, a term commonly used to signify accumulated or inherited wealth held in the form of assets (such as ◊stocks and shares, property, and bank deposits); in more strict terms, capital is defined as the stock of goods (themselves produced) used in the production of other goods, and may be fixed capital (such as plant and machinery) or circulating capital (raw materials and components). All forms of capital require resources being devoted to their creation, and hence the foregoing of ◊consumption at some point.

capitalism economic system in which the principal means of production, distribution, and exchange are in private (individual or corporate) hands. A 'mixed economy', as in Britain, combines the private enterprise of capitalism and a degree of state monopoly, as in the nationalized industries. See also ◊privatization.

capital punishment punishment by death. At the end of the 18th century in England, it was the penalty for more than 200 offences, though not always inflicted, and was carried out by hanging in public until 1866. From 1810 onwards Samuel Romilly (1757–1818) and others conducted a vigorous campaign for the mitigation of the penal laws; several acts were passed, each reducing the number of crimes liable to so drastic a penalty, until an act of 1861 left only murder, treason, piracy with violence, and the firing of government arsenals and dockyards punishable by death. From 1838 capital punishment was in practice almost invariably imposed only for murder; and from 1965 was in effect abolished. In the USA the Supreme Court ruled in 1972 that capital punishment was a violation of the 8th amendment to the constitution (prohibiting cruel and unusual punishment), but the death penalty was subsequently restored by a number of individual states after a further ruling in 1976 by the Court laid down that it was not 'cruel and unusual' in all circumstances. Execution methods vary from state to state and include electrocution, lethal gas, hanging and shooting. Capital punishment is still retained by the majority of countries for ordinary crimes and sanctioned by majority public opinion, for example in the USSR crimes punishable by

Cape Verde

REPUBLIC OF (*República de Cabo Verde*)

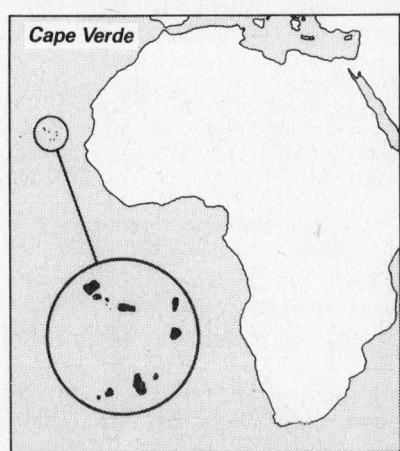

AREA 4,033 sq km/1,557 sq mi
CAPITAL Praia
PHYSICAL archipelago of ten islands 565 km/350 mi W of Senegal
FEATURES strategically important because it dominates the western shipping lanes
HEAD OF STATE AND OF GOVERNMENT Aristides Pereira from 1975
GOVERNMENT one-party republic
EXPORTS bananas, coffee
CURRENCY Cape Verde escudo (147.11 = £1 Sept 1987)
POPULATION (1985) 312,000 (including some 100,000 Angolan refugees); annual growth rate 1.4%
LANGUAGE Creole dialect of Portuguese
RELIGION Roman Catholic 80%
LITERACY 54% male/34% female (1980 est)
GDP $110 million (1983); $300 per head of population
CHRONOLOGY
1974 Moved towards independence through a transitional Portuguese–Cape Verde government.
1975 Full independence achieved. National people's assembly elected. Aristides Pereira became the first president.
1980 Constitution adopted providing for eventual union with Guinea-Bissau.
1981 Union with Guinea-Bissau abandoned and the constitution amended; became one-party state.

Capote 'Death is the central factor of life...I've always held a tragic view of life, which accounts for the side of me that appears frivolous'. (Truman Capote).

death include bribe-taking, thefts and currency offences. All countries tend to invoke it in times of exceptional crisis. France uses the ◊guillotine, Spain garrotting (a form of strangulation), and the USSR shooting.

capitulum in botany, an inflorescence consisting of a flattened or rounded head of numerous, small, stalkless flowers. The capitulum is surrounded by a whorl of bracts, and has the appearance of a large, single flower. It is characteristic of plants belonging to the daisy family (Compositae) such as the daisy (*Bellis perennis*) and the garden marigold (*Calendula officinalis*); but is also seen in parts of other families, such as scabious (*Knautia*) and teasels (Dipsacus) The individual flowers are known as ◊florets.

Capo-di-Monte /'kæpəu di 'mɒnteɪ/ village, N of Naples, Italy, where porcelain known by the same name was first produced under King Charles III of Naples in 1736.

Capone /kə'pəʊn/ Al(phonse) 1898–1947. American gangster, born in Brooklyn, the son of an Italian barber. During the ◊Prohibition Period Capone built up a criminal organization in the city of Chicago. He was imprisoned 1931–39, for income tax evasion, the only charge which could be sustained against him.

Caporetto /ˌkæpə'retəʊ/ former name of ◊Kobarid, Yugoslavia.

Capote /kə'pəʊti/ Truman. Pseudonym of Truman Streckfuss Persons 1924–1984. American novelist, born in New Orleans, he used a Southern setting in *The Grass Harp* 1951; wrote *Breakfast at Tiffany's* 1958; set a trend in 'faction' (non-fiction novels) with *In Cold Blood* 1966, reconstructing a Kansas killing; and mingled recollection and fiction in *Music for Chameleons* 1980. He was a prominent figure in the New York literary world in his later years.

Cappadocia ancient region of Asia Minor, in modern E central Turkey. The area includes over 600 Byzantine cave churches cut into volcanic rock, dating mainly from the 10th and 11th centuries. It was conquered by the Persians in 584 BC but in the 3rd century BC became an independent kingdom. The region was annexed as a province of the Roman Empire in 17 AD.

Capra /'kæprə/ Frank 1897– . American film director. His films, which often have idealistic heroes, include *It Happened One Night* 1934, *Mr Deeds Goes to Town* 1936, and *You Can't Take It With You* 1938.

Capri /kə'priː/ Italian island at the south entrance of the Bay of Naples, 32 km/20 mi S of Naples. It has two towns, Capri and Anacapri,

Capone Alphonse 'Al' Capone (centre) , notorious gangster in Chicago during Prohibition. This photograph was taken whilst he was under indictment in the Chicago Federal Court, 1931. He was imprisoned 1931–39 for tax evasion.

and is famous for its flowers, beautiful scenery, and ideal climate. Area 13 sq km/5 sq mi.

capriccio /kəˈprɪtʃɪəʊ/ (Italian 'caprice') in music, a short, lively instrumental piece, often humorous or whimsical in character.

Capricornus constellation of the ◊zodiac, representing a fish-tailed goat. The Sun is within its boundaries from late Jan to mid-Feb.

Caprivi /kəˈpriːvi/ Georg Leo Count von Caprivi 1831–1899. German imperial chancellor 1890–94.

Caprivi Strip /kəˈpriːvi/ NE access strip for ◊Namibia to the Zambezi river.

capsicum plant of the nightshade family Solanaceae, native to Central and South America. The differing species produce green-to-red fruits which vary from the small ones (used whole to give the hot flavour of chilli, or ground to produce cayenne pepper), to the large pointed or squarish pods of the sweet peppers (mild flavoured and used as a vegetable).

capsule in botany, a dry, usually many-seeded ◊fruit formed from an ovary composed of two or more fused ◊carpels, that splits open to release the seeds. Capsules dehisce in various ways, including lengthwise, by a transverse lid, for example scarlet pimpernel (*Anagallis arvensis*, or by a number of pores, either towards the top of the capsule, for example poppy (*Papaver*), or near the base, as in certain species of *Campanula*. The same term is also used for the spore-containing structure of mosses and liverworts; this is borne at the top of a long stalk or seta.

Capua /ˈkæpjʊə/ Italian town in Caserta province on the Volturno, in a fertile plain N of Naples. There was heavy fighting here in 1943 during World War II, and the Romanesque cathedral was almost destroyed.

Capuchin a member of the Order of ◊Franciscan friars in the Roman Catholic church, instituted about 1520 by Friar Matteo di Bassi, an Italian monk who wished to return to the literal observance of the rule of St Francis. The brown habit with the pointed hood (French *capuche*) which he adopted gave his followers the name. The order was recognized by the Holy See in 1619, and has been remarkable for its missionary activity. Despite stress on poverty and austerity, it has attracted many members of the nobility.

capuchin type of monkey, genus *Cebus* found in Central and South America, so called because the hairs on the head resemble the cowl of a capuchin monk. Capuchins live in small groups, feed on fruit and insects, and have a tail which is semi-prehensile and can give support when climbing through the trees.

capybara largest rodent *Hydrochoerus hydrochaeris*, up to 1.3 m/4 ft long and 50 kg/110 lb in weight. It is found in South America, and belongs to the guinea-pig family. It inhabits marshes, and dense vegetation around water. It has thin yellowish hair, swims well, and can rest underwater with just eyes, ears and nose above.

caracal cat *Felis caracal* of the lynx type with very long black ear-tufts and a short tail. It has short reddish-fawn fur and lives in bush and desert country in Africa, Arabia and India, hunting birds and small mammals at night. Head and body length is about 75 cm/2.5 ft.

Caracalla /ˌkærəˈkælə/ Marcus Aurelius Antoninus 186–217. Roman emperor. He succeeded his father Septimius Severus in 211, ruled with cruelty and extravagance, and was assassinated.

Caracalla The Roman emperor Caracalla murdered his brother to gain sole possession of the throne. His delusions of grandeur extended to having himself represented as a god or pharaoh in statues and coins.

Caracas /kəˈrækəs/ chief city and capital of Venezuela, founded 1860–67; the birthplace of Simon ◊Bolívar. It is situated on the Andean slopes, 13 km/8 mi S of its port La Guaira on the Caribbean coast. It has suffered several severe earthquakes. Its products are cement, textiles, paper, and tobacco, and it has an international airport. Among its many fine buildings is Venezuela University, which forms a city within a city, and has gates guarded by university police. As in most Latin American countries, the university is independent and self-governing, and no state police or soldiers are allowed to enter. Population of metropolitan area (1980) 2,398,000.

Caractacus /kəˈræktəkəs/ died c. 54 AD. British chieftain, who headed resistance to the Romans in the SE 43–51 AD, but was defeated on the Welsh border. Shown in Claudius's triumphal procession, he was released in tribute to his courage and died in Rome.

Caradon /ˈkærədən/ Baron title of Hugh ◊Foot, British Labour politician.

carat (US karat) unit of purity in gold. Pure gold is 24-carat; 22-carat (the purest used in jewellery) is 22 parts gold and two parts alloy (to give greater strength). The metric carat of 0.200 grams is the unit of weight for diamonds and other precious stones.

Caravaggio /ˌkærəˈvædʒɪəʊ/ Michelangelo Merisi da 1573–1610. Italian ◊Baroque painter, born at Caravaggio, near Milan. He killed a man in a brawl in 1606, and had to flee Rome, where the Cardinal del Monte had been his patron, for

Caracas The complex of buildings which forms the University of Venezuela.

Naples. He influenced Neapolitan painting profoundly, introducing a controversial harsh realism in which ordinary people appear as saints, then considered unsuitable for religious paintings. Works include *The Supper at Emmaus* (National Gallery, London), *The Entombment of Christ* (Vatican) and *The Death of the Virgin* (Louvre).

caraway umbelliferous plant *Carum carvi* grown for its aromatic fruit, known as caraway 'seed', used in cookery, medicine, and perfumery.

carbides compounds of carbon and one other chemical element, usually a metal, silicon or boron. Calcium carbide (CaC_2) is particularly important. It can be used as the starting material for many basic organic chemical syntheses, by the addition of water and generation of ◊acetylene. Some metallic carbides are important in engineering because of their extreme hardness and strength. Tungsten carbide is an essential ingredient of carbide tools and 'high-speed' tools. The 'carbide process' was used during World War II to make organic chemicals from coal rather than from oil.

carbohydrates a group of compounds composed of carbon, hydrogen and oxygen, all with the basic formula $Cm(H_2O)n$. The simplest carbohydrates are the sugars (*monosaccharides*), such as glucose and fructose, and *disaccharides*, such as sucrose, which are soluble compounds, some with a sweet taste. When these basic sugar units are joined together in long chains they form *polysaccharides*, such as starch, and glycogen, which often serve as food-stores in living organisms. As such they form an important energy-providing part of the human diet. Even more complex carbohydrates are known, including ◊chitin which is found in the cell walls of fungi and the hard outer skeletons of insects, and ◊cellulose, which makes up the cell walls of plants. Carbohydrates form the chief foodstuffs of herbivorous animals.

carbolic acid more common name for the aromatic compound, ◊phenol.

carbon one of the most widely distributed non-metallic elements; symbol C, atomic weight 12.011, atomic number 6. It occurs on its own

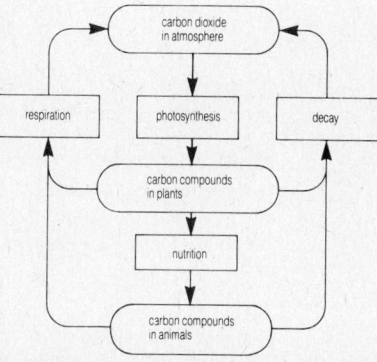

Caravaggio *Supper at Emmaus* by Michelangelo Merisi da Caravaggio. The harsh bright light in the painting is the hallmark of Caravaggio's work. Sometimes it comes from a candle, sometimes as here as if a spotlight is on the apostles.

as diamonds and graphite (crystalline forms), in carbonaceous rocks such as chalk and limestone ($CaCO_3$), as carbon dioxide (CO_2) in the atmosphere, as hydrocarbons in petroleum, coal and natural gas, and as a constituent of all organic substances; see ▷organic chemistry. In its amorphous form it is familiar as coal, charcoal, and soot. Of the inorganic carbon compounds, the most important is *carbon dioxide*, a colourless gas formed when carbon is burned in an adequate supply of air, and *carbon monoxide* (CO), formed when carbon is oxidized in a limited supply of air. *Carbon disulphide* (CS_2) is a dense liquid with a sweetish odour. Another important group of compounds is the *carbon halides*, of which carbon tetrachloride (CCl_4) is the best-known. Being non-inflammable it is used in certain fire appliances, but as it reacts with oxygen at high temperatures to produce phosgene ($COCl_2$), the fumes are dangerous.

When added to steel carbon forms a wide range of alloys with useful properties. In pure form it is widely used as a moderator in nuclear reactors; as colloidal graphite (Dag, Aquadag) it is a good lubricant and, when deposited on a surface in a vacuum, obviates photoelectric and secondary emission of electrons. Carbon is a widespread fuel in the form of coal or coke. The radioactive isotope carbon-14 is widely used as a tracer in biological research.

Carbonari /ˌkɑːbəˈnɑːri/ a political secret revolutionary society in S Italy in the first half of the 19th century. Originally they were republican rebels against Murat, the Bonapartist king of Naples, who hid in the Abruzzi and called

themselves Carbonari ('charcoal burners'). They later played a part in ▷Mazzini's nationalist 'Young Italy' movement.

carbonates an important group of chemical compounds formed by the combination of a carbonate group (CO_3) with a cation. The carbon dioxide (CO_2) dissolved by rain falling through the air, and liberated by decomposing animals and plants in the soil, forms with water carbonic acid (H_2CO_3) which unites with various basic substances to form carbonates. Calcium carbonate ($CaCO_3$) (chalk, limestone, marble) is one of the most abundant carbonates known, being an important constituent of mollusc shells and the hard outer skeletons of crabs and similar creatures.

carbon cycle the sequence by which ▷carbon circulates and is recycled through the natural world. The carbon element from carbon dioxide in the atmosphere is taken up, during the process of ▷photosynthesis, and the oxygen component is released back into the atmosphere. Photosynthesis is carried out by plants and by organisms such as diatoms and dinoflagellates in the oceanic ▷plankton. The carbon they accumulate is later released back into circulation through the ▷decomposition of decaying plant matter, the consumption of plant matter or plankton by herbivores, or the burning of fuels such as ▷coal (fossilized plants). Today, the carbon cycle is being altered by the increased consumption of fossil fuels, and burning of large tracts of tropical forests, as a result of which levels of carbon dioxide are building up in the atmosphere and probably contributing to the ▷greenhouse effect.

carbon dating another name for ▷radiocarbon dating.

carbon fibre a fine, black silky filament of pure carbon produced by heat treatment from a special grade of Courtelle acrylic fibre, used for reinforcing plastics. The resulting ▷composite is very stiff and weight-for-weight has four times the strength of high-tensile steel. It is becoming widely used in aerospace, cars, electrical equipment, and sports gear.

Carboniferous the period of geological time between 345 and 280 million years ago. In the USA it is regarded as two periods – the Mississippian (lower) and the Pennsylvanian (upper). Typical rocks of the lower Carboniferous are shallow-water ▷limestones, while the upper Carboniferous has ▷delta deposits with ▷coal (hence the name). Typical animals of the Carboniferous were fish and the diversifying amphibians.

carbon monoxide a colourless, odourless gas (CO) formed when carbon is oxidized in a limited supply of air. It is a poisonous constituent of car exhaust fumes, forming a stable compound with ▷haemoglobin in the blood thus preventing the haemoglobin from transporting oxygen to the body tissues.

carborundum silicon carbide (SiC), an artificial compound of carbon and silicon, discovered in 1891 by E G Acheson. It is a hard, black substance, used as an abrasive, harder than corundum but not as hard as diamond.

carbuncle in anatomy, a multiple boil.

carbuncle in gemmology, a garnet cut to resemble a rounded knob.

carburation regular combustion, usually in a closed space, of carbon compounds such as petrol, kerosene, or fuel oil; regulated combustion is distinct from much more rapid burning such as explosion or detonation, and the definition applies particularly to combustion in the cylinders of reciprocating petrol engines of the types used in aircraft, road vehicles, or marine vessels. The device by which the liquid fuel is atomized and mixed with air is called a *carburettor*.

Carcassonne /ˌkɑːkəˈsɒn/ city in SW France, capital of Aude *département*, on the river Aude,

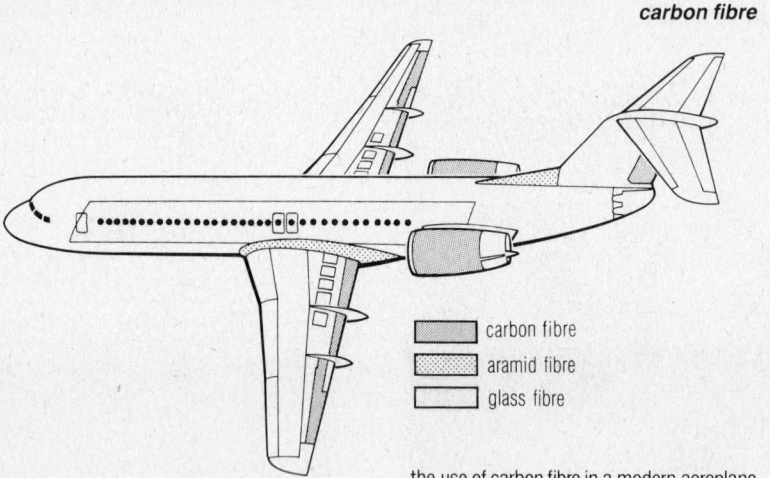

carbon fibre

◼ carbon fibre
▨ aramid fibre
▢ glass fibre

the use of carbon fibre in a modern aeroplane

which divides it into the ancient and modern town. Its medieval fortifications (restored) are the finest in France. Population (1982) 42,450.

Carcassonne The fortifications of Carcassonne, unsuccessfully besieged by the Black Prince in 1356. Viollet-le-Duc carried out a programme of restoration 1850–80.

Carchemish /ˈkɑːkəmɪʃ/ (modern Karkamis, Turkey), on the Euphrates, 80 km/50 mi NE of Aleppo, centre of the New ◊Hittite empire, and taken by Sargon II of Assyria 717 BC. Also site of a battle in which Nebuchadnezzar defeated the Egyptians 605 BC.

Cardano /kɑːˈdɑːnəʊ/ Girolamo 1501–1576. Italian physician, mathematician, philosopher, astrologer and gambler. Born at Pavia, he became professor of medicine there in 1543, and wrote two important works on physics and natural science, *De subtilitate rerum* 1551 and *De varietate rerum* 1557. He is noted for his theory of chance, his use of algebra, and many medical publications, notably the first clinical description of typhus fever.

Cárdenas /ˈkɑːdɪnæs/ Lazaro 1895–1970. Mexican general and statesman, in early life a civil servant, he took part in the revolutionary campaigns 1915–29 that followed the fall of

President Diaz, was president of the republic 1934–40, and introduced many socialist measures. He was minister of national defence 1943–45.

Cardiff /ˈkɑːdɪf/ capital of Wales (from 1955), and administrative headquarters of S and Mid Glamorgan, at the mouth of the Taff, Rhymney and Ely rivers.

history the city dates from Roman times, the later town being built round the Norman castle, which was the residence of the Earls and Marquesses of Bute from the 18th century and was given to the city in 1947 by the fifth marquess.

The docks on the Bristol Channel were opened in 1839 and greatly extended by the second Marquess of Bute (1793–1848). The derelict docks have now been redeveloped for industry. Coal was exported until the 1920s. As coal declined iron and steel exports continued to grow, and an import trade in timber, grain and flour, tobacco, meat, and citrus fruit developed. Besides steelworks, there are automotive component, flour milling, paper, cigar and other industries.

In Cathays Park is a group of public buildings including the Law Courts, City Hall, the National Museum of Wales, the Welsh Office (established 1964), a major part of the University of Wales (Institute of Science and Technology, National School of Medicine and University College of S Wales), and the Temple of Peace and Health. Llandaff, on the right bank of the Taff, seat of an archbishop from the 6th century, was included in Cardiff in 1922; its cathedral, virtually rebuilt in the 19th century and restored 1948–57 after air raid damage in World War II, has Jacob ◊Epstein's sculpture, *Christ in Majesty*. At St Fagan's is the Welsh National Folk Museum, containing small rebuilt historical buildings from rural Wales in which crafts are demonstrated. The city is the headquarters of the Welsh National Opera. Population (1983) 279,800.

Cardiganshire /ˈkɑːdɪɡənʃə/ former county of Wales facing Cardigan Bay, which was in 1974 merged, together with Pembroke and Carmarthen, into Dyfed. Mainly mountainous, the area rises in the NE to Plynlimmon (752 m/2,468 ft), and is drained by the Rheidol, Ystwyth, Teifi and Towy. The county town was Cardigan, population (1980) 3,592.

Cardin /kɑːˈdæŋ/ Pierre 1922– . French fashion designer, the first to show a collection for men, in 1960.

cardinal in the Roman Catholic church, the highest rank next to the Pope. Originally a cardinal was any priest in charge of a major parish; but in 1567 the term was confined to the members of the Sacred College, from whom since 1973, 120 (below the age of 80) elect the Pope and are themselves nominated and elected by him. They must come to Rome for the ceremony within a year, to receive the red hat which is the badge of office. They act as an advisory body to the Papacy on all matters of doctrine, canonizations, convocation of councils, liturgy and temporal business.

cardioid heart-shaped curve traced out by a point on the circumference of a circle which rolls around the edge of another circle of the same diameter. If the two circles have different diameters, the curve is an ◊epicycloid.

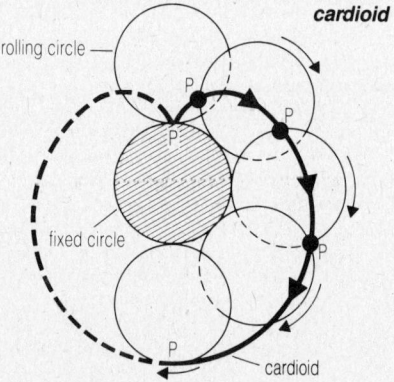

cardioid

rolling circle —
fixed circle
cardioid

Carême /kəˈreɪm/ Antonin 1784–1833. French chef who at various times was chief cook to the Prince Regent in England and Czar Alexander in Russia. He is regarded as the founder of classical French *haute cuisine*.

Carew /kəˈruː/ Thomas ? 1595–? 1640. English poet. Born in Kent, he was in 1628 a gentleman of the privy chamber to Charles I, and was the best lyricist as well as craftsman of the school of ◊'Cavalier Poets'.

Carey /ˈkeəri/ Henry 1690–1743. British poet and musician, remembered for the song 'Sally in Our Alley'. 'God Save the King' (both words and music) has also been attributed to him.

cargo cult Melanesian religious belief, from the 19th century, in the arrival of the trappings of Western life (the cargo) through the agency of some messianic spirit figure. Rituals are performed and 'warehouses' built for the expected goods. It was reinforced by the supplies delivered by air to US troops evicting Japanese troops from the islands.

Carib /'kærɪb/ a member of a group of ◊American Indian aboriginal people of South America and the islands of the West Indies in the Caribbean Sea. The name was given by Columbus. In 1796 the English in the West Indies deported most of them to Roatan Island off Honduras. They have since spread extensively in Honduras and Nicaragua.

Caribbean /ˌkærɪ'biːən/ part of the Atlantic Ocean between the N coasts of South and Central America and the ◊West Indies, about 2,740 km/1,700 mi long and between 650 km/400 mi–1,500 km/900 mi wide. It is here that the ◊Gulf Stream turns towards Europe.

Caribbean Community organization (CARICOM) for economic and foreign policy coordination in the Caribbean region, established by the Treaty of Chaguaramas in 1973. The leading member is Trinidad and Tobago; headquarters Georgetown, Guyana; others are Antigua, Barbados, Belize, Dominica, Grenada, Guyana, Jamaica, Montserrat, St Christopher Nevis, Anguilla, St Lucia and St Vincent. From 1979 a left-wing Grenadan coup led to a progressive regional subgroup including St Lucia and Dominica.

caribou name for the ◊reindeer of North America.

caricature exaggerated artistic representation, for the purpose of ridicule. Grotesque drawings have been discovered in Pompeii and Herculaneum, and Pliny refers to a grotesque portrait of the poet Hipponax. Humorous drawings were executed by the Carracci and their followers (the Italian 'eclectic' school of the 16th century). Caricaturists include Gillray, Hogarth, Rowlandson, Cruikshank, Lear, Doyle, Du Maurier, Beerbohm, Low, 'Vicky', 'Giles', Cummings, Ronald Searle, Lancaster, Calman, Herb Block, Gerald Scarfe, Ralph Steadman (the last two producing grotesque, distorted figures), and Peter Fluck and Roger Law (three-dimensional puppets for the UK television series *Spitting Image*). Charles Philipon 1800–62 founded in Paris in 1830 *La Caricature*, probably the first periodical to specialize in caricature.

CARICOM abbreviation for ◊Caribbean Community, an organization for economic and foreign policy coordination in the Caribbean region, established 1973.

caries disease or deterioration of teeth or bones. Dental caries is erosion of the teeth by bacterial decay. Prevention is by a low sugar diet, good dental hygiene and fluoride.

Carina ◊constellation of the southern hemisphere, representing a ship's keel. Its brightest star is ◊Canopus; it also contains Eta Carinae, a peculiar star embedded in a gas cloud. Eta Carinae is a massive and highly luminous star that has varied unpredictably in the past; some astronomers think it is likely to explode as a supernova within 10,000 years.

Carinthia /kə'rɪnθiə/ an independent duchy from 976, and a possession of the ◊Hapsburgs 1276–1918, now an alpine province of SE Austria, bordering Italy and Yugoslavia in the south. The capital is Klagenfurt. Area 9,533 sq km/3,681 sq mi; population (1981) 536,179.

Carisbrooke /'kærɪzbruk/ village SW of Newport, Isle of Wight. Charles I was imprisoned in its castle 1647–48.

Carissimi /kə'rɪsɪmi/ Giacomo 1605–1674. Italian composer, a pioneer of the oratorio.

Carlisle /kɑː'laɪl/ city and administrative headquarters of Cumbria, England, the county town of the former county of Cumberland, situated on the Eden at the W end of Hadrian's Wall. It is an important railway centre; textiles, engineering, and biscuit making are the chief industries. There is a Norman cathedral and a castle. The bishopric dates from 1133. Population (1981) 70,706.

Carlist a supporter of the claims of the Spanish pretender Don Carlos de Bourbon 1788–1855, and his descendants, to the Spanish crown. He had been excluded by an abrogation of the Salic ◊Law (see ◊Isabella II). The Carlist revolt continued, especially in the Basque provinces, until 1839. In 1977 the Carlist political party was legalised and Carlos Hugo de Bourbon Parma (1930–) renounced his claim as pretender and became reconciled with King Juan Carlos. See also ◊Bourbon.

Carlos /'kɑːlɒs/ Don 1545–1568. Spanish prince. Son of Philip II, he was recognized as heir to the thrones of Castile and Aragon, but became mentally unstable and had to be placed under restraint following a plot to assassinate his father. His story was made the subject of plays by Schiller, Alfieri, Otway, and others.

Carlos I /'kɑːlɒs/ 1863–1908. King of Portugal, of the Braganza-Coburg line, from 1889 until he was assassinated in Lisbon with his elder son Luis. He was succeeded by his younger son Manoel.

Carlow /'kɑːləu/ county in the Republic of Ireland (county town Carlow), in the province of Leinster. The county is a low-lying and undulating plain, except for a long range of heights in the south, rising to 796 m/2,610ft in Mount Leinster. The land, watered by the Barrow and the Slaney, is fertile, and dairy farming is important. Area 896 sq km/346 sq mi; population (1981) 39,820.

Carlsbad /'kɑːlzbæd/ German name of ◊Karlovy Vary, a spa town in W Bohemia, Czechoslovakia.

Carlson /'kɑːlsən/ Chester 1906–1968. American scientist, who invented xerography. A research worker with Bell Telephone, he was sacked from his post in 1930 during the Depression, and set to work on his own to develop an efficient copying machine. By 1938 he had invented the ◊Xerox method.

Carlsson /'kɑːlsən/ Ingvar Gösta 1934– . Swedish socialist politician, leader of the Social Democratic Party, prime minister from 1986. After studying in Sweden and the USA, Carlsson became president of the Swedish Social-Democratic Youth League in 1961. He was elected to the Riksdag (parliament) in 1964 and became a minister in 1969. With the return to power of the Social Democrats in 1982, Carlsson became deputy to Prime Minister ◊Palme and on his assassination in 1986 succeeded him.

Carlyle /kɑː'laɪl/ Thomas 1795–1881. Scottish author and academic, born at Ecclefechan in Dumfriesshire. In 1821 he passed through the spiritual crisis described in *Sartor Resartus*. He married Jane Baillie Welsh (1801–66) in 1826 and they moved to her farm at Craigenputtock, where *Sartor Resartus* 1836 was written. His reputation was established with the *French Revolution* 1837. The series of lectures he gave 1837–40 included *On Heroes, Hero-Worship*, and *The Heroic in History* 1841. He also wrote several pamphlets, including *Chartism* 1839, attacking the doctrine of ◊laissez-faire; the notable *Letters and Speeches of Cromwell* 1845; and the miniature life of his friend *John Sterling* 1851. Carlyle then began his *History of Frederick the Great* 1858–65, and after the death of his wife in 1866 devoted his time to editing her letters 1883 and preparing the *Reminiscences* 1881, which shed an unfavourable light on his character and his neglect of her, for which he could not forgive himself. His house in Cheyne Row, Chelsea, London, is a museum.

Carl XVI /kɑːl/ Gustaf 1946– . King of Sweden from 1973. He succeeded his grandfather ◊Gustaf VI, his father having been killed in an air crash in 1947. Under the new Swedish constitution which became effective on his grandfather's death, the monarchy was effectively stripped of all power at his accession.

Carmarthenshire /kə'mɑːðənʃə/ former county of S Wales, and formerly also the largest Welsh county. It bordered on the Bristol Channel, and was merged in 1974, together with Cardigan and Pembroke, into Dyfed. The county town was Carmarthen, population (1981) 12,302.

Carmelites mendicant order of friars in the Roman Catholic church. Traditionally they originated in the days of Elijah, who according to the Old Testament is supposed to have lived on Mount Carmel in Palestine. Historically the first congregation was founded on Carmel by Berthold, a crusader from Calabria, about 1155. According to the rule which the patriarch of Jerusalem drew up for them about 1210, they lived as hermits in separate huts. About 1240 the Saracen conquests compelled them to move from Palestine, and they took root in the west, particularly in France and England, where the order became cenobitical and mendicant. The most important reform movement was initiated by St ◊Teresa. In 1562 she founded in Avila a convent and with the cooperation of St John of the Cross and others she established a stricter order of barefoot friars and nuns. The Carmelites have devoted themselves largely to missionary work and mystical theology. They were known from their white overmantle (over a brown habit) as White Friars.

Carmichael /kɑː'maɪkəl/ 'Hoagy' (Hoagland Howard) 1899–1981. American composer, pianist, singer and actor. His best known songs include 'Stardust' 1927, 'Rockin' Chair' 1930, 'Lazy River' 1931, and 'In the Cool, Cool, Cool of the Evening' 1951 (Academy Award).

Carmina Burana medieval lyric miscellany compiled from the work of wandering 13th-century scholars, and including secular (love songs and drinking songs) as well as religious verse. A cantata (1937) by Cari ◊Orff was based on the material.

Carnac /'kɑːnæk/ village in Brittany, France, with megalithic remains of tombs and stone alignments of the period 2000–1500BC. The largest of the latter has some 1000 stones up to 4 m/13 ft high arranged in 11 rows, with a circle at the W end. Population (1982) 3,964.

Carnap /'kɑːnæp/ Rudolf 1891–1970. American philosopher of German origin, the world's foremost exponent of logical ◊empiricism. Born at Wuppertal, Germany, he was a member of the Vienna Circle who adopted ◊Mach as their guide, and in 1935 went to the United States, where he was professor of philosophy at the University of California 1954–62. His books include *The Logical Syntax of Language* 1934, and *Meaning and Necessity* 1956.

Carnarvon Range /kə'nɑːvən/ section of the Great Divide, Queensland, Australia, about 900 m/1,000ft high. There are many Aboriginal paintings in the sandstone caves along its 160 km/100 mi length.

Carnatic region of SE India, in Madras state. It is situated between the Eastern Ghats and the Coromandel Coast, and was formerly an important trading centre.

carnation name given to the numerous double-flowered cultivated varieties of the clove-pink *Dianthus caryophyllus*. They are divided into flake, bizarre, and picotees, according to whether the petals exhibit one or more colours on their white ground, or have the colour dispersed strips, or as a border to the petals.

carnauba S American palm *Copernicia cerifera*, which produces fine wax and timber.

Carné /kɑː'neɪ/ Marcel 1909– . French film director, noted for his atmosphere and subtle characterization, for example *Le Jour se lève* 1939, and *Les Enfants du Paradis* 1944.

Carnegie /kɑː'negi/ Andrew 1835–1919. Scottish-American millionaire industrialist. Born at Dunfermline, Scotland, he was taken by his parents to the USA in 1848, and at 14 became a telegraph boy in Pittsburgh. Subsequently he became a railway employee, rose to be superintendent, introduced sleeping-cars and invested successfully in oil. He developed the Pittsburgh iron and steel industries, and built up a vast empire which he disposed of to the United States Steel Trust in 1901. From that time he lived at Skibo castle in Sutherland, Scotland, and devoted his wealth to endowing libraries and universities, the Carnegie Hero Fund, and other good causes. On his death the Carnegie Trusts continued his benevolent activities. *Carnegie Hall* in New York, opened in 1891 as The Music Hall, was renamed in 1898 because of his large contribution to its construction.

Carnegie /kɑː'negi/ Dale 1888–1955. American author and teacher, best known for the book *How to Win Friends and Influence People* 1938.

carnelian semi-precious gemstone consisting of quartz (silica) with iron impurities which give

Carnegie On his retirement, the industrialist Andrew Carnegie devoted his life to the philanthropic distribution of his huge fortune.

it a translucent red colour. Also called cornelian, it comes mainly from Brazil, India and Japan.

Carnera /kɑː'neərə/ Primo 1906–1967. Italian world heavyweight champion boxer 1933–34, known as the 'Ambling Alp' (he was 1.98 m/6 ft 6 in tall).

Carniola /,kɑːni'əʊlə/ a former crownland and duchy of Austria, most of which was included in Slovenia, part of the kingdom of the Serbs, Croats, and Slovenes (later Yugoslavia) in 1919. The westerly districts of Idrija and Postojna, then allocated to Italy, were transferred to Yugoslavia in 1947.

carnivore an animal which eats other animals. Sometimes confined to animals that eat the flesh of ◊vertebrate prey, but often used more broadly, to include animals that eat any other animals, even microscopic ones. Carrion-eaters may or may not be included. Additionally, the name carnivore is sometimes used to refer to members of the mammalian group *Carnivora*, which includes cats, dogs, bears, badgers, and weasels.

Carnot /'kɑːnəʊ/ Lazare 1753–1823. French general. He joined the army as an engineer, and his transformation of French military technique in the Revolutionary period earned him the title of 'Organizer of Victory'. After the coup d'état of 1797 he went abroad, but returned in 1799 and was made War Minister 1800–01. In 1814 as governor of Antwerp he put up a brilliantly successful defence. Minister of the Interior during the Hundred Days, he was proscribed at the Restoration and retired to Magdeburg, where he died. His work on fortification (*De la défense de places fortes* 1810) became a military textbook.

Carnot /'kɑːnəʊ/ Marie François Sadi 1837–1894. French President. Grandson of

Lazare Carnot, he entered the government service, was returned to the Assembly for Côte d'Or in 1871, and in 1887 was elected president. He successfully countered the Boulangist movement, and in 1892 the scandals arising out of French financial activities in Panama. He was assassinated by an Italian anarchist at Lyons.

Carnot /'kɑːnəʊ/ Nicolas Leonard Sadi 1796–1832. French soldier-scientist, son of Lazare Carnot. He founded thermodynamics; his pioneering work was *Réflexions sur la puissance motrice du feu/On the Motive Power of Fire*.

Carnot It is as founder of thermodynamics that the distinguished military engineer and scientist Sadi Carnot is remembered. He died at the age of 36, victim of a cholera epidemic.

Carnot cycle for a reversible heat engine a Carnot cycle consists of the following changes, in the order stated, in the physical condition of a gas: (1) isothermal expansion (i.e. without change of temperature), (2) adiabatic expansion (i.e. without change of heat content), (3) isothermal compression and (4) adiabatic compression. The principles derived from a study of this cycle are important in the fundamentals of heat and ◊thermodynamics.

carnotite important radioactive ore of vanadium (12 per cent) and uranium (53 per cent) with traces of radium. A yellow powdery mineral, it is mined chiefly in the western United States and the Soviet Union.

Caro /'kɑːrəʊ/ Anthony 1924– . British sculptor. Assistant to Henry Moore 1951–53. His works include 'Fathom', outside the *Economist* building in London. He is noted for his bold simplicity of form, use of paint on steel, and for free standing pieces without formal bases.

carob small tree of the Mediterranean region (*Ceratonia siliqua*), often called locust tree. The 20 cm/8 in pods are used as animal fodder. They are also the source of a chocolate substitute.

carol song, in medieval times associated with a round dance. The term came later to be applied to popular songs (as distinct from hymns) associated with the great annual festivals, such as May Day, the New Year, Easter, and Christmas. Christmas carols were popular as early as the 15th century. The custom of singing carols from house to house, collecting gifts, was associated with wassailing. Many of the best-known carols, such as 'God Rest You Merry, Gentlemen' and 'The First Nowell', date back at least as far as the 16th century. Others, such as 'Good King Wenceslas', have modern words but an ancient tune, and still others are completely modern.

Carolina /ˌkærəˈlaɪnə/ two separate states of the USA; see ◊North Carolina and ◊South Carolina.

Caroline of Anspach /ˈkærəlaɪn, ˈænspæx/ 1683–1737. Queen of George II of Great Britain. The daughter of the Margrave of Brandenburg-Anspach, she married George, Electoral Prince of Hanover, in 1705, and followed him to England in 1714 when his father became King George I. As Princess of Wales she held court at Leicester House and was the patron of many of the leading writers and politicians.

Caroline of Brunswick 1768–1821. Queen of George IV of Great Britain. Second daughter of Karl Wilhelm, duke of Brunswick, and Augusta, sister of George III, she married her first cousin the Prince of Wales in 1795, but following the birth of the Princess ◊Charlotte a separation was arranged. When her husband ascended the throne in 1820 she was offered an annuity of £50,000 provided she agreed to renounce the title of queen and to continue to live abroad. She returned forthwith to London, where she assumed royal state. In Jul 1820 the government brought in a bill to dissolve the royal marriage, but Lord ◊Brougham's splendid defence led to the bill's abandonment. On Jul 19, 1821, she was prevented by royal order from entering Westminster Abbey for the coronation. She died on Aug 7, and her funeral was the occasion of popular riots.

Carolines /ˈkærəlaɪnz/ scattered archipelago in Micronesia, Pacific Ocean, consisting of over 500 coral islets; area 1,200 sq km/463 sq mi. The chief islands are Ponape, Kusai, and Truk in the eastern group and Yap and Palau in the western. They are well watered and productive. Occupied by Germany from 1899, by Japan in 1914, and mandated by the League of Nations to that country in 1919, they were fortified, contrary to the terms of the mandate. Under Allied air attack in World War II, they were not conquered. In 1947 they became part of the US Trust Territory of the Pacific ◊Islands. Population (1973) 57,100.

Carolingian dynasty Frankish dynasty descending from ◊Pepin the Short (died 768) and named after his son Charles the Great (◊Charlemagne), and ending with Louis V of France, who reigned 966–87, who was followed by Hugh ◊Capet.

Carol I /ˈkærəl/ 1839–1914. First King of Romania, 1881–1914. A prince of the house of Hohenzollern-Sigmaringen, he was invited to become Prince of Romania, then under Turkish

Caroline of Brunswick The wife of George IV of England, Caroline of Brunswick was paid to renounce the title of queen on her husband's accession. This portrait was painted by J. Lonsdale around 1820.

suzerainty, in 1866. In 1877, in alliance with Russia, he declared war on Turkey, and the Treaty of Berlin recognized Romanian independence.

Carol II /ˈkærəl/ 1893–1953. King of Romania. Son of King Ferdinand, he married Princess Helen of Greece, and had a son, Michael. In 1925 he renounced the succession, and settled in Paris with his mistress, Mme Lupescu. Michael succeeded to the throne in 1927, but in 1930 Carol returned to Romania and was proclaimed king. In 1938 he introduced a new constitution under which he became practically absolute. He was forced to abdicate by the pro-German Iron Guard in Sept 1940, and went to Mexico and married his mistress in 1947.

carotene a naturally occurring pigment of the ◊carotenoid group. There are many different carotenes, and they produce the orange, yellow and red colours of carrots, tomatoes, oranges, shellfish etc. They are also involved in ◊photosynthesis as adjuncts to ◊chlorophyll. In animals, carotenes can be converted to ◊vitamin A if that vitamin is lacking in the diet.

carotenoids a group of yellow, orange, red or brown pigments found in many living organisms, particularly in the ◊chloroplasts and other plastids of plants. There are two main types, the carotenes and the xanthophylls. Both are long-chain lipids (◊fats). Some carotenoids act as accessory pigments in ◊photosynthesis, and in certain algae they are the principal light-absorbing pigments, functioning more efficiently than ◊chlorophyll in low intensity light. Carotenes can also occur in organs such as petals, roots and fruits, giving them their characterisitc colour, as in the yellow and orange petals of wallflowers. They are also responsible for the autumn colours of leaves, persisting longer than the green chlorophyll, which masks them during the summer.

Carothers /kəˈrʌðəz/ Wallace 1896–1937. American chemist, best known for his researches in ◊polymerization. By 1930 he had discovered that some polymers were fibre-forming, and in 1937 produced ◊nylon.

carotid artery a major blood vessel supplying ◊blood to the head. There are two carotid arteries, one on each side of the neck.

carp fish *Cyprinus carpio* found over much of Asia and Europe. Its fast growth, large size, and ability to live in still water with little oxygen have made it a good fish to farm, and it has been cultivated for hundreds of years and spread by human agency. It regularly grows to 50 cm/1.8 ft and 3 kg/7 lb but may be very much larger. It lives in lakes, ponds and slow rivers, and the wild form is drab, but cultivated forms may be golden, or may have few large scales (mirror carp) or be scaleless (leather carp). A large proportion of European freshwater fishes belong to the carp family, Cyprinidae, and related fishes are found in Asia, Africa and North America. Members of this family have a single non-spiny dorsal fin, pelvic fins well back on the body, and toothless jaws, although teeth in the throat form an efficient grinding apparatus. Minnows, roach, rudd and many others including goldfish belong to this family. Chinese **grass carp** *Ctenopharyngodon idella* have been introduced to European rivers for weed control.

Carpaccio /kɑːˈpætʃɪəʊ/ Vittorio 1465–1522. Venetian artist, painter of his native city and of religious works, famous for the cycle of paintings on *The Legend of Saint Ursula* painted from 1490 (Accademia, Venice).

Carpathian Mountains /kɑːˈpeɪθɪənz/ Central European mountain system, forming a semi-circle through Czechoslovakia-Poland-USSR-Romania, 1450 km/900 mi long. The central *Tatra mountains* on the Czech-Polish frontier include the highest peak, Gerlachovka, 2663 m/8737 ft.

Carpeaux /kɑːˈpəʊ/ Jean-Baptiste 1827–1875. French sculptor and painter, who learned his trade at a provincial academy as an artisan, and who after repeated attempts finally won the ◊Prix de Rome in 1854. After visiting Italy, he evolved an intense emotional style, based on the work of ◊Michelangelo. His greatest works are *Ugolino and his sons* 1857–61, and *La Danse* (1865–69).

carpel a female reproductive unit in flowering plants (◊angiosperms). It usually comprises an ◊ovary containing one or more ovules, the stalk or style, and a ◊stigma at its top which receives the pollen. A flower may have one or more carpels, and they may be separate or fused together. Collectively the carpels of a flower are known as the ◊gynoecium.

carpetbagger in US history, derogatory name given by Southerners to the entrepreneurs and politicians from the North who moved to the Southern states during ◊Reconstruction after the ◊Civil War of 1861–65. With the votes of newly enfranchised blacks and some local white people (called ◊scalawags), they won posts in Republican state governments, but were resented by many white Southerners as outsiders and opportunists. The term thus came to mean a corrupt outsider who profits from an area's political instability. They were so called because they were supposed to own no property but what they carried in their carpetbags, or knapsacks.

Carpini /kɑːˈpiːni/ Johannes de Plano 1182–1252. Franciscan friar and traveller. In 1245 Pope Innocent IV placed him in charge of a fact-finding mission to Mongolia, from which he returned in 1247. His history of the Mongols is a valuable piece of practical research and an interesting document of its time.

Carracci /kəˈrɑːtʃi/ Agostino c. 1557–1602. Italian painter, who assisted his cousin Lodovico Carracci (c. 1555–1619) in founding the Academy of Art in Bologna.

Carracci /kəˈrɑːtʃi/ Annibale 1560–1609. Italian painter, the greatest painter of the Carracci family and perhaps of the Bolognese school. In the years around 1600 decorated Cardinal Farnese's gallery of antique sculpture in the Farnese Palace, turning the walls and ceiling into a *trompe l'oeil* Classical picture gallery. He also initiated the landscape as a new category of art with his *Flight into Egypt* 1603, which has as its real subject an idealized vision of the classical Roman countryside, harmonious and calm.

carragheen species of deep reddish branched seaweed *Chondrus crispus*, named after Carragheen in Ireland, and found elsewhere in N Europe. It is exploited commercially in food and medicinal preparations, and as cattle feed.

Carrara /kəˈrɑːrə/ town in Tuscany, Italy, 60 km/37 mi NW of Livorno, with quarries of some of the finest white marble in the world. These were worked by the Romans, abandoned in the 5th century AD, and came into use again with the revival of sculpture and architecture in the 12th century. Population (1977) 56,000.

Carrel /kəˈrel/ Alexis 1873–1944. French surgeon, whose method of suturing blood vessels prepared the way for organ transplants; he was awarded a Nobel prize in 1912.

Carrhae /ˈkæriː/ ancient town near modern Haran, Turkey, where ◊Crassus was defeated by the Parthians in 53 BC.

carriage driving sport in which a two-wheeled carriage is pulled by a horse. Events include ◊dressage and obstacle driving, and the marathon, in which less elegant carriages are used. It has been popularized by Prince Philip of Britain.

carrier /ˈkæriə/ someone whose body harbours disease-causing organisms (such as typhoid bacteria) but shows no symptoms of the disease. He or she can, however, pass the infection to others.

Carrington /ˈkærɪŋtən/ Peter Alexander Rupert, 6th Baron 1919– . British Conservative politician. He was defence secretary 1970–74, and led the opposition in the House of Lords 1964–70 and 1974–79. While foreign secretary 1979–82, he negotiated independence for Zimbabwe, but resigned after failing to anticipate the Falklands crisis. He became secretary-general of NATO in 1984.

Carroll /ˈkærəl/ Lewis, pseudonym of Charles Lutwidge Dodgson 1832–1898. English mathematician and writer of children's books.

Born in Daresbury, Cheshire, he became a mathematics lecturer at Oxford and published books on mathematics under his own name. *Alice's Adventures in Wonderland*, appeared in 1865 under the pseudonym of Lewis Carroll, and quickly became popular. It grew out of a story told by Dodgson to amuse three little girls, including the original 'Alice', the daughter of Dean Liddell, Dean of Christ Church. During his lifetime Dodgson refused to acknowledge any connection with any books not published under his own name, but a sequel, *Through the Looking Glass*, followed in 1872. Among later works was the mock-heroic nonsense poem 'The Hunting of the Snark' 1876. A shy man with a stammer, he never married. He was among the pioneers of portrait photography.

Carroll Charles Lutwidge Dodgson – Lewis Carroll – who, as well as a mathematician and author of the *Alice* books, was a pioneer of portrait photography, pictured here by Rejlander polishing a lens.

carrot hardy European biennial *Daucus carota*, family Umbelliferae, grown since the 16th century for its edible root, which has a high sugar content and also contains carotene, which can be converted by the human liver to vitamin A.

carrying capacity in ecology, the maximum number of animals of a given species that a particular area can support. When the carrying capacity is exceeded, there is insufficient food (or other resources) for all members of the population. The population may then be reduced by emigration, reproductive failure, or death through starvation.

Carse of Gowrie /ˈkɑːs əv ˈɡaʊri/ fertile lowland plain bordering the Firth of Tay. It is 24

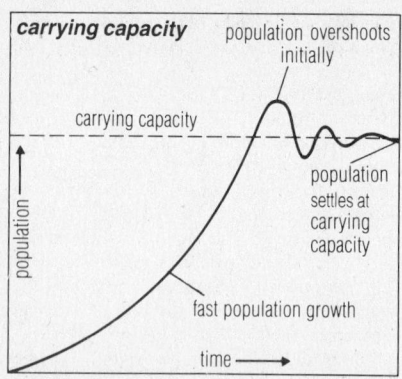

carrying capacity — population overshoots initially — carrying capacity — population settles at carrying capacity — fast population growth — population — time

km/15 mi long, and is one of Scotland's most productive agricultural areas.

Carson /ˈkɑːsən/ Christopher 'Kit' 1809–68. American frontiersman, guide, and Indian agent, who later fought for the Federal side in the Civil War; ◊Carson City was named after him.

Carson /ˈkɑːsən/ Edward Henry, Baron Carson 1854–1935. Irish politician and lawyer. He was a well-known member of both the English and Irish Bars and played a decisive part in the trial of Oscar ◊Wilde. In the years before World War I he led the movement in Ulster to resist Irish ◊Home Rule by force of arms if need be, but on the outbreak of war he campaigned in Ulster in support of the government, and took office under both Asquith and Lloyd George (attorney general 1915, First Lord of the Admiralty 1916, member of the war cabinet 1917–18). He was a Member of Parliament 1892–1921 and a Lord of Appeal in Ordinary, 1921–29.

Carson /ˈkɑːsən/ Rachel 1907–1964. American naturalist. An aquatic biologist with the US Fish and Wildlife Service 1936–49, she then became its editor-in-chief until 1952. In 1951, she published *The Sea Around Us*, and in 1963 *Silent Spring*, attacking the indiscriminate use of pesticides.

Carson City /ˈkɑːsən/ capital of Nevada, USA; population (1980) 30,810. Smallest of the state capitals, it is named after Kit ◊Carson.

Cartagena /ˌkɑːtəˈdʒiːnə/ port and industrial city in N Colombia, capital of the department of Bolívar. Population (1980) 470,000. Founded in 1533, it was taken by ◊Drake in 1586. A pipeline brings petroleum here from the Baranco Dermaja wells.

Cartagena /ˌkɑːtəˈdʒiːnə/ Spanish industrial city, seaport, and naval base in the province of Murcia on the Mediterranean. Population (1981) 172,751.

history It was founded about 225 BC by the Carthaginian ◊Hasdrubal, and was then called New Carthage; it continued to flourish under the Romans and the Moors, and was conquered by the Spanish in 1269. It has a 13th-century cathedral and Roman remains.

cartel (from German *Kartell*, a group) a group of industrial businesses which remain independent but which collectively restrict output or raise prices so as to prevent entrants to the market and increase profits. They therefore represent a form of ◊oligopoly. The growth of organizations such as ◊EFTA and the ◊EC increased the danger of the establishment of cartels and operation of restrictive practices. Both the Treaty of Rome and Stockholm Convention (governing EC and EFTA, respectively) contain provisions for control.

Carter /'kɑːtə/ 'Jimmy' (James Earl) 1924– . 39th president of the USA 1977–81. Born in Plains, Georgia; he served in the Navy, studied nuclear physics, and after a spell as a peanut farmer entered politics as a Democrat in 1953. In 1976 he narrowly wrested the presidency from Ford. Features of his presidency were the ◊Panama Treaty, the ◊Camp David Agreements, and the Iranian seizure of US embassy hostages. He was defeated by Reagan in 1980.

Carter /'kɑːtə/ Angela 1940– . English writer of the ◊magic realist school. Her novels include *The Magic Toyshop* (filmed by David Wheatley 1987) and *Nights at the Circus* 1984. She co-wrote the script for the film *The Company of Wolves* 1984, which was based on one of her stories.

Carter /'kɑːtə/ Elliott (Cook) 1908– . US composer. His early works show the influence of Stravinsky, but his musical language has moved on to become tough and dissonant. His works include four string quartets, the Symphony for Three Orchestras 1967, and *A Mirror on Which to Dwell* 1975.

Carter Doctrine assertion in 1980 by President Carter of a vital US interest in the Gulf region (prompted by Soviet invasion of Afghanistan): any outside attempt at control would be met by force if necessary.

Cartesian coordinates in ◊coordinate geometry, a system used to denote the position of a point on a plane or in space with reference to a set of two or more axes. For a plane defined by two axes at right-angles (a horizontal x-axis and a vertical y-axis), the coordinates of a point are given as its perpendicular distance from the y-axis and its perpendicular distance from the x-axis. For example, a point 3 units from the y axis and 4 units from the x-axis has Cartesian co-ordinates (3,4). A point can also be located with reference to a third, z-axis. This is three-dimensional coordinate geometry, which is particularly useful in creating technical drawings of machines or buildings, and in computer-aided design (◊CAD). The Cartesian coordinate system can be extended to any finite number of dimensions (axes), and is used thus in applications in theoretical mathematics. The system is named after the French mathematician and philosopher René ◊Descartes.

Carthage /'kɑːθɪdʒ/ ancient Phoenician city in N Africa, on the gulf of Tunis, 16 km/10 mi N of modern ◊Tunis. Carthage is said to have been founded in 814 ◊c by Phoenician emigrants from Tyre, led by the princess ◊Dido. It developed an extensive commerce throughout the Mediterranean, and traded with the Tin Islands, whose location is believed to have been either Cornwall or SW Spain. After the capture of Tyre by the Babylonians in the 6th century BC it became the natural leader of the Phoenician

colonies in N Africa and Spain, and there soon began a prolonged struggle with the Greeks which centred mainly in Sicily, the E of which was dominated by Greek colonies, while the W was held by Carthaginian trading stations. About 540 BC the Carthaginians defeated a Greek attempt to land in Corsica, and in 480 a Carthaginian attempt to conquer the whole of Sicily was defeated by the Greeks at Himera. Eventually the Carthaginians came into conflict with Rome, and in the first Punic War 264–241 BC they were defeated at sea and expelled from their strongholds in E Sicily. Under ◊Hamilcar Barca, they next proceeded to build up an empire and army in Spain, whence Hamilcar's son Hannibal launched the second Punic War 218–201 BC; he crossed the Pyrenees and Alps and inflicted crushing defeats upon the Roman armies in Italy before being forced back to Africa and defeated at ◊Zama 202 BC. In the third Punic War 149–146 BC, Carthage was finally defeated, and the city itself destroyed by the Romans in 146 BC. About 45 BC Roman colonists were settled in Carthage by Julius ◊Caesar, and it rose to be the wealthy and important capital of the province of Africa. After its capture by the Vandals in AD 439 it was little more than a pirate stronghold. From 533 it formed part of the Byzantine empire until its final destruction by the Arabs in AD 698. The population of Carthage before its destruction by the Romans is said to have numbered over 700,000. The constitution was an aristocratic republic with two chief magistrates elected annually, and a senate of 300 life-members. The religion was Phoenician, including the worship of the goddess Tanit, the great god Baal-Hammon, and the Tyrian Meklarth: human sacrifices were not unknown. The real strength of Carthage lay in its commerce and its powerful navy; its armies were for the most part mercenaries.

Carthusian order Roman Catholic order of monks and, later, nuns, founded by St Bruno in 1084 at ◊Chartreuse, near Grenoble. Living chiefly in unbroken silence, they ate one vegetarian meal a day and supported themselves by their own labours. The first rule was drawn up by Guigo, the fifth Prior. Between then and 1681 a few important changes were made. The order was introduced into England about 1178, when the first Charterhouse was founded at Witham in Essex. They were suppressed at the Reformation, but there is a Charterhouse at Parkminster, Sussex, established in 1833.

Cartier /ˌkɑːti'eɪ/ Georges Etienne 1814–1873. French-Canadian politician. He fought against the British in the rebellion of 1837, was elected to the Canadian parliament in 1848, and was joint prime minister with Sir John Macdonald 1858–62. He furthered railway development and brought Quebec into the Canadian federation in 1867.

Cartier /ˌkɑːti'eɪ/ Jacques 1491–1557. French navigator, who sailed up the St Lawrence river in 1534, and named the site of Montreal, later exploring Canada further.

Cartier-Bresson /ˌkɑːti'eɪ bre'spŋ/ Henri 1908– . French photographer, considered the greatest of photographic artists. His

documentary work was achieved using a small format camera. He was noted for his ability to structure the image and to capture the decisive moment.

cartilage flexible bluish-white connective ◊tissue made up of the protein collagen. In cartilaginous fish it forms the skeleton; in other vertebrates it forms the embryonic skeleton which is replaced by ◊bone in the adult, except in areas of wear such as bone endings, and the discs between the backbones. It also supports the larynx, nose and external ear of mammals.

Cartland /'kɑːtlənd/ Barbara 1904– . English romantic novelist. She published her first book *Jigsaw* in 1921, and since then has produced a prolific stream of stories of chastely romantic love, usually in idealized or exotic settings, for a mainly female audience (such as *Love Climbs In* 1978 and *Moments of Love* 1981). She is a well-known advocate of health foods.

cartomancy the practice of telling fortunes by cards, often ◊tarot cards.

cartoon traditionally a preliminary design for an oil painting, mosaic, and tapestry. When completed the drawing is transferred by tracing or pouncing to the surface on which the work is to be executed. Many still survive, the most famous being by ◊Leonardo da Vinci and ◊Michelangelo. The term is nowadays more commonly applied to a humorous or satirical drawing, often commenting wittily on political events, or telling a story in a sequence of drawings. Cartoons commenting on political affairs became common in England from the 18th century; many of the greatest cartoonists worked for the satirical magazine *Punch*. Noted cartoonists include Thomas ◊Rowlandson, James ◊Gillray, David ◊Low, and James ◊Thurber.

Cartwright /'kɑːtraɪt/ Edmund 1743–1823. British inventor. Born in Nottinghamshire, he went to Oxford and became a country rector (and was also a farmer). In 1785 he patented a power loom. He invented several other machines, but went bankrupt in 1793.

Caruso /kə'ruːsəʊ/ Enrico 1873–1921. Italian operatic tenor. Born in Naples, he made his first appearance on the stage there at 21. In 1902 he achieved a great success at Monte Carlo, in Puccini's *La Bohème*. He subsequently won world-wide fame and is today chiefly remembered for performances as Canio in *Pagliacci*, and the Duke in *Rigoletto*.

Carver /'kɑːvə/ George Washington 1864–1943. American agricultural chemist. Born a slave in Missouri, he devoted his life to improving the economy of the US South and the condition of blacks. He advocated the diversification of crops in the South, promoted peanut production, and was a pioneer in the field of plastics.

Cary /'keəri/ (Arthur) Joyce (Lunel) 1888–1957. British novelist. In 1918 he entered the Colonial Service, retiring two years later because of ill-health, but Nigeria, where he had served, gave a background to such novels as *Mister Johnson* 1939. Other books are *Castle Corner* 1938 and *A House of Children* 1941, both with autobiographical elements; *The Horse's*

Mouth 1944, about a Bohemian artist, Gulley Jimson, and *The Captive and the Free* 1959, dealing with faith-healing and written when he was progressively paralysed by muscular atrophy.

caryatid building support or pillar in the shape of a woman, the name deriving from the Karyatides, who were the priestesses at the temple of Artemis at Karyai; a male figure is a *telamon* or *atlas*.

caryopsis a dry, one-seeded ◊fruit in which the wall of the seed becomes fused to the carpel wall during its development. It is a type of ◊achene, and therefore develops from one ovary and does not split open to release the seed. The caryopsis is typical of members of the grass family (Gramineae), including the cereals.

Casablanca /ˌkæsəˈblæŋkə/ (Arabic *Dar el-Beida*), port, commercial and industrial centre on the Atlantic coast of Morocco; population (1980) 2,175,000; it was occupied by the French in 1907 and developed by them until Morocco became independent in 1956.

Casablanca Conference World War II meeting of Churchill and Roosevelt, 14–24 Jan 1943, at which the Allied demand for the unconditional surrender of Germany, Italy, and Japan was issued.

Casals /kəˈsɑːlz/ Pablo 1876–1973. Spanish Catalan cellist, composer and conductor. Born in Tarragona, he left Spain in 1939 and lived in Prades, in the French Pyrenees, where he founded an annual music festival. He wrote symphonic, chamber and choral works including the Christmas oratorio *The Manger*. He married three times; his first wife was the Portuguese cellist Guilhermina Suggia.

Casals Spanish cellist, conductor, and composer Pablo Casals in 1943.

Casanova de Seingalt /ˌkæsəˈnəʊvə də sænˈgæ lt/ Giovanni Jacopo 1725–98. Italian adventurer, spy, violinist, librarian, and, according to his *Memoirs*, one of the world's great lovers. Born in Venice, he served in the household of Cardinal Acquaviva, and embarked upon a career of intrigue and adventure which took him into many parts of Europe, especially to Paris, Rome, Berlin, Warsaw, and Madrid. From 1774 he was a spy in the Venetian police service. In 1782 a libel got him into trouble, and after more wanderings he was in 1785 appointed Count Waldstein's librarian at his castle of Dûx in Bohemia, where he wrote his *Memoirs* (published 1826–38, although the expurgated text did not appear until 1960–61).

Cascade Range /kæsˈkeɪd/ volcanic mountains in Washington, USA, 64 km/40 mi NE of Portland. They include Mount St Helens and Mount Rainier (the highest peak, 4,392 m/14,408 ft), which is noted for its glaciers. The mountains are the most active in the USA, excluding Alaska and Hawaii.

case grammar a theory of language structure which proposes that the underlying structure of language should contain some sort of functional information about the roles of its components; thus in the sentence, 'The girl opened the door,' the phrase 'the girl' would have the role of agent, not merely that of grammatical subject.

casein main protein of milk, from which it can be separated by the action of acid, rennin, or bacterial action (souring); it is also the main component of cheese. Commercially casein is used in cosmetics, glues, and as a sizing for coating paper.

Casement /ˈkeɪsmənt/ Roger David 1864–1916. Irish nationalist. While in the British consular service he exposed the ruthless exploitation of the people of the Belgian Congo and in Peru, and was knighted in 1911 (degraded 1916). In 1914 he went to Germany and attempted to induce Irish prisoners of war to form an Irish brigade to take part in a republican rising. He returned to Ireland in a submarine in 1916 (actually to postpone, not start, the Easter rising), was arrested, tried for treason, and hanged. His controversial diaries, revealing his homosexuality, were made available by the British government in 1959. His remains were returned to Ireland by the British government in 1965 and are now in Glasnevin cemetery, Dublin.

Caserta /kəˈzɜːtə/ town in S Italy 33 km/21 mi NE of Naples. The base for Garibaldi's campaigns in the 19th century, it was the Allied headquarters in Italy 1943–45, and the German forces surrendered to Field Marshal Alexander here in 1945. Population (1981) 66,318.

Cash /kæʃ/ Johnny 1932– . US country singer, songwriter, and guitarist. His early hits, recorded for Sun Records in Memphis, Tennessee, include the million-selling 'I Walk the Line' 1956. He has also sung gospel, rockabilly, and blues, and many of his songs have become classics.

cash crop crop grown solely for sale rather than for the farmer's own use, for example coffee, cotton or sugar beet. See ◊agriculture.

cashew tree of tropical America *Anacardium occidentale*, family Anacardiaceae, with an edible kidney-shaped nut in a hard shell, now extensively cultivated in India and Africa.

Caslavska /ˈtʃɑːslævskə/ Vera 1943– . Czech gymnast. The first of the great post-war

Casement British public official and Irish nationalist Roger Casement in 1915. He was arrested on landing in Ireland from a German submarine in 1916, and executed for high treason.

female gymnasts, she won a record 21 Olympic, world, and European titles, beginning with the one she gained on the beam at the 1959 European championship. She ended her international career at the 1968 Olympics, where she won four gold medals which she gave away, one to each of the four leaders of her country, at the time of the Soviet invasion.

Caspian Sea /ˈkæspiən/ world's largest inland sea, divided between Iran and the USSR. An underwater ridge divides it into two halves, of which the shallow N is almost salt-free. There are no tides. Drainage in the N and the damming of tributaries such as the Volga and Ural for hydroelectric power have led to shrinkage over the last 50 years, and the growth of industry along its shores has caused pollution and damaged the Russian and Iranian caviar industries. The chief ports are Astrakhan and Baku. Area about 400,000 sq km/155,000 sq mi. It is now approximately 28 m/90 ft below statute sea level.

Cassandra /kəˈsændrə/ in Greek mythology, the daughter of ◊Priam, king of Troy. Her prophecies (for example of the fall of Troy) were never believed, because she had rejected the love of Apollo. She was murdered with ◊Agamemnon by ◊Clytemnestra.

Cassatt /kəˈsæt/ Mary 1845–1926. American artist. In 1875 she went to Europe and finally settled near Paris. She is best known for her impressionistic renderings of mothers and children.

cassava or manioc. The starch-containing roots of the South American plant, *Manihot utilissima*, now widely grown in the tropics, which belongs to the family Euphorbiaceae. The bitter cassava yields a flower called Brazilian arrowroot, from which tapioca and bread are made.

Cassavetes /ˌkæsəˈveɪtiːz/ John 1929– . American actor and film director. He has

Cassatt *In the Garden*, pastel on paper 1893, by the American artist Mary Cassatt. Cassatt settled in France in her early thirties, where she worked closely with the Impressionists.

appeared in many films, including *The Dirty Dozen* 1967, and *Rosemary's Baby* 1968. He has also directed experimental, apparently improvised films, including *Shadows* 1960, and *The Killing of a Chinese Bookie* 1980.

Cassel /'kæsəl/ alternative spelling of ◊Kassel, an industrial town in West Germany.

cassia bark of a plant *Cinnamomum cassia* of the family Lauraceae. It is aromatic, and closely resembles the true cinnamon, for which it is widely substited.
Cassia is also a genus of plants of the family Leguminosae, many of which have strong purgative properties; *Cassia senna* is the source of the laxative senna.

Cassini /kæ'si:ni/ Jean Dominique 1625–1712. French astronomer, who made pioneering studies of the planets. Born in Italy, he became director of the Paris Observatory in 1671, where he discovered four moons of ◊Saturn and the gap in the rings of Saturn now called Cassini's division. His son, grandson, and great-grandson in turn became directors of the Paris Observatory.

Cassino /kæ'si:nəʊ/ town in S Italy, 80 km/50 mi NW of Naples, at the foot of Monte Cassino. It was the scene of heavy fighting during World War II in 1944, when most of the town was destroyed. It was rebuilt 1.5 km/1 mi to the N. The famous abbey on the summit of Monte Cassino, founded by St Benedict in 529, was rebuilt in 1956. Population (1981) 31,139.

Cassiopeia in Greek mythology, the mother of ◊Andromeda.

Cassiopeia in astronomy, prominent ◊constellation of the northern hemisphere, representing Cassiopeia, mother of Andromeda, It has a distinctive W-shape and contains one of the most powerful radio sources in the sky, Cassiopeia A, the remains of a ◊supernova (star explosion).

cassiterite chief ore of tin, consisting of black stannic oxide (SnO_2). Usually found in granite rocks, it was formerly extensively mined in Cornwall. Today Malaysia is the world's major supplier; other sources of cassiterite (also called tinstone) are in Africa, Indonesia and South America.

Cassius /'kæsiəs/ Gaius died 42 BC. Roman soldier, one of the conspirators who killed ◊Julius Caesar. He fought at Carrhae 53 BC, and with the republicans against Caesar at Pharsalus 48 BC, was pardoned and appointed praetor, but became a leader in the conspiracy of 44 BC, and after Caesar's death joined Brutus. He committed suicide after his defeat at ◊Philippi 42 BC.

Cassivelaunus /ˌkæsɪvə'lɔːnəs/ chieftain of the British tribe, the Catuvellauni, who led the British resistance to Caesar in 54 BC.

Casson /'kæsən/ Hugh 1910– . British architect. Director of architecture for the Festival of Britain 1948–51, he was knighted in 1952, was professor at the Royal College of Art 1953–75, and President of the Royal Academy 1976–84. His books include *Victorian Architecture* 1948.

cassowary large flightless running bird, genus *Casuarius*, found in New Guinea and N Australia, usually in forests. Cassowaries are related to emus, but have a bare head with a horny casque, or helmet, on top, and brightly coloured skin on the neck. The loose plumage is black and the wings are tiny, but cassowaries can run and leap well, and defend themselves by kicking. They stand up to 1.5 m/5 ft tall.

castanets Spanish percussion instrument made of two hollowed wooden shells, held in the hand to produce a rhythmic accompaniment to dance.

caste grouping of Hindu society (Portuguese *casta* 'race') from ancient times into four main classes from which some 3000 subsequent divisions derive: Brahmans (priests), Kshatriyas (nobles and warriors), Vaisyas (traders and farmers), and Sudras (servants), which are said to have originated from the head, arms thighs, and feet respectively of ◊Brahma, the creator; plus a fifth class (probably the aboriginal inhabitants of the country), known variously as Scheduled Castes, Depressed Classes, Untouchables, Harijan (name coined by Gandhi, 'children of God'), who were considered to be polluting by touch, or even by sight, to others. Discrimination against the last-named was made illegal in 1947, but persists.

Castiglione /ˌkæs,tiːli'əʊni/ Baldassare, Count Castiglione 1478–1529. Italian author and diplomat. Born near Mantua, he served the Duke of Milan, and in 1506 was engaged by the Duke of Albino on a mission to Henry VII of England. While in Spain in 1524 he was created bishop of Avila. He published letters, and poems in Latin and Italian, but is best remembered for his picture of the perfect Renaissance gentleman *Il Cortegiano/The Courtier* 1528.

Castile /kæs'tiːl/ kingdom founded in the 10th century, occupying the central plateau of Spain. Its union with Aragon in 1479 was the foundation of the Spanish state. It comprised the two great basins separated by the Sierra de Gredos and the Sierra de Guadarrama, known traditionally as Old and New Castile. The area now forms the modern regions of ◊Castilla-León and ◊Castilla-La Mancha.
history The kingdom of Castile grew from a small area in the N. In the 11th century Old Castile

Castiglione Perhaps the best expression of the Renaissance spirit has come from the Italian author and diplomat, Count Baldassare Castiglione, in his celebrated dialogue on courtly life, *Il Cortegiano*.

was united with León; in 1085 the kingdom of Toledo was captured from the Moors and became New Castile, with Toledo the capital of the whole. The marriage in 1469 of Isabella, heiress of Castile, to Ferdinand, who became king of Aragon in 1479, united Castile and Aragon.

Castilian language a member of the Romance branch of the Indo-European language family originating in NW Spain, in the provinces of Old and New Castile. It is the basis of present-day standard Spanish (see ◊Spanish language) and is often seen as the same language, the terms *castellano* and *español* being used interchangeably in both Spain and the Spanish-speaking countries of the Americas.

Castilla-La Mancha /kæˈstiːljə lɑː ˈmæntʃə/ autonomous region of central Spain; population (1981) 1,628,000.

Castilla-León /kæˈstiːljə leɪˈɒn/ autonomous region of central Spain; population (1981) 2,557,000.

casting the process of producing solid objects by pouring molten material into a shaped mould and allowing it to cool. Casting is used to shape such materials as glass, plastics, and especially metals and alloys. The casting of metals has been practised for more than 6000 years, using first copper, then ◊bronze, and then iron.

The traditional method of casting metal is *sand casting*. Using a model of the object to be produced, a hollow mould is made in a damp sand and clay mix. Molten metal is then poured into the mould, taking its shape when it cools and solidifies. The sand mould is broken up to release the casting. Permanent metal moulds called *dies* are also used for casting, particularly of small items in mass-production processes. Molten

metal is injected under pressure into cooled dies. *Continuous casting* is a method of shaping bars and slabs which involves pouring molten metal into a hollow, water-cooled mould of the desired cross-section.

cast iron a cheap but invaluable constructional material, whose most common use is for car engine blocks. Cast iron is partly refined ◊pig iron, which is very fluid when molten and highly suitable for shaping by ◊casting. It contains too many impurities, especially carbon, to be readily shaped in any other way. Solid cast iron is heavy and can absorb great shock, but it is very brittle.

castle /ˈkɑːsəl/ the private fortress of a king or noble. The earliest castles in Britain were built following the ◊Norman Conquest, and the art of castle building reached a peak in the 13th century. By the 15th century, the need for castles for domestic defence had largely disappeared, while the advent of gunpowder made them largely useless against attack.

The main parts of a typical castle are: the *keep*, a large central tower containing store rooms, soldiers' quarters, and a hall for the lord and his family; the *inner bailey* or walled courtyard surrounding the keep; the *outer bailey* or second courtyard, separated from the inner bailey by a wall; crenellated *embattlements* through which missiles were discharged against an attacking enemy; rectangular or round *towers* projecting from the walls; the *portcullis*, a heavy grating which could be let down to close the main gate; and the *drawbridge* crossing the ditch or moat surrounding the castle. Sometimes a tower called a *barbican* was constructed over a gateway as an additional defensive measure.

11th century the *motte and bailey* castle (the motte was a mound of earth, and the bailey a courtyard enclosed by a wall); the earliest example is on the Loire river in France, dated 1010. The first *rectangular keep* dates from this time; the best known is the White Tower in the Tower of London.

12th century development of more substantial defensive systems, based in part on the Crusaders' experiences of sieges during the First Crusade 1096; the first *curtain walls* with projecting towers were built (as at Framlingham, Suffolk).

13th century introduction of the *round tower*, both for curtain walls (Pembroke, Wales) and for keeps (Conisborough, Yorkshire); *concentric planning* (particularly in the castles of Wales, such as Beaumaris and Harlech); fortified *town walls*.

14th century first use of gunpowder; inclusion of gunports in curtain walls (Bodiam, Sussex).

15th century fortified manor houses now adequate for private dwelling.

16th century end of castle as a practical means of defence; fortified coastal defences, however, continued to be built (Falmouth, Cornwall).

Castle /ˈkɑːsəl/ Barbara, Baroness Castle (born Betts) 1911– . British Labour politician. She was minister of overseas development 1964–65, transport 1965–68, employment 1968–70 (when her white paper 'In Place of Strife', on trade-union reform, was abandoned as

too controversial), and social services 1974–76, when she was dropped from the cabinet by Callaghan (an opponent of her white paper, who was criticized in her *Diaries* 1980). She led the Labour group in the European Parliament from 1979.

Castleford /ˈkɑːsəlfəd/ town in W Yorkshire, England; population (1981) 36,032.

Castle Hill rising Irish convict revolt in New South Wales, Australia, 4 Mar 1804; a number were killed while parleying with the military under a flag of truce.

Castlemaine /ˈkɑːsəlmeɪn/ town in Victoria, Australia, about 105 km/65 mi NW of Melbourne, on the Loddon. Site of the earliest gold strikes in 1851, its population rose to 30,000 at that period. It survives as an agricultural marketing centre.

Castlemaine /ˈkɑːsəlmeɪn/ Lady 1641–1709. Mistress of Charles II of England. Born Barbara Villiers, she was the wife from 1659 of Roger Palmer (1634–1705), created Earl of Castlemaine in 1661. She was the chief mistress of Charles 1660–70, when she was created Duchess of Cleveland. Among her descendants, through her son the Duke of Grafton (1663–90), is ◊Diana, Princess of Wales.

Castlereagh /ˈkɑːsəlreɪ/ Robert Stewart, Viscount Castlereagh 1769–1822. British Tory politician. When his father, an Ulster landowner, was made an earl in 1796, he took the courtesy title of Viscount Castlereagh. In 1821 he succeeded his father as Marquess of Londonderry. He sat in the Irish House of Commons from 1790. As chief secretary 1797–1801, he suppressed the rebellion of 1798, and helped the younger Pitt secure the union of England, Scotland, and Ireland in 1801. In Parliament at Westminster he was war secretary 1805–06 and 1807–09, when he had to resign after a duel with ◊Canning, and foreign secretary from 1812, when he devoted himself to the overthrow of Napoleon and represented Britain at the Congress of Vienna. Abroad his policy favoured the development of material liberalism, but at home he repressed the Reform movement, and popular opinion held him responsible for the Peterloo massacre of peaceful demonstrators in 1819.

Castor and Pollux/Polydeuces in Greek mythology, twin sons of Leda (by ◊Zeus), brothers of ◊Helen and ◊Clytemnestra. Protectors of seamen, they were transformed at death to the constellation Gemini.

castoreum the preputial follicles of the beaver, abbreviated as 'castor', and used in perfumery.

castor oil plant tropical and subtropical tall shrub *Palma Christi Ricinus communis*, family Euphorbiaceae; the seeds yield the purgative castor oil, and also ricin, one of the most powerful poisons known, which can be 'targeted' to destroy cancer cells, while leaving normal cells untouched.

castration the removal of the testicles. It prevents reproduction, and also much modifies the secondary sexual characteristics: for instance, the voice may remain high as in childhood, and growth of hair on the face and body may become weak or cease, owing to the removal of the hormones normally secreted by the testes.

Castration was formerly used to preserve the treble voice of boy singers or, by Muslims, to provide trustworthy harem guards called eunuchs.

Male domestic animals, especially stallions and bulls, are castrated to prevent undesirable sires from reproducing, to moderate their aggressive and savage disposition, and , in the case of bulls, to make them produce more meat. Cockerels are castrated (capons) to improve their flavour and increase their size. The effects of castration can also be achieved by chemical means, by administration of hormones, in humans and animals.

Castro (Ruz) /ˈkæstrəʊ ˈruːs/ Fidel 1927– . Cuban politician. Of wealthy parentage, Castro was educated at Jesuit schools and, after studying law at the University of Havana, he gained a reputation through his work for poor clients. He strongly opposed the Batista dictatorship, and with his brother Raúl took part in an unsuccessful attack on the Army barracks at Santiago de Cuba in 1953. After spending some time in exile in the USA and Mexico, Castro attempted a secret landing in Cuba in 1956 in which all but 11 of his supporters were killed. He eventually gathered an army of over 5,000 which overthrew Batista in 1959 and he became prime minister a few months later. His regime became socialist and he epoused Marxism-Leninism until in 1974 he rejected the Marxian formula 'from each according to his ability and to each according to his need', and decreed that each Cuban should 'receive according to his work'. He became president in 1976, from 1979 was also president of the Non-Aligned Movement, although promoting the line of the Soviet Union, which subsidized his regime. His brother Raúl was appointed minister of armed forces in 1959.

casuarina tree and shrub, with many Australian and New Guinea species, also found in Africa and Asia. It is gracefully handsome, as is the river she-oak *Casuarina cunninghamiana*, with fronded branches resembling cassowary feathers, hence the name.

cat small carnivorous mammal *Felis catus* kept as a pet and for catching small pests such as rodents. The domestic cat is found in many colour variants – tabby, black, white (pure white are often deaf), grey, ginger (usually males), tortoiseshell (usually females) and combinations. Shorthaired, longhaired ('Persian') and even hairless or tailless ('Manx') varieties are bred, but the domestic cat does not show the same plasticity of form as the dog, and the general shape and size remains the same as its ancestor. This is generally believed to be the *African wild cat Felis libyca*, found across Africa and Arabia, which looks like a large tabby. Many scientists think this is simply a race of the *European wild cat Felis silvestris* of Europe and W Asia. Domestic cats can interbreed with either of these wild relatives. Various other species of small wild cat live in all continents except Antarctica and Australia. Large cats such as the

Castro (Ruz) Cuban revolutionary and premier Fidel Castro, photographed in January, 1959. Opposed to the corrupt Batista dictatorship, he joined forces with his brother, Raúl, and Ernesto 'Che' Guevara, and fought a long guerrilla campaign. He eventually gathered an army of over 5,000, and finally toppled the government. When they entered Havana, Castro was given a hero's welcome.

lion and tiger also belong to the cat family Felidae. All cats walk on the pads of their toes, and have retractile claws. The canine teeth are long and well-developed, as are the shearing teeth in the side of the mouth. The limbs are strong and good for springing or short bursts of speed. The eyes are large and forward-facing, the hearing acute. Cats are well-camouflaged and highly adapted for their role as stealthy hunters. They are, of all mammals, one of the most committed to a carnivorous diet.

catacomb underground cemetery. Those of the early Christians beneath the basilica of St Sebastian in Rome, where bodies were buried in niches in the walls of the tunnels, are particularly well-known.

Catalan language a member of the Romance branch of the Indo-European language family, an Iberian language closely related to Provençal in France. It is spoken in Catalonia in NE Spain, the Balearic Isles, Andorra, and a corner of SW France. Since the end of the Franco regime in Spain in 1975, Catalan nationalists have vigorously promoted their regional language as co-equal in Catalonia with Castilian Spanish.

Catalaunian Fields /ˌkætəˈlɔːnɪən/ plain near Troyes, France, scene of the defeat of ◊Attila by the Romans and Goths under the Roman general Aëtius in 451.

catalepsy in medicine, an abnormal state in which the patient is apparently or actually unconscious. There is no response to stimuli, and the rate of heartbeat and breathing is slow. A similar condition can be drug induced, or produced by hypnosis, but catalepsy as ordinarily understood occurs spontaneously. It is essentially an extreme form of resistive stupor, generally considered to be a defence against the environment or reality.

Catal Huyuk /tʃæˈtɑːl huːˈjuːk/ Neolithic site (6,000 BC) discovered by James Mellaart in 1961 in Anatolia, SE of Konya. A fortified city, it had temples with fine wall paintings, and there were rich finds including jewellery, obsidian, mirrors. Together with ◊finds at Jericho, it demonstrated much earlier development of urban life in the ancient world than previously imagined.

Catalonia /ˌkætəˈləʊnɪə/ autonomous region (*Cataluña*) of NE Spain, which includes Barcelona, Lérida, and Tarragona. Area 31,960 sq km/12,340 sq mi; population (1981) 5,938,208. The N is mountainous, but in the S the Ebro basin breaks through the Castellón mountains. The soil is fertile, but the climate in the interior is arid. Hydroelectric power is produced, and Catalonia leads Spain in industrial development, especially in wool and cotton textiles. The capital is Barcelona.
history The region has a long tradition of independence, enjoying autonomy 1932–39, but lost its privileges for supporting the Republican cause in the ◊Spanish Civil War. Autonomy and official use of the Catalan language were restored in 1980. French Catalonia is the adjacent *département* of Pyrénées–Orientales.

catalpa tree found in N America, China, and West Indies, belonging to the Bignoniaceae. The Indian bean tree, *Catalpa bignoniodes*, has been introduced into Europe. It has large, heart-shaped leaves, and white, yellow and purple streaked bell-shaped flowers.

catalyst a substance which alters the speed of a chemical or biochemical reaction but which remains unchanged at the end of the reaction. ◊Enzymes are biochemical catalysts. In practice most catalysts are used to speed up reactions.

catamaran a twin-hulled sailing vessel, based on the aboriginal craft of S America and the Indies, made of logs lashed together, with an outrigger. A similar vessel with three hulls is known as a trimaran.

Catania /kəˈtɑːnɪə/ industrial port in Sicily; population (1981) 380,328. It exports local sulphur.

cataract opacity of the lens of the eye. It sometimes affects children (lamellar cataract), although the commonest form is senile cataracts, occurring chiefly in those over 50. Fluid accumulates between the fibres of the lens and gives place to deposits of albumen; these coalesce into rounded bodies; the lens fibres themselves break down, and areas of the lens become filled with opaque products of degeneration. The condition nearly always affects both eyes, but

usually one more than the other. In most cases the treatment is extraction of the lens. This enables the patient to see, but not to alter focus, but a plastic lens may be implanted with which a change of spectacles will change focus.

catarrh the excessive secretion of mucous fluid, sometimes mixed with pus, from the nose, as the result of a cold, or hay fever.

catastrophe theory mathematical theory developed by René Thom in 1972, in which he showed that the growth of an organism proceeds by a series of gradual changes, which are triggered by, and in turn trigger, large-scale changes or 'catastrophic' jumps. It also has applications in engineering; for example, the gradual strain on the structure of a bridge which eventually results in a sudden collapse, and has been extended to economic and psychological events; for example, a quarrel between two people, which reaches a point where it suddenly comes to a crisis – perhaps of physical violence.

catastrophism geological theory that the features of the earth were formed by violent convulsions, beyond the ordinary workings of nature. The theory was largely the work of Georges ◊Cuvier. It was later replaced by the theories of ◊uniformitarianism and ◊evolution, particularly through the work of Charles ◊Lyell.

catchment area area from which water is collected by a river; hence area from which a school draws pupils, for instance.

catchment area

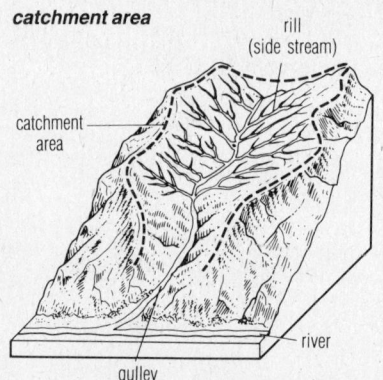

rill
(side stream)

catchment
area

river

gulley

Cateau-Cambresis, Treaty of treaty which ended the dynastic wars between the Valois of France and the Habsburg Empire, 2–3 Apr 1559.

catechism teaching by question and answer on the Socratic method, but especially as a means of instructing children in the basics of the Christian creed. A form of catechism was used for the catechumens in the early Christian Church. Little books of catechism became numerous at the Reformation. Luther published simple catechisms for children and unlearned people, and a larger catechism for the use of teachers. The most popular Roman Catholic catechism was that of Peter Canisius 1555; that with the widest circulation now is the 'Explanatory catechism of Christian Doctrine'. Among the best-known Protestant catechisms are Calvin's Geneva Catechism 1537; that composed by Cranmer and Ridley with additions by Overall 1549–1661, incorporated in the Book

of Common Prayer; The Presbyterian Catechism 1647–48; and the Evangelical Free Church Catechism 1898.

catecholamine a type of chemical that functions as a ◊neurotransmitter or a ◊hormone. They include dopamine, epinephrine (adrenaline) and norepinephrine (noradrenaline).

catechu an extract of the leaves and shoots of *Uncaria gambier*, an East Indian acacia. It is rich in tannic acid, which is released slowly, a property which makes it a useful intestinal astringent in diarrhoea.

category in philosophy, a fundamental concept applied to being, which cannot be reduced to anything more elementary. Aristotle listed ten categories: substance, quantity, quality, relation, place, time, position, state, action, passion. ◊Kant derived a table of 12 categories from the forms of judgement. His categories are applied in experience, although they do not derive from it.

catenary a curve taken up by a flexible cable suspended between two points. The term is used to describe the overhead suspension cables that hold the conductor wire of an electric railway or tramway.

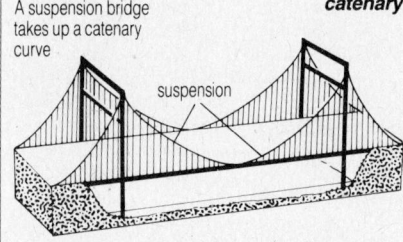

A suspension bridge
takes up a catenary
curve

catenary

suspension

caterpillar larval stage of a butterfly or moth. Worm-like in form the body is segmented. The abdominal segments bear a varying number of 'pro-legs' as well as the six true legs on the thoracic segments. The head has strong biting mandibles, silk glands, and a spinneret. In many species the body is hairy, and the body is often provided with scent and other glands. Many caterpillars resemble the plant on which they feed, dry twigs, or rolled leaves. Others are highly coloured and rely for their protection on their irritant hairs, disagreeable smell, or on their power to eject a corrosive fluid. Yet others take up a 'threat attitude' when attacked.
Caterpillars emerge from eggs which have been laid by the female insect on the food plant and feed greedily, increasing greatly in size and casting their skins several times, until the pupal stage is reached.

caterpillar track the kind of track on which track-laying vehicles such as tanks and ◊bulldozers run, which takes the place of ordinary tyred wheels. The caterpillar track consists of an endless flexible belt of metal plates. A track-laying vehicle has a track each side. Its engine drives small cog wheels that run along the top of the part of the track in contact with the ground. The great advantage of such tracks over wheels is that they distribute the vehicle's weight over a wider area. They are thus ideal for use in soft and waterlogged ground conditions.

catfish one of the many fishes belonging to the order Siluriformes, in which barbels (feelers) on the head are well-developed, so giving a resemblance to the whiskers of a cat. Catfishes are found worldwide, mainly but not exclusively in fresh water, and are especially plentiful in South America. The eastern European *giant catfish* or *wels Silurus glanis* has been introduced to several places in Britain. It grows to 1.5 m/5 ft long or more. The quite unrelated marine *wolf-fish Anarhicas lupus*, a deepsea relative of the blenny growing 1.2 m/4 ft long is sometimes called catfish.

Cathars /'kæθɑːz, 'kæθəriː/ or Cathari (medieval Latin, 'the pure'). A sect in medieval Europe usually numbered among the Christian heretics. They started about the 10th century in the Balkans where they were called Bogomils, spread to the southern countries of W Europe where they were often identified with the ◊Albigenses, and by the middle of the 14th century had been destroyed or driven underground by the Inquisition. They believed that this world is under the domination of Satan, and men and women are the terrestrial embodiment of spirits who were inspired by him to revolt and were driven out of heaven. At death the soul will become again imprisoned in flesh, whether of human or animal, unless it has been united in this life with Christ. If a human has become one of the Cathars, death brings release, the Beatific Vision, and immortality in Christ's presence. Baptism with the spirit – the *consolamentum* – was the central rite, which was held to remedy the disaster of the Fall. The spirit received was the Paraclete, the Comforter, and it was imparted by imposition of hands. Those who received it were included among the Perfect, the ordained priesthood, were implicitly obeyed in everything, and lived lives of the strictest self-denial and chastity, The Believers or *Credentes* could approach God only through the Perfect.

cathedral (Latin *cathedra*, a seat or throne). Christian church containing the throne of a bishop or archbishop, which is usually situated on the south side of the choir. There are cathedrals in most of the important cities of Britain, and formerly they were distinguished as monastic and secular cathedrals, the clergy of the latter not being members of a regular monastic order. The term 'minster' applied to such cathedrals as Lincoln and York does not imply that they were at one time monastic churches, but it originated in the name given to the bishop and cathedral clergy who were often referred to as a *monasterium*. After the dissolution of the monasteries by Henry VIII, most of the monastic churches were re-founded and are called Cathedrals of the New Foundation. Cathedrals of sees founded since 1836 include St Albans, Southwark, Truro, Birmingham, and Liverpool. Among the most famous American cathedrals are: St Patrick's and St John the Divine, both in New York, and the Episcopal Cathedral of St Peter and St Paul, Washington, DC. A cathedral is governed by a dean and chapter.

Cather /'kæðə/ Willa Sibert 1876–1947. American novelist, born in Virginia. She wrote about Western pioneer life, for example in *Death Comes for the Archbishop* 1927, set in New Mexico.

Catherine de' Medici /deɪ 'medɪtʃi/ 1519–1589. French queen consort of Henry II, whom she married in 1533, and mother of Francis II, Charles IX, and Henry III. At first outshone by Diane de ◊Poitiers, she became regent 1560–63 for Charles IX, and was politically powerful until his death in 1574. At first scheming with the ◊Huguenots, she later opposed them. She also patronized the arts.

Catherine de' Medici Catherine was a true Medici in her love of magnificent architecture, and during her regency much work was carried out on the Palace of the Tuileries.

Catherine of Aragon /'ærəgən/ 1485–1536. First queen of Henry VIII of England. She married Henry's elder brother, Prince Arthur, in 1501 (the marriage was allegedly unconsummated), and on his death in 1502 was betrothed to Henry, marrying him on his accession in 1509. Of their six children, only a daughter (later Mary I) lived. Wanting a male heir, Henry sought an annulment in 1526 on the grounds that the union with his brother's widow was invalid despite a papal dispensation. When the Pope demanded that the case be referred to him, Henry married Anne Boleyn, afterwards receiving the desired decree of nullity from Cranmer, the archbishop of Canterbury, in 1533. The Reformation in England followed, and Catherine went into retirement until her death.

Catherine of Braganza /brə'gænzə/ 1638–1705. Queen of Charles II of England, whom she married in 1662, bringing the Portuguese possessions of Bombay and Tangier as her dowry. Her childlessness and practice of her Catholic faith were unpopular, but Charles resisted pressure for divorce. The daughter of João IV of Portugal (1604–56), she returned to Lisbon in 1692.

Catherine of Genoa, Saint /'dʒenəʊə/ 1447–1510. Italian mystic, who devoted herself

to the sick and to meditation. Her feast day is 15 Sept.

Catherine of Siena /si'enə/ 1347–1380. Catholic saint and mystic, born at Siena in Italy. She practised severe mortification while still a child, and at the age of 16 became a Dominican tertiary. She attempted to reconcile the Florentines with the Pope, and persuaded Gregory XI to return to Rome from Avignon in 1376. In 1375 she is said to have received on her body the stigmata, the impression of Christ's wounds. Her *Dialogue* is a classic mystical work. She was canonized in 1461.

Catherine of Valois /væl'wɑː/ 1401–1437. Queen of Henry V of England, whom she married in 1420, becoming the mother of Henry VI. After the death of Henry V, she secretly married Owen Tudor (c. 1400–61) about 1425, and their son became the father of Henry VII.

Catherine I /'kæθrɪn/ 1683–1727. Empress of Russia. A Lithuanian peasant girl, born Martha Skavronsky, she married a Swedish dragoon and eventually became the mistress of Peter the Great. In 1703 she was rechristened as Katarina Alexeievna, and in 1711 the emperor divorced his wife and married Catherine. She accompanied him in his campaigns, and showed tact and shrewdness. In 1724 she was proclaimed empress, and after Peter's death in 1725 she ruled capably with the help of her ministers. She allied Russia with Austria and Spain in an anti-English bloc.

Catherine II /'kæɪrɪn/ the Great 1729–1796. Empress of Russia. Daughter of the prince of Anhalt-Zerbst, she married in 1745 the Russian grand duke Peter, who was an unbalanced weakling, and six months after his becoming Tsar in 1762 he was put out of the way. Henceforth Catherine ruled alone and proved capable and energetic. During her reign Russia extended its boundaries to include territory from Turkey (1774) and Sweden (1790), and profited by the Partitions of Poland. Catherine's private life was notorious throughout Europe, but she did not permit her amours to influence her policy. She admired and aided the Encyclopedists, and corresponded with Voltaire and D'Alembert.

cathode the electrode towards which positive particles (cations) move within a device, such as the cells of a battery, electrolytic cells, diodes.

cathode-ray tube a form of vacuum tube in which a beam of electrons is produced and focused on to a fluorescent screen. It is an essential component of television receivers, computer visual display units (VDU) and of oscilloscopes, instruments widely used in electronics for studying waveforms.

Catholic Church the whole body of the Christian Church, though by those who accept Papal supremacy usually applied only to themselves. Members of other churches add the qualifying term 'Roman' when speaking of them. See also ◊Christianity.

Catholic Emancipation acts passed in Britain 1780–1829 to relieve Catholics of restrictions imposed from the time of Henry VIII.

Catiline /'kætɪlaɪn/ (Lucius Sergius Catilina) c. 108–62 BC. Roman politician. Twice

Catherine II An extremely intelligent ruler and patron of the arts, Catherine the Great of Russia is remembered as a benevolent despot who significantly increased Russia's territory, into Turkey, Sweden and Poland.

failing to be elected to the consulship in 64/63 BC, he planned a military coup, but ◊Cicero exposed his conspiracy. He died at the head of the insurgents

cation an ion carrying a positive charge. During electrolysis, cations in the electrolyte move to the cathode (negative electrode). See also ◊anion.

catkin in flowering plants (◊angiosperms), a pendulous inflorescence, bearing numerous small, usually unisexual flowers. The tiny flowers are stalkless and the petals and sepals are usually absent or much reduced in size. Many types of trees bear catkins, including willows, poplars, and birches. Most plants with catkins are wind-pollinated, so the male catkins produce large quantities of pollen (see ◊arenophily). Some ◊gymnosperms also have catkin-like structures that produce pollen, for example, the swamp cypress *Taxodium*.

Cato /'keɪtəʊ/ Marcus Porcius 234–149 BC. Roman statesman. Appointed censor (senior magistrate) in 184, he excluded from the senate those who did not meet his high standards, and was so impressed by the power of ◊Carthage, on a visit in 157, that he ended every speech by saying 'Carthage must be destroyed.' His farming manual is the earliest surviving work in Latin prose.

Cato Street Conspiracy unsuccessful plot hatched in Cato Street, Edgware Road, London, to murder ◊Castlereagh and his ministers on 20 Feb 1820. The leader, the radical Arthur Thistlewood (1770–1820), who intended to set up a provisional government, was hanged with four others.

CAT scan Computerized Axial Tomography a special X-ray procedure in which the camera 'scans' a body organ, taking hundreds of X-ray pictures from various angles and levels. These are integrated by computer to build up a composite and detailed picture of the organ.

cats' cradle worldwide game played on the fingers with looped string, and linked with magic and folk-tale.

cat's-eyes reflective studs used to mark the limits of traffic lanes. Yorkshireman Percy Shaw invented them as a road safety device in 1934. A cat's-eye stud has two pairs of reflective prisms (the eyes) set in a rubber pad. They reflect the light of a vehicle's head-lamps back to the driver. When a vehicle goes over a stud, it moves down inside an outer rubber case. The surface of the prisms brush against the rubber case and are thereby cleaned.

Catskills /'kætskɪlz/ American mountain range, mainly in SE New York state; the highest point is Slide Mt, 1,281 m/4,204 ft.

Catterick /'kætərɪk/ village near Richmond in N Yorkshire, England, where there is an important military camp.

cattle large ruminant even-toed hoofed mammals of the family Bovidae, including wild species such as buffaloes, bison, yak, gaur, gayal and banteng, as well as the familiar domestic breeds. Fermentation in the four-chambered stomach allows them to make good use of the grass which is the main part of the diet for most. There are two main types of domesticated cattle. The European breeds are variants of *Bos taurus* descended from the ◊aurochs, and the *zebu Bos indicus*, the humped cattle of India, which are useful in the tropics for their ability to withstand the heat and diseases to which European breeds succumb. Modern European breeds include Charolais and Hereford bred for beef, Friesian and Jersey used in dairying, and dual-purpose breeds such as Simmental. A Friesian cow can produce more than 9,000 litres of milk in a year.

Catullus /kə'tʌləs/ Gaius Valerius c. 84–54 BC. Roman lyric poet, born in Verona. He moved in the literary and political society of Rome and wrote lyrics describing his unhappy love affair with Clodia, probably the wife of the consul Metellus. His longer poems include two wedding-songs. Many of his poems are short verses to his friends.

Caucasoid or *Caucasian* former racial classification used for any of the light-skinned peoples; so named because the German anthropologist J F Blumenbach (1752–1840) theorized that they originated in the Caucasus.

Caucasus /'kɔːkəsəs/ series of mountain ranges between the Caspian and the Black Sea, USSR; 1200 km/750 mi long. The highest is Elbruz, 5633 m/18,480 ft. Arabian thoroughbreds are raised at Tersk farm in the N foothills.

caucus in the USA a closed meeting of regular party members, for example to choose a candidate for office. The term was originally used in Boston, Massachusetts, in the 18th century. In England it was first applied to the organization introduced by Joseph ◊Chamberlain in 1878 and is generally used to mean a local party committee.

cauliflower variety of cabbage *Brassica oleracea*, distinguished by its large flattened head of fleshy, aborted flowers, and by being less hardy than is the broccoli.

cautery destroying, or fusing, body tissues using heat, electricity, or chemicals. Cryocautery employs intense cold; a cautery knife uses heat to seal small blood vessels, so reducing bleeding upon surgical incision.

Cavafy /kə'vɑːfi/ Constantinos, pseudonym of Konstantínos Pétrou 1863–1933. Greek poet. An Alexandrian, he throws a startlingly up-to-date light on the Greek past, recreating the classical period with zest. In 1923 E M Forster translated *Pharos and Pharillon*.

cavalier horseman of noble birth, but in particular a supporter of Charles I in the English Civil War, typically with courtly dress and long hair (as distinct from a Roundhead); also a supporter of Charles II after the Restoration.

Cavalier poet a poet of Charles II's court, including Thomas ◊Carew, Robert ◊Herrick, Richard ◊Lovelace, Sir John ◊Suckling.

Cavalli /kə'væli/ (Pietro) Francesco 1602–1676. Italian composer, organist at St Mark's, Venice, and the first to make opera a popular entertainment with, for example, *Xerxes* 1654, later performed in honour of Louis XIV's wedding in Paris. Twenty-seven of his operas survive.

Cavan /'kævən/ inland county of the Republic of Ireland, though in the province of Ulster. The river Erne divides it into a narrow, mostly low-lying peninsula, some 20 mi long, between Leitrim and Fermanagh, and an eastern section of wild and bare hill country. The soil is generally poor, and the climate moist and cold. Agriculture is the chief industry. The chief towns are Cavan, the capital, population about 3,000, Kilmore, seat of Roman Catholic and Protestant bishoprics, and Virginia. Area 1,890 sq km/730 sq mi; population (1981) 53,855.

cave a hollow in the earth's crust produced by the action of underground water or by waves on a sea coast. Caves of the former type commonly occur in limestone, but not in chalk country where the rocks are soluble in water. A *pothole* is a vertical hole in rock caused by water descending a crack. Cave animals often show loss of pigmentation or sight, and under isolation specialized species may develop. The scientific study of caves is called speleology.

Some of the most famous caves are the Mammoth Cave in Kentucky, 6.4 km/4 mi long and 38 m/125 ft high; the Caverns of Adelsberg (Postumia) near Trieste, which extend for many miles; Carlsbad Cave, the largest in America; the Cheddar caves, Somerset; Fingal's Cave, Staffa, Scotland, famous for its range of basalt columns; and Peak Cavern, Derbyshire.

Cave /keɪv/ Edward 1691–1754. British printer, founder under the pseudonym Sylvanus Urban of *The Gentleman's Magazine* 1731–1914, the first periodical to be called a magazine. Dr Samuel ◊Johnson was an influential contributor 1738–44.

cavefish cave-living fish, which may belong to one of several quite unrelated groups, independently adapted to life in underground waters. They have in common a tendency to blindness and atrophy of the eye, enhanced touch-sensitive organs in the skin, and loss of pigment. In the *Kentucky blind-fish Amblyopsis spelaea* the eyes are vestigial and beneath the skin and the body colourless. These small fishes live underground in limestone caves. The Mexican *cave characin* is a blind colourless form of *Astyanax fasciatus* found in surface rivers of Mexico, and all 'stages' of loss of eyes can be seen in different populations.

Cavell /ˈkævəl/ Edith Louisa 1865–1915. British matron of a Red Cross hospital in Brussels in World War I, who helped Allied soldiers escape to the Dutch frontier. She was court-martialled by the Germans and condemned to death. Her last words were: 'Patriotism is not enough. I must have no hatred or bitterness towards anyone'.

Cavendish /ˈkævəndɪʃ/ Frederick Charles, Lord Cavendish 1836–1882. Second son of the 7th duke of Devonshire. He was appointed chief secretary to the lord-lieutenant of Ireland in 1882. On the evening of his arrival in Dublin he was murdered in Phoenix Park with Burke, the permanent Irish undersecretary, by members of the Irish Invincibles, a group of Irish ◊Fenian extremists founded 1881.

Cavendish /ˈkævəndɪʃ/ Henry 1731–1810. British physicist. A grandson of the 2nd Duke of Devonshire, he devoted his life to scientific pursuits, living in rigorous seclusion at Clapham Common. He discoverd hydrogen, which he called 'inflammable air' (1766), the composition of water, and the composition of nitric acid. The ◊Cavendish experiment was a device of his to discover the mass and density of the Earth.

Cavendish /ˈkævəndɪʃ/ Thomas 1555–1592. English navigator; commander of the third circumnavigation of the world. He sailed in July 1586, touched Brazil, followed down the coast to Patagonia, passed through the Straits of Magellan, and sailed back via the Philippines, Cape of Good Hope, and St Helena, reaching Plymouth after two years and 50 days.

Cavendish experiment measurement of the gravitational attraction between lead and gold spheres, which enabled Henry ◊Cavendish to calculate a mean value for the mass and density of Earth, using Newton's Law of Universal Gravitation.

caviar Russian delicacy, obtained from the roes of the sturgeon. It is prepared by beating and straining the ovaries until the eggs are free from fats and then adding salt.

Cavour /kəˈvuə/ Camillo Benso, Count 1810–1861. Italian nationalist statesman. Prime minister of Piedmont 1852–59 and 1860–61, he enlisted the support of Britain and France for the concept of a united Italy, achieved in 1861. Born in Turin, he served in the army in early life, and entered politics in 1847 as editor of *Il Risorgimento*. From 1848 he sat in the Piedmontese parliament, and held cabinet posts

1850–52. Becoming prime minister in 1852, he sought to secure French and British sympathy for the cause of Italian unity by sending Piedmontese troops to fight in the Crimean War. In 1858 he had a secret meeting with Napoleon III at Plombières, where they planned the war of 1859 against Austria, which resulted in the union of Lombardy with Piedmont. The central Italian states also joined the kingdom of Italy, although Savoy and Nice were to be ceded to France. With Cavour's approval Garibaldi overthrew the Neapolitan monarchy, but to prevent him from marching on Rome Cavour occupied part of the Papal States, which with Naples and Sicily were annexed to Italy.

Cavour As prime minister of Piedmont, Cavour was largely responsible for achieving the unification of Italy in 1861.

cavy type of short-tailed S American rodent, family Caviidae, of which the *guinea-pig Cavia porcellus* is the most familiar example. Wild cavies are greyish or brownish with coarse hair. They live in small groups in burrows. They are kept, and have been since ancient times, as food.

Cawnpore /ˌkɔːnˈpɔː/ former spelling of ◊Kanpur, Indian city.

Caxton /ˈkækstən/ William c. 1422–1491. First English printer. Born in Kent, he was apprenticed to a London mercer 1438, and set up his own business in Bruges 1441–70. In 1471 he went to Cologne, where he learned the art of printing, and then set up his own press in Bruges in partnership with Colard Mansion. The first book from his press, and the first book printed in English, was Caxton's own version of a French romance, *Recuyell of the Historyes of Troye* (1474). Returning to England in 1476 Caxton established himself in Westminster, where he produced the first book printed in England, *Dictes and Sayenges of the Philosophers* (1477). Altogether he printed about 100 books, including editions of Chaucer, Gower and Lydgate, and translated many texts from French and Latin, in addition to revising others, such as Malory's *Morte d'Arthur*.

Cayenne /keɪˈen/ capital, chief port, and international airport of French Guiana, on Cayenne island at the mouth of the river

Cayenne. Founded in 1634 and destroyed by Indians, it dates actually from 1664. It was used as a penal settlement from 1854 to 1946. Population (1982) 38,135.

cayenne pepper a condiment derived from the dried fruits of ◊Capsicum, a genus of plants of the family Solanaceae. It is wholly distinct in its origin from black or white pepper, which is derived from a different plant (*Piper nigrum*).

Cayley /ˈkeɪli/ Arthur 1821–1895. British mathematician, who worked in non-Euclidean geometry, and developed matrix algebra, used by Heisenberg in his elucidation of quantum mechanics.

Cayley /ˈkeɪli/ George 1773–1857. British aviation pioneer and inventor, who produced the first piloted glider in 1853.

Cayman Islands /ˈkeɪmən/ British island group in the West Indies
area 260 sq km/100 sq mi
features comprises three low-lying islands, Grand Cayman, Cayman Brac, and Little Cayman
exports farmed green turtle; seawhip coral, a source of ◊prostaglandins
currency CI dollar
population (1983) 18,750
language English
government Governor, Executive Council and Legislative Assembly
history settled by military deserters in the 17th century, the islands became a pirate lair in the 18th century. Administered with Jamaica until 1962, when they became a separate colony, they are now a tourist resort, international financial centre, and tax haven.

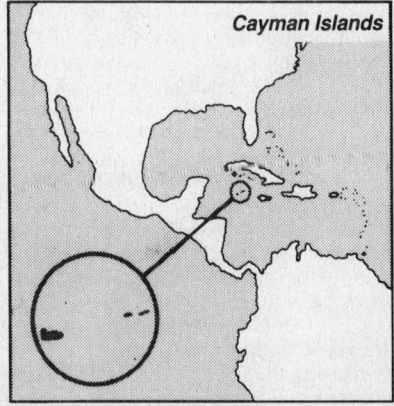

Cayman Islands

Ceauşescu /tʃaʊˈʃesku/ Nicolae 1918– . Romanian politician, leader of Romanian Communist Party (RCP), in power from 1967. Ceauşescu joined the underground RCP in 1933 and was imprisoned for anti-fascist activities 1936–38 and 1940–44. After World War II he was elected to the Grand National Assembly. He was inducted into the party secretariat and Politburo in 1954–55. In 1965 Ceauşescu became leader of the RCP and, in 1967, chair of the state council. He was elected president in 1974. As Romania's leader, Ceauşescu has pursued a policy line independent of and critical of the USSR.

Cebu /seɪˈbuː/ chief city and port of the island of the same name in the Philippines; area 5,086 sq km/1,964 sq mi. The oldest city of the Philippines, founded as San Miguel in 1565. Population (1980) 490,000.

Cecil /ˈsɪsəl/ Robert, 1st Earl of Salisbury 1563–1612. He was chief minister to James I, who created him earl of Salisbury in 1605.

Cecilia /səˈsiːliə/ Christian saint, patron saint of music, martyred in Rome in the 2nd or 3rd century, whose feast day is 22 Nov.

cedar type of coniferous tree. The best-known is the cedar of Lebanon *Cedrus libani*, which grows to a great height in the mountains of Syria and Asia Minor. Of the famous forests on Mount Lebanon only a few groups of trees remain. Together with the Himalayan cedar *Cedrus deodara* and the Atlas cedar *Cedrus atlantica*, it has been introduced into England.

Cedar Rapids town in East Iowa, USA; population (1980) 110,243.

Ceefax one of Britain's two ◊teletext systems (the other is Oracle), or 'magazines of the air', developed by the BBC and first broadcast in 1973. 'Ceefax' is a corruption of 'see facts'.

celandine name given to two plants belonging to different families, and resembling each other only in their bright yellow flowers. The greater celandine *Chelidonium majus* belongs to the Papaveraceae, and is common in English hedgerows. The lesser celandine *Ranunculus ficaria* is a member of the buttercup family, and is a familiar wayside and meadow plant.

Celebes /səˈliːbɪz/ island of the Republic of Indonesia, also known as Sulawesi, which is one of the Great ◊Sunda Islands. It is mountainous and forested, and produces copra and nickel. Area, with dependent islands, 190,000 sq km/73,00 sq mi; population (1980) l0,409,533.

celery plant *Apium graveolens* of the family Umbelliferae. It grows in ditches and salt-marshes, and is coarse and acrid. In cultivation the acrid qualities are removed by blanching.

celestial mechanics the branch of ◊astronomy that deals with the calculation of the orbits of celestial bodies and their gravitational attractions, such as those that produce the tides on Earth. Celestial mechanics is also used to calculate the orbits of artificial satellites and space probes. It is based on the laws of motion and gravity laid down by Isaac ◊Newton.

celestial sphere the imaginary sphere surrounding the Earth, on which the celestial bodies seem to lie. The positions of bodies such as ◊stars, ◊planets and ◊galaxies are specified by their coordinates on the celestial sphere. The equivalents of latitude and longitude on the celestial sphere are called ◊declination and ◊right ascension. The *celestial poles* lie directly above the Earth's poles, and the *celestial equator* lies over the Earth's equator.

celestine, or celestite mineral consisting of strontium sulphate (SrSO4). It is the principal source of ◊strontium; found in Germany, Italy, and the USA.

Céline /seˈliːn/ Louis Ferdinand, pseudonym of Louis Destouches 1884–1961. French novelist, whose writings (the first of which was *Voyage au bout de la nuit/Journey to the End*

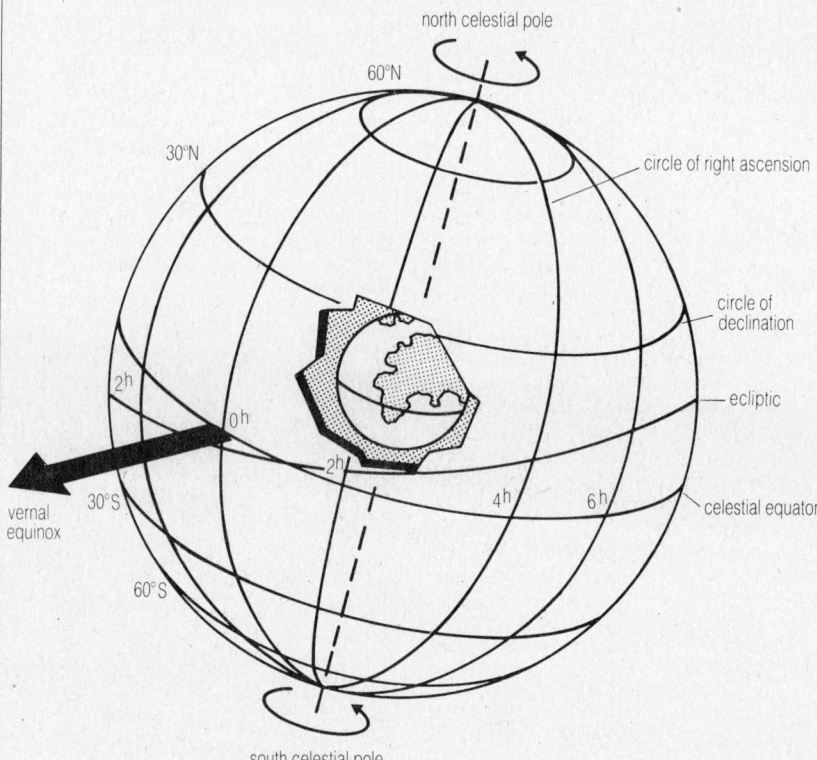

celestial sphere

north celestial pole

60°N

30°N

circle of right ascension

circle of declination

ecliptic

2h

0h

2h

4h   6h

30°S

celestial equator

vernal equinox

60°S

south celestial pole

of the Night 1932, were controversial for their cynicism and misanthropy.

cell in biology, a discrete, membrane-bound portion of living matter, the smallest unit capable of an independent existence. The word 'cell' was first used by Robert Hooke in his *Micrographia*) 1665, to describe the structure of plant tissue.All living organisms consist of one or more cells, with the exception of ◊viruses. Bacteria, protozoa and many other microorganisms consist of single cells, whereas a human is made up of billions of cells. Essential features of a cell are the membrane which encloses it and restricts the flow of substances in and out; the jelly-like material within, often known as ◊protoplasm, the ◊ribosomes that carry out protein synthesis, and the ◊DNA that forms the hereditary material. The composition of the protoplasm varies, but its breakdown products when the cell dies are mostly proteins. It also contains carbohydrates, fats, and the lipoids lecithin and cholesterin, besides inorganic salts such as the phosphates and chlorides of potash, soda, and lime. The cell wall in most animal cells is not a substantial membrane, and the shape of the cell is maintained by surface tension or chemical action.

In protozoa, fungi, and higher animals and plants, DNA is organized into ◊chromosomes and contained within a ◊nucleus; this type of cell is ◊eukaryotic. The only cells of the human body which have no nucleus are the red blood cells. The nuclei of some cells contain a denser spot called the ◊nucleolus, but many kinds of cells do not.

In bacteria and cyanobacteria the DNA forms a simple loop and there is no nucleus; this type is known as ◊prokaryotic. The prokaryotic cell also lacks organelles such as ◊mitochondria, ◊chloroplasts, ◊endoplasmic reticulum, ◊Golgi apparatus and centrioles, which perform specialized tasks in eukaryotic cells. Cells divide by ◊mitosis, or by ◊meiosis when gametes are being formed.

In 1976 the barrier between the plant and animal kingdoms was broken by the achievement in the laboratory (in the UK, USA, and Hungary), of the fusion of a plant and animal cell to form a hybrid, for example, red blood cell from a hen and a yeast cell, using polyethylene glycol as a fusing agent. There has as yet been no development beyond a single cell.

cell, electric in physics, apparatus in which chemical energy is converted into electrical energy; the popular name is 'battery', but this should be reserved for a collection of cells in one unit. Electric cells can be divided into: (a)*primary*, which produce electrical energy by chemical action and require replenishing after this action is complete; and (b)*secondary*, or accumulators, which are so constituted that the action is reversible, and the original condition can be restored by an electric current. The first battery was made by ◊Volta in 1800. Types of primary cells include the ◊Daniell, Lalande, ◊Leclanché, and the so-called dry cells;

animal cell

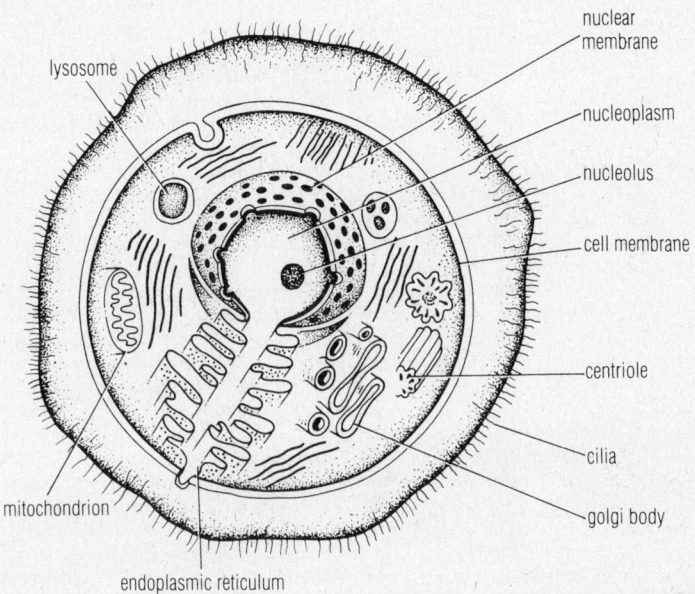

lysosome

nuclear membrane

nucleoplasm

nucleolus

cell membrane

centriole

cilia

golgi body

mitochondrion

endoplasmic reticulum

plant cell

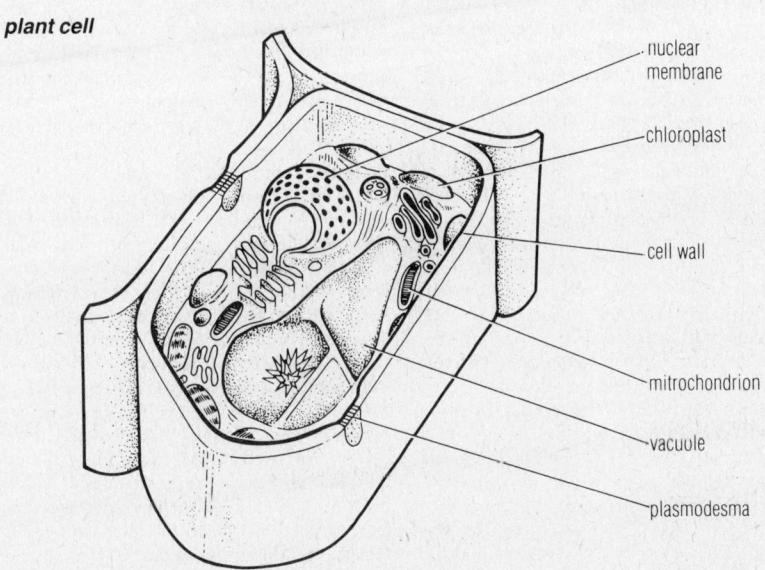

nuclear membrane

chloroplast

cell wall

mitrochondrion

vacuole

plasmodesma

secondary cells include Planté, Faure, Edison. Newer types include the Mallory (mercury depolarizer), which has a very stable discharge curve and can be made in very small units, for example for hearing-aids, and the Venner accumulator, which can be made substantially solid for some purposes.

Cellini /tʃe'liːni/ Benvenuto 1500–1571. Italian artist, sculptor, and silversmith; also famous for his anecdotal autobiography. Born in Florence, he was apprenticed to a goldsmith, and in 1519 went to Rome, where he claimed to have played a historic role defending the city during the siege of 1527 and also to have killed the

Constable de Bourbon. Later Cellini worked for the papal mint, and once was imprisoned on a charge of having embezzled pontifical jewels. He worked for a time in France at the court of Francis I, but finally settled in Florence in 1545, where he died. As a sculptor, his best-known work is the bronze group of Perseus holding the head of Medusa 1546–54, and as a goldsmith, the saltcellar he made for Francis I.

cello short for *violoncello*, a member of the ◊violin family of bowed string musical instruments.

cellophane a transparent wrapping film made from wood ◊cellulose, widely used for packaging.

Swiss chemist Jacques Edwin Brandenberger first produced cellophane in 1908. It is made from woodpulp, in much the same way that the artificial fibre ◊rayon is made. The pulp is dissolved in chemicals to form a viscose solution, which is then pumped through a long narrow slit into an acid bath. In the bath the emergent viscose stream turns into a film of pure cellulose - cellophane.

cellular radio a system of radiotelephony for vehicles that uses an interconnected network of low-powered transmitters. Each transmitter serves a limited area, or cell, about 5 km/3 mi across. The transmitters are linked to the telephone system via a central computer, which switches a telephone call to the receiver car's cell. The cellular system allows the use of the same set of frequencies with the minimum risk of interference. See ◊radio.

cellulite /'seljulaɪt/ fatty compound alleged by some dietitians to be produced in the body by liver disorder and to cause lumpy obesity. Medical opinion generally denies its existence.

cellulitis inflammation of body tissue, accompanied by swelling, redness, and pain.

celluloid transparent or translucent highly inflammable plastic material once used in photographic film, now replaced by the non-inflammable cellulose acetate.

cellulose a complex ◊carbohydrate composed of long chains of glucose units. It is the principal constituent of the cell wall of higher plants. Molecules of cellulose are organized into long, unbranched microfibrils which give support to the cell wall. Cellulose is the most abundant substance found in the plant kingdom.

cellulose nitrate an ◊ester made by the action of nitric acid and sulphuric acid on cellulose, and used to make lacquers and explosives ('gun cotton'). ◊Celluloid is a form of cellulose nitrate.

Celsius /'selsɪəs/ a temperature scale in which one division or degree is taken as one hundredth part of the interval between the freezing point (0°C) and the boiling point (100°C) of water at standard atmospheric pressure. The degree centigrade (°C) was officially renamed Celsius in 1948 to avoid confusion with the angular measure (a hundredth of a grade) known as the centigrade. It is named after the Swedish astronomer Anders Celsius (1701–44), who devised it in 1742, but in reverse (freezing point was 100°; boiling point 0°).

Celt /kelt/ name given, under various forms, by Greek and Roman writers to a people whose first known territory was in central Europe around 1200 BC, in the basin of the upper Danube and southern Germany. They developed a transitional civilization between the Bronze and Iron Ages, 9th–5th century BC (the Hallstatt culture, from its site southwest of Salzburg). Pioneers of iron working, they reached their peak in the period from the 5th century to the Roman conquest (the La Tène culture; see under ◊Celtic art). They overran France, Spain, Portugal, N Italy (sacking Rome in 390 BC), the British Isles, and Greece, though they never established a united empire. Their conquests were made by emigrant bands which made permanent settlements in these areas, as well as in the part of Asia Minor later known as Galatia. Classical authors named the fair, tall people of northern Europe Celts and only gradually distinguished them from German peoples. The Celtic religion was ◊druidism.

Celtic art a style of art which originated in about 500 BC, probably on the Rhine, and spread westwards to Gaul and the British Isles, and southwards to Italy and Asia Minor until it was superseded by Roman influence (2nd–1st century BC. It is known conventionally as La Tène art, from a site at Lake Neuchâtel, Switzerland, where the best examples of the style were found. The chief characteristics are linear designs – developing at a later state into intricate patterns – and the use of enamel and coral in the decoration of bronze objects. A Late Celtic period existed only in the British Isles; it is characterized by a rich decorative art, especially by enamelled horse-trappings and engraved mirrors.

Celtic languages a branch of the Indo-European family, further divided into two groups: the *Brythonic* or *P-Celtic* (Welsh, Cornish, Breton, and Gaulish) and the *Goidelic* or *Q-Celtic* (Irish, Scottish and Manx Gaelic). As their names suggest, a major distinction between the two groups is that where Brythonic has 'p' (as in Old Welsh *map*, 'son') Goidelic has a 'q' sound (as in Gaelic *mac*, 'son'). Celtic languages once stretched from the Black Sea to Britain, but have been in decline for centuries limited to the so-called 'Celtic Fringe' of W Europe. Gaulish is the long-extinct language of ancient Gaul, Cornish died out as a natural language in the late 18th century and Manx in 1974. All surviving Celtic languages have experienced official neglect in recent centuries and have suffered from emigration; currently, however, governments are more inclined than in the past to encourage their use.

Celtic League nationalist organization based in Ireland, aiming at an independent Celtic federation. It was founded 1975 with representatives from Alba (Scotland), Breizh (Brittany), Eire, Kernow (Cornwall), Cymru (Wales) and Ellan Vannin (Isle of Man).

Celtic Sea /'keltɪk/ name coined by workers in the oil industry in the 1970s for the sea area between Wales, Ireland, and SW England, to avoid nationalist significance.

cement a bonding agent used to unite particles in one mass or to cause one surface to adhere to another. The term is applied to a variety of materials, such as fluxes and pastes, and also bituminous products obtained from tar. In general the name is more applicable to Portland cement, a powder obtained from burning together a mixture of lime or chalk, and clay, which is the universal medium for building in brick or stone or for the production of concrete. In 1824 Joseph Aspdin, a Yorkshire bricklayer, discovered and patented the first Portland cement, so named because its colour, in the hardened state resembled that of the famous Portland stone, a ◊limestone used in building.

cenotaph (Greek 'empty tomb'), monument to commemorate a person or persons not actually buried at the site, as in the Whitehall Cenotaph, London, designed by Sir Edwin Lutyens to commemorate the dead of both World Wars.

censor in ancient Rome, either of two senior magistrates, high officials elected every five years to hold office for 18 months. Their resposibilities included public morality, a census of the citizens, and a revision of the Senatorial list.

censor in Freudian psychology, the psychic function which prevents unconscious impulses that are unacceptable from reaching the conscious mind, that is, so-called ◊repression.

censorship the suppression by authority of material considered immoral, heretical, subversive, libellous, damaging to state security, or otherwise offensive. It is generally more stringent under totalitarian or strongly religious regimes and in wartime.
In England under the Tudors and Stuarts, the crown claimed a monopoly on printing presses, and publication could be carried out only under licence until 1695. The British government now uses the ◊D-notice and the ◊Official Secrets Act to protect itself. Laws relating to obscenity, libel, and blasphemy act as a form of censorship; the libel laws in Britain are more rigid than in France or the USA, for example. The media are not automatically subject to official censorship, but a degree of self-censorship is exercised, for example, the British Board of Film Censors was set up by the film industry. There is a similar body, popularly called the Hays Office (after its first president, 1922–45, Will H Hays), in the USA. Censorship of plays in the UK by the Lord Chamberlain (under the Theatres Act 1843, a continuation of the Licensing Act 1737) ended in 1968.

census official count of the population of a country, originally for military call-up, later for assessment of social trends as other information regarding age, sex, and occupation of each individual was included. The first American census was taken in 1790 and the first In Britain in 1801. They may become unnecessary as databanks are built up on computers, and ceased in Denmark in 1982.

centaur in Greek mythology, a creature half man and half horse. They were supposed to live in Thessaly, and be wild and lawless: the mentor of Hercules, Chiron, was an exception. The earliest representation of centaurs (about 1800–1000 BC) were excavated near Famagusta in 1962, and are two-headed. Some female representations are also known.

Centaurus large bright ◊constellation of the southern hemisphere, representing a centaur. It contains the closest star to the Sun, ◊Alpha Centauri. Another prominent feature is Omega Centauri, the largest and brightest globular cluster of stars in the sky, 16,000 light years away. Centaurus A, a peculiar galaxy 15 million light years away, is a strong source of radio waves and X-rays.

centigrade alternative name for the ◊Celsius temperature scale.

centipede jointed-legged animal of the group Chilopoda, members of which have a distinct head and a single pair of long antennae. They are distinguished from insects by their bodies being composed of segments (which may number nearly 200), each of similar form and bearing a single pair of legs. Nocturnal, frequently blind, and all carnivorous, they eat animal food usually when rotten, live in moist, dark places, and protect themselves by a poisonous secretion. They have a pair of poison claws, and strong jaws with poison fangs. The bite of some tropical species is dangerous to humans. Most are small, but the tropical *Scolopendra gigantea* may reach 30 cm/1 ft in length. Several species live in Britain, *Lithobius forficatus* being the most common. *Millipedes*, class Diplopoda, have a lesser number of segments (up to 100), but have two pairs of legs on each.

Central African Republic /'sentrəl 'æfrɪkənrɪ'pʌblɪk/ landlocked country in Central Africa, bordered northeast and east by the Sudan, south by Zaïre and the Congo, west by Cameroon, and northwest by Chad.
government after a coup in Sept 1981, the constitution of Feb the same year was suspended and all executive and legislative powers placed in the hands of a Military Commitee for National Recovery (CMRN). Four years later CMRN was dissolved and a new 22-member council of ministers, composed of both military and civilian members, was established. In Jan 1985 a new constitution, to be appproved by referendum, was announced. The president is head of both state and government and presides over the council of ministers. All political activity has been banned since the coup but the main opposition groups, although passive, still exist. They are the Patriotic Front Ubangi Workers' Party (FPO-PT), the Central African Movement for National Liberation (MCLN), and the Movement for the Liberation of the Central African People (MPLC). Collectively, they comprise the Central African Revolutionary Party (PRC), and this may be reactivated if a new, democratic constitution is adopted. In Dec 1984 a Provisional Government for National Salvation was formed in exile uner the aegis of MPLC.
history a French colony from the late 19th century, the territory of Ubangi-Shari became self-governing within French Equatorial Africa in 1958 and two years later achieved full independence. Barthélémy Boganda, who had founded the Movement for the Social Evolution of Black Africa (MESAN), had been a leading figure in the campaign for independence and became the country's first prime minister. A year before full independence he was killed in an air crash and was succeeded by his nephew, David Dacko, who became president in 1960, and in 1962 established a one-party state, with MESAN as the only political organization. Dacko was overthrown in a military coup in Dec 1965 and the commander-in-chief of the army, Colonel Jean-Bédel Bokassa, assumed power.
Bokassa annulled the constitution and made himself president-for-life in 1972, and marshal of the Republic in 1974. An authoritarian regime was established and in 1976 ex-president Dacko was recalled to be the president's personal adviser. At the end of that year the republic was restyled the Central African Empire (CAE) and

in 1977 Bokassa was crowned emperor at a lavish ceremony his country could ill afford. His rule became increasingly dictatorial and idiosyncratic, leading to revolts by students and, in Apr 1979, by school children who objected to the compulsory wearing of school uniforms, made by a company owned by the Bokassa family. Many of the children were imprisoned and it is estimated that at least 100 were killed, with the emperor allegedly personally involved. In Sept 1979, while Bokassa was in Libya, Dacko ousted him in a bloodless coup, backed by France. The country became a republic again, with Dacko as president. he initially retained a number of Bokassa's former ministers but, following student unrest, they were dropped and in Feb 1981 a new constitution was adopted, with an elected national assembly. Dacko was elected president for a six-year term in Mar but opposition to him grew and in Sept 1981 he was deposed in another bloodless coup, led by the armed forces' chief-of-staff, General André Kolingba. The constitution and all political organizations were suspended, and a military government installed. Undercover opposition to the Kolingba regime continued, with some French support, but relations with France were improved by an unofficial visit by President Mitterrand in Oct 1982.

By 1984 there was evidence of a gradual return to constitutional government. The leaders of the banned political parties were granted an amnesty and at the end of the year the French president paid a state visit. In Jan 1985 proposals for a new constitution were announced and in Sept civilians were included into Kolingba's administration.

Central America /'sentrəl ə'merıkə/ the part of the Americas which links Mexico with the Isthmus of Panama, comprising Belize, Costa Rica, El Salvador, Guatemala, Honduras, Nicaragua, and Panama. It is also an isthmus itself, crossed by mountains that form part of the *Cordillera*. Much of Central America formed part of the ◊Maya civilization. Spanish settlers married indigenous women, and the area remained out of the mainstream of Spanish Empire history. Demand for cash crops (bananas, coffee, cotton), especially from the USA, created a strong landowning class controlling a serf-like peasantry by military means. There has been US military intervention in the area, for example in Nicaragua, where the dynasty of Gen Anastasio Somoza was founded. President ◊Carter reversed support for such regimes; the ◊Reagan administration again favours military and financial aid to selected political groups, including the ◊Contras in Nicaragua.

Central American Common Market ODECA (*Organización de Estados Centroamericanos*), established in 1960 by El Salvador, Guatemala, Honduras (seceded 1970), and Nicaragua; Costa Rica joined in 1962.

Central Criminal Court in the UK, Crown Court in the City of London, able to try all treasons and serious offences committed in the City or Greater London. First established 1834, it is popularly known as the Old Bailey after part

Central African Republic
(République centrafricaine)

AREA 625,000 sq km/240,000 sq mi
CAPITAL Bangui
PHYSICAL most of the country is on a plateau, with rivers flowing N and S. The N is dry and there is rain forest in the SW
HEAD OF STATE AND OF GOVERNMENT André Kolingba from 1981
GOVERNMENT military
EXPORTS diamonds, uranium, coffee, cotton, and timber
CURRENCY CFA franc (498.38 = £1 Sept 1987)
POPULATION 2,664,000 (1985); annual growth rate 1.8%
LANGUAGE Sangho, French (both official)
RELIGION animist over 50%; Christian 35%, both Catholic and Protestant; Muslim 10%
LITERACY 48% male/19% female (1980 est)
GNP $690 million (1983); $310 per head of population
CHRONOLOGY
1960 Central African Republic achieved independence from France with David Dacko elected president.
1962 The republic made a one-party state.
1965 Dacko ousted in a military coup led by Col Bokassa.
1966 Constitution rescinded and national assembly dissolved.
1972 Bokassa declared himself president for life.
1976 Bokassa made himself emperor of the Central African Empire.

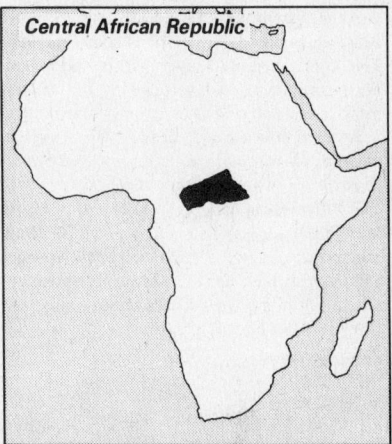

Central African Republic

1979 Bokassa deposed by Dacko following violent repressive measures by the self-styled emperor, who went into exile.
1981 Dacko deposed in a bloodless coup, led by Gen André Kolingba, and an all-military government established.
1983 Clandestine opposition movement formed.
1984 Amnesty for all political party leaders announced. President Mitterrand of France paid a state visit.
1985 New constitution, with some civilians in the government, promised.
1986 Formal trial of Bokassa started. Gen Kolingba re-elected.

of the medieval defences of London; the present building is on the site of Newgate Prison.

central dogma in genetics and evolution, the fundamental belief that ◊genes can affect the nature of the physical body, but that changes in the body (e.g. through use or accident) cannot be translated into changes in the genes. The elements of this idea were outlined by the German biologist August Weismann, in the 1880s when he claimed that the *soma* (body) and *germ* (reproductive) parts were separate lines. In the 1950s, following the discovery of the structure of ◊DNA, Francis ◊Crick formulated the central dogma as we now know it, on the basis that genetic information can only flow out of DNA, not into it, because RNA (and thus proteins) can be made using DNA as a template, but not *vice versa*. The more recent discovery of ◊retroviruses has shown this to be partly untrue: DNA can be copied from RNA. However, the fundamental idea of the central dogma is still valid. See also ◊acquired character.

central heating a system of heating, typically of a house, from a central source, as opposed to heating each room individually with, say, a separate fire. Central heating has its origins in the ◊hypocaust heating system introduced by the Romans nearly 2,000 years ago. The most common type of central heating used in British houses is the hot-water system. Water is heated in a furnace burning oil, gas or solid fuel, and is

then pumped through radiators in each room. The level of temperature can be selected by adjusting a ◊thermostat in one of the rooms. The central heating system is usually switched on and off by a time switch. Another kind of central heating system uses hot air, which is pumped through ducts to grills in the rooms. Underfloor heating is used in some houses, the heat coming from electric elements buried in the floor. It uses cheaper 'off-peak' electricity, as does the heating system using night-storage radiators.

Central Intelligence Agency (CIA) US intelligence organization established in 1947 by President Truman. Developed from the wartime Office of Strategic Services and set up on the lines of the British Secret Service, it was intended solely for use overseas in the cold war. Its active interventions overseas, generally to undermine left-wing regimes or to protect US financial interests, include the restoration of the shah of Iran 1953; South Vietnam (see ◊Vietnam War); ◊Zaïre (when it was still the Congo); Chile (against ◊Allende); Cuba (see ◊Bay of Pigs). On the domestic front, it was illegally involved in ◊Watergate, and in the 1970s lost public confidence when US overseas influence collapsed in Iran, Afghanistan, ◊Nicaragua, Yemen, and elsewhere. The director from 1987 is William Webster; past directors include William Casey, Richard ◊Helms and George ◊Bush. See also ◊Federal Bureau of Investigation.

central nervous system the part of the nervous system with a concentration of ◊nerve cells, which coordinates various body functions. The remainder is known as the peripheral nervous system. In ◊vertebrates the central nervous system consists of a ◊brain and a dorsal nerve cord (the ◊spinal cord) within the spinal column. In worms, insects and crustaceans it consists of two ventral nerve cords with concentrations of nerve cells, known as ◊ganglia in each segment, and a small brain in the head. Some simple invertebrates, such as the sponges and jellyfish, have no central nervous system but a simple network of nerve cells, called a *nerve net*.

central nervous system

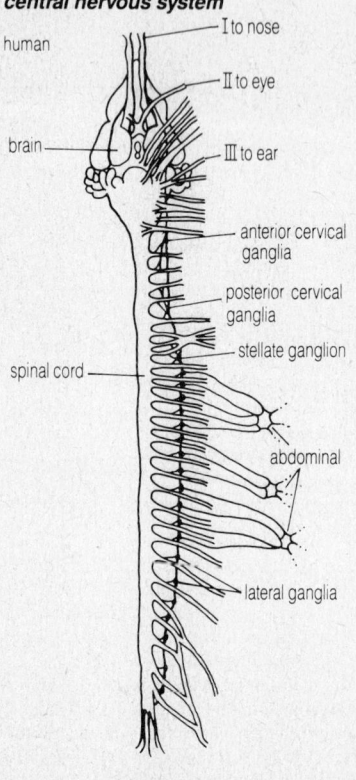

human
- I to nose
- II to eye
brain
- III to ear
- anterior cervical ganglia
- posterior cervical ganglia
spinal cord
- stellate ganglion
- abdominal
- lateral ganglia

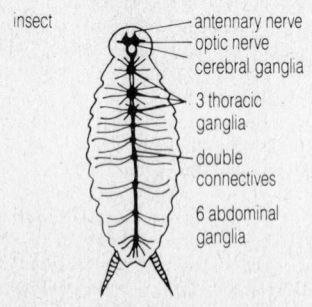

insect
- antennary nerve
- optic nerve
- cerebral ganglia
- 3 thoracic ganglia
- double connectives
- 6 abdominal ganglia

Central Scotland region of Scotland, formed 1975 from the counties of Stirling, S Perth, and W Lothian.
area 2,518 sq km/971 sq mi
towns administrative headquarters Clackmannan; Falkirk, Stirling

features Stirling Castle; field of Bannockburn; Lock Lomond
products agriculture; industries include brewing and distilling; engineering; electronics
population (1981) 271,819
famous people Rob Roy McGreagor (1671–1734).

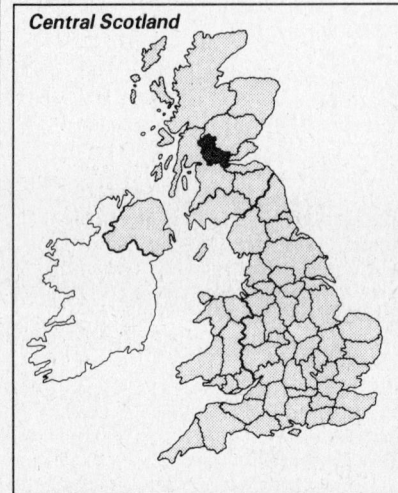

Central Scotland

Central Treaty Organization (CENTO) defence organization which replaced the ◊Baghdad Pact in 1959; it collapsed when the withdrawal of Iran, Pakistan, and Turkey in 1979 left the UK as the only member.

Centre /'sentə/ region of N central France; capital Orléans; population (1982) 2,264,164. There is a Renaissance château at Chambord, and George ◊Sand's home is preserved at Nohant.

Centre, The /'sentə/ region of Central Australia, including the tourist area between the Musgrave and MacDonnell ranges which contains Ayers Rock and Lake Amadeus.

centre of mass also called *centre of gravity* the point in or near an object from which its total weight appears to originate and can be assumed to act. A symmetrical homogeneous object such as a sphere or cube has its centre of mass at its physical centre; a hollow shape (such as a cup) may have its centre of mass in space inside the hollow. For an object to be in stable equilibrium, a perpendicular line down through its centre of mass runs within the boundaries of its base. If tilted until this line falls outside the base, the object becomes unstable and topples over.

Centre party (German *Zentrumspartei*) German political party established 1871 to protect Catholic interests. Although alienated by Bismarck's *Kulturkampf* 1873–78, in the following years the *Zentrum* became an essential component in the government of Imperial Germany. The party continued to play an important part in the politics of Weimar Germany before being barred by Hitler in the summer of 1933.

centrifugal force a useful (but unreal) concept in physics. It may be regarded as a force

that acts radially outwards from a spinning or orbiting object, thus balancing the (real) inwardly-directed ◊centripetal force. For an object of mass m moving with a velocity v in a circle of radius r, the centrifugal force F equals mv^2/r (outwards).

centrifuge apparatus for rotating containers at high speeds. One use is for separating mixtures of substances of different densities. The mixtures are placed in the containers and the rotation sets up centrifugal forces in the whirling substances acting radially outwards, causing them to separate according to their densities. A common example is the separation of the lighter cream from the heavier milk in this way. The ultracentrifuge is a very high-speed centrifuge, used for separating colloids, and in biochemistry, and may operate at several million revolutions per minute. Large centrifuges are used for physiological research, for example in astronaut training: testing bodily response to many times the normal gravitational force.

centriole a structure found in the ◊cells of animals that plays an important role in the processes of ◊meiosis and ◊mitosis (cell division).

centripetal force force that acts radially inwards on an object moving in a curved path. For example, with a weight whirled in a circle at the end of a length of string, the centripetal force is the tension in the string. For an object of mass m moving with a velocity v in a circle of radius r, the centripetal force F equals mv^2/r (inwards). The reaction to this force is an (unreal) equal one, the ◊centrifugal force, which may be regarded as being directed radially outwards.

centromere part of the ◊chromosome where there are no ◊genes. Under the microscope, it usually appears as a constriction in the strand of the chromosome, and is the point at which the spindle fibres are attached during ◊meiosis and ◊mitosis (cell division).

cephalopod type of predatory marine mollusc with the mouth and head surrounded by tentacles. Examples include octopus, squid and cuttlefish. In most shells are rudimentary or absent. They include the most intelligent, the fastest-moving and the largest of all animals without backbones, and there are remarkable luminescent forms which swim or drift at abyssal depths. Typically they move by swimming with the mantle, aided by the arms, but can squirt water out of the siphon (funnel) to propel themselves backwards by jet propulsion. They grow very rapidly and may be mature in a year. In the common octopus the female lays 150,000 eggs after copulation, and stays to brood them for as long as six weeks. After they hatch the female dies, and, although reproductive habits of many cephalopods are not known, it is thought that dying after spawning may be typical. Cephalopods have the most highly developed nervous and sensory systems of all invertebrates, the eye in some paralleling closely that found in vertebrates.

cephalosporin antibiotic, also known as ceporin, extracted from cephalosporium mould. It was developed at Oxford by E P ◊Abraham and others in the 1960s: Dorothy ◊Hodgkin was associated in the early stages. Cephalosporin is capable of destroying penicillin-resistant bacteria.

Cepheid variable an important type of ◊star that varies regularly in brightness every few days or weeks as a result of pulsations in its size. The time that a Cepheid variable takes to pulsate is directly related to its average brightess: the longer the pulsation period, the brighter the star. This relationship, the *period-luminosity law* (discovered by Henrietta ◊Leavitt), allows astronomers to use Cepheid variables, as 'standard candles' to measure distances in our Galaxy and to nearby galaxies. Cepheid variables are supergiant yellow stars, named after their prototype, Delta Cephei, whose light variations were noted in 1784 by English astronomer John Goodricke.

Cepheus constellation of the north polar region, representing King Cepheus in Greek mythology, husband of ◊Cassiopeia and father of ◊Andromeda. It contains the Garnet Star, Mu Cephei, a red supergiant of variable brightness that is one of the reddest-coloured stars known, and Delta Cephei, prototype of the ◊Cepheid variables.

Ceram /sə'ræn/ Indonesian island, in the Moluccas. Area 6,621 sq mi.

ceramic non-metallic mineral used in articles created from powder and sintered at high temperatures. Ceramics are divided into heavy clay products (bricks, roof tiles, drainpipes, sanitary ware), refractories or high-temperature materials (linings for furnaces used in steel-making, fuel elements in nuclear reactors), and ◊pottery, which uses china clay, ball clay, china stone and flint. Pottery ranges from the opaque and porous earthenware well adapted to colour, through translucent white bone china (5% calcined bone) to finest ◊porcelain. Super-ceramics, such as silicon carbide, are lighter, stronger, and more heat-resistant than steel for use in motor and aircraft engines, and have to be cast to shape since they are too hard to machine.

Cerberus /'sɜːbərəs/ in Greek mythology, the three-headed dog guarding the entrance to ◊Hades, the underworld.

cereals grain-bearing plants cultivated for food. The term relates primarily to barley and wheat, but may also be said to cover oats, maize, rye, millet, and rice. Cereals have been of the utmost importance in the history of human society and different grain-bearing plants are characteristic of different civilizations in various parts of the world.

cerebral haemorrhage or *stroke* the bursting of a blood vessel in the brain, caused by factors such as a blood clot, high blood pressure combined with hardening of the arteries, chronic poisoning with lead or alcohol; popularly known as a 'stroke' or apoplectic fit. It may cause death, or damage parts of the brain and lead to paralysis or mental impairment. The effects are usually long-term.

cerebral hemisphere one of the two halves of the ◊cerebrum.

cerebral palsy handicap caused in children (known as *spastic*) by damage to the brain while it is actively growing before birth, at birth, or in the first year of life. It may cause paralysis of the muscles, difficulty in movement, speech, and sometimes mental handicapital

cerebrum part of the vertebrate ◊brain, formed from two paired dorsal extensions of the olfactory region of the hindbrain (cerebral hemispheres). In birds and mammals, it is the largest part of the brain. It is covered with an infolded layer of grey matter, the cerebral cortex which integrates brain function. The cerebrum coordinates the senses, and is responsible for learning and other higher mental faculties.

Ceres /'sɪəriːz/ in astronomy, the largest ◊asteroid, some 1,000 km/600 mi in diameter, and the first asteroid to be discovered (by Giuseppe ◊Piazzi in 1801). Ceres is a rocky body that orbits the Sun every 4.6 years at an average distance of 420 million km/260 million mi. Its mass is about one-sixtieth that of our Moon.

Ceres /'sɪəriːz/ in Roman mythology, the goddess of agriculture, identified with the Greek goddess ◊Demeter.

cerium a chemical element. Symbol, Ce, atomic number 58. It is a metal in the ◊lanthanide series and used as a sparking component in lighter flints.

cermet a heat-resistant material containing ceramics and metal, widely used in jet engines. Cermets behave much like metals but have the great heat resistance of ceramics. Tungsten carbide, molybdenum boride and aluminium oxide are among the ceramics used; iron, cobalt, nickel and chromium are among the metals.

CERN /sɜːn/ European organization which came into being in 1954 as a cooperative enterprise among European governments. It was originally known as the *Conseil Européen pour la Recherche Nucléaire*, but was subsequently renamed *Organisation Européene pour la Recherche Nucléaire*, although still familiarly known as CERN. At the laboratories at Meyrin, near Geneva, research is carried out into the fundamental structure of matter by teams of scientists from the 12 member states. In 1965 the original laboratory was doubled in size by extension across the border from Switzerland into France. Under construction, for completion in the 1990s, is a new large electron-positron collider (LEP).

Cernăuţi /ˌotʃeanə'uts/ Romanian form of ◊Chernovtsy.

Cervantes /sɜː'væntiːz/ Saavedra, Miguel de 1547–1616. Spanish novelist, playwright, and poet. Born at Alcalá de Henares, he entered the army in Italy and in 1571 was wounded in the battle of Lepanto. In 1575, while on his way back to Spain, he was captured by Barbary pirates and was taken to Algiers, where he became a slave until ransomed in 1580. Returning to Spain he began to support himself by writing. He wrote several plays, and in 1585 his pastoral romance *Galatea* was printed. In 1587 he was employed in Seville in provisioning the Armada. While working as a tax collector, he was imprisoned more than once for deficiencies in his accounts. He sank into poverty, and little is known of him until the publication of his masterpiece, *Don Quijote* (in full *El ingenioso hidalgo Don Quijote de la Mancha*) about a knight errant and his servant Sancho Panza, in 1605. It immediately achieved great success and was soon translated into English and French. In 1613 his *Novelas Exemplares/Exemplary Novels* appeared, a collection of short tales; and in 1614 a burlesque poem, *Viaje del Parnaso/The Voyage to Parnassus*. A spurious second part of *Don Quijote* prompted Cervantes to bring out his own authentic second part, considered to be superior to the first in construction and in characterization. His last work was *Pérsiles y Sigismunda* 1616.

cervical cancer ◊cancer of the cervix (the neck of the womb).

cervical smear (PAP smear) a screening test to detect changes in cells rubbed from the cervix (neck of the womb) that might, without treatment, lead to cancer.

Cetewayo /ketʃ'waɪəʊ/ 1836–1884. King of Zululand, South Africa, 1873–83, who defeated the British at Isandhlwana 1879, but was later that year defeated by them at Ulundi. Restored to his throne in 1883, he was then expelled by his subjects.

Cetinje /'tsetiːnjeɪ/ town in Montenegro, Yugoslavia, 19 km/12 mi SE of Kotor. Founded in 1484 by Ivan the Black, it was capital of Montenegro until 1918. Population (1981) 20,213.

Ceuta /'sjuːtə/ Spanish seaport and military base in Morocco, captured in 1580. It is 27 km/17 mi south of Gibraltar and overlooks the Mediterranean approaches to the Straits of Gibraltar. Population (1981) 70,864.

Cevennes /se'ven/ a series of mountain ranges on the southern, south eastern and eastern borders of the Central Plateau of France.

Ceylon /sɪ'lɒn/ former name of ◊Sri Lanka.

Cézanne /seɪ'zæn/ Paul 1839–1906. French painter of landscapes, still-lifes, and portraits, the leader of the ◊Post-Impressionist School. He was born at Aix-en-Provence, where he studied, and was a friend of Emile ◊Zola. In Paris he met ◊Pissarro and other ◊Impressionist painters, with whom at first he was in sympathy. However he broke away from the Impressionists' spontaneous vision to produce a greater sense of permanence. His use of geometrical shapes to form a solid scaffolding for his compositions was to influence later artists and form the basis of ◊Cubism.

c.g.s. system a system of units based on the centimetre, gram and second, as units of length, mass and time. For scientific work it is now replaced by the ◊SI system to avoid inconsistencies in definition of the thermal calorie and electrical quantities.

Chablis /'ʃæbliː/ town in the Yonne département of central France, famous for white burgundy wine of the same name.

Chabrier /'ʃæbrɪeɪ/ (Alexis) Emmanuel 1841–1894. French composer. He made his name with *España* 1883, an orchestral rhapsody.

chacma a type of ◊baboon.

Chaco /'tʃɑːkəʊ/ province of Argentina, until 1951 a territory, part of Gran Chaco, a great zone, mostly level, stretching into Paraguay and Bolivia. The province includes many lakes and swamps, and much of it is forested, producing timber and quebracho (a type of wood used in

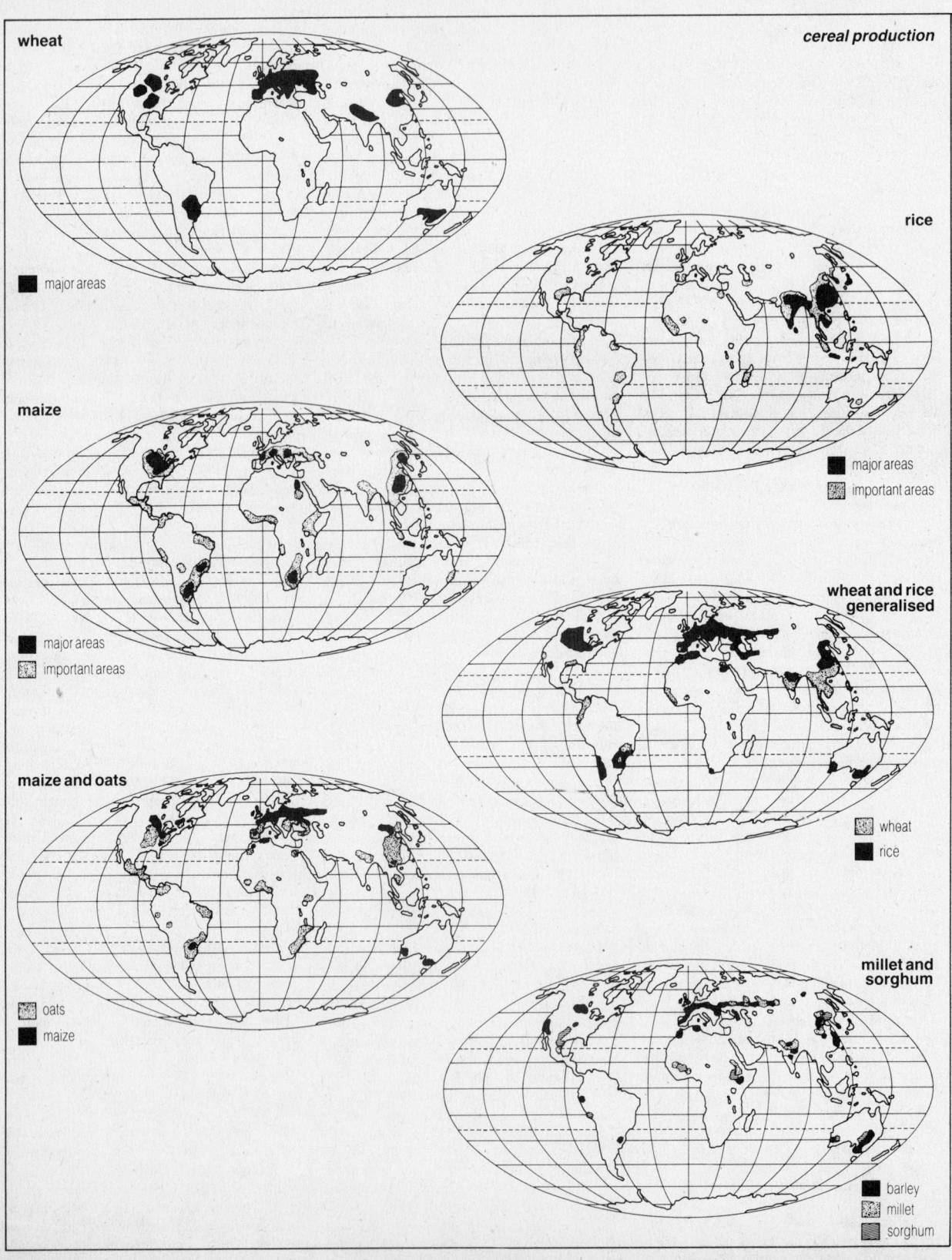

wheat

cereal production

rice

■ major areas

maize

■ major areas
▨ important areas

■ major areas
▨ important areas

wheat and rice
generalised

maize and oats

▨ wheat
■ rice

▨ oats
■ maize

millet and
sorghum

■ barley
▨ millet
▨ sorghum

Cézanne Self-portrait by Paul Cézanne, who pursued his work with agonizing care. The few portraits that he did produce are either of himself or of people whose sittings could be protracted over a long period.

◊tanning); the chief crop is cotton. The capital is Resistencia, in the south east. Area 99,633 sq km/38,479 sq mi; population (1970) 567,000. The north of Gran Chaco was the scene of the Bolivia-Paraguay border dipute of 1932–35, settled by arbitration in 1938.

Chaco War /'tʃɑːkəʊ/ war over boundaries in the North Gran Chaco between Bolivia and Paraguay 1932–35, settled by arbitration in 1938.

Chad, Lake /tʃæd/ lake on the north east boundary of Nigeria, first seen by white explorers in 1823. It varies in extent between rainy and dry seasons from 50,000 sq km/20,000 sq mi to 20,000 sq km/7,000 sq mi. The Lake Chad basin is being jointly developed by Cameroon, Chad, Niger and Nigeria.

Chad /tʃæd/ landlocked country in central N Africa, bounded to the north by Libya, to the east by Sudan, to the south by the Central African Republic, and to the west by Cameroon, Nigeria, and Niger.

government the 1982 provisional constitution provides for a president who appoints and leads a council of ministers which exercises executive and legislative power. In 1984 a new regrouping, the National Union for Independence (UNIR), was undertaken in an attempt to consolidate the president's position, but a number of opposition groups exist.

history called Kanem when settled by Arabs in the 7th–13th centuries, the area later became known as Bornu and in the 19th century was conquered by Sudan. From 1913 a province of French Equatorial Africa, Chad became an autonomous state within the French Community in 1958, with François Tombalbaye as prime minister.

Full independence was achieved in 1960 and Tombalbaye became president. He soon faced disagreements between the Arabs of the north, who saw Libya as an ally, and the black African Christians of the south, who felt more sympathy for Nigeria. In the north the Chadian National Liberation Front (Frolinat) revolted against the government. In 1975 Tombalbaye was killed in a coup led by former army chief-of-staff, Félix Malloum, who became president of a supreme military council and appealed for national unity, but Frolinat continued its opposition, supported by Libya, which held a strip of land in the north, believed to contain uranium.

By 1978 Frolinat, led by General Goukouni Oueddi, had expanded its territory but was halted with French aid. Malloum tried to reach a settlement by making former Frolinat leader, Hissène Habré, prime minister, but disagreements developed between them.

In 1979 fighting broke out again between government and Frolinat forces and Malloum fled the country. Talks resulted in the formation of a provisional government (GUNT), with Goukouni holding the presidency with Libyan support. A proposed merger with Libya was rejected and Libya withdrew most of its forces. The Organization for African Unity (OAU) set up a peacekeeping force but civil war broke out and by 1981 Hissène Habré's Armed Forces of the North (FAN) controlled half the country. Goukouni fled and set up a 'government in exile'. In 1983 a majority of OAU members agreed to recognize Habré's regime but Goukouni, with Libyan support, fought on.

After Libyan bombing, Habré appealed to France for help. 3,000 troops were sent as instructors, with orders to retaliate if attacked. Following a Franco-African summit in 1983, a ceasefire was agreed, with latitude 16° N dividing the opposing forces. Libyan president Colonel Khaddhafi's proposal of a simultaneous withdrawal of French and Libyan troops was accepted. By Dec all French troops had left but Libya's withdrawal was doubtful.

Meanwhile Habré had dissolved the military arm of Frolinat and formed a new party, the National Union for Independence (UNIR), but opposition to his regime grew. In 1987 Goukouni was reported to be under house arrest in Tripoli. Meanwhile Libya intensified its military operations in northern Chad, Habré's government retaliated, and France renewed, if reluctantly, its support. It was announced in Sept 1987 that France, Chad, and Libya had agreed to observe a ceasefire proposed by the Organization of African Unity (OAU).

Chadli /ʃæd'liː/ Benjedid 1929– . Algerian statesman. An army colonel, he supported Boumédienne in the overthrow of ◊Ben Bella, 1965 and succeeded Boumédienne in 1979 (re-elected 1984) pursuing more moderate socialist policies.

chador all-enveloping black garment (Hindi 'square of cloth') for women, originating in the period of Cyrus the Great and the Achaemenian empire in Persia (6th century BC). Together with the purdah (Persian 'veil') and the idea of female seclusion, it persisted under Alexander the Great

and the Byzantine Empire, and was adopted by the Arab conquerors of the Byzantines. It was revived by Khomeini in Iran in response to the Koran request for 'modesty' in dress.

Chadwick /'tʃædwɪk/ James 1891–1974. British physicist. He studied at Cambridge under ◊Rutherford, and in 1932 discovered the particle in an atomic nucleus which became known as the neutron, because it has no electric charge. In 1935 he was awarded a Nobel prize, and in 1940 was one of the British scientists reporting on the atomic bomb. He was Lyon Jones professor of physics at Liverpool 1935–48, and master of Gonville and Caius College, Cambridge, 1948–59.

Chadwick /'tʃædwɪk/ Lynn 1914– . British sculptor of monumental pieces, such as *Couple on a Seat*; and of captured motion, for example his figures striding into the wind.

chafer type of beetle of the family Scarabeidae in which the adults eat foliage or flowers and the underground larvae feed on roots, especially of grasses and cereals, and can be very destructive. Examples include the ◊cockchafer and the *rose chafer Cetonia aurata*, about 2 cm/0.8 in long, bright green, and seen sitting in flowers in summer.

chaffinch bird *Fringilla coelebs* of the finch family, common throughout much of Europe and western Asia. About 15 cm/6 in long, the male is olive-brown above, with a bright chestnut breast, a bluish-grey cap, and two white bands on the upper part of the wing; the female is duller.

Chagall /ʃæ'gæl/ Marc 1887–1985. Russian artist. A precursor of ◊Surrealism, he studied under ◊Bakst. Living mainly in France from 1922 (citizen 1947); he decorated a chapel at ◊Vence, in the south of France, and there is a Chagall National Museum at Nice. His art shows a dream world of floating animals and figures, strange colours and juxtapositions of objects, frequently taken from the Russian Jewish images of his youth. He also produced illustrated books the Bible and La Fontaine's *Fables*, and a series of stained-glass windows in the cathedrals of Chartres, Metz, and Reims.

Chagas' Disease /'ʃɑːgəs/ named after Brazilian doctor Carlos Chagas (1879–1934), a disease caused by a trypanosome parasite transmitted by insects, which results in incurable damage to the heart and brain.

Chagos Archipelago /'tʃɑːgəs ˌɑːkɪ'peləgəʊ/ island group in the Indian Ocean; area 197 sq km/76 sq mi. Formerly a dependency of ◊Mauritius, it now forms the ◊British Indian Ocean Territory. The chief island is Diego Garcia, now a UK/USA strategic base.

Chaillu /ʃaɪ'uː/ Paul Belloni du 1835–1903. American (French-born) explorer. In 1855 he began a four year journey of exploration in West Africa. His *Explorations and Adventures in Equatorial Africa* (1861) describes his discovery of the gorilla in Gabon.

Chain /tʃeɪn/ Ernst Boris 1906–1979. German-born biochemist, who emigrated to England in 1933, and worked at Cambridge. With ◊Florey, he initiated the work on penicillin which led to the discovery of its therapeutic

Chad

REPUBLIC OF (*République du Tchad*)

AREA 1,284,000 sq km/495,753 sq mi

CAPITAL N'djamena

PHYSICAL savanna and part of Sahara Desert in the N; rivers in the S flow N to Lakę Chad in the marshy E

HEAD OF STATE AND OF GOVERNMENT Hissène Habré from 1982

GOVERNMENT republic

EXPORTS cotton; meat, livestock, hides and skins; there are resources of bauxite, uranium, gold, oil

CURRENCY CFA franc (498.38 = £1 Sept 1987)

POPULATION 5,036,000 (1985); annual growth rate 2.3%

LANGUAGE French (official), Arabic

RELIGION Muslim (north); Christian, animist (south)

LITERACY 44% male/8% female (1980 est)

GDP $360 million (1984); $88 per head of population

CHRONOLOGY

1960 Independence from France achieved, with François Tombalbaye as president.

1963 Violent opposition in the Muslim N, led by the Chadian National Liberation Front (Frolinat), backed by Libya.

1968 Revolt quelled with French help.

1975 Tombalbaye killed in military coup led by Felix Malloum. Frolinat continued its resistance.

1978 Malloum tried to find a political solution by bringing the former Frolinat leader Hissenè Habré into his government but they were unable to work together.

1979 Malloum forced to leave the country. An interim government was set up under Gen

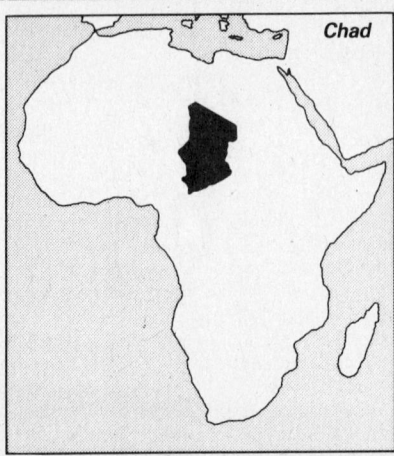

Chad

Goukouni. Habré continued his opposition with his Army of the North (FAN).

1981 Habré was now in control of half the country, forcing Goukouni to flee to Cameroon and then Algeria, where, with Libyan support, he set up a 'government in exile'.

1983 Habré's regime recognized by the Organization for African Unity (OAU) but in the north Goukouni's supporters, with Libyan help, fought on. Eventually a ceasefire was agreed, dividing the country into two halves either side of latitude 16° N.

1984 Libya and France agreed a withdrawal of forces.

1985 Fighting between Libyan-backed and French-backed forces intensified.

1987 Chad, France, and Libya agree on ceasefire proposed by OAU.

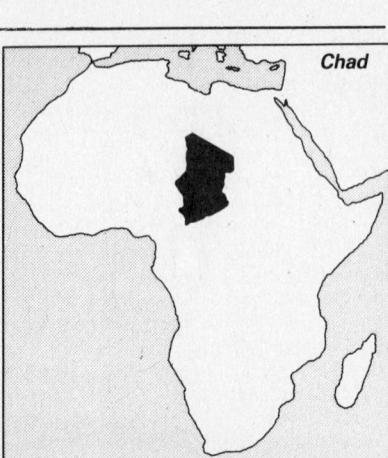

Chadwick The discoverer of the neutron in 1932 (for which he was awarded a Nobel Prize in 1935), James Chadwick was working with Hans Geiger in Germany when World War I broke out; he was interned for its duration.

Chalmers /'tʃɑːməz/ Thomas 1780–1847. Scottish theologian. As minister of Tron Church, Glasgow, from 1815, he became noted for his eloquence and for his proposals for social reform. In 1823 he became professor of moral philosophy at St Andrews, and in 1828 of theology at Edinburgh. At the 'Disruption' of the Church of Scotland in 1843, Chalmers withdrew from the church along with a large body of other divines, and became principal of the Free Church college, thus founding the free church of Scotland.

Châlons-Sur-Marne /ʃɑːˈlɒn sjuə ˈmɑːn/ capital of the *département* of Marne, France, with a fine 13th century cathedral. There is a trade in champagne. Population (1982) 54,359. Tradition has it that Attila was defeated in his attempt to invade France, at the *Battle of Châlons* (451), by the Roman general Aëtius and the Visigoth Theodoric.

Chalon-Sur-Saône /ʃɑːˈlɒn sjuə ˈsəʊn/ town in the *département* of Saône-et-Loire, France, on the river Saône and the Canal du Centre. It has mechanical and electrical engineering, and chemical industries. Population (1982) 57,967.

Chamberlain, Lord /'tʃeɪmbəlɪn/ chief officer of the royal household, who engages staff and appoints tradesmen; until 1968 he licensed and censored plays before their public performance. The office is temporary and appointments are made by the government.

Chamberlain, Lord Great /'tʃeɪmbəlɪn/ the only officer of state whose position survives from Norman times; responsibilities include the arrangements for the opening of Parliament, assisting with the regalia at coronations, and organizing the ceremony when bishops and peers are created.

Chamberlain /'tʃeɪmbəlɪn/ (Arthur) Neville 1869–1940. British Conservative politician,

properties, and shared a Nobel prize with ◊Fleming and Florey in 1945.

chain reaction in nuclear physics, a fission reaction which is maintained because neutrons released by the splitting of some atomic nuclei themselves go on to split others, releasing even more neutrons, and so on. Such a reaction can be controlled (as in a nuclear reactor) by using moderators to absorb excess neutrons. Uncontrolled, a chain reaction produces a nuclear explosion (as in an atomic bomb).

Chaka /'ʃɑːgə/ 1783–1828. Zulu chief, who built up an empire from the border of Cape Colony to the Zambezi in the early 19th Century. Famous for the ruthlessness of his rule, his reign ended when he was himself murdered.

chalcedony a form of ◊quartz, SiO_2, in which the crystals are so fine grained that they are impossible to distinguish with a microscope (cryptocrystalline). It often contains large numbers of semiprecious stones. See also ◊agate.

Chaldaea an ancient region of ◊Babylonia.

Chaliapin /ˌʃæliˈæpɪn/ Fyodor Ivanovich 1873–1938. Russian singer. Born at Kazan of peasant parentage, he became a world-famous bass singer, and made his London debut in 1913.

His greatest role was that of Boris Godunov in ◊Mussorgsky's opera of the same name. Chaliapin left Russia after the rise of the Soviet regime, and died in Paris.

chalice cup, usually of precious metal, used in celebrating the ◊Eucharist in the Christian church.

chalk a soft, fine-grained whitish rock composed of carbonate of lime, $CaCO_3$, formerly thought to derive from the remains of microscopic animal organisms or Foraminifera (foraminiferal ooze theory). In 1953 however it was seen under the electron microscope to be composed chiefly of coccoliths, unicellular lime-secreting algae, and hence to be primarily a vegetable deposit. Chalk was laid down in the later ◊Cretaceous period and covers a wide area in Europe. In England it stretches in a belt from Wiltshire contiuously across Buckinghamshire and Cambridgeshire to Lincolnshire and Yorkshire, and also forms the North and South Downs and the cliffs of South East England. Chalk is extensively quarried for use in cement, lime and mortar. It is also used in the manufacture of cosmetics and toothpaste. It is not used for blackboard chalk, which is ◊gypsum.

Chagall This oil painting, *The Birthday*, dates from 1915, the year Chagall returned to Russia and married. In 1937 he took French nationality, but chose to live in a succession of different countries.

younger son of Joseph Chamberlain, and half-brother of Joseph Austen Chamberlain. Born in Birmingham, of which he was lord mayor in 1915. He was minister of health in 1923 and 1924–29 and worked at slum clearance. In 1931 he was chancellor of the exchequer in the national government, and in 1937 succeeded Baldwin as prime minister. Trying to close the old Anglo-Irish feud he agreed to return to Eire those ports that had been occupied by the navy. He also attempted to 'appease' the demands of the European dictators, particularly Mussolini. In 1938 he went to Munich and negotiated with Hitler the settlement of the Czechoslovak question. He was ecstatically received on his return, and claimed that the Munich agreement brought 'peace in our time'. But he soon agreed that he had been tricked, and Britain declared war on 3 Sept 1939. He resigned 1940.

Chamberlain /'tʃeɪmbəlɪn/ (Joseph) Austen 1863–1937. British Conservative politician, elder son of Joseph Chamberlain. He was elected to parliament in 1892 as a Liberal-Unionist, and after holding several minor posts was chancellor of the exchequer 1903–06. During World War I he was secretary of state for India 1915–17 and member of the war cabinet 1918. He was chancellor of the exchequer 1919–21 and lord privy seal 1921–22, but failed to secure the leadership of the party in 1922, as many Conservatives resented the part he had taken in the Irish settlement of 1921. He was foreign secretary in the Baldwin government 1924–29, and negotiated and signed the ◊Locarno pact, and the Kellog-Briand pact 1928 to ban war and provide for peaceful settlement of disputes. He won the Nobel peace prize in 1925.

Chamberlain Neville Chamberlain returning with the Munich agreement that he had negotiated with Hitler, 1938. His claims that he had brought 'peace in our time' were soon to be refuted, with Britain declaring war against Germany in 1939.

Chamberlain /'tʃeɪmbəlɪn/ Joseph 1836–1914. British Liberal politician. By 1874 he had made sufficient fortune in the Birmingham screw-manufacturing business to devote himself entirely to politics. He adopted radical views, and took an active part in local affairs. Thrice mayor of Birmingham, he carried through many schemes of municipal development. In 1876 he was elected member of parliament for Birmingham as John ◊Bright's colleague, and joined the republican group led by Sir Charles Dilke, the extreme left wing of the

Liberal Party. In 1880 he entered Gladstone's cabinet as president of the board of trade. The climax of his radical period was reached with the unauthorized programme, advocating, among other things, free education, graduated taxation, and small holdings of 'three acres and a cow'. In 1886 he broke with Gladstone over home rule for Ireland, resigned from the cabinet, and led the revolt of the Liberal-Unionists.

In 1895 Chamberlain became colonial secretary in Salisbury's Conservative government, and as such was responsible for relations with the Boer republics up to the outbreak of war in 1899. In 1903 he resigned to campaign for imperial preference or tariff reform as a means of consolidating the empire. From 1906 he was incapacitated by a stroke. Chamberlain was one of the most colourful figures of British politics, and his monocle and orchid made him a favourite subject for political cartoonists.

chamber music music suitable for performance in a small room or chamber, as opposed to that intended for the concert hall. The term is applied to music written for a small combination of instruments, played with one instrument to a part. Many such combinations are possible, but of these the string quartet is one of the most common. A string quartet of G ◊Allegri is believed to be the first example of its kind, while among English composers who wrote 'fantasy trios', or 'fancies', were ◊Byrd and ◊Gibbons. In the 17th and early 18th centuries the harpsichord generally provided a bass line. The chamber sonata with a figured bass accompaniment was established by the great Italian school of violinists – such as ◊Vivaldi, and ◊Corelli. From the 18th century onwards a new type of chamber music was tried out by Haydn, in which members of a string quartet play on equal terms, with no additional keyboard instrument. Haydn also developed the classical ◊sonata form in his chamber music. His quartets influenced those of ◊Mozart, who in turn influenced Haydn's later works. The last quartets of ◊Beethoven show many striking departures from the original classical framework. In the 19th century ◊chamber music found its way into the concert hall, sometimes taking on a quasi-orchestral quality, even in the work of ◊Brahms. The early 20th-century French school of Impressionists, represented by Debussy and Ravel, experimented with chamber music forms, and, during the period which followed, developments such as ◊atonality, ◊polytonality, etc., have found expression in chamber music. Twentieth-century composers of chamber music include Berg, Webern, Hindemith, Stravinsky, Prokoviev, Shostakovich, Kodály, Bartók, Ireland, Bliss, Tippett, Rubbra, Copland, and Roy Harris.

Chambers /'tʃeɪmbəz/ William 1726–1796. British architect, popularizer of Chinese influence (Kew Gardens pagoda) and designer of Somerset House, London.

Chambéry /ʃɒmbeɪˈriː/ former capital of Savoy, now capital of Savoie *département*, France. It is the seat of an archbishopric, and has a railway junction and airport, with some industry; it is also a holiday and health resort. Population (1982) 54,9896.

chameleon type of lizard, some 80 or so species of which form the family Chameleontidae. Most live in Africa and Madagascar, but the *common chameleon Chameleo chameleon* is found in Mediterranean countries, two species live in south west Arabia, and one species in India and Sri Lanka. The tail is long and highly prehensile, assisting the animal when climbing. Most chameleons are entirely arboreal in their habits and move very slowly. The tongue is very long, protrusible, and covered with a viscous secretion; it can be shot out with great rapidity to 20 cm/8 in for the capture of insects. The eyes are on 'turrets', move independently, but can swivel forward to give stereoscopic vision for 'shooting'. Chameleons are noted for their colour-changing abilities, which in some species are highly developed. Their colour changes are caused by changes in the intensity of light, of temperature, and of emotion, which, via the nervous system affect the dispersal of pigment granules in the layers of cells beneath the outer skin.

chamois goat-like mammal *Rupicapra rupicapra* found in the mountain ranges of southern Europe and Asia Minor. It is brown, lighter below, and with dark patches running through the eyes. Standing up to 80 cm/2.6ft high, both sexes have horns, which may be 20 cm/8 in long. The horns are set close together, go up vertically then back at the top to form a hook. Chamois live in herds up to 30 strong and are very sure footed. Chamois skin is very soft and excellent for cleaning glass, but the chamois is now comparatively rare and 'chamois leather' is often made from skin of sheep and goats.

Chamonix /'ʃæməni/ holiday resort at the foot of Mont Blanc, in the French Alps. Population (1982) 9,255.

Champagne /ˌʃæm'peɪn/ ancient province of France, of which the capital was Troyes, famous for its vineyards. The modern region of Champagne-Ardennes comprises the *départements* of Ardennes, Aube, Marne, and Haute-Marne forms the plains east of the Paris basin. Area 25,741 sq km/9,939 sq mi; population (1982) 1,345,935.

champagne /ˌʃæm'peɪn/ French wine, produced from specially fine grapes and blended wines, the former grown in a strictly defined area of the Marne region around Reims and Epernay in Champagne. Unlike other wines, fermentation takes place after the bottle has been sealed, which causes the effervescence.

Champaigne /ˌʃæm'peɪn/ Philippe de 1602–1674. French painter. Of Flemish origin, he settled in Paris at the age of 19, and is noted for his naturalistic portraits, for example, Richelieu, and for his religious art.

champignon edible fungus *Marasmius oreades*, very popular in France. It forms 'fairy rings' on short turf.

Champlain /ʃæm'pleɪn/ lake situated in north east USA, discovered in 1609 by Samuel de ◊Champlain.

Champlain /ʃæm'pleɪn/ Samuel de 1567–1635. French pioneer and soldier-explorer in Canada. Having served in the army of Henry IV and on an expedition to the West Indies, he began his exploration of Canada in 1603. In a third expedition in 1608 he founded and named Quebec, and in 1612 was appointed lieutenant–governor of French Canada.

Champollion /ˌʃɒmpɒl'jɒŋ/ Jean Françdois, le Jeune 1790–1832. French Egyptologist, who in 1822 deciphered Egyptian hieroglyphics with the aid of the Rosetta ◊Stone.

chance the theory of ◊probability. As a science it originated when the Chevalier de Méré consulted Blaise ◊Pascal about how to reduce his gambling losses. In correspondence with another mathematician, Pierre de ◊Fermat, Pascal worked out the foundations of the theory of chance. This underlies the science of statistics, and is particularly important for life assurance and atomic physics.

Chancellor, Lord High British state official, originally the royal secretary, today a member of the cabinet, whose office ends with a change of government. The lord high chancellor acts as speaker of the house of lords, may preside over the court of appeal, and appoints the judges and justices of the peace. Until the 14th century he was always an ecclesiastic, who also acted as royal chaplain and keeper of the great seal. Under Edward III the lord high chancellor became head of a permanent court to consider petitions to the king, the court of chancery. In order of precedence the lord high chancellor comes after the archbishop of Canterbury.

Chancellor of the Duchy of Lancaster honorary post held by a cabinet minister in the British government who has other non-departmental responsibilities. The chancellor of the Duchy of Lancaster was originally the monarch's representative controlling the royal lands and courts within the duchy.

Chancellor of the Exchequer senior cabinet minister in the British government responsible for the national economy. The office, established under Henry III, originally entailed keeping the exchequer seal.

Chancery court in the UK which, until the fusion of the courts in 1875 into the high court of justice and the court of appeal, administered the rules of equity as distinct from the rules of common law. Now a division of the high court it deals with such matters as the administration of the estates of deceased persons, the execution of trusts, the enforcement of sales of land, foreclosure of mortgages, partnerships and the estates of minors.

Chan Chan /'tʃæn 'tʃæn/ capital of the pre-Inca ◊Chimu kingdom in Peru.

Chandelá or *Candella* a Rājput dynasty which ruled the Bundelkand region of central India from the 9th–11th centuries. They fought against Muslim invaders, until they were eventually replaced by the ◊Bundelās.

Chandernagore /ˌtʃʌndənə'gɔː/ Indian city, on the Hooghly, in the state of West Bengal. Formerly a French settlement, it was ceded to India by treaty in 1952. Population (1981) 101,925.

Chandigarh /ˌtʃʌndɪ'gɑː/ city of the Republic of India, in the foothills of the Himalayas north of Ambala. Population (1981) 451,610 (territory).

history Chandigarh was inaugurated in 1953 to replace Lahore (capital of British Punjab), which went to Pakistan under partition in 1947. Planned by the architect Le Corbusier, since 1966 it has been the capital city of both Haryana and Punjab, until a new capital is built for the former.

Chandler /'tʃɑːndlə/ Raymond 1888–1959. American crime writer. Born in Chicago, he was educated at Dulwich College in London. He created the 'private eye' hero Philip Marlowe, a hard-boiled knight errant, in books which include *The Big Sleep* 1939, *Farewell, My Lovely* 1940, and *The Long Goodbye* 1954.

Chandragupta Maurya /'tʃʌndrəˌguptə 'mauriə/ ruler of North India c. 321–c. 296BC, founder of ◊Maurya dynasty; see ◊Asoka, his grandson.

Chandrasekhar /ˌtʃændrə'seɪkə/ Subrahmanyan 1910– . American astrophysicist, made pioneering studies of the structure and evolution of stars (see ◊star). Born in Lahore, he studied in Cambridge, England, before settling in the USA. The *Chandrasekhar limit* of 1.4 suns is the maximum mass of ◊white dwarf before it turns into a ◊neutron star. Awarded 1983 Nobel Prize for physics.

Chanel /ʃæ'nel/ Coco (Gabrielle) 1883–1970. French fashion designer, creator of the 'little black dress', informal cardigan suit, and perfumes.

Chanel The French 'Coco' Chanel in 1929. She liberated women from restrictive clothes designing fashions which combined elegance with comfort, and many of her styles became classics.

Changchiakow /'tʃæŋ ˌtʃɪə 'kaʊ/ former name for ◊Zhangjiakou, trading centre in Hesei province, China.

Changchun /ˌtʃæŋ'tʃʊn/ industrial city in Jilin province, China; a rail junction and centre of an agricultural district. Machinery and motor vehicles are manufactured. As Hsingking ('new capital'), it was the capital of Manchukuo 1932–45. Population (1981) 1,740,000.

change of state in physics, occurs when a gas condenses to a liquid or a liquid freezes to a solid. Similar changes take place when a solid melts to form a liquid or a liquid vaporizes (evaporates) to produce gas. The first set of changes are brought about by cooling, and the second set by heating. In the unusual change of state called sublimation, a solid changes directly to a gas without passing through the liquid state. For example, solid carbon dioxide (dry ice) sublimes to carbon dioxide gas.

Chang Jiang /'tʃæŋ dʒi'æŋ/ greatest river (formerly Yangtze Kiang) of China, flowing about 5,470 km/3,400 mi from Tibet to the Yellow Sea. It has 204 km/127 mi of gorges, below which is Gezhou Ba, the first dam to harness the river.

Changsha /ˌtʃæŋ'ʃɑː/ river port, on the Xiang Jiang, capital of Hunan province, China. It trades in rice, tea, timber and non-ferrous metals; works antimony, lead, and silver; and makes porcelain and embroideries. Population (1982) 1,072,000.

Channel, English stretch of water between England and France, leading in the west to the Atlantic Ocean, and in the east via the Strait of Dover to the North Sea; known as La Manche, 'the sleeve' (from its shape), by the French. It is 450 km/280 mi long W–E; 27 km/17 mi wide at its narrowest (Cap Gris Nez–Dover) and 117 km/110 mi wide at its widest (Ushant–Land's End).
Channel swimming the first to swim the English Channel was Captain Webb on 25 Aug 1875, Dover–Calais 21 hr 45 min; fastest crossing (England to France) was made by Penny Dean (US) in 1978, 7 hr 42 min; and first to swim nonstop in both directions, was the Argentinian Antonio Abertondo in 1961.

Channel Country /'tʃænl/ area of south west Queensland, Australia, in which channels such as Cooper's Creek (where explorers Burke and Wills died in 1861) are cut by intermittent rivers. Summer rains supply rich grass for cattle, and there are the 'beef roads', down which herds are taken in linked trucks for slaughter.

Channel Islands /'tʃænl/ *area* 194 sq km/75 sq mi
features the islands comprise Jersey, Guernsey, Alderney, Great and Little Sark, with the lesser Herm, Brechou, Jethou and Lihou; the climate is very mild, and the soil productive. Financially the islands are a 'tax haven'.
exports flowers, early potatoes, tomatoes, butterflies
currency English pound, also local coinage
population (1981) 128,878
language official language French (◊Norman-French) but English more widely used
religion chiefly Anglican
famous people Lily Langtry
government the main islands have their own parliaments and laws. Unless specially signified, the Channel Islands are not bound by British acts of parliament, though the British government is responsible for defence and external relations.
history originally under the duchy of Normandy, they are the only part still held by Britain. The islands came under the same rule as England in

1066, and are dependent territories of the English Crown, owing allegiance to the monarch. Germany occupied the islands during World War II from Jun 1940–May 1945.

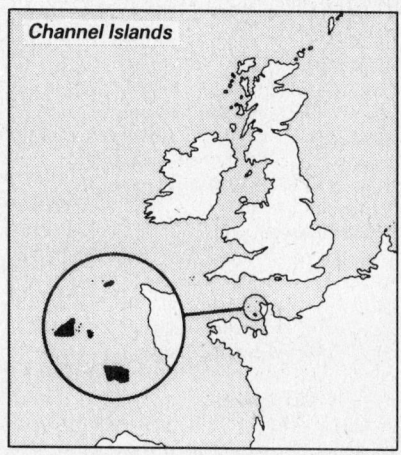

Channel Islands

Channel tunnel a proposed tunnel beneath the English ◊Channel linking Britain with mainland Europe, sometimes called the 'Chunnel'. The latest decision to go ahead with a tunnelling project was taken early in 1986, when a design presented by a consortium called the Channel Tunnel Group was approved by the English and French governments. The project comprises twin rail tunnels some 50 km/30 mi long and 7.3 m/24 ft in diameter located 40 m/130 ft beneath and seabed. Specially designed shuttle trains carrying cars and lorries will run every few minutes between terminals at Cheriton, near Folkestone, Kent, and at Ffethun, near Calais. The cross-Channel link will cost an estimated ◊2,330 million and is scheduled for completion by 1993.
A Chunnel is by no means a new idea. In the 1880s British financier and railway promoter Sir Edward Watkin actually started boring a tunnel near Dover, abandoning it in 1894 because of governmental opposition after driving some 1.6 km/1 mile out to sea. In 1973 Britain and France agreed to back a tunnel, but a year later Britain pulled out following a change of government.

chant word used in common speech to denote any vocal melody or song, especially of a slow and solemn character; but applied specifically to a type of simple melody used in services of the Christian Church, for singing the psalms and canticles and in some forms of Buddhism. The Ambrosian and ◊Gregorian chants are forms of ◊plainsong melody.

chanterelle bright yellow edible fungus *Cantharellus cibarius* growing in woodlands.

Chantilly /ʃæn'tɪli/ town in Oise département, France, north east of Paris. It has a fine chateau, is the centre of French horseracing, and was the headquarters of the French military chief ◊Joffre 1914–17. Population (1982) 10,208.

Chantrey /'tʃɑːntri/ Francis Legatt 1781–1841. British sculptor. He made a reputation with his busts and statues of

Wellington, Wordsworth and Scott, but is most celebrated for his child studies notably the *Sleeping Children* (in Lichfield cathedral). The *Chantrey Bequest* provides for the ◊Royal Academy of Arts to buy works of art for the nation, which are housed in the Tate Gallery, London.

Chao Phraya /'tʃaʊ prə'jɑː/ chief river (formerly Menam) of Thailand, flowing 1,200 km/750 mi into the Gulf of Thailand.

chaos theory branch of mathematics used to deal with chaotic systems, for example, an engineered structure, such as an oil platform, which is subjected to irregular, unpredictable wave stress.

chaparral thick scrub country of south west USA, mainly evergreen oak trees.

Chapel Royal term originally used in the UK for the royal retinue of priests, singers, and musicians (including Tallis, Byrd, and Purcell) of the English court from 1135. There are Chapels Royal, in the sense of Chapel buildings, at the former royal palaces of St James's, Hampton Court, and the Tower of London (St John the Evangelist, and St Peter ad Vincula). Windsor Castle (with a royal chapel also in Windsor Great Park) and a royal church at Sandringham.

Chaplin /'tʃæplɪn/ Charles Spencer ('Charlie') 1889–1977. British actor-director. Born in South London, he first appeared on the stage at the age of five, but made his worldwide reputation as the little tramp with smudge moustache, bowler hat, and cane in silent films for example, *The Gold Rush* 1925. Later came *City Lights* 1931, *Modern Times* 1938, *The Great Dictator* (guying Hitler) 1940, *Monsieur Verdoux* (in which he spoke for the first time) 1947, and *Limelight* (eventually awarded an Oscar for Chaplin's musical theme) 1952. He left the USA to live in Switzerland in 1952 when accused of Communist sympathies. He was four times married, his third wife being Paulette Goddard, and the fourth, Oona, daughter of Eugene O'Neill. Knighted in 1975.

Chapman /'tʃæpmən/ George 1559–1634. English poet-dramatist, who was associated with ◊Marlowe, and collaborated with Ben ◊Jonson. His translations of Homer (completed 1616) were celebrated, and were later the subject of a sonnet by Keats. His plays include the comedy *Eastward Ho!* (with Jonson and Marston), and the tragedy *Bussy d'Amboise*.

char fish *Salvelinus alpinus* allied to the trout, living in the Arctic sea and also in Europe and North America in some freshwaters, especially upland lakes, such as Lake Windermere in England. Numerous variants have been described, but probably all belong to one species. The distribution is probably explained by the fish spreading during the Ice Ages and being left behind, surviving where it could, when the ice retreated. Sometimes spelt *charr*.

characin freshwater fish belonging to the family Characidae. There are over 1300 species, mostly from South and Central America, but some from Africa. Most are carnivores. This family includes the ◊piranhas. Most characins,

Chaplin Charlie Chaplin in *City Lights* 1931. By this time he had been the supreme comic actor of silent films for fifteen years and was reluctant to adapt to the coming of sound films. In this film he used music and effects, but there was no speech until *Modern Times* 1938, which combined mime and dialogue.

however, are small fishes, often colourful, and they include many popular aquarium species such as the ◊tetras. In typical characins, unlike the somewhat similar carp family, the mouth is toothed and there is a small dorsal adipose fin just in front of the tail.

charcoal form of ◊carbon, produced by heating wood in the absence of air, which is used as a fuel, and in making black-and-white drawings.

Charcot /ʃɑːˈkəu/ Jean-Martin 1825–1893. French neurologist, who studied diseases of the nervous system, initiated the scientific study of hypnotism, and influenced Sigmund Freud (one of his students).

Chardin /ʃɑːˈdæn/ Jean Baptiste Siméon 1699–1779. French artist. Born in Paris, he is chiefly celebrated for his interiors and still-lifes of kitchen utensils, baskets of fruit, fish, and game.

Chardonnet /ˌʃɑːdɒˈneɪ/ Hilaire Bernigaud 1839–1924. French chemist, who developed artificial silk in 1883, the first artificial fibre.

Charente /ʃæˈrɒnt/ French river, rising in Haute-Vienne département and flowing past Angoulême and Cognac into the Bay of Biscay below Rochefort. Length 360 km/225 mi. Its wide estuary is much silted up. It gives its name to two départements, Charente and Charente-Maritime (formerly Charente-Inférieure).

charge See ◊electric charge.

charge-coupled device (CCD) ◊semiconductor logic circuit component, employed in computers, which usually consists of alternate layers of metal, silicon dioxide and silicon.

charged particle beam high-energy beam (CPB) of electrons or protons, which does not burn through the surface of its target like a laser,

but cuts through it. Such beams are being developed as weapons. See ◊laser.

Charge of the Light Brigade gallant but disastrous charge of British Light Brigade of cavalry against the Russian entrenched artillery on 25 Oct 1854 during the Crimean War at ◊Balaclava.

Charing Cross /ˈtʃeərɪŋ/ district in Westminster, London, around Charing Cross mainline railway station, deriving its name from the site of the last of twelve stone crosses erected by Edward I in 1290 at the resting-places of the coffin of his queen, Eleanor. The present cross is modern.

Charlemagne /ˌʃɑːləˈmeɪn/ Charles I, the Great 742–814. King of the Franks and Roman emperor. The son of Pepin the Short, mayor of the palace in Merovingian Neustria, he was crowned by the Pope in 754 along with his father and his younger brother Carloman. When Pepin died in 768, Charlemagne inherited the northern part of the Frankish kingdom, and when Carloman died in 771, Charlemagne also took possession of his countries. In 770 he married the daughter of the king of the Lombards, whom he divorced a year later.

He was engaged in his first Saxon campaign when the Pope's call for help against the Lombards reached him; he crossed the Alps, captured Pavia, and took the title of king of the Lombards. The pacification and christianizing of the warlike pagan tribes of Saxons occupied the greater part of Charlemagne's reign. The Westphalian leader Widukind did not submit until 785, when he received baptism. From 792 North Saxony was subdued, and in 804 the country was finally pacified. In 777 the emir of Saragossa asked for Charlemagne's help against the emir of Cordova. Charlemagne crossed the Pyrenees in 778, and reached the Ebro, but had to turn back from Saragossa. The rearguard action of Roncesvalles in which Roland, warden of the Breton March, and other Frankish nobles were ambushed and killed by Basque hordes, became immortal in the *Chanson de Roland*. In 801 the district between the Pyrenees and the Llobregat was organized as the Spanish March. The independent duchy of Bavaria was incorporated in the kingdom in 788, while the Avars, Turko-Finnish nomads inhabiting Hungary, were subdued in 791–96 and accepted Christianity. The supremacy of the Frankish king in the western world found outward expression in the bestowal of the imperial title: in Rome, during Mass on Christmas Day 800, Pope Leo III crowned Charlemagne emperor.

Charlemagne's activities were not confined to warfare. Jury-courts were introduced, the laws of the Franks revised, and other tribal laws written down. A new coinage was introduced, weights and measures were reformed, and communications were improved. Charlemagne also took a lively interest in theology, organized the Church in his dominions, and furthered missionary enterprises and monastic reform. The 'Carolingian Renaissance' of learning began when he persuaded the Northumbrian Alcuin to enter his service in 781. Charlemagne gathered a kind of academy around him. He also collected

the old heroic lays, began a German grammar, and promoted religious instruction in the vernacular. He died on 28 Jan 814, at Aachen, where he was buried. Soon a cycle of heroic legends and romances developed round him including epics of Ariosto, Boiardo, and Tasso.

Charlemagne Statue of the French warrior, who became the legendary hero of medieval romances. He took NE Spain from the Moors and invaded Bavaria and Italy. He restored the papacy to Leo III, who then crowned him emperor. He was also a brilliant administrator and intellectual, who encouraged the arts and codified the law.

Charles /ʃɑːl/ Jacques Alexandre César 1746–1823. French physicist, who studied gases and made the first manned ascent in a hydrogen-filled balloon (1783). His work on the expansion of gases led to the formulation of ◊Charles' law.

Charles /tʃɑːlz/ Ray 1930– . US singer, songwriter, and pianist, blind from childhood, whose first hits were 'I've Got A Woman' 1955 and 'What'd I Say' 1959. Perhaps best known for his recording of Hoagy Carmichael's ballad 'Georgia on My Mind' 1960, he has recorded gospel, blues, rock, soul, country, and rhythm and blues.

Charles /tʃɑːlz/ two kings of Great Britain and Ireland.

Charles I /tʃɑːlz/ 1600–1649. Born at Dunfermline, the son of James I of England (James VI of Scotland), he became heir to the throne on the death of his brother Henry in 1612. He went to Madrid in 1623 to urge his suit to the Infanta of Spain, but without success. In 1625 he became king, and married Henrietta Maria, daughter of Henry IV of France. Friction with Parliament began at once. The parliaments of 1625 and 1626 were dissolved, and that of 1628 refused supplies until Charles had accepted the Petition of Right. In 1629 it attacked Charles's illegal taxation and support of the Arminians (see ◊Arminius) in the church, whereupon he dissolved Parliament and imprisoned its leaders. For 11 years he ruled without a parliament, raising money by expedients that alienated the entire nation, while the ◊Star Chamber suppressed opposition by persecuting the Puritans. When Charles attempted in 1637 to force a prayer book on the English model on Presbyterian Scotland he found himself confronted with a nation in arms. The Short Parliament, which met in April 1640, refused to grant money until grievances were redressed, and was speedily dissolved. The Scots then advanced into England, and forced their own terms on Charles. The ◊Long Parliament met on 3 Nov 1640, and declared extra-parliamentary taxation illegal, abolished the Star Chamber and other prerogative courts, and voted that Parliament could not be dissolved without its own consent. ◊Laud and other ministers were imprisoned, and ◊Strafford condemned to death. After the failure of his attempt to arrest the parliamentary leaders on 4 Jan 1642, Charles withdrew from London, and on 22 Aug declared war on Parliament by raising his standard at Nottingham.

Scottish invasion followed in 1648, and was shattered by ◊Cromwell at Preston. In Jan 1649 the House of Commons set up a high court of justice, which tried Charles and condemned him to death. He was beheaded on 30 Jan before the Banqueting Hall in Whitehall, and was buried in St George's Chapel.

Charles II /tʃɑːlz/ 1630–1685. Born at St James's Palace, the son of Charles I, he lived with his father at Oxford 1642–45, and after the victory of the parliament withdrew to the Continent. Accepting the ◊Covenanters' offer to make him king, he landed in Scotland in 1650, and was crowned at Scone on 1 Jan 1651. An attempt to invade England was ended on 3 Sept by Cromwell's victory at Worcester. Charles escaped, and after many adventures reached the Continent. For nine years he wandered through France, Germany, Flanders, Spain, and Holland until the opening of negotiations by ◊Monck in 1660 offered new hope. In Apr Charles issued the Declaration of ◊Breda, promising a general amnesty and freedom of conscience. Parliament accepted the Declaration; Charles was proclaimed king on 8 May 1660, landed at Dover on the 26th, and entered London three days later.

grew tired of him. The disasters of the Dutch War furnished an excuse in 1667 for banishing Clarendon, and he was replaced by the ◊cabal of ◊Clifford and Arlington (Henry Bennett, 1618–85), both secret Catholics, and ◊Buckingham, ◊Ashley and ◊Lauderdale, who had links with the ◊Dissenters. In 1670 Charles signed the Secret Treaty of Dover, the full details of which were known only to Clifford and Arlington, whereby he promised Louis XIV he would declare himself a Catholic, re-establish Catholicism in England, and support Louis's projected war against the Dutch; in return Louis was to finance Charles and in the event of resistance to supply him with troops. War with Holland followed in 1672, and at the same time Charles issued the Declaration of Indulgence, suspending all penal laws against Catholics and Dissenters.

Parliament forced Charles in 1673 to withdraw the Indulgence and accept a Test Act exluding all Catholics from office, and in 1674 to end the war in Holland. This broke up the cabal, while Ashley (Lord Shaftesbury), who had learned the truth about the treaty, assumed the leadership of the opposition. ◊Danby, the new chief minister, built up a court party in the commons by bribery, while subsidies from Louis relieved Charles from dependence on parliament. In 1678 ◊Oates's announcement of a 'popish plot' released a general panic, which Shaftesbury exploited to introduce his Exclusion Bill, excluding James, Duke of York, from the succession as a Papist; instead he hoped to substitute Charles's illegitimate son ◊Monmouth. Charles played for time, counting on a Royalist reaction and offering compromises which the opposition rejected.

In 1681 his last parliament was summoned at Oxford; the Whigs attended armed, but when Shaftesbury rejected a last compromise, Charles dissolved Parliament and the Whigs fled in terror. Henceforward Charles ruled without a parliament. For money he relied on subsidies from Louis. When the Whigs plotted a revolt their leaders were executed, while Shaftesbury and Monmouth fled to Holland. Before Charles died in 1685 he had achieved his ambition to free himself from parliamentary control. A patron of the arts and science, Charles enjoyed a lively personal life: see Lady ◊Castlemaine, Nell ◊Gwyn, Lady ◊Portsmouth, Lucy ◊Walter.

Charles /tʃɑːlz/ Philip Arthur George 1948– . Prince of the United Kingdom, heir apparent to the British throne, and Prince of Wales since 1958 (investiture 1969). Born at Buckingham Palace on 14 Nov 1948, he is the first-born child of Queen Elizabeth II and the Duke of Edinburgh. He went to Cheam School, Berkshire, in 1957 and in 1962 to his father's school Gordonstoun in Scotland. He studied at Trinity College, Cambridge, 1967–70, before serving in the RAF and Royal Navy. In 1980 he acquired a country home, Highgrove, Doughton, near Tetbury, Gloucestershire, and was the first royal heir since 1659 to choose an English bride, Lady Diana Spencer (1961–) daughter of the 8th Earl Spencer.

Charles /tʃɑːlz/ ten kings of France.

Charles I A portrait by Daniel Mytens, 1631. An inflexible idealist, Charles I of England believed that the king ruled by Divine Right, but many objected to his view of monarchy, to his advisers, to his religion and to his Catholic queen, Henrietta Maria.

Charles's defeat at Naseby in Jun 1645 ended all hopes of victory; in May 1646 he surrendered at Newark to the Scots, who in Jan 1647 handed him over to Parliament. In June the army seized him, and carried him off to Hampton Court. While the army leaders strove to find a settlement, Charles secretly intrigued for a Scottish invasion. In Nov he escaped, but was recaptured and held at Carisbrooke Castle; a

Politically he had three aims: 'not to go on his travels again'; to make himself absolute; and to secure toleration, and if possible supremacy, for Catholicism. He hovered between Catholicism and scepticism, but favoured the former for his subjects as most consistent with absolute monarchy. He entrusted the government to ◊Clarendon, who arranged his marriage in 1662 with ◊Catherine of Braganza, but Charles soon

Charles II The Restoration of the monarchy in 1660 was greeted with joy in England and Charles II showed himself to be an exceptionally affable and energetic king. He had many mistresses, including Nell Gwynn. The portrait by Peter Lely shows the face of the bon vivour.

Charles I /tʃɑːlz/ see ◊Charlemagne.

Charles II /tʃɑːlz/ the Bald; see ◊Charles, rulers of the Holy Roman Empire.

Charles III /tʃɑːlz/ the Simple 879–929. Son of Louis the Stammerer, he was crowned at Reims in 893. In 911 he ceded what later became the duchy of Normandy to the Norman chief ◊Rollo.

Charles IV /tʃɑːlz/ the Fair 1294–1328. Succeeded Philip V in 1322, as the last of the direct Capetian line.

Charles V /tʃɑːlz/ the Wise 1337–80. He was regent during the captivity of his father (John II) in England 1356–60, and became king 1364. He reconquered nearly all France from England 1369–80.

Charles VI /tʃɑːlz/ 1368–1422. Succeeded in 1380, and was under the regency of his uncles until 1388. He went mad in 1392, and civil war broke out between the dukes of Orleans and Burgundy. Henry V of England invaded France in 1415, conquering Normandy, and in 1420 forcing Charles to sign the Treaty of Troyes, recognizing Henry as his successor.

Charles VII /tʃɑːlz/ 1403–61. Son of Charles VI, he was excluded from the succession by the Treaty of Troyes, but recognized by the S of

France. In 1429 Joan of Arc raised the siege of Orleans and had him crowned at Reims. He organised France's first standing army and by 1453 he had expelled the English from all of France except Calais.

Charles VIII /tʃɑːlz/ 1470–98. Succeeded Louis XI in 1483. In 1494 he claimed the Neapolitan crown without success, and when he entered Naples in 1495 was forced to withdraw by a coalition of Milan, Venice, Spain, and the Emperor. He defeated them at Fornovo, but lost Naples. He died while preparing a second expedition.

Charles IX /tʃɑːlz/ 1550–74. Second son of Henry II and Catherine de Medici, he succeeded his brother Francis II in 1560, but remained under the domination of his mother for ten years while France was torn by religious wars. In 1570 he fell under the influence of the Huguenot leader Coligny; alarmed by this, Catherine instigated his order for the Massacre of St ◊Bartholomew, which led to a new religious war.

Charles X /tʃɑːlz/ 1757–1836. Grandson of Louis XV and brother of Louis XVI and XVII, known as the Count of Artois before his accession. He had fled to England at the beginning of the ◊Revolution. When he came to

the throne in 1824, he attempted to reverse the achievements of the Revolution; a revolt ensued in 1830, and he again fled to England. He died at Gorizia.

Charles /tʃɑːlz/ (Karl) 1887–1922. Emperor of Austria and King of Hungary, the last of the Hapsburg emperors. He succeeded his great-uncle, Francis Joseph, in 1916, at the height of the World War I, and in 1919 was forced to withdraw to Switzerland, although he refused to abdicate. In 1921 he attempted unsuccessfully to regain the crown of Hungary; and was deported to Madeira, where he died. He married the Princess Zita of Bourbon-Parma, and their son, the Archduke Otto, maintains the Hapsburg claims.

Charles /tʃɑːlz/ seven rulers of the Holy Roman Empire.

Charles I /tʃɑːlz/ see ◊Charlemagne.

Charles II /tʃɑːlz/ the Bald 823–877. Holy Roman Emperor 875–77, and (as Charles II) King of France 843–77. Younger son of Louis I, the Pious warred against his eldest brother the Emperor Lothais I, until the Treaty of Verdun (843) made him king of the West Frankish Kingdom, that is, modern France and the Spanish March. Crowned Emperor at Rome in 875.

Charles III /tʃɑːlz/ the Fat 832–888. Holy Roman Emperor 881–87, became king of the West Franks in 885, thus uniting for the last time the whole of Charlemagne's dominions, but was deposed.

Charles IV /tʃɑːlz/ 1316–1378. Holy Roman Emperor 1355–78 and King of Bohemia 1346–78. Son of John of Luxemburg, king of Bohemia, was elected king of Germany 1346, ruled all Germany from 1347. He was the founder of the first German university at Prague in 1348.

Charles V /tʃɑːlz/ 1500–1558. Holy Roman Emperor 1519–56. Son of Philip of Burgundy and Joanna of Castile, he inherited the Netherlands from his father in 1506, Spain, Naples, Sicily, Sardinia, and the Spanish dominions in North Africa and America from his maternal grandfather (Ferdinand V) in 1516, and from his paternal grandfather (Maximilian) the Hapsburg dominions in 1519, when he was elected emperor. Such vast possessions led to rivalry from Francis I, whose alliance with the Turks brought Vienna under siege in 1529 and 1532. From 1517 the Empire was split by the rise of Lutheranism, Charles making unsuccessful attempts to reach a settlement at Augsburg in 1530, and being forced by the Treaty of ◊Passau in 1552 to yield most of the Protestant demands. Worn out, he abdicated in favour of his son, Philip II in the Netherlands 1555 and Spain 1556; yielded the imperial crown to his brother Ferdinand, and retired to the monastery of Yuste, Spain.

Charles VI /tʃɑːlz/ 1685–1740. Holy Roman Emperor 1711–40, father of Maria Theresa, whose succession to his Austrian dominions he tried to ensure, and himself claimant in 1700 to the Spanish throne: see Spanish ◊Succession.

Charles VII /tʃɑːlz/ 1697–1745. Holy Roman Emperor 1742–45, opponent of Maria

Theresa's claim to the Austrian dominions of Charles VI.

Charles /tʃɑːlz/ (Spanish *Carlos*) four kings of Spain:

Charles I /tʃɑːlz/ also ◊Charles V, Holy Roman Emperor.

Charles II /tʃɑːlz/ 1661–1700. second son of Philip IV, was the last of the Spanish Hapsburg kings, and succeeded in 1665. Imbecilic from birth, he bequeathed his dominions to Philip of Anjou, grandson of Louis XIV, which led to the War of the Spanish ◊Succession.

Charles III /tʃɑːlz/ 1716–1788. the son of Philip V, he became Duke of Parma in 1732, and in 1734 conquered Naples and Sicily. On the death in 1759 of his half-brother Ferdinand VI he became king of Spain, handing over Naples and Sicily to his son Ferdinand. During his reign Spain was twice at war with Britain – during the Seven Years' War, when he sided with France and lost Florida, and when he backed the Americans in the War of Independence and regained it. At home he carried out a programme of reforms and expelled the Jesuits.

Charles IV /tʃɑːlz/ 1748–1819. succeeded his father, Charles III in 1788, but left the government wholly in the hands of his wife and her lover, Godoy. In 1808 Charles abdicated in favour of his son Ferdinand. He was awarded a pension by Napoleon, and died in Rome.

Charles /tʃɑːlz/ (Swedish *Carl*) name of fifteen kings of Sweden. The first six were merely local chieftains.

Charles VII /tʃɑːlz/ reigned 1161–67.

Charles VIII /tʃɑːlz/ elected king in 1448, was twice expelled by the Danes and twice restored before his death in 1470.

Charles IX /tʃɑːlz/ 1550–1611. Elected regent of Sweden and Poland in 1595, and king in 1604. This involved him in war with Poland and Denmark.

Charles X /tʃɑːlz/ 1622–1660. Succeeded his cousin Christina in 1654. He waged war with Poland and Denmark, and in 1657 invaded Denmark from the S leading his army over the frozen sea.

Charles XI /tʃɑːlz/ 1655–1697. He succeeded in 1660, showed himself a remarkable general, and drastically reformed the administration.

Charles XII /tʃɑːlz/ 1682–1718. Succeeded his father Charles XI in 1697 and from 1700 was involved continuously in war with Denmark, Poland, and Russia. He won a brilliant succession of victories, until in 1709 while invading Russia he was defeated at Poltava, and forced to take refuge in Turkey until 1714. He was killed in 1718 while besieging Frederiksten.

Charles XIII /tʃɑːlz/ 1748–1818. He was elected king in 1809, became the first king of Sweden and Norway in 1814.

Charles XIV /tʃɑːlz/ 1763–1844. Originally Jean Baptiste Jules Bernadotte, he ruled over Sweden and Norway. Born at Pau, he entered the French army, won rapid promotion during the Revolutionary War, and was created a marshal of France by Napoleon. In 1810 he was elected crown prince of Sweden, under the name of Charles John. He brought Sweden into the

Charles V The Holy Roman Emperor and King of Spain, Charles V aimed to preserve the medieval idea of the Empire, and persecuted any separatist political or religious movements in order to achieve this essentially unrealistic end.

alliance against Napoleon in 1813 as a reward for which Sweden received Norway. He succeeded to the throne in 1818, proved a capable ruler, and was the founder of the present dynasty.

Charles XV /tʃɑːlz/ 1826–1872. Reigned over Sweden and Norway from 1859.

Charles Albert /tsɑːlz ˈælbət/ 1798–1849. King of Sardinia. He showed Liberal sympathies in early life, and after his accession in 1831 introduced some reforms. On the outbreak of the 1848 revolution he granted a constitution and declared war on Austria. His troops were defeated at Custozza and Novara. In 1849 he abdicated in favour of his son Victor Emmanuel and retired to a monastery, where he died.

Charles Augustus /tʃɑːlz ɔːˈɡʌstəs/ 1757–1828. Grand duke of Saxe-Weimar. He succeeded his father in infancy, fought against the French in 1792–94 and 1806, and is remembered as the patron and friend of Goethe.

Charles Edward Stuart /tʃɑːlz ˈedwəd ˈstjuːət/ 1720–1788. British prince, known as the Young Pretender. He was born in Rome, the son of James, the Old Pretender, and grandson of James II, and created Prince of Wales at birth. In Jul 1745 he sailed for Scotland, and landed in Invernessshire with seven companions. On 19 Aug he raised his father's standard, and within a week had rallied an army of 2,000 Highlanders. He entered Edinburgh almost without resistance, won an easy victory at Prestonpans, invaded England, and by 4 Dec had reached Derby, where his officers insisted on a retreat. The army returned to Scotland and won a victory at Falkirk, but was forced to retire to the Highlands before ◊Cumberland's advance. On 16 Apr at Culloden Charles Edward's army was

completely routed by Cumberland, and he fled. For five months he wandered through the Highlands with a price of £30,000 on his head before escaping to France. He visited England secretly in 1750, and may have made other visits. In later life he degenerated into a friendless drunkard. He settled in Italy in 1766.

Charles Martel /mɑːˈtel/ known as 'the Hammer' c. 688–741. Frankish ruler. An illegitimate son of Pepin of Heristal, he was grandfather of Charlemagne. He ruled the east of the Frankish kingdom from 717, and the whole kingdom from 731. His victory against the Moors between Poitiers and Toulouse in 732 earned him his nickname and halted the Islamic advance into Europe.

Charles's law law stated by Jacques Charles (1746–1823), French physicist, in 1787 and independently by Gay-Lussac in 1802 which states that the volume of a given mass of gas at constant pressure increases by 1/273 of its volume at 0°C for each degree C rise of temperature, that is, the coefficient of expansion of all gases is the same. The law is only approximately true and the coefficient of expansion is generally taken as 0.003663 per degree C.

Charles the Bold /tʃɑːlz/ Duke of Burgundy 1433–1477. Son of Philip the Good, he inherited Burgundy and the Low Countries from him in 1465. It was his ambition to create a kingdom stretching from the mouth of the Rhine to the mouth of the Rhône. He formed the League of the Public Weal against Louis XI of France, invaded France in 1471, and conquered the country as far as Rouen. The Emperor, Lorraine, and the Swiss united against him; he captured Nancy, but was defeated at Granson, and again at Morat 1476. Nancy was lost and he was killed in battle while attempting to recapture it. His possessions in the Netherlands passed to the Habsburgs by the marriage of his daughter Mary to Maximilian, to the Hapsburgs.

Charleston /ˈtʃɑːlstən/ main port and city of South Carolina, USA, dating from 1670. Fort Sumter, in the sheltered harbour of Charleston, was bombarded by Confederate batteries 12–13 April 1861, thus beginning the Civil War. There are many historic houses and fine gardens. Population (1980) 69,510.

Charleston /ˈtʃɑːlstən/ chief city of West Virginia, USA, on the Kanawha. It is the centre of a district producing coal and natural gas. Home of the pioneer Daniel ◊Boone. Population (1980) 63,968.

Charleston /ˈtʃɑːlstən/ a popular back-kicking dance of the 1920s which originated in Charleston, South Carolina and became a national craze in the USA.

charlock or wild mustard. A plant (*Sinapis arvensis*) of the family Cruciferae. It is a common annual weed in Britain, reaching a height of 60 cm/2 ft and with yellow flowers.

Charlotte /ˈʃɑːlət/ city in North Carolina, USA, on the border with South Carolina. Industries include data processing, textiles, chemicals, machinery, and food products. It was the gold-mining centre of the country until 1849. The Mint Museum of Arts has paintings,

Charles Edward Stuart Prince Charles Edward Stuart, painted c. 1729, was known to the English as the Young Pretender and to the Scots as Bonnie Prince Charlie. His story inspired the well-known 'Skye Boat Song.'

sculpture, and ceramics. Population (1980) 314,447.

Charlotte Amalie /'ʃɑːlət ə'mɑːljə/ capital and tourist resort of the US Virgin Islands; population (1980) 11,756.

Charlotte Augusta /ɔː'gʌstə/ Princess 1796–1817. Only child of George IV and Caroline of Brunswick, and heir to the English throne. In 1816 she married Prince Leopold of Saxe-Coburg (see ◊Leopold, King of the Belgians), but died in childbirth 18 months later.

Charlotte Sophia /'ʃɑːlət sə'faɪə/ 1744–1818. Queen consort. The daughter of the duke of Mecklenburg-Strelitz, she married George III of England in 1761, and bore him nine sons and six daughters.

Charlton /'tʃɑːltən/ Robert (Bobby) 1937– . English footballer, who played for England and Manchester United. He scored a record 49 goals for England in 106 appearances. He won three League championship medals, one FA Cup and one European Cup Winner's medal. He was Footballer of the Year 1966 and European Player of the Year 1967. On retiring from play, he went into football club management.

Charon /'keərən/ in Greek mythology, the boatman who ferried the dead over the river Styx to the underworld.

Charpentier /ʃɑː'pɒntieɪ/ Gustave 1860–1956. French composer, best known for his opera of Paris working-class life *Louise* 1900.

Charpentier /ʃɑː'pɒntieɪ/ Marc-Antoine 1645–1704. French composer. His music is mostly sacred, and includes a number of masses; other works include the operas *Médée*, and *Circé*.

Charrière /ʃæri'eə/ Isabelle Van Zuylen de 1740–1805. Dutch aristocrat, who settled in Colombier, Switzerland, in 1761. Her works

include plays, tracts, and novels, including *Caliste* 1786. She had many early feminist ideas.

Charteris /'tʃɑːtərɪs/ Leslie 1907– . British novelist. Born in Singapore, the son of a surgeon, he had a varied career in many exotic occupations which were to give authentic background to some 40 novels about Simon Templar, the 'Saint', a gentleman-adventurer on the wrong side of the law, which have been translated into 16 languages and adapted for films, radio and television. The first was *The Saint Meets the Tiger* 1928. He became a US citizen in 1946.

chartism radical British democratic movement, mainly of the working classes, which flourished around 1838–50. It derived its name from the People's Charter, a programme comprising six points: universal male suffrage, equal electoral districts, vote by ballot, annual parliaments, abolition of the property qualification for, and payment of, members of parliament.

Chartres /'ʃɑːtrə/ capital of the *département* of Eure-et-Loir, NW France, 96 km/59 mi SW of Paris, on the Eure. Its cathedral of Notre Dame, completed about 1240, is a masterpiece of Gothic architecture. Population (1982) 39,243.

Chartreuse, La Grande /ʃɑː'trɜːz/ the original home of the Carthusian order of Roman Catholic monks, established by St Bruno around 1084, in a remote valley 23 km/14 mi NNE of Grenoble (in modern département of Isère), France. The present buildings date from the 17th century. The monks were expelled at the Revolution, returned 1816, were again expelled in 1903, but, returning in 1940 as refugees from Italy, were allowed to remain.

chartreuse /ʃɑː'trɜːz/ green liqueur distilled since 1607 by the ◊Carthusian monks at La Grande Chartreuse monastery and also in Tarragona, Spain.

Charybdis /kə'rɪbdɪs/ in Greek mythology, a whirlpool formed by a monster of the same name on one side of the narrow straits of Messina, Sicily, opposite the monster Scylla. Homer tells how the ship of Odysseus contrived to pass unscathed 'between Scylla and Charybdis'.

Chase /tʃeɪs/ James Hadley. Pseudonym of René Raymond 1906–1985. He served in the Royal Air Force during World War II, and wrote *No Orchids for Miss Blandish* 1939, and other popular novels.

Chasidim /'hæsɪdiːm/ an 18th-century sect of ◊Judaism.

chasing indentation of a design on metal by small chisels and hammers. This method of decoration was familiar in ancient Egypt, Assyria and Greece.

chasuble the outer garment worn by the priest in the celebration of the Christian Mass. The colour of the chasuble depends on the feast which is being celebrated.

château term originally applied to a French medieval castle, but now used to describe a country house or important residence in France. The château was first used as a domestic building in the late 15th century; by the reign of Louis XIII 1610–43 fortifications such as moats, keeps, etc., were no longer used for defensive purposes, but merely as decorative features.

Chateaubriand /ʃæ,təubri'ɒŋ/ François René, vicomte de 1768–1848. French author, noted as a precursor of ◊Romanticism. He visited the USA in 1791 and, on his return to France, was exiled by the Revolution 1794–99. In exile he wrote *Atala* 1801 (written after his encounters with American Indians); and the autobiographical *René*, which formed part of *Le Génie de Christianisme/The Genius of Christianity* 1802. Having fought on the royalist side during the Revolution, he held diplomatic appointments under Louis XVIII. He later wrote *Mémoires d'outre tombe/Memoirs from Beyond the Tomb* 1849–50.

Châtelet /,ʃɑːtə'leɪ/ Emilie de Breteuil, marquise du 1706–1749. French scientific writer. Her marriage to the Marquis du Châtelet in 1725 gave her the leisure to study physics and mathematics; she became famous as a companion of ◊Voltaire, whom she met in 1733, and with whom she settled at her husband's estate at Cirey, in the Duchy of Lorraine. Her study of Newton was influential on Voltaire's thought; she collaborated with him on various scientific works, and independently produced the first (and only) French translation of Newton's *Principia Mathematica* (published posthumously in 1759).

THE MARCHIONESS
DU CHÂTELET.

Châtelet Writer on science and mistress of Voltaire, the Marquise du Châtelet resided with him at Montjeu and also at Chateau de Cirey. Her works include a translation of Newton's *Principia*.

Chatham /'tʃætəm/ town in Kent, England; population (1983) 146,000. The Royal Dockyard 1588–1984 was from 1985 converted to a 'new town' including an industrial area, marina, and museum as a focus of revival for the whole Medway area.

Chatham Islands /'tʃætəm/ two Pacific islands, forming a county of South Island, New Zealand; area 963 sq km/372 sq mi; population (1981) 750. The chief settlement is ◊Waitangi.

Chattanooga /ˌtʃætə'nuːgə/ city in Tennessee, USA on the Tennessee river; population (1980) 169,565. It is the focus of the Tennessee Valley Authority area.

Chatterton /'tʃætətən/ Thomas 1752–1770. British poet, whose brief life and suicide were to inspire English ◊Romanticism. Born in Bristol, he studied ancient documents he found in the Church of St Mary Redcliffe, and composed poems he ascribed to a 15th-century monk, 'Thomas Rowley', which were accepted as genuine. He sent examples to Horace Walpole but Walpole was advised by friends that they were forgeries. He then began contributing to periodicals in the style of Junius and went to London in 1770. Failing to gain patronage as a writer he poisoned himself with arsenic. His medieval-style poems influenced the Romantics, especially ◊Coleridge.

Chaucer /'tʃɔːsə/ Geoffrey c. 1340–1400. English poet, born in London. Author of *The Canterbury Tales*, he was the greatest and most influential English poet of the Middle Ages. He was taken prisoner in the French wars and had to be ransomed by Edward III in 1360. He married Philippa Roet in 1366, becoming in later life the brother-in-law of John of ◊Gaunt. He gained various appointments, for example, controller of London customs, and was sent on missions to Italy (where he may have met ◊Boccaccio and ◊Petrarch), France, and Flanders. His early work showed formal French influence, as in his adaptation of the French allegorical poem on courtly love *Romance of the Rose*; more mature works reflected the influence of Italian realism, as in his long narrative poem *Troilus and Criseyde*, adapted from Boccaccio. In his masterpiece, *The Canterbury Tales* written about 1387, a collection of tales told by pilgrims on their way to the Thomas Becket shrine, he showed his own genius for metre and characterization. The popularity of his work assured the dominance of southern English in literature.

chauvinism a warlike patriotism as exhibited by Nicholas Chauvin, one of Napoleon I's veterans, and his fanatical admirer. In the mid-20th century the expression 'male chauvinist' was coined to mean the belief in superiority of the male sex over the female.

Chávez (y Ramírez) /'tʃɑːves/ Carlos (Antonio de Padua) 1899–1878. Mexican composer. A student of the piano and of the complex rhythms of his country's folk music, he founded the Mexico Symphony Orchestra. His works include a number of ballets, seven symphonies, and concertos for both violin and piano.

Chayefsky /tʃeɪ'efski/ Sydney 'Paddy' 1923– . American playwright. He established his reputation with the television plays *Marty* and *Bachelor Party*, both successfully filmed (1955 and 1957 respectively). His stage plays include *The Tenth Man* 1959.

Cheapside /'tʃiːpsaɪd/ a street running from St Paul's Cathedral to Poultry, in the City of London, England. The scene of the 13th century 'Cheap', a permanent fair and general market. Christopher Wren's church of St Mary-le-Bow in Cheapside has the famous Bow Bells.

Checheno-Ingush /tʃɪ'tʃenəʊ ɪŋ'guːʃ/ republic in the W USSR, conquered in the 1850s. A major oilfield. Area 19,300 sq km/7,350 sq mi; population (1984) 1,200,000. The capital is Grozny.

Cheddar /'tʃedə/ village in Somerset, England; population (1983) 3,994. It is famous for cheese, its limestone gorge, and caves with stalactites and stalagmites. In 1962 excavation revealed the site of a Saxon palace.

cheese the curd of milk (from cows, goats, sheep, etc.), separated from the whey, and variously treated to produce three main types: *hard-pressed:* Cheddar, Cheshire, Cantal, Parmesan, Gruyère, which are the most important nutritionally and economically. *semi-hard:* Stilton, Gorgonzola, Wensleydale, Roquefort, Pont l'Evêque, Gouda, Lymeswold. *soft:* Cambridge, York, Camembert, Brie, Quark/Fromou. In France (from 1980) cheese has the same *appellation contrôlée* status as wine if made only in a special defined area, for example Cantal and Roquefort, but not Camembert and Brie, which are also made elsewhere

cheesecloth fine muslin or cotton fabric, originally used to press curds.

cheetah large wild cat *Acinonyx jubatus* native to Africa, Arabia and SW Asia, but now rare in some parts of its range. It is yellowish with black spots and has a slim lithe build. The claws do not retract as fully as in most cats. Up to 1 m/3 ft tall at the shoulder, the head and body up to 1.5 m/5 ft long, it is renowned for its speed. It can reach 110 kph/70 mph, but tires after about 400 metres. Cheetahs live in open country where they hunt small antelopes, also hares and birds.

Cheever /'tʃiːvə/ John 1912–1982. American writer. Born in Quincy, Massachusetts, he wrote short stories, and novels which include *The Wapshot Chronicle* 1937, *Bullet Park* 1969, *World of Apples* 1973 and *Falconer* 1977.

Chefoo /ˌtʃiːˈfuː/ former name of part of ◊Yantai in China.

Cheka secret police operating in the USSR 1918–23. The name is formed from the initials *che* and *ka* of the two Russian words meaning 'extraordinary commission', formed for 'the repression of counter-revolutionary activities and of speculation', and extended to cover such matters as espionage and smuggling. It originated from the tsarist Okhrana and became successively the OGPU (GPU) 1923–34, NKVD 1934–46, and MVD 1946–53, before its present form, the ◊KGB.

Chekhov /'tʃekɒf/ Anton Pavlovich 1860–1904. Russian writer. Born at Taganrog, he qualified as a doctor in 1884, but devoted himself to writing short stories rather than medical practice. A collection *Particoloured Stories* 1886 consolidated his reputation, and gave him leisure to develop his style: *My Life* 1895, *The Lady with the Dog* 1898 and *In the Ravine* 1900. His first play *Ivanov* 1887 was a

failure, as was *The Seagull* 1896 until revived by Stanislavsky in 1898 at the Moscow Arts Theatre, for which Chekhov went on to write *Uncle Vanya* 1899, *The Three Sisters* 1901 and *The Cherry Orchard* 1904. His plays concentrate on the creation of atmosphere and delineation of internal development, rather than external action.

Chekiang /ˌtʃeki'æŋ/ former name for ◊Zhejiang province of SE China.

chelate type of chemical compound whose molecules consist of one or more metal atoms or charged ions joined to chains of organic residues by coordinate (or dative covalent) chemical ◊bonds. The parent organic compound is known as a chelating agent (for example EDTA, ethylene-diaminetetraacetic acid, used in chemical analysis).

Chelmsford /'tʃelmzfəd/ town in Essex, England, 48 km/30 mi NE of London; population (1981) 58,000. It is the administrative headquarters of the county, and a market town with radio, electrical, engineering and agricultural machinery industries.

Chelsea /'tʃelsi/ historic area of the Royal Borough of Kensington and Chelsea, London, immediately N of the Thames, where it is crossed by the Albert and Chelsea bridges. The Royal Hospital was founded in 1682 by Charles II for old and disabled soldiers, 'Chelsea Pensioners', and the National Army Museum (1960) covers campaigns 1485–1914. The Physic Garden for botanical research was established in the 17th century; and the home of Thomas Carlyle in Cheyne Row is a museum. The Chelsea Flower Show, held by the Royal Horticultural Society in the grounds of Royal Hospital, is held anually. Ranelagh Gardens 1742–1804 and Cremorne Gardens 1845–77 were celebrated places of entertainment.

Cheltenham /'tʃeltənəm/ spa at the foot of the Cotswolds, Gloucestershire, England; population (1981) 73,000. There are annual literary and music festivals, a racecourse (major race the Cheltenham Gold Cup, held annually), and Cheltenham College (founded 1854). The home of the composer Gustav ◊Holst is now a museum. Cheltenham is also the centre of the British government's electronic surveillance operations (◊GCHQ).

Chelyabinsk /ˌtʃeli'æbɪnsk/ industrial town in the USSR, capital of Chelyabinsk region; population (1985) 1,096,000. It lies E of the Ural Mountains, 240 km/150 mi SE of Sverdlovsk. It has iron and other industries and engineering works, and makes chemicals, motor vehicles, and aircraft.

chemical see ◊ chemistry.

chemical compound see ◊chemistry.

chemical element see ◊element.

chemical equation method of indicating the reactants and products of a chemical reaction using chemical symbols and formulae. These may indicate ◊atoms, ◊ions, radicals or ◊molecules. The equation should balance – that is, the total number of atoms of a particular element among the reactants (on the left-hand side of the equation) must be the same as the number of atoms of that element among the

Chekhov Portrait of the Russian writer. Although trained as a doctor, he devoted himself to writing short stories and plays including *Uncle Vanya* 1899, *The Three Sisters* 1901, and *The Cherry Orchard* 1904.

products (on the right-hand side). For example, the equation

$$2H_2 + O_2 \rightarrow 2H_2O$$

denotes that two molecules of hydrogen combine with one molecule of oxygen to form two molecules of water; there are four atoms of hydrogen and two atoms of oxygen represented on each side of the equation, so it balances. Substituting the molecular weights of the participating substances indicates the proportions of masses involved. In this case $2 \times 2 = 4$ grams of hydrogen $+ 2 \times 16 = 32$ grams of oxygen $- 2 \times 18 = 36$ grams of water. The double arrows in the equation $3H_2 + N_2 \rightarrow 2NH_3$ indicate that the formation of ammonia from hydrogen and nitrogen is a reversible reaction (in this example depending on the temperature and pressure of the reactants).

chemical warfare use of gaseous, liquid, or solid substances with toxic effect to humans, animals, or plants; with biological warfare, it was banned in 1925 although experimentation continues. From 1980 the subject has been under review and there have been Anglo-Soviet negotiations. Chemical weapons are of five types:
irritant gases which may cause permanent injury or death, such as chlorine, phosgene (Cl_2CO) and mustard gas ($C_4H_8Cl_2S$) used in World War I and allegedly in Afghanistan, Laos, and by Iraq against Iran; and tear gases, for example, CS gas used in riot control, which are intended to have less permanent effect.
nerve gases organophosphorus compounds allied to insecticides, which are taken into the body through the skin and lungs and break down the action of the nervous system. Developed by the Germans for World War II, they were not used.
incapacitants drugs designed to put an enemy temporarily out of action by impairing vision, inducing hallucinations, etc. Not so far used.
toxins eaten, drunk, or injected, for example, ricin (see castor ▷oil) or the ▷botulism toxin.
herbicides defoliants used to destroy vegetation sheltering guerrillas and crops of hostile populations. Used in the Malayan Emergency by Britain and by the USA in Vietnam. Agent Orange (see ▷dioxin) became notorious because of later allegations that it had caused cancer and birth abnormalities among Vietnam War veterans and US factory staff. Some stocks are held by a number of countries for retaliation or the development of preventative measures.
binary weapons are those in which the two chemical components become toxic only when mixed, which happens on the battlefield, when the shell is fired. See also ▷biological warfare.

chemiluminescence alternative term for ▷bioluminescence.

chemisorption in chemistry, the reaction between a clean solid surface and a foreign substance, such as occurs with a gas in various forms of corrosion. It is the basis of catalysis and of great importance both to science and industry.

chemistry the science concerned with the composition of matter, and of the changes which take place in it under certain conditions. The ancient civilizations were familiar with certain chemical processes, for example, extracting metals from their ores, and making alloys. The alchemists were concerned with endeavouring to turn base metals into gold, and modern chemistry may be said to have evolved from alchemy towards the end of the 17th century. Robert ▷Boyle defined elements as the simplest substances into which matter could be resolved. The alchemical doctrine of the four elements (earth, air, fire, and water) gradually lost its hold, and the theory that all combustible bodies contained a substance called phlogiston (a weightless 'fire element' generated during combustion) was discredited in the 18th century by the experimental work of ▷Black, ▷Lavoisier, and ▷Priestley, the last-mentioned discovering the presence of oxygen in the air. ▷Cavendish discovered the composition of water, and ▷Dalton put forward the atomic theory, which ascribed a precise relative weight to the 'simple atom' characteristic of each element. Much research then took place leading to the development in modern times of ▷biochemistry, ▷chemotherapy, and ▷plastics.
All matter can exist in three states: gas, liquid, or solid. It is composed of minute particles termed *molecules* which are constantly moving, and may be further divided into ▷atoms. Molecules which contain atoms of one kind only are known as *elements*, while those which contain atoms of different kinds are called *compounds*. The separation of compounds into simpler substances is analysis, and the building up of compounds from their components is synthesis. When substances are brought together without changing their molecular structure they are said to be *mixtures*. Chemical compounds are produced by a chemical action which alters the arrangement of the atoms in the molecule. Heat, light, vibration, catalytic action, radiation or pressure, as well as moisture (for ionization), may be necessary to produce a chemical change. To facilitate the expression of chemical composition, symbols are used to denote the elements. The symbol is usually the first letter or letters of the English or Latinized name of the element, for example C, carbon; Ca, calcium; Fe, iron (ferrum). These symbols represent one atom of the element; molecules containing more than one atom are denoted by a subscript figure, for example, water, H_2O. In some substances a group of atoms acts as a single atom, and these are enclosed in brackets in the symbol, for example $(NH_2)_2SO_4$, ammonium sulphate. The symbolical representation of a molecule is known as a formula. A figure placed before a formula represents the number of molecules of one substance present in another, for example $2H_2O$, two molecules of water. Chemical reactions are expressed by means of equations, as in:

$$NaCl + H_2SO_4 \rightarrow NaHSO_4 + HCl$$

Thus, sodium chloride (NaCl) on being treated with sulphuric acid (H_2SO_4) is converted into sodium bisulphate ($NaHSO_4$) and hydrogen chloride (HCl).
Elements are divided into two classes: metals, having lustre, and being conductors of heat and electricity, and non-metals, which usually lack these properties. The Periodic System developed by Newlands in 1863 and established by ▷Mendeleyev in 1869, classified elements according to their atomic weights, that is, the least weight of the element present in a molecular weight of any of its compounds. Those elements which resemble each other in general properties were found to bear a relation to one another by weight, and these were placed in groups or families. Certain anomalies in this system were removed by classifying the elements according to their atomic number. The latter is the equivalent of the charge on the nucleus of the atom.
▷*Organic chemistry* is that branch of chemistry which deals with carbon compounds. ▷*Inorganic chemistry* deals with the description, properties, reactions, and preparation of the elements and their compounds, with the exception of carbon compounds. *Physical chemistry* treats of the particular changes which materials may undergo in special circumstances. Physical changes are changes of state only, the properties of the material remaining unaltered. This branch studies in particular the movement of molecules, and the effects of temperature and pressure, especially with regard to gases and liquids.

Chemnitz /'kemnɪts/ former name for ◊Karl-Marx-Stadt, industrial city in E Germany.

chemotherapy medical treatment that uses drugs, often restricted to mean the drug treatment of cancer (with cyctotoxic drugs) or of mental illness (such as psycholeptic drugs).

Chemulpo /tʃemul'pəu/ former name for ◊Inchond, port and summer resort on the W coast of South Korea.

Chenab /tʃɪ'næb/ a tributary of the river ◊Indus.

Chengchow /,tʃek'tʃau/ former name of ◊Zhengzhou, capital of Henan province of China.

Chengde /,tʃek'deː/ town, formerly Hehei province, China, NE of Beijing. It was the summer residence of the Manchu rulers and has an 18th-century palace and temples. Population (1973) 200,000.

Chengdu /,tʃek'duː/ ancient city (formerly Chengtu), capital of Sichuan province, China, with well-preserved temples. It is an important rail junction and has railway workshops, textile, electronics and engineering industries. Population (1982) 2,470,000.

Chengteh former name for ◊Chengde.

Chengtu former name for ◊Chengdu.

Chénier /,ʃeɪni'eɪ/ André de 1762–1794. French poet, born in Constantinople. His deeply felt lyrical poetry was later to influence the Romantic movement, but he was best known in his own time for his uncompromising support of the constitutional royalists after the Revolution. In 1793 he went into hiding, but finally he was arrested, and on 25 Jul 1794, guillotined. While in prison he wrote some of his most famous poems, including the *Jeune Captive/Captive Girl* and the political *Iambes*, published after his death.

Chepstow /'tʃepstəu/ market town in Gwent, Wales, on the Wye; population (1980) 10,500. The high tides, sometimes 15 m/50 ft above low level, are the highest in Britain. There is a Norman castle, and the ruins of Tintern Abbey are 6.5 km/4 mi to the N.

cheque (American 'check') a type of ◊bill of exchange, drawn on a ◊bank by a depositor. Usually, though not necessarily, on a special form, it should bear the date on which it is payable, name in words and figures a definite sum of money to be paid, to a named person or body or to the bearer, and be signed by the drawer. It is then payable on presentation at the bank on which it is drawn. If the cheque is 'crossed', as is usual British practice, it is not negotiable and can be paid only through a bank; in the USA a cheque is always negotiable.

cheque card card issued from 1968 by savings and clearings ◊banks in Europe (including the UK), which guarantees payment by the issuing bank when it is presented with a ◊cheque to a bank, or shop. It bears the customer's signature and account number, for comparison with those on the cheque, and payment to the vendor by the issuing bank is immediate, no commission being charged. Unlike the ◊credit card, it cannot be used by itself for the purchase of goods.

Chequers /'tʃekəz/ country seat of the current prime minister of the UK. It is an Elizabethan mansion in the Chiltern hills near Princes Risborough, Buckinghamshire, and was given to the nation by Lord Lee of Fareham under the Chequers Estate Act (1917), which came into effect in Jan 1921.

Cher /ʃeə/ French river which rises in Creuse *département* and flows into the Loire below Tours. Length 355 km/220 mi. It gives its name to a *département*.

Cherbourg /'ʃeəbuəg/ French port and naval station at the N end of the Cotentin peninsula, in Manche *département*; population (1982) 256,189. There is an institute for studies in nuclear warfare, and Cherbourg has large shipbuilding yards. During World War II, Cherbourg was captured in Jun 1944 by the Allies, who thus gained their first large port of entry into France. Cherbourg was severely damaged; restoration of the harbour was completed in 1952. There is a nuclear processing plant at nearby Cap la Hague.

Cherenkov /tʃɪ'reŋkɒf/ Pavel 1904– . Russian physicist. Educated at Vormeah University, in 1934 he discovered **Cherenkov radiation**; this occurs as a bluish light when charged atomic particles pass through water or other media at a speed in excess of that of light in that medium. He shared a Nobel prize in 1958 with his colleagues Ilya Frank and Igor Tamm. The Cherenkov radiation has also been claimed as the discovery of the French scientist Lucien Mallet.

Cherepovets /,tʃErɪpə'vets/ iron and steel city in W USSR, on the Volga-Baltic waterway; population (1985) 299,000.

Chéret /ʃe'reɪ/ Jules 1836–1932. One of the first French ◊poster artists.

Chernenko /tʃɜ'njeŋkəu/ Konstantin 1911–1985. Soviet politician, leader of the Soviet Communist Party (CPSU) and president 1984–85.

Chernenko, born in central Siberia, joined the ◊Komsomol in 1929 and the CPSU in 1931. He was moved to Moscow by Brezhnev in 1956 and was inducted into the Politburo in 1978. Brezhnev sought to establish Chernenko as his successor, but Chernenko was passed over in favour of §Andropov. When Andropov died in Feb 1984 Chernenko was selected as the CPSU's stop-gas leader by cautious party colleagues, and was also elected president. From Jul 1984 he gradually retired from public life because of failing health, and died in Mar 1985.

Chernigov /tʃə'nɪgɒf/ town and river port on the Desna in the N of the Ukrainian SSR, population (1985) 278,000. It has an 11th-century cathedral. Lumbering, textiles, chemicals, distilling, and food-canning are among its industries.

Chernobyl /tʃə'nəubəl/ town in the Ukraine, USSR, site of Europe's worst ever nuclear power station accident in 1986.

Chernovtsy /,tʃɜːnəft'siː/ industrial city in the Ukraine, USSR; population (1985) 244,000. As Cernauti, it was part of Romania 1918–1940.

Cherokee /'tʃerəkiː/ North ◊American Indian people, formerly living in the mountain county of Alabama, the Carolinas, Georgia, and Tennessee. They sided with Britain against France in N America, and fought against the rebel colonists in the American War of Independence. One of them, Sequoyah (c. 1770–1843), devised the syllabary used for writing down the Indian languages. They now live mainly in North Carolina and in Oklahoma, where they established their capital at Tahlequah.

cherry tree of the genus *Prunus* distinguished from the plums and apricots by the fruit, a drupe, being spherical and smooth, and not covered with a bloom. Cultivated cherries are derived from 2 species, the sour cherry *Prunus cerasus*, and the gean *Prunus avium*, which grow wild in Britain. The former is the ancestor of the 'sour cherries' – morello, duke, and Kentish cherries, and the latter of the 'sweet cherries' – hearts, mazzards, and bigarreaus. Besides those varieties which are grown for their fruit, others are well-known ornamental trees.

Cherubini /,keru'biːni/ Luigi (Carlo Zanobi Salvadore Maria) 1760–1842. Italian composer, born in Florence. His first opera *Quinto Fabio* was produced at Alessandria in 1779. In 1784 he went to London and became composer to King George III, but from 1786 Paris became his permanent home. There he produced a number of dramatic works, for example, *Médée* 1797, *Les Deux Journées* 1800, and the ballet *Anacréon* 1803. In 1809 he began his career as a great church composer with his Mass in F. In 1822 he became director of the Conservatoire at Paris. His treatise *Counterpoint and Fugue* was published in 1835 and he wrote his Requiem in D minor in 1838.

chervil genus of umbelliferous plants *Chaerophyllum*. The garden chervil *Chaerophyllum cerefolium* has leaves with a sweetish odour, somewhat resembling parsley. It is used as a garnish, and as a pot-herb.

Cherwell /'tʃɑːwəl/ Frederick Alexander Lindemann, Viscount Cherwell 1886–1957. British physicist. Director of the Physical Laboratory of the RAF at Farnborough in World War I, he was personal adviser to ◊Churchill on scientific and statistical matters during World War II. He was professor of experimental philosophy at Oxford 1919–56.

Chesapeake Bay /'tʃesəpiːk/ largest of the inlets on the Atlantic coast of the USA. Its wildlife is threatened by urban and industrial development.

Cheshire /'tʃeʃə/ county in NW England
area 2,328 sq km/899 sq mi
towns administrative headquarters Chester; Warrington; textile centres of Macclesfield and Congleton.
features It is chiefly a fertile plain with dairy-farming. There are salt mines and geologically rich former copper workings at Alderley Edge (in use from Roman times until the 1920s). Little Moreton Hall; discovery of Lindow Man, the first 'bogman', dating from around 500 BC, to be found in mainland Britain. Chief rivers are the Mersey, Dee and Weaver.
products textiles and chemicals
population (1986) 942,400
famous people Mrs Gaskell lived at Knutsford (the locale of *Cranford*), John Speed.

CHEMISTRY – CHRONOLOGY

1 AD Gold, silver, copper, lead, iron, tin, and mercury were known.

1100 Alcohol was first distilled.

1242 Gunpowder was introduced to Europe from the Far East.

1540 Date of first known scientific observation and experiment.

1604 Italian mathematician, astronomer and physicist Galileo invented the thermometer.

1620 Scientific method of reasoning was expounded by English philosopher Francis Bacon in his *Novum Organum*.

1649 Carbon, sulphur, antimony, and arsenic were known.

1650 Leyden University in the Netherlands set up the first chemistry laboratory.

1660 Law concerning effect of pressure on gas *(Boyle's Law)* was established by English chemist Robert Boyle; definition of the element.

1662 The Royal Society was formed.

1742 Invention of the Centigrade scale.

1746 Lead chamber process developed for manufacturing sulphuric acid; German chemist Andreas Marggraf discovered zinc.

1750 Swedish chemist Axel Cronstedt discovered cobalt and nickel.

1756 Scottish chemist and physicist Joseph Black discovered carbon dioxide.

1772 German chemist Karl Scheele discovered oxygen, two years before Priestley.

1774 Scheele discovered chlorine; Swedish chemist Johan Gahn discovered manganese; Lavoisier demonstrated his *law of conservation of mass*.

1777 Lavoisier explained burning; sulphur was known to be an element.

1779 Dutch scientist Jan Ingenhousz demonstrated photosynthesis.

1781 English scientist Henry Cavendish showed water to be a compound.

1792 Italian physicist Alessandro Volta demonstrated the electrochemical series.

1793 German chemist Hieronymus Richter demonstrated the *law of equivalent proportions*.

1799 Twenty-seven elements were known.

1800 Volta designed his electric battery.

1801 Dalton demonstrated his *law of partial pressures*.

1803 Dalton expounded his atomic theory.

1807 Sodium and potassium were first prepared by Davy.

1808 Gay-Lussac announced his *law of volumes*.

1811 Publication of Italian physicist Amedeo Avogadro's hypothesis on the relationship of volumes of gases and numbers of molecules to temperature and pressure.

1813 French chemist Bernard Courtois discovered iodine.

1818 Berzelius's atomic symbols were elaborated.

1819 French scientists Henri Dulong and Alexis-Thérèse Petit's *law of atomic heats* was demonstrated.

1820 Danish scientist Hans Christian Oersted demonstrated electromagnetism.

1825 French chemist Antoine-Jerôme Balard prepared bromine. Matches were invented.

1928 The first organic compounds, alcohol and urea, were synthesized.

1834 Faraday expounded the *laws of electrolysis*.

1836 Acetylene was discovered.

1840 Liebig expounded the carbon and nitrogen cycles.

1846 Scottish chemist Thomas Graham's *law of diffusion (Graham's Law)* was expounded.

1849 Fifty-seven elements were known.

1850 Ammonia was first made from coal-gas.

1853 German chemist Robert Bunsen invented his burner.

1858 Cannizzaro's method of atomic weights was expounded.

1862 Haemoglobin was crystallized.

1866 Nobel invented dynamite.

1868 The first plastic substance – celluloid – was made.

1869 Mendeleyev expounded his Periodic Table.

1879 Saccharin was discovered.

1886 French chemist Ferdinand Moissan isolated fluorine.

1894 Ramsay and Rayleigh discovered inert gases.

1897 The electron was discovered by English physicist Sir Joseph Thomson.

1898 The Curies discovered radium.

1905 Einstein announced his *theory of relativity*.

1912 Vitamins were discovered by British biochemist Gowland Hopkins; British physicist Lawrence Bragg demonstrated that crystals have a regular arrangement of atoms.

1919 Artificial disintegration of atoms by Rutherford.

1920 Rutherford discovered the proton.

1927 British chemist Neil Sidgwick's *theory of valency* was announced.

1928 Vitamin C was crystallized.

1932 Deuterium (heavy water) was discovered; Chadwick discovered the neutron.

1933 British chemist Norman Haworth synthesized Vitamin C.

1942 Plutonium was first synthesised.

1945 The atomic bomb was exploded.

1953 Hydrogen was converted to helium.

1954 Einsteinium and fermium were synthesized

Cheshire /'tʃeʃə/ Geoffrey Leonard 1917– . British airman. Commissioned with the Royal Air Force on the outbreak of the World War I, he won the Victoria Cross, Distinguished Service Order (with 2 bars) and Distinguished Flying Cross, and in 1945 was an official observer at the dropping of the atom bomb on Nagasaki. He retired in 1946. A devout Roman Catholic, he founded the first Chesire Foundation Home for the Incurably Sick in 1948. He was awarded the Order of Merit in 1981. In 1959 he married Susan Ryder (1923–) who established a foundation for the sick and disabled of all ages and became a life peeress (as Baroness Ryder) in 1978.

Chesil bank /'tʃezəl/ shingle bank extending 19 km/11 mi along the coast of Dorset, England, from Abbotsbury to the Isle of Portland.

chess board game originating at least as early as the 2nd century AD. Two players use 16 pieces each, on a board of 64 squares of alternating

chess

the way each piece can move

arrangement of the chessmen

Chernobyl The damage caused to the nuclear reactor in the 1986 accident at the Chernobyl power station near Kiev, USSR, is clearly visible. Less evident and more sinister is the harm inflicted by raised levels of radiation

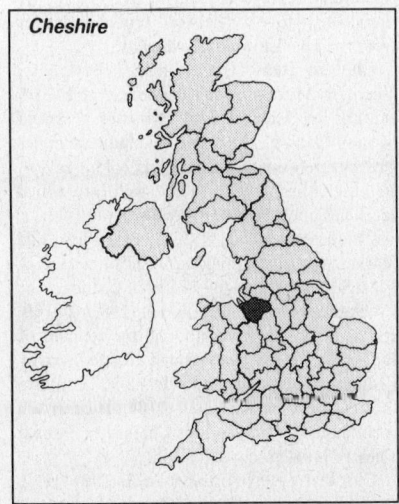

Cheshire

men
1948 Mikhail Botvinnik *(USSR)*
1957 Vassiliy Smyslov *(USSR)*
1958 Mikhail Botvinnik *(USSR)*
1960 Mikhail Tal *(USSR)*
1961 Mikhail Botvinnik *(USSR)*
1963 Tigran Petrosian *(USSR)*
1969 Boris Spassky *(USSR)*
1972 Bobby Fischer *(United States)*
1975 Anatoliy Karpov *(USSR)*
1985 Gary Kasparov *(USSR)*
women
1927 Vera Menchik *(Great Britain)*
1950 Lyudmila Rudenko *(USSR)*
1953 Elizaveta Bykova *(USSR)*
1955 Olga Runtsova *(USSR)*
1958 Elizaveta Bykova *(USSR)*
1962 Nona Gaprindashvili *(USSR)*
1978 Maya Chiburdanidze *(USSR)*

colour, to try and force their opponent into a position where the chief piece cannot be moved or allowed to remain in the same position without its being taken. There are said to be more variations than there are atoms in the universe. The Fédération Internationale des Echecs was established in 1924. Leading players are rated according to the Elo System and Bobby Fischer (United States) is reckoned to be the greatest Grand Master of all time with a rating of 2,785. A world championship was established in 1851. Players of the rank of grand master can now be defeated by a computer. There is a World Chess Federation (FIDE).

World Champions first official world champion recognized 1886
Recent winners:

Chester /'tʃestə/ English city, the administrative headquarters of Cheshire, on the river Dee 26 km/16 mi S of Liverpool; population (1984) 116,657. Its name derives from the Roman *Castra Devana*, 'the camp on the Dee', and there are many Roman and later remains. It is the only English city to retain its city walls (two miles long) intact. The cathedral dates from the 11th century but was restored in 1876. The church of St John the Baptist is one of the finest examples of early Norman architecture. The famous 'Rows' are covered arcades dating from the Middle Ages. From 1070 to the reign of Henry III, Chester was the seat of a ◊county palatine (a county whose lord exercised some of the roles usually reserved for the monarch). The town hall dates from 1869. Although the silting up of the Dee destroyed Chester's importance as a port, navigation has been greatly improved by dredging.

Chesterfield /'tʃestəfiːld/ market town of Derbyshire, England, 40 km/25 mi N of Derby, on the Rother. A coal-mining and industrial centre; population (1981) 78,210. Burial place of the engineer George ◊Stephenson. All Saints' Church is renowned for its crooked spire.

Chesterfield /'tʃestəfiːld/ Philip Dormer Stanhope, 4th Earl of Chesterfield 1694–1773. English statesman and man of letters, remembered chiefly for his *Letters to his Son* 1774 – his illegitimate son, Philip Stanhope (1732–68). Born in London, he sat in Parliament from 1715, and in 1726 succeeded his father as 4th earl. As an opponent of Walpole, he was Lord-Lieutenant of Ireland in 1745 and Secretary of State in 1746. A member of the literary circle of Swift, Pope, and Bolingbroke, he incurred the wrath of Dr Samuel ◊Johnson by failing to carry out an offer of patronage.

Chesterton /'tʃestətən/ G(ilbert) K(eith) 1874–1936. British author. Born in London, he studied art but quickly turned to journalism. Initially a Socialist sympathizer, like Hilaire ◊Belloc he later found his own solution in ◊Distributism. In poetry he is particularly noted for his satire, in the humorous *Wine, Water, and Song* 1915, and in *The Ballad of the White Horse* 1911. The most famous of his novels are the series dealing with the adventures of the naïve priest-detective, who first appeared in *The Innocence of Father Brown* 1911; others include *The Napoleon of Notting Hill* 1904, *The Man who was Thursday* 1908, *The Flying Inn* 1914, and *The Man who knew too Much* 1922. He entered the Catholic Church in 1922. His autobiography was published in 1936.

chestnut tree, genus *Castanea*, belonging to the same family as the oak and beech *Fagaceae*. The Spanish or sweet chestnut, *Castanea sativa*, produces a fruit that is a common article of diet in Europe and USA, and its timber is also valuable. The horse chestnut ('conker tree') or *Aesculus*

Chesterfield This 1765 painting of Philip Stanhope, 4th Earl of Chesterfield, by Allan Ramsay, hangs in London's National Portrait Gallery. An English politician and man of letters, he kept company with great writers of the 18th century, such as Pope and Swift.

Chesterton British journalist, novelist and broadcaster G K Chesterton, seen here with literary friends Belloc and Baring.

hippocastanum is quite distinct, belonging to a different family.

Chetniks Serbian nationalist group which operated underground during the German occupation of Yugoslavia during World War II. Led by Colonel Draza Mihailovič, the Chetniks initially received aid from the Allies, but this was later transferred to the Communist Partisans led by Tito.

Chevalier /ʃəˈvælieɪ/ Maurice 1888–1972. French actor and singer. Born in Paris, he became famous as dancing partner to the revue artiste Mistinguett at the Folies-Bergère, and made numerous films including *The Innocents of Paris*, which revived his song 'Louise', and *Gigi* 1958.

Chevening /ˈtʃiːvnɪŋ/ residence near Sevenoaks, Kent, bequeathed to the nation by the 7th Earl of Stanhope for royal or ministerial use; Prince Charles lived there 1974–80.

Cheviots /ˈtʃiːvɪəts/ range of hills 56 km/35 mi long, mainly in Northumberland, forming the border between England and Scotland for some 48 km/30 mi. The highest point is the Cheviot 816 m/2,676 ft. For centuries the area was a battleground between the English and the Scots.

chewing gum confectionery mainly composed of ◊chicle, sweetened with various flavours. The first patent was taken out in the USA in 1871.

Chiang Ching former name of the Chinese actress ◊Jian Qing, third wife of Mao.

Chiang Ching-Kuo /tʃiˈæŋ ˌtʃɪŋ ˈkwəʊ/ 1910–1988. Taiwanese statesman, son of Chiang Kai-shek. Prime minister from 1971, he became president in 1978.

Chiang Kai-shek /ˈtʃæŋ kaɪ ˈʃek/ 1887–1975. Chinese statesman (Pinyin: *Jiang Jie Shi*). He took part in the Revolution of 1911, and after the death of Sun Yat-sen was made Commander-in-Chief of the Guomindang armies in S China in 1925. The initial collaboration with the Communists, broken in 1927, was resumed following the Xi An incident (see ◊Chinese history), and he nominally headed the struggle against the Japanese invaders, receiving the Japanese surrender in 1945. Civil War then resumed between Communists and Nationalists, and ended in the defeat of Chiang in 1949, and the limitation of his rule to Taiwan. His son is Chiang ◊Ching-Kuo.

Chibchas /ˈtʃɪbtʃɑːz/ South American Indians of Colombia, whose civilization was overthrown by the Spaniards in 1538. Their practice of covering their chief with gold dust, after applying an underlay of gum, fostered the legend of El Dorado, the city of gold.

Chicago /ʃɪˈkɑːgəʊ/ second city of the USA, in Illinois; population (1980) 3,005,072. Situated on the Chicago river, which cuts the city into three 'sides', it contains the world's first skyscraper (built 1887–88), and some of the world's tallest modern skyscrapers, including the Sears Tower, 443 m/1,454 ft. The Museum of Science and Industry, opened in 1893, has 'hands on' exhibits including a coal-mine, a World War II U-boat, an Apollo spacecraft and lunar module; and exhibits by industrial firms, and 50 km/30 mi to the W is the Fermilab, the US centre for particle physics. Industries include iron, steel, chemicals and textiles; the famous stockyards are now closed. It is a major financial centre. Chicago is known as the Windy City, possibly from the breezes of Lake Michigan, and its citizens' (and, allegedly, politicians') voluble talk; the lake shore ('the Gold Coast') is occupied by luxury apartment blocks. There is a renowned symphony orchestra, an art institute, and the University of Chicago.
history The site of Chicago was visited by Jesuit missionaries in 1673, and Fort Dearborn, then a frontier fort, was built here in 1803. The original layout of Chicago was a rectangular grid, but many outer boulevards have been constructed on less rigid lines. As late as 1831 Chicago was still an insignificant village, but railways connected it with the east coast by 1852, and by 1871, when it suffered a disastrous fire, it was a city of more than 300,000 inhabitants. Rapid development began again in the 1920s, and during the years of Prohibition, 1919–33, the city became notorious for activities of its gangsters. The opening of the St Lawrence Seaway in 1959 brought Atlantic shipping to its docks.

Chicago School of Sociology the first university department of sociology was founded in Chicago, in 1892 under Albion Small. He was succeeded by Robert E Park, who with W I Thomas, Ernest Burgess, Louis Wirth, and R McKenzie created an important centre for the social sciences in the 1920s and 1930s, studying modern urban life including crime and deviance in Chicago, with its variety of urban communities, lifestyles, and ethnic subcultures. A neo-Chicagoan school emerged in the 1940s under Erving Goffman and Howard Becker.

Chicano /tʃɪˈkɑːnəʊ/ a Spanish-speaking American of Mexican descent in the SW USA. The term was originally used for those who became US citizens when their territory (including Texas) was acquired from Mexico by the USA 1846–48. The word probably derives from the Spanish word *Mexicanos*.

Chichén Itzá /tʃɪˈtʃen ɪtˈsɑː/ Maya city, Yucatan, Mexico, which flourished 11th–13th century AD. Excavated by Sylvanus Griswold Morley 1924–40, the remains including temples with magnificent sculptures and colour reliefs, an observatory, and a sacred well into which sacrifices, including human beings, were cast.

Chichester /ˈtʃɪtʃɪstə/ English city and market town, the administrative headquarters of West Sussex, 111 km/69 mi SW of London, near Chichester Harbour. Population (1981) 24,189. It was a Roman township, and the remains of the Roman palace built around 80 AD at nearby Fishbourne are unique outside Italy. There is a fine cathedral consecrated 1108, later much rebuilt and restored, and the Chichester Festival Theatre (1962).

Chichester /ˈtʃɪtʃɪstə/ Francis 1901–1972. British yachtsman. Born in Devon, he became famous as a pilot (1931 first E–W crossing of Tasman Sea in *Gipsy Moth*), and was knighted (KBE) for his circumnavigation of the world in *Gipsy Moth IV* 1966–67.

chicken domestic fowl; see under ◊poultry.

chicken pox or varicella. A mild disease, caught especially by children, characterized by crops of small blisters and a rash. It is caused by a virus of the ◊herpes group of viruses, identical with that which causes shingles, the latter representing a re-activation of the chicken pox virus. It chiefly attacks children under 10. The virus is often air-borne, in the spray of coughing or speaking, but may also be transmitted on objects such as clothing or toys. The incubation period is 2–3 weeks.

chickpea seeds of the annual *Cicer arietinum*, family Leguminosae, grown for food in India and the Middle East.

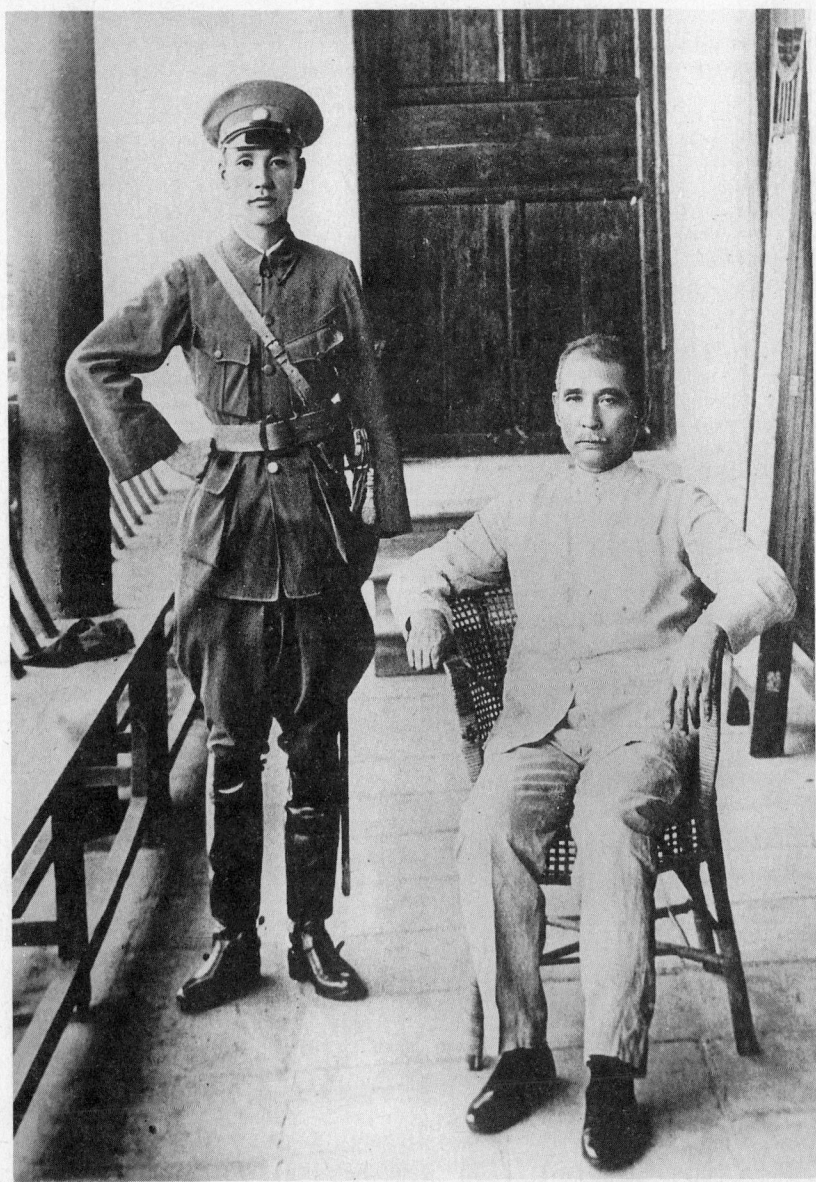

Chiang Kai-shek The Chinese general and politician Chiang Kai-shek (standing) with Sun Yat-Sen in Canton, 1923. After the Communists won control of mainland China, Chiang's rule was limited to Taiwan 1950–75.

chickweed weed *Stellaria media* family Caryophyllaceae, with small white star-like flowers.

chicle juice of the sapodilla tree *Achras zapota* of Central America, which is the basis of chewing gum.

chicory plant *Cichorium intybus* of the family Compositae. It grows wild in Britain, mainly on chalky soils, and has large, usually blue, flowers. Its long tap-root is dried and roasted, to be used as a coffee substitute. The blanched leaves are used in salads.

Chiengmai /dʒiˈeŋˈmaɪ/ town in N Thailand, with a trade in teak and lac (as shellac, a resin used in varnishes and polishes), and many handicraft industries. Population (1979) 105,230.

chiffchaff bird *Phylloscopus collybita* of the warbler family, found in woodlands and thickets in Europe and N Asia during the summer, migrating S for winter. About 11 cm/4.3 in long, olive above, greyish below, with an eyestripe and usually dark legs, it looks similar to a willow-warbler but has a distinctive song.

Chifley /ˈtʃɪfli/ Joseph Benedict 1885–1951. Australian Labour statesman. Minister of Defence under Scullin 1931–32, and Treasurer 1941–49 and Minister of Post-War Reconstruction 1942–45 under Curtin, when he succeeded him as Prime Minister. He united the party in fulfilling a welfare and nationalisation programme 1945–49, initiated the post-Second World War immigration programme, and also the Snowy Mountains hydroelectric scheme.

Chihuahua /tʃɪˈwɑːwə/ Mexican city, capital of Chihuahua state, 1,285 km/800 mi NW of Mexico City. Founded in 1707, it is the centre of a mining district. Population (1984) 375,000.

chihuahua smallest breed of dog, developed in the USA from Mexican origins. It may weigh only 1 kg/2 lb. The domed head and wide set ears are characteristic, and the skull is large compared to the body. It can be almost any colour, and occurs in both smooth (or even hairless) and long-coated varieties.

chilblain painful inflammation of the skin of the feet or hands, due to damp cold. The parts turn red, swell, itch violently, and are very tender. In a bad case the skin cracks, blisters, or ulcerates, or may even become gangrenous.

childbirth the expulsion of a baby from its mother's body: see ◊pregnancy, ◊birth. In a broader sense, the period of time involving labour and delivery of the baby, plus the effort and pain involved.

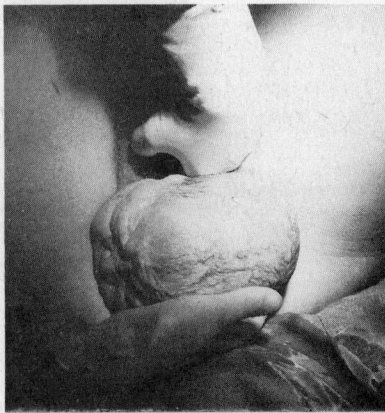

childbirth The head is now out and a nurse helps the shoulders through.

Childe /tʃaɪld/ Gordon 1892–1957. Australian archaeologist, director of the London Institute of Archaeology 1946–57. He discovered the pre-historic village of Skara Brae in the Orkneys, and in 1939 published *The Dawn of European Civilization*.

Childers /ˈtʃɪldəz/ Robert Erskine 1870–1922. Irish Sinn Fein politician and writer. Before turning to Irish politics, he was a clerk in the House of Commons in London and author of the spy novel, *The Riddle of the Sands* (1903). In 1921 he was elected to the Irish Parliament as a supporter of ◊DeValera, and as a Republican took up arms against the Irish Free State in 1922. Shortly afterwards he was captured, court-martialled and shot by the Irish Free State government of William T Cosgrave. His son, *Erskine Childers* (1905–74), although a Protestant, succeeded DeValera as president of Ireland 1973–74.

children's literature in the sense of works specifically written for children is relatively recent; the earliest known illustrated children's book in English is *Goody Two Shoes* 1765, possibly written by Oliver Goldsmith. *Fairy tales* were originally part of a vast range of oral literature, credited only to the writer who first recorded them, such as Charles ◊Perrault. During the 19th century several writers including Hans Christian ◊Andersen wrote original stories in the fairytale genre; others, such as the ◊Grimm brothers, collected (and sometimes adapted) existing stories. Early children's stories were always written with a moral purpose; this was particularly true in the 19th century, apart from the unique case of Lewis Carroll's *Alice* books. The late 19th century was the great era of children's literature in the UK, with Lewis ◊Carroll, Beatrix ◊Potter, Charles ◊Kingsley, and J M ◊Barrie. It was also the golden age of illustrated children's books, with such artists as Kate Greenaway. Among the great 20th-century children's writers in English have been Kenneth Grahame (*The Wind in the Willows* 1908) and A A Milne (*Winnie the Pooh* 1926). *Adventure stories* have often appealed to children even when written for adults – examples include *Robinson Crusoe* by Daniel Defoe, and the satirical *Gulliver's Travels* by Jonathan Swift. *Books about animals* include *Watership Down* 1972 by Richard Adams, and *The Mouse and his Child* by Russell Hoban.

Chile /'tʃɪli/ country in S America, bounded to the N by Peru and Bolivia, to the E by Argentina, and to the S and W by the Pacific Ocean.
government Since 1973 Chile has been ruled by a military junta. A new constitution announced in 1981 will take full effect in 1989. It provides for the election of a president for an eight-year, non-renewable, term and a legislature consisting of a senate with 26 elected and 9 appointed members and a chamber of deputies with 120 elected members, all serving four-year terms. Marxist and 'totalitarian' groups and political activity are all banned until 1989. Strikes in the public services are not allowed and the economy is based on 'free market principles'.
history The area now known as Chile was originally occupied by the Araucanian Indians, and invaded by the ◊Inca in the 15th century. The first European to see it was ◊Magellan, who in 1520 sailed through the strait now named after him. A Spanish expedition under Pedro de Valdivia founded Santiago in 1541, and Chile was subsequently colonized by Spanish settlers who established an agricultural society, though the Indians continued to rebel until the late 19th century. Becoming independent from Spain in 1818, Chile went to war with Peru and Bolivia in 1879 and gained considerable territory from them.
Most of the 20th century has been characterized by left-versus right-wing struggles. The Christian Democrats under Eduardo Frei held power 1964–70, followed by a left-wing coalition led by Dr Salvador ◊Allende, the first democratically elected Marxist head of state. He promised social justice by constitutional means and began nationalizing industries, including US-owned copper mines.

The ◊CIA saw Allende as a pro-Cuban communist and encouraged opposition to him. In 1973 the army, led by Gen Augusto Pinochet, overthrew the government. Allende was killed, or, as the new regime claimed, committed suicide. Pinochet became president and his opponents were tortured, imprisoned or just 'disappeared'. In 1976 he proclaimed an 'authoritarian democracy' and in 1977 banned all political parties. His policies were endorsed by a referendum in 1978.
In 1980 a 'transition to democracy' by 1989 was announced, but imprisonment and torture continued. By 1983 opposition to Pinochet had increased, with demands for a return to democratic government. He attempted to placate opposition by initiating public works. In 1984 an anti-government bombing campaign began, aimed mainly at electricity installations, resulting in a 90-day state of emergency, followed by a 90-day state of siege. In 1985, as opposition grew in the Catholic Church and the army as well as among the public, another state of emergency was declared, but the bombings and killings continued. In 1986 Pinochet was considering another eight-year term. In Sept 1987, opposition groups announced plans to work together to oppose him in the 1988 plebiscite to ratify the choice of a new president.
Chilean Revolution name given to the period between 1970 and 1973 and the Presidency of Salvador ◊Allende, the world's first democratically elected Marxist head of state.
chilli the pod, or powder made from this, of a type of the ◊capsicum, *Capsicum frutescens*.
Chillon /ʃɪ'lɒn/ a fortress on an island rock at the E end of Lake Geneva, Switzerland, dating from the eighth century. The 16th century patriot François Bonward commemorated by Byron, was imprisoned here from 1530–36.
Chiltern Hundreds, stewardship of. In the UK, a nominal office of profit under the Crown. British MPs may not resign; therefore, if they wish to leave office during a Parliament they may apply for this office, a formality which disqualifies them from being an MP.
Chilterns /'tʃɪltənz/ range of chalk hills extending for some 72 km/45 mi in a curve from a point N of Reading to the Suffolk border. Haddington Hill, near Wendover, 261 m/857 ft high, is the highest point.
chimaera fish, also called *rabbit-fish*, of the group Holocephali. These fishes have a cartilaginous skeleton, as do sharks and rays, but have a long fossil history as a group separated from them. They are elongate fishes, larger at the head, with the tail tapering to a long thread. There is only a single gill opening on each side. The skin is smooth. The egg is laid with a horny capsule. Most chimaeras are deep-water fish, and even *Chimaera monstrosa*, a relatively shallow-living form caught commonly round European coasts, is taken mostly between 300 and 500 m/1000 and 1600 ft.
chimera in biology, an organism composed of tissues that are genetically different. Chimeras can develop naturally if a ◊mutation occurs in a cell of a developing embryo but are more commonly produced artificially by implanting

cells from one organism into the embryo of another. The latter has applications in breeding experiments. For example, a chimera comprising a goat embryo surrounded by sheep cells can be reared in a ewe since the foster mother does not recognize the embryo as foreign.
chimpanzee African ape *Pan troglodytes* that ranges from W Africa to W Uganda and Tanzania in the east, mainly in rain forests but sometimes in wooded savannah. It has thin but long black body hair, the youngsters with a white tuft on the rump, and the face is bare, with pink or black skin. Chimpanzees normally walk on all fours, supporting the front of the body on the knuckles of the fingers, but can stand upright or walk upright for a short distance, when they may be 1.4 m/4.5 ft tall. A male may weigh 50 kg/110 lb or more and is much stronger than a human. Chimpanzees climb well, but spend time on the ground. They live in loose social groups. They have a long 'childhood' and adolescence, about two-thirds as long as humans. The bulk of the diet is fruit, with some leaves, insects and occasional meat. Chimpanzees can use 'tools', fashioning twigs to extract termites from their nests. Studies of chromosomes suggest that chimpanzees are the closest apes to humans, perhaps sharing 99% of the same genes. They are highly intelligent, and can 'talk' with the aid of machines or sign language, but even if they were mentally equipped for it are probably precluded from true speech by the position of the voicebox.
Chimu /'tʃiːmuː/ South American pre-Inca civilisation which flourished in Peru AD 1200–c.1470. The Chimu people built enormous adobe brick mounds or *huacas* as the base of temples and palaces, produced fine work in gold, boldly realistic portrait pottery, and savage fanged images in clay, and possibly a system of 'writing' or recording by painting beans in particular patterns. Their agricultural system depended on remarkable irrigation schemes with aqueducts carrying water many miles, defaulting peasants seem to have been ritually mutilated. Their greatest monument is the maze-like city of Chan Chan 36 sq km/14 sq m on the coast near Trujillo. It consists of nine complexes, probably built by successive kings and forming their eventual tombs, where they were buried with much human sacrifice. The Chimu were conquered by the Incas who ensured victory by cutting their aqueducts.
China /'tʃaɪnə/ country in SE Asia, bounded N by Mongolia, NW and NE by the USSR, SW by India and Nepal, S by Bhutan, Burma, Laos, and Vietnam, SE by the South China Sea, and E by the East China Sea, North Korea, and the USSR,
government China is divided into 21 provinces, five autonomous regions and three municipalities (Beijing, Shanghai, and Tianjin), each having an elected local people's government with policy-making power in defined areas.
Ultimate authority resides in the single-chamber *National People's Congress* (NPC), composed of 2,978 deputies indirectly elected every five years through local people's congresses. Deputies to local people's congresses are directly elected through universal suffrage in constituency

Chile

REPUBLIC OF (*República de Chile*)

AREA 741,765 sq km/286,400 sq mi
CAPITAL Santiago
TOWNS Concepción, Vina del Mar, Temuco; ports are Valparaiso, Antofagasta, Arica, Iquique
PHYSICAL Andes mountains along E border, Atacama Desert in N, arable land and forest in the S
TERRITORIES Easter Island, Juan Fernandez Island, half of Tierra del Fuego, and part of Antarctica
HEAD OF STATE AND OF GOVERNMENT Augusto Pinochet from 1973
GOVERNMENT military
EXPORTS copper, iron, nitrate (Chile is the chief mining country of S America); paper and pulp
CURRENCY peso (369.92 = £1 Sept 1987)
POPULATION (1985) 12,042,000 (the majority mestizo, of mixed American Indian and Spanish descent); annual growth rate 1.7%
LANGUAGE Spanish
RELIGION Roman Catholic
LITERACY 94% male/91% female (1980 est)
GNP $21.8 bn (1983); $1,950 per head of population
CHRONOLOGY
1818 Achieved independence from Spain.
1964 Christian Democrats formed government under Eduardo Frei.
1970 Dr Salvador Allende became the first democratically elected Marxist president. He

Chile

embarked on an extensive programme of nationalization and social reform.
1973 Government overthrown by the CIA-backed military, led by Gen Augusto Pinochet. Allende killed. Policy of repression began during which all opposition was put down and political activity banned.
1983 Growing opposition to the regime from all sides, with outbreaks of violence.
1986 Pinochet announced that he might continue for another eight-year term.

Chimu A bottle in the form of a musician, and high on the neck a monkey. Animals were often used to ornament Chimu pottery.

contests. The NPC, the 'highest organ of state power', meets annually and elects a permanent, 133-member committee to assume its functions between sittings. The committee has an inner body comprising a chairman (presently Peng Zhen) and 19 vice-chairmen. The NPC also elects for a five-year term a State Central Military Commission (SCMC), leading members of the judiciary, the vice-president and the state president, who must be at least 45 years of age, is restricted to two terms in office, and whose functions are primarily ceremonial. Executive administration is effected by a prime minister and a cabinet (state council) which includes ten vice-premiers, 39 departmental ministers, eight commission chiefs, an auditor-general and a secretary-general, and is appointed by the NPC.

China's controlling force is the *Chinese Communist Party* (CCP). It has a parallel hierarchy comprising elected congresses and committees functioning from village level upwards and taking orders from above. A national party congress every five years elects a 340-member central committee (210 of whom have full voting powers) which meets twice a year and elects a 20–22-member politbureau and 12-member secretariat to exercise day-to-day control over the party and to frame state and party policy goals. The Politburo meets weekly and is China's most significant political body.

history For early history see ◊China: history. Imperial rule ended in 1911 with the formation of a republic in 1912. After several years of civil war the nationaliist ◊Guomindang, led by ◊Chiang Kai-shek, was firmly installed in power in 1926, with Communist aid. In 1927 Chiang

Kai-shek began a purge of the Communists, who began the 'Long March' (1934–36) to Shaanxi, which became their base.

In 1931 Japan began its penetration of Manchuria, and in 1937 began the second ◊Sino-Japanese War, during which both Communists and Nationalists fought Japan. Civil war resumed after the Japanese surrender in 1945, until in 1949, following their elimination of Nationalist resistance on the mainland, the Communists inaugurated the People's Republic of China, the Nationalists having retired to Taiwan.

To begin with, the communist regime concentrated on economic reconstruction. A centralized Soviet-style constitution was adopted in 1954, industries were nationalized and central planning and moderate land reform introduced. The USSR provided economic aid, while China successfully intervened in the ◊Korean War. Development during this period was based on material incentives and industrialization.

From 1958, under state president and CCP chairman ◊Mao Zedong, China embarked on a major new policy, the Great Leap Forward. This created large self-sufficient agricultural and industrial communes in an effort to achieve classless 'true communism'. The experiment proved unpopular and impossible to co-ordinate, and over 20,000,000 people died in the floods and famines of 1959–62. A breach in Sino–Soviet relations brought a withdrawal of Soviet technical advisers in 1960.

The failure of the 'Great Leap' reduced Mao's influence 1962–65, and a successful 'recovery programme' was begun under President Liu Shaoqi. Private farming plots and markets were re-introduced, communes reduced in size, and income differentials and material incentives restored.

Mao struck back against what he saw as a return to capitalism by launching the Great Proletarian Cultural Revolution (1966 69), a 'rectification campaign' directed against 'rightists' in the CCP which sought to re-establish the supremacy of (Maoist) ideology over economics. During the campaign, Mao, supported by People's Liberation Army (PLA) chief ◊Lin Biao and the Shanghai-based 'Gang of Four' (comprising Mao's wife Jiang Qing, radical intellectuals Zhang Chunqiao and Yao Wenyuan and former millworker Wang Hongwen), encouraged student (Red Guard) demonstrations against party and government leaders.

The chief targets were Liu Shaoqi, ◊Deng Xiaoping (head of the CCP secretariat) and Peng Zhen (Mayor of Beijing). All were forced out of office. The campaign grew anarchic during 1967, necessitating PLA intervention and the dispersal of Red Guards into the countryside to 'learn from the peasants'. Government institutions fell into abeyance during the Cultural Revolution and new 'Three Part Revolutionary Committees', comprising Maoist party officials, trade unionists and PLA commanders, took over administration. By 1970, Mao sided with pragmatic Prime Minister ◊Zhou Enlai and began restoring order and a more balanced system. A number of 'ultra-leftists' were ousted in 1970 and in 1971 Lin Biao died en route to Mongolia after a failed coup. In 1972–73 Deng Xiaoping, finance minister Li Xiannian, and others, were rehabilitated, and a policy of détente towards the USA began. This reconstruction movement was climaxed by the summoning of the NPC in 1975 for the first time in 11 years to ratify a new constitution and approve an economic plan termed the 'Four Modernizations' -agriculture, industry, defence, and science and technology -which aimed at placing China on a par with the West by the year 2000.

The deaths of Zhou Enlai and Mao Zedong in 1976 unleashed a violent succession struggle between the leftist 'Gang of Four', led by Jiang Qing, and moderate 'rightists', grouped around vice-premier Deng Xiaoping. Deng was forced into hiding by the 'Gang'; and Mao's moderate protegé ◊Hua Guofeng became CCP chairman and head of government in 1976. Hua arrested the 'Gang' on charges of treason and held power 1976–78 as a stop-gap leader, continuing Zhou Enlai's modernization programme.

His authority was progressively challenged, however, by Deng Xiaoping, who returned to office in 1977 after campaigns in Beijing. By 1979, after further popular campaigns, Deng had gained effective charge of the government, controlling a majority in the Politburo. State and judicial bodies began to meet again, Liu Shaoqi was rehabilitated as a party hero and economic reforms were introduced. These involved the dismantling of the commune system, the introduction of direct farm incentives under a new 'responsibility system' and the encouragement of foreign investment in 'Special Economic Zones' in coastal enclaves. By Jun 1981 Deng's supremacy was assured when his protegés ◊Hu Yaobang and ◊Zhao Ziyang became party chairman and prime minister and the 'Gang of Four' were sentenced to life imprisonment (Yao Wenyuan received 20 years).

In 1982, Hua Guofeng and a number of senior colleagues were ousted from the Politburo, and the NPC adopted a definitive constitution, restoring the post of state president (abolished since 1975) and establishing a new civil rights code. The new administration was a collective leadership, with Hu Yaobang in control of party affairs, Zhao Ziyang overseeing state administration and Deng Xiaoping (a party vice-chairman and SCMC chairman) formulating long-term strategy and supervizing the PLA.

The triumvirate pursued a three-pronged policy aimed firstly at streamlining the party and state bureaucracies and promoting to power new, younger, and better-educated technocrats. By 1986 half the CCP's provincial-level officers had been replaced. Secondly, they also sought to curb PLA influence by retiring senior commanders and reducing numbers from 4.2 to 3 million. Thirdly, they gave priority to economic modernization by extending market incentives and local autonomy, and by introducing a new 'open door' policy to encourage foreign trade and investment.

These economic reforms met with substantial success in the agricultural sector (output more than doubled 1978–85), but had adverse side effects, widening regional and social income differentials and fuelling a wave of 'mass consumerism' which created balance of payments problems. Contact with the West brought demands for full-scale democratization in China. These calls led in 1986 to widespread student demonstrations, and party chief Hu Yaobang was dismissed in 1987 for failing to check the disturbances. His departure imperilled the future of the post-1978 Dengist reform programme as conservatives sought to slow the pace of change and re-establish central party control.

In foreign affairs, China's 1960 rift with ◊Khrushchev's Soviet Union over policy differences became irrevocable in 1962 when Russia sided with India during a brief Sino-Indian border war. Relations with the Soviet Union deteriorated further in 1969 after border clashes in the disputed Ussuri river region. China pursued a ◊non-aligned strategy, projecting itself as the voice of Third World nations, although it achieved nuclear capability by 1964. During the early 1970s, concern with Soviet expansionism brought rapprochement with the US, bringing China's entry to the UN (at ◊Taiwan's expense) in 1971 and culminating in the establishment of full Sino-American diplomatic relations in 1979. In recent years there has been political decentralization and a diminishing of direct party control over government organs. Competition has been introduced into party and state elections and non-party bodies, such as the broad-front Chinese People's Political Consultative Conference, have been revived and inducted into the policy-making process. Relations with the West have remained warm during the Deng administration, with economic contacts broadening.

china clay a clay mineral formed by the decomposition of ◊feldspars. The alteration of aluminium silicates results in the formation of kaolinite from which ◊kaolin of white china clay is derived. It is important in the manufacture of ceramics, paper, rubber, paint, textiles and medicines. It is mined in the UK, the USA, France and Czechoslovakia.

China, history the earliest human remains found in China are those of 'Peking man' (*Sinanthropus pekingensis*), thought to have lived about 500,000 years ago. Humans of the modern type are first known to have inhabited the region about 20,000 years ago, and to have established a simple agricultural society around 5000 BC.

The earliest Chinese civilizations are known only from legends; these are the so-called *Sage Kings* (c. 2800–c. 2205 BC), a period of agricultural development; and the *Xia* dynasty (c. 2000–c. 1500 BC), a bronze age with further agricultural developments, including irrigation, and the first known use of writing.

The *Shang* dynasty (c. 1500–c. 1066 BC), is the first of which we have documentary evidence; the artistic genius of this period is illustrated in its bronze vases. During the *Zhou* dynasty

(1066–221 BC) which followed, the feudal structure of society broke down in a period of political upheaval, though iron, money, domestic animals, and written laws were all in use, and philosophy flourished (see ◊Confucius, ◊Laozi, ◊Mencius). The dynasty ended in the 'Warring States' period (403–221 BC), with the country divided into small kingdoms.

This was followed by the shortest and most remarkable of the dynasties, the *Qin* (221–206 BC), comprising the reign of Shih Huang Ti, who curbed the feudal nobility and introduced a widespread system of orderly government; he built roads and canals, and began the ◊Great Wall, to keep out invaders from the north.

The next dynasty was the *Han* (206 BC–220 AD), a long period of peace, during which territory was expanded, the keeping of historical records was systematized, and an organized civil service set up. Art and literature flourished, and ◊Buddhism was introduced. During this dynasty the idea of the unity of China was so firmly implanted that, though that unity has often been broken since, it always re-asserted itself.

The Han dynasty gave way to a period of division known as the *Three Kingdoms*. These were the Wei, Chu, and Wu, of which the Wei became the most powerful, eventually founding the *Jin* dynasty (265–439 AD), which expanded to take over from the barbarian invaders who ruled much of China at that time, but lost the territory they had gained to the ◊Tatar invaders from the north. Reunification came with the *Sui* dynasty (581–618); when the government was reinstated and the Great Wall refortified.

Next came the *Tang* dynasty (618–907), when the system of government became more highly developed than ever before, and the empire covered most of SE and much of central Asia. Art and literature (especially poetry) flourished again.

Another period of warfare and disruption followed during the period known as the *Five Dynasties and Ten Kingdoms* (907–960) which, in spite of economic depression and loss of territory, was an important stage in the development of printing. During the *Song* dynasty (960–1279), a period of calm and creativity, central government was restored and printing continued to develop, but ◊Mongol invasions began in the north. The Mongols reigned 1279–1368, (the *Yu*an dynasty) and after widespread revolts were expelled by the first of the *Ming* dynasty (1368–1644). They expanded the empire still further, and in the 16th century Europeans began to arrive in China.

The Portuguese reached Canton in 1517, and were followed by Spanish, Dutch, French, British and Americans. During the 19th century it seemed likely that China would be partitioned amongst the European powers, all trade being conducted through Treaty Ports in their control, and the system not being ended until new agreements were made 1943–47. The last Chinese effort under the Empire to throw off Western influence was the Boxer Rising of 1900, suppressed by European troops.

The last of the dynasties was the *Manchu* (1644–1912) which gave several great rulers to

China

PEOPLE'S REPUBLIC OF (*Zhonghua Renmin Gonghe Guo*)

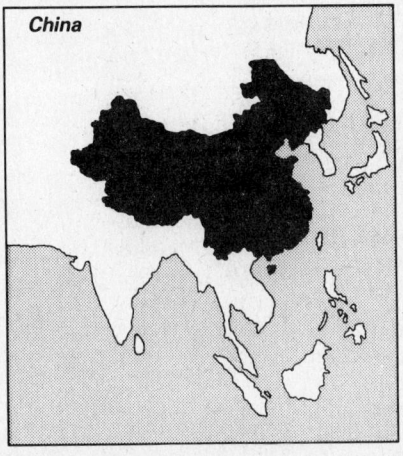

China

AREA 9,569,700 sq km/3,694,000 sq mi
CAPITAL Beijing (Peking)
TOWNS Chongqing (Chungking), Shenyang (Mukden), Wuhan, Nanjing (Nanking), Harbin; ports Tianjin (Tientsin), Shanghai, Qingdao (Tsingtao), Lüda (Lü-ta), Guangzhou (Canton)
PHYSICAL two-thirds of China is mountains (in the N and SW) or desert; the E is irrigated by rivers Huang He (Yellow River), Chang Jiang (Yangtze-Kiang), Xi Jiang (Si Kiang)
FEATURES Great Wall of China; Kongur Shan mountain
HEAD OF STATE Li Xiannian from 1983
HEAD OF GOVERNMENT Zhao Ziyang from 1980
GOVERNMENT communist
EXPORTS tea; livestock and animal products; textiles (silk and cotton); oil, minerals (China is the world's largest producer of tungsten), chemicals; light industrial goods
CURRENCY yuang (6.15 = £1 Sept 1987)
POPULATION (1985) 1,037,588,000 (of whom the majority are Han or ethnic Chinese; the 67 million of other ethnic groups, including Tibetan, Uigur, and Zhuang, live in border areas). By 2000 AD the population is estimated to reach 2,000 million. The number of people of Chinese origin outside China, Taiwan, and Hong Kong is estimated at 15–24 million. Annual growth rate 1.2%
LANGUAGE Chinese
RELIGION officially atheist, but traditionally Taoist, Confucianist, and Buddhist; Muslim 13 million; Catholic 3–6 million (divided between the 'patriotic' church established 1958 and the 'loyal' church subject to Rome); Protestant 3 million
LITERACY 79% male/51% female (1982)
GDP $313 bn (1983); $566 per head of population
CHRONOLOGY
1949 People's Republic of China proclaimed by Mao Zedong.
1954 Soviet-style constitution adopted.
1956–57 Hundred Flowers Movement encouraged criticism of the government.
1958–60 Great Leap Forward commune experiment to achieve 'true communism'.
1960 Withdrawal of Soviet technical advisers.
1962 Sino-Indian border war.
1962–65 Economic recovery programme under Liu Shaoqi; Maoist 'socialist education movement' rectification campaign.
1966–68 Great Proletarian Cultural Revolution and overthrow of Liu Shaoqi.
1969 Ussuri river border clashes with USSR.
1970–76 Reconstruction under Mao and Zhou Enlai; purge of extreme left.
1971 Entry into United Nations.
1972 US president Nixon visited Beijing.
1975 New state constitution. Unveiling of Zhou's Four Modernizations programme.
1976 Death of Zhou Enlai and Mao Zedong; appointment of Hua Guofeng as prime minister and Communist Party chair. Deng in hiding. Gang of Four arrested.
1977 Rehabilitation of Deng Xiaoping.
1979 Economic reforms introduced. Diplomatic relations opened with USA. Punitive invasion of Vietnam.
1980 Zhao Ziyang appointed prime minister.
1981 Hu Yaobang succeeded Hua as party chair. Imprisonment of Gang of Four.
1982 New state constitution adopted.
1984 'Enterprise management' reforms for industrial sector.
1986 Student demonstrations for democracy.
1987 Dismissal of Hu Yaobang as party leader.

China, up to the empress dowager Tz'e Hsi who died 1908. Three years later revolution broke out, and in 1912 the infant emperor (see Henry ◊Pu Yi) was deposed. For history 1911–present, see ◊China.

China Sea /'tʃaɪnə/ area of the Pacific Ocean bordered by China, Vietnam, Borneo, the Philippines, and Japan. N of Taiwan it is known as the *East China Sea* and to the S as the *South China Sea*. Various groups of small islands and shoals in the centre, W and E of the South China Sea, including the Paracels, 500 km/300m E of Vietnam, have been disputed by China and other powers because they lie in oil-bearing areas.

Chincherinchee S African plant *Ornithogalum thyrsoides*, family Liliaceae, with spikes of white or yellow wax-like flowers which are long-lasting.

chinchilla S American rodent *Chinchilla laniger* found in high, rather barren areas of the Andes in Bolivia and Chile. About the size of a small rabbit, it has long ears and a long bushy tail, and shelters in rock crevices. This gregarious animals has a very thick soft siver-grey fur, and was hunted almost to extinction for it. Now chinchillas are farmed, and also given some protection in the wild.

Chindits /'tʃɪndɪts/ name given to the 3rd Indian Division (Long Range Penetration Group) under the command of Brigadier ◊Wingate in World War II. The name derived from the mythical Chinthay – half lion, half eagle – at the entrance of Burmese pagodas to scare evil spirits.

Chinese architecture since early times Chinese buildings have been constructed chiefly of timber, and consequently they do not usually last long. There are few buildings which date back earlier than the Ming dynasty (1368–1644), but there are records, such as the *Ying Tsao Fa Shih*/*Method of Architecture*, published in 1103, which describe and illustrate early Chinese buildings. These records reveal that Chinese architecture has remained very much the same in style throughout the ages. Chinese buildings usually face S, a convention which can be traced back to the 'Hall of Brightness', a famous building of the Zhou dynasty (c. 1050–221 BC). One of the most characteristic features of Chinese architecture is the curved roof, believed to have been imported with Buddhism from India.

The Chinese are also famous for their walls. The Great Wall of China was built, c. 228–210 BC, by the Emperor Shi Huangdi along the northern frontier as a defence against the hostile nomadic tribes of the north. The fine city walls of Beijing (Peking) (of which some sections have been demolished in modernization of the city) date to the Ming dynasty, as also do some of the buildings in or near the city, notably the Altar of Heaven, the ancestral temple of the Ming tombs, and the Five Pagoda Temple. The pagoda with its tiled roofs one above the other is typically Chinese.

Modern Chinese architecture has tended to be functionally Western in construction, with some traditional features.

Chinese art during China's Stone Age painted pottery and jade objects were made, but there was not a Chinese culture until the acquisition of bronze. During the Shang period, which lasted till c. 1050 BC, beautiful bronze vessels were produced, and motifs, such as the dragon, the elephant, and the ogre's mask, were already in use. Under the Chou dynasty a feudal system emerged, together with important developments in the field of art. Buildings were often decorated with mural paintings, and this art is said to have won the praise of ◊Confucius. The brush had been used for painting on pottery, and lacquer workers used brushes as early as 2 or 3 centuries BC. The use of finer brushes resulted in the invention by Mêng T'ien of the writing brush, c. 200 BC, and the development of ◊calligraphy, which the Chinese have long regarded as the greatest of the fine arts.

The Han period (206 BC–220 AD) was very important in art. Silk weavings appeared, glaze was used to brighten pottery, great architectural schemes were carried out, relief sculpture, portrait and other painting developed.

The first of the great painters whose name we know – Ku K'ai Chih – worked c. 3500–400 AD in S China. Some of his illustrations on the inscribed scroll entitled *The Admonitions of the*

CHINA, PEOPLE'S REPUBLIC OF

Province	Former name	Capital	Area sq km	Province	Former name	Capital	Area sq km
Anhui	Anhwei	Hefei	139	Sichuan	Szechwan	Chengdu	567
Fujian	Fukien	Fuzhou	121	Yunnan	Yunnan	Kunming	394
Gansu	Kansu	Lanzhou	454	Zhejiang	Chekiang	Hangzhou	102
Guangdong	Kwangtung	Guangzhou	212				
Guizhou	Kweichow	Guiyang	176	*Autonomous Regions*			
Hebei	Hopei	Shijiazhuang	188	Guangxi Zhuang	Kwangsi Chuang	Nanning	236
Heilongjiang	Heilungkiang	Harbin	469	Nei Monggol	Inner Mongolia	Hohhot	1,183
Henan	Honan	Zhengzhou	167	Ningxia Hui	Ningshia Hui	Yinchuan	66
Hubei	Hupeh	Wuhan	186	Xinjiang Uygur	Sinkiang Uighur	Urumqi	1,600
Hunan	Hunan	Changsha	210	Xizang	Tibet	Lhasa	1,228
Jiangsu	Kiangsu	Nanjing	103	*Municipalities*			
Jiangxi	Kiangsi	Nanchang	169	Beijing	Peking		17
Jilin	Kirin	Changchun	187	Shanghai	Shanghai		6
Liaoning	Liaoning	Shenyang	146	Tianjin	Tientsin		11
Quinghai	Tsinghai	Xining	721				
Shaanxi	Shensi	Xian	206			TOTAL	9,571
Shanxi	Shansi	Taiyuan	156				
Shandong	Shantung	Jinan	153				

Instructress to the Court Ladies are in the British Museum.

During the T'ang period (618–906) the art of painting reached its zenith, and porcelain was perfected. This was a period of great expansion, and Chinese art began to show both oriental and occidental influences; for example the shapes of vessels show the influence of Persian designs. The Sung period (960–1279) is famous for its many animal, flower, and bird paintings, and for its landscape paintings. Seen from a bird's eye view, the space within a landscape was as meaningful as the subject. An Imperial Academy of Painting was founded by the emperor Hui Tsung, who was himself a talented painter of birds. Then with the Mings (1386–1644) there was an outburst of patriotism which was reflected by artists and craftsmen in bold masses, free flowing line, and brilliant colour, expressed in the architecture, pottery, and painting of the period. There was a flourishing trade in porcelain, and typical of the time are the large wine jars of sturdy design, tall and imposing vases with heavily outlined floral designs. Enamelling on metal was perfected.

The Manchu dynasty (1644–1911), who overthrew the Ming dynasty, fostered the arts and encouraged learning. Closer contact was made with western civilization. The two great liberal rulers of the period were K'ang Hsi, whose reign began in 1662, and Ch'ien Lung, who reigned from 1736 till almost the end of the 18th century. Under K'ang Hsi porcelain became the most typical medium of expression. K'ang Hsi wares were chiefly the blue and white (called 'Nanking' in England), and the enamelled porcelains. During the 18th century there was a trend for intricate design, and some fine pieces were produced during the reign of Ch'ien Lung. In the 20th century, painting in traditional styles has continued (a noble exponent being Li K'o-jan), but attempts to incorporate modernist ideas have been frowned on by the authorities.

Chinese language depending upon definition, a language or group of languages of the Sino-Tibetan family, spoken in China, Taiwan, Hongkong, Singapore and Chinese communities throughout the world. Varieties of spoken Chinese differ greatly, but share a written form using thousands of ideographic symbols which have changed little in 2,000 years. Because the writing system has a symbolic form (rather like numbers and road signs) it can be read and interpreted regardless of the reader's own dialect. Nowadays, *putonghua* ('common speech'), based on the educated Peking dialect known as 'Mandarin' Chinese, is promoted throughout China as the national spoken and written language. The Chinese dialects are tonal (i.e., they depend upon the tone of a syllable to indicate its meaning, *ma* with one tone meaning 'mother', with another meaning 'horse'). The characters of Chinese script are traditionally written vertically and read right-left but are now commonly written horizontally and read left-right, using 2,000 simplified characters. A variant of the Roman alphabet has been introduced and used in schools to help with pronunciation. This, *Pinyin*, is prescribed for international use by the People's Republic of China, for personal and place names; as in Beijing rather than Peking. Pinyin spellings are generally used in this volume, but are not accepted by the government of Taiwan.

Chinese literature *Poetry* written in the ancient literary language understood throughout China, Chinese poems, often only four lines long, consist of rhymed lines of a fixed number of syllables, ornamented by parallel phrasing and tonal pattern. The oldest poems are contained in the *Book of Songs* (800–600 BC). Among the most famous Chinese poets are the nature poet T'ao Ch'ien (372–427 AD), the master of technique Li Po (701–62), the autobiographical Po Chüi (772–846), and the wide-ranging Su Tung-p'o (1036–1101); and among the moderns using the colloquial language under European influence and experimenting in free verse are Hsu Chih-mo (1895–1931), and Pien Chih-lin (1910–).

Prose typical Chinese history is less literary than an editing of assembled documents with moral comment, but the essay has long been cultivated under strict rules of form and style. Among the most famous essays is that of Han Yü (768–824) *Upon the Original Way*, recalling the nation to Confucianism. Until the 16th century the short story was confined to the anecdote, startling by its strangeness, related in the literary language, for example, those of the poetic Tuan Ch'eng-shih (died 863), but after that time the more novelistic type in the colloquial tongue developed by its side. The Chinese novel evolved from the street storyteller's art, and has consequently always used the popular language. The early romances *Three Kingdoms*, *All Men are Brothers*, and *Golden Lotus* are anonymous, the earliest known author being Wu Che'ng-en (c. 1505–80); the most realistic of the great novelists is Ts'ao Chan (died 1763).

Twentieth-century Chinese novels have largely adopted European form, and have been particularly influenced by Russia, as have the realistic stories of Lu Hsün. In typical Chinese drama, the stage presentation far surpasses the text in importance (the dialogue was not even preserved in early plays), but the present century has seen experiments in the European manner.

Chinese Revolution a series of major political upheavals which began in 1911 with a nationalist revolt which overthrew the Chiing imperial dynasty in 1912. Led by Sun Yat–Sen (1923–25) and then by Chiang Kai–Shek (1925–49), the nationalists came under increasing pressure form the growing Communist movement. The 6,000 mile 'Long March' of the Chinese Communists (1934–35) to escape from the nationalist forces saw Mao Tse-Tung emerge as leader. After World War II, the conflict expanded into open civil war (1946–49) with the revolutionists finally being defeated at Nanking. This effectively established communist rule in China under the leadership of Mao.

Chinghai /ˌtʃɪŋˈhaɪ/ former name of ◊Qinghai, NW province of China.

chip a complete electronic circuit on a slice of silicon (or other ◊semiconductor) crystal only a few millimetres square. Also called ◊silicon chip and ◊integrated circuit.

chip

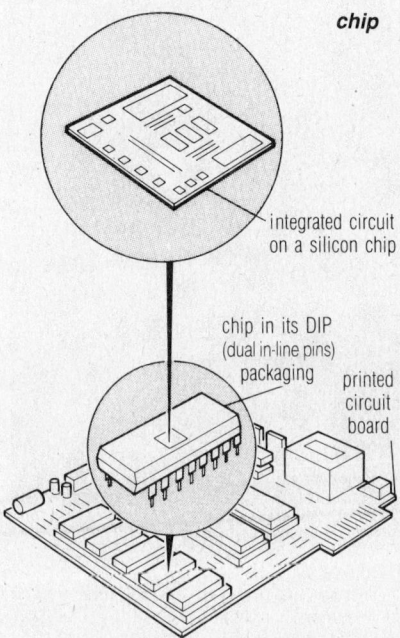

integrated circuit on a silicon chip

chip in its DIP (dual in-line pins) packaging

printed circuit board

chipmunk name for a number of species of small ground squirrel mostly living in N America, but also E Asia, in a variety of habitats, usually wooded. They have pouches in their cheeks for carrying food and stripes along their sides. They climb well but spend most time on or near the ground, and take shelter in burrows. The *Siberian chipmunk Eutamias sibiricus*, about 13 cm/5 in body length, is found through N Russia, N China and Japan.

Chippendale /'tʃɪpəndeɪl/ Thomas c. 1718–79. English furniture designer. The son of a joiner from Otley, Yorkshire, he set up his workshop in St Martin's Lane, London in 1753. His book *The Gentleman and Cabinet Maker's Director* 1754 was a significant contribution to furniture design. He favoured Louis XIV, Chinese, Gothic, and neo-Classic styles, and worked mainly in dark mahogany

Chirac /'ʃɪəræk/ Jacques 1932– . French conservative politician, prime minister 1974–76 and from 1986; he established the neo-Gaullist Rassemblement pour la République (RPR) 1976.
During the ◊Pompidou presidency (1969–74), Chirac held ministerial posts and gained the nickname 'the bulldozer'. In 1974 he became prime minister to President ◊Giscard d'Estaing, but the relationship was uneasy. Chirac became mayor of Paris in 1977, contested the 1981 presidential election and emerged as the National Assembly leader for the parties of the right during the socialist administration of 1981–86.
Following the right coalition's victory in 1986, Chirac was appointed prime minister by

President ◊Mitterrand in a 'cohabitation' experiment. In the autumn of 1986 student demonstrations forced him to scrap controversial plans for educational reform.

Chirac French politician Jacques Chirac, mayor of Paris from 1977. After a vigorous campaign in the 1986 elections he became prime minister under Mitterrand, and has had a rough ride with economic decline, nationality reforms, student unrest and the conflict with Iran.

Chirico /'kɪərɪkəʊ/ Giorgio de 1888–1978. Artist of Italian parentage born in Greece, a ◊Surrealist precursor, as shown by *The Uncertainty of the Poet* (Tate Gallery, London).

Chiron /'kaɪrən/ in Greek mythology, the son of Cronos by a sea nymph. A ◊centaur, he was the wise tutor of Jason and Achilles among others.

Chiron /'kaɪrən/ in astronomy, 'mini-planet' discovered in 1977, orbiting between Saturn and Venus. It appears to have a dark surface resembling that of asteroids in the outer solar system, and probably consists of a mixture of ice and dark stony material.

chiropody the care and treatment of the hands and feet. The first centre to deal with common foot disorders was the Pedic Clinic (1913), which later became the London Foot Hospital; and the Society of Chiropodists was established 1945.

chiropractic manipulation of the spine, etc., to relieve apparently non-related conditions, claimed to be caused by pressure on the nerves. It is not fully recognized by orthodox medicine.

Chissano /ʃɪ'sɑːnuː/ Joaquim 1939– . Mozambique Frelimo politician, president from 1986.
Chissano was active in the Mozambique Liberation Front (Frelimo) from 1963. From independence in 1975, he was foreign minister until his election as president after ◊Machel's death in 1986.

Chita /tʃiː'tɑː/ town in E Siberia, USSR, on the Chita river. It is on the Trans-Siberian

railway, and has engineering works and coal mines. Population (1981) 315,000.

chitin a complex long-chain compound, or ◊polymer; a nitrogenous derivative of glucose. Chitin is found principally in the ◊exoskeleton of insects and other arthropods. It combines with protein to form a covering that can be hard and tough, as in scorpions, or soft and flexible, as in caterpillars. In crustaceans such as crabs it is impregnated with calcium carbonate for extra strength. Chitin also occurs in some ◊protozoans and coelenterates, such as certain jellyfish, in the jaws of annelid worms, and as the cell-wall polymer of fungi.

Chittagong /'tʃɪtəgɒŋ/ town and port in Bangladesh, 16 km/10 mi from the mouth of the Karnaphuli river, on the Bay of Bengal. Industries include steel, engineering, chemicals and textiles. Population (1981) 1,388,476.

chivalry originally the knightly class of the feudal Middle Ages; subsequently the word came to mean the code of gallantry and honour that the knights were supposed to observe. A Court of Chivalry existed in England from Edward III's reign to 1737.

chive plant *Allium schoenoprasum* that grows wild in a few places in Britain, and is cultivated as a vegetable.

chlamydia single-celled organism that can only live parasitically in animal cells. Chlamydias were once thought to be large viruses, but is is now known that they have protein-making machinery which viruses characteristically lack. They are considered to be descendants of bacteria which have lost certain metabolic processes. In humans, chlamydias cause ◊trachoma (a leading cause of blindness), a type of venereal disease found mainly in the tropics, and psittacosis which is contracted from birds by inhaling particles of dried bird droppings, which can contain chlamydias in great numbers.

chloracne eruption of the skin symptomatic of contact with chlorinated organic chemicals and a contaminated environment

chloral *trichloracet-aldehyde*. An oily colourless liquid with a characteristic pungent smell. It is very soluble in water, and its compound chloral hydrate is a powerful sleep-inducing agent.

chlorates in chemistry, salts whose acid contains both chlorine and oxygen (ClO, ClO$_2$, ClO$_3$, and ClO$_4$). Common chlorates are those of sodium, potassium, and barium . Certain chlorates are used in weedkillers.

chlorella single-cell, freshwater alga, 3–10 micrometres in diameter, which obtains its growth energy from light and can increase its weight by four times in 12 hours. Nutritive content: 50% protein, 20% fat, 20% carbohydrate, 10% phosphate, calcium, and other inorganic substances. Unappetizing *au naturel*, it can be flavoured, and may become a food for space travellers.

chlorides salts of hydrochloric acid (HCl) commonly formed by its action on various metals or by the direct combination of the metal and chlorine. Sodium chloride (NaCl) is common table salt.

chlorine a chemical element, a greenish-yellow gas with an irritating, suffocating smell: symbol Cl; atomic number 17; atomic weight, 35.457. It rapidly attacks the membranes of the nose, throat and lungs, producing bronchitis or pneumonia. During World War I, it was used as a weapon. It is never found uncombined in nature, but is widely distributed in combination with the alkali metals, as ◊chlorides or ◊chlorates. Chlorine was discovered in 1774 by Scheele, but Sir Humphrey ◊Davy in 1810 first proved it to be an element. It is an important bleaching agent and is used as a germicide for drinking and swimming-pool water. It is also an oxidizing agent and finds many applications in organic chemistry.

chloroform (*trichloromethane*) a clear, colourless toxic liquid (formula CHCl₃) with a characteristic pungent, sickly-sweet smell and taste, formerly used as an anaesthetic. It is used as a solvent and in the synthesis of organic chemical compounds.

chloromycetin antibiotic which attacks viruses as well as bacteria, used in treatment of scrub-typhus, typhus and psittacosis.

chlorophyll the green pigment present in the majority of plants which is responsible for the absorption of light energy during the light reaction of ◊photosynthesis. It absorbs the red and blue-violet parts of sunlight but reflects the green, thus giving the characteristic colour to most plants. Chlorophyll is found within the ◊chloroplasts, which are present in large numbers especially in the leaves. Cyanobacteria and other photosynthetic bacteria also have chlorophyll, though of a slightly different type. Chlorophyll is similar in structure to ◊haemoglobin, but with magnesium instead of iron as the reactive part of the molecule.

chloroplast a plant cell ◊organelle containing the green pigment ◊chlorophyll. Chloroplasts occur in most cells of the green plant which are exposed to light, often in large numbers. Typically they are flattened and disc-like with a double membrane enclosing the stroma, a gel-like matrix. Within the stroma are stacks of flat vesicles, or grana, where the 'light reactions' of ◊photosynthesis occurs. It is believed that the chloroplasts were originally free-living ◊cyanobacteria, that invaded larger, non-photosynthetic cells and developed a symbiotic relationship with them. Like ◊mitochondria, they contain a small amount of ◊DNA and divide by fission. Chloroplasts are a type of ◊plastid.

chlorosis an abnormal condition of green plants in which the stems and leaves turn pale green or yellow. The yellowing is due to a reduction in the levels of the green chlorophyll pigments. It may be caused by a deficiency in essential elements (such as magnesium, iron or manganese), a lack of light, genetic factors, or virus infection.

chocolate a drink or confectionery. See ◊cocoa.

choir a body of singers, normally divided into two or more parts, and commonly four (◊soprano, ◊alto, ◊tenor, and ◊bass). The words choir and chorus are frequently interchangeable, although all church groups use the former, while

larger groups, which may have several hundred members, invariably use the latter.

choke in physics, a coil employed as an electrical ◊inductance, particularly the type used as a 'starter' in the circuit of ◊fluorescent lighting. See also induction.

cholera intestinal infection by a bacterium (*Vibrio cholerae*), formerly with a high death rate, much reduced by injections or drinks of saline fluid to prevent dehydration and loss of body salts. Transmitted in contaminated water or food, it is still prevalent in many tropical areas.

cholesterol a ◊steroid substance that forms part of all ◊cell membranes, and plays a vital role in stabilizing them. It is made by the body for this purpose and transported in the blood. Cholesterol in foodstuffs is absorbed and boosts the blood concentration, which leads to cholesterol being deposited on the ◊artery walls; this can contribute to a heart attack. Cholesterol is broken down in the liver into ◊bile salts.

Chomsky /'tʃomski/ Noam 1928– . American professor of linguistics. He proposed a theory of transformational generative grammar which attracted widespread interest outside linguistics because of the claims it made about the relationship between language and the mind, and the universality of an underlying language structure. Chomsky was also an active opponent of the American involvement in the ◊Vietnam War.

Chongqing /,tʃʊŋ'tʃɪŋ/ or *Chungking*, also known as *Pahsien* city in Sichuan province, China. Opened to foreign trade in 1891, it stands at the confluence of the Jinsha Jiang and the Jialing Jiang. For over 4,000 years it has been an important commercial centre in one of the most remote and economically deprived regions of China, and it remains a focal point of road, river and rail transport. Industries include iron, steel, chemicals, synthetic rubber, and textiles, and there is a university. When both Beijing and Nanjing were in Japanese hands, it was the capital of China 1938–46. Population (1982) 2,650,000.

Chopin /'ʃopæn/ Frédéric (François) 1810–1849. Polish composer and pianist. Born near Warsaw, the son of a French father and Polish mother, he made his debut as a pianist at the age of eight. From 1831 he made his home in Paris, where he became well known in the fashionable salons, though rarely performed in public. In 1836 Liszt introduced him to Mme Dudevant (George ◊Sand), with whom he had a liaison from 1838–1846. She nursed him in Majorca (he had tuberculosis) and for a time he regained his health. He died on 17 Oct 1849 and was buried in Père Lachaise cemetery in Paris. As a performer Chopin revolutionized the technique of pianoforte-playing. He concentrated on solo piano pieces – sonatas, waltzes, preludes, etudes, nocturnes, ballades, impromptus, fantasias, polonaises, and mazurkas, and was at his best in the intimate atmosphere of a salon, although he also wrote two piano concertos. His pieces for piano solo are characterized by their lyrical and poetic quality; in them Slavonic passion and melancholy are combined with French grace and refinement.

Chopin A daguerrotype of the composer.

chorale /kɒ'rɑːl/ a traditional hymn tune of the German Protestant Church.

chord in geometry, a straight line joining any two points on a curve. In a circle, the chord that passes through the centre of the circle (the longest chord) is the diameter. In an ellipse (a regular oval), the longest and shortest chords are called the major and minor axes.

chordate animal belonging to the phylum Chordata, which includes backboned animals (◊vertebrates), sea squirts, amphioxus and others. All these animals, at some stage of their lives, have a supporting rod of tissue (notochord or backbone) running down their bodies.

chorea a disease of the nervous system marked by involuntary movements of the face muscles and limbs, formerly called St Vitus' dance.

choreography originally, in the 18th century, the art of dance notation. Today it means the art of creating and arranging ballet and dance for performance.

chorion outermost of the three membranes enclosing the embryo of reptiles, birds and mammals. See also ◊amnion.

chorus a group of singers. See ◊choir.

Chou En-lai /'tʃəʊ en 'laɪ/ alternative name for Chinese statesman ◊Zhou En Lai.

chough bird *Pyrrhocorax pyrrhocorax* of the crow family, about 38 cm/15 in long, black-feathered, and with red bill and legs. It lives on some sea-cliffs and in high mountains, but is now rare and confined to W in Britain. It is found from Europe right to E Asia. The *alpine chough Pyrrhocorax graculus* is similar, but has a yellow bill and is found up to the snowline in mountains from the Pyrennees to Central Asia.

chow chow breed of dog originating in China in ancient times. About 45 cm/1.5 ft tall, it has a soft woolly undercoat with a coarse outer coat and a mane. Its coat should be of one colour, and it has an unusual blue-black tongue.

Chrétien de Troyes /ˌkreti'æn də 'trwɑː/ medieval French poet, born in Champagne, about the middle of the 12th century. His epics, which include *Le Chevalier de la Charrette*; *Perceval*, written for Philip, Count of Flanders; *Erec*; *Yvain*, and other Arthurian romances, first introduced the concept of the Holy Grail.

Christ see ◊Jesus Christ.

Christchurch /'kraɪstʃɜːtʃ/ town in Dorset, England, adjoining Bournemouth at the junction of the Stour and the Avon, with a fine Norman and Early English priory church. Population (1983) 40,300.

Christchurch /'kraɪstʃɜːtʃ/ city on South Island, New Zealand, on the Avon, 11 km/7 mi from its mouth. Principal city of the Canterbury plains, it has an Anglican cathedral, designed by Sir Gilbert Scott, and a Roman Catholic cathedral; and is the seat of the University of Canterbury. Industries include fertilizers and chemicals, canning and meat-processing, rail workshops, and shoes. Christchurch uses as its port a bay in the sheltered Lyttelton Harbour on the N shore of the Banks Peninsula, which forms a denuded volcanic mass. Land has been reclaimed for service facilities, and rail and road tunnels (1867 and 1964 respectively) link Christchurch with Lyttelton. Population (1981) 289,000.

christening Christian ceremony of ◊baptism of infants, including giving a name.

Christian /'krɪstjən/ follower of ◊Christianity, the religion derived from the teaching of ◊Jesus Christ. In the New Testament, Acts xi, 26, it is stated that the first to be called Christians were the disciples in Antioch.

Christian /'krɪstjən/ eight kings of Denmark and Norway, including:

Christian I /'krɪstjən/ 1426–1481. Founder of the Oldenburg dynasty. In 1450 he established the union of Denmark and Norway which lasted until 1814.

Christian III /'krɪstjən/ 1503–1559. Under his reign (1535–59) the Reformation was introduced.

Christian IV /'krɪstjən/ 1577–1648. He sided with the Protestants in the Thirty Years War (1618–48), and founded Christiania (now Oslo, capital of Norway).

Christian VIII king of Denmark 1839–48.

Christian IX /'krɪstjən/ 1818–1906. King of Denmark from 1863. His daughter Alexandra married Edward VII of the UK and another married Tsar Alexander III of Russia; his second son George, became king of Greece. In 1864 he lost Schleswig-Holstein following a war with Austria and Prussia.

Christian X /'krɪstjən/ 1870–1947. Succeeded his father Frederick VIII as king of Denmark and Iceland in 1912. He married Alexandrine, Duchess of Mecklenburg-Schwerin and was popular for his democratic attitude. During World War II he was held prisoner by the Germans in Copenhagen.

Christiania /ˌkrɪsti'ɑːniə/ former name of Norwegian capital of ◊Oslo (1624–1924), after King Christian IV who replanned it after a fire in 1624.

Christianity world religion derived from the teaching of ◊Jesus Christ in the first third of the first Christian century; overall membership about 944 million. Belief in an omnipotent God the father is the fundamental concept, together with the doctrine of the Trinity, that is, the union of the three Persons of the Father, Son, and Holy Spirit in one Godhead. Like Buddhism and Islam, it is a universal religion, and has always had a missionary element. In the late 20th century it is spreading most rapidly in Africa and South America. The chief commandment is to love God, and to love one's neighbour as oneself.

divisions

Roman Catholicism which acknowledges the supreme jurisdiction of its head the Pope, infallible when he speaks *ex cathedra* 'from the throne', a tenet which remains the chief difference between Catholicism and Protestantism; the doctrine of the ◊Immaculate Conception (which states that the Virgin Mary, the mother of Jesus, was conceived without the original sin with which all other human beings are born), and the allotment of a special place to the Virgin Mary is also a difference. The final split between Eastern and Western churches was in 1054, and a further schism came with the Reformation in the 16th century, to which the Counter-Reformation was a response. An attempt to update its doctrines in the late 19th century was condemned by Pope Pius X in 1907, and more recent moves have been rejected by Pope John Paul II. Membership 585 million.

Eastern Orthodox a federation of self-governing churches (some founded by the Apostles and their disciples). There is elaborate ritual and singing (no instrumental music) in services, and in the marriage service the bride and groom are crowned. There is a married clergy, except for bishops; the Immaculate Conception is not accepted.

Protestantism originating with the Reformation, and named from the protest of Luther and his supporters at the Diet of Spires 1529 against the decision to reaffirm the Edict of the Diet of ◊Worms against the Reformation. The chief sects are the Anglican Communion, Baptists, Christian Scientists, Lutherans, Methodists, Pentecostal Movement, Presbyterians, Unitarians. Membership about 320 million. There has been a move this century to reunite various Protestant sects and, to some extent, the Protestant churches and the Roman Catholic church, for example the World Council of Churches 1948. See ◊Ecumenical Movement. In the 1970s and 80s there has been a revival of interest in Christianity among young people which is not necessarily connected to the established churches, for example, the Jesus Freaks, Children of God.

history

the Christian Church is traditionally said to have originated on the first Whitsun Day, but was only finally separated from the parent Jewish Church by the declaration of Saints Barnabas and Paul that the distinctive rites of Judaism were not necessary for entry into the Christian Church.

For its first two centuries the Church was not much more than a spasmodically persecuted minority, but in the 3rd century more determined efforts to destroy it were made under Severus, Decius, and Diocletian. Toleration was obtained by Constantine's victory Milvian Bridge outside Rome (312), and Christianity became the established religion of the Roman Empire. In the 4th century there were heresies such as Montanism and Gnosticism, to which the Church opposed a developed creed, a canon of established scriptures, and a threefold ministry with its succession from the Apostles. Questions of discipline also threatened disruption within the Church; to settle these Constantine called the Council of Arles 314, which was followed by the Councils of ◊Nicaea 325, Constantinople 381, Ephesus 431, and Chalcedon 451. A settled doctrine of Christian belief evolved, but failed to prevent the schism of the churches of the East. From the 5th century the Church, especially as represented by the Celtic and Benedictine monks, attempted to preserve features of the Graeco-Roman civilization and took Christianity to the northern peoples via figures such as Saints Colomba and Augustine in England. The Church assisted the growth of the feudal system of which it formed the apex, as recognized by Charlemagne 800 in seeking coronation by the Pope.

The Middle Ages, despite an underlying unity symbolized by the theology of St Thomas Aquinas, saw much controversy between secular and spiritual jurisdiction, for example, Emperor Henry IV and Pope Gregory VII, Henry II of England and Becket. Moreover, increasing worldliness (against which the foundation of the Dominicans and Franciscans was a protest), and other ecclesiastical abuses, led to dissatisfaction in the 14th century and the appearance of the reformers Wycliffe and Huss.

In N Europe the Renaissance brought a re-examination of Christian truth by More, Colet, and Erasmus, and with the advent of Luther, Calvin, and Zwingli came the Reformation, an attempt to return to primitive Christianity. In England Henry VIII and Elizabeth I found a compromise between orthodox Catholicism and reforming Protestantism in the Church of England. During the 18th-century Age of Reason, Christianity was questioned and the Scriptures examined on the same basis as secular literature, the shock to orthodox belief being highlighted still further by the evolutionary theories of the 19th century.

Meanwhile in England the Church of England suffered the loss of large numbers of Nonconformists, who established the denominations known today as the Free churches. The Methodist movement started in the 18th century, and the Oxford movement in the 19th, led by Newman, Keble, and Pusey, eventually developed into present-day Anglo-Catholicism. Of the Presbyterian churches founded in the Reformation period the most important is the Church of Scotland.

Christian Science an interpretation of the Christian religion, originating with Mary Baker ◊Eddy. It is regarded by its adherents as the restatement of primitive Christianity with its full gospel of salvation from all evil, including sickness and disease as well as sin. Christian Scientists believe that since God is good and is Spirit, matter and evil are not truly real. The application of this belief constitutes Christian Science practice. According to its adherents, Christian Science healing is brought about by the operation of truth in human conscience and not by medical treatment, which they refuse. There is no ordained priesthood, but there are public practitioners of Christian Science healing who are officially authorized and listed by the Church of Christ, Scientist, that was established by Mrs Eddy in 1879. The Mother Church – the First Church of Christ, Scientist – is situated in Boston, Massachusetts, USA, and has branches in most parts of the world. The textbook of Christian Science is Mrs Eddy's *Science and Health with Key to the Scriptures,* first published in 1875. Among the Christian Science publications is the *Christian Science Monitor,* an international daily newspaper.

Christians of St Thomas sect of Indian Christians on the Malabar coast; named after the apostle who is supposed to have carried his mission to India, although they were established in the 5th century by Nestorians from Persia. They now form part of the Syrian Church and have their own patriarch.

Christie /'krɪsti/ Agatha (born Miller) 1890–1976. British novelist, writer of detective fiction. Born in Torquay, she married Colonel Archibald Christie in 1914 and served during World War I as a nurse. Her first crime novel, *The Mysterious Affair at Styles* 1920, introduced Hercule Poirot, the Belgian detective. She later created Miss Jane Marple, an elderly spinster detective. She often broke 'purist' rules, as in *The Murder of Roger Ackroyd* 1926 in which the narrator is the murderer, and in *Ten Little Indians* 1939, in which all the suspects are killed. Her plays include *The Mousetrap* 1952, still running in the West End of London in 1988, and a number of her books were filmed, for example *Murder on the Orient Express* 1975. She caused a nationwide sensation in 1926 by disappearing for ten days (possibly because of amnesia) when her husband fell in love with another woman. After a divorce in 1928, she married the archaeologist Sir Max Mallowan (1904–78) in 1930. She was created a DBE in 1971.

Christina /krɪs'tiːnə/ 1626–1689. Queen of Sweden. Succeeding her father Gustavus Adolphus in 1632, she assumed power in 1644, but disagreed with the former regent ◊Oxenstjerna. Refusing to marry, she eventually nominated her cousin Charles Gustavus as her successor. As a secret convert to Rome (Catholicism was then illegal in Sweden), she had to abdicate in 1654. She joined the Catholic Church in Innsbruck and then maintained a court in Rome, twice returning to Sweden unsuccessfully to claim the throne. She ended her life as a pensioner of the Pope.

Christmas 25 Dec, the day on which the birth of Christ is celebrated by Christians. Although the actual birth date is unknown, the choice of a

Christie Among the detective novelists who formed the 'classical' school of the 1920s and 1930s, the name of Agatha Christie remains pre-eminent.

date near the winter solstice owed much to missionary desire to facilitate conversion of pagans, for example in Britain 25 Dec had been kept as a festival long before the introduction of Christianity. Many of its customs also have a non-Christian origin.

Christmas Island /'krɪsməs/ island in the Indian Ocean, 360 km/250 mi S of Java. Area 135 sq km/52 sq mi; population (1982) 3,000. It has phosphate deposits. Found to be uninhabited when reached by Captain W Mynars on Christmas Day 1643, it was annexed by Britain in 1888; occupied by Japan 1942–45, and transferred to Australia in 1958. After a referendum in 1984, it was included in Northern Territory.

Christmas rose see ◊hellebore.

Christmas tree type of tree brought indoors and decorated for Christmas, usually the Norway spruce *Picea abies.* The custom was a medieval German tradition and is now practised in many Western countries.

Christoff /'krɪstɒf/ Boris 1918– . Bulgarian bass singer. Born near Sofia, he gained a scholarship to study singing in Rome, and in 1946 made his debut in opera. His roles include Boris Godunov, Ivan the Terrible, and Mephistopheles.

Christophe /kriːs'tɒf/ Henri 1767–1820. Black slave in the West Indies who was one of the leaders of the revolt against the French in 1790, and in 1812 was crowned king of Haiti. He shot himself when his troops deserted him because of his alleged cruelty.

Christopher, St /'krɪstəfə/ in the Christian church, the patron saint of ferrymen and travellers. Traditionally he was a Christian martyr in Syria in the 3rd century, and the best-known legend concerning him describes his carrying the Christ child over the stream; despite

his great strength he found the burden increasingly heavy, whereupon he was told that this was no wonder as Christ was bearing the sins of all the world. His feast day is 25 Jul.

Christ's Hospital /'kraɪsts 'hɒspɪtl/ English independent school for boys, generally known as the Blue Coat school after the blue gown which forms part of the boys' dress. Founded in 1552, it moved from Newgate Street, London, to Horsham, Sussex, in 1902. There is a girls' school in Hertford which belongs to the same foundation. The English writers Coleridge and Lamb were educated at Christ's Hospital.

chromatic scale a musical scale proceeding by semitones. All 12 notes in the octave are used rather than the seven notes of the diatonic scale.

chromatography an important technique used especially in ◊biochemistry, for separating mixtures into their components for analysis and quantification. For example, if a protein has been broken down into its consistent amino acids, chromatography can be used to separate and identify those amino acids. Chromatography may be carried out by passing solutions of different substances along a column of an absorbent when they will be separated according to their relative affinities for the absorbent, or by putting drops of a mixture of components in solution on filter paper when the different components will be separated by differential diffusion through the paper (paper chromotography). In thin-layer chromato-graphy, a wafer-thin layer of absorbent medium on a glass plate replaces the filter paper. In gas–liquid chromatography, the liquid to be analysed is evaporated and then allowed to flow into a partition column containing a substance such as a high-boiling point liquid. The materials of the sample have different partition coefficients, and separate because they travel at different speeds. These methods are extremely sensitive and enable very small quantities of substances (fractions of parts per million, ppm) to be separated and analysed. The name 'chromatography' comes from the Greek for 'colour', because in the earliest forms of paper chromatography, treatment with coloured reagents was used to identify and locate the separated compounds.

chromium chemical element, symbol Cr, atomic number 24, atomic weight 52.01. A bluish-white metal capable of taking a high polish, and with a high melting-point. It is used decoratively and (alloyed with nickel) for electrical heating wires. Resistant to abrasion and corrosion, it is used to harden steel, and is a constituent of stainless steel and many other useful alloys. It is used extensively in chromium plating and as a ◊catalyst. Its most important compounds are sodium and potassium chromates and dichromates (for tanning leather) and potassium and ammonium chrome alums. It occurs chiefly as chrome-iron ore: the USSR, Zimbabwe and Brazil are important sources.

chromosome a structure in a cell nucleus responsible for the transmission of hereditary characteristics. See ◊genetic code.

chromosphere a layer of gas about 10,000 km deep above the visible surface of the Sun (the

chromatography

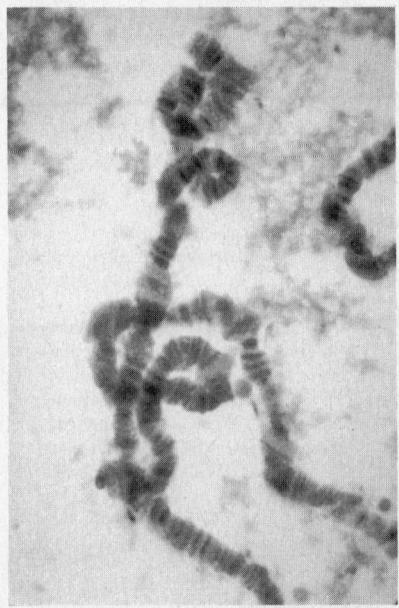

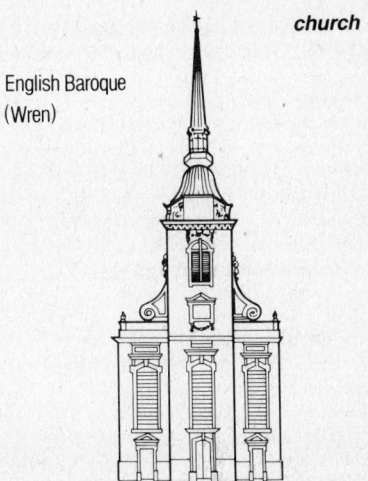

English Baroque (Wren)

than 2,000 years, and it is the national emblem of Japan. The first chrysanthemum was introduced into England in 1789, but the ox-eye daisy *Leucanthemum vulgare*, now placed in a closely related genus, and the corn marigold *Chrysanthemum segetum* are common weeds in Britain. Chrysanthemums may be grown from seed, but are more usually reproduced by cutting or division.

chrysolite an alternative name for the mineral ◊olivine.

chub freshwater fish *Leuciscus cephalus* of the carp family. Rather thickset and cylindrical, it grows up to 60 cm/2 ft but is usually less, is dark greenish or grey on the back, silvery yellow below with metallic flashs on the flanks. It lives generally in clean rivers, from Britain to the USSR.

Chubb Crater /tʃʌb/ crater discovered in 1950 by a prospector, F W Chubb, in N Quebec, 96 km/60 mi from Hudson Strait, Canada. Made by a meteor in prehistoric times, it is 411 m/1,350 ft deep, with its rim 168 m/550 ft above the local land level. In the centre is a lake (Crater Lake) 224 m/800 ft deep.

Chufu /ˌtʃuːˈfuː/ former name for ◊Qufu, town in Jinan province, China.

Chun Doo-Hwan /ˈtʃʌn ˌduːˈhwɑːn/ 1931–. South Korean military ruler from 1979, president from 1981.

Chun, trained in Korea and the USA, served as an army commander from 1967 and was in charge of military intelligence in 1979 when President ◊Park was assassinated by the chief of the Korean Central Intelligence Agency (KCIA). General Chun took charge of the KCIA and, in a coup, assumed control of the army and the South Korean government. In 1981 Chun was appointed president as head of the newly formed Democratic Justice Party.

Chungking /ˌtʃʊŋˈkɪŋ/ former name for ◊Chongqing, city in Sichuan province, China.

church a building designed as a Christian place of worship; see ◊Christianity.

Church /tʃɜːtʃ/ Frederick Edwin 1826–1900. American landscape artist of the Hudson River School. Noted for its effects of light and colour, his work was rediscovered after World War II. His painting *Icebergs* was found in a boys' remand home in Manchester, England, in 1979, after being lost for a hundred years.

Church Army religious organization within the Church of England founded in 1882 by Wilson Carlile (1847–1942), a businessman converted after the failure of his textile firm, who took orders in 1880. Originally intended for evangelical and social work in the Westminster slums, it developed along Salvation Army lines, and has done much work among ex-prisoners and for the soldiers of both world wars.

Churchill /ˈtʃɜːtʃɪl/ town in province of Manitoba, W Canada.

Churchill /ˈtʃɜːtʃɪl/ Caryl 1938– . British playwright, whose works, predominantly radical and feminist in tone, have been performed in association with the Royal Court Theatre, London, and include *Cloud Nine* 1979, *Top Girls* 1982, and *Serious Money* 1987.

Italian Romanesque

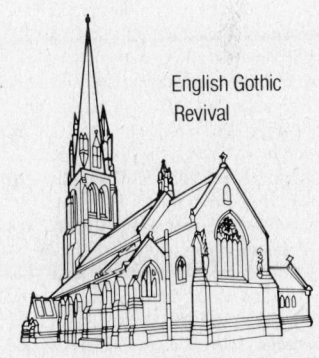

English Gothic Revival

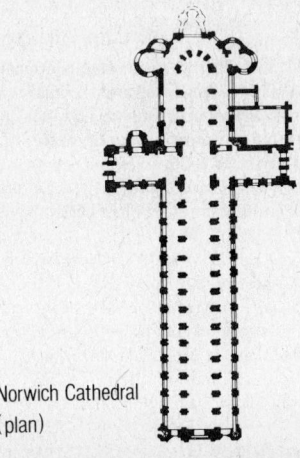

Norwich Cathedral (plan)

chromosome Chromosomes from *Drosophila sp*, the fruit fly magnified 400 times. Chromosomes are the structure in a cell nucleus responsible for the transmission of hereditary characteristics.

photosphere). Its name means 'colour sphere', because it appears pinkish-red during ◊eclipses of the Sun. The colour is caused by hydrogen gas of which the chromsphere is mostly composed.

chronometer an instrument for measuring equal intervals of time with the greatest accuracy, especially one used for determining position in navigation. John Harrison in England built the first accurate marine chronometer in 1761, capable of an accuracy of half a minute a year.

chrysanthemum plant of the family Compositae, with about 200 species, with many cultivated varieties, and there is uncertainty as to the wild species from which they have been evolved. In the Far East the common chrysanthemum has been cultivated for more

Churchill /'tʃɜːtʃɪl/ Randolph Henry Spencer 1849–1895. British Conservative politician. Born at Blenheim, son of the 7th duke of Marlborough, he entered Parliament in 1874. In 1880 he formed a Conservative group known as the Fourth Party with Drummond Wolff (1830 1908), J E Gorst (1835–1916), and Arthur Balfour, and in 1885 his policy of Tory democracy was widely accepted by the party. In 1886 he became Chancellor of the Exchequer, but resigned within six months because he did not agree with the demands made on the Treasury by the War Office and the Admiralty.

Churchill /'tʃɜːtʃɪl/ Winston Leonard Spencer 1874–1965. British politician. A descendant of the great duke of Marlborough, he was born at Blenheim Palace on 30 Nov 1874, the elder son of Lord Randolph ◊Churchill. Educated at Harrow, he was commissioned in the Fourth Hussars in 1895 and saw active service in a series of minor campaigns. During the Boer War he was the *Morning Post's* war correspondent and made a dramatic escape from imprisonment in Pretoria. In 1900 he was elected Conservative Member of Parliament for Oldham, but he disagreed with Chamberlain's tariff-reform policy, and joined the Liberals. In 1908 Asquith made him president of the Board of Trade, where he introduced legislation for the establishment of labour exchanges. In 1910 he became home secretary.

In 1911 Asquith appointed him First Lord of the Admiralty with the instruction to put the fleet into a state of instant readiness for war. Churchill ordered naval mobilization on the eve of war without waiting for cabinet authority, and early in the war sent the Naval Brigade to Antwerp. His sponsorship of the Dardanelles operation led to his exclusion from the first coalition government formed in 1915. Until the autumn of 1916 he served in the trenches in France, but then resumed his parliamentary duties and was minister of munitions under Lloyd George in 1917, when he was concerned with the development of the tank. After the armistice he was secretary for war, 1918–21, and then as colonial secretary played a leading part in the establishment of the Irish Free State. During the postwar years he was active in support of the ◊Whites (anti-Bolshevik) generals in Russia.

In 1922–24 Churchill was out of Parliament. He left the Liberals in 1923, and in 1924 was returned for Epping as a Constitutionalist. Baldwin made him chancellor of the Exchequer, and he brought about Britain's return to the gold standard and was prominent in the defeat of the General Strike of 1926. In 1929–39 he was out of office as he disagreed with the Conservatives on India, rearmament, and Chamberlain's policy of appeasement.

On the first day of World War II he went back to his old post at the Admiralty, and there he remained until 10 May 1940, when he was called to the premiership as head of an all-party administration. On 13 May he made his historic 'blood, tears, toil and sweat' speech to the House of Commons. Another significant turning point was his broadcast announcement on the evening of 22 Jun 1941 that Britain was allying itself with the USSR. He had a close relationship with President Roosevelt of the USA, and in Aug 1941 concluded the ◊Atlantic Charter with him. On 20 Dec 1941 he addressed a joint session of the US Congress. He travelled to Washington, Casablanca, Cairo, Moscow, and Tehran, meeting the other great leaders of the Allied war effort; and at Christmas 1944 he made a dramatic flight to Athens to avert civil war in Greece. In Feb 1945 he met Stalin and Roosevelt in the Crimea, and agreed on the final plans for victory. On 8 May he announced the unconditional surrender of Germany.

On 23 May 1945 the coalition was dissolved, and Churchill formed a 'caretaker' government drawn mainly from the Conservatives. Defeated in the general election in July, he resigned office to become leader of the opposition until the general election of Oct 1951 brought his return to power as prime minister. He received the Order of Merit in 1946, and was created Knight of the Garter in 1953. In Apr 1955 he resigned. He won the Nobel Prize for Literature in 1953. He was buried at Bladon, near Blenheim Palace, and his home from 1922, Chartwell in Kent, was opened as a museum.

In 1908 Churchill married Clementine Hozier (1885–1977), in 1965 created a life peeress as Lady Spencer-Churchill. Their son *Randolph Churchill* (1911–68), Conservative MP 1940–45, was a journalist and author of studies of Eden 1959 and Derby 1960.

Churchill A VE day portrait of British politician Winston Churchill taken in his study in 1945. During World War II he inspired the nation with his powerful oratory and courageous leadership.

Church of England the established form of ◊Christianity in England; member of the ◊Anglican Communion.

Church of Scotland the established form of ◊Christianity in Scotland, first recognized by the State in 1560.

Chuvash /'tʃuːvæʃ/ autonomous Soviet Socialist Republic of the USSR. It lies W of the Volga, 560 km/350 mi E of Moscow. Population (1982) 1,313,000. Area 18,300 sq km /7,100 sq mi. The capital is Cheboksary, population (1985) 389,000. Lumbering and grain-growing are important and there are phosphate and limestone deposits, and electrical and engineering industries.

CIA abbreviation for US ◊Central Intelligence Agency.

Ciano /'tʃɑːnəʊ/ Galeazzo 1903–1944. Italian Fascist politician. Son-in-law of Mussolini, he was Foreign Minister 1936–43, when his loyalty became suspect. He voted against Mussolini at the meeting of the Grand Council on 25 July which overthrew the dictator, and was tried for treason and shot by the Fascists.

Cibachrome in photography, a process of printing directly from transparencies introduced in 1963, now marketed by Ilford UK Ltd. Distinguished by rich, saturated colours, it can be home-processed and is one of the most permanent processes.

cicada type of insect, ◊bug of the family Cicadidae. Most species are tropical, but a few occur in Europe, including one found in the New Forest, England, the rare *Cicadetta montana* about 2 cm/0.8 in long. Young cicadas live underground, for up to 17 years in some species. The adults live on trees, whose juices they suck, and the males produce a loud, almost continuous, chirping by vibrating membranes in resonating cavities in the abdomen.

Cicero /'sɪsərəʊ/ Marcus Tullius 106–43 BC. Roman orator, writer, and statesman. Born in Arpinum, he became an advocate in Rome, spent three years in Greece studying oratory, and after the dictator Sulla's death distinguished himself in Rome on the side of the popular party. In 63 BC he was appointed consul; later in the year he saved the Republic by exposing Catiline's conspiracy in four major orations. When the First Triumvirate of Caesar, Crassus, and Pompey was formed in 59, Cicero was exiled, and devoted himself to literature. On the outbreak of the Civil War in 49 he followed Pompey to Greece, but in 48 returned to Italy where he was well treated by Caesar. After the Caesar's assassination in 44 BC he took the lead in the Senate in an attempt to restore the republican form of government and in 14 great speeches he supported Octavian (the future Augustus) and denounced Mark Antony. These speeches are known as the Philippics after the denunciations of King Philip of Macedon by Demosthenes in the 4th century BC. In the autumn of 43, Antony and Octavian came to terms and Cicero was killed while trying to escape to the East.

As a statesman, Cicero attempted unsuccessfully to carry out a moderate policy. His influence on the future of literature was immense. His speeches were recorded as models of Latin prose, and his philosophical essays are full of common sense and practical sympathies. His letters refer to his wives, both of whom he divorced, and his daughter Tullia, who died young.

cichlid freshwater fish of the family Cichlidae. Cichlids are somewhat perch-like, but

Cicero Sculpture of Roman statesman and writer Cicero. His informal letters, with their references to his wives – both of whom he divorced – and to his beloved daughter, Tullia, who died while still a young woman, show the human side of the public figure.

differ in several characters, such as having a single nostril on each side instead of two. A large group of more than 1000 species found mainly in S and Central America and Africa, a few in India, they are mostly predatory fishes, and have deep bodies, flattened from side to side so that some are almost disc shaped. Many are territorial in the breeding season and may show care of the young. The *discus fish Symphysodon* produces a skin secretion on which the young feed. Other cichlids, such as those of the genus *Tilapia* brood their young in the mouth. Many cichlids have interesting coloration and are popular as aquarium fishes.

Cid /sɪd/ Rodrigo Diaz de Bivar 1040–1099. Legendary Spanish hero, nicknamed *El Cid* ('the lord') by the Moors. Born in Castile of a noble family, he fought against the King at Navarre, and won his nickname 'el Campeadar' (the Champion) by killing the Navarrese champion in single combat. Essentially a mercenary, fighting with or against the Moors, he died while defending Valencia against them, and in subsequent romances became Spain's national hero.

cider fermented drink made from the juice of the apple. As a beverage it has been known for more than 2,000 years, and for many centuries it has been a popular drink in France and England, which are now its main centres of production. The French output is by far the greater, mainly from Normandy and Brittany. In a good year about 30 million gallons are produced in Britain. The West of England from Hereford to Devon has long been famous for its cider. Most of the apple crop is sold to factories in the region and also in Kent and Norfolk. In the USA the term

cider usually refers to unfermented (non-alcoholic) apple juice.

Cienfuegos /ˌsiːenˈfweɪɡɒs/ port and naval base in Cuba; with a tobacco trade; population (1981) 235,293.

Cierva /θiˈeəvə/ Juan de la 1895–1936. Spanish engineer. In trying to produce an aircraft which would not stall and could fly slowly, he invented the autogyro, the forerunner of the helicopter, but differing from it in having unpowered rotors which revolve freely.

cigar originally a sheath of palm leaves filled with tobacco, smoked by the Indians of Central and N America. The modern cigar is a compact roll of tobacco leaves. Cigar smoking was introduced into Spain soon after the discovery of America, and then spread all over Europe. The first cigar factory was opened in Hamburg in 1788, and about that time cigar smoking became popular in England. The first cigars were made by hand – as still are the more expensive cigars, including most of those made in Cuba – but in the USA from about the 1850s various machine methods were employed. From about 1890 cigar smoking was gradually supplanted in popularity in England by cigarette smoking.

cigarette literally, a little cigar. The first cigarettes were the *papelitos* smoked in S America about 1750. The habit spread to Spain, and then throughout the world, and is today the most general form of tobacco ◊smoking. In some countries, through the tax on tobacco, smokers contribute a large part of the national revenue. Following the establishment of a direct link between cigarette smoking and lung cancer in the 1960s, there was concentration by manufacturers on filtering harmful substances, but not with any proven success. In many countries, including the UK, and the USA, governments ban the advertising of cigarettes on television and issue health warnings on cigarette packets, and antismoking organizations campaign to reduce the number of smokers.

cigarette cards card included in packets of cigarettes, bearing a printed view, drawing, portrait, etc. Cigarette cards originated in the USA in the 1870s and are now popular collectors' items.

cilium small thread-like organ on the surface of some cells, composed of a number of contractile fibres which produce rhythmic waving movement. Some single-celled organisms move by means of waving cilia. In multicellular animals they keep lubricated surfaces clear of debris, as in the air passages of many animals. They also move food in the digestive tracts of some invertebrates.

Cimabue /ˌtʃiːməˈbuːeɪ/ Giovanni. Pseudonym of Italian painter Cenni de Peppi c 1240–1302. The master of ◊Giotto, he was styled the 'father of Italian painting'. Among the best-known works attributed to him are a *Madonna and Child* in the Uffizi, Florence, and other paintings of the same subject in the Louvre, Paris, and the National Gallery, London. Cimabue was one of the first artists to paint from a living model.

Cimarosa /ˌtʃiːməˈrəuzə/ Domenico 1749–1801. Italian composer of operas

extremely popular in their day, which include *Il matrimonio segreto/The Secret Marriage* 1792.

Cimino /tʃɪˈmiːnəu/ Michael 1943– . American film director, who established his reputation with *The Deer Hunter* 1978 (which won five Academy Awards). His other films include *Heaven's Gate* 1981, and *The Year of the Dragon* 1986.

cinchona shrub or tree belonging to the family Rubiaceae and growing wild in the Andes. From the bark of some species is produced ◊quinine, and its culture has been introduced into India, Sri Lanka, the Philippines, and Indonesia, with marked success.

Cincinnati /ˌsɪnsɪˈnæti/ city and port in Ohio, USA, on the Ohio river. Population (1980) 385,457. Founded in 1788, it became a city in 1819. It attracted large numbers of European immigrants, particularly Germans, during the 19th century. It has a university, and a major symphony orchestra; there is also a Roman Catholic university. Among the chief industries are machine-tool, clothing, and furniture making, and meat-packing.

Cincinnatus /ˌsɪnsɪˈnɑːtəs/ Lucius Quintus, lived 5th century BC. Early Roman general, known for his frugal simplicity. Appointed dictator in 458 BC he defeated the Aequi in a brief campaign, then resumed life as a yeoman farmer.

ciné camera a camera for taking 'moving pictures'. The whole concept of a 'moving picture', however, is a fallacy. There is no way of recording movement on film without blurring. What the ciné camera does is take a rapid sequence of still photographs – 24 frames (pictures) each second. When the pictures are projected one after the other at the same speed on to a screen, they appear to show movement. This is because of the 'persistence of vision' of our eyes -because they hold on to the image of one picture before the next one appears. The ciné camera differs from an ordinary still camera in having a motor that winds on the film continuously. But the film is held still by a claw mechanism while each frame is exposed. When the film is moved between frames, a semicircular disc slides between the lens and the film and prevents exposure.

cinema a modern form of art and entertainment, consisting of 'moving pictures' projected on to a screen. Cinema borrows from the other arts, such as music, drama, and literature, but is entirely dependent for its origins on technological developments, including the technology of ◊film.

The first moving pictures were shown in the 1890s: Edison persuaded James J Corbett (1866–1933), American world boxing champion 1892–97, to act a boxing match for a film. Lumière in France; R W Paul in England; Latham in the USA and others were making moving pictures of a few minutes' duration of actual events (for example, *The Derby*, shown in London, on the evening of the race, 1896), and of simple scenes such as a train coming into a station.

For a number of years, films even of 'indoor' happenings were 'shot' out of doors by daylight – and Hollywood's sunny climate was the basis of its outstanding success as a centre of film production, though the first film studio was Edison's at Fort Lee, New Jersey. In England, the pioneer company of Cricks and Martin set up a studio at Mitcham (where a romantic domestic drama, *For Baby's Sake*, was made in 1908).

D W ◊Griffith, the great American director, revolutionized film technique and made it in essentials what it is today. He introduced, for example, the close-up, the flashback, the fade-out and the fade-in. His first 'epic' was *The Birth of a Nation* (1915), and his second, *Intolerance*, with spectacular scenes in the Babylonian section, followed in 1916.

At first, the players' names were considered of no importance, though one who appeared nameless in *The Great Train Robbery*, G M Anderson, afterwards became famous as 'Bronco Billy' in a series of cowboy films – the first 'Westerns'. The first 'movie' performer to become a name was Mary Pickford – cinemagoers found this young actress so attractive that they insisted on knowing who she was; and in the Hollywood of the 1920s – helped to pre-eminence by World War I which virtually stopped film production in Europe – many stars were created: Rudolph Valentino, Douglas Fairbanks Sr, Lillian Gish, Gloria Swanson, Richard Barthelmess, and Greta Garbo outstanding among dramatic actors; Charles Chaplin, Harry Langdon, Buster Keaton, Harold Lloyd among comedians.

Concern for artistry began with Griffith; but developed in Europe, particularly the USSR and Germany, where directors exploited film's artistic possibilities, during both the silent and the sound era. Silent films were never completely silent; there was always a musical background, integral to the film, whether played by a solo pianist in a suburban cinema, or a 100-piece orchestra in a big city theatre. The arrival of sound films (*The Jazz Singer* 1927), seen at first as having only novelty value, soon brought about a wider perspective and greater artistic possibilities through the combination of sight and sound. Among the directors who succeeded were Jean Renoir in France, Lang and Murnau in Germany, Hitchcock in Britain and the USA, and Pudovkin and Eisenstein in the USSR. After World War II Japanese films were first seen in the West (although the industry dates back to the silent days), and India developed a thriving cinema industry.

Apart from story films, the industry produced news films: 'documentaries', depicting factual life, of which the pioneers were the American Robert Flaherty (*Nanook of the North*, 1920, *Man of Aran*, 1932–34) and the Scottish John Grierson (for example, *Drifters*, 1929, *Night Mail*, 1936); cartoon films, which achieved their first success with Patrick Sullivan's Felix the Cat (1917), later surpassed in popularity by Walt Disney's Mickey Mouse (1937).

By the 1960s, increasing competition from television, perceived at the time as a threat to the existence of cinema, led the film industry both to make films for the new medium, and to exploit areas of sexuality and violence considered unsuitable for family television viewing, for example, *Last Tango in Paris* 1973. A distinction

was usually made by critics between 'art' films and 'popular' films: the latter included such genres as the Chinese 'western' or kung-fu film, which had a vogue in the 1970s, and films controversial for the amount of violence depicted; the theme of the loner who takes the law into his own hands, epitomized by the character Rambo as played by Sylvester Stallone, spawned a number of imitators in the 1980s. Another popular genre was science fiction, such as *Star Wars* 1977, *Close Encounters of the Third Kind* 1977, and *ET* 1982, with expensive special effects. By the late 1980s cinema both as art and as pure entertainment seemed to be undergoing a revival, partly aided by the growth over the preceding decade of the video industry, which made major films widely available for viewing at home.

CinemaScope trade name copyrighted by Twentieth Century Fox for a wide-screen process using anamorphic lenses, in which images are compressed during filming and then extended during projection over an area wider than the normal screen. The first film to be made in CinemaScope was *The Robe* 1953.

cinema vérité (French 'cinema truth') a style of filmmaking that aims to capture truth on film by observing, recording, and presenting real events and situations as they occur without exercising any directorial, editorial, or technical control.

Cinerama a wide-screen process devised in 1937 by Fred Waller of Paramount's special-effects department. Originally three 35-mm cameras and three projectors were used to record and project a single image. Three aspects of the image were recorded and then projected on a large curved screen with the result that the images blended together to produce an illusion of vastness. The original system underwent many improvements until the release of the first Cinerama story film *How the West Was Won* 1962. It was eventually abandoned in favour of a single-lens 70-mm process.

cinnabar mercuric sulphide, HgS, the only important ore of mercury. It is deposited in veins and impregnations near recent volcanic rocks and hot springs. It is found in Spain (Almaden), the USA (California), Peru, Italy and Yugoslavia. The mineral itself is used as a pigment, commonly known as vermilion

cinnamon bark of a tree *Cinnamomum zeylanicum* grown in India and Sri Lanka. The bark is ground to make the spice used in curries and confectionery. Oil of cinnamon is obtained from waste bark, and is used as flavouring in food and medicine.

cinquefoil plant of a group in the genus *Potentilla* in the rose family Rosaceae. The typical species *Potentilla reptans*, is a creeping perennial, widely distributed throughout the British Isles, growing in pastures and meadows and on banks.

cinque ports /sɪŋk/ group of ports in S England, originally five, Sandwich, Dover, Hythe, Romney, and Hastings, later including Rye, Winchelsea and others. Probably founded in Roman times, they rose to importance after the Norman conquest, and until the end of the

15th century were bound to supply the ships and men necessary against invasion. The office of Lord Warden survives as an honorary distinction (Churchill 1941–65, Menzies 1965–78, the Queen Mother from 1979). The official residence is Walmer Castle.

circadian rhythm the metabolic rhythm found in most organisms, which coincides with the 24 hour day, but may be slightly longer or shorter. The most familiar manifestation of this rhythm is the regular cycle of sleeping and waking, but body temperature and the concentration of many ◊hormones that influence mood and behaviour also vary over the day. In humans, alteration of habits (e.g. a change from day-shift to night-shift working or rapid travel by plane round the world) may result in the circadian rhythm being out of phase with actual activity patterns; as a result, the person may feel out of sorts until the body's circadian rhythm has had time to adjust. See also ◊biological clock and ◊jetlag.

Circassia /sə'kæsiə/ former name of an area of the N Caucasus, ceded to Russia by Turkey in 1829 and now part of the Karachayevo-Cherkess region of the USSR.

Circe in Greek mythology, an enchantress. In the *Odyssey* of Homer she turned the followers of Odysseus into pigs when she held their leader captive.

circle path followed by a point which moves so as to keep a constant distance, the *radius*, from a fixed point, the *centre*. The longest distance from one side of a circle to the other, called the *diameter*, is thus twice the radius. The ratio of the distance all the way round the circle – the *circumference* – to the diameter is an ◊irrational number called π (*pi*), roughly equal to 3.14159. A circle of diameter d has a circumference C equal to πd, or $C = 2\pi r$ and an area $A = \pi r^2$. If a circle is divided up by two radii, then the resulting divisions are termed major and minor *sectors*. The area of a circle (πr^2) can be shown by dividing a circle into very thin sectors and reassembling them to make an approximate rectangle.

circuit breaker a switching device designed to protect an electric circuit from excessive current. It has the same action as a ◊fuse. Many houses now have a circuit-breaker between the incoming mains supply and the domestic circuits. They usually work by means of ◊solenoids. The circuit-breakers at electricity generating stations have to be specially designed to prevent dangerous arcing when the high voltage supply is switched off. They may use an air blast or oil immersion to quench the arc.

circuits in England and Wales the periodic travels by High Court and Circuit Judges to try civil and criminal cases at centres (graded as first, second, and third-tier) on six circuits (Midland and Oxford, N Eastern, Northern, S Eastern, Wales and Chester, and Western). In the USA the Court of Appeals sits in ten judicial circuits – hence circuit courts – and Washington DC.

circulatory system the system of vessels ramifying through an animal's body, carrying ◊blood (or other circulatory fluid) which transports essential substances to and from the

CINEMA CHRONOLOGY

1826-34 Various machines were invented to show moving images: the stroboscope, zoetrope, and thaumatrope.

1872 Eadweard Muybridge demonstrated movement of horses' legs using 24 cameras.

1877 Invention of Praxinoscope; developed as a projector of successive images on screen in 1879 in France.

1878-95 Marey, a French physiologist, developed various forms of camera for recording human and animal movements.

1887 Augustin le Prince produced the first series of images on a perforated film; Thomas Edison, having developed the phonograph, took the first steps in developing a motion-picture recording and reproducing device to accompany recorded sound.

1888 William Friese-Green showed the first celluloid film and patented a movie camera.

1889 Edison invented 35mm film.

1890-94 Edison, using perforated film, perfected his Kinetograph camera and Kinetoscope individual viewer; developed commercially in New York, London, and Paris.

1895 The Lumière brothers, Auguste (1862-1954) and Louis (1864-1948), projected, to a paying audience, a film of a train arriving at a station. Some of the audience fled in terror.

1896 Pathe introduced the Berliner gramophone, using discs in synchronization with film. Lack of amplification, however, made the performances ineffective.

1899 Edison tried to improve amplification by using banks of phonographs.

1900 Attempts to synchronize film and disc were made by Gaumont in France and Goldschmidt in Germany, leading later to the American Vitaphone system.

1902 Georges Méliès (1861–1938) made *Le Voyage dans la lune/A Trip to the Moon.*

1903 The first 'western' was made in the USA: *The Great Train Robbery* by Edwin S Porter.

1906 The earliest colour film (Kinemacolor) was patented in Britain by George Albert Smith.

1908-11 In France, Emile Cohl experimented with film animation.

1910 With the dominating influence of the Hollywood Studios, film actors and actresses began to be recognized as international stars.

1912 In Britain, Eugene Lauste designed experimental 'sound on film' systems.

1914-18 Full newsreel coverage of World War I.

1915 *The Birth of a Nation,* D W Griffith's epic on the American civil war, was released in the USA.

1918-19 A sound system called Tri-Ergon was developed in Germany which led to sound being recorded on film photographically. The photography of sound was also developed by Lee De Forrest in his Phonofilm system.

1923 The first sound film (as Phonofilm) was demonstrated.

1927 Release of the first major sound film, *The Jazz Singer,* Warners in New York. The first Academy Awards (Oscars) were given.

1928 Walt Disney released his first Mickey Mouse cartoon, *Steamboat Willie.*

1932 Technicolor (three-colour) process was used for a Walt Disney cartoon film.

1952 Cinerama (wide-screen presentation) was introduced in New York.

1953 Commercial 3-D (three-dimensional cinema) and wide screen Cinemascope were launched in the USA.

1976-77 Major films became widely available on video for viewing at home.

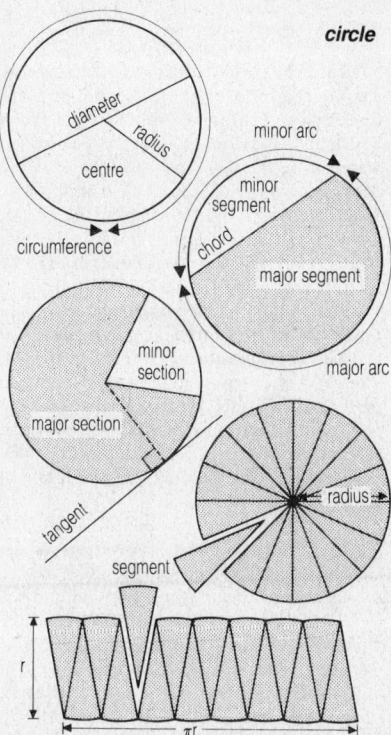

circle

different parts of the body. Except for simple animals such as sponges and coelenterates (including jellyfish, sea anemones, and corals), all animals have a circulatory system. In some small invertebrates (animals with no backbone) normal body movements circulate the fluid, but most animals have a ◊heart or hearts to pump the blood. Two distinct types of circulatory system are found in invertebrates. In the **open system**, as in snails and slugs, the blood (more correctly called ◊haemolymph) passes from the ◊arteries into a body cavity (the haemocoel) and from here is gradually returned to the heart, via the gills, by other blood vessels. In the **closed system** of earthworms, blood flows directly from the main artery to the main vein, via smaller lateral vessels in each body segment. Vertebrates, too, have a closed system with a network of tiny ◊capillaries carrying the blood from arteries to ◊veins. In fish, the circulation is single, blood passing once around the body before returning to a two-chambered heart. In birds and mammals the circulation is double, blood passing to the lungs and back to the heart before circulating around the remainder of the body. In all vertebrates, blood flows in one direction. Valves in the heart, large arteries and veins prevent back-flow, and the muscular walls of the arteries assist in pushing the blood around the body.

circumcision removal of a part of the foreskin of the penis. It is a religious ritual practiced by Jews and Muslims and, to some extent, Australian aboriginal peoples. All Jewish boys must be circumcised on the eighth day after birth as a reminder of the covenant God made with Abraham. Circumcision is also occasionally performed on medical grounds. Female 'circumcision', which includes removal of the clitoris, is performed among some peoples and forms part of a mutilatory method of ensuring the virginity of girls before marriage; it has been illegal in the UK since 1985.

Circumcision, Feast of Roman Catholic and Anglican religious festival, celebrated annually on 1 Jan in commemoration of Christ's circumcision.

circumference in geometry, the curved line that encloses a plane figure, for example, a circle or an ellipse. Its length varies according to the nature of the curve, and may be ascertained by the appropriate formula. Thus the circumference of a circle is $2\pi r$, where r is the radius and $\pi = 3.1415927$ ... or roughly **22/7**.

circumnavigation sailing round the world. The first ship to do so was the *Victoria*, one of the Spanish squadron of five vessels that sailed from Seville in Aug 1519 under Magellan. Four vessels were lost on the way, but the *Victoria* arrived back in Spain in Sept 1522 under Cano. Magellan himself did not complete the voyage, as he died in the Philippines in 1521. The first English circumnavigator was Drake in 1577–80 in the Golden Hind.

circus (Latin 'circle') originally, in Roman times, an arena for chariot races and gladiatorial combats. In modern times, it is an entertainment, often held in a large tent or 'big top', involving performing animals, acrobats and clowns. In 1897 the American Phineas Taylor ◊Barnum created the 'Greatest Show on Earth' which included a circus, menagerie and 'freaks', all transported in 100 rail cars.

Cirencester /'saɪrənˌsestə/ town in Gloucestershire, England, the 'capital' of the Cotswolds; population (1981) 15,620. It was the second largest town in Roman Britain, and has an amphitheatre which seated 8,000, and the Corinium Museum. The Royal Agricultural College is based here.

Cisalpine southern region of the Roman province of Gallia, that is N Italy; the northern, Transalpine Gaul, comprised modern Belgium, France, Netherlands and Switzerland. The *Cisalpine Republic* was the creation of Napoleon in N Italy in 1797, known as the Italian Republic 1802–04 and the Kingdom of Italy 1804–15.

Ciskei /ˌsɪs'kaɪ/ Republic of. Independent Black National State 1981
area 19,943 sq km/7,700 sq mi
capital Bisho
features one of the two homelands of the Xhosa people created by South Africa (the other is Transkei). It declared its independence in 1981, but this is not recognized by any other country
products pineapples, timber, metal products
population (1981) 2,100,000
language Xhosa
government president (Lennox Sebe from 1981), with legislative and executive councils.

Cistercian Order Roman Catholic monastic order established at Cîteaux in 1098 by St Robert de Champagne, abbot of Molesme, as a stricter form of the Benedictine order. Living mainly by agricultural labour, the Cistercians made many advances in farming methods in the Middle Ages. The *Trappists*, so-called from the original house at La Trappe in Normandy (founded by Dominique de Rancé in 1664), follow an even stricter version of the Cistercian rule (including the maintenance of silence, manual labour, and a vegetarian diet); their order has now been absorbed in the former.

cistron in genetics, the segment of ◊DNA that is required to synthesize a complete polypeptide chain. It is the molecular equivalent of a ◊gene.

CITES (*Convention on International Trade in Endangered Species.*) An international agreement signed by 81 countries under the auspices of the ◊IUCN to regulate the trade in ◊endangered species of animals and plants.

Because it was first signed in 1973 at Washington, DC, it is sometimes known as the *Washington Convention*. Member states agree not to permit the export or import of certain highly endangered species except for reasons connected with conservation or science. They also agree to notify a central IUCN monitoring unit known as TRAFFIC (Trades Records Analysis of Fauna and Flora in Commerce) of all exports of other species considered to be at risk.

cithara ancient musical instrument, resembling a lyre but with a flat back. It was strung with wire and plucked with a plectrum or (after the 16th century) with the fingers. The bandurria and laud, still popular in Spain, are instruments of the same type.

citizens' band (CB) shortrange radio communication (around 27 mHz) facility used by members of the public in USA and many European countries to chat or call for assistance in emergency. Use of a form of citizens' band called Open Channel (above 928 mHz) was legalized in the UK in 1980.

citizenship status as a member of a state. In most countries citizenship may be acquired either by birth or by naturalization. Under the British Nationality Act 1981, amended by the British Nationality (Falkland Islands) Act 1983, and the Hong Kong Act 1985, only a person designated as a British citizen has a right of abode in the UK, basically anyone born in the UK to a parent who is a British citizen, or to a parent who is lawfully settled in the UK. Four other categories of citizenship are defined: *British Dependent Territories citizenship*, *British Overseas citizenship*, *British subject*, and *Commonwealth citizen*. Rights of abode in the UK differ widely for each.

Citlaltepec (Aztec 'star mountain') highest mountain in Mexico, height 5,700 m/18,700 ft, N of the city of Orizaba (after which it is sometimes named). A volcano, it erupted 1687 but is now dormant.

citric acid an organic acid, $C_6H_8O_7$, widely distributed in the plant kingdom, especially in citrus fruits. It is a white crystalline powder with a sharp acid taste. At one time it was prepared from concentrated lemon juice, but now the main source is the fermentation of sugar with certain moulds.

citronella the lemon-scented oil obtained from the S Asian grass *Cymbopogon nardus*, used in cosmetics and insect-repellents.

citrus genus of trees and shrubs, belonging to the family Rutaceae, and found in the warmer parts of the world, particularly Asia. They are evergreen and aromatic, and several species (orange, lemon, lime, citron, grapefruit) are cultivated for fruit.

city generally, a large and and important town; in the UK one awarded the title by the Crown, and traditionally a cathedral town. In the ancient world cities were states in themselves. In the early Middle Ages, cities were usually those towns which were episcopal sees (seats of bishops).

City, The the financial centre of ◊London.

city technology college in the UK, a network of some 20 schools, financed jointly by the

government and industry, designed to teach technological subjects in inner–city areas to students aged 11–18. The scheme is a controversial one because of government plans to operate the schools independently of local education authorities. The first college opened in September 1987 at Solihull, West Midlands.

Ciudad Bolívar /θjuː'ðaːð bɒ'liːvɑː/ city in Venezuela, on the Orinoco, 400 km/250 mi from its mouth, and linked with Soledad across the river by the Angostura bridge (1967), the first to span the Orinoco. It was called Angostura 1824–49. Gold is mined in the vicinity. Population (1980) 115,000.

civet type of small to medium-sized carnivorous mammal found in Africa or Asia. There are various kinds of civet, not all very closely related, but all belonging to the family Viverridae, which also includes ◊*mongooses* and ◊*genets*. Distant relations of cats, members of this family generally have longer jaws and more teeth, some walk on the sole of the foot, and all have a scent gland in the inguinal region. Extracts from this gland are taken from the *African civet Civettictis civetta* to be used in perfumery. This civet is 70 cm/2.3 ft long, darkly spotted, and hunts small animals at night. As well as eating animal matter many species, especially *palm civets* such as the SE Asian *Arctogalidia trivirgata*, are fond of fruit.

civil aviation the operation of passenger and freight transport by air.
The ◊International Civil Aviation Organization (1947) has its headquarters in Montreal, and is a UN agency. In the UK there are about 170 airports, those for London (Heathrow and Gatwick) and Prestwick and Edinburgh being managed by the British Airports Authority (1965). The British Airways Board supervises British Airways, formerly British European Airways (BEA) and British Overseas Airways Corporation (BOAC); there are also independent companies.
Close co-operation is maintained with authorities in other countries, including the Federal Aviation Agency, which is responsible for development of aircraft, air navigation, traffic control and communications in the USA: the Civil Aeronautics Board is the American authority prescribing safety regulations and investigating accidents. There are no state airlines in the USA, although many of the private airlines are large. The world's largest airline is the government owned Aeroflot (USSR), which operates some 1,300 aircraft over 1 million km/620,000 mi of routes and carries some 110 million passengers a year.
With increasing traffic, control of air space is a major problem, and in 1963 Eurocontrol was established by Belgium, Britain, France, W Germany, Luxembourg, and the Netherlands to supervise both military and civil movement in the air space over member countries. There is also a tendency to co-ordinate services and pool services and other facilities between national airlines, for example, the establishment of Air Union by France (Air France), W Germany (Lufthansa), Italy (Alitalia) and Belgium (Sabena) in 1963.

civil defence organization of the civilian population of a state to mitigate the effects of enemy attack. In Britain the Ministry of Home Security was constituted 1939 to direct Air Raid Precautions in the World War II, the country being divided into 12 regions, each under a commissioner to act on behalf of the central government in the event of national communications systems being destroyed. Associated with the 'air-raid wardens' were ambulance and rescue parties, gas officers, breakdown gangs, etc., and a National Fire Service, based on existing local services, and about five million people enrolled as firewatchers and firefighters. The Civil Defence Corps and Auxiliary Fire Service were disbanded in 1968. In Britain a new structure of 'Home Defence' is now being created, in which the voluntary services, local authorities and the Territorial Army would co-operate.

In the USA the Office of Civil Defense (1961) of the Department of Defense has a staff college and three warning centres. Public shelter from nuclear fall-out is available for 160 million and special attention is given to incorporating shelter in all new constructions.

China has a comprehensive civil defence system, networks of tunnels in the cities enabling the population to escape nuclear fallout and reach the countryside, although not protecting against the actual blast.

civil disobedience term coined by ◊Thoreau in an essay of that name 1849 to mean the deliberate breaking of laws considered unjust, a form of nonviolent direct action. It was advocated by ◊Gandhi to prompt peaceful withdrawal of British power from India. Civil disobedience has since been employed by, for instance, the US ◊civil rights movement in the 1960s and the ◊peace movement in the 1980s.

civil engineering the branch of engineering that is concerned with the construction of roads, bridges, aqueducts, water-works, tunnels, canals, irrigation works, and harbours. The term is thought to have been used for the first time by British engineer John Smeaton in about 1750, to distinguish civilian from military engineering projects. The professional organization in Britain is the Institution of Civil Engineers, which was founded in 1818 and is the oldest engineering institution in the world.

civil list in Britain, the annual sum provided to meet the expenses of the sovereign (three-quarters being wages for the royal household); consort of a sovereign; children of a sovereign (except the Prince of Wales, who has the revenues from the Duchy of Cornwall); and widows of those children. Payments to other individual members of the royal family are covered by a contribution from the Queen. See also ◊Privy Purse. In the USA there is no equivalent of the civil list, but presidents and vice-presidents have salaries and allowances for expenses. Provision is also made for their widows, and ex-presidents are pensioned and have free office space, with free post and allowances for staff.

civil-list pensions pensions originally paid out of the sovereign's ◊civil list, but granted separately since the accession of Queen Victoria. They are paid to persons in need, who have just claims on the royal beneficence, who have rendered personal service to the crown, or who have rendered service to the public by their discoveries in science and attainments in literature, art, or the like. The recipients are nominated by the prime minister, and the list is approved by Parliament.

civil rights the personal rights of the individual citizen. In many countries they are specified (as in the Bill of Rights of the US Constitution) and guaranteed by law to ensure equal treatment for all citizens. In the USA, the struggle to obtain civil rights for former slaves (who did not have the rights of citizens under the Constitution) and their descendants, both through legislation and in practice, has been a major and continuing theme since the ◊Civil War. The *civil rights movement* is a general term for this aspect of US history, which includes a great number of diverse individuals and organizations. See *history* under ◊black.

civil service the body of administrative staff appointed (not elected) to carry out the policy of a government. In Britain, civil servants were originally in the personal service of the sovereign. They were recruited by patronage, and many of them had only nominal duties. The great increase in public expenditure during the Napoleonic Wars led to a move in Parliament for reform of the civil service, but it was not until 1854 that two civil servants, Charles Trevelyan and Stafford Northcote, issued a report as a result of which recruitment by competitive examination, carried out under the Civil Service Commission 1855, came into force. Its recommendations only began to be effective when nomination to the competitive examination was abolished in 1870. The two main divisions of the British civil service are the Home and Diplomatic services, the latter created in 1965 by amalgamation of the Foreign, Commonwealth and Trade Commission services. All are paid out of funds voted annually for the purpose by Parliament.

Since 1968 the Civil Service Department has been controlled by the prime minister (as minister for the civil service), but everyday supervision is exercised by the Lord Privy Seal. The Head of the Home Civil Service is also permanent secretary to the Civil Service Department. The present emphasis is on the professional specialist, and the Civil Service College (Sunningdale Park, Ascot) was established in 1970 to develop training. Members of the British civil service may not take an active part in politics, and do not change with the government. Their permanence gives those in the upper echelons an advantage over ministers who are in office for a comparatively brief time, and in the 1970s and 1980s it was alleged that ministerial policies in conflict with civil-service views tended to be blocked from being put into practice.

In the USA, until 1883 all civil service posts were given as rewards for political services, and changed hands with a change of the party in power (see ◊spoils system); the Pendleton Act 1883 established competitive examinations and permanency for certain posts, and that system has been steadily extended. The government agency concerned is the Civil Service Commission.

civil war war between rival groups within the same country.

Civil War, American war 1861–65 between the Southern or Confederate States in the USA (South Carolina, Mississippi, Florida, Alabama, Georgia, Louisiana, and Texas; joined later by Virginia, Arkansas, Tennessee, and North Carolina), and the northern or Federal States. The former wished to maintain their 'state rights', in particular the institution of slavery, and claimed the right to secede from the Union; the latter fought to maintain the Union.

1861 seven southern states set up the Confederate States of America (president Jefferson Davis) on 8 Feb; Fort Sumter, Charleston (see ◊Beauregard), captured 12–14 April; Lee (Confederate) was victorious at the first Battle of Bull Run 21 July.

1862 Battle of Shiloh 6–7 Apr was indecisive. Grant captured New Orleans in May, but the Confederates were again victorious at the second Battle of Bull Run 29–30 Aug. Lee's advance was then checked by ◊McClellan at Antietam on 17 Sept.

1863 the Emancipation Proclamation was issued by Lincoln on 1 Jan, freeing the slaves; Battle of Gettysburg (Union victory) on 1–4 Jul marked the turning point of the war; Lincoln delivered the *Gettysburg Address* at the dedication of the national cemetery on 19 Nov; Grant overran the Mississippi states, capturing Vicksburg on 4 July.

1864 Battles of Cold Harbor near Richmond, Virginia; in the first, on 27 Jun 1862, Lee defeated McClellan, and by the second Grant was delayed in his advance on Richmond. Sherman marched through Georgia to the sea, taking Atlanta on 1 Sept and Savannah on 22 Dec.

1865 Lee surrendered to Grant at Appomattox Court House on 9 April; Lincoln was assassinated on 14 April; last Confederate troops surrendered on 26 May. There were 359,528 Union dead and 258,000 Confederate dead. The war, and in particular its aftermath, when the South was occupied by Northern troops in the period known as ◊Reconstruction, left behind lasting bitterness. Industry prospered in the North while the economy of the South, which had been based on slavery, continued to decline.

Civil War, English in English history, the name usually applied to the struggle in the middle years of the 17th century following disputes between the king and the Royalist supporters (cavaliers) on one side, and the Parliamentarians (also called Roundheads) on the other. It falls into two parts. The first civil war began on 22 Aug 1642, when ◊Charles I raised his standard at Nottingham, and was ended on 5 May 1646, when he surrendered to the Scottish army. The most important battles were Edgehill (23 Oct 1642), which was indecisive, Marston Moor (2 July 1644) and Naseby (14 June 1645), both of which were Parliamentary victories won largely by ◊Cromwell. The second civil war was the

Royalist and Presbyterian rising of Mar to Aug 1648, which was soon crushed by Cromwell and his New Model Army.

Extensions of the civil war were Cromwell's invasion of Ireland 1649–50, and the campaign in which he defeated the Royalists under Prince Charles (◊Charles II) at Dunbar 1650, and Worcester 1651.

Civil War, Spanish war 1936–39 precipitated by a military revolt led by General ◊Franco against the Republican government. Franco's insurgents (Nationalists, who were supported by Fascist Italy and Nazi Germany) seized power in the S and NW, but were suppressed in areas such as Madrid and Barcelona by the workers' militia. The loyalists (Republicans) were aided by the USSR, and the volunteers of the International Brigade, for example, George Orwell.

1937 Bilbao and the Basque country were bombed into submission by the Nationalists;

1938 Catalonia was cut off from the main republican territory;

1939 Barcelona fell in Jan and Madrid in April, and Franco established a dictatorship.

cladistics a method of biological ◊classification (taxonomy) which uses a formal step-by-step procedure for objectively assessing the extent to which organisms share particular characters, and for assigning them to taxonomic groups. These taxonomic groups (◊species, ◊genera, families, etc.) are termed *clades*. Cladism developed in an attempt to make taxonomy less subjective, and to avoid assuming particular evolutionary relationships between taxonomic groups when attempting to assess their biological relationships. The problems with making such assumptions is that they may be wrong, so the whole taxonomic scheme is based on error. Cladistics has sometimes been wrongly interpreted as denying the theory of evolution.

cladode a flattened stem that is leaf-like in appearance and function. It is an adaptation to dry conditions because a stem contains fewer ◊stomata than a leaf, and water loss is thus minimized. The true leaves are usually reduced to spines or small scales. Examples of plants with cladodes are butcher's broom (*Ruscus aculeatus*), *Asparagus*, and certain cacti. Cladodes may bear flowers or fruit on their surface and this distinguishes them from leaves.

Clair /kleə/ René, pseudonym of René-Lucien Chomette 1898–1981. French film-maker, originally a poet, novelist, and journalist. His *Sous les Toits de Paris/Under the Roofs of Paris* 1930 was one of the first sound films.

clam name which is sometimes used to include any ◊bivalve mollusc, but used particularly of edible species, such as the N American **hard clam** *Venus mercenaria* used in clam chowder and whose shells were formerly used as money by N American Indians. The **giant clam** *Tridacna gigas* of the Indopacific may weigh, with the shell, 225 kg/500 lb.

clan (Gaelic *clann* 'children') social grouping based on ◊kinship, most familiar in the Highland clans of Scotland, theoretically each descended from a single ancestor from whom the name is derived, e.g. clan MacGregor ('son of Gregor').

cladistics

[cladistics cladogram showing: gibbons, orang-utans, gorrillas, chimpanzees, humans]

Rivalry between clans has often been bitter, and they played a large role in the Jacobite revolts of 1715 and 1745, after which their individual tartan highland dress was banned 1746–82.

Clapton /'klæptən/ Eric 1945– . English blues and rock guitarist, singer, and composer, member of the groups Yardbirds and Cream in the 1960s. One of the pioneers of heavy rock and an influence on younger musicians, he later adopted a more subdued style.

Clare /kleə/ County county in the Republic of Ireland, in the province of Munster; area 3,188 sq km/1,231 sq mi; population (1979) 85,000. Bounded on the W by the Atlantic, with a wild and dangerous coastline. Inland Clare is an undulating plain, with mountains on the E, W, and NW, the chief range being the Slieve Bernagh mountains in the SE rising to over 518 m/1,700 ft. The principal rivers are the Shannon and its tributary, the Fergus. There are over 100 lakes in the county, Lough Derg is on the E border. The county town is Ennis. At Ardnachusha, 5 km/3 mi N of Limerick, is the main power station of the Shannon hydroelectric installations. Shannon (Irish *Rineanna*) Airport, is here. The county is said to be named after Thomas de Clare, an Anglo-Norman settler to whom this area was granted in 1276.

Clare /kleə/ John 1793–1864. English poet. Born at Helpstone, near Peterborough, the son of a farm labourer, he spent most of his life in poverty. His *Poems of Rural Life* 1820, and *The Village Minstrel* 1821 were followed in 1827 by *The Shepherd's Calendar*. He was given an annuity from the Duke of Exeter and other patrons, but had to turn to work on the land and spent his last 20 years in Northampton asylum. His early life is described in his autobiography,

first published in 1931. Clare's work was little read until the 20th century, but he is now generally considered a poet of great power.

Clare The poet John Clare, by William Hilton in 1820. He spent his last years in a mental institution, where he wrote some of his most poignant poetry.

Clare, St /kleə/ c. 1194–1253. Christian saint. Born at Assisi, Italy, she became at 18 a follower of St Francis, who founded for her the convent of San Damiano. Here she gathered the first members of the Order of Poor Clares. She was canonized in 1255, and in 1958 she was proclaimed by Pius XII the patron saint of television, since in 1252 she saw from her convent sickbed the services celebrating Christmas in the Basilica of St Francis at Assisi. Her feast day is 12 Aug.

Clarendon, Constitutions of a code of laws accepted by the royal council of Henry II at Clarendon, near Salisbury, in 1164, and intended to regulate the relations between church and state. Thomas Becket refused to accept the Constitutions, and his ensuing quarrel with Henry II led to his murder.

Clarendon /'klærəndən/ Edward Hyde, 1st Earl of Clarendon 1609–1674. English politician and historian. He sat in the Short Parliament of 1640 and in the ◊Long Parliament, where he attacked Charles I's unconstitutional actions and supported the impeachment of Strafford. In 1641 he broke with the revolutionary party and became one of the royal advisers. When civil war began he followed Charles to Oxford, and was knighted and made chancellor of the Exchequer. On the king's defeat in 1646 he followed Prince Charles to Jersey, where he began his *History of the Rebellion* published 1702–04, which provides memorable portraits of his contemporaries.

In 1651 he became chief adviser to the exiled Charles II. At the Restoration he was created Earl of Clarendon, while his influence was further increased by the marriage of his daughter Anne to James, Duke of York. The 'Clarendon Code' was designed to secure the supremacy of the Church of England, but his moderation earned the hatred of the extremists, and finally he lost Charles's support by openly expressing disapproval of the king's private life. The disasters of 1667, when the Dutch sailed up the Medway, brought about his downfall. His last years were passed in exile in France. He died at Rouen, and was buried in Westminster Abbey.

Clarendon A 1666 portrait by David Logan of Edward Hyde, the 1st Earl of Clarendon. A politician and historian, he changed sides in the run-up to the Civil War in England. After first opposing Charles I's unconstitutional actions, he then became loyal to the Crown.

Clarendon /ˈklærəndən/ George William Frederick Villiers, 4th Earl of Clarendon 1800–1870. British Liberal diplomat. He was Lord-Lieutenant of Ireland 1847–52, and in 1853 became foreign secretary. His diplomatic skill was shown at the Congress of Paris 1855. He was again foreign secretary in 1865–66 and 1868–70, and achieved a settlement of the dispute between Britain and the USA over the ◊Alabama cruiser.

claret English term for the red wines of Bordeaux, since the 17th century.

clarinet a musical ◊woodwind instrument with a single reed, and a cylindrical tube, broadening at the end, developed in Germany in the 18th century. At the lower end of its range it has a rich 'woody' tone, which becomes increasingly brilliant toward the upper register. Equally effective both in fast 'virtuoso' passages and as an expressive melodic instrument, its potential was quickly exploited, and it became a regular member of the orchestra in Beethoven's time. Its ability both to blend and to contrast with other instruments made it popular for chamber music and as a solo instrument. It is also much used in military and concert bands, and as a jazz instrument. Music for the instrument is written in one key, for simplicity, but is played in a different key. There are various types of clarinet, varying in range, of which the bass clarinet has become a regular member of the orchestra.

Clark /klɑːk/ Jim 1936–1968. Scottish motor racing driver. He was world champion 1963 and 1965, and spent all his Formula One career with Colin Chapman's Lotus team. He won 25 Grand Prix races during his career, then a record. He was killed at Hockenheim, West Germany, during a Formula Two race.

Clark /klɑːk/ Joe (Joseph) Charles 1939– . Canadian Progressive Conservative politician. Born in Alberta, he became party leader in 1976, and in May 1979 defeated Trudeau at the polls to become the youngest prime minister in Canada's history. Following the rejection of his government's budget, he was himself defeated in a second election in Feb 1980.

Clark /klɑːk/ Kenneth, Lord Clark 1903–1983. British art historian and critic. As director of the National Gallery, London, 1934–45 he did much to improve relations with the public, and he popularized the arts through his television series *Civilisation* 1969. His books include *Leonardo da Vinci* 1939, *The Nude* 1955, and the autobiography *Another Part of the Wood* 1974.

Clark /klɑːk/ Mark Wayne 1896–1984. American soldier. Born in New York, he fought in France in World War I and between the wars held various military appointments in the USA. In 1942, during World War II, he became chief of staff for ground forces, led a successful secret mission by submarine to get information in North Africa preparatory to the Allied invasion, and commanded the Fifth Army in the invasion of Italy, where his wish to be the first to reach and capture Rome is said to have lead to unnecessary casualties among his troops. He succeeded Ridgway as commander-in-chief of the United Nations forces in Korea 1952–53. He was created an honorary KBE in 1944.

Clarke /klɑːk/ Arthur C(harles) 1917– . British writer and scientist, best known for his work on space exploration. He originated the plan for the modern system of communications satellites in 1945. His science-fiction works include *Childhood's End* 1953 and *2001: A Space Odyssey* 1968. He has also carried out underwater exploration on the coast of Sri Lanka, where he lives, and on the Great Barrier Reef.

Clarke /klɑːk/ Jeremiah 1659–1707. English composer. Organist at St Paul's, he composed 'The Prince of Denmark's March', a harpsichord piece which was arranged by Sir Henry ◊Wood as a 'Trumpet Voluntary' and wrongly attributed to Purcell. Clarke shot himself after an unhappy love affair.

Clarke /klɑːk/ Kenneth (Harry) 1940– . British Conservative politician. Clarke was politically active as a law student at Cambridge. He was elected to Parliament for Rushcliff, Nottinghamshire, in 1970. In 1982 he became a minister of state, in 1985, paymaster general, with special responsibility for employment and a seat in the cabinet, and in 1987 chancellor of the duchy of Lancaster. Clarke was once secretary of the left-of-centre Bow Group.

Clarke /klɑːk/ Marcus Andrew Hislop 1846–1881. Australian writer. Born in London, he went to Australia when he was 18, and worked as a journalist in Victoria. He wrote *For the Term of his Natural Life* in 1874, a novel dealing with life in the early Australian prison settlements.

Clarke orbit an alternative name for ◊geostationary orbit, an orbit 35,900 km/22 300 mi high, in which ◊satellites circle at the same speed as the earth turns. This orbit was first suggested by space writer Arthur C ◊Clarke in 1945.

Clarkson /ˈklɑːksən/ Thomas 1760–1846. British philanthropist. From 1785 he devoted himself to a campaign against slavery. He was one of the founders of the Anti-Slavery Society in 1823 and was largely responsible for the abolition of slavery in British colonies in 1833.

class in sociology, the main form of social stratification in industrial societies, based primarily on economic and occupational factors, but also referring to people's style of living or sense of group identity. Within the social sciences, class has been used both as a descriptive category and as the basis of theories about industrial society. The most widely used descriptive classification in the UK divides the population into five main classes. The main division is that between the manual and non-manual occupations. Such classifications have been widely criticized, however, on several grounds: that they reflect a middle-class bias that brain is superior to brawn; that they classify women according to their husband's occupation rather than their own; that they ignore the upper class, the owners of land and industry. Theories of class may see such social divisions either as a source of social stability (◊Durkheim) or social conflict (◊Marx).

class in biological classification, a group of related ◊orders. For example, all mammals belong to the class Mammalia and all birds to the class Aves. Among plants, all class names end in 'idae' (such as Asteridae) and among fungi in 'mycetes'; there are no equivalent conventions among animals. Related classes are grouped together in a ◊phylum.

Classicism in literature, music, and art, a style that emphasizes the qualities traditionally considered as characteristic of ancient Greek and Roman art, that is, reason, objectivity, restraint, and strict adherence to form. The term Classicism is often used to characterize the culture of 18th century Europe, and contrasted with the 19th century ◊Romanticism.

classification in biology, the arrangement of organisms into a hierarchy of groups, on the basis of their similarities in biochemical, anatomical or physiological characters. Species are assumed to share characters because they acquire them from a common ancestor. (Care is taken to exclude shared characteristics known to be due to ◊convergent evolution.) Such a classification is thus thought to mirror the evolutionary relationships between organisms. The basic grouping is a ◊species, several of which may constitute a ◊genus, which in turn are grouped into families, and so on up through orders, classes, phyla (or, in plants, divisions) to kingdoms. See also ◊cladistics.

clathrates compounds formed by small ◊molecules filling in the holes in the structural

CLASS

British Social Classes as classified by the Registrar-General

	Middle Class
I	professional occupations: accountant, lawyer
II	intermediate occupations: manager, senior administrator
IIIN	skilled occupations (non-manual): policeman, nurse

	Working Class
IIIM	skilled occupations (manual): plumber, electrician
IV	semi-skilled occupations: machinist, mechanic
V	unskilled occupations: dustman, cleaner

	Other
	residual groups: students, armed forces

lattice of another compound, for example, sulphur dioxide molecules in ice crystals. Clathrates are, therefore, intermediate between mixtures and compounds.

Claudel /klɔʊ'del/ Paul 1868–1955. French poet and dramatist. He entered the diplomatic service in 1892, and was ambassador to Tokyo, Washington and Brussels. A fervent Catholic, he was influenced by the Symbolists and achieved an effect of mystic allegory in such plays as *L'Annonce faite à Marie/Tidings Brought to Mary* 1912 and *Le Soulier de satin/The Satin Slipper* 1929, set in 16th-century Spain. His verse includes *Cinq Grandes Odes/Five Great Odes* 1910.

Claude Lorrain /'klɔud lɒ'ræŋ/ properly Claude Gellée 1600–1682. Landscape painter of the French school. Born in Lorraine, he established himself in Rome in 1627, where he executed several pictures for Pope Urban VIII. He was the first painter to specialize entirely in landscapes, of which he painted about 400, reducing the story-telling elements to small foreground figures, and is known for his ability to render light and the atmosphere of a place at a particular time of day. His *Liber Veritatis* contains some 200 drawings after his finished works, useful for dating.

Claudian /'klɔːdiən/ or Claudius Claudianus c. 370–404. Last of the great Latin poets of the Roman empire. He was probably born at Alexandria, and wrote official panegyrics, epigrams, and the epic *The Rape of Proserpine*.

Claudius /'klɔːdiəs/ 10 BC–54 AD. Nephew of ◊Tiberius, made Roman emperor by his troops in 41, after the murder of Caligula, though more inclined to scholarly pursuits. During his reign the Roman Empire was considerably extended, and in 43 he took part in the invasion of Britain. He was long dominated by his third wife, ◊Messalina, whom ultimately he had executed, and is thought to have been poisoned by his fourth wife, Agrippina the Younger.

Clausewitz /'klauzɔvɪts/ Karl von 1780–1831. Prussian soldier and writer on war, born near Magdeburg. He is known mainly for his book *Vom Kriege/On War* translated into English 1873, which gave a new philosophical foundation for the science of war, and put

Claudius One of the most intriguing of the Roman emperors, Claudius wrote historical works and an autobiography, none of which survives. This statue of the deified Claudius is from the Lateran Museum, Rome.

forward a conception of strategy which was dominant up to World War I.

Clausius /'klauziəs/ Rudolf Julius Emaneul 1822–1888. German physicist, one of the founders of the science of thermodynamics. In 1850 he enunciated its second law: heat cannot of itself pass from a colder to a hotter body.

claustrophobia a ◊phobia involving fear of enclosed spaces.

Claverhouse /'kleɪvəhaʊs/ John Graham, Viscount Dundee 1649–1689. Scottish soldier. Employed in the suppression of the ◊Covenanters, he was routed at Drumclog in 1679, but three weeks later won the battle of Bothwell Bridge, in which the rebellion was crushed. Until 1688 he was engaged in continued persecution and became known as 'Bloody Clavers', regarded by the Scottish people as a figure of evil. In 1688 his army supported James II and defeated the loyalist forces in the pass of Killiecrankie, but Claverhouse was mortally wounded.

Clausewitz The Prussian army officer Karl von Clausewitz is most famous for his writings on the theory and tactics of warfare. *Vom Kriege,* which puts forward a concept of military strategy, remains his best-known work.

clavichord stringed keyboard instrument, popular in Renaissance Europe and in 18th century Germany until the early 19th century. Notes are sounded by a metal blade striking the string. It was a forerunner of the pianoforte.

claw a hard, hooked pointed outgrowth of the digits of mammals, birds and some reptiles. Claws are composed of the protein keratin, and grow continuously from a bundle of cells in the lower skin layer. Hooves and ◊nails are modified structures with the same origin as claws.

clay /kleɪ/ a mud that has undergone a greater or lesser degree of consolidation. It may be white, grey, red, yellow, blueish, or black, and consists essentially of hydrated silicates of alumina, together with sand, lime, iron, oxides, magnesium, potassium, soda and organic substances. When moistened it is rendered plastic. It hardens on heating, which renders it impermeable. The more important clays are adobe, alluvial, building, brick, cement, china, ferruginous, fusible, refractory, vitrifiable and fireclays. Clays have an immense variety of uses, some of which, for example, pottery and bricks, date back to prehistoric times. According to international classification, in mechanical analysis of soil clay has a grain size less than 0.002 mm.

Clay /kleɪ/ Cassius. Original name of boxer Muhammad ◊Ali.

Clay /kleɪ/ Henry 1777–1852. American politician, a founder of the Republican party. He stood three times unsuccessfully for the presidency. He supported the war of 1812 against Britain, and tried to hold the Union together on the slavery issue by the Missouri Compromise of 1820. He was secretary of state 1825–29.

clef in music, the symbol used to indicate the pitch of the lines of the staff in musical notation.

cleft palate fissure of the roof of the mouth, often accompanied by a hare lip, the result of a genetic defect.

Cleisthenes /'klaɪsθəniːz/ ruler of Athens. Inspired by Solon, he is credited with the establishment of democracy in Athens in 507 BC.

cleistogamy the production of flowers which never fully open and are automatically self-fertilized. Cleistogamous flowers are often formed late in the year, after the production of normal flowers, or during a period of cold weather, as seen in several species of *Viola*.

Cleland /'kleland/ John 1709–1789. British author. Consul at Smyrna and one-time employee of the East India Company at Bombay, he wrote *Fanny Hill, the Memoirs of a Woman of Pleasure* 1748–49 to extract himself from the grip of his London creditors. His publisher made £10,000 from sales, of which the author received only 20 guineas. The book was considered immoral, and Cleland was called before the Privy Council, but was granted a pension to prevent his falling into more mischief.

clematis genus of temperate woody climbers with showy flowers, family Ranunculaceae; *traveller's joy* or *old man's beard*, *Clematis vitalba*, is the only British species, although many have been introduced, and hybrids bred.

Clemenceau /ˌklemɒn'səʊ/ Georges 1841–1929. French politician. Born in La Vendée, he was mayor of Montmartre, Paris, in the war of 1870, and in 1871 was elected a member of the National Assembly at Bordeaux. He was elected a deputy in 1876, and soon earned the nickname of 'The Tiger' on account of his ferocious attacks on politicians whom he disliked. At this time he was an extreme radical. In 1893 he lost his seat and spent the next ten years in journalism. He was prominent in defence of ◊Dreyfus. In 1902 he was elected senator for the Var, and henceforth was one of the most powerful politicians. He was prime minister 1906 09; and in 1917 at the most difficult point of World War I, he was again called to the premiership. His appointment of Foch as generalissimo was significant to the outcome of the war. Victory won, Clemenceau presided over the Peace Conference in Paris, but failed to secure for France the Rhine as a frontier. In 1920 he resigned, and withdrew his candidature for the presidency of the Republic for lack of support.

Clemens /'klemənz/ Samuel Langhorne, real name of the American writer Mark ◊Twain.

Clement VII /'klemənt/ 1478–1534. Illegitimate son of a brother of Lorenzo the Magnificent (see under ◊Medici), he was Pope 1523–34. He refused to allow the divorce of ◊Henry VIII and ◊Catherine of Aragon. He and Leo X commissioned monuments for the Medici chapel from ◊Michelangelo.

Clementi /kle'menti/ Muzio 1752–1832. Italian pianist and composer. He settled in London in 1782 as a teacher and then as proprietor of a successful pianoforte and music business. He was the founder of the new technique of piano-playing, and his series of studies *Gradus ad Parnassum* 1817 is still in use.

Clement of Alexandria /'klemənt/ c. 150–c. 215 AD. Greek theologian who applied Greek philosophical ideas to Christian doctrine, and was the teacher of ◊Origen.

Clement of Rome, St /'klemənt/ lived about 1st century AD. One of the early Christian leaders and writers known as the 'Fathers of the Church'. He lived in the late 1st century AD, and according to tradition he was the third or fourth bishop of Rome, and a disciple of St Peter. He wrote a letter addressed to the church at Corinth (First Epistle of Clement), and many other writings have been attributed to him.

Cleon /'kliːən/ an Athenian demagogue and military leader in the Peloponnesian War. After the death of Pericles, to whom he was opposed, he won power as representative of the commercial classes and leader of the party advocating a vigorous war policy. He was killed fighting the Spartans at Amphipolis.

Cleopatra /ˌkliːə'pætrə/ c. 68–30 BC. Queen of Egypt, the last ruler of the Macedonian Dynasty, which lasted from 323 BC until annexation by Rome in 31 BC. Upon the death of her father in 51 BC she ascended the throne in Alexandria together with her younger brother Ptolemy XII, whom she was expected to marry according to the tradition of the Pharoahs. In 49 BC Julius Caesar arrived in Egypt and she became his mistress, bore him a son, Caesarion, and returned with him to Rome. After Caesar's murder she returned to Alexandria and resumed her position as queen of Egypt. In 41 BC she met Mark Antony in Cilicia, who, after having married Octavia, sister of Octavian (the future ◊Augustus), in 40 BC, returned to Egypt to live in sumptuous magnificence with Cleopatra, who bore him three sons. In 32 BC open war broke out between Antony and Octavian. In the crucial battle of Actium 31 BC, fought at sea off the W coast of Greece, Cleopatra took to flight with her 60 Egyptian ships, whereupon Antony abandoned the struggle and followed her to Egypt; the next year they were besieged in Alexandria. Antony committed suicide, and Cleopatra killed herself by applying an asp to her bosom. Caesarion was put to death by Octavian. Cleopatra remains one of the great romantic figures of history.

Cleopatra's Needle each of two ancient Egyptian granite obelisks erected at Heliopolis 15th century BC by Thothmes III, and removed to Alexandria by Augustus about 14 BC – so, much older than Cleopatra's reign. One of the pair was taken to London in 1878 and erected on the Victoria Embankment; it is 21 mi/68.5 ft high. The other was given by the Khedive to USA, and erected in Central Park, New York, in 1881.

clerihew humorous verse form invented by Edmund Clerihew ◊Bentley, characterized by a first line consisting of a person's name. The four lines rhyme AABB, but the metre is often distorted for comic effect. An example, from Bentley's *Biography for Beginners* 1905, is: Sir Christopher Wren/ Said, 'I am going to dine with some men./ If anybody calls/ Say I am designing St Paul's'.

Clerk Maxwell /'klɑːk 'mækswel/ James. See ◊Maxwell.

Clermont-Ferrand /'kleəmɒŋ fe'rɒŋ/ city, capital of Puy-de-Dôme *département*, France. Its rubber industry is the largest in France; car tyres are manufactured. Other products include chemicals, preserves, foodstuffs, and clothing, and Clermont-Ferrand is an important agricultural market. The Gothic cathedral is 13th-century. Urban II ordered the First Crusade at a council here in 1095. Population (1983) 155,000.

Cleveland /'kliːvlənd/ county in NE England
area 583 sq km/225 sq mi
towns administrative headquarters Middlesbrough; Stockton on Tees, Billingham, Hartlepool
features river Tees; North Yorkshire Moors National Park
products Teesside, the industrial area at the mouth of the Tees, has Europe's largest steel complex (at Redcar) and chemical site (ICI, using gas and local potash), as well as an oil fuel terminal at Seal Sands and natural gas terminal at St Fergus, 12 miles south of Fraserburgh in the Grampians
population (1986) 561,300.

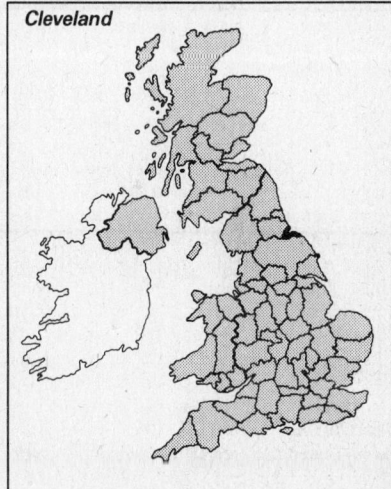

Cleveland

Cleveland /'kliːvlənd/ largest city of Ohio, USA, standing on Lake Erie at the mouth of the river Cuyahoga, where the iron ore from the Lake Superior region is brought to meet the coal from the mines in Ohio and Pennsylvania; population (1981) 574,000. Its chief industries centre round the many great iron and steel works; petroleum refining is also important.

Cleveland /'kliːvlənd/ (Stephen) Grover 1837–1908. 23rd and 24th president of the USA; notable as the first Democratic president elected after the Civil War, and as the only president to hold office for two non-consecutive terms 1885–89 and 1893–97. He attempted to check corruption in public life, and in 1895 settled the Venezuela dispute with Britain.

click-beetle type of ◊beetle which can regain its feet from lying on its back by jumping into the air and turning over, clicking as it does so.

climate weather conditions at a particular place over a period of time. Climate encompasses all the meteorological elements and the factors that influence them. The primary factors that determine the variations of climate over the surface of the earth are: (a) the effect of latitude and the tilt of the earth's axis to the plane of the orbit about the sun (66½°); (b) the difference between land and sea; (c) contours of the ground; and (d) location of the area in relation to ocean currents. The amount of heat received from the sun varies in different latitudes and at different times of the year. In the equatorial region the mean daily temperature of the air near the ground has no large seasonal variation. In the polar regions the temperature in the long winter, when there is no incoming solar radiation, falls far below the summer value. Climate types were first classified by Vladimir Köppen in 1918.

The temperature of the sea, and of the air above it, varies little in the course of day or night, while the surface of the land is rapidly cooled by radiation to a clear sky. In the same way the annual change of temperature is relatively small over the sea and great over the land. Thus the land is colder than the sea in winter and warmer in summer. Winds that blow from the sea are warm in winter and cool in summer, while winds from the central parts of continents are hot in summer and cold in winter.

On an average, air temperature falls off with height at a rate of 1°C/1.8°F per 90 m/300 ft. Thus places situated above mean sea level usually have lower temperatures than places at or near sea level. Even in equatorial regions, high mountains are snow-covered during the whole year. Rainfall is produced by the ascent of air. When an air current blows against a range of mountains so that it is forced to ascend over the high ground, it gives rainfall, the amount depending on the height of the ground and the dampness of the air.

The complexity of the distribution of land and sea, and the consequent complexity of the general circulation of the atmosphere, makes the distribution of the climate extremely complicated. Centred on the equator is a belt of tropical rain forest which may be either constantly wet or monsoonal, that is, seasonal with wet and dry seasons in each year. Bordering each side of this belt is a belt of savannah, with lighter rainfall and less dense vegetation. After this usually comes a transition through ◊steppe (semi-arid) to desert (arid), with a further transition through steppe to ◊Mediterranean climate with dry summer, followed by the moist temperate climate of middle latitudes. Next comes a zone of cold climate with moist winter, but where the desert extends into middle latitudes the zones of Mediterranean and moist temperate climates are missing, and the transition is from desert to a cold climate with moist winter. In the extreme east of Asia a cold climate with dry winters extends from about 70° N to 35° N. The polar caps have ◊tundra and ice-cap climates, with little or no precipitation. Catastrophic variations to climate may be caused by the impact of another planetary body, or clouds resulting from volcanic activity.

climax community an assemblage of plants and animals that is relatively stable in its environment (for example, oak woods in Britain). It is brought about by ecological

◊succession, and represents the point at which succession ceases to occur.

climax vegetation the state of equilibrium that is reached after a series of changes have occured in the vegetation of a particular habitat. It is the final stage in a ◊succession, where the structure and species of a habitat do not develop further, providing conditions remain unaltered.

clinical psychology discipline dealing with the understanding and treatment of health problems, particularly mental disorders. The main problems dealt with include ◊anxiety, ◊phobias, ◊depression, ◊obsessions, sexual and marital problems, ◊drug and alcohol dependence, childhood behavioural problems, ◊psychoses (such as ◊schizophrenia), ◊mental handicap and ◊brain damage (such as ◊dementia). Other areas of work include ◊forensic psychology (concerned with criminal behaviour) and health psychology. The main approaches include: *assessment procedures* which assess intelligence and cognition, for example, in detecting the effects of brain damage. Assessment procedures usually involve the use of psychometric tests. *Behavioural approaches* are methods of treatment which apply learning theories to clinical problems. ◊*Behaviour therapy* helps clients change unwanted behaviours (such as phobias, obsessions, sexual problems) and to develop new skills (such as improve social interactions). *Behaviour modification* relies on operant conditioning, and makes selective use of rewards (such as praise) to change behaviour. This is particularly useful for children, the mentally handicapped and for patients in institutions, such as mental hospitals. *Cognitive therapy* is a new approach to treating emotional problems, such as ◊anxiety and ◊depression, by teaching clients to change negative thoughts and attitudes. *Counselling*, developed by ◊Rogers, is widely used in order to help clients to solve their own problems. *Psychoanalysis*, as developed by ◊Freud and ◊Jung, is little used by clinical psychologists today. It emphasizes childhood conflicts in leading to adult problems.

clinometer hand-held ◊surveying instrument for measuring angles of slope.

Clio in Greek mythology, the inventor of epic poetry and history. One of the nine ◊Muses.

Clive /klaɪv/ Robert, Baron Clive 1725–1774. soldier and politician, adminstrator, known as Clive of India, who established British rule in India as against the French. Born at Market Drayton, in 1743 he became a writer in the East India Company's service in Madras and was given an ensign's commission. In 1751, during a dispute over the succession to the Carnatic in which the French took the side of one claimant and the British of the other, Clive marched from Madras with 500 men, seized Arcot, the capital of the Carnatic, defended it for seven weeks against 10,000 French and Indian troops, and then sallied out and relieved the British besieged in Trichinopoli. In 1753 Clive returned to England a national hero.
In 1755 he went back to India as a lieutenant-colonel and governor of Fort St David. In the next year the Nawab of Bengal, Suraj-ud-Dowlah,

seized Calcutta, and shut up 146 British prisoners in the 'black hole' where all but 23 perished (20 Jun 1756). In Feb 1757 Clive, with 1900 men, defeated the Nawab's army of 34,000 men outside Calcutta, and forced him to make peace. In Europe the Seven Years War had begun; and Clive, discovering that Suraj-ud-Dowlah intended to assist the French, set out from Chandernagore with 3,200 men, and on 23 Jun completely defeated the Nawab's army at Plassey. By this victory Bengal practically fell to the East India Company. In 1760 ill-health forced Clive to return to England. In 1762 he was created Baron Clive of Plassey. He returned to India in 1765 as governor of Bengal and commander-in-chief, and executed many reforms. He made many enemies, however, and on his return to England for the last time, in 1766, was threatened with impeachment. In 1772–73 a parliamentary enquiry was held and he was virtually acquitted, but he remained obsessed by the charges and committed suicide.

Clive Known as the legendary 'Clive of India', Robert Clive has been called the founder of the British Empire in India.

Cliveden /ˈklɪvdən/ country house of Lord Astor, in Buckinghamshire, N of Maidenhead on the Thames, a hotel from 1985. Lady Astor used it for politically influential house-parties.

cloaca the common opening of the digestive, urinary and reproductive tracts; a cloaca is found in all backboned animals (◊vertebrates) except the marsupial and placental mammals. The cloaca forms a chamber in which products can be stored before being voided from the body via a muscular opening.

clock any device that can be used for measuring the passage of time, though customarily a timepiece consisting of a train of wheels driven by a spring or weight controlled by a balance wheel or pendulum. The ◊watch is a portable clock. The purpose of a clock is to subdivide the day into smaller time intervals. In ancient Egypt the time during the day was measured by a shadow-clock, a primitive form of

◊sundial, and at night the water-clock was used. Up to the late 16th century the only clock available for use at sea was the sand-clock, of which the most familiar form is the hour-glass. The Royal Navy kept time by half-hour sand-glasses until 1820. During the Middle Ages various types of sundials were widely used, and portable sundials were in use from the 16th to the 18th century. Watches were invented in the 16th century – the first were made in Nuremberg shortly after 1500 – but it was not until the 19th century that they became cheap enough to be widely available.

The first known public clock was set up at Milan in 1353; the first in England was the Salisbury cathedral clock of 1386, which is still working. The time-keeping of both clocks and watches was revolutionized in the 17th century by the application of pendulums to clocks and of balance-springs to watches.

The marine chronometer is a precision timepiece of special design and of the finest workmanship, used at sea for giving Greenwich mean time (GMT). Electric timepieces were made possible by the discovery early in the last century of the magnetic effects of electric currents. One of the earliest and most satisfactory methods of electrical control of a clock was invented by Matthaeus Hipp in 1842. In the modern mains electric clock, the place of the pendulum or spring-controlled balance-wheel is taken by a small synchronous electric motor which counts up the alternations (frequency) of the mains electric supply, and then by a suitable train of wheels records the time by means of hands on a dial.

The quartz crystal clock (made possible by the ◊piezo-electric property of certain crystals) has great precision, with a short-term accuracy of about one-thousandth of a second per day. More accurate still is the atomic clock. This utilizes the natural resonance of certain atoms, for example, caesium, as a regulator control the frequency of a quartz crystal ◊oscillator. It is accurate to within one millionth of a second per day.

Biological clock. As early as the 18th century endogenous circadian cycles had been discovered, and by 1950 the existence of the circadian clock (see ◊Circadian rhythm) was widely recognized, especially when 'jetlag' was the consequence of a body's internal and external clocks being out of step. Except in organisms without a discrete nucleus, such as bacteria and the majority of algae, such clocks are common to all animals, and also to many plants, fungi and unicellular organisms. Some clocks may control several activities, but in higher organisms, there appears to be a series of clocks of graded importance. For example, although body temperature and activity cycles in human beings are normally 'set' to 24 hours, the two cycles may vary independently, showing that two clock mechanisms are here concerned, and yet other clocks control other functions. Research into the exact nature of these clocks is being directed into enzyme systems and membrane activity.

cloisonné ornamental technique in which strips of metal follow a pattern on a metal surface, and the interstices are filled with coloured ◊enamels.

cloister a convent or monastery, and more particularly a covered walk within these, often opening onto a courtyard.

Cloisters, The branch of the Metropolitan Museum of Art in Fort Tryon Park, New York. A number of medieval buildings transported to the USA from Europe have been carefully reassembled and medieval tapestries, pictures, and books, are among the exhibits.

clone group of cells or organisms arising by asexual reproduction from a single 'parent' individual. Clones therefore have exactly the same genetic make-up. Examples include a group of plants produced from cuttings from one other plant and, more recently, several animals produced from a single denucleated egg cell. The term has been adopted by computer technology, in which it describes a (non-existent) device that mimics an actual one to enable certain software programs to run correctly.

closed circuit television (CCTV) a localized ◊television system in which programmes are sent over relatively short distances, the camera, receiver and controls being linked by cable. Closed-circuit TV systems are used in department stores and large offices as a means of internal security, the cameras monitoring peoples' movement.

closed shop a company or firm, public corporation, or other body that requires its employees to be members of the appropriate trade union. The practice became legally enforceable in the UK in 1976, but was rendered largely inoperable by the Employment Acts of 1980 and 1982. Usually demanded by unions, it may be preferred by employers as simplifying negotiation, but it was condemned by the European Court of Human Rights in 1981. In the USA the closed shop was made illegal by the Taft-Hartley Act 1947, passed by Congress over Truman's veto.

clothes moth type of moth whose larva feeds on clothes, upholstery and carpets. The natural habitat of the larvae is in the nests of animals, feeding on remains of hair and feathers, but they have adapted to human households and can cause considerable damage, especially the common clothes-moth *Tineola bisselliella*.

cloud water vapour condensed into minute water particles that float in masses in the atmosphere. Like fogs or mists, from which clouds are distinguished by the height at which they occur above the ground, they are formed by the cooling of air charged with water vapour which condenses generally on tiny dust particles. Clouds are usually classified according to the height at which they occur and their shape. *Cirrus* and *cirro-stratus* clouds occur at 10,000 m/30,000 ft. The former, sometimes called mare's-tails, consist of minute specks of ice and appear as feathery white wisps, while cirro-stratus clouds stretch across the sky as a thin white sheet. Three types of cloud are found at 3,000–7,500 m/10,000–24,000 ft: cirro-cumulus, alto-cumulus, and alto-stratus. *Cirro-cumulus* clouds occur in small or large rounded tufts, sometimes arranged in the familiar pattern

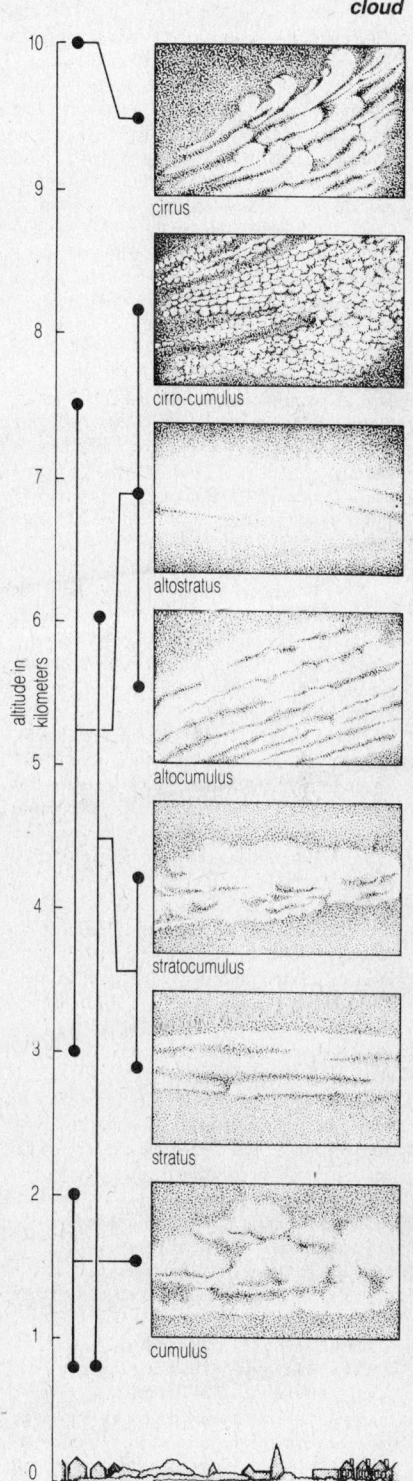

cloud

cirrus

cirro-cumulus

altostratus

altocumulus

stratocumulus

stratus

cumulus

altitude in kilometers

called mackerel sky. *Alto-cumulus* clouds are similar, but larger, white clouds, also arranged in lines. *Alto-stratus* clouds are like heavy cirro-stratus clouds and may stretch across the sky as a grey sheet.

The lower clouds, occurring at heights of up to 2,000 m/6,000 ft, may be of two types, the strato-cumulus or the nimbus. The *strato-cumulus* clouds are the dull grey clouds that give rise to a so-called leaden sky which may not yield rain. *Nimbus* clouds are dark-grey, shapeless rain clouds. Two types of clouds, the *cumulus* and *cumulo-nimbus*, are placed in a special category because they are produced by daily ascending currents which take moisture into the cooler regions of the atmosphere. Cumulus clouds have a flat base generally at 1,500 m/4,500 ft where condensation begins, while the upper part is dome-shaped and extends to about 2,000 m/6,000ft. Cumulo-nimbus clouds have their base at much the same level, but extend much higher, often up to over 6,000 m/20,000 ft. Short heavy showers and sometimes thunder may accompany them. *Stratus* clouds, occurring below 1,000 m/3,500 ft, have the appearance of sheets parallel to the horizon and are like high fogs.

cloud chamber apparatus devised in 1897 by C T R Wilson of Cambridge university for tracking ionized particles. It consists of a vessel filled with air or other gas, saturated with water vapour. When suddenly expanded this cools and a cloud of tiny droplets forms on any nuclei, dust or ions present. If single fast-moving ionizing particles collide with the air or gas molecules, they show as visible tracks. Much information about interactions between such particles and radiations has been obtained from photographs of these tracks. This system has been developed in recent years by the use of liquid hydrogen or helium instead of air or gas.

Clouet /'kluːeɪ/ François c. 1515–1572. French artist. Like his father Jean ◊Clouet, he was also known as Janet and succeeded him as court painter to Francis I, holding the same office under Henry II and Charles IX. His half-nude portrait of Diane de Poitiers *The Lady in her Bath*, is a piece of refined eroticism reflecting the style of the Italian ◊Mannerists.

Clouet /'kluːeɪ/ Jean 1486–1541. French artist, court painter to Francis I, known as Janet. His portraits of Francis and the members of his court express his concern with elegance and decoration, and provide an important pictorial record of the French court of the period.

Clough /klʌf/ Arthur Hugh 1819–1861. British poet. Many of his lyrics are marked by a melancholy scepticism which reflects his struggle with his religious doubt.

clove the unopened flower bud of the clover tree *Eugenia caryophyllus*, a member of the family Myrtaceae. The aromatic quality of cloves is shared to a large degree by the leaves, bark, and fruit of the tree, which is a native of the Moluccas. Cloves are used for flavouring in cookery and confectionery. Oil of cloves, which has tonic and carminative qualities, is employed in medicine.

clover leguminous plant, of which there are great number of species, which mostly belong to the genus *Trifolium* found mainly in the temperate regions; 18 are native to Britain. Herbaceous plants, they have trifoliate leaves and roundish heads or a spike of small flowers. Many are cultivated as fodder plants. The most important is the red clover *Trifolium pratense*. White or Dutch clover *Trifolium repens* is common in pastures.

Clovis /'kləʊvɪs/ 465–511. King of the Franks. One of the Merovingians, he succeeded his father Childeric in 481 as king of the Salian Franks, defeated the Gallo-Romans near Soissons, and also the Alemanni near Cologne in 496, embraced Christianity and subsequently proved a powerful defender of orthodoxy against the Arian Visigoths, whom he defeated at Poitiers 507. He made Paris his capital.

club moss flowerless plant of the order Lycopodiales belonging to the Pteridophyta and allied to the ferns and horsetails. They have a wide distribution, but were far more numerous in Palaeozoic times, the Lepidodendroids of the coal measures being large trees. The living species are all of small size. The common club moss or stag's horn moss *Lycopodium clavatum* is found on upland heaths.

clubroot a disease affecting cabbages, turnips, and allied plants of the Cruciferae family. It is caused by a ◊slime-mould *Plasmodiophora brassicae*. This attacks the roots of the plant, which send out knotty outgrowths, hence the popular name of finger-and-toe disease; eventually the whole plant decays.

Cluj /kluːʒ/ city in Transylvania, Romania, located on the river Somes, Cluj is a communications centre for Romania and the Hungarian plain. There is a 14th-century cathedral, and Romanian (1872) and Hungarian (1945) universities. Industries include machine tools, furniture and knitwear. Population (1979) 274,000.

Clunies-Ross /'kluːnɪz 'rɒs/ family which established a benevolently paternal rule in the ◊Cocos Islands. John Clunies-Ross settled on Home Island in 1827: the family's rule ended in 1978 with the purchase of the Cocos by the Australian government.

Cluny /'kluːnɪ/ town in Saône-et-Loire *département*, France, on the river Grosne. Its abbey, now in ruins, was the foundation house 910–1790 of the ◊Cluniac order, originally a reformed branch of the ◊Benedictines. Cluny, once famous for lace, has an important cattle market. Population (1982) 4,500.

clutch a device for disconnecting rotating shafts, particularly in a car's transmission system. In a car with a manual gearbox, the driver depresses the clutch when he or she wants to change gear. This disconnects the engine from the gearbox. The clutch consists of two main plates, a pressure plate and a driven plate, which is mounted on a shaft leading to the gearbox. When the clutch is engaged, the pressure plate presses the driven plate against the engine ◊flywheel and drive goes to the gearbox. Depressing the clutch springs the pressure plate away, freeing the driven plate. Cars with *automatic transmission* have no clutch. Drive is transmitted from flywheel to the automatic gearbox by a liquid coupling or ◊torque converter.

Clutha /'kluːθə/ longest river in South Island, New Zealand, 338 km/210 mi long. It rises in the Southern Alps, has hydroelectric installations (Roxburgh), and flows out on the east coast.

Clwyd /'kluːɪd/ county in North Wales
area 2427 sq km/937 sq mi
towns administrative headquarters Mold; Flint, Denbigh, Wrexham; seaside resorts Colwyn Bay, Rhyl, Prestatyn
features rivers Dee and Clwyd; Clwydian Range with Offa's Dyke along the main ridge; Chirk, Denbigh, Flint, and Rhuddlan castles; Blaenau Ffestiniog Railway (steam) and the nearby Llechwedd slate 'caverns'; Greenfield Valley, NW of Flint, was the site of one of the generators of the industrial revolution before steam.
products dairy and meat products; optical glass, chemicals, limestone
population (1981) 390,200.
language 19% Welsh-speaking; English

Clyde /klaɪd/ river in Strathclyde, West Scotland; 170 km/106 mi long. The Firth of Clyde and Firth of Forth are linked by the Forth and Clyde canal, 56 km/35 mi long. The shipbuilding yards have declined, but are still important, and there are the nuclear submarine bases of Faslane (Polaris) and Holy Loch (USA Poseidon).

Clyde /klaɪd/ Colin Campbell, 1st Baron Clyde 1792–1863. British field marshal. He commanded the Highland Brigade at ◊Balaclava, and as commander in chief during the Indian Mutiny raised the siege of Lucknow and captured Cawnpore.

Clydebank /'klaɪdbæŋk/ town on the Clyde, Strathclyde, Scotland, 10 km/6 mi NW of Glasgow. At the John Brown yard the famous liners such as the *Queen Elizabeth II*, were built. Population (1981) 51,700.

Clytemnestra /ˌklaɪtəmˈniːstrə/ in Greek mythology, the wife of ◊Agamemnon.

CND abbreviation for ◊Campaign for Nuclear Disarmament.

Cnossus alternative form of ◊Knossos.

coach see ◊bus and coach.

coaching conveyance by a coach – a horse-drawn passenger carriage on four wheels, sprung and roofed in. Famous coaches still in use are those of the Lord Mayor of London 1757 and the state coach built in 1761 for George III. Stage coaches made their appearance in the middle of the 17th century; running the first mail coach in 1784. The golden age of coaching was between that time and 1840 when railways became fashionable. The main roads were kept in good repair by turnpike trusts, and large numbers of inns – many of which still exist – arose to cater for stage-coach passengers and horses. The influence of coach design may be seen in the railway carriage.

coal mineral substance of fossil origin, the result of the transformation of organic matter. It is classified according to a progressive increase in the amount of carbon and a simultaneous decrease in the amount of volatiles it contains: the main types are ◊anthracite (bright and with

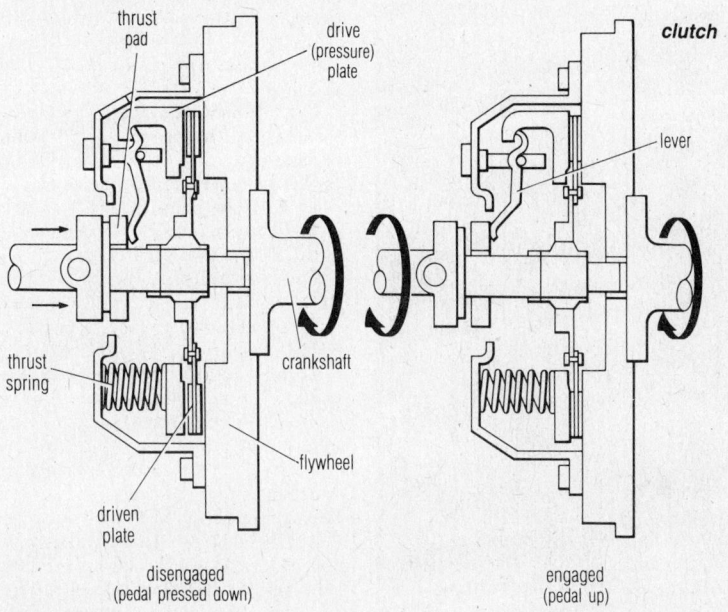

thrust pad

drive (pressure) plate

clutch

lever

thrust spring

crankshaft

thrust spring

flywheel

driven plate

disengaged (pedal pressed down)

engaged (pedal up)

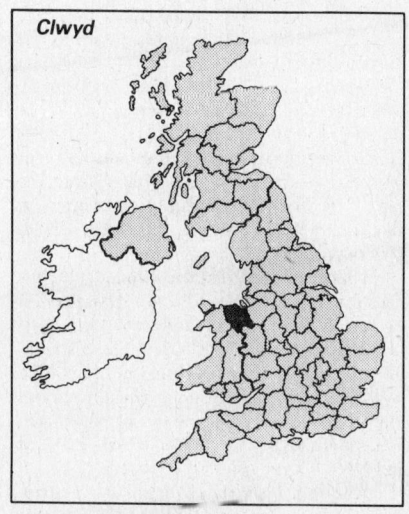

Clwyd

more than 90% carbon), bituminous coal (bright and dull patches) and ◊lignite (woody, grading into peat) and peat (no woody structure but only 70% carbon). Fields are widely distributed in the temperate northern hemisphere, the greatest reserves being in Europe, West Siberia and USA: the York, Derby and Notts is Britain's chief reserve, extending N of Selby. In the Southern hemisphere, Australia is an important producer. Coal has probably been worked in England since Roman times and in the second half of the 18th century became the basis of Britain's rise to industrial power. There was increasing use 1950–70 of cheap natural gas and oil as fuel and for the production of electricity, but the energy crisis of the 1970s led to an expansion of the exploitation of coal resources throughout the world. Under the coal Industry Nationalization Act (1946) Britain's mines are administered by the National Coal Board, now known as British Coal. Extraction is now almost entirely mechanical, whether below ground or by the open-cast method, when the soil is stripped from near-surface deposits and afterwards replaced. However where seams are thick, near the surface and of the bituminous type, which shrinks when heated (allowing air to enter) underground gasification is used, and in the USA this is now the preferred method. Coal is becoming increasingly important as a source of synfuel (synthetic petrol). In the Fischer–Tropsch process (used in Germany in World War II and today in South Africa) the coal is gasified and then catalysts are used to reconstitute it into diesel and jet fuel. In the degradation process (under development in USA for high-octane motor fuel), a liquid fuel is directly produced by adding hydrogen or removing carbon from the coal.

coal gas gas produced when ◊coal is destructively distilled or heated out of contact with the air. Scottish engineer William Murdoch was the first to light a house with coal-gas light in 1792. Today coal gas has been superseded by ◊natural gas for domestic purposes. The main constituents of coal gas are ◊methane, hydrogen and ◊carbon monoxide.

coalition an association of political groups, usually for some limited or short-term purpose, such as fighting an election or forming a government where one party has failed to secure a majority in a legislature following an election.

coaltar black oily material resulting from the destructive distillation of coal. Further distillation of coal tar yields a number of fractions: light oil, middle oil, heavy oil, and anthracene oil; the residue is called pitch. On further fractionation a large number of substances are obtained. About 200 have been isolated and they are used as dyes and in medicines.

coastguard organization to prevent smuggling, assist distressed vessels, watch for oil slicks, etc. In Britain the coastguard was originally formed to prevent smuggling after the Napoleonic Wars, and is now administered by the Department of Trade. The US Coast Guard 1915 has wider duties including enforcement of law and order on the high seas and navigable waters; prevention of smuggling; maintenance of lighthouses, buoys and bells; carrying out of an ice patrol for ships crossing the N Atlantic. It had its beginnings in the revenue cutter service established by Washington in 1790.
The *Coastwatchers* of Australia 1919, a volunteer civilian organisation, were originally formed to maintain a defensive watch on the home coast, but in World War II won distinction in an active role from 1942 in New Guinea and the Pacific Islands against the Japanese.

coati climbing mammal related to the ◊raccoon, with a long flexible pig-like snout used for digging, a good sense of smell, and long claws and long tail. Coatis, sometimes known as *coatimundis*, live in packs in the forests of S and Central America. The *common coati Nasua nasua* of S America is about 60 cm/2 ft long, plus a tail about the same length.

co-axial cable an electric ◊cable that consists of a central conductor surrounded by a conducting tube or sheath. It can transmit the high-frequency signals used in television, telephone and other ◊telecommunications transmissions.

cobalt metallic element, closely resembling nickel in appearance, symbol Co, atomic number 27, atomic weight 58.94. It occurs in a number of ores, though not in great quantities, and is used as a pigment and in alloys: because it maintains its hardness at great heat, it is used to cement carbides in tools in the high-speed machining of metals. Radioactive cobalt-60 (half-life 5.3 years) is produced by neutron radiation in heavy water reactors, and is used in large sources for gamma rays in cancer therapy, substituting for the more costly radium.

cobalt ore cobalt is extracted from a number of minerals, the main ones being smaltite, $CoAs_2$; linnaeite, Co_3S_4; cobaltite, CoAsS; and erythrite, $Co_3As_2O_8.8H_2O$. All commercial cobalt is obtained as a by-product of other metals. Zaire is the major producer of cobalt, and it is obtained there as a by-product of the copper industry. Canada and Morocco also produce cobalt.

Cobbett /'kɒbɪt/ William 1763–1835. British politician and journalist. Born at Farnham in Surrey, the self-taught son of a farmer, he enlisted in the army in 1784 and saw service in Canada. Having obtained his discharge, he lived in USA as a teacher of English, and became known as a vigorous pamphleteer, at this time supporting the Tories. In 1800 he returned to England, and in 1802 launched his *Political Register*, a weekly journal. Gradually Cobbett's views changed to out-and-out Radicalism, largely because of his increasing knowledge of the sufferings of the farm labourers, whose champion he became. In 1809 he was imprisoned for having criticized the flogging of English troops by German mercenaries, and in the postwar years he became the leader of the working-class movement. From 1817 to 1819 he was in America, and on his return wrote the *Rural Rides* for his newspaper, which were collected in book form in 1830. He was a strong advocate of parliamentary reform, and sat in the Reformed Parliament from 1832.

Cobbett An unknown artist's impression of the bucolic William Cobbett, the British journalist and politician. A farmer's son and champion of abused farm labourers, his journeys through S England inspired his Rural Rides, which give an insight into early 19th century society.

Cobden /'kɒbdən/ Richard 1804–1865. British Liberal politician. Born in Sussex, the son of a farmer, he became a calico manufacturer in Manchester. With other businessmen he founded in 1838 the Anti-Corn Law League in 1838 and began his lifelong association with John ◊Bright. In 1841 he was elected Liberal Member of Parliament for Stockport, and until 1845 devoted himself to the repeal of the Corn Laws. A typical early Victorian radical, he believed in the abolition of class and religious privileges, a minimum of government interference, and the securing of international peace by disarmament and arbitration. He opposed trade unionism and most of the factory legislation of his time, because he regarded them as opposed to liberty of contract. His opposition to the Crimean War made him unpopular, but in 1859 Palmerston offered him a seat in the cabinet, which he refused. Cobden was largely responsible for the commercial treaty with France in 1860.

Cobden-Sanderson /'kɒbdən 'saːndəsən/ Thomas James 1840–1922. British bookbinder and painter. Influenced by William ◊Morris and ◊Burne-Jones, he opened his own workshop in Maiden Lane, Strand, in 1884, and soon established a reputation as a bookbinder with a fine technique. Later he founded the Doves Press 1900–16.

Cobh /kəʊv/ Irish seaport and market town on Great Island, in the estuary of the Lee, county

Cobden The British liberal statesman Richard Cobden, captured here in 1869 in a portrait by L Dickinson, courted unpopularity with his radical views in the staid years of the early Victorian era. He was against class and religious privileges and believed in disarmament.

Cork, Republic of Ireland. Population (1978) 11,000.

Coblenz alternative spelling of the German city ◊Koblenz.

Cobol (Common business-oriented language) a computer-programming language, designed in the late 1950s especially for business use. Cobol facilitates the writing of programs that deal with large computer files and handle business arithmetic, and has become the major language for commercial data processing.

cobra type of venomous snake found in Africa and S Asia in which the neck can be stretched into a 'hood' when the snake is alarmed. Cobras have cylindrical bodies, long tails and smooth scales. Their venom contains powerful nerve toxins and, although not normally aggressive, they are responsible for many fatalities in areas where people go barefoot. The *Indian cobra Naja naja* is found over most of S Asia. In some parts of its range individuals have 'spectacle' markings on the hood. Generally about 1.5 m/5 ft long, it is much smaller than the *hamadryad Naja hannah* of S and SE Asia, which can be 4.3 m/14 ft or more, and eats snakes. The *ringhals Hemachatus hemachatus* of S Africa, and the *black-necked cobra Naja nigricollis* found on African savannah, both about 1 m/3 ft long, are able to spray venom towards the eyes of an attacker.

Coburg /'kəʊbɜːg/ town in Bavaria, West Germany, on the Itz, 80 km/50 mi SE of Gotha. Formerly the capital of the duchy of Coburg, it was part of Saxe-Coburg-Gotha 1826–1918, and a residence of its dukes. Population (1984) 44,500.

coca S American shrub *Erythroxylon coca* belonging to the Erythroxylaceae, whose dried leaves are the source of cocaine. It is cultivated in Bolivia.

cocaine chief alkaloid found in the leaves of the coca tree. It was formerly used in medicine to produce local anaesthesia, although its use is now rare. It is a dangerous drug, increasing the heart rate and blood pressure, and in chronic use creates a psychosis resembling delirium tremens as well as psychological dependence.

Cochabamba /,kɒtʃə'bæmbə/ city in Bolivia, SE of La Paz. At 2,550 m/8,370 ft, it has a refinery linked by pipeline with the Camiri oilfields. Population (1982) 281,962.

Cochin /'kəʊtʃɪn/ former princely state lying W of the Anamalai hills in S India. It was part of Travancore-Cochin from 1949 until merged in Kerala in 1956.

Cochin /'kəʊtʃɪn/ Indian town and seaport, also fishing port and naval training base, in Kerala state, on the Malabar coast; population (1981) 513,000. An industrial centre with oil refineries, ropes and clothing are manufactured here. It exports coir, copra, tea, and spices. Vasco da Gama established a Portuguese factory at Cochin in 1502, and 1530 St Francis Xavier made it a missionary centre. The Dutch held Cochin 1663–1795 when it was taken by the English.

Cochin-China /'kɒtʃɪn 'tʃaɪnə/ region of SE Asia. With ◊Kampuchea it formed part of the ancient Khmer empire. In the 17th–18th centuries it was conquered by ◊Annam. Together with Kampuchea it became, 1863–67, the first part of the Indo-China peninsula to be occupied by France. Since 1949 it has been part of ◊Vietnam.

cochineal red dye obtained from the cactus-eating Mexican ◊scale insect *Dactylopius coccus*, used in food and fabrics.

Cochran /'kɒkrən/ Charles Blake ('C.B') 1872–1951. British impresario, who promoted a wide range of forms of entertainment including wrestling, roller-skating and the introduction to London of the Diaghilev Ballet. He was knighted in 1948.

cockatiel small Australian parrot *Nymphicus hollandicus*, with greyish plumage, yellow cheeks, a long tail and a crest like a cockatoo. About 20 cm/8 in long, cockatiels are popular as pets and aviary birds.

cockatoo type of ◊parrot which has an erectile crest on the head, found in Australia, New Guinea and nearby islands. There are about 17 species, one of the most familiar being the Australian *sulphur-crested cockatoo Cacatua sulphurea*, about 30 cm/1 ft long, pure white with a yellow crest.

cockchafer beetle *Melolontha melolontha*, also known as *maybug*, up to 3 cm/1.2 in long, with heavy, clumsy buzzing flight, seen on early summer evenings. They damage trees by feeding on the foliage and flowers, and the larvae, sometimes called *rookworms*, live underground feeding on grass and cereal roots.

Cockcroft /'kɒkrɒft/ John Douglas 1897–1967. British physicist. Born at Todmorden, W Yorkshire, he held an engineering appointment with Metropolitan-Vickers, and took up research work under ◊Rutherford at the Cavendish Laboratory, Cambridge. He succeeded (with E T S Walton) in splitting the nucleus of the atom for the first time in 1932, and in 1951 they were jointly awarded a Nobel prize. Succeeding ◊Appleton as Jacksonian professor of natural philosophy, Cambridge (1939–46), he was engaged in World War II on scientific work for the government, latterly in connection with the atomic bomb. He was director at Harwell atomic research establishment 1946–58, and in 1960 became first Master of Churchill College, Cambridge. Knighted in 1948, he was awarded the Order of Merit in 1957.

Cockerell /'kɒkərəl/ Charles 1788–1863. British architect who built mainly in a Neo-Classical style derived from antiquity and from ◊Wren. He received the first RIBA Gold Medal. His best known surviving buildings are the Ashmolean Museum and Taylorian Institute in Oxford 1841–45.

Cockerell /'kɒkərəl/ Christopher 1910– . British engineer, who invented the ◊hovercraft. From a first interest in radio, he switched to electronics, working with the Marconi Company from 1935 to 1950. In 1953 he began work on the hovercraft, carrying out his early experiments on Oulton Broad, Norfolk. He was knighted in 1969.

cock-fighting the pitting of game-cocks against one another to make sport for onlookers and gamblers – a diversion now, in most countries, illegal because of its cruelty. It was extremely popular in feudal England. A royal cockpit was built in Whitehall by Henry VIII, and royal patronage continued in the next century. During the Cromwellian period it was banned, but at the Restoration it received a new lease of life until it was banned in 1849. Cock-fighting continues surreptitiously in advanced countries, and is still legal in many others. Fighting cocks are 1–2 yrs when matched and steel spurs are attached to their legs.

cockle bivalve mollusc with ribbed, rather heart-shaped shell. The **common cockle** *Cerastoderma edule* is up to 5 cm/2 in across, and is found low on shores and in estuaries around N European and Mediterranean coasts in sand or mud, and is gathered in large numbers for food.

cockney a native of the City of London. According to tradition cockneys must be born within sound of ◊Bow bells in Cheapside. The term cockney is also applied to the dialect of the Londoner, of which a striking feature is rhyming slang.

cock-of-the-rock S American bird genus *Rupicola* of the family Cotingidae which also includes the cotingas and umbrella birds. The male cock-of-the-rock has brilliant orange plumage including the head crest, the female is a duller brown. Males clear an area of ground and use it as a communal display ground, spreading wings, tail and crest to attract mates.

cockroach insect of the family Blattidae, distantly related to the mantises. A very ancient group, and 'primitive' or unspecialized compared

to many insects, there are nevertheless some 3500 species, mainly in the tropics. They have long antennae and biting mouthparts, and can fly but rarely do so. In Britain only two small innocuous species are native, but several species have been introduced with imported food and become severe pests. The **common cockroach** or **black-beetle** *Blatta orientalis* is common in dirty houses, is nocturnal and omnivorous. It contaminates food with a disgusting smell. The **German cockroach** *Blattella germanica* and **American cockroach** *Periplaneta americana* are pests in kitchens, bakeries and warehouses.

cocoa and chocolate food products both made from the cacao (or cocoa) bean, fruit of a tropical tree (*Theobroma cacao*) growing chiefly in W Africa (Ghana, Nigeria), parts of S America, the West Indies, Java, and Sri Lanka. Cacao is believed to be indigenous to the forests of the Amazon and Orinoco, and the use of the beans was introduced into Europe following the conquest of Mexico by Cortez in the 16th century. A 'cocoa-house' was opened in London in 1657; others followed and became centres for the fashionable and the wits. In Mexico *chocolatl* (its native name) was mixed with hot spices, whisked to a froth and drunk cold. Cocoa powder was a later development.

The cacao tree when fully grown is some 6 m/20ft high. It begins bearing fruit about the fifth year; this matures rapidly as a pod, 12.5–22.5 cm/5–9 in long, containing 20 to 40 seeds (beans), embedded in juicy white pulp. The trees bear all the year round and there are two, sometimes three, harvests. Preparation consists chiefly in roasting, winnowing, and grinding the nib (the edible portion of the bean). If drinking cocoa is required, a proportion of the cocoa butter is removed by hydraulic pressure and the cocoa which remains is reduced by further grinding and sieving to a fine powder. Chocolate, on the other hand, contains all the original butter.

coconut fruit of the coconut palm *Cocos nucifera*. The palm grows throughout the tropics in the lowlands, and is salt-tolerant and able to grow by the seashore. It can grow to about 25 m/80 ft, the leaves and fruit being at the top, a bare trunk below. The fruit has a large outer husk of fibres which are split off and used for coconut matting and ropes. Inside this is the 'nut' exported to temperate countries. Inside the hard shell is white 'meat' and 'coconut milk' which makes a nourishing drink. The meat can be eaten or dried to 'copra' prior to the extraction of its oil, which makes up nearly two-thirds of it. The oil can be used for soap, margarine and cooking. The residue can be used in cattlefeed.

Cocos /'kəʊkɒs/ group of 27 small coral islands in the Indian Ocean, aboout 1,770 km/1,720 mi NW of Perth, Australia. Discovered by William Keeling 1609, they were uninhabited till 1826, were annexed by Britain 1857, and transferred to Australia as the Territory of Cocos (Keeling) Islands in 1955. In 1978 the Australian government purchased them from John ◊Clunies-Ross. West Island has an airport. Area 14 sq km/5.5 sq mi; population (1984) 584.

Cocteau /'kɒktəʊ/ Jean 1889–1963. French poet, dramatist, film director, and critic. A leading figure in European modernism, he worked with ◊Picasso, ◊Diaghilev and ◊Stravinsky. He produced many volumes of poetry, ballets such as *Le Boeuf sur le toit/The Nothing Doing Bar* 1920, plays, for example, *Orphée/Orpheus* 1926, and a mature novel of bourgeois French life, *Les Enfants terribles* 1929, which he made into a film in 1950.

Cocteau French playwright, novelist, poet, film director and artist, Jean Cocteau in 1929. Success came to him at 21 and remained with him throughout his life. He was associated with Modernism in all the arts, and sponsored Stravinsky and Picasso.

cod sea fish *Gadus morhua* found in the N Atlantic and Baltic. Brown to grey with spots, white below, it can grow to 1.5 m/5 ft, and is an important food fish. The most important cod fisheries are on the Newfoundland banks, Iceland and the North Sea. Much of the catch is salted and dried. Formerly one of the cheapest fish, decline in numbers from overfishing has made it one of the most expensive.

coda (Italian 'tail') in music, a concluding section of a movement added to indicate finality.

codex an ancient book, with pages stitched together and bound. During the 2nd century AD codices began to replace the earlier rolls.

cod liver oil oil obtained by subjecting fresh cod livers to pressure at a temperature of about 85° C. When prepared by modern methods, it is nearly tasteless and odourless and is highly nutritious, being a valuable source of the vitamins A and D. However overdose has occurred.

codon in ◊genetics, triplet of ◊bases in a molecule of ◊DNA or ◊RNA that codes for a

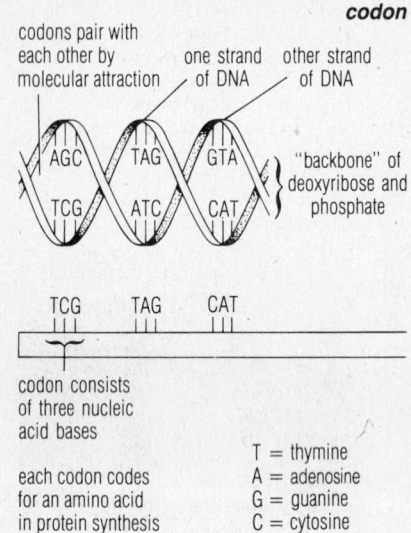

codon

codons pair with each other by molecular attraction

one strand of DNA   other strand of DNA

AGC   TAG   GTA

TCG   ATC   CAT

"backbone" of deoxyribose and phosphate

TCG   TAG   CAT

codon consists of three nucleic acid bases

each codon codes for an amino acid in protein synthesis

T = thymine
A = adenosine
G = guanine
C = cytosine

Coe Britain's Sebastian Coe, seen winning his first Olympic title, the 1500 metres at the Moscow Games in 1980. Jürgen Straub (GDR, No. 338) and Steve Ovett (GB 279) won the silver and bronze medals. Coe came second in the 800 metres, and repeated his medal-winning performances in the Los Angeles Olympics in 1984.

particular ◊amino acid during the process of protein synthesis. See ◊genetic code.

Cody /'kəudi/ Samuel Franklin 1862–1913. Anglo-American aviation pioneer. Born in Texas, USA, he took British nationality in 1909. He spent his early days with a cowboy stage and circus act, and made kites capable of lifting people. He made his first powered flight on 16 Oct 1908 at Farnborough, England, in a machine of his own design. He was killed in a flying accident.

Cody /'kəudi/ William Frederick 1846–1917. American scout and showman, known as 'Buffalo Bill' from his contract to supply buffalo carcases to railway labourers (over 4000 in 18 months). From 1883 he toured USA and Europe with a Wild West show.

Coe /kəu/ Sebastian 1956– . English middle distance runner. He was Olympic 1500 metres champion 1980 and 1984. During 1979–81 he broke seven world records at 800, 1000 and 1500 metres and one mile. In the 1980s he has suffered from a series of injuries and illness.

co-education the education of boys and girls together in one institution. There has been a marked switch away from single sex education and in favour of co-education over the last 20 years in the UK, although there is some evidence to suggest that girls perform better in a single sex institution, particularly in maths and science. In 1954 the USSR returned to its earlier co-educational system, partly abolished in 1944. In the USA 90 per cent of schools and colleges are co-educational. In Islamic practice co-education is discouraged beyond the infant stage.

coefficient the number part in front of an algebraic term, signifying multiplication. For example, in the expression $4x^2 + 2xy - x$, the coefficient of x^2 is 4 (because $4x^2$ means 4 x x^2), that of xy is 2 and that of x is -1 (because -1 x $x = -x$). In some algebraic expressions, coefficients are represented by letters called constants, that stand for numbers, for example,

in the equation $ax^2 + bx + c = 0$, a, b and c are constants.

coefficient of relationship the probability that any two individuals share a given ◊gene by virtue of being descended from a common ancestor. In ◊sexual reproduction of ◊diploid species, an individual shares half its genes with each parent, with its offspring, and (on average) with each sibling, but only a quarter (on average) with its grandchildren or its siblings' offspring, an eighth with its great-grandchildren and so on. In certain species of insects (for example honey bees), females have only one set of chromosomes (inherited from the mother), so that sisters are identical in genetic make-up; this produces a different set of coefficients. These coefficients are important in calculations of ◊inclusive fitness.

coelacanth fish *Latimeria chalumnae* found near the Comoro Islands, up to 2 m/6 ft long with paddle-like fins. It was new to science in 1938, all previous known coelacanths being fossils from the period 370 to 70 million years ago, at which time fossils cease, and this type of fish was believed extinct. Coelacanths are lobe-finned fish, with bone and muscle at the base of the fins, distantly related to the lobefins which were the ancestors of all land animals with backbones. Many specimens have now been caught and investigated, but little is known of the fish's life in the deep sea.

coelom the fluid-filled cavity of all but the simplest animals. It separates the body wall from the gut and associated organs, and allows the gut muscles to contract independently of the rest of the body.

Coetzee /ˌkuːtˈsɪə/ J(ohn) M 1940– . South African author whose novel *In the Heart of the Country* 1975 dealt with the rape of a white

woman by a black man. In 1983 he won the ◊Booker Prize with *Life and Times of Michael K*.

coffee the seeds or berries of cultivated forms of *Coffea arabica*, *Coffea liberica* and allied species – natives of Africa and probably Arabia. Naturally about 5 m/17 ft, the shrub is pruned to about 2 m/7 ft in cultivation, is in full bearing in five to six years and lasts for 30 years. Susceptibility to frost and disease, and the length of time before a tree begins to bear, results in periodic scarcity, as in the late 1970s. Coffee is a tropical crop and does best on frost-free hillsides with moderate rainfall. The largest producer is Brazil; others are Colombia, Ivory Coast, Angola, Uganda, Zaïre, Guyana, Mexico, El Salvador, Guatemala and Indonesia. ◊Chicory is often mixed with coffee to give it a distinctive bitter flavour and rich colour. The species *Coffea robusta*, grown especially in Angola, is that used in most 'instant' coffee.

In Arab countries coffee drinking dates from about the 14th century, but did not become common in Europe until 300 years later. In the 17th century coffee houses were opened in London, but coffee was largely superseded by tea until the 20th century: in USA and on the Continent coffee has always been more popular.

Cognac /'kɒnjæk/ town in Charente département, France, 40 km/25 mi W of Angoulême. Situated in a vine-growing district, Cognac has given its name to a brandy. Population (1982) 21,000.

cognition in psychology, a general term covering the functions involved in dealing with information, for example, perception (seeing, hearing, and so on) attention, memory, and reasoning.

cognitive therapy a treatment for emotional disorders, particularly ◊depression and ◊anxiety, developed by Professor Aaron T Beck in the USA. This approach encourages the client to challenge the distorted and unhelpful thinking that is characteristic of these problems. The treatment includes ◊behaviour therapy and has been particularly helpful for people suffering from ◊depression.

cohesion in physics, a phenomenon in which interaction between two surfaces of the same material in contact makes them cling together (with two different materials the similar phenomenon is called adhesion). According to kinetic theory, cohesion is caused by attraction between particles at the atomic or molecular level. Surface tension, which causes liquids to form spherical droplets, is caused by cohesion.

Coimbatore /ˌkəʊˌɪmbəˈtɔː/ city in Tamil Nadu, India, on the Noyei river. It has textile industries and the Indian Air Force Administrative College. Population (1981) 701,100.

Coimbra /kəʊˈɪmbrə/ city in Portugal, on the Mondego river, 32 km/20 mi from the sea. There is a 12th-century Romanesque cathedral incorporating part of an older mosque, and a celebrated university, founded in Lisbon 1290 and transferred to Coimbra 1537. Coimbra was the capital of Portugal 1139–1385. Population (1981) 71,800.

coin a form of ◊money. See also ◊numismatics.

coke /kəʊk/ a clean, light fuel produced by the carbonization of certain types or blends of coal. When this coal is strongly heated in airtight ovens, in order to release all volatile constituents, the brittle, silver-grey coke is left. It comprises 90 per cent carbon together with very small quantities of water, hydrogen, and oxygen, and makes a most useful industrial and domestic fuel. An inferior grade of coke is produced as a by-product in the manufacture of coal-gas.

Coke /kəʊk/ Edward 1552–1634. Lord Chief Justice of England. He was called to the Bar in 1578, and in 1592 became speaker of the House of Commons and solicitor-general. In 1594 he was appointed attorney-general, and as such conducted the prosecution at the trials of Essex, Raleigh, and the Gunpowder Plot conspirators. In 1606 he became Chief Justice of the Common Pleas, and began his struggle against James I's attempts to exalt the royal prerogative. An attempt to silence him by promoting him to the dignity of Lord Chief Justice proved unsuccessful, and from 1620 he was a leader of the parliamentary opposition. Under Charles I he drew up the Petition of Right, and led the attack on Buckingham. His *Institutes* are a legal classic, and he ranks as the supreme common lawyer.

Coke /kəʊk/ Thomas William 1752–1842. Known as 'Coke of Norfolk', he pioneered agricultural improvement, especially sheep breeding.

cola or *kola* genus of tropical trees, family Sterculiaceae. Their nuts are chewed in West Africa for their high caffeine content, and in the West are used with coca leaves to flavour soft drinks.

Colbert /kɒlˈbeə/ Jean-Baptiste 1619–1683. French statesman. Born at Reims, he entered the service of Mazarin, and succeeded him as chief minister to Louis XIV. In 1661 he set to work to reform the Treasury, and in 1665 was appointed controller-general. The national debt was largely repaid, and the system of tax collection was drastically reformed. Industry was brought under state control, shipbuilding was encouraged by bounties, companies were established to trade with India and America, and colonies were founded in Louisiana, Guiana, and Madagascar. Above all, Colbert tried to make France a naval power equal to England or Holland. He favoured a peaceful foreign policy, but in his later years was supplanted in Louis's favour by Louvois, who supported a policy of conquests.

Colchester /ˈkəʊltʃɪstə/ English town and river port on the Colne, Essex, 80 km/50 mi north east of London; population (1981) 82,000. In an agricultural area, it is a market centre with clothing manufacture and engineering and printing works. The University of Essex (1962) is to the SE at Wivenhoe.

history Colchester dates from the time of ◊Cymbeline (about 10–43 AD). It became a colony of Roman ex-soldiers in 50 AD, it became one of the most prosperous towns in Roman Britain despite its burning by ◊Boudicca (Boadicea) in 61. Most of the Roman walls remain, as well as ruins of the Norman castle, and St Botolph's priory. Holly Tree Mansion (1718) is a museum of 18th–19th century social life.

cold, common minor disease caused by a variety of viruses. Symptoms: headache, chill, nasal discharge, sore throat and occasionally cough. Research at the Common Colds Research Unit at Salisbury indicates that the virulence of a cold depends on psychological factors and either reduction or increase of social or work activity as a result of stress in the previous six months. There is little immediate hope of an effective cure since the viruses transform themselves so rapidly. Colds remain a major cause of industrial absenteeism.

Coldharbor, Battle of /ˈkəʊld ˈhɑːbə/ engagement near Richmond, Virginia, 1–12 June 1864, during the American Civil War in which the Confederate Army under Lee repulsed Union attacks under Grant.

Colditz /ˈkəʊldɪts/ town in East Germany, near Leipzig, site of a castle used as a high-security prisoner-of-war camp (Oflag IVC) in World War II. Among daring escapes was that of Captain Patrick Reid and others in Oct 1942.

Cold War term used to describe the tensions from about 1945 between the USSR and Eastern Europe on the one hand, and the USA and Western Europe on the other. The origins of the Cold War can be seen in the disagreements between the USSR and the Western allies during World War II, especially over the future structure of Eastern Europe. The Atlantic Charter signed by Roosevelt and Churchill in 1941 proposed that the political structure of post-war Europe should be decided on the principle of self-determination, whereas Stalin insisted that the USSR should be allowed to keep the territory obtained as a result of the Hitler-Stalin pact of 1939. While the fate of Eastern Europe was undoubtedly the main cause of friction between the two blocks, there had been a legacy of mistrust between the USSR and the Western allies since the Russian revolution of 1917.

The disagreements between the USA and the USSR resurfaced in the conferences held to decide the future of the post-war world. While the USA was keen to open up all of Europe to Western economic orientated states around the USSR, the Soviets were similarly afraid of being encircled and indeed attacked by their former allies. In addition, the USSR saw Eastern Europe as its own 'sphere of influence' and, in the case of Germany was looking to extract reparations. Thus most of the tension was concentrated on the fate of Poland and the partition of Germany. Berlin became the focal point of East-West tension, culminating in the Soviet blockade of the British, American and French zones of the city in 1948 which was relieved only by a massive airlift of essential supplies. As the USSR increased its hold on the countries of Eastern Europe, the USA pursued a policy of 'containment' (the so-called Truman doctrine) which involved offering material aid to Western Europe (Marshall Aid) and also to Mediterranean countries such as Greece and Turkey.

The increasing divisions between the capitalist and communist world were reinforced by the creation of defensive alliances, the ◊North Atlantic Treaty Organization 1949 (NATO) in the West, and the ◊Warsaw Pact 1955 in the East. Further disputes turned the Cold War into a global conflict – most notably the Korean War of 1950–53, Soviet intervention in Hungary 1956 and Czechoslovakia 1968 and US involvement in Vietnam together with the Cuban missile crisis of 1962. From the early 1970s there was a discernible 'thaw' in the relations between the two powers, known as the period of détente, but this was largely destroyed by the Soviet intervention in Afghanistan and US support for the Solidarity movement in Poland. Since the beginning of the Reagan presidency there has been a return to the state of friction between the two powers -termed the 'New Cold War'. This has been alleviated only by disarmament discussions centred on the future of Strategic Arms Limitation Treaties (SALT) and the US Strategic Defence Initiative (SDI), popularly called ◊Star Wars.

Coleman /ˈkəʊlmən/ Ornette 1930– . US alto saxophonist and composer. He has created controversial new jazz sounds for the symphony orchestra. In a classical manner, he accords priority to the composition and restrains improvisation in performance.

Colenso /kəˈlenzəʊ/ John William 1814–1883. Scholar and mathematician who was Bishop of Natal from 1853. He was the first to write down the Zulu language. He championed the Zulu way of life (including polygamy) in relation to Christianity, and applied Christian morality to race relations in southern Africa. He incurred furious attack from traditionalists by his *Pentateuch and Book of Joshua Critically Examined* 1862. Deposed in 1863 by the bishop of Capetown, he was reinstated on appeal to the Privy Council.

coleoptile the protective sheath which surrounds the young shoot tip of a grass during its passage through the soil to the surface. Although of relatively simple structure, most coleoptiles are very sensitive to light.

Coleridge /'kəʊlərɪdʒ/ Samuel Taylor 1772–1834. British poet, one of the founders of the Romantic movement. While at Cambridge, he was driven by debt to enlist in the Dragoons, and then in 1795, as part of an abortive plan to found a communist colony in America with Robert ◊Southey (see ◊Susquehanna), married Sarah Fricker, from whom he afterwards separated. In 1798 he collaborated with ◊Wordsworth in *Lyrical Ballads*, which include 'The Ancient Mariner', and broke with the Classical tradition of English poetry. 'Kubla Khan' and 'Christabel' were also written at this time. He became addicted to opium and from 1816 lived at Highgate under medical care. As a philosopher, he argued inferentially that even in registering sense-perceptions the mind was performing acts of creative imagination, rather than being a passive arena in which ideas interacted mechanistically. As a critic, he brought the psychological method to bear, as in *Biographia Literaria* 1817.

Coleridge Samuel Taylor Coleridge, the poet who, together with William Wordsworth, signalled the beginning of the romantic era of poetry with their jointly produced *Lyrical Ballads* in 1798. This volume included Coleridge's haunting poem *The Ancient Mariner*.

Coleridge /'kəʊlərɪdʒ/ Sara 1802–1852. Editor of the work of her father Samuel Taylor ◊Coleridge.

Coleridge-Taylor /'kəʊlərɪdʒ 'teɪlə/ Samuel 1875–1912. British composer. Born in London, he was the son of a West African doctor and an English mother. While still a student at the Royal College of Music, he had a symphony performed at St James's Hall in 1896. His choral work *Hiawatha* 1898–1900, a setting in three parts of Longfellow's poem, won immediate popularity. He was a student and champion of traditional black music.

Colet /'kɒlɪt/ John c. 1467–1519. English humanist, influenced by Savonarola and Erasmus. He reacted against the scholastic tradition in his interpretation of the Bible, and founded modern biblical exegesis. In 1505 he became dean of St Paul's.

Colette /kɒ'let/ Sidonie-Gabrielle 1873–1954. French writer. At 20 she married Henri Gauthier-Villars, a journalist known as 'Willy', and under this name her four 'Claudine' novels, based on her own early life, were published. Divorced in 1906, she was a striptease and mime artist for a while, but continued to write, for example, *Chéri* 1920, *La Fin de Chéri/The End of Chéri* 1926, and *Gigi* 1944.

Coligny /,kɔlɪn'jiː/ Gaspard de 1519–1572. French admiral and soldier, and prominent Huguenot. About 1557 he joined the Protestant party, and in 1569 achieved an advantageous peace. He became a favourite of the young king Charles IX, but on the eve of the massacre of St Bartholomew's Day was killed by a servant of the duc de Guise.

colitis inflammation of the walls of the colon. Sulphonamides are among the drugs used in its treatment.

collage in art, ◊Dada technique originated by Max ◊Ernst, and named from the French for 'glueing' or 'pasting'. Disparate items such as fragments of newsprint or photographs are stuck alongside one another, and linked by brush or pencil to create a new artistic whole.

collective farm system of farming developed in the Soviet Union. A collective farm formed by a group of peasant farmers, who pool their land, horses, and agricultural implements, each household retaining as private property a plot of land and domestic animals for its own requirements. The profits of the farm are divided among its members in proportion to work done. The system developed gradually after 1917, and became general after 1930. State farms also exist which are owned and run by the State, and employ their workers for wages. The State supplies the collective farms with stock and equipment, and loans agricultural machinery as required. The system exists in other Communist countries, and was adopted (1953) as an objective in China, but by 1954 had been considerably modified in Yugoslavia. Israel also has a large number of collective farms, of which the best known type is the ◊kibbutz.

collective security a system for achieving international security by an agreement among all states to unite against any aggressor. Such a commitment was embodied in the post-World War I League of Nations and also in the United Nations Organization, although neither body was able to live up to the ideals of its founders.

collective unconscious in psychology, the term used for the shared pool of memories inherited from ancestors which Carl Jung suggested co-existed with individual ◊unconscious recollections, and which might be active both for evil in precipitating mental disturbance or for good in prompting achievements (for example, in the arts).

College of Arms see ◊Heralds' College.

college of higher education in the UK, a college controlled by the local education authorities in which a large proportion of the work undertaken is at degree level or above.

collenchyma a plant tissue composed of somewhat elongated cells with thickened cell walls, especially at the corners where adjacent cells meet. It is a supporting and strengthening tissue found in non-woody plants, particularly in the stems and leaves.

collie type of sheepdog originally bred in Britain. The *border collie* is a working dog, often black and white, about 45 cm/1.5 ft tall, with a dense coat. The *rough* and *smooth collies* are bigger, about 60 cm/2 ft tall, and although originally sheepdogs have been kept as pets and bred as elegant showdogs. These collies have long narrow heads and muzzles. The *bearded collie* is a little smaller, and rather like an Old English sheepdog in appearance, with long hair, and is another working dog that has moved to the show world.

Collier /'kɒlɪə/ Jeremy 1650–1726. British Anglican cleric, a ◊Nonjuror, who was outlawed in 1696 for granting absolution on the scaffold to two men who had tried to assassinate William III. His *Short View of the Immorality and Profaneness of the English Stage* 1698 was aimed at Congreve and Vanbrugh.

Collier /'kɒlɪə/ Lesley 1947– . British ballerina, a principal dancer of the ◊Royal Ballet from 1972. She had major roles in MacMillan's *Anastasia* 1971, and *Four Seasons* 1975, van Manen's *Four Schumann Pieces* 1975, Ashton's *Rhapsody* and Tetley's *Dance of Albiar* both 1980. She was Princess Aurora in *Sleeping Beauty* at the Royal Ballet's 50th anniversary performance 1981.

collimator an optical device for producing a parallel beam of light. A small point source or an illuminated slit is placed at the focal point of a ◊convex lens, from which the rays emerge parallel.

Collingwood /'kɒlɪŋwʊd/ Cuthbert, Baron Collingwood 1750–1810. British admiral. He entered the navy at the age of 11, he formed a close friendship with Nelson while serving in the West Indies. He distinguished himself on the 'glorious 1st June' and at St Vincent was promoted to rear-admiral in 1799. Collingwood was with the Channel fleet blockading Brest 1803–05, until Villeneuve's return from the West Indies, when he blockaded him in Cadiz. Here he was joined by Nelson as his commander in chief, and after Nelson's death he took command at Trafalgar. He was buried beside Nelson in St Paul's.

Collingwood /'kɒlɪŋwʊd/ Robin George 1889–1943. English philosopher, professor of philosophy at Oxford. Collingwood stressed the importance of 'doing philosophy historically'. In effect this meant that any philosophical theory or position could only be properly understood within its own historical context and not from the point of view of the present. He is also significant for his aesthetic theory, outlined in the *Principles of Art* 1938.

Collins /'kɒlınz/ (William) Wilkie 1824–1889. British novelist, author of mystery and suspense novels, including *The Woman in White* 1860 (with its fat villain Count Fosco), often called the first English detective novel, and *The Moonstone* 1868 (with Sergeant Cuff, one of the first detectives in English literature).

Collins /'kɒlınz/ Michael 1890–1922. Irish Sinn Féin leader. Born in County Cork, he became an active member of the Irish Republican Brotherhood, and in 1916 fought in the Easter Rebellion. In 1918 he was elected a Sinn Féin member to the Dáil, and became a minister in the Republican Provisional government. In 1921 he and Arthur Griffith (1872–1922) were mainly responsible for the treaty which established the Irish Free State. In spite of the opposition of De Valera and the Republicans, he persuaded the Dáil to accept the treaty, and in 1922 became minister for finance in the Provisional government. During the ensuing civil war Collins took command of the Free State forces, and crushed the opposition in Dublin and the large towns within a few weeks. When Griffith died on 12 Aug Collins became head of the state and the army, but he was ambushed near Cork by fellow Irishmen ten days later and killed.

Collins /'kɒlınz/ William 1721–1759. British poet. Born at Chichester, he was educated at Winchester and Magdalen College, Oxford. His *Persian Eclogues* 1742 were followed in 1746 by his series 'Odes', the best-known being 'To Evening'.

Collodi /kɒ'ləʊdi/ Carlo, pseudonym of Carlo Lorenzini 1826–1890. Italian writer, born in Florence. He was a journalist, and in 1881–83 wrote *The Adventure of Pinocchio*, the children's story of a wooden puppet who became a human boy.

colloid a substance composed of extremely small particles whose size is between those in suspension and those in true solution (between 1 and 1,000 microns across). The two components are known as the continuous phase, which has the second (dispersed) phase distributed in it. There are various types of colloids. Ones involving gases include an aerosol (a dispersion of a liquid or solid in a gas, as in fog or smoke) and a foam (a dispersion of a gas in a liquid). Liquids form both the dispersed and continuous phases in an emulsion. Milk is a natural emulsion of liquid fat in a watery liquid; synthetic emulsions such as some paints and cosmetic lotions have chemical emulsifying agents to stabilize the colloid and stop the two phases from separating out. Colloidal solutions (a solid dispersed in a liquid) are called sols. A sol in which both phases contribute to the molecular three-dimensional network of the colloid take on a jelly-like form and are known as gels; gelatine, starch 'solution' and silica gel are common examples. Colloids were first studied thoroughly by the British chemist Thomas Graham (1805–1869) who defined them as substances which (in solution) will not diffuse through a semi-permeable membrane (as opposed to crystalloids, solutions of inorganic salts, which will diffuse through).

Colman /'kəʊlmən/ Ronald 1891–1958. British actor. Born in Richmond, Surrey, he went to the USA in 1920 where his charm, good looks and speaking voice soon brought success in romantic Hollywood roles. His films include *Beau Geste* 1924, *The Prisoner of Zenda* 1937, *Lost Horizon* 1937, and *A Double Life* 1947, for which he received an Academy Award.

Colmar /'kɒlmɑː/ capital of Haut-Rhin *département*, France, between the river Rhine and the Vosges mountains; population (1983) 64,200. It is an industrial centre. The church of St Martin is 13th–14th century, and the former Dominican monastery, now the Unterlinden Museum, contains a famed Grünewald altarpiece.

Cologne /kə'ləʊn/ (German *Köln*) German port, and industrial and commercial city in North Rhine-Westphalia, West Germany, on the left bank of the Rhine, 35 km/22 mi from Düsseldorf; population (1981) 973,000. It can be reached by ocean-going vessels and has developed into a great transshipment centre, and is also the headquarters of Lufthansa, the state airline. To the N is the Ruhr coalfield, on which many of Cologne's industries are based. They include motor vehicles, railway wagons, chemicals, and machine tools.

history founded by the Romans 38 BC and made a colony in 50 AD under the name Colonia Claudia Arae Agrippinensis (hence the name Cologne), it became an important Frankish city and during the Middle Ages was ruled by its archbishops. It was a free imperial city from 1288 until the Napoleonic age. In 1815 it passed to Prussia. The great Gothic cathedral was begun in the 13th century but its towers were not built until the 19th century (completed 1880). Cologne university (1388–1797) was refounded 1919. Cologne suffered severely from aerial bombardment during World War II; some 85 per cent of the city was wrecked and its three Rhine bridges were destroyed.

Colombes /kɒ'lɒmb/ industrial suburb of Paris, capital of Hauts-de-Seine *département*. Tyres, electronic equipment, and chemicals are manufactured. Population (1983) 83,260.

Colombey-les-Deux-Eglises /,kɒlɒm'beı/ village (the name means Colombey with the two churches) in Haute-Marne, France. General ◊de Gaulle lived and was buried here.

Colombia /kə'lɒmbiə/ country in South America, bounded N and W by the Caribbean and the Pacific, and having borders with Panama to the NW, Venezuela to the E and NE, Brazil to the SE, and Peru and Ecuador to the SW.

government The 1886 constitution provides for a president, a two-chamber congress of senate of 114 members, and a house of representatives of 199 members, all elected by universal suffrage for a four-year term. The president appoints the cabinet. Although it does not have a fully federal system, Colombia is divided into 32 regions, enjoying considerable autonomy, with governors appointed by the president and locally elected legislatures. Most significant among many political parties are the Liberal Party and the Conservative Party.

history Until it was conquered by Spain in the 16th century, the area was inhabited by the Chibcha. From 1538 Colombia formed part of a colony known as New Granada, comprising Colombia, Panama, and most of Venezuela. In 1819 the area included Ecuador, and became independent as Gran Colombia, a state set up by Simón Bolívar. Colombia became entirely independent in 1886.

In 1948 the left-wing mayor of Bogotá was assassinated and there followed a decade of near civil war, 'La Violencia', during which it is thought that over 250,000 people died. Left-wing guerrilla activity continued into the 1980s. In 1957, in an effort to halt the violence, the Conservatives and Liberals formed a National Front, alternating the presidency between them. They were challenged in 1970 by the National Popular Alliance (ANAPO), with a special appeal to the working classes, but the Conservative-Liberal coalition continued and when in 1978 the Liberals won majorities in both chambers of congress and the presidency, they kept the National Front accord.

In 1982 the Liberals kept their majorities in congress but Dr Belisario Bentacur won the presidency for the Conservatives. He sought a truce with the left-wing guerrillas by granting them an amnesty and freeing political prisoners. He also embarked on a radical programme of public works. His plans suffered a major blow in 1984 when his minister of justice, who had been using harsh measures to curb drug dealing, was assassinated. Betancur reacted by strengthening his anti-drug campaign. In the 1986 elections Liberal Virgilio Barco Vargas won the presidency by a record margin. Three months after taking office, he announced the end of the National Front accord, despite a provision in the constitution that the opposition party always has the opportunity to participate in government if it wishes to.

Colombo /kə'lʌmbəʊ/ capital and principal seaport of Sri Lanka, on the west coast near the mouth of the Kelani; population (1981) 585,750. The chief government offices are here. The University of Sri Lanka (1942), formerly in Colombo, is now at Peradeniya, near Kandy. Colombo was mentioned as Kalambu about 1340, but the Portuguese renamed it in honour of Christopher ◊Columbus. The Dutch seized it in 1656 and it was surrendered to Britain in 1796.

Colombo plan Commonwealth plan for cooperative economic development in S and SE Asia which came into operation in 1951. It covers large-scale irrigation and hydro-electric schemes, technical training, an Asian nuclear centre at Manila, and is not limited to Commonwealth members. A Staff College for Technician Education was established at Singapore in 1974.

colon /kɒ'lɒn/ in punctuation, a mark (:) intended to direct the reader's attention forward, usually because what follows explains or develops what has just been written (for example, the soldiers carried a variety of weapons: rifles,

Colombia
REPUBLIC OF (*República de Colombia*)

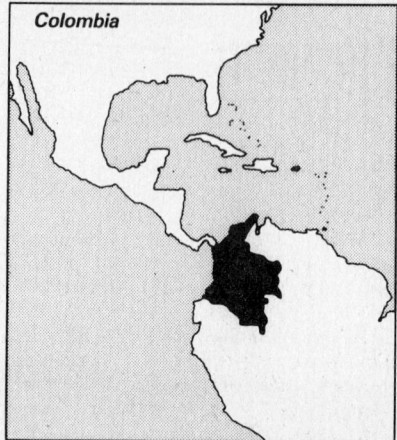

Colombia

AREA 1,139,000 sq km/456,500 sq mi
CAPITAL Bogotá
TOWNS Medellin, Cali, Bucaramanga; ports Barranquilla, Cartagena
PHYSICAL the Andes mountains run N–S; plains in the E; Magdalena river runs N to the Caribbean
HEAD OF STATE AND OF GOVERNMENT Virgilio Barco Vargas from 1986
GOVERNMENT republic
EXPORTS emeralds (world's largest producer), coffee (second largest world producer), bananas, cotton, meat, sugar, oil, skins and hides
CURRENCY peso (419.56 = £1 Sept 1987)
POPULATION (1985) 29,347,000 (mainly of mixed Spanish and American Indian descent); annual growth rate 2.8%
LANGUAGE Spanish
RELIGION Roman Catholic
LITERACY 86% male/84% female (1981 est)
GNP $42.5 bn (1983); $1,112 per head of population
CHRONOLOGY
1886 Full independence achieved. Conservatives in power.
1930 Liberals in power.
1946 Conservatives in power.
1948 Left-wing mayor of Bogotá assassinated. Widespread outcry.
1949 Start of near civil war, La Violencia, during which 280,000 people died.
1957 Hoping to halt the violence, Conservatives and Liberals agreed to form a National Front, sharing the presidency.
1970 National Popular Alliance (ANAPO) formed as a left-wing opposition to the National Front.

1974 National Front accord temporarily ended.
1975 Civil unrest because of disillusionment with the government.
1978 Liberals, under Julio Turbay, revived the accord and began an intensive fight against drug dealers.
1982 Liberals maintained their control of Congress but lost the presidency. The Conservative president, Belisario Betancur, attempted to end the violence by granting left-wing guerrillas an amnesty, freeing political prisoners, and embarking on a large public works programme.
1984 Minister of justice assassinated by, it was suspected, drug dealers. Campaign against them was stepped up.
1986 Virgilio Barco Vargas, Liberal, elected president by a record margin.

capital, was founded in the gold rush which followed the discoveries of 1858. Colorado became a state in 1876.

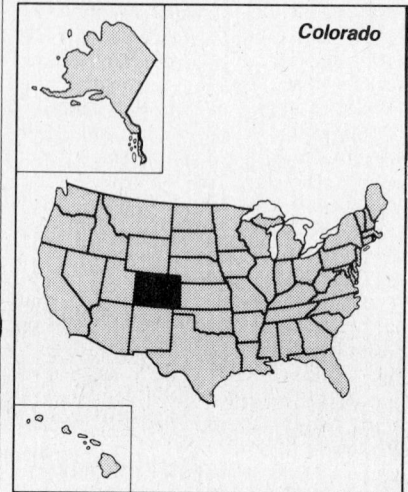

Colorado

Colorado Springs /ˌkɒləˈrɑːdəʊ sprɪŋz/ health resort in Colorado, USA, 120 km/75 mi SE of Denver; population (1980) 215,000. At an altitude of about 1,800 m/6,000 ft, and surrounded by magnificent scenery, it is also a local trade centre.

coloratura in music, a rapid ornamental vocal passage with runs, and trills. A *coloratura soprano* has a light, high voice suited to such music.

Colosseum /ˌkɒləˈsiːəm/ ruined amphitheatre in ancient Rome, begun by the emperor Vespasian to replace the amphitheatre destroyed by fire in the reign of Nero, and completed by Titus in 80 AD, it was 187 m/615 ft long and 49 m/160 ft high, and seated 50,000 people. Early Christians were martyred here by lions and gladiators. It could be flooded for mimic sea battles.

Colossus of Rhodes /kəˈlɒsəs əv ˈrəʊdz/ bronze statue of Apollo erected at the entrance to the harbour at Rhodes 292–280 BC. Said to have been about 30 m/100 ft high, it was counted as one of the Seven Wonders of the World, but in 224 BC fell as a result of an earthquake.

colour blindness an incurable defect of vision which reduces the ability to discriminate one colour from another. In the most common types confusion among the red-yellow-green range of colours is very prevalent – for example, many colour-blind observers are unable to distinguish red from yellow or yellow from green. The cause of congenital colour blindness is not known, although it probably arises from some defect in the retinal receptors. Toxic conditions caused by excessive smoking, and lead poisoning, can lead to colour blindness. Statistics show that from two to six per cent of men suffer from the defect, and less than one per cent of women.

colours, military flags or standards carried by British military regiments, so called because of the various combinations of colours employed to distinguish one regiment from another. Each

hand-guns, several machine-guns and an anti-tank weapon).

colon /ˈkɒlən/ in anatomy, the part of the large ◊intestine, between the caecum and ◊rectum. It is the region where water and mineral salts are absorbed from digested food, and the residue formed into ◊faeces or faecal pellets.

Colón /kɒˈlɒn/ city in Panama, at the Caribbean end of the Panama Canal. Founded in 1850, and named Aspinwall in 1852, it was renamed Colón in 1890 in honour of Christopher ◊Columbus. Population (1980) 60,000.

Colón, Archipélago de /kɒˈlɒn/ official name of the ◊Galapagos Islands.

colophon originally an inscription on the last page of a book giving the writer's or printer's name, and place and year of publication. In modern practice it is a decorative device on the title page or spine of a book, the 'trade-mark' of the individual publisher.

Colorado /ˌkɒləˈrɑːdəʊ/ river in North America, rising in the Rocky Mountains and flowing 2,300 km/1,450 mi to the Gulf of California through Colorado state, Utah and Arizona, and North Mexico. The many dams

along its course, including Hoover and Glen Canyon, provide power and irrigation water, but have destroyed wildlife and scenery, and very little water now reaches the sea. To the west of the river in south east California is the *Colorado Desert*, an arid area of 5,000 sq km/2,000 sq mi.

Colorado /ˌkɒləˈrɑːdəʊ/ mountain state of the central USA; Centennial State
area 270,240 sq km /104,247 sq mi
capital Denver
towns Colorado Springs
features Rocky Mountain National Park; Pike's Peak; prehistoric cliff dwellings of the Mesa Verde National Park; Garden of the Gods (natural sandstone sculptures); Dinosaur and Great Sand Dunes national monuments; 'ghost' mining towns
products cereals, meat and dairy products; oil, coal, molybdenum, uranium; iron, steel, machinery
population (1980) 2,890,000
famous people Jack Dempsey, Douglas Fairbanks
history first settled by the Spanish, Colorado later attracted fur traders, and Denver, the

battalion carries the Sovereign's colour – that is, a Union Jack on a blue ground – and the regimental colour which bears the title, crest, and motto of the regiment with the names of battle honours. Rifle regiments do not carry colours.

Colt /kəʊlt/ Samuel 1814–1862. American gunsmith who invented the revolver 1835 that took his name. At Hartford, Connecticut, his birthplace, and later in England, he built up an immense arms-manufacturing business.

Coltrane /kɒl'treɪn/ John (William) 1926–1967. US jazz saxophonist who rose to fame in 1955 with the Miles ◊Davis quintet. He was a powerful and highly individual artist whose performances were noted for experimentation, and whose quartet was highly regarded for its innovations in melody and harmony.

coltsfoot yellow flower *Tussilago farfara* of the family Compositae. The flowers appear in early spring before the leaves. The solitary flower-heads have many narrow rays and the stems have large purplish scales. The large leaf, up to 22 cm/9 in across, is shaped like a horse's foot and gives the plant its common name. Coltsfoot lives in Europe, N Asia and N Africa, often on bare ground and in waste places.

colugo south east Asian climbing mammal in which a flap of skin extends from head to forelimb to hindlimb to tail, and can be used for gliding between forest trees. It may glide 130 m or more, losing little height. It feeds largely on buds and leaves, and hangs upside down under branches. There are two species, *Cynocephalus variegatus* of Indo-China and Indonesia, and *Cynocephalus volans* of the Philippines, both 60 cm/2 ft or so including tail. Sometimes misleadingly called 'flying lemurs', they cannot fly and are not lemurs. They are so different from other mammals that they form an order of their own, the Dermoptera.

Colum /'kɒləm/ Padraic 1881–1972. Irish poet and playwright. He was associated with the foundation of the Abbey Theatre, Dublin, where his best-known plays *Land* 1905, and *Thomas Muskerry*, were performed. His *Collected Poems* 1932 show his gift for lyrical expression. He and his wife Mary were close friends of James ◊Joyce.

Columban /kə'lʌmbən/ 543–615. Irish saint. Born in Leinster, he studied at Bangor, and about 585 went to the Vosges with 12 other monks and founded the monastery of Luxeuil. Later he preached to the barbarians in Switzerland, then went to Italy, where he built the abbey of Bobbio in the Apennines.

Columba, St /kə'lʌmbə/ 521–597. Latin form of Colum or Colum-cille ('Colum of the cell'). Irish saint and apostle of Scotland. Born in county Donegal of royal descent, he founded monasteries and churches in Ireland. In 563 he sailed with 12 companions to Iona, and built there the monastery famous in the history of the conversion of Britain. He crowned king Aidan. In 1958 his cell, with the broad slab of rock on which he slept, was discovered. His feast day is 9 Jun.

Columbia /kə'lʌmbiə/ river in W North America, famous for salmon. It rises in British Columbia, Canada, and flows through

Washington state, USA, to the Pacific below Astoria. It is harnessed for irrigation and power by the Grand Coulee and other great dams.

Columbia /kə'lʌmbiə/ city, capital of South Carolina, USA, on the Congaree river. A distribution centre and seat of South Carolina university. Textiles, fertilizers, and hosiery are made here. Population (1980) 101,200.

Columbia, District of /kə'lʌmbiə/ seat of the federal government of the USA, coterminous with the capital, ◊Washington. area 178 sq km/69 sq mi. Situated on the Potomac river, it was ceded by Maryland as the national capital site in 1790.

columbine plant *Aquilegia vulgaris* of the family Ranunculaceae. It is a perennial herb, with deeply divided leaves, and purple flowers with spurred petals. It grows wild in woods and is a familiar garden plant.

columbium former name for the chemical element ◊niobium.

Columbus /kə'lʌmbəs/ capital city of Ohio, USA, on the rivers Scioto and Olentangy. Population (1980) 565,000. It is near a coalfield and natural gas resources, and industries include the manufacture of cars, planes, missiles, electrical goods, mining machinery, refrigerators, and telephones. There are three universities and a symphony orchestra.

Columbus /kə'lʌmbəs/ Christopher 1451–1506. Italian navigator and explorer (Spanish name Cristobal Colón). Born at Genoa, he went to sea at an early age, and in 1478 settled in Portugal. Having come to the conclusion that Asia could be reached by sailing westward, he sought for many years a patron to finance such a voyage. After many delays he won the support of King Ferdinand and Queen Isabella of Spain, and on 3 Aug 1492 sailed from Palos with three small ships. On 12 Oct land was sighted, probably Watling Island (now San Salvador Island), and within a few weeks also Cuba and Haiti. On his return to Spain in Mar 1493, Columbus was greatly honoured. During his second voyage 1493–96 he discovered Guadaloupe, Montserrat, Antigua, Porto Rico and Jamaica. On the third voyage in 1498 he discovered Trinidad, and the mainland of South America for the first time. He now became involved in quarrels among the colonists sent to Haiti, and in 1500 the governor sent him back to Spain in chains. Released and compensated by the king, he made his last voyage in 1502–04, during which he explored the coast of Honduras and Nicaragua in the hope of finding a strait leading to India. He died in poverty in Valladolid, and is buried in Seville cathedral. In the USA *Columbus Day* (12 Oct) is a public holiday. In 1968 the site of the wreck of his flagship, *Santa Maria*, sunk off Hispaniola 25 Dec 1492, was located.

column in architecture, a structure, round or polygonal in plan, erected vertically as a support for some part of a building. Cretan paintings reveal the existence of wooden columns in Aegean architecture, about 1500 BC. The Hittites, Assyrians, and Egyptians also used wooden columns, and in modern times they are a feature of the monumental architecture of China

Columbus An engraving of the portrait by Sebastiano del Piombo, of which the original is in the Uffizi, Florence.

and Japan. In classical architecture there are five principal types of column; see ◊order.

Colwyn Bay /'kɒlwɪn 'beɪ/ seaside town in Clwyd, North Wales, known as the 'garden resort of Wales'. Population (1981) 26,300.

coma in medicine, a state of complete unconsciousness caused by head injuries, cerebral haemorrhage, or drug overdose, from which the subject cannot be roused even by powerful stimuli. In optics, one of the geometrical aberrations of a lens, whereby skew rays from a point object make a comet-shaped spot on the image plane instead of meeting at a point, hence the name. In astronomy, the hazy cloud of gas and dust that surrounds the nucleus of a ◊comet.

Combination Laws laws passed in Britain in 1799 and 1800 making trade unionism illegal. Their introduction was the result of the anti-Jacobin panic following the French Revolution, and the fear that the unions would become centres of political agitation. The unions continued to exist, but claimed to be friendly societies or went underground, until the acts were repealed in 1824, largely due to Francis Place.

combine a machine universally used for harvesting cereals and other crops, so called because it combines the actions of reaping – cutting the crop, and threshing – beating the ears so that the grain separates. The first successful combines, drawn by horses, were used in the Californian cornfields in the 1850s. Modern combines are huge self-propelled machines capable of cutting a swathe of up to 9 m/30 ft or more.

combined operations see ◊Commandos.

combustion burning, defined in chemical terms as rapid combination of a substance with oxygen accompanied by the evolution of heat and usually light. Thus a slow-burning candle flame and the explosion of a mixture of petrol vapour and air are extreme examples of combustion. See also ◊oxidation.

Comecon (Council for Mutual Economic Cooperation) established in 1949 in opposition to the ◊Marshall Plan, links the USSR with Bulgaria, Czechoslovakia, Hungary, Poland, Romania, East Germany (from 1950), Mongolia (from 1962), Cuba (from 1972) and Vietnam (from 1978), with Yugoslavia as an associated member. Albania also once belonged (1949–61). It seeks to promote economic co-operation and development among member states, but has no ◊free trade between members. The USSR in particular, because of its need for new technology, has in recent years increased its share of trade with the West.

Comédie Française /ˌkɒmeɪˈdiː frɒnˈseɪz/ The French national theatre (for both comedy and tragedy) in Paris, founded in 1680 by Louis XIV. Its base is the Salle Richelieu on the right bank of the Seine, and the Théatre de l'Odéon, on the left bank, is a testing-ground for avant-garde ideas.

comedy in the simplest terms, a drama with a happy ending, as opposed to tragedy. Since much comedy relies on topical allusion and taste many comedies, successful during their time, have subsequently been forgotten. The comic tradition was established by the Greek dramatists ◊Aristophanes and ◊Menander, and the Roman writers ◊Terence and ◊Plautus. In medieval times, the Vices and Devil of the ◊Morality plays developed into the stock comic characters of the Renaissance *Comedy of Humours* with such notable villains as ◊Jonson's Mosca in *Volpone*. The timeless comedies of ◊Shakespeare and ◊Molière were followed in England during the 17th century by the witty *Comedy of Manners* of Restoration writers such as ◊Etherege, ◊Wycherley and ◊Congreve. Their often coarse but always vital comedies became toned down in the later Restoration dramas of ◊Sheridan and ◊Goldsmith. A fashion for sentimental comedies dominated most of the 19th century and left little that is remembered today until its close brought the realistic tradition of ◊Shaw and the elegant social comedies of ◊Wilde. The polished comedies of ◊Coward and ◊Rattigan from the 1920s to 1940s were eclipsed during the late 1950s and 1960s by a trend towards satire and a more cynical humour as seen in the works of Joe ◊Orton and Peter ◊Nichols. From the 1970s the 'black comedies' of Alan ◊Ayckbourn have dominated the English stage.

comet a small, icy body orbiting the Sun on a highly elliptical path. A comet consists of a central nucleus a few kilometres across, often likened to a dirty snowball because it consists mostly of ice mixed with dust. As the comet approaches the Sun the nucleus heats up, releasing gas and dust which form a tenuous ◊*coma* up to 100,000 km/60,000 mi wide, around the nucleus. Gas and dust stream away from the coma to form the comet's tail, which may extend for millions of kilometres.

Comets are believed to have been formed at the birth of the ◊solar system. Billions of them now reside in the **Oort cloud** (after the Dutch astronomer Jan ◊Oort) beyond the planets. The gravitational effect of passing stars pushes some towards the Sun, when they become visible from Earth. Most comets swing around the Sun and return to distant space, never to be seen again for thousands or millions of years. But some have their orbits altered by the gravitational pull of the planets so that they reappear every 200 years or less. These are termed *periodic comets*. Of the 800 or so comets whose orbits have been calculated, about 1 in 5 is periodic; the only one visible to the naked eye is ◊Halleys comet. That with the shortest known period is Encke's comet, which orbits the Sun every 3.3 years. A dozen or more comets are discovered every year, some by amateur astronomers.

comfrey tall perennial *Symphytum officinale* of the family Boraginaceae. Up to 1.2 m/4 ft tall, hairy, with winged stems and lanceolate leaves, the flowers grow in drooping clusters and are bell-like in shape. They may be white, yellowish, purple or pink. Comfrey was once an important medicinal plant for treating wounds and various ailments, and is still sometimes used as a poultice. It is found throughout Europe. Various other species are found in Europe and W Asia.

comic strip (or *strip cartoon*) a sequence of, usually, four or more frames of drawings in ◊cartoon style. Strips may work independently or form instalments of a serial and are predominantly humorous or satirical in intent. Longer stories in comic-strip form are published separately as comic books (see under ◊magazine).

The first modern comic strip was 'The Yellow Kid' by Richard Felton Outcault, which appeared in the Sunday newspaper *New York World* 1896; it was immediately successful and others soon followed. One of the most admired comic strips has been the US 'Krazy Kat', which began 1910 and ended with the death of its creator, Richard Herriman, 1944. Current notable strip cartoons include the US 'Peanuts' by Charles M Schulz (1922–), which began 1950 and was read daily by 60 million people by the end of the 1960s, and the political 'Doonesbury' by Gary Trudeau; the British 'Andy Capp' by Reginald Smythe (1917–); and the French 'Asterix' by Albert Uderzo and René Goscinny, which began in the early 1960s.

Comines /kɒˈmiːn/ Philippe de c. 1445–1509. French diplomat in the service of Louis XI, author of *Mémoires*.

Cominform (Communist Information Bureau) 1947–56, established by Andrei Zhdanov to exchange information between European communist parties. Yugoslavia was expelled in 1948.

Comintern abbreviation of *Com*munist ◊*Intern*ational.

comma a punctuation mark (,), intended to provide breaks or pauses inside a sentence; commas may come at the end of a clause, after a phrase, or in lists (for example, apples, pears, plums, and pineapples; or, apples, pears, plums and pineapples). Uncertain where sentences properly end, many occasional writers use a comma instead of a period (or full stop), writing *We saw John last night, it was good to see him again*, rather than *We saw John last night. It was* *good to see him again*. The meaning is entirely clear in both cases. One solution in such situations is to use a *semicolon* (;), which combines period and comma and serves well in bridging the gap between the close association of the comma and the sharp separation of the period. See also ◊parenthesis.

command language in computing, a set of commands and the rules governing their use by which ◊end-users (nonspecialists) control a program. For example, an ◊operating system may have commands such as SAVE and DELETE, or a payroll program may have commands for adding and amending staff records.

Commandos British troops of Combined Operations Command who raided enemy-occupied territory in World War II. The term Commando originated in S Africa, where it was used for Boer military reprisal raids against African tribesmen, and later, in the South African War, against the British. At the end of the war the army Commandos were disbanded, but the organization was carried on by the Royal Marines.

commedia dell'arte popular form of Italian improvised drama in the 16th and 17th centuries. It was performed by specially trained troupes of actors with their own stock characters and situations. It exerted considerable influence on writers such as ◊Molière and on the English genres ◊pantomime, harlequinade, and the ◊Punch and Judy show. It laid the foundation for a tradition of mime, particularly in France, which has continued with the contemporary mime of Jean-Louis ◊Barrault and Marcel ◊Marceau.

commensalism a relationship between two ◊species whereby one (the commensal) benefits from the association, while the other neither benefits nor suffers. For example, certain species of millipede and silverfish inhabit the nests of army ants and live by scavenging on the refuse of their hosts, but without affecting the ants.

Commissioner for Oaths in England, a person appointed by the Lord Chancellor with power to administer the oath or take an affidavit; usually a practising solicitor.

committal proceedings in the UK, a hearing before local magistrates of evidence as to whether there is a case to answer before a higher court. From 1967 the proceedings were unreported unless a defendant, or one of them, wished the restriction lifted.

commodity things produced for sale. They may be *consumer goods* like radios, or *producer goods* such as copper bars. *Commodity markets* deal in raw or semi-raw materials which are amenable to grading and which can be stored for considerable periods without deterioration. They developed to their present form in the 19th century, when industrial growth facilitated trading in large, standardized quantities of raw materials. Most markets encompass trading in 'commodity futures', that is trading for delivery several months ahead. Major commodity markets exist in Chicago, Tokyo, London, and elsewhere. Though specialized markets exist, such as silkworm cocoons in Tokyo, most trade relates to cereals and metals. 'Softs' is a term used for most materials other than metals.

INTERNATIONALLY TRADED COMMODITIES

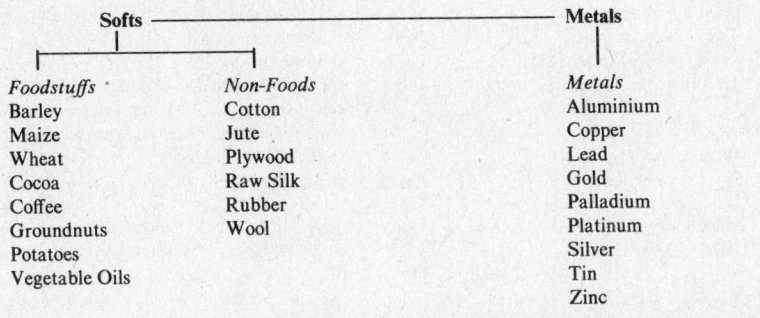

Softs		Metals
Foodstuffs	*Non-Foods*	*Metals*
Barley	Cotton	Aluminium
Maize	Jute	Copper
Wheat	Plywood	Lead
Cocoa	Raw Silk	Gold
Coffee	Rubber	Palladium
Groundnuts	Wool	Platinum
Potatoes		Silver
Vegetable Oils		Tin
		Zinc

Commodus /ˈkɒmədəs/ Lucius Aelius Aurelius 161–192. Roman emperor from 180. Son of Marcus Aurelius, he was a tyrant and was strangled by members of his household.

common unenclosed wasteland and pasture used in common by the inhabitants of a parish or district or the community at large. The common originated in the English manorial system, in the middle ages, when every manor had a large area of unenclosed and uncultivated land over which the freeholders and copyholders had the right to take or use what the soil naturally produced.

common law that part of the English law not embodied in legislation. It consists of rules of law embodied in judicial decisions; described as 'unwritten law' as opposed to the 'written law' of legislation. English common law became the basis of law in the USA.

With the growth of law reports grew the doctrine of 'judicial precedent', that is, that, in deciding a particular case, the courts must have regard to the principles of law laid down in earlier reported decisions which relate to the same point, or to a similar point. This does not prevent the courts from making reasonable extensions of such principles to suit variant facts, or from laying down a new principle if the case before them is unconnected with any existing principle. Hence, the common law (sometimes also called 'case law' or 'judge-made law') is an important agency in keeping the law in harmony with the needs of the community, where no legislation is applicable, or where, if there is, its exact meaning has to be interpreted by the courts.

A narrower meaning of common law is that it comprises the law embodied in decisions of the common law Courts, as opposed to that contained in ◊'Equity', that is, the decisions formerly of the Court of Chancery exclusively.

Common Market popular name for the EEC or European Economic Community; see ◊European Community.

Common Prayer, Book of the service book of the Church of England based very largely on the Roman Breviary. The first Book of Common Prayer in English was that known as the First Prayer Book of Edward VI, published in 1549. The Second Prayer Book of Edward VI appeared in 1552, but was withdrawn in 1553 on Mary's

accession. In 1559 the Revised Prayer Book was issued, closely resembling that of 1549. This was suppressed by parliament in 1645, but its use was restored in 1660 and a number of revisions were made. This is the Book of Common Prayer still officially authorized, but an act of 1968 legalized alternative services, and the Worship and Doctrine Measure 1974 gave the Church control of its worship and teaching. The Church's Alternative Service Book 1980, in modern language, is also in use.

Commons, House of the lower but more powerful of the two parts of the British and Canadian ◊Parliaments.

Commonwealth period in English history 1649–53, between the execution of Charles I and the establishment of the Protectorate governed by Oliver Cromwell. Commonwealth is also used to refer to the period 1649–60, between the execution of Charles I and the re-establishing of the monarchy in 1660 under Charles II.

Commonwealth, the (British) association of states that have been or still are ruled by Britain. On 15 May 1917 ◊Smuts, representing South Africa in the Imperial War Cabinet of World War I, suggested that 'British commonwealth of nations' was the right title for the British Empire. The name was recognized in the Statute of Westminster 1931, but after World War II a growing sense of independent nationhood led to the simplification of the title to the Commonwealth.

It is now a free association of sovereign independent states, the full 'members of the Commonwealth', together with a number of dependent territories, such as colonies and protectorates, which rank as 'Commonwealth countries'. Commonwealth countries that have reached self-governing maturity but are too small to bear the full responsibilities of 'members of the Commonwealth' may have special status, for example, Nauru. See also ◊British Empire.

Commonwealth Conference popular name for a top-level consultation between the prime ministers (or defence, finance, foreign or other ministers) of the sovereign independent members of the Commonwealth. Colonial Conferences had been instituted in 1887, also meeting in 1894, 1897 and 1902. The 1907 Conference resolved that Imperial Conferences be held every four years, and these met regularly

till 1937 (the most notable being in 1926 which defined the relationship of the self-governing members of the Commonwealth). From 1937 the tendency was towards the present more informal discussions now known as Commonwealth Conferences, but although these are purely consultative, the implementation of policies being decided by individual governments, results may be far-reaching.

Notable recent Commonwealth Conferences have been Singapore (1971) the first outside the UK; Sydney (1978) the first regional meeting; Lusaka (1979), the first regular session in Africa; and Vancouver 1987.

Commonwealth Day celebrated on the official birthday of Elizabeth II, it was called Empire Day until 1958 and celebrated on 24 May (Queen Victoria's birthday) until 1966.

Commonwealth Development Corporation organization founded as the Colonial Development Corporation in 1948 to aid the development of dependent Commonwealth territories; the change of name and extension of its activities to include those now independent were announced in 1962.

Commune, Paris two periods of government in France: *The Paris municipal government 1789–94* established after the storming of the Bastille, and powerful in the French Revolution until after the fall of Robespierre. *The provisional national government 18 Mar–May 1871* consisting of Socialist and left-wing Republicans, often considered the first socialist government in history. Elected after the right-wing National Assembly at Versailles tried to disarm the National Guard, it fell when the Versailles troops captured Paris and massacred about 20,000 people 21–28 May.

communication in biology, the signalling of information by one organism to another, usually with the intention of altering the recipient's behaviour. Signals used in communication may be visual (such as a smile, or the flashes of a firefly), auditory (for example, the whines or barks of a dog), olfactory (such as the odours released by the scent glands of a deer), electrical (as in the pulses emitted by electric fish) or tactile (for example, the nuzzling of male and female elephants or horses). In many cases, communication expresses the emotional state of the sender, but may be understood by the recipient as a warning of behaviour about to be performed. Thus, a dog's growl warns of an impending attack. In other cases, signals convey information about the location of important resources. Thus, the figure-of-eight dance of the honey bee tells other members of its hive the direction and distance at which it has found a nectar source.

communications satellite A relay station in space for sending telephone, television, telex and other messages around the world. Messages are sent to and from the satellites via ground stations. The first satellite to carry TV signals across the Atlantic Ocean was Telstar in July 1962. The world is now linked by a system of communications satellites called Intelsat. Other satellites are used by individual countries for their own internal communications, or for

THE COMMONWEALTH

Country and Capital	Area in 1,000 sq km
IN AFRICA	
*Botswana Gaborone	575
British Indian Ocean Terr.	
Victoria	.2
*Gambia Banjul	11
*Ghana Accra	239
*Kenya Nairobi	583
*Lesotho Maseru	30
*Malawi Zomba	117
*Mauritius Port Louis	2
*Nigeria Lagos	924
St Helena Jamestown	.1
*Seychelles Victoria	65
*Sierra Leone Freetown	73
*Swaziland Mbabane	17
*Tanzania Dodoma	943
*Uganda Kampala	236
*Zambia Lusaka	752
*Zimbabwe Salisbury	391
IN THE AMERICAS	
Anguilla The Valley	.09
*Antigua St John's	.4
*Bahamas Nassau	14
*Barbados Bridgetown	.4
*Belize Belmopan	23
Bermuda Hamilton	.05
Brit. Virgin Is. Road Town	.2
*Canada Ottawa	9,976
Cayman Islands Georgetown	.3
*Dominica Roseau	.7
Falkland Is. Stanley	12
*Grenada St George's	.3
*Guyana Georgetown	210
*Jamaica Kingston	12
*Montserrat Plymouth	.1
*St Christopher-Nevis	
Basseterre Charlestown	.4
*St Lucia Castries	.6
*St Vincent and the	
Grenadines Kingstown	.2
*Trinidad and Tobago Port of Spain	.5
Turks and Caicos Is. Grand Turk	.4

Country and Capital	Area in 1,000 sq km
IN THE ANTARCTIC	
Australian Antarctic Terr.	5,403
Brit. Antarctic Terr.	390
Falkland Is. Dependencies	1.6
(N.Z.) Ross Dependency	453
IN ASIA	
*Bangladesh Dacca	143
*Brunei Bandar Seri Begawan	6
*Cyprus Nicosia	9
Hong Kong Victoria	1.2
*India Delhi	3,215
*Malaysia, Rep. of Kuala Lumpur	332
*Maldives Malé	.3
*Singapore Singapore	.6
*Sri Lanka Colombo	66
IN AUSTRALASIA AND THE PACIFIC	
*Australia Canberra	7,704
Norfolk Island	.03
*Fiji Suva	18
*Kiribati Tarawa	.7
*Nauru	.02
*New Zealand Wellington	269
Cook Islands	.2
Niue Island	.3
Tokelau Islands	.01
*Papua New Guinea Port Moresby	475
Pitcairn	.005
*Solomon Islands Honiara	30
Tonga Nuku'alofa	.7
**Tuvalu Funafuti	.02
*Vanuatu Vila	15
*Western Samoa Apia	3
IN EUROPE	
**United Kingdom	
England London	131
Wales Cardiff	21
Scotland Edinburgh	79
N. Ireland Belfast	14
Isle of Man Douglas	.5
Channel Islands	.2
Gibraltar Gibraltar	.006
*Malta Valletta	.3
	33,932

*Independent members of the Commonwealth
**Special members

---

business or military use. Most modern communications satellites are in ◊geostationary orbit so that they appear to hang fixed over one point on the Earth's surface. The new generation of satellites, called *direct broadcast satellites*, will be powerful enough to transmit direct to small domestic aerials, cutting out powerful ground stations such as at Goonhilly.

Communion, Holy another name for the ◊Eucharist.

communism revolutionary ◊socialism based on the idea, expressed by ◊Marx and ◊Engels in the *Communist Manifesto* 1848, that human society, having passed through successive stages of slavery, feudalism, and capitalism, must advance to a communist society based on common ownership of the means of production and a planned economy. This theory combines with a belief in economic determinism to form the central communist concept of 'dialectical materialism'. Marx believed that capitalism had become a barrier to progress and needed to be replaced by a dictatorship of the proletariat (working class), which would build a socialist society.

Only in 1917 in Russia, where the communal basis of feudalism was still strong, was such a system imposed (see ◊Lenin and ◊Stalin) in Europe. The Social Democratic parties formed in Europe in the second half of last century professed to be Marxist, but their outlook gradually became 'reformist' – aiming at reforms of capitalist society rather than at the radical social change envisaged by Marx. The Russian Social Democratic Labour Party, led by Lenin, remained Marxist, and changed its name to Communist Party after the Nov 1917 revolution to emphasize its difference from Social Democratic parties elsewhere. Revolutionary socialist parties and groups united to form Communist parties in other countries (in Britain in 1920).

After World War II, communism was enforced in those countries that came under Soviet occupation, and ◊China, at first under Russian tutelage, emerged after 1961 as a rival to the ◊USSR in world leadership. Both took strong measures to maintain or establish their own types of 'orthodox' communism in countries on their borders (USSR in ◊Hungary and ◊Czechoslovakia, and China in N ◊Korea and ◊Vietnam), and in more remote areas (USSR in the Arab world and ◊Cuba, and China in ◊Albania), and (both of them) in the newly emergent African countries, as the fount of doctrine and source of technological aid.

The denunciation of Stalinism by Khrushchev in 1956 was the first crack in the Soviet communist ideal, and was followed by the Hungarian revolt. See also ◊Poland, ◊Romania, ◊Yugoslavia. During the late 1960s and the 1970s it was debated whether the state requires to be maintained as 'the dictatorship of the proletariat' once revolution on the economic front has been achieved, or whether it may then become the state of the entire people: Engels, Lenin, Khrushchev, and ◊Liu Shaoqi held the latter view, and Stalin and ◊Mao Zedong the former. Many Communist parties inside Europe (for example, the Euro-Communism of France, Italy, and the major part of the British Communist Party) and outside (for example, Japan) have rejected since the 1960s or later any suggestion of automatic Soviet dominance. In the 1980s there was an expansion of economic freedom in E Europe: the USSR, E Germany, Czechoslovakia, and Romania remained strongly socialist, stressing modernization and technical efficiency; whereas Hungary, Bulgaria Poland, and Yugoslavia moved towards decentralization, competition, and the market place. See also ◊Chile, ◊Kampuchea, ◊Libya, ◊Nicaragua.

Communism Peak highest mountain (*Pik Kommunizma*) in the USSR; 7,495 m/24,589 ft.

community in the social sciences, term for the sense of identity, purpose, and companionship that comes from belonging to a particular place, organization, or social group. The concept dominated sociological thinking in the first half of the 20th century, and inspired the academic discipline of *community studies*.

community in ecology, an assemblage of plants, animals and other organisms living within a circumscribed area. Communities are usually named by reference to a dominant feature such as a characteristic plant species (for example, beech wood community), or prominent physical feature (for example, a freshwater pond

Commonwealth Conference The Vancouver conference in 1987. From left to right: back row – A C S Hameed (Sri Lanka); P V Obeng (Ghana); L J Chimango (Milawi); Va'ai Kolone (Western Samoa); Raymond Robinson (Trinidad and Tobago); Paias Wingti (Papua New Guinea); Lloyd Erskine Sandiford (Barbados); B S Dlamini (Swaziland); V C Bird (Antigua and Barbuda); James Fitz-Allen Mitchell (St Vincent and the Grenadines); Ezekiel Alebua (Soloman Islands); Manuel Esquivel (Belize); Kennedy A Simmonds (St Kitts and Nevis); A B Kamara (Sierra Leone); Satcam Boolell (Mauritius); middle row – Herbert A Blaize (Grenada); Augustus Aikhomu (Nigeria); Edward P G Seaga (Jamaica); Desmond Hoyte (Guyana); Ieremia T Tabai (Kiribati); Albert Rene (Seychelles); Mahathir bin Mohamed (Malaysia); Robert G Mugabe (Zimbabwe); Spyros Kyprianou (Cyprus); Q K J Masire (Botswana); Maumoon Abdul Gayoom (Maldives); Ali Hassan Mwingi (Tanzania); Yoweri K Museveni (Uganda); John Compton (St Lucia); Eddie Fenech-Adami (Malta); front row – Hassanal Bolkiah (Brunei Darussalam); David Lange (New Zealand); Daniel T Arap Moi (Kenya); Rajiv Gandhi (India); Margaret Thatcher (Britain); Lee Kuan Yew (Singapore); Lynden O Pindling (Bahamas); Brian Mulroney (Canada); Shridath Ramphal, Commonwealth Secretary-General; K D Kaunda (Zambia); Eugenia Charles (Dominica); Dawda Jawara (Gambia); Hussain Ershad (Bangladesh); Robert Hawke (Australia); King Moshoeshoe II (Lesotho).

community). The same community in different areas is usually characterized by the same (or similar) species.

community council in Wales, name for a ◊parish council.

community school/education the philosophy which asserts that educational institutions are more effective if closely integrated with, and opened up to all members of, the surrounding community. First pioneered by Henry ◊Morris.

community service scheme introduced in Britain by the Criminal Justice Act 1972, under which minor offenders are sentenced to spare time work in the service of the community (aiding children, the elderly or the handicapped), instead of prison. The offender must consent, be 17 or over, and have committed no violence.

commutator a device in a DC (direct current) electric motor that reverses the current flowing in the armature coils as the armature rotates. A DC generator, or ◊dynamo, uses a commutator to convert the AC (alternating current) generated in the armature coils into DC. A commutator consists of opposite pairs of conductors insulated from one another. Contact to an external circuit is provided by carbon or metal brushes.

Como /'kəuməu/ city in Lombardy, Italy, on Lake Como at the foot of the Alps. The river

Adda flows N–S through the lake, and the shores are famous for their beauty. Como has a marble cathedral, built 1396–1732, and is a tourist resort. Population (1981) 95,500.

Comodoro Rivadavia /,kɒmə'dɔːrəu ,rivə'dɑːviə/ port in SE Argentina; population (1984) 120,000. Argentina's main oilfields are nearby.

Comorin /'kɒmərɪn/ the most southerly cape of the Indian sub-continent, in Tamil Nadu, where the Indian Ocean, Bay of Bengal and Arabian Sea meet.

Comoro /'kɒmərəu/ archipelago in the Mozambique Channel, NW of Madagascar, now the *Federal Island Republic of Comoros* except for the island of Mayotte which is still united with France.

Comoros /'kɒmərəuz/ group of islands comprising Njazidja, Nzwani, and Mwali, situated in the Indian Ocean between Madagascar and the E coast of Africa. The fourth island in the group, Mayotte, is a French dependency.

government under the 1978 constitution there is a president, elected by universal adult suffrage for a six-year term, with an appointed council of ministers and a single-chamber federal assembly of 38 members elected for five years. Although each of the four main islands has a degree of autonomy, with its own governor and council, the system is a limited form of federalism, since the

president appoints the governors and the federal government is responsible for the islands' resources. The Comoros is officially Muslim, and since 1979 has been a one-party state although unofficial opposition groups exist

history originally inhabited by Asians, Africans, and Indonesians, The Comoros became a French colony in 1912 and were attached to Madagascar 1914–47, when they were made a French Overseas Territory. Internal self-government was obtained in 1961 but full independence not achieved until 1975, because of Mayotte's reluctance to sever links with France. Although the Comoros joined the United Nations in 1975, with Ahmed Abdallah as president, Mayotte remained under French administration. Relations with France deteriorated as Ali Soilih, who had overthrown Abdallah, became more powerful as president under a new constitution. In 1978 he was killed by French mercenaries working for Abdallah.

A federal Islamic republic was proclaimed, a new constitution adopted and Abdallah elected president, diplomatic relations with France were restored. In 1979 the Comoros became a one-party state and government powers were increased. In the same year a plot to overthrow Abdallah was foiled. In 1984 he was re-elected president and in the following year the constitution was amended, abolishing the post of prime minister and making Abdallah head of government as well as head of state. Mayotte remains an uneasy member of the federation, with its future uncertain.

Comoros
FEDERAL ISLAMIC REPUBLIC OF (*Republique fédérale islamique des Comores*)

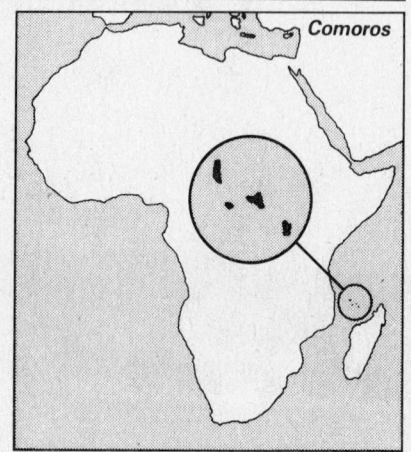

Comoros

AREA 2,170 sq km/838 sq mi
CAPITAL Moroni
PHYSICAL comprises the islands of Njazídja, Nzwani, and Mwali (formerly Grand Comoro, Anjouan, Maheli)
FEATURES active volcano on Njazídja
HEAD OF STATE AND OF GOVERNMENT Ahmed Abdallah Abderemane from 1978
GOVERNMENT one-party federal republic
EXPORTS copra, vanilla, cocoa, sisal, coffee, cloves, essential oils
CURRENCY CFA franc (498.38 = £1 Sept 1987)
POPULATION 469,000 (1985); annual growth rate 3.1%
LANGUAGE French, Arabic (official); Comorian (Swahili dialect)
RELIGION Muslim (official)
LITERACY 15%
GNP $154 million (1982); $339 per head of population
CHRONOLOGY
1975 Independence achieved, but with Mayotte a reluctant member of the new federal state. Ahmed Abdallah elected president. The Comoros joined United Nations.
1976 Abdallah overthrown by Ali Soilih.
1978 Soilih killed by mercenaries working for Abdallah. Islamic republic proclaimed and Abdallah elected president.
1979 The Comoros became a one-party state. Powers of the federal government increased.
1985 Constitution amended to make Abdallah head of government as well as head of state.

largely adopted in the USA. This limitation of liability is essential to commercial expansion when large capital sums must be raised by the contributions of many individuals. The affairs of companies are managed by directors, a public company having at least two, and their accounts must be audited.

The development of ◊multinational corporations, companies that are worldwide in their operations, enabled them to avoid tax laws, affect currency stability, and be independent of elected governments.

comparative advantage law of international trade first elaborated by David ◊Ricardo showing that trade becomes advantageous if the cost of production of particular items differs as between one country and another. At a simple level, if wine is cheaper to produce in country A than in country B, and the reverse is true of cheese, A can specialize in wine and B in cheese and they can trade to mutual benefit.

compass an instrument for finding direction. The most commonly used is a magnetic compass. This consists of a thin piece of magnetic material with the north-seeking pole indicated, free to rotate on a pivot and mounted on a compass card on which the points of the compass are marked. When the compass is properly adjusted and used, the north-seeking pole will point to the magnetic north, from which true north can be found from tables of magnetic corrections.

Compasses not dependent on the magnet are gyrocompasses, dependent on the ◊gyroscope, and radiocompasses, dependent on the use of radio. These are unaffected by the presence of iron and by magnetic anomalies of the earth's magnetic field, and are widely used in ships and aircraft. See ◊magnetism.

competence and **performance** in linguistics, the potential and actual utterances of a speaker. As formulated by the linguist ◊Chomsky, a

compact disc a record disc, only some 12 cm/4.5 in across, which has an hour's playing time on one side. The compact disc looks entirely different from a conventional LP (gramophone) record. It is silvery in colour with a transparent plastic coating. The technology of reproduction is also entirely different. The metal disc underneath the plastic coating is etched by a ◊laser beam with microscopic pits, which carry a digital code that represents the music. During playback, a laser beam reads the code and produces signals that are changed into near-exact replicas of the original sounds.

Companion of Honour British order of chivalry, founded by George V in 1917. It is of one class only, and carries no title, but Companions append 'CH' to their names. The number is limited to 65 and the award is made to both men and women.

company a group of people combined together for business or trade. A company may be either public (to which the general public is invited to subscribe for shares) or, in the case of the great majority, private. (Private companies may not sell shares to the public.) At least seven members are required for the former and two for the latter in the UK. In the majority of companies in Britain the liability of the members is limited liability to the amount of their subscription, under an act of 1855 promoted by Judge Lord Bramwell, by which British law came into line with European practice, which had already been

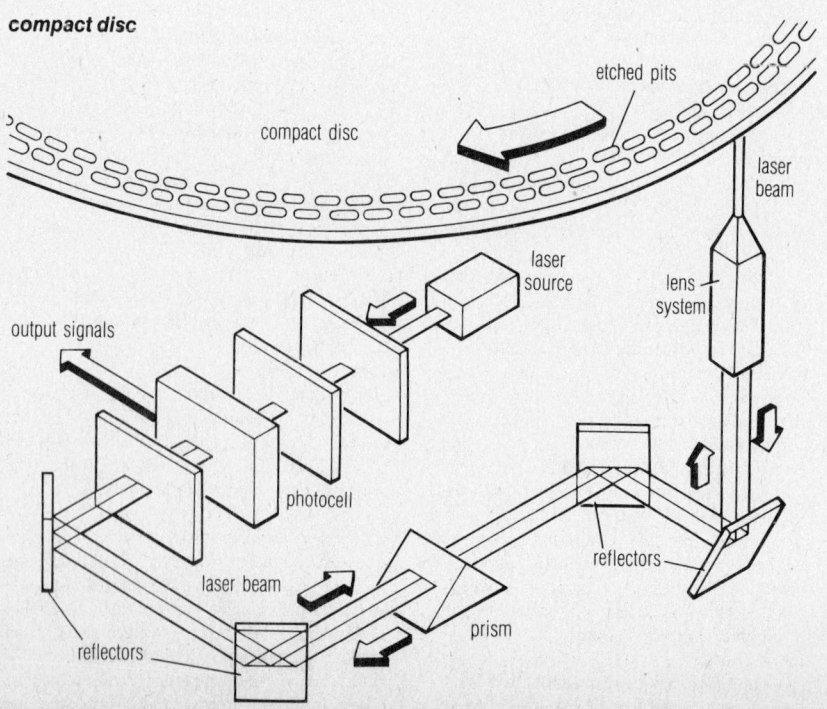

compact disc

compact disc
etched pits
laser beam
laser source
lens system
output signals
photocell
laser beam
reflectors
prism
reflectors

compass

person's linguistic competence is the set of internalized rules in his or her brain that make it possible to understand and produce language - that stipulate, for example, what order words can be put in to form a sentence. A person's performance is the actual phrases and sentences he or she produces on the basis of these rules.

competition in ecology, the interaction between two or more organisms, or groups of organisms (for example, species), that use a common resource which is in short supply. Thus, plants may compete with each other for sunlight, or nutrients from the soil, while animals may compete amongst themselves for food, water or refuges. Because competition invariably results in a reduction in the numbers of one or both competitors, it has played an important role in ◊evolution, contributing both to the decline of certain species, and to the evolution of ◊adaptations (structures or behaviour patterns that allow organisms to compete more effectively).

Compiègne /ˌkɒmpiˈeɪn/ town with an airport in Oise *département*, France, on the Oise near its confluence with the Aisne; population (1983) 37,250. It has an enormous chateau, built by Louis XV. The armistices of 1918 and 1940 were signed (the latter by Hitler and Pétain) in a railway coach in the forest of Compiègne.

compiler a computer program, invented by Grace Murray Hopper at the Remington Rand Corporation in 1951, that translates other programs, written in high-level (easy-to-use) programming languages, into a code executable by the computer. High-level language typically consists of English words and phrases mixed with an algebraic notation to make them easier to write. Compilation is then necessary to convert this source code program, as it is known, into an object code program which the machine can execute.

complement in mathematical ◊set theory, the set consisting of the elements within the universal set that are not in the designated set. For example, if the universal set equals all positive whole numbers and the designated set (S) equals all even numbers, then the complement of S (denoted S') equals all odd numbers. In geometry, the complement of an angle is the number of degrees that need to be added to make it a right-angle (90°). For example, the complement of 60° is 30°; the two (60° and 30°) are termed complementary angles. In number theory, the complement of a number is obtained by subtracting the number from its base. For example, the complement of 1 in numbers to the ◊base 10 is 9, that of 2 is 8, that of 3 is 7, and so on.

Complementary numbers are important in computers, because the only mathematical operation digital computers (including pocket calculators) are directly capable of is addition. However, two numbers can be subtracted by adding one number to its complement; two numbers can be divided by using successive subtraction (which, using complements, becomes successive addition); and multiplication can be performed by using successive addition. The four main operations of arithmetic can thus all be reduced to various types of addition and made with the capability of a digital computer, using the binary number system.

complementation in genetics, the interaction that can occur between two different mutant forms of a ◊gene in a ◊diploid organism, such that they make up for each other's deficiencies and so the organism functions normally.

complex in psychology, a group of ideas and feelings which have become repressed because they are distasteful to the person in whose mind they arose; but which are still active in the depths of the person's unconscious mind, and which continue to affect his or her life and actions, even though he or she is no longer fully aware of their existence. Typical examples of a complex are the ◊Oedipus complex and the inferiority complex.

complex number in mathematics, a number written in the form $a + bi$, where a and b are real numbers and i is the square root of -1 (that is, $i^2 = -1$); b is known as the imaginary part of the complex number. Some equations in algebra, such as those of the form $x^2 + 5 = 0$, cannot be solved without recourse to complex numbers, because the real numbers do not include square roots of negative numbers. The sum of two or more complex numbers is obtained by adding separately their real and imaginary parts, for example,

$$(p + qi) + (r + si) = (p + r) + (q + s)i.$$

Complex numbers can be represented graphically on an Argand diagram, which uses rectangular ◊Cartesian co-ordinates in which the x-axis represents the real part of the number and the y-axis the imaginary part. Thus the number $p + qi$ is plotted as the point (p, q). Complex numbers have important applications in various areas of science, such as the theory of alternating currents in electricity.

componential analysis in linguistics, the analysis of the elements of a word's meaning. The word *boy*, for example, might be said to have three basic meaning elements (or semantic properties): 'human', 'young,' and 'male'; and so might the word *murder*: 'kill', 'intentional', and 'illegal'.

Compositae the daisy family; dicotyledonous flowering plants characterized by flowers borne in composite heads. It is the largest family of flowering plants, the majority being herbaceous. Birds seem to favour the family for use in nest 'decoration', possibly because many species either repel or kill insects (see ◊pyrethrum). Species include the daisy and dandelion; food plants artichoke, lettuce, safflower; and the garden chrysanthemum, dahlia, daisybush, and zinnia.

composite in industry, a purpose-designed engineering material created by combining single materials with complementary properties into a composite form. Most composites have a structure in which one component consists of discrete elements such as fibres (for example, asbestos, glass or carbon steel in continuous or short lengths, or 'whiskers', specially grown crystals a few mm long, such as silicon carbide) dispersed in a continuous matrix, such as plastics, concrete, steel.

Composite in classical architecture, one of the five types of ◊column. See ◊order.

compound in chemistry, a substance formed by the chemical combination of two or more ◊elements in fixed proportions. Thus unlike a mixture, which can be separated by purely physical means, a compound requires chemical manipulation to separate it into its component elements.

comprehensive school a secondary school which admits pupils of all abilities and therefore without any academic selection procedure. Most secondary education in the USA and the USSR has always been comprehensive, but most western European countries, including France and the UK, have switched from a selective to a comprehensive system within the last 20 years. In England the 1960s and 1970s saw a slow but major reform of secondary education, in which the majority of local authorities replaced selective grammar schools (taking only the most academic 20 per cent of children) and secondary modern schools (for the remainder), with comprehensive schools capable of providing suitable courses for children of all abilities. By 1985 only 3.2 per cent of secondary pupils were still in grammar schools. Scotland and Wales have switched completely to comprehensive education, while Northern Ireland retains a largely selective system.

compressor a machine designed to compress a gas, usually air. Compressors are commonly used to power pneumatic tools, such as road drills, paint sprayers and dentists' drills. They are of two main types. Reciprocating compressors use pistons moving in cylinders to compress the air. Rotary compressors use a varied rotor moving eccentrically inside a casing. The air compressor in jet and ◊gas-turbine engines consists of a many-varied rotor rotating at high speed within a fixed casing. The rotor blades slot between fixed, or stator blades on the casing.

Compton-Burnett /ˈkʌmptən ˈbɜːnɪt/ Ivy 1892–1969. English novelist. She used dialogue to show reactions of small groups of characters dominated by the tyranny of family relationships. Set at the turn of the century, her novels include *Pastors and Masters* 1925, *More Women than Men* 1933, *Mother and Son* 1955, and *The Mighty and Their Fall* 1961. She was made a Dame of the British Empire in 1967.

computer a programmable, electronic device for performing calculations and other symbol manipulation tasks.

There are three types, of which by far the most common is the ◊digital computer (this is what is normally meant by 'computer'). Digital computers manipulate information coded as ◊binary numbers. They are true general-purpose computing devices as they perform computations on the basis of a stored program: changing the program changes the computation they perform. The other two types are the ◊analogue computer, which is a task-orientated computer, and the hybrid computer, which has components of both analogue and digital computers.

history the first mechanical computer was conceived by Charles ◊Babbage around 1835, but it never went beyond the design stage. In 1943, more than a century later, Thomas Flowers built Colossus, the first electronic computer. Working with him at the time was Alan ◊Turing, a mathematician who seven years earlier had published a paper on the theory of computing machines which had a major impact on subsequent developments. John von ◊Neumann's computer, EDVAC, built in 1949, was the first to use binary arithmetic and to store its operating instructions internally. In fact, von Neumann's design for EDVAC still forms the basis for today's computers.

basic components a computer is a collection of various components. At the heart is the ◊CPU (central processing unit), which performs all the computations. This is supported by memory which holds the current program and data, and 'logic arrays' which help move information around the system. A main power supply is needed and, in the case of a mini or mainframe computer, a cooling system. The computer's 'device driver' circuits control the ◊peripheral devices which can be attached. These will normally be ◊keyboards and ◊VDU screens for user input and output, ◊disk drive units for mass memory storage, and ◊printers for printed output.

sizes there are four sizes corresponding roughly to their memory capacity and processing speed. ◊Microcomputers are the smallest and the most common and are used in small businesses, at home and in schools. They are usually single-user machines. ◊Minicomputers are generally larger and will be found in medium-sized businesses and university departments. They may support from a dozen to 30 or so users at once. ◊Mainframes, which can often service several hundreds of users all at once, are found in large organizations such as national companies and government departments. ◊Supercomputers are the most powerful of all. There are very few in the world and are mostly used for special highly complex scientific tasks, such as analysing the results of nuclear physics experiments and weather forecasting.

computer game computer-controlled game in which the computer (usually) opposes the human player. Also known as video games, they typically employ fast, animated graphics on a

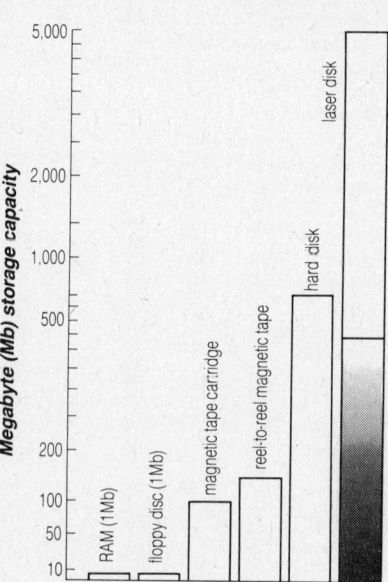

microcomputer system

modem / laser printer / VDU / disk drive / keyboard / tape recorder / disks / joystick / mouse

computer memory

Megabyte (Mb) storage capacity

5,000 / 2,000 / 1,000 / 500 / 200 / 100 / 50 / 10

RAM (1Mb) / floppy disc (1Mb) / magnetic tape carridge / reel-to-reel magnetic tape / hard disk / laser disk

◊VDU (screen) and ◊synthesized sound. Computer games became possible with the advent of the ◊microprocessor in the mid-1970s and rapidly became popular as arcade games, for example Space Invaders.

computer literacy the ability to understand the functions and role of and make use of ◊computer technology in an everyday context.

computer numerical control the control of machine tools, especially milling machines, by a computer. The pattern of work for the machine to follow, which often involves performing repeated

sequences of actions, is described using a special-purpose programming language.

computer simulation representation of a problem or situation mathematically on a computer, possibly involving complex graphics, so that the effects of varying one or more of the definitive parameters can be observed and the problem solved or a design modified. Highly sophisticated computer-graphics simulations are also used in entertainment media, such as video games, and in the training of pilots and astronauts.

computer terminal a screen and a keyboard, sometimes combined in one unit, connected to a computer. It is a ◊peripheral device.

computing device any device built to perform or help perform computations. Probably the earliest known example is the ◊abacus. Mechanical devices with sliding scales (similar to the slide rule) date back to ancient Greece. They were used for performing various calculations, often as an aid to navigation. In 1642, the French mathematician Pascal built a mechanical adding machine, and in 1671 the German philosopher Leibniz produced a machine to perform multiplication. The first mechanical ◊computer, the ◊analytic engine, was designed by Charles Babbage in 1835. A century later Alan ◊Turing developed the mathematical theory of computation, and the digital computer is a direct descendant of his ideas. The basic design for today's computers was developed by John von ◊Neumann in the 1940s.

Comte /kɒmt/ Auguste 1798–1857. French philosopher, generally regarded as the founder of sociology, a term he coined in 1830. In his six-volume *Cours de philosophie positive* 1830–42 he argued that human thought and social development evolve through three key stages: the theological, the metaphysical, and the positive or scientific. He divided human knowledge into a hierarchy, with sociology at the top of the

COMPUTING

1614 Scottish mathematician John Napier invented logarithms.

1625 William Oughtred (1575–1660) invented the slide rule.

1623 Wilhelm Schickard (1592–1635) invented the first mechanical calculating machine.

1645 Blaise Pascal produced a calculator.

1672-74 Leibniz built his first calculator, the Stepped Reckoner.

1801 Joseph-Marie Jacquard developed an automatic loom controlled by punched cards.

1820 First mass-produced calculator (the Arithmometer, by Charles Thomas de Colmar 1785–1870).

1822 Charles Babbage's first model for the Difference Engine.

1830s Babbage created the first design for the Analytical Engine.

1890 Herman Hollerith developed the punched card ruler for the US census.

1936 Alan Turing published the mathematical theory of computing.

1938 Konrad Zuse constructed the first binary calculator, using Boolean algebra.

1943 'Colossus' electronic code-breaker developed at Bletchley Park, England; Harvard University Mark I or Automatic Sequence-Controlled Calculator (partly financed by IBM): the first program-controlled calculator.

1945 ENIAC (Electronic Numerator, Integrator, Analyser, and Computer) completed at the University of Pennsylvania.

1948 Manchester University (England) Mark I completed: first stored-program computer.

1951 Ferranti Mark I: the first commercially produced computer; 'Whirlwind', the first real-time computer, built for the US air-defence system; investigation of transistor.

1952 EDVAC (Electronic Discrete Variable Computer) completed at the Institute for Advanced Study, Princeton,USA (by von Neumann and others).

1953 Magnetic core memory developed.

1957 FORTRAN, the first high-level computer language, developed by IBM.

1958 The first integrated circuit.

1963 The first minicomputer built by Digital Equipment (DEC): the PDP-8; the first electronic calculator (Bell Punch Company).

1964 IBM System/360: the first compatible family of computers.

1965 The first supercomputer: the Control Data CD6600.

1970 The first microprocessor: the Intel 4004.

1974 CLIP-4, the first computer with a parallel architecture.

1975 The first personal computer: Altair 8800.

1981 The Xerox Start system, the first WIMP system (Windows, Icons, Menus and Pointing devices).

1985 The Inmos T414 Transputer, the first 'off the shelf' RISC microprocessor for building parallel computers.

---

academic pyramid. For Comte, positivism offered a method of logical analysis and provided through sociology an ethical and moral basis for predicting and evaluating social progress. Though he originally sought to proclaim society's evolution to a new golden age of science, industry, and rational morality, his radical ideas were increasingly tempered by the political and social upheavals of his time. His influence, however, continued in Europe and the USA until the early 20th century.

Conakry /ˌkɒnəˈkriː/ capital and chief port of the Republic of ◊Guinea on the island of Tombo, linked with the mainland by a causeway and by rail with Kankan 480 km/300 mi to the north-east. Bauxite and iron ore are mined nearby. Population (1980) 763,000.

concave lens a converging lens – that is, a parallel beam of light gets wider as it passes through such a lens. A concave lens is thinner at its centre that at the edges. Common forms include biconcave (with both surfaces curved inwards) and plano-concave (with one flat surface and one concave). The whole lens may be further curved overall (making a convexo-concave or diverging meniscus lens, as in some spectacle lenses). See also ◊lens.

concentration camp prison camp used by the ◊Nazis for the detention, and later for the mass extermination, of the Jews and political opponents. In 1939 some 40,000 Germans were estimated to be in concentration camps and over 200,000 had previously passed through them. During World War II the numbers of inmates were swollen by many millions of Jews and political suspects from occupied Europe. The Allies found 80,000 prisoners at Buchenwald, 30,000 at Belsen, 32,000 at Dachau, 16,000 at Mauthausen and 16,000 at Ebensee – all near to starvation and many severely ill. Conditions were even worse in the Polish camps: at Oswiecim (Auschwitz) the total number sent to the gas-chambers exceeded four million and medical experiments were carried out on living persons. At Maidanek about 1½ million people were exterminated, cremated, and their ashes used as fertilizers. Many camp officials and others responsible were executed by the Allies as war criminals.

concertina a wind musical instrument with free reeds consisting of two keyboards connected by expansible and folding bellows. It is played by compressing and expanding the bellows while at the same time pressing the knobs on the keyboard. By these means air is admitted to the reeds, which are set in vibration. The English concertina, or melodion, was invented by ◊Wheatstone in 1829.

concerto composition, usually in three movements, for solo instrument (or instruments) and orchestra. It developed from the concerto grosso form for string orchestra, in which a group of solo instruments is contrasted with a full orchestra. ◊Corelli and Torelli were early concerto composers, followed by ◊Vivaldi, ◊Handel and ◊Bach (for example, *Brandenburg concertos*) when other instruments were introduced. By the middle of the 18th century the solo concerto had grown in popularity; Mozart wrote some 40. Modern concerto composers include ◊Schoenberg, ◊Berg and ◊Bartók, who have developed it along new lines.

Conchobar in Celtic mythology, king of Ulster whose intended bride, Deirdre, eloped with Nolse. She died of sorrow when Conchobar killed her husband and his brothers.

conclave literally, a room locked with a key. The term is used for any secret meeting, in particular the gathering of cardinals in Rome to elect a new Pope. Wooden cells are erected inside the Vatican Palace near the Sistine Chapel, one for each cardinal, who is accompanied by his secretary and a servant, and all are sworn to secrecy. This section of the palace is then locked and no communication with the outside world is allowed until a new pope is elected, the result of each ballot being announced by a smoke signal – black for an indecisive vote and white when the choice is made.

Concord /ˈkɒŋkəd/ town in Massachusetts, USA; population (1980) 16,300. Site of the first battle of the War of American Independence, 19 Apr 1775. Emerson, Thoreau, Hawthorne, and Louisa Alcott lived here.

concordance book containing an alphabetical list of the words in some important work with references to the places in which they occur. The first concordance was one prepared to the Vulgate by a Dominican in the 13th century.

COMPUTER PROGRAMMING LANGUAGES

Languages	Main Uses	Description	Examples
assembler	jobs needing speed and good control of the machine	fast and efficient but very hard to debug once written	LD B,AH SUB A SUMJ:ADD A,(B) DEC B JR NZ,SUMJ JP [display routine]
BASIC	in education and at home	easy to learn but lacks many of the features of other languages	10 SUM = 0 20 FOR J = 1 TO 10 30 SUM = SUM + J 40 NEXT J 50 PRINT SUM

C	systems programming	fast and efficient; has now largely replaced assembler for such jobs	sum = 0;
			for (j = 1; j = 10; j++)
			  sum = sum +j;
			printf("%d/n", sum)

COBOL	business programming	oriented strongly to commercial work; used almost exclusively for it	SET SUM TO 0. PERFORM SUM-J VARYING J FROM 1 BY 1 UNTIL J = 10. DISPLAY SUM. SUM = J. COMPUTE SUM = SUM + J.
Fortran	scientific programming	at first, lacking in features of other languages; since 1977 has been much improved	SUM = 0; DO 10 J = 1, 10. WRITE (1,100) SUM 10 SUM = SUM + J 100 FORMAT (1X, 16)
Lisp	artificial intelligence systems and research programming	a list processing language with many functional features; the code can look obscure	(SETQ SUM 0) (REPEAT ((UNTIL GREATERP J10)) (PRINT SUM)) (SETQ SUM (PLUS SUM J)) (SETQ J ADDIJ)))

Pascal	education, business, systems and scientific programming	a good all-rounder; easy to learn, with a set of features	sum : = 0;
			for j : = 1 to 10 do
			  sum : = sum + j;
			  writeln (sum);

Prolog	artificial intelligence systems and research programming	the first logic progamming language and the only one in common use	sum—j (11, SUM) :-
			  write (SUM), nl.
			sum—j (J, SUM) :-
			  SUM1 is SUM + J,
			  J1 is J + 1,
			sum—j (J1, SUM1).
			[call using sum—j (1, 0).]

The most famous is A Cruden's concordance of the Bible 1737, of which many editions have appeared. There are also concordances to Shakespeare, Milton, and other writers.

concordat agreement regulating relations between the papacy and a secular government, for example, that for France between Pius VII and Napoleon, which lasted 1801–1905; Mussolini's concordat, which lasted 1929–78 and safeguarded the position of the church in Italy; and one of 1984 in Italy in which Roman Catholicism was no longer the Italian state religion.

Concorde the only successful ◊supersonic airliner, which cruises at Mach 2, or twice the speed of sound, about 2,170 kph/1,350 mph.

Concorde, the result of Anglo-French cooperation, made its maiden flight in 1969, and entered commercial service seven years later. It is 62 m/202 ft long and has a wing span of nearly 26 m/84 ft.

concrete (Latin *concretus* 'compounded') a building material composed of ◊cement, stone, sand, and water. It was used by the Romans and Egyptians, but the technique was forgotten after the Romans.

c. 5600 BC Earliest discovered use of concrete at Lepenski Vir, Yugoslavia (hut floors in Stone Age village).

2500 BC Concrete used in Great Pyramid at Giza by Egyptians.

2nd century BC Romans accidentally discovered

the use of lime and silican/alumina to produce 'pozzolanic' cement.

127 AD Lightweight concrete (using crushed pumice as aggregate) used for walls of Pantheon, Rome.

medieval times Concrete used for castles (infill in walls) and cathedrals (largely foundation work).

1756 John Smeaton produced the first high quality cement since Roman times (for rebuilding of Eddystone lighthouse).

1824 Joseph Aspdin of Wakefield patented Portland cement (so-called because of its resemblance to Portland stone in colour).

1854 William Wilkinson patented reinforced concrete – first successful use in a building.

1880s First continuous-process rotary cement kiln installed (reducing costs of manufacturing cement).

1898 François Hennébique: first multi-storey reinforced concrete building in Britain (factory in Swansea).

1926 Eugène Freysinnet began experiments on pre-stressed concrete in France.

concrete music (French *musique concrète*) term used for music created by reworking natural sounds on record or tape, in particular that of Pierre Schaeffer in 1948.

Condé /kɒn'deɪ/ French family founded by *Louis de Bourbon* 1530–69, an uncle of Henry IV of France, who was prominent as a Huguenot leader in the Wars of Religion. *Louis II*, called the Great Condé,1621–86, won brilliant victories during the Thirty Years' War at Rocroi in 1643 and Lens in 1648, but rebelled in 1651 and entered the Spanish service. Pardoned in 1660, he commanded Louis XIV's armies against the Spaniards and the Dutch.

condenser in optics, a short focal-length convex ◊lens or combination of lenses used for concentrating a light source onto a small area, as used in a slide projector or microscope sub-stage lighting unit. A condenser can also be made using a concave mirror.

Conder /'kɒndə/ Charles 1868–1909. English artist, who painted in watercolour and oil, and executed a number of lithographs including the 'Balzac' 1899 and the 'Carnival' sets 1905.

Condillac /,kɒndiː'æk/ Étienne Bonnot de 1715–1780. French philosopher, Born at Grenoble, of noble parentage, he entered the Church and was appointed tutor to Louis XV's grandson, the Duke of Parma. As a philosopher he mainly followed ◊Locke, but his *Traité de sensations* 1754 claims that all mental activity stems from the transformation of sensations. He was a collaborator in the ◊*Encyclopédie*.

conditioning in psychology, there are two major principles of conditioning. In *classical conditioning*, described by ◊Pavlov, a new stimulus can evoke an automatic response by being repeatedly associated with a stimulus that naturally provokes a response. For example, a bell repeatedly associated with food will eventually trigger salivation, even if presented without food. In *operant conditioning*, described by Thorndike and ◊Skinner, the frequency of a voluntary response can be increased by following it with a reinforcer or reward. For example,

A poor conductor has few free electrons (such as the non-metals glass and porcelain). Carbon is exceptional in being non-metallic and yet (in some of its forms) a relatively good conductor of heat and electricity. Substances such as silicon and germanium, with intermediate conductivities, are known as semiconductors.

cone in geometry, a solid figure having a plane curve as its base and tapering to a point (the vertex). The line joining the vertex to the centre of the base is called the axis of the cone. A circular cone has a circle as its base; a cone that has its axis at right angles to the base is called a right cone. A circular cone of perpendicular height h and base of radius r has a volume $v = 1/3\ \pi r^2 h$. The distance from the edge of the base of a cone to the vertex is called the slant height. In a right circular cone of slant height l, the curved surface area is $\pi r l$, and the area of the base is πr^2. Therefore the total surface area $A = \pi r l + \pi r^2$.

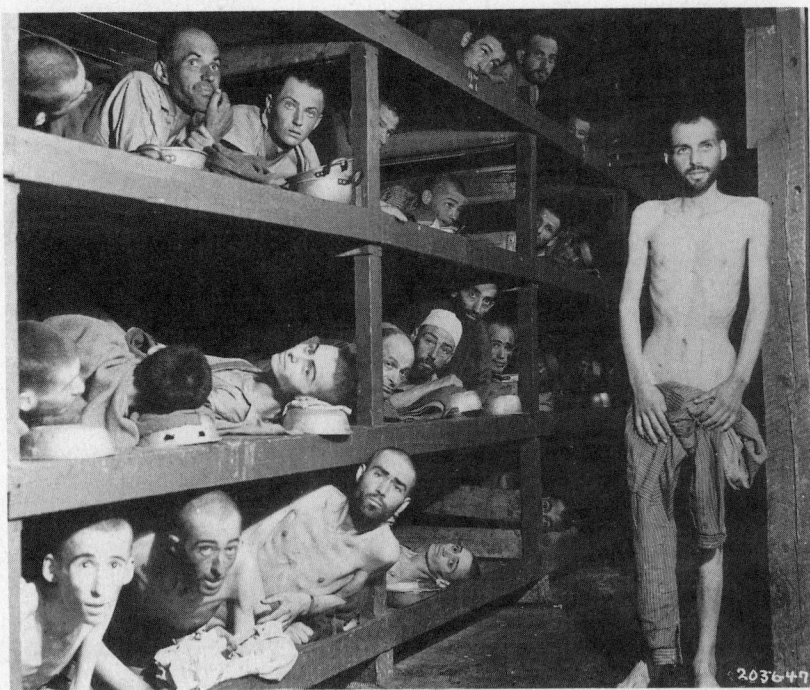

concentration camp Auschwitz. *Above* Starving and diseased prisoners use empty food bowls as pillows in their catacomb-type sleeping shelves. The allies found 32,000 here, many of whom they were unable to save. The total number killed in the gas chambers at Auschwitz exceeded four million. *Below* The most infamous Nazi concentration camp is liberated by the American 7th Army, 3 May, 1945. The scenes they found as they went round the camp appalled the world – thousands of starved corpses were piled up for cremation. The young prisoners wearing the blue and white striped garments were to be next.

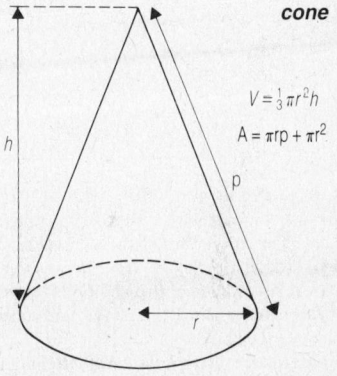

cone

$$V = \tfrac{1}{3}\pi r^2 h$$
$$A = \pi r p + \pi r^2$$

children will be more likely to say 'Thank you' if they have been repeatedly praised for doing so when given something.

condominium the joint rule of a territory by two or more states, for example, Canton and Enderbury islands, in the Phoenix group (under the joint control of Britain and the USA for 50 years from 1939). The term has also come into use in the USA to describe a type of joint property ownership of, for example, a block of flats.

condor one of the largest of all flying birds *Vultur gryphus*, an American ◊vulture, with wingspan up to 3 m/10 ft, weight up to 13 kg/28 lb, and length up to 1.15 m/3.8 ft. It is black, with some white on the wings and a white frill at the base of the neck, which has bare red skin like the head. It is found along the Andes and some South American coasts, and feeds on carrion. The *Californian condor Gymnogyps californianus* is a similar bird, but on the verge of extinction. It only lays one egg at a time and may not breed every year. It is the subject of a special conservation effort.

Condorcet /ˌkɒndɔːˈseɪ/ Marie Jean Antoine Nicolas Caritat, marquis de Condorcet 1743–1794. French philosopher-politician. One of the ◊Girondins, he opposed the execution of Louis XVI, and was imprisoned and poisoned himself. His *Esquisse d'un tableau des progrès de l'esprit humain/ Historical Survey of the Progress of Human Understanding* 1795 envisaged inevitable future progress, though not the perfectibility of human nature.

conductance the ability of a material to carry an electrical current, usually given the symbol G. For a direct current, it is the reciprocal of resistance – that is, a conductor of resistance R has a conductance of $1/R$. For an alternating current, conductance is the resistance (R) divided by the impedence Z – that is, $G = R/Z$. Conductance was formerly expressed in reciprocal ohms (or mhos); the modern SI unit is the Siemens.

conductor in physics, a material that conducts heat or electricity (as opposed to a non-conductor or insulator). The distinction between the two is not clear-cut. A good conductor has a high electrical or thermal conductivity, generally a substance rich in free electrons such as a metal.

cone in botany, the reproductive structure of the ◊conifers, and ◊cycads, also known as a ◊strobilus. It consists of a central axis surrounded by numerous, overlapping, scale-like sporophylls, modified leaves which bear the reproductive organs. Usually there are separate male and female cones, the former bearing pollen sacs containing pollen grains, and the larger female cones bearing the ovules which contain the ova or egg cells. The pollen is carried from male to female cones by wind (◊anemophily). The seeds develop within the female cone, and are released by the opening of the scales in response to dry atmospheric conditions, which favour seed dispersal. In some groups (for example, the pines) the cones take two or even three years to reach this stage. The cones of ◊junipers have fleshy cone scales that fuse to form a berry-like structure. One group of angiosperms, the alders, also bear cone-like structures; these are the woody remains of the short female catkins, and they contain the alder ◊fruits.

In zoology, a type of light-sensitive cell found in the retina of the ◊eye.

Coney Island /ˈkəʊnɪ/ seaside resort on a peninsula in the south west of Long Island, New York, USA. It is popular for its amusement parks.

Confederacy in US history, popular name for the Confederate States of America, the government established by the southern US states 1860 when they seceded from the Union, precipitating the ◊Civil War. Richmond, Virginia, was the capital, and Jefferson Davis the president. The Confederacy fell after its army was defeated 1865 and General Robert E Lee surrendered.

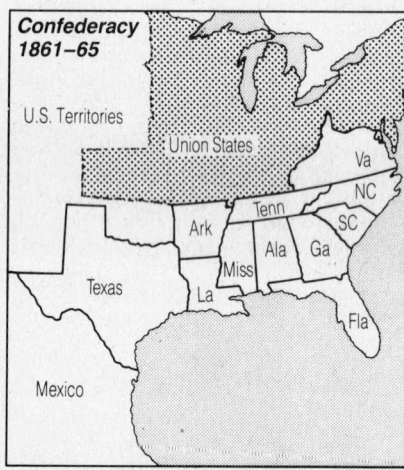

Confederacy 1861–65

Confederation of British Industry (CBI) organization established in 1965, combining the former Federation of British Industries (founded 1916), British Employers' Confederation, and National Association of British Manufacturers. It voices general policy of employers and matters relating to the economy.

Conference system a system of international conferences promoted principally by ◊Bismarck to ease the integration of a new powerful German state into the 'Concept of Europe'. The conferences were intended to settle great power disputes, mainly related to the Balkans, the Middle East and the designation of colonies in Africa and Asia. Most important of these was the congress of Berlin (1878) which determined the boundaries of the Balkan states after the Russo-Turkish war. The system fell into disuse with the retirement of Bismarck and the pressures of new European alliance blocks.

confession a religious practice, the confession of sins, which originated with the Jews. Both John the Baptist's converts and the early Christian church practised public confession. The Lateran Council of 1215 made auricular confession (the accusation by the penitent of himself of his sins to a priest who in Catholic doctrine is divinely invested with authority to give him absolution) obligatory once a year. Auricular confession is practised in Roman Catholic, Orthodox and most Oriental churches and since the early 19th century has been revived in Anglican and Lutheran churches.

The Roman Catholic penitent in modern times has always confessed alone to the priest in a confessional box, but from 1977 such individual confession might be preceded by group discussion, or the confession itself might be made openly by members of the group.

Confindustria a General Confederation of Industry established in Italy in 1920 with the aim of countering working-class agitation. It became a major contributor of funds to the Fascist movement which, in turn, used its *squandristi* against the workers. After Mussolini's takeover of power in 1922, Confindustria became one of the major groups of the fascist corporative state.

confirmation rite by which a previously baptized person is admitted to full membership of the Christian Church. It consists in the laying on of hands by a bishop, in order that the confirmed person may receive the gift of the Holy Spirit. Among Anglicans, the rite is deferred until the child is able to learn a catechism or series of questions and answers, containing the fundamentals of Christian doctrine.

Confucianism the body of beliefs and practices that are based on the Chinese classics and are supported by the authority of ◊Confucius (Kong Zi), although he himself maintained that he was a transmitter rather than a creator. For some 2,500 years Confucianism has been the religion of most of the Chinese people.

The scriptures of Confucius are the five Chinese classics or canonical books, namely the Shu King, or book of historical documents; the Shih King, or ancient poems; the Li Ki, or book of rites and ancient ceremonies and institutions; the Yi King, or book of changes; and the Annals of Lu, otherwise known as Spring and Autumn. Only the last may be attributed with any confidence to Confucius, but the material in the other books may owe something to his editing.

From these scriptures the Chinese in countless generations have derived their ideas of cosmology, political government, social organization, and individual conduct. The origin of things is seen in the union of Yin and Yang, the negative and positive principles. Human relationships follow the patriarchal pattern; until 1912 the emperor was regarded as the father of his people, appointed by heaven to rule. The Superior Man was the ideal human, filial piety was the virtue of virtues, and in general human relationships were to be regulated by the Golden Rule. Accompanying this high morality is a kind of ancestor worship. Under the emperor, sacrifices were offered to heaven and earth, the heavenly bodies, the imperial ancestors, various nature gods, and Confucius himself. These were abolished at the Revolution in 1912, but ancestor worship (better expressed as reverence and remembrance) remained a regular practice in the home.

Under Communism Confucianism continued, Lin ◊Piao being associated with the cult, but Mao Zedong undertook an anti-Confucius campaign 1974–76, which was not pursued by the succeeding regime.

Confucius /kən'fjuːʃəs/ 550–478 BC. Latinized form of Kong Zi (Kong the master), the Chinese sage whose name is given to ◊Confucianism. He was born in Lu, a small state in what is now the province of Shangdong, and his early years were spent in poverty. Married at 19, he worked as a minor official. Then as a teacher, he gradually attracted a number of disciples. In 517 there was an uprising in Lu,

and Confucius spent the next year or two in the adjoining state of Ch'i. When he was nearly 50, he accepted the governorship of a small town and distinguished himself in the suppression of crime and in the promotion of morality. Then for 14 years he wandered from state to state accompanied by a handful of disciples. At last he returned to Lu and devoted himself to the revision of the ancient Chinese scriptures, some parts of which have been attributed, though on slight evidence, to his authorship. At his death he was buried with great pomp, and his grave outside Qufu has remained a centre of pilgrimage.

conga a popular Latin American dance, originally from Cuba, in which the participants, usually in a line, take three steps forwards or backwards and then kick.

conger marine fish *Conger conger*, a large eel found in the N Atlantic and Mediterranean, often 1.8 m/6 ft long and sometimes as much as 2.7 m/9 ft. In shallow water it hides in crevices in the day and is active by night, feeding on fish and other animals. It is valued for food and angling.

conglomerate a coarse ◊sedimentary rock, made up of broken fragments of pre-existing rocks (a clastic sedimentary rock). The fragments in conglomerate are pebble-shape, large and rounded, and the rock can be regarded as a fossilized shingle beach. A ◊bed of conglomerate is often associated with a break in a sequence of rock beds (an unconformity), where it marks the advance of a sea over an old eroded landscape. An oligomict conglomerate contains one type of pebble; a polymict conglomerate has a mixture pebble types.

Congo /'kɒŋgəʊ/ former name 1960–71 of ◊Zaïre.

Congo /'kɒŋgəʊ/ country in W central Africa, bounded to the N by Cameroon and the Central African Republic, to the E and S by Zaïre, to the W by the Atlantic Ocean, and to the NW by Gabon.

government the Congo is a one-party state based on the Marxist-Leninist Congolese Labour Party (PTC). The president of the central committee of PTC is automatically elected state president for a five-year term and chairs the council of ministers. The single-chamber legislature is the 153-member people's national assembly, elected by universal suffrage from a list prepared by PTC.

history occupied from the 15th century by the Bakongo, Bateke, and Sanga, the area was exploited by Portuguese slave traders. From 1889 it came under French administration, becoming part of French Equatorial Africa in 1910.

The Congo became an autonomous republic within the French Community in 1958 and Abbé Fulbert Youlou, a Roman Catholic priest who involved himself in politics and was suspended by the Church, became prime minister and then president when full independence was achieved in 1960. Two years later plans were announced for a one-party state but in 1963, after industrial unrest, Youlou was forced to resign.

A new constitution was approved and Alphonse Massamba-Débat, a former finance minister, became president, adopting a policy of 'scientific socialism'. The National Revolutionary Movement (MNR) was declared the only political party. In 1968 Captain Marien Ngouabi overthrew Massamba-Débat in a military coup and the national assembly was replaced by a national council of the revolution. Ngouabi proclaimed a Marxist state but kept economic links with France.

In 1970 the nation became the People's Republic of the Congo, with the PTC as the only party and in 1973 a new constitution provided for an assembly chosen from a single party list. In 1977 Ngouabi was assassinated and Colonel Joachim Yhombi-Opango took over. He resigned in 1979, after discovering a plot to overthrow him, and was succeeded by Denis Sassou-Nguessou, who has moved away from Soviet influence, strengthening links with France, the US, and China.

In 1982 President Mitterrand of France paid an official visit to the Congo. In 1984 Sassou-Nguessou was elected for another five-year term. He increased his control by combining the posts of head of state, head of government and president of the central committee of PTC.

Congo
PEOPLE'S REPUBLIC OF THE (*République Populaire du Congo*)

AREA 342,000 sq km/132,000 sq mi
CAPITAL Brazzaville
TOWNS chief port Pointe Noire
PHYSICAL Zaïre (Congo) river on the border; half the country is rain forest
HEAD OF STATE AND OF GOVERNMENT Denis Sassou-Nguessou from 1979
GOVERNMENT one-party communist
EXPORTS timber, potash, petroleum
CURRENCY CFA franc (498.38 = £1 Sept 1987)
POPULATION (1985) 1,798,000 (chiefly Bantu); annual growth rate 2.6%
LANGUAGE French (official)
RELIGION animist 50%, Christian 48%
LITERACY 70% male/44% female (1980 est)
GDP $2.1 bn (1983); $500 per head of population
CHRONOLOGY
1960 Achieved full independence from France, with Abbe Youlou as the first president.
1963 Youlou forced to resign. New constitution approved, with Alphonse Massamba-Débat as president.
1964 The Congo became a one-party state.
1968 Military coup, led by Capt Marien Ngouabi, ousted Massamba-Débat.

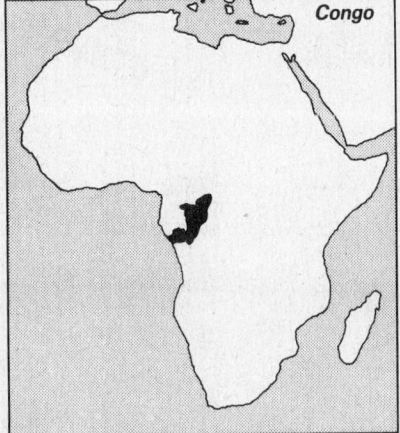

Congo

1970 A Marxist state, the People's Republic of the Congo, was announced, with the Congolese Labour Party (PCT) as the only legal party.
1977 Ngouabi assassinated. Col Yhombi-Opango became president.
1979 Yhombi-Opango handed over the presidency to PCT, who chose Col Denis Sassou-Nguessou as his successor.
1984 Sassou-Nguessou elected for another five-year term.

Brownists, named after Robert Browne, who in 1580 defined the congregational principle. In the next century they were known as Independents, for example, Cromwell and many of his Ironsides, and in 1662 hundreds of their ministers were driven from their churches and established separate congregations. The Congregational Church in England and Wales and the Presbyterian Church in England joined in 1972 to form the United Reformed Church. The latter, like its counterpart the Congregational Union of Scotland, has no control over individual churches but is simply consultative. Similar unions have been carried out in Canada (United Church of Canada, 1925) and USA (United Church of Christ, 1957).

Congress national legislature of the USA, consisting of the House of Representatives (435 members, apportioned to the States of the Union on the basis of population, and elected for two-year terms) and the Senate (100 senators, two for each state, elected for six years, one third elected every two years). Both representatives and senators are elected by direct popular vote. Congress meets at Washington, DC, in the Capitol.

An *Act of Congress* is a bill or resolution that has been passed by the Senate and the House of

Congress of Industrial Organizations (CIO) a branch of the ◊American Federation of Labor and Congress of Industrial Organizations, the federation of US trade unions.

Congress of Racial Equality (CORE) US non-violent civil rights organization, founded in Chicago, 1942.

Congress of Vienna international congress held 1814–15 to discuss the reconstruction of continental Europe after the Napoleonic wars. National representatives included Prince Metternich (Austria), Alexander I (Russia), Castlereagh and Wellington (Britain). The settlement created the basis for the Quadruple Alliance of the Victorious Powers -transformed in 1818 into the Quintuple Alliance with the inclusion of France. The congress also created other attempts at international cooperation.

Congress Party the Indian National Congress, founded by the Englishman A O Hume in 1885, was a moderate body until World War I when, under Gandhi's leadership, it began a campaign of non-violent non-co-operation. Declared illegal 1932–34, under Nehru's guidance, it was recognized as the paramount power in India at the granting of independence in 1947, and won the elections of 1952, 1957, 1962, 1967 and 1971. In 1977 it was defeated for the first time and Indira Gandhi lost the leadership she had held since 1966. Heading a splinter group, known by her initial as Congress (I), she achieved an overwhelming victory in the elections of 1980, and reduced the main Congress party in turn to a splinter group.

Congress system developed from the Congress of Vienna, a series of international meetings at Aix-la-Chapelle (1818), Troppali (1820) and Verona (1822). British opposition to the repressive intentions of the congresses effectively ended them as a system of international arbitration, although congresses continued to meet into the 1830s.

Congreve /ˈkɒngriːv/ William 1670–1729. English dramatist and poet, considered the most brilliant of the Restoration comic dramatists, whose plays are noted for the elegance of their construction and prose style. Born near Leeds, he was a friend of ◊Swift at Trinity College, Dublin, and in 1691 began studying law in London. He won immediate success with his first comedy *The Old Bachelor* 1693, which was followed by *The Double Dealer* 1694, *Love for Love* 1695 and the tragedy *The Mourning Bride* 1697. In 1700 his masterpiece, *The Way of the World*, appeared, but was at the time a failure.

congruence in geometry, having the same shape and size, as applied to two-dimensional or solid figures. With plane congruent figures, one figure will fit on top of the other exactly though this may first require rotation or reflection (making a mirror image) of one of the figures. For example two indentical triangles, one standing on its pointed end (apex), the other flat on its base, are congruent when one is rotated 180° (turned around a half circle).

conic section curve obtained when a ◊cone is intersected by a plane. Conic sections were first discovered by the ancient Greeks and have been of great importance in mathematics. If the

congregationalism form of church government adopted by those Protestant Christians known as Congregationalists, in which each congregation manages its own affairs. The first Congregationalists were the

Representatives and has received the president's assent. Even if the president vetoes it, it may become an Act of Congress if it is returned to Congress again and passed by a majority of two-thirds in each house. It then becomes law.

Congreve Restoration playwright William Congreve, depicted here by G Kneller in 1709, still delights audiences with his brilliant comedies, notably *Love for Love* and *The Way of the World*, which satirize the social affectations of the time.

intersecting plane cuts both extensions of the cone it yields a ◊hyperbola; if it is parallel to the side of the cone it produces a parabola. Other intersecting planes produce a ◊circle or an ◊ellipse.

conidium an asexual spore formed by some fungi at the tip of a specialized hypha or conidiophore. The conidiophores grow erect, and cells from their ends round off and separate into conidia, often forming long chains. Conidia easily become detached and are dispersed by air movements.

conifer plant of the class Coniferales, in the gymnosperm group. These are trees or shrubs, often pyramidal in form, with leaves that are 'needles' or scale-like. The 'flowers' are the male and female cones, and pollen is distributed by the wind. The seeds develop in the female cones. The processes of maturation, fertilization, and seed ripening may extend over several years. Conifers include pines, firs, yews, monkey-puzzles and larches. Most are evergreen.

conjugation in biology, the bacterial equivalent of sexual reproduction. A fragment of the ◊DNA from one bacterium is passed along a thin tube, the pilus, into the cell of another bacterium.

conjunction a grammatical ◊part of speech that serves to connect words, phrases and clauses; for example *and* in 'apples and pears' and *but* in 'we're going but they aren't'.

conjunctivitis inflammation (formerly called ophthalmia) of the conjunctiva or membrane which covers the front of the eye. A severe form of it, *trachoma*, is caused by the bacterium *Chlamydia trachomatis* which flourishes in poor living conditions in tropical and semi-tropical countries. It is the greatest single world cause of blindness.

Connacht /'kɒnɔːt/ province of the Republic of Ireland, comprising the counties of Mayo, Galway, Roscommon, Sligo, and Leitrim. Mainly lowland, it is agricultural and stock-raising country with poor land in the west. The chief rivers are the Shannon, Moy, and Suck, and there are a number of lakes. The chief towns are Galway, Roscommon, Castlebar, Sligo, and Carrick-on-Shannon. The Connacht dialect is the national standard. Area 17,122 sq km/6,611 sq mi; population (1981) 424,410.

Connecticut /kə'netɪkət/ New England state of the USA

area 12,973 sq km/5,009 sq mi

capital Hartford

towns Bridgeport, New Haven

features Highlands in the NW; Connecticut river; Yale University; Mystic Seaport (reconstruction of 19th-century village, with restored ships); Shakespeare Festival at Stratford

products market garden, dairy, and poultry products; tobacco; watches, clocks, silverware; helicopters, jet engines, nuclear submarines

population (1980) 3,107,576

famous people Phineas T Barnum, Katharine Hepburn, Harriet Beecher Stowe, Mark Twain

history settled by Puritan colonists from Massachusetts in 1635, it was one of the Thirteen Colonies, and became a state in 1788.

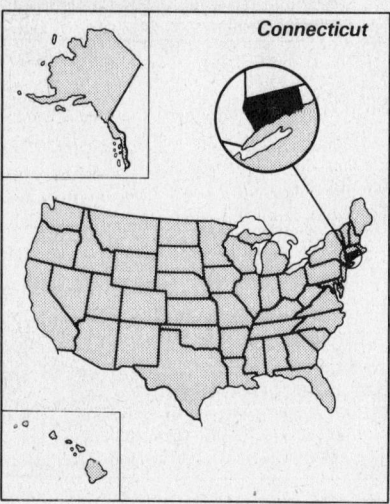

Connecticut

connectionist machine a computing device built from a large number of simple ◊processors all interconnected, which are both able to communicate with each other and process information separately. The underlying model is that of the human brain. These 'massively parallel' computers, as they are sometimes known, are still at the development stage, but some are expected to be in production in the near future.

connective tissue in animals, tissue made up of a noncellular substance, the ◊extracellular matrix, with some cells embedded in it. The skin, bones, tendons, cartilage and adipose tissue (fat) are the main connective tissues. There are also small amounts of connective tissue in organs such as the brain and liver, where they maintain shape and structure.

Connell /'kɒnl/ James. Irish socialist who wrote 'The ◊Red Flag' during the 1889 London strike.

Connemara /ˌkɒnɪ'mɑːrə/ the western division of county Galway, Republic of Ireland, much visited by tourists for its wild scenery.

Connolly /'kɒnəli/ Cyril 1903–1974. English writer. As founder-editor of the literary magazine *Horizon* 1930–50, he exercised considerable critical influence. His books include *The Rock Pool* 1935, a novel of artists on the Riviera, *The Unquiet Grave* 1945.

Connolly /'kɒnəli/ Maureen 1934–1969. American lawn tennis player. Nicknamed 'Little Mo' because she was 5 ft 2 in tall, she was the first woman to perform the Grand Slam by winning all four major titles in one year (1953). Three times Wimbledon champion 1952–54, French champion 1953–54, Australian champion 1953 and US champion 1951–53, she was forced to retire after a riding accident and later died of cancer.

conquistador Spanish word for 'conqueror', applied to such explorers and adventurers in the Americas as Cortes and Pizarro.

Conrad /'kɒnræd/ Joseph 1857–1924. British novelist, of Polish parentage. He was born Teodor Jozef Konrad Korzeniowski in the Ukraine. A merchant seaman, he landed at Lowestoft with no knowledge of English in 1878, but in 1886 gained his master mariner's certificate and became a naturalized British subject. He retired in 1894 to write. His novels include *Almayer's Folly* 1895, *Lord Jim* 1900, *Nostromo* 1904, *The Secret Agent* 1907, and *Under Western Eyes* 1911. His works vividly evoked for English readers the mysteries of sea life and exotic foreign settings, and explored the psychological isolation of the 'outsider'.

Conrad /'kɒnræd/ name of several kings of the Germans.

Conrad I /'kɒnræd/ died 918, succeeded Louis the Child, the last of the German Carolingians in 911, and during his reign the realm was harassed by Magyar invaders.

Conrad II /'kɒnræd/ died 1039, reigned from 1024 and ceded the march Sleswick to Canute.

Conrad III /'kɒnræd/ 1093–1152, the first king of the Hohenstaufen dynasty, was crowned at Aachen in 1138, and throughout his reign a fierce struggle between his followers, the Ghibellines, and the Guelphs, the followers of Henry the Proud, duke of Saxony and Bavaria. His son Henry the Lion, continued the struggle. Conrad took part in the second crusade.

Conrad IV /'kɒnræd/ 1228–54, son of the emperor Frederick II, was elected king in 1237, and had to defend his right of succession against Henry Raspe of Thuringia and William of Holland. His son *Conradin* (1252–68), the last of the Hohenstaufen, was defeated and captured by Charles of Anjou at Tagliacozzo in 1268, and beheaded in Naples.

consanguinity relationship by blood, whether lineal, for example, by direct descent, or collateral, such as by virtue of a common ancestor. The degree of consanguinity is of importance in laws relating to the inheritance of property and also in relation to marriage, which is forbidden in many cultures between parties closely related by blood.

conscientious objector term originally denoting parents who objected to compulsory vaccination of their children, later applied to persons refusing compulsory service, usually military, on moral, religious or political grounds.

conscription system under which all able-bodied male citizens are legally liable to serve with the armed forces. It originated in France in 1792, and in the 19th century it became the established practice in almost all European states. In Britain it was introduced for single men between 18 and 41 in Mar 1916 and for married men two months later, but was abolished after the war. It was introduced for the first time in peace in Apr 1939, when all men aged 20 became liable to six months' military training. The National Service Act, passed in Sept 1939, made all men between 18 and 41 liable to military service, and in 1941 women also became liable to be called up for the women's services as an alternative to industrial service. Men reaching the age of 18 continued to be called up until 1960. In the USA conscription (the 'draft') was introduced during the Civil War – by the Confederates 1862 and by the Union side 1863. In World War I a Selective Service Act was passed in 1917, and again in 1940 in anticipation of America's entry into World War II. It remained in force, except for 15 months 1947–48, until abolished by Nixon following the withdrawal from Vietnam. In 1980 Carter restored registration for a possible military draft for men at 18, but his proposal that it be extended to women was rejected by Congress.

consent, age of the age at which consent may legally be given to sexual intercourse by a girl or boy. In the UK it is 16.

conservation in the life sciences, care for, and protection of, the ◊biosphere. Since the 1950s it has been increasingly realized that the earth, together with its atmosphere, animal and plant life, and mineral and agricultural resources, form an interdependent whole which is in danger of irreversible depletion and eventual destruction unless positive measures are taken to conserve a balance. Action by governments has been supplemented by private agencies, such as the World Wildlife Fund. In attempts to save particular ◊species or habitats, a distinction is often made between *preservation*, that is maintaining the pristine state of nature exactly as it was or might have been, and *conservation*, the management of natural resources in such a way as to allow any of its excess production to be controlled, or to be used for commercial purposes, including integration of the requirements of the local human population with those of the animals, plants or the habitat being conserved.

conservatism an approach to government and economic management identified with a number of Western political parties, such as the British Conservative, West German Christian Democratic and Australian Liberal parties. It tends to be explicitly non-doctrinaire and pragmatic but its central themes may be identified as an emphasis on the importance of national traditions, a belief in free-enterprise capitalism, a minimalist approach to governmental intervention in the economy, and a stress on law and order.

Conservative Party one of the two historic British parties; the name replaced 'Tory' in general use from 1830 onwards. Traditionally the party of landed interests, opposed to the *laissez-faire* of the Liberal manufacturers, it supported, to some extent, the struggle of the working-class against the harshness of conditions arising from the Industrial Revolution. The split of 1846 over Peel's Corn Law policy led to 20 years out of office, or in office without power, until Disraeli 'educated' his party into accepting parliamentary and social change, extended the franchise to the artisan (winning considerable working-class support), launched imperial expansion, and established an alliance with industry and finance. The Irish Home Rule issue of 1886 drove Radical Imperialists and old-fashioned Whigs into alliance with the Conservatives, so that the party had nearly 20 years of office, but fear that Joseph Chamberlain's protectionism would mean higher prices led to a Liberal landslide in 1906. The Conservative Party fought a rearguard action against the sweeping reforms that followed and only the outbreak of World War I averted a major crisis. During 1915–45, except briefly in 1924 and 1929–31, the Conservatives were continually in office, whether alone or as part of a coalition, the main factor in maintaining this ascendancy being the break-up of the traditional two-party system by the rise of Labour.

Labour swept to power after World War II, but the Conservative Party formulated a new policy in their Industrial Charter of 1947, visualizing an economic and social system in which employers and employed, private enterprise and the state, work to mutual advantage. Antagonism to further nationalization reduced the Labour majority in the 1950 election, and in 1951 returned the Conservatives to power with a small majority. This was slightly increased in the general elections of 1955 and 1959 – despite such setbacks as Suez – because of maintained prosperity. Narrowly defeated in 1964 under Douglas Home, the Conservative Party from 1965 elected its leaders, and under Edward Heath in was again defeated 1966, but in 1970 achieved a small majority. The Conservative government's imposition of wage controls led to confrontation with the unions and, when Heath sought a mandate Feb 1974, a narrow defeat, repeated in a further election in Oct 1974. Margaret Thatcher replaced Heath, and under her leadership the Conservative Party returned in to power in May 1979, and was re-elected for a third term in 1987.

Constable /'kʌnstəbəl/ John 1776–1837. English landscape painter. Born at East Bergholt, Suffolk, the son of a miller, he first worked in his father's mills, but in 1795 was sent to study art in London, where he copied Reynolds, painted religious pictures and studied ◊Ruysdael. In 1799 he entered the Royal Academy schools and from 1802 exhibited every year in the ◊Royal Academy of Arts, London. He was elected Associate of the Royal Academy in 1819, and his picture *The Hay Wain* created a sensation when exhibited in the Paris Salon in 1821. From 1830 to 1833 he was mainly occupied with the famous series of mezzotints engraved by David Lucas. His pictures are remarkable for the way in which they evoke a sense of warmth or coolness, according to the kind of weather he is depicting, and for the changing effects of light on the landscape. His technique of broken brush strokes gave great vibrancy and life to his colours and portended the developments of ◊Impressionism. Among his most famous paintings are *Flatford Mill* 1825, *The Leaping Horse* 1825, *The Cornfield* 1826, *Dedham Vale*, and *Salisbury Cathedral* 1831. In 1978 it was recognized that a number of works attributed to him had been produced by other members of the family, including his son Lionel.

Constable A self-portrait of John Constable in pencil and watercolour.

Constance /'kɒnstəns/ town in Baden-Württemberg, Germany, on the section of the Rhine joining Lake Constance and the Untersee. Suburbs stretch across the frontier into Switzerland. Constance has clothing, machinery, and chemical factories and printing works. Population (1978) 65,000.

Constance, Lake /'kɒnstəns/ lake (German *Bodensee*) between Germany, Austria, and Switzerland, through which the Rhine flows. Area 540 sq km/200 sq mi.

Constance, Council of /'kɒnstəns/ 1414–17. Agreement which ended the ◊Great Schism, during which period 1378–1417 there were rival popes at Rome and Avignon.

constant in mathematics, a fixed quantity or one that does not change its value in relation to ◊variables. For example, in the algebraic expression $y^2 = 5x - 3$, the numbers 5 and 3 are constants; so too are a and b in the general equation $ax + b = 0$. In physics, certain quantities are regarded as universal constants that never vary, for example, the speed of light in vacuum, represented by the letter c.

Constanta /kɒn'stæntsə/ chief seaport of Romania on the Black Sea, capital of Constanta region; population (1983) 284,800. The exporting centre for the Romanian oilfields, to which it is connected by pipeline, it has refineries, shipbuilding yards, and food factories.

constantan a high-resistance alloy of approximately 40% nickel and 60% copper with a very low temperature coefficient. It is used in electrical resistors.

Constantine the Great /'kɒnstantaɪn/ 274–337. First Christian emperor of Rome, and founder of Constantinople. Born at Naissus (Nish, Yugoslavia), he was the son of Constantius. He was already well known as a soldier when his father died at York in 306 and he was acclaimed by the troops there as joint-emperor in his father's place. His authority over Britain and Gaul was at first recognized by the other emperors, but a few years later Maxentius, the joint-emperor at Rome (whose sister had married Constantine the Great), mobilized his armies to invade Gaul. Constantine the Great won a crushing victory outside Rome at the Milvian Bridge 312. It was during this campaign that he was said to have seen a vision of the cross of Christ superimposed upon the sun, accompanied by the words, 'In this sign conquer'. By the Edict of Milan 313 he formally recognized Christianity as one of the religions legally permitted within the Roman Empire, and in 314 summoned the bishops of the western world to the Council of Arles. Since 312 Constantine had been sole emperor of the West, and by defeating Licinius, the emperor in the East, he became sole ruler of the Roman world 324. He set to work to consolidate and reorganize his empire. He increased the autocratic power of the emperor, issued legislation which tied the farmers and workpeople to their crafts in a sort of caste system, and enlisted the support of the Christian Church. He summoned, and presided over, the first general council of the Church at ◊Nicaea in 325. Constantine moved his capital to Byzantium on the Bosporus in 330 and renamed it Constantinople. In 337 he set out to defend the Euphrates frontier against the Persians, but died at Nicomedia in Asia Minor.

Constantine II /'kɒnstantaɪn/ 1940– . King of the Hellenes. In 1964 he succeeded his father Paul I and later that year married Princess Anne-Marie of Denmark: his heir is Crown Prince Paul (1967–). He went into exile 1967 and was formally deposed 1973.

Constantinople /,kɒnstæntɪ'nəupəl/ former capital of the Eastern Roman and Turkish Empires, now called by its Turkish name, ◊Istanbul. It was founded by ◊Constantine the Great by the enlargement of the Greek city of Byzantium in 328, and became the seat of the imperial government in 330. Its elaborate fortifications enabled it to resist a succession of sieges, but it was captured by crusaders in 1204, and was the seat of a Latin kingdom until recaptured by the Greeks in 1261. An attack by the Turks in 1422 proved unsuccessful, but after nearly a year's siege, it was taken by another Turkish army on 29 May 1453.

constellation in astronomy, one of the 88 areas into which the sky is divided for the purposes of identifying and naming objects. The first constellations were simple patterns of ◊stars in which early civilizations visualized gods, sacred beasts and mythical heroes. The constellations in general use today have been modified and extended from a list of 48 known to the ancient Greeks, who inherited some from the Babylonians. The modern list of 88 constellations was officially adopted by the International Astronomical Union, astronomy's governing body, in 1930.

constitution the fundamental laws of a state, laying down the system of government and defining the relations of the legislature, executive, and judiciary to each other and to the citizens. Since the French Revolution almost all countries have adopted written constitutions. The constitution of the UK does not exist in the form of a single document but as an accumulation of customs and precedents, together with a number of laws defining certain of its aspects. Among the most important of the latter are Magna Carta 1215, the Petition of Right 1628, and the Habeas Corpus Act 1679, limiting the royal powers of taxation and of imprisonment; the Bill of Rights 1689 and the Act of Settlement 1701, establishing parliamentary supremacy and the independence of the judiciary; and the Parliament Acts 1911 and 1949, limiting the powers of the Lords. The Triennial Act 1694, the Septennial Act 1716, and the Parliament Act 1911 limited the duration of parliament, while the Reform Acts of 1832, 1867, 1884, 1918, and 1928 extended the electorate. The proliferation of legislation during the 1970s, often carried on the basis of a small majority in the Commons and by governments elected by an overall minority of votes, led to demands for the introduction of a written constitution as a safeguard for the liberty of the individual. See also ◊Parliament.

That of the USA, drawn up in 1787, is the oldest written constitution in existence. There have been 26 amendments in the subsequent 200 years, including the first ten (1791), known as the ◊Bill of Rights, to guarantee individual liberties.

constructivism ◊abstract art movement which arose in Moscow in about 1915 out of ◊cubism; it rejected the past and invented images for the new age, having as its aim the creation of works – sculpture, painting, and so on – which exist in their own right and are unrelated to natural forms. The chief exponents of the movement are Naum ◊Gabo, and Vladimir Tatlin, who aimed to create art for the Revolution which, however, rejected them; the movement spread abroad and influenced Ben ◊Nicholson, Barbara ◊Hepworth, and Piet ◊Mondrian.

consul the chief magistrate of ancient Rome following the expulsion of the last king in 510 BC. The Consuls were two annually elected magistrates, both of equal power; they jointly held full civil power at Rome, and the chief military command in the field. After the establishment of the Roman Empire the office became purely honorary. (The term consul is also used for a state official, with political and commercial responsibilities, who looks after their country's citizens in major foreign cities.)

consumer protection laws and measures designed to ensure fair trading for buyers. An early organization attempting consumer protection was the British Standards Institution (1901), which lays down specifications of quality, performance and safety: goods reaching these standards may carry a certification, known from its shape as the 'kitemark'. Legal protection was given by the Trade Descriptions Act (1968), rendering it a criminal offence to describe goods or provisions falsely. More recent legislation includes the Fair Trading Act 1973, the Unfair Contract Terms Act 1977, and the Consumer Safety Act 1978. A more positive approach to consumer protection in the UK was the creation in 1974 of a government department of Prices and Consumer Protection by subdivision of the Department of Trade and Industry. In the USA there is special provision by both federal and state governments for consumer protection, and in 1962 President Kennedy set out the four basic rights of the consumer as the right to safety, to be informed, to choose, and to be heard. There are many private consumer associations, and among the most influential of crusaders for greater protection has been Ralph ◊Nader.

consumption the purchasing and using of goods and services. In economics, it means the total expenditure, in a given economy and over a given period, on goods and services (including expenditure on raw materials). In Britain consumption accounts for about 80 per cent of the ◊national income.

Consumption was also a former name for the disease ◊tuberculosis.

contact lens a lens placed in contact with the eye, separated in most cases only by a film of tears. Contact lenses may be used as a substitute for spectacles for the correction of defective vision or, in special circumstances, as protective shells or for cosmetic purposes, for example, changing eye colour. The earliest use of contact lenses in the late 19th century was protective, or in the correction of corneal malformation, for it was not until the 1930s that simplification of fitting technique by taking eye impressions made their general use possible. The most recent development has been the 'soft' plastic lens which avoids the often severe discomfort suffered by prolonged use of earlier types, and which in some cases enables the contact lenses to be worn night and day for lengthy periods without removal.

contact process the main method of manufacturing sulphuric acid, one of the most important industrial chemicals. The acid is produced by oxidizing sulphur dioxide gas into sulphur trioxide, and then absorbing this in water, according to the outline reactions: $2SO_2 + O_2, 2SO_3 \quad SO_3 + H_2O \quad H_2SO_4$ In the contact process a mixture of sulphur dioxide and air is passed over a hot (450 degrees C) catalyst of vanadium/vanadium oxide (see catalysis). The

contact lens Hard type lens on the forefinger, ready to insert on the eye.

sulphur trioxide produced is then absorbed by a spray of dilute acid.

Contadora Group an alliance formed between Colombia, Mexico, Panama and Venezuela in January 1983 to establish a general peace treaty for Central America. The process was designed to include the formation of a Central American parliament (similar to the European parliament). Support for Contadora has come from Argentina, Brazil, Peru, and Uruguay as well as from the Central American states. The Caraballeda Declaration of Jan 1986 outlined a commitment to continuing the search for a diplomatic solution to the region's problems.

continent any one of the large land masses of the earth, as distinct from ocean. They include Asia, Africa, North and South America, Europe, Australia, and Antarctica. Continents are constantly moving and evolving (see ◊plate tectonics).

At the centre of each continental mass lies a shield or ◊craton, a deformed mass of old metamorphic rocks dating from Precambrian times. The shield is thick, compact and solid (the Canadian shield is the most obvious example), having undergone all the mountain-building activity it is ever likely to, and is usually worn flat. Around the shield is a concentric pattern of fold mountains, with old ranges, such as the Rockies, closest to the shield, and young ranges, such as the coast ranges of North America, farther away. This general concentric pattern is modified when two continental masses have drifted together and they become welded with a great mountain range along the join, the way Europe and N Asia are joined along the Urals. If a continent is torn apart, the new continental edges have no fold mountains, for instance S America has fold mountains along its western flank, the Andes, but none along the east where it tore away from Africa 200 million years ago. A continent does not end at the coastline. Its boundary is the edge of the shallow continental shelf which may extend several hundred kilometres out to sea. See ◊crust, ◊sial, and ◊sima.

Continental Congress in US history, the federal legislature of the original 13 colonies, convened in Philadelphia from 1774 to 1789, when the Constitution was adopted. The second Continental Congress convened May 1775 was responsible for drawing up the Declaration of Independence.

continental drift theory in geology first proposed 1915 by the German meteorologist Alfred Wegener that the earth consisted some 200 million years ago of a single large continent (he called it ◊Pangaea) which subsequently broke apart to form the continents as we know them today. The theory of ◊plate tectonics has provided a convincing explanation of how such vast movement may have occurred.

continental system Napoleon's attempted economic blockade of Britain 1806–12.

continuo in music, short for *basso continuo*, the bass line on which a keyboard player, often accompanied by a bass stringed instrument, built up a harmonic accompaniment in much 17th-century music.

continuum system of coordinates or axes that make up a mathematical frame of reference. For example, in ◊relativity theory the three dimensions of space (height, breadth, and depth) together with the time dimension can be regarded as a four-dimensional continuum.

contraceptive drug (or device or technique) that interferes with reproduction by preventing the ripening and release of an egg cell (ovum), (the Pill); or stopping sperm reaching the egg, or preventing a sperm fertilizing the egg (barrier methods, such as the condom or diaphragm); or halting implantation of the early embryo in the wall of the womb (intrauterine device, also known as the IUD or the coil).

contract agreement between two or more parties which will be enforced by law according to the intention of the parties. It always consists of an offer and an acceptance of that offer. In English law a contract must either be made under seal (in a deed) or there must be consideration to support it, that is, there must be some benefit to

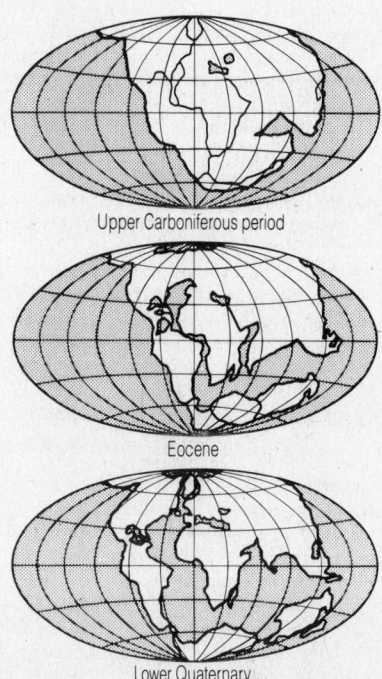

Upper Carboniferous period

Eocene

Lower Quaternary

one party to the contract or some detriment to the other. A contract, even though it is made in the proper form and the parties to it have the necessary capacity, may be unenforceable because it is made under a mistake, misrepresentation, duress, or undue influence. Contracts which are illegal are void. Among illegal contracts are those to commit a crime or civil wrong, to trade with the enemy, immoral contracts, and contracts in restraint of trade, that is, contracts by which a servant binds himself indefinitely not to compete with his master after his service is over. Contracts by way of gaming and wagering are also void.

contract bridge popular card game, played since 1930. It originated in 1925 in a bridge game on a steamer *en route* from Los Angeles to Havannah, and was introduced to New York clubs by H S Vanderbilt, one of the players.

contractile root a thickened root at the base of a corm, bulb or other organ that helps position it at an appropriate level in the ground. Contractile roots are found, for example, on the corms of *Crocus*. After they have become anchored in the soil the upper portion contracts, pulling the plant deeper into the ground.

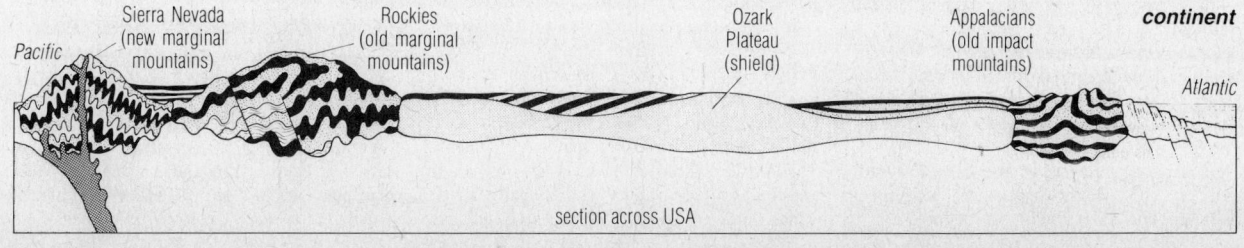

Sierra Nevada (new marginal mountains) Rockies (old marginal mountains) Ozark Plateau (shield) Appalacians (old impact mountains) **continent**

Pacific   Atlantic

section across USA

contralto another name for the female alto voice.

contrapuntal in music, term used to describe a work employing ◊counterpoint.

convection a type of heat energy transfer that involves the movement of a fluid (gas or liquid). According to the kinetic theory, molecules of fluid in contact with the source of heat oscillate faster and farther apart – that is, they expand – and tend to rise within the bulk of the fluid. Less energetic, cooler molecules sink to take their place, setting up convection currents. This is the principle of natural convection in many domestic hot-water systems and room space-heating.

convergence in mathematics, property of a series of numbers in which the difference between consecutive terms gradually decreases. The sum of a converging series approaches a limit as the number of terms tends to ◊infinity.

convergent evolution the independent evolution of similar structures in species (or other taxonomic groups) that are not closely related, as a result of living in a similar way. Thus, birds and bats have wings, not because they are descended from a common winged ancestor, but because their respective ancestors independently evolved flight. In such cases, the structures often differ in their anatomical origins and are only superficially similar. Such structures are said to be 'analogous', in contrast to the ◊homologous organs of related groups.

convergent evolution

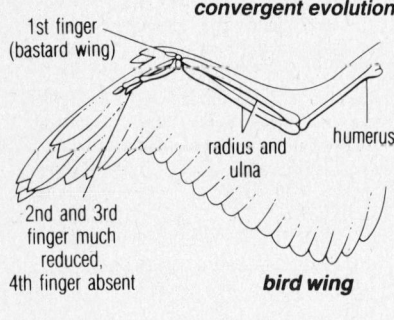

1st finger (bastard wing)
radius and ulna
humerus
2nd and 3rd finger much reduced, 4th finger absent

bird wing

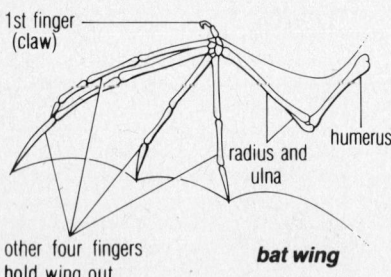

1st finger (claw)
radius and ulna
humerus
other four fingers hold wing out

bat wing

convex lens a converging ◊lens – that is, parallel beam of lights gets narrower as it passes through such a lens and is eventually brought to a focus. It can therefore produce a real image on a screen. Such a lens is wider at its centre than at the edges. Common forms include biconvex (with both surfaces curved towards) and plano-convex (with one flat surface and one convex). The whole lens may be further curved overall, making a concavo-convex or converging meniscus lens, as in some spectacle lenses.

conveyor a device used for transporting materials. Very widely used throughout industry is the *conveyor belt*, usually a rubber or fabric belt running on rollers. Trough-shaped belts are used, for example in mines, for transporting ores and coal. In coal mines too *chain conveyors* are used to remove coal from the cutting machines. Overhead endless chain conveyors are used to carry components and bodies in car assembly works. Other types include *bucket conveyors* and *screw conveyors*, powered versions of ◊Archimedes screw.

convocation in the Church of England, the synods of the clergy of the provinces of Canterbury and York. The General Synod established 1970 took over the functions and authority of the Convocation of Canterbury and York which continued to exist only in a restricted form.

Convolvulus or *bindweed* genus of plants, typical of the family Convolvulaceae. They are characterized by their twining stems, and by having their petals united into a tube. The field bindweed *Convolvulus arvensis*, a trailing plant with handsome white or pink-and-white-streaked flowers, is a common weed in Britain.

convoy system grouping of ships to sail together under naval escort in wartime. In World War I Royal Navy escort vessels were at first used only to accompany troopships, but the convoy system was adopted for merchant shipping when the unrestricted German submarine campaign opened in 1917. In World War II it was widely used by the Allies, and was generally successful, although there were heavy losses.

Conwy /'kɒnwi/ Welsh port on the river Conwy, Gwynedd, known until 1972 by the anglicized form *Conway*; population (1981) 12,950. Conwy has picturesque ruins of a castle rebuilt by Edward I in 1284.

Coober Pedy /'kuːbə 'piːdi/ town (Aboriginal 'white man in a hole') in the Great Central Desert, Australia. Opals were discovered in 1915, and are mined amid a moonscape of diggings in temperatures up to 60°C/140°F.

Cooch Behar /'kuːtʃ bɪ'hɑː/ former princely state in India, it was merged in West Bengal in 1950.

Cook, Mount /kʊk/ highest point, 3,764 m/12,349 ft of Southern ◊Alps, range of mountains running through New Zealand.

Cook /kʊk/ James 1728–1779. British explorer, born at Marton, Yorkshire. He joined the Royal Navy in 1755, and in 1768 was given command of an expedition to the South Pacific to witness the transit of Venus. He sailed in the *Endeavour* with Joseph Banks and other scientists, reaching Tahiti in April 1769. The transit was observed in Jun, after which Cook sailed round New Zealand and charted the coasts. He then went on to make a detailed survey of the E coast of Australia, naming New South Wales, and Botany Bay, and arriving back in England on 12 Jun 1771. Now a commander, Cook set out in 1772 with the *Resolution* and *Adventure* to search for the southern continent. The location of Easter Island was determined, and the Marquesas and Tonga Islands plotted. Among other discoveries were New Caledonia

and Norfolk Island, and New Zealand was revisited. Cook returned on 25 Jul 1775, having sailed 60,000 mi in three years. The object of his third and last voyage with the *Resolution* and *Discovery*, on which he set out 25 Jun 1776, was the discovery of the NW Passage from the Pacific end. On the way to New Zealand, he discovered several of the Cook or Hervey Islands and rediscovered the Hawaiian or Sandwich Islands. The ships sighted the American coast in latitude 45°N and sailed N, making a continuous survey as far as the Bering Strait, when the way was blocked by ice. Cook then surveyed the opposite coast of the strait (Siberia), and returned to Hawaii early in 1779. In Kealakekua Bay, one of the *Discovery's* boats was stolen by the islanders. Cook was clubbed to death from behind on 14 Feb in a scuffle on the beach when trying to recover it, and was buried at sea. Cook made enormous additions to geographical knowledge, was responsible for Britain's acquisition of the Australasian territories, and his accounts of his discoveries are classics.

CAPTAIN JAMES COOK FRS

Cook The British seaman Captain James Cook explored the E coast of Australia. He gave European names to New South Wales and Botany Bay and, in turn, the Cook Islands, Mount Cook and Cook Strait, which all belong to New Zealand, were named after him.

Cook /kʊk/ Peter 1937– . British writer and comedian, who appeared in revue (*Beyond the Fringe* 1959–64), and opened London's first satirical nightclub *The Establishment* in 1960 with *Dudley Moore* (1935–), his partner in comic dialogues.

Cook /kʊk/ Thomas 1808–1892. Pioneer British travel agent, founder of Thomas Cook & Son. He organized his first tour, to Switzerland, in 1863, and introduced travellers' cheques ('circular notes'), in the early 1870s.

Cooke /kʊk/ Alistair 1908– . American journalist. Born in England, he was *Guardian* correspondent in the USA 1948–72, and contributed a weekly *Letter from America* to

BBC radio. He was created Honorary Knight Commander of the Bath 1973.

Cooke /kʊk/ Sam 1931–1964. US soul singer and songwriter, who began his career as a gospel singer and turned to pop music in 1956. His hits, which have become classics, include 'You Send Me' 1957 and 'Wonderful World' 1960 (re-released 1986).

Cookham-on-Thames /'kʊkəm ɒn 'temz/ village in Berkshire, England. The artist Stanley ◊Spencer lived here for many years and a memorial gallery of his work was opened in 1962.

Cook Islands /kʊk/ group of six large and a number of smaller Polynesian islands 2,600 km/1,600 mi NE of Auckland, New Zealand. Area 230 sq km/90 sq mi; population (1981) 17,754. The chief island, Rarotonga, is the site of an international airport and of Avarua, the seat of government. Niue, geographically part of the group, is separately administered. The Cook Islands were visited by Captain Cook in 1773, annexed by Britain 1888, transferred to New Zealand 1901, and became a self-governing overseas territory (with common citizenship with New Zealand) in 1964.

Cook Strait /kʊk/ strait dividing North and South Island, New Zealand. A submarine cable carries electricity from South to North Island.

coolabah Australian riverside tree *Eucalyptus microtheca.*

Coolidge /'kuːlɪdʒ/ (John) Calvin 1872–1933. 30th President of the USA. Born in Vermont, the son of a farmer and storekeeper, he became a lawyer. He was Governor of Massachusetts in 1919, and was responsible for crushing the Boston police strike. A republican, he became Vice-President in 1921 and President, on the death of Harding, in 1923. He was re-elected in 1924, and his period of office was marked by great economic prosperity.

Cooper /'kuːpə/ Gary 1901–62. American actor. Born in Montana, he epitomized the lean, true-hearted Yankee, slow of speech but capable of outdoing the 'badmen' in *Lives of a Bengal Lancer* 1935, *Mr Deeds Goes to Town* 1936, *Sergeant York* 1940 (Academy Award 1941), and *For Whom the Bell Tolls* 1943.

Cooper /'kuːpə/ Henry 1934– . British heavyweight boxer. Noted for his left-hook – 'Henry's hammer' – he held the British and Empire titles 1959–71, and the European 1964 and 1968–71. In 1967 he became the first to win three Lonsdale belts outright.

Cooper /'kuːpə/ James Fenimore 1789–1851. US writer, considered the first great American novelist. He was born in New Jersey, sailed as an apprentice seaman to Europe and in 1808 became a midshipman. Marrying in 1811, he spent most of the rest of his life on the family estate of Cooperstown, New York State. He wrote some 50 novels, first becoming popular with *The Spy* 1821. Most notable were the volumes of *Leather Stocking Tales* (so called because they were linked by the figure of the frontiersman Natty Bumppo, nicknamed Leatherstocking) comprising *The Pioneers* 1823, *The Last of the Mohicans* 1826, *The Prairie* 1827, *The Pathfinder* and *The*

Deerslayer 1841, about settlers and American Indians in the mid-18th century.

Cooper /'kuːpə/ Samuel 1609–1672. English miniaturist. His subjects included Milton, members of Charles II's court and Pepys's wife. He is most famous for his portraits of Oliver Cromwell ('warts and all'). His serious, objective portraits raised the status of his art to that of oil painting.

co-operative movement the banding together of groups of people for mutual assistance in trade, manufacture, the supply of ◊credit, or other services. In Britain the predominant type of co-operative is the ◊Co-operative Wholesale Society (CWS), a retail trading concern whose shops sell at current market prices, but return the bulk of their profits (less any sums placed to reserve) to their members as 'dividends' on the sums spent there. Control is in the hands of a management committee elected by the members. Societies of this type in Britain have several million members, and in Scandinavia the rate is also high – in Denmark they cover some 45 per cent of the population. Usually the local societies are federated nationally in co-operative wholesale societies, which carry on wholesale trade and factory production. The original principles of co-operative movement were laid down in 1844 by the Rochdale Pioneers, under the influence of Robert ◊Owen, and by Charles ◊Fourier in France. Producers' co-operative societies, formed on a basis of co-partnership among the employees, exist on a large scale in France, Italy, Spain and the Soviet Union, but have, until recently been of little importance in Britain. The 1970s and 1980s have, however, seen a growth in the number of ◊workers' co-operatives, set up in factories otherwise threatened by closure due to economic depression. Agricultural co-operative societies have been formed in Britain for the collective purchase of seeds, fertilizers, and other commodities, while societies for co-operative marketing of agricultural produce are prominent in the USA, Ireland, Denmark, the Commonwealth, and many other countries. Agricultural credit societies are strong in rural economies of Europe and Asia, including parts of India. The USA also has a co-operative farm credit system.

Co-operative Party political party founded in Britain in 1918 by the co-operative movement, to maintain its principles in parliamentary and local government. A written constitution was adopted in 1938. The party had strong links with the Labour Party; from 1946 Co-operative Party candidates stood in elections as Co-operative and Labour Candidates, and after the 1959 General Election agreement was reached to limit the party's candidates to 30.

Co-operative Wholesale Society a British concern, the largest co-operative organization in the world, owned and controlled by the numerous co-operative retail societies, who are also its customers. Founded in 1863, it acts as wholesaler, manufacturer, banker, and so on, and owns factories, farms and estates, in addition to offices and warehouses.

Cooper's Creek /'kuːpə/ stretch of water in ◊Channel Country, SW Australia.

coordinate geometry a system of geometry, also called analytical geometry, in which points, lines, shapes, and surfaces are represented by algebraic expressions. In plane (two-dimensional) coordinate geometry, the plane is usually defined by two axes at right angles to each other, the horizontal x-axis and the vertical y-axis, meeting at O, the origin. A point on the plane can be represented by a pair of ◊Cartesian coordinates, which define its position in terms of its distance along the x-axis and along the y-axis from O. These distances are respectively the x and y coordinates of the point. Lines are represented as equations; for example, $y = 2x + 1$ gives a straight line, and $y = 3x^2 + 2x$ gives a ◊parabola (a curve). Different lines and curves can be drawn by plotting the coordinates of points that satisfy their equations and joining up the points. One of the great advantages of coordinate geometry, however, is that geometrical solutions can be obtained without drawing but by manipulating algebraic expressions. For example, the coordinates of the point of intersection of two straight lines can be determined by finding the unique values of x and y that satisfy both of the equations for the lines, that is, by solving them as a pair of ◊simultaneous equations. The curves studied in simple coordinate geometry are the ◊conic sections (circle, ellipse, parabola, and hyperbola) each of which has its own characteristic equation.

Coorg /kʊəg/ district of the state of Karnataka, India. Formerly the princely state of Coorg, it was merged in Karnataka in 1956.

coot water bird *Fulica atra* belonging to the rail family. About 38 cm/1.2 ft long, and mainly black, it has a stark white forehead and big feet with lobed toes. It is found through Europe, Asia and Australia on lakes, ponds and reservoirs, feeding on plants, insects and small fish. Another eight species are distributed around the world, most in the Americas.

cope semicircular cape, without sleeves, worn by priests of the Western Christian church in processions and on some other formal occasions, but not when officiating at Mass.

Copenhagen /ˌkəʊpən'heɪgən/ capital of Denmark: on the islands of Zealand and Amager; population (1985) 1,358,500. To the NE is the royal palace at Amalienborg; the 17th-century Charlottenburg Palace houses the Academy of Arts, and parliament meets in the Christiansborg Palace. The statue of Hans Andersen's 'Little Mermaid' (by Edvard Eriksen) is at the harbour entrance.

history Copenhagen was a fishing village until 1167, when the bishop of Roskilde built the castle on the site of the present Christiansborg palace. A settlement grew up, and it became the Danish capital in 1443. The university was founded in 1479. The city was under German occupation Apr 1940–May 1945.

Copenhagen, Battle of /ˌkəʊpən'heɪgən/ naval victory on 2 Apr 1801 by a British fleet under Sir Hyde Parker (1739–1807) and ◊Nelson over the Danish fleet. Nelson put his telescope to his blind eye and refused to see Parker's signal for withdrawal.

Copepoda sub-class of ◊crustacea, freshwater and marine, mainly microscopic, and found in plankton.

Copernicus /kə'pɜːnɪkəs/ Nicolaus 1473–1543. Polish astronomer. Born at Torun on the Vistula, then under the Polish king, he studied at Cracow and in Italy, and lectured on astronomy at Rome. On his return to Pomerania in 1505 he became physician to his uncle, the bishop of Ermland, and was made canon at Frauenburg, although he did not take holy orders. Living there until his death, he interspersed astronomical work with the duties of various civil offices. For 30 years he worked on the hypothesis that the motion of the Earth was responsible for the apparent movements of the heavenly bodies, but his great work *De revolutionibus orbium coelestium* was not published until the year of his death. In this work he postulated that the Sun is the centre of our system, and he thus became a prime founder of modern astronomy.

Copland /'kəʊplənd/ Aaron 1900– . American composer. Born in New York, he studied in France with Nadia Boulanger, and in 1940 became instructor in composition at the Berkshire Music Center – from 1945 assistant director. Copland's early works, such as the piano concerto of 1926, were in the jazz idiom then popular in the USA, but he gradually developed a gentler style with a regional flavour drawn from American folk music. Later works include the ballets *Billy the Kid* 1939 – with a variant of the cowboy song 'Bury Me Not on the Lone Prairie' – *Rodeo* 1942, and *Appalachian Spring* 1944, based on a poem by Hart Crane; and *Inscape for Orchestra* 1967.

Copland The American composer Aaron Copland often conducts his own works, which use American folk tunes.

Copley /'kɒplɪ/ John Singleton 1737–1815. American artist. Born at Boston, Massachussetts, he became the leading portraitist of the colonial period. From 1774 he lived mainly in England, where he also painted historical scenes including *The Death of Chatham*.

copper a chemical element, and one of the earliest metals used by humans. Chemical symbol Cu; atomic number 29; atomic weight 63.54. It is orange-pink in colour, very malleable and ductile, and used principally on account of its toughness, softness, and pliability, high thermal and electrical conductivity, and resistance to corrosion. When alloyed with tin it forms bronze, a relatively hard metal, the discovery of which opened a new age in human pre-history. Brass is an alloy of copper and zinc. The USA produces about a quarter of the world's output. Other producers are Chile, Canada, Zambia and the Sheba region of Zaïre.

copper ore copper is extracted from a number of minerals including native copper, Cu; chalcocite, Cu_2O; chalcopyrite, $CuFeS_2$; bornite, $FeS.2Cu_2S.CuS$; azurite, $2CuCO_3.Cu(OH)_2$; malachite, $CuCO_3.Cu(OH)_2$; and chrysocolla, $CuSiO_3.2H_2O$. Native copper and the copper sulphides are usually found in veins associated with igneous ◊intrusions. Chrysocolla and the carbonates are products of the ◊weathering of copper-bearing rocks. Native copper was one of the first metals to be worked, because it was available as the metal and needed little refining. Nowadays the main producers are the United States of America, the Soviet Union, Zambia, Chile and Peru, also Canada and Zaïre.

coppicing a severe type of pruning where trees are cut down to near ground level at regular intervals, typically every 3–20 years, to promote the growth of numerous shoots from the base. This form of woodland management used to be commonly practiced, especially on hazel, to produce large quantities of thin branches for firewood, fencing, etc. The resulting thicket was known as a coppice or copse. See also◊pollarding.

Coppola /'kɒpələ/ Francis Ford 1939– . American film director and screenwriter, born in New York. In 1972 he directed *The Godfather*, one of the biggest money-makers of all time. Other successes include *The Godfather Part II* (which, like the original, won several Academy Awards), *Apocalypse Now* 1979, and *The Cotton Club* 1984.

copra dried kernel of the ◊coconut.

Copt one of the descendants of the ancient Egyptians who accepted Christianity in the 1st century and refused to adopt Islam after the Arab conquest. Before the conquest a majority of Christian Egyptians had adopted Monophysite views (that Christ had 'one nature' rather than being human and divine), and when this was condemned by the Council of Chalcedon in 451 they became schismatic and were persecuted by the orthodox party, to which they were opposed on nationalistic as well as religious grounds. They therefore readily accepted Arab rule, but were later subjected to persecution by their new masters. They now form a small minority (about 3,000,000) of the population, mainly town-dwellers, and are distinguishable in dress and customs from their Muslim fellow-countrymen. They rarely marry outside their own sect. The head of the Coptic Church is the Patriarch of Alexandria, currently Shenonda III (1923–), 117th Pope of Alexandria. He was imprisoned by Sadat in 1981 and is opposed by Muslim fundamentalists.

Coptic language a member of the Hamito-Semitic language family and a minority language of Egypt. It is descended from the language of the ancient Egyptians and is the ritual language of the Coptic Christian Church. It is written in the Greek alphabet with some additional characters derived from Demotic script. The Sahidic dialect of Upper Egypt is the medium of a wholly religious literature.

copyright generally speaking, the law of copyright applies to literary, musical or artistic works, including plays, recordings, films, and radio and television broadcasts. It prevents the reproduction of the work, either whole or in part, without the consent of the author. Copyright applies to a work, not an idea. For example, the basic plots of two novels might be identical without infringing the law of copyright, but should details in the descriptions and development of characters make it clear that one author had copied from the other, then copyright would be infringed. Translations of literary works are also protected. The copyright holder may license others to reproduce the work (as in the case of a musical composition or a book), and receives payments (royalties) per performance or copy.

Under the Universal Copyright Convention (1952) each contracting country offers authors of other signatories the same protection it gives its own: it came into force USA 1955, UK 1957 and USSR 1973, when the last-named also established a copyright agency as the sole body to deal with foreign publishers, and made it illegal for an author to do so on his own behalf. Revision of the Convention of Berne (1886, mainly European) at Stockholm 1967 introduced a controversial protocol allowing countries regarded by the UN as 'developing' to modify copyright conditions extensively: Britain did not sign the protocol. Under English law, copyright subsists for 50 years from end of year of author's death, or from date of publication, where posthumous. Duration of copyright in the USA used to be for 28 years from date of publication, with a right to renewal for another 28, but under an act effective 1978 this was amended to the life of the author plus 50 years.

coral marine organism, related to sea anemones and belonging to the class Anthozoa of the phylum Cnidaria, which has a skeleton of lime (calcium carbonate) extracted from the surrounding water. Corals live in a ◊symbiotic relationship with microscopic algae (zooxanthellae) which are incorporated into the structure. The algae receive carbon dioxide from the polyps, and the polyps receive nutrients from the algae. They are also in relationship with the fish which rest or take refuge within their branches, and which excrete nutrients which make them grow faster. Sedentary, the majority of corals are omnivorous and form large colonies. Their accumulated skeletons form large *coral reefs* and atolls. These occur in the warm seas of the world, at moderate depths with sufficient light. *Fringing reefs* are so called because they build up on the shores of continents or islands; the living animals mainly occupying the outer edges of the reef. *Barrier reefs* are separated from the shore by a saltwater lagoon, which may be as much as 30 km/20 mi) wide; there are usually navigable passes through the barrier into the lagoon. The Great Barrier Reef, to the NE of Australia, is about 1600 km/1000 mi) long. *Atolls* resemble a ring surrounding a lagoon, and do not enclose an island; they are usually formed by the gradual subsidence of an extinct volcano, the coral growing up from where the edge of the island once lay. Some coral is valued for decoration or jewellery, for example Mediterranean *red coral Corallum rubrum*.

coral reefs

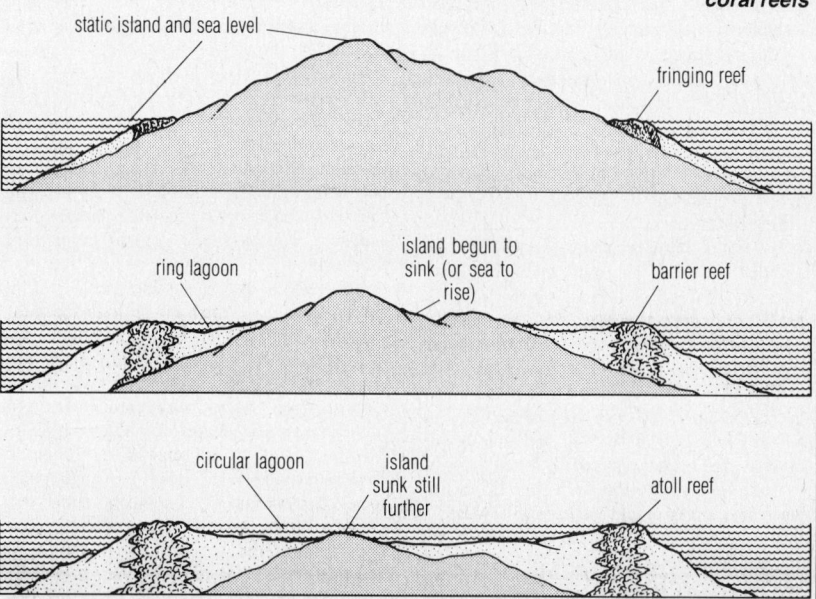

static island and sea level
fringing reef

ring lagoon
island begun to sink (or sea to rise)
barrier reef

circular lagoon
island sunk still further
atoll reef

Coralli /ˌkɒrəˈliː/ Jean 1779–1854. French dancer and choreographer of Italian descent. Born in Paris, he made his debut as a dancer in 1802. He chorographed *Giselle* 1841 and *La Péri* 1843, for the Italina ballerina Grisi; *Le Diable boîteux* 1836 for Fanny Elssler, and many other famous ballets.

Coral Sea /ˈkɒrəl/ part of the Pacific Ocean lying between NE Australia, New Guinea, the Solomon Islands, New Hebrides, and New Caledonia. It contains numerous coral islands and reefs.

coral tree name given to several tropical trees of the genus *Erythrina*, family Leguminosae, with bright red or orange flowers, and producing a particularly light-weight wood.

Coram /ˈkɔːrəm/ Thomas 1668–1751. British philanthropist. Born in Lyme Regis, he became a farmer and shipwright in Massachusetts. He returned to England in 1703 and established the Foundling Hospital for orphaned and abandoned children in Holborn, London, in 1741. The site, now Coram's Fields, is still a children's foundation.

cor anglais or *English horn*. Musical instrument; not a ◊horn, but a woodwind, a member of the ◊oboe family, and its English origin is doubtful. A metal tube, bent backwards to the mouth of the player, contains the double reed. It was introduced into the orchestra in the time of ◊Wagner, has an expressive tone, and is normally used in slow melodic passages.

Corbière /ˌkɔːbiˈeə/ Tristan 1845–1875. French poet. The merits of his *Les Amours jaunes/Yellow Loves* 1873 went unrecognized until Verlaine called attention to it in 1884. Many of his poems, such as *La Rhapsodie Foraine/Wandering Rhapsody*, deal with life in his native Brittany.

Corby /ˈkɔːbi/ town in Northamptonshire, England; population (1981) 52,500. Formerly a major steel centre, it now makes plastics.

Corday /kɔːˈdeɪ/ Charlotte 1768–1793. French ◊Girondist (right-wing republican during the French Revolution). After overthrow of the Girondists by the more extreme Jacobins in May 1793, she stabbed to death the Jacobin leader, Marat, with a bread-knife as he sat in his bath in Jul the same year. She was guillotined.

cordillera a group of mountain ranges and their valleys, all running in a specific direction, formed by the convergence of two ◊tectonic plates along a line. The whole western section of N America, with the Rocky Mountains and the coast ranges parallel to the contact between the N American and the Pacific plates, is called the Western Cordillera.

Córdoba /ˈkɔːdəbə/ city in Argentina, on the Rio Primero; population (1980) 982,000. Founded in 1573, it has a university founded 1613, a military aviation college, an observatory, and a cathedral.

Córdoba /ˈkɔːdəbə/ Spanish city, capital of Córdoba province, on the Guadalquivir; population (1981) 284,750. It has many Moorish remains, the most famous of which is the mosque, now a cathedral, founded by Abder-Rahman I in 785; it is one of the largest Christian churches in the world. Córdoba was probably founded by the Carthaginians, and from 711 until 1236 was held by the Moors.

core the innermost part of the structure of the earth. It is divided into an inner core, the upper boundary of which is 1,600 km/940 mi from the centre, and an outer core, 1,820 km/1,060 mi thick. Both parts are thought to be made of nickel and iron, with the inner core being solid and the outer core being liquid. The temperature may be 3,000°C. These hypotheses are based on seismology (the observation of the paths of earthquake waves through the earth), and calculations of the earth's density.

Corelli /kəˈreli/ Arcangelo 1653–1713. Italian composer and violinist. Born near Milan, he studied in Bologna and in about 1685 settled in Rome, under the patronage of Cardinal Pietro Ottoboni, where he published his first violin sonatas. He was one of the first great violinists and his music, marked by graceful melody, includes a set of concerti grossi and five sets of chamber sonatas.

Corelli /kəˈreli/ Marie, pseudonym of British novelist Mary Mackay 1855–1924. Trained for a musical career, she turned instead to writing and from the appearance of *The Romance of Two Worlds* 1886 was highly popular (she was said to be Queen Victoria's favourite novelist), though her works were later ridiculed for their pretentious style.

Corfe Castle /kɔːf/ village in the Isle of Purbeck, Dorset, England, built around the ruins of a Norman castle destroyed in the Civil War.

Corfu /kɔːˈfuː/ most northerly, second largest of the Ionian islands (Greek Kérkyra), off the coast of Epirus in the Ionian Sea; area 1,072 sq km/414 sq mi, population (1981) 99,500. The chief town, also Corfu (Kérkyra) (population (1981) 33,560), is a port and seat of a Roman Catholic archbishopric. Corfu was colonized by Corinthians about 700 BC, Venice held it 1386–1797, Britain from 1815–64.

Corinna /kəˈrɪnə/ Greek lyric poet of 6th century BC, said to have instructed Pindar. Only fragments of her poetry survive.

Corinth /ˈkɒrɪnθ/ port (Greek Kórinthos) in Greece, on the isthmus connecting the Peloponnesus with the mainland; population (1981) 22,650. The isthmus is rocky, and is now cut by the 6.5 km/4 mi Corinth canal, opened in 1893. The ancient city-state of Corinth was already a place of some importance in the 9th century BC. At the end of the 6th century BC it joined the Peloponnesian League, and took a prominent part in the Persian and the Peloponnesian wars. In 146 BC it was conquered by the Romans. St Paul visited Corinth, and addressed two epistles to its churches. After many changes of ownership it became part of independent Greece in 1822. The most outstanding of Corinth's ancient monuments is the ruined temple of Apollo (6th century BC).

Corinthian in classical architecture, one of the five types of ◊column. See ◊order.

Coriolis effect a result of the deflective force of the earth's W-to-E rotation. Winds and ocean currents are deflected to the right in the N and to the left in the S hemisphere. It has to be allowed for in launching guided missiles, but despite popular belief it has negligible effect on the clockwise or anti-clockwise direction of water running out of a bath. Named after its discoverer, the French mathematician Gaspard Coriolis (1792–1843).

coriolis effect

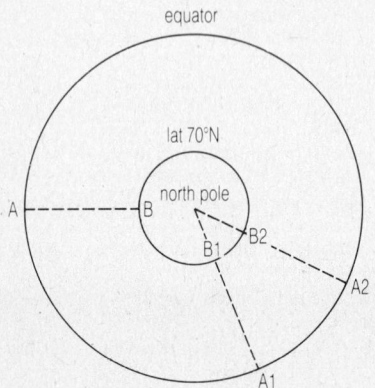

equator

lat 70°N

A — — — — B north pole

B1　B2

A2

A1

point A on equator moves
distance A1–A2 in 3 hrs
　　　　point B at lat 70°N moves
　　　　distance B1–B2 in 3 hrs
　　　　shorter distance moves more slowly

Cork /kɔːk/ largest county (county town Cork) of the Republic of Ireland, in the province of Munster; population (1981) 402,000; area 7,459 sq km/2,880 sq mi. It includes Bantry Bay and the village of Blarney. There is a series of ridges and vales running NE–SW across the county. The Nagles and Boggeraph mountains run across the centre, separating the two main rivers, the Blackwater and the Lee. It is an agricultural county but there is also some copper and manganese mining, marble quarrying, and river and sea fishing. Towns are Cobb, Bantry, Youghal, Fermoy, and Mallow. Natural gas, found off the S coast at Kinsale, is supplied to N Ireland.

Cork /kɔːk/ city, episcopal *see*, and seaport of county Cork , population (1981) 136,350. At the head of the long inlet of Cork Harbour, on the Lee, Cork is the second port of the Republic of Ireland. The lower section of the harbour can berth liners, and the town has distilleries, shipyards, and iron foundries. There is a Protestant cathedral dedicated to St Finbarr, and a Roman Catholic cathedral of St Mary and St Finbarr. University College (1845) beame in 1968 the University of Cork. The city hall was opened in 1937.

St Finbarr's seventh-century monastery was the original foundation of Cork. It was eventually settled by Danes, who were dispossessed by the English in 1172.

cork /kɔːk/ the light cellular outer layers of the bark of the stems and roots of almost all trees and shrubs, which are impermeable to water. In particular, the word is used for the corky outer layers of the bark of the cork oak *Quercus suber*, a native of S Europe and N Africa, which is cultivated in Spain and Portugal and provides the cork for commercial use.

corm a short, swollen, underground plant stem, surrounded by protective scale-leaves, as seen in *Crocus*. It stores food, provides a means of ◊vegetative reproduction, and acts as a ◊perennating organ. During the year the corm gradually withers as the food reserves are used for the production of leafy, flowering shoots formed from axillary buds. Several new corms are formed at the base of these shoots, above the old corm.

cormorant seabird *Phalacrocorax carbo* about 90 cm/3 ft long, with webbed feet, long neck and beak, and glossy black plumage. In W Europe it is mainly coastal, but it has a wide, but broken range across the world and in some places is common by lakes and rivers. It generally feeds on bottom-living fish in shallow water. The *shag Phalacrocorax aristotelis* is smaller. There are some 30 species of cormorant worldwide including a flightless form *Nannopterum harrisi* in the Galapagos Islands.

corn general name given to the main cereal ◊crop of a region, for example, wheat in the UK, oats in Scotland and Ireland, maize in the USA.

corncrake bird *Crex crex* of the rail family. About 25 cm/10 in long, it is drably coloured, and shy, but has a persistent rasping call, often made at night. It lives in meadows and crops, but has become rare where mechanical methods are used in fields. Its summer range includes Europe and W Asia.

Corneille /kɔː'neɪ/ Pierre 1606–1684. French dramatist. Born in Rouen, he had his first play *Mélite* performed in 1629. It was followed by others which were approved by Richelieu, and gained him an appointment as one of the five poets engaged to mould the cardinal's ideas for the stage 1634. But Corneille proved intractable and was dismissed.

His first important play, the tragedy *Médée* 1635, was followed in 1636 by *Le Cid*, a tragi-comedy and his most famous play, which was attacked by Academicians under the influence of Richelieu but achieved huge public success. After three years' retirement, Corneille returned to the cardinal's favour and a pension with *Horace* 1639, which like all his later plays was based on ◊Aristotle's unities. Continuing his success with *Cinna* 1640, *Polyeucte* 1643, the comedy *Le Menteur* 1643, and *Rodogune* 1645, he was elected to the Academy in 1647. He then encountered a run of failures, and retired in 1652 to devote himself to translation and criticism, notably his *Discours du poème dramatique*. He returned with *Oedipe* 1659, approved by Louis XIV, and *La Toison d'or* 1661. His last great play was *Sertorius* 1662, although he continued to write until 1674. His tragedies glorify the strength of will governed by reason, and established the French classical drama of the next two centuries. His younger brother *Thomas Corneille* 1625–1709, wrote some 40 plays, of which the most famous are *Ariane* 1672, and *Comte d'Essex* 1678.

cornet musical instrument. Originally the name of a family of woodwind instruments; it now refers to the *cornet à pistons*. Like a shorter, broader trumpet, with a wider bore, it is without fixed notes, notes of different pitch being obtained by over-blowing and by means of three pistons. It is chiefly used in military and brass bands.

cornflour the purified starch content of maize (Indian corn), used as a thickener in cooking. In the USA it is called cornstarch.

cornflower plant *Centaurea cyanus* belonging to the Compositae. It is distinguished from the knapweeds by its deep azure blue flowers, and was formerly a common weed in cornfields in Britain.

Cornforth /'kɔːnfɔːθ/ John 1917– . Australian chemist. He settled in England in 1941. In 1975 he shared a Nobel prize with Vladimir Prelog for work utilizing ◊radioisotopes as 'markers' to find out how enzymes synthesize chemicals which are mirror images of one another (stereo isomers).

Corniche /kɔː'niːʃ/ *la Grande* (Great) *Corniche* (Italian 'mountain ledge'), a road with superb alpine and coastal scenery, was built between Nice and Menton, S France, by Napoleon: it rises to 520 m/1,700 ft. *La Moyenne* (Middle) and *la Petite* (Little) *Corniche*, are supplementary parallel roads, the latter being nearest the coast.

Cornish language an extinct member of the Celtic language, branch of the Indo-European language family, spoken in Cornwall until 1777. Written Cornish first appeared in 10th century documents, some religious plays were written in Cornish in the 15th and 16th centuries, but later literature is scanty, mainly folk-tales and verses. Members of the Cornish nationalist movement have in recent years 'revived' the language for social purposes and for its symbolic value.

Corn Laws laws to regulate the export or import of cereals, in order to maintain an adequate supply for the consumers and a fair price for the producers. For centuries they formed an integral part of the mercantile system in England, and it was not until after the Napoleonic wars that they aroused any strong opposition because of their tendency to drive up the price. They were modified in 1828, again in 1842, and, partly as a result of the Irish famine, practically repealed by Peel in 1846, as being an unwarranted tax on food.

Cornwall /'kɔːnwɔːl/ county in SW England including Scilly Islands (Scillies)
area (excluding Scillies) 3,548 sq km/1,370 sq mi
towns administrative headquarters Truro; Camborne, Launceston; resorts of Bude, Falmouth, Newquay, Penzance, St Ives
features Bodmin Moor (including Brown Willy 419 m/1,375 ft), Land's End peninsula, St Michael's Mount, rivers Tamar, Fowey, Fal and Camel; ◊Poldhu, site of first transatlantic radio signal 1901. The Stannary or Tinners' Parliament, established in the 11th century, ceased to meet in 1752 but its powers were never rescinded at Westminster, and it was revived in 1974 as a separatist movement. It has six

members from each of the four Stannary towns: Losthwithiel, Launceston, Helston, and Truro. The flag of St ◊Piran, a white St George's cross on a black ground, is used by separatists.

products growing electronics industry; spring flowers; tin (mined since Bronze Age, some workings renewed in 1960s, though the industry has all but disappeared), kaolin (St Austell); fish

population (1986) 441,900

famous people John Betjeman (buried at Trebetherick on the N coast), Humphry Davy, Daphne du Maurier, William Golding.

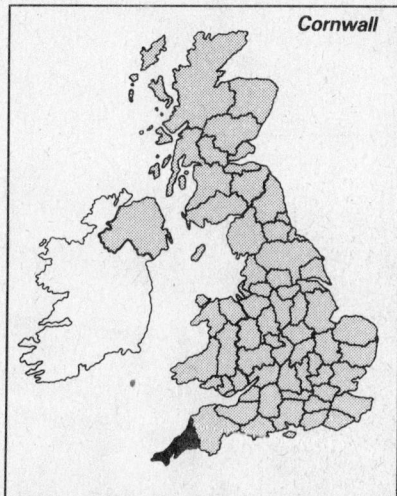

Cornwall

Cornwallis /kɔːnˈwɒlɪs/ Charles, 1st Marquess Cornwallis 1738–1805. British soldier, eldest son of the first Earl Cornwallis. He led the British forces in the War of ◊American Independence until 1781, when his surrender at Yorktown ended the war. Subsequently he was twice governor-general of India, and viceroy of Ireland, and was made a marquess in 1793.

corolla a collective name for the ◊petals of a flower. In some plants the petal margins are partially or completely fused to form a *corolla-tube*, for example in bindweed (*Convolvulus arevensis*).

Coromandel /ˌkɒrəˈmændl/ the cast coast of Tamil Nadu, India.

Coromandel Peninsula /ˌkɒrəˈmændl/ peninsula on North Island, New Zealand, east of Auckland.

corona a faint halo of gas around the Sun, visible at solar ◊eclipses or through a *coronagraph*, an instrument that blocks light from the Sun's brilliant disk. The corona consists of hot (about 2,000,000k) but tenuous gas boiling from the surface of the sun. The gas flows away from the corona to form the ◊solar wind.

coronary artery disease condition in which the fatty deposits of ◊atherosclerosis form in, and therefore narrow, the coronary arteries which supply the heart muscle. (Latin *corona* 'crown', from their encircling of the heart.) These arteries may already be hardened (arteriosclerosis). If the heart's oxygen requirements are increased, as during exercise, the blood supply through the narrowed arteries may be inadequate, and the

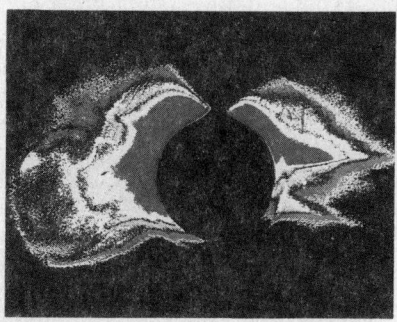

corona A photograph of the sun's hot outer atmosphere, which reaches outwards for millions of miles, retouched to distinguish levels of brightness. Skylab permitted eight months of corona observation, compared with less than 80 hours from all natural eclipses since photography was first used in 1839.

pain of ◊angina results. A heart attack occurs if the blood supply to an area of the heart is cut off, for example because a blood clot (thrombus) has blocked one of the coronary arteries. The subsequent lack of oxygen damages the heart muscle (infarct), and if a large area of the heart is affected, the attack may be fatal. Coronary artery disease tends to run in families, and is linked to smoking, lack of exercise, and a diet high in saturated (mostly animal) fats which increases the level of blood cholesterol. It is a common cause of death in many developed countries, especially among older men.

coronation the ceremony of investing a sovereign with the emblems of royalty, as a symbol of inauguration in office. The British coronation ceremony combines the Hebrew rite of anointing with customs of Germanic origin, for example, the actual crowning and the presentation of the monarch to his or her subjects to receive homage. Its main features are the presentation to the people; the administration of the oath; the presentation of the Bible; the anointing of the sovereign with holy oil on hands, breast, and head; the presentation of the spurs and the sword of state, the emblems of knighthood; the presentation of the armils (a kind of bracelet), robe royal, the orb, the ring, the sceptre with the cross, and the rod with the dove; the coronation with St Edward's Crown; the benediction; the enthroning; and the homage of the princes of the blood and the peerage. A consort is anointed on the head, presented with a ring, crowned, and presented with the sceptre and the ivory rod. Since the coronation of Harold in 1066, English sovereigns have been crowned in Westminster Abbey.

coroner in England an officer appointed by a county council to inquire into the deaths of persons who have died suddenly by acts of violence, under suspicious circumstances, or, formerly, in prison at the hands of the hangman. They may also inquire into instances of treasure trove. The office may date back to the days of King Alfred. A coroner is appointed for life, and must be a barrister, solicitor, or medical practitioner with at least five years' professional

service. Some county councils insist on the double medical and legal qualification. At an inquest, a coroner is assisted by a jury of between seven and 11 persons. Evidence is on oath, and medical and other witnesses may be summoned. If the jury returns a verdict of murder or manslaughter, the coroner can commit the accused for trial. In Scotland similar duties are performed by the procurator-fiscal. In the USA coroners are usually elected by the voters of the county.

coronet a small crown worn by a peer at the Coronation and the state opening of parliament. A duke's coronet consists of a golden circlet, above which are eight strawberry leaves; a marquess's has four strawberry leaves with four points surmounted by pearls between them, an earl's eight strawberry leaves with eight tall points surmounted by pearls between them, a viscount's sixteen small pearls, and a baron's six large pearls.

Corot /ˈkɒrəʊ/ Jean Baptiste Camille 1796–1875. French landscape painter. Born in Paris, he became famous as one of the painters of the ◊Barbizon school, excelling in early morning or twilight scenes. He used his sketches from nature to paint harmonious, classical landscapes, which became increasingly romantic.

corporatism the belief that the state in modern capitalist democracies should intervene to a large extent in the economy in order to ensure social harmony.

corporative state state in which the members are organized and represented not on a local basis as citizens, but as producers working in a particular trade, industry, or profession. The conception first appeared in modern politics in the theories of the syndicalist movement of the early 20th century, which proposed that all industries should be taken over and run by the trade unions, a federation of whom should replace the state. Similar views were put forward in Britain by the guild socialists about 1906–25. Certain features of syndicalist theory were adopted and given a right-wing tendency by the fascist regime in Italy, under which employers' and workers' organizations were represented in the National Council of Corporations, but this was completely dominated by the Fascist Party and had no real powers. Catholic social theory, as expounded in some papal encyclicals, also favours the corporative state as a means of eliminating class conflict. Corporative institutions were set up by the Franco and Salazar regimes in Spain and Portugal, under the influence of fascist and Catholic theories. In Spain representatives of the national syndicates were included in the Cortes (parliament), and in Portugal a corporative chamber existed alongside the National Assembly.

corps de ballet the dancers in a ballet company who usually dance in groups, in support of the soloists. At the Paris Opéra this is the name given to the whole company.

Corpus Christi feast celebrated in the Roman Catholic and Greek Orthodox churches, and to some extent in the Anglican Church, on the Thursday after Trinity Sunday. It was instituted in the 13th century through the devotion of St Juliana, prioress of Mount Cornillon, near Liège, in honour of the Real Presence of Christ in the Eucharist.

corpuscular theory hypothesis about the nature of ◊light championed by Isaac ◊Newton, who postulated that it consists of a stream of particles or corpuscles. The theory was superseded at the beginning of the 19th century by Thomas ◊Young's wave theory. Modern ◊quantum theory and wave mechanics embody both concepts.

Correggio /kɒ'redʒiəu/ Antonio Allegri da c. 1494–1534. Italian Renaissance painter, named after his birthplace near Modena. The son of a prosperous merchant, he came under the influence of ◊Mantegna, ◊Leonardo da Vinci, and ◊Raphael, but developed a style of his own which is remarkable for its fine sense of colouring and its treatment of light and shade. His best-known works include *Adoration of the Shepherds* or *Night* in the Dresden Gallery, *The Marriage of St Catherine* in the Louvre, and *Mercury instructing Cupid before Venus* and *Ecce Homo* in the National Gallery, London. Several of his works are in Parma, including the frescoed dome of the cathedral.

Corregidor /kə'regidɔː/ island at the mouth of Manila Bay, Luzon, Philippine Republic, defended by survivors of the Bataan campaign against the Japanese, 9 Apr–6 May 1942; the USA recaptured it on 15 Feb 1945.

Corrèze /kɒ'reɪz/ river of central France flowing 89 km/55 mi from the Plateau des Millevaches, past Tulle, capital of Corrèze *département* (to which it gives its name), to join the Vézère. It is used for generating electricity at Bar, 9.5 km/6 mi NW of Tulle.

corrie a hollow in the mountainside in a glaciated area representing the source of a melted glacier. The weight of the ice has ground out the bottom and worn back the sides. It is open at the front, and its sides and back are formed of ◊arêtes. There may be a lake in the bottom, known as a tarn. The term is Scottish; the same feature is known in Wales as a cwm and in Europe as a cirque.

Corrientes /ˌkɒri'entes/ city of Argentina, capital of Corrientes province, on the Paraná river, an important river port in a stock-raising district. Population (1980) 180,000.

corroboree Australian aboriginal dance. Some corroborees record events in history; others have a religious significance, connected with fertility and rejuvenation, or are theatrical entertainment.

corrosion the eating away and eventual destruction of metals and alloys by chemical attack. The rusting of ordinary iron and steel is the commonest form of corrosion. Rusting takes place in moist air. The iron combines with oxygen and water to form a brown-orange deposit of ◊rust, hydrated iron oxide. The rate of corrosion is increased where the atmosphere is polluted with sulphur dioxide. Salty roads accelerate the rusting of car bodies. Corrosion is largely an electrochemical process, and acidic and salty conditions favour the establishment of electrolytic cells on the metal which cause it to be eaten away. Other examples of corrosion include the green deposit that forms on copper and

bronze, called ◊verdigris. It is a basic copper carbonate. The tarnish on silver is a corrosion product, a film of silver sulphide.

corsair one of a group of Moorish pirates who from the 16th century onward plundered shipping in the Mediterranean and Atlantic. Although many punitive expeditions were sent against them, they were not suppressed until France occupied Algiers in 1830. Some Englishmen joined the Barbary pirates or corsair, for example, the half-brother of Sir Edmund ◊Verney, Sir Francis Verney.

Corse /kɔːs/ French name for ◊Corsica.

Corsica /'kɔːsɪkə/ island region (French *Corse*) of France, in the Mediterranean off the W coast of Italy, immediately N of Sardinia.
area 8680 sq km/3367 sq mi
capital and port Ajaccio
features ◊maquis vegetation; its mountain bandits were wiped out in 1931, but the tradition of the vendetta or blood feud lingers; it is the main base of the ◊Foreign Legion.
exports wine, olive oil
population (1984) 244,600, of whom just under 50% are native Corsicans; there are about 400,000 *émigrés*, mostly in Mexico and Central America, who return to retire.
language French (official); the majority speak Corsican, an Italian dialect.
religion Roman Catholicism
famous people Napoleon
government its special status involves a regional assembly from 1982 with uncertain powers.
history the first civilized inhabitants of Corsica were the Phocaeans of Ionia, who founded Alalia about 570 BC. They were succeeded in turn by the Etruscans, the Carthaginians, the Romans, the Vandals, and the Arabs. In the 14th century Corsica fell to the Genoese, and in the second half of the 18th century a Corsican nationalist, Pasquale Paoli (1725–1807), led an independence movement. Genoa sold Corsica to France in 1768 and French rule was established. In World War II Corsica was occupied by Italy 1942–43. From 1962 French *pieds noir* (refugees from Algeria), especially vine growers, were settled in Corsica, and their prosperity helped to fan nationalist feeling, which demands an independent Corsica. This fuelled a 'national liberation front' (FNLC), banned in 1983.

Cort /kɔːt/ Henry 1740–1800. British iron manufacturer. He invented the puddling process and developed the rolling mill in the manufacture of wrought iron, both of which were of vast importance early in the Industrial Revolution.

Cortés /'kɔːtez/ Hernándo (Ferdinand) 1485–1547. Spanish conqueror of Mexico. He went to the West Indies as a young man, and in 1518 was given command of an expedition to Mexico. Landing with only 600 men, he was at first received as a god by the Aztec emperor Montezuma, but was finally expelled from Tenochtitlán (Mexico City) by a revolt. With the aid of native allies he recaptured the city in 1521, and overthrew the Aztec empire. His conquests eventually included most of Mexico and northern Central America.

corticosteroid hormones which occur naturally, made in the adrenal cortex.

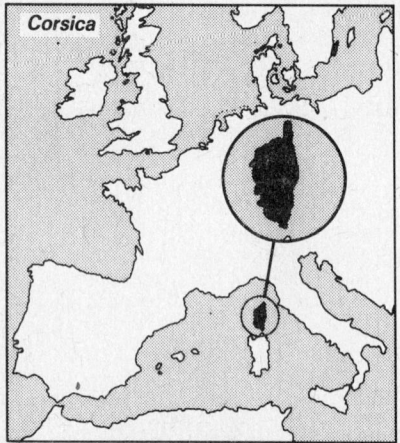

Corsica

Ferdinand Cortez A Spaniard.

Cortés A Spanish soldier and the conqueror of Mexico, Ferdinand Cortés destroyed the powerful Aztec civilization before becoming Mexico's governor.

Synthetically produced corticosteroids reduce inflammation and are also ◊immunosuppressive. They are used to treat several disease groups including rheumatoid arthritis, and some cancers. Over-use causes unpleasant side-effects.

cortisone *(Compound E)* steroid hormone discovered by T Reichstein of Basle, Switzerland, and put to practical clinical use for rheumatoid arthritis by P S Hench and E C Kendall in the USA (all three shared a Nobel prize in 1950). A product of the adrenal gland, it was first synthesized from a constituent of ox-bile, and is now produced commercially from a Mexican yam and from a by-product of the sisal plant. It is used for treating allergies and certain cancers, as well as rheumatoid arthritis.

Cortona /kɔː'təunə/ town in Italy, 22 km/14 mi SE of Arezzo, one of Europe's oldest cities. It is encircled by walls built by the ◊Etruscans, and has a medieval castle, and an 11th century cathedral.

corundum native aluminium oxide (Al_2O_3), occurring in cleavable masses or in pyramidal crystals. It includes the ruby and sapphire, and among naturally occurring materials is 9 on the ◊Mohs scale of hardness, next to diamond. It occurs as crystals distributed through granite, cyanite and schist rocks in many parts of the world.

Corunna /kɒ'rʌnə/ town (Spanish *La Coruña*), capital of Corunna province, in the extreme NW of Spain; population (1981) 232,350. Its activities are for the most part based on the fisheries, but it has tobacco and match factories, sugar refineries, and linen and cotton mills. The ◊Armada sailed form Corunna in 1588 and the town was sacked by Francis ◊Drake in 1589.

Corunna, Battle of /kɒ'rʌnə/ battle held to cover embarkation of British troops during Peninsular War 1809, after their retreat to Corunna; their commander, Sir John Moore was killed after ensuring a British victory over the French.

corvette term, now obsolete, revived from sailing days for small armed vessels, such as those escorting British convoys in World War II.

Corvo /'kɔːvəʊ/ Baron 1860–1913. assumed name of British writer Frederick ◊Rolfe.

Cos alternative spelling of ◊Kos, a Greek island.

cosecant in trigonometry, a measure in a right-angled triangle, the length of hypotenuse (the longest side) divided by the length of the side opposite the angle. Thus a cosecant, usually shortened to *cosec*, is always greater than 1. It is the reciprocal of the sine of the angle, that is, cosec A = 1/sin A, where A is the angle in question.

Cosenza /kəʊ'zentsə/ town in Calabria, Italy, at the junction of the Crati and the Busento, capital of Cosenza province. Population (1981) 106,801. It is an archiepiscopal see, and the burial place of ◊Alaric, king of the Visigoths.

Cosgrave /'kɒzgreɪv/ Liam 1920–   . Leader of the Fine Gael party 1965–77, he was prime minister of a Fine Gael-Labour coalition 1973–77. Improved relations developed between the Irish and British governments under his premiership.

Cosgrave /'kɒzgreɪv/ William Thomas 1880–1965. Irish politician. Born in Dublin, he took part in the Easter Rebellion of 1916, and sat in the Sinn Féin cabinet of 1919–21. Head of the Free State government from 1922 until his defeat by De Valera in 1932, he led the Fine Gael opposition 1933–44. His eldest son is Liam ◊Cosgrave.

cosine in trigonomentry, a measure of an angle in a right-angled triangle found by dividing the length of the side adjacent to the angle by the length of the hypotenuse (the longest side). It is usually shortened to *cos*.

cosmic radiation high-speed particles (atomic nuclei), some of which originate in the Sun, but most coming from beyond the Solar System. Those of low energy seem to be galactic in origin, and detectors (the water-Cherenkov

detector near Leeds has an area of 12 sq km/4.5 sq mi) are in use to detect extra-galactic sources (possibly the rotating discs of infalling matter round black holes) of high-energy rays.

cosmology the study of the origin and evolution of the ◊Universe. Modern cosmology began in the 1920s with the discovery of the expanding Universe, which suggested that it began in an explosion, the ◊Big Bang. The *steady state theory* was an alternative view put forward in 1948 by ◊Hoyle and others which said that the Universe had no origin, but is expanding because new matter is being continually created. Modern evidence supports the Big Bang theory.

cosmonaut Soviet/Eastern term for a person who travels in space; the Western term is ◊astronaut.

cosmonaut The Soviet pioneers of manned space flight for scientific research photographed in 1965. Left to right, seated: Yuri Gagarin, Pavel Belyayev, Valentina Nikolayeva-Tereshkova, Alexei Leonov and Vladimir Komarov, standing: Pavel Popovich, Gherman Titov, Konstantin Feoktistov, Boris Yegorov, Andrian Nikolayev and Valeri Bykovsky.

Cossack /'kɒsæk/ member of that section of the Russian population which once held land in return for military service. Before 1917 a Cossack household had a larger allotment of land than that of the ordinary peasant, and in return all the men were bound to serve in the army for 20 years. They were bitterly opposed to the Soviet regime, and their resistance was brutally suppressed. In World War II some fought for the Germans.

Cossyra ancient name for ◊Pantelleria, Italian island in the Mediterranean.

Costa Rica /'kɒstə 'riːkə/ country in central America, bounded to the N by Nicaragua, to the S by Panama, to the E by the Caribbean, and to the west by the Pacific Ocean.

government the 1949 constitution provides for a president elected for a four-year term by compulsory adult suffrage, two elected vice-presidents, and an appointed cabinet. There is a single-chamber legislature, the 57-member assembly, also serving a four-year term. Most significant among several parties are the

National Liberation Party (PLN), and the Unity Party (PUSC).

history originally occupied by Guaymi Indians, the area was visited by Christopher ◊Columbus, and was colonized by Spanish settlers from the 16th century, becoming independent in 1821. First part of the ◊Mexican empire, then, with El Salvador, Guatemala, Honduras, and Nicaragua, part of the ◊Central American Federation from 1824, Costa Rica became a republic in 1838. Apart from a military dictatorship 1870–82, and a brief civil war in 1948 after a disputed presidential election, it has been one of the most democratically governed states in Latin America.

In 1949 a new constitution abolished the army, defence resting on the Civil Guard. José Figueres, leader of the anti-government forces in the previous year, became president. He co-founded the PLN, nationalized the banks, and introduced a social security system. He was re-elected in 1953.

There followed 16 years of mostly conservative rule, with the reversal of some PLN policies. In 1974 Daniel Oduber won the presidency for the PLN. He returned to socialist policies, extended the welfare state and established friendly relations with communist states. Communist and left-wing parties were legalized.

In 1978 Rodrigo Carazo of the conservative Unity Coalition (CU) became president. His presidency was marked by economic collapse and allegations of his involvement in illegal arms trafficking between Cuba and El Salvador.

In 1982 Luis Alberto Monge, a former trade union official and co-founder of PLN, won a convincing victory in the presidential election. To reverse the damage done by the Carazo government, he introduced a 100-day emergency economic programme.

The Monge government came under pressure from the US to abandon its neutral stance and condemn the left-wing Sandinista regime in Nicaragua. It was also urged to re-establish its army. Monge resisted the pressure and in 1983 reaffirmed his country's neutrality, but relations with Nicaragua deteriorated after border clashes between Sandinista forces and the Costa Rica civil guard. In 1985 Monge agreed to create a US-trained anti-guerrilla guard, increasing doubts about Costa Rica's neutrality. In 1986 Oscar Arias Sánchez became president on a neutralist platform, defeating the pro-US candidate, Rafael Angel Calderón.

Costa Rica

REPUBLIC OF (*República de Costa Rica*)

AREA 50,997 sq km/19,690 sq mi
CAPITAL San José
TOWNS ports Limón, Puntarenas
PHYSICAL high central plateau and tropical coast
FEATURES highest literacy rate in Latin America; there has been no standing army since the civil war of 1948–49
HEAD OF STATE AND OF GOVERNMENT Oscar Arias Sanchez from 1986
GOVERNMENT democratic republic
EXPORTS coffee, bananas, cocoa, sugar
CURRENCY colón (105.31 = £1 Sept 1987)
POPULATION (1985) 2,644,000 (including 1,200 Guaymi Indians); annual growth rate 3.1%
LANGUAGE Spanish
RELIGION Roman Catholic
LITERACY 92% male/92% female (1980 est)
GDP $2 bn (1982); $2,238 per head of population
CHRONOLOGY
1821 Independence achieved.
1949 New constitution adopted. National army abolished. José Figueres, cofounder of the National Liberation Party (PLN), was elected president. He embarked on an ambitious socialist programme.
1958–73 Mainly Conservative administrations returned.
1974 PLN regained the presidency and returned to socialist policies.
1978 Rodrigo Carazo, Conservative, elected

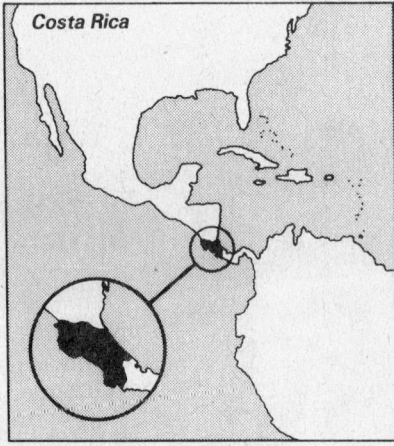

Costa Rica

president. Sharp deterioration in the state of the economy.
1982 Luis Alberto Monge of the PLN elected president. Harsh austerity programme introduced to rebuild the economy. Pressure from the USA to abandon neutral stance and condemn the Sandinista regime in Nicaragua.
1983 Policy of neutrality reaffirmed.
1985 Following border clashes with Sandinista forces, a US-trained anti-guerrilla guard was formed.
1986 Oscar Arias Sanchez won the presidency on a neutralist platform.
1987 Oscar Arias Sanchez won Nobel Peace Prize.

cost of living the cost of goods and services needed for an average standard of living. In Britain the first cost-of-living index was introduced in 1914 and based on the expenditure of a working-class family of man, woman, and three children; the standard is 100. Known from 1947 as the Retail Price Index (RPI), it is revised to allow for inflation, etc. Supplementary are the Consumer's Expenditure Deflator (formerly Consumer Price Index) and the Tax and Price Index (TPI), introduced in 1979. Comprehensive indexation has been advocated as a means of controlling ◊inflation by linking all forms of income (wages, investment, etc), contractual

Costello /kɒˈsteləʊ/ Elvis. Stage name of Declan McManus 1954– . English rock singer, songwriter, and guitarist. A prolific composer, noted for his stylistic range and intricate lyrics. His albums with the group The Attractions include *Armed Forces* 1979, *Trust* 1981, and *Blood and Chocolate* 1986.

Coster /ˈkɒstə/ Laurens Janszoon 1370–1440. Dutch printer, born at Haarlem. According to some sources, he invented movable type, but after his death an apprentice ran off to Mainz with the blocks and, taking Gutenberg into his confidence, began a printing business with him.

debts and tax scales, to the RPI. Index-linked savings schemes were introduced in the UK in 1975.
In the USA a Consumer Price Index, based on the expenditure of families in the iron, steel and related industries, was introduced in 1890. The modern index is based on the expenditure of the urban wage-earner and clerical-worker families in 46 large, medium, and small cities, the standard being 100. Increases in social security benefits are linked to it, as are many wage settlements.

Cosway /ˈkɒzweɪ/ Richard 1742–1821. British artist. Elected Royal Academician in

1771, he was an accomplished miniaturist and painted the chief members of the Prince Regent's court.

cotangent in trigonometry, a measure of angle in a right-angled triangle found by dividing the length of the side adjacent to the angle by that of the side opposite it. It is usually written as *cotan*, or *cot* and it is the reciprocal of the tangent of the angle, so that cotan A = 1/tan A, where A is the angle in question.

cot death death of an apparently healthy baby during sleep, also called Sudden Infant Death Syndrome (SIDS); possible causes include poor heart rhythm and irregular breathing.

Côte d'Azur /ˈkəʊt dæˈzjʊə/ the Mediterranean coast from Menton to St Tropez, France, renowned for its beaches; part of ◊Provence-Côte d'Azur.

Côte d'Ivoire /ˈkəʊt dɪvˈwɑː/ official name for ◊Ivory Coast from 1986.

Cotman /ˈkɒtmən/ John Sell 1782–1842. British landscape painter. Born in Norwich, he went to London to study about 1798, returning to Norwich in 1807 as a drawing master. In 1834 ◊Turner helped him to an appointment at King's College, London. His works, many of which depict bridges, are among the finest English landscapes of the early 19th century. His sons, *Miles Edmund Cotman* (1810–58) and *Joseph John Cotman* (1814–78) were also landscape painters.

cotoneaster genus of trees and shrubs belonging to the Rosaceae and closely allied to the hawthorn and medlar. Its leaves are simple and entire, the fruits, though small and unpalatable, are usually bright red and conspicuous, often persisting through the winter.

Cotonou /ˌkɒtəˈnuː/ chief port of Benin, Nigeria, on the Gulf of Benin. It is a road and rail centre, and has an airport. Palm products and timber are exported. Population (1979) 327,600.

Cotopaxi /ˌkɒtəˈpæksi/ an active ◊volcano, situated to the S of Quito in Ecuador. It is 5,897 m/19,347 ft high, and was climbed first in 1872. Its name is Quechua for 'shining peak'.

Cotswolds /ˈkɒtswəʊldz/ range of hills in Avon-Gloucestershire, England, some 80 km/50 mi long, between Bristol and Chipping Camden. They rise to 330 m/1,083 ft, but average about 200 m/600 ft.

Cottbus /ˈkɒtbʊs/ capital of Cottbus district and industrial city (textiles, carpets) in East Germany; population (1984) 123,000.

cotton /ˈkɒtn/ tropical and sub-tropical herbaceous plant, genus *Gossypium* family Malvaceae, producing fibres round the seeds in the ripened fruit or 'boll', which are spun into yarn for cloth. Cotton disease (byssinosis) caused by cotton dust, affects the lungs of those working in the industry. The seeds are used to produce cooking oil and livestock feed, and the pigment gossypol has potential as a safe male contraceptive in a modified form. See also ◊cotton gin.

Cotton /ˈkɒtn/ Robert Bruce 1571–1631. English antiquary. At his home in Westminster he built up a fine collection of manuscripts and coins, many of which had come from the despoiled monasteries. His son, Thomas Cotton (1594–1662), added to the library, and in 1700 it was given to the nation by Robert Cotton's great-grandson, John Cotton (1679–1731). Its contents are in the British Museum.

cotton gin a machine that separates cotton fibres from the seed boll. The invention of the gin by American Eli Whitney in 1793 was a milestone in ◊textile history. The modern gin consists of a roller carrying a set of circular saws, which project through a metal grill in a hopper containing the seed bolls. As the roller rotates, the saws pick up the cotton fibres, leaving the seeds behind.

cotton-grass type of sedge *Eriophorum angustifolium* and related species, in which fruiting heads form white heads of down in midsummer which break off to carry the fruits long distances on the wind. Cotton-grass is found in wet places throughout the arctic and N temperate region, most species being found in acid bogs.

cotton stainer type of ◊bug, family Pyrrhocoridae, that pierces and stains cotton bolls.

cottonwood name given to several species of N American poplar with fluffy seeds. Also, Australian tree *Bedfordia salaoina* , with downy leaves.

cotyledon a structure in the embryo of a seed plant which may form a 'leaf' after germination and is commonly known as a seed leaf. The number of cotyledons present in an embryo is an important character in the classification of flowering plants (◊angiosperms) ◊Monocotyledons (for example grasses, palms and lilies) have a single cotyledon, whereas ◊dicotyledons (the majority of species) have two. In seeds that also contain ◊endosperm the cotyledons are thin but where they are the primary food-storing tissue, as in peas and beans, they may be quite large. After germination the cotyledons either remain below ground (hypogeal) or, more commonly, spread out above soil level (epigeal) and become the first green leaves. In ◊gymnosperms there may be up to a dozen cotyledons within each seed.

couch grass plant *Elymus repens*, one of the commonest of the grasses Gramineae. It is closely allied to wheat, but is generally regarded as a weed.

Coué /'kuːeɪ/ Emile 1857–1926. French psychological healer, pioneer of auto-suggestion famous for his slogan, 'Every day, and in every way, I am becoming better and better'. 'Couéism' reached the height of its popularity in the 1920s.

cougar alternative name for the ◊puma, a large American cat.

coulomb /'kuːlɒm/ the practical unit of electrical charge – the quantity of electricity conveyed by a current of one ampere in one second.

Coulomb /'kuːlɒm/ Charles Auguste de 1736–1806. French scientist, inventor of the torsion balance for measuring the force of electric and magnetic attraction. The ◊coulomb was named after him.

council in ◊local government in England and Wales, a popularly elected local assembly charged with the government of the area within its boundaries. Under the Local Government Act of 1972, they comprise three types: ◊County Councils, ◊District Councils, and ◊Parish Councils.

Council for Mutual Economic Assistance full name for ◊Comecon, organization established in 1949 by Eastern bloc countries.

Council of Europe body constituted in 1949 to secure 'a greater measure of unity between the European countries'. The first session of the Consultative Assembly opened at Strasbourg (still its headquarters) in August 1949, the members then being Great Britain, France, Italy, Belgium, the Netherlands, Sweden, Denmark, Norway, the Republic of Ireland, Luxembourg, Greece, and Turkey; Iceland, West Germany, Austria, Cyprus, Switzerland, Malta, Portugal, Spain and Liechtenstein joined subsequently. The widest association of European states, it has a Committee of foreign ministers, Parliamentary Assembly (with members from national parliaments), and a European Commission investigates violations of human rights.

counselling an approach to treating problems, particularly psychological problems, in which clients are encouraged to solve their own problems with support from a counsellor. The qualities of the counsellor, such as empathy, warmth and genuineness, are important.

counterfeiting fraudulent imitation, especially of banknotes. It is countered by special papers, elaborate watermarks, and skilled printing, sometimes also insertion of a metallic strip. See also ◊forgery.

counterpoint in music, the simultaneous combination of two or more separate melodies to form a harmonious whole. Originating in ◊plainsong, with two independent vocal lines sung simultaneously (Latin *punctus contra punctum* 'note against note'), it reached its height in the 16th century.

Counter-Reformation movement initiated by the Catholic Church at the Council of Trent 1545–63 to counter activities of the ◊Reformation, extending into the 17th century. Its dominant forces included the rise of the Jesuits as an educating and missionary group and the extension of the Spanish ◊Inquisition to other countries.

countertenor highest natural male voice, favoured by the Elizabethans, ◊Purcell himself singing in this range. It was revived in the UK by Alfred Deller (1912–79).

country and western the popular music of the white US South and Southwest, evolved from the folk music of the English, Irish and Scottish settlers with a strong blues influence. Country music encompasses a variety of regional styles, such as *western swing* (Texas) and *bluegrass* (Kentucky), and ranges from mournful ballads to fast and intricate dance music. Characteristic instruments are slide guitar, Dobro, mandolin, and fiddle. Lyrics typically extol family values and traditional sex roles. Nashville, Tennessee, has been the centre of the country-music industry since the 1930s, with the Grand Ole Opry a showcase for performers.

Early singer-songwriters were Jimmie Rodgers (1897–1933) and Hank Williams (1923–53); later singers include George Jones (1931–), Patsy Cline (1932–63), Johnny ◊Cash, Merle Haggard (1937–), Dolly Parton (1946–), and Emmylou Harris (1947–). Neotraditionalists, rebelling against the Nashville style, have included in the 1970s Willie Nelson (1933–) and Waylon Jennings (1937–) and in the 1980s Dwight Yoakam (1957–).

Country rock was pioneered in the 1960s by the US singer and songwriter Gram Parsons (1946–73) and led in the 1980s to *cowpunk* in Britain and 'moo wave' in the USA.

Country Party Australian party representing the interests of the farmers and people of the smaller towns, which developed from about 1860, and holds the power balance between Liberals and Labor. It gained strength following the introduction of preferential voting in 1918, and formed a coalition with the Liberals in 1949, its leader, Douglas (1929–) being deputy Prime Minister in the Fraser Government. Re-named *National Country Party* 1975.

Countryside Commission an official conservation body, created for England and Wales under the Countryside Act 1968. It replaced the National Parks Commission, and had by 1980 created over 160 Country Parks. Here, as in all other activities, such as its Demonstration Farms Project, it aims at conservation, improvement, and the reconciliation of working activity with public recreational use. There is a separate commission for Scotland.

county in Britain, an administrative unit, nowadays synonymous with 'shire', although historically the two had different origins. Many of the English counties can be traced back to Saxon times. Under the Local Government Act of 1972, which came into effect in 1974, the existing English administrative counties were replaced by 45 new county areas of local government, and the 13 Welsh counties were reduced by amalgamation to eight. Under the Local Government (Scotland) Act of 1973 the 33 counties of Scotland were amalgamated in 1975 in nine new regions and three island areas. Northern Ireland has six geographical counties, but under the Local Government Act of 1973 administration is through 26 district councils (single-tier authorities) each based on a main town or centre. The Republic of Ireland has 26 geographical and 27 administrative counties.

The term is also used in some other countries, for example, the USA, where it is a subdivision of a state; the power of counties differs widely between states.

county council since the Local Government Act of 1972, the county councils in England and Wales consist of a chair and councillors (the former distinction between councillors and ◊aldermen has been abolished). Councillors are elected for four years, the franchise being the same as for parliamentary elections, and elect the chair from among their own number. The revised responsibilities of county councils are defined as including broad planning policy; highways; education, personal social services and libraries; police, fire and traffic control; and refuse disposal.

county court English court of law created by the County Courts Act 1846 and now governed by the Act of 1959. It exists to try civil cases, and actions on contract and most actions on tort may be brought before it if the claim does not exceed £5,000. County courts are presided over by one or more Circuit Judges. An appeal on a point of law lies to the Court of Appeal.

county palatine in England, a county whose lord held particularly important rights, in lieu of the king, such as pardoning treasons and murders. Under William I four counties palatine – Chester, Durham, Kent, and Shropshire – existed, perhaps because of their vulnerability to outside attack. Lancaster became a palatinate in 1357 (Edward III) and Durham remained a palatinate until 1836.

coup or *coup d'état* forcible takeover of the government of a country by elements from within that country. It differs from a revolution in typically being carried out by a small group (for example of army officers or opposition politicians) to install their leader as head of government, rather than being a mass uprising by the population at large.

Notable early examples include the coup of 1799 in which Napoleon overthrew the Revolutionary Directory and declared himself first consul of France, and the coup of 1851 in which Louis Napoleon (then president) dissolved the French national assembly and a year later declared himself emperor. Coups of more recent times include the overthrow of the socialist government of Chile in 1973 by a right-wing, CIA-backed military junta, and the military seizure of power in Fiji by Colonel Rabuka in Sept 1987.

Couperin /'ku:pəræŋ/ François 1668–1733. French composer, called *le Grand*, as the most famous of a distinguished musical family. Born in Paris, he held various court appointments and wrote vocal, chamber, and harpsichord music.

couplet in literature, a pair of lines of verse, usually of the same length and rhymed. The *heroic couplet*, consisting of two rhymed lines in iambic pentameter, was considered particularly suitable for epic poetry, and was a convention of both serious and mock-heroic 18th-century English poetry, as in the work of Alexander ◊Pope. An example, from Pope's *An Essay on Criticism*, is: 'A little learning is a dang'rous thing;/Drink deep, or taste not the Pierian spring'.

Courbet /'kuəbeɪ/ Gustave 1819–1877. French landscape and genre painter, who from 1841 was associated with the ◊Barbizon school. Reacting against both Classicists and Romantics, he set out to establish a new realism, based solely on direct observation of things around him. His *Burial at Ornans* 1850 showed ordinary working people gathered round a village grave and shocked the Establishment art world with its 'vulgarity'. His scientific spirit of realism was to be continued by ◊Manet. In 1871 he became a member of the socialist Paris

Commune and was sentenced to six months' imprisonment and a fine.

Courrèges /ku'reɪʒ/ André 1923–   . French dress designer. Originally with Balenciaga, he founded his own firm in 1961, and is credited with inventing the 'mini-skirt' in 1964.

coursing chasing of hares by greyhounds, not by scent but by sight, as a 'sport', and as a test of the greyhound's speed. It is one of the most ancient of field sports. Since the 1880s it has been practised on enclosed or park courses. The governing body in Great Britain is the National Coursing Club, formed in 1858. The coursing season lasts Sept–Mar: the Altcar or Waterloo meeting, which decides the championship, is held in Feb at Altcar, Lancashire. The Waterloo Cup race is known as the Courser's Derby.

court building where legal cases are held. See ◊law court and particular kinds of court, for example ◊County Court, ◊Small Claims Court.

Courtauld /'kɔːtəuld/ Samuel 1793–1881. British industrialist. He founded the firm of Courtaulds in 1816 at Bocking, Essex, which at first specialized in silk and crepe manufacture, but from 1904 developed the production of viscose rayon and, later, other synthetic fibres. His great-nephew, *Samuel Courtauld* (1876–1947), was chairman of the firm from 1921, and in 1931 gave his house and art collection to the University of London as the Courtauld Institute.

court-martial court convened for the trial of persons subject to military discipline. British courts martial are governed by the code of the service concerned – Naval Discipline, Army, or Air Force Acts – and in 1951 an appeal court was established for all three services by the Courts Martial (Appeals) Act. The procedure prescribed for the US services is similar, being based on British practice.

Courtneidge /'kɔːtnɪdʒ/ Cicely 1893–1980. British actress. Born in Sydney, she was a stage and film comedienne and singer, for example 'Vitality'. She married comedian Jack Hulbert (1892–1978), with whom she formed a successful partnership in musical comedy, variety and revue. She was made a Dame of the British Empire in 1972.

Court of Session the supreme Civil Court in Scotland, established 1532. Cases come in the first place before one of the eight Lords Ordinary, and from their decisions an appeal lies to the Inner House which sits in two divisions called the First and Second Division. From the decisions of the Inner House an appeal lies in the House of Lords.

Court of the Lord Lyon Scottish heraldic body composed of one King of Arms, three Heralds, and three Pursuivants who specialize in genealogical work. It embodies the High Seanachie of Scotland's Celtic kings.

Courtrai /kuə'treɪ/ Belgian industrial town on the Lys, in West Flanders (Flemish *Kortrijk*); population (1985) 76,110. It is connected by canal with the coast, and by river and canal with Antwerp and Brussels. It has a large textile industry, especially damask, linens, and lace.

Courtrai, Battle of /kuə'treɪ/ defeat of French knights by the Flemings of Ghent and Bruges in 1302, also called 'Battle of the Spurs'.

courtship behaviour exhibited by animals as a prelude to mating. The behaviour patterns vary considerably from one species to another, but are often ◊ritualized forms of behaviour quite unrelated to courtship or mating (for example, courtship feeding in birds). Courtship ensures that copulation occurs with a member of the opposite sex of the right species. It also synchronizes the partners' readiness to mate and allows each partner to assess the suitability of the other. In pigeons, for example, males may reject females that respond too quickly to their courtship displays because such females have probably already mated with another male.

Cousin /ku:'zæŋ/ Victor 1792–1867. French philosopher. Born in Paris, he became a lecturer at the Sorbonne when 23, and did much to introduce German philosophical ideas into France. In 1840 he was minister of public instruction and reorganized the system of elementary education.

Cousteau /'ku:stəu/ Jacques-Yves 1910–   . French naval officer. Celebrated for his oceanographic researches in command of the *Calypso* from 1951; he pioneered the invention of the aqualung in 1943 and techniques in underwater filming. *The Silent World* 1953 and other books recount his adventures and his work in underwater archaeology and ecology.

Coutts /ku:ts/ Thomas 1735–1822. British banker. He established with his brother the firm of Coutts & Co (one of London's oldest banking houses, founded in 1692 in the Strand), becoming sole head on the latter's death in 1778. Since the reign of George III an account has been maintained there by every succeeding sovereign and other customers have included ◊Chatham, William ◊Pitt, ◊Fox, ◊Wellington, ◊Reynolds, and ◊Boswell.

couvade custom of a man behaving as if he were about to give birth when his child is being born, which may include feeling or appearing to feel real pain. It has been observed since antiquity in many cultures, and may have begun either as a magic ritual or as a way of asserting paternity.

Covenanter one of the Presbyterians who swore to uphold their forms of worship in a National Covenant, signed on 28 Feb 1638, when Charles I attempted to introduce a liturgy on the English model into Scotland. A general assembly abolished episcopacy, and in 1643 the Covenanters signed with the English parliament the Solemn League and Covenant, promising military aid in return for the establishment of Presbyterianism in England. A Scottish army entered England and fought at Marston Moor. At the Restoration Charles II revived episcopacy in Scotland, evicting resisting ministers, so that revolts followed in 1666, 1679, and 1685. However, Presbyterianism was again restored in 1688.

Covent Garden /'kɒvənt 'gɑːdn/ London square (named from the convent garden once on the site), laid out by Inigo ◊Jones in 1631. The buildings which formerly housed London's fruit and vegetable market (moved to Nine Elms,

courtship display

gulls courting, indulging in neck arching (left) and sky-pointing (right)

Cousteau Concerned with protecting as well as exploring the marine world, the French oceanographer Jacques Cousteau is known for his pioneering work in developing the aqualung, and manned undersea stations.

Wandsworth, in 1973), were adapted for shops and leisure. The Royal Opera House, also housing the Royal Ballet, is here, also the London Transport Museum. The Theatre Museum, opened 1987, is in the Old Flower Market.

Coventry /'kɒvəntri/ industrial city in West Midlands, England; population (1981) 315,000. *history* it originated when Leofric, Earl of Mercia and husband of Lady ◊Godiva, founded a priory in 1043. Its modern industry began with bicycle manufacture in 1870, and today includes cars, electronic equipment, machine tools, agricultural machinery. Notable are the cathedral designed by Basil Spence, and incorporating the steeple of the church built 1373–95 and destroyed in an air raid Nov 1940; St Mary's Hall, built 1394–1414 as a guild centre; two gates of the old city walls 1356; Belgrade Theatre 1958; Art Gallery and Museum; Museum of British Road Transport, and Lanchester Polytechnic.

Coverdale /'kʌvədeɪl/ Miles 1488–1569. Translator of the Bible into English. Born in Yorkshire, he became a Catholic priest, but turned to Protestantism and in 1528 went abroad to avoid persecution. His translation of the Bible appeared in 1535, and was dedicated to Henry VIII – the first complete translation of the Bible to be printed in English. His translation of the psalms is that retained in the Book of Common Prayer. In 1539 he edited the Great Bible which was ordered to be placed in churches. After some years in Germany, he returned to England in 1548, and in 1551 was made bishop of Exeter. Under Mary he again left the country, but in the early part of Elizabeth's reign he held the living of St Magnus near London Bridge.

Coward /'kaʊəd/ Noel 1899–1973. British playwright, actor, producer, director and composer, who epitomized the witty and sophisticated man of the theatre. From his first success with *The Young Idea* 1923, he wrote and appeared in sophisticated plays and comedies *The Vortex*: 1924; *Hay Fever* 1925; *Private Lives* 1930, with Gertrude Lawrence; *Cavalcade* 1931; *Design for Living* 1933; *Blithe Spirit* 1941. His works also include the script for the film *In Which We Serve* 1942, the subtle *Brief Encounter* 1945, and many popular songs including 'Mad Dogs and Englishmen'. He was knighted in 1970.

Cowes /kaʊz/ seaport and resort on the north coast of the Isle of Wight, England, on the Medina estuary, opposite Southampton Water; population (1981) 19,500. It is the headquarters of the Royal Yacht Squadron which holds the annual Cowes Regatta, and has maritime industries. In East Cowes is Osborne ◊House, used as a museum.

cowfish type of ◊boxfish.

Cowley /'kaʊli/ Abraham 1618–1667. British poet. Joining King Charles at Oxford in 1644, he went to Paris with the queen, becoming a royalist secret agent. He introduced the Pindaric ode (based on the Greek poet Pindar) to English poetry, and published metaphysical verse with elaborate 'conceits', as well as essays.

cow parsley tall perennial plant *Anthriscus sylvestris* of the carrot family. Up to 1 m/3 ft tall, its pinnate leaves, hollow furrowed stems and heads of white flowers in early summer are familiar in hedgerows and shady places. Also known as keck, it can be found in Europe, North Asia and North Africa.

Cowper /'kuːpə/ William 1731–1800. British poet, born in Hertfordshire. He trained as a lawyer, but suffered a mental breakdown in 1763 and entered a asylum, where he underwent an evangelical conversion. He later wrote hymns (for example 'God moves in a mysterious way'). His verse includes *Table Talk* 1782, the six books of *The Task* 1785, and the comic poem 'John Gilpin'.

cowrie marine snail-like mollusc, in which the interior spiral form is concealed by a double outer lip. The shells are hard, shiny and often coloured. They have been used as ornaments and fertility charms, and also as currency, especially the *money cowrie Cypraea moneta*. Most cowries are shallow-water forms, and are found in many parts of the world, particularly the tropical Indopacific. In life the shell may be partly covered by the soft parts. One species, the *European cowrie Trivia monacha* is fairly common on British shores. It is about 1.2 cm/0.5 in long, with three spots on the shell.

cowslip plant *Primula veris* belonging to the Primulaceae, being placed in the same genus as the primrose. Once common in English meadows, its numbers have now greatly diminished. The flowers can be made into cowslip wine. The oxlip *Primula elatior* is closely allied to it.

coyote wild dog *Canis latrans*, in appearance like a small wolf, living from Alaska south to Central America. Head and body are about 90 cm/3 ft long, the colour brown flecked with grey or black, and the main foods are rabbits and rodents. Coyotes live in open country and can run at 65 kph/40 mph.

coypu South American water rodent *Myocastor coypus*, about 60 cm/2 ft long plus scaly rat-like tail and weighing up to 9 kg/20 lb. It has webbed hind feet, a blunt-muzzled head, and the large incisors are orange. The fur is yellowish brown. It feeds on vegetation and lives in burrows in river and lake banks. Brought to Europe to farm for their fur ('nutria') many escaped or were released and became established. In 1987, the lack of reliable sightings in Britain's fen country (East Anglia), suggested that the coypu has been eradicated.

Cozens /'kʌzənz/ Alexander c. 1717–1786. British artist. Born in Russia, he was rumoured to be an illegitimate son of Peter the Great, but was probably the son of Richard Cozens,

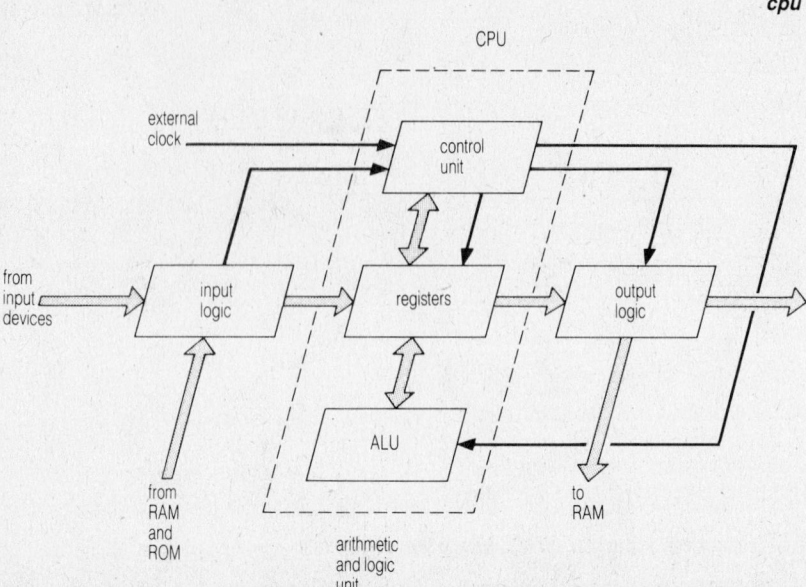

cpu

coypu Once released in Britain, the coypu flourished on root crops and young corn; it also lacked natural enemies to check its numbers. Widespread trapping, however, led to its virtual eradication.

employed by the Tsar as a shipbuilder. Coming to England in 1742, he taught at Eton, and George III's sons were his pupils. He is famous for his watercolour landscapes, and for sometimes using blots in brown, grey or black washes, as the inspiration of a study to be finished with brush or pen. His son, *John Robert Cozens* (c. 1752–97) was also a water-colourist, influencing ◊Girtin and ◊Turner.

CPU central processing unit of a computer: the part that reads the program, fetches data, performs operations on the data in accordance with the program, and outputs its results. It is composed of five main elements: the ◊ALU (arithmetic and logic unit), which contains the basic operations (its 'instruction set') and applies them to data; a program counter to keep track of the program being executed; a number of ◊registers for storing intermediate results and data awaiting processing; (normally) an electronic clock which emits regular pulses that coordinate the CPU's activities; and a control unit for organizing the processing.

CPVE (Certificate of Pre-Vocational Education) in the UK, educational qualification introduced in 1986 for students over 16 in schools and colleges who want a one-year course of preparation for work or further vocational study.

crab name given to many decapod ('ten-legged') crustaceans of the suborder Reptantia ('walking') allied to the ◊lobsters and ◊crayfish. Mainly marine, some crabs live in fresh water or on land. They are alert carnivores that act as scavengers. They have a typical sideways walk and strong pincers on the first pair of legs, the other four pairs being used for walking. Periodically the outer shell is cast to allow for growth. The true crabs (division Brachyura) have a broad, rather round, upper body shell (carapace), and a small ◊abdomen tucked beneath the body. There are many species worldwide. The European *shore crab Carcinus maenas* is common on British shores between the

tidemarks, is dull green, and grows to 4 cm/1.5 in or more. The *edible crab Cancer paqurus* grows 14 cm/5.5 in long or more, lives down to 100 m/325 ft and is extensively fished. Other true crabs include: *fiddler crabs* (*Uca*), in which males have one enlarged claw to wave and attract females; the European *river crab Thelphusa fluviatilis*; and *spider crabs* with small bodies and very long legs, including the Japanese spider crab *Macrocheira kaempferi* with a leg span of 3.4 m/11 ft. *Hermit crabs* (division Anomura) have a soft, spirally twisted abdomen and make their home in empty shells of whelks and winkles for protection. The *common hermit crab Eupagurus bernhardus*, up to 10 cm/4 in long, is found off Atlantic and Mediterranean shores. Some tropical hermit crabs are found a considerable distance from the sea. The *robber crab Birgus latro* grows large enough to climb palm trees and feed on coconuts.

crab apple wild form *Malus sylvestris* from which the cultivated apple has been derived; it differs chiefly in the smaller size and bitter flavour of the fruit, used in crab apple jelly. The tree is common in woods and hedgerows in southern Britain and and varies from a mere bush to 10 m/30 ft in height.

Crabbe /kræb/ George 1754–1832. British poet, born in Aldeburgh. Originally a doctor, he became a clergyman in 1781, and wrote grimly realistic verse of the poor of his own time: *The Village* 1783, *The Parish Register* 1807, *The Borough* 1810 (which includes the story used in the Britten opera *Peter Grimes*), and *Tales of the Hall* 1819.

Crab Nebula cloud of gas in space believed to be the remains of a star that exploded as a ◊supernova. The explosion was observed as a brilliant point of light by astronomers on Earth in 1054. The name comes from its crab-like appearance in large telescopes. It lies 6,000 light years away, in the constellation of ◊Taurus. At

the centre of the crab is a ◊pulsar that flashes 30 times a second.

Cracow /'krækaʊ/ alternative form of ◊Krakow, Polish city.

Craig /kreig/ Edward Gordon 1872–1966. British director and stage designer, the son of actress Ellen ◊Terry. His first stage production was Purcell's *Dido and Aeneas* 1900, and he subsequently staged productions throughout Europe including Ibsen's *The Vikings* 1903, in which his mother appeared. His innovations and theories on stage design and lighting effects, expounded in *On the Art of the Theatre* 1911, have had a huge influence on stage production in Europe and the USA.

Craig /kreig/ James 1871–1940. Ulster Unionist politician, the first prime minister of Northern Ireland from 1921 until his death. A captain in the Boer War, Craig became a Unionist Member of Parliament in 1906, and was a highly effective organizer of Unionist resistance to ◊Home Rule. As prime minister he carried out systematic discrimination against the Catholic minority, abolishing proportional representation in 1929 and redrawing constituency boundaries to ensure Protestant majorities; in an infamous speech he called for Northern Ireland to be a 'Protestant state for Protestant people'. He was created Viscount Craigavon in 1927.

Craigavon /ˌkreig'ævən/ town in Armagh, Northern Ireland, created from 1965 by the merging of Lurgan and Portadown, and intended to become the second city of the region. It was named after the first prime minister of Northern Ireland. Population (1971) 73,100.

Craik /kreik/ Dinah Maria (born Mulock) 1826–1887. British novelist. Born in Stoke-on-Trent, she is best remembered for *John Halifax, Gentleman* 1857, the story of the social betterment of a poor orphan through his own efforts.

Cranach /'krɑːnæx/ Lucas 1472–1553. German artist. Born at Kronach in Bavaria, he settled at Wittenberg in 1504 to work for the elector of Saxony. He was a close friend of ◊Luther, whose portrait he painted several times. He painted courtly female nudes representing classical figures with a gloss-like finish. He produced numerous woodcuts and copperplates. His second son *Lucas Cranach the Younger* (1515–86) had a similar style, and succeeded his father as director of the Cranach workshop.

cranberry plant *Vaccinium oxycoccos* allied to the bilberry, and belonging to the heath family Ericaceae. It is a small evergreen, growing in marshy places, and bearing small, acid, edible, crimson berries.

crane in engineering, a machine for raising, lowering or placing in position heavy loads. The main features of a jib crane are a power winch, a rope or cable, and a moveable arm or jib. The cable, which carries a pulley block, hangs from the end of the jib and is wound up and down by the winch. Most cranes have the machinery mounted on a revolving turntable. They may be mounted on trucks or be self-propelled, often being fitted with ◊caterpillar tracks. The overhead travelling crane, chiefly used in workshops, consists of a fixed horizontal arm, along which runs a trolley carrying the pulley block. Tower cranes, seen on large building sites, have a long horizontal arm able to revolve on top of a tall tower. The arm carries the trolley.

crane in zoology, bird of the family Gruidae, with long legs and neck, and powerful wings. They are marsh and plain-haunting birds, feeding on plants as well as insects and small animals. They fly well and are usually migratory. They are found in all parts of the world except S America. The common crane *Grus grus* is an occasional visitor to Britain, and is still common in many parts of Europe, and winters in Africa and India. It stands over 1 m/3ft high and the plumage of the adult bird is grey, varied with black and white, and a red patch of bare skin on the head and neck.

Crane /kreɪn/ (Harold) Hart 1899–1932. US poet, born in Ohio. He had little education and at 15 was working in his father's sweet factory. His long mystical poem *The Bridge* (1930) uses the Brooklyn Bridge as a symbol. He drowned after jumping overboard from a steamer bringing him back to the USA after a visit to Mexico.

Crane /kreɪn/ Stephen 1871–1900. US writer, who introduced grim realism into the American novel. Born in New Jersey, he became a journalist, and won fame in 1895 with *Red Badge of Courage*, dealing vividly with the American Civil War.

Crane /kreɪn/ Walter 1845–1915. British artist. While apprenticed to W J Linton, the wood engraver, he came under ◊Pre-Raphaelite influence. He excelled as a book illustrator for children and adults, his finest work being for an edition of Spenser's *Faerie Queene* 1894–96.

crane-fly type of fly, often known as *daddy-long-legs*, with long, slender and very fragile legs. The larvae live in the soil, or in water. Some soil-living larvae, *leatherjackets*, cause crop

crane The brolga (*Grus rubicunda*) is the only Australian crane. Its call is trumpet-like.

damage by eating roots, for example the common crane-fly *Tipula paludosa*.

cranesbill plant of the genus *Geranium*, which contains about 400 species and is typical of the family Geraniaceae. They are so called because of the long, beak-like process which is attached to the seed-vessels. When ripe, this splits into spiral, coiling processes which jerk the seeds out, thus assisting in their distribution. The genus includes ten species native to Britain, including *herb Robert, Geranium robertianum* and *bloody cranesbill, Geranium sanguineum.*

Cranko /'kræŋkəʊ/ John 1927–1973. British choreographer. Born in South Africa, he joined Sadler's Wells in 1946, and excelled in the creation of comedy characters, as in the *Tritsch-Tratsch Polka* 1946 and *Pineapple Poll* 1951. He also produced a successful revue *Cranks* 1955.

crankshaft an essential component of piston engines, which converts the up-and-down (reciprocating) motion of the pistons into useful rotary motion. The familiar car crankshaft carries a number of cranks, whose pins are offset from the main axis of rotation like the handle of a brace. The pistons are connected to the cranks by connecting rods and ◊bearings. When the pistons move up and down, the connecting rods force the offset crank pins to describe a circle, thereby rotating the crankshaft.

Cranmer /'krænmə/ Thomas 1489–1556. English churchman, Archbishop of Canterbury from 1533. He had suggested in 1529 that the question of Henry VIII's marriage to Catherine of Aragon should be referred to the universities of Europe rather than the Pope, but in 1533 declared it null and void. A Protestant convert, under Edward VI he helped to shape the doctrines of the Church of England. He was responsible for the issue of the Prayer Books of 1549 and 1552, and supported the succession of Lady Jane Grey. Condemned for heresy under the Catholic Mary Tudor, he at first recanted, but when his life was not spared, resumed his

position and was burnt, first holding to the fire the hand which had signed his recantation.

craps casino game with two dice, originating in the USA in the 19th century; winning throws are 7 or 11 and losers 2, 3, and 12.

Crashaw /'kræʃɔː/ Richard 1613–1649. English religious poet of the metaphysical school. Born in London, he published a book of Latin sacred epigrams in 1634. Developing Catholic leanings, he fled to France, and in Paris joined the Roman Catholic Church, and his *Steps to the Temple* appeared in 1646. In 1649 he became sub-canon of the Holy House at Loretto and died there of fever or possibly of poison.

Crassus /'kræsəs/ Marcus Licinius c. 108–53 BC. Roman general who crushed the ◊Spartacus rising in 71 BC. In 60 BC he joined with Caesar and Pompey in the first Triumvirate and in 55 BC obtained command in the East. Invading Mesopotamia, he was defeated by the Parthians, captured, and put to death.

crater a bowl-shaped topographic feature, usually round and with steep sides. Craters are formed by explosive events such as the eruption of a volcano or by the impact of a meteorite. A ◊caldera is a much larger feature.

Crater Lake lake in the centre of ◊Chubb Crater.

craton the core of a ◊continent. A vast tract of very ancient ◊metamorphic rock, around which the continent has been built. In Precambrian times there may have been mountains here, but now these mountains have been worn down and the land is flat. The rocks of the region are so contorted and compact that no further folding and faulting can take place. Younger mountain ranges usually surround them. Examples exist in the hearts of all the continents, with the typical example being the Canadian Shield.

Crawford /'krɔːfəd/ Joan 1908–1977. American actress. Born in Texas, she was originally a dancer, but made her name from 1925 in dramatic films such as *Mildred Pierce* 1945, and *Whatever Happened to Baby Jane?* 1963.

Crawford /'krɔːfəd/ Osbert Guy Stanhope 1886–1957. British archaeologist. He introduced aerial survey as means of finding and interpreting remains, an idea conceived in World War I, and was founder-editor of *Antiquity* from 1927.

Crawley /'krɔːli/ town in West Sussex, England, NE of Horsham. Chartered by King John in 1202, it was developed as a 'new town' from 1946. Industries include plastics, engineering, and printing. Population (1981) 73,000.

crawling peg in economics, also known as 'sliding parity', a method of achieving a desired adjustment in a currency ◊exchange rate (up or down) by small percentages over a given period, rather than by a major one-off revaluation or devaluation.

Craxi /'kræksi/ Bettino 1934– . Italian socialist politician, leader of the Italian Socialist Party (PSI) from 1976, prime minister 1983–87. Craxi, born in Milan, became a member of the Chamber of Deputies 1968 and in 1976 general secretary of the PSI. In 1983 he became Italy's first socialist prime minister, successfully leading a broad coalition until 1987.

crayfish freshwater type of lobster. The *common crayfish Astacus pallipes*, up to 10 cm/4 in long, is found in rivers in chalky areas of Britain, living in burrows in the mud and emerging, chiefly at night, to feed on small animals. Crayfish are edible, and some species are farmed. The *crawfish* or *spiny lobster Palinurus vulgaris*, sometimes called crayfish, is a marine lobster without pincers, growing up to 50 cm/1.8 ft, and good to eat.

creationism a theory concerned with the origins of matter and life, claiming, as does the Bible in Genesis, that the world and humanity (with no link with the great apes) was created, by a supernatural Creator, only some 6,000 years ago. It is not recognized by scientists as having a scientific basis. After a trial 1981–82 a US judge ruled unconstitutional an attempt to enforce equal treatment to creationism and evolutionary theory in Arkansas schools.

Crécy-en-Ponthieu /'kresi ɒm pɒn'tjɜː/ village in Somme *département*, France, 18 km/11m NE of Abbeville, where in 1346 Philip VI of France was defeated by Edward III.

credit in economics, means by which goods or services are obtained without immediate payment, usually by agreeing to pay interest. The three main forms are consumer credit (usually extended to individuals by retailers), bank credit (such as overdrafts or personal loans) and trade credit (common in the commercial world both within countries and internationally).

credit in education, the system of evaluating courses so that a partial qualification from one institution is accepted by another on transfer to complete a course. Credit transferability is common in higher education in the USA but is just beginning to be developed between institutions in the UK. At school level, the equivalence between an O Level pass and a Grade 1 pass at CSE, and between a BTEC diploma and A Levels is a long-standing one.

credit card card issued by an organization which enables the holder to obtain goods or services on credit (usually to a specified limit). Some credit cards also act as bank cards to enable customers to obtain money more easily from branches of their bank other than their own. Diners Club pioneered the use of the credit card in the USA in 1950. 'Intelligent' credit cards are now being introduced which contain coded information about the customer and the amount of credit still available. This can be 'read' by a terminal connected with the company's central computer. A number of 'intelligent' cards have been introduced in the 1980s, but not all are credit cards. Some require payment in advance (for example, cardphone cards) and others debit the consumer's bank account immediately on use.

creed /kriːd/ in general, any system of belief; in the Christian church the name given to the verbal confessions of faith expressing the accepted doctrines of the church. The oldest is the *Apostles' Creed*, which, though not the work of the apostles, was probably first formulated in the 2nd century. The full version of the Apostles' Creed, as now used, first appeared about 750. The use of creeds as a mode of combating heresy was established by the appearance of the ◊*Nicene Creed*, introduced by the Council of ◊Nicaea in 325, when the ◊Arian heresy was widespread. The Nicene Creed, as used today, is substantially the same as the version adopted at the Church Council at Constantinople in 381.
The so-called *Athanasian Creed* is much later in origin than the time of Athanasius (d. 373) although it represents his views in a detailed exposition of the doctrines of the Trinity and the Incarnation. Some authorities suppose it to have been composed in the 8th or 9th century but others place it as early as the 4th or 5th century. The only creed recognized by the Eastern Orthodox Church is the Nicene.

Creed /kriːd/ Frederick George 1871–1957. Canadian inventor, who developed the teleprinter. Born in Nova Scotia, he went to Britain in 1897 and perfected the Creed telegraphy system (teleprinter), first used in Fleet Street in 1912 and now, usually known as Telex, in offices throughout the world.

creep in physics, the property of a solid – typically a metal – under continuous stress that causes it to deform below its yield point (the point at which any elastic solid normally stretches without any increase in load or stress). Lead, tin, and zinc, for example, exhibit creep at ordinary temperatures, as evidenced by the movement of the lead sheeting on the roofs of old buildings; copper, iron, nickel and their alloys show creep at high temperatures.

Creevey /'kriːvi/ Thomas 1768–1838. British politician and diarist. He was the son of a Liverpool slave-trader. He entered Parliament as a follower of ◊Fox, and in 1830 became Treasurer of the Ordnance. His lively letters and journals give information on early 19th century society and politics.

cremation the method of disposing of the dead by burning. The custom was universal among ancient Indo-European peoples, for example, the Greeks, Romans, and Teutons, but was discontinued among Christians on account of the belief in the bodily resurrection of the dead. Cremation was revived in Italy about 1870, and shortly afterwards introduced into England. The Cremation Society was formed in 1874, but it was not until 1885 that cremation was legalized and the first crematorium in England was opened at Woking. In the UK an application for cremation must be accompanied by two medical certificates. Cremation is usually carried out by means of gas-fired furnaces. Ashes are scattered in Gardens of Remembrance or deposited in urns at the crematorium or in private graves.

Cremona /krɪ'məʊnə/ Italian city, capital of Cremona province, situated in Lombardy, on the river Po, 72 km/45 mi SE of Milan. Population (1981) 81,000. It has a 12th-century cathedral, and was a famous violin-making centre.

Creole in the West Indies and Spanish America, originally someone of European descent born in the New World; but also someone of mixed European and African descent; in Louisiana and other states on the Gulf of Mexico, either someone of French or Spanish descent or (popularly) someone of mixed European and African descent.

Creole languages term for ◊pidgin languages which have ceased to be simply trade jargons in ports and markets and have become the mother tongues of particular communities. The name 'creole' derives through French from Spanish and Portuguese, in which it originally referred both to children of European background born in tropical colonies and to house slaves on colonial plantations. The implication is that such groups picked up the pidgin forms of languages like Portuguese, Spanish, Dutch, French and English as used in and around the Caribbean, in parts of Africa, and in island communities in the Indian and Pacific Oceans. Having begun with the characteristics of pidgin languages (crudely, the vocabulary of the dominant community arranged in accordance with the syntax or grammar of the dependent groups), many creoles have developed into distinct languages with incipient literatures of their own, for example, Jamaican Creole, Haitian Creole, Krio in Sierra Leone, and Tok Pisin in Papua-New Guinea. According to circumstance, there may in such places as Jamaica, Haiti, Mauritius and West Africa be a 'creole continuum' of usage between the strongest forms of a creole and the standard version of the language with which the creole is associated.

creosote name given to several of the fractions of coal-tar; they are used as wood preservatives. Medicinal creosote is derived from wood tar.

crescent term applied to the curved shape of the ◊Moon when it is less than half illuminated. Also applied to any object or symbol resembling the crescent moon. Often associated with Islam, it was first used by the Turks on their standards after the capture of Constantinople in 1453, and appears on the flags of many Muslim countries The *Red Crescent* is the Muslim equivalent of the Red Cross.

cress name given to several plants, mostly belonging to the Cruciferae, and characterized by a pungent taste, but especially to the common garden cress *Lepidium sativum*. This is cultivated in Europe, North Africa, and parts of Asia, the young plants being grown along with white mustard to be eaten while in the seed-leaf stage as 'mustard and cress'.

Cretaceous the period of geological time between about 140 and 65 million years ago. It is the last period of the ◊Mesozoic era, during which ◊angiosperm plants evolved and dinosaurs and other reptiles reached a peak before almost complete extinction at the end of the period. The name comes from the Latin *creta*, chalk; chalk is a typical rock type of the second half of the period.

Crete /kriːt/ Mediterranean island (Greek *Kríti*)
area 8378 sq km/3235 sq mi
capital Khaniá (Canea)
towns largest town Iráklion
features it is the largest of the Greek islands, and has the remains of the ◊Minoan civilization 3000–1400BC (see ◊Knossos)

products citrus fruit, olives, wine
population (1981) 502,000
language Cretan dialect of Greek
history coming successively under Roman, Byzantine, Venetian, and Turkish rule, the island was annexed by Greece in 1913. In 1941, it was captured by German forces from Allied troops who had retreated from the mainland, and retaken by the Allies in 1944.

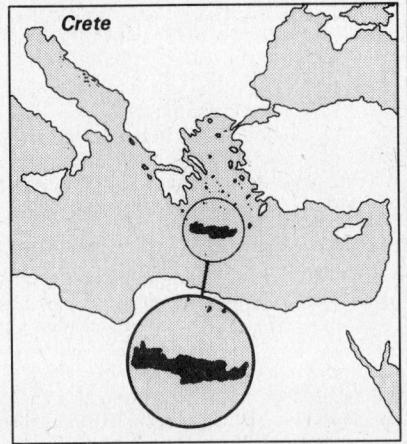

Crete

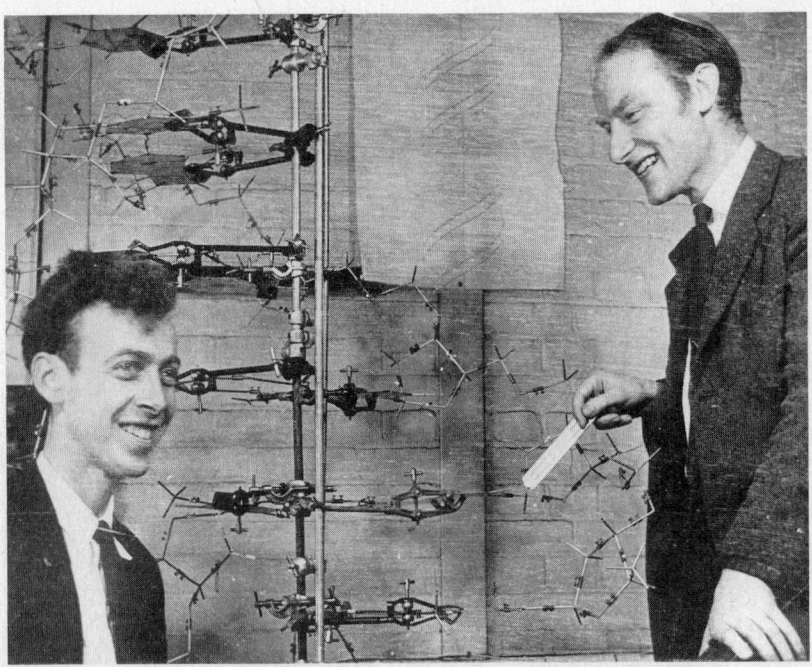

Crick British molecular biologist Francis Crick with his colleague James Watson (left). They were the first to discover the structure of DNA, the molecule that carries genetic information in living organisms. He shared the Nobel Prize for Medicine in 1962 with Watson and Maurice Wilkins.

Creuse /krɜːz/ river in central France flowing 255 km/158 mi generally N from the Plateau des Millevaches to the Vienne river. It traverses Creuse *département*, to which it gives its name.

Creusot, Le /krɜˈzəʊ/ industrial and coal-mining centre in Saône-et-Loire *département*, France. It has foundries, locomotive shops, and armaments factories. Population (1982) 32,100.

Crewe /kruː/ English industrial town in Cheshire, which owes its growth to its position as a railway junction. At Crewe are the chief construction workshops of British Rail. Population (1981) 48,000.

Crichton /ˈkraɪtn/ James c. 1560–1582. Scottish scholar, known as 'the Admirable Crichton' because of his extraordinary gifts as a poet, scholar, and linguist. He was also an athlete and swordsman. According to one account he was killed in a street brawl by his pupil, a son of the Duke of Mantua, whose enmity had been aroused by his master's popularity.

Crick /krɪk/ Francis 1916– . British molecular biologist. During World War II he worked on the development of radar, but from 1949 researched into ⟩DNA at the Cavendish Laboratory, Cambridge. For his discoveries of DNA's molecular structure, and the means whereby characteristics are transmitted from one generation to another, he was awarded a Nobel prize (with Maurice Wilkins of London and James D ⟩Watson then also at Cambridge in 1962). In 1977 he became research professor at the Kieckhefer Center for Molecular Biology at La Jolla, California.

cricket in sport, England's national summer game, played with bat and ball. Its origin is obscure, but some form of bat and ball game has been played since the 13th century. In 1711 Kent played All England, and in 1735 a match was played between teams chosen by the Prince of Wales and the Earl of Middlesex. The Hambledon Club at Broad-Halfpenny Down in Hampshire was the first to be formed, in 1750. The Marylebone Cricket Club (MCC) was established in Thomas Lord's ground in Dorset Square in 1787, and in 1814 it moved to St John's Wood. Since then it has been the controlling authority, and its ground the acknowledged headquarters of the game. The rules of the game have been changed from time to time. The third stump was introduced in the middle of the 18th century. The first rules of the game were drawn up in 1774. Only underhand bowling was allowed at first, but over-arm bowling was introduced in 1865. The game is played between two sides of 11 players each. Wickets are pitched at 20 m/22 yds apart. A batsman stands at each wicket and the object of the game is to score more runs than the opponents. The bowler bowls to the batsman a stipulated number of balls (usually six), after which another bowler bowls from the other wicket. A run is normally scored by the batsman after striking the ball and exchanging ends with his partner, or by hitting the ball to the boundary line for an automatic four runs or six runs if the ball is hit directly over it without first hitting the ground. A batsman is usually got out by being (1) bowled; (2) caught; (3) run out; (4) stumped; (5) l.b.w. – when the ball hits his leg which is placed before the wicket. Games comprise either one or two innings per team. Every year series of Test Matches are played among member countries of the Commonwealth, where the game has its greatest popularity: Australia, India, New Zealand, Pakistan, the UK, Sri Lanka and the West Indies. Famous grounds, besides Lord's, include Kennington Oval, Old Trafford (Manchester), the Melbourne Ground and Sydney Oval (Australia); and the Wanderers' Ground (Johannesburg). Great cricketers have included W G Grace, Sir Jack Hobbs, W R Hammond, and Sir Len Hutton; the Australian Sir Don Bradman; the Indian K S Ranjitsinhji; the South African A D Nourse; and the West Indians Sir Leary Constantine, Sir Frank Worrell, and Sir Gary Sobers. Test matches take several days, but otherwise the majority of matches last one or three days. The Cricket Memorial Gallery at Lord's is a museum.

County Championship first officially held 1890:
1979 Essex
1980 Middlesex
1981 Nottinghamshire
1982 Middlesex
1983 Essex
1984 Essex
1985 Middlesex
1986 Essex
1987 Nottinghamshire
World Cup first held 1975, contested every four years
1975 West Indies
1979 West Indies
1983 India

cricket in zoology, type of insect belonging to the order Orthoptera and allied to grasshoppers. Crickets are somewhat flattened and have long antennae. The males make a chirping note by rubbing together special areas on the wings. The females have a long needle-like egglaying organ (ovipositor). Many species are known in the

cricket

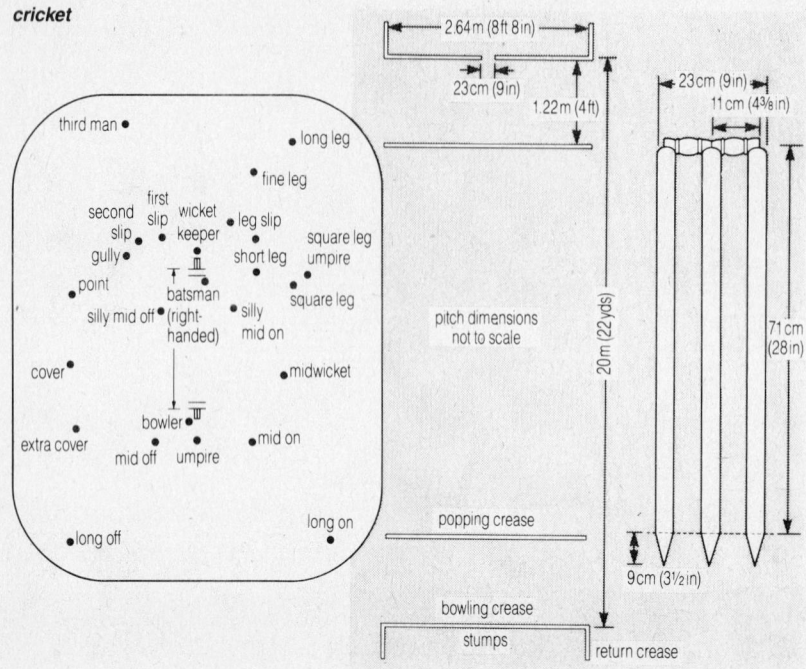

pitch dimensions not to scale

2.64 m (8 ft 8 in)
23 cm (9 in)
1.22 m (4 ft)
23 cm (9 in)
11 cm (4⅜ in)
20 m (22 yds)
71 cm (28 in)
9 cm (3½ in)
popping crease
bowling crease
stumps
return crease

third man · long leg · fine leg · second slip · first slip · wicket keeper · leg slip · square leg umpire · gully · short leg · point · batsman (right-handed) · square leg · silly mid off · silly mid on · cover · midwicket · bowler · mid off · umpire · mid on · extra cover · long on · long off

---

tropics, but just two are native to S England, the larger one, the *field cricket Gryllus campestris*, being about 2.5 cm/1 in long, and unable to fly. The *house cricket Acheta domesticus*, common in warm buildings such as kitchens and bakeries, originated in the Middle East. *Mole crickets* belong to a separate but allied family, and, as the name suggests, tunnel in the soil, having strong specialized front legs to do so. *Gryllotalpa gryllotalpa*, the only British species, is 3.5 cm/1.4 in long, and only found in the south *Bush crickets*, or long-horned grasshoppers, are another related family, living mainly in bushes and having very long antennae.

Crimea /kraɪˈmɪə/ N peninsula on the Black Sea, a region of ▷Ukraine Republic, USSR, from 1954.
area 27,000 sq km/10,400 sq mi
capital Simferopol
towns Sevastopol, Yalta
features mainly steppe, but the S coast is a holiday resort
products iron, oil
recent history Under Turkish rule 1475–1774, a subsequent brief independence was ended by Russian annexation in 1783. It was the republic of Taurida 1917–20, and the Crimean Autonomous Soviet Republic from 1920 until occupied by Germany Jul 1942–May 1944. It was then reduced to a region, its Tatar people being deported to Uzbekistan for collaboration; although they were exonerated in 1967, and some were allowed to return, others were forcibly re-exiled in 1979.

Crimean War war 1853–56 between Russia and the allied powers of England, France, Turkey, and Sardinia. The war arose nominally from a disagreement over the custody of the Holy Places at Jerusalem, actually from British and

French mistrust of Russia's ambitions in the Balkans. Hostilities began in 1853 with a Russian invasion of the Balkans (from which they were compelled to withdraw by Austrian intervention) and the sinking of the Turkish fleet at Sinope. Britain and France declared war on Russia in 1854, and were joined in 1855 by Sardinia. The main military operations were the invasion of the Crimea, the siege of Sevastopol (Sept 1854–Sept 1855), and the battles of the Alma, Balaclava, (including the Charge of the Light Brigade) and Inkerman, fought in 1854. The French lost 62,500 men, the British 19,600 – 15,700 of them by disease, a scandalous state of affairs that led to the organization of proper military nursing services by Florence ▷Nightingale. Conflict was settled by the Treaty of Paris, Feb 1856.

Criminal Injuries Compensation Board in Britain, board established in 1964 to administer financial compensation for victims of crimes of violence.

Criminal Investigation Department (CID) detective branch of the London Metropolitan Police, established in 1878, and comprising a force of about 4,000 men and women, which is recruited entirely from the uniformed police and controlled by an Assistant Commissioner.
Some 1,000 are stationed at New Scotland Yard, which houses: the *Central Office*, which deals with international offences and serious crimes in London and the provinces, and controls the Flying Squad; the *Criminal Intelligence Department*, which studies criminals and their methods; the *Fingerprint Department*, which contains about 2,000,000 prints of convicted persons; the *Criminal Record Office*, which information on all known criminals, and publishes the 'Police Gazette' and a pawn list daily; the *Scientific Laboratory*, which also

serves police forces in the Home Counties; the *Stolen Car Squad*; and the *Special Branch*, which deals with offences against the State. The remaining 3,000 detectives are stationed locally in the Metropolitan Police District.
Developed outside London in the later 19th century, such departments now exist in all UK forces. In practice they had been autonomous, but in 1979 new administrative arrangements were introduced so that all police officers, including CID, came under the uniformed chief superintendent of the division, so putting into practice the former theoretical position. Around the country from 1965 are Regional Crime Squads. These comprise detectives drawn from the various local forces of region to deal with major crime, and are kept in touch by a London-based national co-ordinator.

criminal law the body of ▷law reflecting the aim of a state to preserve public order by defining offences against the state (crimes) and establishing methods of prosecution and punishment. It is distinct from civil law, which deals with private matters between individuals.
In England before the Norman Conquest, machinery for the enforcement of criminal law was rudimentary, and rested on the organization of the local territorial unit, for example, the hundred. The principal court was the shire court, at which the freemen of the county were represented, and in which the law was declared from oral tradition. The main tendency of Saxon times was to extend money penalties for all offences, except for those that were *botless*, for example, murder, arson, and rape.
After the Norman Conquest the Saxon conception of the king's peace, at first limited to the vicinity of the king's person, was extended to include the whole kingdom, and offences against this, together with the crimes that were *botless*, form the basis of modern English criminal law. Under Henry II more modern procedure was introduced into criminal law by the institution of a formal 'presentation' of persons suspected of felonies, such as homicide, treason, arson, before a grand jury, and their ultimate trial before one of the king's justices. Lesser offences or misdemeanours were for a time dealt with by the county courts, and later by the Justices of the Peace. The distinction between felonies and misdemeanours was afterwards lost, when, owing to the extreme penalties inflicted for the former, new crimes created by statute were commonly placed in the latter class.
The Criminal Justice Act (1972) made provision in Britain for non-custodial penalties for minor offences. It also introduced life imprisonment as the maximum penalty for the use of firearms; reparation for personal injury or loss of/damage to property of the victim; and criminal bankruptcy proceedings to recover the proceeds of crime.
In the USA, in addition to federal (national) law, each of the states has its own individual body of criminal law; all have a common origin in English practice.

Crippen /ˈkrɪpən/ Henry Hawley 1861–1910. American murderer of his wife, variety artist Belle Elmore. He buried her

Crimean War The English and French allies fighting in the Crimean War share a drink together. The photograph is by Roger Fenton.

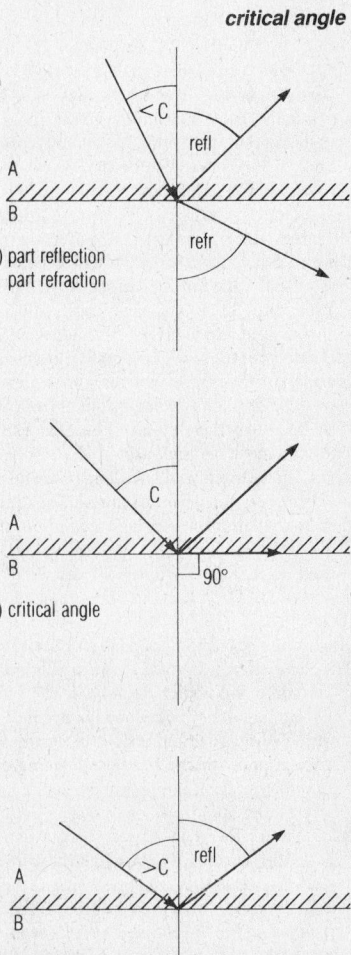

a) part reflection
part refraction

b) critical angle

c) total internal
reflection

remains in the cellar of his London home and tried to escape to the USA with his mistress Ethel le Neve (dressed as a boy). He was arrested on board ship following a radio message, the first criminal captured 'by radio', and was hanged.

Cripps /krɪps/ (Richard) Stafford 1889–1952. British Labour statesman, nephew of Beatrice ◊Webb. A founder of the Socialist League, he was expelled from the party 1939–45 for supporting a 'Popular Front' of all opposed to Chamberlain's appeasement policy. He was ambassador to Moscow 1940–42, Minister of Aircraft Production 1942–45, and Chancellor of the Exchequer 1947–50.

Crispi /'krɪspi/ Francesco 1819–1907. Italian Prime Minister (1887–91) and (1893–96). He advocated the ◊Triple Alliance of Italy with Germany and Austria, but was deposed in 1896.

critical angle in optics, for a ray of light passing from a denser to a less dense medium (such as from glass to air), the smallest angle of incidence at which the emergent ray grazes the surface of the denser medium – at an angle of refraction of 90°. The ray does not pass out into the less dense medium (when the angle of incidence has to be less than the critical angle), nor is it internally reflected back into the denser medium (when the angle of incidence has to be greater than the critical angle).

critical mass in nuclear physics, the minimum mass of fissile material that can undergo a continuous ◊chain reaction. Below this mass, too many ◊neutrons escape from the surface for a chain reaction to carry on; above the critical mass, the reaction may accelerate into a nuclear explosion.

critical temperature temperature above which a particular gas cannot be converted into

Crispi Resolutely anti-French and anti-clerical, Francesco Crispi was Italian Premier 1887–91 and 1893–96. An advocate of the Triple Alliance of Germany, Italy and Austria, he was deposed in 1896.

a liquid by pressure alone. It is also the temperature at which a magnetic material loses its magnetism (the Curie point).

Crivelli /krɪ'veli/ Carlo 1430–1493. Venetian painter of religious subjects, noted for his use of detail and colour.

Croatia /krəʊ'eɪʃə/ constituent republic of Yugoslavia;
area 56,538 sq km/21,824 sq mii
capital Zagreb

features Adriatic coastline with large islands; very mountainous, with part of the Karst region and the Julian and Styrian Alps; some marshland
population (1981) 4,578,109 including 3,455,000 Croats, 531,500 Serbs, 25,500 Hungarians
language the Croatian variant of Serbo-Croat
religion Roman Catholic 75% Greek Orthodox 25%
history Croatia was in Roman times part of Pannonia, but in the 7th century was settled by Carpathian Croats. From 1102 it was for 800 years an autonomous kingdom under the Hungarian Crown. An Austrian crownland 1849, a Hungarian crownland 1868, it was included in the kingdom of the Serbs, Croats, and Slovenes (called Yugoslavia from 1931) in 1918. In the 1970s Croatia became the chief hotbed for violent nationalist separatism in Yugoslavia, and there were demands for complete autonomy.

Croce /'krəʊtʃi/ Benedetto 1866–1952. Italian philosopher and literary critic, an opponent of ◊Fascism. Like Hegel, he held that ideas do not *represent* reality but *are* reality; but unlike his master he rejected every kind of transcendence.

Crockett /ˈkrɒkɪt/ Davy 1786–1836. American folk-hero. Tennessee-born, he was a Democrat Congressman 1827–31 and 1833–35. A series of books, of which he may have been part-author, made him into a mythical hero of the frontier, but their Whig associations cost him his office. He died defending the Alamo during the war for Texan independence.

Crockford /ˈkrɒkfəd/ William 1775–1844. British gambler, founder in 1827 of Crockford's Club in St James's Street, which became the fashionable place for London society to gamble.

crocodile large aquatic reptile, allied to alligators and caimans, but distinguished from them by the notch in the upper jaw into which the fourth tooth in the lower jaw fits. Crocodiles date back to 200 million years ago, and survived when their relations the dinosaurs became extinct. They can move on land, usually sluggishly, but fast when required, and have long powerful tails which propel them when swimming. They ballast themselves with stones to adjust their buoyancy. They can stay underwater for long periods, but surface to breathe. The nostrils can be closed underwater. They bask in the sun, and cool themselves by opening the mouth wide, which also enables scavenging birds to pick their teeth. They are active by night, and fierce hunters, the larger specimens attacking animals the size of large antelopes or, occasionally, people. The hardshelled eggs are laid in holes or nestmounds of vegetation, with the female remaining close by. She may assist in hatching and take the young to water in her mouth. About a dozen species of crocodile are found in Africa, Asia, Australia and Central America. The largest is the *saltwater crocodile Crocodylus porosus*, which can grow 6 m/20 ft or more, and is found from E India to Australia and the W Pacific. The *Nile crocodile Crocodylus niloticus* is found in Africa and Madagascar. The *gharial Gavialis gangeticus* is an Indian species with a very long narrow snout, specialized for fish-eating, and growing 4.5 m/15 ft long or more.

crocus genus of plants of the family Iridaceae, natives of the N parts of the Old World, especially S Europe and Asia Minor. During the dry season of the year they remain underground in the form of a 'corm', and produce fresh shoots and flowers in spring or autumn. At the end of the season of growth fresh corms are produced. Several species are cultivated as garden plants, the familiar mauve, white and orange forms being varieties of *Crocus vernus*, *Crocus versicolor*, and *Crocus aureus*. To the same genus belongs the saffron *Crocus sativus*. The so-called autumn crocus or meadow saffron *Colchicum* is not a true crocus, but belongs to the Liliaceae.

Croesus died c. 546 BC. Last king of Lydia, famed for his wealth. His court included ◊Solon, who warned him that no man could be called happy until his life had ended happily. When Croesus was overthrown by Cyrus the Great in 546 and condemned to be burnt to death, he called out Solon's name. Cyrus, having learnt the reason, spared his life.

Croker /ˈkrəʊkə/ Richard 1841–1922. American politician, 'Boss' of Tammany Hall, the Democratic party political machine in New York, from 1886 to 1902.

Cro-magnon name given to a type of prehistoric human, the first skeletons of which were found in 1868 in the Cro-magnon cave near Les Eyzies, in the Dordogne region of France. They superseded the Neanderthals, and lived between 40,000 and 35,000 years ago. Although biologically modern, they were larger in build than modern humans. Their culture produced flint and bone tools, jewellery, and remarkable cave paintings.

Crome /krəʊm/ John 1768–1821. British painter, born Norwich. He drew from nature, his work showing Dutch influence, and in 1803 founded the Norwich Society. He worked mainly in oils, but also produced water-colours and etchings, and is important in the development of English landscape art. His works include *Mousehold Heath* (National Gallery), *The Poringland Oak*, and *Carrow Abbey*.

Crompton /ˈkrɒmptən/ Richmal, pen name of British writer R C Lamburn 1890–1969. She is best remembered for her stories about the mischievous schoolboy 'William'.

Crompton /ˈkrɒmptən/ Samuel 1753–1827. British inventor at the time of the ◊Industrial Revolution. Born in Lancashire, he invented in 1779 the 'spinning mule', combining the ideas of ◊Arkwright and ◊Hargreaves. Though widely adopted, his invention brought him little return.

Cromwell /ˈkrɒmwel/ Oliver 1599–1658. English general and statesman. Born at Huntingdon, son of a small landowner, he entered parliament and was active in events leading to the Civil War. He raised cavalry forces (later called Ironsides) which aided the victories at Edgehill and Marston Moor, and organized the New Model Army, which he led (with ◊Fairfax) to victory at Naseby. Failing to secure a constitutional settlement with Charles I 1646–48, he defeated the 1648 Scottish invasion at Preston. A special commission, of which Cromwell was a member, tried the king and condemned him to death, and a republic was set up. The ◊Levellers wished to go further, but he executed their leaders in 1649; used terror to crush Irish clan resistance 1649–50 (see ◊Drogheda), and defeated the Scots (who had acknowledged Charles II) at Dunbar and Worcester. Having forcibly expelled the corrupt 'Rump' Parliament, he summoned a convention ('Barebone's Parliament'), soon dissolved as too radical, and under a constitution (Instrument of Government) drawn up by the army leaders, became Protector (king in all but name). The Parliament of 1654–55 was dissolved as uncooperative, and after a period of military dictatorship, his last parliament offered him the crown: he refused because he feared the army's republicanism. He established religious toleration, and Britain's prestige in Europe on the basis of an anachronistic alliance with France against Spain. At the Restoration his body was removed from Westminster Abbey.

Cromwell /ˈkrɒmwel/ Richard 1626–1712. son of Oliver ◊Cromwell. He succeeded his father as Protector, but resigned in May 1659, living in

Cromwell Oliver Cromwell became king in all but name when he assumed the role of Protector – he had been a member of the special commission which had condemned Charles I to death. This portrait is after Samuel Cooper.

exile after the Restoration until 1680, when he returned to England.

Cromwell /ˈkrɒmwel/ Thomas, Earl of Essex c. 1485–1540. English politician. Originally in Wolsey's service, he became secretary to Henry VIII in 1534 and the real director of government policy. He had Henry proclaimed head of the Church, suppressed the monasteries, ruthlessly crushed all opposition, and favoured Protestantism, which upheld the divine right of the Pope. His mistake in arranging Henry's marriage to ◊Anne of Cleves (to cement an alliance with the German Protestant princes against France and the Empire) led to his being accused of treason and beheaded.

Cronkite /ˈkrɒŋkaɪt/ Walter 1916– . American broadcast journalist, who became a household name and face throughout the USA as anchorman of the national evening news programme for CBS, a leading US television network, from 1962 to 1981.

Crookes /krʊks/ William 1832–1919. British scientist, whose many chemical and physical discoveries included the metal ◊thallium 1861, the radiometer 1875, and Crooke's high vacuum tube used in X-ray techniques. Elected Fellow of the Royal Society in 1863, he was awarded the Order of Merit in 1910.

crop in ◊birds, the thin-walled enlargement of the digestive tract between the oesophagus and stomach. It is an effective storage organ especially in seed eating birds; a pigeon's crop can hold about 500 cereal grains. Digestion begins in the crop, by the moisturizing of food. A crop also occurs in insects and annelid worms.

EARL OF ESSEX.

Cromwell Thomas Cromwell's loyalty to Henry VIII and support of Protestantism were rewarded first with the earldom of Essex, but finally with his execution. This is a portrait after Holbein.

crop a plant grown for human use. Over 80 crops are grown worldwide, providing people with the majority of their food, and supplying fibres, rubber, pharmaceuticals, dyes and other materials. Four main groups of crops are readily identifiable: food crops, forage crops, fibre crops, and miscellaneous crops.

food crops are grown specifically to feed people, and provide the bulk of human food worldwide. The major types are cereals, roots, pulses, vegetables, fruits, oil crops, tree nuts, sugar, beverages and spices. Cereals make the most important contribution to human nutrition. Though most food crops are carefully cultivated, crop production techniques and yields vary enormously from one part of the world to another.

cereal crops are grasses which are grown for their edible starch seeds. All major civilizations have depended upon them for food, and in 1985 world production exceeded 1.8 billion tonnes. Cereals are an attractive foodstuff as they are easy to store and contain about 75 per cent carbohydrate and 10 per cent protein. In recent years research has led to dramatic increased in cereal yields; in the decade 1975–85 cereal yields in Britain almost doubled and now commonly exceed six tonnes per hectare. If all the world's cereal crop was consumed directly by humans everybody could obtain an adequate dietary intake of protein and carbohydrate. However a large proportion of cereal production, particularly in affluent nations, is used as animal feeds to boost the production of meat, milk, butter, and eggs.

root crops in agriculture the term refers to turnips, swedes, and beets which are actually enlarged hypocotyls and contain little root, while in trade statistics it refers essentially to the tubers of potatoes, cassava, and yams. These three crops are second in importance to cereals as human food, and in the mid-1980s world production was just under 600 million tonnes. Food production per hectare from roots is higher than for cereals.

Roots have a high carbohydrate content, but their protein content rarely exceeds 2 per cent. Consequently communities relying too heavily upon roots may suffer from protein deficiency. *Potatoes* are the major temperate root crop. The major tropical root crops are cassava – a shrub which produces starchy tubers, yams, and sweet potatoes.

Pulses are crops such as peas and beans. They are grown primarily for their seeds which provide a concentrated source of vegetable protein and make a vital contribution to human diets, especially in poor countries where meat is scarce. In the mid-1980s world production was about 50 million tonnes a year. *Soyabeans* are the major temperate protein crop. Most are used for oil production or for animal feeds, though some are processed into 'meat substitutes'. Peanuts dominante pulse production in the tropical world, and are mostly consumed directly as human food. Pulses play a useful role in crop rotation as they help to raise soil nitrogen levels as well as acting as break crops.

vegetable crops are a diverse group of plants eaten for their leaves, stems, flower clusters, and buds. Some fruits such as pumpkins and tomatoes are also considered vegetables because of the manner in which they are consumed. Most vegetables are annuals, that is plants that live for one year or less. Though vegetables are not major sources of protein or energy, they add variety to human diets and are an important source of vitamins A and C, as well as providing dietary fibre and minerals. Vegetables are succulent, easily damaged, and rapidly decompose. Consequently until recent years there was little international trade in them, and even today the bulk of production will be consumed close to where it is grown. As a high proportion never enters the commercial market, statistics probably underestimate the amount grown. In the mid-1980s world production certainly exceeded 380 million tonnes.

fruits the seeds of plants together with the tissues which enclose them. These fleshy tissues have evolved to aid seed dispersal and are often colourful, sweet, juicy, and very palatable. The word fruit comes from the Latin *frui* meaning 'to enjoy'. Most fruits are borne by perennial plants. Like vegetables, they provide vitamins and minerals but little protein, and are often regarded as a semi-luxury. Recorded world production in the mid-1980s was approximately 300 million tonnes per year. Broadly fruits are divided into three types: *temperate fruits*, which require a cold season for satisfactory growth; *sub-tropical fruits*, which require warm conditions but can survive light frosts; and *tropical fruits*, which succumb if temperatures drop close to freezing point. In order of abundance the principal temperate fruits are apples, pears, plums, peaches and apricots, cherries, and soft fruits like raspberries and strawberries. Sub-tropical fruits include oranges and other citrus fruits, dates, pomegranates, and avocados, while bananas, mangoes, pineapples, papaya, and litchis are typical tropical fruits. In recent decades technical advances have improved the storage

and transportablilty of fruits and increasingly new trade routes are being established.

oil crops vegetable oils are pressed from the seeds of many crops. All arable agricultural regions have their characteristic oil crops. Cool temperate areas grow rapeseed and linseed; warm temperate regions produce sunflowers, olives and soyabeans; tropical areas produce groundnuts, oil palm and coconuts. Some of the major vegetable oils such as soyabean oil, groundnut oil, and cottonseed oil are derived from crops grown primarily for other purposes. Most vegetable oils are used as both edible oils and ingredients in industrial products such as soaps and varnishes, printing inks, and paints.

tree nuts nut is the common name for seeds which are enclosed in 'woody' shells. The kernels of most nuts provide a concentrated food with about 50 per cent fat and a protein content of 10 per cent to 20 per cent, though a few, such as chestnuts, are high in carbohydrates and have only a moderate (5 per cent) protein content. Most nuts are produced by perennial trees and bushes. While the majority are obtained from plantations, considerable quantities of Brazil and pecan nuts are still collected from the wild. Records of production are incomplete but current estimates suggest that world production in the mid-1980s was only about four million tonnes per year. Besides being a useful food for people, nuts also provide edible and industrial oils.

sugar in the mid-1980s world production of refined sugar averaged approximately 100 million tonnes per year. The major sources are tropical cane sugar which accounts for about two-thirds of production, and temperate sugar beet. Sugar cane, which is a tropical grass, commonly yields over 20 tonnes of sugar per hectare per year, whereas sugar beet rarely exceeds seven tonnes per hectare per year. Beet sugar is more expensive to produce and its cultivation is often subsidized by governments which wish to support the agricultural sector and avoid over-dependence on the volatile world sugar market. Minor quantities of sugar are produced from maple trees (maple syrup) and from sorghum and date palms.

beverages and spices tea, coffee, cocoa, cola nuts, and hops are plant products which are widely used to impart pleasant flavours and stimulants to people's fluid intake. The juice of grapes and other fruits is fermented to produce wines, while fermented cereals form the basis of most beers. Spices are used to impart flavours and aromas to food. They have little food value.

forage crops are crops like grass, clover and kale which are grown to feed livestock. Forage crops cover a greater area of the world than food crops, and grass, which dominates this group, is the world's most abundant crop, though much of it is still in an unimproved state. In areas where intense agriculture occurs forage crops often form break crops in a predominantly arable rotation.

fibre crops produce vegetable fibres. Temperate areas produce flax and hemp, but the most important fibre crops are cotton, jute, and sisal which are grown mostly in the tropical world. Cotton dominates fibre crop production.

crop rotation in agriculture, the system of changing the crop grown on a piece of ground each year and growing the different crops in a particular order to fully utilize the nutrients in the soil and to prevent the build-up of insect and fungal pests. Originally, in the 18th century, a four-year rotation was introduced with autumn-sown cereal, followed by a root crop, then spring cereal, and ending with a leguminous crop. Later, rotation on a three-year basis became more usual.

croquet open-air game played with mallets and balls on a level grass lawn 27 m/90 ft by 18 m/60 ft. Two or more players drive the balls through a series of hoops set to a pattern on the ground, and a player may have his ball advanced by his partner or retarded by his opponent. Played in France 16th–17th centuries, it was popular in England in the 1850s and revived from the 1950s. The headquarters is the Croquet Association, established in 1897, at the Hurlingham Club, London.

Crosby /'krɒzbi/ 'Bing' (Harry Lillis) 1904–1977. American singer, born Tacoma, Washington. He started singing with dance bands in 1925 and achieved world success with such songs as 'Pennies from Heaven', 'Blue Skies', 'White Christmas', 'The Bells of St Mary's' – which were featured in films with the same titles. He also made a series of 'road' film comedies with Dorothy Lamour and Bob Hope, the last being *Road to Hong Kong* 1962.

crossbill type of ◊finch *Loxia curvirostra* in which the hooked tips of the upper and lower beak cross one another, an adaptation for extracting the seeds from conifer cones. It is found in the N, and in mountains, in Europe, Asia and N America. The *parrot crossbill Loxia pytopsittacus* of Europe, and the *white-winged crossbill Loxia leucoptera* of N Asia and America specialize in pine and larch respectively.

crossing over in biology, a process that occurs during ◊meiosis, a type of cell division. While the ◊chromosomes are lying alongside each other in pairs, each partner may break, and then link up with the segment from the other partner, so exchanging corresponding sections. This process is one form of genetic ◊recombination, which increases variation and thus provides the raw material of ◊evolution.

Crossman /'krɒsmən/ Richard (Howard Stafford) 1907–1974. British Labour politician. A follower of Aneurin ◊Bevan, he was minister of housing and local government 1964–66, and of health and social security 1968–70. His posthumous *Crossman Papers* 1975 revealed confidential cabinet discussion.

croup inflammation (usually viral) of a child's larynx and trachea, with croaking breathing and a cough.

crow bird *Corvus corone*, found across Europe and N Asia. 45 cm/1.5 ft long, with a strong bill, feathered at the base, and omnivorous with a bias towards animal food, the crow exists in two colour forms. The *carrion crow*, found in S Britain and W Europe, is all black. The *hooded*

crow is found further E, also in N Scotland and Ireland, and has black head, wings and tail, but the body is greyish. The two forms may mix and interbreed where they overlap. Another 35 or so species of the genus *Corvus* are found worldwide, known as crows or ravens.

crowding out in economics, a situation in which an increase in government expenditure, by generating price rises and thus a reduction in the real ◊money supply, results in a fall in private ◊consumption and/or ◊investment. Crowding out has been used in recent years as a justification of privatization of state-owned industries.

crowfoot name applied to aquatic plants of the genus *Ranunculus*, with white flowers, with only a touch of yellow at the base of the petals.

Crowley /'krəʊli/ Aleister (Edward Alexander) 1875–1947. British mystic and dabbler in drugs, sex, and magic. He called himself the 'Great Beast', and the 'wickedest man alive', and established the Abbey of Théléme, a shrine devoted to pleasure, in 1920 at Cefalu, Sicily.

crown an official head-dress worn by a king or queen. The modern crown originated with the diadem, an embroidered fillet worn by eastern rulers, for which a golden band was later substituted. A laurel crown was granted by the Greeks to a victor in the games, and by the Romans to a triumphant general. Crowns came into use among the Byzantine emperors and the European kings after the fall of the Western Empire. Perhaps the oldest in Europe is the Iron Crown of Lombardy, made in 591. The crown of Charlemagne, preserved in Vienna, consists of eight gold plates. Before the Norman Conquest, kings of England certainly wore crowns, and from the Conquest to the Commonwealth each king had two crowns. The old ◊regalia was broken up under the Commonwealth, and a new set was made after the Restoration.

Crown Colonies British colonies which are under the direct legislative control of the Crown, and do not possess their own systems of fully responsible or representative government. They are administered either by a Crown-appointed governor or by elected or nominated legislative and executive councils with an official majority. Usually the Crown retains rights of veto and of direct legislation by orders in Council.

Crown Courts on the abolition of quarter sessions and assizes in England and Wales by the Courts Act 1971, Crown Courts were established which may sit at any number of different centres. They are presided over by a High Court judge, for more serious cases, and by Circuit judges or Recorders for lesser ones. Appeals against conviction or sentence at magistrates' courts may be heard in Crown Courts.

crown jewels popular name for ◊regalia.

Crown Proceedings Act an Act of Parliament which provided that the Crown (for example, government departments) could from 1948 be sued like a private person.

Croydon /'krɔɪdn/ borough of S London. *features* 11th-century Lanfranc's palace, former residence of Archbishops of Canterbury; Ashcroft Theatre, founded 1962; overspill office development from central London

population (1981) 316,557.

crucifixion death by fastening to a cross, a form of capital punishment used by the ancient Romans, Persians, and Carthaginians, and abolished by the Emperor ◊Constantine. Specifically, the Crucifixion refers to the death of ◊Jesus Christ in this manner.

Cruelty, Theatre of a theory advanced by Antonin ◊Artaud in his book *Le Théâtre et son double* 1938 and adopted by a number of writers and directors including Peter Brook. It aims to shock the audience into an awareness of basic, primitive human nature, through the release of feelings usually repressed by conventional behaviour.

Cruft /krʌft/ Charles 1852–1938. British dog expert. He organized his first dog show in 1886, and from that year annual shows were held in Islington – Cruft's being the premier event of the dog year in Britain.

Crusades a series of wars (1096–1291) undertaken by various European rulers to recover the Holy Land from the Muslims. Motivated by religious zeal and the desire for more land, and by the trading ambitions of the major Italian cities, the Crusades were varied in their effects.

1st Crusade 1095–99 motivated by occupation of Asia Minor and Jerusalem by the Seljuk Turks. Crusade succeeded in recapturing Jerusalem and establishing a series of Latin kingdoms on the Syrian coast.

2nd Crusade 1147–49 led by Louis VII of France and Emperor Conrad III; a complete failure.

3rd Crusade 1189–92 led by Philip Augustus of France and Richard I of England. Failed to recapture Jerusalem, which had been seized by Saladin in 1187.

4th Crusade 1202–04 directed against Egypt but diverted by the Venetians to sack and divide Constantinople.

5th Crusade 1218–21 captured and then lost Damietta.

6th Crusade 1228–29 led by Frederick II. Recovered Jerusalem by negotiation with the Sultan of Egypt. City finally lost in 1244.

7th and 8th Crusades 1249–54, 1270–72 both led by Louis IX of France. Acre, the last Christian fortress in Syria, was lost in 1291.

crust the outermost part of the structure of the ◊Earth, consisting of two distinct parts, the oceanic crust and the continental crust. The *oceanic* crust is on average about 10 km/6.2 mi thick and is fairly even in composition. Beneath a surface sediment lies a layer of basalt, then a layer of gabbro. The composition of the whole oceanic crust shows a high proportion of *si*lica and *mag*nesia, hence named *sima* by geologists. In contrast the *continental* crust is extremely complex. It varies in thickness between about 40 and 70 km/25 and 44 mi, being deeper beneath mountain ranges. It consists of a great many rock types, including a surface layer of sedimentary and volcanic rocks overlying a zone of metamorphic rocks built on a thick layer of granodiorite. *Si*lica and *al*umina dominate the composition and the name sial is given to continental crustal material. Because of the movements of ◊plate tectonics, the ocean crust

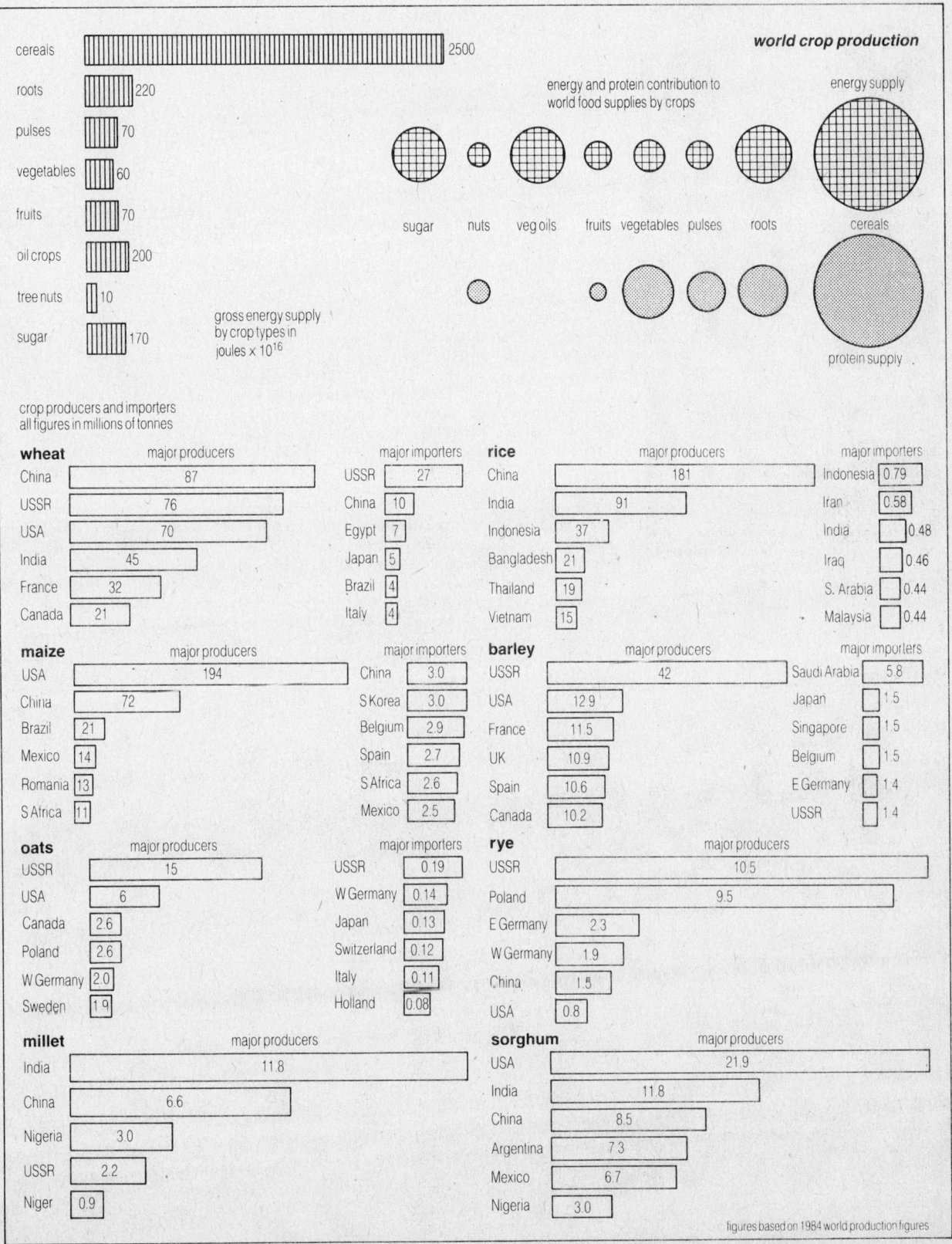

world crop production

	joules
cereals	2500
roots	220
pulses	70
vegetables	60
fruits	70
oil crops	200
tree nuts	10
sugar	170

gross energy supply by crop types in joules x 10^16

energy and protein contribution to world food supplies by crops

energy supply

sugar nuts veg oils fruits vegetables pulses roots cereals

protein supply

crop producers and importers all figures in millions of tonnes

wheat

major producers		major importers	
China	87	USSR	27
USSR	76	China	10
USA	70	Egypt	7
India	45	Japan	5
France	32	Brazil	4
Canada	21	Italy	4

rice

major producers		major importers	
China	181	Indonesia	0.79
India	91	Iran	0.58
Indonesia	37	India	0.48
Bangladesh	21	Iraq	0.46
Thailand	19	S. Arabia	0.44
Vietnam	15	Malaysia	0.44

maize

major producers		major importers	
USA	194	China	3.0
China	72	S Korea	3.0
Brazil	21	Belgium	2.9
Mexico	14	Spain	2.7
Romania	13	S Africa	2.6
S Africa	11	Mexico	2.5

barley

major producers		major importers	
USSR	42	Saudi Arabia	5.8
USA	12.9	Japan	1.5
France	11.5	Singapore	1.5
UK	10.9	Belgium	1.5
Spain	10.6	E Germany	1.4
Canada	10.2	USSR	1.4

oats

major producers		major importers	
USSR	15	USSR	0.19
USA	6	W Germany	0.14
Canada	2.6	Japan	0.13
Poland	2.6	Switzerland	0.12
W Germany	2.0	Italy	0.11
Sweden	1.9	Holland	0.08

rye

major producers	
USSR	10.5
Poland	9.5
E Germany	2.3
W Germany	1.9
China	1.5
USA	0.8

millet

major producers	
India	11.8
China	6.6
Nigeria	3.0
USSR	2.2
Niger	0.9

sorghum

major producers	
USA	21.9
India	11.8
China	8.5
Argentina	7.3
Mexico	6.7
Nigeria	3.0

figures based on 1984 world production figures

Crowley Notorious British mystic and dabbler in drugs, sex, and magic, Aleister Crowley called himself 'the wickedest man alive.' He established a shrine devoted to pleasure in Sicily.

is nowhere older than about 200 million years. However, parts of the continental crust are more than ten times that age.

crustacean one of the class of arthropods that includes crabs, lobsters, shrimps, woodlice, barnacles and many less familiar forms. The external skeleton is made of protein and chitin hardened with lime. Each segment bears a pair of appendages which may be modified as antennae, for feeding, swimming, walking or grasping. Most breathe with gills. There are 30,000+ species, varying from 0.025 cm/0.001 in to 3 m/10 ft across. Most are marine and they are very important in the 'food-chains' of the sea.

Crux ◊constellation of the southern hemisphere, popularly known as the Southern Cross. Crux is the smallest of all the 88 constellations; its brightest star, Alpha Crucis, is a ◊double star. Near Beta Crucis lies a glittering star cluster known as the Jewel Box. The constellation also contains the Coalsack, a dark cloud of dust silhouetted against the bright starry background of the ◊Milky Way.

cryolite a rare crystalline mineral (Na_3AlF_6) found in Greenland, comprising fluoride of sodium and aluminium, used in refining aluminium.

cryonics process of freezing at the moment of clinical death with the aim of enabling eventual resuscitation. The first human treated was James H Bedford, a lung cancer patient of 74, in the USA in 1967. The body, drained of blood, is indefinitely preserved in a thermos-type container filled with liquid nitrogen at -196°C.

cryptogam an obsolete name applied to the lower plants. It included the algae, liverworts, mosses and ferns (plus the fungi and bacteria in very early schemes of classification). In such classifications the ◊seed plants were known as phanerogams.

cryptography science of codes, for example, that produced by the Enigma coding machine used by the Germans in World War II (see ◊Ultra), and those used in commerce by banks encoding electronic fund transfer messages, business firms sending computer-conveyed memos between headquarters, and in the growing field of electronic mail. No method of encrypting is completely unbreakable, but decoding can be made so complex that the time and equipment needed is difficult to arrange.

crystal a substance with an orderly three-dimensional arrangement of its atoms or molecules, thereby creating an external surface of clearly defined smooth faces having characteristic angles between them. Examples are common salt, a cubic arrangement, and quartz. Each geometrical figure or form, many of which may be combined in one crystal, consists of two or more faces, for example, dome, prism, pyramid. A mineral can often be identifed by the shape of its crystals and the system of crystallization determined. A single crystal can vary in size from a sub-microscopic particle to a huge mass some 30 m/100 ft in length.

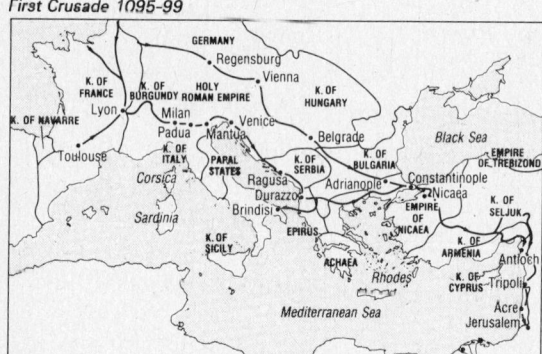

First Crusade 1095-99

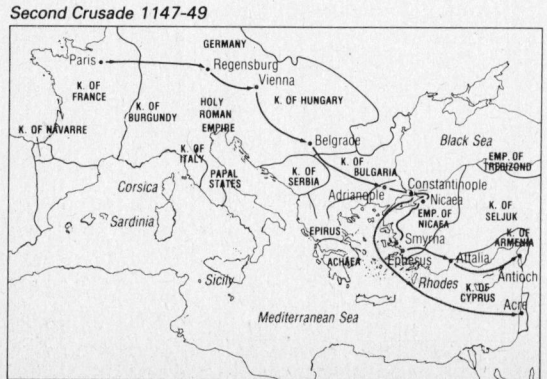

Second Crusade 1147-49

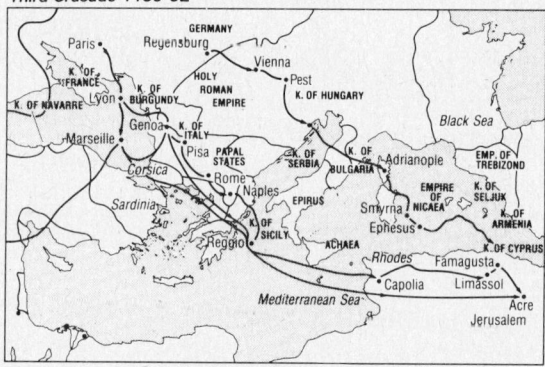

Third Crusade 1189-92

Fourth Crusade, Venice–Constantinople 1202-04

crust

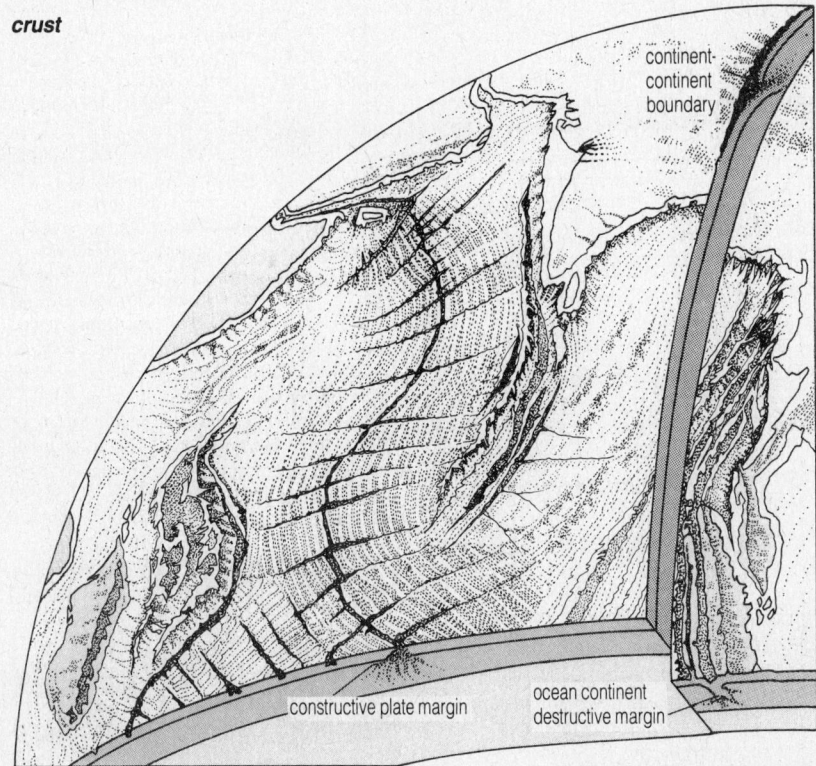

continent-
continent
boundary

constructive plate margin

ocean continent
destructive margin

crystal

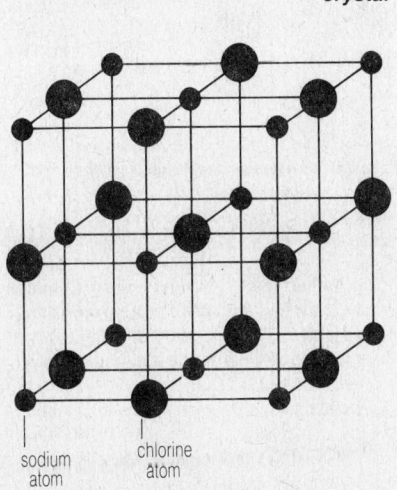

sodium
atom

chlorine
atom

crystallography the scientific study of ⊳crystals. In 1912 it was found that the shape and size of the unit cell of a crystal can be discovered by ⊳X-rays, thus opening up an entirely new way of 'seeing' atoms. This means of determining the atomic patterns in a crystal is known as X-ray diffraction. By this method it has been found that many substances have unit cells or boxes which are exact cubes, for example ordinary table salt (sodium chloride). It has been shown that even purified biomolecules, such as proteins and DNA, can form crystals, and such compounds may now be studied by the same method. Another field of application of X-ray analysis lies in the study of metals and alloys. Crystallography is also of use to the geologist studying rocks and soils. Many materials were not even suspected of being crystals until they were examined by X-ray crystallography.

Crystal Palace glass and iron building designed by ⊳Paxton, housing the Great Exhibition of 1851 in Hyde Park, London; later rebuilt in modified form at Sydenham Hill in 1854 (burnt down in 1936). The site is partly filled by the National Sports Centre.

CSE (Certificate of Secondary Education) the examinations taken by the majority of secondary school pupils in the UK, who were not regarded as academically capable of GCE ⊳O Level, until the introduction of the common secondary examination system, ⊳GCSE, in 1988

Ctesiphon /ˈtesɪfən/ ruined city of the Sassanians 19 km/12 mi SE of Baghdad. A palace of the 4th century still has its throne-room standing, spanned by a single vault of unreinforced brickwork some 24 m/80 ft across.

Cuba /ˈkjuːbə/ island in the Caribbean, the largest of the West Indies, off the south coast of Florida.

government the 1976 constitution created a socialist state with the national assembly of people's power as its supreme organ. It consists of 500 deputies elected by universal suffrage for a five-year term and elects 31 of its members to form the council of state. It also elects the head of state who is president of the council, head of government, and first secretary and chairman of the political bureau of the only party, the Cuban Communist Party (PCC). Fidel ⊳Castro thus occupies all the key positions within the state and the party.

history the first European to visit Cuba was Christopher ⊳Columbus in 1492. From 1511 Cuba was a Spanish colony, its economy based on sugar plantations worked by slaves, who were first brought from Africa in 1523. Slavery was not abolished until 1886. Cuba was ceded to the USA in 1898, at the end of the ⊳Spanish-American War. A republic was proclaimed in 1901, though the USA retained its naval bases and a right to intervene in internal affairs until 1934.

In 1933 an army sergeant, Fulgencio ⊳Batista, seized and held power until he retired in 1944. In 1952 he regained power in a bloodless coup and began another period of rule which many Cubans found oppressive. In 1953 a young lawyer and son of a sugar planter, Dr Fidel ⊳Castro, tried to overthrow him but failed. He went into exile to prepare for another coup in 1956 but was again defeated. He fled to the hills with Dr Ernesto 'Che' ⊳Guevara and ten others, to form a guerrilla force.

In 1959 Castro's force of 5,000 men deposed Batista, to great popular acclaim. The 1940 constitution was suspended and replaced by a 'Fundamental Law', power being vested in a council of ministers with Castro as prime minister, his brother Raul as his deputy and Che Guevara, reputedly, as the next in command. In 1960 the USA broke off diplomatic relations after all US businesses in Cuba were nationalized without compensation. In 1961 it went further, sponsoring a full-scale, but abortive, invasion, the ⊳'Bay of Pigs' episode. In Dec of that year Castro proclaimed a communist state whose economy would develop along Marxist-Leninist lines.

In 1962 Cuba was expelled from the Organization of American States (OAS), originally formed as a regional agency of the UN, but increasingly dominated by the USA, which initiated a full political and economic blockade. Castro responded by tightening relations with the USSR which, in the same year, supplied missiles with atomic warheads for installation in Cuba. A crisis was averted when they were dismantled at the US president's insistence.

In 1965 Guevara left Cuba, ostensibly to fight causes abroad, and the country's only political party changed its name to the Cuban Communist Party (PCC). With Soviet help, Cuba made substantial economic and social progress 1965–72, in 1972 becoming a member of the Council for Mutual Economic Assistance (CMEA), a Moscow-based organization linking communist states.

In 1976 a referendum approved a socialist constitution and Fidel Castro and his brother were elected president and vice-president. During the following five years Cuba played a larger role in world affairs, particularly in Africa, to the disquiet of the USA.

Re-elected in 1981, Castro offered to discuss foreign policy with the USA but Cuba's support for ◊Argentina, against Britain, cooled relations and drew it closer to other Latin American countries. The 1983 US invasion of ◊Grenada lowered the diplomatic temperature still further, though Cuba has since adopted a more conciliatory posture towards the USA.

Cuba

REPUBLIC OF (*República de Cuba*

AREA 121,464 sq km/46,736 sq mi
CAPITAL Havana
PHYSICAL comprises Cuba, the largest and westernmost of the West Indian islands, and smaller islands including Isle of Youth; low hills; Sierra Maestra mountains in E
FEATURES US base (on perpetual lease since 1934) at Guantánamo Bay (Gitmo), and Soviet base at Cienfuegos
HEAD OF STATE AND OF GOVERNMENT Fidel Castro Ruz from 1959
GOVERNMENT one-party communist
EXPORTS sugar (largest producer after USSR), tobacco, coffee; iron, copper, nickel
CURRENCY Cuban peso (1.30 = £1 Sept 1987, official rate)
POPULATION (1985) 10,105,000 (plus 125,000 refugees from the Cuban port of Mariel, hence *marielitos* in USA); 66% are of Spanish descent, and a large number are of African origin; annual growth rate 0.7%
LANGUAGE Spanish
RELIGION Roman Catholic 45%
LITERACY 96% male/95% female (1979)
DISPOSABLE NATIONAL INCOME $15.8 bn (1983); $1,590 per head of population
CHRONOLOGY
1901 Cuba achieved independence.
1933 Fulgencia Batista seized power.
1944 Batista retired.
1952 Batista seized power again to begin an oppressive regime.
1953 Fidel Castro led an unsuccessful coup against Batista.
1956 Castro led a second unsuccessful coup.
1959 Batista overthrown by Castro. Constitution of 1940 replaced by a 'Fundamental Law', making Castro prime minister, his brother Raul Castro his deputy, and Che Guevara his number three.
1960 All US businesses in Cuba appropriated without compensation. USA broke off diplomatic relations.
1961 USA sponsored an unsuccessful invasion,

Cuba

the Bay of Pigs episode. Castro announced that Cuba had become a communist state, with a Marxist-Leninist programme of economic development.
1962 Cuba expelled from the Organization of American States (OAS). Soviet nuclear missiles removed from Cuba at US insistence.
1965 Cuba's sole political party renamed Cuban Communist Party (PCC). With Soviet help, Cuba began to make considerable economic and social progress.
1972 Cuba became a full member of the Moscow-based Council for Mutual Economic Assistance (CMEA).
1976 New socialist constitution approved and Castro elected president.
1976–81 Castro became involved in extensive international commitments, assisting Third World countries, particularly in Africa.
1982 Cuba joined other Latin American countries in giving moral support to Argentina in its dispute with Britain.
1984 Castro tried to improve US-Cuban relations by discussing the exchange of US prisoners in Cuba with Cuban 'undesirables' in the USA.

techniques as collage, with cut-up photographs, printed texts, and objects included in the painting. Cubists avoided emotional and narrative expression to depict almost colourless shapes split up into a series of semi-geometric facets overlapping, interlocking and semi-transparent as though seen from different viewpoints. The aim was to show objects as they are known to be rather than as they happen to look at a particular moment. Cubism announced that a work of art exists in its own right rather than as a representation of the real world, and it attracted such artists as Juan Gris, Albert Gleizes, Fernand ◊Léger, Jean Metzinger, and Robert ◊Delauney.

Cuchulain /ku'hulɪn/ legendary Celtic hero, the chief figure in an important cycle of Irish legends. He is associated with his uncle Conchobar, king of Ulster, and his most famous exploits are described in the epic saga *Cowreiving of Cuailgne*.

cuckoo bird *Cuculus canorus*, breeding in Europe and N Asia and migrating south in winter. Its name derives from its characteristic call. The adult somewhat resembles a hawk, being about 33 cm/1.1 ft long, bluish-grey and barred beneath (females sometimes reddish), and has a long rounded tail. It is a 'brood parasite', laying its eggs singly, at intervals of about 48 hours, in the nests of small insectivorous birds. As soon as the young cuckoo hatches it ejects all other young birds or eggs from the nest, and is tended by 'foster-parents' until fledging. Cuckoos feed on insects, particularly hairy caterpillars which are distasteful to most birds. The cuckoo has played a great part in European folklore and literature, and has often been introduced into music and song. There are about 130 species of the cuckoo family worldwide, including cuckoos and roadrunners.

cuckoo A young cuckoo *Cuculus canorus* ejects a tree pipit's eggs and establishes itself in the nest. Its foster parents will have to work hard to feed the cuckoo, which will quickly grow to several times their size.

cucumber plant *Cucumis sativus*, family ◊Cucurbitaceae, producing long, green-skinned fruit with crisp translucent flesh; small cucumbers, especially the fruit of *Cucumis anguria*, are pickled as 'gherkins'.

Cuenca /'kwɛŋkə/ city in Ecuador, capital of Azuay province; population (1980) 140,000. It was founded by the Spanish in 1557.

Cuenca /'kwɛŋkə/ Spanish city, capital of Cuenca province, at the confluence of the Jaúcar and Huécar, 135 km/84 mi SE of Madrid; population (1981) 40,000. It has a 13th-century cathedral.

Culdees /'kʌldiːz/ name given to an ancient order of Christian monks which existed in Ireland and Scotland from before the 9th century to about the 12th century AD, when the Celtic Church, to which they belonged, was forced to conform to Roman usages. Some survived until the 14th century, while at Armagh in Northern Ireland they remained until the dissolution of the monasteries in 1541.

cube in geometry, a solid figure whose faces are all squares. It has six equal-area faces and 12 equal-length edges. If the length of one edge is l, the volume of the cube $V = l^3$ and its surface area $A = 6l^2$.

cubic measure a measure of volume, either by the prefix 'cubic' followed by the term for linear measure, as in 'cubic foot' or the suffix 'cubed', as in 'metre-cubed'.

Cubism ◊abstract art movement arising out of ◊Post-Impressionism, developed by Georges ◊Braque and ◊Picasso, who introduced such

Culham /'kʌləm/ village near Oxford, England, site of a British nuclear research establishment.

Culloden /kə'lɒdn/ stretch of moorland in Inverness-shire, where the Young Pretender, ◊Charles Stuart, was defeated in 1746 by the Duke of ◊Cumberland.

Culshaw /'kʌlʃɔ:/ John 1924–1980. British record producer, who developed recording techniques. Managing Decca's classical recordings in the 1950s and 1960s, he introduced echo chambers, the speeding and slowing of tapes, and so on, to achieve effects not possible in live performance. He produced the first complete recordings of Wagner's *Ring* cycle.

cultivar a variety of a plant developed by horticultural or agricultural techniques. The term is derived from 'cultivated variety'.

culture in sociology, the way of life of a particular society or group of people, including patterns of thought, beliefs, behaviour, customs, traditions, rituals, dress, and language, as well as art, music, and literature. Sociologists and anthropologists see culture as a key concept in describing and analysing human societies.

culture in biology, the growing of living cells, and tissues in laboratory conditions.

Cumae /'kju:mi:/ ancient city in Italy, on the coast 16 km/10 mi W of Naples. A Greek colony founded about 740 BC, it was famous in the ancient world as the seat of the oracle of the Cumaean Sibyl.

Cuman /'kju:mənz/ member of a powerful Turki federation of the Middle Ages, which dominated the steppes in the 11th and 12th centuries and built an empire reaching from the Volga to the Danube. For a generation they held up the Mongol advance on the Volga, but in 1238 a Cuman and Russian army was crushingly defeated near Astrakhan, and 200,000 Cumans took refuge in Hungary, where they settled and where their language died out only about 1775. The Mameluke dynasty of Egypt was founded by Cuman ex-slaves. Most of the so-called Tartars of South Russia were of Cuman origin.

Cumberland /'kʌmbələnd/ former county of NW England, adjacent to the Scottish border on the N, and in the S including part of the Lake District. After the Roman withdrawal, Cumberland became part of Strathclyde, a British kingdom. In 945 it passed to Scotland, in 1157 to England, and until the union of the English and Scottish crowns in 1603 Cumberland was the scene of frequent battles between the two countries. In 1974 Cumberland was merged in ◊Cumbria.

Cumberland /'kʌmbələnd/ Ernest Augustus, Duke of Cumberland; King of Hanover 1771–1851. The fifth son of George III, he served in the Hanoverian army against the French 1793–95. In 1799 he was created Duke of Cumberland. He was intensely unpopular, being a high Tory and an opponent of all reforms. On the death of William IV in 1837 he became king of Hanover, Victoria being excluded by the Salic Law, and had a stormy reign.

Cumberland /'kʌmbələnd/ William Augustus, Duke of Cumberland 1721–1765. British general. Third son of George II, he was

created Duke of Cumberland in 1726. He fought at Dettingen in 1743, was defeated by Marshal Saxe at Fontenoy in 1745, and in 1746 ended the Jacobite rising in Scotland by his victory at Culloden. His brutal repression of the Highlands earned him the nickname of 'Butcher'. In the ◊Seven Years' War he surrendered with his army at Kloster-Zeven (1757).

Cumbernauld /,kʌmbə'nɔ:ld/ new town in Strathclyde, Scotland, 18 km/11 mi from Glasgow, and founded 1956 to take the city's overspill; population (1981) 47,000. In 1966 it won a prize as the world's best-designed community.

Cumbria /'kʌmbriə/ county in NW England
area 6,810 sq km/2,629 sq mi
towns administrative headquarters Carlisle; Barrow, Kendal, Whitehaven, Workington
features Lake District National Park, including Scafell Pike 978 m/3,210 ft, highest mountain in England; Helvellyn 950 m/3,118 ft; Lake Windermere, the largest lake in England, 17 km/10.5 mi long, 1.6 km/1 mi wide; other lakes including Derwentwater, Ullswater; Furness peninsula; atomic stations at Calder Hall and Sellafield (reprocessing plant), formerly Windscale.
products the traditional coal, iron, and steel of the coast towns has been replaced by newer industries including chemicals, plastics, and electronics; in the N and E there is dairying, and West Cumberland Farmers is the country's largest agricultural cooperative.
population (1986) 483,600
famous people birthplace of ◊Wordsworth at Cockermouth, and home at Grasmere; homes of ◊Coleridge and ◊Southey at Keswick.

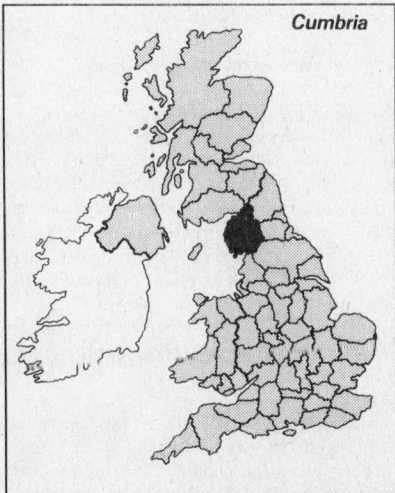

Cumbria

cumin spice, the seed-like fruit of the plant *Cuminum cyminum*, with a bitter flavour.

Cummings /'kʌmɪŋz/ E(dward) E(stlin) 1894–1962. American poet, born in Massachusetts. He first achieved fame with the novel *The Enormous Room* 1922, about life in a French prison camp, but his reputation rests on his poetry (for example, the collection *Tulips and Chimneys* 1923). At first the poems gained

notoriety for their idiosyncratic punctuation and typography (he always wrote his name 'e.e. cummings', for example), but their lyric power has gradually been recognized.

cuneiform an ancient system of writing formed of combinations of wedge-shaped strokes, usually impressed on clay. It was probably invented by the Sumerians, and was in use in Mesopotamia as early as the middle of the 4th millennium BC. It was adopted and modified by the Assyrians, Babylonians, Elamites, Hittites, Persians, and many other peoples with different languages. In the 5th century BC it fell into disuse, but sporadically reappeared in later centuries BC. The decipherment of the cuneiform scripts was due to the efforts of G F Grotefend (1802) and H C Rawlinson (1846).

Cunningham /'kʌnɪŋəm/ Merce 1919– . American dancer and choreographer. Influenced by Martha ◊Graham, with whose company he was soloist from 1939–45, he formed his own dance company and school in New York in 1953. His works include *The Seasons* 1947, *Antic Meet* 1958, *Squaregame* 1976, and *Arcade* 1985.

Cunninghame Graham /'kʌnɪŋəm 'greɪəm/ Robert Bontine 1852–1936. Scottish writer and politician. Of Scottish and Spanish descent, he travelled widely in Central and South America, Spain, and Morocco. He was a Liberal member of parliament 1886–92, became president of the Scottish Labour Party in 1888, and in later life was associated with the Scottish Nationalist movement.

Cuno /'ku:nəu/ Wilhelm 1876–1933. German industrialist and politican who was briefly chancellor of the Weimar Republic in the inflationary year of 1923.

Cupid /'kju:pɪd/ in Roman mythology, the god of love, identified with the Greek god ◊Eros.

cuprite a red oxide of copper, Cu_2O, in crystalline form.

cupro-nickel a copper alloy (75% copper and 25% nickel) substituted in the UK in 1946 for the 'silver' (50% silver, 40% copper, 5% nickel and 5% zinc) previously used in coins.

Curaçao /,kjuərə'sɔu/ island in the West Indies, one of the ◊Netherlands Antilles. Area 338 sq km/210 sq mi); population (1983) 165,000.
Willenstad, the capital, has a fine harbour. There is some agriculture,but the principal industry, dating from 1918, is the refining of petroleum from Venezuela. Curaçao was first visited by Europeans in 1499, colonized by Spain 1527, annexed by the Dutch West India Company 1634, and gave its name from 1924 to the group of islands renamed Netherlands Antilles in 1948.

curaçao /,kjuərə'sɔu/ liqueur, originally the produce of the island of Curaçao, but now made in other countries, notably Latvia. Both dry and sweet Curaçao is produced and marketed, the alcohol content varying between 36 and 40 per cent.

curare South American native poison obtained from the bark of the tree *Strychnos toxifera* by macerating in water: used on arrow tips it paralyses the victim. An alkaloid derivative, curarine, is used as a muscle relaxant in surgical operations.

curate literally, a priest who has the cure of souls in a parish, and so used in Europe. In England, however, it is generally applied to an unbeneficed clergyman who acts as assistant to a parish priest, more exactly an 'assistant curate'.

curia romana the judicial and administrative bodies through which the Pope carries on the government of the Roman Catholic Church. It includes certain tribunals; the chancellery which issues papal bulls, and various offices including that of the Cardinal Secretary of State; and the Congregations, or councils of cardinals, each with a particular department of work.

Curie /əkjʊəri/ Marie (born Sklodovska) 1867–1934. Polish scientist. Born in Warsaw, she went to study in Paris in 1891, where she married the scientist *Pierre Curie* (1859–1906), in 1895. Impressed by the publication of Becquerel's experiments, Marie Curie decided to investigate the nature of uranium rays; and in 1898 she reported the possible existence of some new powerful radioactive element in pitchblende ores. Her husband abandoned his own researches to assist her, and in the same year the existence of polonium and radium was announced, the pure elements being isolated in 1902. Both scientists refused to take out a patent on their discovery, and were jointly awarded the Davy Medal (1903) and the Nobel Prize for physics (1903; with Becquerel). In 1904 Pierre was appointed to a chair in physics at Sorbonne, and on his death in a street accident was succeeded by his wife. She wrote a *Treatise on Radioactivity* in 1910, and was awarded the Nobel Prize for chemistry in 1911. She died a victim of the radiations among which she had worked in her laboratory. The curie, the unit of radioactivity equal to that emitted by 1 gramme of radium, is named after her.

Curie Madame Curie in her Paris laboratory.

curium a metallic element, atomic number 96, atomic weight 247. It is radioactive and does not occur naturally, but is produced from ◊americium; it is named after the ◊Curies.

curlew wading bird *Numenius arquata* 55 cm/1.8 ft long, with mottled brown plumage, long legs and a long thin downcurved bill. Nesting in N Europe and Asia on moors, fields and marshes, it moves S in winter. It is also seen on mudflats. The name derives from its haunting flute-like call. There are seven other species of curlew around the world.

curling game played on ice with stones; sometimes described as 'bowls on ice'. One of the most distinctive national games of Scotland, where it probably originated, it has spread to many countries. It can also be played on artificial (cement or tarmacadam) ponds.

Curnonsky pseudonym of Maurice Edmond Sailland 1872–1956. French gastronome and cookery writer, who was a leading pioneer of the cataloguing of French regional cuisine.

Curragh, The /'kʌrə/ plain in County Kildare, Republic of Ireland, headquarters of Irish racing and site of the national stud.

Curragh 'Mutiny' demand in Mar 1914 by Gen Hubert Gough and his officers, stationed at the army camp in Curragh, Ireland, that they should not be asked to take part in forcing Protestant Ulster to participate in Home Rule. They were subsequently allowed to return to duty, and after World War I the solution of partition was adopted.

currant variety of grape first cultivated near Corinth (hence the name), with a small round seedless berry. Dried, these are used extensively in cakes and are grown on a large scale in Greece and California. Because of the similarity of the fruit, the same name is given to several species of shrubs in the genus *Ribes* family Grossulariaceae. The red currant *Ribes rubrum* is a native of S Europe, Asia and North America, occasionally growing wild in Britain. The white currant is a cultivated, less acid variety, but the black currant *Ribes nigrum* is the most favoured for cooking. The flowering currant *Ribes sanguineum* is a native of N America.

current the flow of a body of water or air moving in a definite direction. Oceanic currents may be:

drift currents, broad and slow-moving;
stream currents, narrow and swift-moving, e.g. ◊Gulf Stream and ◊Kuroshio/Japan Current;
upwelling currents, which bring cold, nutrient-rich water from the ocean bottom to provide food for plankton, which in turn supports fish and sea birds, such as Gulf of Guinea Current and the ◊Peru (Humboldt) Current. Once in ten years or so, the latter, which runs from the Antarctic up the W coast of South America, turns warm, with heavy rain and rough seas, and has disastrous results (as in 1982–83) for the Peruvian anchovy industry and wildlife. The phenomenon is called ◊*El Niño* (Spanish 'the Child') because it occurs towards Christmas.

curriculum in education, the range of subjects offered within an institution or course. The only part of the school curriculum prescribed by law in the UK is religious education. General responsibility for overseeing the curriculum in England and Wales rests with the local education authority and school governors; however, growing concern about the low proportion of 14- and 16-year-olds opting to study maths, science, and technology, with a particularly low take-up rate among girls, has strengthened moves towards increasing central government control over the curriculum with the provision of a 'national' or 'core' curriculum proposed in an education bill 1987 to ensure basic subjects are studied by all school students at least up to the age of 16. The 'core' would include maths, English, science and technology, religious education, and physical education.

Curtin /'kɜːtɪn/ John 1885–1945. Australian Labour statesman. Born in Victoria, he rose to prominence as a trade union leader and journalist, entered the House of Representatives in 1928, and was elected leader of the Labour Party in 1935. Becoming prime minister in 1941, he organized the mobilization of Australia's resources to meet the danger of Japanese invasion, and was confirmed in office in 1943.

curve in geometry, the ◊locus of a point moving according to specified conditions. The best-known of all curves is the circle, which is the locus of all points equidistant from a given point (the centre). Other common geometrical curves are the ellipse, parabola, and hyperbola, which are also produced when a cone is cut by a plane at different angles. Many curves have been invented for the solution of special problems in geometry and mechanics, for example, the cissoid (the inverse of a parabola) and the ◊cycloid.

Curwen /'kɜːwɪn/ John 1816–1880. British musician, who around 1840 established the *tonic sol-fa* system of music notation (originated in the 11th century by Guido d'Arezzo) in which the notes of a scale are named by syllables (doh, ray, me, fah, soh, lah, te, with the ◊key indicated) to simplify singing by sight.

Curzon /'kɜːzən/ George Nathaniel, 1st Marquess Curzon of Kedleston 1859–1925. British Conservative politician. Viceroy of India from 1899, he resigned in 1905 following a controversy with Kitchener, and was foreign secretary 1919–22. On Bonar Law's resignation in 1923 he was bitterly disappointed when passed over for the premiership in favour of Baldwin. He was the lover of the romantic novelist Elinor ◊Glyn.

Curzon Line Polish-Russian frontier proposed by the territorial commission of the Versailles conference in 1919, based on the eastward limit of areas with a predominantly Polish population. It acquired its name after Lord ◊Curzon suggested in 1920 that the Poles, who had invaded Russia, should retire to this line pending a Russo-Polish peace conference. The frontier established in 1945 in general follows the Curzon Line.

Cusack /'kjuːsæk/ Cyril 1910– . Irish actor, who joined the Abbey Theatre, Dublin, in 1932 and appeared in many of its productions including ◊Synge's *The Playboy of the Western World*. In Paris he won an award for his solo performance in ◊Beckett's *Krapp's Last Tape* and has played many roles as a member of the Royal Shakespeare Company and the National Theatre Company in Britain.

custard apple name give to several tropical fruits, produced by trees and shrubs belonging to the genus *Annona*, of the family Annonaceae. *Annona reticulata*, the 'bullock's heart', bears a large dark-brown fruit, containing a sweet reddish-yellow pulp. It is a native of the West Indies.

Curzon British politician Lord Curzon with Lady Curzon in India; he became viceroy in 1899. Foreign Secretary from 1919, he was disappointed in his ambitions for the premiership.

Custer /'kʌstə/ George Armstrong 1839–1876. American Civil War general. He subsequently campaigned against the Sioux from 1874, and was killed with his troops, by the forces of Sitting Bull, in the Battle of Little Big Horn, Montana: 'Custer's last stand', 25 Jun 1876.

custodianship in the UK, legal status granted to an adult for the care of children not one's own by birth, separate from adoption. In 1984 in the UK effect was given to the provision under the Children's Act of 1975 for 'custodianship' by step-parents, or foster-parents. It transfers many parental rights needed by a permanent guardian without affecting the legal status of the real parents.

Customs and Excise custom duties are taxes levied on certain imports, for example, tobacco, wine and spirits, perfumery and jewellery; excise duties are levied on certain goods produced (such as beer) and include VAT; or on licences to carry on certain trades (such as sale of wines and spirits) or other activities (theatrical entertainments, betting, and so on) within a country. In the UK both come under the Board of Customs and Excise, which also administrate VAT generally, although there are independent tax tribunals for appeal against the decisions of the commissioners; in the USA Excise duties are classed as Internal Revenue and Customs are controlled by the Customs Bureau.

Cuthbert /'kʌθbət/ died 687. Christian saint, who was a shepherd of Northumbria until after a vision he entered the monastery of Melrose, travelled widely as a missionary and because of

his miracles was known as the 'wonderworker of Britain'. He became prior of Lindisfarne, but retired in 676 to Farne Island. In 684 he became bishop of Hexham and later of Lindisfarne. His body was removed to Durham in 995.

cuticle in zoology, the horny noncellular surface layer of many ◊invertebrates such as insects; in botany, the waxy surface layer on those parts of plants that are exposed to the air, continuous except for the ◊stomata and ◊lenticels. All these different types of cuticle are secreted by the cells of the ◊epidermis. A cuticle serves to reduce water loss and, in arthropods, acts as an ◊exoskeleton.

Cuttack /kʌ'tæk/ Indian city and minor port in Orissa state, of which it was the capital until 1950. It is on the Mahanadi river delta. The old fort (Kataka) from which the town takes its name is in ruins. Population (1981) 327,500.

cuttle-fish small squid with an internal calcareous shell (cuttlebone). The *common cuttle Sepia officinalis* of the Atlantic and Mediterranean, is up to 30 cm/1 ft long, swims actively by means of the fins into which the sides of its oval, flattened body are expanded, and also jerks itself backwards by shooting a jet of water from its 'siphon'. It is capable of rapid changes of colour and pattern. The large head has conspicuous eyes, and the ten arms are provided with suckers. Two arms are very much elongated, and with them the cuttle seizes its prey. It has an 'ink-sac' from which a dark fluid can be discharged into the water, distracting predators from the cuttle itself. From this is obtained sepia, the dark brown pigment.

Cutty Sark most famous of the tea clippers that used to compete in the 19th century to bring their cargoes home first from China to Britain. The name, meaning 'short chemise', comes from that of the witch in Robert Burns's poem 'Tam O'Shanter'. The ship, built 1869, was permanently preserved in dry dock at Greenwich in 1957. The biennial Cutty Sark International Tall Ships Race commemorates it.

Cuvier /'kjuːvieɪ/ Georges, Baron Cuvier 1769–1832. French comparative anatomist. In 1798 he produced *Tableau élémentaire de l'histoire naturelle des animaux*, in which his scheme of classification is outlined. In 1799 he proved extinction (the phenomenon that some species have ceased to exist) by reconstructing extinct giant animals which he believed were destroyed in a series of giant deluges. These ideas are expressed in *Recherches sur les ossamens fossiles/Essay on the Theory of the Earth* 1817 (see also ◊catastrophism). He was professor of natural history in the Collège de France from 1799, and at the Jardin des Plantes from 1802; and at the Restoration in 1815 he was elected Chancellor of the University of Paris. Cuvier was the first to relate the structure of ◊fossil animals to that of their living allies. His great work, *Le Règne animal*, embodies a systematic survey of the animal kingdom.

Cuzco /'kuskəu/ city in S Peru, capital of Cuzco department, in the Andes, over 3,350 m/11,000 ft above sea level some 560 km/350 mi SE of Lima. Population (1981) 181,500.

Cuvier Georges Cuvier, the founder of paleontology and comparative anatomy, believed that the earth was periodically flooded, and explained fossils as remnants of life which had escaped the most recent deluge.

history Cuzco was the ancient capital of the ◊Inca empire, and has many Inca remains as well as a fine Renaissance cathedral and other relics of the early Spanish conquerors. Founded in the 11th century by the Incas, it was captured by ◊Pizarro in 1533. The university was founded in 1598. In the 1970s and 1980s the Inca irrigation canals and terracing nearby were being restored to increase cultivation.

Cwmbran /kum'braːn/ administrative headquarters of Gwent, Wales, NW of Newport, on the Afon Lywel, a tributary of Usk. Population (1981) 45,000. It was established in 1949, the name meaning 'Vale of the Crow', to provide a focus for new industrial growth in a depressed area, producing car components, nylon, and biscuits.

cyanide in chemistry, a salt of hydrocyanic acid (or hydrogen cyanide, HCN) produced when this is neutralized by alkalis, for example potassium cyanide, KCN. The principal cyanides are potassium, sodium, calcium, mercuric, gold and cupric. Certain cyanides are infamous as poisons.

Cybele /'sɪbəli/ in Phrygian mythology, an earth goddess, identified by the Greeks with ◊Rhea and honoured in Rome. The Corybantes (eunuch priests) celebrated her worship with orgiastic dances.

cybernetics science concerned with how systems organize, regulate, and reproduce themselves, and also how they evolve and learn. It was founded and named by Norbert Wiener (1894–1964), a US mathematician. The name is derived from the Greek 'steersman'. In the laboratory inanimate objects are created that behave like living systems. Uses range from the creation of electronic artificial limbs to the running of the fully automated factory where decision-making machines operate at up to managerial level.

cycad plant of the order Cycadales belonging to the Gymnosperms. Some have a superficial resemblance to palms, others to ferns. there are ten genera and about 80–100 species, natives of tropical and sub-tropical countries. The stems of many species yield an edible starchy substance resembling sago.

Cyclades /'sıklədi:z/ group of about 200 Greek islands (Greek *Kiklādhes*) in the Aegean Sea, lying between Greece and Turkey. They include Andros, Melos, Paros, Naxos, and Siros, on which is the capital Hermoupolis. Area 2,579 sq km/996 sq mi; population (1981) 88,500.

cyclamate derivative of cyclohexysulphamic acid, formerly used as an artificial sweetener. Its use in foods was banned in UK and USA from 1970, when studies showed that massive doses caused cancer in rats.

cyclamen genus of perennial plants of the Primulaceae, with heart-shaped leaves and the lobes of the corolla twisted and bent back. The flowers are usually white or pink, and several species are cultivated.

cyclic compounds organic chemicals that have rings of atoms in their molecules. They may be alicyclic, aromatic, or heterocylic. Alicyclic compounds have localized bonding, that is all the electrons are confined to their own particular ◊bond, in contrast to aromatic compounds, where certain electrons have free movement between different bonds in the ring. Alicyclic compounds include cyclopentare (C_5H_{10}) and cyclohexanol ($C_6H_{11}OH$). Their chemical properties are similar to their straight-chain (aliphatic) counterparts. ◊Aromatic compounds, because of their special structure, undergo entirely different chemical reactions. Heterocyclic compounds have a ring of ◊carbon atoms with one or more carbons replaced by another element, usually nitrogen, oxygen or sulphur. For instance pyridine is a six-membered ring with five carbons and one nitrogen (C_5H_5N). Furan is a five-membered ring containing one oxygen (C_4H_4O). Uracil contains two nitrogens in a six-membered ring ($C_4H_4N_2O_2$). These heterocyclic compounds may be aliphatic or aromatic in nature.

cycling riding a bicycle for sport, pleasure, or transport. The bicycle derived from the hobby-horse, which consisted of two wheels connected by a wooden beam carrying a saddle. Propulsion was attained by thrusting the feet against the ground. By the 1860s it had assumed a practical form; being driven from the front wheel by pedals and cranks. Structural improvements, including wire wheels, metal frames, and solid rubber tyres followed in the 1870s and 1880s, and an increase in the diameter of the front wheel to gain extra speed, gave rise to the graceful 'penny-farthing'. Further developments led to the chain drive 'safety' bicycle, equipped with pneumatic tyres (J B Dunlop, 1888), which exists virtually unchanged to the present day. Slight variants are the small-wheel Molton bicycle, and folding machines for carriage in a car boot.

Cycle racing is on oval artificial tracks: or on the road, for example, the French ◊Tour de France or the British Milk Race; or across country (cyclo-cross). There are several main types of races.

Stage races are run over gruelling terrain and can last anything from three to five days up to three and a half weeks, like the Tour de France, Tour of Italy, and Tour of Spain. *Criteriums* are fast, action-packed races around the closed streets of town or city centres. Each race lasts about an hour. *Road races* are run over a prescribed circuit, which the riders will lap several times. Such a race will normally cover a distance of approximately 100 miles. *Track racing* takes place on either a concrete or wooden banked circuit, either indoors or outdoors. In *time trialling* each rider races against the clock.

Tour de France first held 1903
1983 Laurent Fignon *(France)*
1984 Laurent Fignon *(France)*
1985 Bernard Hinault *(France)*
1986 Greg LeMond *(USA)*
1987 Stephen Roche *(Ireland)*
World Professional Road Race Champions first held at the Nuburgring *(West Germany)* 1927
1982 Giuseppe Saroni *(Italy)*
1983 Greg LeMond *(USA)*
1984 Claude Criquielon *(Belgium)*
1985 Joop Zoetemelk *(Holland)*
1986 Moreno Argentin *(Italy)*

---

cycloid in geometry, a curve resembling a series of arches traced out by a point on the circumference of a circle that rolls along a straight line. It has such applications as studying the motion of wheeled vehicles along roads and tracks.

cycloid

rolling circle   cycloid

cyclone an area of low atmospheric ◊pressure. Cyclones are formed by the mixture of cold, dry polar air with warm, moist equatorial air. These masses of air meet in temperate latitudes; the warm air rises over the cold, resulting in rain. Winds blow in towards the centre in an anti-clockwise direction in the northern hemisphere, clockwise in the southern hemisphere; the systems are characterized by variable weather, and are common over the British Isles. They bring rain or snow, winds up to gale force, low cloud, and sometimes fog. Tropical cyclones are a great danger to shipping (the tornado is a rapidly moving cyclone). In middle and high latitudes low-pressure systems are referred to as depressions or lows, rather than cyclones.

cyclops /'saɪ'kləupi:z/ in Greek mythology, one of a legendary nation of giants who lived in Sicily, had a single eye, and lived as shepherds; Odysseus encountered them in the *Odyssey*.

cyclotron type of particle ◊accelerator.

Cygnus large and prominent ◊constellation of the northern hemisphere, representing a swan.

Its brightest ◊star is first-magnitude Deneb. Beta Cygni (Albireo) is a well know yellow-and-blue ◊double star, plainly visible in small telescopes. The constellation contains two beautiful gas clouds: the North America ◊nebula, so named because its shape resembles the continent, and the Veil nebula, the remains of a ◊supernova that exploded about 50,000 years ago. Within the constellation is a powerful radio source, Cygnus A, apparently two distant galaxies in collision, and the x-ray source Cygnus X-1, thought to mark the position of a black hole.

cylinder in geometry, a tubular solid figure with a circular base, ordinarily understood to be a right cyclinder, that is, having its curved surface at right angles to the base. The volume of a cylinder is given by: $V = \pi r^2 h$ where V is the volume, r is the radius, and h is the height. Its total surface area A has the formula: $A = 2\pi r(h + r)$ where A is the total area and $2\pi r h$ is the curved surface area, and $2\pi r^2$ is the area of both ends.

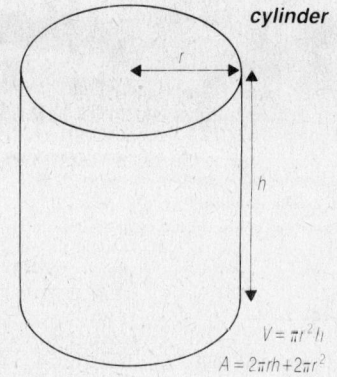

cylinder

$V = \pi r^2 h$
$A = 2\pi r h + 2\pi r^2$

cymbal musical instrument of percussion, consisting of a round metal plate with a drumstick, struck or clashed against another cymbal.

Cymru /'kʌmri/ Celtic name for ◊Wales.

Cynewulf /'kınıwʊlf/ lived early 8th century. Anglo-Saxon poet. He is thought to have been a Northumbrian monk, and ıs the undoubted author of 'Juliana' and part of the 'Christ' in the Exeter Book, and of the 'Fates of the Apostles' and 'Elene' in the Vercelli Book, in all of which he inserted his name in the form of runic acrostics.

cynic originally the name of a school of ancient Greek philosophy, founded at Athens about 400 BC by Antisthenes, a disciple of Socrates, who advocated a stern and simple morality, and a complete disregard of pleasure and comfort. His followers, led by ◊Diogenes (fl.340 BC), not only showed a contemptuous disregard for pleasure, but despised all human affection as a source of weakness. Their 'snarling contempt' for ordinary people earned them the name of Cynic, which in Greek means 'dog-like'.

cypress coniferous tree of the genera *Cupressus* and *Chamaecyparis* of the family Cupressaceae. There are about 20 species, which are evergreen trees or rarely shrubs, found mainly in the warm temperate regions of the northern hemisphere. They have minute scale-like leaves and small globular cones, made up of peltate woody scales, and exude an aromatic resin.

Cyprian, St /'sıprıən/ c. 210–258. Christian saint and martyr, one of the earliest Christian writers and bishop of Carthage about 249. He wrote a treatise on the unity of the Church.

Cyprus /'saıprəs/ island in the Mediterranean, off the S coast of Turkey.

government under the 1960 constitution, power is shared between Greek and Turkish Cypriots, but in 1963 the Turks ceased participating and in 1964 set up a separate community in N Cyprus, refusing to acknowledge the Greek government in the S.

The Greek Cypriot government claims to be the government of all Cyprus and is generally accepted as such, except by the Turkish community. There are, therefore, two republics, each with a president, council of ministers, legislature and judicial system. The 'Turkish Republic of Northern Cyprus' has its own representatives overseas.

Greek Cyprus has a president who appoints and heads a council of ministers, elected for five years by universal adult suffrage, and a single-chamber legislature, the 56-member house of representatives, also elected for five years.

The four main political parties are the Democratic Front (DIKO), the Progressive Party of the Working People (AKEL) the Democratic Rally (DISY), and the Socialist Party (EDEK).

Under the separate constitution adopted by Turkish Cyprus in 1985, there is a president, council of ministers and legislature similar to that in the south. Turkey is the only country to have recognized this government.

history for early history, see ◊Greece, ancient. The strategic position of Cyprus has long made it a coveted territory, and from the 15th century BC it was colonized by a succession of peoples from the mainland. In the 8th century it was within the ◊Assyrian empire, then the ◊Babylonian, ◊Egyptian, and ◊Persian. As part of Ptolemaic Egypt, it was seized by ◊Rome in 58 BC. From 395 AD it was ruled by ◊Byzantium, until taken in 1191 by England during the Third ◊Crusade. In 1489 it was annexed by ◊Venice, and became part of the ◊Ottoman empire in 1571. It came under British administration in 1878, and was annexed by Britain in 1914. In 1955 a guerrilla war against British rule was begun by Greek Cypriots seeking 'Enosis', or unification with Greece. The chief organization in this campaign was the National Organization of Cypriot Combatants (EOKA) and its political and military leaders were the Head of the Greek Orthodox Church in Cyprus, Archbishop Makarios, and General Grivas. See also◊Greece. In 1956 Makarios and other Enosis leaders were deported by the British government. After years of negotiation, Makarios was allowed to return to become president of a new, independent Greek-Turkish Cyprus, retaining British military and naval bases.

In 1963 the Turks withdrew from power-sharing and fighting began. The following year a UN peace-keeping force was set up to keep the two sides apart. After a prolonged period of mutual hostility, relations improved and talks were resumed, with the Turks arguing for a federal state and the Greeks wanting a unitary one.

In 1971 General Grivas returned to the island and began a guerrilla campaign against the Makarios government, which he believed had failed the Greek community. Three years later he died and his supporters were purged by Makarios, who was himself deposed in 1975 by Greek officers of the National Guard and an Enosis extemist, Nicos Sampson, who became president. Makarios fled to Britain.

At the request of the Turkish Cypriot leader, Turkey sent troops to the island, taking control of the N and dividing Cyprus along what became known as the 'Attila Line', cutting off about a third of the total territory. Later in 1975 Sampson resigned, the military regime which had appointed him collapsed, and Makarios returned. The Turkish Cypriots established an independent government for what they called the 'Turkish Federated State of Cyprus' (TFSC), with Rauf Denktaş as president.

In 1977 Makarios died and was succeeded by Spyros Kyprianou, who had been president of the house of representatives. In 1980 UN-sponsored peace talks were resumed. The Turkish Cypriots offered to hand back about 4 per cent of the 35 per cent of the territory they controlled and to resettle 40,000 of the 200,000 refugees who had fled to the N, but stalemate was reached on a constitutional settlement.

The Turks wanted equal status for the two communities, equal representation in goverment and firm links with Turkey. The Greeks, on the other hand, favoured an alternating presidency, strong central government and representation in the legislature on a proportional basis.

Between 1982 and 1985 several attempts by the Greek government in Athens and the UN to find a solution failed and the Turkish Republic of Northern Cyprus (TRNC), with Denktaş as president, was formally declared, but recognized only by Turkey.

In 1985 a meeting between Denktaş and Kyprianou failed to reach agreement and the UN secretary-general drew up proposals for a two-zone federal Cyprus, with a Greek president and a Turkish vice-president, but this was not found acceptable. Meanwhile, both Kyprianou and Denktaş had been re-elected.

The dispute between the communities remains unresolved but, because of its strategic importance in the Mediterranean, Cyprus is a problem which causes concern among leading nations.

Cyrano de Bergerac /'sırənəu də 'baːʒəræk/ Savinien de 1619–1655. French writer. Born in Paris, he joined a corps of guards at 19, and performed heroic feats which made him famous. He wrote plays and is the hero of a classic play by ◊Rostand, in which his notoriously long nose is used as a counterpoint to his chivalrous character.

Cyrenaic member of a school of ancient Greek philosophy founded c. 400 BC by ◊Aristippus of Cyrene. He regarded pleasure as the only absolutely worthwhile thing in life, but taught that self-control and intelligence were necessary to choose the best pleasures. See also ◊hedonism.

Cyrenaica /ˌsaırə'neııkə/ Area of E Libya, N Africa. The Greeks established colonies here in the 7th century BC which passed under the rule of Ptolemys in 322 BC, and in 174 BC became a Roman province. It was conquered by the Arabs in the 7th century, by Turkey in the 16th and by Italy in 1912, when it was developed as a colony which became a province of the new kingdom of Libya from 1951 until it was split into a number of smaller divisions under the constitutional reorganization of 1963. Modern cities, rapidly growing following discoveries of oil, include Benghazi, Derna and Tobruk, and there are magnificent ruins at Cyrene, and Apollonia.

Cyril of Alexandria, Saint /'sırəl/ 376–444. Archbishop of Alexandria from 412, persecutor of Jews and other non-Christians, and hated for his suspected share in the death of ◊Hypatia the woman philosopher.

Cyrus /'saırəs/ the Great died 529 BC. Founder of the Persian Empire. King of Persia, originally as vassal to the ◊Medes, whose empire he overthrew in 550 BC, he captured ◊Croesus in 546 BC, and conquered all Asia Minor, adding Babylonia (including Syria and Palestine) to his empire in 539 BC. The exiled Jews were allowed to return to Jersualem. He died fighting in Afghanistan.

cystic fibrosis genetic disorder of the exocrine glands causing thickening of the mucus throughout the body, and resultant blockage, e.g. in the lungs, and in the pancreatic duct, where it prevents enzymes for digestion being formed. Although as yet incurable, it can be treated by diet and antibiotics. In 1985 the identification of the small region of the chromosomes in which a defect occurs brought closer the prospect of a cure.

cystitis inflammation of the bladder, usually caused by bacterial infection, and resulting in frequent and painful urination.

cytochrome a type of protein, responsible for part of the process of ◊respiration by which food molecules are broken down in ◊aerobic organisms. The cytochromes make up a sequence called the electron transport chain, which uses energized electrons to reduce molecular oxygen (O_2) to oxygen ions (O^-). These then combine with hydrogen ions (H^+) to form water (H_2O), the end product of aerobic respiration. As electrons are passed from one cytochrome to another energy is released and used to make ◊ATP.

cytokin a type of ◊plant hormone which stimulates cell division. Cytokin affects several different aspects of plant growth and development, but only if ◊auxin is also present. It may delay the process of senescence, break the dormancy of certain seeds and buds, and induce flowering.

cytology the study of ◊cells, especially in relation to their functions. Major advances have been made possible in this field by the development of ◊electron microscopes.

Cyprus

Mediterranean island, divided between the southern Republic of Cyprus (Greek *Kypriaki Dimokratia*), and the Turkish Republic of Northern Cyprus (Turkish *Kibris Cumhuriyeti*)

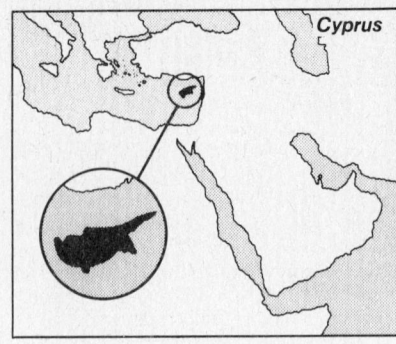
Cyprus

AREA 9,251 sq km/3,572 sq mi, 40% in Turkish hands

CAPITAL Nicosia (divided between the Greeks and Turks)

TOWNS ports Paphos, Limassol, and Larnaca (Greek); and Morphou, and ports Kyrenia and Famagusta (Turkish)

PHYSICAL central plain between two E–W mountain ranges

FEATURES Attila Line; two British military enclaves on the S coast at Episkopi (includes Royal Air Force Akrotiri) and Dhekelia; there is also an outpost of British Government Communications Headquarters in the mountains

HEADS OF STATE AND OF GOVERNMENT Spyros Kyprianou (Greek) from 1977, Rauf Denktaş (Turkish) from 1976

GOVERNMENT republic

EXPORTS citrus, grapes, Cyprus sherry, potatoes; copper, pyrites

CURRENCY Cyprus pound (0.78 = £1 Sept 1987)

POPULATION (1985) 665,600 (Greek Cypriot 80%, Turkish Cypriot 20%); annual growth rate 1.2%

LANGUAGE Greek and Turkish (official); English

RELIGION Greek Orthodox, Sunni Muslim

LITERACY 99% (1984)

GNP $2.11 bn (1983); $3,986 per head of population

CHRONOLOGY

1955 Guerrilla campaign for enosis, or union with Greece, started by Archbishop Makarios and Gen Grivas.

1956 Makarios and enosis leaders deported.

1959 Compromise agreed and Makarios returned to be elected president of an independent Greek-Turkish Cyprus.

1960 Full independence achieved, with Britain retaining its military bases.

1963 Turks set up their own government in N Cyprus. Fighting broke out between the two communities.

1964 UN peacekeeping force installed.

1971 Grivas returned to start a guerrilla war against the Makarios government.

1974 Grivas died.

1975 A military coup deposed Makarios, who fled to Britain. Nicos Sampson appointed president. Turkish army sent to N Cyprus to confirm the Turkish Cypriots' control. The military regime in S Cyprus collapsed and Makarios returned. N Cyprus declared itself the Turkish Federated State of Cyprus (TFSC), with Rauf Denktaş as president.

1977 Makarios died and was succeeded by Spyros Kyprianou.

1983 An independent Turkish Republic of Northern Cyprus (TRNC) was proclaimed but was recognized only by Turkey.

1984 UN peace proposals rejected.

1985 Summit meeting between Kyprianou and Denktaş failed to reach agreement.

---

cytoplasm in cells with a ◊nucleus (◊eukaryotic cells) the part of the cell outside the nucleus. Strictly speaking, this includes all the ◊organelles (mitochondria, chloroplasts etc.) but often the word cytoplasm is just used to mean the jelly-like matter in which the organelles are embedded (correctly termed the cytosol). In many cells, the cytoplasm is made up of two parts, the ◊ectoplasm or plasmagel, a dense gelatinous outer layer concerned with cell movement, and the endoplasm or plasmasol, a more fluid inner part where most of the organelles are found.

cytoskeleton in a living ◊cell, a matrix of protein filaments and tubules that occurs within the cytosol (the liquid part of the ◊cytoplasm). It gives the cell a definite shape, transports vital substances around the cell, and may also be involved in cell movement.

cytotoxic drug drug that kills or damages cells. Although used specifically to kill the multiplying cells of a tumour, or as an ◊immunosuppressive, it may damage healthy cells as well and therefore have dangerous side-effects.

czar alternative form of tsar, an emperor of Russia.

Czechoslovakia /ˌtʃekəʊsləˈvækiə/ landlocked country in E central Europe, bounded to the NE by Poland, E by the USSR, S by Hungary and Austria, W by West Germany, and NW by East Germany.

government since 1968 Czechoslovakia has been a federation of two, Czech and Slovak, national republics. The supreme legislative body in the CSR is the federal assembly *Federalni Shromazdeni*, composed of two chambers of equal rights, the 200-deputy chamber of the people and the 150-deputy chamber of nations. The first is elected for five-year terms and has a 2:1 Czech majority. The second is divided equally between members chosen by each of the Czech and Slovak National Councils.

The federal assembly elects, for a five-year term, the president of the CSR, who appoints a prime minister and federal government accountable to the federal assembly. The federal government has authority in defence and foreign affairs. In other areas, power is shared with the national councils elected by the national republics.

The controlling force in the CSR is the Communist Party of Czechoslovakia (CCP). It works with the Czechoslovak Socialist Party, Czechoslovak People's Party (both based in the Czech National Republic), Slovak Freedom Party and Slovak Revival Party (both based in the Slovak National Republic) in the National Front, which, headed by the CCP, puts up agreed single lists of candidates in state elections.

history Czechoslovakia came into existence as an independent republic in 1918, after the break-up of the ◊Austro-Hungarian empire at the end of World War I It consisted originally of the Bohemian crownlands (◊Bohemia, ◊Moravia, and part of ◊Silesia) and ◊Slovakia, the area of Hungary inhabited by Slavonic peoples; to which was added as a trust part of Ruthenia when the Allies and Associated Powers recognized the new republic under the treaty of St Germain-en-Laye. Besides the Czech and Slovak peoples, the country included substantial minorities of German origin, long settled in the N, and of Hungarian (or Magyar) origin in the S. But despite the problems of welding into a nation such a mixed group of people, until the troubled 1930s Czechoslovakia made considerable political and economic progress.

The rise to power of ◊Hitler in Germany brought a revival of opposition among the German-speaking population, and irredentism among the Magyar speakers. In addition, the Slovakian clerical party demanded autonomy for Slovakia. These difficulties led on to crisis in 1938 and the ◊Munich agreement between Britain, France, Germany, and Italy, made without consultation with or the consent of Czechoslovakia, which detached from Czechoslovakia the Sudetenland and gave it to Germany. Six months later Hitler occupied all Czechoslovakia. A government-in-exile was established in London under Eduard ◊Benes 3 until the liberation in 1945 by Russian and US troops. In the same year some 2,000,000 Sudeten Germans were expelled, and Czech Ruthenia was transferred to the Ukraine republic of the USSR. Elections in 1946 gave the Left a slight majority and in Feb 1948 the communists seized power, winning an electoral victory in May. The country was divided into 19 and then, in 1960, into ten regions plus Prague and Bratislava.

There was a Stalinist regime during the 1950s, under Presidents Gottwald (1948–53), Zapotocky (1953–57) and Novotný (1957–68). Pressure from students and intellectuals brought about policy changes from 1965, and in 1968, following Novotný's replacement as CCP leader by Alexander ◊Dubček and as president by war hero General Ludvík Svoboda (1895–1979) and the appointment of Oldřich Černik as prime minister, a liberalization programme ('Socialist Democratic Revolution') began, promising the return of freedom of assembly, speech and movement, and the imposition of restrictions on the secret police.

Czechoslovakia

SOCIALIST REPUBLIC OF (*Československá Socialistická Republika*)

Czechoslovakia

AREA 127,895 sq km/49,381 sq mi
CAPITAL Prague
TOWNS Brno, Bratislava, Ostrava
PHYSICAL Carpathian Mountains, rivers Morava, Labe (Elbe), Vltava (Moldau); hills and plateau; Danube plain in S
FEATURES divided by valley of the Morava into the W densely populated area with good communications, and the E sparsely populated, comparatively little-developed Slovak area
HEAD OF STATE Milos Jakes from 1987
HEAD OF GOVERNMENT Lubomir Strougal from 1970
GOVERNMENT communist
EXPORTS machinery, timber, ceramics, glass, textiles
CURRENCY koruna (8.9 commercial rate, 15.05 tourist rate = £1 Sept 1987)
POPULATION (1985) 15,502,000 (60% Czech, 30% Slovak, with Hungarian, Polish, German, Russian, and other minorities); annual growth rate 0.2%
LANGUAGE Czech and Slovak (official)
RELIGION Roman Catholic with Protestant minority
LITERACY 99% (1981)
GNP $85.8 bn (1982); $5,800 per head of population

CHRONOLOGY
1945 Liberation of Czechoslovakia.
1948 Communists assumed power in coup and new constitution framed.
1968 Prague Spring experiment with liberalization ended by Soviet invasion.
1969 Czechoslovakia became a federal state. Husak elected Communist Party leader.
1977 Emergence and suppression of Charter 77 human-rights movement.
1985–86 Criticism of Husak rule by new Soviet leadership.
1987 Following Soviet criticism, Husak resigned as Communist party leader; replaced by Milos Jakes.

Despite assurances that Czechoslovakia would remain within the Warsaw Pact, the USSR viewed these events with suspicion and in Aug 1968 sent 600,000 troops from Warsaw Pact countries to restore the orthodox line. After the invasion a purge of liberals began in the CCP, with Gustáv ◊Husák (a Slovak Brezhnevite) replacing Dubček as CCP leader in 1969 and Lubomír Štrougal (a Czech) becoming prime minister in 1970. General Svoboda remained as president until 1975 and negotiated the Soviet withdrawal.

In 1968 a new constitution transformed unitary Czechoslovakia into a federal state. In 1973 an amnesty was extended to some of the 40,000 who had fled after the 1968 invasion, signalling a slackening of repression. In 1977, following the signature of a human rights manifesto ('Charter 77') by over 700 intellectuals and former party officials in response to the 1975 ◊Helsinki Agreements, a new crackdown commenced. The arrest of dissidents continued during the events of 1981 in ◊Poland. Czechoslovakia under Dr Husák has been a loyal ally of the USSR. In recent years, however, following the accession of Mikhail ◊Gorbachev to the Soviet leadership in 1985, pressure for economic and administrative reform has grown. Dr Husák was replaced as CCP secretary (leader) in Dec 1987 by Mr Milos Jakes (1922–   ).

Częstochowa /ˌtʃenstəˈxəʊvə/ industrial town in Poland, 193 km/120 mi SW of Warsaw, making iron goods, chemicals, paper, and cement. It is a railway junction. Population (1981) 237,500.

D fourth letter of the alphabet, it corresponds to the Semitic *daleth* and the Greek *delta*.
In the Latin numeral system D stands for 500. In UK currency d was the sign for a penny (Latin *denarius*), until decimalization of the currency in 1971.

dab marine flatfish *Limanda limanda* of the plaice family found in the NE Atlantic. Light brown or grey, with dark brown spots and rough-scaled on the coloured side, it grows to about 25 cm/10 in.

Dacca /'dækə/ former spelling (until 1984) of ◊Dhaka, capital of Bangladesh.

dace freshwater fish *Leuciscus leuciscus* of the carp family. Common in England, and also in Europe, it is silvery and reaches a length of 30 cm/1ft.

Dachau /'dæxau/ town in Bavaria, West Germany; site of a World War II ◊concentration camp.

dachshund small hound of German origin (German 'badger-dog') bred originally for badger digging. It is long in body and short legged. Several varieties are bred, standard size (up to 10 kg/22 lb) and miniature (5 kg/11 lb or less), and long-haired, smooth-haired and wire-haired.

dacoit member of an armed gang of robbers in India; also used in Burma.

Dadaism literary and artistic movement developed between 1915 and 1922, born of reaction and disillusion during World War I. Dadaism appeared almost simultaneously in New York, with Marcel Duchamp's exhibition of 'ready-made' sculptures, and in Zürich. The Romanian poet Tzara with German writers Ball and Hillsenbeck founded the 'Cabaret Voltaire' in 1916, where works by Jean ◊Arp, Max ◊Ernst, ◊Klee, ◊Modigliani and ◊Picasso were exhibited. The movement aimed to question established artistic rules and values by provoking outrage. Dadaism was an early phase in the development of ◊Surrealism.

Dadd /dæd/ Richard 1817–1886. British artist. In 1844 he murdered his father and was confined as insane, but continued to paint haunting, detailed pictures. His figures have a great intensity, and his choice of colour and subject matter is vivid and at times disturbing, as in *The Fairy Feller's Master-Stroke*.

daddy-long-legs popular name for a ◊cranefly.

Dadra and Nagar Haveli /də'drɑː,'nʌgə ɹ'veli/ since 1961 a Union Territory of West India; capital Silvassa; population (1981) 103,700. Formerly part of ◊Daman.

Daedalus /'diːdələs/ in Greek mythology, an Athenian craftsman supposed to have constructed for King Minos the labyrinth in which the ◊Minotaur was imprisoned. He fled from Crete with his son ◊Icarus using wings made from feathers fastened with wax; Icarus flew too near the sun, and fell into the Aegean and was drowned.

Daedalus in space travel, a futuristic project put forward by the British Interplanetary Society to send a ◊robot probe to nearby stars. The probe, 20 times the size of the Saturn V moon rocket, would be propelled by thermo-nuclear fusion, or in effect a series of mini ◊H-bomb explosions. Interstellar cruise speed would be about 40,000 km/25,000 mi per second.

daffodil name given to several species of plants of the genus *Narcissus*, distinguished by their trumpet-shaped corollas. The common daffodil of northern Europe *Narcissus pseudonarcissus*, has large yellow flowers, and grows from a large bulb. There are numerous cultivated forms.

Dagestan /,dægɪ'stɑːn/ republic of western USSR, situated in the extreme east of the ◊Caucasus, bordering the Caspian Sea. Capital Makhachkala; area 50,300 sq km/14,700 sq mi; population (1982) 1,700,000. It is mountainous, with deep valleys, and its numerous ethnic groups speak a variety of distinct languages. Annexed from Iran in 1723, which strongly resisted Russian conquest (see ◊Shamyl), it became an autonomous republic in 1921.

Daglish /'dæglɪʃ/ Eric Fitch 1892–1966. British artist and author. He wrote a number of natural history books, and illustrated both these and classics by Izaac Walton, Thoreau, Gilbert White, and W H Hudson with exquisite wood engravings.

Daguerre /dæ'geə/ Louis Jacques Mande 1787–1851. French pioneer of photography. Together with Niepce, he is credited with the invention of photography (though others were reaching the same point simultaneously). He invented the ◊daguerreotype in 1838, a one-off image process, superseded ten years later by Fox ◊Talbot's negative/positive process.

Daguerre Frenchman Louis Daguerre discovered how to produce a one-off photographic image as a result of accidentally spilt iodine on some of his silvered plates.

daguerreotype a one-off photographic image taken by using mercury vapour and iodine sensitized silvered plates; discovered by ◊Daguerre in 1838.

Dahl /dɑːl/ Roald 1916– . British writer, celebrated for short stories with a twist, for example, *Tales of the Unexpected* 1979; and for children's books including *Charlie and the Chocolate Factory* 1964.

dahlia genus of plants of the family Compositae, named after Andrew Dahl, a

Swedish botanist. There are 20 species of the genus, which is a native of Mexico, but was introduced to England in 1789. There are many cultivated forms.

Dahomey /dəˈhəʊmi/ the former name (until 1975) of the People's Republic of ◊Benin.

Dahrendorf /ˈdɑːrəndɔːf/ Ralf (Gustav) 1929– . German sociologist, director of the London School of Economics from 1974–84. His works include *Life Chances* 1980, which sees the aim of society as the improvement of the range of opportunities open to the individual.

Dáil Eireann /ˈdɔɪl ˈeərən/ the lower house of the legislature of Eire. It consists of 148 members elected by adult suffrage on a basis of proportional representation.

Daimler /ˈdeɪmlə/ Gottlieb 1834–1900. German engineer who pioneered the modern motor car. Born in Württemberg, he had engineering experience at the Whitworth works, Manchester, before joining in 1872 N A Otto of Cologne in the production of an internal combustion gas engine. In 1886 he produced his first motor vehicle and a motor-bicycle. He later joined forces with Karl ◊Benz and was one of the pioneers of the high-speed 4-stroke petrol engine.

Dairen /ˌdaɪˈren/ former name for the Chinese port of ◊Lüda.

dairying the business of producing and handling ◊milk and milk products. In England and Wales, over 70 per cent of the milk produced is consumed in its liquid form, consequently dairying is dominated by the needs of the home liquid milk market, whereas countries such as New Zealand rely on easily transportable milk products such as butter, cheese, condensed and dried milk. It is now usual for dairy farms to concentrate on the production of milk and for factories to take over the handling, processing, and distribution of milk as well as the manufacture of dairy products. In Britain the Milk Marketing Board (1933), to which all producers must sell their milk, forms a connecting link between farms and factories. Research is carried out at the National Institute for Research in Dairying at Reading, and the Hannah Dairy Research Institute in Scotland.

daisy genus *Bellis* of hardy perennials, family ◊Compositae, for example *common daisy Bellis perennis*, an abundant wild flower with a single white or pink flower head rising from a rosette of leaves. It opens during daylight, hence its name, a corruption of 'day's eye'.

daisybush genus of Australian and New Zealand shrubs *Olearia*, family ◊Compositae, with flowers like daisies, and felted or holly-like leaves.

Dakar /ˈdækɑː/ capital and chief port (with artificial harbour) of Senegal; population (1979) 978,560. It is an industrial centre, and there is a university (1957). Founded in 1862, it was formerly the seat of government of ◊French West Africa. In Jul 1940 an unsuccessful naval action was undertaken by British and Free French forces to seize Dakar as an Allied base.

Dakota /dəˈkəʊtə/ see ◊North Dakota and ◊South Dakota.

Daladier /ˌdæˈlædˈjeɪ/ Edouard 1884–1970. French Radical politician. As prime minister

Apr 1938–Mar 1940, he was largely responsible both for the Munich Agreement and France's declaration of war on Germany. Arrested on the fall of France (see ◊Riom), he was a prisoner in Germany 1943–45. He was re-elected to the Chamber 1946–58.

Dalai Lama /ˈdælaɪ ˈlɑːmə/ 14th Incarnation 1935– . Spiritual and temporal head of the Tibetan State until 1959. Enthroned in 1940, he temporarily fled 1950–51 when the Chinese overran Tibet, and in Mar 1959 made a dramatic escape from Lhasa to India, following a local uprising against Chinese rule. He then settled at Dharmsala, in the Punjab. His people continued to demand his return and the Chinese made unavailing overtures to him in 1980. See ◊Lamaism and also ◊Panchen Lama.

Dalcroze Emile Jaques see ◊Jaques-Dalcroze, Emile.

Dale /deɪl/ Henry Hallett 1875–1968. British physiologist, who in 1936 shared a Nobel prize with Otto Loewi for work on the chemical transmission of nervous effects. Order of Merit in 1944.

D'Alembert see ◊Alembert.

Dalgarno /dælˈgɑːnəʊ/ George 1626–1687. Scottish schoolmaster and inventor of the first deaf-and-dumb alphabet in 1680.

Dalhousie /dælˈhaʊzi/ James Andrew Broun Ramsay, 1st Marquess and 10th Earl of Dalhousie 1812–1860. British administrator. He worked with Gladstone at the board of trade, succeeding him as president from 1845 until his appointment as governor-general of India 1847. For his successful handling of the second Sikh War he received a marquessate; he annexed the Punjab 1849 and, after the Burmese War (see ◊Burma), Lower Burma 1853. He reformed the Indian army and civil service and furthered social and economic progress. He retired 1856.

Dali /ˈdɑːli/ Salvador 1904– . Spanish artist. Born near Barcelona, he came under the influence of the Italian ◊Futurists, but in 1929 joined the ◊Surrealists. A student of ◊Freud, he claimed that his work could be appreciated only by the unconscious and used photographic clarity to depict contorted landscapes and figures which seem both familiar and disconcertingly nightmarish, as in his limp pocket watches or giant ants. His later work shows a reversion to classicism. He collaborated with Luis ◊Buñuel in surrealist films, and has designed ballet costumes and scenery. *Secret Life of Salvador Dali* and *Diary of a Genius* 1966 are autobiographical.

Dalian /ˌdɑːliˈæn/ one of the two cities comprising the Chinese port of ◊Lüda.

Dallapiccola /ˌdæləˈpɪkələ/ Luigi 1904–1975. Italian composer. In his early years he was a ◊neoclassicist in the manner of Stravinsky, but he soon turned to ◊serialism, which he adapted to his own style. His works include the operas *Il Prigioniero/The Prisoner* 1949 and *Ulisse/Ulysses* 1968, as well as many vocal and instrumental compositions.

Dallas /ˈdæləs/ commercial city in Texas, USA; population (1980) 904,000. Its industries include banking, insurance, oil, aviation, aerospace, electronics, machinery, clothing, food, printing, and publishing. It is a cultural

centre, with a symphony orchestra, opera, ballet, and theatre. Dallas–Fort Worth Regional Airport (opened 1973) is one of the world's largest, and there is an annual Texas State Fair.
history founded as a trading post in 1844, it developed as the focus of a cotton area, and then as a mineral and oil-producing centre, with banking and insurance operations. After World War II growth increased rapidly. There is a Memorial to John F ◊Kennedy, who was assassinated there in 1963.

Dalmatia /dælˈmeɪʃə/ region of Croatia, Yugoslavia. The capital is Split. It lies along the eastern shore of the Adriatic and includes a number of islands. The interior is mountainous. Important products are wine, olives, and fish. Notable towns in addition to the capital are Zadar, Sibenik, and Dubrovnik.
history Dalmatia became Austrian in 1815, and by the treaty of Rapallo, 1920, became part of the kingdom of the Serbs, Croats, and Slovenes (Yugoslavia from 1931), except for the town of Zadar (Zara), and the island of Lastovo (Lagosta), which, with neighbouring islets, were given to Italy until transferred to Yugoslavia in 1947. Dalmatia was made a region of Croatia in 1949.

dalmatian breed of dog, the 'spotted' or 'plum-pudding' dog, formerly used as a coach dog; about 60 cm/2 ft tall. The spots on the white background can be black or liver-brown.

dalmatic the outer liturgical vestment of the deacon in the Roman Catholic Church; a mantle worn at Mass and in solemn processions.

Dalton /ˈdɔːltən/ Hugh, Baron Dalton 1887–1962. British economist and Labour politician. Chancellor of the Exchequer in 1945, he resigned in 1947 following an indiscreet disclosure to a Lobby correspondent before a budget speech. His name is associated with the 2½ per cent Irredeemable Treasury Stock known as Daltons, introduced in 1946 and bought by many savers, but which rapidly depreciated in value. In 1960 he was created a life peer.

Dalton /ˈdɔːltən/ John 1776–1844. British chemist, the first to propose the existence of ◊atoms, which he considered to be the smallest parts of matter. From experiments with gases he noted that the proportions of two components combining to form another were always consistent. From this he suggested that if substances combine in simple numerical ratios then the macroscopic weight proportions represent the relative atomic masses of those substances. Extending the range of compounds, he produced the first list of relative atomic masses, *Absorption of Gases* 1805. He was also the first scientist to note and record colour-blindness.

Dalton: atomic weights

	1803	1808	modern
hydrogen	1	1	1.008
azote (nitrogen)	4.2	5	14.007
carbon	4.3	5	12.011
oxygen	5.5	7	15.999
phosphorous	7.2	9	30.974
sulphur	14.4	13	32.064

Dalton The Labour Chancellor of the Exchequer, Hugh Dalton oversaw nationalization of the Bank of England, but was forced to resign in 1947 following a disclosure to a lobby correspondent before a budget speech.

Daly /'deɪli/ Augustin 1838–1899. American theatre manager. He began as a drama critic and playwright before building his own theatre in New York in 1879 and another, Daly's, in Leicester Square, London (1893–1937).

Dalziel /'dælziel/ **family** British wood-engravers. George (1815–1902), Edward (1817–1905), John (1822–60), and Thomas Bolton (1823–1906), were all sons of Alexander Dalziel of Wooler, Northumberland. George went to London in 1835 and was joined in due course by his brothers. They produced a large number of illustrations for the classics and magazines.

dam a structure built to hold back water, so as to prevent flooding, provide water for ◊irrigation and storage, and to provide ◊hydroelectric power. All the world's biggest dams are of the earth-and-rock-fill type, also called *embankment dams*. Such dams are generally built on broad valley sites. Deep, narrow gorges, however, dictate a *concrete dam*, the enormous strength of reinforced ◊concrete being able to withstand the enormous water pressures involved. Many concrete dams are triangular in cross-section, with their vertical face pointing upstream. Their sheer weight holds them in position, and they are called gravity dams. Some concrete dams, however, are more slightly built in the shape of an arch, with the curve facing upstream. The *arch dam* derives its strength from the arch shape, just as an arch bridge does. A valuable development in arid regions, as in parts of Brazil, is the *underground dam*, where water is stored among sand and stones on a solid rock base, with a wall

to ground level, so avoiding rapid evaporation. Major dams include: *Rogun* (USSR), the world's highest at 325 m/1,067 ft; *New Cornelia Tailings* (USA), the world's biggest in volume, 209 million m³; *Owen Falls* (Uganda), the world's largest reservoir capacity, 204.8 billion m³; and *Itaipu* (Brazil/Paraguay), the world's most powerful, 12,700 megawatts.

dam

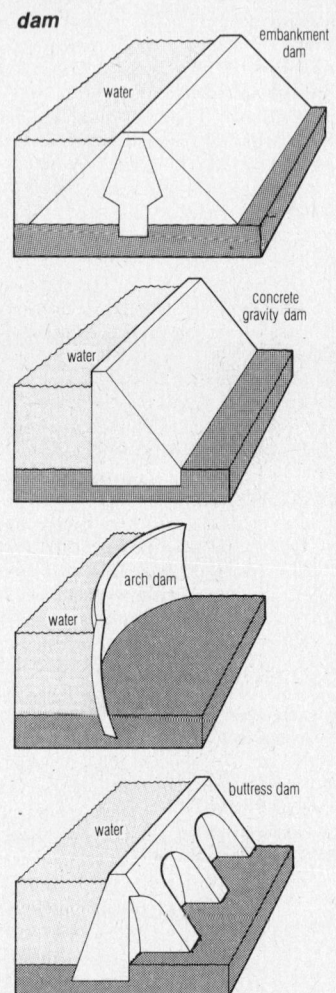

Daman /də'mɑːn/ or *Damão* port on west coast of India, some 160 km/100 mi north of Bombay. A Portuguese settlement (area 386 sq km/149 sq mi) from the 16th century, it was annexed by India in 1961 and incorporated in the Union Territory of ◊Goa, Daman and ◊Diu.

Damaraland /də'mɑːrəlænd/ central region of Namibia, home of the nomadic Bantu-speaking ◊Hereros.

Damascus /də'mæskəs/ capital of Syria; population (1981) 1,251,028, on the river Barada, south east of Beirut. It is situated on the edge of a highly fertile area, and has road, rail and air links.

history said to be the oldest still inhabited city of the world, Damascus was an ancient city even in Old Testament times. The Assyrians destroyed

it in about 733 BC. In 332 BC it fell to one of the generals of ◊Alexander the Great; in 63 BC it came under Roman rule. In 635 AD it was taken by the Arabs, and has since been captured many times, by Egyptians, Mongolians, and Turks. In 1918, during World War I it was taken from the Turks by the British with Arab aid, and in 1920 became the capital of French-mandated Syria. The 'street which is called straight' is associated with St ◊Paul, who was converted while on the road to Damascus. The tomb of ◊Saladin is here. The most notable of the old buildings is the Great Mosque, completed as a Christian church in the 5th century. The fortress dates from 1219. A Syrian university was founded in 1924.

damask reversible textiles: linen, cotton, and silk, with a figured pattern. The name derives from the city of ◊Damascus.

Dame title of a woman who has been awarded the Order of the British Empire. Legal title of the wife (or widow) of a ◊knight or ◊baronet, placed before her name.

Damien, Father /,dæmi'æn/ 1840–1889. Belgian missionary, original name Joseph de ◊Veuster.

Damietta /,dæmi'etə/ English name for the Egyptian port of ◊Dumyat.

Damocles /'dæməkliːz/ (fl. 4th century BC) a courtier of the elder Dionysius, ruler of Syracuse. Having extolled the happiness of his sovereign, Damocles was invited by him to a great feast, and in the midst of his enjoyment beheld above his head a sword suspended by a single hair. He recognized this as a symbol of the insecurity of the great.

Damodar /'dæmədɑː/ Indian river flowing 560 km/350 mi from Chota Nagpur plateau in Bihar, through Bihar and West Bengal states to join the ◊Hooghli 40 km/25 mi SW of Calcutta. The Damodar Valley is an industrial centre with a hydroelectric project, combined with irrigation works.

damper incorrectly called shock absorber, a device for reducing the vibration of, say, a spring. Dampers are used in conjunction with coil springs in most car suspension systems. They are usually of the telescopic type, consisting of a piston in an oil-filled cylinder. The resistance to movement of the piston through the oil creates the damping effect.

Dampier /'dæmpiə/ William 1652–1715. English explorer, born in Somerset, who went to sea in 1668. He led a life of buccaneering adventure, circumnavigated the globe, and published his *New Voyage Round the World* in 1697. In 1699 he was sent by the government on a voyage to Australia and New Guinea, and again circled the world. He accomplished a third circumnavigation 1703–07, and on his final voyage 1708–11 rescued Alexander ◊Selkirk, the original of Robinson Crusoe, from Juan Fernandez. Named after him are: *Dampier*, a newly developed port on the remote north coast of Western Australia, where salt from sea water is exported to Japan's soda industry; *Dampier Archipelago* in the Indian Ocean, NW of the coast of Western Australia, of which Enderby Island is the largest (area 54 sq km/21 sq mi; and

Mount Dampier, a peak of the Southern Alps in South Island, New Zealand (3,440 m/11,287ft).

damselfly type of ◊dragonfly. Damselflies differ from 'true' dragonflies in having two pairs of similar wings which are generally folded back over the body when at rest, having smaller eyes and very slender bodies.

damson type of small plum *Prunus damascena*, distinguished by its small, oval fruit, which is dark purple or blue to black in colour.

Dana /'deɪnə/ Richard Henry 1815–1882. American author. Son of Richard Henry Dana, poet and essayist, he went to sea and worked his passage round Cape Horn to California and back, writing an account in *Two Years before the Mast* 1840.

Danaë /'dæneɪiː/ in Greek mythology, daughter of Acrisius, king of Argos. He shut her up in a brazen tower because of a prophecy that her son would kill his grandfather. Zeus became enamoured of her and descended in a shower of gold, and by him she became the mother of ◊Perseus.

Da Nang /'dɑː 'næŋ/ port and second city (formerly Tourane) of South Vietnam, 80 km/50 mi SE of Hué; population (1975) 500,000. Following the reunion of N and S Vietnam, the major part of the population was dispersed in 1976 to rural areas. An American base in the ◊Vietnam War, it is now used by the USSR.

Danby /'dænbi/ Thomas Osborne, Earl of Danby 1631–1712. British Tory politician. He entered Parliament in 1665, acted 1673–78 as Charles II's chief minister, and in 1674 was created earl of Danby. He endeavoured to strengthen the crown, although his foreign policy was hostile to France. In 1678 he was impeached and sent to the Tower until 1684. In 1688 he signed the invitation to William of Orange that led to the Revolution; he was again chief minister 1690–95, and in 1694 was created duke of Leeds.

dance rhythmic movement of the body, usually performed in time to music. Its primary purpose may be religious, magical, martial, social or artistic – the last two being characteristic of contemporary societies. European dance history is relatively recent in comparison to that of the rest of the world. The first Indian book on dancing, the 'Natya Sastra', existed a thousand years before its European counterpart. The remarkable *bugaku* dances of Japan were being performed, with *gaguku* orchestra accompaniment, from around the 7th century. When the Peking (Beijing) Opera dancers first astonished Western audiences during the 1950s, they were representatives of a tradition stretching back to 740, the year in which Emperor Ming Huang established the renowned Pear garden academy. The first comparable European institution, *L'Académie royale de dance*, was founded by Louis XIV in 1661.

Social dances have always tended to rise upward through the social scale, for example, the medieval court dances derived from peasant country dances. One form of dance tends to typify a whole period, thus the galliard represents the 16th century, the minuet the 18th, the waltz the 19th, and the quickstep the 20th. In this century new dances have tended to reach Britain from the Americas, the pioneers in popularizing them being Vernon and Irene Castle and the ◊Astaires. The nine dances of the modern World Championships in ◊ballroom dancing are the standard four (◊waltz, ◊foxtrot, ◊tango and quick-step), the Latin-American styles (samba, rumba, cha-cha-cha, and paso doble), and the Viennese waltz. A British development since the 1930s, which has spread to some extent abroad, is 'formation' dancing in which each team (usually eight couples) performs a series of ballroom steps in strict coordination. Popular dance crazes, usually American imports, have included the jitterbug in the 1940s, ◊jive in the 1950s, the twist in the 1960s, 'disco dancing' in the 1970s, and break dancing in the 1980s. In general, popular dance in the West since the 1960s has moved away from any prescribed sequence of movements and physical contact between participants, the dancers performing as individuals with no distinction between the male and female role. Dances were developed requiring skilled athletic performance, for example the Grapevine, Hustle, and New Yorker. A key figure was John Travolta in his films *Grease* 1977 and *Saturday Night Fever* 1978.

In classical dance, the post-war world has also produced a great cross-fertilization from dances of different cultures. Troupes have visited the West, not only from Russia and Eastern Europe, but from Afro-Asia, for example India (notably Kathakali from Kerala state), Indonesia, Japan, South Korea (Little Angels), Nigeria, and Senegal. In the 1970s Jazz Dance, pioneered in the USA by Matt Mattox, which included elements of ballet, modern dance, tap, Indian classical, Latin American and Afro-American, and may be summed up as 'free-style dance'. See also ◊ballet.

dance of death (German *Totentanz*, French *danse macabre*) a popular theme in painting of the late medieval period, depicting an allegorical representation of death (usually a skeleton) leading the famous and the not-so-famous to the grave. One of the best known representations is a series of woodcuts by Hans ◊Holbein the younger.

dandelion perennial British wild flower *Taraxacum officinale* belonging to the Compositae. The stout stalk rises from a rosette of leaves, deeply indented like a lion's teeth, hence the name (from French *dent de lion*). The flower-heads are bright yellow. The fruit is surmounted by the hairs of the calyx which constitutes the familiar dandelion 'puff'. The milky juice of the dandelion has laxative properties, and the young leaves are sometimes eaten in salads. In the Russian species *Taraxacum koksaghyz* the juice forms an industrially usable latex, relied upon especially during World War II.

Dandie Dinmont breed of ◊terrier which originated in the Scottish border country, and named after the character Dandie Dinmont in Walter Scott's novel *Guy Mannering*. It is short-legged, long-bodied, with drooping ears and a long tail, only about 25 cm/10 in tall. Its hair, about 5 cm/2 in long, can be greyish or yellowish.

Dandolo /'dændələʊ/ celebrated Venetian family which produced four doges, of whom the most outstanding was Enrico Dandolo (c. 1120–1205) who became doge in 1193. He greatly increased the dominions of the Venetian republic and accompanied the crusading army which took Constantinople in 1203.

dangling participle see ◊participle.

Daniel /'dænɪəl/ Glyn 1914– . British archaeologist. A pioneer in the development of the subject, he was Disney professor of archaeology, Cambridge, 1974–81. His books include *Megaliths in History* 1973, and *A Short History of Archaeology* 1981.

Daniel /'dænɪəl/ Samuel 1562–1619. English sonneteer best known for the sonnet collection *Delia* 1592, master of the revels at court from 1603, for which he wrote masques.

Daniell /'dænɪəl/ John Frederic 1790–1845. British chemist and meteorologist, who in 1836 invented a primary electrical cell. In its original form, the Daniell cell consists of a central zinc cathode dipping into a porous pot containing zinc sulphate solution. The porous pot is, in turn, immersed in a solution of copper sulphate contained in a copper can, which acts as the cell's anode. The use of a porous barrier prevents polarization (the covering of the anode with small bubbles of hydrogen gas) and allows the cell to generate a continuous current of electricity.

Daniell cell

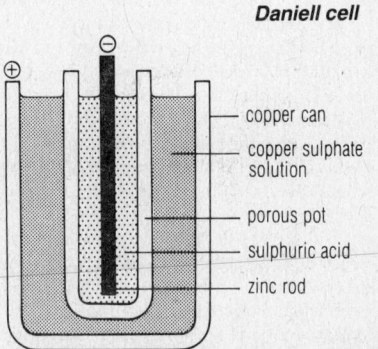

copper can
copper sulphate solution
porous pot
sulphuric acid
zinc rod

Daninos /ˌdænɪ'nəʊ/ Pierre 1913– . French author. Originally a journalist, he was liaison agent with the British Army at Dunkirk in 1940, and created in *Les Carnets du Major Thompson/The Notebooks of Major Thompson* 1954 a humorous-type Englishman who caught the French imagination.

Danish language a member of the North Germanic group of the Indo-European language family, spoken in Denmark and Greenland and related to Icelandic, Faroese, Norwegian, and Swedish. As one of the languages of the Vikings, who invaded and settled in parts of Britain during the 9th to 11th centuries, Old Danish had a strong influence on English. *They*, *their*, and *them* as well as such *sk*-words as *sky*, *skill*, *skin*, *scrape*, and *scrub* are among the language gifts of the Danelaw, along with such placename endings as *by* (a farm or town) as in Derby, Grimsby and Whitby.

Danish literature writers of world fame emerged in the 19th century: Hans Andersen, the philosopher Søren ◊Kierkegaard, and the critic Georg Brandes (1842–1927), who played a major part in the Scandinavian literary awakening, encouraging Ibsen and others. The novelists Henrik Pontoppidan (1857–1943), Karl Gjellerup (1857–1919), and Johannes Jensen (1873–1950) were all Nobel prizewinners, but have not achieved an enduring reputation outside Scandinavia.

Dankworth /'dæŋkwɔːθ/ John 1927– British jazz musician. Influential in the development of British jazz after World War II, he formed a large orchestra in 1953. His film scores include *Saturday Night and Sunday Morning* and *The Servant*, and he composed television music, for example, for the series *The Avengers*, all in the 1960s.

d'Annunzio /dæ'nʊntsiəʊ/ Gabriele 1863–1938. Italian poet, novelist and playwright. His first volume of poetry, *Primo Vere/In Early Spring* 1879, was followed by further collections of verse, short stories, novels, and plays, such as *La Gioconda* which he wrote for the actress Duse in 1898, and *Francesca da Rimini* 1902. After serving in World War I, he led an expedition in 1919 to capture Fiume, which he held until 1921. He prepared the way for Fascism by his mystic nationalism, and was created Prince of Montenevoso in 1924.

Dante Alighieri /'dænti ˌælɪ'gjeəri/ 1265–1321. Italian poet. Born in Florence, he first met Beatrice (Portinari) in 1274 and conceived a love for her which survived her marriage to another and her death in 1290, as he described in *Vita Nuova/New Life* c. 1295. In 1289 Dante fought in the battle of Campaldino, won by Florence against Arezzo, and from 1295 took an active part in Florentine politics. In 1300 he was one of the six Priors of the Republic, and since he favoured the moderate White Guelphs rather than the Black, was convicted in his absence of misapplication of public moneys in 1302 when the latter became predominant. He spent the remainder of his life in exile, in central and northern Italy. His works include the prose philosophical treatise *Convivio* 1306–08; *Monarchia* 1310–13, expounding his political theories; *De vulgari eloquentia/Concerning the Vulgar Tongue* 1304–06, an original Latin work on Italian, its dialects, and kindred languages; *Canzoniere/Lyrics*, containing his scattered lyrics; and his masterpiece *Divina Commedia/The Divine Comedy* c. 1300–21 an imaginary journey through Hell, Purgatory, and Paradise, under the guidance of Reason and Faith, represented by Virgil and Beatrice respectively. It is generally considered the greatest poem of the Middle Ages.

Danton /dɒn'tɒŋ/ Georges Jacques 1759–1794. French revolutionary. Born at Arcis-sur-Aube, he practised law, and during the early years of the ◊French Revolution he was one of the most influential men in Paris. He organized the rising of 10 Aug 1792 which overthrew the monarchy, roused the country to expel the

Dante Alighieri Italian poet Dante Alighieri by Andrea del Castagno. His *Divine Comedy* c. 1300–21 describes Hell as a funnel of descending cities where sinners are punished, Purgatory as a mountain of repentant sinners in circles ascending to Paradise, which contains his beloved Beatrice.

Prussian invaders, and procured the formation in Apr 1793 of the revolutionary tribunal and the Committee of Public Safety, of which until Jul he was the real leader. Thereafter he lost power, and when he attempted to recover it, he was arrested and guillotined.

Danube /'dænjuːb/ second longest of European rivers. It rises on the east slopes of the Black Forest, and flows 2,820 km/1,750 mi across Europe to enter the Black Sea in Romania by a swampy delta. The head of river navigation is Ulm, in Baden-Württemberg; Braila, Romania, is the limit for ocean-going ships. Cities on the Danube include Linz, Vienna, Bratislava, Budapest, Belgrade, Ruse, Braila, and Galati. A canal connects The Danube with the ◊Main, and thus with the Rhine system.

Danzig /'dæntsɪg/ German name for the Polish port of ◊Gdansk.

Daphne /'dæfni/ in Greek mythology, a nymph, changed into a laurel tree to escape from Apollo's amorous pursuit.

Daqing oilfield near ◊Harbin, China.

D'Arblay, Madame /'dɑːbleɪ/ married name of Fanny ◊Burney.

Darby /dɑːbɪ/ Abraham 1677–1717. English ironmaster who developed a process for smelting iron ore using coke instead of the more expensive charcoal. At his works at Coalbrookdale he employed the cheaper iron to cast strong thin pots for domestic use as well as the huge cylinders required by the new steam pumping-engines. His son (also Abraham) in 1779 constructed the world's first iron bridge, over the river Severn at Coalbrookdale.

Dardanelles /ˌdɑːdə'nelz/ Turkish strait connecting the Sea of Marmara with the Aegean Sea (ancient name Hellespont, Turkish name ◊Canakkale Boğazi); its shores are formed by the ◊Gallipoli peninsula on the NW and the mainland of Turkey-in-Asia on the SE. It is 75 km/47 mi long and 5–6 km/3–4 mi wide.

Dar El-Beida /'dɑːr el 'beɪdə/ Arabic name for the port of ◊Casablanca, Morocco.

Dar es Salaam /'dɑːr es sə'lɑːm/ (Arabic 'haven of peace'). Seaport in Tanzania, on mainland Tanganyika, and capital of Tanzania until its replacement by ◊Dodoma. It is the Indian Ocean terminus of the TanZam Railway, and a line also runs to the lake port of Kigoma; a road links it with Ndola in the Zambian copperbelt, and oil is carried to Zambia by pipeline from Dar es Salaam's refineries; there is also an international airport. University College (1963) became the University of Dar es Salaam in 1970. Population (1985) 1,394,000.

Darfur /dɑː'fʊə/ province in the west of the

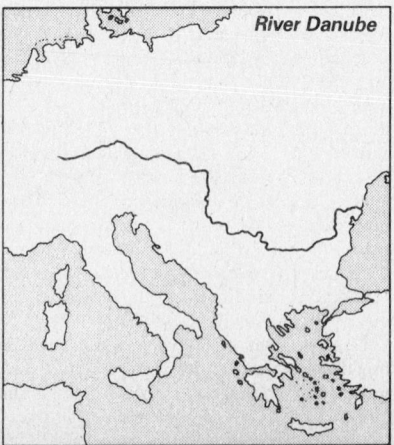

River Danube

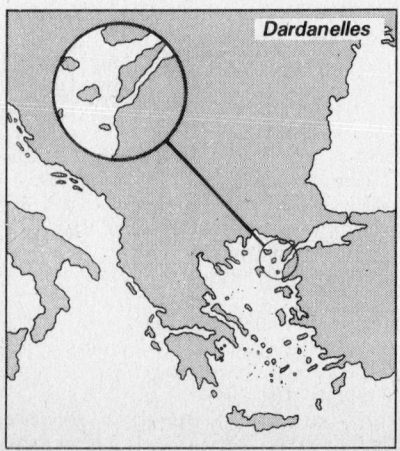

Dardanelles

DANTON DÉPUTÉ DE PARIS

A LA CONVENTION NATIONALE,

Jugé le 6 Avril 1794.

Danton The French revolutionary leader Georges Jacques Danton, organizer of the uprising in France 1792, was overthrown and guillotined in the following year by Robespierre and the leaders of the Reign of Terror.

Republic of Sudan. Area 357,806 sq km/138,150 sq mi; population (1983) 3,093,699. The capital is El Fasher (population 30,000). The area is a vast rolling plain producing ◊gum arabic, and there is also some stock raising. Darfur was an independent sultanate until conquered by Egypt in 1874.

Darien /'deəriən/ former name for the Panama isthmus as a whole, and still the name of an eastern province of Panama. The *Gulf of Darien*, part of the Caribbean, lies between Panama and Colombia. The *Darien Gap* is the complex of swamp, jungle and ravines, which long prevented the linking of the North and South American sections of the Pan-American Highway, stretching about 300 km/200 mi between Canitas, Panama, and Chigorodo, Colombia. At the Colombian end is the Great Atrato Swamp, 60 km/35 mi across and over 300 m/1,000 ft deep. The *Darien Expedition* was a Scottish attempt to colonize the isthmus 1698–99, which failed disastrously owing to the climate and Spanish hostility. The British Trans-Americas Expedition, led by John ◊Blashford-

Snell, made the first motorized crossing in 1972.

Darío /dæ'riːəʊ/ Rubén, pseudonym of Nicaraguan poet Félix Rubén Sarmiento 1867–1916. He established *modernismo*, the Spanish-American modernist literary movement, with an idiosyncratic and deliberately frivolous style that broke away from the prevailing Spanish provincialism and adapted French poetic models. His vitality and eclecticism influenced every poet writing in Spanish after him, both in the New World and in Spain.

Darío led a bohemian and nomadic life, travelling widely and living in Chile, then Buenos Aires, and Spain. His first important book, *Azul/ Azure* 1888, a collection of prose and verse, created a sensation. In *Prosas profanas/ Profane Prose* 1896 he played erotically with cultural allusions. Greatest of the later works is *Cantos de vida y esperanza/ Songs of Life and Hope* 1905, lush, musical poems mixed with confessions about his own failure to live up to his high ideals and his concept of poetry as salvation.

Darius I /də'raɪəs/ the Great c. 558–486 BC.

King of Persia 521–485 BC. A member of a younger branch of the royal family of the Achaemenidae, he won the throne from the usurper Gaumata, reorganized the government, and in 512 BC marched against the ◊Scythians and subjugated Thrace and Macedonia. An expedition in 492 BC to crush a rebellion in Greece failed, and the army sent into Attica (490 BC) was defeated at ◊Marathon. Darius had an account of his reign inscribed on the mountain at Behistun, Persia.

Darjeeling /dɑː'dʒiːlɪŋ/ town and health resort in West Bengal, India. It is situated 2,150 m/7,000 ft above sea level, on the southern slopes of the Himalayas, and is connected by rail with Calcutta, 595 km/370 mi to the south. It is the centre of a tea-producing district. Population (1981) 57,603.

Darkhan /dɑː'kɑːn/ industrial town in Outer Mongolia, near the border with the USSR. Cement and bricks are made, and to the south is Erdenet, where copper and molybdenum are mined. Population (1984) 63,600.

Darlan /dɑː'lɒŋ/ Jean Francois 1881–1942. French admiral and politician. He entered the navy in 1899, and in 1939 was appointed admiral and commander-in-chief. He commanded the French navy 1939–40, took part in the evacuation of Dunkirk, and entered the Pétain cabinet as naval minister. In 1941 he was appointed vice-premier, and became strongly anti-British and pro-German, but in 1942 he was dropped from the cabinet by Laval and was sent to North Africa. He was recognized as chief of state by the Americans when they landed in French North Africa, and was assassinated by a young Frenchman.

Darling /'dɑːlɪŋ/ river in SE Australia, a tributary of the Murray, which it joins at Wentworth. It is 3,075 km/1,910 mi long and its waters are conserved in Menindee Lake 155 sq km/60 sq mi, and others nearby. The name comes from Sir Ralph Darling (1775–1858), governor of New South Wales 1825–31. The *Darling Range*, a ridge in W Australia, has a highest point of about 582 m/1,669. The *Darling Downs* in SE Queensland is an agricultural and stockraising area.

Darling /'dɑːlɪŋ/ Grace 1815–1842. British heroine. She was the daughter of a lighthouse keeper on the Farne Islands. On 7 Sept 1838 the *Forfarshire* was wrecked, and Grace Darling and her father rowed through a storm to the wreck, saving nine lives. She was awarded a medal for her bravery.

Darlington /'dɑːlɪŋtən/ town in Durham, England, on the Skerne, near its junction with the Tees. It has coal and ironstone mines, and produces iron and steel goods, and knitting wool. The world's first passenger railway was opened between Darlington and Stockton on 27 Sept 1825. Population (1981) 85,396.

Darmstadt /'dɑːmstæt/ town in the *Land* of Hessen, West Germany, 29 km/18 mi south of Frankfurt-am-Main. It has a ducal palace and a technical university. Its industries include iron founding and the manufacture of chemicals. Population (1983) 138,577.

Darnley /'dɑːnli/ Henry Stewart or Stuart, Lord Darnley 1545–1567. Second husband of Mary, Queen of Scots. He was born in England, the son of the 4th Earl of Lennox (1516–71) and Lady Margaret Douglas (1515–78), through whom he inherited a claim to the English throne. In 1565 he married Mary, who was his first cousin. By the advice of her secretary, David ◊Rizzio, Mary refused Darnley the crown matrimonial; in revenge Darnley led a band of nobles who murdered Rizzio in Mary's presence. Within a few days Mary and Darnley were reconciled, and a son, later James I of England, was born in Jun 1566, but soon Darnley alienated all parties and a plot was formed against him by ◊Bothwell. While he was lying ill on 10 Feb 1567 at Kirk o'Field, a lonely house in Edinburgh, it was blown up. Darnley's body was found strangled in a neighbouring garden. Mary's share in the plot remains a subject of controversy.

Darrow /'dærəʊ/ Clarence Seward 1857–1938. American lawyer, known as a champion of radical causes and defender of the underdog. Born in Ohio, he appeared on behalf of trade union leaders in many famous cases, notably in the trial of Eugene Debs in 1895. He was counsel for the defence in the Loeb and Leopold murder trial of 1924, and in the Dayton 'monkey' trial of 1925, in which a teacher was tried for teaching ◊Darwin's theory of evolution. He was also an early opponent of capital punishment.

Dart /dɑːt/ Raymond 1893–1985. Australian anthropologist. His discovery of the fossil remains of the 'southern African ape' *Australopithecus africanus* in 1924, near Taungs in Botswana, was a landmark in the study of early humans. See also ◊human species

Dartford /'dɑːtfəd/ industrial town in Kent, England, 27 km/17 mi SE of London. Cement, chemicals, and paper are manufactured. The *Dartford Tunnel* (1963) runs under the Thames to Purfleet, Essex. Population (1981) 42,000.

Dartmoor /'dɑːtmʊə/ plateau of SW Devon, England, over 1,000 sq km/400 sq mi in extent, of which half is some 300 m/1,000 ft above sea level. Most of Dartmoor is a National Park. The moor is noted for its wild aspect, and rugged blocks of granite, or 'tors', crown its higher points, the highest being *Yes Tor* 618 m/2,028 ft and *High Willhays* 621 m/2,039 ft. Devon's chief rivers have their sources on Dartmoor. There are numerous prehistoric remains. Near Hemerdon there are tungsten reserves.
Dartmoor Prison, opened in 1809 originally to house French prisoners-of-war, is at Princetown in the centre of the moor, 11 km/7 mi east of Tavistock.

Dartmouth /'dɑːtməθ/ English seaport at the mouth of the Dart, 43 km/27 mi east of Plymouth, on the Devon coast. It is a centre for yachting, and has an excellent harbour. The Britannia Royal Naval College dates from 1905. Population (1981) 62,298.

Dartmouth /'dɑːtməθ/ port in Nova Scotia, Canada, on the NE of Halifax harbour, and virtually part of the capital city itself. It has engineering industries. Population (1981) 62,277.

darts game possibly derived from target practice with broken arrow-hafts, in the days when archery was a compulsory military exercise for all able-bodied men. The shortening of the dart and segmentation of the board date from the 17th century. During the 1970s the game became popular in the USA, and it has become a television sport. Some seven million players take part in the World Cup.

Darwin /'dɑːwɪn/ capital and port in Northern Territory, Australia, in NW Arnhem Land. It serves the uranium mining site at Rum Jungle to the south, and commercial fruit and vegetable growing is being developed in the area. Darwin is the north terminus of the rail line from Birdum, and has an airport.
history founded in 1869, under the name of Palmerston, and renamed after Charles ◊Darwin in 1911, it was destroyed in 1974 by a cyclone, but rebuilt on the same site. Population (1981) 56,500.

Darwin /'dɑːwɪn/ Charles Robert 1809–1882. British scientist; founder of the modern theory of ◊evolution, and discoverer of the principle of ◊natural selection. He also made important discoveries in many other areas, including the fertilization mechanisms of plants, the classification of barnacles, and the formation of coral reefs. Born at Shrewsbury, the grandson of Erasmus ◊Darwin, he studied medicine at Edinburgh and theology at Cambridge. As naturalist of the surveying voyage of HMS *Beagle* 1831–36, he made many observations, especially in South America and the nearby Galapagos Islands, which led to his theory of modification of species. Having married his cousin Emma Wedgwood in 1839, he settled in Down House, Downe, Kent, for the rest of his life. By 1844 he had enlarged his sketch of ideas to an essay of his conclusions, but then left his theory for eight years while he studied barnacles. In 1858 he was forced into action by the receipt of a memoir from A R ◊Wallace, embodying the same theory. In 1859 Darwin published *On the Origin of Species by Means of Natural Selection or the Preservation of Favoured Races in the Struggle for Life* which set out the huge amounts of evidence Darwin had collected to show that evolution had occurred, and explained the principles of natural and sexual selection. It refuted earlier evolutionary theories, such as those of ◊Lamarck. Inevitably, the book aroused bitter controversy because it did not agree with the literal sense of the Book of Genesis. Darwin himself played little part in the debates, but his *Descent of Man* 1871 added fuel to the theological discussion in which T H ◊Huxley and Haeckel took leading parts. Darwin then devoted himself chiefly to botanical studies till his death. He had inherited £40,000 on the death of his father, and Darwin's own estate at death was valued at £282,000. He was buried in Westminster Abbey. Down House is maintained as a museum by the Royal College of Surgeons. Darwinism alone is not enough to explain the evolution of sterile worker bees, or altruism. ◊Neo-Darwinism, the current theory of evolution, is a synthesis of Darwin and genetics based on the work of ◊Mendel.

CHARLES ROBERT DARWIN, LL.D., F.R.S.

In his *Descent of Man* he brought his own Species down as low as possible—*i.e.*, to "A Hairy Quadruped furnished with a Tail and Pointed Ears, and probably *Arboreal* in its habits"—which is a reason for the very general Interest in a "Family Tree." He has lately been turning his attention to the "Politic Worm."

Darwin Cartoon of Charles Robert Darwin by Linley Sambourne which is typical of those published following Darwin's *Origin of Species by Means of Natural Selection* (1859) and the Oxford Debate of 1860 on his theory of evolution.

Darwin /'dɑːwɪn/ Erasmus 1731–1802. British poet, physician and naturalist, and grandfather of Charles ◊Darwin. He wrote *The Botanic Garden* 1792, which included a versification of the Linnaean system 'The Loves of the Plants', and *Zoonomia* 1794–96, which anticipated some aspects of evolutionary theory, but tended to ◊Lamarck's interpretation.

Dasht-e-Kavir Desert /'dæʃti kæ'vɪə/ or Dasht-i-Davir Desert. Salt desert SE of Tehran, Iran; US forces landed here in 1980 in an abortive mission to rescue hostages held at the American Embassy in Tehran.

Dassault /dæ'səʊ/ Marcel 1892–1986. French aircraft designer and manufacturer. Active in World War I, he refused to collaborate with the Nazis in World War II, and was imprisoned in Buchenwald. After the war he produced the Mystère and Mirage jet fighter aircraft.

dasyure type of marsupial, also known as a 'native cat', found in Australia and New Guinea. Various species have body lengths from 25 cm/10 in to 75 cm/2.5 ft plus a long bushy tail, and have dark coats with white spots. They are agile nocturnal carnivores, able to move fast and climb.

data information, often in tabular or graphic form, especially that stored on computers.

database in computing, a structured, centralized collection of data, organized to allow access by several or many different user programs. The data is held in ◊files and arranged into hierarchies, networks, or relations -the three main types of database structure. For example, a telephone directory stored as a database might allow all the people whose names start with the letter B to be selected by one program, and all those living in London by another. A database management system (DBMS) program ensures that the integrity of the data is maintained by controlling the degree of access of the ◊application programs using the data. Databases are normally used by large organizations with mainframes or minicomputers. A collection of databases is known as a databank.

data-flow diagram in computing, another name for ◊flow diagram.

data processing (DP) the commercial use of computers, typically to handle access to a database and the manipulation of large volumes of data, or for ◊batch processing of homogeneous (of similar nature) data on a large scale. DP (sometimes called EDP, electronic data processing) is normally carried out on a mainframe computer. A large organization usually has a special department to support its DP activities, which might include the writing and maintenance of software (programs), control and operation of the computers, and an analysis of the organization's information requirements.

data protection the safeguarding of information about individuals stored on computers. The Council of Europe adopted in 1981 a Data Protection Convention which led in the UK to the ◊Data Protection Act 1986. This requires computer databases containing personal information to be registered, and users to process only accurate information and to retain the information only for a necessary period and for specified purposes. Individuals have a right of access, and sometimes of correction or erasure. See also under ◊privacy.

date palm, genus *Phoenix*, of which *Phoenix dactylifera*, a native of North Africa, SW Asia, and parts of India, is the most important. It is up to 25 m/80 ft high. The fruit are produced by the female tree in bunches, weighing 9–11 kg/20–25 lb and with 1,000 fruit. Dates are an important source of food in the Near and Middle East, being exceedingly rich in sugar, and when dried are exported. Their juice is made into a kind of wine. The tree also supplies timber, and materials for baskets, rope, and animal feed.

dating the science of determining the age of geological structures, rocks, and fossils, and placing them in the context of geological time. Dating can be carried out by identifying fossils of creatures that only lived at certain times (marker fossils), by looking at the physical relationships of rocks to other rocks of a known age, or by measuring how much of a rock's radioactive elements (usually the ◊isotope of carbon C14) have changed since the rock was formed (see under ◊radiocarbon dating).

datura genus of plants, family Solanaceae, such as the thorn apple, with handsome trumpet-shaped blooms. They have narcotic properties.

Daudet /'dəʊdeɪ/ Alphonse 1840–1897. French novelist. He became a journalist in Paris. Best known for his works about his native Provence, *Lettres de mon moulin/Letters from My Mill* 1866, and creation of character

Tartarin, a hero epitomizing southern temperament, in *Tartarin de Tarascon* 1872 with its two sequels; *Fromont jeune et Risler aîné/Young Froment and Old Risler* 1874; the play *L'Arlêsienne/The Woman from Arles* 1872, for which Bizet composed the music; and *Souvenirs d'un homme de lettres/Recollections of a Literary Man* 1889.

Daudet /'dəʊdeɪ/ Léon 1867–1942. French writer and journalist, son of Alphonse ◊Daudet, who founded the militant right-wing royalist periodical *Action française* in 1899 after the ◊Dreyfus case. He wrote novels and philosophical treatises, and frank *Souvenirs* 1914. During World War II he was a collaborator with the Germans.

Daugavpils /'daʊgəfpɪlz/ town (Russian Dvinsk) in Latvia, USSR, on the Daugava (west Dvina). A fortress of the Livonian Knights 1278, it became the capital of Polish ◊Livonia. There is a timber industry. Population (1983 est.) 122,000.

Daulaghiri /ˌdaʊlə'gɪəri/ a mountain in the ◊Himalayas.

Daumier /ˌdəʊmi'eɪ/ Honoré 1808–1879. French artist. Born at Marseilles, he was taken to Paris as a child and entered a lithographer's studio. He became famous for his sharply realized cartoons, dissecting Parisian society, for *La Caricature, Charivari* and other periodicals, once being imprisoned for an attack on ◊Louis Philippe. His output was enormous and included 4,000 lithographs, but his popular success hindered appreciation of his work as a painter, for example his realistic *Les Bohêmiens de Paris, Christ Mocked* and illustrations of incidents from Cervantes.

dauphin title of the eldest sons of the kings of France, derived from the personal name of a count, whose lands, the *Dauphiné* (capital Grenoble), traditionally passed to the heir to the throne from 1349 to 1830.

Dauphiné old province of France, comprising the *départements* of Isère, Drôme, and Hautes-Alpes. After the collapse of Rome it belonged to Burgundy, then was under Frankish domination; afterwards part of Arles, it was sold by its ruler to France in 1349. The capital was Grenoble.

Davao /'daːvaʊ/ town in the Philippine Republic, capital of Davao province, at the mouth of the Davao river on the island of Mindanao. It is the centre of a fertile district and is a busy port. Population (1980) 611,310.

Davenant /'dævənənt/ William 1606–1668. English poet and dramatist. Born at Oxford, he was rumoured to be an illegitimate son of Shakespeare. In 1638 he became Poet Laureate. An active supporter of Charles I, he was imprisoned in the Tower of London during the ◊Civil Wars. His *Siege of Rhodes* 1656 is sometimes considered the first English opera.

Daventry /'dævəntri/ town in Northamptonshire, England, 19 km/12 mi west of Northampton. Because of its central position, it became in 1925 the site of the BBC high-power radio transmitter. Originally specializing in footwear manufacture, it received London and Birmingham overspill from the 1950s, and

developed varied light industries. Population (1981) 16,178.

David /'deɪvɪd/ c. 1060–970 BC. Second king of Israel, successor to ◊Saul. Youngest son of Jesse of Bethlehem, while still a shepherd boy he was anointed by Samuel. According to the Bible he played the harp before Saul to banish his melancholy, and later slew the ◊Philistine giant, Goliath, with a sling and stone. Saul's son, Jonathan, became his friend, but Saul, jealous of his prowess, schemed to murder him. David married Michal, Saul's daughter, but following further attempts on his life went into exile until Saul and Jonathan fell in battle with the Philistines at Gilboa. David was anointed king at ◊Hebron, took ◊Jerusalem, made it his capital, and housed the Ark there. ◊Absalom, his favourite son, led a rebellion but was defeated and slain. David sent Uriah to his death in order that he might marry his widow, Bathsheba. Their son was ◊Solomon. David probably wrote a few of the psalms, was a skilled harpist, and was celebrated as a secular poet.

David /'deɪvɪd/ Elizabeth 1914– . British cookery writer, whose *Mediterranean Food* (1950), and *French Country Cooking* (1951) helped to spark off an increased interest in foreign cuisine in Britain, and also inspired a growing school of deeply researched, highly literate writing on food and wine.

David /dæ'viːd/ Félicien César 1810–1876. French composer. He travelled in Palestine, and became famous with the performance of his symphonic fantasy *Desert* 1844. He was one of the first Western composers to introduce oriental scales and melodies into his music.

David /dæ'viːd/ Gerard c. 1450–1523. Flemish painter. The last great artist of the Bruges school, he is famous chiefly for his altar-pieces.

David /dæ'viːd/ Jacques Louis 1748–1825. French painter. He studied under ◊Boucher, won the Prix de Rome in 1774, and during the Revolution he was an ardent supporter of the republicans; he was elected to the Convention and a member of the Committee of Public Safety, and narrowly escaped the guillotine. His most famous paintings are *The Sabine Women* and *Mme Récamier*, fine examples of neoclassicism. In his *Death of Marat*, he turned political murder into a classical tragedy. Later under Napoleon, to whom he became court painter, he produced heroic portraits and scenes celebrating the glory of the Empire. He was banished by the ◊Bourbons and settled in Brussels.

David /'deɪvɪd/ or Dewi (5th–6th century). Patron saint of Wales, traditionally the son of a prince of Cardiganshire and uncle of King Arthur. He founded a monastery at Menevia, and presided over a synod at Brefi and condemned the Pelagian heresy. It is said that David was responsible for the adoption of the leek as the national emblem of Wales.

Davidson /'deɪvɪdsən/ John 1857–1909. Scottish poet whose modern, realistic idiom as in 'Thirty bob a week' influenced T S ◊Eliot.

David /'deɪvɪd/ two kings of Scotland.

David I /'deɪvɪd/ 1084–1153. King of Scotland from 1124. The youngest son of

◊Malcolm Canmore and St ◊Margaret, he was brought up in the English court of Henry I, married in 1113 Matilda, widow of the first earl of Northampton, and in 1124 became king. He invaded England in 1138 in support of Queen ◊Matilda, daughter of Henry I, but was defeated at Northallerton in the Battle of the Standard, and again in 1141.

David II /'deɪvɪd/ 1324–1371. King of Scotland from 1329. Son of Robert the Bruce, he was married at the age of four to Joanna, daughter of Edward II of England, and in 1329 succeeded to the throne. After the defeat of the Scots by Edward III at Halidon Hill, David and Joanna were sent to France for safety. They returned in 1341; in 1346 David invaded England, was captured at the battle of Neville's Cross and imprisoned for 11 years. On Joanna's death in 1362 David married Margaret Logie, but divorced her in 1370.

Davies /'deɪvɪs/ Henry Walford 1869–1941. English composer. Born in Shropshire of Welsh parentage, he was knighted in 1922, and was organist at St George's Chapel, Windsor 1927–32. From 1934 he was Master of the King's Musick, and he was influential in the musical education of Britain through his radio talks. His compositions include the cantata *Everyman* 1904, the 'Solemn Melody' 1908 for organ and strings, chamber music and part songs.

Davies /'deɪvɪs/ Peter Maxwell 1934– . British composer and conductor, a pioneer of British music-theatre. He has composed much music for chamber ensembles, and has a particular interest in the work of the 16th-century composer John Taverner, whose life is the basis of his opera *Taverner* 1972. Other works include the opera *The Lighthouse* 1980. His more recent music reflects the sounds of his island home in ◊Orkney. His music is often dramatic and disturbing.

Davies /'deɪvɪs/ Robertson 1913– . Canadian novelist. He gained an international reputation with *Fifth Business* 1970, the first novel of his Deptford trilogy, a panoramic work blending philosophy, humour, the occult, and ordinary life. Other works include *A Mixture of Frailties* 1958, *The Rebel Angels* 1981 and *What's Bred in the Bone* 1986.

Davies /'deɪvɪs/ W(illiam) H(enry) 1871–1940. British poet. Born in Monmouth, he went to America, where he lived the life of a 'hobo', and lost his right foot 'riding the rods'. Returning to England he raised the money to publish his first volume of poems, *Soul's Destroyer* 1906, as a wandering pedlar. He published further volumes of simple direct verse and the prose *Autobiography of a Super-Tramp* 1908.

Da Vinci see ◊Leonardo da Vinci.

Davis /'deɪvɪs/ Angela 1944– . American black activist, prominent in the US student movement of the 1960s. At the University of California, she studied under Marcuse, and was assistant professor of philosophy at UCLA 1969–70. Later in 1970 she went into hiding after being accused of supplying guns used in the murder of a judge seized as a hostage in an attempt to secure the release of three black convicts (known as the Soledad brothers from the name of their prison), but was captured, tried, and acquitted. In 1980 she stood as the Communist vice-presidential candidate.

Davis /'deɪvɪs/ Bette 1908– . American actress. Born in Massachusetts, she entered films in 1930, established a reputation with *Of Human Bondage* as a forceful dramatic actress. Later films included *Dangerous* 1935 and *Jezebel* 1938, both winning her Academy Awards, *Private Lives of Elizabeth and Essex*, and *Whatever happened to Baby Jane* 1963.

Davis A Hollywood legend who had to claw her way to the top, Bette Davis was at her peak in the 1930s and 1940s with her powerful portrayals of independent women.

Davis /'deɪvɪs/ Colin 1927– . British conductor, musical director at Sadler's Wells 1961–65, chief conductor of the BBC Symphony Orchestra 1967–71, musical director of the Royal Opera 1971–86, and chief conductor of the Bavarian Radio Symphony Orchestra from 1983. He was knighted in 1980.

Davis /'deɪvɪs/ Dwight Filley 1879–1945. American tennis player, donor in 1900 of the Davis Cup, more properly the Dwight Davis International Bowl, for a tennis competition.

Davis /'deɪvɪs/ Jefferson 1808–1889. American politician, president of the short-lived Confederate States of America 1861–65. Born in Kentucky, he served in the US army before becoming a cotton planter in Mississippi. He sat in the US Senate 1847–51, and was secretary of war 1853–57. He returned to the Senate in 1857 as a leader of the Southern Democrats, and a defender of 'humane' slavery; in 1860 he issued a declaration in favour of secession from the US, and early in 1861 he was elected president of the ◊Confederacy. During the Civil War he assumed strong political leadership, but often disagreed with military policy (Robert E Lee surrendered without his approval). He left Richmond on its fall in 1865, and shortly after was captured in Georgia, and spent two years in prison.

Davis /'deɪvɪs/ Joe 1901–1978. British billiards and snooker player. He was world snooker champion 1927–46, and virtually the creator of the sophisticated modern game.

Davis /'deɪvɪs/ John 1550–1605. English navigator and explorer, born near Dartmouth, England. He sailed in search of the Northwest Passage through the Canadian Arctic to the Pacific Ocean in 1585, and in 1587 sailed to Baffin Bay through the straits named after him. In 1588 he fought against the Spanish Armada, and discovered the Falkland Islands in 1592. He was killed by Japanese pirates in the straits of Malacca.

Davis /'deɪvɪs/ Miles (Dewey Jr) 1926– . US jazz trumpeter, composer, and band leader. He recorded bebop with Charlie Parker in 1945, pioneered cool jazz in the 1950s and jazz-rock fusion from the late 1960s. His influential albums include *Birth of the Cool* 1949, *Sketches of Spain* 1959, and *Bitches Brew* 1970.

Davis /'deɪvɪs/ Steve 1957– . English snooker player. He won his first major professional title in 1980 (Coral UK Championship), and has since won over 30 major events including the world professional title 1981, 1983, 1984, and 1987.

Davis During the 1986–87 season, Britain's Steve Davis became the first man to win more than a million pounds sterling in prize money from snooker. He has won all the major tournaments, including the world professional title four times.

Davison /'deɪvɪsən/ Emily 1872–1913. English militant suffragette, who died while trying to stop the King's horse at the Derby at Epsom (she was trampled by the horse). A teacher with degrees from Oxford and London Universities, she joined the Women's Social and Political Union in 1906 and served several prison sentences for militant action such as stone throwing, setting fire to pillar boxes, and bombing Lloyd George's country house.

Her coffin was carried through London draped in the colours of the suffragette movement, purple, white and green, and escorted by 2,000 uniformed suffragettes.

Davison A militant suffragette who had served prison sentences for stone throwing, setting fire to pillar boxes and bombing, Emily Davison was trampled on and killed by the King's horse at the Epsom Derby in 1913.

Davisson /'deɪvɪsən/ Clinton 1881–1958. American physicist. Born in Illinois, he worked under O W Richardson at Princeton before joining the Bell Telephone organization in 1917, and proved ◊de Broglie's theory that electrons – and therefore all matter – have wave structure. G P Thompson carried through the same research independently and in 1937 the two men shared a Nobel prize.

Davitt /'dævɪt/ Michael 1846–1906. Irish revolutionary, born in County Mayo. He began work in a factory at the age of ten, joined the ◊Fenians in 1865, and was sentenced in 1870 to 15 years' imprisonment for treason. After his release in 1877 he and ◊Parnell founded the Land League in 1879, and Davitt was imprisoned several times for his share in the land-reform agitation. He served as a Member of Parliament 1895–99.

Davos /dɑː'vəʊs/ town at 1,559 m/5,115 ft above sea level in an Alpine valley in Grisons canton, Switzerland, famous as a health resort and as a winter sports centre.

Davy /'deɪvi/ Humphry 1778–1829. British chemist. While a laboratory assistant at Bristol, he discovered the respiratory effects of 'laughing gas' (nitrous oxide) in 1799, and in 1802 became professor at the Royal Institution, London. There he discovered, by electrolysis, the metals sodium, potassium, calcium, magnesium, strontium, and barium. He invented the 'safety lamp' for use in mines where methane was present, in effect enabling the miners to work in previously unsafe conditions. He was elected President of the Royal Society in 1820.

Davy English chemist Sir Humphrey Davy began to experiment with the respiration of gases whilst employed as a laboratory assistant and almost died from the effects. He went on to isolate metals such as potassium and magnesium and to invent the miners' safety lamp.

Davy Jones sailor's name, generally occurring in the phrase 'gone to Davy Jones's locker', applied to those drowned at sea, and taken as the name of a sea-spirit or devil.

Dawes /dɔːz/ Charles Gates 1865–1951. American statesman. In 1923 he was appointed by the Allied Reparations Commission president of the committee which produced the 'Dawes Plan' – aiming at securing that Germany should pay as much as possible as war debts. It was superseded as unworkable by the Young Plan in 1929. Dawes was elected vice-president of the USA in 1924, received the Nobel peace prize in 1925, and was ambassador to Britain 1929–32.

Dawkins /'ɔːkɪnz/ Richard 1941– . British zoologist whose book *The Selfish Gene* popularized the theories of ◊sociobiology. A second book, *The Blind Watchmaker*, explains the modern theory of evolution.

Dawson /'dɔːsən/ Canadian 'ghost town', capital until 1953 of the ◊Yukon Territory, at the junction of the Yukon and Klondike rivers; population (1981) 1320. It was founded in 1896, at the time of the Klondike gold rush, when its population was 25,000.

Dawson /'dɔːsən/ Peter 1882–1961. Australian baritone, noted for marching songs and ballads.

Dawson Creek /'dɔːsən/ town in British Columbia, Canada. It is the south east terminus of the Alaska Highway; population (1981) 11,500.

day the time taken for the Earth to rotate once on its axis. There are two kinds. The *solar day* is the time that the Earth takes to rotate once relative to the Sun. It is divided into 24 hours, and is the basis of our civil day. The *sidereal day* is the time that the Earth takes to rotate once relative to the stars. It is four minutes shorter than the solar day, because the Sun's position against the star background as seen from Earth changes as the Earth orbits it.

Day /deɪ/ Robin 1923– . British broadcasting journalist. A barrister, he pioneered the probing political interview, notably when he questioned Harold Macmillan on the composition of his cabinet in 1958. Knighted 1981.

Dayak or *Dyak* an indigenous people of Borneo, noted for arts and crafts, who live communally. They hunt with blowpipes, fish, and cultivate rice.

Dayan /daɪ'æn/ Moshe 1915–1981. Israeli general. As minister of defence 1967 and 1969–74, he was largely responsible for the victory in the 1967 Six Day War, but was criticized for Israel's alleged unpreparedness in the 1973 October War, and resigned with Golda Meir. Foreign minister from 1977, he resigned in 1979 in protest over the refusal of the Begin government to negotiate with the Palestinians.

Day Lewis /'deɪ 'luːɪs/ Cecil 1904–1972. British poet, poet laureate 1968–72. Born at Ballintubber, Ireland, he was educated at Oxford and then taught at Cheltenham College 1930–35. With ◊Auden and ◊Spender he was one of the influential left-wing poets of the 1930s, and first showed an individual quality in *From Feathers to Iron* 1931. In maturity he developed a gift for tangy accomplished lyrics, and sustained narrative power, for example 'The Loss of the Nabara' in *Overtures to Death* 1938. Professor of poetry at Oxford 1951–56, he published critical works, translations of the Georgics and Aeneid, and detective novels under the pseudonym Nicholas Blake. In 1968 he succeeded Masefield as poet laureate. His autobiography, *The Buried Day* 1960, was followed by a biography written by his eldest son Sean 1980.

Dayton /'deɪtn/ city in Ohio, USA; population (1980) 193,500. It produces precision machinery, household appliances, and electrical equipment. It has an aeronautical research centre and a Roman Catholic university, and was the birthplace of the aviator Orville Wright.

Dayton /'deɪtn/ small town in Tennessee, USA, notorious as the scene of the trial (1925) of John T Scopes, a science teacher at the high school. He was accused of teaching, contrary to a law of the State, that 'man is descended from the lower animals'. Scopes was fined $100, but this was waived on a technical point.

Daytona Beach /deɪ'təʊnə/ popular US resort and motor-racing centre on the Atlantic coast of Florida. Population (1980) 54,176.

Dazai /'dɑːzaɪ/ Osamu, pseudonym of Shuji Tsushima 1909–1948. Japanese novelist. The title of his novel *The Setting Sun* 1947 has become in Japanese synonymous with the dead of World War II. He committed suicide.

D-Day name given to the day – 6 June 1944 – when the Allied invasion of Europe took place during World War II. It was originally fixed for 5 June, but owing to unfavourable weather the invasion was postponed for 24 hours. Originally military jargon for any day on which a crucial operation was planned, it has also acquired this sense in ordinary usage.

DDT *dichloro-diphenyl-trichloroethane* an insecticide discovered in 1939 by Swiss chemist Paul Müller. It is useful in control of insects that spread malaria, but resistant strains develop. DDT is highly toxic and persists in the environment and in animal tissue, so that its use is now banned in most countries.

deacon third order of the Christian ministry; in the Anglican Communion a candidate for holy orders is ordained deacon, proceeding to the priesthood after a year. The lay order of women deaconesses was revived in 1962 (legally recognized 1968); in England they may not administer the sacraments, but may conduct public worship and preach. In 1985 the General Synod voted to allow ordination of women as deacons, enabling them to perform marriages and baptisms, but not to take communion, or give absolution and the blessing. In the Presbyterian and Free Churches a deacon is a lay assistant.

Dead Sea large lake, partly in Israel and partly in Jordan; area 1,020 sq km/394 sq mi. It lies 394 m/1,292 ft below sea-level. The chief river entering it is the Jordan; it has no outlet to the sea, and the water is very salty. Since both Israel and Jordan are using the waters of the Jordan river, the Dead Sea is now dried up in the centre and divided into two halves, but in 1980 Israel announced a plan to link it by canal with the Mediterranean. The Dead Sea Rift is part of the fault between the African and Arab plates.

Dead Sea Scrolls collection of ancient scrolls (some intact in their jars) and fragments of scrolls found 1947–56 in caves on the W side of the Jordan 12 km/7 mi S of ◊Jericho and 2 km/1 mi from the N end of the Dead Sea. See ◊Qumran. The most valuable date from c. 150 BC to AD 68, when the monastic community which owned them was destroyed by the Romans because of its support for a revolt against their rule from AD 66. They include scripts of Old Testament books a thousand years earlier than those previously known.

deafness lack or deficiency in the sense of hearing, either because of an inborn deficiency, or caused by injury or disease of the inner ear. It is often accompanied by an inability to speak if deafness was present at, or soon after, birth. Of assistance are hearing aids, lip-reading, a cochlear implant in the ear in combination with a special electronic processor, sign language (signs for concepts), and 'cued speech' (phonetic).

Deakin /'diːkɪn/ Alfred 1856–1919. Australian Liberal statesman. He was attorney-general in the first Federal Cabinet of 1901, and prime minister 1903–04, 1905–08, and 1909–10. In his second administration, legislation on defence, protection and the provision of pensions was wide-reaching and long-lasting. His posthumous *The Federal Story* 1944 described the negotiations which established the Commonwealth and the drafting of its constitution.

Deal /diːl/ English port and resort on the east coast of Kent, one of the ◊Cinque ports. Julius Caesar is said to have landed here in 55 BC. The

Dead Sea Scrolls Among the leather scrolls from Quman were two of bronze, of which only metallic salts remained. Professor H Wright Baker of Manchester College of Science and Technology solved the problem by bonding the salts together and cutting them into strips with a tiny circular saw. They record the location of the treasures of the temple at Jerusalem.

Deakin Alfred Deakin was a leading figure in the negotiations to establish the Australian Commonwealth, and in drafting the constitution.

castle was built by Henry VIII and houses the town museum. Population (1981) 25,989.

dean *Anglican Communion* head of the chapter of a cathedral or collegiate church; a rural dean presides over a division of an archdeaconry;

Roman Catholic senior cardinal bishop, head of the college of cardinals.

There are also deans in the colleges of Oxford and Cambridge, who are fellows charged with the maintenance of discipline; and in medical schools, and universities.

Dean /diːn/ Basil 1888–1978. British founder and director-general of ◊ENSA in 1939, which provided entertainment for the Allied forces in World War II.

Dean /diːn/ James. Stage-name of James Byron 1931–1955. American actor. Killed in a road accident when only his first film, *East of Eden*, 1955, had been shown, he posthumously became the focus of a cult with *Rebel Without a Cause*, 1955, and *Giant*, as the a symbol of teenage rebellion against American middle-class values.

Dearborn /'dɪəbɔːn/ motor manufacturing city in Michigan, USA, 16 km/10 mi SW of Detroit; population (1980) 158,366. Settled in 1795, it was the birthplace and home of Henry ◊Ford, who built his first car factory here. Dearborn also makes aircraft parts, steel, and bricks.

death a permanent ending of all the functions needed to keep an organism alive. Death used to be pronounced when a person's breathing and heartbeat stopped. The advent of mechanical aids has made this point difficult to determine, and a person is now pronounced dead when the brain ceases to control the vital functions. For a donor in transplant surgery the World Health Organization definition 1968 is that there should be no brain–body connection, muscular activity, blood pressure, or ability to breathe unaided by machine. In religious belief it may be seen as the prelude to rebirth (see ◊Hinduism, ◊Buddhism); under ◊Islam and ◊Christianity, there is the concept of a Day of Judgment, and consignment to Heaven or Hell; ◊Judaism tends to concentrate more on survival through descendants.

death cap poisonous fungus *Amanita phalloides*, the most poisonous mushroom known.

Death Valley /'deθ 'væli/ depression 225 km/140 mi long and 6–26 km/4–16 mi wide, in SE California, USA. At 85 mi/280 ft below sea level, it is the lowest point in North America. Bordering mountains rise to 3,000 mi/10,000 ft. It is one of the world's hottest places, with an average annual rainfall of 35 mm/1.4 in.

death-watch beetle *Xestobium rufovillosum* of the 'woodworm' family. The larva lives in oaks and willows, and can also cause damage by boring in old furniture or structural timbers. The male produces a ticking sound to attract the female, by striking its head upon a wooden surface, and this is taken by the superstitious as a warning of approaching death.

Deauville /'dəʊvɪl/ holiday resort of Normandy in Calvados *département*, France, on the English Channel and at the mouth of the Touques, opposite Trouville; population (1982) 5,769.

de Bono /də 'bəʊnəʊ/ Edward 1933– . British doctor. Lecturer at the Department of Investigative Medicine, Cambridge University, from 1976, he is best known for his concept of lateral thinking (*The Use of Lateral Thinking* 1967), which involves thinking round a problem rather than tackling it head on.

Debray /də'breɪ/ Régis 1941– . French Marxist theorist. He was associated with Che Guevara in the revolutionary movement in Latin

Dean The American heartthrob of the fifties, James Dean, photographed at 24, shortly before his fatal car crash in 1955. After some small roles on Broadway, he became a star overnight with the success of *East of Eden* (1955) and *Rebel Without a Cause* (1955).

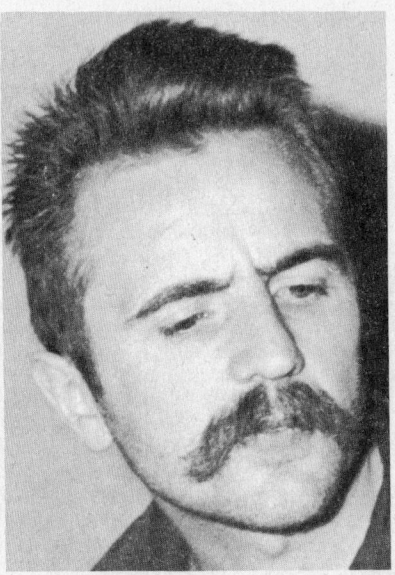

Debray One of the influential theorists of the revolutionary liberation movements in Latin America, Debray was a friend of Che Guevara and was imprisoned in Bolivia in the 1960s.

de Broglie The Nobel prizewinner for physics in 1929, Louis de Broglie was a prominent member of the French Academy of Science, an Honorary Doctor of Oxford University, and technical adviser to the French atomic energy commission.

America in the 1960s, and in 1967 was sentenced to 30 years' imprisonment in Bolivia, but was released after three years. His writings on Latin American politics include *Strategy for Revolution* 1970. He is a specialist adviser to President Mitterrand of France on Latin American affairs.

Debrecen /ˈdebrətsen/ Hungarian town, 193 km/120 mi east of Budapest; population (1980) 193,000. ◊Kossuth declared Hungary independent of the ◊Hapsburgs here in 1849. It is a commercial centre, and has a university founded in 1912.

Debrett /dəˈbret/ John 1753–1822. London publisher of a directory of the Peerage 1802, followed by a *Baronetage* in 1808, still called by his name.

de Broglie /də ˈbrəʊli/ Louis, 7th Duc de Broglie 1892–1987. French theoretical physicist. His distinguished ancestors include Victor, 2nd Duc de Broglie (1718–1804) who was a Marshal of France, he campaigned in the Seven Years' War, and headed an emigré army in the Revolution. In 1929 the 7th Duc was awarded a Nobel Prize, having established that all particles can be described either by particle equations or by wave equations. thus laying the foundations of wave mechanics.

de Broglie /də ˈbrəʊli/ Maurice, 6th Duc de Broglie 1875–1960. French physicist, brother of the 7th Duc de Broglie. He worked on X-rays and gamma rays, and helped to establish the Einsteinian description of light in terms of photons.

Debs /debz/ Eugene Victor 1855–1926. American labour organizer and founder of the US Socialist party. Born in Indiana, he organized the American Railway Union in 1893, and was Socialist candidate for the presidency in every election from 1900 to 1920, except that of 1916. He opposed US intervention in World War I and was imprisoned 1918–21.

debt something which is owed, usually money, goods, or services. The ◊*national debt* of a country is the total money owed by the government to private individuals, banks, and so on; *international debt*, the money owed by one country to another, began on a large scale with the investment in foreign countries by newly industrialized countries like Britain in the late 19th–early 20th centuries. As a result of the ◊Bretton Woods conference in 1944, the ◊World Bank (officially called the International Bank for Reconstruction and Development) was established in 1945 as an agency of the United Nations to finance international development, by providing loans where private capital was not forthcoming. Loans were made largely at prevailing market rates ('hard loans') and therefore generally to the developed countries, who could afford them.

In 1960 the ◊International Development Association (IDA) was set up as an offshoot of the World Bank to provide interest-free ('soft') loans over a long period to finance the economics of developing countries and assist their long-term developments. International debt became a global problem as a result of the oil crisis of the 1970s. The resulting cash surpluses of Middle Eastern oil-producing countries was channelled by western banks to Third World countries. However, a slump in the world economy, and rises in interest rates, have resulted in the debtor countries paying an ever-increasing share of their national output in *debt-servicing* (paying off the interest on a debt, rather than paying off the debt itself). As a result, many loans had to be *rescheduled* (renegotiated so that repayments were made over a longer term). In 1980–81 Poland ceased making repayments on international debts. Today, the countries most at risk include Mexico and Brazil, both of which have a *debt-servicing ratio* (proportion of export earnings which is required to pay off the debt) of more than 50%. In May 1987 the world's largest bank, Citibank of New York, announced that it was writing off $3 billion of international loans, mainly due to Brazil's repeated rescheduling of debt repayments. The dangers of the current scale of international debt (the so-called *debt crisis*) is that the debtor country can only continue to repay its existing debts by means of further loans; for the western countries, there is the possibility of a confidence crisis causing panic withdrawals of deposits and consequent collapse of the banking system.

debugging finding and removing errors (called ◊bugs) from a computer program or system. The behaviour of a particular program can be investigated using a software device called a debugging tool, which allows examination and if necessary modification of the program at predetermined breakpoints.

Debussy /də'bu:si/ (Achille-) Claude 1862–1918. French composer. Born at St Germain-en-Laye, he studied in Paris, and won the Grand Prix de Rome with his cantata *L'Enfant prodigue* 1884. After studying in Rome, he returned to Paris and won fame with his *Prélude à l'après-midi d'un faune* 1894. His opera *Pélleas et Mélisande* was first performed in 1902. He wrote orchestral music and numerous piano pieces, chamber music, ballets, songs, etc. His style reflects impressionist paintings and poetry in orchestral colour - *La Mer*

is a vivid description of moods of the sea. For his rejection of classical diatonic harmony he is often considered the first of the modern composers.

Debye /də'baɪ/ Peter 1884–1966. Dutch-American physicist. In 1940 he went to the US where he was professor of chemistry at Cornell university 1940–52. A pioneer of X-ray powder crystallography, and famed for his work on polar molecules, dipole moments and molecular structure, he was awarded a Nobel prize in 1936.

Decalogue the ten commandments which, according to the Bible, were delivered by ◊Jehovah to ◊Moses, and stated in Exodus xx, 1–17, and Deuteronomy v, 6–21. The Decalogue is recognized as the basis of morality by both Jews and Christians.

decathlon an athletics competition for men in the Olympic games which consists of ten different events: 100m, 400m and 1,500m running races, 110m hurdles, javelin, discus, shot put, pole vault, high jump and long jump. The competition takes place over two days

Decatur /dɪ'keɪtə/ city in central Illinois, USA, on Lake Decatur, population (1980) 94,000. It has engineering, food processing, and plastics industries. It was founded in 1829 and named after Stephen ◊Decatur.

Decatur /dɪ'keɪtə/ Stephen 1779–1820. American naval hero. He was born in Maryland and greatly distinguished himself in the war with Tripoli (1801–05), when he succeeded in burning the *Philadelphia*, which the enemy had captured. During the war of 1812 with England he surrendered only after a desperate resistance in 1814, and in 1815 was active against the Algerian pirates. He was killed in a duel. His well known toast includes the phrase 'our country, right or wrong'.

decay, radioactive the process of continuous disintegration undergone by the nuclei of radioactive elements, such as radium and various isotopes of uranium and the transuranic elements. Certain lighter artificial (non-naturally occurring) isotopes also undergo radioactive decay. The associated radiation consists of alpha-rays, beta-rays, or gamma-rays (or a combination of these) and it takes place with a characteristic half-life, which is the time taken for half of any mass of a radioactive isotope to decay completely. The original nucleotide is known as the parent substance, and the produce is a daughter nucleotide (which may or may not be radioactive). After a time t, the number of daughter atoms from an original number N of parent atoms is equal to $Ne^{-\gamma t}$, where γ is the decay, or disintegration, constant.

Deccan /'dekən/ triangular tableland in eastern India, stretching between the Vindhya Hills in the north, and the Western and Eastern Ghats in the south.

decibel symbol dB, a unit that was used originally to compare sound intensities (loudness), but is now also employed to compare electrial or electronic power outputs. A tenth of a bel, a decibel is a logarithmic unit, so that an increase of 1 on the decibel scale represents a tenfold increase in sound intensity or power. In mathematical terms, two sources of power (or sound) of levels L_1 and L_2 differ by $10\log_{10}L_1/L_2$

decibels. One decibel therefore corresponds to a difference of roughly 25 per cent.

deciduous describing trees and shrubs that shed their leaves before the onset of winter or a dry season (see ◊abscission). In temperate regions there is little water available during winter and leaf-fall is an adaptation to reduce ◊transpiration. Examples of deciduous trees are oak and beech. Most deciduous trees belong to the ◊angiosperms, and the term 'deciduous tree' is sometimes used to mean 'angiosperm tree', despite the fact that many angiosperms are evergreen, especially in the tropics, and a few ◊gymnosperms (such as larches) are deciduous. The term ◊broad-leaved is now preferred to 'deciduous tree' for this reason.

decimal fractions the system of ◊fractions expressed by the use of the decimal point, which are in fact all those fractions where the denominator is 10, 100, 1,000 or any higher power of 10. Thus 3/10, 51/100, 23/1,000 are decimal fractions and are normally expressed as 0.3, 0.51, 0.023. The regular use of the decimal point appears to have been introduced about 1585, but the occasional use of decimal fractions can be traced back as far as the 12th century. The use of decimals greatly simplifies addition and multiplication of fractions, though not all fractions can be expressed exactly as decimal fractions.

decimal system a system of weights and measures, or coinage, based on one standard unit (for example the metre, the dollar) which is divided into or multiplied by multiples of 10. Since the USA and France set the example in the late 18th century, many countries of the world have adopted the decimal system for their coinage. Canada early adopted decimal coinage, but it was not until after World War II that many other Commonwealth countries did so, such as India 1957, Australia 1966, New Zealand 1967, and the UK 1971. The decimal system of weights and measures was first suggested in the 18th century by the Scottish engineer James Watt and first adopted by France during the Revolution (see ◊metric system). It is almost universally used throughout the world, especially by scientists and technologists, and was adopted in the UK from 1975. See also ◊SI unit.

decision table in computing, a method of describing a procedure for a program to follow, based on comparing possible decisions and their consequences. The top part of the table contains the conditions for making decisions (for example if a number is negative rather than positive and is less than 1), the bottom part describes the outcomes when those conditions are met (then either end or repeat the operation). Used as an aid in systems design.

Decius /'diːsiəs/ Gaius Messius Quintus Traianus 201–251. Roman emperor from 249. He fought a number of campaigns against the ◊Goths, but was finally beaten and killed by them near Abritum. He ruthlessly persecuted the Christians.

Declaration of Independence historic American document stating the theory of government on which the USA was founded, based on human natural rights. The statement was issued by the American Continental Congress on 4 July 1776, renouncing all allegiance to the British Crown, and ending the political connection with Britain. Following a resolution moved on 7 June, 'that these United Colonies are, and of right ought to be, free and independent States', a committee including Thomas Jefferson and Benjamin Franklin was set up to draft a declaration; most of the work was done by Jefferson. The resolution was adopted by the representatives of 12 colonies, New York at first abstaining, on 2 July, and the Declaration on 4 July; the latter date has ever since been celebrated as Independence day in the USA. The representatives of New York announced their adhesion on 15 July, and the Declaration was afterwards signed by the members of Congress on 2 August.

Declaration of Independence The committee who were appointed to draft the document – John Adams, Roger Sherman, Robert Livingston, Jefferson and Franklin – are seen at the table in 'The Signing of the Declaration of Independence' by John Trumbull.

Declaration of Rights in England, the statement issued by the Convention Parliament in February 1689, laying down the conditions under which the crown was to be offered to ◊William and Mary. Its clauses were later incorporated in the ◊Bill of Rights.

declination in astronomy, the coordinate on the ◊celestial sphere (imaginary sphere surrounding the Earth) that is equivalent to latitude on Earth. Declination runs from 0° at the celestial equator to 90° at the north and south celestial poles.

decomposer in biology, an organism that feeds on excreta, dead plant or animal matter. Decomposers include dung-beetle larvae, earthworms, certain bacteria and fungi. They play a vital role in ecological systems by freeing important chemical substances, such as nitrogen compounds, locked up in dead organisms or excreta. These are returned to the environment where they can once more be used by living organisms. See also ◊carbon cycle, ◊decomposition, ◊nitrogen cycle, and ◊saprotroph.

decomposition the process whereby a chemical compound is reduced to its component substances. In biology, the destruction of dead

organisms either by chemical reduction or by the action of ◊decomposers.

decompression sickness an illness brought about by a sudden and substantial change in atmospheric pressure. It is caused by a too rapid release of nitrogen which has been absorbed into the bloodstream under pressure. It causes breathing difficulties, joint and muscle pain, and cramp, and is experienced mostly by deep-sea divers who surface too quickly. It is popularly known as 'the bends'.

decorated name given in architecture to the second period of English Gothic, covering the latter part of the 13th century and the 14th century. Its chief characteristics are highly ornate window tracery, the window itself being divided into several lights by vertical bars called mullions; sharp spires ornamented with crockets and pinnacles; complex church vaulting; and slender arcade piers. Exeter cathedral is a notable example.

Dedekind /'deɪdəkɪnd/ Richard 1831–1916. German mathematician who made contributions to number theory. In 1872 he introduced the Dedekind cuts (which divide a line of infinite length representing all ◊real numbers) to categorize ◊irrational numbers as fractions, and thus increase their usefulness.

dedicated computer a computer built into another device for the purpose of controlling or supplying information to it. Their use has increased dramatically since the advent of the ◊microprocessor: washing machines, digital watches, cars and video recorders all have their own processors. A dedicated system is a general-purpose computer system confined to performing only one function for reasons of efficiency or convenience, for instance, a word processor.

deduction in philosophy, a form of argument in which the conclusion necessarily follows from the premises: it would be inconsistent to accept the premises but deny the conclusion.

Dee /diː/ John 1527–1608. English alchemist and mathematician. Born in London, he lived for many years in Europe and claimed to have transmuted metals into gold. He long enjoyed the favour of Elizabeth I, and was employed as a secret diplomatic agent, but died in poverty.

deed a legal document serving to pass an interest in property or to bind a person to perform or abstain from some action. Deeds are of two kinds: indentures and Deeds poll. Indentures are those which bind two parties in mutual obligations; Deeds poll concern one party only, as where a person changes their name.

deep freezing method of preserving food by rapid freezing, and storage at −18°C/0°F. Rapid freezing avoids structural change destructive of palatability, for example, the shrinkage and distortion of cells by formation of enlarged ice crystals in the extra-cellular spaces. Some 'quick-frozen' foods require pre-thawing before use, and cooking must then be prompt. Commercial freezing is usually by blast, circulation of air at −40°C/−40°F; contact, in which a refrigerant is circulated through hollow shelves; immersion, for example, fruit in a solution of sugar and glycerol; or cryogenic, for example, by liquid nitrogen spray. *Accelerated*

Dee The alchemist, astrologer, and mathematician John Dee enjoyed Elizabeth I's favour, and was also employed as a secret agent. He claimed to have turned base metal to gold, but nevertheless died in poverty.

freeze drying (AFD) involves rapid freezing followed by heat drying in a vacuum, for example, prawns for later rehydration. The product does not have to be stored in frozen condition.

Deep-Sea Drilling Project a research project initiated by the USA in 1968 to sample the rocks of the ocean ◊crust. In 1975 the operation became international, with Britain, France, Germany, Japan, and the USSR involved. Over 800 boreholes were drilled in all the oceans using the ship *Glomar Challenger*, and knowledge of the nature and history of the ocean basins was increased dramatically. The difficulties of drilling the seabed at a depth of 2,000 m/6,500 ft were overcome by keeping the ship on position with side-thrusting propellers and satellite navigation, and guiding the drill into its hole by using a radiolocation system.

deer ruminant even-toed hoofed mammal belonging to the family Cervidae, in which the male typically has a pair of ◊antlers, shed and regrown each year. Most species of deer are forest-dwellers, and the family is distributed throughout Europe, Asia, and America, but is absent from Australia and Africa south of the Sahara. Native to Britain are *red deer Cervus elaphus* and *roe deer Capreolus capreolus*. Red deer are found across Europe and can be 1.2 m/4 ft or more at the shoulder, plain dark brown with yellowish rump, and may have many points to the antlers. The roe deer is smaller, only about 75 cm/2.5 ft at the shoulder, with small erect antlers with three points or less. The *fallow deer Dama dama* came originally from the Mediterranean region but was introduced to Britain in ancient times. It typically has a spotted coat, and flattened 'palmate' antlers, and stands about 1 m/3 ft high. The little ◊muntjac has been introduced in more recent years from East Asia, and is spreading. Other species in the deer family include the ◊elk, ◊wapiti, ◊reindeer, and the *musk deer Moschus moschiferus* of Central Asia which yields musk and has no antlers.

deerhound large rough-coated dog used formerly used for hunting and killing deer. Slim and long-legged, it is 75 cm/2.5 ft or more tall, usually with a bluish-grey coat.

de Falla Spanish composer. See ◊Falla, Manuel de.

defamation in law, an attack on a person's reputation by ◊libel or ◊slander.

Defence, Ministry of British government department created in 1964 from a temporary Ministry of Defence established after World War II together with the Admiralty, Air Ministry, and War Office. It is headed by the secretary of state for defence undersecretaries for the Royal Navy, Army, and RAF. This centralization was influenced by the example of the USA, where the army, navy, and air force were unified by the National Security Act 1947, under the *Department of Defense*, presided over by a secretary of defense with a seat in the president's cabinet; each of the three services has a civilian secretary, not of cabinet rank, at its head. See also ◊NATO, and ◊war.

Defender of the Faith one of the titles of the English sovereign, conferred on Henry VIII in 1521 by Pope Leo X in recognition of the king's treatise against Luther. It appears on British coins in the abbreviated Latin form *F. D.*

deflation in economics, a decrease in the supply of money (as opposed to ◊inflation) leading to a reduction in the level of economic activity in an economy.

Defoe /dɪˈfəʊ/ Daniel 1660–1731. English novelist and journalist, best known for his adventure novel *Robinson Crusoe.* Born in Cripplegate, the son of a butcher, James Foe, he was educated for the Nonconformist ministry, but became a hosier. He took part in Monmouth's rebellion, and joined William of Orange in 1688. After his business had failed, he held a Civil Service post (1695–99). He wrote numerous pamphlets, and first achieved fame with the satire *The True-Born Englishman* 1701, followed in 1702 by the ironic *The Shortest Way with Dissenters*, for which he was fined, imprisoned, and pilloried. In Newgate he wrote his 'Hymn to the Pillory' and started a paper, *The Review* 1704–13. Released in 1704 he travelled in Scotland 1706–07, working to promote the Union, and published in 1709 *A History of the Union.* During the next ten years he was almost constantly employed as a political controversialist and pamphleteer. His version of the contemporary short story 'True Relation of the Apparition of one Mrs Veal' 1706 had revealed a gift for realistic narrative, and *Robinson Crusoe*, based on the story of Alexander Selkirk, appeared in 1719. It was followed among others by the pirate story *Captain Singleton* 1720, *A Journal of the Plague Year*, and picaresque novels *Moll Flanders* and *Colonel Jack* in 1722, and *Roxanna* 1724.

Degas /ˈdeɪgɑː/ (Hilaire Germain) Edgar 1834–1917. French ◊Impressionist painter and sculptor. Born in Paris, he abandoned law in order to study at the ◊Ecole des Beaux-Arts, where he came under the influence of ◊Ingres.

Defoe English novelist Daniel Defoe in 1706. A prolific writer, he produced over 500 books, pamphlets and journals, and had an enormous influence on the development of the novel. He is chiefly remembered for the work of his later years *Robinson Crusoe* 1719.

He worked in Italy for five years, and in 1870, during the Franco-Prussian War, he served in the National Guard. He avoided the Paris Salon, and became one of the chief exponents of the French Impressionist technique, working almost exclusively in pastel, and devoting himself to studies of ballet, horses and jockeys, and representations of contemporary life. He became blind, and died in Paris.

de Gaulle /də ˈɡəʊl/ Charles 1890–1970. French politician. Born at Lille, he graduated from Saint-Cyr in 1911 and in 1916 was severely wounded and captured by the Germans. In his *The Army of the Future* (1934) he attacked French dependence on an 'impregnable' Maginot Line, and in 1940 refused to accept ◊Pétain's truce with the Germans, becoming leader of the ◊Free French in England. In 1944 he entered Paris in triumph and was briefly head of the provisional government before resigning in protest at the defects of the new constitution of the Fourth Republic in 1946. In 1947 he founded the Rassemblement du Peuple Français (RPF) a non-party constitutional reform movement, and when bankruptcy and civil war loomed in 1958 de Gaulle was called by Coty to form a government. As premier he promulgated a constitution subordinating the legislature to the presidency and in 1959 took office as president. Economic recovery and eventual solution of colonial problems followed, but in pursuit of his Grand Design he opposed 'Anglo-Saxon' influence in Europe. Re-elected president in 1965, he quelled student-worker unrest which endangered the economy in 1968, and the Gaullist party, reorganized as *Union des*

Degas This print (probably dating from 1890) of a nude figure dressing is an example of the way in which Degas demonstrated that the unposed figure, even while performing simple and homely acts, was beautiful.

democrats pour la Cinquième République, won an overwhelming majority in the elections of the same year. In 1969 he resigned after the defeat of the government in a referendum on constitutional reform. His *Mémoires* cover the war and his years of political power. He retired to Colombey-les-Deux-Eglises.

de Gaulle Paris, 1954. Soldier and wartime leader of the Free French who entered Paris in triumph in May 1944. In 1958 the national assembly asked him to resume the presidency during France's economic recovery, and to solve the crisis in Algeria.

degaussing neutralization of the magnetic field of a body by encircling it with a conductor through which a current is maintained. Ships were degaussed in the World War II to avoid them detonating magnetic mines.

degree in mathematics, a unit of measurement of an angle, written as °. A circle is 360°. A quarter-turn (90°) is a right angle; a half-turn (180°) is the angle on a straight line. A degree is subdivided into 60 minutes. A degree of latitude is the length along a meridian such that the difference between its north and south ends is 1°. A degree of longitude is the length between two meridians making an angle of 1° at the centre of the earth. *Temperature* is also measured in degrees, but in this case the degree is divided decimally, not into minutes and seconds. See also under ◊Celsius and ◊circle.

de Havilland /də 'hævɪlənd/ Geoffrey 1882–1965. British aircraft designer who in 1920 founded the De Havilland Aircraft Company. He had already designed planes for World War I. Later came the *Moth*, the *Mosquito* fighter-bomber of World War II, and the post-war *Comet* – the world's first jet-driven airliner to enter commercial service. He was knighted in 1944 and received the Order of Merit in 1962.

Dehra Dun /'deərə 'duːn/ town in Uttar Pradesh, India, capital of Dehra Dun district. It has a military academy, a college, and a Sikh temple built in 1699. Population (1981) 220,530.

dehydration a process developed commercially in France c. 1795 for sliced vegetables using a hot air blast. Cereals have been dried naturally since earliest times and the process is now applied to legumes, nuts and some fruits. Moisture content is reduced to 10–20 per cent of fresh produce and this provides good protection against moulds. Bacteria are not inhibited by drying so the quality of raw materials is vital. The earliest large-scale application was to starch products such as spaghetti and pasta, but after 1945 it was extended to milk, potato, soups, instant coffee, and prepared baby and pet foods. A major benefit to food manufacturers is reduction of weight and volume of the food products, lowering distribution cost.

Deighton /'deɪtn/ Len 1929– . British author of spy fiction, including *The Ipcress File* 1963 and the trilogy *Berlin Game, Mexico Set, London Match* 1983–85, featuring the spy Bernard Samson.

Deimos one of the two moons of the planet Mars; see ◊Phobos and Deimos.

deindustrialization reduction in the proportion of a country's or other area's wealth production which is contributed by manufacturing industry, as opposed to service industries. It is typified by the closing down and non-replacement of industrial plants.

Deirdre in Celtic mythology, beautiful intended bride of ◊Conchobar.

deism literally, belief in a supreme being; but the term is usually used to refer to a movement of religious thought in England in the 17th–18th centuries, characterized by belief in the 'religion of nature' as opposed to the revealed religion of Christianity. The father of English deism was Lord Herbert of Cherbury (1583–1648), and the chief writers were John Toland (1670–1722),

Anthony Collins (1676–1729), Matthew Tindal (1657–1733), Thomas Woolston (1670–1733), Thomas Chubb (1679–1747). Later, deism came to mean a belief in a personal deity who is distinct from the world and not very intimately interested in its concerns. See also ◊theism.

Dekker /'dekə/ Thomas c. 1572–c. 1632. English dramatist and pamphleteer, who wrote mainly in collaboration with others. His best known play *The Shoemaker's Holiday* 1600, was followed by *The Honest Whore* and *Roaring Girl* (both with Middleton); *Sir Thomas Wyat* (with Webster), *Virgin Martyr* (with Massinger), and *The Witch of Edmonton* (with Ford and Rowley). His pamphlets include *The Gull's Hornbook* 1609, a lively satire on the fops and fashions of the day.

Delacroix /ˌdelə'krwɑ/ Eugène 1798–1863. French artist, one of the best known ◊Romantic painters. Possibly the son of ◊Talleyrand, whom he resembled, he was born near Paris. His *Massacre at Chios* 1824 (Louvre) shows Greeks enslaved by wild Turkish horsemen, a contemporary atrocity. Admired as a colourist, he used a technique of divided brushwork – adjacent brush marks of contrasting colour which the eye mixes as it scans – which anticipates the Impressionists. He learned this from seeing Constable's *Hay Wain* when it was exhibited in Paris in 1824. His prolific output includes religious and historical subjects, animal studies, illustrations from Shakespeare, Dante and Byron, and portraits of friends such as Paganini and Chopin. His *Journal* is interesting as much for the insight it gives on the social and artistic world of Paris as on his own life and works.

Delafield /'deləfiːld/ E M, pen name of Edmée Elizabeth Monica de la Pasture 1890–1931. British writer, best remembered for her amusing *Diary of a Provincial Lady* 1931, skilfully exploiting the foibles of middle-class life.

de la Mare /'delə 'meə/ Walter 1873–1956. English poet, best known for his verse for children, such as *Songs of Childhood* 1902, which appeared under the pseudonym Walter Ramal. Later volumes of poetry include *The Listeners* 1912 and *Collected Poems* 1942. He was also a gifted anthologist, as in *Come Hither* 1923 and *Behold this Dreamer* 1939, and wrote attractive prose, including *The Memoirs of a Midget* 1921. He had a gift for the weirdly mysterious, as in *The Return* 1910. He received the Order of Merit in 1953.

Delane /də'leɪn/ John Thaddeus 1817–1879. British journalist. As editor of *The Times* (1841–77), he first gave it international standing.

de la Ramée /də lɑ 'rɑːmeɪ/ Louise. British novelist who wrote under the name of ◊Ouida.

de la Roche /ˌdelə'rɒʃ/ Mazo 1885–1961. Canadian novelist, author of the 'Whiteoaks' family saga.

Delaroche /ˌdelə'rɒʃ/ Paul 1797–1856. French historical artist. Born in Paris, he first exhibited in the Salon of 1822, and with his friends ◊Géricault and ◊Delacroix was in the forefront of the revolt against the classicism of

Delacroix A self-portrait by the leader of the French Romantic school – Eugène Delacroix. He shocked his contemporaries by departing from classical tradition, exhibiting vivid paintings of scenes which were often violent or macabre.

◊David and his followers. Delaroche's paintings achieved great contemporary popularity.

Delaunay /də,ləʊ'neɪ/ Robert 1885–1941. French painter. Born in Paris, he experimented with the constructive use of colour in non-representational works and in subject pictures of runners. His *Windows* 1912 is believed to be the first ◊Cubist painting in colour.

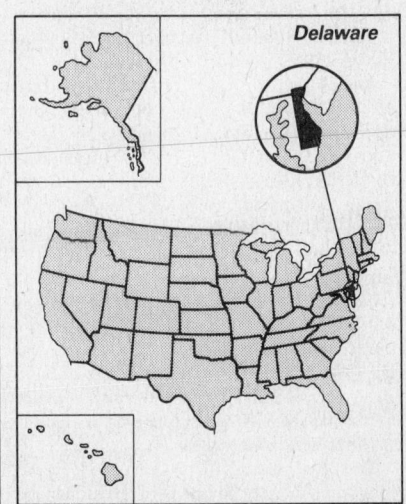

Delaware /'deləweə/ state of the northeast USA
area 5,328 sq km/2,057 sq mi
capital Dover
physical divided into two physical areas, one hilly and wooded, and the other gently undulating.

towns Wilmington
features one of the most industrialized states; headquarters of the Dupont chemical firm (see ◊nylon)
population (1980) 595,225
products dairy, poultry and market garden produce; chemicals, motor vehicles, textiles
history the first settlers were Dutch and Swedes about 1638, but in 1664 the area was captured by the British. Delaware was made a separate colony in 1702, organized as a state in 1776. It was one of the original 13 states of the USA.
famous people J P Marquand

de la Warr /'deləweə/ Thomas West, Baron de la Warr 1577–1618. known as Delaware. American colonial governor. Appointed Governor of Virginia in 1609, he arrived in 1610 just in time to prevent the desertion of the Jamestown colonists and by 1611 had reorganized the settlement. Both the river and state of Delaware are named after him.

Declassé /,delkæ'seɪ/ Théophile 1852–1923. French politician. He became foreign minister in 1898, but had to resign in 1905 because of German hostility; he held that post again in 1914–15. To a large extent he was responsible for the ◊*Entente Cordiale* with Britain.

De Lesseps /dəle'seps/ Ferdinand, Vicomte 1805–1894. French engineer, who constructed the ◊Suez Canal 1859–1869. He reluctantly began the ◊Panama Canal in 1881, but failed when he tried to construct it without locks.

Delft /delft/ town in the Netherlands in the province of S Holland, 14 km/9 mi NW of Rotterdam, famous for its china. William the ◊Silent was murdered here in 1584; population (1984) 87,000.

Delhi /'deli/ union territory of the Republic of India from 1956. Area 1,484 sq km/573 sq mi; population (1981) 6,196,400. The chief town is Delhi, capital of the Republic. Grains, sugar cane, fruits, and vegetables are the chief crops.

Delilah in the Old Testament, the Philistine mistress of ◊Samson.

Delius /'diːlɪəs/ Frederick (Theodore Albert) 1862–1934. British composer. Born at Bradford, he tried orange-growing in Florida, before going to study music in Leipzig in 1887. Encouraged by ◊Grieg, he settled in Paris to work in 1888, and in 1903 married the artist Jelka Rosen, the couple making their home at Grez-sur-Loing, near Paris. From 1925 he was blind and paralysed. His works include choral works (*Appalachia, Sea Drift, A Mass of Life, A Song of the High Hills*); the opera *A Village Romeo and Juliet* 1906 and music for the very popular play *Hassan* 1923; orchestral works such as *Brigg Fair* and *In a Summer Garden*; chamber music and songs. His reputation owes much to the untiring advocacy of Sir Thomas ◊Beecham.

Dell /del/ Ethel M(ary) 1881–1939. British romance writer, who achieved great popular success with her novels in which the heroes were usually ugly: *Way of an Eagle* 1912, *The Keeper of the Door* 1915, and *Storm Drift* 1930.

Deller /'delə/ Alfred 1912–1979. British ◊countertenor, founder of the Deller Consort, 1950, and particularly noted for performances of 16th–18th century music.

Delius British composer Frederick Delius painted by Ernst Proctor as he listens to his *A Mass of Life*. For ten years before his death he was paralysed and totally blind, but was able to contine his work with the help of an amanuensis, Eric Fenby.

Delos /'diːlɒs/ Greek island, smallest in the ◊Cyclades group, in the SW Aegean; area about 5 sq km/2 sq mi. The great temple of Apollo (4th century BC) is still standing.

Delphi /'delfi/ city of ancient Greece, situated in a rocky valley to the north of the gulf of Corinth, on the southern slopes of Mount Parnassus, site of a famous oracle. Here in the temple of Apollo was the *Omphalos* or conical stone supposed to stand at the centre of the earth; the oracle was interpreted by priests from the inspired utterances of the Pythian priestess until it was closed down by Emperor ◊Theodosius in 390 AD. A European Cultural Centre was built nearby 1966–67.

delphinium plant belonging to the Ranunculaceae. There are some 150 species in the N hemisphere including the *great flowered larkspur Delphinium grandiflorum*, an Asian form, one of the ancestors of the garden delphinium.

del Sarto /del 'saːtəʊ/ Andrea 1486–1531. See ◊Andrea del Sarto.

delta a triangular tract of land at a river's mouth, formed by deposited silt or sediment. Familiar examples of large deltas are those of the Mississippi, Ganges and Brahmaputra, Rhône, Po, Danube, and Nile; the shape of the Nile delta is like the Greek letter Δ, and thus gave rise to the name.
The *arcuate delta* of the Nile is only one form. Others are *birdfoot deltas*, like that of the Mississippi, which is a seaward extension of the river's ◊levee system; and *tidal deltas*, like that of the Mekong in which most of the material is swept to one side by sea currents.

Delta Force US anti-terrorist force, based at Fort Bragg, N Carolina, and modelled on the British ◊SAS.

Delta rocket a US rocket used to launch many scientific and communications satellites

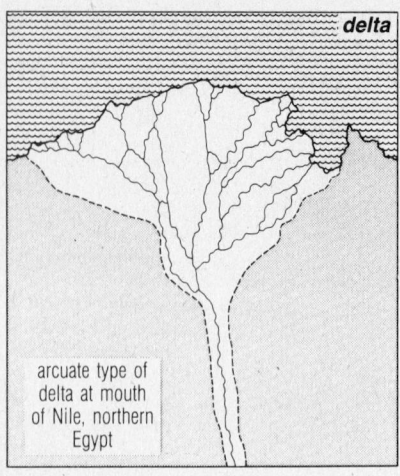

delta

arcuate type of delta at mouth of Nile, northern Egypt

since 1960, based on the Thor ballistic missile. Several increasingly powerful versions have been produced as satellites have become larger and heavier. Solid-fuel boosters are attached to the first stage to increase lifting power.

delta wing an aircraft wing shaped like the Greek letter Δ. It is a design that enables an aircraft to pass through the ◊sound barrier with little effect. The supersonic airliner ◊Concorde and the ◊space shuttle have delta wings.

dementia a state of mental deterioration accompanied by emotional disturbance. It is usually associated with old age and may be caused by faulty blood supply to the brain. A proportion of younger people showing signs of dementia suffer from *Alzheimer's disease* (loss of brain cells, tangling and distortion of those remaining, and biochemical imbalance). It is as yet untreatable.

Demerara /,demə'reərə/ river in Guyana, 174 km/180 mi long, which gives its name to the country's chief sugar cane growing area, after which Demerara sugar is named.

Demeter /dɪ'miːtə/ in Greek mythology, goddess of agriculture (identified with Roman ◊Ceres), daughter of Kronos and Rhea, and by Zeus mother of ◊Persephone. She is identified with the Egyptian goddess ◊Isis and had a temple dedicated to her at ◊Eleusis where ◊mystery religions were celebrated.

Demetrius /dɪ'miːtriəs/ Donskoi 1350–1389. Grand Prince of Moscow from 1363. He achieved the first Russian victory over the Tatars on the plain of Kulikovo, next to the Don (hence his nickname) in 1380.

de Mille /də 'mɪl/ Cecil B(lount) 1881–1959. American film director. Born in Massachusetts, he entered films with Jesse L Lasky in 1913 (with whom he later established Paramount), and was one of the founders of Hollywood's long supremacy. He specialized in biblical epics, for example *The Sign of the Cross* 1932 and *The Ten Commandments* 1956.

Demirel /,demɪ'rel/ Suleyman 1924– . Turkish politician. Leader from 1964 of the Justice Party (JP), he was prime minister 1965–71, 1975–77, and 1979–80. He favoured links with the West, full membership of the EEC and foreign investment in Turkish industry.

democracy from ancient Greek *demokratia*, a compound of *demos* (the community) and *kratos* (sovereign power). Government by the people, or, as defined by Abraham Lincoln, 'government of the people, by the people, for the people'. A distinction may be made between direct democracy, where the whole people meet for the making of laws or the direction of executive officers, and indirect democracy, where the people entrust such power to elected representatives. The most famous example of direct democracy is that of Athens in the 5th century BC (and allegedly modern ◊Libya). Direct democracy today is represented mainly by the use of the ◊referendum, as in the UK, Switzerland, and certain states of the USA.
In the modern world democracy has developed from the American and French revolutions. Representative parliamentary government has existed in England since the 13th century, but the working classes were excluded almost entirely from the ◊vote until 1867, and women were admitted and property qualifications abolished only in 1918.
Recent controversy has centred on the Western conception of democracy, as accepted in Britain, France, and the USA, and the Eastern, as in the USSR and communist Asia and Europe. The former emphasizes the control of the government by the electorate and freedom of speech and the press. The latter envisages economic control by the government for the benefit of the community, both political and economic power resting in the Communist Party under a single-party system.

Democratic Party one of the two main political parties of the USA. Founded by Jefferson in 1792 (originally called Democratic Republicans) to defend the rights of the individual states against the centralizing policy of the Federalists, it now tends to be the party of the working person, as opposed to the Republicans, the party of 'big business', but the divisions between the two are not clear-cut. Its stronghold has traditionally been the Southern states. The Democratic Party held power almost continuously 1800–60, and later returned Cleveland, Wilson, F D Roosevelt, Truman, Kennedy, Johnson, and Carter. In the 20th century it has become associated with more liberal policies than the Republican. In the 1960s the Northern Democrats ('Presidential wing') pressed for civil rights reform, while Southern Democrats ('Congressional wing') voted against the President on social issues.

Democritus /dɪˈmɒkrɪtəs/ c. 460–361 BC. Greek philosopher and speculative scientist. Born in Thrace, he travelled widely in the East in search of knowledge. His most important contribution to philosophy is the atomic theory of the universe.

demodulation the technique in ◊radio of separating a transmitted audio frequency signal from its modulated radio carrier wave. At the transmitter the audio frequency signal (representing speech or music, for example) may be made to modulate the amplitude (AM broadcasting) or frequency (FM broadcasting)

of a continuously transmitted radiofrequency carrier wave. At the receiver, the signal from the aerial is demodulated to extract the required speech or sound component. In early radio systems, this process was called detection.

demography the study of the size, structure, and development of human populations to establish reliable statistics on such factors as birth and death rates, marriages and divorces, life expectancy, and migration. Demography is important in the social sciences as the basis for government planning in such areas as education, housing, welfare, transport, and taxation.

demonstration public show of support for or opposition to a particular political or social issue, typically by a group of people holding a rally, displaying placards, making speeches, and so on. The aim is usually to seek some change in official policy, either directly by impressing the authorities with the weight of opinion in favour of such change, or indirectly (for example by provoking disorder that will embarrass the authorities into giving way). Demonstrations can be static (such as the nonstop anti-apartheid demonstration in front of South Africa House in London, which began in Apr 1986, or the continuous presence of women at ◊Greenham Common) or take the form of elementary street theatre or processions (such as the ◊hunger marches organized in the 1920s–30s in Britain). A specialized type of demonstration is the *picket*, in which striking or dismissed workers try to dissuade others from using or working in the premises of the employer. An example is the picketing of the News International complex in Wapping, East London, by print workers in 1986. In Britain, official response to demonstrations was first codified by the Public Order Act 1936. This was provoked by the Cable Street riot of that year, when an anti-Jewish march through East London by Oswald Mosley and 2,500 of his Blackshirts gave rise to violent clashes. The Public Order Act 1986 gave police extensive new powers to restrict demonstrations and pickets. It requires those organizing a demonstration to give seven days' notice to the police and gives the police the power to say where demonstrators should stand, how long they can stay and in what numbers, if they believe the protest could cause 'serious disruption to the life of the community' (traffic and shoppers) even though no disorder is anticipated. Penalties for disobeying a police officer's instruction are three months' imprisonment for organizers and a heavy fine for followers. Police power to ban processions that they believe might result in serious public disorder has been used with increasing frequency in recent years (11 banning orders 1970–80 and 75 in 1981–85).

Demosthenes /dɪˈmɒsθəniːz/ c. 384–322 BC. Athenian orator and statesman. From 351 BC he led the party which advocated resistance to the growing power of ◊Philip of Macedon and in his 'Philippics' incited the Athenians to war. This policy resulted in the defeat of Chaeronea in 338, and the establishment of Macedonian supremacy. After the death of Alexander he organized a revolt, and when it failed took poison to avoid capture by the Macedonians.

Demosthenes The greatest of Greek orators, the Athenian Demosthenes, was said to have acquired his rhetorical powers in a series of lawsuits against the trustees who had seriously mismanaged his inheritance.

Demotic Greek the common or vernacular variety of the modern ◊Greek language.

demotic script a form of cursive (joined) writing derived from Egyptian hieratic script, itself a cursive form of ◊hieroglyphic. Demotic documents are known from the 6th century BC to about 470 AD. It was written horizontally, from right to left.

Dempsey /ˈdempsi/ 'Jack' (William Harrison) 1895–1983. American boxer, known from his birthplace in Colorado as the Manassa Mauler. In 1919 he defeated Jess Willard to become world heavyweight champion until he lost to Gene Tunney in 1926.

Denbighshire /ˈdenbiʃə/ former county of Wales, largely merged in 1974, together with Flint and part of Merioneth, in Clwyd, although a small area along the W border was included in Gwynedd. Denbigh, in the Clwyd valley (population (1981) 9,000) was the county town.

Dench /dentʃ/ Judi 1934– . British actress, who made her debut as Ophelia in *Hamlet* in 1957 with the Old Vic Company. She is noted for her many Shakespearean and classical roles including Portia in *Twelfth Night*, *Major Barbara*, *The Duchess of Malfi*, Lady Macbeth, and Cleopatra. She is also a versatile comedy actress, as in the television series *A Fine Romance* 1985, and her recent films include *A Room with a View* and *84 Charing Cross Road*. Dame of the British Empire 1988.

dendrochronology the analysis of the ◊annual rings of trees to date past events. Samples of ◊wood can be obtained by means of a narrow metal tube that is driven into a tree to remove a core extending from the bark to the centre. Samples taken from timbers at an

Dempsey A fearless, aggressive fighter, 'Jack' Dempsey, known as the Manassa Mauler, was world heavyweight boxing champion from 1919–26.

archaelogical site can be compared with cores from old, living trees, and the year when they were felled can be determined by locating the point where the rings of the two samples correspond. Since annual rings are formed from the varying sizes of water-conducting cells produced by the plant in different seasons of the year, they also provide a means of determining past climatic conditions in a given area. In North America, sequences of tree rings extending back over 8,000 years have been obtained by using cores from the bristle-cone pine (*Pinus aristata*) which can live for over 4,000 years.

dengue viral fever transmitted by mosquitoes and accompanied by joint pains, a rash and glandular swelling. A more virulent form, dengue haemorrhagic fever, thought to be caused by a second infection on top of the first, also causes internal bleeding.

Deng Xiao Ping /ˈdʌŋ ˌʃaʊˈpɪŋ/ formerly *Teng Hsiao-ping* 1904– . Chinese political leader. A member of the Chinese Communist Party (CCP) from the 1920s, he took part in the Long March 1934–36. He was in the Politburo from 1955 until ousted in the Cultural Revolution 1966–69. Reinstated in the 1970s, he gradually seized power and introduced a radical economic modernization programme.

Deng, born in Sichuan province into a middle-class landlord family, joined the CCP as a student in Paris, where he adopted the name Xiaoping (Little Peace), in 1925, and studied in Moscow in 1926. After the Long March, he served as a political commissar to the People's Liberation Army during the civil war of 1937–49. He entered the CCP Politburo in 1955 and headed the secretariat during the early 1960s, working closely with President ◊Liu Shaoqi. During the Cultural Revolution Deng was dismissed as a 'capitalist roader' and sent to work in a tractor factory in Nanchang for 're-education'.

Deng was rehabilitated by his patron ◊Zhou Enlai in 1973 and served as acting prime minister after Zhou's heart attack in 1974. On Zhou's death in Jan 1976 he was forced into hiding but returned to office as vice premier in Jul 1977. By Dec 1978, although nominally a CCP vice chair, state vice premier, and Chief of Staff to the PLA, Deng was the controlling force in China. He helped to oust ◊Hua Guofeng in favour of his protégés ◊Hu Yaobang and ◊Zhao Ziyang.

Deng, despite repeated suggestions of retirement, remains the dominant decision maker in China. His policy, misinterpreted in the West as a drift to capitalism, is 'socialism with Chinese characteristics'.

Den Haag /den ˈhɑːx/ Dutch form of The ◊Hague.

Den Helder /den ˈheldə/ fishing port and naval base in North Holland province, Netherlands, 65 km/40 mi N of Amsterdam, on the entrance to the North Holland Canal from the North Sea. Population (1985) 63,538.

denier system of measuring fine yarns, both natural and synthetic, derived from the old French silk industry. The denier was an old French silver coin. Thus 9,000 metres of 15 denier nylon, commonly used in nylon stockings, weighs 15 g/0.5 oz, and in this case the thickness of thread would be 0.00425 mm/0.0017 in.

Denikin /dɪˈniːkɪn/ Anton Ivanovich 1872–1946. Russian general. He distinguished himself in the Russo-Japanese war and World War I After the outbreak of the Bolshevik Revolution he organized a volunteer army of 60,000 Whites (Russian counter-revolutionaries), but in 1919 was routed and escaped to France. He wrote a history of the Revolution and the Civil War.

De Niro /dəˈnɪərəʊ/ Robert 1943– . American actor, best known for his sensitive portrayal of strong and often complex characters. His films include *Mean Streets* 1973, *Taxi Driver* 1976, and *The Deer Hunter* 1978, also *The Godfather Part II* 1974 and *Raging Bull* 1979, for both of which he won Academy Awards, and *The Untouchables* 1987.

Denis, Saint /ˈdenɪs/ (Dionysius) first bishop of Paris and one of the patron saints of France. He was martyred by the Romans in about 275 AD.

Denmark /ˈdenmɑːk/ peninsula and islands in N Europe, bounded to the north by the Skagerrak, to the east by the Kattegat, to the south by West Germany, and to the west by the North Sea.

government under the 1849 constitution, last revised in 1953, there is an hereditary monarch with no personal political power, and a single-chamber parliament, the *Folketing*. The prime minister and cabinet are drawn from and responsible to the *Folketing*, which has 179 members elected by adult franchise, 175 representing metropolitan Denmark, two the Faroe Islands and two Greenland. Voting is by proportional representation and the *Folketing* has a life of four years, but may be dissolved within this period if the government is defeated on a vote of confidence. The government, however, need only resign on what it itself defines

as a 'vital element' of policy. Most significant of the 12 political parties are the Social Democrats, the Conservative People's Party, the Liberals, the Socialist People's Party, the Radical Liberals, the Centre Democrats, the Progress Party, the Christian People's Party, and the Left Socialists.

history the original home of the Danes was Sweden, whence they migrated in the 5th and 6th centuries. Ruled by local chieftains, they terrified Europe by their piratical raids during the 8th–10th centuries, until Harald Bluetooth (c. 940–85) unified Denmark and established Christianity. Canute (ruled 1014–35) founded an empire embracing Denmark, England, and Norway, which fell to pieces at his death. After a century of confusion Denmark again dominated the Baltic under Valdemar I, Canute VI, and Valdemar II (1157–1241). Domestic conflict then prodduced anarchy, until Valdemar IV (1340–75) restored order. Denmark, Norway, and Sweden were united under one sovereign in 1397. Sweden broke away in 1449 and after a long struggle had its independence recognized in 1523. Christian I (1448–81) secured the duchies of Schleswig and Holsstein, fiefs of the ◊Holy Roman Empire, in 1460; and they were held by his descendants until 1863. Christian II (ruled 1513–23) was deposed in favour of his uncle Frederick whose son Christian III (ruled 1534–59) in 1536 made Lutheranism the established religion. Attempts to regain Sweden led to disastrous wars with that country 1563–70, 1643–45, 1657–60; equally disastrous was Christian V's intervention, 1625–29, on the Protestant side of the ◊Thirty Years War. Frederick III (ruled 1648–70) made himself absolute monarch in 1665, and ruled through a burgher bureaucracy. Serfdom was abolished in 1788. Denmark's adherence in 1780 to the Armed neutrality against Britain resulted in the naval defeat of Copenhagen in 1801, and in 1807 the British bombarded Copenhagen and seized the Danish fleet to save it from ◊Napoleon. This incident drove Denmark into the arms of France, and the Allies at the Congress of Vienna took Norway from Denmark and gave it to Sweden, in 1815. A liberal movement then arose, which in 1848–49 compelled Frederick VII (ruled 1848–63) to grant a democratic constitution. The Germans in Schleswig-Holstein revolted with Prussian support 1848–50, and Prussia seized the provinces in 1864, after a short war. North Schleswig was recovered after a plebiscite in 1920.

Neutral in World War I, Denmark tried to preserve its neutrality in 1939 by signing a pact with Hitler, but was occupied by Germany 1940–45. Although traditionally neutral, Denmark joined ◊NATO in 1949 and the ◊European Free Trade Association (EFTA) in 1960, but resigned in 1973 to join the EEC. ◊Iceland was part of the Danish kingdom until 1945 and the other parts of non-metropolitan Denmark, the Faroe Islands and Greenland, were given special recognition by a constitution which has been adapted to meet changing circumstances. In 1953 provision was made for a daughter to succeed to the throne in the absence

Denmark
KINGDOM OF (*Kongeriget Danmark*)

AREA 43,075 sq km/16,631 sq mi
CAPITAL Copenhagen
TOWNS Aarhus, Odense, Aalborg, Esbjerg, all
ports
PHYSICAL the land is flat and cultivated; sand
dunes and lagoons on the W coast and long
inlets on the E
TERRITORIES Faeroe Islands and Greenland
FEATURES comprises the peninsula of
Jylland/Jutland, plus the main island Sjaelland
(English ZEALAND), Fünen, Lolland, Bornholm,
and smaller islands
HEAD OF STATE Margarethe II from 1972
head of government Paul Schluter from 1982
GOVERNMENT constitutional monarchy
EXPORTS bacon, dairy produce, eggs, fish, mink
pelts; car and aircraft parts, electrical
equipment, textiles
CURRENCY krone (11.49 = £1 Sept 1987)
POPULATION 5,105,000 (1985); annual growth
rate -0.1%
LANGUAGE Danish (official)
RELIGION Lutheran
LITERACY 99% (1983)
GNP $50.4 bn (1983); $12,956 per head of
population
CHRONOLOGY
1940–45 Occupied by Germany.

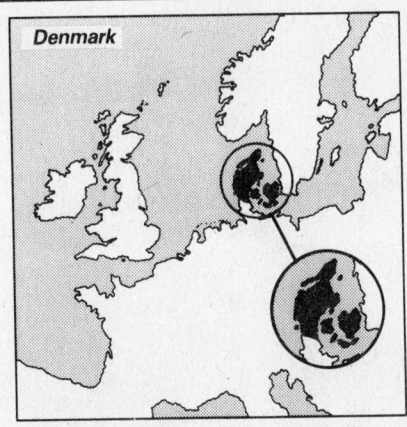

Denmark

1945 Iceland's independence recognized.
1947 Frederik IX succeeded Christian X.
1948 Home rule granted for Faeroe Islands.
1949 Became a founder member of NATO.
1960 Joined EFTA.
1972 Margrethe II became Denmark's first
queen for nearly 600 years.
1973 Left EFTA and joined EEC.
1979 Home rule granted for Greenland.
1985 Strong non-nuclear movement in
evidence.

of a male heir, and a system of voting by
proportional representation was introduced.
Left-wing policies have dominated Danish
politics, and proportional representation, often
resulting in minority or coalition governments,
has encouraged this moderate approach. In the
Sept 1987 general election, the centre-right
coalition lost seven seats, but Prime Minister
Schluter decided to continue with a minority
government, holding 70 of the *Folketing* seats.

Denning /'denɪə Alfred Thompson, Baron
Denning 1899– . British judge, Master of the
Rolls 1962–82. In 1963 he conducted the inquiry
into the ◊Profumo scandal. A vigorous and
highly innovatory civil lawyer, he was
controversial in his defence of the rights of the
individual against the state, the unions and big
business.

density measure of the compactness of a
substance; its mass per unit volume, measured in
kg per cubic metre/lb per cubic foot. *Relative
density* is the ratio of the density of a substance
to that of water at 4°C.

dentistry the care and treatment of the teeth
and their supporting tissues. The bacteria which
start the process of dental decay are normal, non-
pathogenic members of a large and varied group
of micro-organisms present in the mouth. They
are strains of oral streptococci, but it is only in
the presence of sucrose (from refined sugar) in
the mouth that they become damaging to the
teeth. ◊Fluoride in the water supply is one
attempted solution, but in 1979 a vaccine was
developed from a modified form of the bacterium
Streptococcus mutans. *Orthodontics* deals with

the straightening of the teeth, and
periodontology with care of the supporting
tissue.
The earliest dental school was opened at
Baltimore, Maryland, in 1839; in Britain the
predecessors of the modern University College
Hospital Dental School and Royal Dental
Hospital and School, both within the University
of London, were established 1859 and 1860.
There is an International Dental Federation
(1900).

denudation general term for the natural loss
of soil and rock debris, blown away by wind or
washed away by running water, that lays bare the
rock below. Over millions of years, denudation
causes a general levelling of the landscape.

Denver /'denvə/ city in Colorado, USA, on
the South Platte river, near the foothills of the
Rocky Mountains. Population (1980) 492,365.
It was founded in 1858, with the discovery of
gold, becoming a mining camp supply centre.
Coal is also mined nearby, and Denver became a
big industrial centre with rubber, mining
machinery, canning and meat packing, brewing,
and many other varied manufactures. In the
1970s oil and gas finds in the Rocky Mountains
made it a rival oil capital to Houston, and it is also
important as a communications and distribution
centre for the western USA. There is a university,
a mining school, and many medical institutions,
and the US mint is sited here.

deodar Himalayan cedar tree *Cedrus
deodara*, often planted as rapid-growing
ornamental. It has valuable timber.

deoxyribonucleic acid the full name of
◊DNA.

**Department of Education and Science
(DES)** UK government department responsible
for education policy making in England, and for
the universities throughout the UK.

depilatory instrument (such as electrolytic
needle) or substance used to eradicate growing
hair, usually for cosmetic reasons. Permanent
eradication is by destruction of each individual
hair root by an electrolytic needle or an
electrocautery, but there is a danger of scarring.

depreciation in economics, the decline or
erosion of the value of a ◊currency in relation to
other currencies; also, the fall in value of an asset
(such as factory machinery) resulting from age,
wear and tear, or other factors.

depression an emotional state characterized
by sadness, unhappy thoughts, apathy, and
dejection. Sadness is a normal response to major
losses such as bereavement, and unemployment.
However, clinical depression, which is prolonged
or unduly severe, often requires treatment, such
as anti-depressant medication, cognitive therapy
or, in very rare cases, electro-convulsive therapy
(ECT), in which an electrical current is passed
through the brain.

Depression term used to describe two periods
of crisis in the European and world economies.
The Depression of 1873–96 centred on falling
growth rates in the British economy but also
affected industrial activity in Germany and the
USA. Recent research has suggested that the
crisis in the British economy lasted longer than
these dates suggest.
The name Depression more often refers to the
world economic crisis precipitated by the Wall
Street crash of 29 Oct 1929 when millions of
dollars were wiped off US share values in a matter
of hours. This forced the closure of many US
banks involved in stock speculation and led to the
recall of US overseas investments. This loss of US
credit had serious repercussions on the European
economy, especially that of Germany, and led to
a steep fall in the levels of international trade
as countries attempted to protect their domestic
economies. Although most European countries
experienced a slow recovery during the mid-
1930s, the main impetus for renewed economic
growth was provided by rearmament
programmes later in the decade.

depression of freezing point a lowering of the
◊freezing point of a solution, below that of the
pure solvent, which depends on the number of
molecules of solute dissolved in it.

Deptford district in SE London in the
borough of Lewisham, mainly residential, with
industries including engineering and chemicals.
It was an important Royal naval dockyard from
1513 to 1869, on the south bank of the river
Thames.

de Tocqueville Alexis 1805–1859. French
politician, see ◊ Tocqueville, Alexis de.

de Quincey /də'kwɪnsi/ Thomas 1785–1859.
British author. Born in Manchester, he ran away
from school there to wander and study in Wales.
He then went to London where he lived in
extreme poverty, but with the constant
companionship of the young orphan Ann, of

Depression A soup kitchen in Chicago during the Depression.

whom he writes in the *Confessions*. In 1803 he was reconciled to his guardians and was sent to Oxford, entering the Middle Temple in 1808. In 1809 he settled with the ◊Wordsworths and ◊Coleridge in the Lake District, and in 1816 married Margaret Simpson. His addiction to opium had begun while he was at college. He published his *Confessions of an English Opium-eater* in 1821 in the *London Magazine*. Among his best essays are *On the Knocking at the Gate in Macbeth* 1823, and *Murder Considered as One of the Fine Arts* 1827. He was obliged to devote the rest of his life to miscellaneous journalism. In 1828 he moved to Edinburgh, where he eventually died. De Quincey's work had a powerful influence on ◊Baudelaire and ◊Poe amongst others. His biography was written by E Sackville West, 1936.

Derain /dəˈræ̃/ André 1880–1954. French Post-Impressionist artist. He established himself as a leader of ◊Fauvism, with landscapes and studies of Paris suburbs. His gift for fantasy emerged in his costumes and scenery for Diaghilev's ballet *La Boutique Fantasque*.

Derby /ˈdɑːbi/ industrial city in ◊Derbyshire, England; population (1981) 216,000. Rail locomotives, Rolls-Royce cars and aero-engines, chemicals, paper, electrical, mining and engineering equipment are manufactured here. Noted are the museum collections of Crown Derby china; the Rolls-Royce collection of aero engines; and the Derby Playhouse. British Rail has research laboratories, and training and technical centres here.

Derby chief English horse race, established by the 12th Earl of Derby 1780, over 2.4 km/1.5 mi at Epsom. The American equivalent is the

Kentucky Derby 1875, at Churchill Downs, Louisville over 2 km/1.25 mi

Recent Derby Winners (year, horse, jockey)
1983 *Teenoso* (L Piggott)
1984 *Secreto* (Christy Roche)
1985 *Slip Anchor* (Steve Cauthen)
1986 *Shahrastani* (Walter Swinburn)
1987 *Reference Point* (S Cauthen).

Derby /ˈdɑːbi/ Edward Geoffrey Smith Stanley, 14th Earl of Derby 1799–1869. British politician. Originally a Whig, he became secretary for the colonies in 1830, and introduced the bill for the abolition of slavery. He joined the Tories in 1834, and the split in the Tory Party over Peel's free-trade policy gave him the leadership for 20 years. He was prime minister 1852, 1858–59, and 1866–68, with ◊Disraeli as his lieutenant in the Commons.

Derby /ˈdɑːbi/ Edward George Villiers Stanley, 17th Earl of Derby 1865–1948. British Conservative politician. He became a member of parliament in 1892. In 1915 he was appointed director-general of recruiting and was responsible for the system known as the Derby Scheme. In the Lloyd George coalition of 1916–18 he was secretary of war, and held the same post in 1922–24. In 1918–20 he was ambassador to France.

Derbyshire /ˈdɑːbiʃə/ county in N central England
area 2,631 sq km/1,016 sq mi
towns administrative headquarters Matlock; Derby, Chesterfield, Ilkeston
features Peak District National Park (including Kinder Scout 636 m/2,088 ft); rivers Derwent,

Dove, Rother, Trent; Chatsworth House, Bakewell (seat of Duke of Devonshire), Haddon Hall
products cereals are grown in the S and E, and there is dairy and sheep farming on the hills. There have been pit and factory closures, but the area is being redeveloped, and there are large reserves of fluorspar.
population (1986) 911,700.

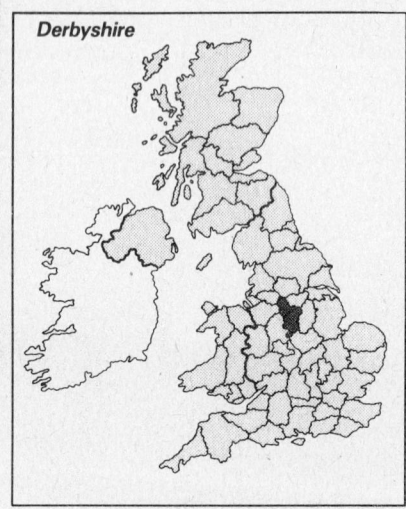

Derbyshire

Derbyshire Chatsworth House, Bakewell, the chief seat of the Duke of Devonshire, with a valuable collection of paintings and other treasures.

deregulation action to abolish or reduce state controls and supervision over private economic activities, as with the deregulation of the US airline industry in 1978. In Britain the major changes in the City of London in 1986 (the ◊big bang) were in part deregulation.

dermatitis inflammation of the skin caused by allergy, industrial processes, disease, and so on. It may occur in nearly any skin disease, but the best-known varieties are those caused in people whose occupations bring them into contact with irritating substances such as dyes, paints, solvents or even flour, or in people wearing clothing, such as woollen garments or fur coats, to which their skin is sensitive.

derrick a simple lifting machine, consisting in essence of a pole carrying a block and tackle. Derricks are commonly to be seen on ships such as freighters. In the oil industry the tower used for hoisting the drill pipes is known as a derrick.

derris climbing plant of SE Asia *Derris elliptica* family Leguminosae, its roots contain rotenone, a strong insecticide.

Derry /'deri/ another name for ◊Londonderry.

dervish in Iran and Turkey, a religious mendicant, and throughout the rest of Islam a member of an Islamic religious brotherhood, not necessarily mendicant in character. The Arabic equivalent is *fakir*. There are various orders of dervishes, each with its 'rule', and a special ritual. The 'whirling dervishes' claim close communion with the deity through ecstatic dancing; the 'howling dervishes' gash themselves with knives and claim miraculous healing powers.

Desai /de'saɪ/ Morarji 1896– . Indian statesman. An early follower of Mahatma Gandhi, he was prime minister, as leader of the Janata Party 1977–79, after toppling Indira Gandhi. Party in-fighting led to his resignation of both the premiership and party leadership.

desalination the removal of salt, especially from sea water, to produce fresh water for irrigation, etc. Distillation has usually been the method adopted, but in the 1970s a cheaper process, using certain polymer materials which filter the molecules of salt from the water by reverse ◊osmosis, was developed.

Descartes /deɪ'kɑːt/ René 1596–1650. French philosopher, generally regarded as the founder of modern philosophy. Born near Tours, he served in the army of Prince Maurice of Nassau, and in 1619, while travelling through Europe, he experienced an illumination which determined him to apply the certain methods of mathematics to metaphysics and science. He settled in Holland in 1628, where he was likely to be free from interference by the ecclesiastical authorities. In 1649 he visited the court of Queen Christina of Sweden, and died in Stockholm.

Descartes exposed the doubtful nature of commonly accepted 'knowledge' (such as that acquired through the senses). He then attempted to rebuild human knowledge using a foundation 'Cogito ergo sum' ('I think, therefore I am'). The 'thinking thing' (*res cogitans*) or mind Descartes identified with the human soul or consciousness; the body, though somehow interacting with the soul, was a physical machine, secondary to, and in principle separable from the soul. He held that everything has a cause; nothing can result from nothing; and matter is extended substance. He aimed at showing that the entire material universe can be completely explained in terms of mathematical physics, on the basis of the fewest possible ultimates – his 'clear ideas' of extended substance and its ultimate properties, divisibility, and mobility. But although all matter

is in motion, matter does not move of its own accord – the initial impulse comes from God; and he also postulated two quite distinct substances – spatial substance or matter, and thinking substance or mind. This is called Cartesian Dualism and it preserved him from serious controversy with the Church. Descartes is regarded as the discoverer of analytical geometry and the founder of the science of optics. His works include *Discourse on Method* (1637), *Meditations on the First Philosophy* (1641), and *Principles of Philosophy* (1644), and numerous books on physiology, optics, and geometry.

Descartes An engraving of French philosopher and mathematician René Descartes from a portrait by Frans Hals. Descartes is generally considered the founder of modern philosphy.

Deschamps /deɪ'ʃɒŋ/ Eustache 1346–1406. French poet. Born in Champagne, he was the author of more than 1,000 ballades, and the *Miroir de Mariage/The Mirror of Marriage*, an attack on women.

deselection in Britain, removal or withholding of a sitting Member of Parliament's official status as a candidate for a forthcoming election. The term came into use in the 1980s with the efforts of many local Labour parties to revoke the candidature of MPs viewed as too right-wing.

desert area without sufficient vegetation to support human life. Scientifically this term includes the ice areas of the polar regions, although a desert is generally thought of as restricted to the earth's warmer zones particularly at the latitudes of the tropics. The *tropical desert* belts are caused by the descent of dry air that has already risen and dropped its water at the equator. Other natural desert types are the *continental deserts*, like the Gobi, that are too far from the sea to receive any moisture; *rain-shadow deserts*, such as California's Death Valley, that lie in the lee of mountain ranges, all rain having been dropped on the windward

slopes; and *coastal deserts*, such as the Namib, where cold ocean currents cause the local dry air masses to descend. Desert surfaces are usually rocky or gravelly, with only a small proportion being covered with sand.

Almost 33 per cent of the earth's land surface is desert, and this proportion is increasing. Deserts are created by changes in climate, or by the human-aided process of desertification, including overgrazing, destruction of timber shelter belts, and the overpopulation which leads to exhaustion of the soil by too intensive cultivation without restoration of fertility. Some 135 million people are affected, chiefly in Africa, the Indian subcontinent, and South America. The process can be reversed by special planting (marram grass, trees) and by the use of water-absorbent plastic grains with the sand, a polymer absorbent of 40 times its own weight of water, which enables crops to be grown.

Desert Rats nickname of the British 8th Army, in North Africa in World War II, originating in a military shoulder-flash of a ◊jerboa (capable of great leaps forward).

de Sica /deɪ 'siːkə/ Vittorio 1901–1974. Italian director and actor. Born in Sora, Caserta, he achieved international fame in 1946 with *Bicycle Thieves*, a film of subtle realism. Later films included *Umberto D* 1952 and *The Garden of the Finzi-Continis* 1972.

Design Centre, The British official body, established in the Haymarket, London, in 1956 by the Council of Industrial Design (an official body set up in 1944 to improve standards in British products). The centre displays goods such as building fittings, furniture, and cutlery, and includes in a Design Index selected examples of good design. Since 1957 Design Awards have been given annually for 20 outstanding specimens. The Scottish Design Centre in Glasgow is run on similar lines.

Des Moines /dɪ 'mɔɪn/ capital and largest town in Iowa, USA, on the Des Moines river, a tributary of the Mississippi. It is an important road, railway, and air centre with many manufactures. Population (1980) 371,800.

Desmoulins /ˌdeɪmuː'læŋ/ Camille 1760–1794. French revolutionary, who summoned the mob to arms on 12 Jul 1789, so precipitating the revolt that culminated in the storming of the Bastille. A prominent Jacobin, he was elected to the National Convention in 1792, and his *Histoire des Brissotins* was largely responsible for the overthrow of the ◊Girondins. But shortly after he was sent to the guillotine as too moderate.

de Soto /'sautəu/ Hernando c. 1496–1542. Spanish explorer. In his expedition of 1539, he explored Florida, Georgia, and the Mississippi.

Desprez /deɪ'preɪ/ Josquin c. 1440–1521. Franco-Flemish composer. See ◊Josquin Desprez.

Dessalines /ˌdesæ'liːn/ Jean Jacques 1758–1806. Emperor of Haiti. Born in Guinea, he was taken to Haiti as a slave, where he succeeded ◊Toussaint-L'Ouverture as leader of a revolt against the French, and made himself emperor in 1804. He was killed when trying to suppress a revolt provoked by his cruelty.

J.J.DESSALINES
Kaiser auf St. Domingo

Dessalines Brought to Haiti as a slave, Jean Jacques Dessalines became Emperor under the title of Jean Jacques I. A tyrannical and cruel ruler, he was murdered while trying to suppress a revolt.

Dessau /ˈdesaʊ/ town of Halle district, East Germany, on the Mulde, 115 km/70 mi SW of Berlin, the former capital of Anhalt duchy and state; population (1981) 103,000. It manufactures chemicals, machinery, and chocolate, and was the site of the Junkers aeroplane works.

destroyer small, fast warship, originally introduced as a 'torpedo boat destroyer.' In World War I they were developed for anti-submarine work, serving in this capacity with convoys in World War II. Modern guided-missile destroyers weigh 3,700–5,650 tonnes, and in 1977 the last of the Royal Navy's conventional destroyers, the 2,600-tonne *Cavalier*, was preserved at Southampton as a museum. See also §warship.

detective fiction novels or short stories in which a mystery is solved mainly by the action of a professional or amateur detective. Where the mystery to be solved concerns the commission of a crime, the work is called *crime fiction*. The earliest work of detective fiction as understood today was *Murders in the Rue Morgue* 1841 by Edgar Allen Poe, and his detective Dupin became the model for those who detected by deduction from a series of clues. The most popular deductive sleuth was Sherlock Holmes in the stories by Sir Arthur Conan Doyle. The height of the genre was the 'golden age': the period from the 1920s to the 1940s, when the most famous writers were women – Agatha Christie, Margery Allingham, Dorothy L Sayers. Types of detective fiction include the *police procedural*, where the mystery is solved by detailed police work, as in the work of Swedish writers Maj Sjowall and Per Wahloo; the *inverted novel*, where the identity of the criminal is known from the beginning, only

the method or the motive remaining to be discovered, as in *Malice Aforethought* by Francis Iles; the *hard-boiled school* of private investigators begun by Raymond Chandler and Dashiell Hammett, which became known for its social realism and explicit violence. More recently, the form and traditions of the genre are used as a framework within which to explore other concerns, as in *Innocent Blood* and *A Taste for Death* by P D James, *The Name of the Rose* by Umberto Eco, and the works of many women writers who explore feminist ideas, for example Barbara Wilson with *Murder in the Collective*. As with most genres, crime fiction has produced its oddities: *Murder in Pastiche* by Marion Mainwaring is written in the styles of nine famous writers; Agatha Christie, Georgette Heyer and Ellis Peters have all written detective novels with historical settings; *Murder Off Miami* by Dennis Wheatley was a dossier containing real clues such as photographs, ticket stubs, and hairpins for the reader to solve the mystery. The solution was in a closed envelope at the back of the book.

détente in politics, relaxation of tension in relations between the main power blocs.

detention centre in Britain, an establishment for the short-term detention of young offenders (aged 14–21). In 1980 those at New Hall (Wakefield, Yorkshire) and Send (Woking, Surrey) were selected to give 'short, sharp shock' treatment to those sentenced to three months by the courts.

detergent a surface-active cleansing agent. The common detergents are made from fats (hydrocarbons) and sulphuric acid, and their long-chain molecules have a type of structure similar to that of soap molecules – a salt group at one end attached to a long hydrocarbon 'tail'. The mechanism of removing dirt, which is generally attached to materials by oil or grease, is that the hydrocarbon 'tails' (soluble in oil or grease) penetrate the oil or grease drops, while the 'heads' (soluble in water but insoluble in grease) remain in the water, and, being salts, become ionized. Consequently the oil drops become negatively charged and tend to repel one another; thus they remain in suspension and are washed away with the dirt. They have the advantage over soap in that they do not produce scum by forming insoluble salts with the calcium and magnesium ions present in hard water.

Detergents were first developed from ◊coal tar in Germany during World War I, and synthetic organic detergents came into ever-increasing use after World War II. Domestic powder detergents for use in hot water have alkyl benzene as their main base, but also include bleaches and fluorescers as whiteners, perborates to free stain-removing oxygen, and water softeners. Liquid detergents for washing dishes are based on ethylene oxide. Cold-water detergents consist of a mixture of various alcohols, plus an ingredient for breaking down the surface tension of the water, so enabling the liquid to penetrate fibres and remove the dirt. Problems of pollution are caused by detergents when surface-active materials escape the normal processing of sewage and cause troublesome foam in rivers.

determinant in mathematics, a number that follows the manipulation of a matrix (a set of quantities in a rectangular array). For the matrix $(p\ q)\ (r\ s)$ the determinant is $(p\ q)\ (r\ s)$ and is equal to $ps - qr$ (the difference between the products of the diagonal terms). Determinants can be used to solve sets of ◊simultaneous equations.

determinism in philosophy and theology, the view that denies human freedom of action, arguing that because everything in the natural world is strictly governed by the principle of cause and effect, human action is no exception. It is the opposite of free will, and rules out moral choice and responsibility; the causes which determine human actions are not limited to their external circumstances, but include also their own past mental states and their motives. In antiquity the theory of determinism was held by the ◊Stoics. In Christian theology the Calvinist doctrine of Predestination is deterministic. Psychoanalysis provided support for determinism, but quantum mechanics and the ◊'uncertainty principle' lends support to the other side of the argument.

deterrence the underlying conception of the nuclear ◊arms race: the belief that a potential aggressor will be deterred from launching a 'first strike' nuclear attack by the knowledge that the adversary is capable of striking back. This doctrine is widely known as that of Mutual Assured Destruction (MAD). See also ◊war.

detonator also called blasting cap, a small explosive charge used to trigger off a main charge of high explosive. The relatively unstable compounds mercury fulminate and lead acid are often used in detonators, being set off by a lighted ◊fuse, or more commonly by an electric current.

detritus in biology, the organic debris produced during the ◊decompositon of animals and plants.

Detroit /dɪˈtrɔɪt/ city of Michigan, USA, situated on Detroit river. Population (1980) 1,203,339. It was founded in 1701 and is the oldest city of any size west of the original colonies of the east coast. In 1805 it was completely destroyed by fire, but was soon rebuilt and is today an industrial centre with the headquarters of Ford, Chrysler and General Motors, which give it its nickname, Motown (from 'motor town'). A recent major development is the waterfront Renaissance Center complex. Once a famous centre for jazz, Detroit became in the 1960s and 1970s noted for the 'Motown Sound', the rock and soul music of such artists as Diana Ross, Stevie Wonder and Aretha Franklin. The fine reputation of its symphony orchestra was established by Antal Dorati.

Detskoye Selo /ˈdetskɔɛ selˈɔ/ former name of ◊Pushkin, near Lenigrad, which was renamed after the Russian poet in 1937.

Dettingen, Battle of /ˈdetɪŋən/ battle in the Bavarian village of that name where on 27 June 1743, in the War of the Austrian Succession, an army of British, Hanoverians, and Austrians under George II defeated the French under Noailles. It was the last battle in which a British sovereign took part.

deuterium a heavy isotope of ◊hydrogen, mass number 2 (one proton and one neutron), discovered in 1932 by Urey. Combined with oxygen, it produces 'heavy water', used in the nuclear industry.

deuteron the ◊ion of ◊deuterium ('heavy hydrogen'). It consists of one proton and one neutron, and thus has a positive charge.

Deutschmark the standard currency of West Germany.

de Valera /də vəˈleərə/ Éamon 1882–1975. Irish politician. He was born in New York, the son of a Spanish father and an Irish mother, and sent to Ireland as a child, where he became a teacher of mathematics. He was sentenced to death for his part in the Easter Rebellion, but the sentence was commuted, and in 1917 he was released under an amnesty. In the same year he was elected member of parliament for E Clare, and president of ◊Sinn Féin. In May 1918 he was rearrested, but in 1919 escaped to the USA. Elected president of the Irish Republic, he returned to Ireland in 1920 and directed the struggle against the British government from a hiding place in Dublin. He authorized the negotiations of 1921, but refused to accept the ensuing treaty which divided Ireland into the Free State and the North.

Civil war followed. In 1923 de Valera was arrested by the Free State government and spent a year in prison. In 1926 he formed a new party, ◊Fianna Fáil, which in 1932 secured a majority. De Valera became prime minister and foreign minister, and at once abolished the oath of allegiance and suspended payment of the annuities due under the Land Purchase Acts. In 1938 he negotiated an agreement with Britain, under which all outstanding points were settled. Throughout World War II he maintained a strict neutrality. He resigned after his defeat at the 1948 elections, but was again prime minister 1951–54 and 1957–59, and was president of the republic 1959–73.

de Valois /də ˈvælwɑː/ Ninette 1898– . Irish dancer, choreographer and teacher. A pioneer of British national ballet, she worked with Diaghilev in Paris before opening a dance academy in London in 1926. Collaborating with Lilian Baylis, she founded the Vic-Wells Ballet in 1931 and continued to work with the company and school, which later became the ◊Royal Ballet and Royal Ballet School. Among her most important works are *Job* 1931 and *Checkmate* 1937.

devaluation the lowering of the value of a currency in the international market, which makes exports cheaper and imports dearer. Used in a financial crisis, when a country is badly in deficit in its balance of payments, it results in the goods the country produces being made cheaper abroad, so that the economy is stimulated, but in the longer term imports of food, raw materials and manufactured goods become dearer. Hence prices at home may rise, and chronic inflation may set in with further devaluations, especially when commodities are rising in price because of increased world demand. *Revaluation* is the opposite process. Devaluations upset the balance of the world's money markets and allow

de Valera At 70, the leader of the opposition in Eire was still a dominant figure in Irish politics. A fighter for Irish independence, he repeatedly paid for his views by imprisonment, and was regarded by both sides of the House with respect.

speculators to operate, so that in an attempt to promote greater stability, many countries have allowed the value of their currencies to 'float', that is, to fluctuate in value.

developing in photography, the process which produces a visible image on exposed photographic ◊film. When film is exposed, invisible changes take place in the silver salts of the emulsion. It holds a latent or invisible image. Developing involves treating the emulsion with chemical developer, a reducing agent (such as hydroquinone) that changes the light-altered salts into dark metallic silver. The developed image is a negative – darkest where the strongest light hit the emulsion, lightest where the least light hit it.

development in the social sciences, the term generally refers to economic development, the acquisition by a society of industrial techniques and technology; hence the common classification of the 'developed' nations of the First World and the poorer 'developing' or 'underdeveloped' nations of the Third World. The assumption that development in the sense of industrialization was inherently good has been increasingly questioned since the 1960s. Many universities today have academic departments of *development studies* which address the theoretical questions involved in proposing practical solutions to the problems of development in the Third World.

development aid financial and other assistance given by richer, usually industrialized, countries to developing states. Official development aid (ODA) may be given for idealistic, commercial, or political reasons, or a combination of the three, as through the ◊International Development Association and ◊International Finance Corporation.

developmental psychology the study of development of cognition and behaviour from birth to adulthood.

Deventer /ˈdeɪvəntə/ town in Overijssel province, the Netherlands, on the Ijssel, 45 km/28 mi S of the Ijssel Meer; population (1984) 64,800. It is an agricultural and transport centre.

deviance abnormal behaviour; that is, behaviour that deviates from the norms or laws of a particular society or group, and so invokes social sanctions, controls, or stigma. The term may refer to minor abnormalities (such as nail-biting) as well as to criminal acts. Deviance is a relative concept: what is considered deviant in some societies is normal in others; and in a particular society the same act (killing someone, for example) may be either normal or deviant depending on the circumstances (in wartime or for money, for example). Some sociologists, for example Howard Becker, argue that the reaction of others, rather than the act itself, is what determines whether an act is deviant – that deviance is merely behaviour other people so label.

devil in Christian theology, the supreme spirit of Evil (Beelzebub, Lucifer), or an evil spirit generally. The devil or Satan is mentioned only in the later books of the Old Testament, written after the Exile, but the later Jewish doctrine is that found in the New Testament. Jesus recognized as a reality the kingdom of evil, of which Satan or Beelzebub was the prince. The conception of the devil thus passed into the early Church; and theology until at least the time of St Anselm represented the Atonement as primarily the deliverance, through Christ's death, of mankind from the bondage of the devil. In the Middle Ages the devil in popular superstition assumed the attributes of the horned fertility gods of paganism, and was regarded as the god of the witches. The belief in a personal devil continued at the ◊Reformation; ◊Luther regarded himself as the object of a personal Satanic persecution. With the development of liberal ◊Protestant theology in the 19th century came a strong tendency to deny the existence of a positive spirit of evil, and to explain the devil as merely a personification. However the traditional conception was never abandoned by the Roman Catholic Church, and such theologians as C S Lewis have maintained the assumption of the existence of a power of positive evil.

devil ray name given to large rays of the genera *Manta* and *Mobula*, in which two 'horns' project forward from the sides of the huge mouth. These flaps of skin guide the plankton on which the fish feeds into the mouth. The largest of these rays can be 7 m/23 ft across. They live in warm seas.

devil's coach horse large black long-bodied beetle *Ocypus olens*, about 3 cm/1.2 in long. It has powerful jaws and is capable of giving a painful bite.

Devil's Island /ˈdevəlz ˈaɪlənd/ smallest (Ile du Diable) of the Iles du Salut, off French Guiana, 43 km/27 mi NW of Cayenne. The group of islands was collectively and popularly known by the name Devil's Island, and formed a penal colony notorious for its terrible conditions. Alfred ◊Dreyfus was imprisoned there 1895–99. Political prisoners were held on Devil's Island, and dangerous criminals on St Joseph, where they were subdued by solitary confinement in tiny cells or subterranean cages. The largest island, Royale, now has a tracking station for the French rocket site at Kourou.

Devil's Marbles area of granite boulders, S of Tennant Creek, off the Stuart Highway in Northern Territory, Australia.

Devil's Marbles About 1450 million years old and up to some 3 m/10 ft in diameter, this strange rock formation plays its part in Aborigine legend.

devil wind minor form of tornado, occurring usually in fine weather, and formed from rising thermals of warm air (see also ◊cyclone). A fire creates a similar updraught, and a *fire devil* or *firestorm* may occur in oil-refinery fires, or in the firebombings of cities, for example Dresden, Germany, in World War II.

devolution the delegation of authority and duties, especially in the later 20th century the movement to decentralize governmental power, as in the UK where a bill for the setting-up of Scottish and Welsh assemblies was introduced in 1976. See ◊Scotland and ◊Wales. The word was first widely used in this sense in connection with Ireland, with ◊Redmond claiming in 1898 that the Liberals wished to diminish 'Home Rule' into 'some scheme of devolution or federalism'.

Devolution, War of 1667–68. Waged by Louis XIV to gain Spanish territory in the Netherlands, of which ownership had allegedly 'devolved' on his wife Maria Theresa. It was ended by the treaty of Aix-la-Chapelle. During the course of the war Turenne conducted a remarkable series of sieges.

Devon /'devən/ county in SW England
area 6,711 sq km/2,590 sq mi
towns administrative headquarters Exeter; Plymouth, and the resorts Paignton, Torquay, Teignmouth, and Ilfracombe.
features rivers Dart, Exe, Tamar; Dartmoor and Exmoor National Parks.
products mainly agricultural, with sheep and dairy farming; cider and clotted cream; kaolin in the south; Honiton lace; Dartington glass
population (1986) 988,400

famous people Sir Francis Drake, Sir John Hawkins, Charles Kingsley, Robert F Scott.

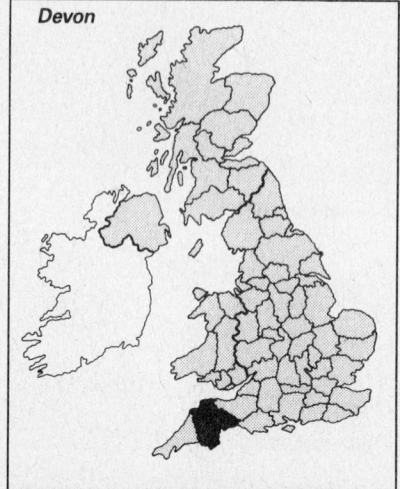

Devon

Devonian the period of geological time between 395 and 345 million years ago. Many desert sandstones from N America and Europe date from this time. The first land plants flourished in the Devonian, corals were abundant in the seas, vertebrates left the water for the first time. The name comes from the county of Devon in SW England, where Devonian rocks were first studied.

Devonshire /'devənʃə/ Spencer Compton Cavendish, 8th Duke of Devonshire 1833–1908. British Liberal politician, known as Lord Hartington 1858–91, and leader of the Liberal Party 1874–80. He broke with Gladstone over Irish Home Rule 1885, and was president of the council 1895–1903 under Salisbury and Balfour. As a free trader, he resigned from Balfour's cabinet.

Devonshire /'devənʃə/ William Cavendish, 7th Duke of Devonshire 1808–1891. British nobleman, whose development of Eastbourne was an early example of town planning.

dew moisture that collects on the ground during clear, calm nights, particularly after a warm day. As temperature falls during the night the air and the water vapour in it become chilled. Condensation takes place on the cooled surfaces of grass, and leaves. When the moisture begins to form, the surrounding air is said to have reached its ◊dew point. If the temperature falls below freezing point during the night, the dew will freeze, or if the temperature is low and the dew point is below freezing point, the water vapour condenses directly into ice; in both cases hoar frost is formed.

Dewar /'dju:ə/ James 1842–1923. British chemist and physicist who in 1872 invented the vacuum flask during his researches in the properties of matter at extremely low temperatures. The flask consists of a double-walled vessel containing a vacuum and silvered on the inside, all in an outer insulating container. This arrangement reduces the three forms of heat

transfer: radiation (prevented by the silvering), conduction and convection (prevented by the vacuum and insulation). A vacuum flask – often called by its trademark Thermos flask – is therefore equally efficient at keeping cold liquids cold, or hot liquids hot.

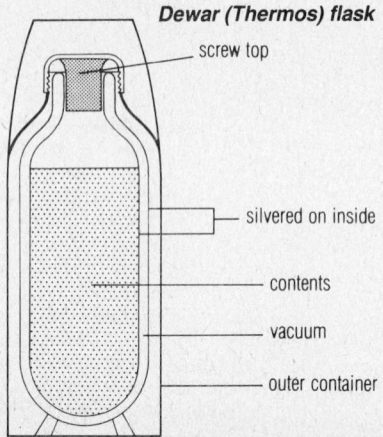

Dewar (Thermos) flask
screw top
silvered on inside
contents
vacuum
outer container

de Wet /də 'vet/ Christian 1854–1922. Boer general and politician. Born in the Orange Free State, he served in the Boer Wars of 1880 and 1899; in 1907 became Minister of Agriculture in the Orange River Colony; and when World War I broke out in 1914 he headed a pro-German rising that was soon suppressed by Prime Minister Louis ◊Botha.

Dewey /'dju:i/ John 1859–1952. American philosopher, born in Vermont. From 1904 he was professor of philosophy at Columbia university. Dewey believed that the exigencies of a modern democratic and industrial society demand new educational techniques. He expounded his ideas in numerous writings, especially in *School and Society* (1899), and founded a progressive school in Chicago. A pragmatist thinker, influenced by William James, Dewey maintained that there is only the reality of experience, and made 'inquiry' the essence of logic. His other writings include *Experimental Logic* 1916, *Reconstruction in Philosophy* 1920, *Quest for Certainty* 1929, *Problems of Men* 1946.

Dewey /'dju:i/ Melvil 1851–1931. American librarian. He devised the Dewey decimal system of classification for books in 1876, now widely used in libraries.

de Wint /də 'wınt/ Peter 1784–1849. English landscape artist. Born in Staffordshire, of Dutch descent, he was a notable water-colourist.

dew point the temperature at which air is just completely saturated with water vapour. At temperatures below the dew point, water vapour condenses out of the air as droplets, which if small form a suspension as mist or fog or if larger become deposited on objects on or near the ground as ◊dew.

dharma (from Sanskrit 'habit, usage') in Hinduism, consciousness of forming part of a cosmologically ordered world, and hence the moral duty of accepting one's station in life.

Dhofar /'dəʊfɑː/ mountainous western province of ◊Oman, population (1982) 40,000; on the border with South Yemen. The latter supported guerrilla activity here in the 1970s, while Britain and Iran supported the government's military operations. The capital is Salalah, which has a port at Rasut.

dhole species of wild dog *Cuon alpinus* found in Asia from Siberia to Java. With head and body up to 1 m/3 ft long, variable in colour but often reddish above and lighter below, the dhole lives in groups from three up to 30 individuals. These can chase prey for long distances and are capable of pulling down deer and cattle as well as smaller prey. They are even known to have attacked tigers and leopards.

diabetes disease (*diabetes mellitus*) in which a deficiency in the islets of the pancreas prevents the body producing the hormone insulin, so that it cannot use sugars properly. Adult diabetes (frequently inherited) can often be controlled by diet, though dosage with ◊insulin may also be needed; juvenile diabetes, which is possibly viral and may eventually be treated by vaccine, needs daily injections of insulin. Unless treated, diabetes causes incapacity, weakens resistance to infection, and ends in death in a coma.

diagenesis in geology, the physical and chemical processes by which a ◊sediment becomes a ◊sedimentary rock. The main processes involved include compaction of the grains, and the cementing of the grains together by the growth of new minerals deposited by percolating groundwater.

Diaghilev /di'ægəlef/ Sergei Pavlovich 1872–1929. Russian ballet impresario, who produced Chaliapin in *Boris Godunov* in 1908 in Paris, and in 1909 founded the *Ballets Russes* (headquarters Monte Carlo), which he directed for 20 years, and which went to London in 1911. Through the company he brought Russian ballet to the West, introducing and encouraging a dazzling array of dancers, choreographers and composers, such as ◊Pavlova, ◊Nijinsky, ◊Fokine, ◊Massine, ◊Balanchine, ◊Stravinsky, and ◊Prokofiev, who together revolutionized ballet.

dialect a variety of a language, either as spoken in a particular area ('Yorkshire dialect'), by a particular social group ('the dialect of educated Standard English'), or both ('the black American dialects of English'). The term is used both neutrally, as above, and in a judgemental and often dismissive way ('the locals have a harsh, ugly dialect; few of them have been properly educated'). In the latter case, the standard language of a community is not seen as a dialect itself, but as the 'proper' form of that language, dialects being considered in some way corrupt. This is a matter of social attitude, not of scientific study.

dialectic a Greek term, originally associated with Socrates's method of argument through dialogue and conversation. The word was taken over by 19th-century German thinkers, notably ◊Hegel and ◊Marx. For Hegel, dialectic refers to thought which develops through contradiction.

Diaghilev Russian impressario Sergei Diaghilev (seated) with Serge Lifar in Venice, 1928. The lavish *Ballets Russes* which he ran in Paris for 20 years became a hot-house of talented dancers, musicians, choreographers and designers which revolutionized ballet.

dialectical materialism the political, philosophical, and economic theory of Marx and Engels, also known as ◊Marxism.

dialysis a way of separating colloidal particles from other non-colloidal ones in solution using a semi-permeable membrane (which allows the passage of the smaller non-colloidal particles but not the larger colloidal particles; see also ◊colloid). Dialysis can thus separarate, for example, salts from proteins in blood, which is the natural process in the filtration system of the kidneys and the engineered equivalent in a dialysis (artificial kidney) machine.

diamond a precious gem stone, the hardest natural substance known (10 on ◊Mohs scale). Composed of carbon and with a chemical formula C, it crystallizes in the cubic system; other common crystals are octahedra and dodecahedra. The high refractive index of 2.42 and the high dispersion of light or 'fire' account for the displays of colours seen in cut diamonds. Rough diamonds are dull or greasy before being cut, and only some 20% are suitable as gems. They are valued by weight (◊carat), cut (which highlights the stone's optical properties), colour and clarity (which is on a six-point scale from P ('pique', showing a flaw visible to the naked eye) to FL ('flawless')). There are four chief varieties: well-crystallized transparent stones, colourless or only slightly tinted, valued as gems; *bort*, poorly crystallized or inferior diamonds; *balas*, an industrial variety, extremely hard and tough; and *carbonado*, or industrial diamond also called black diamond or carbon, which is opaque, black or grey, and very tough. Industrial diamonds are used for cutting (for example the tungsten carbide tools used in steel mills are themselves cut with diamond tools), grinding, polishing.

Industrial diamonds (20 tonnes per annum) are also produced synthetically from graphite. Diamonds act as perfectly transparent windows, and do not absorb infra-red radiation, hence their use aboard NASA space-probes to Venus in 1978.

Diamonds were known before 3000 BC; and until their discovery in Brazil in 1725 India was the principal source of supply. Modern sources are Angola, Ghana, Guyana, Sierra Leone, South Africa, Namibia, Tanzania, and Yakutia; Brazil and Zaïre are noted for industrial diamonds. They may be found as alluvial diamonds on or close to the earth's surface in river beds or dried water-courses, or on the sea bottom (off W Africa); or else in pipes composed of blue ground or ◊kimberlite, where the original matrix has penetrated the earth's crust from great depths. They are sorted from the residue of washed blue ground, etc., by X-ray. Natural diamonds may be exhausted by 2000 unless new deposits are found: see ◊gem.

Famous rough diamonds include the Cullinan (3,106 carats/over 20 oz, South Africa 1905); Excelsior (995.2 carats, South Africa 1893) and Star of Sierra Leone (968.9 carats, Yengema 1972). Diamonds are cut by the use of diamond dust. The two most frequent forms of cutting gem diamonds are the brilliant (for thicker stones) and the rose for shallower ones. By 1980 India was on the way to replacing Antwerp and Tel Aviv as the world's major cutting and polishing centres.

Diana /daɪˈænə/ in Roman mythology, goddess of hunting and the moon (Greek ◊Artemis), daughter of Jupiter and twin-sister of Apollo.

Diana /daɪˈænə/ Princess of Wales 1961– . popularly known as Princess Di. The daughter of the 8th Earl Spencer, she married Prince Charles at St Paul's cathedral in 1981, the first English bride of a royal heir since 1659. She is descended from the only sovereigns from whom Prince Charles is not descended, Charles II and James II.

DIANE the collection of information suppliers or 'hosts' for the European computer network, *D*irect *I*nformation *A*ccess *N*etwork for *E*urope.

dianetics a form of psychotherapy developed by L Ron Hubbard in the USA, which formed the basis for ◊scientology.

diapause a period of suspended development that occurs in some species of insects, characterized by greatly reduced metabolism. Periods of diapause are often timed to coincide with the winter months, and improve the insect chances of surviving adverse conditions.

diarrhoea excessive action of the bowels so that the motions are fluid or semi-fluid. It is usually due to irritation by a poisonous substance taken with the food or generated by bacteria in the food itself (food poisoning), or by a disease organism, as in dysentery or cholera.

diary a daily record of personal events. The earliest diary extant in English is that of Edward VI.

diaspora a dispersal, especially of the Jews from Palestine from the time of the Babylonian Captivity in 586 BC. See ◊Israel.

diathermy the generation of heat in body tissues by the passage of high-frequency electric currents between two electrodes placed on the body. It is used to relieve arthritic pain. In diathermic surgery one electrode is very much reduced for cutting purposes and the other correspondingly enlarged and placed at a distance on the body. The high-frequency current produces, at the tip of the cutting electrode, sufficient heat to cut tissues, or to coagulate and kill tissue cells, with less bleeding than in normal surgical methods.

diatom microscopic alga of the division Bacillariophyta found in all parts of the world. They consist of single cells, sometimes in colonies; the cell-wall is made up of two overlapping valves known as *frustules*, which are usually impregnated with silica, and which fit together like the lid and body of a pill-box. Diatomaceous earths (diatomite) are made up of the valves of fossil diatoms, and are used in the manufacture of dynamite, and in the rubber and plastics industries.

diatonic in music, a diatonic scale consists of the seven notes of any major or minor key.

Diaz /'diːes/ Bartolomeu c.1450–1500. Portuguese explorer. First European to reach the Cape of Good Hope 1488 and to establish a route round the S extremity of Africa.

Dick /dɪk/ Philip K(endred) 1928–1982. American science-fiction writer, whose works often deal with religion and the subjectivity of reality; his novels include *The Man in the High Castle* 1962 and *Do Androids Dream of Electric Sheep?* 1968.

Dickens /'dɪkɪnz/ Charles 1812–1870. British novelist, noted for his memorable characters and his portrayals of the social evils of Victorian England. Born on 7 Feb 1812, in Portsea, the son of a clerk, he received little systematic education, although a short period spent working in a blacking factory in S London, while his father was imprisoned for debt in the Marshalsea prison during 1824, was followed by three years in a private school. In 1827 he became a lawyer's clerk, and then after four years a reporter for the *Morning Chronicle*, to which he contributed the *Sketches by Boz*. In 1836 he married Katherine Hogarth, three days after the publication of the first number of the *Pickwick Papers*. Originally intended merely as an accompaniment to a series of sporting illustrations, the adventures of Pickwick outgrew their setting and established Dickens' position as a writer.

This success was followed by *Oliver Twist* 1838, the first of his 'reforming' novels; *Nicholas Nickleby* 1839; *Barnaby Rudge* 1840, set in the period of the Gordon Riots; and *The Old Curiosity Shop* 1841. In 1842 he visited the USA, where his attack on the pirating of English books by American publishers chilled his welcome; his experiences are reflected in *American Notes* and *Martin Chuzzlewit* 1843. In 1843 he published the first of his Christmas books, *A Christmas Carol*, followed in 1844 by

DICKENS, MAJOR WORKS

Title	Date	Well-known characters
The Pickwick Papers	1837	Mr Pickwick, Sam Weller, Mr Snodgrass, Mr Jingle, Mrs Bardell
Oliver Twist	1838	Oliver Twist, Fagin, Mr Bumble, Dodger
Nicholas Nickleby	1839	Nicholas Nickleby, Mr Squeers, Madame Manatalini, Smike
The Old Curiosity Shop	1841	Dick Swiveller, Little Nell, Daniel Quilp
Barnaby Rudge	1841	Simon Tappertit (Sim), Miggs, Gashford
A Christmas Carol	1843	Ebenezer Scrooge
Martin Chuzzlewit	1844	Martin Chuzzlewit (Junior), Mr Pecksniff, Mrs Gamp, Tom Pinch
Dombey and Son	1848	Paul Dombey, Edith Dombey, Mr James Carker, Major Bagstock, Mrs Skewton, Mr Toots
David Copperfield	1850	Mr Micawber, Mr Dick, Uriah Heap, Little Em'ly, David Copperfield
Bleak House	1853	John Jarndyce, Esther Summerson, Mr Turveydrop, Lady Dedlock, Mrs Jellyby
Hard Times	1854	Gradgrind, Tom and Louisa Gradgrind, Josiah Bounderby, Bitzer, 'Sissy' Jupe
Little Dorrit	1857	Amy Dorrit, Flora Finching, Mr Merille
A Tale of Two Cities	1859	Dr Manette, Charles Darnay, Sydney Carton, Jerry Cruncher, Madame Defarge
Great Expectations	1861	Pip, Estella, Miss Havisham, Joe Gargery, Wemmick, Magwitch
Our Mutual Friend	1865	Noddy, Silas Wegg, Mr Podsnap, Betty Higden, Bradley Headstone, Reginald Wilfer
The Mystery of Edward Drood (*unfinished*)	1870	Rosa Bud, John Jasper

The Chimes, written in Genoa during his first long sojourn abroad, and in 1845 by the even more successful *Cricket on the Hearth*. A venture as editor of the Liberal newspaper, *The Daily News*, in 1846 was short-lived, and *Dombey and Son* 1848 was largely written abroad. *David Copperfield*, his most popular novel, appeared in 1849, and contains many autobiographical incidents and characters. Reverting to journalism, Dickens inaugurated the weekly magazine *Household Words* in 1850, reorganizing it in 1859 as *All the Year Round*; many of his later stories were published serially in these periodicals. His married life had long been unsatisfactory, and in 1856 he agreed with his wife on a separation: his sister-in-law remained with him to care for his children, while Dickens himself formed an association with the actress Ellen Ternan. In 1858 he began making public readings from his novels, which proved such a success that he was invited to make a second tour of America in 1867. Among his later books are *Bleak House* 1853, which mirrors his legal experience; *Hard Times* 1854; *Little Dorrit* 1857, in which he evoked his memories of the Marshalsea prison; *A Tale of Two Cities* 1859, about the French Revolution; *Great Expectations* 1861; and *Our Mutual Friend* 1864. He died at ◊Gadshill, his home near Rochester, on 9 Jun 1870. *Edwin Drood*, a mystery story influenced by the style of his friend, Wilkie ◊Collins, was left incomplete.

Dickinson /'dɪkɪnsən/ Emily 1830–1886. American poet. Born in Amherst, Massachusetts, she lived in complete seclusion there from 1862. She wrote a large number of short poems of an increasingly mystical character, of which very few were published during her lifetime. Her work includes *Bolts of Melody* 1947.

dicotyledon a sub-class of the ◊angiosperms, containing the great majority of flowering plants. Dicotyledons are characterized by the presence of two seed-leaves or ◊cotyledons in the embryo, which is usually surrounded by an ◊endosperm. They generally have broad leaves with net-like veins. Dicotyledons may be small plants such as daisies and buttercups, shrubs, or trees such as oak and beech. The other sub-class of the angiosperms is the ◊monocotyledons.

dictator originally a Roman magistrate invested with emergency powers for six months, but in modern usage an absolute ruler, overriding the constitution. Although dictatorships were common in Latin America during the 19th century, the only European example during this period is the rule of Napoleon III. The crises following World War I produced many dictatorships, including the régimes of ◊Atatürk, ◊Mussolini, ◊Hitler, ◊Pilsudski, ◊Primo de Rivera, ◊Franco, and ◊Salazar. Dictatorships also arise in communist regimes, for instance under ◊Stalin, and in the Third World after World War II there were many with both right-wing and left-wing characteristics.

dictatorship of the proletariat Marxist term for a revolutionary dictatorship established during the transition from capitalism to ◊communism after a socialist revolution.

dictionary a book that contains a selection of the words of a language, with their pronunciations and meanings, usually arranged in alphabetical order. The first dictionaries of English ('glossa collectae') served to explain

Dickens English Victorian novelist Charles Dickens, whose childhood included working as a drudge in a blacking factory. Most of his novels were serialized before publication. His unique genius at drawing memorable characters made him perhaps the best loved novelist of his age, but his works have a darker undercurrent in their portrayal of the social evils of Victorian England — particularly cruelty to children.

Diego Garcia /diˈeɪgəʊ gɑːˈsiːə/ island in the ◊Chagos Archipelago, named after its Portuguese discoverer in 1532. See ◊**British Indian Ocean Territory**.

dielectric substance (an insulator such as ceramics, glass, etc,) capable of supporting electric stress. The dielectric constant or relative permittivity of a substance is the ratio of the capacity of a capacitor with the medium as dielectric to that of a similar capacitor in which the dielectric is replaced by a vacuum.

Diels /diːls/ Otto 1876–1954. German chemist. He was professor of chemistry at the Berlin University Institute 1906–15, and at Kiel University 1916–45. In 1950 he and his former assistant, Kurt Alder, were jointly awarded the Nobel Prize for Chemistry for their research into carbon synthesis.

Diemen /ˈdiːmən/ Anthony van 1593–1645. Dutch admiral, born at Kuilenberg. In 1636 he was appointed Governor-General of Dutch settlements in the E Indies, and wrested Ceylon and Malacca from the Portuguese. In 1636 and 1642 he supervised expeditions to Australia, on the second of which Abel Tasman discovered land which he named Van Diemen's Land, now ◊Tasmania.

Dien Bien Phu /ˈdiːen ˈbiːen ˈfuː/ town in North Vietnam, near the Laotian border, 320 km/200 mi from Hanoi. The battle of Dien Bien exerted an enormous influence on contemporary social thinking with his ◊materialism and anti-clericalism. His materialism, most articulately expressed in *D'Alembert's Dream*, sees the natural world as nothing more than matter and motion. He gave an account of the origin and development of life which is purely mechanical.

didjeridu musical wind instrument, made from a hollow bamboo section 1.5 m/4 ft long, and blown to produce rhythmic, booming notes. First developed and played by Australian Aborigines.

Dido /ˈdaɪdəʊ/ Phoenician princess, legendary founder of Carthage, who committed suicide rather than marry a local prince. However Virgil records that it was because ◊Aeneas deserted her.

diecasting a major form of ◊casting, in which molten metal is injected into permanent metal moulds, or dies.

Diefenbaker /ˈdiːfənˌbeɪkə/ John George 1895–1979. Canadian Progressive Conservative statesman, born in Ontario, he became known as the 'prairie lawyer' because of his brilliance as a defence counsel. He became leader of his party in 1956 and prime minister in 1957. In 1958 he went to the country to get an absolute majority and achieved the greatest landslide in Canadian history. In 1963 he was defeated after criticism of the proposed manufacture of nuclear weapons in Canada, and resigned the party leadership in 1967, following his repudiation of a 'two nations' policy for Canada. A 'radical' Tory, he was also a strong supporter of Commonwealth unity. Phu proved decisive in the ◊Indochina War. During this General de Castries and some 10,000 troops were besieged in the French Union fortress 13 Mar–7 May 1954 by the communist Vietminh. Its fall resulted in the end of French

'hard' Latin and Greek words in everyday English. Samuel Johnson's dictionary of 1755 was one of the first dictionaries of standard English, and the first to give extensive coverage to phrasal verbs, to which Noah Webster in 1828 offered an American alternative. The many-volume *Oxford English Dictionary*, begun in 1884 and subject to continuous revision (and now computerization), provides a detailed historical record of the vocabulary of the language.
10th century Byzantine *Lexicon* of Suidas (first A–Z)
1225 John Garland used the term 'dictionarus'
1530 first English–English dictionary (appendix to William Temple's *Pentateuch*)

16th century first vernacular–vernacular dictionaries: William Salesbury, Welsh–English 1547; John Florio, Italian–English 1599
1604 Robert Cawdrey *Table Alphabeticall of hard usuall English wordes* (aimed at converting Latin to Latinate English)
1755 Samuel Johnson's dictionary of standard English
1828 Noah Webster's American dictionary
1852 Peter Mark Roget's *Thesaurus of English Words*
1884 the *Oxford English Dictionary* was begun.

Diderot /ˈdiːdərəʊ/ Denis 1713–1784. French philosopher of the ◊Enlightenment and editor of the celebrated ◊*Encyclopédie* (1751–1780). He

Diderot A portrait, by L M Loo, of the French philosopher and encyclopedist Denis Diderot. His account of the origin and nature of life anticipated evolutionary theories.

control of Indochina and of the Fourth Republic in France.

Dieppe /diːˈep/ channel port at the mouth of the Arques, Seine-Maritime *département*, N France; population (1983) 39,500. It has an airport and a good harbour, with ferry services to Newhaven and elsewhere, and fishing, shipbuilding and pharmaceutical industries.

diesel engine a kind of ◊internal combustion engine that burns a lightweight oil. The principle of the diesel was first put forward in England by Herbert Akroyd (1864–1937), in 1890, and applied practically by Rudolf Diesel (1858–1913) in Germany two years later. Diesel engines are piston-in-cylinder engines like the car ◊petrol engine, and many work like it in a ◊four-stroke engine cycle, stroke referring to an upward or downward movement of a piston. The first two strokes of the diesel cycle are different,

differential

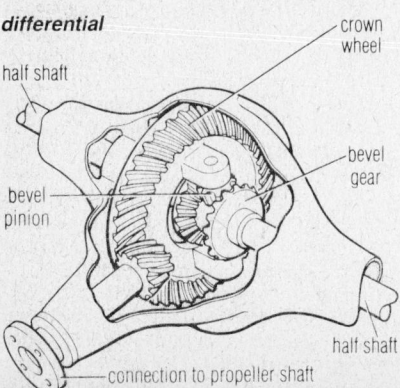

half shaft
crown wheel
bevel gear
bevel pinion
half shaft
connection to propeller shaft

Dietrich A cultivated enigma in life as well as on celluloid, Marlene Dietrich first won international fame with *The Blue Angel* 1930, and was known as 'the world's most glamorous grandmother' in 1948.

however. In the diesel engine just air (not an air/fuel mixture) is taken into the cylinder on the first piston stroke (down). Then the piston moves up and compresses the air until it is at a very high temperature. The fuel oil is then injected into the hot air, whereupon it burns, driving the piston down on its power stroke. For this reason the diesel engine is called a compression-ignition engine (as opposed to the spark in a petrol engine).

diet a meeting or convention of the princes and other dignitaries of the ◊Holy Roman (German) Empire.

diet a particular selection of ◊food, usually recommended for medical reasons.

dietetics a specialized branch of human nutrition, dealing with the promotion of health through good nutrition. Therapeutic dietetics is important in the treatment of certain illnesses

differentiation

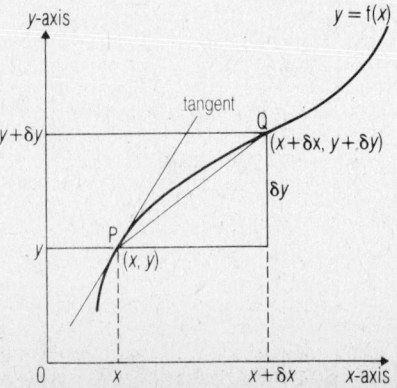

y-axis
$y = f(x)$
tangent
Q
$y + \delta y$
$(x + \delta x, y + \delta y)$
δy
P
y
(x, y)
0
x
$x + \delta x$
x-axis

such as diabetes; it is sometimes used alone, but often in conjunction with drugs. See ◊food.

Dietrich /ˈdiːtrɪk/ Marlene. Stage-name of the German-American actress Magdalene von Losch 1904– . Born in Berlin, she first won fame by her appearance with Emil Jannings in *The Blue Angel* 1930, and went to Hollywood, becoming a US citizen in 1937. Her husky, sultry singing voice added to her appeal.

difference engine a mechanical calculating machine designed, but never built, by the British mathematician Babbage about 1830. It was to calculate mathematical functions by solving the differences between values given to ◊variables within equations. Babbage designed the calculator so that once the initial values for the variables were set it would produce the next few thousand values without error.

differential an arrangement of gears in the final drive of a vehicle's transmission system that allows the driving wheels to turn at different speeds when cornering. The differential consists of sets of bevel gears and pinions within a cage attached to the crown wheel. When cornering, the bevel pinions rotate to allow the outer wheel to turn faster than the inner.

differential calculus method of calculating continuously varying quantities, using ◊differentiation. See also ◊calculus, ◊integration.

differentiation in mathematics, a procedure for finding the rate of change of one variable quantity relative to another. Together, differentation and ◊integration of functions make up ◊calculus. When a ◊function $f(x)$ is differentiated, the result is a derived function (or derivative) written $f'(x)$. It may be regarded as the limit of the expression $[f(x + h) - f(x)]/h$ as h tends to zero. Graphically this is equivalent to the gradient (slope) of the curve represented by $y = f(x)$ at any point x.

differentiation in ◊embryology, the process whereby cells become increasingly different and specialized, giving rise to more complex structures which have particular functions in the adult organism. For instance, embryonic cells may develop into nerve, muscle or bone cells.

diffraction the interference phenomena observed at the edges of opaque objects, or discontinuities between different media in the path of a wave train. The phenomena give rise to slight spreading of light into light and dark bands at the shadow of a straight edge. The diffraction grating is a device for separating a wave train such as a beam of incident light into its component frequencies (white light results in a spectrum). The regular spacing of atoms in crystals are used to diffract X-rays, and in this way the structure of many substances has been elucidated, including recently that of proteins. Sound waves can also be diffracted by a suitable array of solid objects.

diffusion term used in physical chemistry to describe at least three processes: the spontaneous mixing of gases or liquids (classed together as *fluids* in scientific usage) when brought into contact without mechanical mixing or stirring; the spontaneous passage of fluids through membranes; and the spontaneous passage of dissolved materials both through the material in which they are dissolved and also through membranes.

One important application of the diffusion principle is for the separation of isotopes, particularly those of uranium. When uranium hexafluoride is forced through a porous plate the ratio of the 235 and 238 isotopes is changed slightly. With sufficient number of passages, the separation is nearly complete. There are large plants both in UK and USA for obtaining enriched fuel for fast reactors and the fissile uranium-235, originally required for the first atom bombs. Another application is the diffusion pump, used extensively in vacuum work, in which the gas to be evacuated diffuses into a chamber where it is carried away by the vapour of a suitable medium, usually oil or mercury.

digestion the process whereby food eaten by an animal is broken down physically, and chemically by ◊enzymes, usually in the ◊stomach and ◊intestines, so as to make the nutrients available for absorption and cell metabolism. In some single-celled organisms, such as amoebae, a food particle is engulfed by the cell itself, and digested in a ◊vacuole within the cell. See ◊digestive system.

digestive system the mouth, stomach, gut and associated glands of animals, which are responsible for digesting food. The food is broken down by physical and chemical means in the ◊stomach and the soluble products absorbed in the ◊intestines. In birds, additional digestive organs are the ◊crop and ◊gizzard. In smaller, simpler animals such as jellyfish, the digestive system is simply a cavity (coelenteron or enteric cavity) with a 'mouth' into which food is taken; the digestive portion is dissolved and absorbed in this cavity and the remains are ejected back through the mouth.

Diggers also called *true ◊Levellers*. An English 17th-century socialist sect which became prominent in Apr 1649, when, headed by Gerrard Winstanley (c. 1609–60), it set up communal colonies near Cobham, Surrey, and elsewhere. They were broken up by mobs and, being pacifists, made no resistance. Their ideas considerably influenced the early ◊Quakers.

digital in electronics and computing, a term meaning 'coded as numbers'. A digital system uses two-state, either on/off or high/low voltage pulses, to encode, receive, and transmit information.

A *digital computer* is a computing device that operates on a two-state system, using symbols that are internally coded as binary numbers (numbers made up of combinations of the digits 0 and 1), allowing very low-power circuits and very small electronic components.

A *digital display* shows discrete values as numbers (as opposed to an analogue signal such as the continuous sweep of a pointer on a dial).

digital recording is a technique whereby the pressure of sound waves is sampled more than 30,000 times a second and the values recorded as numbers which, during playback, are reconverted to sound waves. This gives very high-quality reproduction.

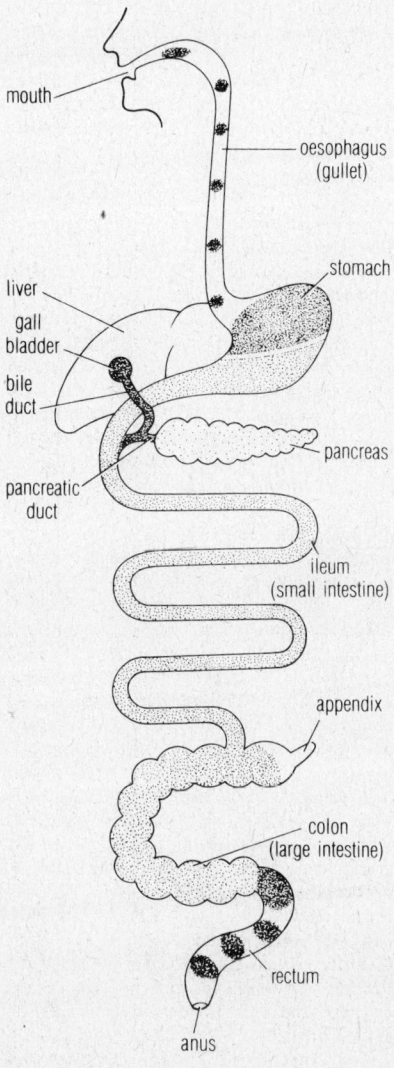

human digestive system

mouth
oesophagus (gullet)
stomach
liver
gall bladder
bile duct
pancreas
pancreatic duct
ileum (small intestine)
appendix
colon (large intestine)
rectum
anus

digital data transmission converts all signals (whether pictures, sounds, or words) into numeric (normally binary) codes before transmission and then reconverts them on receipt. This virtually eliminates any distortion or degradation of the signal during transmission, storage, or processing.

digital electronics is the technology that underlies digital techniques. Low-power, miniature, integrated circuits (chips) provide the means for the coding (sometimes with analogue-to-digital conversion), storage, transmission, processing, and reconstruction (sometimes through digital-to-analogue conversion) of information of all kinds.

digital computer a general-purpose electronic ◊computing device, which is based on a two state sytem of on/off pulses (as opposed to a ◊analogue computer, which is based on continuous varying physical quantities).

digitalis plant of the genus *Digitalis*, family Scrophulariaceae, including the foxgloves. The leaves of the common foxglove *Digitalis purpurea* are the source of the drug *digitalis* used in the treatment of heart trouble.

digital sampling an electronic process used in ◊telecommunications for transforming a constantly varying, or analogue, signal into one composed of discrete units, a digital signal. For example, a telephone microphone changes sound waves into an analogue signal that fluctuates up and down like a wave. In the digitizing process the waveform is sampled thousands of times a second and each part of the sampled wave is given a number related to the height of the wave at that point. The numbers are then converted into ◊binary code (which uses only the numbers 0 and 1 to represent values), which is transmitted along the telephone line. At the receiving end of the line the process is reversed. Using digital signals, messages can be transmitted faster, more accurately and more economically.

Dijon /'diːʒɒn/ industrial city and capital of Burgundy, France; population (1983) 150,500. As well as metallurgical, chemical and other industries, it is famed for its mustard.

dik-dik one of several species of tiny antelope, genus *Madoqua* found in Africa south of the Sahara in dry areas with scattered brush. About 60 cm/2 ft long and 35 cm/1.1 ft tall, dik-diks are often seen in pairs. Males only possess short pointed horns. The name is derived from the alarm call of the animal.

dilatation and curettage (D and C) a procedure in which the cervix (neck-shaped entrance of the womb) is widened or dilated, to access the inside of the womb, so that its lining can be scraped away (curettage). It may be carried out to terminate a pregnancy, treat an incomplete miscarrriage or discover the cause of heavy menstruation.

Dilke /dɪlk/ Charles Wentworth 1843–1911. British Liberal politician, member of parliament 1868–86 and 1892–1911. A Radical, he supported a minimum wage and legalization of trade unions.

dill umbelliferous European herb *Anethum graveolens* used for culinary and medicinal purposes.

Dilthey /'ɪltaɪ/ Wilhelm 1833–1911. German philosopher, a major figure in the tradition of ◊hermeneutics.

Dimbleby /'dɪmbəlbi/ Richard 1913–1965. British broadcaster and provincial newspaper owner. He joined the BBC in 1936 and established himself as the foremost commentator on royal and state events, and current affairs (*Panorama*), on radio and television. He is commmemorated by the Dimbleby lectures.

dimension basic physical quantity such as mass (M), length (L) and time (T), which can be combined by multiplication or division to give the dimensions of derived quantities. For example, acceleration (the rate of change of velocity) has dimensions (LT^{-2}), and is expressed in such units as km sec^{-2}. A quantity that is a ratio, such as relative density or humidity, is dimensionless.

dimethyl sulphoxide by-product of the processing of wood to paper, used as an anti-freeze and industrial solvent.

diminishing returns, law of in economics, the hypothesis that additional application of money and/or labour, which at first results in rapidly increasing output, eventually yields declining returns unless other factors are modified to sustain the increase. For example, additional employees may increase output, but eventually the increase will become less for each employee added, unless a new machine is also installed. Generally, the law tends to be true only in the short term.

Dimitrov /ˌdɪmɪˈtrɒf/ Georgi 1882–1949. Bulgarian communist. He was elected a deputy in 1913, and from 1919 was a member of the executive of the Comintern. In 1933 he was arrested in Berlin and tried with others at Leipzig, for allegedly setting fire to the Reichstag. So forceful was his defence that he was acquitted, and he went to the USSR, where he became general secretary of the Comintern until its dissolution in 1943. He was prime minister of Bulgaria from 1946.

Dinan /diːˈnɒŋ/ town in Côtes-du-Nord *département*, N France, on the river Rance, which is harnessed for tidal hydroelectric power. Population (1982) 14,150.

Dinant /diːˈnɒŋ/ ancient town in Namur province, Belgium, on the Meuse, a tourist centre for the Ardennes.

Dinaric Alps /dɪˈærɪk/ extension of the European ◊Alps in Western Yugoslavia.

Dinesen /ˈdɪnɪsən/ Isak 1885–1962. Pen name of Danish writer Karen ◊Blixen, born Karen Christentze Dinesen.

Dingaan /ˈdɪŋɡɑːn/ ruled 1828–1840. Zulu king. Obtaining the throne in 1828 by murdering his predecessor, he was noted for his cruelty. In warfare with the Boer immigrants into Natal he was defeated on 16 Dec 1838 – 'Dingaan's Day'. He escaped to Swaziland, where he was subsequently murdered.

Ding Ling /ˈdɪŋ ˈlɪŋ/ 1904–1986. Chinese novelist. She was imprisoned by the Guomindang (Chiang Kai-Shek's Nationalists) in the 1930s, wrongly labelled as rightist and expelled from the Communist Party 1957, imprisoned in the 1960s and intellectually exiled for not keeping to Maoist literary rules; she was rehabilitated in 1979. Her works include *Wei Hu* 1930 and *The Sun Shines over the Sanggan River* 1951. Her husband was the writer Hu Yepin, executed by Chiang Kai-Shek's police in 1931.

dingo wild dog of Australia. Descended from domestic animals brought from Asia by aborigines thousands of years ago, it belongs to the same species *Canis familiaris* as other domestic dogs. Reddish-brown, and with a bushy tail, it often hunts at night. It cannot bark.

Dinorwig /dɪˈnɔːwɪɡ/ the location of Europe's largest pumped-storage ◊hydroelectric scheme, completed in 1984, in Gwynedd, North Wales. Six turbogenerators are involved, which have a maximum output of some 1,880 megawatts. The main machine hall is twice as long as a football field and as high as a 16-storey building. The working head of water for the station is 530 m/1,740 ft.

dinosaur one of the group of extinct reptiles living between about 215 million and 65 million years ago. The name dinosaur, meaning 'terrible lizard', was given to the first specimens discovered, but the dinosaurs were not lizards. They form a group (or rather groups, for there are at least two main lines) of their own, their closest living relations being crocodiles and birds, the latter perhaps descended from the dinosaurs. There was an enormous variety of dinosaurs and they kept evolving and changing for all the millions of years they were the dominant large land animals. They all disappeared 65 millon years ago. The reason is not known, but some have theorized that it was due to a catastrophic change in climate, perhaps after the earth was hit by a large meteorite. Not all dinosaurs were large. *Brachiosaurus*, a long-necked plant-eating member of the sauropod group, was about 12.6 m/40 ft to the top of its head, and weighed 80 tonnes. *Compsognathus* was only the size of a chicken, and ran on its hind legs. Not all dinosaurs had small brains. *Stegosaurus*, an armoured plant-eater 6 m/20 ft long, had a brain of only about 3 cm/1¼ in long. At the other extreme the hunting dinosaur *Stenonychosaurus*, 2 m/6 ft long, had a brain size comparable to a mammal or bird of today, stereoscopic vision, and grasping hands. Many dinosaurs appear equipped for a high activity level. Eggs are known of some species. In 1982 a number of nests and eggs were found in 'colonies' in Montana, suggesting that some bred together like modern seabirds. In 1987 major new finds were made in China, which may change much of traditional knowledge of dinosaurs, chiefly gleaned from North American specimens.

Diocletian /ˌdaɪəˈkliːʃən/ (Gaius Valerius Diocletianus) 245–313. Roman emperor 284–305, when he abdicated in favour of Galerius. He reorganized and sub-divided the Empire, with two joint and two subordinate emperors, and in 303 initiated severe persecution of the Christians.

diode a thermionic valve (vacuum tube) with two electrodes (negative cathode and positive anode) or its semi-conductor equivalent, which incorporates a *p–n* junction. Either device allows the passage of direct current in one direction only, and so is commonly used to rectify alternating current (AC), converting it to direct current (DC).

dioecious describing plants that have male and female flowers borne on separate individuals of the same species. Dioecy occurs, for example, in the willows (*Salix*) and is a way of avoiding self-fertilization.

Diogenes /daɪˈɒdʒəniːz/ c. 412–323 BC. Ascetic Greek philosopher of the Cynic school, born at Sinope. The story of his having lived in a barrel arose only from Seneca having said that was where a man so crabbed ought to have lived. He was captured by pirates and sold as a slave to a Corinthian named Xeniades, who appointed Diogenes tutor to his two sons. He spent the rest of his life in Corinth and won a great reputation for cynical wisdom.

Diomede /ˈdaɪəmiːd/ two islands off the tip of the Seward peninsula, Alaska. *Little Diomede* 6.2 sq km/2.4 sq mi, belongs to the USA, and is only 3.9 km/2.4 mi from *Big Diomede* 29.3 sq km/11.3 sq mi, owned by the USSR. They were first sighted by Vitus Bering 1728.

Dion Cassius /ˈdaɪən ˈkæsiəs/ 150–235. Roman historian. He wrote in Greek a Roman History in 80 books (of which 26 survive), covering the period from the foundation of the city to AD 229 including the only surviving account of Claudius's invasion of Britain.

Dionysia /ˌdaɪəˈnɪziə/ festivals of ◊Dionysus (◊Bacchus) celebrated in ancient Greece, especially in Athens. The most important were the lesser Dionysia in Dec, chiefly a rural festival and the greater Dionysia, at the end of Mar, when new plays were performed.

Dionysius /ˌdaɪəˈnɪziəs/ name of two tyrants of the ancient Greek city of Syracuse in Sicily. *Dionysius the Elder* (432–367 BC) seized power in 405. His first two wars with Carthage further extended the power of Syracuse, but in a third (383–378 BC) he was defeated. He was a patron of ◊Plato (see also ◊Damocles). He was succeeded by his son, *Dionysius the Younger*. Driven out of Syracuse by Dion in 356, he was tyrant again in 353, but in 343 returned to Corinth.

Dionysus /ˌdaɪəˈnaɪsəs/ in Greek mythology, god of wine (son of Semele and ◊Zeus), and also of orgiastic excess (an animal, or on occasion a child, being torn to pieces alive and eaten). He was identified with ◊Bacchus, whose rites were less savage. His festivals, the *Dionysia*, were particularly associated with Athens; see ◊theatre. Attendant on him were wild women (*maenads*) and goatlike men (*satyrs*) with pointed ears, horns and a tail.

Diophantus /ˌdaɪəˈfæntəs/ fl. c. 250. Greek mathematician at Alexandria, whose *Arithmetica* is one of the first known works on problem-solving by algebra, in which both words and symbols were used.

dioptre an optical unit in which the power of a lens is expressed as the reciprocal of its focal length in metres. The usual convention is that convergent lenses are positive and divergent lenses negative.

Dior /ˈdiːɔː/ Christian 1905–1957. French couturier. He established his own Paris salon in 1947, and made an impact in 1947 with the 'New Look' – long and full-skirted after war-time austerity.

dioxin common name for tetra-chlorodibenzodioxin, one of a family of organic chemicals called dioxins. A highly toxic chemical, it was produced as a by-product of a defoliant used in the Vietnam War, and of the weedkiller 245-T. It causes a disfiguring skin complaint, chloracne, and has been linked with birth defects, miscarriages, and cancer. Disasters involving release of dioxin into the environment have occurred at Seveso in Italy and Times Beach in the USA. Smaller amounts of dioxin are released from rubbish incinerators, especially if these are operated at insufficiently high temperatures, and from other fires, including garden bonfires. See also ◊hexachlorophene.

dip magnetic, the angle between the horizontal and that taken up by a freely pivoted magnetic needle mounted vertically in the Earth's magnetic field. It is also called the angle of inclination. The dip needle parallels the lines of force of the magnetic field at any point. Thus at the north and south magnetic poles, the needle dips vertically and the angle of dip is 90°.

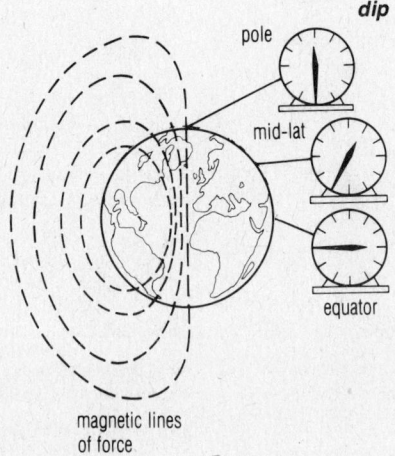

dip

pole

mid-lat

equator

magnetic lines of force

diphtheria infectious disease in which an occlusive membrane forms in the throat, possibly causing death by asphyxia. It is preventible by immunization. The ◊Schick test detects susceptibility.

Diplock court in Northern Ireland, a type of court established in 1972 by the British government under Lord Diplock (1907–) to try offences linked with terrorism. The right to jury trial was suspended and the court consisted of a single judge, since it was alleged that potential jurors were being intimidated and were unwilling to serve. Despite widespread criticism, the Diplock courts have remained in operation.

diplodocus plant-eating dinosaur that lived about 145 million years ago, whose remains have been found in the western USA. Up 27 m/88 ft long, most of this neck and tail, it weighed about 11 tonnes. It walked on four elephant-like legs, had nostrils on top of the skull, and peg-like teeth only at the front of the mouth.

diploid having two sets of ◊chromosomes in each cell. In sexually reproducing species, one set is derived from each parent, the ◊gametes, or sex cells, of each parent being ◊haploid (having only one set of chromosomes) due to ◊meiosis (cell division).

diplomacy the process in which states attempt to settle their differences through peaceful means such as negotiation or ◊arbitration. See ◊foreign relations.

dipole in chemistry, a pair of equal and opposite charges located apart, as in some ionic ◊molecules. The product of one charge and the distance between them is the dipole moment. In radio, a dipole is a rod ◊aerial, usually one half-wavelength or a whole wavelength long.

dipper bird *Cinclus cinclus* found in hilly and mountainous regions across Europe and Asia, where there are clear fast-flowing streams. It can swim, dive, or walk along the bottom using the pressure of water on its wings and tail to keep it down, while it searches for insect larvae and other small animals. About 18 cm/7 in long, it has chestnut plumage with white on chin and breast, and a shape and cocked tail like a wren.

Dirac /dɪ'ræk/ Paul Adrien Maurice 1902–1984. British physicist who worked out a version of ◊mechanics quantum consistent with special ◊relativity. The existence of the ◊positron was one of its predictions. He shared a Nobel prize 1933.

Dirichlet /,dɪrɪ'kleɪ/ Peter Gustav Lejeune 1805–1859. German mathematician and physicist who made major contributions to number theory. He is best known for the theorem named after him, which states that there is an infinite series of prime numbers of the form $an + b$, where a and b are primes and n is an integer (whole number). He also introduced the modern form of representing a function in the form $y = f(x)$. Dirichlet applied his mathematical knowledge to various aspects of physics, such as an analysis of vibrating strings, and to astronomy in a critique of the ideas about the stability of the solar system as proposed by the French mathematician Laplace.

Dis in Roman mythology, god of the underworld (Greek Pluto); ruler of Hades.

disarmament the reduction of a country's weapons of war. ◊League of Nations attempts to achieve disarmament failed in the 1930s. After World War II President Johnson's proposals 1967 for *Strategic Arms Limitation* (SALT) were delayed by the Soviet invasion of Czechoslovakia, but Salt I was operative 1972–77; Salt II, signed by Brezhnev and Carter to operate 1979–85, was never ratified, but both the US and the USSR abided by it. In 1986 Reagan revoked this pledge, against the advice of his European NATO partners. See ◊nuclear arms verification. Biological and chemical weapons, as well as conventional weapons, have also come under discussion at the United Nations. In Mar 1985 US/USSR negotiations reopened on intermediate range nuclear weapons, strategic arms, and weapons in outer space. In Britain the *Campaign for Nuclear Disarmament* (CND, see ◊Aldermaston), with which Lord Brockway, Canon Collins, Michael Foot, and Tony Benn were associated, enjoyed a spectacular revival in the 1980s

Disch /dɪʃ/ Thomas M(ichael) 1940– . US writer and poet, noted for science-fiction novels such as *Camp Concentration* 1968 and *334* 1972.

discharge tube usually takes the form of a glass tube from which virtually all the air has been removed (so that it 'contains' a near vacuum), with electrodes at each end. When a high-voltage current is passed between the electrodes, the few remaining gas atoms in the tube (or some deliberately introduced ones) ionize and emit coloured light as they conduct the current along the tube. The light originates as electrons change energy from higher to lower levels in the ionized atoms. By coating the inside

of the tube with a phosphor, invisible emitted radiation (such as ultraviolet light) can produce visible light; this is the principle of the fluorescent lamp.

discotheque club for dancing to pop music on records, which originated in the 1960s. The most famous, Studio 54 (1977–80) in Manhattan, New York, gained notoriety when its owner, Steve Rubell, operated a policy of selective admission. Its shortened form, *disco*, was used for an international style of recorded dance music of the 1970s with heavily emphasized beat, derived from ◊funk.

Discovery the ship in which Captain ◊Scott, commanding the National Antarctic Expedition in 1900–04, sailed to the Antarctic and back. In 1980 it moved to St Katharine's Dock, London, for a new life as a Maritime Trust museum of exploration.

discrimination unequal distinction (social, economic, political, legal) between individuals or groups such that one has the power to treat the other unfavourably. Discrimination may be on grounds of difference of colour, nationality, religion, politics, culture, class, sex, age, or a combination of such factors. Legislation has been to some degree effective in forbidding *racial discrimination*, against which there is a United Nations convention 1969 and national legislation in the UK (Race Relations Act from 1965) and USA (Civil Rights Acts 1964 and 1968, Voting Rights Act 1965). Positive discrimination, or 'affirmative action' is sometimes practised in an attempt to counteract the effects of previous long-term discrimination against a minority group. See also ◊antisemitism, ◊apartheid, ◊caste, ◊racism, ◊sexism, ◊slavery, ◊stereotype.

discus circular disc thrown by athletes in ancient times at gymnastic contests, especially at the Olympic Games, and also in modern Olympic and other athletic games. See ◊throwing events.

disinfectant agent which kills, or prevents the growth of, bacteria and other microorganisms. Chemical disinfectants include carbolic acid (phenol) used by Lister in surgery in the 1870s, ethyl alcohol, formaldehyde, chlorine and iodine.

disinvestment the practice of withdrawing investment from a country for political reasons. Most generally applied to the ostensive removal of funds from South Africa in recent years by such multinational companies as General Motors and Barclays Bank. Disinvestment may be motivated by fear of loss of business in the home market caused by adverse publicity, or by fear at loss of foreign resources if the local government loses power.

disk in computing, a common medium for storing large volumes of data. (The alternative is ◊magnetic tape.) A magnetic disk is rotated at high speed in a disk drive unit as a read/write (playback or record) head passes over its surfaces to record or to 'read' the magnetic variations that encode the data.
Fixed disks provide the most storage: up to 600 megabytes (million bytes) is quite common, though the *hard disks* of this type used with microcomputers may hold only 10 or 20 megabytes. Fixed or hard disks are built into the drive unit, stacked on top of one another.

Removable disks, which are common in minicomputer systems, and hold about 80 megabytes of data, are contained in a rigid plastic case which can be taken out of the drive unit. A *floppy disk* (also called diskette) is very much smaller in size and capacity. Normally holding less than one megabyte of data, it is flexible, mounted in a card envelope or rigid plastic case, and can be removed from the drive unit.

Recently, ◊laser disks have been used to store computer data. These have an enormous capacity (about 400 megabytes on a compact disk and billions of bytes on a single 12-inch disk) but once written onto the disk data cannot be erased.

Disney /'dɪznɪ/ 'Walt' (Walter Elias) 1901–66. American film-maker, whose name has become almost a keyword for family entertainment. Born in Chicago, he established his own studio in Hollywood in 1923, and his first Mickey Mouse cartoon (*Plane Crazy*) appeared in 1928: among other notable creations was Donald Duck. He developed the 'Silly Symphony', a new type of cartoon based on a musical element conceived in close association with the visual image, of which *Fantasia* 1940, made with ◊Stokowski was the culmination. His first feature-length cartoon was *Snow White and the Seven Dwarfs* 1938, followed by *Pinocchio* 1940, *Dumbo* 1940 and others. From 1953, when *The Living Desert* was shown, Disney also made some remarkable nature-study films as well as features with human casts such as *The Swiss Family Robinson* 1960, and *Mary Poppins* 1964. He also originated the concept of pleasure parks, of which Disneyland, California, was the first. Walt Disney World, Florida, 1972 includes the Epcot (Experimental Prototype Community of Tomorrow) Centre, a cross between a science museum and a theme park, opened in 1982.

dispersion describes two phenomena in science. In optics, dispersion describes the splitting of white light into a spectrum, for example when it passes through a prism or a diffraction grating. It occurs because the prism (or grating) bends each component wavelength to a slightly different extent. The natural dispersion of light through suspended raindrops creates a rainbow. Dispersion also refers to the distribution of microscopic particles in a ◊colloid.

displacement activity in animal behaviour, an action that is performed out of its normal context, while the animal is in a state of stress, frustration or uncertainty. Birds, for example, often peck at grass when uncertain whether to attack or flee from an opponent; similarly, humans scratch their heads when nervous. See ◊ethology.

Disraeli /dɪz'reɪlɪ/ Benjamin, Earl of Beaconsfield 1804–1881. Conservative politician and novelist. His father Isaac ◊D'Israeli, who was Jewish, had him baptized at the age of 13. After a period in a solicitor's office, Disraeli wrote the novel *Vivian Grey* 1826, and others, and the brilliant pamphlet *Vindication of the English Constitution* 1835. Entering Parliament in 1837 after four unsuccessful attempts he was laughed at as a dandy, but when

Disney 'Steamboat Willie' (1928) was the world's first talking cartoon. 'Walt' Disney, Mickey Mouse's creator, remains the most famous name in film animation and family entertainment, even since his death in 1966.

his maiden speech was shouted down, he said: 'The time will come when you will hear me.'

Excluded from Peel's government of 1841–46, Disraeli formed his Young England group to keep a critical eye on Peel's conservatism. Its ideas were expounded in the novels *Coningsby* 1844, *Sybil* 1845, and *Tancred* 1847. When Peel decided in 1846 to repeal the Corn Laws, Disraeli opposed the measure in a series of witty and effective speeches; Peel's government fell soon after, and Disraeli gradually came to be recognized as the leader of the Conservative Party in the Commons. He gave his own account of these events in his *Life of Lord George Bentinck* 1852.

During the next 20 years the Conservatives formed short-lived minority governments in 1852, in 1858–59, and in 1866–68, with Lord Derby as prime minister and Disraeli as chancellor of the Exchequer and leader of the Commons. In 1852 Disraeli first proposed discrimination in income tax between earned and unearned income, but without success. The 1858–59 government legalized the admission of Jews to Parliament, and transferred the government of India from the East India Company to the crown. In 1866 the Conservatives took office after defeating a Liberal Reform Bill, and then attempted to secure the credit of widening the franchise by the Reform Bill of 1867. On Lord Derby's retirement in 1868 Disraeli became prime minister, but a few months later he was defeated at a general election. During the six years of opposition that followed he published another novel, *Lothair* 1870, and established a Conservative Central Office, the prototype of modern party organizations.

In 1874 Disraeli took office with a majority of 100. Some useful reform measures were carried, such as the Artisans' Dwelling Act, which empowered local authorities to undertake slum clearance, but the outstanding feature of the government's policy was its imperialism. It was Disraeli's personal initiative that purchased from the Khedive of Egypt a controlling interest in the Suez Canal, conferred on the Queen the title of Empress of India, and sent the Prince of Wales on the first royal tour of that country. He accepted an earldom 1876. The Bulgarian revolt of 1876 and the subsequent Russo-Turkish War of 1877–78 provoked the most famous of the political duels between Disraeli and Gladstone. The crisis was concluded by the Congress of Berlin (1878), where Disraeli was the principal British delegate, and whence he brought home 'peace with honour'. The government was defeated in 1880, and a year later Disraeli died after writing *Endymion*. He was the founder and chief inspiration of the modern Conservative Party.

D'Israeli /dɪz'reɪlɪ/ Isaac 1766–1848. British scholar, father of Benjamin ◊Disraeli and author of *Curiosities of Literature* 1791–93 and 1823.

Disruption, The split in the Church of Scotland 1843 when its Evangelical wing formed the Free Church of Scotland, hoping to recreate the spirit of John Knox and early Protestantism.

Dissenter historically, one of those Protestants dissenting from the Established Church, for example, Baptists, Presbyterians, and Independents (who are now known as Congregationalists).

dissident in one-party states, one intellectually dissenting from the official line. In the USSR dissidents comprise communists who advocate a more democratic and humanitarian approach; religious proselytizers; Jews wishing to emigrate; and those who support ethnic or national separatist movements within the USSR (among them Armenians, Lithuanians, Ukrainians, and Tatars). Their views are expressed through ▷samizdat and sometimes published abroad. They may be sent into exile, prison, labour camps, and mental institutions, or deprived of their jobs. Among them are ▷Sakharov and ▷Solzhenitsyn.

distemper contagious virus disease in young dogs, which is also found in wild animals, such as foxes. It is characterized by catarrh, cough, and general weakness, and is prevented by vaccination.

distributive law in mathematics, the law that states that one operation is independent of being carried out before (or after) another. Multiplication distributes over addition or subtraction; for example, $3 \times (4 + 5)$ is the same as $(3 \times 4) + (3 \times 5)$. See also ▷associative law.

distributor a device in a car engine's ▷ignition system that distributes pulses of high-voltage electricity to the ▷spark plugs in the cylinders. The electricity is passed to the plug leads by the tip of a rotor arm, driven by the engine camshaft. Current is fed to the rotor arm from the ignition coil. The distributor also houses the contact-breaker, which opens and closes to interrupt the battery current to the coil, thus triggering off the high-voltage pulses. In modern cars with electronic ignition, it is absent.

district council in England and Wales, under the Local Government Act 1972, 300 district councils were created to replace the former county borough, borough, and urban and rural district councils. The district councils are headed by an annually elected chair or, in an honorary borough or city, mayor or lord mayor. Councillors are elected for four years, and one-third retire at a time, so that district elections are held in three out of four years, county-council elections taking place in the fourth. Their responsibilities cover housing, local planning and development, roads (excluding trunk and classified), bus services, environmental health (refuse collection, clean air, food safety and hygiene, and enforcement of the Offices, Shops and Railway Premises Act), rating, museums and art galleries, parks and playing fields, swimming baths, cemeteries, and so on. In Metropolitan District Councils education, personal social services, and libraries are also included. See ▷local government.

District of Columbia /kə'lʌmbiə/ federal district of the USA, see ▷Washington.

Diu /'diːuː/ island 11 km/7 mi long, and town, off the Kathiawar peninsular, NW India. Part of the Union Territory of ▷Goa, ▷Daman and Diu.

diuretic drug that rids the body of excess fluid by increasing the output of urine by the kidneys. Used to treat high blood pressure and kidney disease.

diver type of bird specialized for swimming and diving found in the northern N Hemisphere. The legs are set so far back that walking is almost impossible, and they come to land only to nest, but divers are powerful swimmers and good

flyers. Most breed in fresh water, but at other times of the year are largely marine. They have straight bills and long bodies, and feed on fish, crustaceans, and some water plants. There are just four species, the largest, the **white-billed diver** *Gavia adamsii*, being an Arctic species 75 cm/2.5 ft long. Divers are also called *loons*.

Djibouti
REPUBLIC OF (*Jumhouriyya Djibouti*)

AREA 23,000 sq km/8,880 sq mi
CAPITAL and chief port Djibouti
PHYSICAL mountains divide an inland plateau from a coastal plain; hot and arid
HEAD OF STATE AND OF GOVERNMENT Hassan Gouled Aptidon from 1977
GOVERNMENT one-party republic
EXPORTS acts mainly as a transit port for Ethiopia
CURRENCY Djibouti franc (290 = £1 Sept 1987)
POPULATION (1985) 297,000 (Issa 40%, Afar 35%, Arab 25%); annual growth rate 3.4%
LANGUAGE Somali, Afar, French, Arabic
RELIGION Sunni Muslim
LITERACY 17% (1985)
GNP $307 (1984); $400 per head of population
CHRONOLOGY
1977 Full independence achieved. Hassan Gouled elected president.

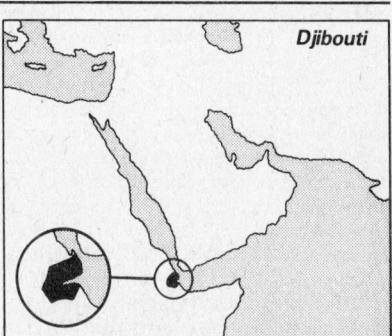
Djibouti

1979 All political parties combined to form the People's Progress Assembly (RPP).
1981 New constitution made RPP the only legal party. Gouled re-elected. Treaties of friendship signed with Ethiopia, Somalia, Kenya, and Sudan.
1984 Policy of neutrality reaffirmed.

diverticulitis inflammation of hernias of the large intestine, it may be caused by lack of bulk in the diet.

divertissement (French 'entertainment') a dance, or group of dances, within a ballet or opera that have no connection with the plot, such as the character dances in the last act of *Coppélia*.

divination art of ascertaining future events or eliciting other hidden knowledge by supernatural or non-rational means. There are two main types of divination. The first depends on the interpretation of the mechanical operations of chance or natural law, and includes the casting of lots and ordeals by water, fire, and single combat; consultation of texts obtained by a random opening of such books as the Bible, etc.; omens drawn from the behaviour of birds and animals; examination of the entrails of sacrificed animals; and the observation of the stars in astrology. On the borderline of the subjective forms of divination are fortune-telling by cards and palmistry; manipulation of a Bible and key or the reaction of a suspended ring; and the use of the divining rod in finding water, or metals. To the second or almost entirely subjective class, which uses external aids only to a minor extent, belongs clairvoyance by crystal gazing; oracular trance-speaking and automatic writing; necromancy, or the raising of the spirits of the dead; and dreams, often specially induced.

Divination played a large part in the ancient civilizations of the Egyptians, Greeks, and Romans, and is still practised throughout the world by users of such methods as ▷astrology, and the ▷Tarot. See also ▷Sibyl.

divine right of kings Christian political doctrine that monarchy is divinely ordained as in the Bible, hereditary right cannot be forfeited, monarchs are accountable to God alone for their actions, and rebellion against the lawful sovereign is thus a sin against God. The doctrine had its origins in the anointing of Pepin in 751 by the Pope after he had usurped the throne of the Franks. It was at its peak in 16th-and 17th-century Europe (notably in the court of Louis XIV of France) as a weapon against the claims of the papacy, and in 17th-century England was maintained by the supporters of the Stuarts in opposition to the democratic theories of the Puritans and Whigs.

diving the sport of entering the water either from a springboard (3 m/10 ft) above the water, or from a highboard (10 m/33 ft) above the water. Various differing starts are adopted, and twists and somersaults performed in mid-air.

diving apparatus any apparatus used to enable a person to spend time underwater. Diving bells were in use in the 18th century, the diver breathing air trapped in a bell-shaped chamber. The first diving suit, with a large metal helmet and supplied with air by pipeline, was invented by the brothers John and Charles Deane in 1828. Complete freedom of movement came with the ▷aqualung, invented by Jacques ▷Cousteau in the early 1940s. For depths of several hundred metres the technique of saturation diving was developed in the 1970s, particularly for working in the offshore oilfields in the North Sea and elsewhere. Divers live for a week or more breathing a mixture of helium and oxygen at the pressure existing on the seabed where they work. When they are not diving, they live in a compression chamber on board a support ship. They are ferried down to the work site by a lock-out ▷submersible. By this technique they aoid the need for lengthy periods of decompression after every dive. Slow decompression is necessary to avoid the dangerous consequences of an attack of the ◊bends. See ◊decompression sickness.

divorce the legal dissolution of a lawful marriage. In England, divorce could be secured only by the passing of a private Act of Parliament until the Matrimonial Causes Act, 1857, set up the Divorce Court and enacted that a wife could be divorced for adultery, a husband for adultery only when combined with other offences including cruelty or desertion. Under the *Divorce Reform Act* (1969) the sole ground for divorce from 1971 is the irretrievable breakdown of the marriage. Emphasis is on provision for the children, and in 1984 further legislation put a time limit on maintenance payments.

In the USA divorce laws differ from state to state, although adultery is a ground everywhere, in New York until 1967 the only ground; other grounds are cruelty, desertion, alcoholism, drug addiction and insanity. Minimum periods of residence before a divorce is granted are from 6 weeks, and the Supreme Court ruled in 1949 that quick divorces instituted by one side without notification to the partner may be challenged. The so-called *Enoch Arden Laws* prescribe the number of years which must elapse before remarriage in instances where one partner disappears and is not known to be dead: they are named after the sailor of Tennyson's poem who returned after many years to find his wife remarried. In the USSR, under laws introduced in the 1960s, divorce is easy and cheap. Maintenance for a wife after divorce is decreasing in importance, but she is likely to benefit by a more equitable division of property. Custody and maintenance of children is tending to become a joint responsibility. In the USA unmarried couples cohabiting are increasingly negotiating 'pre-cohabitation agreements' which make an advance settlement of division of property and assets, in anticipation of a break-up, the woman sometimes stipulating for subsequent financial payments based on the number of years the arrangement lasts.

The Roman Catholic Church does not permit divorce among its members, and under Pope John Paul II conditions for 'annulment' have been tightened. Among Muslims a wife cannot divorce her husband, but he may divorce her by repeating the formula 'I divorce you' three times: property settlements by careful parents make this a right not too frequently exercised.

Diwali festival of ◊Lakshmi, Hindu goddess of light.

Dixie /'dɪksi/ word of uncertain origin, denoting the southern states of the USA.

Dixieland jazz name given to early jazz style which originated in New Orleans in the early 20th century.

Diyarbakir /dɪ'jɑːbəkɪə/ town in Asiatic Turkey, on the Tigris; population (1980) 235,600. It has a trade in gold and silver filigree work, copper, wool and mohair, and manufactures textiles and leather goods.

Djakarta variant spelling of ◊Jakarta, capital of Indonesia.

Djibouti /dʒɪ'buːti/ country on the E coast of Africa, at the S end of the Red Sea, bounded to the E by the Gulf of Aden, to the SE by the Somali Republic, and to the S, W, and N by Ethiopia.

government the 1981 constitution made Djibouti a one-party state, the only legal party being the People's Progress Assembly (RPP). The constitution also provides for a single-chamber legislature, the 65-member chamber of deputies, elected by universal suffrage for a five-year term, and a president, nominated by the party, who is elected for six years and may not serve more than two terms.

history first colonized by France in 1862, Djibouti was part of French Somaliland 1896–1945, after which it was declared an overseas territory. In 1967 it was renamed the French Territory of the Afars and the Issas. Calls for independence were frequent, sometimes violent. It was achieved in 1977, with Hassan Gouled as president. In 1979 all political parties combined to form the RPP and the government embarked on the task of uniting the two main ethnic groups, the Issas, who traditionally had strong links with Somalia, and the Afars, who had been linked with Ethiopia.

In 1981 a new constitution was adopted, making RPP the only party and providing for the election of a president after nomination by RPP. President Gouled was re-elected and in 1982 a chamber of deputies was elected from a list of RPP nominees. Under Gouled, Djibouti has pursued a largely successful policy of amicable neutralism with its neighbours, concluding treaties of friendship with Ethiopia, Somalia, Kenya and the Sudan, and has tried to assist the peace process in E Africa. Although affected by the 1984–85 droughts, it managed to maintain stability with EEC aid.

DNA a complex two-stranded molecule that contains, in chemically coded form, all the information needed to build, control and maintain a living organism. DNA is a double-stranded ◊nucleic acid that forms the basis of genetic inheritance in all organisms, except for a few viruses that depend on ◊RNA. In ◊eukaryotic organisms, it is organized into ◊chromosomes and contained in the cell nucleus. DNA is made up of two strands of ◊nucleotide sub-units which contain purine or pyrimidine ◊bases; these form base pairs that link the two strands of the DNA molecule like the rungs of a twisted ladder. The specific way in which the pairs form means that the base sequence is preserved from generation to generation. The hereditary information is stored as a specific sequence of the various bases. A set of three bases is known as a ◊codon and it specifies a particular ◊amino acid, the sub-unit of a protein molecule. (Proteins are the chief structural molecules of living matter.) The codons are represented by the initial letters of the bases involved, for example, CAG for the base sequence cytosine-adenine-guanine. The meaning of each of the codons in the ◊genetic code has been worked out by molecular geneticists. There are four different bases, which means that there are $4 \times 4 \times 4 = 64$ different codons. Proteins are usually made up of multiple combinations of 20 different amino acids, so many amino acids have more than one

DNA

how a cell divides

1 original double helix

2 forms ladder

3 unzips

4 new bases join onto opened zip teeth

5 two new identical double strands

Key
S sugars
P phosphates
C cytosine
G guanine
A adenine
T thymine

codon (for example, GGT, GGC, GGA and GGG all code for the same amino acid, glycine.) By specifying protein sequences, DNA can build a whole organism. All aspects of the functioning of an organism depend on ◊enzymes, and enzymes are proteins also, so DNA controls the rates of protein production. DNA is 'translated' into protein by means of messenger RNA. See also ◊mutation.

Dneprodzerzhinsk /ˌnɪprədzə'ʒɪnsk/ industrial port in the Ukraine, USSR, on the Dnieper, 48 km/30 mi NW of ◊Dnepropetrovsk; population (1985) 271,000. It produces chemicals, iron, and steel.

Dnepropetrovsk /ˌnɪprəpɪ'trɒfsk/ industrial city in the Ukraine, USSR; population (1985) 1,153,000. On the right bank of the Dnieper, it is the centre of an important industrial region, with iron, steel, chemical, and engineering industries. It is linked with the Dnieper Dam, 60 km/37 mi downstream. Founded in 1786, it was originally named Ekaterinoslav (Catherine's glory) after Catherine the Great.

Dnieper /'niːpə/ Russian river, and Europe's third largest, rising in the Smolensk region and flowing S past Kiev, Dnepropetrovsk, and Zaporozhe, to enter the Black Sea E of Odessa. Total length 2,250 km/1,400 mi.

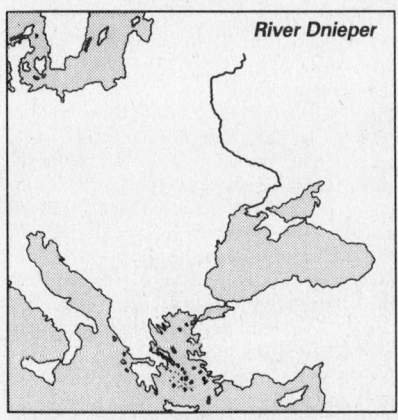

River Dnieper

D-notice in the UK, a censorship notice issued by the Department of Defence to the media to prohibit the publication of information on matters of national security. The system dates from 1922.

Dobell /dəu'bel/ William 1899–1970. Australian portraitist and genre painter, born in New South Wales. He worked as an architect until, in 1929, he won a travelling scholarship, and went to study art in England and Holland. He returned to Australia in 1939, and during World War II became an official war artist. His best-known portraits include *Joshua Smith*, *Margaret Olley*, and *Helena Rubinstein*. He was knighted in 1966.

Dobermann streamlined smooth-coated breed of dog with a docked tail, much used as a guard dog. Standing up to 70 cm/2.2 ft tall, often black with brown markings, the dog takes its name from the man who bred it in 19th century Germany.

Döblin /'dɜːbliːn/ Alfred 1878–1957. German novelist. He practised as a doctor in Berlin until 1933 when his books were banned and he was exiled; he moved first to France and from 1941 lived in the USA. His *Berlin-Alexanderplatz* 1929 owes much to Joyce in its minutely detailed depiction of the inner lives of a

city's inhabitants, and is considered by many to be the finest 20th-century German novel. Other works include *November 1918: Eine deutsche Revolution/A German Revolution* 1939–50 (published in four parts), a study of Germany in the aftermath of World War I and the formation of the Weimar Republic.

Dobruja /'dɒbruːdʒə/ district in the Balkans, bounded to the N and W by the Danube, and to the E by the Black Sea. It is low-lying, partly marshland, partly fertile steppe land. Constanta is the chief town. Dobruja was divided between Romania and Bulgaria in 1878. In 1913, after the second Balkan War, Bulgaria ceded its part to Romania, but received it back in 1940, a cession confirmed by the peace treaty of 1947.

dock port accommodation for commercial and naval vessels, usually simple linear quayage adaptable to ships of any size, but with specialized equipment for handling bulk cargoes, refrigerated goods, container traffic, and oil tankers. Flexible 'floating' docks are used for repairs.

dock in botany, name applied to a number of plants of the genus *Rumex*, belonging to the Polygonaceae. They are annual to perennial herbs, natives of the temperate parts of the world, often with lance-shaped leaves and small, greenish-coloured flowers. There are several British species and some 30 N American.

dodder genus of parasitic plants, *Cuscuta*, family ◊Convolvulaceae, without leaves or roots. The thin stem twines round the host, and penetrating suckers withdraw nourishment.

Dodds /dɒdz/ Charles 1899–1973. British biochemist. Courtauld professor of biochemistry at London university 1927–65, and president of the Royal College of Physicians 1962, he was largely responsible for the discovery of stilboestrol, the powerful synthetic hormone used in treating prostate conditions and also for fattening cattle. He was knighted in 1954.

Dodds /dɒdz/ Johnny 1892–1940. US clarinettist, generally ranked among the top New Orleans jazz clarinettists. He was most successful with the New Orleans Wanderers and noted for his warmth of tone and improvisation.

Dodecanese /ˌdəʊdekə'niːz/ (Greek *Dhodhekánisosê*) group of islands in the Aegean sea; area 1,028 sq m/2,663 sq km. Once Turkish, the islands were Italian 1912–47, when they were ceded to Greece. They include ◊Rhodes, and ◊Kos.

dodecaphonic in music, a term applied to the 12-note system of composition.

Dodge City /dɒdʒ/ city in S W Kansas, USA, on the Arkansas; population (1980) 18,000. On the Santa Fé Trail, it was a noted frontier cattle town in the days of the Wild West.

Dodgson /'dɒdsən/ Charles Lutwidge, real name of writer Lewis ◊Carroll.

dodo extinct bird *Raphus cucullatus* formerly found on Mauritius but exterminated before the end of the 17th century. Related to the pigeons, it was larger than a turkey, with a bulky body and very short wings and tail. Flightless and trusting, it was easy prey to humans and the animals they introduced.

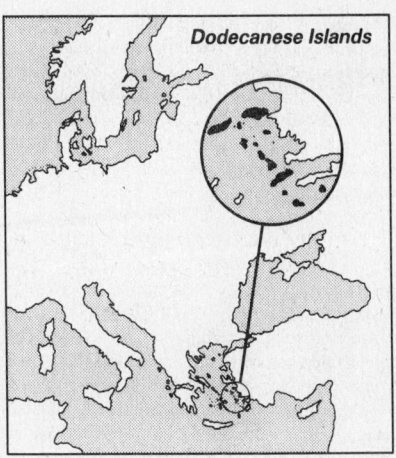

Dodecanese Islands

Dodoma /'dəʊdəmə/ capital of Tanzania from 1975; population (1985) 1,171,000. It replaced Dar-es-Salaam as capital in 1975, chosen for its position in the approximate centre of the country, 1,132 m/3,713 ft above sea level. It is a hub of communications, linked by rail with Dar-es-Salaam and Kigoma on Lake Tanganyika, and by road with Kenya to the N, and Zambia and Malawi to the S.

dog meat-eating mammal *Canis familiaris* domesticated by humans, and bred into many different varieties for use as working animals and pets. Domestic dogs have existed since prehistoric times, and may have originally descended from the wolf, but some authorities favour jackals or a mixed parentage for the ancestor. There are some 400 different breeds of dog throughout the world, the Kennel Club (1873) grouping those eligible for registration (150 breeds) into sporting breeds (hound, gundog and terrier) and non-sporting (utility, working and toy). The premier event of the dog year is Crufts Show in London. As well as domestic dogs there are many species of wild dog in the dog family Canidae. Found in all continents except Antarctica, wild dogs are mostly running hunters, going on the toes of the feet, and with long faces and keen noses. Some are solitary such as the long-legged *maned wolf Chrysocyon brachurus* of S America but others hunt in groups, such as the *African wild dog Lycaon pictus* or the ◊*wolf*. Some scavenge, such as the *jackals* and many include plant as well as animal food in the diet, as does the *raccoon dog Nyctereutes procyonoides* of E Asia. The latter, with a head and body about 50 cm/1.6 ft and a bushy tail, is farmed for its fur in the USSR and escapers have spread across Europe.

Doge the chief magistrate in the ancient constitutions of Venice and Genoa. The first Doge of Venice was appointed in 697 with absolute power (modified in 1297), and from his accession dates Venice's prominence in history. The last Venetian Doge, Lodovico Manin, retired in 1797.

dogfish small shark *Scyliorhinus caniculus* found in the NE Atlantic and Mediterranean. It is caught in some numbers and finds its way to the table as 'rock eel' or 'rock salmon'. Bottom-living, it is sandy brown and covered with spots, and grows to about 75 cm/2.5 ft. Various other species of small shark may also be called dogfish.

Dogger Bank /'dɒgə/ submerged sandbank in the North Sea, about 115 km/70 mi off the coast of Yorkshire. In places the water is only 11 m/36 ft deep, but the general depth is 18–36 m/60–120 ft; it is a well-known fishing ground.

Doggett /'dɒgɪt/ Thomas c. 1670–1721. British comedy actor for whom ◊Congreve wrote parts. In 1714 Doggett instituted the prize of 'Doggett's Coat and Badge', which is still given to the winner of a sculling race on 1 Aug, open to Thames watermen in the year following their apprenticeship.

Dogs, Isle of /dɒgz/ district of E London, England, part of the Greater London borough of Tower Hamlets.

dog's mercury plant *Mercurialis perennis* of the family Euphorbiaceae. Growing about 30 cm/1ft tall, dog's mercury carpets woodland floors in patches consisting of a single sex. Male flowers are small, greenish yellow, and held on upright spike above the leaves. Female flowers droop below the upper leaves. Leaves are oval and light green. It is found across Europe.

dogwood deciduous shrub *Cornus sanguinea* growing up to 4 m/12 ft, normally with red twigs. The oval green leaves also redden in the autumn. Heads of small white flowers, each with four petals joined as a tube, are produced in midsummer, followed by black berries. The dogwood is characteristic of lime soils in the S of England, and is found over much of S Europe. Various other species of dogwood are planted in gardens.

Doha /'dəuhɑ:/ capital and chief port of Qatar; population (1980) 180,000. The Doha regional training centre provides vocational training for all the Gulf states. The Gulf (football) Tournament is played in Khalifa Stadium.

Doldrums area of low atmospheric pressure along the equator, largely applied to oceans at the convergence of the NE and SE ◊trade winds. To some extent the area affected moves N and S with the sun. The Doldrums are characterized by calm or very light westerly winds, during which there may be sudden squalls and stormy weather. For this reason the areas are avoided as far as possible by sailing ships.

dolerite an ◊igneous rock formed below the earth's surface, and containing little silica (basic in composition). It is a medium-grained (hypabyssal) form of ◊basalt and forms in minor intrusions such as dykes, that cut across the rock strata, and sills, that push between beds of sedimentary rock. When exposed at the surface dolerite (also called diabase in the USA) weathers into spherical lumps.

Dolgellau /dɒl'geθli/ tourist centre and market town at the foot of Cader Idris in Gwynedd, Wales; population (1981) 2,400. Nearby are the Gwynffynydd ('White mountain') and Clogau goldmines; a nugget from the latter has supplied gold for the wedding rings of royal brides since 1923.

Dolin /'dɒlɪn/ Anton, stage name of Patrick Healey-Kay 1904–1983. British dancer and choreographer. After studying under ◊Nijinsky, he was a leading member of ◊Diaghilev's company from 1923, before becoming principal of the Vic-Wells Ballet 1935–37. Later he formed the Markova-Dolin Ballet with Alicia ◊Markova.

Doll /dɒl/ William Richard 1912– . British physician, Professor of medicine at Oxford and late Master of Greene College, Oxford. Working with Professor Bradford Hill, he provided the first statistical proof, in 1950, of the link between smoking and lung cancer. In a later, prospective study of the smoking habits of doctors, they were able to show that stopping smoking immediately reduces the risk of cancer.

dollar (from the German *thaler*) a monetary unit containing 100 cents adopted as the standard unit in the USA in 1785; Australia, Canada, Hong Kong, and a number of other countries have also adopted the name for their standard unit.

Eurodollar Following World War II, a large American dollar reserve accumulated in Europe and London, became the centre of this Eurodollar market.

Asian dollar Large reserves of US dollars accumulated in Asia and Singapore, became from 1968, the centre of the Asian dollar market, working in co-operation with London.

Following the depreciation of the US dollar after the Vietnam War expenditure and the oil crisis of 1973, the European monetary system became anchored to the German mark, and in Asia the Japanese yen became important as a trading currency.

Dollfuss /'dɒlfu:s/ Engelbert 1892–1934. Austrian politician. A Christian Socialist, he was appointed Chancellor in 1932, and in 1933 suppressed parliament and ruled by decree. Negotiations for an alliance with the Austrian Nazis broke down. On 12 Feb 1934 he crushed the Social Democrats by force, and in May Austria was declared a corporative state. The Nazis attempted a coup d'état on 25 Jul; the Chancellery was seized and Dollfuss murdered. He was known as the 'pocket chancellor' because of his small stature.

dolmen type of prehistoric monument, taking the form of a chamber built of large stone slabs, which are roofed over by a flat stone which they support. Dolmens are grave chambers of the Neolithic period, found in Europe and Africa, and occasionally in Asia as far as Japan. In Wales they are known as cromlechs.

dolphin type of marine mammal, a small toothed whale, of which many species exist. The *common dolphin Delphinus delphis* is found in all temperate and tropical seas. It is up to 2.5 m/8 ft long, and is dark above, white below, with bands of grey, white and yellow on the sides, and has up to 100 teeth in its jaws which make the 15 cm/6 in 'beak' protruding forwards from the rounded head. It feeds on fish and squid. Of high intelligence, dolphins are popular performers in oceanaria. The usual species exhibited is the *bottle-nosed dolphin Tursiops truncatus*, found in all warm seas, mainly grey in colour and

growing to a maximum 4.2 m/14 ft. Dolphins emit many sounds, some audible to humans, others too high, and use sound in echolocation to navigate and find prey, as well as for communication. Some species can swim at up to 56 kph/35 mph, helped by special streamlining modifications of the skin. All power themselves by beating the tail up and down. The flippers, which betray dolphin's land mammal ancestry with their typical five-toed limb bone structure, are used to steer and stabilize. Also known as *dolphin* is the totally unrelated true fish *Coryphaena hippurus*, up to 1.5 m/5 ft long.

Domenico Veneziano / də'menɪkəu vɪˌnetsi'ɑːnəu/ c. 1400–1461. Italian painter, probably from Florence. He worked in Sant'Egidio, Florence, on frescoes now lost. Piero della ◊Francesca trained under him; Domenico was one of the most influential artists after Masaccio and was largely concerned with the mutation of colour by light. His works include the *Carnesecchi Madonna and two saints* and the *Saint Lucy alterpiece*, now divided between Florence (Uffizi), Berlin, Cambridge (Fitzwilliam), and Washington (National Gallery).

Domesday Book record of the survey of England carried out in 1086 by officials of William the Conqueror, in order to assess land tax and other dues, ascertain the value of the crown lands, and enable the king to estimate the power of his vassal barons. Northumberland and Durham were omitted, and also London, Winchester, and certain other towns. The Domesday Book is preserved in two volumes at the Public Record Office, London. The name is derived from the belief that its judgement was as final as that of Doomsday.

domestic animal an animal tamed, or otherwise brought under people's control for exploitation in respect of their labour; use of their feathers, hides or skins; consumption of their eggs, milk, or meat. Almost coexistent with the emergence of humans themselves, the use of domestic animals has only since World War II developed to factory farming and the inclusion of an increasing number of formerly wild species, with increasing stress on scientific breeding for desired characteristics.

domestic service paid employment in the household of another person, as maid, butler, cook, gardener, and so on. Before the Industrial Revolution it was virtually the only form of employment open to women, and has traditionally been an occupation of the lower classes, generally badly paid and little esteemed. It was at its peak in Victorian times with the increase in prosperity that created a wealthy new middle class, whose ostentatious households demanded a number of servants for their upkeep. In Victorian times domestic service was seen as a more 'respectable' occupation for women than industrial employment such as work in factories, but after World War I the shortage of available men meant that more women were able to choose employment other than domestic. The mobilization of women in World War II, the increase in labour-saving devices, and the growth of employment opportunities for women since

domestic service Domestic staff on the garden steps at Erddig Park, 1912 (above), and gardeners at Polesden Lacey, 1925 (below). Senior domestic staff would include the butler, housekeeper, personal maid, and head gardener.

the war, have meant that domestic service hardly exists today as a full-time occupation except for a tiny proportion of working people, generally in aristocratic households.

dominance in genetics, the concept that certain characteristics are dominant, that is, they mask the expression of other characteristics, known as ◊recessives. For example if a person has one ◊allele (gene variant) for blue eyes and one for brown eyes, the brown colour will predominate. See also ◊heterozygous and ◊gene.

dominant in music, the fifth degree of the scale, for example G in C major.

Domingo /də'mɪŋgəʊ/ Placido 1941– . Spanish tenor, also a skilled pianist. Born in Madrid, of a celebrated musical family, he emigrated with them to Mexico as a boy. He excels in romantic operatic roles.

Dominica /ˌdɒmɪ'niːkə/ island in the West Indies, between Guadeloupe and Martinique, the largest of the Windward Islands, with the Atlantic to the E and the Caribbean to the W.

government Dominica is an independent republic within the ◊Commonwealth. The constitution dates from independence in 1978, and provides for a single-chamber, 30-member, house of assembly. 21 are representatives elected by universal suffrage, and 9 are appointed senators, 5 on the advice of the prime minister and 4 on the advice of the leader of the opposition. The assembly serves a five-year term, as does the president, who is elected by it and acts as constitutional head of state, appointing the prime minister on the basis of assembly support. The prime minister chooses the cabinet and all are responsible to the assembly. The two main political parties are the Dominica Freedom Party (DFP) and the Labour Party of Dominica.

history Dominica was named by Christopher ◊Columbus, who visited it in 1493. It became a British possession in the 18th century, and was part of the Leeward Islands federation until 1939. In 1940 it was transferred to the Windward Islands and remained attached to that group until 1960, when it was given separate status, with a chief minister and legislative council.

In 1961 the leader of the Dominica Labour Party (DLP), Edward leBlanc, became chief minister and after 13 years in office, retired and was succeeded as prime minister by Patrick John. The DLP held office until full independence was achieved in 1978 and its leader, John, became the first prime minister under the new constitution. Opposition to John's increasingly authoritarian style of government soon developed and in the 1980 elections the DFP won a convincing victory on a free enterprise policy programme. Its leader, Eugenia Charles, became the Caribbean's first woman prime minister.

In 1981 John was thought to be implicated in a plot against the government and a state of emergency was imposed. The next year he was tried and acquitted. He was retried in 1985, found guilty and given a 12-year prison sentence. Left-of-centre parties regrouped, making the Labour Party of Dominica (LPD) the main opposition to the DFP. In the 1985 elections Eugenia Charles was re-elected. Under her leadership, Dominica has developed links with France and the USA and in 1983 sent a small force to the US-backed invasion of ◊Grenada.

Dominican Order the order of friars founded by St ◊Dominic; they are also known as Friars Preachers, Black Friars, or Jacobins. The first house was established at Toulouse in 1215; in 1216 the order received papal recognition, and their rule was drawn up in 1220–21. They soon spread all over Europe, the first house in England being established at Oxford in 1221. The English Dominicans were suppressed in 1559, but were restored to a corporate existence in 1622. Today the order is worldwide and there is also an order of contemplative nuns; the habit is black and white. Dominicans have included Thomas ◊Aquinas, ◊Savonarola, and Las ◊Casas.

Dominican Republic /də'mɪnɪkən/ country in the West Indies, occupying the E of the island of Hispaniola, with Haiti to the W. The island is surrounded by the Caribbean Sea.

government although not a federal state, the Dominican Republic has a highly devolved system of 26 provinces, each administered by an appointed governor, and a national district, which includes the capital, Santo Domingo. The 1966 constitution provides for a popularly

Domingo Spanish opera singer Placido Domingo at the Royal Opera House, Covent Garden, in 1985.

120 members, one per 50,000 inhabitants. The president is head of both government and state and chooses the cabinet. Most significant of a wide range of political parties are the left-wing Dominican Revolutionary Party (PRD) and the centrist Christian Social Reform Party (PRSC).

history The first European to visit the island was Christopher ◊Columbus in 1492; he named it Hispaniola ('Little Spain'). It was divided between France and Spain in 1697, and in 1795 the Spanish part (Santo Domingo) was ceded to France. After a revolt it was retaken by Spain in 1808. Following a brief independence in 1821 it was occupied by Haiti until the establishment of the Dominican Republic in 1844.

Spain occupied the country again 1861–65, and after independence was restored, it was in such financial difficulties that in 1904 the USA took over its debts and intervened militarily 1916–24. In 1930 the elected president was overthrown in a military coup and General Rafael Trujillo Molina became dictator. He was assassinated in 1961, and in 1963 Dr Juan Bosch, founder and leader of the left-wing PRD, who had been in exile for over 30 years, won the country's first free elections. Within a year he was overthrown by the military, who set up a three-man junta.

his links with Trujillo, proved a popular leader, being re-elected in 1970 and 1974.

The 1978 election was won by the PRD candidate, Silvestre Antonio Guzmán. The PRD was again successful in the 1982 election and Salvador Jorge Blanco, the party's left-wing nominee, became president-designate. After allegations of fraud by his family, Guzmán committed suicide before he had finished his term, and an interim president was chosen before the start of Blanco's term.

Blanco steered a restrained course in foreign policy, maintaining good relations with the USA and avoiding too close an association with Cuba. The economy deteriorated, and in 1985 the Blanco administration was forced to adopt harsh austerity measures in return for ◊IMF help. The PRD became increasingly unpopular and it was no suprise that the PRSC, under Joaquín Balaguer, returned to power in 1986.

Dominic, St /'dɒmɪnɪk/ 1170–1221. Founder of the Roman Catholic ◊Dominican Order of preaching friars. Born in Old Castile, he was sent by Pope Innocent III on a mission to the Provençal Albigenses, and remained preaching among them 1205–15. In 1208 the Pope substituted the Albigensian crusade to suppress the heretics by force, and this was supported by Dominic. From Dominic's mission grew the ◊Dominican Order, and in 1215 it was given premises at Toulouse. Pope Honorius III, in 1218, permitted Dominic to constitute his 'holy preaching' as an order, and by the time of his death it was established all over W Europe. Dominic was canonized in 1234.

Dominions name formerly applied to self-governing divisions of the British Empire, for example Canada, now members of the ◊Commonwealth.

Domitian /də'mɪʃən/ (Titus Flavius Domitianus) 51–96 AD. Roman emperor. Born in Rome, he became emperor in 81 AD. He finalized the conquest of Britain (see ◊Agricola), strengthened the Rhine–Danube frontier, and suppressed immorality as well as freedom of thought in philosophy (see ◊Epictetus), and religion (Christians were persecuted). His reign of terror led to his assassination.

Don /dɒn/ Russian river, rising to the S of Moscow and entering the NE extremity of the Sea of Azov: length 1,900 km/1,200 mi. In its lower reaches the Don is 1.5 km/1 mi wide, and for about four months of the year it is closed by ice. Its upper course is linked with the Volga by a canal.

Donat /'dɒnət/ Robert 1905–1958. British actor, especially remembered for the films *The Thirty-Nine Steps* 1935 and *Goodbye Mr Chips* 1939.

Donatello /ˌdɒnə'teləu/ or Donato di Niccolo di Betto Bardi 1386–1466. Italian sculptor born in Florence. With ◊Brunelleschi he revived the classical style, and exercised a profound influence on the masters of the Italian Renaissance. Donatello used perspective in his relief sculptures. His bronze statues like the youthful *David* 1430–32, the first free-standing nude since antiquity, or his equestrian statue of the mercenary General Gattamelata (Padua,

Dominica
COMMONWEALTH OF

AREA 750 sq km/290 sq mi
CAPITAL Roseau, with a deepwater port
PHYSICAL largest of the Windward Islands, mountainous, tropical
FEATURES of great beauty, it has mountains of volcanic origin rising to 1,620 m/5,315 ft; Boiling Lake, an effect produced by escaping subterranean gas
HEAD OF STATE Clarence Seignoret from 1983
HEAD OF GOVERNMENT Mary Eugenia Charles from 1980
GOVERNMENT democratic republic
EXPORTS bananas, coconuts, citrus, lime, and bay oil
CURRENCY E Caribbean dollar (4.46 = £1 Sept 1987), pound sterling, French franc
POPULATION (1984) 74,000 (mainly black African in origin, but with a small Carib reserve of some 500); annual growth rate 1.3%
LANGUAGE English (official), but the Dominican *patois* still reflects earlier periods of French rule
RELIGION Roman Catholic 80%
LITERACY 80%
GNP $79 million (1983); $460 per head of population
CHRONOLOGY
1978 Dominica achieved full independence within the Commonwealth. Patrick John,

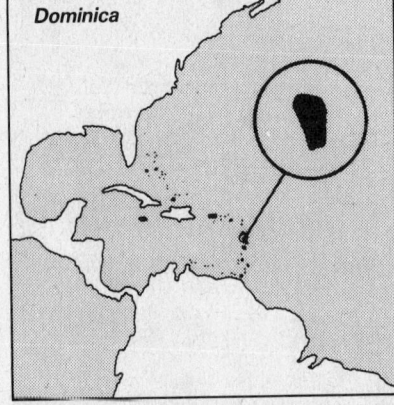

Dominica

leader of the Dominica Labour Party (DLP), elected prime minister.
1980 Dominica Freedom Party (FDP),led by Eugenia Charles, won a convincing victory in the general election.
1981 Patrick John was implicated in a plot to overthrow the government.
1982 John tried and acquitted.
1985 John retried and found guilty. Regrouping of left-of-centre parties resulted in the new Labour Party of Dominica (LPD). DFP, led by Eugenia Charles, re-elected.

elected president and a two-chamber congress, comprising a senate and a chamber of deputies, all elected for a four-year term. The senate has 27 members, one for each province and one for the national district, and the chamber of deputies

An attempt to re-establish Bosch in 1965 was defeated with US help, and in 1966 Joaquín Balaguer, a protégé of Trujillo and leader of the PRSC, won the presidency. A more democratic constitution was adopted and Balaguer, despite

Dominican Republic
(República Dominicana)

AREA 48,430 sq km/18,700 sq mi
CAPITAL Santo Domingo
PHYSICAL comprises E part of island of
Hispaniola; central mountain range; fertile
valley in N
FEATURES Pico Duarte 3,174 m/10,417 ft,
highest point in the Caribbean islands
HEAD OF STATE AND OF GOVERNMENT Joaquin
Balaguer from 1986
GOVERNMENT parliamentary democracy
EXPORTS sugar, gold, coffee, ferro-nickel
CURRENCY peso (5.27 = £1 Sept 1987)
POPULATION 6,614,000 (1985); annual growth
rate 2.9%
LANGUAGE Spanish (official)
RELIGION Roman Catholic
LITERACY 75% male/73% female (1980 est)
GNP $8.7 bn (1983); $1,221 per head of
population
CHRONOLOGY
1930 Military coup established the
dictatorship of Rafael Trujillo.
1961 Trujillo assassinated.
1962 First democratic elections resulted in
Juan Bosch, founder of the Dominican
Revolutionary Party (PRD) becoming
president.

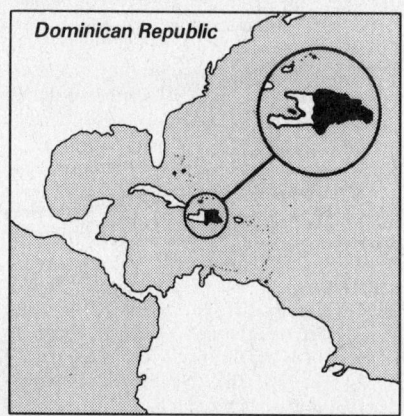

Dominican Republic

1963 Bosch overthrown in military coup.
1966 New constitution adopted. Joaquín
Balaguer, leader of the Christian Social
Reform Party (PRSC), became president.
1978 PRD returned to power, with Silvestre
Antonio Guzmán as president.
1982 PRD re-elected, with Jorge Blanco as
president.
1985 Blanco forced by IMF to adopt austerity
measures to save the economy.
1986 PRSC returned to power, with Joaquín
Balaguer re-elected president.

1443) look back to Classical prototypes but have
the alert liveliness of all early Renaissance art.
In his later work, such as his wood-carving of the
aged Mary Magdalene 1445, he sought dramatic
expression through distortion, even ugliness.

Donbas /ˌdɒn'bæs/ abbreviation of ◊Donets
Basin, a coal-rich area in the USSR.

Doncaster /'dɒŋkəstə/ town in South
Yorkshire, England, on the Don; population
(1981) 81,600. It has a racecourse, famous races
here are the St Leger (1776) in Sept and the
Lincolnshire Handicap in Mar.
history Doncaster was originally a Roman
station. Conisbrough, a ruined Norman castle to
the SW, features in Scott's *Ivanhoe* as
Athelstan's stronghold. Coal, iron, and steel have
been the dominant industries in this area for
hundreds of years, though they have recently
declined and are being replaced by other
manufactures, such as synthetic textiles.

Donegal /ˌdɒnɪ'gɔːl/ county in Ulster, in the
extreme NW of the Republic of Ireland;
population (1981) 125,112. Area 4,830 sq
km/1,865 sq mi. The county town is Lifford. The
market town and port of Donegal is at the head
of Donegal Bay in the SW. Donegal is
surrounded on three sides by the Atlantic, and
most of it is mountainous, being geologically a
continuation of the Highlands of Scotland.
Agriculture consists mainly of sheep and cattle
raising. There is little industry, but tweed and
linen are made, and there is some deep-sea
fishing. The river Erne hydro-electric project
(1952) involved the building of large power
stations at Ballyshannon.

Donets /dɒ'nets/ river of the USSR rising in
Kursk region and flowing 1,080 km/670 mi to
join the Don 100 km/60 mi E of Rostov. See
◊Donets Basin.

Donets Basin /dɒ'nets/ area in the bend
formed by the rivers Don and Donets, which
holds one of Europe's richest coalfields, together
with salt, mercury, and lead, so that the *Donbas*,
as the name is abbreviated, is one of the greatest
industrial regions of the USSR.

Donetsk /dɒ'nets/ city in the Ukrainian SSR,
capital of Donetsk region, 600 km/380 mi SE of
Kiev, USSR; population (1981) 1,140,000.
Situated in the Donbas, Donetsk is a rail centre
and has an airport. It has blast furnaces, rolling
mills, and other heavy industries. It developed
from 1871 when a Welshman, John Hughes,
established a metallurgical factory, and the town
was first called Yuzovka after him; renamed
Stalino in 1924, and Donetsk in 1961.

Dongola /'dɒŋgələ/ town in the Republic of
the Sudan, on the Nile. It was founded about
1812 to replace *Old Dongola*, 120 km/75 mi up
river, which was destroyed by the ◊Mamelukes.
The latter was the capital of the Christian
kingdom of ◊Nubia between the 6th–14th
centuries.

Dongting /ˌduŋtɪŋ/ lake in Hunan province,
China; area 10,000 sq km/4,000 sq mi.

Dönitz /'dɜːnɪts/ Karl 1891–1980. German
admiral, originator of the wolf-pack submarine
technique which sank 15 million tonnes of Allied
shipping in World War II. He succeeded Hitler
in 1945, capitulated and was imprisoned
1946–56.

Donizetti /ˌdɒnɪd'zeti/ Gaetano 1797–1848.
Italian composer, born in Lombardy. He
composed more than 60 operas, of which the best
known are *Lucrezia Borgia* 1833, *Lucia di
Lammermoor* 1835, *La Fille du régiment* 1840,
La Favorite 1840, and *Don Pasquale* 1843. They
show the influence of Rossini and Bellini, and
their chief feature is their flow of expressive
melodies.

Don Juan /'dʒuːən, Spanish xwɑːn/ character
of Spanish legend, Don Juan Tenorio, supposed
to have lived in the 14th century, and notorious
for his debauchery. Tirso de Molina, Molière,
Mozart, Byron and G B Shaw have featured the
legend.

donkey alternative name for ◊ass.

Donne /dʌn/ John 1571–1631. British
metaphysical poet, famous for his use of subtle
imagery and figurative language. He was
brought up in the Roman Catholic faith, and
matriculated early at Oxford to avoid taking the
oath of supremacy. Before entering Lincoln's Inn
as a law student in 1592 he travelled in Europe.
During his four years at the law courts he was
notorious for his wit and reckless living. In 1596
he sailed as a volunteer with Essex and Raleigh,
and on his return became private secretary to
Sir Thomas Egerton, Keeper of the Seal. This
appointment was ended by his secret marriage
to Ann More, niece of Egerton's wife, and they
endured many years of poverty. The more
passionate and tender of his love poems were
probably written to her. In 1615 Donne took
orders in the Church of England. His wife died
two years later; from 1621 to his death he was
Dean of St Paul's. His sermons rank him with
the century's greatest orators, and his passionate
poems of love and hate, violent, tender, or
abusive, give him a unique position among
English poets. His verse was not published in
collected form until after his death, and was long
out of favour, but he is now recognized as one of
the greatest English poets. Many of his sonnets
are popularly known by their first lines, such as
'No man is an island' and 'Death, be not proud'.

Donnybrook /'dɒnibrʊk/ former village,
now part of Dublin, Republic of Ireland,
notorious until 1855 for riotous fairs.

Donoghue /'dɒnəhjuː/ Stephen ('Steve')
1884–1945. British jockey. Between 1915 and
1925 he rode six Derby winners, thus beating
Fred Archer's record of five Derby victories, and
1921–23 achieved the 'hat-trick' by winning
three successive Derbys.

Doolittle /'duːlɪtl/ Hilda 1886–1961.
American poet. She went to Europe in 1911, and
was associated with Ezra ◊Pound and the British
writer Richard ◊Aldington (to whom she was
married 1913–37), in founding the ◊Imagist
school of poets, whose members advocated the
presentation of a clear-cut visual image in poetry,
and the writing of short, concentrated poems in
free rhythms. She signed her work 'HD'.

Doomsday Book a variant spelling of
◊Domesday Book.

Doone /duːn/ family of freebooters who
according to legend lived on Exmoor, Devon,
until they were exterminated in the 17th century.

They feature in R D ◊Blackmore's novel *Lorna Doone* 1869. The Doone Valley is near Lynton.

Doors, The US psychedelic and hard rock group, formed 1965 in Los Angeles. Original members were Jim Morrison (1943–71), Ray Manzarek, Robby Krieger, and John Densmore. Their first hit was 'Light My Fire' from their debut album *The Doors* 1967. They were noted for Morrison's poetic lyrics and their raw energy in performance.

Doppler /'dɒplə/ Christian Johann 1803–1853. Austrian physicist. He became professor of experimental physics at Vienna, and described the ◊Doppler effect.

Doppler effect change in observed frequency (or wavelengths) of waves due to relative motion between wave source and observer. Responsible for the perceived change in pitch of an ambulance siren as it approaches and then recedes, and, on a somewhat grander scale, for the ◊red shift of light from distant stars. Named after the Austrian physicist Christian Doppler (1803–53).

DORA in the UK, short for the Defence of the Realm Act, passed in Nov 1914, which conferred extraordinary powers on the Government with a view to the proper prosecution of the war.

Dorati /dɒ'rɑːti/ Antal 1906– . American conductor, born in Budapest. Conductor Laureate of the Royal Philharmonic Orchestra.

Dorchester /'dɔːtʃɪstə/ town (administrative headquarters) in Dorset, England, on the river Frome population (1985) 14,000.
history There are Roman remains, including an amphitheatre, and Thomas ◊Hardy was born nearby. *Maiden Castle* to the SW, occupied as a settlement from about 2000 BC, became an Iron Age ◊hillfort with a rampart 18 m/60 ft high enclosing an area of 18 ha/45 acres, which was stormed by the Romans in 43 AD.

Dordogne /dɔː'dɔɪn/ river in SW France, rising in Puy-de-Dôme *département* and flowing 490 km/300 mi to join the Garonne, 23 km/14 mi N of Bordeaux. It gives its name to a *département* and is harnessed for power.
The valley of the Dordogne is a popular tourist area and the caves of the wooded valleys of its tributary, the Vézére, have signs of early human occupation. Famous sites include Cromagnon, Moustier, and the Lascaux caves, discovered in cave art. Images of bulls, bison and deer were painted by the Cromagnon people (named from skeletons found 1868 in Cromagnon Cave, near Les Eyzies). The opening of the caves to tourists led to deterioration of the paintings; the caves were closed in 1963 and a facsimile opened in 1983.

Dordrecht /'dɔːdrext/ industrial river port on an island in the Maas, South Holland, Netherlands, 19 km/12 mi SE of Rotterdam; population (1985) 107,300. It is an inland port with shipbuilding yards and makes heavy machinery and plastics.

Doré /'dɔːreɪ/ Gustave 1832–1883. French illustrator. Born at Strasbourg, he was a skilled lithographer at 11, and was also active as a painter, etcher, and sculptor. His lasting reputation rests on his wood-engraved book illustrations for Rabelais 1854, Dante,

Cervantes, the Bible, Milton and Poe, which range from the sardonically humorous to the dark and harrowing.

Dorian /'dɔːriənz/ member of a people of ancient Greece. They entered Greece from the N and conquered most of the Peloponnese from the Achaeans and destroyed the ◊Mycenean civilization; this invasion appears to have been completed before 1000 BC. Their chief cities were Sparta, Argos, and Corinth.

Doric in classical architecture, one of the five types of ◊column. See ◊order.

dormancy in botany, a phase of reduced physiological activity exhibited by certain buds, seeds and spores. Dormancy can help a plant to survive unfavourable conditions, as in annual plants that pass the cold winter season as dormant seeds, and plants which form dormant buds. However, for various reasons many seeds exhibit a period of dormancy even when conditions are favourable for growth. Sometimes this can be broken by artificial methods, such as penetrating the seed coat to facilitate the uptake of water (chitting) or exposing the seed to light, ◊after-ripening.

dormouse small rodent, akin to a mouse, with a hairy tail. It derives its name from French *dormir*, (to sleep) because of its hibernating habit. There are about ten species, living in Europe, Asia and Africa. They are arboreal, nocturnal, and in cold latitudes hibernate in winter. The *common dormouse Muscardinus avellanarius* lives from England to W Russia and Asia Minor in thickets and forests with undergrowth. It is reddish-fawn and 15 cm/6 in long, including tail. The *fat* or *edible dormouse Glis glis* lives in continental Europe and is 30 cm/1 ft including tail. It was a delicacy at Roman feasts, and has been introduced to SE England.

Dorneywood / country house near Burnham Beeches, Buckinghamshire, England. Presented to the nation by Lord Courtauld-Thomson (1865–1954), as an official residence or a minister of the Crown, it is used by the Foreign Secretary. Administered by the National Trust, it is open to the public.

Dornier /,dɔːni'eɪ/ Claude 1884–1969. German aircraft designer. Born in Bavaria, he founded the Dornier Metallbau works at Friedrichshafen, Lake Constance, in 1922. He invented the seaplane and during World War II supplied the Luftwaffe with the 'flying pencil' bomber.

Dorpat /'dɔːpæt/ German name for the Estonian city of ◊Tartu.

d'Orsay /'dɔːseɪ/ Alfred Guillaume Gabriel, Count d'Orsay 1801–1857. French dandy. After serving in the French army, he accompanied the Earl and Countess of ◊Blessington on a tour of Italy. For 20 years he resided with Lady Blessington in London at Gore House, where he became known as an arbiter of taste.

Dorset /'dɔːsɪt/ county in SW England
area 2,654 sq km/1,024 sq mi
towns administrative headquarters Dorchester; Poole, Shaftesbury, Sherborne; resorts Bournemouth, Lyme Regis, Weymouth
features Chesil Bank (shingle bank along the coast 19 km/11 mi long); Isle of Purbeck, a

peninsula where china clay and Purbeck 'marble' are quarried, and which includes Corfe Castle and the holiday resort of Swanage; Dorset Downs; Cranborne Chase; rivers Frome and Stour; Maiden Castle; Tank Museum at Royal Armoured Corps Centre, Bovington, where the cottage of TE ◊Lawrence is a museum.
products Wytch Farm is the largest onshore oilfield in the UK.
population (1986) 627,700
famous people Thomas Hardy, the novelist, born at Higher Bockhampton (Dorchester is Casterbridge, the heart of Hardy's Wessex).

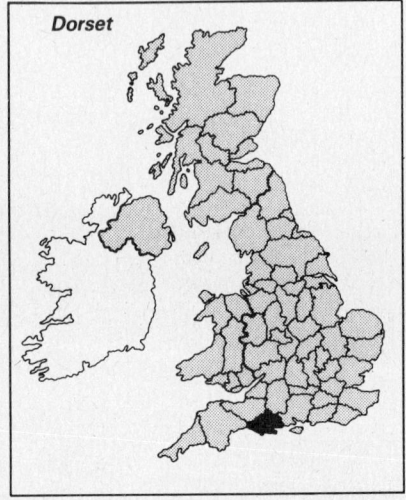

Dorset

Dorset /'dɔːsɪt/ first Earl of Dorset 1536–1608. title of English poet Thomas ◊Sackville.

Dort /dɔːt/ another name for ◊Dordrecht, a port in the Netherlands.

Dortmund /'dɔːtmʊnd/ industrial centre in the ◊Ruhr, West Germany, 58 km/36 mi NE of Düsseldorf; population (1984) 584,800. It is the S terminus of the Dortmund-Ems canal, and has large docks and an airport. Dortmund owes its importance to the Westphalian coalfield, of which it is the largest mining town.

dory /'dɔːri/ marine fish *Zeus faber* found in the Mediterranean and Atlantic. It has nine or ten long spines at the front of the dorsal fin, and four at the front of the anal fin. It is olive brown or grey, with a conspicuous black spot ringed with yellow on each side. It is a stalking predator, shooting out its mobile jaws to catch fish. It is an excellent food fish and grows up to 60 cm/2 ft. Also known as *John Dory*.

dos Passos /dəs 'pæsəs/ John 1896–1970. American author, born in Chicago. He made a reputation with the war novels *One Man's Initiation* 1919, and *Three Soldiers* 1921. His greatest work is the *USA* trilogy 1930–36, which gives a panoramic view of American life through the device of placing fictitious characters against the real setting of newspaper headlines and contemporary events.

Dostoievsky /,dɒstɔɪ'efski/ Fyodor Mihailovich 1821–1881. Russian novelist. Born in Moscow, the son of a physician, he was for a short time an army officer. His first novel, *Poor Folk*, appeared in 1846. In 1849 Dostoievsky was arrested as a member of a free-thinking literary circle during a period of intense Tsarist censorship, and after being reprieved from death at the last moment was sent to the penal settlement at Omsk for four years, where the terrible conditions increased his epileptic tendency. Finally pardoned in 1859, he published the humorous *Village of Stepanchikovo*; *The House of the Dead* 1861, recalling his prison experiences; and *The Insulted and the Injured* 1862. Meanwhile he had launched two unsuccessful liberal periodicals, in the second of which his *Letters from the Underworld* appeared. Compelled to work by pressure of debt he quickly produced *Crime and Punishment* 1866, an analysis of a murderer's reactions, and *The Gambler* 1867, before fleeing abroad from his creditors. He then wrote *The Idiot* 1868–69, in which the hero is an epileptic like himself; *The Eternal Husband* 1870; and *The Possessed* 1871–72.

Returning to Russia in 1871 he again entered journalism and issued the personal miscellany *Journal of an Author* in which he discussed contemporary problems. In 1875 he published *A Raw Youth*, but the great work of his last years is *The Brothers Karamazov* 1880.

Dostoievsky Russian novelist Fyodor Dostoievsky read Dickens and shared his concern for urban poverty, crime and the exploitation of children. He was later to visit London, and was horrified by the condition of the poor.

dotterel bird *Eudromias morinellus* of the plover family, nesting on high moors and tundra in Europe and Asia and going S for the winter. About 23 cm/9 in it is clad in a pattern of black, brown and white in summer, duller in winter, but always with white eyebrows and breastband.

Females are larger than males, and the male incubates and rears the brood.

Dou /daʊ/ Gerard 1613–1675. Dutch painter of interiors, born at Leyden, a student of Rembrandt.

Douai /duː'eɪ/ French town on the river Scarpe, Nord *département*.; population (1982) 44,515. It has coal-mines, iron foundries, and breweries. In the English Roman Catholic college (founded 1568 and removed to England 1903), the Douai Bible was prepared, which influenced the King James Version.

double bass a bowed string musical instrument of the ◊violin family.

double coconut tree-like ◊palm plant, *Lodoicea maldivica*, also known as 'coco de mer', of the Seychelles, with a two-lobed edible nut, one of the largest known fruits.

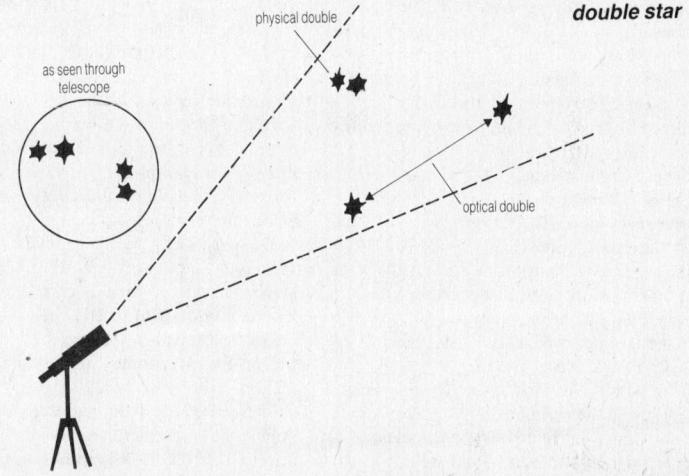

double star

double star pair of stars close together as seen from earth. Most double stars are held close together by gravity, and orbit each other, forming a genuine ◊binary star. In other cases the two stars are at different distances from earth, and lie in the same line of sight only by chance.

Doubs /duː/ French river rising in the Jura mountains and flowing 430 km/265 mi to join the Saône. It gives its name to a *département*.

doughboy nickname for US soldiers in the two world wars. One derivation is from the large buttons on the uniforms of the soldiers of the American Civil War, which were so called.

Douglas /'dʌgləs/ capital of the Isle of Man, on the E coast of the island, in the Irish Sea; population (1981) 20,000. It is a holiday resort, and terminus of the shipping routes to and from Fleetwood and Liverpool.

Douglas /'dʌgləs/ Alfred (Bruce) 1870–1945. British poet. The third son of the 8th Marquess of Queensbury, he became closely associated in London with Oscar ◊Wilde. This friendship led to Wilde's action for libel against Douglas's father, who strongly disapproved of the relationship, which ultimately resulted in Wilde's own imprisonment.

Douglas /'dʌgləs/ Gavin (or Gawain) 1475–1522. Scottish poet. A son of the Earl of Angus, he became bishop of Dunkeld in 1515, and was active in Scottish politics. He wrote two allegories, *The Palace of Honour* and *King Hart*, but is best known for his translation of Virgil's *Aeneid*, the first English version of one of the great classical poets.

Douglas /'dʌgləs/ Norman 1868–1952. British diplomat and travel writer (*Siren Land* 1911 and *Old Calabria* 1915, dealing with Italy); his novel *South Wind* 1917 is set in his adopted island of Capri.

Douglas-Home /'dʌgləs 'hjuːm/ William 1912– . British playwright, younger brother of Lord ◊Home of the Hirsel. His plays include *The Chiltern Hundreds* 1947 and *Lloyd George Knew My Father* 1972.

Douglas of Kirtleside /'kɜːtlsaɪd/ William Sholto Douglas, 1st Baron Douglas of Kirtleside 1893–1969. British air marshal. During World War II he was air officer commander in chief of Fighter Command 1940–42, Middle East Command 1943–44, and Coastal Command 1944–45.

Douglass /'dʌgləs/ Frederick c. 1817–1895. US anti-slavery campaigner. Born a slave in Maryland, he escaped 1838. His autobiographical *Narrative of the Life of Frederick Douglass* 1845 aroused support for the abolition of slavery; supporters purchased his own freedom for him as a result of it. In 1847 he founded the abolitionist weekly *North Star* in Rochester, New York, and after the ◊Civil War he held several US government offices.

Doukhobor member of a Russian religious sect, also known as 'Christians of the Universal Brotherhood'. Some of the Doukhobor teachings resemble those of the Quakers. They were long persecuted, mainly for refusing military service – Tolstoy organized a relief fund for them – but in 1898 were permitted to emigrate and settled in Canada where they number about 13,000, mainly in British Columbia and Saskatchewan. An extremist group, 'The Sons of Freedom', staged demonstrations and terrorism in the 1960s leading to the imprisonment of about 100 members of the sect.

Doulton /'dəultən/ Henry 1820–1897. British ceramicist. He developed special wares for the chemical, electrical and building industries and in 1846 established the world's first stoneware drainpipe factory. From 1870 he created at Lambeth and Burslem a reputation for art pottery and domestic tablewares.

Doumer /duː'meə/ Paul 1857–1932. French politician. He was elected president of the Chamber in 1905, president of the Senate in 1927, and President of the Republic in 1931. He was assassinated by Gorgulov, a mad White Russian emigré.

Doumergue /duː'meəg/ Gaston 1863–1937. French prime minister during the time leading up to World War I and again after the fall of Léon Blum's Popular French government *in 1937.*

Douro /'duərəu/ (Spanish *Duero*) river rising in N central Spain and flowing through N Portugal to the Atlantic at Oporto; length 800 km/500 mi. Navigation at the river mouth is hindered by sand bars. There are hydro-electric installations.

dove type of ◊pigeon.

Dover /'dəuvə/ one of the ◊Cinque Ports, a market town and seaport on the SE coast of Kent, England; population (1981) 33,000. It is Britain's nearest point to the Continent, being only 34 km/21 mi from Calais. Dover's modern development has been chiefly due to the cross-Channel traffic, which includes train, ferry, hovercraft, and other services.

history Under Roman rule, Dover (Portus Dubris) was the terminus of ◊Watling Street, and the beacon or 'lighthouse' in the grounds of the Norman castle dates from about 50 AD, making it one of the oldest buildings in Britain. The Lord Warden of the Cinque Ports is Constable of Dover Castle.

Dover, Strait of /'dəuvə/ (French: Pas-de-Calais) stretch of water separating England from France, and connecting the English Channel with the North Sea. It is about 35 km/22 mi long and 34 km/21 mi wide at its narrowest part. It is one of the world's busiest sea lanes, and by 1972 increasing traffic, collisions, and shipwrecks had become so frequent that traffic-routeing schemes were enforced.

Dowding /'daudıŋ/ Hugh Caswall Tremenheere, 1st Baron Dowding 1882–1970. British air chief marshal. He was chief of Fighter Command at the outbreak of World War II in 1939, a post he held through the Battle of Britain. He retired in 1942 and was created a baron in 1943. He wrote works on spiritualism.

Dowell /'dauəl/ Anthony 1943– . British ballet dancer. Noted for the classical perfection of his style, he was principal dancer with the ◊Royal Ballet 1966–86, and director from 1986. His noted performances include those in *Enigma Variations*, *Sleeping Beauty* and *Four Schumann Pieces*. He was made a Commander of the British Empire in 1973.

Dowland /'daulənd/ John 1563–1626. English composer. He failed to establish himself

at the court of Queen Elizabeth – he was a Roman Catholic convert – but later reverted to Protestantism and from 1612 was patronized by the ◊Stuarts. He is remembered for his songs to lute accompaniment.

Down /daun/ county in the SE of Northern Ireland, facing the Irish Sea on the east. In the S are the Mourne mountains, in the E Strangford sea lough. Area 2,465 sq km/952 sq mi. The county town is Downpatrick. The town of Hillsborough was the site of signature of the ◊Hillsborough Agreement. The main industry is dairying.

Downing Street /'daunıŋ/ street in Westminster, London, leading from Whitehall to St James's Park, named after Sir George Downing (died 1684), a diplomat under Cromwell and Charles II. Number 10 is the official residence of the prime minister, number 11 is the residence of the chancellor of the Exchequer, and number 12 the office of the government whips.

Downs, North and South /daunz/ two lines of chalk hills in SE England. They form two scarps which face each other across the Weald of Kent and Sussex, and are much used for sheep pasture. The *North Downs* run from Salisbury Plain across Hampshire, Surrey, and Kent to the cliffs of S Foreland. The *South Downs* run across Sussex to Beachy Head.

Downs, The /daunz/ · roadstead (partly sheltered anchorage) off E Kent, England between Deal and the Goodwin Sands. Several 17th-century naval battles took place here, including a defeat of Spain by the Dutch in 1639.

Down's syndrome chromosomal abnormality (the presence of an additional chromosome in all the sufferer's cells) which produces a rather flattened face and fold of skin at the inner edge of the eye (hence the former name 'mongolism'), as well as mental handicap in children.

dowsing ascertaining the presence of water or minerals with a forked twig, pendulum. Unconscious muscular action by the dowser moves the twig, usually held with one fork in each hand, possibly in response to a local change in the pattern of electrical forces. The ability has been known since at least the 16th century, and though not widely recognized by science, it has been used commercially.

Dowson /'dausən/ Ernest 1867–1900. British poet, one of the 'decadent' poets of the 1890s. He is best remembered for the lyric with the refrain: 'I have been faithful to thee, Cynara! in my fashion'.

Doxiadis /,dɒksi'ɑːdiːs/ Constantinos 1913–1975. Greek architect and town planner; designer of ◊Islamabad.

Doyle /dɔıl/ Arthur Conan 1859–1930. British writer, creator of the detective Sherlock Holmes. Born in Edinburgh, he qualified as a doctor, and during the Boer War was senior physician of a field hospital in South Africa. He wrote *The Great Boer War* 1900, and was knighted in 1902.

The first of Conan Doyle's books, *A Study in Scarlet*, appeared in 1887 and introduced the private detective Sherlock Holmes, and his

ingenuous companion, Dr Watson. Other books featuring the same characters followed, including *The Sign of Four* 1889, *The Hound of the Baskervilles* 1902, and *The Valley of Fear* 1915, as well as several volumes of short stories, first published in the *Strand Magazine*. Conan Doyle also wrote historical romances (*Micah Clarke* 1889, and *The White Company* 1891) and the scientific romance *The Lost World* 1912 with an irascible hero Professor Challenger. In his later years he became a spiritualist.

Doyle Creator of the popular fictional duo of Sherlock Holmes and Dr Watson, Arthur Conan Doyle was originally a doctor. In his later years, he became increasingly interested in psychic phenomena.

Doyle /dɔıl/ Richard 1824–1883. British caricaturist and book illustrator. In 1849 he designed the original cover for *Punch*.

D'Oyly Carte /'ɔıli 'kɑːt/ Richard 1844–1901. British producer of the Gilbert and Sullivan operas at the Savoy Theatre, London, which he built.

Drabble /'dræbəl/ Margaret 1939– . British writer. Her novels include *The Millstone* 1966, filmed as *The Touch of Love*, *The Middle Ground* 1980, and *The Radiant Way* 1987. She also edited the 1985 edition of the *Oxford Companion to English Literature*.

Draco /'dreıkəu/ 7th century BC. Athenian statesman, the first to codify the laws of the Athenian city-state. These were notorious for their severity; hence draconian, meaning particularly harsh.

Draco /'dreıkəu/ in astronomy, large but faint ◊constellation representing a dragon coiled around the north celestial pole. The star Alpha Draconis (Thuban) was the pole star 4,800 years ago, when the Great Pyramid of Egypt was built.

Dracula /'drækjulə/ in the novel *Dracula* 1897, by Bram ◊Stoker, the caped count who, as a ◊vampire, drinks the blood of beautiful women. The man on whom the character was based, was a 15th-century prince of ◊Romania, Vlad V, known as 'the impaler' because he slowly impaled the Turkish invaders of his country, and was no less cruel to his own people. The name Dracula derives from his father, who was known as Vlad Drakul (the Devil), and Castle Dracula, N of Bucharest in the Carpathians, is a tourist attraction.

draft in the USA, to select for compulsory military service; also known as ◊conscription.

drag the resistance to motion a body experiences when passing through a fluid – gas or liquid. The aerodynamic drag aircraft experience when travelling through the air represents a great waste of power. So they must be carefully shaped, or streamlined to reduce drag to a minimum. Even cars benefit from streamlining. Aerodynamic drag is used to slow down spacecraft returning from space. Boats travelling through water experience hydrodynamic drag on their hull, which should also be carefully shaped to reduce power loss. The fastest vessels are ◊hydrofoils, whose hulls lift out of the water while cruising, thus minimizing hydrodynamic drag.

dragon a mythical reptilian beast, often portrayed as breathing fire; the name is popularly given to various sorts of lizard. These include the ◊*flying dragon*; the *komodo dragon Varanus komodoensis* of Indonesia, at over 3 m/10 ft the largest living lizard; and some Australian lizards with bizarre spines or frills.

dragonfly type of insect with a long narrow body, two pairs of almost equal glassy wings with a network of veins, very large compound eyes and short bristle-like antennae. They are predators on other insects, both as adults and as aquatic nymphs, and adults have powerful 'toothed' mouthparts. They hunt by sight and the eyes may have up to 30,000 facets. Dragonflies are a very ancient group. The largest modern species have a wingspan of 18 cm/7 in but fossils with wings up to 70 cm/2.3 ft across are known.

dragoon name derived from the 'dragon' or short musket used by the French in the 16th century, and applied to a mounted soldier who carried this or some other infantry weapon. The name was retained by some later regiments after the original meaning became obsolete.

Drake /dreɪk/ Francis c. 1545–1596. English sea captain, who sailed around the world and fought against the Spanish Armada. He was born near Tavistock and apprenticed to the master of a coasting vessel, who left him the ship at his death. He accompanied Sir John ◊Hawkins in 1567 and 1572 to plunder the Spanish Main, and returned to England in 1573 with considerable booty. After serving in Ireland as a volunteer, he suggested to Queen Elizabeth I an expedition to the Pacific, and in Dec 1577 he sailed in the *Pelican* with four other ships and 166 men. In Aug 1578 the fleet passed through the Straits of Magellan in 16 days and was then blown S to Cape Horn. The ships became separated and returned to England, leaving the *Pelican*, now renamed the *Golden Hind*, alone in the Pacific. Drake sailed N along the coast of Chile and Peru, plundering Spanish ships as far N as California, and then, in Jul 1579, SW across the Pacific. He rounded the Cape in Jun 1580, and reached England in Sept. Thus the second voyage around

the world, and the first made by an Englishman, was completed in a little under three years. When the Spanish ambassador demanded Drake's punishment, the Queen knighted him on the deck of the *Golden Hind* at Deptford.

In 1582 Drake was chosen mayor of Plymouth, and in 1584–85 he represented Bosinney in Parliament. In a raid on Cadiz in 1587 he burnt 10,000 tons of shipping, 'singed the King of Spain's beard', and delayed the Armada for a year. He was stationed off Ushant in 1588 to intercept the Armada, but was driven back to England by unfavourable winds. During the fight in the Channel he served as a vice-admiral in the *Revenge*. Drake sailed on his last expedition to the West Indies with Hawkins in 1595, and in Jan 1596 died on his ship off Nombre de Dios. Today a national park at San Francisco marks the approximate site where he anchored the *Golden Hind* off the Californian coast in 1579.

Drakensberg /'drɑːkənsbɜːg/ mountain range in South Africa (Sesuto name *Quathlamba*), on the boundary of Lesotho and the Orange Free State with Natal; highest point is Mont aux Sources, 3,482 m/10,822 ft, near which is Natal National Park.

drama as a term applied to a play performed by actors for an audience, drama is an element of ◊theatre. The term is also used collectively to group plays into historical or stylistic periods, for example Greek drama, Restoration drama, as well as referring to the whole body of work written by dramatists for performance. Drama is distinct from literature. It is a living art open to infinite interpretation, since it is the product not merely of the playwright but also of the collaboration of directors, designer, actors and many others. No two performances, even by the same actor, can ever be the same. Shakespeare's *Hamlet* for example, is generally regarded as 'good' literature, but a performance with poor direction or acting can turn it into 'bad' drama. It is not surprising therefore that drama, even more than literature, is subject to the tastes and fashion of its day both in content and in presentation.

See also ◊comedy, ◊tragedy, ◊mime, ◊pantomime, ◊theatre.

draughts board game (also known as in the USA and Canada as *checkers* because of the 'chequered' board of 64 squares) which has elements of a simplified form of chess. Each of the two players has 12 men (discs), and attempts either to capture all of the opponent's men or to block their moving.

Dravidian name applied to a group of non-Indo-Aryan peoples of the Deccan region of India and in N Sri Lanka. They generally are of darker skin and shorter stature than the Aryan types of the N, and developed their own style of temple architecture. The Dravidian languages include Tamil, Telugu, Malayalam, and Kannada.

Drayton /'dreɪtn/ Michael 1563–1631. English poet. Born in Warwickshire, he came to London in 1590, where he published a volume of poems, *The Harmony of the Church* 1591, which was destroyed by order of the Archbishop of Canterbury. His greatest poetical work was the

topographical survey of England, *Polyolbion* 1613–22, in 30 books. He was buried in Westminster Abbey.

dream a series of events, or images, which occurs during sleep. For the purposes of (allegedly) foretelling the future, dreams fell into disrepute in the scientific atmosphere of the 18th century, but were given importance by ◊Freud who saw them as wish fulfilment (nightmares being failed dreams prompted by fears of 'repressed' impulses). Dreams occur in periods of rapid eye movement (REM) by the sleeper, when the cortex of the brain is approximately as active as in waking hours, and they occupy a fifth of sleeping time. They could be a means of forgetting, so as to clear an 'overloaded network', a nightmare being brought to conscious attention so that the anxiety causing it can be dealt with. If a high level of acetylcholine is present (see under ◊brain) dreams occur too early in sleep, causing wakefulness, confusion, and ◊depression, which suggests that a form of memory search is involved. Prevention of dreaming, by taking sleeping tablets, for example, has similar unpleasant results. The surrealistic progression of some dreams could be caused by the brain desperately trying to make sensible links between fragments of what is passing before it as waking consciousness gradually returns. Some people achieve a degree of control of their dreams.

Dreikaiserbund (German 'Three Emperors League') (1872) an informal alliance between the Emperors of Russia, Germany, and Austria-Hungary. It was effectively at an end by 1879.

Dreiser /'draɪsə/ Theodore 1871–1945. American realistic novelist, best-remembered for *An American Tragedy* 1925, based on the real life crime of a man who in 'making good' becomes a murderer.

Dresden /'drezdən/ city of East Germany, capital of Dresden district, formerly capital of Saxony; population (1981) 516,285. Manufactures include chemicals, machinery, glassware, and musical instruments.

history Dresden became one of the most beautiful German cities under the elector Augustus II the Strong (1694–1733), who made it a centre of art and culture. The manufacture of Dresden china, started at Dresden in 1709, was transferred to Meissen in 1710. The city was devastatingly bombed by the Allies on the night 13–14 Feb 1945, 15.5 sq km/6 sq mi of the inner town being destroyed, and deaths being estimated at 35,000–135,000. The Russians took the city on 8 May.

Dreyfus /'dreɪfəs/ Alfred 1859–1935. French soldier. Born in Mulhouse of a Jewish family, he was employed in the War Ministry, and in 1894 was accused of betraying military secrets to Germany, court-martialled, and sent to Devil's Island. In 1896 it was discovered that the real criminal was Major Esterhazy; the High Command nevertheless attempted to suppress the facts, and used forged documents to strengthen their case. After a violent controversy, in which Clemenceau and Zola championed Dreyfus, a re-trial in 1899 found him guilty with extenuating circumstances and he received a pardon. In 1906 the Court of Appeal declared him innocent, and he was reinstated in his military rank.

Dreyfus French army officer Alfred Dreyfus who was convicted of treason in 1894 on forged evidence and imprisoned. His case was taken up by Zola and grew into a bitter issue in France, even dividing families, involving anti-semitism and national pride.

drill large monkey *Mandrillus leucophaeus* from the forests of W Africa, that spends much of the day on the ground. Sombre-coated, black-faced and stoutly built, with a very short tail, the male can have a head and body up to 75 cm/2.5 ft long, although females are smaller.

drilling a common woodworking and metal machinery process, which involves boring holes with a drill ◊bit. The commonest kind of drill bit is the fluted drill, which has spiral grooves around it to allow the cut material to escape. In the oil industry rotary drilling is used to bore oil wells. A drill bit is fixed to the end of a length of drill pipe and rotated by a turning mechanism called the rotary table. More lengths of pipe are added as the hole deepens. The drill bit consists usually of a number of toothed cutting wheels, which grind their way through the rock as the drill pipe is turned. Mud is pumped through the pipe to lubricate the bit and flush the ground-up rock to the surface. The long drill pipes are handled by lifting gear in a steel tower ◊derrick.

Drinkwater /'drɪŋk,wɔːtə/ John 1882–1937. British poet and playwright. He was a prolific writer of lyrical and reflective verse, and also wrote many historical plays, including *Abraham Lincoln* 1918.

Drogheda /'drɔɪdə/ seaport near the mouth of the Boyne, county Louth, Republic of Ireland. In 1649 the town was stormed by Oliver ◊Cromwell, who massacred most of the garrison, and in 1690 it surrendered to William III after the battle of the Boyne.

Drôme /drəʊm/ French river rising in Dauphiné Pre-Alps and flowing NW for 101

km/63 mi to join the Rhône below Livron. It gives its name to Drôme *département*.

dromedary type of Arabian ◊camel.

drosera Latin name for the plant ◊sundew.

drought period of prolonged dry weather: in the UK absolute drought is defined as the passing of 15 days with less than 0.2 mm of rain. The area of the world subject to serious droughts, as in the ◊Sahel, is increasing because of destruction of forests and so on (see ◊desert).

drowning death by immersion in liquid. Unless spasm of the muscles of the larynx prevents the entry of water to the lungs, death is caused by hindrance of the passage of oxygen to the bloodstream, as well as direct effects on the blood itself. The latter occur more rapidly in the case of fresh water (3 min) than sea water (8 min). Death can sometimes be prevented by ◊artificial respiration.

drug and alcohol dependence individuals can become dependent on addictive drugs such as alcohol, nicotine (in cigarettes), tranquillizers, heroin, or stimulants (for example, amphetamines). Such substances can alter mood or behaviour. When dependence is established, sudden withdrawal from the drug can cause an unpleasant reaction, which can be dangerous.

drug misuse the abuse of medicinal drugs. Under the UK Misuse of Drugs Acts they comprise: (1) *most harmful* heroin, morphine, opium, and other narcotics; hallucinogens, such as mescalin and LSD, and injectable amphetamines, such as methedrine; (2) *less harmful* narcotics such as codeine and cannabis; stimulants of the amphetamine type, such as Benzedrine and barbiturates; (3) *least harmful* milder drugs of the amphetamine type. *Designer drugs* are variants of illegal narcotics made by criminal chemists to evade the law, and may be many times more powerful and dangerous. Crack, a variant of cocaine, has recently become available to drug abusers. Sources of traditional drugs include the 'Golden Triangle' (where Burma, Laos and Thailand meet), Mexico, Colombia, China and the Middle East.

Druidism religion of the Celtic peoples of pre-Christian Britain and Gaul. The word is usually derived from Greek *drus* oak, and they regarded this tree as sacred, one of their chief rites being the cutting from it of mistletoe with a golden sickle. They taught the immortality of the soul and a reincarnation doctrine, and were also expert in astronomy. The Druids are supposed to have offered human sacrifices.
Druidism was stamped out in Gaul after the Roman conquest. In Britain their stronghold was Anglesey, where they were extirpated by Agricola. They also existed in Scotland and Ireland until the coming of the Christian missionaries. What are often termed Druidic monuments – cromlechs, and stone circles – are of Neolithic origin, though they may later have been used for religious purposes by the Druids.

drum ◊percussion instrument, essentially a piece of skin (parchment, plastic or nylon) stretched over a resonator and struck with a stick, or the hands.

Drummond /'drʌmənd/ William 1585–1649. Scottish poet, laird of his native Hawthornden,

hence known as Drummond of Hawthornden. He was the first Scots poet of note to use southern English.

Drummond de Andrade /druːˈmɒŋ di ænˈdrɑːdə/ Carlos 1902–1987. Brazilian poet and journalist. Generally considered the greatest modern Brazilian poet, he was born in Itabira, a small town in the interior. He was a prominent member of the Brazilian Modernist school; his verse, often seemingly casual, continually surprises and confounds the reader's expectation of the 'poetical'.

drupe a fleshy ◊fruit containing one or more seeds that are surrounded by a hard, protective layer, for example cherry, almond and plum. The wall of the fruit (◊pericarp) is differentiated into the outer skin (exocarp), the fleshy layer of tissues (mesocarp), and the hard layer surrounding the seed (endocarp). The coconut is another drupe, but here the pericarp becomes dry and fibrous at maturity. Blackberries are an aggregate fruit composed of a cluster of small drupes.

Drury Lane Theatre /'drʊəri/ theatre first opened 1663 on the site of earlier London playhouses. It was twice burnt; the present building dates from 1812.

Druse or *Druzea* religious sect of some 500,000 people, founded in Egypt in the 11th century, which then fled to Palestine to avoid persecution; they today occupy areas of Syria, Lebanon, and Israel. They are monotheists, preaching that the Fatimid caliph al-Hakim/996–1021 is God; their scriptures are drawn from the Christian gospels, the Pentateuch (the first five books of the Old Testament), the Koran, and from Sufi allegories. Druse militia groups form one of the three main factions involved in the Lebanese civil war (the others being ◊Amal Shi'ite Muslims and Christian Maronites). The Druse military leader (since his father's assassination in 1977) is Walid Jumblatt.

Dr Who hero of a science-fiction television series of the same name, created in 1962 by Sidney Newman and Donald Wilson; his space vehicle is the *Tardis* (*T*ime and *R*elative *D*imensions in *S*pace).

dryad /'draɪæd/ in Greek mythology, a forest nymph or tree spirit.

dry cleaning a method of cleaning textiles based on the use of volatile solvents which dissolve grease, for example, trichloroethylene. First developed in France in 1849, the method is termed 'dry' because no water is used.

Dryden /'draɪdn/ John 1631–1700. British poet and dramatist, born at Aldwinkle, Northamptonshire. His plays include *The Conquest of Granada* 1669–70, the bombastic height of 'heroic tragedy'; the comedy *Marriage à la mode* 1671; and *All for Love* 1678, a reworking of Shakespeare's *Antony and Cleopatra*. Their prefaces, and his *Essay of Dramatic Poesy* 1668, contain sound criticism. As a verse satirist, he is best remembered for *Absalom and Achitophel* 1681; other poems include 'Annus Mirabilis', and his odes on 'St Cecilia's Day' 1687 and to the 'Memory of Mrs Anne Killigrew'. On occasion, he trimmed his politics and his religion to the prevailing wind, and, as a Roman Catholic convert under James II, lost the laureateship (to which he had been appointed in 1688) at the Revolution of 1688. Later ventures to support himself include a translation of Virgil in 1697. He was a master of all verse forms, but especially of the heroic couplet.

Dryden English poet, satirist, dramatist and biographer John Dryden, painted in 1693 by Kneller.

dry-point a means of ◊print engraving.

dry rot infection of timber in damp conditions by fungi, such as *Merulius lacrymans*, which forms a thread-like surface whitish at first, later reddening where it forms reproductive spores. Dry rot also spreads fungoid 'tentacles' though the fabric of the timber, rendering it dry-looking and brittle. The spores are rapidly spread though a building.

Drysdale /'draizdeil/ George Russell 1912–1969. Australian artist. Born in Sussex, England, he went to Australia as a child. He studied art in Melbourne, London and Paris, and became known particularly for his drawings and paintings of the Australian Outback. He was knighted in 1969.

Dual Entente (1893) an alliance between France and Russia which lasted until the Bolshevik Revolution of 1917.

dualism in philosophy, the belief that reality is essentially dual in nature. ◊Descartes, for example, refers to thinking and material substance. These entities interact, but are fundamentally separate and distinct. Dualism is contrasted with ◊monism.

Dubai /duː'baɪ/ one of the ◊United Arab Emirates.

Du Barry /djuː 'bæri/ Marie Jeanne Bécu, Comtesse Du Barry 1743–93. Mistress of Louis ◊XV of France from 1768. At his death in 1774 she was banished to a convent, and at the

Revolution fled to London. Returning to Paris in 1793, she was guillotined.

Dubček /'dʊbtʃek/ Alexander 1921– Czech politician. As first secretary of the Communist Party 1967–69, he launched a liberalization campaign (the Prague spring). He was arrested by invading Soviet troops, and expelled from the party in 1970.

Dublin /'dʌblɪn/ capital and county borough on the E coast of the Republic of Ireland, at the mouth of the Liffey, facing the Irish Sea. Population (1981) 525,500. The official Gaelic name is ◊Baile Atha Cliath.

With roads, railways, and canals converging on it, and an airport to the north, Dublin is the greatest port of the republic, and is the largest collecting and distributing centre, handling exports from the whole state. It has one of the world's largest breweries (Guinness), and other industries include textiles, biscuits, pharmaceuticals, electrical goods, and machine tools.

history the city was founded in 840 by the invading Danes, who were finally defeated in 1014 at Clontarf, now a N suburb of the city. From 1171, when Henry II landed in Ireland, Dublin became the centre of English rule (exercised from Dublin Castle (1220) until 1922. In the Georgian period many fine squares were laid out, and the Custom House (damaged in the 1921 rising but later restored) survives. There is a Roman Catholic pro-Cathedral, St Mary's (1816), two Protestant cathedrals; and two universities: the University of Dublin and the National University of Ireland. Trinity College library contains the Book of Kells, a splendidly illuminated 8th-century gospel book produced at the monastery of Kells in county Meath, founded by St Columba. Other buildings are the City Hall (1779), the Four Courts (1796), the National Gallery, Dublin Municipal Gallery, National Museum, Leinster House (where the *Dáil Eireann* sits), and the Abbey and Gate theatres.

Dublin /'dʌblɪn/ county of the Republic of Ireland, facing the Irish Sea. Area 922 sq km/356 sq mi; population (1981) 915,000. It is mostly level and low-lying, though in the south it rises to 753 m/2,473 ft in Kippure, part of the Wicklow mountains. The only large river is the Liffey, which enters Dublin Bay. Agriculture is chiefly directed towards supplying the needs of Dublin city. Dun Laoghaire is the only other large town.

Dubna /dʊb'nɑː/ town in USSR, 40km/25 mi W of Tula. Population (1977) 45,000. It is a metal-working centre, and has the Volga Nuclear Physics Centre.

Dubrovnik /duː'brɒvnɪk/ (Italian Ragusa) picturesque Yugoslav port on the Adriatic; population (1985) 35,000. Once a Roman station, it was for a long time an independent republic, but passed to Austrian rule 1814–1919.

Dubuffet /ˌdjuːbʊ'feɪ/ Jean 1901–1985. French artist and sculptor. He originated *l'art brut* or 'raw art' in the 1940s, using materials such as coal or steel wool, advocating the naively primitive, and being inspired by graffiti and the work of children and psychotic mental patients.

Duccio di Buoninsegna /'duːtʃəʊ diː ˌbwɒnɪn'seɪnjə/ c. 1255–1319. Italian painter, the earliest of the Sienese school. His greatest work is his altarpiece for Siena cathedral (1308–11). His *Virgin and Child with Four Angels*, one wing of a diptych, is in the National Gallery.

Duce (Italian 'leader'). title bestowed on Mussolini by his followers, and later adopted as his official title.

Duchamp /djuː'ʃɒŋ/ Marcel 1887–1968. French artist. He achieved fame with his *Nude Descending a Staircase* exhibited at the ◊Armory Show in New York 1913, which used schematized human forms. He produced humorous pastiches of other artists, reduced the creative act to one of choice by putting everyday items like a bicycle wheel mounted on a kitchen stool on display and calling them 'ready-mades'. With ◊Picabia he founded the ◊Dada movement, and was associated with the ◊Surrealists.

duck short-legged waterbird with webbed feet and flattened bill of the family Anatidae, which also includes the geese and swans. Ducks have the three front toes in a web, the hind toe free, and have a skin-covered bill with a horny tip and provided with little plates (lamellae) through which the birds are able to strain their food from water and mud. Most species of duck live in fresh water, feeding on worms and insects as well as vegetable matter. A typical species is the *mallard Anas platyrhynchos*, 58 cm/1.9 ft, found over most of the northern hemisphere, which is also the ancestor of our domestic ducks. The male (drake) has a glossy green head, brown breast, grey body and yellow bill. The female (duck) is speckled brown, with a duller bill. The male moults and resembles the female for a while just after the breeding season. There are many other species of duck including ◊teal, ◊eider, ◊merganser, ◊shelduck and ◊shoveler.

duckweed tiny plant *Lemna minor* found floating on the surface of still water such as ponds and ditches throughout most of the world except polar regions and tropics. Each plant consists of a flat circular leaf-like structure 0.4 cm/0.15 in or less across, with a single thin root below up to 15 cm/6 in long. The plant buds off new individuals, and can soon cover the surface of the water. Flowers are rarely needed, but when they appear are minute, sited in a pocket at the edge of the plant.

ductless gland another name for an ◊endocrine gland.

Dudley /'dʌdli/ town NW of Birmingham, West Midlands, England. Industries include light engineering and clothing manufacture. Population (1981) 187,000.

Dufay /djuː'feɪ/ Guillaume 1400–1474. French composer. After early musical training as a choirboy at Cambrai Cathedral, he went on to work in Cambrai, then in Italy at the papal chapel, and at the court of Savoy. He is recognized as the foremost composer of his time, both of secular songs and sacred music, including 84 songs, eight masses, motets, and antiphons. His work marks a transition between the music of the Middle Ages and that of the Renaissance, and is characterized by expressive melodies and rich harmonies.

Duccio di Buoninsegna Triptych *Father and Child* by Italian painter Duccio di Buoninsegna. Many of his ideas were developed from Byzantine art.

Du Fu another name for the Chinese poet ▷Tu Fu.

Dufy /'duːfi/ Raoul 1877–1953. French painter and designer. He was noted for his calligraphic style, varied use of colour, and for his pictures of sport and recreation.

dugong marine mammal *Dugong dugon* found along shores of the Indian Ocean and West Pacific. It grows 2.5 m/8 ft long or more, and has a tapering body with a notched tail and two foreflippers. It is herbivorous, feeding on sea grasses and seaweeds. Leather and oil can be obtained from it, and its flesh is edible.

Dukas /djuːˈkɑːs/ Paul (Abraham) 1865–1935. French composer. Born in Paris, he was professor of composition at the Paris Conservatoire, and composed the opera *Ariane et Barbe-Bleue* 1907, and the ballet *La Péri* 1912. His orchestral scherzo *L'Apprenti Sorcier/The Sorcerer's Apprentice* 1897 is full of the colour and energy which characterizes much of his work.

duke highest title in the English peerage. It originated in England in 1337, when Edward III created his son Edward duke of Cornwall. The oldest Scottish duchy is Hamilton, 1643.

dulcimer musical instrument, consisting of a shallow box strung with wire strings which are struck with small wooden hammers.

Dulles /'dʌlɪs/ Alan 1893–1969. American lawyer, brother of John Foster Dulles, and director of the Central Intelligence Agency (CIA) 1953–61.

Dulles /'dʌlɪs/ John Foster 1888–1959. American politician. Senior US adviser at the founding of the United Nations, he largely drafted the Japanese peace treaty of 1951, and as Secretary of State 1952–59 was critical of

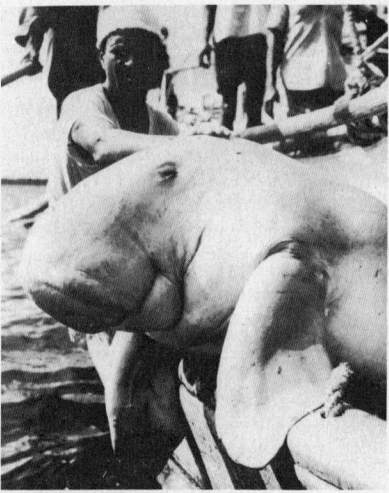

dugong Slow-moving and harmless, the dugong is herbivorous and becoming rare. It is sometimes suggested as the original of the mermaid legend, but a close-up view can be disillusioning.

Britain in the Suez crisis. He was the architect of US ▷Cold War foreign policy.

dulse red seaweed *Rhodymenia palmata* found on the middle and lower shore. It may have a single broad blade up to 30 cm/1 ft long arising direct from the holdfast, or often, as the name suggests, a palmate or fan shape. The frond is tough and dark red, sometimes with additional small 'leaflets' at the edge. This seaweed is edible.

Duluth /dəˈluːθ/ US port on Lake Superior, by the mouth of the St Louis river, Minnesota.

Population (1980) 92,000. It manufactures steel, flour, timber, and dairy produce.

Dulwich /'dʌlɪdʒ/ suburb, part of the inner London borough of Southwark, England. It contains Dulwich College (founded in 1619 by Edward Alleyn, an Elizabethan actor), the Horniman Museum/1901 with a fine ethnological collection, Dulwich Picture Gallery (1814), rebuilt in 1953 after being bombed during World War II, Dulwich Park, and Dulwich Village.

Duma in Russia, before 1917, an elected assembly which met four times following the abortive 1905 Revolution. With progressive demands the government could not accept, the Duma was largely powerless. After the abdication of Nicholas II the Duma directed the formation of a provisional government.

Dumas /'djuːmɑː/ Alexandre 1802–1870. French author, known as Dumas *père* (the father). His play *Henri III et sa cour/Henry III and his Court* 1829 established French romantic historical drama, but today he is remembered for his romances, the reworked output of a 'fiction-factory' of collaborators. They include *Les Trois Mousquetaires/The Three Musketeers* 1844 and its sequels; *Le Comte de Monte Cristo/The Count of Monte Cristo* 1844, and *Les Frères corses/The Corsican Brothers* 1845. Dumas *fils* was his illegitimate son.

Dumas /'djuːmɑː/ Alexandre 1824–1895. French author, known as Dumas *fils* (the son), son of Dumas *père* and remembered for the play *La Dame aux camélias/The Lady of the Camellias* 1852, based on his own novel, and source of Verdi's opera *La traviata*.

Dumas French dramatist and novelist Alexandre Dumas. Some of his exciting works have been made into successful films, such as *The Count of Monte Cristo* and *The Three Musketeers*.

Du Maurier /duː ˈmɒrieɪ/ Daphne 1907– . British novelist, daughter of actor-manager Sir

Gerald Du Maurier, and granddaughter of George ◊Du Maurier. Best-known of her romantic works are *Jamaica Inn* 1936, *Rebecca* 1938, and *My Cousin Rachel* 1951.

Du Maurier /duː 'mɒrieɪ/ George Louis Palmella Busson 1834–1896. French-born British author, best remembered for his novel *Trilby* 1894 – the story of a natural singer able to perform only under the hypnosis of Svengali, her tutor.

Dumbarton /dʌm'bɑːtn/ industrial town (marine engineering, whisky distilling) in Strathclyde, Scotland; population (1981) 23,204.

Dumbarton Oaks an 18th-century mansion near Washington, DC, USA, used as a centre for conferences and seminars. It was the scene of a conference held in 1944 between Britain, the USA, and the USSR to plan a new international league to enforce peace. After the Russians had left, a Chinese delegation arrived. The conference led to the foundation of the United Nations.

Dumfries /dʌm'friːs/ administrative headquarters of Dumfries and Galloway region, Scotland; population (1981) 32,000. It has knitwear, plastics and other industries.

Dumfries and Galloway /dʌm'friːs, 'gæləweɪ/ region of Scotland
area 6,369 sq km/2,458 sq mi
towns administrative headquarters Dumfries
features Solway Firth; Galloway Hills, setting of John Buchan's *The Thirty-Nine Steps*; Glen Trool National Park; Ruthwell Cross, a runic cross of about 800 at the village of Ruthwell; Stranraer provides the shortest sea route to Ireland
products horses and cattle, for which the Galloway area was especially famous; sheep; timber
population (1981) 145,000
famous people home of Robert Burns at Dumfries; birthplace of Thomas ◊Carlyle at Ecclefechan.

Dumfriesshire /dʌm'friːsʃə/ former county of southern Scotland, merged in 1975 in the region of Dumfries and Galloway.

Dumouriez /djuː,mʊəri'eɪ/ Charles François du Périer 1739–1823. French general. In 1792 he was appointed foreign minister, supported the declaration of war against Austria, and after the fall of the monarchy was given command of the army defending Paris; he won the battle of Jemappes, but was defeated at Neerwinden in 1793, and after intriguing with the Royalists he had to flee for his life. From 1804 he lived in England.

Dunant /djuː'nɒŋ/ Jean Henri 1828–1910. Swiss philanthropist; the originator of the Red Cross. Born at Geneva, he became a physician and witnessed the Battle of Solferino (1859). He helped to tend the wounded, and described their distress in *Un Souvenir de Solferino* 1862, in which he proposed the establishment of an international body for the aid of the wounded – an idea that was realized in the Geneva Convention of 1864.

Dunbar /dʌn'bɑː/ port and resort in Lothian region, Scotland; population (1971) 4,500.

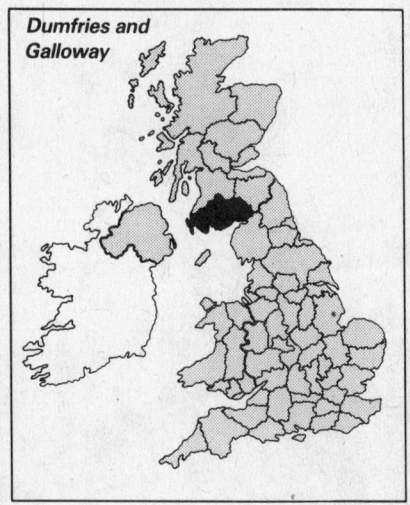

Dumfries and Galloway

Oliver ◊Cromwell defeated the Scots here in 1650.

Dunbar /dʌn'bɑː/ William c. 1460–c. 1520. Scottish poet at the court of James IV.

Dunbartonshire /dʌn'bɑːtnʃə/ former county of Scotland, bordering the north bank of the Clyde estuary, on which stand Dumbarton (the former county town), Clydebank and Helensburgh. It was merged in 1975 in the region of Strathclyde.

Duncan /'dʌŋkən/ Isadora 1878–1927. American dancer and teacher. An influential pioneer of American modern dance, she adopted an expressive, free form, dancing barefoot and wearing a loose tunic, inspired by the ideal of Hellenic beauty. She toured extensively, often returning to Russia after her initial success there in 1905, but died in an accident when her long scarf was caught in the wheel of a car.

Duncan-Sandys /'dʌŋkən 'sændz/ Duncan Edwin Sandys, Baron Duncan-Sandys 1908–1987. British Conservative politician. As minister for Commonwealth Relations 1960–64, he negotiated the independence of Malaysia 1963. He was created a life peer in 1974.

Dundas /dʌn'dæs/ Henry, 1st Viscount Melville 1742–1811. British Tory politician. In 1791 he became home secretary, and carried through the prosecution of the English and Scottish reformers. After holding other high cabinet posts, he was impeached in 1806 for corruption, and although acquitted on the main charge held no further office.

Dundee /dʌn'diː/ city and fishing port, administrative headquarters of Tayside, Scotland, on the north side of the Firth of Tay. Population (1981) 175,000. There are jute, marine engineering, watch and clock, textile, and fruit canning industries, and marmalade and confectionery are made. An important shipping and rail centre, Dundee benefitted from the North Sea oil discoveries of the 1970s. There is a university (1967) derived from Queen's College (founded 1881), and other notable buildings

include the Albert Institute (1867) and Caird Hall.

dune a bank or a hill of wind-drifted sand. Loose sand is blown and bounced along by the wind, up the windward side of a dune. The sand particles then fall to rest on the lee side, while more are blown up from the windward. In this way a dune moves gradually downwind. Dunes are seen in sandy deserts and along beaches. The typical crescent-shaped dune is called a barchan, seif dunes are longitudinal and lie parallel to the wind direction, and star-shaped dunes are formed by irregular winds.

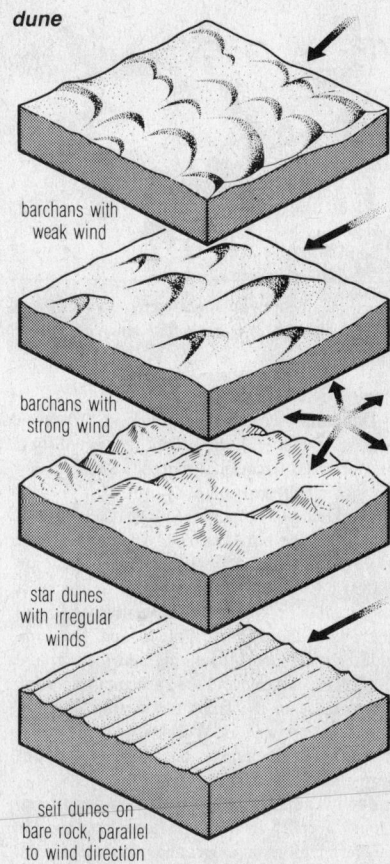

dune

barchans with weak wind

barchans with strong wind

star dunes with irregular winds

seif dunes on bare rock, parallel to wind direction

Dunedin /dʌn'iːdn/ port on Otago harbour, South Island, New Zealand; population (1983) 105,700. It is also a road, rail and air centre. There are engineering and textile industries, and Otago university was established 1869. The city itself was founded in 1848 by members of the Free Church of Scotland.

Dunfermline /dʌn'fɜːmlɪn/ industrial town near the Firth of Forth in Fife region, Scotland; population (1981) 52,000. It includes the naval base of Rosyth. Many Scottish kings, including Robert the Bruce, are buried in Dunfermline Abbey. Industries include engineering, shipbuilding and textiles.

Dungeness /,dʌndʒə'nes/ shingle headland on the south coast of Kent, England. It has nuclear power stations, a lighthouse, and a bird sanctuary.

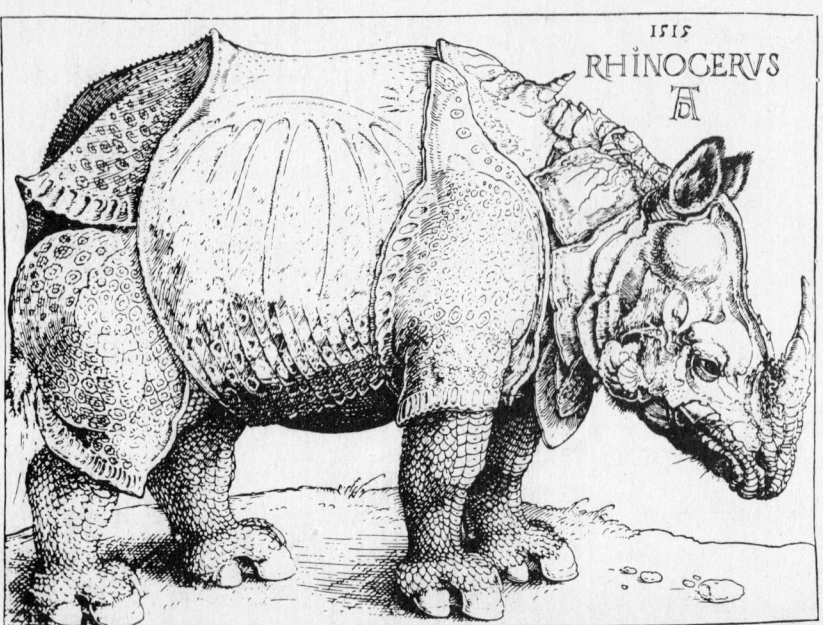

Dürer Woodcut of a rhinoceros by Albrecht Dürer. The rhinoceros was described to him by a Portuguese artist in 1515. This was the foundation of most representations of the Indian rhinoceros until the mid-18th century.

Dunham /'dʌnəm/ Katherine 1912– . American dancer, born in Chicago, noted for a free, strongly emotional method. She founded her own school and company in 1945.

Dunkirk /dʌn'kɜːk/ (French *Dunkerque*) seaport on the north coast of France, in Nord *département*, on the Strait of Dover; population (1983) 83,760. Its harbour is one of the most important in France, and it has widespread canal links with the rest of France and Belgium. Industries include oil refining and fishing; and textiles, machinery, and soap are manufactured. It was close to the front line during much of World War I, and in World War II, 337,131 Allied troops (including about 110,000 French) were evacuated from the beaches.

dunlin small wading bird *Calidris alpina* about 18 cm/7 in long, nesting along the far northern regions on moors and marshes. It is the commonest small sandpiper and may be seen on all British shores. Chestnut above and black below in summer, it is greyish in winter.

Dunlop /'dʌnlɒp/ John Boyd 1840–1921. Scottish inventor, who founded the rubber company that bears his name. In 1887, to help his child win a tricycle race, he bound on inflated rubber hose to the wheels. The same year he developed commercially practical pneumatic tyres (first patented by Thompson in 1846) for bicycles and cars.

Dunmow, Little /'dʌnməʊ/ village in Essex, England, scene every four years of the Dunmow Flitch trial (dating from 1111), in which a side of bacon is presented to any couple who 'will swear that they have not quarrelled nor repented of their marriage within a year and a day after its celebration'; they are judged by a jury whose members are all unmarried.

dunnock European bird *Prunella modularis* similar in size and colouring to the sparrow, but with slate-grey head and breast, and more slender bill. It nests in bushes and hedges, and is often called 'hedge sparrow'.

Duns Scotus /'dʌnz 'skəʊtəs/ John c. 1265–c. 1308. Franciscan monk known as Doctor Subtilis, born in Scotland, and an important figure of medieval ◊scholasticism. On many points he turned against the orthodoxy of ◊Aquinas; for example, he rejected the idea of a necessary world, favouring a conception of God as absolute freedom capable of spontaneous activity. However the Church rejected his ideas, hence the word 'dunce'. In the medieval controversy over universals he advocated ◊nominalism.

Dunstable /'dʌnstəbəl/ English town in SW Bedfordshire, 48 km/30 mi NW of London. Population (1981) 31,000. Whipsnade Zoo is nearby. Industries are printing and engineering.

Dunstable /'dʌnstəbəl/ John c. 1385–1453. English composer. Little is known of his life, though he may have had some connection with St Albans Cathedral, and seems to have travelled widely in Europe, achieving a reputation also as mathematician and astrologer. He wrote songs and anthems, and is generally considered one of the founders of Renaissance music.

Dunstan, Saint /'dʌnstən/ c. 924–988. Archbishop of Canterbury from 960. As Abbot of Glastonbury from 945, he made it an educational centre and was chief minister under Edred and Edgar. Feast day 19 May.

duodecimal system system of arithmetic notation using 12 as a base, often considered superior to the decimal system in that 12 has a high divisibility (2, 3, 4, 6) and the gross (12

dozen) also has numerous divisors. Duodecimal societies exist for its promotion in the UK and US.

Duparc /dju:'pɑːk/ (Marie Eugène) Henri Fouques 1848–1933. French composer. Born in Paris, he studied under César Franck. His songs, though only 15 in number, are of great importance for their craftsmanship and their place in the history of French song-writing.

Du Pré /du:'preɪ/ Jacqueline 1945–1987. British cellist. Noted for her extraordinary technique and powerful interpretations of the classic cello repertory, particularly of Elgar. She had an international concert career while still in her teens, and made many recordings. She married Daniel ◊Barenboim in 1967, and worked with him in concerts as a duo and in a conductor-soloist relationship until her playing career was ended by multiple sclerosis. Although confined to a wheelchair for the last 14 years of her life, she continued to work as a teacher and to campaign on behalf of the other sufferers of the disease.

duralumin a lightweight aluminium ◊alloy widely used in aircraft construction, containing copper, magnesium and manganese.

Duras /dju'rɑː/ Marguerite 1914– . French writer. Educated at the Sorbonne, she graduated in law, and her works include short stories (*Des Journées entières dans les arbres*), plays (*La Musica*), film scripts (*Hiroshima Mon Amour* 1960), and novels such as *Le Vice-Consul* 1966, evoking an existentialist world from the actual setting of Calcutta. Her autobiographical novel, *La Douleur*, is set in Paris in 1945.

Durazzo /du'rætsəʊ/ Italian form of ◊Dürres, Albanian port.

Durban /'dɜːbən/ principal port of Natal, South Africa, and second port of the republic; population (1980) 506,000. Founded in 1824 as Port Natal, it was renamed in 1835 after General Sir Benjamin d'Urban (1777–1849), lieutenant-governor of the east district of Cape Colony 1834–37. Durban's exports consist of coal, maize, and wool, whilst heavy machinery and mining equipment is imported. It is also an important holiday resort. Natal university (1949) is divided between Durban and Pietermaritzburg.

Dürer /'djʊərə/ Albrecht 1471–1528. German engraver and painter. Born at Nuremberg, in 1486 he was apprenticed to Michael Wohlgemuth, a distinguished artist, and at the age of 13 he drew a portrait of himself from the mirror, the first known self-portrait in the history of European art. After some years of travel he returned to Nuremberg and executed a number of copperplates, and also his famous series of woodcuts of the *Apocalypse* 1498. His first important painting, *The Adoration of the Magi*, is dated 1504. In 1505 he went to Venice, where he painted *The Feast of the Rosary* and *The Martyrdom of St Bartholomew*. His intellectual powers put him in line with the great Italian masters and their influence introduced a new solidity of form into his basically Gothic style. He worked for the Emperor Maximilian I 1512–19, for example the engraving *The Knight, Death and the Devil* 1513, and in 1520 went to

Durham The Norman cathedral at Durham, which dates from 1093. The remains of the venerable Bede were transferred here in 1370.

the Netherlands, and became court painter to Charles V He was a friend of Luther, and was greatly influenced by the Reformation.

Durga /'duəgə/ Hindu goddess; one of the many names for Siva's wife.

Durham /'dʌrəm/ city (administrative headquarters) of the county of Durham, England; population (1981) 26,550. Founded in 995, it has a superb Norman cathedral dating from 1093, where the remains of ◊Bede were transferred in 1370; the castle was built by William I in 1072, and the university was founded in 1832. Annual events include the Miners' Gala.

Durham /'dʌrəm/ county in NE England
area 2,436 sq km/6,309 sq mi
towns administrative headquarters Durham; Darlington, and the new towns of Peterlee and Newton Aycliffe
features Beamish open-air industrial museum
products sheep and dairy produce; the county lies on one of Britain's richest coalfields.
population (1986) 603,700.

Durham /'dʌrəm/ John George Lambton, 1st Earl of Durham 1792–1840. British politician. Appointed Lord Privy Seal in 1830, he drew up the first Reform Bill of 1832, and as governor-general of Canada briefly in 1837 drafted the Durham Report which led to the union of Upper and Lower Canada.

Durkheim /'dɜːkhaɪm, French djuə'kem/ Emile 1858–1917. French sociologist, one of the founders of modern sociology, who also influenced social anthropology. He was the first lecturer in social science at Bordeaux University 1887–1902, professor of education at the Sorbonne in Paris from 1902 and the first professor of sociology there in 1913. He examined the bases of social order and the effects of industrialization on traditional social and moral order, and attempted to establish sociology as a respectable and scientific discipline, capable of diagnosing social ills and recommending possible cures. His four key

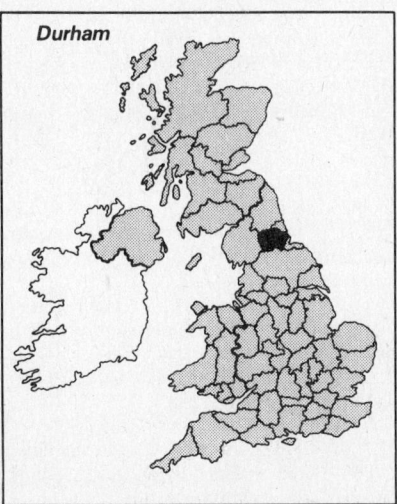

Durham

works are *The Division of Labour in Society* 1893, comparing social order in small-scale societies with that in industrial ones; *The Rules of Sociological Method* 1895, outlining his own brand of functionalism and proclaiming positivism as the way forward for sociology as a science; *Suicide* 1897, showing social causes of this apparently individual act; and *The Elementary Forms of Religion*, a study of the beliefs of Australian aborigines showing the importance of religion in social solidarity.

durra or *dourra* grass of the genus *Sorghum*, also known as Indian millet, grown as cereals in parts of Asia and Africa. *Sorghum vulgare* is the chief cereal of many parts of Africa.

Durrell /'dʌrəl/ Gerald Malcolm 1925– . British naturalist, brother of Lawrence ◊Durrell. Director of Jersey Zoological Park, he is the author of travel and natural history books, and the humorous memoir *My Family and Other Animals* 1956.

Durrell /'dʌrəl/ Lawrence George 1912– . British novelist and poet. Born in India, he joined the Foreign Service, and has lived mainly in the East Mediterranean, the setting of his novels, including the Alexandria Quartet: *Justine*, *Balthazar*, *Mountolive* and *Clea* 1957–60; in turn interlinked with the Avignon Quintet (in progress); he has also written travel books. He is the brother of Gerald ◊Durrell.

Dürrenmatt /'djuərənmæt/ Friedrich 1921–. Swiss dramatist, author of grotesquely farcical tragi-comedies, for example *The Physicists* 1962, in which three sane nuclear physicists flee to a Swiss asylum.

Durrës /'durəs/ chief port of Albania, population (1981) 70,000, and also its main commercial and communications centre, with flour mills, soap and cigarette factories, distilleries, and an electronics plant.

Duse /'duːzeɪ/ Eleonora 1859–1924. Italian actress. She was the mistress of D'Annunzio from 1897, as recorded in his novel *Il Fuoco/The Flame of Life*, and he wrote the play *La Gioconda* for her.

Dushanbe /duː'ʃænbeɪ/ capital (known 1929–69 as Stalinabad) of Tadzhik Republic, USSR; population (1981) 510,000. Situated 160

Durham John, first Earl of Durham, became a Whig MP in 1817. He later went to Canada as Governor General and put down a revolt of the French in Lower Canada.

km/100 mi N of the Afghan frontier, it is an important road, rail and air centre. Dushanbe has cotton mills, tanneries, meat-packing factories, and printing works, and is the seat of Tadzhik state university.

Düsseldorf /'dusəldɔːf/ city of West Germany, on the right bank of the Rhine, 26 km/16 mi NW of Cologne, capital of North Rhine-Westphalia; population (1980) 592,200. It is a river port, and the commercial and financial centre of the Ruhr area, with large exhibition facilities. There are food processing, brewing, agricultural machinery, textile, and chemical industries. It is also a university city.

dust bowl area in the Great Plains region of North America (Texas to Kansas) that has suffered extensive wind erosion as the result of bad farming practice in the once fertile soil. Much of the topsoil was blown away in the 1930s. Similar dust bowls are being formed in many areas today, especially across Africa, because of the same overcropping and overgrazing, resulting in ◊desert conditions.

Dutch art With the rise of the Dutch nation in the second half of the 16th century came the full emergence of Dutch art with Frans Hals, Pieter Lastman (1585–1633) – the teacher of ◊Rembrandt – and Gerard van Honthorst. Among the many masters of the 17th century are Rembrandt and his pupil Gerard Douw (1613–75); Adriaen van Ostade (1610–84), who painted Flemish peasant scenes; Gerard Ter Borch the Younger (1617–81), first painter of characteristic Dutch interiors; Albert ◊Cuyp; Jan ◊Steen; Jakob van ◊Ruysdael, greatest of the landscapists; Pieter de ◊Hooch; Jan ◊Vermeer van Delft; Willem van de ◊Velde, sea painter to Charles II of England; Jan van der Heyden (1637–1712); and Meindert ◊Hobbema. The houses, market and town halls of this period were also a consummate expression of the Dutch genius. In the 18th and 19th centuries there was a marked decline, except for the genre painters Cornelis Troost (1697–1750) and Jozef Israels (1824–1911), and the outstanding genius of Vincent van ◊Gogh.

Dutch East Indies former Dutch colony which in 1945 became independent as ◊Indonesia.

Dutch elm disease a disease of elm trees (*Ulmus*), principally English elm and Dutch elm, caused by the fungus *Certocystis ulmi*. It was first described in the Netherlands and by the early 1930s had spread across Britain and continental Europe, as well as occuring widely in North America. In the 1970s, a new epidemic was caused by a much more virulent form of the fungus, probably brought to Britain from Canada. The fungus is usually spread from tree to tree by the elm bark beetle which lays its eggs beneath the bark. The disease has no cure and control methods involve injecting insecticide into the trees annually to prevent infection, or the destruction of all elms in a broad band around an infected area, to keep the beetles out.

Dutch Guiana /gɪˈɑnə/ former Dutch colony which in 1948 became independent as ◊Suriname.

Dutch language a member of the Germanic branch of the Indo-European language family, often referred to by scholars as Netherlandic and taken to include not only the standard language and dialects of the Netherlands (excluding Frisian) but also Flemish (in Belgium and northern France) and, more remotely, its offshoot Afrikaans in South Africa. Many, however, regard Flemish and Afrikaans as distinct languages. Dutch is also spoken in Suriname in South America and the Netherlands Antilles, in the South Caribbean.

Dutch literature the earliest known poet to use the Dutch dialect was Henric van Veldeke in the 12th century, but the finest example of early Gothic literature is *Van Den Vos Reinaarde* (About Reynard the Fox) by a poet known as 'Willem-who-made-the-Madoc'. To the Golden Age belong Pieter C Hooft (1581–1647), lyricist, playwright and historian; Constantijn Huygens (1596–1687), who was knighted by James I in 1622; Gerbrand A Bredero (1585–1618), gifted in comedy and light verse; the great lyric, satiric and dramatic poet Joost van den Vondel (1587–1679), and the moralizing poet Father Jacob Cats (1577–1660). As in art, the 18th century was generally a period of decline, although the epic poet Willem Bilderdijk (1756–1831) ranks high. The Romantic movement found its fullest expression in the nationalist periodical *De Gids* (The Guide) founded 1837. Among the best-known writers of the period were Nicolas Beets (1814–1903), with his famous sketches *Camera Obscura*, and Eduard Douwes Dekker (1820–87), who wrote novels under the pseudonym 'Multatuli' and was a forerunner of the movement grouped round a second periodical *De Nieuwe Gids* (The New Guide, established 1885) which marked the late 19th century revival. Among writers of the period were lyricist Herman Gorter (1864–1927), the

staider poet Albert Verwey (1865–1937), the poet, playwright and novelist Frederick van Eeden (1860–1932), the novelist Louis Couperus (1863–1923), Marcellus Emants (1848–1923), and Arthur van Schendel (1874–1946). After World War I Hendrik Marsman (1899–1940), a rhetorical 'vitalist' influenced by German expressionism, led a school counterbalanced by the more sober *Forum* group led by critic Menno Ter Braak (1902–40). See also ◊Flemish literature.

Duval /djuːˈvæl/ Claude 1643–1670. English highwayman. He was born in Normandy and moved to England at the Restoration as a valet, but turned highwayman, and his gallantry was as famous as his robberies. He was hanged at Tyburn.

Duvalier /djuːˈvælieɪ/ Jean Claude 1951– . Haitian statesman. His father François Duvalier (1907–71), known as 'Papa Doc', became president of Haiti in 1957 and ruled till his death with the aid of a private army of Tontons Macoute 'bogeymen'. Under Jean Claude, who succeeded his father in the presidency, and is known as 'Baby Doc', they were replaced, as presidential bodyguard, by the less aggressive Les Léopards, trained by American veterans, and the modernization of Haiti by agricultural and industrial development was speeded. In 1973 he held the first elections since 1961, and in 1979 allowed the formation of other political parties. Censorship remained strict.

Duve /djuːv/ Christian de 1917– . Belgian scientist, who shared a Nobel Prize for Medicine in 1974 for his work on the structural and functional organization of the cell.

Duvivier /djuːˈvɪvieɪ/ Julien 1896–1967. French film director, whose work included *Un Carnet de Bal 1937 and La Fin du Jour* 1938.

Duwez /ˈduːvəz/ Pol 1907– . American scientist, born in Belgium, who in 1959 developed with his team ◊metallic glass at the California Institute of Technology.

Dvořák /ˈdvɔːʒɑːk/ Antonin (Leopold) 1841–1904. Czech composer. Born near Prague, the son of a butcher, he played the viola in cafés before joining the orchestra of the Prague National Theatre in 1862, and later became a church organist. He achieved international success with his series of Slavonic dances 1877–86, and was Director of the National Conservatory, New York, 1892–95, his *New World Symphony* 1893 and such works as the *American Quartet* 1893 showing his interest in black music. He wrote operas, including *Rusalka* 1901; large-scale choral works, the *Carnival* and other overtures, violin and cello concertos, chamber music, piano pieces, and songs. His music is in the classical tradition of Beethoven and Brahms, and strongly influenced by Czech folk music.

Dyck /ˈdaɪk/ Anthony van 1599–1641. Flemish painter. Born at Antwerp, he was for four years an assistant to ◊Rubens. He visited England 1620–21, and was painter to James I. He then worked for a time in Italy, but in 1628 returned to Antwerp where he painted many religious works and portaits. In 1632 he was

Dvořák Czech composer Antonin Dvořák, sponsored by Brahms, won international popularity and became director of the National Conservatory in New York, where he wrote his *New World Symphony*.

invited to England by Charles I, became court painter, and was knighted.

dye substance which, applied in solution to fabrics, imparts a colour resistant to washing. Direct dyes combine with the material of the fabric, yielding a coloured compound; indirect dyes require the presence of another substance (a mordant), with which the fabric must first be treated, and which will cause precipitation of the coloured compound in the fibres; vat dyes are colourless soluble substances which on oxidation by exposure to air yield an insoluble coloured compound. Naturally occurring dyes include indigo, madder (alizarin), logwood and cochineal, but industrial dyes are usually synthetic, and are classified according to the substances from which they are produced, or the characteristic chemical groupings in the molecules, for example the azo-dye-stuffs, acridine, anthracene and aniline.

Dyfed /ˈdʌvɪd/ county of SW Wales
area 5766 sq km/2226 sq mi
towns administrative headquarters Carmarthen; Aberystwyth, Cardigan, Lampeter
features Pembrokeshire Coast National Park, part of the Brecon Beacons National Park, including the Black Mountain, and part of the Cambrian Mountains, including Plynlimon Fawr 752 m/2,468 ft; the village of Laugharne, at the mouth of the Towey, was the home of Dylan Thomas, and features in his work as 'Milk Wood'; Museum of the Woollen Industry at Drefach Felindre, and of Welsh religious life at Tre'rddôl.
population (1981) 330,000
language English, Welsh (46% Welsh-speaking)
famous people Taliesin.

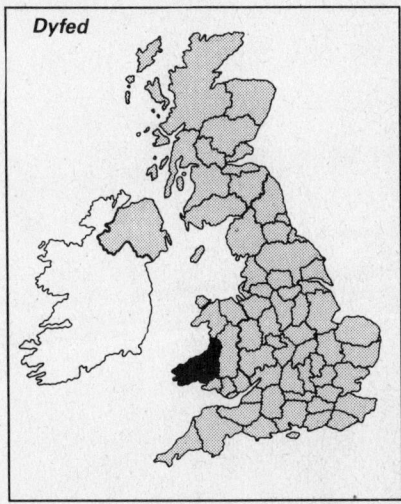

Dyfed

Dylan /'dɪlən/ Bob. Stage name of Robert Allen Zimmerman 1941– . US singer and songwriter. His early songs, on his albums *Freewheelin'* 1963 and *The Times They Are A-Changin'* 1964, were in the 1960s folk music tradition, associated with the US civil-rights movement and anti-war protest. When he first used an electric rock band 1965 he was accused by some early fans of selling out, but the albums *Highway 61 Revisited* 1965 and *Blonde on Blonde* 1966 are often cited as his best work. His increasingly obscure lyrics provided catchphrases for a generation and influenced innumerable songwriters. He later became a Christian.

dynamics branch of mechanics that deals with the mathematical and physical study of the behaviour of bodies under the action of forces which produce changes of motion in them.

dynamite an explosive consisting of a mixture of nitroglycerine and kieselguhr; it was first devised by Alfred Nobel.

dynamo also called generator. A machine for transforming mechanical energy into electrical energy. Present-day dynamos work on the principles described by ◊Faraday in 1830, that an electromotive force (e.m.f.) is developed in a conductor when it is moves in a magnetic field. A simple form of dynamo consists of a powerful field magnet, between the poles of which a suitable conductor, usually in the form of a coil (armature), is rotated. The mechanical energy of rotation is thus converted into an electric current in the armature.

dyscalculus a disability with figures, named on analogy with ◊dyslexia.

dysentery infective bleeding and ulceration of the large bowel, causing diarrhoea containing blood and mucus, and usually caused by either amoebae or bacillae microorganisms. Treatment is by drugs, and in the more serious amoebic dysentery the amoebae must be killed. It is spread by infected water and foods, and remains common in some tropical areas.

dyslexia (Greek 'bad', 'pertaining to words'), a malfunction in the brain's synthesis and interpretation of sensory information, popularly 'word blindness'. It results in poor ability to read and write, though the person may otherwise excel, for example, in mathematics. A similar disability with figures is called ◊dyscalculus.

dyspepsia disturbance of digestion, which may be caused by faulty diet, nervous tension, or disease, such as cancer of the stomach.

dysprosium one of the yttrium group of rare earths (symbol Dy, atomic number 66, atomic weight 162.51) discovered in 1886 by Lecoq de Boisbaudran (1838–1912).

Dzerzhinsk /dzə'ʒɪnsk/ city in central USSR, on the Oka river, 32 km/20 mi W of Gorki. There are engineering, chemical, and timber industries. Population (1981) 263,000.

Dzhambul /dʒæm'bʊl/ city in Kazakhstan, USSR, in a fruit-growing area. Industries include fruit canning, sugar refining, and the manufacture of phosphate fertilizers. Population (1981) 277,000.

Dzungarian Gates /dzuŋ'geəriən/ ancient route in central Asia on the border of Kazakh Republic (USSR) and Xinjiang Uygur region (China), 470 km/290m NW of Urümqi. The route was used by the Mongol hordes on their way to Europe.

E the second vowel and fifth and most often used letter of our alphabet. In Lloyd's Register of Shipping it formerly represented a 2nd-class rating.

eagle name given to a number of genera of large birds of prey of the family Accipitridae. The typical genus *Aquila* includes the golden eagle *Aquila chrysaetos*. It has a 2 m/6 ft wingspan and is dark brown; in Britain it is found in the Highlands of Scotland with a few recolonizing the Lake District. The larger spotted eagle *Aquila clanga* lives in Central Europe and Asia.
The sea eagles *Haliaetus* include the white-tailed sea eagle *Haliaetus albicilla* which has been renaturalized in Britain in the 1980s, having died out there in 1916. Mainly a carrion-feeder, it breeds on sea cliffs. The American white-headed sea eagle or bald eagle *Haliaetus leucocephalus* is the symbol of the USA; rendered infertile through the ingestion of agricultural chemicals, it has become very rare.

Eagling /'iːglɪŋ/ Wayne 1950– . Canadian dancer. With an English father and Canadian mother, he grew up in California. He joined the ◊Royal Ballet in London, appearing in *Gloria* 1980, and other productions.

Ealing /'iːlɪŋ/ borough of Greater London, England. Population (1981) 280,000. The first British sound-film studio was built here in 1931, and 'Ealing comedies' became a noted genre in British film-making.

Eanes /eɪˈɑːneʃ/ Antonio dos Santos Ramalho 1935– . Portuguese politician. He helped plan the 1974 coup which ended the ◊Caetano regime, and as Army Chief of Staff put down a left-wing revolt in November 1975. He was president 1976–86.

ear the organ of hearing in animals. In many animals, ears are not necessarily on the head; in some insects they are found on the legs, thorax, or abdomen. However, the principle behind all ears is the same. A sensitive organ responds to the air or water vibrations that constitute sound, and these are translated into nerve signals and passed to the brain. In mammals the ear consists of three parts. The *outer ear* is a funnel which collects sound, directing it down a tube to the *ear drum* or tympanic membrane which separates the outer and *middle ear*. Sounds vibrate this membrane, the mechanical movement of which is transferred to the membrane of the *inner ear* by three small bones, the auditory ossicles. Vibrations of the inner ear membrane move fluid contained in the snail-shaped cochlea, which vibrates hair cells that stimulate the auditory nerve, connected to the brain. The fluid-filled labyrinth of the inner ear detects changes of position which, with other sensory inputs, is responsible for the sense of balance.

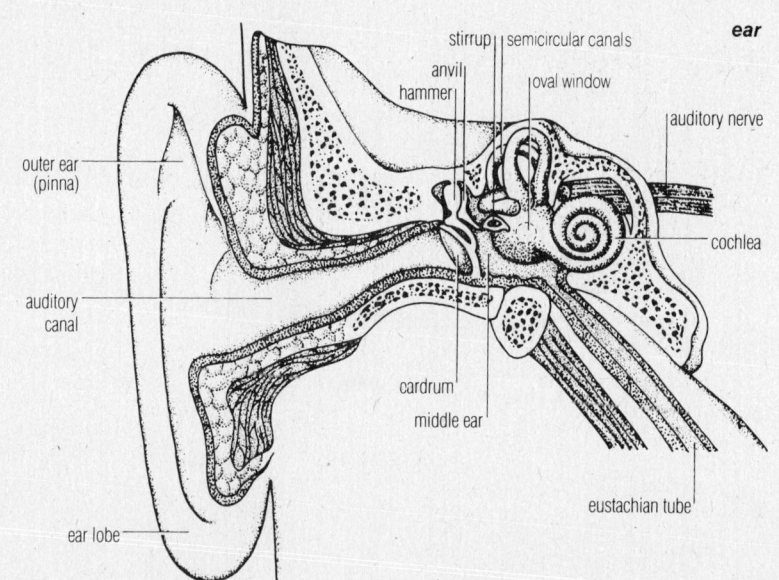

ear

stirrup | semicircular canals
anvil | oval window
hammer
auditory nerve
outer ear (pinna)
cochlea
auditory canal
eardrum
middle ear
eustachian tube
ear lobe

Earhart /'eəhɑːt/ Amelia 1898–1937. American airwoman, born in Kansas. In 1932 she was the first woman to fly the Atlantic alone, and in 1937 disappeared without trace while making a Pacific flight.

earl in the British peerage, the third title in order of rank, coming between marquess and viscount; it is the oldest of British titles, being of Scandinavian origin. The premier earldom is Arundel, now united with the dukedom of ◊Norfolk. An earl's wife is a countess.

Earl Marshal in England, one of the Officers of State; the office has been hereditary since 1672 in the family of Howard, the dukes of Norfolk. The Earl Marshal is head of the College of Arms, and arranges state processions and ceremonies.

Early English in architecture, name given by Thomas Rickman (1776–1841) to the first of the three periods of the English Gothic style. It covers the period from about 1189 to about 1280, and is characterized by tall, elongated windows (lancets) without mullions (horizontal bars), often grouped in threes, fives, or sevens; the pointed arch; pillars of stone centres surrounded by shafts of black Purbeck marble; and dog-tooth (zig-zag) ornament. Salisbury Cathedral is almost entirely Early English.

Earth the third planet from the sun
mean distance from the sun 149,500,000 km/93,000,000 mi

diameter 12,756 km
rotation period 23 hr 56 min 4.1 sec
year (complete orbit, or sidereal period) 365 days
5 hr 48 min 46 sec. The Earth's average speed
round the sun is 30 km/18.5 mi a second; the
plane of its orbit is inclined to its equatorial plane
at an angle of 23.5°, the reason for the changing
seasons
atmosphere nitrogen 78.09 per cent, oxygen
20.95 per cent, argon 0.93 per cent, carbon
dioxide 0.03 per cent, and less than 0.0001 per
cent neon, helium, krypton, hydrogen, xenon,
ozone, radon.
surface land surface 150,000,000 sq
km/57,500,000 sq mi (greatest height Mount
Everest); water surface 361,000,000 sq
km/139,400,000 sq mi (greatest depth
◊Mariana Trench in Pacific). The interior is
thought to be an inner core about 1,300 km/800
mi from the centre of solid iron and nickel; an
outer core about 2,250 km/1,400 mi molten iron
and nickel; and a ◊mantle of solid rock about
2,900 km/1,800 mi thick, separated by the
◊Mohorovičić Discontinuity from the ◊Earth's
crust. The crust and the topmost layer of the
mantle form about 12 major plates (on top of
which the ◊continents slowly drift). The Earth is
an oblate spheroid, spherical but slightly
flattened at the poles.
age 4,600 million years. The Earth was formed
with the rest of the ◊solar system by consolidation
of interstellar dust. Life began about 4,000
million years ago.
satellites see ◊Moon.

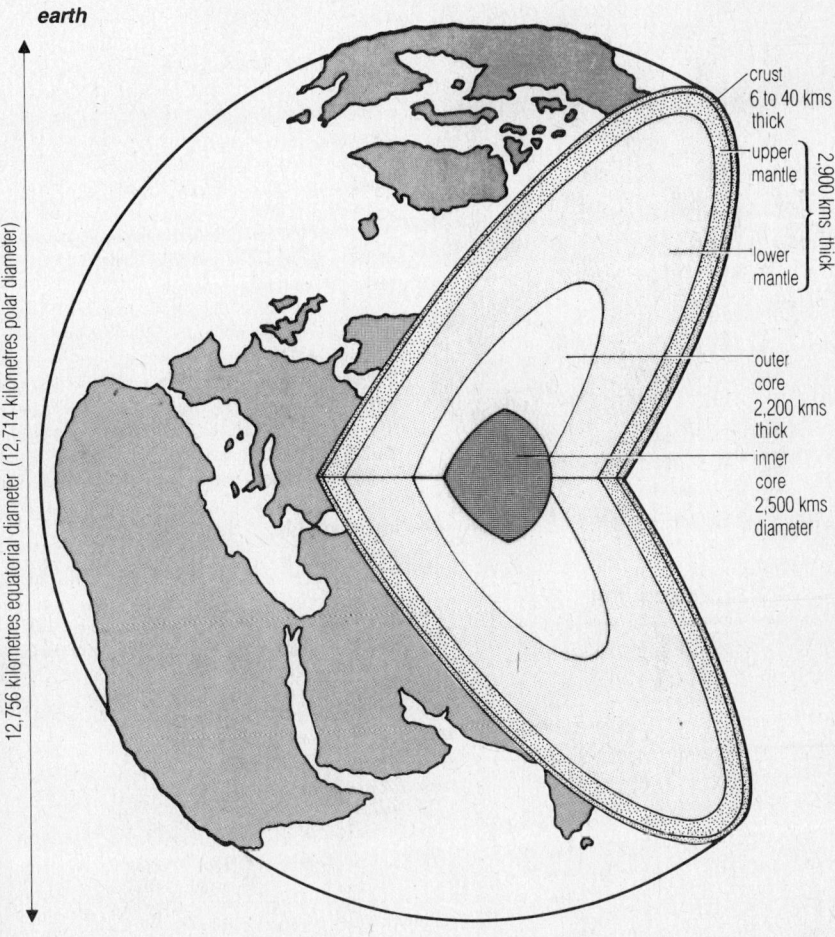

earth

crust 6 to 40 kms thick
upper mantle
2,900 kms thick
lower mantle
outer core 2,200 kms thick
inner core 2,500 kms diameter

12,756 kilometres equatorial diameter (12,714 kilometres polar diameter)

Earth Most of Africa and portions of Europe and Asia can be seen in this photograph taken from the Apollo 11 spacecraft. Astronauts Neil Armstrong, Edward Aldrin and Michael Collins were 170,000 km from Earth when this shot was obtained.

earth in electricity, a connection between an appliance and the ground. The potential of the Earth (planet) is taken to be zero. In the event of a fault in an electrical appliance, for example, involving connection between the live part of the circuit and the outer casing, the current flows to earth, causing no harm to the user. In most domestic installations, earthing is achieved by a connection to a metal water supply pipe buried in the ground before it enters the premises.

earthquake a shaking or convulsion of the earth's surface, the scientific study of which is called ◊seismology. Earthquakes result from a build-up of stresses within rocks until strained to fracturing point. Most occur along ◊faults (fractures or breaks) in the earth's strata. These tectonic earthquakes are the greatest and most widespread in their effects. The great majority are under the sea. The force of an earthquake is measured on the ◊Richter scale. The point at which an earthquake originates is the *seismic focus*. The point on earth's surface directly above this is the *epicentre*. In 1987 a California earthquake was successfully predicted by measurement of underground pressure waves; prediction attempts have also involved the study of such phenomena as the change of gases in the ◊crust, the level of water in wells, and the behaviour of animals. The possibility of earthquake prevention is remote. However, rock slippage might be slowed at movement points, or promoted at stoppage points by the extraction or injection of huge quantities of water underground, which serves as a lubricant. This would ease overall pressure.

earth sciences term for the scientific study of the planet Earth as a whole, a new synthesis of several traditional disciplines such as ◊geology, ◊meteorology, oceanography, ◊geophysics, and ◊geochemistry. The mining and extraction of minerals and gems, the prediction of weather and earthquakes, the pollution of the atmosphere, and the forces that shaped the physical world all fall within its scope of study. The emergence of the discipline reflects scientists' concern that an understanding of the global aspects of Earth's structure and its past will hold the key to how humans affect its future, ensuring that its resources are used in a sustainable way.

earthworm annelid worm of the class Oligochaeta which is mainly terrestrial in its habits. Earthworms are hermaphrodite, and deposit their eggs in cocoons. They live by burrowing in the soil, feeding on the organic matter it contains. They play a most important role in the formation of humus, by irrigating the soil, and levelling it by transferring earth from the deeper levels to the surface as castings. The

earthquake Mexico City, 19th Sept 1985. In the space of a few minutes, 10,000 people lost their lives and more than 200 buildings were razed.

building which would exclude light from existing windows.

east one of the four cardinal points of the compass, indicating that part of the horizon where the sun rises; when facing north, east is to the right. The sun, and hence the east, has held an important place in various religions; ancient temples had their altars at the east end so that sacrifices and other rituals could be made facing the rising sun. In the 2nd century it became customary for Christians to worship facing the east, and also to bury the dead with their feet towards the east, so that on the morning of the Resurrection they would be facing the direction from which Christ was to come in glory.

East Africa /ˈiːst ˈæfrɪkə/ territorial region of ◊Africa comprising Djibouti, Ethiopia, Kenya, Madagascar, Mauritius, Republic of Somali, Tanzania, and Uganda.

East Anglia /ˈiːst ˈæŋgliə/ district of E England, formerly a Saxon kingdom, and including Norfolk, Suffolk, and parts of Essex and Cambridgeshire. The University of East Anglia was founded at ◊Norwich in 1962, and the Sainsbury Centre for the Visual Arts, opened in 1978, has a collection of ethnographic art and sculpture. East Anglian ports such as Harwich

First reached by Europeans on Easter Sunday 1722, it is famous for its huge carved statues and stone houses, the work of neolithic peoples of unknown origin. The chief centre is Hanga-Roa.

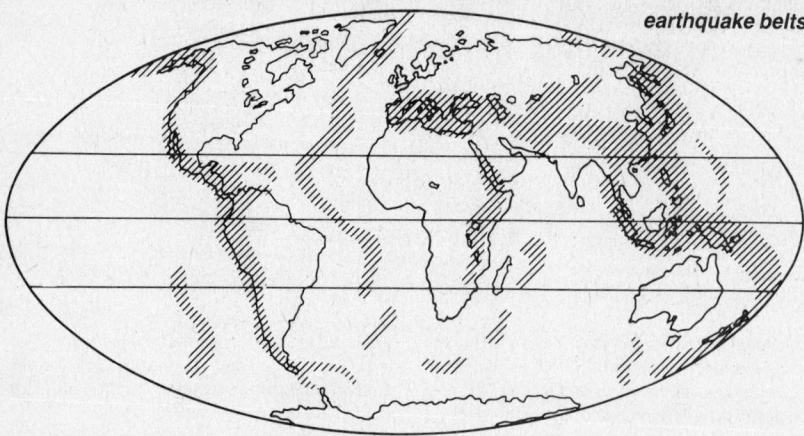

Easter Island The giant figures, raised on stepped ceremonial platforms of beautifully carved and fitted stone masonry, look out over the Pacific ocean. They are the work of neolithic peoples of unknown origin.

Eastern Orthodox Church the Christian Church (see ◊Christianity) of many countries of eastern Europe and the N and W of Asia, including Greeks, Russians, Romanians, Serbians, Bulgarians, Georgians, and Albanians; in the last 200 years it has spread into China, Korea, Japan, and Alaska, as well as among the people of Siberia and central Asia. Today it is a federation of self-governing churches, some of which were founded by the Apostles and their disciples, which conduct services in their own languages, and follow their own customs and traditions, but are in full communion with one another. The senior Church of Eastern Christendom is that of Constantinople (modern Istanbul), whose chief bishop bears the title of ecumenical patriarch, and has primacy of honour.

The Church's teaching is based on the Bible, and the ◊Nicene creed, as modified by the Council of Constantinople in 381, is the only confession of faith used. The centre of Eastern worship is the ◊Eucharist, celebrated with little change since the 6th century. The ritual is elaborate, and accompanied by singing in which both men and women take part, but no instrumental music is used. Besides the seven sacraments, the prayer book contains many other services for daily life. There is an impressive marriage service during which the bride and groom are crowned. There are many monasteries, the most famous being Mount Athos in Greece, which has flourished since the 10th century. During the past century contacts between Eastern and Anglican Christians have become more frequent, and several societies have been started for its promotion, for example, the Fellowship of St Alban and St Sergius.

East Germany /ˈiːst ˈdʒɜːməni/ see ◊Germany, East.

earthquake belts

common British earthworms belong to the genera *Lumbricus* and *Allolobophora*. These are comparitively small, but some tropical forms reach over 1 m/3 ft and *Megascolides australis*, of Queensland, over 3 m/11 ft.

earwig nocturnal insect of the order Dermaptera. Most species are tropical, but a number are found in Britain, such as the common European earwig *Forficula auricularia*. The fore-wings are short and leathery, and serve to protect the hind-wings, which are large and are folded like a fan when at rest; the insects seldom fly. They are regarded as pests because they feed on flowers, fruit, etc, but they also eat other insects, dead or alive. Eggs are laid beneath the soil, and the female cares for the young even after hatching.

easement in law, rights which a person may have over the land of another. The commonest example is a right of way; others are rights to bring water over another's land, and to prevent

and Felixstowe have greatly developed as trade with the rest of Europe increases.

Eastbourne /ˈiːstbɔːn/ English seaside resort in East Sussex, 103 km/64 mi SE of London; population (1981) 77,500. The old town was developed in the early 19th century as a model of town planning, largely due to the seventh Duke of Devonshire. The modern town extends along the coast for 5 km/3 mi. To the E the South Downs terminate in ◊Beachy Head.

Easter feast of the Christian Church, commemorating the Resurrection of Christ. The English name derives from Eostre, Anglo-Saxon goddess of spring, who was honoured in April. Eggs are given at this time as a symbol of new life.

Easter Island /ˈiːstə/ Chilean island (known as Rapa Nui, Spanish name Isla de Pascua), area about 166 sq km/64 sq mi, in the S Pacific Ocean, part of Polynesia, about 5,960 km/2,300 mi W of Chile. Population (1982) 1,931.

East India Company an English commercial company that was chartered by Queen Elizabeth I in 1600 and given a monopoly of trade between England and the Far East. In the 18th century it became in effect the ruler of a large part of India, and a form of dual control by the company and a committee responsible to Parliament in London was introduced by Pitt's India Act, 1784. The end of the monopoly of China trade came in 1834 and, following the ◊Indian Mutiny in 1857, the Crown took complete control of the government of British India; the India Act of 1858 abolished the company.

East India Company, Dutch (VOC, or Vereenigde Oost-Indische Compagnie). A company 1602–1798, chartered by the States-General of the Netherlands, which was granted a monopoly on Dutch trade in the Far East. In the 17th century some 100 ships were regularly trading between the Netherlands and the East Indies. Its main base was Batavia in Indonesia; ships sailed there via the Cape of Good Hope, a colony founded by the company in 1652 as a staging post. On the winding-up of the company in 1798 its possessions became part of the Dutch Empire.

East Kilbride /ˈiːst kɪlˈbraɪd/ old village in Strathclyde, Scotland; population (1985) 72,000. It was developed as a 'new town' from 1947 to take overspill from Glasgow, 11 km/6 mi to the NE. It is the site of the National Engineering Laboratory. There are various light industries and some engineering, including jet engines.

East London /ˈiːst ˈlʌndən/ port and resort on the SE coast of Cape Province, South Africa. Population (1980) 160,582. It has a good harbour, is the terminus of a railway from the interior, and is a leading wool-exporting port.

East Lothian /ˈiːst ˈləʊðɪən/ former county of SE Scotland, merged with West Lothian and Midlothian in 1975 in the new region of ◊Lothian. Haddington was the county town.

Eastman /ˈiːstmən/ George 1854–1932. American businessman and inventor who founded the Kodak photographic company. From 1888 he marketed daylight-loading flexible roll films (to replace the glass plates used previously) and portable cameras for use with them. By 1900 his company was selling a pocket camera for as little as $1. Today the Eastman-Kodak company is the 28th largest in the United States, employing more than 127,000 people.

East River /ˈiːst/ tidal strait 26 km/16 mi long, between Manhattan and the Bronx, and Long Island, in New York, USA. It links Long Island Sound with New York Bay, and is also connected, via the Harlem river, with the Hudson. There are both commercial and naval docks, and most famous of its many bridges is the Brooklyn.

East Siberian Sea /ˈiːst saɪˈbɪərɪən/ part of the ◊Arctic Ocean, off the N coast of USSR, between the New Siberian Islands and Chukchi Sea.

East Sussex /ˈiːst ˈsʌsɪks/ county in SE England
area 1,795 sq km/693 sq mi

towns administrative headquarters Lewes; cross-channel port of Newhaven; Brighton, Eastbourne, Hastings, Bexhill, Winchelsea, Rye
population (1986) 678,900.
features Beachy Head, highest headland on the S coast at 180 m/590 ft, the E end of the South ◊Downs; the Weald (including Ashdown Forest); the modern Friston Forest; rivers Ouse, Cuckmere, East Rother; Romney Marsh; the 'Long Man' chalk hill figure at Wilmington, near Eastbourne; Herstmonceux, with a 15th-century castle (conference and exhibition centre) and adjacent modern buildings housing, from 1958, Greenwich Royal Observatory; other castles at Hastings, Lewes, Pevensey, and Bodiam; Battle Abbey and the site of the Battle of Hastings; Michelham Priory; Sheffield Park garden; University of Sussex at Falmer, near Brighton, founded in 1961.
famous people former homes of Henry James at Rye, Rudyard Kipling at Burwash, Virginia Woolf at Rodmell.

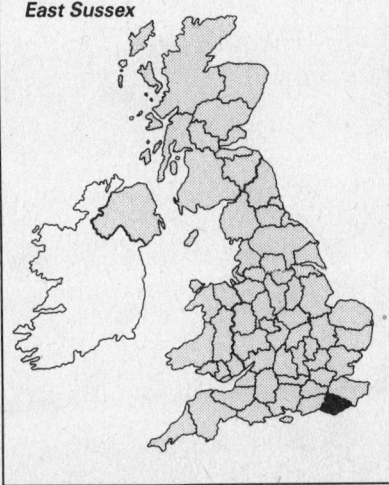

East Sussex

East Timor /ˈtiːmɔː/ former Portuguese colony with a predominantly Roman Catholic population. Following the Portuguese revolution (1974), Portugal withdrew from the island and the left-wing Revolutionary Front of Independent East Timor (Fretilin) occupied the capital, Dili, calling for independence. Opposed to this course, troops of neighbouring Indonesia immediately invaded the territory and established control, declaring East Timor (*Loro Sae*) the 17th province of Indonesia in Jul 1976. The Indonesian occupation has, however, always been opposed by the local population and Fretilin guerrillas, and has not been recognized by the United Nations. Since 1975 more than 100,000 are thought to have died from disease, starvation, and intermittent warfare, and 7,000 Indonesian troops remain stationed there.

Eastwood /ˈiːstwʊd/ Clint 1930– . American film actor. As the 'man with no name' caught up in Wild West lawlessness in *A Fistful of Dollars* 1964, he started the vogue for 'spaghetti westerns'.

eau de cologne a refreshing scent, weaker than perfume, whose invention is ascribed to Giovanni Maria Farina (1685–1766), who moved from Italy to Cologne in 1709 to manufacture it.

Ebbw Vale /ˈebuː ˈveɪl/ town in Gwent, Wales; population (1978) 25,710. The iron and steel industries ended in the 1970s, but tin-plate manufacture continues. Aneurin ◊Bevan was Member of Parliament for Ebbw Vale 1929–60. To the east is Blaenavon, where the Big Pit (no longer working) is a tourist attraction.

EBCDIC (*extended binary coded decimal interchange code*) in computing, a code used for storing and communicating alphabetic and numeric characters. It is an eight-digit code, representing up to 256 different characters by a ◊binary number system. It is still used in many mainframe computers but almost all mini-and microcomputers now use ◊ASCII code.

ebony tropical hardwood tree, genus *Diospyros* of the family Ebenaceae. Its very heavy, hard black timber takes a fine polish; and is used in cabinet-making, inlaying, and also for piano-keys and knife-handles.

Eboracum /iːˈbɒrəkəm/ Roman name for ◊York. The archbishop of York signs himself 'Ebor'.

Ebro /ˈiːbrəʊ/ river in NE Spain, which rises in the Cantabrian Mountains and flows some 800 km/500 mi SE to meet the Mediterranean SW of Barcelona. Zaragoza is on its course, and ocean-going ships can sail as far as Tortosa, 35 km/22 mi from its mouth. It is a major source of hydro-electric power.

EC abbreviation for ◊European Community.

eccentricity in geometry, a property of a ◊conic section (circle, ellipse, parabola, or hyperbola). It is the distance of any point on the curve from a fixed point (the focus) divided by the distance of that point from a fixed line (the directrix). A circle has an eccentricity of zero; for an ellipse it is less than one, for a parabola equal to one, and for a hyperbola greater than one.

Eccles /ˈeklz/ town near Manchester, England, 8 km/5 mi W of Manchester, on the river Irwell and Manchester Ship Canal. Population (1981) 37,166. Industries include cotton textiles, machinery, and pharmaceuticals. Eccles cakes, rounded pastries with a dried fruit filling, originated here.

Eccles /ˈeklz/ John Carew 1903– . Australian physiologist, who in 1963 shared a Nobel prize (with Alan ◊Hodgkin and Andrew ◊Huxley) for work on conduction in the central nervous system. He argued that the mind has an existence independent of the brain.

ecdysis the periodic shedding of the ◊exoskeleton, the outer covering or skin of insects and other arthropods to allow growth. Prior to shedding, a new soft and expandable layer is first laid down underneath the existing one. The old layer then splits, the animal moves free of it, and the new layer expands and hardens.

Echegaray /ˌetʃɪɡəˈraɪ/ José 1832–1916. Spanish dramatist. His dramas include *O locura o santidad*/*Madman or Saint* 1877, and *El gran*

Galeoto/The World and his Wife 1881, and he received the Nobel Prize for Literature in 1904.

echidna or *spiny ant-eater*. Several species of toothless egg-laying mammals, in the order Monotremata, found in Australia and New Guinea. They have spines like the hedgehog, are terrestrial in their habits, and feed entirely upon ants and termites which they dig out with their powerful claws and lick up with their prehensile tongue. When attacked echidnas roll themselves into a ball, or try to hide by burrowing in the earth.

echinoderm marine invertebrate which has a basic body structure divided into five sectors. The phylum Echinodermata ('spiny-skinned') includes the starfish, brittlestars, sea-lilies, sea urchins and sea-cucumbers. The skeleton is external, made of a series of limy plates, and echinodermata generally move using tube-feet – small water-filled sacs which can be protruded or pulled back to the body.

echo a reflection of a ◊sound wave, or of a ◊radar or ◊sonar signal. By accurately measuring the time taken for a echo to return to the transmitter, and from the knowledge of the speed of a radar signal (the speed of light) or a sonar signal (the speed of sound in water), it is possible to calculate the range of the object causing the echo. A similar technique is used in echo-sounders to estimate the depth of water under a ship's keel or the depth of a shoal of fish.

echolocation a method used by certain animals, notably bats and dolphins, to detect the positions of objects using sound. The animal emits a stream of high-pitched sounds, generally at ◊ultrasonic frequencies, and listens for the returning echoes reflected off objects ahead. As with ◊radar, the distance of an object can be determined by the time difference between the emitted sound and its return as an echo. Echolocation is of particular value under conditions when normal vision is poor (at night in the case of bats, in murky water for dolphins). A few species of bird can also echolocate.

echo-sounder a device that detects objects under water by means of ◊sonar bouncing sound waves off them. Most boats are equipped with echo-sounders to measure the water depth beneath them. The echo-sounder comprises a transmitter, which emits an ◊ultrasonic pulse, and a receiver, which detects its echo after being reflected from the seabed. The time between transmission and receipt of the reflected signal is a measure of the depth of water. Fishing boats also use echo-sounders to detect shoals of fish.

Eckhart /'ekhɑːt/ Johannes, called Meister Ekhart c. 1260–1327. German mystic. Born near Gotha, he became a Dominican friar, and was provincial of the order for Saxony 1304–11. He taught in Paris, Strasbourg, and Cologne, where in 1326 he was accused of heresy; in 1329 a number of his doctrines were condemned by the pope as heretical.

eclipse the event when one astronomic body passes into the shadow of another. A *solar eclipse* occurs when the Moon passes in front of the Sun as seen from Earth, and covers it either partially or totally. A solar eclipse can happen only during a new Moon. During a total eclipse the Sun's ◊corona can be seen. A total solar eclipse can last just over 7.5 minutes. When the Moon is at its farthest from Earth it does not completely cover the face of the Sun, leaving a ring of sunlight visible. This is an *annular eclipse* (from the Latin word *annulus*, ring). Between two and five solar eclipses occur each year.

A *lunar eclipse* occurs when the Moon passes into the shadow of the Earth, so that the Moon's surface becomes dim until emerging from the shadow. Lunar eclipses may be partial or full, and they can happen only at full Moon. Total lunar eclipses last for up to 100 minutes; the maximum number each year is three.

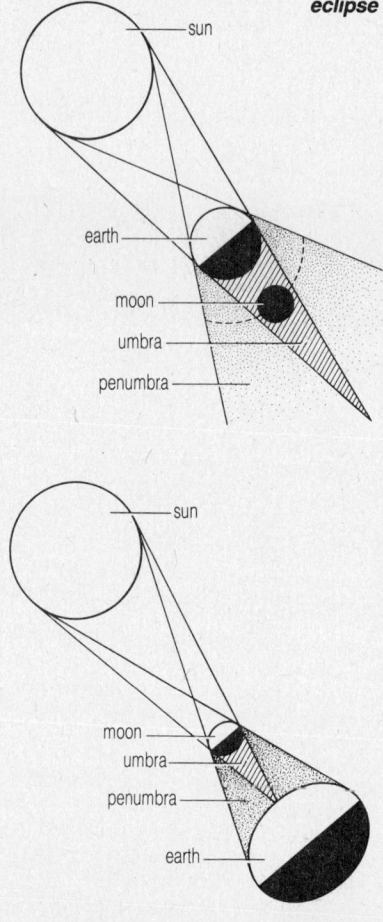

eclipse

eclipsing binary a ◊binary (double) star in which the two stars periodically pass in front of each other as seen from Earth. When one star crosses in front of the other the total light received on Earth from the two stars declines. The first eclipsing binary to be noticed was ◊Algol.

ecliptic the path against the star background that the Sun appears to follow each year as the Earth orbits the Sun. It can be thought of as the plane of the Earth's orbit projected on to the ◊celestial sphere (imaginary sphere around the Earth). The ecliptic is tilted at about 23.5° with respect to the celestial equator, a result of the actual tilt of the Earth's axis with regard to the Sun.

Eco /'ekəʊ/ Umberto 1932– . Italian semiologist and literary critic (*The Role of the Reader* 1979), and author of the 'philosophical thriller' *The Name of the Rose* 1983.

Ecole Nationale d'Administration French government school (ENA) established in Paris in 1945 to train apolitical top administrators. ◊Giscard d'Estaing and ◊Chirac were students.

ecology (from Greek *oikos*, house) the study of the relationship between an organism and the ◊environment in which it lives, including other living organisms and the non-living surroundings. The term was first introduced by the biologist Ernst Haeckel in 1866. Ecology may be concerned with individual organisms (for example, behavioural ecology, foraging strategies), with ◊populations or ◊species (for example, population dynamics) or with entire ◊communities (for example, competition between species for access to resources in an ◊ecosystem, or predator-prey relationships). Applied ecology is concerned with the management and ◊conservation of habitats and the consequences and control of ◊pollution.

ecology

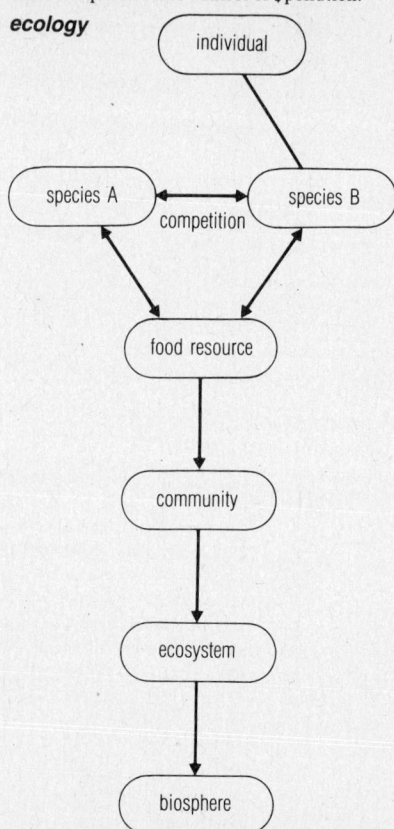

econometrics in economics, the use of mathematical and statistical approaches to the study of economic relationships, including testing economic theories and making quantitative predictions.

economic community or *common market* an organization of autonomous countries formed to promote trade. Examples include: ◊Caribbean

Community (Caricom) 1973, Central African Economic Community 1985, European Economic Community (EEC) 1957 (see ◊European Community), ◊Latin American Economics System 1975 (see ◊Latin America).

economics the study of how, in a given society, choices are made on the allocation of resources to produce goods and services for consumption, and the mechanisms and principles that govern this process. Economics seeks to apply scientific method to construct theories about the processes involved and to test them against what actually happens. Its two central concerns are the efficient allocation of available resources, and the problem of reconciling finite resources with a virtually infinite desire for goods and services. Economics analyses the ingredients of economic efficiency in the production process, and the implications for practical policies, and examines conflicting demands or resources and the consequences of whatever choices are made, whether by individuals, enterprises, or governments.

The subject is usually divided into the disciplines of ◊*microeconomics*, studying individual producers, consumers or markets, and ◊*macroeconomics*, studying whole economies or systems (in particular, areas such as ◊taxation and public spending). These spheres often overlap, but in practice it is useful to distinguish between the two main levels at which economic phenomena are studied.

Straddling both spheres is the sub-discipline of *econometrics*, which analyses economic relationships using mathematical and statistical techniques. Increasingly sophisticated econometric methods are today being used for such topics as economic forecasting.

Economics aims to be either *positive*, presenting objective and scientific explanations of how an economy works, or *normative*, offering prescriptions and recommendations on what should be done to cure perceived ills. However, almost inevitably, value judgements are involved in all economists' formulations.

Economics came of age as a separate area of study with the publication of Adam ◊Smith's *The Wealth of Nations* in 1776; the economist Alfred Marshall (1842–1924) established the orthodox position of 'neo-classical' economics, which, as modified by J M ◊Keynes (1883–1946) remains the standard today. Major economic thinkers include ◊Ricardo, ◊Malthus, J S ◊Mill, Karl ◊Marx, ◊Pareto, and Milton ◊Friedman.

ecosystem an integrated unit in ◊ecology comprising the ◊community of living organisms and the physical environment in a particular area. Energy and nutrients pass through the organisms in an ecosystem in a particular sequence: energy is captured through ◊photosynthesis, and nutrients are taken up from the soil or water by plants; both are passed to the herbivores that eat the plants and so to the carnivores that feed on the herbivores (see ◊food chain). These nutrients are later returned to the soil through the ◊decomposition of excreta and dead organisms, thus completing a cycle which is crucial to the continued stability and survival of the ecosystem. The relationships between

species in an ecosystem can be complex and finely balanced, so that removal of one species may be disastrous. If a major predator is removed, for example, this can result in the destruction of the ecosystem through overgrazing by herbivores.

ectoparasite a ◊parasite that lives on the outer surface of its host.

ectoplasm part of a cell's ◊cytoplasm.

ectotherm an animal such as a lizard that relies on external warmth (ultimately from the sun) to raise its body temperature so that it can become active; commonly called 'cold-blooded'. See also ◊endotherm, ◊poikilotherm.

ECU acronym for European Currency Unit, a unit derived from the value of several different currencies used in the ◊Common Market and in international trade. See also ◊European Monetary System.

Ecuador /'ekwədɔː/ country in South America, bounded to the north by Colombia, to the east and south by Peru, and to the west by the Pacific Ocean.

government Ecuador is not a fully federal state, but has a devolved system of 20 provinces, each administered by an appointed governor. The 1979 constitution provides for a president and a single-chamber national congress, the 71-member chamber of representatives, both popularly elected for a four-year term. The president is not eligible for re-election. Seven of the 16 political parties formed a left-wing coalition in 1984.

history conquered by the ◊Inca in the 15th century, Ecuador was invaded and colonized by Spain from 1532, becoming part of Gran Colombia in 1819. After joining other South American colonies in a revolt against Spain, Ecuador was liberated in 1822 by Antonio José de ◊Sucre, and became fully independent in 1830. Since independence, Peru has repeatedly invaded Ecuador because of boundary disputes, which remain unresolved.

From independence onwards the political pendulum has swung from the Conservatives to the Liberals, from civilian to military rule, and from democracy to dictatorship. By 1948 some stability was evident and eight years of Liberal government ensued. In 1956, Dr Camilo Ponce became the first Conservative president for 60 years. Four years later a Liberal, Dr José Maria Velasco (president 1933–35, 1944–47 and 1952–56), was re-elected. He was deposed in 1961 by the vice-president, who was himself replaced by a military junta the following year. In 1968 Velasco returned from exile and took up the presidency again. Another coup in 1972 put the military back in power until, in 1978, when it seemed as if Ecuador had returned permanently to its pre-1948 political pattern, a new, democratic constitution was adopted.

The 1979 constitution has survived, though economic deterioration has caused strikes, demonstrations and, in 1982, a state of emergency. In the 1984 elections there was no clear majority in the national congress, and the Conservative León Febres Cordero became president on a promise of 'bread, roofs and jobs'. With no immediate support in congress, his policies seemed likely to be blocked but in 1985

he won a majority when five opposition members shifted their allegiance to him.

ecumenical movement movement for reunification of the various branches of the Christian Church. It began in the 19th century with the extension of missionary work to the Third World, where the divisions created in Europe were incomprehensible, and gathered momentum from the need for unity in the face of growing secularism in Christian countries and of the challenge of such faiths as Islam. The *World Council of Churches* was founded 1948.

eczema an inflammatory skin condition marked by dryness, rashes and itching, the formation of blisters, and the exudation of fluid. It may sometimes be allergic in origin, and in some cases is complicated by infection.

Edam /'iːdəm/ town in the Netherlands on the river Ij, North Holland province, Population (1984) 24,019. It is famous for its round cheeses covered in red wax.

Edda name given to two collections of early Icelandic literature, which together constitute our chief source for the old Scandinavian mythology. The term strictly applies to the *Younger* or *Prose Edda*, compiled by Snorri Sturluson, a priest, about 1230. The *Elder* or *Poetic Edda* is the name given to a collection of poems, discovered by Brynjólfr Sveinsson, about 1643, and written by unknown Norwegian poets of the 9th to 12th centuries.

Eddington /'edɪŋtən/ Arthur Stanley 1882–1944. British astrophysicist. Professor of astronomy at Cambridge from 1913, he worked on the motions and equilibrium of stars, their luminosity and atomic structure. In 1919 his observation of stars during an ◊eclipse confirmed Einstein's prediction that light is bent when passing near the Sun. In his *Expanding Universe* 1933 he expressed the theory that in the spherical universe the outer galaxies or spiral nebulae are receding from one another. Knighted 1930, Order of Merit 1938.

Eddison /'edɪsən/ Eric Rucker 1882–1945. British author of heroic fantasies, notably *The Worm Ouroboros* 1922.

Eddy /'edi/ Mary Baker 1821–1910. American founder of the Christian Science movement. Born in New Hampshire, she was brought up as a ◊Congregationalist. Her faith in divine healing was confirmed by her recovery from injuries caused by a fall in 1866. Her pamphlet *Science of Man* 1869 was followed by *Science and Health* 1875, which she constantly revised until her death. In 1876 she founded the Christian Science Association. She married A G Eddy, one of her disciples, in 1877. In 1879 the Church of Christ, Scientist, was established, and although living in retirement after 1892 she continued to direct the activities of the movement until her death.

eddy current an electric current induced, in accordance with ◊Faraday's laws, in a conductor sited in a changing magnetic field. Eddy currents can cause much wasted energy in the cores of transformers and other electrical machines.

Eddystone Rocks /'edɪstən/ rocks in the English Channel, 23 km/14 mi S of Plymouth.

Ecuador
REPUBLIC OF (*República del Ecuador*)

AREA 301,150 sq km/116,270 sq mi
CAPITAL Quito
TOWNS Cuenca; chief port Guayaquil
PHYSICAL Andes mountains, divided by a
central plateau, or Valley of the Volcanoes,
including Chimborazo and Cotopaxi, which
has a large share of the cultivable land and is
the site of the capital
FEATURES the untouched rain forest of the
Amazon basin has a wealth of wildlife;
Ecuador is crossed by the equator, from which
it derives its name; Galapagos Islands
HEAD OF STATE AND OF GOVERNMENT León Febres
Cordero from 1984
GOVERNMENT democratic republic
EXPORTS bananas, cocoa, coffee, sugar, rice,
balsa wood, fish
CURRENCY sucre (263.84 = £1 Sept 1987,
official rate)
POPULATION 9,378,000 (1985); annual growth
rate 2.9%
LANGUAGE Spanish (official); Quechuan,
Jivaroan
RELIGION Roman Catholic
LITERACY 82% male/76% female (1980 est)
GNP $11.6 bn (1983); $1,428 per head of
population
CHRONOLOGY
1830 Ecuador became an independent
republic.
1930–48 Great political instability.
1948–55 Liberals in power.
1956 First Conservative president for 60 years.
1960 Liberals returned, with José Velasco as
president.

Ecuador

1961 Velasco deposed and replaced by the
vice-president.
1963 Military junta installed.
1968 Velasco returned as president.
1972 A coup put the military back in power.
1978 New democratic constitution adopted.
1979 Liberals in power but opposed by right-
and left-wing parties.
1982 Deteriorating economy provoked strikes,
demonstrations and a state of emergency.
1983 Austerity measures introduced.
1985 No party with a clear majority in the
national congress. Febres Cordero narrowly
won the presidency for the Conservatives.

Eden British politician Anthony Eden delivers an
election speech at Nottingham in 1955, the year
he became prime minister. He was widely criticized
for his handling of the Suez crisis in 1956, which
led to his resignation.

by David I. It remained separate from Edinburgh
until 1856. Robert ◊Bruce made Edinburgh a
burgh in 1329, and established its port at Leith.
In 1544 the town was destroyed by the English.
After the union with England in 1707, Edinburgh
lost its political importance, but remained
culturally pre-eminent. Edinburgh University,
established in 1583, has a famous medical school
and the Koestler chair of parapsychology
(instituted 1985), the only such professorship in
the UK. The Heriot-Watt University
(established 1885; university status 1966) is
mainly a technical institution.
Edinburgh castle contains the 12th-century St
Margaret's chapel, the oldest building in
Edinburgh. The palace of Holyrood House was
built in the 15th and 16th centuries on the site of
a 12th-century abbey; it is the British sovereign's
official Scottish residence. ◊Rizzio was murdered
here in 1566, in the apartments of Mary Queen
of Scots. The *Parliament House*, begun in 1632,
is now the seat of the supreme courts. The
episcopal cathedral of St Mary, opened in 1879,
and St Giles parish church (mostly 15th-
century) are the principal churches. The Royal
Observatory has been at Blackford Hill since
1896. The two best known thoroughfares are
Princes Street and the Royal Mile. Development
of the area known as New Town was started in
1767.
Edinburgh is not a major industrial city, but
printing, publishing, banking, and insurance are
carried on and there are chemical manufactures,
distilling and brewing, and some shipbuilding. It
attracts many tourists, especially to the annual
Edinburgh festival of music and the arts.
Edirne /e'dɪəneɪ/ town in European Turkey,
on the Maritza, about 225 km/140 mi NW of
Istanbul. It was formerly known as Adrianople.
Population (1975) 54,000.

The lighthouse, built in 1882, is the fourth on this
exposed site.
edelweiss perennial alpine plant
Leontopodium alpinum family Compositae,
with a white woolly star-shaped flower, found in
Eurasia and the Andes.
Eden /'iːdn/ in the Old Testament book of
Genesis, the 'garden' in which Adam and Eve
were placed after their creation, and from which
they were expelled for disobedience. It is usually
assumed that it was in Mesopotamia, part of
modern Iraq, and that two of its rivers were the
Euphrates and the Tigris.
Eden /'iːdn/ Anthony, 1st Earl of Avon
1897–1977. British Conservative politician. In
1935 he became foreign secretary, resigning in
Feb 1938 in protest against Chamberlain's
decision to open conversations with Mussolini,
and was foreign secretary again Dec 1940–45
and 1951–Apr 1955, when he succeeded
Churchill as prime minister. He negotiated an
interim peace in Vietnam 1954. His military
intervention in ◊Suez led to his resignation in Jan
1957. He received an earldom in 1960.
Edgar /'edgə/ c. 1050–c. 1130. English
prince, known as 'the Atheling', meaning 'of
royal blood'. Grandson of Edmund Ironside, he
was supplanted as heir to Edward the Confessor

by William the Conqueror. He led two rebellions
against William in 1068 and 1069, but made
peace with him in 1074.
Edgar /'edgə/ the Peaceful 944–975. King of
all England from 959. He was the younger son of
Edmund I, and strove successfully to unite
English and Danes as fellow subjects.
Edgehill /,edʒ'hɪl/ ridge in S Warwickshire,
England, where the first battle of the Civil War
took place in 1642, between Royalists under
Charles I and Parliamentarians under the Earl
of Essex. The result was indecisive.
Edgeworth /'edʒwɜːθ/ Maria 1767–1849.
Irish novelist. Her first novel, *Castle Rackrent*
1800, dealt with Anglo-Irish country society, and
was followed by the similar *The Absentee* 1812
and *Ormond* 1817.
Edinburgh /'edɪnbərə/ city and capital of
Scotland in the region of ◊Lothian (of which it is
the administrative town), near the S shores of the
Firth of Forth; population (1982) 447,741.
history in Roman times the site was occupied by
Celtic peoples, and about 617 was captured by
Edwin of Northumbria, from whom the town
took its name. The early settlement grew up
round a castle on Castle Rock, while about a mile
to the east another burgh, Canongate, developed
round the abbey of Holyrood, founded in 1128

Edison /'edɪsən/ Thomas Alva 1847–1931. American scientist, one of the great inventors of his age. Born in Ohio, of Dutch-Scottish parentage, he became first a newsboy and then a ◊telegraph operator. His first invention was an automatic repeater for telegraphic messages. Later came the carbon transmitter (used as a microphone in the production of the Bell ◊telephone); the ◊phonograph; the electric filament lamp; a new type of storage ◊battery; and the kinetoscopic camera, an early form of cinematography. He also anticipated the Fleming thermionic valve. He supported direct current transmission (DC), but alternating current (AC) was eventually found to be more efficient and economic.

Edison In his physics laboratory at West Orange, New Jersey, the inventor Thomas Edison holds one of his 'Edison Effect' lamps. By his discovery of this 'effect' in 1880 he revealed one of the fundamental principles on which modern electronics rests.

Edmonton /'edməntən/ locality, once a town, part of the London borough of Enfield. John ◊Keats lived at Edmonton, and Charles ◊Lamb lived and died here. The Bell Inn is referred to in William ◊Cowper's poem *John Gilpin*.

Edmonton /'edməntən/ capital of Alberta Province, Canada, on the N Saskatchewan river. Population (1982) 560,085. It is the centre of an oil and mining area to the N and also of an agricultural and dairying region. Petroleum pipelines link Edmonton with Superior, Wisconsin, the USA, and Vancouver, British Columbia.

Edmund Ironside /'aɪənsaɪd/ c. 989–1016. King of England. The son of ◊Ethelred the Unready, he led the resistance to ◊Canute's invasion in 1015, and on Ethelred's death in 1016 was chosen as king by the citizens of London, while the Witan (the king's council) elected Canute. Edmund was defeated by Canute at Assandun (Ashington), Essex, and they divided the kingdom between them.

Edmund, St /'edmənd/ c. 840–870. King of East Anglia from 855. In 870 he was defeated and captured by the Danes at Hoxne, Suffolk, and martyred on refusing to renounce Christianity. He was canonized and his shrine at Bury St Edmunds became a place of pilgrimage.

Edom /'iːdəm/ in the Old Testament, a mountainous area of S Palestine, which stretched from the Dead Sea to the Gulf of Aqaba. Its people, supposedly descendants of Esau, were enemies of the Israelites.

education the process, beginning at birth, of developing people's intellectual capacity, manual skill, and social awareness, especially by giving instruction. In its more restricted sense, the term refers to the process of imparting literacy, numeracy, and a generally accepted body of knowledge.

history of education the earliest known European educational systems are those of ancient Greece – in Sparta devoted mainly to the development of military skills, in Athens to politics, philosophy and public speaking, but both accorded only to the privileged few.

In ancient China, formalized education received a decisive impetus from the imperial decree of 165 BC, which set up open competitive examinations for the recruitment of members of the civil service, based mainly on a detailed study of literature.

Rome adopted the Greek system of education, and spread it through western Europe. Following the disintegration of the Roman Empire, widespread education vanished from Europe, though monks preserved both learning and the Latin tongue. Charlemagne's monastic schools which taught the 'seven liberal arts' – grammar, logic, rhetoric, arithmetic, geometry, music, and astronomy – produced the theological philosophers of the Scholastic Movement, which in the 11th to 13th centuries led to the foundation of the universities of Paris (◊Sorbonne), Bologna, Padua, ◊Oxford and ◊Cambridge. The capture of Constantinople by the Turks in 1453 sent the Christian scholars who had congregated there into exile across Europe, and revived European interest in learning. Compulsory attendance at primary schools was first established in the mid-18th century in Prussia, and has since spread almost worldwide.

UK education it was not until the 19th century in England that attempts were made to spread literacy throughout society. The Factory Act of 1802 required that during the first four years of their apprenticeship children employed by the owners of the newly arising factories were taught reading, writing, and arithmetic. The requirement was not always observed, but it embodied a new principle. The British and Foreign Schools Society (1808) and the National Society for Promoting the Education of the Poor in the Principles of the Established Church (1811) set up schools in which basic literacy and numeracy as well as religious knowledge were taught. In 1862 government grants became available for the first time for schools attended by children up to 12. The Elementary Education Act of 1870 (Forster's Act) established district school boards all over the country whose duty was to provide facilities for the elementary education of all children not otherwise receiving it. Once the principle of elementary education for all was established, the idea of higher education being widely available began to be accepted. The Education Act of 1944 introduced a system of secondary education for all, and formed the foundation of much education policy today. This has been revised by two further acts in 1980, which repealed previous legislation (1976) enforcing ◊comprehensive reorganization, and gave new rights to parents; by the 1981 Education Act which made new provisions for the education of children with special needs, and by legislation in 1986 giving further powers to school governors as part of a move towards increased parental involvement in schools, and in 1987 on the remuneration of teachers. An education bill 1987 proposes further reorganization.

In the UK the Department of Education and Science (DES), established in 1964 and headed by a Cabinet Minister, is responsible for non-military scientific research and for universities throughout Great Britain, and school education in England. In Wales primary and secondary education is the responsibility of the Welsh Education Office. There is a Scottish Education Department, under the Secretary of State for Scotland, and until direct rule (1972) Northern Ireland had its own Ministry of Education. Local education authorities (LEAs) are education committees of metropolitan or county councils, responsible for providing educational services locally under the general oversight of the DES. There are 104 LEAs in England and Wales. In Northern Ireland the responsibility for education is held by the Education and Library Boards.

US education in the USA, education is mainly the responsibility of the states, but the Department of Health, Education, and Welfare (1953), headed by a Secretary who is a member of the president's Cabinet, includes a commissioner of education responsible for federal aspects. Education is normally divided into (optionally) nursery or kindergarten (to age 5), elementary or grammar school (6 to 11), junior high school (12 to 14), and high school (15 to 18). The basic school-leaving qualification is the high school diploma, normally awarded by the individual school or local school district on successful completion of a broad secondary school curriculum. There is no national school-leaving examination, although there is a national examination used to help select students for college (university) entrance, the Scholastic Aptitude Test (SAT). A large proportion of US high-school graduates goes on to higher education, either at a state-funded or private college or university.

educational psychology the work of psychologists primarily in schools, including the assessment of children with achievement problems and advising on problem behaviour in the classroom.

Edward, Lake /'edwəd/ lake in Uganda, at about 900 m/3,000 ft above sea level in the Albertine rift valley. From 1973–79 it was known as Lake Idi Amin Dada, after President ◊Amin of Uganda.

Edward /'edwəd/ Prince 1964– . Prince of the UK, third son of Queen Elizabeth II.

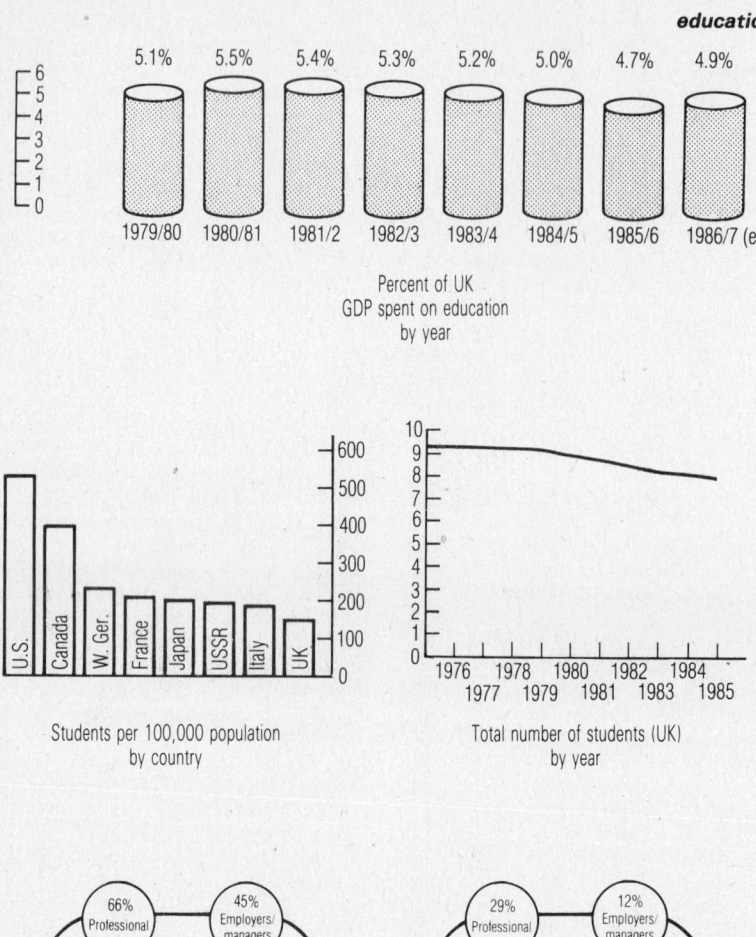

education

5.1% 5.5% 5.4% 5.3% 5.2% 5.0% 4.7% 4.9%

1979/80 1980/81 1981/2 1982/3 1983/4 1984/5 1985/6 1986/7 (est)

Percent of UK
GDP spent on education
by year

U.S. Canada W. Ger. France Japan USSR Italy UK

Students per 100,000 population
by country

1976 1977 1978 1979 1980 1981 1982 1983 1984 1985

Total number of students (UK)
by year

66% Professional   45% Employers/ managers
16 to 18 year olds
43% Other white collar   25% Skilled manual   18% Other manual

29% Professional   12% Employers/ managers
20 to 24 year olds
13% Other white collar   2% Skilled manual   3% Other manual

Participation in education (UK)
according to
parents' social class

Edward A coin stamped with the head of the pious English king Edward the Confessor. His death in 1066 triggered off the events leading to the Norman Conquest, for William the Conqueror claimed the English throne had been bequeathed him by Edward.

Edward /'edwəd/ the Black Prince 1330–1376. Prince of Wales, eldest son of Edward III. The epithet supposedly derived from his black armour. During the Hundred Years' War he served at the Battle of Crécy; defeated and captured the French king at Poitiers 1356, and in 1367 invaded Castile and restored to the throne the deposed king, Pedro the Cruel (1334–69). Ill health kept him from public life after 1371.

Edward /'edwəd/ eleven kings of England or the UK:

Edward, St /'edwəd/ (the Confessor) c. 1003–1066. King of England from 1042. The son of Ethelred II, he lived in Normandy until shortly before his accession. During his reign power was held by Earl ◊Godwin and his son ◊Harold while the king devoted himself to religion. He was buried in Westminster Abbey, which he had rebuilt; canonized 1161.

Edward, St /'edwəd/ (the Martyr) c. 963–978. King of England from 975. Son of King Edgar, he was murdered at Corfe Castle, probably at his stepmother Aelfthryth's instigation (she wished to secure the crown for her son, Ethelred). He was canonized in 1001.

Edward I /'edwəd/ 1239–1307. King of England from 1272. Son of Henry III, he led the royal forces in the ◊Barons' War 1264–67, and was on a crusade when he succeeded to the throne. He established English rule over all Wales 1282–84, and secured recognition of his overlordship from the Scottish king, though the Scots (under Wallace and Bruce) fiercely resisted actual conquest. In his reign Parliament took its approximate modern form with the Model Parliament of 1295.

Edward II /'edwəd/ 1284–1327. King of England from 1307. Son of Edward I, and born at ◊Caernarvon, he was created the first prince of Wales in 1301. Incompetent and frivolous, and entirely under the influence of his favourites, he struggled throughout his reign with discontented barons. His invasion of Scotland in 1314 to suppress Bruce's revolt resulted in defeat at ◊Bannockburn. He was deposed in 1327 by his wife Isabella (1292–1358), daughter of Philip IV of France, and her lover ◊Mortimer, and murdered in Berkeley Castle, Gloucestershire.

Edward III /'edwəd/ 1312–1377. King of England from 1327. Son of ◊Edward II, he assumed the government from his mother in 1330. He began his reign by attempting to force his rule on Scotland, winning a victory at Halidon Hill 1333. In 1337 he began the Hundred Years' War by claiming the French throne by right of his mother. During the first stage of the war, the English defeated the French at Crécy 1346, won naval victories at Sluys 1340 and Winchelsea 1350, and captured Calais 1347, while Edward's son, the Black Prince, defeated and captured the French king at Poitiers 1356. The war ended temporarily in 1360 with the Treaty of Brétigny, by which Edward surrendered his claim to the throne in return for Calais, Aquitaine, and Gascony. After its renewal in 1369 the French recaptured all the English gains in France except Calais, Bordeaux and Bayonne.

Edward IV /'edwəd/ 1442–1483. King of England from 1461. Son of Richard, Duke of York, he was known as Earl of March until his accession. After his father's death Edward occupied London in 1461, and was proclaimed king in place of Henry VI by a council of peers. His position was secured by the defeat of the Lancastrians at Towton (1461) and by the capture of Henry. He quarrelled, however, with Warwick, his strongest supporter, who in 1470–71 temporarily restored Henry, until

Edward recovered the throne by his victories at Barnet and Tewkesbury.

Edward V /'edwəd/ 1470–1483. King of England 1483. Son of Edward IV, he was deposed three months after his accession in favour of his uncle (◊Richard III), and is traditionally believed to have been murdered (with his brother) in the Tower of London on Richard's orders.

Edward VI /'edwəd/ 1537–1553. King of England from 1547, son of Henry VIII and Jane Seymour. The government was entrusted to his uncle the Duke of Somerset, and after his fall in 1549 to the Earl of Warwick, later created Duke of Northumberland. While still a child, Edward became a Protestant, and strongly supported the policy of advancing the Reformation adopted by both Somerset and Northumberland. He died of tuberculosis.

Edward VI A portrait after Holbein painted c. 1542 of Prince Edward. Only son of Henry VIII, he became King Edward VI at the age of ten, and died of tuberculosis before reaching adulthood.

Edward VII /'edwəd/ 1841–1910. King of Great Britain and Ireland from 1901. Born at Buckingham Palace, the eldest son of Queen Victoria and Prince Albert. In 1860 he made the first tour of Canada and the USA ever undertaken by a British prince. After his father's death in 1861 he undertook many public duties, but the Queen considered him too frivolous to take part in political life. Nevertheless, he took a close interest in politics, and was on friendly terms with the party leaders. In 1863 he married Princess Alexandra of Denmark, by whom he had six children. He toured India in 1875–76, was a prominent social figure, had several mistresses, and was a keen yachtsman and sportsman. He succeeded to the throne in 1901, and was crowned in 1902. Although he overrated his political influence, he contributed to the Entente Cordiale of 1904 with France, and the Anglo-Russian agreement of 1907.

Edward VIII /'edwəd/ 1894–1972. King of Great Britain and Ireland from 1936. Eldest son

Edward VII The Prince of Wales, as he was known until crowned, contemplates his prize, a wild bull shot by him during a visit to Chillingham Castle, Northern Ireland.

of George V, he was created Prince of Wales in 1910 and succeeded to the throne on 20 Jan 1936. As king he showed concern for the problems of the Glasgow slums and the distressed areas of South Wales.

In Nov 1936 a constitutional crisis arose when Edward wished to marry Mrs Wallis Warfield (Simpson) (1896–1986), an American, since it was felt that, as a divorcee, she would be unacceptable as queen. On 11 Dec Edward abdicated and left for France, where the couple were married in in 1937. He received the title of duke of Windsor and was governor of the Bahamas 1940–45, subsequently settling in France.

Edwards /'edwədz/ George 1908– . British civil and military aircraft designer. He was associated with the *Viking, Viscount, Valiant V-bomber, VC-10* and *Concorde*. Order of Merit 1971.

Edwards /'edwədz/ Jonathan 1703–1758. American theologian, who took a ◊Calvinist view of predestination, and initiated a religious revival, the 'Great Awakening'. His *The Freedom of the Will* (defending determinism) 1754 received renewed attention in the 20th century.

Edwards Air Force Base /'edwədz/ military USAF centre in California, situated on a dry lake bed. Often used as a landing site by the ◊Space Shuttle.

Edwin /'edwin/ c. 585–633. king of Northumbria from 617. He captured and fortified Edinburgh, which was named after him, and was killed in battle with Penda of Mercia.

EEC abbreviation for European Economic Community; part of the ◊European Community.

eel order of fish Anguilliformes including: Europoean eel *Anguilla anguilla*, freshwater family Anguillidae; its snakelike body has some 260 vertebrae, weighs 75 kg/15 lb, and is valued as food. Capable of travelling long distances overland, eels die after spawning in special

Edward VIII The Duke and Duchess of Windsor in a Sussex village, Sept 1939. He came to the British throne in 1936, but abdicated eleven months later after a crisis over his wish to marry Mrs Wallis Simpson.

grounds at a depth of 7,000 m/23,000 ft in the ◊Sargasso Sea; the fry return after a period of years to European rivers, helped by the North Atlantic Drift.

Common Moray *Muraena helena*, of the Mediterranean, family Muraenidae, is brightly coloured and aggressive, reaching 2.5 m/8 ft. The flesh, poisonous till cooked, was thought a delicacy by the Romans.

Conger eel, family Congridae, of the Mediterranean and Atlantic, is also aggressive, and reaches 3 m/9 ft, 65 kg/140 lb.

eel Mature common eels, (*Anguilla anguilla*), caught in an eel trap built into the river, on their downward migration to the sea.

eel-grass or *glass wrack* flowering plant of tidal mud flats, *Zostera marina*, family Zosteraceae, one of the few flowering plants to adapt to marine conditions, being completely submerged at high tide.

efficiency in physics, the output of a machine (work done by the machine) divided by the input (work put into the machine), usually expressed as a percentage. Since the *mechanical advantage* or force ratio is the ratio of the load (the output force) to the effort (the input force), and the *velocity ratio* is the distance moved by the effort divided by the distance moved by the load, for certain machines the efficiency can also be defined as the mechanical advantage divided by the velocity ratio. Because of losses caused by friction, efficiency is always less than 100 per cent, although it can approach this for electrical machines with no moving parts (such as a transformer).

EFT abbreviation for ◊electronic funds transfer.

EFTA acronym of ◊European Free Trade Association.

Egbert /'egbɜːt/ d. 839, king of the West Saxons from 802. The son of Ealhmund, an under-king of Kent. By 829 he had united England for the first time under one king.

egg in animals, the ovum, or female ◊gamete (reproductive cell). After ◊fertilization by a sperm cell, it begins to divide to form an ◊embryo. Eggs may be deposited by the female (◊ovipary) or they may develop within her body (◊vivipary and ◊ovovivipary). In the oviparous reptiles and birds, the egg is protected by a shell, and well supplied with nutrients in the form of ◊yolk. In plants, the ovum is called an egg-cell.

eggplant another name for ◊aubergine, a plant with dark purple fruits which are cooked and eaten as a vegetable.

Egmont, Mount /'egmɒnt/ symmetrical extinct volcano in North Island, New Zealand; 2,517 m/8,260 ft high.

Egmont /'egmɒnt/ Lamoral, Count of Egmont 1522–1568. Flemish patriot. Born in Hainault, he defeated the French at St Quentin in 1557 and Gravelines in 1558, and became stadtholder (chief magistrate) of Flanders and Artois. From 1561 he helped to lead the movement against Spanish misrule, but in 1567 the Duke of Alva was sent to crush the resistance, and Egmont was beheaded.

ego (Latin 'I') in psychology, a general term for the processes concerned with the self and a person's conception of himself or herself, such as values and attitudes. In Freudian psychology, the term refers specifically to the element of the human mind that represents the conscious processes, concerned with reality, in conflict with the ◊id and the ◊superego.

egret type of heron. The great white egret *Egretta alba* of SE Europe and other parts of the Old World, which grows to a length of 1 m/3 ft, develops snowy-white plumes, used for hat ornaments until the practice was made illegal. The little egret *Egretta garzetta*, 0.6 m/2 ft, is found in Asia, Africa, S Europe and Australia.

Egypt /'iːdʒɪpt/ country in NE Africa, bounded to the north by the Mediterranean, to the east by the Suez Canal and Red Sea, to the south by Sudan, and to the west by Libya.
government the 1971 constitution provides for a single-chamber people's assembly of 458, ten nominated by the president and 448 elected for a five-year term by 48 constituencies. The president is nominated by the assembly and then elected by popular referendum for a six-year term, and is eligible for re-election. At least one vice-president and a council of ministers are appointed by the president.
history for early history see ◊Egypt, ancient. After its conquest by ◊Augustus in 30 BC Egypt passed under the rule of Roman, and later of Byzantine, governors, and Christianity superseded the ancient religion. The Arabs conquered Egypt 639–42, introducing ◊Islam and ◊Arabic to the area, and the country was ruled by successive Arab dynasties until 1250, when the ◊Mamelukes seized power. Mameluke rule lasted until 1517, when Egypt became part of the Turkish ◊Ottoman Empire.
Contact with Europe began with ◊Napoleon's invasion and the French occupation of 1798–1801. A period of anarchy followed, until in 1805 an Albanian officer, Mehemet Ali, was appointed pasha, a title which later became hereditary in his family. Under his successors Egypt met with economic difficulties over the building of the ◊Suez Canal (1859–69), to the extent that an Anglo-French commission was placed in charge of its finances. After subduing a nationalist revolt 1881–82, Britain occupied Egypt, and the government was from then on mainly in the hands of British civilian agents who directed their efforts particularly to the improvement of the Egyptian economy. On the outbreak of World War I in 1914, nominal Turkish suzerainty was abolished and the country was declared a British protectorate.
Post-war agitation by the nationalist Wafd party led to the granting of nominal independence in 1922, under King Fuad I. He was succeeded in 1936 by King Farouk and Britain agreed to recognize Egypt's full independence, announcing a phased withdrawal of its forces, except from the Suez Canal and Alexandria and Port Said, where it had naval bases. The start of World War II delayed the British departure, as did the consequent campaign in Libya which ended in the defeat of the German and Italian forces which had threatened the Canal Zone.
In 1946 all British troops except the Suez Canal garrison were withdrawn. In the immediate post-war years a radical movement developed, calling for an end to the British presence and opposing Farouk for his extravagant life style and his failure to prevent the growth of ◊Israel. This led, in 1952, to a bloodless coup by a group of army officers, led by Col Gamal ◊Nasser, who replaced Farouk with a military junta. The 1923 constitution was suspended and all political parties banned. The following year Egypt declared itself a republic, with Gen Mohammed Neguib as president and prime minister. In 1954 Nasser became prime minister and an agreement was signed for the withdrawal of British troops from the Canal Zone by 1956.
After a dispute with Neguib, Nasser took over as head of state and embarked on a programme of social reform. He became a major force for the creation of Arab unity. In 1956 the presidency was strengthened by a new constitution, and Nasser was elected president, unopposed. Later that year, British forces were withdrawn, in accordance with the 1954 agreement.
When the US and Britain cancelled their offers of financial aid for the ◊Aswan High Dam, Nasser responded by nationalizing the Suez Canal. In a contrived operation, Britain, France and Israel invaded the Sinai ◊Peninsula and two days later Egypt was attacked. US pressure brought a cease-fire and an Anglo-French withdrawal. The effect of the abortive Anglo-French operation was to push Egypt towards the USSR and to enhance Nasser's reputation in the Arab world. In 1958 Egypt and Syria merged to become the ◊United Arab Republic (UAR), with Nasser as president, but three years later Syria withdrew, though Egypt retained the title of UAR until 1971. The 1960s saw several unsuccessful attempts to federate Egypt, Syria and Iraq. Despite these failures Nasser's prestige among his neighbours grew, while at home, in 1962, he founded the Arab Socialist Union (ASU), as Egypt's only recognized political organization.
In 1967 Egypt led an attack on Israel which developed into the 'Six Day War', in which Israel defeated all its opponents, including Egypt. One result of the conflict was the blocking of the Suez Canal, which was not reopened until 1975. After Egypt's defeat, Nasser offered to resign but was persuaded to stay on. In 1969, aged 52, he died of a heart attack and was succeeded by Vice-President Col Anwar ◊Sadat.
In 1971 a new constitution was approved and the title Arab Republic of Egypt adopted. Sadat continued Nasser's policy of promoting Arab unity but proposals to create a federation of Egypt, Libya, and Syria again failed.
In 1973 an attempt was made to regain territory from Israel. After 18 days' fighting, US Secretary of State Henry ◊Kissinger arranged a cease-fire, resulting in Israel's evacuation of parts of Sinai, with a UN buffer zone separating the rival armies. This US intervention strengthened ties between the two countries while relations with the USSR cooled.
In 1977 Sadat went to Israel to plead for peace. Other Arab states were dismayed by this move and diplomatic relations with Syria, Libya, Algeria, and the Yemen, as well as the ◊Palestinian Liberation Organisation (PLO), were severed. Despite this opposition, Sadat pursued his peace initiative and at the ◊Camp David talks in the US, he and the Israeli prime minister, Menachem ◊Begin, signed two agreements. The first laid a framework for peace in the Middle East and the second a framework for a treaty between the two countries. In 1979 a treaty was signed and Israel began a phased withdrawal from Sinai. Egypt was, in consequence, expelled from the ◊Arab League. After acceding to the presidency, Sadat had begun to introduce a more liberal regime. In 1981 he was assassinated by a group of ◊Muslim fundamentalists who opposed him. and was succeeded by Lieut-Gen Hosni Mubarak, who had been vice-president since 1975.
Just as Sadat had continued the policies of his predecessor, so did Mubarak. In the 1984 elections the National Democratic Party, formed by Sadat in 1948, won an overwhelming victory

in the assembly, strengthening Mubarak's position. Although Egypt's treaty with Israel remains intact, relations between the two countries have been strained, mainly because of Israel's activities in ◊Lebanon. Egypt's relations with other Arab nations have improved and only Libya and Syria maintain their trade boycott. At home problems with Muslim fundamentalists have increased Mubarak's dependence on military support. President Mubarak was re-elected in Oct 1987.

Egypt *The Banquet*, a fragment of wall painting, is in the British Museum, London. Dating from c. 1400 BC, it comes from the ancient Egyptian city of Thebes and shows two rows of guests waited on by serving girls.

Egypt, ancient the Egyptian state was founded c. 3200 BC by the semi-legendary ◊Menes, who united Lower Egypt, in the delta, to his own kingdom of Upper Egypt in the Nile valley. Following the Archaic Period of the 1st and 2nd Dynasties (32nd–29th centuries), the 'Old Kingdom' reached the height of its power under the 4th Dynasty kings, who built the great pyramids at Gizeh (c. 26th century BC), and then gradually sank into anarchy. Unity was recovered under the 11th and 12th Dynasties (the 'Middle Kingdom', c. 22nd–18th centuries BC); there followed another period of anarchy resulting in the conquest of Egypt by the Semitic Hyksos. Their expulsion in 1580 BC marks the beginning of the 'New Kingdom'. Under the 18th Dynasty (1580–1370) a succession of able kings, notably Thothmes III (reigned 1484–1451), founded an empire in Palestine and Syria extending to the Euphrates. The golden age of Amenhotep III was probably continued under ◊Ikhnaton – although it is thought by some historians that his neglect of imperial defence for religious reforms led to the loss of most of Egypt's possessions in Asia – and also under the 19th Dynasty (Ramses II and Ramses III). However, during the 20th Dynasty there was undoubtedly a decline in Egyptian strength, and power within the country passed from the pharaohs to the priests of Ammon. Under the Late New Kingdom (1090–663 BC) Egypt was often divided between two or more dynasties; the nobles

became virtually independent, and in the 7th century the Assyrians established their suzerainty over Egypt. Psammetichus I (663–609) and his successors restored Egypt's independence, and attempted to restore the empire. This national revival ended when Cambyses in 525 brought Egypt under Persian rule, which survived, except for a period of independence c. 405–340, until Alexander conquered Egypt in 332. When his empire was divided Egypt went to Ptolemy, whose descendants ruled until Cleopatra's death in 30 BC.

Egyptian art see under ◊Ancient art.

Egyptian religion prehistoric Egyptian religion was based on the worship of totemic animals believed to be the ancestors of the clan. Totems later developed into gods, represented by the heads of the animals sacred to them; thus, the hawk was sacred to Ra and Horus, the ibis to Thoth, the jackal to Anubis. The cult of Osiris, who was murdered, mourned by his sister and wife Isis, and then rose again, was a fertility ritual similar to those of Tammuz and Dionysus; by a natural development Osiris became the god of the underworld. Under the 18th Dynasty a local deity of Thebes, Ammon, came to be regarded as supreme, a reflection of rediscovered national unity. Ikhnaton attempted, without success, to establish the monotheistic cult of Aton, the solar disc, as the one national god. Immortality, conferred by the magical rite of mummification, was originally the sole prerogative of the king, but was extended under the New Kingdom to all who could afford it.

egyptology the study of ancient Egypt. Interest in the subject was first stimulated by Napoleon's expedition of 1798, during which the Rosetta Stone was discovered. This contained the same inscription in Greek as well as the hieroglyphic and demotic scripts, and made possible the decipherment of the Egyptian inscriptions. Excavation continued throughout

the 19th century, and gradually assumed a more scientific character, largely as a result of the work of Sir Flinders Petrie from 1880 onwards, and the formation of the Egyptian Exploration Fund in 1892. The most celebrated discovery so far has been that of Tutankhamen's tomb by Howard Carter in 1922, the only royal tomb with all its treasures intact. Special branches of egyptology developed in more recent years are the study of prehistoric Egypt, and the search for papyri (ancient documents) preserved by the dryness of the climate; besides ancient Egyptian writings, many lost Greek and early Christian works have been recovered.

Ehrenburg /'erənbɜːg/ Ilya Grigorievich 1891–1967. Russian writer. Born in Kiev, he is noted particularly for the controversial *The Thaw* 1954, which depicts artistic circles in the USSR, and contributed to the growing of literary freedom in the 1950s.

Ehrlich /'eəlɪk/ Paul 1854–1915. German bacteriologist, concerned mostly with immunology. He developed the arsenic compounds used in the treatment of syphilis before the discovery of antibiotics. He shared a Nobel prize 1908.

Eichendorff /'aɪkəndɔːf/ Joseph Freiherr von 1788–1857. German poet and novelist. Born in Upper Silesia, he held various judicial posts, and wrote romantic stories, but is chiefly remembered as a lyric poet. His work was set to music by Schumann, Mendelssohn and Wolf.

Eichmann /'aɪkmən/ Karl Adolf 1906–1962. Austrian Nazi war criminal. As an SS official during ◊Hitler's regime he was responsible for atrocities against Jews and others, including the implementation of the ◊Final Solution. He managed to escape at the fall of Germany in 1945. Discovered in Argentina in 1960, he was abducted from Argentina by Israeli agents, tried in Israel during 1961 for the extermination of six million Jews, and executed.

eider large marine duck, *Somateria mollissima*, highly valued for its soft down, used in stuffing quilts and cushions. It breeds in northern latitudes, from the Farne Islands to Spitzbergen, and in Iceland and Norway it is bred for its down.

Eiffel Tower /'aɪfəl/ iron tower 320 m/1,050 ft designed by Gustave Alexandre Eiffel 1832–1923 for the Paris Exhibition of 1889, now in the Champ de Mars, Paris.

Eiger /'aɪgə/ mountain peak in the Swiss ◊Alps.

Eighth Route Army the Chinese 'Red Army' formed in 1927 when the Communists broke away from ◊Kuomintang (the Chinese Nationalist Party), and established a separate government in Kiangsi, in South East China. When the Japanese invaded China in 1937 it was recognized as a section of the national forces under the name Eighth Route Army.

Eijkman /'aɪkmən/ Christiaan 1858–1930. Dutch bacteriologist, who identified vitamin B_1 deficiency as the cause of beri-beri, and pioneered the recognition of vitamins as essential to health. Nobel prize 1929.

Eilat /eɪˈlɑːt/ alternative spelling of ◊Elat, a port in Israel.

Egypt

ARAB REPUBLIC OF (*Jumhuriyat Misr al-Arabiya*)

AREA 1,000,000 sq km/386,198 sq mi
CAPITAL Cairo
TOWNS Gîza; ports Alexandria, Port Said
PHYSICAL mostly desert; hills in E; fertile land along river Nile
FEATURES Aswan High Dam and Lake Nasser; Sinai; remains of Ancient Egypt (Pyramids, Sphinx, Luxor, Karnak, Abu Simbel, El Faiyum)
HEAD OF STATE AND OF GOVERNMENT Hosni Mubarak from 1981
GOVERNMENT (F12) DEMOCRATIC SOCIALIST
(F14) EXPORTS cotton and textiles
CURRENCY Egyptian pound (3.63 = £1 Sept 1987)
POPULATION 49 million (1985); annual growth rate 1.9%
LANGUAGE Arabic (ancient Egyptian survives to some extent in Coptic)
RELIGION Sunni Muslim 95%, Coptic Christian 5%
LITERACY 66% male/28% female (1980 est)
GDP $32 bn (1983); $686 per head of population
CHRONOLOGY
1914 Egypt became a British protectorate.
1936 Independence recognized. King Fuad succeeded by his son Farouk.
1946 Withdrawal of British troops except from Suez Canal Zone.
1952 Farouk overthrown by the army in a bloodless coup.
1953 Egypt declared a republic, with Gen Neguib as president.
1956 Neguib replaced by Col Gamal Nasser. Nasser announced nationalization of Suez Canal; Egypt attacked by Britain, France and Israel. Ceasefire agreed because of US intervention.
1958 Short-lived merger of Egypt and Syria as United Arab Republic (UAR). Subsequent

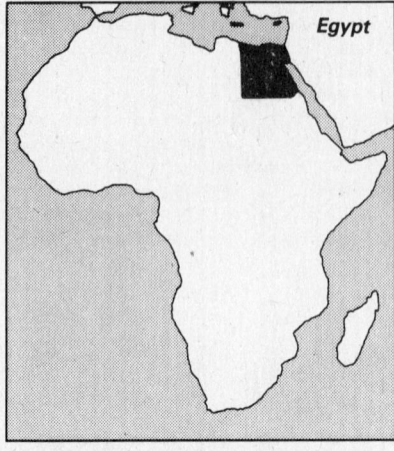

Egypt

attempts to federate Egypt, Syria, and Iraq failed.
1967 Six-Day War with Israel ended in Egypt's defeat and Israeli occupation of Sinai and the Gaza strip.
1970 Nasser died suddenly and was succeeded by Anwar Sadat.
1973 Attempt to regain territory lost to Israel led to fighting. Ceasefire arranged by US secretary of state Henry Kissinger.
1977 Visit by Sadat to Israel to address the Israeli parliament was criticized by Egypt's Arab neighbours.
1978–79 Camp David talks in the USA resulted in a treaty between Egypt and Israel. Egypt expelled from the Arab League.
1981 Sadat assassinated and succeeded by Hosni Mubarak.
1983 Improved relations between Egypt and the Arab world; only Libya and Syria maintained a trade boycott.
1984 Mubarak's party victorious in the people's assembly elections.
1987 Mubarak re-elected.

Eindhoven /'aɪndhəʊvən/ town in N Brabant province, Netherlands, on the river Dommel. Population (1985) 191,725. It is a manufacturing centre, chiefly of electrical equipment and electronics.

Einstein /'aɪnstaɪn/ Albert 1879–1955. German-Swiss physicist, who formulated the theories of ◊relativity and did important work in radiation physics and thermodynamics. Born at Ulm, in Württemberg, he lived with his parents in Munich and then in Italy. After teaching at the polytechnic school at Zürich he became a Swiss citizen and was appointed an inspector of patents at Berne. In his spare time he took his degree of PhD at Zürich, and some of his papers on physics were of such a quality that in 1909 he was given a chair of theoretical physics at the university. After holding a similar post at Prague 1911, he returned to teach at Zürich 1912, and in 1913 took up a specially created post as

director of the Kaiser Wilhelm Institute for Physics, Berlin. He received the Nobel Prize for Physics in 1921. After being deprived of his post at Berlin by the Nazis, he emigrated in 1933 to the USA and became professor of mathematics and a permanent member of the Institute for Advanced Study at Princeton, New Jersey. During World War II he worked for the US Navy Ordnance Bureau. In 1905 he had published his first theory – the so-called special theory of relativity – and in 1915 issued his general theory of relativity. His latest conception of the basic laws governing the universe was outlined in his unified field theory made public in 1953; and of the 'relativistic theory of the non-symmetric field', completed 1955. Einstein wrote that this simplified the derivations as well as the form of the field equations and the whole theory becomes thereby more transparent, without changing its content.

einsteinium metallic element (symbol Es, atomic number 99), one of the ◊lanthanide series, created by irradiation of uranium 238 with neutrons in the first thermonuclear explosion. Einsteinium has no present use.

Einthoven /'aɪnthəʊvən/ William 1860–1927. Dutch physiologist, inventor of the electrocardiograph, used in detecting heart disease.

Eire /'eərə/ Gaelic name for the Republic of ◊Ireland.

Eisenach /'aɪzənæx/ industrial town (pottery, vehicles, machinery), Erfurt district, East Germany; population (1972) 51,000. Martin ◊Luther made the first translation of the Bible into German in Wartburg Castle and J S ◊Bach was born here.

Eisenhower, Mount /'aɪzən,haʊə/ Rocky Mountain peak in Alberta, Canada, included in Banff National Park, 2,862 m/9,390 ft.

Eisenhower /'aɪzən,haʊə/ Dwight David ('Ike') 1890–1969. 34th president of the USA, born at Denison, Texas. In World War II he became commander-in-chief of the American and British forces for the invasion of North Africa Nov 1942; commanded the Allied invasion of Sicily Jul 1943, and announced the surrender of Italy on 8 Sept 1943. In Dec he became commander of the Allied invasion of Europe, and from Oct 1944 commanded all the Allied armies in the West. He resigned from the army in 1952 to campaign for the presidency as a Republican; he was elected, and re-elected in 1956, with Richard Nixon as vice-president. A popular hero, Eisenhower held office during a period of domestic and international tension, with the growing civil rights movement at home and the Cold War dominating international politics. Much criticized at the time for his lack of strong leadership, his presidency has since been favourably reassessed as maintaining stability in a time of crisis.

Eisenstein /'aɪzənstaɪn/ Sergei Mikhailovich 1898–1948. Soviet film director. He pioneered the use of montage (a technique of deliberately juxtaposing shots to create a particular meaning) as a means of propaganda, as in *The Battleship Potemkin* 1925. His *Alexander Nevsky* 1938 was the first part of an uncompleted trilogy, the second part, *Ivan the Terrible* 1944, being banned in Russia.

eisteddfod /aɪ'steðvɒd/ (Welsh 'sitting'). Traditional Welsh gathering for the encouragement of the bardic arts of music, poetry, and literature. Towns and rural communities often hold their own annual eisteddfod. The national eisteddfod traditionally dates from pre-Christian times, but it was discontinued from the late 17th century until the beginning of the 19th century, since when it has been held annually. The meetings last three to four days, and bardic degrees are awarded. The eisteddfod ends with the ceremony of 'chairing' the bard (the best contestant in verse).

Ekaterinburg /e,kætərinˈbɜːg/ pre-revolutionary name of ◊Sverdlovsk, a town in the western USSR, the site of the assassination of Tsar Nikolai II and his family in 1918.

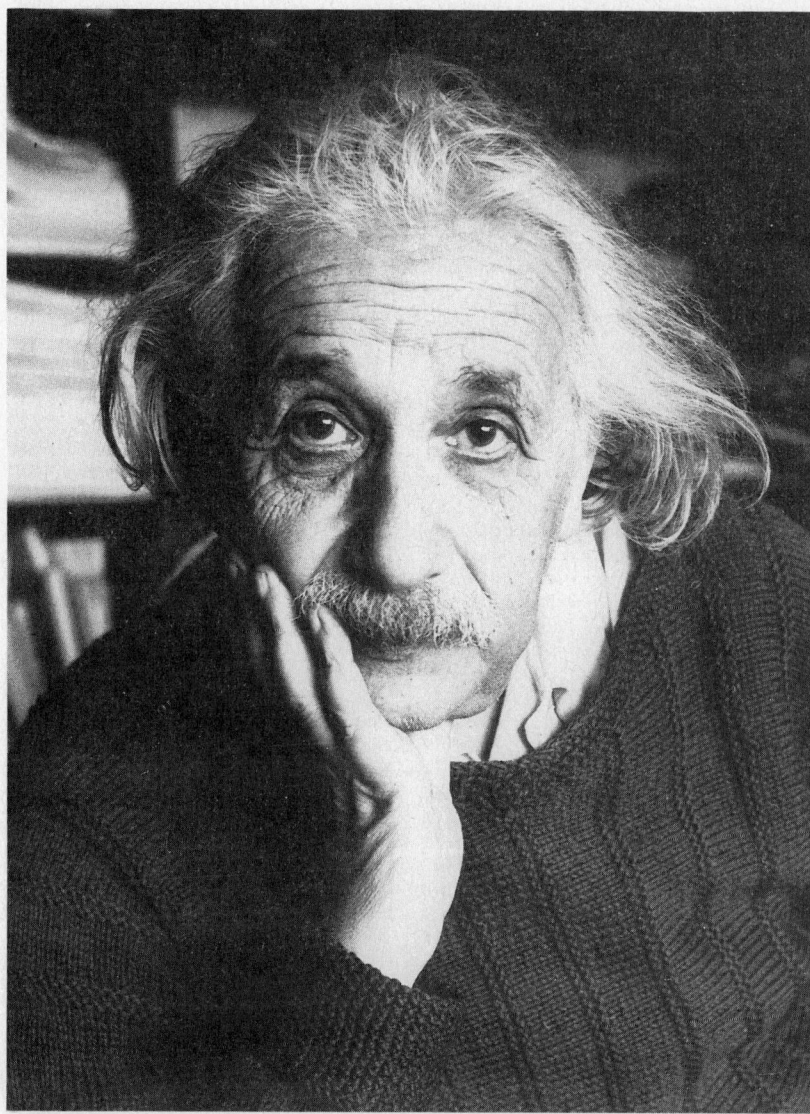

Einstein Physicist Albert Einstein is best-known for his theory of relativity, outlining the relationship between time and the universe, and for his work in radiation physics and thermodynamics.

Ekaterinodar /eˌkætəriːnəuˈdɑː/ pre-revolutionary name of ◊Krasnodar, an important industrial town in the USSR.

Ekaterinoslav /eˌkætəriːnəuˈslɑːv/ pre-revolutionary name of ◊Dnepropetrovsk, centre of an industrial region in the Ukraine, USSR.

Ekman spiral effect /ˈekman/ an application of the ◊Coriolis effect to ocean currents, whereby the currents flow at an angle to the winds that drive them. It derives its name from Swedish oceanographer Vagn Ekman (1874–1954). In the northern hemisphere, the surface current is deflected to the right of the wind direction. The surface current then drives the sub-surface layer at an angle to that, and so on, so that the effect decreases with increasing depth. The net result is that most water is transported at about right angles to the wind direction. Directions are reversed in the southern hemisphere.

El Aaiún /el aɪˈuːn/ capital of Western Sahara; population (1974) 20,000. Phosphates are exported from the port 20 km/12 mi away. The city was formerly the capital of ◊Spanish Sahara.

eland largest species of antelope *Taurotragus oryx*. Pale fawn in colour, it is about 2 m/6 ft high, and both sexes have spiral horns about 45 cm/18 in long. It is found in central and southern Africa.

elasticity ability of a solid to recover its shape once deforming forces (stresses modifying its length or shape) are removed. Metals are elastic up to a certain stress (the elastic limit), beyond which greater stress gives them a permanent deformation. See ◊Hooke's Law.

Elat /eɪˈlɑːt/ port at the head of the Gulf of Aqaba, Israel's only outlet to the Red Sea; population (1982) 19,500. Founded in 1948, on the site of the Biblical Elath, it is linked by road with Beersheba. There are copper mines and granite quarries nearby, and a major geophysical observatory opened in 1968 is 16 km/10 mi to the N.

Elba /ˈelbə/ island in the Mediterranean, 10 km/6 mi off the W coast of Italy; population (1971) 27,500; area 223 sq km/86 sq mi. Iron ore is exported from the capital, Portoferraio, to the Italian mainland, and there is a fishing industry. The small uninhabited island of *Monte Cristo* 40 km/25 mi to the S, supplied the title of Alexandre ◊Dumas' hero in *The Count of Monte Cristo*. Elba was Napoleon's place of exile 1814–15.

Elbe /elb/ one of the principal rivers of Germany, 1,166 km/725 mi long. It rises on the S slopes of the Riesengebirge in Czechoslovakia, and flows NW across the German plain to the North Sea.

Elberfeld /ˈelbəfelt/ West German industrial town, merged with ◊Wuppertal in 1929.

Elbing /ˈelbɪŋ/ German name for ◊Elblag, a Polish port.

Elblag /ˈelblɒŋk/ Polish port 11 km/7 mi from the mouth of the river Elblag which flows into the Vistula Lagoon, an inlet of the Baltic; population (1981) 112,000. It has shipyards, engineering works, and car and tractor factories.

Elbruz /elˈbruːs/ highest mountain in Europe, 5,642 m/18,510 ft, in the ◊Caucasus, Georgian Republic, USSR.

Elburz /elˈbuəz/ volcanic mountain range in NW Iran, close to the S shore of the Caspian Sea, rising in Mount Demavend to 5,770 m/18,934 ft.

elder in the Presbyterian Church, the elders or ruling elders are lay members who assist the minister (or teaching elder) in running the church.

elder in botany, small tree or shrub, genus *Sambucus* of the family Caprifoliaceae. The common *Sambucus nigra*, found in Europe, N Africa, and W Asia, has pinnate leaves, and in early summer bears heavy heads of small, sweet-scented, white flowers, which are succeeded by clusters of small, black berries. The scarlet-berried *Sambucus racemosa* is found in parts of Europe, Asia and N America.

Eldon /ˈeldən/ John Scot, 1st Earl of Eldon 1751–1838. British lord chancellor 1801–05 and 1807–27. He became an member of parliament in 1782. During his period the rules of the lord chancellor's court governing the use of the injunction and precedent in ◊equity finally became fixed.

El Dorado /ˈel dəˈrɑːdəu/ fabled city of gold believed by 16th-century Spaniards to exist somewhere in the Americas. See also ◊Chibchas.

Eleanor of Aquitaine /ˈelɪnər əv ˌækwɪˈteɪn/ c. 1122–1204. Daughter of the Duke of Aquitaine, and Queen of ◊Henry II of England. She was married 1137–51 to ◊Louis VII of France, but the marriage was annulled on grounds of consanguinity. Shortly after she married Henry of Anjou, who became King of England in 1154. Henry imprisoned her 1174–89 for supporting their sons, the future Richard I and King John, in revolt against him.

Eleanor of Castile /'elɪnər əv kæs'tiːl/ died 1290. Queen of Edward I of England. The daughter of Ferdinand III of Castile, she married Prince Edward in 1254, and accompanied him on his crusade in 1270. She died at Harby, Nottinghamshire, and Edward erected stone crosses in towns where her body rested on the funeral journey to London. Several *Eleanor Crosses* are still standing, for example at Northampton.

Eleactic philosophy school of philosophical thought founded at Elea, S Italy, based around the philosophers ◊Parmenides and ◊Zeno in the early 5th century BC. It was characterized by its ◊monism (belief in the essential unity of all things).

elector (German *kurfürst*) any of originally seven (later ten) princes of the ◊Holy Roman Empire who had the prerogative of electing the emperor (in effect, the king of Germany). Their constitutional status was formalized in 1356 in the document known as the Golden Bull, which granted them extensive powers within their own domains: such as acting as judges, issuing coins and imposing tolls.

electoral college the indirect system of voting for the president and vice-president of the USA. The people of each state officially vote not for the presidential candidate, but for a list of electors nominated by each party. The whole electoral-college vote of the state then goes to the winning party (and candidate). Each state has as many electors as it has senators and representatives in Congress, so that the electoral college numbers 538, and a majority of 270 electoral votes is needed to win. The system can lead to a presidential candidate being elected with a minority of the total vote over the whole country, and it has been proposed, for example by Carter in 1977, to substitute a direct popular vote. A constitutional amendment to this effect failed in 1979, partly because minority groups argued that this would deprive them of their politically influential block vote in key states.

electoral system see under ◊vote, ◊proportional representation.

Electra /ɪ'lektrə/ in ancient Greek legend, the daughter of Clytemnestra and ◊Agamemnon, king of Mycenae, and sister of Iphigenia and Orestes. Her story is the subject of two plays of the 5th century BC by Sophocles and Euripides, which explore her role in the complex family tragedy which involved the deaths of her sister, both parents, and finally her brother.

electrical engineering the branch of engineering which deals with applications of electricity, such as design and construction of electrical generators, motors, and so on. In the UK, the Institution of Electrical Engineers (1888) began as the Society of Telegraph Engineers, 1871.

electrical relay electromagnetic switch. See ◊relay.

electric arc a continuous electric discharge of high current between two electrodes, giving out a brilliant light and heat. The phenomenon is exploited in the carbon-arc lamp, once widely used in film projectors. In the electric-arc furnace an arc struck between huge carbon electrodes and the metal charge provides the heating. In arc ◊welding an electric arc provides the heat to fuse the metal. The discharges in low-pressure gases, as in neon and sodium lights, can also be broadly considered as electric arcs.

electric bell a bell that makes use of electromagnetism. At its heart is a wire-wound coil on an iron core (an electromagnet) which, when a direct current (from a battery) flows through it, attracts an iron ◊armature. The armature acts as a switch, whose movement causes contact with an adjustable contact point to be broken, so breaking the circuit. A spring rapidly returns the armature to the contact point, once again closing the circuit. In this way, the armature oscillates back and forth, and the clapper or hammer fixed to the armature strikes the bell. A slightly different arrangement of magnet and armature allows a bell to employ low-voltage ◊alternating current (from a ◊transformer).

electric charge property of some bodies that causes them to exert forces on each other. Two bodies both with positive or negative charges repel each other, while oppositely or 'unlike' charged bodies attract each other, since each is in the ◊*electric field* of the other. ◊Electrons possess a negative charge, and ◊protons an equal positive charge, the unit of charge being the *coulomb* (C). ◊Atoms have no charge but can sometimes gain electrons to become negative *ions* or lose them to become positive ions. So-called ◊*static electricity*, seen in such phenomena as the charging of nylon shirts when they are pulled on or off, or in brushing hair, is in fact the gain or loss of electrons from the surface atoms. A flow of charge (such as electrons through a copper wire) constitutes an *electric current*; the flow of current is measured in *amperes*.

electric current rate of flow of ◊electric charge. Measured in amperes (coulombs per second).

electric energy in physics, the ◊energy of a body that is due to its position in an ◊electric field. See also ◊electric charge and ◊energy.

electric field in physics, a region in which an ◊electric charge experiences a force due to the presence of another electric charge. See also ◊electromagnetic field.

electric fish name given to certain fish that have electricity-producing powers. The best-known example is the South American 'electric eel' *Electrophorus electricus*, in which the lateral tail muscles are modified to form electric organs capable of generating 650 volts; current passing from tail to head is strong enough to stun another animal. Other fish such as the electric ray *Torpedo* and the electric catfish *Malapterurus* of Africa also produce big discharges, but more important to them and other electric fish (some skates, knifefish and mormyrids) is the ability to navigate and detect nearby objects using an electric field generated from weak pulses.

electricity fundamental constituent of matter. A general term used for all phenomena caused by ◊electric charge whether static or in motion. The fact that amber has the power, after being rubbed, of attracting light objects, such as bits of straw and feathers, is said to have been known to ◊Thales of Miletus (600 BC) and to Pliny (700 AD). William ◊Gilbert (1544–1603), Queen Elizabeth I's physician, found that many substances possessed this power, and he called it electric after the Greek word meaning amber. The attracting power may be transferred by contact from one body to another by conductors, such as metals. On the other hand, paraffin wax, hard rubber and dry glass do not transmit the power; they are called insulators. In the early 1700s it was recognized that there are two types of electricity; and that unlike kinds attract each other and like kinds repel. The charge on glass rubbed with silk came to be known as positive electricity, and the charge on amber rubbed with wool as negative electricity. These two charges were found to cancel each other when brought together.

In 1800, ◊Volta found that a series of little cells containing brine, in which were dipped plates of zinc and copper, gave an electric current, which later in the same year was shown to evolve hydrogen and oxygen when passed through water (known as ◊electrolysis). Humphry ◊Davy, in 1807, decomposed soda and potash (both thought to be elements) and isolated the metals sodium and potassium; a discovery which led the way to ◊electroplating. Other properties of electric currents discovered were the heating effect, now used in lighting and warming our homes, offices, and so on, and the deflection of a magnetic needle, described by ◊Oersted in 1820 and elaborated by ◊Ampère in 1825. This work made possible the electric telegraph.

For Michael ◊Faraday the fact that an electric current passing through a wire caused a magnet to move suggested that moving a wire or coil of wire rapidly between the poles of a magnet would induce an electric current. He demonstrated this in 1831, producing the first ◊dynamo, which became the basis of electrical engineering. The characteristics of currents were crystallized by G S ◊Ohm about 1827 who showed that the current passing along a wire was equal to the electromotive force (emf) across the wire multiplied by a constant, which was the conductivity of the wire. The unit of resistance is named after Ohm, emf is named after Volta (volt), and current after Ampère (amp).

The work of the late 1800s indicated the wide interconnections of electricity (with magnetism, heat and light), and about 1855 J C Maxwell formulated a single electromagnetic theory. The universal importance of electricity was decisively proved, by the discovery that the ◊atom itself, up till then thought to be the ultimate particle of matter, is composed of a positively charged central core, the nucleus, about which negatively charged electrons rotate in various orbits. Electricity generated on a commercial scale was available from the early 1880s and used for electric motors driving all kinds of machinery; and for lighting, first by carbon arc, but later by incandescent filaments, first of carbon and then of tungsten, enclosed in glass bulbs partially filled with inert gas under vacuum. Light is also produced by passing electricity through a gas or metal vapour, or a fluorescent lamp. Other practical applications include telephone, radio, television, and X-ray machines. See also ⍁electronics.

electricity generation and supply electricity is the most useful and most convenient form of energy there is. It can readily be converted into heat and light and used to power machines. Because electricity flows readily through wires, it can be made, or generated, in one place and distributed to anywhere it is needed. Electricity is generated at power stations, where a suitable energy source is made to drive ⍁turbines that spin the electricity generators. The generators produce alternating current (AC), and the producing units are generally called turboalternators. The main energy sources for electricity generation are coal, oil, water power (hydroelectricity), natural gas, and ⍁nuclear power, with limited contributions from wind power, ⍁tidal power and ⍁geothermal power. Nuclear fuel provides the cheapest form of electricity generation in Britain, but environmental considerations may limit its future development.

Electricity is generated at power stations at a voltage of about 25,000 volts, which is not a suitable voltage for long-distance transmission. For minimal power loss, transmission must take place at very high voltage – 400,000 volts or more. The generated voltage is therefore increased, or stepped up, by a ⍁transformer. The resulting high voltage electricity is then fed into the main arteries of the ⍁grid system. This is an interconnected network of power stations and distribution centres covering a large area, sometimes (as in Britain) countrywide, or even (as in Europe) from country to country. After transmission to a local substation, the line voltage is reduced by a step-down transformer and distributed to consumers.

use conventional fuels such as propane gas, as in portable military power packs, or, if refuelling is to be avoided, radioactive fuels, as in unmanned navigational aids, and spacecraft.

electric light-bulb the most common device for producing light from electricity. It has its origins in the incandescent filament lamp first demonstrated by Joseph Swan in England in 1878 and Thomas Edison in the United States in 1879. See ⍁incandescence. The modern light-bulb is a thin glass bulb filled with an inert mixture of nitrogen and argon gas. It contains a filament made of fine tungsten wire. When electricity is passed through the wire, it glows white hot.

electric motor a machine that converts electrical ⍁energy into mechanical energy. There are various types, most of which produce rotary motion. A simple direct-current motor consists of a horseshoe-shaped permanent ⍁magnet with a wire-wound coil (⍁armature) mounted so that it can rotate between the pole-pieces of the magnet. A ⍁commutator reverses the current (from a battery) fed to the coil on each half-turn, which rotates because of the mechanical force exerted on a conductor carrying a current in a magnetic field. An induction motor employs ⍁alternating current. It comprises a stationary current-carrying coil (stator) surrounding another coil (rotor), which rotates because of the current induced in it by the magnetic field created by the stator; it thus requires no commutator. A linear induction motor uses a similar principle to produce linear (sideways) rather than rotary motion.

electric power the rate at which an electrical machine uses electrical ⍁energy or converts it into other forms of energy, for example, light, heat, mechanical energy. Usually measured in watts (equivalent to joules per second), it is equal

– in ordinary terms it is a 100-watt lamp. An electric motor that requires 6 amps at the same voltage consumes 1,500 watts (1.5 kilowatts), equivalent to delivering about 2 horse-power of mechanical energy.

electrocardiogram (ECG) a recording on a chart of the electrical impulses from the heart, detected by metal sensors attached to the chest, and used to diagnose heart disorders. The process is known as electrocardiography.

electroconvulsive therapy or *ECT* a treatment for ⍁schizophrenia, and ⍁depression, given under anaesthesia and with a muscle relaxant. An electric current is passed through the brain to induce alterations in the brain's electrical activity. The treatment can cause distress, and there is some controversy about its use and effectiveness.

electrocution death caused by electric current. It is used as a method of execution in some of the states of the USA. The criminal is strapped in a special electric chair and an electric shock at 1,800–2,000 volts administered.

electrode conductor by which an electric current passes in or out of a substance, for example, in an electric furnace or neon tube.

electrodynamics study of the interaction between charged particles and their emission and absorption of electromagnetic ⍁radiation. *Quantum electrodynamics* (QED) applies quantum ⍁mechanics and ⍁relativity theory, making exceedingly accurate predictions about subatomic processes involving charged particles, for example, electrons and protons.

electroencephalogram (EEG) a recording on a chart of the electrical discharges of the brain, detected using metal sensors on the scalp, used in diagnosis of brain conditions such as epilepsy. The process is known as electro-encephalogy.

electrolysis the production of chemical changes by passing an ⍁electric current through a solution (the ⍁electrolyte) resulting in the migration of the ions to the electrodes: cations to the negative electrode, or cathode, and anions to the positive electrode, or anode. The ions react with the electrode, either receiving, or giving up, electrons. The resultant atoms may be liberated as a gas, or deposited as a solid on the electrode, in amounts that are proportional to the amount of current passed, as discovered by Faraday. One important application of electrolysis is ⍁electroplating, in which a solution of a salt, such as silver nitrate, is used and the object to be plated acts as the negative electrode, thus attracting silver ions, Ag+. Electrolysis is used in many industrial processes such as coating metals for vehicles and ships (electroplating), and refining bauxite into aluminium.

electrolyte a conducting medium or solution in which an electric current flows because of the movement and discharge of ions in accordance with Faraday's laws of ⍁electrolysis. The term electrolyte is frequently used to denote a substance which, when dissolved in a specified solvent, usually water, produces an electrically conducting medium.

electromagnetic field in physics, a region of space in which a particle with an ⍁electric charge experiences a force. If it does so only when

electricity generation
coal-fired power station (highly simplified)

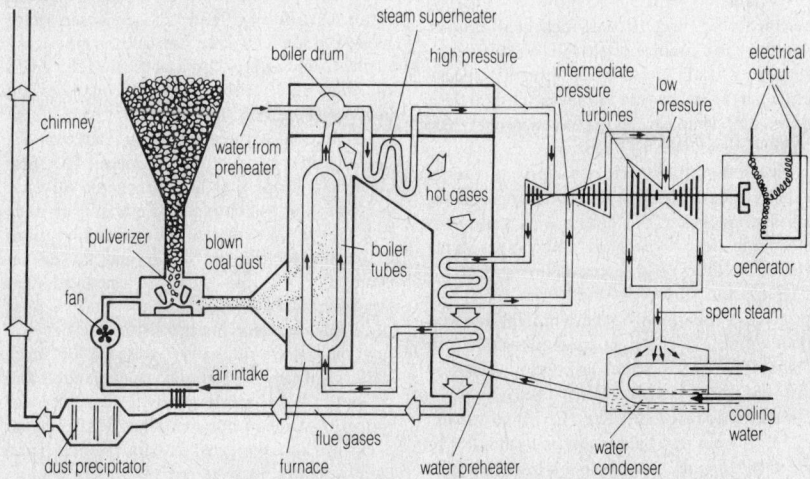

Among specialized power units which convert energy directly to electrical energy without the intervention of any moving mechanisms, the most promising are thermionic converters. These

to the product of the voltage and the current flowing (measured in amps). Thus an electric lamp that passes 0.4 amps at 250 volts uses 100 watts of electrical power and converts it into light

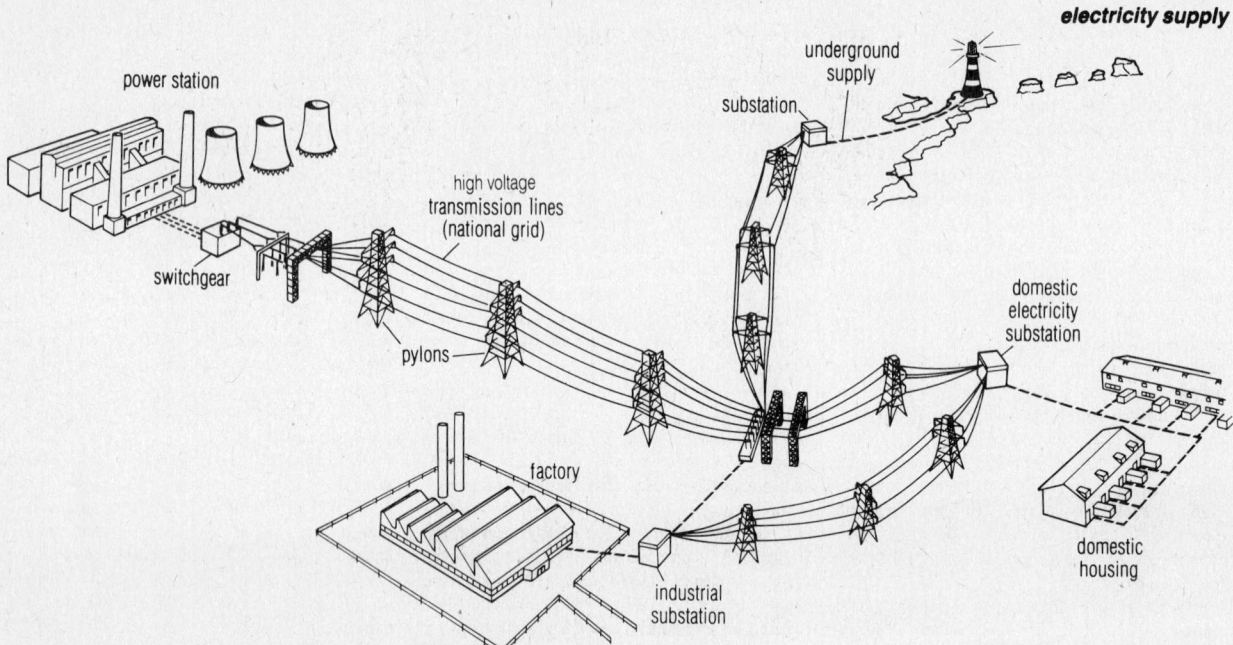

moving, it is in a pure ◊*magnetic field*, if it does so when stationary, it is in an ◊*electric field*. Both can be present simultaneously.

electromagnetic induction in physics, the production of an ◊electromotive force (emf) in a circuit by a change of ◊magnetic flux through the circuit. The emf so produced is known as an induced emf, and any current that may result from there as an induced current. If the change of magnetic flux is due to a variation in the current flowing in the same circuit, the phenomenon is known as self-induction; if due to a change of current flowing in another circuit, as mutual induction. See ◊electric bell, ◊induction coil.

electromagnetic spectrum see ◊electromagnetic waves.

electromagnetic system of units a system of absolute electromagnetic units (emu) based on the ◊CGS system and having, as its primary electrical unit, the unit magnetic pole. Now superseded by ◊SI units.

electrolysis

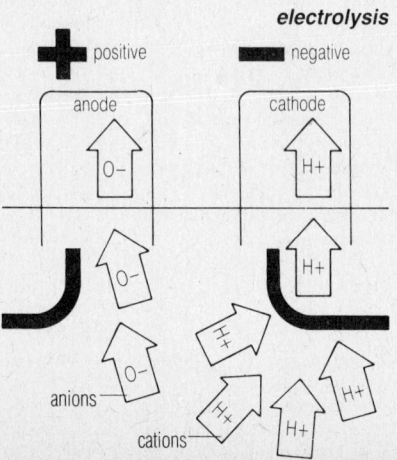

electromagnetic waves oscillating electric and magnetic fields travelling together through space at a speed of nearly 300 million metres per second. The (limitless) range of possible ◊frequencies of electromagnetic waves, which can be thought of as making up the *electromagnetic spectrum*, include radio waves, infrared radiation, visible light, ultraviolet radiation, and X-rays and gamma rays. Dividing 300 million by the frequency (number of cycles per second, or hertz) gives the wavelength of the waves in metres.

electromotive force or *emf* agency causing the movement of charge in a circuit, measured by the work done per unit charge flowing. The unit is the volt.

electron stable, negatively charged ◊elementary particle, a constituent of all ◊atoms, and the basic particle of electricity. Diffraction (passing a beam of electrons through a special lattice, in a similar way to that in which light is diffracted) demonstrates the wave aspect of these particles. See Joseph ◊Thomson.

electron gun a structure comprising a series of ◊electrodes, including a cathode for producing an electron beam. An essential part of many electronic devices such as cathode-ray tubes (television tubes) and ◊electron microscopes.

electronic flash a discharge tube that produces a high-intensity flash of light, used for photography in dim light conditions. The tube contains an inert gas such as krypton. The flash lasts only a few thousandths of a second.

electronic funds transfer (EFT) the transfer of funds from one bank account to another by electronic means. For example, a bank customer inserts a plastic card in a point-of-sale computer terminal in a supermarket, and telephone lines are used to make an automatic debit from the customer's bank account to settle the bill. See also ◊credit card.

electronic mail a ◊telecommunications system that sends messages to people or machines (such as computers) via computers and the telephone network rather than by letter. Subscribers to an electronic mail system type messages in ordinary letter form on their ◊word processor, or microcomputer, and 'drop' the letters into a central computer's memory bank by means of a computer/telephone connector (a modem). The person to whom the letter is addressed 'collects' the letter by calling up the central computer and feeding a unique password into the system. ◊British Telecom operates an electronic mail system called Telecom Gold.

electronic music music produced since the 1950s in which composers work with electronically assembled or arranged sounds. ◊Varèse, ◊Boulez, and ◊Stockhausen have pioneered the technique. See also ◊synthesizer.

electronics a branch of science that deals with the emission of ◊electrons from conductors and ◊semiconductors, with the subsequent manipulation of these electrons, and with the construction of electronic devices. The first electronic device was the ◊thermionic valve, or vacuum tube, which involved electrons moving in a vacuum. This device led to such inventions as ◊radio, ◊television, ◊radar and the digital ◊computer. Electronics entered a new era after the invention of the ◊transistor in 1948 because of its minute size. Tiny transistors the size of a fingernail replaced valves the size of torch batteries. Transistors were also more reliable and consumed less power than valves. The process of miniaturization in electronics has been going on ever since, in the design of integrated circuits and ◊silicon chips, water-thin crystal slices holding tens of thousands of electronic components. Using such solid-state devices, electronic circuits can be constructed of a complexity previously only dreamed of, leading to such modern-day miracles as ◊digital watches, pocket

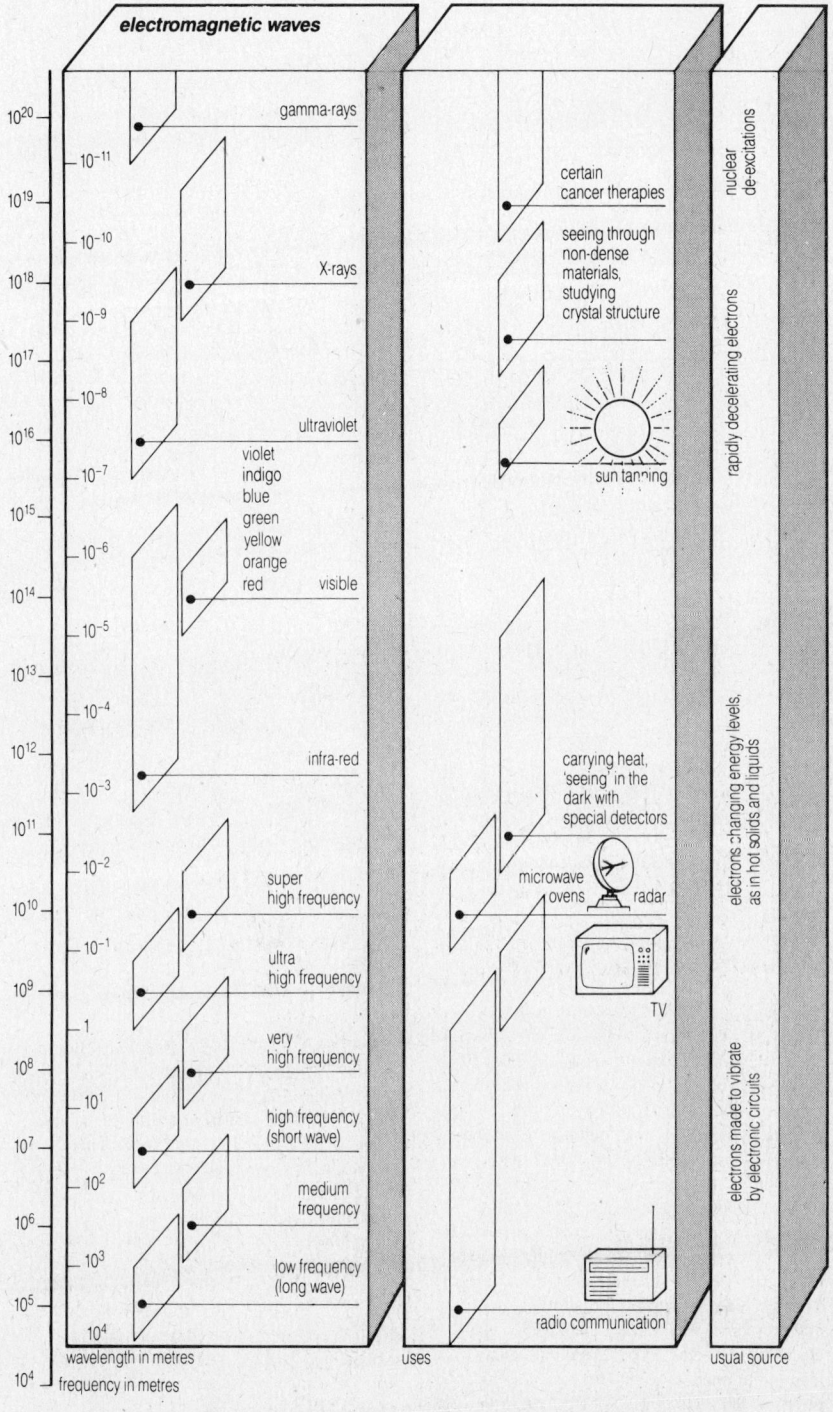

electromagnetic waves

frequency	wavelength		uses	usual source
10^{20}	10^{-11}	gamma-rays		nuclear de-excitations
10^{19}	10^{-10}		certain cancer therapies	
10^{18}	10^{-9}	X-rays	seeing through non-dense materials, studying crystal structure	rapidly decelerating electrons
10^{17}	10^{-8}			
10^{16}	10^{-7}	ultraviolet		
10^{15}	10^{-6}	violet indigo blue green yellow orange red	sun tanning	
10^{14}	10^{-5}	visible		
10^{13}	10^{-4}			electrons changing energy levels, as in hot solids and liquids
10^{12}	10^{-3}	infra-red	carrying heat, 'seeing' in the dark with special detectors	
10^{11}	10^{-2}			
10^{10}	10^{-1}	super high frequency	microwave ovens radar	
10^{9}	1	ultra high frequency	TV	
10^{8}	10^{1}	very high frequency		electrons made to vibrate by electronic circuits
10^{7}	10^{2}	high frequency (short wave)		
10^{6}	10^{3}	medium frequency		
10^{5}		low frequency (long wave)		
10^{4}			radio communication	

wavelength in metres
10^{4} frequency in metres

Dcalculators, powerful Dmicrocomputers, and Dword processors.

electron microscope an instrument that produces a magnified image using a beam of Delectrons instead of light rays as in an optical Dmicroscope. It uses electron lenses rather than optical lenses. An electron lens is an arrangement of electromagnetic coils that controls and focuses the beam. Electrons are not visible to the eye, so

instead of an eyepiece there is a fluorescent screen or a photographic plate on which the electrons form an image. Since the wavelength of the electron beam is very much shorter than that of light, it is possible to achieve much greater magnification and resolution (ability to distinguish detail). A high-resolution electron microscope (HREM) can produce a 7 million times magnification. The development of the

electron microscope has made possible the observation of very minute organisms, viruses, and even large molecules. A transmission electron microscope passes the electron beam through a very thin slice of a specimen. A scanning electron microscope looks at the exterior of a specimen.

electron volt in atomic physics, the energy $(1.602,19 \times 10{-19}$ J) acquired by an electron in passing through a potential difference of 1 volt.

electrophoresis the Ddiffusion of charged particles through a fluid under the influence of an electric field. It can be used in the biological sciences to separate Dmolecules of different sizes, which diffuse at different rates. In industry electrophoresis is used in paint-dipping operations to ensure that paint reaches awkward corners.

electroplating the deposition of metals upon metallic surfaces by Delectrolysis for decorative and/or protective purposes. A current is passed through a bath containing a solution of a salt of the plating metal, the object to be plated being the cathode (negative terminal); the anode is either an inert substance or the plating metal. Among the metals most commonly used for plating are zinc, nickel, chromium, cadmium, copper, silver, and gold. Electroplating is used in the preparation of printers' blocks, 'master' audio discs, and in many other processes.

In electropolishing the object to be polished is made the anode in an electrolytic solution and by carefully controlling the conditions the high spots on the surface are dissolved away leaving a high-quality stain-free surface. This technique is useful in polishing irregular stainless steel articles.

electroscope an apparatus for detecting Delectric charge. The simple gold-leaf electroscope consists of a vertical conducting (metal) rod ending in a pair of rectangular pieces of gold foil, mounted inside and insulated from an earthed metal case. An electric charge applied to the end of the metal rod makes the gold leaves diverge, because they each receive a similar charge (positive or negative) and so repel each other. The polarity of the charge can be found by bringing up another charge of known polarity and applying it to the metal rod. A like charge has no effect on the gold leaves, whereas an opposite charge neutralizes the charge on the leaves and causes them to collapse.

electrostatics study of electric charges from stationary sources (not currents), for example in amber, and Dlightning. See also Delectricity.

electrum a naturally occurring alloy of gold and silver used by early civilizations to make the first coins, about the 6th century BC.

element a substance which cannot be split chemically into simpler substances. Of the 109 known elements, 92 occur naturally. Elements consist of atoms having the same number of protons in their nuclei. Hydrogen and helium were produced in the 'Big Bang'. Of the rest, those up to atomic number 56 (iron) are produced by nuclear fusion within the stars, but the more massive, such as lead and uranium, are produced when an old Dstar explodes and its gravitational energy as it collapses squashes

shell	number of subshells	number of orbitals in each subshell					total number of orbitals in shell	maximum number of electrons in shell
		s	p	d	f	g		
$n = 1$ (K)	1	1					1	2
$n = 2$ (L)	2	1	3				4	8
$n = 3$ (M)	3	1	3	5			9	18
$n = 4$ (N)	4	1	3	5	7		16	32
$n = 5$ (O)	5	1	3	5	7	9	25	50

electronic configuration: the arrangement of atomic shells and subshells   *electron*

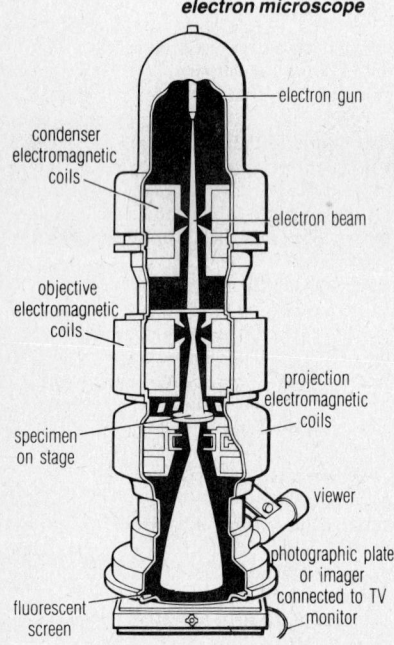

electron microscope

- electron gun
- condenser electromagnetic coils
- electron beam
- objective electromagnetic coils
- projection electromagnetic coils
- specimen on stage
- viewer
- photographic plate or imager connected to TV monitor
- fluorescent screen

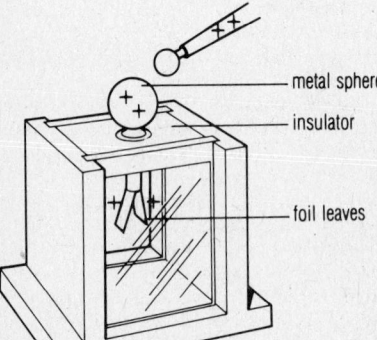

electroscope

- metal sphere
- insulator
- foil leaves

nuclei together. The transuranium elements are artificially made by bombarding uranium or other substances with various atomic particles. See also ◊periodic table.

To facilitate the expression of chemical composition, symbols are used to denote the elements. The symbol is usually the first letter or letters of the English or Latinized name of the element, for example C, carbon; Ca, calcium; Fe, iron (ferrum). These symbols represent one atom of the element; molecules containing more than one atom are denoted by a subscript figure, for example water, H_2O. The symbolic representation of a molecule is known as a formula. A figure placed before a formula represents the number of molecules present for example $2H_2O$, two molecules of water. Chemical reactions are expressed by means of equations, for example $NaCl + H_2SO_4 = NaHSO_4 + HCl$. This equation states that when sodium chloride (NaCl) is treated with sulphuric acid (H_2SO_4) it is converted into sodium hydrogen sulphate, or bisulphate ($NaHSO_4$) and hydrogen chloride (HCl).

elementary particle a subatomic particle which together with others makes up an ◊atom. They are the fundamental components of all matter. About 200 different ones have been identified. The best-known are protons and neutrons (in an atom's nucleus) and electrons (which may be regarded as orbiting the nucleus). Others include short-lived particles such as the mesons, which skip and interchange between neutrons and protons and thus hold them together in the nuclei of atoms, and photons, which represent packets or quanta of electromagnetic energy such as light. Elementary particles which undergo strong interactions within the atom are called hadrons. They include, among others, protons, neutrons and mesons. Elementary particles such as electrons, which take part in weak or electromagnetic interactions, belong to the group called leptons. Photons belong to neither of the two groups. See also ◊particle (subatomic) and ◊quark.

elephant name given to the two surviving species of the Proboscidea, the Asiatic *Elephas maximus* and African *Loxodonta africana* elephants. Elephants reach 2.5–3 m/8–10 ft up to a maximum 3.4 m/11 ft and 6 tonnes in African males, have a thick, grey, wrinkled skin, a large head, and a long trunk used to obtain food and water. The upper incisors or tusks, which

grow to a considerable length, are a source of ivory. The African elephant has very large ears and a flattened forehead, and the Indian species has smaller ears and a convex forehead. Elephants are herbivorous, and live in herds. With a reputation for intelligence, elephants are quickly tamed, and in India, Burma and Thailand are widely used for transport and logging. The period of gestation is about 19–22 months (the longest amongst mammals) and the life span is probably about 60–70 yrs. Elephants do not breed readily in captivity, and this, together with the (now illegal) slaughter of African elephants for ivory, is leading to their extinction. They have one of the lowest metabolic rates amongst placental mammals. Elephants are rightly credited with long memories.

elephant

Asiatic Elephant

African Elephant

Elephanta /ˌelɪˈfæntə/ island in Bombay harbour, Maharashtra, India, some 8 km/5 mi from Bombay. The Temple Caves (6th century), cut out of solid rock, have sculptures of many Hindu deities executed 450–740. There was formerly a large stone elephant near the island's landing place.

elephant bird see ◊aepyornis.

elephantiasis in the human body, a gross local enlargement and deformity, especially of a leg, the scrotum, a labium of the vulva, or a breast. The commonest is the tropical variety due to infestation by the parasite filaria; the enlargement is due to chronic blocking of the lymph channels and consequent overgrowth of the skin and tissues.

Eleusinian Mysteries /ˌeljuːˈsɪnɪən/ ceremonies in honor of ◊Demeter, ◊Persephone, and ◊Dionysus, celebrated in the remains of the temple of Demeter at Eleusis, Greece, Worshippers saw visions in the darkened temple, possibly connected with the underworld.

elevation of boiling point a raising of the boiling point of a liquid above that of the pure solvent, caused by a substance being dissolved in it. How much it is raised depends on the number of molecules or substance dissolved. For a single solvent, such as pure water, all substances in the same molecular concentration (expressed in ◊moles) produce the same elevation of boiling point (measured using the very accurate Beckmann thermometer). The elevation *e* for a molar concentration *C* is given by the equation *e* = *KC*, where K is a constant for the particular solvent (called the ebullioscopic constant). The phenomenon is readily observed during cooking – when salt is added to boiling water the water ceases to boil because its boiling point has been elevated.

elevator mechanical device for raising or lowering goods or materials on a ◊conveyor belt. Such a device used for lifting people in buildings is known as an elevator in the USA, but in Britain is known as a ◊lift. In 1979 a 'space elevator' was advocated by Arthur C ◊Clarke as eventually the most economical method of carrying people or freight into high orbit.

Eleven Plus examination test designed to select children for grammar school education in the UK, at the time when local authorities provided separate grammar, secondary modern, and occasionally technical schools for children over the age of 11. The examination became defunct on the introduction of ◊comprehensive schools in Scotland, Wales, and most of England during the 1960s and 1970s.

El Faiyûm /el faɪˈjuːm/ city in N Egypt; population (1976) 167,000. A centre of prehistoric culture; the crocodile god Sobek used to be worshipped nearby, and famous realistic mummy portraits of 1st–4th centuries AD were found in the area.

El Ferrol /el feˈrɒl/ city and port (full name El Ferrol del Caudillo), on the NW coast of Spain; population (1981) 92,000. It is a naval base, and has a deep, sheltered harbour and shipbuilding industries.

Elgar /ˈelgɑː/ Edward 1857–1934. British composer. Born at Broadheath, Worcestershire, the son of a church organist and music-seller, Elgar had little formal musical education and gained his first experience in conducting when appointed bandmaster of the staff of a mental asylum in 1879. He gained fame as a composer with his *Enigma Variations* in 1899, and although his most celebrated choral work, the oratorio setting of Newman's *The Dream of Gerontius*, was a failure when performed in Birmingham the following year, it was a great success at Düsseldorf in 1902. Many of his earlier works were then performed, including the popular *Pomp and Circumstance* marches. He was knighted in 1904, was awarded the Order of Merit in 1911, and became Master of the King's Musick in 1924. Among his later works are oratorios, two symphonies, a violin concerto and a cello concerto, chamber music, songs, and the tone-poem *Falstaff* 1913.

Elgin /ˈelgɪn/ town in Grampian region, Scotland, on the river Lossie 8 km/5 mi S of its port of Lossiemouth on the south shore of the Moray Firth; population (1983) 20,065. There are sawmills and whisky distilleries. ◊Gordonstoun public school is nearby.

Elgar The composer of several oratorios, Edward Elgar is best remembered as the composer of the *Dream of Gerontius*, which is now recognized as a masterpiece, although its first performance in 1900 was badly received.

Elgin marbles collection of ancient Greek sculptures mainly from the Parthenon at Athens, assembled by the seventh earl of Elgin. Sent to England in 1812, bought for the nation in 1816 for £35,000, they are now in the British Museum. Greece has asked for them to be returned to Athens.

Elijah /ɪˈlaɪdʒə/ in the Old Testament, a Hebrew prophet during the reigns of the Israelite kings Ahab and Ahaziah (about the mid-9th century BC). He came from Gilead. He defeated the prophets of ◊Baal, and was said to have been carried up to heaven in a fiery chariot in a whirlwind.

Eliot /ˈeliət/ George, pen name of Mary Ann Evans 1819–1880. British novelist, who portrayed rural Victorian society, particularly its intellectual hypocrisy, with realism and irony. Born at Chilvers Coton, Warwickshire, she had a strict evangelical upbringing, but on moving to Coventry with her father in 1841 was converted to free thinking (see ◊freethought). As assistant editor of the *Westminster Review* under John Chapman (1851–53), she made the acquaintance of Carlyle, Harriet Martineau, Herbert Spencer, and the philosopher and critic George Henry Lewes (1817–1878). Lewes was married but separated from his wife, and from 1854 he and Eliot lived together in a relationship which she regarded as a true marriage and which continued until his death. In 1857 she published the story 'Amos Barton', the first of the *Scenes of Clerical Life*, under the name of George Eliot. These were successful, and in the following years she won fame with her novels *Adam Bede* 1859 which like its successors, *Mill on the Floss* 1860 and *Silas Marner* 1861, was set in Warwickshire. *Middlemarch* 1872, her masterpiece, is now considered one of the greatest novels of the 19th century. Her final book *Daniel Deronda* 1876 was concerned with anti-semitism. She also wrote poetry. In 1880 she married John Cross (1840–1924).

Eliot /ˈeliət/ John 1592–1632. English politician. Born in Cornwall. He became an member of parliament in 1614, and with the

Eliot The true identity of the English novelist George Eliot is revealed in this old photograph. 'He' was really Mary Ann Evans, whose novels portray rural Victorian society and its intellectual hypocrisy.

Duke of Buckingham's patronage was made a vice admiral in 1619. In 1626 he was sent to the Tower for demanding Buckingham's impeachment. In 1628 he was primarily responsible for the ◊Petition of Right opposing Charles II, and with other parliamentary leaders was again imprisoned in the Tower in 1629, where he died.

Eliot /ˈeliət/ T(homas) S(tearns) 1888–1965. American-born poet and critic; a British subject from 1927. Born at St Louis, Missouri, he was educated at Harvard, Paris, and Oxford. He settled in London in 1915 and was for a time a bank clerk, later lecturing and entering publishing. In 1917 Eliot's first book of verse, *Prufrock and other Observations*, expressed the disillusionment of the generation affected by World War I and caused a sensation by its experimental verse form and rhythms. His reputation was established by the desolate modernity of *The Waste Land* 1922. *The Hollow Men* 1925 renewed the same note, but *Ash Wednesday* 1930 revealed the change in religious attitude which led him to become an Anglo-Catholic. Among his other works are *Four Quartets* 1944, a religious sequence in which he seeks the eternal reality, and the poetic dramas *Murder in the Cathedral* 1935 about Thomas ◊Becket, *The Cocktail Party* 1949, *The Confidential Clerk* 1953, and *The Elder Statesman* 1958. His collection *Old Possum's Book of Practical Cats* has become a classic, and was used for the ◊Lloyd Webber musical *Cats* 1981. His critical works include *The Sacred Wood* 1920 and *Notes toward the Definition of Culture* 1949, and as editor of *The Criterion* 1922–39, he exercised a moulding influence on the thought of his generation. In 1948 he received the Order of Merit and the Nobel Prize for Literature.

Elisabethville /ɪˈlɪzəbəθvɪl/ former name of ◊Lubumbashi, a town in Zaïre.

Elisha /ɪˈlaɪʃə/ in the Old Testament, a Hebrew prophet of the mid-9th century BC, successor of ◊Elijah.

elite a small group in a society with power, privileges, and status above others. An elite may be cultural, educational, religious, political, or social. Sociological interest has centred on how such minorities get, use, and hold on to power, and on what distinguishes elites from ordinary members of society.

Elizabeth /ɪˈlɪzəbəθ/ city in New Jersey, USA; population (1980) 106,205. It was the first English settlement in New Jersey, established in 1664. It has motor car, sewing machine, and tool factories, oil refineries, and chemical works.

Elizabeth /ɪˈlɪzəbəθ/ the Queen Mother 1900– . Wife of King George VI of England. Born the Lady Elizabeth Angela Marguerite Bowes-Lyon, she is the third daughter of the 14th Earl of Strathmore and Kinghorne (died 1944), through whom she is descended from Robert Bruce, king of Scotland. On 26 April 1923, she married Albert Duke of York, and their two children, Queen Elizabeth II and Princess Margaret, were born in 1926 and 1930 respectively. When her husband became King George VI in 1936 she became Queen Consort, and was crowned with him in 1937. She adopted the style Queen Mother after his death.

Elizabeth /ɪˈlɪzəbəθ/ two queens of England or the UK.

Elizabeth I /ɪˈlɪzəbəθ/ 1533–1603. Queen of England from 1558. The daughter of Henry VIII and Anne Boleyn, she was born at Greenwich on 7 Sept 1533. During her Catholic half-sister Mary's reign, Elizabeth's Protestant sympathies brought her under suspicion, and she lived in seclusion at Hatfield, Hertfordshire, until on Mary's death she became queen. Her first task was to bring about a broad religious settlement. Many unsuccessful attempts were made by Parliament to persuade Elizabeth to marry or settle the succession. Courtship she found a useful political weapon, and she maintained friendships with a succession of favourites, among them ◊Leicester, ◊Raleigh, and ◊Essex. The arrival in England in 1568 of Mary, Queen of Scots, and her imprisonment by Elizabeth caused a political crisis and a rebellion of the feudal nobility of the north followed in 1569. Friction between English and Spanish seamen hastened the breach with Spain. When the Dutch rebelled against Spanish tyranny Elizabeth secretly encouraged them; Philip II retaliated by aiding Catholic conspiracies against her. This undeclared war continued for many years, until the landing of an English army in the Netherlands in 1585, and Mary's execution in 1587, brought it into the open. Philip's Armada, in 1588, met with total disaster.

The war with Spain continued with varying fortunes to the end of the reign, while events at home foreshadowed the conflicts of the 17th century. Among the ◊Puritans discontent was developing with Elizabeth's religious settlement,

and several were imprisoned or executed. Parliament showed a new independence, and in 1601 forced Elizabeth to retreat on the monopolies question. Yet her prestige remained unabated, as was shown by the failure of Essex's rebellion in 1601. In literature and the arts, the reign of the 'Virgin Queen' was outstanding.

Elizabeth I 'I have the body of a weak and feeble woman, but I have the heart and stomach of a king', Elizabeth I told her troops. This portrait, attributed to John Bettes the Younger, emphasizes her regality.

Elizabeth II /ɪˈlɪzəbəθ/ 1926–. Queen of Great Britain and Northern Ireland from 1952. The elder daughter of George VI, Princess Elizabeth Alexandra Mary was born in London on 21 Apr 1926, educated privately, and assumed official duties at 16. During World War II she served in the Auxiliary Territorial Service, and by an amendment to the Regency Act she became a state counsellor on her 18th birthday. She married her third cousin, Philip, the Duke of Edinburgh, in 1947. They have four children, Prince ◊Charles Philip Arthur George, born 14 Nov 1948, Princess ◊Anne Elizabeth Alice Louise, born 15 Aug 1950, Prince ◊Andrew Albert Christian Edward, born 19 Feb 1960, and Prince ◊Edward Antony Richard Louis, born 10 Mar 1964. On the death of George VI she succeeded to the throne while in Kenya with her husband at the beginning of a projected tour of Ceylon, Australia, and New Zealand. In 1977 she celebrated her silver jubilee as monarch.

Elizabeth /ɪˈlɪzəbəθ/ Empress of Russia 1709–1762. Daughter of Peter the Great, she carried through a palace revolution in 1741 and supplanted her cousin, the infant Ivan VI, on the throne. She was an able and energetic leader. She continued the policy of westernization begun by Peter, and allied herself with Austria against Prussia.

Elizavetpol /ˌɪlɪzəˈvetpɒl/ former name of ◊Kirovabad, industrial town in Azerbaijan Republic, USSR.

elk largest deer (*Alces alces*) inhabiting N Europe, Asia, Scandinavia, and America, where it is known as the moose. It is brown in colour,

stands about 2 m/6 ft at the shoulders, has very large palmate antlers, a fleshy muzzle, short neck, and long legs; it feeds on leaves and shoots.

Ellesmere /ˈelzmɪə/ second largest island of the Canadian Arctic archipelago, Northwest Territories. Area 212,687 sq km/82,119 sq mi. It is for the most part glacier-covered.

Ellesmere Port /ˈelzmɪə ˈpɔːt/ oil port and industrial town in Cheshire, England, on the river Mersey and the Manchester Ship Canal. Population (1983) 81,900. Formerly the biggest transshipment canal port in NW England, it now has the National Waterways Museum, 1976, with old narrow boats and a blacksmith's forge.

Ellice Islands /ˈelɪs/ former name of ◊Tuvalu, a group of islands in the W Pacific Ocean.

Ellington /ˈelɪŋtən/ 'Duke' (Edward Kennedy) 1899–1974. US pianist, who had an outstanding career as a composer and orchestrator of jazz. He played in New York's Cotton Club, and wrote numerous pieces for his own jazz orchestra, with which he achieved great success, becoming one of the most important figures in jazz over a 55-year span. Numbers include 'Mood Indigo', 'Sophisticated Lady', 'Solitude', and 'Black and Tan Fantasy'.

ellipse a curve joining all points (loci) around two fixed points (foci) so that the sum of the distances from those points is always constant. An ellipse is one of a series of curves known as ◊conic sections; it can also be produced, for example, by imagining a slice taken parallel with the base from a solid cone with an oval base. The diameter passing through the foci is the major axis, and the diameter bisecting this at right angles is the minor axis.

Ellis /ˈelɪs/ (Henry) Havelock 1859–1939. British writer. He is chiefly known as the author of many works on the psychology of sex, including *Studies in the Psychology of Sex* (seven volumes) 1898–1928. He was also a literary critic and essayist.

Ellis Island /ˈelɪs/ island off the shore of New Jersey, USA, former reception centre for steerage class immigrants on arrival in New York between 1892 and 1943. No longer used, it was declared a National Historic Site in 1965 by President Johnson. Sam Goldwyn, Irving Berlin, and Elia Kazan were among the 16 million people who entered the USA through Ellis Island.

Ellora /eˈlɔːrə/ archaeological site in the north west Deccan, ◊Maharashtra State, India, with 35 cave temples – Buddhist, Hindu and Jain – varying in date from the late 6th century to the 9th century. They include some of the greatest of India's architectural treasures: Visvakarma (a hall about 26 m/86 ft long containing a huge image of the Buddha), Tin Thal (a three-storeyed Buddhist monastery cave), the Rameswara cave (with beautiful sculptures) and Siva's Paradise, the great temple of Kailasa.

elm tree of the family Ulmaceae, distributed throughout the temperate latitudes of the northern hemisphere, and in mountainous parts of the tropics. The common English elm *Ulmus procera* is distributed widely in W and S Europe and reaches 35 m/115 ft; its small, purplish-brown flowers are borne in tufts and appear

Elizabeth II Her Majesty Queen Elizabeth II of the United Kingdom and head of the Commonwealth. In 1947 when in Africa with her parents, she broadcast a pledge to serve the Commonwealth, and this has remained one of her chief concerns. This portrait was taken in Canada, 1987.

Ellora Goddesses in stone, in the porch of the Rameswara cave temple.

Ellington The jazz musician 'Duke' Ellington at 75, shortly before his death. His career as a pianist-composer spanned more than 50 years and he performed in every continent.

before the leaves. Other species are the wych elm *Ulmacaceae glabra* found in Britain, where it is indigenous, and the N American white elm *Ulmacaeae americana* and red or slippery elm *Ulmacaeae fulva*. The fungus disease *Ceratocystis ulmi*, known as Dutch elm disease, because of a severe outbreak in that country 1924, has reduced the numbers of elm trees in Europe and N America. It is carried by a beetle from tree to tree, and although individual trees

ellipse

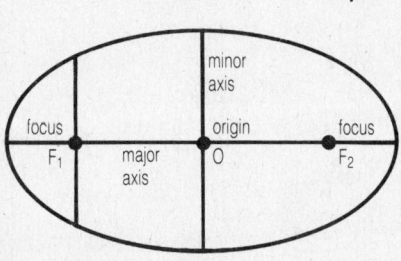

may be saved by chemical injection, the process is expensive.

El Niño /el 'ni: njɒ/ (Spanish 'the child') warm ocean surge of the Peru (◊Humboldt) Current, so called because it tends to occur at Christmas, recurrent every ten years or so in the East Pacific off South America. It can disrupt the climate of the area disastrously, and has played a part in causing famine in Indonesia 1983, bush fires in Australia because of drought, rainstorms in California and South America, and the destruction of Peru's anchovy harvest and wildlife 1982–83.

El Obeid /el əʊ'beɪd/ capital of Kordofan province, Sudan; population (1984) 140,025. Linked by rail with Khartoum, it is a market for cattle, ◊gum arabic and durra (Indian millet).

El Paso /el 'pæsəʊ/ city in Texas, USA; population (1980) 425,260. It is situated at the base of the Franklin Mountains, on the Rio Grande, opposite the Mexican city of Ciudad Juárez. It is the centre of an agricultural and cattle raising area, and has industries based on local iron and copper mines, as well as oil refineries, and electronic, food processing and packing, and leather industries.

El Salvador /el 'sælvədɔː/ country in central America, bounded N and E by Honduras, S and SW by the Pacific Ocean, and NW by Guatemala.

government the 1983 constitution, amended in 1985, provides for a president elected by universal suffrage for a five-year term, assisted by an appointed vice-president and a council of ministers. There is a single-chamber national assembly of 60, elected by universal suffrage for a three-year term.

history conquered by Spain in 1523, El Salvador achieved independence in 1829. Since then there have been frequent coups and political violence. After a coup in 1961 the conservative Party of National Conciliation (PCN) was established, winning all the seats in the national assembly. PCN stayed in power, with reports of widespread human rights violations, until challenged in 1979 by a socialist guerrilla movement, the Farabundo Martí Liberation Front. A civilian-military junta deposed the president and promised to introduce democracy and free elections, though these were postponed as the violence continued. In 1980 the Archbishop of San Salvador, Oscar Romero, a well known champion of human rights, was shot dead in his cathedral. The murder of three American nuns and a social worker prompted US President ◊Carter to suspend economic and military aid. In 1980 José Duarte, leader of a left-of-centre coalition, became president. The ◊Reagan administration supported him, as an anti-communist, and encouraged him to call elections in 1982. The left-wing parties refused to participate, and the elections were held amidst great violence, at least 40 people being killed on election day. The extreme right-wing ARENA party eventually won.

During 1982 some 1,600 Salvadorean troops were trained in the USA and US military advisers were said to be actively involved in the country's internal conflict. It was estimated that about 35,000 people were killed between 1979 and 1982.

Despite a new constitution in 1983, guerrilla activity continued. Duarte won the 1984 presidential election and in 1985 the anti-imperialist PDC won a convincing victory in the assembly, with 33 seats. The right-wing groups ARENA and PCN won 13 and 12 seats respectively, fighting the election on a joint platform. In 1984 the president's daughter was abducted by guerrillas, forcing him to negotiate with them, in the face of criticism from opposition parties and the military. The guerrilla war continued, Duarte again attempting, in 1986, to negotiate a settlement with the rebels. In Aug 1987 they agreed to meet and discuss the Regional Peace Plan with him.

El Salvador

REPUBLIC OF (*República de El Salvador*)

AREA 21,393 sq km/8,236 sq mi
CAPITAL San Salvador
PHYSICAL flat in S, rising to mountains in N
FEATURES smallest and most thickly populated Central American country
HEAD OF STATE AND OF GOVERNMENT José Napoleon Duarte from 1984
GOVERNMENT republic
EXPORTS coffee, cotton
CURRENCY colón (8.25 = £1 Sept 1987)
POPULATION (1985) 4,981,000 (mainly of Spanish-Indian extraction, including some 500,000 illegally in the USA); annual growth rate 3.2%
LANGUAGE Spanish
RELIGION Roman Catholic
LITERACY 70% male/63% female (1980 est)
GDP $4.3 bn (1984); $854 per head of population
CHRONOLOGY
1829 Achieved independence.
1961 Right-wing coup.
1972 Allegations of human-rights violations and growth of left-wing guerrilla activities. Gen Carlos Romero elected president.
1979 A coup replaced Romero with a military-civilian junta.
1980 Archbishop Oscar Romero assassinated.

El Salvador

Country on verge of civil war. José Duarte became president.
1981 The Mexican and French governments recognized the guerrillas as a legitimate political force but the USA actively assisted the government in its battle against them.
1982 Assembly elections boycotted by left-wing parties and held amid considerable violence.
1985 Right-wing majority in the national assembly elections.
1986 Duarte sought a negotiated settlement with the guerrillas.

Elsinore /'elsinɔ:/ another form of ◊Helsingøør, a port on the NE coast of Denmark.

Elton /'eltən/ Charles 1900– . British ecologist. He was a pioneer of the study of animal and plant life in their natural settings, and of animal behaviour as part of a complex whole. He published *Animal Ecology and Evolution* 1930 and *The Pattern of Animal Communities* 1966. He was director of the Bureau of Animal Population at Oxford 1932–67. He originated the 'pyramid of numbers', the concept that in an

◊ecosystem a large number of minute animals at the bottom are eaten by a smaller number of bigger ones; the pyramid of the ◊food chain continues successively until it ends in a small number of large animals.

Eluard /,eɪluː'ɑː/ Paul, pseudonym of Eugène Grindel 1895–1952. French poet. Born in Paris, he expressed the suffering of poverty in his verse, and was a leader of the Surrealists. He fought in World War I, the inspiration for *Poèmes pour la paix/Poems for Peace* 1918, and was a member of the Resistance in World War II. His books include *Poésie et vérité/Poetry and Truth* 1942 and *Au Rendezvous allemand/To the German Rendezvous* 1944.

Ely /'iːli/ city in Cambridgeshire, England, on the Great Ouse river 24 km/15 mi NE of Cambridge; population (1983) 11,030. It has sugar beet factories.
history It was the chief town of the former administrative district of the *Isle of Ely*, so-called because the area was once cut off from the surrounding countryside by the fens. ◊Hereward

the Wake had his stronghold here. The 11th-century cathedral is one of the largest in England. At the annual feast of St Ethelreda (Audrey), founder of a religious community at Ely in the 7th century, cheap, low-quality souvenirs were sold; the word 'tawdry', a corruption of St Audrey, derives from this practice.

Elyot /'eliət/ Thomas 1490–1546. English diplomat and scholar. In 1523 he was made clerk to the Privy Council by Wolsey, and in 1531 published *The Governour*, the first treatise on education in English.

Elysée Palace /e'liːzeɪ/ (Palais de l'Elysée) building in Paris erected in 1718 for Louis d'Auvergne, Count of Evreux. It was later the home of Mme de Pompadour, Napoleon I and Napoleon III, and in 1870 became the official residence of the presidents of France.

Elysium /ɪ'lɪziəm/ or the *Elysian Fields*. In classical mythology, an afterworld or paradise (sometimes called the Islands of the Blessed) for the souls of those who found favour with the gods; it was situated near the river Oceanus.

Elytis /'elitiːs/ Odysseus, pseudonym of Odysseus Alepoudelis 1911– . Greek poet. Born in Crete, he celebrates the importance of the people's attempts to shape an individual existence in freedom. His major work *To Axion Esti/Worthy It Is* 1959, is a lyric cycle, parts of which have been set to music by ◊Theodorakis. He was awarded the Nobel Prize for Literature 1979.

Elzevir /'elzəvɪə/ Louis 1540–1617. Founder of the Dutch printing house of Elzevir in the the 17th century. Born at at Louvain, he was obliged to leave Belgium in 1580 because of his Protestant and political views. He settled at Leyden as a bookseller and printer. Of his seven sons, five joined the printing business. Among the firm's publications were editions of Latin, Greek, and Hebrew works, French and Italian classics.

Emba /'embə/ river 612 km/380 mi long in the Kazakh Republic, USSR, draining into the N part of the Caspian Sea.

embroidery the art of decoration by means of a needle and thread. Ancient Egypt, Greece, Phrygia, Babylon, and China were renowned for their embroidery. The earliest emboidery that survives in England is the stole and maniple, (a decorative strip of silk worn over the arm) found in the tomb of St Cuthbert at Durham dating from 905. The ◊Bayeux 'Tapestry' is an embroidery dating from 1067–70. Embroidery has been used for the adornment of costumes, gloves, book covers, curtains, and ecclesiastical vestments. In Britain, early in the 20th century, embroidery on canvas and linen for household purposes, together with appliqué, was popular, usually in conventional designs. From the 1950s there was a revival of creative embroidery as a craft by designers in many countries.

embryo early development stage of animals and plants following fertilization of an ovum (egg cell), or ◊parthenogenetic activation of an ovum. In animals the embryo exists either within an egg (where it is nourished by food contained in the yolk), or in mammals, in the ◊uterus of the mother. In mammals (except marsupials) the embryo is fed through the ◊placenta. In humans the term embryo describes the fertilized egg during its first seven weeks of existence; from the eighth week it is referred to as the foetus. The plant embryo is found within the seed in higher plants. It sometimes consists of only a few cells, but usually includes a root, a shoot (or primary bud), and one or two ◊cotyledons, which nourish the growing seedling.

embryology the study of the changes undergone by living matter from its conception as a fertilized ovum (egg) to its emergence into the world at hatching or birth. It is mainly concerned with the changes in cell organization in the ◊embryo and the way in which these lead to the structures and organs of the adult (◊differentiation). Applications of embryology include embryo transplants, both in commercial applications (for example, in building up a prize dairy cow herd quickly at low cost) and in obstetric medicine (as a method for helping couples with fertility problems to have children). This usually involves the surgical removal of eggs from a woman, their fertilization under laboratory conditions and, once normal development is under way, their replacement in the womb. See also ◊embryo research.

embryology

bird   human

1 hour

fertilization
(1 day)

zona
pellucida

two cells
(1–2 days)

10 hours

eight cells
(2–3 days)

subgerminal
space   cell {outer
mass {inner

20 hours

blastocyst
(7 days)

archenteron

3½ days   28 days

8 days   8 weeks

embryo research the study of human embryos at an early stage, in order to detect hereditary disease, and genetic defects, and to investigate the problems of subfertility and

infertility. The UK Medical Research Council laid down in 1982 that experiments on human embryos were acceptable for approved research purposes, provided that both donors agreed. There must also be no intent to transfer the embryo to the uterus, or to culture it beyond the stage when implantation was possible. The Warnock Report 1984 proposed to limit experiment to up to 14 days after fertilization (the point at which the embryo 'decides' to become a single individual or a multiple birth). It also recommended strict controls on AID (artificial insemination by donor); IVF (*in vitro* fertilization), fertilization outside the body ('test-tube baby') when either the sperm or the egg (or both) do not necessarily come from the couple involved as eventual parents; and condemned surrogate motherhood, or 'womb leasing', in which a woman is artificially inseminated and bears a child for another couple.

embryo sac a large cell within the ovule of flowering plants which represents the female ◊gametophyte when fully developed. It typically contains eight nuclei. Fertilization occurs when one of these nuclei, the egg nucleus, fuses with a male ◊gamete.

Emden /'emdən/ port in W Germany at the mouth of the river Ems; population (1984) 50,500. It is an important export outlet for the ◊Ruhr, with which it is connected by the Dortmund-Ems canal. There are oil refineries here.

emerald green variety of the mineral ◊beryl, $Be_3Al_2Si_6O_{18}$.

emergence or *emergent evolution*. A philosophical theory, propounded in the 20th century by C Lloyd Morgan, Samuel ◊Alexander, and C ◊Broad, who maintain that life 'emerges' or 'grows naturally' out of matter, and mind emerges out of life.

emergent properties features of a system that are due to the way in which its components are structured in relationship to each other, rather than to the individual properties of those components. Thus, the distinctive characteristics of chemical ◊compounds are emergent properties of the way in which the constituent elements are organized, and cannot be explained by the particular properties of those elements taken in isolation. In biology, ◊ecosystem stability is an emergent property of the interaction between the constituent species, and not a property of the species themselves.

Emerson /'eməsən/ Ralph Waldo 1803–1882. American poet and essayist. Born at Boston, Massachusetts, and educated at Harvard, he became a ◊Unitarian minister at Boston. In 1832 he resigned and travelled to Europe, meeting Carlyle in England, who had a deep and lasting influence on his thought. On his return to America in 1833 he settled at Concord, where he led the ◊Transcendentalists. He made a second visit to England in 1847, and incorporated his impressions in *English Traits* 1856. This had been preceded by two volumes of *Essays* 1841, 1844, and *Representative Men* 1850. Later works include *The Conduct of Life* 1860, *Society and Solitude* 1870, and *Letters and Social Aims* 1876. Much of his verse was published in the

literary magazine *The Dial*, including two of his best-known poems 'The Problem' and 'Woodnotes'.

Emerson The American poet and essayist Ralph Waldo Emerson. His lucid style and clarity of thought made his writings eminently quotable, although he claimed to 'hate quotations'.

emery /'eməri/ a variety of ◊corundum, greyish-black and opaque, containing a quantity of haematite and magnetite. Its hardness is second only to diamond, and it is much used as an ◊abrasive. It occurs on the island of Naxos (Greece).

Emery /'eməri/ Walter Bryan 1903–1971. British archaeologist, who in 1929–34 in Nubia excavated the tumuli at Ballana and Qustol, rich royal tombs of the mysterious X-group (3rd to 6th centuries AD). He also surveyed the whole region 1963–64 before it was flooded as a result of the building of the Aswan High Dam.

Emilia-Romagna /e'miːljərəʊ'mænjə/ region of N central Italy including much of the Po valley; population (1981) 3,957,400. The capital is Bologna; other towns include Reggio, Rimini, Parma, Ferrara, and Ravenna.

éminence grise /'eminɒns 'griːz/ (French 'grey eminence') name given to the Capuchin friar François Leclerc du Tremblay 1577–1638 (also known as Père Joseph), who from 1612 was the close friend and behind-the-scenes adviser of Cardinal Richelieu. Since his time the term has been applied to other manipulators of power without immediate responsibility.

Eminent Persons Group group of seven distinguished Commonwealth statesmen and women deputed by Commonwealth leaders in Dec 1985 to visit South Africa to report on the political situation there and suggest solutions. It was chaired jointly by Malcolm ◊Fraser of Australia and Olusegun Obasanjo, former head of the Nigerian government. Its report, *Mission to South Africa* 1986, proposed among other things that ◊apartheid should be abolished.

Emmental /'eməntɑːl/ district in the valley of the Emme river, Berne, Switzerland, where a hard cheese of the same name has been made since the mid 15th century.

Emmet /'emɪt/ Robert 1778–1803. Irish nationalist leader. In 1803 he led an unsuccessful revolt in Dublin against British rule, and was captured, tried, and hanged. His youth and courage made him an Irish hero.

emotivism a philosophical position in the theory of ethics which came to prominence during the 1930s, largely under the influence of *Language, Truth and Logic* by A J ◊Ayer, 1936. Emotivists deny that moral judgements can be true or false: they merely express an attitude or an emotional response.

Empedocles /em'pedəkliːz/ c. 490–430 BC. Greek philosopher and scientist. He lived at Acragas (Agrigentum) in Sicily, and is famous for his analysis of the universe into the four elements – fire, air, earth, and water – which through the action of love and discord are eternally constructed, destroyed, and constructed anew. According to tradition, he committed suicide by throwing himself into the crater of Mount Etna.

emphysema lung disease (often linked to smoking, and also to playing brass instruments, such as the trumpet) in which the air spaces lose their elasticity, and are unable to expel air sufficiently. The result is progressive shortness of breath.

empiricism (from Greek *empeiria*, experience or experiment) a long-established tradition in British philosophy, frequently contrasted with ◊rationalism. The principal tenet of empiricism is the belief that all knowledge is ultimately derived from sense experience. It suspects metaphysical schemes based on *a priori* propositions, which are claimed to be true irrespective of experience. Empiricism developed in the 17th and early 18th centuries through the work of ◊Locke, ◊Berkeley, and ◊Hume, traditionally known as the British empiricist school.

employers' association an organization of employers formed for purposes of collective action. In the UK there were formerly three main organizations, which in 1965 combined as the ◊Confederation of British Industry; one of the largest in the USA is the National Association of Manufacturers.

employment exchange agency for bringing together employers requiring labour and workers seeking employment. Employment exchanges may be organized by central government or a local authority (these are known in the UK as Job Centres); or as a business venture, when they are usually called employment agencies. A similar system operates in the USA.

employment law although in Britain common law governs relations between employer and employee in circumstances not covered by special enactments, the latter cover an increasingly large field. Conditions in factories have been covered since the 19th century, but the Offices, Shops and Railway Premises Act 1963 extended protection to workers in previously neglected areas. The Equal Pay Act 1970, in force from 1975, prevents unequal pay for men and women in similar jobs. Redundancy payments were provided for under

an act of 1965, and the Contracts of Employment Act 1972 compels employers to set out details of their contract with employees including wage rates, hours of work, holiday entitlement, injury and sick pay, and length of notice to be given by both parties to end the contract. The Sex Discrimination Act 1975 attempted to secure equality of opportunity in employment for both sexes. Conditions at work are also governed by the Health and Safety at Work Act 1974 and through such bodies as the Health and Safety Commission and the Factories and Nuclear Installations Inspectors.

Empson /'empsən/ William 1906–1984. English poet and critic, born in Yorkshire. He was professor of English literature at Tokyo and Beijing (Peking), and from 1953–71 at Sheffield University. His critical work examined the potential variety of meaning in poetry, as in *Seven Types of Ambiguity* 1930 and *The Structure of Complex Words* 1951. His verse was published in *Collected Poems* 1955. He was knighted in 1979.

emu flightless running bird *Dromaius novaehollandiae*. The largest of living birds with the exception of the ostrich, it is a native of Australia and stands about 2 m/6 ft high. The emu has small rudimentary wings, short feathers on the head and neck, and a curious bag or pouch in the windpipe of the female that enables it to emit the characteristic loud booming note. In appearance it is dull and dowdy.

emulsion a type of ◊colloid, consisting of a stable dispersion of a liquid in another liquid, for example, oil and water in some cosmetic lotions.

enamel vitrified (glass-like) coating of various colours used for decorative purposes on a metallic or porcelain surface. In ◊cloisonné the various sections of the design are separated by thin metal wires or strips soldered to the metal base. In *champlevé* the enamel is fused in holes in the base.

The art of enamelling dates back to ancient times, and is believed to be of Western Asiatic origin. The Egyptians, Greeks, and Romans enamelled their jewellery, and enamel-work dating from between the 6th and the 9th centuries has been found in the British Isles. Byzantium was famed for enamels from about the 9th to the 11th centuries, and the altar-piece at St Mark's, Venice, which was brought from Constantinople, still survives. Byzantine work was emulated in Europe, particularly in Saxony, Brunswick, and in the Rhine valley. German enamellers were later employed in France, and during the 13th and 14th centuries the art was introduced into Italy. The chief centres of enamelling during the 15th and 16th centuries. were the cities of Lorraine and Limoges. Enamelling was introduced into China in about the 13th century.

encaustic painting a process of wall painting, commonly used in ancient times by the Egyptians, Greeks, and Romans, in which the coloured pigments were mixed with molten wax.

encephalin a naturally-occurring ◊peptide produced by nerve cells which has the same effect as morphine, acting as a natural painkiller. Unlike morphine, encephalins are quickly

degraded by the body, so there is no build-up of tolerance to them, and hence no 'addiction'. ◊Endorphins, larger peptides, have similar effects.

encephalitis inflammation of the brain, such as may occur with, for example, malaria, rabies, and occasionally herpes. *Japanese encephalitis* is a virus disease found in migrating birds, and transmitted by mosquitoes who first bite the birds and then humans.

◊*Sleeping sickness* or *encephalitis lethargica*, causes headache, vomiting and fever, and results in coma. There was a worldwide epidemic between 1917 and 1924.

enclosure appropriation of common land as private property, or the changing of open-field systems to enclosed fields (often used for sheep). This process began in Britain in the 14th century, and became widespread in the 15th and 16th centuries. It caused poverty, homelessness, and rural depopulation, and resulted in revolts in 1536, 1569, and 1607. Numerous government measures to prevent depopulation were introduced during 1489–1640, but were sabotaged by landowning magistrates at local level. A new wave of enclosures 1760–1820 reduced the yeoman class of small landowning farmers to agricultural labourers, or forced them to leave the land. From 1876 the enclosure of common land was limited by statutes.

encyclical a letter addressed by the pope to Roman Catholic bishops for the benefit of the people. The first was issued by Benedict XIV in 1740, but encyclicals became common only in the 19th century. They may be doctrinal (condemning errors), exhortative (recommending devotional activities), or commemorative. Among the most important recent encyclicals are *Pacem in terris* (Pope John XXIII, 1963), *Sacerdotalis celibatus* (on the celibacy of the clergy, Pope Paul VI, 1967), and *Humanae vitae* (Pope Paul VI, 1967, on methods of contraception).

encyclopedia a work of reference, usually alphabetical, covering either all fields of knowledge or one specific subject. The earliest extant encyclopedia is the *Historia Naturalis/Natural History* 23–79 AD of ◊Pliny the Elder. The first alphabetical encyclopedia in English was the *Lexicon Technicum/Technical Lexicon* 1704, compiled by John Harris. In 1728 Ephraim Chambers published his *Cyclopaedia*, which co-ordinated the scattered articles by a system of cross–references, and was translated into French 1743–45. This translation formed the basis of the *Encyclopédie* edited by Diderot and d'Alembert, published 1751–72. By this time the system of engaging a body of expert compilers and editors was established, and in 1768–71 the *Encyclopaedia Britannica* first made its appearance.

Famous encyclopedias include the Chinese encyclopedia printed 1726; the German *Conversations-Lexikon/Conversation Lexicon* of Brockhaus; and the French *Grand Dictionnaire Universel du XIXᵉ Siècle/Great Universal Dictionary of the 19th Century* of Pierre Larousse 1866–76.

Encyclopédistes a group of French scholars including D'◊Alembert and ◊Diderot who, inspired by the English encyclopedia produced by Ephraim Chambers in 1728, wrote their own 1751–72. Religious scepticism and ◊Enlightenment social and political views were a feature of the work.

endangered species a plant or animal species whose numbers are so few that it is at risk of becoming extinct. Thus, there are only about 50 Javan rhino alive today and, unless active steps are taken to promote this species' survival, it will probably be extinct within a few decades. Officially designated endangered species are listed by ◊IUCN. See also ◊CITES.

Enders /'endəz/ John Franklin 1897– . American virologist. With Thomas Weller and Frederick Robbins, he discovered the ability of the polio virus to grow in cultures of different tissues, which led to the perfection of an effective vaccine: they were awarded the Nobel Prize for Medicine in 1954. He also succeeded in isolating the measles virus.

endive hardy annual plant *Cichorium endivia* family Compositae, grown in England since the 16th century for its leaves, used in salads and cooking. It is related to ◊chicory.

endocrine gland

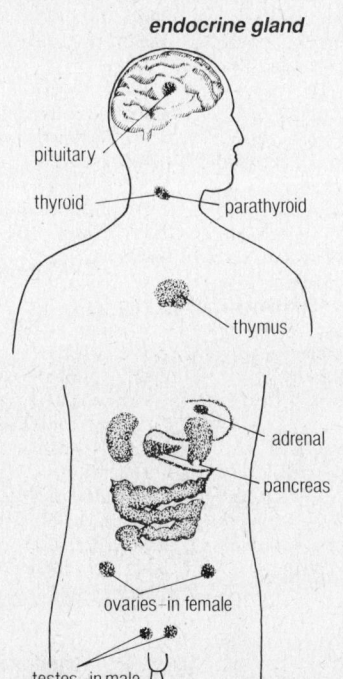

pituitary

thyroid

parathyroid

thymus

adrenal

pancreas

ovaries – in female

testes – in male

endocrine gland a type of ◊gland which secretes ◊hormones into the bloodstream, to regulate body processes. Endocrine glands are best developed in vertebrates, but are also found in other animals, notably insects. In humans, the main endocrine glands are the ◊pituitary, ◊thyroid, ◊parathyroid, ◊adrenal ◊pancreas, ◊ovary and ◊testis.

endoparasite a type of ◊parasite.

endoplasm part of a cell's ◊cytoplasm.

endoplasmic reticulum a membranous structure in ◊eukaryotic cells, often referred to as ER. Under the electron microscope it looks like a series of channels and vesicles, but it is in fact a large, sealed, bag-like structure crumpled and folded into a convoluted mass. The interior of the 'bag', the ER lumen, stores various proteins needed elsewhere in the cell, then organizes them into transport vesicles formed by a small piece of ER membrane budding from the main membrane. ER also carries various enzymes needed for the synthesis of ◊fats and it often bears ◊ribosomes which carry out protein synthesis.

endorphin a natural substance (a polypeptide) that modifies the action of ◊nerve cells. Endorphins are produced by the ◊pituitary gland and ◊hypothalamus of vertebrates. They lower the perception of pain by reducing the transmission of signals between nerve cells. Discovered in the 1970s, endorphins not only regulate pain and hunger, but are also involved in the release of sex hormones from the pituitary gland. Drugs such as morphine, heroin and opium act in a similar way to endorphins but they are not rapidly degraded by the body, as natural endorphins are, and thus have a long-lasting effect on pain-perception and mood. See also ◊encephalin.

endoscope an optical instrument for looking inside the body, without the need for surgery. A modern type of endoscope consists of a bundle of optical fibres, some of which carry light to illuminate the target, while the rest are used for viewing (see ◊fibre optics). It can be inserted in the body to view, say, the stomach or, via a vein, the heart. Advanced endoscopes are fitted with scalpel devices so that they can be used for minor operations internally. Similar endoscopes are used to examine inside machines or any small confined spaces.

endoskeleton the internal supporting structure, or ◊skeleton, of vertebrates, made up of ◊cartilage or ◊bone. It provides support, and acts as a system of levers to which muscles are attached to provide movement. Certain parts of the skeleton (the ◊skull and ◊ribs) give protection to vital body organs. Some simple animals also have an endoskeleton, although of a very much simpler type. ◊Sponges are supported by a network of rigid or semi-rigid, spiky structures called spicules; a bath sponge is the proteinaceous skeleton of a sponge. See also ◊exoskeleton.

endosperm a nutritive tissue in the seeds of most flowering plants. It surrounds the embryo and is produced by an unusual process that parallels the ◊fertilization of the ovum by a male gamete. A second male gamete from the pollen grain fuses with two female nuclei within the ◊embryo sac. Thus the endosperm cells are triploid (having three sets of chromosomes). They contain food reserves such as starch, fat and protein which are utilized by the developing seedling. In 'non endospermic' seeds, absorption of these food molecules by the embryo is completed early, so that the endosperm has disappeared by the time of germination.

endotherm a 'warm-blooded' animal; see ◊homeothermy.

end user a user of a computer program, in particular someone who uses a program to perform a task (such as accounting or playing a computer game) rather than someone who writes programs (a programmer).

energy the capacity for doing ◊work. Potential energy (PE) is energy deriving from position: thus a stretched spring has elastic PE; an object raised to a height above the earth's surface, or the water in an elevated reservoir, has gravitational PE; a lump of coal and a tank of petrol, together with the oxygen needed for their combustion, have chemical PE (due to relative positions of atoms). Other sorts of PE include electrical and nuclear. Moving bodies possess kinetic energy (KE).

Energy can be converted from one form to another, but the total quantity stays the same (in accordance with the conservation laws that govern many natural phenomena). For example, as an apple falls it loses gravitational PE but gains KE. Einstein's special theory of ◊relativity 1905 correlates any gain, E, in KE with a loss, m, in 'rest mass', by the equation $E = mc^2$, in which E is energy and c is the speed of light. The equation applies universally, not just to nuclear reactions, though it is only for these that the percentage change in rest mass is large enough to detect. Although energy is never lost, after a number of conversions it tends to finish up as KE of random motion of molecules (e.g. of the air) at lowish temperatures. This is 'degraded' energy in that it is difficult to convert it back to other forms.

So-called energy resources are stores of convertible energy. Non-renewable resources include the fossil fuels (coal, oil, and gas) and ◊nuclear fission 'fuels' for example uranium-235. Burning fossil fuel causes ◊acid rain and is gradually increasing the carbon dioxide content in the atmosphere, with unknown consequences for future generations. Coal-fired power stations also release significant amounts of radioactive material, and the potential dangers of nuclear power stations are greater still.

Renewable resources, which have so far been less exploited, depend ultimately on the Sun's energy. Hydroelectric schemes are well established, and wind turbines and tidal systems are being developed. The ultimate non-renewable but almost inexhaustible energy source would be nuclear fusion (the way in which energy is generated in the Sun), but controlled fusion is a long way off. (The hydrogen bomb is a fusion bomb.) Harnessing resources generally implies converting their energy into electrical form, because electrical energy is easy to convert to other forms and to transmit from place to place, though not to store.

Enfield /'enfiːld/ borough of NE Greater London. Population (1981) 259,000. Industries include engineering – the Royal Small Arms factory was famous for its production of the Enfield rifle – textiles, furniture, and cement. Little remains of ◊Edward VI's palace, but the royal hunting ground of Enfield Chase partly survives in the 'green belt'. The borough includes the district of Edmonton, where John ◊Keats and Charles and Mary ◊Lamb once lived (the Lambs are buried there); and the Bell Inn, referred to in

William ◊Cowper's poem 'John Gilpin'. From the 1970s the Lea Valley has been developed as London's first regional park.

Engadine /'eŋgədiːn/ the upper valley of the river Inn in Switzerland, famous as a winter sports resort.

Engels /'eŋglz/ Friedrich 1820–1895. German social and political philosopher. In 1842 his father sent him to work in the cotton-factory owned by his family in Manchester, England. There he established contact with the ◊Chartists, and collected material for his *The Condition of the Working Class in England in 1844* 1845. In 1844 began his lifelong friendship with Karl ◊Marx, in collaboration with whom he worked out the materialist interpretation of history and in 1847–48 wrote the *Communist Manifesto*. Returning to Germany during the 1848–49 revolution, Engels worked with Marx on the *Neue Rheinische Zeitung/New Rhine Newspaper*, and fought on the barricades in Baden. After the defeat of the revolution he returned to Manchester, and for the rest of his life largely supported the Marx family. The lessons of 1848 he summed up in his *The Peasants' War in Germany* 1850 and *Revolution and Counter-Revolution in Germany* 1851. After Marx's death Engels was largely responsible for the wider dissemination of his ideas; he edited the second and third volumes of Marx's *Capital* in 1885 and 1894. Although Engels himself regarded his ideas as identical with those of Marx, discrepancies between their works are the basis of many modern Marxist debates.

Engels The German socialist philosopher Friedrich Engels was also manager of a family cotton factory in Manchester. He collaborated with his lifelong friend Karl Marx on the *Communist Manifesto*, while his later works helped to popularize Marxist beliefs.

engineering broadly speaking, engineering is the application of science for the benefit of human beings. It involves the design, construction and maintenance of works, machinery, roads, railways, bridges, harbour installations, engines, ships, aircraft and airports, spacecraft and space stations, and the generation, transmission and use of electrical power. To practise engineering professionally a university or college training in addition to practical experience is required, but technician engineers usually receive their training through apprenticeships or similar training schemes. The main divisions of engineering are aeronautical, chemical, civil, electrical, electronic, gas, marine, mechanical, metallurgical, mining, production, radio and structural engineering.

engineering drawing a technical drawing that forms the plans for the design and construction of engineering components and structures. Engineering drawings show different projections, or views of objects, with the relevant dimensions, and show how they fit together.

England /'ɪŋglənd/ largest division of the ◊United Kingdom.
area 130,763 sq km/50,487 sq mi
capital London
towns Birmingham, Cambridge, Coventry, Leeds, Leicester, Manchester, Newcastle-upon-Tyne, Nottingham, Oxford, Sheffield, York; ports Bristol, Dover, Felixstowe, Harwich, Liverpool, Portsmouth and Southampton
features variability of climate and diversity of scenery; among European countries, only the Netherlands is more densely populated
exports agricultural (cereals, rape, sugar beet, potatoes); meat and meat products; electronic (especially software), and telecommunications equipment (main centres Berkshire and Cambridge); scientific instruments; textiles and fashion goods; ◊North Sea oil and gas, petrochemicals, pharmaceuticals, fertilizers; beer; china clay, pottery, porcelain, and glass; film and television programmes, and sound recordings. Tourism is important. There are worldwide banking and insurance interests.
currency pound sterling
population (1981) 46,229,955
language English, with more than 100 minority languages
religion Christian, with the ◊Anglican Communion as the established church, 31,500,000; plus various Protestant sects, of which the largest is the ◊Methodist 1,400,000; Roman Catholic about 5,000,000; Jewish 410,000; Muslim 900,000; Sikh 175,000; Hindu 140,000.
For *government* and *history*, see ◊United Kingdom.

England: history BC
Old Stone Age Traces of human occupation at Cheddar Caves, Somerset. *New Stone Age* Long barrows; remains of flint mining can be seen at Grimes Graves, Norfolk.
Bronze Age Round barrows.
c. 1800 Invasion of the Beaker people, who left traces of their occupation at Avebury and Stonehenge.
c. 450 Iron Age begins.
c. 400 Invasion by the Celts, who built hillforts, and left burial sites containing chariots.
55–54 Julius Caesar first visited England.

ENGLAND: COUNTIES

County	Area sq km	Administrative headquarters
Avon	1,338	Bristol
Bedfordshire	1,235	Bedford
Berkshire	1,256	Reading
Buckinghamshire	1,883	Aylesbury
Cambridgeshire	3,409	Cambridge
Cheshire	2,332	Chester
Cleveland	583	Middlesborough
Cornwall	3,546	Truro
Cumbria	6,809	Carlisle
Derbyshire	2,631	Matlock
Devon	6,715	Exeter
Dorset	2,654	Dorchester
Durham	2,436	Durham
East Sussex	1,795	Lewes
Essex	3,674	Chelmsford
Gloucestershire	3,117	Gloucester
Hampshire	3,772	Winchester
Hereford & Worcester	3,925	Worcester
Hertfordshire	1,634	Hertford
Humberside	3,512	Kingston upon Hull
Kent	3,730	Maidstone
Lancashire	3,005	Preston
Leicestershire	2,553	Leicester
Lincolnshire	5,885	Lincoln
London, Greater	1,580	
Manchester, Greater	1,284	
Merseyside	648	Liverpool
Norfolk	5,515	Norwich
Northamptonshire	2,367	Northampton
Northumberland	5,034	Newcastle-upon-Tyne
North Yorkshire	8,316	Northallerton
Nottinghamshire	2,108	Nottingham
Oxfordshire	2,612	Oxford
Shropshire	3,490	Shrewsbury
Somerset	3,458	Taunton
South Yorkshire	1,562	Barnsley
Staffordshire	2,660	Stafford
Suffolk	3,807	Ipswich
Surrey	1,655	Kingston upon Thames
Tyne & Wear	567	Newcastle
Warwickshire	1,980	Warwick
West Midlands	958	Birmingham
West Sussex	2,017	Chichester
West Yorkshire	2,039	Wakefield
Wiltshire	3,481	Trowbridge

AD
43 Beginning of Roman conquest; surviving remains can be seen at Bath, Fishbourne (near Chichester), Hadrian's Wall, Watling Street, London (Temple of Mithras), Dover, St Alban's, and Dorchester.
407 Romans withdrew, but partially reoccupied the country c. 417–27 and c. 450.
5th–7th centuries Anglo-Saxons overran all England except Cornwall and Cumberland, forming independent kingdoms including Northumbria, Mercia, Kent, and Wessex.
c. 597 England converted to Christianity by St Augustine.

829 Egbert of Wessex accepted as overlord of all England.

878 Alfred ceded N and E England to the Danish invaders but kept them out of Wessex.

1066 Norman Conquest; England passed into French hands under William the Conqueror.

1172 Henry II became King of Ireland.

1215 King John forced to sign Magna Carta.

1284 Conquest of Wales, begun by the Normans, completed by Edward I.

1295 Model Parliament set up.

1338–1453 Hundred Years War with France enabled parliament to secure control of taxation, and, by impeachment, of the king's choice of ministers.

1348–49 Black Death killed about 30% of the population.

1381 Social upheaval led to the Peasants' Revolt, which was brutally repressed.

1399 Richard II deposed by parliament for absolutism.

1414 Lollard revolt repressed.

1455–85 Wars of the Roses.

1497 Henry VII ended the power of the feudal nobility with the suppression of the Yorkist revolts.

1529 Henry VIII became head of the English Church after breaking with Rome.

1536–43 Acts of Union united England and Wales after conquest.

1547 Edward VI adopted Protestant doctrines.

1553 Reversion to Roman Catholicism under Mary I.

1558 Elizabeth I adopted a religious compromise.

1588 Attempted invasion of England by the Spanish Armada.

1603 James I united the English and Scottish crowns; parliamentary dissidence increased.

1642-52 Civil War between royalists and parliamentarians.

1649 Charles I executed and the Commonwealth set up.

1653 Oliver Cromwell appointed Lord Protector.

1660 Restoration of Charles II.

1685 Monmouth rebellion.

1688 William of Orange invited to take the throne; flight of James II.

1707 Act of Union between England and Scotland under Queen Anne, after which the countries became known as Great Britain.

Engleheart /'eŋgəlhɑːt/ George 1752–1829. English miniature painter. Born at Kew, he studied under Joshua ◊Reynolds and in 40 years painted nearly 5,000 miniatures including copies of many of Reynolds' portraits.

English art *painting* English ◊medieval art included illuminated manuscripts and wall paintings. Some of the surviving wall paintings were deliberately damaged on religious grounds or have been incompetently restored, but recent discoveries show a well-established tradition.

In Tudor times for the first time painting became mainly secular, and the first well-known artist is Hans ◊Holbein, who came from Germany to paint the court of Henry VIII. Among his followers was the miniaturist Nicholas ◊Hilliard, who established a tradition of English excellence in this field which was continued by Samuel ◊Cooper, Richard ◊Cosway and George ◊Engleheart. The Flemish Anthony ◊van Dyck, employed as a court painter by Charles I from 1632, greatly influenced English portrait painters, as did Peter ◊Lely and Godfrey ◊Kneller.

In the 18th century William ◊Hogarth and Thomas ◊Rowlandson used art as a vehicle for social satire, The German-born Johann ◊Zoffany and Arthur Devis were painters of portraits and conversation pieces. An indigenous form is the sporting picture, George ◊Stubbs being the great 18th-century master, although the Sartorius and ◊Alken families also produced fine work, as did Edwin ◊Landseer in the next century and Alfred ◊Munnings in the 20th. George ◊Morland's pictures of rural life have a similar vigorous realism. Among English portrait painters Joshua ◊Reynolds, Thomas ◊Gainsborough – also a landscape artist – and Thomas ◊Lawrence are the best-known of the late 18th and early 19th centuries. Rather apart were the visionary William ◊Blake, the water-colourist Samuel ◊Palmer, who came under his influence, and John ◊Martin. Among painters specializing in landscape in the same period were Richard ◊Wilson, Paul Sandby, Alexander ◊Cozens, J R ◊Cozens, John ◊Crome, Thomas ◊Girtin, J S ◊Cotman, David ◊Cox, Peter ◊de Wint and – the best known and most influential – J W M ◊Turner and John ◊Constable.

In Victorian times the subject picture was popular and there was a domestic school which included J C ◊Horsley. An outstanding group were the ◊Pre-Raphaelites – ◊Millais, Holman ◊Hunt and ◊Rossetti, together with G F Watts, Ford Madox ◊Brown, Frederick ◊Leighton and Edward ◊Burne-Jones. J M ◊Whistler, the American who introduced the doctrine of 'art for art's sake' and settled in Chelsea, had as his disciple W R ◊Sickert, who also admired the French painter ◊Degas and with Wilson ◊Steer introduced Impressionism to England. Sickert headed the ◊Camden Town group which included Spencer Gore and Harold Gilman. Among artists of the 20th century are Duncan ◊Grant, Frank ◊Brangwyn, William ◊Nicholson, Augustus ◊John, Gwen ◊John, Paul ◊Nash, Ben ◊Nicholson, Christopher Wood, Graham ◊Sutherland, Ivon ◊Hitchens, Stanley ◊Spencer, John ◊Bratby, Francis ◊Bacon, Victor ◊Pasmore, and Lucian ◊Freud.

In more recent years there has been a tendency to individualism divorced from schools and particular genres, of which the multi-figure townscapes of L S ◊Lowry and work of David ◊Hockney are disparate examples.

sculpture some early Celtic work has survived. From medieval times there are ecclesiastical sculptures, for example in Wells Cathedral and the Henry VII chapel in Westminster Abbey. In the 18th century foreign sculptors such as Louis Roubillac were popular, but John Flaxman is the first widely known English name. Well-known in the 19th century were Francis ◊Chantrey, Alfred Stevens, and Frederick Leighton, and George ◊Frampton at the turn of the century. The 20th century has seen the work of Jacob ◊Epstein, Eric ◊Gill, Frank Dobson, Henry ◊Moore, Barbara ◊Hepworth, Anthony ◊Caro and Reg ◊Butler.

architecture the main styles in English architecture are: Saxon, Norman, Early English (of which Westminster Abbey is an example), Decorated, Perpendicular (15th century), Tudor (a name chiefly applied to domestic buildings of the period about 1485–1558), Jacobean, Stuart (including the Renaissance and Queen Anne styles), Georgian, and the Gothic revival of the 19th century. Notable architects include Christopher ◊Wren, Inigo ◊Jones, ◊Vanbrugh, ◊Hawksmoor, Charles ◊Barry, Edwin ◊Lutyens, Hugh ◊Casson, Basil ◊Spence, Frederick ◊Gibberd, Denys ◊Lasdun and Richard ◊Rogers.

English Channel stretch of water off S coast of England, see ◊Channel.

English Civil War see ◊Civil War, English.

English language a member of the Germanic branch of the Indo-European language family, traditionally described as having passed through four major stages over about 1,500 years: *Old English* or *Anglo-Saxon* (c. 500–1050), *Middle English* (c. 1050–1550), *Early Modern English* (c. 1550–1700), and *Late Modern English* (from c. 1700 onward). The ancestral forms of English were dialects brought from the NW coastlands of Europe to the island of Britain by Angle, Saxon and Jutish invaders who gained footholds in the SE in the 5th century and over the next 200 years extended and consolidated their settlements from the Channel to the Firth of Forth. Scholars distinguish four main early dialects: of the Jutes in Kent, the Saxons in the south, the Mercians or S Angles in the Midlands, and the Northumbrians or N Angles north of the Humber. Until the Danish invasions of the 9th to 11th centuries, Old English was a highly inflected language, but appears to have lost many of its grammatical endings in the interaction with Danish, creating a more open or analytic style of language that was further changed by the influence of Norman-French after the Conquest of 1066. For several centuries English was in competition with other languages: first the various Celtic languages of Britain, then Danish, then French as the language of Plantagenet England and Latin as the language of the Church. In Scotland, English was in competition with Gaelic and with the Welsh of the Strathclyde Britons, as well as French and Latin (see Scots). In 1362 English at last replaced French as the language of the law courts of England, although the records continued for some time to be kept in Latin. Geoffrey Chaucer was a court poet at this time and strongly influenced the literary style of the London dialect. When William Caxton set up his printing press in London in 1477 the new hybrid language (vernacular English mixed with courtly French and learned Latin) became increasingly standardized, and by 1611, when the Authorized Version of the Bible was published, the educated English of the Home Counties and London had become the core of what is now called 'Standard English'. At the same time, however, dialect variation remained, and still remains, very great throughout Britain. By the end of the 16th century, English was firmly established in four

ENGLISH SOVEREIGNS FROM 900

West Saxon Kings

Edward the Elder	901	son of Alfred the Great
Athelstan	925	son of Edward I
Edmund	940	half-brother of Athelstan
Edred	946	brother of Edmund
Edwy	955	son of Edmund
Edgar	959	brother of Edwy
Edward the Martyr	975	son of Edgar
Ethelred II	978	son of Edgar
Edmund Ironside	1016	son of Ethelred

Danish Kings

Canute	1016	son of Sweyn
Hardicanute	1040	son of Canute
Harold I	1035	son of Canute

West Saxon Kings (restored)

Edward the Confessor	1042	son of Ethelred II
Harold II	1066	son of Godwin

Norman Kings

William I	1066	
William II	1087	son of William I
Henry I	1100	son of William I
Stephen	1135	son of Adela (daughter of William II)

House of Plantagenet

Henry II	1154	son of Matilda
Richard I	1189	son of Henry II
John	1199	son of Henry II
Henry III	1216	son of John
Edward I	1272	son of Henry III
Edward II	1307	son of Edward I
Edward III	1327	son of Edward II
Richard II	1377	son of the Black Prince (son of Edward III)

House of Lancaster

Henry IV	1399	son of John of Gaunt
Henry V	1413	son of Henvy IV
Henry VI	1422	son of Henry V

House of York

Edward IV	1461	son of Richard, Duke of York
Richard III	1483	brother of Edward IV
Edward V	1483	son of Edward IV

House of Tudor

Henry VII	1485	son of Edmund Tudor, Earl of Richmond
Henry VIII	1509	son of Henry VII
Edward VI	1547	son of Henry VIII
Mary I	1553	daughter of Henry VIII
Elizabeth I	1558	daughter of Henry VIII

House of Stuart

James I	1603	great-grandson of Margaret
Charles I	1625	son of James I

The Commonwealth

House of Stuart (restored)

Charles II	1660	son of Charles I
James II	1685	son of Charles I
William III and Mary	1689	son of Mary (daughter of Charles I)/daughter of James II
Anne	1702	daughter of James II

House of Hanover

George I	1714	son of Sophia (granddaughter of James I)
George II	1727	son of George I
George III	1760	son of Frederick (son of George II)
George IV	1820	son of George III
William IV	1830	son of George III
Victoria	1837	daughter of Edward (son of George III)

House of Saxe-Coburg

Edward VII	1901	son of Victoria

House of Windsor

George V	1910	son of Edward VII
Edward VIII	1936	son of George V
George VI	1936	son of George V
Elizabeth II	1952	daughter of George VI

---

countries: England, Scotland, Wales and Ireland, and with the establishment of the colonies in North America in the early 17th century took root in what are now the United States, Canada and the Caribbean islands. Seafaring, exploration, commerce and colonial expansion in due course took both the standard language and other varieties to every corner of the world. By the time of Johnson's world-famous Dictionary in 1755 and the American Declaration of Independence in 1776 English was no longer confined to one off-shore European island, and was recognizably the language we use today. The orthography of English was more or less established by 1650, and in England in particular a form of standard educated speech (known as 'Received Pronunciation') spread out in the 19th century from the major public (= private) schools. This accent was adopted in the early 20th century by the BBC for its announcers and readers, and is variously known as RP, BBC English, Oxford English and the King's or Queen's English. It was also the socially dominant accent of the British Empire, and retains great prestige, especially as a model for foreigners acquiring the language. Outside Britain, however, especially in N America, it has no more status than any other educated accent of English, and in the UK is no longer so assiduously sought after by the upwardly mobile as it once was. By and large, Standard English today is not dependent on accent, but rather on shared educational experience, especially of the printed language. Today English is an immensely varied language, having absorbed material from many other tongues. It is currently used in a spectrum of varieties from British English, American English, Canadian English, Indian English and so on, through to such new 'Englishes' as Singapore English and Nigerian English and many pidgins and creoles. It is spoken by more than 300 million 'native speakers', and between 400 and 800 million 'foreign users'. It is the official language of aircraft and shipping, the leading language of science, technology, computers and commerce, and a major medium of education, publishing and international negotiation. For this reason scholars frequently refer to its latest phase as 'World English'.

English law one of the major European legal systems, Roman law being the other. English law has spread to the USA, Canada, Australia, and New Zealand, and has greatly influenced Indian law. It has a continuous history dating from the local customs of the Anglo-Saxons, traces of which survived until 1925. After the Norman Conquest there grew up, side by side with the Saxon shire courts, the feudal courts of the barons and the ecclesiastical courts. From the king's council developed the royal courts, presided over by professional judges, which gradually absorbed the jurisdictions of the baronial and ecclesiastical courts. By 1250 the royal judges had amalgamated the various local customs into the system of ◊Common Law, that is, law common to the whole country. A second system known as ◊Equity developed in the Court of Chancery, in which the Lord Chancellor considered petitions.

In the 17th–18th centuries, Common Law absorbed the Law Merchant, the international code of mercantile customs. During the 19th century virtually the whole of English law was reformed by legislation, for example, the number of capital offences was greatly reduced. The Judicature Acts 1873–75 abolished a multiplicity of courts, and in their place established the Supreme Court of Judicature, organized in the Court of Appeal and the High Court of Justice; the latter has three divisions – the Queen's Bench, Chancery, and Family Divisions. All Supreme Court judges may apply both Common Law and Equity in deciding cases. From the Court of Appeal there may be a further appeal to the House of Lords.

A unique feature of English law is the doctrine of judicial precedents, whereby the reported decisions of the courts form a binding source of law for future decisions. A judge is bound by decisions of courts of superior jurisdiction, but not necessarily by those of inferior courts.

English literature the earliest surviving English literature is in the form of Old English poems – *Beowulf* and the epic fragments *Finnesburh*, *Waldhere*, *Deor* and *Widsith* – which reflect the heroic age and Germanic legends of the 4th–6th centuries, although probably not written down until the 7th century. Heroic elements survive in several elegiac lyrics, for example *The Wanderer*, *The Seafarer*, and in many poems with a specifically Christian content, such as *The Dream of the Rood*; the Saints' Lives, for example *Elene*, by the 8th-century poet Cynewulf; and biblical paraphrases, for example *Genesis*, formerly attributed to Caedmon. These poems are all written in unrhymed alliterative metre. The great prose writers of the early period were the Latin scholars Bede, Aldhelm, and Alcuin, and King Alfred founded the tradition of English prose with his translations and his establishment of the Anglo-Saxon Chronicle; other prose writers of the time are Aelfric and Wulfstan.

With the arrival of a Norman ruling class at the end of the 11th century, the ascendancy of Norman-French in cultural life began, and it was not until the 13th century that the native literature regained its strength. Prose was concerned chiefly with popular devotional use, but verse emerged most typically in the metrical chronicles, such as Layamon's *Brut*, and the numerous romances based on the stories of Charlemagne, the Arthurian legends, the classical episodes of Troy, and so on. First of the great English poets was Chaucer, whose early work reflected the predominant French influence, but later that of Renaissance Italy. Of purely native inspiration was *The Vision of Piers Plowman* of Langland in the old alliterative verse, and the anonymous *Pearl*, *Patience*, and *Gawayne and the Grene Knight*. Chaucer's mastery of versification was not shared by his much less effective successors, Lydgate, Hoccleve, and Hawes; most original of them was Skelton. More successful were the anonymous authors of ◊songs and ◊carols, and of the ◊ballads, which (for example those concerned with Robin Hood) often formed a complete cycle. Drama flowered in the form of ◊miracle and ◊morality plays, and ◊prose, although still awkwardly handled by Wycliffe in his translation of the Bible, rose to a great height with Malory in the 15th century.

The Renaissance, which had first touched the English language through Chaucer, came to delayed fruition in the 16th century. Wyatt and Surrey used the sonnet and blank verse in typically Elizabethan forms, and prepared the way for Spenser, Sidney, Daniel, Campion, and others. With Kyd and Marlowe drama emerged into theatrical form; it reached the highest level in Shakespeare and Jonson. Elizabethan prose is represented by Hooker, North, Ascham, Holinshed, Lyly, and others, but English prose reached full richness in the 17th century, with the Authorized Version of the Bible 1611, Bacon, Milton, Bunyan, Taylor, Browne, Walton, and Pepys. Most renowned of the 17th-century poets were Milton and Donne; others include the religious writers Herbert, Crashaw, Vaughan, and Traherne, and the Cavalier poets Herrick, Carew, Suckling, and Lovelace. To the Restoration belong the poet Butler, and Dryden, poet, dramatist, and critic, the founders of religious and political satire; the best of the court poets, Rochester; and the once popular Cowley, Waller, and Denham. Drama is represented by Dryden; Otway and Lee in tragedy; Etherege, Wycherley, Congreve, Vanbrugh, and Farquhar in comedy.

The 18th century is known as the Augustan Age in English literature. Pope developed the poetic technique of Dryden; while in prose Steele and Addison evolved the polite essay, Swift achieved supremacy in satire, and Defoe exploited his journalistic ability. This century also saw the development of the ◊novel through the epistolary style of Richardson to the robust narrative of Fielding and Smollett, the comic genius of Sterne, and the Gothic 'horror' of Horace Walpole. The Neoclassical standards established by the Augustans were maintained by Johnson and his circle – Goldsmith, Burke, Reynolds, Sheridan, and others – but the romantic element present in the work of poets Thomson, Gray, Young, and Collins was soon to overturn them. The forgeries of Chatterton and Macpherson's *Ossian* foreshadowed the new Romantic movement.

The *Lyrical Ballads* 1798 of Wordsworth and Coleridge were the manifesto of the new Romantic age. Byron, Shelley, and Keats form a second generation of Romantic poets. In fiction Scott took over the Gothic tradition from Mrs Radcliffe, to create the ◊historical novel, and Jane Austen established the novel of the comedy of manners. Criticism gained new prominence in Coleridge, Lamb, Hazlitt, and De Quincey.

During the 19th century the novel was further developed by Dickens, Thackeray, the Brontës, George Eliot, Trollope, and others. The principal poets of the reign of Victoria were Tennyson, Robert and Elizabeth Browning, Arnold, the Rossettis, Morris and Swinburne, and the solitary Fitzgerald.

A lone voice in poetry, Victorian by birth date but belonging to the 20th century for his experimentation with verse forms, was Gerard Manley Hopkins. Poets of World War I include Sassoon, Brooke, Owen, and Graves. Poets of the succeeding years include T S Eliot, Auden, Day Lewis, MacNeice and Spender. New elements entered the novel with Henry James, Conrad, Kipling, and George Moore. A middle-class realism developed in the novels of Wells, Bennett, Forster, and Galsworthy. Maugham, James Joyce, D H Lawrence, Aldous Huxley, Virginia Woolf, Christopher Isherwood, Evelyn Waugh, and Graham Greene are later writers of fiction. Writers for the stage include Shaw, Galsworthy, J B Priestley, Coward, Rattigan, Emlyn Williams, and the writers of poetic drama, such as T S Eliot, Fry, Auden, Isherwood, and Dylan Thomas. The 1950s and 1960s produced the 'kitchen sink' dramatists, including Osborne and Wesker. The following decade saw the rise of Harold Pinter, John Arden, Tom Stoppard, Peter Schaffer, Joe Orton, and Alan Ayckbourn. Poets since 1945 include Thom Gunn, Roy Fuller, Philip Larkin, and John Betjeman; novelists include William Golding, Iris Murdoch, Angus Wilson, Muriel Spark, Lawrence Durrell, John Braine, Kingsley Amis, C P Snow, Anthony Powell, Alan Sillitoe, Anthony Burgess, John Fowles, Ian McEwan, Angela Carter and Doris Lessing.

English-Speaking Union society for promoting the fellowship of the English-speaking peoples of the world, founded in 1918 by Sir Evelyn Wrench.

engraving the art of incising marks of any kind upon any hard substance, especially on blocks of metal or wood for purposes of reproducing the design by printing. Three main types of prints are produced in this way: (1) relief prints made by means of wood-cutting and wood engraving; (2) intaglio prints made by means of engraving and etching upon metal, of which the main processes are line engraving, stipple engraving, ◊aquatint, ◊dry-point, ◊etching, ◊print, and ◊mezzotint; and (3) surface prints made by means of ◊lithography.

enhanced radiation weapon another name for the ◊neutron bomb.

Eniwetok /ˌenɪˈwiːtɒk/ atoll in the ◊Marshall Islands, in the central Pacific Ocean, Population (1980) 453. In 1944 it was taken from Japan by the USA, which made the island a naval base and conducted 43 atomic tests there from 1947. The inhabitants were re-settled at Ujelang, but insisted on returning home in 1980 though radiation danger persisted in spite of nuclear debris and contaminated soil having been removed to the islet of Runit and restoration work having been carried out.

Enlightenment a broad European intellectual movement, reaching its high point in the 18th century. Enlightenment thinkers were believers in social progress and in the liberating possibilities of science. They were often critical of existing society and were hostile to religion, which they saw as keeping the human mind chained down by superstition. The American and French revolutions were justified by Enlightenment principles of human natural rights. Leading representatives of the Enlightenment are ◊Voltaire, ◊Lessing, and ◊Diderot.

Ennis /ˈenɪs/ county town of County Clare, Republic of Ireland, on the river Fergus, 32 km/20 mi NW of Limerick; population (1971) 5,975. There are distilleries, flour mills, and furniture manufacturing.

Enniskillen /ˌenɪsˈkɪlən/ county town of Fermanagh, Northern Ireland, between Upper and Lower Lough Erne; population (1981) 10,500. There is some light industry, and it has been designated for further industrial growth. A bomb exploded there at a Remembrance Day service in Nov 1987, causing many casualties.

Ennius /'eniəs/ Quintus 239–169 BC. Earliest Roman poet. Born near Tarentum in S Italy, he wrote tragedies based on Greek models. His epic poem, the *Annales*, deals with Roman history.

enosis the movement, developed from 1930, for the union of ◊Cyprus with Greece.

ENSA (English National Service Association) an organization formed in 1938–39 to provide entertainment for the British and allied forces during World War II. Directed by Basil ◊Dean from headquarters in the Drury Lane Theatre, it provided a variety of entertainment throughout the UK and also in all war zones abroad.

Enschede /'enskədeɪ/ textile manufacturing centre in Overijssel province, the Netherlands; population (1982) 144,600.

Ensor /'ensɔ:/ James 1860–1949. Belgian artist, noted for macabre satire and dissonant colour, for example *Entrance of Christ into Brussels* 1888.

entail in law, the settlement of land on a successive line of people, usually succeeding generations of the original owner's family. An entail can be either (1) general, in which case it descends to the eldest child, or (2) special, when it descends according to a specific arrangement, for example, to the eldest male child or the eldest female child. Such settlements are increasingly rare in modern times, and the power to make them has often been destroyed by legislation, for example, restrictions in certain states of the USA.

Entebbe /en'tebi/ town in Uganda, on the NW shore of Lake Victoria, 20 km/16 mi SW of Kampala, the capital; population (1977) 22,000. It lies 1,779 m/3,863 ft above sea level. Founded in 1893, it was the administrative centre of Uganda from 1894–1962. An incident here in 1976 involved the hijacking of a French aircraft by a Palestinian liberation group. It was flown to Entebbe airport, where the hostages on board were rescued six days later by Israeli aircraft.

Entente Cordiale (French 'friendly understanding') the agreement reached by Britain and France in 1904 recognizing British interests in Egypt and French interests in Morocco.

enteric a general term applied to infective fevers of the intestine, especially typhoid and paratyphoid.

enterprise zone in the UK, a special zone designated by the government in which there is total exemption from rates on industrial and commercial property, from development land tax, and from certain other restrictions. Enterprise zones were introduced in 1980 to encourage regional investment, particularly in depressed inner city areas.

entomology the study of ◊insects.

entrechat a spring into the air during which the dancer criss-crosses his legs and feet a number of times. Wayne ◊Sleep broke ◊Nijinsky's record of an *entrechat dix* (ten

times) with an *entrechat douze* (12 times) in 1973.

entropy in ◊thermodynamics (the study of heat as related to other forms of energy), a parameter representing the state of disorder of a system at the atomic, ionic or molecular level; the greater disorder, the higher the entropy. Thus the fast-moving disordered molecules of water vapour have higher entropy than those of more ordered liquid water, which in turn have more entropy than the molecules in solid crystalline ice. At ◊absolute zero (−273°C/0 K), when all molecular motion ceases and order is assumed to be complete, entropy is zero.

Enugu /ɛ'nuːguː/ town in Nigeria, capital of East Central state. Population (1975) 187,000. It is a coal mining centre, with steel and cement works, and is linked by rail with Port Harcourt.

E number any of various numbers preceded by the letter E (standing for European) which represent food additives and which under EEC regulations must be displayed on the packaging of food which contains such additives. They cover preservatives, flavourings, and colourings (for example E150 is caramel colouring).

envelope in geometry, a curve that touches all the members of a family of curves. For example, a family of three equal circles all touching each other and forming a triangle (like a clover leaf) has two envelopes: a small circle that fits in the triangular space in the middle, and a large circle that encompasses all three circles.

Enver Pasha /'envə 'pɑːʃə/ 1881–1922. Turkish politician and soldier. He led the military revolt in 1908 which resulted in the Young Turk revolution (see ◊Turkey). He was killed fighting the Bolsheviks in Turkestan.

environment in ◊ecology, the sum of conditions affecting a particular organism, including physical surroundings, climate and influences of other living organisms; see also ◊biosphere and ◊habitat. In common usage, 'the environment' often means the total global environment, without reference to any particular organism. In genetics, it is the external influences that affect an organism's development, and thus its ◊phenotype.

environment-heredity controversy a long-standing dispute among philosophers, psychologists, and scientists over the relative importance of environment (upbringing, experience, and learning) and heredity (genetic inheritance) in determining the make-up of an organism, especially as related to human personality and intelligence. It has also been called the nature-nurture controversy. A particularly controversial aspect of the debate has to do with the reasons for differences between individuals, for example, in performance in ◊intelligence tests. The environmentalist position assumes that individuals do not differ significantly in their inherited mental abilities and that subsequent differences are due to learning, or to differences in early experiences. Opponents insist that certain differences in the capacities of individuals (and hence their behaviour) can be attributed to differences in the genetic material inherited from their parents. In most cases, however, it is almost impossible to

distinguish clearly between the influence of the two factors because an individual organism is the product of the interaction between genes and a specific environment.

enzyme a biological ◊catalyst which converts one chemical to another, usually very swiftly, without itself being destroyed in the process. Enzymes are all large, complex ◊proteins. They digest food, convert food energy into ◊ATP, help to manufacture all the molecular components of the body, produce copies of ◊DNA when the cell divides, and control the movement of substances into and out of cells. Enzymes have many medical and industrial uses, from washing powders to drug production, and as research tools in molecular biology. They can be extracted from bacteria and moulds, and ◊genetic engineering now makes it possible to tailor the enzyme for a specific purpose, and greatly increase the rate of production.

Eocene the second division of the Tertiary period of geological time, between 54 and 38 million years ago. The name means 'early recent', referring to the early forms of mammals evolving at the time, following the extinction of the dinosaurs.

EOKA (Greek *Ethnikí Organósis Kipriakóu Agónos*/National Organization of Cypriot Struggle) an underground organization formed by George ◊Grivas in 1955 to fight for the independence of Cyprus from Britain and ultimately its union (enosis) with Greece. In 1971, 11 years after Cyprus's independence, Grivas returned to the island to form EOKA B, to resume the fight for enosis which had not been achieved by the Cypriot government.

eoliths the simplest and most primitive form of stones specially shaped by humans for use as implements, mainly rudimentary chopping tools, dating from the Tertiary period. Their recognition as artifacts was largely due to Benjamin Harrison in 1899.

Eos /'iːɒs/ in Greek mythology, the goddess of the dawn, better known by the Roman name of ◊Aurora.

Eötvös /'ɜːtvɜːʃ/ Roland von, Baron 1848–1919. Hungarian scientist, born in Budapest, who investigated problems of gravitation, and constructed the double-armed torsion balance for determining variations of gravity.

Epaminondas /e,pæmɪ'nɒndæs/ c. 420–362 BC. Theban general and politician, who won a decisive victory over the Spartans at Leuctra in 371, and was killed at the moment of victory at Mantinea.

Epernay /,epeə'neɪ/ town in Marne *département*, France, centre of the champagne industry. Population (1986) 29,000.

ephedrine a member of a group of drugs, called sympathomimetic amines, which includes adrenalin and benzedrine. It occurs in the *Ephedra* genus of shrubs, found in warm temperate zones, and is used in the treatment of asthma and hay fever.

ephemeral plant a plant with a very short life cycle, sometimes as little as six or eight weeks. It may complete several generations in one growing season. A number of common weeds are

E-NUMBERS: FOOD ADDITIVES AUTHORIZED BY THE EUROPEAN COMMISSION

COLOURS

number	name	typical use
E100	circumin	flour confectionery; margarine
E101	riboflavin	sauces
E102	tartrazine	soft drinks
E104	quinoline yellow	
E110	sunset yellow FCF	biscuits
E120	cochineal	alcoholic drinks
E122	carmoisine	jams and preserves
E123	amaranth	
E124	ponceau 4R	dessert mixes
E127	erythrosine	glacé cherries
E131	patent blue V	
E132	indigo carmine	
E140	chlorophyll	
E141	copper complexes of chlorophyll and chlorophyllins	
E142	green S	pastilles
E150	caramel	beer, soft drinks, sauces, gravy browning
E151	black PN	
E153	carbon black (vegetable carbon)	liquorice
E160(a)	alpha-carotene; beta-carotene; gamma-carotene	margarine; soft drinks
E160(b)	annatto; bixin; norbixin	crisps
E160(c)	capsanthin; capsorubin	
E160(d)	lycopene	
E160(e)	beta-apo-8' carotenal	
E160(f)	ethyl ester of beta-apo-8'-carotenic acid	
E161(a)	flavoxanthin	
E161(b)	lutein	
E161(c)	cryptoxanthin	
E161(d)	rubixanthin	
E161(e)	violaxanthin	
E161(f)	rhodoxanthin	
E161(g)	canthaxanthin	
E162	beetroot red (betanin)	ice-cream, liquorice
E163	anthocyanins	yoghourt
E171	titanium dioxide	sweets
E172	iron oxides; iron hydroxides	
E173	aluminium	
E174	silver	
E175	gold	cake decorations
E180	pigment rubine (lithol rubine BK)	

ANTIOXIDANTS

number	name	typical use
E300	L-ascorbic acid	fruit drinks; also used to improve flour and bread dough
E301	sodium L-ascorbate	
E302	calcium L-ascorbate	
E304	ascorbyl palmitate	scotch eggs
E306	extracts of natural origin rich in tocopherols	vegetable oils
E307	synthetic alphatocopherol	cereal-based baby foods
E308	synthetic gammatocopherol	
E309	synthetic deltatocopherol	
E310	propyl gallate	vegetable oils; chewing gum
E311	octyl gallate	
E312	dodecyl gallate	
E320	butylated hydroxynisole (BHA)	beef stock cubes; cheese spread
E321	butylated hydroxytoluene (BHT)	chewing gum
E322	lecithins	low fat spreads; also as an emulsifier in chocolate

EMULSIFIERS AND STABILIZERS

number	name	typical use
E400	alginic acid	ice-cream; soft cheese
E401	sodium alginate	cake mixes
E402	potassium alginate	
E403	ammonium alginate	
E404	calcium alginate	
E405	propane-1,-2-diol alginate (propylene glycol alginate)	salad dressings; cottage cheese
E406	agar	ice-cream
E407	carageenan	quick setting jelly mixes; milk shakes
E410	locust bean gum (carob gum)	salad cream
E412	guar gum	packet soups and meringue mixes
E413	tragacanth	salad dressings; processed cheese
E414	gum arabic (acacia)	confectionery
E415	xanthan gum	sweet pickle; coleslaw
E440(a)	pectin	
E440(b)	amidated pectin, pectin extract	jams and preserves
E460	microcrystalline cellulose; alphacellulose	high-fibre bread; grated cheese
E461	methylcellulose	low fat spreads
E463	hydroxypropyl-cellulose	
E464	hydroxypropyl-methylcellulose	edible ices
E465	ethylmethylcellulose	gateaux
E466	carboxymethylcellulose, sodium salt (CMC)	jelly, gateaux
E470	sodium, potassium and calcium salts of fatty acids	cake mixes
E471	mono- and di-glycerides of fatty acids	frozen desserts
E472(a)	acetic acid esters of mono- and di-glycerides of fatty acids	mousse mixes
E472(b)	lactic acid esters of mono- and di-glycerides of fatty acids	dessert topping
E472(c)	citric acid esters of mono- and di-glycerides of fatty acids	continental sausages
E472(e)	mono and diacetyltartaric acid esters of mono- and di-glycerides of fatty acids	bread; frozen pizza
E473	sucrose esters of fatty acids	
E474	sucroglycerides	edible ices
E475	polyglycerol esters of fatty acids	cakes and gateaux
E477	propane-1,2-diol esters of fatty acids	instant desserts
E481	sodium stearoyl-2-lactylate	bread; cakes and biscuits
E482	calcium stearoyl-2-lactylate	gravy granules
E483	stearyl tartrate	

PRESERVATIVES

numbers	name	typical use
E200	sorbic acid	soft drinks; fruit yoghourt; processed cheese slices
E201	sodium sorbate	
E202	potassium sorbate	
E203	calcium sorbate	frozen pizza; flour confectionery
E210	benzoic acid	
E211	sodium benzoate	beer, jam, salad cream,
E212	potassium benzoate	soft drinks, fruit pulp,
E213	calcium benzoate	fruit-based pie fillings,
E214	ethyl para-hydroxy benzoate	marinated herring and
E215	sodium ethyl para-hydroxbenzoate	mackerel
E216	propyl para-hydroxy-benzoate	
E217	sodium propyl para-hydroxybenzoate	
E218	methyl para-hydroxy-benzoate	
E220	sulphur dioxide	
E221	sodium sulphate	dried fruit, dehydrated
E222	sodium bisulphite	vegetables, fruit juices
E223	sodium metabisulphate	and syrups, sausages,
E224	potassium metabisulphite	fruit-based dairy desserts,
E226	calcium sulphite	cider, beer and wine; also
E227	calcium bisulphite	used to prevent browning of raw peeled potatoes and to condition biscuit doughs
E230	diphenyl	
E231	orthophenylphenol	surface treatment of
E232	sodium orthophenyl-phenate	citrus fruit
E233	thiabendazole	surface treatment of bananas
E239	hexamine	marinated herring and mackerel
E249	potassium nitrite	
E250	sodium nitrite	bacon, ham, cured meats,
E251	sodium nitrate	corned beef and some
E252	potassium nitrate	cheeses
E280	propionic acid	
E281	sodium propionate	bread and flour
E282	calcium propionate	confectionery, Christmas
E283	potassium propionate	pudding

SWEETENERS

	name	typical use
E421	mannitol	sugar-free confectionery
E420	sorbitol; sorbitol syrup	sugar-free confectionery, jams for diabetics

OTHERS

	name	typical use
E170	calcium carbonate	base, firming agent, release agent, diluent; nutrient in flour
E260	acetic acid	
E261	potassium acetate	acid/acidity regulators
E262	sodium hydrogen diacetate	(buffers) used in pickles, salad cream and bread; they contribute to flavour and provide protection against mould growth
E263	calcium acetate	firming agent; also provides calcium in quick-set jelly mix

number	name	typical use
E270	lactic acid	acid/flavouring protects against mould growth; salad dressing, soft margarine
E290	carbon dioxide	carbonating agent/packing gas and propellant; used in fizzy drinks
E325	sodium lactate	buffer, humectant; used in jams, preserves, sweets, flour confectionery
E326	potassium lactate	buffer; jams, preserves and jellies
E327	calcium lactate	buffer, firming agent; canned fruit pie filling
E330	citric acid	
E331	monosodium citrate disodium citrate trisodium citrate	acid/flavourings, sequestrants, emulsifying salts; used in soft drinks,
E332	monopotassium citrate tripotassium citrate	jams, preserves, sweets, UHT cream, processed
E333	monocalcium citrate dicalcium citrate tricalcium citrate	cheese, canned fruit, dessert mixes, ice-cream
E334	L-(+)-tartaric acid	
E335	monosodium L-(+) -tartrate; disodium L-(+) -tartrate	acid/flavourings, buffers, emulsifying salts, sequestrants; used in soft
E336	monopotassium L-(+) -tartrate (cream of tartar); dipotassium L-(+) -tartrate	drinks; biscuits creams and fillings, sweets, jams, dessert mixes and
E337	potassium sodium L-(+) -tartrate	processed cheese
E338	phosphoric acid	acid/flavourings; soft drinks, cocoa
E339	sodium dihydrogen orthophosphate; disodium hydrogen orthophosphate; trisodium orthophosphate	buffers, sequestrants, emulsifying salts; used in dessert mixes, non-dairy creamers, processed
E340	potassium dihydrogen orthophosphate; dipotassium hydrogen orthophosphate; tripotassium orthophosphate	cheese
E341	calcium tetrahydrogen diorthophosphate; calcium hydrogen orthophosphate; tricalcium diorthophosphate	firming agent, raising agent; cake mixes, baking powder, dessert mixes
E450(a)	disodium dihydrogen diphospate; trisodium diphosphate; tetrasodium diphosphate; tetrapotassium diphosphate	buffers, sequestrants, emulsifying salts, stabilisers, texturisers,
E450(b)	pentasodium triphosphate; pentapotassium triphosphate	raising agents, used in whipping cream, fish and meat products, bread,
E450(c)	sodium polyphosphates; potassium polyphosphates	processed cheese, canned vegetables

ephemerals, for example, groundsel (*Senecio vulgaris*) as are many desert plants. The latter take advantage of short periods of rain to germinate and reproduce, passing the dry season as ◊dormant seeds.

Ephesus /'efɪsəs/ ancient Greek seaport in Asia Minor, a centre of the Ionian Greeks, with a temple of ◊Artemis destroyed by the Goths in 262 AD. St Paul visited the city, and addressed a letter (◊epistle) to the Christians there.

epic a narrative poem or cycle of poems dealing with some great action, often the founding of a nation or the forging of national unity, and often using religious or cosmological themes. In the Western tradition, the crucial works are the *Iliad* and *Odyssey* attributed to Homer, works probably intended to be chanted in sections at feasts. Greek and later criticism, which considered the Homeric epic the highest form of poetry, produced a genre of *secondary epic*, notably the *Aeneid* of Virgil, Tasso's *Jerusalem Delivered* and Milton's *Paradise Lost*, which attempt to emulate Homer, often for a patron or a political cause. The term epic is also applied to narrative poems of other traditions in Europe: the Anglo-Saxon *Beowulf* and the Finnish *Kalevala*; in India the *Ramayana* and *Mahabharata*; the Babylonian *Gilgamesh*.

epicentre the point on the earth's surface immediately above the ◊focus of an ◊earthquake. Most damage usually takes place at an earthquake's epicentre.

Epictetus /ˌepɪk'tiːtəs/ c. 60–110 AD. Greek Stoic philospher of the 1st century AD. Born at Hierapolis in Phrygia, he lived for many years in Rome as a slave, but eventually secured his freedom, attended the lectures of a Stoic, and became a Stoic philosopher himself. Banished by ◊Domitian from Rome in 89 AD, he taught people to give up self-interest and to promote the common good of humanity. He believed that people were in the hands of an all-wise providence, and that they should endeavour to do their duty in the position to which they were called.

epicureanism system of philosophy named after the Greek philosopher ◊Epicurus. He taught that soundly based human happiness is the highest good, so that its rational pursuit is to be adopted. The most distinguished Roman Epicurean was ◊Lucretius.

Epicurus /ˌepɪ'kuərəs/ 341–270 BC. Greek philosopher, founder of ◊Epicureanism, who taught at Athens from 306 BC.

epicyclic gear a gear system which consists of one or more gear wheels moving around another. This arrangement is also called a sun-and-planet gear. Epicyclic gears are found in bicycle hub gears and in automatic gearboxes.

epicycloid in geometry, a curve resembling a series of arches traced out by a point on the circumference of a circle that rolls around another circle of a different diameter. If the two circles have the same diameter, the curve is a ◊cardioid. Greek mathematicians thought that planets moved in small circles (epicycles) while completing a large circle (the deferent) round the Earth.

epicycloid

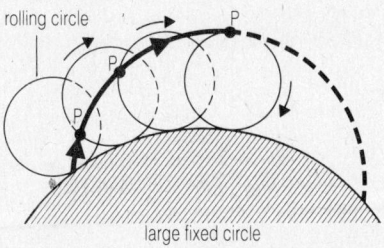

large fixed circle

Epidaurus /ˌepɪ'dɔːrəs/ ancient Greek city and port on the E coast of Argolis, in the NE Peloponnese. Originally famous for the temple of the god of healing, Aesculapius, Epidaurus is now noted for its beautiful and well-preserved amphitheatre of the 4th century BC.

epidermis the outermost layer of ◊cells on an organism's body. In plants and many invertebrates such as insects, it consists of a single layer of cells, often with an outer ◊cuticle that protects the organism from desiccation. In vertebrate animals, it consists of several layers of cells. The outermost of these is dead in reptiles, birds and mammals, forming a tough, waterproof layer known as ◊skin.

epigeal seed germination in which the ◊cotyledons are borne above the soil.

epigram a short poem, originally a religious inscription but later a short, witty, and pithy saying. The form was popular among writers of ancient Rome, the best-known Latin epigrammatists being Catullus and Martial. In English literature the epigram has been employed by Ben Jonson, Herrick, Pope, Swift, Prior, Landor, and Yeats.

epigraphy (Greek *epigráphein* 'to write on') the art of writing with a sharp instrument on hard, durable materials such as stone, and also the scientific study of epigraphical writings or inscriptions.

epilepsy disorder of the nervous system involving attacks of loss or alteration of consciousness, sometimes with convulsions (fits). It is controlled by anticonvulsant drugs. There are several different forms, and a percentage of young sufferers outgrow the condition.

Epinal /ˌeɪpɪ'næl/ capital of Vosges *département*, on the Moselle, France. Population (1982) 40,954. A cotton textile centre, it dates from the 10th century.

Epiphany annual festival (6 Jan) of the Christian Church, celebrating the coming of the ◊Magi or Wise Men to Bethlehem with gifts for the infant Jesus, and symbolizing the manifestation of Christ to the world. It is the 12th day after Christmas, and marks the end of the Christmas festivities. In many countries the night before, called *Twelfth Night*, is marked by the giving of gifts.

epiphyte plant which grows on another plant or object above the surface of the ground, and which has no roots in the soil. An epiphyte does not parasitize the plant it grows on, but merely uses it for support. Its nutrients are obtained from rainwater, organic debris such as leaf litter, or from the air. The greatest diversity of epiphytes is found in tropical areas and includes many orchids. The family Bromeliaceae is predominantly epiphytic and contains the genus *Tillandsia*, several of which are sold as 'air plants'. Although there are few specialized epiphytes in temperate regions, mosses and lichens are often found growing epiphytically on trees.

Epirus /e'paɪrəs/ (Greek 'mainland') country of ancient Greece; the N part is in modern Albania; the remainder, in NW Greece, is divided into four provinces -Arta, Thesprotia, Yanina, Preveza.

episcopacy in the Christian church, a system of church government in which administrative and spiritual power over a district (diocese) is held by a bishop. The Roman Catholic, Eastern Orthodox, Anglican, and Episcopal (USA) churches are episcopalian; episcopacy also exists in some branches of the Lutheran Church, for example, in Scandinavia.

Episcopalianism is the US term for the ◊Anglian Communion.

epistemology the study of knowledge. It is a branch of ◊philosophy that examines the nature of knowledge and attempts to determine the limits of human understanding. How knowledge is derived, how it is to be validated and tested are central issues in epistemology.

epistle a letter; in the New Testament, any of the 21 letters to individuals or to the members of various churches written by Christian leaders. The best known are the 13 written by St ◊Paul. The term is also used for a letter addressed to someone in the form of a poem, as in the epistles of ◊Horace and ◊Pope. The *epistolary novel*, a story told as a series of (fictitious) letters, was popularized by Samuel ◊Richardson in the 18th century. In modern usage the word is applied to letters with a suggestion of pomposity and literary affectation.

epoxy resin a synthetic ◊resin used as an ◊adhesive and as an ingredient in paints. Household epoxy resin adhesives come in component form as two separate tubes of chemical, one tube containing resin, the other a curing agent, or hardener. The two chemicals are mixed just before application, and the mix soon sets hard.

Epping Forest /'epɪŋ/ a forest in ◊Essex, SE England.

EPROM (erasable programmable read-only memory) a computer memory device in the form of a chip that can record data and retain it indefinitely. The data can be erased by exposing it to ultraviolet light and new data added. Other kinds of memory are ROM, PROM, and RAM.

Epsilon Aurigae a binary star in the constellation Auriga. It consists of a huge star some 15 times the mass of the Sun eclipsing a companion about the same size. The eclipsing object is thought to be a ring or shell of gases, while its invisible companion is believed to be a true star.

Epsom /'epsəm/ town in Surrey, England; population (1981) 68,535. In the 17th century it was a spa producing Epsom salts. There is a racecourse, where the Derby and the Oaks are held. The site of Henry VIII's palace of Nonsuch was excavated in 1959.

Epsom Salts hydrated magnesium sulphate, $MgSO_4.7H_2O$, known as a saline purgative. The name is derived from a bitter saline spring at Epsom, Surrey, which contains the salt in solution.

Epstein /'epstain/ Jacob 1880–1959. American-born British sculptor. Born in New York, in 1904 he moved to England, where most of his major work was done. In 1907–08 his series of figures for the British Medical Association building in the Strand, London, provoked much criticism for their apparent lack of the conventional aesthetics of form, as did the tomb of Oscar Wilde in Paris 1909. These were followed by the *Rima* memorial to W H Hudson in Hyde Park 1925; *Genesis* 1931; *Ecce Homo* 1933; *Adam* 1939; *Lucifer* 1945; the aluminium *Christ in Majesty* 1957 for Llandaff Cathedral; and *St Michael and the Devil* 1959 for Coventry Cathedral. Epstein became equally well known for his portrait busts, for example of Vaughan Williams, Einstein and Blake. He was knighted in 1954.

Epstein British sculptor who worked in stone and marble. He is photographed next to his statue *Lazarus*.

equation mathematical expression or formula that represents an equality, and thus always includes an equals sign (=). For example, the equation $A = \pi r^2$ is the formula for the area of a circle of radius r, the algebraic equation $y = mx + c$ is the general one in coordinate geometry for a straight line, and the chemical equation $2H_2O = 2H_2 + O_2$ represents the decomposition of water by electrolysis into its constituent elements. A chemical equation must 'balance', that is, a given element must have the same total number of atoms on one side of the equation as on the other (thus there are four atoms of hydrogen on each side of the above equation). Chemical equations are often written with an arrow or arrows (instead of an equals sign) to indicate the direction of the reaction; thus $2H_2O + \rightarrow 2H_2 + O_2$. An *indeterminate* equation is an equation for which there is an infinite set of solutions, for example, $2x = y$. A *diophantine* equation is an indeterminate equation in which the solution and terms must be whole numbers (after Diophantos of Alexandria, c. 250 AD).

equator the *terrestrial equator* is the ◊great circle whose plane is perpendicular to the Earth's axis (the line joining the poles). Its length is 40,076 km/24,901.8 mi, divided into 360° of longitude. The *celestial equator* is the circle in which the plane of the Earth's equator intersects the ◊celestial sphere.

Equatorial Guinea /ˌekwə'tɔːriəl 'gini/ country in W central Africa, bounded north by Cameroon, east and south by Gabon, and west by the Atlantic Ocean; also several small islands off the coast and the larger island of Bioko off the coast of Cameroon.
government the 1973 constitution was suspended in a military coup of 1979, after which a supreme military council ruled by decree. In 1982 a new constitution was approved by referendum, providing for a president and a house of representatives of the people, elected by universal suffrage for a five-year term. The house of representatives sat for the first time in 1983, its 41 members all nominated by the president and elected unopposed. The president governs with the supreme military council and a transition to civil, constitutional government is promised. All political parties have been banned.
history reached by Portuguese explorers in 1472, Bioko was ceded to Spain in 1778. The mainland territory of Rio Muni (now Mbini) came under Spanish rule in 1885, the whole colony being known as Spanish Guinea. From 1959 the territory was a Spanish Overseas Province, with internal autonomy from 1963.
After 190 years of Spanish rule, Equatorial Guinea became fully independent in 1968, with Francisco Macias Nguema as president with a coalition government. In 1970 he banned all political parties and replaced them with one, the United National Party (PUN). Two years later he declared himself president-for-life and established a dictatorship, controlling press and radio and forbidding citizens to leave the country. There were many arrests and executions 1976–77. He also established close relations with the Soviet bloc.
In 1975 he was overthrown in a coup by his nephew, Col Teodoro Obiang Nguema Mbasogo, with at least the tacit approval of Spain. Macias was tried and executed. Obiang expelled the Soviet advisers and technicians and renewed economic and political ties with Spain. He banned PUN and other political parties and ruled through a supreme military council. Coups against him in 1981 and 1983 were unsuccessful. In 1982 a new constitution promised a return to civilian rule.

equestrianism skill in horse riding, especially as practised under International Equestrian Federation rules, when it is an Olympic sport. *Showjumping* is horse jumping over a course of fences. The winner is usually the competitor with fewest 'faults' (penalty marks given for knocking down or refusing fences), but in time competitions it is the competitor completing the course most quickly, additional seconds being added for mistakes.

World Championship first held 1953 for men, 1965 for women; since 1978 for both concurrently
1978 Gerd Wiltfang *(West Germany)*
1982 Norbert Koof *(West Germany)*
1986 Gail Greenough *(Canada)*
European Championship first held 1957 as separate competition for men and women; since 1975 they have competed together
1977 Johan Heins *(Holland)*
1979 Gerd Wiltfang *(West Germany)*
1981 Paul Schockemohle *(West Germany)*
1983 Paul Schockemohle *(West Germany)*
1985 Paul Schockemohle *(West Germany)*
British Showjumping Derby first held 1961 and staged annually at Hickstead, Sussex
1982 Paul Schockemohle *(West Germany)*
1983 John Whitaker *(UK)*
1984 John Ledingham *(Ireland)*
1985 Paul Schockemohle *(West Germany)*
1986 Paul Schockemohle *(West Germany)*

Three-Day Eventing horse trials testing the all-round abilities of a horse and rider in: *dressage* testing a horse's response to control; *cross-country*, testing speed and endurance; and *showjumping* in a final modified contest.

World Championship first held 1966
1970 Mary Gordon-Watson *(UK)*
1974 Bruce Davidson *(USA)*
1978 Bruce Davidson *(USA)*
1982 Lucinda Green (born Prior-Palmer) *(UK)*
1986 Virginia Leng (born Holgate) *(UK)*

Equiano /ˌekwi'ɑːnəʊ/ Olaudah 1745–1797. African anti-slavery campaigner and writer. He was born near the Niger River in what is now Nigeria, captured at the age of ten and sold to slavers, who transported him to the West Indies. He learnt English and was able to buy his freedom at the age of 21. He subsequently sailed on voyages to the Mediterranean and the Arctic, before being appointed commissary of stores for freed slaves returning to Sierra Leone. He was an active campaigner against slavery. His autobiography, *The Interesting Narrative of the Life of Olaudah Equiano or Gustavus Vassa the African* 1789, is the earliest significant work by an African written in English.

equilateral in geometry, a figure having all sides of equal length. For example, a square and a rhombus are both equilateral four-sided figures. An equilateral triangle, to which the term is most

Equatorial Guinea
REPUBLIC OF (*República de Guinea Ecuatorial*)

AREA 28,100 sq km/10,852 sq mi
CAPITAL Malabo
PHYSICAL comprises mainland Rio Muni, plus the small islands of Corisco, Elobey Grande and Elobey Chico, and Bioko Island (formerly Fernando Po) together with Pagalu Island (formerly Annobon)
FEATURES volcanic mountains on Bioko
HEAD OF STATE AND OF GOVERNMENT Teodoro Obiang Nguema Mbasogo from 1979
GOVERNMENT military
EXPORTS cocoa, coffee, bananas, timber
CURRENCY ekuele; CFA franc (498.38 = £1 Sept 1987)
POPULATION 350,000 (1985); annual growth rate 2.1%
LANGUAGE Spanish (official); pidgin English is widely spoken, and on Pagalu (whose people were formerly slaves of the Portuguese) a Portuguese dialect
RELIGION nominally Christian, mainly Catholic, but in 1978 Roman Catholicism was banned
LITERACY 55% (1984)
GDP $60 million (1983); $250 per head of population
CHRONOLOGY
1968 Achieved full independence from Spain.

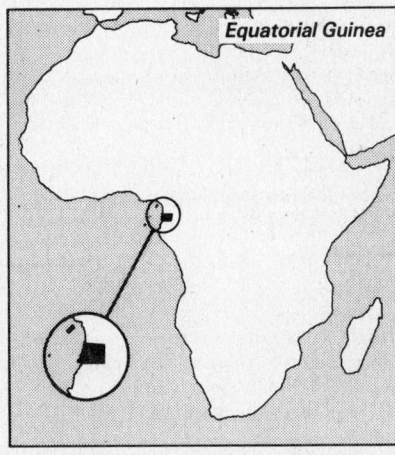
Equatorial Guinea

Francisco Macias Nguema became first president, soon assuming dictatorial powers. 1979 Macias overthrown and replaced by his nephew, Teodoro Obiang Nguema Mbasogo, who established a military regime. Macias tried and executed.
1982 Obiang elected president for another seven years. New constitution, promising a return to civilian government, adopted.

often applied, has all three sides equal and all three angles equal (at 60°).

equilibrium in physics and chemistry, the state of a system in which the energy is balanced among the components in the most probable way, and there is no overall interaction between the components. After a slight displacement from rest, an object in stable equilibrium returns to its rest position, for example, a cube of wood, lifted slightly at one corner, falls back on its base when it is released. By contrast, a coin balanced on edge is in unstable equilibrium and topples over when pushed slightly sideways (see ⍭centre of mass). An object is in thermal equilibrium when no heat enters or leaves it. Substances are in chemical equilibrium when the products of a reversible chemical reaction are formed at the same rate at which they decompose to form the reactants.

equinox the point in spring (vernal) and autumn at which the sun crosses the celestial equator (see ⍭celestial sphere), so that the day and night are of approximately equal length on about 21 Mar and 23 Sept each year.

equity in law, a term denoting the mitigation of the ordinary rules of law where the application of these would operate harshly in a particular case; sometimes it is regarded as an attempt to achieve 'natural justice'. So understood, equity appears as an element in most legal systems, and in a number of modern codes the judge is instructed to apply to the decision of particular cases both the rules of strict law and the principles of equity.

In England equity originated in decisions of the Lord Chancellor's court, the Court of Chancery, on matters that were remitted to it because there was no remedy available in the Common Law courts, or the remedy there was inadequate. Gradually it assumed the appearance of a distinct system of legal rules, as precise and limited in their operation as the rules of ⍭Common Law, and developed by the same method as the Common Law, that is, by the doctrine of judicial precedent. Thus, in the 19th century, there existed two systems of ⍭English Law – Common Law and Equity – side by side, and applied in separate law courts, until the Judicature Acts 1873–75 established a single High Court of Justice, in which judges were given full powers to apply both Common Law and equity to the decision of any case. Equitable principles exist side by side with principles of Common Law in many branches of the law, and particularly in the law of contracts, of real and personal property, and of torts (or civil wrongs).

equity in economics, a company's assets less its liabilities. Popularly, equities are ⍭stocks and shares which, unlike debentures and preference shares, do not pay interest at fixed rates.

Equity in the UK theatre, a shortened term for the British Actors' Equity Association, the trade union for professional actors in the theatre, film and television, founded in 1929. In the USA, its counterpart is the American Actors' Equity Association which, however, deals only with performers in the theatre.

Erasmus /ɪ'ræzməs/ Desiderius c. 1466–1536. Dutch scholar and humanist. Born at Rotterdam, the illegitimate son of Rogerius Gerardus (whose story is told in Charles Reade's novel *The Cloister and the Hearth* 1861), he adopted the Latin-Greek name which means 'beloved'. As a youth he was a monk in an Augustinian monastery near Gouda, but in 1495 after becoming a priest, he went to study at Paris and in 1499 paid the first of a number of visits to England. Here he met ⍭Linacre, ⍭More, and ⍭Colet, and for a time he was professor of Divinity and of Greek at Cambridge University. His pioneer edition of the Greek New Testament was published in 1516, and an edition of the writings of St Jerome and his own *Colloquia*, dialogues on contemporary subjects, in 1519. In 1521 he went to Basle, where he edited the writings of the early Christian leaders. The *Erasmus Prize* 1958 is awarded annually to outstanding contributors to international understanding, usually in social or cultural fields, for example, Martin ⍭Buber, Herbert Read, Robert ⍭Schuman, Jan ⍭Tinbergen.

Erasmus An engraving by the German painter Dürer of Desiderius Erasmus, the Renaissance Dutch scholar and theologian. His Biblical criticism contributed to the European Reformation.

Erastianism the belief that the Church should be subordinated to the State. The name is derived from Thomas Erastus (1534–83), a German-Swiss theologian, an opponent of Calvinism, who maintained in his writings that the Church should not have the power of excluding people as a punishment for sin.

Eratosthenes /ˌerə'tɒsθəniːz/ c. 276–194 BC. Greek geographer, whose map of the ancient world was the first to contain lines of latitude and longitude, and who calculated the earth's circumference with an error of less than 200 mi.

erbium a metallic element; symbol Er, atomic number 68, atomic weight 167.27. It is one of the rare earths, and was discovered in 1843 by Mosander.

Erebus, Mount /'erɪbəs/ the world's southernmost active volcano 3,794 m/12,520 ft high, on Ross Island, Antarctica. It contains a lake of molten lava which scientists are investigating in the belief that it can provide a 'window' on to the magma beneath the Earth's crust.

Erebus /'erɪbəs/ in Greek mythology, the god of darkness and the intermediate region between upper earth and ◊Hades.

Erfurt /'eəfʊət/ city in East Germany on the river Gera, capital of Erfurt district, in a rich agricultural area; population (1983) 214,000. The 12th–15th-century cathedral has fine stained glass, and the Augustinian monastery where Martin ◊Luther spent some years is now an orphanage. Manufactures include textiles, typewriters and electrical goods.

erg in physics, the unit of energy in the cgs system. It is the energy expended when a force of 1 dyne is exerted through a distance of 1 cm. It is exactly equal to 10^{-7}J (see ◊joule).

ergonomics the study of the relationship between people and the furniture, tools, and machinery they use at work. The object is to improve work performance by removing sources of muscular stress and general fatigue, for example, by presenting data and control panels in easy-to-view form, making office furniture comfortable, and creating a pleasant environment.

ergosterol a substance which, under the action of the sun's ultraviolet rays on the skin, gives rise to the production of vitamin D – a vitamin which promotes bone-formation and deficiency of which produces ◊rickets. The sterol occurs in ergot (hence the name), in yeast, in other fungi, and in some animal fats. The principal source of commercial ergot is yeast.

ergot parasitic fungus, *Claviceps purpurea*, which attacks the rye plant. It forms large grains usually dark violet in colour from which alkaloids (used to induce childbirth) are extracted. Infected bread causes ergotism, with gangrene or convulsions.

Erhard /'eəhɑːt/ Ludwig 1897–1977. West German politician. He succeeded Konrad Adenauer as chancellor of the Federal Republic 1963–66. The 'economic miracle' of West Germany's recovery after World War II is largely attributed to Erhard's policy of social free enterprise (German *Marktwirtschaft*).

erica in botany, more commonly known as the heathers; the typical genus of the family Ericaceae. There are about 500 species, distributed mainly in South Africa and also Europe.

Ericsson /'erɪksən/ Leif lived about 1000 AD. Norse explorer, son of Eric 'the Red', who according to tradition sailed W from Greenland in about 1000 to find a country first sighted by Europeans in 986. Landing with 35 companions in N America, he called it 'Vinland', because he discovered grape vines growing, and spent a winter there. The story was confirmed in 1963 when a Norwegian expedition, led by Helge Ingstad, discovered remains of a Viking settlement (dated about 1000) near the fishing village of L'Anse-aux-Meadows at the northern tip of Newfoundland.

Eric 'the Red' /'erɪk/ 940–1010. (fl. 982–1000) allegedly the first European to find Greenland. According to a 13th-century saga, he was the son of a Norwegian chieftain, who was banished from Iceland about 982 for murder, sailed westward, and discovered a land which he called Greenland.

Eridanus the sixth-largest ◊constellation, representing a river which meanders from the celestial equator deep into the southern hemisphere of the sky. Its most brilliant star, Achernar, is the ninth-brightest star in the entire sky.

Eridu /'eərɪduː/ ancient city of Mesopotamia about 5000 BC, according to tradition the cradle of Sumerian civilization. On its site is the modern village of Tell Abu Shahrain, ◊Iraq.

Erie /'ɪəri/ city and port on the Pennsylvania bank of Lake Erie, USA, population (1981) 120,000. It has heavy industries and a trade in iron, grain, and freshwater fish.

Erie, Lake /'ɪəri/ fourth largest of the 'Great Lakes' of North America, connected to Lake Ontario by the Niagara river, on which are the famous falls, by-passed by the Welland Canal. Area 25,718 sq km/9,930 sq mi.

Erigena /ɪ'rɪdʒɪnə/ Johannes Scotus 815–877. Medieval philosopher. He was probably Irish and according to tradition travelled in Greece and Italy before the French king Charles II the Bald invited him to France (before 847), where he became head of the court school. He is said to have visited Oxford, to have taught at Malmesbury, and to have been stabbed to death by his pupils. As a thinker he tried to combine Christianity with ◊Neo-Platonism.

Erin /'ɪərɪn/ poetic name for Ireland derived from the dative case Érinn of the Gaelic name Ériu, possibly derived from Sanskrit 'western'.

Eritrea /ˌerɪ'treɪə/ province of N Ethiopia.
area 118,500 sq km/45,745 sq mi
capital Asmara
towns ports Assab and Massawa are Ethiopia's outlets to the sea
features coastline on the Red Sea 1,000 km/670 mi
exports coffee, salt
currency birr
population (1980) 2,426,200
language Amharic (official)
religion Muslim
recent history an Italian colony 1889–1941, when it came under British military administration until 1952. Eritrea was then federated with Ethiopia by United Nations decision. It enjoyed autonomy 1952–62, but its reduction to a region prompted a demand for independence, and the various Eritrean Liberation fronts continued resistance in 1986 (aided by the conservative Gulf states), and some cooperation with guerrillas in Tigré province.

Erivan alternative transliteration of ◊Yerevan, capital of Armenian Republic, USSR.

Erlangen /'eəlæŋən/ town in Bavaria, West Germany; population (1980) 101,900. It produces textiles and electrical goods.

ermine name given to the ◊stoat when in its white winter coat. In northern latitudes the coat becomes completely white, except for a black tip to the tail, but in warmer regions the back may remain brownish. The fur is used commercially.

Ernie /'ɜːni/ (Electronic Random Number Indicator Equipment). In the UK, machine designed and produced by the Post Office Research Station to select a series of random 9-figure numbers to indicate prizewinners in premium-bond draws.

Ernst /eənst/ Max 1891–1976. German ◊Surrealist painter, who worked mostly in France. Born in Brühl, near Cologne, he studied philosophy at the University of Bonn and first exhibited in Berlin in 1916. He was an active ◊Dadaist and in 1922 went to Paris where he helped found the Surrealist movement in 1924.

Eros /'ɪərɒs/ in Greek mythology, boy-god of love (Roman *Cupid*), son of ◊Aphrodite, and armed with bow and arrows; he fell in love with ◊Psyche.

Eros /'ɪərɒs/ in astronomy, an ◊asteroid, discovered in 1898, that passes 22 million km/14 million mi from the Earth at closest. Eros was the first asteroid to be discovered whose orbit comes within that of Mars. It is elongated, measures about 36×12 km/22×7 mi, rotates around it shortest axis every 5.3 hours, and orbits the Sun every 1.8 years.

erosion the processes whereby the rocks and soil of the earth's surface are loosened, worn away, and transported (◊weathering does not involve transportation). There are two forms – chemical and physical. Chemical erosion involves the alteration of the mineral component of the rock, by means of rainwater or the substances dissolved in it, and its subsequent movement. The decay of granite by the conversion of its feldspar minerals into china clay by carbonic acid in rainwater, and the dissolving of limestone into caves and potholes, are examples. Physical erosion involves the breakdown and transportation of exposed rocks by physical forces. The shattering of cliff-faces in mountainous areas by the expansion of frost in the rock cracks, and the movement of boulders in an avalanche, are examples. In practice the two work together. Water, consisting of sea waves and currents, rivers and rain; ice, in the form of glaciers, frost and melting snow; and wind, hurling sand fragments against exposed rocks and moving dunes along, are the most potent forces of erosion. People may also contribute to erosion by bad farming practices such as thoughtless deforestation and the creation of dust bowls.

Erse /ɜːs/ originally a Scottish form of the word 'Irish', a name applied by Lowland Scots to Scottish Gaelic and also sometimes used as a synonym for Irish Gaelic.

Ershad /'eəʃəd/ Hussain Mohammad 1930– . Military ruler of Bangladesh from 1982. He became chief of staff in the Bangladesh army in 1979 and assumed power in a military coup in 1982. As president from 1983, Ershad introduced a successful rural-orientated economic programme. He was re-elected in 1986 and lifted martial law, but faced continuing political opposition.

Erskine /'ɜːskɪn/ Thomas, 1st Baron Erskine 1750–1823. British barrister and Lord Chancellor. Born in Edinburgh. He was called to the Bar in 1778 and appeared for the defence in a number of trials of parliamentary reformers for sedition. When the Whigs returned to power in 1806 he became Lord Chancellor and a baron. Among his most famous speeches were those in defence of Lord George Gordon, Thomas Paine, and Queen Caroline.

erysipelas an acute disease of the skin due to infection by a streptococcus. Starting at some point where the skin is broken or injured, the infection spreads, producing a swollen red patch with small blisters, and general fever.

Erzebirge /'eətsgə,bɪəgə/ mountain range (German 'ore mountains') on the German-Czech frontier, where the rare metals uranium, cobalt, bismuth, arsenic, and antimony are mined. Some 145 km/90 mi long, its highest summit is Mount Klinovec (Keilberg) 1,244 m/4,080 ft, in Czechoslovakia.

Erzurum /'eəzurum/ town and military base in NE Turkey; population (1980) 190,240.

Esarhaddon /,iːsɑːˈhædn/ died 669 BC. King of Assyria from 680, when he succeeded his father ◊Sennacherib. He conquered Egypt 671–74.

Esau /'iːsɔː/ in the Old Testament, the son of Isaac and Rebekah, and the elder twin brother of Jacob, who tricked Isaac into giving him the blessing intended for Esau by putting on goatskins. Earlier Esau had sold his birthright to Jacob for a 'mess of red pottage'. He was the ancestor of the Edomites.

Esbjerg /'esbjɜːg/ port of Denmark on the W coast of Jutland; population (1981) 70,250. It is the terminus of the rail-ferry link with Stockholm, Sweden.

escalator a moving staircase which carries people between floors or levels. The first escalator was exhibited in Paris in 1900.

escape velocity minimum velocity which an object such as a rocket must reach for it to escape from the gravitational pull of a planet or moon. In the case of the Earth, the escape velocity is 11.2 km/6.9 mi per sec; the Moon 2.4 km/1.5 mi; Mars 5 km/3.1 mi; and Jupiter 59.6 km/37 mi per second.

Escher /'eʃə/ Maurits Cornelis 1902–1972. Dutch graphic artist. His drawings, often based on mathematical principles of symmetry or pattern, usually originate in paradox, illusion, or double meaning. Especially notable are such lithographs as 'Relativity' 1953 and 'Ascending and Descending' 1960.

escrow (from Old French *escroe* 'scroll') in law, a document sealed and delivered to a third party and not released or coming into effect until some condition has been fulfilled or performed; whereupon the document takes full effect.

Esenin /je'senɪn/ Sergey 1895–1925. Soviet poet. Born in Konstantinovo (renamed Esenino in his honour), he went to Petrograd in 1915, attached himself to the Symbolists, greeted the Revolution, revived peasant traditions and folklore, and initiated the Imaginist group of poets 1919. After a brief and unsuccessful marriage to the American dancer, Isadora Duncan 1922–23, he suffered from depression, took to drink, and finally committed suicide.

Eskilstuna /'eskɪlz,tuːnə/ town W of Stockholm, Sweden; population (1981) 90,000. It has iron foundries, steel and armament works.

Eskimo /'eskɪməʊ/ member (or language) of a people of the Arctic. The Eskimos of Greenland and Canada are ◊Inuit and their language Inuktitut; the Eskimos of South Alaska and Siberia are Yupik and their language Yuk.

Eskimo dog semi-domesticated dog kept by Eskimos in Alaska for drawing sledges. They are strong and fierce, and are also known as *huskies*.

Eskişehir /es'kiːʃəhɪə/ city in Turkey, 200 km/125 mi W of Ankara; population (1979) 295,500. It produces meerschaum, chromium, magnesite, cotton goods and tiles, and also assembles aircraft.

esparto grass *Stipa tenacissima*, native to S Spain, S Portugal and the Balearics, now widely grown in dry, sandy situations throughout the world. The plant is just over 1 m/3 ft high, producing greyish-green leaves, which are used for paper-making, ropes, baskets, mats, and cables.

Esperanto /,espə'ræntəʊ/ an artificial language devised in 1887 by Dr Ludwig L Zamenhof, a Warsaw oculist (1859–1917), as an international auxiliary language. For its structure and vocabulary it draws upon various European languages. Esperantists refer to Esperanto as a 'planned language' and to the natural languages of the world as 'ethnic languages'. Its spelling is phonetic, its accents varying according to the ethnic backgrounds of its users. For its centenary in 1987, Esperantists have claimed some 10 to 15 million users worldwide, and say that *Esperanto estas tre facile lernebla lingvo* ('Esperanto is a very easily learnable language').

espionage the practice of spying; a way to gather ◊intelligence.

Espronceda /,esprɒnˈθeɪðə/ José de 1808–1842. Spanish poet. Originally one of the Queen's guards, he lost his commission because of his political activity, and was involved in the Republican risings of 1835 and 1836. His lyric poetry and life style both owed much to Byron.

Esquivel /,eskɪ'vel/ Adolfo 1932– . Argentinian sculptor and architect. As leader of the Servicio de Paz y Justicia (Peace and Justice Service), a Catholic-Protestant human rights organization, he was awarded a Nobel peace prize in 1980.

ESS (evolutionary stable strategy) in ◊sociobiology, an assemblage of behavioural or physical characters (collectively termed a 'strategy') that is resistant to replacement by any forms bearing new traits, because these individuals will be unable to reproduce as successfully. ESS analysis is based on ◊game theory and can be applied both to genetically determined physical characters (such as horn length) and to learned behavioural responses (for example, whether to fight or retreat from an opponent). An ESS may be conditional on the context, as in the rule 'fight if the opponent is smaller, but retreat if the opponent is larger'.

essay short, literary piece of prose, dealing often from a fairly personal point of view with some particular subject. The essay first became a recognized genre and name with the first edition of the French writer Montaigne's *Essais* 1580. Bacon's essays 1597 are among the most famous in English. Abraham Cowley, whose essays appeared in 1668, brought a greater ease and freedom to the genre than it had possessed before in England, but it was with the development of periodical literature in the 18th century that the essay became a widely used form. The great names are Addison and Steele, with their *Tatler* and *Spectator* papers, and later Johnson and Goldsmith. A new era was inaugurated by Lamb's *Essays of Elia* 1820; to the same period belong Leigh Hunt, Hazlitt, the French Sainte Beuve and De Quincey and the Americans Emerson and Thoreau; Hazlitt may be regarded as the originator of the modern critical essay, and his successors include Arnold and Gosse. Macaulay, whose essays began to appear shortly after those of Lamb, presents a strong contrast in his vigorous but less personal tone. There was a considerable revival of the form during the closing years of the 19th and beginning of the 20th century, in the work of R L Stevenson, Anatole France, Gautier, Sir Max Beerbohm, and later of Chesterton and Belloc. The literary journalistic tradition of the essay was continued by E V Lucas, Robert Lynd, the American James Thurber, Sir Desmond MacCarthy, and others, and the critical essay by George Orwell, Cyril Connolly, F R Leavis, T S Eliot, and others. The essay was largely used in 19th-century Europe as a vehicle for literary criticism, but the personal essay is usually regarded as being particularly English in spirit. However, its leisured approach made it a less often used form by the mid-20th century, although its spirit survived in the radio 'essays' of Alistair Cooke, and in newspapers and magazines as 'opinion pieces'.

Essen /'esən/ city in North Rhine-Westphalia, West Germany; population (1980) 647,500. Administrative centre of the Ruhr, it has textile, chemical, electrical, and other industries.

Essene /'esiːn/ one of a body of pre-Christian Jewish ascetics in Palestine who regulated their life according to rules resembling those of later monasticism, and practised community of goods. It has been claimed that both St John the Baptist and Christ himself may possibly have lived for a time among the Essenes, perhaps at ◊Qumran, and sayings of Jesus seem to reflect both the influence of Essene teaching and antipathy to certain aspects.

Essequibo /,esɪ'kwiːbəʊ/ chief river of ◊Guyana, length 960 km/600 mi. The Kaietur Fall is the chief feature of the Kaietur National Park.

Essex /'esɪks/ county in SE England.
area 3,672 sq km/1,417 sq mi
towns administrative headquarters Chelmsford; Colchester; ports Harwich, Tilbury; resorts Southend, Clacton
features former royal hunting ground of Epping Forest (controlled from 1882 by the City of

London); the marshy coastal headland of The Naze; birdlife at Maplin Sands; since 1111 at Great Dunmow the Dunmow flitch (side of cured pork) can be claimed every four years by any couple proving to a jury they have not regretted their marriage within the year (winners are few); Stansted, site of London's third airport
products dairying, cereals, fruit
population (1986) 1,504,700
famous people William Harvey.

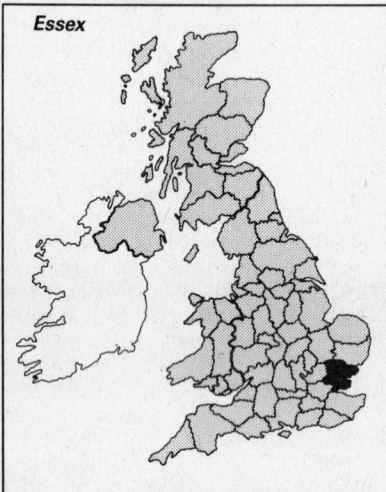
Essex

Essex /'esɪks/ Robert Devereux, 2nd Earl of Essex 1566–1601. English soldier and politician. He saw service in the Netherlands in 1585–86 and distinguished himself by his courage at the Battle of Zutphen. From 1587 he became a favourite with Elizabeth I, who created him Master of the Horse and a Knight of the Garter. In 1599 he became Lieutenant of Ireland and led an army against Irish rebels under the Earl of Tyrone in Ulster, but was unsuccessful, made an unauthorized truce with Tyrone, and returned without permission to England. He was forbidden to return to Court, and when he marched into the City at the head of a body of supporters, he was promptly arrested, tried for treason, and beheaded on Tower Green.

Essex /'esɪks/ Robert Devereux, 3rd Earl of Essex 1591–1646. English soldier. Eldest son of the 2nd earl, he commanded the Parliamentary army in the inconclusive English Civil War Battle of Edgehill in 1642. Following a disastrous campaign in Cornwall, he resigned his command in 1645.

estate in law, the interest which a person has in any property. *Real estate* is an interest in any freehold land; *personal estate* the interest in any other kind of property.

ester an organic compound formed by the reaction between an alcohol and an acid, with the elimination of water. Esters are the organic equivalent of salts in inorganic chemistry.

Esther /'estə/ in the Old Testament, the wife of the Persian king ◊Ahasuerus, who prevented the extermination of her people by the vizier Haman, a deliverance celebrated in the Jewish

Essex Robert Devereux, 2nd Earl of Essex, a favourite of Elizabeth I. His earlier career was crowned with success, culminating in the capture of Cadiz, but ended in imprisonment and execution.

festival of Purim. Her story is told in the Old Testament book *Esther*.

Estonia /es'təʊnɪə/ constituent republic of the Soviet Union from 1940.
area 45,000 sq km/17,400 sq mi
capital Tallinn
features mild climate, lakes and marshes in a partly forested plain
products oil from shale, wood products, flax, dairy and pig products
population (1982) 1,500,000
language Estonian, allied to Finnish
religion traditionally Lutheran
history an independent republic 1920–40, Estonia was then incorporated in the USSR. As in the other Baltic republics, there has been nationalist dissent since 1980, influenced by Poland's example, and prompted by the influx of Soviet workers and officials.

estradiol a type of ◊oestrogen (female sex hormone).

estrogen alternative spelling of ◊oestrogen.

estuary a river mouth widening into the sea, where both fresh and salt water are found and tidal effects are felt.

Esztergom /'estəgɒm/ city on the Danube, NW of Budapest, Hungary; population (1986) 31,000. It was the birthplace of St Stephen, and the former ecclesiastical capital of Hungary, with a fine cathedral.

Etaples /eɪ'tɑːplə/ fishing port and seaside resort on the Canche estuary, Pas de Calais *département*, France; population (1985) 11,500.

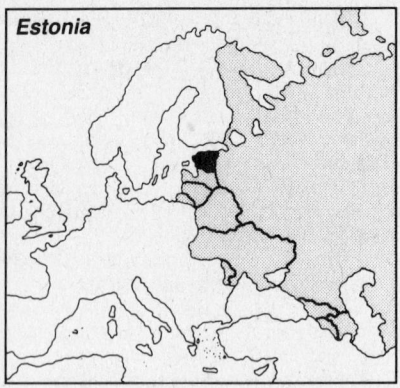
Estonia

During World War I it was an important British base and hospital centre.

etching a print or impression on paper, taken from a metal (usually copper) plate, in which the picture has been 'etched', or bitten in, by means of some corrosive acid or chemical. The method was invented in Germany about 1500, the earliest dated print being of 1513. Whereas in the earlier method of engraving on metal the picture is cut into the metal surface by means of a sharp instrument called a burin or graver, used with a pushing action, in etching it is drawn on the plate by means of a sharp delicate metal point, which allows much greater freedom of action. Among the earliest etchers were ◊Dürer, ◊van Dyck, ◊Hollar, and ◊Rembrandt. Since then great interest has been shown in it by many artists, for example ◊Whistler, and ◊Sickert.

ethane a colourless, odourless gas, C_2H_6. It is the second member of the series of paraffin hydrocarbons, the first being methane.

Ethelbert /'eθəlbɜːt/ c. 552–616. King of Kent, England. Succeeding his father Eormenric in 560, he extended his rule over all England south of the Humber. Married to a Christian (Bertha), he received St Augustine in 597, and was later baptized.

Ethelred II /'eθəlred/ 968–1016. King of England from 978; nicknamed the Unready, that is, lacking in foresight. The son of King Edgar, he became king after the murder of his half-brother, Edward the Martyr. He tried to buy off the Danish raiders by paying Danegeld, and in 1002 ordered the massacre of the Danish settlers – so provoking an invasion by ◊Sweyn of Denmark. War with Sweyn and Sweyn's son, Canute, occupied the rest of Ethelred's reign.

ether or *diethyl ether*, $C_2H_5OC_2H_5$. A colourless, volatile inflammable liquid, slightly soluble in water, miscible with alcohol. It is prepared by treatment of ethyl alcohol with excess concentrated sulphuric acid at 140°C. It is used as an anaesthetic by vapour inhalation and as an external cleansing agent before surgical operations. It is also used as a solvent, and in the extraction of oils fats, waxes, resins, and alkaloids.

ether in physics, a hypothetical concept introduced by early physicists to explain some of the properties of light. It was supposed that light and other electromagnetic radiation – even in outer space – needed a medium in which to travel, and this was called the ether. Its existence was disproved in 1887 by the classic Michelson-Morley experiment, which showed that light travels at the same speed in the direction of the Earth's motion through space as it does at right angles to the motion. The abandonment of the other hypothesis later led to ◊Einstein's formulation of special relativity.

Etherege /'eθərɪdʒ/ George c. 1635–c. 1691. British Restoration dramatist whose play *Love in a Tub* 1664 was the first attempt at the 'comedy of manners' (a genre further developed by his successor ◊Congreve). *She Would If She Could* 1668, was followed by his best comedy *The Man of Mode* in 1676, and contains his most famous character Sir Fopling Flutter, the epitome of the Restoration dandy.

Ethical Movement movement designed to further the moral or ethical factor as the real substance and fundamental part of religion, influential in the late 19th and early 20th centuries. It first came to prominence in the USA in 1876, when Felix Adler founded an Ethical Society in New York. In 1888 the first English Ethical Society was founded by Dr Stanton Coit.

ethics the area of philosophy concerned with human conduct, also referred to as moral philosophy. As well as investigating the meanings of moral terms, ethics studies theories of conduct and goodness. In Europe, it may be said to have originated as a systematic intellectual study with the Greek philosopher ◊Socrates in the 5th century BC, but considerably earlier there was intense ethical speculation in India and China. ◊Plato's *Republic* is an exposition of the nature of justice or righteousness, and ethical theory was advanced by ◊Aristotle's *Nicomachean Ethics* and similar writings. The ◊Cyrenaics, ◊Epicureans, and ◊Stoics advanced theories that have been many times revived. The 'Christian ethic' is mainly a combination of New Testament moral teaching with ideas drawn from Plato and Aristotle. ◊Hobbes, ◊Hume, and Bishop ◊Butler are notable 17th–18th century British ethical philosophers. One of the greatest individual contributors to ethical theory was ◊Kant, with his 'categorical imperative' (the obligation to obey absolute moral law). The utilitarian ethic was ably expounded by ◊Bentham, J S Mill, Sidgwick, and Herbert Spencer; they were opposed by such thinkers as F H Bradley and T H Green, who linked ethics with metaphysics, and emphasized the place of the individual in organized society. Ethicists of the 20th century include G E Moore, C D ◊Broad, John Dewey, Nicolai ◊Hartmann, R M Hare and Stephen Toulmin 1922– , whose *Place of Reason in Ethics* 1950 first put forward the viewpoint of modern linguistic analysis.

Ethiopia /ˌiːθiˈəʊpiə/ country in E Africa, bounded NE by the Red Sea, E and SE by Somalia, S by Kenya, and W and NW by Sudan. *government* a traditional monarchy until 1974, Ethiopia has since been ruled by a Provisional Military Administrative Council (PMAC), chaired by the head of state, who also presides over a council of ministers and is secretary-general of the only political party, the Marxist-Leninist Workers' Party of Ethiopia (WPE). Parliament was suspended in 1974 when the king was deposed and Ethiopia was proclaimed a socialist state. The council of ministers is mainly civilian but is under military control.

history long subject to Egypt, the area became independent about the 11th century BC. The kingdom of ◊Aksum flourished from the 1st–10th century AD, reaching its peak around the 4th century with the introduction of ◊Coptic Christianity from Egypt, and declining from the 7th century as ◊Islam expanded. The ◊Arab conquests isolated Aksum from the rest of the Christian world.

During the 10th century there emerged a kingdom which formed the basis of Abyssinia, reinforced in 1270 with the founding of a new dynasty. Although it remained independent throughout the period of European colonization of Africa, Abyssinia suffered civil unrest and several invasions from the 16th century, and was eventually reunited in 1889 under ◊Menelik II, with Italian support. In 1896 Menelik put down an invasion by Italy, which claimed he had agreed to make the country an Italian protectorate, and annexed ◊Ogaden and several provinces to the W.

Ethiopia was dominated for over 50 years by ◊Haile Selassie, who became regent in 1916, king in 1928, and emperor in 1930. The country was occupied by Italy 1935–41, and Haile Selassie went into exile in Britain. Ogaden was returned to ◊Somalia, which was also under Italian control.

Haile Selassie returned from exile in 1941 and ruled until 1974, when he was deposed by the armed forces, after famine, high inflation, growing unemployment and demands for greater democracy. His palace and estates were nationalized, parliament dissolved and the constitution suspended. He died in 1975, aged 83, in a small apartment in his former palace in Addis Ababa.

Gen Teferi Benti, who had led the uprising and been made head of state, was killed in 1977 by fellow officers and replaced by Col Mengistu Haile Mariam. The Ethiopian empire had been built up by Haile Selassie and Menelik, and annexed regions had made frequent attempts to secede. The 1975 revolution encouraged secessionist movements to increase their efforts and the military government had to fight to keep Eritrea and the SE region of Ogaden, where Somalian troops were assisting local guerrillas. The USSR, having adopted Ethiopia as a new ally, threatened to cut off aid to Somalia, and Cuban troops assisted Mengistu in ending the fighting there. Eritrea and its neighbour, Tigré, continued their struggle for independence.

In the midst of this confusion there was acute famine in the N, including Eritrea, when the rains failed for three successive seasons. In addition to a massive emergency aid programme from many Western nations, the Ethiopian government tried to alleviate the problem by resettling people from the N to the more fertile S. By 1986 more than 500,000 had been resettled.

Meanwhile, the military regime had re-established normal relations with most of its neighbours, promising a return to civilian rule, and in 1986 publishing the draft of a new constitution for the People's Democratic Republic of Ethiopia (PDRE), which would include a Soviet-style assembly. In Sept 1987 the new constitution was adopted, ending 12 years of military rule and electing Col Mengistu Mariam as the country's first president.

ethnicity from Greek *ethnos*, 'a people', a term that overlaps with such social concepts as race, nation, class, and religion. Social scientists use the term *ethnic group* to refer to groups or societies who feel a common sense of identity, often based on a similar culture, language, religion, and customs. It may or may not include common territory, skin colour, or common descent. Whereas the concept of race was used from the outside to label people according to perceived biological features, ethnicity refers to people's own sense of cultural identity. The USA, for example, is often described as a *multi-ethnic society* because many members would describe themselves as members of an ethnic group (Jewish, black, or Irish, for example) as well as their national one (American).

ethnology branch of anthropology concerned with the characteristics and distribution over the globe of the ethnic groups of humankind; also of their cultural conditions and achievements.

ethnomethodology the study of social order and routines used by people in their daily lives, to explain how everyday reality is created and perceived. Ethnomethodologists tend to use small-scale studies and experiments to examine the details of social life and structure (such as conversations) that people normally take for granted, rather than construct large-scale theories about society.

ethology the comparative study of ◊animal behaviour in its natural setting, pioneered during the 1930s by K ◊Lorenz and K von ◊Frisch who, along with N ◊Tinbergen, received the Nobel prize in 1973. Ethology is concerned with the causal mechanisms (both the stimuli that elicit behaviour and the physiological mechanisms controlling it), as well as the development of behaviour, its function and evolutionary history. Ethologists believe that the significance of an animal's behaviour can be understood only in its natural context, and emphasize the importance of field studies and an evolutionary perspective. A recent development within ethology is ◊sociobiology, the study of the evolutionary function of ◊social behaviour.

ethyl alcohol or *ethanol*, C_2H_5OH. The chemical term for the alcohol found in beer, wine, cider, spirits and other 'alcoholic drinks'. (Chemically, the term alcohol denotes a whole family of compounds.) When pure, it is a colourless liquid with a pleasant odour, miscible with water or ether, and burning in air with a pale blue flame. The vapour forms an explosive mixture with air and may be used in high-compression internal combustion engines.

It is produced naturally by the fermentation of carbohydrates by yeast cells. Industrially, it can be made by ◊absorption of ethylene and

Ethiopia

PEOPLE'S DEMOCRATIC REPUBLIC OF (Amharic *Hebretesebawit Ityopia*, formerly also known as Abyssinia)

AREA 1,000,000 sq km/395,000 sq mi
CAPITAL Addis Ababa
TOWNS Asmara (capital of Eritrea), Dire Dawa; ports are Massawa, Assab
PHYSICAL a high plateau with mountains; plains in E; Blue Nile river
FEATURES Danakil and Ogaden deserts; ancient remains at Aksum, Gondar, Lalibela among other places; only African country to retain its independence during the colonial period
HEAD OF STATE AND OF GOVERNMENT Mengistu Haile Mariam from 1977
GOVERNMENT one-party communist; military rule 1974–87; civilian rule restored 1987 with elected assembly
EXPORTS coffee, pulses, oilseeds, hides and skins
CURRENCY birr (3.41 = £1 Sept 1987)
POPULATION (1985) 42,266,418 (Oromo 40%, Amhara 25%, Tigré 12%, Sidama 9%); annual growth rate 3.3%
LANGUAGE Amharic (official); Tigré, Galla, Arabic
RELIGION Christian (Ethiopian Orthodox church, which has had its own patriarch since 1976) 50%, Sunni Muslim 50%
LITERACY 18% (1985)
GNP $4.7 bn (1984); $141 per head of population
CHRONOLOGY
1974 Haile Selassie deposed and replaced by a

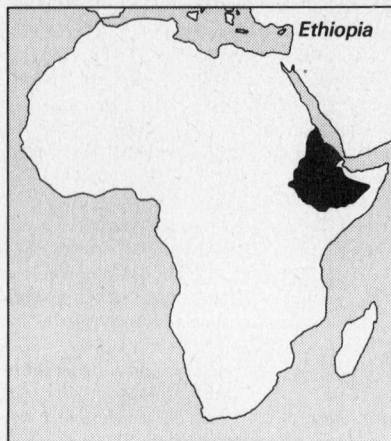
Ethiopia

military government led by Gen Teferi Benti. Ethiopia declared a socialist state; parliament suspended.
1977 Teferi Benti killed and replaced by Col Mengistu Haile Mariam.
1984 The Workers' Party of Ethiopia (WPE) declared the only legal party.
1986 Worst famine for more than a decade. Western aid sent and internal resettlement programmes undertaken.
1987 New constitution adopted, Mengistu Mariam elected president. Provisional Military Administrative Council dissolved and elected National Assembly introduced. New famine; food aid hindered by guerrillas.

subsequent reaction with water, or by the reduction of acetaldehyde in the presence of a catalyst, and is widely used as a solvent.
When consumed, ethanol is rapidly absorbed from the stomach and upper intestine and affects nearly every tissue, particularly the central nervous system. Tests have shown that the feeling of elation usually associated with drinking alcoholic liquors is due to the loss of inhibitions through removal of the restraining influences of the higher cerebral centres. It also results in dilatation of the blood vessels, particularly of the skin. This loss of heat from the skin actually produces a physical cooling inside the body, despite the feeling of warmth experienced.

ethylene a colourless, flammable gas (C_2H_4), the first member of the alkene series of hydrocarbons. It is the most widely used synthetic organic chemical and is used to produce polyethylene (polythene), ethylene dichloride and polyvinyl chloride (PVC). It also occurs naturally in plants, helping to promote growth, and the ripening of fruit. It is applied to fruit that has been picked and shipped in an unripe state, to promote ripening.

ethylene glycol another name for ◊glycol (OHCH₂CH2OH).

etiolation in botany, a form of growth seen in plants receiving insufficient light. It is characterized by long, weak stems, small leaves, and a pale yellowish colour (◊chlorosis) owing to a lack of chlorophyll. The rapid increase in height

enables a plant which is surrounded by others to quickly reach a source of light, when a return to normal growth usually occurs.

Etna /'etnə/ volcano on the E coast of Sicily, 3,323 m/10,902 ft – the highest in Europe. Its most recent eruptions were in Dec 1985.

Eton /'iːtn/ town in Berkshire, England, on the N bank of the Thames, opposite Windsor; population (1981) 3,500.

Etruscan /ɪ'trʌskən/ member of an ancient people of N Italy. Their chief settlements were the twelve cities of Etruria, including Volaterrae, Tarquinii, Clusium, Caere, and Vetulonia, each of which seems to have been independent. The height of their power was reached about 500 BC. In 474 BC they were defeated by the Carthaginians in a naval battle off Cumae, and about 400 BC their northern conquests were lost by the irruption of the Celts into N Italy. Thereafter the Etruscans entered into a period of decline, and they gradually succumbed to the rising power of Rome.
Some knowledge of their art, religion, and language has been obtained from excavated tombs. The principal medium is sculpture, but pottery, bronzeware, and mural painting are also noteworthy. Etruscan religion seems to have been derived from Asia Minor, and shows many signs of Greek influence. The language, despite the discovery of a large number of inscriptions, mainly funerary, and a certain number of words

derived by the Romans from Etruscan, is still very imperfectly known.

Etty /'eti/ William 1787–1849. British artist. Born at York, he served seven years' apprenticeship to a Hull printer before becoming a student of Sir Thomas ◊Lawrence in 1807, and first gained success at the Royal Academy in London with *Telemachus rescuing Antiope* in 1811. In his work Etty aimed to paint great moral truths and regarded his numerous nude paintings as a dedication to 'God's most glorious work'.

étude (French 'study') a musical exercise designed to develop technique.

etymology the study of the origin and history of words within and across languages. It has two major aspects: the study of the phonetic and written forms of words, and the semantics or meanings of those words. Etymological research has been particularly successful in tracing the development of words and word elements within the Indo-European language family. Standard dictionaries of a language like English typically contain etymological information within square brackets at the end of each entry.

Euboea /juː'biə/ largest of the Greek islands; area 3,755 sq km/1,480 sq mi. It lies off the E coast of Greece, in the Aegean Sea, and is about 177 km/110 mi long. It is mountainous, Mount Delphi reaching 1,743 m/5,718 ft. The chief town is Chalcis, connected by a bridge to the mainland.

eucalyptus tree of the Myrtaceae family, practically confined, in the natural state, to Australia and Tasmania, where they are commonly known as gum trees. About 90 per cent of Australian timber belongs to the eucalyptus group, which comprises about 500 species.

Eucharist chief Christian sacrament, in which bread is eaten and wine drunk in memory of the death of Christ. The word comes from the Greek for 'thanksgiving', and refers to the statement in the Gospel narrative that Christ gave thanks over the bread and the cup. Other names for it are the Lord's Supper, Holy Communion, and (among Roman Catholics, who believe that the bread and wine are transubstantiated, that is, converted to the body and blood of Christ) the Mass. The doctrine of *transubstantiation* was rejected by Protestant Churches at the Reformation. In Britain, members of the Church of England are required to participate in the Eucharist at least three times a year, with Easter as one.

Euclid /'juːklɪd/ c. 330–c. 260 BC. Greek mathematician, who lived at Alexandria and wrote the *Stoicheia/Elements* in 13 books, of which nine deal with plane and solid geometry, and four with arithmetic. His main work lay in the systematic arrangement of previous discoveries, and the geometrical books remained a standard textbook for over 2,000 years and are still in regular use today.

Eugène /juː'dʒiːn/ Prince of Savoy 1663–1736. Austrian general. The son of Prince Eugène Maurice of Savoy-Carignano, he was born in Paris. When Louis XIV refused him a commission he entered the Austrian army, and served against the Turks at the defence of Vienna in 1683, and against the French on the Rhine and in Italy ten years later. In 1697 he expelled the Turks from Hungary by his triumph at Zenta. In the War of the Spanish Succession 1701–14 he shared with Marlborough in his great victories against the French (battles of Blenheim, Oudenarde, and Malplaquet), and won many successes as an independent commander in Italy. He again defeated the Turks in 1716–18, and fought a last campaign against the French in 1734–35.

eugenics the study of ways in which the physical and mental quality of a people can be controlled and improved by selective breeding, and the belief that such a situation should occur. The term was coined by Sir Francis ◊Galton in 1883, and comes from the Greek 'well-born'. Originally developed in the late 19th century with a view to improving the intelligence and behaviour of humanity, its ideas were later used by the ◊Nazis in Germany during the 1930s to justify the extermination of entire groups of people. In 1986 Singapore became the first democratic power to adopt an openly eugenic policy by guaranteeing pay rises to female university graduates when they give birth to a child, while offering grants towards house purchase for non-graduate married females on condition that they are sterilized after the first or second child. Eugenics can serve the more useful purpose of trying to control the spread of inherited genetic abnormalities by counselling prospective parents.

Eugénie /ˌɜːʒeɪˈniː/ 1826–1920. Empress of the French. Daughter of the Spanish count of Montijo, she married in 1853 Louis Napoleon, soon after he became French emperor as Napoleon III. She encouraged his intervention in Mexico and after his surrender to the Germans at ◊Sedan 1870 she fled to England, and settled with him at Chislehurst. Later she lived at Farnborough, where she built a mausoleum in which she, her husband, and her son, who was killed in the Zulu War, were buried.

eukaryote one of the two classes into which all living organisms (except viruses) are divided. The ◊cells of eukaryotes possess a clearly defined nucleus, bounded by a membrane, within which ◊DNA is formed into distinct ◊chromosomes. Their cells contain ◊mitochondria, chloroplasts and other organelles which are lacking in the cells of the alternative class, the ◊prokaryotes. All organisms other than bacteria and cyanobacteria are eukaryotic.

Euler /ˈɔɪlə/ Leonhard 1707–1783. Swiss mathematician. He became professor of physics at the University of St Petersburg in 1730. In 1741 he was invited to Berlin by Frederick the Great, where he spent 25 years before returning to Russia. He developed the theory of differential equations, the calculus of variations, and did important work in astronomy and optics.

Eumenides /juːˈmenɪdiːz/ ('kindly ones') in Greek mythology, appeasing name for the ◊Furies.

eunuch a castrated male. Originally eunuchs were simply bed-chamber attendants in harems in the East (*eunoukhos* is Greek for 'one in charge of a bed') but as these were usually castrated so that they should not take too great an interest in their charges, the term became applied more generally. Eunuchs often filled high offices of state in China, India and Persia. The Italian *castrati* were singers castrated as boys to preserve their high voices, but on the accession of pope Leo XIII in 1878 this practice ceased.

Eupen-et-Malmédy /ˈɜːpen eɪ ˌmælmeˈdiː/ region of Belgium around the towns of Eupen and Malmédy. It was Prussian from 1814 until it became Belgian in 1920 after a plebiscite; there was fierce fighting here in the German Ardennes offensive in Dec 1944.

euphemism a ◊figure of speech whose name in Greek means 'speaking well (of something)'. When people speak or write euphemistically they use a milder, more polite, less direct or even less honest expression rather than one that is considered too blunt, vulgar, direct or revealing. Thus, 'He passed away' is preferred to *he died*; 'sleep with someone' substitutes for *have sex with someone*; and 'liquidate the opposition' softens the impact of 'kill one's enemies'.

euphonium type of ◊brass instrument, like a small tuba.

Euphrates /juːˈfreɪtiːz/ river, rising in E Turkey and flowing through Syria and Iraq to join the Tigris above Basra to form the Shatt-el-Arab, at the head of the Persian/Arabian Gulf; 3,600 km/2235 mi in length. The ancient cities of Babylon, Eridu and Ur were situated along its course.

Eurasian /juːˈreɪʒən/ in India and the East Indies a term formerly used to denote a person born of mixed European and Asian parentage or ancestry; it was almost exclusively derogatory and often insulting.

Euratom /juərˈætəm/ European Atomic Energy Commission, founded in 1957 and forming part of ◊European Community organization.

Eure /ɜː/ river rising in Orne *département*, France, and flowing SE, then N, to the Seine; length 115 km/70 mi. Chartres is on its banks. It gives its name to two *départements*, Eure and Eure-et-Loire.

Eureka 1) exclamation (Greek 'I've got it!') allegedly made by ◊Archimedes on his discovery of fluid displacement. 2) a plan for European Technological Cooperation, 1985. 3) alternative name for the copper-nickel alloy ◊constantan which is used in electrical equipment.

Eureka Stockade /juːˈriːkə/ incident at Ballarat, Australia, when about 150 goldminers or 'diggers', rebelled against authority. They took refuge behind a wooden stockade, which was taken in a few minutes by the military on 3 Dec 1854. Some 30 diggers were killed, and a few soldiers were killed or wounded, but the majority of the rebels were taken prisoner. Among those who escaped was Peter Lalor, their leader. Of the 13 tried for treason, all were acquitted; the Eureka Stockade is regarded as marking the emergence of Australian democracy.

eurhythmics practice of coordinated bodily movement as a help to musical development. It was founded in about 1900 by the Swiss musician ◊Jaques-Dalcroze, professor of harmony at the Geneva conservatoire. He devised a series of

'gesture' songs, to be sung simultaneously with certain bodily actions.

Euripides /juːˈrɪpɪdiːz/ c. 484–407 BC. Greek dramatist. His influence on later drama was probably more important than either of the two other great tragedians, Aeschylus and Sophocles. A realist, he was bitterly attacked for his unorthodox 'impiety' and sympathy for the despised: slaves, beggars, and women. His plays reflect his concern with individual passions and social issues, dealing with ordinary people rather than the idealized heroes and higher principles felt at the time to be appropriate subjects for tragedy. He went into voluntary exile from Athens to Macedonia at the end of his life. He wrote more than 80 plays, of which 19 survive, the most famous being: *Alcestis* 438 BC, *Medea* 431, *Andromache* 420, *Trojan Women* 415, *Electra* 413, *Iphigenia in Tauris* 413, *Iphigenia in Aulis* 405, *Bacchae* 405.

Euripides A bust of the ancient Greek dramatist Euripides. His tragedies, concerned with individual passions and social issues rather than higher principles, exerted incalculable influence on later drama.

Europa /juːˈrəʊpə/ in astronomy, the fourth-largest moon of the planet ◊Jupiter, diameter 3,100 km/1,900 mi, orbiting 671,000 km/417,00 mi from the planet every 3.5 days. It is covered by ice and criss-crossed by thousands of thin cracks, each some 50,000 km/30,000 mi long.

Europa /juːˈrəʊpə/ in Greek mythology, the daughter of the king of Tyre, carried off by ◊Zeus (in the form of a bull); she personifies the continent of Europe.

Europa Nostra international federation established in 1963 by the representatives of 18 organizations (including Italia Nostra, National Trust, Irish Georgian Society, Vieilles Maisons Françaises) in 11 European countries for the preservation of historic sites, buildings, and monuments.

Europe /'juərəp/ second smallest continent, comprising the land W of the Ural mountains; it has 8 per cent of the earth's surface, with 14.5 per cent of world population.

area 10,400,000 sq km/4,000,000 sq mi

largest cities (over 2,000,000 inhabitants) Moscow, London, Istanbul, Leningrad, Madrid, Rome, Athens, Kiev, Budapest, Paris

features North European Plain on which stand London, Paris, Berlin, and Moscow; Central European Highlands (Sierra Nevada, Pyrenees, Alps, Apennines, Carpathians, Balkans); and Scandinavian highland, which takes in the Scottish Highlands; highest point Mount Elbruz in Caucasus mountains. Rivers (over 1,000 mi) Volga, Don, Dnieper, Danube; lakes (over 2,000 sq mi) Ladoga, Onega, Vanern. The climate ranges from the variable NW, modified by the ◊Gulf Stream, through the Central Zone with warm summers and cold winters, becoming bitterly cold in E Europe, to the Mediterranean zone with comparatively mild winters and hot summers. The last is the richest zone for plant life, but animal species have long been reduced everywhere by the predominance of humans.

population (1985) 492,000,000 (excluding Turkey and USSR)

languages mostly of Indo-European origin, with a few exceptions, including Finno-Ugrian (Finnish and Hungarian) and Basque

religion Christianity (Protestantism, Roman Catholicism, Greek Orthodox), Islam

history see ◊Europe: history.

European Atomic Energy Commission (EURATOM) organization established by the second treaty of Rome 1957, which seeks the cooperation of member states of the European Community in nulear research and the rapid and large-scale development on non-military nuclear energy.

European Coal and Steel Community (ECSC) organization established by the treaty of Paris 1951, establishing a single authority for

European Community The signing of the Rome Treaties on 25 Mar 1957 in Palazzo dei Conservatori on the Capitoline Hill, which established the European Economic Community and Euratom.

EUROPE: HISTORY

3000BC	Bronze Age civilizations: Minoan, Mycenaean.
6th–4th cent.	Greek civilization at its height; Alexander.
3rd cent.	Rome in control of the Italian peninsula.
146	Greece a Roman province, and Carthage destroyed.
1st cent.	Augustus made the Rhine and Danube the Roman Empire's northern frontiers; see Celts.
1st cent. AD	Britain brought within the Roman Empire.
2nd cent.	Roman Empire ceased to expand.
4th cent.	Christianity the established religion of the Roman Empire.
4th–6th cent.	W Europe overrun by Anglo-Saxons, Franks, Goths, Lombards.
7th–8th cent.	Christendom threatened by the Moors (Arabs).
800	Charlemagne given title of emperor by the Pope.
1073	Gregory VII begins 200 years of conflict between Empire and Papacy.
1096–1272	Crusades.
12th cent.	Setting-up of German, Flemish, and Italian city states, which in the 14–15th centuries fostered the Renaissance.
1453	Constantinople captured by the Turks.
16th–17th cent.	Dominated by rivalry of France and the Hapsburgs, the Protestant Reformation, and the Catholic Counter-Reformation.
17th cent.	Absolute monarchy came to prevail (Louis XIV) in Europe, although in England supremacy of Parliament established by Civil War.
18th cent.	War of the Austrian Succession and Seven Years' War ended in the loss of the French colonial empire to Britain, and the establishment of Prussia as Europe's emergent power.
1789–95	French Revolution led to the united opposition of the rest of Europe in the Revolutionary and Napoleonic Wars.
1821–29	Greek War of Independence marked the end of Turkish control of the Balkans.
1848	Year of revolutions (see Louis Philippe, Metternich, Risorgimento).
1914–1918	World War I arose from the Balkan Question, Franco-German rivalry, and colonial differences; it destroyed the Austrian and Turkish empires and initiated that of the USSR.
1933	Hitler came to power.
1939–45	World War II resulted in decline of European colonial rule in Africa and Asia; full emergence of Soviet power, and Western forces organized under the aegis of the USA (NATO); the Cold War.
1957	Establishment of the European Economic Community, the 'Common Market'.
1973	Enlargement of the European Community to include Britain.
1979	First direct elections to the European Parliament.
1985	Accession to power in the USSR of Mikhail Gorbachev marked an apparent relaxation of political and economic bureaucracy.

the coal and steel industries of France, West Germany, Italy, Belgium, Holland, and Luxembourg, eliminating tariffs and other restrictions; it later became part of the ◊European Community.

The ECSC arose out of the ◊Schuman plan of 1950, which proposed a union of the French and German coal and steel industries so as to make future was between the two countries impossible. The ECSC was, in effect, a prototype institution for the European Community itself, under whose authority it came in 1967. Subsequent members of the EC automatically became ECSC members also.

European Community (EC) political and economic alliance consisting of the European Coal and Steel Community (1952), European Economic Community (EEC, popularly called the Common Market 1957), and the European Atomic Energy Community (Euratom, 1957). These three shared from 1967 the following institutions: the Commission of 13 members pledged to independence of national interests, who initiate Community action; the Council of Ministers, which makes decisions on the Commission's proposals; the ◊European Parliament, directly elected from 1979, which is mainly a consultative body but can dismiss the

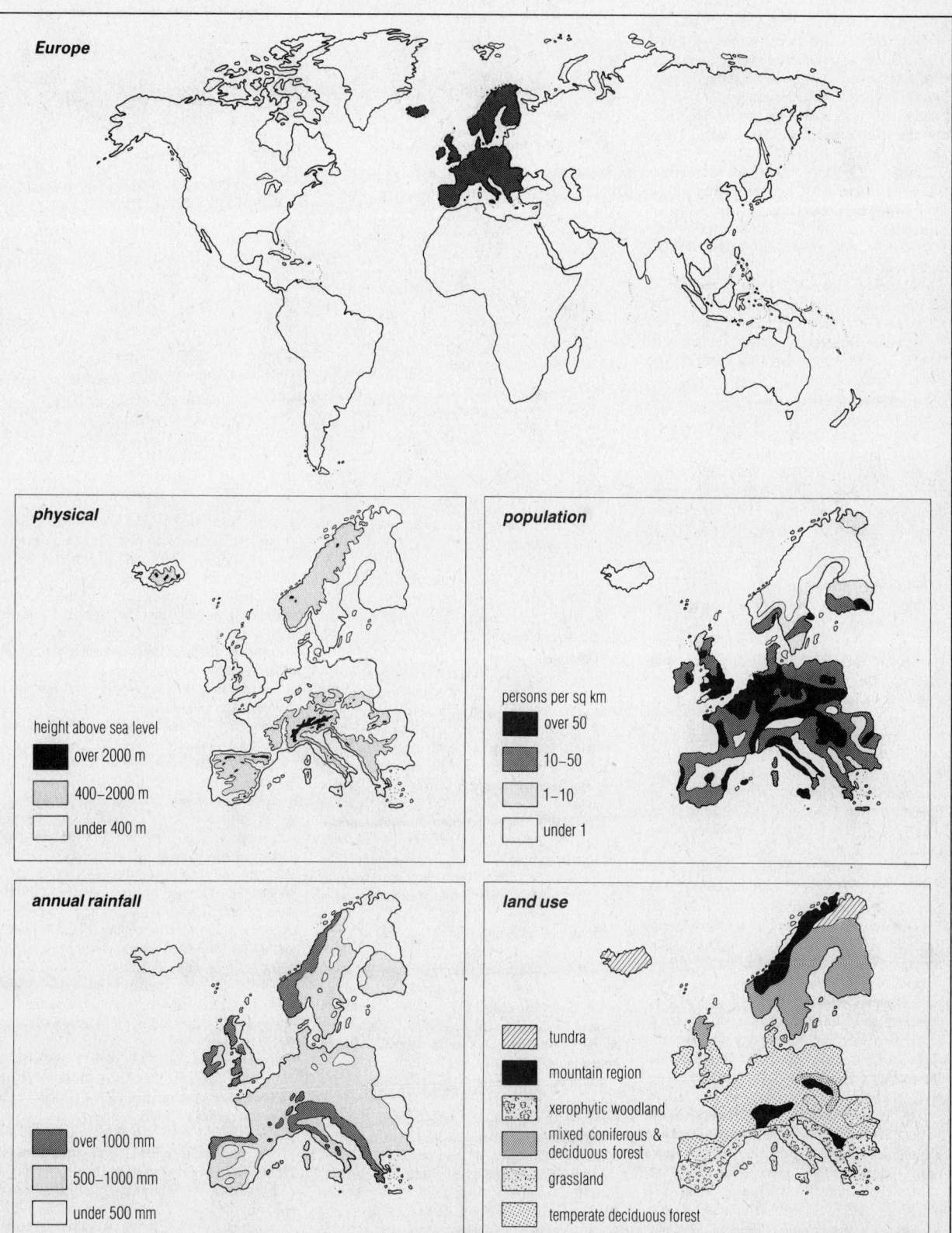

Europe

physical

height above sea level

- over 2000 m
- 400–2000 m
- under 400 m

population

persons per sq km

- over 50
- 10–50
- 1–10
- under 1

annual rainfall

- over 1000 mm
- 500–1000 mm
- under 500 mm

land use

- tundra
- mountain region
- xerophytic woodland
- mixed coniferous & deciduous forest
- grassland
- temperate deciduous forest

Commission; and the ▷European Court of Justice, to safeguard interpretation of Rome Treaties (1957) that established the Community. The original six members, Belgium, France, West Germany, Italy, Luxembourg, and the Netherlands were joined by Britain, Denmark and the Irish Republic (1974), Greece (1981) and Spain and Portugal (1985).

European Court of Justice the court of the European Community (EC) which is responsible for interpreting Community law and ruling on breaches by member states and others of such law. It sits in Luxembourg with judges from the member states.

The European Court of Human Rights sits in Strasbourg to adjudicate on breaches of the European Convention of Human Rights.

European Democratic Group the group of British ▷Conservative Party members of the European Parliament.

European Economic Community (EEC) part of the ▷European Community.

European Free Trade Association (EFTA) an organization established 1960 and as of 1987 consisting of Austria, Finland, Iceland, Norway, Sweden, and Switzerland. There are no import duties between members. Of the original members, Britain and Denmark left (end 1972) to join the ▷European Community, as subsequently did Portugal (end 1985).

European Monetary System (EMS) established 1979, a voluntary system of semi-fixed ▷exchange rates based on the ECU (*European currency unit*), which is a weighted average of all EEC currencies (including sterling). Most EEC countries (except the United Kingdom and Greece) are members. EMS replaced the earlier 'European Currency Snake' system, which did not tie exchange rates to the ECU.

European Parliament the parliament of the European Community, which meets in Luxembourg or Strasbourg to comment on the legislative proposals of the Commission of the European Communities. Henry Plumb (UK) is president (from 1987). Members are elected for a five-year term (last election 1984). The European Parliament has 518 seats, of which the UK, France, Germany, and Italy have 81 each, Spain 60, Netherlands 25, Belgium, Greece, and Portugal 24 each, Denmark 16, Ireland 15 and Luxembourg 6.

European Space Agency (ESA) an organization of European nations to engage in space research and technology for peaceful purposes. ESA was founded in 1975 by Belgium, Denmark, France, West Germany, Ireland, Italy, Netherlands, Spain, Sweden, Switzerland and the United Kingdom, with headquarters in Paris. ESA has developed various scientific and communications satellites, the ▷Giotto space probe, the ▷Ariane rocket and has built ▷Spacelab for the USA. ESA plans to build its own space station, Columbus, for attachment to the US space station, and is working on its own shuttle project, Hermes.

europium a rare element, symbol Eu; atomic number 63; atomic weight 152. One of the

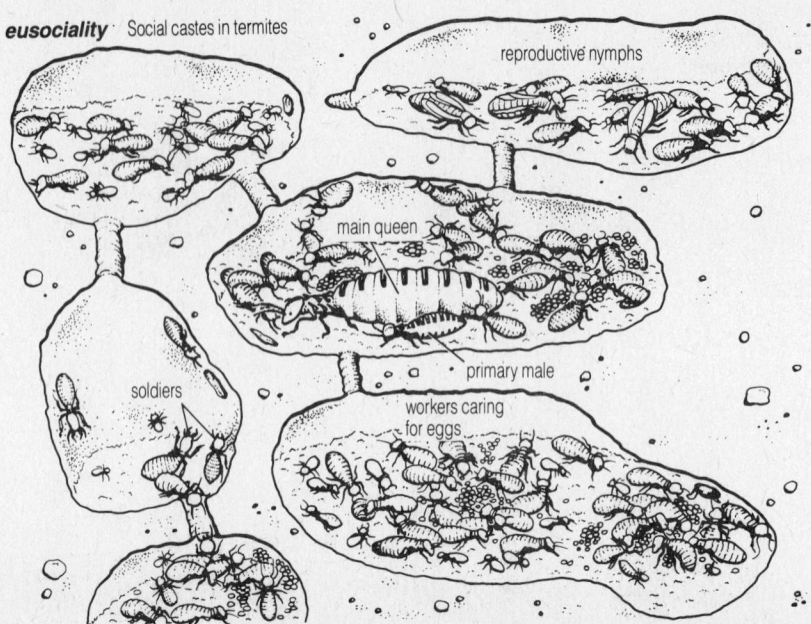

eusociality Social castes in termites

reproductive nymphs

main queen

primary male

soldiers

workers caring for eggs

lanthanide series of metals, it is used in lasers and in colour television.

Eusebius /juːˈsiːbiəs/ c. 260–c. 340. Bishop of Caesarea: author of a history of the Christian Church to 324.

Euskadi /ˌeɪuːsˈkɑːdi/ the Basque name for the ▷Basque Country.

eusociality a form of social life found in insects such as honey bees and termites, in which the colony is made up of special castes (for example, workers, drones and reproductives) whose membership is biologically determined. The worker castes do not usually reproduce. Only one mammal, the naked mole rat, has a social organization of this type. See also ▷social behaviour.

Eustachio /juːˈstɑːkiəu/ Bartolommeo 1520–1574. Italian anatomist, the discoverer of the Eustachian tube, leading from the middle ear to the pharynx, and of the Eustachian valve in the right auricles of the heart. He was physician to the Popes.

Euston Road School an art school in Euston Road, London, England, 1937–39, which included as teachers the painters William Coldstream (1908–) and Victor Pasmore (1908–). Despite its brief existence, the school influenced many recent British painters with its emphasis on careful, often measured, subdued figurative paintings.

Euterpe in Greek mythology, one of the ▷Muses (nine minor divinities) who inspired lyric poetry.

euthanasia the painless killing of a patient suffering from painful and incurable illness, especially the old, and usually with their consent. Bills for voluntary euthanasia failed to pass Parliament in the UK in 1969 and 1976, it being argued that modern drugs control pain, and that such a measure would bring to bear intolerable pressures on the patient and destroy trust between doctor and patient.

eutrophication the over-enrichment of lake waters, primarily by nitrate fertilizers washed from soil by rain, and phosphates from detergents in municipal sewage. These encourage the growth of ▷algae to the extent of eliminating oxygen, thereby making the water uninhabitable for fish and other animal life.

evangelicalism the beliefs of some Protestant sects which stress fundamental Biblical authority, faith, and the personal commitment of the 'born-again' experience.

evangelist person travelling to spread the Christian gospel, and especially the authors of the four Gospels.

Evans /ˈevənz/ Arthur John 1851–1941. British archaeologist. Born in Hertfordshire, he was the son of Sir John Evans (1823–1908), an authority on the Neolithic and Bronze Age periods in Europe. His excavation of ▷Knossos on Crete resulted in the discovery of the pre-Phoenician Minoan script and proved the existence of the Minoan civilization of which all trace had disappeared except in legend. Notable among his published works are *Scripta Minoa* 1909 and four volumes on the *Palace of Minos*.

Evans /ˈevənz/ Edith 1888–1976. British actress, best remembered as Lady Bracknell in the film of Oscar Wilde's *The Importance of Being Earnest* 1939.

Evans /ˈevənz/ Walker 1903–1975. American photographer, best known for his documentary photographs of the people in the rural American south during the Great Depression of the 1930s. Many of his photographs appeared in James Agee's book *Let Us Now Praise Famous Men* 1941.

Evansville /ˈevənzvɪl/ industrial city (pharmaceuticals, plastics) in Indiana, USA; population (1980) 130,500. Abraham ▷Lincoln spent his boyhood in nearby Spencer County.

Eve /iːv/ in the Old Testament, the first woman, wife of ▷Adam; see also ▷Lilith.

Evans A portrait study by Karsh of Ottawa of British actress Edith Evans. A versatile performer, she was probably most famous for her formidable portrayal of Lady Bracknell in Oscar Wilde's comedy *The Importance of Being Earnest*.

Evelyn /'iːvlɪn/ John 1620–1706. English diarist and author. Born in Surrey, he enlisted for three years in the Royalist army 1624, but withdrew on finding his estate exposed to the enemy and lived mostly abroad until 1652. He declined all office under the Commonwealth, but after the Restoration enjoyed great favour, received court appointments, and was one of the founders of the Royal Society. He was a friend of Pepys, and like him remained in London during the Plague and the Great Fire. Of his more than 305 books the most important is his diary, first published in 1818, which covers the period 1640–1706.

evening primrose American plant naturalized in Europe of the family Onagraceae, especially *Oenothera biennis* of which the bright yellow flowers die the next day. It is grown as a field crop for the oil it produces, which is used in treating eczema and premenstrual tension.

eventing sport (horse trials) giving an all-round test of a horse in a three-day event: dressage, testing a horse's response to control; speed and endurance across country; and finally a modified showjumping contest.

Everest, Mount /'evərɪst/ the highest mountain in the world – 8,848 m/29,028 ft – situated in the most northerly range of the ◊Himalayas.

Everglades /'evəgleɪdz/ area of swamps and lakes in ◊Florida, USA.

everlasting flower flower head with coloured bracts which retains its colour when cut and dried, as some *Ammobium, Helichrysum, Xeranthemum* species.

Evershed /'evəʃed/ John 1864–1956. British astronomer, born in Surrey. He devoted himself to solar observations, surveying solar prominences in particular detail, and in 1909 discovered the radial movements of gases in sunspots ('Evershed effect'). He also gave his name to a spectroheliograph, the 'Evershed' spectroscope.

Everest, Mount The world's highest mountain seen from Nepal. It was first climbed by Edmund Hilary and Sherpa Tensing in 1953. The more dangerous SW face was climbed by a British expedition led by Chris Bonington in 1975.

Evesham /'iːvʃəm/ town in Hereford and Worcester, England, on the Avon SE of Worcester; population (1981) 15,250. Fruit and vegetables from the fertile *Vale of Evesham* are canned. In the Battle of Evesham, 4 Aug 1265, Edward, Prince of Wales, defeated Simon de Montfort, who was killed. See ◊Barons' Wars.

evolution a slow process of change from one form to another, as in the evolution of the ◊universe from its formation in the ◊Big Bang to its present state, or in the evolution of ◊life on earth. With respect to the living world, the idea of continuous evolution can be traced as far back as ◊Lucretius in the 1st century BC, but it did not gain wide acceptance until the 19th century following the work of Sir Charles ◊Lyell, J B ◊Lamarck, Charles ◊Darwin and T H ◊Huxley. Darwin assigned the major role in evolutionary change to ◊natural selection acting on genetic variation, which is ultimately produced by spontaneous changes (◊mutations) in the genetic material of organisms. Natural selection occurs because those individuals that are better adapted to their particular environments reproduce more effectively, thus contributing more ◊genes to future generations. Darwin's theory was later combined with ◊Mendel's discoveries in ◊genetics, to give the modern theory of evolution, often called ◊neo-Darwinism. Although neither the general concept of evolution nor the importance of natural selection is doubted by biologists, there remains dispute over other possible processes involved in evolutionary change. Besides natural selection and ◊sexual selection, chance may play an important role in deciding which genes become characteristic of a population, a phenomenon sometimes referred to as 'genetic drift'. In addition, it is now clear that evolutionary change does not always occur at a constant rate, but that the process sometimes shows long periods of relative stability interspersed with periods of rapid change. This has led to new theories, such as ◊punctuated equilibrium model. See also ◊adaptive radiation.

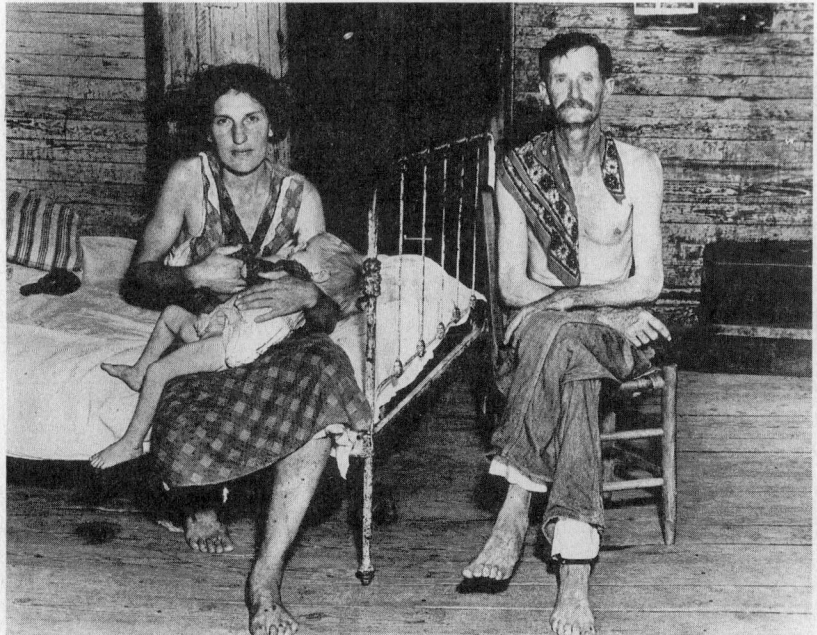

Evans The poverty of the American Depression and the stoical dignity of its victims is sympathetically recreated in this photograph by Walker Evans. Entitled *Depression: Bud Fields and Wife; Alabama, 1935*, it is typical of Evans's social documentary pictures of the 1930s.

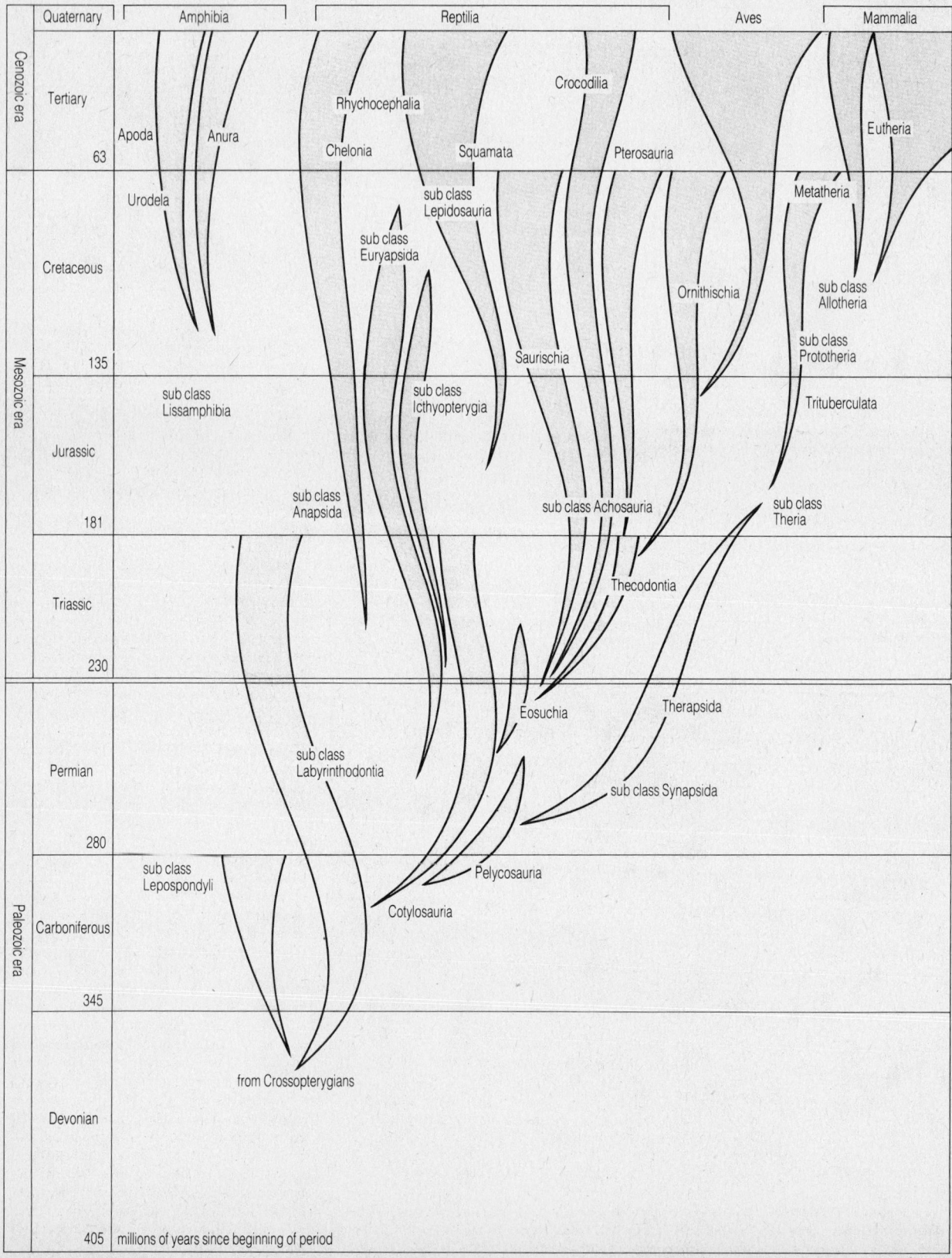

Quaternary | Amphibia | Reptilia | Aves | Mammalia

Cenozoic era — Tertiary — 63

Apoda | Anura | Rhychocephalia | Crocodilia | Eutheria
Chelonia | Squamata | Pterosauria

Mesozoic era

Cretaceous

Urodela | sub class Lepidosauria | Metatheria
sub class Euryapsida | Ornithischia | sub class Allotheria
Saurischia | sub class Prototheria

135

Jurassic

sub class Lissamphibia | sub class Icthyopterygia | Trituberculata

181

sub class Anapsida | sub class Achosauria | sub class Theria
Thecodontia

Triassic

230

Eosuchia | Therapsida

Permian

sub class Labyrinthodontia | sub class Synapsida

280

Carboniferous

sub class Lepospondyli | Pelycosauria
Cotylosauria

345

Devonian

from Crossopterygians

405 | millions of years since beginning of period

Evreux /ev'rɜː/ capital of Eure *département* in NW France; population (1983) 46,250. It produces pharmaceuticals and rubber.

excavator a machine designed for digging in the ground, or for earth-moving in general. Diggers using hydraulically powered digging arms are widely used on building sites. The largest excavators are the draglines used in mining to strip away earth covering the coal or mineral deposit. They are called draglines because they cast their digging bucket away like a fisherman casts a line and then drag the bucket back along the ground, so filling it with earth. Britain's 'Big Geordie' walking dragline, in the Northumberland coalfields, has a digging bucket a capacity to 50 cu m/65 cu yd.

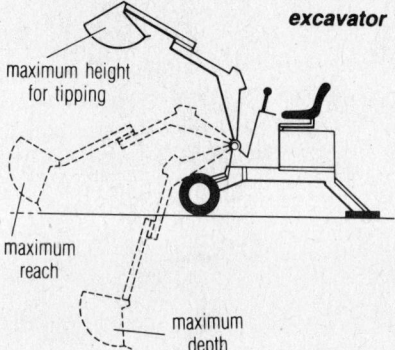

excavator

maximum height for tipping

maximum reach

maximum depth

exchange rate the price at which one currency is bought, sold or valued in terms of other currencies, gold or accounting units such as the special drawing right (SDR) of the ◊International Monetary Fund. Exchange rates may be fixed by international agreement or as a matter of government policy; or they may be wholly or (more commonly) partly allowed to 'float' (that is, find their own level) in world currency markets, as has been the case with most major currencies since the 1970s.

excise duties levied on certain goods produced within a country. See under ◊Customs and Excise.

exclamation mark or *exclamation point* a punctuation mark (!), used to indicate emphasis or strong emotion ('What a surprise!'). Usually the emphasis or emotion is built directly into the text, as part of a story, or dialogue, but the exclamation can also be placed in brackets to indicate that the writer is surprised by something, especially by something in a quotation.

exclusion principle in physics, a principle of atomic structure originated by Wolfgang ◊Pauli.

excommunication exclusion of an offender from the rights and privileges of the Roman Catholic Church; famous offenders included King John, Henry VIII, and Elizabeth I.

excretion the removal of waste products from the cells of living organisms. In plants and simple animals, waste products are removed by diffusion, but in higher animals by specialized organs. In mammals, for example, carbon dioxide and water are removed via the lungs, and nitrogenous compounds and water via the ◊liver, ◊kidneys and ◊urinary system.

executor in law, person appointed in a will to carry out the instructions of the deceased. A person so named has the right to refuse to act. The executor also has a duty to bury the deceased, prove the will and obtain a grant of probate (that is, establish that the will is genuine and obtain official approval of his or her actions).

Exeter /'eksɪtə/ city, administrative headquarters of Devon, England; population (1981) 96,000. It has medieval, Georgian and Regency architecture, including a cathedral, 1280–1369, a modern market centre, and a university, 1955. It manufactures agricultural machinery.

existentialism a trend in modern philosophy, whose origins are usually traced back to ◊Kierkegaard and which was popularized about 1943 by J P ◊Sartre. Existentialists argue that philosophy must begin from the concrete situation of the individual in the world, and that this situation cannot be comprehended by any purely rational system.

Exmoor /'eksmʊə/ moorland in Devon and Somerset, England, forming (with the coast from Minehead to Combe Martin) a National Park since 1954. It includes Dunkery Beacon 520 m/1,707 ft, and the ◊Doone Valley.

exobiology the study of possible life-forms that may exist elsewhere in the Universe.

Exodus in the Old Testament, the book telling of the departure of the Israelites from slavery in Egypt, under the leadership of ◊Moses, for the Promised Land of Canaan. The journey included the miraculous parting of the Red Sea, Pharaoh's pursuing forces being drowned as the waters returned. Modern research questions the historical basis for the Biblical account.

exorcism rite, as in the Roman Catholic and Pentecostal churches, for the expulsion of so-called 'evil spirits'.

exoskeleton the hardened external ◊skeleton of insects, spiders, crabs and other arthropods. It provides attachment for muscles and protection for the internal organs, as well as support. To permit growth it is periodically shed in a process called ◊ecdysis. See also ◊endoskeleton.

exosphere the uppermost layer of the ◊atmosphere. It is an ill-defined zone above the thermosphere, beginning at about 700 km and fading off into the vacuum of space.

expansion or *expansivity* in physics, increase in size due to increase in temperature, also called ◊thermal expansion.

experiment in science, a practical test carefully designed so that the results are relevant to a particular theory or set of theories. Although some experiments may be used merely for gathering more information about a topic which is already well understood, others may be of crucial importance in confirming a new theory or indeed in undermining long-held beliefs. Of central importance therefore is the manner in which experiments are performed, and the relation between the design of an experiment and its value. In general an experiment is of most value when the factors which might affect the results (variables) are carefully controlled; for this reason most experiments take place in a well-

managed environment such as a laboratory or clinic.

experimental psychology the application of rigorous and objective scientific methods to the study of mental processes and behaviour. This covers a wide range of fields of study including: *human and animal learning* in which learning theories describe how new behaviours are acquired and modified; *cognition*, the study of a number of functions, such as perception, attention, memory and language; *physiological psychology*, which relates the study of cognition to different regions of the brain. *Artificial intelligence* refers to the computer simulation of cognitive processes, such as language and problem-solving.

expert system a computer program for giving advice which incorporates knowledge derived from human expertise. It is a kind of ◊knowledge-based system containing rules that can be applied to find the solution to a problem. See also ◊artificial intelligence.

explanation in science, an attempt to make clear the cause of any natural event, by reference to physical laws and to observations. The extent to which any explanation can be said to be true is one of the chief concerns of philosophy, partly because observations may be wrongly interpreted, partly because explanations should help us predict how nature will behave. Although it may be reasonable to expect that a physical law will hold true in the future, that expectation is problematic in that it relies on ◊induction, a much-criticized feature of human thought; in fact no explanation, however 'scientific', can be held to be true for all time, and thus the difference between a scientific and a common-sense explanation remains the subject of intense philosophical debate.

Explorer Satellite one of a series of US scientific ◊satellites. Explorer 1, launched on January 31, 1958 was the first US satellite in orbit and discovered the ◊Van Allen belts around the Earth.

explosive any material capable of a sudden release of energy and the rapid formation of a large volume of gas, leading when compressed to the development of a high-pressure wave (blast). Combustion and explosion differ essentially only in rate of reaction, and many explosives are capable of undergoing relatively slow combustion under suitable conditions. The explosive violence of atomic and hydrogen bombs arises from the tremendous amount of energy released by the conversion of mass into energy, according to Einstein's mass-energy equivalence, $E = mc^2$, where c is the velocity of light.

exponential in mathematics, a ◊function in which the variable quantity is an exponent, that is, an ◊index or power to which another number or expression is raised. For example, $f(x) = a^x$ is an exponential function in which a is typically a number, say 5, and x is the exponent. Such functions are always positive and their values get closer and closer to 0 with increasingly large negative values of x. The term 'exponential function' usually refers to $f(x) = e^x$, the basis of natural or Naperian ◊logarithms and definitive of many natural phenomena of growth and decay (such as the radioactive decay of various isotopes). In this expression *e* is an ◊irrational number equal to 2.7283. *Exponential growth* is not constant; instead, it occurs by raising the last term to some power. It applies, for example, to uncontrolled population growth where the population doubles in short time period. A graph of population number against time produces a curve that is characteristically rather flat at first but then shoots almost directly upwards.

export product or service prepared in one country and sold to another. Exports may be visible (goods which are physically exported) or invisible (services such as tourism or insurance, provided in the exporting country but paid for in another country).

export credit loan, finance, or guarantee provided by a government or a financial institution enabling companies to export goods and services in situations where payment for them may be delayed or subject to risk.

exposure meter an instrument used in photography for indicating the correct exposure – the length of time the camera shutter should be open in given light conditions. Meters use substances such as cadmium sulphide and selenium as light sensors. These materials change electrically when light strikes them, the change being proportional to the intensity of the incident light. Many modern cameras have a built-in exposure meter, which sets the camera controls automatically as the light conditions change.

Expressionism term applied to a style of painting, sculpture, or theatre, music or literature composition which is concerned with the inner world of feeling rather than the outer world as observed, and in particular to a movement in art of the first 30 years of this century in Germany, Austria, and N Europe. It is allied to ◊Romanticism rather than ◊Classicism. An expressionist painter does not imitate nature but distorts or exaggerates natural appearance in order to give a greater emotional impact. Some of Van Gogh's paintings may be described as 'expressionist' in his use of simplified form and strong colour unrelated to nature. ◊Picasso in his painting of *Guernica* expresses all the horror of war by means of distorted forms. ◊Matisse's works are (in his own words) expressions of 'balance, of purity and serenity, devoid of any troubling subject matter'. The most prominent painters associated with the movement were ◊Klee, ◊Marc, ◊Kandinsky, and ◊Chagall. Leading expressionist writers included ◊Strindberg, ◊Wedekind, and ◊Brecht. Other movements related to Expressionism include ◊Blaue Reiter, die ◊Brücke, and ◊Fauvism.

extinction in biology, the complete disappearance of a species. In the past extinctions generally occurred because species were unable to adapt quickly enough to a changing environment. Today, most extinctions are due to human activity. Some species, such as the ◊dodo of Mauritius, the ◊moas of New Zealand and the passenger ◊pigeon of North America have been exterminated by hunting. Others become extinct

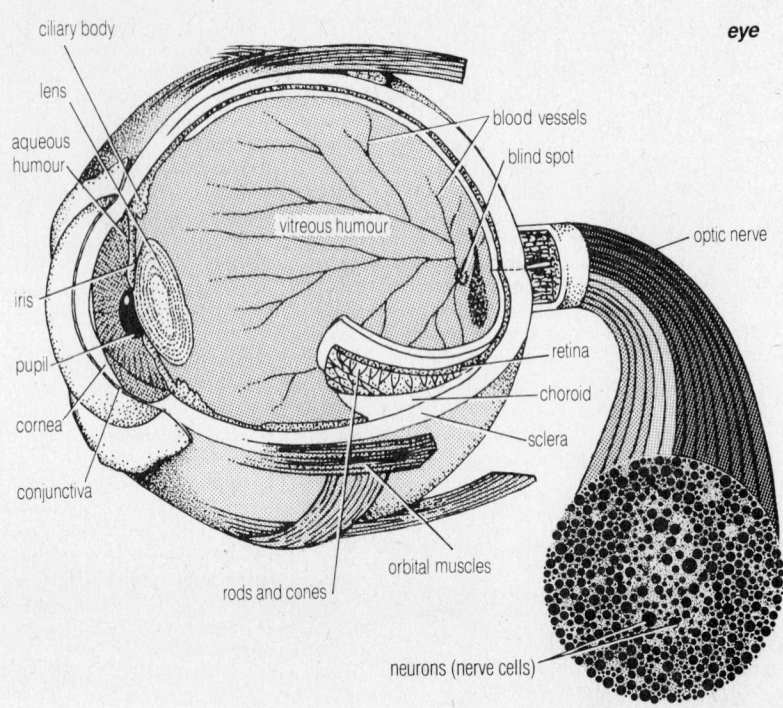

eye

when their habitat is destroyed. Mass extinctions are episodes during which whole groups of species have become extinct, the best known being that of the dinosaurs, other large reptiles and various marine invertebrates some 65 millions years ago. Another mass extinction occurred about 10,000 years ago when many giant species of mammal died out. This is known as the 'Pleistocene overkill' because their disappearance was probably hastened by the hunting activities of prehistoric humans.

extracellular matrix a strong material naturally occurring in animals and plants, made up of protein and long-chain sugars (polysaccharides) in which cells are embedded. It is often called a 'biological glue', and forms an important part of ◊connective tissues such as bone and skin. The cell walls of plants and bacteria, and the ◊exoskeletons of insects and other arthropods, are also formed by types of extracellular matrix.

extraversion or *extroversion* a personality dimension described by ◊Jung and later by Eysenck. The typical extravert is sociable, impulsive and carefree. The opposite of extraversion is introversion; the typical introvert is quiet, inward-looking and reliable.

Extremadura /e,streɪmə'dʊərə/ autonomous region of W Spain (including Badajoz); population (1970) 1,600,000.

extrusion a common method of shaping metals, plastics and other materials. The materials, usually hot, are forced through the hole in a metal die and take its cross-sectional shape. Rods, tubes and sheets may be made in this way.

Eyck /aɪk/ Jan van c. 1390–1441. Flemish artist, who with his brother *Hubert van Eyck* (c. 1370–1426) was one of the earliest masters of Flemish oil painting. He is best known for his portraits, which are full of realistic detail and remarkable for their brilliant, jewel-like colours. In his *Arnolfini Wedding* 1434 (National Gallery, London) the bride and groom appear in a domestic interior crammed with disguised symbols, as a kind of pictorial marriage certificate. He served as court painter to Philip the Good, Duke of Burgundy.

eye the organ of vision. The human eye is a roughly spherical structure contained in a bony socket. Light enters it through the *cornea*, and passes through the circular opening (*pupil*) in the ◊iris (the coloured part of the eye). The light is focused by the combined action of the curved cornea, the internal fluids, and the *lens* (the rounded transparent structure behind the iris). The ciliary muscles act on the lens to change its shape, so that images of objects at different distances can be focused on the *retina*. This is at the back of the eye, and is packed with light-sensitive cells (rods and cones), connected to the brain by the optic nerve. In contrast, the insect eye is compound, that is, made up of many separate facets which each collect light and direct it separately to a receptor to build up an image. Lower ◊invertebrates, such as worms and snails, have much simpler eyes, with no lens.

eyebright common wild flower of the genus *Euphrasia*, family Scrophulariaceae, found in fields throughout Britain. It is 2–30 cm/1–12 in high, bearing whitish flowers streaked with purple. The name indicates its former use as an eye-medicine.

Eyre, Lake /eə/ a lake in S Australia, named after E J ⬦Eyre who reached it in 1840; area about 7,770 sq km/3,000 sq mi. It becomes a salt marsh in dry seasons.

Eyre /eə/ Edward John 1815–1901. British explorer (*Expeditions into Central Australia* 1845), and Governor of Jamaica 1864, where he was suspended in 1865 for harshly suppressing a black riot.

Eyre Peninsula /eə/ peninsula in S Australia.

Ezekiel /ɪˈziːkɪəl/ born c. 622 BC. In the Old Testament, a Hebrew prophet. Carried into captivity in Babylon by ⬦Nebuchadnezzar in 597, he preached that Jerusalem's fall was due to the sins of Israel.

Ezra /ˈezrə/ in the Old Testament, a Jewish scribe who was allowed by Artaxerxes to lead his people back to Jerusalem from Babylon in 458 BC. He re-established the Mosaic Law, and eradicated intermarriage.

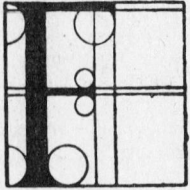

F the sixth letter of the alphabet. Its capital form has changed little from that of the earlier Semitic alphabets.

Fabergé /'fæbəʒeɪ/ Peter Carl 1846–1920. Russian goldsmith. Of Huguenot descent, he was born at St Petersburg, and his workshops there and in Moscow were celebrated for the exquisite delicacy of their products, especially the use of gold in different shades. Among Fabergé's masterpieces was the series of jewelled Easter eggs, the first of which was commissioned by Alexander III for the Tsarina in 1884.

Fabian Society socialist organization for research, discussion and publication, founded in London in 1884. Its name is derived from the Roman commander ◊Fabius Maximus, and refers to the evolutionary methods by which it hopes to attain socialism by a succession of gradual reforms. Early members included Bernard ◊Shaw, Beatrice and Sidney ◊Webb.

Fabius /'feɪbiəs/ Laurent 1946– . French socialist politician, prime minister 1984–86. Fabius, became economic adviser to the Socialist Party (PS) leader ◊Mitterrand in 1976. In 1984, at a time of economic crisis, he was appointed prime minister and introduced a liberal, freer-market economic programme. Fabius was personally damaged by the 1985 ◊Greenpeace sabotage scandal. He resigned after his party's electoral defeat in Mar 1986.

Fabius Maximus /'feɪbiəs 'mæksɪməs/ name of an ancient Roman family of whom the best known is Quintus Fabius Maximus died 203 BC, Roman general, known as Cunctator or 'Delayer' because of his tactics against ◊Hannibal 217–214BC, when he continually harassed his armies, but never risked a set battle.

fable a story, either in verse or prose, in which animals or inanimate objects are endowed with the mentality and speech of human beings in order to point a moral. The best-known fables include those of ◊Aesop Phaedrus and Avianus, ◊La Fontaine, and ◊Lessing.

Fabricius /fə'brɪsiəs/ Geronimo 1537–1619. Italian anatomist. He was professor of surgery and anatomy at Padua from 1562, and did pioneer work that won him the title of the 'father of embryology'.

facsimile transmission also called **fax** or **telefax**; the transmission of images over a ◊telecommunications link, usually the telephone network. The original image is scanned by a transmitting device and converted into coded signals, which travel via the telephone lines to the receiver. There an image is created that is a copy of the original. Photographs ('wire photos') as well as printed material can be sent.

factor a number which divides into another number exactly. All numbers have 1 and themselves as factors, and many have others. For example, the factors of 64 are 1, 2, 4, 8, 16, 32 and 64; those of 99 are 1, 3, 9, 11, 33 and 99. In algebra, certain kinds of polynomials (expressions consisting of several or many terms) can be factorized. For example, the factors of $x^2 + 3x + 2$ are $x + 1$ and $x + 2$; those of $x^3 + 6x^2 + 11x + 6$ are $x + 1$, $x + 2$ and $x + 3$. See also ◊prime number.

factorial the factorial of a number, is the product of all the whole numbers (integers) inclusive between 1 and the number itself. A factorial is indicated by the symbol !. For example, $6! = 1 \times 2 \times 3 \times 4 \times 5 \times 6 = 720$. Factorial zero, 0!, is defined as 1.

factory act in Britain, an act of parliament governing conditions of work, hours of labour, safety, and sanitary provision in factories and workshops. The first was the Health and Morals of Apprentices Act 1802, followed in 1819, by the Cotton Mills Act, which forbade the labour of children under 9 and reduced the hours of labour of those under 16 to 72 per week. Ashley's Act of 1845 forbade night work to women, and in 1847 Ashley (later the 7th earl of ◊Shaftesbury) was responsible for passing a bill fixing a ten-hour day for factory workers. The first factory inspectors were appointed in 1833. Legislation was subsequently extended and consolidated, and by an act of 1963 offices, shops, and railway premises, in which conditions had often been unsatisfactory, were covered. See ◊employment law.

factory farming the intensive rearing of poultry or animals for food on high-protein foodstuffs in confined quarters. Chickens for eggs and meat and calves for veal are commonly factory farmed. Some people question the use of antibiotics and growth hormones as aids to factory farming, because they can persist in the flesh of the animals after they are slaughtered; others, such animal liberation activists, object to the practice on moral grounds.

factory system the basis of manufacturing in the modern world. In the factory system workers are employed at a place where they carry out specific tasks, which together result in a product. This is called the division of labour. Usually these workers will perform their tasks with the aid of machinery. Such ◊mechanization is another feature of the modern factory system, which leads to ◊mass production. Richard ◊Arkwright pioneered the system in England in 1771, when he set up a cotton-spinning factory.

faeces remains of food and other debris passed out of the digestive tract of animals. Faeces consist of quantities of fibrous material, ◊bacteria and other microorganisms, rubbed-off lining of the digestive tract, ◊bile fluids, undigested food, minerals, and water.

Faenza /faɪ'entsə/ city on the river Lamone in Ravenna province, Emilia-Romagna, Italy; population (1971) 55,000. It gave its name to 'faience' pottery, a type of tin-glazed earthenware first produced there.

Faeroe Islands alternative spelling of ◊Faroe Islands, a group of islands in the N Atlantic.

Fahd /faːd/ 1921– King of Saudi Arabia. He succeeded his half-brother Khaled in 1982, also becoming prime minister. He has been active in trying to bring about a solution to the Middle East conflicts.

Fahrenheit /'faːrənhaɪt/ Gabriel Daniel 1686–1736. German physicist who devised the Fahrenheit temperature scale.

Fahrenheit scale a temperature scale invented in 1714, no longer in scientific use. Intervals are measured in degrees (°F). Zero was set at the lowest temperature obtainable at the time in the laboratory, and body temperature was taken as 98.4°F. In modern terms, water freezes at 32°F and boils at 212°F. °F = (°C × 9/5) + 32.

fainting a sudden and temporary suspension of consciousness and movement, due to failure of the supply of blood, and consequently of oxygen, to the brain. The cause is generally a fall in blood pressure because of shock, illness, fatigue.

Fairbanks /'feəbæŋks/ town in Alaska, USA; population (1980) 22,645. It is situated on the Chena Slough, a tributary of the river Tanana, and is the terminus of the Alaska Railroad and of the Pan-American Highway.

Fairbanks /'feəbæŋks/ Douglas 1883–1939. American actor, born in Denver, Colorado. He starred in silent films such as *The Three Musketeers* 1921, *The Thief of Baghdad* 1925, and *Don Quixote* 1925, and was the most famous of the silent screen's swashbuckling heroes. He and Mary Pickford, whom he married in 1920, were idolized as 'the world's sweethearts'.

Fairbanks /'feəbæŋks/ Douglas, Jnr 1909– . American actor, son of Douglas ◊Fairbanks. He achieved screen renown in *Catherine the Great* 1934, and *The Prisoner of Zenda* 1937. He was created an honorary KBE in 1949 for his efforts in the Allied cause during World War II.

Fairbanks American film actor Douglas Fairbanks Junior excelled in the type of swashbuckling role in movies that made his father famous on the silent screen.

Fairfax /'feəfæks/ Thomas, 3rd Baron Fairfax of Cameron 1612–1671. English general, Commander in chief of the parliamentary army in the English ◊Civil War. With Cromwell he formed the New Model Army, defeated Charles I at Naseby, and suppressed the Royalist and Presbyterian risings of 1648.

Faisal /'faisəl/ Ibn Abdul Aziz 1905–1975. king of Saudi Arabia. The younger brother of King Saud, on whose accession in 1953 he was declared Crown Prince. He was prime minister 1953–60 and from 1962 until his death. In 1964 he emerged victorious from a lengthy conflict with his brother and adopted a policy of steady modernization of his country. He was assassinated by his nephew.

fakir originally a Muslim mendicant of some religious order, but in India a general term for an ascetic.

Falaise /fə'leiz/ town 32 km/20 mi SE of Caen, in Calvados *département* Normandy, France; population (1982) 8,820. The castle was that of the first dukes of Normandy, and ◊William the Conqueror was born here.

Falange Española /fæ'læŋxei ,espæn'joulə/ (Spanish 'phalanx'). Former Spanish Fascist Party, founded in 1933 by José Antonio de Rivera, son of Miguel Primo ◊de Rivera. It was closely modelled in programme and organization on the Italian Fascists and on the Nazis. In 1937, when ◊Franco assumed leadership, it was declared the only legal party, and altered its name to Traditionalist Spanish Phalanx.

Falasha a member of a small community of black Jews in Ethiopia. They suffered discrimination, but, after being accorded Jewish status by Israel, in 1975 a gradual process of resettlement in Israel began, so that now only about 30,000 Falashas remain in Ethiopia.

falcon genus of birds of prey *Falco*, family Falconidae, order Falconiformes. The *peregrine falcon Falco peregrinus* up to about 50 cm/1.8 ft long, has become re-established in North America and Britain, after near extinction by pesticides, and human predation by falconers (for whom it is the prime bird) and egg collectors. When 'stooping' on its intended prey it is the fastest creature in the world, timed at 240 kph/150 mph. About 30 cm/1 ft maximum in length are the *hobby Falco subbuteo*; and the *merlin Falco columbarius,* called pigeon-hawk in North America, steel-blue above and reddish below, which nests on moors. The *kestrel Falco tinnunculus*, just over 30 cm/1 ft long with grey head and tail, and light chestnut back with black spots, has an unmistakeable quivering hover.

falconry the use of specially trained falcons and hawks to capture birds or small mammals. It has been practised since ancient times in the Middle East, and was introduced from the Continent to Britain in Saxon times. The Normans, the Tudors and Stuarts were all fond of falconry, but it fell into disuse after the English Civil War: in modern times there has been some revival of interest in it in the West.

Falkender /'fɔːlkəndə/ Marcia, Baroness Falkender 1932– . British political secretary to Harold ◊Wilson as Marcia Williams, from 1956, she was influential in the 'kitchen cabinet' of the 1964–70 Labour ministry, as described in her book *Inside No 10* 1972. Life peer 1974.

Falkirk /'fɔːlkɜːk/ town in Central Region, Scotland, overlooking the fertile Carse (plain) of Falkirk; population (1981) 37,734.

Falkland /'fɔːklənd/ Lucius Cary, 2nd Viscount Falkland c. 1610–1643. English soldier and politician. Elected to the ◊Long Parliament, he was nevertheless opposed to absolute monarchy, but was alienated by Puritan extremism, in particular a proposal to abolish episcopacy, and tried hard to secure a compromise peace between royalists and parliamentarians. He was killed at the battle of Newbury in the Civil War. The Falkland Islands are named after him.

Falkland Islands /'fɔːklənd/ British Crown Colony in the S Atlantic

area 12,173 sq km/4,700 sq mi, made up of two main islands: E Falkland 6,760 sq km/2,610 sq mi, and W Falkland 5,413 sq km/2,090 sq mi

capital Port Stanley; new port facilities were opened in 1984, and Mount Pleasant airport in 1985

features in addition to the two main islands, there are about 200 small islands, all with wild scenery and rich bird life

exports wool, alginates (used as dyes and as a food additive) from seaweed beds. There may also be oil in resources in the sea nearby.

currency pound sterling

population (1980) 1,813

government there is a Governor (Gordon Jewkes from Oct 1985) advised by an executive council, and a mainly elected legislative council. Administered with the Falklands, but separate dependencies of the UK, are South Georgia and the South ◊Sandwich Islands.

history the first European to visit the islands was Englishman John Davis in 1592, and at the end of the 17th century they were named after Lord ◊Falkland, treasurer of the British navy. The first British settlers arrived in 1765; Spain bought out a French settlement in 1766, and the British were ejected 1770–71, but British sovereignty was never ceded, and from 1833, when a few Argentines were expelled, British settlement was continuous. Argentina asserts its succession to the Spanish claim to the 'Islas Malvinas', but the inhabitants oppose cession. The islands were occupied by Argentina Apr 1982, and recaptured by British military forces in May–June of the same year.

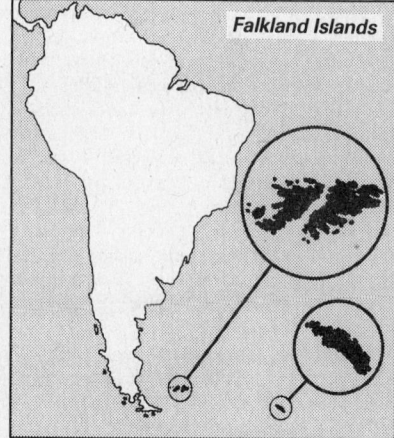

Falkland Islands

Falkland Islands /'fɔːklənd/ **Battle of the** British naval victory (under Admiral Sturdee) 8 Dec 1914 over German Admiral von Spee.

Falla /'fæljə/ Manuel de 1876–1946. Spanish composer. Born in Cadiz, he lived in France where he was influenced by the impressionists, especially ◊Debussy and ◊Ravel. His first work of importance, the opera *La vida breve/Brief Life* 1905 (performed 1913) was followed by the ballets *El amor brujo/Love the Magician* 1915 and *El sombrero de tres Picos/The Three-*

Cornered Hat 1919, and his most ambitious concert work, *Noches en los jardines de España/Nights in the Gardens of Spain* 1916. The folk-idiom of southern Spain is an integral part of his compositions.

Fallopian tube in mammals, a tube which carries eggs from the ◊ovary to the ◊uterus (also called an oviduct). There are two Fallopian tubes, one from each ovary. Each tube is lined with cells whose ◊cilia move the egg towards the ovary. Eggs are fertilized by ◊sperm in the Fallopian tube.

Fallopius /fə'ləupiəs/ Gabriel 1523–1562. Latinized name of Gabriello Fallopio. Italian anatomist. He taught at Ferrara, Pisa, and Padua, and made a particular study of the reproductive organs; the ◊Fallopian tubes are named after him.

fall-out radioactive material released into the atmosphere in the debris of a nuclear explosion.

Fall River /fɔːl/ city and port in Massachusetts, USA; population (1980) 95,900. It stands at the mouth of the Taunton river, over the Little Fall river which gave it its name.

Falmouth /'fælməθ/ port on the S coast of Cornwall, England, on the estuary of the Fal; population (1981) 18,525.

false-colour imagery a modern graphic technique that displays images in false (not true to life) colours so as to enhance certain features. It is widely used in displaying electronic images taken by spacecraft, such as earth-survey satellites like *Landsat*. Any colours can be selected by a computer processing the received data.

falsetto in music, a male voice singing in the female (soprano or alto) register.

falsificationism in philosophy of science, the belief that a scientific theory must be under constant scrutiny, and that its merit lies only in how well it stands up to rigorous testing. First expounded by the philosopher Karl ◊Popper in his *Logic of Scientific Discovery* (1934), falsificationism in its crudest form suggests that a theory must be rejected or modified as soon as contradictory evidence emerges. It is also suggested that a theory can only be held to be scientific if it makes predictions which are clearly testable. Critics of this belief acknowledge the strict logic of this process, but doubt whether the whole of scientific method can be subsumed into so narrow a programme.

Famagusta /,fæmə'gustə/ seaport on the E coast of Cyprus, the chief port of the island; population (1982) 39,500.

family in biological classification, a group of related genera (see ◊genus). Thus all the different genera of hummingbirds are grouped together in the hummingbird family, Trochilidae. Family names are not shown in italic (unlike genus and species names) and by convention they all have the ending -idae (animals) or -aceae (plants and fungi). Related families are grouped together in an ◊order.

family planning spacing or preventing the birth of children; see ◊contraceptive.

Fancy The, formerly the popular name for ◊boxing.

Fangio /'fændʒiəu/ Juan Manuel 1911– . Italian racing driver, born in Argentina. He was five times world champion 1951–57.

fan jet also called turbofan and by-pass turbojet, the jet engine used by most airliners, so called because of its huge front fan. The fan sends air not only into the engine itself, but also around the engine. This results in a faster and more efficient propulsive jet. See ◊jet propulsion.

Fanon /fæ'nɒŋ/ Frantz 1925–1961. French political writer. His experiences in Algeria during the war for liberation in the 1950s led to the writing of *Les damnés de la terre/The Wretched of the Earth* 1964, which calls for violent revolution by the peasants of the Third World.

fantail type of domestic dove, often white, bred as an ornamental bird with a large widely fanning tail.

fantasy non-realistic fiction. Much of the world's fictional literature could be subsumed under this term, but as a commercial and literary genre fantasy started to thrive in the aftermath of the success of ◊Tolkien's *Lord of the Rings* 1954–55 in the late 1960s. Dominant themes, drawn from the stock of world literature, are those of the quest for a cure for evil and the reconciliation of the demands of the poetically bizarre fantasy world and the more domestic claims of the mundane world. Much fantasy is pseudo-medieval in subject matter and tone, following the spirit rather than substance of Tolkien; much of what is better in the field is equally influenced by the work of Mervyn ◊Peake in its grotesquerie and passion. Important works since Tolkien are Ursula LeGuin's *Earthsea Trilogy* and Stephen Donaldson's *Thomas Covenant*. Important works in the more urban tradition of Peake are John Crowley's *Little Big*, Michael Moorcock's *Gloriana* and Gene Wolfe's *Free, Life Free*. Much of the matter of such books overlaps with that of ◊magic realist writers like Gabriel García Márquez and Angela Carter.

Fantin-Latour /fɒn'tæn læ'tuə/ Henri 1836–1904. French artist. Born at Grenoble, he excelled in lightly delicate still-lifes and flower paintings, and portraiture such as *Homage à Delacroix* 1864, a portrait group of Baudelaire, Champfleury, Legros, Whistler, and himself.

farad the ◊SI unit of electrical capacitance (symbol F). Defined as the capacitance of a capacitor that, if charged with 1 ◊coulomb, has a potential difference of 1 volt between its plates. Named after Michael ◊Faraday.

Faraday /'færədeɪ/ Michael 1791–1867. British chemist and physicist. He became a laboratory assistant to Sir Humphry ◊Davy at the Royal Institution in 1813, and in 1833 succeeded him as professor of chemistry there. In 1812 he began researches into electricity, and made his first electric battery. In 1821 he began experimenting on ◊electromagnetism, and ten years later discovered the induction of electric currents and made the first dynamo. Many more discoveries in electricity followed. In 1845 he began a second great period of research in which he discovered what he announced as the magnetization of light. He delivered highly popular lectures at the Royal Institution, and

published many treatises on scientific subjects. Deeply religious, he was a member of the Sandemanian sect.

Faraday One of ten children of a blacksmith, Michael Faraday had little formal education before becoming assistant at the age of 22 to Humphry Davy, whom he succeeded as professor of chemistry at the Royal Institution in 1833.

Faraday's laws two laws of electromagnetic induction, and three laws of ◊electrolysis, all proposed originally (in a slightly different form) by Michael ◊Faraday.

induction (1) a changing magnetic field induces an electromagnetic force in a conductor; (2) the electromagnetic force is proportional to the rate of change of the field; (3) the direction of the induced electromagnetic force depends on the orientation of the field.

electrolysis (1) the amount of chemical change during electrolysis is proportional to the charge passing through the liquid; (2) the amount of chemical change produced in a substance by a given amount of electricity is proportional to the electrochemical equivalent of that substance.

farandole an old French dance in six-eight time originating in Provence. The dancers join hands in a chain and follow the leader to the accompaniment of tambourine and pipe. There is a farandole in Act II of Tchaikovsky's *The Sleeping Beauty*.

farce a broad form of comedy involving stereotyped characters in complex, often improbable situations frequently revolving around extra-marital relationships, hence the term 'bedroom farce'. Originating from the physical knockabout comedy of Greek satyr plays and the broad humour developed from medieval religious drama, the farce was developed and perfected during the 19th century by Labiche and Feydeau in France, and ◊Pinero in England. In modern times two notable English series have been the Aldwych farces of Ben ◊Travers in the 1920s and 1930s and the Whitehall farces produced by Brian Rix during the 1950s and 1960s.

Far East geographical term for all Asia east of the Indian subcontinent.

Fargo /'fɑːgəʊ/ William George 1818–81. American pioneer expressman. In 1844 he established with Henry Wells (1805–78) and Daniel Dunning the first express company to carry freight west of Buffalo. Its success led to his appointment in 1850 as secretary of the newly established American Express Company, of which he was president 1868–81. He also established Wells Fargo & Company (1851) carrying goods express between New York and San Francisco via Panama.

Fargo, a town on the Red river in North Dakota, is named after him; population (1980) 66,040.

Farman /fɑː'mɒŋ/ Henry 1874–1958. Anglo-French air pioneer. Making his first flying experiments in 1907, he designed and flew his classic biplane in 1909. With his brother Maurice he founded an aircraft works at Billancourt, important as a source of machines for the French army, and other countries, including England, which also made use of Farman's inventions, for example, air-screw reduction gears, in World War II.

Farnaby /'fɑːnəbi/ Giles 1563–1640. English composer. He is thought to have been born in Truro, Cornwall, and studied at Oxford. He composed pieces for the virginals (an early keyboard instrument), psalms for Ravens croft's Psalter 1621, and madrigals for voices.

Farnborough /'fɑːnbərə/ town in Hampshire, England, N of Aldershot; population (1981) 45,500. The mansion of Farnborough Hill was occupied by Napoleon III and the Empress Eugénie, and she, her husband and her son, are buried in a mausoleum at the Roman Catholic church she built. Experimental work is carried out at the Royal Aircraft Establishment.

Farne /fɑːn/ rocky island group in the North Sea, off Northumberland, England. A chapel stands on the site of the hermitage at St ◊Cuthbert on Inner Farne; there are two lighthouses, the Longstone lighthouse being the scene of the rescue of shipwrecked sailors by Grace ◊Darling. The islands are a sanctuary for birds and grey seals.

Farnese /fɑː'neɪseɪ/ an Italian family who held the duchy of Parma 1545–1731.

Farnham /'fɑːnəm/ town in Surrey, England on the river Wey; population (1981) 35,250.

Faroe Islands, Faroes /'feərəʊ/ or *Faeroe Islands, Faeroes* island group (18 out of 21 inhabited) in the North Atlantic, forming an outlying part of ◊Denmark.

area 1,399 sq km/540 sq mi. The largest islands are Stromo, Ostera, Vaego, Sudero and Sando.

capital Thorshavn on Stromo

features the name means 'Sheep Islands'; they do not belong to the EEC

exports fish, crafted goods

currency Danish Krone

population (1986) 45,728

government since 1948 the islands have had full self-government.

history first settled by Norsemen in the 9th century, they were a Norwegian province 1380–1709.

Farouk /fə'ruːk/ 1920–1965. King of Egypt. The son of ◊Fuad, he succeeded him in 1936. In 1952 he was compelled to abdicate, his own son Fuad being temporarily proclaimed in his stead.

Farquhar /'fɑːkə/ George 1677–1707. Irish dramatist. He became an actor in Dublin, but in 1698 went to London, where in 1699 his first play *Love and a Bottle* was produced. *The Constant Couple* 1700 was followed by a sequel *Sir Harry Wildair* 1701. His most famous plays *The Recruiting Officer* 1706, and *The Beaux' Stratagem* 1707, are in the tradition of the Restoration comedy of manners but less robust.

Farragut /'færəgʌt/ David Glasgow 1801–70. American seaman and first admiral. Born near Knoxville, Tennessee, son of a Spanish emigrant. During the American civil war he took New Orleans in 1862, after destroying the Confederate fleet, and in 1864 effectively put an end to blockade-running at Mobile.

Farrell /'færəl/ J(ames) G(ordon) 1935–1979. British historical novelist, born in Liverpool. He is best remembered for *Troubles* 1970, set in Ireland; and *The Siege of Krishnapur* 1973.

Farrell /'færəl/ James T(homas) 1904–1979. American novelist, born in Chicago. He worked as a clerk, filling-station assistant, and reporter. In his trilogy *Young Lonigan*, *The Young Manhood of Studs Lonigan*, and *Judgement Day* (1932–35) he described a youth growing up in Chicago during the depression.

Fars /fɑːs/ province of Iran, comprising fertile valleys among mountain ranges running NW–SE. The capital is Shiraz, and there are imposing ruins of Cyrus the Great's city of Parargardae and of ◊Persepolis.

farthing formerly the smallest English coin, a quarter of a penny. It was introduced as a silver coin in Edward I's reign. The copper farthing became general in Charles II's time, and the bronze in 1860. It was dropped from use 1961.

fasces in ancient Rome, bundles of rods carried in procession by the lictors in front of the chief magistrates, as a symbol of the latter's power over the lives and liberties of the people. An axe was included in the bundle. The fasces were revived as the symbol of ◊fascism.

Fasching /'fæʃɪŋ/ period preceding Lent in German-speaking towns, particularly Munich, Cologne, and Vienna, devoted to masquerades, formal balls and street parades.

fascism the totalitarian nationalist movement founded in Italy 1919 by ◊Mussolini. The units were originally called *fasci di combattimento* (combat groups), from ◊fasces. Fascism was essentially a product of the economic and political crisis of the years after World War I. It protected the existing social order by forcible suppression of the working-class movement and by providing scapegoats for popular anger in the Jew, the foreigner, or the

black person; it also provided the machinery for the economic and psychological mobilization of both nations for war. Its ideology denied all rights to individuals in their relations with the state, personified in the infallible leader (*Duce, Führer*). The atrocities committed by Nazi Germany and other fascist countries discredited fascism but small neofascist groups still exist in many Western European countries.

Fashoda Incident dispute in 1898, in a town in the Sudan, now known as Kodok, then called Fashoda, in which French forces clashed with British, under ◊Kitchener. Originally just a disagreement over local territorial claims, it almost led the two countries into war.

Faslane /fæz'leɪn/ a nuclear submarine base on the river ◊Clyde in Scotland.

Fassbinder /'fæsbɪndə/ Rainer Werner 1946–1982. German film director, noted for enormous productivity (over 30 films) and stylized films about love, hate, and prejudice, for example *Angst essen Seele auf/Fear Eats the Soul* 1974.

Fassbinder German firm director Rainer Werner Fassbinder, who was noted for his enormous output of films (more than 30) and for his stylized treatment of love, hate and prejudice.

fast reactor a ◊nuclear reactor that makes use of fast neutrons to bring about fission. It is also called a *breeder reactor* because it produces more fuel than it consumes. The world's first commercial fast reactor, the Super Phénix, has been built at Creys-Malville in SW France. The fast reactor uses a mixture of plutonium and uranium oxides as fuel. It has no ◊moderator, present in other reactors to slow down neutrons. The reactor core is surrounded by a 'blanket' of uranium carbide. When operating, some of this uranium is converted into plutonium that can be extracted and later used as fuel. Heat is removed from the reactor by a coolant of liquid sodium.

fat in the broadest sense, an organic compound that is soluble in alcohol, but not in water; when used in this way, 'fat' is synonymous with lipid. The term is also used more specifically to denote triglycerides, and other esters of glycerol with ◊fatty acids. Glycerides that are liquid at room temperature are called oils; only those that are solid at this temperature are called fats. Boiling fats in alkali forms soaps (saponification). Fats are essential constituents of food in many animals. In humans too much fat in the diet (especially saturated fats from animal products) is linked with heart disease:

Boethius, Jerome, Gregory of Tours, Pope Gregory the Great, and Bede.

fathom (Anglo-Saxon *faethm* 'to embrace') in mining, seafaring, and handling timber, unit of depth measurement (6 ft/1,829 m) used before metrication; it approximates to the distance between the hands when the arms are outstretched, hence its derivation.

Fatimite member of a Muslim Shi'ite dynasty which was founded by Obaidallah, who claimed to be a descendant of Fatima, ◊Muhammad's daughter, and her husband, Ali, in North Africa in 909. In 969 the Fatimites conquered Egypt,

rated as his finest work; *As I Lay Dying* 1930, *Light in August* 1932, a study of segregation; *The Unvanquished* 1938, stories of the Civil War; and *The Hamlet* 1940, *The Town* 1957, and *The Mansion* 1959, a trilogy covering the rise of the materialist Snopes family.
His experimental stream-of-consciousness style – sentences sometimes running over a page – hindered popular recognition. He was awarded a Nobel Prize for Literature 1949.

fault in geology, a crack in a rock along which the two sides have moved as a result of differing strains in the adjacent rock bodies. Displacement of rock masses horizontally or vertically along a fault may be microscopic, or it may be massive, causing major ◊earthquakes.

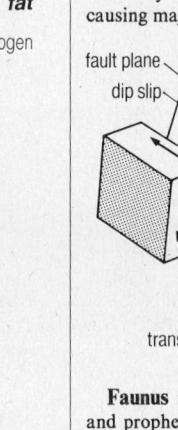

fault

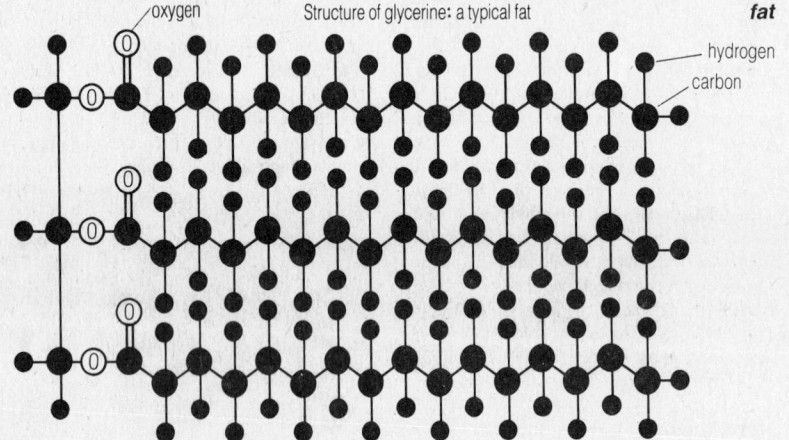

Structure of glycerine: a typical fat — oxygen, hydrogen, carbon — *fat*

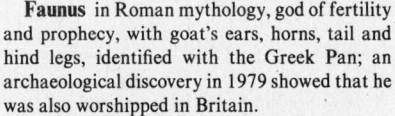

fault plane, dip slip, strike slip, transcurrent fault

Fates in Greek mythology, the three female spirits who determined the destiny of each newborn child, and in particular the length of its life. They are analogous to the Roman ◊Parcae and Norse ◊Norns. They are pictured as three old women spinning, their names being Clotho, Lachesis, and Atropos.

fat-hen plant *Chenopodium album* found as a weed on waste places and in fields. Up to 1 m/3 ft tall, with lance- or diamond-shaped leaves, with packed heads of small inconspicuous flowers arising from the leaf junctions in late summer. The stem may be reddish, and the leaves are deep green, but often with a white mealy covering. Now considered a weed, fat-hen was once valued for its fatty seeds and edible leaves.

Father of the Church name applied to certain teachers and writers of the early Christian Church, particularly eminent for their learning and orthodoxy, experience, and sanctity of life, who lived from the end of the 1st to the end of the 7th century, a period divided by the Council of ◊Nicaea (325) into the Ante-Nicene and Post-Nicene Fathers. The most important of the Ante-Nicene Fathers are the Apostolic Fathers – Clement of Rome, Ignatius of Antioch, Polycarp of Smyrna, and 'Barnabas' – Justin Martyr, Tatian, Irenaeus, Clement, Origen, Tertullian, Cyprian, and Gregory Thaumaturgus. Of the Post-Nicene Fathers, the most memorable are Cyril of Alexandria, Athanasius, John Chrysostom, Eusebius of Caesarea, Cyril of Jerusalem, Basil the Great, Ambrose of Milan, Hilary of Poitiers, Augustine, Pope Leo I,

and the dynasty continued until overthrown by Saladin in 1171.

fatty acid an organic compound consisting of a hydrocarbon chain, up to 24 carbon atoms long, with a carboxyl group (-COOH) at one end. The bonds between the carbon atoms may be single or double; where a double bond occurs the carbon atoms concerned carry one instead of two hydrogen atoms. Chains with some double bonds in are therefore said to be *unsaturated* with hydrogen, whereas chains with single bonds only have all the hydrogen they can carry, and are said to be *saturated*. Saturated fatty acids include acetic, butyric, palmitic and stearic acid; and unsaturated include oleic and linoleic.
Fatty acids are generally found combined with glycerol, in triglycerides and other fats and oils. The melting point of these is determined by the type of fatty acids they contain: the more unsaturates, the lower the melting point.

Faulkner /'fɔːknə/ Brian 1921–1977. Northern Ireland Unionist politician. He was the last prime minister of Northern Ireland 1971–72 before the Stormont Parliament was prorogued.

Faulkner /'fɔːknə/ William 1897–1962. American novelist, born in Mississippi. He served in World War I and his first novel, *Soldier's Pay* 1926, is about a war veteran. After the war Faulkner returned to Oxford, Mississippi, on which he was to model Jefferson in the county of Yoknapatawpha, the setting of his major novels. These began with *Sartoris* 1929, *The Sound and the Fury* 1929, dealing with a Southern family in decline and sometimes

Faunus in Roman mythology, god of fertility and prophecy, with goat's ears, horns, tail and hind legs, identified with the Greek Pan; an archaeological discovery in 1979 showed that he was also worshipped in Britain.

Fauré /'fɔːreɪ/ Gabriel (Urbain) 1845–1924. French composer. A pupil of ◊Saint-Saëns, he became professor of composition at the Conservatoire in 1896, and was director 1905–20. He is remembered for his songs, chamber music, and *Requiem* 1888.

Faust /faʊst/ legendary magician. The historical Georg Faust appears to have been a wandering scholar and conjurer in Germany during the opening decade of the 16th century. But earlier figures such as Simon Magus (1st century AD Middle Eastern practitioner of magic arts) contributed to the Faust legend. In 1587 the first of a series of Faust books appeared. Marlowe's tragedy of *Dr Faustus* was acted in 1594. In the 18th century the story was a subject for pantomime in England and puppet plays in Germany. In Germany the serious possibilities of the theme were first pointed out by Lessing; Goethe made Faust a symbol of humanity's striving after the infinite. Heine, Thomas Mann, Lunarcharski, Dorothy Sayers, and Paul Valéry have also used the legend. Faust has also inspired musical works by Schumann, Berlioz, Gounod, Boito, and Busoni.

Fauvism art movement originating in Paris with the founding of the Salon d'automne in 1903 by ◊Matisse and his friends. Their chief source of inspiration was the work of ◊van Gogh. Others who participated in the movement were ◊Rouault, ◊Derain, ◊Bonnard, and ◊Vlaminck. Their name originated in 1905 when the art critic Louis Vauxcelles called their exhibition gallery 'une cage aux fauves' (cage of wild beasts). The Fauves exaggerated reality, contorted shapes and heightened colour.

Fawcett /ˈfɔːsɪt/ Millicent Garrett 1847–1929. English suffragette, younger sister of Elizabeth Garrett ◊Anderson. A non-militant, she rejected the violent acts of some of her contemporaries in the suffrage movement. She joined the first Women's Suffrage Committee in 1867 and emerged as the leader of the women's suffrage movement in 1890. She was president of the National Union of Women's Suffrage Societies from 1897 to 1918.

Fawcett An educational reformer and leader of the women's suffrage movement, Dame Millicent Garrett Fawcett was one of the founders of Newnham College, Cambridge.

Fawcett /ˈfɔːsɪt/ Percy Harrison 1867–1925. British explorer. After several expeditions to delineate frontiers in South America during the rubber boom, he set off in 1925, with his eldest son John and a friend, into the Mato Grosso to find the the legendary 'lost cities' of the ancient Indians, the 'cradle of Brazilian civilization'. They were never seen again.

Fawkes /fɔːks/ Guy 1570–1606. English conspirator, born in York. He converted to Roman Catholicism as a youth, served in the Spanish army in 1593, and in 1604 joined in the Gunpowder Plot to blow up King James I and the members of both Houses of Parliament. He was arrested in the cellar underneath the House on 4 Nov 1605, tortured, and executed. The event is still commemorated in Britain with bonfires and fireworks on 5 Nov.

fax an alternative name for ◊facsimile transmission.

FBI abbreviation of ◊Federal Bureau of Investigation, agency of the Department of Justice in the USA.

feather a rigid outgrowth of the outer layer of the skin of ◊birds, made of the ◊protein keratin.

Fawkes Britain's most famous terrorist, Guy Fawkes, joined the Gunpowder Plot to blow up James I and both Houses of Parliament in 1604. Fireworks and bonfires on which his effigy, the guy, is burned still celebrate the failure of the plot on 5 Nov every year.

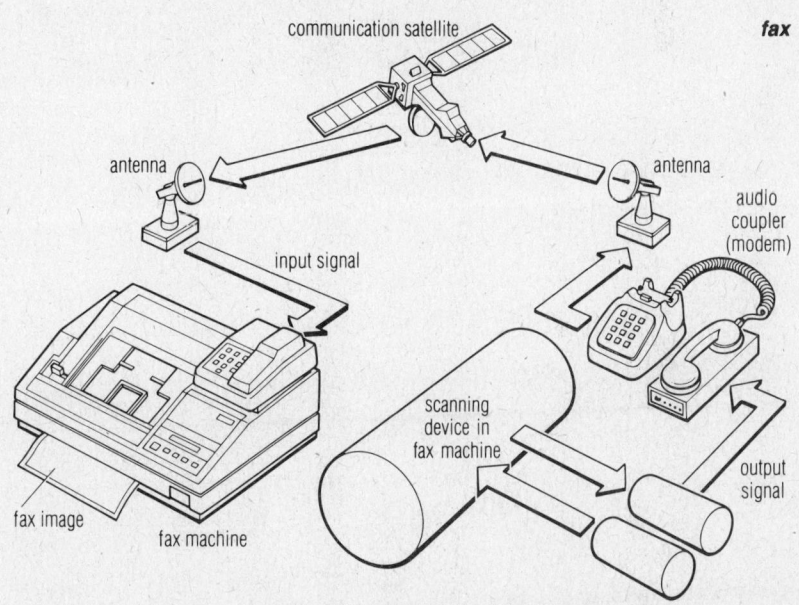

fax

Feathers provide insulation and facilitate flight. Several types occur, including long quill feathers on the wings and tail, fluffy down feathers for retaining body heat, and contour feathers covering the body. The colouring of feathers is often important in camouflage or in courtship and other displays. Feathers are replaced at least once a year.

feather star type of ◊echinoderm belonging to the class Crinoidea. The arms are branched into numerous projections (hence 'feather' star) and grow from a small cup-shaped body. Below the body are appendages which can hold on to a surface, but the feather star is not permanently attached. *Antedon bifida* is a species about 15 cm/6 in across found in NW European seas. It is reddish brown and has ten arms.

fecundity the rate at which an organism reproduces, as distinct from its ◊fertility, or ability to reproduce. In vertebrates, it is usually measured as the number of offspring produced by a female each year.

Federal Bureau of Investigation (FBI) agency of the Department of Justice in the USA which investigates violations of federal law not specifically assigned to other agencies, being particularly concerned with internal security, that is, the monitoring and suppression of subversives. Field divisions are maintained in more than 60 US cities. Its special agents, known as G-men from the department's code letter, are qualified in law, accounting, or auditing. The

feather Scanning electron micrograph (SEM) of a feather from the head of a bullfinch. Extending from the central shaft are the barbs which are interlined with comb-like rows of barbules. This structure is strong and light, ideal for flight.

feather

secondary coverts
smaller contour feathers
greater coverts
primary feathers
secondary feathers
semi-plume feather
filoplume feather
barbs
barbules
shaft
hooks
down feather
calamus
lower umbilicus

federation should be distinguished from a confederation, a looser union of states for mutual assistance. Switzerland, the USSR, the USA, Canada, Australia, and Malaysia are all examples of federal government, and many supporters of the ◊European Community see it as the forerunner of a federal Europe.

Federal Reserve System ('Fed') US central banking system and note issue authority, established in 1913 to regulate the country's credit and monetary affairs and to contribute to its economic wellbeing. The Fed consists of the 12 federal reserve banks and their 25 branches and other facilities throughout the country; it is headed by a board of governors in Washington, appointed by the US President with Senate approval.

feedback a principle used in self-regulating control systems from a simple ◊thermostat and steam-engine ◊governor to automatic computer-controlled machine tools. In such systems, information about what *is* happening in a system (level of temperature, engine speed, size of workpiece) is fed back to a controlling device, which compares it with what *should* be happening. If the two are different, the device takes suitable action (say, switching on a heater, allowing more steam to the engine, resetting the tools).

Feininger /'faɪnɪŋə/ Lyonel 1871–1956. American artist, born in New York. The son of German immigrants, he returned to Germany for a time, and worked at the ◊Bauhaus, a key centre of modern design, and later helped to found the Bauhaus in Chicago.

Feisal /'faɪsəl/ two kings of Iraq:
Feisal I 1885–1933. Elected king from 1921.
Feisal II 1935–58, Feisal I's grandson. He succeeded his father, King Ghazi, in 1939, and following the regency of his uncle Abdul Illah was king of Iraq 1935–38. He was assasssinated with his uncle when an army revolt established a republic.

feldspar or **felspar** a type of rock-forming mineral, the chief constituent of ◊igneous rock. Feldspars contain aluminium silicate with varying proportions of silicates of sodium, potassium, calcium, and barium. These are white, grey, or pink, and may form striking crystals. The three main types of feldspar are orthoclase, $KAlSi_3O_8$; albite, $NaAlSi_3O$; and anorthite, $CaAld2Si_2O_8$. Other feldspar types are intermediate between these compositions. The type known as moonstone has a pearl-like effect, and is used in jewellery. Approximately 4000 tonnes of feldspar are used in the ceramics industry annually.

Felixstowe /'fiːlɪkstəʊ/ port and resort opposite Harwich in Suffolk, England, between the Orwell and Deben estuaries; population (1981) 21,000.

Fellini /fe'liːni/ Federico 1920– . Italian film director, noted for his strongly subjective poetic imagery. His films include *I Vitelloni/The Young and the Passionate* 1953, *La Strada/The Street* 1954, *La Dolce Vita/The Sweet Life* 1960, *Otto e Mezzo/8½* 1963, *Casanova* 1975, and *La Città delle Donne/City of Women* 1981.

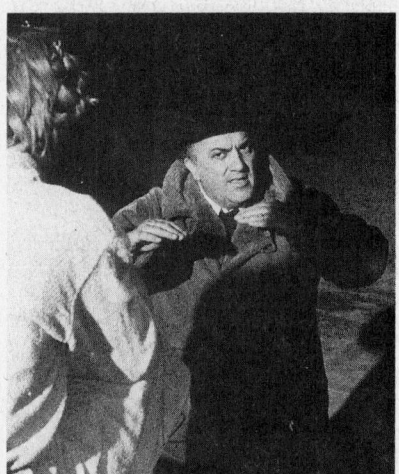

Fellini Italian film director Federico Fellini was a cartoonist and journalist before he began directing neorealistic films in the 1950s. *La Dolce Vita* caused a scandal when it won the Grand Prix at the 1960 Cannes Film Festival.

felony in UK law, former term for an offence which is more serious than a misdemeanour; in the US, a felony is a crime punishable by imprisonment of a year or more. See ◊criminal law.

felt matted fabric of wool, hair, etc., made by working fibres together under pressure, heat or by chemical action.

department built up a position of powerful autonomy during the autocratic directorship of J Edgar Hoover 1924–72. In 1964 the FBI was criticized by the Warren Commission into the assassination of President Kennedy, and in 1973 L Patrick Gray, the acting director, resigned when it was revealed that he had destroyed relevant material in the ◊Watergate investigation. Clarence M Kelley was director 1973–78, William Webster 1978–87 and Judge William Sessions from 1987.

federalism a system of government where two or more separate states unite under a common central government while retaining a considerable degree of local autonomy. A

fencing sport using the *foil*, derived from the light weapon used in practice duels; *épée*, a heavier weapon derived from the duelling sword proper; and *sabre*, in which cuts (it has two cutting edges) count as well as thrusts. Masks and protective jackets are worn, and hits are registered electronically in competitions.

Fénelon /ˌfenɪˈlɒŋ/ François de Salignac de la Mothe 1651–1715. French writer and ecclesiastic. He entered the priesthood in 1675 and in 1689 was appointed tutor to the Duke of Burgundy, grandson of Louis XIV. For him he wrote his *Fables* and *Dialogues des Morts/Dialogues of the Dead* 1690, *Télémaque/Telemachus* 1699, and *Plans de Gouvernement/Plans of Government*. Télémaque, with its picture of an ideal commonwealth, had the effect of a political manifesto, and Louis banished Fénelon to Cambrai, where in 1695 he had been consecrated archbishop. Fénelon's mystical *Maximes des Saints/Sayings of the Saints* 1697 had also led to a quarrel with the Jansenists, and condemnation by Pope Innocent XII.

Fenian a member of an Irish-American republican secret society, founded in 1858 and named after the ancient Irish legendary warrior band of the Fianna. It failed to achieve its aim of an independent Irish republic by a rising in Ireland 1867, but continued to exist till 1922. It was succeeded by the ◊Irish Republican Army.

fennec small nocturnal desert ◊fox *Fennecus zerda* found in North Africa and Arabia. With head and body only 40 cm/1.3 ft long, it has enormous ears which help it find insects and small animals to eat, and also act as radiators to lose excess heat.

fennel perennial plant with feathery green leaves, family Umbelliferae. Fennels have an aniseed flavour and the thickened leafstalks of *sweet fennel Foeniculum dulce* are eaten, while the leaves and seeds of *Foeniculum vulgare* are used in seasoning.

Fens /fenz/ level, low-lying tracts of land in E England, W and S of the Wash, about 115 km/70 mi N–S and about 55 km/35 mi E–W. They fall within the counties of Lincolnshire, Cambridgeshire, and Norfolk, consisting of a huge area, formerly a bay of the North Sea, but now crossed by numerous drainage canals and forming some of the most productive agricultural land in Britain. The first drainage attempts were made by the Romans, but later attempts were unsuccessful until in 1634 the fourth earl of Bedford brought over the Dutch water-engineer Vermuyden, who introduced Dutch methods.

Fenton /ˈfentən/ Roger 1819–1869. British photographer. The world's first war photographer, he went to the Crimea in 1855; he also founded the Royal Photographic Society in London.

Ferber /ˈfɜːbə/ Edna 1887–1968. American novelist and playwright. Her novel *Show Boat* 1926 was adapted as an operetta by Jerome Kern and Oscar Hammerstein II, and her plays, in which she collaborated with G S Kaufmann, included *Stage Door* 1936.

Ferdinand /ˈfɜːdɪnænd/ five kings of Castile, including:

Ferdinand I the Great c.1016–65. King of Castile from 1035, he began the reconquest of Spain from the Moors and united all NW Spain under his and his brothers' rule.

Ferdinand V becoming **Ferdinand III** of Naples in 1504 and also

Ferdinand II of Aragon. 1452–1516. First king of all Spain. In 1469 he married his cousin Isabella, who in 1474 succeeded to the throne of Castile. When in 1479 Ferdinand inherited the throne of Aragon, the two great Spanish kingdoms were brought under a single government for the first time. The outstanding events of his reign included the introduction of the ◊Inquisition in 1480, the expulsion of the Jews and the surrender of the Moors at Granada in 1492 and Columbus's expedition to America, which he financed. He conquered Naples 1500–03.

Ferdinand /ˈfɜːdɪnænd/ three Holy Roman Emperors: *Ferdinand I* 1503–64, who succeeded his brother Charles V in 1556.

Ferdinand II 1578–1637, king of Bohemia and Hungary, succeeded his uncle Matthias as emperor in from 1619; he was a fanatical Catholic who provoked the Bohemian revolt which led to the ◊Thirty Years' War.

Ferdinand III 1608–57, son of Ferdinand II, whose reign saw the end of the Thirty Years' War in 1648. He was king of Hungary 1625–57.

Ferdinand /ˈfɜːdɪnænd/ 1861–1948. King of Bulgaria. Son of Prince Augustus of Saxe-Coburg-Gotha, he was elected prince of Bulgaria in 1887, and in 1908 proclaimed Bulgaria's independence of Turkey and assumed the title of Tsar. In 1915 he entered World War I as Germany's ally, and in 1918 abdicated.

Ferdinand /ˈfɜːdɪnænd/ 1865–1927. King of Romania. He succeeded his uncle Charles I in 1914, and in 1916 declared war on Austria. The Allied victory was followed by the acquisition of Transylvania and Bukovina from Austria–Hungary and Bessarabia from Russia, and in 1922 Ferdinand was crowned king of All Romanians.

Ferghana /fəˈgɑːnə/ town in Uzbekistan, USSR, in the fertile Ferghana valley; population (1985) 195,000. It is the capital of the important cotton and fruit-growing Ferghana region; nearby are petroleum fields.

Ferguson /ˈfɜːgəsən/ Harry 1884–1960. Irish engineer, born in County Down. A farmer's son, he pioneered the development of the tractor, joining forces with Henry Ford in 1938 to manufacture in America. He also experimented in automobile and aircraft development.

Fermanagh /fəˈmænə/ county in the southern part of Northern Ireland
area 1,701 sq km/657 sq mi
towns Enniskillen (county town) Lisnaskea, Irvinestown
features in the centre is a broad trough of low-lying land, in which lie Upper and Lower Lough Erne
products mainly agricultural; livestock, tweeds, clothing
population (1981) 51,600

Fermat /feəˈmɑː/ Pierre de 1601–1665. French mathematician, who with Pascal founded

the theory of ◊probability and the modern theory of numbers. His *last theorem*, a proof of simple relations of the form $3^2 + 4^2 = 5^2$ (or, more generally, $ax^n + bx^m = cx^p$), believed to be true, may have been proved by him, but no one else since has succeeded in doing so.

fermentation the breakdown of sugars by bacteria and yeasts using ◊anaerobic respiration. These processes have long been utilized in baking bread, making beer and wine, and producing cheese, yoghurt, soy sauce and many other foodstuffs. In baking and brewing, yeasts ferment sugars to produce ◊ethyl alcohol and carbon dioxide; the latter makes bread rise and puts bubbles into beers and champagne.

Fermi /ˈfɜːmi/ Enrico 1901–1954. Italian-American physicist, who proved the existence of new radioactive elements produced by bombardment with neutrons and discovered nuclear reactions produced by slow neutrons. Born in Rome, he was professor of theoretical physics there from 1926 to 1938, when he settled in the USA. The same year he was awarded a Nobel prize for his discoveries. He was professor at Columbia University, New York, from 1939 to 1942 and from 1946 at Chicago. In 1954 the US Atomic Energy Commission made a special award to him for outstanding work in nuclear physics, and these annual awards have subsequently been known as Fermi awards.

Fermilab the US centre for ◊particle physics in Chicago, named after ◊Fermi.

fermium a metallic element, symbol Fm, atomic number 100. One of the actinide series, it was named after ◊Fermi and has been produced only in minute quantities.

fern plant of the class Filicales, related to horsetails and clubmosses. Ferns are spore-bearing, not flowering, plants, and most are perennial herbs spreading by low-growing roots. The leaves, known as fronds, vary widely in size and shape. Some taller types, such as tree-ferns, grow in the tropics. There are over 7,000 species. Ferns found in Britain include the polypody *Polypodium vulgare*, shield fern *Polystichum*, and male fern *Dryopteris filix-mas*, hart's-tongue *Phyllitis scolopendrium*, maidenhair *Adiantum capillus-veneris*, and bracken *Pteridium aquilinum*, an agricultural weed.

Fernandez /fəˈnændez/ Juan c. 1536–c. 1604. Spanish explorer and navigator. As a pilot on the Pacific coast of South America, he discovered in 1563 the islands off the coast of Chile that now bear his name; on one of these Alexander Selkirk, the original Robinson Crusoe, lived.

Fernando Po /fəˈnændəʊ ˈpəʊ/ former name (until 1973) of ◊Bioko.

Ferrara /fəˈrɑːrə/ industrial city and archbishopric in Emilia-Romagna region, N Italy, on a branch of the Po delta 52 km/32 mi W of the Adriatic Sea; population (1981) 149,640.
history It has the Gothic castle of its medieval rulers, the House of Este, palaces, museums, and a cathedral, consecrated in 1135. The university was founded in 1391. ◊Savonarola was born here, and the poet ◊Tasso was confined in the asylum 1579–86.

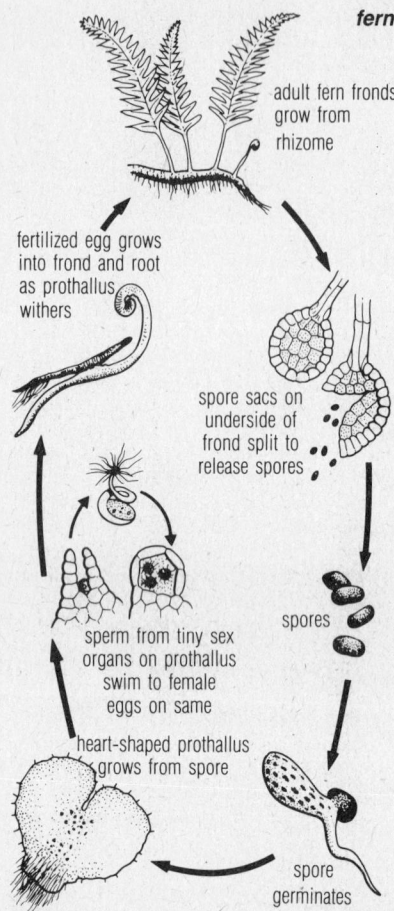

fern

adult fern fronds grow from rhizome

fertilized egg grows into frond and root as prothallus withers

spore sacs on underside of frond split to release spores

spores

sperm from tiny sex organs on prothallus swim to female eggs on same

heart-shaped prothallus grows from spore

spore germinates

fern Tree ferns in the New Zealand 'bush'.

Ferraro /fə'rɑːrəʊ/ Geraldine 1935– . US Democrat politician, vice-presidential candidate in the 1984 election.

ferret domesticated variety of ◊polecat. About 35 cm/1.2 ft long, it usually has yellowish-white fur and pink eyes, but may be the colour of a wild polecat. It is used to hunt rabbits and rats.

Ferrier /'feriə/ Kathleen (Mary) 1912–1953. British contralto singer, born in Lancashire and originally a student of the piano. She made her reputation in oratorio and opera. Notable appearances were in Britten's *The Rape of Lucretia* 1946 in which she created the role of Lucretia. She died of cancer.

Ferrier /'feriə/ Susan Edmundstone 1782–1854. Scottish novelist, born in Edinburgh. Her anonymously published books include *Marriage* (1818), *Inheritance* (1824), and *Destiny* (1831), all of which give a lively picture of Scottish manners and society.

ferro-alloy an alloy of iron with a high proportion of manganese, silicon, chromium, molybdenum. Ferro-alloys are used in the manufacture of alloy steels.

Ferrol /fe'rəʊl/ alternative name for ◊El Ferrol, a city and port in NW Spain.

Ferry /'feri/ Julies François Camille 1832–1893. French politician. He was mayor of Paris during the siege of 1870–71. As a member of the republican governments of 1879–85 (prime minister 1880–81 and 1883–85) he was responsible for the famous law of 1882 making primary education free, compulsory, and without any religious teaching.

fertility an organism's ability to reproduce. Individuals become infertile (unable to reproduce) when they cannot generate gametes (eggs or sperm) or when their gametes cannot yield a viable ◊embryo after ◊fertilization. See also ◊fecundity.

fertility drug any of a range of drugs taken to increase a female's fertility, developed in Sweden in the mid-1950s. The best-known is gonadotrophin, which is made from hormone extracts (FSH and LH) taken from the human pituitary gland, and stimulates ovulation in women. Multiple births are a risk, and in 1974 the first sextuplets to survive were born to Susan Rosenkowitz of S Africa.

fertilization in ◊sexual reproduction, the union of two ◊gametes (sex cells, often called egg and sperm) to produce a ◊zygote, which combines the genetic material contributed by each parent. In terrestrial insects, mammals, reptiles and birds, fertilization occurs within the female's body; in the majority of fish and amphibians, and most aquatic invertebrates, it occurs externally, when both sexes release their gametes freely into the water. In most fungi, gametes are not released, but the hyphae of the two parents grow towards each other and fuse to achieve fertilization. In higher plants, ◊pollination precedes fertilization. In self-fertilization the male and female gametes come from the same plant; in cross-fertilization they come from different plants. Self-fertilization occurs rarely in ◊hermaphrodite animals.

fertilizer a substance containing a range of the twenty-odd chemical elements necessary for healthy plant growth, used to compensate the deficiencies of poor soil or of soil depleted by repeated cropping. Fertilizers may be (a) **organic**, for example, farmyard manure, composts, bonemeal, blood and fishmeal. (b) **inorganic**, in the form of compounds, mainly of nitrogen, phosphate and potash, which have come into use on a tremendously increased scale since World War II. The compounds are most frequently administered in solid form, but 'non-pressure' liquid fertilizers are used in market gardening and 'pressure' liquids, such as anhydrous ammonia (containing 82 per cent nitrogen), are being increasingly used on larger farms and by contractors. The cost of fertilizers, greatly increased by rises in the prices of fuels needed to make them, and also the fact that externally applied fertilizers tend to be in excess of plant requirements and leach away to affect lakes and rivers (see ◊eutrophication), have turned attention to the modification of crop plants themselves. Plants of the pea family, including the bean, clover and lupin, live in symbiosis with bacteria, *Rhizobia*, located in root nodules, which fix nitrogen from the atmosphere. Research is now directed to producing a similar relationship between such bacteria and crops such as wheat.

Fès /fez/ religious centre (formerly *Fez*) and former capital of Morocco 808–1062, 1296–1548, and 1662–1912, in a valley N of the Great Atlas Mountains, 160 km/100 mi E of Rabat; population (1973) 321,460. Kairwan Islamic University dates from 859; the second university was founded in 1961. The fez, a brimless hat worn in S and E Mediterranean countries, is traditionally said to have originated here.

Fessenden /'fesəndən/ Reginald Aubrey 1866–1932. Canadian-born American physicist, who patented the ◊modulation of radio waves (transmission of a signal using a carrier wave), an essential technique for voice transmission. Early radio communications relied on telegraphy by using bursts of single-frequency signals in morse code. In 1900, Fessenden devised a method of making audio-frequency speech (or music) signals modulate the amplitude of a transmitted radio-frequency carrier wave – the basis of AM radio ◊broadcasting.

fetishism in anthropological usage, belief in the supernormal power of some inanimate object which is known as a fetish. Fetishism in some form is common to most civilizations, and often has religio-magical significance. In psychology, the term is used for the practice of associating an object with the sexual act, and transferring desire to the object (such as clothing) rather than the person.

feudalism a form of social stratification which arose in Europe during the 4th – 10th centuries under which the monarch owned all land. In return for military service the monarch allowed powerful vassals to hold land, and often also to administer justice and levy taxes. They in turn 'sub-let' such rights. At the bottom of the system were the serfs, who worked on their lord's manor in return for being allowed to cultivate some land for themselves, and so underpinned the system. They could not be sold as if they were slaves, but also could not leave the estate. The system declined from the 13th century, partly because of the growth of a money economy, with commerce, trade, and industry, and partly because of the many peasants' revolts of 1350 – 1550. Serfdom ended in England in the 16th century, but lasted in France until 1789, and in the rest of Western Europe until the early 19th century. In Russia it continued until 1861.

fever disorder due to raising of the body temperature from the normal 36.9°C/98.4°F; if over 41°C/106°F it can lead to death. It is generally the reaction of the organism to the presence in the blood stream of a foreign substance, usually a protein. This is most often produced by invading micro-organisms.

Feyerabend /'faɪərɑːbənd/ Paul K 1924– . American philosopher of science, who rejected the attempt by certain philosophers (for instance ◊Popper) to find a methodology common to all scientific research. Although his work relies on historical evidence, he argues that successive theories which apparently concern the same subject (for instance the motion of the planets) cannot in principle be subjected to any comparison that would aim at finding the 'truer' explanation. According to this notion of 'incommensurability' there is no neutral or objective standpoint by which theories can be compared, and therefore no rational way by which one theory should be chosen over another.

Fez /fez/ alternative spelling of ◊Fès, a city in Morocco.

Fezzan /fe'zɑːn/ former province of Libya, split into smaller divisions in 1963; situated in a desert region, with many oases.

Fianna Fáil /'fiənə 'fɔɪl/ (Gaelic: Soldiers of Destiny) Irish Republican Party, founded by De Valera in 1926. It has been the governing party in the Republic of Ireland 1932–48, 1951–54, 1957–73, 1977–81, 1982, and 1987– . It aims at the establishment of a united and completely independent all-Ireland republic.

Fibonacci /ˌfɪbə'nɑːtʃi/ Leonardo c. 1170–c. 1230. Italian mathematician. He published his *Liber abaci* in Pisa in 1202, which led to the introduction of Arabic notation into Europe. From 1960 interest increased in his discovery of the *Fibonacci numbers*, in their simplest form a series in which each number is the sum of its two predecessors (1, 1, 2, 3, 5, 8, 13). They have unusual characteristics with possible applications in botany, psychology, and astronomy (for example, a more exact correspondence than ◊Bode's Law to the distances between the planets and the Sun).

fibreglass glass that has been formed into fine fibres. It can be produced as long continuous filaments or as a fluffy short-fibred glass wool. The long filament form is made by forcing molten glass through the holes of a spinneret. It has exciting applications in the field of ◊fibre optics, and as a strengthener for plastics in ◊GRP (glass-reinforced plastics), commonly called fibreglass. Glass wool is made by blowing streams of molten glass in a jet of high-pressure steam. It is used as thermal insulation for the roof space in houses.

fibre optics transmission of light through glass or plastic fibres, known as ◊optical fibres.

fibres natural and synthetic; see ◊textile.

Fichte /'fɪxtə/ Johann Gottlieb 1762–1814. German philosopher. Born in Silesia and educated at Jena and Leipzig, he was an admirer of ◊Kant and in 1792 published a *Critique of Religious Revelation*, a critical study of the Kantian doctrine of the thing-in-itself as dogmatic, and developed a comprehensive form of subjective idealism, expounded in his *The Science of Knowledge* (1794). For Fichte, the absolute ego posits both the external world (the non-ego) and finite self. Morality consists on a striving of this finite self to rejoin the absolute. In 1799 he was accused of atheism, and was forced to resign his post. He moved to Berlin, where he lectured and devoted himself to public affairs.

Fichtelgebirge /'fɪxtəlgə,bɪəgə/ chain of mountains in Bavaria, West Germany, on the Czechoslovak border. The highest peak is the *Schneeberg* 1,051 m/3,448 ft.

fiction in literature, any work or type of work whose content is completely or largely invented. In the 20th century the term is usually used to refer to imaginative works of narrative prose (such as the ◊novel or the ◊short story), and contrasted with *non-fiction* such as history, biography, or works on practical subjects, and with *poetry*. This usage reflects the dominance in contemporary Western literature of the novel as a vehicle for imaginative literature: strictly speaking, poems can also be fictional (as opposed to factual). Genres such as the ◊historical novel often combine a fictional plot with real events; ◊biography may also be 'fictionalized' through the use of imagined conversations or events.

Fidei Defensor /'fɪdiaɪ dɪ'fensɔː/ title of 'defender of the faith' (still retained by British sovereigns) conferred by Pope Leo X on Henry VIII of England to reward his writing of a treatise against Martin ◊Luther.

field in physics, a region in which an object exerts a force on another non-touching object because of certain properties they both possess. For example, there is a force of attraction between any two objects that have mass, one of which is in the gravitational field of the other. Other fields of force include an ◊electric field (caused by electric charges) and a ◊magnetic field (caused by magnetic poles), either of which can involve attractive or repulsive forces.

fieldfare bird *Turdus pilaris* of the thrush family, a winter migrant in Britain, breeding in Scandinavia, N Russia, and Siberia. It has a pale-grey lower back and neck with a dark tail.

Fielding /'fiːldɪŋ/ Henry 1707–1754. English novelist, whose individual genius at narrative influenced the form and technique of the novel and helped to make it the most popular form of literature in England. In 1742 he parodied Richardson's novel *Pamela* in *Joseph Andrews*, then took seriously to the craft with *Jonathan Wild the Great* 1743; his masterpiece *Tom Jones* 1749, which he described as a 'comic epic in prose'; and *Amelia* 1751. As Justice of the Peace for Middlesex and Westminster (appointed 1748), he exercised the same compassion as appears in his novels. In failing health, he went

to recuperate in Lisbon in 1754, writing on the way *A Journal of a Voyage to Lisbon*. He died and was buried there two months later.

Fielding Henry Fielding's concern for social justice, seen in his best-known novel *Tom Jones*, was also a feature of his term as a magistrate.

Field-Marshal the highest rank in certain armies. It was introduced to Britain from Germany by George II in 1736.

Field of the Cloth of Gold site between Guînes and Ardres near Calais, France, where a meeting took place between Henry VIII of England and Francis I of France in Jun 1520, remarkable for the lavish clothes worn and tent pavilions erected. Francis hoped to gain England's support in opposing the Holy Roman Emperor, Charles V, but failed.

Fields /fiːldz/ Gracie. Stage-name of British comedian and singer Grace Stansfield 1898–1979. Born in Rochdale, she was originally a mill-girl. Her films include *Sally in our Alley* and *Sing as We Go* 1934. Dame of the British Empire 1979.

Fields /fiːldz/ W(illiam) C(laude) 1879–1946. American actor and screenwriter, one of the most original comedians to appear in films. His distinctive speech and professed anti-establishment attitudes such as hatred of children and dogs gained him enormous popularity in films such as *The Bank Dick* 1940 and *Never Give a Sucker an Even Break* 1941.

field studies the study of ecology, geography, geology, history, archaeology, and allied subjects, in the natural environment, with emphasis on promoting a wider knowledge and understanding of the natural environment among the public. The Council for the Promotion of Field Studies was established in Britain in 1943, and Flatford Mill, Suffolk, was the first research centre to be opened.

fife a kind of small flute. Originally from Switzerland, it was known as the Swiss pipe and has long been used by British Army bands.

Fife /faɪf/ region of E Scotland (formerly the county of Fife), facing the North Sea and Firth of Forth

area 1,305 sq km/504 sq mi

towns administrative headquarters Glenrothes; Dunfermline, St Andrews, Kirkcaldy, Cupar

features the only high land is the Lomond Hills, in the northwest. Chief rivers Eden and Leven; Rosyth naval base and dockyard on N shore of the Firth of Forth; Tentsmuir, possibly the earliest settled site in Scotland. The ancient palace of the Stuarts was at Falkland, and eight Scottish kings are buried at Dunfermline

products potatoes, cereals, sugar beet; electronics, petrochemicals (Mossmorran)

population (1981) 326,500.

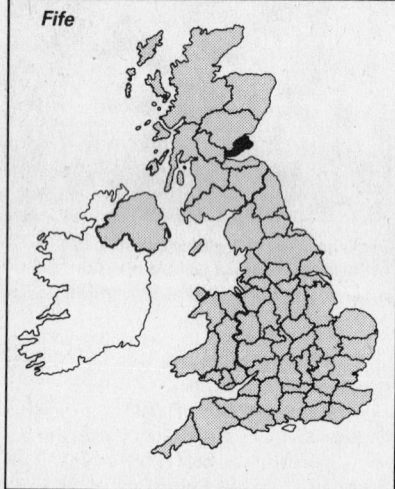

Fife

Fifteen, the Jacobite rebellion of 1715, led by the 'Old Pretender' (◊James Edward Stuart) and the Earl of Mar, in order to place the former on the throne. Mar was checked at Sheriffmuir, and the revolt collapsed.

fifth column a group within a country secretly aiding an enemy attacking from without. The term originated in 1936, during the Spanish Civil War, when General Mola boasted that Franco supporters were attacking Madrid with four columns, and that they had a 'fifth column' inside the city.

fifth-generation computer an anticipated new type of computer based on emerging microelectronic technologies. The basis will be very fast computing machinery, with many processors working in parallel. These will be possible because of very large-scale integration (◊VLSI) which can put many more circuits onto a ◊silicon chip. Such computers will run advanced 'intelligent' programs.

The other four generations are usually said to be:

first generation: 1943–59 based on valves and wire circuits

second generation: 1959–64 based on transistors and printed circuits

third generation: 1964–72 many interconnected circuits incorporated into one integrated circuit.

fourth generation: from 1972 based on large-scale integration (◊LSI) of circuits.

The **Fifth-Generation Project** is a ten-year research programme begun in Japan in 1982 to develop the new type of computer systems. It has been a spur for several other programmes, including ESPRIT in Europe and Alvey in the UK.

fig fruit of the W Asian tree *Ficus carica*, family Moraceae, produced in two or three crops a year, and eaten fresh or dried; it has a high sugar content and laxative properties. In the wild they are totally dependent on the fig wasp for pollination, and the wasp is completely parasitic on the flowers. The tropical *banyan Ficus benghalensis* has less attractive edible fruit, and roots which grow down from its branches, looking like separate 'trunks'. The *bo tree* under which Buddha became 'enlightened' is the Indian peepul or wild fig *Ficus religiosa*.

fighting fish small fish *Betta splendens* and related species found in SE Asia. It can breathe air using an accessory breathing organ above the gill and can live in poorly oxygenated water. The male builds a nest of bubbles at the water surface and displays to a female to induce her to lay. Rival males are attacked, and in a confined space fights may occur. In Thailand public contests are held. About 6 cm/2 in long, the male has large fins, and various colours occur, including shining greens, reds and blues. The female is yellowish brown with short fins.

figure of speech a poetic, imaginative or ornamental expression used for purposes of comparison, emphasis, stylistic effect, etc., usually one of a list of such forms dating from discussions of literary and rhetorical style in Greece in the 5th century BC. These figures include ◊euphemism, ◊hyperbole, ◊metaphor, ◊metonymy, ◊onomatopoeia, ◊oxymoron, ◊personification, the ◊pun, ◊simile and ◊synecdoche.

figwort plant of the genus *Scrophularia*. These are perennial herbs with square stems, opposite leaves, and open two-lipped flowers in a cluster at the top of the stem. *Common figwort Scrophularia nodosa* lives across Europe and N Asia. It grows in damp woods and by hedges, and is up to 80 cm/2.6 ft long, with small reddish-brown flowers with green sepals in late summer. It is pollinated by wasps.

Fiji /ˈfiːdʒiː/ group of 332 islands in the SW Pacific, about 100 of which are inhabited.

government Fiji is a constitutional monarchy within the ◊Commonwealth, with the British monarch as head of state, represented by a resident governor-general (but see below). The constitution dates from independence in 1970. The government is modelled on the British system, with a two-chamber parliament (senate and house of representatives) and a prime minister and cabinet drawn from and responsible to the house of representatives. The senate has 22 appointed members, eight on the advice of the great council of Fijian chiefs, seven on the advice of the prime minister, six on the advice of the leader of the opposition, and one on the advice of the council of Rotuma Island, which is a Fijian dependency. It has a life of six years. The house of representatives has 52 members, elected for five years through a cross-voting system which ensures that all ethnic groups are represented.

history Originally inhabited by ◊Melanesian and ◊Polynesian peoples, Fiji's first European visitor was Abel ◊Tasman in 1643. Fiji became a British possession in 1874, and achieved full independence within the Commonwealth in 1970. Before independence there had been racial tension between Indians, descended from workers brought to Fiji in the late 19th century, and Fijians, so the constitutution incorporated an electoral system which would ensure racial balance in the house of representatives.

The leader of the Alliance Party, Ratu Sir Kamisese Mara, became prime minister at the time of independence and has held office ever since. The Alliance Party has traditionally been supported by Fijians and the National Federation Party (NFP), led by Siddiq Koya, by Indians. The main divisions between the two have centred on land ownership, with the Fijians owning more than 80% of the land and defending their traditional rights, and the Indians claiming greater security of land tenure. The Fijian Labour Party was formed in 1985 but has so far made little impact at the polls.

An attempted coup in May 1987, led by Lt-Col Sitivina Rambuka, was abandoned after intervention by the Governor-General and the Great Council of Chiefs. Another coup by Rambuka in Sept seemed, despite indecision by its leader, more likely to succeed. On this occasion the Queen, at the instigation of the Governor-General, condemned the coup in an unprecedented fashion. Nevertheless, the coup went ahead and in Oct 1987 the Queen accepted the resignation of the Governor-General, thereby relinquishing her role as head of state and making Fiji a republic.

filariasis collective term for several diseases, prevalent in tropical areas, caused by roundworm (nematode) parasites. Symptoms include blocked and swollen lymph vessels leading to grotesque swellings of the legs and genitals (Bancroftian filariasis, elephantiasis); and blindness and dry, scaly skin (onchocerciasis). These diseases are spread mainly by insects, notably mosquitoes and blackflies.

file in computing, a collection of data or a program stored in a computer's external memory, for example on disk. It might include anything from information on a firm's employees to a program for an adventure game. Usually consists of a set of records, each having a number of fields for specific items of data. For example, the file for a class of schoolchildren might have five fields containing each child's family name (1) first name (2) house name or number (3) street name (4) and town (5). To find out which children live in the same street one would look in field 4. *Serial files* hold information as a sequence of characters, so that to read any particular item of data the sequence before it must first be read. *Random access files* allow the required record to be reached directly.

file transfer in computing, the transmission of a file (data stored for example on disk) from one machine to another. For this to be possible,

Fiji

AREA 18,272 sq km/7,055 sq mi
CAPITAL Suva on Viti Levu
PHYSICAL comprises some 800 Melanesian
islands (about 100 inhabited), the largest being
Viti Levu (10,386 sq km/400 sq mi) and Vanua
Levu (5,535 sq km/2,137 sq mi); mountainous,
with tropical forest
FEATURES Nadi airport is an international
Pacific staging post
HEAD OF STATE Sir Penaia Ganilau from 1987
HEAD OF GOVERNMENT Sir Kamisese Mara from
1987
GOVERNMENT republic
EXPORTS sugar, coconut oil, ginger, timber,
canned fish; tourism is important
CURRENCY Fiji dollar (2.09 = £1 Sept 1987)
POPULATION (1985) 700,000 (44% Fijian,
holding 80% of the land communally, and 50%
Indians introduced in the 19th century to work
the sugar crop); annual growth rate 1.5%
LANGUAGE English (official); Fijian, Hindi
RELIGION Hindu 50%, Methodist 44%
LITERACY 88% male/77% female (1980 est)
GDP $1.2 bn (1984); $1,086
CHRONOLOGY
1970 Full independence achieved. Ratu Sir
Kamisese Mara elected as first prime minister.
1987 General election in Apr brought to power
an Indian-dominated coalition led by Dr
Timoci Bavadra. Military coup in May by Col
Sitiveni Rambuka removed new government at

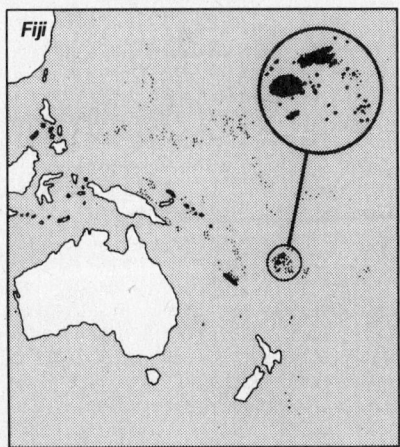

Fiji

gunpoint. Governor General Ratu Sir Penaia
Ganilau regained control within weeks. A
second military coup by Rambuka in Sept
proclaimed Fiji a republic and suspended the
constitution. It was feared that ethnic rivalry
would escalate and people of Indian extraction
be forced to emigrate. In Oct Fiji ceased to be
a member of the Commonwealth. In Dec a
civilian government was restored with
Rambuka retaining control of security as
minister for home affairs.

both machines must be part of a computer
◊network, and both must be running appropriate
communications software, so that the sending
and receiving of the data can be coordinated.

Fillmore /'fɪlmɔː/ Millard 1800–74. 13th
President of the USA. As Vice-President to
Zachary Taylor from 1848, he succeeded on
Taylor's death. A Whig, he advocated a
compromise on slavery to reconcile North and
South, and failed to be renominated.

film, art of see ◊cinema.

film noir (French 'black film') a term
originally used by French critics to describe any
film characterized by pessimism, cynicism, and
a dark, sombre tone. It has since been used to
describe Hollywood films of the 1940s and early
1950s protraying the dark and seedy side of the
criminal underworld and, by extension, later
films made in the same style. Typically the *film
noir* is shot with lighting that emphasizes shadow
and stark contrasts, abounds in night scenes, and
contains a cynical antihero – an example is the
character of Philip Marlowe in *The Big Sleep*.

film, photographic a strip of transparent
material (usually cellulose acetate) coated with a
light-sensitive emulsion, used in cameras to take
pictures. The emulsion contains a mixture of
light-sensitive silver halide salts (for example
bromide or iodide) in gelatin. Films differ in their
sensitivity to light, this being reflected in their
speed. When the emulsion is exposed to light, the
silver salts are invisibly altered, giving a latent

image, which is then made visible by the process
of ◊developing.
Colour film consists of several layers of emulsion,
each of which records a different colour in the
light falling on it. The front emulsion records
blue light, then comes a yellow filter, followed by
layers that record green and red light
respectively. In the developing process the
various images in the layers are dyed yellow,
magenta and cyan, respectively. When they are
viewed, either as a see-through transparency or
as a colour print, the colours merge to produce the
true colour of the original scene photographed.

Financial Times (FT) Index the London
Financial Times's industrial ordinary ◊index
measuring the daily movement of 30 major
industrial share prices on the London ◊Stock
Exchange (1935 = 100). Other FT indices cover
government securities, fixed-interest securities,
goldmine shares, and Stock Exchange activity.

finch bird of the family Fringillidae, in the
order Passeriformes, which are seed-eaters with
stout conical beaks.

Fine Gael /'fɪnə 'geɪl/ Irish political party
(United Ireland), founded by W J ◊Cosgrave,
and led by Garrett ◊FitzGerald 1977–87.

Fingal's Cave /'fɪŋɡəlz/ cave on the island of
Staffa, Inner Hebrides, Scotland. It is lined with
natural basalt columns and is 60 m/200 ft long
and 20 m/65 ft high. Fingal, based on the Irish
hero Finn mac Cumhaill, was the leading
character in ◊Macpherson's Ossianic forgeries.

Visited by ◊Mendelssohn in 1829, the cave was
the inspiration of his *Hebrides* overture,
otherwise known as Fingal's Cave.

fingerprint the ridge pattern of the skin on a
person's fingertips; this is constant through life
and no two are exactly alike. Fingerprinting was
first used as a means of identifying suspects in
India, and adopted by the English police in 1901.

Finistère /ˌfɪnɪs'teə/ *département* of
◊Brittany, NW France; area 7030 sq km/2740
mi; population (1982) 828,500.

Finisterre /ˌfɪnɪs'teə/ Cape promontory in the
extreme NW of Spain.

Finland /'fɪnlənd/ country in Scandinavia,
bounded N by Norway, E by the USSR, S and
W by the Baltic Sea, and NW by Sweden.
government Finland is a republic which combines
a parliamentary system with a strong presidency.
The single-chamber parliament, the *Eduskunta*,
has 200 members, elected by universal suffrage,
through a system of proportional representation,
for a four-year term. The president is elected for
six years by a 301-member electoral college,
chosen by popular vote in the same way as the
parliament. The president appoints a prime
minister and a cabinet, called a council of state,
whose members are collectively responsible to
the *Eduskunta*.
The relationship between the president and the
prime minister and the council of state is unusual,
the nearest equivalent being in France. The
president has supreme executive power, and can
ignore even a unanimous decision reached in the
council of state, but the prime minister is
concerned with the day-to-day operation of the
government so that to some extent they can, at
times, both act as heads of government. Both the
president and the *Eduskunta* can initiate
legislation and the president has a right of veto,
though this can be overruled by a newly
appointed parliament.
Because of the system of proportional
representation, there is a multiplicity of parties,
and the prime minister invariably heads a
coalition council of state, typically between four
parties. The main parties are: the Social
Democratic Party (SDP), the National Coalition
Party (KOK), the Centre Party (KP), the
Finnish People's Democratic League (SKDL),
the Finnish Rural Party (SMP) and the Swedish
People's Party (SFP).
history The Lapps, who once inhabited the area
now known as Finland, were driven by Finnic
nomads from Asia into the far northern region
they occupy today from about the 1st century BC.
The area was conquered in the 12th century by
Sweden, and for much of the next 200 years the
country was the scene of wars between Sweden
and Russia. As a duchy of Sweden, Finland was
allowed a measure of autonomy, becoming a
grand duchy in 1581. In 1809, during the
Napoleonic Wars, Finland was annexed by
Russia; nationalist feeling grew, and the country
proclaimed its independence during the 1917
Russian revolution. The Soviet regime initially
tried to regain control but acknowledged
Finland's independence in 1920.
In 1939 the USSR's request for military bases in
Finland was rejected and the two countries were

involved in the 'Winter War', which lasted for 15 weeks. Finland was defeated and forced to cede territory. In the hope of regaining it, in 1941 it joined Nazi Germany in attacking the USSR, but agreed a separate armistice in 1944. It was again forced to cede territory and in 1948 signed the Finno-Soviet Pact of Friendship, Co-operation and Mutual Assistance (the YYA Treaty). This was extended in 1955, 1970 and 1983. Although the Treaty requires it to repel any attack on the USSR through Finnish territory by Germany or its allies, Finland has maintained a policy of strict neutrality. It signed a trade treaty with the EEC in 1973 and a 15-year trade agreement with the USSR in 1977. Finnish politics have been characterized by instability in governments, over 60 having been formed since independence, including many minority coalitions. The presidency, on the other hand, has been very stable, with only two presidents in over 30 years.

The Social Democratic and Centre parties have dominated Finland's coalition politics for many years but the 1987 general election resulted in the Social Democrats entering government with their arch-enemies, the Conservatives, and the Centre Party being forced into opposition.

Finland
REPUBLIC OF (*Suomen Tasavalta*)

AREA 337,050 sq km/130,125 sq mi
CAPITAL Helsinki
TOWNS Tampere, and the port of Turku
PHYSICAL archipelago in S; most of the country is forest, with some 60,000 lakes; one third is within the Arctic Circle; mountains in the N
HEAD OF STATE Mauno Koivisto from 1982
HEAD OF GOVERNMENT Kalevi Sorsa from 1982
GOVERNMENT parliamentary democracy
EXPORTS metal, chemical and engineering products (icebreakers and oil rigs); paper, timber, and textiles; fine ceramics, glass, and furniture
CURRENCY Finnish mark (7.24 = £1 Sept 1987)
POPULATION 4,908,000 (1985); annual growth rate 0.5%
LANGUAGE Finnish, Swedish (official); Lapp
RELIGION Lutheran 90%
LITERACY 99%
GNP $50.6 bn (1984); $10,477 per head of population
CHRONOLOGY
1917 Independence declared.
1939 Defeated by USSR in Winter War.

Finland

1941 Joined Hitler in invasion of USSR.
1944 Concluded separate armistice with Allies.
1948 Finno-Soviet Pact of Friendship, Co-operation, and Mutual Assistance signed.
1973 Trade treaty with EEC signed.
1977 Trade agreement with USSR signed.

Finland /'finlənd/ Gulf of eastern arm of the ◊Baltic Sea.

Finlandization political term invented by the Austrian politician Karl Gruber in 1953 to signify the limits set on the autonomy of a small state by a much more powerful neighbour, as with Finland and the USSR. Finns resent the term as implying that their sovereignty is under threat.

Finney /'fini/ Albert 1936– . British stage and film actor. He created the title roles in *Billy*

Liar 1960, and ◊Osborne's *Luther* 1961, and was artistic director of the Royal Court Theatre from 1972–75. His films include *Saturday Night and Sunday Morning 1960, Murder on the Orient Express* 1974, and *The Dresser*1984.

Finnish architecture little survives of the earliest Finnish architecture, which was built of timber. The oldest buildings are ecclesiastical, dating from the 15th century (Turku cathedral, Lohja church). Classically detailed wooden churches from the late 18th century by Jakob Rijf survive in northern and western Finland. The elegantly neo-Classical monumental centre to Helsinki, by the Prussian architect Carl Ludvig Engel, dates from the 1820s. A truly individual Finnish style emerged in the 1890s with architects such as Lars Sonck and the Saarinen – Gesellius – Lindgren practice (Eliel ◊Saarinen later gained an internation reputation in the United States), fusing the elastic lines of Art Nouveau with the chunkier outlines of vernacular architecture and using typically Finnish motifs such as pine cones, squirrels, bears and characters from legend. All this activity laid the foundation for the work of the modernist Alvar ◊Aalto, and for urban planning such as that of the visionary garden suburb of Tapiola,

outside Helsinki, built in the 1950s. Contemporary architecture includes the organic designs of Raimo and Raili Pietilaa – for instance, their Tampere City Library, opened 1987 – and Finland's first example of Postmodernism, the Yhtyneet Kuvalehdet (United Magazines) building in Helsinki, by Ilmo Valjakka, also opened 1987.

Finnish language a member of the Finno-Ugric language family, the national language of Finland and closely related to neighbouring

Estonian, Livonian, Karelian and Ingrian languages. At the beginning of the 19th century Finnish had no official status, Swedish being the language of education, government and literature in Finland. The publication of the *Kalevala*, a national epic poem, in 1835, contributed greatly to the arousal of Finnish national and linguistic feeling.

Finnish literature some fragments in Finnish literature survive from the 12th century; the first book was an ABC published 1544. A complete Bible in Finnish was issued at Stockholm 1642. But the predominance of Swedish in Finland inhibited the growth of Finnish literature until the 19th century, when it was launched with the publication in 1835 of Elias Lönnrot's epic folk verse compilation *Kalevala*. The earliest Finnish writer was Aleksis Kivi, whose comedy *Seitsemän veljestä/Seven brothers* was published in 1870. The turn of the century saw a crop of realist writers, including Juhani Aho (1861–1921), Ilmari Kianto (1874–1970), and Joel Lehtonen (1881–1943), and the lyric poet Eino Leino (1878–1926). Mika Waltari (1908–79) has attracted the greatest attention abroad with his *Sinuhe egyptiläinen/Sinuhe the Egyptian*. Frans Emil Sillanpää (1888–1964) received a Nobel prize in 1939. Väinö Linna's *Tuntematon sotilas/The Unknown Soldier* is the definitive account of the Winter War of 1939. Modern writers include the poets Pentti Saarikoski (1937–83) and Paavo Haavikko (1931–), and the novelists Veijo Meri (born 1928), Antti Tuuri (1944–), and Leena Krohn (1947–).

Finnish music besides folk music and compositions by foreign musicians living in Finland, there was little Finnish music until the generation of Jean ◊Sibelius. His contemporaries include Toivo Kuula (1883–1918), composer of darkly passionate solo songs; the orchestral composer Uuno Klami (1900–1961); Selim Palmgren (1878–1951), who produced sparkling, Debussy-like piano music; and the modernist Leevi Madetoja, whose neglected opera *Juha* was revived at the 1987 Edinburgh Festival. In modern Finnish music opera dominates, with works such as Joonas Kokkonen's *Viimeiset kiusaukset/The Last Temptations*, dealing with the first universal suffrage elections in Finland in 1907, and Aulis Sallinen's popular *Punainen viiva/The Red Line* and his abstruse *The King Goes forth to France*, premiered at Covent Garden, London, in 1987. Younger composers include the rigorously intellectual Paavo Heininen and Magnus Lindberg.

Finn Mac Cumhaill /'fin mə'ku:l/ legendary Irish hero, identified with a general who organized an Irish regular army in the mid-3rd century. James Macpherson (1736–96) featured him (as Fingal) and his followers in the verse of his popular epics 1762–63, which were supposedly written by a 3rd-century bard, Ossian. Although challenged by the critic Dr Johnson, the poems were influential in the Romantic movement. ◊Fingal's Cave in the Hebrides was fancifully linked with him.

Finno-Ugric a group or family of more than 20 languages spoken by some 22 million people in scattered communities from Norway in the W to Siberia in the E and to the Carpathian mountains in the S. Speakers of these languages tend to live in enclaves surrounded by Germanic, Slavonic and Turkish speakers, all of whom exercise influence upon the local Finno-Ugric varieties. The best-known members of the family are Finnish, Lapp, and Hungarian.

Finsen /'fɪnsən/ Niels Ryberg 1860–1904. Danish physician, the first to use ultraviolet light treatment for skin diseases; Nobel prize for medicine 1903.

Finsteraarhorn the highest mountain, 4,725 m/14,020 ft, in the Bernese Alps, Switzerland.

fiord /fiː'ɔːd/ alternative spelling of ◊fjord.

fir general term applied to ◊conifers, but correctly applied only to a few species, such as *silver fir Abies alba*, which may produced dense growths of small branches, 'witches' brooms', after attack by ◊rust fungi; other *Abies* species; and the *Douglas fir Pseudotsuga menziesii*. *Canada balsam* is the resin obtained from certain N American species.

Firbank /'fɜːbæŋk/ Ronald 1886–1926. English novelist. His work, set in the Edwardian decadent period, has a malicious humour, and includes *Caprice* 1916, *Valmouth* 1918, and the posthumous *Concerning the Eccentricities of Cardinal Pirelli* 1926.

Firdawsî /fɪəˈdausi/ Abdul Qasim Mansur c. 935–c./1020. Persian poet, whose epic *Shahnama/The Book of Kings* relates the history of Persia in 60,000 verses. Among other episodes, it tells how Rustum unwittingly killed his son Sohrab in battle; this was used by Matthew ◊Arnold in his poem 'Sohrab and Rustum'.

firearm a weapon from which missiles are discharged by the combustion of an explosive. Firearms are classified in two groups: ◊artillery, (ordnance or cannon) which have a bore greater than 2.54 cm/1 in, and small ◊arms, with a bore of less than 2.54 cm/1 in. Although gunpowder was known 60 years previously, the invention of guns dates from 1300–25, and is attributed to Berthold Schwartz, a German monk.

firebrat insect of the order Thysanura (◊bristletail).

fireclay a clay that is resistant to very high temperatures, and is therefore suitable for lining furnaces. Its refractory characteristics are due to its chemical composition, which contains a high percentage of silica and alumina and a low percentage of oxides of sodium, potassium, iron, and calcium. Fireclays underlie the coal seams in the British Isles.

firedamp a gas which occurs in coal-mines and is explosive when mixed with air in certain proportions. It consists chiefly of methane CH_4 (natural gas or marsh gas) but always contains small quantities of other gases, such as nitrogen, carbon dioxide and hydrogen, and sometimes ethane and carbon monoxide.

fire extinguisher a device for putting out a fire. Many domestic extinguishers contain liquid carbon dioxide under pressure. When the handle is pressed, carbon dioxide is released as a gas which blankets the burning material and prevents oxygen reaching it. Other dry extinguishers spray powder, which then releases carbon dioxide gas. Wet extinguishers are often of the soda-acid type. When activated, sulphuric acid mixes with sodium bicarbonate, producing carbon dioxide. The gas pressure forces the solution out of a nozzle. A foaming agent may be added to produce foam.

firefly winged nocturnal ◊beetle which emits light.

Firenze /fɪˈrentseɪ/ Italian form of ◊Florence, a city in Italy.

fire protection methods available for fighting fires. They have always depended on a combination of public service and private enterprise. In Britain, Acts of 1707 and 1774 required every parish to provide engines (horse-drawn), hoses and ladders, but insurance companies established their own more efficient brigades for the benefit of buildings bearing their own firemarks. The latter amalgamated in the 19th century to form the basis of the present-day service which is run by the local authorities who co-operate closely: experimentation in new methods is carried out at the Fire Research Station at Boreham Wood, in Hertfordshire. Similar services operate in other countries. Since early detection enhances the chance of success, a valuable method of protection for industrial and commercial buildings is by automatic sprinkler system: heat or smoke opens the sprinkler heads on a network of water pipes and immediately sprays the seat of the fire. In certain circumstances water is ineffective and may be dangerous, for example, for oil and petrol storage tank fires, foam systems are used; for plant containing inflammable vapours, carbon dioxide is used; where electricity is involved, vaporizing liquids create a non-inflammable barrier; and for some chemicals only varoius dry powders can be used. Fire-resistant materials are also increasingly used in building construction. Forest fires and oilwell fires are among the worst disasters, the latter often being tackled by international specialists.

Firestone /'faɪəstəun/ Shulamith 1945– . Canadian feminist writer, whose book *The Dialectic of Sex* 1970 had a great influence on feminist thought in the early 1970s. She was also one of the most influential early organizers of the Women's Liberation Movement in the USA.

firework a device for producing a display of coloured lights (and sometimes also noises) by burning chemicals. A firework consists of a container or 'case', usually cylindrical in shape and of rolled paper, enclosing a mixture capable of burning independently of the oxygen of the air, since it includes an ingredient holding a supply of oxygen which it readily gives up to the other burnable ingredients. Fireworks are particularly popular in China, where they originated, and Japan. In Britain they are traditionally used on 5 Nov, Guy Fawkes' Night, and in the USA on 4 Jul, Independence Day. The art of firework-making is called pyrotechny.

firmware a computer program held permanently in the machine in ◊ROM (read-only memory) chips. So called because a piece of normally ephemeral ◊software resident permanently in a piece of ◊hardware needed a special name.

first aid action taken immediately after an accident in order to save the life of a victim, prevent further damage, or facilitate later treatment. A practicable technique is taught by the Red Cross and the Order of St John of Jerusalem.

First World War See ◊World War I.

fiscal policy the range of measures by which government revenue is raised (notably by taxation) and the priorities and purposes governing its expenditure. Post-war British governments have customarily made frequent adjustments to fiscal policy in order to regulate the level of economic activity. However, since 1979 the Conservative administration has placed greater emphasis on ◊monetary policy (control of the money supply).

fiscal year UK government term for the financial year, running from 6 Apr in one year to 5 Apr in the following year. In the USA, the fiscal year runs from 1 Jul to 30 Jun.

Fischer /'fɪʃə/ Emil 1852–1919. German chemist. Working with Julius Tufel, he produced synthetic sugars and from these the various enzymes. He was a pioneer biochemist and received a Nobel prize in 1902.

Fischer /'fɪʃə/ Hans 1881–1945. German chemist who received the Nobel Prize for Chemistry in 1930 for his discovery of haemoglobin in blood.

Fischer-Dieskau /'fɪʃə 'diːskau/ Dietrich 1925– . German baritone and conductor, particularly noted for his interpretation of Schubert songs.

fish aquatic vertebrate which breathes using gills. There are three main groups, not very closely related: the jawless fishes; the sharks and rays; and the bony fishes. In the latter, the majority of living fishes (about 20,000 species), the skeleton is bone, movement is controlled by mobile fins, and the body is usually covered with scales. The gills are covered by a single flap. Many have a swim bladder which the fish uses to adjust its buoyancy. Most lay eggs, sometimes in vast numbers. The ◊ling can produce as many as 28,000,000. Those species that produce small numbers of eggs very often protect them in nests, by brooding them in their mouths and so on. Some fishes are internally fertilized and retain eggs until hatching inside the body, so giving birth to live young. Most living bony fishes, from goldfish to cod and tuna, are rayfinned fishes. A few, including the lungfish and coelacanth, are fleshy-finned, belonging to groups whose heyday was in the geological past, but which gave rise to the land vertebrates. The cartilaginous fishes include the sharks and rays. The former in particular retain an ancient type of body plan, but are still efficient hunters. There are fewer than 600 known species of cartilaginous fishes. The skeleton is cartilage, the mouth is generally beneath the head, the nose is large and sensitive, and there is a series of gill slits along the neck region. They may lay eggs ('mermaid's purses') or bear live young. Jawless 'fishes' include hagfishes and lampreys, and have a body plan like that of some of the earliest vertebrates that existed before true fishes evolved. There is no true backbone but a ◊notochord. The lamprey attaches itself to fishes on which it feeds by a sucker-like rasping mouth. Hagfishes are entirely marine, that is, they live in the sea. They are very slimy, and feed on carrion and injured fishes.

FISH CLASSIFICATION

Class Agnatha	JAWLESS FISHES	
	Order Petromyzoniformes	Lampreys *30*
	Order Myxiniformes	Hagfishes *15*
Class Chondrichthyes	CARTILAGINOUS FISHES	
	1 Elasmobranchii (Sharks and rays)	
	Order Hexanchiformes	Frilled shark, comb-toothed shark
	Order Heterodontiformes	Port Jackson sharks *10*
	Order Lamniformes	'Typical' sharks *200*
	Order Rajiformes	Skates, rays *300*
	2 Holocephali (Rabbitfishes)	
	Order Chimaeriformes	Chimaeras, rabbitfishes *20*
Class Osteichthyes	BONY FISHES	
	1 Sarcopterygii (Fleshy-finned fishes)	
1 COELACANTHS	Order Coelacanthiformes	Coelacanth *1*
2 LUNGFISHES	Order Ceratodontiformes	Australian lungfish *1*
	Order Lepidosireniformes	S American and African lungfish *4*
	2 Actinopterygii (Ray-finned fishes)	
1 CHONDROSTEANS	Order Polypteriformes	Bichirs and reedfish *11*
	Order Acipenseriformes	Paddlefish and sturgeons *25*
2 HOLOSTEANS	Order Amiiformes	Bowfin and garpikes *8*
3 TELEOSTS	Order Elopiformes	Tarpons and tenpounders *12*
	Order Anguilliformes	Eels *300*
	Order Notacanthiformes	Spiny eels *20*
	Order Clupeiformes	Herrings and anchovies *350*
	Order Osteoglossiformes	Arapaima, African butterfly fish *16*
	Order Mormyriformes	Elephant-trunk fishes, featherbacks *150*
	Order Salmoniformes	Salmon, trout, smelt, pike *500*
	Order Gonorhynchiformes	Milkfish *15*
	Order Cypriniformes	Carp, barbs, characins, loaches *350*
	Order Siluriformes	Catfishes *200*
	Order Myctophiformes	Deep-sea lantern-fishes, Bombay ducks *300*
	Order Percopsiformes	Pirate perches, cave dwelling amblyopsids *10*
	Order Batrachoidiformes	Toadfishes *10*
	Order Gobiesociformes	Clingfishes *100*
	Order Lophiiformes	Anglerfishes *150*
	Order Gadiformes	Cod, pollack, pearl-fishes, eelpout *450*
	Order Atheriniformes	Flying fishes, toothcarps, halfbeaks *600*
	Order Lampridiformes	Opah, ribbon-fishes *50*
	Order Beryciformes	Squirrel-fishes *150*
	Order Zeiformes	John Dory, boarfish *60*
	Order Gasterosteiformes	Sticklebacks, pipefishes, seahorses *150*
	Order Channiformes	Snakeheads *5*
	Order Synbranchiformes	Cuchia *7*
	Order Scorpaeniformes	Gurnards, miller's thumb, stonefish *700*
	Order Dactylopteriformes	Flying gurnard *6*
	Order Pegasiformes	Sea-moths *4*
	Order Pleuronectiformes	Flatfishes *500*
	Order Tetraodontiformes	Puffer fishes, trigger fishes, sun fish *250*
	Order Perciformes	Perches, cichlids, damsel fishes, gobies, wrasses, parrot-fishes, gouramis, marlin, mackerel, tunny, sword-fish, spiny eels, mullets, barracudas, sea bream, croakers, ice fishes and butter-fishes *6500*

numbers of living species in italic; e.g. Lampreys *30*

he went to Australia in 1885, and entered the Australian parliament in 1901. He was prime minister in 1908, 1910–13, and 1914–15, and then Australian High Commissioner in London until 1921.

Fisher /'fɪʃə/ John Arbuthnot, 1st Baron Fisher 1841–1920. British admiral. Joining the navy in 1854, he served in the Crimean War, held various commands and was First Sea Lord

1904–10, when he carried out many radical reforms and innovations, including the introduction of the Dreadnought battleship. He returned to the post in 1914, but resigned in the following year, disagreeing with Churchill over the invasion of the ◊Dardanelles.

Fisher /'fɪʃə/ John, St c. 1469–1535. English bishop. Born at Beverley, he was created Bishop of Rochester in 1504, and was an enthusiastic supporter of the revival in the study in Greek, and a friend of ◊More and ◊Erasmus. In 1535 he was tried on a charge of denying the royal supremacy and beheaded. Together with More he was canonized in 1935.

fish farming also called *aquaculture* raising fish under controlled conditions in tanks and ponds, sometimes in offshore pens. It has been practised for centuries in the Far East, where Japan alone produces some 100,000 tonnes of fish a year. In the 1980s one tenth of the world's fish requirements (either for the table or restocking) were farmed, notably trout and Atlantic salmon, turbot, eel; and the shellfish, mussels and oysters.

Fishguard /'fɪʃgɑːd/ seaport on an inlet on the S side of Fishguard Bay, Dyfed, Wales; population (1981) 5,000. There is a ferry service to Rosslare in the Republic of Ireland.

fishing the catching of fish. The greatest proportion of the world's catch comes from the oceans (marine fishing). The primary production area is the photic zone, the relatively thin surface layer (50 m/166 ft) of water that can be penetrated by light, allowing photosynthesis by plant ◊plankton to take place. Nutrients in this layer are constantly both depleted, as dead plankton sinks to the bottom, and enriched by deeper waters welling up to the surface.

Plankton-eating fish tend to be small in size, and include herrings, pilchards and sardines. As plankton is plentiful, these are too, and form the basis of substantial fisheries. Herring travel in immense schools several kilometres long and wide. Demersal fishes, such as haddock, halibut and cod, live primarily near the ocean floor. They feed on various invertebrate marine animals and are caught by trawling. Pelagic fish, such as herring and tuna, live in the open sea, near the surface, and purse seine nets are used to catch them.

Freshwater fishing is carried out on a large scale for such fish as salmon, trout, carp, eel, whitefish, pike, perch and catfish. These inhabit ponds, lakes, rivers or swamps, and some species have been successfully cultivated (◊fish farming). Carp and eel have traditionally been raised in rice fields.

Fish populations may be increased by stocking from hatcheries, or reduced to increase the size of the remaining fish. Line fishing, seine nets and lift nets are the most common commercial methods used. Fisheries can be classified by (1) type of water: Freshwater – lake, river, pond; Ocean – inshore, midwater, deep sea, (2) by catch: for example salmon fishing, (3) by the particular method used to catch the fish – diving, fish poisoning, harpooning, trawling, drifting, and so on.

fish

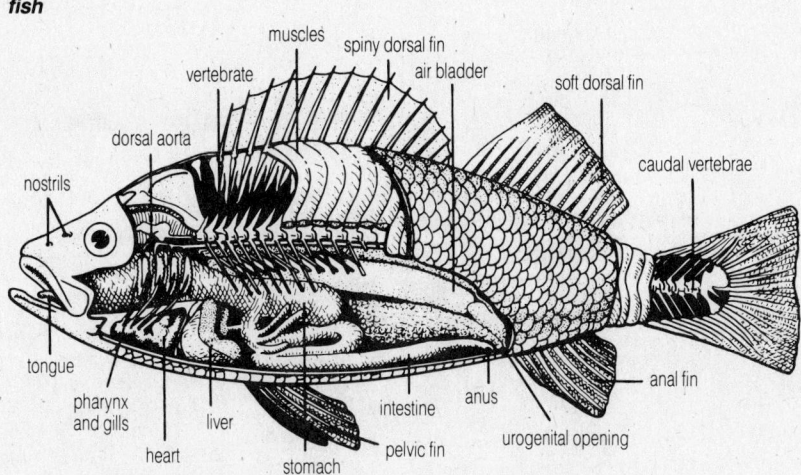

The increasing demand for fish as food has led to the development of improved marketing organizations for the catches, and of powerful ships with special refrigerating equipment, or fish-factory ships which enable filleting and processing, to be done at sea, designed to exploit the deep-water resources out of reach of the smaller, older-type boats. Japan (where fish is a mainstay of the diet) has evolved new techniques for locating shoals (for example, sonar and radar methods) and catching them (for example, electrical charges and chemical baits); and the North Sea countries have experimented less successfully with the artificial breeding of fish eggs and release of small fry into the sea. The future seems to lie with intensive breeding and farming in controlled areas for high quality fish. Over-fishing had by the later 20th century led to serious depletion of stocks, for example, off British coasts by continental trawlers using methods designed to take all fish, even immature

Fisher John Fisher, bishop of Rochester, was beheaded in 1535 for denying the royal supremacy. The portrait is after a painting by Hans Holbein (c. 1528).

specimens, and in the case of Iceland competition for the remaining catch led to 'Cod wars'. A partial solution was the extension of fishing limits to 320 km/200 mi.

Ancillary industries include net manufacture, oil, fishmeal (nearly one-quarter of fish caught annually are turned into meal for animal feed), pet food, glue, manure, and drugs such as insulin and other pharmaceutical products.

fission in physics, the splitting of the atomic nucleus. See ◊nuclear fission.

fitness in ◊genetic theory, a measure of the success with which a genetically determined character can spread in future generations. By convention, the normal character is assigned a fitness of one and variants (determined by other ◊alleles) are then assigned fitness values relative to this. Those with fitness greater than one will spread more rapidly and ultimately replace the normal allele; those with fitness less than one will gradually die out. See also ◊inclusive fitness.

Fitzgerald /fɪts'dʒerəld/ Edward 1809–1883. British poet and translator, born in Suffolk. In 1859 he published his poetic version of the *Rubaiyat of Omar Khayyam*, which is generally considered less a translation than an original creation.

Fitzgerald /fɪts'dʒerəld/ Ella 1918– . US jazz singer, recognized as one of the greatest voices of jazz, both in solo work and with big bands. She is noted for her interpretations of Gershwin and Cole Porter songs.

Fitzgerald /fɪts'dʒerəld/ F(rancis) Scott (Key) 1896–1940. American novelist, born in Minnesota. *This Side of Paradise* 1920 reflected his experiences at Princeton and made him known in the bright postwar society of the east. In *The Great Gatsby* 1925, which epitomizes the jazz age, the narrator resembles his author, and Gatsby, the self-made millionaire, is lost in the soulless 'society' he enters. His wife Zelda Sayre (1900–47), a schizophrenic, entered an asylum in 1930. Her descent into madness forms the subject of *Tender is the Night* 1934.

FitzGerald /fɪts'dʒerəld/ Garret 1926– . Irish politician. As *Taoiseach* (prime minister)

1981–82 and again 1982–86, he was noted for his attempts to solve the Northern Ireland dispute, ultimately by participating in the Anglo-Irish agreement 1985. He tried to remove some of the overtly Catholic features of the constitution to make the Republic more attractive to nothern Protestants. He retired as leader of the Fine Gael Party in 1987.

Fitzherbert /fɪts'hɑːbət/ Maria Anne 1756–1837. Morganatic wife of the Prince of Wales, later George IV. She became Mrs Fitzherbert by her second marriage in 1778 and, after her husband's death in 1781, entered London society. She secretly married the Prince of Wales in 1785, and finally parted from him in 1803. Henceforward she lived in retirement in Brighton.

Fitzroy /'fɪtsrɔɪ/ Robert 1805–1865. British vice admiral and meteorologist, born in Suffolk. He entered the navy in 1819, and in 1828 succeeded to the command of HMS *Beagle*, then engaged on a survey of the Patagonian coast, and in 1831 was accompanied by Charles Darwin on a five-year survey. In 1843–45 he was governor of New Zealand.

fives a game resembling squash played by two or four players in a court enclosed on three or four sides: the ball is struck with the hand. It dates from the 14th century, and was probably derived from the French *jeu de paume*. The name fives may refer to the five fingers, or to there originally being five players, who had to make five points to win. In Britain the game is practically confined to public schools and colleges, and there are three main forms, namely, Eton fives, Rugby fives, and Winchester Fives.

Five-Year Plan an economic plan for an extended period with specific targets. From 1928 the basis of economic planning in the USSR, aimed particularly at developing heavy and light industry in a primarily agricultural country, the idea has been adopted by other Eastern bloc countries, and also in the West, to increase agricultural as well as industrial production.

fjord or fiord name given to narrow sea inlets in Norway, enclosed by high cliffs, and now to similar formations elsewhere. *Fiordland* is the deeply indented SW coast of South Island, New Zealand: one of the most magnificent inlets is Milford Sound.

flag a piece of cloth used as an emblem or symbol, since ancient times, for religious, nationalistic, or military displays or as a means of signalling.

The British national flag, the Union Jack, unites the crosses of St George, St Andrew, and St Patrick, representing England, Scotland, and Ireland; the merchant flag places the national flag in the canton of a red flag; similarly placed on a large St George's Cross it becomes the distinguishing flag of the Royal Navy. The Stars and Stripes, 'Old Glory', is the flag of the United States; the 50 stars represent the 50 states now in the union, the 13 stripes the 13 original states. The flag of the USSR places the crossed hammer and sickle, representing the workers of town and country, on the red flag, the emblem of revolution. The flags of the Scandinavian countries bear crosses; the Danish 'Dannebrog'

drag net

trawl net

fishing

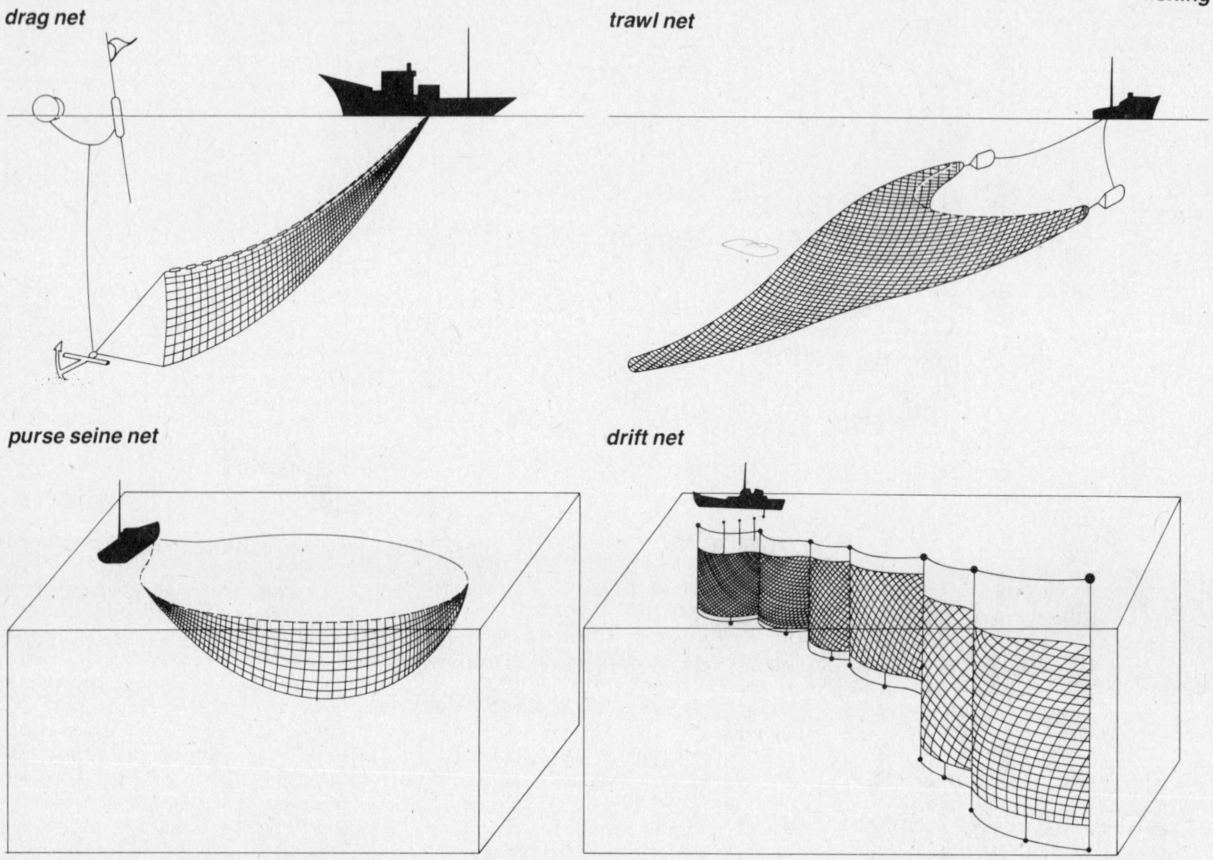

purse seine net

drift net

Fitzgerald American novelist F Scott Fitzgerald and his wife Zelda on their honeymoon.

(strength of Denmark) is the oldest national flag, used for 700 years. The Red Cross originated in Switzerland, and its emblem is the Swiss flag with its colours reversed. Muslim states often incorporate in their flags the crescent emblem of Islam and the colour green, also associated with their faith.

The flags of Australia and New Zealand both incorporate the Union Jack, together with symbols of the Southern Cross constellation. The Canadian flag has a maple leaf design.

A flag is flown upside down as a signal of distress; is dipped as a salute; and when flown a little below the masthead is a sign of mourning. The 'Blue Peter', blue with a white centre, announces that

a vessel is about to sail; a flag half red and half white that a pilot is on board.

The British royal standard combines the emblems of England, Scotland, and Ireland; the United States presidential standard displays the American eagle, surrounded by 50 stars.

flag in botany, plant of the *Iris* genus; *yellow flag Iris pseudacorus* which grows in damp places and in marshes in Britain and throughout Europe. It has a thick rhizome, from which arise stiff, blade-like monocotyledonous leaves, and stems up to 150 cm/5 ft high. The flowers are large and yellow. Cultivated varieties include the purple garden flag.

flagellant a religious fanatic who uses a whip as a means of self-discipline and penance. Flagellation is known in many religions from ancient times, and there were notable outbreaks of this type of extremist devotion in Christian Europe in the 11th–16th centuries.

flagellum a small hair-like organ on the surface of certain cells. Flagella are the motile organs of certain ◊protozoa and single-celled algae, and of the ◊sperm cells of higher animals. Water movement inside sponges is also produced by flagella. Each flagellum consists of contractile filaments producing snake-like movements which propel cells through fluids, or fluids past cells. Unlike ◊cilia, flagella usually occur single or in pairs; they are also longer and have a more

complex whip-like action. Some ◊bacteria have flagella which, although superficially similar to the flagella of other cells, are simpler in construction with an entirely different form of movement.

flag of convenience a flag flown by a ship registered in a country not its own in order to avoid legal or tax commitments. Applied especially to the merchant fleets of Liberia and Panama; ships registered in these countries avoid legislation governing employment of seamen and minimum rates of pay, for example.

Flagstad /'flægstæd/ Kirsten (Malfrid) 1895–1962. Norwegian soprano, who specialized in Wagnerian opera.

Flaherty /'flɑːəti/ Robert 1884–1951. American film director, born in Michigan. He exerted great influence by his pioneer documentary of (Eskimo) life *Nanook of the North* 1920. Later films include *Man of Aran* 1934, and *Elephant Boy* 1937.

flamboyant in ◊architecture, term applied to the late Gothic style of French architecture, contemporary with the ◊Perpendicular style in England. It is characterized by flame-like decorative work in windows, balustrades, and other projecting features.

flamen a sacrificial priest in ancient Rome. The office was held for life, but was terminated by the death of the flamen's wife (who assisted him at ceremonies) or by some misdeamour. At first there were three flamens, but another 12 were later added.

flame tree smooth-stemmed semi-deciduous tree *Sterculia acerifolia* with red/orange flowers, native to Australia, but spread throughout the tropics.

flamingo long-legged and long-necked wading bird, family Phoenicopteridae, of the stork order Ciconiiformes, and having some features in common with the waterfowl. Largest of the family is the **greater** or **roseate flamingo** *Phoenicopterus ruber*, of both Africa and South America, with delicate pink plumage, and 1.25 m/4 ft high. They sift the mud for food with their downbent bills, and build colonies of high, conelike mud nests, with a little hollow for the eggs at the top.

Flaminius /flə'mɪnɪəs/ Gaius died 217 BC. Roman consul and general. He constructed the Flaminian Way northward from Rome to Rimini 220 BC, and was killed at the battle of Lake Trasimene fighting ◊Hannibal.

Flamsteed /'flæmstiːd/ John 1646–1719. First Astronomer Royal of England. Born near Derby, he was appointed astronomer to Charles II in 1675, and began systematic observations of the positions of the stars, Moon, and planets at Greenwich in the following year. His observations were posthumously published in 1725.

Flamsteed After petitioning Charles II for a national observatory, John Flamsteed, a painstaking perfectionist, was made the first Astronomer Royal in 1675.

Flanagan /'flænəgən/ Bud. Stage name of British comedian Robert Winthrop 1896–1968. Leader of the 'Crazy Gang' (1931–62), he also played in variety all over the world and, with his partner Chesney Allen, popularized such songs as 'Underneath the Arches'.

Flanders /'flɑːndəz/ a region of the Low Countries which in the 8th and 9th centuries extended from Calais to the Scheldt, and is now covered by the Belgian provinces of Oost Vlaanderen and West Vlaanderen (E and W

Flanders), the French department of Nord, and part of the Dutch province of Zeeland. The language is ◊Flemish.

flare, solar a brilliant eruption on the Sun above a ◊sunspot, thought to be caused by release of magnetic energy. Flares reach maximum brightness within a few minutes , then fade away over an hour or so. They eject a burst of atomic particles into space at up to 1,000 km/600 mi per second. When these particles reach Earth they can cause radio blackouts, disruptions of the Earth's ◊magnetic field, and ◊aurorae; they may endanger the health of astronauts in space.

flash point in physics, the temperature at which a liquid heated under standard conditions gives off sufficient vapour to ignite on the application of a small flame. Flash point tests are carried out with the Pensky-◊Martens instrument. The fire point of the material itself is obtained by continuing the test and noting the temperature at which full combustion occurs. For safe storage (of fuel, or oil) the flash and fire points must be high enough to reduce fire risks to a minimum, and such that no appreciable quantity of oils are driven off during exposure to the weather.

flatfish bony fish of order Pleuronectiformes having a characteristically flat, asymmetrical body with both eyes (in adults) on the upper side. Species include turbot, halibut, plaice, sole, and flounder.

flatworm invertebrate of the phylum Platyhelminthes. Some are free-living, but many are parasitic – the tapeworms and flukes. The body is simple and bilaterally symmetrical. The gut has a mouth but no anus or, in tapeworms, is absent. Many are hermaphrodite (male and female), with complex sex organs, the parasitic forms producing large numbers of eggs.

Flaubert /fləʊ'beə/ Gustave 1821–1880. French novelist, born in Rouen. He entered Paris literary circles in 1840, but in 1846 retired to Rouen, where he remained for the rest of his life. His masterpiece *Madame Bovary* appeared in 1857 and aroused much controversy by its portrayal of the wife of a country doctor, driven to suicide by a series of unhappy love affairs. *Salammbô* 1862 earned him the Legion of Honour in 1866, and was followed by *L'Education sentimentale/Sentimental Education* 1869, and *La Tentation de Saint Antoine/The Temptation of St Anthony* 1874. Flaubert established himself as the master of the short story by his *Trois Contes/Three Tales* 1877.

flax plant of the family Linaceae which yields valuable commercial products. The common flax or linseed plant *Linum usitatissimum* is of almost worldwide distribution. It has a stem up to 60 cm/2 ft high, bearing small leaves and bright blue flowers. The seeds yield **linseed oil** used in paints and varnishes, the residue being fed to cattle; the stems are steeped in water to separate out the long fibres, which are then spun into **linen** thread, twice as strong, yet more delicate than cotton, and especially suitable for lace; shorter ones make twine or paper. The USSR, Belgium, Netherlands, and N Ireland, where cultivation has recently been revived, are producers. The

Flaubert French novelist Gustave Flaubert. His masterpiece *Madame Bovary* caused considerable controversy when it first appeared because of the its subject, adultery. The publicity arising out of an attempt to have it banned ensured the novel's success.

New Zealand flax *Phormium tenax*, is unrelated to the true flax. It belongs to the Liliaceae, and is commercially grown for the fibre in its sword-shaped leaves which may be 2 m/6 ft long.

flax The flax harvest at Courtrai in Belgium. Flax yields valuable commercial products, such as linseed oil, used in paints and varnishes, and linen thread.

Flaxman /'flæksmən/ John 1755–1826. British sculptor, born at York. He studied at the Royal Academy in London and for 12 years was employed by Wedgwood as a designer. He became a Royal Academician in 1800, and in 1810 he was appointed first professor of sculpture. His best-known works include the portrait sculptures of Reynolds in St Paul's Cathedral, London, and of Burns and Kemble in Westminster Abbey.

flea wingless insect, order Siphonaptera, with blood-sucking mouthparts. Fleas are parasitic on warm-blooded animals, and leave when the host dies. Species include *Pulex irritans*, which lives on humans; the rat flea *Xenopsylla cheopsis*, the transmitter of plague and typhus; and (fostered by central heating) the cat and dog fleas *Ctenocephalides felis* and *canis*. Some fleas can jump 130 times their own height. Britain's largest flea *Histricopsylla talpae* lives on the mole and is about 8 mm/0.25 in long.

fleabane plant of the genera *Erigeron* or *Pulicaria* belonging to the Compositae family. Common fleabane *Pulicaria dysenterica*, with golden yellow flower-heads, is common in wet and marshy places throughout Britain.

Flecker /'flekə/ James Elroy 1884–1915. British poet. He entered the consular service, and went to Constantinople in 1910 and in 1911 to Smyrna. He published several volumes of verse, including *The Bridge of Fire* 1907, *The Golden Journey to Samarkand* 1913 and *The Old Ships* 1915. He also wrote the dramas *Don Juan* and *Hassan*, the latter performed in 1923 with incidental music by Delius.

Fleet Street /fliːt/ street in London, England (named after the subterranean river Fleet), traditionally the centre of British journalism. It runs from Temple Bar eastwards to Ludgate Circus. With adjoining streets it contained the offices and printing works of many leading British newspapers until the mid-1980s, when most moved to sites farther from the centre of London (for example, Times Newspapers in ◊Wapping).

Fleetwood /'fliːtwʊd/ port and seaside resort in Lancashire, England, at the mouth of the river Wyre; population (1981) 28,530.

Fleming /'flemɪŋ/ Alexander 1881–1955. British bacteriologist, discoverer in 1928 of the antibiotic drug ◊penicillin. He shared a Nobel prize 1945 with E B Chain and Sir Howard ◊Florey, who developed it for practical use. Knighted 1944.

Fleming /'flemɪŋ/ Ian 1908–1964. British author, creator of the secret agent James Bond. Son of an army officer, he was educated at Eton, Sandhurst, and Munich and Geneva universities. After a number of years with Reuters news agency, he worked successively with banking and stockbroking firms, and in World War II was personal assistant to the director of naval intelligence. From 1953 he became famous as the author of suspense novels featuring the ruthless, laconic 'James Bond', Secret Service agent, No. 007 – the prefix '00' meaning licensed to kill.

Fleming /'flemɪŋ/ John Ambrose 1849–1945. British electrical physicist and engineer, who invented the thermionic valve (1904).

Fleming's rules a way of remembering on the fingers of one's hands the relation between the directions of the magnetic field, current and motion in an electric generator or motor. The three directions are represented by the thuMb (for Motion), Forefinger (for magnetic Field) and seCond finger (Current), all held at right angles to each other. The right-hand rule – using one's right hand – applies to generators, such as a dynamo, and the left-hand rule applies to

motors. They were named after the British physicist John ◊Fleming.

Flemish /'flemɪʃ/ a branch of the West Germanic division of the ◊Germanic languages, spoken in the northern half of Belgium and in the Nord *département* of France. In opposition to the introduction of French as the official language in the Flemish provinces of Belgium after 1830 there arose a strong Flemish movement, led by scholars like J F Willems (1793–1846) and writers such as H Conscience (1812–83), and although equality of French and Flemish was not achieved until 1898, it brought about a cultural and political revival of Flemish. The Flemish movement was promoted for political reasons by the Germans in both world wars, and by the 1970s had become a threat to Belgian unity. The great figures of Flemish literature are the poet Guido Gezelle, and the novelists Cyriel Buysse, Stijn Streuvels, and Felix Timmermanns.

Flemish art the style of painting developed and practised in ◊Flanders (Belgium) from the 14th to the 17th century and distinguished by colourful realism, keen observation, and masterful technique. Hubert and Jan van ◊Eyck made Bruges the first centre of Flemish art; other schools arose in Tournai, Ghent, and Louvain. The great names of the early period were Rogier van der ◊Weyden, Dierick ◊Bouts, Hugo van der ◊Goes, Hans ◊Memling, and Gheerardt ◊David. In the 16th century Italian influences were felt, and the centre shifted to Antwerp, where Quinten ◊Matsys worked. Hieronymus ◊Bosch painted creatures of his own wild imagination, but the pictures of Pieter ◊Brueghel are faithful reflections of Flemish life. The Italian influence was strong in ◊Mabuse, Jan Massys, and others. In the 17th century Peter Paul ◊Rubens and his school created a new powerful style, continued by van ◊Dyck, ◊Jordaens, and others, while ◊Brouwer and ◊Teniers kept up the earlier tradition.

Flemish literature Flemish literature in Belgium, in its written form the same as Dutch, was stimulated by the declaration following the revolution of 1830–39, that French was the only official language (it remained so until 1898). J F Willems (1793–1846) brought out a magazine which revived medieval Flemish works; H Conscience (1812–83) and J T van Ryswyck (1811–49) published novels in Flemish; K L Ledeganck (1805–47), Prudens van Duyse (1804–59), and Jan de Beers (1821–88) wrote poetry. Later writers include Albrecht Rodenbach (1856–80), Pol de Mont (1857–1931), and Cyriel Buysse (1859–1932).

Fletcher /'fletʃə/ John 1579–1625. English dramatist. Of the 50 plays once attributed to his partnership with ◊Beaumont, only seven are now generally recognized as being the result of their collaboration, most notably *Philaster* 1609 and *The Maid's Tragedy* 1610–11. The remainder are divided between Fletcher and collaborators such as Massinger, and he is alleged to have collaborated with Shakespeare on *The Two Noble Kinsmen* and *Henry VIII* in 1612. Among those credited to Fletcher alone are the pastoral drama *The Faithful Shepherdess* 1610, the

tragedy *Bonduca* c. 1614, and *Rule a Wife and Have a Wife* c. 1624.

fleur-de-lis (French 'flower of the lily') heraldic device in the form of a stylized iris flower borne on coats of arms since the 12th century and adopted by the ◊Bourbons.

flight people first took to the air in ◊balloons and began powered flight in ◊airships. But the history of flying is dominated by the ◊aeroplane. The aeroplane is a development of the model glider, first flown by Sir George Cayley (1773–1857) in 1804. But not until the invention of the petrol engine did powered flight become feasible. The ◊Wright brothers of the USA first achieved success, when they flew their biplane *Flyer* on 17 Dec 1903. In Europe, inspired by the Wrights, France led in aeroplane design (Voisin brothers) and Louis Blériot brought aviation much publicity by crossing the Channel in 1909, as did the Reims air races of that year. The first powered flight in England was made by S F Cody in 1908. In 1912 Sopwith and Bristol both built small biplanes. The first big twin-engined aeroplane was the Handley Page bomber in 1917. The stimulus of World War I and rapid development of the petrol engine led to increased power and speeds rose to 320 kph/200 mph. Streamlining the body of planes then became imperative: the body, wings, and exposed parts were reshaped to reduce drag. Eventually the biplane was superseded by the internally braced monoplane structure, for example, the Hawker Hurricane and Supermarine Spitfire fighters and Avro Lancaster and Boeing Flying Fortress bombers of World War II.
The flight of the German Heinkel 178 (1939) ushered in a new era in aviation. It was the first ◊jet plane, propelled, not as all planes before it with a ◊propeller, but by a jet of hot gases. The first British jet aircraft, the Gloster E.28/39 flew from Cranwell, Lincolnshire, on 15 May 1941, powered by a jet engine invented by Frank ◊Whittle. Twin-jet Meteor fighters were in use by the end of the war. The rapid development of the jet power plane led to enormous increases in power and speed until air-compressability effects were felt near the speed of sound, which at first seemed to be a flight speed limit (the sound barrier). To exceed sonic speed, simply streaming the aircraft body became insufficient, and wings were swept back, engines buried in wings and tail units, and even bodies were eliminated in all-wing, delta designs.
In the 1950s the first jet airliners, such as the Comet, were introduced into service. Today jet planes dominate both military and civilian aviation, although many light planes still use piston engines and propellers for propulsion. The late 1960s saw the introduction of the ◊jumbo jet and the ◊supersonic airliner, notably the Anglo-French ◊Concorde. The former paved the way for more economic air travel, while the latter brought to reality a transatlantic crossing in under three hours.
During the 1950s and 60s much research was done on V/STOL (vertical and/or short take-off) aircraft. The British Harrier jet fighter has been the only VTOL aircraft to achieve commercial success, but STOL technology has

Fleming Nobel-prizewinning British bacteriologist Alexander Fleming first discovered the antibiotic penicillin by chance in 1928, but had to wait 11 years until a method of producing the volatile drug had been perfected.

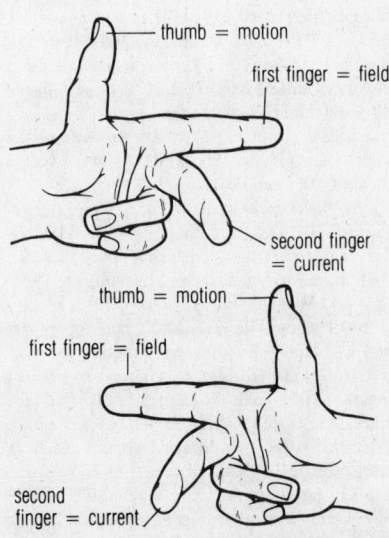

Fleming's rules

thumb = motion
first finger = field
second finger = current

thumb = motion
first finger = field
second finger = current

fed into subsequent generations of aircraft. The 1960s and 70s also saw the development of variable geometry ('swing-wing') aircraft, whose wings can be swept back in flight to achieve higher speeds. In the 1980s much progress has

been made in 'fly-by-wire' aircraft with computer aided controls.
Concorde has also demonstrated another aspect of the way ahead – the need for international partnerships to develop new aircraft. Other examples of partnerships include the *Panavia Tornado*, a joint project of British, German, and Italian aircraft companies. It is an advanced swing-wing craft of multiple roles – interception, strike, ground support, and reconnaissance. Another joint project is the Airbus, a wide-bodied airliner built by companies from France, Germany, Britain, the Netherlands, and Spain.

Flinders /ˈflɪndəz/ Matthew 1774–1814. British navigator, born in Lincolnshire. He joined the Navy in 1789, and explored the Australian coasts, 1795–99 and 1801–03. Named after him are *Flinders Island*, NE of Tasmania, Australia, in Bass Strait, area 2,080 sq km/800 sq mi; the *Flinders Range* in S Australia, which reaches 1,165 m/3,822 ft in St Mary Peak and has copper, lead and uranium; and *Flinders River* in Queensland, Australia, which rises in the Great Dividing Range and flows NW to the Gulf of Carpentaria 840 km/520 mi.

flint /flɪnt/ a compact, hard, brittle mineral, brown, black, or grey in colour, found in nodules in chalk deposits. It consists of fine-grained silica, SiO_2, compressed into a homogeneous mass. When broken, the nodule has a shell-like fracture

and a sharp cutting edge. Owing to their hardness, flint splinters are used for abrasive purposes and, when ground into powder, for pottery manufacture.
Flint implements made by chipping one flint against another were widely used by Palaeolithic and Neolithic people. The earliest flint implements, belonging to Palaeolithic cultures, are simple, while those of the Neolithic are more expertly cut, and often ground or polished. In historic times flints were used for making fire by striking the flint against steel, which produces a spark, and for discharging guns. Cigarette-lighter flints are made from cerium alloy.

Flintshire /ˈflɪntʃə/ former county of Wales, and smallest of the Welsh counties. It was merged in 1974, with Denbigh and part of Merioneth, into the new county of Clwyd: the county town of Mold became the administrative headquarters of the new region.

Flodden /ˈflɒdn/ battle site 5 km/3 mi SE of Coldstream, Northumberland, England where the Scots under James IV were defeated by the English under the Earl of Surrey 9 Sept 1513; Scots casualties, which included James, were heavy.

Flood, The in the Old Testament, disaster alleged in Genesis to have obliterated all humanity except a chosen few (see ◊Noah). It may represent memories of a major local flood, for example, excavations by ◊Woolley at ◊Ur in

flight The pioneer aviator Sam Cody came to England from America and experimented with flying devices and the first dirigibles. He built this aeroplane in 1908 and he and his passengers, who totalled 334.8 kg/738 lbs, flew at Aldershot at a height of 21.3 m/70 ft for about seven miles. He was killed in a flying accident three years later.

Flinders British navigator and explorer Captain Matthew Flinders. Most of his ventures were around the coast of Australia, where an island, a mountain range and a river are all named after him.

modern Iraq revealed 2.5 m/8 ft of water-laid clay dating before 4000 BC, over an area of about 645 km/400 mi by 160 km/100 mi.

Flora in Roman mythology, goddess of flowers, youth, and of spring. Festivals were held in her name.

floral diagram a diagram showing the arrangement and number of parts in a flower, drawn in cross-section. An ovary is drawn in the centre, surrounded by representations of the other floral parts, indicating the position of each at its base. If any parts such as the petals or sepals

are fused, this is also indicated. Floral diagrams allow the structure of different flowers to be compared, and are usually presented with the ◊floral formula.

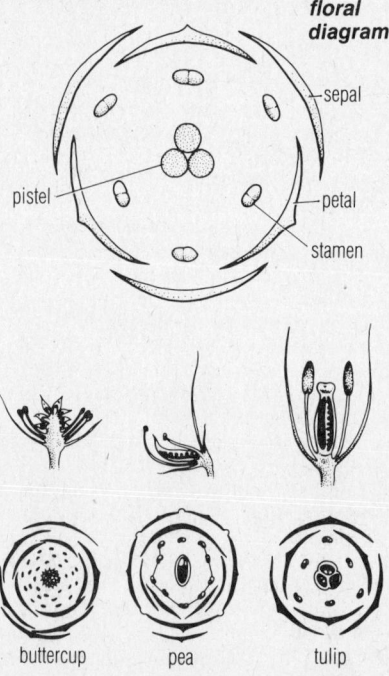

floral diagram

sepal
pistel
petal
stamen

buttercup   pea   tulip

floral formula a symbolic representation of the structure of a flower. Each kind of floral part is represented by a letter (K for ◊calyx, C for ◊corolla, P for ◊perianth, A for ◊androecium, G for ◊gynoecium), followed by a number to indicate the quantity of the part present, for example, C5 for a flower with five petals. The number is put in brackets if the parts are fused. If the parts are arranged in distinct whorls within the flower this is also shown by giving two separate figures, such as A5 + 5 indicating two whorls of five stamens each. A flower with radial symmetry is known as *actinomorphic*, a flower with bilateral symmetry *zygomorphic*.

Florence /'florəns/ (Italian *Firenze*) city, capital of ◊Tuscany, Italy, 88 km/55 mi from the mouth of the river Arno; population (1981) 448,330. It has printing, engineering, and optical industries, and many crafts, including leather, gold and silver work, and embroidery.

history The Roman town of Florentia was founded in the 1st century BC on the site of the Etruscan town of Faesulae. It was besieged by the Goths in 405 AD, and visited by Charlemagne in 786.

In 1052 Florence passed to Countess Matilda of Tuscany (1046–1115), and from the 11th century onwards gained increasing autonomy. In 1198 it became an independent republic, with new city walls, and governed by a body of 12 citizens. In the 13th–14th centuries the city was the centre of the strruggle between the ◊Guelphs (papal supporters), and Ghibellines (supporters of the Holy Roman emperor).

From the 15th–18th centuries the ◊Medici family, originally bankers, were the predominant power in Florence, in spite of their having been twice expelled by revolutions. In the first of these, in 1493, a year after Lorenzo de' Medici's death, a republic was proclaimed (with ◊Machiavelli as secretary) which lasted until 1512. From 1494–98 the city was under the control of ◊Savonarola. In 1527 the Medicis again proclaimed a republic, which was to last though many years of gradual decline until 1737 when the city passed to Maria Theresa of Austria. From 1737 the city was ruled by the ◊Hapsburgs. Notable Medieval and Renaissance Florentines include ◊Dante, ◊Boccaccio, ◊Giotto, ◊Leonardo da Vinci, and ◊Michelangelo.

Florence's architectural treasures include the Ponte Vecchio, 1345; the Pitti and Vecchio palaces; the churches of Santa Croce and Santa Maria Novella; the cathedral of Santa Maria del Fiore, 1314; and the Uffizi Gallery, which has one of Europe's finest art collections, based on that of the Medici. The city was badly damaged in World War II, and by floods in 1966.

floret a small flower, usually making up part of a larger, composite inflorecence (or ◊capitulum) where numerous florets are grouped together into one flower-head. Florets are characteristic of the daisy family (Compositae). There are often two different types present on one flower-head: disc florets in the central area, and ray florets around the edge which usually have a single petal known as the ligule. In the common daisy, for example the disc florets are yellow, while the ligules are white.

Florey /'flɔːri/ Howard Walter, Baron Florey 1898–1968. British pathologist, born in Australia. He was professor of pathology at Oxford University. For his work on making penicillin available for use, he shared a Nobel

Prize for Medicine with ◊Fleming and Chain in 1945. He was made a life peer and was awarded the Order of Merit 1965.

Florida /'flɒrɪdə/ most southerly state of the USA; mainly a large peninsula jutting into the Atlantic, which it separates from the Gulf of Mexico; known as the Sunshine State.
area 151,700 sq km/58,560 sq mi
capital Tallahassee
towns Miami, Tampa, Jacksonville
features 50% forested; lakes (including Okeechobee 1,800 sq km/700 sq mi); Everglades National Park (5,000 sq km/2,000 sq mi, rich birdlife, cypresses, alligators); Palm Beach, an island resort between the lagoon of Lake Worth and the Atlantic; John F Kennedy Space Center at Cape Canaveral; Disney World theme park
products citrus fruit, melons, vegetables; fish and shellfish; phosphates (one third of world supply), chemicals; largest US producer of uranium.
population (1980) 9,750,000, including 500,000 Cubans and many Haitian refugees
history under Spanish rule from 1513 until its cession to England in 1763, Florida was returned to Spain in 1783, and purchased by the USA in 1819, becoming a state in 1845.

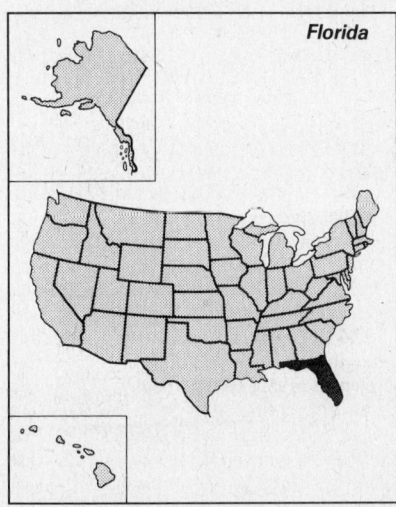

Florida

Florida Keys /'flɒrɪdə/ series of small coral islands which curve over 160 km/100 mi SW from the southern tip of Florida. The most important are Key Largo and Key West (with a US naval and air station); they depend on fishing and tourism.

florin coin, common to many European lands, first minted in Florence in 1252. The obverse bore the image of a lily, which led to the coin being called *fiorino* (from *fiore*, flower). This florin was a gold coin. The British silver florin of two shillings was first struck 1849, and continued in use after decimalization as the equivalent of 10p.

Florio /'flɒrɪəʊ/ Giovanni c. 1553–1625. English translator, born in London, the son of Italian refugees. He taught French and Italian at Oxford, but is best known for his translation of ◊Montaigne (1603).

flotation process a common method of mineral dressing, or preparing ores for subsequent processing. It makes use of the different wetting properties of different ores. In the process the ore is finely ground and then mixed with water and a specially selected wetting agent. Air is bubbled through the mixture, forming a froth. The desired ore particles attach themselves to the bubbles and are skimmed off. Unwanted dirt or other ores remain behind.

flotsam, jetsam and lagan *flotsam* goods found floating at sea after a shipwreck; *jetsam* those thrown overboard to lighten a sinking vessel; *lagan* those on the sea bottom, or secured to a buoy. Under British law all belong to the Crown unless the owner is known.

flounder small edible ◊flatfish *Platichthys flesus* of North East Atlantic and Mediterranean, which sometimes penetrates estuaries. Dully coloured, it grows to 50 cm/1.6 ft.

flow chart a diagram, often used in computing, to show the possible paths through the logical structure of a sequence of events (or a computer program). Different symbols are used to indicate processing, decision-making, input, and output. These are connected by arrows showing the flow of control through the program, that is, the paths the computer can take when executing the program. See also ◊algorithm.

flower the reproductive unit of an ◊angiosperm or flowering plant, typically consisting of four whorls of modified leaves: the sepals, petals, stamens, and carpels. These are borne on a central axis or ◊receptacle. The sepals and petals are collectively known as the *calyx* and *corolla* respectively and together comprise the perianth with the function of protecting the reproductive organs and attracting pollinators. The *stamens* lie within the corolla, each having a slender stalk, or filament, bearing the pollen-containing anther at the top. Collectively they are known as the *androecium*. The inner whorl of the flower comprises the *carpels*, each usually consisting of an ◊ovary in which are borne the ◊ovules, and a stigma borne at the top of a slender stalk, or style. Collectively the carpels are known as the *gynoecium*. There are many different forms of flower varying in size, colour, number and arrangement of parts, and this is usually closely related to the method of pollination. Flowers adapted for wind-pollination typically have reduced or absent petals and sepals and long, feathery stigmas which hang outside the flower to trap air-borne pollen. In contrast, the petals of insect-pollinated flowers are usually conspicious and brightly-coloured. In size, flowers range from the tiny blooms of duckweeds scarcely visible with the naked eye to the gigantic flowers of the Malaysian *Rafflesia* which can reach over 1 m/3 ft across. Flowers may either be borne singly or grouped together in ◊inflorescences. The stalk of the whole inflorescence is termed a peduncle, and the stalk of an individual flower is termed a pedicel. A flower may contain both male and female reproductive organs, termed ◊hermaphrodite, or male and female organs may be carried in separate flowers, termed ◊monoecious if on the same plant and ◊dioecious when on separate plants.

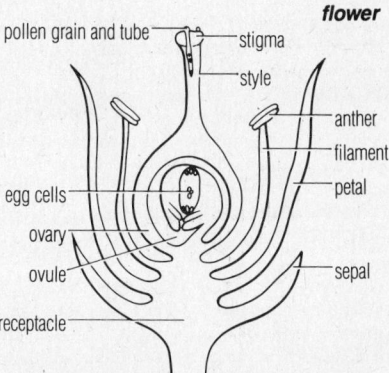

flower

flowering plant a term generally used for the ◊angiosperms, which bear ◊flowers with various parts, including sepals, petals, stamens and carpels. Sometimes the term is used more broadly, to include both angiosperms and ◊gymnosperms, in which case the ◊cones of conifers and cycads may be refered to as 'flowers'. Usually, however, the angiosperms and gymnosperms are referred to collectively as ◊seed plasts, or spermatophytes.

flower power a youth movement of the 1960s; see ◊hippie.

flugelhorn type of ◊brass musical instrument.

fluid a liquid or gas, where the molecules are relatively mobile and can 'flow'.

fluid, supercritical fluid brought by a combination of heat and pressure to the point at which, as a near vapour, it combines the properties of a gas and a liquid. Supercritical fluids are used as solvents in chemical processes, such as the extraction of lubricating oil from refinery residues or the decaffeination of coffee because they avoid the energy-expensive need for phase changes (from liquid to gas and back again) required in conventional distillation processes.

fluke parasitic flatworm such as *Fasciola hepatica* that causes rot and dropsy of the liver, in sheep, cattle, horses, dogs, and humans. Only the adult encysted stage of its life history is passed within the body, after ingestion by the host. The cyst dissolves in the stomach and the young fluke passes to the liver.

fluorescence the process of emission of ◊electromagnetic radiation resulting from the absorption of certain types of energy, in which case it is a luminescence lasting a minute fraction of a second after the exciting energy is removed. Fluorescence is also used to mean the radiation emitted as well as the emission process, and in X-ray fluorescence is the characteristic X-rays emitted when X-rays of a higher frequency are absorbed. This is used in analysis. Fluorescence is made use of in strip and other lighting, and was developed rapidly during World War II because of its greater efficiency of illumination, compared with the incandescent lamp. Other important applications are in fluorescent screens for television, and cathode-ray tubes.

fluoride salt of hydrofluoric acid. Fluorides occur naturally in all water to a differing extent. Experiments in Britain, the USA and elsewhere have indicated that a concentration of fluoride of

1 part per million in water retards the decay of teeth in children by more than 50 per cent. If the natural concentration of fluoride is less than 1 part per million, the recommended policy in Britain is to add sufficient sodium fluoride to the water to bring it up to this amount, but implementation is entirely up to each local authority.

fluorine chemical element, symbol F, atomic number 9, atomic weight 19. Discovered by Scheele in 1771 and isolated by Moissan in 1886. It occurs naturally as the minerals fluorspar (CaF_2) and cryolite (Na_3ALFe_6) and is the first member of the ◊halogen group of elements. At ordinary temperatures it is a pale yellow, highly poisonous and reactive gas and it unites directly with nearly all the elements. Hydrogen fluoride is used in etching glass, and the freons, which all contain fluorine, are widely used as refrigerants and aerosol propellants. Combined with uranium as UF_6, it is used in the separation of uranium isotopes. Minute quantities of sodium fluoride are added to some water supplies to help prevent tooth decay.

fluorocarbon compound formed by replacing the hydrogen atoms of ◊hydrocarbon with fluorine. They are used as inert coatings, refrigerants, synthetic resins, and as a propellants in aerosols. There is concern that their release into the atmosphere may deplete the ozone layer, allowing more ultraviolet light to reach the cell from the Sun, and increasing skin cancer.

fluorspar or *fluorite*. A cubic mineral, CaF_2, usually violet-tinted. The *Blue John* from Derbyshire is a fibrous variety used as an ornamental stone. Colourless fluorspar is used in the manufacture of microscope lenses, for the glaze on pottery and in the Bessemer process of steel manufacture. Fluorspar is also used in the manufacture of fluorine and hydrofluoric acid.

Flushing /ˈflʌʃɪŋ/ port (Dutch *Vlissingen*) on Walcheren Island, Zeeland, Netherlands; population (1982) 46,500. It stands at the entrance to the Scheldt estuary, one of the principal sea routes into Europe. Industries include fishing, shipbuilding and petrochemicals, and there is a ferry service to Harwich. De ◊Ruyter was born at Flushing and is commemorated in the Jacobskerk.

flute member of a group of ◊woodwind musical instruments, including the piccolo, the concert flute, the bass or alto flute. They are cylindrical in shape, with a narrowed end, containing an aperture, across which the player blows. The air vibrations produce the note, which can be altered by placing fingers over lateral holes. Certain keys can be depressed to extend the range of the flute to three octaves. The modern orchestral flute is at concert pitch - middle C to C sharp an octave higher. The alto (sometimes known as the 'bass') flute has a range the same as that of the concert flute, but a fourth lower. There is a special 'Bass Flute in B Flat' which is usually only played in drum and fife bands.

fly /flaɪ/ two-winged insect of the order Diptera, which includes some 90,000 species; the hindwings are represented only by a pair of knob-like organs on slender stalks (halteres) which balance the fly in flight. The mouth-parts project from the head as a proboscis used for sucking fluids, and in some species are modified to pierce a victim's skin and enable blood to be withdrawn. They can to walk up a window by using discs at the ends of the hairs on their feet, which secrete a fluid enabling them to adhere to the glass. Flies undergo complete metamorphosis; their larvae (maggots) are without true legs, and the pupae are rarely enclosed in a cocoon. The sexes are similar, coloration rarely vivid, though some are remarkable for being metallic green or blue. The fruitfly, *Drosophila*, is much used in genetic experiments as it is easy to keep, fast-breeding, and has easily visible chromosomes.

fly An adult blowfly (*Calliphora*) encountered head-on.

flying dragon ◊lizard *Draco volans* of SE Asia, which can glide on flaps of skin spread and supported by its ribs. Arboreal, this small (7.5 cm/3 in head and body) lizard can glide between trees for 6 m/20 ft or more.

flying fish Atlantic fish *Exocoetus volitans*, family Exocoetidae, of order Beloniformes, which can glide 100 m/325 ft, over the surface of the sea with expanded pectoral fins.

flying fox ◊bat of the order Megachiroptera.

flying lemur alternative name for ◊colugo.

flying lizard another name for ◊flying dragon.

flying squirrel ◊squirrel in which there is a gliding membrane along the side of the body from forelimb to hindlimb, in some species running to neck and tail too. There are many species, not all closely related, with this adaptation, and they are found in the Old and New World, but most species are East Asian. The giant flying squirrel *Petaurista* grows up to 1.1 m/3.5 ft including tail, and can glide 65 m/210 ft.

Flynn /flɪn/ Errol 1909–1959. Australian actor, born in Tasmania. His films, in which he played daring swashbuckling heroes include *Captain Blood* 1935 and *The Master of Ballantrae* 1953.

Flynn /flɪn/ John 1880–1951. Australian missionary. Inspired by the use of aircraft to transport the wounded of World War I, he instituted in 1928 the 'flying doctor' service in

Flynn Australian film actor Erroll Flynn. Famous for his good looks and reckless personality, he usually played dashing heroes.

Australia, which can be summoned to the outback by radios in individual homesteads.

flywheel a heavy wheel in an engine, which helps keep it running and smooths its motion. The ◊crankshaft in a petrol engine has a flywheel at one end. It keeps the crankshaft turning in between the intermittent power strokes of the pistons. It also comes into contact with the ◊clutch, serving as the connection between the engine and the car's transmission system.

FM (Frequency Modulation), a method of altering or modulating a radio carrier wave for broadcasting. See ◊modulation.

Fo /fəʊ/ Dario 1926– . Italian playwright and actor. His plays are predominantly political satires combining black humour with slapstick. They include *Morte accidentale di un anarchio/Accidental Death of an Anarchist* 1970, and *Non si paga non si paga/Can't Pay? Won't Pay!* 1975/1981.

focal length the distance from the centre of a spherical mirror or lens to the focal point. For a concave mirror or ◊convex lens, it is the distance at which parallel rays of light are brought to a focus to form a real image (and in the case of a mirror is half the radius of curvature). For a convex mirror or ◊concave lens, it is the distance from the centre to the point at which a virtual image (an image produced by diverging light) is formed. With lenses, the more powerful the lens the shorter its focal length (see ◊dioptre).

Foch /fɒʃ/ Ferdinand 1851–1929. Marshal of France, born at Tarbes. He was largely responsible for the Allied victory of the ◊Marne during World War I, and commanded on the northwest front Oct 1914–Sept 1916. He was appointed chief of general staff in 1917 and commander-in-chief of the Allied armies in the

focal length

C = centre of curvature
F = focus
P = pole
f = focal point

concave mirror

convex mirror

concave lens

convex lens

and cold currents meet, and the air above them mixes. Fog frequently forms on calm nights over the land, as the land surface cools more rapidly than the air immediately above it. In drought areas, for example, Baja California, Canary Islands, Cape Verde islands, Namib Desert, and Peru/Chile, coastal fogs enable plant and animal life to survive without rain and are a potential source of water for human use by means of water collectors exploiting the effect of condensation. Officially, fog refers to a condition when visibility is reduced to 1 km/0.62 mi or less, and mist or haze to that giving a visibility of 1–2 km. A mist is produced by condensed water particles, and a haze by smoke or dust. Industrial areas uncontrolled by pollution laws have a continual haze of smoke over them, and if the temperature falls suddenly, a dense yellow smog forms. Fog dispersal at airports and over motorways is too expensive for normal use and aeronautic research has concentrated on navigation by electronic means. Since 1975 it has been possible for aircraft at certain airports to land and take off blind in fog, using radar navigation.

Foggia /ˈfɒdʒə/ city and episcopal see of Apulia region, S Italy; population (1981) 156,500. The cathedral, dating from about 1170, was rebuilt after an earthquake in 1731. Natural gas is found nearby.

föhn /fɜːn/ warm wind which blows through the valleys of the European Alps.

Fokine /ˈfɔːkiːn/ Mikhail 1880–1942. Russian dancer-choreographer, born in St Petersburg. He became chief choreographer to the Ballets Russes 1909–14, and with ◊Diaghilev revitalized the art of ballet, promoting the idea of artistic unity between dramatic, musical and stylistic elements. His creations include the 'Dying Swan' for ◊Pavlova; and for ◊Diaghilev *Les Sylphides* 1907, *Carnival* 1910, *The Firebird* 1910, *Le Spectre de la Rose* 1911, and *Petrushka* 1911.

fold in geology, a bend in rock ◊beds. If the bend is arched up in the middle it is called an anticline. If it sags downwards in the middle it is called a syncline.

folk dance a dance characteristic of a particular people, nation, or region. Many European folk dances are derived from the dances accompanying the customs and ceremonies of pre-Christian times, and are sometimes taken up at a more formal level (for example, the minuet, waltz, and polka were originally peasant dances). Folk dance has tended to die out in industrialized countries; its preservation in England was promoted by the work of Cecil ◊Sharp. See also ◊Morris dance, ◊farandole, and ◊jota.

Folkestone /ˈfəʊkstən/ port and holiday resort on the SE coast of Kent, England, 10 km/6 mi SW of Dover; population (1983) 44,200. There are ferry and hovercraft services to and from Boulogne.

folklore the oral traditions and culture of a people. The term folklore was coined in 1846 by W J Thoms (1803–85), but the founder of the systematic study of the subject was Jacob ◊Grimm. The approach to folklore has varied greatly: the German scholar Max Müller (1823–1900) interpreted it as evidence of nature myths; J G ◊Frazer was the exponent of the comparative study of early and popular folklore as mutually explanatory; Sir Laurence Gomme (1853–1916) adopted the historical method; and Bronislaw ◊Malinowski and Alfred Radcliffe-Brown (1881–1955) examined the material as an integral element in a living culture. See also ◊oral literature.

folk music body of traditional music, originally transmitted orally and seen as the spontaneous musical expression of a people. Many folk songs originated as a rhythmic accompaniment to manual work. Folk song is usually melodic, not harmonic, and the modes used are distinctive of the country of origin. The interest in ballad poetry in the later 18th century led to the discovery of a rich body of folk song in Britain and in Europe. The multi-ethnic background of the USA has brought forth a wealth of material derived from European, African, and South American sources. A great revival of interest, starting in the 1950s, was led

spring of 1918. He launched the Allied advance in Jul which ended the war.

foetus a stage in mammalian ◊embryo development, in which body features can be distinguished. The human embryo is usually termed a foetus after the eighth week of development, when the limbs and external features of the head are recognizable.

fog ◊cloud that collects at the surface of the earth, composed of water vapour which has condensed on particles of dust in the atmosphere. Cloud and fog are both caused by the air temperature falling below ◊dew point. The thickness of fog is dependent on the number of water particles it contains. Usually, fog is formed by the meeting of two currents of air, one cooler than the other, or by warm air flowing over a cold surface. Sea fogs commonly occur where warm

fold

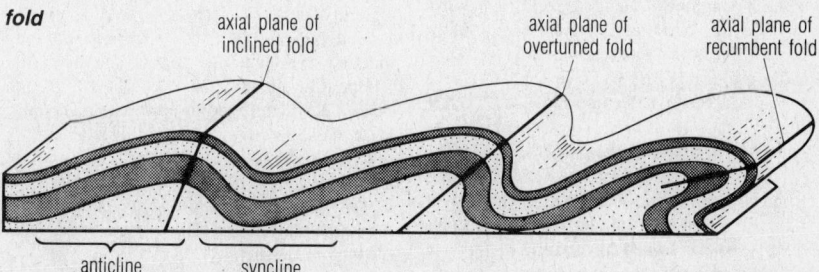

axial plane of inclined fold

axial plane of overturned fold

axial plane of recumbent fold

anticline   syncline

folic acid a ◊vitamin of the B-complex. Found in liver and green leafy vegetables, it is also synthesized by the intestinal bacteria. It is essential for growth, and has many other roles in the body. Lack of folic acid causes anaemia.

Folies-Bergère /ˈfɒli beəˈʒeə/ music-hall in Paris built in 1869, named after its original proprietor and famous for its lavish productions and striptease acts.

by Alan Lomax, John Jacob Niles, Theo Bikel, Pete Seeger, Woody Guthrie and Bob Dylan, who wrote new material in folk-song style, dealing with contemporary topics such as atomic warfare and racial prejudice. In Britain the folk revival of the 1980s was furthered by the virtuoso rock guitarist Richard Thompson (1949-) and groups such as the Pogues (1983-).

follicle in botany, a dry, usually many-seeded

◊fruit which splits along one side only to release the seeds within. It is derived from a single ◊carpel and examples include the fruits of *Delphinium* and columbine (*Aquilegia*). It differs from a pod which always dehisces along both sides.

In zoology, a small group of cells that surrounds and nourishes a structure such as a hair (hair follicle) or a cell such as an egg (Graafian follicle; see ◊menstrual cycle).

Fonda /'fɒndə/ Henry 1905–1982. American actor, born in Omaha, Nebraska, whose engaging sincerity made him ideal in the role of the American pioneer and honourable man. He appeared in both stage and screen versions of *Mister Roberts*, and the films *Grapes of Wrath* 1940, *My Darling Clementine* 1946, and *On Golden Pond* 1982. He was acclaimed for his production of the film *12 Angry Men* 1957. He is the father of actress Jane ◊Fonda and actor/director *Peter Fonda* (1939-), best known for *Easy Rider* 1969.

Fonda American actor Henry Fonda receiving Hollywood's Life Achievement Award photographed with his famous children, Jane and Peter. Fonda's career spanned more than 50 years, culminating with the film *On Golden Pond* made the year he died.

Fonda /'fɒndə/ Jane 1937– . American actress, daughter of Henry ◊Fonda, also active in left-wing politics and in promoting physical fitness. She won Academy Awards for *Klute* 1971, and *Coming Home* 1979.

Fontainebleau /'fɒntɪnbləu/ town to the south east of Paris, in Seine-et-Marne *département*; population (1982) 18,753. The palace was built by Francis I in the 16th century. Mme de ◊Montespan lived there in the reign of Louis XIV, and Mme ◊du Barry in that of Louis XV. Napoleon signed his abdication there in 1814. Nearby is the village of ◊Barbizon, famous as the haunt of several 19th-century painters.

Fontana /fɒn'tɑːnə/ Domenico 1543–1607. Italian architect. He was employed by Pope Sixtus V, and his principal works include the Vatican library, the completion of the dome of St Peter's, and the royal palace at Naples.

Fontanne /fɒn'tæn/ Lynn 1887–1983. American actress, one half of the American husband-and-wife acting partnership known as the 'Lunts' with her husband Alfred Lunt.

Fontenoy /'fɒntənwɑː/ village in Hainaut province, Belgium, south east of Tournai, where in the War of the ◊Austrian Succession, Marshal Saxe and the French defeated the British, Dutch, and Hanoverians under the Duke of Cumberland in 1745.

Fonteyn /'fɒnteɪn/ Margot (born Margaret Hookham) 1919– . British ballet dancer. She made her debut with the Vic-Wells Ballet in *Nutcracker* in 1934 and first appeared as Giselle in 1937, eventually becoming prima ballerina of the ◊Royal Ballet. Renowned for her perfect physique, musicality and interpretive powers, she created several roles in ◊Ashton's ballets and formed a famous partnership with ◊Nureyev.

Fonteyn One of the greatest partnerships in the history of ballet – Margot Fonteyn and Rudolf Nureyev in *Giselle*.

Foochow /ˌfuː'tʃau/ former name of ◊Fuzhou, port and capital of Fujian province, SE China.

food general term for anything eaten by human beings and other animals to sustain life. Essential for humans are:

protein for body building and repair (sources: meat, milk, fish, eggs, and some vegetables);

◊*fats* (in moderation) to provide energy (sources: butter, oil, and lard);

carbohydrates also provide energy and are found in bread, potatoes, cereals and sugar, which form the bulk of the diet;

◊*vitamins* required only in small quantities to assist the body to make full use of its food;

minerals which are also required in small quantities: salt; calcium (bone building) from milk; and iron (blood formation) from meats and green vegetables.

Essential foods also include water and fibre (for example, bran, green leaves for digestion) although these give little nourishment. The energy value of food is expressed in joules or calories.

Food and Agriculture Organization (FAO) United Nations agency founded in 1945 with headquarters in Rome to coordinate activities to improve food and timber production and levels of nutrition throughout the world.

food chain or *food web* the sequence of organisms through which energy and other nutrients are successively transferred in an ecological system. The main components of the sequence are the ◊autotrophs or *primary producers*, principally plants and photosynthetic micro-organisms, the ◊herbivores that feed on them, the ◊carnivores that feed on the herbivores, and the ◊decomposers that break down the dead bodies and waste products of all three groups, ready for recycling. Many organisms, however, feed at several different levels (for example, omnivores such as bears and badgers, feed on both fruit and meat), so that the relationships often form a complex web rather than a simple chain. See also ◊ecosystem and ◊heterotroph.

food chain

[Diagram: food chain showing hawk and fox as tertiary consumers (carnivores); snake and frog as secondary consumers (carnivores); grasshopper and mouse as primary consumers (herbivores); grass as producers; beetle and worm as decomposers]

food poisoning acute illness caused by harmful bacteria; poisonous food (for example, certain mushrooms, puffer fish); poisoned food (for example, lead, arsenic introduced accidentally during manufacture).

Uncooked meat may carry harmful organisms. Pork may carry the round-worm *Trinchinella*, and rye the parasitic fungus ergot. The most dangerous food poison is the bacillus which causes ◊botulism.

The most frequent cause of food poisoning, however, is the *salmonella* bacterium. This comes in many forms, and strains are found in a high percentage of cattle, pigs and poultry. There they develop resistance to the ◊antibiotics which are used not merely to treat sick animals but as growth promoters to produce more meat more quickly. Consequently food poisoning is becoming more common and more lethal, and spreads quickly from human to human by contact with faeces or unwashed hands.

food technology the application of scientific and engineering knowledge to the commercial processing and manufacture of foodstuffs.

Food technology is closely connected with the general development of technology within society. Many Third World societies still process foods in ways that were commonplace in western Europe centuries ago. Many modern processes developed from the principles used in the earliest times, for example, brewing, drying, freezing.

Early food technology, and much of modern-day activity, is concerned with prolonging the storage life of crops and meat. Urban society has made this requirement more important since many foods are consumed a great distance from where they were grown and harvested. New Zealand lamb is readily available in the UK, for example. Modern food technology also concerns itself with the processing of a wider range of ingredients and combining them in order to produce new foods. Spun vegetable protein, modified starch and gum arabic are all commonly used, especially in 'convenience' foods. Additives may be used to modify the natural properties of the foods.

All food, once harvested, is subject to spoilage processes, for example, infestation, enzyme action, micro-organisms, oxidation and dehydration. Preservation techniques concentrate on the factors to which the food is most vulnerable.

Refrigeration (below 4°C) slows the processes of decay. It is good for meat, less good for foods with high water content. It tends to dehydrate the food so humidity control may be necessary.

Freezing (between 0° and −4°C) was developed by the Inuit (Eskimo) people to store meat and fish. It drastically slows decay processes and effectively stops micro-organism action. Usually accomplished in less than 30 minutes by means of a cold air blast, direct immersion in liquefied air, nitrogen or carbon dioxide, or contact with refrigerated plates. Fast freezing results in smaller ice crystals, less cell damage and better reconstitution. Not all foods freeze well; soft fruits may be damaged, and cream, sauces and the like separate out. Freezing destroys parasites and protects from infestation.

Drying/dehydration was developed commercially in France c. 1795 for sliced vegetables using a hot air blast. Cereals have been dried naturally since earliest times and the process is now applied to legumes, nuts and some fruits. Moisture content is reduced to 10–20% of fresh produce and this provides good protection against moulds. Bacteria are not inhibited by drying so the quality of raw materials is vital. The earliest large-scale application was to starch products such as spaghetti and pasta, but after 1945 it was extended to milk, potato, soups, instant coffee, and prepared baby and pet foods. A major benefit to food manufacturers is reduction of weight and volume of the products, lowering distribution cost.

Freeze-dehydration is carried out under vacuum. It is less damaging to food. Developed for premium instant coffee and now extended to pre-packed ready meals.

Canning involves the sealing of food into a metal container and the use of high temperature to inhibit decay. Beverages may also be canned to preserve the carbon dioxide that gives the drinks their fizzy character.

Pickling and fermentation are among the oldest of techniques and use the natural action of salt, acid or vinegar to provide good protection against moulds. Especially popular for onions, cucumbers, sauerkraut and olives. For meat products the treatment (with salts) may be combined with smoking to produce hams.

Concentration is used to make jams and jellies. Sugar is added to raise the concentration of acid to a point where micro-organisms no longer function.

Chemical treatments act to destroy micro-organisms or delay their action and hence prevent deterioration during manufacture and distribution of food. Many organic acids act against yeasts. Sulphur compounds act against moulds and are commonly used to treat fruits, vegetables and wines, being added in low concentrations that do not affect flavour. Nitrates are oxidizing agents that are used in the curing of meats.

Radiation treatments are held to offer the promise of treatments that destroy micro-organisms, parasites, insect contaminants and inhibit the sprouting of produce (potatoes, onions) in storage and distribution. Energy consumption is about 2% of thermal techniques but many chemical changes may take place in the food, leading to oxidation and reduction processes that may be deleterious. Debate continues about the desirability of the techniques; radiation treatment is permitted in some countries but banned in others.

Packaging technology regulates the immediate environment of the food while also offering protection, convenience and enhancing the appearance and ease of handling of the product. It includes sealing foods in plastic containers, paper wrappers and so on.

See also ▷additives and ▷pasteurization.

foot /fʊt/ an Imperial unit of length (ft), equivalent to 0.3048 m. Twelve inches comprise a foot, three feet make a yard.

Foot /fʊt/ Dingle 1905–1978. British lawyer and Labour politician, brother of Michael Foot. He was solicitor-general 1964–67. Knighted 1964.

Foot /fʊt/ Hugh, Baron Caradon 1907– . British Labour politician, son of Isaac ▷Foot and brother of Michael ▷Foot. As governor of Cyprus 1957–60, he guided the independence negotiations, and he represented the UK at the United Nations 1964–70.

Foot /fʊt/ Isaac 1880–1960. British Liberal politician. A staunch Nonconformist, he held office (minister of mines 1931–32) only briefly. Father of Dingle, Hugh, and Michael Foot.

Foot /fʊt/ Michael 1913– . British Labour politician. A leader of the left-wing Tribune Group; he was secretary of state for employment 1974–76, Lord President of the Council and leader of the House 1976–79, and succeeded Callaghan as Labour Party leader 1980–83.

foot and mouth disease contagious eruptive viral fever which causes deterioration of milk yield and abortions in cattle. In the UK affected herds are destroyed; inoculation is practised in Europe, and in the US a vaccine has recently been developed.

football a team game involving kicking a ball. The earliest form of the game is *Association football* or *soccer* originating in rural football in the UK. It is now played worldwide, under rules of the Football Association 1863. It is played betwen two teams each of 11 players, on a field 90–120 m/100–130 yds long and 45–90 m/50–100 yds wide with a spherical, inflated (traditionally leather) ball, circumference 0.71–0.68 m/27–28 in.

The object of the game is to send the ball with the feet or head into the opponents' goal, an area 7.32 m/8 yds wide and 2.44 m/8 ft high. A team is broadly divided into defence (including the goalkeeper and defenders); midfield (whose players collect the ball from the defence and distribute it to the attackers); and attack (forwards or strikers). The number of players assigned to each role varies according to the tactics adopted, but a typical formation is 4–4–2 (four defenders, excluding goalkeeper, four midfield, and two forwards). The field has a halfway line, marked with a centre circle, two penalty areas, and two goal areas. Corner kicks are taken from a 1 m/1 yd segment, when the ball goes behind the goal-line off a defender; a ball kicked over the touch-lines is thrown in by one of the opposing side. Only the goalkeeper is allowed to touch the ball with his hands and then only in his own penalty area. For major offences committed within the defenders' penalty area, a penalty kick may be awarded by the referee to the attacking team. This is taken 11 m/12 yds from the goal centre, with only the goalkeeper inside the area and stood still on his line. The game is started from the centre spot. It is played for two periods of 45 minutes each, the teams changing ends at half-time. The game is controlled by a referee; two linesmen indicate when the ball is kicked into touch and bring other rule infringements to the referees attention.

The Football Association Cup competition was inaugurated in Britain in 1872. The Football League was founded in 1888. The Fédération Internationale de Football Association (FIFA) (1904) organized in 1930 the first of the quadrennial competitions for the World Cup.

World Cup first contested 1930, held every four years
1970 Brazil
1974 West Germany
1978 Argentina
1982 Italy
1986 Argentina
European Championship instituted 1958, first final 1960; held every four years
1968 Italy
1972 West Germany
1976 Czechoslovakia
1980 West Germany
1984 France
European Champions Cup first held 1955
1982 Aston Villa *(England)*

1983 SV Hamburg *(West Germany)*
1984 Liverpool *(England)*
1985 Juventus *(Italy)*
1986 Steau Bucharest *(Romania)*
FA Cup knockout club competition, first held 1872; held annually in the UK
1982 Tottenham Hotspur
1983 Manchester United
1984 Everton
1985 Manchester United
1986 Liverpool
Division One Champions Football League founded 1888–9
1982–83 Liverpool
1983–84 Liverpool
1984–85 Everton
1985–86 Liverpool
1986–87 Everton
Scottish Premier Division Champions
Scottish League formed 1890–91, reformed into three divisions in 1975–6
1981–82 Celtic
1982–83 Dundee United
1983–84 Aberdeen
1984–85 Aberdeen
1985–86 Celtic

1983 Washington Redskins
1984 Los Angeles Raiders
1985 San Francisco 49ers
1986 Chicago Bears
1987 New York Giants.

football, Australian Australia has its own code of football. It is played with 18 men a side, 2 reserves being allowed for each team. Each side is placed in 5 lines of 3 men each. Three men follow the ball all the time. The 2 goal-posts, at each end, are 6m high and 6.4 apart. On either side are 2 smaller posts. The football is oval, and weighs a little more than a rugby ball. A goal (6 points) is scored when the ball is kicked between the goalposts, if it is not touched on the way. If the ball passes between a goal-post and one of the smaller posts, or hits a post, the score is a 'behind', or one point. There are no scrums, line-outs, or off-side rules. A player must get rid of the ball as soon as he starts to run, by kicking, punching or bouncing it every 10m. No tackling is allowed as in rugby. This code originated on the Australian goldfields in the 1850s.

footpad a thief, operating on foot, who robbed travellers on the highway in the 18th and 19th

sea bottom.

force in physics, that which tends to change the state of rest or the uniform motion of a body in a straight line. It is measured by the rate of change of momentum of the body on which it acts, that is, the mass of the body multiplied by its acceleration $f=ma$.

forces, fundamental in physics, the four fundamental interactions believed to be at work in the physical universe. ◊*Gravity*, which keeps the planets in orbit around the Sun, acts between all ◊particles with mass. *Electromagnetic forces*, which stop solids from falling apart, act between all particles with ◊electric charge. In addition to those long-range forces, there are two very short-range forces: the *weak*, responsible for the reactions which fuel the Sun, and for the emission of ◊beta particles from certain nuclei; and the *strong*, which binds together the protons and neutrons in the nuclei of ◊atoms. By 1971 a theory developed by Steven Weinberg, Sheldon Glashow (USA), Abdus Salam (UK) and others, suggested that the weak and electromagnetic forces were linked; experimental support came from observation at ◊CERN in the 1980s. Physicists are now working on theories to unify all four forces.

Ford /fɔːd/ Ford Madox 1873–1939. English writer (originally Ford Madox Hueffer), a grandson of Ford Madox ◊Brown. He is best-remembered as editor of the *English Review* 1908 to which ◊Hardy, D H ◊Lawrence, and ◊Conrad contributed, and for his novel *The Good Soldier* 1915.

Ford /fɔːd/ Gerald R(udolph) 1913– . 38th president of the USA. He was born in Omaha, Nebraska; played football at college, and graduated from Yale Law School. He was elected to the House of Representatives as a Republican in 1949, was nominated to the vice-presidency by ◊Nixon in 1973, and in 1974, when Nixon resigned, succeeded him as president. His decisions to give his predecessor a free pardon, and to give amnesty to draft resisters in the Vietnam War, were controversial. A visit to Vladivostok in 1974 resulted in agreement with the USSR on strategic arms limitation. He was defeated by Carter in the 1976 election by a narrow margin.

Ford /fɔːd/ Henry 1863–1947. American motor car manufacturer, born in Michigan. He built his first car in 1893 and ten years later founded the Ford Motor Company. His model T (1908–27) was the first to be constructed by purely mass-production methods, and 15 million of these historic cars were made. A pacifist, he visited Europe 1915–16 in an attempt to end World War I, and in 1936 he founded, with his son Edsel Ford (1893–1943), the philanthropic Ford Foundation.

Ford /fɔːd/ John 1586–1640. English poet and dramatist, born in Devon. He was noted for an imaginative and dramatic study of incest between brother and sister in *'Tis Pity She's a Whore* 1633. The best of his other pieces are *The Broken Heart* 1633 and the chronicle play *Perkin Warbeck* 1634.

Ford /fɔːd/ John. Assumed name of Sean O'Fearn 1895–1973. Irish-American film

football

American football

football, American formally originated in a Princeton University/Rutgers University game in 1869. The goals and ball are those of English rugby, but the players are kitted out in protective suits against rough tackling, and the two teams of 11 men play on a field marked out in 'gridiron intervals', much closer together than those of the rugby pitch. The scoring rules are complex. It is strenuous and games are divided into four 15-minute periods.
Super Bowl first held 1967, an annual meeting between the winners of the National and American Football Leagues

centuries in England. Thieves on horseback were termed ◊highwaymen.

foot-poundal an Imperial unit of energy (ft, lb). Defined as the work done when a force of 1 lb moves through a distance of 1 ft. Superseded for scientific work by the joule. Equivalent to 0.04214 joule.

foraminifera single-celled marine animals, often classified as an order of Protozoa. They are enclosed by a thin shell. Some form part of ◊plankton, for example the many-chambered *Globigerina* whose shells eventually form the chalky ooze of the ocean floor, others live on the

Ford Henry Ford, who pioneered the mass-production methods of car manufacture. He is photographed with his son Edsel in a model F Ford, the first car he built in 1893.

director. Active since the silent days, he was one of the original creators of the 'western', *Stagecoach* 1939 being a masterpiece of the genre. His other films include the socially-aware *The Informer* 1935, *The Grapes of Wrath* 1940, and *Two Rode Together* 1961. He was co-director of the first cinerama story film *How the West was Won* 1962.

Foreign Legion a volunteer corps of foreigners within a country's army. The French Légion Etrangère, formed 1831, is the most famous of a number of such forces. Enlisted volunteers are of any nationality (about half are now French), but the officers are usually French. Headquarters until 1962 were Sidi Bel Abbés, Algeria; the main base is now Corsica, with reception headquarters at Aubagne, near Marseilles.

foreign relations a country's dealings with other countries. In medieval England foreign affairs were dealt with, together with home affairs, by the king's principal secretary, an office split into two under Henry VIII. Irish and colonial affairs and relations with Mediterranean countries became the responsibility of the secretary of state for the Southern Department, the rest of Europe of the Northern Department. In 1782 the Southern Department became the Home Office and the Northern Department the Foreign Office, and colonial affairs, growing in importance, became separate departments – Colonial Office 1854, India Office 1858, Dominions Office 1925, Commonwealth Office 1947. By 1968, so many members of the Commonwealth had achieved independence that the Foreign Office was renamed the Foreign and Commonwealth Office,

the staffs being merged in the new HM Diplomatic Service.

In the USA foreign relations are the responsibility of the State Department (from 1789). Thomas Jefferson, then minister to France, was appointed secretary of state by Washington in 1789 and took office in 1790. The secretary of state is charged, under the direction of the president, 'with the duties appertaining to correspondence with the public ministers and the consuls of the United States, and with representatives of foreign powers accredited to the United States, and to negotiations of whatever character relating to the foreign affairs of the United States.'

In the USSR foreign relations are handled by the Foreign Ministry.

After World War II there was a great increase, partly owing to newly created states, in the number of countries represented by diplomats of ambassadorial rank, rather than by a minister, envoy or chargé d'affaires. Consuls are state agents with commercial and political responsibilities in foreign towns.

Instantaneous communications systems have in recent years lessened the importance of the career diplomat as the person on the spot. Professionally trained spies (see ◊intelligence) often inflate the numbers of 'diplomats' accredited to foreign countries.

Foreland /ˈfɔːlənd/ North and South headlands on the Kent coast, England. *North Foreland*, with one lighthouse, lies 4 km/2.5 mi E of Margate; *South Foreland*, with two, lies 4.8 km/3 mi NE of Dover.

Forest /ˈfɒrɪst/ Lee de 1873–1961. American inventor, born in Iowa, and educated at Yale and

Chicago universities. He perfected the audion tube (triode valve) and contributed to the development of radio, radar, and television.

Forester /ˈfɒrɪstə/ C(ecil) S(cott) 1899–1966. British novelist. His reputation rests on his series of historical novels set in the Napoleonic era which, beginning with *The Happy Return* 1937, covers the career – from midshipman to admiral – of Horatio Hornblower. He also wrote *Payment Deferred* 1926, a subtle crime novel; *Brown on Resolution* 1938, a study of patriotism; *The African Queen* 1938; and *The Earthly Paradise* 1940, dealing with Columbus.

forestry the science of forest management. In the past three centuries forest areas throughout the world have been drastically reduced, with consequent soil erosion and adverse modification of the climate, as in the Sahel region, and potential danger to the atmosphere we breathe, as with the increasing destruction of the Amazonian forest. Too often the practice of forestry has in effect reduced the total yield of a natural forest, having been confined to the planting of a single species, such as one of the rapid-growing conifers providing 'softwood' for paper pulp and construction timber, for which world demand is greatest. In Britain there has been much criticism of the neglect of native, more slow-growing 'hardwoods', to the detriment of the landscape and elimination of the varied wildlife which does not survive in the new plantations. The recommended modern forestry practice aims at multipurpose cropping, preserving the forest as an ecological entity, and allowing the preservation of varied plant species, animal life, and human crafts dependent on them. A tropical forest may thus yield medicinal plants, oils (cedar, juniper, cinnamon, and sandalwood), spices, gums, resins (pines, and others used in inks, lacquers, and linoleum) tanning and dyeing materials, forage for animals, beverages, insect and rodent poisons, green manure, rubber, and animal products (feathers, hides, honey, ivory and musk).

Forfarshire /ˈfɔːfəʃə/ former name (from 16th century–1928) of Angus, which was absorbed in Tayside in 1975.

forgery the making of a fake document, painting, or object with deliberate intention to deceive or defraud. Financial gain is not the only motive for such deception. Hans van ◊Meegeren, the most famous of modern art forgers, probably began painting in the style of ◊Vermeer to make fools of the critics, but found such a ready market for his creations that he became a rich man before he was forced to confess. The technical merit of his early forgeries was such that some experts continued to believe they had bought genuine Vermeers. In the best-known archaeological hoax a mixture of human and ape skull fragments discovered in 1912 was believed until 1953 to be an early human ancestor, ◊Piltdown Man. The Drake Brass Plate (supposedly set up in California by Sir Francis Drake in 1579 and discovered in 1936) and the Vinland Map (indicating that Vikings discovered America before Columbus) were both denounced as forgeries after modern scientific analysis. The

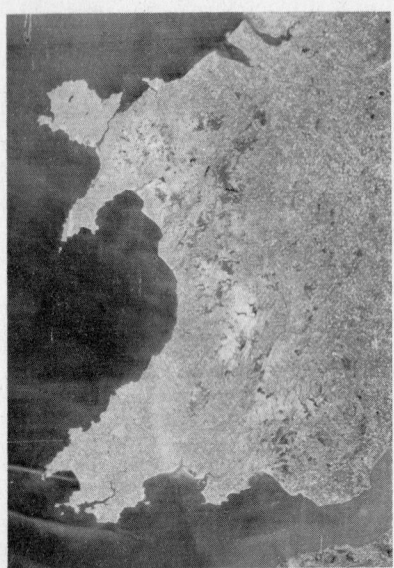

forestry Landsat mosaic of Wales, showing the forested regions darker. These are mostly confined to mountain slopes. In Britain forestry practices have been criticised for concentrating too much on softwood conifers to the neglect of native hardwoods.

1760s saw two literary hoaxes of considerable influence: the teenage poet Thomas ◊Chatterton passed off his own poems as the work of a fictitious 15th century monk Thomas Rowley and James ◊Macpherson created the works of ◊Ossian. Literary forgers proper include William Henry Ireland (1777–1835), who wrote two 'lost' Shakespearean plays, *Vortigern* and *Henry II* in the 1790s, and Thomas ◊Wise, an eminent 20th century collector who concocted his own 'first editions'. Forged letters sold to *The Times* in 1886 by Richard ◊Pigott had considerable impact on Irish politics and the ◊Zinoviev Letter helped the Conservatives to power in the 1924 General Election.

forget-me-not several plants of genus *Myosotis*, family Boraginaceae; the annual *common forget-me-not* has bright blue flowers. There are many others of the genus.

forging one of the main methods of shaping metals, which involves hammering or the more gradual application of pressure. A blacksmith hammers red-hot metal into shape on an anvil, and the traditional place of work is called a forge. The blacksmith's mechanical equivalent is the drop forge. The metal is shaped by the blows from a falling hammer or ram, which is usually accelerated by steam or air pressure. Hydraulic presses forge by applying pressure gradually in a squeezing action.

Forli /fɔːˈliː/ city and market centre in Emilia-Romagna region, Italy, south of Ravenna; population (1981) 111,000. It has a cathedral, churches, and a citadel. Felt, ◊maiolica, and paper are manufactured.

formaldehyde *methanal* a gas, HCHO, at ordinary temperatures, condensing to a liquid at – 21 °C. It has a powerful penetrating smell. In aqueous solution it is used as a biological preservative and is used in manufacture of plastics, dyes, foam (for example urea-formaldehyde foam, used in insulation), and in medicine.

Formby /ˈfɔːmbi/ George 1904–1961. English comedian. Son of the music-hall star of the same name, who established a stage and screen reputation as the apparently simple working lad, and sang such songs as 'Mr Wu' and 'Cleaning Windows', accompanying himself on the ukelele.

Formby Most famous for his ukulele and the song 'Cleaning Windows', George Formby, the Lancashire comedian, achieved a popular stage and screen reputation as the archetypal Northern lad.

Formentor, Cape /ˌfɔːmenˈtɔː/ northern extremity of ◊Majorca, in the Balearic Islands of the West Mediterranean.

Formica trade name for a heat-proof plastic laminate, widely used for wipe-down kitchen surfaces. It is made from formaldehyde resins akin to ◊Bakelite.

formic acid *methanoic acid* a colourless, slightly fuming liquid, HCOOH, that melts at 8 °C and boils at 101 °C. It occurs in stinging ants, nettles, sweat and pine needles, and is used in dyeing, tanning and electroplating.

Formosa /fɔːˈməʊsə/ former name of ◊Taiwan, main island of the Republic of China, off the SE coast of mainland China.

Forrest /ˈfɒrɪst/ John, 1st baron Forrest 1847–1918. Australian explorer, born in Western Australia. He is best-known for his dual crossing of the state from west to east in 1870, when he went along the southern coast route of Eyre and in 1874, when he crossed much further north, exploring the Musgrave Ranges. He was the first premier of the state in 1890–1901.

Forrestal /ˈfɒrɪstl/ James Vincent 1892–1949. American Democratic politician. As secretary of the Navy from 1944, he organized its war effort, accompanying the US landings on the Japanese island Iwo Jima. He was the first Secretary of the Department of National Defense (1947–49), a post created to unify the three services at the end of World War II.

Forssmann /ˈfɔːsmæn/ Werner 1904–1979. West German heart specialist. In 1929 he originated, by experiment on himself, the technique of cardiac catheterization (passing a thin tube from an arm artery up into the heart itself for diagnostic purposes). In 1956 he was awarded a joint Nobel Prize for Medicine.

Forster /ˈfɔːstə/ E(dward) M(organ) 1879–1970. British author, born in London and educated at King's College, Cambridge. He published his first novel *Where Angels Fear to Tread* in 1905. He undermines the superficial situations of his plots with unexpected insights in *The Longest Journey* 1907, *A Room with a View* 1908, and *Howard's End* 1910. *A Passage to India* 1924, his most famous book, explores the relationship between the English and the Indians through the incident of a possibly imagined assault on a stolid Englishwoman by the charming Indian, Dr Aziz. *Maurice*, published 1971, has a homosexual theme. Forster was concerned with the interplay of personality and the contrast between the conventional and the instinctive. His critical work includes *Aspects of the Novel* 1927. Order of Merit 1969.

Forster British novelist Edward Morgan Forster photographed by Cecil Beaton. His many years spent in India and as secretary to the Maharajah of Dewas in 1921 provided him with the material for his best-known novel *A Passage to India*.

Forster /ˈfɔːstə/ William Edward 1818–1886. British Liberal reformer. A Bradford woollen manufacturer, he entered Parliament in 1861. In Gladstone's government of 1868–74 he was vice president of the council, and secured the passing of the Education Act 1870 and the Ballot Act 1872. He was chief secretary for Ireland, 1880–82.

Forsyth /fɔːˈsaɪθ/ Frederick 1938– . British thriller writer, born at Ashford, Kent. He was a Reuters correspondent, and BBC radio and television reporter before making his name with *The Day of the Jackal* 1970, dealing with an attempted assassination of president de Gaulle of France. Later novels were *The Odessa File* 1972, *The Dogs of War* 1974, *The Devil's*

Alternative 1979, and *The Fourth Protocol* 1984.

forsythia genus of temperate E Asian shrub, family Oleaceae, which in spring bears yellow flowers before the leaves appear.

Forth /fɔːθ/ river in SE Scotland, with its headstreams rising on the NE slopes of Ben Lomond. It flows approximately 72 km/45 mi to Kincardine where the *Firth of Forth* begins. The Firth is approximately 80 km/50 mi long, and is 26 km/16 mi wide where it joins the North Sea. At Queensferry near Edinburgh are the Forth rail (1890) and road (1964) bridges. The *Forth and Clyde Canal* (1768–90) across the lowlands of Scotland links the Firth with the river Clyde, Grangemouth to Bowling (53 km/33 mi). A coalfield was located beneath the Firth of Forth in 1976.

Fortin /fɔːˈtæŋ/ Jean 1750–1831. French physicist and instrument-maker who invented a mercury barometer that bears his name. It measures atmospheric pressure by means of a column of mercury, formed by filling a closed tube with mercury and updating it in a reservoir of the metal. This leaves a gap (Torricellian vacuum) at the upper end of the tube, which changes size with variations in atmospheric pressure, expressed as the height of the column of mercury in millimetres. On this scale, normal atmospheric pressure is 760 mm.

Fort Knox /nɒks/ US army post and gold depository in Kentucky.

Fort Lamy /læˈmiː/ former name of ◊N'djaména, capital of Chad.

Fortran (from 'formula translation') computer-programming language particularly suited to mathematical and scientific computations. Developed in the mid-1950s, and one of the earliest languages, it is still widely used today. ◊BASIC was very strongly influenced by Fortran and is similar in many ways.

Fort Sumter /ˈsʌmtə/ fort in ◊Charleston harbour, South Carolina, USA, 6.5 km/4 mi SE of Charleston. The first shots of the American Civil War were fired here on 12 Apr 1861, after its commander had refused the call to surrender made by the Confederate Gen Beauregard.

Fortuna /fɔːˈtjuːnə/ in Roman mythology, goddess of chance and good fortune (Greek *Tyche*).

Fort Wayne /weɪn/ town in Indiana, USA; population (1980) 172,000. Industries include electrical goods, electronics, and farm machinery. A fort was built here against the North American Indians in 1794 by Gen Anthony Wayne (1745–96), hero of a surprise attack on a British force at Stony Point, New York, in 1779, which earned him the nickname 'Mad Anthony'.

Fort Worth /wɜːθ/ city in Texas, USA; population (1980) 385,164. It is a grain, petroleum, and railway centre serving the southern USA.

Forty-Five the name given to the ◊Jacobite rebellion of 1745, led by Prince ◊Charles Edward Stuart. With his army of Highlanders 'Prince Charlie' occupied Edinburgh and advanced into England as far as Derby, but then turned back.

The rising was crushed by the duke of Cumberland at ◊Culloden in 1746.

fossil remains of an animal or plant from an earlier geological period (Latin *fossilis* dug up) preserved in rocks. Fossils may be formed by refrigeration (Siberian ◊mammoths), preservation of the skeleton only, carbonization (for example, leaves in coal), formation of a cast (dinosaur or human footprints in mud), and mineralization of bones or teeth. They are tantalizingly incomplete for the study of evolution.

Fos-sur-Mer /ˈfɒs sjuə ˈmeə/ harbour near Marseille, France, forming the southern focus of a direct Rhone–Rhine route to the North Sea.

Foster /ˈfɒstə/ Norman 1935– . British architect of the high-tech school. His works include the Willis Faber office, Ipswich 1978, the Sainsbury Centre for Visual Arts at the University of East Anglia 1979, and the headquarters of the Hongkong and Shanghai Bank, Hong Kong 1986.

Foster /ˈfɒstə/ Stephen Collins 1826–1864. American songwriter, author of 'The Old Folks at Home' 1851, 'My Old Kentucky Home' 1853, and several others, mostly drawing on the black minstrel style.

Foucault /ˈfuːkəʊ/ Jean Bernard Léon 1819–1868. French physicist who, in 1851, produced the pendulum (named after him) which demonstrates the rotation of the Earth on its axis, and invented the gyroscope.

Foucault /ˈfuːkəʊ/ Michel 1926–1984. French philosopher, one of the generation that came to maturity in the 1950s, and who rejected ◊phenomenology and ◊existentialism. His work is concerned with how forms of knowledge and forms of human subjectivity are constructed by specific institutions and practices, and is largely historical in character. Foucault was deeply influenced by ◊Nietzsche, and developed a novel analysis of the operation of power in modern society using Nietzschean concepts.

Fouché /ˈfuːʃeɪ/ Joseph, Duke of Otranto 1759–1820. French politician, born near Nantes. He was elected to the National Convention (the post-Revolutionary legislature), and organized the conspiracy which overthrew ◊Robespierre. Napoleon employed him as Police Minister.

Fou-Liang /ˈfəʊ liˈæŋ/ former name of ◊Jingdezhen, a town in China.

Fountains Abbey /ˈfaʊntənz/ Cistercian abbey situated 13 km/8 mi north of Harrogate, in ◊N Yorkshire, England. It was founded c. 1132, and suppressed in 1540. The ruins were incorporated into a Romantic landscape garden 1720–40 with lake, formal water garden, and temples, and a deer park. beautifully preserved.

Fouquet /ˈfuːkeɪ/ Jean c 1420–81. French artist. The major French painter of the 15th century, he became court painter to Charles VIII in 1475. His miniatures and altarpieces show Italian influence.

Fouquet /ˈfuːkeɪ/ Nicolas 1615–1680. French politician, a famous rival to ◊Colbert. Fouquet became *procureur général* of the Paris parliament in 1650 and in 1651 *surintendant des finances*, where he was responsible for raising funds for the long war against Spain, a post he

Fouché Joseph Fouché was minister of police under Napoleon. He was also instrumental in organizing the conspiracy that overthrew Robespierre.

held until arrested and imprisoned (for peculation, at the instigation of Colbert, who succeeded him) from 1661 until his death.

four-colour process the method by which colour ◊printing is done, using four printing plates. It relies on the principle that any colour is made up of different proportions of the three primary colours blue, red, and green. The first stage in preparing a colour picture for printing is to have colour separations made, that is, film representing the amount of blue, red and green respectively in the picture. From these separations three printing plates are made. A fourth plate is made for black. Printing is done from the colour plates in an ink colour complementary to that of the colour it represents -yellow for the blue plate, cyan for the red and magenta for the green.

Fourdrinier machine a papermaking machine, patented by the Fourdrinier brothers Henry and Sealy in England in 1803. On the machine liquid pulp flows onto a moving wire-mesh belt. Water drains and is sucked away, leaving a damp paper web. This is next passed first through a series of steam-heated rollers, which dry it, and then between heavy calendar rollers, which give it a smooth finish. The machine can measure up to 90 m/300 ft in length. The type is still in use.

Four Freedoms The four kinds of liberty essential to human dignity as defined in address to the American Congress by Franklin D Roosevelt 6 Jan 1941: freedom of speech and expression, freedom of worship, freedom from want, freedom from fear.

Fourier /ˈfʊrieɪ/ François Charles Marie 1772–1837. French socialist, born at Besançon. He spent most of his life as a clerk, and died in Paris. In his *Le Nouveau monde industriel/The New Industrial World* 1829–30, he advocated that society should be organized in cooperative units of approximately 1,800 people.

four-stroke cycle or the *Otto cycle* the engine-operating cycle of most ◊petrol and

Fourier The French socialist François Fourier. One of his major theories was to reorganize society into self-sufficient units of some 1800 people, living and working in co-operation. Conventional marriage was to be abandoned.

◊diesel piston engines. The 'stroke' refers to an upward or downward movement of a piston in a cylinder. In a petrol engine the cycle begins with intake, or induction, of fuel mixture as the piston goes down on its first stroke. On the second stroke (up) the piston compresses the mixture in the top of the cylinder. An electric spark then ignites the mixture, and the gases produced force the piston down on its third, power stroke On the fourth stroke (up) the piston expels the burnt gases from the cylinder into the exhaust. Then the cycle begins again. The diesel engine cycle works in a slightly different way.

Fourteen Points the terms proposed by President Wilson of the USA in his address to Congress on 8 Jan 1918, as a basis for the settlement of World War I that was about to reach its climax. They included: open diplomacy; freedom of the seas; removal of economic barriers; international disarmament; adjustment of colonial claims; German evacuation of Russian, Belgian, French, and Balkan territories; the restoration of Alsace-Lorraine to France; autonomy for the Austro-Hungarian peoples and those under Turkish rule; an independent Poland; and a general association of nations. Many of the 'points' were embodied in the peace treaties following the war.

fourth estate name applied to the Press and coined by the British politician Edmund ◊Burke.

fourth-generation language in computing, a programming language aimed at producing straightforward, commercial programs far more quickly than a more conventional language such as ◊Cobol. A fourth-generation language has facilities to support rapid screen design and easy use of databases. So called because it follows three other generations of programming language: machine code (first generation), assembly language (second), and currently used languages such as ◊BASIC and Pascal (third).

Fourth of July in the USA, the anniversary of the day in 1776 when the ◊Declaration of Independence was adopted by the ◊Continental Congress. It is a public holiday, officially called Independence Day.

Fourth Republic the French regime of 3 Jun 1944–44 Oct 1958.

fowl name for a chicken or chicken-like bird. The *red jungle fowl Gallus gallus* is the ancestor of all domestic chickens. It is a forest bird of South Asia, without the size or egg-laying ability of many domestic strains. ◊*Guinea fowl* are African.

Fowler /ˈfaʊlə/ Henry Watson 1858–1933. and his brother Francis George 1870–1918. British scholars and authors of a number of English dictionaries. *Modern English Usage* 1926, the work of Henry Fowler, has become a classic reference work for advice on matters of style and disputed usage.

Fowler /ˈfaʊlə/ (Peter) Norman 1938– . British Conservative politician, social services secretary from 1981.
Fowler was chair of the Cambridge University Conservative Association in 1960. He worked as correspondent for *The Times* until 1970, when he became a member of Parliament. He was a junior minister in Edward ◊Heath's government, transport secretary in Margaret ◊Thatcher's first administration, in 1979, and became social services secretary in 1981.

Fowler /ˈfaʊlə/ William 1911– . American astrophysicist. In 1983 he was awarded a Nobel prize for physics, with Subrahmanyan Chandrasekhar for their work on the life-cycle of stars, and the origin of chemical elements.

Fowles /faʊlz/ John 1926– . English writer. His complex novels, often concerned with illusion and reality, and with the creative process, include *The Collector* 1963, *The Aristos* 1965, *The French Lieutenant's Woman* 1969, *Daniel Martin* 1977, and *A Maggot* 1985.

fox name given to many of the smaller species of wild dog of the family Canidae. The *common* or *red fox Vulpes vulpes* of Britain and Europe is about 60 cm/2 ft long plus a tail ('brush') 40 cm/1.3 ft long. The fur is reddish with black patches behind the ears and a light tip to the tail. It feeds on a wide range of animals from worms to rabbits, scavenges for food, and also eats berries. Largely nocturnal, it makes an underground den or 'earth'. Very adaptable, it maintains high populations in some towns. Other species of the genus *Vulpes* live in N America, Asia and Africa. The *Arctic fox Alopex lagopus* is valued for its fur. Other 'foxes' include the ◊*fennec*, the *gray foxes* genus *Urocyon* of N and Central America, and the S American genus *Dusicyon* to which the extinct *Falkland Islands dog* belonged.

Fox /fɒks/ Charles James 1749–1806. English Whig politician. The son of the 1st baron Holland, he entered Parliament in 1769 as a supporter of the court, but in 1774 went over to the opposition. In 1782 he became secretary of state in Rockingham's government, but resigned when Shelburne succeeded Rockingham. He allied with North in 1783 to overthrow Shelburne, and formed a coalition ministry. When the Lords threw out Fox's bill to reform the government of India, George III dismissed the ministry, and in their place installed Pitt.
Fox now became leader of the opposition, although cooperating with Pitt in the impeachment of Hastings. He welcomed the French Revolution, but the 'Old Whigs' deserted to the government in 1792, leaving Fox and a small group of 'New Whigs' to oppose Pitt's war of intervention and his persecution of the reformers. On Pitt's death in 1806 a ministry was formed with Fox as foreign secretary, which at Fox's insistence abolished the slave trade. He opened peace negotiations with France, but died before their completion.

Fox /fɒks/ George 1624–1691. English founder of the Society of ◊Friends, born in Leicestershire. He became a travelling preacher

four-stroke cycle the internal combustion engine

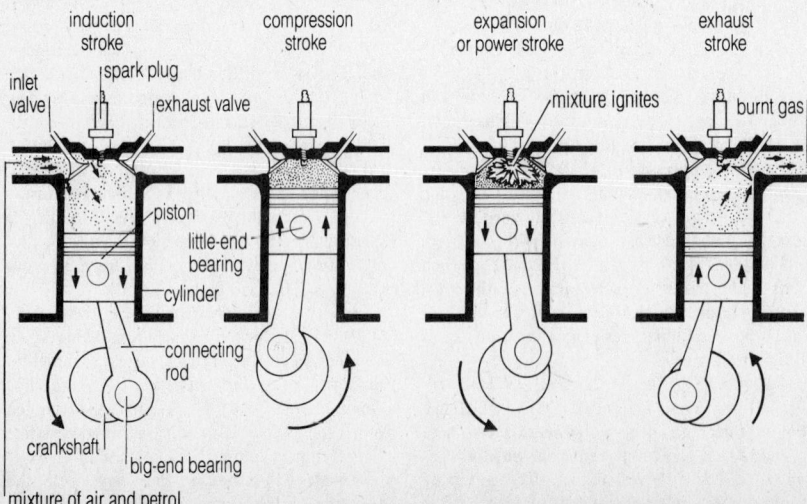

induction stroke — compression stroke — expansion or power stroke — exhaust stroke

inlet valve, spark plug, exhaust valve, mixture ignites, burnt gas, piston, little-end bearing, cylinder, connecting rod, crankshaft, big-end bearing, mixture of air and petrol

Fox One of the founders of British parliamentary Radicalism, Charles James Fox, an ardent Whig, opposed all abuses and restrictions of liberty. The portrait is by K A Hickel.

in 1647, and in 1650 was imprisoned for blasphemy at Derby, where the name Quakers was first applied derogatorily to him and his followers, supposedly because he enjoined Judge Bennet to 'quake at the word of the Lord'. He suffered further imprisonments, made missionary journeys, and wrote a *Journal*, published 1694.

Foxe /fɒks/ John 1516–1587. English Protestant propagandist, born at Boston, Lincolnshire. His *Book of Martyrs* 1563 luridly described persecutions under Queen ◊Mary, reinforcing popular hatred of Roman Catholicism.

foxglove flowering plant, of genus *Digitalis* of the family Scrophulariaceae. found in Europe and the Mediterranean region; they bear showy spikes of bell-like flowers, up to 1.5 m/5 ft high. The wild species *Digitalis purpurea*, native to Britain, produces purple to reddish flowers. It was originally a source of digitalis, a drug used for some heart problems.

fox-hunting the pursuit of a fox across country on horseback, aided by a pack of foxhounds, specially trained dogs that track the fox's scent. The aim is to catch and kill the fox. It dates from the late 17th century, and arose as a practical method of limiting the fox population, but by the early 19th century it was indulged in as a sport.

Among the most famous 'hunts' are the Quorn, Pytchley, Belvoir, and Cottesmore. There is a recognized fox-hunting season from the first Monday in November until the following April. Fox-hunting was introduced into the USA by early settlers from England, and continues in the south and middle-eastern regions.

In recent years opposition to fox-hunting has become more vehement; anti-blood-sport protesters condemn it as involving excesssive cruelty, and groups such as the Hunt Saboteurs seek to disrupt meets. In draghunting, hounds pursue a prepared trail rather than a fox.

fox-trot ballroom dance originating in the USA about 1914. Its name derives from the alternate rapid and slow movements of the fox.

Foyle /fɔɪl/ sea-lough on the N coast of Ireland, traversed by the frontier of Northern Ireland and the Irish Republic.

f.p.s. system the Imperial system of units based on the foot, pound, and second as units of length, mass, and time. Now replaced for scientific work by the ◊SI system.

fractal name given by the French mathematician Benoit Mandelbrod (from Latin *fractus* meaning broken) to irregular shapes or surfaces outside the rules of conventional geometry. Sets of curves with such discordant properties were developed in Germany by Georg Cantor (1845–1918) and Karl Weierstrass (1815–1897). Generated on a computer screen, fractals are used in creating models for geographical or biological processes (for example, the creation of a coastline by erosion or accretion, or the growth of plants). They are also used for computer art.

fraction in mathematics, a number that indicates one or more equal parts of a whole (from Latin *fractio* meaning to break). The usual way of denoting this is to place below a horizontal line the number of equal parts into which the unit is divided (denominator), and above the line the number of these parts comprising the fraction (numerator); thus ⅔ or ¾. Such fractions are called *vulgar* or *simple fractions*. A *proper fraction* is one in which the numerator is less than the denominator. A combination such as ⅚ is not regarded as a fraction however (an object cannot be divided into zero equal parts), and mathematically any number divided by 0 is equal to infinity. An *improper fraction* is one in which the numerator is larger than the denominator, for example, ³⁄₂. An improper fraction can therefore be expressed as a mixed number, for example, 1½. A *decimal fraction* is one in which the fraction is expressed by figures written to the right of the units figure (which may be 0) after a dot or point (the decimal point), for example 0.04, which is ⁴⁄₁₀₀. The digits to the right of the decimal point indicate the numerators of vulgar fractions whose denominators are 10, 100, 1,000, and so on.

fractionation also known as *fractional distillation*, a process used to split complex mixtures (such as crude oil) into its components, usually by repeated heating, boiling, and condensation.

Fra Diavolo /ˈfrɑː diˈævələʊ/ name by which the Italian brigand Michele Pezza (1771–1806) was known. A renegade monk, he led a gang in the mountains of Calabria for many years, but was eventually executed at Naples.

Fragonard /ˌfrægəʊˈnɑː/ Jean Honoré 1732–1806. French artist. He studied under ◊Boucher in Paris, and is famous chiefly for his light-hearted ◊rococo paintings of love in scenes such as *The Swing* c. 1766.

Frame /freɪm/ Janet. Pen name of New Zealand novelist Janet Paterson Frame Clutha 1924– . After being wrongly diagnosed as schizophrenic, she reflected her experiences 1945–54 in her work, for example, the novel *Faces in the Water* 1961, and the autobiographical *An Angel at My Table* 1984.

Frampton /ˈfræmptən/ George James 1860–1928. British sculptor. His most famous statues are *Peter Pan* in Kensington Gardens and the Nurse Cavell memorial near St Martin's, London.

franc French coin, so-called from 1360 when it was a gold coin inscribed *Francorum Rex*, 'King of the Franks'. The *franc CFA* is the currency of the French Community in Africa; in France's Pacific territories the *franc CFP* (Communauté française du pacifique) is used. The currency unit of Belgium, Luxembourg, and Switzerland is also called a franc.

France /frɑːns/ country in W Europe, bounded NE by Belgium and West Germany, E by Switzerland and Italy, S by the Mediterranean, SW by Spain and Andorra, and W by the Atlantic Ocean.

government Under the 1958 Fifth Republic constitution, amended in 1962, France has a two-chamber legislature and a 'shared executive' government. The legislature comprises a national assembly, whose 577 deputies are elected for five-year terms from single-member constituencies following a two-ballot, 'run-off' majority system (proportional representation was adopted for the 1986 elections but was later rescinded), and a senate, whose 319 members are indirectly elected, a third at a time, triennially for nine-year terms from groups of local councillors. 22 national assembly and 13 senate seats are elected by overseas *départements* and territories and ten senate seats by French nationals abroad. The national assembly is the dominant chamber, from whose ranks the prime minister is drawn and upon whose support the government rests. The senate can temporarily veto legislation. Its vetoes, however, can be overridden by the national assembly.

France's executive is functionally divided between the president and prime minister. The president, elected for a seven-year term by direct universal suffrage after gaining a majority in either a first or second 'run-off' ballot, functions as head of state, commander-in-chief of the armed forces and guardian of the constitution. The president selects the prime minister, presides over cabinet meetings, countersigns government bills, negotiates foreign treaties, and can call referenda and dissolve the national assembly. According to the constitution, however, ultimate control over policy making rests with the prime minister and council of ministers.

The president and prime minister work with ministers from political and technocratic backgrounds, assisted by a skilled and powerful civil service. A nine-member Constitutional Council (selected triennially in a staggered manner by the state president and the presidents of the senate and national assembly) and a *Conseil d'Etat*, staffed by senior civil servants, rule on the legality of legislation passed.

At the local level there are 22 regional councils concerned with economic planning. Below these are 96 *département* councils and almost 36,000 town and village councils. Corsica has its own directly elected 61-seat parliament with powers to propose amendments to national assembly legislation. French politics are dominated by four parties, divided into two broad right and left ideological and electoral coalitions.

There are four overseas *départements* (◊French Guiana, ◊Guadeloupe, ◊Martinique, and ◊Réunion) with their own elected general and regional councils, two overseas 'collective territories' (◊Mayotte and ◊St Pierre and Miquelon) administered by appointed commissioners, and four overseas territories (◊French Polynesia, the ◊French Southern and Antarctic Territories, ◊New Caledonia, and the ◊Wallis and Futuna Islands) governed by appointed high comissioners, which form constituent parts of the French Republic, returning deputies to the national legislature. The 'right coalition', which was pre-eminent 1958–81, is divided between the Rassemblement (Rally) pour la République (RPR), formed in 1976 by Jacques Chirac as the successor to ◊de Gaulle's Union pour la Nouvelle République (UNR), and the Union pour la Démocratie Française (UDF), formed by President Valéry ◊Giscard d'Estaing, Prime Minister Raymond ◊Barre and Jean Lecanuet in 1978 to unite several centre-right parties. The two major parties on the left are the pro-Moscow French Communist Party (PCF), and the Socialist Party (PS). The fifth significant party is the extreme right-wing National Front, which, although excluded from electoral coalitions, has gained ground campaigning for immigrant repatriation and the return of capital punishment.

history For history before 1945, see ◊France, history. A 'united front' provisional government headed by ◊de Gaulle, and including communists, assumed power in the re-established republic before a new constitution was framed and adopted for a Fourth Republic in Jan 1946. This provided for a weak executive and powerful national assembly which, being elected under a generous system of proportional representation, was to be divided between numerous small party groupings. With 26 impermanent governments being formed 1946–58, real power passed to the civil service, which, by introducing a new system of 'indicative economic planning', engineered rapid economic reconstruction. Decolonization of French ◊Indochina 1954, Morocco and Tunisia 1956, and entry into the EEC 1957 were also effected. The Fourth Republic was overthrown in 1958 by a political and military crisis over Algerian independence, which threatened to lead to a French army revolt. De Gaulle was recalled from retirement to head a government of national unity, and supervized the framing of the new Fifth Republic constitution, which strengthened the president and prime minister.

De Gaulle, who became president in 1959, restored domestic stability and presided over the decolonization of Francophone Africa, including Algerian independence in 1962. Close economic links were maintained with former colonies. De Gaulle also initiated a new foreign policy, withdrawing France from ◊NATO in 1966 and developing an autonomous nuclear deterrent force. The de Gaulle era was one of economic growth and large scale rural-urban migration. Politically, however, there was tight censorship

France
FRENCH REPUBLIC (*République Française*)

AREA (including Corsica) 551,553 sq km/212,960 sq mi
CAPITAL Paris
TOWNS Lyon, Lille, Bordeaux, Toulouse, Nantes, Strasbourg; ports Marseille, Nice
PHYSICAL rivers Seine, Loire, Garonne, Rhône, Rhine; mountain ranges Alps, Massif Central, Pyrenees, Jura, Vosges, Cévennes
TERRITORIES Guadeloupe, French Guiana, Martinique, Réunion, St Pierre and Miquelon, Southern and Antarctic Territories, New Caledonia, French Polynesia, Wallis and Futuna
FEATURES Ardennes forest, Auvergne mountain region, caves of Dordogne with relics of early humans, Riviera
HEAD OF STATE François Mitterrand from 1981
HEAD OF GOVERNMENT Jacques Chirac from 1986
GOVERNMENT parliamentary democracy
EXPORTS fruit (especially apples), wine, cheese; cars, aircraft, chemicals, jewellery, silk, lace; tourism is very important
CURRENCY franc (9.97 = £1 Sept 1987)
POPULATION (1985) 55,166,000 (including 4,500,000 immigrants, chiefly from Portugal, Algeria, Morocco, and Tunisia); annual growth rate 0.6%
LANGUAGE French (regional languages include Breton)
RELIGION mainly Roman Catholic; Muslim 2 million, Protestant 750,000
LITERACY 99% (1984)
GNP $568 bn (1983); $7,179 per head of population

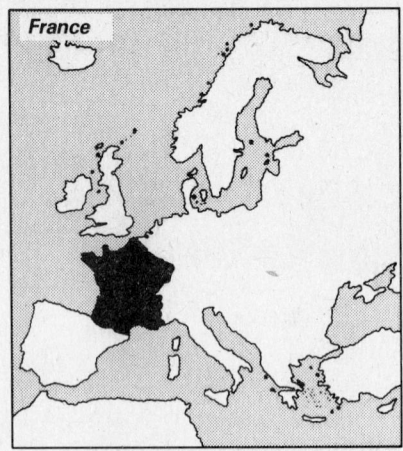
France

CHRONOLOGY
1944–46 De Gaulle provisional government. Commencement of Fourth Republic.
1954 Independence granted to Indochina.
1956 Moroccan and Tunisian independence.
1957 Entry into EEC.
1958 Recall of de Gaulle following Algerian crisis. Commencement of Fifth Republic.
1959 De Gaulle became president.
1962 Algerian independence granted.
1966 France withdrew from NATO.
1968 'May events' crisis.
1969 De Gaulle resigned following referendum defeat. Pompidou became president.
1974 Giscard d'Estaing elected president.
1981 Mitterrand elected Fifth Republic's first socialist president.

and strong centralization, and in 1967 the public reacted against de Gaulle's paternalism by voting the 'right coalition' a reduced majority. A year later, in 1968, the nation was paralyzed by students' and workers' demonstrations in Paris which spread to the provinces and briefly threatened the government. De Gaulle called elections and won a landslide victory. In 1969, however, he was defeated in a referendum over proposed senate and local government reforms and resigned. De Gaulle's former prime minister, Georges ◊Pompidou, was elected president and pursued Gaullist policies until his death in 1974. Pompidou's successor as president, Valéry ◊Giscard d'Estaing, leader of the centre-right Independent Republicans, introduced liberalizing domestic reforms and played a more active and co-operative role in the EEC. Giscard faced opposition, however, from his 'right coalition' partner, Jacques ◊Chirac, who was prime minister 1974–76, and deteriorating external economic conditions. France performed better than many of its European competitors between 1974–81, with the president launching a major nuclear power programme to save on energy imports and, while Raymond ◊Barre was

prime minister (1976–81), a new liberal 'freer market' economic strategy. However, with 1,700,000 unemployed, Giscard was defeated by the Socialist party leader, François ◊Mitterrand, in the 1981 presidential election.

Mitterrand's victory was the first presidential success for the 'left coalition' during the Fifth Republic and was immediately succeeded by a landslide victory for the PS and PCF in elections to the national assembly in 1981. The new administration, which included four Communist ministers, introduced a radical programme of social reform, decentralization and nationalization, and passed a series of reflationary budgets aimed at reducing unemployment.

Financial constraints, however, forced a switch towards a more conservative policy of 'rigueur' (austerity) in 1983. A U-turn in economic policy was completed in 1984 when prime minister Pierre ◊Mauroy was replaced by Laurent ◊Fabius, prompting the resignation of communist members of the cabinet. Unemployment rose to over 2,500,000 in 1985–86, increasing racial tension in urban areas. The extreme right-wing National Front,

FRANCE: REGIONS AND *DEPARTEMENTS*

Region and Département	Capital	Area sq km	Region and Département	Capital	Area sq km
Alsace			**Limousin**		
Bas-Rhin	Strasbourg		Corrèze	Tulle	
Haut-Rhin	Colmar	8,324	Creuse	Guéret	
Aquitaine			Haute-Vienne	Limoges	17,049
Dordogne	Périgueux		**Lorraine**		
Gironde	Bordeaux		Meurthe-et-Moselle	Nancy	
Landes	Mont-de-Marsan		Meuse	Bar-le-Duc	
Lot-et-Garonne	Agen		Moselle	Metz	
Pyrénées-Atlantiques	Pau	42,411	Vosges	Épinal	23,677
Auvergne			**Midi-Pyrénées**		
Allier	Moulins		Ariège	Foix	
Cantal	Aurillac		Aveyron	Rodez	
Haute-Loire	Le Puy		Haute-Garonne	Toulouse	
Puy-de-Dôme	Clermont-Ferrand	26,178	Gers	Auch	
Bourgogne			Lot	Cahors	
Côte-d'Or	Dijon		Hautes-Pyrénées	Tarbes	
Nièvre	Nevers		Tarn	Albi	
Saône-et-Loire	Mâcon		Tarn-et-Garonne	Montauban	45,603
Yonne	Auxerre	31,763	**Nord—Pas-de-Calais**		
Bretagne			Calvados	Caen	
Côtes-du-Nord	St. Brieuc		Manche	St. Lô	
Finistère	Quimper		Orne	Alençon	18,249
Ille-et-Vilaine	Rennes		**Haute-Normandie**		
Morbihan	Vannes	28,331	Eure	Evreux	
Centre			Seine-Maritime	Rouen	12,379
Cher	Bourges		**Pays de la Loire**		
Eure-et-Loir	Chartres		Loire Atlantique	Nantes	
Indre	Châteauroux		Maine-et-Loire	Angers	
Indre-et-Loire	Tours		Mayenne	Laval	
Loir-et-Cher	Blois		Sarthe	Le Mans	
Loiret	Orléans	39,542	Vendée	La Roche-sur-Yon	32,671
Champagne-Ardennes			**Picardie**		
Ardennes	Charleville-Mézières		Aisne	Laon	
Aube	Troyes		Oise	Beauvais	
Marne	Châlons-sur-Marne		Somme	Amiens	19,592
Haute-Marne	Chaumont	25,741	**Poitou-Charentes**		
Corsica			Charente	Angoulême	
Haute Corse	Bastia		Charente-Maritime	La Rochelle	
Corse du Sud	Ajaccio	8,772	Deux-Sèvres	Niort	
Franche-Comté			Vienne	Poitiers	26,302
Doubs	Besançon		**Provence-Côte d'Azur**		
Jura	Lons-le-Saunier		Alpes-de-Haute-Provence	Digne	
Haute Saône	Vesoul		Hautes-Alpes	Gap	
Terre de Belfort	Belfort	16,298	Alpes-Maritimes	Nice	
Île de France			Bouches-du-Rhône	Marseille	
Essonne	Évry		Var	Draguignan	
Val-de-Marne	Créteil		Vaucluse	Avignon	31,778
Val d'Oise	Cergy-Pontoise		**Rhône-Alpes**		
Ville de Paris			Ain	Bourg-en-Bresse	
Seine-et-Marne	Melun		Ardèche	Privas	
Hauts-de-Seine	Nanterre		Drôme	Valence	
Seine-Saint-Denis	Bobigny		Isère	Grenoble	
Yvelines	Versailles	12,022	Loire	St. Étienne	
Languedoc-Roussillon			Rhône	Lyon	
Aude	Carcassone		Savoie	Chambéry	
Gard	Nimes		Haute-Savoie	Annecy	44,624
Hérault	Montpellier				
Lozère	Mende				551,553
Pyrénées-Orientales	Perpignan	27,771			

led by Jean Marie ◊Le Pen, benefitted from this and gained seats in the Mar 1986 National Assembly elections, held under a new proportional representation system. The RPR gained 148 seats, the UDF 129, the Socialists and allied groupings 216, the PCF 35 and the National Front 35. The 'left coalition' lost its majority, the PCF having been in decline in recent years. The PS, however, has emerged as France's single most popular party.

From 1958–1986 the president and prime minister came from the same party coalition and the president was allowed to dominate in both home and foreign affairs. In 1986, however, President ◊Mitterrand was obliged to appoint a prime minister from the opposition coalition, Jacques Chirac, who emerged as the dominant force in the 'shared executive' and introduced a right-wing programme of denationalization, deregulation and 'de-socialization'. His reforms in the educational and economic sphere, however, encountered serious opposition from students and workers in 1986, necessitating policy concessions.

France /frɒns/ Anatole, pen name of Jacques Anatole Thibault 1844–1924. French writer, born in Paris. He published a critical study of Alfred de Vigny in 1868, which was followed by several volumes of poetry and short stories. His earliest novel was *Le Crime de Sylvestre Bonnard*/*The Crime of Sylvestre Bonnard* 1881; later books include *Thaïs* 1890, the satiric *L'Ile des pingouins*/*Penguin Island* 1908, and the autobiographical series beginning with *Le Livre de mon ami*/*My Friend's Book* 1885. He was elected to the French Academy in 1896, and in 1921 was awarded the Nobel Prize for Literature. He was a socialist and supporter of ◊Dreyfus.

France, history before its conquest by Julius ◊Caesar (57–51 BC), France, then called Gaul, was occupied by independent peoples, mostly Celtic. During the five centuries of Roman rule they accepted Roman civilization and the Latin language. As the empire declined in the 5th century Germanic tribes overran the country, until a Frankish chief, ◊Clovis (481–511), brought the other tribes under his rule and accepted Christianity. Under his successors, the ◊Merovingians, the country sank into anarchy, until unity was restored by Pepin (741–68), founder of the Carolingian dynasty. ◊Charlemagne (768–814) made France the centre of a great empire, but under his weak successors the great nobles became semi-independent, and Norsemen invaded France and settled in Normandy (◊William the Conqueror was of this descent). The first kings of the House of ◊Capet, which assumed the crown in 987, established rule in the district round Paris, but were surrounded by vassals stronger than themselves. During the 11th–13th centuries their power was gradually extended, with the support of the Church and the townspeople, but progress was later retarded by the ◊Hundred Years' War (1337–1453). Charles VII expelled the English from France (see ◊Joan of Arc). The restoration of the royal power was finally achieved by 1500, through the policies of Louis XI (1461–83) and

the annexation of Burgundy and Brittany (1483) to the crown. ◊Charles VIII's Italian wars initiated a struggle with Spain for supremacy in W Europe which lasted two centuries (1503–1697). Protestantism made considerable progress in France, and was adopted by a party of the nobles for political reasons; the result was a succession of civil wars, fought under religious slogans (1592–98). ◊Henry IV (1589–1610) restored peace, established religious toleration, and made the monarchy absolute. His work was continued by the great ministers ◊Richelieu and ◊Mazarin, who by their intervention in the ◊Thirty Years' War secured Alsace and made France the leading power in Europe. ◊Louis XIV (1643–1715) embarked on an aggressive policy which united Europe against him; in his reign began the conflict with Britain which lost France its colonies in Canada and India (see War of the ◊Spanish Succession (1701–14), War of the Austrian Succession (1756–58), ◊Seven Years War (1756–63). Misgovernment and unsuccessful wars aroused increasing discontent and resulted in the ◊French Revolution.

The revolution abolished feudalism and absolute monarchy, but failed to establish democracy. Foreign attempts at intervention led to wars (1792–1802, 1803–15), which gave Napoleon his opportunity to set up his military dictatorship. After Waterloo the Bourbon monarchy was restored (1814), see ◊Louis XIV. ◊Charles X's attempt in 1830 to substitute absolute for limited monarchy provoked a revolution which placed his cousin, Louis Philippe, on the throne; he was overthrown in the revolution of 1848, and the Second Republic set up. Its president, Louis Napoleon, Napoleon I's nephew, restored the empire in 1852, with the title of Napoleon III. His ambitious foreign policy ended in defeat in the Franco-Prussian War (1870–71) and the foundation of the Third Republic.

The new republic had an uneasy career, and on several occasions conflict between the clerical and militarist right and the radical and socialist left threatened civil war. Meanwhile a new colonial empire was being built up in Africa and Indochina. After 1900 politics were largely dominated by the approach of World War I. The war left France exhausted, and desperately seeking security in a system of E European alliances. An unsuccessful Fascist coup in 1934 prepared the way for the victory in 1936 of a radical-socialist-communist alliance, which introduced many social reforms; this broke down in 1938, and it was an alliance of the radicals with the right which declared war on Germany in 1939. The German invasion of 1940 allowed the extreme right to set up a puppet dictatorship under ◊Pétain, but resistance was maintained by the Free French under de Gaulle and the *maquis* until the liberation of 1944. For postwar history see ◊France.

Francesca /fræn'tʃeskə/ Piero della see ◊Piero della Francesca.

Franche-Comté /'frɒnʃ kɒn'teɪ/ region of E France; capital Besançon; population (1981) 1,100,000. Once independent and ruled by its own count, it was disputed by France, Burgundy, Austria, and Spain from the 9th century until it

became a French province under the Treaty of ◊Nijmegen in 1678. In the mountainous Jura there is farming and forestry, and elsewhere there are engineering and plastics industries.

Francis /'frɑːnsɪs/ or *François* two kings of France:

Francis I /'frɑːnsɪs/ 1494–1547. King of France. He succeeded his cousin Louis XII, and from 1519 European politics turned on the rivalry between him and Charles V, which led to war in 1521–29, 1536–38, and 1542–44. In 1525 Francis was defeated and captured at Pavia, and released only on signing a humiliating treaty. At home Francis developed absolute monarchy.

Francis II /'frɑːnsɪs/ 1544–1560. King of France. He married Mary, Queen of Scots, in 1558, and succeeded his father, Henry II, in 1559. He was completely under the influence of his mother, Catherine de' ◊Medici.

Francis II /'frɑːnsɪs/ Holy Roman Emperor. He succeeded his father, ◊Leopold II, in 1792. During his reign Austria was five times involved in war with France, in 1792–97, 1798–1801, 1805, 1809, and 1813–14. He assumed the title Francis I, Emperor of Austria in 1804, and abandoned that of Holy Roman Emperor in 1806.

Franciscan a member of one of the Catholic orders of friars (*Friars Minor* or *Grey Friars*), founded 1209 by ◊Francis of Assisi. Subdivisions were the strict Observants; the Conventuals, who were allowed to own property corporately; and the Capuchins, founded in 1520 to return to the simple way of life of the early Franciscans, and noted for missionary activity, and their habit with a pointed hood (French *capuche*). The Franciscans were noted for their preaching and ministrations amongst the poor, and included such scholars as Roger ◊Bacon.

A second (female) order the *Poor Clares* was founded by St ◊Clare in 1215, and lay people who adopt a Franciscan regime without abandoning the world form a third order (*Tertiaries*).

Francis of Assisi, St /ə'siːzi/ 1182–1226. Italian saint. The son of a wealthy merchant, he changed his life after two dreams during an illness following spells of military service when he was in his early 20s. He resolved to follow literally the behests of the New Testament and live a life of poverty and service while preaching a simple form of the Christian gospel. Francis attracted many followers, and in 1209 founded the Franciscan Order of friars.

Many stories are told of his ability to charm wild animals and to influence people in all walks of life. In 1219 he went to Egypt to convert the Sultan, and lived for a month in his camp. Returning to Italy, he resigned his leadership of the friars, and in 1224 he suffered a mystical experience during which he is said to have received the *stigmata* or five wounds of Christ. He died at Assisi, and was canonized in 1228.

Francis of Sales, St /seɪlz/ French bishop and theologian. Born in Savoy, he became bishop of Geneva 1602, and in 1602, and in 1610 founded the Order of the Visitation, an order of nuns. His writings include *Introduction à la vie dévote*/*Introduction to a Devout Life* 1609,

FRANCE: FORMER COLONIES

Current Name	Colonial Names and History	Colonized	Independent
Kampuchea	Cambodia to 1970	1863	1953
Laos	French Indo-China (protectorate)	1893	1954
Vietnam	Tonkin, Annam, Cochin-China to 1954; N&S Vietnam 1954–76	1858	1954
Burkina Faso	Upper Volta to 1984	1896	1960
Central African Republic	Ubangi-Shari	19th cent.	1960
Chad	French Equatorial Africa	19th cent.	1960
Côte d'Ivoire	Ivory Coast to 1986	1883	1960
Madagascar		1896	1960
Mali	French Sudan	19th cent.	1960
Niger		1912	1960
Algeria	Colonized in 19th cent. — incorporated into France 1881	c. 1840	1962

written to reconcile the Christian life with living in the real world. He was canonized 1665.

francium a metallic element, symbol Fr, atomic number 87, atomic weight 223. Discovered by Mlle Perey in 1939, it is a highly radioactive metal – the most stable isotope has a half-life of only 21 minutes.

Franck /fræŋk/ César Auguste 1822–1890. Belgian composer, born at Liège. His music is mainly religious and Romantic in style, and includes the symphony in D minor 1866–68, *Symphonic Variations* 1885 for piano and orchestra, the violin sonata 1886, the oratorio *Les Béatitudes/The Beatitudes* 1879, and many organ pieces.

Franco (Bahamonde) /'fræŋkəu ˌbɑː'mɒndeɪ/ Francisco 1892–1975. Spanish dictator, born in Galicia. He entered the army in 1910, served in Morocco, and was appointed Chief of Staff in 1935 but demoted to Governor of the Canary Islands in 1936. Dismissed from this post by the Popular Front (Republican) government, he plotted an uprising with German and Italian assistance, and on the outbreak of the Spanish Civil War organized the invasion of Spain by Moorish troops and foreign legionaries. After the death of General Sanjurjo, he took command of the insurgents (Nationalists), proclaiming himself *Caudillo* (leader) of Spain, and the defeat of the Republic with the surrender of Madrid in 1939 brought all Spain under his government. On the outbreak of World War II, in spite of Spain's official attitude of 'strictest neutrality', his pro-Axis sympathies led him to send aid, later withdrawn, to the German side. At home, he curbed the growing power of the ◊*Falange* (the Fascist party), and in 1942 reinstated the *Cortes* (Spanish parliament), which in 1947 passed an act by which Franco became head of state for life.
In later years Franco slightly liberalized his regime. In 1969 he nominated Juan ◊Carlos as his successor and future king of Spain, and relinquished the premiership in 1973. During his time in power he had presided over considerable economic growth in Spain.

Franco-German entente rapprochement between France and Germany, designed to erase the enmities of successive wars. It was initiated by the French president de Gaulle's personal mission to West Germany in 1962, followed by the Franco-German Treaty of Friendship and Co-operation 1963.

François /frɒn'swɑː/ French form of ◊Francis, name of two kings of France.

Franco-Prussian War 1870–71. War caused by rivalry between France and Prussia. The Prussian chancellor Bismarck put forward a German candidate for the vacant Spanish throne with the deliberate, and successful, intention of provoking the French emperor Napoleon III into declaring war. The Prussians trounced the French at ◊Sedan and went on to successfully besiege Paris. The Treaty of Frankfurt in May 1871 brought Prussia Alsace and Lorraine, plus a large French indemnity, and established Prussia as Europe's leading power.

frangipani tropical American tree *Plumeria rubra*, family Apocynaceae; perfume is made from its strongly scented flowers.

Franglais the French language when mixed with (unwelcome) elements of modern, especially American, English.

Frank /fræŋk/ a member of the Germanic people who overran Belgium and N France in the 4th–5th centuries. Their king, ◊Clovis, became Christian, founded the French monarchy, and all France and West Germany was temporarily united under his descendants. One branch of the Franks gave its name to France, and was fused by the 9th century into a single people with the Gallo-Romans, speaking the modified form of Latin which became modern French.

Frank /fræŋk/ Anne 1929–1945. German diarist, born at Frankfurt-am-Main. She fled to Holland with her family in 1933 to escape Nazi anti-Semitism. Under the occupation they remained in a sealed-off room in Amsterdam

1942–44, when betrayal resulted in Anne's death in Belsen concentration camp. The house in which the family took refuge is preserved as a museum. Her diary during her period in hiding was published in 1947.

Frankenstein Law in the USA, popular name for the ruling by the Supreme Court (1980) that new forms of life created in the laboratory may be patented.

Frankfurt-am-Main /'fræŋkfət æm 'maɪn/ city in Hesse, West Germany, 72 km/45 mi NE of Mannheim; population (1980) 630,000. Frankfurt is an important commercial and banking centre, university city, and inland port. There are electrical and machine industries, and an international Book Fair is held annually.
history Frankfurt was a free imperial city 1372–1806, when it was incorporated in ◊Prussia. It was the headquarters of the US zone of occupation in World War II and of the Anglo-US zone 1947–49.

Frankfurt-an-der-Oder /'fræŋkfət æn deə 'əudə/ city in East Germany 80 km/50 mi SE of Berlin, capital of Frankfurt district; population (1972) 65,072. It is linked by the river Oder and its canals to the Vistula and Elbe. Industries include chemicals, engineering, paper, and leather.

Frankfurt School in the social sciences, term used to refer to the work of the members of the Institute of Social Research, set up at Frankfurt University in Germany in 1923 as the first Marxist research centre. In the 1930s, under its second director Max Horkheimer, a group which included Erich Fromm, Herbert Marcuse, and T W Adorno attempted to update Marxism and create a coherent social theory, drawing on the work of a variety of disciplines as well as Marx and Freud, and producing major works such as *Authority and the Family* 1936 and a Marxist perspective known as *critical theory* . With the rise of Hitler, many of its members went to the US and set up the Institute at Columbia University, New York. After World War II the Institute returned to Frankfurt, although Marcuse and some others remained in the US. The German and American branches diverged in the 1950s, and the Institute was dissolved in 1969 after Adorno's death, although Jurgen Habermas and others have since attempted to revive its theory and research programme.

frankincense resin of trees of the Old World genus *Boswellia*, burnt as incense. Costly in ancient times, it was one of the three gifts traditionally brought by the Magi to the Christ child.

Franklin /'fræŋklɪn/ Benjamin 1706–1790. American scientist and politician. Born in Boston, he combined a successful printing business with scientific experiment. He proved that lightning is a form of electricity by the very dangerous experiment of flying a kite in a storm, distinguished between positive and negative electricity, and invented the lightning-conductor. A member of the Pennsylvania Assembly 1751–64, he was sent to England to lobby Parliament about tax grievances, and later helped to draft the Declaration of Independence. As ambassador to France, 1776–85, he

FRANCE: RULERS

Kings	Pepin III/Childerich III	751	*Kings*	Henri IV	1574
	Pepin III	752		Louis XIII	1610
	Charlemagne/Carloman	768		Louis XIV	1643
	Charlemagne (Charles I)	771		Louis XV	1715
	Louis I	814		Louis XVI	1774
	Lothair I	840		National Convention	1792
	Charles II (the Bald)	843		Directory (five members)	1795
	Louis II	877	*First Consul*	Napoléon Bonaparte	1799
	Louis III	879	*Emperor*	Napoléon I	1804
	Charles III (the Fat)	882	*King*	Louis XVIII	1814
	Odo	888	*Emperor*	Napoléon I	1815
	Charles III (the Simple)	893	*Kings*	Louis XVIII	1815
	Robert I	922		Charles X	1824
	Rudolf	923		Louis XIX	1830
	Louis IV	936		Henri V	1830
	Lothair II	954		Louis-Philippe	1830
	Louis V	986	*Heads of*	Philippe Buchez	1848
	Hugues Capet	987	*State*	Louis Cavaignac	1848
	Robert II	996	*President*	Louis Napoléon Bonaparte	1848
	Henri I	1031	*Emperor*	Napoléon III	1852
	Philippe I	1060	*Presidents*	Adolphe Thiers	1871
	Louis VI	1108		M. Patrice MacMahon	1873
	Louis VII	1137		Jules Grevy	1879
	Philippe II	1180		François Sadi-Carnot	1887
	Louis VIII	1223		Jean Casimir-Périer	1894
	Louis IX	1226		François Faure	1895
	Philippe III	1270		Émile Loubet	1899
	Philippe IV	1285		Armand Fallières	1913
	Louis X	1314		Raymond Poincaré	1913
	Jean I	1316		Paul Deschanel	1920
	Philippe V	1328		Alexandre Millerand	1920
	Charles IV	1322		Gaston Doumergue	1924
	Philippe VI	1328		Paul Doumer	1931
	Jean II	1350		Albert Le Brun	1932
	Charles V	1356		H. Philippe Pétain (Vichy government)	1940
	Charles VI	1380		provisional government	1944
	Charles VII	1422		Vincent Auriol	1947
	Louis XI	1461		René Coty	1954
	Charles VIII	1483		Charles de Gaulle	1959
	Louis XII	1498		Alain Poher	1969
	François I	1515		Georges Pompidou	1969
	Henri II	1547		Alain Poher	1974
	François II	1559		Valéry Giscard d'Estaing	1974
	Charles IX	1560		François Mitterrand	1981
	Henri III	1574			

Francis I Unstable and vacillating as a ruler, he is remembered for the brilliance of the artists and writers of his court.

negotiated an alliance with France and the peace settlement with Britain. As a delegate from Pennsylvania 1785–88, he helped draw up the American constitution.

Franklin /'fræŋklɪn/ John 1786–1847. British naval explorer. He took part in expeditions to Australia, the Arctic, and N Canada, and in 1845 commanded an expedition to look for the ◊North West Passage, on which he and his men perished. In 1984 two of its members buried on King Edward Island were found to be perfectly preserved in the frozen ground of their graves. The expedition had virtually found the Passage, but then become trapped in the ice, and no trace of them was discovered until 1859.

Franklin /'fræŋklɪn/ Rosalind 1920–1958. British biophysicist, whose research on ◊X-ray diffraction of DNA crystals helped ◊Crick and ◊Watson to deduce the chemical structure of ◊DNA.

Franz Ferdinand /'frænts 'fɜːdɪnænd/ or Francis Ferdinand 1863–1914. Archduke of Austria. He became heir to his uncle, the Emperor ◊Franz Joseph, from 1884 but while visiting Sarajevo on 28 Jun 1914, he and his wife were assassinated by Scrb nationalists; Austria used the episode as an excuse for attacking Serbia, precipitating World War I.

Franz Josef Land /'frænts 'jəuzef/ archipelago of some 85 islands in the Arctic Ocean, E of Spitsbergen and NW of Novaya Zemlya, USSR. Area 20,720 sq km/8,000 sq mi. There are scientific stations.

Franz Joseph /'frænts 'jəuzef/ or Francis Joseph 1830–1916. Emperor of Austria-Hungary. He succeeded his uncle, Ferdinand I,

Francis of Assisi, St Portrait of the saint, believed to date from 1225. He renounced all property and founded the Franciscan Order of friars.

Franklin One of 17 children, the American scientist and diplomat Benjamin Franklin invented the lightning conductor and helped to draw up the American constitution.

Franz Joseph The life of Franz Joseph, Emperor of Austria, was marred by a series of personal tragedies; the suicide of his only son, and the assassinations of Empress Elizabeth in 1898 and of his heir and nephew Franz Ferdinand in 1914.

on his abdication in 1848, and after the suppression of the 1848 revolution set out to establish an absolute monarchy. But he was defeated in the Italian War of 1859 and the Prussian War of 1866, and had to grant Austria a parliamentary constitution in 1861 and Hungary equality with Austria in 1867. His only son committed suicide in 1889, and the empress was assassinated in 1897. In 1914 he made the assassination of his nephew, ◊Franz Ferdinand, the excuse for attacking Serbia, precipitating World War I.

Frasch process a process used to extract underground deposits of ◊sulphur, developed in the USA by German-born Herman Frasch in 1891. In the process superheated steam is piped to the sulphur deposit and melts it. Compressed air is then pumped down to force the molten sulphur to the surface.

Fraser /'freɪzə/ Antonia 1932– . British author of biographies, for example, *Mary Queen of Scots* 1969; history, for example, *The Weaker Vessel* 1984; and a series of detective novels featuring investigator Jemima Shore.

Fraser /'freɪzə/ Dawn 1937– . Australian swimmer. The only person, male or female, to win the same event at three consecutive Olympic Games. She won 100 metres freestyle 1956, 1960, 1964, broke 27 world records and was the first woman to break the one-minute barrier for the 100 metres.

Fraser /'freɪzə/ Malcolm 1930– . Australian Liberal politician (nicknamed the 'Prefect' because of a supposed disregard of subordinates). Educated at Oxford, he became a millionaire sheep farmer. In Mar 1975 he replaced Snedden as Liberal Party leader. In Nov, following the Whitlam government's economic difficulties, he blocked finance bills in the Senate, became prime minister of a caretaker government and in the consequent general

election won a large majority. He lost to Hawke in the 1983 general election.

Fraser /'freɪzə/ Peter 1884–1950. New Zealand Labour politician, born in Scotland. He joined the Independent Labour Party in 1908. In 1910 he went to New Zealand and soon became prominent in the Labour movement there. He held various cabinet posts 1935–40, and was prime minister 1940–49.

fraternity and sorority a student society (fraternity for men; sorority for women) in US universities and colleges. Usually named with Greek letters, they are nominally secret, with badge, passwords, motto, and initiation rites. They have a central governing body and a 'chapter' at each college. Although mainly social and residential, some are purely honorary, membership being on the basis of scholastic distinction, for example, Phi Beta Kappa, earliest of the fraternities, founded at William and Mary College, Virginia, in 1776.

fraud in law, an act of deception. To establish fraud it has to be demonstrated that : (1) a false representation (for example, a factually untrue statement) has been made, with the intention that it should be acted upon; (2) the person making the representation knows it is false or does not attempt to find out whether it is true or not; and (3) the person to whom the representation is made acts upon it to their detriment. A contract based on fraud can be declared void, and the injured party can sue for damages.

Fraunhofer /'fraʊnhəʊfə/ Joseph von 1787–1826. German physicist, who did important work in optics. Born in Bavaria, he was apprenticed to a glass cutter, and in 1807 founded an optical institute. The dark lines in the solar spectrum (Fraunhofer lines), which

revealed the chemical composition of the sun's atmosphere, were accurately mapped by him.

Fray Bentos /'fraɪ 'bentɒs/ river port in Uruguay; population (1970) 14,000. Linked by a bridge over the Uruguay with Puerto Unzue in Argentina (1976), it is famous for its meat-packing industry, particularly corned beef.

Frazer /'freɪzə/ James George 1854–1941. Scottish anthropologist, born in Glasgow. He was educated at Glasgow and Cambridge universities, and in 1890 won acclaim with *The Golden Bough*. This study of the origins of religion and sociology on a comparative basis was a pioneer work: by the standards of modern anthropology many of its methods and findings are unsound, but it had a considerable influence on writers such as T S Eliot and D H Lawrence.

Frederick /'fredrɪk/ two Holy Roman Emperors:

Frederick I c. 1123–90. Emperor from 1152, known as Barbarossa 'red-beard'. Originally duke of Swabia, he was elected emperor in 1152, and was engaged in a struggle with the papacy (◊Alexander III) 1159–77, which ended in his submission; the Lombard cities, headed by Milan, took advantage of this to establish their independence of imperial control. Frederick joined the Third Crusade, and was drowned in Asia Minor.

Frederick II 1194–1250. Called 'the Wonder of the World'. Son of Henry VI, he was elected emperor in 1212. He led a crusade in 1228–29 which recovered Jerusalem by treaty without fighting. At the same time he quarrelled with the pope who three times excommunicated him, and a feud began which lasted at intervals until the end of his reign. Frederick, who was a complete sceptic in religion, is often considered the most cultured man of his age.

Frederick /'fredrɪk/ three kings of Prussia:

Frederick I 1657–1713. He became Elector of Brandenburg in 1688, and assumed the title of King of Prussia in 1701.

Frederick II, called *the Great* 1712–86. King from 1740. He received a Spartan education from his father, ◊Frederick William I, and in 1730 was threatened with death for attempting to run away. Soon after his accession he started the War of the ◊Austrian Succession by his attack on Austria. In the peace of 1745 he secured Silesia. The struggle was renewed in the Seven Years' War 1756–63 and, in spite of assistance from Britain, Frederick had a hard task holding his own against the Austrians and their Russian allies; the skill with which he did so proved him to be one of the great soldiers of history. In his domestic policy he was one of the first and most famous 'enlightened despots' of the Age of Reason: he encouraged industry and agriculture, reformed the judicial system, fostered education, and established religious toleration. He was also a great patron of the arts, and himself a talented musician. He acquired West Prussia in the first partition of Poland 1772, and left Prussia as Germany's foremost state.

Frederick III 1831–88. King and German Emperor in 1888. The son of ◊William I, he married Queen Victoria of England's eldest

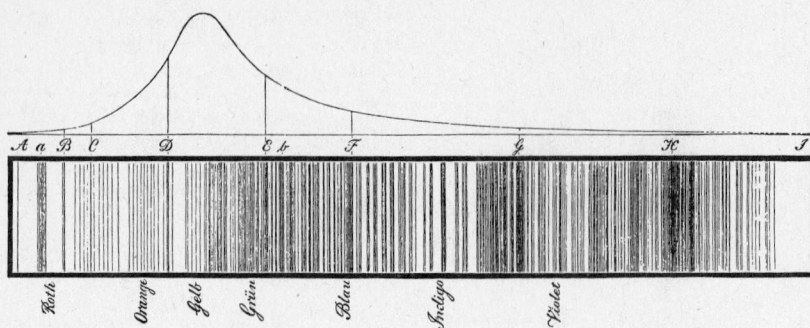

Rath — Orange — Gelb — Grün — Blau — Indigo — Violet

Fraunhofer Drawing of the dark lines of the solar spectrum by the German physicist Joseph von Fraunhofer, the first to accurately map the chemical composition of the sun's atmosphere. The curve shows the intensity of sunlight in different parts of the spectrum.

daughter (Victoria) in 1858, and, as a liberal, frequently opposed ◊Bismarck. He died of cancer three months after his accession.

Frederick William /ˈfredrɪk ˈwɪljəm/ 1620–1688. Elector of Brandenburg from 1640, 'the Great Elector'. By successful wars with Sweden and Poland, he prepared the way for Prussian power in the 18th century.

Frederick William /ˈfredrɪk ˈwɪljəm/ 1882–1951. Last Crown Prince of Germany, eldest son of Wilhelm II. During World War I he commanded a group of armies on the western front. In 1918 'Little Willie', as he was called in England, retired into private life.

Frederick William /ˈfredrɪk ˈwɪljəm/ four kings of Prussia:

Frederick William I 1688–1740. King from 1713, he developed Prussia's military might and commerce.

Frederick William II 1744–97. Nephew of ◊Frederick II and king from 1786, he was unsuccessful in waging war on the French 1792–95, and lost all Prussia west of the Rhine.

Frederick William III 1770–1840. King from 1797, he was defeated by Napoleon 1806, but in 1813–15 contributed to his final overthrow, and profited in territory allotted at the Congress of ◊Vienna.

Frederick William IV 1795–1861. King from 1840, he believed in the ◊divine right of kings, but had to grant a constitution in 1850 after the Prussian revolution of 1848. He became insane in 1857.

Fredriksstad /ˈfredrɪkstæd/ Norwegian port at the mouth of the river Glomma, dating from 1570; population (1980) 27,893. It is a centre of the timber trade, and has shipyards.

Free Church name given to protestant denominations in England and Wales which are not part of the Church of England, for example, the Methodist Church, Baptist Union, and United Reformed Church (Congregational and Presbyterian). These churches joined for common action in the Free Church Federal Council in 1940.

Free Church of Scotland the body of Scottish Presbyterians who seceded from the Established Church of Scotland in 1843. In 1900 all but a small section that retains the old name combined with the United Presbyterian Church to form the United Free Church, which reunited with the Church of Scotland in 1929.

Freedom, Presidential Medal of the highest peacetime civilian honour in the USA. Instituted by Kennedy in 1963, it is awarded to those 'who contribute significantly to the quality of American life' and a list of recipients is published each Independence Day. It replaced the Medal of Freedom, instituted 1945, which had been conferred on no regular basis, with only 24 awards having been made.

free fall a state in which a body is falling freely under the influence of ◊gravity, as in free-fall parachuting. In orbit we normally use the term *weightless* to describe a body in free fall. In orbit astronauts and spacecraft are still held by gravity, and are in fact falling towards the Earth. Because of their speed (orbital velocity), the amount they fall towards the Earth just equals the amount the Earth's surface curves away. So in effect they remain at the same height, apparently weightless.

free falling sport also known as ◊skydiving, which entails falling from an aircraft and then, by a correct positioning of the body, gliding down from anything up to 3,650 m/12,000 ft until the level at which a parachute must be opened – 600 m/2,000 ft.

Free French movement formed by General ◊de Gaulle in England in Jun 1940, consisting of French soldiers who continued to fight against the Axis after the Franco-German armistice. They took the name Fighting France in 1942 and served in many campaigns, among them General Leclerc's advance from Chad to Tripolitania 1942, the Syrian campaigns 1941, the campaigns in the Western Desert, the Italian campaign, the liberation of France, and the invasion of Germany. Their emblem was the Cross of Lorraine (with two 'bars').

freehold in the UK, ownership of land which is for an indefinite period and is therefore contrasted with a leasehold, which is always for a fixed term of years. In practical effect, a freehold is absolute ownership.

freemasonry the beliefs and practices of a group of linked national organizations open to men over 21, united by the possession of a common code of morals, and of certain traditional 'secrets'. Freemasons believe in God, whom they call the 'Great Architect of the Universe'. Freemasonry is descended from an operative guild of masons which existed in the 14th century, and by the 16th was admitting men unconnected with the building trade. The name 'freemason' may mean a full member of the guild, or one working in free-stone, that is, a mason of the highest class. Modern freemasonry originated with the formation of the first Grand Lodge, or governing body, in 1717, and during the 18th century spread from Britain to America, Europe, and elsewhere. In France and other European countries, freemasonry assumed a political and anticlerical character; it has been condemned by the papacy, and in certain countries was suppressed by the state. Freemasons do much charitable work, but have been increasingly criticized in recent years for their secrecy, their male exclusivity, and particularly their alleged use of influence within and between organizations (for example, the police or local government) to further each others' interests.

free port a port allowed to operate without the application of usual Customs duties; for example, if foreign firms land goods for assembly, which are then exported. Duties and tax become payable only if the products are then imported into the country to which the free port belongs. The UK's free ports are Cardiff, Liverpool, Southampton, and, linked to airports, Belfast, Birmingham, and Prestwick.

freesia genus of South African plants, family Iridaceae; commercially grown for their scented funnel-shaped flowers.

free thought post-Reformation movement opposed to Christian dogma, represented in Britain by the 17th–18th century deists, in the 19th century by the radical thinker Richard Carlile (1790–1843), (a pioneer of a free press), Charles ◊Bradlaugh, Lord ◊Morley, and J B Bury (1861–1927), and in the 20th by Bertrand ◊Russell. The tradition is upheld by the Rationalist Press Association and Secular Society.

Freetown /ˈfriːtaʊn/ capital of Sierra Leone, W Africa; population (1975) 274,000. It is a commercial port and also a naval station, and has an excellent harbour. There is an international airport at Lungi.

free trade international trade free from all tariffs (import taxes) except those levied for revenue purposes only. The case for free trade, first put forward in the 17th century, received its classic statement in Adam ◊Smith's *Wealth of Nations* 1776. The movement towards free trade began with ◊Pitt's commercial treaty with France in 1786, and triumphed with the repeal of the ◊Corn Laws in 1846. According to traditional economic theory, free trade allows nations to specialize in those commodities which can be produced most efficiently. In Britain, superiority to all rivals as a manufacturing country in the Victorian age made free trade an advantage, but when that superiority was lost the demand for protection was raised, notably by Joseph Chamberlain. The ◊Ottawa Agreements of 1932 marked the end of free trade until in 1948 an international treaty, the ◊*General Agreement on Tariffs and Trade* (GATT), came into operation. A drastic series of resultant international tariff reductions was agreed in the Kennedy Round Conference 1964–67, and the Tokyo Round 1973–79 made substantial special concessions to developing countries. In the 1980s long-continued recession swung the pendulum back towards *protectionism* which discourages by heavy duties foreign imports likely to compete with home products.

free verse poetry without metrical form. At the beginning of the 20th century, under the very different influences of ◊Whitman and ◊Mallarmé, many poets became convinced that the 19th century had done most of what could be done with regular metrical forms, and rejected regular metre in much the same spirit as Milton had rhyme, preferring irregular metres which made it possible to express thought clearly and without distortion. This was true of T S ◊Eliot and the Imagists; it was also true of poets who, like the Russians ◊Esenin and ◊Mayakovsky, placed emphasis on public performance. Poets including Robert Graves and the later Auden have criticized free verse on the ground that it lacks the difficulty of true accomplishment, but their own metrics would have been considered loose much of the time by earlier critics. The freeness of free verse is largely relative.

free will the doctrine that human beings are free to control their own actions and that these actions are not fixed in advance by God or fate. This doctrine is hard to reconcile convincingly with the view that people are part of a world governed by either physical laws or God's will. Some Christian theologians assert that God gave humanity free will to choose between good and evil; others that God has decided in advance the outcome of all human choices (◊predestination, as in Calvinism).

freezing change from a liquid to a solid state, as when water becomes ice. For a given substance, freezing occurs at a definite temperature, known as the freezing point, that is invariable under similar conditions of pressure, and the temperature remains at this point until all the liquid is frozen. The amount of heat per unit mass that has to be removed to freeze a substance is a constant for each particular substance and is known as the latent heat of fusion. Since ice is lighter than water, water expands just before its freezing point is reached. If pressure is applied, expansion is retarded and the freezing point will be lowered. The presence of dissolved substances in a liquid also lowers the freezing point, the amount of lowering being proportional to the molecular concentration of the solution (see ◊freezing point depression). Antifreeze mixtures for car radiators and the use of salt to melt ice on roads are common applications of this principle. In physical terms, freezing and melting are the same phenomenon - one involves lowering temperature and the other involves raising it. Animals in arctic conditions, for example, insects or fish, cope with the extreme cold either by manufacturing natural 'antifreeze' and staying active, or by allowing themselves to

freeze in a controlled fashion, that is, they manufacture proteins to act as nuclei for the formation of ice crystals in areas that will not produce cellular damage, and so enable themselves to thaw back to life again.

freezing point depression of a solution, below that of the pure solvent, depends on the number of molecules of solute dissolved in it. Thus for a single solvent, such as pure water, all substances in the same molecular concentration produce the same lowering of freezing point. The depression d for a molar concentration C is given by the equation $d = KC$, where K is a constant for the particular solvent (called the cryoscopic constant). Measurement of freezing point depression is a useful method of determining molecular weights of solutes.

Frege /'freɪgə/ Gottlob 1848–1925. German philosopher. The founder of modern mathematical logic, he published in 1884 *Grundgesetze der Arithmetik/The Foundations of Arithmetic* which was to influence ◊Russell and ◊Wittgenstein. His work, neglected for a time, has attracted renewed attention in recent years in Britain and the USA.

Freiburg-im-Breisgau /'fraɪbʊəg ɪm 'braɪsgaʊ/ industrial city (pharmaceuticals, precision instruments) in Baden-Württemberg, West Germany; population (1980) 175,800. It is the seat of an archbishopric and university, and has a fine 12th-century cathedral.

Frelimo (Front for the Liberation of Mozambique) nationalist group aimed at gaining independence for Mozambique from the occupying Portuguese. It began operating out of Southern Tanzania 1963, and continued until victory in 1975.

Fremantle /'friːmæntl/ chief port of W Australia, at the mouth of the Swan river, SW of ◊Perth; population (1981) 23,780. It has shipbuilding yards, sawmills, and iron foundries, and exports wheat and timber. The America's Cup yacht races (Australia v USA) were held there in 1987.

French /frentʃ/ John Denton Pinkstone, 1st Earl of Ypres 1852–1925. British field marshal. In the ◊South African War, he relieved Kimberley and took Bloemfontein; in World War I he was commander in chief of the British Expeditionary Force in France 1914–15; he resigned after being criticized as indecisive.

French Antarctica /frentʃ ænt'ɑːktɪkə/ territory, in full *French Southern and Antarctic Territories*, created 1955; area 10,100 sq km/3,900 sq mi; population about 200 research scientists. It includes Adélie Land, on the antarctic continent (136–142 km long), the Kerguelen and Crozet archipelagos, and Saint Paul and Nouvelle Amsterdam islands in the southern seas. It is administered from Paris, but Port-aux-Français on Kerguelen is the chief centre, with several research stations. There are also research stations on Nouvelle Amsterdam and in Adélie Land; and a meteorological station on Possession Island in the Crozet archipelago. Saint Paul is uninhabited.

French art before the 15th century the main forms of artistic expression in France were architecture and sculpture. The miniatures of

Jean Fouquet and the *Très riches heures* (a book of hours) of the Limbourg brothers, manuscript illuminators, stand out in the 15th century. The 16th century artists were influenced by the Italians, but the miniature tradition was kept up by the Clouets and Corneille de Lyons. A great sculptor of the age was Jean Goujon. The most famous names of the 17th century include Poussin, Claude Lorrain, Philippe de Champaigne, Blanchard, and Bourdon.

In the 18th century French painting and sculpture became dominant throughout Europe. The great masters were Watteau, Chardin, Fragonard, Lancret, Boucher, and the sculptor Houdon. The Neo-Classical school was founded by David. He was followed by Ingres. Delacroix was the leader of the Romantic movement. Géricault excelled as a history and animal painter.

The 19th century produced two famous schools of painting – the *Barbizon* and the *Impressionist*. The landscape painters of the Barbizon school include Millet, Corot, Daubigny, and Theodore Rousseau; the most famous Impressionists were Monet, Manet, Pissarro, Sisley, Degas, and Renoir. More subjective painters were Toulouse-Lautrec and van Gogh, and it was the latter, with Cézanne and Gauguin, whose Expressionist approach to the technique of painting prepared the way for many 20th century developments. In the 1850s the graphic artists Daumier and Guys were notable; other outstanding artists were Courbet, Henri Rousseau, Bonnard, the *Pointillist* Seurat, and the sculptor Rodin. In the 20th century Paris became the home of two schools of painting in particular: Fauvism, showing the influence of Gauguin with his emphasis on pure colour, for example, Matisse, Derain, Vlaminck, Dufy, and Friesz; and Cubism, deriving from Cézanne, and with exponents as diverse as Matisse and Derain, Picasso, Braque, and Juan Gris. Other notable artists were Chagall, the Dadaist Duchamp, the Surrealist Max Ernst, Rouault, Soutine, Utrillo, Modigliani, and Maillol the sculptor.

French Canadian literature F-X Garneau's *Histoire du Canada* (1845–48) inspired a school of patriotic verse led by Octave Crémazie (1827–79) and continued by Louis Fréchette (1838–1908). A new movement began after 1900 with such poets as André Lozeau (1878–1924), Paul Morin, Robert Choquette (1862–1941), Alain Grandbois, St Denys Garneau, Eloi de Grandmont, and Pierre Trottier. Fiction reached a high point with Louis Hémon (1880–1914) whose *Maria Chapdelaine* inspired many genre works. Outstanding later novelists are Germaine Guèvremont, Gabrielle Roy, 'Ringuet' (Philippe Panneton, 1895–), Robert Elie, Roger Lemelin, and Yves Thériault.

French Community former association comprising France and those overseas territories joined with it by the constitution of the Fifth Republic, following the 1958 referendum. Many of the constituent states withdrew during the 1960s, and it no longer formally exists, but in practice all former French colonies have close economic and cultural as well as language links with France.

French Guiana /giː'ɑːnə/ overseas region of France from 1976, in the north of South America, adjoining Suriname
area 91,000 sq km/34,740 sq mi
capital Cayenne
towns St Laurent
features Eurospace rocket launch pad at Kourou; Îles du Salut, which include ◊Devil's Island
exports timber, shrimps, gold
currency franc
population (1982) 73,000
language French
religion Roman Catholic
famous people Capt ◊Dreyfus
history first settled by France 1604, the territory became a French possession 1817.

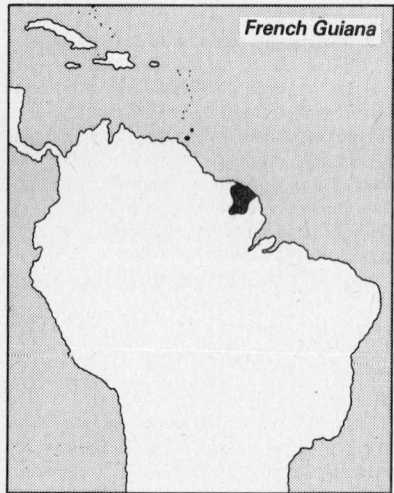

French Guiana

French horn musical instrument. See ◊brass.

French India former French possessions in India (Pondichéry, Chandernagore, Karikal, Mahé, and Yanaon (Yanam)), all transferred to India by 1954.

French language a member of the Romance branch of the Indo-European language family, spoken in France, Belgium, Luxembourg and Switzerland in Europe, Canada (especially the province of Quebec) in North America, such islands as Haiti and Martinique in the Caribbean, Reunion and Mauritius in the Indian Ocean, New Caledonia in the Pacific, and the Francophone (French-speaking) countries of N and W Africa (for example, Mali, the Cote d'Ivoire and Senegal). French developed from the Latin spoken in Gaul and was established as a distinct language by the 9th century. Varieties used north of the river Loire formed the *Langue d'oil* (*oui*) while those to the south formed the *Langue d'oc*, according to their word for 'yes'. However, by the 13th century, the dialect of the Ile de France was supreme and became in 1539 the official medium of the courts and administration of France. Its literary form still serves as the basis of *le bon français* ('correct French'), which is officially protected by the Academie Francaise (founded in 1635 at the behest of Cardinal Richelieu) and by occasional legislation in both France and Quebec.

French literature *The Middle Ages*
The *Chanson de Roland* (c. 1080) is the greatest of the early *chansons de geste* (epic poems about deeds of chivalry) which were superseded by the Arthurian romances (seen at their finest in the work of Chrétien de Troyes in the 12th century), and by the classical themes of Alexander, Troy, and Thebes. Other aspects of French medieval literature are represented by the charming anonymous *Aucassin et Nicolette* of the early 13th century, the allegorical *Roman de la Rose/Romance of the Rose*, the first part of which was written by Guillaume de Lorris (c. 1230) and the second by Jean de Meung (c. 1275), and the satiric *Roman de Renart/Story of Renard* of the late 12th century, the historians Villehardouin, Joinville, Froissart, and Comines, and the first great French poet, François Villon.
Renaissance to the 18th century
Most notable poet of the Renaissance was Ronsard, leader of the ◊Pléiade (a group of seven writers); others included Marot at the beginning of the 16th century and Régnier at its close. In prose the period produced the broad genius of Rabelais and the essayist Montaigne. In the 17th century came the triumph of form with the great classical dramatists Corneille, Racine, and Molière, and the graceful brilliance of La Fontaine, and the poet-critic Boileau. Masters of prose in the same period include the philosophers Pascal and Descartes; the preacher Bossuet; the critics La Bruyère, Fénelon and Malebranche; and La Rochefoucauld, Cardinal de Retz, Mme de Sévigné, and Le Sage.
The 18th century was the age of the ◊Enlightenment and an era of prose, with Montesquieu, Voltaire, Rousseau; the scientist Buffon; the encyclopaedist Diderot; the ethical writer Vauvenargues; the novelists Prévost and Marivaux; and the memoir writer Saint-Simon.
19th and 20th centuries
In the 19th and 20th centuries poetry came to the fore again with the Romantics Lamartine, Hugo, Vigny, Musset, Leconte de Lisle, and Gautier; novelists of the same school were George Sand, Stendhal and Dumas *père*, while criticism is represented by Sainte-Beuve, and history by Thierry, Michelet, and Taine. The realist novelist Balzac was followed by the school of Naturalism, whose representatives were Flaubert, Zola, the Goncourt brothers, Alphonse Daudet, Maupassant, and Huysmans. 19th-century dramatists included Hugo, Musset, and Dumas *fils*. Symbolism, a movement of experiment and revolt against classical verse and the materialist attitude, with the philosopher Bergson as one of its main exponents, found its first expression in the work of Gérard de Nerval, who was later followed by Baudelaire, Verlaine, Mallarmé, Rimbaud, Corbière, and the prose writer Villiers de l'Isle Adam; later writers in the same tradition were Henri de Régnier and Laforgue.
In the late 19th and early 20th centuries drama and poetry revived with Valéry, Claudel, and Paul Fort, who advocated 'pure poetry'; other writers were the novelists Gide and Proust, and the critics Thibaudet (1874–1936) and later St John Perse, also a well-known poet. The Surrealist movement, which developed from 'pure poetry' through the work of Eluard and Apollinaire, influenced writers as diverse as Giraudoux, Louis Aragon, and Cocteau. The literary reaction against the Symbolists included Charles Péguy, Rostand, Mme de Noailles, and Romain Rolland. 20th-century novelists in the Naturalist tradition were Henri Barbusse, Jules Romains, Julian Green, François Mauriac, Francis Carco, and Georges Duhamel. Other prose writers are Maurois, Malraux, Montherlant, Anatole France, Saint-Exupéry, Alain-Fournier, Pierre Hamp, and J R Bloch, while the theatre flourished with plays by J J Bernard, Anouilh, Beckett, and Ionesco. World War II had a profound effect on French writing, and distinguished post-war writers include the Existentialist Sartre, and Camus, 'Vercors' (pen name of Jean Bruller), Simone de Beauvoir, Alain Robbe-Grillet, Romain Gary, Nathalie Sarraute and Marguerite Duras.

French Polynesia /ˌpɒlɪ'niːzɪə/ French overseas territory (from 1961) in the S Pacific
total area 3,940 sq km/1,520 sq mi
capital Papeete on Tahiti
features comprises five archipelagos (see below)
exports cultivated pearls, coconut oil, vanilla; tourism is important
total population (1983) 166,000
languages French, Tahitan (official)
government a High Commissioner (Alain Ohrel) and Council of Government; two deputies are returned to the National Assembly in France
recent history first visited by Europeans 1595, the Polynesian islands became famous as living 'proof' of ◊Rousseau's theory of the noble savage when visited by Louis ◊Bougainville in 1768. They became a French Protectorate 1843, self-governing 1977. Following demands for independance in ◊New Caledonia 1984–85, agitation increased also in Polynesia.
major divisions
Society Islands, divided into Leeward and Windward groups; area 1,685 sq km/650 sq mi; population (1977) 117,000. Administrative headquarters Papeete on *Tahiti*, the largest island, area 1,040 sq km/402 sq mi, population (1977) 96,000. Tahiti was visited by Capt James ◊Cook 1769 and by Capt ◊Bligh of the *Bounty* 1788, and has attracted artists such as ◊Gauguin and modern tourists. Claimed by France 1768, the group became a French protectorate 1843.
Marquesas Islands, area 1,270 sq km/490 sq mi; population (1977) 5,420. Administrative headquarters Atuona on Hiva Oa. Annexed by France 1842.
Tuamotu Islands, area 1,064 sq km/411 sq mi; population (1977) 8,540. Administrative headquarters Apataki. Mururoa Atoll has been a controversial French nuclear test site since 1966. The *Gambier Islands* are grouped with them.
Tubuai/Austral Islands, area 163 sq km/63 sq mi; population (1977) 5,208. They form a chain of volcanic islands and reefs 1,300 km/812 mi long.

French Revolution the forcible abolition of the *Ancien Régime* 'old order of things' (feudalism and absolute monarchy) 1789–99.

1789 5 May the States General (an assembly of the three 'estates', nobles, clergy, and commons) met at Versailles, bent on establishing a new constitution; 17 Jun National Assembly formed by the Third Estate (commons); 14 Jul ◊Bastille was taken by the mob when ◊Louis XVI attempted repressive moves; see also first Paris ◊Commune.

1791 20 Jun flight of the royal family to Varennes; 14 Sept Louis, brought back as a prisoner, accepted the new constitution.

1792 20 Apr war declared on Austria, which threatened to suppress the revolution; 10 Aug royal palace stormed by the French mob; 21 Sept First Republic proclaimed.

1793 21 Jan Louis XVI executed; 2 Jun overthrow of the moderate ◊Girondists by the ◊Jacobins; rule of the dictatorial Committee of Public Safety; 5 Sept the mass executions of the ◊Terror began.

1794 27 Jul (9 Thermidor under the Revolutionary calendar) fall of Robespierre and end of the Terror; the Directory (a body of five directors) established to hold a middle course between Royalism and Jacobinism. It ruled until ◊Napoleon seized power in 1799.

French Somaliland /sə'mɑːlilænd/ former name, until 1967, of ◊Djibouti, in E Africa.

French Sudan /suː'dɑːn/ former name (1898–1959) of ◊Mali, NW Africa.

French West Africa /frentʃ west 'æfrɪkə/ group of French colonies administered from Dakar 1895–1958, they have become the modern Senegal, Mauritania, Sudan, Burkina Faso, Guinea, Niger, Ivory Coast, and Benin.

Freneau /frɪ'nəʊ/ Philip Morin 1752–1832. American poet, whose *A Political Litany* 1775 was a mock prayer for deliverance from British tyranny.

frequency in physics, the number of cycles of a vibration occurring per unit of time. The unit of frequency is the hertz (Hz); 1 Hz = 1 cycle per second, 1 kHz (1 kilohertz) = 1,000 Hz, 1 MHz (1 megahertz) = 1,000,000 Hz. Human beings can hear sounds from objects vibrating in the range 20 Hz to 15,000 Hz. Ultrasonic frequencies are above that range.

Frere /frɪə/ John 1740–1807. British archaeologist; high sheriff of Suffolk and member of parliament for Norwich. He discovered palaeolithic tools at Hoxne, Suffolk, in 1790 and recognized from their situation that they must antedate the conventional biblical timescale.

fresco term applied to a process of painting on plaster walls before the plaster is dry, or the picture or design produced in this way. Some of the earliest frescoes (about 1750–1400 BC) are found on the walls of the palace of Knossos in Crete. They reached their finest expression in Italy during the 16th century with the frescoes of ◊Michelangelo and ◊Raphael.

Freud /frɔɪd/ Clement 1924– . British journalist, television personality, and (until 1987) Liberal member of parliament; a grandson of Sigmund Freud.

Freud /frɔɪd/ Lucian 1922– . British artist, a grandson of Sigmund Freud. A realist painter, he is noted for his nudes and incisive, dispassionate portraits of friends and acquaintances in the art world such as Francis ◊Bacon.

Freud /frɔɪd/ Sigmund 1865–1939. Austrian psychiatrist, born in Freiberg, Moravia. He was an originator of ◊psychoanalysis. Influenced by the French physiologist ◊Charcot and the researches into hysteria of the Viennese physician ◊Breuer, he developed the method of free association and interpretation of dreams which are still techniques of psychoanalysis. His theory of the repression of infantile sexuality as the root of neuroses in the adult (see ◊Oedipus complex) was controversial, and his associates ◊Adler and ◊Jung parted company with him. In 1938, following the Nazi occupation, he left Vienna for London.

His books include *The Interpretation of Dreams* 1900, *The Psychopathology of Everyday Life* 1901, *Totem and Taboo* 1913, and *The Ego and the Id* 1923. His work, long accepted as definitive by many, has been increasingly questioned in recent years.

Freud Sigmund Freud is often thought of as the father of modern psychology, having pioneered the technique of psychoanalysis.

friar a monk of any order, but originally specifically the title of members of the mendicant orders, the chief of which were the Franciscans or Minors (Grey Friars), the Dominicans or Preachers (Black Friars), the Carmelites (White Friars), and Austin Friars (Augustinians).

Fribourg /'friːbʊə/ city in Switzerland, on the river Sarine, capital of the canton of the same name; population (1980) 37,400. It is noted for its food products, particularly the famous cheese of the Gruyère district.

friction in physics, the force preventing one body sliding over another, which occurs in solids, liquids, and gases. The coefficient of friction between two solid surfaces is equal to the force required to move one surface over the other, divided by the total force pressing the two surfaces together. Friction is greatly reduced by the use of lubricants such as oil, grease, and graphite, and air bearings are now used to minimize the friction in high-speed rotational machinery. In other instances friction is deliberately increased by making the surfaces rough, for example, brake linings, driving belts, soles of shoes, and tyres.

Friedan /'friːdn/ Betty 1921– . American liberal feminist, influential in the women's movement in the 1970s. Her book *The Feminine Mystique* 1963 was one of the earliest and most influential books for the women's movement both in the USA and in Britain.

Friedman /'friːdmən/ Milton 1912– . American economist, professor of economics at the University of Chicago from 1948, and Nobel prizewinner 1976. The foremost exponent of ◊monetarism, he argues that a country's economy, and hence inflation, can be controlled through its ◊money supply, although governments lack the 'political will' to control inflation by cutting government spending and thereby increasing unemployment.

Friedrich /'friːdrɪk/ Caspar David 1774–1840. German landscape painter, whose evocative paintings of distant mountain peaks and moonlit shores are classic examples of the European Romantic movement.

friendly society or in the USA *benefit society*. Association designed to meet the needs of sickness and old age by money payments. In Britain the movement was the successor in this field of the great medieval guilds, but the period of its greatest expansion was in the late 18th and early 19th centuries, following the passing in 1797 of the first legislation providing for the registration of friendly societies. There are now some 6,500 registered societies and their funds total about £385,000,000: among the largest are the National Deposit, Odd Fellows, Foresters, and Hearts of Oak. In the USA there are similar 'fraternal insurance' bodies including the Modern Woodmen of America 1883 and the Fraternal Order of Eagles 1898.

Friends, Society of Christian sect (popularly known as Quakers, possibly because of George ◊Fox's injunction to 'quake at the word of the Lord'), founded by Fox in England in the 17th century. Originally marked out by their sober dress, and use of 'thee' and 'thou' to all as a sign of equality, they incurred penalties by their pacifism, and refusal to take oaths or pay tithes. Many emigrated to form communities abroad, for example, in Pennsylvania and New England, USA. In the 19th century many Friends were prominent in social reform, for example, Elizabeth ◊Fry. They now form a worldwide movement of about 200,000, and worship is marked by its stress on meditation, and by the freedom of all to take an active part in the service (called a meeting). They have no priests or ministers, and 'meeting houses' rather than churches.

Friends of the Earth (FOE or FoE) environmental pressure group, established in the UK in 1971, which aims to promote the rational and sustainable use of the earth's resources. Its 220 UK local groups campaign on environmental issues such as acid rain, nuclear power, the use of pesticides and motorway projects. FoE has branches in 30 countries.

Friese-Greene /'friːz 'griːn/ William 1855–1921. British photographer and early experimenter in cinematography.

Friesland /'friːzlənd/ northern maritime province (capital Leeuwarden) of the Netherlands, in which land is still being reclaimed from the former Zuyder Zee. Friesian (black and white) cattle originated here. The *Eleven Cities Tour* 1909 is a 210 km/124 mi skating marathon on the canals of the province held only in the rare years when the ice is hard enough. The inhabitants of the province are called ◊Frisians.

frigate originally a small swift undecked sailing vessel, used in the Mediterranean. The name was first applied to a type of warship in the 18th century, and in modern times frigates are the most numerous type of larger surface vessel in the British Royal Navy. They are essentially general purpose anti-aircraft, anti-submarine escort vessels of up to 3,000 tonnes. Britain's type-23 (1988) is armoured, heavily armed (4.5 inch naval gun, 32 Sea Wolf anti-missile and anti-aircraft missiles and a surface-to-surface missile), and, for locating submarines, has a large helicopter and a hydrophone array towed astern. Engines are diesel-electric up to 17 knots, with gas turbines for spurts of speed to 28 knots.

Frigga /'frɪgə/ or *Freya* in Scandinavian mythology, wife of Odin and mother of Thor, goddess of married love and the hearth. Friday is named after her.

fringe theatre in Britain, a term derived in the 1960s from the activities held on the 'fringe' of the Edinburgh Festival, and now denoting plays which are less commercial, (often as a result of their anti-establishment content or experimental nature), less formal and expensive than conventional theatre. Fringe groups which tour the country include Belt and Braces, Hull Truck, and Joint Stock. Notable writers who began writing for the theatre include Howard ◊Brenton and David ◊Hare. The American equivalent is off-off-Broadway (off-Broadway is mainstream theatre which is not on Broadway).

fringing reef a ◊coral reef which is attached to the coast without an intervening lagoon.

Frink /frɪŋk/ Elisabeth 1930– . British sculptor. Among her works are the *Horseman* (opposite the Ritz hotel in London), *In Memoriam* (heads), and *Running Man* 1980. Dame of the British Empire 1982.

Frisch /frɪʃ/ Karl von 1886–1982 German zoologist, founder with Konrad Lorenz of ◊ethology, the study of animal behaviour. Specializing in bees, he discovered how they communicate the location of sources of nectar by 'dances' (see ◊communication). He shared a Nobel prize in 1973 with Lorenz and N ◊Tinbergen.

Frisch /frɪʃ/ Max 1911– . Swiss dramatist. Influenced by ◊Brecht, his early plays such as *Als der Krieg zu Ende War/When the War is Over* 1949, and *Santa Cruz* 1944 are more romantic

in tone than his later symbolic dramas which deal with questions of identity such as *Don Juan* 1953, and *Andorra* 1962. His best known play is *Biedermann und die Brandstifter/The Fire Raisers* 1958, showing the trivial beginnings of large disasters.

Frisch /frɪʃ/ Otto 1904–1979. Austrian physicist, who coined the term 'nuclear fission'. A refugee from Nazi Germany, he worked from 1943 at Los ◊Alamos, then at Cambridge. He was the nephew of Lise ◊Meitner.

Frisch /frɪʃ/ Ragnar 1895–1973. Norwegian economist, the inventor of ◊econometrics; he shared the first Nobel Prize for Economics in 1969 with Jan ◊Tinbergen.

Frisch-Peierls memorandum one of the crucial documents in the development of the atomic bomb, written by Otto ◊Frisch and Rudolf Peierls (1907–) at the University of Birmingham in 1940. The memo reveals for the first time how small (about 500g/1lb the ◊critical mass (the minimum quantity of substance required for a chain nuclear reaction to begin) of uranium needed to be if the isotope U-235 was separated from naturally occurring uranium; the memo thus implied the feasibility of an atomic bomb using this isotope, but warned that its lethal power 'may make it unsuitable as a weapon'.

Frisian a member of a Germanic people of NW Europe. In Roman times they occupied the coast of Holland, and may have taken part in the Anglo-Saxon invasions of Britain. Their language was closely akin to Anglo-Saxon, with which it formed the Anglo-Frisian branch of the West Germanic languages.It is almost extinct in the German districts of East Friesland, has attained some literary importance in the North Frisian Islands and Schleswig, and developed a considerable literature in the West Frisian dialect of the Dutch province of Friesland.

Frisian Islands /'friːzɪən/ chain of low-lying islands 5–32 km/3–20 mi off the north west coasts of the Netherlands and Germany, with a northerly extension off the west coast of Denmark. They were formed by the sinking of the intervening land. *Texel* is the largest and most westerly.

fritillary in entomology, type of butterfly of the family Nymphalidae. There are many species, most with a checker-board (Latin *fritillaria*) pattern of black on orange.

fritillary in botany, plant, genus *Fritillaria* of the family Liliaceae. The snake's head fritillary, *Fritillaria meleagris*, has bell-shaped flowers marked in a checkered pattern. It is rare in Britain.

Friuli-Venezia Giulia /fri'uːli vɪ'netsiə 'dʒuːliə/ autonomous region of Italy, bordered on the east by Yugoslavia; area 7,844 sq km/3,030 sq mi; population (1981) 1,234,000. Formed in 1947 from the province of Venetian Fruli and part of Eastern Friuli, to which Trieste was added after its cession to Italy in 1954, it was granted autonomy in 1963. The Slav minority numbers about 100,000, and in Friuli there is a movement for complete independence.

Frobisher /'frəʊbɪʃə/ Martin 1535–1594. English navigator. Born in Yorkshire, he made his first voyage to Guinea, West Africa in 1554.

In 1576 he set out in search of the North West Passage; and visited Labrador, and Frobisher Bay, in Baffin Land. A second and third expedition sailed in 1577 and 1578. Frobisher served as vice-admiral in Drake's West Indian expedition of 1585, and in 1588 was knighted for helping to defeat the Armada. He was mortally wounded in 1594 fighting against the Spanish off the coast of France.

Froebel /'frəʊbəl/ Friedrich August Wilhelm 1782–1852. German educationist. Born in Thuringia, he came into contact with ◊Pestalozzi, and evolved a new system of education using instructive play, described in *Education of Man* 1826, and other works. In 1836 he founded the first kindergarten ('garden for children') in Blankenburg.

frog amphibian of the order Anura (Greek 'without a tail' – because the adult forms are tailless). Squat-bodied, they have hind legs which may be specialized for jumping or by webbed feet for swimming. The *flying frogs* of Malaysia, using webbed fore and hind feet, can achieve a 12 m/40 ft glide. Many frogs and ◊toads use their long extensible tongues to capture insect prey, and are useful to farmers, and gardeners. The males attract the females in great gatherings, usually by croaking. In some tropical species the inflated vocal sac may exceed the rest of the body in size. Other courtship 'lures' include thumping on the ground and 'dances'. Eggs (spawn, laid in large masses) may be left to float in water to hatch into tadpoles, which then develop gradually to frogs; or nests may be constructed, some South American frogs build little mud pool 'nests' and African *tree frogs* make foam nests from secreted mucus. In other species the eggs may be carried in 'pockets' on the mother's back, or brooded by the male in his vocal sac, or, as with the midwife toad *Alytes obstetricans*, carried by the male wrapped round his hind legs until hatching. Certain species of frog have powerful skin poisons (alkaloids). They vary in size from the smallest *Sminthillus limbatus*, 12 mm/under 0.5 in long, to the giant frog *Telmatobius culeus* of Lake Titicaca 50 cm/20 in, which is edible.

True frogs family Ranidae, includes the common frog *Rana temporaria*, becoming rare in Britain as small ponds disappear; the edible frog *Rana esculenta* (only the legs are eaten); and bullfrog *Rana catesbeiana*, with a far-reaching croak that carries for miles, and able to jump nine times its own length (annual jumping races are held at Calaveras, California).

frogbit small water plant *Hydrocharis morsus-ranae* with submerged roots, floating leaves, and small green and white flowers. It is locally common in England.

frog-hopper type of leaping plant-bug, family Cercopidae, which sucks the juice from plants. The larvae are pale green and protect themselves (from drying out and from predators) by secreting froth ('cuckoo-spit') from their anus.

frogmouth nocturnal bird, related to the nightjar, of which the commonest species, *Podargus strigoides*, is found throughout

Australia, including Tasmania. Well-camouflaged, it sits and awaits its prey.

Froissart /frwæ'saː/ Jean 1338–1410. French chronicler, secretary to Queen Philippa, wife of Edward III of England. He travelled in Scotland and Brittany, went with the ◊Black Prince to Aquitaine, and in 1368 was in Milan with ◊Chaucer and ◊Petrarch. He recorded in his *Chronicles* events of 1326–1400, often at first hand. Later he entered the Church and died, a canon, at Chimay.

Fromm /from/ Erich 1900–1980. German-American psychoanalyst, driven from Germany in 1933. His *The Fear of Freedom* 1941 and *The Sane Society* 1955 were source books for modern alternative lifestyles.

frond a large leaf or leaf-like structure, especially of ferns where it is often pinnately divided. The term is also applied to the leaves of palms, and less commonly to the plant bodies of certain seaweeds, liverworts and lichens.

Fronde French revolts 1648–53 against the administration of ◊Mazarin during Louis XIV's minority. In 1648–49 the Paris *parlement* attempted to limit the royal power, its leaders were arrested, Paris revolted, and the rising was surpressed by the royal army under ◊Condé. Condé then (1650) led a new revolt of the nobility, but this was surpressed by 1653.

front in meteorology, the interface between two air masses of different temperature or humidity. Fronts are usually found when warm air from one region of the Earth's surface meets cold air from another. Warm air, being lighter, tends to rise above the cold; its moisture is carried upwards and usually falls as rain or snow - hence the changeable weather conditions at fronts. Fronts are rarely stable but move with the air masses. A warm front brings warm air into an area occupied by cold air; a cold front does the reverse.

governor of Canada in 1672. Although efficient, he quarrelled with the local bishop and his followers and was recalled in 1682. A disastrous war with the Iroquois followed, and Frontenac was reinstated in 1689.

front line states term applied to those black nations of southern Africa in the 'front line' (both as victim and aggressor) of the struggle against the racist policies of South Africa. They are Mozambique, Tanzania, and Zambia; during the 1970s the term was particularly associated with their respective presidents: Samora Machel, Julius Nyerere, and Kenneth Kaunda respectively. All three actively supported Robert Mugabe and Joshua Nkomo in their struggle for independence in what was to become Zimbabwe.

frost condition of the weather when the air temperature is below freezing 0°C/32°F. Water in the atmosphere then freezes and crystallizes on the ground or exposed objects. As cold air is heavier than warm, *Ground frosts* are more common than *hoar frost*, which is formed by the condensation of water particles in the same way as ◊dew collects.

Frost /frost/ Robert (Lee) 1874–1963. American poet. Born in San Francisco, he became an unsuccessful farmer in New ◊Hampshire. In 1912–15 he was in England, where he published *A Boy's Will* 1913, and *North of Boston* 1914, which established his reputation. His verse, in traditional form, is written with an individual voice and penetrating vision; his best-known poems include 'Mending Wall' ('Something there is that does not love a wall'), 'The Road Not Taken', and 'Stopping by Woods on a Snowy Evening'.

frostbite the freezing of body tissues, caused by ice crystals forming within them. There is the danger of subsequent damage (such as gangrene) after thawing because of disrupted blood supply. The treatment is slow warming of the affected

Froude /fruːd/ James Anthony 1818–1894. British historian, whose *History of England from the Fall of Wolsey to the Defeat of the Spanish Armada* 1856–70 was a classic Victorian work. He was Carlyle's literary executor. He was influenced by the ◊Oxford Movement, in which his brother, *Richard Hurrell Froude* (1803–36), collaborated with ◊Newman.

fructose a fruit sugar, $C_6H_{12}O_6$, which occurs in honey, the nectar of flowers and many sweet fruits. It is a monosaccharide, whereas the more familar cane or beet sugar is a disaccharide, made up of two monosaccharide units: fructose and glucose. Sweeter than cane sugar, it is prepared from the latter on a large scale.

fruit in botany, the structure that develops from the carpel of a ◊flower, and encloses one or more seeds, except in cases of ◊parthenocarphy. Its function is to protect the seeds during their development and to aid in their dispersal. It consists of the ◊pericarp or fruit wall which is usually divided into a number of distinct layers. Sometimes parts other than the ovary are incorporated into the fruit structure, resulting in a false fruit or ◊pseudocarp, such as the apple and strawberry. Fruits may open to shed their seeds (dehiscent), or remain unopened and be dispersed as a single unit (indehiscent). There are two main groups of fruits, those that are dry (such as the ◊capsule, ◊follicle, ◊schizocarp, ◊nut, ◊caryopsis, pod or ◊legume, ◊lomentum and ◊achene), and those that become fleshy (such as the ◊drupe and ◊berry). Simple fruits (for example, peaches) are derived from a single ovary, whereas composite or multiple fruits (for example, blackberries) are formed from the ovaries of a number of flowers. In ordinary usage, 'fruit' includes only sweet, fleshy items; it excludes many botanical fruits such as acorns, bean pods, thistledown and cucumbers (see

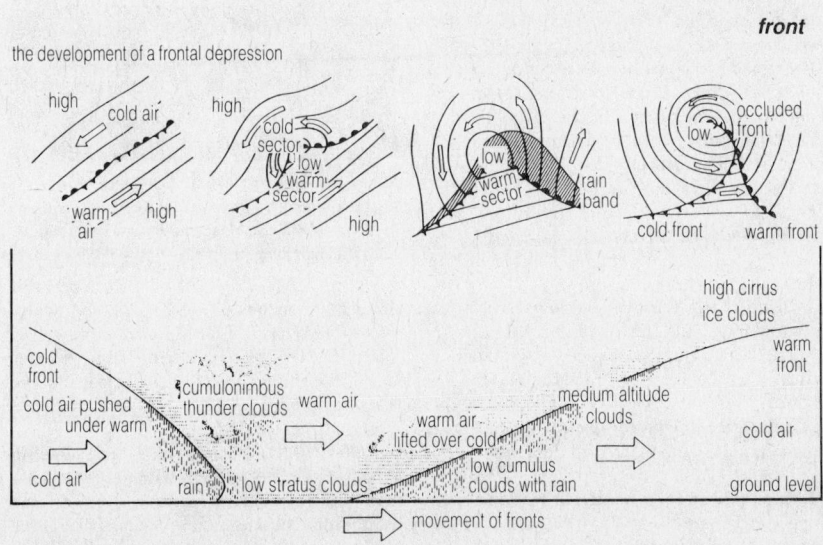

the development of a frontal depression

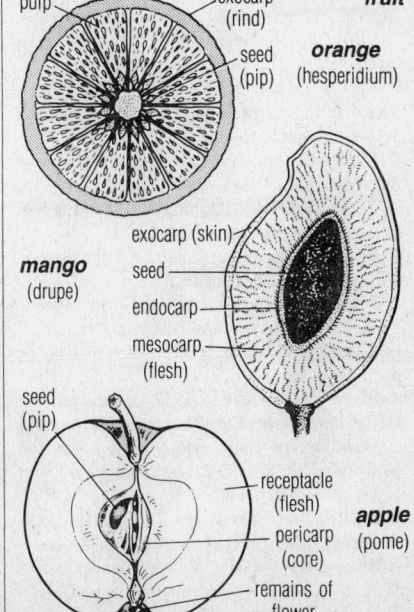

front

pulp — exocarp (rind)
seed (pip)
fruit
orange (hesperidium)

mango (drupe)
exocarp (skin)
seed
endocarp
mesocarp (flesh)
seed (pip)

receptacle (flesh)
pericarp (core)
remains of flower
apple (pome)

Frontenac et Palluau /ˌfrɒntəˈnæk eɪ ˌpæljuˈəʊ/ Louis de Buade, Comte de 1620–1698. Governor of French Canada. He began his military career in 1635, and was appointed

area, for example by skin to skin contact, and warm coverings of lukewarm water. Sufferers of frostbite should always receive hospital treatment.

◊vegetable), but is often used for foodstuffs such as rhubarb, that are not fruits in a botanical sense.

Frunze /'fru:nzi/ capital (formerly Pishpek) of Kirghiz Republic, USSR; population (1981) 552,000. It produces textiles, farm machinery, and metal goods.

frustule the cell wall of a ◊diatom. Frustules are intricately patterned on the surface with spots, ridges, and forrows, each pattern being characteristic of a particular species.

frustum in geometry, a 'slice' taken out of a solid figure by a pair of parallel planes; from the Latin for 'a piece cut off'. A conical frustum, for example, resembles a cone with the top cut off. The volume and area of a frustum are calculated by subtracting the volume or area of the 'missing' piece from those of the whole figure.

Fry /fraɪ/ Christopher 1907– . British dramatist. He was a leader of the revival of verse drama after World War II, notably *The Lady's Not for Burning* 1948, *Venus Observed* 1950, and *A Sleep of Prisoners* 1951. He has also written screen plays and successful translations of ◊Anouilh and ◊Girardoux.

Fry /fraɪ/ Elizabeth (born Gurney) 1780–1845. British Quaker philanthropist. She formed an association for the improvement of

frustrum

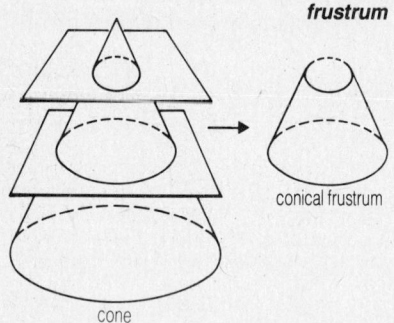

conical frustrum

cone

female prisoners in 1817, and worked with her brother, Joseph Gurney (1788–1847), on an influential report (1819) on prison reform.

Fry /fraɪ/ Roger Elliott 1866–1934. British artist and art critic, who introduced ◊Post-Impressionism to England.

f-stop in photography, one of a series of numbers on the lens barrel designating the size of the variable aperture; altering the f-stop also changes the appearance of the image.

FT Index short for ◊Financial Times Index, a list of leading share prices.

Fuad /'fu:ɑːd/ two kings of Egypt. *Fuad I* 1868–1936 was the son of the Khedive Ismail, and succeeded his elder brother, Hussein Kiamil, as sultan of Egypt in 1917, and when Egypt was declared independent in 1922 he assumed the title of king. *Fuad II* 1952– , grandson of Fuad I, was king of Egypt 1952–53 between the abdication of his father ◊Farouk and the establishment of the republic.

Fuchs /fuks/ Klaus Emil Julius 1911–1988. German spy, who worked on atom bomb research in Britain in World War II, and was imprisoned 1950–59 for passing information to the USSR. He resettled in East Germany.

Fuchs /fuks/ Vivian 1908– . British explorer and geologist. Before World War II he accompanied several Cambridge expeditions to Greenland, Africa, and Antarctica. In 1957–58 he led the Commonwealth Trans-Antarctic Expedition and was knighted on his return.

fuchsia exotic plant of the Onagraceae family. A number of shrubs, small trees or herbaceous plants native to South and Central America and New Zealand, are frequently cultivated in Britain. The genus was named in 1703 after Leonhard Fuchs (1501–66), German botanist. The red, purple, or pink flowers hang downwards, and are bell-shaped.

Fuehrer /'fjuərə/ German for 'leader'; the name adopted by Adolf ◊Hitler as leader of the National Socialist German Workers' Party (Nazi).

fuel any source of heat or energy, embracing the entire range of all combustibles and including anything that burns.

fuel cell cell converting chemical energy directly to electrical energy. It works on the same principle as a battery, but is continually fed with fuel, usually hydrogen. Hydrogen is passed over an ◊electrode (usually nickel or platinum) containing a ◊catalyst, which strips electrons off the atoms. These pass through an external circuit while hydrogen ◊ions (charged atoms) pass through the electrolyte to the other electrode, over which oxygen is passed. Water is formed at this electrode (as a by-product) in a chemical reaction involving electrons, hydrogen ions, and oxygen atoms. If the spare heat also produced is used for hot water and space heating, some 80% efficiency in fuel is achieved. Fuel cells are silent, reliable (no moving parts), but expensive to produce.

fuel injection injecting fuel directly into the cylinders of an internal combustion engine. It is the standard method used in ◊diesel engines, and is now becoming popular for ◊petrol engines. In the diesel engine oil is injected into the hot compressed air at the top of the second piston stroke and explodes to drive the piston down on its power stroke. In the petrol engine petrol is injected into the cylinder at the start of the first induction stroke of the ◊four-stroke cycle. Such engines need no ◊carburettor.

Fuentes /fu'entes/ Carlos 1928– . Mexican novelist, whose first novel *La región más transparente/Where the Air is Clear* 1958 encompasses the history of the country from the Aztecs to the present day.

fugue (Latin 'flight') in music, a complicated contrapuntal form for a number of parts or 'voices' which enter successively in imitation of each other. It was used, for example, by J S ◊Bach.

Fujairah /fu:'dʒaɪərə/ one of the constituent members of the ◊United Arab Emirates.

Fujian /,fu:dʒi'æn/ province (formerly *Fukien*) of SE China, bordering Taiwan Strait, opposite Taiwan.
area 123,100 sq km/47,516 sq mi
capital Fuzhou
features dramatic mountainous coastline being developed for tourists; designated in 1980 as pace-setting province for modernization

products sugar, rice, special aromatic teas, tobacco, timber
population (1982) 25,800,000.

Fujiyama /,fu:dʒi'jɑːmə/ volcano on Honshu Island, Japan; height 3,778 m/12,390 ft. Extinct since 1707, it has a ◊Shinto shrine and a weather station on its summit.

Fukien /,fu:'kjen/ former name of ◊Fujian, a province of SE China.

Fukuoka /,fu:ku:'əukə/ Japanese industrial town and port on the NW coast of Kyushu island; population (1980) 1,010,000.

Fulbright /'fulbraɪt/ William 1905– . American statesman. A ◊Rhodes Scholar, he was responsible for the *Fulbright Act* (1946) which provided grants for thousands of Americans to study overseas and overseas students to enter the US. Chairman of the Senate Foreign Relations Committee 1959–74, he was a strong internationalist and supporter of the United Nations.

Fuller /'fulə/ (Richard) Buckminster 1895–1983. American architect and theorist. He invented the lightweight geodesic dome, a half-sphere of triangular components independent of buttress or vault, for example, the headquarters of the American Society of Metals in Cleveland and the St Louis climatron.

Fuller American architect Buckminster Fuller is best known for his invention of the geodesic dome in 1947, which combined the maximum strength with the minimum structure.

Fuller /'fulə/ Roy 1912– . British poet and novelist. A London solicitor, he published his first *Poems* 1939, and 1968–73 was professor of poetry at Oxford University. Later volumes included *Epitaphs and Occasions* 1951, and *The Reign of Sparrows* 1980; and the novel *My Child, My Sister* 1965.

Fuller /'fulə/ Thomas 1608–1661. English author. He served as a chaplain to the Royalist army during the Civil War, and at the Restoration became the king's chaplain; he wrote the biographical *Worthies of England* 1662.

fuller's earth a soft, greenish-grey rock resembling clay, but without clay's plasticity. It is formed largely of clay minerals, particularly montmorillonite, but a great deal of silica, SiO_2, is also present. Its absorbent properties made it suitable for removing oil and grease from wool (known as 'fulling'), but nowadays it is important in the purification of oils. Beds of fuller's earth are found in the southern USA, Germany, Japan and in England, where it may represent a bed of volcanic ash dating from ◊Jurassic times.

fulmar name given to two species of petrels of the family Procellariidae, which are similar in size and colour to the common gull. The northern fulmar (*Fulmarus glacialis*) is found in the North Atlantic and visits land only to nest, laying a single egg.

fulminates the salts of fulminic (cyanic) acid (HOCN), the chief being silver and mercury. The fulminates detonate, that is, they are exploded by a blow.

Fulton /'fʊltən/ Robert 1765–1815. American engineer and inventor, who designed the first successful steamships. Born in Pennsylvania, he went to England in 1787 where he devoted himself to engineering in connection with inland navigation. In 1797 he moved to Paris where he produced a submarine, the *Nautilus*. After experimenting in steam navigation on the Seine in 1803, he returned to the USA and the first steam vessel of note, the *Clermont*, appeared on the Hudson in 1807, sailing between New York and Albany. The first steam warship was the *Fulton* of 38 tonnes, built in 1814–1815 and named after its designer.

fumitory plant, genus *Fumeria*, family Fumariaceae, native to Europe and Asia. The common fumitory grows abundantly as a weed in Britain, and produces pink flowers tipped with blackish-red.

Funafuti /ˌfuːnəˈfuːti/ one of the ◊Tuvalu group of islands in the West Pacific.

Funchal /fʊnˈʃɑːl/ capital and chief port of the Portuguese island of Madeira; population (1980) 100,000. It is on the S coast. Tourism and the wine trade are the main industries.

function in computing, those statements in a programming language that generate one value from another. *Function code* is a computer instruction in two parts: its function or operation code states what is to be done (add, subtract, and so on); the second part indicates on what (numbers, addresses). A *function key* on a keyboard performs a specific task when depressed: clear the screen, say, or shift to lower-case letters. Not every programming language supports function definition (Prolog, for one, does not) whereas others are based very largely on the concept of function.

function in mathematics, a procedure that defines a relationship between quantities, usually ◊variables. For example, in the algebraic expression $y = 4x^3 + 2$, the variable y is a function of the variable x, generally written as $f(x)$. Commonly used in applied mathematics, physics and science generally: for example, the formula $2\pi(1/g)^{-1}$ shows that for a simple pendulum the time of swing t is a function of its length l and of no other variable quantity (π and g, the acceleration due to gravity, are ◊constants).

functionalism in the social sciences, the view of society as a system comprising a number of interrelated parts, all functioning on the basis of a common value system or consensus about basic values and common goals. Every social custom and institution is seen as having a function in ensuring that society works efficiently; deviance and crime are seen as a form of social sickness. Functionalists often describe society as an organism with a life of its own, above and beyond the sum of its members. ◊Comte, ◊Durkheim, and ◊Parsons have taken functionalist approaches.

functionalism in architecture and design, a 20th-century school, also called modernism and International Style, characterized by a desire to exclude everything that serves no practical purpose. It was a reaction against the 19th century practice of imitating earlier styles, and its finest achievements are in the realm of industrial building. Its leading exponents were the German ◊Bauhaus school, and the Dutch group de ◊Stijl; architects in the field were Le Corbusier and Walter ◊Gropius.

fundamentalism in religion, an emphasis on basic principles or articles of faith; in particular a Christian religious movement arising in the USA just after World War I which insisted on belief in the literal truth of everything in the Bible – the Virgin Birth, the physical resurrection of Christ, the Atonement, and the Bible miracles which were regarded as fundamental to the Christian faith. It confronted evolutionary theory in 1925 (see ◊Dayton, Tennessee), and underlies modern ◊Creationism. There is a similar modern movement in Islamic countries.

Fundy, Bay of /'fʌndi/ Canadian Atlantic inlet between New Brunswick and Nova Scotia, with a rapid tidal rise and fall of 18 m/60 ft (harnessed for electricity since 1984). In summer fog increases the dangers to shipping.

fungicide a chemical used to treat fungus diseases in plants and animals. Inorganic and organic compounds containing sulphur are widely used.

fungus one of the group of organisms formerly included within the division Thallophyta, along with algae and bacteria, but now placed in the kingdom Fungi, separate from green plants. Unlike the green plants they have no chlorophyll, and hence must get food from organic substances. They are either ◊parasites, existing on living plants or animals, or ◊saprophytes living on dead matter. Some 50,000 different species have been recognized to date, and include slime moulds, mildews, rusts and smuts, mushrooms, toadstools and puff-balls. Fungi reproduce by means of spores. Some fungi are edible, but many are highly poisonous.

funk a style of dance music of black American origin, relying on heavy percussion in polyrhythmic patterns. Leading exponents include James Brown (1928–   ).

fur pelts of animals used as clothing, mainly as a luxury trade, which had its modern origin in the furs of North America, exploited by the Hudson's Bay Company from the late 17th century. The chief centres of the fur trade are London, New York, Leningrad, and Kastoria. Mink, chinchilla and sable are among the most valuable, the wild furs being finer than the farmed; it is illegal to import furs or skins of endangered species such as leopard. Since World War II synthetic fibres have been widely used as substitutes.

Furies in Greek mythology, the Erinyes, appeasingly called the Eumenides, or 'kindly ones'. They were the daughters of Earth or of Night, represented as winged maidens, with serpents twisted in their hair. They punished such crimes as filial disobedience, murder, and inhospitality.

furlong traditional measure of length – 220 yds/201 m, or 40 rods, poles, or perches: 8 furlongs made one statute ◊mile. Originally it was the length of the furrow in the common field characteristic of medieval husbandry.

furnace a structure in which fuel such as coal, coke, gas or oil is burned to produce heat for various purposes. Furnaces are used in conjunction with ◊boilers to produce hot water, for heating, and steam for driving turbines – in ships for propulsion and in power stations for generating electricity. The largest furnaces are those used for smelting and refining metals, such as the ◊blast furnace, ◊electric furnace and ◊open-hearth furnace.

Furness /'fɜːnɪs/ peninsula in England, formerly a detached northern portion of Lancashire, separated from the main part by Morecambe Bay. In 1974 it was included in the new county of ◊Cumbria. Barrow is its ship-building and industrial centre.

Fürth /'fjʊət/ town in Bavaria, West Germany, adjoining Nuremberg; population (1984) 98,500. It has electrical, chemical, textile and toy industries.

further education college college in the UK for students over school-leaving age which provides courses of a vocational or pre-vocational nature and general education at a level below that of a degree course.

Furtwängler /'fʊətvɛŋglə/ (Gustav Heinrich Ernst Martin) Wilhelm 1886–1954. German conductor. He succeeded Nikisch at Leipzig, and was with the Berlin Philharmonic Orchestra 1922–54. His interpretations of the German romantic composers, especially Wagner, were regarded as classically definitive. A postwar tribunal cleared him of Nazism charges.

fuse in electricity, *fuse wire* is a wire designed to melt when excessive current passes through. It is a safety device to prevent surges of current that could damage equipment and cause fires.
In ◊explosives, a fuse is a cord impregnated with chemicals so that it burns slowly at a predetermined rate. It is used to set off a main explosive charge, sufficient length of fuse being left to allow the person lighting it to get away to safety.

Fuseli /'fjuːzəli/ Henry Johann Heinrich 1741–1825. Swiss-born British artist, influenced by ◊Blake. Fancifully macabre, he plundered the depths of his subconscious for grotesque and dream-like images in such paintings as *The Nightmare* 1782. He was admired by the ◊Surrealists.

fusel oil a liquid with a characteristic unpleasant smell, obtained as a by-product when distilling the product of any alcoholic fermentation, and used in paints, varnishes, essential oils, and plastics. Fusel oil is a mixture of fatty acids, alcohols and esters.

Fushun /ˌfuːˈʃʌn/ coal-mining centre in Liaoning province, China, 40 km/25 mi E of Shenyang; population (1984) 636,000. It has aluminium, steel, and chemical works.

fusion in physics, the fusing of the nuclei of light elements. The Sun works on the principle of nuclear fusions; so does the hydrogen bomb. So far no successful fusion reactor – able to produce the required energy and contain the reaction under control – has been built.

futurism a literary and artistic movement, 1909–14, originating in Paris. The Italian poet ◊Marinetti published the *Futurist Manifesto* in 1909 urging Italian artists to join him in Futurism. They eulogized the modern world and the 'beauty of speed and energy' in their works, trying to capture the dynamism of a speeding motor car or train by combining the shifting geometric planes of ◊Cubism with vibrant colours. Gino Severini painted a topsy-turvy landscape as if seen from the moving window of a *Suburban Train Arriving at Paris* 1915 (Tate Gallery) and Giacomo Balla represented the abstract idea of speed by the moving object in such pictures as *Abstract Speed-wake of a Speeding Car* 1919 (Tate Gallery). Umberto Boccioni, a sculptor, froze his figures as if they were several frames of a film moving at once. ◊Vorticism was a similar movement in Britain from 1909. As a movement it died out during World War I, but Futurists' exultation in war and violence was seen as an early manifestation of ◊Fascism.

Fuzhou /ˌfuːˈdʒəʊ/ industrial port (formerly Foochow), capital of Fujian province in SE China; population (1980) 800,000. There are joint foreign and Chinese factories. The Mazu (Matsu) island group, occupied by the Nationalist Chinese, is offshore.

Fyfe /faɪf/ David Maxwell, 1st Earl of British lawyer and Conservative politician; see ◊Kilmuir.

Fyffe /faɪf/ Will 1885–1947. Scots music-hall comedian remembered for his vivid character sketches, and for his song 'I Belong to Glasgow'.

Fylingdales /ˈfaɪlɪŋdeɪlz/ site in the North Yorkshire Moors National Park, England, of an early-warning radar station, linked with similar stations in Greenland and Alaska, to give a four-minute warning of nuclear attack.

Fyn /fjuːn/ island (German *Fünen*) forming part of Denmark and lying between the mainland and Zealand: area 2,976 sq km/1,149 sq mi; capital Odense; population (1984) 454,000.

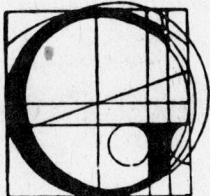

G the seventh letter of the alphabet. It was formed by the Romans by adding a 'tail' to the letter C which represented the K sound.

gabbro an ◊igneous rock formed deep in the Earth's crust, and containing little silica (basic in composition). It contains ◊pyroxine and calcium-rich ◊feldspar with smaller amounts of ◊olivine and ◊amphibole. Its coarse crystals of dull minerals give it a speckled appearance. Gabbro is the plutonic version of ◊basalt (that is, derived from ◊magma that has solidified below the earth's surface), and forms in large, slow-cooling intrusions.

gabelle (Arabic *qabālāh* 'tribute') term used orginally for a tax on various items, but which came to be used exclusively for a tax on salt, first levied in France by Philip the Fair in 1286, and abolished 1790.

Gabès /'gɑːbes/ port in Tunisia; population (1975) 40,585. Fertilizers and dates are exported. The town stands on the site of the Roman town of Tacapae.

Gable /'geɪbəl/ Clark 1901–60. American actor. A star for more than 30 years in 90 films; he was celebrated for his romantic nonchalance and tough-with-women roles, for example as Rhett Butler in *Gone with the Wind* 1939. He was nicknamed the 'King' of Hollywood.

Gabo /'gɑːbəʊ/ Naum 1890–1977. Russian sculptor. One of the leading exponents of ◊Constructivism, he left Russia in 1923 and settled first in England, then in the USA from 1946. He used modern synthetic materials.

Gabon /gæ'bɒn/ country in central Africa, bounded N by Cameroon, E and S by the Congo, W by the Atlantic Ocean, and NW by Equatorial Guinea.

government The 1961 constitution, revised in 1976, 1975 and 1981, provides for a president elected by universal suffrage for a seven-year term. As head of both state and government, the president appoints and presides over a prime minister and council of ministers, and is also founder and secretary-general of the Gabonese Democratic Party (PDG). There is a single-chamber legislature, the National Assembly, of 120 members, 111 elected and nine nominated for a five-year term. Gabon became a one-party state in 1968, the party being the PDG.

history Gabon was colonized by some of its present inhabitants (the Fang and the Omiéné) during the 16th–18th centuries. Its first European visitors were the Portuguese in the late 15th century. They began a slave trade which lasted almost 500 years. In 1889 Gabon became part of the French Congo, and was a province of French Equatorial Africa from 1908.

Gabon achieved full independence in 1960. There were then two main political parties, the Gabonese Democratic Bloc (BDG), led by Léon M'ba, and the Gabonese Democratic and Social Union (UDSG), led by Jean-Hilaire Aubame. Although the two parties were evenly matched in popular support, on independence M'ba became president and Aubame foreign minister.

In 1967 the BDG wanted the two parties to merge but the UDSG resisted, and M'ba called a general election. Before the elections M'ba was deposed in a military coup by supporters of Aubame but was restored to office with French help. Aubame was tried and imprisoned for treason. The UDSG was outlawed and most of its members joined the BDG.

In 1967 M'ba, although in failing health, was re-elected. He died later that year and was succeeded by Albert-Bernard Bongo, who the following year established the Gabonese Democratic Party (PDG) as the only legal party. Bongo was re-elected in 1973 and was converted to Islam, changing his first name to Omar. In 1979 Bongo, as the sole presidential candidate, was re-elected for a further seven years.

Gabon's reserves of uranium, manganese, and iron make it the richest per capita country in Black Africa, and both M'ba and Bongo have successfully exploited these resources, gaining control of the iron-ore ventures once half-owned by the Bethlehem Steel Corporation of the USA, and concluding economic and technical agreements with China as well as maintaining ties with France. Although he has operated an authoritarian regime, Gabon's prosperity has diluted any serious opposition to President Bongo. He was again re-elected in Nov 1986.

Gabor /'gɑːbɔː/ Dennis 1900–1979. Hungarian-British physicist. In 1958 he invented a type of colour TV tube of greatly reduced depth, and in 1971 was awarded a Nobel prize for his invention of the ◊holographic method of three-dimensional photography in 1947.

Gaborone /ˌgæbə'rəʊni/ capital of Botswana from 1964, mainly an administrative centre; population (1981) 59,700.

Gabriel /'geɪbrɪəl/ in the New Testament, the archangel who foretold the birth of John the Baptist to Zacharias and of Christ to the Virgin Mary. Also mentioned in the Old Testament in the book of Daniel.

Gabrieli /ˌgæbri'eli/ Giovanni c. 1555–1612. Italian composer and organist. After several years in Munich, working under ◊Lassus, he became organist at St Mark's, Venice, where he remained until his death. Although he gained a reputation as a composer of secular music, particularly madrigals, he is best known for his motets, which are frequently dramatic and often use several choirs and groups of instruments.

Gadamer /'gɑːdəmə/ Hans-Georg 1900– . German philosopher, a major contributor to the tradition of ◊hermeneutics in the 20th century. In his masterpiece, *Truth and Method* 1960, he argued that 'understanding' is fundamental to human existence, and that all understanding takes place within a tradition. The relation between text and interpreter can be viewed as a dialogue, in which the interpreter must remain open to the truth of the text.

Gaddafi alternative form of ◊Khaddhafi, Libyan leader.

Gaddi /'gædi/ surname of three Florentine religious painters: *Gaddo* (c. 1260–1333); his son *Taddeo* (1300–66), who was influenced by ◊Giotto, his most famous work being the fresco cycle *Life of the Virgin* in Santa Croce, Florence; and grandson *Agnolo* (c. 1333–96), who also painted a series of frescoes in Santa Croce.

gadfly a ◊fly which bites cattle, such as a ◊bot-fly, or ◊horse-fly.

gadolinium an element, symbol Gd, atomic number 64, atomic weight 157.25. A silvery-white metal, one of the Lanthanide series. It is found in the products of nuclear fission and used

Gabon

GABONESE REPUBLIC (*République Gabonaise*)

AREA 266,700 sq km/103,000 sq mi
CAPITAL Libreville
PHYSICAL virtually the whole country is
tropical rain forest; mountains alternate with
lowlands; Ogooué River flows S–W
FEATURES Schweitzer hospital at Lambaréné
HEAD OF STATE AND OF GOVERNMENT Omar
Bongo from 1967
GOVERNMENT one-party republic
EXPORTS petroleum; manganese, iron,
uranium; timber
CURRENCY CFA franc (498.38 = £1 Sept
1987)
POPULATION 988,000 (1985); annual growth
rate 1.6%
LANGUAGE French (official), Bantu
RELIGION animist 60%, Roman Catholic 35%,
small Muslim minority
LITERACY 62% male/44% female (1980 est)
GNP $3 bn (1983); $2,613 per head of
population
CHRONOLOGY
1960 Independence from France achieved.
Léon M'ba became the first president.

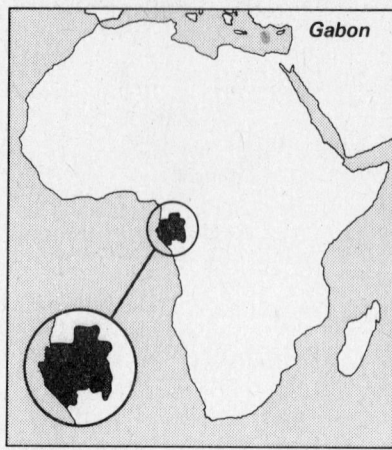
Gabon

1967 Attempted coup by rival party foiled
with French help. M'ba died and was
succeeded by his protégé, Albert-Bernard
Bongo.
1968 One-party state established.
1973 Bongo re-elected; converted to Islam, he
changed his first name to Omar.

in electronic components, alloys, and products
needing to withstand high temperatures.

Gaelic language a member of the Celtic
branch of the Indo-European language family,
spoken in Ireland, Scotland and (until 1974) the
Isle of Man. It is, along with English, one of the
national languages of the Republic of Ireland,
with over half a million speakers, and is known
there as both Irish and Irish Gaelic. In Scotland,
speakers of Gaelic number around 90,000 and
are concentrated in the Western Isles, in parts of
the NW coast and in the city of Glasgow. Gaelic
has been in decline for several centuries, subject
until quite recently to neglect within the British
state. There is a small Gaelic-speaking
community in Nova Scotia, Canada.

Gagarin /gə'gɑːrɪn/ Yuri 1934–1968.
Russian cosmonaut. Born in the Smolensk
Region, son of a collective farmer, he qualified
as a foundryman. He became a pilot 1957 and
completed the first manned space flight on 12
Apr 1961, orbiting the Earth once, taking 108
minutes from launch to landing. He died in a
plane crash while training for another flight.

Gaia /'geɪə/ or *Ge* in Greek mythology, the
goddess of the Earth. She sprang from primordial
Chaos and herself produced ◊Uranus, by whom
she was the mother of the ◊Cyclopes and ◊Titans.

Gainsborough /'geɪnzbərə/ market town in
Lincolnshire, England; population (1985)
18,715. It stands on the river Trent, which
periodically rises in a tidal wave, the 'eagre'.

Gainsborough /'geɪnzbərə/ Thomas
1727–88. British artist. Born in Sudbury,
Suffolk, he began to paint while still at school,
and in 1741 went to London where he learnt
etching and studied at the Academy of Arts, but
remained largely self-taught. In 1759 he settled

in Bath, becoming famous as a painter of high
society – his portraits of Sir Charles Holte,
Garrick, and the *Blue Boy* belong to this period.
In 1768 he became one of the original members of
the Royal Academy, and in 1774 went to London
where his sitters included the royal family, Mrs
Siddons, Dr Johnson, Burke, and Sheridan. His
work is clear-toned, graceful, and naturalistic,
and in his preferred subject, landscapes, he was
one of the first English artists to follow the Dutch
in painting real scenes rather than using
imaginary Italian scenery.

Gaitskell /'geɪtskəl/ Hugh Todd Naylor
1906–1963. British Labour politician. In 1950 he
succeeded ◊Cripps first as minister of economic
affairs and then as chancellor of the Exchequer
until Oct 1951. In 1955 he defeated ◊Bevan for
the succession to Attlee as party leader, and tried
to reconcile internal differences on
nationalization and disarmament. He was re-
elected in 1960.

Galápagos Islands /gə'læpəgɒs/ group of 15
islands (official name Archipiélago de Colón) in
the Pacific, belonging to Ecuador; area 7,800 sq
km/3,000 sq mi; population (1980) 6,000. The
capital is San Cristóbal on the island of the same
name. The islands are a nature reserve. Their
unique fauna (including giant tortoise, iguana,
penguin, flightless cormorant, and Darwin's
◊finches) are under threat from introduced
species.

Galatea /ˌgælə'tiːə/ in Greek mythology, a sea
nymph who loved Acis, and when he was killed
by Polyphemus transformed his blood into the
river Acis. ◊Pygmalion made a statue (later
named Galatea) which he married after it was
brought to life by Aphrodite.

Galati /gæ'læts/ port on the river Danube in
Romania; population (1983) 254,636. Industries
include ship-building, iron and steel, textiles,
food processing, perfume, and cosmetics.

Galatia /gə'leɪʃə/ ancient province of Asia
Minor occupying part of the inland plateau; it
was occupied in the 3rd century BC by the ◊Gauls,
and a Roman province from 25 BC.

galaxy a congregation of millions or billions
of ◊stars, held together by ◊gravity. There are
two main shapes. *Spiral* galaxies are flattened in
shape, with a central bulge of old stars
surrounded by a disc of younger stars, arranged
in spiral arms like a catherine wheel. Barred
spirals are a class of spiral galaxies that have a
straight bar of stars across their centre, from the
ends of which the spiral arms emerge. The arms
of spiral galaxies contain gas and dust from
which new stars are still forming. *Elliptical*
galaxies contain old stars and very little gas. They
include the most massive galaxies known,
containing a million million stars. Some elliptical
galaxies are thought to be merged spiral galaxies.
Most galaxies occur in clusters, containing
anything from a few to thousands of members.
Although the ◊Universe is expanding, individual
clusters do not expand: rather, the space between
clusters expands.
Our own Galaxy, the Milky Way, is a spiral type
about 100,00 light years in diameter, containing
at least 100,000 million stars. It is a member of a
small cluster, the ◊Local Group. The ◊Sun lies in
one of its spiral arms, about 25,000 light years
from the centre.

Galaz /gæ'læts/ German name for the port of
◊Galati in Romania.

Galbraith /gæl'breɪθ/ John Kenneth
1908– . Canadian economist of the Keynesian
school (see ◊Keynes). Professor of Harvard
University, USA, 1949–75, his major works
include *The Affluent Society* 1958 and
Economics and the Public Purpose 1974. In the
former he argued that advanced industrialized
societies like the USA were suffering from
private affluence accompanied by public squalor.

Galen /'geɪlən/ c 130–200. Graeco-Roman
physician. Born at Pergamum in Asia Minor, he
personally attended ◊Marcus Aurelius. He was
skilled in anatomy and physiology. His treatises
(some 80 out of his 500 have survived) remained
the encyclopedic authority until the
Renaissance.

galena chief ore of lead, consisting of lead
sulphide (PbS), which occurs mainly among
limestone deposits in Australia, Mexico, the
USSR, and the USA. It may contain up to 1 per
cent silver, and so the ore is sometimes mined for
both metals.

Galicia /gə'lɪsɪə/ mountainous but fertile
region of NW Spain, formerly an independent
kingdom. It includes La Coruña, El Ferrol,
Santiago de Compostela, and Cape Finisterre.
The language is close to Portuguese.

Galicia /gə'lɪsɪə/ former province of central
Europe, extending from the N slopes of the
Carpathians to the Czech-Romanian border.
Once part of the Austrian Empire, it was
included in Poland after World War I, and
divided in 1945 between Poland and the USSR.

Gainsborough *Mr and Mrs Andrews* by British artist Thomas Gainsborough hangs in the National Gallery, London. It combines the portraiture that earned him his living and the landscape painting he preferred.

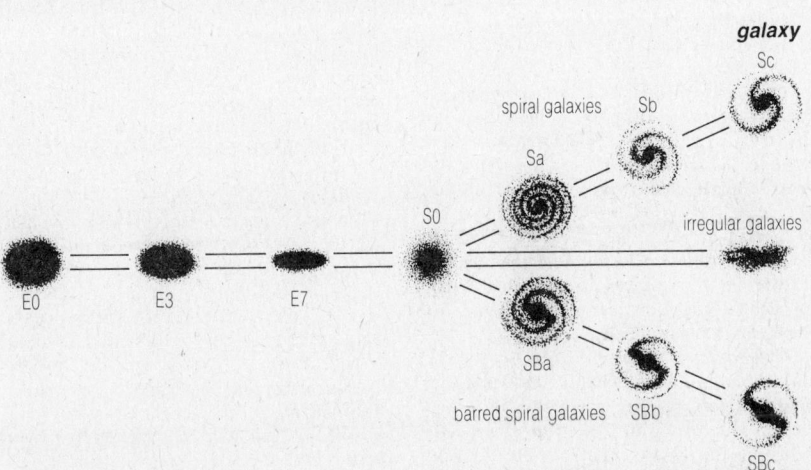

galaxy

spiral galaxies — Sa, Sb, Sc

S0 — E0, E3, E7

irregular galaxies

barred spiral galaxies — SBa, SBb, SBc

Galilee /'gælɪliː/ region of N Israel (once a Roman province), which includes Nazareth and Tiberias. Frequently mentioned in the Gospels of the New Testament.

Galilee, Sea of /'gælɪliː/ alternative name for Lake ▷Tiberias in N Israel.

Galileo /ˌgælɪ'leɪəʊ/ Galilei 1564–1642. Italian mathematician, astronomer, and physicist, who revolutionized the scientific thinking of his time and paved the way for ▷Newton. He was born in Pisa, and at 25 he became professor of mathematics at the University there; in 1592 he became a professor at Padua; and in 1610 he was appointed chief mathematician to the Grand Duke of Tuscany, Florence. He developed the astronomical telescope and was the first to see the four main satellites of Jupiter, mountains and craters on the Moon, and Venus's appearance going through 'phases' as would be expected if it were orbiting the Sun. In mechanics, Galileo argued convincingly that freely-falling bodies, heavy or light, had the same, constant acceleration (though the story of his dropping cannon balls from the Leaning Tower of Pisa is probably apocryphal), and that a body moving on a perfectly smooth horizontal surface would neither speed up nor slow down. Galileo's observations and arguments were an unwelcome refutation of the ideas of ▷Aristotle taught at the (Church-run) universities, especially because they made plausible for the first time the heliocentric (Sun-centred) theory of ▷Copernicus. Galileo's persuasive *Dialogues on the Two Chief Systems of the World* 1632 was banned by the Church authorities at Rome, he was made to recant by the ▷Inquisition and put under house arrest for his last years.

gall an abnormal outgrowth on a plant which develops as a result of attack by insects, or less commonly, by bacteria, fungi, mites or nematodes. The attack causes an increase in the number of cells, or an enlargement of existing cells in the plant. Gall-forming insects generally pass the early stages of their life inside the gall. A gall wasp is responsible for the conspicuous bud galls forming on oak trees, 2.5–4 cm across, and popularly known as 'oak apples'.

Gall /gæl/ Franz Joseph 1758–1828. Instigator of the discredited theory of ▷phrenology.

Galla a people of E Africa, especially Ethiopia, who speak a Hamito-Semitic language.

gall bladder a small muscular sac attached to the underside of the liver and connected to the small intestine by the bile duct. It stores ▷bile from the liver.

Galle /'gælə/ Johann Gottfried 1812–1910. German astronomer, who in 1846 discovered the planet ▷Neptune, close to the position predicted by the French mathematician Urbail Levernier.

Galileo The Italian mathematician, astronomer, and physicist, Galilei Galileo, who revolutionized scientific thought in his day, and prepared the ground for Newton.

galley ship powered by oars, and usually also with sails. Galleys typically had a crew of hundreds of oarsmen arranged in rows; they were used in warfare from antiquity until the 18th century. Louis XIV of France maintained a fleet of some 40 galleys, crewed by over 10,000 convicts, until 1748. The maximum speed of a galley is estimated to have been only four knots, while only 20 per cent of the oarsmens' effort was effective, and galleys could not be used in stormy weather because of their very low waterline. In 1987 a reconstructed trireme (three-tiered galley) was commissioned in the Greek navy.

Gallico /ˈgælɪkəʊ/ Paul (William) 1897–1976. American author, born in New York. Originally a sports columnist, he began writing fiction in 1936, and his books include *The Snow Goose* 1941.

Gallipoli /gəˈlɪpəli/ port in European Turkey, giving its name to the peninsula (ancient name *Chersonesus*) on which it stands. In World War I under Sir Ian ◊Hamilton there was an unsuccessful and costly attempt Feb 1915–Jan 1916 (with British Empire and French troops) to force the narrows and link up with Russia. See also ◊Anzac.

gallium an element, symbol Ga; atomic weight 69.75; atomic number 31. A grey metal, liquid at room temperatures. It is very scarce and was discovered in 1875 by Lecoq de Boisbaudran. Gallium arsenide crystals are used in microelectronics, since electrons travel a

Gallipoli Men of the British Royal Naval Division and Australian troops sharing a trench. One man is using a periscope (left) and another a 'sniperscope'.

thousand times faster through them than through silicon.

gallon imperial liquid or dry measure, equal to 4.546 litres, and subdivided into 4 quarts or 8 pints.

Galloway /ˈgæləweɪ/ ancient area of SW Scotland, now part of the region of ◊Dumfries and Galloway.

gallstone a hard, insoluble, pebble-like accretion formed in the human gall bladder or bile duct from substances, chiefly cholesterol, in the bile. The size varies from a grain of sand to a walnut. It is technically called a biliary calculus.

Gallup /ˈgæləp/ George Horace 1901–1984. American journalist and statistician, founder in 1935 of the American Institute of Public Opinion and deviser of the *Gallup Polls*, in which public opinion is gauged by questioning a number of representative individuals.

Galsworthy /ˈgɔːlzwɜːði/ John 1867–1933. British novelist and dramatist, best known for *The Forsyte Saga*. Born in Kingston, Surrey, he achieved success with *The Man of Property* 1906, the first instalment of *The Forsyte Saga* 1922, which included *In Chancery* and *To Let*. Soames Forsyte is the embodiment of Victorian values and feeling for property, and the wife whom he also 'owns' – Irene – was based on Galsworthy's wife. Later additions to the series are *A Modern Comedy* 1929, which contained *The White Monkey*, *The Silver Spoon*, and *Swan Song*, and the short stories *On Forsyte Change* 1930.

Galt /gɔːlt/ John 1779–1839. Scottish novelist. Born in Ayrshire, he moved to London in 1804 and lived in Canada from 1826–29. He is probably best known for the *Annals of the Parish* 1821 in which he portrays the life of a Lowlands village, using the local dialect. He founded the

Canadian town of ◊Guelph, and Galt, on the Grand river in Ontario, was named after him.

Galtieri /ˌgaeltiˈeəri/ Leopoldo Fortunato 1926– . Argentinian general, leading member of the military junta 1979–82 which ordered the seizure of the Falkland Islands 1982. He and his fellow junta members were tried for abuse of human rights, and also court-martialled for their conduct of the war; he was sentenced to 12 years in prison in 1986.

Galtieri President Leopoldo Galtieri of Argentina condemning Britain during the Falklands crisis of 1982.

Galton /ˈgɔːltən/ Francis 1822–1911. British scientist, born in Birmingham, England. After discovering the existence of ◊anticyclones, he turned from meteorology to study the inheritance of physical and mental attributes in humans. He traced family trees and 'proved' that genius was inherited, and was concentrated in the British. He was an advocate of ◊eugenics.

Galvani /gælˈvɑːni/ Luigi 1737–1798. Italian physiologist. Born in Bologna, where he taught anatomy, he discovered galvanic or voltaic electricity in 1762, when investigating the contractions produced in the muscles of dead frogs by contact with pairs of different metals. His work led quickly to ◊Volta's invention of the electric battery, and eventually to an understanding of how nerves control muscles.

galvanizing process for rendering iron rust-proof, by plunging it into molten zinc (the dipping method), or by ◊electroplating it with zinc.

galvanometer instrument for detecting small electric currents by their magnetic effect.

Galveston /ˈgælvəstən/ city and port in Texas, USA; population (1980) 61,902. In 1900, 8,000 people died in a hurricane.

Galway /ˈgɔːlweɪ/ county of the Republic of Ireland on the W coast, in the province of Connacht; area 5,939 sq km/2,293 sq mi; population (1981) 172,018. The E part is low-lying. In the S are the Slieve Aughty mountains and Galway Bay, with the Aran islands. W of Lough Corrib is Connemara, a wild area of moors, hills, lakes, and bogs. The Shannon is the principal river. Towns include Galway (the county town), Ballinasloe, Tuam, Clifden, and Loughrea, near which deposits of lead, zinc and copper were found in 1959.

Galway /'gɔːlweɪ/ fishing port and county town of county Galway, Republic of Ireland; population (1981) 37,835. Galway Theatre stages Irish Gaelic plays.

Galway /'gɔːlweɪ/ James 1939– . British flautist. Born in Belfast, he was a member of the Berlin Philharmonic Orchestra 1969–75, before taking up a solo career.

Gama /'gɑːmə/ Vasco da 1460–1524. Portuguese navigator. Born at Sines, he was chosen by king Emanuel I to command an expedition sent in 1497 to discover the Cape route to India. The land he touched on Christmas Day, 1497, he named Natal. Crossing the Indian Ocean, he arrived at Calicut in May 1498, and arrived back in Portugal in Sept 1499. In 1502 he founded a Portuguese colony at Mozambique, and attacked and plundered Calicut in revenge for the murder of some Portuguese seamen. After 20 years of retirement, he was despatched to India again as Portuguese viceroy in 1524, but died two months after his arrival in Goa.

Gama An engraving of the Portuguese navigator Vasco da Gama. He discovered Natal, now a province of South Africa, on Christmas Day 1497.

Gambetta /gæm'betə/ Léon Michel 1838–1882. French politician, organizer of resistance in the ◊Franco–Prussian War, and founder in 1871 of the Third Republic. In 1881–82 he was prime minister for a few weeks.

Gambia /'gæmbiə/ river in W Africa, which gives its name to ◊Gambia; 1,000 km/620 mi long.

Gambia, The /'gæmbiə/ country in W Africa, surrounded to the N, E, and S by Senegal, and bordered to the W by the Atlantic Ocean.

government The Gambia is an independent republic within the ◊Commonwealth. Its constitution dates from 1970 and provides for a single-chamber legislature, the house of representatives, consisting of 49 members, 35 directly elected by universal suffrage, five elected by the chiefs, eight non-voting, nominated members, and the attorney-general, ex-officio. It serves a five-year term, as does the president, who is elected by direct universal suffrage and appoints a vice-president, who also leads the house of representatives, and a cabinet. There are two main political parties, the Progressive People's Party (PPP) and the National Convention Party.

history The Gambia was formerly part of the ◊Mali empire, whose decline coincided with the arrival of the Portuguese in 1455. In the late 16th century commerce was taken over from Portugal by England, and trading posts established on the Gambia River were controlled from Sierra Leone. In 1843 Gambia was made a Crown Colony, becoming an independent British colony in 1888.

Political parties were formed in the 1950s, internal self-government granted in 1963, and full independence within the Commonwealth achieved in 1965, with Dawda K Jawara as prime minister. It declared itself a republic in 1970, with Jawara as president, replacing the British monarch as head of state. He was re-elected in 1972 and 1977.

With the PPP the dominant political force, there was pressure to make The Gambia a one-party state but Jawara resisted this. When an attempted coup against him in 1981 was thwarted with Senegalese military aid, ties between the two countries were strengthened to the extent that plans were announced for their merger into a confederation of Senegambia. The process is not yet complete and there are signs that Senegal has doubts about the wisdom of the idea. In economic terms The Gambia would seem to have more to gain. In 1982 Jawara was re-elected for another five-year term.

Gambier Islands /'gæmbiə/ part of one of the five archipelagos of ◊French Polynesia.

gamelan orchestra a type of Indonesian orchestra, mainly using tuned metal percussion instruments, the music of which has influenced Western composers.

Gamelin /'gæmələ̃/ Maurice Gustave 1872–1958. French commander-in-chief of the Allied armies in France in 1939. Replaced by Weygand after the German breakthrough at Sedan in 1940, he was tried as a scapegoat before the ◊Riom 'War Guilt' court in 1942. He refused to defend himself, and was detained in Germany until released by the Allies in 1945.

gamete a cell generated for sexual reproduction. In most organisms, the gametes are ◊haploid, that is they contain half the number of chromosomes of the parent, due to reduction division or ◊meiosis. In higher organisms, gametes are of two distinct types, large immobile ones known as eggs or egg-cells (see ◊ovum) and small ones known as ◊sperm. They come together at ◊fertilization. In some lower organisms the gametes are all the same, or they may belong to different mating strains but have no obvious differences in size or appearance.

game theory branch of mathematics that deals with strategic problems (such as those that arise in business, commerce, and warfare) by assuming that the people involved invariably try to win – that is, they are assumed to employ strategies that should give the greatest gain and the smallest loss. The theory was developed by Oscar ◊Morgenstern and John von ◊Neumann during World War II.

Gambia

REPUBLIC OF THE

AREA 11,000 sq km/4,000 sq mi
CAPITAL Banjul
PHYSICAL banks of the river Gambia
FEATURES the smallest state in black Africa
HEAD OF STATE AND OF GOVERNMENT Dawda Kairaba Jawara from 1970
GOVERNMENT democratic republic
EXPORTS groundnuts, palm oil, fish
CURRENCY dalasi (12.29 = £1 Sept 1987)
POPULATION 751,000 (1985); annual growth rate 1.2%
LANGUAGE English (official)
RELIGION Muslim 70%, with animist and Christian minorities
LITERACY 29% male/12% female (1980 est)
GNP $200 million (1983); $330 per head of population
CHRONOLOGY
1965 Achieved independence as a constitutional monarchy within the Commonwealth, with Dawda K Jawara as prime minister.
1970 Declared itself a republic, with Jawara as president.

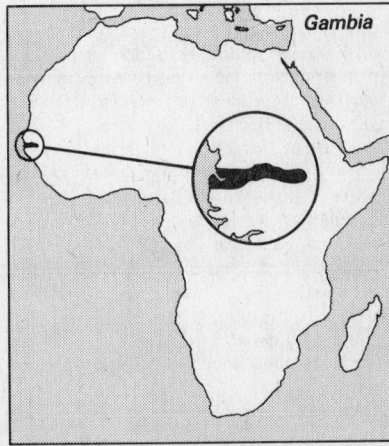

1972 Jawara re-elected.
1981 Attempted coup foiled with the help of Senegal. Plans announced for a merger with Senegal.
1982 Jawara re-elected.

gametophyte the haploid generation in the lifecycle of a plant that produces gametes; see ◊alternation of generations.

gamma radiation very high-frequency ◊electromagnetic radiation emitted by the nuclei of radioactive substances during decay, similar in nature to X-rays, but of shorter wavelength. It is used to kill bacteria and other microorganisms, sterilize medical devices, change the molecular structure of plastics to modify their properties (for example, to improve heat and abrasion resistance for insulation purposes) Most cosmic gamma rays cannot pass through the Earth's atmosphere and telescopes to detect them must be placed above it. Only a few of the many sources have been identified, including pulsars, radio galaxies, and quasars.

Gance /gɒns/ Abel 1889– . French film director, whose *Napoléon* 1927 was a silent epic.

Gandhi /'gændi/ Indira 1917–1984. Indian politician and prime minister of India 1966–77, and 1980–84. A daughter of ◊Nehru, she married Feroze Gandhi in 1942 (died 1960). not related to M K ◊Gandhi, and had two sons, *Sanjay Gandhi* (1946–80), who died in an air crash, and Rajiv ◊Gandhi. She became leader of the Congress Party and prime minister in 1966. In 1975 her election to parliament was declared invalid and she declared a state of emergency. During this time her son, Sanjay, was implementing a social and economic programme (including a ruthless family planning policy) which led to her defeat in 1977, though he masterminded her return to power in 1980. She was assassinated by members of her Sikh bodyguard, resentful of her use of troops to clear malcontents from the temple at ◊Amritsar.

Gandhi /'gændi/ Mohandas Karamchand 1869–1948. Indian leader, called Mahatma ('Great Soul'). Born in Porbandar, he studied in London, and then led the Indian community in South Africa in opposition to racial discrimination. Returning to India in 1915, he led the struggle for Indian independence by 'non-violent non-cooperation' (*satyagraha*, defence of and by truth), which included several 'fasts unto death'. He was several times imprisoned by the British authorities, was influential in the Congress (nationalist) Party, and in the independence negotiations in 1947. His fasts were less effective against his fellow-countrymen, and he was assassinated by a Hindu nationalist in the violence which followed Partition.

Gandhi /'gændi/ Rajiv 1944– . Prime minister of India from 1984 and Congress (I) Party leader.
Son of Indira ◊Gandhi and grandson of ◊Nehru, Rajiv Gandhi displayed little interest in politics and became an airline pilot. But after the death in a plane crash of his brother Sanjay (1946–80), he was elected to his brother's Amethi parliamentary seat in 1981. When Indira Gandhi was assassinated in Oct 1984, he was appointed Congress (I) leader and Indian prime minister and in the Dec 1984 parliamentary elections won a record majority. In 1985 he reached a settlement with the moderate ◊Sikhs.

Ganesa /gæ'neɪsə/ Hindu god, represented as

Gandhi Indira Gandhi, Nehru's daughter, had a controversial political career, during which she was twice prime minister of India. This photograph was taken during the 1983 summit meeting of the non-aligned countries. She was assassinated as she left her New Delhi home on the morning of 31 Oct 1984.

elephant-headed, and worshipped as a remover of obstacles.

Ganges /'gændʒiːz/ (Hindi *Ganga*) major river of India and Bangladesh, the most sacred river of the ◊Hindus; length 2,506 km/1,557 mi. Its chief tributary is the *Yamuna* (Jumna); length 1,385 km/860 mi, which joins the Ganges near Allahabad, where there is a sacred bathing place. M K ◊Gandhi, ◊Nehru, and Indira ◊Gandhi were all cremated on the banks of the Yamuna at Delhi. The Ganges is joined in its delta in Bangladesh by the ◊Brahmaputra, and its most commercially important and westernmost channel to the Bay of Bengal is the *Hooghly*.

Gang of Four (1) a name given to the chief members of the radical faction that tried to seize power in China after the death of Mao Zedong in 1976. It included his widow, ◊Jiang Qing, and the other members were Zhang Chunjao, Wang Hungwen, and Yao Wenyuan. The coup failed, and they were soon arrested.
(2)in Britain the name was subsequently applied to the four members of the Labour Party who in 1981 resigned to form the new ◊Social Democratic Party (SDP): Roy ◊Jenkins, David ◊Owen, Shirley ◊Williams, and William Rodgers.

gangrene death and decay of tissues by bacterial action due to injury, burning, freezing, poisoning, or failure of the blood supply, as where a bandage is too tight or the vessels are abnormally contracted, or where a vessel is blocked with a blood clot (◊thrombosis). The affected parts are at first painful and sensitive

and feel cold, and their skin turns brownish or violet. Amputation may be necessary.

gannet or *solan goose*. Sea-bird *Sula bassana* in the family Sulidae, found in the N Atlantic. When full-grown it is white with black-tipped wings with a span of 1.7 m/5.6 ft, but the young are speckled. It breeds on cliffs, the nest being roughly made of grass and seaweed. Only one (white) egg is laid.

Gansu /ˌgæn'suː/ province (formerly Kansu) of NW China
area 530,000 sq km/204,633 sq mi
capital Lanzhou
features subject to earthquakes; the 'Silk Road' (now a motor road) passed through it in the Middle Ages, carrying trade to central Asia
products coal, oil, hydroelectric power from the Yellow River
population (1982) 19,569,261, including many Muslims.

Ganymede /'gænɪmiːd/ in Greek mythology, a youth so beautiful he was chosen as cupbearer to Zeus (Roman Jupiter).

Ganymede /'gænɪmiːd/ in astronomy, the largest moon of the planet ◊Jupiter, and the largest moon in the ◊solar system, 5,300 km/3,300 mi in diameter (larger than the planet Mercury). It orbits Jupiter every 7.2 days at a distance of 1.1 million km/0.7 million mi.

Gaoxiong /'gau ʃi 'ʊŋ/ mainland Chinese form of ◊Kaohsiung, a port in W Taiwan.

Garbo /'gɑːbəʊ/ Greta. Stage-name of the Swedish actress Greta Lovisa Gustafsson 1905– . Trained at the Royal Theatre drama school, Stockholm, she made her first film *The Story of Gosta Berling* in 1924, then went to the USA, where she played in *The Torrent* 1926, becoming one of Hollywood's first 'stars'. Her later films include *Anna Christie* 1930, her first 'talkie', *Mata Hari* 1931, *Queen Christina* 1933, *Anna Karenina* 1935, and *Ninotchka* 1939.

García Lorca /gɑː'θiːə 'lɔːkə/ Federico. See ◊Lorca.

Garcia Márquez /gɑːsiːə 'mɑːkes/ Gabriel 1928– . Colombian novelist, whose *Cien años de soledad/One Hundred Years of Solitude* 1967, the story of six generations of a family, initiated a renaissance of Latin American literature and awakened interest in it from the English-speaking world. Politically on the left, he is perhaps the best-known exponent of magic realism, a technique for heightening the intensity of realistic portrayal of social and political issues by introducing grotesque or fanciful material. He was awarded the Nobel Prize for Literature in 1982.

Garcilaso de la Vega /ˌgɑːθɪ'lɑːsəʊ/ 1539–1616. Spanish writer, called *el Inca*. Son of a Spanish conquistador and an Inca princess, he wrote an account of the conquest of Florida and *Commentarios* on the history of Peru.

Garcilaso de la Vega /ˌgɑːθɪ'lɑːsəʊ/ 1503–1536. Spanish poet. A soldier, he was a member of ◊Charles V's expedition in 1535 to Tunis; he was killed in battle at Nice. His verse, some of the greatest of the Spanish Renaissance, includes sonnets, songs, and elegies, often on the model of ◊Petrarch.

Gandhi The political rise of Indian prime minister Rajiv Gandhi was built on family tragedy. In 1981, he won the parliamentary seat of his brother Sanjay, killed in a flying accident, and became premier in 1984 on the assassination of his mother Indira Gandhi.

Gandhi After spending his youth opposing discrimination against Indians in South Africa, Mahatma ('Great Soul') Ghandi returned to India and campaigned for 30 years by civil disobedience and 'fasts unto death' for independence, which Britain finally granted in 1947.

Garbo The film star Greta Garbo, photographed by Cecil Beaton in 1969. The Swedish-born actress began her career in silent movies and became a screen legend, starring in more than 25 films.

Gard /gɑː/ French river, 133 km/83 mi long, a tributary of the Rhône, which it joins above Beaucaire. It gives its name to Gard *département*.

Garda, Lake /'gɑːdə/ The largest lake in Italy; 370 sq km/143 sq mi.

garden city in the UK, name for a town built in a rural area and designed to combine town and country advantages, with its own industries, controlled developments, private and public gardens, and cultural centre. The idea was proposed by Sir Ebenezer Howard (1850–1928), who in 1899 formed the Garden City Association, which established the first garden city, Letchworth (in ◊Hertfordshire). A second, Welwyn, 35 km/22 mi from London, was started in 1919. The New Towns Act, 1946, provided machinery for developing ◊new towns on some of the principles advocated by Howard (for example Stevenage, begun in 1947), and there

have been similar schemes in Europe and in the USA, but on the whole these have not kept the economic structure, or the industrial self-sufficiency of the rural belt which formed an integral part of Howard's original idea.

gardenia genus of subtropical and tropical trees and shrubs of Africa and Asia, family Rubiaceae, with evergreen foliage and flattened rosettes of fragrant waxen-looking blooms, often white.

Garden of the Gods natural sandstone 'sculptures' in ◊Colorado, USA.

Gardiner /'gɑːdnə/ Stephen c. 1493–1555. English priest and politician. After being secretary to Wolsey, he became bishop of Winchester in 1531. An opponent of Protestantism, he was imprisoned under Edward VI, and as lord chancellor 1553–55 under Mary he tried to restore Roman Catholicism.

Gardner /'gɑːdnə/ Erle Stanley 1889–1970.

American author of crime fiction. He created the character of lawyer-detective Perry Mason, who later featured in film and television versions.

Garfield /'gɑːfiːld/ James Abram 1831–1881. 20th president of the USA. Born in a log cabin in Ohio, he entered politics as a Republican and served in the ◊Civil War on the side of the North. He was inaugurated as president in 1881, but a few months later was assassinated in a Washington station.

Garcia Márquez The Colombian writer Gabriel Garcia Márquez, whose novels have become widely known since he was awarded the Nobel Prize for Literature in 1982.

garfish type of fish with a long spear-like snout. The *common garfish Belone belone*, order Beloniformes, family Belonidae, has an elongated body 75 cm/2.5 ft long and, despite its green bones, has excellent flesh.

gargoyle spout projecting from the roof-gutter of a building with the purpose of directing water away from the wall. The term is usually applied to the ornamental forms found in Gothic architecture; these were carved in stone and took the shape of fantastic animals, angels, or human heads.

Garibaldi /ˌgærɪˈbɔːldi/ Giuseppe 1807–1882. Italian patriot. Born in Nice, he became a sailor, and in 1834 joined ◊Mazzini's Young Italy Society. Condemned to death for treason, he escaped to South America where he became a mercenary. He returned to Italy during the 1848 revolution, served with the Sardinian army against the Austrians, and commanded the army of the Roman republic in its defence of the city against the French. He subsequently lived in exile until 1854, when he settled on the island of Caprera. He again fought against the Austrians in the war of 1859; and in 1860, at the head of his 1,000 *redshirts*, he conquered Sicily and Naples for the new kingdom of Italy. He led two unsuccessful expeditions to liberate Rome from papal rule in 1862 and 1867.

Garland /ˈgɑːlənd/ Judy 1922–69. American singer and actress, born Frances Gumm. Her films include *The Wizard of Oz* 1939 (including the song 'Over the Rainbow'), *Meet Me in St Louis* 1944, and *A Star is Born* 1954.

garlic perennial plant *Allium sativum*, family Liliaceae, with white flowers. The bulb, made of small segments, 'cloves', is used in cookery, and its pungent essence has an active medical ingredient allyl methyl trisulphide which prevents blood clotting.

Garibaldi Italian hero of the *Risorgimento*, Giuseppe Garibaldi. In 1860 he made a spectacular conquest of Naples and Sicily with his thousand redshirts.

garnet a group of silicate minerals with the formula $X_3Y_2 (SiO_4)_3$, when X is calcium, magnesium, iron, or manganese, and Y is iron, aluminium, chromium, or titanium, used as semi-precious ◊gems (usually pink to deep red) and ◊abrasives. They occur in ◊metamorphic rocks such as ◊gneiss and ◊schist.

Garrick /ˈgærɪk/ David 1717–1779. British actor-manager. Born in Hereford, he was a pupil of Samuel ◊Johnson at Lichfield, and both set out for London together in 1737. His naturalistic acting style and brilliant mimicry soon made him famous. From 1747 he became joint patentee of the Drury Lane theatre with his own company, during which time he was responsible for the institution of a number of significant theatrical conventions including concealed stage lighting

and banishing spectators from the stage. He was noted for his Shakespearean performances as Richard III, Lear, Hamlet, and Benedick. With Colman he wrote the play *The Clandestine Marriage* 1766 and made numerous adaptations.

Garter, Order of the Senior British order of knighthood, founded by Edward III in about 1347. Its distinctive badge is a garter of dark blue velvet, with the motto of the order, *Honi soit qui mal y pense* ('Shame be to him who thinks evil of it'), in gold letters, worn below the left knee. Its sash is also dark blue. Membership is limited to 25 knights, and to members of the royal family and foreign royalties; appointments are made by the sovereign alone. St George's Chapel, Windsor, is the chapel of the order. The ◊Blue Riband is derived from the order's garter.

Garrick David Garrick, portrayed by William Hogarth as Shakespeare's Richard II, waking from a nightmare before the fatal Battle of Bosworth.

Garvey /'gɑːvi/ Marcus (Moziah) 1887–1940. Jamaican political thinker and activist, an early advocate of black nationalism. He founded the UNIA (Universal Negro Improvement Association) in 1914, and moved to the USA in 1916, where he established branches in New York and other northern cities. Aiming to achieve human rights and dignity for black people through black pride and economic self-sufficiency, he campaigned for a 'Back to Africa' movement for black Americans to establish a black-governed country in Africa. ◊Rastafarianism was largely based on his ideas.

Garvey Jamaican-born Marcus Garvey, pictured here at a New York parade in 1922, was the founder of the 'Back to Africa' movement.

Gary /'gæri/ city in Indiana, USA; population (1980) 151,953. It contains the steel and cement works of the United States Steel Corporation, and was named after E H Gary (1846–1927), its chairman.

gas a form of matter in which the molecules move randomly in otherwise empty space, filling any size or shape of container into which the gas is put; see also ◊liquid, ◊solid, ◊fluid. A sugar-lump sized cube of air at room temperature contains 30 million million million molecules moving at an average speed of 500 metres per second (1,800 kph/1,200 mph). Gases can be liquefied by cooling, which lowers the speed of the molecules and enables attractive forces between them to bind them together.

Gascony /'gæskəni/ ancient province of SW France. Henry II of England gained possession of it through his marriage to Eleanor of Aquitaine in 1152, and it was often in English hands until 1451. It was united with the French royal domain in 1607 under Henry IV.

gas-cooled reactor see ◊advanced gas-cooled reactor.

gas engine type of internal combustion engine in which gas (coal, producer, natural, or gas from a blast furnace) is used as the fuel. The first practical gas engine was built in 1860 by Jean Etienne Lenoir, and the type was subsequently developed by Mikolaus August Otto, who introduced the ◊four-stroke cycle.

gas exchange in biology, the exchange of gases between living organisms and the atmosphere. In humans, and other tetrapods, the air is drawn into ◊lungs and is there brought into contact with blood in very thin-walled capillary vessels. The blood takes up oxygen, while giving up carbon dioxide, together with water and small quantities of ammonia and waste matter. The entire process is called ◊respiration. Many adult amphibia and terrestrial invertebrates can absorb oxygen from the atmosphere directly through the skin. Insects and some spiders have a system of air-filled tubes known as ◊tracheae ramifying through the body, while fish and most other aquatic organisms have ◊gills. In plants, gas exchange generally takes place via the ◊stomata, specialized pores in the epidermis that can be opened and closed.

Gaskell /'gæskəl/ Elizabeth Cleghorn (born Stevenson) 1810–1865. British novelist. Her books include *Mary Barton* (set in industrial Manchester) 1848, *Cranford* (set in the town in which she was brought up, Knutsford, Cheshire) 1853, *North and South* 1855, *Sylvia's Lovers* 1863–64, the unfinished *Wives and Daughters* 1866, and a life of her friend Charlotte ◊Brontë.

gas laws physical laws concerning the behaviour of gases. They include ◊Boyle's law and ◊Charles' law, which are concerned with the relationships between pressure, temperature and volume of a (hypothetical) ideal gas. ◊Graham's law concerns gaseous diffusion, and ◊Van der Waals' law includes corrections for the non-ideal behaviour of real gases.

gasohol a type of motor fuel that is 90 per cent petrol and 10 per cent ethanol (alcohol). The ethanol is usually obtained by fermentation, followed by distillation, using maize, wheat, potatoes or sugar cane.

gasolene a mixture of hydrocarbons derived from petroleum, whose main use is as a fuel for internal combustion engines. It is colourless and highly volatile. In the USA petrol is called gasoline.

Gaspé Peninsula /gæs'peɪ/ mountainous peninsula in SE Quebec, Canada; area 29,500 sq km/11,390 sq mi. It has fishing and lumbering industries.

Gasperi /'gæspəri/ Alcide de 1881–1954. Italian statesman. A founder of the Christian Democrat party, he was prime minister 1945–53, and worked for European unification.

gastritis inflammation of the lining of the stomach. It may be caused by corrosive poisons (such as lysol, caustic soda, strong acids), too high a concentration of alcohol, or infection.

gastroenteritis inflammation of the stomach and intestines leading to vomiting and diarrhoea, usually caused by food poisoning.

gastropod very large class (Gastropoda) of ◊molluscs; single-shelled (in a spiral or modified spiral form), in some cases with eyes on stalks, and moving with a flattened, muscular foot. Gastropods have a well-developed head and rough tongue. Some are marine, some freshwater, and others land creatures, but all tend to inhabit damp places. They include snails, slugs, limpets, and periwinkles.

gas turbine an engine in which burning fuel supplies hot gas to spin a ◊turbine. The most widespread application of gas turbines has been in aviation. All ◊jet engines are modified gas turbines. A few locomotives and ships also use gas turbines as a power source. They are also used in industry for generating and pumping duties. In a typical gas turbine a multi-vaned compressor draws in and compresses air. The compressed air enters a combustion chamber at high pressure, and fuel is sprayed in and ignited. The hot gases produced escape through the blades of (typically) two turbines and spin them round. One of the turbines drives the compressor, the other provides the external power which can be harnessed.

gas warfare use of gas to produce a toxic effect on the human body; see ◊chemical warfare.

Gateshead /'geɪtshed/ port in Tyne and Wear, England; population (1981) 81,000. Industries include engineering, chemicals, and glass.

Gatling /'gætlɪŋ/ Richard Jordan 1818–1903. American inventor of a rapid-fire gun. Patented in 1862, the Gatling gun had ten barrels arranged as a cylinder rotated by a hand crank. Cartridges from an overhead hopper or dum dropped into the breech mechanism, which loaded, fired and extracted them at a rate of 320 rounds per minute. The Gatling gun was used in the France-Prussian War of 1870. By 1882 rates of fire of up to 1,200 rounds per minute were achieved, but the weapon was soon superseded by Hiram Maxim's ◊machine gun (1889).

Gatwick /'gætwɪk/ site of Gatwick Airport, Surrey, England, constructed 1956–58.

gaucho /'gaʊtʃəʊ/ part Indian, part Spanish cattle herder, formerly working on the Argentine and Uruguayan pampas.

Gaudí /gaʊ'diː/ Antonio 1852–1926. Spanish architect, noted for his flamboyant Art Nouveau-influenced style. He was also influenced by Moorish and medieval architecture. His spectacular Church of the Holy Family, Barcelona, begun 1883, was still under construction when he died.

Gaudier-Brzeska /'gəʊdɪeɪ 'bʒeskə/ Henri 1891–1915. French sculptor. He studied art at Bristol, Nuremberg, and Munich, and became a member of the English ◊Vorticist movement. His sculptures include *The Dancer* and *The Embracers*.

Gaudier-Brzeska A 1912 self-portrait of the French sculptor Henri Gaudier-Brzeska. He was a member of the Vorticist movement which aimed to reflect the modern industrial world in art and which was led by the British artist Percy Wyndham Lewis.

gauge scientific measuring instrument, for example, wire-gauge, pressure-gauge. The term is also applied to the width of a railway or tramway track.

Gauguin /'gəʊgæŋ/ Paul 1848–1903. French artist. Born in Paris, he joined a banking firm, but gave up his career in 1881 in order to paint. After a visit to Martinique in 1887, he went to Pont Aven in Brittany, becoming the leading artist in the movement known as *Synthesism*. In 1891 he left Paris for Tahiti, where he remained from 1895 until his death. Going beyond the ◊Impressionists' notion of reality, he sought a more direct experience of life in the magical rites of the people and rich colours of the islands. A friend of ◊Van Gogh, he disliked theories and rules of painting, and his pictures are ◊Expressionist compositions characterized by his use of pure, unmixed colours. Among his most famous paintings is *Le Christe Jaune* 1889.

Gaul /gɔːl/ member of the Celtic-speaking peoples who inhabited France and Belgium in Roman times. They were divided into several groupings, but united by a common religion controlled by the Druid priesthood. Certain Gauls invaded Italy c. 400 BC, sacked Rome, and settled between the Alps and the Apennines; this

Gauguin *Nave Nave Fenua*, a woodcut by the French artist Paul Gauguin made c. 1894, in Tahiti, where he made his home in his later years.

district, known as Cisalpine Gaul, was conquered by Rome c. 225 BC. The Romans conquered S Gaul between the Mediterranean and the Cevennes c. 125 BC and the remaining Gauls up to the Rhine were conquered by ◊Caesar 58–51 BC.

gaur Asiatic wild ox *Bos gaurus* which is dark grey-brown with white stockings, and 2 m/6 ft tall at the shoulders. Its original range was from India to Indo-China and Malaya, but its numbers and range are now diminished.

Gauss /gaʊs/ Karl Friedrich 1777–1855. German mathematician who worked on the theory of numbers, non-Euclidian geometry, and on the mathematical development of electric and magnetic theory; in World War II the method of countering magnetic mines was called degaussing. The old measure of magnetic flux density was named after him; it has now been replaced by the SI unit, the ◊tesla.

Gautier /'gəʊtieɪ/ Théophile 1811–1872. French Romantic poet, whose later work emphasized the perfection of form and the 'polished' beauty of language and imagery (for example, *Émaux et Camées/Enamels and Cameos* 1852). He was also a novelist (*Mlle de Maupin* 1835) and later in his life turned to journalism.

Gay /geɪ/ John 1685–1732. British poet, born in Barnstaple. He was the friend of ◊Pope and Arbuthnot, and wrote *Trivia* 1716, a verse picture of 18th-century London. His *The Beggar's Opera* 1728, 'a Newgate pastoral' using traditional songs and telling of the love of Polly for highwayman Captain Macheath, was an extraordinary popular success. Its satiric

political touches led to the banning of *Polly*, a sequel.

Gaya /'gaɪə/ ancient city in Bihar state, India; population (1981) 344,941. It is famous for its association with Buddhism and includes ◊Buddh Gaya, with a temple dating back to 543 BC.

Gaye /geɪ/ Marvin 1939–1984. US soul singer and songwriter, whose songs were classic examples of the Detroit ◊Motown sound in the 1960s. A leading solo vocalist (hits include 'How Sweet It Is' 1964 and 'I Heard It Through The Grapevine' 1968).

Gay-Lussac /'geɪ luːˈsæk/ Joseph Louis 1778–1850. French physicist and chemist, born near Limoges. He made balloon ascents to study the weather in 1804 and in 1808 became professor of physics at Paris. He investigated the physical properties of gases and discovered new methods of producing sulphuric and oxalic acids. See also ◊Charles's law and ◊gas laws.

Gaza /'gɑːzə/ capital of the ◊Gaza Strip, once a ◊Philistine city, and scene of three World War I battles; population (1967) 120,000.

Gaza Strip strip of Palestine under Israeli administration; capital Gaza; area 260 sq km/100 sq mi; population (1967) 365,000. It was invaded by Israel in 1956; reoccupied in 1967, and retained in 1973. See ◊Arab–Israeli Wars.

gazelle name given to various species of lightly-built fast-running antelopes found on the open plains of Africa and South Asia, especially those of the genus *Gazella*.

Gaziantep /ˌgæziænˈtep/ town 185 km/115 mi NE of Adana in Turkey; population (1980) 374,290. It has textile and tanning industries.

GCE (General Certificate of Education) in the UK, the public examination usually taken at the age of 16 at Ordinary Level (O Level) and at 18 at Advanced Level (A Level). The GCE O Level examination, which was aimed at the top 20% of the ability range, was superseded in 1988 by the General Certificate of Secondary Education (◊GCSE).

GCHQ (Government Communications Headquarters) the centre of the British Government's electronic surveillance operations, in Cheltenham, Gloucestershire. It monitors broadcasts of various kinds from all over the world. In addition there are six listening stations: at Bude, Cornwall; Culm Head, Somerset; Brora and Hawklaw, Scotland; Irton Moor, N Yorkshire; and Cheadle, Greater Manchester. There is an outpost in Cyprus. It was established in World War I, and was successful in breaking the German Enigma code in 1940. In 1982 Geoffrey Prime (1939–), a linguist there, was convicted of handing the secrets of US spy satellites to the USSR.

GCSE (General Certificate of Secondary Education) in the UK, from 1988, the new examination for 16-year old pupils, which superseded both GCE O Level and CSE, and offers qualifications for up to 60 per cent of school leavers in any particular subject. The GCSE is intended to be more practically biased than O Level and is organized in the light of national criteria laid down by the Secondary Examinations Council.

Gdańsk /gdænsk/ port (German *Danzig*) in Poland; population (1980) 454,000. Formerly a member of the ◊Hanseatic League, it was in almost continuous Prussian possession 1793–1919, when it again became a free city under the protection of the League of Nations. Annexed by Germany in 1939, at the beginning of World War II, it reverted to Poland in 1945, when the churches and old merchant houses were restored. The shipyard strikes of 1980 were symptomatic of growing resistance to Communist rule.

GDP abbreviation for ◊Gross Domestic Product.

Gdynia /'gdɪnjə/ port in Poland; population (1980) 234,500. It was established in 1920 to give newly constituted Poland a sea outlet to replace lost ◊Gdańsk. It has a naval base and shipyards.

Ge /dʒiː/ in Greek mythology, an alternative name for ◊Gaia, goddess of the Earth.

Geber /'dʒiːbə/ full name Jabir ibn Hayyan c. 721–c. 776. Arabian alchemist. His influence lasted for more than 600 years, and in the late 1300s his name was adopted by a Spanish alchemist whose writings spread the knowledge and practice of alchemy throughout Europe. This Geber probably discovered nitric and sulphuric acids, and he propounded a theory that all metals are composed of various mixtures of mercury and sulphur.

gecko small soft-skinned lizard in the family Gekkonidae. They are common in warm climates, and have a large head, and short, stout body. Their adhesive toe pads enable them to walk up windows and across ceilings in their search for flies, spiders, and other prey. Gecko is derived from the clicking sound which the animal makes.

Geddes /'gedɪs/ Patrick 1854–1932. A pioneering British town planner, who established the current theory of town planning, in particular the importance of surveys and research work, and properly planned 'diagnoses before treatment'. His major work is *City Development*, 1904.

Geiger counter device for detecting and/or counting nuclear radiations and particles. Geiger-Müller, Geiger-Klemperer and Rutherford-Geiger counters are all devices often referred to loosely as Geiger counters, after Hans Geiger (1882–1945), one-time student of ◊Rutherford and professor of physics at Kiel, who was active in their development. The principle on which the Geiger counter operates is the detection of the momentary current which passes between ◊electrodes in a suitable gas when a nuclear particle or a radiation pulse causes ionization in the gas. The electrodes are connected to electronic devices which enable the intensity of radiation or the number of particles passing to be measured.

geisha female entertainer (music, singing, dancing, and so on), in Japanese teahouses and private parties. Geishas survive mainly as a tourist attraction.

Geissler tube high-voltage ◊discharge tube in which traces of gas ionize and conduct electricity, glowing with coloured light (such as the neon tubes used in advertising signs). It is named after the German physicist Heinrich Geissler (1814–1879), who developed it in 1858.

gelatine water-soluble protein prepared from boiled hide and bone, used in cookery to set jellies, and in ◊glues and photographic emulsions.

Gelderland /'geldəlænd/ also *Guelders*, E province of the Netherlands. The capital is Arnhem; area 5,014 sq km/1,955 sq mi; population (1982) 1,791,000. In the NW is the Veluwe, a favourite holiday district.

Geldof /'geldɒf/ Bob 1954– . Irish rock musician and philanthropist; singer with the Boomtown Rats (1975–86). He was the instigator of Band Aid and Live Aid 1984–86. Band Aid made a record, and Live Aid was a combination of two concerts, one in London and one in Philadelphia, broadcast live. Both were charity events raising large sums of money for famine relief, especially in Ethiopia. He was made Knight Commander of the British Empire 1986.

gelignite type of ◊dynamite.

Gell-Mann /'gel 'mæn/ Murray 1929– . American physicist. R A Millikan professor of theoretical physics at the Californian Institute of Technology from 1967, he was awarded a Nobel prize 1969 for his work on elementary particles and their interaction. He formulated in 1964 the theory of the ◊quark as the fundamental constituent of all matter and smallest particle in the universe. See also ◊particle physics.

Gelsenkirchen /ˌgelzən'kɪəkən/ industrial city in the ◊Ruhr, West Germany; population (1985) 295,000. It has iron and steel, chemical, and glass industries.

gem a mineral precious by virtue of its composition, hardness and rarity, cut and polished for ornamental use, or engraved. Of 120 minerals known to have been used as gemstones, only about 25 are in common use in jewellery; of these, the ◊diamond, ◊emerald, ◊ruby, and ◊sapphire are classified as precious, and the ◊topaz, ◊amethyst, ◊opal, and ◊aquamarine, as semi-precious. Among synthetic precious stones to have been produced successfully are rubies, sapphires, emeralds, and diamonds (first produced by GEC in the USA in 1955). Pearls are not technically gems.

Gemara in ◊Judaism, part of the Talmud, the compilation of ancient Jewish law.

Gemayel /ˌgemaɪ'el/ Amin 1942– . Lebanese (Maronite Christian) president from 1982. He succeeded his brother, president-elect *Bechir Gemayel*, on his assassination on 14 Sept 1982.

Gemeinschaft and Gesellschaft German terms (roughly, 'community' and 'association') used by Ferdinand ◊Tönnies (1855–1936) to contrast social relationships in traditional rural societies with those in modern industrial societies. He saw *gemeinschaft* as intimate and positive, and *gesellschaft* as impersonal and negative. In small-scale societies where everyone knows everyone else, the social order is seen as stable and the culture homogeneous. In large urban areas life is faster and more competitive, and relationships are seen as more superficial, transitory, and anonymous.

Gemini prominent constellation of the ◊zodiac, representing the twins Castor and Pollux. The Sun passes through it from late June to late July; its brightest star is Pollux, an orange giant 36 light years away. Castor is a system of six stars linked by ◊gravity. Each December, the Gemini meteors radiate from this constellation.

Gemini project US space programme (1965–66) in which astronauts practised rendezvous and docking of spacecraft, and working outside their spacecraft, in preparation for the Apollo Moon landings (see ◊Apollo project). Gemini spacecraft carried two astronauts and were launched by Titan rockets.

gemma a unit of ◊vegetative reproduction, comprising a small group of undifferentiated green cells. Gemmas are found in certain mosses and liverworts, forming on the surface of the plant, often in cup-shaped structures, or gemmae cups. Gemmae are dispersed by splashes of rain, and can then develop into new plants. In many species gemmation is more common than reproduction by ◊spores.

gender in grammar, one of the categories into which nouns are divided in many languages, such as masculine, feminine, and neuter (as in Latin, German, and Russian), masculine and feminine (as in French, Italian, and Spanish), or animate and inanimate (as in the North American Indian languages).
Grammatical gender may or may not correspond with sex: in French, *la soeœur* (the sister) is feminine, but so is *la plume* (the pen). In German, *das Mädchen* (the girl) is neuter.
English nouns have only *natural gender*; that is, their grammatical gender reflects the sex of the referent of the noun rather than the form of the word itself. (For example, the name Katharine is a feminine noun because it refers to a particular girl.)

gene a unit of inherited material, situated on a strand of nucleic acid (◊DNA or ◊RNA). In higher organisms, genes are located on the ◊chromosomes. The term 'gene' was first used in 1909 by the Danish geneticist Wilhelm Johannsen (1857–1927) to refer to the inherited factor that consistently affects a particular character in an individual that bears it, for example, the gene for eye colour. Also termed a Mendelian gene, after Gregor ◊Mendel, it may have several variants or ◊alleles, each of which specifies a particular form of that character, for example, the alleles for blue eyes or brown eyes. Some alleles show ◊dominance, that is they mask the effect of others, known as ◊recessive alleles. In the 1940s, it was established that a gene could be identified with a particular length of DNA, which coded for a complete ◊protein molecule, leading to the 'one-gene-one-enzyme' principle. Later it was realized that proteins might be made up of several ◊polypeptide chains, each with a separate gene, so this principle was modified to 'one-gene-one-polypeptide'. However, the fundamental idea remains the same, that genes produce their visible effects simply by coding for proteins; they control the structure of those proteins via the ◊genetic code, as well as the amounts produced and the timing of production. In modern ◊genetics, the gene is identified either with the ◊cistron (a set of ◊codons that determines a complete polypeptide) or with the unit of selection (a Mendelian gene that determines a particular character in the organism on which ◊natural selection can act). Genes undergo ◊mutation and ◊recombination to produce the variation on which natural selection operates.

genealogy the study and tracing of family histories. The Society of Genealogists in London (established 1911) with its library, thousands of family papers, marriage index (6,000,000 names of persons married before 1837), and collection of parish register copies, undertakes and assists research.

Genée /ʒɔˈneɪ/ Adeline 1878–1970. Stage-name of Danish-British dancer Anina Jensen. She was president of the Royal Academy of Dancing 1920–54. She was created a Dame in 1950.

gene pool the total sum of ◊alleles (variants of ◊genes) possessed by all the members of a given ◊population or ◊species alive at a particular time.

general senior military officer commanding a body of troops larger than a regiment, the ascending grades being in Britain (and the USA) lieutenant general, major general, and general; in the USA the rank of general of the army is equivalent to a British field ◊marshal.

General Agreement on Tariffs and Trade (GATT) an organization within the ◊United Nations which was begun in 1948 with the aim of encouraging ◊free trade between nations through low tariffs, abolitions of quotas, curbs on subsidies, and the like.

General Assembly supreme court of the Church of ◊Scotland.

generator a machine that produces electrical energy from mechanical energy. A dynamo, for example, is a simple generator consisting of a wire-wound coil (◊armature) which is rotated between the pole-pieces of a permanent magnet. The movement (of the wire in the magnetic field) induces a current in the coil, which can be fed by means of a commutator as a continuous direct current into an external circuit. Slip rings instead of a commutator produce an alternating current, when the generator is called an alternator. See also ◊electric motor, ◊electromagnetic induction.

gene-splicing technique invented in 1973 by Stanley Cohen and Herbert Boyer (Stanford University/University of California) for inserting a foreign gene into bacteria in order to generate commercial biological products, for example, synthetic insulin, hepatitis-B vaccine, and interferon. It was patented in the USA in 1984.

genet small nocturnal meat-eating mammal, genus *Genetta*, related to the mongooses and civets. Most species live in Africa, but *Genetta genetta* is also found in Europe and the Middle East. It is about 50 cm/1.6 ft long plus a 45 cm/1.5 ft tail, greyish yellow in colour with rows of black spots, and climbs well, preying on birds as well as small animals on the ground.

Genet /ʒɔˈneɪ/ Jean 1910–1986. French dramatist, novelist, and poet, an exponent of the Theatre of ◊Cruelty. His turbulent life and early years spent in prison are reflected in his drama. His plays are characterized by a sense of ritual, role-play and illusion in which his characters come to act out their bizarre and violent fantasies in actuality as in *Les Bonnes/The Maids* 1947, and *Le Balcon/The Balcony* 1957. Later plays include *Les Nègres/The Blacks* 1959, and *Les Paravents/The Screens* 1961 dealing with the Algerian situation.

gene therapy a proposed medical technique for curing or alleviating inherited diseases or defects. Although not yet a practical possibility, some of the basic techniques are available as a result of intensive research in ◊genetic engineering. It may be useful for diseases such as ◊haemoglobin irregularities, where only a relatively small group of cells – those in the bone marrow, which produce the red blood cells – need to be treated. The normal gene would be ◊cloned in bacterial cells to obtain many copies. Bone marrow cells taken from the patient would then be exposed to these cloned normal genes. Cells that had taken up the normal gene could be identified and a batch of them returned to the patient's bone marrow. The existing bone marrow cells would be destroyed beforehand, to give the introduced cells a chance to multiply. The possibility of gene therapy for reproductive cells, to prevent genetic defects being passed on to the next generation, is more remote.

genetic code the way in which instructions for building ◊proteins, the basic structural molecules of living matter, are 'written' in the genetic material ◊DNA. This relationship between the sequence of ◊bases, the sub-units in a DNA molecule, and the sequence of ◊amino acids, the sub-units of a protein molecule, is the basis of heredity. The code employs ◊codons of three bases each; it is the same in almost all organisms, except for a few minor differences recently discovered in some bacteria.

genetic diseases disorders caused at least partly by defective genes or chromosomes, of which there are some 3,000, including arthritis, autism, cleft palate, cystic fibrosis, Down's syndrome, haemophilia, Huntington's chorea, some forms of anaemia, spina bifida, and ◊Tay-Sachs disease.

genetic engineering the natural course of heredity is interfered with by any ◊breeding programme, but true genetic engineering is direct manipulation of genetic material by biochemical techniques. This is often achieved by introduction of new ◊DNA, ordinarily by means of an infecting ◊virus. This transplantation of genes is used to increase our knowledge of cell function and reproduction, but it can also achieve practical ends, for example, plants grown for food could be given the ability to fix nitrogen, found in some bacteria, and so reduce the need for expensive fertilizers, or simple bacteria may be enabled to produce rare drugs. However, there is a risk that when transplanting genes between different types of bacteria (*Escherichia coli*, which lives in the human intestine, is often used) new and harmful bacteria might be produced, which, on escape from the laboratory, might start an uncontrollable epidemic. One solution, apart from strict safety precautions, is to render the bacteria genetically unable to exist outside the laboratory.

genetic fingerprinting a technique used in genetic studies to investigate how ◊genes are mixed and matched during cell division. It can accurately distinguish humans from one another just like skin fingerprinting, with the exception of identical twins. It involves isolating the genetic material of cells, ◊DNA, then comparing and contrasting the sequences of component chemicals between individuals. The DNA pattern can be ascertained from a sample of skin, hair, or semen. Although differences are minimal – only 0.1 per cent between unrelated people – certain regions for the DNA are unique. Genetic fingerprinting was discovered by Dr Alec Jeffries, and was first allowed as a means of legal identification at a court in Britain in 1987. It may soon be used for paternity testing, in forensic medicine, and in inbreeding studies.

genetics the study of inheritance and of ◊genes, which are the units of inheritance. The founder of genetics was Gregor ◊Mendel. From his experiments with plants such as peas he realized that inheritance takes place by means of discrete 'particles', which later came to be called genes. Before Mendel, it had been assumed that the characteristics of the two parents were blended during inheritance, but Mendel showed that the genes remained intact although their combinations change. In the century since Mendel genetics has advanced greatly, first by means of breeding experiments and light-microscope observations (classical genetics), later by means of biochemical and electron-microscope studies (molecular genetics). An important advance was the elucidation of the structure of ◊DNA by Watson and Crick, and the subsequent cracking of the ◊genetic code. These discoveries opened up the possibility of deliberately manipulating genes, or ◊genetic engineering.

Geneva /dʒɪˈniːvə/ Swiss city, capital of Geneva canton, on the shore of Lake Geneva; population (1983) 370,000. It is a natural route focus, and is a cultural and commercial centre. Industries include the manufacture of watches, scientific and optical instruments, foodstuffs, jewellery, and musical boxes.

history the site on which Geneva now stands was the chief settlement of the Allobroges, a central European tribe who were annexed to Rome in 121 BC; Caesar built an entrenched camp here. In the Middle Ages Geneva was controlled by the prince-bishops of Geneva and the rulers of Savoy. Under ◊Calvin it became a centre of the Reformation 1536–64; the Academy, which he founded in 1559, became a university in 1892. Geneva was annexed by France in 1798; it was freed in 1814 and entered the Swiss Confederation in 1815. In 1864 the International ◊Red Cross Society was established at Geneva. It was the headquarters of the ◊League of Nations, whose properties at Geneva passed in 1946 into the possession of the ◊United Nations.

Geneva, Lake /dʒɪˈniːvə/ Largest of the central European lakes (French *Lac Léman*),

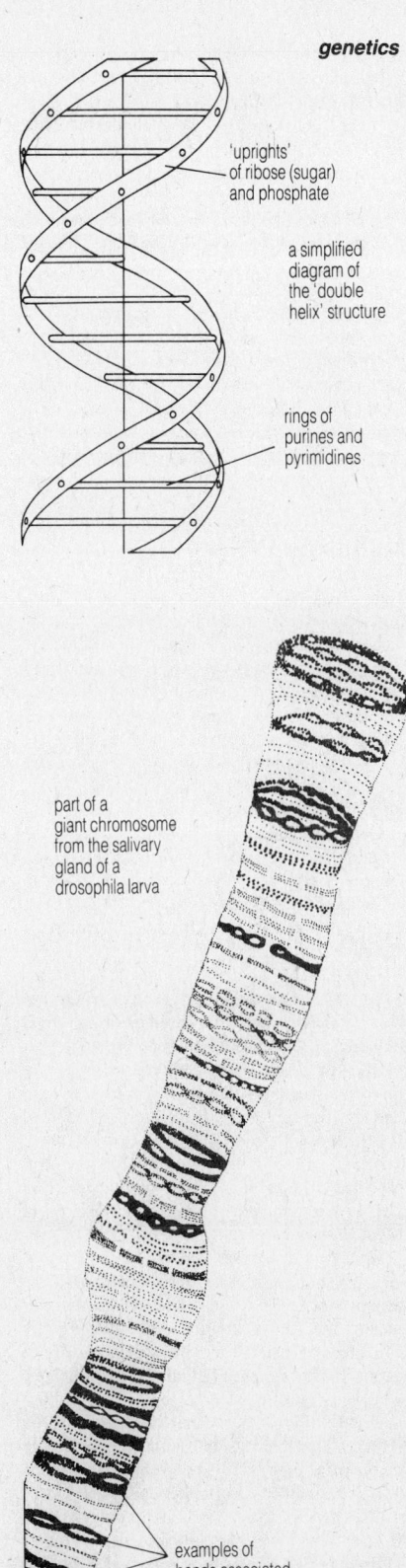

genetics

'uprights'
of ribose (sugar)
and phosphate

a simplified
diagram of
the 'double
helix' structure

rings of
purines and
pyrimidines

part of a
giant chromosome
from the salivary
gland of a
drosophila larva

examples of
bands associated
with genes

between Switzerland and France; area 580 sq km/225 sq mi.

Geneva Convention an international agreement, regulating the treatment of those wounded in war, reached at a conference held in 1864 and later extended to cover the treatment of the sick and prisoners and the protection of civilians in war-time. The rules were revised at conventions held in 1906, 1929, and 1949.

Geneva Protocol international agreement made in 1925, designed to prohibit the use of poisonous gases, chemical weapons, and bacteriological methods of warfare. It came into force in 1928 but was only ratified by the US in 1974.

Genf /genf/ German form of ◊Geneva, a city in Switzerland.

Genghis Khan /ˈdʒeŋgɪs/ 1162–1227. Mongol conqueror. Temujin, as he was originally called, was the son of a local chieftain. After a long struggle he established his supremacy over all the Mongol tribes by 1206, when he assumed the title of Chingis or 'perfect warrior'. He began the conquest of North China in 1213, overran the empire of the shah of Khiva 1219–25, and invaded North India, while his lieutenants advanced as far as the Crimea. When he died his empire ranged from the Yellow Sea to the Black Sea. See ◊Golden Horde and ◊Karakoram.

genitalia the reproductive organs of sexually reproducing animals, particularily the external/visible organs of mammals: in males, the ◊penis and the scrotum which contains the ◊testes, and in females, the clitoris and vulva.

Gennesaret, Lake of /gɪˈnezərɪt/ Another name for the Sea of ◊Galilee in N Israel.

Genoa /ˈdʒenəʊə/ city (Italian *Genova*) in NW Italy, capital of Liguria; population (1981) 763,000. Giuseppe ◊Mazzini was born here. It is Italy's largest port; industries include oil-refining, chemicals, engineering, and textiles.

genome the full complement of ◊genes carried by a single set of ◊chromosomes for a given species.

genotype the particular set of ◊alleles (variants of ◊genes) possessed by a given organism. The term is usually used in conjunction with ◊phenotype, which is the product of the genotype and all environmental effects. See also ◊environment-heredity controversy.

Genova /ˈdʒenəvɑː/ Italian form of ◊Genoa, a city in Italy.

genre French word meaning 'kind' or 'type', and originally used in conjunction with an adjective to describe certain 'kinds' of painting, for example *genre du paysage* (landscapes) or *genre historique* (historical paintings). But *genre* is now usually applied specifically to paintings in which scenes of everyday life are depicted. The most famous genre pictures were painted by Flemish artists such as Pieter ◊Brueghel and Adriaen ◊Brouwer, and by Dutch artists such as ◊Teniers and Frans ◊Hals. Of the English genre painters the best-known include ◊Hogarth, William ◊Mulready, and Sir David ◊Wilkie. The term is used in other arts, such as literature, for a category (for example, science fiction).

Genscher /ˈgenʃə/ Hans-Dietrich 1927– . West German liberal politician, chair of the Free Democratic Party (FDP) 1974–85, foreign minister from 1974. Born in Halle, Genscher settled in West Germany in 1952. He served as interior minister 1969–74 and then as foreign minister, committed to ◊Ostpolitik and European cooperation. As FDP leader, Genscher masterminded the party's switch of allegiance from the Social Democratic Party to the Christian Democratic Union which resulted in the downfall of the ◊Schmidt government in 1982.

Gentileschi /ˌdʒentɪˈleski/ Artemisia 1593–1652. Italian painter, born in Rome. She trained under her father Orazio ◊Gentileschi, but her own work is more in the intense, dramatic style of ◊Caravaggio, with a macabre choice of subject such as *Judith decapitating Holofernes* (Naples).

Gentileschi /ˌdʒentɪˈleski/ Orazio 1563–1637. Italian painter, born in Pisa. His early work was done in Rome, which he left in 1613. From 1626 until his death he lived in London, painting for King Charles I. Although greatly influenced, like most of his contemporaries, by ◊Caravaggio's dramatic treatment of light and shade, Gentileschi's work remains simple and direct in composition. His masterpiece is perhaps *The Annunciation* 1623 (Turin).

Gentili /dʒenˈtiːli/ Alberico 1552–1608. Italian jurist. He practised law in Italy, but having adopted Protestantism was compelled to flee to England, where he lectured on Roman Law in Oxford. His *De Jure Belli libri tres/On The Law Of War, Book Three* 1598 constitutes the foundation of international law.

Gentlemen-at-arms Honourable Corps of. Established in 1509, the Corps is, next to the Yeomen of the Guard, the oldest in the British Army; it was reconstituted in 1862. It consists of army officers of distinction under a captain, a peer, whose appointment is political. Theoretically the main bodyguard of the Sovereign, its functions are ceremonial.

genus a set of ◊species that share a large number of characteristics in common. Thus, all dog-like species (including dogs, wolves, and jackals) belong to the genus *Canis* (Latin 'dog'). Species of the same genus are thought to be descended from a common ancestor species. Related genera are grouped into ◊families.

geochemistry the science of chemistry as it applies to geology. It deals with the relative and absolute abundances of the chemical ◊elements and ◊isotopes in the earth, and also with chemical changes that take place there.

geodesy methods of surveying the Earth for making maps and correlating geological, gravitational, and magnetic measurements. Geodesic surveys, formerly carried out by means of various measuring techniques on the land's surfaces, are now commonly made using radio signals and laser beams from orbiting satellites.

geography the science of the Earth's surface; its topography, climate, and physical conditions, especially as these factors affect civilization and society. It is usually divided into *physical* *geography*, dealing with landforms and climates, *biogeography*, dealing with the conditions that affect the distribution of animals and plants, and *human geography*, dealing with the distribution and activities of peoples on the Earth.

geology the science of the ◊Earth, its origin, composition, structure, and history. It is divided into several branches: ◊mineralogy deals with the minerals of the Earth: ◊petrology deals with rocks; ◊stratigraphy deals with the deposition of successive beds of sedimentary rocks; ◊palaeontology deals with fossils; and ◊tectonics deals with the deformation and movement of the Earth's crust. Nowadays geology is regarded as part of earth science, a more widely embracing subject that brings in meteorology, oceanography, geophysics, and geochemistry.

Geometric series can be generalized as $a + ar + ar^2 + ar^3 + ar^4 + ... ar^{n-1}$, where a is the first term and r is the common ratio and ar^{n-1} is the nth term. The sum S of n terms is given by $S_n = a(r^n - 1)/(r - 1)$. For the above example, $S_n = 3(4^5 - 1)/(4 - 1) = 1023$.

In nature many single-celled organisms reproduce by splitting in two such that one cell gives rise to 2 then 4 then 8 cells and so on, forming a geometric series, 1, 2, 4, 8, 16, 32 in which the common ratio is 2.

geometry branch of mathematics concerned with the properties of space, usually in terms of plane (two-dimensional) and solid (three-dimensional) figures. It probably originated in Egypt, in land measurements necessitated by the periodic inundations of the river Nile, and was

which embraces roughly the plane and solid geometry dealt with in Euclid's *Elements*, and *analytical* or ◊*coordinate geometry*, in which problems are solved using algebraic methods. From the 19th century various non-Euclidean geometries were devised by Gauss and Rieman in Germany, Lobachevsky in Russia, and others. These proved significant in the development of the theory of relativity and in the formulation of atomic theory.

geophysics branch of geology using physics to study Earth's surface, interior, and atmosphere.

George /geɪˈɔːgə/ Stefan 1868–1933. German poet. His early poetry was influenced by the French ◊Symbolists but his conception of himself as regenerating the German spirit first appears in *Des Teppich des Lebens/The Tapestry of Life* 1899 and later in *Der Siebente Ring/The Seventh Ring* 1907 which deifies the young man whom he sees as a substitute for God. *Das Neue Reich/The New Empire* 1928 shows his realization that World War I had not had the right purifying effect. He rejected Nazi overtures and emigrated in 1933 to Switzerland.

George /dʒɔːdʒ/ six kings of Great Britain:

George I /dʒɔːdʒ/ 1660–1727. King of Great Britain from 1714. The son of the elector of ◊Hanover, Ernest Augustus, and his wife ◊Sophia, and a great-grandson of James I. He succeeded to the electorate in 1698 and spent most of his reign in Hanover. He married Sophia Dorothea of Zell (1666–1726) in 1682.

George II /dʒɔːdʒ/ 1683–1760. King of Great Britain from 1727, when he succeeded his father, George I. His victory at Dettingen in 1743, in the War of the Austrian Succession, was the last battle commanded by a British king. He married Caroline of Anspach 1705.

George III /dʒɔːdʒ/ 1738–1820. King from 1760, when he succeeded his grandfather George II. Although bent on strengthening royal influence, his alleged domination of parliament by corrupt 'King's friends' is a discredited Whig invention. He supported his ministers in a hard line towards the American colonies, and opposed Catholic emancipation and other reforms. Possibly suffering from ◊porphyria, he had repeated attacks of insanity, permanent from 1811. He married Princess Charlotte of Mecklenburg-Strelitz.

George IV /dʒɔːdʒ/ 1762–1830. King of Great Britain from 1820, when he succeeded his father George III, for whom he had been regent during the king's insanity 1811–20. Strictly educated, he reacted by entering into a life of debauchery, and in 1785 married a Catholic widow, Mrs ◊Fitzherbert, but in 1795 also married Princess ◊Caroline of Brunswick, in return for payment of his debts. Attempting to divorce Caroline after his accession in 1820, he had to desist for fear of revolution.

George V /dʒɔːdʒ/ 1865–1936. King of Great Britain from 1910, when he succeeded his father ◊Edward VII. He was the second son, and became heir only in 1892 on the death of his elder brother ◊Albert Victor, Duke of Clarence (1864–92). He married in 1893 Princess May of Teck (Queen ◊Mary), formerly engaged to his

THE GEOLOGICAL TIME CHART

Millions of Years ago	Begins Period		Era	Eon
1.8	Quaternary			
5	Plicocene			
22.5	Miocene		Cenezoic	
38	Oligocene	Tertiary		
54	Eocene			
65	Palaeocene			
141	Cretaceous			Phanerozoic
195	Jurassic		Mesozoic	
230	Triassic			
280	Permian			
345	Carboniferous			
395	Devonian		Palaeozoic	
435	Silurian			
500	Ordovician			
570	Cambrian			
2500	Pre-Cambrian			Proterozoic
				Archaean

GEOLOGY

'Hard rock' geology	petrology – igneous and metamorphic rocks
	mineralogy – minerals
	geochemistry – matter
	geophysics – energy
'Soft rock' geology	petrology – sedimentary rocks
	palaeontology – fossils
	stratigraphy – dating and sequence of beds (strata)
	sedimentology – deposition of sediments
Structural geology	the structures of rock
Geomorphology	landscapes, their formation and destruction

geometric series a sequence of numbers (progression) in which each term is a constant multiple (called the common ratio) of the one preceding it. For example, 3, 12, 48, 192, 768 is a geometric series with a common ratio 4.

soon extended into surveying and navigation. Early geometers were Thales, Pythagoras and Euclid. Analytical methods were introduced and developed by Descartes in the 17th century. The subject is usually divided into *pure geometry*,

George IV Prince Regent of Great Britain from 1811, when his father George III was deemed unfit to rule, George IV acceded to the throne in 1820. As regent he built the Royal Pavilion, Brighton.

brother. During World War I he made several visits to the front.

George VI /dʒɔːdʒ/ 1895–1952. King of Great Britain from 1936, when he succeeded after the abdication of his brother ◊Edward VIII. Created duke of York in 1920, he married in 1923 Lady Elizabeth Bowes-Lyon (1900–   ), and their children are Elizabeth II and Princess Margaret. During World War II he visited the Normandy and Italian battlefields.

George II /dʒɔːdʒ/ 1890–1947. King of Greece from the expulsion of his father Constantine in 1922, and himself overthrown in 1923. Restored by the military in 1935, he set up a dictatorship under ◊Metaxas, and went into exile during the German occupation 1941–46.

George Cross/Medal the George Cross is the supreme civilian award in Britain for acts of the greatest courage in circumstances of extreme danger, insituted in 1940. It consists of a silver cross with a medallion in the centre bearing a design of St George and the Dragon, and is worn on the left breast before all other medals except the Victory Cross. The George Cross was conferred on the island of Malta in 1942. The *George Medal*, also instituted in 1940, is a civilian award for acts of great courage. The medal is silver and circular, bearing on one side a crowned effigy of the sovereign, and on the reverse St George and the Dragon.

George, St /dʒɔːdʒ/ Patron saint of England. He is said to have been martyred at Lydda in Palestine in 303, probably under ◊Diocletian, but

George VI Called unexpectedly to the throne after the abdication of his brother, George VI won the affection of his people by his devotion to duty.

the other elements of his legend are of doubtful historicity. The story of St George rescuing a girl by slaying a dragon, evidently derived from the ◊Perseus legend, first appears in the 6th century. The cult of St George was introduced into Western Europe by the Crusaders, and his feast day is 23 Apr.

Georgetown /'dʒɔːdʒtaʊn/ capital and port of Guyana; population (1980) 183,000. Founded in 1781 by the British, it was held 1784–1812 by the Dutch who renamed it Stabroek, and was ceded to Britain in 1814.

Georgetown, Declaration of call in 1972, at a conference of non-aligned countries in Guyana, for a multipolar system to replace the two world power blocks and for the Mediterranean and Indian Ocean to be neutral.

George Town /'dʒɔːdʒtaʊn/ (also called Penang) chief port of the Federation of Malaysia, and capital of Penang, on the Island of Penang; population (1980) 250,600.

Georgia /'dʒɔːdʒɪə/ state of the southern USA; Empire State of the South/Peach State
area 152,500 sq km/58,880 sq mi
capital Atlanta
towns Columbus, Savannah
features Okefenokee National Wildlife Refuge (1,700 sq km/60 sq mi)
products poultry, livestock; tobacco, maize, peanuts, cotton; china clay, crushed granite; textiles, carpets, aircraft
population (1980) 5,464,265
famous people James Bowie, Erskine Caldwell, Jimmy Carter, Martin Luther King, Margaret Mitchell

history named after George II of England, Georgia was founded in 1733 and was one of the original ◊Thirteen States of the USA.

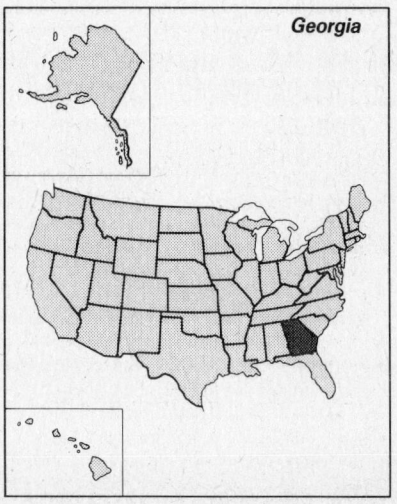

Georgia

Georgia /'dʒɔːdʒɪə/ constituent republic of the southwestern USSR, from 1936
area 69,700 sq km/26,900 sq mi
capital Tbilisi
features holiday resorts and spas on the Black Sea; good climate
products subtropical, such as tea, citrus, orchard fruits, tung oil, tobacco, vines, silk
population (1982) 5,000,000
language Georgian
religion Georgian Church, independent of the Russian Orthodox Church since 1917
famous people Stalin
recent history an independent republic 1918–21, it was invaded by the USSR in 1921, and was linked with Armenia and Azerbaijan as the Transcaucasian Republic within the southwestern USSR in 1922–36.

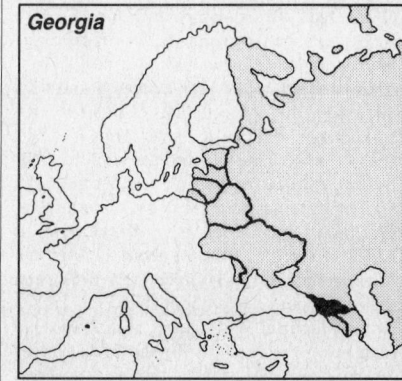

Georgia

geostationary orbit the circular path 35,900 km/22,300 mi above the Earth's equator on which a ◊satellite takes 24 hours to complete an orbit, thus appearing to hang stationary over one place on the Earth's surface. It is particularly used for communications satellites.

geothermal energy either subterranean hot water pumped to the surface and converted to steam or run through a heat exchanger, or dry steam, directed through turbines to produce electricity.

geranium or **crane's bill** plant of the family Geraniaceae. Many of the geraniums cultivated in Britain are not members of the *Geranium* genus but of *Pelargonium*.

gerbil rodent of the family Cricetidae of a group which has elongated back legs and good hopping or jumping ability. They range from rat to mouse size and have haired tails. Many of the 13 genera live in dry, sandy or sparsely vegetated areas of Africa and Asia. The *Mongolian jird* or *gerbil Meriones unguiculatus* has become a popular pet in recent years.

gerenuk East African antelope *Litocranius walleri* about 1 m/3 ft at the shoulder, but with a greatly elongated neck. It browses on leaves picked with lips and tongue, often balancing on its hind legs to do so. Sandy brown in colour, it is well camouflaged in its habitat of dry scrub.

Géricault /ˌʒerɪˈkəʊ/ (Jean Louis André) Théodore 1791–1824. French artist. A keen horseman himself (he was killed in a riding accident), he is noted for pictures including horses, for example *The Derby at Epsom*. His *Raft of the Medusa* 1816, showing an incident in which shipwrecked seamen had deliberately been set adrift, had political repercussions.

germ a colloquial term for a micro-organism that causes disease, such as certain ◊bacteria and ◊viruses. Once it also used to mean something that is capable of developing into a complete organism (such as a fertilized egg, or the ◊embryo of a seed), and survives still in terms such as ◊germ layer.

Germain /ʒeəˈmæŋ/ Sophie 1776–1831. French mathematician, born in Paris. Although not allowed to study at the newly opened École Polytechnique, she corresponded with ◊Lagrange and ◊Gauss. She is remembered for work she carried out in studying ◊Fermat's last theorem.

German /ˈdʒɜːmən/ Edward 1862–1936. Name used by British composer German Edward Jones. He is best remembered for his operettas *Merrie England* 1902 and *Tom Jones* 1907.

German art in the 13th century German art first emerged in the sculptures of Bamberg and Naumberg cathedrals, the wood carvings of Veit ◊Stoss, sometimes claimed as Polish (Wit Swosz), and the bronzes of Peter Vischer. The earliest paintings resembled the miniatures of illuminated manuscripts but with the series of panels of the life of Christ about 1350 by the Master of Hohenfurth (Czech *Vissy Brod*), and the altar about 1380 for the monastery of Trebon by the Master of Wittingau (Czech *Trebon*), a high level was reached. To the 15th century belong Stefan ◊Lochner, the realists Hans Multscher (c. 1400–57) and Konrad Witz (c. 1400–46), and the painter-sculptor Michael Pacher (c. 1435–98). The incarnation of the Renaissance in Germany was Albrecht ◊Dürer: other 16th century masters include Hans Baldung Grien (c. 1484–1545), Lucas ◊Cranach, Albrecht ◊Altdorfer, ◊Grünewald,

and Hans ◊Holbein. The only notable name in the 17th century is that of Adam Elsheimer (1578–1610). Among the Romantics are the almost 'expressionist' portrait painter Philipp Otto Runge (1777–1810) and the landscapist Caspar David ◊Friedrich. Max Liebermann (1847–1935) was the first to feel the influence of such foreign developments as ◊Impressionism. At the turn of the century came Jugendstil (corresponding to French Art Nouveau), and then parallel with ◊Fauvism the movement known as Die ◊Brücke (The Bridge) which include Emil ◊Nolde. Also important were the ◊Blaue Reiter (Blue Rider) group – named for a painting by ◊Kandinsky – and in architecture and the arts generally the ◊Bauhaus was influential abroad. Later artists include Max ◊Ernst and Käthe ◊Kollwitz.

Germanic languages a branch of the Indo-European language family, divided into *East Germanic* (Gothic, now extinct), *North Germanic* (Danish, Faroese, Icelandic, Norwegian and Swedish), and *West Germanic* (Afrikaans, Dutch, English, Flemish, Frisian, German and Yiddish). The Germanic languages differ from the other Indo-European languages most prominently in the consonant shift known as Grimm's Law. In it, the sounds *p, t, k* became either (as in English) *f, th, h* or as in Old High German *f, d, h*. Thus, the typical Indo-European of the Latin *pater* is *father* and *Fater* in Old High German. In addition, the Indo-European *b, d, g* moved to become *p, t, k*, or in Old High German *f, ts, kh*; compare Latin *duo*, English *two*, and German *zwei* ('tsvai').

Germanicus Caesar /dʒɜːˈmænɪkəs ˈsiːzə/ 15 BC–19 AD. Roman general. Adopted son of ◊Tiberius, he married Augustus' granddaughter Agrippina. Though he refused the suggestion of his troops that he claim the throne on the death of ◊Augustus, his military successes in Germany made Tiberius jealous. Sent to the east, he died near Antioch, possibly murdered at the instigation of Tiberius. He was the father of ◊Caligula, and of Agrippina, mother of ◊Nero.

germanium a metallic element, symbol Ge; atomic number 32; atomic weight 72.6. It was discovered in 1886. A grey-white, brittle, crystalline metal, it is in the silicon group, and its chemical and physical properties lie between those of silicon and tin. Germanium is a semiconductor material and is widely used in the manufacture of transistors and integrated circuits. The oxide is transparent to infra-red radiation, and is used in defence applications.

German language a member of the Germanic group of the Indo-European language family, the national language of West Germany, East Germany and Austria, and an official language of Switzerland. There are many spoken varieties of German, the best known distinction being between High German (*Hochdeutsch*) and Low German (*Plattdeutsch*). 'High' and 'low' refer to geography rather than social status, Hochdeutsch originating in the central and southern highlands of Germany, Austria and Switzerland, Plattdeutsch being used in the lowlands of N Germany. However, modern standard and literary German is based on High

German, in particular on the Middle German dialect used by Martin Luther for his translation of the Bible in the 16th century. Low German is closer to English in its sound system, the verb 'to make' being *machen* in High German but *maken* in Low German. Such English words as *angst, blitz, frankfurter, hamburger, poltergeist, sauerkraut* and *schadenfreude* are borrowings from High German.

German literature the fragmentary alliterative poem the *Hildebrandslied* (c. 800), the most substantial relic of the *Old High German* period, bears no comparison with the Old English literature of the same era. In the *Middle High German* period there was a great flowering in the vernacular which had been forced into subservience to Latin since the early attempts at encouragement by Charlemagne. The court epics of Hartmann von Aue, Gottfried von Strassburg, and Wolfram von Eschenbach in the early 13th century were modelled on the French in style and material, but the folk-epic, the *Nibelungenlied*, revived the spirit of the old heroic Germanic sagas. Adopted – in the more limited meaning – from France and Provence, the *Minnesang* reached its height in the lyric poetry of Walther von der Vogelweide.

Modern German literature begins in the 16th century with the standard of language set by Luther's Bible. In this century also came the climax of popular drama in the *Fastnachtsspiel* as handled by Hans Sachs. In the later 16th and early 17th centuries French influence was renewed and English influence, notably by troupes of players, was introduced: Martin Opitz's *Buch von der deutschen Poeterey* 1624, in which he advocates the imitation of foreign models, epitomizes the German Renaissance which was followed by the Thirty Years' War vividly described in Grimmelshausen's *Simplicissimus*.

In the 18th century French Classicism predominated, extolled by Gottsched but opposed by Bodmer and Breitinger, whose writings prompted the Germanic *Messias* of Klopstock. Both Lessing and Herder were admirers of Shakespeare, and Herder's enthusiasm inaugurated the *Sturm und Drang* phase which emphasized individual inspiration, and his collection of folk songs was symptomatic of the feeling which inspired Bürger's modern ballad *Lenore*. Greatest representatives of the Classical period at the end of the century were Goethe and Schiller, but their ideals were combatted by the new Romantic school which based its theories on the work of the brothers Schlegel, and Tieck, and which included Novalis, Arnim, Brentano, Eichendorff, Chamisso, Uhland, and Hoffmann.

With Kleist and Grillparzer in the early 19th century stress on the poetic in drama ends, and with Hebbel the psychological aspect becomes the more important. Notable about 1830 was the 'Young German' movement led by Heine, Gutzkow, and Laube, which the authorities tried to suppress. Other writers of the century include the masters of the *Novelle*, Gottfried Keller and Theodor Storm, also both fine poets; and Wilhelm Raabe and Theodor Fontane, novelists of realism. Naturalistic drama found its chief exponents in Hauptmann and Sudermann. Influential in literature, as in politics and economics, were Marx and Nietzsche.

Outstanding in the early years of the 20th century were the lyric poets Richard Dehmel, Stefan George, and Rainer Maria Rilke; von Hofmannsthal, both poet and dramatist, and the novelists Thomas and Heinrich Mann, Ludwig Renn, E M Remarque, and Hermann Hesse. Just before World War I Expressionism emerged in the poetry of Georg Trakl, dominated the novels of Franz Kafka and the plays of Ernst Toller, Franz Werfel, Georg Kaiser and Karl Sternheim, and was later to influence Bertolt Brecht. Under National Socialism many major writers left the country, others were silenced or ignored: to the period after World War II belong the Swiss dramatists Max Frisch and Friedrich Dürrenmatt, the novelists Heinrich Böll and Heimito von Doderer, and the poets Paul Celan and Günter Grass.

german measles (**rubella**) virus disease, usually of children, having an incubation period of 10–15 days, marked by a sore throat, pinkish rash, and slight fever. If contracted in the first three months of pregnancy, it may affect a woman's unborn child, and immunization between the ages of 10 and 13 is advised.

German Ocean German name for the ◊North Sea.

German silver or **nickel silver** a silvery alloy of nickel, copper and zinc widely used for cheap jewellery and the base metal for silver plating. The letters EPNS on silverware stand for *electroplated nickel silver*.

Germany /ˈdʒɜːmənɪ/ single state of central Europe, which was divided after ◊World War II into East and West Germany, and land to the east of the Oder and western Neisse rivers, which was shared between Russia and Poland. Restoration of these 'lost territories' (◊Silesia, ◊Pomerania, the ◊Sudetenland and East ◊Prussia), a third of the former area, remains a political issue, as does the reunion of the two Germanies. See also ◊Germany, history

Germany, East /ˈdʒɜːmənɪ/ country in E Europe, bounded to the north by the Baltic Sea, east by Poland, south by Czechoslovakia, and southwest and west by West Germany.

government East Germany is a centralized unitary state, the five *Länder* (Brandenburg, Mecklenburg, Saxony, Saxony-Anhalt and Thuringia) which existed 1945–52 having been divided into 14 districts (*Bezirke*). Under the 1968 constitution the supreme legislative and executive body in the German Democratic Republic is the people's chamber *Volkskammer*, whose 500 members (including 66 from East Berlin) are elected every five years by universal suffrage. The *Volkskammer* debates and passes laws and chooses the members and chair of the 25-member council of state *Staatsrat*.

Day-to-day government executive administration is conducted by the council of ministers *Ministerrat*, headed and selected by a prime minister drawn from the largest single party within the *Volkskammer*. East Germany's dominating force is the Communist Party

(Socialist Unity Party of Germany). It provides the major grouping within the *Volkskammer* and is supported by four allied parties – the Democratic Farmers' Party, the Christian Democratic Union, the Liberal Democratic Party and the National Democratic Party – to form the National Front of the German Democratic Republic.

history for history before 1949, see ◊Germany, history. Formerly the Russian zone of occupation, the German Democratic Republic was established in 1949, becoming a sovereign state in 1954. It was recognized at first only by the Communist powers. In 1973, however, following the adoption by the Federal Republic of the new policy of ◊Ostpolitik, a Basic Treaty governing relations between East and West Germany was ratified by both states. The treaty fell short of full recognition by the Federal Republic, permanent missions rather than ambassadors being stationed in the respective nations. It led, however, to East Germany's admission to the ◊UN and to its full recognition by other Western states.

The years immediately after 1949 saw the rapid establishment of a Communist regime on the Soviet model, involving the creation of a one-party political system, the nationalization of industry and the formation of agricultural collectives. Opposition to such Sovietization led, during food shortages, to demonstrations and a general strike in 1953, which was suppressed by Russian troops.

Eight years later, in 1961, the ◊Berlin Wall was erected to stem the growing movement of

refugees to the Federal Republic. Economic reforms boosted the East German growth rate in the 1960s, significantly improving living conditions. During the following decade, with the replacement of the Stalinist Socialist Unity Party leader Walther ◊Ulbricht by the pragmatic Erich ◊Honecker, a more moderate political approach was adopted at home, while economic and diplomatic relations with the West were extended.

The German Democratic Republic is a loyal and vital member of ◊Comecon and the ◊Warsaw Pact (Soviet medium range nuclear missiles being stationed on its soil). Foreign relations remain circumscribed, however, by opinion in Moscow: the planned inaugural official visit of Erich Honecker to West Germany being postponed 1983–84 and 1985–86 following Soviet pressure. It eventually took place in Sept 1987.

Germany, history the west Germanic tribes, originating in Scandinavia, early overran the region between the Rhine, Elbe, and Danube, where they were confined by the Roman power. In the 4th–5th centuries the Franks occupied Belgium and France, and there founded a kingdom which by Charlemagne's day had extended its authority over Germany. Under the Frankish kings the Germans accepted Christianity. After Charlemagne's death Germany was separated from France under its own kings while the local officials or dukes became virtually independent until the central power was restored by the Saxon dynasty (919–1002). Otto I, who in 962 revived the title

Germany, East
GERMAN DEMOCRATIC REPUBLIC (*Deutsche Demokratische Republik*)

AREA 108,180 sq km/41,768 sq mi
CAPITAL East Berlin
TOWNS Leipzig, Dresden, Karl-Marx-Stadt, Magdeburg; chief port Rostock
PHYSICAL N flat, mountains in S; rivers Elbe, Oder, and Neisse; many lakes, including Müritz
FEATURES Harz mountains, Erzgebirge, Fichtelgebirge, Thüringer Wald
HEAD OF STATE Erich Honecker from 1976
HEAD OF GOVERNMENT Willi Stoph from 1976
GOVERNMENT communist
EXPORTS lignite; rare minerals (uranium, cobalt, and others); coal, iron, and steel; fertilizers; plastics
CURRENCY GDR Mark, or Ostmark (2.99 = £1 Sept 1987, not free rate)
POPULATION 16,686,000 (1985); annual growth rate -0.1%
LANGUAGE German
RELIGION Protestant 80%, Catholic 11%
LITERACY 99% (1985)
GNP $86 bn (1983); $8,000 per head of population
CHRONOLOGY
1949 The German Democratic Republic established as an independent state.

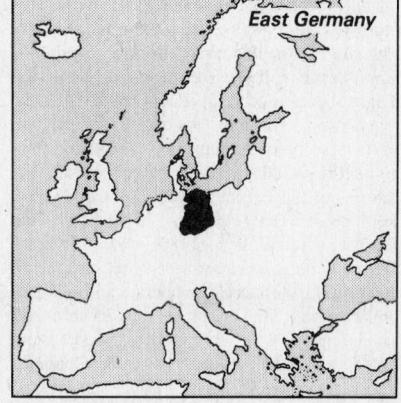

East Germany

1953 Riots in East Berlin suppressed by Soviet troops.
1961 The Berlin Wall erected to stem flow of refugees.
1964 Treaty of Friendship annd Mutual Assistance signed with USSR.
1971 Erich Honecker elected Socialist Unity Party (SED) leader.
1973 Basic Treaty ratified, normalizing relations with Federal Republic.
1975 Friendship Treaty with USSR renewed for 25 years.

GERMANY: REGIONS

Democratic Republic of (East) Germany Bezirke	Capital Berlin (East)	Area in sq km	Federal Republic of (West) Germany Länder	Capital Bonn	Area in sq km
Berlin (East)		400	Baden-Württemberg	Stuttgart	35,751
Dresden	Dresden	6,740	Bavaria	Munich	70,552
Erfurt	Erfurt	7,350	Bremen	Bremen	404
Frankfurt-on-Oder	Frankfurt	7,185	Hamburg	Hamburg	755
Gera	Gera	4,005	Hesse	Wiesbaden	21,115
Halle	Halle	8,770	Lower Saxony	Hanover	47,447
Karl-Marx-Stadt	Karl-Marx-Stadt	6,010	North-Rhine-Westphalia	Düsseldorf	34,061
Cottbus	Cottbus	8,260	Rhineland-Palatinate	Mainz	19,848
Leipzig	Leipzig	4,970	Saarland	Saarbrücken	2,571
Magdeburg	Magdeburg	11,525	Schleswig-Holstein	Kiel	15,721
Neubrandenburg	Neubrandenburg	10,790	West Berlin	West Berlin	480
Potsdam	Potsdam	12,570			
Rostock	Rostock	7,075			
Schwerin	Schwerin	8,670			
Suhl	Suhl	3,860			
		108,180			248,206

of emperor, began the colonization of the Slav lands east of the Elbe. This period of progress was ended by the feud between emperors and popes (1075–1250), which enabled the princes to recover their independence. A temporary revival of imperial power took place under Maximilian I (1493–1519), but he and his successor, Charles V (1519–56), were mainly concerned with dynastic interests outside Germany which brought them into conflict with France. The reformation increased Germany's disunity, and led to the Thirty Years' War (1618–48). The war not only reduced the Empire to a mere name, but destroyed Germany's economic and cultural life. The rise of Brandenburg-Prussia as a military power began in the 17th century, and reached its height under Frederick II (1740–86). Germany's regeneration was due, however, to Napoleon, who united West Germany in the Confederation of the Rhine (1806) and introduced the ideas and reforms of the French Revolution: his reforms were subsequently imitated in Prussia. The Empire was abolished in 1806, and after 1815 Germany became a loose federation. In spite of persecution, the ideas of democracy and national unity spread, and inspired the unsuccessful revolutions of 1848. The growth of industry from 1850 also made national unity an economic necessity. Under Bismarck's leadership Prussia united Germany in 1871, after victorious wars with Austria and France. In the following years industry expanded greatly; the beginnings of a colonial empire and a fleet were made, and at home a powerful socialist movement arose. Political, industrial, and colonial rivalries with Britain, France, and Russia all combined to produce World War I.

In 1918 a revolution overthrew the monarchy, and the Socialists seized power, and established the democratic Weimar republic. The economic crisis of 1929–33 brought Germany near to revolution, until in 1933 the reaction manoeuvred the Nazis into power. At home they solved the unemployment problem by a vast rearmament programme, abolished the democratic constitution, and ruthlessly destroyed all opposition; abroad, the policy of aggression led to eventual defeat in World War II. Germany was then divided, within its 1937 frontiers, into British, American, French, and Russian occupation zones until 1952.

Subsequent German history is overshadowed by partition into the rival German Democratic Republic (East ◊Germany) under a Communist regime and German Federal Republic (West ◊Germany) under a Christian Democrat coalition, tension being heightened by the anomalous position of ◊Berlin.

Germany, West /'dʒɜːməni/ country in W Europe, bounded to the north by the North Sea and Denmark, east by East Germany and Czechoslovakia, south by Austria and Switzerland, and west by France, Belgium, Luxembourg, and the Netherlands.

government West Germany's constitution (the Basic Law) was drafted 1948–49 by the Allied military governors and German provincial leaders in an effort to create a stable, parliamentary form of government, diffuse authority and safeguard liberties, borrowing from British, American and neighbouring European constitutional models. It established, firstly, a federal system of government built around ten *Länder* (states), each with its own constitution and elected parliament and government headed by a minister-president.

The *Länder* have original powers in education, police and local government and are responsible for the administration of federal legislation through their own civil services. They have local taxation powers and are assigned shares of federal tax revenues.

The constitution, secondly, created a new federal parliamentary democracy, built around a two-chamber legislature comprising a directly elected 520-member lower house *Bundestag* (federal assembly), and an indirectly elected 45-member upper house *Bundesrat* (federal council). *Bundestag* representatives are elected for four-year terms by universal suffrage under a system of 'personalized proportional representation' in which electors have one vote for an ordinary constituency seat and one for a *Länder* party list, enabling adjustments in seats gained by each party to be made on a proportional basis.

Political parties must win at least 5 per cent of the national vote to qualify for shares of 'list seats'. *Bundesrat* members are nominated and sent in blocs by *Länder* governments, each state being assigned between three and five seats depending on population size. The *Bundestag* is the dominant parliamentary chamber, electing from the ranks of its majority party or coalition a chancellor (prime minister) and cabinet to form the executive government. Once appointed, the chancellor can only be removed by a 'constructive vote of no confidence' in which a majority votes positively in favour of an alternative leader.

Legislation is effected through all-party committees. The *Bundesrat* has few powers to initiate legislation, but has considerable veto authority. All legislation relating to *Länder* responsibilities requires its approval, constitutional amendments need a two-thirds *Bundesrat* (and *Bundestag*) majority, while the *Bundesrat* can temporarily block bills or force amendments in joint *Bundestag-Bundesrat* 'conciliation committees'. *Bundestag* members also join an equal number of representatives elected by *Länder* parliaments in a special Federal Convention *Bundesversammlung* every five years to elect a federal president as head of state. The president, however, has few powers and is primarily a titular figure.

The 1949 constitution is a written document. Adherence to it is policed by an independent federal constitutional court based at Karlsruhe which is staffed by 16 judges, who are selected, a half each, by all-party committees from the *Bundestag* and *Bundesrat*, judges serving terms

Germany, West

FEDERAL REPUBLIC OF GERMANY (*Bundesrepublik Deutschland*)

AREA 248,651 sq km/95,984 sq mi
CAPITAL Bonn
TOWNS West Berlin, Cologne, Munich, Essen, Frankfurt-am-Main, Dortmund, Düsseldorf; ports Hamburg, Kiel, Cuxhaven, Bremerhaven
PHYSICAL flat in N, mountainous in S with Alps; rivers Rhine, Weser, Elbe flow N, Danube flows SE
FEATURES Black Forest
HEAD OF STATE Richard von Weizsacker from 1984
HEAD OF GOVERNMENT Helmut Kohl from 1982
GOVERNMENT parliamentary democracy
EXPORTS machine tools (world's leading exporter); cars and commercial vehicles, electronics, industrial goods, textiles, chemicals, iron and steel; wine
CURRENCY Deutschmark (2.99 = £1 Sept 1987)
POPULATION (1985) 60,950,000 (including 4,400,000 guest workers, *Gastarbeiter*, of whom 1,600,000 are Turks; the rest are Yugoslavs, Italians, Greeks, Spanish, and Portuguese); annual growth rate -0.2%
LANGUAGE German
RELIGION Protestant 49%, Roman Catholic 47%
LITERACY 99% (1985)
GNP $655 bn (1983); $9,450 per head of population

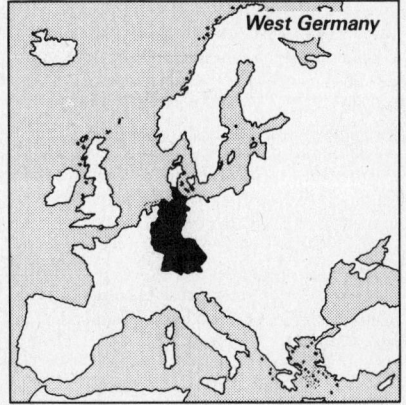

CHRONOLOGY
1945 German surrender and division into four (US, French, British, Soviet) occupation zones.
1948 Berlin crisis.
1949 Establishment of Federal Republic under the 'Basic Law' Constitution with Adenauer as chancellor.
1954 Grant of full sovereignty.
1957 Entry into EEC. Recovery of Saarland.
1961 Construction of Berlin Wall.
1963 Retirement of Chancellor Adenauer.
1969 Willy Brandt became chancellor.
1972 Basic Treaty with East Germany.
1974 Resignation of Brandt. Helmut Schmidt became chancellor.
1982 Kohl became chancellor.

and reconstruction during the 1950s and 1960s, an era termed the 'miracle years'.

During this period, West Germany was also reintegrated into the international community. It gained full sovereignty in 1954, entered ◊NATO in 1955, emerging as a loyal supporter of the USA, and, under Adenauer's lead, joined the new ◊European Economic Community in 1957. Close relations with France enabled the ◊Saarland to be transferred to German sovereignty in 1957.

In 1961, East Germany's construction of the ◊Berlin Wall to prevent refugees from leaving the East created a political crisis which vaulted West Berlin's mayor, Willy ◊Brandt, to international prominence. Domestically, Brandt played a major role in shifting the SPD away from its traditional Marxist affiliation towards a more moderate position following the party's 1959 Bad Godesberg conference. Support for the SPD steadily increased after this policy switch and the party joined the CDU in a 'Grand Coalition' 1966–69, before gaining power itself, with the support of the FDP, under Brandt's leadership in 1969. As chancellor, Brandt introduced the foreign policy of ◊Ostpolitik, which sought reconciliation with Eastern Europe as a means of improving contacts between East and West Germany.

Treaties in 1970 normalized relations with the Soviet Union and Poland and recognized the Oder-Neisse border line, while in 1972 a basic treaty was effected with East Germany, acknowledging the Democratic Republic's borders and separate existence, enabling both countries to enter the UN in 1973. Brandt resigned as chancellor in 1974, following the revelation that his personal assistant had been an East German spy. His successor, the former finance minister, Helmut ◊Schmidt, adhered to Ostpolitik and emerged as a leading advocate of European cooperation, while at home introducing important social reforms.

The SPD-FDP coalition only narrowly defeated the CDU-CSU in the 1976 federal election, but gained a comfortable victory in 1980 when the controversial Franz-Josef ◊Strauss headed the CDU-CSU ticket. Between 1980–82, however, the left wing of the SPD and the liberal FDP were divided over defence policy (particularly the proposed stationing of US nuclear missiles in West Germany) and economic policy, during a period of recession.

Chancellor Schmidt fought to maintain a moderate, centrist course but the FDP eventually withdrew from the federal coalition in 1982 and joined forces with the CDU, led by Dr Helmut ◊Kohl, to unseat the chancellor in a 'positive vote of no confidence'. Helmut Schmidt immediately retired from politics and the SPD, led by the colourless Hans-Jochen Vögel, was heavily defeated in the *Bundestag* elections of 1983, losing votes on the left to the new environmentalist Green Party. The new Kohl administration, with the FDP's Hans-Dietrich ◊Genscher remaining as foreign minister, adhered closely to the external policy of the previous chancellorship.

At home, however, a freer market approach was

of up to 12 years. The court functions as a guarantor of civil liberties and adjudicator in Federal-*Land* disputes. (Similar courts function at the *Land* level).

West German politics have been dominated since 1949 by two major parties, the Christian Democratic Union (CDU) and Social Democratic Party (SPD), and one minor party, the Free Democratic Party (FDP). The conservative CDU has gained the most support at the national level, forming the principal party of government 1949–69 and after 1982. It is represented in Bavaria by a more right-wing sister party, the Christian Social Union (CSU). The SPD is the dominant party of the left and, after adopting a more moderate policy programme, became the principal party of federal government between 1969–82. The FDP liberal party has averaged 8 per cent of the national vote since 1949, but has regularly held the balance of power in the *Bundestag* and been a coalition partner, with a 20 per cent share of cabinet portfolios, in all but seven years (1957–61 and 1966–69) since 1949. In recent years a fourth significant party, the ◊Green Party, has emerged, surmounting the 5 per cent federal electoral barrier in both 1983 and 1987. West Berlin has its own elected parliament and government and sends 22 'honorary representatives' to the federal *Bundestag* and

four to the *Bundesrat*. The three Allied powers, the USA, France, and Britain, continue to exercise supreme authority over West Berlin.
history for history before 1949, see ◊Germany, history. The Federal Republic was formed in 1949 from the British, American and French occupation zones in the W of the German Empire which were under Allied military control following Germany's surrender in 1945. A policy of demilitarization, decentralization and democratization was instituted by the Allied control powers and a new, intentionally provisional, constitution framed, which included eventual German re-unification.
West ◊Berlin was blockaded by the Soviet Union 1948–49, but survived to form a constituent *Land* in the Federal Republic, after an airlift operation by the Allied powers. Politics during the Federal Republic's first decade were dominated by the CDU, led by the popular Konrad ◊Adenauer.
Chancellor Adenauer and his economics minister, Ludwig ◊Erhard, established a successful approach to economic management, termed the 'social market economy', which combined the encouragement of free market forces with strategic state intervention on the grounds of social justice. This new approach, combined with ◊Marshall Aid and the enterprise of the labour force (many of whom were refugees from the partitioned East), brought rapid growth

introduced. With unemployment rising to 2.5 million in 1984, problems of social unrest emerged, while violent demonstrations greeted the installation of US nuclear missiles on German soil in 1983–84. Internally, the Kohl administration was rocked by scandals over illegal party funding, which briefly touched the chancellor himself. However, a strong recovery in the German economy from 1985 enabled the CDU-CSU-FDP coalition to gain re-election in the federal election of 1987, with 269 *Bundestag* seats. The opposition SPD meanwhile won 186 seats, and was divided over its future and whether or not to seek alliance with the Greens, who won 42 seats.

germination the changes that occur in a seed, spore or pollen grain immediately preceding and including the initial stages of growth. Germination occurs in seeds when they are exposed to favourable external conditions of moisture, light, and temperature and when any factors causing ◊dormancy have been removed. The process begins with the uptake of water by the seed. The embryonic root, or radicle, is normally the first organ to emerge, followed by the embryonic shoot, or plumule. Food reserves, either within the endosperm or from the cotyledons, are broken down to nourish the rapidly growing seedling. Germination is considered to have ended with the production of the first true leaves.

Germiston /'dʒɜːmɪstən/ town in the Transvaal, South Africa; population (1980) 155,435. Industries include gold refining, chemicals, steel, textiles.

germ layer in ◊embryology, a layer of cells that can be distinguished during the development of a fertilized egg. Most animals have three such layers. The inner one (*endoderm*) later gives rise to the gut, the middle one (*mesoderm*) develops into most of the other organs, while the outer one (*ectoderm*) gives rise to the skin and nerves. Simple animals, such as sponges, lack a mesoderm.

Gerona /xe'rəunə/ town in NE Spain, capital of Gerona province; population (1980) 87,648.

Geronimo /dʒə'rɒnɪməu/ 1829–1909. Apache Indian chief and war leader. He led raids on US soldiers after his Chiricahua reservation was abolished in 1876. He was captured in 1886,

following a hard-fought campaign against General George Crook, but escaped. He later surrendered, on condition that his men returned to their homes in Florida. Instead they were imprisoned, and later settled elsewhere. He became a Christian and a successful farmer in Oklahoma.

gerrymander in politics, the rearranging of constituency boundaries to give an unfair advantage to the ruling party. The term is now used more generally to describe various kinds of political trickery. The term derives from US politician Elbridge Gerry (1744–1814), who while governor of Massachusetts reorganized an electoral district (shaped like a salamander) in favour of the Republicans.

Gers /ʒeə/ river in France, 178 km/110 mi in length; it rises in the Lannemezan Plateau and flows north to join the Garonne 8 km/5 mi above Agen.

Gershwin /'gɜːʃwɪn/ George 1898–1937. American composer. Born in Brooklyn, he wrote popular songs, to many of which his brother *Ira Gershwin* (1896–1983) wrote the lyrics, and more serious music, in which he incorporated the essentials of jazz, for example the tone poem *An American in Paris* 1928, *Rhapsody in Blue* 1924, and the opera *Porgy and Bess* 1935.

Gertler /'gɜːtlə/ Mark 1891–1939. British painter. He was a pacifist and a non-combatant during World War I; his masterpiece *Merry-Go-Round* 1916 (in the Tate Gallery, London) has been seen as an evocation of the horrors of the war machine through its portrayal of a carousel on which the human riders wear identical mask-like expressions of terror. His later works were more traditional in manner and theme.

gestalt term first used in psychology in Germany about 1910, which has been adopted from German into English because there is no exact equivalent. It refers to the concept of a unified whole which is greater than, or different from, the sum of its parts; that is, a complete structure whose nature is not explained simply by analysing its constituent elements. A chair, for example, will generally be recognized as a chair despite great variations between individual chairs in such attributes as size, shape, colour, and so on. *Gestalt psychology* regarded all mental phenomena as being arranged in

Gershwin Jazz pianist and composer George Gershwin photographed in 1937, the year of his death.

Gertler *Merry-Go-Round* by British artist Mark Gertler, painted in 1916. Using bright colours and bold lines, Gertler used the image of a carousel from which the terrified riders are unable to escape.

organized, structured wholes. For example, learning was seen as a reorganizing of a whole situation (often involving insight), as opposed to the behaviourists' view that it consisted of associations between stimuli and responses. Gestalt psychologists' experiments showed that the brain is not a passive receiver of information,

germination

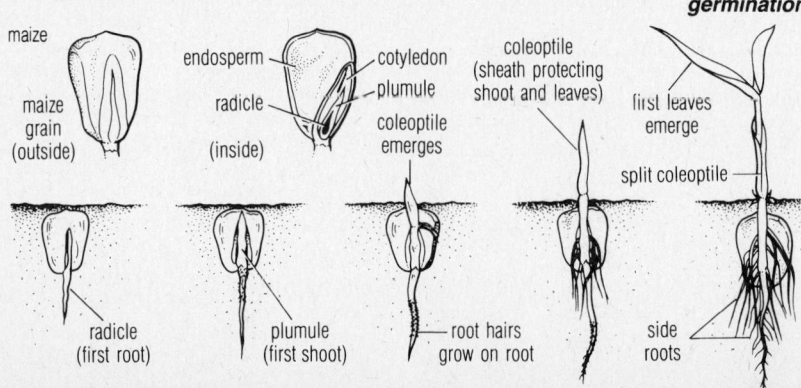

maize

maize grain (outside)

endosperm
radicle

cotyledon
plumule
coleoptile

(inside)

coleoptile (sheath protecting shoot and leaves)
coleoptile emerges

first leaves emerge

split coleoptile

radicle (first root)

plumule (first shoot)

root hairs grow on root

side roots

but that it structures all of its input in order to make sense of it, a belief which is now generally accepted. The concept and the term gestalt have since been applied in other fields, including philosophy and literary criticism.

Gestapo abbreviated form of *Geheime Staatspolizei*, the Nazi secret political police, formed in 1933 and condemned at the ◊Nuremberg trials in 1946.

gestation in all mammals except the monotremes (duck-billed platypus and spiny anteater), the period of development of the young in the uterus/womb of the female from the time of ◊implantation of the embryo in the uterus to birth. This period varies between species; in humans it is about 40 weeks. See also ◊menstrual cycle.

Gethsemane /geθ'semǝni/ site on the Mount of Olives, east of Jerusalem, of the garden where Judas Iscariot, according to the New Testament, betrayed Jesus. When Jerusalem was divided in 1948 between Israel and Jordan, Gethsemane fell within Jordanian territory.

Getty /'geti/ John Paul 1892–1976. American oil millionaire, president of the Getty Oil Company from 1947, and founder of the Getty Museum (the world's richest) at Malibu, California. In 1985 *John Paul Getty jr* established an endowment fund of £50 million for the National Gallery, London. He received an honorary knighthood in 1986.

Gettysburg, Battle of battle of the ◊American Civil War at Gettysburg, Pennsylvania, USA, in 1863. It was won by the North and was a turning point in the war. The site is now a national cemetery, at the dedication of which President Lincoln delivered the Gettysburg Address on 19 Nov 1863.

Getz /gets/ Stan(ley) 1927– . US tenor saxophonist of the 1950s cool school. He was also the first American musician to be closely identified with the Latin American influenced *bossa nova* sound.

geyser a natural spring which, at more or less regular intervals, explosively discharges a column of steam and hot water into the air. One of the best-known geysers is Old Faithful, in Yellowstone National Park, Wyoming, USA; geysers also occur in New Zealand and Iceland.

Gezira, El /gɪ'zɪǝrǝ/ plain in the Republic of Sudan, between the Blue and White Niles. The cultivation of cotton, sorghum, wheat, and groundnuts is made possible by irrigation.

G-forces the forces pilots and astronauts experience when their craft accelerate or decelerate rapidly. One G is the ordinary pull of gravity we all experience. Early astronauts were subjected to launch and re-entry forces up to six-Gs or more. Pilots and astronauts wear G-suits that prevent their blood 'pooling' too much under severe G-forces, which can lead to unconciousness, or blackouts.

Ghaghara or *Gogra* /'gɑːgǝrǝ/ river in N India, a tributary of the ◊Ganges, which rises in Tibet and flows through Nepál and the state of Uttar Pradesh. Length 1,000 km/600 mi.

Ghana /'gɑːnǝ/ country in W Africa, bounded N by Burkina Faso, E by Togo, S by the Gulf of Guinea, and W by the Ivory Coast.

government the 1979 constitution was suspended in 1981 when Flight-Lieutenant Jerry Rawlings seized power and set up a Provisional National Defence Council (PNDC), with himself as chairman. Parliament and the council of state were abolished and the government now rules by decree. All political parties were banned but opposition groups still operate from outside the country.

history the area now known as Ghana was once made up of several separate kingdoms, including those of the Fanti on the coast and the ◊Ashanti further inland.

The first Europeans to arrive in the region were the Portuguese in 1471. Their coastal trading centres, dealing in gold and slaves, flourished alongside Dutch, Danish, British, Swedish, and French traders until about 1800, when the Ashanti, having conquered much of the interior, began to invade the coast. Denmark and the Netherlands abandoned their trading centres, and the Ashanti were defeated by Britain and the Fanti in 1874. The coastal region became the British colony of The Gold Coast, and after continued fighting, the inland region to the N of Ashanti in 1898, and the Ashanti kingdom in 1901, were made British protectorates. After 1917 the W part of Togoland, previously governed by Germany, was administered with The Gold Coast. Britain thus controlled both coastal and inland teritories, and in 1957 they, together with British Togoland, were granted independence as the Republic of Ghana.

Dr Kwame Nkrumah, a former prime minister of The Gold Coast, became president. He embarked on a policy of what he called 'African socialism' and established an authoritarian regime. In 1964 he declared Ghana a one-party state, with the Convention People's Party (CPP), which he led, as the only political organization. He then dropped his stance of ◊non-alignment and forged links with the USSR and other communist countries. In 1966, while visiting China, he was deposed in a coup led by Gen Joseph Ankrah, whose national liberation council purged CPP supporters.

In 1969 Ankrah was replaced by Gen Akwasi Afrifa, who announced plans for a return to civilian government. A new constitution established an elected national assembly and a non-executive presidency. The Progress Party (PP) won a big majority in the assembly and its leader, Kofi Busia, became prime minister. In 1970 Edward Akufo-Addo became the civilian president.

Following economic problems, the army seized power again in 1972. The constitution was suspended and all political institutions replaced by a National Redemption Council (NRC), under Col Ignatius Acheampong. In 1978 he was replaced by his deputy, Frederick Akuffo, in a bloodless coup. Like his predecessors, he announced a speedy return to civilian government but before elections could be held he, in turn, was deposed by junior officers led by Flight-Lt Jerry Rawlings, claiming that previous governments had been corrupt and had mismanaged the economy.

Civilian rule was restored in 1979 but two years later Rawlings led another coup, again complaining of the government's incompetence. He established a Provisional National Defence Council (PNDC), with himself as chairman, again suspending the constitution, dissolving parliament and banning political parties. Although Rawlings' policies were initially supported, particularly by workers and students, his failure to revive the economy caused discontent and he has had to deal with a number of demonstrations and attempted coups.

Ghana Empire an empire which flourished in NW Africa during the 5th–13th centuries. Founded by the Soninke people, the Ghana Empire was based, like the ◊Mali empire which superseded it, on the Saharan gold trade. From its capital at Kumbi Saleh most trade routes ran north across the Sahara and west to the coast. Trade consisted mainly of the exchange of gold from inland deposits for salt from the coast. At its peak in the 11th century, it occupied the area which includes parts of present-day Mali, Senegal, and Mauritania.

Ghats, Eastern and Western /gɔːts/ twin mountain ranges in S India, to the E and W of the central plateau; a few peaks reach about 3,000 m/9,000 ft. The name is a European misnomer, the Indian word *ghat* meaning pass, not mountain.

Ghent /gent/ city and port in E Belgium; population (1982) 237,500. Industries include textiles, chemicals, and metallurgy. The cathedral of St Bavon (12th–14th centuries), has paintings by van ◊Eyck and ◊Rubens, and there is a university established in 1816.

gherkin a young or small green ◊cucumber.

ghetto area of a town where under a law enforced by papal bull in 1555 Jews were compelled to live. Ghettos were abolished, except in E Europe, in the 19th century, but the concept was revived by the Germans and Italians 1940–45. The term is now used generally for any deprived area occupied by a minority group.

Ghibelline in medieval Germany and Italy, member of a rival party to the ◊Guelphs.

Ghiberti /gɪ'beǝti/ Lorenzo 1378–1455. Italian sculptor. A goldsmith by training, the bronze doors which he made with ◊Pollaiuolo for the baptistery of his native Florence are one of the finest works of the Renaissance. He also wrote *Commentarii/Commentaries* on art history.

Ghirlandaio /ˌgɪǝlæn'daɪǝu/ Domenico c. 1449–1494. Name by which the Florentine fresco painter Domenico Bigordi is known.

Giacometti /ˌdʒækǝ'meti/ Alberto 1901–1966. Swiss sculptor and painter, who trained in Italy and Paris. After an early surrealist period, he developed in the 1940s his characteristic mature style of emaciated, single figures, based on wire frames, almost always monochromatic, and so elongated that they seem almost without volume. There are many examples in the Tate Gallery, London.

Giant's Causeway stretch of columnar basalt forming a promontory on the north coast of county Antrim, Northern Ireland. It was formed by an outflow of lava in Tertiary times which has solidified in polygonal columns.

Ghana
REPUBLIC OF

AREA 238,537 sq km/92,100 sq mi
CAPITAL Accra
TOWNS Kumasi, and ports Sekondi-Takoradi, Tema
PHYSICAL mostly plains; bisected by river Volta
FEATURES artificial Lake Volta; relics of traditional kingdom of Ashanti
HEAD OF STATE AND OF GOVERNMENT Jerry Rawlings from 1981
GOVERNMENT military
EXPORTS cocoa, coffee, timber; gold, diamonds, manganese, and bauxite
CURRENCY cedi (282.58 = £1 Sept 1987)
POPULATION 13,004,000 (1985); annual growth rate 3.1%
LANGUAGE English (official)
RELIGION Christian 43%, animist 38%, Muslim 12%
LITERACY 59% male/37% female (1980 est)
GNP $3.9 bn (1983); $420 per head of population
CHRONOLOGY
1957 Independence achieved, within the Commonwealth, with Kwame Nkrumah as president.
1960 Ghana became a republic and a one-party state.
1966 Nkrumah deposed and replaced by Gen Joseph Ankrah.

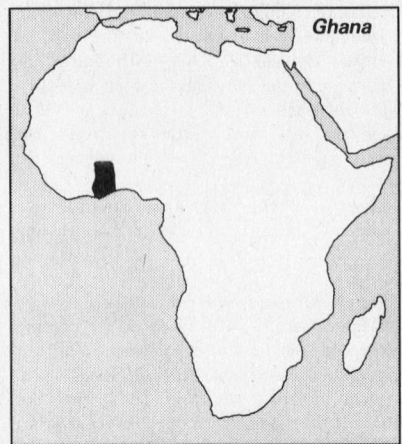

1969 Ankrah replaced by Gen Akwasi Afrifa, who initiated a return to civilian government.
1970 Edward Akufo-Addo elected president.
1972 Another coup placed Col Acheampong at the head of a military government.
1978 Acheampong deposed in a bloodless coup led by Frederick Akuffo. Another coup put Flight Lt Jerry Rawlings in power.
1979 Return to civilian rule under Hilla Limann.
1982 Rawlings seized power again, complaining about the incompetence of previous governments.

Gibbon A portrait of the historian Edward Gibbon, painted c. 1773 by Henry Walton. Gibbon is best-known for *The History of the Decline and Fall of the Roman Empire,* a work which occupied a major part of his life; the first volume appeared in 1776, and the last in 1788.

Gibberd /'gɪbəd/ Frederick 1908–1984. British architect and town planner. His works include the new towns of Harlow, England and Santa Teresa, Venezuela, the Catholic Cathedral, Liverpool, and the Central London mosque at Regent's Park. He was knighted in 1967.

gibberellin plant growth substance (see also ◊auxin) which mainly promotes stem growth but may also affect several other aspects of growth and development, including the breaking of dormancy in certain buds and seeds, and the induction of flowering. Application of gibberellin can stimulate the stems of dwarf plants to additional growth, delay senescence of ageing leaves, and promote the production of seedless fruit (◊parthenocarpy).

gibbon type of small ape, genus *Hylobates,* of which there are several species, the *common* or *black-handed gibbon Hylobates lar* being about 60 cm/2 ft tall. The body is hairy except for the buttocks, which distinguishes them from other types of apes. They have long limbs, no tail, and are arboreal in habit, but when on the ground walk upright. They are found from Assam, through the Malay peninsula to Borneo.

Gibbon /'gɪbən/ Edward 1737–1794. British historian, born in Putney. He was withdrawn from Oxford owing to his conversion to Roman Catholicism in 1753, was sent to Lausanne by his father and reconverted in 1754. He conceived the idea of *The History of the Decline and Fall of the Roman Empire* while in Rome in 1764. The first volume appeared in 1776, and was immediately successful, although he was compelled to reply to attacks on his account of the early development of Christianity by a *Vindication* 1779. The work was completed in 1788. From 1783 he had lived in Lausanne, but returned to England and died in London.

Gibbon /'gɪbən/ Lewis Grassic, pen name of James Leslie Mitchell 1901–1935. Anglo-Scottish novelist, author of the trilogy *A Scots Quair: Sunset Song, Cloud Howe and Grey Granite* 1932–34, set in the area S of Aberdeen, the Mearns, where he was born and brought up.

Gibbons /'gɪbənz/ Grinling 1648–1721. English wood-carver, born in Rotterdam. Recommended to royal patronage by ◊Evelyn, he produced detailed delicate work (especially birds, flowers, and fruit) for St Paul's Cathedral and Petworth House, Sussex.

Gibbons /'gɪbənz/ Orlando 1583–1625. English composer. Born in Oxford, he was the most distinguished of a family of musicians, and was appointed organist at Westminster Abbey in 1623. His finest works are his madrigals and motets.

Gibbons /'gɪbənz/ Stella Dorothea 1902– . British novelist. Born in London, she became a journalist, and is best known for her *Cold Comfort Farm* 1932, a classic satire on the regional novel.

Gibbs /gɪbz/ James 1682–1754. Scottish Neo-Classical architect whose works include St Martin's-in-the-Fields, London 1722–26, Radcliffe Camera, Oxford 1737–49, and Bank Hall, Warrington 1750.

Gibbs' function in ◊thermodynamics (the study of heat and other forms of energy), an expression representing part of the energy content of a system that is available to do external work, also known as the free energy G. In an equilibrium system at constant temperature and pressure, $G = H - TS$, where H is the enthalpy (heat constant), T the temperature, and S the ◊entropy (decrease in energy availability). The function was named after the American physicist Josiah Willard Gibbs (1839–1903).

Gibraltar, Strait of /dʒɪˈbrɔːltə/ strait between N Africa and Spain, with Gibraltar on the north side and ◊Ceuta on the south, the so-called Pillars of Hercules.

Gibraltar, city of /dʒɪˈbrɔːltə/ *area* 6.5 sq km/2.5 sq mi
features strategic naval and air base, with NATO underground headquarters and communications centre; colony of Barbary ◊apes; the frontier zone is adjoined by the Spanish port of La Línea
exports mainly a trading centre for the import and re-export of goods.
currency Gibraltar government notes and UK coinage
population (1981) 30,500
language English
religion mainly Roman Catholic
government the governor has executive authority, with the advice of the Gibraltar council, and there is an elected house of assembly (chief minister Sir Joshua Hassan 1964–69 and from 1972)

recent history captured from Spain in 1704 by English admiral Sir George Rooke (1650–1709), it was ceded to Britain in 1713 under the Treaty of Utrecht. A referendum in 1967 confirmed the wish of the people to remain in association with Britain, but Spain continues to claim sovereignty, and closed the border 1969–85.

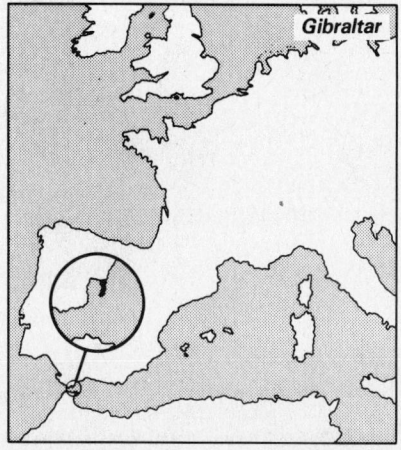

Gibraltar

Gibson /'gɪbsən/ Charles Dana 1867–1944. American illustrator. Born in Massachusetts, he became famous for his portrayal of an idealized type of American young woman, known as the 'Gibson Girl'.

Gibson /'gɪbsən/ William 1948– . US writer, whose science-fiction debut *Neuromancer* 1984, with its computer-using 'cyberspace' adventurers, won both the Hugo and the Nebula awards.

Gibson Desert /'gɪbsən/ desert in central Western Australia; area 220,000 sq km/85,000 sq mi.

Gide /ʒiːd/ André 1869–1951. French novelist, born in Paris. His work is largely autobiographical and concerned with the themes of self-fulfilment and renunciation between which he swung. It includes *L'Immoraliste/The Immoralist* 1902, *La Porte étroite/Strait is the Gate 1909, La Symphonie pastorale/The Pastoral Symphony* 1919, *Les Caves du Vatican/The Vatican Cellars* 1914, and *Les Faux-Monnayeurs/The Counterfeiters* 1926; and an almost lifelong *Journal*. He was awarded the Nobel Prize for Literature in 1947.

Gielgud /'giːlgʊd/ John 1904– . British actor and producer. A great-nephew of the actress Ellen ◊Terry, he made his debut at the Old Vic in 1921, attracted notice as Romeo in 1924, and created his most famous role as Hamlet in 1929. Although best known as a Shakespearean actor, his numerous stage appearances include performances in plays by Chekhov and Sheridan, and in works by modern playwrights. Film roles include Clarence in Shakespeare's *Richard III* 1955 and the butler in *Arthur* 1981 (for which he won an Oscar).

Giessen /'giːsən/ manufacturing town on the Lahn, Hesse, West Germany, with a university 1605; population (1984) 71,800.

Gide Parisian André Gide was acclaimed as one of the most brilliant writers of his generation, winning the Nobel Prize for Literature in 1947. Although primarily a novelist, he also co-founded the *Nouvelle Revue Française*.

Giffard /ʒiˈfɑː/ Henri 1825–1882. French inventor of the first passenger-carrying steerable airship. Built in 1852 and called a dirigible, the hydrogen-filled airship was 45 m/150 ft long, had a 3 hp steam engine which drove a propellor, and was steered using a sail-like rudder. It flew at a speed of 5 kph/8 mph.

giga- prefix signifying 10^9 (multiplying by a factor of one thousand million or 1,000,000,000, or in current scientific terminology, one billion), as in *gigabyte*, which is 1,000,000,000 bytes of digital information.

Gigli /'dʒiːlji/ Beniamino 1890–1957. Italian lyric tenor. From his operatic debut in 1914 he was especially successful in roles from ◊Puccini, ◊Gounod, and ◊Massenet.

Gigli Italian opera singer Beniamino Gigli.

Gijón /xiˈxɒn/ port on the Bay of Biscay, Oviedo province, N Spain; population (1981)

255,969. It produces iron, steel, chemicals, and oil.

gila monster lizard *Heloderma suspectum* of SW USA and Mexico. Belonging to the only venomous genus of lizards, it has poison glands in its lower jaw, but the bite is not usually fatal to humans.

Gilbert /'gɪlbət/ Alfred 1854–1934. British sculptor, whose best known work is the statue of *Eros* in Piccadilly Circus, London erected as a memorial to the 7th Earl of Shaftesbury.

Gilbert /'gɪlbət/ Cass 1859–1934. American architect born in Ohio, he became known for his skyscrapers, including the Woolworth Building in New York, 1913.

Gilbert /'gɪlbət/ Humphrey c. 1539–1583. English soldier and navigator, half-brother of Sir Walter ◊Raleigh, born at Dartmouth. In 1583 he claimed Newfoundland (landing at St John's) for Elizabeth I; he died when his ship sank on the return voyage.

Gilbert /'gɪlbət/ W(illiam) S(chwenk) 1836–1911. British humourist and dramatist, who collaborated with Arthur ◊Sullivan, providing the libretti for their series of light comic operas from 1871. Born in London, he was called to the Bar in 1863, but in 1869 published a collection of his humorous verse and drawings, *Bab Ballads* – 'Bab' being his own early nickname – which was followed by a second volume in 1873. He was knighted in 1907.

Gilbert British humorist and dramatist W S Gilbert best-known for his collaboration with Arthur Sullivan.

Gilbert /'gɪlbət/ William 1544–1603. English doctor and scientist who was physician to Queen Elizabeth I and (briefly) King James I. He studied magnetism and static electricity, deducing that the Earth's magnetic field behaves as if there were a huge bar magnet between the north and south poles. He erroneously thought that the planets were held in their orbits by magnetic forces.

Gilbert and Ellice Islands former British colony, a protectorate, known since independence in 1978 as ◊Tuvalu and ◊Kiribati.

Gilbert and George /'gɪlbət, dʒɔːdʒ/ Gilbert Proesch 1943– and George Passmore 1942– . British painters and performance artists. They became famous in the 1960s for their presentation of themselves as works of art, 'living sculpture'. They received the Turner Award 1986.

Giles /dʒaɪlz/ Carl Ronald 1916– . British cartoonist for the *Daily* and *Sunday Express*

Gilbert and George The British artists Gilbert and George first captured the public imagination in the 1960s when they offered themselves as works of art, and they also feature prominently in their more recent large-scale emblematic photoworks.

from 1943, noted for his creation of a family with a formidable 'Grandma' who finds herself in a number of exciting adventures.

Gilgamesh /ˈɡɪlɡəmeʃ/ hero of Sumerian, Hittite, Akkadian and Assyrian legend. The 12 verse 'books' of the *Epic of Gilgamesh* were recorded on 12 cuneiform tablets by Ashurbanipal's scholars in the 7th century BC; the epic itself is older than the *Iliad* by at least 1,500 years. Part mortal and part divine, Gilgamesh is Lord of Uruk, and his friend Enkidu (half beast, half man) dies for him: the incident of the Flood is similar to the Old Testament account.

Gilgit /ˈɡɪlɡɪt/ town and region on the NW frontier of Kashmir, under the rule of Pakistan.

gill in biology, the main respiratory organ of most fish and immature amphibians, and of many aquatic ◊invertebrates. Gills are generally branched, comb-like or feathery structures. In all types, water passes over the gills, and oxygen diffuses across the gill membrane into the ◊circulatory system while carbon dioxide passes from the system out into the water. In aquatic

insects these gases diffuse into and out of an air-filled ◊trachea ('windpipe').

gill in the imperial system of measurement, a unit of volume for liquid measure, equal to one-quarter of a pint, used in selling alcoholic drinks.

Gill /ɡɪl/ Eric 1882–1940. British sculptor and engraver. He began his career carving inscriptions for tombstones. Interested in lettering and book production, he devised the famous type faces Perpetua 1925 and Gill Sans 1927, that is 'sans serif', without serifs. His sculptures include those on Broadcasting House, London (1933).

Gillette /dʒɪˈlet/ King Camp 1855–1932. American inventor of the Gillette safety-razor.

Gillray /ˈɡɪlreɪ/ James 1757–1815. English caricaturist. His 1,500 cartoons, 1779–1811, satirized the the French, George III, politicians, and social follies of his day.

gillyflower archaic name for the ◊carnation and related plants, used in Chaucer, Shakespeare, and Spenser.

Gilpin /ˈɡɪlpɪn/ William 1724–1804. British artist. Vicar of Boldre from 1777 and a keen educationist, he is remembered as the inventor of the 'picturesque', establishing precise rules for the production of this effect in his essays.

gilt-edged stock securities issued by the British Government to raise funds and traded

Gill Not only was Eric Gill an accomplished sculptor and engraver, as shown in this 1927 self-portrait in wood, but he also made his mark on the printing industry, devising several new type faces.

on the ◊Stock Exchange. A relatively risk-free investment, gilts bear fixed interest and are usually redeemable on a specified date.

gin alcoholic drink made by distilling a mash of maize, malt, and rye, with juniper flavouring.

ginger SE Asian reed-like perennial *Zingiber officinale*, family Zingiberaceae; the underground root is used as a 'hot' condiment and in preserves.

ginger ale and beer sweetened, carbonated drinks containing ginger flavouring, sugar, and syrup; ginger beer also contains bitters.

gingko tree *Ginkgo biloba*, related to the conifers and also known, from the resemblance of its leaves to those of the maidenhair fern (though much enlarged), as the maidenhair tree. It is a 'living fossil', unchanged since prehistoric times, and cultivated in China for many hundreds of years. First planted in England in the 18th century, it does well in towns. In 200 years it may reach 30 m/100 ft, and the fruits have edible kernels, although the pulp is poisonous.

Ginner /ˈdʒɪnə/ Charles 1878–1952. British painter. Born at Cannes, he settled in London in 1910, and was one of the London Group (set up in 1913 and including followers of ◊Vorticism and the ◊Camden Town Group) from 1914. He was noted for the treatment of buildings in his landscapes.

Ginsberg /ˈɡɪnzbɜːɡ/ Allen 1926– . American poet. His *Howl* 1956 was the most influential poem produced by the ◊Beat Generation, criticizing the materialism of modern American society. In the 1960s Ginsberg travelled widely in Asia, and was a key figure in introducing Eastern thought to students of that decade. Later poems were published in the collection *Planet News* 1968.

ginseng plant *Panax ginseng*, family Araliaceae, used in medicine in China. It has been used, as by Russian cosmonauts, to increase resistance to fatigue and stress, but the effects are controversial.

Giolitti /dʒəʊˈlɪti/ Giovanni 1842–1928. Italian politician. Born in Mondovi, he was prime minister in 1892–93, 1903–05, 1906–09, 1911–14, and 1920–21. He opposed Italian intervention in World War I. A Liberal, he pursued a policy of broad coalitions, which was ineffective in the face of the rise of Fascism.

Giorgione /dʒɔːˈdʒəʊni/ 1478–1511. name by which Giorgio of Castelfranco, Veneto, Italy, is known, although few details of his life are certain. He created the Renaissance poetic landscape, with rich colours and a sense of intimacy. His most famous works are the *Tempest* Venice, and the *Madonna and Child Enthroned with Two Saints*, an altar piece for the church of Castelfranco. He influenced ◊Titian.

Giotto di Bondone /ˈdʒɒtəʊ/ c. 1266–1337. Italian artist and architect. Born in Vespignano, N of Florence, he introduced a naturalistic style, painting saints as real people. He is chiefly famous for his frescoes in churches at Assisi, Florence, and Padua. In one of the series of frescoes he painted for the Cappella dell' Arena, Padua, he made the Star of Bethlehem appear as a comet (◊Halley's comet had appeared in 1303, just two years before). From 1334 he was official architect to Florence; he collaborated with Andrea ◊Pisano in decorating the cathedral facade with statues, and designing the campinile (bell-tower), which was completed after his death.

Giotto a space probe built by the ◊European Space Agency to study ◊Halley's comet. Launched by an ◊Ariane rocket in Jul 1985, Giotto passed within 600 km/375 mi of the comet's nucleus on 13 Mar 1986. Its colour photographs showed that the nucleus resembled a lumpy potato, 15 km long and 8 km wide. Other instruments analysed gas and dust given off by the comet, finding it to be a 'dirty snowball' as predicted.

Gippsland Lakes /ˈgɪpslænd/ series of shallow lagoons on the coast of Victoria, Australia: the chief are Wellington, Victoria and King (broadly interconnected), and Reeve.

giraffe tallest mammal, *Giraffa camelopardalis*. It measures over 5.5 m/15 ft, the neck accounting for nearly half this amount. The giraffe has two small skin-covered horns on the head and a long tufted tail. The skin has a mottled appearance and is reddish brown and cream. Giraffes are now found only in Africa, south of the Sahara Desert.

Giraldus Cambrensis /dʒɪˈrældəs kæmˈbrensɪs/ c. 1146–1220. Welsh bishop and historian. Born in Pembrokeshire, he was elected bishop of St David's in 1198. He wrote a history of the conquest of Ireland by Henry II and *Itinerarium Cambriae* 1191.

Giraudoux /ˌʒɪrəʊˈduː/ (Hippolyte) Jean 1882–1944. French diplomat and writer of novels, including *Suzanne et la Pacifique/Suzanne and the Pacific* 1921, and plays including *Amphitryon 38* 1929, *La Guerre de Troie n'aura pas lieu/Tiger at the Gates* 1935

and *La Folle de Chaillot/The Madwoman of Chaillot* 1945.

Girgenti /dʒɪəˈdʒenti/ former name of ◊Agrigento, a town in Sicily, Italy.

Girl Guides scouting organization founded in the UK in 1910 by ◊Baden-Powell and his sister Agnes. There are three branches: Brownie Guides, 7–11 year-olds; Guides, 10–16 year-olds; Ranger Guides, 14–20 year-olds, and adult leaders – Guiders. The World Association of Girl Guides and Girl Scouts (as they are known in the USA) has over 6,500,000 members.

Giro system of making payments by direct transfer between one bank or post office account and another. Originating in Austria in 1883, the idea was introduced in the UK in 1968, the beginning of the present National Girobank run by the Post Office (headquarters Bootle, Merseyside).

Gironde /ʒɪˈrɒnd/ navigable estuary 80 km/50 mi long, formed by the mouths of the ◊Garonne, length 580 km/360 mi, and ◊Dordogne rivers, in SW France. The Lot, length 480 km/300 mi, is a tributary of the Garonne.

Girondins /dʒɪˈrɒndɪn/ the right-wing republican party in the French Revolution, so called because a number of their leaders came from the Gironde *département*. They were driven from power by the ◊Jacobins in 1793.

Girtin /ˈgɜːtɪn/ Thomas 1775–1802. English painter of watercolour landscapes, a friend of ◊Turner.

Gisborne /ˈgɪzbən/ port on the east coast of North Island, New Zealand, exporting dairy products, wool and meat. Population (1984) 31,300.

Giscard d'Estaing /ˈʒiːskɑː desˈtæŋ/ Valéry 1926– . French conservative politician, president 1974–81. Giscard was active in the wartime Resistance. After a distinguished academic career, he worked in the Ministry of Finance and entered the National Assembly for Puy de Dôme in 1956 as an Independent Republican. He was finance minister to ◊de Gaulle 1962–66 and ◊Pompidou 1969–74. After Pompidou's death he was narrowly elected president in 1974, in difficult economic circumstances; he was defeated by the socialist ◊Mitterrand in 1981. He returned to the National Assembly in 1984. As leader of the Union pour la Démocratie Française, which he formed in 1978, Giscard has sought to project himself as leader of a 'new centre'.

Gissing /ˈgɪsɪŋ/ George Robert 1857–1903. British author. Born in Yorkshire, he taught for many years in London and the USA. Among his later books are *New Grub Street* 1891 (perhaps his best-known novel), the autobiographical *Private Papers of Henry Ryecroft* 1903, and a study of Dickens.

Giulini /dʒuːˈliːni/ Carlo Maria 1914– . Italian conductor. Principal conductor at La Scala, Milan, 1953–55, and musical director of the Los Angeles Philharmonic 1978– , he is renowned as an interpreter of Verdi.

Giza /ˈgiːzə/ site of the Great Pyramids and Sphinx at ◊Cairo, Egypt.

gizzard a muscular grinding organ of the digestive tract, below the ◊crop of birds,

earthworms and some insects, and forming part of the ◊stomach. The gizzard of birds is lined with a hardened horny layer of the protein keratin, preventing damage to the muscle layer during the grinding process. Most birds swallow sharp grit which aids maceration of food in the gizzard.

glacier a mass of ice which originates in mountains in the snowfields above the snowline, where the annual snowfall exceeds the annual melting and drainage. Under the weight of the layers above, the snow compacts to ice, and under pressure the ice can move (glacier flow). It moves slowly down a valley or depression, and is constantly replenished from its source. The scenery produced by the passing of glaciers is characteristic and includes U-shaped valleys, ◊corries, ◊arêtes and various features formed by the deposition of ◊moraine (rocky debris). When a glacier moves over an uneven surface crevasses are formed in it; if it reaches the sea or a lake it breaks up to form icebergs. A glacier that is formed by the confluence of several valley glaciers as they leave the mountains is called a *piedmont* glacier. A glacier that covers a continent, for example Greenland and Antarctica, and moves outwards rather than downwards is called an *ice sheet*.

gladiator Roman professional fighter, recruited mainly from slaves, criminals, and prisoners of war, who fought to the death for the entertainment of the ancient Romans. The custom, which originated in the practice of slaughtering slaves on a chieftain's grave, was introduced into Rome from Etruria in 264 BC and survived until the 5th century AD.

gladiolus genus of South European and African cultivated perennials, family Iridaceae, with brightly-coloured funnel-shaped flowers, borne in a spike; the sword-like leaves spring from a corm.

Gladstone /ˈglædstən/ William Ewart 1809–1898. British Liberal politician. Born in Liverpool, the son of a rich merchant. He entered parliament as a Tory in 1833. In Peel's government he was president of the Board of Trade 1843–45, and colonial secretary 1845–46. He left the Tory Party with the Peelite group in 1846, and after 1859 identified himself with the Liberals. He was chancellor of the Exchequer in Aberdeen's government 1852–55, and in Palmerston's and Russell's governments 1859–66. As prime minister 1868–74, he carried through a series of important reforms, including the disestablishment of the Church of Ireland, the Irish Land Act, the abolition of the purchase of army commissions and of religious tests in the universities, and the introduction of elementary education and of vote by ballot.

During Disraeli's government of 1874–80 Gladstone strongly resisted his imperialist and pro-Turkish policy, and by his Midlothian campaign of 1879 helped to overthrow him. Gladstone's second government of 1880–85 was confronted with difficult problems in Ireland, Egypt, and South Africa, and lost prestige through its failure to relieve General ◊Gordon. Returning to office in 1886, Gladstone introduced his Home Rule Bill, which was defeated by the secession of the Liberal

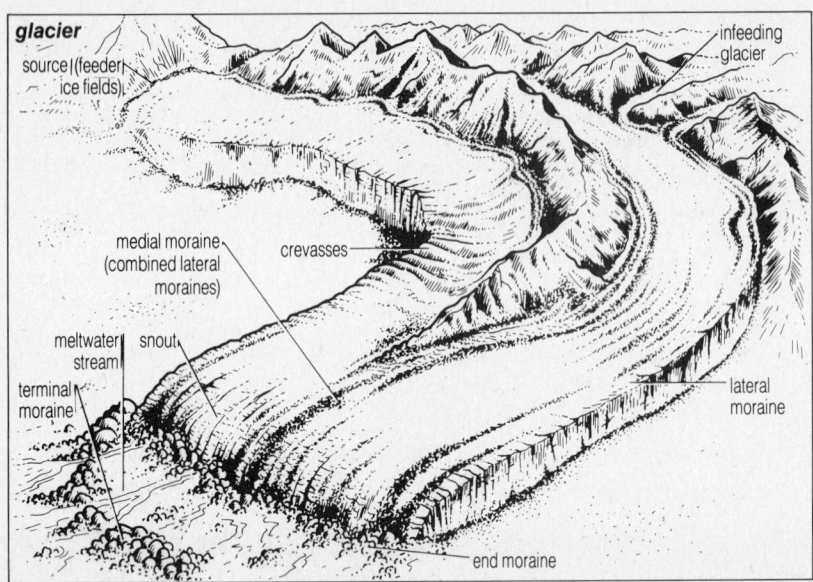

glacier

source (feeder ice fields)

infeeding glacier

medial moraine (combined lateral moraines)

crevasses

meltwater stream

snout

terminal moraine

lateral moraine

end moraine

Unionists, and he thereupon resigned. After six years' opposition he formed his last government in 1892; his second Home Rule Bill was rejected by the Lords, and in 1894 he resigned.

Gladstone The 19th-century British Liberal politician William Gladstone photographed in his later years. Four times prime minister, he made a significant impact on policies concerned with reform in Ireland. At home, he introduced elementary education and vote by ballot.

Glamorgan /glə'mɔːgən/ three counties of S Wales – Mid, South and West Glamorgan – created in 1974 from the former county of Glamorganshire. All are on the Bristol Channel, and the administrative headquarters of Mid and South Glamorgan is Cardiff; the headquarters of West Glamorgan is Swansea. *Mid Glamorgan*, which also takes in a small area of the former county of Monmouthshire to the east, contains the important coalmining towns of Aberdare and Merthyr Tydfil, and the Rhondda in the valleys. The mountains are in the northern part of the county; area 1,019 sq km/394 sq mi; population (1983) 536,400. In *South Glamorgan*, there is mixed farming in the fertile Vale of Glamorgan, and towns include Cardiff, Penarth, and Barry; area 416 sq km/161 sq mi; population (1983) 391,700. *West Glamorgan* includes Swansea, with tin-plating and copper industries, Margam, with large steel rolling mills, Port Talbot, and Neath; area 815 sq km/315 sq mi; population (1983) 366,600.

gland a specialized organ of the body that manufactures and secretes enzymes, hormones or other chemicals. In animals, glands vary in size from small (for example, tear glands) to large (for example, pancreas), but in plants they are always small, and may consist of just a single cell. Some discharge their products internally (◊endocrine glands) others externally (◊exocrine glands). ◊Lymph nodes are sometimes wrongly called glands.

glandular fever viral disease (also known as *infectious mononucleosis*: in the ◊herpes group of viruses), causing fever, painfully swollen lymph nodes (in the neck), and changes in the blood cells (lymphocytes) which produce antibodies.

American physicist. In 1960 he was awarded a Nobel prize for his invention of the ◊bubble chamber for observing high-energy nuclear phenomena. By using a pressurized liquid medium instead of a gas, it overcomes drawbacks inherent in the earlier ◊cloud chamber.

Glasgow /'glæzgəʊ/ city and administrative headquarters of Strathclyde, Scotland; population (1983) 740,000. Industries include engineering, chemicals, printing, and distilling. Buildings include the 12th-century cathedral of St Mungo, and the Cross Steeple (part of the historic Tolbooth); the universities of Glasgow, established in 1450 (modern buildings by Sir Gilbert ◊Scott) and Strathclyde, established in 1963; the Royal Exchange, the Stock Exchange, Kelvingrove Art Gallery (◊Impressionist collection); the Glasgow School of Art, designed by ◊Mackintosh; the Burrell Collection at Pollock Park, bequeathed by shipping magnate Sir William Burrell (1861–1958).

Glasgow /'glæzgəʊ/ Ellen (Anderson Gholton) 1873–1945. US novelist. Her books, set mainly in her native Virginia, often deal with the survival of tough heroines in a world of adversity. Among the best-known are *Barren Ground* 1925, *The Sheltered Life* 1932, and *Vein of Iron* 1935.

glasnost (Russian 'openness') term applied by the Soviet leader ◊Gorbachev to his policy of liberalizing various aspects of Soviet life and opening up Soviet relations with Western countries.

glass a brittle, usually transparent or translucent substance which is physically neither a solid nor a liquid. Glass is made by fusing certain types of sand (silica); this fusion occurs naturally in the case of volcanic glass (see ◊obsidian). In the industrial production of common types of glass, the type of sand used and the particular chemicals added to it (for example lead, potassium, barium), as well as refinements of technique, make the difference between the cheap product (soda glass), flint glass (used in cut-crystal ware), optical glass, stained glass, heat resistant glass, and glasses that exclude certain ranges of the light spectrum. Methods of processing include: *blown glass*, which is either blown individually from molten glass using a tube 1.5 m/4.5 ft long for expensive, crafted glass, or automatically blown into a mould, for example, light bulbs, and bottles; *pressed glass*, which is simply pressed into moulds, for jam jars, cheap vases, and light fittings; *sheet glass* for windows, which is made by putting the molten glass through rollers to form a 'ribbon' or by floating molten glass on on molten tin in the 'float glass' process. ◊*Fibreglass* comprises of fine glass fibres. In bulk it can be used as insulation material in construction work or woven into material or made into glass-reinforced plastic (GRP). See also ◊metallic glass.

Glass /glɑːs/ Philip 1937– . American composer. Strongly influenced by Indian music, his work is characterized by repeated rhythmic figures that are continually being expanded and modified as if by organic growth. His compositions include the operas *Einstein on the Beach* 1975 and *Akhnaten* 1984.

Glasse /'glæsə/ Hannah 1708–1770. British cookery writer whose *The Art of Cookery made Plain and Easy* 1747 is widely regarded as the first classic recipe book in Britain.

Glastonbury /'glæstənbəri/ market town in Somerset, England; population (1981) 6,773. Nearby are two excavated lake villages thought to have been occupied for about 150 years before the Romans came to Britain.

The first church on the site was traditionally founded in the 1st century by ◊Joseph of Arimathea. The ruins of the Benedictine abbey built in the 10th–11th centuries by ◊Dunstan and his followers were excavated in 1963 and the site of the grave of King ◊Arthur and Queen Guinevere was thought to have been identified.

Glauber's salt /'glaubəz/ crystalline sodium sulphate decahydrate, which melts at 31°C; the latent heat stored as it solidifies makes it a convenient thermal energy store. Used in medicine.

glaze a transparent vitrified ◊enamel used as a coating for pottery and porcelain.

Glencoe /glen'kəʊ/ glen in ◊Strathclyde region, Scotland, where members of the Macdonald clan were massacred in 1692. John Campbell, Earl of Breadalbane, was the chief instigator. It is now a winter sports area.

Glendower /glen'daʊə/ Owen c. 1359–1415. Welsh leader of a revolt against the English in North Wales, who defeated Henry IV in three campaigns 1400–02, though Wales was reconquered 1405–13.

Gleneagles /glen'iːgəlz/ glen in Tayside, Scotland, famous for its golf course and for the *Gleneagles Agreement*, formulated in 1977 at the Gleneagles Hotel by Commonwealth heads of government, that 'every practical step (should be taken) to discourage contact or competition by their nationals' with South Africa, in opposition to apartheid.

Glenn /glen/ John (Herschel) 1921– . US astronaut and politician, first American to orbit the Earth. On 20 Feb 1962 he orbited Earth three times in the Mercury spacecraft Friendship 7, in a flight lasting 4 hr 55 min. After retiring from ◊NASA he subsequently entered politics, becoming a senator for Ohio in 1974, and unsuccessfully seeking the Democratic presidential nomination in 1984.

Glenrothes /glen'rɒθɪs/ town and administrative headquarters of Fife, Scotland, 10 km/6 mi N of Kirkcaldy, developed as a 'new town' from 1948; population (1981) 32,700.

gliding the art of using air currents to fly unpowered aeroplanes. Technically speaking gliding involves the gradual loss of altitude; gliders designed for soaring flight (utilizing air rising up a cliff face or hill, warm air rising as a 'thermal' above sun-heated ground, and so on) are known as sail-planes. Pioneers include George ◊Cayley, ◊Lilienthal, Octave Chanute (1832–1910), and the ◊Wright brothers, the latter perfecting gliding technique in 1902. The British Gliding Association dates from 1929. Launching may be by rubber catapult from a hilltop; by a winch which raises the glider like a kite; or by aircraft tow. In World War II towed troop-carrying gliders were used by the Germans in Crete and the Allies at Arnhem. In hang gliding, perfected by US engineer Rogallo in the 1970s, the aeronaut is strapped into a carrier, attached to a sail wing of nylon stretched on an aluminium frame shaped like a paper dart, and jumps into the air from a high place.

Glinka /'glɪŋkə/ Mikhail Ivanovich 1804–1857. Russian composer. Born near Smolensk, he broke away from the prevailing Italian influence, and turned to Russian folk-music as the inspiration for his opera *A Life for the Tsar (Ivan Susanin)* 1836. His later works include another opera *Ruslan and Lyudmila* 1842, and the orchestral *Kamarinskaya* 1848.

glissando in music, a rapid uninterrupted scale produced by sliding the finger across the keys or strings.

Gliwice /glɪ'viːtseɪ/ town in Poland, formerly in German Silesia, population (1982) 202,000. It has coal-mining, iron, steel, and electrical industries.

globefish another name for ◊puffer fish.

Globe Theatre octagonal theatre open to the sky, built by Cuthbert ◊Burbage in 1599 on the Bankside, ◊Southwark, London. It was the site for the first productions of most of ◊Shakespeare's plays by Richard ◊Burbage and his company. It was burnt down in 1613. In 1987 planning permission was granted to the American film producer Sam Wanamaker (1919–) to build a working replica of the theatre on its original site.

globular cluster a ball-shaped group of ◊stars, containing approximately 10,000 to a million stars. More than a hundred globular clusters are distributed in a spherical halo around our ◊Galaxy. They consist of old stars, formed early in our Galaxy's history. Observations of other galaxies show they too are surrounded by globular clusters. (See also ◊star cluster.)

Glomma /'glɒmə/ river in Norway, 570 km/350 mi long. The largest river in Scandinavia, it flows into the Skaggerak at Frederiksstad.

Gloucester /'glɒstə/ city, port, and administrative headquarters of Gloucestershire, England; population (1983) 92,200. Its 11th–14th century cathedral has a Norman nucleus and additions in every style of Gothic.

Gloucester /'glɒstə/ Richard Alexander Walter George, Duke of Gloucester 1944– . Prince of the United Kingdom. Grandson of ◊George V, he succeeded his father owing to the death of his elder brother Prince William (1941–72) in an air crash. He married in 1972 Birgitte van Deurs, daughter of a Danish lawyer.

Gloucestershire /'glɒstəʃə/ county in SW England
area 2,643 sq km/1,020 sq mi
towns administrative headquarters Gloucester; Stroud, Cheltenham, Tewkesbury, Cirencester
features Cotswold Hills; river Severn and tributaries; Berkeley Castle, where ◊Edward II was murdered
products cereals, dairy products; engineering, coal in the Forest of Dean
population (1986) 513,000
famous people Edward Jenner.

glove-box a form of protection used when handling certain dangerous materials, such as radioactive substances. Gloves fixed to ports in the walls of a box allow manipulation of objects within the box. Contamination through inhalation of fine air-borne particles of poisonous materials is prevented by maintaining a slight vacuum inside the box, so that any airflow is inwards.

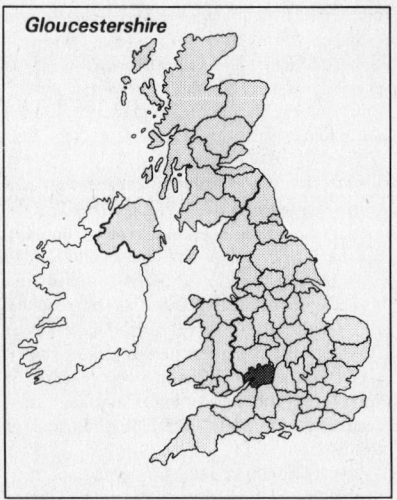

Gloucestershire

glow-worm the wingless female of various luminous beetles in the family Lampyridae. The luminous organs are situated under the abdomen, and the light has usually attracts winged males for mating. The species are distributed throughout Europe and Siberia.

Glozel /glɒ'zel/ village near Vichy, France. An archaeological find here in 1924 was attacked as a hoax because of the disparate age of the objects. It included bones with drawings of animals 10,000 BC, axes 4,000–2,000 BC, inscribed clay tablets 700 BC–100 AD, and a glass kiln, possibly medieval.

Glubb /glʌb/ John Bagot 1897–1986. British soldier, founder of the modern Arab Legion (the Jordanian army) which he commanded from 1939 until he was dismissed in 1956 as a result of anti-British sentiment in Jordan. He was customarily known by the title Glubb Pasha.

Gluck /glʊk/ Christoph Willibald von 1714–1787. German composer. Born in Erasbach, Bavaria, he studied music at Prague, Vienna, and Milan, went to London in 1745 to compose operas for the Haymarket, but returned to Vienna in 1746. He was knighted by the Pope, and in 1754 settled at Vienna as Kapellmeister (director of court music) to Maria Theresa. In 1762 his *Orfeo ed Euridice/Orpheus and Eurydice* revolutionized the 18th-century conception of opera by giving free scope to dramatic effect. *Orfeo* was followed by *Alceste/Alcestis* 1767 and *Paris ed Elena/Paris and Helen* 1770. *Iphigénie en Aulide/Iphigenia in Aulis* 1774, produced in Paris, gave rise to furious controversies in which Gluck had the support of Marie Antoinette, while his Italian rival Piccini was patronized by Mme Du Barry. With *Armide* 1777 and *Iphigénie en Tauride/Iphigenia in Tauris* 1779 Gluck won a complete victory over Piccini. He died in Vienna.

glucose a type of sugar or carbohydrate, $C_6H_{12}O_6$. also known as grape-sugar or dextrose. It is present in the blood and is found in honey and fruit juices. It is a source of energy for the body, being produced from other sugars and starches to form the 'energy curency' of many biochemical reactions (see also ◊ATP). It is usually prepared by hydrolysis from cane sugar or starch. Generally a yellowish syrup, it may be purified to a white crystalline powder. Glucose is a monosaccharide, that is, it is made up of a single sugar unit.

glue a kind of ◊adhesive.

glycerine a non-technical name for glycerol *trihydroxypropane* (HOCH₂CH(OH)CH₂OH) a thick, colourless, odourless sweetish liquid. It can be mixed with water and alcohol, but is insoluble in either. Glycerine is obtained from vegetable and animal oils and fats (by treatment with acid, alkali, superheated steam or an enzyme), or by fermentation of glucose, and is used in the manufacture of high explosives, in antifreeze solutions, to maintain moist conditions in fruits and tobacco, and in cosmetics.

glycerol another name for ◊glycerine.

glycine the simplest amino acid, and one of the main components of proteins, CH₂(NH₂)COOH. When purified, it is a sweet, colourless crystalline compound.

glycogen polymer (a polysaccharide) of the sugar ◊glucose made and retained in the liver as a carbohydrate store, for which reason it is sometimes called animal starch. It is a source of energy when needed by muscles, in which it is converted back into glucose and metabolized under the action of the hormone ◊insulin.

glycol *dilydroxyethane* a thick, colourless, odourless, sweetish liquid also called ethylene glycol or ethanediol (CH₂OH)₂. It can be mixed with water and alcohol. Glycol is used in antifreeze solutions, in the preparation of ethers and esters, especially for explosives, as a solvent, and as a substitute for glycerine.

Glyndebourne /ˈɡlaɪndbɔːn/ estate in East Sussex, England, site of an opera house established in 1934 by John Christie 1882–1962. Operas are staged at an annual summer festival, and a touring company is also based there.

GMT abbreviation for ◊Greenwich Mean Time.

gnat small fly, especially of the family Culicidae, the mosquitoes. The eggs are laid in water, where they hatch into worm-like larvae, which after passing through a pupal stage emerge as perfect insects. Well-known species are *Culex pipiens* abundant in England: the carrier of malaria *Anopheles maculipennis*; and the banded mosquito *Aedes aegypti* which transmits yellow fever. Only the female is capable of drawing blood, since the male possesses no piercing mandibles.

gneiss a ◊metamorphic rock, formed under conditions of extreme pressure, and often found in association with schists and granites. It has a foliated structure, consisting of an alternation of micaceous and granular bands. ◊Garnets commonly occur in gneiss.

gnome in fairy tales, a small, mischievous spirit of the earth. The males are bearded, wear tunics and hoods, and often guard an underground treasure. The *garden gnome*, an ornamental representation of these spirits, was first was brought from Germany to England in 1850 by Sir Charles Isham for his mansion, Lamport Hall, Northamptonshire.

Gnosticism esoteric cult of Divine Knowledge (a synthesis of Christianity, Greek philosophy, Hinduism, Buddhism, and the mystery cults of the Mediterranean), which was a rival to early Christianity, as shown by the 4th-century codices discovered in Egypt in the 1940s. They include the *Gospel of St Thomas* (unconnected with the disciple), a Gnostic collection of 114 of Christ's sayings, discovered in Egypt 1945, and probably originating c. AD 135. Gnosticism envisaged the world as a series of emanations from the highest of several gods, emphasized the distinction between spirit (good) and matter (evil), gave women cult-equality with men, and opposed private property. It influenced the development of Christianity; and the French ◊Cathars and the modern ◊*Mandeans* in South Iraq descend from it.

GNP abbreviation for ◊Gross National Product.

gnu African antelope, also known as *wildebeest*, with a cow-like face, a beard and mane, and heavy curved horns in both sexes. The body is up to 1.3 m/4.2 ft at the shoulder and slopes away to the hindquarters. The *brindled gnu Connochaetes taurinus* is silver-grey with dark face, mane and tail tuft, and occurs from Kenya southwards. Vast herds move together on migration. The *white-tailed gnu Connochaetes gnou* of South Africa almost became extinct, but was saved by breeding on farms.

go game first played in China 3,000 years ago, and now the national game of Japan. The board, squared off by 19 horizontal and 19 vertical lines, begins empty and gradually fills up with black and white flattish, rounded stones, as the players win territory by surrounding areas of the board with 'men' and capturing the enemy armies by surrounding them. A handicapping system enables expert and novice to play against each other. It is far more complex and subtle than chess, the mathematical possibilities being 10 to the power of 720.

Goa, Daman, and Diu /ˈɡəʊə, dɑːˈmɑːn, ˈdiːuː/ Union Territory of India comprising the former Portuguese coastal possessions of Goa and Daman, and the island of Diu, forcibly seized by India in 1961; population (1981) 1,086,730. The capital is Panaji.

goat ruminant mammal, genus *Capra*, family Bovidae, closely related to the sheep. Domestic varieties are kept for milk, or for mohair (the ◊angora and ◊cashmere); males are usually bearded and smell strongly. Noted wild species are the *ibex Capra ibex*, of the Alps, and *markhor Capra falconeri* of the Himalayas, 1 m/3 ft high and with long twisted horns. The *Rocky mountain goat, Oreamnos americanus*, is a 'goat-antelope' and not closely related to true goats.

Gobbi /ˈɡɒbi/ Tito 1913–1984. Italian baritone singer, noted for his opera characterizations, especially Figaro, Scarpia, and Iago.

Gobelin /ˈɡəʊbələŋ/ French tapestry factory, originally founded as a dyeworks in Paris by Gilles and Jean Gobelin about 1450. The firm began to produce tapestries in the 16th century, and in 1662 the establishment was bought by Colbert for Louis XVI. With the support of the French government it still continues to make tapestries.

Gobi /ˈɡəʊbi/ Asian desert divided between the Mongolian People's Republic and Inner Mongolia, China; 800 km/500 mi N–S, and 1,600 km/1,000 mi E–W. It is rich in fossil remains of extinct species.

God the concept of a supreme being, a unique personal creative entity, assumed to be completely good. *Monotheism* is the belief in one God; *polytheism* is the belief in more than one God. The rise of science since the 17th century, and the belief that the only valid statements were those verifiable by the senses, has had a complex influence on human beings' belief in God. See ◊deism, ◊theism, and ◊pantheism; ◊religion and ◊theology, and entries on individual religions.

Godalming /ˈɡɒdlmɪŋ/ town in Surrey, England; population (1981) 18,200.

Godavari /ɡəʊˈdɑːvəri/ river in the Republic of India; length 1,450 km/900 mi. It is sacred to Hindus.

Goddard /ˈɡɒdəd/ Robert Hutchings 1882–1945. American pioneer of rocketry. His first liquid-fuelled rocket was launched at Auburn, Massachusetts, USA, in Mar 1926. By 1935 his rockets had gyroscopic control and carried cameras to record instrument readings. Two years later a Goddard rocket gained the world altitude record with an ascent of 3 km/1.9 mi.

Gödel /ˈɡɜːdl/ Kurt 1906–1978. Austrian-born US mathematician and philosopher, who proved that a mathematical system always contains statements that can be neither proved nor disproved within the system; in other words, as a science mathematics can never be totally consistent and totally complete. He was a friend of Einstein and worked on relativity, constructing a mathematical model of the Universe which made travel back through time theoretically possible.

Godfrey de Bouillon /ˈɡɒdfri də buːˈjɒŋ/ c. 1060–1100. Crusader. Second son of Count Eustace II of Boulogne, he and his brothers (Baldwin and Eustace) led 40,000 Germans in the first Crusade in 1096. When Jerusalem was taken in 1099, he was elected its ruler, but refused the title of king.

Godiva /ɡəˈdaɪvə/ Lady c. 1140–1180. Wife of Leofric, earl of Mercia (died 1057), who founded a Benedictine monastery at Coventry, where she is buried. Legend has it that he promised to reduce the heavy taxes on the townspeople of Coventry if she rode naked through the streets at noon. Everyone remained indoors, but 'Peeping Tom' bored a hole in his shutters, and was struck blind.

God Save the King/Queen British national anthem. The tune resembles a composition by John Bull (1563–1628), and similar words are found from the 16th century. In its present form it dates from the 1745 Rebellion, when it was used as an anti-Jacobite Party song. In the USA the song 'America', with the first line, 'My country, 'tis of thee' is sung to the same tune.

Godthaab /ˈɡɒdhɔːb/ capital (Greenlandic *Nuuk*) of Greenland; population (1982) 9,700.

Godunov /ˈɡɒdənɒv/ Boris 1552–1605. Tsar of Russia from 1598, who died during a revolt led by Dmitri, brother and rightful heir of the previous tsar Fyodor I, whom Boris was said to have murdered. ◊Mussorgsky wrote an opera based on his life.

Godwin /ˈɡɒdwɪn/ died 1053. Earl of Wessex from 1020. He secured the succession to the throne in 1042 of ◊Edward the Confessor, to whom he married his daughter Edith, and whose chief minister he became. King ◊Harold was his son.

Godwin /ˈɡɒdwɪn/ William 1756–1836. British philosopher and novelist. At first a Nonconformist minister, he later became an atheist. His *Enquiry concerning Political Justice* 1793 advocated an anarchic society based on a faith in people's essential rationality. His novel *Caleb Williams* 1794 promoted his views. His first wife was Mary ◊Wollstonecraft.

Goebbels /ˈɡɜːbəlz/ Paul Josef 1897–1945. German Nazi leader. Born in the Rhineland, he became a journalist, joined the Nazi Party in its early days, and was given control of its propaganda in 1929. On becoming minister of propaganda in 1933, he brought all cultural and educational activities completely under Nazi control, and built up sympathetic movements abroad to carry on the 'war of nerves' against Hitler's intended victims. On the capture of Berlin by the Allies he poisoned himself.

Goehr /ɡɜː/ (Peter) Alexander 1932– . British composer, born in Berlin. A lyrical but often hard-edged serialist, he has nevertheless usually remained within the forms of the symphony and traditional chamber works, and more recently has turned to tonal and even Neo-Baroque models.

Goering /ˈɡɜːrɪŋ/ Hermann Wilhelm 1893–1946. German field marshal from 1938 and Nazi leader. Born in Bavaria, he was a renowned fighter pilot in World War I, and joined the Nazi party in 1922. He became commander of the SA (◊Storm Troops), and in 1933, as minister of the interior, allegedly arranged the ◊Reichstag fire, directing the reign of terror which followed. As commissioner for aviation he built up the ◊Luftwaffe and in 1936 he became director of the four year plan for war preparations. Appointed successor to Hitler 1939, he later lost favour, and was expelled from the party in 1945. Tried at Nuremberg, he poisoned himself before he could be executed.

Goes /xuːs/ Hugo van der c. 1440–1482. Flemish artist, whose work is noted for its emotional intensity; for example Portinari altarpiece (Uffizi) and the *Death of the Virgin* (Bruges).

Goethe /ˈɡɜːtə/ Johann Wolfgang von 1749–1832. German poet, novelist, and dramatist, generally considered the founder of modern German literature. Born at Frankfurt-am-Main, he went on to study law. He was inspired by Shakespeare, to whom he was introduced by ◊Herder, to write the play *Götz von Berlichingen* 1773, and became the leader of the Romantic ◊*Sturm und Drang* movement. His

works include the autobiographical *The Sorrows of the Young Werther* 1774, which made him a European figure, and his masterpiece the poetic play *Faust* 1808, completed in a second part in 1831. He was prime minister at the court of Weimar 1775–85. A visit to Italy 1786–88 inspired the classical dramas *Iphigenie auf Tauris* 1787 and *Tasso* 1790. Also memorable are the *Wilhelm Meister* novels 1796–1829. He was a friend of ◊Schiller. Many of his lyrics were set to music.

Goffman /ˈɡɒfmən/ Erving 1922–1982. American social scientist, born in Canada. He studied the ways people try to create, present, and defend a particular self-image and the social structures surrounding, controlling, and defining human interaction; works include *The Presentation of Self in Everyday Life* 1956, *Gender Advertisements* 1979, and *Forms of Talk* 1981.

Gogarty /ˈɡɔːɡəti/ Oliver St John 1878–1957. Irish writer. A successful Dublin physician, he was a member of the literary circle which included Yeats, George Moore, and Joyce, and figures in *Ulysses* as Buck Mulligan. A wit and a poet, he wrote several books including the autobiographical *As I was going down Sackville Street* 1937.

Gogh /ɡɒx/ Vincent van 1853–1890. Dutch painter. Born in Zundert, he tried various careers, working for a time as a schoolmaster in England, before he took up painting. He studied under Van Mauve at The Hague. In 1886 he went to Paris where he became a friend of ◊Gauguin, and the two painters worked together for a short time in Arles, Provence. One of the leaders of the Post-Impressionist painters, he executed still-lifes and landscapes, some of the best-known being *A Cornfield with Cypresses, The Yellow Chair, Sunflowers*, and striking self-portraits, for example when he cut off part of his earlobe, following a quarrel with Gauguin. He spent the last years of his life in asylums, and committed suicide.

Gogol /ˈɡɔːɡɒl/ Nicolai Vasilyevich 1809–1852. Russian writer. Born near Poltava, he tried several careers before entering the St Petersburg Civil Service. His first collection of stories, *Evenings on a Farm near Dikanka* 1831–32, had an immediate success, and his second, *Mirgorod*, was warmly praised by ◊Pushkin. Later came *Arabesques* 1835, the short story, 'The Overcoat', and the comedy *The Inspector General* 1836, an attack on bureaucracy. From 1835 he had travelled in Europe, and it was in Rome that he completed the earlier part of his best-known work, the picaresque novel *Dead Souls* 1842, depicting Russian provincial society.

Gogra alternative transcription of river ◊Ghaghara in India.

goitre swelling on the front of the neck caused by an enlargement of the thyroid gland, simple goitre, due to iodine deficiency. It may arise from lack of iodine in the water in certain areas, for example Derbyshire (potassium iodide is now added to salt sold for use in the home) or by under-or over-activity of the gland. In exophthalmic goitre, also known as Graves's

disease, the enlargement of the thyroid gland is accompanied by protrusion of the eyeballs and palpitation, among other symptoms.

Golan Heights /ˈɡəʊlæn/ plateau on the Syrian border with Israel, bitterly contested in the ◊Arab-Israeli Wars, and annexed by Israel on 14 Dec 1981.

gold a heavy, precious, yellow metallic element; symbol Au, atomic number 79, atomic weight 197.0. It occurs naturally in veins, but following erosion it can be transported and redeposited. Gold has long been valued for its durability, malleability, and ductility. It is unaffected by temperature changes and is highly resistant to acids. The major producers are South Africa, the USSR, Canada, the USA, and Australia. It is used in dentistry and making jewellery and electronic devices. For manufacture, gold is alloyed with another strengthening metal, its fineness being measured by the parts of pure gold on a scale of 24. See ◊carat, ◊mining.

Gold Coast /ˈɡəʊld kəʊst/ historically, the W coast of Africa from Cape Three Points to the Volta river, where alluvial gold is washed down. Portuguese and French navigators visited this coast in the 14th century and in 1618 a British trading settlement developed into the colony of the Gold Coast; with its dependencies of Ashanti and Northern Territories plus the trusteeship territory of Togoland, it became ◊Ghana in 1957. The name is also used for many coastal resort areas; for example, in Queensland, Australia, and Florida, USA.

goldcrest smallest British bird, *Regulus regulus*, about 9 cm/3.5 in long. Olive green, with a bright yellow streak across the crown, this warbler frequents conifers and builds its nest in them.

Golden Calf in the Old Testament, image made by ◊Aaron in response to the request of the Israelites for a god, when they despaired of Moses' return from Mount Sinai.

Golden Fleece in Greek mythology, fleece of the winged ram Chrysomallus, which hung on an oak tree at Colchis guarded by a dragon. It was stolen by ◊Jason and the Argonauts; the story may have had its origin in the ancient use of greasy sheep fleeces to recover alluvial gold.

Golden Fleece in European history, former order of knighthood in Spain and Austria which was instituted by Philip the Good, Duke of Burgundy, in 1429, and freshly inaugurated in Vienna in 1713 by Charles VI.

Golden Gate strait in California, USA, linking ◊San Francisco Bay with the Pacific, spanned by a bridge which was completed in 1937. The longest span is 1,280 m/4,200 ft.

Golden Horde the invading Mongol-Tatar army which first terrorized Europe from 1237 under the leadership of Batu, a grandson of ◊Genghis Khan. ◊Tamerlane broke their power in 1395, and ◊Ivan III ended Russia's payment of tribute to them in 1480.

goldenrod tall, leafy N American perennial, *Solidago virgaurea*, family Compositae, with heads of many small yellow flowers.

golden section a proportion, known intuitively by most artists, which forms an aesthetically satisfying relation between the parts of a painting. It approximates to the proportion 13:8 (it cannot be shown as a exact fraction).

golden section

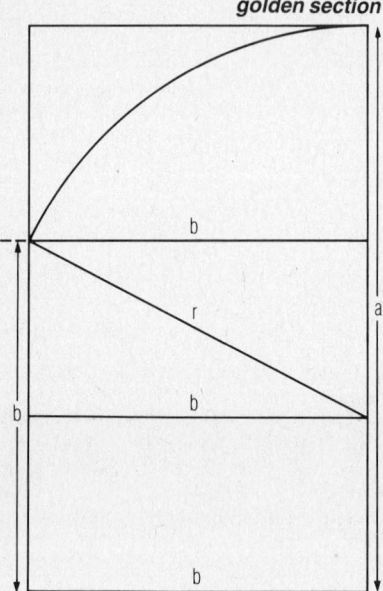

goldfinch songbird *Carduelis carduelis* commonly found in Europe, W Asia and N Africa. It is brilliantly coloured – black, white, and red about the head, and gold and black wings.

goldfish fish of the carp family *Carassius auratus* found in E Asia. Greenish-brown in its natural state, it has for centuries been bred by the Chinese, taking on highly coloured and freakishly shaped forms. In Japan goldfish breeding developed rapidly among low-class warriors dismissed by their feudal lords on the Emperor's restoration in 1868, and keeping them became an almost universal Japanese hobby: today enormous quantities are shipped abroad.

Golding /ˈɡəʊldɪŋ/ William 1911– . British novelist, best known for his first book, *Lord of the Flies* 1954, in which savagery takes over among a group of English schoolboys on a Pacific island. Later novels include *The Spire* 1964, *Rites of Passage* 1980, and *The Paper Men* 1984. He was awarded the Nobel Prize for Literature in 1983.

Goldoni /ɡɒlˈdəʊni/ Carlo 1707–1793. Italian dramatist. Born in Venice, he wrote popular comedies for the Sant'Angelo theatre, including *La putta onorata/The Respectable Girl* 1749, *I Pettegolezzi delle donne/Women's Gossip* 1750, and *La locandiera/Mine Hostess* 1753. In 1761 Goldoni moved to Paris, where he directed the Italian theatre, wrote several more plays, including *L'Eventail/The Fan* 1763, gave Italian lessons at the court, and died in extreme poverty.

Goldsmith /ˈɡəʊldsmɪθ/ Oliver 1728–1774. British author. Born in Ireland, the son of a clergyman, he was educated at Trinity College, Dublin, and went to Edinburgh to study medicine in 1752. After travelling extensively in Europe, he returned to England and became a hack

writer. His earliest work of literary importance was *The Citizen of the World* 1762, a series of letters by an imaginary Chinese traveller. In 1761 he met ◊Johnson, and became a member of his 'club'. In 1764 he established his reputation with his poem *The Traveller*, and followed it with his collected essays in 1765, and his novel, *The Vicar of Wakefield* 1766, sold according to Johnson's account to save him from imprisonment for debt. A further poem, *The Deserted Village* 1770, was followed by his dramatic masterpiece, *She Stoops to Conquer* 1773.

Goldsmith The life of Oliver Goldsmith was characterized by eccentricity. He failed at many things, including his ambitions to become a teacher and physician, and was always in debt. His writing career, however, was much more successful, in particular his play *She Stoops to Conquer*.

gold standard system under which a country's ◊currency is exchangeable for gold on demand at the central bank. The system broke down in World War I, and attempted revivals were undermined by the Great Depression. After World War II the par values of the currency units of the ◊International Monetary Fund (which includes nearly all members of the United Nations not in the immediate Soviet bloc) were fixed in terms of gold and the US and East European dollar, but by 1976 floating exchange rates (already unofficially operating from 1971) were legalized. Holdings of gold are still retained because it is an internationally recognized commodity money, which cannot be legislated upon or manipulated by interested countries.

Goldwater /ˈɡəʊldˌwɔːtə/ Barry 1909– . US Republican politician, presidential candidate in the 1964 election, when he was heavily defeated by Lyndon ◊Johnson. Many of Goldwater's ideas have been adopted by the Republican right and the ◊Reagan administration.

Goldwyn /ˈɡəʊldwɪn/ Samuel 1882–1974. American film producer. Born in Warsaw, he

emigrated to the USA in 1896 and became a pioneer film-maker. He was famed for his illogical aphorisms known as 'goldwynisms', for example 'Anyone who visits a psychiatrist should have his head examined'.

golf game in which a small rubber-cored ball is hit with any of 14 clubs (woods or irons, according to the clubhead) from a platform tee into a series of 18 holes, usually about 275 m/300 yd distant, round a landscaped course. In *medalplay* the object is to take fewer strokes than an opponent, but in *match-play* the result depends on the winner of individual holes. The main fairway has short grass, and the green surrounding the hole is almost manicured, but sand bunkers or water at strategic points provide obstacles to progress, and the ball is also more difficult to extricate from the long bordering grass and shrubs, the 'rough.' A course measures some 5,500 m/6,000 yd, for which a good player will have a score of under 70 strokes; handicaps match unequal opponents. Golf originated in the 15th century in Scotland, where the Royal and Ancient Club at St Andrews dates from 1754. Major events include the British and US Open, US Masters, and US Professional Golfers Association. Famous winners of the Open include Jack Nicklaus, Lee Trevino, and Tom Watson (all USA), Gary Player (South Africa), and Severiano Ballesteros (Spain).

British Open first held 1860
1983 Tom Watson *(USA)*
1984 Severiano Ballesteros *(Spain)*
1985 Sandy Lyle *(Great Britain)*
1986 Greg Norman *(Australia)*
1987 Nick Faldo *(Great Britain)*
United States Open first held 1895
1983 Larry Nelson *(USA)*
1984 Fuzzy Zoeller *(USA)*
1985 Andy North *(USA)*
1986 Ray Floyd *(USA)*
1987 Scott Simpson *(USA)*
US Masters first held 1934
1983 Severiano Ballesteros *(Spain)*
1984 Ben Crenshaw *(USA)*
1985 Bernhard Langer *(West Germany)*
1986 Jack Nicklaus *(USA)*
1987 Larry Mize *(USA)*

Golgi apparatus or *Golgi body* a membranous structure found in the cells of ◊eukaryotes. It produces the membranes that surround the cell vesicles or ◊lysosomes.

Goliath /ɡəˈlaɪəθ/ in the Old Testament, champion of the ◊Philistines, who was said (*I Samuel*) to have been slain with a stone from a sling by ◊David in single combat in front of the opposing armies of Israelites and Philistines.

Gollancz /ɡəˈlænts/ Victor 1893–1967. British left-wing writer and publisher. Founder in 1936 of the influential Left Book Club.

gonadotrophin a ◊fertility drug.

Goncharov /ˌɡɒntʃəˈrɒf/ Ivan Alexandrovitch 1812–1891. Russian novelist. Born in Simbirsk, he became a civil servant. His first novel, *A Common Story* 1847, was followed in 1858 by his humorous masterpiece, *Oblomov*,

golf Since the Spanish golfer Severiano Ballesteros won the Dutch Open in 1976, he has won more than 50 tournaments worldwide. He has twice won both the British Open and the US Masters.

which satirized the indolent Russian landed gentry.

Goncourt /gɒŋˈkuə/ de, the brothers Edmond 1822–96 and Jules 1830–1870. French writers. They produced a compendium, *L'Art du XVIIIe Siècle/18th-Century Art* 1859–75, historical studies, and a *Journal* 1887–96, which depicts French literary life of their day. Edmond de Goncourt founded the *Académie Goncourt*, opened in 1903, which awards an annual prize to the author of the best French novel of the year. Equivalent to the ◊Booker Prize in prestige, the monetary value however is only 50 francs.

Gondar /ˈgɒndɑː/ town in Ethiopia about 2,300 m/7,500 ft above sea level and 40 km/25 mi N of Lake Tana; population (1980) 76,950.

Gondwanaland /gonˈdwɑːnəlænd/ southern continent of the ancient (Mesozoic) land mass which included modern South America, Africa, Australia, and Antarctica. See ◊Baobab, ◊Wegener.

gonorrhoea infection by the gonococcus, the commonest form of venereal disease. It is usually transmitted by sexual intercourse, but sometimes, especially in children, by contact with an infected person. A copious opaque discharge from the infected part appears in a few days and infection of the eyes may follow. Gonorrhoea became increasingly resistant to penicillin and streptomycin, but in 1963 a new antibiotic actinospectacin effected cures by a single injection.

González Márquez /gonˈθɑːleθ ˈmɑːkeθ/ Felipe 1942– . Spanish socialist politician, leader of the Socialist Workers' Party (PSOE), prime minister from 1982.
After studying law in Spain and Belgium, in 1966 he opened the first labour-law office in his home city of Seville. In 1964 he had joined the PSOE, and he rose rapidly to the position of leader. In

1982 PSOE won a sweeping electoral victory and González became prime minister.

Good Friday (probably a corruption of God's Friday). In the Christian Church, the Friday before Easter, which is kept in memory of the Crucifixion (the death of Jesus on the cross).

Good King Henry perennial plant *Chenopodium bonus-henricus* growing up to 50 cm/1.6 ft, with triangular leaves which are mealy when young. Above the leaves spikes of tiny greenish-yellow flowers appear in midsummer. The young shoots were formerly eaten as a vegetable, and the plant was probably introduced to the British Isles from S Europe. It is now found on roadsides and wasteland.

Goodman /ˈgudmən/ 'Benny' (Benjamin David) 1909–1986. US clarinettist, nicknamed 'the King of Swing' for the new jazz idiom he introduced. Leader of his own band from 1934, he is remembered for numbers such as 'Blue Skies' and 'King Porter Stomp'. Bartók's *Contrasts* 1939 and Copland's *Clarinet Concerto* 1950 were written for him. He led racially integrated bands, thus breaking down racial barriers in the world of jazz musicians.

Goodman /ˈgudmən/ Paul 1911– . US writer and social critic, whose many writings (novels, plays, essays) express his anarchist, anti-authoritarian ideas. He studied youth offenders in *Growing up Absurd* 1960.

Goodwin Sands /ˈgudwɪn/ sandbanks off the coast of Kent, England, exposed at low tide, and famous for wrecks. According to legend, they are the remains of the island of Lomea, owned by Earl Godwin in the 11th century.

Goodwood /ˈgudwud/ racecourse, NE of Chichester, West Sussex, England. There was a motor-racing track there 1948–66.

Goodyear /ˈgudjɪə/ Charles 1800–1860. American inventor, who developed vulcanized

rubber in 1839, which was to prove of great importance for motor vehicle tyres.

Goonhilly /gunˈhɪli/ British Telecom satellite tracking station in Cornwall, England. It is equipped with a communications satellite transmitter-receiver in permanent contact with most parts of the world.

goose name given to birds forming the genus *Anser*. Both sexes are similar in appearance: they have short, webbed feet, placed nearer the front of the body than in other members of the order Anatidae, and the beak is slightly hooked. They feed entirely on grass and plants, 'grey' geese being very destructive to young crops. The *greylag goose Anser anser* is the ancestor of the tame goose. This is the only species which nests in the British Isles. The genus also includes the *bean goose Anser fabalis*, the *pink-footed goose Anser brachyrhynchus*, and the *white-fronted goose Anser albifrons*, all of which breed in the Old World, and visit Britain in winter. The goose builds a nest of grass and twigs on the ground, and from five to nine eggs are laid, white or cream-coloured, according to the species.

gooseberry edible fruit of *Ribes uva-crispa*, a low-growing bush allied to the currant bushes. The bush is straggling in its growth, bearing straight sharp spines in groups of three, and rounded, lobed leaves. The flowers are green, and hang on short stalks. The fruits are generally globular, green, and hairy, but there are reddish and white varieties.

goosefoot plants of the family Chenopodiaceae, including *fat-hen* or *white goosefoot Chenopodium album* of which the seeds were used as food in Europe from Neolithic times, and also from early times in the Americas. The green part is a ◊spinach substitute.

gopher burrowing rodent of the family Geomyidae of North and Central America, remarkable for its cheek pouches, and harmful to crops.

Gorakhpur /ˈgɔːrəkpuə/ town in Uttar Pradesh, N India; population (1981) 290,814.

Gorbachev /ˌgɔːbəˈtʃof/ Mikhail Sergeevich 1931– . Soviet leader. A member of the Politburo from 1980 and general secretary of the Communist Party (CPSU) from 1985, he introduced radical liberal reforms at home and attempted to halt the arms race abroad.
Born in the N Caucasus, Gorbachev studied law at Moscow University and joined the CPSU in 1952. In 1955–62 he worked for the ◊Komsomol, before being appointed regional agriculture secretary. As Stavropol party leader from 1970 he impressed ◊Andropov, and was brought into the CPSU secretariat in 1978.
Gorbachev was promoted into the Politburo, and in 1983, when Andropov was general secretary, took broader charge of the Soviet economy. During the ◊Chernenko administration (1984–85), Gorbachev, as chair of the Foreign Affairs Commission, was sent on diplomatic tours overseas. On Chernenko's death in 1985 he was appointed party leader. He introduced campaigns against alcoholism, corruption, and inefficiency, and a policy of ◊glasnost, openness. Gorbachev radically changed the style of Soviet

leadership, despite opposition to the pace of change.

Gorbachev Russian leader Mikhail Gorbachev on a visit to Britain. He is seen as the initiator of *glasnost*, an unprecedented movement towards increased openness and freedom of opinion in the Soviet Union.

Gordian knot /ˈgɔːdiən/ in Greek myth, the knot tied by King Gordius of Phrygia, only to be unravelled by the future conqueror of Asia. According to tradition, Alexander cut it with his sword in 334 BC.

Gordimer /ˈgɔːdɪmə/ Nadine 1923– . South African novelist, an opponent of apartheid. Her first novel, *The Lying Days*, appeared in 1953, and other works include *The Conservationist* 1974, and *July's People* 1981. Her books are banned in South Africa.

Gordon /ˈgɔːdn/ Charles George 1833–1885. British general. Born in Woolwich, he joined the Royal Engineers in 1852, and served in the Crimean War, and in the Chinese War of 1860. In the latter he suppressed the Taiping rebellion and became known as 'Chinese Gordon'. In 1874 he went to Egypt, and 1877–79 was governor of the Sudan. He spent the next few years in India, China, Ireland, Mauritius, the Cape, and Palestine. He was sent back to the Sudan in 1884 to rescue English garrisons which were under attack by the ◊Mahdi, but was himself besieged by the Mahdi's army in Khartoum. A relief expedition under ◊Wolseley arrived on 28 Jan 1885, to find that Khartoum, after a siege of ten months, had been captured, and Gordon killed, two days before. Gladstone's government was toppled largely as a result.

Gordon /ˈgɔːdn/ George 1751–1793. British organizer of the so-called Gordon Riots of 1778 in protest against removal of penalties imposed

Gordon British general Charles George Gordon achieved almost mythical status for his distinguished army career, entering popular legend as Gordon of Khartoum in a film of the same name.

on Roman Catholics in the Catholic Relief Act of 1778; he was acquitted on a treason charge.

Gordon /ˈgɔːdn/ Richard 1921– . Pen name of British author Gordon Ostler. He published a series of light-hearted novels on the career of a young doctor beginning with *Doctor in the House* 1952. Many of them were filmed.

Gordonstoun /ˈgɔːdnztən/ public school near Elgin, Grampian, Scotland, founded by Kurt ◊Hahn in 1935, which emphasizes a spartan outdoor life and achievement of objectives, for example, in mountain-climbing and sailing.

Gorgon /ˈgɔːgən/ in Greek mythology, any of three sisters, Stheno, Euryale and Medusa, who had wings, claws, enormous teeth, and snakes for hair. Medusa, the only one who was mortal, was killed by ◊Perseus, but her head was still so frightful, it turned the onlooker to stone. The winged horse ◊Pegasus was supposed to have sprung from her blood.

Gorgonzola /ˌgɔːgənˈzəʊlə/ small town NE of Milan, Italy, famous for cheese.

gorilla largest of the anthropoid apes found in the dense forests of West Africa and mountains of Central Africa. There are three races of one species, *Gorilla gorilla*, these being the Western lowland, Eastern lowland and Mountain gorillas. The male stands about 2 m/6 ft, the female being much smaller, and the body is covered with blackish hair, silvered on the back in the male in a 'saddlemark'. Almost entirely vegetarian, they travel in search of food in family parties of a senior male, several females, some younger males, and a number of infants. They construct stoutly built nests in trees for overnight use. The breast-beating movement, once thought to indicate rage, actually signifies only nervous excitement, and gorillas will not attack except in self-defence. They are dwindling in numbers, being shot for food by some local people, or by

poachers seeking young for zoos, but protective measures are having some effect.

gorilla Guy the gorilla arrived at Regent's Park Zoo, London, on 5 Nov 1947 aged 18 months; by the time he died in 1978, of a heart attack – at that time the world's oldest gorilla – he had a huge following of fans. He stood 1.7 m/5 ft 8 in high, with a chest measurement of 1.8 m/6 ft. His body is now in the Natural History Museum, London.

Gorizia /gɒˈrɪtsiə/ town in Friuli-Venezia-Giulia region, N Italy, on the Isonzo, SE of Udine; population (1981) 41,500. It was a cultural centre during ◊Hapsburg rule.

Gorky /ˈgɔːki/ city in central USSR; population (1985) 1,399,000. Cars, locomotives, and aircraft are manufactured here. Formerly known as Nizhi-Novgorod, it was renamed in honour of Maxim ◊Gorky in 1932.

Gorky /ˈgɔːki/ Arshile 1904–1948. American artist. Born in Armenia, he went to the USA in 1920 and was an initiator of Abstract Impressionism.

Gorky /ˈgɔːki/ Maxim, pseudonym of Russian writer Alexei Peshkov 1868–1936. Born in Nizhi-Novgorod (renamed Gorky in 1932 in his honour), he was exiled 1906–13 for his revolutionary principles. His works include the play *The Lower Depths* 1902, and the recollections *My Childhood* 1913, and combine realism and faith in the potential of the industrial proletariat.

Görlitz /ˈgɜːlɪts/ manufacturing town in East Germany; population (1978) 87,500.

Gorlovka /ˈgɔːləvkə/ industrial town on the ◊Donbas coalfield, Ukraine, USSR; population (1985) 342,000.

gorse furze, or whin, genus of plants *Ulex* of the family Leguminosae, consisting of thorny shrubs with spine-shaped leaves densely clustered along the stems, and bright yellow

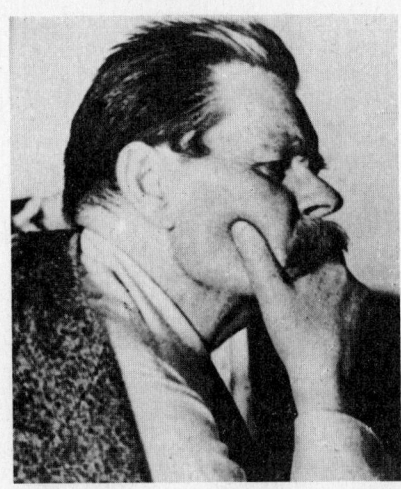

Gorky A committed, lifelong revolutionary, Maxim Gorky attracted official disapproval both before and after the 1917 Revolution.

flowers. The gorse bush *Ulex europaeus* is an evergreen, and grows on heaths and sandy areas throughout western Europe, and abundantly in Britain.

Gorshkov /ˈgɔːʃkɒv/ Sergei 1910– . Russian admiral, commander in chief of the Soviet navy 1956–85, and responsible for its major development since the period of Khrushchev.

Gorst /gɔːst/ J(ohn) E(ldon) 1835–1916. English Conservative Party administrator. Gorst was largely responsible for the transformation of the Victorian Conservative Party electoral base to a position of widespread middle- and working-class support. Appointed Conservative Party agent in 1870, he established the Conservative Central Office, and became secretary of the National Union in 1871.

Gort /gɔːt/ John Vereker, First Viscount Gort 1886–1946. British general, awarded a Victoria Cross after World War I, who commanded the British Expeditionary Force 1939–40, conducting a fighting retreat to ◊Dunkirk.

Gorton /ˈgɔːtn/ John Grey 1911– . Australian Liberal statesman. He was minister for education and science 1966–68, and then prime minister on the death of ◊Holt until he resigned in 1971.

Goschen /ˈgəʊʃən/ George Joachim, 1st Viscount Goschen 1831–1907. British Liberal politician. He held several cabinet posts under Gladstone 1868–74, but broke with him in 1886 over Irish Home Rule. In Salisbury's Unionist government of 1886–92 he was chancellor of the Exchequer after Lord Randolph Churchill's resignation.

goshawk bird *Accipiter gentilis* used in falconry; similar in appearance to the peregrine falcon, but with short wings and short legs.

Gospel word used in the New Testament generally to signify the message of Christian salvation; later it was applied to the four written accounts of ◊Jesus Christ's life by Matthew,

Mark, Luke, and John. Although the first three give approximately the same account or synopsis (thus giving rise to the name Synoptic Gospels), their differences from John have raised many problems.

The so-called fifth Gospel, or Gospel of St Thomas, is a 2nd century collection of 114 sayings of Jesus found in a Coptic translation in one of 13 papyrus codices, discovered in Upper Egypt in 1945, which were apparently the library of a ◊Gnostic community. Strongly influenced by Gnostic teaching, it is nevertheless interesting for comparison with the canonical Gospels: there is no reason to believe that it was written by St Thomas the disciple, the name being used merely to give authority.

gospel music a type of music, developed in the 1920s in the black Baptist churches of the US South, from spirituals, which were 18th and 19th century hymns joined to the old African pentatonic (five-note) scale. Most outstanding of the early gospel singers was Mahalia Jackson (1911–72), but from the 1930s to the mid-1950s male harmony groups predominated, among them the Dixie Hummingbirds, the Swan Silvertones, and the Five Blind Boys of Mississippi.

Gosport /ˈgɒspɔːt/ naval port opposite ◊Portsmouth, Hampshire, England; population (1981) 77,250.

Gossamer Albatross the first human-powered aircraft to fly across the English Channel, in Jun 1979. It was designed by Paul MacCready and piloted and pedalled by Bryan Allen. The same team was behind the first successful human-powered aircraft (*Gossamer Condor*) two years earlier. The Channel crossing took 2 hours 49 minutes.

Gosse /gɒs/ Edmund William 1849–1928. English author. Son of a marine biologist, who was a member of the ◊Plymouth Brethren, Gosse's strict Victorian upbringing is reflected in his masterpiece of autobiographical work *Father and Son* (published anonymously in 1907). Gosse worked as a librarian, first at the British Museum, and from 1904–19 in the House of Lords, and was knighted in 1925. He was influential as a critic.

Göteborg /jɜːtəˈbɔːri/ port (German Gothenburg) in Sweden, on the Göta Canal (built in 1832), which links it with Stockholm; population (1983) 424,186.

Goth /gɒθ/ East Germanic people who settled near the Black Sea around the 2nd century AD. The eastern branch, the *Ostrogoths*, were conquered by the ◊Huns about 370, while the western, the *Visigoths*, migrated to Thrace. Under ◊Alaric the latter raided Greece and Italy 395–410, sacked Rome, and established a kingdom in southern France. Expelled from there by the Franks, they established a Spanish kingdom which lasted until the Moorish conquest of 711. The Ostrogoths regained their independence in 454, and under ◊Theodoric conquered Italy in 488–93; they disappeared as a nation after ◊Justinian reconquered Italy 535–55.

Gotha /ˈgəʊtə/ town in East Germany, former capital of the duchy of Saxe-Coburg-Gotha; population (1973) 57,098.

Gotha, Almanach de /ˈgəʊtə/ Annual survey of the European royalty, aristocracy and diplomatic ranks, published in Gotha 1763–1944; a smaller scale successor, *Le Petit Gotha/The Little Gotha* was revived in Paris from 1968.

Gothenburg /ˈgɒθənbɜːg/ German form of ◊Göteborg.

Gothic architecture the various styles of architecture which are grouped under the heading of Gothic have certain features in common, the vertical lines – tall pillars, and spires – which take the place of the horizontal lines of previous styles, the pointed arch, rib vaulting, and the flying buttress. Gothic architecture originated in Normandy and Burgundy in the 12th century, and prevailed in western Europe until the 16th century when classic architecture was revived. The term Gothic was at first used disparagingly of medieval art by Renaissance architects.

In France, Gothic architecture may be divided into four periods, namely (a) early Gothic, 1130–90, when ogival vaults were introduced; (b) lancet Gothic, 1190–1240, when pointed arches were tall and narrow; (c) radiating Gothic, 1240–1350, which takes its name from the series of chapels which radiate from the cathedral apse; and (d) late Gothic or the Flamboyant style, 1350–1520. Examples of the different periods are (a) Notre Dame, Paris begun 1160; (b) Chartres begun 1194; Bourges begun 1209; Rheims begun 1211; and Amiens begun 1221; (c) Sainte Chapelle, Paris 1226–30; and (d) St Gervais, Paris.

In Italy Gothic had a classical basis. A notable example of Italian Gothic is Milan cathedral. The Gothic style in Germany, until the end of the 13th century was at first heavily influenced by that of France, for example Cologne Cathedral, the largest in N Europe, was built after the model of Amiens.

In England the Gothic style is divided into ◊Early English 1200–75, for example Salisbury Cathedral, ◊Decorated 1300–75, for example York Minster, and ◊Perpendicular 1400–1575, for example Winchester Cathedral. A *Gothic Revival*, imitating the medieval style, took place in the late 18th and the 19th centuries, for example the House of Commons.

gothic novel genre established by Horace Walpole's *The Castle of Otranto* 1765, and marked by mystery, violence, and horror; other exponents of the genre were Mrs ◊Radcliffe, Bram ◊Stoker, and E A ◊Poe.

Gotland /ˈgɒtlənd/ Swedish island in the Baltic Sea; area 3,160 sq km/1,220 sq mi. The capital is Visby.

Gottfried von Strassburg /ˈgɒtfriːd fɒn ˈstrɑːsbʊəg/ lived c. 1210. German poet, author of the unfinished epic *Tristan und Isolde* which inspired ◊Wagner.

Göttingen /ˈgɜːtɪŋən/ town in Lower Saxony, West Germany; population (1983) 132,700. Its university was founded by George II of England in 1734.

Gouda /'gaʊdə/ town in W Netherlands; population (1984) 60,026. It produces round flat cheeses.

Gough /gɒf/ Hubert 1870–1963. British general. He was initially blamed, as commander of the Fifth Army 1916–18, for the German breakthrough on the Somme, but his force was later admitted to have been too small for the length of the front.

Goulburn /'ɡəʊlbɜːn/ town in New South Wales, Australia; population (1983) 22,500. It is an agricultural centre, and manufactures bricks, tiles, and pottery.

Gould /guːld/ Jay 1836–1892. American financier. Born in New York, he is said to have caused a financial panic on 'Black Friday', 24 Sept 1869, through his speculations in gold.

Gounod /'ɡuːnəʊ/ Charles François 1818–1893. French composer. Born in Paris, he studied at the Conservatoire and in Rome. His first opera, *Sappho*, was produced in Paris in 1851, and was followed by *Faust* 1859, *Philêmon et Baucis/Philemon and Baucis* 1860, and *Roméo et Juliette/Romeo and Juliet* 1867. His music has great lyrical appeal and emotional power, and influenced many French composers of the later 19th century.

gourd name applied to the various members of the family Cucurbitaceae, including the melon, and pumpkin. In a narrower sense, the name applies only to the genus *Lagenaria*, of which the bottle gourd *Lagenaria siceraria* is best known.

gout disease marked by an excess of uric acid in the blood and inflammation of the joints (especially the big toe), and largely confined to older men. If it becomes chronic, it affects the kidneys: diet and drugs are used to prevent the deposit of urate crystals in the system.

government system whereby political authority is exercised.

Aristotle was the first to attempt a systematic classification of governments. His main distinctions were between government by one person, by few, and by many (monarchy, oligarchy, and democracy) although the characteristics of each may vary between states and each may degenerate into tyranny (rule by an oppressive elite in the case of oligarchy or by the mob in the case of democracy).

Later writers attempted a refinement of Aristotle's definitions, including the French philosopher ◊Montesquieu who distinguished between constitutional governments – whether monarchies or republics -which operated under various legal and other constraints, and despotism, which was not constrained in this way. A more modern distinction is between liberal democracies, totalitarian states, and autocracies. The term 'liberal democracy' was coined to distinguish Western types of democracy from the many other political systems that claimed to be 'democratic'. Its principal characteristics are the existence of more than one political party, open processes of government and political debate, and a separation of powers. Totalitarian is a more disputed term. It has been applied to both fascist and communist states and denotes a system where all power is centralized in the state, which

in turn is controlled by a single party which derives its legitimacy from an exclusive ideology. Autocracy describes a form of government that has emerged in a number of Third World countries, where state power is in the hands either of an individual or of the army; normally ideology is not a central factor, individual freedoms tend to be suppressed where they may constitute a challenge to the authority of the ruling group; and there is a reliance upon force.

Other useful distinctions are between federal governments (where important powers are dispersed among various regions which in certain respects are self-governing) and unitary governments (where powers are concentrated in a central authority); and between presidential (where the head of state is also the directly elected head of government, not part of the legislature) and parliamentary systems (where the government is drawn from an elected legislature which can dismiss it).

Government Communications Headquarters centre of the British Government's electronic surveillance operations, popularly known as ◊GCHQ.

governor in engineering, a device that controls the speed of a machine or engine. James ◊Watt invented the steam-engine governor in 1788. It works by means of heavy balls, which rotate on the end of linkages and move in or out because of ◊centrifugal force according to the speed of rotation. The movement of the balls closes or opens the steam valve to the engine. When the engine speed increases too much, the balls fly out, and cause the steam valve to close, so the engine slows down. The opposite happens when the engine speed drops too much.

Gower /'ɡaʊə/ John c. 1330–1408. English poet. Born in Kent, friend of Chaucer, remembered for his tales of love *Confessio Amantis* 1390 written in English, and other poems in French and Latin. He is buried in Southwark Cathedral.

Gower Peninsula /'ɡaʊə/ peninsula in West ◊Glamorgan, S Wales.

Gowon /ɡəʊ'ɒn/ Yakubu 1934– . Nigerian statesman. Educated at Sandhurst, he became chief of staff and in the military coup of 1966 became head of state. After the Biafran civil war 1967–70, he reunited the country with his policy of 'no victor, no vanquished'. In 1975 he was overthrown by a military coup.

Goya y Lucientes /'ɡɔɪə iː ˌluːsi'entes/ Francisco José de 1746–1828. Spanish artist, born in Aragon, who was for a time a bullfighter, the subject of some of his etchings. After studying in Italy, he returned to Spain, was employed on a number of paintings for the royal tapestry factory and from 1786 he was court painter to Charles IV. His later works include portraits of four successive kings of Spain, other great personages and his etchings include *The Disasters of War*, depicting the French invasion of Spain 1808–14.

GPU former name for ◊KGB, the Russian secret police.

Graaf /ɡrɑːf/ Regnier de 1641–1673. Dutch physician at Delft, who wrote a treatise in 1663 on the pancreatic secretions, and in 1672

discovered the *Graafian follicles* of the female ovary which contain the developing egg.

Gracchus /'ɡrækəs/ the brothers *Tiberius Sempronius* 163–133 BC and *Gaius Sempronius* 153–121 BC. Roman agrarian reformers. As ◊tribune in 133 BC, Tiberius tried to prevent the ruin of small farmers by making large slave-labour farms illegal, but was murdered. Gaius, tribune in 123 and 122 BC, revived his brother's legislation, and introduced other reforms, but was outlawed by the Senate and committed suicide.

Grace /ɡreɪs/ W(illiam) G(ilbert) 1848–1915. British cricketer and physician. Born in Downend, Gloucestershire, he began playing in first-class matches at 15, and helped to establish cricket as England's national game. In 1871 he scored 2,739 runs in the season, and by 1908, when his career as a first-class cricketer ended, he had scored over 54,000 runs.

Grace The British cricketer W G Grace, who helped establish cricket as England's national sport. His cricketing career spanned 60 years.

Graces in Greek mythology, three goddesses (Aglaia, Euphrosyne, and Thalia), daughters of Zeus and Hera, the personification of grace and beauty and the inspirers of the arts and the sciences.

grafting the operation by which a piece of living tissue is removed from one organism and transplanted into the same or a different organism where it continues growing.

In horticulture, it is a technique widely used for propagating plants, especially woody species. A bud or shoot on one plant, termed the scion, is inserted into another, the stock, so that they continue growing together, the tissues combining at the point of union. Grafting is usually only successful between species that are closely related and is most commonly practised on roses and fruit trees. Grafting of non-woody species is more difficult but sometimes used to propagate tomatoes, and cacti. See also ◊transplant.

grafting

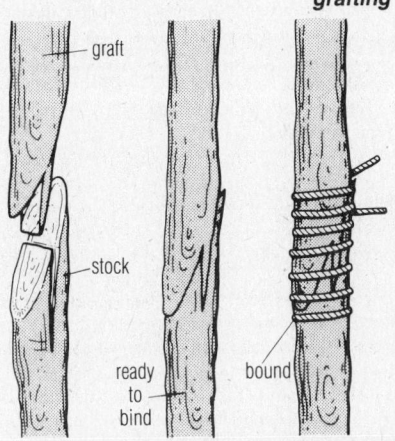

graft

stock

ready to bind

bound

Grafton /ˈgrɑːftən/ town in New South Wales, Australia; population (1985) 17,600. It is a sugar and dairy farming centre.

Grafton /ˈgrɑːftən/ Augustus Henry, 3rd Duke of Grafton 1735–1811. British politician. Grandson of the first duke, who was the son of Charles II and Barbara Villiers (1641–1709), Duchess of Cleveland. He became First Lord of the Treasury in 1766 and acting prime minister 1767–70.

Graham /ˈgreɪəm/ Billy 1918– . American evangelist. Of Scottish-Irish parents, he was brought up in N Carolina, and at 17 was converted at a revival. His Evangelistic Association conducts worldwide 'crusades'.

Graham /ˈgreɪəm/ Martha 1894– . American choreographer. An innovative exponent of American modern dance, she had a major influence on choreographers such as Robert Cohan, Glen Tetley, Norman Morrice, Paul Taylor and Robert North. She has created over 150 ballets, including *Appalachian Spring* 1944 (score by Aaron Copland) and *Clytemnestra* 1958 (music by Halim El-Dabh), the first full-length modern dance work.

Graham /ˈgreɪəm/ Thomas 1805–1869. Scottish chemist, who by his work on the diffusion of gases and liquids laid the foundations of physical chemistry (the branch of chemistry concerned with changes in energy during a chemical transformation). *Graham's Law* states that the diffusion rate of two gases varies inversely as the square root of their density. His work on colloids was equally fundamental: he discovered the principle of ◊dialysis, that colloids can be separated from solutions containing smaller molecules by the differing rates at which they pass through a semi-permeable membrane (a process he termed ◊osmosis).

Grahame /ˈgreɪəm/ Kenneth 1859–1932. British author. Born in Edinburgh, son of a lawyer, he worked at the Bank of England

Graham Thomas Graham, one of the founders of physical chemistry and formulator of Graham's Law on the diffusion of gases. He also worked on alcoholates and was the first to suggest adding poison to alcohol that was not intended for consumption to prevent unauthorized drinking.

1878–1908. The early volumes of sketches of childhood, *The Golden Age* 1895 and *Dream Days* 1898, were followed by his masterpiece *The Wind in the Willows* 1908, an animal fantasy originally created for his young son which was dramatized by A A Milne as *Toad of Toad Hall*.

Graham Land /ˈgreɪəm/ mountainous peninsula in Antarctica, formerly a dependency of the ◊Falkland Islands, and from 1962 part of the ◊British Antarctic Territory. It was discovered by John Biscoe in 1832, and until 1934 was thought to be an archipelago.

Grahamstown /ˈgreɪəmztaʊn/ town in Cape Province, South Africa; population (1985) 75,000. It has two bishops, Anglican and Roman Catholic, and is the seat of Rhodes University, founded in 1904 as Rhodes University College.

Grail, Holy in Christian legend, the dish or cup used by Christ at the Last Supper, which, together with the spear with which he was wounded at the Crucifixion, appears as an object of quest by King Arthur's knights in certain stories incorporated in the Arthurian legend. According to one story, the blood of Christ was collected in it by ◊Joseph of Arimathea at the Crucifixion, and he brought it to Britain.

Grainger /ˈgreɪndʒə/ Percy Aldridge 1882–1961. Australian composer. Born in Melbourne, he was a concert pianist and is remembered for a number of songs and short

instrumental pieces drawing on folk idioms, particularly *Country Gardens* 1925.

gram metric unit of weight; one thousandth of a ◊kilogram.

grammar as an aspect of language and the study of language, grammar has traditionally been seen as dealing with the rules of combining words into phrases and clauses, phrases and clauses into sentences, and sentences into paragraphs. In this view, 'good grammar' is the result of an adequate education in one or more classical language, in the mother tongue, in one or more foreign languages, or a combination of these. As a consequence, people with 'bad grammar' have tended to be seen as uneducated, poorly educated, inattentive while being educated, and/or inclined toward sloppy thinking and slovenly style. This widespread view has emerged out of 2,500 years of educational procedures and social attitudes relative to the classical Greek *grammatike tekhne* ('art of letters').

This original 'grammar' was an analytical approach to writing, intended to improve the understanding and the skills of scribes, philosophers and litterateurs. Because of a traditional emphasis on writing and (since the 15th century) on the standardizing impact of print, spoken or colloquial language has often been perceived as less grammatical than written - especially literary - language. In addition, when compared with Latin, English has also been widely regarded as having 'less' grammar or at least a simpler grammar; it would be truer, however, to say that English and Latin have *different* grammars, each complex in its own way.

In linguistics, the contemporary study of language, grammar or syntax is generally understood to refer to the arrangement of the elements in a language, for the purposes of acceptable communication in speech, writing and print. All forms of a language, standard or otherwise, have their grammars or grammatical systems, which children acquire as they mature; a child may acquire several overlapping systems within one language (especially a non-standard form for everyday life and a standard form linked with writing, school and national life). Not even the most comprehensive grammar book (or grammar) of a language like English, French, Arabic or Japanese completely covers or fixes the implicit grammatical system that people use in their daily lives. The rules and tendencies of natural grammar operate largely in non-conscious ways, but can, for many social and professional purposes, be studied and explicitly developed as conscious as well as inherent skills. See also ◊parts of speech.

Recent theories of the way language functions include ◊*phrase structure grammar*, ◊*transformational grammar*, and ◊*case grammar*.

grammar school in the UK, a secondary school catering for children of high academic ability, usually measured by the ◊Eleven Plus examination. Most grammar schools have now been replaced by ◊comprehensive schools. In the USA the term is sometimes used for a primary school (also called elementary school).

gramophone an old-fashioned English name for what is now called a ◊record player. Inventor Thomas ◊Edison's original name for the machine, and the traditional US name, was *phonograph*.

Grampian /'græmpiən/ region of Scotland
area 8,702 sq km/3,359 sq mi
towns administrative headquarters Aberdeen
features part of the Grampian Mountains (the Cairngorms); valley of the river Spey, with its whisky distilleries; Balmoral Castle (royal residence); Braemar Highland Games in Aug
products beef cattle (Aberdeen Angus and Beef Shorthorn); fishing, including salmon; North Sea oil service industries; tourism is important, with winter skiing
population (1984) 497,272.

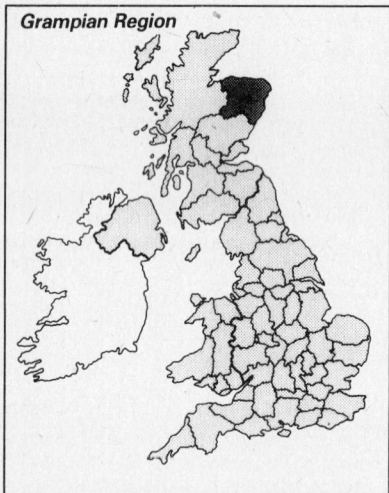

Grampian Region

Grampian Mountains /'græmpiən/ a range which separates the Highlands from the Lowlands of Scotland, running NE from Strathclyde. It takes in the S Highland region (which includes *Ben Nevis*, the highest mountain in the British Isles at 1,340 m/4,406 ft), northern Tayside, and the S border of Grampian region itself, the Cairngorms, which include *Ben Macdhui* 1,309 m/4,296 ft. The region includes Aviemore, Britain's first complete winter holiday and sports centre, and the Highland Wildlife Park at Kincraig.

Grampians /'græmpiənz/ western end of Australia's eastern highlands, in Victoria; the highest peak is Mount William 1,167 m/3,829 ft.

grampus another name for the killer ◊whale.

Gramsci /'græmʃi/ Antonio 1891–1937. Italian Marxist theorist, who attempted to unify social theory and political practice. He helped to found the Italian Communist party in 1921, and was elected to parliament in 1924, but was imprisoned by Mussolini in 1926 and spent the rest of his life in prison. His *Prison Notebooks* argued that politics and ideology were independent of the economic base, that no ruling class could dominate by economic factors alone, and that the working class could achieve liberation by political and intellectual struggle.

His concept of *hegemony* argued that real class control in capitalist societies is ideological and cultural rather than physical, and that only the working class 'educated' by radical intellectuals could see through and overthrow such bourgeois propaganda. His humane and gradualist approach to Marxism, particularly his emphasis on the need to overthrow bourgeois ideology, influenced European Marxists in their attempt to distance themselves from orthodox determinist Soviet Communism.

Granada /grə'nɑːdə/ city in Andalucia, Spain; population (1981) 246,500.
history founded by the ◊Moors high in the Sierra Nevada in the 8th century, it became the capital of an independent kingdom 1236–1492, when it was the last Moorish stronghold to surrender to the Spaniards. ◊Ferdinand and ◊Isabella, the first sovereigns of a united Spain, are buried in the cathedral (built 1529–1703). The *Alhambra*, a fortified hilltop palace, was built in the 13th–14th centuries by the Moorish kings.

Granada /grə'nɑːdə/ city in Nicaragua; population (1980) 42,500. It has shipyards, and manufactures sugar, soap, clothing and furniture. Founded in 1523, it is the oldest city in Nicaragua.

Granados /grə'nɑːdɒs/ Enrique 1867–1916. Spanish composer-pianist. His piano-work *Goyescas* 1911, inspired by the work of Goya, was converted to an opera in 1916.

Granby /'grænbi/ John Manners, Marquess of Granby 1721–1770. British soldier. His head appears on many inn-signs in England as a result of his popularity as a commander of the British forces fighting in Europe in the ◊Seven Years' War.

Gran Chaco /græn 'tʃɑːkəu/ large plain in Argentina, Paraguay, and Bolivia. It consists mainly of swamps and forests, a source of ◊quebracho timber.

Grand Banks /'grænd 'bæŋks/ continental shelf of the N Atlantic off SE Newfoundland, where the shallow waters are rich fisheries, especially for cod.

Grand Canal (Chinese Da Yunhe /'dɑː jʊn'hɜː/) the world's longest canal. It is 1,600 km/1,000 mi long, 30–61 m/100–200 ft wide, and 0.6–4.6 m/2–15 ft deep, and runs N from Hangzhou to Tianjin, China. The earliest section was completed in 486 BC, and ◊Kublai Khan built the northern section 1282–92 AD.

Grand Canyon /'grænd 'kænjən/ vast gorge in ◊Arizona, USA. It is 6–29 km/4–18 mi in width, it reaches depths of over 1.5 km/1 mi, and is 350 km/217 mi long. It was made a national park in 1919. The Colorado river flows between its cliffs of multi-coloured rock.

Grand Design in history, a plan attributed to the French statesman ◊Sully to ◊Henry IV of France, and rendered abortive by his assassination, for a great Protestant Union against the Holy Roman Empire; the term was also applied to President de Gaulle's vision of France's place in a united Europe.

Grande Dixence dam /grɒnd diːk'sɒns/ the world's highest dam, located in Switzerland, which measures 285 m/935 ft from base to crest.

Completed in 1961, it contains 6 million cu m/nearly 8 million cu yds of concrete.

Grand Falls /'grænd 'fɔːlz/ town in Newfoundland, Canada; population (1976) 8,800. It is the site of large paper and pulp mills.

Grand Guignol /'grɒŋ 'giːnjɒl/ genre of short horror play produced at the Grand Guignol theatre in Montmartre, Paris (called after the bloodthirsty character 'Guignol' in late 18th-century marionette plays).

Grand National the name given to several famous steeplechases, the most famous being run at Aintree, Merseyside during the Liverpool meeting in Mar or Apr over 7 km 242 m/4 mi 880 yards with 30 formidable jumps. It was first run in 1839.

Grand Rapids /'grænd 'ræpɪdz/ city in Michigan, USA; population (1980) 182,000. It produces furniture, motor bodies, plumbing fixtures, and electrical goods.

Grand Remonstrance petition passed by the English parliament in Nov 1631 which listed all the alleged misdeeds of Charles I and demanded parliamentary approval for the king's ministers and the reform of the Church. Charles refused to accept the Grand Remonstrance and countered it by trying to arrest five leading members of the House of Commons (Pym, Hampden, Holles, Hesilrige, and Strode). The worsening of relations between king and Parliament led to the outbreak of the English Civil War in 1642.

granite a plutonic ◊igneous rock, acidic in composition, that is, containing a high proportion of silica, SiO_2, occurring in large-scale intrusions. The rock is coarse-grained, the characteristic minerals being quartz, feldspars, particularly orthoclase, and mica. It often comprises the core of a range of mountains, the surrounding rocks having been metamorphosed by the heat of the intrusion. Granite may be pink or grey, depending on the composition and hence the colour of the feldspars. Orthoclase gives a pink granite, whereas albite and anorthite give a grey granite. Granitic areas produce a very characteristic scenery type, consisting of rounded blocks that appear to have been stacked one upon another on exposed hillsides. This is the result of weathering along regular cracks or joints in the solid rock. See ◊feldspar.

Grant /grɑːnt/ Cary 1904–1986. Stage-name of Anglo-American actor Archibald Leach, born in Bristol (US citizen in 1942). His first stage appearances were as an acrobat and juggler. His screen personality as the witty, debonair man made him a favourite for more than three decades. Films include *Bringing Up Baby* 1937, *The Philadelphia Story* 1940, *Arsenic and Old Lace* 1944, *Notorious* 1946, and *North by Northwest* 1959.

Grant /grɑːnt/ Duncan 1885–1978. Scottish painter. A member of the ◊Bloomsbury group which included Roger ◊Fry and ◊Virginia Woolf and Vanessa ◊Bell. Later works, such as *Snow Scene* 1921, showed the influence of the ◊Post-impressionists, especially Cézanne.

Grant /grɑːnt/ Ulysses Simpson 1822–1885. American general and 18th president of the USA. The son of an Ohio farmer, he had an unsuccessful career in the army 1839–54 and in

Grant Born in England, Cary Grant went to the USA in 1921 to make a career in films. His screen personality was that of the witty, debonair man, an image that made him an enduring favourite for more than 30 years.

business, and on the outbreak of the Civil War received a commission on the Mississippi front. He took command there in 1862, and by his capture of Vicksburg in 1863 brought the whole Mississippi front under Northern control. Appointed commander-in-chief in 1864, he slowly wore down ◊Lee's resistance, and in 1865 received his surrender at Appomattox. He was elected President in 1868 and 1872, and carried through a liberal ◊reconstruction policy in the south, although he failed in his attempts to suppress political corruption.

Grantham /'grænθəm/ market town in SE Lincolnshire, England; population (1981) 30,084. It is an agricultural centre, dating from Saxon times. Margaret ◊Thatcher was born here.

Gran Vilaya /'græn vɪ 'laɪə/ 'lost city' of a 9th-century South American civilization which came under ◊Inca domination in the 15th century. It lies 2,620 m/8,600 ft above sea level, in the Peruvian Andes, 485 km/300 mi N of Lima. It is built of stone with striking pyramids.

Granville-Barker /'grænvɪl 'bɑːkə/ Harley 1877–1946. British theatre director and author. Although he wrote plays including *The Madras House* 1910 and *Waste* 1907, his major contribution was to the development of British theatre as director-manager with J E Vedrenne at the Royal Court Theatre from 1904–18, directing plays by Shaw, Yeats, Ibsen, Galsworthy, and Masefield.

graph method of showing the mathematical relationship between two or more variables by drawing a diagram. There are often two axes or ◊coordinates at right-angles intersecting at the origin – the zero point from which values of the variables (say they are distance and time for a moving object) are assigned along the axes. Pairs of simultaneous values (the distance moved after a particular elapsed time) are plotted as points in

Grant General Ulysses Simpson Grant, photographed in Jun 1864 at City Point – his headquarters during the American Civil War.

the area between the axes, and the points then joined by a smooth curve to produce a graph.

graphics tablet in computing, also known as a bit pad, an input device consisting of a pressure-sensitive tablet on which marks can be made with a stylus. The position of any mark is automatically identified and communicated to a computer for interpretation. A graphics tablet is often used with a form overlaid for users to tick boxes in positions that each relate to specific registers in the computer, but some recent development in handwriting recognition may increase its versatility in the future.

graphite a blackish-grey laminar crystalline form of ◊carbon, also known as ◊plumbago or ◊black lead. The carbon atoms are strongly bonded together in sheets, but the bonds between the sheets are weak and so the sheets are free to slide over one another. It is widely used as a lubricant and as the active component of pencil lead. It has a very high melting point (3,500°C) which gives it mechanical strength and makes it a good conductor of heat and electricity. In its very pure form it is used as a moderator in nuclear reactors.

Grasmere /'grɑːsmɪə/ English lake and village in the Lake District, Cumbria. William ◊Wordsworth lived at Dove Cottage (now a Wordsworth Museum) 1799–1808, Thomas ◊de Quincey later made his home in the same house, and both Samuel Taylor ◊Coleridge and Wordsworth are buried here.

grass plant of the large family, Gramineae, of monocotyledons with about 9,000 species distributed worldwide except in the Arctic regions. The majority are perennial, with long and narrow leaves, hollow stems, and hermaphroditic flowers borne in spikelets. Usually the growing point remains close to the ground, growth continuing when the grass is grazed. They are well represented in Britain, many being economically important.

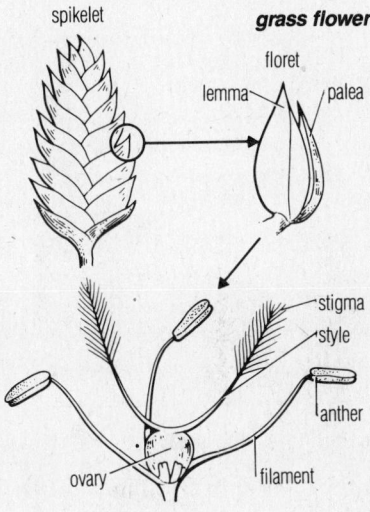

Grass /grɑːs/ Günter 1927– . German writer. Born in Danzig, he studied at the art academies of Düsseldorf and Berlin, worked as a writer and sculptor, first in Paris and later in Berlin, and in 1958 won the coveted 'Group 47' prize. The grotesque humour of his novel *Die Blechtrommel/The Tin Drum* 1963 characterizes many of his poems. His political stance is socialist.

Grasse /grɑːs/ town near Cannes, SE France; population (1982) 38,360. It is the centre of a perfume-manufacturing region, and flowers are grown on a large scale for this purpose.

grasshopper insect of the order Orthoptera, usually with strongly developed hind legs which enables it to leap. The *short-horned grasshoppers* Acrididae include the locust, and all members of the family feed voraciously on vegetation. The femur of each hind leg in the male usually has a row of protruding joints which produce the characteristic chirping when rubbed against the hard wing veins. Eggs are laid in a small hole in the ground, and the unwinged larvae become adult after about six moults. There are several sober-coloured, small and harmless species in Britain. The *long-horned grasshoppers* or *bush crickets* Tettigoniidae have a similar life-history, but differ from the Acrididae in having long antennae, and in producing their chirping by the friction of the wing covers over one another (stridulation). The *great green bush cricket* *Tettigonia viridissima* 5 cm/2 in long, is a British species of this family, which also comprises the North American katydids, notable stridulators.

---

grass flower (diagram labels: spikelet, floret, lemma, palea, stigma, style, anther, filament, ovary)

grass of Parnassus flower *Parnassia palustris* unrelated to grasses, growing in marshes and on wet moors in Europe and Asia. Low-growing, with a rosette of heart-shaped stalked leaves, it has five white petals with conspicuous veins, the flowers growing singly on stem tips in late summer.

grass-tree Australian plant of the genus *Xanthorrhoea*. The tall, thick stems have a grass-like tuft at the top, and are surmounted by a flower-spike resembling a spear.

grass-tree The characteristic tufts of the Australian grass-tree.

Grattan /'grætn/ Henry 1746–1820. Irish politician. He entered the Irish parliament in 1775. As leader of the opposition he secured the abolition of all claims by the British parliament to legislate for Ireland in 1782, but failed to prevent the Act of Union, and sat in the British parliament from 1805.

gravel mineral consisting of pebbles or small fragments of rock, originating in the beds of lakes and streams or on beaches. Gravel is commonly obtained from quarries known as gravel pits (where it is often found mixed with sand or clay) and is used to build roads, make tarmac, ballast railway lines and as an aggregate in concrete. Some gravel deposits also contain metal ores (particularly tin) or free metals (such as gold and silver).

Graves /greɪvz/ Robert Ranke 1895–1985. English poet and author. Born in London, he was severely wounded on the Somme in World War I and his frank autobiography *Goodbye to All That* 1929 is one of the outstanding war books. His first book of verse was *Over the Brazier* 1916 and other volumes followed, including *Collected Poems* 1959. Of particular note are his historical novels of Imperial Rome, *I Claudius* and *Claudius the God* 1934. He also wrote books on myth, for example *The White Goddess* 1948. He was professor of poetry at Oxford 1961–66. He lived on Majorca from 1946 until his death.

Graves Robert Graves came to prominence as the author of World War I poems and a memoir, *Goodbye to All That.*

Gravesend /ˌgreɪvz'end/ town on the Thames, Kent, England, linked by ferry with Tilbury opposite; population (1981) 52,963.

gravimetry the study of the Earth's gravitational field. Small variations in the gravitional field can be caused by varying densities of rocks and structure beneath the surface (see ◊Bouguer anomaly). These variations can provide information about inaccessible subsurface conditions.

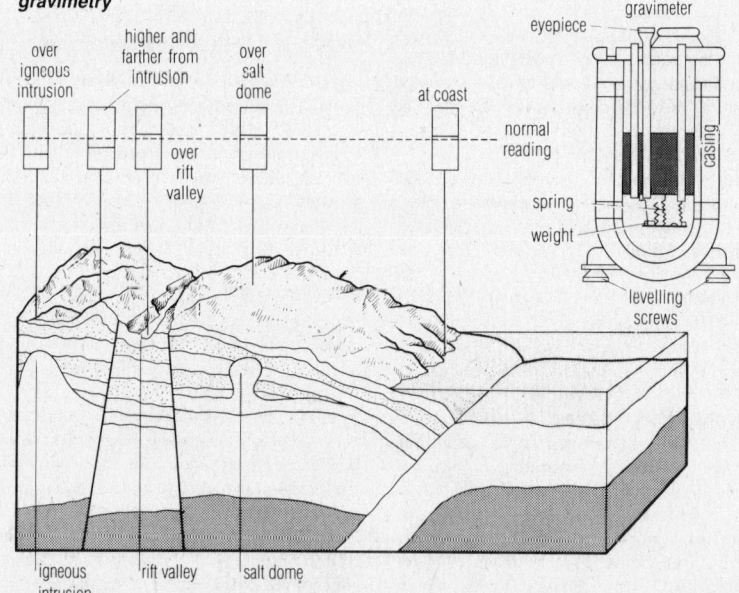

gravimetry

gravity the force of attraction between two objects because of their masses; for instance, the force we call gravity on Earth is the force of attraction between any object in the Earth's gravitational field and the Earth itself. According to Newton's law of gravitation (relativity), for an object of mass m at a distance d from the centre of the Earth (mass M), the force of gravity F equals GmM/d^2, where G is the gravitational constant. According to Newton's second law of motion, F also equals mg, where g is the acceleration due to gravity. Therefore $g = GM/d^2$ and is independent of the mass of the object; at the Earth's surface it equals 9.806 m s^2-2 (metres per second per second). In other words, all objects fall to Earth with the same acceleration, regardless of mass.

The general theory of relativity treats gravitation not as a force but as a curvature of space and time around a body. Relativity predicts the bending of light and the ◊redshift of light in a gravitational field; both have been observed. Another prediction of relativity is *gravitational waves*, which should be produced when massive bodies are violently disturbed. These waves are so weak that they have not yet been detected with certainty, although observations of a ◊pulsar (emits energy at regular intervals) in orbit around another star have shown that the stars are spiralling together at the rate that would be expected if they were losing energy in the form of gravitational waves. See also gravitational ◊lens.

gravure one of the three main ◊printing methods, in which printing is done from a recessed surface. It is an intaglio method. It is an economical process for high-volume printing and reproduces illustrations well.

gray the derived SI unit of absorbed radiation dose (Gy). It is defined as the dose absorbed when the energy per unit mass imparted to matter by ionizing radiation is 1 joule/kg.

Gray /greɪ/ Thomas 1716–1761. English poet. A close friend of Horace ◊Walpole at Eton, he made a continental tour with him 1739–41, which he cut short when they quarrelled; an account of the tour is given in his vivid letters. In 1748 his first poems appeared anonymously in Dodsley's *Miscellany*. His 'Elegy Written in a

Country Churchyard' (written, according to tradition, at Stoke Poges) 1750 is one of the most quoted poems in the language. Others include the 'Ode on a Distant Prospect of Eton College', 'The Progress of Poesy', and 'The Bard'. Found by critics, such as Johnson, to be obscure, these poems are now seen as precursors of ◊Romanticism.

grayling freshwater fish *Thymallus thymallus* of the family Salmonidae. It is found locally in England and has been introduced into Scotland. It exhibits a coloration shading from purple to pink, and may be distinguished by its long dorsal fin.

Graz /grɑːts/ city, capital of Styria province, Austria: population (1981) 243,401. Industries include chemicals, iron and steel. It has a 15th-century cathedral and a university founded in 1573.

Graziani /ˌgrætsiˈɑːni/ Rodolfo 1882–1955. Italian general. He was general-in-chief of Italian forces in N Africa during World War II, but was defeated by ◊Wavell 1940, and subsequently superseded. Later, as defence minister in the new Mussolini government, he failed to reorganize a Republican Fascist army, was captured by the Allies 1945, tried by an Italian military court, and finally released in 1950.

Great Australian Bight broad bay in S Australia, notorious for storms.

Great Barrier Reef chain of coral reefs and islands about 2,000 km/1,250 mi long, at a distance of 15–45 km/10–30 mi from the E coast of ◊Queensland, Australia. It forms an immense natural breakwater, and is rich in wildlife.

Great Barrier Reef A collection of variously formed corals and shells from the reef.

Great Bear popular name for the constellation ◊Ursa Major.

Great Britain official name from 1603 for ◊England, ◊Scotland, and ◊Wales, and the adjacent islands, when the English and Scottish crowns were united in the person of ◊James VI of Scotland, I of England. With ◊Northern Ireland it forms the ◊United Kingdom.

great circle a plane cutting through a sphere, and passing through the centre point of the sphere, cuts the surface along a great circle. Thus, on the Earth, all meridians of longitude are half great circles; of the parallels of latitude, only the equator is a great circle. The shortest route between two points on the Earth's surface is along the arc of a great circle, and these are used extensively in air routes (although on maps, due to vagaries of their projection, they are not straight lines).

great dane large, usually fawn, dog, formerly used for hunting boar and stags. The minimum height for a dog is 75 cm/2.5 ft, bitches a little smaller.

Great Divide or *Great Dividing Range*. Mountain range in Australia, extending 3,700 km/2,300 mi from Cape York Peninsula, Queensland, to Victoria. It includes the Carnarvon Range, Queensland, which has many Aboriginal cave paintings, the Blue Mountains in New South Wales, and the Australian Alps.

Greater London Council (GLC) in the UK, local authority that governed London 1965–86. It was established under the London Government Act 1963, and not only took over the administration of what was then the London County Council area, but also incorporated almost all of Middlesex and parts of Surrey, Kent, Essex, and Hertfordshire. It came into force on 1 Apr 1965. The existing 85 local authorities in the area covered by the new GLC were merged into 32 boroughs (excluding the City of London, which remained independent). The Labour Party had a majority of seats on the council after the 1964, 1973, and 1981 elections; the Conservative Party had a majority after the 1967, 1970, and 1977 elections. When the GLC was abolished in 1986 (see under ◊local government) its powers either devolved back to the borough councils or were transferred to certain non-elected bodies.

Great Lake Australia's largest freshwater lake, 1,025 m/3,380 ft above sea level, in Tasmania; area 114 sq km/44 sq mi. It is used for hydroelectric power and is a tourist attraction.

Great Lakes series of five freshwater lakes along the USA–Canada border, comprising Lakes Superior, Michigan, Huron, Erie, and Ontario; area 245,000 sq km/94,600 sq mi. By means of interconnecting canals they are navigable by large ships. The lakes are drained by the ◊Saint Lawrence River.

Great Leap Forward the change in Chinese economic policy introduced under the second five-year plan of 1958–62. The basic idea, instigated by Mao Zedong (Mao Tse-Tung) was to convert China into an industrially based economy by transferring resources away from agriculture. This coincided with the creating of people's communes but the inefficient and poorly planned allocation of state resources led to the effective collapse of the strategy by 1960 and a return to more adequate support for agricultural production.

Great Rift Valley longest 'split' in the Earth's surface, 8,000 km/5,000 mi, running S from the Dead Sea (Israel/Jordan) to Mozambique.

Great Sandy Desert desert in northern Western Australia; area 415,000 sq km/160,000 sq mi.

Great Schism period 1378–1417 in which there were rival popes at Rome and Avignon; it was ended by the election of ◊Martin V during the Council of Constance 1414–17.

Great Wall of China continuous defensive wall stretching from W Gansu to the Gulf of Liaodong (2,250 km/1,450 mi), though surveys in remote areas show it once to have been even longer. It was built under the Ch'in dynasty from 214 BC to prevent incursions by the Turkish and Mongol tribesmen. Some 8 m/25 ft high, it consits of a brick-faced wall of earth and stone, has a series of square watch towers, and has been carefully restored.

Great Yarmouth alternative name for the resort and port of ◊Yarmouth in Norfolk, England.

Greco, El /'grekəʊ/ 1541–1614. Spanish artist, Doménico Theotocopuli 1541–1614, called 'the Greek' because he was born in Crete. He studied under ◊Titian, and finally settled in Toledo c. 1575. Paintings such as *The Burial of Count Orgaz* and *The Agony in the Garden* illustrate his use of intense colours and exaggeratedly elongated forms.

Greece /griːs/ country in SE Europe, comprising the S Balkan peninsula, bounded north by Yugoslavia and Bulgaria, northeast by Turkey, east by the Aegean Sea, south by the Mediterranean Sea, west by the Ionian Sea, and northwest by Albania, and numerous islands to the south and east.

government the 1975 constitution provides for a parliamentary system of government, with a president, who is head of state, a prime minister, who is head of government, and a single-chamber parliament. The president, elected by parliament for a five-year term, appoints the prime minister and cabinet. Parliament has 300 members, all elected by universal suffrage for a four-year term, and the prime minister and cabinet are collectively responsible to it. Bills passed by parliament must be ratified by the president, whose veto can be overridden by an absolute majority of the total number of members. The two main political parties are the Panhellenic Socialist Movement (PASOK), and the New Democracy Party (ND).

history for ancient history, see ◊Greece, ancient. Except for the years 1686–1715, when the Morea was occupied by the Venetians, Greece remained Turkish until the outbreak of the War of Independence in 1821. British, French, and Russian intervention in 1827, which brought about the destruction of the Turkish fleet at Navarino, led to the establishment of Greek independence 1829. Prince Otto of Bavaria was placed on the throne 1832; his despotic rule provoked a rebellion 1843, which set up a parliamentary government, and another 1862, when he was deposed and replaced by Prince George of Denmark. Relations with Turkey were embittered by the Greeks' desire to recover Macedonia, Crete, and other Turkish territories with Greek populations. A war in 1897 ended in disaster, but the ◊Balkan Wars 1912–13 won most of the disputed areas for Greece.

In a period of internal conflict from 1914, two monarchs were deposed, and there was a republic 1923–25, when a military coup restored ◊George

II, who in the following year established a dictatorship under Joannis ◊Metaxas.

An Italian invasion in 1940 was successfully resisted, but an intensive attack by Germany in 1941 overwhelmed the Greeks. During the German occupation of Greece 1941–44, a communist-dominated resistance movement armed and trained a guerrilla army, and after World War II the National Liberation Front, as it was called, wanted to create a socialist state. If the Greek royalist army had not had massive assistance from the USA, this undoubtedly would have happened. As it was, the monarchy, in the shape of King Paul, was re-established, and in 1964 he was succeeded by his son, Constantine. Dissatisfaction with the government and conflicts between the king and his ministers resulted in a coup in 1967, replacing the monarchy with a new regime, which, despite its democratic pretensions, was little more than a military dictatorship, with Col George Papadopoulos as its head. All political activity was banned and opponents of the government forced out of public life.

In 1973 Greece declared itself a republic and Papadopoulos became president. A civilian cabinet was appointed but before the year was out another coup brought Lieut-Gen Phaidon Ghizikis to the presidency, with Adamantios Androutsopoulos as prime minister. The government's failure to prevent the Turkish invasion of Cyprus led to its downfall and a former prime minister, Constantine Karamanlis, was recalled from exile to form a new Government of National Salvation. He immediately ended martial law, press censorship, and the ban on political parties, and in the 1974 general election his New Democracy Party (ND) won a decisive majority in parliament.

A referendum the same year rejected the return of the monarchy and in 1975 a new constitution for a democratic 'Hellenic Republic' was adopted, with Constantine Tsatsos as president. ND won the 1977 general election with a reduced majority and in 1980 Karamanlis resigned as prime minister and was elected president.

The following year Greece became a full member of the EEC, having been an associate since 1962. Meanwhile, the ND was faced with a growing challenge from the Panhellenic Socialist Movement (PASOK), which won an absolute majority in parliament in the 1981 general election. Its leader, Andreas Papandreou, became Greece's first socialist prime minister.

PASOK had been elected on a radical socialist platform, which included withdrawal from the EEC, the removal of US military bases, and a programme of domestic reform. Important social changes, such as lowering the voting age to 18, the legalization of civil marriage and divorce, and an overhaul of the universities and the army, were carried out, but instead of withdrawing from Europe, Papandreou was content to obtain a modification of the terms of entry, and, rather than close US bases, he signed a five-year agreement on defence and economic cooperation. In 1983 he also signed a ten-year

economic cooperation agreement with the USSR.

Despite introducing austerity measures to deal with rising inflation, PASOK won a comfortable majority in the 1985 elections. In 1986 the constitution was amended, limiting the powers of the president in relation to those of the prime minister.

Greece

HELLENIC REPUBLIC (*Elliniki Dimokratia*)

AREA 131,944 sq km/50,944 sq mi
CAPITAL Athens
TOWNS ports Thessaloniki, Patras, Larisa, Heraklion
PHYSICAL mountainous; a large number of islands, notably Crete, Corfu and Rhodes
FEATURES Corinth canal; Mount Olympus; archaeological sites; there are US military bases at Hellenikon, Nea Makri (both near Athens), and (on Crete) at Souda Bay near Iraklion
HEAD OF STATE Christos Sartzetakis from 1985
HEAD OF GOVERNMENT Andreas Papandreou from 1981
GOVERNMENT parliamentary democracy
EXPORTS tobacco, fruit (including currants) and vegetables, olives and olive oil, textiles
CURRENCY drachma (228.52 = £1 Sept 1987)
POPULATION 9,921,000 (1985); annual growth rate 0.6%
LANGUAGE Greek
RELIGION Greek Orthodox Christian 97%
LITERACY 96% male/89% female (1985)
GNP $32.4 bn (1984); $3,260 per head of population
CHRONOLOGY
1946 Civil war broke out between royalists and communists. Communists defeated.
1949 Monarchy re-established with Paul as king.
1964 King Paul succeeded by his son Constantine.
1967 Army coup removed the king and Col George Papadopoulos became prime minister. Martial law imposed and all political activity banned.

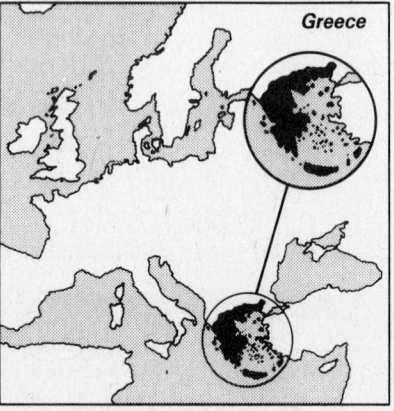

Greece

compelled them to take to the sea. During the years 750–550 BC the Greeks not only became great traders, but founded colonies around the coasts of the Mediterranean and the Black Sea, in Asia Minor, Sicily, S Italy, S France, Spain, and N Africa. The main centres of Greek culture in the 6th century BC were the wealthy Ionian ports of Asia Minor, where Greek philosophy,

1973 Republic proclaimed, with Papadopoulos as president.
1974 Former premier Constantine Karamanlis recalled from exile to lead government. Martial law and ban on political parties lifted. Restoration of the monarchy rejected by a referendum.
1975 New constitution adopted, making Greece a republic.
1980 Karamanlis resigned as prime minister and was elected president.
1981 Greece became a full member of the EEC. Andreas Papandreou elected Greece's first socialist prime minister.
1983 Five-year defence and economic cooperation agreement signed with the USA. Ten-year economic cooperation agreement signed with USSR.
1985 Papandreou re-elected.

Greece, ancient the first Greek civilization, that known as Mycenaean (fl. c. 1600–1200 BC) owed much to the Minoan civilization of Crete, and may have been produced by the intermarriage of Greek-speaking invaders with the original inhabitants. From the 14th century BC a new wave of invasions began. The Achaeans overran Greece and Crete, destroying the Minoan and Mycenaean civilizations, and penetrated Asia Minor; to this period belongs the siege of Troy (c. 1180 BC). The latest of the invaders were the Dorians (c. 1100 BC), who settled in the Peloponnese and founded Sparta; the great city-state arose during the obscure period which followed (1100–800 BC). The mountainous geography of Greece prevented the cities from attaining any national unity, and

science, and lyric poetry originated.

Most of the Greek cities passed from monarchy to the rule of a landowning or merchant oligarchy, and thence to democracy. Thus Athens passed through the democratic reforms of Solon (594 BC), the enlightened 'tyranny' of Pisistratus (560–527 BC), and the establishment of democracy by Cleisthenes (c. 507 BC). Sparta remained unique, a state in which a ruling race, organized on military lines, tyrannized over the original population.

After 545 BC the Ionian cities fell under the suzerainty of the Persian empire. Aid given them by Athens in an unsuccessful revolt in 499–494 BC provoked Darius of Persia to invade Greece in 490 BC, only to be defeated by the Athenians at Marathon and forced to withdraw. Another invasion by Xerxes, after being delayed by the heroic defence of Thermopylae by 300 Spartans, was defeated at sea off Salamis in 480 BC, and on land at Plataea in 479 BC. The Ionian cities were liberated, and formed a naval alliance with Athens, the Confederacy of Delos. Pericles, the real ruler of Athens 461–429 BC, attempted to convert this into an Athenian empire, and in addition to form a land empire in Greece. Mistrust of his ambitions led to the Peloponnesian War (431–404 BC), which destroyed the political power of Athens. In 5th-century BC Athens, Greek tragedy, comedy, sculpture, and architecture were at their peak, and Socrates and Plato founded moral philosophy.

After the Peloponnesian War, Sparta became the leading Greek power, until overthrown by Thebes (378–371 BC). The constant wars between the cities gave Philip II of Macedon (358–336 BC) the opportunity to establish his supremacy over Greece. His son Alexander overthrew the decadent Persian empire, conquered Syria and Egypt, and invaded the Punjab. After his death in 323 BC his empire was divided among his generals, but his conquest had nevertheless spread Greek culture all over the Near East.

During the 3rd century BC the cities attempted to maintain their independence against Macedon, Egypt, and Rome by forming federations, for example the Achaean and Aetolian Leagues. Roman intervention began in 212 BC, and ended in the annexation of Greece in 146 BC. Under Roman rule Greece remained important mainly as a cultural centre, until Justinian closed the university of Athens in 529 AD.

Greek architecture the architecture of ancient Greece underpins virtually all architectural developments in Europe. The Greeks invented the entablature, which allowed roofs to be hipped (inverted V-shape), and perfected the design of columns. There were three styles, or orders of these, namely, Doric, Ionic, and Corinthian; see under ◊column and ◊order. Of these the Doric is the oldest; it is said to have evolved from a former timber prototype. The finest example of a Doric temple is the Parthenon at Athens (447–438 BC). The origin of the Ionic is uncertain. The earliest building in which the Ionic capital appears is the temple of Diana at Ephesus (530 BC). The famous gateway to the Acropolis at Athens (known as the Propylaea) has internal columns of the Ionic order. The most perfect example is the Erechtheum in Athens. The Corinthian order belongs to a later period of Greek art. The most important example of the order is the temple of Jupiter (Zeus) Olympus in Athens (174 BC), completed under Roman influence in AD 129. The Mausoleum in Halicarnassus (353 BC) was one of the Seven Wonders of the World.

Greek art the major periods of Greek art can be divided into the Archaic (late 8th century–480 BC), Classical (480–323 BC), and Hellenistic (323 – 27 BC). No large-scale painting survives, although colour was very important, and even the white marble sculptures we admire today were originally brightly painted.

In the *Archaic* period the statues of naked standing men *kouroi* and draped females *korai* show an Egyptian influence in their rigid frontality. By about 500 BC the figure was allowed to relax its weight onto one leg and immediately seemed to come alive. The archaic smile which gave these early figures a certain cheerful sameness vanished in the *Classical* period when expressions assumed a dignified serenity. Further movement was introduced in new poses such as in Myron's bronze *Diskobolus/The Discus Thrower* 460–50 BC, and in the rhythmic Parthenon reliefs of men and horses supervised by Pheidias. Artists were no longer anonymous and among sculptors whose work is known are ◊*Praxiteles*, *Scopas*, ◊*Lysippus*, and *Polykleitos*, whose *Doryphoros/The Spear Carrier* 450–440 was of such harmony and poise that it set a standard for beautiful proportions which is still in use today. Praxiteles introduced the female nude into the sculptural repertory with the graceful *Aphrodite of Knidos*, c. 350 BC. It was easier to express movement in bronze, hollow-cast by the lost wax method, but few bronze sculptures survive and many are known only through Roman copies in marble. The *Hellenistic* period, when the Greek Empire under Alexander the Great spread to Egypt and beyond Iraq, produced such sculptures as the *Winged Victory of Samothrace* with its dramatic drapery, the expressive *Dying Gaul* and the tortured *Laocoon*, which explored the effects of movement and of deeply-felt emotion.

Vase painting is the one form of Greek painting which has survived the centuries. Artists worked as both potters and painters until the 5th century BC and the works they signed were exported throughout the Empire. Made in several standard shapes and sizes, the pottery served as functional containers for wine, water, and oil. The first decoration took the form of simple lines and circles, from which the *Geometric style* emerged near Athens in the 10th century BC. It consisted of precisely drawn patterns, the most characteristic being the key meander. Gradually the bands of decoration multiplied and the human figure, geometrically stylized, was added. About 700 BC the potters of Corinth invented the *Black Figure* technique in which the unglazed red clay was painted in black with mythological scenes, gods and battles in a narrative frieze. About 530 BC Athenian potters reversed the process and developed the more sophisticated *Red Figure* pottery, which allowed for more detailed and elaborate painting of the figures in red against a black background. This grew increasingly naturalistic, with lively scenes of daily life. The finest examples date from the mid-6th to the mid-5th century BC at Athens. Later painters tried to follow major art trends and represent spatial depth, dissipating the unique quality of their fine linear technique.

The ancient Greeks excelled in carving gems and cameos, and in jewellery and metalwork. They also invented the pictorial mosaic and from the 5th century BC onwards floors were paved with coloured pebbles depicting mythological subjects. Later, specially cut cubes of stone and glass called *tesserae* were used, and Greek craftsmen working for the Romans reproduced famous paintings such as that of *Alexander at the Battle of Issus* from Pompeii, giving us some idea of these lost masterpieces.

Greek language a well-documented member of the Indo-European language family which has passed through at least five distinct phases since the 2nd millennium BC: *Ancient Greek*, including Mycenaean, around the 14th to 12 centuries BC; *Archaic Greek*, which included the language of the Homeric epics, coming to an end around 800 BC; the *Classical Greek* of Athens (Attic Greek), Sparta (Doric Greek) and Ionia (Ionian Greek), until around 400 BC; the *Hellenistic Greek* or *Koine* ('common language') of Greece, Asia Minor, W Asia and Egypt from around the 4th century BC to the 4th century AD, first spread by the campaigns of Alexander the Great; *Byzantine Greek*, the language of the Eastern Roman or Byzantine Empire, 5th to 15th centuries AD; and *Modern Greek*, with a variety of dialects but most noticeably divided into the general vernacular (Demotic Greek or Demotiki) and the so-called 'pure' language of education and traditional literature (*Katharevousa*). In its earlier phases Greek was spoken mainly in Greece proper, the islands, the W coast of Asia Minor and in colonies in Sicily, the Italian mainland and S France. Hellenistic Greek was an important language not only in the Near East but also in the Roman Empire generally, and is the form also known as *New Testament Greek* (in which the Gospels and other books of the New Testament of the Bible were first written). Byzantine Greek was not only an imperial but also an ecclesiastical language, the medium of the Greek Orthodox Church, and Modern Greek, in both its forms, is spoken in Greece and in Cyprus, as well as wherever Greeks have settled throughout the world (especially Canada, the USA and Australia). Classical Greek word-forms continue to have a great influence in the world's scientific and technical vocabulary, and make up a large part of the technical vocabulary of English.

Greek literature *Ancient*. The three greatest names of early Greek literature are those of ◊Homer, reputed author of the epic *Iliad* and *Odyssey*; ◊Hesiod, whose *Works and Days* deals with agricultural life; and the lyric poet ◊Pindar. Prose came to perfection with the historians ◊Herodotus and ◊Thucydides. The 5th century saw the development of the Athenian drama through the works of the tragic dramatists ◊Aeschylus, ◊Sophocles, ◊Euripides, and the comic genius of ◊Aristophanes. After the fall of Athens came a period of prose with the historian ◊Xenophon, the idealist philosopher ◊Plato, the orators ◊Isocrates and ◊Demosthenes, and the scientific teacher ◊Aristotle.

After 323 BC Athens lost its political importance, but was still a university town with teachers such as ◊Epicurus, Zeno, and Theophrastus, and the comic dramatist Menander. Meanwhile Alexandria was becoming the centre of Greek culture: the court of Philadelphus was graced by scientists such as Euclid and the poets Callimachus, Apollonius, and Theocritus. During the 2nd century BC Rome became the new centre for Greek Literature, and Polybius, the historian, spent most of his life there; in the 1st century BC Rome also sheltered the poets Archias, Antipater of Sidon, Philodemus the Epicurean, and Meleager of Gadara, who compiled the first *Greek Anthology*. In the 1st century AD Latin writers overshadow the Greek, but there are still the geographer Strabo, the critic Dionysius of Halicarnassus (fl. 10 BC), the Jewish writers Philo Judaeus and Josephus, the New Testament writers, and the biographer Plutarch. A revival came in the 2nd century with Lucian. To the 3rd century belong the historians Cassius Dio and Herodian, the Christian fathers Clement and Origen, and the Neo-Platonists. For medieval Greek Literature, see ◊Byzantine Literature.

Modern. After the fall of Constantinople, the Byzantine tradition was perpetuated in the classical Greek writing of, for example, the 15th-century chronicles of Cyprus, various historical works in the 16th and 17th centuries, and educational and theological works in the 18th century. The 17th and 18th centuries saw much controversy over the various merits of the Greek vernacular ('demotic'), the classical language (*Katharevousa*), and the language of the Church, as a literary medium. Adamantios Korais (1748–1833), the first great modern, produced a compromise language, and was followed by the prose and drama writer, and poet, Alexandros Rhangavis ('Rangabe') (1810–92), and many others. The 10th-century epic of *Digenis Akritas* is usually considered to mark the beginnings of modern Greek vernacular literature, and the demotic was kept alive in the flourishing Cretan literatire of the 16th and 17th centuries, in numerous popular songs, and in the Klephtic ballads of the 18th century. With independence in the 19th century the popular movement became prominent with the Ionian poet Dionysios Solomos (1798–1857), Andreas Kalvos (1796–1869), and others, and later with Iannis Psichari(1854–1929), short-story writer and dramatist, and the prose writer Alexandros Papadiamandis (1851–1911), who influenced many younger writers, for example, Konstantinos Hatzopoulos (1868–1921), poet and essayist. After the 1920s, the novel began to emerge with Stratis Myrivilis (1892–1969) and Nikos Kazantzakis (1885–1957), author of *Zorba the Greek* 1946 and also a poet. There were also the Nobel poets George ◊Seferis and Odysseus ◊Elytis.

Green /griːn/ Henry, pen name of Henry Vincent Yorke 1905–1974. British novelist, whose works (for example *Loving* 1945, and *Nothing* 1950) are characterized by an experimental colloquial prose style and extensive use of dialogue.

Green /griːn/ Thomas Hill 1836–1882. British philosopher. Born in Yorkshire, he was professor of moral philosophy at Oxford from 1878. He gave a new direction to 19th-century philosophical thought by showing the limitations of ◊Spencer and ◊Mill, and advocated the study of ◊Kant and ◊Hegel. His chief works are *Prolegomena to Ethics* 1883 and *Principles of Political Obligation* 1895.

Greenaway /'griːnəweɪ/ Kate 1846–1901. British artist and illustrator of children's books. Born in London, she became famous for her drawings of children. In 1877 she first exhibited at the Royal Academy, and began her collaboration with the colour-printer Edmund Evans, with whom she produced a number of children's books, including *Mother Goose*.

green belt area surrounding a large city designated by the authorities not to be built on but preserved as open space (for agricultural and recreational use). In the UK, the term has been used widely to refer to the 'outer ring' proposed in the 1944 Greater London Plan by Patrick Abercrombie (1879–1957).

Greene /griːn/ (Henry) Graham 1904– . British novelist. Born at Berkhamsted, son of a headmaster, he became a literary journalist, and in World War II served in the Foreign Office. A Catholic convert from 1926, he is deeply concerned with religious issues. His books include *The Man Within* 1929, *Brighton Rock* 1938, *The Power and the Glory* 1940, *The Heart of the Matter* 1948, *The Third Man* 1950, *Our Man in Havana* 1958, *The Honorary Consul* 1973, and *Monsignor Quixote* 1982.

Greene British author Graham Greene by the Canadian photographer Karsh. Greene is preoccupied with people's motives for committing themselves to a cause, faith, or ideal and the testing of their commitment as they mature.

greenfinch bird *Carduelis chloris*, common in Europe and North Africa. The male is green with a yellow breast and the female a drab greenish-brown.

greenfly plant-sucking insect, a type of ◊aphid.

Greenham Common /'griːnəm/ site of a continuous peace demonstration on common land near Newbury, Berkshire, UK, outside a US airbase. The women-only camp was established in Sept 1981 in protest against the siting of US ◊Cruise missiles in the UK. The protestors have

worked closely with the *Cruisewatch* organization monitoring the US Air Force's excursions with missile launchers to nearby Salisbury Plain.

greenhouse effect a phenomenon of the Earth's atmosphere by which solar radiation is absorbed by the Earth and, although emitted again, is prevented from escaping from the atmosphere by ozone and carbon dioxide in the air. The result is to raise the Earth's temperature; in a garden greenhouse, the glass walls have the same effect. Controversy surrounds predictions that atmospheric pollution and ozone layer depletion will causea gradual rise in our planet's average temperature, with catastrophic results.

Greenland /'griːnlənd/ world's largest island. It lies between the North Atlantic and Arctic Oceans.
area 2,175,600 sq km/840,000 sq mi
capital Godthaab on the W coast
features the whole of the interior is covered by a vast ice-sheet; the island has importance in civil aviation and strategically, and defence responsibilities are shared with the US; there are lead and cryolite deposits, and offshore oil is being explored
exports fishing and fish processing industries are important.
population (1983) 51,903; Inuit, Danish and other European
language Greenlandic
history Greenland was discovered c. 982 by ◊Eric the Red, who founded colonies on the W coast. Christianity was introduced c. 1000. In 1261 the colonies accepted Norwegian sovereignty; but early in the 15th century all communication with Europe ceased, and by the 16th century the colonies had died out. Greenland became a Danish colony in the 18th century, and following a referendum in 1979 was granted full internal self-government in 1981.

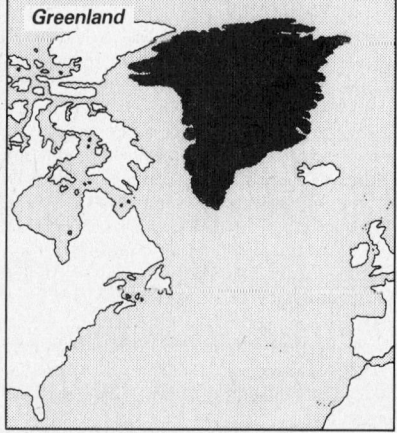

Greenland

Greenland Sea area of the ◊Arctic Ocean between Spitsbergen and Greenland, and N of the Norwegian Sea.

green monkey disease another name for ◊Marburg disease, a virus originating in Central Africa.

Green Mountain Boys irregular troops who fought to keep ◊Vermont free from New York interference, and in the War of American Independence captured Ticonderoga. Their leader was Ethan Allen (1738–89), who was later captured by the British. Vermont is popularly called the Green Mountain State.

Greenock /ˈgriːnək/ port in Strathclyde, Scotland; population (1981) 57,324. Industries include shipbuilding, engineering, and electronics.

Green Paper a publication issued by a British government department setting out various aspects of a matter on which legislation is contemplated, and inviting public discussion and suggestions. In due course it may be followed by a ◊White Paper, giving actual details of proposed legislation. The first Green Paper was published in 1967 by the Department of Economic Affairs.

Green Party political party aiming to 'preserve the planet and its people'. The British Green Party, founded 1973 as the Ecology Party, has policies based on the premise that incessant economic growth is unsustainable. The leaderless party structure reflects a general commitment to decentralization. Green parties have sprung up in W Europe in the 1970s and the 1980s. In countries with ◊proportional representation the Greens had a number of parliamentary seats by 1987: Austria eight, Belgium 15, Finland four, Italy 13, Switzerland four, West Germany 44; and nine members of the European Parliament.

Greenpeace international environmental pressure group, founded 1971, with a policy of nonviolent direct action. During a protest against French atmospheric nuclear testing in the S Pacific 1985, its ship *Rainbow Warrior* was sunk by French intelligence agents, killing a crew member.

green pound the ◊European Community exchange rate for the conversion of EEC farm prices to sterling.

Green Revolution change in agricultural methods of arable farming in developing countries to provide more and better food for their populations, instigated in the 1940s and 1950s. Measures include the increased use of tractors and other machines, artificial fertilizers and pesticides, as well as the breeding of new strains of crop plants and farm animals. Much of the work is coordinated by the ◊FAO of the United Nations. The Green Revolution has been highly successful in SE Asia, less so in Africa, where yields have levelled off in many areas, and some countries, which cannot afford the fertilizers and machinery envisaged in the original Green Revolution idea, have adopted less sophisticated, intermediate technologies.

greenshank greyish bird *Tringa nebularia* of the sandpiper group. The name is derived from its long olive-green legs, which distinguish it from the redshank. It breeds in Scotland and N Europe.

Greenwich /ˈgrɪnɪdʒ/ inner borough of London, England
features the *Queen's House* 1637, designed by Inigo ◊Jones, since 1937 housing part of the *National Maritime Museum*; the *Royal Naval College*, designed by Christopher ◊Wren in 1694 as a naval hospital to replace a palace previously on this site (the birthplace of Henry VIII, Mary and Elizabeth I), and used as a college since 1873; the *Royal Greenwich Observatory* (founded here in 1675). The source of Greenwich Mean Time has been moved to ◊Herstmonceux, but the Greenwich meridian (0°) remains unchanged. The *Cutty Sark*, most celebrated of the great tea clippers, is preserved as a museum of sail, and Francis ◊Chichester's *Gipsy Moth IV* is also here. The borough also includes *Woolwich* with the Royal Arsenal.
population (1981) 212,000.

Greenwich Mean Time (GMT) local time on the zero line of longitude (the *Greenwich meridian*) that passes through the Old Royal Observatory at Greenwich, London. It was replaced in 1986 by Coordinated Universal Time (UTC); see ◊time.

Greenwood /ˈgriːnwʊd/ Walter 1903–1974. British novelist of the Depression, born in Salford. His own lack of a job gave authenticity to *Love on the Dole* 1933.

Greer /grɪə/ Germaine 1939– . Australian feminist, who gained overnight fame and notoriety with the publication of *The Female Eunuch* 1970. She became a familiar figure in the British media through television appearances and as a newspaper columnist. Later works include *The Obstacle Race* 1979, a study of contemporary women artists, and *Sex and Destiny: The Politics of Human Fertility* 1984.

Gregg /greg/ Norman 1892–1966. Australian opthalmic surgeon, who discovered in 1941 that german measles in a pregnant woman could cause physical defects in her child. He was knighted in 1953.

Gregorian chant plainsong choral chants associated with Pope Gregory the Great (540–604), which became standard in the Roman Catholic Church.

Gregory /ˈgregəri/ Isabella Augusta (born Persse) 1852–1932. Irish playwright, associated with W B ◊Yeats in creating the ◊Abbey Theatre in 1904. Born in Galway, she married Sir William Gregory in 1881. She wrote many plays including the comedies *Spreading the News* 1904, and *Rising of the Moon* 1907, and the tragic *Gaol Gate* 1906, and *Grania* 1912.

Gregory /ˈgregəri/ name of 16 popes, including:

Gregory I /ˈgregəri/ St, the Great c. 540–604. Pope from 590, who asserted Rome's supremacy, and exercized almost imperial powers. In 596 he sent St ◊Augustine to England. He introduced Gregorian chant (see under ◊music) into the liturgy. Feast day 12 Mar.

Gregory VII /ˈgregəri/ c. 1023–1085. or *Hildebrand*. He acted as chief minister to several popes before his election 1073. He claimed power to depose kings, denied lay rights to make clerical appointments, and attempted to suppress simony and enforce clerical celibacy, making enemies with both rulers and the church. In 1077 he forced the emperor Henry IV to wait in the snow at Canossa for four days, dressed as a penitent, before receiving pardon. He was driven from Rome and died in exile. Feast day 25 May.

Gregory XIII /ˈgregəri/ 1502–1585. Pope from 1572, who introduced the reformed Gregorian ◊calendar.

Gregory of Tours, St /tuə/ 538–594. French bishop of Tours from 573, author of a *History of the Franks*.

Grenada /grəˈneɪdə/ island in the Caribbean, the southernmost of the Windward Islands.
government the constitution, which dates from full independence in 1974, creates a system modelled on that of Britain, with a resident governor-general, representing the British monarch, as the formal head of state, and a prime minister and cabinet drawn from and collectively responsible to parliament. Parliament consists of two chambers, a 15-member house of representatives, elected by universal suffrage, and a senate of 13, appointed by the governor-general, seven on the advice of the prime minister, three on the advice of the leader of the opposition and three after wider consultation.
history prior to the arrival of Christopher ◊Columbus in 1498, Grenada was inhabited by ◊Carib Indians. The island was eventually colonized by France in 1650, and ceded to Britain in 1783. Grenada remained a British colony until 1958, when it joined the Federation of the West Indies until its dissolution in 1962. Internal self-government was achieved in 1967 and full independence within the Commonwealth in 1974. The early political life of the nation was dominated by two figures, Eric Gairy, a trade union leader who founded the Grenada United Labour Party (GULP) in 1950, and Herbert Blaize, of the Grenada National Party (GNP). On independence, in 1974, Gairy was elected prime minister. He was knighted in 1977 but his rule became increasingly autocratic and corrupt and in 1979 he was replaced in a bloodless coup by the leader of the left-wing New Jewel Movement (NJM), Maurice Bishop. He suspended the 1974 constitution, established a People's Revolutionary Government (PRG) and announced the formation of a people's consultative assembly to draft a new constitution. Bishop promised a ◊non-aligned foreign policy but became convinced that the USA was involved in a plot to destabilize his administration. This was strongly denied.
Grenada's relations with Britain and the USA deteriorated while links with Cuba and the USSR grew stronger. In 1983 Bishop tried to improve relations with the USA and announced the appointment of a commission to draft a new constitution. His conciliatory attitude was opposed by the more left-wing members of his regime, resulting in a military coup, during which Bishop and three of his colleagues were executed.
A Revolutionary Military Council (RMC), led by Gen Hudson Austin, took control. In response to the outcry caused by the executions, Austin promised a return to civilian rule as soon as possible but on 25 Oct about 1,900 US troops, accompanied by 300 from Jamaica and Barbados, invaded the island. It was not clear whether the invasion was in response to a request from the governor-general or on the initiative of the Organization of Eastern Caribbean States

(OECS). In any event, concerned that Grenada might become a Cuban base, the USA agreed to take part. Neither Britain nor other members of the Commonwealth appear to have been consulted. The RMC forces were defeated and Austin and his colleagues arrested.

In Nov the governor-general appointed a non-political interim council and the 1974 constitution was reinstated. Several political parties emerged from hiding, including Sir Eric Gairy's GULP and Herbert Blaize's GNP. After considerable manoeuvring, an informal coalition of centre and left-of-centre parties resulted in the formation of the New National Party (NNP), led by Blaize. In the 1984 general election NNP won 14 of the 15 seats in the house of representatives and Blaize became prime minister. The USA withdrew most of its forces by the end of 1983 and the remainder by Jul 1985.

Grenada

AREA (including the Grenadines, notably Carriacou) 344 sq km/133 sq mi
CAPITAL St George's
PHYSICAL southernmost of the Windward Islands; mountainous
FEATURES smallest independent nation in the western hemisphere
HEAD OF STATE Elizabeth II from 1974 represented by Paul Scoon from 1978
HEAD OF GOVERNMENT Herbert A Blaize from 1984
GOVERNMENT constitutional monarchy
EXPORTS cocoa, nutmeg, bananas, mace
CURRENCY Eastern Caribbean dollar (4.46 = £1 Sept 1987)
POPULATION 113,000 (1984); annual growth rate 1.2%
LANGUAGE English
RELIGION Roman Catholic
LITERACY 85% (1985)
GDP $116 million (1983); $500 per head of population
CHRONOLOGY
1974 Full independence achieved, with Eric Gairy elected prime minister.
1979 Gairy was removed in a bloodless coup led by Maurice Bishop. Constitution suspended and a people's revolutionary government established.
1982 Relations with the USA and Britain

passed the Stamp Act 1765 which precipitated the American War of Independence.

Grenville /'grenvɪl/ Richard 1541–1591. English sailor. He commanded the fleet sent by his cousin, Sir Walter Raleigh, to colonize Virginia in 1585, and organized the defence of W England against the Spanish Armada in 1586–88. In 1591, he sailed to the Azores as second-in-command to Lord Thomas Howard in an attempt to capture a Spanish treasure fleet, and was cut off from the main English fleet. Aboard *Revenge*, he fought for 15 hours against 15 Spanish ships, and was fatally wounded.

Grenville /'grenvɪl/ William Wyndham, Baron Grenville 1759–1834. British Whig politician, son of George ◊Grenville. He was foreign secretary in 1791 and resigned along with Pitt in 1801 over King George III's refusal to assent to Catholic emancipation. He headed the

Grenada

deteriorated as ties with Cuba and USSR strengthened. Bishop feared impending US invasion.
1983 After Bishop's attempt to improve relations with the USA, he was overthrown by left-wing opponents. A coup established the Revolutionary Military Council (RMC) and Bishop and some of his colleagues were executed. The USA, accompanied by troops from some other E Caribbean countries, invaded Grenada, overthrowing the RMC. The 1974 constitution was reinstated.
1984 The newly formed New National Party (NNP) won 14 of the 15 seats in the house of representatives and its leader, Herbert Blaize, became prime minister.

Grenadines /'grenədi:nz/ chain of about 600 small islands in the Caribbean, part of the group known as the Windward Islands. They are divided between ◊St Vincent and ◊Grenada.

Grenoble /grə'nəubəl/ town in SE France; population (1982) 166,000. Industries include computers and technology. It was the birthplace of ◊Stendhal, commemorated by a museum. There is a fine 12th–13th century cathedral, a university, established in 1339, and the Institut Laue-Langevin for nuclear research.

Grenville /'grenvɪl/ George 1712–1770. British Whig politician, prime minister and chancellor of the Exchequer 1763–65. His government prosecuted ◊Wilkes in 1763, and

parties to be resident in Scotland for a minimum of 21 days before the marriage, and marriage by declaration was abolished in 1940.

Greuze /grɜːz/ Jean Baptiste 1725–1805. French genre painter, born in Tournuse whose sentimental paintings include *A Father explaining the Bible to his Children* 1755.

Greville /'grevɪl/ Charles (Cavendish Fulke) 1794–1865. British diarist. He was Clerk of the Council in Ordinary 1821–59, an office which brought him into close contact with all the noted personalities of the court and of both political parties. They provided him with much of the material for his *Memoirs* 1817–60.

Grey /greɪ/ Beryl 1927– . British ballerina. Making her debut with the Sadler's Wells Company in 1941, she was their prima ballerina 1942–57, and was artistic director of the London Festival Ballet 1968–79.

Grey /greɪ/ Charles, 2nd Earl Grey 1764–1845. British Whig politician. He entered Parliament in 1786 and in 1806 became First Lord of the Admiralty in the 'All the talents' ministry, succeeding Fox as foreign secretary soon afterwards. As prime minister 1830–34, he carried the Great Reform Bill in 1832.

Grey /greɪ/ Edward, 1st Viscount Grey of Fallodon 1862–1933. British Liberal politician, nephew of the 2nd Earl Grey. As foreign secretary 1905–16 he negotiated an entente with Russia in 1907, and backed France against Germany in the ◊Agadir Incident of 1911. In 1914 he said: 'The lamps are going out all over Europe; we shall not see them lit again in our lifetime.'

Grey /greɪ/ Henry, 3rd Earl Grey 1802–1894. British politician, son of Charles ◊Grey. He served under his father as undersecretary for the colonies 1830–33, resigning because the cabinet would not back the immediate emancipation of slaves; he was secretary of war 1835–39, and colonial secretary 1846–52. He was unique among politicians of the period in maintaining that the colonies should be governed for their own benefit, not that of Britain, and in his policy of granting self-government wherever possible. Yet he advocated convict transportation, and was opposed to Gladstone's Home Rule policy.

Grey /greɪ/ Lady Jane 1537–1554. Queen of England 9–19 July 1553. She was born in Leicestershire, the daughter of Henry Grey, duke of Suffolk (died 1554), and a great-granddaughter of Henry VII. She was married in 1553 to Lord Guildford Dudley (died 1554), son of the duke of ◊Northumberland. Since she was a protestant, Edward VI was persuaded by Northumberland to set aside the claims to the throne of his sisters Mary and Elizabeth. When Edward died on 6 Jul Jane reluctantly accepted the crown and was proclaimed queen four days later. ◊Mary, however, received the people's support and Grey was executed on Tower Green.

Grey /greɪ/ Zane 1875–1939. American author of westerns, such as *Riders of the Purple Sage* 1912.

greyhound ancient breed of dog, with a long narrow muzzle, slight build, and long legs,

'All the Talents' coalition of 1806–07 which abolished the slave trade.

Gresham /'greʃəm/ Thomas c. 1519–1579. English economist, who paid for the building of the first Royal Exchange, founded Gresham College, and propounded *Gresham's Law* that 'bad money tends to drive out good money from circulation'.

Gretna Green /'gretnə 'gri:n/ village in ◊Dumfries and Galloway region, Scotland. It was famous for runaway marriages after they were banned in England in 1754; all that was necessary was the couple's declaration, before witnesses, of their willingness to marry. From 1856 Scottish law required at least one of the

renowned for its swiftness. Up to 75 cm/2.5 ft tall, it can exceed 60 kph/40 mph.

greyhound racing sport of watching greyhounds pursue a mechanically propelled dummy hare round a circular track. Invented in the USA in 1919, it is popular in Britain and Australia.

grid the network by which electricity is generated and distributed over a region or country. It involves many power stations and switching centres and allows, for example, high demand in one area to be met by surplus power generated in another. Britain has the world's largest grid system, with over 140 power stations able to supply up to 55,000 megawatts. The term is also used for any grating system, as in a cattle grid for controlling the movement of livestock across roads and a conductor in a storage battery or electron gun. In trigonometry, a grid is a network of uniformly spaced vertical and horizontal lines as used to locate points on a map or to construct a graph.

Grieg /griːg/ Edvard Hagerup 1843–1907. Norwegian composer, born in Bergen. He studied at Leipzig Conservatoire, and in Copenhagen, and settled as a teacher and conductor in Oslo in 1867. He was determinedly Norwegian in his musical inspiration. Much of his best music is small scale, particularly his songs, dances and piano works. Among orchestral works are the *Piano Concerto* 1869, one of the most popular in the concert repertoire, and the incidental music for Ibsen's *Peer Gynt* 1876.

Grierson /'griəsən/ John 1898–1972. Scottish film producer. Born in Perthshire, he was a sociologist who pioneered the documentary film in Britain. He directed *Drifters* 1929 and produced 1930–35 *Industrial Britain*, *Song of Ceylon*, and *Night Mail*. During World War II he created the National Film Board of Canada.

griffin mythical monster, the supposed guardian of hidden treasure, with the body, tail and hind legs of a lion, and the head, forelegs and wings of an eagle. It is often found in heraldry, for example the armorial crest of the City of London.

Griffith /'grifiθ/ D(avid) W(ark) 1875–1948. American film director. Son of a Kentucky colonel, he was an actor and then a director, making many hundreds of 'one reelers' (12 minutes) 1908–13, in which he pioneered the techniques of the flash-back, cross-cut, close-up and longshot. His masterpiece as a director was *Birth of a Nation* 1915, which was followed by *Intolerance* 1916, and *Broken Blossoms* 1919.

griffon small breed of dog originating in Belgium, red, black, or black and tan in colour and weighing up to 5 kg/11 lb. Square-bodied and round-headed, there are rough and smooth-coated varieties.

griffon vulture *Gyps fulvus* a bird found in S Europe, W and Central Asia, and parts of Africa. It has a bald head with a neck ruff, and is 1.1 m/3.5 ft long with a wingspan of up to 2.7 m/9 ft.

Grignard /'griːnjɑː/ François Auguste-Victor 1871–1935. French chemist who shared the 1912 Nobel Prize for Chemistry for his work on organometallic compounds. The so-called

Griffith Director D W Griffith (in the hat), with the couple known as 'the world's sweethearts', Douglas Fairbanks Sr and Mary Pickford, and comic actor Charlie Chaplin.

Grignard reagents (compounds containing a hydrocarbon radical, magnesium and a halogen such as chlorine) found important applications as some of the most versatile in organic synthesis.

Grillparzer /'grɪlpɑːtsə/ Franz 1791–1872. Austrian poet and dramatist. His historical tragedies *König Ottokars Glück und Ende/King Ottocar, his Rise and Fall* 1825 and *Ein treuer Diener seines Herrn/A True Servant of his Master* 1826 both involved him with the censor. Two of his greatest dramas followed, *Des Meeres und der Liebe Wellen/The Waves of Sea and Love* 1831, returning to the Hellenic world, and *Der Traum, ein Leben/A Dream is Life* 1834. The bitter cycle of poems *Tristia ex Ponto* 1835 followed an unhappy love-affair.

Grimaldi /grɪ'mɔːldi/ Joseph 1779–1837. British clown, born in London, the son of an Italian actor, who appeared on the stage at two years old. He gave his name 'Joey' to all later clowns, and excelled as 'Mother Goose' performed at Covent Garden in 1806.

Grimm /grɪm/ Jacob 1785–1863. Pioneer philologist (see ◊Grimm's Law) and collaborator with his brother Wilhelm (1786–1859) in the *Fairy Tales* 1812–14, based on folk tales collected from informants. Jacob's chief work was his *Deutsche Grammatick/German Grammar* 1819, which gave the first historical treatment of the ◊Germanic languages.

Grimm's Law in linguistics, the rule by which certain historical sound changes have occurred in some related European languages: for example Latin 'p' became English and German 'f', as in *pater/father, vater*.

Grimond /'grɪmənd/ Jo(seph), Baron Grimond 1913– . British Liberal politician. As leader of the party 1956–67, he aimed at making it 'a new Radical Party to take the place of the Socialist Party as an alternative to Conservatism'. He was made a life peer in 1983.

Grimsby /'grɪmzbi/ fishing port in Humberside, England; population (1985) 95,000. It declined in the 1970s when Icelandic waters were closed to British fishermen.

Grisons /griː'zɒŋ/ French name for the Swiss canton of ◊Graubünden, largest of the cantons of Switzerland; area 7,110 sq km/2,746 sq mi; population (1980) 164,641. The inner valleys are the highest in Europe, and the main sources of the river Rhine rise here. It also includes the resort of

Grimaldi Joseph Grimaldi, the clown who gave the name 'joey' to all later clowns.

Davos, and, in the Upper Engadine, St Moritz. The capital is Chur. ◊Romansh is still widely spoken. It entered the Swiss Confederation in 1803.

Grivas /'griːvəs/ George 1898–1974. Greek Cypriot general who led ◊Eoka's attempts to secure the union (Greek *enosis*) of ◊Cyprus with Greece.

Grodno /'grɒdnəu/ industrial town in the Byelorussian republic, USSR; population (1985) 247,000. Part of Lithuania from 1398, it passed to Poland after its union with Lithuania in 1569. The 1795 partition of Poland gave it to Russia, it was ceded to Poland in 1920, and became Russian again in 1939.

Gromyko /grə'miːkəu/ Andrei 1909– . President of the USSR from 1985. Ambassador to the USA from 1943, he took part in the Tehran, Yalta, and Potsdam conferences; as United Nations representative 1946–49, he exercised the Soviet veto 26 times, and as foreign minister 1957–85 returned from the thaw to the Stalinist line.

Groningen /'grəunɪŋən/ town in NE Netherlands; population (1984) 167,866. Industries include textiles and sugar refining. It has a university, established in 1614.

grooming in biology, the use by an animal of teeth, tongue, feet or beak to remove parasites, dead skin and other debris from fur or feathers. Grooming also helps to spread essential oils for waterproofing. In many social species, notably monkeys and apes, grooming of other individuals is used to maintain social relationships. The term is also used for general care of a pet's coat or fur by a human by brushing, combing and other such methods.

Gropius /'grəupiəs/ Walter Adolf 1883–1969. German architect, who lived in the USA from 1937. A founder-director of the

⊳Bauhaus school in Weimar 1919–28, he was an advocate of team architecture, and artistic standards in industrial production. In the USA he was professor of architecture at Harvard, and designed the Harvard Graduate Centre 1949–50.

grosbeak name given to several thick-billed birds. The pine grosbeak *Pinicola enucleator*, also known as the pinefinch, breeds in Arctic forests; its plumage is similar to that of the crossbill.

Gross Domestic Product (GDP) a measure (normally annual) of the total domestic output of a country; including exports, but not imports. See ⊳Gross National Product.

Grosseteste /'grəʊsteɪt/ Robert c. 1169–1253. Scholar and bishop. Born in Stow, Suffolk, he was a student at Oxford and perhaps Paris, later becoming tutor and subsequently Chancellor of Oxford University. He was Bishop of Lincoln from 1235 to his death. His books include translations of Aristotle, commentaries on the Bible, and many scientific works. He was a forerunner of the empirical school, being one of the earliest to suggest testing ancient Greek theories by practical experiment.

Grossmith /'grəʊsmɪθ/ George 1847–1912. British actor and singer. From journalism he turned to the stage, and in 1877 began his long association with the Gilbert and Sullivan operas, in which he created a number of parts. He collaborated with his brother *Weedon Grossmith* (1853–1919) in the comic *Diary of a Nobody* 1894.

Gross National Product (GNP) the most commonly used measurement of the wealth of a country. GNP is the ⊳Gross Domestic Product plus income from abroad, minus income earned during the same period by foreign investors within the country. The ⊳national income of a country is the GNP minus whatever sum of money needs to be set aside to replace ageing capital stock.

Grosz /grəʊs/ Georg 1893–1959. German artist. A founder of the ⊳Dada movement, Grosz excelled at savagely satirical cartoons and engravings, which soon led to official disapproval. He emigrated to the USA in 1932. His works include the series *The Face of the Ruling Class* and *Ecce Homo*, executed in the 1920s.

Grotefend /'grəʊtəfent/ George Frederick 1775–1853. German scholar. Although a student of the classical rather than the oriental languages, he nevertheless solved the riddle of the ⊳cuneiform script as used in ancient Persia: decipherment of Babylonian cuneiform followed on the basis of his work.

Grotius /'grəʊtiəs/ Hugo 1583–1645. Dutch jurist and politician, born at Delft. He became a lawyer, and later received political appointments. In 1618 he was arrested as a republican and sentenced to imprisonment for life: his wife contrived his escape in 1620, and he settled in France, where he composed the *De Jure Belli et Pacis/On the Law of War and Peace* 1625, the foundation of international law.

groundnut S American annual plant, also known as the *peanut, earthnut* or *monkey nut Arachis hypogaea*, family Leguminosae. After

Grosz *Vergneugt/Pleasure*, from *The Face of the Ruling Class*, was drawn in 1920 and is typical of the work of the German-born caricaturist and satirist Georg Grosz. He suffered numerous prosecutions and in 1932 he fled his native Berlin and became a naturalized American.

flowering, the flowerstalks bend and force the pods into the earth so that they can ripen without desiccation, or drying out, in near desert conditions. The nuts are now a staple food in many tropical countries and also yield a valuable edible oil; they can also make cattle food.

grouper name given to a number of species of sea perch (Serranidae) found in warm waters off the Atlantic coast of the USA. The spotted giant grouper *Promicrops itaiara* is 2–2.5 cm/6–8 ft long, may weigh over 300 kg/700 lb and is sluggish in movement. Formerly primarily game fish, they are now commercially exploited.

grouse game bird of the family Tetraonidae

common in N America and northern Europe. Among the most familiar are the *red grouse Lagopus scoticus*, a native of Britain; the ⊳ptarmigans; the *ruffed grouse Bonasia umbellus*, common in North American woods; and the *capercaillie Tetrao urogallus* and *blackcock Tetrao tetrix*, both known in Britain. Grouse are shot over dogs or by driving in Britain 12 Aug–10 Dec.

Grozny /'grɒznɪ/ capital of the Chechen-Ingush republic, USSR; population (1985) 393,000. It is an oil-producing centre.

GRP *glass-reinforced plastic*. Although usually known as ⊳fibreglass, this material is only

Grotius a portrait of Hugo Grotius, the 17th-century founder of international law, by A Moro.

strengthened by glass fibres, the rest being plastic. Products are usually moulded, mats of glass fibre being sandwiched between layers of a polyester plastic, which sets hard when mixed with a curing agent. GRP is now a favoured material for boat hulls and the bodies and some structural components of cars.

Grundy, Mrs /'grʌndi/ a character first mentioned in Thomas Martin's play *Speed the Plough* 1798, who though she does not actually appear, is constantly appealed to as one who knows the proprieties.

Grünewald /'gruːnəvælt/ identified in 1938 as Mathias Gothardt Neihardt, c. 1460–1528. Chief and last of the German ◊Gothic artists. A tragic visionary, he used colour symbolically in the Isenheim altar in Colmar 1512–15, painted for hospital patients to see his crucified Christ, covered with festering wounds, sharing their suffering.

Gruyère /gruː'jeə/ district in W Switzerland, famous for pale yellow cheese with large holes.

Guadalajara /ˌgwɑːdələ'hɑːrə/ industrial city in W Mexico; population (1980) 2,244,715. A key communications centre, it has a fine 16th–17th century cathedral, the Governor's Palace, and an orphanage with murals by the Mexican painter José ◊Orozco.

Guadalcanal /ˌgwɑːdlkə'næl/ largest of the ◊Solomon Islands.

Guadeloupe /ˌgwɑːdə'luːp/ an island group in the Leeward Islands, forming an overseas region of France; area 1,702 sq km/657 sq mi; population (1982) 328,400. The main islands are Basse-Terre, on which is the chief town of the same name, and Grande-Terre.

Guam /gwɑːm/ largest island in the ◊Mariana group in the W Pacific.

guan type of large bird, genus *Penelope* and others, found in S and Central America. Somewhat like pheasants, to which they are distantly related, guans spend much time on the ground.

guanaco wild member of the camel family *Lama guanacoe* found in S America on pampas and mountain plateaux. It is sandy-brown in colour, white below with a blackish face, and has fine wool. Up to 1 m/3 ft at the shoulder and with head and body about 1.5 m/5 ft long, it lives in small herds and is the ancestor of the domestic llama.

Guanch Republic /gwɑːntʃ/ proposed name for an independent state in the ◊Canary Islands.

Guangdong /ˌgwæŋ'dʊŋ/ province (formerly Kwantung) of S China
area 231,400 sq km/90,246 sq mi
capital ◊Guangzhou
features tropical climate; Hainan, Leizhou peninsula, and the foreign enclaves of Hong Kong and Macao in the Xi Jiang delta
products rice, sugar, tobacco; minerals; fish
population (1982) 59,299,220

Guangxi Zhuang /'gwæŋ,ʃiː dʒu'æŋ/ autonomous region (formerly Kwangsi Chuang) in S China
area 220,400 sq km/85,074 sq mi
capital Nanning
features Zhuang people are allied to the Thai, and form China's largest ethnic minority
products rice, sugar, fruit
population (1982) 36,420,960

Guangzhou /ˌgwæŋ'dʒəʊ/ (formerly Kwangchow/Canton), capital of ◊Guangdong province, China; population (1982) 59,299,220. Sun Yat-sen Memorial Hall, a theatre, commemorates the statesman, who was born nearby and founded the university. There is a rail link with Peking and one is planned with Liuzhai.
history it was the first Chinese port opened to foreign trade, the Portuguese visiting it in 1516, and was a treaty port from 1842 until its occupation by Japan in 1938.

Guanyin in Chinese Buddhism, the goddess of mercy. In Japan she is worshipped as Kwannon. Her origins were in India, as a male god, Avalokiteshvara.

guarana Brazilian woody climbing plant *Paullinia cupana*, family Sapindaceae; a drink made from it contains caffeine, and it is the source of the drug known as zoom in the USA. Its more commercial uses include the extraction of starch, gum, and several oils.

Guaraní /ˌgwɑːrə'niː/ a South ◊American Indian people of modern Paraguay, S Brazil, and Bolivia.

Guardi /'gwɑːdi/ Francesco 1712–1793. Italian artist. He was once regarded merely as a follower of ◊Canaletto, but his atmospheric evocations of his native Venice, using an almost impressionist technique, are now highly valued in comparison with Canaletto's static observations of the city.

Guareschi /gwə'reski/ Giovanni 1909–1968. Italian author of short stories of the friendly feud between parish priest Don Camillo and the Communist village mayor.

Guarneri /gwɑː'neəri/ celebrated family of violin-makers at Cremona, Italy, of whom (Bartolomeo) Giuseppe Guarneri 'del Gesù' (1698–1744) produced the finest models.

Guatemala /ˌgwɑːtə'mɑːlə/ country in central America, bounded N and NW by Mexico, E by Belize and the Caribbean Sea, SE by Honduras and El Salvador, and SW by the Pacific Ocean.
government the 1985 constitution provides for a single-chamber national assembly of 100 deputies, 75 elected directly by universal suffrage, and the rest on the basis of proportional representation. They serve a five-year term. The president, also directly elected for a similar term, appoints a cabinet and is assisted by a vice-president, and is not eligible for re-election. There is a multiplicity of political parties, the most significant being the Guatemalan Christian Democratic Party (PDCG), the Centre Party (UCN), the National Democratic Co-operation Party (PDCN), the Revolutionary Party (PR), the Movement of National Liberation (MLN), and the Democratic Institutional Party (PID).
history formerly part of the ◊Maya empire, Guatemala became a Spanish colony in 1524. Independent from Spain in 1821, it then joined Mexico, becoming independent in 1823. It was part of the ◊Central American Federation 1823–39, and was then ruled by a succession of dictators until the presidency of Juan José Arévalo, in 1944, and his successor, Col Jacobo Arbenz. Their socialist administrations both followed programmes of reform, including land appropriation, but Arbenz's nationalization of the United Fruit Company's plantations, in 1954, so alarmed the US government that it sponsored a revolution, led by Col Carlos Castillo Armas, who then assumed the presidency. He was assassinated in 1963 and the army continued to rule until 1966. There was a brief return to constitutional government until the military returned in 1970.
The next ten years saw much political violence, in which it was estimated that over 50,000 people died. In the 1982 presidential election the government candidate won but opponents complained that the election had been rigged, and before he could take office, there was a coup by a group of young right-wing officers, who installed Gen Rios Montt as head of a three-man junta. He soon dissolved the junta, assumed the presidency, and began fighting corruption and ending violence.
The anti-government guerrilla movement was, however, growing, and was countered by repressive measures by Montt, so that by 1983 opposition to him was widespread. After several unsuccessful attempts to remove him, a coup led by Gen Mejia Victores finally succeeded. Mejia Victores declared an amnesty for the guerrillas, and the preparation of a new constitution. This was adopted in 1985 and in the elections which followed, the PDCG won a majority in the congress as well as the presidency, Vinicio Cerezo becoming president.

Guatemala
REPUBLIC OF (*República de Guatemala*)

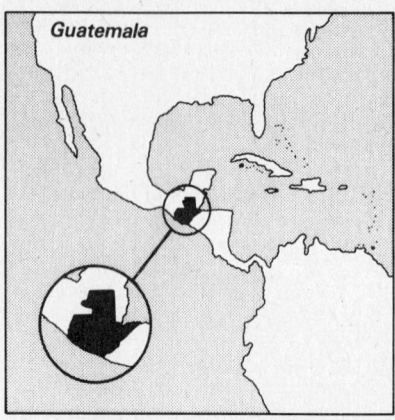
Guatemala

AREA 108,889 sq km/42,042 sq mi
CAPITAL Guatemala City
TOWNS Quezaltenango, Puerto Barrios (naval base)
PHYSICAL mountainous, tropical
FEATURES earthquakes are frequent
HEAD OF STATE AND OF GOVERNMENT Mario Vinicio Cerezo Arevalo from 1986
GOVERNMENT democratic
EXPORTS coffee, bananas, cotton
CURRENCY quetzal (1.65, free rate 4.49 = £1 Sept 1987)
POPULATION (1985) 8,346,000 (Mayaquiche Indians 54%, mestizos 42%); annual growth rate 2.4%
LANGUAGE Spanish
RELIGION Roman Catholic
LITERACY 59% male/44% female (1980 est)
GDP $9.9 bn (1984); $1,085 per head of population
CHRONOLOGY
1839 Independent republic.
1954 Col Carlos Castillo became president in a US-backed coup, halting land reform.
1963 Military coup made Col Enrique Peralta president.
1966 Cesar Méndez elected president.
1970 Carlos Araña elected president.
1974 Gen Kjell Laugerud became president. Widespread political violence.

1978 Gen Fernando Romeo became president.
1981 Growth of anti-government guerrilla movement.
1982 Gen Angel Anibal became president. An army coup installed Gen Ríos Montt as head of a junta and then as president. Political violence continued.
1983 Montt removed in a coup led by Gen Mejía Victores, who declared amnesty for the guerrillas.
1985 New constitution adopted; Guatemalan Christian Democratic Party (PDCG) won congressional elections; Vinicio Cerezo elected president.

Guatemala City /ˌgwɑːtəˈmɑːlə/ capital of Guatemala; population (1983) 1,300,000. It was founded in 1776 when its predecessor (Antigua) was destroyed in an earthquake.

guava tropical American tree *Psidium guajava*, family Myrtaceae; the astringent yellow pear-shaped fruit is used to make guava jelly, or it can be stewed or canned.

Guayaquil /ˌgwaɪəˈkiːl/ city and chief port of ◊Ecuador; population (1982) 1,300,868.

Guderian /gʊˈdeəriən/ Heinz 1888–1954. German general. He created the Panzer armoured divisions of the German army which formed the ground spearhead of Hitler's *Blitzkrieg* strategy, and achieved the breakthrough at ◊Sedan in 1940 and the advance to Moscow in 1941.

gudgeon freshwater cyprinid fish *Gobio gobio* found in Europe and N Asia on the gravel bottoms of streams. Olive-brown, spotted with black and attaining 20 cm/8 in, it has a distinctive barbel at each side of the mouth.

guelder rose European shrub or small tree *Viburnum opulus*, with white flowers and shiny red berries.

Guelders /ˈgeldəz/ another name for ◊Gelderland, a region of the Netherlands.

Guelph /gwelf/ industrial town and agricultural centre in Ontario, Canada; population (1981) 71,250.

Guelph and Ghibelline rival parties in medieval Germany and Italy, which supported the papal party and the German emperors respectively. They originated in the 12th century as partisans of the rival German houses of Welf (hence Guelph or Guelf), dukes of Bavaria, and of the lords of ◊Hohenstaufen (whose castle at Waiblingen gave the Ghibellines their name), who struggled for the imperial crown after the death of Henry VI in 1197, until the Hohenstaufen dynasty died out in 1268.

Guernica /geəˈniːkə/ town in the ◊Basque country of Spain, where the Castilian kings formerly swore to respect the rights of the Basques. It was destroyed in 1937 by German bombers aiding ◊Franco in the Spanish Civil War, and rebuilt in 1946. The bombing inspired a painting by ◊Picasso.

Guernsey /ˈgɜːnzi/ second largest of the ◊Channel Islands; area 63 sq km/24.5 sq mi; population (1981) 53,500. The capital is St Peter Port. Products include tomatoes, flowers, and more recently butterflies; electronics; and from 1975 it has been a major international financial centre. Guernsey cattle are a pale fawn colour, and give rich creamy milk. Guernsey has belonged to the English Crown since 1066, but was occupied by German forces 1940–45.

guerrilla irregular soldier fighting in a small unofficial unit, typically against an established or occupying power, and engaging in sabotage, ambush, and the like, rather than pitched battles against an opposing army. The term was first applied to the Spanish and Portuguese resistance to French occupation during the ◊Peninsular War, and guerrilla techniques were widely used in World War II (for example in Greece and the Balkans) and in the Vietnam War. In modern times guerrilla tactics have been extensively adopted by national liberation groups and militant political extremists, particularly so-called 'urban guerrillas' who operate in cities rather than in the open country traditionally favoured for guerrilla warfare. Such guerrillas tend to be called 'freedom fighters' by those who support their cause, 'terrorists' by those who oppose it. Groups active in recent years include:
Action Directe French group in alliance with Red Army Faction (see below). Carries out bombings in Paris and elsewhere.
Amal Shi'ite Muslim militia in ◊Lebanon.
Armed Revolutionary Nuclei NAR, neo-fascist; 1980 bomb in Bologna railway station, Italy, killed 76.
Black September Palestinian group named from the month when PLO guerrillas active in Jordan were suppressed by the Jordanian army; killed 11 Israelis at the Munich Olympic Games 1972.
Contras right-wing guerrillas in ◊Nicaragua opposing the Sandinista government (see below); they receive funding from the USA.
ETA ◊Basque separatist movement in N Spain.
Hezbollah pro-Khomeini Shi'ite Muslim militia in ◊Lebanon, the extremist wing of Amal (see above); backed by Syria and Iran.
Irish Republican Army IRA, organization committed to the formation of a unified Irish republic; see under ◊Irish Republican Army.
Palestine Liberation Organization PLO, organization committed to the creation of a separate Palestinian state; see under ◊Palestine Liberation Organization.
Quebec Liberation Front separatist organization in Canada committed to the creation of an independent French-speaking Quebec; kidnapped and killed minister Pierre Laporte 1970.
Red Army Faction RAF, opposing 'US imperialism', formerly led by Andreas Baader and Ulrike Meinhof, active in West Germany from 1968; Meinhof committed suicide during her trial 1976.
Red Brigades Italy: kidnap and murder of Prime Minister Aldo Moro 1978; kidnap of US Brigadier-General James Lee Dozier 1981.
Sandinista National Liberation Front Marxist organization which overthrew the fascist dictatorship in ◊Nicaragua 1978–79 to form its own government.
Symbionese Liberation Army USA: kidnap of Patricia Hearst, granddaughter of W R ◊Hearst, 1974.
Tamil Tigers Tamil separatist organization in Sri Lanka.
Tupamaros left-wing urban guerrillas founded by Raoul Sendic in Montevideo, Uruguay, 1960; named after the Peruvian Indian leader ◊Tupac Amaru.

Ulster Defence Association UDA Protestant anti-IRA organization in Northern Ireland, formed 1971.

Violent activities (bombings, kidnappings, ◊hijackings, and so on) by such groups as these have proliferated considerably in recent years; in 1984 there were 600 international terrorist incidents, a 20 per cent increase on the average over the previous five years. Cooperation between the groups (for example in arms supply) has developed, as has state support (such as the USA's for the Contras and Libya's for many groups, including the IRA). Efforts by governments to put a stop to their activities have had only sporadic success. The Council of Europe has set up the European Convention on the Suppression of Terrorism, to which many governments are signatories. In Britain the Prevention of Terrorism Act 1984 is aimed particularly at the IRA. The Institute for the Study of Terrorism was founded in London 1986.

Guesdes /ged/ Jules 1845–1922. French socialist leader from the 1880s who espoused Marxism and revolutionary change. His movement, the *Partie Ouvrier Français*, was eventually incorporated in the foundation of the SFIO (*Section Française de l'International Ouvrière*) in 1905.

Guevara /gɪˈvɑːrə/ Ernesto 'Che' 1928–1967. Argentinian revolutionary. Born in Argentina, he was trained as a doctor, but in 1953 left the country because of his opposition to Perón. In effecting the Cuban revolution of 1959, he was second only to ◊Castro and his brother, but in 1965 moved on to fight against white mercenaries in the Congo, and then to Bolivia, where he was killed in an unsuccessful attempt to lead a peasant rising. He was an orthodox Marxist, and his guerrilla techniques were influential.

Guiana /giːˈɑːnə/ the NE part of South America, which includes ◊French Guiana, ◊Guyana, and ◊Suriname.

Guido /ˈɡiːdəʊ/ Reni Italian painter, see ◊Reni.

Guienne /giːˈèn/ old province of SW France which formed the duchy of Aquitaine with Gascony in the 12th century. Its capital was Bordeaux. It became English in 1154 and passed to France in 1451.

guild or *gild* in commercial and labour history, medieval association particularly of craftsmen or merchants, formed for mutual aid and protection and the pursuit of a common purpose, religious or economic. They became politically powerful in Europe. Guilds fulfilling charitable or religious functions, such as the maintenance of schools, roads, or bridges, the assistance of members in misfortune, or the provision of masses for the souls of dead members, flourished in England from the 9th century down to 1547, when they were suppressed.

The earliest form of economic guild, the *guild merchant* arose in the 11th–12th centuries; this was an organization of the traders of a town, who had been granted a practical monopoly of its trade by charter. As the merchants often strove to exclude craftsmen from the guild, and to monopolize control of local government, the

Guinea
REPUBLIC OF (*République de Guinée*)

AREA 245,860 sq km/95,000 sq mi
CAPITAL Conakry
TOWNS Labe, N'Zerekore, KanKan
PHYSICAL mainly mountainous; sources of rivers Niger, Gambia, and Senegal; forest in SE
FEATURES Fouta Djallon, area of sandstone plateaux, cut by deep valleys
HEAD OF STATE AND OF GOVERNMENT Lansana Conté from 1984
GOVERNMENT military
EXPORTS coffee, rice, palm kernels; alumina, bauxite, diamonds
CURRENCY syli or franc (561.85 = £1 Sept 1987)
POPULATION (1985) 5,597,000 (chief peoples are Fulani 40%, Mandingo 25%); annual growth rate 2.3%
LANGUAGE French (official)
RELIGION Muslim 62%, Christian 15%, local 35%
LITERACY 44% male/14% female (1980)
GNP $1.6 bn (1983); $305 per head of population
CHRONOLOGY
1958 Full independence from France achieved. Sékou Touré elected president.

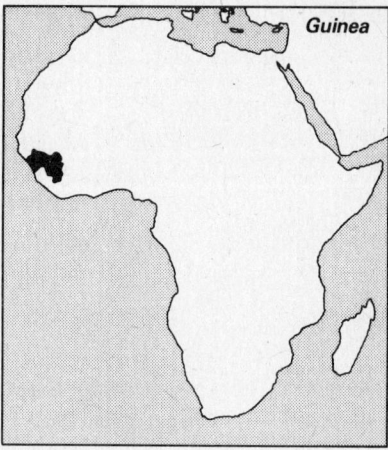

1977 Strong opposition to Touré's policies of rigid Marxism forced him to accept the return to a mixed economy.
1980 Touré returned unopposed for a fourth seven-year term of office.
1984 Touré died. A bloodless coup established a military committee for national recovery, with Col Lansana Conté at its head.
1985 Attempted coup against Conté while he was out of the country was foiled by loyal troops.

craft guilds came into existence in the 12th–13th centuries. These, which included journeymen and apprentices as well as employers, regulated prices, wages, working conditions and apprenticeship, prevented unfair practices, and maintained high standards of craftmanship; they also fulfilled many social, religious and charitable functions. By the 14th century they had taken control of local government, ousting the guild merchant.

After the 16th century the position of the guilds was undermined by the growth of capitalism. The beginning of trade unionism is sometimes traced back to the guilds.

Guildford /ˈɡɪlfəd/ city, administrative headquarters of Surrey, England; population (1981) 56,650. It has a ruined Norman castle; a cathedral designed by Sir Edward ◊Maufe (1936–61); the University of Surrey 1966, and a theatre (1964) named after the comedy actress Yvonne Arnaud (1895–1958).

Guild Socialism an early 20th-century movement in Britain whose aim was to organize and control the industrial life of the country through self-governing democratic guilds of workers. The National Guilds League was founded in 1915, and at the movement's height there were over 20 guilds, but it did not achieve success, and in 1925 the League dissolved.

guillemot diving seabird of the auk family, which breeds in large numbers on the rocky N Atlantic coasts. The *common guillemot Uria aalge* has a sharp bill and short tail, and sooty-brown and white plumage. Guillemots build no

nest, but lay one large, almost conical, egg on the rock.

guillotine beheading device consisting of a metal blade that descends between two posts. It was commonly in use in the Middle Ages, but was introduced in an improved design (by physician Joseph Ignace Guillotin 1738–1814) in France in 1792 during the Revolution. It is still in use in some countries.

guillotine in politics, a device used by governments in the UK of restricting the time allowed for a bill's debate in the House of Commons, to ensure its speedy passage to receiving the royal assent (that is, to becoming law). The tactic of guillotining was introduced during the 1880s to overcome attempts by Irish members of parliament to obstruct the passing of legislation.

guinea /ˈɡɪni/ English gold coin, notionally worth 21 shillings (£1.05). It has not been minted since 1817, when it was superseded by the gold ◊sovereign, but was used until 1971 in billing professional fees.

Guinea /ˈɡɪni/ country in W Africa, bounded to the N by Senegal, NE by Mali, SE by the Ivory Coast, SW by Liberia and Sierra Leone, W by the Atlantic, and NW by Guinea-Bissau.
government the 1982 constitution, which provided for an elected national assembly, was suspended in 1984, after a military coup. A military committee for national recovery assumed power. The president is head of both state and government and leads an appointed council of ministers. The sole political party, the

Democratic Party of Guinea (PDG), was dissolved after the coup and opposition groups now operate from abroad.

history formerly part of the Muslim ◊Mali empire, which flourished in the region between the 7th and 15th centuries, Guinea's first European visitors were the Portuguese in the mid-15th century, who, together with France and Britain, established the slave trade in the area. In 1849 France proclaimed the Boké region in the E a French protectorate and expanded its territory until by the late 19th century most of W Africa was united under French rule as ◊French West Africa.

French Guinea became fully independent in 1958, under the name of Guinea, after a referendum rejected a proposal to remain a self-governing colony within the French Community. The first president was Sekou Touré, who made the PDG the only political organization and embarked upon a policy of socialist revolution. There were unsuccessful attempts to overthrow him in 1961, 1965, 1967, and 1970 and, suspicious of conspiracies by foreign powers, he put his country for a time into virtual diplomatic isolation. By 1975, however, relations with most of his neighbours had returned to normal.

Initially rigidly Marxist, crushing opposition to his policies, Touré gradually moved towards a mixed economy, private enterprise becoming legal in 1979. His regime was, nevertheless, authoritarian and harsh. He sought closer relations with Western powers, particularly France and the USA, and was re-elected unopposed in 1980. In 1984 he died while undergoing heart surgery in the USA.

Before the normal machinery for electing his successor could be put into operation, the army staged a bloodless coup, suspending the constitution and setting up a military committee for national recovery, with Col Lansana Conté at its head. He pledged to restore democracy and respect human rights, releasing hundreds of political prisoners and lifting press restrictions. Conté then made efforts to restore his country's international standing through a series of overseas visits. He succeeded in persuading some 200,000 Guineans who had fled the country during the Touré regime to return. In 1985 an attempt to overthrow him while he was out of the country was foiled by loyal troops.

Guinea-Bissau /'gɪni bɪ'saʊ/ country in W Africa, bounded to the N by Senegal, E and SE by Guinea, and SW by the Atlantic.

government Guinea-Bissau is a one-party state, the 1984 constitution describing the African Party for the Independence of Portuguese Guinea and Cape Verde (PAIGC) as 'the leading force in society and in the nation'. Although Cape Verde chose independence, the title of the original party which served the two countries has been retained. The constitution also provides for a 150-member national people's assembly, all nominees of PAIGC. The assembly elects the president, who is head of both state and government. Policy is determined by PAIGC and it is there that ultimate political power lies, the president being its secretary-general.

history Guinea-Bissau was first reached by Europeans when the Portuguese arrived in 1446, and became a slave trading centre. Until 1879 it was administered with the Cape Verde islands, but then became a separate colony under the name of Portuguese Guinea.

Nationalist groups began to form in the 1950s and PAIGC was established in 1956. Portugal refused to grant independence, fighting broke out, and by 1972 PAIGC claimed to control two thirds of the country. The following year the 'liberated areas' were declared independent and in 1973 a national people's assembly was set up and Luiz Cabral appointed president of a state council. Some 40,000 Portuguese troops were engaged in trying to put down the uprising and were suffering heavy losses but, before a clear outcome was reached, a coup in Portugal ended the fighting and PAIGC negotiated independence with the new government in Lisbon.

In 1974 Portugal formally acknowledged Guinea-Bissau as a sovereign nation. PAIGC began to lay the foundations of a socialist state, intended to include Cape Verde, but in 1980, four days before approval of the constitution, Cape Verde withdrew, feeling that Guinea-Bissau was being given preferential treatment. A coup deposed Cabral and João Vieira became chairman of a council of revolution.

At its 1981 congress, PAIGC decided to retain its name, despite Cape Verde's withdrawal, and its position as the only party was confirmed, with Vieira as secretary-general. Normal relations between the two countries were restored in 1982.

In 1984 a new constitution made Vieira head of government as well as head of state.

Guinea Coast /'gɪni/ the coast of W Africa between Gambia and Cape Lopez.

guinea fowl African game bird, family Numididae, especially the *helmet guinea fowl Numida meleagris* which has a horny growth on the head, white-spotted feathers, and fleshy cheek wattles, and is the ancestor of the domestic form.

guinea pig a species of ◊cavy, a type of rodent.

Guinness /'gɪnɪs/ Alec 1914– . British actor. He joined the Old Vic in 1936. His stage appearances include Shakespeare's Hamlet in modern dress in 1938 and Lawrence of Arabia (in *Ross* in 1960); and in 1979 he gained a 'lifetime achievement' Oscar (films include *Kind Hearts and Coronets* 1949 and *The Bridge on the River Kwai* 1957). Television includes *Tinker, Tailor, Soldier, Spy* 1979, and *Smiley's People* 1981. He was knighted in 1959.

Guise /gwiːz/ French noble family active in the 16th-century religious wars:

Francis, 2nd Duke of Guise (1519–63), combatted the ◊Huguenots and was assassinated; his son *Henri* 3rd Duke of Guise (1550–88), also assassinated, was largely responsible for the Massacre of St Bartholomew in 1572.

guitar six-stringed, flat-backed musical instrument plucked or strummed with the fingers, a later development of the ◊lute, and derived from a Moorish orginal. Popular

17th–mid 19th century, it was revived for concert purposes by Andrés ◊Segovia. From 1890 it was an instrument of American mountain folk musicians; from 1930 electrically amplified versions were used in jazz and dance bands; and from the 1950s the solid-bodied *electric guitar* became the dominant instrument of pop music. The *Hawaiian guitar* has a 'singing tone' achieved by sliding up and down the metal bar across the strings, which is used (instead of the fingers) to 'stop' them.

Guiyang /ˌgweɪ'jæn/ capital (formerly Kweiyang) and industrial city of Guizhou province, China; population (1985) 784,000.

Guizhou /ˌgweɪ'dʒəʊ/ province (formerly Kweichow) of S China

area 174,000 sq km/67,164 sq mi

capital Guiyang

features includes many minority groups which have often been in revolt

products rice, maize; non-ferrous minerals

population (1982) 28,552,997.

Guizot /giː'zəʊ/ François Pierre Guillaume 1787–1874. French statesman and historian. Born at Nîmes, he was a Protestant, and 1812–30 was professor of modern history at the Sorbonne. He wrote on the history of civilization, and became prime minister in 1847. His resistance to all reforms led to the Revolution of 1848.

Gujarat /ˌgʊdʒə'rɑːt/ state of W India

area 195,984 sq km/75,668 sq mi

capital Gandhinagar

features heavily industrialized; includes most of the Rann of Kutch; the Gir Forest is the last home of the wild Asian lion

population (1984) 34,085,799

languages Gujarati, Hindi.

Gujarati or Gujerati language a member of the Indo-Iranian branch of the Indo-European language family, spoken in and around the state of Gujarat in India. It is written in its own script, a variant of the Devanagari script used for Sanskrit and Hindi.

gulf name given to any large sea inlet.

Gulf States oil-rich countries sharing the coastline of the Arabian/Persian Gulf (Iran, Iraq, Bahrein, Kuwait, Oman, Qatar, Saudi Arabia, and the United Arab Emirates). The last six formed a Gulf Co-operation Council (GCC) in 1981.

In the USA, those states bordering the Gulf of Mexico (Alabama, Florida, Louisiana, Mississippi, and Texas).

Gulf Stream ocean ◊current arising from the warm waters of the equatorial current, which flows N from the Gulf of Mexico. It slows to a broadening 'drift' off Newfoundland, splitting as it flows E across the Atlantic, and tempering the harshness of the climate of the British Isles and Western Europe.

Gulf War another name for the ◊Iran-Iraq War.

gull seabird of the family Laridae. A typical gull of the genus *Larus* is the *black-headed gull Larus ridibundus*, common in Britain, which is grey and white with (in summer) dark brown head and red beak; it breeds in large colonies on marshland, making a nest of dead rushes, averaging three eggs. Allied are the larger

Guinea-Bissau
(*Republica da Guiné-Bissau*)

AREA 36,125 sq km/14,000 sq mi
CAPITAL and chief port Bissau
PHYSICAL flat lowlands
FEATURES the archipelago of Bijagos
HEAD OF STATE AND HEAD OF GOVERNMENT João
Bernardo Vieira from 1980
GOVERNMENT one-party socialist
EXPORTS rice, coconuts, peanuts; fish; salt
CURRENCY peso (1,074.13 = £1 Sept 1987)
POPULATION 860,000 (1985); annual growth
rate 2%
LANGUAGE Crioulo, Cape Verdean dialect of
Portuguese
RELIGION Muslim 40%, Christian 4%
LITERACY 25% male/13% female (1980 est)
GDP $177 million (1982); $165 per head of
population
CHRONOLOGY
1956 African Party for the Independence of
Portuguese Guinea and Cape Verde (PAIGC)
formed to secure independence from Portugal.
1973 Two-thirds of the country declared
independent, with Luiz Cabral as president of
a state council.
1974 Portugal recognized independence of
Guinea-Bissau.

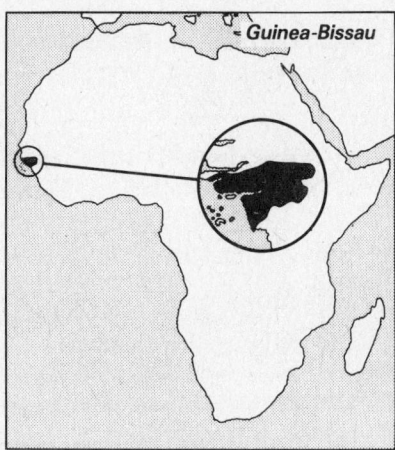

- Guinea-Bissau

1980 Cape Verde decided not to join a unified
state. Cabral deposed amd João Vieira became
chair of a council of revolution.
1981 PAIGC confirmed as the only legal
party, with Vieira as its secretary general.
1982 Normal relations with Cape Verde
restored.
1984 New constitution adopted, making
Vieira head of government as well as head of
state.

gull The herring gull is often seen on beaches, but
its nests are usually hidden in sheltered spots high
up on the cliffs.

Guinness One of Alex Guinness's best-known
character portrayals is George Smiley in the
award-winning television series Smiley's People,

laughing gull of America, and the *great black-
headed gull Larus ichthyaetus* of Asia. Other
notable gulls are the *herring gull Larus
argentatus*, often known in the USA as the
harbour gull, which has white and pearl-grey
adult plumage and yellow beak; and the oceanic
great black-backed gull Larus marinus, found
in the Atlantic and over 75 cm/2.5 ft long.

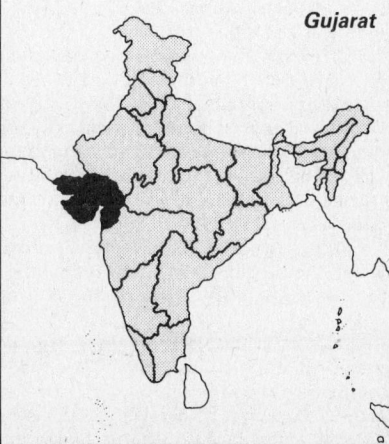

Gujarat

gum in botany, complex polysaccharides
(carbohydrates) formed by many plants and
trees, particularly by those from dry regions.
Tasteless, odourless substances, insoluble in
alcohol and ether but generally soluble in water,
gums are used for adhesives, sizing fabrics, in
confectionery, medicine, and calico printing.
They form five main groups: plant exudates, for
example, gum arabic; marine plant extracts, for
example, agar; seed extracts; fruit and vegetable
extracts; and synthetic gums. Also, a common
name for the ⟡eucalyptus tree.

gum in mammals, the soft tissues surrounding
the base of the tooth. They are liable to
inflammation or to infection by microbes from
food deposits (gingivitis or periodontal disease).

gum arabic substance obtained from certain
species of ⟡acacia, with uses in medicine,
confectionery and adhesive manufacture.

gun the name given to all kinds of firearms.
See⟡artillery,⟡machine-gun,⟡pistol, and⟡small
arms.

gun metal a high copper (88%) alloy, also
containing tin and zinc, so called because it was
once used to cast cannon. It is tough,
hardwearing and resists corrosion.

gunpowder the oldest known ⟡explosive, a
mixture of sulphur, sodium or potassium nitrate
($NaNO_3$ or KNO_3) and charcoal. Though no
longer used as a propellant, it is in wide use for
blasting and fireworks.

Gunpowder Plot in England, the Catholic
conspiracy to blow up James I and his parliament
on 5 Nov 1605. It was discovered through an
anonymous letter sent to Lord Monteagle
(1575–1622), and Guy⟡Fawkes was found in the
cellar beneath the Palace of Westminster, ready
to fire a store of explosives. Several of the
conspirators were killed, and Guy Fawkes and
seven others were executed. The event is
commemorated in England by fireworks and
burning 'guys' on bonfires. The searching of the
vaults of parliament before the opening of each
new session, however, was not instituted until the
'Popish Plot' of 1678.

Guomindang Chinese National People's
Party, founded 1894 by ⟡Sun Zhong Shan (Sun
Yat-sen), which overthrew the Manchu Empire
in 1912. By 1927 the right wing, led by ⟡Jiang Jie
Shi (Chiang Kai-shek), was in conflict with the
left, led by ⟡Mao Zedong until the Communist
victory in 1949 (except for the period of the

Japanese invasion 1937–45). It survives in ◊Taiwan, where it is still spelt Kuomintang.

Gurdjieff /'gɜːdʒief/ George Ivanovitch 1877–1949. Russian occultist. He used stylized dance to 'free' people to develop their full capabilities, and influenced the modern human-potential movement. The mystic ◊Ouspensky was a disciple, who expanded his ideas.

Gurkha /'gɜːkə/ member of the ruling Hindu caste in Nepál. Renowned soldiers, Gurkha men have been recruited since 1815 for the British army, and the Brigade of Gurkhas has its headquarters in Hong Kong.

gurnard genus of coastal fish (*Trigla*) in the family Trigilidae, which creep along the sea bottom by means of three finger-like appendages detached from the pectoral fins. They are both tropic and temperate zone fish, several species being found in British waters, where they are trawled for food.

guru (Hindi *gurū*) name for Hindu or Sikh leader, or religious teacher.

Gush Emunim /'guʃ e'muːnɪm/ Israeli fundamentalist group (Bloc of the Faithful), founded in 1973, who claim divine right to the West Bank, Gaza Strip, and Golan Heights as part of Israel through settlement, sometimes extending the claim to the Euphrates.

Gustaf V /'gustɑːv/ 1858–1950. King of Sweden. Son of Oscar II, he married Princess Victoria, daughter of the Grand Duke of Baden, in 1881, thus uniting the reigning Bernadotte dynasty with the former royal house of Vasa. He succeeded his father in 1907. *Gustaf VI* (1882–1973), son of Gustaf V, was an archaeologist and expert on Chinese art. His first wife was Princess Margaret of Connaught (1882–1920), and in 1923 he married Lady Louise Mountbatten (1889–1965), sister of the Earl of Mountbatten of Burma. He was succeeded by his grandson ◊Carl XVI Gustaf.

Gustavus Adolphus /gu'stɑːvəs ə'dɒlfəs/ 1594–1632. King of Sweden. Son of Charles IX, whom he succeeded in 1611, he waged successful wars with Denmark, Russia, and Poland, and in the Thirty Years' War became a champion of the Protestant cause. Landing in Germany in 1630, he defeated Wallenstein at Lützen on 6 Nov 1632, but was killed in the battle. He was known as the 'Lion of the North'.

Gustavus Vasa /'vɑːsə/ 1496–1560. Leader of the Swedish revolt against Danish rule, he was elected king of Sweden in 1523, and established Lutheranism as the State religion.

Gutenberg /'guːtnbɜːg/ Johann c. 1400–1468. German printer, considered the inventor of printing from metal moveable type. Born at Mainz, he lived at Strasbourg, but about 1448 set up a printing business in Mainz with Johann Fust as a partner. The partnership was dissolved through monetary difficulties, but Gutenberg set up another printing press. He is believed to have printed the Mazarin and the Bamberg Bibles.

Guthrie /'gʌθri/ Tyrone 1900–1971. British theatre director. Administrator of the Old ◊Vic and Sadler's Wells 1939–45, he helped found the Ontario (Stratford) Shakespeare Festival in 1953 and the Minneapolis theatre now named

Gutenberg The earliest illustration of a printing-press, as invented by Johann Gutenberg. It is from the *Dance Macabre* printed by Mathias Lyons, 1499. Note the compositor with case of type, the press-man, his colleague inking a form with ink-balls, and the bookseller in the adjoining shop.

after him. He is notable for the first modern-dress *Hamlet* in 1938 with Alec Guinness.

gutta percha juice of tropical trees, such as the Malayan *Palaquium gutta*, which is hardened to form a flexible, rubbery substance used for insulating electrical cables, but is now largely replaced by synthetics.

guttation the secretion of water onto the surface of leaves through specialized pores, or ◊hydathodes. The process occurs most frequently during conditions of high humidity when the rate of transpiration is low. Drops of water found on grass in early morning are often the result of guttation, rather than dew. Sometimes the water contains minerals in solution, such as calcium, which leaves a white crust on the leaf surface as it dries.

Guyana /gaɪ'ænə/ country in S America, bounded to the N by the Atlantic Ocean, E by Suriname, S and SW by Brazil, and NW by Venezuela.

government Guyana is a sovereign republic within the ◊Commonwealth. The 1980 constitution provides for a single-chamber national assembly of 65 members, 53 elected by universal suffrage and 12 elected by the regions, for a five-year term. The president is the nominee of the party winning most votes in the national assembly elections and serves for the life of the assembly, appointing a cabinet which is collectively responsible to it. The main political parties are the People's National Congress (PNC), and the People's Progressive Party (PPP).

history the area now known as Guyana was a Dutch colony 1621–1796, when it was seized by Britain. In 1814 it was made a British colony under the name of British Guiana, and became part of the Commonwealth from 1831 until full independence in 1966.

The move from colonial to republican status was gradual and not entirely smooth. In 1953 a constitution providing for free elections to an assembly was introduced and the left-wing PPP, led by Dr Cheddi Jagan, won the popular vote. Within months, however, the UK government suspended the constitution and put in its own interim administration, claiming that the PPP threatened to become a communist dictatorship. In 1957 a breakaway group from the PPP founded a new party, the PNC, which was supported mainly by African-descended Guyanans, while PPP followers were mainly of Indian descent. Fresh elections, under a revised constitution, were held in 1967 and PPP won again, with Jagan becoming chief minister. Internal self-government was granted in 1961 and, with PPP again the successful party, Jagan became prime minister. Proportional representation was introduced in 1963 and in the 1964 elections, under the new voting procedures, PPP, although winning most votes, did not have an overall majority so a PPP-PNC coalition was formed, with PNC leader Forbes Burnham as prime minister.

This coalition took the country through to full independence in 1966. PNC won the 1968 and 1973 elections and in 1970 Guyana became a republic within the Commonwealth. In 1980 a new constitution was adopted, making the president head of both state and government and as a result of the 1981 elections, which opposition parties claimed were fraudulent, Burnham became executive president. The rest of his administration was marked by economic deterioration, necessitating austerity measures, and cool relations with the Western powers, particularly the US, whose invasion of Grenada he condemned. He died in 1985 and was succeeded by Prime Minister Desmond Hoyte.

Guyana
COOPERATIVE REPUBLIC OF

AREA 210,000 sq km/83,000 sq mi
CAPITAL and port Georgetown
PHYSICAL mostly tropical rain forest
FEATURES Mount Roraima; Kaietur National
Park including Kaietur Fall on the Potaro
(tributary of Essequibo) 250 m/822 ft (five
times height of Niagara)
HEAD OF STATE AND OF GOVERNMENT Desmond
Hoyte from 1985
GOVERNMENT democratic
EXPORTS sugar, rice, rum, timber, diamonds
CURRENCY Guyana dollar (14.85 = £1 Sept
1987)
POPULATION (1985) 768,000 (50% E Indians,
introduced to work the sugar plantations after
the abolition of slavery, 30% black, 5%
Amerindian); annual growth rate 2%
LANGUAGE English (official), Hindi
RELIGION Christian 57%, Hindu 33%, Sunni
Muslim 9%
LITERACY 96% male/93% female (1980 est)
GNP $419 million (1983); $457 per head of
population
CHRONOLOGY
1953 Assembly elections won by left-wing
party. Britain installed interim administration,
claiming fear of communist takeover.

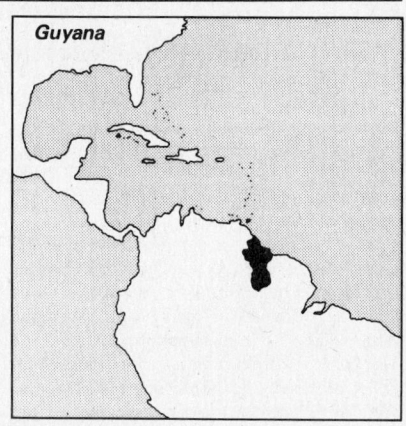

1961 Internal self-government granted.
1966 Full independence achieved.
1970 Guyana became a republic within the
Commonwealth.
1980 Forbes Burnham became the first
executive president under new constitution.
1985 Burnham died and was succeeded by
Desmond Hoyte.

Gwyn Formerly an orange-seller outside London's
Drury Lane Theatre, Nell Gwyn became the
mistress of Charles II, and had two sons by him.
This portrait by Sir Peter Lely is in Raby Castle,
County Durham.

Guys /gwiːs/ Constantin 1805–1892. French
artist. He was with ◊Byron at Missolonghi, and
is noted for sketches of the Crimean War for the
Illustrated London News and realistic drawings
of Parisian life.
   Gwalior /'gwaːliɔː/ city in Madhya Pradesh,
India; population (1981) 543,862. Formerly a
small princely state, it has Jain and Hindu
monuments.
   Gwent /gwent/ county of S Wales
area 1,376 sq km/531 sq mi
towns administrative headquarters Cwmbran;
Abergavenny, Newport, Tredegar
features Wye Valley; Tintern Abbey; Legionary
Museum of Caerleon, and Roman amphitheatre;
Chepstow and Raglan castles
products salmon and trout on the Wye and Usk;
iron and steel at Llanwern, tinplate at Ebbw Vale
population (1985) 438,500
language 2.5% Welsh-speaking; English
famous people Aneurin ◊Bevan and Neil
◊Kinnock, both born in Tredegar; Alfred Russel
◊Wallace.
   Gwyn /gwɪn/ Eleanor ('Nell') 1651–1687.
English comedy actress from 1665, formerly an
orange-seller at Drury Lane Theatre. ◊Dryden
wrote parts for her, and from 1669 she was the
mistress of Charles II (the elder of her two sons
by him was created Duke of St Albans in 1684),
almost his last wish being 'Let not poor Nellie
starve'.
   Gwynedd /'gwɪnəð/ county of NW Wales
area 3,867 sq km/1,493 sq mi
towns administrative headquarters Caernarfon;
Bangor; resorts Pwllheli, Barmouth

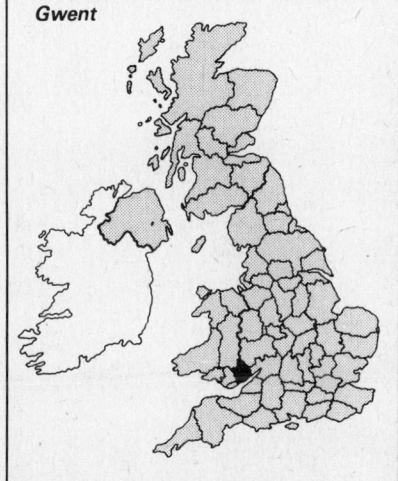

features Snowdonia National Park including
Snowdon (Welsh *Yr Wyddfa*; the highest
mountain in Wales) 1,085 m/3,559 ft, Cader
Idris 892 m/2,928 ft, and the largest Welsh lake,
Llyn Tegid (Bala) 6 km/4 mi long, 1.6 km/1 mi
wide; Caernarfon Castle; ◊Anglesey is across the
Menai Straits; Segontium Roman Fort Museum,
Caernarfon; Criccieth and Harlech castles.
products cattle and sheep, gold (at ◊Dolgellau)
population (1984) 232,000
language 61% Welsh-speaking; English

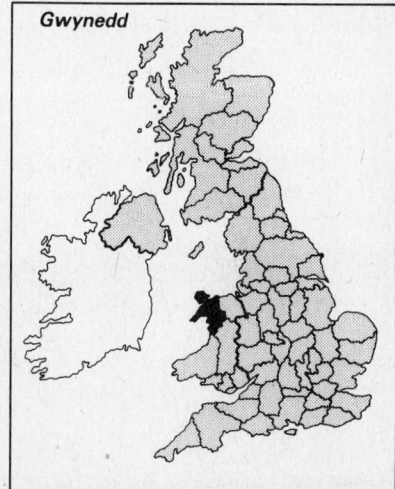

gymnastics physical exercises, originally just
for health and training (so-named from the way
in which men of ancient Greece trained *gymnos*
'naked'). The *gymnasia* were schools for training
competitors for public games. It was first revived
in 19th-century Germany as an aid to military
strength, and was also taken up by educationists
including Froebel and Pestalozzi, becoming a
recognized part of the school curriculum. Today
it is an increasingly popular spectator sport.

World Championships first held 1903, now
biennial
Overall Champions
men: individual/team
1978 Nikolai Adrianov *(USSR)*/Japan
1979 Aleksandr Ditiatin *(USSR)*/USSR
1981 Yuri Korolev *(USSR)*/USSR

1983 Dimitri Belozertchev *(USSR)*/China
1985 Yuri Korolev *(USSR)*/USSR
women: individual/team
1978 Elena Mukhina *(USSR)*/USSR
1979 Nelli Kim *(USSR)*/Romania
1981 Olga Bitcherova *(USSR)*/USSR
1983 Natalia Yurchenko *(USSR)*/USSR
1985 Elena Shoushounova *(USSR)* and Oksana Omeliantchik *(USSR)*/USSR

Men's gymnastics includes horizontal and parallel bars, horse vault, rings, pommel horse and floor exercises.

Women's gymnastics includes asymmetrical bars, side horse vault, balance beam and floor exercises. The advantages conferred by extreme suppleness and lightness has resulted in the best executants being young and immature in physique, for example, Olga Korbut and Nadia Comaneci. Also popular are *sports acrobatics* performed by gymnasts in pairs, trios, or fours to music, where the emphasis is on dance, balance, and timing, and *rhythmic gymnastics* choreographed to music and performed by individuals of six-girl teams, with small hand apparatus including ribbons and hoops.

gynoecium or *gynaecium* the collective term for the female reproductive organs of a flower, comprising one or more ◊carpels, either free or fused together.

gypsum a mineral of common occurrence, composed of hydrated calcium sulphate, $CaSO_4.2H_2O$. It has a number of commercial uses. A fine-grained gypsum, called alabaster, is used for ornamental work. Burnt gypsum is known as plaster of Paris, because for a long time it was obtained from the gypsum quarries of the Montmartre district, and it is used for making casts and moulds, and for setting broken bones.

gypsy English name for a member of the ◊Romany people.

gyre a circular flow of ocean water. Gyres are large and permanent, typically occupying half an ocean. Their movements are dictated by the prevailing winds and the ◊Coriolis effect. They move clockwise in the northern hemisphere and anticlockwise in the southern hemisphere. They tend to be narrower and faster on their W sides and are centred on the subtropical belts of high atmosphere pressure. See ◊current.

gyroscope mechanical instrument, used as a stabilizing device, and consisting, in its simplest form, of a heavy wheel mounted on an axis fixed in a ring that can be rotated about another axis, which is also fixed in a ring capable of rotation about a third axis. The whole is arranged so that the three axes of rotation in any position pass through the wheel's centre of gravity. The wheel is thus capable of rotation about three mutually perpendicular axes, and its axis may take up any direction. If the axis of the spinning wheel is displaced, a restoring movement develops returning it to its initial direction. Important applications of the gyroscope principle include the gyro-compass, the gyropilot for automatic steering, and gyro-directed torpedoes.

H eighth letter of the Roman alphabet, representing an aspirate in all modern alphabets derived from the Latin except in those languages, especially the Romance languages, where the aspirate is lost. It is used in several digraphs (conventional two-letter sequences with special values), such as ch, ph, sh, th. The 'dropping of initial h', often regarded as a corruption in modern dialects, is a phenomenon traceable at least as far back as Tudor times.

Haakon VII /'hɔːkɒn/ 1872–1957. King of Norway. Born Prince Charles, the second son of Frederick VIII of Denmark, in 1896 he married Princess Maud (1869–1938), youngest daughter of Edward VII of England. He was elected king of Norway in 1905 on the separation of the country from Sweden, and at his coronation in 1906 he took the name of Haakon. When the Germans invaded Norway in 1940 he refused to surrender and, when armed resistance in Norway was no longer possible, carried on the struggle from Britain until his triumphant return in 1945.

Haarlem /'hɑːləm/ industrial town in the W Netherlands, 20 km/12 mi W of Amsterdam; population (1984) 152,511. At Velsea to the N a road-rail tunnel runs under the North Sea Canal, linking N and S Holland. Industries include textiles and printing. Haarlem has a 15th–16th-century cathedral and a Frans ◊Hals Museum.

habanera or *havanaise* a slow dance in two-four time originating in Havana, Cuba, which became very popular when introduced into Spain during the 19th century. There is a famous example in Bizet's opera *Carmen.*

habeas corpus (Latin 'have the body'). In English law since 1679, a writ directed to a person who has custody of a prisoner, ordering him to produce the prisoner before the court issuing the writ, and to explain why the prisoner is detained in custody. Traditional rights were enforced, mainly due to Lord Shaftesbury, under the Habeas Corpus Act (1679); the Scottish equivalent is the Wrongous Imprisonment Act (1701). The main principles were also adopted in the US constitution.

Haber /'hɑːbə/ Fritz 1868–1934. German chemist, whose conversion of atmospheric nitrogen to ammonia opened the way for the synthetic fertilizer industry. His study of the combustion of hydrocarbons led to the commercial 'cracking' or ◊fractionating of natural oil into its components, for example diesel, petrol, and paraffin. In electrochemistry he was the first to demonstrate that oxidation and reduction take place at the ◊electrodes; from this he developed a general electrochemical theory. In World War I he worked on poison gas and devised gas masks, hence there were protests against his Nobel prize in 1918.

habitat in ecology, the localized ◊environment in which an organism lives. Habitats are often described by the dominant plant type or physical feature, thus an oak-wood habitat or rocky seashore habitat.

Habsburg /'hæpsbɜːɡ/ alternative form of ◊Hapsburg, European royal family and former imperial house of Austria-Hungary.

Hackney /'hækni/ inner borough of N central Greater London.
features Hackney Downs and Hackney Marsh, formerly the haunt of highwaymen, now a leisure area; includes *Shoreditch*, site of England's first theatre (The Theatre) in 1576; *Stoke Newington*, where Daniel ◊Defoe once lived.
population (1984) 187,900.

Haddingtonshire /'hædɪŋtənʃə/ name until 1921 of the Scottish county of East Lothian, since 1975 part of the region of ◊Lothian.

haddock important food fish *Melanogrammus aeglefinus*, one of the cod family found off the North Atlantic coasts. Haddock may be eaten fresh, but split and smoked haddock, especially from Finnan, near Aberdeen, is a delicacy.

Hades /'heɪdiːz/ in Greek mythology, the underworld where the spirits of the departed went after death, usually depicted as a cavern or pit underneath the earth. It was presided over by the god Hades or ◊Pluto (Roman ◊Dis). He was the brother of Zeus, and married ◊Persephone, daughter of Demeter and ◊Zeus. She was allowed to return to the upper world for part of the year, bringing spring with her. The entrance to Hades was guarded by the three-headed dog ◊Cerberus. ◊*Tartarus* was the section where the wicked were punished, for example ◊Tantalus.

Hadhramaut /ˌhɑːdrəˈmaʊt/ district of the People's Democratic Republic of Yemen (South Yemen), which was formerly ruled by Arab chiefs in protective relations with Britain. A remote plateau region at 1,400 m/4,500 ft, it was for a long time unknown to westerners and later attracted such travellers as Harry St John Philby and Freya Stark.

Hadrian /'heɪdrɪən/ 76–138 AD. Roman emperor. Born in Spain, he was adopted by his kinsman, the emperor Trajan, whom he succeeded in 117. He abandoned Trajan's conquests in Mesopotamia, and adopted a defensive policy which included the building of ◊Hadrian's Wall in Britain.

Hadrian The Canopus pool of the emperor's villa in Rome, built 118–138 AD. The building in the background, now a museum, was built to house Hadrian's servants and guards.

Hadrian's Wall Roman fortification built 122–26 AD to mark Britain's northern boundary and abandoned about 383; it runs 185 km/115 mi from Wallsend on the Tyne to Maryport, W

Cumbria, and possibly then goes further south. The fort at South Shields, Arbeia, built to defend the eastern end, is being reconstructed as a unique experiment. At least in part, the wall was covered with a glistening, white coat of mortar. In 1985 Roman letters (on paper-thin sheets of wood), the earliest and largest collection of Latin writing, were discovered at Vindolanda Fort.

Haeckel /'hekəl/ Ernst Heinrich 1834–1919. German scientist and philosopher. Born at Potsdam, he became professor of zoology at Jena in 1865. A supporter of ◊Darwin, he worked for more than 50 years on his own 'recapitulation' theory (that embryonic stages represent past stages in the organism's evolution). Although the theory has been superseded, it stimulated much research in ◊embryology.

haematite a valuable red or red-black mineral containing 70 per cent of iron and a low proportion of phosphorus. It is the principal ore of iron, and consists mainly of ferric oxide, Fe_2O_3.

haemoglobin a ◊protein which carries oxygen. In vertebrates it occurs in red blood cells, giving them their colour. Oxygen attaches to haemoglobin when the amount dissolved in the blood is high, in the ◊lungs or ◊gills. This process effectively increases the amount of oxygen that can dissolve in the blood. The oxygen is later released where it is at low concentration, in the body tissues.

haemolymph the circulatory fluid of those molluscs and insects that have an 'open' ◊circulatory system. Haemolymph contains water, amino acids, sugars, salts, and white cells like those of ◊blood. Circulated by a pulsatile heart, its main functions are to transport digestive and excretory products around the body. In molluscs, it also transports oxygen and carbon dioxide.

haemophilia a tendency to uncontrollable bleeding through deficiency in the blood of the normal clotting substances – in most cases, that known as Factor VIII. It is hereditary, occurs only in males, and is transmitted through the mother. A degree of control by drugs and injections of Factor VIII is possible. Tests can ascertain the sex of a child before birth, so that parents with relatives who are or have been known to be haemophiliacs can be offered the option of termination.

haemorrhage loss of blood from the circulation. It is 'manifest' when the blood can be seen, as when it flows from a wound, and 'occult' when the blood is lost internally, as from an ulcer or cancer of the stomach or an internal injury. Severe haemorrhage may cause shock, with possible eventual death, and must be remedied by blood transfusion.

haemorrhagic fever any of several virus diseases of the tropics, in which high temperatures over several days end in haemorrhage from nose, throat, and intestines, with up to 90 per cent mortality. The causative organism lives in rats in the case of West African ◊Lassa fever, but in ◊Marburg disease and ◊Ebola fever, the host animal, which betrays no symptoms, is unknown.

haemorrhoids ◊varicose veins of the anus, popularly called piles.

Hâfiz /'hɑːfɪz/ Shams al-Din Muhammad c. 1326–1390. Persian poet, generally considered the greatest lyric poet of Persia. Born in Shiraz, he taught in a Dervish college there. His *Diwan*, a collection of short odes, contains some extolling the pleasures of life and others satirizing his fellow Dervishes.

hafnium a metallic element; symbol Hf, atomic number 72, atomic weight 178.6. It was discovered by the Danish chemists Coster and von Hevesy. It occurs in zircon, and its properties and compounds closely resemble those of ◊zirconium. It is highly absorbent of neutrons, and is used in control rods in nuclear reactors.

Haganah /ˌhɑːgəˈnɑː/ Zionist military organization in Palestine. It originated under Turkish rule before World War I to protect Jewish settlements, and many of its members served in the British forces in both world wars. After World War II it condemned guerrilla activity, opposing the British authorities only passively. It formed the basis of the Israeli army after Israel was established in 1948.

Haggadah /həˈgɑːdə/ in ◊Judaism, the part of the Talmudic literature not given to religious law (the *Halacha*), but devoted to stories of heroes, and folklore.

Haggard /'hægəd/ H(enry) Rider 1856–1925. British novelist. Born in Norfolk, he held colonial service posts in Natal and the Transvaal 1875–79. He used his South African experience in his romantic adventure tales, including *King Solomon's Mines* 1885 and *She* 1887.

haggis Scottish dish made from a sheep's or calf's heart, liver, and lungs, minced up with onion, oatmeal, suet, spice, pepper and salt, and boiled in the animal's stomach.

Hague, The /heɪg/ (Dutch *'s Gravenhage*) seat of the Netherlands government, linked by canal with Rotterdam and Amsterdam; population (1984) 672,127. It is also the seat of the United Nations International Court of Justice, and the seaside resort of Scheveningen (patronized by Wilhelm II and Churchill), with its Kurhaus, is virtually incorporated.

ha-ha in landscape and architecture, a sunken boundary wall permitting an unobstructed view beyond a garden; a device much used by Capability ◊Brown.

Hahn /hɑːn/ Kurt 1886–1974. German educationist. Founder and headmaster 1920–33 of Salem School in Germany, after his expulsion from Germany by Hitler he founded ◊Gordonstoun School in Scotland and was headmaster 1934–53.

Hahn /hɑːn/ Otto 1879–1968. West German physical chemist, who discovered ◊nuclear fission. Born at Frankfurt-am-Main, he worked with Rutherford and Ramsay, becoming director of the Kaiser-Wilhelm Institute for Chemistry in 1928. With Strassmann 1938 he discovered that uranium nuclei split when bombarded with neutrons, which led to the development of the atomic bomb (first used in 1945). He received the Nobel Prize for Chemistry in 1944.

hahnium the former name for the element ◊unnilpentium.

Haifa /'haɪfə/ port in NE Israel; population (1984) 227,000. Industries include oil refining and chemicals.

Haig /heɪg/ Alexander Meigs 1924– . US general. He became President Nixon's White House chief of staff at the height of ◊Watergate, was ◊NATO commander 1974–79, and was secretary of state to President Reagan 1981–82. He announced in 1987 that he would seek the Republican nomination for the presidency in 1988.

Haig /heɪg/ Douglas, 1st Earl Haig 1861–1928. British soldier, born in Edinburgh. He served in the Omdurman and South African campaigns, and in World War I commanded the 1st Army Corps 1914–15, and the 1st Army in 1915 until he succeeded Sir John French as commander-in-chief the same year. His Somme offensive in the summer of 1916 made considerable advances only at heavy cost, and his Passchendaele offensive (Jul–Nov 1917) achieved little at huge loss. He then loyally supported the French Marshal Foch in his appointment as supreme commander of the Allied armies and in his victorious 1918 offensive, and it was Haig's foresight that persuaded Foch to extend his attack north, so breaking the Hindenburg Line. He has been stringently criticized by some modern historians for the appalling losses on the Somme and at Passchendaele.

Haig The British soldier Douglas Haig, whose Allied offensives during World War I gained little ground with huge loss of life.

haiku 17-syllable Japanese verse form, usually divided into three lines of 5, 7, and 5 syllables. ◊Bashō popularized the form in the 17th century.

hail precipitation in the form of pellets of ice, typically of a few millimetres' diameter (with records of over 400 mm). It is caused by the circulation of moisture in strong convection currents, usually within cumulo-nimbus cloud. Water droplets freeze as they are carried upwards. Further layers of ice are deposited around this nucleus as the circulation continues, until they become too heavy to be supported by the currents and they fall as a hailstorm.

Haile Selassie /ˈhaɪli sɪˈlæsi/ Ras Tafari (The Lion of Judah) 1930–1974. Emperor of Ethiopia. Appointed heir to the empress Zauditu in 1916, he became emperor on her death in 1930. He pleaded unavailingly to the League of Nations against Italian conquest of his country 1935–36, and lived in England until his restoration in 1941. In 1974 he was deposed by a military coup and died in captivity. ◊Rastafarians believe that he was the Messiah, the incarnation of God (Jah).

Haile Selassie Haile Selassie was emperor of Ethiopia until deposed in a military coup in 1974.

Hailsham /ˈheɪlʃəm/ Quintin Hogg, Baron Hailsham of St Marylebone 1907– . British lawyer and Conservative politician. Grandson of Quintin Hogg (1845–1903), a merchant philanthropist who founded in 1882 the institution that developed into the Regent Street Polytechnic, he succeeded his father in 1950 as 2nd Viscount Hailsham. He renounced the title in 1963 to re-enter the Commons, but took a life peerage in 1970 on his appointment as lord chancellor 1970–74. He was the first minister for science and technology 1959–64. He was lord chancellor again 1979–87.

Hainan /ˌhaɪˈnæn/ ' island, part of Guangdong province of China, in the South China Sea; area 34,000 sq km/13,000 sq mi; population (19 6) 2,700,000. The capital is Haikou. It is China's second largest offshore island.

Hainaut /eɪˈnəʊ/ industrial province of SW Belgium; population (1981) 1,297,000. The capital is Mons. It produces coal, iron, and steel.

Haiphong /ˌhaɪˈfɒŋ/ industrial port in N Vietnam; population (1980) 1,305,163. It has shipyards, and industries include cement and textiles. Its harbour was heavily bombed during the Vietnam War.

hair a thread-like structure growing from mammalian skin. Each hair grows from a pit-shaped follicle of outer skin-layer (epidermal cells) embedded in the second layer of the skin, the dermis. It consists of dead cells impregnated with the protein ◊keratin. A coat of hair helps to insulate terrestrial mammals by trapping air next to the body. It also aids camouflage and protection, and its colouring or erection may be used for communication. The average human head has about a million hairs.

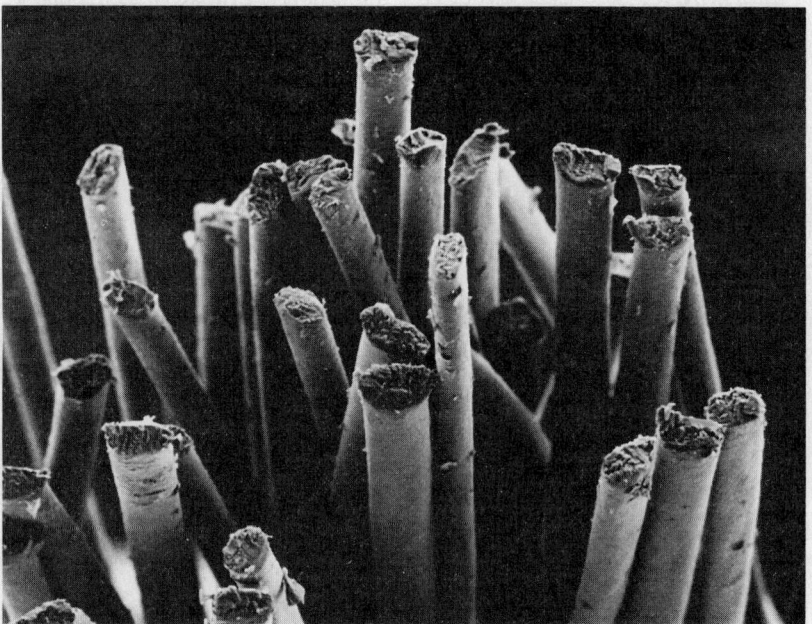

hair Human hairs, cut by scissors, shown magnified 220 times in the scanning electron microscope. There are some 1,000,000 hairs on the average person's head. Each grows at the rate of 5–10 mm per month, lengthening for about three years before being replaced by a new one.

hairstreak one of a group of butterflies, belonging to the Blues (Lycaenidae), and represented in both temperate and tropical regions. Most of them are brownish in their adult form, and they are nearly all tailed.

Haiti /ˈheɪti/ country in the Caribbean, occupying the W part of the island of Hispaniola, to the E is the ◊Dominican Republic.
government the 1950 constitution was revised in 1957, 1964, 1971, 1983, and 1985. The Duvaliers, father and then son, ruled Haiti 1957–86 with absolute power, using private armies to maintain their positions and manipulating the constitution. The leader of the 1986 coup, Lt-Gen Henri Namphy, established a governing council, with himself as its head. Although the constitution provides for an elected national assembly, under the Duvaliers it became a façade for their own dictatorships.
In the 1984 elections about 300 government candidates contested the 59 seats, with no opposition at all. In 1985, political parties were legalized, provided they conformed to strict guidelines, but only one registered, the National Progressive Party (PNP), which supported Duvalier's policies. Since the 1986 coup the future of democracy in Haiti is again under test.

history the island of Hispaniola was once inhabited by ◊Arawak indians. They were driven out in the 14th century by ◊Caribs, 300,000 of whom were wiped out by Europeans in the 50 years following the arrival of Christopher ◊Columbus in 1492. The island was made a Spanish colony under the name of Santo Domingo, but the W part was colonized by France from the mid-16th century. In 1697 it was divided between France and Spain, and in 1795 the E of the island was ceded to France by Spain.

The period 1790–1804, when Haiti became independent, was fraught with rebellions against France, tension between blacks, whites, and mulattos, and military intervention by France and Britain. In one such rebellion the island was taken over by slaves, under Toussaint ◊L'Ouverture, and slavery was abolished, but was reinstated after he was killed by the French. After independence the instability continued, with Santo Domingo repossessed by Spain and then by Haiti, and self-proclaimed kings ruling Haiti. In 1844 Haiti and the Dominican Republic became separate states.
Friction between Haitians of African descent and mulattos, and the country's political instability, brought a period of US rule 1915–34. In the 1940s and 1950s there were several coups, the last being in 1956, which resulted in Dr François Duvalier, a physician, being elected president. After an encouraging start, his administration degenerated into a personal dictatorship, maintained by a private army. In 1964 'Papa Doc' Duvalier made himself life-president, with the power to nominate his son as his successor.
On his father's death in 1971 Jean-Claude Duvalier came to the presidency at the age of

19 and soon acquired the name of 'Baby Doc'. Although the young Duvalier repeatedly promised a return to democracy, and his rule was judged to be less despotic than his father's, there was little change. In 1985 he announced further reform of the constitution, including the legalization of political parties and the eventual appointment of a prime minister, but these were not enough to prevent his overthrow in 1986. The task of establishing democratic government fell to the new military regime led by Lt-Gen Henri Namphy. The regime offered no protection to the electoral council, however, and the US government has withdrawn aid. Elections on 30 Nov 1987 were sabotaged by armed gangs of Duvalierists who massacred voters, and set fire to polling stations and to vehicles delivering ballot papers in the country.

Haiti
REPUBLIC OF (*République d'Haïti*)

AREA 27,740 sq km/10,710 sq mi
CAPITAL Port-au-Prince
PHYSICAL mainly mountainous
FEATURES only French-speaking republic in the Americas; the island of La Tortuga off the N coast was formerly a pirate lair; US military base at Môle St Nicolas, the nearest point to Cuba
HEAD OF STATE AND OF GOVERNMENT Leslie Manigat from 1988
GOVERNMENT authoritarian
EXPORTS coffee, sugar, sisal, cotton, cocoa, rice
CURRENCY gourde (8.24 = £1 Sept 1987)
POPULATION 5,762,000 (1985); annual growth rate 0.9%
LANGUAGE French (official, spoken by the bourgeoisie), creole (spoken by 90% black majority)
RELIGION Roman Catholic (official, but opposed to the regime)
LITERACY 44% male/24% female (1980 est)
GNP $1.6 bn (1983); $300 per head of population
CHRONOLOGY
1804 Independence from France achieved.
1957 Dr François Duvalier (Papa Doc) elected president.

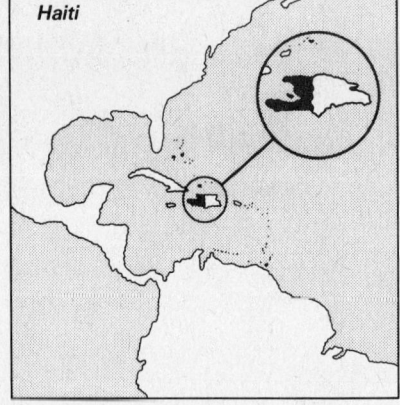

Haiti

1964 Duvalier pronounced himself president for life.
1971 Constitution amended to allow the president to nominate his successor. Duvalier died and was succeeded by his son, Jean-Claude (Baby Doc).
1986 Duvalier deposed and replaced by Lt-Gen Henri Namphy, as head of a governing council.
1988 Leslie Manigat became president under a new constitution despite allegations of fraudulent elections.

Haitink /'haɪtɪŋk/ Bernard 1929– . Dutch conductor of the Concertgebouw Orchestra, Amsterdam, from 1964, and music director of the Royal Opera House, Covent Garden, London, from 1986.

hake important food fish *Merluccius merluccius* of the cod family, found in N European waters. Its silvery, elongated body attains 1 m/3 ft.

Hakluyt /'hæklu:t/ Richard 1553–1616. English geographer. Born in London, he entered the Church and became archdeacon of Westminster in 1603. He lectured on cartography at Oxford, became geographical adviser to the East India Company, and was an original member of the Virginia Company. His chief work is his great compilation, *The Principal Navigations, Voyages and Discoveries of the English Nation* 1589–1600, in which he was assisted by Raleigh. The *Hakluyt Society* established in 1846 publishes later accounts of exploration.

Hakodate /,hækəʊ'dɑːteɪ/ port in Hokkaido, Japan; population (1983) 320,000. It was the earliest port opened to the West, in 1854.

Haldane /'hɔːldeɪn/ Richard Burdon, Viscount Haldane 1856–1928. British Liberal politician. As secretary for war 1905–12, he sponsored the army reforms that established an expeditionary force, backed by a territorial army and under the unified control of an imperial general staff. He was lord chancellor 1912–15 and in the Labour government of 1924.

Hale /heɪl/ George Ellery 1868–1938. US astronomer, who made pioneer studies of the Sun. Born in Chicago, he invented the spectroheliograph in 1889, a device for photographing the Sun at particular wavelengths. In 1897 he founded the ◊Yerkes Observatory in Wisconsin, with a 102 cm/40 in refracting ◊telescope, the largest refractor ever built. In 1904 he moved to Mount Wilson, California, where he discovered that ◊sunspots are cooler areas on the Sun, associated with strong ◊magnetic fields. In 1917 he established a 2.5 m/100 in reflector on Mount Wilson. This was the world's largest telescope until superseded in 1948 by the 5 m/200 in reflector on Mount Palomar, which was also planned by Hale before he died.

Hale /heɪl/ Nathan 1755–1776. American patriot. Hanged by the British as a spy in the War of American Independence, he is remembered for his final words: 'I regret that I have but one life to give for my country'.

Hale /heɪl/ Sarah Josepha Buell 1788–1879. American poet, author of 'Mary had a Little Lamb' 1830.

Halévy /,æleɪ'viː/ Ludovic 1834–1908. French novelist and librettist. He collaborated with Hector Crémieux in the libretto for Offenbach's *Orpheus in the Underworld*; and with Henri Meilhac on librettos for Offenbach's *La Belle Hélène* and *La Vie parisienne*, and for Bizet's *Carmen*.

Haley /'heɪlɪ/ Bill 1927–1981. US pioneer of rock and roll, originally a western swing musician. His songs 'Rock Around the Clock' 1954 (recorded with his group the Comets and featured in the 1955 film *Blackboard Jungle*) and 'Shake, Rattle and Roll' 1955 came to symbolize the beginnings of the rock and roll era.

half-life time in which the strength of a radioactive source decays to half its original value. It may vary from millionths of a second to thousands of millions of years. See ◊radioactive decay.

half-tone process a technique used in printing to reproduce the full range of tones in a photograph or other illustration. The intensity of the printed colour is varied from full strength to the lightest shades, although only one colour of ink and one of paper is used.
The picture to be reproduced is photographed through a screen ruled with a rectangular mesh of fine lines, which breaks up the tones of the original into dots which vary in size according to the intensity of the tone. In the darker shades the dots are large and run together, in the lighter shades they are small and separate.
Colour pictures are broken down into a pattern of dots in the same way, the original being photographed through a number of colour filters. The process is known as colour separation. Plates made from the separations are then printed in sequence, yellow, magenta (blue-red), cyan (blue-green) and black, which combine to give the full colour range.

halibut valuable food fish *Hippoglossus hippoglossus* of the family Pleuronectidae. Largest of the flatfish, it may reach over 2 m/6 ft and weigh 90–135 kg/200–300 lb, and is very dark mottled brown or green above and pure white beneath. It prefers the colder seas from the English Channel to the Arctic.

Halicarnassus /,hælɪkɑː'næsəs/ ancient city of Asia Minor (now Bodrum in Turkey), where the tomb of Mausolus, built about 350 BC by widowed Queen Artemisia, was one of the seven wonders of the world. ◊Herodotus was born here.

Halifax /'hælɪfæks/ capital and naval station of Nova Scotia, Canada's chief winter port; population (1981) 115,882. Founded in 1749, its industries include lumber, steel, and sugar refining. It is the terminus of North America's two transcontinental railways.

Halifax /'hælɪfæks/ woollen textile town in W Yorkshire, England; population (1981) 87,500. The Town Hall is by Sir Charles ◊Barry;

and the Piece Hall of 1779 (former cloth market) has been adapted to modern use.

Halifax /'hælɪfæks/ Charles Montagu, Earl of Halifax 1661–1715. British financier. Appointed commissioner of the Treasury in 1692, he raised money for the French war by instituting the National Debt, and in 1694 carried out William Paterson's plan for a national bank (the Bank of England), and became chancellor of the Exchequer. In 1695 he reformed the currency and issued the first 'Exchequer Bills', and in 1696 inaugurated the Consolidated Fund, used to pay interest on foreign loans. He was created a baron in 1700, and at the accession of George I became again first Lord of the Treasury and was made an earl.

Halifax /'hælɪfæks/ Edward Frederick Lindley Wood, Earl of Halifax 1881–1959. British Conservative politician. He was viceroy of India 1926–31 when he worked with ◊Gandhi and did much to further independence. As foreign secretary 1938–40 he was associated with Chamberlain's 'appeasement' policy, and was in line to succeed him as prime minister in 1940, but stood aside in favour of Churchill. He received an earldom in 1944 for services to the Allied cause while ambassador to the USA 1941–46.

Halifax A portrait of Charles Montagu, Earl of Halifax, founder of the Bank of England, by Godfrey Kneller.

Halifax /'hælɪfæks/ George Savile, 1st Marquess of Halifax 1633–1695. English politician. He entered parliament in 1660, and was raised to the peerage by Charles II, by whom he was also later dismissed. He strove to steer a middle course between extremists, and became known as 'the trimmer'. He played a prominent part in the revolution of 1688.

halitosis offensive breath, which may be caused by poor oral hygiene, disease of the mouth, throat, nose, or lungs, or disturbance of the digestion.

Hall /hɔːl/ (Marguerite) Radclyffe 1883–1943. English novelist. She is best remembered for *The Well of Loneliness* 1928, whose lesbian theme brought it considerable notoriety.

Hall /hɔːl/ Peter (Reginald Frederick) 1930– . British theatre, opera and film director. A much-respected figure of the British stage, from 1960–68 he was director of the Royal Shakespeare Theatre at Stratford and developed the Royal Shakespeare Company as director from 1968 until appointed director of the National Theatre in 1973, in succession to Olivier (to be replaced by Richard Eyre from 1988). His productions include *Waiting for Godot* 1955, *The Wars of the Roses* 1963, *The Homecoming* stage 1967 and film 1973, *Amadeus* 1979, and *Yonadab* 1985. He was also appointed artistic director at Glyndebourne in 1984. He was knighted in 1977.

Hallam /'hæləm/ Henry 1777–1859. British historian. He was called to the Bar, but a private fortune enabled him to devote himself to historical study from 1812 and his *Constitutional History of England* (1827) established his reputation.

Halle /'hælə/ capital of Halle district and industrial city in East Germany; population (1982) 236,139. Industries include the production of salt from brine springs, and lignite mining. The university was founded in 1694. The composer ◊Handel was born here.

Hall effect production of a voltage across a conductor or semiconductor carrying a current at right-angles to a surrounding magnetic field, discovered in 1897 by the American physicist Edwin Hall (1855–1938). It is characteristic of the material, and is used in the Hall probe for measuring the strengths of magnetic fields and in magnetic switches.

Halley /'hæli/ Edmund 1656–1742. English Astronomer Royal from 1720, a friend of ◊Newton, whose *Principia* he financed. In 1682 he observed ◊Halley's comet, predicting its return in 1759.

Halley's comet a ◊comet that orbits the Sun every 76 years, named after Edmund ◊Halley who calculated its orbit. It is the largest and brightest comet that reappears regularly and orbits the Sun in the opposite direction to the planets. At its closest to the Sun it comes within the orbit of Venus, receding to beyond the orbit of Neptune at its farthest. Its last appearance, in 1986, was studied by the ◊Giotto space probe. It was found to have an elongated nucleus 15 km/10 mi by 8 km/5 mi covered with a dark crust of dust, through which jets of gas shoot at high speeds to produce its glowing head and tail. Records of Halley's comet go back to 240 BC, although the comet itself is much older. It will reappear in 2061.

hallmark official marks (on gold, silver, and from 1913 platinum) instituted in the UK in 1300 for the prevention of fraud. Tests of the metal content are carried out at authorized Assay Offices at Goldsmiths' Hall, London, Birmingham, Sheffield, and Edinburgh, each of which has its distinguishing mark, to which is added a maker's mark, date letter, and mark guaranteeing standard.

Halley's comet Optical image of Halley's comet taken in Jan 1986 when it was close to the Sun. The head of the comet is thought to be composed of ice and dust which the sun evaporates and ionizes by ultraviolet rays. The released gas and dust are swept into a tail by the solar wind.

Hallowe'en the evening of 31 Oct, immediately preceding Hallowmas or All Saints' Day, the Christian festival kept in honour of all the saints. Customs associated with the festival in the UK and the USA include wearing masks or costumes and 'trick or treating', going from house to house collecting sweets or money; these customs are said to date from pre-Christian times.

Hallstatt /'hælʃtæt/ village in Upper Austria, SW of Salzburg. The salt workings date from prehistoric times, and archaeological finds include the discovery in 1846 of over 3,000 graves, belonging to a 9th–5th century BC Celtic civilization transitional between the Bronze and Iron ages.

hallucinogen a drug which induces hallucinations.

halogen one of a group of five elements with similar chemical bonding properties, and showing a gradation of physical properties. In order of reactivity, the elements are flourine, F, chlorine, Cl, bromine, Br, iodine, I, and astatine, At. Together, they form a linked group in the ◊Periodic Table of elements. Salts containing a metal and a halogen are termed halides, for example table salt, NaCl.

halophyte a plant adapted to live where there is a high concentration of salt in the soil, for example, in saltmarshes and mudflats. Halophytes contain a high percentage of salts in their root cells, so that water can still be taken up by the process of ◊osmosis. Some species also have succulent leaves for storing water, such as *seablite Suaeda maritima*, and *sea rocket Cakile maritima*.

Hals /hæls/ Frans 1581/5–1666. Dutch portrait and genre painter. Though some have placed him next to Rembrandt for his skill as a portrait painter, others have criticized him for his lack of insight in delineating character. In his ability to seize and set down a passing mood he anticipated the French ◊Impressionists, on whom he had a great influence. His principal works are at Haarlem, but his famous *Laughing Cavalier* is in the Wallace Collection, London.

Halsey /'hɔːlsi/ William Frederick 1882–1959. American admiral. Entering the navy in 1905, he was appointed to command of the Third Fleet in the South Pacific in 1942. He compelled the Japanese to withdraw 1943–44, and they signed the surrender document ending World War II on his flagship *Missouri*.

Hamadán /ˌhæməˈdɑːn/ city in NW Iran on the site of the ancient Ecbatana, capital of the ◊Medes; population (1982) 234,500.

Hamburg /'hæmbɜːg/ largest port of West Germany and capital of the *Land* of ◊Hamburg; population (1982) 1,645,100. An archbishopric from 834. In alliance with Lübeck it founded the ◊Hanseatic League. It is the site of Deutsches Elektron Synchroton (DESY), the German accelerator laboratory.

Hamburg /'hæmbɜːg/ *Land* of West Germany

area 756 sq km/292 sq mi

capital Hamburg

features comprises the city and surrounding districts; the *hamburger*, a fried and seasoned patty of chopped beef, said to have been invented by medieval Tatar invaders of this Baltic area, was taken to the USA in the 19th century, from where it was reintroduced to Europe in the 1960s

products refined oil, chemicals, electrical goods, ships, processed food

population (1982) 1,645,000

religion Protestant 74%, Roman Catholic 8%

history in 1510 the emperor Maximilian I made Hamburg a free imperial city, and in 1871 it became a state of the German Empire. There is a university, established in 1919, and the Hamburg Schauspielhaus is one of the republic's leading theatres.

Hameln /'hæməln/ (English form Hamelin) town in West Germany; population (1984) 56,300. Old buildings include the *Rattenhaus* rat-catcher's house, and the town is famous for the Pied Piper legend.

Hamersley Range /'hæməzli/ range of hills above the Hamersley Plateau, Western Australia, with coloured rocks and river gorges, as well as iron reserves.

Hamilcar Barca /hæ'mɪlkɑː 'bɑːkə/ c. 270–228 BC. Carthaginian general, father of ◊Hannibal. From 247 to 241 BC he harassed the Romans in Italy, and then led an expedition to Spain where he died in battle.

Hamilton /'hæməltən/ capital of Bermuda, on Bermuda Island; population (1980) 1,617.

Hamilton /'hæməltən/ port in Ontario, Canada; population (1981) 542,095. Linked with Lake Ontario by the Burlington Canal, it has a hydro-electric plant, and heavy machinery, electrical, chemical, and textile industries.

Hamilton /'hæməltən/ industrial and university town on North Island, New Zealand; population (1983) 100,500. Waikato University was established here in 1964.

Hamilton /'hæməltən/ Alexander 1757–1804. American politician, who influenced the adoption of a constitution with a strong central government, and was the first secretary of the treasury 1789–95. Born in the West Indies, he served during the War of Independence as captain and from 1777–81 was Washington's secretary and aide-de-camp. After the war he practised as a lawyer. He was a member of the Constitutional Convention of 1787, and in the *Federalist* influenced public opinion in favour of the ratification of the constitution. As first secretary of the treasury, he proved an able controller of the national finances. He led the Federal Party, and incurred the bitter hatred of Aaron ◊Burr when he cast the deciding vote against Burr and in favour of ◊Jefferson for the presidency in 1801. Eventually he fought a duel with Burr, was wounded, and died the next day.

Hamilton /'hæməltən/ Emma (born Amy Lyon) 1765–1815. British courtesan, the daughter of a Cheshire blacksmith. She obtained employment in London, and in 1782 became the mistress of Charles ◊Greville, and in 1786 of his uncle Sir William ◊Hamilton, the British envoy at Naples. She at once became a leading figure in the society of Naples, and Hamilton married her in 1791. After Admiral ◊Nelson's return from the Nile in 1798 she became well known as his mistress and her daughter by him, Horatia, was born in 1801. After the death of Hamilton and Nelson, Lady Hamilton was imprisoned for debt, but later escaped to Calais where she died in poverty.

Hamilton /'hæməltən/ Iain Ellis 1922– . Scottish composer. Glasgow-born, he worked as an aircraft engineer 1939–46, and studied at the Royal Academy of Music 1947–51. Intensely emotional and harmonically rich, his works include striking viola and cello sonatas, a ballet, the operas *Pharsalia* 1968 and *The Royal Hunt of the Sun* 1967–69, which renounced melody for inventive chordal formations, and symphonies.

Hamilton /'hæməltən/ Ian 1853–1947. Scottish soldier. He was chief of staff and deputy to Lord ◊Kitchener, commander-in-chief in the South African War. In 1914 he was commander-in-chief of the Home Defence Army and became a full general. In 1915 he directed the land operations in ◊Gallipoli.

Hamilton /'hæməltən/ James, 1st Duke of Hamilton 1606–1649. Scottish adviser to Charles I, he led an army against the ◊Covenanters 1639, and subsequently took part in the negotiations between Charles and the Scots. In the second ◊Civil War he led the Scottish invasion of England, but was captured at Preston and executed.

Hamilton /'hæməltən/ William 1730–1803. British diplomat, envoy to the court of Naples 1764–1800, whose collection of Greek vases was bought by the British Museum. Fragments of his second collection, wrecked off the Scillies, were recovered in 1974.

Hamilton /'hæməltən/ William D 1936– . New Zealand biologist who has worked mostly in England. By developing the concept of ◊inclusive fitness, he was able to solve the theoretical problem of explaining ◊altruism in animal behaviour in terms of ◊neo-Darwinism (an evolutionary theory).

Hamilton /'hæməltən/ William Rowan 1805–1865. Irish mathematician, whose formulation of Isaac Newton's mechanics proved adaptable to quantum theory, and whose 'quarternion' theory was a forerunner of the branch of mathematics known as vector analysis.

Hamite /'hæmaɪt/ member of an African people, descended, according to tradition, from Ham, son of ◊Noah in the Bible: they include the ancient Egyptians, the modern ◊Berbers of North Africa, and the Tuareg of Sudan.

Hamito-Semitic languages a family of languages spoken widely throughout the world but commonly associated with North Africa and Western Asia. It has two main branches, the *Hamitic* languages of North Africa and the *Semitic* languages originating in Syria and Mesopotamia, Palestine and Arabia but now found from Morocco in the west to the Arabian or Persian Gulf in the east. The Hamitic languages include ancient Egyptian, Coptic and Berber, while the Semitic languages include the most numerous, Arabic, and such other culturally significant languages as Hebrew, Aramaic, and Syriac. The scripts of the two best known Hamito-Semitic languages, Arabic and Hebrew, run from right to left.

Hamm /hæm/ industrial town in North Rhine-Westphalia, West Germany; population (1985) 178,000. There are coal mines, chemical and engineering industries.

Hammarskjöld /'hæməʃəʊld/ Dag 1905–1961. Swedish secretary-general of United Nations 1953–58. He dealt with the ◊Suez Crisis 1956, in which he opposed Britain, and his attempts to solve the problem of Congo (now Zaïre), where he was killed in a plane crash, were attacked by the Soviet Union.

hammer in athletics, one of the ◊throwing events.

Hammerfest /'hæməfest/ fishing port in NW Norway, northernmost town of Europe; population (1985) 7,500.

hammerhead several species of shark in the genus *Sphyrna*, characterized by a hammer-shaped head, and found in tropical seas. The eyes are at the ends of the double-headed 'hammer'.

Hammerstein /'hæməstaɪn/ Oscar (Greeley Clendenning) II 1895–1960. Lyricist and librettist, particularly for American musicals, who collaborated with Richard ◊Rodgers.

Hammett /'hæmɪt/ Dashiell 1894–1961. American crime novelist, who was himself a former ◊Pinkerton detective agent. His works *The Maltese Falcon* 1930, *The Glass Key* 1931, and the *The Thin Man* 1932 introduced the hard-bitten 'private eye' character. In 1951 he was imprisoned for contempt of court for refusing to testify during the ◊McCarthy era.

Hammond /'hæmənd/ Joan 1912– . Australian soprano, known in oratorio and opera, for example, *Madame Butterfly*, *Tosca*, and *Martha*.

Hammurabi /ˌhæmʊˈrɑːbi/ c. 1792–1750 BC. King of Babylon (reigned c. 1792–50 BC) who united his country and took it to the peak of civilization, although his consolidation of the legal code was bloodthirsty in its punishments.

Hampden /'hæmpdən/ John 1594–1643. English politician. He sat in the parliaments of 1621, 1625, and 1626, and became conspicuous when in 1627 he was imprisoned for refusing to pay a forced loan. His refusal in 1636 to pay ◊ship money made him a national figure. In the Short and ◊Long parliaments he proved himself a skilful debater and parliamentary strategist. Charles's attempt to arrest him and four other leading MPs made the ◊Civil War inevitable. He raised his own regiment on the outbreak of hostilities, and on 18 Jun 1643 was mortally wounded at the skirmish of Chalgrove Field.

Hampshire /'hæmpʃə/ county of S England
area 3,777 sq km/1,458 sq mi
towns administrative headquarters Winchester; Southampton, Portsmouth, Gosport
features New Forest, area 373 sq km/144 sq mi, a Saxon royal hunting ground; Hampshire Basin, where Britain has onshore and offshore oil; Danebury, 2,500-year-old Celtic hillfort; Beaulieu (including National Motor Museum); Highclere (home of the Earl of Carnarvon, with gardens by Capability ◊Brown).
products agricultural; oil from refineries at Fawley
population (1986) 1,509,500
famous people Jane Austen, Charles Dickens, Gilbert White.

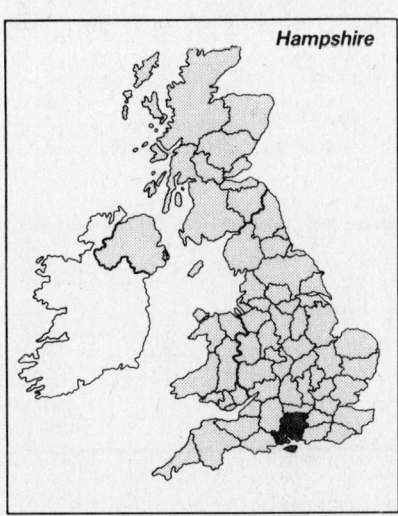

Hampshire

Hampstead /'hæmpstɪd/ district of N London, part of the borough of ◊Camden.

Hampton /'hæmptən/ Christopher 1946– . British dramatist, resident at the Royal Court Theatre 1968–70. His plays include the comedy *The Philanthropist* 1970 and *Savages* 1973.

hamster type of rodent of the family Cricetidae with a thickset body, short tail and cheek pouches to carry food. A number of species are found across Asia and into SE Europe, including the *black-bellied hamster Cricetus cricetus* about 25 cm/10 in long which can be a crop pest and stores up to 90 kg/200 lb of seeds in its burrow. The *golden hamster Mesocricetus auratus* lives in W Asia and SE Europe. All the

domesticated stock originated from a female and 12 young captured in Syria in 1930.

Hamsun /'hæmsuːn/ Knut 1859–1952. Norwegian novelist whose first novel *Sult/Hunger* 1890 was largely autobiographical. Other works include *Pan* 1894, *Look Back on Happiness* 1912 and possibly his best novel, *The Growth of the Soil*, which was mainly responsible for his Nobel prize in 1920. His hatred of capitalism made him sympathize with Nazism, and he was fined in 1946 for collaboration.

Hancock /'hænkɒk/ John 1737–1793. American revolutionary politician. He advocated resistance to the British as president of the Continental Congress 1775–77, and was the first to sign the ◊Declaration of Independence in 1776. Because he signed it in a large, bold hand (according to legend, so that it would be big enough for King George III to see), his name became a colloquial term for a signature in the USA. He was governor of Massachusetts 1780–85 and 1787–93.

Hancock /'hænkɒk/ Tony (Anthony John) 1924–1968. British radio and television comedian. 'Hancock's Half Hour' from 1954 showed him always at odds with everyday life, and became a cult in the 1980s.

handball game in which the ball is hit with the gloved hand, as in *English fives* (chiefly a public school game), on an enclosed court, with 2–4 players; or (in a team version with 7 or 11 players, popular in continental Europe) in which the ball is thrown or punched from one player to another until a goal is scored.

Handel /'hændl/ Georg Friedrich 1685–1759. German-born composer, who became a British subject in 1726. Born in Halle, he abandoned the study of law at the university in 1703, to become a violinist at Keiser's Opera House in Hamburg, where his first opera *Almira* was performed in 1705. Visits to Italy (1706–10) inspired a number of operas and oratorios, and in 1711 his opera *Rinaldo* was performed in London. Appointed Kapellmeister to the elector of Hanover in 1710, he left in 1712 to settle in England, and was for a time in disgrace when the elector succeeded as George I in 1714. However, he wrote for him the 'Water Music' 1717 and from 1720 directed the opera at the King's Theatre, Haymarket. The rivalry of the fashionable Italian composer Bononcini, and ◊Gay's ridicule in *The Beggar's Opera* 1728, led him to abandon Italianate opera for English oratorio. *Saul* and *Israel in Egypt* (both 1739) were unsuccessful, but his masterpiece *Messiah* was acclaimed on its first performance in Dublin in 1742. His great contribution is to choral music, later oratorios including *Samson* 1743, *Belshazzar* 1745, *Judas Maccabaeus* 1747, and *Jephtha* 1752. Other works include the pastoral *Acis and Galatea* 1718 and the set of variations, in his 1720 suite for harpsichord, which were later nicknamed 'The Harmonious Blacksmith'. From 1751 he became totally blind.

Handke /'hæntkə/ Peter 1942– . Austrian novelist and playwright, whose first play *Insulting the Audience* 1966 was an example of 'anti-theatre writing'. His novels include *Die Hornissen/The Hornets* 1966 and *The Goalie's*

Handel A British subject from 1726, the German-born composer Georg Friedrich Handel dominated English musical life. His classics, such as the *Water Music* 1717, are still well loved by audiences today. His portrait is by Thomas Hudson, 1756.

Anxiety at the Penalty Kick 1970. He directed and scripted the film *The Left-handed Woman* 1979.

Handley /'hændli/ Tommy 1896–1949. British radio comedian, born in Liverpool. His popular programme 'ITMA' (It's That Man Again) with its catch-phrases, such as, 'After you, Claud', and characters, for example, 'Mrs Mop' and 'Mona Lot,' ran from 1939 until his death.

Hangchow /,hæŋ'tʃaʊ/ former name for ◊Hangzhou, port in Zhejiang province, China.

hanging execution by suspension, usually with a drop of 0.6–2 m/2–6 ft, so that the powerful jerk of the tightened rope breaks the neck.

hanging participle see ◊participle.

Hangzhou /,hæŋ'dʒaʊ/ port (formerly Hangchow), capital of Zhejiang province, China; population (1982) 4,020,000. It has jute, chemical, tea, and silk industries, and fine landscaped gardens. It was the capital of China 1127–1278 under the Sung dynasty.

Hanley /'hænli/ one of the old Staffordshire pottery towns in England, now part of ◊Stoke-on-Trent.

Hannibal /'hænɪbəl/ 247–182 BC. Carthaginian general from 221 BC, son of ◊Hamilcar Barca. His siege of Saguntum (modern Sagunto, near Valencia) precipitated the 2nd ◊Punic War. Following a brilliant campaign in Italy (after crossing the Alps in 218 BC with 57 elephants), Hannibal was the victor at Trasimene in 217 BC and Cannae in 216 BC, but failed to take Rome. In 203 BC he returned to Carthage to meet a Roman invasion, but was defeated at Zama in 202 BC, and was exiled in 196 BC at Rome's insistence. He fled first to Syria, then to Bythinia (on the Black Sea), Rome always seeking his extradition, and poisoned himself rather than fall into their hands.

Hanoi /hæˈnɔɪ/ capital of Vietnam, on the Red river; population (1979) 2,570,905. It is a trade and communications centre, and has an airport. Industries include textiles, paper, and engineering. Captured by the French in 1873, it was the capital of French Indochina 1902–40; and the capital of North Vietnam 1954–76. Hanoi University was founded in 1918.

Hanover /ˈhænəʊvə/ industrial city, capital of Lower ◊Saxony, West Germany; population (1984) 517,900. Industries include machinery, vehicles, electrical goods, rubber, textiles, and oil refining.

history from 1386 it was a member of the ◊Hanseatic League, and from 1692 capital of the electorate of Hanover (created a kingdom in 1815). ◊George I of England was also Elector of Hanover, and the two countries shared the same monarch until the accession of Victoria in 1837. Then, since a woman could not rule in Hanover, the throne passed to her uncle, Ernest, Duke of Cumberland. His son was forced by ◊Bismarck to abdicate in 1866, and Hanover became a Prussian province. In 1946 Hanover was merged with Brunswick and Oldenburg to form the *Land* of Lower Saxony.

Hanover /ˈhænəʊvə/ German royal dynasty which ruled Great Britain and Ireland 1714–1901. Under the Act of Succession 1701, the succession passed to the ruling family of the principality of Hanover, Germany, on the death of Queen Anne. On the death of Queen Victoria the crown passed to the house of Saxe-Coburg in the person of Edward VII.

Hansard /ˈhænsɑːd/ the official report of the proceedings of the British parliament. Named after Luke Hansard 1752–1828, printer of the House of Commons *Journal* from 1774. The first official reports were published from 1803 by ◊Cobbett, who during his imprisonment of 1810–12 sold the business to his printer, Thomas Curson Hansard, son of Luke Hansard. The publication of the debates remained in the hands of the family until 1889, and is now the responsibility of the Stationery Office. The name *Hansard* was officially adopted 1943.

Hanseatic League A medieval confederation of N German trading cities. The earliest association had its headquarters at Wisby; it included over 30 cities, but was gradually supplanted by that headed by Lübeck. Hamburg and Lübeck established their own trading-stations in London in 1266 and 1267 respectively, which coalesced in 1282 with that of Cologne to form the so-called Steelyard. There were three other such stations: Bruges, Bergen, and Novgorod. At its height in the later 14th century the Hanseatic League included over 70 towns, among them Lübeck, Hamburg, Cologne, Breslau, and Cracow. The basis of its power was its monopoly of the Baltic trade and its relations with Flanders and England. The decline of the Hanseatic League from the 15th century was due to the movement of trade routes, and to the development of national states. The last general assembly (1669) marks the end of the League.

Hansom /ˈhænsəm/ Joseph Aloysius 1803–1882. British architect. His works include the Birmingham town hall 1831, but he is remembered as the introducer of the Hansom cab in 1834.

Hanuman /ˌhʌnuˈmɑːn/ in the Sanskrit epic ◊Ramayana, the monkey god and king of Hindustan. He assisted Rama to recover his wife Sita, abducted by Ravana of Lanka (modern Sri Lanka).

Hanyang /ˌhænˈjæn/ former Chinese city, now merged in ◊Wuhan, in Hubei province.

haploid having one set of ◊chromosomes in each cell. Most higher organisms are ◊diploid, that is they have two sets, but most plants and many seaweeds are haploid, as are female honey bees (because they develop from eggs that have not been fertilized). See also ◊meiosis.

Hapsburg /ˈhæpsbɜːg/ European royal family, former imperial house of Austria-Hungary. The name comes from the family castle in Switzerland. The Hapsburgs held the title ◊Holy Roman Emperor 1273–91, 1298–1308, 1438–1740, and 1745–1806. They ruled Austria from 1278, under the title emperor 1806–1918. The Archduke Otto Hapsburg-Lothringen, son of the last emperor, Charles, became a member of the European parliament in 1979.

hara-kiri ritual suicide of the Japanese samurai, from the 12th century onwards. It was carried out to avoid dishonour or disgrace and could be carried out voluntarily or on the order of a feudal lord. The correct Japanese term is *seppuku*.

Harappa /həˈræpə/ ruined city of a prehistoric Indian culture; see ◊Indus Valley Civilization.

Harare /həˈrɑːri/ capital of Zimbabwe, on the Mashonaland plateau about 1,525 m/5,000 ft above sea level. The British occupied the site in 1890, and named it Fort Salisbury in honour of Lord Salisbury, then prime minister of the UK. It was capital of the Federation of Rhodesia and Nyasaland 1953–63. It is the centre of a rich farming area (tobacco and maize), with tobacco, metallurgical, food processing and other industries. Population (1982) 656,000.

Harcourt /ˈhɑːkət/ William Vernon 1827–1904. British Liberal politician. Under Gladstone he was home secretary 1880–85, and chancellor of the Exchequer 1886 and 1892–95. He is remembered for his remark in 1892: 'We are all Socialists now.'

hard copy output from a computer that is printed on paper rather than displayed on a screen.

Hardenberg /ˈhɑːdnbɜːg/ Karl August von 1750–1822. Prussian politician, foreign minister to King Frederick William III of Prussia during the Napoleonic Wars. He later became chancellor.

Hardicanute /ˈhɑːdɪkənjuːt/ c. 1019–1042. King of England from 1040. Son of ◊Canute, he was king of Denmark 1028. In England he was known as a harsh ruler.

Hardie /ˈhɑːdi/ James Keir 1856–1915. Scottish socialist. Born in Lanarkshire, he worked in the mines as a boy, and in 1886 became secretary of the Scottish Miners' Federation. In 1888 he was the first Labour candidate to stand for Parliament; he entered Parliament independently as a Labour member in 1892 and was a chief founder of the ◊Independent Labour Party in 1893. A pacifist, he strongly opposed the Boer War, and his idealism in his work for socialism and the unemployed made him a popular hero. He was Member of Parliament for West Ham 1892–95 and for Merthyr Tydfil from 1900.

Hardie A former miner, the British socialist James Keir Hardie was a chief founder of the Independent Labour Party and the party's first candidate to stand for Parliament.

Harding /ˈhɑːdɪŋ/ John, 1st Baron Harding of Petherton 1896– . British field marshal. Chief of staff to ◊Alexander in Italy in World War II, he was commander-in-chief of the British Army of the Rhine 1951–52, and chief of the imperial general staff 1952–55. As governor of Cyprus 1955–57, during part of the period of political agitation prior to independence (1960), he was responsible for the controversial deportation of ◊Makarios from Cyprus in 1955, and for the reorganization of the security forces to combat the guerrillas fighting for union with Greece.

Harding /ˈhɑːdɪŋ/ Warren Gamaliel 1865–1923. 29th President of the USA 1921–23. Born in Ohio, he entered the US Senate in 1914 as a Republican, and opposed the Peace Treaty of 1919. In 1920 he was elected president of the USA; he was inaugurated 1921 but died in office. He concluded the peace treaties of 1921 with Germany, Austria, and Hungary, and in the same year called the Washington Conference. After the conference there were charges of corruption among members of his cabinet.

hardness a physical property of materials that governs their use. Methods of heat treatment can increase the hardness of metals. A scale of hardness was devised by Friedrich ◊Mohs in the 1800s, based upon the hardness of certain minerals from soft talc (Mohs hardness 1) to diamond (10), the hardest of all materials. (See also ◊Brinell hardness test).

The hardness of water refers to the presence in it of dissolved minerals which prevent soap lathering. Compounds of calcium and magnesium are mainly to blame. Treatment with a ◊water softener may remove them.

Hardwar /hə'dwɑː/ town in Uttar Pradesh, India, on the right bank of the Ganges; population (1981) 115,513. The name means 'door of Hari' (or Vishnu). It is one of the holy places of the Hindu religion and a pilgrimage centre. The *Kumbhmela* festival, held every 12th year in honour of the god Siva, is the most important and attracts about 1,000,000 pilgrims.

hardware in computing, the mechanical, electrical and electronic components of a computer system, as opposed to the various programs or ◊software (see also ◊firmware). In a microcomputer this might include the circuit boards, the power supply and housing of the processor unit, the VDU (screen), external memory devices such as disk drives, a printer, the keyboard, and so on.

Hardy /'hɑːdi/ Oliver 1892–1957. American film comedian, member of the duo ◊Laurel and Hardy with Stan Laurel.

Hardy /'hɑːdi/ Thomas 1840–1928. British poet and novelist. Born near Dorchester in the heart of the 'Wessex' which was to form the background of his novels, he was trained as an architect. His first success was *Far From the Madding Crowd* 1874, followed among others by *The Return of the Native* 1878, *The Mayor of Casterbridge* 1886 and *The Woodlanders* 1887 – all remarkable for the background contrast of richly humorous rustic characters, for the brooding intensity of human loves and hates played out before the harshly indifferent force of the natural world. *Tess of the D'Urbervilles* 1891 – subtitled 'A Pure Woman' – outraged public opinion by portraying as its heroine a woman who had been seduced, and the even greater outcry which followed *Jude the Obscure* 1895 helped to reinforce Hardy's decision to confine himself to verse. Beginning with *Wessex Poems* 1898, he published several volumes of lyrics and a gigantic blank-verse panorama of the Napoleonic wars, *The Dynasts* 1904–08. In 1910 he was awarded the Order of Merit.

Hardy /'hɑːdi/ Thomas Masterman 1769–1839. British sailor. He entered the navy in 1781, and at Trafalgar was ◊Nelson's flag captain in the *Victory*, attending him during his dying moments. He became First Sea Lord in 1830.

Hardy-Weinberg equilibrium in population genetics, the relative frequency of different ◊alleles within a given population of a species, when the stable end-point of evolution in an undisturbed environment is reached.

hare lagomorph *Lepus capensis*, family Leporidae, larger than the ◊rabbit, and with very long black-tipped ears. Throughout the long breeding season Jan–Aug, there are chases and

Hardy The novelist and poet Thomas Hardy, son of a master mason, a trade which appears in several of his novels, of which the most famous example is *Jude the Obscure*, where the hero, Jude Fawley, is a stonemason.

'boxing-matches' among males; the saying 'mad as a March hare' arises from their behaviour when lack of cover makes them more visible. They do not burrow. The young are termed leverets and live in a grassy depression called a form.

Hare /heə/ David 1947– . British dramatist, whose plays include *Slag* 1970, *Teeth 'n' Smiles* 1975, *Pravda* 1985 (with Howard ◊Brenton).

harebell perennial plant *Campanula rotundifolia*, with bell-shaped blue flower, found on dry grassland and heaths. Known in Scotland as the bluebell.

Hare Krishna popular name for a member of the ◊International Society for Krishna Consciousness, derived from their chant.

hare-lip facial deformity, a cleft in the upper lip and jaw, which may extend back into the palate (see ◊cleft palate), and is remedied by surgery.

Hare's apparatus in physics, an apparatus used to compare the relative densities of two liquids, or to find the density of one if the other is known. It was invented by the US chemist Robert Hare (1781–1858). It consists of a vertical E-shaped glass tube, with the long limbs dipping into the two liquids and a tap on the short limb. Operating the tap removes air, pushing the liquids up the tubes by atmospheric pressure. When the tap is closed, the heights of the liquids are inversely proportional to their relative densities. Thus if a liquid of relative density d_1

rises to a height h_1, and liquid d_2 rises to h_2, d_1/d_2 = h_2/h_1. See ◊hydrometer.

Hare's apparatus

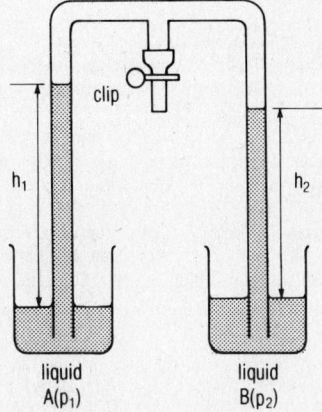

Harewood /'hɑːwʊd/ George Henry Hubert Lascelles, 7th Earl of Harewood 1923– . Artistic director of the Edinburgh Festival 1961–65, director of the English National Opera 1972–85, and a governor of the BBC from 1985.

Harfleur /ɑː'flɜː/ port in NW France; population (1985) 9,700. Important in medieval times, it was superseded by ◊Le Havre.

Hargeisa /hɑː'geɪsə/ trading centre in NW Somalia; population (1985) 150,000.

Hargraves /'hɑːgreɪvz/ Edward Hammond 1816–1891. British discoverer of the Australian goldfields. Born in Hampshire, he found gold in the ◊Blue Mountains of New South Wales in 1851, was made Commissioner of Crown Lands and given a government award of £10,000.

Hargreaves /'hɑːgriːvz/ James died 1778. British inventor. Born near Blackburn, he became a weaver, and in 1760 was co-inventor of a carding machine. About 1764 he invented his 'spinning-jenny', which enabled a number of threads to be spun simultaneously by one person.

harijan /'hʌrɪdʒən/ Hindi 'children of god', name coined by Mahatma ◊Gandhi for members of the caste of untouchables.

Haringey /'hærɪŋgeɪ/ borough of N Greater London.

features Alexandra Palace, with a park; Finsbury Park; includes *Tottenham* with Bruce Castle, originally built in the 16th century on a site belonging to Robert ◊Bruce's father.

population (1984) 200,100.

Harlech /'hɑːlex/ town in Gwynedd, N Wales; population (1980) 1,250. The song 'March of the Men of Harlech' originated in the siege when the town was captured in 1468 by the Yorkists in the Wars of the ◊Roses.

Harlem /'hɑːləm/ commercial and residential district of Manhattan, New York City, USA.

Harlem Renaissance name given to a movement in American literature in the 1920s which used black life and traditional black culture as its subject matter. The centre of the movement was the Harlem area of New York City, where black culture, including jazz, flourished among migrants to the industrial north from the southern states and attracted a new white audience. The magazine *Crisis*, edited by W E B DuBois, was a forum for the new black consciousness; writers associated include Langston Hughes, Zora Neale Hurston, James Weldon Johnson, and Countee Cullen.

Harley /'hɑːli/ Robert, 1st earl of Oxford 1661–1724. British Tory politician, chief minister to Queen Anne 1711–14, when he negotiated the Treaty of Utrecht in 1713. Accused of treason as a Jacobite after the accession of George I, he was imprisoned 1714–17.

Harlow /'hɑːləʊ/ Jean, born Harlean Carpentier 1911–1937. American film actress, the first 'platinum blonde'. Her films include *Hell's Angels* 1930 and *Saratoga* 1937.

Harlow The American film star Jean Harlow, popularly known as the 'platinum blonde'. She appeared in a film of the same name in 1931.

harmattan in meteorology, a dry and dusty NE wind which blows over W Africa.

harmonica either *musical glasses* graded and filled with water, playable with small hammers, for which Mozart and Beethoven composed, or *mouth organ* invented by ◊Wheatstone in 1829, in which small metal reeds of varied size, affixed to small slots in a narrow box, produce the notes when blown upon.

harmonics in music, the series of sounds of different pitches generated naturally by the vibration of a pipe or string when a note is played. This gives tone colour or timbre to an instrument.

harmonium portable pipeless, reed-vibrated organ, worked by air compression with a five-octave keyboard and an air chamber filled by the action of foot-worked pedals.

harmony in music, any simultaneous combination of sounds, as opposed to melody, which is a succession of sounds. Although the term 'harmony' suggests a pleasant or agreeable sound, it is properly applied to any combination of notes, whether consonant or dissonant.

Harmony deals with the formation of chords, their interrelation and logical progression. The founder of modern harmonic theory was Jean-Philippe ◊Rameau. In his *Traité de l'harmonie/Treatise on Harmony* 1722, he established a system of chord classification on which subsequent methods of harmony have been based.

Harold I /'hærəld/ king of England from 1035, died 1040. Known as Harefoot. He was the illegitimate son of ◊Canute, whom he succeeded, and claimed the throne in 1035. In 1037 he was elected king.

Harold II /'hærəld/ c. 1022–1066. King of England, elected in Jan 1066. Son of Earl ◊Godwin, he succeeded his father in 1053 as earl of Wessex. In 1063 ◊William of Normandy tricked him into swearing to support his own claim to the English throne, and when the ◊Witan elected Harold to succeed ◊Edward the Confessor, William prepared to invade. Meanwhile, Harold's treacherous brother Tostig (died 1066) joined the king of Norway, Harald III Hardrada (1015–66), in invading Northumbria: Harold routed and killed them at Stamford Bridge on 25 Sept. Three days later William landed at ◊Pevensey; Harold was killed at the Battle of ◊Hastings 14 Oct 1066.

Harold II After Edward the Confessor's death, Harold, Earl of Wessex, was crowned king in Jan 1066. Harold's short but eventful rule came to an abrupt end with his death at the Battle of Hastings in Oct of that year.

harp plucked musical string instrument, with the strings stretched vertically within a wooden frame, normally triangular. Its origins are obscure, but there is evidence of its existence in the West in the 9th century, and it was popular with medieval minstrels. At that time it was quite small, and was normally placed on the knees. The need for greater volume, however, particularly following its introduction into the orchestra in the 19th century, was met by increasing its size, and the modern concert harp is now the largest musical instrument to be plucked by hand. It has up to 47 strings, and seven pedals set into the soundbox at the base to alter pitch. The harp has also been used in folk music, as both a solo and accompanying instrument, and is associated with Wales and Ireland in this respect.

Harper's Ferry /'hɑːpəz 'feri/ village in W Virginia, USA, where the Potomac meets the Shenandoah. It is famous for the incident in 1859 when anti-slavery leader John ◊Brown seized the government's arsenal here.

Harpies in early Greek mythology, wind spirits; in later legend they have horrific women's faces and the bodies of vultures.

harpsichord keyboard musical instrument popular in the 16th–18th centuries, until its supercession by the piano. The strings are plucked by quills, not struck by hammers. It has been revived in the 20th century for authentic performance of early music.

harrier bird of prey of the genus *Circus* of the family Accipitridae. They are found throughout the world, and three species occur in Britain: the *moorland hen harrier Circus cyaneus*, *Montagu's harrier Circus pygargus*, and the *marsh harrier Circus aeruginosus*.

harrier a dog hunting the hare by scent. It resembles a foxhound, though smaller.

Harrier the only truly successful vertical take-off and landing fixed-wing aircraft, often called the *jump jet*. Built in Britain, it made its first flight in 1966. It has a single ◊jet engine and a set of swivelling nozzles, These deflect the jet exhaust vertically downwards for take-off and landing, and to the rear for normal flight.

Harrier An RAF Harrier jet takes off from aircraft carrier *Hermes*. Designed to fly from confined spaces with minimal ground support, it refuels in mid-air.

Harriman /'hærɪmən/ (William) Averell 1891–1986. American administrator of Lease-Lend in World War II; negotiatior of the nuclear test ban treaty with the USSR in 1963, and governor of New York 1955–58.

Harris /'hærɪs/ southern part of Lewis-with-Harris, in the ◊Hebrides.

Harris /'hærɪs/ Arthur Travers 1892–1984. British marshal of the RAF, 'Bomber Harris', commander-in-chief Bomber Command 1942–45.

Harris /'hærɪs/ Frank 1856–1931. Irish journalist, who wrote colourful biographies of Wilde and Shaw, and an autobiography, *My Life and Loves* 1926, originally banned in the UK and USA.

Harris /'hærɪs/ Joel Chandler 1848–1908. American author, born in Georgia, of the folktales of 'Uncle Remus', based on black folklore, about Br'er Rabbit and the Tar-Baby, from 1879.

Harris /'hærɪs/ Paul P 1878–1947. American lawyer, born in Wisconsin. In 1896 he became a lawyer in Chicago, where he founded the first ◊Rotary Club in 1905, and the International Association in 1912.

Harris /'hærɪs/ Roy 1898–1979. American composer, born in Oklahoma, who used American folk tunes. Notable are the 'Abraham Lincoln' symphony (10th) 1965, and the orchestral *When Johnny Comes Marching Home* 1935.

Harrison /'hærɪsən/ Benjamin 1833–1901. 23rd president of the USA 1889–93. A Republican, he called the first Pan-American Conference.

Harrison /'hærɪsən/ Reginald Carey 'Rex' 1908– . British actor. Lancashire-born, he had his first big success in *French Without Tears* 1936, and subsequently often appeared in London and New York, notably as Professor Higgins in the stage and film musical *My Fair Lady* 1956. His films include *Blithe Spirit* 1944, and Caesar in *Cleopatra* 1962.

Harrison /'hærɪsən/ William Henry 1773–1841. 9th president of the USA, elected 1840, but died a month after taking office; Benjamin ◊Harrison was his grandson.

Harrisson /'hærɪsən/ Tom 1911–1976. British anthropologist. After working among the people of Borneo, he decided to apply the same study techniques among Bolton cotton-mill operators, and set up with Charles Madge in 1937 Mass Observation, earliest of the organizations for the analysis of public opinions and attitudes.

Harrogate /'hærəgət/ resort and spa in N Yorkshire, England; population (1981) 66,500.

harrow /'hærəʊ/ an agricultural implement used to break up the furrows left by the ◊plough and reduce the soil to a fine tilth. It is also used after sowing to cover the seeds. The traditional harrow consists of spikes set in a frame. Other harrows use sets of discs.

Hart /hɑːt/ Gary 1936– . US Democrat politician, senator for Colorado from 1974. In 1980 he unsuccessfully contested the Democratic nomination for the presidency, and stepped down from his Senate seat in 1986 to stand in the 1988 presidential campaign. Early in 1987 he withdrew because of a scandal involving an alleged affair with a model, but in Dec 1987 he resumed his campaign.

Hart /hɑːt/ Judith 1924– . British Labour politician and sociologist. She was minister of overseas development 1967–70. She returned as minister of state 1974–75 and to overseas development 1977–79.

Harte /hɑːt/ Francis Bret 1839–1902. American author, he became a gold-miner at 18 before founding the *Overland Monthly* 1868 in which he wrote short stories of the pioneer West, for example *The Luck of Roaring Camp* and poems such as *The Heathen Chinee*. From 1885 he settled in England.

hartebeest type of large African antelope *Alcelaphus buselaphus* with lyre-shaped horns set close on top of the head in both sexes. It may reach 1.5 m/5 ft at the rather humped shoulders, and up to 2 m/6 ft long. Clumsy-looking runners, hartebeest can still reach 65 kph/40 mph.

hartebeest A group of Coke's hartebeest (*Alcelaphus buselaphus Cokei*) in East Africa. They can achieve running speeds of 65 kph/40 mph.

Hartley /'hɑːtlɪ/ L(eslie) P(oles) 1895–1972. British novelist, noted for his exploration of the sinister. He established his name with the trilogy *The Shrimp and the Anemone* 1944, *The Sixth Heaven* 1946, and *Eustace and Hilda* 1947, on the intertwined lives of a brother and sister. Later books include *The Go-Between* 1953 and *The Hireling*, both successfully filmed.

hart's-tongue fern *Phyllitis scolopendrium* with strap-like undivided fronds up to 60 cm/2 ft long, with prominent brown spore-bearing organs in parallel lines on the underside of the leaf. It is found on walls, shady rocky places and in woods, especially in wetter districts.

Hartz Mountains /hɑːts/ range running N to S in Tasmania, Australia, with two remarkable peaks: Hartz Mountain 1,254 m/4,113 ft, and Adamsons Peak 1,224 m/4,017 ft.

Harun al-Rashid /hæ'ruːn æl ræ'ʃiːd/ 763–809. Caliph of Baghdad from 786, a lavish patron of music, poetry, and letters.

Harvard University /'hɑːvəd/ oldest educational institution in the USA, founded in 1636 at New Towne (later Cambridge), Massachusetts, and named after John Harvard (1607–38), who bequeathed half his estate and his library to it. Women were first admitted in 1969; they had previously been admitted to *Radcliffe College*, the women's college of the university.

harvestman arachnid of the order Opiliones found in late summer and early autumn. Distinguished from true spiders by the absence of a waist or constriction in the oval body, they are carnivorous, and are found from the Arctic to the tropics. The *long-legged harvestman Phalangium opilio* is often found in Britain.

harvest-mite scarlet or rusty brown ◊mite. Common in summer and autumn. They are parasitic, and their bites are intensely irritating to humans.

Harvey /'hɑːvɪ/ William 1578–1657. English physician, who discovered the circulation of blood. In 1609 he became physician to St. Bartholomew's Hospital in London, and in 1615 lecturer at the College of Physicians. His theory of circulation was published in 1628. He was physician to James I and Charles I, and was in attendance on the latter at the battle of Edgehill.

Harvey Court physician to James I and Charles I, William Harvey published his theory of the circulation of the blood in 1628.

Harwell /'hɑːwəl/ the main research establishment of the United Kingdom Atomic Energy Authority, close to the village of Harwell in Oxfordshire.

Harwich /'hærɪdʒ/ seaport in Essex, England; with ferry services to Scandinavia and the North Continent; population (1981) 15,076.

Haryana /ˌhærɪ'ɑːnə/ NW state of India
area 44,222 sq km/17,074 sq mi
capital Chandigarh
features part of the Ganges plain, and a centre of Hinduism
population (1981) 12,850,900
language Hindi.

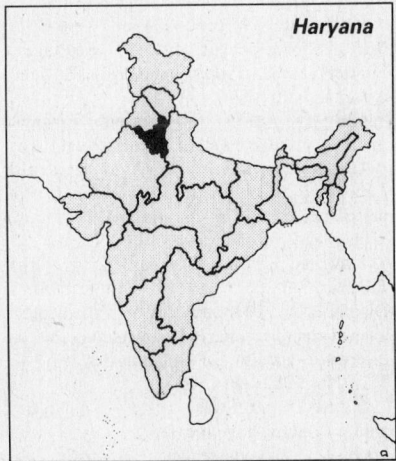

Haryana

Hašek /'hæʃek/ Jaroslav 1883–1923. Czech writer, who in 1915 deserted to the Russians, and eventually joined the Bolsheviks. His comic masterpiece is the unfinished *The Good Soldier Schweik* 1920–23.

hashish form of ◊cannabis.

Hassan II /hæ'sɑːn/ 1930–. King of Morocco from 1961; from 1976 he undertook the occupation of Western Sahara.

Hastings /'heɪstɪŋz/ resort in East Sussex, England; population (1981) 74,803. The chief of the ◊Cinque Ports, it has ruins of a Norman castle. It is adjoined by St Leonard's, developed in the 19th century.

Hastings /'heɪstɪŋz/ Warren 1732–1818. British administrator. A protégé of ◊Clive, he carried out major reforms, and became governor of Bengal in 1772, and governor-general of India in 1774. Impeached for corruption on his return to England in 1785, he was acquitted in 1795.

Hastings Governor-general of India Warren Hastings was impeached for corruption on his return to England in 1785, and was acquitted in 1795. His portrait is by Joshua Reynolds (c. 1766–68).

Hathaway /'hæθəweɪ/ Anne 1556–1623. Wife of ◊Shakespeare from 1582; her cottage at Shottery, near Stratford-upon-Avon, England, is a tourist attraction.

Hathor /'hæθɔː/ in ancient Egyptian mythology, the sky-goddess, identified with ◊Isis.

Hattersley /'hætəzli/ Roy 1932– . British Labour politician. On the right wing, he was prices secretary 1976–79, and in 1983 became deputy leader of the party.

Haughey /'hɔːhi/ Charles 1925– . Irish Fianna Fail politician of Ulster descent. Dismissed in 1970 from Jack Lynch's cabinet for alleged complicity in IRA gun-running, he was afterwards acquitted. Prime minister 1979–81, Mar–Nov 1982, and 1986– .

Hausa /'hausə/ Muslim people of N Nigeria, whose Hamitic language (see ◊Hamito-Semitic language) is a lingua franca of W Africa.

Haussmann /əʊs'mæn/ Georges Eugène, Baron Haussman 1809–1891. French administrator, who replanned medieval Paris 1853–70, with wide boulevards and parks.

haustorium a specialized organ produced by a parasitic plant or fungus which penetrates the cells of its host to adsorb nutrients. It may be either an outgrowth of hyphae, as in the case of parasitic fungi, or of the stems of flowering parasitic plants, as seen in dodders (*Cuscuta*). The sucker-like haustoria of a dodder penetrate the vascular tissue of the host plant without killing the cells.

Havana /hə'vænə/ capital and port of Cuba; population (1981) 1,924,866. The palace of the Spanish governors, and the stronghold of La Fuerza (1583), survive. In 1898 the blowing up of the US battleship *Maine* in the harbour began the Spanish–American ◊war. Cigars and tobacco are made here.

Havel /'hævel/ Vaclav 1936– . Czech satiric playwright, for example, *The Garden Party* 1963, and *Largo Desolato* 1985, about a dissident intellectual. He was imprisoned 1979–83 for support of Charter 77 (see ◊Czechoslovakia).

Havre, Le /'ɑːvrə/ see ◊Le Havre, port in France.

Hawaii /hə'waiiː/ Pacific island state of the USA; nicknamed Aloha State
area 16,705 sq km/6450 sq mi
capital Honolulu on Oahu
towns Hilo
features Hawaii consists of a chain of some 20 volcanic islands, of which the chief are: *Hawaii* itself, noted for *Mauna Kea* 4201 m/13,784 ft, the world's highest island mountain (site of a UK infrared ◊telescope) and Mauna Loa, 4170 m/13,680 ft, the world's largest active volcanic crater;
Maui second largest island;
Oahu third largest, with the greatest concentration of population and tourist attractions, for example, Waikiki beach, and site of ◊Pearl Harbor; *Kauai* and *Molokai*
products sugar, coffee, pineapples, bananas and flowers; there are offshore cobalt, nickel and manganese deposits
population (1980) 964,691 of whom about 30% are European, 30% Japanese, 15% Filipino, and 5% Chinese
language English
religion Christianity; minority Buddhism
famous people Father Joseph Damien
history Captain Cook, who called them the Sandwich Islands, was the first known European visitor in 1778. A kingdom until 1893, Hawaii became a republic in 1894, ceded itself to the USA in 1898, and became a state in 1959.

hawfinch European finch *Coccothraustes coccothraustes* with a large powerful bill. About 18 cm/7 in long it is rather uncommon and spends most of its time in the treetops. It feeds on berries and seeds, and can crack stones of cherries with its bill.

hawk name of various small to medium-sized birds of prey, other than eagles and vultures, of the family Accipitridae. They have an untoothed bill and short wings. The term is also applied metaphorically to people with aggressive ideas on foreign policy, in contrast to moderate *doves*; it was originally used for US advocates of continuation and escalation of the Vietnam War.

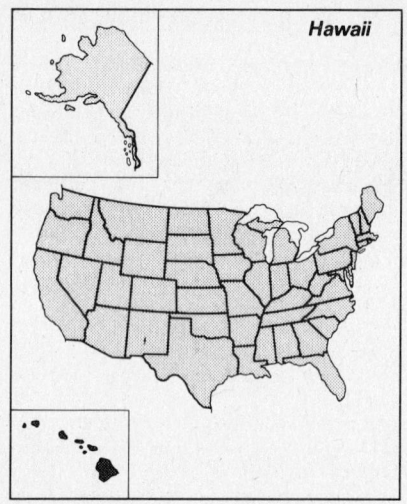

Hawaii

Hawke /hɔːk/ Bob (Robert) 1929– . Australian Labour politician, on the right wing of the party. He was president of the Australian Council of Trade Unions 1970–80, and became prime minister in 1983.

Hawkesbury /'hɔːksbəri/ river in New South Wales, Australia; length 480 km/300 mi. It is a major source of Sydney's water.

Hawking /'hɔːkɪŋ/ Stephen 1942– . British physicist, who has conducted important research into ◊black holes and gravitational field theory. Professor of gravitational physics at Cambridge from 1977, he has discovered, among other things, that the strong gravitational field around a black hole can radiate particles of matter. Commenting on Einstein's remark, 'God does not play dice with the Universe,' he said: 'God not only plays dice, he throws them where they can't be seen.' Confined to a wheelchair because of a muscular disease, he is forced to perform complex mathematical calculations entirely in his head.

Hawkins /'hɔːkɪnz/ Anthony Hope. Real name of British novelist Anthony ◊Hope.

Hawkins /'hɔːkɪnz/ Coleman (Randolph) 1904–1969. US virtuoso tenor saxophonist. He became a soloist with Fletcher Henderson's Orchestra, and was the most influential figure in bringing the jazz saxophone to prominence as a solo instrument.

Hawkins /'hɔːkɪnz/ John 1532–1595. English navigator, born in Plymouth. Treasurer to the navy 1573–89, he was knighted for his services as a commander against the Armada.

Hawkins /'hɔːkɪnz/ Richard c. 1562–1622. English navigator, son of John ◊Hawkins. He held a command against the Spanish Armada in 1588; was captured in an expedition against Spanish possessions 1593–94 and not released till 1602; knighted in 1603.

hawk moth family of moths (Sphingidae) with some 1,000 species distributed throughout the world, but mainly tropical. The death's head hawk-moth *Acherontia atropos* is the largest of British moths. Some South American hawk

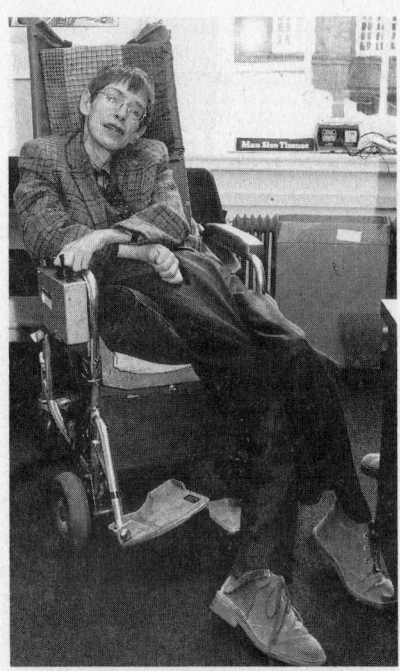

Hawking The British physicist and mathematician Professor Stephen Hawking helped to confirm the big bang theory of creation and made important discoveries on the nature of black holes.

moths closely resemble humming birds and the humming bird hawk moth *Macroglossum stellatarum* is found in southern England.

Hawks /'hɔːks/ Howard 1896–1977. American director and producer of a wide range of films with popular appeal, including *The Big Sleep* 1946.

Hawksmoor /'hɔːksmɔː/ Nicholas 1661–1736. English architect, assistant to ◊Wren in London churches and St Paul's; joint architect with ◊Vanbrugh of Castle Howard and Blenheim Palace. The original west towers of Westminster Abbey, long attributed to Wren, are his.

Haworth /'hauəθ/ village in W Yorkshire, home of the ◊Brontë family. It is now part of ◊Keighley.

Haworth /'hauəθ/ Norman 1883–1950. British organic chemist, he was the first to synthesize a vitamin (vitamin C), in 1933. He shared a Nobel prize in 1937.

hawthorn common name for shrubs and trees of the *Crataegus* genus, of the Rosaceae family. The common hawthorn, may or whitethorn *Crataegus monogyna*, a thorny shrub or small tree 2–10 m/6–30 ft in height, bears clusters of white or pink flowers followed by groups of red berries. It is indigenous to Britain and much of Europe, North Africa and Western Asia, and has been naturalized in North America and Australia.

Hawthorne /'hɔːθɔːn/ Nathaniel 1804–1864. American author, born at ◊Salem. He worked as a customs official, but won fame with *The Scarlet Letter* 1850, *The House of the Seven Gables* 1851, and with his classic legends retold for

children, *Tanglewood Tales* 1853. He was a friend of ◊Melville.

Hayden /'heɪdn/ William 1933– . Australian Labor politician. Born in Brisbane, he was leader of the Australian Labor Party and of the opposition 1977–83, and became minister of foreign affairs 1983.

Haydn /'haɪdn/ Franz Joseph 1732–1809. Austrian composer. Born in Lower Austria, he was Kapellmeister 1761–90 to Prince Esterházy at Eisenstadt and Esterház. He visited London twice, in 1791–92 and again in 1794–95. A teacher of both Mozart and Beethoven, he was a major exponent of the classical sonata form in his numerous chamber and orchestral works (he wrote over 100 symphonies). He also wrote much choral music, the best-known including the oratorios *The Creation* 1798 and *The Seasons* 1801. He was the first great master of the string quartet. His work also includes operas, church music, and songs, and he composed the 'Emperor's Hymn', adopted as the Austrian – and later, German – national anthem.

Haydon /'heɪdn/ Benjamin Robert 1786–1846. British artist. Born in Plymouth, he settled in London and became celebrated for his gigantic canvases. Attempts at 'high art' include *Christ's Entry into Jerusalem* (1820, now in Philadelphia). He is now better appreciated in genre pictures, for example *The Mock Election* and *Chairing the Member*; and for his lively *Autobiography and Memoirs* 1853.

Hayek /'haɪek/ Friedrich August von 1899– . Austrian economist. Born in Vienna, he taught at the London School of Economics 1931–50, and was professor of social and moral science at the University of Chicago 1950–62. His *The Road to Serfdom* 1944 was a critical study of socialistic trends in Britain. He was awarded a Nobel prize in 1974.

Hayes /'heɪz/ Rutherford Birchard 1822–1893. 19th president of the USA (1877–81). Born in Ohio, he was a major-general in the Civil War and prominent Republican politician. During his presidency federal troops (see ◊reconstruction) were withdrawn from the southern states and the Civil Service reformed.

hay fever a common allergic reaction to pollen, causing sneezing and asthmatic symptoms. In those who are specially sensitive, powerful body chemicals, related to ◊histamine, are produced at the site of entry, causing irritation. Treatment is by antihistamine drugs.

hazardous substances waste substances, for the most part generated by industry, which represent a hazard to the environment or to people living or working nearby, for example, radioactive wastes, acidic resins, arsenic residues, residual hardening salts, lead, mercury, nonferrous sludges, organic solvents and pesticides. Their economic disposal or recycling is the subject of research.

hazel genus *Corylus* of northern temperate trees, family Corylaceae, including *common hazel* or *cobnut Corylus avellana* of which the *filbert* is the cultivated variety.

Hazlitt /'hæzlɪt/ William 1778–1830. British essayist and critic, noted for his invective, scathing irony and gift for epigram. Born in

Maidstone, he worked for the daily press and magazines in London, writing from the liberal viewpoint. He was a superb controversialist, with a unique, clear, hard-hitting prose style which served him equally well in his critical essays: *Characters of Shakespeare's Plays* 1817–18, *English Comic Writers* 1819, and *Dramatic Literature of the Age of Elizabeth* 1820. Other notable works are his *Table Talk* 1821–22; *The Spirit of the Age* 1825, and the curious *Liber Amoris* 1823, a record of his infatuation with the daughter of a tailor with whom he lodged.

Hazlitt A master of invective and irony, British essayist William Hazlitt was encouraged to take up journalism by S T Coleridge.

Head /'hed/ Edith 1900–1981. American costume designer for Hollywood films, who won eight Oscars, including *The Heiress* 1949, *All About Eve* 1950, and *The Sting* 1972.

headache pain in the head, which has causes ranging from minor eye strain, stress, infection and neck or jaw muscle strain to severe physical illness, for example brain tumour. It is marked by dilution of the cerebral blood vessels and irritation of the brain linings (meninges) and of the nerves.

Healey /'hiːli/ Denis Winston 1917– . British Labour politician. While minister of defence 1964–70 was in charge of the reduction of British forces east of Suez. As chancellor of the Exchequer 1974–79, he attempted to control inflation and in his 1976 budget made reduction in personal income tax dependent on union agreement to minimum wage increases. In 1980 he contested the party leadership with Callaghan, and was deputy to Michael Foot 1980–83. In 1987 he resigned from the shadow cabinet.

health care life expectancy is determined by overall efficiency of the body's vital organs and the rate at which these organs deteriorate. The fundamental rules of health care are concerned with:

smoking this is linked to heart disease, stroke, bronchitis, lung cancer and other serious diseases.

exercise regular physical exercise, provided it is vigorous and taken regularly (such as for 20–30 minutes, 3–5 times a week) improves fitness, slows down the gradual decline in efficency of the heart and lungs, and so helps to prolong life.

alcohol recommended maximum intake is no more than 21 units of alcohol a week for men, no more than 14 for women. (Half a pint of beer, one glass of wine or single measure of spirits is equivalent to one unit.) Doctors recommend at least two alcohol free days a week. Excessive alcohol intake can cause liver damage and may lead to dependence.

diet a healthy diet contains plenty of vegetable fibre, vitamins, with protein and carbohydrate, and substitutes polyunsaturated fats (which lower the level of blood cholesterol) for saturated (animal) fats. Too much food causes obesity.

weight obesity (defined as being 10 kg/20 lb or more above the desirable weight for the person's age, sex and height) is associated with many potentially dangerous conditions, such as coronary heart disease, diabetes, and stroke, as well as muscular and joint problems, and breathing difficulties.

health education teaching and advice on healthy living, including nutrition, sex education, and advice on drink, drugs, and other threats to health, offered by most secondary schools in the UK. Health education is often included within a course of personal and social education, or alternatively integrated into subjects such as biology, home economics, or physical education.

health psychology a new development within ◊clinical psychology which applies psychological principles to promote physical well-being. For example, people with high blood pressure can learn methods such as relaxation, meditation, and life-style changes.

health service government provision of medical care on a national scale. From 1948 the UK has had a National Health Service which includes hospital care, but charges are made for ordinary doctors' prescriptions, spectacles, and dental treatment, except for children and people on very low incomes. Private health schemes such as BUPA have become increasingly used. In the USA the Medicare health insurance scheme provides care (towards which patients pay a share) out of hospital for the elderly and disabled, and the Medicaid state scheme (to which the federal government contributes) for people unable to afford private care. Many Americans have personal subscriptions to private health schemes, such as Blue Cross (established 1929) and Blue Shield (established 1917), and from 1985 fees for Medicare patients to join health maintenance organizations (HMOs, covering visits to a group of doctors and hospital fees) have been paid for them. See also ◊social security.

Heaney /'hi:ni/ Seamus (Justin) 1939– . Irish poet, born in Londonderry, who has written powerful verse about the polical situation in Northern Ireland. Collections include *North* 1975, *Field Work* 1979, and *Station Island* 1984.

Heard and MacDonald Islands /hɜːd, mək'dɒnld/ group of islands in the S Indian Ocean, about 4,000 km/2,500 mi SW of Fremantle. They were discovered in 1833, annexed by Britain in 1910, and transferred to Australia in 1947. *Heard Island* 42 km by 19 km/26 mi by 12 mi is glacier-covered, although the volcanic mountain *Big Ben* 2,743 m/9,000 ft, is still active: there is a weather station (1947).

hearing aid a device to improve the hearing of partially deaf people. The earliest aid was an ear trumpet. A typical modern aid consists of a battery-powered transistorized microphone/amplifier unit and earpiece. Some miniaturized aids are compact enough to fit in the ear or be concealed in the frame of spectacles.

Hearst /hɜːst/ Patty (Patricia) 1955– . American granddaughter of William R ◊Hearst, who was kidnapped in 1974, by the Symbionese Liberation Army. She joined her captors in a bank raid, and was imprisoned 1976–79.

Hearst /hɜːst/ William Randolph 1863–1951. American newspaper proprietor, celebrated for his introduction of banner headlines, lavish illustration, and the sensational approach known as 'yellow journalism'. A campaigner in numerous controversies, and a strong isolationist, he was said to be the model for Citizen Kane in the film of that name by Orson Welles. He collected art treasures, antiques, and castles – one of which, San Simeon (Hearst Castle) in California, is a state museum.

heart a muscular organ that rhythmically contracts to force blood around the body of animals with a ◊circulatory system. Annelid worms and some other invertebrates have simple hearts consisting of thickened sections of main blood vessels that pulse regularly. An earthworm has ten such hearts. Vertebrates have one heart. In fish the heart has two chambers – the thin-walled *atrium* (once called the auricle) that expands to receive blood and the thick-walled *ventricle* which pumps it out; amphibians and most reptiles have two atria and one ventricle; birds and mammals have two atria and two ventricles creating a double circulation, one to the ◊lungs and one to the rest of the body. The beating of the heart is controlled by the ◊autonomic nervous systems, and by ◊hormones.

heartburn popular name for irritation of the lower oesophagus (gullet) by excessively acid stomach contents, as sometimes happens during pregnancy and in cases of duodenal ulcer or obesity. It may be due to a weak valve at the entrance to the stomach that allows its contents to well up into the oesophagus.

heart-lung machine apparatus used during heart surgery to take over temporarily the functions of the heart and the lungs. It has a pump to circulate the blood around the body and facility for adding oxygen to the blood and removing carbon dioxide from it. A heart-lung machine was first used for open-heart surgery in the USA in 1953.

heat form of energy which when it is added to or removed from an object usually causes a rise or fall in its temperature. Heat always flows from a region of higher temperature to one of lower temperature. Its effect on a substance may be simply to raise its temperature, to cause it to expand, to melt it if a solid, to vaporize it if a liquid, or to increase its pressure if a confined gas. The *specific heat* of a substance is the ratio of the quantity of heat required to raise the temperature of a given mass of the substance through a given range of temperature, to the heat required to raise the temperature of an equal mass of water through the same range (see ◊calorimeter, ◊temperature, ◊entropy). Quantities of heat are usually measured in units of energy, such as joules (J) or calories (C).

There are three ways by which heat may be transferred from one place to another: (a) *convection* – transmission through a fluid (liquid or gas) by currents, for example when the air in a room is warmed by a fire or radiator, or water is heated in a domestic hot-water system; (b) *conduction* – heat passing from one part of a medium to neighbouring parts with no visible motion of the medium accompanying the transfer of heat, as when the whole length of a metal rod is heated when one end is held in a fire; (c) *radiation* – heat transfer by infra-red rays. Radiant heat is of the same nature as light. It can pass through a vacuum, travels at the same speed as light, can be reflected and refracted, and does not affect the medium through which it passes.

heat capacity in physics, the quantity of heat required to raise the temperature of a substance by one degree. The *specific heat capacity* of a substance is the heat capacity per unit of mass, measured in joules per kilogram per ◊kelvin (J kg^{-1} K^{-1}).

heath plant of the family Ericaceae of low-growing woody evergreen shrubs also known as *heathers* of Europe and Africa. With bell-shaped pendant flowers, they are popular garden plants. The *bell heather Erica cinerea* is often found with common ◊heather.

Heath /hiːθ/ Edward Richard George 1916– . British Conservative politician. He entered parliament in 1950, was minister of labour 1959–60, and as Lord Privy Seal 1960–63 conducted abortive negotiations for Common Market membership. He succeeded Home as Conservative leader in 1965 – the first elected leader of his party. Defeated in the general election of 1966, he achieved a surprise victory in 1970, but his confrontation with the striking miners as part of his campaign to control inflation led to his defeat in Feb 1974 and again in Oct 1974. He was replaced as party leader by Margaret Thatcher in 1975.

heather low-growing evergreen shrub, common on sandy or acid soil, especially *common heather* or *ling Calluna vulgaris*, with pale purple flowers and small leaves on a shrubby stem. See also ◊heath.

Heathrow /,hiːθ'rəʊ/ site of Heathrow Airport, ◊London, England.

heat pump machine run by electricity or other power source, on a similar principle to a ◊refrigerator, for example, to cool the interior of a building or, conversely, by extracting energy from the atmosphere to provide space heating.

heat shield a material on the external surface of a spacecraft, which protects the astronauts and equipment inside from the searing heat of re-

heart

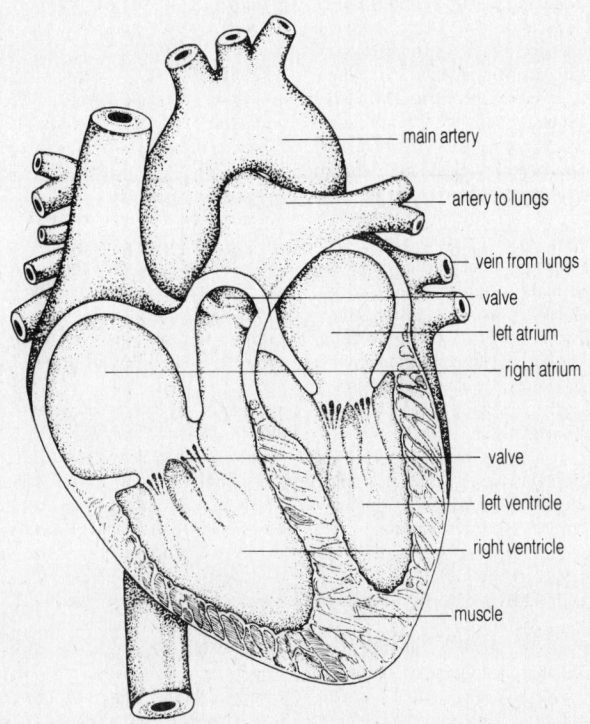

- main artery
- artery to lungs
- vein from lungs
- valve
- left atrium
- right atrium
- valve
- left ventricle
- right ventricle
- muscle

entry when returning to Earth. Air friction can generate temperatures of up to 1,500°C upon re-entry to the atmosphere, which a heat shield must withstand.

heat storage means of storing heat for release later. It is usually achieved by using materials which undergo phase changes, for example, ◊Glauber's salt, and sodium pyrophosphate, which melts at 70°C. The latter is used to store off-peak heat in the home, the salt being liquefied by cheap heat during the night, and then freezing to give off heat during the day. Other developments include the use of plastic crystals, which change their structure rather than melting when they are heated. They could be incorporated in curtains or clothing.

heat stroke condition caused in human beings when the body temperature rises above 40°C (104°F). The brain swells, resulting in confusion of thought; the body becomes dehydrated, blood circulation slows, and organs, such as the kidneys, fail to function. Coma may ensue, and possibly cardiac arrest. Treatment is by cooling the body carefully and giving fluids to relieve dehydration.

heat treatment subjecting metals and alloys to controlled heating and cooling after fabrication to relieve internal stresses and improve their physical properties. Methods include ◊annealing, ◊quenching, and ◊tempering.

heaven in the theology of Christianity and some other religions, the destination of the virtuous after death. Many attempts have been made, particularly by Christian and Muslim writers, to describe its physical joys, but modern theologians usually describe it as a place or state in which the soul sees God as he really is.

Heaviside /'hevɪsaɪd/ Oliver 1850–1925. British physicist whose theoretical work had important implications for radio transmission. His studies of electricity published in *Electrical Papers* 1892 had considerable influence on long-distance telephony. In 1902 he predicted the existence of an ionized layer of air in the upper atmosphere, which was verified by Kennelly and was later known as the ◊Kennelly-Heaviside or Heaviside layer but is now called the E-layer. Deflection from it makes possible the transmission of radio signals round the world, which would otherwise be lost in outer space, and its presence is connected with the phenomenon of radio fading. See ◊ionosphere.

heavy metal a metallic element of high ◊atomic mass, for instance platinum, gold, lead. Heavy metals are poisonous and tend to persist in living systems, causing, for example, gradual mercury poisoning in shellfish.

heavy metal in music, a style of rock characterized by loudness, blood-and-thunder imagery, and guitar solos. The British group Led Zeppelin (1968–80) pioneered the form; later bands include Motorhead (1975–) and Van Halen (1974–). The usage comes from *The Naked Lunch* by the US author William Burroughs.

heavy metal poisoning illness caused by exposure to toxic heavy metals, for example, plutonium and cadmium, to which workers in industry may be exposed. Some heavy metals, however, such as zinc and copper, are essential to living cells. Treatment of the condition is difficult

because it is not yet possible to produce a drug which can distinguish, when removing heavy metals from the body cells, between those which are vital and those which are poisonous.

heavy water deuterium oxide (D_2O), that is water containing the isotope deuterium instead of hydrogen (molecular weight 20 against 18 for ordinary water). Its chemical properties are identical with those of ordinary water, while its physical properties differ slightly. It occurs in ordinary water in the ratio of about one part by weight of deuterium to 5,000 parts by weight of hydrogen and can be concentrated by ◊electrolysis, the ordinary water being more readily decomposed by this means than the heavy water. It has been used in the nuclear industry.

Hebe /'hiːbi/ in Greek mythology, the goddess of youth, daughter of ◊Zeus and ◊Hera, and handmaiden of the gods.

Hebei /ˌhʌ'beɪ/ province (formerly *Hopei* or *Hupei*) of N China
area 202,700 sq km/79,053 sq mi
capital Shijiazhuang
features include special municipalities of Beijing and Tianjin
products cereals, textiles, iron and steel
population (1982) 60,770,000.

Hebrew language a member of the ◊Hamito-Semitic language family spoken in W Asia by the ancient Hebrews, sustained for many centuries as the liturgical language of Judaism, and revived and developed in the 20th century as modern Israeli Hebrew, the national language of the State of Israel. It is the original language of the Old Testament of the Bible. Such English words as *cherub*, *Jehovah/Yahweh*, *kosher*, *rabbi*, *seraph* and *shibboleth* are borrowings from Hebrew. The Hebrew alphabet is written from right to left.

Hebrides /'hebrɪdiːz/ group of over 500 islands (fewer than 100 inhabited) off W Scotland; total area 2,900 sq km/1,120 sq mi. The Hebrides were settled by Scandinavians in the 6th–9th centuries, and passed under Norwegian rule from about 890–1266.
The *Inner Hebrides* are divided between the Highland and Strathclyde regions. The largest is Skye, area 1,665 sq km/643 sq mi, capital Portree, where Bonnie Prince Charlie (◊Charles Edward Stuart) took refuge after ◊Culloden. The others include ◊Mull (chief town Tobermory), ◊Jura, ◊Islay (which produces the finest of malt whisky, and whose wildlife includes eagles and rare wintering geese), and uninhabited ◊Staffa. Of special interest is ◊Iona, where in 563 St ◊Columba founded a monastery. The *Outer Hebrides* form the islands area of the ◊Western Isles administrative area, separated from the Inner group by the Little Minch. The largest is ◊Lewis-with-Harris 2,225 sq km/859 sq mi, capital Stornoway, others being N and S Uist, all of which are famous for tweeds. To the W of Harris is ◊St Kilda, a small island group uninhabited since 1930.

Hebron /'hebrən/ (Arabic *El Khalil*) city on the West Bank of the Jordan, occupied by Israel from 1967; population (1967) 43,000, including 4,000 Jews. Within the mosque is the traditional site of the tombs of Abraham, Isaac, and Jacob.

Heb-Sed royal festival in ancient Egypt, apparently commemorating ◊Menes's union of Upper and Lower Egypt.

Hecate /'hekəti/ in Greek mythology, the goddess of witchcraft and magic, sometimes identified with ◊Artemis and the moon.

hectare unit of area in the metric system (Greek *hekaton* 100) equalling 100 acres (square decametres) or 10,000 square metres or 2.471 acres. Trafalgar Square, London's only 'metric square', was laid out as one hectare.

Hector /'hektə/ in Greek mythology, a Trojan prince, son of ◊Priam who, in the siege of Troy, was the foremost warrior on the Trojan side until he was killed by ◊Achilles.

Hecuba /'hekjubə/ in Greek mythology, the wife of ◊Priam, and mother of ◊Hector and ◊Paris, captured by the Greeks after the fall of Troy.

hedgehog mammal *Erinaceus europaeus* common in Europe, western Asia, Africa, and India. The body, including the tail, is 30 cm/1 ft long. It is speckled-brown in colour, has a pig-like snout, and is covered with sharp spines. When alarmed it can roll the body into a ball. Hedgehogs feed on insects, slugs and carrion.

hedgehog Its spines not fully developed, this young hedgehog is only a week old. There is now concern over the dwindling number of hedgehogs in the British countryside.

hedge sparrow another name for ◊dunnock, a small bird.

hedonism the ethical theory that pleasure or happiness is, or should be, the chief end of life. Hedonist sects in Greece were the ◊Cyrenaics, who held that the sentient pleasure of the moment is the only human good, and the ◊Epicureans, who advocated the pursuit of pleasure under the direction of reason. Modern hedonistic philosophies, such as those of ◊Bentham and ◊Mill, regard the happiness of society as the aim, and not that of the single individual.

Hefei /ˌhʌ'feɪ/ capital (formerly Hofei) of Anhui province, China; population (1982) 815,000.

Hegel /'heɪgəl/ Georg Wilhelm Friedrich 1770–1831. German philosopher, author of *The Phenomenology of Spirit* 1807, *Encyclopaedia of the Philosophical Sciences* 1817, and *Philosophy of Right* 1821. He was professor of philosophy at Heidelberg 1817–18, and at Berlin 1818–31. Hegel conceived of consciousness and the external object as forming a unity, in which neither factor can exist independently. Mind and nature are two abstractions of one indivisible whole. Thus the world is the unfolding and expression of one all-embracing absolute idea, an organism constantly developing by its own internal necessity so as to become the gradual embodiment of reason. Each system by its own development brings about its opposite (antithesis), and finally a higher synthesis unifies and embodies both. As a rightist Hegel championed religion, the Prussian State and the existing order, but leftist followers include Marx, who used Hegel's dialectic to attempt to show the inevitability of radical change and attacked both religion and the social order.

hegemony (from Greek *hegemonia*, authority) political dominance of one power over others in a group in which all are supposedly equal. The term was first used for the dominance of Athens over the other Greek city states; later applied to Prussia within Germany, and, in modern times, to the USA and USSR throughout the world.

Hegira Arabic 'flight', applied to Muhammad's flight from Mecca to Medina on 16 Jul 622 AD. The Muslim era is dated from this event, and Islamic dates are preceded by AH *anno hegirae* (Latin, 'in the year of the Hegira').

Heidegger /'haɪdegə/ Martin 1889–1976. German philosopher, one of the most influential of the 20th century. In his major work, *Being and Time* 1927, he used the methods of ◊Husserl's phenomenology to develop an account of the concrete structures of human existence, *Dasein*. Throughout his work, he argued that Western philosophy had forgotten the basic question of the 'meaning of being', and his later writings meditated on the fate of a world dominated by science and technology.

Heidelberg /'haɪdlbɜːg/ town on the S bank of the Neckar, 19 km/12 mi SE of Mannheim, in Baden-Württemberg, West Germany; population (1984) 133,500. Heidelberg university, the oldest in Germany, was established in 1386.

Heidelberg /'haɪdlbɜːg/ village near Melbourne, Australia, which gave its name to the *Heidelberg School* – a group of Impressionist artists (including Roberts, Streeton, and ◊Conder) working in teaching camps in the neighbourhood. Flourishing 1888–90, the school had its most famous exhibition in 1889, the '9 by 5', from the size of the cigar-box lids used.

Heifetz /'haɪfɪts/ Jascha 1901–1987. Russian-born American violinist. One of the great virtuosos of the 20th century, he first performed at the age of five, and before he was 17 had played in most European capitals, and in the USA, where he settled in 1917. ◊Walton's concerto was written for him.

Heilongjiang /ˌheɪˌluŋdʒi'æŋ/ province (formerly Heilungkiang) of NE China, in ◊Manchuria
area 710,000 sq km/274,060 sq mi
capital Harbin
features China's largest oilfield, near Anda
products cereals, gold, coal
population (1982) 32,665,546.

Heilungkiang former name of ◊Heilongjiang, a province of NE China.

Heine /'haɪnə/ Heinrich 1797–1856. German revolutionary and romantic poet. His *Reisebilder*, which announced his revolutionary sympathies, appeared in 1826, and the *Buch der Lieder/Book of Songs* in 1827. From 1831 he lived mainly in Paris, as a correspondent for German newspapers. Schubert and Schumann set many of his songs to music.

Heinkel /'haɪŋkəl/ Ernst 1888–1958. German aircraft designer who pioneered jet aircraft. He founded his firm in 1922, and built the first jet aircraft 1939 (developed independently of the Whittle jet of 1941). During World War II he was Germany's biggest producer of warplanes.

Heinlein /'haɪnlaɪn/ Robert A(nson) 1907– . American science-fiction writer, associated with the pulp magazines of the 1940s; best known for the militaristic novel *Starship Troopers* 1959 and the utopian cult novel *Stranger in a Strange Land* 1961.

Heisenberg /'haɪzənbɜːg/ Werner Carl 1901–1976. German physicist. He was an originator of quantum mechanics (see ◊quantum theory) and the formulator of the ◊uncertainty (indeterminacy) principle, which states that the motion and position of a ◊particle cannot be measured precisely because the act of measuring disturbs the system. He was awarded a Nobel prize in 1932.

Hejaz /hiː'dʒæz/ former independent kingdom, merged in 1932 with Nejd to form ◊Saudi Arabia; population (1970) 2,000,000; the capital is Mecca.

Hel /hel/ or *Hela* in Norse mythology, the goddess of the underworld.

Helen /'helən/ in Greek mythology, the daughter of ◊Zeus and ◊Leda, and the most beautiful of women. She married Menelaus, king of Sparta, but during his absence eloped with ◊Paris, prince of Troy, which precipitated the Trojan War. Afterwards she returned to Sparta with her husband.

Helena, Saint /'helɪnə/ c. 248–328. Roman empress, mother of the emperor Constantine the Great, and a convert to Christianity. According to legend, she discovered the true cross of Christ at Jerusalem. Her feast day is 18 Aug.

helicopter an aircraft which achieves both lift and propulsion by means of a rotary wing, or rotor on top of the fuselage. It can take off and land vertically, move in any direction or remain stationary in the air. Igor Sikorsky in the USA built the first practical single rotor craft in 1939. The rotor of a helicopter has two or more blades, which are of aerofoil cross-section, like an aeroplane's wings. Lift and propulsion are achieved by angling the blades as they rotate. A single rotor helicopter must also have a small tail rotor to counter the tendency of the body to spin in the opposite direction to this main rotor. Twin-rotor helicopters like the Boeing Chinook have their rotors turning in opposite directions and this prevents the body spinning.

In war they carry troops and equipment in difficult terrain, and make aerial reconnaissance and attacks. Naval carriers are being increasingly built, helicopters with depth charges and homing ◊torpedoes being guided to submarine or surface targets beyond the carrier's attack range. The helicopter may also use dunking ◊sonar to find targets beyond the carrier's own radar horizon. See also ◊autogiro.

neutrons, and is thus identical to alpha-particles ejected by many radioactive isotopes. Helium-oxygen atmospheres are used in high-pressure breathing work, as required by divers; being less soluble than nitrogen in blood, helium does not give rise to the 'bends' (see ◊decompression sickness). Liquid helium is very important in cryogenics (low-temperature physics). Airships use helium because of its non-inflammability.

Heller /'helə/ Joseph 1923– . American novelist. In World War II, he served in the US Air Force and then entered advertising. Best known is his *Catch-22* 1961, satirizing war and bureaucratic methods.

Hellespont /'helɪspont/ former name of the ◊Dardanelles, separating Europe from Asia.

Hellman /'helmən/ Lillian 1907–1984. American playwright. Born in New Orleans, she

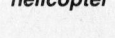

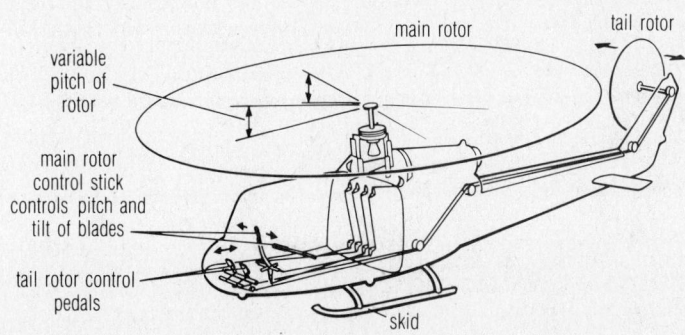

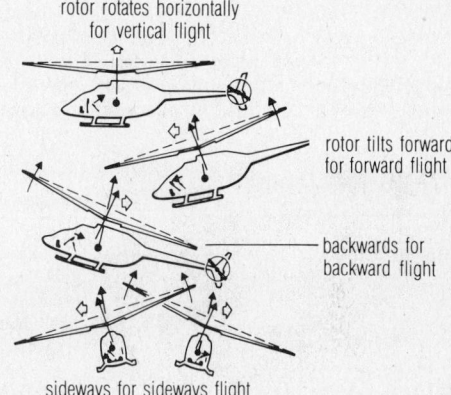

sideways for sideways flight

Heligoland /'helɪgəʊlænd/ island in the North Sea, one of the North Frisian Islands; area 0.6 sq km/150 acres. It is administered by the state of Schleswig-Holstein, West Germany, having been ceded to Germany by Britain in 1890 in exchange for ◊Zanzibar. It was used as a naval base in both world wars.

heliograph old method of signalling, used by armies in the late 19th century, which employed sunlight reflected from a mirror to pass messages. By working a shutter to create long and short flashes of light, the sender could transmit messages in ◊Morse code. On a clear day, a heliograph could send over distances in excess of 50 km/30 mi.

Heliopolis /ˌhiːli'ɒpəlɪs/ ancient Egyptian centre (biblical On) of the worship of the sun-god Ra, NE of Cairo and near the modern village of Matariah.

Helios /'hiːliɒs/ in Greek mythology, the sun-god and father of ◊Phaethon, thought to make his daily journey across the sky in a chariot.

heliotrope genus *Heliotropium* of decorative plants, family Boraginaceae, with distinctive spikes of blue, lilac, or white flowers, especially the *Peruvian* or *cherry pie heliotrope Heliotropium peruvianum*.

helium a gaseous element, symbol He, atomic weight 4.003, atomic number 2. Helium is colourless, odourless, inert, non-inflammable and very light. It is present in the Sun, in gases issuing from the Earth (in Kansas and other parts of North America), in radioactive minerals, and in small quantities in the atmosphere. Helium is obtained by compression and fractionation of naturally occurring gases. When ionized, by losing its two electrons in a high electric field, helium consists of just two protons and two

helix in mathematics, a curve resembling a spring, corkscrew or screw thread. It is generated by a line that encircles a cylinder or cone at a constant angle.

hell in the Bible, a word used to translate Hebrew and Greek words all meaning the place of departed spirits, the abode of the dead. In medieval Christian theology and popular speech, however, hell is the place in which unrepentant sinners suffer the eternal torments of the damned. During the last century the tendency has been to regard hell as a state of damnation rather than a place. The idea of hell is also contained in Islam and most other religions.

hellebore herbaceous plant of the genus *Helleborus*, family Ranunculaceae. The poisonous *stinking hellebore Helleborus foetidus* has greenish flowers early in the spring; the *Christmas rose Helleborus niger*, originally from South and Central Europe, has white flowers from Dec onwards.

helleborine temperate orchids of genera *Epipactis* and *Cephalanthera*, including the British *marsh helleborine Epipactis palustris*, with pink and white flowers.

Hellenic (from *Hellas*, Ancient Greek name for Greece) the classical period of Ancient Greek civilization, from the first Olympic Games in 776 until the death of Alexander the Great in 323 BC.

Hellenistic period (Greek *Hellenizo*, to speak Greek) term for the period in Greek civilization, from the death of Alexander in 323 BC, when Greek culture spread through the Mediterranean, until the accession of the Roman emperor Augustus in 27 BC. ◊Alexandria in Egypt was the centre of culture and commerce during the Hellenistic period.

worked as a journalist in New York. Her plays, concerned with contemporary political and social issues, include *The Children's Hour* 1934, *The Little Foxes* 1939, *Watch on the Rhine* 1941, and *Toys in the Attic* 1960. She lived some 31 years with Dashiell ◊Hammett, and in her will founded a fund to promote Marxist doctrine.

Helmholtz /'helmhəʊlts/ Hermann Ludwig Ferdinand von 1821–1894. German scientist, particularly noted for his work in ◊thermodynamics. Born at Potsdam, he became professor of physics at Berlin. In 1847 he published an epoch-making treatise on the conservation of ◊energy. He investigated the mechanics of vision, wrote a *Manual of Physiological Optics* 1856–66, invented the ophthalmoscope, and in his *Doctrine of the Sensations of Tone* 1862 gave a complete study of sound.

Helmont /'helmɒnt/ Jean Baptiste van 1577–1644. Belgian doctor. The first to realize that gases exist apart from the atmosphere, he claimed to have coined the word 'gas' (from the Greek 'chaos').

Helms /helmz/ Richard 1913– . US secret agent. Originally with the Office of Strategic Services, he was director of the ◊Central Intelligence Agency 1966–73, when he was dismissed by Nixon. In 1977 he was convicted of lying before a congressional committee because his oath as chief of intelligence compelled him to keep secrets from the public.

helot a class of slaves in ancient Sparta, who probably represented the aboriginal inhabitants. Their cruel treatment by the Spartans became proverbial.

Helpmann /'helpmən/ Robert 1909–1986. Australian dancer, choreographer, and actor. He was the leading male dancer with the Sadler's Wells Ballet 1933–50, successfully partnering Margot ◊Fonteyn in the war years. He was noted for his gift for mime and for his dramatic sense, also apparent in his choreographic work, for example *Miracle in the Gorbals* 1944. He was knighted in 1968.

Helsingborg /'helsɪŋbɔːg/ port in SW Sweden, linked by ferry with Helsingör across the Sound; population (1983) 103,870. Industries include copper-smelting, rubber and chemical manufacture, and sugar refining.

Helsingfors /ˌhelsɪŋ'fɔːʃ/ Swedish name for ◊Helsinki.

Helsingör /ˌhelsɪŋ'ɜː/ port in NE Denmark; population (1980) 56,566. It is linked by ferry with ◊Helsingborg across the Sound; Shakespeare made it the scene of *Hamlet*.

Helsingör (English name Elsinore) Kronborg Castle, about 45 km/28 mi north of Copenhagen, built by Frederik II 1574–85, the setting for Shakespeare's *Hamlet*.

Helsinki /'helsɪŋki/ capital and port (kept open by ice-breakers in winter) of Finland; population (1984) 780,456. It has the homes of the architect Eliel ◊Saarinen and the composer ◊Sibelius outside the town.

Helsinki Conference international conference in 1975 at which 35 countries including the USSR and the USA supposedly reached agreements on cooperation in security, economics, science, technology and human rights. Often regarded as marking the end of the Cold War.

Helvellyn /hel'velɪn/ peak of the English Lake District in ◊Cumbria, 950 m/3,118 ft high.

Helvetia /hel'viːʃə/ region, corresponding to W Switzerland, occupied by the Celtic Helvetii 1st century BC – 5th century AD. In 58 BC Caesar repulsed their invasion of southern Gaul at Bibracte (near Autun) and Helvetia became subject to Rome.

Helvetius /ˌelver'sjuːs/ Claude Adrien 1715–1771. French philosopher. Born in Paris, he became a farmer-general of taxes in 1738. In *De l'Esprit* 1758 he maintained that self-interest, however disguised, is the mainspring of all human action, that since conceptions of good and evil vary according to period and locality there

is no absolute good or evil; and the intellectual differences are only a matter of education.

Hemel Hempstead /'heməl 'hempstɪd/ 'new' town in Hertfordshire, England; population (1981) 80,000.

Hemingway /'hemɪŋweɪ/ Ernest 1898–1961. American novelist. Born in Illinois, the son of a doctor, he became a newspaper correspondent in Kansas City. Wounded while serving as a volunteer ambulance man in Italy during World War I, he used these experiences for his war book *Farewell to Arms* 1929. He was much influenced by Gertrude ◊Stein who introduced him to bull-fighting, the theme of his first novel *The Sun Also Rises* 1926 and of *Death in the Afternoon* 1932. *For Whom the Bell Tolls* 1940 has a Spanish Civil War setting, and he served as a correspondent both in this conflict and in World War II. His passion for big-game hunting emerges in short stories, such as 'The Snows of Kilimanjaro' and 'The Short Happy Life of Francis Macomber', and *The Old Man and the Sea* 1952, telling of the duel between a Cuban fisherman and an enormous fish. In 1954 he was awarded a Nobel prize. His style of simple sentences attracted imitators, and was widely parodied. He committed suicide in a fit of depression.

Hemingway American novelist Ernest Hemingway on a fishing expedition. The author had a passion for bull-fighting, big-game hunting, and fishing, and physical courage is a prominent theme in many of his short stories and novels.

hemlock plant of genus *Conium* of the Umbelliferae, one important species being **common hemlock** *Conium maculatum*, found in Britain and Europe, and naturalized in the Americas. Reaching up to 2 m/6 ft high, it bears umbels of small white flowers, and the whole plant, but especially the root and fruit, is poisonous, causing paralysis of the nervous system. The ancient Greeks used it as a mode of capital punishment. Also, name of type of

conifer, genus *Tsuga*, whose crushed leaves have a similar smell.

hemp annual plant *Cannabis sativa* of the family Cannabaceae cultivated in most temperate countries for its fibres, produced in the outer layer of the stem 1–2.5 m/3–7.5 ft high, and used in ropes, twines and, occasionally, in a type of linen or lace. The drug cannabis (marijuana) is obtained from certain varieties of hemp, principally from the young leaves and shoots. The name hemp is extended to similar types of fibre, for example, sisal hemp or henequen obtained from the leaves of *Agave sisalana* and other species native to Yucatan and cultivated in many tropical countries and manila hemp from *Musa textilis*, a plant native to the Philippines and Moluccas.

Henan /ˌhʌ'næn/ province (formerly Honan) of E central China
area 167,000 sq km/64,462 sq mi
capital Zhengzhou
features comprises river plains of the Huang Ho; in the 1980s the ruins of Xibo, the 16th-century BC capital of the Shang dynasty were discovered here.
products cereals and cotton
population (1982) 74,422,739.

henbane wild plant *Hyoscyamus niger*, found on waste ground in Britain and almost through Europe, and W Asia. A branching plant, up to 80 cm/2.6 ft high, it has hairy leaves and a nauseous smell. The yellow flowers are bell-shaped. It is sometimes grown for medicinal purposes, but its use is dangerous.

Henderson /'hendəsən/ Arthur 1863–1935. British Labour politician. Born in Glasgow; he worked 20 years as an iron-moulder in Newcastle, entered Parliament in 1903 and did much for Labour's political organization. He was home secretary in the first Labour government, and was foreign secretary 1929–31, when he accorded the Soviet government full recognition. He was awarded a Nobel Peace Prize in 1934.

Hendon /'hendən/ residential district in the borough of ◊Barnet, Greater London, England. Its airport (1910–57) was important in the early days of flying.

Hendrix /'hendrɪks/ Jimi (James Marshall) 1942–1970. US rock guitarist, songwriter, and singer, who influenced a generation of musicians with his flamboyance (he burned his guitar at the 1967 Monterey Pop Festival) as well as his legendary technique.

Hengist legendary leader, with his brother Horsa, of the ◊Jutes who settled in Kent about 450, the first Anglo-Saxon settlers in Britain.

Henie /'heni/ Sonja 1912–1969. Norwegian skater. Norwegian champion at 11, she won ten world championships and three Olympic titles, turning professional in 1936 and making numerous films.

Henlein /'henlaɪn/ Konrad 1898–1945. Sudeten-German leader of the Sudeten National Socialist party inside Czechoslovakia and closely allied with Hitler's German Nazis. He was partly responsible for the destabilization of the Czech state in 1938 which led to the Munich settlement and secession of the Sudetenland to Germany.

Henley-on-Thames /ˈhenli ɒn ˈtemz/ town in Oxfordshire, England; population (1984) 10,976. The regatta, held here annually since 1839, is in Jul; Henley Management College, established in 1946, was the first in Europe.

henna small shrub *Lawsonia inermis* found in Iran, India, Egypt and N Africa. The leaves and young twigs are ground to powder, mixed with hot water to a paste and applied to the fingernails and hair of women, and beards of men, giving an orange-red hue. The colour may then be changed to black by applying a preparation of indigo.

Henrietta Maria /ˌhenriˈetə məˈriːə/ 1609–1669. Queen of England 1625–49. The daughter of Henry IV of France, she married Charles I in 1625. As she used her influence to encourage him to aid Roman Catholics and make himself absolute, she became highly unpopular and had to go into exile 1644–60. She returned to England at the Restoration.

henry the ◊SI unit of inductance (H). Defined as the inductance of a closed circuit in which an electromotive force of 1 volt is produced when the electric current in the circuit varies uniformly at a rate of 1 ampere per second. Named after Joseph ◊Henry.

Henry /ˈhenri/ Joseph 1797–1878. American physicist, inventor of the electromagnetic motor in 1829, and a telegraphic apparatus. He also discovered the principle of electromagnetic induction, roughly at the same time as ◊Faraday, and the phenomenon of self-induction. A unit of inductance (henry) is named after him.

Henry /ˈhenri/ O 1862–1910. Pen name of the American short-story writer William Sydney Porter. Born in North Carolina, he worked in Texas as a bank clerk and a journalist, and was imprisoned for three years on a charge of embezzlement. After his release he lived in New York, and published several collections of short stories, beginning with *Cabbages and Kings* 1904 and *The Four Million* 1906. His stories, which deal mainly with New York or southern and western life, are in a colloquial style and noted for their skilled construction with 'twist' endings.

Henry /ˈhenri/ Patrick 1736–1799. American politician, who in 1775 supported the arming of the Virginia militia against George III by a speech ending: 'Give me liberty or give me death!' He was governor of the state 1776–79 and 1784–86.

Henry /ˈhenri/ William 1774–1836. British chemist. In 1803 he formulated *Henry's law*: when a gas is dissolved in a liquid at a given temperature, the amount (that is the mass) which dissolves is in direct proportion to the gas pressure.

Henry /ˈhenri/ eight kings of England.

Henry I /ˈhenri/ 1068–1135. King of England from 1100. Youngest son of William I, he succeeded his brother William II. He won the support of the Saxons by granting them a charter and marrying a Saxon princess. An able administrator, he established a professional bureaucracy and a system of travelling judges.

Henry II /ˈhenri/ 1133–1189. King of England from 1154, when he succeeded ◊Stephen. He was the son of ◊Matilda and Geoffrey of Anjou (1113–51). He curbed the power of the barons, but his attempt to bring the church courts under control had to be abandoned after the murder of ◊Becket. During his reign the English conquest of Ireland began.

Henry III /ˈhenri/ 1207–1272. King of England from 1216, when he succeeded ◊John, but he did not assume royal power until 1227. His subservience to the papacy and his foreign favourites led to de ◊Montfort's revolt in 1264. Henry was defeated at Lewes and imprisoned. He was restored to the throne after royalist victory at Evesham in 1265.

Henry IV /ˈhenri/ (Bolingbroke) 1367–1413. King of England from 1399. He was the son of ◊John of Gaunt. In 1398 he was banished by ◊Richard II for political activity, and returned in 1399 to head a revolt and be accepted as king by Parliament. He had difficulty in keeping the support of Parliament and the clergy, and had to deal with baronial unrest and ◊Glendower's rising in Wales. In order to win support he had to conciliate the church by a law for the burning of heretics, and to make many concessions to Parliament.

Henry V /ˈhenri/ 1387–1422. King of England from 1413, son of Henry IV. Invading Normandy in 1415, he captured Harfleur, and defeated the French at ◊Agincourt. He invaded again 1417–19, capturing Rouen, and in 1420 married ◊Catherine de Valois to gain recognition as heir to the French throne by his father-in-law Charles VI.

Henry VI /ˈhenri/ 1421–1471. King of England from 1422. Son of Henry V. He assumed royal power in 1442. He identified himself completely with the party opposed to the continuation of the French war, and after his marriage in 1445 was dominated by his wife, ◊Margaret of Anjou. The unpopularity of the government, especially after the loss of the English conquests in France, encouraged Edward, Duke of ◊York to claim the throne, and though York was killed in 1460, his son Edward proclaimed himself king in 1461 (see Wars of the ◊Roses). Henry was captured in 1465, temporarily restored in 1470, but again imprisoned 1471 and then murdered.

Henry VII /ˈhenri/ 1457–1509. King of England from 1485, son of Edmund Tudor, Earl of Richmond (c. 1430–56) and a descendant of John of ◊Gaunt. He spent his early life in Brittany until 1485, when he landed in Britain to lead the rebellion against Richard III which ended with Richard's defeat and death at ◊Bosworth. Yorkist revolts continued till 1497, but he restored order after the Wars of the ◊Roses by the ◊Star Chamber, and achieved independence from Parliament by amassing a private fortune through confiscations.

Henry VIII /ˈhenri/ 1491–1547. King of England from 1509, when he succeeded his father Henry VII and when he married ◊Catherine of Aragon, the widow of his brother. During the period 1513–29 he pursued an active foreign policy, largely under the guidance of ◊Wolsey. In 1529, Wolsey was disgraced for failing to persuade the Pope to grant Henry a divorce. With Parliament's approval Henry renounced the papal supremacy, proclaimed himself head of the Church, and dissolved the monasteries; in this policy his chief assistant was Thomas ◊Cromwell. Henry divorced Catherine in 1533 and married Anne ◊Boleyn, who in 1536 was beheaded for adultery. Henry's third wife, Jane ◊Seymour, died in 1537. ◊Anne of Cleves he married in 1540 in pursuance of Cromwell's policy of allying with the German Protestants, but rapidly abandoned this policy, divorced Anne, and beheaded Cromwell. His fifth wife, Catherine ◊Howard, was beheaded in 1542, and the following year he married Catherine ◊Parr, who survived him.

Henry never lost his popularity, but wars with France and Scotland towards the end of his reign sapped the economy, and in religion he not only executed Roman Catholics for refusing to acknowledge his supremacy in the Church (see Thomas ◊More), but burned Protestants who maintained his changes had not gone far enough.

Henry VIII A king of imperious will, Henry VIII proclaimed himself head of the English Church, dissolved the monasteries, and beheaded two of his six wives: Anne Boleyn in 1536 and Catherine Howard in 1542.

Henry /ˈhenri/ four kings of France.

Henry I /ˈhenri/ 1008–1060. King of France from 1031, who spent much of his reign in conflict with ◊William the Conqueror, then Duke of Normandy.

Henry II /ˈhenri/ 1519–1559. King of France from 1547. He captured Metz and Verdun from the emperor, and Calais from the English. He was killed in a tournament.

Henry III /ˈhenri/ 1551–1589. King of France from 1574. He fought both the ◊Huguenots (headed by his successor, Henry of Navarre), and the Catholic League, headed by the Duke of Guise. He expelled Henry from Paris in 1588 but was assassinated. Catholic fury was at fever pitch and Henry allied with the Huguenots under Henry of Navarre to besiege the city, but was assassinated by a monk.

Henry IV /'henri/ 1553–1610. King of France from 1589. Son of Antoine de Bourbon and Jeanne, queen of Navarre, he was brought up as a Protestant, and from 1576 led the ◊Huguenots. On his accession he settled the religious question by adopting Catholicism while tolerating Protestantism. He restored peace and strong government to France, and brought back prosperity by measures for the promotion of industry and agriculture and the improvement of communications. He was assassinated by a Catholic fanatic.

Henry /'henri/ seven Holy Roman Emperors.

Henry I /'henri/ the Fowler c. 876–936. Duke of Saxony 912. King of Germany from 919, about to claim the imperial crown at his death.

Henry II /'henri/ the Saint 973–1024. Emperor from 1002, a defender of the Papacy.

Henry III /'henri/ 1017–1056. Emperor from 1093, who raised the empire to the height of its power, and extended its authority over Poland, Bohemia, Hungary.

Henry IV /'henri/ 1050–1106. Emperor from 1056, who was involved from 1075 in a struggle with the Papacy (see ◊Gregory VII).

Henry V /'henri/ 1081–1125. Emperor from 1106. He continued the struggle with the Church until the settlement of the investitures question in 1122.

Henry VI /'henri/ 1165–1197. Emperor from 1190. As part of his plan for making the empire universal he captured and imprisoned Richard I of England, and compelled him to do homage.

Henry VII /'henri/ 1269–1313. Emperor from 1308. He attempted unsuccessfully to revive the imperial supremacy in Italy.

Henry the Navigator /'henri/ 1394–1460. Portuguese prince. The son of John I, he devoted himself largely to the promotion of exploration and colonization. Under his patronage Portuguese seamen explored and colonized Madeira and the Azores, and sailed down the African coast almost to Sierra Leone.

Henty /'henti/ G(eorge) A(lfred) 1832–1902. British war correspondent, whose books for children, such as *With the Allies to Peking* 1904, became a 1980s cult.

Henze /'hentsə/ Hans Werner 1926– . German composer. Although thought of as avant-garde, and showing the influence of ◊Schoenberg, his music often uses traditional forms such as symphony and concerto, and parodies or incorporates a wide range of styles. His output includes orchestral, vocal, and chamber music. He is also a major composer of operas, including *Boulevard Solitude* 1952 (based on Prévost's *Manon Lescaut*), *The Bassarids* 1966 (based on the *Bacchae* of Euripides), *We Come to the River* 1976 with libretto by Edward Bond, and *The English Cat* 1983.

hepatitis inflammation of the liver. Hepatitis B is a long-term viral disease of the Third World, causing jaundice and linked with liver cancer, but preventable by vaccine. It is carried by the blood and other body fluids; a small proportion

Henze German composer Hans Werner Henze. One of the most prolific modern composers of opera, he lives in Italy, and his love of Italian opera is evident in his own work.

of recovered patients become carriers (the virus remains in the liver).

Hepburn /'hepbɜːn/ Katharine 1909– . American actress, born in Connecticut. Her gangly grace and husky voice brought stardom in such films as *Morning Glory* 1933, *The African Queen* 1951, *Guess Who's Coming to Dinner* 1967, *The Lion in Winter* 1968, and *On Golden Pond* 1981. Winner of four Academy Awards.

Hephaestus /hɪ'fiːstəs/ in Greek mythology, the god of fire and metalcraft (Roman ◊Vulcan), son of ◊Zeus and ◊Hera; he was lame, and married ◊Aphrodite.

Hepplewhite /'hepəlwaɪt/ George died 1786. British furniture-maker. In his workshop at St Giles, Cripplegate, London, he developed a simple elegant style, especially in his chairs, often with shield or heart-shaped backs. He worked mainly in mahogany or satinwood, and his decorations of feathers, shells, or wheat-ears were inlaid or painted, rather than carved.

heptarchy term coined by 16th-century historians to denote the seven Saxon kingdoms thought to have existed before 800 AD: Northumbria, Mercia, East Anglia, Essex, Kent, Sussex, and Wessex.

Hepworth /'hepwɜːθ/ Barbara 1903–1975. British sculptor. Born in Wakefield, she studied at Leeds School of Art and the Royal College of Art, and from 1939 lived at St Ives, Cornwall, where her studio is a museum. She worked in concrete, bronze, wood and aluminium, but her favourite medium was stone. She married first sculptor John Skeaping, and second Ben ◊Nicholson. Under Nicholson's influence she became more interested in abstract form.

Hera /'hɪərə/ in Greek mythology, a goddess, sister-consort of ◊Zeus, mother of ◊Hephaestus, ◊Hebe, and ◊Ares; protector of women and marriage, and identified with Roman Juno.

Heracles /'herəkliːz/ in Greek mythology, a hero (Roman Hercules), son of ◊Zeus and ◊Alcmene, famed for strength. While serving Eurystheus, king of Argos, he performed 12 labours, including the cleansing of the Augean stables.

Heraclitus /ˌhɪərə'klaɪtəs/ c. 544–483 BC. Greek pre-Socratic philosopher who saw everything in the universe as fire. Fire was the fundamental material which accounted for all change and motion in the world; it also explained the contradictory, ever-changing, nature of things. Nothing in the world ever stays the same, hence the famous dictum, 'one cannot step in the same river twice'.

Heraclius /ˌhɪərə'klaɪəs/ c. 575–641. Byzantine emperor. His reign as emperor from 610 marked a turning point in the empire's fortunes. Himself of Armenian descent, he recaptured Armenia from the Persians in 622, successfully defended Constantinople in 626 from the Persians, and finally eliminated the Persian threat in 629. In his later years he faced growing attacks from Arabs, while devoting much of his time to religious controversy.

Heraklion /hɪ'rækliən/ alternative name for ◊Iraklion, largest city of Crete, Greece, formerly known as ◊Candia; population (1981) 101,500.

Heralds' College or *College of Arms* an English heraldic body formed in 1484 by Richard III incorporating the heralds attached to the Royal Household; reincorporated by Royal Charter of Philip and Mary in 1555. There are 3 Kings of Arms, 6 Heralds, and 4 Pursuivants, who specialize in genealogical and heraldic work. The College establishes the right to bear Arms, and the Kings of Arms grant Arms by letters patent. In Ireland the office of Ulster King of Arms was transferred in 1943 to the College of Arms in London and placed with that of Norroy King of Arms, who now has jurisdiction in Northern Ireland as well as in the north of England.

Herat /he'ræt/ capital of Herat province, Afghanistan, on the N banks of the Hari Rud; population (1980) 160,000. A principal road junction, it was a great city in ancient and medieval times.

Hérault /e'rəu/ river in S France, 160 km/100mi long, rising in the Cévennes and flowing into the Gulf of Lyons near Agde. It gives its name to a *département*.

herb any plant (usually a flowering plant) tasting sweet, bitter, aromatic, or pungent used in cookery, medicine, or perfumery.

herbarium a collection of dried, pressed plants used as an aid to identification of unknown plants and by taxonomists in the ◊classification of plants. The plant specimens are accompanied by important information, such as the date and place of collection, the collector's name and an

Hepworth British sculptor Barbara Hepworth before her 1930 exhibition with her stone *Mother and Child*. With the sculptors Henry Moore and Ben Nicholson, she was a leading figure in the abstract movement of the 1930s.

identifying number, details of habitat, flower colour and local names. Herbaria range from small collections containing plants of a particular county or region, to the large national herbaria containing millions of specimens from all parts of the world, such as that at the Royal Botanic Gardens, Kew.

Herbert /ˈhɜːbət/ Edward, 1st Baron Herbert of Cherbury 1583–1648. English philosopher, brother of George ◊Herbert. His *De veritate* 1624, with its theory of natural religion, founded English ◊Deism.

Herbert /ˈhɜːbət/ Frank (Patrick) 1920–1986. American science fiction writer, noted for the Dune saga from 1965 onwards (filmed 1984), adventure stories containing serious ideas about ecology and religion.

Herbert /ˈhɜːbət/ George 1593–1633. English poet. He became a prebendary in Huntingdonshire 1625, where his friends included Donne, Walton, and Bacon. After ordination in 1630 he became vicar of Bemerton, Wiltshire, and died of consumption. His volume of religious poems, *The Temple*, appeared in 1633. He was the brother of Lord Edward ◊Herbert of Cherbury.

Herbert /ˈhɜːbət/ Wally (Walter) 1934– . British surveyor-explorer. His first surface crossing by dog sledge of the Arctic Ocean 1968–69, from Alaska to Spitzbergen, was the

longest sustained sledging journey (6,000 km/3,800 mi) in polar exploration.

Herbert of Lea /liː/ Sidney Herbert, 1st Baron Herbert of Lea 1810–1861. British politician. He was secretary for war in Aberdeen's Liberal-Peelite coalition of 1852–55, and during the Crimean War was responsible for sending Florence Nightingale to the front. After the war he supported army reforms and became a peer in 1861.

herbicide a type of ◊weedkiller.

herbivore an animal which feeds on green plant material. In a broader sense, any animal that lives by eating plants or their products, including seeds, fruit and nectar, as well as ◊photosynthetic organisms in the plankton. Herbivorous animals are more numerous than other types because their food is the most abundant. They form a vital link in the food chain between plants and ◊carnivores (meat eaters).

herb Robert common wild flower *Geranium robertianum* found throughout Europe, central Asia, and naturalized in N America. About 30 cm/1 ft high, it bears hairy leaves and small purplish flowers, and has a reddish hairy stem. When rubbed, the leaves have an unpleasant smell.

Hercegovina /ˌheətsəɡəˈviːnə/ or *Herzegovina* part of Yugoslavia, see ◊Bosnia and Herzegovina.

Herculaneum /ˌhɜːkjuˈleɪniəm/ ancient city of Italy between ◊Naples and ◊Pompeii. Herculaneum was overwhelmed during the eruption of Vesuvius AD 79, which also destroyed Pompeii. It was excavated from the 18th century onwards.

Hercules /ˈhɜːkjuliːz/ Roman form of ◊Heracles.

Hercules /ˈhɜːkjuliːz/ in astronomy, the fifth-largest ◊constellation, lying in the northern hemisphere. Despite its size it contains no prominent stars. Its most important feature is M 13, a globular cluster of stars 22,500 light years away, one of the best examples of a ◊globular cluster in the sky.

Hercules, Pillars of /ˈhɜːkjuliːz/ rocks (at Gibraltar and Ceuta) which guard the entrance to the Mediterranean.

Herder /ˈheədə/ Johann Gottfried von 1744–1803. German poet, critic, and philosopher. Born in E Prussia, he studied at Königsberg where he was influenced by Kant, became pastor at Riga, and in 1776 was called to Weimar as court preacher. Herder's critical writings indicate his intuitive rather than reasoning trend of thought. He gave considerable impulse to the ◊*Sturm und Drang/Storm and Stress* movement in German literature. He collected folk songs of all nations 1778 and in the *Ideen zur Philosophie der Geschichte der Menschheit/Outlines of a Philosophy of the History of Man* 1784–91 he outlined the stages of human cultural development.

heredity in biology, the transmission of traits from parent to offspring. See also ◊genetics.

Hereford /ˈherɪfəd/ town in the county of Hereford and Worcester, England; population (1981) 630,000. The cathedral was begun in 1079, and the Three Choirs Festival is held in Hereford every third year. Products include cider, beer, and metal goods.

Hereford and Worcester /ˈherɪfəd, ˈwustə/ county in W central England
area 3,927 sq km/1,516 sq mi
towns administrative headquarters Worcester; Hereford, Kidderminster, Evesham, Ross-on-Wye, Ledbury
features rivers Wye and Severn; Malvern Hills (high point Worcester Beacon 425 m/1,395 ft) and Black Mountains; Droitwich, once a Victorian spa, reopened its baths in 1985
products mainly agricultural, apples, pears, and cider; hops and vegetables; Hereford cattle
population (1986) 653,900
famous people Samuel Butler (author of *Hudibras*), Edward Elgar, A E Housman, William Langland, John Masefield.

Herero /həˈreərəu/ nomadic Bantu-speaking people living in Namibia, SW Africa.

heresy doctrine opposed to orthodox belief, especially in religion. Those holding ideas considered heretical by the Christian church have included Gnostics, Arians, Pelagians, Montanists, Albigenses, Waldenses, Lollards and Anabaptists. Among modern dissidents in the Catholic church is Hans ◊Kung.

Hereward /ˈherɪwəd/ the Wake active c. 1070. English leader of a revolt against the Normans in 1070, whose stronghold in the Isle of

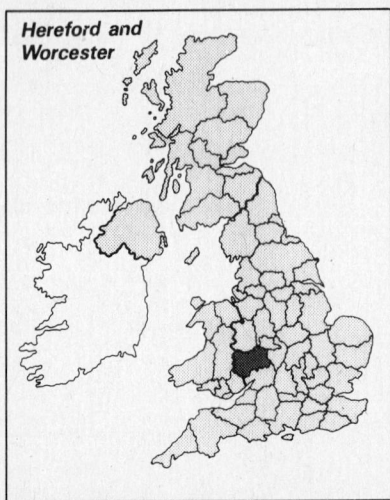

Hereford and Worcester

Ely was captured by William the Conqueror in 1071. Hereward escaped, but his fate is obscure.

Herman /'hɜːman/ Woody (Woodrow Wilson) 1913–1987. US band leader and clarinettist. A child prodigy, he was leader of his own orchestra at 23, and after 1945 formed his famous Herd band. Soloists in this or later versions of the band included Lester Young and Stan Getz.

hermaphrodite an organism which has both male and female sex organs; pseudo-hermaphrodites have the internal sex organs of one sex, but the external appearance of the other. The true sex of the latter becomes apparent at adolescence when the normal hormone activity appropriate to the internal organs begins to function. Hermaphroditism can be the norm in species such as snails and oysters, and is standard in flowering plants.

Hermaphroditus /hɜːˌmæfrə'daɪtəs/ in Greek mythology, the son of ◊Hermes and ◊Aphrodite. He was loved by a nymph who prayed for eternal union with him, so that they became one body with dual sexual characteristics, hence the term ◊hermaphrodite.

hermeneutics a philosophical tradition concerned with the nature of understanding and interpretation. From its origins in problems of biblical interpretation, hermeneutics has expanded to cover many fields of enquiry, including aesthetics, literary theory, and social science. ◊Dilthey, ◊Heidegger, and ◊Gadamer are influential contributors to this tradition.

Hermes /'hɜːmiːz/ in Greek mythology, a god, son of ◊Zeus and ◊Maia, and messenger of the gods; he has winged sandals and a staff around which serpents coil. Identified with the Roman Mercury and ancient Egyptian Thoth, he protected thieves, travellers, and merchants.

Hermes Trismegistus /ˌtrɪsmə'gɪstəs/ supposed author of the *Hermetica* (2nd–3rd centuries AD), writings inculcating a cosmic religion, in which the sun is regarded as the visible manifestation of God. In the Renaissance they were thought to be by an Egyptian priest

contemporary with Moses, and it is possible they do contain some Egyptian material.

hermit religious votary living in seclusion, often practising extremes of mortification, such as ◊Simeon Stylites; modern hermits, for example, the Anglican community at Bede house, Kent, have bungalow 'cells'.

hermit crab a type of ◊crab.

Hermon /'hɜːmən/ snow-topped mountain (Arabic Jebel esh-Sheikh), 2,814 m/9,232 ft high, on the Syria-Lebanon border. According to tradition, Jesus was transfigured here.

Herne Bay /'hɜːn/ seaside resort in Kent, England; population (1981) 27,528.

hernia or *rupture* protrusion of part of an internal organ through a weakness in the surrounding muscular wall, usually in the groin or navel. The appearance is that of a rounded soft lump or swelling.

Hero /'hɪərəʊ/ of Alexandria, a Greek mathematician and writer, probably of the 2nd century AD, who invented an automatic fountain, and perhaps a kind of stationary steam-engine.

Hero and Leander /'hɪərəʊ, li'ændə/ in Greek mythology, a pair of lovers. Hero was a priestess of Aphrodite at Sestos on the ◊Hellespont, in love with Leander on the opposite shore at Abydos. When he was drowned while swimming across during a storm, she threw herself into the sea out of grief.

Herod /'herəd/ the Great 74 BC–4 BC. The son of Antipater, he was declared King of Judaea by the Romans in 40 BC, and with the aid of Mark Antony established his government in Jerusalem in 37 BC. He rebuilt the Temple at Jerusalem, but his Hellenizing tendencies made him suspect to orthodox Jewry. His last years were akin to a reign of terror, and St Matthew in the New Testament alleges that he ordered the slaughter of all the infants in Bethlehem to ensure the death of Christ, whom he foresaw as a rival. He was the father of ◊Herod Antipas.

Herod Agrippa I /ə'grɪpə/ died AD 44. Jewish ruler of Palestine under the Romans. Grandson of ◊Herod the Great, he was made tetrarch of Palestine by ◊Caligula, and king by ◊Claudius. He put St James to death and imprisoned St Peter. His son was ◊Herod Agrippa II.

Herod Agrippa II /ə'grɪpə/ died AD 100. King of Chalcis (now South Lebanon), son of Herod Agrippa I. He helped ◊Titus take Jerusalem in AD 70, then went to Rome where he died. In AD 60 he tried St ◊Paul.

Herod Antipas /'æntɪpæs/ 21 BC–39 AD. governor (tetrarch) of Galilee 4 BC–9 AD, son of ◊Herod the Great. He divorced his wife to marry his niece Herodias, and the latter got her daughter Salome to ask for St ◊John the Baptist's head when he reproved Herod's action. Jesus Christ was brought before him on Pontius Pilate's discovery that he was a Galilean and hence of Herod's jurisdiction, but Herod returned him without giving any verdict. In 38 AD Herod Antipas went to Rome to try to get Caligula to make him 'king', but was banished for his pains. Remains of one of his royal palaces were excavated at Masada 1963–64.

Herodotus /he'rɒdətəs/ c. 484 BC–424 BC. Greek historian and prose writer, who travelled

widely, recording in his history observations of habits and creeds of many peoples. After four years in Athens, he settled in S Italy in 443 BC at Thurii, apparently staying there the rest of his life. His history, written lucidly and with charm, deals with the Greek-Persian struggle which culminated in the defeat of the Persian invasion attempts in 490 BC and 480 BC. Herodotus was the first historian to apply critical evaluation to his material.

heroin the pain-killing drug diamorphine hydrochloride, an alkaloid obtained from ◊morphine. A white crystalline powder, it depresses the nerve centres controlling breathing and is valuable as a sedative, but the danger of addiction means that it is rarely used in medical treatment.

heron large bird in the family Ardeidae, which also includes bitterns, egrets, night-herons, and boatbills. *The common heron Ardea cinerea* nests in Europe, Asia and parts of Africa in large colonies at the tops of trees. The bird is about 1 m/3 ft long, and has a long neck and long legs. The plumage is chiefly grey, but there are black patches on the sides and a black crest. The legs are olive-green, and the beak yellow, except during the breeding season when it is pink. It is a wading bird, but is rarely seen to swim or walk. It feeds on fish, frogs, and rats.

herpes group of viruses, including *Herpes simplex* (type 1), which causes *fever blisters* or *cold sores*; the virus remains within the body (in nerve ganglia at the base of the spine) and is triggered by sunburn, stress, etc. Serious outbreaks of sores on the genitals are caused by *Herpes simplex* (type 2) (*Herpes genitalis*), treatable in some cases by drugs. Also caused by herpes viruses are *chicken pox* or *varicella* marked by fever, small blisters and a rash (there is a vaccine); *shingles* (caused by a reactivation of the chicken pox virus, *Herpes zoster*), and marked by blisters at nerve endings, sometimes over the ribs in a 'girdle'; and *glandular fever* or *infectious mononucleosis* (feverish sore throat, painful lymph nodes, and changes in the blood). ◊Encephalitis may also be caused by a herpes virus.

Herrera /e'reərə/ Francisco de 1576–1656. Named El Viejo (the Elder). Spanish painter, born in Seville. A master of chiaroscuro (the artistic representation of light and shadow), he may have taught ◊Velazquez.

Herrera /e'reərə/ Francisco de 1622–1685. Called El Mozo (the Younger). Spanish painter, son of the elder Herrera, he was remarkable for still lifes.

Herrick /'herɪk/ Robert 1591–1674. English poet and cleric. Born in Cheapside, London, he was a friend of Ben Jonson. In 1629 he became vicar of Dean Prior, near Totnes. He published *Hesperides* in 1648, a collection of sacred and pastoral poetry admired for its lyric quality, including 'Gather ye rosebuds' and 'Cherry ripe'.

herring one of the most important food fish *Clupea harengus*, of the family Clupeidae. A salt-water fish, it swims close to the surface and may be 25–40 cm/10–16 in long. A silvered greenish-blue, it has only one dorsal fin and one short ventral fin. Young herrings about 5 cm/2 in long can be cooked and eaten whole as a delicacy known as 'whitebait'.

The herring is found in large quantities off the shores of Britain, Scandinavia, the E coast of North America and the White Sea, but not in the Mediterranean. Shoals have recently diminished, partly due to over-fishing, and pollution.

Herriot /ˌeriˈəʊ/ Édouard 1872–1957. French Radical politician. An opponent of Poincaré, especially his advocacy of French occupation of the Ruhr, he was briefly prime minister in 1924–25, 1926, and 1932. As President of the Chamber in 1940 he opposed the policies of the ◊Vichy government, was arrested and later taken to Germany until released in 1945 by the Russians.

Herriott /ˈheriət/ James, pen name of British writer James Alfred Wright 1916– . A practising veterinary surgeon in Thirsk, Yorkshire from 1940, he began writing of his experiences only at the age of 50, in a popular series of books including *If Only They Could Talk* 1970, *All Creatures Great and Small* 1972, and *The Lord God made Them All* 1981.

Herschel /ˈhɜːʃəl/ Caroline Lucretia 1750–1848. British astronomer, sister of William ◊Herschel. Born in Hanover, she had no formal education. She came to England in 1772 and became assistant to her famous brother. Apart from her extensive achievements in collaboration with him, in 1786 she independently discovered a comet (she discovered a total of nine), and the following year was granted an annual salary by King George III. On her brother's death in 1822 she returned to Hanover.

Herschel /ˈhɜːʃəl/ John Fredrick William 1792–1871. English scientist and astronomer who became director of the Cape of Good Hope observatory in South Africa in 1834, where he discovered thousands of close ◊double stars, clusters and ◊nebulae, reported in 1847. His inventions include astronomical instruments, sensitized photographic paper, and the use of sodium hyposulphite for fixing it.

Herschel /ˈhɜːʃəl/ William 1738–1822. British astronomer. Born at Hanover, he went to England in 1757, earning his living as a musician, while instructing himself in mathematics and astronomy. In 1781 he discovered ◊Uranus, and later several of its satellites. During his appointment as astronomer to George III from 1782 he discovered the motion of the ◊double stars round one another, and recorded it in his *Motion of the Solar System in Space* 1783. He constructed a 1.2 m/4 ft telescope, of 12 m/40 ft focal length, at Slough, in 1789, and discovered ◊infra-red solar rays in 1800. He was the father of John ◊Herschel.

Herstmonceux /ˌhɜːstmənˈsuː/ village 11 km/7 mi N of Eastbourne, East Sussex, England. Since 1958 the buildings of the Royal Greenwich Observatory have been here, alongside the 15th-century castle. The Observatory is to move from Herstmonceux to Cambridge by 1991.

Hertford /ˈhɑːfəd/ administrative headquarters of Hertfordshire, England, on the

Herstmonceux First built by Roger de Fiennes, a hero of Agincourt, in 1446, Herstmonceux castle has been greatly restored. From 1958 Herstmonceux has been the site of the Royal Greenwich Observatory.

Lea; population (1981) 21,412. There are brewing and brick industries.

Hertfordshire /ˈhɑːfədʃə/ county in SE England
area 1,634 sq km/631 sq mi
towns administrative headquarters Hertford; St Albans, Watford, Hatfield, Hemel Hempstead, Bishop's Stortford, Letchworth (the first ◊garden city, followed by Welwyn in 1919, and Stevenage in 1947)
features rivers Lea, Stort, Colne; part of the Chiltern Hills; Hatfield House; Knebworth House (home of Lord ◊Lytton); home of G B ◊Shaw at Ayot St Lawrence; Rothamsted agricultural experimental station
products engineering, aircraft, electrical goods, paper and printing; general agricultural
population (1986) 986,500
famous people Graham ◊Greene.

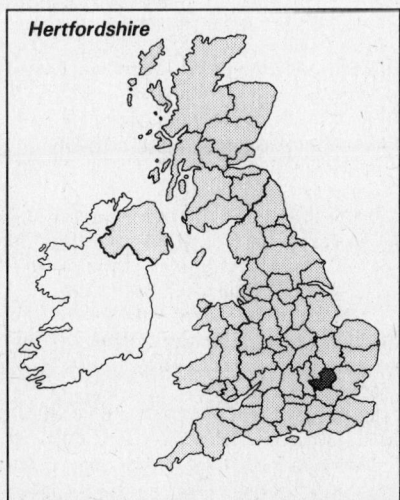

Hertfordshire

Hertling /ˈheətlɪŋ/ Count Georg von 1843–1919. German politician who was appointed imperial chancellor in Nov 1917. He maintained a degree of support in the Reichstag but was powerless to control the military leadership under Ludendorff. His term of office was ended in Sept when a more broadly based civilian government was appointed under Max von Baden.

Hertogenbosch city in the Netherlands. See ◊'s-Hertogenbosch.

hertz derived SI unit (Hz) of frequency (the number of repetitions of a regular occurrence in one second), named after Heinrich ◊Hertz.

Hertz /heəts/ Heinrich 1821–1894. German physicist who continued the work of ◊Maxwell in electromagnetic waves, preparing the way for radio communication, and showed that their behaviour resembled that of light and heat waves. The unit of frequency, the ◊hertz, is named after him.

Hertzog /ˈhɜːtsɒg/ James Barry Munnik 1866–1942. South African politician. Born in Cape Colony, of Boer descent, he was a general in the South African War, and in 1910 became minister of justice under Botha. In 1913 he formed the Nationalist Party, and in 1914 opposed South African participation in World War I After the 1924 elections Hertzog became prime minister, and in 1933 his party and General Smuts's South African Party were merged as the United South African National Party. In Sept 1939 his motion against participation in World War II was rejected, and he resigned.

Hertzsprung-Russell diagram in ◊astronomy, a graph on which the surface temperatures of stars are plotted against their luminosities. It is named after Dane Ejnar Hertzsprung and the American Henry Norris Russell who independently devised it in the years 1911–1913, and is a major tool for understanding the evolution of ◊stars. Most stars, including the Sun, fall into a narrow band called the *main sequence*. A star's position on this sequence depends on its mass, with the least massive stars at the bottom right and the most massive at the top left. When a star grows old it moves from the main sequence to the upper right part of the graph, into the area of the giants and supergiants. At the end of its life, as the star shrinks to become a white dwarf, it moves again, to the bottom left area.

Herzl /ˈheətsəl/ Theodor 1860–1904. Austrian journalist and founder of the Zionist movement. Born in Budapest, he became a successful playwright and journalist, but the Dreyfus case convinced him that the only solution to the problem of the Jews was their resettlement in a state of their own. His book *Jewish State* 1896 launched political Zionism, and he was the first president of the World Zionist Organization 1897.

Heseltine /ˈhesəltaɪn/ Michael 1933– . British Conservative politician, MP for Henley. Secretary of state for the environment 1979–83, he succeeded John Nott as minister for defence in Jan 1983 but resigned in Jan 1986 over the ◊Westland affair.

Hesiod /ˈhiːsiəd/ c. 700 BC. One of the earliest of the poets of ancient Greece. He is supposed to have lived a little later than Homer, and

Hertzsprung-Russell diagram

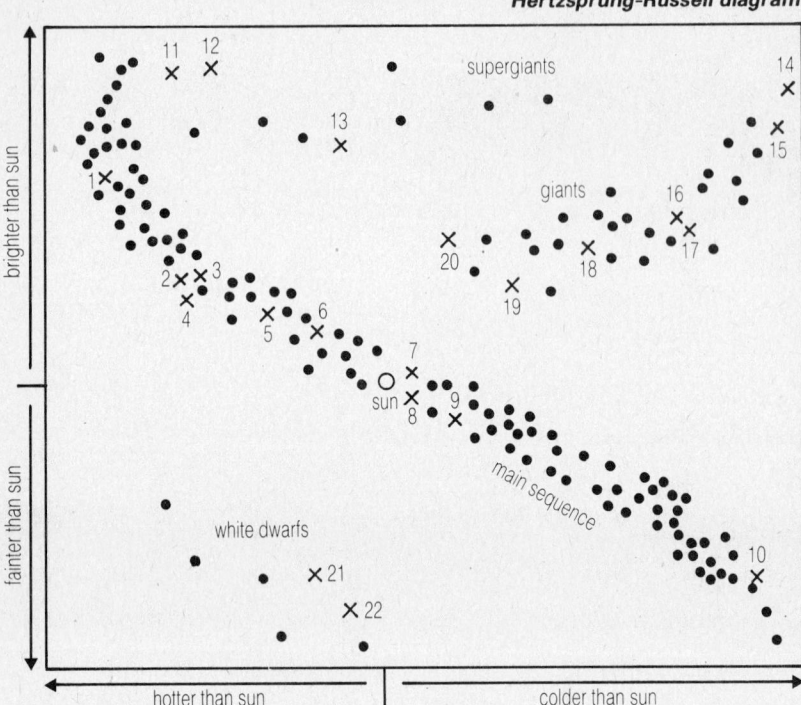

Hesse German novelist Hermann Hesse. The main themes in his work are self-knowledge, and the opposition of emotion and intellect.

heterostyly in botany, having ◊styles of different lengths. Certain flowers, such as primroses (*Primula vulgaris*), have different-sized ◊anthers and ◊styles to ensure cross-fertilization (through ◊pollination) by visiting insects.

heterostyly

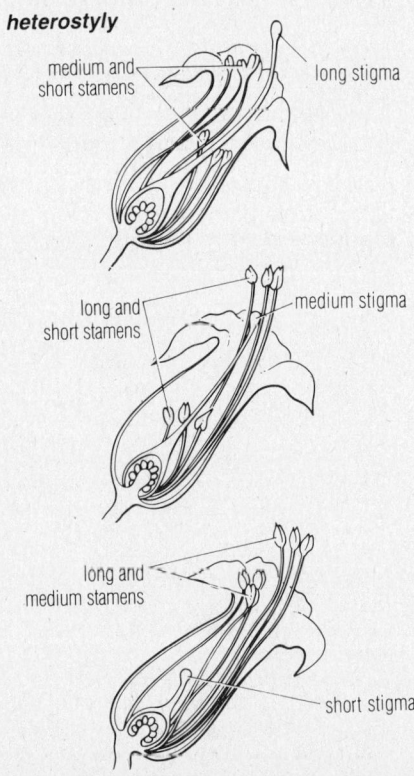

heterotroph any living organism that obtains its energy from organic substances which have been produced by other organisms. All animals

according to his own account he was born in Boeotia. He is the author of *Works and Days*, a poem that tells of the country life, and the *Theogony*, an account of the origin of the world and of the gods.

Hesperides /hes'peridiːz/ in Greek mythology, the mythical Greek maidens who guarded a tree bearing golden apples in the Islands of the Blessed.

Hess /hes/ (Walter Richard) Rudolf 1894–1987. German Nazi leader. Imprisoned with Hitler 1923–25, he became his private secretary, taking down *Mein Kampf* from his dictation. In 1932 he was appointed deputy to the Führer, and in 1939 was nominated as Hitler's successor after Göring. He was head of the *Ausland* organization responsible for fifth-column activities abroad. On 10 May 1941 he landed by air in Britain with compromise peace proposals, and was held a prisoner-of-war till 1945, when he was tried at ◊Nuremberg, as a war criminal, and was sentenced to life imprisonment, in Spandau prison, where he died.

Hess /hes/ Myra 1890–1965. British pianist. She is remembered for her interpretations of Beethoven.

Hess /hes/ Victor 1883–1964. American physicist. Born in Austria, he was professor at Fordham University, New York, from 1938. In 1936 he shared a Nobel prize for his discovery of cosmic radiation.

Hesse /'hesə/ former German state divided into two by a strip of Prussian territory, the S portion consisting of the valleys of the Rhine and the Main, the N being dominated by the Vogelsberg (744 m/2,539 ft). Its capital was Darmstadt.

Hesse /'hesə/ Hermann 1877–1962. German-born writer who became a Swiss citizen in 1923. A conscientious objector in World War I and a pacifist opponent of Hitler, he published short stories, poetry and novels, including *Peter Camenzind* 1904, *Siddharta* 1922, and *Steppenwolf* 1927. Later works, such as *Das Glasperlenspiel/The Glass Bead Game* 1943, tend towards the mystical. He received a Nobel prize in 1946.

Hessen /'hesən/ administrative region (German *Land*) of West Germany
area 21,125 sq km/8,156 sq mi
capital Wiesbaden
towns Frankfurt-am-Main, Darmstadt, Kassel
features valleys of the Rhine and Main; Taunus mountains, rich in mineral springs
products wine, timber; chemicals, cars, electrical engineering
population (1981) 5,612,925
religion Protestant 61%, Roman Catholic 33%

Hestia /'hestiə/ in Greek mythology, the goddess (Roman Vesta) of the hearth, daughter of ◊Chronos (Roman Saturn) and ◊Rhea.

heterosexuality sexual preference for, or attraction mainly to, persons of the opposite sex.

heterosis or *hybrid vigour* an improvement in physical capacities that sometimes occurs in the ◊hybrid produced by mating two genetically different parents. The parents may be of different strains or varieties within a species, or they may be of different species, as in the mule, which is stronger and has a longer life span than either of its parents (donkey and horse). Heterosis is also exploited in hybrid varieties of maize, tomatoes and other crops.

and fungi are heterotrophs, and they include ◊herbivores (which feed on ◊autotrophs), ◊carnivores (which feed on other heterotrophs), and ◊saprotrophs (which feed on dead animal and plant material). See also ◊food chain.

heterozygous in a living organism, having two different ◊alleles of the ◊gene for a given trait. In ◊homozygous organisms, by contrast, both chromosomes carry the same allele. An individual organism will generally be heterozygous for some genes but homozygous for others. For example in humans the allele for eye colour is heterozygous. A person who inherits an allele for brown eyes and an allele for blue eyes will be brown-eyed as a result of ◊dominance.

Hewish /'hjuːʃ/ Antony 1924– . British radio-astronomer. Professor at Cambridge from 1971, he was awarded a Nobel physics prize, with Sir Martin Ryle, in 1974. In 1967–68 he discovered ◊pulsars, now known to be flashes from rapidly rotating ◊neutron stars.

hexachlorophene bactericide, used in minute quantities in soaps and surgical disinfectants. Trichlorophenol is used in its preparation, and without precise temperature control, the highly toxic TCDD or ◊dioxin (tetrachlorodibenzo-p-dioxin) may form as a by-product.

hexadecimal number system a number system to the base 16, used in computing. In hex (as it is commonly known) the decimal numbers 0–15 are represented by the characters 0, 1, 2, 3, 4, 5, 6, 7, 8, 9, A, B, C, D, E, F. Each place in a number increases in value by a power of 16 going from right to left, for instance, 8F is equal to 15 + (8×16)= 143 in decimal. Hexadecimal numbers relate more closely than ◊decimal numbers to a computer's internal ◊binary code.

Heydrich /'haɪdrɪk/ Reinhard 1904–1942. German Nazi. While deputy 'protector' of Bohemia and Moravia from 1941, he was ambushed and killed by three members of the Czech forces in Britain, who had landed by parachute. Reprisals followed including several hundred executions and the massacre of Lidice.

Heyerdahl /'haɪədɑːl/ Thor 1914– . Norwegian ethnologist. In 1947 he sailed on the raft Kon-Tiki from Peru to the ◊Tuamotu Islands along the ◊Humboldt Current, proving that Polynesians could have been migrants from S America; in 1969–70 he used ancient-Egyptian-style papyrus-reed boats to cross the Atlantic, so possibly explaining the presence in the New World of a sun-orientated ◊pyramid culture.

Heywood /'heɪwʊd/ Thomas c. 1570–c. 1650. English dramatist. Born in Lincolnshire, he became an actor in London, and wrote or adapted over 220 plays, including the domestic tragedy, A Woman kilde with kindnesse 1607.

Hezekiah /ˌhezɪ'kaɪə/ died c. 699 BC. In the Old Testament, King of Judah from 719 BC until his death. He was the son of Ahaz, and father of Manasseh. Against the advice of ◊Isaiah he rebelled against Assyrian suzerainty in alliance with Egypt, but was defeated by Sennacherib. He carried out religious reforms.

Hiawatha /ˌhaɪə'wɒθə/ legendary 16th century North American Indian teacher and Onondaga chieftain, who is said to have welded the Six Nations of the ◊Iroquois into the league

of the Long House. Longfellow's epic Hiawatha 1855 was based on the data collected by Henry R Schoolcraft (1793–1864).

hibernation a state of ◊dormancy in which certain animals spend the winter. It is associated with a dramatic reduction in body temperature, breathing, pulse rate and other metabolic processes.

hibiscus plant of the mallow family Malvaceae. They range from large herbaceous plants to trees. Favourite ornamental plants because of their brilliantly coloured red through to white bell-shaped flowers, they include Hibiscus syriacus and Hibiscus rosa-sinensis. Some tropical species are also useful, such as Hibiscus esculentus, of which the edible fruit is okra or 'lady's fingers'; Hibiscus tiliaceus, which supplies timber and fibrous bark to S Sea islanders; and Hibiscus sabdariffa, cultivated in the W Indies and elsewhere for its fruit.

hiccup sharp noise caused by a sudden spasm of the diaphragm with closing of the windpipe, commonly due to digestive disorder. One remedy for ordinary hiccups is to cause a feeling of breathlessness by breathing into a paper bag.

Hickey /'hɪki/ William 1749–1830. British writer. He was intended to follow his father as an attorney in England but dissipation led to his being sent first to the East Indies and then to Jamaica, before he finally made good at the Indian Bar. His Memoirs give one of the raciest accounts of the age.

Hickok /'hɪkɒk/ James Butler 'Wild Bill' 1837–1876. American frontiersman, a legendary figure in the tradition of the 'Wild West'. In the Civil War he was a sharpshooter and scout for the Union army, and then served as marshal in Kansas, killing many desperadoes. He was shot from behind in Deadwood, S Dakota.

hickory common tree, genus Carya, native to N America. It provides a valuable timber, and all species bear nuts, although some are inedible. The pecan Carya pecan is widely cultivated in the S, and the shagbark Carya ovata in the N.

hieroglyphic Egyptian writing system mid 4th millennium BC–3rd century AD, which combined picture signs with those indicating letters. The direction of writing is normally from right to left, the signs facing the beginning of the line. It was deciphered (in 1822 by J F ◊Champollion) with the aid of the Rosetta Stone of 197 BC, which was found by one of Napoleon's officers at the Delta town of Rosetta (modern Rashid), but later fell into British hands and was placed in the British Museum in 1802. The stone has the same inscription carved in hieroglyphic, demotic, and Greek. Demotic is a cursive script (for quick writing) derived from Egyptian hieratic, which in turn is a more easily written form of hieroglyphic.

hi-fi the high-fidelity, or faithful reproduction of sound from a ◊record player, ◊compact disc player, ◊tape recorder or ◊radio. Modern advances in mechanical equipment and electronics, such as digital recording techniques and the introduction of compact discs, have made it possible to eliminate most distortions in the sound reproductive processes. Two loudspeakers located in the front to the left and right of the

listener give a ◊stereophonic effect. Two more speakers behind produce a quadrophonic, or 'surround-sound' effect.

Higgins Jack pseudonym of British novelist Harry ◊Patterson.

high commissioner representative of one independent Commonwealth country in the capital of another, ranking with ambassador.

High Country New Zealand name for the generally mountainous land above the 750–51,000 m/2,500–30,000 ft level, most of which is in South Island. The lakes, fed by melting snow, are used for hydro-electric power, and it is a skiing, mountaineering, and tourist area.

higher education in most countries, ◊education beyond the age of 18 leading to a degree or similar qualification. It is provided in the UK mainly in ◊universities, ◊polytechnics, and ◊colleges of higher education, and by distance learning through the ◊Open University.

Highland Games traditional Scottish outdoor gathering including such events as tossing the caber (a tree trunk), dancing, and bagpipe playing.

Highland Region /'haɪlənd/ administrative region of Scotland
area 25,141 sq km/9,704 sq mi
towns administrative headquarters Inverness; Thurso, Wick
features comprises almost half the country; ◊Grampian Mountains; Loch Ness, Caledonian Canal; Inner Hebrides; John O'Groats's House; Dounreay (with Atomic Energy Authority's prototype fast reactor, and a nuclear processing plant)
products provision of winter sports, grouse and deer shooting and salmon fishing
population (1980) 200,000

Highlands /'haɪləndz/ general name for the plateau of broken rock which covers almost all of Scotland, and extends S of the Highland region itself.

Highsmith /'haɪsmɪθ/ Patricia 1921– . American crime novelist. Her first book Strangers on a Train 1950 was filmed by Hitchcock, and she excels in tension and psychological exploration of character. Notable is her series dealing with the amoral Tom Ripley, including The Talented Mr Ripley 1956, Ripley Under Ground 1971, and Ripley's Game 1974.

highway in Britain, any ◊road over which there is a right of way. In the USA, a term for a ◊motorway.

highwayman term applied to a thief on horseback who robbed travellers on the highway; those who did so on foot were known as footpads. With the development of regular coach services in the 17th and 18th centuries, the highwaymen's activities became notorious, and the Bow Street Runners were organized to suppress them. Favourite haunts were Hounslow and Bagshot heaths and Epping Forest. They continued to flourish well into the 19th century. Among the best-known highwaymen were Jonathan ◊Wild, Claude ◊Duval, John Nevison (1639–84), Dick ◊Turpin, and his partner Tom King, and Jerry Abershaw (c. 1773–95).

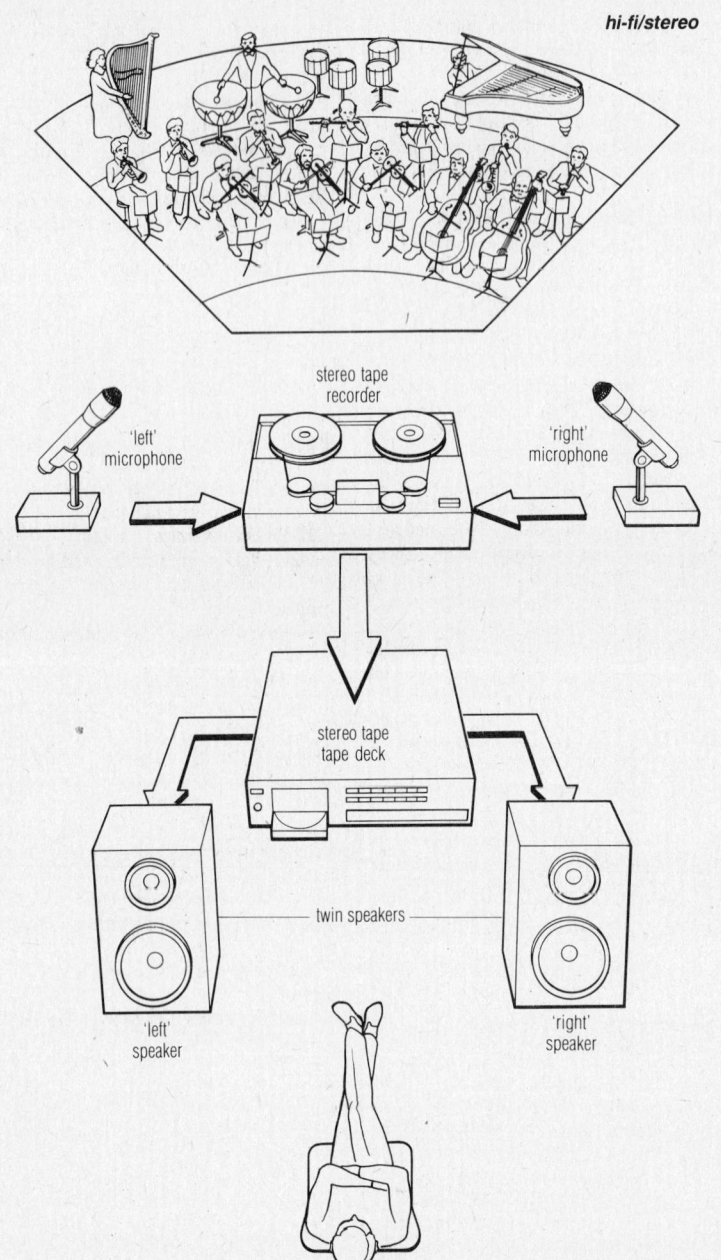

hi-fi/stereo

stereo tape recorder

'left' microphone

'right' microphone

stereo tape tape deck

twin speakers

'left' speaker

'right' speaker

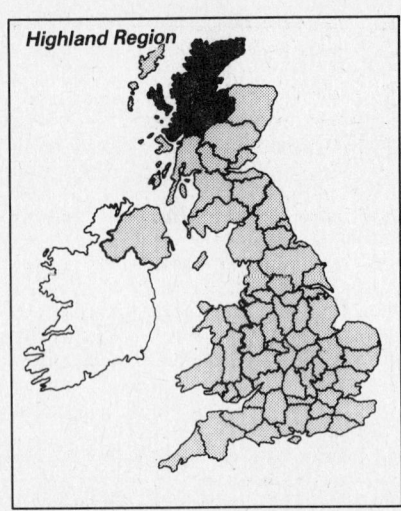

Highland Region

Hildesheim /'hɪldəshaɪm/ industrial town in Lower Saxony, West Germany; population (1984) 101,600. A bishopric from the 9th century, Hildesheim became a free city of the ◊Holy Roman Empire in the 13th century. It was under Prussia 1866–1945.

Hill /hɪl/ David Octavius 1802–1870. Scottish photographer who, in collaboration with ◊Adamson, made extensive use of the ◊calotype process invented by Fox ◊Talbot, in their large

Hill The Scots photographers David Octavius Hill and Robert R Adamson produced some 2,500 calotypes in five years from 1843. The portrait by Hill and Adamson (c. 1843) is an example of this early photography.

High Wycombe /'wɪkəm/ market town in Buckinghamshire, England; population (1981) 60,500. It is famous for furniture.

hijacking the illegal seizure or taking control of a vehicle and/or its passengers or goods. The term is first recorded from 1923, and was originally used to refer to the robbing of freight lorries. In recent times it (and its derivative, _skyjacking_), has been applied to the seizure of aircraft, usually in flight, by an individual or group, often with some political aim; for example the hijacking of a TWA jet by Shia Muslim gunmen in Jun 1985. They diverted the plane to Beirut, killed one passenger, and held the rest hostage for the release of 766 Lebanese and

Palestinian detainees in Israel, precipitating an international crisis. The term has also spread to ships, as when the Italian cruise ship _Achille Lauro_ was hijacked by guerrillas in Oct 1985.

Hildebrand /'hɪldəbrænd/ Benedictine monk who became ◊Gregory VII.

Hildegard of Bingen /'hɪldəgɑːd, 'bɪŋən/ 1098–1179. Abbess and scientific writer. From the age of eight she lived in the Benedictine convent of Mount St Disibode, near the Rhine, and became abbess 1136. She is remembered for an encyclopedia of natural history, _Liber Simplicis Medicinae_ 1150–60, giving both Latin and German names for the species described, as well as their medicinal uses.

collection of portraits taken between 1843 and 1848 in Edinburgh.

Hill /hɪl/ Rowland 1795–1879. British post office official who invented adhesive stamps, and in a pamphlet 'Post Office Reform' prompted the introduction of the penny prepaid post in 1840 (previously the recipient paid, according to distance, on receipt). He was secretary to the Post Office 1854–64.

Hill British reformer Rowland Hill, remembered for his development and introduction of the pre-paid postal service – the penny post.

Hillary /'hɪləri/ Edmund 1919– . New Zealand mountaineer and apiarist. Born in Auckland, ne was one of the reconnaissance party to ◊Everest in 1951, and in 1953, together with Norgay ◊Tenzing, conquered the summit.

Hiller /'hɪlə/ Wendy 1912– . British stage and film actress. An excellent character actress, she has played parts as varied as Sally Hardcastle in *Love on the Dole* 1935, Catherine Sloper in *The Heiress* 1947, and Eliza in the film of *Pygmalion* 1938. Later films include *The Kingfisher* 1982.

hill figure in Britain, any of a number of ancient figures, usually of animals, cut from downland turf to show the underlying chalk. Examples are the White Horse on Bratton Hill, Wiltshire, said to commemorate Alfred the Great's victory over the Danes at Ethandun in 878; and the White Horse at Uffington, Berkshire, 110 m/360 ft long, and probably a tribal totem of the Early Iron Age, 1st century BC. One of the rarer human figures is the Long Man of Wilmington, East Sussex.

hill fort European Iron Age site with massive banks and ditches for defence, used not only as a military camp, but as a permanent settlement. One of the most striking is Maiden ◊Castle.

Hilliard /'hɪliəd/ Nicholas c. 1547–1619. The earliest English miniaturist, and the first great painter of the English school. Born in Exeter, he became miniaturist and goldsmith to Queen Elizabeth. His delicate and refined

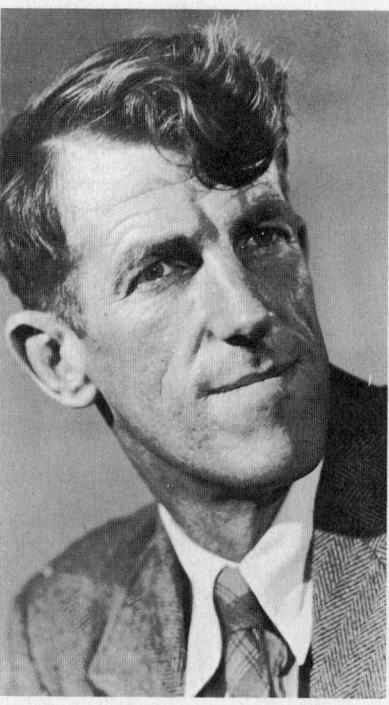

Hillary New Zealand mountaineer and explorer Edmund Hillary. He climbed Everest with the Sherpa Norgay Tenzing in 1953, and crossed Antarctica with Vivian Fuchs in 1958.

technique can be seen in jewel-like work, such as *Young Man Amid Roses* c. 1590 (Victoria and Albert Museum, London).

Hilliard A self-portrait of Nicholas Hilliard at the age of 30 in 1577. The impression of detail in the ruff is created by a series of disparate strokes.

Hillingdon /'hɪlɪŋdən/ borough of W London.
features London Airport at Heathrow; Jacobean mansion (Swakeleys) at Ickenham; ◊Brunel University (technical)
population (1984) 232,200.

Hillsborough Agreement another name for the ◊Anglo-Irish Agreement.

Hilton /'hɪltən/ James 1900–1954. British novelist. Lancashire-born, he was to settle in Hollywood as one of its most successful script writers, for example *Mrs Miniver*. His books include *Lost Horizon* 1933, envisaging Shangri-la, a remote district of Tibet where time stands still; *Mr Chips* 1934, a portrait of an old schoolmaster; and *Random Harvest* 1941.

Hilversum /'hɪlvəsum/ town in N Holland province of the Netherlands, 27 km/17 mi SE of Amsterdam; population (1985) 87,190. Besides being a summer resort, Hilversum is the chief centre of Dutch broadcasting.

Himachal Pradesh /hɪ'mɑːtʃəl prə'deʃ/ NW state of India
area 55,673 sq km/21,700 sq mi
capital Simla
features mainly agricultural state, a third forested, with softwood timber industry
population (1981) 4,237,818, chiefly Hindu
language Pahari
history created as a union territory in 1948, it attained full statehood in 1971. Certain hill areas were transferred from the Punjab to Himachal Pradesh in 1966.

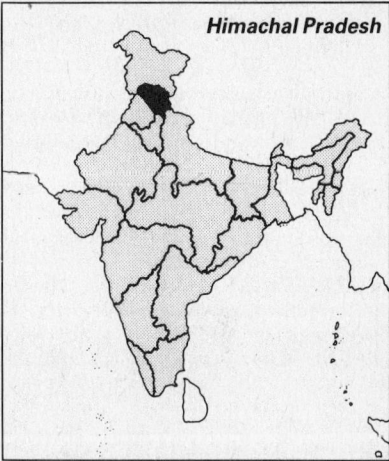

Himachal Pradesh

Himalayas /ˌhɪmə'leɪəz/ mountain system of central Asia, covering part of Tibet and the small states of Bhutan, Nepál, and Sikkim. The two highest peaks are:
Mount Everest (Nepalese name Sagarmatha, 'Head of the Earth'; the English name comes from Sir George Everest (1790–1866), Surveyor-General of India), the world's highest mountain, on the China-Nepál frontier; height 8,848 m/29,028 ft. It was first climbed by Edmund ◊Hillary and Norgay ◊Tenzing in 1953. *Kangchenjunga* third highest mountain in the world, on the Nepál-Sikkim border; height 8,597 m/28,208 ft; first climbed 1955. Other peaks include Makalu, Annapurna, and Nanga Parbat, all over 8,000 m/26,000 ft.

Himes /haɪmz/ Chester 1909–1984. American novelist. After serving seven years in prison for armed robbery, he gained success with his first novel *If He Hollers Let Him Go* 1945, a depiction of the drudgery and racism in a Californian shipyard. Other novels include *Blind Man with a Pistol* 1969.

Himmler /'hımlə/ Heinrich 1900–1945. German Nazi leader. Born in Munich, he joined the Nazi Party in its early days, and became leader of the SS in 1929, and chief of the Bavarian police in 1933. His accumulation of offices meant he had command of all German police forces by 1936, including the ◊Gestapo. This made him one of the most powerful men in Germany, and during World War II he replaced Göring as Hitler's second-in-command. In 1945 he was captured and committed suicide.

Hindemith /'hındəmıt/ Paul 1895–1963. German composer. A fine viola player, he led the Frankfurt Opera Orchestra at 20, and taught composition at the Berlin Hochschule for music 1927–33, when the modernity of his work, for example the *Philharmonic Concerto*, led to a Nazi ban. In 1939 he went to the USA, and in 1951 became professor of musical theory at Zürich. His works include many for chamber ensemble and for orchestra, such as the *Symphonic Metamorphosis on Themes of Carl Maria von Weber* 1944, and the operas *Cardillac* 1926, revised 1952, and *Mathis der Maler* 1938.

Hindenburg /'hındənbɜːg/ German name 1915–45 of the Polish city of ◊Zabrze, in honour of German soldier General ◊Hindenburg.

Hindenburg /'hındənbɜːg/ Paul Ludwig Hans von Beneckendorf und 1847–1934. German soldier and president. Born in Posen of a Prussian Junker (aristocratic landowner) family, he was commissioned in 1866, served in the Austro-Prussian and Franco-German wars, and retired in 1911. Given the command in E Prussia in Aug 1914, he received the credit for the defeat of the Russians at Tannenberg, and was promoted to supreme commander and made a field marshal. Henceforward he and Ludendorff practically directed Germany's policy until the end of the war. He was elected President of the German republic in 1925, and re-elected in 1932. He was compelled to invite Hitler to assume the Chancellorship in Jan 1933, and his last public act was to congratulate him on the 'blood-bath' of Jun 1934. He died on his Prussian estate, and was buried at Tannenberg.

Hindenburg Line German western line of World War I fortifications built 1916–17.

Hindi language a member of the Indo-Iranian branch of the Indo-European language family, the official language of the Republic of India, although resisted as such by the Dravidian-speaking states of the south. Hindi is a N Indian language with many varieties. Hindi proper is used by some 30% of Indians, in such N states as Uttar Pradesh and Madhya Pradesh. Bihari, Punjabi and Rajasthani, the dominant language varieties in the states of Bihar, Punjab and Rajasthan, are claimed by some to be varieties of Hindi, by others to be distinct languages. Hindi has close historical and cultural links with Sanskrit, the classical language of Hinduism, and is written (from left to right) in Devanagari script.

Hinduism religion of the Hindus, which has a triad of three chief gods (the Trimurti):
Brahma the Supreme Spirit, or *Atman*, who works creatively, as one of the triad, and brought into being the cosmos which is both real and an illusion (*'maya'*), since its reality is not lasting; the cosmos is itself personified as the goddess Maya.
Vishnu the preserver, who is thought to have taken various human forms including *Krishna* (hero of the epic ◊*Mahabharata*, the guise in which he receives most popular adoration); and *Rama* (see ◊*Ramayana*). As *Jagganath* 'Lord of the World' he has a famous temple at ◊Puri.
There are numerous lesser divinities, for example ◊Ganesa, ◊Hanuman, and ◊Lakshmi, demons, ghosts, and spirits, who are also reverenced. Important ideas in Hinduism include the ◊transmigration of souls and ◊karma.
The practice of Hinduism is a complex of rites and ceremonies performed within the framework of the caste system under the supervision of the Brahman priests and teachers. Temple worship is almost universally performed, and there are many festivals. In India and the rest of Asia there are over 475 million Hindus.

Hindu Kush /'hındu: 'kuʃ/ mountain range in central Asia; length 800 km/500 mi; greatest height Tirich Mir 7,690 m/25,230 ft, Pakistan. The *Khyber Pass*, a narrow defile (53 km/33 mi long), separates Pakistan from Afghanistan, and was used by Baber and other invaders of India. The present road was built by the British in the ◊Afghan Wars.

Hindustani /ˌhındu'stɑːni/ a member of the Indo-Iranian branch of the Indo-European language family, closely related to Hindi and Urdu and originating in the bazaars of Delhi. It serves as a lingua franca in many parts of the Republic of India, and was the contact language during the British Raj between many of the British in India and their servants and shopkeepers. It is sometimes known as Bazaar Hindi.

Hine /haın/ Lewis 1874–1940. American sociologist. He recorded in photographs child labour conditions in US factories at the beginning of this century.

Hinkler /'hıŋklə/ Herbert John Louis 1892–1933. Australian pilot who in 1928 made the first solo flight from England to Australia. He was killed while making another attempt to fly to Australia.

hip-hop a style of popular music originating in New York in the early 1980s. It uses scratching (a percussive effect obtained by manually rotating a vinyl record) and heavily accented electronic drums behind a usually boastful ◊rap vocal. The term 'hip-hop' also comprises the allied manifestations of break dancing and graffiti.

Hipparchus /hı'pɑːkəs/ c. 555–514 BC. Greek tyrant. Son of ◊Pisistratus, he was associated with his elder brother Hippias as ruler of Athens 527–514 BC. His affection being spurned by Harmodius, he insulted her sister, and was assassinated by Harmodius and Aristogiton.

Hipparchus /hı'pɑːkəs/ fl. 160–145 BC. Greek astronomer, a native of Nicaea in Bithynia. He invented trigonometry, calculated the lengths of the solar year and the lunar month, discovered the precession of the equinoxes, made a catalogue of 800 fixed stars, and advanced Eratosthenes's method of determining the situation of places on the Earth's surface by lines of latitude and longitude.

hippie a member of a youth movement of the mid to late 1960s, also known as flower power, which originated in San Francisco, California, and was characterized by non-violent anarchy, concern for the environment, and rejection of Western materialism. The hippies formed an artistically prolific counterculture in the USA and Britain, and sometimes used psychedelic drugs such as LSD; the style was seen in graphic art and music by bands such as Love (1965–71), The Grateful Dead (1965–), Jefferson Airplane (1965–74), and Pink Floyd (1966–).

Hippocrates /hı'pɒkrəti:z/ c. 460–c. 357 BC. Greek physician, often called the founder of medicine. Little is known of his life except that he was born and practised on the island of Kos, discovered aspirin in willow bark, and died at Larissa. The *Corpus Hippocraticum*, a grouping of some 70 works, is attributed to him, on little evidence; it covers most areas of medicine, including the famous *Aphorisms* and the *Hippocratic Oath* which embodies the essence of medical ethics. The *Aphorisms* include 'Ars longa, vita brevis' (life is short but art and learning last a long time). Hippocrates' ideas on the origin of disease were superseded by the germ theory in the 18th and 19th centuries.

Hippolytus /hı'pɒlıtəs/ in Greek mythology, the son of ◊Theseus, who cursed him for his supposed dishonourable advances to his stepmother Phaedra. Killed by ◊Poseidon as he rode near the sea in his chariot, he was restored to life when his innocence was proved.

hippopotamus (Greek river-horse). Large mammal of the family Hippopotamidae. The common hippopotamus *Hippopotamus amphibius* is found in Africa. It is over 4 m/13 ft long, 1.2 m/4 ft high, weighs between 3 and 4 tonnes, and has a slate-grey skin. The pygmy hippopotamus *Hippopotamus liberiensis* inhabits West Africa. Hippopotamuses are good swimmers, but leave the water at night to graze.

hire purchase in the UK, a system of retail trading under which the buyer makes instalment payments at fixed intervals over a certain period for a particular item. The item is not owned by the buyer until the final instalment has been paid. It has largely been superseded by ◊credit cards, 'budget accounts' offered by shops, and bank loans.

Hirohito /ˌhıərəu'hi:təu/ 1901– . Emperor of Japan. In 1921 he was the first Japanese crown prince to visit Europe, and in 1926 succeeded his father Yoshihito. After the defeat of Japan in 1945 he formally rejected belief in the divinity of the emperor and Japanese racial superiority, and accepted the 1946 constitution greatly curtailing his powers. The Imperial Palace, destroyed by fire in air raids 1945, was rebuilt within the same spacious wooded compound in 1969.

Hiroshige /ˌhıərəu'ʃi:geı/ Ando 1797–1858. Japanese artist. Born in Tokyo, he produced paintings, but was best known for his colour prints of landscapes which influenced the Impressionists, for example, ◊Whistler.

Hiroshima /hı'rɒʃımə/ city and port on the S coast of Honshu, Japan. During World War II

Hirohito Emperor Hirohito of Japan in ceremonial robes.

the city was devastated on 6 Aug 1945 by the first atom bomb to be used in wartime. Over 10 sq km/4 sq mi was obliterated, with heavy damage outside that area. Casualties totalled 136,989 out of a population of 343,000: 78,150 were found dead, others died later. The Peace Memorial Park has hauntingly tragic sculptures and a museum of atomic relics. Population (1980) 899,394.

Hiroshima The total devastation that was Hiroshima towards the end of World War II after it became the first city on which an atom bomb was dropped.

Hispanic /hɪˈspænɪk/ a Spanish-speaking person in the USA, either native-born or immigrant from Mexico, Cuba, Puerto Rico, or any other Spanish-speaking country.

Hispaniola /ˌhɪspæniˈəʊlə/ (Spanish *little Spain*) West Indian island, first landing place of Columbus in the New World, 6 Dec 1492; now divided into ◊Haiti and the Dominican ◊Republic.

Hispano-Suiza /hɪˈspænəʊ ˈswiːzə/ car designed by a Swiss engineer Marc Birkigt (1878–1947), who emigrated to Barcelona, where he founded a factory which produced cars (c. 1900–38) which became legendary for their handling, elegance, and speed.

Hiss /hɪs/ Alger 1904– . US politician, controversially imprisoned in 1950 for perjury. Hiss, one of President Roosevelt's advisors at the 1945 ◊Yalta conference, was accused in 1948 by a former Soviet agent of having passed information to the Soviet Union. He was convicted of perjury for swearing before the Committee on Un-American Activities that he had not spied for the Soviet Union. Richard Nixon was a leading member of the prosecution. Doubts about the justice of his conviction have increased in recent years.

histamine a substance (an amine) which dilates blood vessels, stimulates gastric secretions, and so on, and is formed at the site of an injury or in allergic reactions such as hay fever. Drugs used to neutralize such effects are antihistamines.

histogram diagram for displaying and comparing statistical information, similar to a bar chart except that values are represented by the areas of the bars rather than merely by their lengths.

histology study of the microscopic structure of the tissues of organisms.

historical novel a fictional prose narrative set in the past. Literature set in the historic rather than immediate past has always abounded, but Sir Walter Scott began the modern tradition by

setting imaginative romances of love, impersonation, and betrayal in a past based on known fact; his use of historical detail, and that of European imitators such as Manzoni, gave rise to the genre. Some historical novels of the 19th century were overtly nationalistic, but most were merely novels set in the past to heighten melodrama while providing an informative framework; the genre was used by Victor Hugo and Charles Dickens, among many others. In the 20th century the historical novel also became concerned with exploring psychological states and the question of the difference in the mentality of the past. Successful examples of this are Robert Graves' novels about the Roman Emperor Claudius *I, Claudius* and *Claudius the God* and Margaret Yourcenar's *Memoirs of Hadrian*. The less serious possibilities of the historical novel were exploited by writers including Jeffery Farnol, Stanley Weyman, and Rafael Sabatini in the early 20th century as *historical romance*; Dorothy Dunnett and George MacDonald Fraser revived the historical romance with some success in the late 1960s. The historical novel acquired sub-genres – the stylized *Regency novel* of Georgette Heyer and her imitators; the Napoleonic War sea story, notably those of C S Forester and Patrick O'Brien. These forms have developed their own conventions, particularly when imitating a massively popular ancestor – this has happened in large degree to the *western*, many of which use gestures from Owen Wister's classic *The Virginian*, and to the novel of the American South in the period of the Civil War in the wake of Margaret Mitchell's *Gone With the Wind*.

history the record of the development of human societies. The earliest surviving historical records are the inscriptions denoting the achievements of Egyptian and Babylonian kings. As a literary form in the Western world, historical writing or *historiography* began with the Greek Herodotus (c. 484–425 BC), who first passed beyond the limits of a purely national outlook. Thucydides (c. 471–401 BC) brought to history not only literary gifts but the interests of a scientific investigator and political philosopher. Later Greek history and Roman history tended towards rhetoric; Sallust (86–35 BC) preserved the scientific spirit of Thucydides, but Livy (59–17 BC) and Tacitus (c. AD 54–118), in spite of their insight and literary distinction, tended to subordinate factual accuracy to patriotic or party considerations. Medieval history was dominated by a religious philosophy imposed by the Church. English chroniclers of this period are Bede (673–735), William of Malmesbury (d. 1143), and Matthew Paris (d. 1259). France produced great chroniclers of contemporary events in Froissart (1337–1401) and Comines (1447–1511).

The Renaissance revivified historical writing both by restoring classical models and by creating the science of textual criticism. A product of the new secular spirit is Machiavelli's *History of Florence* 1520–23. The Reformation, especially in Germany, furthered the cause of scientific history by sending controversialists back to the original documents, while in England the constitutional controversies of the 17th century performed a similar function. The 18th century ◊Enlightenment disposed of the attempt to explain history in theological terms, and produced one masterpiece in Gibbon's individual interpretation *Decline and Fall of the Roman Empire* (1776–88). An attempt to formulate a **historical method** and a philosophy of history, that of Vico (1668–1744), remained almost unknown until the 19th century. Romanticism left its mark on historical writing in the tendency to exalt the contribution of the individual 'hero', and in the introduction of a more colourful and dramatic style and treatment, illustrated in the works of Michelet, Carlyle, and Macaulay.

During the last century the study of history has been revolutionized, partly through the contributions of other disciplines, such as the sciences and anthropology. The deciphering of the Egyptian and Babylonian inscriptions opened up a new world. Archaeologists have enabled us to trace the development of prehistoric human beings, and have revealed forgotten civilizations such as that of Crete. Anthropological studies of primitive society and religion, which began with Frazer's *Golden Bough*, have analysed the bases of later forms of social organization and belief. The changes brought about by the Industrial Revolution, and the accompanying perception of economics as a science, forced historians to turn their attention to economic questions. Marx's attempt to find in economic development the most important determining factor in social change, an argument partly paralleled in Buckle's *History of Civilization* 1857, has influenced all serious historians since. A comparative study of civilizations is offered in A J Toynbee's *Study of History 1934–54*, and on a smaller scale by J M Roberts' *History of the World* 1976.

Hitachi /hɪˈtɑːtʃi/ city on Honshu, Japan; population 204,000. The chief industry is the manufacture of electrical goods.

Hitchcock /ˈhɪtʃkɒk/ Alfred 1899–1980. British film director, naturalized American in 1955. He is noted for creating suspense in his mystery films, his camera work, and his hallmark of making 'walk-ons' in his own films: *The Thirty-Nine Steps* 1935, *The Lady Vanishes* 1939, *Rebecca* 1940, *Strangers on a Train* 1951, *Psycho* 1960, and *The Birds* 1963.

Hitchens /ˈhɪtʃɪnz/ Ivon 1893–1979. British painter of abstracts, landscapes, and murals, for example, *Day's Rest, Day's Work* 1963 (Sussex University).

Hitchin /ˈhɪtʃɪn/ market town in Hertfordshire, England, 48 km/30 mi NW of London; population (1985) 30,000.

Hitler /ˈhɪtlə/ Adolf 1889–1945. German dictator. Born at Braunau-am-Inn, in Austria, the son of a customs official, he spent his early years in poverty in Vienna and Munich. After serving as a volunteer in the German army during World War I, he was employed as a spy by the military authorities in Munich, and in 1919 joined in this capacity the German Workers' Party, founded by Anton Drexler. By 1921 he had assumed its leadership, renamed it the National Socialist German Workers' Party,

Hitchcock Suspense, melodrama and fleeting personal appearances are the hallmarks of Alfred Hitchcock's films. His popular cameos were initially motivated by superstition and later continued as an 'in-joke' with the audience.

provided it with a programme, and rallied a following. Having led an unsuccessful rising at Munich in 1923, he was sentenced to nine months' imprisonment, during which he wrote his political testament, *Mein Kampf/My Struggle*. The party did not achieve national importance until the elections of 1930; by 1932, although Hindenburg defeated Hitler in the presidential elections, it formed the largest group in the Reichstag. As the result of an intrigue directed by von Papen, Hitler became Chancellor in a Nazi-Nationalist coalition on 30 Jan 1933.

The opposition were rapidly suppressed, the Nationalists removed from the government, and the Nazis declared the only legal party. In 1934 Hitler succeeded Hindenburg as head of the state. Meanwhile, the drive to war began; Germany left the League of Nations, conscription was reintroduced, and in 1936 the Rhineland was reoccupied. Hitler and Mussolini, who were already both involved in Spain, formed an alliance in 1936. 1938 saw the annexation of Austria, and the occupation of Sudetenland under the Munich agreement. The rest of Czechoslovakia was annexed in Mar 1939. The ◊Hitler-Stalin pact was followed in Sept by the invasion of Poland and the declaration of war by Britain and France. Hitler narrowly escaped death in 1944 from a bomb explosion prepared by high-ranking officers. On 29 Apr 1945, when Berlin was largely in Russian hands, he married Eva Braun in his bunker under the chancellory building, and on the following day committed suicide with her. See also ◊Fascism, ◊anti-semitism, ◊Nazism, ◊World War II.

Hitler-Stalin pact non-aggression treaty between Germany and the USSR signed in Aug

Hitler German Nazi leader Adolf Hitler at Berchtesgaden, his fortified mountain retreat in Bavaria. By oratory, political intrigue and manic drive he became 'Führer' in 1934. He plunged the world into the most devastating war of its history, which ended in the genocide of six million people.

1939. It secretly allowed for the partition of Poland between the two countries and formed a sufficient security in the east for Hitler's declaration of war on France on 1 Sept 1939. This alliance of two apparently inimical ideologies was ended only by the German invasion of the USSR on 22 Jun 1941.

Hittites /ˈhɪtaɪts/ a group of peoples who inhabited Asia Minor and North Syria from the 3rd to the 1st millennium BC. The original Hittites, a people of Armenoid type, inhabited a number of city-states in East Asia Minor, one of which, Hatti, gained supremacy over the others. An Indo-European people invaded the country about 2000 BC, made themselves the ruling class, and intermarried with the original inhabitants. The city of Hattusas (modern Bogharzköy in central Turkey) became the capital of a strong kingdom, which overthrew the Babylonian empire. After a period of eclipse the Hittite New Empire became a great power (about 1400–1200 BC) which successfully waged war with Egypt, until it was overthrown by the so-called ◊Sea Peoples. Small Hittite states then arose in North Syria, the most important of which was ◊Carchemish; these were conquered by the Assyrians in the 8th century BC, Carchemish in 717. The Hittites used a cuneiform script, modelled on the Babylonian for ordinary purposes, and a 'hieroglyphic' script for monumental inscriptions. The Hittite royal archives were discovered at Hattusas in 1906–07, and deciphered in 1915 by Hrozñay.

Hoare-Laval Pact plan for a peaceful settlement to the Italian invasion of Ethiopia in Oct 1935. It was devised by Samuel Hoare (1880–1959), British Foreign Secretary, and Pierre ◊Laval, French Premier, at the request of the ◊League of Nations. Realizing no European country was willing to go to war over Ethiopia, Hoare and Laval proposed official recognition of Italian claims. Public outcry in Britain against the Pact's seeming approval of Italian aggression was so great that the pact had to be disowned and Hoare was forced to resign.

hoatzin tropical South American bird *Opisthocomus hoatzin*, the only representative of its family and resembling a small pheasant in size and appearance: adults are olive with white markings above and red-brown below. The young are hatched naked, and have well-developed claws on the 'thumb and index fingers' of the wing, so that they can crawl reptilian-fashion about the tree – a possible reminder of their ancestry.

Hoban /'həubən/ James C 1762–1831. Irish-born architect who emigrated to the USA. His best known building is the White House, Washington DC, and he also worked on the Capitol and other public buildings.

Hobart /'həubɑːt/ capital and port of Tasmania, Australia; population (1984) 175,660. Founded in 1804, it was named after Lord Hobart, then Secretary of State for the Colonies, and has the University of Tasmania, established 1890.

Hobbema /'hɒbɪmə/ Meindert 1638–1709. Dutch landscape painter. Born in Amsterdam, he came under the influence of ◊Ruysdael, and his pictures show the peace and charm of the Dutch countryside. Most of his best works, including his masterpiece, *Avenue at Middelharnis* (National Gallery, London) are in English galleries.

Hobbes /hɒbz/ Thomas 1588–1679. English political philosopher, tutor to the exiled Prince Charles. The first thinker since Aristotle to attempt to develop a comprehensive theory of nature, including human behaviour. His political thinking was much influenced by the anarchic age in which he lived and he is best remembered for *The Leviathan* 1651, in which he advocates absolutist government as the only means of ensuring order and security.

hobby bird of prey *Falco subbuteo* found across Europe and N Asia. About 30 cm/1 ft long, with grey back, streaked front and chestnut thighs, it is found in open woods and heaths. It feeds mainly on large insects, but also catches small birds.

Hochhuth /'həuxhuːt/ Rolf 1931– . Swiss dramatist, whose controversial play *Soldaten*/*Soldiers* 1968 implied that Churchill was involved in a plot to assassinate ◊Sikorski.

Ho Chi Minh /ˌhəu tʃiː 'mɪn/ 1892–1969. North Vietnamese politician. Born in North Vietnam, he was trained in Moscow, headed the Communist Vietminh from 1941, and, having campaigned against the French 1946–54, became president and prime minister of the Democratic Republic at the armistice. Aided by

Hobbes Best known for his notion of the social contract, the English political philosopher Thomas Hobbes made the radical assertion that absolutist government was the only means of ensuring order and security.

the Communist bloc, he did much to develop industrial potential, and although he relinquished the premiership in 1955, he was re-elected president in 1960.

Ho Chi Minh Ho Chi Minh -'The Enlightener' -who gave his name to Ho Chi Minh City, formerly Saigon, the capital of modern-day Vietnam. A campaigner against French colonial rule of North Vietnam, he became president on its independence.

Ho Chi Minh City /ˌhəu tʃiː 'mɪn/ (former name *Saigon*) chief port and industrial city of southern Vietnam; population (1985) 3,500,000. Industries include shipbuilding, textiles, and rubber.

Saigon was the capital of the Republic of Vietnam (South Vietnam) 1954–76, when it was renamed.

Ho Chi Minh Trails North Vietnamese troop and supply routes to South Vietnam via Laos, especially during the ◊Vietnam War.

hockey a game played with hooked sticks and a ball, the object being to hit the ball into the goal. It is played between two teams, each of not more than 11 players. The ground is 91.50 m/100 yd long and 54.90 m/60 yd wide. Goals 2.13 m/7 ft high and 3.65 m/4 yd wide, are placed within a striking circle of 14.64 m/16 yd radius, from which all shots at goal must be made. The white ball weighs about 155 grams/5.5 oz, circumference about 228 mm/9 in, and the stick must not exceed 50 mm/2 in diameter. The game is started by a 'push-back'. The ball may be stopped with the hand, but not held, picked up, thrown or kicked, except by the goalkeeper in his or her own striking circle. If the ball is sent into touch, it is returned to play by a 'push-in'. The game is divided into two 35 minute periods; it is controlled by two umpires, one for each half of the field.

A game using hooked sticks, not unlike the modern ones, was played by the ancient Greeks, and under the names of 'hurley' and 'shinty' a primitive form of the game was played in Ireland and Scotland. Modern hockey in Britain dates from 1886 when the Men's Hockey Association rules were drafted. The women's game is governed by the All England Women's Hockey Association founded in 1895. In the USA it is known as 'field hockey', to distinguish it from ◊ice hockey.

hockey

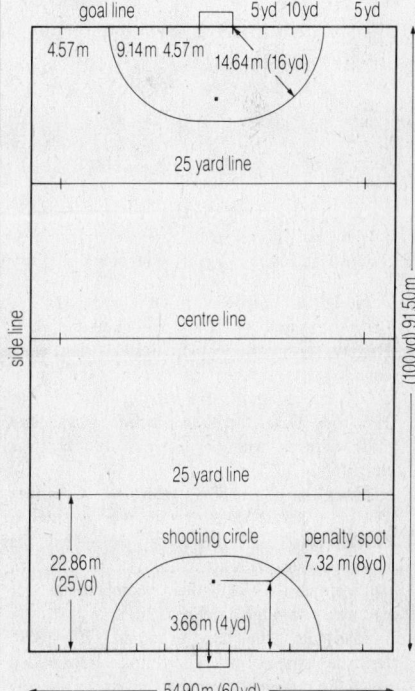

Hockney /'hɒkni/ David 1937– . British artist. Trained at Bradford School of Art and the Royal College of Art, he played an important part in the establishment of the ◊Pop Art movement. His work has a bright, childlike sense of colour. He has also designed sets for opera houses including ◊Glyndebourne, La Scala, Milan, and the Metropolitan Opera House, New York, and produced a film *The Bigger Splash* in 1975.

Hockney The work of the English painter David Hockney is deliberately childlike and characterized by a gentle wit. This painting, 'Peter Getting out of Nick's Pool', is typical of his Californian style: flat and shadowless and showing his interest in depicting moving water.

Hodgkin /ˈhɒdʒkɪn/ Alan Lloyd 1914– . British physiologist. Both Hodgkin and A F Huxley, former students of Lord Adrian, were engaged in research on the mechanism of conduction in peripheral nerves 1946–60. In 1963 they shared the Nobel Prize for Physiology and Medicine with Sir John Eccles. He was knighted in 1972.

Hodgkin /ˈhɒdʒkɪn/ Dorothy Crowfoot 1910– . British chemist. She was awarded a Nobel prize in 1964 for work on the determination, by X-ray studies, of the structure of important biochemical compounds, for example vitamin B_2 and penicillin.

Hodgkin /ˈhɒdʒkɪn/ Thomas 1798–1856. British physician, who first recognized *Hodgkin's disease* (lymphadcnoma), a cancer-like enlargement of the lymphatic glands.

Hodza /ˈhɒdʒə/ Milan 1878–1944. Slovak politician and prime minister of Czechoslovakia from Feb 1936. He and President Beneš were forced to agree to the secession of the Sudeten areas of Czechoslovakia to the Germans before resigning on 22 Sept 1938.

Hofei /ˌhəʊˈfeɪ/ former name of ◊Hefei, a city in China.

Hoffa /ˈhɒfə/ James Riddle 'Jimmy' 1913–?1975. American labour leader, president of the Teamsters Union (truckdrivers), jailed 1964–71 for attempted bribery of a Federal Court Jury after he was charged with corruption. In 1975 he disappeared, and is generally believed to have been murdered.

Hoffman /ˈhɒfmən/ Dustin 1937– . American actor who popularized the role of the anti-hero in the 1960s and 1970s. His films include *The Graduate* 1967, *Midnight Cowboy* 1969, and *Kramer vs Kramer* 1979, for which he won an Academy Award.

Hoffmann /ˈhɒfmən/ E(rnst) T(heodor) A(madeus) 1776–1822. German composer and writer. A lawyer in Berlin, he enjoyed great success with his opera *Undine* 1816, and his *Fantastic Tales* inspired Offenbach's *Tales of Hoffmann*.

Hoffmann /ˈhɒfmən/ Josef 1870–1956. Austrian architect, one of the founders of the Wiener Werkstätte, and a pupil of Otto ◊Wagner.

hog general name for a member of the pig

Hodgkin Nobel prizewinner in chemistry, Professor Dorothy Crowfoot Hodgkin is the first woman since Florence Nightingale to be awarded the Order of Merit.

family. The *river hog Potamochoerus porcus* lives in Africa S of the Sahara. Reddish or black, up to 1.3 m/4.2 ft long plus tail, and 90 cm/3 ft at the shoulder, these gregarious animals root for food in many types of habitat. The *giant forest hog Hylochoerus meinerzthageni* lives in thick forests of Central Africa and is up to 1.9 m/6 ft long.

Hogarth /ˈhəʊgɑːθ/ William 1697–1764. British artist and engraver. Born in London, he was apprenticed to an engraver, and from 1720 studied painting with Sir James Thornhill whose daughter he clandestinely married in 1729. His *A Harlot's Progress* 1731, a series of six pictures, engraved in 1732, established his fame and was followed by *A Rake's Progress* 1735; his masterpiece *Marriage à la Mode* 1745; *Industry and Idleness* 1749 and *The Four Stages of Cruelty* 1751. His penetrating satire of the follies and vices of his age, command of group composition and skill in genre painting are uniquely English in tone.

Hogg /hɒg/ James 1770–1835. Scottish poet, known as the 'Ettrick Shepherd'. Born in Ettrick Forest, Selkirkshire, he worked as a shepherd at Yarrow 1790–99, and until the age of 30, he was illiterate. His novel *Confessions of a Justified Sinner* 1824 is a masterly portrayal of personified evil.

Hogg /hɒg/ Quintin. British politician; see Lord ◊Hailsham.

Hoggar /ˈhɒgə/ another form of ◊Ahaggar, a plateau in the Sahara.

hogmanay Scottish name for the last day of the year and also for the oatmeal cakes given to children as they go from house to house singing carols.

hogweed genus of plants *Heracleum*, family Umbelliferae, of which the *giant hogweed Heracleum mantegazzianum* grows over 3 m/9 ft; in certain individuals, skin exposed to the sap in sunlight develops a rash.

The Company *of* Undertakers

Bearch Sable, an Urinal *proper, between 12* Quack-Heads *of the second &* 19 Cane Heads *Or, Consul-tant. On a* Chief *Nebulæ, Ermine, One Compleat* Doctor *issuant, checkie Sustaining in his Right Hand a* Baton *of the Second. On his* Dexter & Sinister *sides two* Demi-Doctors, *issuant of the second, & two* Cane Heads *issuant of the third; The first having One Eye conchant, to-wards the* Dexter *Side of the Escocheon; the Second* Faced *per pale proper & Gules, Guardent. —— With this Motto.* —— Et Plurima Mortis Imago.

Published by W. Hogarth March the .... Price Six pence

Hogarth The English painter and engraver William Hogarth revived the art of medieval morality pictures, often in a series, such as *A Rake's Progress* (1733). His canvases were crowded with detail and subplots. He published his own engravings; this one is a bitter attack on the medical men of his time.

Hohenlinden /ˌhəʊənˈlɪndən/ Battle of, in the French ◊Revolutionary Wars, a defeat of the Austrians by the French on 3 Dec 1800 which, in conjunction with ◊Marengo, led the Austrians to make peace at the Treaty of Lunéville 1801.

Hohenlohe-Schillingsfürst /ˈhəʊənləʊəˈʃɪlɪŋsfʊəst/ Prince von 1819–1901. German imperial chancellor from Oct 1894 until his replacement by Prince von Bülow in Oct 1900.

Hohenstaufen /ˌhəʊənˈʃtaʊfən/ German family of princes, several members of which were Holy Roman Emperors 1138–1208 and 1214–54. They were the first German emperors to make use of associations with Roman law and tradition to aggrandize their office. Among the most notable were Conrad III, ◊Frederick I (Barbarossa), the first to use the title Holy Roman Emperor, ◊Henry VI, and ◊Frederick II.

Hohenzollern /ˌhəʊənˈzɒlən/ German family, originating in Württemberg, the main branch of which held the titles of elector of Brandenburg from 1415, king of Prussia from 1701, and German Emperor from 1871. The last emperor, William II, was dethroned in 1918. Another branch of the family were kings of Romania 1881–1947.

Hohhot /ˌhɒˈhɒt/ city and capital (formerly Huhehot) of Inner Mongolia (*Nei Monggol*) autonomous region, China; population (1975) 697,000.

Hokkaido /hɒˈkaɪdəʊ/ most northerly of the four main islands of Japan, separated from Honshu to the S by Tsugaru Strait and from Sakhalin to the N by Soya Strait; area 78,508 sq km/30,265 sq mi, population (1970) 5,171,000 including 16,000◊Ainus. The capital is Sapporo. Snow-covered for half the year, Hokkaido was little developed until the Meiji Restoration of 1868 when disbanded Samurai were settled here. Natural resources include coal, mercury, manganese, oil and natural gas, timber, and fisheries. Intensive exploitation followed World War II, including heavy and chemical industrial plants, development of electric power, and dairy farming. An artificial harbour has been constructed at Tomakomai, and an undersea rail tunnel links Hakodate with Aomori (Honshu).

Hokusai /ˌhəʊkʊˈsaɪ/ 1760–1849. Japanese artist. He was born in Yedo, (now Tokyo) and studied engraving. Very prolific, he produced interpretations of everyday Japanese life in prints, water-colours and book illustrations.

Holbein /ˈhɒlbaɪn/ Hans, the Elder c. 1460–1524. German painter, born at Augsburg. His masterpiece is the altarpiece of St Sebastian, 1515 (Munich, Pinakothek).

Holbein /ˈhɒlbaɪn/ Hans, the Younger 1497–1543. German painter. Born at Augsburg, he was the son and pupil of Hans ◊Holbein the Elder. In 1515 Holbein went to Basel, where he became friendly with ◊Erasmus, and in 1517 to Lucerne, where he painted the facades of houses. He was working in Basel again 1519–26, and to this period belong the wood engravings for the *Dance of Death*. He also executed title pages for ◊Luther's translation of the New Testament and ◊More's *Utopia*, and did a number of woodcuts of Old Testament subjects. One of his most famous works is the '*Meyer Madonna*', a fine altarpiece at Darmstadt. In 1527 he came to England, and in 1536 became court painter to ◊Henry VIII. His piercing portraits of the king and his wives, and his delicate portrait drawings, given an excellent pictorial record of the Tudor court. His paintings of small portraits on playing cards began the English vogue for the miniature.

Holborne /ˈhəʊlbɔːn/ Anthony 1584–1602. English composer. He wrote a book of *Pauans, Galliards, Almains and Other Short Aeirs* 1599.

Holden /ˈhəʊldən/ Edith 1871–1920. British artist and naturalist. Daughter of a Birmingham manufacturer, she made most of her observations near her native city, and her illustrated journal was published in 1977 as *The Country Diary of an Edwardian Lady*. In 1911 she married, and was drowned, in a Thames backwater, having overbalanced while reaching for a botanical specimen.

holdfast an organ found at the base of many seaweeds. It may be a flattened, sucker-like structure, or dissected and finger-like, growing into rock crevices and firmly anchoring the plant.

Holford /ˈhɒlfəd/ William, Baron Holford 1907–1975. British architect. Born in Johannesburg, he was the most influential architect-planner of his generation, and was professor of Town Planning at University College, London, 1948–70. He was responsible for much redevelopment after World War II.

Holiday /'hɒlɪdeɪ/ Billie. Stage name of Eleanor Gough McKay 1915–1959. US jazz singer, also known as 'Lady Day'. She made her debut in Harlem clubs, and was famous for the depth of feeling she conveyed with the swing style. Although not a blues singer as such, she brought an individual blues sound to everything she sang. Addicted to drugs, she died of their effects. She published her autobiography *Lady Sings the Blues* 1956.

Holiday Acknowledged as the supreme jazz singer of her day, Billie Holiday brought an individual blues sound to all her songs. Her intensely personal style of diction and phrasing has never been matched.

Holinshed /'hɒlɪnʃed/ Ralph c. 1520–c. 1580. English historian. He published in 1578 two volumes of the *Chronicles of England, Scotland and Ireland*, which were largely used by Shakespeare for his history plays.

holism philosophically, the concept that the whole is greater than the sum of its parts, but in the 1980s specifically the idea that human well-being, physical and mental, is inextricably mingled, and that therefore in attempting a cure for illness it is not enough simply to prescribe drugs – relevant mental and social aspects of the patient's life must be taken into account too.

Holland, Parts of /'hɒlənd/ former separate administrative county of SE Lincolnshire, England.

Holland /'hɒlənd/ Henry Richard Vassall Fox, 3rd Baron 1773–1840. British Whig politician. He was Lord Privy Seal 1806–07. His seat at Holland House was for many years the centre of Whig political and literary society.

Holland /'hɒlənd/ John Philip 1840–1914. Irish-born American engineer who developed some of the first submarines. He began work in Ireland in the late 1860s and emigrated to the USA in 1873. His first successful boat was launched in 1881 and, after several failures, he built the *Holland* in 1893 which was bought by the US Navy two years later. He died in poverty after his company failed because of financial difficulties.

Holland /'hɒlənd/ N two provinces of the ◊Netherlands:
North Holland occupies the peninsula jutting northwards between the North Sea and the Ijsselmeer. Most of it is below sea-level, protected from the sea by a series of sand dunes and artificial dykes. The capital is Haarlem; other towns are Amsterdam, the largest and most important, Hilversum, Den Helder, and the cheese centres Alkmaar and Edam. Area 2,656 sq km/1,025 sq mi; population (1982) 2,312,266. *South Holland* is also low-lying. The Hague is its capital; other important towns are Rotterdam, Leiden, Gouda, and Delft. Dairy cattle are reared and dairy products are important; there are petroleum refineries at Rotterdam, and distilleries at Schiedam. Area 2,867 sq km/1,107 sq mi; population (1982) 3,121,471.

Hollar /'hɒlə/ Wenceslaus 1607–1677. Bohemian engraver. Born at Prague, he went to England in 1637, and was appointed drawing master to the Prince of Wales. He made numerous plates of views of cities, including London before the Great Fire of 1666.

Hollerith /'hɒlərɪθ/ Herman 1860–1929. US inventor of a mechanical tabulating machine, which was effectively the first device for data processing. After attending the Columbia University School of Mines, Hollerith worked on the 1880 US census and witnessed the huge task of processing so much information. In 1882 he became an instructor at the Massachusetts Institute of Technology, where he developed a machine for counting and collating census data. Hollerith's tabulator was widely publicized after being successfully used in the 1890 census. He established, the Tabulating Machine Company, one of the founding companies of International Business Machines (IBM).

Hollis /'hɒlɪs/ Roger 1905–1973. British civil servant, head of the secret intelligence service MI5, 1956–65. See under Kim ◊Philby.

holly tree or shrub of genus *Ilex*, family Aquifoliaceae, including the *English Christmas holly Ilex aquifolium,* an evergreen with spiny, glossy leaves, small white flowers, and poisonous scarlet berries on the female tree, and the *Brazilian holly Ilex paraguayensis*, from the leaves of which the tea *yerba maté* is made.

Holly /'hɒli/ Buddy. Stage name of Charles Hardin Holley 1936–1959. US rock-and-roll singer, guitarist, and composer, born in Lubbock, Texas. His songs include 'That'll Be the Day' 1957, 'Peggy Sue' 1957, and 'Maybe Baby' 1958.

hollyhock garden perennial *Althaea rosea* of the family Malvaceae. Originally a native of Asia, the hollyhock was introduced into Britain some four centuries ago. The flower spikes are 3 m/10 ft high.

Hollywood /'hɒliwʊd/ suburb of Los Angeles, California, USA, from 1911 the centre of the US film industry.

Holmes /'həʊmz/ Oliver Wendell 1809–1894. American writer. Born at Cam-bridge, Massachusetts, he became professor of anatomy at Dartmouth 1838–40 and at Harvard 1847–82. In 1857 he founded with Lowell the *Atlantic Monthly*, in which were published the essays and verse collected in 1858 as *The Autocrat of the Breakfast-Table*, a record of the imaginary conversation of boarding-house guests.

holmium chemical element, symbol Ho, atomic number 67, atomic weight 164.94, discovered by Cleve in 1897. Holmium is one of the ◊rare earth metals and occurs in various minerals such as gadolinite. It is used in electronic devices.

holocaust wholesale destruction, from the Greek word meaning the burning of a sacrificed animal in its entirety. It is especially applied today to the annihilation of about six million Jews under the Hitler regime 1933–45 at the concentration camps of Auschwitz, Belsen, Buchenwald, Dachau and Maidanek.

holography a method of producing three-dimensional (3D) images by means of laser light. British scientist Denis Gabor suggested the possibility of holography as early as 1947, but it could not be demonstrated practically until a pure coherent light source – the ◊laser – became available in 1963. Holography uses a photographic technique to produce a picture, or hologram, which contains 3D information about the object photographed. Some holograms show meaningless patterns in ordinary light and produce a 3D image only when laser light is shone through them. Reflection holograms, however, produce images when ordinary light is reflected from them. They are commonly to be found on credit cards. The technique of holography is also applicable to sound, and it is thought possible that bats navigate by ultrasonic holography. Holographic techniques also have applications in storing dental records, detecting stresses and strains in construction and in retail goods, and in detecting forged paintings and documents.

Holst /həʊlst/ Gustav(us Theodore von) 1874–1934. British composer. Born at Cheltenham, of Swedish descent, he studied at the Royal College of Music under Stanford, became a trombonist, and was a teacher in London and Reading. He composed operas including *Savitri* 1916, *At the Boar's Head* 1925, ballets, choral works including *Hymns from the Rig Veda* 1911, *The Hymn of Jesus* 1920, orchestral suites (among which is *The Planets*, 1918), and songs.

Holstein /'həʊlstaɪn/ Friedrich von 1839–1909. German diplomat and foreign affairs expert. Although he refused the post of foreign minister, Holstein played a key role in German diplomacy from the late 19th century until his death.

Holt /həʊlt/ Harold Edward 1908–1967. Australian politician. Born in Sydney, son of a teacher, he was minister of labour 1940–41 and 1949–58, and federal treasurer 1958–66, when he succeeded Menzies as prime minister. He was drowned in a swimming accident.

Holtby /'həʊltbi/ Winifred 1898–1935. British novelist, poet, and journalist. An ardent advocate of women's freedom and racial

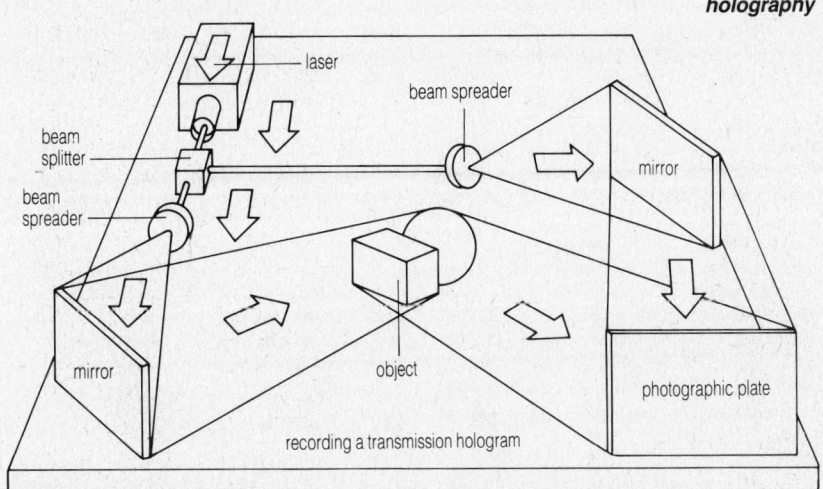

holography

recording a transmission hologram

(labels: laser, beam spreader, beam splitter, beam spreader, mirror, mirror, object, photographic plate)

Queen of Scots and Charles Edward, the Young Pretender.

Holy See the diocese of the ◊Pope.

Holy Shroud ancient piece of linen bearing the imprint of a body, claimed to be that of Jesus Christ. Extensive tests have failed so far to prove or disprove the claim. The shroud, property of the Pope, is kept in Turin cathedral, Italy.

Homburg /ˈhɒmbɜːg/ town and spa at the foot of the Taunus mountains, West Germany; population (1984) 41,800. It has given its name to a soft felt hat for men, made fashionable in Homburg by Edward VII of England.

Home /hjuːm/ Alex Douglas-Home, Baron Home of the Hirsel 1903– . British Conservative politician. Foreign secretary 1960–63. Succeeding Macmillan as prime minister in 1963, he renounced his peerage (as 14th Earl of Home) to fight (and lose) the general election of 1964; he resigned as party leader in 1965. He was again foreign secretary 1970–74, when he received a life peerage. His brother is the playwright William ◊Douglas-Home.

---

equality, she is best known for her novel *South Riding* 1936, set in her native Yorkshire.

Holy Communion another name for the ◊Eucharist, a Christian sacrament.

Holyhead /ˌhɒlɪˈhed/ seaport on the N coast of Holyhead Island, off Anglesey, N Wales; population (1981) 10,467. Holyhead Island is linked bridges with Anglesey, and there are regular sailings between Holyhead and Dublin.

Holy Island /ˈhəʊli/ or *Lindisfarne*. Island in the North Sea, 3 km/2 mi off Northumberland, England, with which it is connected by a causeway. St ◊Aidan founded a monastery here in 635.

Holy Land the name often used to refer to ◊Palestine in Biblical times.

Holy Loch /ˈhəʊli ˈlɒx/ western inlet of the Firth of Clyde, W Scotland, with a US nuclear submarine base.

Holyoake /ˈhəʊlɪəʊk/ Keith Jacka 1904–1983. New Zealand National Party politician. He succeeded Sidney Holland as prime minister for two months in 1957. Favouring a property-owning democracy, he was returned to power in 1960, 1963, 1966, 1969, and retired in 1972.

Holy Office tribunal of the Roman Catholic Church that deals with ecclesiastical discipline; see ◊Inquisition.

Holy Orders Christian priesthood, as conferred by the 'laying on of hands' by a bishop. The Anglican church has three orders (bishop, priest, and deacon); the Roman Catholic Church includes also sub-deacons, acolytes, exorcists, readers, and door-keepers. See also ◊Tertiaries.

Holy Roman Empire name applied to the empire of ◊Charlemagne and his successors, and to the German Empire 962–1806, both being regarded as a revival of the Roman Empire. At its height it comprised much of western and central Europe. See ◊German History, ◊Hapsburg.

Holyrood House /ˈhɒlɪruːd/ royal residence in Edinburgh, Scotland. The palace was built 1498–1503 on the site of a 12th-century abbey by James IV. It has associations with Mary

HOLY ROMAN EMPERORS

Carolingian Kings and Emperors	
Charlemagne, Charles the Great	800–14
Louis I, the Pious	814–40
Lothair I	840–55
Louis II	855–75
Charles II, the Bald	875–77
Charles III, the Fat	881–87
Guido of Spoleto	891–94
Lambert of Spoleto (co-emperor)	892–98
Arnulf (rival)	896–901
Louis III of Provence	901–05
Berengar	905–24
Conrad I of Franconia (rival)	911–18

Saxon Kings and Emperors	
Henry I, the Fowler	918–36
Otto I, the Great	936–73
Otto II	973–83
Otto III	983–1002
Henry III, the Saint	1002–24

Franconian (Salian) Emperors	
Conrad II	1024–39
Henry III, the Black	1039–56
Henry IV	1056–1106
Rudolf of Swabia (rival)	1077–80
Hermann of Luxembourg (rival)	1081–93
Conrad of Franconia (rival)	1093–1101
Henry V	1106–25
Lothair II	1126–37

Hohenstaufen Kings and Emperors	
Conrad III	1138–52
Frederick I Barbarossa	1152–90
Henry VI	1190–97
Otto IV	1198–1215
Philip of Swabia (rival)	1198–1208
Frederick II	1215–50
Henry Raspe of Thuringia (rival)	1246–47
William of Holland (rival)	1247–56
Conrad IV	1250–54

The Great Interregnum	1254–73

Rulers from Various Noble Families	
Richard of Cornwall (rival)	1257–72
Alfonso X of Castile (rival)	1257–73
Rudolf I (Hapsburg)	1273–91
Adolf I of Nassau	1292–98
Albert I (Hapsburg)	1298–1303
Henry VII (Luxembourg)	1308–13
Louis IV of Bavaria	1314–47
Frederick of Hapsburg (co-regent)	1314–25
Charles IV (Luxembourg)	1347–78
Wenceslas of Bohemia	1378–1400
Frederick III of Brunswick	1400
Rupert of the Palatinate	1400–10
Sigismund (Luxembourg)	1411–37

Hapsburg Emperors	
Albert II	1438–39
Frederick III	1440–93
Maximilian I	1493–1519
Charles V	1519–56
Ferdinand I	1556–64
Maximilian II	1564–76
Rudolf II	1576–1612
Matthias	1612–19
Ferdinand II	1619–37
Ferdinand III	1637–57
Leopold I	1658–1705
Joseph I	1705–11
Charles VI	1711–40
Charles VII of Bavaria	1742–45

Hapsburg-Lorraine Emperors	
Francis I of Lorraine	1745–65
Joseph II	1765–90
Leopold II	1790–92
Francis II	1792–1806

Home /hju:m/ Daniel Dunglas 1833–1886. British spiritualist medium whose demonstrations of levitation were vouched for by the scientist William Crookes and others. In 1864 he was expelled from Rome as a sorcerer.

Home Counties name given to the counties in close proximity to London, England: Hertfordshire, Essex, Kent, Surrey, and formerly Middlesex.

Home Guard unpaid force formed in Britain in May 1940 to repel the expected German invasion, and known until Jul 1940 as the Local Defence Volunteers. It consisted of men aged 17–65 who had not been called up, formed part of the armed forces of the crown, and was subject to military law. Over 2 million strong in 1944, it was disbanded 31 Dec 1945, but revived in 1951, then placed on a reserve basis in 1955, and ceased activities in 1957.

Home Office British government department established in 1782 to deal with all the internal affairs of England except those specifically assigned to other departments. Specific responsibilities include the police, the prison service, immigration, race relations, and broadcasting. The home secretary, the head of the department, holds cabinet rank. There is a separate secretary of state for Scotland, and, since 1964, for Wales. The home secretary has certain duties in respect of Northern Ireland, the Channel Islands, and the Isle of Man.

homeopathy or **homoeopathy**. A system of medicine, introduced by the German physician Samuel Hahnemann (1755–1843), based on the treatment of a given disease by administering small quantities of a drug which produces the symptoms of that disease in a healthy person. It is contrasted with ◊allopathy.

homeostasis the maintenance of a constant state in an organism's internal environment. It includes regulation of the chemical composition of body fluids, as well as temperature and pressure. See also ◊homeothermy.

homeothermy the maintenance of a constant body temperature in endothermic or 'warm-blooded' animals, by the use of chemical body processes to compensate for heat loss or gain when external temperatures change. They can generate heat by the breakdown of food and the contraction of muscles, and lose heat by sweating, panting and other means. Homeotherms generally have a layer of insulating material to keep heat in, such as fur, feathers or fat (see ◊blubber). Homeothermy makes animals much more efficient metabolically and enables them to remain active under most climatic conditions. Mammals and birds are homeotherms, whereas invertebrates, fish, reptiles and amphibians are 'cold-blooded' ◊poikilotherms.

Homer /'həʊmə/ legendary Greek ◊epic poet, the traditional author of the *Iliad* and the *Odyssey*. According to tradition he was a blind wandering minstrel; seven cities claimed to be his birthplace, while he has been given dates ranging from the 11th to 7th centuries BC.

The *Iliad* tells of an incident during the siege of Troy, the wrath of Achilles and the death of Hector; the *Odyssey* of the wanderings of Odysseus after the siege and his return to Ithaca. Both formed part of a cycle of epics on the siege of Troy, the remainder of which has been lost. The capture of Troy about 1200 BC was an episode in the Greek invasions of Asia Minor. Songs glorifying princely houses, combining historical elements with myth and folklore, arose at the courts of chieftains, and assumed artistic form at the hands of professional bards, possibly in the Ionian trading cities. In the course of transmission they were greatly modified, for example, only slight traces of human sacrifice remain. Peisistratus, tyrant of Athens, is said to have first collected the complete texts from reciters at the Panathenaian festival about 550 BC and committed them to writing. Early quotations show many variations from the received texts, which may have been produced by Alexandrian editors 3rd–2nd centuries BC.

Modern Homeric criticism began in 1795 with Wolf's *Prolegomena*, which attempted to prove that the *Iliad* was derived from earlier ballads. The origin of the poems remains a subject of controversy; they show many characteristics of traditional oral epic, and some objects described in them have been dated archaeologically to pre-1200 BC.

Homer /'həʊmə/ Winslow 1836–1910. American artist. Born in Boston, he established his reputation as a realist genre painter with *Prisoners from the Front* 1866.

home rule the slogan of the Irish nationalist movement 1870–1914; it stood for the repeal of the Act of ◊Union, and the establishment of an Irish parliament within the framework of the British Empire. The slogan was popularized after 1870 by Isaac Butt (1813–79) and ◊Parnell, his successor in the nationalist leadership. Gladstone's Home Rule bills of 1886 and 1893 were both defeated; Asquith's Home Rule bill became law in 1914, but was suspended during World War I. After 1918 the demand for an independent Irish republic replaced that for home rule.

home service force (HSF) force established in the UK in 1982, linked to the Territorial ◊Army, and recruited from volunteers of ages 18–60. It was introduced to guard key points and installations likely to be the target of enemy 'special forces' and saboteurs, so releasing other units for mobile defence roles.

homologous in biology, an organ or structure possessed by members of different taxonomic groups (for example, species, genera, families, orders) which, although now different in form or usage, originally derived from the same structure in a common ancestor. The wing of a bat, the arm of a monkey and the flipper of a seal are homologous, because they all derive from the forelimb of an ancestral mammal. The wing of a bird and the wing of an insect are not homologous, even though they are both used for flying, because they are not derived from the same structure.

homologous series various organic chemicals which form series whose consecutive members differ by a constant molecular weight. Alkanes (paraffins), alkenes (olefins) and alkynes (acetylenes) form such series whose members differ in weight by 14, 12, and 10 atomic mass units, respectively. For example, the alkane homologous series begins with methane (CH_4), ethane (C_2H_6), propane (C_3H_8), butane (C_4H_10), pentane (C_5H_12), and so on.

homonymy an aspect of language in which, through historical accident, two or more words may sound and look alike (*homonymy* proper; for example, a farmer's bull and a papal bull), may sound the same but look different (*homophony*; for example, air and heir; gilt and guilt), and may look the same but sound different (*homography*; for example the wind in the trees and roads that wind). Homonyms , homophones and homographs seldom pose problems of comprehension, because they usually belong in different contexts. Even when brought into the same context for effect ('The heir to the throne had an air of self-satisfaction'), they are clear. They may, however, be used to make puns (for example, talking about a papal bull in a china shop).

homosexuality sexual preference for, or attraction mainly to, persons of one's own sex; in women it is usually referred to as ◊lesbianism. Men or women who are both homosexual and heterosexual are referred to as bisexual.

homozygous in a living organism, having two identical ◊alleles of the ◊gene for a given trait. Homozygous individuals always breed true, that is they produce offspring that resemble them in appearance, when bred with a genetically similar individual. ◊Recessive alleles are only expressed in the homozygous condition. See also ◊heterozygous.

Homs /hɒms/ city, capital of Homs district, Syria, near the Orontes river; population (1979) 325,724. Silk, cereals and fruit are produced in the area, and industries include silk textiles, oil refining, and jewellery. ◊Zenobia, Queen of Palmyra, was defeated at Homs by the Roman emperor ◊Aurelian in 272.

Honan /ˌhəʊ'næn/ former name of ◊Henan, a province of China.

Hondecoeter /'hɒndəku:tə/ Melchior 1636–1695. Dutch artist. Born at Utrecht, he became famous for his paintings of birds.

Hondo /'hɒndəʊ/ another name for ◊Honshu, an island of Japan.

Honduras /hɒn'djʊərəs/ country in central America, bounded to the N by the Caribbean, to the SE by Nicaragua, to the S by the Pacific, to the SW by El Salvador, and to the W and NW by Guatemala.

government the 1982 constitution, which underwent a major revision in 1985, provides for the election of a president, who is head of both state and government, by universal suffrage for a four-year term, and may not serve two terms in succession. A single-chamber national assembly of 134 members is elected in the same way for a similar term.

There is a range of political parties which sometimes unite to form broad alliances for election purposes. The most significant are the Liberal Party of Honduras (PLH) and the National Party (PN).

history formerly inhabited by ◊Maya Indians, and reached by Christopher ◊Columbus in 1502, the area was colonized by Spain from 1526. Independent from Spain in 1821, Honduras was part of the ◊Central American Federation until 1838, when it achieved full independence. From 1939–49 it was a dictatorship under the PN.

The government changed in a series of military coups, until the return of civilian rule in 1980. The army, however, controlled security and was able to veto cabinet appointments, and although the 1981 general election was won by the PLH and its leader, Dr Roberto Suazo, became president, power was in the hands of Gen Gustavo Alvarez, the commander-in-chief of the army. In 1982 Alvarez secured an amendment to the constitution, reducing government control over the armed forces, and was virtually in charge of foreign policy, agreeing in 1983 to the establishment of US military bases in the country. The ◊CIA was also active in assisting Nicaraguan counter-revolutionaries based in Honduras.

In 1984 Alvarez was ousted by a group of junior officers and the country's close relationship with the USA came under review. In the same year divisions arose in the PLH over selection of presidential candidates and in 1985 the electoral law was changed. Suazo was not eligible to stand in the 1985 presidential elections and the main PLH candidate was José Azeona. Although the PN nominee won most votes, the revised constitution made Azeona the eventual winner.

Honduras
REPUBLIC OF (*República de Honduras*)

AREA 112,088 sq km/43,227 sq mi
CAPITAL Tegucigalpa
TOWNS San Pedro Sula; ports Henecan (on Pacific), La Ceiba
PHYSICAL mountainous; 45% forest
FEATURES areas still unexplored
HEAD OF STATE AND OF GOVERNMENT José Simeon Azeona del Hoyo from 1986
GOVERNMENT democratic
EXPORTS coffee, bananas, timber (including mahogany, rosewood)
CURRENCY lempira (3.30 = £1 Sept 1987)
POPULATION (1985) 4,499,000 (90% mestizo, 10% Indians and Europeans); annual growth rate 3.5%
LANGUAGE Spanish
RELIGION Roman Catholic
LITERACY 44% male/42% female (1980 est)
GNP $2.8 bn (1983); $590 per head of population
CHRONOLOGY
1838 Honduras achieved independence.
1980 After more than a century of mostly military rule, a civilian government was elected, with Dr Roberto Suazo as president. The commander in chief of the army, Gen Gustavo Alvarez, retained considerable power.

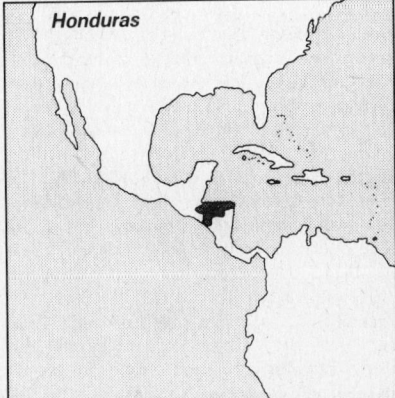

Honduras

1983 Close involvement with the USA in providing naval and air bases and allowing Nicaraguan counter-revolutionaries to operate from Honduras.
1984 Alvares ousted in a coup led by junior officers, resulting in a review of policy towards the USA and Nicaragua.
1985 José Azeona elected president after the electoral law was changed, making Suazo ineligible for presidency.

Litany, in which he expounded the journalist's right to free expression.

Honecker /'hɒnekə/ Erich 1912– . East German communist politician, in power from 1973. Honecker, the son of a miner, joined the German Communist Party in 1929 and was imprisoned for anti-fascist activity 1935–45. He was elected to the East German parliament (*Volkskammer*) in 1949 and became a member of the Socialist Unity Party (SED) Politburo during the 1950s. A security specialist, during the 1960s he served as a secretary of the National Defence Council before being appointed first secretary of the SED in 1971. After ◊Ulbricht's death in 1973, Honecker became effective leader of East Germany and was elected chair of the council of state (head of state) in 1976. He has governed in an austere and efficient manner and, while favouring East-West detente, has been a loyal ally of the USSR.

Honegger /'hɒnegə/ Arthur 1892–1955. Swiss composer. Born at Le Havre, he was educated at Zürich and Paris, and in the 1920s joined the group of French composers known as ◊Les Six. Later his work became more deeply expressive, and is very varied in form, for example, oratorio (*Le Roi David/King David* 1921), programme music ('Pacific 231' 1923 inspired by a railway engine), and the *Symphonie liturgique/Liturgical Symphony* 1946.

Hone /həʊn/ William 1780–1842. British journalist and publisher. He attacked many contemporary abuses in print, and in 1817 was unsuccessfully prosecuted for his *Political

honey sweet food substance made by honey ◊bees from nectar collected from flowers. It is made in excess of their needs as food for the winter. It comprises various sugars, especially

laevulose and dextrose, with enzymes, colouring matter, acids, and pollen grains.

honey-eater or **honey-sucker**. Australasian bird of the family Meliphagidae. They use their long tongues to sip nectar from flowers.

honey guides in botany, lines or spots on the petals of a flower which indicate to pollinating insects the position of the nectaries within the flower. The orange dot on the lower lip of the toadflax flower (*Linaria vulgaris*) is an example. Sometimes the markings reflect only ultra-violet light and are therefore invisible to the human eye, although they can be seen by many insects.

honeysuckle popular name for plants of the *Lonicera* genus of the Caprifoliaceae family. The commmon British honeysuckle or **woodbine** *Lonicera periclymenum*, is a climbing plant with sweet-scented flowers, reddish and yellow-tinted outside and creamy-white inside. The N American **trumpet honeysuckle** *Lonicera sempervirens* has scarlet and yellow varieties.

Hong Kong /'hɒŋ 'kɒŋ/ crown colony in SE Asia, comprising Hong Kong island, the Kowloon peninsula, and the mainland New Territories.
area 1,243 sq km/404 sq mi
capital Victoria (popularly Hong Kong City)
towns Kowloon, Tsuen Wan (in the New Territories)
features an enclave of Kwantung province, China, it has one of the world's finest natural harbours; Hong Kong Island is connected with Kowloon by undersea railway; a world financial centre, its stock market has four exchanges.
exports textiles, clothing, electronic goods, clocks, watches, cameras, plastic products; a large proportion of the exports and imports of S China are transshipped here, and the Chinese special economic zone of Shenzen is only 25 miles away; tourism is important
currency Hong Kong dollar
population (1981) 5,109,812; 57% Hong Kong Chinese, most of the remainder refugees from the mainland
languages English and Chinese
religion Confucianist, Buddhist, Taoist, with Muslim and Christian minorities
government Hong Kong is a British dependency administered by a Crown-appointed governor who presides over an unelected executive council, composed of four ex-officio and 11 nominated members, and a legislative council composed of three ex-officio members, 29 appointees and 24 indirectly elected members.
history formerly part of ◊China, Hong Kong Island was occupied by Britain 1841, during the first of the ◊Opium Wars, and ceded by the Chinese government under the 1842 Treaty of Nanking. The Kowloon Peninsula was acquired under the 1860 Peking (Beijing) Convention and the New Territories secured on a 99-year lease from 1898.

The colony, which developed into a major *entrepôt* for Sino-British trade during the late 19th and early 20th centuries, was occupied by Japan 1941–45. The restored British administration promised, after 1946, to increase self-government. These plans were shelved, however, after the 1949 Communist revolution in ◊China. During the 1950s almost 1,000,000 Chinese (predominantly Cantonese) refugees fled to Hong Kong. Immigration continued during the 1960s and 1970s, raising the colony's population from 1,000,000 in 1946 to 5,000,000 in 1980, and forcing the imposition of strict border controls during the 1980s.

Hong Kong's economy expanded rapidly during the corresponding period, however, and the colony became one of Asia's major commercial, financial, and industrial centres. As the date (1997) for the termination of the New Territories' lease approached, negotiations on Hong Kong's future were opened between Britain and China during the early 1980s. These culminated in a unique agreement, signed in Beijing in 1984, in which Britain agreed to transfer full sovereignty of the Islands and New Territories to China in 1997 in return for a Chinese assurance that Hong Kong's social and economic freedom and capitalist lifestyle would be preserved for at least 50 years.

Under this 'one country, two systems' agreement, in 1997 Hong Kong would become a special administrative region within China, with its own laws, currency, budget and tax system, and would retain its free port status and authority to negotiate separate international trade agreements. In preparation for its withdrawal from the colony, the British government introduced indirect elections to select a portion of the new legislative council in 1984, and direct elections for seats on lower tier local councils in 1985. A Sino-British joint liaison group was also established to monitor the functioning of the new agreement and a 59-member basic law drafting committee (including 25 representatives from Hong Kong) formed in Beijing in 1985 to draft a new constitution.

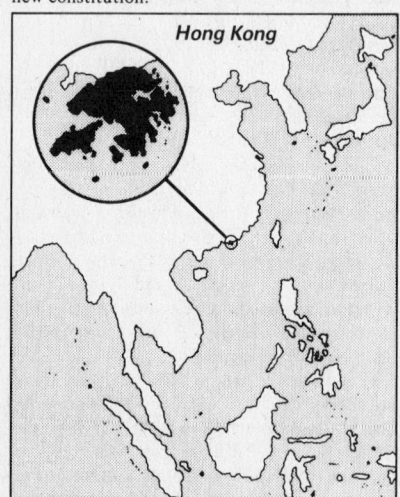

Hong Kong

Honiton /'hɒnɪtən/ market town in Devon, England, on the river Otter; population (1981) 6,627. Its hand-made pillow-lace industry is undergoing a revival.

Honolulu /ˌhɒnə'luːluː/ (Hawaiian 'sheltered bay'), capital city and port of ◊Hawaii, USA, on the S coast of Oahu; population (1980) 365,048. 11 km/7 mi SW is Pearl Harbor with naval and military installations. Waikiki Beach and the

extinct volcano Diamond Head are tourist attractions.

honours list military and civil awards approved by the Sovereign of the UK at New Year, and on her official birthday in Jun. Many Commonwealth countries have their own.

Honshu /'hɒnʃuː/ principal island of Japan. It lies between Hokkaido and Kyushu; area 230,448 sq km/88,839 sq mi, including 382 smaller islands; population (1970) 82,559,580. A chain of volcanic mountains runs along the island, which is subject to frequent earthquakes. Tokyo and Yokohama stand on a triangular plain. On the Inland Sea in the S are the ports of Osaka, Kobe, Kure, and Hiroshima. Honshu is linked by bridges and tunnels with the islands of Hokkaido, Kyushu and Shikoku.

Honthorst /'hɒnthɔːst/ Gerard van 1590–1656. Dutch artist. Influenced by ◊Caravaggio, he is especially noted for his portraits, and for his night scenes.

Hooch /həux/ Pieter de 1629–c. 1684. Dutch painter. Born in Rotterdam, he came under the influence of ◊Vermeer. He is famous for courtyard and garden scenes and interiors, in which the effect of light plays an important role.

Hood /hʊd/ Samuel, 1st Viscount Hood 1724–1816. British admiral. A masterly tactician, he defeated the French at Dominica in 1783, and as commander in the Mediterranean 1793–94 captured Toulon and Corsica.

Hood /hʊd/ Thomas 1799–1845. British poet and humorist. Born in London, he entered journalism, and edited periodicals, for example, *Hood's Monthly Magazine* 1843. Although best known for his comic verse, for example, 'Miss Kilmansegg', he also wrote serious poems such as 'Song of the Shirt' 1843, a protest against poorly paid labour, and 'Bridge of Sighs' 1843.

Hooghly /'huːglɪ/ river and town, in West Bengal, India; population (1981) 125,193. The river is the western stream of the Ganges delta. The town is on the site of a factory set up by the ◊East India Company in 1640, which was moved to Calcutta, 40 km/25 mi downstream, 1686–90.

Hooke /hʊk/ Robert 1635–1703. British experimental physicist and inventor, who furthered the sciences of mechanics and microscopy. He was elected to the Royal Society in 1663, and also became its curator for the rest of his life. He discovered that the tension in a lightly-stretched spring is proportional to its extension from its natural length (Hooke's Law), and he helped improve such scientific instruments as the light microscope, telescope, and barometer. His inventions included a double-barrelled air-pump, the spirit-level, marine barometer, and sea gauge. He studied ◊elasticity, and coined the term 'cell' in biology.

Hooker /'hʊkə/ Joseph Dalton 1817–1911. British botanist who travelled to the Antarctic and made many botanical discoveries, documented in his *Flora Antarctica* 1844–47. Among his other works are *Flora of British India* 1875–97 and *Genera Plantarum* 1862–63. He was a great friend of Charles Darwin; in 1865 he succeeded his father, *William Jackson Hooker* (1785–1865), as Director of the Royal Botanic Gardens, Kew.

Hooker /'hʊkə/ Richard 1554–1600. English theologian. Born near Exeter, in 1585 he became Master of the Temple and in 1591 rector of Boscombe, near Salisbury, where he commenced *The Laws of Ecclesiastical Polity* 1594, a defence of the episcopalian system of the Church of England. He became rector of Bishopsbourne, near Canterbury, in 1595, and died there.

Hook of Holland /'hʊk əv 'hɒlənd/ (Dutch, *Hoek van Holland*, meaning 'corner of Holland') a small peninsula and village in South Holland, the Netherlands, the terminus for ferry services with Harwich and Parkeston Quay, England.

hookworm parasitic ◊roundworm *Necator* which lives in the intestines of humans when adult. The young bore in through the skin. It causes much ill health in tropical regions.

Hooper /'huːpə/ John c. 1495–1555. English Protestant reformer and martyr. Born in Somerset, he adopted Zwinglian views, was appointed bishop of Gloucester 1550, and in 1555 was burnt for heresy.

hoopoe bird *Upupa epops* in the order Coraciiformes. About the size of a mistle thrush, it has a long thin bill and a bright buff-coloured crest which expands into a fan shape as the bird alights. The wings are banded with black and white and the rest of the plumage is black, white, and buff. It is found in Europe, Asia, and Africa.

Hoover /'huːvə/ Herbert Clark 1874–1964. 31st President of the USA 1929–33. As a mining engineer he travelled widely before World War I, during which he organized relief work in occupied Europe; a talented administrator, he was subsequently associated with numerous international relief organizations, and became food administrator for the USA 1917–19. Secretary of commerce 1921–28, he then stood as a Republican and defeated the Democratic candidate for the presidency, 'Al' Smith, but lost public confidence after the stock-market crash of 1929, when he opposed direct government aid for the unemployed in the depression that followed, and in 1933 was succeeded by Roosevelt.

Hoover /'huːvə/ J(ohn) Edgar 1895–1972. American lawyer. As director of the Federal Bureau of Investigation (FBI) from 1924, he built up a powerful network for the detection of organized crime. His drive against alleged Communist activities after World War II has brought much criticism over abuse of power.

Hoover /'huːvə/ William Henry 1849–1932. American manufacturer who is best known for his association with the ◊vacuum cleaner. Threatened in his business as a leather manufacturer for carriages and wagons by the advent of the motor car, he concentrated on developing a primitive existing cleaner into an effective tool for domestic use. The Hoover vacuum cleaner soon became a generic name for the type.

Hoover dam the highest concrete dam in the USA, 221 m/726 ft, on the Colorado River at the Arizona-Nevada border. Known as Boulder Dam 1933–47, its name was restored by President Truman as Herbert Hoover's reputation revived. It has a hydroelectric power capacity of some 1,300 megawatts.

1894 introduced the imaginary Balkan state of Ruritania.

Hope /həʊp/ Bob. Stage-name of comedian Leslie Townes Hope 1904– . He was born in Britain, but taken to the USA in 1907. He has appeared in many films, including a series with Bing Crosby and Dorothy Lamour, for example, *The Road to Rio*, 1947. He has received several Special ◊Academy Awards.

Hopei /ˌhəʊˈpeɪ/ former name of ◊Hebei, a province of China.

Hope's apparatus in physics, an apparatus used to demonstrate the temperature at which water has its maximum density. It consists of a vertical cylindrical vessel fitted with horizontal thermometers through its sides near the top and bottom, and surrounded at the centre by a ledge that holds freezing mixture (ice and salt). When the cylinder is filled with water, this gradually cools, the denser water sinking to the bottom, and eventually the upper thermometer records 0°C/32°F (the freezing point of water) and the lower one has a constant reading of 4°C/39°F (the temperature at which water is densest). The apparatus is named after Thomas Charles Hope (1766–1844).

Hopewell North American Indian culture about 200 AD, noted for burial mounds up to 12 m/40 ft high, and also for Serpent Mound, ◊Ohio. See ◊moundbuilders.

Hopkins /ˈhɒpkɪnz/ Anthony 1937– . British actor. After taking up acting in 1961, he appeared on stage in *As You Like It Equus, Macbeth*, and *Pravda*; films include *All Creatures Great and Small* and *A Bridge Too Far*, and leading parts in the television series *War and Peace* and *A Married Man*.

Hopkins /ˈhɒpkɪnz/ Frederick Gowland 1861–1947. British biochemist. Professor at Cambridge from 1914 and Sir William Dunn professor 1921–43, he revolutionized the conception of the sources of muscular energy and oxidation of tissues, and did fundamental research on vitamins. In 1929 he was awarded the Nobel Prize for Medicine, and in 1935 the Order of Merit. Jacquetta ◊Hawkes is his daughter.

Hopkins /ˈhɒpkɪnz/ Gerard Manley 1844–1889. British poet. Born at Stratford, Essex, he was converted in 1866 to Roman Catholicism, and in 1868 began training as a Jesuit. He preached and ministered as a priest in Ireland and England and subsequently taught. He died of typhoid. His poetry is profoundly religious and records his struggle to gain faith and peace, but also shows great freshness of feeling and delight in nature. A complete edition (including the perhaps best-known poems, 'The Wreck of the Deutschland' 1876 and 'The Windhover' 1877) was issued by Robert Bridges in 1918. His employment of 'sprung rhythm', allied to the Old and Middle English alliterative verse, has greatly influenced later 20th-century poetry. His *Journals and Papers* were published in 1959, and three volumes of letters 1955–56.

Hopkins /ˈhɒpkɪnz/ Harry L(loyd) 1890–1946. American politician. Born in Iowa, he became in 1935 head of WPA (Works Progress Administration), which was concerned with Depression relief work. After a period as Secretary of Commerce 1938–40 he was appointed supervisor of the Lend-Lease programme in 1941, and undertook wartime missions to Britain and Russia.

hoplite in ancient Greece, a heavily-armed infantry soldier.

Hopper /ˈhɒpə/ Edward 1882–1967. American artist, whose work evoked the loneliness of big cities, particularly New York, for example, the street scene *Early Sunday Morning* 1930.

Hoppner /ˈhɒpnə/ John 1758–1810. British artist. Born in London, he was educated at the Royal Academy, and specialized in portraits, notably of the royal princesses, William ◊Pitt, Lord ◊Grenville, ◊Rodney, and ◊Nelson. He became portrait painter to the Prince of Wales in 1789 and Royal Academician in 1795.

hops female fruit-heads of the hop plant *Humulus lupulus*, family Cannabiaceae; these are dried and used as a tonic and in flavouring beer. In designated areas in Europe, no male hops may be grown, since seedless hops produced by the unpollinated female plant contain a greater proportion of alpha acid which gives beer its bitter taste.

Horace /ˈhɒrɪs/ (*Quintus Horatius Flaccus*) 65–8 BC. Roman poet. Born at Venusia, S Italy, the son of a freedman, he fought with the republicans at Philippi, lost his estate, and was reduced to poverty. Virgil introduced him about 38 to Maecenas, who gave him a small estate and procured him the friendship and patronage of

Hoover American Republican Herbert Hoover was president 1929–33 during the Depression. He was criticized for his decision to aid financial institutions and public works, leaving the unemployed masses to depend on charity.

Hoover As director of the FBI, J Edgar Hoover served under eight American presidents, and under his leadership the powers of the bureau were greatly extended.

Hoovervilles colloquial term for shanty towns built by the unemployed and destitute in the USA during the Depression 1929–33, named after the American president, Herbert ◊Hoover.

Hope /həʊp/ Anthony, pseudonym of Anthony Hope Hawkins 1863–1933. British novelist, whose romance *The Prisoner of Zenda*

Hopkins English poet Gerard Manley Hopkins, painted in 1859 by A E Hopkins. He experienced a life-long tension between being a poet and a Jesuit priest. His poetry was written in secret, and published 30 years after his death by his friend Robert Bridges.

Augustus. His *Satires*, published 35–30 BC, survey the follies of contemporary society. His lyrical poems, the *Epodes* and the four books of *Odes* (about 24–25 BC), written in a variety of metres, deal with both personal and political themes. In later life Horace wrote his *Epistles*, a series of verse letters, and the critical treatise in verse *De Arte Poetica/On the Art of Poetry*.

Hordern /'hɔːdən/ Michael 1911– . British actor, noted for such roles as Shakespeare's Lear and Prospero.

Hore-Belisha /'hɔː bə'liːʃə/ Leslie, Baron Hore-Belisha 1895–1957. British politician. A National Liberal, he was minister of transport 1934–37, introducing Belisha beacons to mark pedestrian crossings. As war minister 1937–40 he introduced peace-time conscription in 1939. He was created a peer in 1954.

horehound genus of plants (*Marrubium*) of the family Labiatae. The *white horehound Marrubium vulgare*, found in Europe, North Africa and Western Asia and naturalized in North America, has a thick hairy stem and clusters of dirty-white flowers:

horizon the distance to which one can see across the surface of the sea or a level plain, that is, about 5 km/3 mi at 1.5 m/5 ft above sea level, and about 65 km/40 mi at 300 m/1,000 ft.

hormone product of the ◊endocrine glands, concerned with control and coordination of body functions. The chief glands are the thyroid, parathyroid, pituitary, adrenal, pancreas, uterus, ovary, and testis. Hormones have been called 'chemical messengers of the blood', bringing about changes in the functions of various organs according to the body's requirements. Their combined actions and interactions are delicately balanced and closely bound up with those of the nervous system. Generally speaking, the ◊pituitary gland, at the base of the brain, is the centre for overall coordination of hormone secretion; the ◊thyroid hormones determine the rate of general body chemistry; the ◊adrenal hormones prepare the organism for stressed situations such as 'fight or flight'; and the sexual hormones such as ◊oestrogen govern reproductive functions. Most hormones are complex chemical substances, including ◊proteins and ◊peptides (such as insulin) and ◊steroids (such as testosterone). See also ◊plant hormones.

Hormuz /hɔː'muːz/ small island, 41 sq km/16 sq mi, in the *Strait of Hormuz*, belonging to Iran. It is strategically important because oil tankers leaving the Gulf for Japan and the West have to pass through the strait.

horn family of musical instruments originating in animal horns, of which the French horn is most widely used. See ◊brass.

Horn /hɔːn/ Philip de Montmorency, Count of Horn 1518–1568. Flemish politician. He held high offices under Charles V and Philip II, and from 1563 he was one of the leaders of the opposition to the rule of Cardinal Granvella and to the introduction of the Inquisition. In 1567 he was arrested together with Egmont, and both were beheaded in Brussels.

hornbeam genus *Carpinus*, of the Betulaceae family. The *common hornbeam Carpinus*

betulus is found in woods and hedges throughout the temperate parts of Europe and Asia, and is native to parts of Britain. It has a twisted stem and smooth grey bark. The leaves are oval and hairy on the undersurface. The flowers are borne in catkins, and the fruits are small nuts borne in groups.

hornbill bird of the family of Bucerotidae, found in Africa, India and Malaysia, and so called from the powerful bill surmounted by a bony growth. Hornbills nest in holes in trees.

hornet a type of ◊wasp.

hornfels a ◊metamorphic rock formed by the heating of rocks in contact with a hot ◊igneous body. It is fine-grained and brittle. Hornfels may contain minerals only formed under conditions of great heat, such as andalusite, Al_2SiO_5, and cordierite, $(Mg,Fe)_2Al_4Si_5O_{18}$. This rock, originated from sedimentary rock strata, is found in contact with large igneous ◊intrusions where it represents the heat-altered equivalent of the surrounding clays and limestones. Its hardness makes it suitable for road 'metal' and railway ballast.

Horniman /'hɔːnɪmən/ Annie Elizabeth Fredericka 1860–1937. British pioneer of repertory theatre, who subsidized the Abbey Theatre, Dublin, and founded the Manchester company; she was the daughter of Frederick Horniman (1835–1906), founder of the Horniman Museum in ◊Southwark.

Hornung /'hɔːnəŋ/ E(rnest) W(illiam) 1866–1921. British novelist, who at the prompting of Conan ◊Doyle created A J Raffles, the gentleman-burglar, and his assistant Bunny Manders in *The Amateur Cracksman* 1899.

horoscope the relative position of the stars and planets at the moment of birth, used by astrologers to forecast a person's future. See ◊astrology.

Horowitz /'hɒrəwɪts/ Vladimir 1904– . American pianist. Born in Kiev, he made his debut in the USA in 1928 with the New York Philharmonic Orchestra. He is a leading interpreter of Liszt, Schumann, and Rachmaninov.

Horrocks /'hɒrəks/ Brian Gwynne 1895–1985. British general. He served in World War I, and in World War II under Montgomery at Alamein and with the British Liberation Army in Europe.

horror a modern genre of fiction and film, devoted primarily to scaring the reader, but often also aiming at a catharsis of common fears through their exaggeration into the bizarre and grotesque. Horror is derived from the Gothic novel, which dealt in shock effects, as well as from folk tales and ghost stories throughout the ages. Dominant figures in the horror tradition are Mary Shelley (*Frankenstein* 1818), Bram Stoker, and H P Lovecraft and, among contemporary writers, Stephen King and Clive Barker. Horror writing tends to use motifs such as vampirism, the eruption of ancient evil, and monstrous transformation, which often derive from folk traditions, as well as more modern concerns such as psychopathology.

horse hoofed odd-toed grass-eating mammal, *Equus caballus* of the family Equidae (which

Horowitz Born in Kiev, Vladimir Horowitz has enjoyed world acclaim as a virtuoso pianist, particularly with his interpretations of the Romantic repertoire.

also includes zebras and asses). The *domestic horse* of Euro-Asian derivation ranges in colour through white, brown, and black. The yellow-brown *Mongolian wild horse Equus przewalskii* (named after its Polish 'discoverer' in about 1880) is the only surviving species of wild horse. Notable breeds are: the *Arab* small and agile; *thoroughbred* derived from the Arab via English mares, used in ◊horse-racing for its speed (the present stock is descended from three Arab horses introduced to Britain in the 18th century, especially the Darley Arabian); *quarter horse* used by cowboys for herding; *hackney* high-stepping harness horse; *Lippizaner* pure white horses, named after their place of origin in Yugoslavia, as used in the Spanish Riding School in ◊Vienna; *shire* largest draught horse in the world at 17 hands (descended from the medieval war horses which carried knights in armour), marked by long hair or 'feathering' round its 'ankles'; *Suffolk punch* sturdy all-round working horse.

The *Pony* combines the qualities of various types of horse with a smaller build (under 14.2 hands, or 1.47 m/58 in). Breeds include the large *Welsh cob*, the rather smaller *New Forest*, and, smaller again, the *Exmoor* and *Dartmoor*. The smallest is the hardy *Shetland* about 70 cm/27 in high, popular with children.

The *mule* is the usually sterile offspring of a female horse and male ass, and a hardy pack-animal; the *hinny* is a similarly sterile offspring of a male horse and female ass, but less useful as a beast of burden.

Horse, Master of the head of the department of the British royal household responsible for the royal stables.

horse chestnut tree *Aesculus hippocastanatum*, originally from SE Europe, but widely planted, particularly in the UK, whose fruit contains the familiar 'conker'. Several other related species may also be planted. They are not related to the true chestnut.

horse fly fly of the family Tabanidae. The females suck blood from horses, cattle, and humans. Males live on plants and suck nectar. Also known as clegs or gadflies.

Horse Guards name given to a building in Whitehall, London, England, erected in 1753 by Vardy from a design by Kent, on the site of the Tilt Yard of Whitehall palace. This spot has been occupied by the Household Cavalry or 'Horse Guards' since the Royal Horse Guards were formed in 1661.

horsepower an Imperial unit of power (hp) equivalent to 550 foot-pound force per second or 745.7 watts. It is a standard US unit equal to 746 watts.

horse racing the sport of racing mounted or driven horses. *Flat racing* is for thoroughbreds only. It was first popularized by the Stuarts; the classic English races are the Derby, first run 1780, the Oaks 1779 (both at Epsom), St Leger 1776 (at Doncaster), 2,000 Guineas 1809, and 1,000 Guineas 1814 (both at Newmarket). The Jockey Club (established in 1751) is the governing body. Other major races are the French Prix de ◊l'Arc de Triomphe 1920 (at Longchamp), the Australian Melbourne Cup 1861 (at Flemington Park, Victoria), and the US Triple Crown Kentucky Derby 1875 (at Churchill Downs, Louisville), Preakness Stakes 1873 (at Pimlico, Baltimore), and Belmont Stakes 1867 (at New York). *Steeplechasing* is a development of foxhunting, of which the *point-to-point* is the amateur version, and *hurdling* a version with only modest obstacles. The outstanding race is the Grand National 1839 (at Aintree, Liverpool) with 30 formidable jumps. The governing body in England is the National Hunt Committee. *Harness racing* is for standard-bred horses pulling a two-wheeled 'sulky' on which the driver sits.

The Derby
horse/jockey
1983 Teenoso/Lester Piggott
1984 Secreto/Christy Roche
1985 Slip Anchor/Steve Cauthen
1986 Shahrastani/Walter Swinburn
1987 Reference Point/Steve Cauthen
The Oaks
horse/jockey
1983 Sun Princess/Willie Carson
1984 Circus Plume/Lester Piggott
1985 Oh So Sharp/Steve Cauthen
1986 Midway Lady/Ray Cochrane
1987 Unite/Walter Swinburn
1,000 Guineas
horse/jockey
Grand National first held 1836 at Maghull, now run at Aintree
horse/jockey
1983 Corbiere/Ben De Haan
1984 Hallo Dandy/Neale Doughty
1985 Last Suspect/Hywel Davies
1986 West Tip/Richard Dunwoody
1987 Maori Venture/Steve Knight
Prix de L'Arc de Triomphe
horse/jockey
1983 All Along/Walter Swinburn
1984 Sagace/Yves Saint-Martin

1985 Rainbow Quest/Pat Eddery
1986 Dancing Brave/Pat Eddery
1987 Lieutenant's Lark/Robbie Davis.

horseradish hardy perennial of SE Europe *Armoracia rusticana*, but naturalized elsewhere, family ◊Cruciferae; the thick, cream-coloured root is made into a condiment to eat with meat.

horsetail plant of the class Equisetales, related to ferns and clubmosses. There are about 35 living species, bearing their spores on cones at the stem tip. The upright stems are ribbed, and often have spaced whorls of branches. Today they are of modest size, but hundreds of millions of years ago giant tree-like forms existed.

Horsham /'hɔːʃəm/ town in West Sussex, England, 26 km/16 mi SE of Guildford; population (1985) 30,000. The public school Christ's Hospital is about 3 km/2 mi to the SW.

Horsley /'hɔːzli/ John Calcott 1817–1903. English artist. Born in London, he was a skilled painter of domestic scenes. He was also responsible for the frescoes in the Houses of Parliament, and is credited with designing the first Christmas card.

Horst-Wessel-Lied /ˌhɔːst 'vesəl liːt/ song introduced by the Nazis as a second German national anthem. The text was written by Horst Wessel 1907–30, a Nazi 'martyr', to a traditional tune.

Horthy de Nagybánya /'hɔːti də 'nɒdʒbɑːnjə/ Nicholas 1868–1957. Hungarian politician. Leader of the counter-revolutionary 'White' government, he became regent in 1920, on the overthrow of the Communist Bela Kun regime by Romanian intervention. He pursued a moderate policy, trying (although allied to Hitler) to retain independence of action: in 1944 his country was taken over by the Nazis and he was deported to Germany.

horticulture the branch of ◊botany dealing with the cultivation of garden plants.

Horus /'hɔːrəs/ in ancient Egyptian mythology, the hawkheaded sun god, son of ◊Isis and ◊Osiris, of whom the pharaohs were thought to be the incarnation.

hospice a hospital which specializes in the care of those who are terminally ill. Mother Theresa in India and Cicely Saunders in the UK have pioneered this form of care.

hospital institution for the care of the sick and injured. In ancient times temples of deities such as ◊Aesculapius offered facilities for treatment, and the Church had by the 4th century founded hospitals for lepers, cripples, the blind, the sick, and the poor. The oldest surviving hospital in Europe is the 7th-century Hôtel Dieu, Paris; in Britain, the most ancient are St Bartholomew's 1123 and St Thomas's 1200; and in America the Hospital of Jesus of Nazareth, Mexico 1524. Medical knowledge advanced during the Renaissance and hospitals became increasingly secularized following the Reformation. In the 19th century further progress was made in hospital design, administration and staffing, and in the 20th century there has been a dominant trend to specialization.

In Britain hospitals have formed part of the National Health Service since 1948 and give free

treatment, but there are a number of private hospitals, nursing homes, and clinics. In the USA hospitals may be public (federal or state) or private (voluntary – non-profitmaking, and proprietary – profitmaking). From 1966 people over 65 have come under the state Medicare hospital insurance scheme, extended 1973 to needy younger people with long-term disability. Many other Americans belong to voluntary hospital insurance schemes, for example, the non-profitmaking Blue Cross 1929 and Blue Shield 1917.

host an organism that is parasitized by another. In ◊commensalism, the partner that does not benefit may also be called the host.

hostage person taken prisoner as a means of exerting pressure on a third party, usually with threats of death or injury.

HOTOL (*Horizontal Take-Off and Landing*) craft. A British concept for a hypersonic transport and satellite launcher, which could be operational before the end of the century. It will be a single-stage vehicle with no boosters and will take off and land on a runway. It will feature a revolutionary air-breathing rocket engine which will enable it to carry much less oxygen than a conventional space plane. HOTOL has an American rival known as the *Orient Express*.

hot spot in geology, a hypothetical region of high thermal activity in the Earth's ◊mantle. It is believed to be the origin of many chains of ocean islands, such as Polynesia (including Hawaii) and the Galapagos. A volcano forms on the ocean crust immediately above the hot spot, is carried away by ◊plate-tectonic movement, and becomes extinct. A new volcano forms beside it, above the hot spot. The result is an active volcano and a chain of increasingly old and eroded volcanic stumps stretching away in the direction of plate movement.

Hottentot South African people inhabiting the SW corner of the continent when Europeans first settled there. They were a pastoral people, composed of Bushmen and Bantu, who have now largely interbred with Afrikaaners and others; the Namaqua ethnic group approximates nearest to the original Hottentots. The language bears a resemblance to Bushman, and has mainly monosyllabic roots with explosive consonants which produce clicking sounds.

Houdini /huː'diːni/ Harry 1874–1926. Stage name of Erich Weiss, American escapologist and conjuror, born in Wisconsin. He attained fame by his escapes from ropes and handcuffs, and also reproduced some of the phenomena of spiritualist séances by purely mechanical means to expose fakes.

Houdon /uː'dɒŋ/ Jean Antoine 1741–1828 French sculptor. His busts of some of the greatest men of his time, Voltaire, Rousseau, Napoleon, are famous for their realism.

Hounsfield /'haunzfiːld/ Godfrey 1919– . British pioneer of ◊tomography, who shared a Nobel prize in 1979 with independent researcher Allan Cormack, a South African-born American. He was knighted in 1981.

Hounslow /'haunzləu/ borough of W Greater London

features London Airport (established 1946 at Heathrow) *Chiswick*, with the Palladian villa by ◊Burlington, and ◊Hogarth's home (now a museum); *Brentford*, reputed site of Caesar's crossing of the Thames in 54 BC, and the Duke of Northumberland's seat at Syon House, and *Isleworth*, Osterley, home of Sir Thomas ◊Gresham (both with work by ◊Adam) *population* (1981) 199,782.

Houphouët-Boigny /uːˈfweɪ bwɑːnˈjiː/ Felix 1905– . Ivory Coast politician. He held posts in French ministries, and became president of the republic on independence in 1960. He was re-elected for a sixth term in 1985.

hour a period of time comprising 3,600 seconds; 24 hours make 1 calendar day.

housefly the most common type of ◊fly.

Household, Royal see ◊Royal Household.

Houseman /ˈhaʊsmən/ John 1902– . US theatre, film, and television producer and actor, born in Romania. He collaborated with Orson ◊Welles and Nicholas ◊Ray as directors, and won an Academy Award in 1973 for his acting debut in *The Paper Chase*, which became a television series.

housing the provision of residential accommodation. Legislation in Britain began with measures passed in 1851 and the Housing of the Working Classes Act 1890. The introduction of rent control in 1915 began a long-term decline in the amount of rented accommodation, and tax relief on mortgages encourages private ownership: 14 million Britons were home-owners 1986. Flats and houses to rent (intended for people with low incomes) are also built by local authorities under the direction of the Secretary of State for Environment. In 1980 controversial legislation was introduced to enable council tenants to buy their homes, and nearly 1 million council houses had been sold 1987. All modern states have found some degree of state housing provision or subsidy essential, even in free-enterprise economies such as the USA.

Housman /ˈhaʊsmən/ A(lfred) E(dward) 1859–1936. English poet, born in Worcestershire. In 1896 he published *A Shropshire Lad*, a series of deceptively simple nostalgic ballad-like poems, many inspired by his passionate homosexual attachment to Moses Jackson. They caught the popular mood during World War I.

Houston /ˈhjuːstən/ port in Texas, USA; population (1981) 1,560,000; linked by canal to the Gulf of Mexico. It is an agricultural centre, and industries include petrochemicals, chemicals, plastics, synthetic rubber, and electronics. The Lyndon Johnson Space Centre is nearby, hence its nickname 'Space City'. It was named after Sam ◊Houston.

Houston /ˈhjuːstən/ Sam 1793–1863. American general who won Texan independence from Mexico; Houston, Texas, is named after him.

Hove /həʊv/ seaside resort in East Sussex, England, adjoining Brighton; population (1981) 66,612.

Hovell, /ˈhɒvəl/ William Hilton 1786–1875. Explorer of Australia with Hamilton ◊Hume.

hovercraft a vehicle that rides on a cushion of high-pressure air, free from all contact with the surface beneath. Although hovercraft need a smooth terrain when operating overland, it need not be metalled, and snow and ice present no difficulties. At present hovercraft are best adapted to use on lakes, sheltered coastal waters, river estuaries and swamps, and places where harbours have not been established.

British engineer Christopher Cockerell invented the hovercraft in 1959, when he demonstrated the SR-N1. The first experimental hovercraft passenger ferry service, between Rhyl and Wallasey, was operated in the summer of 1962. Today large hovercraft (SR-N4) operate a swift car-ferry service across the English Channel, taking only about 35 minutes between Dover and Calais. They are fitted with a flexible 'skirt' that helps maintain the air cushion.

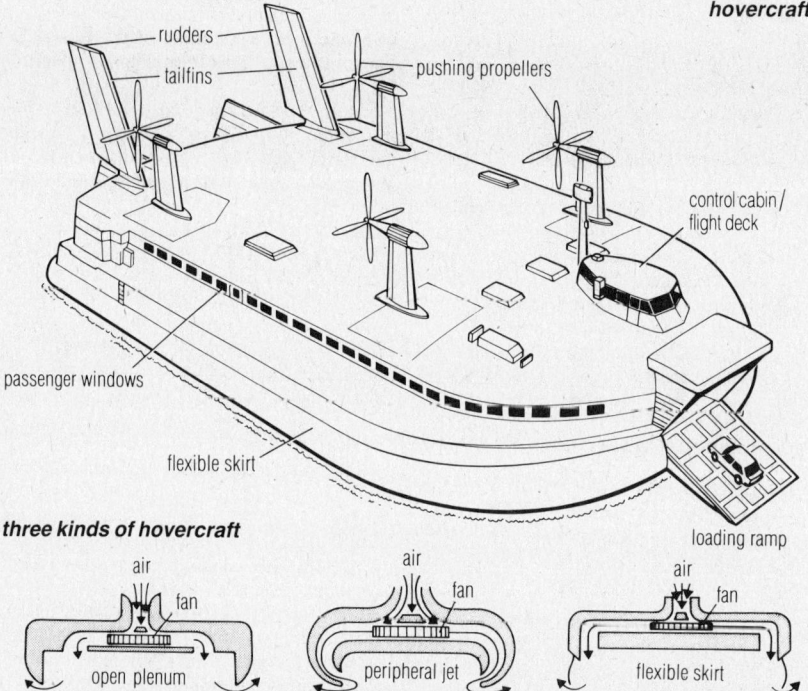

hovercraft

rudders

tailfins

pushing propellers

control cabin / flight deck

passenger windows

flexible skirt

loading ramp

three kinds of hovercraft

air — fan — open plenum

air — fan — peripheral jet

air — fan — flexible skirt

Howard /ˈhaʊəd/ Alan 1937– . British actor, noted for his roles with the Royal Shakespeare Company which include *Henry V*, *Henry VI*, *Coriolanus*, and *Richard III*.

Howard /ˈhaʊəd/ Catherine c. 1520–1542. Queen consort of ◊Henry VIII of England from 1540. In 1541 ◊Cranmer accused her of unchastity before marriage to Henry, and she was beheaded when Cranmer made further charges of adultery.

Howard /ˈhaʊəd/ Charles, 2nd Baron Howard of Effingham and 1st Earl of Nottingham 1536–1624. English admiral, a cousin of Queen Elizabeth, he commanded the fleet against the Armada while Lord High Admiral 1585–1618; and co-operated with the Earl of Essex in the attack on Cádiz in 1596.

Howard /ˈhaʊəd/ Constance 1919– . British embroiderer, born in Northampton. She was influential in the revival of creative work that followed World War II. Her work included framed pictures with fabrics outlined in bold black threads.

Howard /ˈhaʊəd/ Ebenezer 1850–1928. British town planner and founder of the ideal of the ◊Garden City, through his book *Tomorrow* 1898 (republished as *Garden Cities of Tomorrow* in 1902).

Howard /ˈhaʊəd/ John 1726–1790. British philanthropist. On his appointment as high sheriff for Bedford county in 1773, he undertook a tour of English prisons which led to two acts of parliament in 1774, making gaolers salaried officers and setting standards of cleanliness. After touring Europe in 1775 he published his *State of the Prisons in England and Wales, with an account of some Foreign Prisons* 1777. He died of typhus fever while visiting Russian military hospitals at Kherson in the Crimea. The *Howard League for Penal Reform* 1866 exists to continue his work.

Howard /ˈhaʊəd/ Leslie. Stage-name of British film actor Leslie Stainer 1893–1943. Star of *The Scarlet Pimpernel* 1935, *Pygmalion* 1938, and *Gone with the Wind* 1939.

Howard /ˈhaʊəd/ Trevor (Wallace) 1916–1988. British film actor, whose work ranged from the quiet impact of *Brief Encounter* 1945, to the bravura of *Conduct Unbecoming* 1975.

Howe /haʊ/ Elias 1819–1867. American who in 1846 invented a ◊sewing machine using double thread.

Howe /haʊ/ Geoffrey 1926– . British Conservative politician. Under Heath he was solicitor-general 1970–72 and minister for trade 1972–74; as chancellor of the Exchequer 1979–83 under Thatcher, he put into practice the monetarist policy which reduced inflation at the cost of a rise in unemployment. In 1983 he became foreign secretary.

Howe /haʊ/ Julia Ward 1819–1910. American feminist and anti-slavery campaigner, who in 1862 wrote the 'Battle Hymn of the Republic', sung to the tune of 'John Brown's Body'.

Howe /haʊ/ Richard Earl 1726–1799. British admiral. He cooperated with his brother William against the Americans in the War of Independence, and was in command 1792–6 against the French, winning the victory of the Glorious First of June in 1794 off Ushant.

Howe /haʊ/ William, 5th Viscount Howe 1729–1814. British general, brother of Richard. In the American War of Independence he won the Battle of Bunker Hill in 1775, and as commander-in-chief in America 1776–78, captured New York, and defeated Washington at Brandywine and Germantown. He resigned in protest at lack of home government support.

howitzer an artillery weapon in use since the 16th century for the steep angle of its projectile's descent in sieges, and much developed in World War I for demolishing the fortresses of the trench system. The multi-national NATO FH70 field howitzer is mobile, with its own engine, and fires under computer control three 43 kg/95 lb shells at 32 km/20 mi range in 15 seconds.

Howrah /ˈhaʊrə/ city of West Bengal, India, on the right bank of the Hooghli, opposite Calcutta; population (1981) 742,298. The capital of Howrah district, it has jute and cotton factories, rice, flour, and saw mills, chemical factories, and engineering works. Howrah suspension bridge, opened in 1943, spans the river.

Hoxha /ˈhɒdʒə/ Enver 1908–1985. Albanian politician. Once a schoolmaster, he founded the Albanian Communist Party in 1941, and headed the liberation movement of 1939–44. He was prime minister 1944–54, combining with foreign affairs 1946–53, and from 1954 was first secretary of the Albanian Party of Labour. In policy he was a Stalinist, and independent of both Chinese and Soviet Communism.

Hoyle /hɔɪl/ Fred(erick) 1915– . British astronomer, pioneer worker on the evolution of stars and the formation of chemical elements. Born in Bingley, Yorkshire, he studied at Cambridge, where in 1948 he joined with Hermann Bondi and Thomas Gold in developing the steady state theory of ◊cosmology, which suggested that matter is continuously created in the Universe. In 1957, with Geoffrey and Margaret Burbidge and William Fowler, he showed that chemical elements heavier than hydrogen and helium are built up by nuclear reactions inside stars. He has created controversy by suggesting, with Chandra Wickramasinghe, that life originates in the gas clouds of space and is delivered to the Earth and planets by passing comets (*Lifecloud*, 1978). He was knighted in 1972.

Hoyle British astronomer Professor Fred Hoyle is popularly known for his radio talks and science fiction novels. In academic circles he is renowned for his contribution to cosmological theory.

Hsuan Tung name adopted by Henry ◊Pu Yi on becoming emperor of China in 1908.

Hua /ˈhwɑː ˌgwəʊˈfʌŋ/ Guofeng (formerly Hua Kuofeng) 1920– . Chinese politician, leader of the Chinese Communist Party (CCP) 1976–81, premier 1976–80. Hua, born in Shanxi into a peasant family, fought under ◊Zhu De during the liberation war of 1937–49. He entered the Chinese Communist Party (CCP) Central Committee in 1969 and the Politburo in 1973. An orthodox, loyal Maoist, Hua was selected to succeed ◊Zhou Enlai as prime minister in Jan 1976 and became party leader on ◊Mao Zedong's death in Sept 1976. He dominated Chinese politics during 1976–77, seeking economic modernization without major structural reform. From 1978 he was gradually eclipsed by ◊Deng Xiaoping; he was replaced as prime minister by ◊Zhao Ziyang in Sept 1980 and as CCP chair by ◊Hu Yaobang in Jun 1981. Hua was ousted from the Politburo in Sept 1982, but remains a member of the CCP Central Committee.

Huambo /ˈwɑːmbəʊ/ town in central Angola; population (1973) 18,000. It was founded in 1912, and known as Nova Lisboa 1928–73, when it was designated by the Portuguese as the future capital. It is an agricultural centre, with railway repair shops and an airport.

Huang He /ˈhwæŋ ˈhəʊ/ river in China (formerly Hwang-ho), which gained its name (meaning 'yellow river') from its muddy waters; length 4,410 km/2,740 mi. Formerly known as 'China's sorrow' because of disastrous floods, it is now largely controlled through hydroelectric works and flood barriers.

Huangshan Mountains /ˌhwæŋˈʃɑːn/ mountains in S Anhui province, China; the highest peak is Lotus Flower 1,873 m/5,106 ft.

Huáscar /ˈwɑːskə/ c. 1495–1532. King of the ◊Incas, he shared the throne with his half brother ◊Atahualpa from 1525, but the latter overthrew and murdered him.

Huáscaran /ˌwɑːskəˈrɑːn/ extinct volcano in the Andes, the highest mountain in Peru, 6,768 m/22,205 ft.

Hubbard /ˈhʌbəd/ L(afayette) Ron(ald) 1911–1986. American science fiction writer of the 1930s–1940s, founder in 1954 of ◊Scientology.

Hubble /ˈhʌbəl/ Edwin Powell 1889–1953. American astronomer, who discovered the existence of other galaxies outside our own, classified them according to their shape, and proposed the expansion of the ◊Universe, since confirmed. Born in Marshfield, Missouri, Hubble originally studied law before joining ◊Yerkes Observatory in 1914, subsequently moving to Mount Wilson where in 1923, using the 2.5 m/100 in telescope, he discovered ◊Cepheid variable stars outside our own Galaxy. In 1925 he introduced the classification of galaxies as spirals, barred spiral and ellipticals (see ◊galaxy). In 1929 he announced *Hubble's law*, that is, that the galaxies are moving apart at a rate that increases with their distance.

Hubble's constant in astronomy, a measure of the rate at which the Universe is expanding, named after Edwin ◊Hubble. Modern observations suggest that galaxies are moving apart at a rate of between 50 and 100 km/30 to 60 mi per second for every million parsecs of distance. This would mean that the Universe, which began at one place in the ◊Big Bang, is between 10,000 million and 20,000 million years old.

Hubei /ˌhuːˈbeɪ/ province of central China (formerly Hupei), through which flow the Chang Jiang and its tributary the Han Shui; area 187,500 sq km/72,375 sq mi; population (1982) 47,804,150. The capital is Wuhan. In the west the land is high, the Chang breaking through from Sichuan in gorges, but elsewhere the province is low-lying fertile land, and there are many lakes. In summer rice and cotton are grown, and in winter cereals, beans, and vegetables.

huckleberry name for berry-bearing bush of the genus ◊*Vaccinium*, including the *bilberry Vaccinium myrtillus* in Britain, and various blueberries in the USA.

Huddersfield /ˈhʌdəzfiːld/ industrial town in West Yorkshire, on the Colne, linked by canal with Manchester and other north of England centres; population (1981) 123,888. A village in Anglo-Saxon times, it was a thriving centre of woollen manufacture by the end of the 18th century.

Hudson /ˈhʌdsən/ river of the USA; length 485 km/300 mi. First reached by European settlers in 1524, it was explored in 1609 by Henry

◊Hudson, and named after him; New York stands at its mouth.

Hudson A festival gathering of old sailing ships on the Hudson River, New York.

Hudson /'hʌdsən/ Henry died 1611. English explorer. Under the auspices of the Muscovy Company in 1607 and 1608 he made unsuccessful attempts to reach China by way of the NE passage along the north of Asia. In 1609 he was commissioned by the Dutch East India Company, and in Sept reached New York Bay and sailed 240 km/150 mi up the river which now bears his name. In 1610 he sailed from London in the *Discovery* and entered what is now the Hudson Strait. The ship was icebound for the winter in the present Hudson Bay. Next spring some of the crew mutinied, and Hudson and eight others were turned adrift.

Hudson /'hʌdsən/ W(illiam) H(enry) 1841–1922. Anglo-American author. Born at Florencio near Buenos Aires, of American parents, he was inspired by recollections of early days in Argentina to write his romances *The Purple Land* 1885 and *Green Mansions* 1904, and his autobiographical *Far Away and Long Ago* 1918. In 1900 he became British by naturalization. He wrote several books on the English countryside, for example, *Nature in Down-Land* 1900 and *A Shepherd's Life* 1910.

Hudson Bay /'hʌdsən/ inland sea of NE Canada, linked with the Atlantic by **Hudson Strait**, and with the Arctic by Foxe Channel; area 1,233 sq km/476,000 sq mi. It is named after Henry ◊Hudson.

Hudson's Bay Company a chartered company founded by Prince Rupert in 1670 to trade in furs with the North American Indians. In 1783 the rival North-West Fur Company was formed, but in 1851 this became amalgamated with the Hudson's Bay Company which lost its monopoly in 1859. It is still Canada's biggest fur company, but today also sells general merchandise, and has oil and natural-gas interests.

Hue /huː'eɪ/ town in southern Vietnam, formerly capital of Annam (Central Vietnam), 13 km/8 mi from the China Sea; population (1973) 209,043. The Citadel, within which is the Imperial City enclosing the palace of the former emperor, lies to the west of the Old City on the north bank of the Huong (Perfume) River; the New City, including the university, is on the south bank. Hue was once an architecturally beautiful cultural and religious centre, but large areas were devastated, with many casualties, during the *Battle of Hue* 31 Jan–24 Feb 1968, when US and South Vietnamese forces retook the city after Vietcong occupation by infiltration.

Huelva /'welvə/ port in Andalusia, SW Spain, near the mouth of the Odiel, capital of Huelva province; population (1981) 127,822. Columbus began and ended his voyage to America at nearby Palos de la Frontera.

Huesca /'weskə/ capital of Huesca province in Aragon, northern Spain, with the former palace of the kings of Aragon; population (1981) 41,455.

Huggins /'hʌgɪnz/ William 1824–1910. British astonomer. He built a private observatory at Tulse Hill, London, in 1856, where he embarked on research in spectrum analysis that marked the beginning of astrophysics: he was also a pioneer in photographic astronomy. Knighted in 1897, he was awarded the Order of Merit in 1902.

Hughes /hjuːz/ Howard 1905–1976. American tycoon. Inheriting wealth from his father, who had patented a successful oil-drilling bit, he created a legendary financial empire. A skilled pilot, he manufactured and designed aircraft, and made the classic film *Hell's Angels* about airmen of World War I: later successes include *Scarface* and *The Outlaw*. From his middle years he was a recluse.

Hughes /hjuːz/ Richard (Arthur Warren) 1900–1976. British author, chiefly known for his study of childhood, *High Wind in Jamaica* 1929, and the trilogy *The Human Predicament* 1961–73.

Hughes /hjuːz/ Ted 1930– . British poet, Poet Laureate from 1984. He was born in Mytholmroyd, West Yorkshire. His work includes *The Hawk in the Rain* 1957, *Lupercal* 1960, *Wodwo* 1967, and *River* 1983, and is characterized by its harsh portrayal of the crueller aspects of nature. In 1956 he married the poet Sylvia ◊Plath.

Hughes /hjuːz/ Thomas 1822–1896. British author, chiefly remembered for his children's book *Tom Brown's School Days* 1857, a story of Rugby under Thomas ◊Arnold.

Hughes /hjuːz/ William Morris 1864–1952. Australian politician. Born in London, he emigrated to Australia in 1884, and in 1915 succeeded Fisher as prime minister, proving a vigorous war leader. Originally Labor, he headed a national Cabinet. He represented Australia at Versailles, resigned in 1923, but held many other Cabinet posts 1934–41. His dominant personality provoked strong reactions from colleagues and opponents.

Hugo /'hjuːgəʊ/ Victor (Marie) 1802–1885. French poet, novelist, and dramatist, born at Besançon, son of one of Napoleon's generals. His *Odes et poésies diverses* appeared in 1822, and his verse play *Hernani* 1830 established him as the leader of French Romanticism. More volumes of grandiloquent verse followed between his series of dramatic novels which included

Hughes Ted Hughes, who succeeded John Betjeman as British Poet Laureate.

Hughes The Australian prime minister William Morris Hughes (right), seen here with P G Stewart, was one of the most controversial Australian politicians.

Notre Dame de Paris 1831 and *Les Misérables* 1862, and another play *Ruy Blas* 1838. Banished in 1851 for opposing Louis Napoleon's coup d'état, he lived in Guernsey until the fall of the empire in 1870, later becoming a senator.

Huguenot French Protestant (mainly Calvinist) in the 16th century. Severely persecuted under Francis I and Henry II, the Huguenots survived both the Massacre of St Bartholomew on 24 Aug 1572 (when numbers were killed by the order of ◊Catherine de' ◊Medici) and the religious wars of the next 30 years. In 1598 Henry IV (himself formerly a Huguenot) granted them toleration under the Edict of Nantes. They lost military power after the revolt at La Rochelle 1627–29, but were still tolerated by Richelieu and ◊Mazarin. Louis XIV, however, revoked the Edict, attempted their forcible conversion, and 400,000 emigrated (taking their industrial skills with them), 40,000 settling in England, where their descendants include David Garrick and Samuel Courtauld.

Huhehot former name of ◊Hohhot, a city in Inner Mongolia.

Hull /hʌl/ city and port (officially *Kingston upon Hull*), administrative headquarters of Humberside, England; population (1981) 268,100. It is linked with the south bank of the estuary by the Humber Bridge. Industries include fish processing (fishmeal and fish fingers, with imported fish), vegetable oils, flour milling, and aircraft. There are ferries to Rotterdam and Zeebrugge.

Hull /hʌl/ Cordell 1871–1955. American politician. Born in Tennessee, he was a member of Congress 1907–33, and, as Roosevelt's secretary of state 1933–44, was identified with the 'good neighbour' policy, and opposed German and Japanese aggression. In his last months of office he paved the way for an international security system and was called 'father' of the United Nations. He was awarded the Nobel Peace Prize in 1945.

Hulme /hjuːm/ Keri 1947– . New Zealand novelist. She won the Booker Prize with her first novel *The Bone People* 1985.

Hulme /hjuːm/ Thomas Edward 1881–1917. British philosopher, critic and poet. He was killed on active service in the World War I, but his *Speculations* 1924 influenced T S ◊Eliot, and his few poems influenced the ◊Imagist movement.

human body the physical structure of the human being. It develops from the single cell of the fertilized ◊ovum, is born at 40 weeks, and usually reaches sexual maturity between 12 and 18 years of age.

The bony framework (◊skeleton) consists of more than 200 ◊bones, over half of which are in the hands and feet. The ◊skull is mounted on the spinal column, or ◊spine, a chain of 24 vertebrae. The ◊ribs, 12 on each side, are articulated (jointed) to the spinal column behind, and the upper 7 meet the breast-bone (sternum) in front. The lower end of the spine rests on the pelvic girdle, composed of the triangular sacrum, to which are attached the hip-bones (ilia), which are fused in front. Below the sacrum is the tail-bone (coccyx). The shoulder blades (scapulae) are held in place behind the upper ribs by muscles, and connected in front to the breast-bone by the two collar-bones (clavicles). Each carries a cup (glenoid cavity) into which fits the upper end of the arm-bone (humerus). This articulates below with the two forearm-bones, the radius and the ulna. The radius is articulated at the wrist to the bones of the hand.

The upper end of each thigh-bone (femur) fits into a depression in the hip-bone (acetabulum); its lower end is articulated at the knee to the shin bone (tibia) and calf bone (fibula), which are articulated at the ankle to the bones of the foot. Bones are held together by ◊joints (articulations). Some, but not all, of these allow movement of one bone on the other. At a moving joint the end of each bone is formed of tough, smooth ◊cartilage, lubricated by ◊synovial fluid. Points of special stress are reinforced by bands of fibrous tissue (◊ligaments).

Movements of the body, whether of bones or of organs, are produced by ◊muscles. Muscles are bundles of fibres wrapped in thin, tough layers of connective tissue (fascia); these are usually prolonged at the ends into strong, white cords (◊tendons, sinews) or sheets (aponeuroses), which connect the muscles to bones and organs, and through which the muscles do their work. Membranes of connective tissue also wrap the organs and line the interior cavities of the body. The blood vessels of the ◊circulatory system, branching into multitudes of very fine tubes (◊capillaries), supply all parts of the muscles and organs with blood, which carries oxygen and food necessary for life. The food passes out of the blood to the cells in a clear fluid (◊lymph); this returns with waste matter through a system of lymphatic vessels to the large ◊veins below the collar-bones and thence to the ◊heart. Capillaries join together to form veins which return blood, depleted of oxygen, to the heart. A finely branching ◊nervous system regulates the function of the muscles and organs, and makes their needs known to the controlling centres in the ◊central nervous system, which consists of the ◊brain and ◊spinal cord. The former is located in the ◊skull, the latter in the spinal column. The inner spaces of the brain and the cord contain cerebro-spinal fluid. The body processes are regulated both by the nervous system and by ◊hormones secreted by the endocrine glands.

The upper part of the trunk, enclosed by the ribs (◊thorax), contains the ◊lungs and the heart. The thorax has a stout muscular floor, the diaphragm, which with the rib muscles expands and contracts the lungs in the act of breathing. The part of the trunk below the diaphragm, the abdomen, contains the ◊digestive system (stomach and intestines), the ◊liver, ◊spleen and ◊pancreas, the ◊urinary system (kidneys, ureters and bladder), and, in the woman, the reproductive organs (◊ovaries, ◊uterus, and vagina). In the man the prostate gland and seminal vesicles only of the reproductive system are situated in the abdomen, the ◊testes or testicles being housed in the scrotum, which, with the ◊penis, is suspended in front of and below the abdomen. The bladder empties through a small channel (urethra); this in the female opens in the upper end of the vulval cleft, which also contains the opening of the vagina, or birth canal. In the male the urethra is continued into the penis. In both sexes the lower bowel terminates in the anus, a ring of strong muscle situated between the buttocks.

Cavities of the body that open on to the surface are coated with ◊mucous membrane, which secretes a lubricating fluid (mucus). The exterior

suface of the body is coated with ◊skin. Within the skin are the sebaceous glands, which secrete sebum, an oily fluid that makes the skin soft and pliable, and the sweat glands, which secrete water and various salts. From the skin grow hair, chiefly on the head, in the armpits, and around the sexual organs; and nails shielding the tips of the fingers and toes; both these structures are modifications of skin tissue. The skin also contains ◊nerves of touch, pain, heat and cold.

The human body derives energy from the combination of carbon compounds, supplied in the food, with oxygen supplied in the air.

The human digestive system is non-specialized, that is, it can break down a wide variety of foodstuffs. Food is mixed with saliva in the mouth by chewing and is swallowed. It enters the ◊stomach, where it is gently churned for some time and mixed with acidic gastric juice. It then passes into the small ◊intestine. In the first part of this, the duodenum, it is broken down further by the juice of the pancreas and duodenal glands, and mixed with ◊bile from the liver, which splits up the fat. The jejunum and ileum continue the work of digestion and absorb nutritive substances from the food. The large intestine (◊colon) completes the process and reabsorbs water into the body, and ejects the useless residue as faeces. The body, to be healthy, must contain water and various salts in the right proportions; see ◊osmoregulation. The blood is therefore filtered in the two kidneys, which remove excess water and salts. These, with a yellow pigment derived from bile, are the urine, which passes down through two fine tubes (ureters) into the bladder, a reservoir, from which the urine is emptied at intervals (micturition) through the urethra.

Heat is constantly generated by the combustion of food in the muscles and glands, and dissipated through the skin by conduction and evaporation of sweat, through the lungs in the expired air, and in the other excreted substances. Average body temperature is about 38°C/100°F (37°C/98.4°F in the mouth), maintained by a nerve centre in the brain, which regulates the activity of the skin and lungs: see ◊homeothermy. See also ◊human species.

Human Rights, Universal Declaration of (by the United Nations in 1948). They include the right to life, liberty, education, and equality before the law; to freedom of movement, religion, association, and information; and to a nationality. Under the European Convention of Human Rights of 1950, the Council of Europe established the *European Commission of Human Rights* (headquarters in Strasbourg), which investigates complaints by states or individuals, and whose findings are examined by the *European Court of Human Rights* (established 1959), whose compulsory jurisdiction has been recognized by a number of states including the UK.

human species, origins of evolution of modern humans from ancestral ◊primates. The African apes (gorilla and chimpanzee) are shown by anatomical and molecular comparisons to be our closest living relatives. The date of the split between the human and African ape lines is not known from fossil finds, but molecular clock

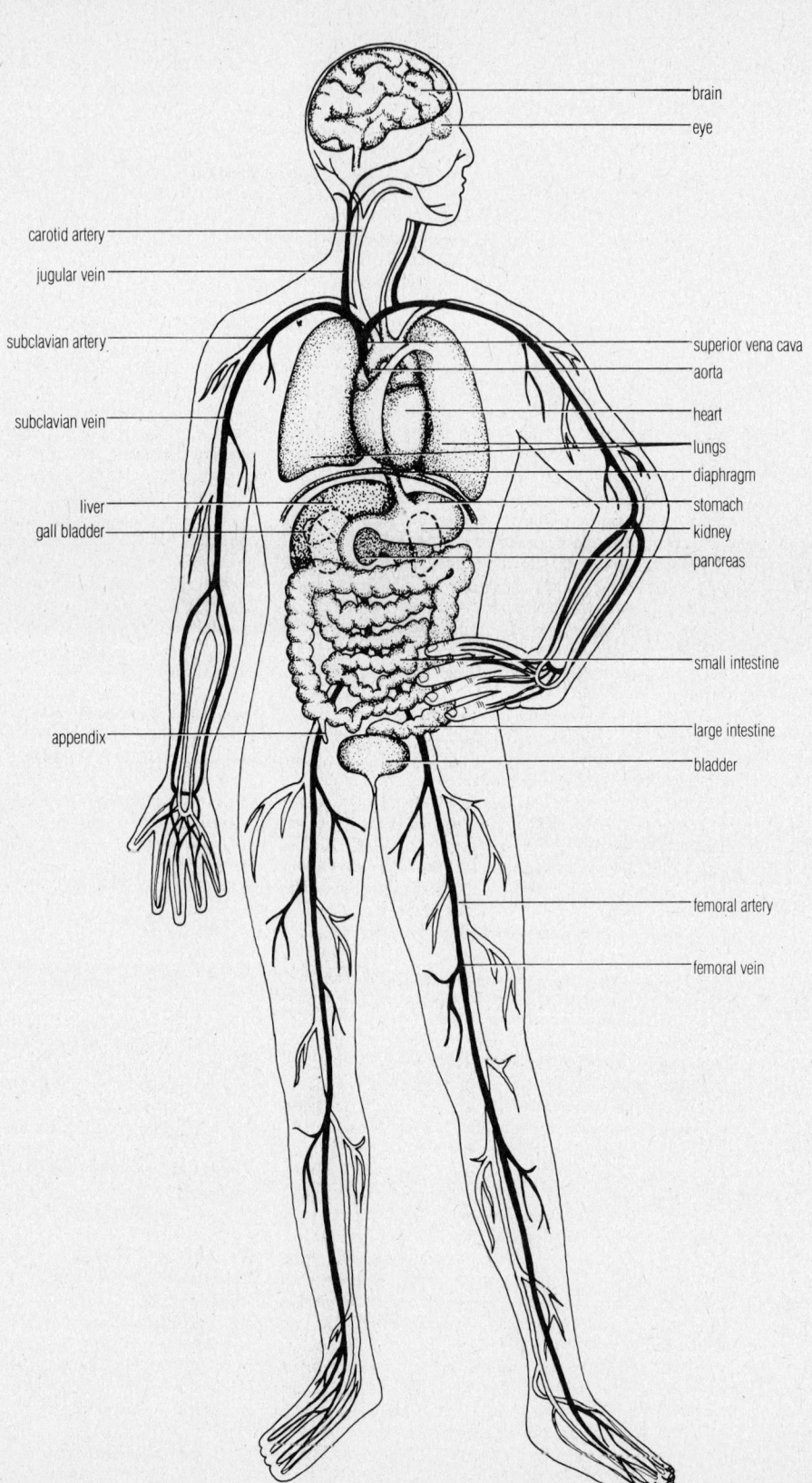

human body

brain

eye

carotid artery

jugular vein

subclavian artery

subclavian vein

liver

gall bladder

appendix

superior vena cava

aorta

heart

lungs

diaphragm

stomach

kidney

pancreas

small intestine

large intestine

bladder

femoral artery

femoral vein

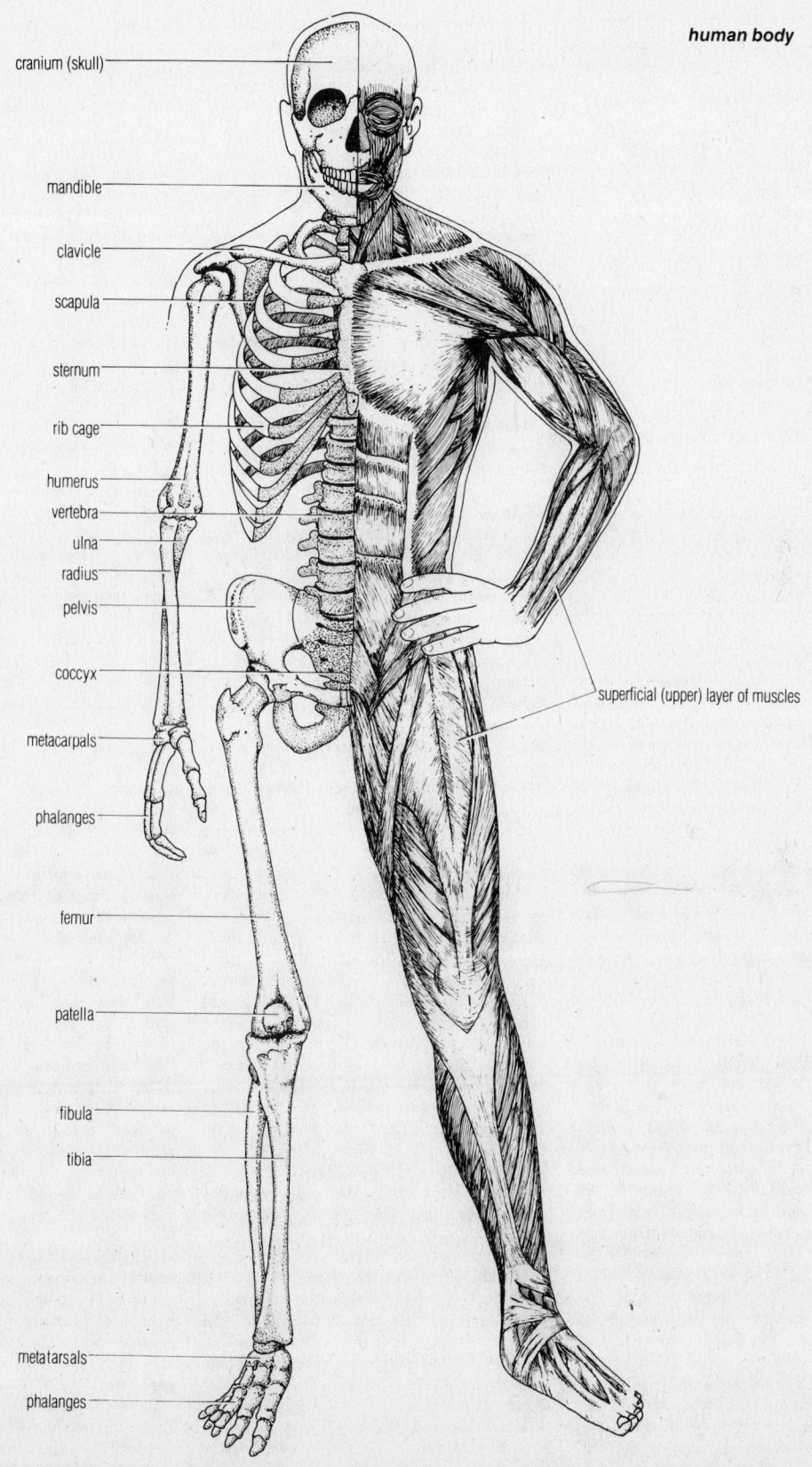

cranium (skull)

mandible

clavicle

scapula

sternum

rib cage

humerus

vertebra

ulna

radius

pelvis

coccyx

metacarpals

phalanges

femur

patella

fibula

tibia

metatarsals

phalanges

superficial (upper) layer of muscles

HUMAN BODY: COMPOSITION BY WEIGHT

Class	Chemical/element or substance	% body weight
As pure elements or as minerals, salts, and so on	Oxygen	65
	Carbon	18
	Hydrogen	10
	Nitrogen	3
	Calcium	2
	Phosphorus	1.1
	Inorganic molecules	1
	Potassium	0.35
	Sulphur	0.25
	Sodium	0.15
	Chlorine	0.15
	Magnesium, Iron, Manganese, Copper, Iodine, Cobalt, Zinc	Traces
As water and solid matter	Water	60–80
	Total solid material	20–40
As organic molecules	Protein	15–20
	Lipid	3–20
	Carbohydrate	1–15
	Small organic molecules	0–1

studies put it at 5 to 10 million years ago or more. There are no ape or *hominid* (of the human group) fossils from this period. The oldest known hominid remains date from 3.5 million years ago, from Ethiopia and Tanzania. They show hominids were already walking upright at this time. There is disagreement over the status of these creatures, known as *Australopithecus afarensis*. Some believe they were our direct ancestors, other that they were an off-shoot of the line that led to modern humans. The first stone tools date from about a million years later, probably made by the hominid *Homo habilis*, who had a slightly larger body and brain than *Australopithecus afarensis*. Other *Australopithecus* hominids, among them *Australopithecus robustus* and *Australopithecus gracilis*, lived in Africa at the same time as *Homo habilis*, but these are not generally considered to be our ancestors. Over 1.5 million years ago a new hominid species, *Homo erectus*, with a much larger brain, appeared in Africa. It is not clear if *Homo habilis* evolved from *Australopithecus afarensis*, but it is generally believed that *Homo erectus* evolved from *Homo habilis*. The erectus people were probably the first to use fire, and the first to move out of Africa. Their remains are found as far afield as China, Spain and southern Britain. Modern humans, *Homo sapiens sapiens*, and the Neanderthals *Homo sapiens neanderthalensis*, are probably descended from *Homo erectus*. Neanderthals were large-brained but heavily-built, probably adapted to the cold conditions of the ice ages. They lived in Europe and the Middle East, and died out about 40,000 years ago, leaving *Homo sapiens sapiens* as the only remaining species of the hominid group.

Humber bridge completed 1980, when it was the ◊bridge with the world's longest span, 1,410 m/4,626 ft. It is a suspension bridge with twin towers 163 m/533 ft high, and spans the estuary of the river Humber in NE England.

Humberside /'hʌmbəsaɪd/ NE county of England
area 3,512 sq km/1,356 sq mi
towns administrative headquarters Beverley; Hull, Grimsby, Scunthorpe, Goole, Cleethorpes
features ◊Humber Bridge; fertile Holderness peninsula
products petrochemicals and refined oil; processed fish; cereals, root crops, cattle
population (1981) 847,666
famous people Amy Johnson, Andrew Marvell, John Wesley.

Humbert /'hʌmbət/ anglicized form of ◊Umberto, name of two kings of Italy.

Humboldt /'hʌmbəʊlt/ Friedrich Heinrich Alexander, Baron von Humboldt 1769–1859. German botanist and geologist, born in Berlin. He explored the regions of the Orinoco and the Amazon, 1800–04, and gathered 60,000 plant specimens. One of the first popularizers of science, his published works include *Cosmos* 1845–62, an account of the physical sciences.

Humboldt /'hʌmbəʊlt/ Wilhelm 1767–1835. German philologist, brother of Friedrich ◊Humboldt. His stress on the identity of thought and language influenced ◊Chomsky.

Humboldt Current /'hʌmbəʊlt/ former name of ◊Peru ocean current.

Hume /hjuːm/ Basil, Cardinal Hume. 1923– . British Roman Catholic cleric. He was born in Newcastle upon Tyne, and became a Benedictine monk. He was abbot of Ampleforth in Yorkshire 1963–76, and in 1976 succeeded Heenan as Archbishop of Westminster, the first monk to hold the office. He was also made Cardinal in 1976.

Hume /hjuːm/ David 1711–1776. Scottish moral and political philosopher a figure of the ◊Enlightenment. His *History of Great Britain* 1754–62 was very popular within his own lifetime but his indifferently-received philosophical work *A Treatise of Human Nature* 1740 has proved to be a lasting stimulus. He shared many of the beliefs of the 'British ◊Empiricist' School, especially ◊Locke (see ◊empiricism). *Hume's Law* in moral philosophy states that it is never possible to deduce statements about what one ought to do, purely from those about what is the case.

Hume /hjuːm/ Fergus 1859–1932. British writer. Educated in New Zealand, he returned to his native England in 1888; his *Mystery of a Hansom Cab* 1887 was one of the first popular detective stories.

Hume /hjuːm/ Hamilton 1797–1873. Australian explorer. Born in the country, he headed an expedition from Sydney in 1824 in company with William ◊Hovell, which discovered the Murray river, and reached Port Phillip. The Melbourne-Sydney *Hume Highway* is named after him.

Hume /hjuːm/ Joseph 1777–1855. British Radical politician. Born at Montrose, he went out to India as an army surgeon in 1797, made a

fortune, and on his return bought a seat in parliament. In 1818 he secured election as a Philosophic Radical and supported many progressive measures.

humidity the quantity of water vapour in a given volume of the atmosphere (absolute humidity), or the ratio of the amount of water vapour in the atmosphere to the saturation value at the same temperature (relative humidity); at dew-point the latter is 100%. Relative humidity is measured by various types of *hygrometer*.

hummingbird name given to many birds forming the family Trochilidae and found in America. They derive their name from the sound produced by the rapid vibration of their wings, and are the only birds able to fly backwards. They are brilliantly coloured, and have a long tongue with which they obtain nectar from flowers and capture insects. The Cuban *bee hummingbird Mellisuga helenae* is the world's smallest bird at 5.5 cm/2 in long, and weighs 2 g/less than 1/10 oz.

humours, theory of theory prevalent in classical and medieval times that the human body was composed of four kinds of humour: phlegm, blood, choler or yellow bile, and melancholy or black bile. Different human characteristics could be accounted for by a different balance of humours in an individual.

Humperdinck /'hʊmpədɪŋk/ Engelbert 1854–1921. German composer. Born at Siegburg, he studied music in Munich and in Italy and assisted Richard◊Wagner at Bayreuth. Fame came to him with his musical fairy operas, *Hänsel und Gretel* 1893, *Königskinder/King's Children* 1910, and others.

humus component of ◊soil consisting of decomposed or partly decomposed organic matter, dark in colour and usually richer towards the surface. It has a higher carbon content than the original material and a lower nitrogen content, and is an important source of minerals in soil fertility.

Hun a member of any of a number of nomad Mongol peoples who first appeared in history in the 2nd century BC raiding across the Great Wall into China. They entered Europe about 372 AD, settled in Hungary, and imposed their supremacy on the Ostrogoths and other Germanic peoples. Under the leadership of Attila they attacked the Eastern Empire, invaded Gaul, and threatened Rome, but after his death in 453 their power was broken by a revolt of their subject peoples. The White Huns or Ephthalites, a kindred people, raided Persia and N India in the 5th–6th centuries.

Hunan /ˌhuːˈnæn/ province of S central China
area 210,500 sq km/81,253 sq mi
capital Changsha
features Dongting Lake; Shaoshan village, where ◊Mao Zedong was born
products rice, tea, tobacco, cotton; non-ferrous minerals
population (1982) 54,008,851.

hundred a subdivision of a shire, once used in England, Ireland, and parts of the USA. Originally the area occupied by 100 families or equalling 100 hides (one hide being the amount

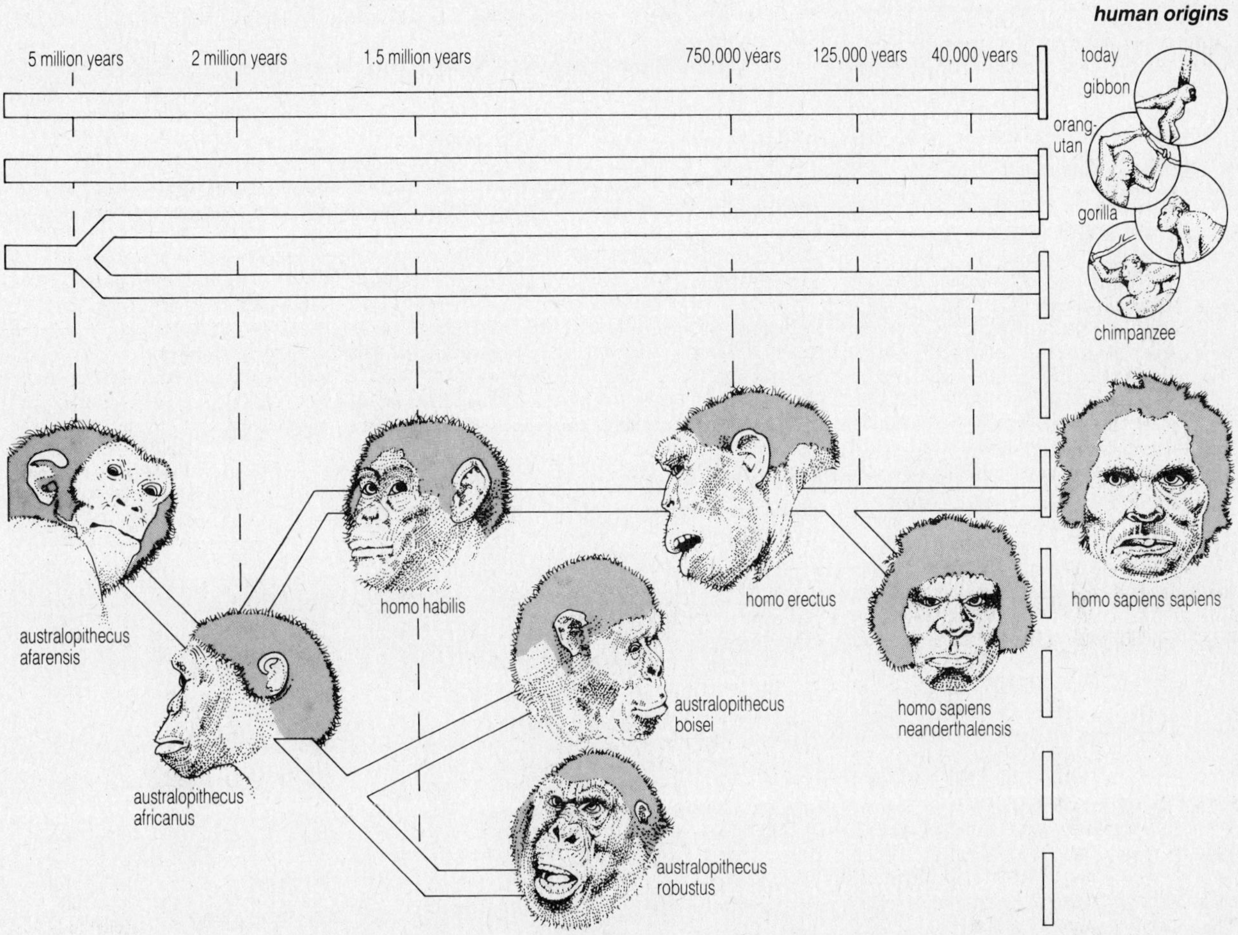

human origins

| 5 million years | 2 million years | 1.5 million years | 750,000 years | 125,000 years | 40,000 years | today |

gibbon

orang-utan

gorilla

chimpanzee

australopithecus afarensis

homo habilis

homo erectus

homo sapiens sapiens

australopithecus africanus

australopithecus boisei

homo sapiens neanderthalensis

australopithecus robustus

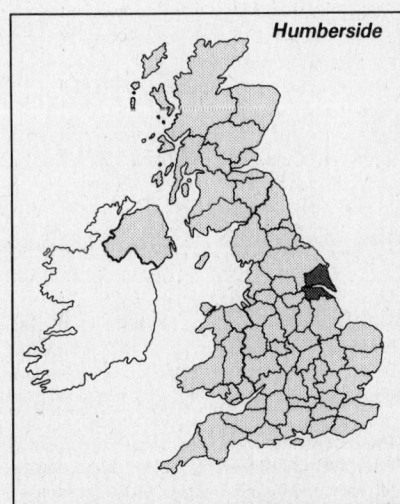

Humberside

of land necessary to support a peasant family). The hundred remained the basic military and administrative division of England until its abolition in 1867.

hundred days the period 20 Mar–28 Jun 1815, from ◊Napoleon's escape from imprisonment on Elba until his departure from Paris after losing the battle of Waterloo on 18 Jun.

Hundred Years' War name given to the struggle between England and France that was carried on from 1337 to 1453. It began with the claim of Edward III, through his mother, to the crown of France, and at the outset the English were victorious at the naval battle of Sluys in 1340 and on land at Crécy in 1346 and Poitiers in 1356. After 1369 the tide turned in favour of the French, and when Edward III died in 1377 only Calais, Bordeaux, and Bayonne were in English hands. A state of half-war continued for many years until Henry V invaded France in 1415 and won a victory at Agincourt. After his death his brother Bedford was generally successful until Joan of Arc raised the siege of Orléans in 1429. Even after her capture and death the French continued their successful counter-offensive, and in 1453 only Calais was left in English hands.

Hungarian language a member of the Finno-Ugric language group, spoken principally in Hungary but also in Czechoslovakia, Romania and Yugoslavia. Known as *Magyar* among its speakers, Hungarian is written in a form of the Roman alphabet in which *s* corresponds to English *sh*, and *sz* to *s*. Like the Turks, the Magyars originated in NE Asia; the term 'Hungarian' appears to derive from the Turkish *on ogur* ('ten arrows'), describing their ten tribes, which may also be the origin of the English 'ogre'.

Hungary /'hʌŋgəri/ country in central Europe, bordered to the N by Czechoslovakia, NE by the USSR, E by Romania, S by Yugoslavia, and W by Austria.

government Hungary is a unitary state with a one-chamber, 387-member legislature, the national assembly *Orszaggyules*. Thirty-five of the assembly's deputies are political, trade union and church figures, elected on a national slate. The remaining 352 are elected for five-year terms by universal adult suffrage.

Following amendments to the original 1949 constitution in 1983, competition has been introduced into candidate selection, with at least two candidates now being required to contest the nomination for seats. The national assembly elects a 21-member presidential council (presidium) to exercise legislative powers between parliamentary sessions, its chair acting as head of state, and a council of ministers, headed by a prime minister, which functions as the executive government.

Hungary's only political party is the Communist Party (Hungarian Socialist Workers Party, HSWP). It dominates the broader Patriotic

People's Front, which draws up lists of approved candidates for elections.

history once inhabited by Celts and Slavs, the region later became a Roman province. After the Roman era it was overrun by Germanic invaders, until the establishment of a ◊Magyar kingdom in the late 9th century, under a chief named Árpád. Hungary's first king was St Stephen (997–1038), who established a kingdom in 1001 and converted the inhabitants to Christianity.

After the Árpádian line died out, Hungary was ruled 1308–86 by the ◊Angevins, and after this by other foreign princes. From 1396, successive rulers fought to keep out Turkish invaders, but were finally defeated at Mohács in 1526, and the S and centre of the country came under Turkish rule for 150 years, while the E was ruled by semi-independent Hungarian princes. By the end of the 17th century the Turks had been driven out by the ◊Hapsburgs, bringing Hungary under Austrian rule.

After 1815 a national renaissance began, under Louis ◊Kossuth. The revolution of 1848–49 proclaimed a republic and abolished serfdom, but Austria suppressed the revolt with Russian help. In 1867 the ◊Austro-Hungarian empire was established, giving Hungary self-government.

During World War I, Hungary fought on the German side, and after the collapse of the Austro-Hungarian empire, became an independent state in 1918. For 133 days in 1919, Hungary was a communist republic under Béla ◊Kun, but this was brought to an end by intervention from Romania and Czechoslovakia. From 1920–44, Hungary was ruled by Admiral ◊Horthy. After 1933, he fell more and more under German influence and, having joined Hitler in the invasion of Russia in 1941, was overrun by Communist forces 1944–45.

Horthy fled and a provisional government, including the Communist agriculture minister, Imre ◊Nagy, was formed, distributing land to the peasants. An elected assembly inaugurated a republic in 1946, but it soon fell under Soviet domination, although only 70 Communists had been returned out of a total of 409 deputies.

Under Communist Party leader Matyas Rakosi (1892–1971), a Stalinist regime was imposed 1946–53, a Soviet-style constitution being adopted in 1949, industry nationalized, land collectivized and a wave of secret police terror launched.

Liberalization in the economic sphere was experienced 1953–55 when Imre Nagy, supported by Soviet premier ◊Malenkov, replaced Rákosi as prime minister. Nagy was removed from office in 1955, after the fall of Malenkov, but in 1956, in the wake of ◊Khrushchev's denunciation of Stalin in his 'secret speech', pressure for democratization mounted. Rakosi stepped down as Communist Party leader and, following student and worker demonstrations in Budapest, Nagy was recalled as prime minister and János ◊Kádár appointed HSWP general-secretary.

Nagy lifted restrictions on the formation of political parties, released the anti-communist primate Cardinal ◊Mindszenty, announced plans for Hungary to withdraw from the ◊Warsaw Pact and become a neutral power. These changes were, however, opposed by Kádár, who set up a counter-government in E Hungary before returning to Budapest with Soviet tanks to overthrow the Nagy government on 4 Nov. 200,000 fled to the West during the 1956 'Hungarian National Rising'.

After a period of repression, Kádár proceeded to introduce pragmatic liberalizing reforms after 1960, including decentralization in economic planning (1968), giving Hungary a reputation as one of the freest and most market-orientated E European states. Hungary has remained, however, a loyal member of the ◊Warsaw Pact and ◊Comecon and its relations with Moscow have improved during the post-Brezhnev era. Kádár was re-elected HSWP leader in 1985. In 1987, to deal with economic difficulties, Hungary introduced VAT and Income Tax.

Hungary

HUNGARIAN PEOPLE'S REPUBLIC (*Magyar Népköztársaság*)

AREA 93,000 sq km/35,920 sq mi
CAPITAL Budapest
TOWNS Miskolc, Debrecen, Szeged, Pécs
PHYSICAL Great Hungarian Plain covers E half of country; Bakony Forest; rivers Danube, Tisza; Lake Balaton
HEAD OF STATE Károly Németh, chair of presidium from 1987
HEAD OF GOVERNMENT Károly Grosz, prime minister from 1987
GOVERNMENT one-party communist
EXPORTS machinery, vehicles, chemicals, textiles
CURRENCY forint (78.48 = £1 Sept 1987)
POPULATION (1985) 10,644,000 (Magyar 92%, Romany 3%, German 2.5%. A Hungarian minority in Romania is the cause of some friction between the two countries); annual growth rate -0.1%
LANGUAGE Hungarian (or Magyar), one of the few languages of Europe with non-Indo-European origins. It is grouped with Finnish and Estonian in the Finno-Ugrian family
RELIGION Roman Catholic 50%, other Christian denominations 25%
LITERACY 99.3% male/98.5% female (1980)

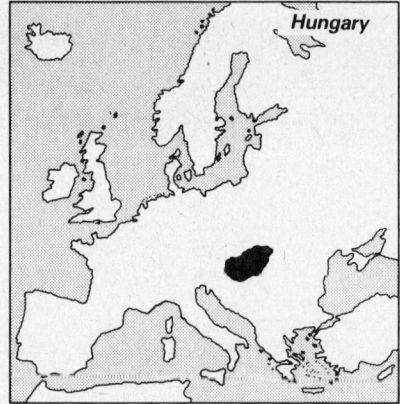
Hungary

GNP $18.6 bn (1983); $4,180 per head of population
CHRONOLOGY
1946 Republic proclaimed.
1949 Soviet-style constitution adopted.
1956 Hungarian national rising: workers' demonstrations in Budapest, democratization reforms by Imre Nagy overturned by Soviet tanks, Kádár installed as party leader.
1968 Economic decentralization reforms.
1983 Competition introduced into elections.
1987 VAT and income tax introduced.

hunger march procession of the unemployed, a feature of social protest in interwar Britain. The first took place from Glasgow to London in 1922 and another in 1929. In 1932 the National Unemployed Workers' Movement organized the largest demonstration, with groups converging on London from all parts of the country, but the most emotive was probably the Jarrow Crusade of 1936, when 200 unemployed shipyard workers marched to the capital.

Hunt /hʌnt/ (James Henry) Leigh 1784–1859. British poet and essayist. Convicted for libel against the Prince Regent in his Liberal newspaper *The Examiner*, he was imprisoned in 1813. The friend, and later enemy of Byron, he also knew Keats and Shelley. His verse is little appreciated today, but he influenced the Romantics, and his book on London *The Town* 1848, and his *Autobiography* 1850, survive.

Hunt /hʌnt/ John, Baron Hunt 1910–   . British army officer and mountaineer, leader of the successful ◊Everest expedition of 1953.

Hunt /hʌnt/ William Holman 1827–1910. British artist. Born in Cheapside, London, he in 1848 helped to found the Pre-Raphaelite Brotherhood. In 1854 Hunt travelled to Syria and Palestine to paint realistic pictures of Biblical subjects. His most famous work, *The Light of the World* 1854, is in Keble College, Oxford.

Hunter /'hʌntə/ river in New South Wales, Australia, which rises in the Mount Royal Range and flows into the Pacific near Newcastle, after a course of about 465 km/290 mi. It is liable to flooding, but there is dairying and market gardening, and Hunter Valley wines are famous.

Hunter /'hʌntə/ John 1728–1793. British surgeon and physiologist. Born in Lanarkshire, he became house-surgeon at St George's hospital, London, in 1756, collaborated with his brother William in the anatomical school; and from 1768 was surgeon. He experimented extensively on animals, collected a large number of specimens and preparations (Hunterian Collections), and greatly furthered the art of surgery.

His brother *William Hunter* (1718–83), anatomist and obstetrician, became professor of anatomy in the Royal Academy in 1768, and president of the Medical Society in 1781. His collections are now in the Hunterian museum of Glasgow university.

THE LADY OF SHALOTT.

PART I.

I.

Oɴ either side the river lie
Long fields of barley and of rye,
That clothe the wold and meet the sky;
And thro' the field the road runs by
To many-tower'd Camelot;

Hunt The English painter William Holman Hunt was a member of the Pre-Raphaelites who chose subjects from the Bible, Greek mythology, and English literature. Hunt illustrated Dickens and Scott and (as above) Tennyson's poem *The Lady of Shalott*.

Huntingdon /ˈhʌntɪŋdən/ town in Cambridgeshire, on the Ouse, 26 km/16 mi NW of Cambridge; population (1981) 17,467. A bridge built in 1332 connects Huntingdon with Godmanchester on the S bank of the river. Samuel ◊Pepys and Oliver ◊Cromwell attended the grammar school founded in 1565.

Huntingdonshire /ˈhʌntɪŋdənʃə/ former English county, merged in 1974 in a much enlarged Cambridgeshire.

Huntington's chorea genetic neurological disease causing paralysis and mental deterioration in middle life.

Huntsville /ˈhʌntsvɪl/ town in NE Alabama, USA; population (1981) 142,513. It is an aerospace research centre.

Hunyadi /ˈhunjɒdi/ János Corvinus 1387–1456. Hungarian politician and general. Born in Transylvania, reputedly the natural son of the emperor Sigismund, he campaigned successfully against the Turks. In 1456 he defeated them before Belgrade, but shortly afterwards died of the plague.

Hunza /ˈhunzə/ small state on the NW frontier of Kashmir, under the rule of Pakistan.

Hupei /ˌhuːˈpeɪ/ former name of ◊Hebei, province of China.

Hurd /hɜːd/ Douglas (Richard) 1930– . British Conservative politician, home secretary from 1986.

Hurd was in the diplomatic service 1952–66, then became a secretary to Edward ◊Heath. He entered the House of Commons 1974. He was given a junior post by Margaret ◊Thatcher, and the sudden resignation of Leon Brittan projected Hurd into the home secretary's post early in 1986.

Huron /ˈhjʊərən/ one of the ◊Great Lakes of North America.

Huron French nickname (*hure*, head of pig) for a member of the Wyandot, nomadic North American Indian tribes related to the Iroquois, and living near Lakes Huron, Erie and Ontario in the 16th–17th centuries. They were almost wiped out by the Iroquois but some still survive in Quebec and Oklahoma.

hurricane a revolving storm in tropical regions. A hurricane begins between 10° and 20° N or S of the equator and moves westwards. A central calm area, called the eye, is surrounded by inwardly spiralling winds of up to 320 kph/200 mph. A hurricane is accompanied by lighting and torrential rain and can cause extensive damage and loss of life along the western shores of tropical oceans. In meteorology a hurricane is a wind of force 12 or more on the Beaufort scale. In Oct 1987 hurricane-force winds were experienced in SE England – the strongest winds there for three centuries.

Husak /ˈhusɑːk/ Gustav 1913– . Leader of the Communist Party of Czechoslovakia (CCP) from 1969 and president 1975–1987.

Husak, a lawyer, was active in the resistance movement during World War II and afterwards in the Slovak Communist Party (SCP), and was imprisoned on political grounds 1951–60. Rehabilitated, he was appointed first secretary of the SCP in 1968 and CCP leader 1969. Husak's task, after the so-called Prague Spring of 1968, was to restore order, purge the CCP, and oversee the implementation of a new, federalist constitution. As state president pursued a policy of cautious reform.

husky sledge dog used by the Inuit in Alaska, about 70 cm/2 ft high, with pricked ears, thick fur and a bushy tail.

Huss /hʌs/ John c. 1373–1415. Bohemian reformer, rector of Prague University from 1402, who was excommunicated for attacks on ecclesiastical abuses. He defended Wycliffe when summoned before the Council of Constance in 1413, rejected the Pope's authority, and was burnt at the stake. His followers were called ◊Hussites.

Hussein /huˈseɪn/ ibn Ali c. 1854–1931. Arab leader of the Arab revolt 1916–18, who became King of the Hejaz in 1916, but was deposed in 1924 by ◊Ibn Saud.

hurricane Satellite picture of Hurricane Gladys off Florida, USA, in Feb 1975. The term is now widely used to mean any violent revolving storm, although at one time it was only applied to those occurring in the West Indies. In the East they are usually referred to as typhoons.

Hurstmonceux alternative spelling of ◊Herstmonceux, a village in ◊East Sussex.

Hurston /ˈhɜːstən/ Zora Neale 1901–1960. American novelist and short story writer, associated with the ◊Harlem renaissance. She collected traditional black American folk tales in *Mules and Men* 1935; her novels include *Their Eyes Were Watching God* 1937.

Hussein /huˈseɪn/ ibn Talal 1935– . King of Jordan. Great-grandson of Hussein ibn Ali, he became king in 1952 (after the mental incapacity of his father Talal). By 1967 he had lost all his kingdom west of the Jordan in the ◊Arab–Israeli Wars, and in 1970 suppressed the ◊Palestinian Liberation Organization acting as a guerrilla force against his rule on the remaining East Bank territories (see Black September under ◊terrorism). By 1984 there was some rapprochement with Yasser ◊Arafat, and Hussein proposed peace with Israel on condition of return of all territories occupied since 1967, including East Jerusalem.

Husserl /'husəl/ Edmund (Gustav Albrecht) 1859–1938. German philosopher, regarded as the founder of ◊phenomenology, a philosophy concentrating on what is consciously experienced (phenomena), which he hoped would become the science of all sciences. He influenced ◊Heidegger, and was influential in sociology through the work of Alfred Schutz. His main works are *Logical Investigations* 1900, 1901, *Phenomenological Philosophy* 1913.

Hussite a follower of John ◊Huss, Bohemian religious reformer. Opposed to both German and Papal influence in Bohemia, the Hussites waged successful war against the Holy Roman Empire for some years from 1419, but in 1620 Roman Catholicism was re-established.

Huston /'hjuːstən/ John 1906–1987. US film director, screenwriter, and actor. He was an impulsive and individualistic filmmaker, and his work often deals with the themes of greed, treachery, human relationships, and the loner. His films as a director include *The Maltese Falcon* 1941 (his debut), *The Treasure of the Sierra Madre* 1947 (for which he won an Academy Award), *The African Queen* 1952, and *The Misfits* 1960.

Hutterian Brethren a Christian sect; see under ◊Mennonites.

Hutton /'hʌtn/ Barbara 1912–1979. American heiress, grand-daughter of F W ◊Woolworth. Notorious in her day as the original 'poor little rich girl', she had seven husbands, including Cary Grant.

Hutton /'hʌtn/ James 1726–1797. Scottish geologist, known as the 'founder of geology'. In 1785 he developed the Huttonian theory of the igneous origin of many rocks. His *Theory of the Earth* 1788 proposed that the Earth was indefinitely old. His main contribution to the science was his concept of 'uniformitarianism', in which he suggested that past events could be explained in terms of processes that work today. For example, the kind of river current that produces a certain settling pattern in a bed of sand today must have been operating many millions of years ago, if that same pattern is visible in ancient sandstones.

Hutton /'hʌtn/ Leonard 1916– . British cricketer. Born in Yorkshire, he captained England in 23 test matches and was the first professional to captain England 1952–56. In 1938 he made 364 against Australia, the highest score by an Englishman in test cricket.

Huxley /'hʌksli/ Aldous 1894–1963. British writer, best known as the author of *Brave New World*, grandson of Thomas Huxley and brother of Julian Huxley. The satirical disillusion of his witty first novel, *Crome Yellow* 1921, continued throughout *Antic Hay* 1923, *Those Barren Leaves* 1925, and *Point Counter Point* 1928. The fantasy *Brave New World* 1932 dealt with the reproduction of the unlikeable human race by mass production in the laboratory. Huxley's pessimism about human nature led him to a retreat, symbolized by his emigration to California in 1938 and a devotion to mysticism which ended in his experiments with the hallucinogenic drug mescalin recorded in *The Doors of Perception* 1954.

Huxley Aldous Huxley, author of the futuristic novel *Brave New World*. Later he became devoted to mysticism and was an early experimenter with drugs, described in *The Doors of Perception* 1954.

Huxley /'hʌksli/ Andrew 1917– . British physiologist, the half-brother of Julian and Aldous Huxley. He was Jodrell professor 1960–69 and from 1969 Royal Society Research professor at University College, London. In 1963 he was awarded the Nobel Prize for Medicine (with Hodgkin and Eccles) for work on nerve impulses. He was knighted in 1974.

Huxley /'hʌksli/ Julian 1887–1975. British biologist, grandson of Thomas Huxley and first director-general of UNESCO.

Huxley /'hʌksli/ Thomas Henry 1825–1895. British scientist, humanist, and agnostic thinker. Following the publication of Charles Darwin's *On The Origin of Species* in 1859, he won fame as 'Darwin's bulldog', and for many years was the most prominent and popular champion of evolution. He wrote *Man's Place in Nature* 1863, textbooks on physiology, and innumerable scientific papers. In 1869 he coined the word 'agnostic' to express his own religious attitude; and his later books, such as *Lay Sermons* 1870, *Science and Culture* 1881, and *Evolution and Ethics* were expositions of scientific humanism. His grandsons include Aldous, Andrew and Julian Huxley.

Hu Yaobang /'huː ˌjaʊ'bæŋ/ 1915– . Chinese Communist Party (CCP) chair 1981–87. Hu, born into a peasant family in Hunan province, joined the Red Army at the age of 14 and was a political commissar during the 1934–36 Long March. In 1941 he served under

Huxley Biologist and humanist Thomas Henry Huxley was the foremost British exponent of Darwin's theory of evolution.

◊Deng Xiaoping and later worked under him in provincial and central government. Hu was purged as a 'capitalist roader' during the 1966–69 Cultural Revolution and sent into the countryside for 're-education'. He was rehabilitated in 1975, but disgraced again when Deng fell from prominence in 1976. In Dec 1978, with Deng established in power, Hu was inducted into the CCP Politburo and became head of the revived secretariat in 1980. As CCP chair from 1981, Hu presided over a radical overhaul of the party structure and personnel 1982–86. He was dismissed in Jan 1987 for his relaxed handling of a wave of student unrest during Dec 1986.

Huygens /'haɪgənz/ Christiaan 1629–1695. Dutch physicist who propounded the wave theory of light. Born in The Hague, he also developed several of ◊Galileo's ideas, observed Saturn's rings, developed the pendulum clock and discovered polarization.

Huysmans /wiːs'mɒns/ J(oris) K(arl) 1848–1907. French novelist. Born in Paris of Dutch ancestry, he spent 30 years as a civil servant. His best-known work is *A rebours/Against Nature* 1884, a novel of self-absorbed aestheticism which symbolized the 'decadent' movement.

Hwange /'hwæŋgeɪ/ coalmining town (Wankie until 1982) in Zimbabwe; population (1982) 39,200. Hwange National Park is nearby.

Hwang-Ho /ˌhwæŋ'həʊ/ former name of the ◊Huang He, a river in China.

hyacinth SE European bulb producing plant. *Hyacinthus orientalis* family Liliaceae, is the ancestor of the garden flowers with large, scented cylindrical heads of pink, white, or blue flowers. Other species grow around the Mediterranean. The ◊water hyacinth, genus *Eichhornia*, is unrelated, a floating plant from South America.

Huygens Dutch physicist Christiaan Huygens's design for an 'aerial' telescope, published in 1724 in his *Opera Varia*. The telescope, which has no tube, worked by refracting light.

Hyades V-shaped cluster of stars that form the face of ◊Taurus, the bull. The Hyades cluster lies 150 light years away and contains about 200 stars, although only a dozen are visible to the naked eye.

hyaline membrane disease (HMD) disorder of prematurely born children, who are unable to produce enough pulmonary surfactant (lung surface conditioner) to enable them to breathe properly; the lungs become hard and glassy (Latin *hyalinus* 'glassy'). A synthetic replacement for surfactant has been developed.

hybrid the offspring from a cross between individuals of two different species, or two inbred lines within a species. In most cases, hybrids between species are infertile and unable to reproduce sexually. In plants, however, doubling of the chromosomes (◊polyploidy) can restore the fertility of such hybrids. Hybrids between different genera are extremely rare; an example is the leylandii cypress which, like many hybrids, shows exceptional vigour, or ◊heterosis. In the wild, a 'hybrid zone' may occur where the ranges of two related species meet.

hybridization the production of a ◊hybrid.

Hydaspes /haɪˈdæspiːz/ classical name of river ◊Jhelum, a river in Pakistan and Kashmir.

hydathode a specialized pore, or less commonly, a hair, through which water is secreted by hydrostatic pressure from the interior of a plant leaf onto the surface. Hydathodes are found on many different plants and are usually situated around the leaf margin at vein endings. Each pore is surrounded by two crescent-shaped cells and resembles an open ◊stoma, but the size of the opening cannot be varied as a stoma. The process of water secretion through hydathodes is known as ◊guttation.

Hyde /haɪd/ Douglas 1860–1949. Irish scholar and politician, known in Gaelic as 'the lovely little branch'. Founder-president of the Gaelic League 1893–1915, he was President of Eire 1938–45. His works include *Love Songs of Connacht* 1894.

Hyde Park /haɪd/ one of the largest open spaces in London, England. It occupies about 146 ha/350 acres in Westminster. It adjoins Kensington Gardens, and includes the Serpentine, a boating lake with a 'lido' for swimming. In 1851 the Great Exhibition was held here. Rotten Row (a corruption of French *route du roi*) is a famous riding track.

Hyderabad /ˈhaɪdərəbæd/ capital city of the Indian state of Andhra Pradesh, on the Musi, a tributary of the Kistna; population (1981) 2,142,087. Most famous of its buildings is the Jama Masjid mosque. Hyderabad was formerly capital of the princely state of Hyderabad which occupied the greater part of the region known as the◊Deccan, and was by far the largest of India's princely states. In 1956 Hyderabad was divided between Maharashtra, Mysore, and Andhra Pradesh.

Hyder Ali /ˈhaɪdər ˈɑːli/ c. 1722–1782. Indian Muslim warrior. In command of the army in Mysore from 1749, he became the actual ruler of the state 1759 and rivalled British power in the area until his triple defeat by Sir Eyre Coote in 1781 during the Anglo-French wars. He was the father of ◊Tippoo.

hydra in zoology, genus of freshwater animals, of the phylum Cnidaria (coelenterates). The body is a double-layered tube (with 6–10 hollow tentacles round the mouth) 1.25 cm/0.5 in extended but capable of contracting to a small knob. Multiplication is by the formation of buds, by division into two or more pieces, and by sexual reproduction (there are no organs except those of reproduction). Usually fixed to waterweed, the hydra feeds on minute animals which are caught and paralysed by the stinging cells on the tentacles.

Hydra in astronomy, largest ◊constellation in the sky, snaking across 100 degrees of arc. Hydra represents the multi-headed monster slain by Hercules. Despite its huge size, it is not prominent, its brightest star is second-magnitude Alphard.

hydra in Greek mythology, a huge monster with nine heads. If one were cut off, two would grow in its place. One of the 12 labours of Heracles was to kill it.

hydrangea flowering shrub *Hydrangea macrophylla* of the Hydrangeaceae family and native to Japan, so named from the Greek for water vessel, after its cup-like seed capsules. It normally produces round heads of pink flowers, but these may be blue if certain chemicals, such as alum or iron, are in the soil.

hydraulics a field of study concerned with utilizing the properties of liquids, particularly the way they flow and transmit pressure. It applies the principles of ◊hydrostatics and hydrodynamics. The oldest type of hydraulic machine is the hydraulic press, invented by Joseph ◊Bramah in England in 1795. It consists in essence of two connected pistons in cylinders, one of narrow bore, one of large bore. A force applied to the narrow piston applies a certain pressure (force per unit area) to the liquid, which is transmitted to the larger piston. Because the area of this piston is larger, the force exerted on it is larger. So the original force has been magnified, although the smaller piston must move a great distance to move the larger piston only a little, hence mechanical efficiency is gained in force but lost in movement. This same principle is used in the hydraulic braking system of cars, the forging press and the hydraulic system of aircraft and excavators.

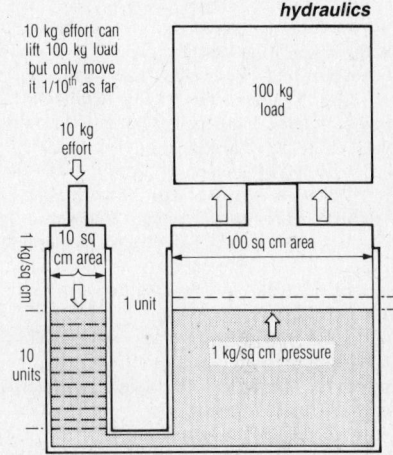

hydraulics

10 kg effort can lift 100 kg load but only move it 1/10th as far

10 kg effort

100 kg load

10 sq cm area

1 kg/sq cm

1 unit

100 sq cm area

10 units

1 kg/sq cm pressure

hydrocarbons one of a class of chemical compounds containing only hydrogen and carbon, for example paraffin. Hydrocarbons are important in ◊organic chemistry.

hydrocephalus blockage of the flow of cerebrospinal fluid, with various consequent dangers to the brain, and in young children causing the enlargement of the head. It may resolve itself or need surgery.

hydrochloric acid highly corrosive aqueous solution of hydrogen chloride (a colourless, corrosive gas HCl). It has many industrial uses, for example recovery of zinc from galvanized scrap iron, and the production of chlorides and chlorine. The acid produced in the stomachs of animals, for the purposes of digestion, is hydrochloric acid.

hydrocyanic acid also called 'prussic acid', a solution of ◊hydrogen cyanide gas (HCN) in water. It is a colourless, highly poisonous, volatile liquid, smelling of bitter almonds.

hydrodynamics the science of non-viscous fluids (water, alcohol, ether, and so on) in motion.

hydroelectric power electricity generated by moving water. In a typical hydroelectric power (HEP) scheme water stored in a reservoir, often created by damming a river, is piped into water ◊turbines, coupled to electricity generators. In ◊pumped-storage plants water flowing through the turbines is recycled. A ◊tidal power station is a HEP plant that exploits the rise and fall of the tides.

Today about one-fifth of the world's electricity comes from hydroelectric power. Such plants have a prodigious generating capacity. The Grand Coulee plant in Washington State, USA, has a power output of some 10,000 megawatts. The Itaipu power station on the Parana river

(Brazil/Paraguay) has a potential capacity of 12,000 megawatts.

hydrofoil boat a boat whose hull rises out of the water when it travels at speed. The boat gets its 'lift' from a set of hydrofoils, underwater 'wings' that develop lift in the water in much the same way that an ◊aeroplane wing develops lift in the air. One of the most advanced hydrofoil boats is the Boeing ◊jetfoil.

hydrogen gaseous element, symbol H, atomic number 1, atomic weight 1.00797. The lightest element known, it occurs chiefly in combination with oxygen as water. Hydrogen is the most common element in the ◊Universe, and the fuel of fusion reactions which take place in the Sun and stars. It has many commercial and industrial uses, from the hardening by hydrogenation (addition of hydrogen) of fats and oils in producing margarine, to creating high-temperature flames for welding, and use as a component in rocket fuel. Its isotopes, deuterium and tritium, have been used to produce the hydrogen bomb. If subjected to a pressure 500,000 times greater than that of Earth's atmosphere, hydrogen becomes a solid metal.

hydrogen bomb ◊bomb that works on the principle of nuclear ◊fusion. Large-scale explosion resulting from the thermo nuclear release of energy when hydrogen nuclei are condensed to helium nuclei. This is the continuing reaction in the Sun and other stars, but on Earth may result from the triggering of tritium (hydrogen isotope of atomic weight 3.0170) by an ordinary atom bomb. The first hydrogen bomb was exploded at Eniwetok Atoll by the USA in 1952. See also ◊weapons.

hydrogen cyanide a poisonous gas (HCN), formed by the reaction of sodium cyanide with dilute sulphuric acid; it is used for fumigation. The salts formed from it are cyanides, for example sodium cyanide, used in hardening steel and extracting gold and silver from their ores. If dissolved in water, hydrogen cyanide gives ◊hydrocyanic acid.

hydrography study and charting of Earth's surface waters in seas, lakes, and rivers.

hydrology study of the location and movement of inland water, both frozen and liquid, above and below the surface of the ground. It is applied to major civil engineering projects such as irrigation schemes, dams and hydroelectric power, and in helping to plan measures for flood control and the supply of water for homes and industry.

hydrolysis a chemical reaction in which decomposition into simpler forms is effected by the action of water or its ions. Hydrolysis occurs in certain inorganic salts in solution, in nearly all non-metallic chlorides, in esters and in other organic substances. It plays an important part in the breakdown of food by the body.

hydrometer in physics, an instrument used to measure the density of liquids compared with that of water, usually expressed in grams per cubic centimetre. The hydrometer is based on ◊Archimedes' principle, that any body floating in a liquid equals in weight the volume of the displaced liquid. It consists of a thin glass tube ending in a sphere which leads into a smaller sphere, the latter being loaded so that the hydrometer floats upright, sinking deeper into lighter liquids than heavier. The density of the liquid is inversely proportional to the volume immersed. The instrument is also used in brewing.

hydrophily a form of ◊pollination in which the pollen is carried by water. Hydrophily is very rare but occurs in a few aquatic species. In *Canadian pondweed Elodea* and *tape grass Vallisneria* the male flowers break off whole and rise to the water surface where they encounter the female flowers which are borne on long stalks. In *eel grasses Zostera*, which are coastal plants growing totally submerged, the filamentous pollen grains are released into the water and carried by currents to the female flowers where they become wrapped around the stigmas.

hydrophobia another name for the disease ◊rabies.

hydrophone an underwater ◊microphone and ancillary equipment capable of picking up water-borne sounds. It was originally developed to detect enemy submarines, but is now also used, for example, for listening to the sounds made by whales. See also ◊sonar.

hydrophyte a plant adapted to live in water, or in waterlogged soil. Hydrophytes may have leaves with a very reduced or absent ◊cuticle and no ◊stomata (since there is no need to conserve water), a reduced root and water-conducting system, and less supporting tissue since water buoys plants up. There are often numerous spaces between the cells in their stems and roots to make gas exchange with all parts of the plant body possible. Many living in water have highly divided leaves, which lessens resistance to flowing water, for example *spiked water milfoil Myriophyllum spicatum*.

hydroplane a specially designed motorboat or ◊hydrofoil boat that skims over the surface of the water when driven at high speed. The water the craft is highly manoeuvrable.

On a ◊submarine, a hydroplane is a moveable fin angled downwards or upwards when the vessel is descending or ascending.

hydroponics the cultivation of plants without soil, using specially prepared solutions of mineral salts. J von Sachs in 1860 and W Knop in 1865 developed a system of plant culture in water whereby the relation of mineral salts to plant growth could be determined, but it was not until about 1930 that the term was first coined by Professor W F Gericke, an American scientist. Beginning in the 1930s, large crops were grown by hydroponic methods, at first in California, but since then in many other parts of the world.

hydrosphere the water component of the Earth, usually encompassing the oceans, seas, rivers, streams, swamps, lakes, groundwater, and atmosphere water vapour.

hydrostatics in physics, the branch of ◊statics dealing with the mechanical problems of fluids in equilibrium, that is, in a static condition. An important practical application concerns the problems connected with floating bodies, as in shipbuilding. Another is concerned with the design of dams.

hydroxides inorganic compounds containing one or more hydroxyl (OH) groups and generally combined with a metal. The most important hydroxides are caustic soda, or sodium hydroxide (NaOH), caustic potash, or potassium hydroxide (KOH), and slaked lime, or calcium hydroxide ($Ca(OH)_2$).

hyena type of carnivorous mammal of which there are three living species, the *striped hyena Hyaena hyaena* found in India and northern Africa; the *brown hyena Hyaena brunnea* found on the South African coasts; and the *spotted hyena Hyaena crocuta* common south of the Sahara. Remarkably strong, both in its bone-cracking jaws and muscular power, the hyena is a useful scavenger, though it will also attack and capture live prey. The ◊aardwolf also belongs to the hyena family.

Hyères /iː'eə/ town in the *département* of Varennes, France; population (1982) 41,739.

Hygieia /haɪ'dʒiːə/ in Greek mythology, the goddess of health (Roman Salus), daughter of Aesculapius.

hygiene the science of the preservation of health and prevention of disease. It is chiefly concerned with such external conditions as the purity of air and water, bodily cleanliness, cleanliness in the home and workplace, and so on. See also ◊health care.

hygrometer in physics, an instrument for measuring the humidity of a gas. A wet and dry bulb hygrometer consists of two vertical thermometers, with one of the thermometer bulbs covered in absorbent cloth dipped into a beaker of water. As the water on the cloth evaporates, the bulb cools producing a temperature difference between the two thermometers. The amount of evaporation, and hence cooling of the wet bulb, depends on the relative humidity of the air. Other hygrometers work on the basis of a length of natural fibre such as hair or a fine strand of gut changing with variations in humidity. In a dew-point hygrometer, a polished metal mirror gradually cools until a fine mist of water (dew) forms on it. This gives a measure of the ◊dew point, from which the air's relative humidity can be calculated.

Hyksos /'hɪksəʊz/ ('shepherd kings' or 'princes of the desert'). A Semitic people which invaded Egypt in the 18th century BC and established their own dynasty, which lasted till 1580 BC.

Hymen /'haɪmen/ in Greek mythology, the son of Apollo and one of the Muses. He was the god of marriage and in art is represented as a youth carrying a bridal torch.

hymn song in praise of a deity: celebrated examples include ◊Ikhnaton's hymn to the ◊Aton in ancient Egypt; the ancient Greek Orphic hymns; Old Testament psalms, and extracts from the New Testament (such as Ave Maria); later Christian hymn-writers have included John ◊Bunyan ('Who would true valour see'); William ◊Blake ('And did those feet in ancient time'), Charles ◊Wesley ('Hark the herald-angels sing'), Henry Francis Lyte (1793–1847) ('Abide with me'), John S B Monsell (1811–75) ('Fight

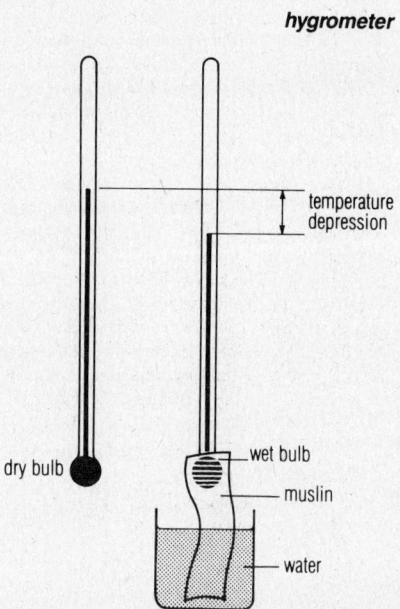

hygrometer

temperature depression

dry bulb — wet bulb — muslin — water

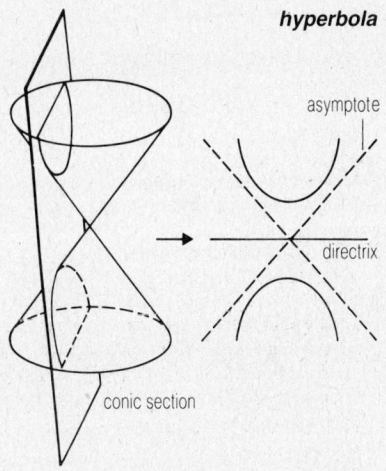

hyperbola

asymptote

directrix

conic section

the good fight'), and Sabine Baring-Gould (1834–1924) ('Onward Christian soldiers').

hyoscine alkaloid extracted from plants of the Solanaceae family, and used in surgery as a sedative.

Hypatia /haɪˈpeɪʃiə/ 370–415. Greek philosopher, born at Alexandria. She studied Neo-Platonism at Athens, and succeeded her father Theon as professor of philosophy at Alexandria. St Cyril, bishop of Alexandria, becoming jealous of her influence, denounced her as a pagan enchantress, and allegedly inspired a mob of monks to murder her.

hyperactivity condition of excessive activity in children, combined with inability to concentrate and difficulty in learning. Modification of the diet may help, and in the majority of cases there is improvement at puberty. The cause is not known, although certain food additives have come under suspicion.

hyperbola in geometry, a curve formed by cutting a right circular cone with a plane so that the angle between the plane and the base is greater than the angle between the base and the side of the cone. A member of the family of curves known as ◊conic sections. A hyperbola can also be defined as a path traced by a point that moves such that the ratio of its distance from a fixed point (focus) and a fixed straight line (directrix) is always greater than 1, that is, it has an ◊eccentricity greater than 1.

hyperbole a ◊figure of speech whose Greek name suggests 'going over the top'. When people speak or write hyperbolically they exaggerate, usually to emphasize a point ('If I've told you once I've told you a thousand times not to overdo things').

hypercharge property of certain ◊elementary particles, analogous to electric charge, that accounts for the absence of some expected behaviour (such as decay) in terms of the short-range strong interaction force, which holds atomic nuclei together. ◊Protons and ◊neutrons, for example, have a hypercharge of +1 whereas a π meson has a hypercharge of zero.

hyperinflation rapid and uncontrolled ◊inflation, or increases in prices, usually associated with political and/or social instability (as in Germany in the 1920s).

hypermarket a very large ◊supermarket.

hypertension abnormally high ◊blood pressure, the smooth muscle cells making up the walls of the arteries being constantly contracted. It increases the risk of several illnesses including kidney disorder, stroke, and heart attacks.

hypha a delicate, usually branching filament, many of which collectively form the mycelium and fruiting bodies of a ◊fungus. Hyphae of the higher fungi (the ◊ascomycetes and ◊basidiomycetes) are divided by cross-walls or septa at intervals, whereas those of lower fungi (for example, bread mould) are undivided. However, even the higher fungi are not truly cellular, as each septum is pierced by a central pore, through which cytoplasm, and even nuclei, can flow. The hyphal walls contain ◊chitin, a polysaccharide which is also found in arthropods. Typically hyphae grow by increasing in length from the tips and by the formation of side-branches. Food molecules and other substances are transported along hyphae by the movement of the cytoplasm, known as 'cytoplasmic streaming.'

Hyphasis /ˈhɪfəsɪs/ classical name of the river ◊Beas, in India.

hyphen a punctuation mark (-) with two functions: (1) to join words, parts of words, syllables, and so on, for particular purposes, and (2) to mark the break in a word continued from the end of one line to the beginning of the next line. The hyphenation of compound words in English is by no means clearcut; the same writer may in one article write, for example *world view*, *worldview* and *world-view*. Broadly speaking, conventional hyphenation is a first stage in bringing two words together; if their close association is then generally agreed, the two words are written or printed as one (*teapot*, as opposed to *tea-pot* or *tea pot*), or are kept apart for visual and aesthetic reasons (*coffee pot* rather than *coffee-pot* or ◊*coffeepot*). Practice does, however, vary greatly. There is a growing tendency in the use of certain prefixes towards omitting the hyphen (*coworker* rather than *co-worker*), often in order to economize in space.

hypnosis a state in which consciousness and will are suspended but other functions are not impaired. The subject is then extremely susceptible to suggestion and will carry out orders at once or long after being awakened, and may be made insensible to pain. Discovered by ◊Mesmer, it was used by charalatans and entertainers until laws such as the Hypnosis Act 1952 in the UK controlled exploitation of hypnosis as entertainment. Hypnotherapists use it to treat disorders such as addictions to tobacco or overeating.

hypnotic any of various drugs which produce a state like natural sleep. They depress the brain centres governing consciousness and mental activity. Taken in excess they suspend sensation and the power of movement, or even the action of the lungs and heart. The best-known are the alcohols, barbiturates and benzodiazepines.

hypo in photography, a term for sodium thiosulphate, discovered in 1819 by Sir John ◊Herschel and used as a fixative for photographic images from 1837.

hypocycloid in geometry, a cusped curve traced by a point on the circumference of a circle that rolls round the inside of another larger circle. Compare with ◊epicycloid.

hypodermic an instrument used for injecting fluids beneath the skin. It consists of a small graduated tube of glass, metal or plastic, with a close-fitting piston and a nozzle on to which a hollow needle can be fitted.

hypogeal a type of seed germination in which the ◊cotyledons remain below ground. The term can also refer to fruits which develop underground, for example peanuts (*Arachis hypogea*).

hypoglycaemic drug that lowers the level of glucose sugar in the blood. Diabetics who do not require insulin can control their blood sugar level by diet and hypoglycaemic tablets.

hyponymy in semantics, a relationship in meaning between two words such that one (for example, *sport*) includes the other (for example, *baseball*) but not vice versa.

hypothalamus the region of the brain below the ◊cerebrum which regulates rhythmic activity and physiological stability within the body, including water balance and temperature. It controls the part of the ◊nervous system which regulates the involuntary muscles. It is also connected to the ◊pituitary gland and regulates the production of its ◊hormones, by means of releasing or inhibiting hormones that affect the pituitary.

hypothermia use of cooling anaesthesia – also known as hibernation – to lower the temperature of the body for heart surgery and to tide over a dangerous phase of illness. The body's metabolism slows down at low temperatures, and less strain is imposed upon the vital organs, particularly the brain and the heart. Also refers to accidental lowering of body temperature below 35.5°C/95°F, and tends to occur among the elderly in poorly heated homes, causing death directly or by giving rise to broncho-pneumonia.

hypothesis in science, an idea concerning an event and its possible explanation, whether in the past (for example, how life on Earth began) or in the future (predictions about life in the 22nd century). The term is one favoured especially by the followers of the philosopher ◊Popper who argue that the merit of a scientific hypothesis lies in its ability to make testable predictions, rather than in any apparent plausibility.

hypothyroidism poor functioning of the thyroid gland, which results in slowed mental and physical performance, sensitivity to cold and infection. This may be due to lack of iodine or a defect of the thyroid gland, both being productive of ◊goitre; or to the pituitary gland providing insufficient stimulus to the thyroid gland. Treatment of thyroid deficiency (also called *myxoedema*) is by hormone thyroxine (either synthetic or from animal glands).

hypsometer (Greek *hypsos*, height) instrument for testing the accuracy of a thermometer at the boiling point of water. It was originally used for determining heights by comparing changes in the boiling point with changes in atmospheric pressure.

hyrax type of mammal (order Hyracoidea) found in Africa, Arabia, and Syria. It is about the size of a rabbit, with a plump body, short legs, short ears and brownish fur. There are four toes on the front limbs, and three on the hind, each of which has a hoof. They are good climbers. Some species live among rocks and in desert places, others live in forests and climb trees. They are believed to be among the nearest living relatives of elephants, and have hoof-like claws.

hyssop aromatic herb *Hyssopus officinalis*, family Labiatae, originally from S Europe but naturalized elsewhere.

hysterectomy surgical removal of the womb, usually because of fibroid or malignant tumours.

hysteria in psychology, a general term for a reaction (which is involuntary and largely unrealized) to a situation that a person is otherwise unable to face. Symptoms are produced which are normally associated with physical illness, such as paralysis, blindness, recurrent cough, vomiting, and general malaise. The term is little used today in diagnosis.

I ninth letter of the Roman alphabet, deriving, in form, from the sign for one of the several breathings of the Semitic languages. Its vocalic value was first given by the Greeks.

Iaşi /ˈjæʃi/ (German name *Jassy*) city in NE Romania, capital of Moldavia; population (1979) 262,493. It has chemical, machinery, and textile industries.

Ibadan /ɪˈbædn/ city in SW Nigeria; capital of Oyo state; population (1975) 847,000. Industries include the manufacture of plastics and vehicles. Part of its ancient protective walls still stand.

Ibáñez /iˈbɑːnjeθ/ Vincente Blasco 1867–1928. Spanish novelist and politician. Born in Valencia, he was actively involved in revolutionary politics. His novels include *La barraca/The Cabin* 1898, the best of his regional works; *Sangre y arena/Blood and Sand* 1908, the story of a famous bullfighter; and *Los cuatro jinetes del Apocalipsis/The Four Horsemen of the Apocalypse* 1916, a product of the effects of World War I.

Ibarruri /iˈbæruri/ Dolores 1895– . Spanish Basque politician, journalist, and orator. She joined the Spanish Socialist Party in 1917 and wrote for a workers' newspaper under the pseudonym 'La Pasionaria' ('the passion flower'). Elected to Parliament 1936, she helped to establish the Popular Front government, and was a Loyalist leader in the Civil War. After Franco came to power in 1939 she left Spain for the USSR, where she was active in the Communist Party. She returned to Spain in 1977 after Franco's death, and was re-elected to Parliament (at the age of 81) in the first elections for 40 years. Her autobiography was published in 1985.

Iberia /aɪˈbɪərɪə/ name given by ancient Greek navigators to the Spanish peninsula, derived from the river Iberus (Ebro). Anthropologists have given the name *Iberian* to a Neolithic people, traces of whom are found in the Spanish peninsula, southern France, the Canary Isles, Corsica, and part of North Africa.

ibex wild goat *Capra ibex*, native to the snowy regions of the Alps. Other species live in Spain, NE Africa, and Central Asia.

ibis type of wading bird related to the storks and herons, but having a long curved beak. Various species occur in the warmer regions of the world, including the scarlet ibis of America and the glossy ibis found in all continents except South America. The sacred ibis of ancient Egypt *Threskiornis aethiopica* is still found in the Nile basin.

Ibiza /ɪˈbiːθə/ one of the ◊Balearic Islands, a popular tourist resort; area 596 sq km/230 sq mi; population (1986) 45,000. The capital and port, also called Ibiza, has a cathedral.

Ibn Battuta /ˈɪbən bəˈtuːtə/ 1304–1368. Arab traveller. Born at Tangiers, he set off in 1325 on an extraordinary journey via Mecca to Egypt, East Africa, India and China, returning some thirty years later. He subsequently travelled to Spain and Mali. The narrative of his travels, *The Adventures of Ibn Battuta*, was written together with an assistant, Ibn Juzayy.

Ibn Saud /ˈɪbən ˈsaʊd/ 1880–1953. First king of Saudi Arabia from 1932. His father was the son of the sultan of Nejd, at whose capital, Riyadh, Ibn Saud was born. In 1891 a rival group seized Riyadh, and Ibn Saud went into exile with his father, who resigned his claim to the throne in his favour. In 1902 Ibn Saud recaptured Riyadh and recovered the kingdom, and by 1921 he had brought all central Arabia under his rule. In 1924 he invaded the Hejaz, of which he was proclaimed king in 1926. Nejd and the Hejaz were united in 1932 in the kingdom of Saudi Arabia. He introduced programmes for modernization with revenue from oil, which was discovered in 1936.

Ibn Sina /ˈɪbən ˈsiːnə/ Arabic name of ◊Avicenna, scholar and translator.

Ibsen /ˈɪbsən/ Henrik (Johan) 1828–1906. Norwegian poet-dramatist. Driven into exile 1864–91 by the opposition roused by his satirical *Love's Comedy* 1862, he wrote the verse dramas *Brand* 1866 and *Peer Gynt* 1867, and then the series of realistic social plays which revolutionized the course of European drama: *Pillars of Society* 1877, *A Doll's House* 1879, *Ghosts* 1881, *An Enemy of the People* 1882, *The Wild Duck* 1884, *Rosmersholm* 1886, *The Lady from the Sea* 1888 and *Hedda Gabler* 1890. In 1891 Ibsen returned to Norway and was recognized as the country's greatest living writer. His later plays are more symbolic: *The Master Builder* 1892, *Little Eyolf* 1894, *John Gabriel Borkman* 1896 and *When We Dead Awaken* 1899.

Ibsen The Norwegian dramatist Henrik Ibsen, whose realistic and often controversial plays revolutionized European theatre.

Icarus /ˈɪkərəs/ in Greek mythology, the son of ◊Daedalus, who died when he flew too near the sun using wings made from feathers fastened with wax.

Icarus /ˈɪkərəs/ in astronomy, an Apollo asteroid 1.5 km/1 mi in diameter, discovered in 1949. It orbits the Sun every 409 days at a distance of between 2.0 and 0.19 astronomical units. It is the only asteroid known to move closer to the Sun than the planet ◊Mercury. In 1968 it passed 6 million km/4 million mi from the Earth.

ice the solid formed by water when it freezes. It is colourless and its crystals are hexagonal. The freezing point, adopted as a thermometric standard, is 0 for the Celsius and Réaumur scales, and 32 for the Fahrenheit. Ice expands in the act of freezing (hence burst pipes), becoming less dense than water (0.9175 at 0 C).

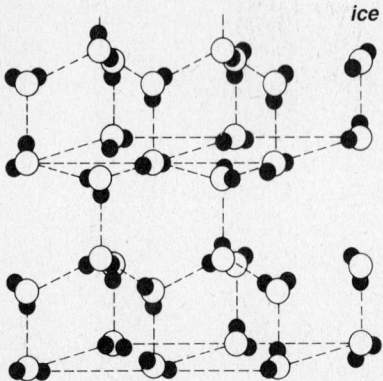

ice

the crystal structure of ice in which water molecules are held together by hydrogen bonds

Ice Age any period of glaciation occurring in the Earth's history but particularly in the Pleistocene epoch, immediately preceding historic times. Other ice ages have occurred throughout geological time: there were three in the Precambrian era, one in the Ordovician, and one at the end of the the Carboniferous and beginning of the Permian. During the Pleistocene Europe and America underwent glacial conditions similar to those of the polar regions today. On the North American continent the ◊glaciers reached as far south as the Great Lakes and the ice sheet spread over northern Europe, leaving its remains as far south as Switzerland. There were several glacial advances separated by interglacial stages during which the ice melted and temperatures were higher than now. Formerly there were thought to have been only three or four glacial advances, but recent research has shown about 20 major incidences. For example, ocean-bed cores record the absence or presence in their various layers of such cold-loving small marine animals as radiolaria, which indicate a fall in ocean temperature at regular intervals.

The occurrence of an ice age is governed by a combination of factors (the Milankovitch hypothesis): (1) the Earth's change of attitude in relation to the Sun, that is, the way it tilts in a 41,000-year cycle and at the same time wobbles on its axis in a 22,000-year cycle, making the time of its closest approach to the Sun come at different seasons; and (2) the 92,000-year cycle of eccentricity in its orbit round the Sun, changing it from an elliptical to a near circular orbit, the severest period of an ice age coinciding with the approach to circularity. There is a possibility that the ice age is not yet over. It may reach another maximum in another 60,000 years.

Major Ice Ages
Name (European/US) date (years ago)
Pleistocene: Riss and Wurm/Wisconsin 80,000–10,000
Mindel/Illinoian 550,000–400,000
Gunz/Kansan 900,000–700,000

Danube/Nebraskan 1.7–1.3 million
Permo-Carboniferous 330–250 million
Ordovician 440–430 million
Verangian 615–570 million
Sturtian 820–770 million
Gnejso 940–880 million
Huronian 2,700–01,800 million

iceberg a floating mass or hill of ice, rising sometimes to 100 m/300 ft above sea level. Polar glaciers that reach the coast become extended into a broad foot; as this enters the sea, masses break off and drift towards temperate latitudes, becoming a menace to shipping. About ⅛th of an iceberg's volume is submerged. The sinking of the liner *Titanic* in 1912 was caused by collision with an iceberg.

ice hockey

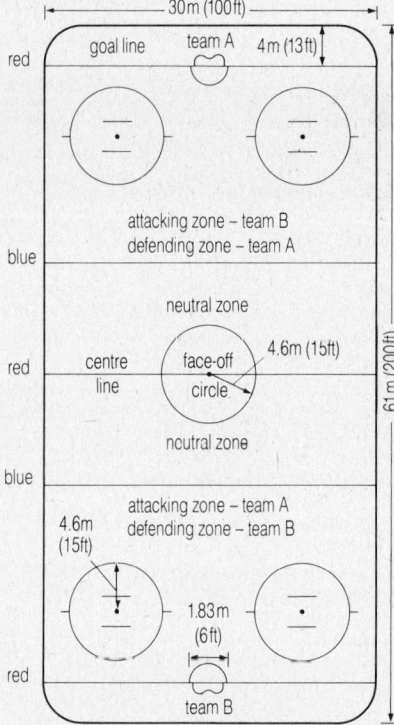

ice cream a frozen liquid, ideally made of cream, eggs, and sugar whipped together and frozen, with various flavourings of syrup and fruit. Ice cream is commercially made from various milk products and sometimes with 'non-milk' fat (that is, vegetable oils) and sugar, with artificial additives to give colour, flavour, and improve its keeping qualities and ease of serving. It became a mechanized industry first in the USA and then in the 1920s in Britain. Technical developments from the 1950s made possible the mass distribution of a 'soft' ice cream resembling the original type in appearance.

ice hockey game on ice between two teams of six players, developed from hockey in Canada (where it is the national sport) in 1867. Protective clothing is worn, and the puck, a flattened rubber disc (with which goals are scored), is kept in continual motion.

Iceland /ˈaɪslənd/ island in the N Atlantic, situated S of the Arctic Circle, between Greenland and Norway.
government The 1944 constitution provides for a president, as head of state, and a legislature, the 60-member *Althing*, both elected by universal suffrage for a four-year term. Voting is by a system of proportional representation which ensures, as nearly as possible, an equality between proportions of the votes cast and seats won.

Once elected, the *Althing* divides into an upper house of 20 members and a lower house of 40. The upper house members are chosen by the *Althing* itself and the residue of 40 automatically constitute the lower house. Members may speak in either house but only vote in the one for which they have been chosen. Legislation must pass through three stages in each house before being submitted to the president for ratification. On some occasions the *Althing* sits as a single house. The president appoints the prime minister and cabinet on the basis of parliamentary support and they are collectively responsible to the *Althing*. The main political parties are the Independence Party, the Progressive Party, the People's Alliance, the Social Democratic Party, the Social Democratic Alliance and the Women's League.
history Iceland was first occupied in 874 by Norse settlers, who founded a republic and a parliament, the *Althing* in 930. In 1000 the inhabitants adopted Christianity, and about 1263 submitted to the authority of the king of Norway. In 1380 Norway, and with it Iceland, came under Danish rule.

Iceland remained attached to Denmark after Norway became independent in 1814. From 1918 it was independent but still recognized the Danish monarch. During World War II Iceland was occupied by British and US forces, and voted in a referendum for complete independence in 1944.

In 1949 it joined ◊NATO and the ◊Council of Europe and in 1953 the Nordic Council. Since independence it has been governed by coalitions of the leading parties, sometimes right-and sometimes left-wing groupings, but mostly moderate.

The centre and right-of-centre parties are the Independents and Social Democrats, while those to the left are the Progressives and the People's Alliance. More recent additions have been the Social Democratic Alliance and the Women's Alliance.

Most of Iceland's external problems have been connected with over-fishing of the waters around its coasts, while domestically governments have been faced with the recurring problem of inflation. The administration formed in 1983 is a coalition of Progressives and Independents, representing a fairly solid, centrist grouping. In 1985 the *Althing* unanimously declared the country a 'nuclear free zone', banning the entry of all nuclear weapons.

The 1987 elections ended control of the *Althing* by the Independence and Progressive parties, giving more influence to the minor parties, including the Women's League, which doubled its seat tally.

Iceland The eruption of the volcano Helgafell lights up the sky over Heimsey Island.

Iceland
REPUBLIC OF (*Lýdveldið Ísland*)

AREA 103,000 sq km/ 39,758 sq mi
CAPITAL Reykjavik
PHYSICAL warmed by the Gulf Stream; glaciers and lava fields cover 75% of the country
FEATURES active volcanoes (Hekla was once thought the gateway to Hell), geysers, hot springs, and new islands being created offshore (Surtsey in 1963); subterranean hot water heats Iceland's homes
HEAD OF STATE Vigdís Finnbogadóttir from 1980
HEAD OF GOVERNMENT Steingrímur Hermannsson from 1983
GOVERNMENT parliamentary democracy
EXPORTS cod and other fish products
CURRENCY krona (64.18 = £1 Sept 1987)
POPULATION 241,000 (1985); annual growth rate 1.2%
LANGUAGE Icelandic, the most archaic Scandinavian language, in which some of the finest sagas were written
RELIGION Evangelical Lutheran
LITERACY 99.9% (1984)
GDP $2.1 bn (1983); $9,000 per head of population

Icelandic language a member of the N Germanic branch of the Indo-European language family, spoken only in Iceland and the most conservative in form of the Scandinavian languages. Its early literature is largely anonymous and seems to have originated in Norse colonies in the British Isles (around 9th-10th centuries). This literature consists mainly of the two Eddas and several Sagas. Despite seven centuries of Danish rule, Icelandic has remained virtually unchanged since the 12th century, being assured survival by the existence of written law and Bishop Gudbrand's vernacular Bible of 1584. After independence in 1918, Icelandic has experienced a revival, as well as governmental protection against such outside linguistic influences as English-language broadcasting. Halldor ◊Laxness (1902—), writing about Icelandic life in the style of the Sagas, was awarded a Nobel prize in 1955.

Iceland spar a form of ◊calcite, $CaCO_3$, originally found in Iceland. The crystals cleave into perfect rhombohedra. In its purest form, which is not uncommon, Iceland spar is quite transparent, and exhibits the peculiar phenomenon of producing two images of anything seen through it. It is used in optical instruments.

Iceni /aɪˈsiːnaɪ/ a people of E England, who revolted against occupying Romans under ◊Boudicca.

Ichang /ˌiːˈtsæŋ/ alternative form of ◊Yichang, a port in China.

ichneumon name given to parasitic wasps in the family Ichneumonidae. There are several

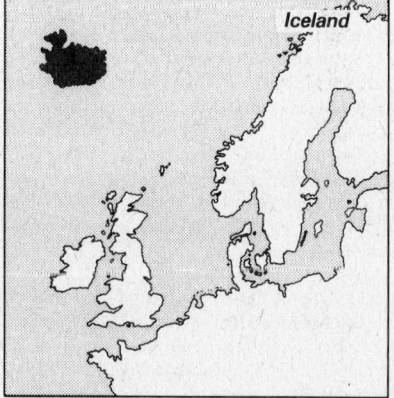

CHRONOLOGY
1944 Independence from Denmark achieved.
1949 Joined NATO and the Council of Europe.
1953 Joined the Nordic Council.
1976 'Cod War' with the United Kingdom.
1979 Iceland announced a 200-mile exclusive fishing zone.
1983 Steingrimur Hermannsson appointed to lead a coalition government.
1985 Iceland declared a nuclear-free zone.

thousand species in Europe, North America and other regions. The eggs are laid in the eggs, larvae or pupae of other insects, usually butterflies or moths.

icon in the Greek or Orthodox Eastern Church, a representation of Christ, an angel or a saint, in painting, low relief or mosaic. A *riza*, or gold and silver covering which leaves only the face and hands visible, and often adorned with jewels presented by the faithful in thanksgiving, is often added as protection.

icon in computing, a small picture on a VDU (computer screen) representing an object or function that the user may manipulate or otherwise use. Icons serve to facilitate ◊human-computer interaction by allowing the user to point with the mouse arrow to pictures rather than type commands.

icon

disk

printer

drawing on screen

file

Iconium /aɪˈkəʊniəm/ city of ancient Turkey; see ◊Konya.

iconoclast (Greek 'image-breaker') literally, a person who attacks religious images; the Iconoclastic doctrine, rejecting the use of icons in churches, was given to the Christian party by Byzantine emperor ◊Leo III in 726. The same name was applied to those opposing the use of images at the Reformation. Their greatest opponent was St ◊John of Damascus. Iconoclastic ideas had much in common with Islam and Judaism. Figuratively, the term is used for a person who attacks established ideals or principles.

id in Freudian psychology, the instinctual element of the human mind, concerned with pleasure, which demands immediate satisfaction. It is regarded as the ◊unconscious element of the human psyche, and is said to be in conflict with the ◊ego and the ◊superego.

Idaho /ˈaɪdəhəʊ/ mountain state of the NW USA; nicknamed Gem State
area 216,412 sq km/ 83,557 sq mi
capital Boise
towns Pocatello
features Rocky mountains; Snake river, which runs through Hell's Canyon, at 2,330 m/7,000 ft the deepest in North America, and has the National Reactor Testing Station on the plains of its upper reaches; Sun Valley, ski and summer resort
products potatoes, wheat; livestock; timber; silver, lead, zinc, antimony
population (1980) 943,935
religion Christian, predominantly Mormon

history first permanently settled in 1860, Idaho became a state in 1890.

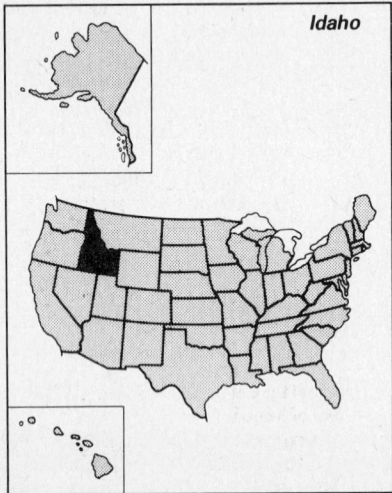

Idaho

idealism in philosophy, theory which states that what we ordinarily refer to as the external world is fundamentally immaterial and a dimension of mind. Objects in the world exist but, according to this theory, they lack substance.

identikit a set of drawings of different parts of the face used to compose a likeness of a person for identification, first used by the police in Britain in 1961. It has largely been replaced by ◊photofit, based on photographs, which produces a more realistic likeness.

ideology a set of ideas, beliefs, and opinions about the nature of people and society providing a framework for a theory about how society is or should be organized. The term is used by philosophers and social scientists in an analytical and neutral way, but it has more popularly been used to describe beliefs based on fanatical faith rather than rational argument.

Ides in the Roman calendar, the 15th day of Mar, May, Jul and Oct, and 13th day of all other months (the word originally indicated the full moon); Julius Caesar was assassinated on the Ides of Mar 44 BC.

Idi Amin Dada, Lake /'ɪdi æ'miːn 'dɑːdɑː/ former name 1973–79 of Lake ◊Edward in Uganda/Zaïre.

Ifni /'ɪfni/ province in Morocco, Spanish territory from 1860–1969; area 1,920 sq km/740 sq mi. The chief town is Sidi Ifni.

Iglesias /iː'gleɪsiəs/ Pablo 1850–1925. Spanish politician, founder of the Spanish Socialist Party (*Partido Socialista Obrero Español*, PSOE) in 1879 and in 1911 the first socialist deputy to be elected to the Cortés.

Ignatius Loyola, St /ɪg'neɪʃəs lɔɪ'əʊlə/ 1491–1556. Spanish soldier converted 1521 to the religious life after being wounded at Pampeluna, and founder of the ◊Jesuits in 1540. Feast day 31 Jul.

Ignatius of Antioch, St /ɪg'neɪʃəs, 'æntiok/ 1st–2nd century AD. Traditionally a disciple of St John, he was bishop of Antioch, and was thrown to the wild beasts at Rome. He wrote seven Epistles, important documents of the early Christian Church. Feast day 1 Feb.

igneous rock a ◊rock formed from cooling magma or ◊lava, and solidifying from a molten state. Igneous rocks are classified according to their ◊feldspar character, grain size, texture and chemical composition.

IGNEOUS ROCKS

Oxygen content	PARTICLE SIZES		
	Coarse (plutonic)	Medium	Fine (volcanic)
less than 45% (ultrabasic)	peridotite kimberlite		
45–52% (basic)	gabbro	dolerite	basalt
52–66% (intermediate)	diorite seyenite		andesite trachyte
more than 66% (acid)	granite		chyolite

ignis fatuus light sometimes seen over marshy ground, thought to be burning ◊methane from decomposing organic material.

ignition coil a kind of ◊transformer that is an essential part of a car's ignition system. It consists of two wire coils wound around an iron core. The primary coil, which is connected to the car battery, has only a few turns. The secondary coil, connected via the ◊distributor to the ◊spark plugs, has many turns. When the engine is running, the battery current (usually at 12 volts) is periodically interrupted by means of the contact-breaker in the distributor. The collapsing current in the primary coil induces a current in the secondary coil, a phenomenon known as ◊electromagnetic induction. The induced current in the secondary coil is at very high voltage, typically about 15,000–20,000 volts. This passes to the spark plugs to create sparks.

iguana lizard of the family Iguanidae, which includes about 700 species and is chiefly confined to the Americas. The common iguana *Iguana iguana* of Central and South America may reach 2 m/6 ft and is a favourite food of the Indians.

iguanodon plant-eating ◊dinosaur whose remains are found in strata of the Lower Cretaceous age. *Iguanodon* varied in length from 5–10 m/16–32 ft, and when standing upright was 4 m/13 ft tall. It walked on its hind legs, balancing its body by its long tail.

Ijsselmeer /'aɪsəlmɪə/ lake in the Netherlands, formed 1932 after the Zuider Zee was cut off by a dyke from the North Sea; freshwater since 1944. Area 1217 sq km/470 sq mi.

IKBS intelligent knowledge-based system; an alternative for the more usual ◊KBS (knowledge-based system).

ikebana the Japanese art of flower arrangement. It dates from the 7th century when arrangements of flowers were placed as offerings in Buddhist temples, a practice learned from China. In the 15th century, ikebana became a favourite pastime of the nobility. Oldest of modern Japanese ikebana schools is Ikenobo at Kyoto (7th century).

Ikhnaton /ɪk'nɑːtn/ or *Akhenaton* 1379–1362. King of Egypt (18th dynasty), who may have ruled jointly for a time with ◊Amenhotep III. His favourite wife was Nefertiti, whose portrait head (now in the Berlin Museum) is the most beautiful known from ancient times, and two of his six daughters by her were married to his successors Smenkhare and Tutankaton (later known as ◊Tutankhamen). He developed the cult of the ◊Aton rather than the rival cult of ◊Ammon.

Île-de-France /'iːl də 'frɒns/ region of N France; capital Paris; population (1982) 10,073,059. From here the early French kings extended their authority over the whole country. It includes Sèvres and St ◊Cloud.

Ilfracombe /'ɪlfrəkuːm/ resort on the N coast of Devon, England; population (1981) 10,479.

Ilkeston /'ɪlkɪstən/ town in SE Derbyshire, England; population (1981) 33,031.

Ilkley /'ɪlkli/ town in W Yorkshire, England, noted for nearby *Ilkley Moor*; population (1981) 24,082.

Ille /iːl/ French river 45 km/28 mi long, which rises in Lake Boulet and enters the Vilaine at Rennes. It gives its name to the *département* of Ille-et-Vilaine.

illegitimacy in law, the birth of a child to a mother who is not legally married; a child may be legitimated by subsequent marriage of the parents. Otherwise the mother has custody and may apply for maintenance from the father through the courts. Nationality of child is usually that of the mother. In the UK, recent acts have removed many of the historic disadvantages of illegitimacy, for example, as regards inheritance, and the Law Commission has recommended reforms to remove the remaining disadvantages.

Illich /'ɪlɪtʃ/ Ivan 1926– . Radical philosopher and activist, born in Vienna, who has lived in the US and Latin America, and whose works are a critique against modern economic development, especially in the Third World. Arguing that true liberation can only be achieved by de-institutionalizing society, his radical solution is to abolish the institutions on which authority rests, such as schools and hospitals. Major works include *Deschooling Society* 1971, *Towards a History of Need* 1978, and *Gender* 1983. His ideas have influenced development strategies in the Third World.

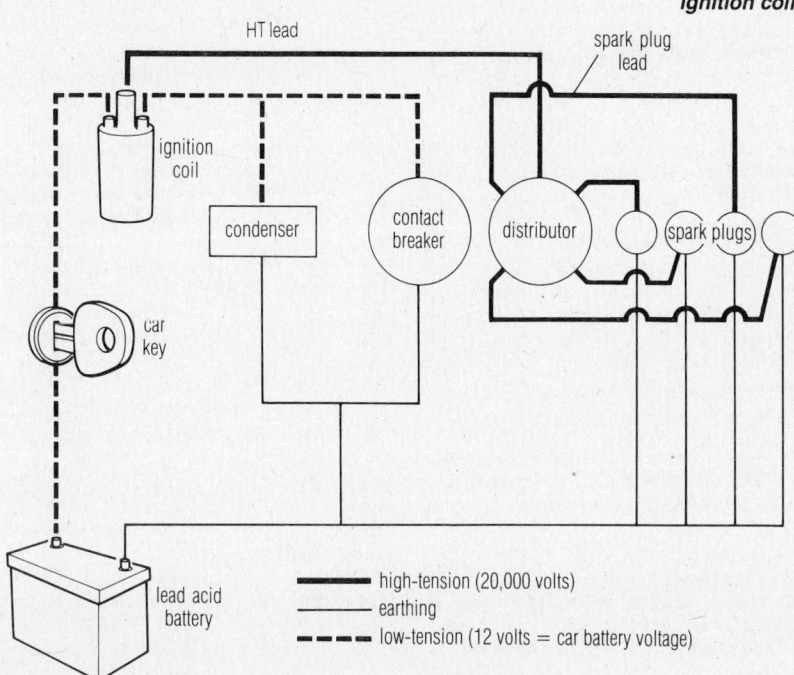

ignition coil

HT lead

spark plug lead

ignition coil

spark plug lead

condenser

contact breaker

distributor

spark plugs

car key

lead acid battery

▬▬▬ high-tension (20,000 volts)
——— earthing
▬ ▬ ▬ low-tension (12 volts = car battery voltage)

Illinois /ˌɪləˈnɔɪ/ midwest state of the USA; nicknamed Inland Empire
area 146,075 sq km/54,600 sq mi
capital Springfield
towns Chicago, Rockford, Peoria, Decatur
features Lake Michigan, the Mississippi, Illinois, Ohio and Rock rivers; Cahokia Mounds, the largest group of prehistoric earthworks in the USA; in Des Plaines, the restaurant where the first McDonald's hamburger was served in 1955 became a museum in 1985
products mainly agricultural, soybeans, cereals, meat and dairy products; also machinery, electric and electronic equipment
population (1980) 11,426,500
famous people Walt Disney, James T Farrell, Ernest Hemingway, Edgar Lee Masters, Ronald Reagan, Frank Lloyd Wright
history originally explored by the French in the 17th century, it was ceded to Britain in 1763, passed to American control in 1783, and became a state in 1818.

Illyria /ɪˈlɪrɪə/ ancient name for the eastern coastal region on the Adriatic, north of the Gulf of Corinth, conquered by Philip of Macedon and a Roman province from 9 AD. The Albanians are survivors of its ancient peoples.

ilmenite an ore of ◊iron and titanium, composed of the oxides, $FeOTiO_2$, with some magnesia. The mineral is black, with a metallic lustre, and closely resembles the iron ore ◊haematite.

ILS *i*nstrument *l*anding *s*ystem, the usual system for assisting aircraft landing at airports.

imaginary number number that is obtained by multiplying a real number by *i*, which is the square root of –1 (that is, $i^2 = -1$). For example, it is impossible to find a real number that multiplied

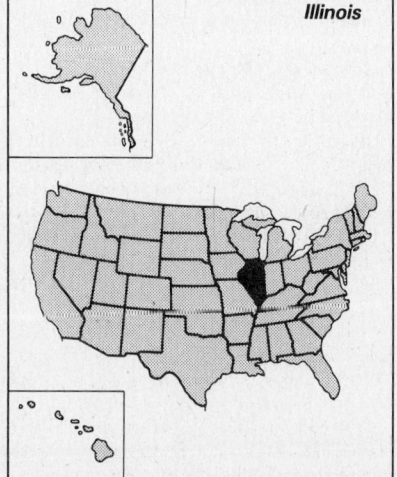

Illinois

by itself gives –4 (since –2 x –2 equals +4), although when this quantity (+*t*N–4) is needed in a mathematical calculation it is ascribed the imaginary value 2*i*; thus $(2i)^2 = -4$. There is also an imaginary component in all ◊complex numbers; in general, the complex number $a + bi$ has the imaginary part *b*. See ◊number.

Imagist School Anglo-American group of poets 1909–17, including T E Hulme, T S Eliot, Ezra Pound and Amy Lowell, who in a revolt against the decadence of late Romanticism advocated clear-cut images, brief poems and free rhythms.

imago the sexually mature stage of an insect.

imam /ɪˈmɑːm/ in a mosque, the leader of congregational prayer, but generally any notable Islamic leader.

Imbros /ˈɪmbrɒs/ island in the Aegean (Turkish Imroz); area 280 sq km/108 sq mi. Occupied by Greece in World War I, it became Turkish under the Treaty of ◊Lausanne 1923. Population (1970) 6,786.

Imhotep /ɪmˈhəʊtep/ c. 2800 BC. Egyptian physician and architect, adviser to King Zoser (3rd dynasty). He is thought to have designed the step-pyramid at Sakkara, and his tomb (believed to be in the North Sakkara cemetery) became a centre of healing. He was deified as the son of ◊Ptah, and was identified with ◊Aesculapius.

Immaculate Conception in the Roman Catholic church, the belief that the Virgin Mary was, by a special act of grace, preserved free from ◊original sin from the moment she was conceived. This article of the Catholic faith was for centuries the subject of heated controversy, opposed by St Thomas Aquinas and other theologians, but generally accepted from about the 16th century. It became a dogma in 1854.

Immingham /ˈɪmɪŋəm/ town on the River Humber, Humberside, England; population (1971) 10,259. It is a bulk cargo handling port, with petrochemical works.

immunity the protection which animals have against the effects of foreign organisms and toxins on their body functions. Immunity is provided by a range of physical barriers, such as the ◊skin or ◊exoskeleton, acid in the stomach, and mucus in the respiratory tract. If these barriers are breached, other defence systems come into operation. In vertebrates, these consist of the white blood cells (◊leucocytes) some of which (◊phagocytes and ◊macrophages) engulf bacteria and other invading organisms, while others (natural killer cells) destroy body cells that have become infected. A third group of white blood cells, the T-lymphocytes (see ◊lymphocytes), are responsible for binding to specific invading organisms and killing them, or rendering them harmless. Another type, the B-lymphocytes, produce ◊antibodies that are specific to particular micro-organisms; they bind them and thus inactivate them. In the case of ◊viruses, there is an additional form of defence, based on ◊interferons, which prevent them from replicating in the host's cells. ◊AIDS is one of many viral diseases in which the immune system is affected.

immunosuppressive drug (usually ◊cytotoxic or ◊corticosteroid) that suppresses the body's normal immune reaction to infection or foreign tissue. Used for treating auto-immune diseases (in which the body attacks its own tissues) and to help prevent rejection of organ transplants.

impala African antelope *Aepyceros melampus* found from Kenya to South Africa in savannas and open woodlands. The body is sandy-brown. Lyre-shaped horns up to 75 cm/2.5 ft long are found only in males. Up to 1.5 m/5 ft long and 90 cm/3 ft tall, impala live in herds and spring high in the air when alarmed.

impeachment in the UK, a judicial procedure by which the House of Commons from 1376 brought ministers and officers of state to trial before the House of Lords, for example Bacon 1621, Strafford 1641, and Warren Hastings 1788. In the USA the House of Representatives similarly may impeach offenders to be tried before the Senate, for example President Andrew Johnson 1868. Richard ◊Nixon was forced to resign the US presidency 1974 following the threat of impeachment.

impedance (symbol Z) the total opposition of a circuit to the passage of electric current. For a direct current (DC) it is the total ◊resistance R of all the components in the circuit. For an ◊alternating current (AC) it includes also the reactance X (caused by ◊capicitance or ◊inductance); the impedance can be found using the equation $Z^2 = R^2 + X^2$.

Imperial College of Science and Technology institution established at South Kensington, London, in 1907, for advanced scientific training and research, applied especially to industry. Part of the University of London, it comprises three separate colleges, the City and Guilds College (engineering faculty), the Royal College of Science (pure science), and the Royal School of Mines (mining).

imperialism the attempt by one country to dominate others. In the 19th century this was synonymous with the establishment of colonies (see ◊British Empire) but contemporary leftist thinkers believe that the role of Western (especially US) finance capital in the Third World constitutes a form of imperialism.

Imperial system system of measurement based on the foot, pound and second (◊f.p.s.).

Imperial War Museum British military museum, founded in 1917, originally as a memorial to the men and women of the Empire in World War I. It now includes records of all operations fought by British forces since 1914. Its present building (formerly the Royal Bethlehem, or Bedlam, Hospital) in Lambeth Road, London, was opened 1936.

impetigo contagious bacterial infection (*Staphylococcus aureus*) of the skin which forms yellowish crusts; it is curable with antibiotics.

Imphal /ɪmˈfɑːl/ capital of Manipur state, India; population (1981) 156,622, a communications and trade centre. It was besieged Mar–Jun 1944, when Japan invaded Assam, but held out with the help of supplies dropped by air.

implantation in mammals, the process by which the developing ◊embryo (at this stage simply a ball of cells) attaches itself to the wall of the mother's uterus (womb) and stimulates the development of the ◊placenta. In some species, such as seals and bats, implantation is delayed for several months, during which time the embryo does not grow; thus the interval between mating and birth may be a year, although the ◊gestation period is only seven or eight months.

import product or service which one country purchases from another for domestic consumption. If an importing country does not have a counterbalancing value of ◊exports, it may experience ◊balance-of-payments difficulties and accordingly consider restricting imports by some form of ◊protection (such as an import tariff or imposing import quotas).

Impressionism movement in painting which originated in France in the 1860s, its chief exponents being ◊Manet, ◊Monet, ◊Degas, ◊Renoir, and ◊Pissarro. The Impressionists depicted real life, but the scenes and objects they painted became increasingly less important than the way they were affected by the ever-changing play of light. The Impressionist group painted out-of-doors, capturing the immediacy and freshness of light on rippling water or on moving leaves. They broke up the forms they painted into fragments of pure colour which they laid side by side directly on the canvas, rather than mixing them on a palette. Their technique was influenced by the work of ◊Constable and ◊Turner, and also by contemporary spectroscopic discoveries.
The starting-point of the movement was the *Salon des Refusés*, an exhibition in 1863 of work rejected by the official Salon, followed by their own exhibitions 1874–86. Their work aroused fierce opposition; the term Impressionism was first used abusively to describe Monet's painting 'Impression, Sunrise' 1872. Among their followers were the American ◊Whistler, who introduced the term into England, and the English painters ◊Sickert and Wilson ◊Steer.

imprinting in ◊ethology, the process whereby a young animal learns to recognize both specific individuals (for example, its mother) and its own species. Imprinting is characteristically an automatic response to certain specific stimuli at a time when the animal is especially sensitive to those stimuli (the *sensitive period*). Thus, goslings learn to recognize their mother by following the first moving object they see after hatching; as a result, they can easily become imprinted on to other species or even inanimate objects if these happen to move near them at this time. In chicks, imprinting occurs only between ten and 20 hours after hatching. In mammals the mother's attachment to her infant may be a form of imprinting made possible by a sensitive period; this period may be as short as the first hour after giving birth.

impromptu in music, a short instrumental piece that suggests spontaneity.

Imroz /ˈɪmrɒz/ Turkish form of ◊Imbros, an island in the Aegean.

inbreeding in ◊genetics, the mating of closely related individuals. It is considered to be undesirable because it increases the risk that an offspring will inherit copies of rare deleterious ◊recessive alleles from both parents, and so suffer from disabilities.

Inca ruling class of South American Indian people of medieval Peru, who established the only empire of the Old World type ever to have existed in the Americas (estimated population 8 million at its zenith). The first emperor or 'Inca' (believed to be a descendant of the sun) was Manco Capac about 1200 AD. Inca rule eventually extended from Quito in Ecuador to beyond Santiago in S Chile (4000 km/2500 mi). Their creator god was Viracocha (identified with ◊Kon-Tiki). Their priesthood ran a uniquely efficient socialist state, allotting labour for irrigation, building temples and fortresses (made of stone blocks, fitted together without mortar),

according to family groups. Produce was collected and similarly distributed (numerical records of stores being kept by means of knotted cords, 'quipus', writing being unknown). Excellent roads maintained communication and foot soldiers were easily sent to ensure order. Medicine and advanced surgery were practised and the dead were mummified. The civilization was destroyed by the Spanish conquest in the 1530s. The descendants of the Incas are the ◊Quechua. The Inca ruin of Machu Picchu, a mountain sanctuary built about 1500, is near Cuzco. In 1987 a contemporary chronicle describing the Inca empire by the Spanish writer Juan de Betanzos was rediscovered after 400 years.

incandescence emission of light from a substance in consequence of its high temperature. The colour of the emitted light from liquids or solids depends on their temperature, and for solids generally the higher the temperature the whiter the light. Gases may become incandescent through ionization (the formation of charged atoms) as in the glowing vacuum ◊discharge tube. The oxides of cerium and thorium are highly incandescent and for this reason are used in gas mantles. The light from an electric filament lamp is due to the incandescence of the filament, rendered white-hot when a current passes through it.

incarnation assumption of living form (plant, animal, human) by a deity, for example the gods of Greece and Rome, Hinduism, Christianity (Jesus Christ as the second person of the Trinity). See also ◊reincarnation.

incendiary bomb a bomb containing inflammable matter. Usually dropped by aircraft, incendiary bombs were used in World War I, and in World War II were a major weapon in attacks on cities. To hinder firefighters, delayed-action high-explosive bombs were usually dropped with them.

incest sexual intercourse between persons thought to be too closely related to marry; the exact relationships which fall under the incest taboo vary widely between societies. A biological explanation for the incest taboo has been the avoidance of ◊inbreeding. However, within groups in which ritual homosexuality is practised, for example in New Guinea, an incest taboo applies also to these relations, suggesting that the taboo is as much social as biological in origin.

inch ◊imperial measure of length, a twelfth of a ◊foot.

Inchon /ˌɪnˈtʃɒn/ port in South Korea. Formerly Chemulpo; population (1983) 1,220,311. It is the chief port of Seoul, and produces steel and textiles.

inclusive fitness in ◊genetics, the success with which a given variant of a ◊gene (or allele) is passed on to future generations by a particular individual, when additional copies of the allele in the individual's relatives and their offspring are taken into account, as well as those in its own offspring. The concept was first recognized by W D ◊Hamilton as a way of explaining the evolution of ◊altruism in terms of ◊natural selection. See also ◊fitness and ◊kin selection.

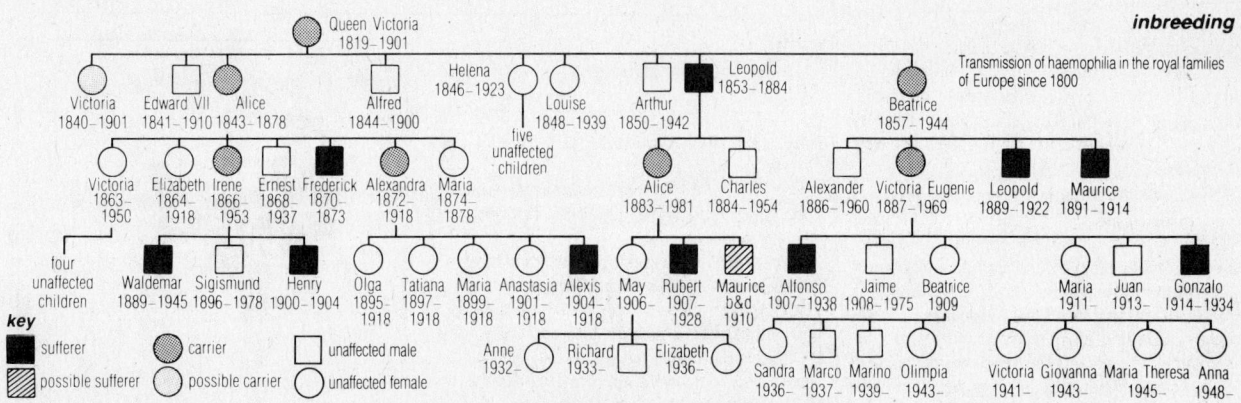

Transmission of haemophilia in the royal families
of Europe since 1800

key
- ■ sufferer
- ▨ possible sufferer
- ◉ carrier
- ◔ possible carrier
- □ unaffected male
- ○ unaffected female

Inca Civilization

MEXICO
HONDURAS
Caribbean Sea
COSTA RICA
Panama
PANAMA
VENEZUELA
COLOMBIA
ECUADOR
Pacific Ocean
PERU
Lima
Cuzco
BOLIVIA
CHILE
Santiago
ARGENTINA

☐ Inca Empire in
11th century

▨ Inca Empire in 1533

Inca Inti-Rayni, the festival of the Sun-god at
Cuzco, held in June as in the time of the ancient
Incas: the descendant of the Inca rulers is borne
along on this throne.

incomes policy government-initiated
exercise to curb ◊inflation by restraining rises in
incomes, on either a voluntary or a compulsory
basis; often linked with action to control prices,
in which case it becomes a prices and incomes
policy. In Britain incomes policies have been
applied at various times since the 1950s with
limited success. An alternative to incomes policy,
employed by the post-1979 Conservative
government in Britain, is ◊monetary policy,
which attempts to manage the economy by
controlling the quantity of money in circulation
(◊money supply).

income tax direct tax levied on annual
income, which may include the value of receipts
other than in cash. In the UK the rate of tax and
allowances is set out yearly in the annual Finance

Act which implements the recommendations
agreed to by the House of Commons in the
budget presented by the chancellor of the
exchequer. William Pitt introduced an income
tax 1799–1801 to finance the wars with
revolutionary France; it was re-imposed 1803–16
for the same purpose, and was so unpopular that
all records of it were destroyed when it was
abolished. Peel reintroduced the tax in 1842 and
it has been levied ever since, forming an
important part of government finance. At its
lowest, 1874–76, it was 0.83 per cent; at its
highest, 1941–46, the standard rate was 50 per
cent. In the UK, employees' tax is deducted
under the ◊PAYE system.

In the USA every citizen or resident (with certain
exemptions on the grounds of age or low income)
must file a report for federal income-tax
consideration. Rate of tax, which is calculated on
a percentage basis, and allowances, are fixed by
Congress from year to year. A state income tax
is also levied in many states, the amount of tax
and allowances varying from state to state; and
in many instances there is a city income tax as
well.

Most countries levy income tax, generally
considered as bearing less heavily on the poor
than indirect taxes: see ◊taxation. However, in
the USSR, where the salaries of most workers
are fixed by the state, income tax began to be
phased out from 1960. Factory and office workers
were exempt, and higher grades – to reduce
differentials – had tax equivalents deducted from
their salaries at source.

incubus male spirit who in the popular belief
of the Middle Ages cohabited with women in
their sleep. Witches and demons were supposed
to result from such intercourse. *Succubus* is the
female equivalent.

incunabula technical term for the earliest
printed books, that is those printed before 1500,
in the infancy of ◊Gutenberg's invention of
moveable type.

indemnity in law, an undertaking to
compensate another for damage, loss, trouble,
or expenses, or the money paid by way of such
compensation, for example under fire insurance
agreements.

indenture in law, a ◊deed between two or more
people.

Independence /ˌɪndɪˈpendəns/ city in
Missouri, USA; population (1980) 111,806.
Industries include steel, Portland cement,
petroleum refining, and flour milling. President
Harry S ◊Truman spent his childhood here, and
later made it his home.

Independence Day in the USA,
commemoration of the ◊Declaration of
Independence 4 Jul 1776. It is a public holiday.

Independent Labour Party (ILP) British
socialist party, founded at Bradford in 1893,
precursor of the ◊Labour Party. In 1900 it joined
with trade unions and Fabians in founding the
Labour Representation Committee, the nucleus
of the Labour Party. Many members left the

Independent Labour Party to join the Communist Party in 1921, and in 1932 all connections with the Labour Party were severed. After World War II it consistently dwindled, eventually becoming extinct. James Maxton (1885–1946) was its chair 1926–46; see also Keir ◊Hardie.

independent school a school run privately without direct assistance from the state. Just over 6% of children in the UK attend private fee-paying schools. The sector includes most ◊boarding education in the UK. Although a majority of independent secondary schools operate a highly selective admissions policy for entrants at the age of 11 or 13, some specialize in the teaching of slow learners or difficult children and a few follow particular philosophies of progressive education. A group of old-established and prestigious independent schools are known as ◊public schools. The Labour Party is committed to their integration into the state system; the Conservatives have encouraged state funding of selected students within certain independent schools under the ◊Assisted Places Scheme.

index (also known as *power* or *exponent*; plural *indices*) in mathematics, a number that indicates a function, as in the terms X^2, Y^5, and 4^7; the indices are 2, 5, and 7, and indicate respectively $X \times X$, $y \times y \times y \times y \times y$, $4 \times 4 \times 4 \times 4 \times 4 \times 4$. Such terms are multiplied by adding the indices, for example, $X^2 \times X^5 = X^7$; and divided by subtracting the indices, for example, $y^5 \div y^3 = y^2$. Any number with the index 0 is equal to 1, for example, $X^0 = 1$ and $99^0 = 1$. The term is from the Latin 'sign, indicator'.

index in economics, an indicator of a general movement in wages, prices, etc. over a specified period. For example, the retail price index (RPI) records changes in the ◊cost of living. The *Financial Times* share index indicates the general movement of the London ◊Stock Exchange market; the USA equivalent is the Dow Jones Index.

Index Librorum Prohibitorum (Latin 'Index of Prohibited Books') the list of books formerly officially forbidden to members of the Roman Catholic church. The process of condemning books and bringing the Index up to date was executed by a congregation of cardinals, consultors, and examiners from the 16th century until it was finally abolished in 1966.

India /'ɪndɪə/ country in S Asia, having borders to the N with Afghanistan, China, Nepál, and Bhutan, to the E with Burma, and to the NW with Pakistan. Situated within the NE corner of India, N of the Bay of Bengal, is ◊Bangladesh, and India is surrounded to the SE, S, and SW by the Indian Ocean.

government India is a federal republic whose 1949 constitution contains elements from both the American and British systems of government. It comprises 24 self governing states, administered by a governor appointed by the federal president, and a council of ministers (headed by a chief minister) drawn from a legislature (legislative assembly) which is popularly elected for a five-year term. Eight of

India
(Hindi *Bharat*)

AREA 3,208,274 sq km/1,175,410 sq mi
CAPITAL New Delhi
TOWNS Bangalore, Hyderabad, Ahmedabad; ports Calcutta, Bombay, Madras, Kanpur, Pune, Nagpur
PHYSICAL Himalaya mountains on the N border; plains around rivers Ganges, Indus, Brahmaputra; Deccan peninsula S of the Narmada River, a plateau between the W and E Ghats mountain ranges
TERRITORIES Andaman and Nicobar Islands, Lakshadweep
FEATURES the Taj Mahal monument; cave paintings (Ajanta); advanced communications via satellite TV (weather forecasting, agricultural information, and education)
HEAD OF STATE Ramaswami Iyer Venkataraman from 1987
HEAD OF GOVERNMENT Rajiv Gandhi from 1984
GOVERNMENT federal democracy
EXPORTS tea, coffee, fish; iron ore; leather, textiles, polished diamonds
CURRENCY rupee (21.30 = £1 Sept 1987)
POPULATION 767,681,000 (1985); annual growth rate 2%
LANGUAGE Hindi (official), English, and 14 other recognized languages: Assamese, Bengali, Gujarati, Kannada, Kashmiri, Malayalam, Marathi, Oriya, Punjabi, Sanskrit, Sindhi, Tamil, Telugu, Urdu
RELIGION Hindu 80%, Sunni Muslim 10%, Christian 2.5%, Sikh 2%
LITERACY 47% male/25% female (1981 est)
GNP $190 bn (1983); $150 per head of population

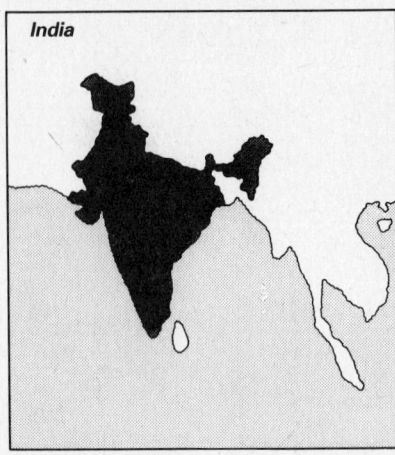

India

CHRONOLOGY
1947 Independence achieved from Britain.
1950 Federal republic proclaimed.
1962 Border skirmishes with China.
1964 Death of Prime Minister Nehru. Border war with Pakistan over Kashmir.
1966 Indira Gandhi became prime minister.
1971 War with Pakistan leading to creation of Bangladesh.
1975–77 State of emergency proclaimed.
1977–79 Janata party government in power.
1980 Indira Gandhi returned in landslide victory.
1984 Assassination of Indira Gandhi. Rajiv Gandhi elected with record majority.
1987 Signing of 'Tamil' Colombo peace accord with Sri Lanka.

the larger states have a second chamber (legislative council). The states have primary control over education, health, police, and local government, and work in consultation with the centre in the economic sphere. In times of crisis, central rule ('president's rule') can be imposed. There are also seven union territories, administered by a lieutenant-governor appointed by the federal president. The central (federal) government has sole responsibility in defence and foreign affairs and plays a key role in economic affairs.

The titular, executive head of the federal government is the president, who is elected for five-year terms by an electoral college composed of members from both the federal parliament and the state legislatures. However, real executive power is held by a prime minister and cabinet drawn from the majority party or coalition within the federal parliament.

The two-chamber federal parliament has a 544-member lower house, *Lok Sabha* (house of the people), which has final authority over financial matters and whose members are directly elected for terms of a maximum of five years from single-member constituencies by universal suffrage, and a 244-member upper house, *Rajya Sabha* (council of states), whose members are indirectly elected, a third at a time for six-year terms, by state legislatures on a regional quota basis. (Two seats in the *Lok Sabha* are reserved for Anglo-Indians, while the president nominates eight representatives of the Rajya Sabha.) Bills to become law must be approved by both chambers of parliament and receive the president's assent. The dominant national-level party in India, which has held power for all but three years (1977–79) since independence, is the ◊Congress Party. After splits in 1969, 1978, 1981, 1987, the main body of the party is today termed Indian National Congress (I or Indira). It is a broad, secular-based, cross-caste and religion coalition which advocates a moderate socialist approach and is based most strongly in N and central India. The principal national-level opposition parties are the Janata (People's) Party; the Bharatiya Janata Party (a conservative Hindu grouping); the Dalit Mazdoor Kisan Party (orientated towards middle peasants); the Rashtriya Sanjay Manch; and the Communist Party of India and Communist Party of India (Marxist). There are also numerous regional-level parties, the most

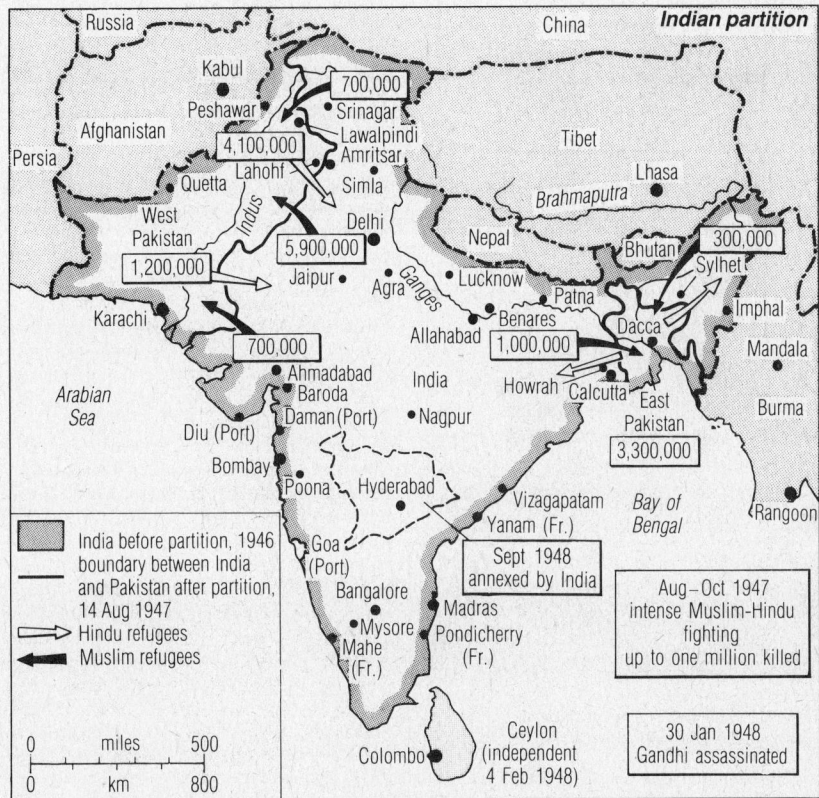

Indian partition

India before partition, 1946
boundary between India
and Pakistan after partition,
14 Aug 1947
Hindu refugees
Muslim refugees

Sept 1948
annexed by India

Aug–Oct 1947
intense Muslim-Hindu
fighting
up to one million killed

30 Jan 1948
Gandhi assassinated

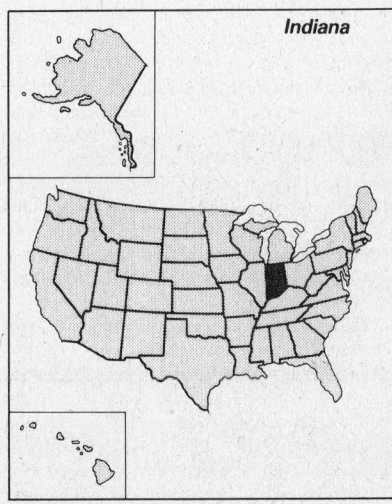

Indiana

Indianapolis /ˌɪndɪəˈnæpəlɪs/ capital and largest city of Indiana, USA. Population (1980) 700,800. It is an industrial centre.

Indian art the painting, sculpture, and architecture of India. The history of Indian art may be traced back to the ancient Indus valley civilization of about 3000 BC, which influenced the Brahmanical art of later periods. The Maurya period (3rd century BC) has its most notable example in the palace of Asoka, and was characterized by sculptured gateways and reliefs. The Kusana and Andhra periods (1st–4th centuries AD) led to the mature and voluptuous art of the Gupta period, which spread widely over SE Asia. Mathura, Sarnath, Ajanta, and Aurangabad were centres of Buddhist sculpture. Images of the Buddha followed a symbolic pattern: his plumpness signified well-being, his posture relaxation, his expression tranquillity. Remarkable examples of Brahmanical art were also produced. The same tradition led in the 6th and 7th centuries to the painting of frescoes, usually depicting incidents in the legends of the Buddhist, Hindu, and Jain religions. The 7th century saw the highest peak of Indian art; for example the magnificent rock sculpture of the descent of the Ganges at Mamallapuram. By the 13th century Hinduism became the major religion. The figures of its many exotic deities are rounded and sensuous, their poses based on religious dance movements. Eroticism enters with exuberantly amorous couples symbolizing the unity of the divine. Sculpture was generally of a religious character, but the Gujarat school also excelled in decorating dwelling houses. A brilliant school of miniature paintings beginning in the 11th century reached its peak in 16th century Rajputana. The Moguls introduced a school of painting based on Persian forms; Indian artists absorbed and expanded this art with great technical virtuosity. After a period of decline Indian art has enjoyed a renaissance in modern times, for example the work of Abanindranath ◊Tagore, Amrita Sher-Gil, Jamini Roy, and

Sailoz Mookherjee. Prehistoric cave paintings were discovered near ◊Bhopal in 1973.

Indian corn an alternative name for ◊maize.

Indian languages traditionally, the languages of the subcontinent of India; since 1947, the languages of the Republic of India. These number some 200, depending on whether a variety is classified as a language or a dialect, and divide into five main groups, the two most widespread of which are the Indo-European languages (mainly in the north) and the Dravidian languages (mainly in the south). The Indo-European languages include the two classical languages, Sanskrit and Pali, and such vernaculars as Bengali, Hindi, Gujarati, Marathi, Oriya, Punjabi and Urdu. The Dravidian languages include Kannada, Malayalam, Tamil and Telugu. A wide range of scripts are used, including Devanagari for Hindi, Arabic for Urdu, and distinct scripts for the various Dravidian languages. The Sino-Tibetan group of languages occurs widely in Assam and along the Himalayas.

Indian literature there has been a wealth of literature in India through medieval to modern times. In the last century Bengali has emerged as an important literary tongue, for example in the work of philologist Ram Mohan Roy, founder of Brahma ◊Samaj, who paved the way for such writers as novelist Bankim Chandra ◊Chatterji and Romesh Chunder Dutt (1848–1909). A sign of the reputation of Bengali among literatures of the modern world was the award to Rabindranath ◊Tagore of a Nobel prize in 1913: notable among later writers are the poets Buddhadeva Bose (1908–) and Amiya Chakravarty. Also important as literary languages are Urdu (the novelist Prem Chand and poet-philosopher ◊Iqbal) and Gujarati (the poet Nanalal Devi and the writings of Gandhi). The long association with Britain has established English as an important literary language, and writers in English – though wholly Indian in the character of their work – include the novelist Dhan Gopal Mukerji, the poet Sarojini Naidu (1879–1949), Sri Aurobindo (1872–1950), and Dom Moraes (1938–), and Nehru. Tagore wrote little creatively in English, but translated many of his own works. Among overseas writers of Indian descent, the most famous is V S ◊Naipaul. For the literature of ancient India see ◊Sanskrit, ◊Veda, ◊Pali, and ◊Prakrit.

Indian Mutiny the revolt against the British in India of the Bengal army in 1857–58. The movement was confined to the north, from Bengal to the Punjab, and Central India; it drew its main support from the army and the recently dethroned princes, but in certain areas it developed into a general revolt. The Indian Mutiny led to the substitution in 1858 of direct administration by the Crown for the rule of the East India Company.

Indian National Congress (INC) the official name for the ◊Congress Party of India.

Indian Ocean ocean between Africa and Australia, with India to the N, and the S boundary being an arbitrary line from Cape Agulhas to S Tasmania; area 73,500,000 sq km/28,350,500 sq mi. The greatest depth is the

Indian Mutiny An Early war photograph of the Indian Mutiny, which drew its main support from the army and the recently dethroned princes, but developed into a general revolt in some areas.

Java Trench 7,725 m/25,344 ft; average depth 3,872 m/12,704 ft. Since the 1970s Soviet-American military competition has enhanced the value of island bases.

India of the Princes name applied to the 562 Indian states ruled by princes during the period of British control. Occupying an area of 715,964 sq mi (45 per cent of the total area of pre-partition India) and with a population of over 93 million they were inextricably mixed up with the former British provinces. Most of the states were Hindu, and their rulers mainly ◊Rajputs. When India was overwhelmed by the Muslims, the Rajput states in the north west deserts of the outer Himalayas, and the central highlands, were saved by their isolation and by the fighting qualities of their inhabitants. As the Mogul empire disintegrated other states were set up by mercenaries, for example Baroda, Hyderabad, Gwalior, Indore, Bhopal, Patiala, Bahawalpur, and Kolhapur. Mysore, Travancore, and Cochin were also non-Rajput states. At partition of British India in 1947 the princes were given independence by the British government, but were advised to adhere to either India or Pakistan. Between 1947 and 1950 all except ◊Kashmir were incorporated in either country.

indicator species a plant or animal whose presence or absence in an area indicates certain environmental conditions. For example, some lichens are sensitive to sulphur dioxide in the air, and absence of these species indicates atmospheric pollution. Many plants show a preference for either alkaline or acid soil conditions, while certain plants, mostly trees, require aluminium, and are only found in soils where it is present.

indigenous native to a country, but especially describing its people and those peoples whose territory has been colonized by Europeans, such as the Australian Aboriginals, the Maori, and American Indians. A World Council of Indigenous Peoples is based in Canada.

indigo violet-blue vegetable dye obtained from genus *Indigofera*, family Leguminosae, but now replaced by a synthetic product. Once a chief export crop of India.

indium a soft, silvery, rare metallic element; symbol In, atomic weight 114.82, atomic number 49. Discovered in 1863 by Reich and Richter, it was named indium after its indigo-blue spectrum. It occurs in minute traces in zinc ores, and is obtained by ◊electrolysis from solutions of complex salts. On account of its large neutron capture cross-section, indium is used to monitor the neutron emission from reactors. Other uses include the manufacture of junctions in ◊semiconductor devices, and as corrosion-resistant coatings for aircraft sleeve bearings.

Indo-Aryan languages another name for the ◊Indo-European languages.

Indo-China /ˈɪndəʊ ˈtʃaɪnə/ French former collective name for ◊Kampuchea, ◊Laos, and ◊Vietnam, which became independent after World War II.

Indo-China War war 1946–1954 between France, the occupying colonial power, and nationalist forces of what was to become Vietnam. In 1945 Vietnamese nationalist Communist leader Ho Chi-Minh proclaimed an independent Vietnamese republic, which soon began an armed struggle against French forces. France in turn set up a non-Communist state in 1949. After the siege of ◊Dien Bien Phu in 1954,

a ceasefire was agreed between France and China which resulted in the establishment of two separate Vietnamese states, North and South Vietnam, divided by the 17th parallel. Attempts at reunification of the country led subsequently to the ◊Vietnam War.

Indo-European languages a family of languages whose members are now distributed throughout every inhabited continent of the world but which were once located along a geographical band from India through Iran into NW Asia, E Europe, the northern Mediterranean lands, N and W Europe and the British Isles. When first discussed and described in the 19th century this family was known as the Aryan and then the Indo-Germanic language family. However, because of an unwelcome association with ideas of 'Aryan' racial purity and superiority and with the ideology of Nazi Germany, both titles have been abandoned by scholars in favour of the neutral 'Indo-European'. The family includes some of the world's leading classical languages (Sanskrit and Pali in India, Zend Avestan in Iran, and Greek and Latin in Europe) as well as several of the most widely spoken languages of the modern world (English worldwide; Spanish in Iberia, Latin America and elsewhere; and the Hindi group of languages in N India). In general terms, many Indo-European languages (such as English, French and Hindi) have shown a tendency to evolve from the highly inflected to a more open or analytic grammatical style that depends less on complex grammatical endings to nouns, verbs and adjectives. Eastern Indo-European languages are often called the *satem* group (Zend, 'a hundred') while western Indo-European languages are the *centum* group (Latin, 'a hundred'); this illustrates a split that occurred over 3,000 years ago, between those which had an *s*-sound in certain words and those which had a *k*-sound. Scholars have reconstructed a Proto-Indo-European ancestral language by comparing the sound systems and historical changes within the family, but continue to dispute the original homeland of this ancient form, some arguing for N Europe, others for Russia N of the Black Sea.

Indo-Germanic languages former name for the ◊Indo-European languages.

Indonesia /ˌɪndəʊˈniːzɪə/ country in SE Asia, made up of over 3,000 islands situated on the equator, between the Indian and Pacific Oceans. *government* Under the 1945 constitution, amended in 1950 and 1969, the supreme political body in Indonesia is, in theory, the 920-member people's consultative council (*Majelis Permusyawaratan Rakyat*). This comprises the 460 members of the legislature (house of representatives), as well as 460 appointed representatives from regional assemblies and functional groups (including 230 from the armed forces). It sits at least once every five years to elect an executive president and vice-president, and determines the constitution.
The house of representatives *Dewan Perwakilan Rakyat* functions as a single-chamber legislature, comprising 364 directly elected members and 96 presidential appointees. It

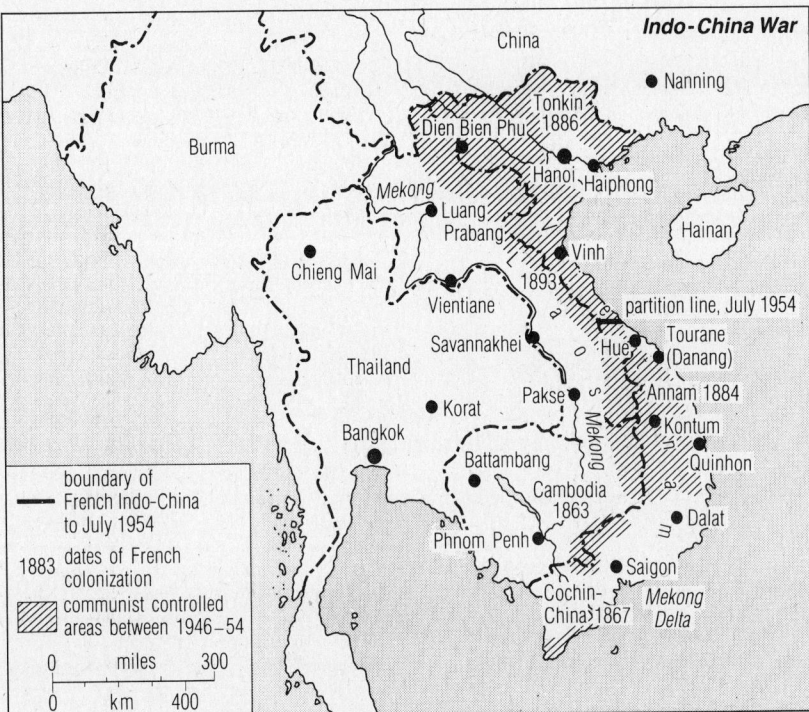

Indo-China War

boundary of
French Indo-China
to July 1954
1883 dates of French
colonization
communist controlled
areas between 1946–54

0 ——— miles ——— 300
0 ——— km ——— 400

---

meets at least once a year, with elections every five years. At the head of the executive, and the most powerful political figure in Indonesia, is the president, elected by the people's consultative council for five-year terms. The president works with an appointed cabinet, exercises the right of veto over house of representatives' bills and appoints governors to supervise local government in each of Indonesia's 27 provinces.
Indonesia's dominant political party is the Golkar. The Islamic Party Persatuan Pembangunan and Christian-orientated Party Demokrasi Indonesia also operate, holding seats in the House of Representatives and People's Consultative Assembly. Parties opposed to Pancasila and which are regionally based are debarred from functioning.
history Between 3000–500 BC, immigrants from S China displaced the original Melanesian population of Indonesia. Between 700 and 1450 AD, two Hindu empires developed, to be superseded by Islam from the 13th century. During the 16th century English and Portuguese traders were active in Indonesia, but in 1595 Holland took over trade in the area. In the 17th century the Dutch only managed to establish trading centres, while Indonesian kingdoms dominated the region, but by the 18th–19th centuries their control was complete, and the islands were proclaimed a Dutch colony in 1816. A nationalist movement developed during the 1920s under the pro-Communist Indonesian Nationalist Party (PNI), headed by Achmed ◊Sukarno. This was suppressed by the Dutch, but in 1942, after Japan's occupation of the islands, the PNI were installed in power as an anti-Western puppet government. When Japan

surrendered to the Allies in 1945, President Sukarno proclaimed Indonesia's independence. The Dutch challenged this by launching military expeditions, before agreeing to transfer sovereignty in 1949. A 'special union' was established between the two countries, but was abrogated by Indonesia in 1956.
The new republic was planned as a federation of 16 constituent regions, but was made unitary in 1950. This led to dominance by Java (which has two-thirds of Indonesia's population), provoking revolts in ◊Sumatra and the predominantly Christian ◊South Moluccas. The paramount political figure in the new republic was President Sukarno, who ruled in an authoritarian manner and pursued an ambitious and expansionist foreign policy. He effected the transfer of Netherlands ◊New Guinea (Irian Jaya) to Indonesia in 1963, but failed in a confrontation with ◊Malaysia over claims to ◊Sabah and ◊Sarawak.
With the economy deteriorating, in 1965 an attempted coup against Sukarno by groups connected with the Indonesian Communist Party was firmly put down by army chief-of-staff Gen ◊Suharto, who then assumed power as emergency ruler in 1966. He ended hostility over Sabah and Sarawak and formally replaced Sukarno as president in 1967. He proceeded to institute what was termed a 'New Order'. This involved the concentration of political power in the hands of a coterie of army and security force officers, the propagation of a new secular state philosophy of Pancasila, which stressed unity and social justice, the pursuit of a liberal economic programme, and the fierce suppression of Communist activity.

Rising oil exports brought significant industrial and agricultural growth to Indonesia during the 1970s, self-sufficiency in rice production being attained by the 1980s. In addition, its borders were extended by the forcible annexation of the former Portuguese colony of ◊East Timor in 1976. However, Suharto's authoritarian approach has met with opposition from left-wing groups, from radical Muslims, and from separatist groups in outlying islands, most especially in Irian Jaya.
In recent years, economic problems have mounted as a result of the fall in world prices of oil, which provides 70% of Indonesia's foreign exchange earnings). Indonesia has long pursued a ◊non-aligned foreign policy, hosting the ◊Bandung Conference of Third World nations in 1955, and is a member of ◊ASEAN. Under Gen Suharto, however, its relations with the West have become closer.
Indore /ɪnˈdɔː/ city in Madhya Pradesh, India; population (1981) 829,327.
Indra /ˈɪndrə/ Hindu god of the sky, shown as a four-armed man on a white elephant, carrying a thunderbolt. The intoxicating drink ◊soma is associated with him.
Indre /ˈændrə/ river rising in the Auvergne mountains, France, and flowing NW for 170 km/115 mi to join the Loire below Tours. It gives its name to the *départements* of Indre and Indre-et-Loire.
indri largest living lemur *Indri indri* of Madagascar. Black and white, almost tailless, it has long arms and, especially, hind limbs and is good at leaping from one upright branch to another. Diurnal and highly arboreal, it has a body 70 cm/2.3 ft long. Its howl is doglike or human in tone.
inductance in physics, that property of an electronic circuit or circuit component which when carrying a current is characterized by the formation of a magnetic field and the storage of magnetic energy. Also a measure of the capability of a circuit or circuit component to store magnetic energy when carrying a current. Symbol L, unit henry.
induction in philosophy, the process of examining and observing particular instances of things, in order to derive general statements and laws. It is the opposite of ◊deduction, which moves from general statements and principles to the particular. The principle of induction was criticized by ◊Hume because it relied upon belief rather than valid reasoning. In the philosophy of science, the 'problem of induction' is a crucial area of debate: however much evidence there is for a proposition, there is a chance that in the future a counter-instance will appear, which will make the explanation untrue. Therefore, it is argued, no scientific statement can be said to be true.
induction in medicine, the use of ◊hormones to initiate childbirth. In biology, a term used for various processes, including the production of an ◊enzyme in response to a particular chemical in the cell, and the ◊differentiation of cells in an ◊embryo.
induction coil type of electrical transformer that produces an intermittent high voltage from

THE INDO-EUROPEAN LANGUAGES

The Indo-European languages An outline diagram of the historical relationships among the Indo-European languages, followed by lists of languages in each branch of the family tree. Extinct languages are marked with an asterisk (*).

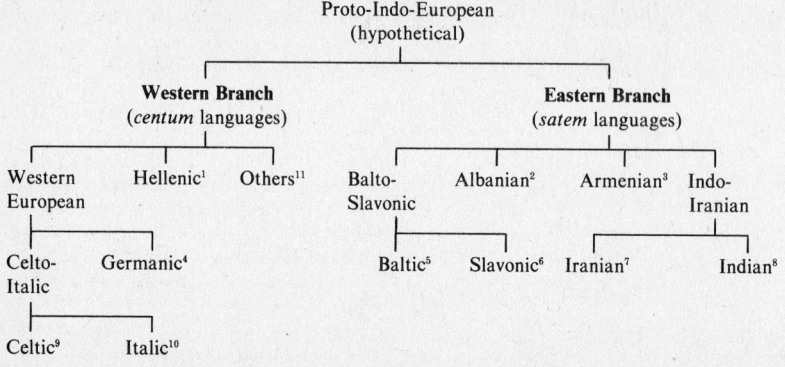

1 Hellenic: Greek (including *Ancient, *Archaic, *Classical, *Koine, *Byzantine and the modern forms *Demotiki* and *Katharevousa*)
2 Albanian: Albanian
3 Armenian: Armenian
4 Germanic: Afrikaans, *Anglo-Saxon (Old English), Bavarian, Danish, Dutch/Flemish, English/Scots, Faroese, Frisian, German (Low, High, Swiss, etc), *Gothic, Icelandic, Luxemburgish, *Old Norse, *Old High German, Norwegian, Swedish, Yiddish
5 Baltic: Latvian, Lithuanian, *Old Prussian
6 Slavonic: Bulgarian, Byelorussian, Croatian, Czech, Kashubian, Macedonian, Polish,
  (or Slavic)   Pomeranian, Russian, Serbian, Slovak, Slovene, Sorbian, Ukrainian
7 Iranian: *Avestan (Zend or Zand), *Bactrian, Baluchi, Kurdish, *Median, Ossetic, *Pahlavi, *Parthian, Pashto, Persian (Farsi), Tadzhik
8 Indian: Assamese, Bengali, Bhili, Bihari, Gujarati, Hindi, Kashmiri, Konkani, Marathi, Oriya, Pahari, *Pali, Punjabi, Rajasthani, *Sanskrit, Sindhi, Sinhalese, Urdu
9 Celtic: Breton, *Brythonic, *Cornish, Gaelic (Irish, *Manx and Scottish), *Gaulish, *Goidelic, Welsh
10 Italic: (1) *Latin, *Oscan, *Umbrian
     (2) Romance: Catalan, French, Gallego (Galician), Italian, Portuguese, Provençal, Romanian (Rumanian), Romansh, Spanish (Castilian)
11 others   *Anatolian (including Hittite), *Tocharian

---

a low-voltage supply. It has a primary coil consisting of a few turns of thick wire wound round an iron core and passing a low voltage (usually from a battery). Wound on top of this is a secondary coil made up of many turns of thin wire. An iron armature and make-and-break mechanism (similar to that in an ⟩electric bell) repeatedly interrupts the current to the primary coil, producing a high, rapidly pulsing current in the secondary circuit. See ⟩ignition coil.

inductor an element possessing the characteristic of ⟩inductance (electromagnetic property).

indulgence in the Roman Catholic church, the total or partial remission of temporal punishment for sins which remain to be expiated after penitence and confession has secured exemption from eternal punishment. The doctrine of indulgence began as the commutation of the church penances for sin, such as fasting, for suitable works of charity or money gifts to the church, and became a great source of church revenue. The system was much criticized, for example, when archbishop Albert of Mainz and Magdeburg sold indulgences through the agency of the Dominican Tetzel. This trade in indulgences roused Luther in 1517 to draw up his 95 'Theses' and initiate the Reformation. The Council of Trent in 1563 recommended moderate retention of indulgences, and they continue, notably in 'Holy Years'.

Indus /'ɪndəs/ river in Asia, rising in Tibet and flowing 2,900 km/1,800 mi to the Arabian Sea. In 1960 the use of its waters, including those of its five tributaries, were divided between India (rivers Ravi, Beas, Sutlej) and Pakistan (rivers Indus, Jhelum, Chenab).

industrial relations relationship between employers and employed, and their dealings with each other (in the latter's case usually through trade unions). In most industries wages and conditions are determined by 'free collective bargaining' between employers and trade unions. When agreement cannot be reached, outside arbitration is often sought (in Britain the Advisory Conciliation and Arbitration Service, ACAS, was set up in 1975). Trade unions' powers are legally restricted in various ways (see under ⟩trade union), but there is no single legal authority that oversees them: the government proposals *In Place of Strife* 1969 favoured the setting up of a Commission on Industrial Relations, but this was shelved. However, under the Industrial Relations Act 1971 an Industrial Court was established, with High Court status, to give judgment on matters relating to industrial disputes; it was abolished in 1974.

Another major aspect of industrial relations is worker participation, through both profit-sharing and industrial democracy. It was introduced in West Germany by law in 1952, giving the 'works councils' of a firm a right of veto in hirings and redundancies, and making at least one-third of the 'supervisory board' workers' representatives, the rest being 'shareholders'. A variation on this system was advocated for Britain by the Bullock Report 1977, which proposed the placing of union-nominated worker-directors on the main boards of companies. The suggestion was not taken up, nor to any extent has been the concept of co-ownership, in which a company is entirely owned by its employees, with any profits not ploughed back being distributed as a bonus to the workers. Another approach to industrial relations in recent years has been that of the Japanese, who encourage a feeling of belonging among their workers amounting almost to family membership.

Industrial Revolution the sudden acceleration of technical development that took place in Britain from the second half of the 18th century. It transferred the balance of political power from the landowner to the industrial capitalist and created an urban industrial working class.

The great achievement of the first phase (to 1830) was the invention of the steam engine, originally developed for draining mines (see ⟩Newcomen) but rapidly put to use in factories and on the railways (see ⟩Watt, ⟩Arkwright, ⟩Crompton, ⟩Trevithick). In the second phase, from 1830 to the early 20th century, the Industrial Revolution spread to Europe, its colonies, and the USA. The internal combustion engine and electricity were developed, and in 1911 Rutherford split the atom at Manchester, opening up the prospect of nuclear power. Electronic devices were developed which made automation possible, with the eventual prospect of even managerial decision-making being in the hands of 'machines'.

industry the extraction and conversion of raw materials, the manufacture of goods, and the provision of services.

British industry The most prominent trends in industrial activity in Britain during the 1970s and 1980s have been the growth of the offshore oil and gas industries, the rapid growth of electronic and microelectronic technologies, and a continuous rise in the share of total employment

Indonesia
REPUBLIC OF (*Republik Indonesia*)

AREA 1,925,000 sq km/741,000 sq mi
CAPITAL Jakarta
TOWNS ports Surabaya, Semarang
PHYSICAL comprises 1,400 tropical islands,
including the greater part of the Sunda Islands
to the W of the Moluccas, both the Greater
Sundas (including Java and Madura, part of
Kalimantan/Borneo, Sumatra, Sulawesi and
Belitung) and the Lesser Sundas/Nusa
Tenggara (including Bali, Lombok, Sumba,
Timor), as well as Malaku/Moluccas and part
of New Guinea (Irian Jaya)
FEATURES world's largest Islamic state; Java is
one of the world's most densely populated
areas
HEAD OF STATE AND OF GOVERNMENT T N J
Suharto from 1967
GOVERNMENT authoritarian
EXPORTS coffee, rubber, palm oil and coconuts,
tin, tea, tobacco; oil and liquid natural gas
CURRENCY rupiah (2,727 = £1 Sept 1987)
POPULATION (1985) 173,103,000 (including
300 ethnic groups); annual growth rate 2.2%
LANGUAGE Indonesian, closely allied to Malay
RELIGION Muslim 90%, Buddhist, Hindu, and
Pancasila (a secular official ideology)
LITERACY 77% male/68% female (1980 est)
GNP $87 bn (1983); $560 per head of
population
CHRONOLOGY
17th century Dutch rule established.
1942 Occupied by Japan. Nationalist
government established.
1945 Japanese surrender. Nationalists declare
independence under Sukarno.

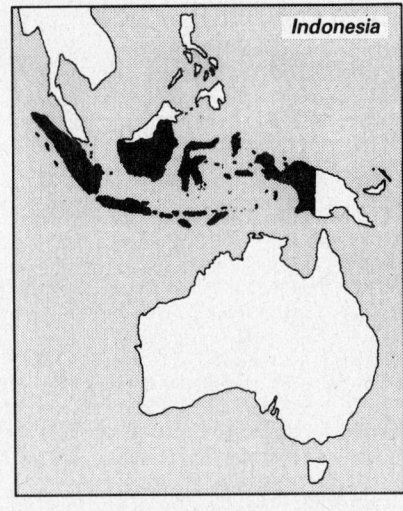

Indonesia

1949 Formal transfer of Dutch sovereignty.
1950 Unitary constitution established.
1963 Western New Guinea (Irian Jaya) ceded
by Holland.
1965–66 Attempted communist coup: Gen
Suharto emergency administration.
1967 Sukarno replaced as president by
Suharto.
1976 Annexation by force of the former
Portuguese colony of E Timor.

of service industries. Recessions in 1974–75 and
1980–81, due in part to fluctuating energy costs,
have been offset by marked increases in
productivity, but these gains mean that the
increased output was achieved with fewer
workers, and unemployment has been a
persistent feature of the period.
Electronics and automated controls are applied
extensively throughout industry, particularly in
steel mills, oil refineries, coal mines and chemical
plants. Britain is now the sixth largest user of
industrial robots in the world. Another area of
technological strength is ◊biotechnology, using
fermentation techniques for food, beverage and
antibiotic production. The main areas of
research and development expenditure are
electronics, chemicals, aerospace, mechanical
engineering and motor vehicles.
The government-owned public sector includes
electricity and water supply, coal, steel, British
Rail and the Post Office. These account for over
6% of total employment. Government policy is
to encourage economic recovery by improving
performance in the face of the open market, and
◊privatization (selling shares to the public) is
planned for a number of companies; British
Telecom was sold in this way in 1985, British Gas
in 1986 and British Airways in early 1987.

As a member of the European Economic
Community (EEC), Britain has received grants
from the European Regional Development Fund,
which was established in 1975 to assist in the
conversion of declining industrial regions, and
developing areas seen to be lagging behind the
rest of the Community.
Manufacturing, construction and the service
industries account for 88% of gross domestic
product, and employed 26%, 5% and 65% of the
labour force respectively in 1985. For
manufacturing, the highest growth in the past
decade has been in the chemicals, electrical and
instrument engineering sectors.
Mineral products the British Steel Corporation
accounts for 82–85% of Britain's steel output by
volume, and is the world's fourth largest steel
company. The private sector is strong in the
manufacture of special steels, alloys and finished
products for the engineering industries.
Manipulation of materials by smelting, casting
rolling, extruding and drawing techniques, is also
carried out.
Chemicals accounting for about 10% of
manufacturing net output, this industry
produces a complete range of products including
fertilizers, plastics, pharmaceuticals, soap,
toiletries and explosives.

Mechanical engineering machine tools,
industrial engines, mechanical handling
equipment, construction equipment and
industrial plant are all significant products in this
area. Britain is the Western world's largest
producer of agricultural tractors.
Motor vehicles recent years have seen a large
increase in the volume of imports in this sector,
notably from Europe and Japan. However,
British manufacturers still provide a major
export.
Aerospace in order to compete with the USA in
this area, Britain has resorted to European and
multinational cooperative ventures, including
the Airbus passenger airliner and the Ariane
rocket for the launching of satellites; however, in
1987 it pulled out of both Airbus and Ariane. The
space industry's major strength at present is the
manufacture of satellites. Aircraft (civil and
military), helicopters, aero engines and guided
weapons are major products, supported by a
comprehensive range of aircraft and airfield
equipment and systems.
Construction building, repair, alteration and
maintenance of buildings, highways, bridges,
tunnels, drainage and sewage systems, docks,
harbours and offshore structures are included,
together with ancillary services such as wiring,
heating, ventilation and air conditioning.
Service industries the fastest growing sectors
during the 1970s, measured by employment,
were financial and business services, professional
and scientific services (including health and
education) and leisure. In the 1980s finance
continued to grow strongly, and franchising,
particularly in labour-intensive areas such as
hotel, catering and cleaning businesses, became
a popular new form of organization.
World industry on the global scale, the period
after World War II has been marked by the
development of traditional industry such as
shipbuilding and motor manufacture in the low-
cost countries, particularly Japan, Korea and the
Pacific region generally. This has been followed
by moves into newer industrial products, most
notably electronics and computers, in which
these countries may be said to have dominated
the world. In the West, the USA has been most
successful due in part to the great size of its home
market, while the USSR, and to a lesser extent
Europe, have resorted to protectionist tariff and
quota barriers, and attempts to implement
economic planning as a tool for increased
economic growth.

Indus Valley Civilization prehistoric culture
existing in the NW Indian subcontinent from
about 2500–1600 BC, of which the most famous
city ruins are those of the latter date: Harappa
(Punjab) excavated by Sir Mortimer ◊Wheeler
in 1946, and Mohenjo Daro (Sind) in Pakistan,
which had advanced sanitary facilities. Most
striking artistic remains are their soapstone seals
with engravings of elephants, snakes, and other
animals. Mystery surrounds their disposal of
their dead.

Indy /æn'diː/ (Paul Marie Théodore)
Vincent 1851–1931. French composer. Born in
Paris, he studied under César ◊Franck, and was
one of the founders of the *Schola Cantorum*. His

works include operas (*Fervaal* 1897), symphonies, tone poems (*Istar* 1896), and chamber music.

inert gases the group of six gaseous elements, so named because of their unreactivity: argon, helium, krypton, neon, radon and xenon. They are also called the noble gases. Some of them are used in strip lighting and ◊lasers.

inertia in physics, the property of an object that causes it, if at rest, to tend to remain at rest, or if moving to keep moving at a constant speed in a straight line. An external force has to be applied to overcome inertia, as postulated by ◊Newton's first law of motion.

INF abbreviation for ◊Intermediate Nuclear Forces Treaty.

infant see ◊minor.

infante /ɪnˈfænteɪ/ and *infanta* (from Latin *infans*, an infant) title given in Spain and Portugal to the sons (other than the heir-apparent) and daughters respectively of the sovereign. The heir-apparent in Spain bears the title of Prince of ◊Asturias.

infanticide killing of offspring, among human beings usually as a method of population control, and most frequently of girls (India and China), though boys are killed in countries where bride-prices are high.

infantile paralysis former term for ◊poliomyelitis.

infant mortality rate a measure of the number of infants dying under one year of age. Improved sanitation, nutrition and medical care have considerably lowered figures throughout much of the world; for example in the 18th century in the UK 50 per cent died, compared with under two per cent in 1971. In much of the Third World, however, the infant mortality rate remains high.

infection invasion of the body by microorganisms. These may be ◊protozoa, ◊viruses, or ◊bacteria including cocci and bacilli. Diseases caused by viruses include AIDS, smallpox, chickenpox, shingles, measles, mumps, german measles, poliomyelitis, influenza, colds, and sleeping sickness; cocci cause diseases with short incubation periods and acute fever, for example scarlet fever, meningitis, and gonorrhoea; bacilli cause diseases with long incubation periods and course, for example diphtheria, whooping cough, and typhus. Both cocci and bacilli tend to be carried by immune persons. The effects of infection are due to the body's reaction to the poisons (toxins) produced by the organisms. Infection may be contracted from a sufferer from the disease; or from a carrier who may be immune or developing the disease or convalescent; or from contaminated objects, such as food, drink, bedclothes, or books; or from discharges, such as spray expelled in coughing or sneezing (common cold), or faeces (typhoid). Some infections are carried by insects (malaria by the mosquito, typhus by the louse), or on the feet of flies (food poisoning). Some may be introduced through a wound in the skin, for example gonorrhoea and lockjaw (tetanus). Contagion is infection by direct contact. Defences against infection include ◊immunity.

inferiority complex in psychology, a

◊complex described by ◊Adler. Based on physical inferiority; the term has been popularly used to refer to general feelings of inferiority.

infinite series in mathematics, the sum of an ordered sequence of numbers or algrebraic terms that go on for ever, for example, the series of ordinary numbers beginning 1 + 2 + 3 + 4 + 5... Such a series is divergent, that is, its terms get larger, and can be summed over a infinite number of terms. Some infinite series, however, are convergent, that is, the terms get smaller, and 'tend to a limit' (approach a sum but never quite reach it), as successive terms approach zero. Thus, the sum of the infinite series 8 + 4 + 2 + 1 + ½ + ¼ + ... tends to the limit 16.

infinity mathematical quantity that is larger than any fixed assignable quantity, given the symbol ∞. By convention, the result of dividing any number by zero is regarded as infinity.

inflammation reaction of living tissue (heat, swelling, redness, pain, and loss of function) to injury. White blood cells and lymph pour into the affected region to combat the injurious agent and repair damage; white cells killed in doing so form yellow pus.

inflation in economics, a rise in the general level of prices, caused by an excess of demand over supply (*cost-push inflation* such as the world price rise in oil in 1974), and related to an increase in the supply of money (*demand-pull inflation*). Deflation is the reverse, a fall in the general level of prices.

inflation accounting ◊accountancy methods that allow for the changing purchasing power of money.

inflation tax tax imposed on companies that increase wages by more than an amount fixed by law (except to take account of increased profits or because of a profit-sharing scheme). Proposed at various times during the 1970s, but not introduced to Britain, it is based on the notion that excessive wage rises contribute to inflation.

inflection or *inflexion* in grammatical analysis, an ending or other element in a word which indicates its grammatical function (whether it is plural or singular, masculine or feminine). In a highly inflected language like Latin, nouns, verbs and adjectives have a whole battery of inflectional endings (for example, in the word *amabunt* the base *am* means 'love', and the complex *abunt* indicates the kind of verb, the future tense, indicative mood, active voice, third person and plurality). English is not a highly inflected language, but does have inflections for plural and for certain forms of the verb (for example, the *s* in 'He run*s*' indicates the third person singular , while in 'the book*s*' it indicates plurality).

inflorescence a flower-bearing branch, or system of branches, in plants. It is usually separated from the leaves by a stalk or peduncle and comprises two, three or more individual flowers. The stalk of each individual flower is called a pedicel.

Inflorescences can be divided into two main types. In a cymose inflorescence, the terminal growing point produces a single flower and subsequent flowers arise on lateral branches farther down, as in forget-me-not (*Myosotis*)

and chickweed (*Stellaria*); the oldest flowers are found at the apex. A racemose inflorescence consists of a main axis, bearing flowers along its length, with an active growing region at the apex; the oldest flowers are found near the base or, where the inflorescence has become flattened, towards the outside. Some examples of this type include the raceme as seen in lupins, a spike which is similar but has stalkless flowers, for example, plantain (*Plantago*); and a corymb, which is rounded or flat-topped, as in candytuft (*Iberis*). A panicle is a branched inflorescence comprising a number of racemes, as seen in many grasses for example, oats (*Avena*). An umbel, as in cow parsley (*Anthriscus sylvestris*), is a special type of racemose inflorescence with all the flower stalks arising from the same point on the main stem. Other types of racemose inflorescence include the ◊catkin, ◊spadix, and ◊capitulum.

influenza acute viral respiratory infection, which sets in sharply with fever, shivering and aching. The 'Spanish flu' epidemic of 1918 killed approximately twice as many as were killed in World War I.

infra-red astronomy study of infra-red radiation produced by relatively cool gas and dust in space, such as in the areas around forming stars. In 1983 the Infra-Red Astronomy Satellite, IRAS, surveyed the entire sky at infra-red wavelengths. It found five new ◊comets, possible forming planetary systems around several dozen stars, and thousands of galaxies undergoing bursts of star formation.

infra-red radiation (IR) invisible electromagnetic radiation of wavelength between about 0.75 micrometres (millionths of a metre) and 1 millimetre, that is, between the limit of the red end of the visible spectrum and the shortest microwaves. All bodies above the ◊absolute zero of temperature absorb and radiate infra-red radiation. Infra-red absorption spectra are made use of in chemical analysis, particularly for organic compounds, and objects which radiate infra-red radiation can be photographed or made visible in the dark, or through mist or fog, on specially sensitized emulsions. This is important for military purposes and in saving life (for example the detection of people under rubble after an explosion). Infra-red radiation is also used in medical photography and treatment, in industry, astronomy and criminology. The strong absorption by many substances of infra-red radiation is a useful method of applying heat, as in baking and toasting.

Ingres /ˈæ̃grə/ Jean Auguste Dominique 1780–1867. French painter, a student of ◊David, and leading exponent of the French ◊neo-Classical style in opposition to the romanticism of ◊Delacroix. Famous for his female nudes *Odalisque* 1814 and *La Source/The Fountain* 1856.

inheritance tax in the UK, a tax imposed on large amounts of money or property passed on from one person to another, by gift, inheritance, and so on. It replaced capital transfer tax in 1986 (which in turn replaced estate duty in 1974).

inhibition, *neural* in biology, the process whereby activity in one ◊nerve cell suppresses

inflorescence

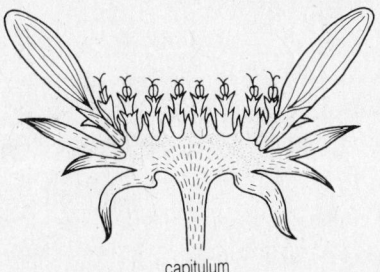
capitulum

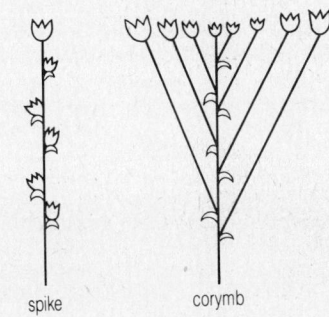
spike   corymb

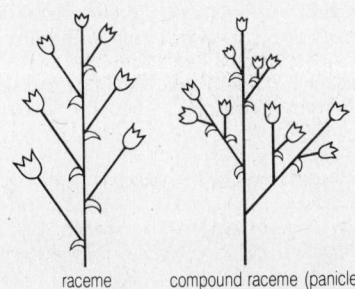
raceme   compound raceme (panicle)

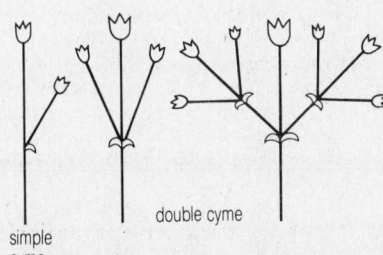
simple
cyme   double cyme

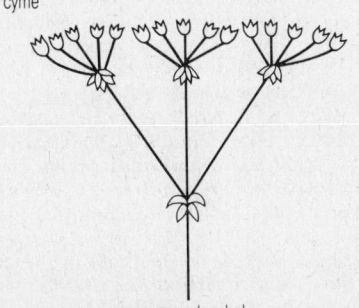
compound umbel

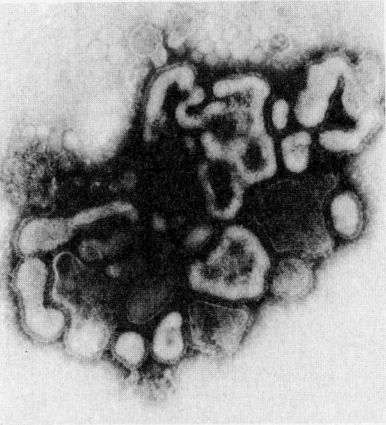

influenza An influenza virus, magnified under an electron microscope over 132,000 times.

activity in another. Neural inhibition in networks of nerve cells leading from sensory organs, or to muscles, plays an important role in allowing an animal to make fine sensory discriminations and in the fine control of movements.

initiative and *referendum* devices whereby the voters may play a direct part in making laws. In the *initiative* a proposed law is drawn up and signed by petitioners, and submitted to the legislature. A *referendum* may be taken on a law that has been passed by the legislature but that will not become operative until the people have expressed their will concerning it. If the referendum gives an affirmative vote, then the law is confirmed and comes into force. Switzerland was the pioneer in these devices, but both have been introduced into a number of states and cities of the USA, and a referendum on membership of the Common Market was held in Britain in 1975. It is argued that referenda undermine parliamentary authority, but they do allow the elector to participate directly in government. Another device is the *recall*, whereby the voters are given the opportunity of demanding the dismissal from office of officials.

ink coloured liquid used for writing, drawing and printing. Traditional ink was produced from gallic acid and tannic acid, but modern inks are based on synthetic dyes.

Inkatha South African political organization formed by Chief Gatsha Buthelezi (1928–), leader of six million Zulus, the country's biggest ethnic group. Because Inkatha has tried to work with the white regime, Buthelezi has been regarded as a collaborator by blacks and the United Democratic Front.

Inkerman /ˈɪŋkəmən/ a battle of the ◊Crimean War, fought on 5 Nov 1854, during which an attack by the Russians on Inkerman ridge, occupied by the British army besieging Sebastopol, was repulsed.

INLA abbreviation for ◊Irish National Liberation Army.

Inland Sea (Japanese *Seto Naikai*), 390 km/240 mi long, almost enclosed by the Japanese islands of Honshu, Kyushu and Shikoku. It has about 300 small islands.

Innocent III /ˈɪnəsənt/ 1161–1216. Pope from 1198, he asserted papal power over secular princes, especially over the succession of ◊Holy Roman Emperors. He also made King ◊John of England his vassal, compelling him to accept ◊Langton as archbishop of Canterbury. He promoted the fourth Crusade, and crusades against the pagan Livonians and Letts, and Albigensian heretics.

Innocents' Day or *Childermas* festival of the Catholic church, celebrated on 28 Dec in memory of the children who were slaughtered by Herod following the birth of Jesus Christ.

Innsbruck /ˈɪnzbrʊk/ city in W Austria, population (1981) 116,100. It is a tourist and winter sports centre, and a route junction for the Brenner Pass.

Inns of Court four private societies in London which have the power to call law students to the English Bar: Lincoln's Inn, Gray's Inn, Inner Temple, and Middle Temple. Each pursues its separate existence, though joint lectures are given, and there is a common examination board. Each is under the administration of a body of Benchers.

inoculation injection into the body of dead disease-carrying organisms, toxins, antitoxins, and so on, to produce immunity by inducing a mild form of a disease.

inorganic chemistry the branch of chemistry dealing with the elements and their compounds, excluding the more complex carbon compounds which are considered in ◊organic chemistry . Many types of inorganic compounds exist, the oldest known being acids, bases and salts. Acids change blue vegetable colours (for example litmus) to red, and react with alkalis to form salts. Alkalis restore the colours of indicators changed by acids, and react with acids to form salts. All acids contain hydrogen. Acids containing one, two or three atoms of replaceable hydrogen are called mono, di or tri-basic, respectively. Salts are formed by the replacement of the acidic hydrogen by a metal or radical. If only part of the hydrogen is replaced, an acid salt is formed. Another important group of compounds is the oxides, in which oxygen is combined with another element. Oxides are classified into: (i) acidic oxides, forming acids with water; (ii) basic oxides, forming bases (containing the hydroxyl group OH) with water; (iii) neutral oxides; and (iv) peroxides (containing more oxygen than the normal oxide). Acidic and basic oxides combine to form salts.
Other groups are the compounds of metals with ◊halogens (fluorine, chlorine, bromine, and iodine), called halides (fluorides, chlorides, and so on), and with sulphur (sulphides).
The basis of the modern description of the elements is the ◊Periodic Table. In this, the elements are arranged in order of increasing ◊atomic number (nuclear charge). The continuous sequence of elements then breaks up into 7 periods and 9 groups, the members of a group, and the sub-groups (a) and (b) into which each is divided, showing similar chemical properties. The Roman numeral at the top of each ◊group is equal to some ◊valency (sometimes the minimum, as in group I,

sometimes the maximum, as in groups VI and VII, of the elements it contains). See also ◊chemistry.

input device a device for entering information into a computer. Input devices include the electronic ◊keyboard (the most common), ◊joysticks, touch-sensitive screens and surfaces (such as the ◊graphics tablet), ◊speech recognizers, ◊vision systems, and others.

inquest an inquiry held by a ◊coroner, especially into an unexplained death.

Inquisition tribunal of the Catholic Church established 1229 to suppress heresy. It operated in France, Italy, Spain and the Holy Roman Empire, and was especially active following the ◊Reformation: it was later extended to the Americas. Its trials were conducted in secret, under torture, and penalties ranged from fines, through flogging and imprisonment, to death by burning. The Inquisition or Holy Office (renamed Sacred Congregation for the Doctrine of the Faith 1965) still deals with ecclesiastical discipline.

insanity popular and legal term for mental disorder. In medicine the corresponding term is ◊psychosis.

insect small invertebrate animal whose body is divided into head, thorax, and abdomen. The head bears a pair of feelers or antennae, and attached to the thorax are three pairs of legs and usually two pairs of wings. The scientific study of insects forms that branch of zoology termed entomology. More than one million species are known, and several thousand new ones are discovered every year. Insects vary in size very considerably from 0.02 cm/0.007 in to 35 cm/13.5 in in length.

The skeleton is almost entirely external and is composed of chitin. It remains membranous at the joints, but elsewhere is hard.

The head is the feeding and sensory centre. It bears the antennae, eyes, and mouth-parts. By means of the *antennae*, the insect detects odours and experiences the sense of touch. The *eyes* comprise *compound eyes* and simple eyes or *ocelli*. The compound eyes are formed of a large number of individual facets or lenses. There are about 4,000 lenses to each compound eye in the house-fly. The mouth-parts include a *labrum* or upper lip; a pair of principal jaws or *mandibles*; a pair of accessory jaws or *maxillae*; and a *labium*, or lower lip. These mouth-parts are modified in insects which feed upon a fluid diet. The *thorax* is the locomotory centre, and is made up of three segments: the *pro-*, *meso-*, and *metathorax*. Each bears a pair of legs and, in flying insects, the second and third of these segments also bears a pair of wings.

Wings are composed of an upper and a lower membrane, and between these two layers they are strengthened by a framework of chitinous tubes known as *veins*. The hind-body or abdomen is the metabolic and reproductive centre: it is here that digestion, excretion, and the sexual functions take place. In the female there is very commonly an egg-laying instrument or *ovipositor*, and many insects have a pair of tail feelers or *cerci*. Most insects breathe by means of

fine airtubes called *tracheae* which open to the exterior by a pair of breathing pores or *spiracles*.
Growth and metamorphosis when ready to hatch from the egg the young insect forces its way through the *chorion*, or egg-shell, and growth takes place in cycles that are interrupted by successive moults. After moulting the new cuticle is soft and pliable and able to adapt itself to increase in size and change of form.

Most of the lower orders of insects pass through a direct or incomplete metamorphosis. The young closely resemble the parents and are known as nymphs.

The higher groups of insects (Endopterygota) undergo indirect or complete metamorphosis. They hatch at an earlier stage of growth than nymphs and are termed *larvae*. The life of the insect is interrupted by a resting *pupal* stage when no food is taken. During this stage the larval organs and tissues are transformed into those of the *imago* or adult. Before pupating the insect protects itself by selecting a suitable hiding place, or making a cocoon of some material which will merge in with its surroundings. When an insect is about to emerge from the pupa, or protective sheath, it undergoes its final moult, which consists of shedding the pupal cuticle.

Reproduction is by diverse means. In most insects mating occurs once only, and death soon follows.

Many insects are pests which may be controlled by chemical insecticides (which may also kill useful insects), importation of natural predators (which may themselves become pests), or, more recently, use of artificially reared sterile insects, either the males only or in 'population flushing' both sexes, so sharply reducing succeeding generations.

The classification of insects is largely based upon characters of the mouth-parts, wings and metamorphosis. Insects are classed in two subclasses (one with two divisions), and 29 orders.

insecticide a chemical used to kill insects. Among the most effective insecticides are synthetic organic chemicals such as ◊DDT and dieldrin, which are chlorinated hydrocarbons. These chemicals, however, have proved very persistent and can also poison higher animals. They are now banned in some countries. Other synthetic insecticides include organic phosphorus compounds such as malathion. Insecticides prepared from plants, such as derris and pyrethrum, are also effective. They are safer to use, but need to be applied more frequently.

insectivore an animal whose diet is made up largely or exclusively of insects. In particular the name is applied to mammals of the order Insectivora, which includes the shrews, hedgehogs and moles.

insectivorous plant a plant that can capture and digest animals, to obtain nitrogen compounds which are lacking in its usual marshy habitat. Some are passive traps, for example, *pitcher plants Nepenthes*. One pitcher plant species has container-traps holding 2 litres/3.5 pints of the liquid which 'digests' its insect food, and may even trap rats: see ◊kinibalu. Others, for example, **sundews** *Drosera*, **butterworts**

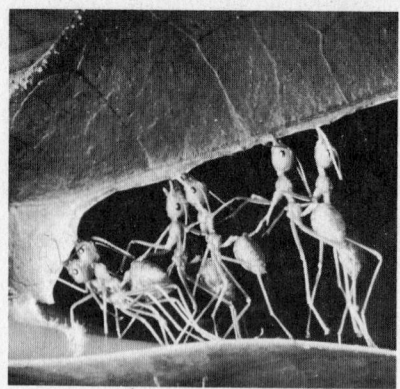

insect Ants close ranks to repair a hole in their nest. Worker weaving ants (Oecophylla smaragdina) combine to pull the edges together. They then prod their larvae (held in their jaws) to make them produce silk, and pass them to and fro as living shuttles to join the edges and close the breach.

Pinguicula and **Venus fly trap** *Dionaea muscipula*, have an active trapping mechanism; see ◊leaf.

inselberg a prominent steep-sided hill of resistant solid rock, such as granite, rising out of a plain, usually in a tropical area. Its rounded appearance is caused by so called onion-skin ◊weathering, in which the surface is eroded in successive layers. The Sugar Loaf in Rio de Janeiro harbour in Brazil, and Ayers Rock in Northern Territory, Australia, are famous examples. The word is German, 'island mountain'.

insemination, artificial artificial introduction of semen into the female reproductive tract to bring about fertilization. Originally used by animal breeders to improve stock by the use of high-quality males, in the 20th century it has been developed for use in humans, to help the infertile. The sperm may come from the husband (AIH) or a donor (AID); an AID child is illegitimate under British law.

A development of artificial insemination is 'in vitro' fertilization ('test-tube' babies), in which the egg is fertilized externally and then reimplanted in the womb; the first successful birth using this method was of Louise Brown in the UK in 1978. Recent extensions of the technique have included the birth of a baby from a frozen embryo (Australia 1984) and from a frozen egg (Australia 1986). Pioneers in the field have been the British doctors Robert Edwards (1925–) and Patrick Steptoe (1913–). As yet the success rate is relatively low; only 15–20 per cent of in vitro fertilizations result in babies.

insider trading or *insider dealing* illegal use of privileged information in dealing on the stock exchanges, for example when a company takeover bid is imminent. Insider trading is in theory detected by the *Securities and Exchange Commission* (SEC) in the USA, and by the *Securities and Investment Board* (SIB) in the UK. Neither agency, however, has any legal powers other than public disclosure.

INSECT CLASSIFICATION

Class Insecta

Subclass Apterytgota – *Wingless insects (considered by some not true insects, and put in other classes)*

Order Thysanura	Three-pronged bristle-tails, silverfish *350*	
Order Diplura	Two-pronged bristle-tails, mostly tiny soil-living insects *400*	
Order Protura	Minute insects living in soil *50*	
Order Collembola	Springtails *1500*	

Subclass Pterygota – *Winged insects, or forms secondarily wingless*

1 EXOPTERYGOTA Young stages (nymphs) largely resemble adults, but are smaller, with externally developing wings.

Order Ephemeroptera	Mayflies *1000*
Order Odonata	Dragonflies, damselflies *5000*
Order Plecoptera	Stoneflies *3000*
Order Grylloblattodea	Wingless soil-living insects of N America *12*
Order Orthoptera	Crickets, grasshoppers, locusts *20000*
Order Phasmida	Stick insects, leaf insects *2000*
Order Dermaptera	Earwigs *1000*
Order Embioptera	Web-spinners *150*
Order Dictyoptera	Cockroaches, praying mantises *5000*
Order Isoptera	Termites *2000*
Order Zoraptera	Tiny insects living in decaying plants *16*
Order Psocoptera	Booklice *1600*
Order Mallophaga	Biting lice, mainly parasitic on birds *2500*
Order Anoplura	Sucking lice, mainly parasitic on mammals *250*
Order Hemiptera	True bugs, including aphids, shield- and bedbugs, froghoppers, pond skaters, water boatmen *55000*
Order Thysanoptera	Thrips *5000*

2 ENDOPTERYGOTA There is a sudden change (metamorphosis) in the life history. Young may look totally unlike adults.

Order Neuroptera	Lacewings, alder flies, snake flies *4500*
Order Mecoptera	Scorpion flies *300*
Order Lepidoptera	Butterflies and moths *165000*
Order Trichoptera	Caddis flies *3000*
Order Diptera	True flies, including bluebottles, mosquitoes, leather jackets *70000*
Order Siphonaptera	Fleas *1400*
Order Hymenoptera	Bees, wasps, ants *100000*
Order Coloeoptera	Beetles, including weevils, ladybirds, glow-worms, wood-worms, chafers *350000*

instalment credit see ◊hire purchase.

instinct in ◊ethology, behaviour found in all equivalent members of a given ◊species (for example, all the males, or all the females with young) that is presumed to be genetically determined. Examples include a male robin's tendency to attack other male robins intruding on its territory and a female mammal's tendency to care for her offspring. Instincts differ from ◊reflexes in that they involve very much more complex actions, and learning often plays an important part in their development.

Institution of Civil Engineers the first national body concerned with the engineering profession in England, founded in 1828. The celebrated builder of roads, bridges and canals, Thomas ◊Telford, became its first president.

instrument landing system a landing aid for aircraft that uses ◊radio beacons on the ground and instruments on the flight deck. One beacon (localizer) sends out a vertical radio beam along the centre line of the runway. Another beacon (glide slope) transmits a beam in the plane at right-angles to the localizer beam at the ideal approach-path angle. The pilot can tell from the instruments what manoeuvres he or she must make to attain the correct approach path.

insulator poor ◊conductor of heat, sound or electricity. Most substances lacking free (mobile) ◊electrons, such as non-metals, are electrical or thermal insulators.

insulin a ◊hormone that promotes utilization of glucose (blood sugar), the body's chief energy source; it is used in the treatment of ◊diabetes.

insurance contract indemnifying the payer of a premium against loss by fire, death, accident, and so on, which is known as assurance in the case of a fixed sum (in Britain especially when the event is inevitable, for example payment of a fixed sum on death), and insurance where the indemnity is proportionate to the loss.

intaglio term applied to an engraving which is cut into some material. It is applied more specifically to a gem which has a pattern cut into one surface, as in an engraved seal-ring. In printing, the term is applied to a process in which ink is laid in incisions and hollows on the plate, as in ◊etching, ◊photogravure, and so on.

integer a positive or negative whole number. Fractions, such as ½ and 0.35, are known as non-integral numbers.

integral calculus branch of mathematics using the process of ◊integration. It is concerned with finding volumes and areas and summing infinitesimally small quantities.

integrated circuit a complete electronic circuit produced on a single crystal of a semiconductor (intermediate between an insulator and a conductor of electricity) such as silicon. The circuit might contain more than a million transistors, resistors, and capacitors and yet measure only 8 mm/0.3 in across. The discovery in the early 1970s of the means to produce such circuits, superseding the printed circuit, began what has been called the computer revolution.

integration in mathematics, method in ◊calculus of finding the sum of a ◊function (or mapping) between certain specified limits. In geometric terms, integration can be thought of as finding the area under a curve (as represented by an algebraic expression or function) between particular values of the function's variable. For example, if a curve is represented by the function $y = f(x)$, the area A under the curve between $x = a$ and the larger value $x = b$ is given by $A = \int f(x)dx$. This method of finding areas is equivalent to splitting the area into an infinite number of small parts and adding all the parts together. By extension, the method can also be used to find the volumes of solids that have an axis of symmetry such as a cube or sphere. In mathematical terms, integration provides a way of finding the limit of the sum S of n values as n gets closer and closer to infinity.

In practice, integral calculus provides scientists with a powerful tool for doing calculations that involve a continually varying quantity (such as determing the position at any given instant of a space rocket that is accelerating away from Earth). Its basic principles were discovered in the late 1660s independently by the German philosopher Leibniz and the British scientist Newton.

intelligence in psychology, a general concept that summarizes the abilities of an individual in reasoning and problem solving, particularly in novel situations. These consist of a wide range of verbal and non-verbal skills and therefore some psychologists dispute a unitary concept of intelligence. See ◊intelligence test.

intelligence in military and political affairs, information, usually covertly or illegally obtained, about other countries.

The British secret intelligence service is M(ilitary) I(ntelligence) 6 and its agents operate abroad; the US equivalent is the ◊Central Intelligence Agency.

Counter-intelligence is information on the activities of hostile agents. In Britain MI5 has as its executive arm Scotland Yard's ◊Special Branch. For the USA, see ◊Federal Bureau of Investigation; for the USSR, see ◊KGB.

Double agents increase their income, but may decrease their lifespan, by working for both sides (◊Mata Hari); *moles* are those within the service who betray their own side, usually defecting (fleeing to the other side) when in danger of discovery (see Kim ◊Philby); a *sleeper* is a spy who is inactive, sometimes for many years, until needed.

intelligence test test which attempts to measure innate intellectual ability, rather than acquired ability. Workers in this field have included Sir Francis ◊Galton, the Frenchman Alfred ◊Binet, Cyril ◊Burt, and Hans ◊Eysenck. Binet devised the first intelligence test in 1905. The concept of intelligence quotient (IQ) was adopted by US psychologist Lewis Terman in 1915. The IQ is calculated according to the formula: $IQ = MA/CA \times 100$, in which MA is 'mental age' (the age at which an average child is able to perform given tasks) and CA is 'chronological age', hence the average person would have an IQ of 100. Intelligence tests were first used on a large scale in World War I in 1917 for two million drafted men in the USA. They were also widely used in UK education as part of the Eleven Plus selection procedures, in the early days of which it was assumed that inborn intelligence was unalterable. It is now generally believed that children's ability to score at a particular level in an intelligence test can be affected by their environment, cultural background, and teaching. There is also considerably more scepticism now about the accuracy of intelligence tests than there was when they were first introduced in the 1930s, but they are still widely used as a diagnostic tool when children display learning difficulties.

'Sight and sound' intelligence tests, developed by Christopher Brand in 1981, avoid the pitfalls of improvement by practice, and cultural bias. Subjects are shown a series of lines being flashed on a screen at increasing speed, and are asked to identify in each case the shorter of the two; and also, when two notes are relayed over headphones, are asked to identify in the same way which is the higher. There is a close correlation between the results and other intelligence test scores.

Intelsat International Telecommunications Satellite Organization, established in 1964 to operate a worldwide system of communications satellites. More than 100 countries are members of Intelsat, with headquarters in Washington DC, USA. Intelsat satellites are stationed in ◊geostationary (maintaining their positions relative to the Earth) orbit over the Atlantic, Pacific and Indian Oceans. The first Intelsat satellite was *Early Bird*, launched in 1965.

intendant official appointed by the French crown under Louis XIV to administer a territorial *département*. Their powers were extensive but counteracted to some extent by other local officials. The term was also used for certain administrators in Spain, Portugal, and Latin America.

intentionality in philosophy, the property of consciousness whereby it is directed towards an object, even when this object does not exist in reality (such as 'the golden mountain'). Intentionality is a key concept in ◊Husserl's philosophy.

interest in finance, a sum of money paid by a borrower to a lender in return for the loan, usually expressed as a percentage per annum. *Simple interest* is interest calculated as a straight percentage of the amount loaned or invested. Thus, a sum of £100 invested at 10 per cent simple interest for five years earns £10 a year, giving a total of £50 interest (and at the end of the period the investor receives a total of £150). In *compound interest*, the interest earned over a period of time (for example, per annum) is added to the investment, so that at the end of the next period interest is paid on that total. It is thus a way of paying interest on the accumulated interest. The same sum of £100 invested for five years at 10 per cent compound interest earns a total of £61.05 interest (with £161.05 returned at the end of the period). Generally, for a sum S invested at x per cent simple interest for y years, the total amount returned is $S + xyS/100$. If it is invested at x per cent compound interest for y years, the total amount returned is $S\,[(100 + x)/100]y$.

interference in physics, the phenomenon of two or more wave motions interacting and combining to produce a resultant wave of larger or smaller amplitude (depending on whether the combining waves are in or out of phase with each other). With monochromatic light (of a single wavelength), interference produces patterns of light and dark bands. This is the basis of ◊holography, for example. Interference of white light (multi-wavelength) results in spectral coloured fringes, for example, the iridescent colours of oil films seen on water or soap bubbles (see also ◊Newton's rings). Interference of sound waves of similar frequency produces the phenomenon of beats, often used by musicians when tuning an instrument. Interferometry can also be applied to radio waves, and is a powerful tool in modern astronomy.

interferon a ◊protein substance produced by the cells of vertebrate animals, in response to ◊virus infection. There are several different types but they work in the same way, by stimulating production of certain ◊enzymes that inhibit the protein-synthesizing mechanisms in the cell, so that the virus cannot produce copies of itself. Interferons confer ◊immunity against a range of viruses, rather than being specific for one type of infection (as ◊antibodies are). Efforts are being made to produce human interferons by means of ◊genetic engineering, for treating viral disesases and possibly for preventing the growth of cancer cells.

interior decoration design, decoration and furnishing of the inside of a building. Among early names associated with interior decoration in England are those of Inigo ◊Jones and Grinling ◊Gibbons, but the first architects to design a building as an integrated whole were the ◊Adam brothers, for example Syon House, Middlesex. Craftsmen who have given their names to different styles of furniture design include ◊Chippendale, ◊Hepplewhite and ◊Sheraton. In Victorian times William ◊Morris became famous for his designs of carpets, wallpaper, and furniture. In more recent times the trend has been to a less ornate and more functional style, fostered by the interaction of architects and designers working in teams.

Interlaken /'ɪntə,lɑːkən/ chief town of the Bernese Oberland, on the river Aar between lakes Brienz and Thun, Switzerland; population (1985) 13,000. The site was first occupied in 1130 by a monastery, suppressed in 1528.

Intermediate Nuclear Forces Treaty (INF) treaty signed 8 Dec 1987 between the USA and the USSR eliminating all ground-based intermediate nuclear missiles by 1989. The treaty, seen as perhaps the most important ◊strategic arms-limitation treaty signed since nuclear weapons were first developed, also included provisions for each country to inspect the other's nuclear installations to check that totals were not being exceeded.

intermediate technology the application of mechanics, electrical engineering, and other technologies, based on inventions and designs developed in scientifically sophisticated cultures, but utilizing materials, assembly, and maintenance methods found in technologically less advanced regions (known as the ◊Third World). Intermediate technologies aim to allow developing countries to benefit from newly developed techniques and inventions of the 'First World', without the burdens of costly maintenance and supply of fuels and spare parts that would represent an enormous and probably uneconomic overhead for the Third World country.

intermezzo in music, a short orchestral interlude often used between the acts of an opera to denote the passage of time.

internal combustion engine a heat engine in which fuel is burned inside the engine, contrasting with an external combustion engine like the ◊steam engine in which fuel is burned in a separate boiler. The ◊petrol and diesel engine are both internal combustion engines. They are reciprocating piston engines in which pistons move up and down in cylinders to effect the engine operating cycle. This may be a ◊four-stroke cycle or a ◊two-stroke cycle. Gas turbines, jet and rocket engines are sometimes also considered to be internal combustion engines since they burn their fuel inside their combustion chambers.

International, the coordinating body established by labour and socialist organizations, including: *International Working Men's Association* 1864–72, formed in London under Karl ◊Marx. *(Socialist) International* or *Comintern* 1919–43, formed in Moscow (see ◊Lenin), advocating from 1933 a popular front (communist, socialist, liberal) against Hitler. *Trotskyist International* 1936, somewhat indeterminate, and anti-Stalinist. Revived *Socialist International* 1951, formed in

Frankfurt, West Germany, a largely anti-communist association of social democrats.

International Atomic Energy Agency organization that advises and assists member states in the development and application of nuclear power and guards against its misuse. Established 1957, it has its headquarters in Vienna, and is responsible for research centres in Austria and Monaco, and the International Centre for Theoretical Physics 1964 in Trieste.

International Bank for Reconstruction and Development official name of the ◊World Bank.

International Brigade international volunteer force on the republican side in the ◊Spanish Civil War 1936–39.

International Civil Aviation Organization see under ◊United Nations.

International Court of Justice the main judicial organ of the ◊United Nations, at The Hague, the Netherlands.

International Date Line a modification of the 180th meridian which marks the difference in time between E and W. The date is put forward a day when crossing the line going W, and back a day when going E. The IDL was chosen at the International Meridian Conference in 1884.

International Development Association (IDA) an agency of the United Nations, and affiliated to the ◊World Bank.

Internationale international communist anthem (words Eugène Pottier 1871, music Pierre Degeyter about 1891), used as the Soviet national anthem 1917–43.

International Finance Corporation arm of the ◊World Bank set up in 1956 to facilitate loans for private investment to developing countries.

International Fund for Agricultural Development see under ◊United Nations.

International Geophysical Year (IGY) a research project sponsored by the International Council of Scientific Unions to find out as much as possible about the physical nature of our planet. It lasted between 1 Jul 1957 and 31 Dec 1958, to coincide with a period of intense sunspot activity, but was extended into 1959 as the International Geophysical Cooperation (IGC). 66 countries were involved, and 40,000 scientists and technicians. The headquarters were in Uccle, Belgium.

Highlights included the launching of the first satellites by the USA and the USSR, and several expeditions into Antarctica and the Arctic ice cap. Scientific knowledge of the Earth was expanded greatly during this time: in astronomy, the Van Allen radiation belts were discovered; in oceanography, the deep ocean currents were found; in gravimetry, the presence of mountain roots in the crust was confirmed.

International Labour Organization see under ◊United Nations.

international law body of rules generally accepted as governing the relations between countries, pioneered by Hugo ◊Grotius, especially in matters of human rights, territory, and war. Neither the League of Nations nor United Nations proved able to enforce it, successes being achieved only when the law coincided with the aims of a predominant major power, for example ◊Korean War. The scope of the law is now extended to space, for example the 1967 treaty banning nuclear weapons from space.

International Maritime Organization a ◊United Nations agency concerned with world shipping. Established in 1958, it has its headquarters in London.

International Monetary Fund (IMF) specialized agency of the ◊United Nations, established under the 1944 ◊Bretton-Woods agreement and operational since 1947. It seeks to promote international monetary co-operation, the growth of world trade, and to smooth multilateral payment arrangements among member states. IMF stand-by loans are available to members in ◊balance-of-payments difficulties (the amount being governed by the member's quota), usually on the basis of acceptance of instruction on stipulated corrective measures. The Fund also operates other drawing facilities, including several designed to provide preferential credit to developing countries with liquidity problems. Having previously operated in US dollars linked to gold, since 1972 the IMF has used the special drawing right (SDR) as its standard unit of account, valued in terms of a weighted 'basket' of major currencies. Since the 1971 Smithsonian agreement permitting wider fluctuations from specified currency parities, IMF rules have been progressively adapted to the increasing prevalence of fully floating ◊exchange rates.

International Settlements, Bank for (BIS) forum for European central bank, established 1930, which acts as a bank to the central banks, to prevent currency speculation. It has been superseded in some of its major functions by the ◊International Monetary Fund.

International Society for Krishna Consciousness (ISKON) a Hindu sect introduced to the West by Swami Prabhupada (1896–1977), based on the demonstration of intense love for ◊Krishna, especially by chanting the mantra 'Hare Krishna'. Members believe that by chanting the mantra and meditating on it, they may achieve enlightenment and so remove themselves from the cycle of reincarnation. They wear distinctive yellow robes and men often have most of their heads shaven. Members of the movement are expected to live ascetic lives, avoiding meat and eggs, alcohol, tea, coffee and other drugs and gambling; sexual relationships should only take place within marriage and solely for procreation. Their holy books are the Hindu scriptures and particularly the *Bhagavad Gita*, which they study daily.

International Telecommunication Union (ITO) a body belonging to the Economic and Social Council of the ◊United Nations.

international trade unionism worldwide cooperation between unions. Modern organizations are the International Confederation of Free Trade Unions (ICFTU 1949), including the American Federation of Labor and Congress of Industrial organizations and in Britain the Trades Union Congress, and the World Federation of Trade Unions (WFTU 1945).

International Union for Conservation of Nature the full name of the ◊IUCN.

internment the detention of suspected criminals without trial. Common with foreign citizens during wartime, internment has been used for the detention of suspected terrorists in Northern Ireland by the UK Government since 1971.

interplanetary matter gas and dust thinly spread through the ◊solar system. The gas flows outwards from the Sun as the ◊solar wind. Fine dust lies in the plane of the solar system, scattering sunlight to cause the zodiacal light. Swarms of dust shed by comets enter the Earth's atmosphere to cause ◊meteor showers.

Interpol /ˈɪntəpɒl/ *Inter*national Criminal *Poli*ce Commission, founded following the Second International Judicial Police Conference 1923 with its headquarters in Vienna, but reconstituted after World War II with its headquarters in Paris. It has an international criminal register, fingerprint file and methods index.

interpreter a computer program that translates statements from a ◊programming language into ◊machine code and causes them to be executed one by one. Unlike a ◊compiler, which translates the whole program at once to produce an executable machine code program, an interpreter translates the programming language each time the program is run. BASIC is an example of an interpreted language.

intersex an individual that is intermediate between a normal male and a normal female in its appearance (for example, a genetic male that lacks external genitalia and so resembles a female). Intersexes are usually the result of an abnormal hormone balance during development (especially during ◊gestation) or of a failure of the ◊genes controlling sex determination. The term ◊hermaphrodite is sometimes used for intersexes, but should be confined to animals that normally have both male and female organs.

interstellar molecules over 50 different ◊molecules (types of particle) exist in gas clouds in the Galaxy. Most have been detected by their radio emissions, but some have been found by the absorption lines they produce in the spectra of starlight. The most complex molecules, many of them based on ◊carbon, are found in the dense clouds where stars are forming. They may be significant for the origin of life elsewhere in space.

interval in music, the pitch difference between two notes, usually measured in terms of the diatonic scale.

intestine the digestive tract of ◊vertebrates, from the stomach outlet to the anus. It is made up of two parts. The *small intestine* measures 6 m/20 ft in humans, and consists of the duodenum, jejunum, and ileum; the *large intestine* measures 1.5 m/5 ft and includes the caecum, ◊colon, and ◊rectum. Both are muscular tubes comprising an inner lining which secretes alkaline digestive juice, a submucous coat containing fine blood vessels and ◊nerves, a muscular coat, and a serous coat covering all. The muscle contracts in a series of waves (◊peristalsis) so as to pass the contents slowly along. The whole tract is supported by a strong band or sling of connective tissue (◊peritoneum) carrying the blood and lymph vessels, and the nerves. The term intestine may also be applied to the lower digestive tract of invertebrates.

intrusion a mass of ◊igneous rock that has formed by 'injection' of molten rock into existing cracks beneath the surface of the Earth, as distinct from a volcanic rock mass which has erupted from the surface.

iron, gold, lead, zinc and copper, and the sea has oil and natural gas. The federal government approved the claim in principle in 1985.

Their language, Inuktitut, belongs to the Eskimo-Aleut group. The conditions of their life make rather for individualism than distinctive tribal organization. The Inuit religion postulates survival after death, has a rich mythology and a shaman (*angakok*) tradition; but Christianity has been adopted by many.

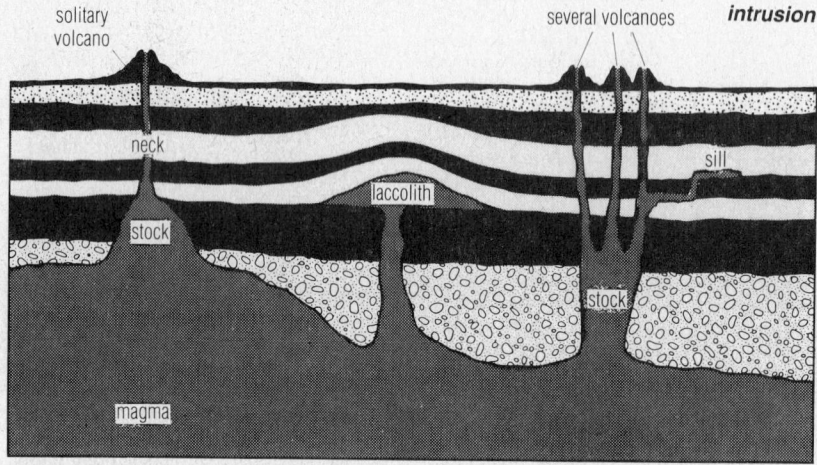

intrusion

intuition in philosophy, that knowledge of an concept which does not derive directly from the senses. Thus, we may be said to have an intuitive idea of God, beauty, or justice. The concept of intuition is similar to Bertrand ◊Russell's theory of knowledge by acquaintance. In both cases, it is contrasted with empirical knowledge (see ◊empiricism).

intuitionism in mathematics, the theory that propositions can only be built up from intuitive concepts which we all recognize easily, such as unity or plurality. The concept of ◊infinity, of which we have no intuitive experience, is thus not allowed.

Inuit people inhabiting the Arctic coasts of N America, the E islands of the Canadian Arctic, and the ice-free coasts of Greenland.

They refer to themselves as Inuit, and were first called Eskimos ('eaters of raw meat') by the N American Algonquin Indians. Traditionally, they construct their homes from stones, peat, bones, driftwood, and skins – snow igloos are used only for temporary camps in winter travel – and get their food by hunting seals, whales, caribou, and other animals (often using their skin-covered canoes, kayaks). In practice this picture has become increasingly modified as patterns of western social organization have increasingly impinged on the Arctic, and many Inuit have abandoned their traditional way of life.

In 1975 the Inuit of the Canadian Arctic (about 14,500) demanded the creation of an autonomous state, Nunavut (Our Land), to comprise part of the mainland of the Northwest Territories and many Arctic islands, including Baffin Island. The area claimed (2,400,000 sq km/930,000 sq mi) is rich in minerals, including

Invalides, Hôtel des building in Paris, S of the Seine, founded in 1670 as a home for disabled soldiers. The church Dôme des Invalides contains the tomb of Napoleon I. The military government of Paris has its headquarters at the Invalides.

invar an alloy of iron containing 36% nickel, which expands or contracts scarcely at all when the temperature changes. It is used to make precision instruments (such as pendulums and tuning forks) whose dimensions must not alter.

Invergordon Mutiny incident in the British Atlantic Fleet, Cromarty Firth, 15 Sept 1931. Ratings refused to prepare the ships for sea following the government's cuts in their pay; the cuts were consequently modified.

Inverness /ˌɪnvəˈnes/ town in Highland region, Scotland; population (1985) 57,800. It lies in a sheltered site at the mouth of the Ness, and until 1975 was the county town of Inverness-shire. It is a tourist centre. Besides tweed manufacture, there are tanning, engineering, and distilling industries.

Inverness-shire /ˌɪnvəˈnesʃə/ largest of the former Scottish counties, it was merged in Highland region in 1975.

inverse square law in physics, the statement that the magnitude of an effect (usually a force) at a point is inversely proportional to the square of the distance between that point and the point location of its cause. ◊Light, ◊sound, electrostatic force (◊Coulomb's law), gravitational force (◊Newton's law) and magnetic force (see ◊magnetism) all decrease in intensity in accordance with the inverse square law.

Invalides, Hôtel des Established by Louis XIV, the Hôtel des Invalides was mainly executed by Jules Hardouin-Mansart. Napoleon was buried beneath the dome of its church in 1840.

invertebrate an animal without a backbone. The invertebrates form a major division of the animal kingdom, and include the sponges, coelenterates, flatworms, nematodes, annelid worms, arthropods, molluscs, echinoderms and primitive aquatic chordates such as sea-squirts and lancelets.

investment in economics, commonly used to signify the purchase of any asset with the potential to yield future financial benefit to the purchaser (such as a house, a work of art, ◊stocks and shares, or even a private education); more strictly, it denotes expenditure on the stock of capital goods or resources of an enterprise or project, with a view to achieving profitable production for consumption at a later date.

investment trust a public company which makes ◊investments on behalf of its shareholders. See ◊trust.

involute of a circle, a ◊spiral that can be thought of as being traced by a point at the end of a taut non-elastic thread being wound onto or unwound from a spool. The name comes from the Latin meaning 'rolled in'.

Io /ˈaɪəʊ/ in Greek mythology, a princess loved by ◊Zeus, who transformed her to a heifer to hide her from the jealousy of ◊Hera.

Io /ˈaɪəʊ/ in astronomy, the third-largest moon of the planet ◊Jupiter, 3,600 km/2,250 mi in diameter, orbiting every 1.77 days at a distance of 413,000 km/256,000 mi. It is the most volcanically active body in the ◊solar system, covered by hundreds of vents that erupt not lava but sulphur, giving Io an orange-coloured surface.

iodine a non-metallic element (Greek *iodes*, violet) discovered by Courtois in 1811: symbol I, atomic weight 126.91, atomic number 53. It is a violet-black lustrous solid, volatilizing at ordinary temperatures to a bluish-violet gas with an irritating odour, and forming a characteristic blue colour with starch. Not found in the free state, it occurs in saltpetre and as iodides in sea-water. It is taken up by seaweeds and sponges and may be extracted from their ashes. Iodine is used in photography, in medicine as an antiseptic, and in chemicals and dyes. It collects in the thyroid gland, lack of it producing goitre. Iodine-131 (a radioactive isotope) is widely used in medical diagnosis, research and treatment.

iodoform an antiseptic (CHI_3) which crystallizes into yellow hexagonal plates. It is soluble in ether, alcohol, and chloroform, but not in water.

ion atom, or group of atoms, which are either positively charged (*cation*) or negatively charged (*anion*), as a result of the loss or gain of electrons.

Iona /aɪˈəʊnə/ an island in the Inner ◊Hebrides.

ion engine a rocket engine that uses ◊ions rather than hot gas for propulsion. Ion engines have already been successfully tested in space, where they will eventually be used for gradual rather than sudden velocity changes. In an ion engine atoms of mercury (say) are ionized – given an electric charge by an electric field, and then accelerated at high speed by a more powerful electric field.

Ionesco /ˌiːəˈneskəʊ/ Eugène 1912– . Romanian-born French dramatist, a leading exponent of the Theatre of the ◊Absurd movement. Most of his plays are in one act and express his concern with the futility of language as a means of communication, as in *La Cantatrice chauve/The Bald Prima Donna* 1950, *Leçon/The Lesson* 1951 and *Les Chaises/The Chairs* 1951. His full-length plays include *Rhinocéros* 1958 and *Le Roi se meurt/Exit the King* 1961.

Ionia /aɪˈəʊnɪə/ in Classical times the W coast of Asia Minor, settled about 1000 BC by the ◊Ionians; it included the cities of Ephesus, Miletus, and later Smyrna.

Ionian member of a Hellenic people from beyond the Black Sea who crossed the Balkans around 1980 BC and invaded Asia Minor. Driven back by the ◊Hittites, they spread over mainland Greece, later being supplanted by the ◊Achaeans.

Ionian Islands /aɪˈəʊnɪən/ island group off the W coast of Greece; area 332 sq km/860 sq mi. A British protectorate from 1815 till their cession to Greece in 1864, they include:
Cephalonia (Kefallínia);
Corfu (Kérkyra, a Venetian possession 1386–1797);
Cythera (Kíthira);
Ithaca (Itháki), the traditional home of ◊Odysseus;
Leukas (Levkás);
Paxos (Paxoí), and *Zante* (Zákynthos).

Ionian Sea /aɪˈəʊnɪən/ the part of the Mediterranean which lies between Italy and Greece, to the S of the Adriatic, and containing the Ionian islands.

Ionic in classical architecture, one of the five types of ◊column. See ◊order.

ionization chamber device for measuring the amount of ionizing radiation. The radiation ionizes gas in the chamber and the ions are collected and measured as an electric charge.

ionizing radiation radiation which knocks electrons from atoms during its passage, thereby leaving ions in its path. Electrons and alpha-particles are much more ionizing than are neutrons or ◊gamma-radiation.

ionosphere ionized layer of Earth's outer ◊atmosphere (60–1000 km/38–620 mi) that contains sufficient free electrons to modify the way in which radio waves are propagated, for instance by reflecting them back to Earth. The ionosphere is thought to be produced by absorption of the Sun's ultraviolet radiation.

ion plating method of applying corrosion-resistant metal coatings. The article is placed in argon gas, together with some coating metal, which vaporizes on heating and becomes ionized (acquires charged atoms) as it diffuses through the gas to form the coating. It has important applications in the aerospace industry.

IOU short for 'I owe you'. A written acknowledgment of debt, signed by the debtor. See ◊Bill of Exchange.

Iowa /ˈaɪəwə/ state of the midwest USA; nicknamed Hawkeye State
area 145,790 sq km/56,290 sq mi
capital Des Moines
towns Cedar Rapids, Davenport, Sioux City
features Grant ◊Wood Gallery in Davenport and Herbert ◊Hoover birthplace and library in West Branch
products cereals, soya beans; meat and wool; industrial products
population (1980) 2,908,800
famous people Buffalo Bill Cody
history part of the Louisiana ◊Purchase in 1803, it remains an area of small farms; it became a state in 1846.

ipecacuanha South American plant *Psychotria ipecacuanha*, family Rubiaceae, is used as an emetic and in treating amoebic dysentery.

Iphigenia /ɪˌfɪdʒɪˈnaɪə/ in Greek mythology, the daughter of ◊Agamemnon and Clytemnestra.

Ipswich /ˈɪpswɪtʃ/ river port on the Orwell estuary, administrative headquarters of Suffolk, England; population (1981) 120,500. Industries include engineering and general manufacturing.

IQ intelligence quotient: the score achieved as the result of an ◊intelligence test, with a score of 100 being regarded as average ability.

Iqbal /ˈɪkbæl/ Muhammad 1875–1938. Islamic poet and thinker, generally considered the greatest modern Islamic poet. His literary works, in Urdu and Persian, were mostly verse in the classical style, suitable for public recitation. His most celebrated work is the Persian *Asrā-e khūdī/Secrets of the Self* 1915, in which he put forward a theory of the self which was the

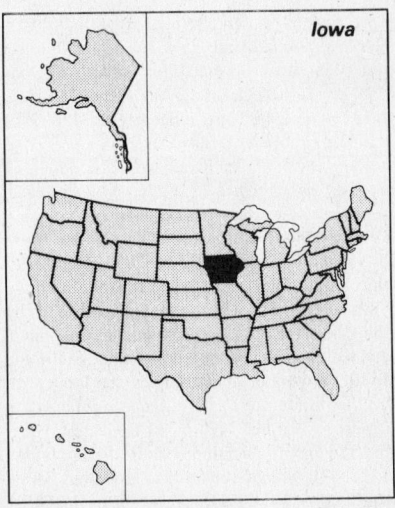

Iowa

opposite of the traditional abnegation of Islam. He sought through his writings to arouse Muslims to take their place in the modern world, and was an influence on the movement which led to the creation of Pakistan.

Iquique /ɪˈkiːkeɪ/ city and seaport of Chile, capital of the province of Tarapaca; population (1982) 109,000. It exports nitrate of soda, from its desert region.

Iquitos /ɪˈkiːtɒs/ river port on the Amazon, Peru, also a tourist centre for the rainforest; population (1981) 173,500.

IRA abbreviation for ◊Irish Republican Army.

Iran /ɪˈrɑːn/ country in SW Asia, bounded to the N by the USSR and the Caspian Sea, to the E by Afghanistan and Pakistan, to the S and SW by the Gulf of Oman, to the W by Iraq, and to the NW by Turkey.
government the constitution, which came into effect on the overthrow of the Shah in 1979, provides for a president elected by universal suffrage, and a single-chamber legislature, the Islamic Consultative Assembly *Majlis*, of 270 members, similarly elected. The president and the assembly serve a four-year term. All legislation passed by the assembly must be sent to the council for the protection of the constitution, consisting of six religious and six secular lawyers, to ensure that it complies with Islamic precepts. The president is the executive head of government but his authority, and that of the assembly, are ultimately subject to the will of the religious leader. The successor to the present leader, Ayatollah Khomeini, has already been chosen by an elected council of experts. Although a number of political parties exist, Iran is fundamentally a one-party state, the Islamic Republican Party having been founded in 1978 to bring about the Islamic revolution. Ayatollah Khomeini is its secretary-general.
history the name Iran is derived from the Aryan tribes, including the Medes and Persians, who overran Persia (see ◊Persia, Ancient) from 1600 BC. ◊Cyrus II, who seized the Median throne in

550, formed an empire including Babylonia, Syria, and Asia Minor, to which Egypt, Thrace, and Macedonia were later added. It was conquered by ◊Alexander the Great 334–328, then passed to his general Seleucus (c. 358–280) and his descendants until overrun in the 3rd century BC by the Parthians. The Parthian dynasty was overthrown in 226 AD by Ardashir, founder of the ◊Sassanian empire.

During 633–41 Persia was conquered for Islam by the Arabs, and then in 1037–55 came under the ◊Seljuk Turks. Their empire broke up in the 12th century and was conquered in the 13th by the ◊Mongols. After 1334 Persia was again divided until its conquest by ◊Tamerlane in the 1380s. A period of anarchy in the later 15th century was ended by the accession of the Safavi dynasty, who ruled 1499–1736, but were deposed by the great warrior Nadir Shah (ruled 1736–47), whose death was followed by a confused period until the accession of the Qajar dynasty (1794–1925).

During the 18th century Persia was threatened by Russian expansion, culminating in the loss of Georgia in 1801 and a large part of Armenia in 1828. Persian claims on Herat, Afghanistan, led to war with Britain 1856–57. Revolutions in 1905 and 1909 resulted in the establishment of a parliamentary regime. During World War I the country was occupied by British and Russian forces. An officer, Col Reza Khan, seized power in 1921, and a coup in 1925 made him the Shah, allowing him to carry out a massive programme of modernization to bring Persia, as it was then called, into the 20th century.

During World War II Iran, as it had become, was occupied by British, US and Russian troops until 1946. Anti-British and anti-American feeling grew and in 1951 the newly elected prime minister, Dr Muhammad Mussadeq, obtained legislative approval for the nationalization of Iran's largely foreign-owned petroleum industry. With American connivance, he was deposed in a 1953 coup and the dispute over nationalization was settled the following year when oil drilling concessions were granted to a consortium of eight companies. The Shah took complete control of the government and between 1965–77 Iran enjoyed a period of political stability and economic growth, based on oil revenue.

In 1975 the Shah had introduced a one-party system, based on the Iran National Resurgence Party *Rastakhis*, but opposition to his regime was growing. The most effective opposition came from the religious leader, Ayatollah ◊Khomeini, who campaigned from exile in France. He demanded a return to the principles of Islam and pressure on the Shah became so great that in 1979 he left the country, leaving the way open for Khomeini's return. He appointed a provisional government but power was placed essentially in the hands of the 15-member Islamic Revolutionary Council, controlled by Khomeini. Iran was declared an Islamic Republic and a new constitution, based on Islamic principles, was adopted. Relations with the US were badly affected when a group of Iranian students took 63 American hostage at the US embassy in Tehran, demanding that the Shah return to face trial.

Even the death of the Shah, in Egypt in 1980, did little to resolve the crisis, which ended when all the hostages were released in Jan 1981.

In its early years several rifts developed within the new Islamic government and although by 1982 some stability had been attained, disputes between factions developed again in the years that followed. Externally, the war with Iraq which broke out in 1980 after a border dispute, continued, with considerable loss of life on both sides. Two peace proposals were put forward in 1984 by President Mubarak of Egypt but neither was found acceptable. The secretary-general of the UN also tried unsuccessfully to find a peace formula. Meanwhile, Islamic law was becoming stricter, with amputation as the penalty for theft and flogging for minor sexual offences. By 1985 the failure to end the Gulf War and the harshness of the Islamic codes were increasing opposition to Khomeini's regime but his position remained secure. By 1987 both sides in the war had increased the scale of their operations, each apparently believing that outright victory was possible.

Iran

ISLAMIC REPUBLIC OF (*Jomhori-e-Islami-e-Irân*; until 1935 PERSIA)

AREA 1,648,000 sq km/636,000 sq mi
CAPITAL Tehran
TOWNS Isfahan, Mashhad, Tabriz, Shiraz, Ahwaz; chief port Abadan
PHYSICAL plateau surrounded by mountains, including Elburz and Zagros; Lake Rezayeh; Dasht-Ekavir Desert
FEATURES ruins of Persepolis
RELIGIOUS LEADER Sayed Ruholla Moussavi Khomeini from 1979
HEAD OF STATE AND OF GOVERNMENT
Hojatoleslam Sayed Ali Khomeini from 1981
GOVERNMENT fundamentalist Islamic
EXPORTS carpets, cotton textiles, metalwork, leather goods; oil and petrochemicals
CURRENCY rial (117.5 = £1 Sept 1987)
POPULATION (1985) 45,191,000 (including minorities in Azerbaijan, Baluchistan, Khuzestan/Arabistan, and Kurdistan); annual growth rate 3.2%
LANGUAGE Farsi, Kurdish, Turk, Arabic, English, French
RELIGION Shi'ite Muslim (official)
LITERACY 55% male/30% female (1980 est)
GDP $76.37 bn (1977); $2,160 per head of population
CHRONOLOGY
1946 British, US, and Soviet forces left Iran.
1951 Oilfields nationalized by Prime Minister Mohammed Mussadeq.

profits to supply right-wing Contra guerrillas in ◊Nicaragua with arms, as well as channelling donations to the Contras from individual donations and from other countries, contravening a law passed by Congress to prohibit military assistance to the Contras (the Boland amendment 1984).

The arms, including Hawk missiles, were sold to Iran via Israel, violating the law prohibiting the sale of US weapons for resale to a third country listed as a 'terrorist nation', as well as the law requiring sales above $14 million to be reported to Congress. The negotiator in the field was Oliver North, a military aide to the National Security Council, reporting in the White House to Rear Admiral John Poindexter.

The Congressional hearing found that the president was not responsible for the actions of his subordinates.

Iranian language the main language of Iran, more commonly known as ◊Persian or Farsi.

Iran-Iraq War or *Gulf War* 1980– . War between Iran and Iraq, claimed by the former to have begun with the Iraq offensive of 21 Sep

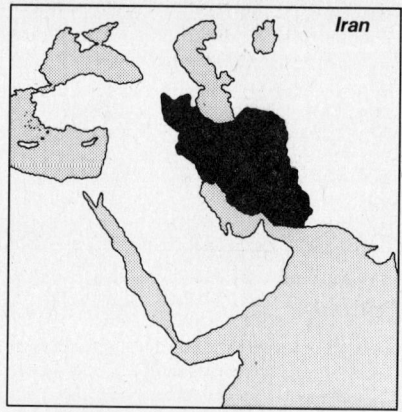

1953 Mussadeq deposed and the shah took full control of the government.
1975 The shah introduced a single-party system.
1978 Opposition to the shah organized from France by Ayatollah Khomeini.
1979 Shah left the country and Khomeini returned to create an Islamic state. Students seized US hostages in Tehran.
1980 Start of Gulf War against Iraq.
1981 US hostages finally released.
1984 Egyptian peace proposals rejected.
1985 Gulf War fighting intensified. UN secretary general's peace moves were unsuccessful.
1987 Further intensification of the war.

Irangate or *Contragate* the revelation in congressional hearings 1986–87 that the US government had secretly sold weapons to Iran in 1985 (at a time when the USA was publicly calling for a worldwide ban on sending arms to Iran) and traded them for hostages, and used the

1980, and by the latter with the Iranian shelling of border posts 4 Sep 1980. Occasioned by a boundary dispute over the ◊Shatt al'Arab waterway, it arose from Iran's encouragement of the Shi'ite majority in Iraq to rise against the Sunni government of Saddam Hussein.

The war's course has been marked by offensive and counter-offensive, interspersed with extended periods of stalemate. Chemical weapons have been used, cities and the important oil installations of the area have been the target for bombing raids and rocket attacks, and international shipping has come under fire in the Persian Gulf (including in 1987 the US frigate *Stark*, which was attacked by the Iraqi airforce). Among Arab states, Iran has been supported by Libya and Syria, the remainder supporting Iraq. Iran has also benefited from secret American arms shipments, the disclosure of which in 1986 led to considerable scandal in the USA (the so-called ◊Irangate affair). The intervention of the USA in 1987, ostensibly to keep the sea lanes open, but seen by Iran as support for Iraq, has heightened, rather than reduced, tension in the Gulf and attempts by the United Nations to obtain a ceasefire between the warring nations have failed. The imposition of a universal arms embargo and the establishment of a genuine United Nations naval peacekeeping force are seen as possible, but not probable, solutions.

Iraq /ɪ'rɑːk/ almost landlocked country in SW Asia, bounded to the N by Turkey, E by Iran, S by the Gulf, Kuwait and Saudi Arabia, SW by Jordan, and W by Syria.

government the 1970 constitution, amended in 1973, 1974 and 1980, provides for a president who is head of state, prime minister and chair of a Revolutionary Command Council RCC). Day-to-day administration is under the control of a council of ministers over which the president also presides. He is also regional secretary of the Arab Ba'ath Socialist Party which, although not the only political party in Iraq, so dominates the country's institutions as to make it virtually a one-party state. In 1980 elections took place for the first 250-member national assembly. Elections for a second assembly were held in 1984. On both occasions the Ba'ath Party dominated the results. In effect, therefore, Iraq is ruled by the Arab Ba'ath Socialist Party through its regional secretary and other leading members.

history the area now occupied by Iraq was formerly ancient ◊Mesopotamia, and was the centre of the ◊Sumerian, ◊Babylonian, and ◊Assyrian civilizations between 6000 BC and 100 AD. It was conquered in 114 by the Romans, and was ruled 266–632 by the native ◊Sassanids before being invaded in 633 by the Arabs. In 1065 the country was taken over by the Turks, and was invaded by the ◊Mongols in 1258, Baghdad being destroyed in 1401 by ◊Tamerlane. Annexed by ◊Suleiman the Magnificent in 1533, Iraq became part of the Turkish ◊Ottoman Empire in 1638. Occupied by Britain in World War I, Iraq was placed under British administration by the League of Nations in 1920. It was the start of a long and generally amicable relationship. In 1932 Iraq became a fully independent kingdom and in 1933 the reigning king, Faisal I, died and was succeeded by his son, Ghazi. The leading figure behind the throne was the strongly pro-Western Gen Nuri-el-Said, who was prime minister 1930–58. In 1939 King Ghazi was killed

in a motor accident and Faisal II became king at the age of three, his uncle Prince Abdul Ilah acting as regent until 1953 when the king assumed full powers.

In 1955 Iraq signed the Baghdad Pact, a regional collective security agreement, with the USSR seen as the main potential threat, and in 1958 joined Jordan in an Arab Federation, with King Faisal as head of state. In Jul of that year, a revolution overthrew the monarchy and King Faisal, Prince Abdul Ilah and Gen Nuri were all killed. The constitution was suspended and Iraq was declared a republic, with Brig Abdul Karim Kassem as head of a left-wing military regime. He withdrew from the Baghdad Pact in 1959 and, after tenuously holding power for five years, was killed in 1963 in a coup led by Col Salem Aref, who established a new government, ended martial law, and within two years had introduced a civilian administration. He died, however, in an air crash in 1966 and his brother, who succeeded him, was ousted in 1968 and replaced by Maj-Gen al-Bakr. He concentrated power in the hands of a Revolutionary Command Council (RCC), and made himself head of state, head of government, and chair of the RCC. In 1979 Saddam Hussein, who for several years had been the real power in Iraq, replaced al-Bakr as RCC chair and state president. In 1980 he introduced a 'National Charter', reaffirming a policy of ◊non-alignment and a constitution which provided for an elected national assembly. The first elections took place that year.

Iraq had, since 1970, enjoyed a fluctuating relationship with Syria, sometimes distant and sometimes close enough to contemplate a complete political and economic union. By 1980, however, the atmosphere was cool. Relations between Iraq and Iran had been tense for some years, with disagreement about the border between them, which runs down the Shatt-al-Arab waterway. The 1979 Iranian revolution made Iraq more suspicious of Iran's intentions and in 1980 a full-scale war broke out. Despite Iraq's inferior military strength, Iran gained little territory and by 1986 it seemed as if a stalemate might have been reached. The fighting intensified however, in late 1986 and early 1987, by which time hundreds of thousands of lives had been lost on both sides and incalculable damage to industry and property sustained.

IRCAM (French *Institut de recherche et de coordination acoustique-musique*) organization in Paris for research into electronic music, using computers, synthesizers, and so on; founded 1976. Its director is Pierre ◊Boulez.

Ireland /'aɪələnd/ one of the British Isles, lying to the W of Great Britain, from which it is separated by the Irish Sea. It comprises the provinces of Ulster, Leinster, Munster, and Connacht, and is divided between the Republic of Ireland, which occupies the S, central, and NW of the island, and Northern Ireland, which occupies the NE corner and forms part of the United Kingdom.

The centre of Ireland is a lowland, about 60–120 m/200–400 ft above sea level, hills are mainly around the coasts, though there are a few peaks

over 1,000 m/3,000 ft high, the highest being Carrantuohill ('the inverted reaping hook'), 1,040 m/3,415 ft, in Macgillicuddy's Reeks, County Kerry. The entire W coastline is an intricate alternation of bays and estuaries. Several of the rivers flow in sluggish courses through the central lowland, and then cut through fjord-like valleys to the sea. The ◊Shannon in particular falls 30 m/100 ft in its last 26 km/16 mi above Limerick, and is used to produce hydroelectric power.

The lowland bogs which cover parts of central Ireland are intermingled with fertile limestone country where dairy farming is the chief occupation. The bogs are an important source of fuel, in the form of ◊peat, Ireland being poorly supplied with coal.

The climate is mild, moist, and changeable. The annual rainfall on the lowlands varies from 76 cm/30 in in the E to 203 cm/80 in in some W districts, but much higher falls are recorded in the mountains.

history In prehistoric times Ireland underwent a number of invasions from Europe, the most important of which was that of the Gaels in the 3rd century BC. Gaelic Ireland was divided into kingdoms, nominally subject to an *Ardri* or High King; the chiefs were elected under the tribal or Brehon law, and were usually at war with one another. Christianity was introduced by St ◊Patrick about 432, and during the 5th and 6th centuries Ireland became the home of a civilization which sent out missionaries to Britain and Europe. From about 800 the Danes began to raid Ireland, and later founded Dublin and other coastal towns, until they were defeated by Brian Boru (king from 976) at Clontarf 1014.

Anglo-Norman adventurers invaded Ireland 1167, but by the end of the medieval period English rule was still confined to the Pale, the territory around Dublin. The Tudors adopted a policy of conquest, confiscation of Irish land, and plantation by English settlers, and further imposed the ◊Reformation and English law on Ireland. The most important of the plantations was that of Ulster, carried out under James I in 1610. The Irish in 1641 took advantage of the developing struggle in England between king and parliament to begin a revolt which was crushed by Oliver ◊Cromwell 1649, the estates of all 'rebels' being confiscated. Another revolt 1689–91 was also defeated, and the Roman Catholic majority held down by penal laws. The subordination of the Irish parliament to that of Engalnd, and of Irish economic interests to English, led to the rise of a Protestant patriot party, which in 1782 forced the British government to remove many commercial restrictions and grant the Irish parliament its independence. This did not satisfy the population, who in 1798, influenced by French revolutionary ideas, rose in rebellion, but were again defeated; and in 1800 Wiliam ◊Pitt induced the Irish parliament to vote itself out of existence by the Act of ◊Union, effective 1 Jan 1801, which gave Ireland parliamentary representation at Westminster. For history since

Iraq
REPUBLIC OF (*Al Jumhouriya al 'Iraqia*)

AREA 444,000 sq km/172,000 sq mi
CAPITAL Baghdad
TOWNS Mosul and port of Basra
PHYSICAL mountains in N, desert in W; wide valley of rivers Tigris and Euphrates NW–SE
FEATURES reed architecture of the marsh Arabs; sites of Eridu, Babylon, Nineveh, Ur, Ctesiphon
HEAD OF STATE AND OF GOVERNMENT Saddam Hussein At-Takriti from 1979
GOVERNMENT one-party socialist
EXPORTS dates (80% of world supply); wool; oil
CURRENCY Iraqi dinar (0.51 = £1 Sept 1987)
POPULATION 15,507,000 (1985); annual growth rate 3.5%
LANGUAGE Arabic (official)
RELIGION Shi'ite Muslim 60%, Sunni Muslim 30%, Christian 3%
LITERACY 68% male/32% female (1980 est)
GNP $31 bn (1981); $2,410 per head of population
CHRONOLOGY
1920 Iraq became a British League of Nations protectorate.
1921 Hashemite dynasty established, with Faisal I as king.

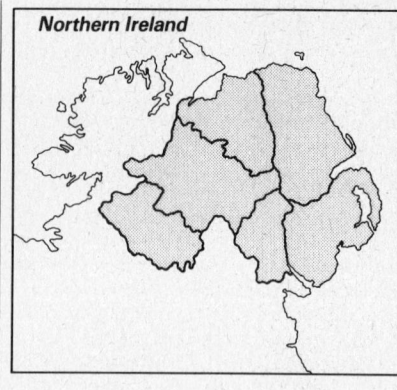

1932 Achieved full independence.
1958 Monarchy overthrown and Iraq became a republic.
1968 Military coup puts Gen al-Bakr in power.
1979 Al-Bakr replaced by Saddam Hussein.
1980 Gulf War between Iraq and Iran broke out.
1985 Gulf War fighting intensified. UN secretary general's peace moves were unsuccessful.
1987 Fighting in the war further intensified.

that date, see ◊Ireland, Republic of; ◊Ireland, Northern.

Ireland, Northern /'aɪələnd/
area 14,147 sq km/5,462 sq mi
capital Belfast
towns Londonderry, Enniskillen, Omagh, Newry, Armagh, Coleraine
features Mourne mountains, Belfast Lough and Lough Neagh; Giant's Causeway; comprises the six counties (Antrim, Armagh, Down, Fermanagh, Londonderry and Tyrone) which form part of Ireland's northernmost province of Ulster
exports engineering, especially shipbuilding including textile machinery, aircraft components; linen and synthetic textiles; processed foods, especially dairy and poultry products – all affected by the 1980s depression and political unrest
currency as for the rest of the UK
population (1983) 1,572,700
language English
religion Protestant 54%, Roman Catholic 31%
famous people Montgomery, Alanbrooke
government because of the outbreak of violence, there has been direct rule from the UK since 1972. Northern Ireland is entitled to send 12 members to the Westminster Parliament.
Under the Anglo-Irish Agreement of 1985, the Republic of Ireland was given a consultative role (via an Anglo-Irish conference) in the government of Northern Ireland, but agreed that there should be no change in its status except by majority consent, and that there should be

greater cooperation against terrorism. The agreement was approved by Parliament, but all 12 Ulster members gave up their seats, so that by-elections could be fought as a form of 'referendum' on the views of the province itself. A similar boycotting of the Northern Ireland Assembly since the Anglo-Irish agreement led to its dissolution in 1986 by the UK government.
recent history the creation of Northern Ireland dates from 1921 when the mainly Protestant counties of Ulster withdrew from the newly established Irish Free State. Spasmodic outbreaks of violence by the ◊IRA continued, but only in 1968–69 were there serious disturbances arising from Protestant political dominance and discrimination against the Roman Catholic minority in employment and housing. British troops were sent to restore peace and protect Catholics, but disturbances continued and in 1972 the parliament at Stormont was prorogued, and superseded by direct rule from Westminster.

Ireland, Republic of /'aɪələnd/ country in NW Europe, occupying almost all of the island of Ireland, to the W of England, Scotland, and Wales.
government the 1937 constitution provides for a president, elected by universal suffrage for a seven-year term, and a two-chamber national parliament, consisting of a senate *Seanad Eireann* and a house of representatives *Dail Eireann*, serving a five-year term. The senate has 60 members, 11 nominated by the prime minister and 49 elected by panels representative of most aspects of Irish life. The *Dail* consists of 166

members elected by universal suffrage through a system of proportional representation.
The president appoints a prime minister who is nominated by the *Dail*, and chooses the cabinet. All are collectively responsible to the *Dail*, which is subject to dissolution by the president if the cabinet loses its confidence within the five-year term. Proportional representation encourages the existence of several parties, the most significant being Fianna Fail (literally translated as 'Soldiers of Destiny'), Fine Gael (United Ireland Party), and the Labour Party.
history Ireland was joined to Great Britain by the 1801 Act of Union, but by the 1880s there was a strong movement for home rule. This was conceded in 1914 but its implementation was delayed by World War I, resulting in fierce riots in Dublin in 1916, the Easter Rebellion. Guerrilla activities continued after the war, through the ◊Irish Republican Army (IRA), formed by Michael ◊Collins in 1919.
In 1921 a treaty gave S Ireland dominion status within the Commonwealth, while the nine northern counties of Ulster remained part of the UK, with limited self-government. The Irish Free State, as S Ireland was formally called in 1922, was accepted by IRA leader, Michael Collins, but not by many of his colleagues, who shifted their allegiance to the *Fianna Fail* leader, Eamonn ◊De Valera. He too, eventually acknowledged the partition, in 1937 when a new constitution established the country as a sovereign state under the name of Eire.
The IRA continued its fight for an independent, unified Ireland through a campaign of violence mainly in N Ireland but also on the British mainland and, to a lesser extent, in the Irish republic. Eire remained part of the Commonwealth until 1949, when it left, declaring itself the Republic of Ireland, while N Ireland remained a constituent part of the UK. Despite the sympathy of governments in Dublin for reunification, all have dealt strongly with IRA violence within the republic. In 1973 Ireland's traditional party, *Fianna Fail*, having held office for over 40 years, was defeated and Liam Cosgrave formed a coalition of the *Fine Gael* and Labour parties. In 1977 *Fianna Fail* returned to power, with Jack Lynch as prime minister. In 1979 IRA violence intensified, with the murders of Earl Mountbatten of Burma in

Ireland and 18 British soldiers in N Ireland. Lynch resigned later the same year and was succeeded by Charles Haughey, leader of *Fianna Fail*. His aim was a united Ireland, with cosiderable independence for the six northern counties. After the 1981 general election Garrett FitzGerald, leader of the *Fine Gael* party, formed another coalition with the Labour Party but was defeated the following year on budget proposals and resigned. Haughey returned to office with a minority government, but he, too, had to resign later that year, resulting in the return of FitzGerald.

Since then various ideas have been explored in an effort to resolve the Irish question. In 1983 all the main Irish and N Irish political parties initiated the New Ireland Forum as a vehicle for discussion. Its report was rejected by Margaret ◊Thatcher's government but discussions between London and Dublin eventually resulted in the signing of the Anglo-Irish Agreement, in 1985, providing for regular consultation and exchange of information on political, legal, security and cross-border matters. The Agreement also said that the status of N Ireland would not be changed without the consent of a majority of the people. The Agreement has been criticised by the leaders of Ulster's two main Protestant Unionist parties, who, early in 1987, sent a petition to the British monarch asking for it to be rescinded. At the end of 1986 FitzGerald's coalition reached the end of its life and the election in Feb 1987 was won by *Fianna Fail*, led by Charles Haughey.

Ireland /ˈaɪələnd/ John (Nicholson) 1879–1962. British composer, born in Cheshire. Works include the mystic orchestral prelude *The Forgotten Rite* 1917 and the piano solo *Sarnia* 1941. ◊Britten was his pupil.

Irene /aɪˈriːni/ in Greek mythology, goddess of peace (Roman Pax).

Irene, St /aɪˈriːni/ c. 752–c. 803. Byzantine emperor. The widow of Leo IV, she became regent for their son Constantine on Leo's death in 780. In 797 she deposed her son, had his eyes put out, and assumed full title of basileus (emperor), ruling in her own right until deposed and exiled to Lesvos by a revolt of 802. She was made a saint by the Greek Orthodox Church for her attacks on the ◊iconoclasts.

Ireton /ˈaɪətən/ Henry 1611–1651. English Civil War general. He joined the Parliamentary forces and fought at ◊Edgehill 1642, Gainsborough 1643, and ◊Naseby 1645. He married ◊Cromwell's daughter in 1646. After the Battle of Naseby, Ireton, who was opposed to the extreme republicans and ◊Levellers, strove for a compromise with Charles I, but then played a leading role in his trial and execution. Lord Deputy in Ireland from 1650, he died after the capture of Limerick.

Irgun short for *Irgun Zvai Leumi* (National Military Society), a Jewish guerrilla group active against the British administration in Palestine 1946–48. Their bombing of the King David Hotel in Jerusalem on 22 Jul 1946 cost 91 lives.

Irian Jaya /ˈɪriən ˈdʒaɪə/ Indonesian name for ◊New Guinea.

Ireland

REPUBLIC OF (Irish *Éire*)

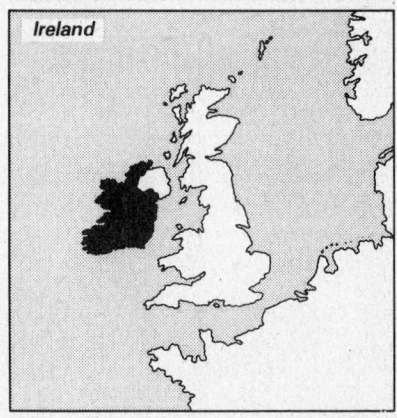

Ireland

AREA 68,892 sq km/26,601 sq mi
CAPITAL Dublin
TOWNS ports Cork, Dun Laoghaire, Limerick, Waterford
PHYSICAL central plateau with hills; rivers Shannon, Liffey, Boyne
FEATURES Bog of Allen, source of domestic and national power; Magillicuddy's Reeks, Wicklow Mountains; Lough Corrib, lakes of Killarney; Galway Bay and Aran Islands; heavy rainfall
HEAD OF STATE (nominal) Patrick J Hillery from 1976
HEAD OF GOVERNMENT Charles Haughey from 1987
GOVERNMENT parliamentary democracy
EXPORTS livestock, dairy products; Irish whiskey; microelectronic components and assemblies; mining and engineering products, chemicals, tobacco, clothing; tourism is important
CURRENCY punt (1.11 = £1 Sept 1987)
POPULATION 3,588,000 (1985); annual growth rate 1%
LANGUAGE Irish and English (both official)
RELIGION Roman Catholic
LITERACY 99% (1984)
GNP $16.5 (1983); $4,750 per head of population
CHRONOLOGY
1739–41 Famine killed about 400,000, or about one-third of population.
1845–46 Great Potato Famine: nearly 1 million died; about 1.5 million emigrated, most to the USA.
1916 Easter Rising: nationalists seized the Dublin general post office and proclaimed a republic. The revolt was suppressed by the British army and most of the leaders were executed.
1918–21 Guerrilla warfare (the 'Troubles') against British army led to split in rebel forces.
1921 Anglo-Irish Treaty resulted in creation of the Irish Free State (Southern Ireland).
1937 Eire established as an independent state.
1949 Eire left the Commonwealth and became the Republic of Ireland.
1973 Fianna Fáil defeated after 40 years in office. Liam Cosgrave formed a coalition government.
1977 Fianna Fáil returned to power, with Jack Lynch as prime minister.
1979 Lynch resigned and was succeeded by Charles Haughey.
1981 Garret FitzGerald formed a coalition.
1983 New Ireland Forum formed, but rejected by the British government.
1985 Anglo-Irish Agreement signed.
1986 Protests by Ulster Unionists against the agreement.
1987 General election won by Charles Haughey.

iridium an element, symbol Ir, atomic weight 192.2, atomic number 77. Discovered by Tennant in 1803, iridium is a metal of the ◊platinum family; white, very hard and brittle, and usually alloyed with platinum or osmium. It is used for points of fountain-pen nibs, compass bearings, parts of scientific apparatus, surgical tools and electrical goods. Under neutron bombardment iridium becomes a most useful source of ◊gamma radiation for industrial radiography, especially for steel up to 5 cm/2 in thick, the half-life being 74 days. Layers in the Earth's crust which are rich in iridium are thought to be due to the impact of meteorites.

iris in physiology, the coloured muscular diaphragm that controls size of the pupil in the vertebrate ◊eye. It contains radial muscle which increases the pupil diameter and circular muscle which constricts pupil diameter. Both types of muscle respond involuntarily to light intensity.

iris in botany, perennial northern temperate flowering plants of marshes, family Iridaceae, which include the wild British *yellow iris* or *flag Iris pseudoacorus*. Many cultivated varieties derive from *Iris germanica*. *Orris root*, used in perfumery, is the violet scented underground stem of the S European iris *Iris florentina*. The ◊crocus also belongs to this family.

Irish Gaelic first official language of the Irish Republic, but much less widely used than the second official language, English. See ◊Gaelic language.

Irish language a common name for Irish ◊Gaelic. At one time, especially in the form 'Erse', also a name for the ◊Gaelic of Scotland.

Irish literature early Irish literature, in Gaelic, consists of the sagas, which are mainly in prose, and a considerable body of verse. The chief cycles are that of Ulster, which deals with the mythological ◊Conchobar and his followers, and the Ossianic, which has influenced European literature through ◊MacPherson's version. Early Irish poetry has a unique lyric quality and consists mainly of religious verse and nature

IRELAND: COUNTIES

	Administrative Headquarters	Area sq. km.
Ulster		
Antrim	Belfast	2,906
Armagh	Armagh	1,266
Down	Downpatrick	2,465
Fermanagh	Enniskillen	1,701
Londonderry	Londonderry	2,082
Tyrone	Omagh	3,155
	N. IRELAND	13,575
Cavan	Cavan	1,890
Donegal	Lifford	4,830
Monaghan	Monaghan	1,290
Munster		
Clare	Ennis	3,188
Cork	Cork	7,459
Kerry	Tralee	4,701
Limerick	Limerick	2,686
Tipperary (N)	Nenagh	1,997
Tipperary (S)	Clonmel	2,258
Waterford	Waterford	1,839
Leinster		
Carlow	Carlow	896
Dublin	Dublin	922
Kildare	Kildare	1,694
Kilkenny	Kilkenny	2,061
Laoighis	Portlaoghise	1,720
Longford	Longford	1,044
Louth	Dundalk	821
Meath	Trim	2,339
Offaly	Tullamore	1,997
Westmeath	Mullingar	1,764
Wexford	Wexford	2,352
Wicklow	Wicklow	2,025
Connacht		
Galway	Galway	5,939
Leitrim	Carrick-on-Shannon	1,525
Mayo	Castlebar	5,397
Roscommon	Roscommon	2,463
Sligo	Sligo	1,795
	IRISH REPUBLIC	68,892

poetry, for example St Patrick's hymn, Ultán's hymn to St Brigit. A large amount of pseudo-historical verse is also extant, ascribed to such poets as Mael Mura (9th century), Mac Liac (10th century), Flann Mainistrech (11th century). Religious literature in prose includes sermons, saints' lives, for example, those in the *Book of Lismore* and in the writings of Michael O'Clery (17th century), and visions. History is represented by annals and by isolated texts like the *Cogad Gaedel re Gallaib*, an account of the Viking invasions by an eye-witness. The 'official' or 'court' verse of the 13th to 17th centuries was produced by a succession of professional poets, notably Tadhg Dall O' Huiginn (died about 1617) and Donnchadh Mór O'Dálaigh (died 1244); and Geoffrey Keating (died 1646) who wrote in both verse and prose.

Ireton A supporter and son-in-law of Oliver Cromwell, English general Henry Ireton fought at several major Civil War battles. He sought a compromise with Charles I after the Roundhead victory at Naseby, but later helped to bring the king to trial and, finally, to the block.

The bardic schools ceased to exist by the end of the 17th century. Metre became accentual, and not as before syllabic. The greatest exponents of the new school were Egan O'Rahilly (early 18th century), and the religious poet Tadhg Gaelach O'Súilleabháin.

Irish National Liberation Army (INLA) guerrilla organization committed to the end of British rule in Northern Ireland and the incorporation of Ulster into the Irish Republic. The INLA was an off-shoot of the ◊Irish Republican Army. Among the INLA's activities was the killing of the politician Airey Neave (1916–79).

Irish Republican Army (IRA) militant Irish nationalist organization, whose aim is to create a united Irish republic including Ulster. It was founded in 1919, and fought a successful war against Britain 1919–21. It came to the fore again in 1939, with a bombing campaign in Britain, and was declared illegal in Eire. Its activities intensified from 1968 onwards, as the civil rights disorders in Northern Ireland developed. In 1970 a group in the north broke away, to become the Provisional IRA; their commitment is to the expulsion of the British from Northern Ireland. The policy of the main IRA (and of ◊Sinn Fein, the political party that represents their views) is more broadly to create a single socialist republic of all 32 Irish counties. In 1974 a further breakaway occurred, of the left-wing Irish Republican Socialist Party with its paramilitary wing, the ◊Irish National Liberation Army (INLA).

The IRA is committed to the use of force in trying to achieve its objectives, and it regularly carries out bombings and shootings. In 1979 it murdered Lord ◊Mountbatten, and its bomb attacks in Britain have included: Birmingham, Guildford,

and Woolwich pub bombs 1974; Chelsea barracks 1981; Harrods department store, London, 1983; and Brighton 1984 (an attempt to kill members of the British cabinet during the Conservative Party conference). The IRA admitted responsibility for the Remembrance Day bomb explosion in Enniskillen in 1987.

Irish Sweepstake ◊lottery, run by the Irish government, on three horse races each year, on behalf of nursing services.

Irkutsk /ɪəˈkutsk/ city in the southern USSR; population (1985) 597,000. It produces coal, iron, steel, and machine tools. Founded in 1652, it began to grow after the Trans-Siberian railway reached it in 1898.

iron the most widely found metal, after aluminium; symbol Fe (Latin *ferrum*), atomic weight 55.85, atomic number 26. Iron is said to have first been worked into implements by the Egyptians about 3000 BC. It is extracted from four main ores: magnetite, a black oxide; haematite or kidney ore, another oxide, red in colour; limonite, a brown oxide; and siderite, a carbonaceous ore. Iron is the basis of all steel, and as well as its constructional uses, when mixed with carbon and other elements, it is most important chemically. In electrical equipment, it forms the basis of all permanent ◊magnets and electromagnets, and the cores of transformers and magnetic amplifiers. Iron is used for anodes in electronic ◊rectifiers, because it is not corroded by mercury. Traces of iron salts in glass give a sharp cut-off for ultraviolet rays. Iron is also an essential component of ◊haemoglobin, the molecule in the blood of animals which helps absorb oxygen. A deficiency of iron in the diet causes a form of anaemia.

Iron Age the period when weapons and tools were made from iron. Iron was produced in Thailand by c. 1600 BC but was considered inferior in strength to bronze until c. 1000 BC when metallurgical techniques improved and steel was produced by adding carbon during the smelting process.

ironbark any species of ◊eucalyptus tree with a hard tough bark.

Ironbridge Gorge /ˈaɪənbrɪdʒ/ site, near Telford New Town, Shropshire, England, of the Iron Bridge (1779), one of the first and most striking products of the Industrial Revolution in Britain: it is now part of an open-air museum of industrial archaeology.

ironclad a wooden warship covered with armour plate. The first to begin construction was the French *Gloire* in 1858, but the first to be launched was the British HMS *Warrior* 1859. The design was replaced by battleships of all-metal construction in the 1890s.

Iron Cross ◊medal awarded for valour in the German armed forces. Instituted in Prussia in 1813, it consists of a Maltese cross of iron, edged with silver.

Iron Curtain in Europe after World War II the division between democratic West and Communist East: first used by Churchill in a speech at Fulton, Missouri, 1946.

Iron Gate (Romanian *Porţile de Fier*) narrow gorge, interrupted by rapids, in Romania. A hydro-electric scheme undertaken

Ironbridge Gorge The iron bridge at Telford, Shropshire, England, was erected over the river Severn by Abraham Darby in 1779 from castings made at Coalbrookdale. It was the first iron bridge to be constructed, and still stands today.

1964–70 by Romania and Yugoslavia transformed this section of the river Danube into a 145 km/90 mi long lake and eliminated the rapids as a navigation hazard. Before flooding, in 1965, an archaeological survey revealed Europe's oldest urban settlement, ◊Lepenski Vir.

Iron Guard pro-fascist group controlling ◊Romania in the 1930s.

iron ore iron ores are found in a number of different forms, including distinct layers in igneous ◊intrusions, as components of contact ◊metamorphic rocks, and as sedimentary ◊beds. Much of the world's iron is extracted in the USSR. Other important producers are the USA, Australia, France, Brazil and Canada; over 40 countries produce significant quantities of ore. See also ◊iron, and ◊iron pyrites.

iron pyrites a common iron ore FeS_2; brassy yellow, and occuring in cubic crystals; it resembles gold nuggets and is often called 'fool's gold'.

Iroquois /ˈɪrəkwɔɪ/ confederation of North American Indians, the Six Nations (Cayuga, Mohawk, Oneida, Onondaga, and Seneca, with the Tuscarora from 1715), traditionally formed by Hiawatha (actually a priestly title) in 1570. Always friendly to the British and Dutch, they played a most important part in the Anglo-French American wars. They now live in reservations on the Canadian–US border.

irradiation in science, subjecting anything to radiation, even cancer tumours. Food can be sterilized by bombarding it with low-strength gamma rays. Although the process is now legal in several countries (and recommended for legalization in Britain), there remains fear about the possible long-term dangers to consumers of irradiated food.

irrationalism a feature of many philosophies rather than a philosophical movement. Irrationalists deny that the world can be comprehended by conceptual thought, and often see the human mind as determined by unconscious forces.

irrational number a number that cannot be expressed as an exact fraction (or a complete decimal fraction) and so cannot be expressed completely. Irrational numbers include some square roots (for example, $\sqrt{12}$, $\sqrt{13}$ and $\sqrt{15}$ are irrational) and numbers such as π (the ratio of the circumference of a circle to its diameter, which is approximately equal to 3.14159) and e, the base of natural logarithms (which is approximately 2.71828). A favourite way of

comparing the speed of operation of computers is to measure the time taken to calculate, say, the first 1,000 decimal places of π.

Irrawaddy /ˌɪrəˈwɒdi/ chief river of Burma. Its sources are the Mali and N'mai rivers. It crosses the centre of Burma, and flows roughly N-S, for 2,090 km/1,300 mi into the Bay of Bengal. Its chief tributaries are the Chindwin and Shweli.

irrigation artificial water supply for dry agricultural areas, as in the channelling of the annual ◊Nile flood from the earliest times, and its modern control by the ◊Aswan High Dam. Its drawbacks are that continuous controlled irrigation tends to concentrate salts causing infertility, and rich river silt is retained at the dam, to the impoverishment of the land and fisheries in the estuary area. The Colorado, USA, now barely reaches the sea through over-exploitation.

Irvine /ˈɜːvɪn/ new town in Strathclyde, Scotland; population (1984) 57,000. It overlooks the Isle of Arran, and is also a holiday resort.

Irving /ˈɜːvɪŋ/ Henry. Stage name of English actor John Brodribb 1838–1905. From 1871 he established his reputation, chiefly at the Lyceum Theatre in London, where he became manager from 1878. He staged a series of successful Shakespearean productions there, including *Romeo and Juliet* 1882, with himself and Ellen ◊Terry playing the leading roles. In 1895 he was the first actor to be knighted.

Irving British actor-manager Henry Irving, the first member of his profession to be knighted, dominated the London stage for the last 30 years of Victoria's reign.

Irving /ˈɜːvɪŋ/ Washington 1783–1859. American essayist and short-story writer. Born in New York City, of English parents, he published a mock-heroic *History of New York* in 1809, supposedly written by the Dutchman 'Diedrich Knickerbocker'. In 1815 he went to England where his publications include the *Sketch Book of Geoffrey Crayon, Gentleman* 1820, which contained such stories as 'Rip van

Winkle' and 'Legend of Sleepy Hollow'. He was US ambassador to Spain 1842–46.

Isaac /ˈaɪzək/ in the Old Testament, Hebrew patriarch, son of Abraham and Sarah, and father of Esau and ◊Jacob.

Isaacs /ˈaɪzəks/ Rufus Daniel, 1st Marquess of Reading 1860–1935. Liberal lawyer and politician. As Lord Chief Justice he tried the Irish nationalist Roger ◊Casement in 1916. Viceroy of India 1921–26; foreign secretary 1931.

Isabella /ˌɪzəˈbelə/ name of two Spanish queens:

Isabella I /ˌɪzəˈbelə/ the Catholic 1451–1504. Queen of Castile from 1474, after the death of her brother Henry IV. By her marriage with Ferdinand of Aragon 1469, the crowns of two of the Christian states in the Spanish peninsula were united. In her reign the Moors were finally driven out of Spain; she introduced the ◊Inquisition into Castile, and the persecution of the Jews, and gave financial encouragement to ◊Columbus.

Isabella II /ˌɪzəˈbelə/ 1830–1904. Queen of Spain from 1822, when she succeeded her father Ferdinand VII. The ◊Salic Law banning a female sovereign had been abrogated by the *Cortes* (Spanish parliament), but her succession was disputed by her uncle Don Carlos. After seven years of civil war the Carlists were defeated. She abdicated in favour of her son Alfonso XII in 1870.

Isaiah /aɪˈzaɪə/ 8th century BC. In the Old Testament, first major Hebrew prophet. The son of Amos, he was probably of high rank, and lived largely in Jerusalem.

Ischia /ˈɪskiə/ volcanic island about 26 km/16 mi SW of Naples, Italy, in the Tyrrhenian Sea; population (1985) 26,000. It has mineral springs known to the Romans, beautiful scenery, and is a holiday resort.

Ise /iːˈseɪ/ city SE of Kyoto, on Honshu, Japan. It is the site of the most sacred Shinto shrine, dedicated to sun-goddess ◊Amaterasu. It has been rebuilt every 20 years in the form of a perfect thatched house of the 7th century BC, and contains the octagonal mirror of the goddess.

Isère /ɪˈzeə/ river of SE France, 290 km/180 mi long, a tributary of the Rhône. It gives its name to the *département* of Isère.

Isfahan /ˌɪsfəˈhɑːn/ industrial city in central Iran; population (1982) 926,600. The ancient capital (1598–1722) of ◊Abbas the Great, its features include the Grand Mosque.

Isherwood /ˈɪʃəwʊd/ Christopher (William Bradshaw) 1904–1986. English novelist. Educated at Cambridge, he lived in Germany 1929–33 just before Hitler's rise to power, a period which inspired *Mr Norris Changes Trains* 1935 and *Goodbye to Berlin* 1939, creating the character of Sally Bowles (the basis of the musical *Cabaret* 1968). Returning to England, he collaborated with ◊Auden in three verse plays, and went to the USA with him in 1939, becoming a US citizen in 1946.

Ishiguro /ˌɪʃɪˈgʊrəu/ Kazuo 1954– . British novelist. Born in Japan, he settled in Britain in 1960. His novel *An Artist of the Floating World* won the 1986 Whitbread Prize.

Isherwood Lifelong friend of W H Auden, English novelist Christopher Isherwood was a leading intellectual of the 1930s.

Ishmael /ˈɪʃmeɪəl/ in the Old Testament, son of ◊Abraham and his wife Sarah's Egyptian maid; traditional ancestor of Muhammad and the Arab people. He and his mother were driven out by Sarah's jealousy.

Ishtar /ˈɪʃtɑː/ goddess of love and war worshipped by the Babylonians and Assyrians, and personified as the legendary queen Semiramis.

isinglass pure form of gelatin obtained from the cleaned and dried swim bladder of various fish, particularly the sturgeon. Isinglass is used in the clarification of wines and beer, and in cookery.

Isis /ˈaɪsɪs/ name sometimes given to the upper stretches of the river Thames, England, above Oxford.

Isis /ˈaɪsɪs/ the principal goddess of ancient Egypt. She was the daughter of Geb and Nut (earth and sky), and as the sister-wife of ◊Osiris searched for his body after his death at the hands of his brother Set. Her son Horus then defeated and captured Set, but cut off his mother's head because she would not allow Set to be killed. She was later identified with ◊Hathor. The cult of Isis ultimately spread to Greece and Rome.

Iskenderun /ɪsˈkendəruːn/ port, naval base and steel town in Turkey; population (1980) 125,000. It was founded by ◊Alexander the Great in 333 BC.

Islam religion (Arabic 'submission' to the will of Allah, the Muslim name for God), of which the creed declares: there is no God but Allah, and ◊Muhammad is the Prophet or Messenger of Allah. Beliefs include Creation, Fall of Adam, Angels and the ◊Jinn, Heaven and Hell, Day of Judgment, God's predestination of good and evil, and the succession of scriptures revealed to the prophets, including Moses and Jesus, but of

which the perfect, final form is the *Koran* or *Quran* divided into 114 *suras* or chapters, said to have been divinely revealed to Muhammad, the original being preserved beside the throne of Allah in heaven.

sects there are two main Muslim sects:

Sunni whose members hold that the first three caliphs were all Muhammad's legitimate successors, and are in the majority. The name derives from the *Sunna*, Arabic 'rule', the body of traditional law evolved from the teaching and acts of Muhammad.

Shi'ite or *Shia* whose members believe that ◊Ali was Muhammad's first true successor; they number some 85 million, and are found in Iran, ◊Iraq, Lebanon, and Bahrain. Holy men have greater authority in the Shi'ite sect. Breakaway sub-sects include the *Alawite* sect to which the ruling party in Syria belongs; and the *Ismaili* sect with the *Aga Khan* IV 1936– as its spiritual head. There is an Ismaili Centre (1985) in Kensington, London. Later schools include *Sufism*, a mystical movement in 17th-century Iran. Generally speaking, Islam has not been a missionary religion, but after World War II a missionary movement, backing the militant organizations for the 'true Islamic state'.

Islamic law Islam embodies a secular Islamic Law (the Shari'a or 'Highway'), which is clarified for Shi'ites by reference to their own version of the *sunna*, 'practice' of the Prophet as transmitted by his companions; the Sunni sect also take into account *ijma'*, the endorsement by universal consent of practices and beliefs among the faithful. A *mufti* is a legal expert who guides the courts in their interpretation, and in Turkey (until the establishment of the republic in 1924) had supreme spiritual authority.

organization there is no organized church or priesthood, though Muhammad's descendants (the Hashim family) and popularly recognized holy men, mullahs and ayatollahs are accorded respect.

observances the 'Five Pillars of the Faith' are: recitation of the creed; worship five times a day facing the holy city of ◊Mecca (the call to prayer is given by a muezzin, usually from the minaret or tower of a ◊mosque); almsgiving; fasting sunrise to sunset through Ramadan (ninth month of the year, which varies with the calendar); and the pilgrimage to Mecca at least once in a lifetime.

Islamabad /ɪzˈlæməbæd/ capital of Pakistan from 1967, in the Potwar district, at the foot of the Margala Hills and immediately NW of Rawalpindi; population (1981) 340,000. The city was designed by Constantinos ◊Doxiadis.

Islamic art is one of ornament, for under the Muslim religion artists may not usurp the divine right of creation by portraying living creatures. Intricate, interlacing patterns based on geometry, Arabic ◊calligraphy, and stylized plant motifs (including the swirling 'Arabesque') swarm over surfaces, structured by a rigid sense of symmetry. Lustreware pottery, ceramic tiles, and carpets were primary art forms. In Islamic Persia miniature painting illustrating literary or historical scenes, often in a lovingly detailed Paradise Garden setting, flourished during the

Safavid period 1502–1736 and after 1526 under the Moghul Empire in India.

Islay /'aɪleɪ/ most southerly island of the Inner ◊Hebrides, Scotland, in Strathclyde region, separated from Jura by the Sound of Islay; area 609 sq km/235 sq mi. The principal towns are Bowmore and Port Ellen.

Isle of Ely /'iːli/ former county of England, in East Anglia. It was merged with Cambridgeshire in 1965.

Isle of Man /mæn/ island in the Irish Sea, off the coast of Cumbria; see ◊Man, Isle of.

Isle of Wight /waɪt/ island off the coast of Hampshire, S England; see ◊Wight, Isle of.

Islington /'ɪzlɪŋtən/ borough of N Greater London
features 19th-century squares and terraces at Highbury, Barnsbury, Canonbury; Wesley Museum in City Road. Mineral springs (Sadler's Wells) in Clerkenwell were exploited in conjunction with a music-hall in the 17th century, and Lilian ◊Baylis developed a later theatre as an 'Old Vic' annexe.
population (1981) 159,754.

Ismail /ˌɪzmɑːˈiːl/ 1830–1895. Khedive of Egypt. A grandson of Mehemet Ali, he became viceroy of Egypt in 1863 and in 1866 received the title of Khedive from the Sultan. In 1875 Britain, at Disraeli's suggestion, bought the Khedive's Suez Canal shares for £3,976,582, and Anglo-French control of Egypt's finances was established. In 1879 Britain and France persuaded the Sultan to appoint Tewfik, his son, Khedive in his place.

Ismail I /ˌɪzmɑːˈiːl/ 1486–1524. Shah of Persia from 1501, founder of the Safavi dynasty, who established the first national government since the Arab conquest, and Shi'ite Islam as the national religion.

Ismaili a set of Shi'ite Muslims. See under ◊Islam.

Ismailia /ˌɪzmaɪˈliːə/ city in NE Egypt; population (1976) 145,978. It was founded in 1863 as the headquarters for construction of the Suez Canal, and was named after the Khedive ◊Ismail.

ISO in photography, a numbering system for rating the speed of films, devised by the International Standards Organization, which now supersedes the ASA.

isobar a line drawn on maps and weather charts linking all places with the same atmospheric pressure (usually measured in millibars). When used in weather forecasting, the distance between the isobars is an indication of the barometric gradient. Where they are close together cyclonic weather is indicated, bringing strong winds and a depression, and where far apart anticyclonic, bringing calmer, settled conditions.

Isocrates /aɪˈsɒkrətiːz/ 436–338 BC. Athenian orator, a pupil of Socrates. He was a professional speechwriter and teacher of rhetoric.

isolation in medicine, segregation of persons exposed to or suffering from an infectious disease, to prevent its spread.

isolationism in politics, concentration on internal rather than foreign affairs. In the USA,

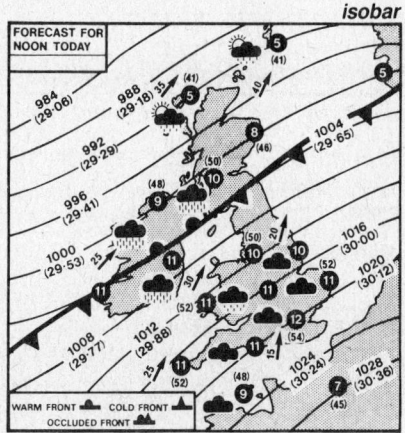

isobar

charts for British Isles (4mm steps)
and North Atlantic (8mm steps)

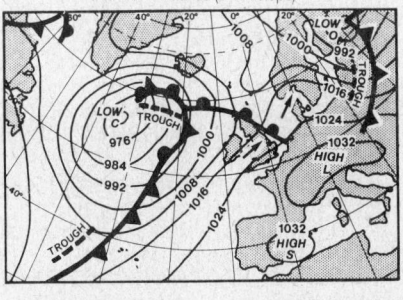

it is usually associated with the Republican Party, especially politicians of the Midwest. Intervention in both world wars was initially resisted, and after ◊Korea and ◊Vietnam, there was resistance to further involvement in Europe, the Pacific, or the Middle East.

isomer a chemical compound having the same molecular composition and mass as another, but with different properties, because of the different structural arrangement of the atoms in the molecules (for example, one being a 'mirror image' of another). The study of isomers is an important branch of ◊organic chemistry.

isomerism the existence of chemical compounds (◊isomers) having the same molecular composition but with different properties.

isometrics system of muscular exercises without apparatus, for example by contracting particular sets of muscles. These exercises, some of which can be performed without visible movement, have been advocated as a means whereby sedentary workers can attain fitness, but can be damaging when practised by the unskilled.

isomorphism the existence of substances of different chemical composition but with similar crystalline form.

isoprene (*methylbutadiene*) a volatile fluid $CH_2:CH.C(CH_3):CH_2$ obtained from petroleum and coal, which is used to make synthetic rubber.

isostasy the theoretical balance in buoyancy of all parts of the Earth's ◊crust, as though they were floating on a denser layer beneath. High mountains, for example, have very deep roots,

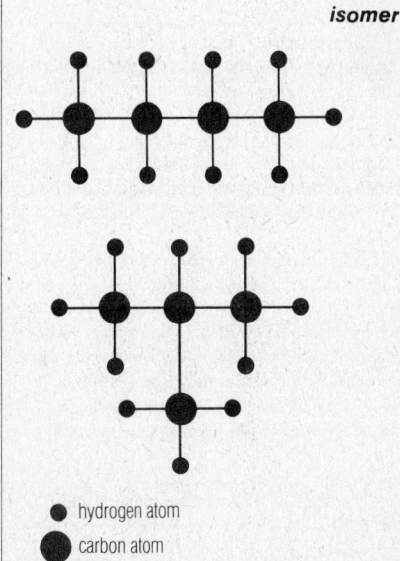

isomer

● hydrogen atom
● carbon atom
— atomic bond

just as an iceberg floats with most of its mass submerged. Similarly, during an ice age the weight of the ice sheet pushes that continent into the earth's mantle; once the ice has melted, the continent rises again. This accounts for shoreline features being found some way inland in regions that were heavily glaciated during the Pleistocene.

isotherm a line on a map linking all places having the same temperature at a given time. See also ◊isobar.

isotopes two or more forms of an element; they have the same number of protons, so share the same atomic number, but contain a different number of neutrons, so differ in their atomic weight. They may be stable or radioactive; see ◊atom, ◊radioisotope. As well as the naturally occuring radioisotopes, such as carbon-14, many synthetic isotopes can be made in the laboratory by bombardment with neutrons. When the atomic weight of an element is quoted, it is that of the most stable isotope.

Israel /'ɪzreɪl/ ancient kingdom of N ◊Palestine, formed after the death of ◊Solomon by Jewish peoples seceding from the rule of his son Rehoboam, and electing ◊Jeroboam in his place.

Israel /'ɪzreɪl/ country in SW Asia, bounded to the N by Lebanon, to the E by Syria and Jordan, to the S by the Gulf of Aqaba, and to the W by Egypt and the Mediterranean.
government Israel has no written constitution. In 1950 the single-chamber legislature, the *Knesset*, voted to adopt a state constitution by evolution over an unspecifed period of time. As in the UK, certain laws are considered to have particular constitutional significance and could, at some time, be codified into a single written document.
Supreme authority rests with the *Knesset*, whose 120 members are elected by universal suffrage, through a system of proportional representation, for a four-year term. It is subject to dissolution

within that period. The president is constitutional head of state and is elected by the *Knesset* for a five-year term. The prime minister and cabinet are mostly drawn from, and collectively responsible to, the *Knesset*, but occasionally a cabinet member may be chosen from outside. There are several political parties, the two most significant being the Israel Labour Party, and the Consolidation Party (Likud).

history the Zionist movement, calling for an independent community for Jews in their historic homeland of Palestine, began in the 19th century, and in 1917 Britain declared its support for the idea. In 1920 the League of Nations placed Palestine under British administration and the British government was immediately faced with the rival claims of Jews who wished to settle and the indigenous Arabs who opposed them. In 1937 Britain proposed separate Arab and Jewish communities, this was accepted by the Jews but not by the Arabs, and fighting broke out between them.

In 1947 this plan for partition was supported by the UN and when, in 1948, Britain ended its Palestinian mandate, an independent State of Israel was proclaimed, with David ◊Ben Gurion as prime minister. Neigbouring Arab states sent forces to crush Israel but failed, and when a cease-fire agreement was reached, in 1949, Israel controlled more land than had been originally allocated to it. The non Jewish-occupied remainder of Palestine, known as the West Bank, was incorporated into ◊Jordan. The creation of this state encouraged Jewish immigration on a large scale, about 2,000,000 having arrived from all over the world by 1962. Hundreds of thousands of Arab residents fled from Israel to neigbouring countries, such as Jordan and Lebanon. In 1964 a number of exiled Palestinian Arabs founded the ◊Palestine Liberation Organisation (PLO), aiming to overthrow Israel. During the 1960s there was considerable tension between Israel and Egypt, which, under President ◊Nasser, had become a leader in the Arab world. His nationalization of the ◊Suez Canal in 1956 provided an opportunity for Israel, with Britain and France, to attack Egypt and occupy a part of Palestine which it had controlled since 1949, the Gaza Strip, Israel being forced by UN and US pressure to withdraw in 1957. Ten years later, in the Six Day War, Israel gained the whole of Jerusalem, the West Bank area of Jordan, the Sinai Peninsula in Egypt, and the Golan Heights in Syria. All were incorporated into the State of Israel.

Ben Gurion resigned in 1963 and was succeeded by Levi Eshkol, leading a coalition government, and in 1968 three of the coalition parties combined to form the Israel Labour Party. In 1969 Golda Meir became Labour Party prime minister. Towards the end of her administration another Arab-Israeli war broke out, coinciding with ◊Yom Kippur, the holiest day of the Jewish year. Israel was attacked by Egypt and Syria and after nearly three weeks of fighting, with heavy losses, a cease-fire was agreed. Golda Meir resigned in 1974 and was succeeded by Gen Itzhak Rabin, heading a Labour-led coalition.

Israel
STATE OF (*Medinat Israel*)

AREA 20,770 sq km/8,017 sq mi (as at 1949 armistice)

CAPITAL Jerusalem (not recognized by the United Nations)

TOWNS ports Tel Aviv/Jaffa, Haifa, Eilat; Bat-Yam, Holon, Ramat Gan, Petach Tikva, Beersheba

PHYSICAL coastal plain of Sharon between Haifa and Tel Aviv noted since ancient times for fertility; high arid region in S and centre; river Jordan Rift Valley along the E is below sea level

FEATURES Dead Sea, Lake Tiberias, Negev Desert, Golan Heights; historic sites: Jerusalem, Bethlehem, Nazareth; Masada, Megiddo, Jericho; caves of the Dead Sea scrolls

HEAD OF STATE Chaim Herzog from 1983

HEAD OF GOVERNMENT Itzhak Shamir from 1986

GOVERNMENT parliamentary democracy

EXPORTS citrus and other fruit, avocados, chinese leaves; fertilizers, plastics, petrochemicals, textiles; electronics (military, medical, scientific, industrial), electro-optics, precision instruments, aircraft and missiles

CURRENCY shekel (2.63 = £1 Sept 1987)

POPULATION (1985) 4,128,000 (including some 750,000 Arabs as Israeli citizens and over 1 million Arabs in the occupied territories); under the Law of Return 1950, 'every Jew shall be entitled to come to Israel as an immigrant', those from the East and E Europe are *Ashkenazim*, and from Spain, Portugal, and Arab N Africa are *Sephardim* (over 50% of the population is now of Sephardic descent). An Israeli-born Jew is a *Sabra*; about 500,000 Israeli Jews are resident in the USA. Annual growth rate 2%

LANGUAGE Hebrew and Arabic (official); Yiddish, European and W Asian languages

RELIGION Israel is a secular state, but the predominant faith is Judaism; also Sunni Muslim, Christian, and Druze

LITERACY 96% male/91% female (1980)

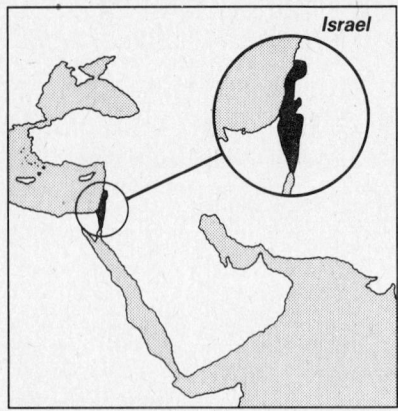

GNP $23 bn (1983); $5,609 per head of population

CHRONOLOGY

1948 Independent state of Israel proclaimed with Ben Gurion as prime minister.

1963 Ben Gurion resigned and was succeeded by Levi Eshkol.

1964 Palestine Liberation Organization (PLO) founded with the aim of overthrowing the State of Israel.

1967 Israel victorious in the Six-Day War.

1968 Israel Labour Party formed, led by Golda Meir.

1969 Golda Meir became prime minister.

1974 Yom Kippur War. Golda Meir succeeded by Itzhak Rabin.

1977 Menachem Begin elected prime minister. Egyptian president addressed the Knesset.

1978 Camp David talks.

1979 Egyptian-Israeli agreement signed.

1982 Israel pursued PLO fighters into Lebanon.

1983 Agreement reached for withdrawal from Lebanon.

1985 Israeli prime minister Shimon Peres had secret talks with King Hussein of Jordan.

1986 Itzhak Shamir took over from Peres under power-sharing agreement.

1988 Criticism of Israel's handling of Palestinian uprising in occupied territories.

In the 1977 elections the Consolidation (Likud) bloc, led by Menachem ◊Begin, won an unexpected victory and Begin became prime minister. Within five months relations between Egypt and Israel changed dramatically, mainly due to initiatives by President ◊Sadat of Egypt, encouraged by US President Jimmy ◊Carter. Sadat visited Israel to address the *Knesset*, and the following year the Egyptian and Israeli leaders met at ◊Camp David, in the US, to sign agreements for peace in the Middle East. A treaty was signed in 1979, and in 1980 Egypt and Israel exchanged ambassadors, to the dismay of most of the Arab world.

Israel withdrew from Sinai by 1982 but continued to occupy the Golan Heights. In the same year Israel, without consulting Egypt, entered Lebanon and surrounded W Beirut, in pursuit of 6,000 PLO fighters who were trapped there. A split between Egypt and Israel was avoided by the efforts of the US special negotiator, Philip Habib, who secured the evacuation from Beirut to other Arab countries of about 15,000 PLO and Syrian fighters, in Aug 1982.

Israel's alleged complicity in massacres in two Palestinian refugee camps increased Arab hostility. Talks between Israel and Lebanon, between Dec 1982 and May 1983, resulted in an agreement, drawn up by US Secretary of State George Shultz, calling for the withdrawal of all foreign forces from Lebanon within three months. Syria refused to acknowledge the agreement and left some 30,000 troops, with

Israel Towards the end of the British mandate over the lands that are now Israel, Jewish immigration was restricted. In 1947, the year before the Jewish state of Israel was proclaimed, the *Theodor Herzl* carrying immigrants to their promised land was shot at by the British Navy.

about 7,000 PLO members, in the NE, and Israel retaliated by refusing to withdraw its forces from the S.

During this time Begin faced growing domestic problems, including rapidly rising inflation and growing opposition to his foreign policies. In 1983 he resigned and Itzhak Shamir formed a shaky coalition. Elections in Jul 1984 proved inconclusive, with the Labour Alignment, led by Shimon Peres, winning 44 seats in the *Knesset*, and Likud, led by Shamir, 41. Neither leader was able to form a viable coalition, so after weeks of negotiation, it was agreed that a government of national unity would be formed, with Peres as prime minister for the first 25 months, until Oct 1986, and Shamir as his deputy, and then a reversal of the positions.

Meanwhile, the problems in the Lebanon continued. In 1984, under pressure from Syria, President Gemayel of the Lebanon rejected the 1983 treaty with Israel, but the government of national unity in Tel Aviv continued to plan the withdrawal of its forces, even though it might lead to outright civil war in S Lebanon. Guerrilla groups of the Shı'ite community of S Lebanon took advantage of the situation by attacking the departing Israeli troops. Israel replied by attacking Shı'ite villages. Most of the withdrawal was complete by Jun 1985. Several peace initiatives by King Hussein of Jordan failed, largely because of Israeli and US suspicions about the PLO, some of whose supporters were alleged to have been involved in terrorism in the Mediterranean area. There were, however, signs of improvement in 1985.

Prime Minister Peres met King Hussein secretly in the S of France and later, in a speech to the UN, Peres said he would not rule out the possibility of an international conference on the Middle East. PLO leader Yasser ◊Arafat also had talks with Hussein and later, in Cairo, denounced PLO guerrilla activity outside Israeli-occupied territory. Domestically, the government of national unity was having some success with its economic policies, inflation falling in 1986 to manageable levels.

Issigonis /ˌɪsɪ'gəʊnɪs/ Alec 1906– . Palestine-born British engineer who designed the Morris Minor (1948) and the Mini-Minor (1959) cars, and so created modern economy motoring and added the word 'mini' to the English language.

Istanbul /ˌɪstæn'bʊl/ city and chief seaport of Turkey; population (1980) 2,772,708.

features the harbour of the Golden Horn; Hagia Sophia (◊Justinian's church of the Holy Wisdom, 537, now a mosque); Sultan Ahmet Mosque, known as the Blue Mosque, from its tiles; Topkapi Palace of the Sultans (with a harem of 400 rooms), now a museum. The Selimye Barracks in the suburb of *Uskuᵃdar* (Scutari) was used as a hospital in the Crimean War. The rooms used by Florence Nightingale, with her personal possessions, are preserved as a museum.

history founded as *Byzantium* about 660 BC, it was renamed *Constantinople* by ◊Constantine the Great in 330, and was the capital of the ◊Byzantine Empire until captured by the Turks 1453. As *Istamboul* it was the capital of the

◊Ottoman Empire until 1922.

isthmus a narrow strip of land joining two larger land masses. The Isthmus of Panama joins North and South America.

Italian art Italy is rich in examples of the Byzantine style of architecture which is a mixture of oriental and classical elements; such are the monuments of Justinian in Ravenna and the later church of St Mark's in Venice. The ◊Romanesque style was developed in Italy from the 10th to the 13th centuries. Examples of this style are the churches of Lombardy; the baptistery, cathedral, and Leaning Tower of Pisa; and the cathedrals of Sicily. The ◊Gothic period in Italy developed from the 13th to the 15th centuries. It is based on Romanesque and differs a great deal from the Gothic style of northern Europe. Facades were elaborately decorated; mosaics and coloured marble were used, and sculpture – delicately carved – was placed around windows and doors.

The history of Italian painting begins in the latter half of the 13th century (the *Duecento* in Italian). ◊Giotto is usually regarded as the first great Italian painter. He broke away from the traditional formal style, and set a new standard of naturalism. An earlier painter, ◊Cimabue, may have been Giotto's master. Other great artists of the *Duecento* were the sculptors Niccola ◊Pisano and his son, Giovanni, and the painter ◊Duccio. The most famous names of the 14th century – the *Trecento* – include the Florentines Bernardo Daddi (about 1290–1348); Taddeo ◊Gaddi and his son Agnolo; the Sienese Ambrogio and Pietro Lorenzetti; and the Veronese painter, Vittore ◊Pisano.

The next period in Italian art is called the *Renaissance* (Italian *rinascimento*)(15th and 16th centuries), that is 'rebirth' of the classical spirit. The architectural style was developed by ◊Brunelleschi and his contemporaries. The most famous achievement is the basilica of St Peter's, Rome, with which ◊Michelangelo's name is associated.

The great artists of the Renaissance include ◊Ghiberti, the sculptor of the 'Doors of Paradise' of the Florentine baptistery; Donatello, the greatest sculptor of the period; Luca della ◊Robbia; ◊Masaccio, famous for his paintings in the Carmelite church, Florence; Fra ◊Angelico; ◊Uccello who achieved fame as a pioneer in scientific perspective; ◊Pollaiuolo, another famous experimenter; the ◊Bellini family; ◊Mantegna; Andrea del ◊Verrocchio, sculptor of the Colleoni memorial, the greatest equestrian statue of the Renaissance; Sandro ◊Botticelli; ◊Leonardo da Vinci, the great mind of the Renaissance; ◊Michelangelo, the greatest artistic genius of the period; ◊Raphael, painter of the 'Sistine Madonna'; ◊Titian, who was supreme as a colourist; ◊Tintoretto, who was Titian's pupil; ◊Correggio; and ◊Veronese. The most famous names of the following *Baroque* period are those of the sculptor and architect ◊Bernini, and in painting ◊Caravaggio and the ◊Caracci. The 18th and earlier 19th centuries were dominated by the ◊Neo-Classic movement, seeking inspiration from the works of the past rather than life itself, and it was not until the rise of the ◊Futurist school, for example Gino Severini (1883–1966), and succeeding Metaphysical school, for example Carlo Carra (1881–1966) that a revival came. ◊Modigliani is an outstanding figure at the beginning of the 20th century. In more recent years sculptors including Giacomo Manzù (1908–), Marino Marini (1901–80), and Emilio Greco (1913–), and the portrait painter ◊Annigoni have risen to prominence.

Italian language a member of the Romance branch of the Indo-European language family. Its development parallels the integration of the Italian peninsula and the plains S of the Alps into a cultural and national unity. The standard language originates in the Tuscan dialect of the Middle Ages, particularly as used for literary purposes by ◊Dante Alighieri. With a strong infusion of Latin for religious, academic and educational purposes, the written standard has tended to be highly formal and divorced from the many regional dialects (often mutually unintelligible) that are still largely the everyday usage of the general population. Italian has provided English with much of the vocabulary of music *(e.g. adagio, arpeggio, cello, crescendo, diminuendo, mezzo-soprano, pianoforte)*, Italian cuisine *(e.g. lasagne, macaroni, pasta, pizza, ravioli, spaghetti, tagliatelle)*, and an assortment of social comment *(e.g. extravaganza, graffiti, imbroglio, mafia, seraglio)*.

Italian literature originated in the 13th century with the Sicilian school, which imitated Provençal poetry. The contemporary works of St Francis of Assisi and Jacopone da Todi reflect the religious faith of the time. Guido Guinicelli (1230–c. 1275) and Guido Cavalcanti (c. 1250–1300) developed the spiritual conception of love and influenced ◊Dante Alighieri, whose *Divina Commedia/Divine Comedy* 1300–21 is generally recognized as the greatest work of Italian literature. ◊Petrarch was a humanist and a poet, while ◊Boccaccio is principally known for his tales.

The 14th-century *Divina Commedia* marked the beginning of the Renaissance. ◊Boiardo dealt with the Carolingian epics in his *Orlando Innamorato/Roland in Love* 1480–94 which was completed and transformed by Lodovico ◊Ariosto as *Orlando Furioso/The Frenzy of Roland* 1516. Their contemporaries Niccolo ◊Machiavelli and Francesco Guicciardini (1483–1540) are historians of note. Torquato ◊Tasso wrote his epic *Gerusalemme Liberata/The Liberation of Jerusalem* 1575 in the spirit of the Counter-Reformation.

The 17th century was characterized by the exaggeration of the poets Giovanni Battista Marini (1569–1625) and Gabriello Chiabrera (1552–1638). In 1690 the 'Academy of Arcadia' was formed: its members included Innocenzo Frugoni (1692–1768) and ◊Metastasio. Other writers include Salvator ◊Rosa, the satirist.

During the 18th century Giuseppe Parini (1729–99) ridiculed the abuses of his day, while Vittorio ◊Alfieri attacked tyranny in his dramas. Carlo ◊Goldoni wrote comedies and Ugo Foscolo (1778–1827) is chiefly remembered for his patriotic verse. Giacomo ◊Leopardi is not only the greatest lyrical poet since Dante, but also a master of Italian prose; the Romantic, Alessandro ◊Manzoni, is best known as a novelist. A later outstanding literary figure and poet, Giosuè ◊Carducci, was followed by the verbose Gabriele ◊d'Annunzio, writing of sensuality and violence, and Benedetto ◊Croce, historian and philosopher, who between them dominated Italian literature at the turn of the century.

Other writers were the realist novelist Giovanni ◊Verga, the dramatist Luigi ◊Pirandello, and the novelists Ignazio ◊Silone and Italo ◊Svevo. Poets of the period include Dino ◊Campana, Giuseppe ◊Ungaretti and among the modern school are Nobel prizewinner Eugenio ◊Montale. Novelists of the post-Fascist period, preoccupied with political and moral problems, include Alberto ◊Moravia, Carlo ◊Levi, Cesare Pavese (1908–50), Elsa Morante (1916–), Giuseppe ◊Tomasi, Prince of Lampedusa, and the younger writers Italo ◊Calvino, and Leonardo ◊Sciascia.

italic style of printing in which the letters slope to the right, introduced by Aldus Manutius of Venice from 1501. Very similar is the handwriting style developed in 1522 by Vatican chancery scribe Ludovico degli Arrighi for popular use (the basis for modern italic script). It is usually used side by side with the erect Roman type, for purposes of emphasis and citation.

Italy /ˈɪtəli/ country in S Europe, bounded N by Switzerland and Austria, E by Yugoslavia and the Adriatic Sea, S by the Ionian and Mediterranean Seas, and W by the Tyrrhenian Sea and France. It includes the Mediterranean islands of Sardinia and Sicily.

government the 1948 constitution provides for a two-chamber parliament consisting of a senate and a 630-member chamber of deputies. Both are elected for a five year-term by universal suffrage, through a system of proportional representation, and have equal powers. The senate's 315 elected members are regionally representative and there are also seven life senators. The president is constitutional head of state and is elected for a seven-year term by an electoral college consisting of both houses of parliament and 58 regional representatives. The president appoints the prime minister and cabinet, (council of ministers), and they are collectively responsible to parliament. Although Italy is not a federal state, each of its 20 regions enjoys a high degree of autonomy, with a regional council elected for a five-year term by universal suffrage. The voting system encourages a multiplicity of political parties, the most significant being the Christian Democrats (DC), the Communists (PCI), the Socialists (PSI), the Italian Social Movement – National Right (MSI-DN), the Republicans (PRI), the Social Democrats (PSDI) and the Liberals (PLI).

history the varying peoples inhabiting Italy – Etruscans in Tuscany, Latins and Sabines in middle Italy, Greek colonies in the S and Sicily, and Gauls in the N – were united under Roman rule during the 4th–3rd centuries BC. With the decline of the Roman empire, and its final extinction in 476 AD, Italy became exposed to barbarian attacks, and passed in turn under the rule of the Ostrogoths and the Lombards.

The 8th century witnessed the rise of the papacy as a territorial power, the annexation of the Lombard kingdon by ◊Charlemagne, and his coronation as emperor of the West in 800. From then until 1250 the main issue in Italian history is the relations, at first friendly and later hostile, between the papacy and the ◊Holy Roman Empire. During this struggle the Italian cities seized the opportunity to convert themselves into self-governing republics.

By 1300 five major powers existed in Italy: the city-republics of Milan, Florence, and Venice; the papal states; and the kingdom of Naples. Their mutual rivalries and constant wars laid Italy open 1494–1559 to invasions from France and Spain; as a result Naples and Milan passed under Spanish rule. After 1700 Austria secured Milan and replaced Spain as the dominating power, while Naples passed to a Spanish Bourbon dynasty, and Sardinia to the dukes of Savoy.

The period of French rule (1796–1814) temporarily unified Italy, and introduced the principles of the French Revolution, but after ◊Napoleon's fall Italy was again divided between Austria, the Pope, the kingdoms of Sardinia and Naples, and four smaller duchies. Nationalist and democratic ideals nevertheless remained alive, and inspired attempts at revolution in 1820, 1831, and 1848–49. After this last failure the Sardinian monarchy assumed the leadership of the national movement. With the help of Napoleon III, the Austrians were expelled from Lombardy in 1859; the duchies joined the Italian kingdom; ◊Garibaldi overthrew the Neapolitan monarchy; and Victor Emmanuel II of Sardinia was proclaimed king of Italy at Turin in 1861. Venice and part of Venetia were secured by another war with Austria in 1866; in 1870 Italian forces occupied Rome, thus completing the unification of Italy, and the Pope ceased to be a temporal ruler until 1929 (see ◊Vatican City).

In 1878 Victor Emmanuel II died, and was succeeded by Humbert (Umberto) I, his son, who was assassinated in 1900. The formation of a colonial empire began in 1869 with the purchase of land on the Bay of Assab, on the Red Sea, from the local sultan. In the next 20 years the Italians occupied all ◊Eritrea, which was made a colony in 1889. An attempt to seize Ethiopia was decisively defeated at Adowa in 1896. War with Turkey 1911–12 gave Tripoli and Cyrenaica. Italy's intervention on the Allied side in World War I secured her Trieste, the Trentino, and S Tirol.

The post-war period was marked by intense political and industrial unrest, culminating in 1922 in the establishment of ◊Mussolini's Fascist dictatorship. The regime embraced a policy of aggression with the conquest of Ethiopia 1935–36, and of Albania 1939, and Italy entered World War II in 1940 as an ally of Germany. Defeat in Africa 1941–43, and the Allied conquest of Sicily 1943 resulted in Mussolini's downfall; the new government declared war on Germany, and until 1945 Italy was a battlefield

In 1946 Victor Emmanuel III, who had been king since 1900, abdicated in favour of his son Humbert (Umberto) II. The monarchy was abolished after a referendum in 1946 and the country became a republic, adopting a new constitution in 1948. Between 1946–86 there were nine parliaments and 45 administrations. The Christian Democrats were dominant until 1963, and after this participated in most coalition governments. In 1976 the Communists became a significant force, winning over a third of the votes for the chamber of deputies and pressing for what they called the 'historic compromise', a broad-based government with representatives from the Christian Democratic, Socialist and Communist parties, which would, in effect, be an alliance between Communism and Roman Catholicism. The Christian Democrats rejected this. Apart from a brief period 1977–78, the other parties excluded the Communists from power sharing, forcing them to join the opposition. In 1980 the Socialists returned to share power with the Christian Democrats and Republicans, and participated in a number of subsequent coalitions.

In 1983, the leader of the Socialist Party, Bettino Craxi, became the republic's first Socialist prime minister, leading a coalition of Christian Democrats, Socialists, Republicans, Social Democrats, and Liberals. Despite criticism of Craxi's strong-willed style of leadership, the coalition parties could find no acceptable alternative so continued to support him.

Under Craxi's government the state of the economy improved, although the N-S divide in productivity and prosperity persists, despite attempts to increase investment in the S In foreign affairs Italy has demonstrated its commitment to the EEC, NATO and the UN, and in 1983 played an important part in the multinational peace-keeping force in ▷Beirut. In 1987 the Christian Democrat Giovanni Goria formed a coalition government which fell when the Liberal Party withdrew some three months later.

itch irritation of nerve endings in skin or mucous membrane. The disorder scabies, an eruption produced by the burrowing into the skin of the female of the minute parasite *Acarus scabiei*, is popularly called 'the itch'.

iteroparity in biology, the repeated production of offspring at intervals throughout the life cycle. It is usually contrasted with ▷semelparity, where each individual reproduces only once during its life. Most vertebrates (animals with backbones) are iteroparous.

Iturbide /ˌiːtʊəˈbiːdeɪ/ Augustin de 1783–1824. Mexican revolutionary leader. The leader of Mexican royalist troops, Iturbide published in 1821 a plan promising independence, protection for the church, and the establishment of a monarchy. As no European came forward, in 1822 he proclaimed himself emperor. Forced to abdicate, he went into exile; on his return to Mexico he was shot by republican leaders Guadalupe Victorai and Santa Anna.

IUCN (International Union for the Conservation of Nature) an organization established by the United Nations to promote

Italy
REPUBLIC OF (*Repubblica Italiana*)

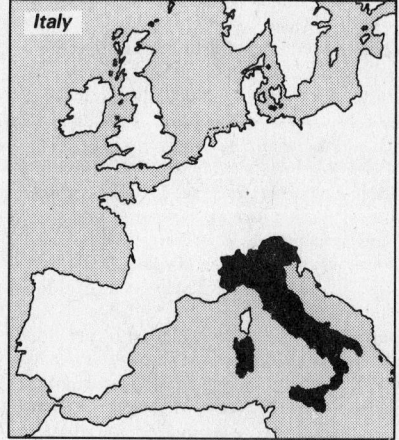
Italy

AREA 301,245 sq km/116,300 sq mi
CAPITAL Rome
TOWNS Milan, Turin; ports Naples, Genoa, Palermo, Bari, Catania
PHYSICAL mountainous (Maritime Alps, Dolomites, Apennines); rivers Po, Adige, Arno, Tiber, Rubicon; islands of Sicily, Sardinia, Elba, Capri, Ischia
FEATURES lakes Como, Maggiore, Garda; Europe's only active volcanoes: Vesuvius, Etna, Stromboli; historic towns include Venice, Florence, Siena
EXPORTS wine, fruit and vegetables; textiles (Europe's largest silk producer), leather goods, motor vehicles, electrical goods, chemicals, marble (Carrara), sulphur and mercury, iron and steel
HEAD OF STATE Francesco Cossiga from 1985
HEAD OF GOVERNMENT Giovanni Goria from 1987
GOVERNMENT parliamentary democracy
CURRENCY lira (2160 = £1 Sept 1987)
POPULATION 57,116,000 (1985); annual growth rate 0.3%
LANGUAGE Italian, derived from Latin
RELIGION Roman Catholic 90%
LITERACY 96% male/95% female (1980 est)
GNP $350 bn (1983); $6,914 per head of population
CHRONOLOGY
1946 Monarchy replaced by a republic.
1948 New constitution adopted.

1954 Trieste returned to Italy.
1976 Communists proposed the establishment of a broad-based, left-right government, the 'historic compromise'. Idea rejected by the Christian Democrats.
1978 Christian Democrat Aldo Moro, architect of the historic compromise, kidnapped and murdered by Red Brigades guerrillas.
1983 Bettino Craxi became the socialist leader of a broad coalition government.
1987 Craxi resigned, and the succeeding coalition fell within months.

ITALY: REGIONS

	Capital	Area sq. km.
Abruzzi	Aquila	10,794
Apulia (Puglia)	Bari	19,346
Basilicata	Potenza	9,992
Calabria	Catanzaro	15,080
Campania	Naples	13,594
Emilia Romagna	Bologna	22,119
Friuli-Venezia Giulia*	Udine	7,844
Latium (Lazio)	Rome	17,202
Liguria	Genoa	5,413
Lombardy	Milan	23,797
Marches (Marche)	Ancona	9,690
Molise	Campobasso	4,438
Piedmont (Piemonte)	Turin	25,399
Sardinia* (Sardegna)	Cagliari	24,089
Sicily* (Sicilia)	Palermo	25,709
Trentino-Alto Adige*	Trento**	13,613
Tuscany (Toscana)	Florence	22,991
Umbria	Perugia	8,456
Valle d'Aosta*	Aosta	3,262
Veneto	Venice	18,367
		301,195

* special autonomous regions
** also Bolzano-Bozen

the conservation of wildlife and habitats in the national policies of member states. It has formulated guidelines and established a number of research programmes (for example, International Biological Programme, IBP) and advisory bodies (such as Survival Services Commissions, SSC).

Ivan /ˈaɪvən, Russian iːˈvɑːn/ name of several rulers of Russia, including:

Ivan III the Great 1440–1505. Grand Duke of Moscovy from 1462, who revolted against Tatar overlordship by refusing tribute to the Grand Khan Ahmed in 1480. He claimed the title of tsar, and used the double-headed eagle as the Russian state emblem.

Ivan IV called 'the Terrible', 1530–84. Grand Duke of Moscovy from 1533, he assumed power 1544, and was crowned as first tsar of Russia 1547. He conquered Kazan 1552, Astrakhan 1556, and Siberia 1581. His last years alternated between debauchery and religious austerities.

Ivanovo /iːˈvɑːnəvəʊ/ capital of Ivanovo region, USSR, 240 km/150 mi NE of Moscow; population (1981) 470,000. Industries include textiles, chemicals and engineering.

Ives /aɪvz/ Charles (Edward) 1874–1954. American composer. Working largely in isolation from the musical mainstream of his day, he produced compositions of extraordinary individuality and inventiveness, experimenting

between German occupying forces and the advancing Allies.

early on with ◊atonality, quarter tones, clashing time signatures, and quotation from popular music of the time. He wrote five symphonies, including *Holidays Symphony* 1904–13, and is also well known for his songs, for the orchestral *Three Places in New England* 1903–14 and for *The Unanswered Question* 1908 for trumpet, four flutes and strings. His work anticipated many developments in modern music.

Ives /aɪvz/ Frederic Eugene 1856–1937. American inventor who developed the ◊halftone method of printing photographs.

Born in Connecticut, he became manager of the photography laboratory at Cornell University, where in 1878 he invented a halftone process (using a screen to break up light and dark areas into different-sized dots). By 1886 he had evolved the halftone process now generally in use. Among his many other inventions was a three-colour process of colour printing.

Iviza alternative spelling of ◊Ibiza, one of the ◊Balearic islands.

ivory /'aɪvərɪ/ the hard white substance of which the teeth of certain animals are composed. Most valuable are the tusks of the African and Indian elephants, in which the dentine is of unusual hardness and density. Ivory has been used in carving and other decorative work from prehistoric times, and is today so valuable that poachers continue to destroy the remaining wild elephant herds in Africa to obtain it illegally.

Vegetable ivory is used for buttons, toys, and cheap ivory goods. It consists of the hard albumen of the seeds of a tropical palm *Phytelephas macrocarpa*, which is imported from Colombia.

Ivory /'aɪvərɪ/ James 1928– . American director best known for his collaboration with Indian producer Ismael ◊Merchant. Merchant-Ivory productions include *Shakespeare Wallah* 1965, *The Europeans* 1979, *Heat and Dust* 1983, and *Room with a View* 1986.

Ivory Coast /'aɪvərɪ 'kəʊst/ country in W Africa, bounded to the N by Mali and Burkina Faso, E by Ghana, S by the Gulf of Guinea, and W by Liberia and Guinea.

government the 1960 constitution, amended in 1971, 1975, 1980 and 1985, provides for a president who is head of both state and government, elected by universal suffrage for a five-year term, and a single-chamber national assembly of 175 members, also popularly elected and serving a five-year term. The president chooses and heads a council of ministers. The only political party is the Democratic Party of the Ivory Coast (PDCI) and its chair is the state president.

history the area now known as the Ivory Coast was once made up of several separate kingdoms. From the 16th century the Portuguese, French, and British established trading centres along the

Ivory Coast
REPUBLIC OF (*République de la Côte d'Ivoire*)

AREA 322,463 sq km/127,000 sq mi
CAPITAL Abidjan
TOWNS Bouaké
PHYSICAL tropical rain forest (diminishing as it is exploited) in the S; savanna and low mountains in the N
HEAD OF STATE AND OF GOVERNMENT Félix Houphouët-Boigny from 1960
GOVERNMENT one-party republic
EXPORTS coffee, cocoa, timber, petroleum
CURRENCY CFA franc (498.38 = £1 Sept 1987)
POPULATION 10,090,000 (1985); annual growth rate 3.5%
LANGUAGE French (official)
RELIGION animist 65%, Muslim 24%, Christian 11%
LITERACY 45% male/24% female (1980 est)
GNP $6.7 bn (1983); $1,100 per head of population

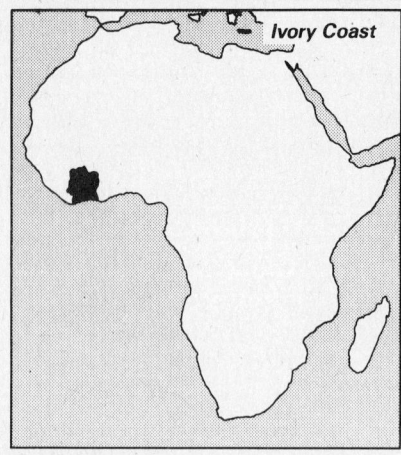
Ivory Coast

CHRONOLOGY
1958 Achieved internal self-government.
1960 Achieved full independence, with Félix Houphouët-Boigny as president of a one-party state.

coast, dealing in slaves and ivory. During the 19th century France acquired the region by means of treaties with local leaders, eventually incorporating it into ◊French West Africa in 1904.

The Ivory Coast was given self-government within the French Community in 1958 and full independence in 1960, when a new constitution was adopted. Félix Houphouët-Boigny has been the country's only president. He has maintained close links with France since independence and this support, combined with a good economic growth rate, has given his country a high degree of political stability. He has been criticized by some other African leaders for maintaining links with South Africa, but has argued that a dialogue between blacks and whites is essential. He has denounced Communist intervention in African affairs, and has travelled extensively to improve relations with Western powers.

ivy tree and shrub of the genus *Hedera* family Araliaceae. The European ivy *Hedera helix* has shiny, evergreen, triangular or oval-shaped leaves and its clusters of small, yellowish-green flowers, are followed by poisonous black berries. It climbs by means of root-like suckers put out from its stem, and is injurious to trees. Ground ivy *Glechoma hederacea* is a small, creeping plant of the Labiatae family found in Britain; and the N American poison ivy *Rhus toxicodendron*, also known as poison oak, belongs to the Anacardiaceae.

Ivy League a collective term for eight long-

established East Coast private universities in the USA (Harvard, Yale, Princeton, Pennsylvania, Columbia, Brown, Dartmouth and Cornell) with academic and social prestige similar to that of ◊Oxford and ◊Cambridge in the UK.

IWW (Industrial Workers of the World) US labour movement founded 1905, popularly known as the Wobblies. The IWW was dedicated to the overthrow of capitalism but divided on tactics and gradually declined in popularity after 1917. At its peak 1912–15 the organization claimed to have 100,000 members.

Ixion /ɪk'saɪən/ in Greek mythology, a king whom Zeus punished for his crimes by binding him to a fiery wheel rolling endlessly through the underworld.

Izhevsk /iː'ʒefsk/ industrial city in the E USSR; population (1985) 611,000. Industries include steel, agricultural machinery, and machine tools.

Izmir /ɪz'mɪə/ port and naval base (formerly *Smyrna*) in Turkey; population (1980) 757,854. An annual trade fair is held there, the largest in the Middle East. It is the headquarters of ◊North Atlantic Treaty Organization SE Command.

history originally Greek (founded about 1000 BC), it was of considerable importance in ancient times, vying with Ephesus and Pergamum as the first city of Asia. It was destroyed by ◊Tamerlane in 1402, and became Turkish in 1424. It was occupied by the Greeks in 1919 but retaken by the Turks in 1922; in the same year it was largely destroyed by fire.

J tenth letter of the modern Roman alphabet. The modern English value of *j* is that of a compound consonant, *d* followed by the sound *zh* (as in pleasure, pronounced plez*h*'ur). Also the symbol for joule, SI unit of energy.

Jabalpur /ˌdʒʌbəl'puə/ industrial city in Madhya Pradesh, India; population (1981) 615,000. It has textile, oil, and flour mills, and produces armaments.

jabiru species of stork *Jabiru mycteria* found in Central America. It is 1.5 m/5 ft high with white plumage. The head is black and red.

jaborandi South American plant *Pilocarpus microphyllus*, family Rutaceae, source of pilocarpine, used to contract the pupil of the eye.

jacamar small bird of the family Galbulidae of Central and South America. They have long sharp-pointed bills, long tails and paired toes. The plumage is brilliantly coloured.

jacana one of seven species of wading birds, family Jacanidae, with very long toes and claws enabling it to walk on the flat leaves of river plants, thus the name 'Lily trotter'. They are found in South America, Africa, South Asia and Australia. In the *pheasant-tailed jacana Hydrophasianus chirurgus*, of Asia, the female has a 'harem' of two to four males.

jacaranda genus of tropical American ornamental trees with fragrant wood and showy blue/violet flowers, family Bignoniaceae.

jacinth or *hyacinth*. Red or yellowish-red gem which is a variety of zircon.

jack a machine for lifting. A *screw jack* uses the principle of the screw to magnify an applied effort. In a car jack, for example, turning the handle many times causes the lifting screw to rise slightly. In this way the effort is magnified to lift heavy weights. A *hydraulic jack* uses a succession of piston strokes to increase pressure in a liquid and force up a lifting ram.

jackal small member of the dog family adapted for scavenging. The *golden jackal Canis aureus* of S Asia, S Europe and N Africa is 45 cm/1.5 ft high and 60 cm/2 ft long. It is greyish-yellow, darker on the back. Nocturnal, it preys on smaller mammals and poultry, though packs will attack larger animals. It has a reputation as a scavenger and will follow lions and tigers to finish off the carcases of their kill. The *side-striped jackal (Canis adustus)* is found over much of Africa, the *black-backed jackal (Canis mesomelas)* only in the S of Africa.

jackdaw bird *Corvus monedula* of the crow family, found in Europe and W Asia. It is mainly black, but greyish on sides and back of head, and about 33 cm/1.1 ft long. It nests in tree holes or on buildings.

Jackson /'dʒækson/ city, capital of Mississippi, USA, on the Pearl River; population (1980) 203,000. It dates from 1821 and was almost destroyed by William ◊Sherman 1863.

Jackson /'dʒækson/ Andrew 1767–1845. 7th president of the USA, born in S Carolina, he defeated the British at New Orleans in 1815, and was elected president in 1828. In 1832 he vetoed the renewal of the US bank charter, and was re-elected, whereupon he continued his struggle against the power of finance.

Jackson /'dʒækson/ Glenda 1936– . British actress, born in Birkenhead, near Liverpool. Her films include the Oscar-winning *Women in Love* 1971, *A Touch of Class* 1973, and *Return of the Soldier* 1982. On television she played Queen Elizabeth I in *Elizabeth R* 1971.

Jackson /'dʒækson/ Jesse 1941– . US Democrat politician, campaigner for minority rights.

Born in North Carolina and educated in Chicago, Jackson emerged as a powerful Baptist preacher and black activist politician, working first with Martin Luther ◊King, then on building the political machine in Chicago that gave the city a black mayor in 1983. Jackson contested the Democratic Party's 1984 presidential nomination in an effort to increase black voter registration and to put black issues on the national agenda. He sought to construct what he called a rainbow coalition, comprising ethnic minority and socially deprived groups. After the election, Jackson took the lead in successfully campaigning for US disinvestment in South Africa in 1986.

Jackson /'dʒækson/ Lady title of British economist Barbara ◊Ward.

Jackson /'dʒækson/ Thomas Jonathan, known as 'Stonewall' Jackson 1824–63.

Jackson British actress Glenda Jackson has starred on stage, in films, and on television. She is also a director of United British Artists, an acting company which believes that established artists should set up their own projects.

American Confederate general. In the American Civil War he acquired his nickname and his reputation at the Battle of ◊Bull Run, from the firmness with which his brigade resisted the Northern attack. In 1862 he organized the Shenandoah valley campaign, and assisted Lee's invasion of Maryland. He helped to defeat Hooker's army at Chancellorsville, but was accidentally shot by his own men.

Jacksonville /'dʒæksonvɪl/ port, resort, and commercial centre in Florida, USA; population (1980) 541,000. Founded in 1822, it was named after President Andrew ◊Jackson. To the N the Cross-Florida Barge Canal links the Atlantic with the Gulf of Mexico.

Jackson American Confederate general 'Stonewall' Jackson was so nicknamed in recognition of his tenacity in resisting attack at Bull Run, during the American Civil War.

Jack the Ripper /dʒæk/ popular name for unidentified mutilator and murderer of five women prostitutes in the Whitechapel area of London in 1888.

Jacob /'dʒeɪkəb/ in the Old Testament, Hebrew patriarch, son of ◊Isaac and Rebecca, who obtained the rights of seniority from his twin brother Esau by trickery. He married his two cousins Leah and Rachel, serving their father Laban seven years for each, and at the time of famine in Canaan joined his son ◊Joseph in Egypt. His 12 sons were the traditional ancestors of the 12 tribes of Israel.

Jacob /'dʒeɪkəb/ François 1920– . French biochemist who, with Jacques ◊Monod, did pioneering research in molecular genetics and showed how the production of ◊proteins from ◊DNA is controlled. He shared the Nobel Prize for medicine and physiology in 1965.

Jacobabad /ˌdʒeɪkəbə'bæd/ town in Pakistan, 400 km/250 mi NE of Karachi; population (1972) 130,000. It has a very low annual rainfall (about 5 cm/2 in) and temperatures are among the highest in the Indian subcontinent – up to 53°C/127°F.

Jacobean /ˌdʒækə'biːən/ term applied to a style in the arts, particularly in architecture and furniture, during the reign of James I (1603–25) in England. Following the general lines of Elizabethan design, it used classical features more widely, adopting many motifs from Italian ◊Renaissance design.

Jacobin /'dʒækəbɪnz/ member of an extremist republican club of the French Revolution founded at Versailles 1789, which later used a former Jacobin (Dominican) friary as its headquarters in Paris. It was led by ◊Robespierre, and closed after his execution 1794. The name 'Jacobin' passed into general

use for any supporter of revolutionary or leftist opinions.

Jacobite /'dʒækəbaɪts/ a supporter of the ◊Stuarts after the deposition of James II in 1688 (Latin *Jacobus* 'James'). They included the Scottish Highlanders, who rose unsuccessfully under ◊Claverhouse in 1689; and those who rose in Scotland and N England under the leadership of ◊James Edward, the 'Old Pretender', in 1715, and followed his son ◊Charles Edward in an invasion of England which reached Derby in 1745–46. After the defeat of ◊Culloden, Jacobitism disappeared as a political force.

Jacobs /'dʒeɪkəbz/ W(illiam) W(ymark) 1863–1943. British author. He excelled in the macabre, for example, 'The Monkey's Paw' 1902.

Jacquard /"dʒækɑːd/ Joseph Marie 1752–1834. French textile manufacturer, who invented a punched-card system for programming designs on a carpet-making loom. Beginning in 1804 at the Paris Conservatoire des Arts et Métiers, he constructed looms that used a series of punched cards which controlled the pattern of longitudinal warp threads depressed before each sideways passage of the shuttle. On later machines the punched cards were joined to form an endless loop which represented the 'program' for the repeating pattern of a carpet.

Jacquard The Jacquard loom revolutionized the art of weaving, but was originally faced with violent opposition from silk weavers, and once its French inventor Joseph Marie Jacquard narrowly escaped with his life.

Jacquerie /ˌʒækə'riː/ French peasant rising 1358, the word deriving from the nickname for French peasants, Jacques Bonhomme.

Jacuzzi /dʒə'kuːzi/ Candido 1903–1986. American inventor and engineer, born in Italy. He invented the Jacuzzi, a pump that enabled a whirlpool to be emulated in a domestic bath; he

developed it for his 15-month-old son, a sufferer from rheumatoid athritis.

jade the name given to various glassy silicate minerals, most commonly jadeite, $NaAl(Si_2O_6)$, and nephrite, $Ca_2(Mg,Fe)_5Si_8O_{22}(OH)$, ranging from white to dark green according to the iron content. One of the hardest minerals known, it was used by early civilizations. The Chinese discovered and used jade, bringing it from E Turkestan, and carried the art of jade carving to its peak. The Aztecs and Maoris have also used jade for ornaments, weapons and utensils since prehistoric times.

Jaén /xɑː'en/ capital of Jaén province, S Spain; population (1981) 95,800. It has remains of its Moorish walls and citadel.

Jaffa /'dʒæfə/ port (Biblical name *Joppa*) in W Israel, part of Tel-Aviv-Jaffa from 1949. It was captured by the ◊Crusaders in the 12th century, by ◊Napoleon in 1799, and by ◊Allenby 1917.

Jagan /'dʒeɪgən/ Cheddi 1918– . Guyanese politician. Educated in British Guyana and the USA. Leader of the People's Progressive Party from 1950, in 1961–64 he was the first prime minister of British Guyana.

Jagan /'dʒeɪgən/ Janet 1920– . Guyanese politician. Wife of Cheddi ◊Jagan. She was general secretary of the People's Progressive Party 1950–70.

jaguar largest species of cat in America *Panthera onca*. It is about 1.2 m/4 ft long excluding the tail. The ground colour of the fur varies from creamy white to brown or black, and is covered with black spots in rosettes.

jaguarundi wild cat *Felis yaguouaroundi* found in forests in Central and S America. Up to 80 cm/2.6 ft long plus 40 cm/1.3 ft tail, it is very slim, rather short in the leg, and with short rounded ears. It is uniformly coloured dark brown or chestnut. A good climber, it feeds on birds and small mammals, and, unusually for a cat, has been reported to eat fruits.

Jahangir /dʒə'hɑːngɪə/ 'Conqueror of the World'. Name adopted by the tyrannical Salim 1569–1627, son of ◊Akbar the Great, and 3rd Mogul emperor of Delhi, India, from 1605. In 1622 he lost Kandahar to Persia, and his addiction to alcohol and opium gave power to his wife Nur Jahan; he designed the Shalimar Gardens in Kashmir and buildings and gardens in Lahore.

Jahweh /'jɑːweɪ/ another spelling of ◊Jehovah.

jai alai another name for the ball-game ◊pelota.

Jainism a religion professed by about two and a half million Hindus, and sometimes regarded as an offshoot from Hinduism. Its sacred books record the teachings of Mahavira (599–527 BC), the latest of a long series of Tirthankaras, or omniscient saints and seers. Born in Vessali, now Bessarh, he became an ascetic at the age of 30, acquired omniscience (all-knowing) at 42, and preached for 30 years. Jains believe that non-injury to living beings is the highest religion and their code of ethics is based on sympathy and compassion. They also believe in ◊'karma'. In Jainism there is no deity, and like Buddhism it is

jaguar Even at two months, the heaviest leather gloves are needed to handle this young specimen.

Jamaica

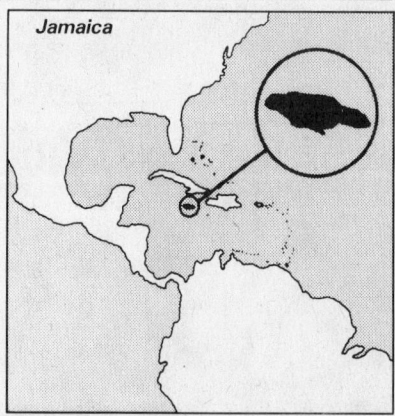

AREA 11,525 sq km/4,411 sq mi
CAPITAL Kingston
TOWNS Montego bay, Spanish Town, St Andrews
PHYSICAL mountainous
FEATURES Blue Mountains (so called because of the haze over them, and famous for their coffee); partly undersea remains of the pirate city of Port Royal, destroyed by an earthquake in 1692
HEAD OF STATE Elizabeth II from 1962 represented by Florizel Glasspole from 1973
HEAD OF GOVERNMENT Edward P G Seaga from 1980
GOVERNMENT parliamentary democracy
EXPORTS sugar, bananas, bauxite, rum, coffee, coconuts, liqueurs, cigars
CURRENCY Jamaican dollar (8.9 = £1 Sept 1987)
POPULATION (1985) 2,366,000 (a mixture of several ethnic groups); annual growth rate 1.3%
LANGUAGE English, Jamaican creole
RELIGION Protestant 70%, Rastafarian
LITERACY 90% male/93% female (1980 est)
GNP $2.9 bn (1983); $1,340 per head of population

CHRONOLOGY
1959 Granted internal self-government.
1962 Achieved full independence, with Sir Alexander Bustamente of the Jamaica Labour Party (JLP) as prime minister.
1967 JLP re-elected under Hugh Shearer.
1972 Michael Manley of the People's National Party (PNP) became prime minister.
1980 JLP elected, with Edward Seaga as prime minister.
1983 JLP re-elected, winning all 60 seats.

a monastic religion. There are two main sects: the Digambaras, who originally went about completely naked, and the Swetambaras.

Jaipur /ˌdʒaɪˈpuə/ capital of Rajasthan, India; population (1981) 966,700. Formerly the capital of the state of Jaipur, it was merged with Rajasthan in 1949. It was founded in 1728 by Jai Singh II.

Jakarta /dʒəˈkɑːtə/ capital of Indonesia on the NW coast of Java; population (1980) 6,480,000. Industries include textiles, chemicals, and plastics. Founded by the Dutch in 1619, and known as Batavia until 1949, it has the president's palace and government offices, and is a tourist centre. A canal links it with its port at Tanjung Priok.

Jalgava /ˈjælgɑːva/ (former name *Mitau*) town in Latvian republic, USSR, 48 km/30 mi S of Riga; textile and sugar-refining industries; population about 57,000. The town was founded in 1265 by Teutonic knights.

Jamaica /dʒəˈmeɪkə/ island in the Caribbean, to the S of Cuba, and to the W of Haiti.
government The 1962 constitution follows closely the unwritten British model, with a resident constitutional head of state, the governor-general, representing the British monarch and appointing a prime minister and cabinet, collectively responsible to the legislature. This consists of two chambers, an appointed, 21-member, senate and a 60-member, elected house of representatives. Normally 13 of the senators are appointed on the advice of the prime minister and eight on the advice of the leader of the opposition, but as the Jamaica Labour Party won all the seats in the 1983

general election there was no opposition leader, so all 21 senators were nominated by the prime minister. Members of the house are elected by universal suffrage for a five-year term, but it is subject to dissolution within that period. The main political parties are the Jamaica Labour Party (JLP), and the People's National Party (PNP).
history Before the arrival of Christopher ◊Columbus in 1494, the island was inhabited by ◊Arawak Indians. From 1509–1655 it was a Spanish colony, and after this was in British hands until 1959, when it was granted internal self-government, achieving full independence within the Commonwealth in 1962.
The two leading political figures in the early days of independence were Sir Alexander Bustamante, leader of the JLP, and Norman Manley, leader of the PNP. The JLP won the 1962 and 1967 elections, led by Bustamante's successor, Hugh Shearer, but the PNP, under Norman Manley's son Michael, was successful in 1972. He advocated social reform and economic independence from the developed world. Despite high unemployment, Manley was returned to power in 1976 with an increased majority but by 1980 the economy had deteriorated and, rejecting the conditions attached to an IMF loan, Manley sought support for his policies of economic self-reliance.
The 1980 general election campaign was extremely violent, despite calls by Manley and the leader of the JLP, Edward Seaga, for moderation. The outcome was a decisive victory for the JLP, with 51 of the 60 seats in the house of representatives. Seaga thus received a

mandate for a return to a renewal of links with the US and an emphasis on free enterprise. He severed diplomatic links with Cuba in 1981. In 1983 Seaga called an early, snap election, with the opposition claiming they had been given insufficient time to nominate their candidates. The JLP won all 60 seats. There were violent demonstrations when the new parliament was inaugurated and the PNP said it would continue its opposition outside the parliamentary arena.

James /dʒeɪmz/ Henry 1843–1916. Anglo-American novelist. Born in New York, he was the brother of William ◊James. He spent much of his youth in Europe, the chief theme of his novels being the impact of European culture upon the American soul. They include *Roderick Hudson* 1876, *The American* 1877, *The Portrait of a Lady* 1881, *Washington Square* 1881, *The Bostonians* 1886, *The Tragic Muse* 1890, *The Spoils of Poynton* 1897, *The Awkward Age* 1899, *The Wings of the Dove* 1902, *The Ambassadors* 1903, and *The Golden Bowl* 1904. The supernatural tale *The Turn of the Screw* 1898 was the basis of an opera by ◊Britten. After 1875 he lived in Europe, becoming a naturalized British subject 1915.

James /dʒeɪmz/ Jesse 1847–1882. American folk hero, a bank and train robber, born in Missouri and a leader (with his brother Frank) of the ◊Quantrill gang. Jesse was killed by an accomplice; Frank remained unconvicted and became a farmer.

James /dʒeɪmz/ M(ontague) R(hodes) 1862–1936. British writer and theologian. Provost of King's College, Cambridge, 1905–18, and of Eton 1918–36, he published numerous

James The novels of Henry James reflect his own background in their preoccupation with the influence of European culture on the American consciousness. Born to a prominent, intellectual American family, James lived in Paris and London, before finally settling in Rye, Sussex.

biblical studies, including the *Apocryphal New Testament* 1924. He also wrote *Ghost Stories of an Antiquary* 1904.

James /dʒeɪmz/ P(hyllis) D(orothy) 1920– . British detective novelist, generally considered one of the best modern crime writers. She created the characters Superintendent Adam Dalgliesh and private investigator Cordelia Gray. She was a tax official, hospital administrator, and civil servant before turning to writing. Her books include *Death of an Expert Witness* 1977, *The Skull Beneath the Skin* 1982, and *Taste for Death* 1986.

James /dʒeɪmz/ William 1842–1910. American psychologist and philosopher, brother of Henry James. He turned from medicine to psychology and taught at Harvard 1872–1907. His books include *Principles of Psychology* 1890, *Will to Believe* 1897, and *Varieties of Religious Experience* 1902, one of the most important works on the psychology of religion. He expounded his pragmatic approach to metaphysics in *Pragmatism* 1907 and *Meaning of Truth* 1909.

James I /dʒeɪmz/ 1208–1276. King of Aragon, called 'the Conqueror'. Succeeding his father in 1213, he conquered the Balearic Islands and took Valencia from the Moors, dividing it with Alfonso X of Castile by a treaty of 1244. Both of these exploits are recorded in his autobiography *Llibre deis feyts*. He largely established Aragon as the major power in the Mediterranean.

James /dʒeɪmz/ two kings of Britain:

James I /dʒeɪmz/ 1566–1625. King of England from 1603 and Scotland (*James VI*) from 1567. The son of ◊Mary Queen of Scots and Lord ◊Darnley, he succeeded on his mother's abdication from the Scottish throne, assumed

power 1583, established a strong centralized authority, and married ◊Anne of Denmark 1589. As successor to Elizabeth in England, he alienated the Puritans by High Church views and Parliament by his assertion of divine right, and was generally unpopular because of his favourites, for example, ◊Buckingham, and because of his schemes for an alliance with Spain.

James I The son of Mary Queen of Scots, James I of England was already James VI of Scotland when he came to the throne in England in 1603. He was successor to Elizabeth I and the first of the Stuart kings of England.

James II /dʒeɪmz/ 1633–1701. King of England and Scotland (*James VII*) from 1685, second son of Charles I. He married Anne Hyde 1659 (1637–71, mother of Mary and Anne) and ◊Mary of Modena 1673 (mother of ◊James Edward, the 'Old Pretender'). Appointed Lord High Admiral at the Restoration, he was successful both as an administrator and as a commander in the Dutch wars. His conversion to Roman Catholicism led to attempts to exclude him from the succession, and though after his accession the failure of ◊Monmouth's and ◊Argyll's rebellions strengthened his position, his attempted arbitrary rule and favour to Catholics led Whig and Tory leaders to invite William of Orange to take the throne in 1688. James fled to France, led a rising in Ireland 1689, but after defeat at the Battle of the Boyne 1690 remained in exile in France.

James /dʒeɪmz/ seven kings of Scotland:

James II /dʒeɪmz/ 1430–1460. King of Scotland from 1437, assumed power 1449. He was accidentally killed while besieging Roxburgh Castle.

James III /dʒeɪmz/ 1451–1488. King of Scotland from 1460, assumed power 1469. He was murdered during a rebellion.

James IV /dʒeɪmz/ 1473–1513. King of Scotland from 1488, who married Margaret

James II The Duke of York, later to become James II, painted by Sir Peter Lely. His reign was not a stable one, due largely to his conversion to Roman Catholicism. There were uprisings, including the 1685 rebellion led by his nephew the Duke of Monmouth which culminated in the Battle of Sedgemoor.

(1489–1541, daughter of Henry VII) in 1503. He invaded England 1513, but was defeated and killed at Flodden.

James V /dʒeɪmz/ 1512–1542. King of Scotland from 1513, who assumed power 1528. He was defeated by the English at Solway Moss 1542.

James Edward /dʒeɪmz/ 1688–1766. The 'Old Pretender' or (for ◊Jacobites) James III. Son of James II, he was born at St James's Palace and after the revolution of 1688 was taken to France. He landed in Scotland in 1715 to head a Jacobite rebellion, but withdrew owing to lack of support. In his later years he settled in Rome.

Jameson /'dʒeɪmɪsən/ Leander Starr 1853–1917. British colonial administrator. He practised medicine in Kimberley, Cape Province, South Africa, where he became a friend of Cecil ◊Rhodes. Early in 1896 he led the *Jameson Raid* from Mafeking into Transvaal, in support of the non-Boer colonists there. In an attempt to overthrow the government, for which he served some months in prison. Returning to South Africa, he succeeded Rhodes as leader of the Progressive Party of Cape Colony, where he was prime minister 1904–08.

James, St /dʒeɪmz/ name of several Christian saints.

James, St /dʒeɪmz/ the Great. New Testament apostle, the son of Zebedee and brother of ◊John. A Galilean fisherman, he was put to death by ◊Herod Agrippa in 44 AD. Patron saint of Spain.

James, St /dʒeɪmz/ the Just. The New Testament brother of Jesus. Jesus appeared to him after the Resurrection; leader of the Church in Jerusalem, and author of the biblical *Epistle of James*.

James, St /dʒeɪmz/ the Little. In the New Testament, a disciple of Christ, son of Alphaeus.

Jamestown /'dʒeɪmztaʊn/ first permanent British settlement in N America, established by Captain John Smith 1607, capital of ◊Virginia

1624–99. In the nearby Jamestown Festival Park there is a replica of the original Fort James, and models of the ships (*Discovery, Godspeed* and *Constant*) that carried the 105 pioneers.

Jammu /'dʒʌmuː/ winter capital of the state of ◊Jammu and Kashmir, India; population (1971) 155,400. It stands on the Tavi and was linked to India's rail system in 1972.

Jammu and Kashmir /'dʒʌmuː, ˌkæʃˈmɪə/ state of N India
area 222,236 sq km/85,800 sq mi, of which some 30% is currently occupied by Pakistan, and 20% by China.
capital Srinagar (summer); Jammu (winter)
towns Leh
population (1981) 5,982,000 (Indian-occupied territory)
history part of the Mogul Empire from 1586, Jammu came under the control of Gulab Singh in 1820. In 1947 it was attacked by Pakistan and chose to become part of the new state of India; there were further hostilities between India and Pakistan in 1971 (ended by the Simla agreement 1972).

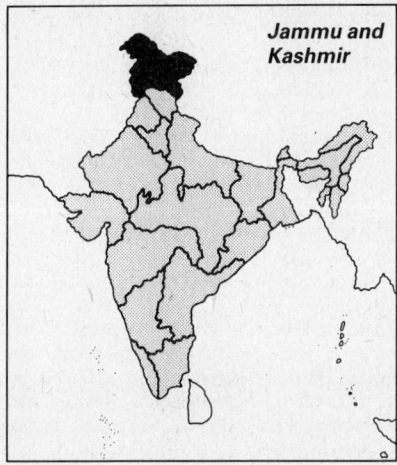

Jammu and Kashmir

Jamnagar /dʒæmˈnʌgə/ port in Gujarat, India, on the Gulf of Kutch, SW of Ahmedabad; population (1981) 317,000.

Jamshedpur /ˌdʒʌmʃedˈpʊə/ city in Bihar, India; population (1981) 439,000. It was built in 1909, and takes its name from the industrialist Jamsheedji Tata, who founded the Tata iron and steel works here and in Bombay.

Janáček /'jænətʃek/ Leoš 1854–1928. Czech composer. He became director of the Conservatoire at Brno in 1919, and professor at the Prague Conservatoire in 1920. His music, highly original and influenced by Moravian folk music, includes arrangements of folk songs, operas (*Jenůfa* 1904, *The Cunning Little Vixen* 1924), and the choral *Glagolitic Mass* 1927.

Janata alliance of opposition parties in India formed 1971 to oppose Indira Gandhi's Congress Party. Victory in the election brought Morarji Desai (1896–   ) to power as prime minister but he was unable to control the various groups within the alliance and resigned 1979. His successors fared little better and the elections of

1980 overwhelmingly returned Mrs Gandhi to office.

Janissary (Turkish *yenicheri* 'new force') bodyguard of the Sultan, the Turkish standing army 1330–1826. Until the 16th century Janissaries were Christian boys forcibly converted to Islam; after this time they were allowed to marry and recruit their own children. The bodyguard ceased to exist when it revolted at the decision of the Sultan in 1826 to raise a regular force.

Jan Mayen /'jæn 'maɪən/ Norwegian island in the Arctic, between Greenland and Norway. It is named after a Dutchman who visited it about 1610. Area 373 sq km/144 sq mi.

Jansen /'dʒænsən/ Cornelius 1585–1638. Dutch Roman Catholic theologian. He became professor at Louvain, Belgium in 1630, and Roman Catholic bishop of Ypres, Belgium, in 1636. Founder of ◊Jansenism with *Augustinus* 1640.

Jansenism teaching of ◊Jansen, which divided the church in France in the mid-17th century. Emphasizing the more predestinatory approach of Augustine's teaching, as opposed to that of the Jesuits, Jansenism was supported by ◊Pascal and Antoine Arnauld (a theologian linked with the Abbey of Port Royal, south west of Paris). In 1713 a Jansenist work by Quesnel, the leader of the party, was condemned by Pope Clement XI as heretical, and after Quesnel's death in 1719 Jansenism as an organized movement in France disappeared. However it survived in Holland where in 1723 a regular Jansenist church was established under the bishop of Utrecht.

Jansky /'dʒænski/ Karl Guthe 1905–1950. US radio engineer, founder of ◊radio-astronomy. Born in Norman, Oklahoma, he joined Bell Telephone Laboratories in New Jersey in 1928, where he investigated causes of static that created interference on radio telephone calls. Jansky found that the centre of our ◊Galaxy was giving out radio waves; he did not follow up his discovery, but it marked the birth of radio-astronomy. The unit of signal strength in radio–astronomy, the Jansky, is equal to 10^{-26} watts per square metre per hertz.

Januarius, St /ˌdʒænjuˈeərɪəs/ patron saint of Naples, Italy; also called San Gennaro. Traditionally, he suffered martyrdom under Diocletian. Two phials of his blood are alleged regularly to liquefy miraculously.

Janus /'dʒeɪnəs/ in Roman mythology, god of doorways and passageways, the patron of the beginning of the day, month, and year, after whom January is named; he is represented as two-faced, looking in opposite directions.

Japan /dʒəˈpæn/ country in E Asia, occupying a group of islands of which the four main ones are Hokkaido, Honshu, Kyushu, and Shikoku. Japan is situated in the N Pacific, to the E of North and South Korea.
government Japan's 1946 constitution was framed by the occupying Allied forces with the intention of creating a consensual, parliamentary form of government and avoiding an over-concentration of executive authority. The emperor, whose functions are purely

ceremonial, is head of state. The Japanese parliament is a two-chamber body composed of a 252-member house of councillors and a 512-member house of representatives. The former chamber comprises 152 representatives elected in single-member constituencies and 100 elected by proportional representation. Each member serves a six-year term, the chamber being elected half at a time every three years. Representatives to the lower house are elected by universal suffrage for four-year terms in multi-member constituencies. The house of representatives is the most powerful chamber, being able to override (if a two-thirds majority is gained) vetoes on bills imposed by the house of councillors and enjoying paramountcy on financial questions. Legislative business is effected through a system of standing committees. Executive administration is entrusted to a prime minister chosen by parliament, who selects a cabinet which is collectively responsible to parliament.

The major political parties are: on the right, the Liberal Democratic Party (LDP), the New Liberal Club, the Democratic Socialist Party; in the centre, the Komeito (Clean Government) Party; and on the left, the Japan Socialist Party, and the Japan Communist Party.

The LDP has dominated postwar Japanese politics, monopolizing government power. It is divided into five powerful, clan-like factions – the Tanaka, Suzuki, Fukuda, Nakasone and Komoto – which compete and bargain for cabinet portfolios. The ultimate prize is the position of prime minister, which each faction seeks to capture by succeeding in the biennial contests for presidency of the LDP.

history the Japanese nation probably arose from the fusion of two peoples, one from the Malay Peninsula or Polynesia, the other from Asia, who conquered the original inhabitants, the ◊Ainu. Japanese history remains legendary until the 5th century AD, when the art of writing was introduced from Korea. After the introduction of Buddhism, also from Korea, in the 6th century, Chinese culture became generally accepted, but although attempts were made in the 7th century to diminish the power of the nobles and set up a strong centralized monarchy on the Chinese model, real power remained in the hands of the great feudal families until modern times.

In 1192 the ruling noble Yoritomo assumed the title of *shogun* (commander-in-chief), which until 1867 was usually borne by the real ruler of Japan. Contact with Europe began in 1542, when Portuguese traders arrived; they were followed by the Spanish, and in 1609 by the Dutch. Christianity was introduced by Francis ◊Xavier in 1549. During the 15th–16th centuries Japan sank into a state of feudal anarchy, until order was restored 1570–1615 by three great rulers, Nobunaga, Hideyoshi, and Iyeyasu; the family of the latter, the Tokugawa, held power until the abolition of the shogunate.

The fear that Roman Catholic propaganda was intended as a preparation for Spanish conquest led to the expulsion of the Spanish in 1624, and the Portuguese in 1639, and to the almost total extermination of Christianity by persecution;

only the Dutch were allowed to trade with Japan, under irksome restrictions, while Japanese subjects were forbidden to leave the country. This isolation continued until 1853, when the USA insisted on opening trade relations; during the next few years this example was followed by the European powers. Consequently the isolationist party compelled the *shogun* to abdicate in 1867, and executive power was restored to the Emperor. During the next 30 years the privileges of the feudal nobility were abolished, a uniform code of law was introduced, and a constitution was established in 1889. The army was modernized, and a powerful navy founded. Industry developed steadily and a considerable export trade was built up.

In 1894 a war with China secured Japanese control of Formosa and S Manchuria, as well as Korea, which was formally annexed in 1910. A victory over Russia 1904–05 gave Japan the S half of Sakhalin, and compelled the Russians to evacuate Manchuria. Japan formed an alliance with Britain in 1902, and joined the Allies in World War I. At the peace settlement it received the German islands in the N Pacific as mandates. The 1920s saw an advance towards democracy and party government, but after 1932 the government assumed a semi-Fascist form. As a result of successful aggression against China 1931–32, a Japanese puppet monarchy under Pu Yi, the last emperor of China, was established in Manchuria (see ◊Manchukuo); war with China was renewed in 1937. Japan entered World War II with the attack on Pearl Harbor on 7 Dec 1941, and at first won a succession of victories in the Philippines, the Malay Peninsula, Burma, and the Netherlands Indies.

Japan was finally compelled to surrender on 15 Aug 1945, following the detonation of American atomic bombs at ◊Hiroshima and ◊Nagasaki. An allied control commission took charge and Japan was placed under military occupation by Allied (chiefly American) troops under Gen Douglas ◊MacArthur until 1952 when the Japanese Peace Treaty came into force and full sovereignty was regained.

After Japan's defeat, Korea was made independent; Manchuria and Formosa (◊Taiwan) were returned to China; and the islands mandated to Japan after World War I were placed by the UN under American trusteeship. Japan regained the ◊Ryukyu Islands (1972) and the ◊Bonin and Volcano Islands (1968) from the US, and continues to agitate for the return of the Northern Territories (the islands of the Shikotan and Habomai Group) and the southernmost ◊Kurils (Kunashiri and Etorofu).

During Allied rule, Aug 1945–Apr 1952, a major 'democratization campaign' was launched, involving radical land, social and educational reform and the framing of a new 'Peace Constitution' (1946) in which Emperor ◊Hirohito renounced his claims to divinity and became a powerless figurehead ruler, and the nation committed itself to a pacific foreign policy. Japan concentrated during the early postwar years on economic reconstruction, tending towards neutralism in foreign affairs under the protection provided by the 1951 Security Pact.

Postwar politics in Japan were dominated by the LDP, formed in 1955 from the merger of existing conservative parties and providing a regular succession of prime ministers. Real decision-making, however, centred around a broader, consensual grouping of politicians, senior civil servants and directors of the major Zaibatsu finance and industrial houses. Through a paternalist, guided approach to economic development, epitomized by the operations of the Ministry for International Trade and Industry (MITI), the Japanese economy expanded dramatically during the 1950s and 1960s, with ◊gross national product (GNP) increasing by 10% per annum.

During this period, Japan was rehabilitated within the international community, entering the UN in 1958 and establishing diplomatic relations with Western nations and, following the lead taken by America's ◊Nixon presidency, with Communist China in 1972. Japan's internal politics were rocked in 1960 and 1968–69 by violent demonstrations involving the anarchic 'Red Army' guerrilla organization against American domination, and in 1974 by the resignation of Prime Minister Kakuei Tanaka after a bribery scandal involving the American Lockheed Corporation. This scandal tarnished the image of the LDP and led to the loss of its majority in the house of representatives in 1976 and the formation of the New Liberal Club as a breakaway grouping. The LDP remained in power, however, as the largest single party in parliament.

Japanese economic growth was maintained during the 1970s, though at a reduced annual rate of 4.5%, and the country made a major impact in the markets of the US and Europe as an exporter of electrical goods, machinery and motor vehicles. The growth in the Japanese trade surplus and the concentration of the country's export activity in a few sensitive sectors created resentment overseas as economic recession began to grip Europe and the US during the later 1970s. This led to calls for Japan to open up its internal market to foreign exporters and to assume a greater share of the defence burden for the Asia-Pacific region. Prime Ministers Miki, Fukuda, Ohira and Suzuki resisted these pressures, and the Japanese government, in 1976, placed a rigid 1% of GNP limit on the level of defence spending permissible.

A review of policy was instituted, however, by Prime Minister Yasuhiro ◊Nakasone, who assumed power in 1982. Nakasone favoured a strengthening of Japan's defence capability, a re-evaluation of attitudes towards the country's past and the introduction of a more liberal, open-market economic strategy at home. His policy departures have been controversial and have been only partially implemented. Nakasone emerged, however, as a popular national figure, gaining a landslide victory in the 1986 elections, and became the first prime minister since Sato (1964–72) to be re-elected by the LDP for more than one term in office. In Oct 1987, after months of back-room bargaining, Mr Noburo Takeshita was chosen as the next prime minister.

Japan /dʒə'pæn/ **Sea of** Sea which lies between Japan and the mainland of Asia.

Japan Current warm ocean current flowing from Japan to America; also called Kuroshio.

Japanese art the main periods are:

Pre-Buddhist (before 580): examples of Pre-Buddhist art and simplicity are the *haniwa*, clay grave figures, and *dôtaku*, bronze bells decorated with engravings.

Suiko period (580–650): Korean temple builders, painters, etc., came with Buddhism.

Hakuohô period (650–720): strong influence by Chinese.

Tempyô period (720–810): still a strong Chinese influence, but an indigenous art developed, and a great amount of sculpture was produced.

Jogan period (810–980): chief influences were the religious sects of Shingon and Tendai.

Fujiwara period (980–1170): elaborate temples and mansions were built.

Kamakura period (1170–1350), sculpture was characterized by great strength and solidity and a more vigorous style of art was adopted.

Ashikaga period (1350–1570): Zen Buddhist influence. The rapid ink sketch in line and wash introduced by Zen priests from China became popular. Pottery gained in importance from the introduction of the tea ceremony.

Momoyama period (1570–1630): the Kano artists produced beautiful screens to decorate palaces and castles.

Tokugawa period (1630–1867): the introduction of the colour print (*Ukiyo-e*), perhaps the most important contribution by Japan to world art. Originating in genre paintings of 16th and 17th century theatre scenes, actors, and bathhouse women, it developed into the woodcut, and after 1740 the true colour print, while its subject matter expanded beyond the amusements of daily life to include flowers, birds, animals, and landscapes. Their brilliant combination of flat decorative colour and expressive pattern influenced 19th century European art. Notable painters included **Utamaro** 1753–1806 and **Hokusai** 1760–1849. Distinguished artists also worked in miniature sculpture, producing tiny carved *netsuke* figures.

Meiji period (1868–1912): the influence of Western art, especially Impressionism; well-known artists were Gaho (1835–1908) and Kogyo (1866–1919).

Showa period (1926–): attempts were made by, for example, Seiho (1864–1942), to adapt the Western methods of objective realism to the traditional Japanese variety, and by painters such as Taikan (1868–1958) to revive the traditional subjective style; younger painters, for example, Kokei (1883–1957) tried to combine traditional and foreign styles. Related art forms are ◊bonsai (dwarf tree cultivation), ◊ikebana (flower arrangement) and ◊origami (paper folding).

Japanese language a traditionally isolated language of E Asia, spoken almost exclusively in the islands of Japan. It may be related to ◊Korean. Japanese has a well-defined structure of syllables generally ending with a vowel (*dojo,*

Japan
(*Nippon*)

AREA 370,000 sq km/142,680 sq mi
CAPITAL Tokyo
TOWNS Fukuoka, Kitakyushu, Kyoto,
Sapporo; ports Osaka, Nagoya, Yokohama,
Kobe, Kawasaki
PHYSICAL mountainous, volcanic; comprises
over 1,000 islands, of which the chief are
Hokkaido, Honshu, Shikoku, Kyushu
FEATURES Mount Fuji
HEAD OF STATE (figurehead) Emperor Hirohito
from 1926
HEAD OF GOVERNMENT Noburo Takeshita from
1987
GOVERNMENT parliamentary democracy
EXPORTS televisions, cassette and video
recorders, radios, cameras, computers, robots,
and other electronic and electrical equipment;
cars and other vehicles, ships; iron and steel;
chemicals, textiles
CURRENCY yen (236.5 = £1 Sept 1987)
POPULATION 120,731,000 (1985); annual
growth rate 0.7%
LANGUAGE Japanese
RELIGION Shinto, Buddhist, Christian
(minority)
LITERACY 99% (1985)
GNP $1,200 bn (1984); $10,266 per head of
population
CHRONOLOGY
1945 Japanese surrender. Allied control
commission in power.

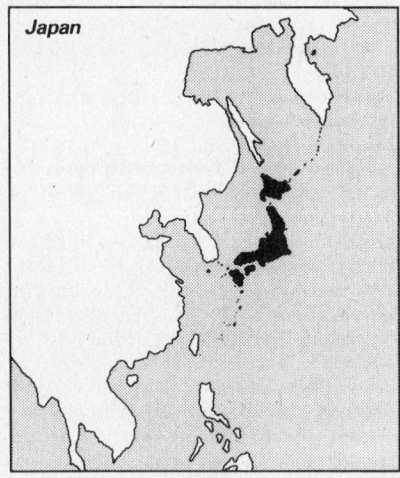

Japan

1946 Framing of 'Peace Constitution'.
1952 Full sovereignty regained.
1958 Joined United Nations.
1972 Ryukyu Islands regained.
1974 Resignation of Prime Minister Tanaka
over Lockheed bribes scandal.
1982 Election of Yasuhiro Nakasone as prime
minister.
1987 Noburo Takeshita chosen to succeed
Nakasone.

*judo, hiragana, samurai, Honshu, kimono,
Mitsubishi, teriyaki*). Culturally and
linguistically influenced by Mandarin Chinese,
Japanese is written in a triple system that has
evolved from Chinese ideograms: its *Kanji*
ideograms are close to their Chinese originals,
while the *Hiragana* system is a syllabary for the
general language, and *Katakana* a syllabary for
foreign borrowings. In print, the three systems
blend on the page in a manner comparable to
the distinct typefaces of the Roman alphabet.
Japanese has an extensive religious and secular
literature, including such terse poetic forms as
◊haiku. English words adapted into Japanese
belong in *gairaigo*, the foreign vocabulary
expressed in the syllable signs of Katakana: e.g.,
fairu ('file') *ereganto* ('elegant'), and
purutoniumu ('plutonium'). Shorter forms are
common: *fainda* ('viewfinder') and *wapuro*
('word-processor').

   Japanese literature earliest survivals include
the 8th-century *Collection of a Myriad Leaves*,
with poems by Hitomaro and Akahito (the
principal form being the *tanka*, 5-line stanza of
5, 7, 5, 7, 7, syllables), and the prose *Record of
Ancient Matters*. The late 10th and early 11th
centuries produced the writers Sei Shōnagon and
◊Murasaki Shikibu. During the 14th century the
Nō drama developed from ceremonial religious
dances, combined with monologues and
dialogues. The 17th century brought such
scholars of Chinese studies as Fujiwara Seikwa

(1560–1619) and Arai Hakuseki (1657–1725).
To this period belongs the origin of *kabuki*, the
popular drama of Japan, of which Chikamatsu
Monzaemon (1653–1724) is the chief exponent;
of *haiku* (the stanza of 3 lines of 5, 7, 5 syllables),
popularized by ◊Bashō, and of the modern novel,
as represented by Ibara Saikaku (1642–93).
Among those reacting against Chinese influence
was the poet-historian Motoori Norinaga
(1730–1801). The late 19th and early 20th
centuries saw the replacement of the obsolete
Tokugawa style as a literary medium by the
modern colloquial language, and the influence of
Western and Russian literature produced writers
such as the 'Realist' Tsubouchi Shōyo
(1859–1935), followed by the 'Naturalist' and
'Idealistic' novelists, whose romantic
preoccupation with self-expression gave rise to
the still popular 'I-novels' of, for example, Osamu
Dazai (1909–48).
Reacting against the autobiographical school
were Natsume Sōseki (1867–1916), Nagai Kafū
(1879–1959), and Junichirō Tanizaki
(1886–1965), who found inspiration in past
traditions or in self-sublimation; later novelists
include Yasunari Kawabata (1899–1972) and
Yukio ◊Mishima. Shimazaki Tōson
(1872–1943) introduced Western-style poetry
for example, 'Symbolism', but the traditional
forms of *haiku* and *tanka* are still widely used.
Western-type, modern drama (Shingeki),

inspired by Ibsen and Strindberg, has been
growing since the turn of the century.
   Jaques-Dalcroze /ˈʒæk dælˈkrəuz/ Emile
1865–1950. Swiss composer and teacher. He is
best remembered for his system of physical
training by rhythmical movement to music
(◊eurhythmics), and founded the Institut
Jaques-Dalcroze, Geneva, in 1915.
   jargon language usage that irritates because
it is complex and hard to understand, usually
because it is (1) technical or occupational, (2)
may seem more technical and complicated than
necessary, (3) used in the wrong contexts, or (4)
intended to impress or confuse ('technical
jargon'; 'writing in pseudoscientific jargon';
'using a meaningless and barbarous jargon').
Jargon is often also known as
gobbledygook/gobbledegook and *bafflegab*, and
is sub-categorized as e.g. *bureaucratese* and
officialese (the usage of bureaucrats and
officials), *journalese* (the languages of
newspapers), and *medicalese* (the often
impenetrable usage of doctors), etc. In writing,
jargon may be highly formal, while in speech it
often contains ◊slang expressions.
   Järnefelt /ˈjeənəfelt/ (Edvard) Armas
1869–1958. Finnish composer. Born at Vyborg,
he became court conductor at Stockholm, and is
chiefly known for his 'Praeludium' and the lyrical
'Berceuse'.
   jarrah type of ◊eucalyptus tree of W
Australia, with durable timber.
   Jarrow /ˈdʒærəu/ town in Tyne and Wear,
NE England, on the S bank of the Tyne, 10 km/6
mi E of Newcastle and connected with the N
bank by the Tyne Tunnel (1967); population
(1981) 27,075. The closure of Palmer's shipyard
in Jarrow in 1933 prompted the unemployed to
march to London, a landmark of the
◊Depression.
   Jarry /ˈʒæri/ Alfred 1873–1907. French
satiric dramatist, whose *Ubu Roi* 1896,
foreshadowed the Theatre of the ◊Absurd, and
the French surrealist movement.
   Jaruzelski /jæruːˈzelski/ Wojciech
1923– . Polish communist military ruler, in
power from 1981. He was defence minister
1968–83 and entered the Politburo in 1971. At
the height of the crisis of 1980–81 he assumed
power as prime minister and PUWP first
secretary and imposed martial law. In 1985
Jaruzelski resigned as prime minister to become
president, but remained the dominant political
figure in Poland.
   Jarvik 7 the first successful artificial heart
intended for permanent implantation in a human
being. Made from polyurethane plastic and
aluminium, it is powered by compressed air. Dr
Barney Clark became the first person to receive
a Jarvik 7 in Salt Lake City in Dec 1982. It kept
him alive for 112 days. In 1986 a similar heart
was implanted temporarily in a British patient
waiting for a human heart transplant.
   jasmine genus of plants *Jasminium*, family
Oleaceae, with fragrant white/yellow flowers,
and yielding jasmine oil, used in perfumes.
Common jasmine is *Jasminium officinale*, and
the Chinese *winter jasmine Jasminium
nudiflorum* flowers before the leaves appear.

jasper hard, compact variety of ◊quartz, SiO_2, usually coloured red, brown or yellow. Jasper is opaque, and has been used as a gem.

Jaspers /'jæspəz/ Karl 1883–1969. German philosopher. HIs works include *General Psychopathology* 1913, and *Philosophy* 1932, in which he anticipated ◊existentialism.

Jassy /'jæsi/ German name for the Romanian city of ◊Iaşi.

Jataka name given to a collection of Buddhist legends giving an account of 547 previous incarnations of Buddha.

jaundice yellowing of the skin and eyes. The usual cause is the presence of bile in the deeper layers of skin, due to obstruction of the common bile duct (for example, by gallstones), pressure of a growth on the duct, or swelling of the duct walls through catarrh; or to some disturbance of liver function which prevents the bile from ever reaching the ducts. It is common in newborn babies (neonatal jaundice), where the immature liver may not be able to cope, but soon clears in the majority of cases.

Jaurès /'ʒɔures/ Jean Léon 1859–1914. French Socialist politician and advocate of international peace. In 1893 he joined the Socialist Party, established a united party, and in 1904 founded *L'Humanité*, becoming its editor until he was assassinated in 1914.

Jaurès French socialist, politician and journalist Jean Jaurès, assassinated in 1914, was an advocate of international peace. He was shot outside the Café du Croissant in Paris, where his admirers still meet, faithful to his memory.

Java /'dʒɑːvə/ the most important island of Indonesia, situated between Sumatra and Bali.
area (with the island of Madura) 132,000 sq km/51,000 sq mi
capital Jakarta (also capital of Indonesia)
towns ports include Surabaja and Semarang
features a chain of mountains, some of which are volcanic, runs along the centre, rising to 2,750 m/9,000 ft. The highest mountain, Semeru 3,676 m/12,060 ft, is in the east. About half the island is

under cultivation, the rest being thickly forested. Mountains and sea breezes keep temperatures down, but humidity is high, as is rainfall Dec–Mar
exports include rice, coffee, cocoa, tea, sugar, rubber, quinine, teak, and petroleum
population (with Madura) (1980) 91,270,000; including people of Javanese, Sundanese, and Madurese origin, with differing languages
religion predominantly Muslim
history fossilized early human remains (*Homo erectus*) were discovered 1891–92. In central Java there are ruins of magnificent Buddhist monuments and of the Sivaite temple in Prambanan. The island's last Hindu kingdom, Majapahit, was destroyed about 1520 and followed by a number of short-lived Javanese kingdoms. The Dutch East India company founded a factory in 1610. Britain took over during the Napoleonic period, 1811–16, and Java then reverted to Dutch control. It was occupied by Japan 1942–45, and then became part of the republic of ◊Indonesia.

javelin a type of spear used in sports events. See ◊throwing events.

jaws the bony structures that form the framework of the mouth in all vertebrates except lampreys and hagfish (the agnathous or jawless vertebrates). They consist of the upper jaw bone or maxilla, and the lower jawbone, or mandible; the latter is hinged at each side to the bone of the temple by ◊ligaments.

jay genus of birds *Garrulus* of the crow family, confined to the Old World and common in Europe except in the far N. In the common jay *Garrulus glandarius* the body is fawn with patches of white, blue and black on the wings and tail. Its own cry is a harsh screech, but it has considerable powers as a mimic. Allied is the common blue jay *Cyanocitta cristata*, of North America, found in the pine forests.

Jay /dʒeɪ/ Peter 1937– . British Labour economist. He is the son of Douglas Jay (1907–), who was president of the Board of Trade 1964–67, and campaigned zealously against the Common Market. He married in 1961 Margaret, daughter of James ◊Callaghan, during whose premiership he was ambassador to Washington 1977–79.

Jayawardene /ˌdʒaɪəˈwɑːdɪnə/ Junius Richard 1906– . Sri Lankan politician. Leader of the United Nationalist Party from 1973, he became prime minister in 1977, and the country's first president.

jazz polyphonic, syncopated music characterized by improvisation, which developed in the USA at the turn of this century out of black American and other indigenous popular music.
1880–1900 originated chiefly in New Orleans
1917 centre of jazz moved to Chicago (Louis ◊Armstrong) and St Louis
1920s growth of 'swing' music
1930s New York jazz and swing orchestras: Paul Whiteman, Fletcher Henderson, Glenn Miller, the Dorsey brothers
1940s the 'big bands': Duke ◊Ellington, Woody Herman, Benny ◊Goodman, Stan Kenton, Count ◊Basie

1950s increasing diversity of styles: Charlie ◊Parker, Dizzy Gillespie, Miles ◊Davis, Stan ◊Getz, Thelonius ◊Monk, ◊Modern Jazz Quartet
1960s 'free form' jazz: Ornette ◊Coleman, John ◊Coltrane
1970s jazz rock: Weather Report
1980s diversity of styles and traditions; e.g. jazz funk, Grover Washington jr; traditional, Wynton Marsalis; Caribbean, Courtney Pine; anarchic, Loose Tubes.

jazz dance dance which combines African and American techniques and rhythms, introduced into modern dance by choreographers including Jerome ◊Robbins and Alvin Ailey.

jeans denim trousers, traditionally blue, originating in jean cloth (from 'jene fustian', a heavy canvas material made in Genoa), which was first used in Liverpool, England, about 1850 to make working clothes. Levi Strauss (1830–1902), a Bavarian immigrant to the USA, made trousers for goldminers in San Francisco out of jean material intended for waggon covers. Hence they became known as 'Levis'. Later a French fabric *serge de Nîmes* (corrupted to 'denim') was used. Until the 1950s they were exclusively working clothes, but they were then adopted by US and European teenagers and became fashionable throughout the world.

Jeans /dʒiːnz/ James Hopwood 1877–1946. British mathematician and scientist, whose original contributions included work in physics, on the kinetic theory of gases, and forms of energy radiation; and in astronomy, on giant and dwarf stars, the nature of spiral nebulae, and the origin of the cosmos. He also did much to popularize astronomy.

Jedburgh /'dʒedbərə/ small town in the Borders region, SE Scotland, on Jed Water; population (1981) 4,000. It has the remains of a 12th-century abbey.

Jedda /'dʒedə/ alternative spelling for the Saudi Arabian port ◊Jidda.

jeep the popular name for the general purpose (GP) vehicle of the US Army. It is a small open vehicle which can be driven over rough ground.

Jefferies /'dʒefrɪz/ (John) Richard 1848–1887. British naturalist and writer, noted for his books on the countryside, including *Gamekeeper at Home* 1878, *Wood Magic* 1881, *Life of the Fields* 1884.

Jeffers /'dʒefəz/ (John) Robinson 1887–1962. American poet. His volumes include *Tamar and Other Poems* 1924, *The Double Axe* 1948, and *Hungerfield and Other Poems* 1954.

Jefferson /'dʒefəsən/ Thomas 1743–1826. 3rd president of the USA. Born in Virginia, he published *A Summary View of the Rights of America* 1774 and as a member of the Continental Congresses of 1775–76 was largely responsible for the drafting of the Declaration of Independence. He was governor of Virginia 1779–81, ambassador to Paris 1785–89, and secretary of state 1789–93. Jefferson was the founder of the Democratic Party. He was elected vice-president 1796–1801 and president 1801–09.

Jeffrey /'dʒefri/ Francis, Lord 1773–1850. Scottish lawyer and literary critic. Born at Edinburgh, he was a founder and editor of the *Edinburgh Review* 1802–29. In 1830 he was made Lord Advocate, and in 1834 a Scottish law lord. He was hostile to the ◊Romantic poets, and wrote of Wordsworth's *Excursion*: 'This will never do.'

Jeffreys /'dʒefrɪz/ George, 1st Baron 1648–1689. British judge. Born in Denbighshire, Scotland, he became Chief Justice of the King's Bench in 1683, and presided over many political trials, notably those of Sidney, Oates, and Baxter, becoming notorious for his brutality. In 1685 he was made a peer and conducted the 'bloody assizes' after ◊Monmouth's rebellion, during which 320 rebels were executed and hundreds more flogged, imprisoned or transported. Created Lord Chancellor in 1685, he was captured when attempting to flee the country after the revolution of 1688, and died in the Tower.

Jehol /ˌdʒʌ'hɒl/ region and Former province (to 1956) of NE China, N of the Great Wall.

Jehovah /dʒɪ'həʊvə/ also *Jahweh* name of God in the biblical Old Testament; in Hebrew YHVH, to which the vowels 'a o a' were later added.

Jehovah's Witness a member of a religious organization originating in the USA in 1872 under Charles Taze Russell (1852–1916). Jehovah's Witnesses attach great importance to Christ's second coming, which Russell predicted would occur in 1914, and which Witnesses still believe is imminent. The ensuing Armageddon and Last Judgment, which entail the destruction of all except the faithful, is to give way to the Theocratic Kingdom. Earth will continue to exist as the home of mankind, apart from 144,000 chosen believers who will reign with Christ in heaven. When Russell died in 1916, he was succeeded by Joseph Rutherford (died 1942). Witnesses believe that they should not become involved in the affairs of this world, and their tenets, involving rejection of obligations such as military service, have often brought them into conflict with authority. Because of Biblical injunction against eating blood, Witnesses will not give or receive blood transfusions. Adults are baptized by total immersion. All Witnesses are expected to take part in house-to-house preaching; there are no clergy. The Watch Tower Bible and Tract Society and the Watch Tower Students' Association form part of the movement. Membership (1986) about 1,000,000.

Jekyll /'dʒiːkl/ Gertrude 1843–1932. English landscape gardener. Originally a painter and embroiderer, her worsening eyesight led her at the age of 48 to gardening. She created over 200 gardens, many in collaboration with the architect Edwin ◊Lutyens, and wrote many books, including *A Gardener's Testament* 1937. She advocated natural gardens of the cottage type, with plentiful herbaceous borders.

jellyfish marine animal of the phylum Cnidaria (coelenterates) with an umbrella-shaped body composed of a semi-transparent gelatinous substance, with a fringe of stinging

Jekyll Using such native plants as honeysuckle and pinks, British horticulturalist Gertrude Jekyll, often working in partnership with architect Edwin Lutyens, introduced the 'wild' garden style to Britain in the early years of this century. The portrait was painted by Sir William Nicholson in 1920.

tentacles. Most jellyfish move freely, but some are attached by a stalk to rocks or seaweed. They feed on small animals which are paralysed by the stinging threads.

Jena /'jeɪnə/ town SE of Weimar, East Germany; population (1981) 104,300. Industries include the Zeiss firm of optical-instrument makers, founded 1846. Here in 1806 Napoleon defeated the Prussians, and ◊Schiller and ◊Hegel taught at the university which dates from 1558.

Jencks /dʒeŋks/ Charles 1939– . American architectural theorist and furniture designer. He coined the term 'post-modern architecture' and wrote the influential book *The Language of Post-Modern Architecture*.

Jenkins /'dʒeŋkɪnz/ Roy (Harris) 1920– . British politician. Educated at Oxford, he was a close friend of ◊Gaitskell, and has published studies of ◊Attlee, ◊Asquith, and others. Elected a Labour Member of Parliament in 1948, he was minister of aviation 1964–65, home secretary 1965–67, and chancellor of the Exchequer 1967–70. In 1970 he became deputy leader of the Labour Party, but in 1972 resigned because of disagreement with Harold ◊Wilson on the Common Market issue. He was again home secretary 1974–76 and president of the Common Market Commission 1977–80. In 1981 he became one of the founders of the ◊Social Democratic Party and was elected SDP Member of Parliament in 1982, but lost his seat in 1987. He was elected Chancellor of Oxford University in 1987.

Jenkins's Ear, War of war between Britain and Spain 1739 which later became part of the war of ◊Austrian Succession 1740–48. The name derives from an incident in which Robert Jenkins, a merchant captain, claimed his ear had been cut off by Spanish coastguards near Jamaica. The incident was seized on by opponents of Robert ◊Walpole seeking to

embarrass his government's anti-war policy and to force war with Spain.

Jenner /'dʒenə/ Edward 1749–1823. British physician. He studied in London under John Hunter and practised all his life in Gloucestershire. From 1775 he made a special study of cowpox, and in 1796 successfully inoculated a boy against smallpox with matter taken from cowpox vesicles, publishing his work on vaccination in 1798.

Jenner /'dʒenə/ Henry ('Gwas Myhal') 1849–1934. English poet. He attempted to revive Cornish as a literary language, and in 1904 published a handbook of the Cornish language.

Jerablus /'dʒerəbləs/ ancient Syrian city, adjacent to ◊Carchemish.

jerboa several genera of rodents, found chiefly in Africa and Asia, and mainly herbivorous and nocturnal. Typical is the common North African jerboa *Jaculus orientalis* with a body about 15 cm/6 in long and slightly longer tail. At speed it moves in a series of long jumps with its fore-feet held close to the body.

Jeremiah /ˌdʒerɪ'maɪə/ 7th century BC. In Old Testament, Hebrew prophet born near Jerusalem, whose ministry continued 626–586 BC. He was imprisoned during ◊Nebuchadnezzar's siege of Jerusalem on suspicion of intending to desert to the enemy. On the city's fall, he retired to Egypt.

Jerez de la Frontera /xe'reθ deɪ lɑː frɒn'teərə/ city in Andalusia, SW Spain; population (1981) 175,700. It is famed for sherry, the fortified wine to which it gave its name.

Jericho /'dʒerɪkəʊ/ Israeli-administered town in Jordan, N of the Dead Sea. It was settled by 8000 BC, and by 6000 BC had become a walled city with 2,000 inhabitants. In the Old Testament it was the first Canaanite stronghold captured by the Israelites, its walls, according to the Book of ◊Joshua, falling to the blast of Joshua's trumpets. Successive archaeological excavations since 1907 show that the walls of the city were destroyed many times.

Jerome /dʒə'rəʊm/ Jerome K(lapka) 1859–1927. British journalist and essayist. His works include the humorous essays *Idle Thoughts of an Idle Fellow* 1889, the novel *Three Men in a Boat* 1889, and the play *The Passing of the Third Floor Back* 1907.

Jerome, St /dʒə'rəʊm/ c. 340–420. Christian saint and scholar, and a father of the Church. Born at Strido, Italy, he was baptized at Rome in 360, and subsequently travelled in Gaul, Asia Minor, and Syria. Summoned to Rome as adviser to Pope Damasus, he revised the Latin translation of the New Testament and the Latin psalter. On the death of Damasus in 384 he travelled to the east, and settling at Bethlehem translated the Old Testament into Latin from the Hebrew. His Latin versions form the basis of the Roman Catholic Vulgate. Feast day 30 Sept.

Jersey /'dʒɜːzi/ largest of the ◊Channel Islands, area 117 sq km/45 sq mi; population (1981) 76,000. Its capital is St Helier. Like Guernsey, it is famous for cattle. Government is by a lieutenant-governor representing the

English Crown and an assembly. The island was occupied 1940–45 by German forces.

Jersey City /ˈdʒɜːzi/ city of New Jersey, USA; population (1980) 223,500. It faces Manhattan Island, to which it is connected by tunnels. A former port, it is now an industrial centre.

Jerusalem /dʒəˈruːsələm/ ancient city of Palestine, divided 1948 between Jordan and the new republic of Israel; area (pre-1967) 37.5 sq km/14.5 sq mi, (post-1967) 108 sq km/42 sq mi, including areas of the West Bank; population (1983) 472,900. In 1950 the western New City was proclaimed as the Israeli capital, and following its capture from Jordan of the eastern Old City in 1967, Israel affirmed in 1980 that the united city was the country's capital, but the United Nations does not recognize the claim.

history by 1400 BC Jerusalem was ruled by a king subject to Egypt, but c. 1000 BC ◊David made it the capital of a united Jewish kingdom. It was captured 586 BC by ◊Nebuchadnezzar, who deported its inhabitants. Under ◊Cyrus a new settlement was made and in about 445 BC the walls were rebuilt. Later conquerors include Alexander the Great and ◊Pompey (63 BC), and it was under the Roman governor ◊Pontius Pilate that ◊Jesus Christ was executed. In 70 AD a Jewish revolt led to the complete destruction of the city by ◊Titus. On its site was founded in 130 the Roman city of Aelia Capitolina, which was pillaged by the Persian Chosroës II in 615 while under Byzantine rule. It was first conquered by Islam in 637; captured by the ◊Crusaders 1099, and recaptured by ◊Saladin 1187, remaining under almost unbroken Muslim rule until the British occupation of Palestine in 1917. Jerusalem was the capital of the British mandate 1922–48.

There are seven gates into the old city through the walls built by Selim I (1467–1520). Notable buildings include the Church of the Holy Sepulchre (built by ◊Constantine 335), and the mosque of the Dome of the Rock. The latter was built on the site of the temple built by ◊Solomon in the 10th century BC, and the Western ('wailing') Wall, held sacred by Jews, is part of the walled platform on which the Temple once stood. The Hebrew University of Jerusalem opened in 1925. Religions are Christian, Hebrew, and Muslim, with Roman Catholic, Anglican, and Greek bishops, and a Coptic metropolitan. In 1967 Israel guaranteed freedom of access of all faiths to their holy places.

Jerusalem artichoke a type of ◊artichoke.

Jervis /ˈdʒɑːvɪs/ John, Earl of St Vincent 1735–1823. British admiral. A rigid disciplinarian, he secured the blockage of Toulon in 1795, and the defeat of the Spanish fleet off Cape St Vincent 1797, in which Captain ◊Nelson played a key part.

Jervis Bay /ˈdʒɑːvɪs/ deep bay on the coast of New South Wales, Australia, 145 km/90 mi SW of Sydney. The Federal Government in 1915 acquired 73 sq km/28 sq mi here to create a port for ◊Canberra. It forms part of the Australian Capital Territory and is the site of the Royal Australian Naval College.

Jesuit a member of the largest and most influential Roman Catholic religious order, also known as the Society of Jesus. The order has about 29,000 members including 15,000 priests, the remainder being students and lay members. Their head (general) is known as the 'Black Pope' from the colour of his cassock; the head from 1983 was Pieter-Hans ◊Kolvenbach.

history Founded by Ignatius ◊Loyola in 1534, it received papal approval in 1540. Its main objects were defined as educational work, the suppression of heresy, and missionary work among non-believers (its members were not confined to monasteries). Loyola infused into the order a spirit of military discipline, with long and arduous training. During the 16th and 17th centuries Jesuits achieved success as missionaries to Japan and China, in Paraguay and among the North American Indians. Their political influence resulted in their expulsion during 1759–68 from Portugal, France, and Spain, and papal suppression in 1773. The order of Jesuits was revived in 1814, but has since been expelled from many of the countries of Europe and America, and John Paul II attacked them in 1981 for support of revolution in South America.

Jesus Christ /ˈdʒiːzəs ˈkraɪst/ c. 4 BC–29 or 30 AD. In the New Testament, Jesus (Hebrew *Messiah*, Greek *the Christ*) was the Jewish preacher and healer on whose teachings ◊Christianity was founded, based on the account of his life in the four ◊Gospels. Born in ◊Bethlehem, son of the Virgin ◊Mary of the tribe of Judah and the family of ◊David, he was brought up as a carpenter by ◊Joseph at ◊Nazareth. In 26/27 AD his cousin ◊John the Baptist began a preparatory mission, and baptized Jesus, whose Galilean ministry included two missionary journeys through the district, and the calling of the 12 ◊apostles. His teaching, summarized in the Sermon on the Mount, aroused both religious opposition from the ◊Pharisees and secular opposition from the Herodian (see ◊Herod Antipas) party. When he returned to Jerusalem (probably in 29 AD) a week before the ◊Passover, he was greeted by the people as the ◊Messiah, and the Jewish authorities (aided by ◊Judas) had him arrested and condemned to death (after a hurried trial) by the ◊Sanhedrin. The sentence was confirmed by the Roman procurator, ◊Pontius Pilate, by stressing the threat to imperial authority of his teaching; but three days after the ◊Crucifixion there came reports of his resurrection, and later ascension to heaven.

jet in geology a mineral substance similar in composition to ◊lignite and ◊anthracite; it occurs in quantity near Whitby and along the Yorkshire coast. Ornaments made of jet have been found in Bronze Age tombs.

JET *Joint European Torus.* Machine of the type called a ◊tokamak which has been built at Culham, near Abingdon in Berkshire, to conduct experiments on ◊nuclear fusion. It is the focus of the European effort to produce a practical fusion power ◊reactor.

jeté (French 'thrown') in dance, a jump from one foot on to the other. A *grand jeté* is a big jump in which the dancer pushes off on one foot, holds

a brief pose in mid-air and lands lightly on the other foot.

jetfoil an advanced kind of ◊hydrofoil boat built by Boeing, which is propelled by water jets. It features horizontal fully submerged hydrofoils fore and aft, and has a sophisticated computerized control system to maintain its stability in all waters. Jetfoils have been in service worldwide since 1975. A jetfoil service currently operates between Dover and Ostend, with a passage time of about 1½ hours. Cruising speed of the jetfoil is about 80 kph/50 mph.

jetlag effect of a sudden switch of time-zones in jet air travel, resulting in tiredness and feeling 'out of step' with day and night. See ◊circadian rhythm.

jet propulsion a method of propulsion in which an object is propelled in one direction by a jet, or stream of gases, moving in the other. This follows from ◊Newton's celebrated third law of motion 'to every action, there is an equal and opposite reaction'. The most widespread application of the jet principle is in the jet engine, the commonest kind of aero-engine.

The jet engine is a kind of ◊gas turbine. Air, after passing through a forward-facing intake, is compressed by a compressor or fan, and fed into a combustion chamber. Fuel (usually kerosene) is sprayed in and ignited. The hot gas produced expands rapidly rearwards, spinning a ◊turbine that drives the compressor before being finally ejected from a rearward-facing tail pipe, or nozzle, at very high speed. Reaction to the jet of gases streaming backwards produces a propulsive thrust forwards which acts on the aircraft through its engine-mountings. It does not come from any pushing of the hot gas stream against the static air. Thrust is proportional to the mass of the gas ejected times the acceleration imparted to it, and is stated in units of pounds force (lbf) or kilograms force (kgf), both now being superseded by the international unit, the Newton (N).

◊*Turbojet* the simplest form of gas turbine, used in aircraft well into the ◊supersonic range. ◊*Turboprop* for moderate speeds and altitudes (up to 725 kph/450 mph and 10,000 m/30,000 ft). It incorporates extra stages of turbine that absorb most of the energy from the gas stream to drive the propeller shaft via a speed reduction gear. ◊*Turbofan* best suited to high subsonic speeds. It is fitted with an extra compressor or fan in front, and some of the airflow bypasses the core engine, and mixes with the jet exhaust stream, to give it lower temperature and velocity. This results in greater economy, efficiency and quietness compared with the turbojet, and a higher speed than the turboprop. *Turboshaft* used to drive the main and tail rotors of ◊helicopters; and in ◊hovercraft, ships, trains, and in power stations and pumping equipment. It is effectively a turboprop without its propeller, power from an extra turbine being delivered to a reduction gearbox or directly to an output shaft. Most of the gas energy drives the compressors and provides shaft power, so residual thrust is low. Turboshaft power is normally quoted as shaft horsepower (shp) or kilowatts (kW). *Ramjet* used for some types of missiles. At twice the speed of sound (Mach 2), pressure in the forward-facing intake of a jet engine is seven times that of the outside air, a compression ratio which rapidly mounts with increased speed (to Mach 8), with the result that no compressor or turbine is needed. The ramjet comprises merely an open-ended rather barrel-shaped tube, burning fuel in its widest section. It is cheap, light and easily made. However, fuel consumption is high and it needs rocket-boosting to its operational speed.

Variants and additional capabilities of jets include 1) multi-spool engines, in which the compressors may be split into two or three parts or stages driven by independent turbines, so that each runs at its own optimum speed. 2) vectored thrust, a swivelling of the jet nozzles from vertical to rearward horizontal to achieve vertical take-off followed by level flight (as in the ◊*Harrier*). 3) reverse thrust, used to slow down a jet plane on landing, and achieved by blocking off the jet pipe with special doors and re-directing the gases forward through temporarily opened cascades. 4) reheat (afterburning), used especially in military aircraft to obtain short-duration thrust increase of up to 70% by the controlled burning of fuel in the gas stream after it has passed through the turbine, but which increases fuel consumption.

altitudes of 10–16 km/6–10 mi in the upper troposphere or lower stratosphere. Jet streams usually occur about the latitudes of the Westerlies (35–60°). They may be used by high flying aircraft to speed their journeys.

Jevons /'dʒevənz/ William Stanley 1835–1882. British economist. He introduced into economic theory the concept of final or marginal utility, that is the increase in total utility, satisfaction or pleasure of consumption relative to a unit increase of the goods consumed.

Jew a follower of ◊Judaism, the Jewish religion. The term is also used to refer to members or supposed members of the ethnic group, who may or may not practise the religion or identify with the cultural tradition. See also ◊anti-semitism.

Jewish Agency body created by the British mandate power in Palestine in 1929 to oversee the administration of the Jewish population and immigration. In 1948 it took over as the government of an independent Israel.

Jewish Autonomous Region part of the Khabarovsk Territory, USSR, on the river Amur; capital Birobidzhan; area 36,000 sq km/13,900 sq mi; population (1983) 200,000. It was established as a Jewish National District in 1928, and became an Autonomous Region in 1934, but became only nominally Jewish after

with the fingers. Different notes are obtained by changing the shape of the mouth.

Jezebel /'dʒezəbel/ in the Old Testament, daughter of the King of Sidon. She married King Ahab, and was brought into conflict with Elijah by her introduction of the worship of Baal.

Jhansi /'dʒɑːnsi/ city in Uttar Pradesh, India, 286 km/178 mi SW of Lucknow; population (1981) 246,172. It is a railway and road junction, and a market centre. It was founded in 1613, and was the scene of a massacre of British civilians in 1857.

Jhelum /'dʒiːləm/ river rising in Kashmir and flowing into Pakistan; length about 720 km/450 mi. The Mangla Dam 1967, one of the world's largest earth-filled dams, stores flood waters for irrigation and hydroelectricity. The Jhelum is one of the five rivers which give Punjab its name, and was known in the ancient world as the Hydaspes, on whose banks Alexander the Great won a great victory in 326 BC.

Jiang Jie Shi /dʒiˈæŋ ˌdʒeɪ ˈʃiː/ alternative transcription of Chinese leader ◊Chiang Kai-shek.

Jiang Qing /dʒiˈæŋ ˈtʃɪŋ/ (formerly Chiang Ching) 1913– . Chinese communist politician, wife of Mao Zedong, arrested 1976 as member of Gang of Four.

Jiang was a Shanghai actress when she met ◊Mao Zedong at ◊Yan'an in 1937; she became his third wife in 1939. She emerged as a radical, egalitarian Maoist. In 1960 she became minister for culture, and played a key role in the 1966–69 Cultural Revolution as the leading member of the Shanghai-based Gang of Four. Jiang's influence waned during the early 1970s and her relationship with Mao became embittered. On Mao's death in Sept 1976, the Gang of Four sought to seize power by organizing militia coups in Shanghai and Beijing. They were arrested for treason by ◊Hua Guofeng and tried during 1980–81. The Gang were blamed for the excesses of the Cultural Revolution, but Jiang asserted during her trial that she had only followed Mao's orders as an obedient wife. This was rejected and Jiang received a death sentence in Jan 1981, which was subsequently commuted to life imprisonment.

Jiangsu /dʒiˌæŋˈsuː/ province (formerly Kiangsu) on the coast of E China.
area 102,200 sq km/39,450 sq mi
capital Nanjing
features includes the swampy mouth of the Chang Jiang, and the special municipality of Shanghai
products cereals, rice, tea, cotton, soya; silk; ceramics, textiles; coal, iron and copper; cement
population (1982) 60,521,115.

Jiangxi /dʒiˌæŋˈʃiː/ province (formerly Kiangsi) of SE China
area 164,800 sq km/63,600 sq mi
capital Nanchang
features the province was ◊Mao Zedong's original base in the first phase of the Communist struggle against the Nationalists
products rice, tea, cotton, tobacco; porcelain; coal, tungsten, uranium
population (1982) 33,185,000.

jet propulsion

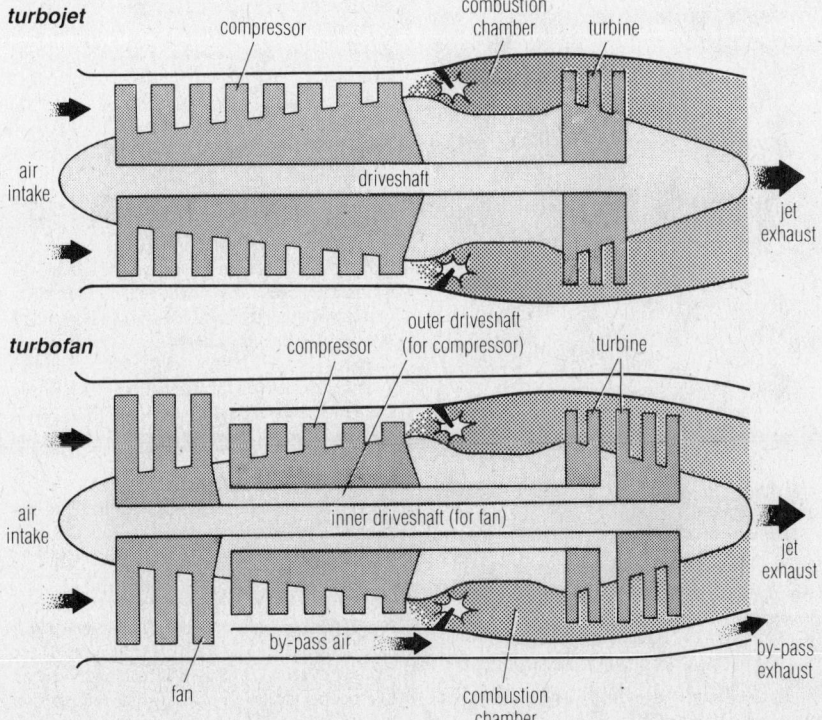

turbojet — compressor, combustion chamber, turbine, air intake, driveshaft, jet exhaust

turbofan — compressor, outer driveshaft (for compressor), turbine, air intake, inner driveshaft (for fan), jet exhaust, by-pass air, by-pass exhaust, fan, combustion chamber

jetsam goods deliberately sunk in the sea to lighten a vessel in a storm, or wreck. See under ◊flotsam.

jet stream a narrow band of very fast wind (velocities of over 150 kph/95 mph) found at

the Stalinist purges of 1936–47 and 1948–49. Industries include textiles, leather, metallurgy, light engineering, agriculture, and timber.

Jew's harp musical instrument, an iron frame held in the teeth, which has a steel strip twanged

Jiangsu Massed silkworm cocoons are gathered from the cut branches by a member of a commune which is striving to diversify the local economy.

Jibuti /dʒɪˈbuːti/ variant spelling of ◊Djibouti, republic of NE Africa.

Jidda /ˈdʒɪdə/ also *Jedda* port in Hejaz, Saudi Arabia; population (1982) 1,200,000. Industries include cement, steel, oil refining. It is linked by road to Medina, Riyadh and Taif and has an airport. Pilgrims pass through en route to Mecca.

jihad Arabic 'struggle', used in the Koran for the Muslim duty of opposition to those who reject Islam. In the *Mecca Declaration* 1981, the Islamic powers pledged a jihad against Israel, though not necessarily military attack.

Jilin /ˌdʒiːˈlɪn/ province (formerly Kirin) of NE China in Central ◊Manchuria.
area 290,000 sq km/111,940 sq mi
capital Changchun
population (1982) 22,560,000.

Jim Crow originally a derogatory US term for a black person, the term historically refers to the systematic practice of segregating black Americans, which was common in many areas of the USA until the 1960s. *Jim Crow laws* is a general term for the body of laws designed to deny civil rights to blacks or to enforce the policy of segregation, which existed in parts of the USA until Supreme Court decisions and civil rights legislation of the 1950s and 1960s denied their legality. See also *history* under ◊black.

Jiménez /xɪˈmeɪneθ/ Juan Ramón 1881–1958. Spanish lyric poet. Born in Andalusia, he left Spain during the civil war to live in exile in Puerto Rico. Nobel prize 1956.

Jinan /ˌdʒiːˈnæn/ city (formerly Tsinan) and capital of Shandong province, China; population (1982) 1,333,000. It has food processing and textile industries.

Jindyworobaks name for an Australian literary group 1938–53, derived from Aboriginal 'take-over'. Founded by Reginald Ingamells

(1931–55), it encouraged an individual Australian character in the country's literature.

Jingdezhen /ˌdʒɪŋdəˈdʒen/ town (formerly Chingtechen or Fou-liang) in Jiangxi, China. Ming blue-and-white ware was produced here, the name of the clay ◊kaolin coming from Kaoling, a hill east of Jingdezhen; some of the best Chinese porcelain is still made here.

jingoism truculent and blinkered patriotism. The term originated in 1878, when ◊Disraeli's pro-Turkish policy nearly involved Britain in war with Russia. His supporters' war-song included the line, 'We don't want to fight, but by jingo if we do ...'.

Jinja /ˈdʒɪndʒə/ town in Eastern Province, Uganda, on the Victoria Nile; population (1980) 45,000. Nearby is the Owen Falls Dam 1954.

jinn in Muslim mythology, a spirit able to assume human or animal shape.

Jinnah /ˈdʒɪnə/ Muhammad Ali 1876–1948. Indian politician. He was educated at Karachi and in England being called to the English Bar in 1896, and became president of the Muslim League in 1916. From 1934 he was elected annually as president. His views on the citation of a separate state of Pakistan were recognized by the Cripps mission of 1942, and at the 1946 conferences in London he insisted on the partition of British India into Indian and Muslim states. He became first governor-general of Pakistan on the transfer of power on 15 Aug 1947.

Jinnah Indian politician Muhammad Ali Jinnah was president of the Muslim League from 1916. He opposed Gandhi's policies, insisting on the creation of a separate Muslim state, and was made the first governor-general of Pakistan in 1947.

Jinsha Jiang /ˌdʒɪnˈʃɑː dʒiˈæn/ greatest river (formerly Yangtze Kiang) of China, rising in Tibet and flowing into the Yellow Sea. Length about 5,470 km/3,400 mi.

Jivaro /hɪˈvɑːrəʊ/ American Indian peoples of Ecuador and Peru, formerly famous for keeping the shrunken heads of their enemies as battle trophies.

jive an energetic dance popular in the USA from the 1940s and a forerunner of rock and roll.

Joachim /ˈjəʊəkɪm/ Joseph 1831–1907. Hungarian violinist and composer. He studied under Mendelssohn, first performed in England in 1844, and was the founder of the Joachim Quartet (1869–1907). He was closely associated with the music of his friend ◊Brahms. His compositions include the 'Hungarian Concerto' and orchestral works.

Joan /dʒəʊn/ mythical Englishwoman supposed to have become pope in 855, as John VIII, and to have given birth to a child during a papal procession. The myth was exposed in the 17th century.

Joan of Arc, Saint /ɑːk/ 1412–1431. French heroine, born at Domrémy, daughter of a well-to-do farmer. In 1429 at Chinon, she persuaded Charles VII she had a divine mission to expel the English from France, and secure his coronation. She raised the siege of Orléans, defeated the English at Patay, and Charles was crowned at Reims. However, she failed to capture Paris, was captured in May 1430 by the Burgundians, who sold her to the English. She was found guilty of witchcraft and heresy, and was burned at Rouen on 30 May 1431. In 1920 she was canonized.

Job /dʒəʊb/ in the Old Testament, chieftain who in the *Book of Job* (c. 5th century BC) questioned God's infliction of suffering on the righteous and endured great sufferings himself. Although he comes to no final conclusion, his book is one of the first attempts to explain the problem of human suffering in a world created and governed by God, who is all-powerful and all-good.

Job Centre in the UK, a state-run ◊employment exchange.

Jockey Club governing body of English ◊horse racing.

Jodhpur /ˌdʒɒdˈpʊə/ city in Rajasthan, India, formerly capital of Jodhpur princely state, founded in 1459 by Rao Jodha; population (1981) 493,600. It is a market centre and has the training college of the Indian Air force, an 18th-century Mughal palace, and a red sandstone fort. A style of riding breeches is named after it.

Jodl /ˈjəʊdl/ Alfred 1892–1946. German general. He headed the delegation which signed Germany's surrender at Reims on 7 May 1945. He was tried at Nuremberg in 1945–46, and hanged.

Jodrell Bank /ˈdʒɒdrəl ˈbæŋk/ site in Cheshire, England, of the Nuffield Radio Astronomy Laboratories of the University of Manchester. Its largest instrument is the 76 m/250 ft radio dish, completed in 1957 and modified in 1970. A 38 m × 25 m/125 ft × 83 ft elliptical radio dish was introduced in 1964, capable of working at shorter wavelengths. These ◊radio telescopes are used in conjunction with five smaller dishes to produce detailed maps of radio sources.

Joffre /ˈʒɒfrə/ Joseph Jacques Césaire 1852–1931. Marshal of France. The German invasion of Belgium 1914 took him by surprise, but his stand on the Marne resulted in appointment as supreme commander of all the French armies 1915. His failure to make adequate preparations at Verdun in 1916, and the disasters on the Somme, led to his replacement by Nivelle in Dec 1916.

Jogjakarta /ˌjɒɡjə'kɑːtə/ alternative spelling of ◊Yogyakarta, a city in Indonesia.

Johannesburg /dʒəʊ'hænɪsbɜːg/ largest city of South Africa, situated on the Witwatersrand in Transvaal; population (1983) 1,713,000. It is the centre of the world's gold-mining industry. Founded after the discovery of gold in 1886, the town was probably named after Jan (Johannes) Meyer, the first mining commissioner. Notable buildings include the law courts, Escom House (Electricity Supply Commission), the South African Railways Administration Building, the City Hall, Chamber of Mines and Stock Exchange, the Witwatersrand (1921) and Rand Afrikaans (1966) universities, and the Union Observatory. It is an important rail centre and has engineering works, meat-chilling plants, and clothing factories. The Jan Smuts international airport, to the NE, came into use in 1954.

John /dʒɒn/ Augustus Edwin 1878–1961. British artist. Born in Tenby, Wales, the son of a solicitor, he studied at the Slade, and in 1903 first exhibited at the New English Art Club. Elected Royal Academician in 1928, he was awarded the Order of Merit in 1942. His portraits include *The Smiling Woman* (his second wife, Dorelia), and *Galway*. He was president of the Gypsy Lore Society, and in 1952 published a fragmentary autobiography *Chiaroscuro*. Gwen ◊John was his sister.

John /dʒɒn/ Elton. Stage name of Reginald Dwight 1947– . English pop singer, pianist, and composer, noted for his elaborate costumes and stage manner.

John /dʒɒn/ Gwen 1876–1939. British artist, sister of Augustus ◊John. A Catholic convert, she lived in France for most of her life and many of her paintings depict the Dominican nuns of a French convent. For many years she was the mistress of ◊Rodin.

John /dʒɒn/ 1167–1216. King of England. The youngest son of Henry II, he attempted to seize the kingdom during his brother Richard I's absence at the Crusades. On Richard's death in 1199, he was recognized as king by England and Normandy, while Anjou and Brittany supported the claim of his nephew Arthur. He murdered Arthur, but consequently lost his French possessions. He was forced by Innocent III to accept Langton as Archbishop of Canterbury and in 1213 he surrendered his kingdom to the Pope and became his vassal. However, King John's tyranny led to the barons forcing him to sign the Magna ◊Carta in 1215 and he died at Newark during the civil war which ensued when he repudiated the charter.

John /dʒɒn/ several kings of France:

John II /dʒɒn/ 1319–1364. King from 1350. He was defeated and captured by the Black Prince at Poitiers 1356. Released 1360, he failed to raise the money for his ransom and returned in 1364 to England, where he died.

John /dʒɒn/ name of 23 popes including:

John XXII /dʒɒn/ 1249–1334. Pope 1316–34. He spent his papacy at Avignon, France, engaged in a long conflict with the

emperor, Louis of Bavaria, and the Spiritual Franciscans, who preached the absolute poverty of the clergy.

John XXIII /dʒɒn/ died 1419. Pope (antipope) 1410–1415. In an attempt to end the Great Schism he was elected pope by a council of cardinals at Bologna, but was deposed by the Council of Constance in 1415, together with the popes of Avignon and Rome. His papacy is not recognized by the church.

John XXIII /dʒɒn/ Angelo Giuseppe Roncalli 1881–1963. Pope from 1958. Born near Bergamo, Italy, and one of a peasant family of 13, he was elected pope in 1958. He improved relations with the USSR in line with his encyclical *Pacem in Terris/Peace on Earth* 1963; established Roman Catholic hierarchies in newly emergent states, and summoned the Second Vatican Council, which reformed church liturgy, backed the ecumenical movement, and made the pope more 'one among equals'.

John /dʒɒn/ several kings of Poland including:

John III /dʒɒn/ 1642–1696. Called *Sobieski*. Elected king of Poland from 1674, he saved Vienna from the besieging Turks 1683.

John /dʒɒn/ six kings of Portugal, including:

John I /dʒɒn/ 1357–1433. Elected king of Portugal from 1385 by the Cortes, although a natural son of Pedro I. His claim was supported by an English army against the rival king of Castile, thus establishing the Anglo-Portuguese Alliance 1386. He married Phillippa of Lancaster, daughter of ◊John of Gaunt.

John IV /dʒɒn/ 1603–1656. Originally Duke of Braganza, elected king 1640 when the Portuguese rebelled against Spanish rule.

John VI /dʒɒn/ 1769–1826. Regent for his insane mother *Maria I* (1792–1816), he fled to Brazil when the French invaded Portugal in 1807, and did not return until 1822. On his return Brazil declared its independence, with John's elder son Pedro as emperor.

John Bull an imaginary figure used as a personification of England. The name was popularized by Dr ◊Arbuthnot's *History of John Bull* 1712. He is represented as a prosperous farmer of the 18th century.

John Chrysostom, St /'krɪsəstəm/ 345–407. Born at Antioch, he was a hermit before being appointed Eastern Orthodox bishop of Constantinople 398–404.

John of Austria /dʒɒn/ Don 1545–1578. Spanish soldier, the illegitimate son of ◊Charles V, who defeated the Turks at ◊Lepanto in 1571.

John of Damascus, St /dʒɒn/ c. 676–c. 754. Eastern Orthodox theologian. Born at Damascus, he was a defender of image-worship against the iconoclasts.

John of Gaunt /dʒɒn/ 1340–1399. English nobleman, born at Ghent, fourth son of Edward III, Duke of Lancaster from 1362. During Edward's last years and the minority of Richard II, he acted as head of government, and parliament protested against his corrupt rule. He supported ◊Wycliffe. ◊Henry VII's mother, Margaret Beaufort, was a descendant of John of Gaunt through his marriage with his mistress Catherine Swynford. ◊John I of Portugal

married John of Gaunt's daughter, Phillippa of Lancaster.

John of the Cross, St /dʒɒn/ 1542–1591. Spanish Carmelite friar from 1564, who was imprisoned several times for attempting to impose the reforms laid down by St Teresa. His verse is full of spiritual ecstasy. Feast day 24 Nov.

John o' Groats /ə'grəʊts/ village in NE Highland region, Scotland, about 3 km/2 mi W of Duncansby Head, proverbially Britain's most northerly point. It is named after the Dutchman John de Groot who built a house there in the 16th century.

John Paul /dʒɒn/ name of two popes:

John Paul I /dʒɒn/ (Albino Luciani) 1912–1978. Known from his smile as 'the happy pope', held the office only 26 Aug–28 Sept 1978. He chose his name as the combination of his two immediate predecessors.

John Paul II /dʒɒn/ (Karol Wojtyla) 1920– . Pope 1978– . The first non-Italian pope since 1522, he was born near Kraków, Poland. In 1939 he was conscripted for forced labour by the Germans, working in quarries and a chemical factory, but from 1942 studied for the priesthood at a seminary illegally open in Kraków. After the war he taught ethics and theology at the universities of Lublin and Kraków, becoming archbishop of Kraków in 1964, and was created a cardinal in 1967. Despite personal charisma, he has been criticized for his upholding of the tradition of papal infallibility, and condemnation of artificial contraception, women priests, married priests, and modern dress for monks and nuns. He has warned against involvement of priests in political activity. He was shot and wounded by a Turk in 1981.

John Paul II The first pope to come from Poland, John Paul is an accomplished linguist and author. His works translated into English include *Easter Vigil and other Poems*.

Johns /dʒɒnz/ 'Captain' W(illiam) E(arl) 1893–1968. British author, from 1932, of popular novels of World War I flying ace Captain James Bigglesworth ('Biggles'), now sometimes criticized for chauvinism, racism, and sexism. He retired from the RAF in 1930.

John, St /dʒɒn/ New Testament apostle, identified with the unnamed 'disciple whom

Jesus loved'. Son of Zebedee, born in Judaea, he and his brother ◊James were Galilean fishermen. Jesus entrusted his mother to John at the Crucifixion. Traditionally, he wrote the fourth Gospel and the Johannine Epistles, when bishop of Ephesus, and the Revelation while imprisoned on ◊Patmos.

John the Baptist, St /dʒɒn/ in the New Testament, son of Zacharias and Elizabeth (a cousin of Christ's mother), he was a Nazarene from birth. After preparation in the wilderness, he proclaimed the coming of Christ, baptized Jesus in the Jordan, and was executed by ◊Herod Antipas at the instigation of Salome.

Johnson /'dʒɒnsən/ Amy 1904–1941. British aviator. Born at Hull, she made a solo flight from Croydon to Australia, 1930, in 19½ days, and in 1932 she made the fastest ever solo flight to Cape Town. She married J A Mollison in 1932, with whom she flew the Atlantic in 1933. Her plane disappeared over the Channel in World War II while she was serving with the Air Transport Auxiliary.

Johnson Amy Johnson, British flyer of the 1930s, when 'record flights' were one of the excitements of the period, broke many records.

Johnson /'dʒɒnsən/ Andrew 1808–1875. 17th president of the USA 1865–69. Born in North Carolina, he was elected to Congress in 1843 as a Democrat, became vice-president in 1864, and succeeded to the presidency on Lincoln's assassination. His conciliatory policy to the defeated South after the Civil War involved him in a feud with the radical Republicans, culminating in his impeachment before the Senate in 1868, which failed to convict him by one vote.

Johnson /'dʒɒnsən/ Celia 1908–1982. British actress, she made her debut in 1928 as *Major Barbara*, but is best remembered for her starring role in the film *Brief Encounter* 1946.

Johnson /'dʒɒnsən/ Lyndon Baines 1908–1973. 36th president of the USA 1963–69; born in Stonewall, Texas. He was elected to Congress (1937–49), and to the Senate (1949–60). He stood as vice-president in 1960, so bringing crucial Southern votes to Kennedy, whom he then succeeded. After the ◊Tonkin Gulf incident, the escalation of US involvement in the ◊Vietnam War eventually dissipated the support won by his Great Society legislation (civil rights, education, alleviation of poverty), so that he declined to stand again in 1968.

Johnson Lyndon B Johnson became president of the USA after Kennedy's assassination in 1963. He is remembered for his Great Society legislation, especially in civil rights. He declined to stand again in 1968 after failing to end the increasingly unpopular war in Vietnam.

Johnson /'dʒɒnsən/ Pamela Hansford 1912–1981. British novelist, born in London, who in 1950 married C P ◊Snow; her works include the novels *Too Dear for my Possessing* 1940, and *The Honours Board* 1970, and the play *Corinth House* 1948.

Johnson /'dʒɒnsən/ Philip Cortelyou 1906– . American architect, who invented the term 'international style'. He began designing in the style of ◊Mies van der Rohe (house at New Canaan, 1949) but became one of the early, and spectacular, exponents of ◊Post-Modernism. His best known building is the giant AT&T building in New York 1978, a pink skyscraper with a Chippendale-style cabinet top.

Johnson /'dʒɒnsən/ Pierre-Marc 1946– . Canadian lawyer and politician. Leader of the Parti Québecois and prime minister of Quebec from 1985, fighting not for independence, but for greater control of provincial affairs.

Johnson /'dʒɒnsən/ Samuel, known as 'Dr Johnson' 1709–1784. English lexicographer, author, and critic, also noted as a brilliant conversationalist and the dominant figure in

Johnson The Crystal Cathedral, Los Angeles, by Johnson and Burgee. Philip Johnson was director of architecture and design at the Museum of Modern Art in New York 1932–54, where he built the annexe and sculpture court.

18th-century London literary society. Born in Lichfield, Staffordshire, he became first an usher and then a literary hack. In 1735 he married Elizabeth Porter and opened a private school. When this proved unsuccessful he went to London with his pupil David Garrick, becoming a regular contributor to the *Gentleman's Magazine* and publishing the poem *London* in 1738. In 1755 he published his *Dictionary*, a classic work which remained authoritative for over a century and which is still interesting for the vigour of its definitions. Other works include the satire imitating Juvenal, *Vanity of Human Wishes* 1749, the philosophical romance *Rasselas* 1759, an edition of Shakespeare 1765 and the classic *Lives of the Most Eminent English Poets* 1779–81. His first meeting with his biographer ◊Boswell in 1763 was followed by the formation of the 'Literary Club' in 1764, to which Reynolds, Burke, Goldsmith, and Garrick belonged. A visit with Boswell to Scotland and the Hebrides in 1773 was recorded in *Journey to the Western Isles of Scotland* 1775. He was buried in Westminster Abbey and his house in Gough Square, London, is preserved as a museum; his wit and humanity are documented in Boswell's classic biography *Life of Samuel Johnson* 1791.

Johnson /'dʒɒnsən/ Uwe 1934– . German novelist, who left East Germany for West Berlin in 1959, and writes of the division of Germany, for example, *Anniversaries* 1977.

Johore /dʒəʊ'hɔː/ state of Malaysia; capital Johore Bahru; area 18,960 sq km/7,320 sq mi; population (1980) 1,601,500. The southernmost point of mainland Asia, it is joined to Singapore by a causeway.

joint in any animal with a ◊skeleton, a point of movement or articulation. In vertebrates, the point where two bones meet. Some joints allow no motion (for example, the sutures of the skull),

Johnson 'Lexicographer; a writer of dictionaries, a harmless drudge', said Samuel Johnson. He published his famous *Dictionary* in 1755, and it remained an authoritative work for over a century. His portrait is by Joshua Reynolds, c. 1772.

joint

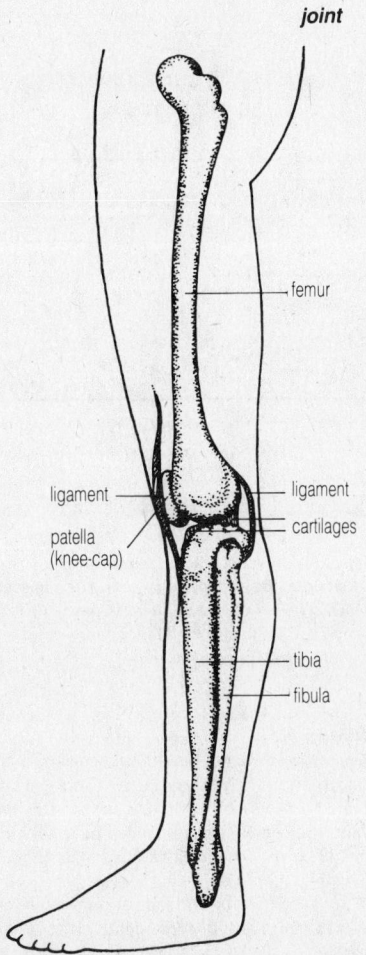

femur

ligament

patella
(knee-cap)

ligament

cartilages

tibia

fibula

Jones A drawing after Robert Van Voerst of English architect Inigo Jones, in the National Portrait Gallery, London. The foremost practitioner of English Renaissance architecture, he also designed scenery for masques.

others allow a very small motion (for example, the sacro-iliac joints in the lower back), but most allow a relatively free motion. Of this third class some allow a gliding motion (for example, one vertebra of the spine on another), some have a hinge action (for example, those of the elbow and knee), and others allow motion in all directions (for example, the hip and shoulder joints), by means of a ball-and-socket arrangement. The ends of the bones at a moving joint are covered with ◊cartilage for greater elasticity and smoothness, and enclosed in an envelope (capsule) of tough white fibrous tissue lined with a membrane which secretes lubricating (◊synovial) fluid. The joint is further strengthened by ◊ligaments.

In invertebrates with an ◊exoskeleton, the joints are places where the exoskeleton is replaced by a more flexible outer covering, the arthrodial membrane, which allows the limb (or other body part) to bend at that point.

Joint European Torus an experimental nuclear fusion machine, known as ◊JET.

joint intelligence committee a weekly British ◊cabinet meeting held to discuss international ◊intelligence.

Joinville /ʒwæn'viːl/ Jean, Sire de 1224–1317. French chronicler. Born in Champagne, he accompanied Louis IX on the crusade of 1248–54, which he described in his *History of St Louis*.

Jolson /'dʒəʊlsən/ Al. Stage name of Asa Yoelson 1886–1950. US singer, born in Russia. He became famous as a stage performer, in

recordings, and as a star of the early sound-films, *The Jazz Singer* 1927 and *The Singing Fool*.

Jonah /'dʒəʊnə/ Hebrew prophet whose name is given to a book in the Old Testament. He fled by ship to evade his mission to prophesy the destruction of Nineveh. The crew threw him overboard in a storm, as a bringer of ill fortune, and he spent three days and nights in the belly of a whale before coming to land.

Jonathan /'dʒɒnəθən/ Chief (Joseph) Leabua 1914–1987. Lesotho politician. As prime minister of Lesotho 1965–86, he played a pragmatic role, allying himself in turn with South Africa, then the Organization of African Unity. His rule was ended by a coup in 1986.

Jones /'dʒəʊnz/ Bobby 1902–1971. American golfer. He dominated the game from 1923 until he retired in 1930 after achieving the grand slam, US and British amateur and open championships all in one year. He was the originator of the Masters Tournament.

Jones /'dʒəʊnz/ Inigo 1573–c. 1652. English architect. Born in London, he studied in Italy, and was influenced by the works of Palladio. He was employed by James I in designing the scenery for Ben Jonson's masques, and in 1619 he designed his masterpiece, the banqueting-room at Whitehall; and the church of St Paul, Covent Garden, London.

Jones /'dʒəʊnz/ John Paul 1747–1792. American naval officer, born in Kirkcudbright, Scotland. He was originally a trader and slaver but became an American privateer in the War of Independence in 1775. Heading a small French-sponsored squadron in the *Bonhomme Richard* he captured the British warship *Serapis* 23 Sept 1799 in a bloody battle off Scarborough. He joined the Russian navy as a rear-admiral in 1788, fighting against Turkey, but lost Catherine's favour and died in France.

Jonestown /'dʒəʊnztaʊn/ commune of the People's Temple Sect, NW of Georgetown, Guyana, established 1974 by Jim Jones (1933–78), who originally founded the sect among San Francisco's black community. Complaints of oppression of his black subjects led to a visit by a US congressman who was shot, with his companions. After this Jones enforced mass suicide on his followers by drinking cyanide; 914 died, including over 240 children.

Jönköping /'jɜːntʃɜːpɪŋ/ town at the S end of Lake Vättern, Sweden; population (1980) 107,600. It is an industrial centre.

jonquil a species of small daffodil *Narcissus jonquilla*, family Amaryllidaceae, which has yellow flowers, native to Spain and Portugal but often cultivated elswhere.

Jonson /'dʒɒnsən/ Ben(jamin) 1572–1637. English dramatist, poet, and critic. Born at Westminster, he entered the theatre as actor and dramatist in 1597. In 1598 he narrowly escaped the gallows for killing a fellow-player in a duel, and in the same year his *Every Man in his Humour* established the English 'comedy of humours', in which each character embodies a 'humour' or vice such as greed, lust, or avarice. This was followed by *Every Man out of his Humour* 1599, *Cynthia's Revels* 1600 and *Poetaster* 1601. His first extant tragedy is *Sejanus* 1603, with Burbage and Shakespeare as members of the original cast. He collaborated with Marston and Chapman in *Eastward Hoe* 1605, and shared their imprisonment when official exception was taken to the satirization of

James I's Scottish policy. The great plays of his middle years include *Volpone, or The Fox* 1606, *Epicene, or The Silent Woman* 1609, *The Alchemist* 1610, and *Bartholomew Fair* 1614. He also produced some 30 masques, before a quarrel with his associate Inigo ◊Jones in 1630 lost him court favour.

Jonson The poet and dramatist Ben Jonson started out as a bricklayer and once narrowly escaped the gallows after killing a man in a duel.

Joplin /'dʒɒplɪn/ Janis 1943–1970. US blues and acid-rock singer, born in Texas, who became a symbol and a victim of the 1960s drug culture. She was lead singer with the San Francisco group Big Brother and the Holding Company from 1966, and started a solo career in 1969 with the album *Kozmic Blues*. Her biggest hit, Kris Kristofferson's 'Me and Bobby McGee', was released in 1971 after her death.

Joplin /'dʒɒplɪn/ Scott 1868–1917. US ◊ragtime pianist and composer in Chicago. His 'Maple Leaf Rag' 1899 was the first instrumental sheet music to sell a million copies, and 'The Entertainer', as the theme tune of the film *The Sting* 1973, revived his popularity. He was an influence on Jelly Roll ◊Morton and other early jazz musicians.

Joppa /'dʒɒpə/ ancient name of ◊Jaffa, a port in W Israel.

Jordaens /jɔː'dɑːns/ Jakob 1593–1678. Flemish Baroque painter, born in Antwerp, and assistant to ◊Rubens. He was noted for exuberant, large-scale works, including scenes of peasant life.

Jordan /'dʒɔːdn/ river rising on Mount Hermon, Syria at 550 m/1,800 ft above sea level and flowing S for about 320 km/200 mi via the Sea of Galilee to the Dead Sea, 390 m/1,290 ft below sea level. It occupies the northern part of the Great Rift Valley; its upper course forms the boundary of Israel with Syria and the kingdom of Jordan; its lower course runs through Jordan – the West Bank has been occupied by Israel from 1967.

Jordan /'dʒɔːdn/ country in SW Asia, bordered to the N by Syria, NE by Iraq, E and

Joplin The cover of a songsheet containing 'The Entertainer', Scott Joplin's ragtime masterpiece which provided the theme tune for the 1973 film *The Sting*. Joplin was the first ragtime composer to write down his compositions.

SE by Saudi Arabia, S by the Gulf of Aqaba, and W by Israel.

government Jordan is not a typical constitutional monarchy on the Western model, since the king is effectively head of both state and government. The 1952 constitution, amended in 1974, 1976 and 1984, provides for a two-chamber national assembly comprising a senate (house of notables) of 30, appointed by the king for an eight-year term, and a house of representatives (house of deputies), elected by universal suffrage for a four-year term. The house is subject to dissolution within that period. In each chamber there is equal representation for the E and W (occupied) Banks. Three of Jordan's eight administrative provinces have been occupied by Israel since 1967. The king governs with the help of a council of ministers whom he appoints and who are responsible to the assembly. Political parties were banned in 1963, partially restored in 1971, and then banned again in 1976.

history the area forming the kingdom of Jordan was occupied by the independent Nabataeans from the 4th century BC and perhaps earlier, until 106AD when it became part of the Roman province of Arabia. It was included in the Crusaders' kingdom of Jerusalem 1099–1187. Palestine, which included the W Bank of present-day Jordan, and Transjordan, which is the present-day E Bank, were part of the Turkish ◊Ottoman Empire until its dissolution after World War I Both were then placed under British administration by the League of Nations. Transjordan acquired greater control of its own affairs, separating from Palestine in 1923 and achieving full independence when the British mandate expired in 1946. The mandate for Palestine ran out in 1948, whereupon Jewish leaders claimed it for a new state of ◊Israel. Fighting broke out between Jews and Arabs until

a cease-fire was agreed in 1949. By then Transjordan forces had occupied part of Palestine to add to what they called the new state of Jordan. The following year they annexed the W Bank. In 1953 Hussein ibn Talai came to the Jordanian throne at the age of 17. He was to rule his country for over 30 years. In 1958 Jordan and ◊Iraq formed an Arab Federation which ended five months later when the Iraqi monarchy was overthrown.

King Hussein has survived many upheavals in his own country and neighbouring states, including attempts on his life, and has kept control of Jordan's affairs as well as playing an important role in Middle East affairs. Relations with his neighbours have fluctuated but he has generally been a moderating influence. After Israel's invasion of Lebanon, in 1982, Hussein played a key role in attempts to bring peace to the area, establishing a relationship with ◊Palestine Liberation Organization (PLO) leader, Yasser ◊Arafat. By 1984 the Arab world was split into two camps, with the moderates represented by Jordan, Egypt and Arafat's PLO, and the militant radicals by Syria, Libya and the rebel wing of the PLO. In 1985 Hussein and Arafat put together a framework for a Middle East peace settlement. It would involve bringing together all interested parties including the PLO, but Israel objected to the PLO representation. Further progress was hampered by the PLO's alleged complicity in a number of guerrilla operations in that year. Hussein tried to revive the search for peace by secretly meeting the Israeli prime minister in France and persuading Yasser Arafat to publicly denounce PLO violence in territories not occupied by Israel. The role of Jordan, through King Hussein, could be vital in any future peace-making moves.

Jordan /'dʒɔːdn/ Dorothea 1762–1816. British actress. She made her debut in 1777, and retired in 1815. She was a mistress of the Duke of Clarence (later William IV), by whom she had ten children with the name FitzClarence.

Joseph /'dʒəuzɪf/ in the New Testament, the husband of the Virgin Mary, a descendant of David, and a carpenter by trade. Although Jesus was not the son of Joseph, Joseph was his legal father. According to Roman Catholic tradition, he had a family by a previous wife, and was an elderly man when he married Mary.

Joseph /'dʒəuzɪf/ in the Old Testament, the 11th and favourite son of ◊Jacob, sold into Egypt by his jealous half-brothers. After he had risen to power there, they and his father joined him to escape from famine.

Joseph /'dʒəuzɪf/ Keith Sinjohn 1918– . British Conservative politician. A barrister; he entered Parliament in 1956. He held ministerial posts 1962–64, 1970–74, 1979–81, and (education and science) 1981–86.

Joseph /'dʒəuzɪf/ Père 1577–1638. Religious name of Capuchin friar Francis Le Clerc du Tremblay. Influential secretary-agent to Cardinal Richelieu, hence nicknamed 'Grey Eminence' in reference to his grey habit.

Joseph name of two Holy Roman Emperors:
Joseph I /'dʒəuzɪf/ 1678–1711. Holy Roman Emperor from 1705, and king of Austria. A

Jordan

HASHEMITE KINGDOM OF (*Al Mamlaka al Urduniya al Hashemiyah*)

AREA 98,000 sq km/38,000 sq mi
CAPITAL Amman
TOWNS Aqaba, the only port
PHYSICAL mostly desert
FEATURES Dead Sea, river Jordan, archaeological sites including Jerash, Roman forum
HEAD OF STATE AND OF GOVERNMENT King Hussein ibn Talai from 1952
GOVERNMENT constitutional monarchy
EXPORTS potash, phosphates, citrus
CURRENCY Jordanian dinar (0.57 = £1 Sept 1987)
POPULATION (1985) 2,668,000 (including Palestinian refugees); annual growth rate 3.7%
LANGUAGE Arabic
RELIGION Sunni Muslim
LITERACY 31% (1980)
GDP $4.2 bn (1984); $552 per head of population
CHRONOLOGY
1946 Achieved full independence as Transjordan.
1949 New state of Jordan declared.

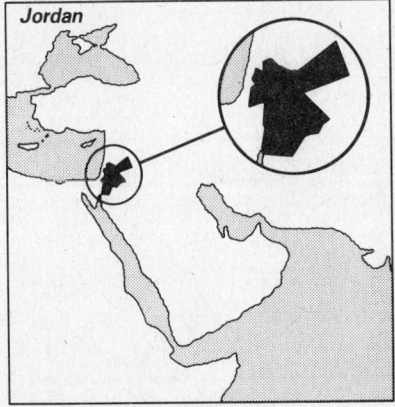

Jordan

1953 Hussein ibn Talai became king of Jordan.
1958 Jordan and Iraq formed Arab Federation which ended when the Iraqi monarchy was deposed.
1982 Hussein tried to mediate in Arab-Israeli conflict.
1985 Hussein put forward a framework for a Middle East peace settlement. Secret meeting between Hussein and Israeli prime minister.

◊Hapsburg, he spent most of his reign involved in fighting the War of Spanish Succession.

Joseph II /'dʒəʊzɪf/ 1741–1790. Holy Roman Emperor from 1765, son of ◊Francis I. The reforms he carried out after the death of his mother, Maria ◊Theresa, in 1780, provoked revolts from those who lost privileges.

Josephine /'dʒəʊzɪfiːn/ Marie Josèphe Rose Tascher de la Pagerie 1763–1814. Empress of France. Born on Martinique, she married in 1779 the Vicomte de Beauharnais, and in 1796 Napoleon, who divorced her in 1809 because she had not produced children. She spent the rest of her life in retirement near Paris. Her chateau at Malmaison, Paris, is a museum.

Joseph of Arimathaea, St /,ærɪmə'θiːə/ in the New Testament, a wealthy Jew, member of the Sanhedrin, and a secret supporter of Jesus, who on the evening of the Crucifixion asked Pilate for Jesus' body and buried it in his own tomb. According to tradition he brought the Holy Grail to England about 63 AD and erected the first Christian church to be built in Britain at Glastonbury. Feast day 17 Mar.

Josephs /'dʒəʊzɪfs/ Wilfred 1927– . British composer, born in Newcastle-upon-Tyne. He first became known for television music, but has also written symphonies, including a *Pastoral Symphony*, and an opera *Rebecca* 1983.

Josephson /'dʒəʊzɪfsən/ Brian 1940– . British physicist, a leading authority on superconductivity. Working at Cambridge, in 1973 he shared a Nobel prize for his theoretical predictions of the properties of a supercurrent through a tunnel barrier, especially the phenomenon named after him, the Josephson effect.

Josephine A portrait of Empress Josephine at Malmaison, her favourite residence, which Napoleon gave her after their divorce.

Josephson junction a device used in 'superchips' to speed the passage of signals by a phenomenon called 'electron tunnelling'. Though these superchips respond a thousand times faster than the ◊silicon chip, they have the disadvantage that the components of the Josephson junctions operate only at temperatures close to ◊absolute zero. They are named after Brian ◊Josephson.

Josephus /dʒəʊ'siːfəs/ Flavius 37–c. 100 AD. Jewish historian. Born in Jerusalem, he became

a Pharisee, and commanded the Jewish forces in Galilee in the revolt against Rome from 66 (which ended with the mass suicide at Masada). When captured, he gained the favour of Vespasian and settled in Rome as a citizen. He wrote *Antiquities of the Jews* to 66 AD; *The Jewish War*, and an autobiography.

Joshua /'dʒɒʃuə/ in the Old Testament, successor of ◊Moses, who led the Jews in their conquest of the land of ◊Canaan. The city of ◊Jericho fell under his leadership.

Josiah /dʒəʊ'saɪə/ c. 647–609 BC. King of Judah. Grandson of Manasseh and son of Amon, he succeeded to the throne when eight. The discovery of a Book of Instruction (probably Deuteronomy) during repairs of the Temple in 621 BC stimulated thorough reform, which included the removal of all sanctuaries except that of Jerusalem. He was killed in a clash at Megiddo with Pharaoh-nechoh, king of Egypt.

Josquin Desprez /ʒɒ'skæŋ deɪ'preɪ/ or *des Prés* 1440–1521. Franco-Flemish composer, generally considered the finest composer of his time. Possibly a pupil of ◊Ockeghem, he spent the early part of his life in Milan, first at the cathedral and then in the service of the Sforza family. In 1484, already highly renowned, he moved to Rome, and went from there to France, Ferrara, and the Low Countries. Josquin's music combines a technical mastery with the feeling for words which became a hallmark of Renaissance vocal music. His works, which include 18 masses, over 100 motets, and secular vocal works, are characterized by their vitality and depth of feeling.

jota a traditional northern Spanish dance in lively triple time for one or more couples who play the castanets, accompanied by guitar and singing. There is a *jota* in de ◊Falla's *The Three-Cornered Hat*.

Jotunheim /'jəʊtʊnhaɪm/ mountainous region of S Norway, containing the highest mountains in Scandinavia, *Glittertind* 2,453 m/8,048 ft and *Galdhøpiggen* 2,468 m/8,097 ft. In Norse myth it is the home of the giants.

Joubert /ʒuː'beə/ Petrus Jacobus 1831–1900. Boer general. He opposed British annexation of the Transvaal in 1878, proclaimed its independence in 1880, led the Boer Commandos against the British 1880–81, defeated ◊Jameson in 1896, and fought in the ◊South African War.

joule /dʒuːl/ unit (symbol J) of work and energy in mks and SI units. It is the work done – the energy transferred – when the point of application of 1 Newton is displaced a distance of 1 metre in the direction of the force, also expressed as the work done in one second by the current of 1 amp across a potential difference of 1 volt. It is equal to 10^7 ergs, or 0.239 calories, or 2.78×10^{-7} kWh, or 0.000948 BTUs. 1 ◊watt is equivalent to 1 joule per second.

Joule /dʒuːl/ James Prescott 1818–1889. British physicist whose work on the relations between electrical, mechanical, and chemical effects led to the discovery of the first law of ◊thermodynamics. He was a brewery owner, and dedicated to precise scientific research. He determined the mechanical equivalent of heat

GENᵗ JOUBERT ᴀɴᴅ STAFF ᴀᴛ NEWCASTLE, NATAL. Oct 17ᵗʰ 1899.
PHOTO ʙʏ GELL.

Joubert The Boer general and politician Petrus Joubert, also known as 'Slim Piet', opposed British annexation of the Transvaal in 1878, and proclaimed its independence in 1880. He commanded the Transvaal's forces in the first Boer War 1880–81.

Irish writer James Joyce, whose innovative use of language in works such as *Ulysses* 1922 was a major step in the development of the English novel.

(Joule's equivalent), and the SI unit of energy, the ◊joule, is named after him.

Joule-Thomson effect in physics, the fall in temperature of a gas it expands adiabatically (without loss or gain of heat to the system) through a narrow jet. (It can be felt when, for example, compressed air escapes through the valve of an inflated bicycle tyre.) Only hydrogen does not exhibit the effect. It is the basic principle of most refrigerators and was named after the British scientists James Prescott ◊Joule and William Thomson (Lord Kelvin) (1824–1907).

journalism the profession of reporting, photographing or editing news for ◊newspapers, ◊magazines, ◊radio, and ◊television. Professional bodies include the NUJ (National Union of Journalists) in the UK, and the ANG (American Newspaper Guild) in the USA. In the UK the NCTJ (National Council for the Training of Journalists) sets standards and awards proficiency certificates. Standards are also set by awards such as those founded by J ◊Pulitzer.

Jovian /ˈdʒəʊvɪən/ 331–364. Roman emperor from 363. Captain of the imperial bodyguard, he was chosen emperor by the troops after ◊Julian's death in battle with the Persians. He concluded an unpopular peace, and restored Christianity as the state religion.

Joyce /dʒɔɪs/ James (Augustine Aloysius) 1882–1941. Irish writer, born in Dublin, who revolutionized the form of the English novel with his 'stream of consciousness' technique. His works include *Dubliners* 1914 (short stories), *Portrait of the Artist as a Young Man* 1916 (semi-autobiographical), and *Ulysses* 1922, which records the events of a single Dublin day, mingling direct narrative with the unspoken and

unconscious reactions of the characters and experimenting with language. The book, banned at first for obscenity in England and the USA, was enormously influential. *Finnegans Wake* 1939 continued Joyce's experiments with language, attempting a synthesis of all existence.

Joyce /dʒɔɪs/ William 1906–1946. Born in New York, son of a naturalized Irish-born American, he carried on Fascist activity in Britain as a 'British subject'. During World War II he made broadcasts from Germany to Britain, his upper-class accent earning him the nickname 'Lord Haw-Haw'. He was hanged for treason.

joystick in computing, an input device, similar to a joystick used to control the flight of an aircraft, which signals to a computer the direction and extent of displacement of a hand-held lever. Often used to control the movement of a cursor (marker) on a VDU (computer screen), joysticks are most popular for moving predetermined specific shapes or icons (such as space-invader characters) in computer games. They allow fast and direct input.

Juan Carlos /ˈhwæn ˈkɑːlɒs/ 1938– . King of Spain. The son of Don Juan, pretender to the Spanish throne, he married in 1962 Princess Sophia, eldest daughter of King Paul of Greece. In 1969 he was nominated by Franco to succeed on the restoration of the monarchy intended to follow Franco's own death: his father was excluded because of his known liberal views. He became king in 1975 and has sought to steer his country from dictatorship to democracy.

Juan Fernández Islands /ˈdʒuːən fəˈnændez, Spanish ˈxwæn feəˈnændeθ/ three small volcanic Pacific islands belonging to Chile; almost uninhabited. The largest is Más-a-Tierra (also sometimes called Juan Fernández Island) where

Juan Carlos Photograph taken in 1982 of King Juan Carlos of Spain, who succeeded the Spanish dictator Franco on his death in 1975. He is wearing the uniform of Captain General of the Navy.

Alexander ◊Selkirk was marooned 1704–09. The islands were named after the Spanish navigator who discovered them about 1565.

Juárez /ˈxwɑːreθ/ Benito 1806–1872. Mexican politician, president 1861–64 and

1867–72. In 1861 he suspended payouts on Mexico's foreign debts, which prompted a joint French, British and Spanish expedition to exert pressure. French forces invaded the country and an empire was created for ◊Maximilian, brother of the Austrian emperor. The empire was only sustained by French troops and their withdrawal in 1867, together with the animosity of the USA after the American ◊Civil War, led to Maximilian's defeat and death by firing squad, and the return of Juárez to the presidency.

Juba /'dʒuːbə/ river in E Africa, formed at Dolo, Ethiopia, by the junction of the Ganale Dorya and Dawa rivers. It flows S for about 885 km/550 mi through the Somali Republic (of which its valley is the most productive area) into the Indian Ocean.

Juba /'dʒuːbə/ capital of Equatoria province, Sudan Republic; population (1970) 45,500. It stands on the left bank of the White Nile, at the head of navigation above Khartoum, 1,200 km/750 mi to the north.

Jubbulpore /,dʒʌbəl'puə/ (or Jabalpur). City of Madhya Pradesh, India; population (1981) 615,000. It has textile, oil, and flour mills, and a university 1957.

Judaea /dʒuː'diːə/ southern division of ancient Palestine, see ◊Judah.

Judah /'dʒuːdə/ district of South Palestine, which after the death of Solomon adhered to his son Rehoboam and the Davidic line, whereas the rest of Israel elected Jeroboam as ruler of the northern Kingdom. In New Testament times, Judah was the Roman province of Judaea, and in modern Israeli usage refers to the S area of the West Bank.

Judaism the religion of the Jews, founded on the Torah ('direction for living'), combining the Mosaic code and its oral interpretation. This comprises the first five books of the Bible, also known as the Pentateuch. It was retained when the Jews were in exile in Babylon from 586 BC, and was reconstituted by Ezra on the return to Jerusalem. The ultimate destruction of the Temple at Jerusalem was countered by greater stress on the synagogue (in continental and US non-orthodox usage 'temple'), the local building for worship (originally simply the place where the Torah was read and expounded; its characteristic feature is still the Ark, or cupboard, where the Torah scrolls are kept) and home observance. The work of lay rabbis (teachers) skilled in the Jewish law and ritual also grew in importance, and in modern times they either act as spiritual leaders and pastors of their communities, or devote themselves to study. The *Talmud* compiled c. 200 AD combines the *Mishnah*, rabbinical commentary on the law handed down orally from 70 AD, and the *Gemara* legal discussions in the schools of Palestine and Babylon. The *Haggadah* is that part of the Talmud which deals with stories of heroes. The *Midrash* is the collection of commentaries on the scriptures written 400–1200 AD, mainly in Palestine. The *creed* rests on the concept of one God, whose will is revealed in the Torah, and who has a special relationship with the Jewish people. *Observances* include: circumcision, daily services in Hebrew, observance of the *Sabbath* (sunset on

Friday to sunset Saturday) as a day of rest, and, among orthodox Jews, strict dietary laws (see ◊kosher). Holy days are ***Rosh Hashanah*** Jewish New Year (first new moon after the autumn equinox, announced by blowing a ram's horn) and, a week later, the religious fast ***Yom Kippur***. *history* led by Abraham, the Israelites emigrated from Mesopotamia to Canaan c. 2000 BC. During the Hyksos period some settled on the borders of Egypt and were put to forced labour, from which they were rescued by Moses, founder of the religion, who aimed at their establishment in Palestine. The main invasion c. 1274 BC was led by Joshua and during the period of Judges ascendancy was established over the Canaanites. Complete conquest of Palestine and the union of all Israel was achieved under David c. 1000 BC, and Jerusalem became the capital. Solomon, David's son, succeeded and enjoyed a reputation for great wealth and wisdom, but his lack of a constructive policy led after his death to the secession of the north (Israel) under Jeroboam, only Judah remaining under the house of David. A new factor was introduced with the rise of Assyria: Israel purchased safety by tribute, and under Jeroboam II c. 785 reached its highest pitch of luxury, but the basis of the society was corrupt, and prophets such as Amos, Isaiah, and Micah predicted destruction. At the hands of Tiglathpileser and his successor Shalmaneser IV, the northern kingdom was organized as Assyrian provinces after the fall of Samaria in 721 BC, although Judah was spared as an ally. When the power of Assyria waned, its place was taken by Babylonia, and in 586 BC Nebuchadnezzar took Jerusalem and carried off the major part of the population to Babylon. Under Cyrus, the founder of the Persian Empire, the Jews were allowed to return to Palestine; the Temple was restored in 520, and in about 444 Ezra promulgated the legal code which was to govern the future of the Jewish people. Alexander's conquest of the Persian Empire was followed by a struggle for Palestine between the Syrian Seleucids and Egyptian Ptolemies, and until the end of the 3rd century BC Palestine remained under the government of Egypt with a large measure of freedom. But with the advance of Syrian power Antiochus IV attempted intervention in Jewish internal quarrels, thus prompting the Maccabean revolt in 165 BC. For a short time Judaea was practically an independent kingdom, but internal dissension led to Pompey's intervention in 63 BC, and Roman suzerainty was established. After the death of Herod in 4 BC there were several unsuccessful governments until the revolt of 66–70 AD led to the destruction of the Temple by Titus. Further revolts followed, but a new focus of Jewish national sentiment was found in the work of the Rabbi Johanan ben Zakkai (c. 20–90), and after his day the President of the Sanhedrin was recognized as the Patriarch of Palestinian Jewry. Greatest of these presidents was Rabbi Judah (c. 135–220), who codified the traditional law in the *Mishnah*. As the Roman Empire adopted Christianity, the intellectual leadership of Judaism passed to the descendants of the 6th-century exiles in Babylonia, who compiled the

Babylonian Talmud. Judaism enjoyed a golden era during the period of Islamic conquest in Europe, producing the philosopher Saadiah, the poet Jehudah Ha-levi, the codifier Moses Maimonides, and others. In medieval Europe, however, where Christianity was the dominant religion, the Jews were increasingly segregated from mainstream life and trade by ◊anti-semitism which included restrictive legislation. Outbreaks of persecution increased with the rise of European nationalism, eventually culminating in the ◊Nazi regime 1939–45. The Reform movement, a rejection of religious orthodoxy and an attempt to interpret Judaism for modern times, began in Germany in 1810 and reached England in 1842; the more radical Liberal Judaism developed in the USA and founded its first London synagogue in 1911. ◊Zionism was an attempt to create a homeland where the Jewish people would be free from persecution (see also ◊Israel). In the 20th century, particularly in the USA, many people who would call themselves Jews prefer to identify Judaism with a historical and cultural tradition rather than strict religious observance, and a contemporary debate (complicated by the history of non-Jewish attitudes towards Jews) centres on the question of how to define a Jew. As with other religions, including Christianity and Islam, there have also been fundamentalist movements in recent times, for example, ◊Gush Emunim. Outside Israel, there are large Jewish populations today in the USA (5,834,650), USSR (2,200,000), and the UK (385,000), and Jewish communities throughout the world.

Judas Iscariot /'dʒuːdəs ɪ'skæriət/ in the New Testament, he was the apostle who betrayed Jesus. He was the treasurer of the group, and at the last Passover arranged with the chief priests to betray Jesus for 30 pieces of silver. After the betrayal he was overcome with guilt and committed suicide.

judge a person invested with power to hear and determine legal disputes. In the UK, judges are chosen from barristers of long standing (for higher courts), and solicitors. See ◊Law Courts. Judges of the High Court, the Crown Courts, and the County Courts are nominated by the Lord Chancellor, and those of the Court of Appeal and the House of Lords by the Prime Minister. In the USA, apart from the Federal judiciary which are executive appointments, judges in most states are elected by popular vote.

judicial separation in the UK, a suit before a magistrate's court by either husband or wife, in which it is not necessary to prove an irreconcilable breakdown of a marriage, but in which the grounds are otherwise the same as for divorce. It does not end a marriage, but a declaration may be obtained that the complainant need no longer cohabit with the defendant, and is entitled to maintenance. A similar procedure exists in the USA.

judo synthesis of the most valuable methods – judo meaning 'gentle way' – from the many forms of jujitsu, 'the soft art', the traditional Japanese skill of self-defence and offence without weapons, which was originally practised as a secret art by the feudal Samurai. In modern times judo has been adopted throughout the world in the armed forces, the police, and in many schools. When it is practised as a sport the two combatants wear special loose-fitting, belted jackets and trousers to facilitate holds, and the falls are broken by a special square mat: when one has established a painful hold that the other cannot break, the latter signifies his surrender by slapping the ground with a free hand. Degrees of proficiency are indicated by the colour of the belt: for novices white; after examination, brown (three degrees); and finally, black (nine degrees).

World Championships first held 1956, now contested biennially
open class
1981 Yasuhiro Yamashita *(Japan)*
1983 Angelo Parisi *(France)*
1985 Yoshimi Masaki *(Japan)* ·
over 95 kg
1981 Yasuhiro Yamashita *(Japan)*
1983 Yasuhiro Yamashita *(Japan)*
1985 Yong-Chul Cho *(South Korea)*
under 95 kg
1981 Tengiz Khubuluri *(USSR)*
1983 Valeriy Divisenko *(USSR)*
1985 Hitoshi Sugai *(Japan)*
under 86 kg
1981 Bernard Tchoullouyan *(France)*
1983 Detlef Ultsch *(East Germany)*
1985 Peter Seisenbacher *(Austria)*
under 78 kg
1981 Neil Adams *(Great Britain)*
1983 Nobutoshi Hikage *(Japan)*
1985 Nobutoshi Hikage *(Japan)*
under 70 kg
1981 Chon Hak Park *(South Korea)*
1983 Hidetoshi Nakanichi *(Japan)*
1985 Ahn Byeong-Keun *(South Korea)*
under 65 kg
1981 Katsuhiko Kashiwazaki *(Japan)*
1983 Nikolai Soludkhin *(USSR)*
1985 Yuri Sokolov *(USSR)*
under 60 kg
1981 Yasuhiko Mariwaki *(Japan)*
1983 Khazret Tletseri *(USSR)*
1985 Shinji Hosokawa *(Japan)*

Juggernaut /'dʒʌgənɔːt/ or *Jagannath* a name for Vishnu, the Hindu god, meaning 'Lord of the World'. His temple is at Puri, Orissa, India.

Jugoslavia /juːgəʊˈslɑːviə/ alternative spelling of ◊Yugoslavia.

jugular vein a vein in the neck of vertebrates; there are two jugular veins and they return blood from the head to the superior (or anterior) vena cava and thence to the heart.

Jugurtha /dʒuːˈgɜːθə/ died 104 BC. King of Numidia, North Africa, who, after a long resistance, was betrayed to the Romans in 107 BC, and put to death.

jujitsu traditional Japanese form of self-defence; see ◊judo.

jujube tree of the *Zizyphus* genus in the family Thamnaceae, and also its berry-like fruits. The Chinese jujube (*Zizyphus jujuba*), cultivated in S Europe, and frequently naturalized in the Mediterranean region, has fruit the size of small plums, known when

preserved in syrup as 'Chinese dates', but the Indian (*Zizyphus mauritiana*) has a more mediocre fruit. The name is also given to a type of sticky sweet.

Julian /'dʒuːliən/ c. 331–363. Roman emperor, called the 'Apostate'. Born in Constantinople, the nephew of Constantine the Great, he was brought up as a Christian, but in early life became a convert to paganism. Sent by Constantius to govern Gaul in 355, he was proclaimed emperor by his troops in 360, and in 361 was marching on Constantinople when Constantius's death allowed him to succeed peacefully. He revived pagan worship, and refused to persecute heretics. He was killed in battle against the Persians.

Juliana /ˌdʒuːliˈɑːnə/ 1909– . Queen of the Netherlands. The daughter of Queen Wilhelmina (1880–1962), she married Prince Bernhard of ◊Lippe-Biesterfeld in 1937 and ruled 1948–80, when she abdicated and was succeeded by her daughter ◊Beatrix.

Julius II /'dʒuːliəs/ 1443–1513. Pope 1503–13, a politician who wanted to make the papal states the leading power in Italy, and formed international alliances first against Venice and then against France. He began the building of St Peter's, Rome, in 1506, and was the patron of Michelangelo and Raphael.

July Revolution the Parisian revolution of 27–29 Jul 1830 which overthrew the restored Bourbon monarchy of Charles X, and substituted the constitutional monarchy of Louis Philippe, whose rule (1830–48) is sometimes referred to as the July Monarchy.

jumbo jet name given to huge wide-bodied airliners, particularly the *Boeing 747* which is 71 m/232 ft long, has a wing span of 60 m/196 ft, a maximum take-off weight of nearly 380 tonnes, and can carry over 400 passengers.

Jumna /'dʒʌmnə/ river in India, rising in the Himalayas, in Uttar Pradesh, and joining the Ganges near Allahabad, where it forms a sacred bathing place. Agra and Delhi are also on its course. Length 1385 km/860 mi.

jumping hare long-eared S African rodent *Pedetes capensis*, similar in appearance and habits to the ◊jerboa, but with head and body about 40 cm/1.3 ft long, with a bushy tail about as long again.

Juneau /'dʒuːnəʊ/ ice-free port of Alaska, USA, on Gastineau Channel in the remote Alaska panhandle; population (1980) 19,500. It was the capital 1906–80, when it was replaced by Willow South. There is salmon fishing, and gold and furs are exported.

Jung /jʊŋ/ Carl Gustav 1875–1961. Swiss psychiatrist, who collaborated with ◊Freud until their disagreement in 1912 about the importance of sexuality in causing psychological problems. He studied religion and dream symbolism, and saw the unconscious as a source of spiritual insight. He also distinguished between introversion and extraversion. Works include *Modern Man in Search of a Soul* 1933.

Jungfrau /'jʊŋfraʊ/ (German 'maiden') mountain in the Bernese Oberland, Switzerland: 4,166 m/13,669 ft high. A railway ascends to the

Jung Swiss psychiatrist Carl Jung was an early collaborator with Freud, but they disagreed about the importance of human sexuality in causing psychological problems. Jung went on to develop the theory of the collective unconscious.

plateau of the Jungfraujoch, 3,456 m/11,340 ft, where there is a winter sports centre.

juniper aromatic evergreen trees or shrubs found throughout Britain, Europe, America, and temperate countries of the world. They are members of the family Cupressaceae, genus *Juniperus*. Its berries are used to flavour gin.

junk bond derogatory term for a security, officially rated as 'below investment grade', that is issued in order to raise a lot of capital in a short peiod, typically to finance a takeover. Junk bonds have a high yield, but are a high-risk investment.

junker name applied to a class of landed gentry in Prussia, who were traditionally the source of most of the Prussian civil service and officer corps.

Junkers /'jʊŋkəs/ Hugo 1859–1935. German aeroplane designer. In 1919 he founded in Dessau the aircraft works named after him. Junkers planes, including dive bombers, night fighters and troop carriers, were used by the Germans in World War II.

Juno /'dʒuːnəʊ/ in Roman mythology, principal goddess (identified with the Greek Hera). The wife of Jupiter, the queen of heaven, she was concerned with all aspects of women's life.

junta Spanish word meaning a council, and usually applied to the military rulers of a country after an army takeover, as in Turkey in 1980.

Jupiter /'dʒuːpɪtə/ in astronomy, largest planet in the ◊solar system, with a mass over twice that of all the other planets combined. Its equatorial diameter is 142,800 km/88,700 mi, 11 times that of the Earth, and it has 318 times the Earth's mass. Jupiter is largely composed of hydrogen and helium, liquefied by pressure in its interior, and probably with a rocky core larger than the Earth. Its visible surface consists of clouds of white ammonia crystals, drawn out into belts by the planet's high speed of rotation (9 hr 51 min at the equator, the fastest of any planet).

Darker orange and brown clouds are at lower levels and may contain sulphur as well as simple organic compounds. Jupiter is warm inside, a result of heat left over from its formation, which drives the turbulent weather patterns of the planet. The only permanent cloud feature is the great 'red spot', a swirling formation of rising gas 14,000 km/8,500 mi wide and some 30,000 km/20,000 mi long, first observed in 1665. The top of the red spot is higher than the surrounding clouds; its red colour is thought to be due to red phosphorus. Jupiter takes 11.9 years to orbit the Sun, at an average distance of 778 million km/484 million mi. Its strong ◊magnetic field gives rise to a large surrounding magnetic 'shell', or magnetosphere, from which bursts of radio waves are detected. There are 16 known moons. The four largest, ◊Io, ◊Europa, ◊Ganymede and ◊Callisto, are the *Galilean satellites*, discovered in 1610 by Galileo (Ganymede is the largest moon in the solar system). The three most recently discovered moons, all small, were found in 1979 by the ◊Voyager space probes, as was a faint ring of dust around Jupiter's equator, 55,000 km above the cloud tops.

Jupiter A photograph of the largest planet in the solar system. Towards the top left is the great red spot, and above it the shadow of the satellite Ganymede which can be seen top right.

Jupiter /'dʒuːpɪtə/ or *Jove* in mythology, chief god of the Romans, identified with the Greek ◊Zeus. He was god of the sky, associated with lightning and thunderbolt, protector in battle and bestower of victory. He was the son of Saturn, married his sister Juno, and reigned on Olympus as lord of heaven.

Jura /'dʒuərə/ island of the Inner Hebrides: separated from the mainland by the Sound of Jura. The whirlpool Corrievrekin (Gaelic 'Brecan's cauldron') is off the N coast.

Jura mountains /'dʒuərə/ series of parallel mountain ranges running SW–NE along the French-Swiss frontier between the Rhône and the Rhine, a distance of 250 km/156 mi. The highest peak is *Crête de la Neige*, 1,723 m/5,650 ft. The Jura mountains give their name to a *département* of France; and in 1979 a Jura canton was established in Switzerland, formed from the French-speaking areas of Berne, where

a separatist movement, in existence since the 19th century, has grown stronger since 1947.

Jurassic the period of geological time between 195 and about 140 million years ago. It is the middle period of the ◊Mesozoic era, when climates worldwide were equable, dinosaurs roamed the continents, and limestones and iron ores were deposited. The name comes from the Jura mountains in France and Switzerland, where the rocks formed during this period were first studied.

jurisprudence the science of law in the abstract; that is, not the study of any particular laws or legal system, but of the principles upon which legal systems are founded.

jury a body of lay persons sworn to reach a verdict in a court of law. Of generally Germanic origin, the British jury probably derives most directly from the custom of the Franks, introduced into England by the Normans. Under the Plantagenets it developed from a body of neighbours, familiar with the people and background of the case – almost appearing in the character of witnesses – to an impartial panel rendering a verdict based solely on evidence heard in court.

In England jurors are selected from men and women 18–65 on the electoral roll (peers, doctors, MPs, and ministers of religion are exempt; and under the Juries Disqualification Act 1984, anyone who has received a prison sentence in the last ten years or a probation order in the last five years may not serve). They may be challenged (without explanation) by either the prosecution or defence. Their verdict is by majority (10 out of 12 secures a decision). There have been recent unsuccessful attempts to restrict jury trial to serious criminal cases, because of its high cost, and because of the technical complexity of some crimes, for example, fraud.

The basic principles of the British system have been adopted in the US, most Commonwealth countries, and in some European countries, for example France. In the USA the use of a Grand Jury (abolished in England in 1933) has been retained, both at federal and state level: consisting of 23 persons, it hears only evidence for the prosecution to decide on an indictment, that is, whether there is a case to be referred for trial. Hearings are in secret, with the jury's findings presented subsequently to a judge. Immunity is frequently given to witnesses providing evidence which enables a criminal indictment to be made.

justice of the peace in England, an unpaid magistrate appointed by the Lord Chancellor. Two or more sit to dispose of minor charges (formerly their jurisdiction was much wider), to commit more serious ones for trial by a higher court, to grant licences for the sale of intoxicating liquor. In the USA, where they receive fees and are usually elected, their courts are the lowest in the States, and deal only with minor offences, such as traffic violations; they may also conduct marriages.

Justinian I /dʒʌ'stɪnɪən/ 483–562. Byzantine emperor. Born in Illyricum, he was associated with his uncle Justin I in the government from

518. He married the actress Theodora, and succeeded Justin in 527. He recovered North Africa from the Vandals, south east Spain from the Visigoths, and Italy from the Ostrogoths, largely owing to his great general Belisarius. The greater part of his reign was also taken up by an indecisive struggle with the Persians. He built St Sophia at Constantinople, and closed the university at Athens in 529. He ordered the codification of Roman law, which has exercised a great influence on European jurisprudence.

Justin Martyr /'dʒʌstɪn/ c. 100–c. 163. Christian apologist, and a father of the Church. Born in Palestine, he was converted to Christianity at Ephesus, and spent the rest of his life as an itinerant Christian missionary-philosopher. He was martyred in Rome.

Jute /dʒuːt/ member of a Germanic people who originated in Jutland but later settled in Frankish territory. They occupied Kent, England, about 450, according to tradition under Hengist and Horsa, and conquered the Isle of Wight and the opposite coast of Hampshire in the early 6th century.

jute fibre obtained from two plants of the genus *Corchorus – Corchorus capsularis* and *Corchorus olitorius*. Jute is used for sacks and sacking, upholstery, webbing, twine, stage canvas, but in uses such as bulk packaging, and tufted carpet backing, tends to be replaced by synthetic polypropylene. The world's largest producer of jute is Bangladesh.

Jutland /'dʒʌtlənd/ a peninsula of N Europe between the North Sea and the Kattegat. The S belongs to West Germany, while the N part (Danish name ◊Jylland) forms the mainland portion of Denmark.

Jutland, Battle of /'dʒʌtlənd/ naval battle of World War I, fought between England and Germany on 31 May 1916, off the W coast of Jutland. Its outcome was indecisive, but the German fleet remained in port for the rest of the war.

Juvenal /'dʒuːvənl/ c. 60–140 AD. Roman satirist and poet, born probably at Aquinum. His genius for satire brought him to the unfavourable notice of the emperor Domitian. Sixteen of his satires are extant, and they give an explicit and sometimes brutal picture of the decadent Roman society of his time.

juvenile delinquency term for offences against the law committed by young people. The Children and Young Persons Act 1969 introduced in Britain the gradual abolition of the prosecution of children up to the age of 14, and provided three options for Juvenile Courts in respect of all care and criminal proceedings involving children up to the age of 17: binding over of parents, supervision orders, and care orders. Community homes were to have replaced the former approved schools, remand homes and probation hostels. The Criminal Justice Act 1982 introduced new types of short-term youth custody and detention.

Jylland /'juːlæn/ Danish name for the mainland of Denmark, the N section of the ◊Jutland peninsula. The chief towns are Aalborg, Aarhus, Esbjerg, Fredericia, Horsens, Kolding, Randers, and Vejle.

K 11th letter of the Roman alphabet, representing the voiceless velar stop. It is silent before *n* at the beginning of a word (for example, in *knee*), a change accomplished, probably, in the 17th century. K is also the chemical symbol for ◊potassium and the symbol for degrees ◊Kelvin, a scale of temperature.

K2 second highest mountain in the world, 8,611 m/28,250 ft, in the Karakoram range, Kashmir, N India; it is also known as Dapsang (Hidden Peak) and formerly as Mount Godwin-Austen (after the son of a British geologist). It was first climbed in 1954 by an Italian expedition.

Kaaba /'kɑːbə/ (Arabic 'chamber') the oblong building in the quadrangle of the Great Mosque at ◊Mecca, into the NE corner of which is built the black stone declared by Muhammad to have been given to Abraham by Gabriel, and revered by Muslim pilgrims.

Kabardino-Balkar /ˌkæbə,diːnəʊ'bælkə/ autonomous republic of the USSR, capital Nalchik. Area 12,500 sq km/4,825 sq mi; population (1984) 708,000. Under Russian control from 1557, it was annexed in 1827, and became an autonomous republic 1936.

Kabbala /kə'bɑːlə/ ancient esoteric Jewish mystical tradition of philosophy containing strong elements of Pantheism, and akin to Neo-platonism. Among its earliest documents are the *Sefir Jezirah/The Book of Creation*, attributed to Rabbi Akiba (died 120). The *Zohar/Book of Light* was first written in Aramaic about the 13th century, and Kabbalistic writing reached its peak period between the 13th and 16th centuries. It was largely rejected by modern rationalist Judaism as medieval superstition.

Kabinda part of Angola. See ◊Cabinda.

kabuki Japanese 'music-dance-play', popular drama on legendary themes, first developed about 1603 by the shrine maiden Okuni who gave performances with a chiefly female troupe: from 1629 only men were allowed to act, in the interests of 'propriety'. It was influenced by ◊Nō, but in kabuki, though the scripts are ancient, they are of less importance than the staging and the virtuoso ability of the actors. The art has been modernized and its

following revived in the 1980s by Ennosuke III (1940–).

Kabul /'kɑːbʊl/ capital of Afghanistan, 2,100 m/6,900 ft above sea level, on the river Kabul; population (1979) 1,036,400. It commands the strategic routes to Pakistan via the ◊Khyber Pass.

Kabwe /'kɑːbweɪ/ town in central Zambia (formerly Broken Hill); mining industry (copper, cadmium, lead, and zinc); population (1980) 143,635.

Kabyle group of Muslim peoples in N Africa, chiefly Algeria. They formerly served as soldiers in the French forces under the name ◊Zouave.

Kádár /'kɑːdɑː/ János 1912– . Hungarian Communist leader, in power from 1956.
Kádár was a mechanic before joining the outlawed Communist Party and working as an underground resistance organizer in World War II. After the war he was elected to the National Assembly, served as minister for internal affairs (1948–50), and became a prominent member of the Hungarian Workers' Party (HSP). Imprisoned 1951–53 for deviation from Stalinism, Kádár was rehabilitated in 1955, becoming party leader in Budapest, and in Nov 1956, at the height of the Hungarian national rising, he was appointed head of the new Hungarian Socialist Workers' Party (HSWP). With the help of Soviet troops, he suppressed the revolt and served as prime minister 1956–58 and 1961–65.
As HSWP leader and the dominant figure in Hungary, Kádár has introduced a series of market-socialist economic reforms, while retaining cordial political relations with the USSR.

Kaduna /kə'duːnə/ town in Nigeria, on the Kaduna river, a market centre for grain and cotton; industry (textiles, cars, timber, pottery; oil refinery); population (1975) 202,000.

kaffir /'kæfə/ a South African English term for a black person, regarded as offensive by many people. It derives from the former designation of various Bantu-speaking peoples, including the Xhosa and Pondo of Cape Province, living in much of SE Africa.

Kafka /'kæfkə/ Franz 1883–1924. Czech novelist. Born in Prague, he worked for a time in

an insurance office. He wrote in German and is chiefly remembered for his three unfinished, allegorical novels *Der Prozess/The Trial* 1925, *Der Schloss/The Castle* 1926 and *Amerika/America* 1927. His work is marked by themes of oppression. The best known of his short stories is 'Die Verwandlung/The Metamorphosis' 1915, in which a man turns into a beetle.

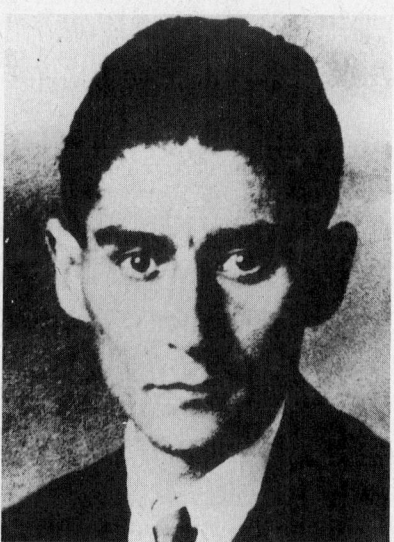

Kafka Czech novelist Franz Kafka wrote complex allegorical novels in German.

Kafue /kə'fuːeɪ/ river in central Zambia, a tributary of the Zambezi: 965 km/600 mi long.

Kafue /kə'fuːeɪ/ town 44 km/27 mi S of Lusaka, centre of Zambia's heavy industry; population (1980) 35,000.

Kagoshima /ˌkægə'ʃiːmə/ industrial city (Satsumayaki porcelain) and port on Kyushu Island, SW Japan; population (1980) 505,000.

kagu crested bird *Rhynochetos jubatus* found in New Caledonia. About 50 cm/1.6 ft long, it is virtually flightless and nests on the ground. Introduced cats and dogs have endangered its survival.

Kahlo /'kɑːləʊ/ Frida 1907–1954. Mexican artist, who mingled Mexican folk art with classical and modern style.

Kahn /kɑːn/ Louis 1901–1974. American architect. A follower of ◊Mies van der Rohe, he developed a romantically classical style, marked by 'service' towers surrounding the main working spaces. His works include the Salk Laboratories, La Jolla, California, and the Palace of Congresses, Venice.

Kaieteur /ˌkaɪə'tʊə/ waterfall on the river Potaro, a tributary of the Essequibo, Guyana. At 250 m/822 ft it is five times as high as Niagara.

Kaifeng /ˌkaɪ'fʌŋ/ former capital of China, 907–1127, and of Honan province; population (1975 est) 600,000. It has lost its importance because of the silting-up of the nearby Huang He river.

Kaikouras /kaɪ'kʊərəz/ double range of mountains in the NE of South Island, New Zealand, separated by the Clarence river, and reaching 2,885 m/9,465 ft.

Kaingaroa /ˌkaɪŋə'rəʊə/ forest NE of Lake Taupo in North Island, New Zealand, one of the world's largest planted forests.

Kairwan /ˌkaɪə'wɑːn/ Muslim holy city in Tunisia, N Africa, S of Tunis; population (1975) 54,546. Kairwan, said to have been founded 617 AD, ranks after Mecca and Medina as a place of pilgrimage.

Kaiser /'kaɪzə/ a title formerly used by the Holy Roman Emperors, Austrian Emperors 1806–1918, and German Emperors 1871–1918. The word, like Tsar, is derived from the Latin *Caesar*.

Kaiser /'kaɪzə/ Georg 1878–1945. German playwright, the principal writer of German ◊Expressionist drama. His large output includes *Die Bürger von Calais/The Burghers of Calais* and *Gas* 1918–20.

Kaiser /'kaɪzə/ Henry J 1882–1967. American industrialist. He built up steel and motor industries, and his shipbuilding firms mass-produced vessels, including the 'Liberty ships' – cheap transport ships – built for the UK in World War II.

Kaiserslautern /ˌkaɪzəz'laʊtən/ town in West Germany, in the Rhineland Palatinate, 48 km/30 mi W of Mannheim; industry (textiles, cars); population (1978) 98,700.

history it dates from 882; the castle from which it got its name was built by Frederick Barbarossa in 1152, destroyed by the French in 1703.

kakapo an almost flightless parrot *Strigops habroptilus* which lives in burrows in New Zealand. Nocturnal, and a dullish green-brown, it is in danger of extinction.

Kalahari Desert /ˌkælə'hɑːri/ semi-desert area forming most of Botswana, but extending into Namibia, Zimbabwe, and South Africa (which has a nuclear site there); area about 900,000 sq km/347,400 sq mi. The only permanent river, the Okavango, flows into a delta in the NW forming marshes rich in wildlife but under threat from drainage. Its inhabitants are the nomadic Bushmen.

Kaldor /'kældɔː/ Nicholas 1908–1986. British economist, born in Hungary, adviser to several Third World governments on economic and tax reform. He was the prime architect of selective employment tax in the first ◊Wilson administration in the UK in the 1960s, and a fierce critic of monetarism. He was made a life peer in 1974.

kale a type of ◊cabbage.

kaleidoscope optical toy invented by the British physicist David Brewster in 1816. In its usual form it consists of a pair of long mirrors at an angle to each other and arranged inside a triangular tube, containing pieces of coloured glass, paper or plastic. An axially symmetrical (hexagonal) pattern is seen by looking along the tube, which can be varied infinitely by rotating or shaking the tube.

Kalevala /ˌkɑːlə'vɑːlə/ Finnish national epic poem compiled from legends and ballads by Elias Lönnrot in 1835; its hero is Väinamöinen, god of music and poetry.

Kalgan /ˌkɑːl'gɑːn/ city in NE China, now known as ◊Zhangjiakou.

Kalgoorlie /kæl'gʊəli/ town in Western Australia, 545 km/340 mi NE of Perth, amalgamated with Boulder in 1966; population (1981) 19,800. Gold has been mined since 1893.

Kali /'kɑːli/ in Hindu mythology, the goddess of destruction and death. She is the wife of ◊Siva.

Kalidāsa /ˌkɑːlɪ'dɑːsə/ lived c. 5th century AD. Indian epic poet and dramatist, who according to tradition served at the court of King Vikramaditya at Ujjain. His works, in Sanskrit, include the classic drama *Sakuntala*, the love story of King Dushyanta for the nymph Sakuntala.

Kalimantan /ˌkælɪ'mæntən/ the province of the republic of Indonesia that occupies part of Borneo

area 543,900 sq km/210,000 sq mi

towns Banjermasin, at the mouth of the Negara river, and Balikpapan, both ports

physical for the most part low-lying, with mountains in the NW rising in Mt Raya to 2,274 m/7,462 ft

products petroleum

population (1980) 6,723,086.

Kalinin /kə'liːnɪn/ city of the USSR, capital of Kalinin region, a transport centre on the Volga, 160 km/100 mi NW of Moscow; population (1985) 438,000. Called Tver until 1933, it was renamed in honour of President Kalinin.

Kalinin /kə'liːnɪn/ Mikhail Ivanovich 1875–1946. Soviet politician, founder of the newspaper *Pravda*. He was prominent in the October Revolution, and in 1919 became head of state (president of the Central Executive Committee of the Soviet government until 1937, then president of the Presidium of the Supreme Soviet until 1946).

Kaliningrad /kə'liːnɪngræd/ Baltic naval base (formerly Königsberg) in USSR; population (1985) 385,000. It was the capital of East Prussia until the latter was divided between the USSR and Poland 1945 under the Potsdam Agreement, when it was renamed in honour of President Kalinin.

Kalmar /'kælmɑː/ port on the SE coast of Sweden; industry (paper, matches, and the Orrefors glassworks); population (1983) 53,516.

Kalmuck /'kælmək/ or *Kalmyk* steppe area of the southern USSR, on the Caspian Sea; area 75,900 sq km/29,300 sq mi; population (1984) 315,000; capital Elista. It was settled by migrants from China in the 17th century, and abolished 1943–57 because of alleged collaboration of the people with the Germans during the siege of Stalingrad.

Kaltenbrunner /'kæltən,brʊnə/ Ernst 1901–1946. Austrian Nazi leader, head of the Security Police (SD) from 1943. He was responsible for the murder of Allied soldiers, and millions of Jews. He was tried at Nuremberg, and hanged.

Kaluga /kə'luːgə/ town in the USSR, on the river Oka, 160 km/100 mi SSW of Moscow, capital of Kaluga region; industry (hydro-electric installations and engineering works, telephone equipment, measuring devices); population (1985) 297,000.

Kamakura /ˌkæmə'kʊərə/ city on Honshu island, Japan; population 175,000. It was the seat of the first shogunate 1192–1333, which established the rule of the samurai class, and the Hachimangu Shrine is dedicated to the gods of war. From the 19th century artists and writers, for example Kawabata, settled here.

Kamanev /'kæmənev/ Lev Borisovich 1883–1936. Russian leader of the Bolshevik movement after 1917 who, with Stalin and Zinoviev, formed a ruling triumvirate in the USSR after Lenin's death in 1924. His alignment with the Trotskyists led to his dismissal from office and from the Communist Party by Stalin in 1926. In 1935 he was arrested, tried for plotting to murder Stalin and given a five-year sentence. Retried in Aug 1936, he confessed to the crime, was condemned and shot.

Kamara'n /ˌkæmə'rɑːn/ island in the Red Sea, formerly belonging to South Yemen, but occupied by North Yemen in 1972; area 180 sq km/70 sq mi. The former RAF station is controlled by the USSR.

Kamchatka /kæm'tʃætkə/ mountainous peninsula separating the Bering Sea and Sea of Okhotsk, forming (together with the Chukchi and Koryak national districts) a region of the USSR. Its capital Petropavlovsk is the only town; agriculture is possible only in the south. Most of the inhabitants are fishers and hunters.

Kamet /'kʌmeɪt/ Himalayan mountain 7,756 m/25,447 ft high on the Tibet–India border. The Britons F S Smythe and Eric Shipton were in the group that made the first ascent in 1931.

kamikaze term applied to the pilots of the Japanese air force in World War II – the name means 'divine wind' – who deliberately crash-dived their planes, loaded with bombs, usually on ships of the US navy.

Kampala /kæm'pɑːlə/ capital of Uganda; population (1980) 458,400. It is linked by rail with Mombasa. Makerere University (1961).

Kamperduin Dutch spelling of ◊Camperdown, village in the Netherlands.

Kampuchea /ˌkæmpu'tʃiːə/ country in SE Asia, bordered N and NW by Thailand, N by Laos, E and SE by Vietnam, and SW by the South China Sea.

government under the 1981 constitution, the sole and supreme legislative body in Kampuchea is the national assembly, whose 117 members are elected for five-year terms by universal suffrage. The assembly elects from within its ranks a smaller, permanent council of state, headed by the state president. In addition, it appoints a council of ministers, headed by a prime minister, to carry out day-to-day government. The dominating force in Kampuchea is the Communist Party (Kampuchean People's Revolutionary Party) supported by the mass organization, the Kampuchean United Front for National Construction and Defence.

history the area now known as Kampuchea was once occupied by the Khmer empire, an ancient civilization which flourished during the 6th–15th centuries. After this the region was ruled by Siam (Thailand), and in 1863 became a French protectorate. During World War II it was occupied by Japan. France regained control of the country, then known as Cambodia, in 1946, but granted it semi-autonomy within the French Union in 1949 and full independence in 1953. Prince Norodom Sihanouk (1922–   ), who had been elected king in 1941, abdicated in favour of his parents and became prime minister as leader of the Popular Socialist Community in 1955. In 1960, when his father died, he became head of state.

Sihanouk remained neutral during the ◊Vietnam War and was overthrown by a right-wing revolt led by pro-US Lt-Gen Lon Nol in 1970. Lon Nol first became prime minister (1971–72) and then president (1972–75) of what was termed the new Khmer Republic. His regime was opposed by the exiled Sihanouk and by the Communist Khmer Rouge (backed by N Vietnam and China) who merged to form the National United Front of Cambodia. A civil war developed and despite substantial military aid from the US during its early stages, Lon Nol's government fell in 1975. The country was renamed Kampuchea, with Prince Sihanouk as head of state.

The Khmer Rouge proceeded to ruthlessly introduce an extreme Communist programme, forcing urban groups into rural areas, which led to over 2,500,000 deaths from famine, disease and maltreatment. In 1976 a new constitution removed Prince Sihanouk from power, appointed Khieu Samphan (the former deputy prime minister) president and placed the Communist Party of Kampuchea, led by ◊Pol Pot, in control. The Khmer Rouge developed close links with China and fell out with its former sponsors Vietnam and the Soviet Union.

In a Vietnamese invasion of Kampuchea launched in 1978, Pol Pot was overthrown and a pro-Vietnamese puppet government was set up under Heng Samrin, head of the newly formed Kampuchean National United Front for National Salvation. The defeated regime kept up guerrilla resistance under Pol Pot, causing over 125,000 Kampuchean refugees to flee to Thailand in 1979.

In 1982 the resistance movement broadened with the formation in Kuala Lumpur (Malaysia) of an anti-Vietnamese coalition and Democratic Kampuchea government-in-exile with Prince Sihanouk (then living in N Korea) as president, Khieu Samphan (political leader of the now less extreme Khmer Rouge) as vice-president, and Sonn Sann (an ex-premier and contemporary leader of the non-communist Khmer People's National Liberation Front) as prime minister. The coalition received sympathetic support from ◊ASEAN countries and China. However, its 60,000 troops were outnumbered by the 170,000 Vietnamese who supported the Heng Samrin government. With the resistance coalition's base-camps being overrun in 1985, a military victory appeared unlikely.

Hopes of a political settlement were improved by the retirement of the reviled Pol Pot as Khmer Rouge military leader in 1985. The Vietnamese say they intend to withdraw their forces by 1990. The position of the Heng Samrin regime has been strengthened by the influx of 500,000 Vietnamese settlers to SE Kampuchea, but it still lacks official UN recognition.

Kampuchea
PEOPLE'S REPUBLIC OF

AREA 181,000 sq km/71,000 sq mi
CAPITAL Phnom Penh
TOWNS Battambang, and the seaport Kompong Som
PHYSICAL mostly forested; flat, with mountains in S; Mekong river runs N–S
FEATURES ruins of ancient capital Angkor
HEAD OF STATE Heng Samrin from 1979
HEAD OF GOVERNMENT Hun Sen from 1985
GOVERNMENT communist
EXPORTS rubber, rice
CURRENCY Kampuchean riel
POPULATION 6,249,000 (1985); annual growth rate 2.8%
LANGUAGE Khmer (official), French
RELIGION Theravada Buddhist
LITERACY 78% male/39% female (1980 est)
GDP $100 per head of population (1984)
CHRONOLOGY
1863–1941 Vietnam became a French protectorate.
1941–45 Occupied by Japan.
1946 Recaptured by France.
1953 Granted full independence.

Kampuchea

1970 Prince Sihanouk overthrown by US-backed Lon Nol.
1975 Lon Nol overthrown by Khmer Rouge.
1978–79 Vietnamese invasion and installation of Heng Samrin government.
1987 Partial withdrawal of Vietnamese troops.

Kandinsky /kæn'dɪnski/ Wassily 1866–1944. Russian ◊Expressionist artist. Born in Moscow, he travelled widely abroad and by 1910 was producing the first abstract or non-objective work. In 1912 he published the influential *Concerning the Spiritual in Art* and was joint-originator with Franz Marcof the ◊*Blaue Reiter* movement 1911–12. For some years he taught at the ◊Bauhaus and, after its closure by the Nazis, settled in Paris. His use of colour, and ordered arrangement of spheres and rectangles, influenced the work of many other artists.

Kandy /'kændi/ town in Sri Lanka, formerly capital of the ancient kingdom of Kandy 1480–1815; population (1985) 140,000. One of its temples contains an alleged tooth of Buddha and is one of the most sacred Buddhist shrines. At Peradenia, 5 km/3 mi away, is the chief campus of the University of Sri Lanka (1942).

kangaroo marsupial mammal of the family

Kanaka /kə'nækə/ Hawaiian word for a person; applied to the indigenous people of the South Sea islands.

Kanazawa /ˌkænə'zɑːwə/ industrial city (textiles and porcelain) on Honshu island, Japan, 160 km/100 mi NNW of Nagoya; population (1983) 412,000.

Kanchenjunga /ˌkæntʃən'dʒʊŋgə/ a variant spelling of ◊Kangchenjunga, a Himalayan mountain.

Kandahar /ˌkændə'hɑː/ city in Afghanistan, 450 km/280 mi SW of Kabul, capital of Kandahar province and a trading centre, with wool and cotton factories; population (1979) 191,300. It is surrounded by a 8 m/25 ft high mud wall. It was the first capital of Afghanistan when it became independent in 1747.

Macropodidae found in Australia, Tasmania and New Guinea. Kangaroos are plant-eaters and highly adapted to hopping, most species having very large back legs and feet compared to the small forelimbs. At speed they hop on the hind limbs, the largest types jumping 9 m/30 ft at a single bound. When moving slowly they may use the tail and front limbs to support the weight while moving the back legs. Species vary from small rat kangaroos, with head and body only 30 cm/1 ft long, through the medium sized wallabies, to the large red and great grey kangaroos which are the largest living marsupials. These may have head and body 1.6 m/5.2 ft long plus 1.1 m/3.5 ft tail. In New Guinea and N Queensland tree kangaroos occur. These climbers have comparatively short hind limbs. The **great grey kangaroo** *Macropus giganteus* produces a single young ('joey') about 2 cm/1 in long after a very short gestation, usually in early summer. It remains in the pouch, with excursions as it matures, for about 280 days.

kangaroo paw bulbous plant *Anigozanthos manglesii*, family Hameodoraceae, with a row of small white flowers emerging from velvety green tubes with red bases; floral emblem of Western Australia.

Kangchenjunga /ˌkæntʃən'dʒuŋgə/ Himalayan mountain on the Nepál–Sikkim border (8,598 m/20,208 ft), 120 km/75 mi SE of Everest: the name means 'five treasure houses of the great snows'. Kangchenjunga was first climbed by a British expedition 1955.

Kano /'kɑːnəu/ capital of Kano state in N Nigeria, trade centre of an irrigated area; population (1975) 399,000. Founded about 1000 BC, Kano is a walled city where goods still arrive by camel train to a market place holding 20,000 people. New Kano extends beyond the walls and products include cycles, glass, furniture, textiles, chemicals.

Kanpur /ˌkɑːn'puə/ Indian city, formerly Cawnpore, on the Ganges, SW of Lucknow, in Uttar Pradesh, capital of Kanpur district; an important commercial and industrial centre (cotton, wool, jute, chemicals, plastics, iron, steel); population (1981) 1,486,522.

Kansas /'kænzəs/ state of central USA; nicknamed Sunflower State
area 213,063 sq km/82,264 sq mi
capital Topeka
towns Kansas City, Wichita, Hutchinson
features rivers Missouri, Kansas, and Arkansas
products wheat, cattle; coal, petroleum, natural gas; aircraft
population (1980) 2,364,236

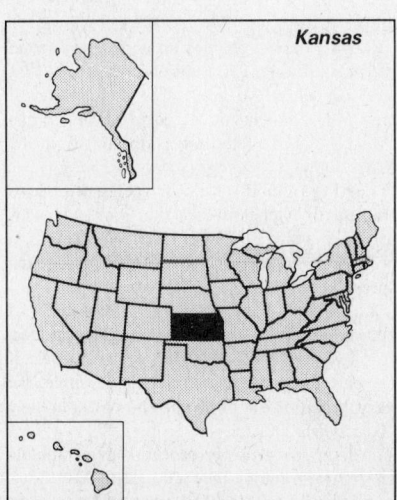

Kansas

Kansas City /'kænzəs/ twin city in the USA at the confluence of the Missouri and Kansas rivers, partly in Kansas and partly in Missouri; a market and agricultural distribution centre and, next to Chicago, the chief livestock centre of the USA. Kansas City, Missouri, has car assembly plants and Kansas City, Kansas, has offices;

population (1980) of Kansas City (Kansas) 161,087, Kansas City (Missouri) 448,159.
history founded c. 1826 by French fur trappers as a trading post. In the 1920s and 1930s Kansas City was run by boss Tom Pendergast, of the Ready-Mix Concrete Company, and in the nightclubs on Twelfth Street under his 'protection' jazz musicians such as Lester Young, Count Basie, and Charlie Parker performed.

Kansu alternative spelling for Chinese province ◊Gansu.

Kant /kænt/ Immanuel 1724–1804. German philosopher. Born at Königsberg, he attended the university there, and in 1770 was appointed professor in logic and metaphysics. Best-known of his works is the *Kritik der reinen Vernunft/Critique of Pure Reason* 1781, which was followed by the *Prolegomena* 1783, *Metaphysik der Sitten/Metaphysic of Ethics* 1785, *Metaphysische Anfangsgründe der Naturwissenschaft/Metaphysic of Nature* 1786, *Kritik der practischen Vernunft/Critique of Practical Reason* 1788 and *Kritik der Urtheilskraft/Critique of Judgment* 1790. Kant argued that our knowledge of the world cannot be the mere aggregate of impressions impinging on our consciousness from our senses (roughly the view of ◊Locke), but that it is dependent upon the conceptual apparatus of the human understanding – which is not itself derived from experience. In ethics, Kant stressed that the right action is objectively determinable and must conform to a moral law he called 'the Categorical Imperative'; feelings and inclinations are not a basis for moral decisions.

Kant An 1812 engraving of the German moral philosopher Immanuel Kant.

Kantorovich /ˌkæntə'rəuvɪtʃ/ Leonid 1912–1986. Russian mathematical economist, whose theory that decentralization of decisions in a planned economy could only be made with a rational price system earned him a Nobel prize in 1975.

Kanu (Kenya African National Union) political party led by Jomo ◊Kenyatta from 1947. It formed his political power base in 1963 when he became prime minister and in 1964 when he

became the first president of Kenya.

Kaohsiung /ˌkau ʃi'uŋ/ city and port on the W coast of Taiwan; industry (aluminium ware, fertilizers, cement, oil refineries, iron and steel works, shipyards, food-processing); population (1984) 1,280,000.
history Kaohsiung began to develop as a commercial port after 1858; its industrial development came about while it was occupied by Japan, 1895–1945.

kaoliang variety of sorghum. See under ◊cereals.

Kapitza /kə'pɪtsə/ Peter 1894–1984. Russian physicist who in 1978 shared a Nobel prize for his work on magnetism and low-temperature physics.

Kaplan /'kæplən/ Viktor 1876–1934. Austrian engineer who invented a water turbine with adjustable rotor blades. In the machine patented in 1920, the rotor was on a vertical shaft and could be adjusted to suit any rate of flow of water. Horizontal Kaplan turbines are used at the installation on the estuary of the river Rance in France, the world's first tidal power station.

kapok silky hairs produced round the seeds of certain trees, particularly the kapok tree *Bombax ceiba* of India and Malaysia, and the silk-cotton tree *Ceiba pentandra*, a native of tropical America. Kapok is used for stuffing cushions, mattresses, and for sound insulation. Oil obtained from the seeds is used in food and soap preparation.

Kara Bogaz Gol /kə'rɑː bə'gæz 'gɒl/ shallow gulf of the Caspian Sea, USSR; area 20,000 sq km/8,000 sq mi. Rich deposits of sodium chloride, sulphates, and other salts formed by evaporation.

Karachi /kə'rɑːtʃi/ chief seaport of Pakistan, in Sind, N of the Indus delta; industry (engineering, chemicals, plastics, textiles); population (1981) 5,208,000. Natural gas is brought to Karachi by pipeline from Sui, 563 km/350 mi to the N, and there is an oil refinery at nearby Korangi. Formerly the capital, 1947–59.

Karafuto /ˌkɑːrə'fuːtəu/ Japanese name for ◊Sakhalin island.

Karaganda /ˌkærəgən'dɑː/ industrial town (coal, copper, tungsten, manganese) in Kazakh republic of USSR, capital of Karaganda region; population (1985) 617,000.

Karaites 8th-century sect of ◊Judaism which denied the authority of rabbinic tradition, recognizing only the authority of the scriptures.

Karajan /'kærəjæn/ Herbert von 1908– . Austrian conductor. He was conductor of the Berlin Philharmonic Orchestra from 1955. He directed the Salzburg Festival from 1964, and became director of the Vienna State Opera (artistic director 1956–64) in 1976. He is particularly associated with the Classical and Romantic repertoire.

Kara-Kalpak /kə'rɑː kæl'pɑːk/ republic of Uzbekistan, USSR
area 158,000 sq km/61,000 sq mi
capital Nukus
towns Munyak
products cotton, rice, wheat, fish
population (1984) 1,044,000

history called after the Kara-Kalpak people whose name means black bonnet. They live south of the Sea of Aral and were conquered by Russia in 1867. An autonomous Kara-Kalpak region was formed in 1926 within Kazakhstan, transferred to the Soviet republic in 1930, made a republic in 1932, and attached to Uzbekistan in 1936.

Karakoram /ˌkærəˈkɔːrəm/ mountain range in central Asia, divided among China, Pakistan, and India. Peaks include K2, Masharbrum, Gasharbrum, and Mustagh Tower. *Ladakh* subsidiary range is in NE Kashmir on the Tibetan border.

Karakoram highway /ˌkærəˈkɔːrəm/ road constructed by China and Pakistan and completed 1978; runs 800 km/500 mi from Havelian (NW of Rawalpindi), via ◊Gilgit in Azad Kashmir and the Khunjerab Pass 4,800 m/16,000 ft, to ◊Kashi in China.

Karakorum /ˌkærəˈkɔːrəm/ ruined capital of ◊Genghis Khan, SW of Ulaan Baataar in Mongolia.

Kara-Kum /kəˈrɑː ˈkuːm/ sandy desert occupying most of ◊Turkmenistan, USSR. Area about 310,800 sq km/120,000 sq mi.

Karamanlis /ˌkærəmænˈliːs/ Constantinos 1907– . Greek politician. A lawyer and an anti-Communist, he was prime minister Oct 1955–Mar 1958; May 1958–Sept 1961; and Nov 1961–June 1963, when he went into self-imposed exile. He was recalled as prime minister on the fall of the regime of the 'colonels' in July 1974, and was president 1980–85.

Kara Sea /ˈkɑːrə/ part of the Arctic Ocean off the N coast of the USSR, bounded to the NW by the island of Novaya Zemlya and to the NE by Severnaya Zemlya. Novy Port on the Gulf of Ob is the chief port, and the Yenisei flows into it.

karate one of the ◊martial arts.

Karbala alternative spelling for ◊Kerbela, holy city in Iraq.

Karelia /kəˈriːliə/ autonomous republic of the NW USSR
area 172,400 sq km/66,500 sq mi
capital Petrozavodsk
towns Vyborg
physical mainly forested; Lake Ladoga
population (1982) 753,000
history under the tsars, political exiles were sent here. The present republic was formed in 1956 from the Karelo-Finnish Soviet Socialist Republic set up in 1940.

Karelian Isthmus /kəˈriːliən ˈɪsməs/ strip of land between Lake Ladoga and the Gulf of Finland, USSR, with Leningrad at the S extremity and Vyborg at the N. Finland ceded it to the USSR 1940–41 and from 1947.

Karen /kəˈren/ a people of the Far East, numbering perhaps 1.5 million in all. Most of them live in E Burma, some across the border in Thailand, some in the Irrawaddy delta. Their language belongs to the Sino-Thai family, and it is believed that they are descended from the Chinese driven south by the Shan people.
The Karen strongly resisted integration in Burma after its independence in 1948, and Kantarawaddy, Bawlake, and Kyebogyi, three divisions of Burma formerly called the Karenni

states, were in 1954 formed into the Kayah state (area about 11,900 sq km/4,600 sq mi) while parts of the districts of Toungoo, Thaton, and Amherst became the Karen state (area 30,000 sq km/11,600 sq mi); both states have a measure of autonomy.

Kariba dam /kəˈriːbə/ concrete dam on the Zambia–Zimbabwe border, about 386 km/240 mi downstream from the Victoria Falls, constructed 1955–60 to supply power to both countries. The dam crosses Kariba Gorge, and the reservoir, Lake Kariba, has fisheries.

Karikal /ˌkærɪˈkɑːl/ small port in India, 250 km/155 mi S of Madras, at the mouth of the right branch of the Cauvery delta. On a tract of land acquired by the French in 1739, it was transferred to India in 1954, confirmed by treaty in 1956. See also ◊Pondicherry.

Karl-Marx-Stadt /ˈkɑːl ˈmɑːks ʃtæt/ town in East Germany, capital of Karl-Marx-Stadt district, on the river Chemnitz, 65 km/40 mi SSE of Leipzig; industrial centre (engineering, textiles, chemicals); population (1982) 318,917. Formerly called Chemnitz, it came within the Soviet zone of occupation after World War II and was renamed in 1953.

Karlovy Vary /ˈkɑːləvi ˈvɑːri/ spa in the Bohemian Forest, Czechoslovakia, famous from the 14th century for its alkaline thermal springs; population (1983) 59,696.

Karlsbad /ˈkɑːlzbæd/ German name of ◊Karlovy Vary.

Karlsruhe /ˈkɑːlzruːə/ industrial town (nuclear research, oil refining) in Baden-Württemberg, West Germany; population (1980) 272,000.

karma (Sanskrit 'fate'). In Hinduism, the sum of a human being's actions, carried forward from one life to the next to result in an improved or worsened fate. Buddhism has a similar belief, except that no permanent personality is envisaged, the karma relating only to the physical and mental elements carried on from birth to birth, until the power holding them together disperses in the attainment of Nirvana.

Karmal /ˈkɑːməl/ Babrak 1929– . Afghani Communist politician, president 1979–86. Karmal was imprisoned for anti-government activity in the early 1950s. He was a member of the government 1957–62 and of the national assembly 1965–72. In 1965 he formed what in 1977 became the banned People's Democratic Party of Afghanistan (PDPA). In Dec 1979 he returned from brief exile in Eastern Europe with Soviet support to overthrow President Hafizullah Amin and was installed as the new head of state. Karmal sought to broaden the appeal of the PDPA but encountered wide resistance from the ◊mujahadeen guerrillas. He was persuaded to step down as president and PDPA leader in May 1986 as the administration's Soviet backers began to search for a compromise settlement with opposition groupings.

Karnak /ˈkɑːnæk/ village of modern Egypt, on the E bank of the Nile, which gives its name to the temple of Ammon (constructed by Seti I and Rameses (I) around which the major part of the city of ◊Thebes was built. An avenue of rams

leads to ◊Luxor.

Karnataka /kəˈnɑːtəkə/ state of SW India (formerly Mysore)
area 191,773 sq km/740,024 sq mi
capital Bangalore
products mainly agricultural, but its minerals include India's only sources of gold and silver
population (1981) 37,000,000
language Kannada
famous people Hyder Ali, Tippoo Sahib.

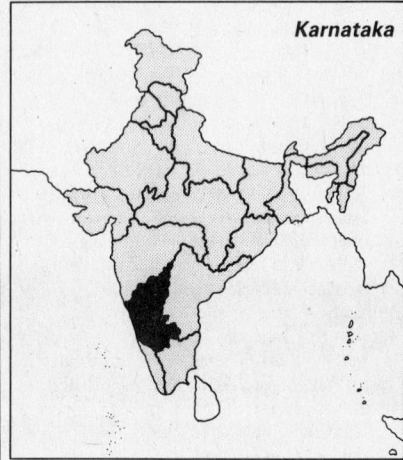

Karnataka

karri giant eucalyptus tree *Eucalyptus diversifolia* which grows in the extreme SW of Western Australia. It may reach over 120 m/400 ft. Exceptionally strong, the timber is used for girders.

Karroo /kəˈruː/ two areas of semi-desert in Cape Province, South Africa, divided into the Great Karroo and Little Karroo by the Swartberg mountains. The two Karroos together have an area of about 260,000 sq km/100,000 sq mi.

karst /kɑːst/ a barren limestone landscape in which all drainage is underground. Rocks that were originally flat are carved and weathered into gullies called grikes and pinnacles or ribs called clints. The feature gets its name from the Karst region in W Yugoslavia.

karting miniature motor racing with low-framed, light chassis cars (karts or go-karts), originating in the USA c. 1955. With standard production two-stroke engines, karts reach speeds of approximately 240 km/150 mph.

karyotype in biology, the set of ◊chromosomes characteristic of a given species. It is described by the number, shape and size of the chromosomes. In humans for example, the karyotype consists of 46 chromosomes, in mice 40, crayfish 200, and in fruit flies 8.
The diagrammatic representation of a complete chromosome set is called a karyogram.

Kasai /kɑːˈsaɪ/ river that rises in Angola and forms the frontier with Zaïre before entering Zaïre and joining the Zaïre river, of which it is the chief tributary. It is rich in alluvial diamonds. Length 2,100 km/1,300 mi.

Kashgar /ˌkæʃˈgɑː/ former name of ◊Kashi in China.

Kashi /ˌkɑːˈʃiː/ oasis town (formerly Kashgar) in Xinjiang Uyghur autonomous

karyotype

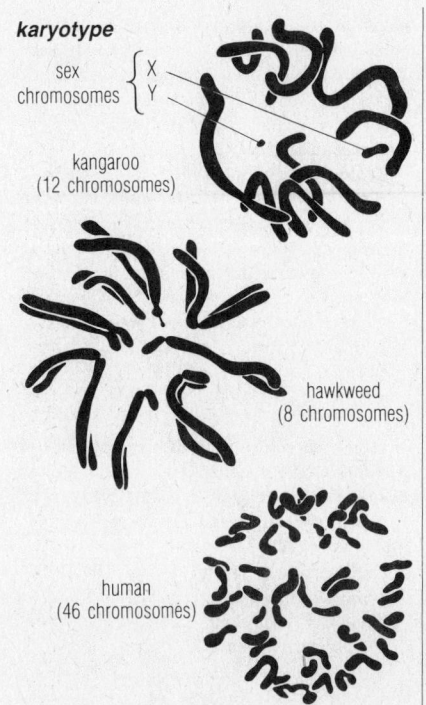

sex chromosomes { X Y }

kangaroo
(12 chromosomes)

hawkweed
(8 chromosomes)

human
(46 chromosomes)

region, China, on the Kaxgar He, capital of Kashi district which adjoins the Kirghiz and Tadzik republics, Afghanistan and Kashmir; population (1973) 180,000. It is a trading centre, the Chinese terminus of the ◊Karakoram Highway, and a focus of Muslim culture.

Kashmir /kæʃ'mɪə/ former Muslim state of North British India, ruled by a Hindu maharajah, the latter acceding to the Republic of India in 1947. There was fighting between pro-India and pro-Pakistan factions, and open war between the two countries 1965–66, and 1971. A plebiscite decreed by the United Nations in 1949 for the state has never been held, and it remains divided: the north west is occupied by Pakistan, and the rest by India.

Kashmir /kæʃ'mɪə/ Azad ('Free'). Pakistan-occupied area in the NW of the former state of ◊Kashmir
population 1,500,000
administrative headquarters Muzaffarabad
features W Himalayan peak Nanga Parbat 8,126 m/26,660 ft. See also ◊Northern Areas.

Kassel /'kæsəl/ industrial town (engineering, chemicals, electronics) in Hessen, West Germany; population (1984) 186,100. There is the Wilhelmshöhe mountain park, and the ◊Grimm Museum commemorates the folklorists.

Kassem /kæ'sem/ Abdul Karim 1914–1963. Iraqi politician. He became prime minister of the republic in 1958, adopting a pro-Soviet policy. He pardoned the leaders of the pro-Egyptian party who tried to assassinate him in 1959, but was executed after the 1963 coup.

Katanga /kə'tæŋgə/ former name of the ◊Shaba region in Zaïre.

Kathiawar /ˌkætiə'wɑː/ peninsula on the W coast of India. Formerly occupied by a number of princely states, all Kathiawar (60,723 sq km/23,445 sq mi) had been included in Bombay state by 1956, but was transferred to Gujarat in 1960. Mahatma Gandhi was born in Kathiawar at Porbandar.

Katmai /'kætmaɪ/ active volcano in Alaska, USA, 2,046 m/6,715 ft. Its eruption in 1912 created the Valley of Ten Thousand Smokes.

Katmandu /ˌkætmən'duː/ capital of the Himalayan state of Nepál; population (1981) 393,500. Founded in the 8th century, it has the restored royal palace, Buddhist shrines, and many monasteries.

Katowice /ˌkætəʊ'viːtseɪ/ industrial city (anthracite and iron mining, iron foundries, smelting works, machine shops) in S Poland; population (1981) 366,000.

Kattegat /'kætɪgæt/ sea passage between Denmark and Sweden. It is about 240 km/150 mi long and 135 km/85 mi wide at its broadest.

Katyn Forest /kæ'tɪn/ forest near ◊Smolensk, USSR, where 4,500 Polish officer prisoners of war (captured in the German-Soviet partition of Poland in 1940) were shot; 10,000 others were killed elsewhere. The crime was disclosed by the Germans 1943, and attributed to the Soviet secret police; the Russians attribute it to the Germans.

Katz /kæts/ Bernard 1911– . British biophysicist. In 1970 he shared a Nobel prize with Ulf von Euler of Stockholm and Julius Axelrod of Maryland for work on the biochemistry of the transmission and control of signals in the nervous system, vital in the search for remedies for nervous and mental disorders.

Kauffmann /'kaʊfmən/ Angelica 1741–1807. Swiss artist. Born in Grisons, she lived in Italy until 1765 and in England 1765–81, where her Neo-Classical paintings became popular. She became one of the first Royal Academicians in 1796 and returned to Rome in 1781.

Kaunas /'kaʊnəs/ industrial river port (Russian *Kovno*) (textiles, chemicals, agricultural machinery) in the Lithuanian republic of the USSR, on the Niemen river; population (1985) 405,000. Capital of independent Lithuania 1910–40.

Kaunda /kɑː'ʊndə/ Kenneth David 1924– . Zambian politician. Imprisoned in 1958 as founder of the Zambia African National Congress (released 1960), he became in 1964 first prime minister of North Rhodesia, then first president of Zambia. From 1973 he introduced one-party rule.

kauri pine New Zealand timber conifer *Agathis australis*, family Araucariaceae, whose fossilized gum deposits are especially valued in varnishes; the wood is used for carving and handicrafts.

Kautsky /'kaʊtski/ Karl 1854–1938. German socialist theoretician, who opposed the reformist ideas of Edouard ◊Bernstein from within the Social Democrat Party. In spite of his Marxist ideas he remained in the party and did not join its left wing in affiliating to the Third International and forming the German Communist Party (KPD).

Kaunda Zambian president Kenneth Kaunda.

kava non-alcoholic, intoxicating beverage prepared from the roots or leaves of a variety of pepper plant, *Piper methysticum*, in the S Pacific islands.

Kawabata /ˌkaʊə'bɑːtə/ Yasunari 1899–1972. Japanese novelist, author of *Snow Country* 1947 and *A Thousand Cranes* 1952. Nobel Prize for Literature 1968.

Kawasaki /ˌkaʊə'sɑːki/ industrial city (iron and steel, chemicals, textiles) on Honshu island, Japan; population (1980) 1,041,000.

Kay /keɪ/ John 1704–c. 1764. British inventor who developed the flying-shuttle, a machine to speed up the work of hand-loom weaving. In 1733 he patented his invention but was ruined by the litigation necessary to defend his patent. In 1753 his house at Bury was wrecked by a mob, who feared the use of machinery would cause unemployment. He is believed to have died in poverty in France.

Kayah State division of Burma; see ◊Karen.

kayak long light sealskin-covered boat used by Inuit fishermen and sealers.

Kaye /keɪ/ Danny. Stage-name of Daniel Kominski 1913–1987. American film and stage comedian, born in Brooklyn, New York. He appeared in many films, including *Wonder Man* 1944, *The Secret Life of Walter Mitty* 1946, and *Hans Christian Andersen* 1952.

Kazakhstan /ˌkæzæk'stɑːn/ constituent republic of the USSR from 1936, part of Soviet Central Asia
area 2,717,300 sq km/1,049,150 sq mi
capital Alma-Ata
towns Karaganda, Semipalatinsk, Petropavlovsk
physical largest republic in the USSR; Caspian and Aral seas, Lake Balkhash; Steppe region
features it includes the Baikonour Cosmodrome (official name for the Soviet space launch site at Tyuratam, near the coalmining town of Baikonour), and a weapons-testing area near the Chinese border

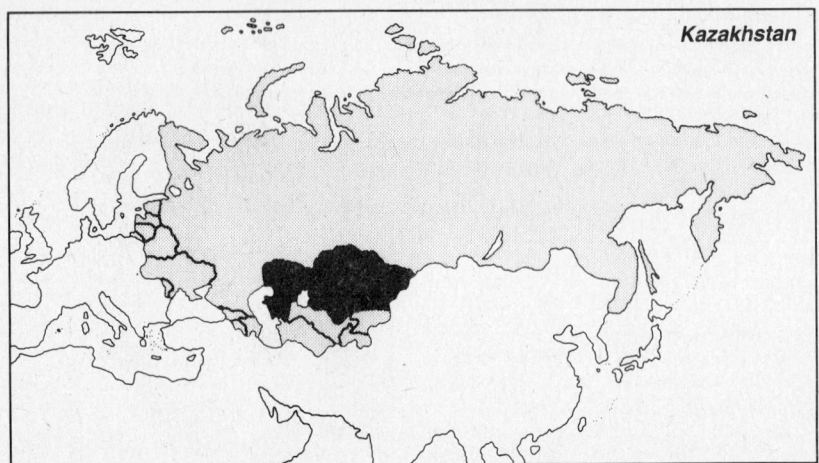

Kazakhstan

products second only to Ukraine as a grain producer; copper, lead, zinc, manganese, coal and oil
population (1982 est) 15,262,000, Russian 42%, Kazakh 33% (see ◊Kirghizia), Ukrainian 7%
language Russian, Kazakh, related to Turkish
religion Sunni Muslim.

Kazan /kə'zæn/ capital of the Tatar Republic, USSR; a transport, commercial and industrial centre (engineering, oil refining, petrochemical, textiles, large fur trade); population (1985) 1,047,000. There is a university (1804).
history Kazan was until 1552 capital of a Tatar khanate, which was conquered by Tsar Ivan IV. The 'Black Virgin of Kazan', an icon so called because blackened with age, was removed to Moscow (1612–1917), where the great Kazan Cathedral was built to house it in 1631; it is now in the USA. Among miracles attributed to its presence were the defeat of Poland (1612) and of Napoleon (1812) at Moscow.

Kazan /kə'zæn/ Elia 1909– . American stage and film director, who established his reputation by his stage direction of *Skin of Our Teeth* 1942, *A Streetcar Named Desire* 1947, and *Death of a Salesman* 1949. He helped to found the ◊Actor's Studio. His films include *On the Waterfront* 1954, *East of Eden* 1954, and *The Visitors* 1972.

Kazantzakis /ˌkæzænd'zɑːkɪs/ Nikos 1885–1957. Greek writer of poems, for example, *I Odysseia/The Odyssey* 1938, which continues Homer's *Odyssey*, and novels, for example, *Zorba the Greek* 1946.

kea a hawk-like greenish parrot *Nestor notabilis* found in New Zealand, which sometimes strikes the back of sheep, eating the fat round their kidneys. The Maori name imitates its cry.

Kean /kiːn/ Edmund 1787–1833. British tragic actor, noted for his portrayal of villainy in Shakespearean roles.

Keaton /'kiːtn/ Buster. Stage-name of American comedian Joseph Frank Keaton 1896–1966. A sophisticated, deadpan actor, he began his screen career after World War I as stooge to 'Fatty' Arbuckle in the Keystone Kops comedies, and became one of the great silent-film comedians; his films include *The General* 1926 and *The Cameraman* 1928.

Keats /kiːts/ John 1795–1821. British poet, a leading figure of the Romantic movement. Born in London, he studied at Guy's Hospital 1815–17, but then abandoned medicine for

Keaton The American comedy star Buster Keaton in a scene from *The General*.

poetry, publishing his first volume in 1817, and *Endymion* in 1818. The latter was harshly reviewed by the Tory *Blackwood's Magazine* and the *Quarterly*, largely owing to Keats' friendship with the Radical, Leigh ◊Hunt. In 1818 he wrote *Isabella*, and the first version of *Hyperion*; took a walking tour in Scotland which increased his tubercular tendency; and nursed his brother Tom, who died of the same disease. To 1819 belong 'The Eve of St Agnes', 'The Eve of St Mark', his 'Odes' ('To Autumn', 'On a Grecian Urn', 'To a Nightingale'), 'Lamia', and the new version of *Hyperion*. In this year also he fell in love with Fanny Brawne. In 1820 he published a final volume of poems, and in Sept sailed for Italy in an effort to recover his health. He died in Rome. Valuable insight into Keats's poetic development is provided by his *Letters*, published in 1848.

Keble /'kiːbəl/ John 1792–1866. Anglican cleric and religious poet. He was professor of poetry at Oxford, 1831–41; and his sermon on the decline of religious faith in Britain, preached in 1833, is taken as the beginning of the ◊Oxford Movement, a Catholic revival in the Church of England. Keble College, Oxford, was founded in 1870 in his memory.

Kedah /'kedə/ state in Malaysia
area 9,480 sq km/3,660 sq mi
capital Alor Star
products rice, rubber, tapioca, tin, tungsten
population (1980) 1,102,200
history Kedah was transferred by Thailand to Britain in 1909, and was one of the Unfederated Malay States till 1948.

Keeling Islands /'kiːlɪŋ/ another name for the ◊Cocos islands, an Australian territory.

Keelung /ˌkiː'lʊŋ/ industrial port (shipbuilding, chemicals, fertilizer) on the N coast of Taiwan, 24 km/15 mi NE of Taipei; population (1985) 351,904.

Keeper of the Great Seal an officer who had charge of the Great Seal of England (the official seal authenticating state documents). During the Middle Ages the great seal was entrusted to the Chancellor. Later a special Lord Keeper was appointed to take charge of it, but since 1761 the posts of Chancellor and Keeper have been combined.

Keewatin /kiː'weɪtɪn/ eastern district of Northwest Territories, Canada, including the islands in Hudson and James Bays

Keats The Romantic poet John Keats.

area 590,935 sq km/228,160 sq mi
towns (trading posts) Chesterfield Inlet, Eskimo Point, and Coral Harbour, the last with an air base set up during World War II
physical the N is an upland plateau, the S low and level, covering the greater part of the Barren Grounds (Arctic prairies) of Canada; there are a number of lakes
products trapping for furs is the main occupation
history Keewatin District was formed in 1876, under the administration of Manitoba; it was transferred to Northwest Territories in 1905, and in 1912 lost land S of 60 degrees N to Manitoba and Ontario.

Kefallinia /ˌkefəliˈniːə/ largest of the Ionian Islands (formerly Cephalonia), off the W coast of Greece; area 935 sq km/360 sq mi; population (1981) 31,300. It was devastated by an earthquake in 1953 which destroyed the capital Argostolion.

Keflavik /ˈkepləvɪk/ fishing port in Iceland, 35 km/22 mi SW of Reykjavik, with a large international airport; population (1978) 6,500. The airport was built during World War II by US forces (who called it Meeks Field). Keflavik became a NATO base in 1951.

Keighley /ˈkiːθli/ industrial (wool, engineering) town in W Yorkshire, England; population (1981) 57,800. Haworth, home of the Brontë family of writers, is now part of Keighley.

Keitel /ˈkaɪtl/ Wilhelm 1882–1946. German field marshal, chief of the supreme command from 1938, who signed the unconditional surrender at Berlin 8 May 1945. Tried at ◊Nuremberg, he was hanged.

Kekulé /ˈkekjʊleɪ/ Freidrich August 1829–1896. German chemist, whose theory (1858) of molecular structure revolutionized organic chemistry. He proposed two resonant forms of the ◊benzene ring.

Kelantan /keˈlæntən/ state of Malaysia

area 14,882 sq km/5,746 sq mi
capital Kota Bharu
products rice, rubber, copra, tin, manganese, gold
population (1980) 877,575
history Kelantan was transferred by Siam to Britain in 1909, and until 1948 was one of the Unfederated Malay States.

Keller /ˈkelə/ Helen (Adams) 1880–1968. American author. Born in Alabama, she became blind and deaf through an illness when 19 months old. Only the tuition of Anne Sullivan Macy enabled her to speak. She graduated from Radcliffe College in 1904 and published several books including *The Story of My Life* 1902.

Kellogg-Briand pact an agreement between the USA and France 1927 to renounce war and seek settlement of disputes by peaceful means. It took its name from the US secretary of state Frank B Kellogg (1856–1937) and the French foreign minister Aristide Briand (1862–1932). Other powers signed in Aug 1928, making a total of 67 signatories. The pact made no provision for measures against aggressors and became ineffective in the 1930s.

Kells /kelz/ Book of. An 8th-century illuminated manuscript of the gospels. See under ◊Dublin.

Kelly /ˈkeli/ Edward 'Ned' 1854–1880. Australian bushranger. The son of an Irish convict, he wounded a constable in 1878 while resisting the arrest of his brother Daniel for horse-stealing. The two brothers escaped and with two confederates carried out bank-robberies on the Victoria–New South Wales border. In 1880 he was captured and hanged.

Kelly /ˈkeli/ Grace (Patricia) 1928–1982. American film actress and later Princess of Monaco. Born in Philadelphia, she made her film début in 1951 in *Fourteen Hours*, and later starred in *High Noon* 1952, *The Country Girl* 1954 for which she received an Academy Award, and *High Society* 1955. In 1956 she married Prince Rainier of ◊Monaco.

kelp collective name for large sea-weeds, particularly the Fucaceae and Laminariaceae. The brown kelp *Macrocystis pyrifera*, abundant in Antarctic and sub-Antarctic waters, is one of the fastest growing organisms known, reaching 100 m/320 ft. It is farmed for the alginate industry, rapid surface growth allowing cropping several times a year, but is an alien pest in European waters.
Kelp is also a term for the powdery ash of burned seaweeds, a source of iodine.

Kelvin /ˈkelvɪn/ William Thomson, 1st Baron Kelvin 1824–1907. British physicist, who pioneered the absolute scale of temperature. His work on the conservation of energy 1851 led to the second law of ◊thermodynamics. Popularly known for his contributions to telegraphy, he developed stranded cables and sensitive receivers, greatly improving transatlantic communications. Maritime endeavours led to a tide gauge and predictor, an improved compass, and simpler methods for fixing a ship's position at sea. He was president of the Royal Society 1890–95.

Kelvin British physicist William Kelvin pioneered the Kelvin scale of temperature used by scientists.

Kelvin scale of temperature (used by scientists) begins at ◊absolute zero (–273°C) but increases in the same way as the Celsius scale, that is, 0°C becomes 273°K and 100°C becomes 373°K.

Kemal Atatürk Mustafa. Turkish politician; see ◊Atatürk.

Kemble /ˈkembəl/ Charles 1775–1854. British actor-manager, younger brother of Philip ◊Kemble, whose greatest successes were in romantic roles with his daughter Fanny ◊Kemble.

Kemble /ˈkembəl/ Frances Anne ('Fanny') 1809–1893. British actress, daughter of Charles ◊Kemble. She first appeared as Shakespeare's Juliet in 1829.

Kemble /ˈkembəl/ (John) Philip 1757–1823. British actor-manager, second of the 12 children of strolling player Roger Kemble, who also included Charles ◊Kemble and Mrs ◊Siddons. He was famous for tragic roles, especially Shakespeare, including Hamlet and Coriolanus. He was manager of Drury Lane, London 1788–1803, and Covent Garden 1803–17, and introduced a number of innovations in theatrical management, costume and scenery.

Kemerovo /ˈkemɪrəʊvəʊ/ coalmining town in the USSR, in W Siberia and centre of Kuznetz coal basin; it has chemical and metallurgical industries; population (1985) 507,000.

Kempe /kemp/ Margery c. 1373–c. 1439. English Christian mystic. She was converted to the religious life after a period of mental derangement, travelled widely as a pilgrim, and in the 1420s dictated her *Boke of Margery Kempe*, describing her life and experiences, both religious and worldly. It has been called the first autobiography in English.

Kempe /ˈkempə/ Rudolf 1910–1976. German conductor. Noted for the clarity and fidelity of his interpretations, especially of Richard Strauss and Wagner's *Ring* cycle, he conducted the Royal Philharmonic Orchestra from 1961 and was musical director of the Munich Philharmonic from 1967.

Kempis Thomas à. Medieval German monk and religious writer; see ◊Thomas à Kempis.

kendo Japanese martial art, in which combatants fence with bamboo replicas of samurai swords. Masks and padding are worn.

Keneally /kɪ'niːli/ Thomas Michael 1935– . Australian novelist, who won the ◊Booker Prize with *Schindler's Ark* 1982, a novel based on the true account of Polish Jews saved from the gas chambers in World War II by a German industrialist.

Kenilworth /'kenlwɜːθ/ castle and small town in Warwickshire, England. The Norman castle became a royal residence and was enlarged by John of ◊Gaunt and later by the Earl of ◊Leicester, who lavishly entertained Elizabeth I here in 1575. It was dismantled after the Civil War; the ruins were given to the British nation by the 1st Lord Kenilworth in 1937.

Kennedy /'kenədi/ Edward (Moore) 1932– . US Democrat politician. He aided his brothers John and Robert ◊Kennedy in the presidential campaign of 1960, and entered politics as a senator from Massachusetts in 1962. He failed to gain the presidential nomination in 1980, largely because of feeling about his delay in reporting a car crash at Chappaquiddick Island, near Cape Cod, in 1969, in which his passenger, Mary Jo Kopechne, was drowned.

Kennedy /'kenədi/ John Fitzgerald 1917–1963. 35th President of the USA. Son of Joseph Kennedy, he was born at Brookline, Massachusetts, and served in the navy in the Pacific during World War II. In 1960 he defeated ◊Nixon for the presidency, the first Roman Catholic and the youngest man to be elected, he brought academics and intellectuals to Washington as advisers. In foreign policy he carried through the unsuccessful Bay of Pigs invasion of Cuba, and in 1963 secured the withdrawal of Soviet missiles from the island. His programme for reforms at home, called the New Frontier, was posthumously executed by Lyndon ◊Johnson. He married *Jacqueline Lee Bouvier* (1929–) in 1953. Kennedy was assassinated on a visit to Dallas 22 Nov 1963 by Lee Harvey Oswald, who was in turn shot dead by Jack Ruby.

Kennedy /'kenədi/ Joseph Patrick 1888–1969. American industrialist and diplomat; US ambassador to Great Britain 1937–40. A self-made millionaire, he groomed his four sons from an early age for careers in politics. Joseph Kennedy Junior (1915–44) was killed in action with the naval air force in World War II. His younger sons were John ◊Kennedy, Robert ◊Kennedy, and Edward ◊Kennedy.

Kennedy /'kenədi/ Robert Francis 1925–1968. US politician, younger brother of John F Kennedy. He was campaign manager for his brother in 1961, and as Attorney-General 1961–64 pursued a 'racket-busting' policy and promoted the Civil Rights Act of 1964. When Johnson preferred Hubert H Humphrey for the 1964 Vice-President nomination, Kennedy resigned and was elected Senator for New York. In 1968 he campaigned for the presidential

Kennedy President Kennedy at a press conference in 1962.

nomination, but was assassinated by Sirhan Bissara Sirhan, a Jordanian Arab.

Kennedy Space Center the ◊NASA installation at ◊Cape Canaveral, Florida. Headquarters of the Center are on Merritt Island. ◊Apollo spacecraft and the ◊Space Shuttle have been launched from here. The Center is dominated by the Vehicle Assembly Building, 160 m/525 ft tall, used for assembly of ◊Saturn rockets and space shuttles.

Kennelly /'kenəli/ Arthur Edwin 1861–1939. American engineer, who gave his name to the ◊Kennelly-Heaviside layer of the ◊ionosphere. An assistant of ◊Edison and later professor at Harvard, he verified the existence of an ionized layer in the upper atmosphere in 1902, shortly before it had been predicted by ◊Heaviside.

Kennelly-Heaviside layer /'kenəli 'hevɪsaɪd/ the lower regions of the ◊ionosphere which refract radio waves allowing their reception round the surface of the Earth. The Kennelly-Heaviside layer approaches the Earth by day, and recedes from it at night.

Kenneth I /'kenɪθ/ Kenneth McAlpin king of Scotland, died 858. Traditionally, he is regarded as the founder of the Scottish kingdom by virtue of his final defeat of the Picts about 844, after which he reigned until his death.

Kensington and Chelsea /'kenzɪŋtən, 'tʃelsi/ Borough of Greater London
features Kensington Gardens; museums – Victoria and Albert, Natural History, Science; Imperial College of Science and Technology 1907; Commonwealth Institute; Kensington Palace; Holland House
population (1986) 137,600.

Kent /kent/ county in SE England, the 'garden of England'
area 3,731 sq km/1,440 sq mi
towns administrative headquarters Maidstone; Canterbury, Chatham, Rochester, Tunbridge Wells; resorts Folkestone, Margate, Ramsgate
features traditionally, a 'man of Kent' comes from E of the Medway and a 'Kentish man' from W Kent; New Ash Green, a new town; Romney

Marsh; the Isles of Grain, Sheppey (on which is the resort of Sheerness, formerly a royal dockyard) and Thanet; Weald (agricultural area); rivers Darent, Medway, Stour; Leeds Castle (converted to a palace by Henry VIII), Hever Castle (where Henry VIII courted Anne Boleyn), Chartwell (Churchill's country home), Knole, Sissinghurst Castle and gardens
products hops, apples, soft fruit (on the weald); sheep (on Romney Marsh); coal, cement, paper
population (1986) 1,495,200
famous people Charles Dickens, Christopher Marlowe.

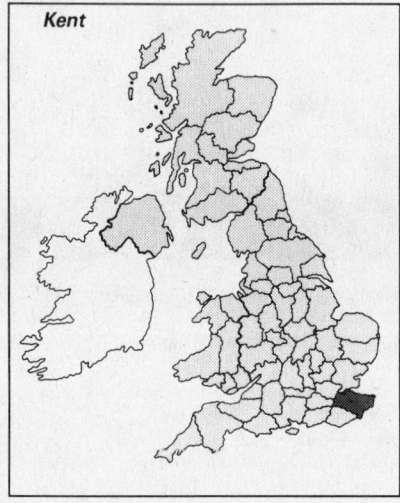

Kent

Kent /kent/ Bruce, Monsignor 1929– . English Catholic priest and peace campaigner who acted as general secretary for the Campaign for Nuclear Disarmament (CND) 1980–85.

Kent /kent/ Edward George Alexander Edmund, 2nd Duke of Kent 1935– . British prince, grandson of George V. His father, George (1902–42), was created Duke of Kent just before his marriage in 1934 to Princess Marina of Denmark and Greece (1906–68). The second duke, who succeeded when his father was killed in an air crash on active service with the RAF, was educated at Eton and Sandhurst, and then commissioned in the Royal Scots Greys. In 1961 he married Katharine Worsley (1933–) and his heir is George (1962–), earl of St Andrews. His brother, Prince Michael (1942–) became an officer with the Hussars in 1962. His sister, Princess Alexandra (1936–), married in 1963 Angus Ogilvy, son of the 12th earl of Airlie; they have two children, James (1964–) and Marina (1966–).

Kent /kent/ William 1685–1748. British architect, interior decorator, and landscape gardener. In architecture he played a leading part in introducing the Palladian style into Britain from Italy. As a gardener, he freed garden design from its earlier formalism; Horace Walpole called him 'the father of modern gardening'.

Kent and Strathearn /stræθ'ɜːn/ Edward Augustus, Duke of Kent and Strathearn 1767–1820. British general. The fourth son of

George III, he married Victoria Mary Louisa 1786–1861, widow of the Prince of Leiningen, in 1818, by whom he had one child, the future Queen Victoria.

Kent William Kent, the British landscape gardener and architect. His portrait is by B Dandridge.

Kentigern, St /'kentɪgən/ c. 518–603. Also called 'Mungo', a nickname meaning 'dear friend'. First bishop of Glasgow, he was born at Culross. Anti-Christian factions forced him to flee to Wales, where he founded the monastery of St Asaph. In 573 he returned to Glasgow and founded the cathedral there.

Kenton /'kentən/ Stan 1912–1979. US exponent of progressive jazz, who broke into West Coast jazz in 1941 with his 'wall of brass' sound; helped introduce Afro-Cuban rhythms to US jazz; and combined jazz and classical music in, for example, *Artistry in Rhythm* 1943.

Kentucky /ken'tʌki/ border state of the USA; nicknamed Blue Grass State
area 104,623 sq km/40,395 sq mi
capital Frankfort
towns Louisville, Lexington-Fayette
features horse racing at Louisville (Kentucky Derby); Mammoth Cave National Park (main cave 6.5 km long/4 mi long, up to 38 m/125 ft high, where Indian councils once held); President Lincoln's birthplace at Hodgenville; Fort Knox, US Gold Bullion Depository
products tobacco, cereals, steel goods, textiles, transport vehicles
population (1980) 3,660,777
famous people Kit Carson, Henry Clay, Jefferson Davis
history originally part of Virginia, Kentucky was first permanently settled after Daniel Boone had blazed his Wilderness Trail, and became a state in 1792.

Kenya /'kenjə/ country in E Africa, bordered N by the Sudan and Ethiopia, E by the Somali

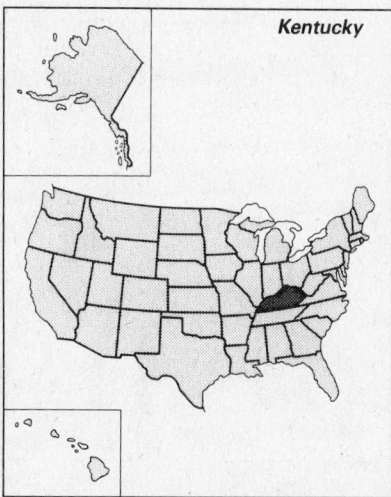

Kentucky

Republic, SE by the Indian Ocean, SW by Tanzania, and W by Uganda.
government the 1963 constitution, amended 1964, 1969 and 1982, provides for a president, elected by universal suffrage for a five-year term, and a single-chamber national assembly, serving a similar term. The assembly has 172 members, 158 elected by universal suffrage, 12 nominated by the president, and the attorney-general and speaker as 'ex officio' members. From 1969–82 Kenya was a one-party state in fact and since then it has become one in law, the only legitimate party being the Kenya African National Union (KANU), whose leader is the state president.
history archeological evidence shows that the area now known as Kenya was first inhabited about 2,000,000 years ago. During the 8th century the coast was settled by Arabs, and from the 15th–18th centuries the region was under Portuguese rule.
Kenya was a British colony 1895–1964, when it achieved full independence within the Commonwealth. There was near civil war during the 20 years before independence, as pro-nationalist groups carried out a campaign of violence. The Kenya African Union (KAU) was founded in 1944 and in 1947 Jomo ◊Kenyatta, a member of Kenya's largest ethnic group, the Kikuyu, became its president. Three years later a secret society of young Kikuyu militants was formed, called Mau Mau, which had the same aims as KAU but sought to achieve them by violent means. Although Kenyatta dissociated himself from Mau Mau, the British authorities distrusted him and imprisoned him in 1953. By 1956 the guerrilla campaign had largely ended, the state of emergency was lifted and Kenyatta was released.
Kenya was granted internal self-government in 1963 and Kenyatta, who had become leader of the Kenya African National Union (KANU), became prime minister and then president after full independence in 1964. Kenyatta continued as president until his death in 1978, during which time the country achieved considerable stability.

He was succeeded by Vice-President Daniel arap Moi.
An attempted coup by junior air force officers in 1982 was foiled and resulted in political detentions and press censorship. The air force and Nairobi University were temporarily dissolved. In the same year the national assembly declared Kenya a one-party state. President Moi was re-elected in 1983 and has had some success in tackling corruption and inefficiency in the public services and, externally, has re-established good relations with most of his E African neighbours.

Kenya, Mount /'kenjə/ extinct volcano from which Kenya takes its name, 5200 m/17,058 ft; it was first climbed by Sir Halford Mackinder in 1899.

Kenyatta /ken'jætə/ Jomo c. 1889–1978. Name assumed by Kenya politician Kamau Ngengi, *kenyatta* meaning 'beaded belt'. A member of the Kikuyu tribe, he joined the Kikuyu Central Association, devoted to recovery of Kikuyu lands from white settlers, of which he became president. He spent some years in Britain, and returning to Kenya in 1946 as president of the Kenya African Union (successor to the banned KCA), he was in 1953 sentenced to seven years' imprisonment for his management of ◊Mau Mau, though some doubt has been cast on his complicity. Released to exile in N Kenya in 1958, he was allowed to return to Kikuyuland in 1961 and in 1963 became prime minister (also president from 1964) of independent Kenya. His policy was summarized by his slogans 'Uhuru na Moja' (Freedom and Unity) and 'Harambee' (Let's get going), and entailed collaboration with the white population of Kenya to ensure unbroken economic progress.

Kenyatta The first president of independent Kenya, Jomo Kenyatta. His slogan was 'Harambee' (Let's get going).

Kenyon /'kenjən/ Kathleen 1906–1978. British archaeologist, whose work at ◊Jericho showed that the double walls associated with the Biblical ◊Joshua belonged to an earlier period, and that a Neolithic settlement had existed about 6,800 BC.

Kepler /'keplə/ Johann 1571–1630. German mathematician and astronomer, who proved that the planets orbit the Sun in ellipses, and discovered the three laws of planetary motion

Kenya

REPUBLIC OF (*Jamhuri ya Kenya*)

AREA 583,000 sq km/224,960 sq mi
CAPITAL Nairobi
TOWNS Kisumu, port Mombasa
PHYSICAL mountains and highlands in the W
and centre; coastal plain in S; the N is arid
FEATURES Great Rift Valley, Mount Kenya,
Lake Nakuru (flamingos), Lake Turkana
(Rudolf), national parks with wildlife,
Malindini Marine Reserve, Olduvai Gorge
HEAD OF STATE AND OF GOVERNMENT Daniel arap
Moi from 1978
GOVERNMENT one-party republic
EXPORTS coffee, tea, sisal, pineapples
CURRENCY Kenya shilling (27.45 = £1 Sept
1987)
POPULATION (1985) 20,194,000 (the dominant
ethnic group is the Kikuyu); annual growth
rate 4.1%
LANGUAGE Swahili, but English is in general
use
RELIGION indigenous religions with Christian
and Muslim minorities
LITERACY 60% male/45% female (1980 est)
GDP $5.6 bn (1983); $309 per head of
population
CHRONOLOGY
1950 Mau Mau campaign began.
1953 Nationalist leader Jomo Kenyatta
imprisoned.

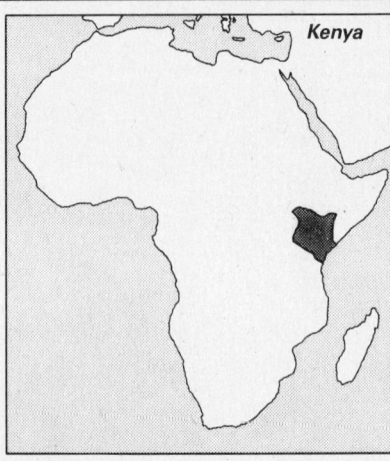

Kenya

1956 Mau Mau campaign defeated, Kenyatta
released.
1963 Granted internal self-government, with
Kenyatta as prime minister.
1964 Achieved full independence as a republic,
within the Commonwealth, with Kenyatta as
president.
1978 Death of Kenyatta. Succeeded by Daniel
arap Moi.
1982 Attempted coup against Moi foiled.
1983 Moi re-elected.

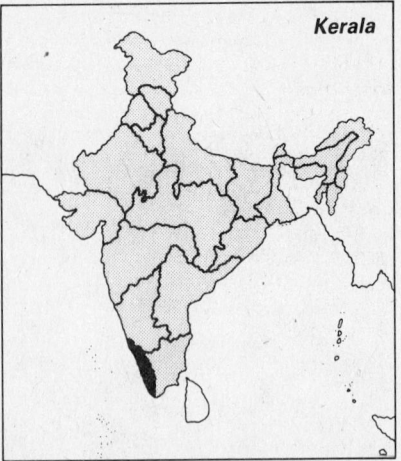

Kerala

French Southern and Antarctic Territories.
Uninhabited except for scientists (centre for
joint study of geomagnetism with USSR); the
islands support a unique wild cabbage containing
a pungent oil.
    Kerkyra /'keəkırə/ Greek form of ◊Corfu, an
island in the Ionian Sea.
    Kermadec Islands /kə'mædək/ volcanic
group, a dependency of New Zealand; area 34 sq
km/13 sq mi. Uninhabited except for a
meteorological station on the largest, Raoul.
    Kerman /kə'mɑːn/ town in SE Iran, a road
centre (shawls, carpets); population (1976)
140,309.
    Kermanshah /ˌkɜːmæn'ʃɑː/ town in Iran,
capital of Kermanshahan province (carpets,
weaving, petroleum refining); population (1976)
290,861. The province, on the border with Iraq,
is very fertile and inhabited mainly by Kurds.
    Kern /kɜːn/ Jerome (David) 1885–1945.
American composer. He wrote the popular
operetta *Show Boat* 1927, which includes the
song 'Ol' Man River'.
    kernel the inner, softer part of a ◊nut, or of a
seed within a hard shell.
    Kernow /'kɜːnəu/ Celtic name for ◊Cornwall,
England.
    kerosene a petroleum distillate, known in the
UK as *paraffin*; a more highly refined form is
used in jet aircraft fuel. It is a mixture of different
◊hydrocarbons of the paraffin series.
    Kerouac /'keruæk/ Jack 1923–1969.
American novelist, who epitomized the 'beat
generation' of the 1950s. Of French-Canadian
extraction, he was born in Lowell,
Massachusetts. Jack Duluoz, king of the
beatniks, is the hero of his books, including *On
the Road* 1958 and *Big Sur* 1963.
    Kerry /'keri/ county in the province of
Munster, Republic of Ireland
county town Tralee
physical W coastline deeply indented, N part
low-lying, but in the S occur the highest
mountains in Ireland; many rivers and lakes
features ◊Macgillycuddy's Reeks; Lakes of
Killarney
products engineering, woollens, shoes, cutlery;
tourism is important

that bear his name. Born in Württemberg, he
became assistant to Tycho ◊Brahe in 1600 and
succeeded him as Imperial Mathematician in
1601. His analysis of Tycho's observations of the
planets led him to discover *Kepler's laws*, the first
two of which he published in *Astronomia Nova*
1609 and the third in *Harmonices Mundi* 1619.
The laws are: (1) the orbit of each planet is an
ellipse with the Sun at one of the foci; (2) the
radius vector of each planet describes equal areas
in equal times; (3) the squares of the periods of
the planets are proportional to the cubes of their
mean distances from the Sun.
    Kerala /'kerələ/ SW state of India, formed in
1956 from the former princely states of
Travancore and Cochin
area 38,864 sq km/15,002 sq mi
capital Trivandrum
features most densely populated, and most
literate (60%) state of India; strong religious and
caste divisions make it politically unstable
population (1981) 25,453,680
language Kannada, Malayalam, Tamil.
    Kerbela /'kɜːbələ/ holy city of the Shi'ite
Muslims, 96 km/60m SW of Baghdad, Iraq;
population (1972) 100,000. Kerbela is built on
the site of the battlefield where Husein, son of Ali
and Fatima, was killed in AD 680 while defending
his succession to the Khalifate. His tomb in the
city is visited every year by many pilgrims.
    Kerch /keətʃ/ port in the Crimea, Ukraine,
USSR, at the E end of Kerch peninsula;
population (1985) 168,000. Kerch, built on the
site of an ancient Greek settlement, became
Russian in 1783.

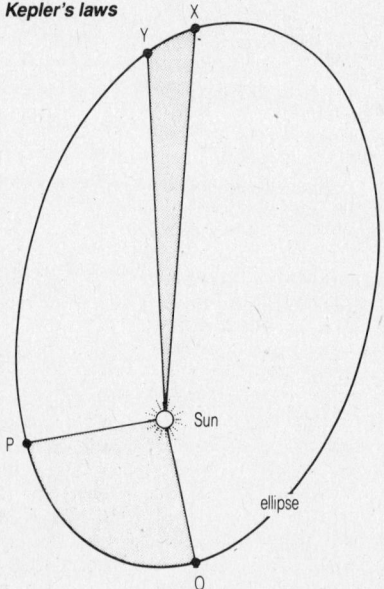

Kepler's laws

X
Y
P
Sun
ellipse
O

Kerensky /kə'renski/ Alexander
Feodorovich 1881–1970. Russian politician,
premier of the second provisional government,
before its collapse in Nov 1917, during the
◊Bolshevik revolution led by Lenin. He lived in
the USA from 1918.
    Kerguelen Islands /'kɜːgəlɪn/ volcanic
archipelago in the Indian Ocean, part of the

population (1981) 122,800.

Kertesz /'kɜːtes/ Andre 1894–1986. American photographer. A master of the ◊35 mm format camera, he recorded his immediate environment (Paris, New York) with wit and style.

Kesselring /'kesəlrɪŋ/ Albert 1885–1960. German field marshal, commander of the Luftwaffe 1939–40, during the invasions of Poland and the Low Countries and the early stages of the Battle of Britain. He later served under Rommel in N Africa, took command in Italy in 1943, and was commander-in-chief on the western front in Mar 1945. His death sentence for war crimes (1947) at the ◊Nuremberg trials was commuted to imprisonment (released 1952).

Kesteven /kes'tiːvən/ **Parts of**. SW area of Lincolnshire, England, formerly an administrative unit with county offices at Sleaford 1888–1974.

kestrel hawk *Falco tinnunculus* of the family Falconidae, which breeds in the British Isles and Europe, Asia and Africa. About 30 cm/1 ft long, the male has a head and tail of blueish-grey, and its back is a light chestnut-brown with black spots. The female is slightly larger and reddish-brown above, with bars. The kestrel hunts mainly by hovering.

Ketch /ketʃ/ Jack, died 1686. English executioner, who included ◊Monmouth in 1685 among his victims; his name became a common nickname for an executioner.

ketones organic compounds containing the carbonyl group, CO, bonded to two atoms of carbon (instead of one carbon and one hydrogen as in ◊aldehydes). They are liquids or low melting point solids, slightly soluble in water, and form derivatives in acid solutions. An example is acetone, $CH_3.CO.CH_3$.

Kew Gardens /kjuː/ the popular name for the ◊Royal Botanic Gardens, Kew, Surrey, England.

key in music, the ◊diatonic scale around which a piece of music is written; that is, a passage in the key of C major will mainly use the notes of the C major scale. The term is also used for the lever activated by a keyboard player, such as a piano key.

Key /kiː/ Francis Scott 1779–1843. American lawyer, who wrote the song 'The Star-Spangled Banner' while Fort McHenry was besieged by the British 1814; from 1931 it has been the national anthem of the USA.

keyboard in computing, an input device resembling a typewriter keyboard, which sends signals to a computer indicating which keys have been depressed. There are many variations on the layout of keys and the labelling of keys for different purposes. Extra numeric keys may be added, as can special-purpose function keys, such as LOAD, SAVE, PRINT, whose effect can be defined by programs in the computer.

Keynes /keɪnz/ John Maynard, 1st Baron Keynes 1883–1946. British economist. Fellow of King's College, Cambridge. He held a Treasury appointment during World War I, and took part in the peace conference as chief Treasury representative, but resigned in protest against the financial terms of the treaty. He justified his action in *The Economic Consequences of the Peace* 1919. His later economic works, for example *The General Theory of Employment, Interest, and Money* 1936, aroused much controversy by their proposals to prevent crises by control of credit and currency.

Keynes led the British delegation at the ◊Bretton Woods Conference 1944, which set up the ◊International Monetary Fund, and his theories were widely accepted in the aftermath of World War II. He was one of the most influential economists of the 20th century, responsible for that part of economics now known as ◊macroeconomics (the economics of large systems, for example nations).

Keynesian economics economic theory formulated by J M ◊Keynes which advocates that a fall in national income, lack of demand for goods, and rising unemployment should be countered by increased government expenditure to stimulate the economy. It is the reverse of ◊monetarism.

Key West /'kiː 'west/ town at the tip of the Florida peninsula, USA; population (1980) 24,382. As a tourist resort, it was popularized by the novelist Hemingway. In 1967 it became the first town in America to take all its fresh water from the sea.

KGB the Russian secret police, the *Komitet Gosudarstvennoye Bezhopaznosti* (Committee of State Security), in control of frontier and general security and the forced-labour system. Earlier names for the secret police were the Okhrana under the tsars; ◊Cheka 1918–23; GPU or OGPU (*Obedinyonnoye Gosudarstvennoye Polititcheskoye Upravleniye/Unified State Political Administration*) 1923–34; NKVD (*Narodny Komisariat Vnutrennykh Del/People's Commissariat of Internal Affairs*) 1934–46; and ◊MVD 1946–53. ◊Smersh was a subsection. The headquarters is in Dzerzhinsky Square, Moscow, and the Lubyanka Prison is located behind it. KGB officers hold key appointments in all fields of daily life, reporting to administration offices in every major town. Many KGB officers are also said to hold diplomatic posts in embassies abroad.

Khabarovsk /ˌkæbə'rɒfsk, Russian xə'bæ rəfsk/ industrial city (oil refining, saw milling, meat packing) in E USSR; population (1981) 545,000.

Khachaturian /ˌkætʃə'tʊəriən/ Aram Il'yich 1903–1978. Russian composer, noted for folk-like themes, for example in the ballets *Gayaneh* 1942, which includes the 'Sabre Dance', and *Spartacus* 1956.

Khaddhafi /kə'dæfi/ or *Gaddafi* or *Qaddafi*, Moamer al 1942– . Libyan revolutionary leader. Overthrowing King Idris 1969, he became virtual president of a republic, although he nominally gave up all except an ideological role in 1974. He favours territorial expansion in North Africa (see under ◊Chad) reaching as far as Zaïre. His theories, based on those of Chairman ◊Mao, are contained in a *Green Book*.

Khajuraho /ˌkædʒʊ'rɑːhəʊ/ town in Madhya Pradesh, central India, the former capital of the Candella kings. It has 35 sandstone temples, built

Khaddhafi Colonel Moamer al Khaddhafi. The photograph was taken at Sebha on the fourth anniversary of the establishment of the 'Power of the People', Mar 1981.

in the 10th and 11th centuries, Jain, Buddhist, and Hindu. The temples are covered inside and out with erotic sculpture symbolizing mystic union with the deity.

khaki the dust-coloured uniform of British and Indian troops in India from about 1850, adopted as camouflage in the South African War 1899–1902, and later standard for military uniforms worldwide.

Khalifa /kɑː'liːfə/ the Sudanese dervish leader *Abdullah el Taaisha* 1846–1899. Successor to the Mahdi as Sudanese ruler from 1885, he was defeated by ◊Kitchener at Omdurman 1898, and later killed at Kordofan.

Khalistan /ˌkɑːlɪ'stɑːn/ projected independent Sikh state. See ◊Sikhism.

Khama /'kɑːmə/ Seretse 1921–1980. Botswana politician. Son of the Bamangwato chief Sekoma II (died 1925), he studied law in Britain and married an Englishwoman, Ruth Williams. This marriage was strongly condemned by his uncle Tshekedi Khama, regent during his minority, as contrary to tribal custom, and Seretse Khama was banished in 1950, returning in 1956 on his renunciation of any claim to the chieftaincy, but in 1965 he became prime minister of Bechuanaland, and was president of the new republic of Botswana 1966–80.

khamsin a hot ◊wind that blows in Egypt.

Khan /kɑːn/ Jahangir 1963– . Pakistani squash player. After losing to Geoff Hunt (Australia) in the final of the 1981 British Open, he did not lose again until Nov 1986 when Ross Norman (New Zealand) beat him in the World Open championship final. He was world amateur champion 1979, 1983, 1985, and British Open champion 1982–86. His father, Roshan Kahn, won the British Open in 1956.

Khan /kɑːn/ Liaquat Ali 1895–1951. Indian politician. Educated at Allahabad and Oxford, he studied law, and in 1923 joined the Muslim League. He was deputy leader of the Muslim League Party 1941–47, and in 1947 became first prime minister of Pakistan. He was assassinated by a Muslim fanatic.

Kharga /'kɑːgə/ oasis in the Western Desert of Egypt, known to the Romans, and from 1960 headquarters of the New Valley irrigation scheme. An area twice the size of Italy is watered from natural underground reservoirs.

Kharkov /'kɑːkɒf/ industrial city (engineering, tractors) and railway junction in the Ukraine, USSR, capital of Kharkov region, 400 km/250 mi E of Kiev; population (1985) 1,554,000. Kharkov, founded in 1654, has a university.

Khartoum /kɑː'tuːm/ capital and trading centre of Sudan, at the junction of the Blue and White Nile; population (1984) 476,218, and of Khartoum North, across the Blue Nile, 150,000. Besides Khartoum University, there is also a branch of Cairo University.

history Khartoum was founded in 1830 by ◊Mehemet Ali. General ◊Gordon was killed at Khartoum by the Mahdist rebels in 1885. A new city was built after the site was recaptured by British troops under Kitchener in 1898.

Khazar /kə'zɑː/ people of Turkish origin from Central Asia, who formed a buffer state in the 7th–12th centuries between the Arabs and the Byzantine empire, and later between the Byzantine empire and subsequent Russian pressure from the north. Converted to Judaism about 740, they died out in the 13th century; it has been suggested they were the ancestors of the E European Jews, themselves the ancestors of the majority of modern Jewry, and hence of Aryan rather than Semitic origin.

Khedive title granted by the Turkish sultan to his Egyptian viceroy 1867, retained by succeeding rulers till 1914.

Kherson /kɑː'sɒn/ port in Ukraine, USSR, on the Dnieper river, capital of Kherson region. Industries include shipbuilding, soap and tobacco manufacture. It was founded in 1778 by army commander ◊Potemkin as the first Russian naval base on the Black Sea.

Khe Sanh /'keɪ 'sæn/ US Marine outpost near the Laotian border and just S of the demilitarized zone in North Vietnam in the Vietnam war. Garrisoned by 4,000 Marines, it was attacked by 20,000 North Vietnamese troops 21 Jan–7 Apr 1968.

Khirbet Qumran see ◊Qumran, archaeological site in Jordan.

Khiva /kiː'vɑː/ town in Uzbek Republic, USSR. Carpets and textiles are made. Capital of Khiva khanate (modern Khorezm) till its submission to Russia in 1873.

Khmer Republic /kmeə/ former name of ◊Kampuchea, country in SE Asia.

Khmer Rouge communist movement in ◊Kampuchea which allied with the exiled Prince Sihanouk to oppose the US-backed regime led by Lon Nol 1970–76. By 1974 the Khmer Rouge controlled the countryside and in 1975 the capital Phnom Penh was captured and Sihanouk installed as head of state. Internal disagreements led to the creation of the Pol Pot government and widespread terror. In 1978 Vietnam invaded the country and installed a regime under Heng Samrin. The Khmer Rouge was forced to conduct a guerrilla campaign against the Vietnamese forces.

Khomeini /kɒ'meɪni/ Ayatollah Ruhollah 1900– . Iranian ◊Shi'ite Muslim leader, born in Khomein, central Iran. Exiled for opposition to the shah from 1964, he returned when the shah left the country in 1979, and established a fundamentalist Islamic republic.

Khomeini The Ayatollah Khomeini giving his final press conference in Paris before returning to Iran to establish the new Islamic republic 1979.

Khorana /kɔː'rɑːnə/ Har Gobind 1922– . American biochemist, born in India. In 1968 he shared a Nobel prize for research on the interpretation of the genetic code and its function in protein synthesis, and in 1976 led the team which first synthesized a biologically active gene.

Khrushchev /kruʃ'tʃɒf/ Nikita Sergeyevich 1894–1971. Soviet politician. Born near Kursk, the son of a miner, he fought in the post-Revolutionary Civil War 1917–21, and in World War II organized the guerrilla defence of his native Ukraine. As secretary general of the Communist Party 1953–64, he denounced Stalinism in a secret session of the Party in Feb 1956. Many victims of the purges of the 1930s were either released or posthumously rehabilitated, but when Hungary revolted in Oct against Soviet domination, there was immediate Soviet intervention. In 1958 Khrushchev succeeded ◊Bulganin as chair of the council of ministers (prime minister), and maintained a policy of peaceful co-existence and competition with capitalism, the space achievements of the USSR being outstanding under his leadership. His attitude in foreign policy, however, conflicted with that of China, so that he developed a personal feud with ◊Mao Zedong, and when he hastily despatched missiles to Cuba, US pressure compelled their withdrawal. He was consequently compelled to resign in 1964, although by 1965 his reputation was to some extent officially restored.

Khrushchev The Soviet politician Nikita Khrushchev at the Quai d'Orsay, Paris. He was ousted by Brezhnev in 1964.

Khufu /'kuːfuː/ c. 3000 BC. Egyptian king of Memphis, who built the largest of the Pyramids, known to the Greeks as the pyramid of Cheops. The Greek form of Khufu is *Cheops*.

Khuzestan /'kuːzɪstɑːn/ SW province of Iran, which includes the chief Iranian oil resources. Towns include Ahwaz (capital), and the ports of Abadan and Khuninshahr. There have been calls for Sunni Muslim autonomy, under the name ◊Arabistan.

Khyber Pass /'kaɪbə/ pass 53 km/33 mi long through the mountain range that separates Pakistan from Afghanistan. The Khyber Pass was used by Mahmud of Ghazni, Baber, Nadir Shah, and other invaders of India. The present road was constructed by the British during the Afghan Wars.

Kiangsi former spelling of ◊Jiangxi, province of China.

Kiangsu former spelling of ◊Jiangsu, province of China.

kibbutz Israeli communal collective settlement, with collective ownership of all property and earnings, collective organization of work, and communal housing for children; a modified version, the *Moshav Shitufi*, is similar to the ◊collective farms of Soviet Russia. Other Israeli co-operative rural settlements include the *Moshav Ovdim* which has equal opportunity, and the similar but less strict *Moshav* settlement.

Kidd /kɪd/ William c. 1645–1701. British pirate, popularly known as Captain Kidd. He was born in Greenock, Scotland, and settled in New York. In 1696 he was commissioned by the governor of New York to suppress pirates, but he became a pirate himself. Arrested in 1699, he was taken to England and hanged. His execution marked the end of some 200 years of semi-official condoning of piracy by the British government.

Kidderminster /'kɪdə,mɪnstə/ market town in the West Midlands of England, on the river Stour; population (1981) 51,300. Famous for carpets from about 1735.

kidnapping the abduction of a person in order to gain money for their safe release. The practice arose in the 17th century with the abduction of young people to become indentured labourers in colonial plantations, from which they could be rescued by a ransom. In English common law it is an offence which carries a maximum sentence of life imprisonment.

kidney an organ of vertebrates which is responsible for water regulation, ◊excretion of waste products, and maintaining the composition of the ◊blood. In mammals, there is a pair of kidneys situated on the rear wall of the abdomen. Each one consists of a number of long tubules; the outer parts filter the aqueous components of blood, and the inner parts selectively reabsorb vital salts, leaving waste products in the remaining fluid (urine) which is collected at the ends of the ducts and passed through the ureter to the bladder. The action of the kidneys is vital to life, although if one is removed, for example, because of a tumour, the other enlarges to take over its function. A patient with two defective kidneys may continue near-normal life with the aid of a kidney machine or continuous ambulatory peritoneal ◊dialysis (CAPD), in which the peritoneal membrane lining the inside of the abdomen takes over kidney function with the aid of dialysis solution, that is replaced at regular intervals via a small plastic tube inserted into the peritoneal cavity.

Kiel /kiːl/ Baltic port (fishing, shipbuilding, engineering), in West Germany, capital of Schleswig-Holstein; population (1984) 246,900. *Kiel Week* in June is a yachting meeting.

Kiel Canal /kiːl/ waterway that connects the Baltic with the North Sea. Built by Germany in the years before World War I, the canal allowed the German navy to move from Baltic bases to the open sea without travelling through international waters.

Kielce /ki'eltseɪ/ city in central Poland, NE of Krakow, industrial rail junction (chemicals, metals); population (1982) 192,000.

Kierkegaard /'kɪəkəgɑːd/ Søren Aabye 1813–1855. Danish philosopher. Born in Copenhagen, where he spent most of his life, he was the son of a Jewish merchant, but was converted to Christianity in 1838, although he became hostile to the established Church, and his beliefs caused much controversy. Kierkegaard is usually considered to be the founder of ◊existentialism. He was a consistent opponent of ◊Hegel's philosophy, arguing that no system of thought could explain the unique experience of the individual. He defended Christianity, suggesting that God cannot be known through reason, but only through a 'leap of faith'. A

prolific author, he published his first important work *Enten-Eller/Either-Or* in 1843, and notable later works are *Begrebet Angest/Concept of Dread* 1844, and *Efterskrift/Post-script* 1846, which summed up much of his earlier writings. His many pseudonyms were sometimes used to argue with himself.

Kierkegaard A portrait of the philosopher sketched by his cousin, Christian Kierkegaard.

Kiev /'kiːef/ capital of the Ukrainian republic, industrial centre and third largest city of the USSR, on the confluence of the Desna and Dnieper rivers; population (1985) 2,248,000. The Kiev opera and ballet are renowned.
history the Slav domination of Russia began with the rise of Kiev (see also under ◊Vikings) the 'mother of Russian cities', founded in the 5th century. It replaced ◊Novgorod as the capital in 882, and was the original centre of the Orthodox Christian faith in 988. St Sophia cathedral (11th century) and Kiev-Pechersky Monastery (both now museums) survive, and also remains of the Golden Gate. It was occupied by Germany 1941.

Kigali /kɪ'gɑːli/ capital of the central African republic of Rwanda; population (1981) 156,650.

Kigoma /kɪ'gəumə/ town and port on the E shore of Lake Tanganyika, Tanzania; population (1978) 50,044.

Kildare /kɪl'deə/ county of Leinster province, Republic of Ireland, S of Meath
area 1,694 sq km/654 sq mi
county town Naas
physical the north is wet and boggy, but in the east and west oats, barley, and potatoes, are grown and cattle are reared
features includes part of the Bog of Allen; the village of Maynooth, with a training college for Roman Catholic priests; and the Curragh, a plain which is the site of the national stud and headquarters of Irish racing
population (1979) 104,100.

Kilimanjaro /,kɪlɪmæn'dʒɑːrəu/ volcano in ◊Tanzania, the highest mountain in Africa.

Kilkenny /kɪl'keni/ county in Leinster province, Republic of Ireland, E of Tipperary
area 2,061 sq km/796 sq mi
county town Kilkenny
features river Nore
products agricultural; coal
population (1981) 70,800.

Killarney /kɪ'lɑːni/ market town in County Kerry, Republic of Ireland; population (1981) 7,693. Most famous beauty spot in Ireland, it has ◊Macgillycuddy's Reeks (a range of mountains) and the Lakes of Killarney to the SW.

killer-whale a type of ◊whale.

Killy /kɪ'liː/ Jean-Claude 1943– . French skier. He won all three gold medals (slalom, giant slalom, and downhill) at the 1968 winter Olympics in Grenoble. The first World Cup winner 1967, he retained the title 1968 and also won six world titles.

Kilmarnock /kɪl'mɑːnək/ town in Strathclyde region, Scotland, 32 km/20 mi SW of Glasgow, producing carpets, agricultural machinery, and whisky; population (1981) 46,612. It was here that Burns's first book of poems was published in 1786.

Kilmuir /kɪl'mjuə/ David Patrick Maxwell Fyfe, 1st Earl of Kilmuir 1900–1967. British lawyer and Conservative politician. He was solicitor-general 1942–45 and attorney-general in 1945 during the Churchill governments. At the ◊Nuremberg trials he was deputy to Sir Hartley Shawcross and for most of the time conducted the British prosecution. He was home secretary 1951–54 and lord chancellor 1954–62. In 1954 he was created viscount and in 1962 earl.

kiln high-temperature furnace used commercially for drying timber, roasting metal ores, or for making cement, bricks, pottery and other ceramics. Oil- or gas-fired kilns are used to bake ceramics at temperatures of up to 1,760°C/3,200°F; electric kilns are generally not so hot.

kilo prefix denoting in the metric system 1,000 units, hence *kilogram* unit of mass equal to 1,000 grams/2.2 lb, *kilometre* unit of length equal to 1,000 metres/3,280.89 ft (approx ⅝ of a mile), *kiloton* unit of explosive force equivalent to 1,000 tons of TNT, used in describing nuclear bombs, *kilowatt* unit of power equal to about 1,000 watts/1.34 horsepower.

kilowatt-hour the commercial unit of electrical energy (kWh). Defined as the work done by a power of 1,000 watts in 1 hour. Used to calculate the cost of electrical energy taken from the mains.

Kilvert /'kɪlvət/ Francis 1840–1879. British clergyman, noted for a diary recording social life on the Welsh border 1870–79 published in 1938–39.

Kimberley /'kɪmbəli/ diamond-mining town in Cape Province, South Africa, 153 km/95 mi NW of Bloemfontein; population (1980) 144,923. Its mines have been controlled by De Beers Consolidated Mines since 1887.

Kimberley /'kɪmbəli/ diamond site in Western Australia, found in 1978–79, estimated to have 5 per cent of world's known gem-quality stones and 50 per cent of its industrial diamonds.

kimberlite an igneous rock which is ultrabasic (containing very little silica). It is similar to ◊peridotite (another ultrabasic rock) and contains ◊olivine and ◊mica. Kimberlite is found in carrot-shaped ◊intrusions called diatremes where mobile material from very deep in the earth's ◊crust has forced itself upwards, expanding in its ascent. The material brought upwards from near the boundary between crust and ◊mantle, often altered and fragmented, includes diamonds, and kimberlites represent the world's principal diamond source. Diatremes are found principally near Kimberley, South Africa, from which the name of the rock is derived, and in the Yakutia area of Siberia.

Kim Il Sung /'kɪm ˌiːl 'sʊŋ/ 1912– . North Korean marshal and politician. He became prime minister in 1948, and president in 1972, but retained the presidency of the Communist Workers' Party; he has campaigned constantly for the reunification of Korea. His son Kim Chong Il (1942–) has been named as his successor.

kimono traditional Japanese costume, still retained by women for formal wear – the *homongi* or 'visiting dress'. For the finest kimonos a rectangular piece of pure silk (about 11 m/36 ft × 0.5 m/1.5 ft) is cut into seven pieces for tailoring, the brilliant colouring of the design (which must match perfectly over the seams and for which flowers are the favourite motif) then being painted by hand and enhanced by embroidery or gilding. The accompanying *obi* or sash is also embroidered. The kimono is also worn informally by men.

Kincardineshire /kɪn'kɑːdɪnʃə/ former county of E Scotland, merged in 1975 in Grampian region. Stonehaven was the county town.

kinetic energy a form of ◊energy possessed by moving bodies. It is contrasted with ◊potential energy.

kinetics branch of ◊dynamics dealing with the action of forces producing or changing the motion of a body, as distinguished from kinematics, which deals with motion without reference to force or mass.

kinetics the branch of chemistry which investigates the rates at which chemical ◊reactions take place at various temperatures, pressures, and so on.

kinetic theory theory describing the physical properties of matter in terms of the behaviour – principally movement – of its component atoms or molecules. A gas consists of rapidly moving atoms or molecules and, according to kinetic theory, it is their continual impact on the walls of the containing vessel that accounts for the pressure of the gas. By making various assumptions about the nature of gas molecules (which define a so-called ideal gas) it is possible to derive from the theory the various gas laws (such as ◊Avogadro's, ◊Boyle's and ◊Charles' law). The slowing down of molecular motion as temperature falls, according to kinetic theory, accounts for the physical properties of liquids and solids, culminating in the concept of no

molecular motion at ◊absolute zero (0°K/–273°C).

King /kɪŋ/ Billie Jean (born Moffit) 1943– . American tennis player. She won her first Wimbledon title 1961 (doubles with Karen Hantze), and broke Elizabeth Ryan's record when she won her 20th title in 1979 (doubles with Martina Navratilova). She won the singles title six times, and the singles titles at the other Grand Slam tournaments, the French, Australian and US Opens.

King /kɪŋ/ Martin Luther, Jr 1929–1968. American black ◊civil rights leader. Born in Atlanta, Georgia, son of a Baptist minister, he also became a pastor. He first came to national attention as leader of the ◊Montgomery, Alabama, bus boycott in 1955, and he founded the ◊Southern Christian Leadership Conference in 1957. A brilliant and moving speaker and a passionate advocate of non-violence, he was the symbol of, and leading figure in, the campaign for integration and equal rights in the late 1950s and early 1960s, which culminated in the massive march on Washington DC 1963. He was awarded the Nobel Peace Prize 1964. In the mid-1960s his moderate approach was criticized by black militants. Always a target of segregationists and right-wing extremists, he was shot and killed in 1968 by James Earl Ray in Memphis, Tennessee. The third Monday in Jan is now celebrated as Martin Luther King day, a public holiday in the USA.

King 'I have a dream...' began the most famous speech of civil rights campaigner Martin Luther King Jr.

King /kɪŋ/ Stephen 1946– . US writer of horror novels in a small-town or rural American setting. Many of his works have been filmed, including *Carrie* 1974, *The Shining* 1978, and *Christine* 1983.

King /kɪŋ/ William Lyon Mackenzie 1874–1950. Canadian Liberal politician. Born in Ontario, he was prime minister 1921–Jun 1926, Sep 1926–1930 and 1935–48. He took part in the 1926 Imperial Conference which recognized the

Dominion's equal status with Britain, and his proposals, that self-governing countries maintain close cooperation with, but be linked only by, allegiance to the British Crown, were included in the Statute of Westminster. He received the Order of Merit in 1947.

king crab or *horseshoe crab* marine arthropod, subclass Xiphosura, class Arachnida, which frequents the Atlantic coast of N America, and the coasts of India and SE Asia. The upper side of the body is entirely covered with a rounded shell, and it has a long spine-like tail; up to 60 cm/2 ft long, it burrows in the sand.

kingcup another name for ◊marsh marigold.

kingdom in biology, the primary division in biological ◊classification. At one time only two kingdoms were recognized: animals and plants. Any organism with a rigid cell wall was a plant, and so bacteria and fungi were considered as plants, despite their many differences from true plants. Anything that was not a plant was in the animal kingdom. However some organisms, such as the ◊photosynthetic euglenoids, were claimed by both kingdoms. The unsatisfactory nature of the two-kingdom system became evident during the 19th century, and the biologist Ernst ◊Haeckel was among the first to try to reform it. High-power microscopes have revealed more about the structure of cells; it has become clear that there is a fundamental difference between cells without a nucleus (◊prokaryotes) and those with a nucleus (◊eukaryotes). However, these differences are larger than those between animals and higher plants, and are unsuitable for use as kingdoms. In fact there is no agreement on how many kingdoms there are in the natural world. Some modern schemes have as many as 20, but most biologists prefer a five-kingdom system, even though it involves grouping together organisms that are probably unrelated. One widely accepted scheme is: Kingdom Animalia (all multicellular animals); Kingdom Plantae (all plants, all seaweeds and other algae, including unicellular algae); Kingdom Fungi (all fungi, including the unicellular yeasts, but not slime moulds); Kingdom Protista or Protoctista (protozoa, diatoms, dinoflagellates, slime moulds, and various other lower organisms with eukaryotic cells) and Kingdom Monera (all prokaryotes – the bacteria and cyanobacteria). The first four of these kingdoms comprise the eukaryotes.

kingfisher European bird *Alcedo atthis* also found in parts of Africa and Asia. The plumage is brilliant blue-green on the back and chestnut beneath. Kingfishers feed upon fish and aquatic insects. The nest is made of fishbones in a hole in a river bank. There are about 90 species of kingfisher in the world, the largest being the Australian ◊kookaburra.

King's Counsel in England, a ◊barrister of senior rank; the term is used when a king is on the throne; and ◊Queen's Counsel when the monarch is a queen.

King's County older name of ◊Offaly, an Irish county.

King's English see ◊English language.

Kingsley /'kɪŋzli/ Charles 1819–1875. British author, historian, cleric, and father of

Mary ◊Kingsley. He was known as the 'Chartist clergyman' because of such social novels as *Alton Locke* 1850 which were influential in their time. His historical novels include *Westward Ho!* 1855 and for children, *The Water-Babies* 1863 which has become a classic. His controversy with J H ◊Newman prompted the latter's *Apologia*.

Kingsley /'kɪŋzli/ Mary Henrietta 1862–1900. British ethnologist. The daughter of Charles Kíngsley, she made extensive expeditions in W Africa, and published lively accounts of her findings, for example, *Travels in West Africa* 1897. She died while nursing Boer prisoners during the South African War.

King's Proctor in England, the official representing the Crown in matrimonial cases; the term is used when a king is on the throne; and ◊Queen's Proctor when the monarch is a queen.

Kingston /'kɪŋstən/ capital of Jamaica, West Indies; the cultural and commercial centre of the island, with an excellent harbour on the S coast; population (1983) 100,637.

history Kingston was rebuilt after an earthquake in 1907. It was founded 1693–1703, and made capital of Jamaica in 1872.

Kingston /'kɪŋstən/ city of Ontario, Canada, on Lake Ontario, seat of Queen's University, with shipbuilding yards, engineering works, and grain elevators; population (1981) 60,313. It grew from 1782 around the French Fort Frontenac, was captured by the English in 1748, and renamed in honour of George III.

Kingston-upon-Hull /'kɪŋstən əpɒn 'hʌl/ official name of ◊Hull, city in NE England.

Kingston upon Thames /'kɪŋstən əpɒn 'temz/ borough of Greater London, England, on the S bank of the Thames, 16 km/10 mi SW of London; administrative headquarters of Surrey; population (1983) 133,600. Industries include metalworking, plastic and paint. The coronation stone of the Saxon kings is still preserved here.

Kingstown /'kɪŋztaʊn/ former name for ◊Dun Laoghaire, port near Dublin, Ireland.

King-Te-Chen former spelling of ◊Jingdezhen, town in China.

kinkajou Central and S American mammal *Potos flavus* of the raccoon family. Yellowish-brown, with a rounded face and slim body, the kinkajou is up to 55 cm/1.8 ft long plus 50 cm/1.6 ft tail, and has short legs with sharp claws. It spends its time in the trees and has a prehensile tail. It feeds largely on fruit.

Kinnock /'kɪnək/ Neil 1942– . British Labour politician. Born and educated in Wales, he was elected to represent a Welsh constituency in Parliament in 1970 (Islwyn from 1983). A noted orator, he was markedly to the left of ◊Wilson and ◊Callaghan, but as party leader from 1983 (in succession to ◊Foot) adopted a more moderate position. He initiated the expulsion of the left-wing ◊Militant Tendency members from the Labour Party in 1986.

Kinross /kɪn'rɒs/ former county of Scotland, merged in 1975 in Tayside region.

kin selection in biology, the idea that ◊altruism shown to genetic relatives can be worthwhile, because those relatives share some genes with the individual that is behaving altruistically; see ◊inclusive fitness. Alarm

Kinnock British Labour Party leader Neil Kinnock with his wife Glenys, at the Labour party conference in Blackpool, Sept 1986.

calling in response to predators is an example of a behaviour that may have evolved through kin selection: relatives that are warned of danger can escape and continue to breed, even if the alarm caller is caught.

Kinsey /'kɪnzi/ Alfred 1894–1956. American researcher, whose studies of male and female sexual behaviour 1948–53, based on questionnaires, were the first serious published research on this topic.

Kinshasa /kɪn'ʃɑːsə/ capital (formerly Léopoldville) of Zaïre on the river Zaïre, 400 km/250 mi inland from Matadi; population (1976) 2,443,876. It has chemical, textile, engineering, food processing, and furniture industries, and the National University. Founded by the explorer Stanley 1887.

kinship human relationship based on blood or marriage, and sanctified by law and custom. Kinship forms the basis for most human societies and for such social groupings as the family, clan, or tribe. Kinship is universal, although its social significance varies from society to society. Most human societies have evolved strict social rules, customs, and taboos regarding kinship, particularly to do with sexual behaviour (such as the prohibition of ◊incest).

Kipling /'kɪplɪŋ/ (Joseph) Rudyard 1865–1936. British writer. Enjoying in his heyday an enormous popularity, and subsequently denigration for alleged 'jingoist imperialism', he is now generally recognized as a highly skilled writer, especially of short stories for children. As a poet he was the author of many quotable lines, from 'Boots', 'If', 'Gunga Din', 'Mandalay', and others. Born in Bombay, he was educated at the United Services College at Westward Ho, England, which provided the background for *Stalky and Co* 1899. He worked as a journalist in India 1882–89; during these years he wrote *Plain Tales from the Hills*, *Soldiers Three*, *Wee Willie Winkie*, and others. Returning to London he published *The Light that Failed* 1890 and *Barrack Room Ballads* 1892. He lived largely in the USA 1892–96, where he produced the two *Jungle Books*

1894–95, and *Captains Courageous* 1897. Back in Britain, living in Sussex (first in Rottingdean, later in Burwash), he published *Kim* 1901, the *Just So Stories* 1902, *Puck of Pook's Hill* 1906, and *Rewards and Fairies* 1910; and in 1907 was awarded a Nobel prize. Later works include the autobiographical *Something of Myself* 1937.

Kipling British poet and author Rudyard Kipling, who enjoyed great popularity. Much of his life was spent in India, and many of his writings reflect this colonial way of life.

Kirchhoff /'kɪəkhɒf/ Gustav Robert 1824–1887. German physicist, who with ◊Bunsen used the spectroscope to show that all elements, heated to incandescence, have their individual spectra.

Kirchner /'kɪəknə/ Ernst Ludwig 1880–1938. German ◊Expressionist artist. With a number of other painters he formed the movement Die ◊Brücke/The Bridge in 1905, which was established in Berlin from 1911. Harsh, angular and distorted, his work changed from portraiture and city scenes to mountain landscapes when he settled in Switzerland on being invalided from the army in 1917. His work was attacked as degenerate under Hitler and many paintings were destroyed.

Kirgizia /kɜː'gɪzɪə/ republic of the USSR from 1936, part of Soviet Central Asia
area 198,500 sq km/76,100 sq mi
capital Frunze
features mountainous, an extension of the Tyan Shan range
products cereals, sugar, cotton, especially by irrigation; coal and other minerals; sheep, yaks and hardy horses
population (1984) 3,886,000, Kirghiz 44% (related to the Kazakhs, they are of Mongol-Tatar origin), Russian 29%, Uzbek 11%
language Kirghiz
religion Sunni Islam
history annexed by Russia in 1864, it was part of an independent Turkestan republic 1917–24, when it was reincorporated in the USSR.

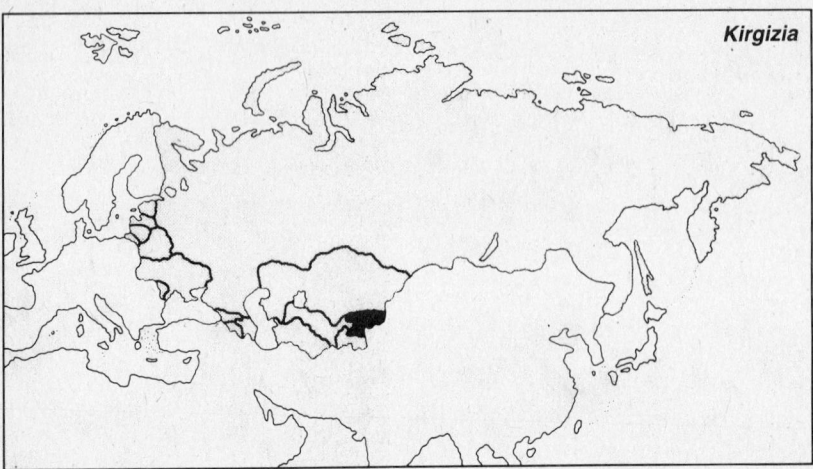

Kirgizia

Kiribati /ˈkɪrɪbæs/ republic in the central Pacific, comprising three groups of coral atolls: the 16 Gilbert Islands, eight uninhabited Phoenix Islands, eight of the 11 Line Islands, and the volcanic island of Banaba.

government Kiribati's 1979 constitution provides for a president, the *Beretitenti*, who is head of both state and government, and is elected by universal suffrage for a four-year term, and a single-chamber legislature, the *Maneaba ni Maungatabu*. The president may not serve more than three terms. The *Maneaba* has 38 members, 36 popularly elected, one elected to represent Banaba, and the attorney-general 'ex officio'. It also serves a four-year term. The president governs with the help of a vice-president and cabinet chosen from and responsible to the *Maneaba*. There are no formal political parties, all candidates for the *Maneaba* fighting as independents.

history the first Europeans to visit the area were the Spanish in 1606. The 16 Gilbert Islands and nine Ellice Islands became a British protectorate in 1892, and then the Gilbert and Ellice Islands Colony (GEIC) in 1916. The colony was occupied by Japan 1942–43 and was the scene of fierce fighting between Japanese and US forces. In preparation for self-government, a legislative council was set up in 1963, and in 1972 a governor took over from the British high commissioner. In 1975 the legislative council was replaced by an elected house of assembly and in 1976, when the Ellice Islands separated and became Tuvalu, GEIC was renamed the Gilbert Islands. The islands achieved internal self-government in 1977 and full independence within the Commonwealth in 1979, under the name of Kiribati, with Ieremia Tabai as their first president. The island of Banaba has tried to become independent or join Fiji.

Kirin former name for ◊Jilin, Chinese province.

Kirkcudbright /kəˈkuːbri/ former county of S Scotland, merged in 1975 in Dumfries and Galloway region. Kirkcudbright was formerly the county town. The name means 'chapel of Cuthbert'.

Kirk /kɜːk/ Norman 1924–1974. New Zealand Labour politician, known as 'Big Norm'. Once an engine-driver, he led the Labour party from 1965, and was prime minister 1972–74.

Kirkpatrick /kɜːkˈpætrɪk/ Jeane 1926– . US politician and professor of political science. She was an outspoken anti-Marxist permanent representative to the United Nations (as a Democrat) 1981–85, then registered as a Republican 1985.

Kirkuk /kɜːˈkʊk/ town in NE Iraq, centre of a major oilfield. Formerly it was served by several pipelines providing outlets to Lebanon, Syria, and other countries, but closures caused by the Iran–Iraq war left only the pipeline to Turkey operational.

Kirkwall /ˈkɜːkwɔːl/ administrative headquarters and port of the Orkneys, Scotland, on the N coast of the largest island, Mainland; population (1985) 6,000. The Norse cathedral of St Magnus dates in part from 1137.

Kirov /ˈkɪərɒf/ town NE of Gorky, on the Vyatka river, USSR; rail centre (rolling stock, machine tools); population (1985) 411,000.

Kirov /ˈkɪərɒf/ Sergei Mironovich 1886–1934. Russian Bolshevik leader, who joined the party in 1904 and took a prominent part in the 1918–20 civil wars. His assassination in 1934, possibly engineered by ◊Stalin, led to the political trials held during the next four years.

Kirovabad /ˌkɪrəvəˈbæd/ industrial city (cottons, woollens, processed foods) in Azerbaijan Republic, USSR; population (1985) 261,000.

Kirovograd /ˌkɪrəvəˈgræd/ industrial city (agricultural machinery, food processing) on a lignite field in Ukrainian Republic, USSR; population (1985) 263,000.

Kisangani /ˌkɪsænˈɡɑːni/ town in NE Zaïre (formerly Stanleyville), on the upper Zaïre river, below Stanley Falls; communications centre; population (1978) 297,900.

Kishinev /ˌkɪʃɪˈnjɒf/ capital of the Moldavian Republic, USSR (cement and food factories); population (1985) 624,500.

history founded in 1436, it became Russian in 1812. It was taken by Romania in 1918, by the USSR in 1940, by Germany in 1941, when it was totally destroyed; the USSR recaptured the site in 1944, and rebuilding soon began.

Kissinger /ˈkɪsɪndʒə/ Henry 1923– . American statesman. Born in Bavaria, he emigrated to the USA in 1938. After work in army counter-intelligence, he won a government scholarship to Harvard, and subsequently

Kiribati
REPUBLIC OF

AREA 655 sq km/253 sq mi
CAPITAL and port Tarawa
PHYSICAL comprises 33 Pacific islands: the Gilbert, Phoenix, and Line Islands, and Banaba (Ocean Island)
HEAD OF STATE AND OF GOVERNMENT Ieremia T Tabai from 1979
GOVERNMENT democratic
EXPORTS copra
CURRENCY Australian dollar (2.24 = £1 Sept 87)
POPULATION 61,000 (1985); annual growth rate 1.7%
LANGUAGE English and Gilbertese (official)
RELIGION Christian, both Roman Catholic and Protestant
LITERACY 90% (1982)
GNP $30 million (1983)
CHRONOLOGY
1977 Gilbert Islands granted internal self-government.

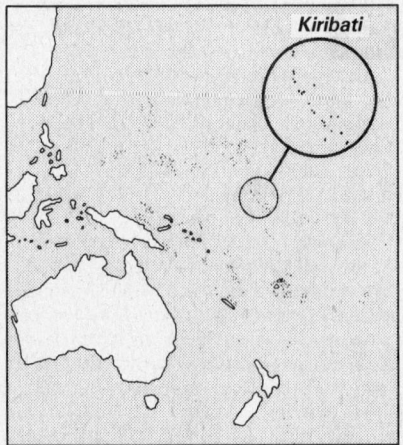

Kiribati

1979 Achieved full independence, within the Commonwealth, as the Republic of Kiribati, with Ieremia Tabai as president.
1983 Tabai re-elected.

became a government consultant. In 1969 he was appointed assistant for National Security Affairs (Secretary of State 1973–77) by President Nixon, and went on secret missions to Beijing and Moscow which led to Nixon's visits to both countries and a general détente. In 1973 he shared a Nobel Peace Prize with Le Duc Tho, the North Vietnamese Politburo member, for his part in the Vietnamese peace negotiations. In 1973–75 he was active in the Arab-Israeli peace negotiations, and in furthering détente between the USSR and the West, and in 1976 was involved in the negotiations in Africa arising from the Angola and Rhodesia crises. In 1983 Reagan appointed him to head a bipartisan commission on Central America.

Kiswahili see ◊Swahili language.

Kitakyushu /ˌkiːtəˈkjuːʃuː/ Japanese industrial city and port (coal, steel, chemicals, cotton thread, plate glass, alcohol) on the Hibiki Sea, N Kyushu, formed 1963 by the amalgamation of Moji, Kokura, Tobata, Yawata, and Wakamatsu; population (1983) 1,055,000. A tunnel (1942) links it with Honshu. Moji was opened to foreign trade in 1887.

Kitchener /ˈkɪtʃɪnə/ industrial city (foundries, furniture) in Ontario, Canada; population (1981) 139,750.

Kitchener /ˈkɪtʃɪnə/ Horatio Herbert, Earl Kitchener of Khartoum 1850–1916. British field marshal from 1909. Born in County Kerry. He was commissioned in 1871, and transferred to the Egyptian Army in 1882. Promoted commander in chief in 1892, he defeated the Sudanese dervishes at ◊Omdurman in 1898, re-occupied Khartoum, and also forced a French expedition to withdraw from ◊Fashoda. During the South African War he acted as Lord Roberts's chief of staff, and as commander in chief 1900–02 brought the war to a successful conclusion. He subsequently commanded the forces in India and acted as British agent in Egypt, and in 1914 received an earldom. He was appointed war minister on the outbreak of World War I, and drowned when his ship was sunk on the way to Russia.

kite name of several birds of prey in the family Accipitridae. The red kite *Milvus milvus* is found in Europe, including W Britain. It has a forked tail and buoyant flight, and is about 60 cm/2 ft long. The darker and slightly smaller black kite *Milvus migrans* is found over most of the Old World. It scavenges in addition to hunting.

Kitwe /ˈkɪtweɪ/ commercial centre for the Zambian copperbelt; population (1980) 314,800. To the south are Zambia's emerald mines.

Kitzbühel /ˈkɪtsbjuːəl/ winter-sports resort in the Austrian Tirol, NE of Innsbruck; population (1985) 9,000.

Kivu /ˈkiːvuː/ lake in the Great Rift Valley between Zaïre and Rwanda, about 105 km/65 mi long. The chief port is Bukavu.

kiwi native name for a genus of nocturnal flightless birds *Apteryx* confined to New Zealand. It has long and hair-like brown plumage, a very long beak, and the egg is larger, in relation to the bird's size (similar to a domestic chicken), than that of any other bird.

kiwi fruit or *Chinese gooseberry Actinidithia chinensis* family Actinidiaceae, with oval fruit flavoured similarly to a gooseberry, and with a fuzzy brown skin. They are commercially grown on a large scale in New Zealand.

Klaipeda /ˈklaɪpɪdə/ industrial port (iron foundries, shipbuilding) in the Lithuanian Republic of the USSR, on the Baltic coast at the mouth of the Dange river; population (1985) 195,000.

history formerly called Memel, it was founded in 1252 as the castle of Memelburg by the Teutonic Knights, joined the ◊Hanseatic League soon after, and has changed hands between Sweden, Russia, and Germany. Lithuania annexed Klaipeda in 1923, and after German occupation 1939–45, it was restored to Lithuania.

Klaproth /ˈklæprəʊt/ Martin Heinrich 1743–1817. German chemist famous for his discovery of the elements uranium, zirconium, cerium and titanium.

Klee /kleɪ/ Paul 1879–1940. Swiss painter, who painted semi-abstract pictures, often humorous in effect, to evoke reactions from the subconscious. He was associated with Der ◊Blaue Reiter, and taught at the ◊Bauhaus 1920–26.

Kleist /klaɪst/ (Bernd) Heinrich (Wilhelm) von 1777–1811. German dramatist, whose comedy, *Der zerbrochene Krug/The Broken Pitcher* 1808, and dramatic *Prinz Friedrich von Homburg/The Prince of Homburg* 1811, achieved success only after his suicide.

Klemperer /ˈklempərə/ Otto 1885–1973. German conductor, noted for his interpretation of contemporary and classical music (especially ◊Beethoven and ◊Brahms). He was director of the Los Angeles Orchestra 1933–39 and Philharmonia Orchestra, London, from 1959.

kleptomania (Greek *kleptēs* 'thief') a behavioural disorder characterized by an overpowering desire to steal. In kleptomania, as opposed to straightforward theft, there is no obvious need or use for what is stolen.

Kliegl /ˈkliːgəl/ John 1869–1959 and Anton 1872–1927. American brothers, born in Germany, who invented the brilliant carbon-arc (klieg) lights used in television and films.

Klimt /klɪmt/ Gustav 1862–1918. Austrian painter, influenced by ◊Art Nouveau; founder of the Vienna ◊Sezession group 1897. His works include the mosaic *The Kiss* 1909 (Musée des Beaux-Arts, Strasbourg).

Klondike /ˈklɒndaɪk/ former gold-mining area in ◊Yukon, Canada. The name is taken from the river valley where in 1896 gold was found; some 30,000 people moved there during the following 15 years. Silver is still mined today.

Klopstock /ˈklɒpʃtɒk/ Friedrich Gottlieb 1724–1803. German poet whose religious epic *The Messiah* 1745–73 and lyric odes prepared the way for the great age of 18th-century German literature.

knapweed N temperate wild flower *hardhead Centaurea nigra*, family Compositae. The hard, bract-covered buds break into purple composite heads.

Knaresborough /ˈneəzbərə/ English market town in N Yorkshire, 6 km/4 mi NE of Harrogate, with a castle dating from about 1070.

Kneller /ˈnelə/ Godfrey 1646–1723. British court portrait painter (of German descent) to Charles II, William III, and George I. Famous series are the Hampton Court *Beauties* and 42 portraits of the members of the Whig 'Kit Cat Club' (1702–17) in the National Portrait Gallery, London. He was knighted in 1692.

Knesset the Israeli parliament, consisting of a single chamber of 120 members elected for a period of four years.

knife fish genus *Gymnotus* and allied forms, in which the body is deep at the front, drawn to a narrow or pointed tail at the rear, the main fin being the well-developed long ventral which completes the knife-like shape. The ventral fin is rippled for forward or backward locomotion. Knife fish produce electrical fields which they use for navigation.

Knight /naɪt/ Laura 1877–1970. British artist. She excelled in detailed, narrative painting of Romany, fairground, and circus life, and of ballet, as well as nudes and landscapes. She was created Dame of the British Empire in 1929.

knighthood, order of fraternity carrying with it the rank of knight, admission to which is granted as a mark of royal favour or as a reward for public services. During the Middle Ages such fraternities fell into two classes, religious and secular. The first class, including the ◊Templars and the *Knights of St John*, consisted of knights who had taken religious vows and devoted themselves to military service against the Saracens or other non-Christians. The secular orders probably arose from bands of knights engaged in the service of a prince or great noble, who wore his badge or the emblem of his patron saint.

British orders The *Order of the Garter*, founded about 1347, is the oldest now in existence: there are eight other British orders, those of the *Thistle* founded 1687, *St Patrick* 1788, the *Bath* 1725, the *Star of India* 1861, *St Michael and St George* 1818, the *Indian Empire* 1878 (no conferments since 1947), the *Royal Victorian Order* 1896, and the *Order of the British Empire* (OBE) 1917. The *Order of Merit*, founded 1902, comprises the sovereign and no more than 24 prominent individuals.

Most of the ancient European orders, such as the *Order of the Golden Fleece*, have disappeared as a result of political changes. A *knight bachelor* belongs to the lowest stage of knighthood, not being a member of any specially named order. See also ◊medal.

Knipper /ˈknɪpə/ Lev Konstantinovich 1898–1974. Russian composer. After 1932 he wrote in a more popular idiom, as in the symphony *Poem of Komsomol Fighters* 1933–34 with its mass battle songs. Best known in the West is his song 'Cavalry of the Steppes'.

knitting method of making fabric by twining yarn with needles. Knitting may have been developed from *crochet* which uses a single hooked needle, or from *netting* with a shuttle. A mechanized process for stockings was developed in the 16th century, but it was not until after World War II that machine knitting was revolutionized with the introduction of synthetic yarns, coloured dyes, and methods of texturing, elasticizing, and so on.

knocking phenomenon that occurs in a spark-ignition petrol engine when the unburnt fuel-air mixture explodes in the combustion chamber before being ignited by the spark. The resulting shock waves produce a characteristic metallic knocking sound. Loss of power occurs, which can be prevented by reducing the compression ratio, re-designing the geometry of the combustion chamber or increasing the octane number of the petrol (usually by the use of lead tetraethyl anti-knock additives).

Knossos /'knɒsɒs/ site near Iráklion of the chief city of ◊Minoan Crete. Excavation of the palace of the legendary King Minos by Sir Arthur ◊Evans showed that the story of Theseus' encounter with the Minotaur in a labyrinth possibly derived from the ritual 'bull-leaping' by youths and girls shown in the frescoes, and the maze-like layout of the palace.

knot bird *Calidris canutus* of the sandpiper family. A wader, about the size of a thrush, it is brick-red below and on the face in summer, drab in winter, and feeds on insects and molluscs. Breeding in the Arctic, knots travel widely in winter, to be found as far afield as Java, South Africa, New Zealand and Britain.

knot the unit by which a ship's speed is measured, corresponding to 1 nautical mile per hour. The nautical mile is one minute of latitude, and although varying over the Earth's surface, is in practice taken to be 1,853 m/6,080 ft (1 kn = about 1⅐ of a mile). It is also used in aviation and has not so far been replaced by the ◊SI measurement in m/s (metres per second).

knot an intertwinement of parts of one or more ropes, cords, and strings, used to bind them together or to other objects. It is constructed so that the strain borne serves to draw it tighter. 'Bends' or 'hitches' are knots used to fasten ropes together or to other objects; when two ropes are joined end to end, they are 'spliced'. The craft of ◊macramé uses knots to form decorative fringes.

knotgrass annual plant *Polygonum aviculare* of the dock family, that grows on bare ground of all kinds including seashores. Often low-growing, but with stems up to 2 m/6 ft, the small lance-shaped leaves have bases that sheathe the stem, giving the superficial resemblance to grass. The small pinkish flowers grow in small clusters in the leaf axils in late summer, followed by seeds which are a favourite with birds. Knotgrass grows worldwide except in the polar regions.

knowledge-based system (KBS) a computer program that uses an encoding of human knowledge to improve its problem-solving performance. It was first discovered in ◊artificial-intelligence research that adding heuristics (rules of thumb) enabled programs to tackle problems that were insoluble by the usual techniques of computer science. Recently chess-playing programs (to take one example) have been strengthened enormously by including knowledge of what makes a good position, or

about overall strategies, rather than relying solely on the computer's ability to calculate variations.

Knox /nɒks/ John c. 1505–1572. Scottish Protestant reformer, originally a Roman Catholic priest. After the death of ◊Wishart, he went into hiding, but later preached the reformed doctrines and when taken by French troops in Scotland in 1547 was first imprisoned in France, then sentenced to the galleys, being released only by intercession of the British government 1549. In England he assisted in compiling the Prayer Book, as a royal chaplain from 1551. On Mary's accession he fled abroad, but in 1559 returned to Scotland where he was the chief founder of the Church of Scotland, and published a *History of the Reformation in Scotland* 1586.

Knox An engraving showing the 16th-century Scottish Protestant reformer John Knox.

Knoxville /'nɒksvɪl/ city in Tennessee, USA, the centre of a mining and agricultural region of great beauty, seat of a university founded in 1794; population (1981) 175,000. Administrative headquarters of the ◊Tennessee Valley Authority.

koala marsupial *Phascolarctos cinereus* of the family Phalangeridae, found only in E Australia and not easily kept in zoos because it feeds almost entirely on eucalyptus shoots. Resembling a bear 60 cm/2 ft long, it has greyish fur which led to its almost complete extermination by hunters. Under protection from 1936 it has rapidly increased in numbers.

Kobe /'kəʊbeɪ/ port in S Honshu, Japan; population (1980) 1,367,400. *Port Island* created from the rock of nearby mountains 1960–68, area 5 sq km/2 sq mi, is one of the world's largest construction projects.

Koblenz /'kəʊblents/ city in the Rhineland-Palatinate, West Germany, at the junction of the Rhine and Mosel, dating back to Roman times; population (1980) 113,700. It is a centre of communications and the wine trade, with industries (shoes, cigars, paper).

Koch /kɒx/ Robert 1843–1910. German bacteriologist, who isolated the tubercle (TB or tuberculosis) bacillus in 1882, and devised the tuberculin test for cattle; he also worked on the bubonic plague and malaria; Nobel Prize for Medicine 1905.

Kodály /'kəʊdaɪ/ Zoltán 1882–1967. Hungarian composer. With ◊Bartók he collected Magyar folk music, and wrote much chamber and instrumental music, including the comic opera, *Háry János* 1926, and 'Dances of Galanta'.

Kodiak /'kəʊdiæk/ island off the S coast of Alaska, site of a US naval base; area 9,505 sq km/3,670 sq mi. It is the home of the world's largest ◊bear. The town of Kodiak is the largest US fishing port (mainly salmon).

Koestler /'kɜːstlə/ Arthur 1905–1983. Hungarian-born British author. Born in Budapest, he became a journalist and Communist, and was sentenced to death as a spy while in Spain during the Civil War (*Spanish Testament* 1938). Imprisoned by the Nazis in France in 1940 (*Scum of the Earth* 1941), he escaped to England, becoming a British subject after World War II. By 1941 (in the novel *Darkness at Noon*), he had shown his disillusion with Communism. Later books were attempted syntheses of all aspects of knowledge, for example *The Roots of Coincidence* 1972. He endowed Britain's first chair of parapsychology at Edinburgh, established 1984. He was joined in suicide by his wife.

Koestler Hungarian-born writer Arthur Koestler was imprisoned in Spain by Franco, in France by the Nazis, and briefly in Britain, where he later settled.

Koh-i-noor (Persian 'mountain of light') a famous diamond, originally part of the Aurangzeb treasure, seized by the Shah of Iran from the Moguls in India in 1739, taken back by Sikhs, and acquired by Britain in 1849 when the Punjab was annexed.

Kohl /kəʊl/ Helmut 1930– . West German conservative politician, leader of the Christian Democratic Union (CDU) from 1973, chancellor from 1982.
Kohl, a practising Catholic, studied law and history before entering the chemical industry. Elected to the Rhineland-Palatinate *Land* (state) parliament in 1959, he became state premier in 1969. After the 1976 Bundestag

(federal parliament) elections Kohl led the CDU in opposition. He became federal chancellor (prime minister) in 1982, when the Free Democratic Party (FDP) withdrew their support from the ◊Schmidt government, and was elected at the head of the new CDU-CSU-FDP coalition. From 1984 Kohl was implicated in the Flick bribes scandal over the illegal business funding of political parties, but he was cleared of all charges by the Bonn public prosecutor in May 1986. Kohl was re-elected as chancellor in Jan 1987 after engineering a healthy economic recovery.

Kohl Chancellor Helmut Kohl addresses the Bundestag, the lower house of the West German parliament.

kohlrabi a variety of kale *Brassica oleracea*. The leaves shoot from a swelling on the main stem. The globular portion is used for food, and resembles a turnip.

Kokand /kə'kænd/ industrial oasis town (fertilizers, cotton, silk) in Uzbek Republic of USSR; population (1981) 156,000. It was the capital of Kokand khanate when annexed by Russia 1876.

Kokhba /'kɒxbə/ Bar. Name adopted by Simeon bar Koziba (died 135). Jewish leader of the revolt against the Hellenization campaign of the Roman emperor ◊Hadrian 132–35, which led to the razing of Jerusalem. He was killed in battle at Bethar.

Koko Nor /'kəʊkəʊ 'nɔː/ Mongolian form of ◊Qinghai, province of China.

Kokoschka /kə'kɒʃkə/ Oskar 1886–1980. Austrian-born ◊Expressionist artist, whose early work caused a sensation in Vienna during the first decade of this century. He fled from the Nazis to England in 1938, taking British citizenship 1947. He was noted for brilliantly coloured portraits, and panoramic townscapes.

kola an alternative spelling of ◊cola, genus of tropical trees.

Kola /'kəʊlə/ peninsula in N USSR, bounded by the White Sea on the S and E, and by the Barents Sea on the N; area 129,500 sq

km/50,000 sq mi; coterminous with Murmansk region. Apatite and other minerals are exported. To the NW the low-lying granite plateau adjoins Norway's thinly populated county of Finnmark, and Soviet troops are heavily concentrated here.

Kolchak /kɒl'tʃæk/ Alexander Vasilievich 1875–1920. Russian admiral, commander of the White forces in Siberia, who proclaimed himself Supreme Ruler of Russia 1918, but was shot by the Bolsheviks.

Kolchugino /kɒl'tʃuːgɪnəʊ/ former name (to 1925) of ◊Leninsk-Kuznetsky, town in USSR.

Kolhapur /ˌkəʊlə'pʊə/ industrial city in Maharashtra, India, noted as a film production centre; population (1981) 346,000.

kolkhoz Russian term for a ◊collective farm, as opposed to a ◊*sovkhoz* or state-owned farm.

Kollontai /ˌkɒlən'taɪ/ Alexandra 1872–1952. Russian revolutionary, politician, and writer. In 1896 she saw the appalling conditions for factory workers in Russia while on a tour of a large textile factory with her husband. She was so enraged by his view that only small improvements were necessary that she left him and devoted herself to improving conditions for working women; in 1905 she published *On the Question of the Class Struggle*. She was harassed by the police for her views and in 1914 she went into exile in Germany. On her return to Russia she joined the Bolsheviks and toured the USA to argue against its involvement in World War I.

She was the only female member of the first Bolshevik government as Commissar for Public Welfare. In 1918 she organized the first all-Russian Congress of Working and Peasant Women. A controversial figure in government, she was sent abroad by Stalin, first as Trade Minister, then as Ambassador to Sweden in 1943. She took part in the armistice negotiations ending the Soviet-Finnish war in 1944. She also campaigned for domestic reforms such as acceptance of free love, simplification of divorce laws and collective childcare . Her book *The Love of Worker Bees* 1923 aroused great controversy.

Kollwitz /'kɒlvɪts/ Käthe 1867–1945. German artist, noted for woodcuts and engravings on themes such as maternal affection and death.

Köln /kɜːln/ German form of ◊Cologne, city in West Germany.

Kolwezi /kɒl'weɪzi/ mining town in Shaba province, Zaïre, important for copper and cobalt. Population (1985) 82,000. In 1978 former police of the province invaded from Angola and massacred some 650 of the inhabitants.

Kommunizma, Pik /'piːk ˌkɒmu'nɪzmə/ the highest mountain in the USSR, in the Akademiya Nauk range of the Pamirs, in Tadzhikistan. Communism Peak (7,495 m/24,590 ft) was formerly known as Stalin Peak and Garmo Peak.

Komsomol Russian name for the All-Union Leninist Communist Youth League. Membership is open to all between the ages of 14 and 26, and numbers several millions. Founded in 1918, it acts as the youth section of the Communist Party, and its activities include all

forms of national service, for example the rebuilding of Stalingrad in 1942.

Kong Zi Pinyin form of ◊Confucius, Chinese philosopher.

Koniev /'kɒnjef/ Ivan Stepanovich 1898–1973. Soviet marshal who liberated the Ukraine from the invading German forces 1943, and advanced from the south on Berlin to link with the Anglo-US forces.

Königsberg /'kɜːnɪgzbeəg/ German name of ◊Kaliningrad, port in USSR.

Konstanz /'kɒnstænts/ German form of the town of ◊Constance.

Kon-tiki /'kɒn 'tiːki/ legendary Sun King who ruled the country later occupied by the ◊Incas, and was supposed to have migrated, with certain whiteskinned and bearded followers, out into the Pacific. The name was used by explorer Thor ◊Heyerdahl for his raft which sailed from Peru to the Pacific Islands.

Konya /'kɒnjə/ city (Roman *Iconium*) in SW central Turkey; population (1980) 329,200. Carpets and silks are made here, and the city contains the monastery of the dancing ◊Dervishes.

kookaburra the largest of the world's kingfishers *Dacelo novaeguineae*, the kookaburra, or laughing jackass, has an extraordinary laughing note, one of the most familiar sounds of the bush of eastern Australia. It is an opportunistic feeder, taking mainly insects and other small creatures, including fish from garden ponds. Body and tail measure 45 cm/18 in; the head is greyish with a dark eye stripe, the back and wings are flecked brown, with grey underparts.

Koran (alternatively transliterated as *Quran*) the sacred book of ◊Islam. Written in the purest Arabic, it contains 114 suras or chapters, and is stated to have been divinely revealed to the prophet Muhammad; the original is supposed to be preserved beside the throne of Allah in heaven.

Korda /'kɔːdə/ Alexander 1893–1956. Hungarian-born British film producer and director, a dominant figure during the 1930s and 1940s. His films include *The Private Life of Henry VIII* 1933, *The Third Man* 1950, and *Richard III* 1956.

Kordofan /ˌkɔːdə'fɑːn/ province of central Sudan, known as the 'White Land'. Although never an independent state, it has a character of its own. It is mainly undulating plain, with acacia scrub producing gum arabic, marketed in the chief town ◊El Obeid. Formerly agricultural, it has been overtaken by desertification.

Korea, history the foundation of the Korean state traditionally dates back about 2,000 years BC, to the dynasty of Tangun, followed by that of the Chinese Kija, which ruled from about 1122 until the 4th century BC. Korea was then distracted by internal war and invasion until the 10th century, when it was united within the boundaries it subsequently retained. In the 16th century, Japan invaded Korea for the first time, later withdrawing from a country it had devastated. In 1905 Japan began to treat Korea as a protectorate, and in 1910 annexed it. Many Japanese colonists settled in Korea, introducing both industrial and agricultural development. At

DiE LEBENDEN DEM TOTEN . ERiNNERUNG AN DEN 15.JANUAR 191⁹

Kollwitz One of a series of large lithographs called *Death* by German artist Käthe Kollwitz. Many of her best works are tragic in theme and have pacifist overtones as a result of the death of her sons in World War I and her grandson in World War II.

the end of World War II, the Japanese in Korea surrendered, but the occupying forces at the ceasefire – the USSR north of the ◊38th parallel, and the USA south of it – resulted in a lasting division of the country as North and South Korea (see ◊Korea, North, and ◊Korea, South for history since 1945).

Korea, North /kəˈrɪə/ country in e asia, bounded N by China, E by the Sea of Japan, S by South Korea, and W by the Yellow Sea.

government under the 1972 constitution, which replaced the 1948 Soviet-type constitution, the leading political figure is the president, who is head of the armed forces and executive head of government. The president is appointed for four-year terms by the 615-member supreme people's assembly, which is directly elected by universal suffrage. The supreme people's assembly meets for brief sessions once or twice a year, its regular legislative business being carried out by a smaller permanent standing committee (Presidium). The president works with and presides over a powerful policy-making and supervisory central people's committee (which is responsible to the assembly for its activities) and an administrative and executive cabinet (Administration Council). The controlling force in North Korea is the Communist Party (Workers' Party of Korea), headed since 1945 by Kim Il Sung. It leads the broader Democratic Front for the Reunification of the Fatherland (which includes the minor North Korean Democratic Party and the Religious Chungwoo Party) in putting forward single slates of candidates for election contests.

history for early history, see ◊Korea, history. The Democratic People's Republic of Korea was formed from the zone N of the 38th parallel of latitude, occupied by Soviet troops after Japan's surrender in 1945. The Soviet Union installed in

power an 'Executive Committee of the Korean People', staffed by Soviet-trained Korean Communists, before North Korea was declared a People's Republic in 1948 under the leadership of the Workers' Party, with ◊Kim Il Sung as president. The remaining Soviet forces withdrew in 1949.

In 1950 North Korea, seeking unification of the Korean peninsula, launched a large-scale invasion of South Korea. This began the three-year-long ◊Korean War, which, after intervention by the USA (on the side of the S) and China (on the side of the N), ended in stalemate. The 38th parallel border between N and S was re-established by the armistice agreement of Jul 1953 and a UN-patrolled de-militarized buffer zone was created. North Korea has never accepted this agreement and remains committed to re-unification.

Relations with the S have remained tense and hostile, despite the establishment in 1972 of a N-S co-ordinating committee to promote peaceful unification. Border incidents have been frequent and in Oct 1983 four South Korean cabinet ministers were assassinated in Rangoon (Burma) following a bombing incident organized by two North Korean army officers.

Factories were nationalized and agriculture collectivized in the 1950s, and priority in investment programmes has been given to heavy industry and rural mechanization. North Korean economic growth has, however, lagged behind that of its richer and more populous southern neighbour. In foreign affairs, North Korea has adopted a neutral stance in the Sino-Soviet dispute, signing a friendship and mutual assistance treaty with China in 1961 while at the same time receiving economic and military aid from the Soviet Union.

In recent years, North Korean politics have been dominated by the 'succession question', with Kim Il Sung seeking to establish his son, Kim Jong-Il (1941–   ), as sole heir designate. Kim Jong-Il has accompanied Kim Il Sung on diplomatic and factory tours, been designated 'Armed Forces Supreme Commander', begun to preside over key party and state government meetings, and his portrait has been placed on public display across the country. Elements within the Workers' Party and armed forces appear, however, to oppose Kim's succession aims.

Korea, South /kəˈrɪə/ country in E Asia, bordered to the N by North Korea, E by the Sea of Japan, S by the E China Sea, and W by the Yellow Sea.

government under the 1987 constitution, executive power in the Republic of Korea is held by the president, who is elected directly by popular vote. The president is restricted to one seven-year term of office, and governs with a cabinet (state council) headed by a prime minister. Legislative authority resides in the single-chamber, 276-deputy national assembly, two-thirds of whose members are directly elected for four-year terms by universal suffrage in 92 double-member constituencies, and the remainder of whom are appointed following a formula designed to reward the largest single assembly party. The assembly's powers of debate are restricted.

The dominant party in South Korea is the Democratic Justice Party, which holds a majority in the national assembly and is supported by the business community. The principal opposition party is the left-of-centre New Korea Democratic Party led by ◊Kim Dae Jung and Kim Yung Sam. Two other parties captured seats in the 1985 national assembly elections, the Democratic Korea Party and the Korea National Party.

history for early history, see ◊Korea, history. The Republic of Korea was formed out of the zone S of the 38th parallel of latitude which was occupied by US troops after Japan's surrender in 1945. The American military government controlled the country until, following national elections, an independent republic was declared in 1948. Dr ◊Syngman Rhee, leader of the rightist Liberal Party, was the nation's first president in a constitution based on the US model. To begin with, the republic had to cope with a massive influx of refugees fleeing the Communist regime in the N, then came the 1950–53 ◊Korean War.

President Syngman Rhee, whose regime had been accused of corruption, resigned in 1960 as a result of student-led disorder. A new parliamentary-style constitution gave greater power to the legislature, and the ensuing political instability precipitated a military coup led by Gen ◊Park Chung-Hee in 1961. A presidential system of government was re-established, with Gen Park Chung-Hee elected president in 1963, and a major programme of industrial development began, involving government planning and financial support. This programme, utilizing the nation's plentiful supply of well-educated and industrious workers, was

Korea, North

DEMOCRATIC PEOPLE'S REPUBLIC OF (*Chosun Minchu-chui Inmin Konghwa-guk*)

AREA 121,250 sq km/46,815 sq mi
CAPITAL Pyongyang
PHYSICAL mountainous
FEATURES the richest of the two Koreas in mineral resources
HEAD OF STATE Kim Il Sung from 1972 (also head of Communist Party)
HEAD OF GOVERNMENT Li Gun mo from 1986
GOVERNMENT communist
EXPORTS coal, iron, copper, textiles, chemicals
CURRENCY won (1.55 = £1 Sept 1987)
POPULATION 20,082,000 (1985); annual growth rate 2.4%
LANGUAGE Korean
RELIGION traditionally Buddhist and Confucian
LITERACY 99% (1984)
GNP $18.1 bn (1982 est); $570 per head of population
CHRONOLOGY
1948 Democratic People's Republic of Korea declared.
1950 North Korea invaded South to begin Korean War.
1953 Armistice agreed to end Korean War.

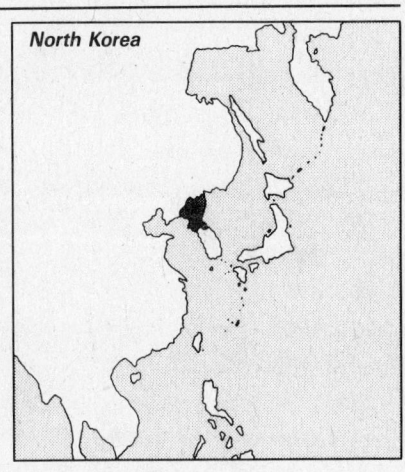

North Korea

1961 Friendship and mutual assistance treaty signed with China.
1972 New constitution, with executive president, was adopted.
1983 Four South Korean cabinet ministers assassinated in Rangoon, Burma, by North Korean army officers.

remarkably successful, with rapid industrial growth during the 1960s and 1970s as South Korea became a major exporter of light and heavy industrial goods.

Opposition to the repressive Park regime mounted during the 1970s. In response, martial law was imposed and in 1972 a new constitution, strengthened the president's powers. A new clampdown on political dissent, launched in 1975, was partially relaxed for the 1978 elections, but brought protests in 1979, as economic conditions briefly deteriorated. President Park was assassinated later that year by the chief of the South Korean Central Intelligence Agency, and martial law was re-imposed.

An interim government, led by former Prime Minister Choi Kyu-Hah, introduced liberalizing reforms, releasing opposition leader Kim Dae Jung in 1980. However, as anti-government demonstrations developed, a new dissident clampdown began, involving the arrest of 30 political leaders, including Kim Dae Jung. After riots in Kim's home city of Kwangju, President Choi resigned in 1980 and was replaced by the leader of the army, Gen Chun Doo-Hwan. A new constitution was adopted and, after Chun Doo-Hwan was re-elected president in 1981, the new Fifth Republic was proclaimed.

Under President Chun economic growth resumed, but internal and external criticism of the suppression of civil liberties continued. Cautious liberalization was seen prior to the 1985 assembly elections, with the release of many political prisoners and the return from exile of Kim Dae-Jung. The opposition parties emerged in a strengthened position after the 1985 assembly election, but the 1987 presidential election was won by the ruling party's candidate, Roh Tae Woo, amid opposition charges of fraud. Since 1953 the constant threat of invasion from the N has been a key factor in South Korean politics, helping to justify stern rule. South Korea has been forced to devote large resources to modernizing its armed forces, which are supported in addition by US troops.

Korean language the language of Korea, written from the 5th century AD in Chinese characters until the invention of an alphabet by King Sejong in 1443. This alphabet was discouraged as 'vulgar letters' (*onmun*) and banned by the colonizing Japanese. After World War II it has been revived as 'top letters' (*hangul*). The linguistic affiliations of Korean are unclear, but it appears to be distantly related to Japanese.

Korean War 1950–53, between North Korea (supported by China) and South Korea, aided by the United Nations (including the UK, though the troops were mainly US). North Korean forces invaded the South 25 Jun 1950, and the Security Council of the United Nations, owing to a walk-out by the USSR, voted to oppose them. After a 'concertina' campaign up and down the peninsula, which ended in the restoration of the original boundary on the 38th parallel, an armistice was signed with the North, although South Korea did not participate.

Korinthos /'kɒrɪnθɒs/ Greek form of ⟩Corinth.

Korolev /kə'rɒljef/ Sergei Pavlovich 1906–1966. Soviet designer of rockets and spacecraft, responsible for the early Soviet lead in space exploration. Born in Zhitomir, Ukraine, Korolev became an aircraft designer before turning to rocketry. After World War II he designed the first Soviet intercontinental missile, used in 1957 to launch the first ⟩Sputnik satellite, and in 1961 to launch the ⟩Vostok spacecraft (also designed by Korolev) in which Yuri ⟩Gagarin made the world's first space flight.

Kortrijk /'kɔːtraɪk/ Flemish form of ⟩Courtrai, town in Belgium.

Kos /kɒs/ or *Cos* fertile Greek island, one of the Dodecanese, in the Aegean Sea; area 287 sq km/111 sq mi. It gives its name to the Cos lettuce.

Kosciusko /ˌkɒsi'ʌskəʊ/ highest mountain in Australia (2,229 m/7,316 ft), in New South Wales. Sir Paul Strzelecki, who was born in Prussian Poland, named it after a Polish revolutionary hero in 1839.

Kościuszko /kɒs'tʃuʃkəʊ/ Tadeusz 1746–1817. Polish revolutionary leader, defeated by combined Russian and Prussian forces in 1794, and imprisoned till 1796.

kosher (Hebrew 'proper') term applied by Jews to food prepared according to Mosaic law. There are several Jewish dietary laws: only animals that chew their cud and have cloven hooves (that is, cows and sheep, but not pigs) are kosher; there are rules governing their slaughter and preparation (such as complete draining of blood), which also apply to fowl. Only fish with scales and fins are kosher (not shellfish). Milk products may not be cooked or eaten with meat or poultry. There have been various explanations for the origins of these laws, particularly hygiene (pork and shellfish spoil quickly in a hot climate), and many Reform Jews no longer feel obliged to observe them.

Košice /'kɒʃɪtseɪ/ town in SE Czechoslovakia; textile industry and road centre; a large part of the population (1980) 204,700 is Magyar-speaking, and Kosiče was in Hungary until 1920 and 1938–45.

Kosovo autonomous region in Serbia, Yugoslavia. Inhabited by Albanians and bordering on Albania, it has demands for unification with that country.

Kossuth /'kɒʃuːt/ Lajos 1802–1894. Hungarian patriot. He proclaimed Hungarian independence of Hapsburg rule in 1849, and when the Hungarians were later defeated, fled first to Turkey, then England.

Kosygin /kə'siːgɪn/ Alexei Nikolaievich 1904–1980. Soviet politician, prime minister 1964–80.

Born in Leningrad, he was elected to the Supreme Soviet in 1938, and became a member of the Politburo 1946. Deputy prime minster from 1960, he succeeded Khrushchev as prime minister.

Kota Bharu /'kəʊtə 'bɑːruː/ capital of Kelantan, Malaysia; population (1980) 170,600.

Kota Kinabalu /'kəʊtə ˌkɪnəbə'luː/ capital and port (formerly Jesselton) in Sabah, Malaysia; population (1980) 59,500.

koto rectangular 13-stringed musical instrument, plucked with the fingers, the chief traditional instrument of Japan. It rests

Korea, South

REPUBLIC OF (*Han Kook*)

AREA 99,999 sq km/38,450 sq mi
CAPITAL Seoul
TOWNS Taegu, ports Pusan, Inchon
PHYSICAL mountainous
HEAD OF STATE Roh Tai Woo from 1987
HEAD OF GOVERNMENT Kim Chung Yul from 1987
GOVERNMENT right-wing authoritarian
EXPORTS steel, ships, chemicals, electronics, textiles, plastics
CURRENCY won (1,335 = £1 Sept 1987)
POPULATION 42,643,000 (1985); annual growth rate 2.2%
LANGUAGE Korean
RELIGION traditionally Buddhist and Confucian
LITERACY 96% male/87% female (1980 est)
GNP $78.9 bn (1984); $1,187 per head of population
CHRONOLOGY
1948 Republic proclaimed.
1950–53 War with North Korea.
1960 President Syngman Rhee resigned amid unrest.
1961 Military coup by Gen Park Chung-Hee.

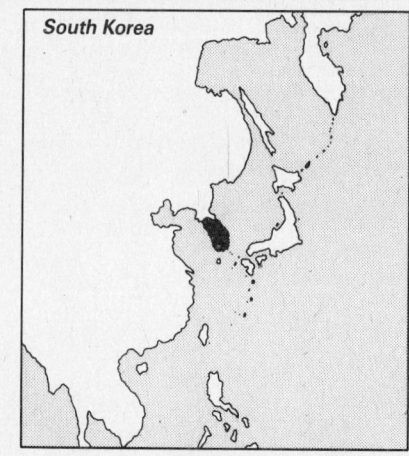

South Korea

Industrial growth programme.
1979 Assassination of President Park.
1980 Military coup by Gen Chun Doo-Hwan.
1987 Adoption of more democratic constitution following student unrest. Roh Tai Woo elected president.

horizontally on the floor, the musician being seated behind it.

Kottbus /'kɒtbʊs/ alternative spelling of ◊Cottbus, town in East Germany.

kouprey type of wild cattle *Bos sauveli* native to the forest of northern Kampuchea. Only known to science since 1937. It is in great danger of extinction.

Kourou /ku'ru:/ river and second-largest town of French Guiana, NW of Cayenne. It is the site of the Guiana Space Centre engaged in work for the ◊European Space Agency. Situated near the equator, it is an ideal site for launches of satellites into ◊geostationary orbit (a fixed position relative to the Earth).

Kovalevsky /,kɒvə'lefski/ Sophia Vasilevna 1850–1891. Russian mathematician. Her dissertation on partial differential equations was accepted by Göttingen University in 1874 for a doctorate, and she became professor of mathematics at the University of Stockholm in 1884. In 1886 she won the *Prix Bordin* of the French Academy of Sciences for a paper on the rotation of a rigid body about a point, a problem the 18th-century mathematicians Euler and Lagrange had both failed to solve.

Kovno /'kɒvnə/ Russian form of ◊Kaunas, port in Lithuania, USSR.

Kowloon /,kaʊ'lu:n/ peninsula on the Chinese coast forming part of the British crown colony of Hong Kong; the town of Kowloon is a residential area.

Krafft-Ebing /'kræft 'eɪbɪŋ/ Baron Richard von 1840–1902. German pioneer psychiatrist. A neurologist, he published his best-known work *Psychopathia Sexualis* in 1886.

Kragujevac /'kræguːjeɪvæts/ garrison town and former capital (1818–39) of Serbia, Yugoslavia; population (1981) 165,000.

Krakatoa /,krækə'təʊə/ (Indonesian *Krakatau*) volcanic island in Sunda strait, Indonesia, which erupted in 1883, causing 36,000 deaths on Java and Sumatra by the tidal waves which followed. The island is now uninhabited.

Kraków /'krækaʊ/ city in Poland, on the Vistula, important industrially (railway wagons, paper, chemicals, tobacco, food processing) and historically (Kraków was the capital of Poland from about 1300 to 1595); population (1984) 735,000. Its university, at which the astronomer ◊Copernicus was a student, is one of the oldest in central Europe (1400); there is a fine 14th-century Gothic cathedral.

Kramatorsk /,kræmə'tɔːsk/ industrial town (coalmining machinery, steel, ceramics, railway repairs) in the Ukraine, USSR, in the Donbas, N of Donetsk; population (1981) 183,000.

Krasnodar /,kræsnəu'dɑː/ industrial town at the head of navigation of the Kuban river, in SW USSR; population (1981) 581,000. It is linked by pipeline with the Caspian oilfields.

Krasnoyarsk /,kræsnəu'jɑːsk/ industrial city (locomotives, paper, timber, cement, gold refining, large hydroelectric works) in central USSR; population (1981) 820,000. There is a large early-warning and space-tracking radar phased array device at nearby Abalakova. See also ◊Novosibirsk.

Krebs /krebz/ Hans 1900–1981. British biochemist, born in Germany. In 1953 he shared a Nobel Prize for medicine for discovering the citric acid cycle, also known as ◊Krebs's cycle, by which food is converted into energy in living tissues.

Krebs's cycle or *citric acid cycle* part of the chain of biochemical reactions whereby organisms break down food ◊aerobically (using oxygen) to release energy (◊respiration). It breaks down food molecules in a series of small steps, producing energy-rich molecules of ◊ATP.

Krefeld /'kreɪfelt/ industrial town (textiles) on the Westphalian coalfield near the Rhine, 52 km/32 mi NW of Cologne, West Germany; population (1980) 224,000.

Kreisler /'kraɪslə/ Fritz 1875–1962. Austrian violinist and composer, renowned as an interpreter of ◊Brahms and Beethoven.

Kremenchug /,kreɪmen'tʃuːg/ industrial town (road-building machinery, rail wagons, processed food) on the river Dnieper, in Ukraine Republic, USSR; population (1981) 215,000.

kremlin /'kremlɪn/ citadel or fortress of Russian cities. The Moscow kremlin dates from the 12th century, and the name 'the Kremlin' is used as synonymous with the Soviet government.

Kreutzer /'krɔɪtsə/ Rodolphe 1766–1831. French violinist and composer of German descent, to whom Beethoven dedicated his violin sonata Opus 47, known as the *Kreutzer Sonata*.

krill Antarctic crustacean, the most common species being *Euphausia superba*. Shrimp-like, it is about 6 cm/2.5 in long, with two antennae, five pairs of legs, seven pairs of light organs along the body, and is coloured orange above and green beneath. Moving in enormous swarms, krill constitute the chief food of the baleen whales, and have been used to produce a protein concentrate for human consumption and meal for animal feed.

Krishna /'krɪʃnə/ incarnation of the Hindu god ◊Vishnu.

Krishna Consciousness Movement popular name for the ◊International Society for Krishna Consciousness.

Kristallnacht the 'night of [broken] glass' 9–10 Nov 1938 when the Nazi Sturm Abteilung in Germany and Austria mounted a concerted attack on Jews, their synagogues and their property. This *pogrom* served to convince nearly all the Jews that there was no future for them in the Third Reich and precipitated a rush for visas for other countries. Restrictive immigration policies throughout the world and Nazi restrictions made it impossible for most of them to leave.

Krivoi Rog /krɪ'vɔɪ 'rɒg/ town in the Ukraine, USSR, 130 km/80 mi SW of Dnepropetrovsk; population (1981) 663,000. The surrounding district is rich in iron ore, and there is a metallurgical industry. The name means 'crooked horn'.

Kronos or *Cronus* in Greek mythology, one of the ◊Titans, ruler of the world, and father of Zeus, who overthrew him.

Kronstadt /'krɒnstæt/ Russian naval base, founded by Peter the Great 1703, on Kotlin island, Gulf of Finland, commanding the sea approach to Leningrad, whose defence under siege was aided by its guns 1941–43.

Kronstadt uprising revolt in Mar 1921 by sailors of the Russian Baltic Fleet at their headquarters in Kronstadt, outside Petrograd (now Leningrad). Following a strike by Petrograd workers in Feb 1921, the Kronstadt sailors reaffirmed their demands for the rights obtained in theory by the Revolution of 1917.

The sailors were thus labelled the 'conscience of the Revolution' for demanding what had been promised, but not delivered, by the Bolsheviks. They were seen as a threat by the Bolsheviks because of their detection and resentment of the growing monopoly of power held by the Bolsheviks. On the orders of ◊Trotsky, Red Army troops, dressed in white camouflage, crossed the ice to the naval base and captured it on 18 Mar. The leaders were subsequently shot. The Kronstadt uprising was one of the immediate causes of the ◊New Economic Policy begun by Lenin in Mar of the same year.

Kropotkin /krɒ'pɒtkɪn/ Peter Alexeivich, Prince 1842–1921. Russian anarchist. Born in Moscow, he served in the army, did important survey work in Asia, joined the revolutionary party in St Petersburg, and in 1874 was imprisoned. He escaped to England in 1876, and later moved to Switzerland. Expelled from Switzerland, he went to France, where he was imprisoned 1883–86. He then lived in England until 1917, when he returned to Moscow. Among his principal works are *Modern Science and Anarchism* and *Mutual Aid*.

Kruger /'kruːgə/ Stephanus Johannes Paulus 1825–1904. President of the Transvaal 1883–1900. He refused to remedy the grievances of the Uitlanders (English and other non-Boer white residents), and so precipitated the ◊South African War.

Kruger National Park game reserve in NE Transvaal, South Africa, between the Limpopo and Crocodile rivers; it is the largest in the world (about 21,000 sq km/8,000 sq mi), established 1898 by President Kruger.

Krugersdorp /'kruːgəzdɔːp/ mining town (manganese, uranium, gold) in the Witwatersrand district, Transvaal, South Africa; population (1980) 103,000.

Kruger telegram message sent by Kaiser Wilhelm II of Germany to President ◊Kruger on 3 Jan 1896 congratulating him on defeating the ◊Jameson raid of 1895. The text of the telegram provoked a good deal of indignation, especially in Britain, and represented a worsening of Anglo-German relations, in spite of a German government retraction.

Krupp /krʊp/ German armaments firm, which developed the long distance artillery used in World War I, and supported Hitler's regime in preparation for World War II, after which the head of the firm was imprisoned.

krypton a colourless, odourless, inert gas. It is an element, symbol Kr, atomic number 36, atomic weight 83.8. It was discovered in 1898 by ◊Ramsay and Travers in the residue from liquid air. It occurs in the atmosphere at about 1½ parts per million, and is used to enhance brilliance in miners' electric lamps, and in some gas-filled electronic valves.

Kuala Lumpur /'kwɑːlə 'lʊmpʊə/ capital of Malaysia, with a large trade in tin and rubber; it has the University of Malaya (1962) and the National Institute of Technology; population (1985) 1,103,200. Formerly within the state of Selangor, of which it was also the capital, it was created a federal territory in 1974.

Kuanyin /ˌkwæn'jɪn/ the 'goddess of mercy' of the Chinese Buddhists; the Japanese know her as Kwannon.

Kuban /kuː'bɑːn/ river in the USSR, rising in Georgia (see ◊Krasnodar); length 906 km/563 mi to the Sea of Azov.

Kubelik /'kuːbəlɪk/ Jan 1880–1940. Czech violinist. He performed in Prague at the age of 8, and was one of the world's greatest virtuosos; he also wrote six violin concertos.

Kubelik /'kuːbəlɪk/ Rafael 1914– . Czech conductor-composer (symphonies, operas, for example *Veronika* 1947).

Kublai Khan /'kuːblaɪ 'kɑːn/ 1216–1294. Mongol emperor of China, grandson of Genghis Khan. He succeeded his brother Mangu in 1259, established himself as emperor of the whole of China, and with little success attempted to extend his rule still further.

Kubrick /'kuːbrɪk/ Stanley 1928– . American-born British film director, producer, and screenwriter. After initial success in Hollywood, he moved to Britain in 1961 where he made films including *Dr Strangelove* 1964 and *2001: A Space Odyssey* 1968.

Kuching /'kuːtʃɪŋ/ capital and port of Sarawak, Malaysia, on the Sarawak river; population (1980) 74,200.

kudu African antelope *Tragelaphus strepsiceros*. Fawn with thin white vertical stripes, only males have the large spiral horns. They may be 1.3 m/4.2 ft at the shoulder and have head and body 2.4 m/8 ft long. The secretive kudu is found in bush country from Angola to Ethiopia. The similar *lesser kudu Tragelaphus imberbis* lives in E Africa and is 1 m/3 ft at the shoulder.

kudzu Japanese creeper *Pueraria lobata*, family Leguminosae, which helps fix nitrogen (see ◊nitrogen cycle) and can be used as fodder, but became a pest in USA when introduced to check soil erosion.

Kufra /'kuːfrə/ group of oases in the Libyan Desert, N Africa, SE of Tripoli. By the 1970s the vast underground reservoirs were being used for irrigation.

Kuhn /kuːn/ Thomas S 1922– . American historian and philosopher of science, who argued that social and cultural conditions affect the directions of science. *The Structure of Scientific Revolutions* 1962 argued that all knowledge, even scientific knowledge, is relative, dependent on the ◊paradigm (theoretical framework) that dominates a particular scientific field at a particular point in time. Such paradigms (such as Darwinism or Newtonian theory) are so dominant that they are uncritically accepted as true, until a 'scientific revolution' creates a new orthodoxy. His ideas have also been influential in the social sciences.

Kuibyshev /'kuːɪbɪʃɛv/ capital of Kuibyshev region, USSR, a port at the junction of the rivers Samara and Volga; population (1981 est) 1,238,000. Kuibyshev is the centre of the fertile middle Volga plain; industries include aircraft, locomotives, cables, synthetic rubber, textiles; petroleum refining, quarrying, and the manufacture of fertilizers in a complex built with US cooperation from 1973. Founded as Samara,

the town was renamed Kuibyshev in 1935, and was the provisional capital of the USSR 1941–43.

Kuibyshev Sea is an artificial lake about 480 km/300 mi long, created in the 1950s by damming the Volga river.

Ku Klux Klan US secret society dedicated to white supremacy, founded in 1866 in the southern states of the USA to oppose ◊Reconstruction after the Civil War and to deny political rights to the black population. Members wore hooded white robes to hide their identity, and burned crosses as a symbol. Their violence led the government to pass the restrictive Ku Klux Klan Acts of 1871. The society re-emerged in 1915 in Atlanta, Georgia, and increased in strength during the 1920s as a racist, antisemitic, anti-Catholic, and anti-Communist organization. It was particularly active in the 1960s in terrorizing civil rights activists. Although small in size, it remains a focus for occasional racist demonstrations.

kulak Russian term for a peasant who could afford to hire labour, and often acted as village usurer. The kulaks resisted the Soviet government's policy of collectivization, and in 1930 they were 'liquidated as a class', about a million families being banished to eastern USSR.

Kulturkampf policy introduced by Chancellor ◊Bismarck in Germany in 1873 which isolated the Catholic interest and attempted to reduce its power in order to create a political coalition of liberals and agrarian conservatives. The alienation of such a large section of the German population as the Catholics could not be sustained and the policy was abandoned after 1876 and replaced by an anti-Socialist policy.

Kumasi /kuː'mɑːsi/ town in Ghana, W Africa, capital of Ashanti region, with trade in cocoa, rubber, and cattle; university (1961); population (1984) 350,000.

history in the Fourth Ashanti War, in 1900, Sir Frederic Hodgson, governor of the Gold Coast Colony, with his wife, staff, and a small garrison were besieged in the fort at Kumasi Mar–Jun, when they fought their way out. Soon afterwards the kingdom of Ashanti, of which Kumasi had been the capital since the 17th century, was annexed by the British.

Kun /kuːn/ Bela 1885–1937. Hungarian politician, who created a Soviet republic in Hungary in Mar 1919, which was overthrown in August of the same year by a western blockade and Romanian military actions. The succeeding regime under Admiral Horthy effectively liquidated both socialism and liberalism in Hungary.

Küng /kʊŋ/ Hans 1928– . Swiss Roman Catholic theologian. He was in 1979 barred by the Vatican from teaching 'in the name of the Church' because he had cast doubt on papal infallibility, and on whether Christ was the son of God.

kung-fu popular name for the Chinese art of unarmed combat (Manadarin *ch'üan fa*), one of the ◊martial arts. Of many varied styles, the best-known is *wing chun* 'beautiful springtime', of which the film actor Bruce Lee was an exponent. This is said to have been founded in the 16th century by a woman, and is marked by constantly flowing movement to sense in advance moves by an opponent, and the use of offence as a means of defence.

Kuniyoshi /ˌkuːniˈjəuʃi/ Yasuo 1893–1953. Japanese-born American artist. A member of the Utagawa family, who specialized in theatrical prints, Kuniyoshi was regarded as a specialist in the warrior-print. His series *108 Heroes of the Suikoden*, depicting heroes of the Chinese classic, the *Water Margin*, was particularly popular.

Kuniyoshi The American artist Yasuo Kuniyoshi, born in Japan, was Oriental in spirit and subject matter, although he employed Western techniques. This is typical of his warrior prints, *Negoro Komizucha amid a Hail of Weapons*.

Kunlunshan /ˈkunlunˈʃɑːn/ Chinese mountain range on the edge of the great Tibetan plateau, 4,000 km/2,500 mi E–W; highest peak Muztag (7,282 m/23,900 ft).

Kunming /ˌkunˈmɪŋ/ capital of Yunnan province, China, on Lake Dian Chi, about 2,000 m/6,300 ft above sea level; population (1975) 1,284,000. It is the Chinese terminus of the Burma Road, seat of Yunnan University, and an important communications centre. Chemicals and textiles are manufactured, and copper smelted with nearby hydroelectric power.

Kuomintang /ˌkwəʊmɪnˈtæŋ/ original name of Chinese nationalist party, now known (outside ◊Taiwan) as ◊Guomindang.

kurdaitcha shoes shoes made of emu feathers which leave no tracks: worn by Australian Aborigines when escaping their enemies and by sorcerers.

Kurdistan /ˌkɜːdɪˈstɑːn/ hilly region in SW Asia in the neighbourhood of Mt Ararat, where the borders of Iran, Iraq, Syria, Turkey, and the USSR meet. The Kurds, divided among all five countries, have nationalist aspirations, and

number about 7 million. They are Sunni Muslims.

The Kurds of *Iraq* live in the mountainous NE province of Kirkuk, rich in oil, and were in revolt 1961–75 to obtain a fully autonomous Kurdish state. Many Kurds were then moved to S Iraq, a policy which led to further revolt in 1977.

The Kurds of *Iran* number about 4 million in the provinces of W Azerbaijan, Kurdistan, Kermanshah, and Ilam. In 1946 they briefly achieved a Kurdish representative with Soviet backing, were repressed under the shah, and when they revolted against the regime of Ayatollah Khomeini were savagely put down 1979–80.

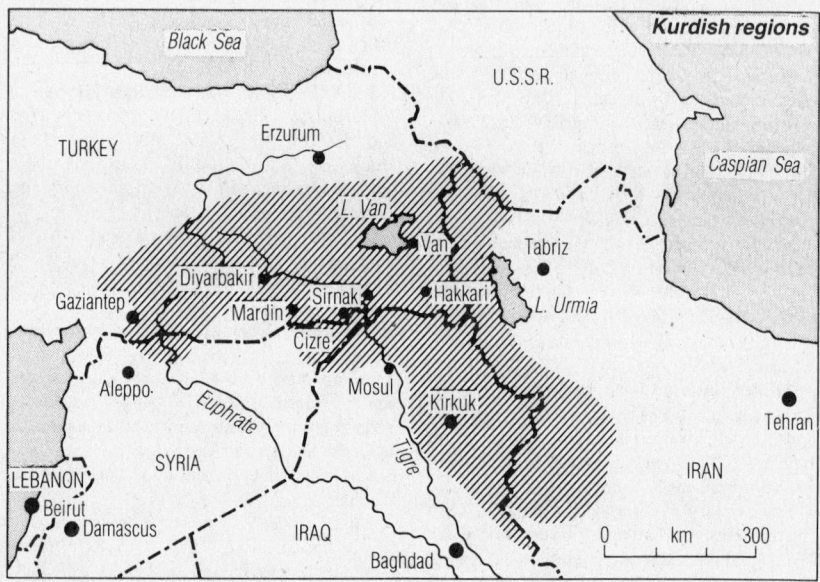

Kure /ˈkuərei/ naval base and port (shipyards, engineering works) 32 km/20 mi SE of Hiroshima, on the S coast of Honshu, Japan; population (1980) 234,500.

Kuria Muria /ˈkuəriə ˈmuəriə/ group of five islands in the Arabian Sea, off the S coast of Oman; area 72 sq km/28 sq mi.

Kurils /kuˈriːlz/ chain of about 50 small islands stretching from the NE of Hokkaido, Japan, to the S of Kamchatka, USSR; area 14,765 sq km/5,700 sq mi; population (1970) 15,000. Some of them are of volcanic origin. The Kurils were discovered in 1634 by a Russian navigator and were settled by Russians. Japan seized them 1875–1945, when under the Yalta agreement they were returned to the USSR. Japan still claims the southernmost (Etorfu and Kunashiri), and also the nearby small islands of Habomai and Shikotan (not part of the Kurils). The USSR agreed to the latter in 1972, but the question of Etorofu and Kunashiri prevents signature of a Japan-Soviet peace treaty.

Kuropatkin /ˌkuərəˈpætkɪn/ Alexei Nikolaievich 1848–1921. Russian general. He won a high reputation during the Russo-Turkish War of 1877–78, was commander-in-chief in Manchuria in 1903, and resigned after his defeat at Mukden. During World War I he commanded

the armies on the N front until 1916, when he was appointed governor of Turkestan.

Kuroshio /kəˈrəʊʃiəu/ also called Japan Current, a warm ocean current flowing from Japan to America.

Kursk /kuəsk/ industrial town (chemicals, machinery, alcohol, tobacco) dating from the 9th century, capital of Kursk region of the USSR; population (1981) 390,000.

Kut-al-Imara /ˈkuːt æl ɪˈmɑːrə/ town on the Tigris, Iraq, a grain market and carpet-manufacturing centre; population (1970) 70,000.

Kutch, Rann of /kʌtʃ/ salt, marshy area in Gujarat state, India, which forms two shallow lakes, the Great Rann and the Little Rann, in the wet season, and is a salt-covered desert in the dry. It takes its name from the former princely state of Kutch, which it adjoined. An international tribunal in 1968 awarded 90% of the Rann of Kutch to India and 10% (about 800 sq km/300 sq mi) to Pakistan, the latter comprising almost all the elevated area above water the year round.

Kutuzov /kuːˈtuːzɒf/ Mikhail Larionovich, Prince of Smolensk 1745–1813. Russian field marshal. He commanded an army corps at Austerlitz, and the retreating army in 1812. After the burning of Moscow he harried the French throughout their retreat, and later took command of the united Prussian armies.

Kuwait /kuˈweɪt/ country in SW Asia, bordered N and NW by Iraq, E by the Gulf, and S and SW by Saudi Arabia.

government the 1962 constitution vests executive power in the hands of the Emir, who governs through an appointed prime minister and council of ministers. The current prime minister is the Emir's eldest son, the crown prince. There is a single-chamber national assembly of 50 members, elected on a restricted suffrage for a four-year term. Political parties are not permitted and, despite the appearance of

Kuwait
STATE OF (*Dowlat al Kuwait*)

AREA 19,000 sq km/7,400 sq mi
CAPITAL Kuwait (also chief port)
PHYSICAL hot desert
FEATURES oil revenues make it one of the world's best equipped states in public works, medical and educational services
HEAD OF STATE AND OF GOVERNMENT Jaber al-Ahmad al-Sabah from 1977
GOVERNMENT authoritarian monarchy
EXPORTS oil
CURRENCY Kuwait dinar (0.46 = £1 Sept 1987)
POPULATION (1985) 1,710,000 (40% Kuwaitis, some 30% Palestinians); annual growth rate 6.8%
LANGUAGE Arabic
RELIGION Sunni Muslim, with Shi'ite minority
LITERACY 72% male/64% female (1980 est)
GNP $22 bn (1984); $11,431 per head of population

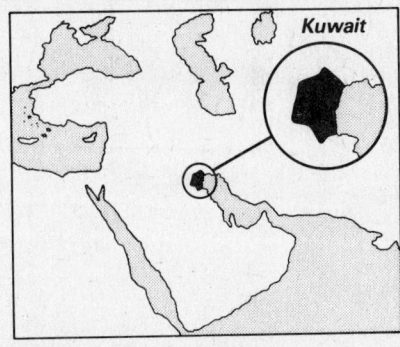
Kuwait

CHRONOLOGY
1961 Achieved full independence, with Sheikh Abdullah al-Salem al-Sabah as emir.
1965 Sheikh Abdullah died and was succeeded by his brother, Sheikh Sabah.
1977 Sheikh Sabah died and was succeeded by Crown Prince Jaber.

constitutional government, Kuwait is, in effect, a personal monarchy.

history part of the Turkish ◊Ottoman Empire from the 16th century, the ruling family founded the sheikhdom of Kuwait in 1756. The ruler made a treaty with Britain in 1899 enabling it to become a self-governing protectorate until it achieved full independence in 1961.

Oil was first discovered in 1938 and its large-scale exploitation began after 1945, transforming Kuwait City from a small fishing port into a thriving commercial centre. The oil revenues have enabled ambitious public works and education programmes to be undertaken. Sheikh Abdullah al-Salem al-Sabah took the title of Emir in 1961 when he assumed full executive powers. He died in 1965 and was succeeded by his brother, Sheikh Sabah al-Salem al-Sabah. He, in turn, died in 1977 and was succeeded by Crown Prince Jaber, who appointed Sheikh Saad al-Abdullah al-Salem al-Sabah as his heir apparent.

Kuwait has used its considerable wealth not only to improve its infrastructure and social services but also to secure its borders, making, for example, substantial donations to Iraq, which in the past had made territorial claims on it. It has also been a strong supporter of the Arab cause generally.

Kuzbas /ˌkʊzˈbæs/ industrial area in Kemerovo region, S USSR, lying on the Tom river to the N of the Altai mountains. Development began in the 1930s. It takes its name from the old town of Kuznetsk.

Kuznets /ˈkʌznets/ Simon 1901–1985. American economist, born in Russia. He developed theories of national income and economic growth, used to forecast the future, in *Economic Growth of Nations* 1971. He was awarded a Nobel prize in 1971.

Kuznetsov /ˌkʊznɪtˈsɒf/ Anatoli 1930–1979. Russian writer. His novels *Babi Yar* 1966, describing the wartime execution of Jews at Babi Yar, near Kiev, and *The Fire* 1969, about workers in a large metallurgical factory, were seen as anti-Soviet. When he visited Britain in 1969, he was given permission to settle there.

Kwangchow former name of ◊Guangzhou, city in China.

Kwangsi-Chuang former name of ◊Guanxi Zhuang, region of China.

Kwangtung former name of ◊Guangdong, province of China.

kwashiorkor Ghanaian name for the severe malnutrition common among children in W Africa, resulting in retarded growth. The term was introduced to medical literature by Dr Cicely Williams in the 1930s.

Kweichow former name of ◊Guizhou, province of China.

Kyd /kɪd/ Thomas c. 1557–1595. English dramatist. He followed his father's profession of scrivener, and about 1588 wrote *The Spanish Tragedy*, which anticipated elements present in *Hamlet*.

Kyoga /kiˈəʊɡə/ lake in central Uganda: area 2,600 sq km/1,000 sq mi.

Kyoto /kiˈəʊtəʊ/ former capital of Japan (794–1868) on Honshu island, linked by canal with Biwa Lake; university town, with industry (silk weaving and manufacture, embroidery, porcelain, bronze and lacquer ware); population (1980) 1,473,000.

Kyrenia /kaɪˈrɪniə/ port in Cyprus, about 20 km/12 mi N of Nicosia. Population (1970) 32,700.

Kyushu /ˈkjuːʃuː/ most southerly of the main islands of Japan, separated from Shikoku and Honshu by Bungo Channel and Suo Bay, but connected to Honshu by bridge and rail tunnel
area 42,079 sq km/16,170 sq mi including about 370 small islands
capital Nagasaki
towns Kagoshima, Kumamoto, Fukuoka
physical mountainous; the coast is very broken
features the active volcano Aso-take (1,592 m/5,223 ft) has the world's largest crater
products coal, gold, silver, iron, tin, rice, tea
population (1970) 13,000,000.

Kyzyl-Kum /kɪˈziːl ˈkuːm/ desert in Kazakhstan and Uzbekistan, USSR, between the Sur-Darya and Amu-Darya rivers; area about 300,000 sq km/116,000 sq mi. It is being reclaimed for cultivation by irrigation and protective tree-planting.

L twelfth letter of the Roman alphabet. The sound represented is one of the most stable in all languages; in some languages it tends to be lost between a back vowel and a consonant, as in English 'half', 'should', and so on.

laager term used by Boers in South Africa to describe an enclosed encampment; now more widely applied to the siege mentality of sections of the Afrikaner population.

Labanotation a comprehensive system of accurate and precise dance notation (*Kinetographie Laban* 1928) devised by Rudolf von Laban (1879–1958), dancer, choreographer and dance theorist.

labelled compound a chemical compound in which an ◊isotope (usually a radioactive one) is substituted for a normal atom. Thus labelled, the path taken by the compound through a system can be followed, for instance through measuring the radiation emitted. This powerful and sensitive technique is used in medicine, chemistry (especially biochemistry) and industry.

labelling in sociology, defining or describing a person in terms of his or her behaviour; for example, describing someone who has broken a law as a criminal. In sociology, labelling theory deals with human interaction, behaviour, and control, particularly in the field of deviance. Social labelling has been seen as a form of social control in that labels affect both a person's self image and other people's reactions. Crucial factors include who labels a person (for example, only a court can convict a criminal), and whether the label sticks.

labellum the lower petal of an orchid flower, which is more elaborate and usually larger than the other petals; it often has a distinctive patterning which attracts insects which use it as a landing platform when visiting the flower.

Labor Party in Australia, political party based on socialist principles. It was founded in 1891 and first held office in 1904. It formed governments 1929–31 and 1939–49, but in the intervening periods internal discord provoked splits, and reduced its effectiveness. It returned to power under Gough ◊Whitlam 1972–75, and again under Bob ◊Hawke 1983–   .

Labour Day annual festival of the Labour movement, often linked with 1 May, for example in England first Monday in May, and a ◊bank holiday since 1976. In the USA, *Labor Day* is celebrated on the first Monday in Sept, and is a public holiday.

Labour Party in the UK, political party based on socialist principles, originally formed to represent the working class. Although Keir ◊Hardie and John ◊Burns entered Parliament independently as Labour members of parliament in 1892, it was not until 1900 that a conference representing the trade unions, the ◊Independent Labour Party (ILP), and the ◊Fabian Society founded the Labour Party, known until 1906, when 29 seats were gained, as the Labour Representation Committee. All but a pacifist minority of the Labour Party supported World War I, and in 1918 a socialist programme was first adopted, with local branches of the party being set up to which individual members were admitted.

By 1922 the Labour Party was recognized as the official opposition, and in 1924 formed a minority government (with Liberal support) for a few months under J R ◊MacDonald. A second minority government in 1929 followed a conservative policy, and in 1931 MacDonald and other leaders, faced with a financial crisis, left the party to support the national government. The ILP seceded in 1932. In 1936–39 there was internal dissension on foreign policy: the leadership's support of nonintervention in Spain was strongly criticized, and Sir Stafford ◊Cripps, Aneurin ◊Bevan, and others were expelled for advocating an alliance of all left-wing parties against the Chamberlain government.

The Labour Party supported Churchill's wartime coalition, but then withdrew and took office for the first time as a majority government under ◊Attlee after the 1945 elections. The welfare state was developed by ◊nationalization of essential services and industries, a system of national insurance (1946), and the National Health Service (1948). Defeated in 1951, the Labour Party was split by disagreements on further nationalization and unilateral or multilateral disarmament, but achieved unity

under ◊Gaitskell's leadership 1955–63, and under ◊Wilson returned to power 1964–70 and, very narrowly, 1974–79. ◊Callaghan, who had been elected by Labour members of parliament to succeed Wilson in 1976, was forced to a general election in 1979 and lost. Michael ◊Foot was elected to the leadership by members of parliament in 1980; Neil ◊Kinnock succeeded him 1983 after Labour had lost another general election. The party adopted a policy of unilateral nuclear disarmament 1986 but lost the general election 1987.

The Labour Party, the Trades Union Congress and the Co-operative movement together form the National Council of Labour, whose aims are to co-ordinate political activities and take joint action on specific issues. The Fabian Society is the most important affiliated political body.

Labrador /ˈlæbrədɔː/ peninsula in NE Canada, lying between Ungava Bay on the NW, the Atlantic on the E, and the Strait of Belle Isle on the SE. Part of it is in the province of Quebec, part forms a division of the province of Newfoundland, with the area 285,000 sq km/110,000 sq mi; population (1976) 557,725. Labrador consists for the most part of a plateau sloping gently from the mountains that fringe the irregular coastline. There are important fisheries, especially for cod. Large forests support a timber and pulp industry, and there are rich mineral resources, especially iron. Hydroelectric resources include Churchill Falls on Churchill river.

La Bruyère /ˌlæbruːˈjeə/ Jean de 1645–1696. French essayist. Born in Paris, he studied law, took a post in the revenue office, and in 1684 entered the service of the house of Condé. His *Caractères* 1688, satirical portraits of contemporaries, made him many enemies.

Labuan /ləˈbuːən/ a flat, wooded island off NW Borneo; chief town and port Victoria; area 90 sq km/35 sq mi. Labuan was ceded to Great Britain in 1846, and from 1963 included in Sabah, Federation of Malaysia.

laburnum flowering tree *Laburnum anagyroides*; a member of the family Leguminosae, native to the mountainous parts of central Europe. The flowers, in long drooping clusters, are bright yellow and appear in early spring; some varieties have purple or reddish flowers. The seeds are poisonous.

lac resinous incrustation exuded by the female lac-insects *Coccus lacca*, which eventually covers the twigs of trees in India and the Far East. The gathered twigs are known as stick-lac, which yields a useful crimson dye; shellac is manufactured commercially by melting the separated resin and spreading it into thin layers or flakes.

Laccadive, Minicoy and Amindivi Islands /'lækədɪv,'mɪnɪkɔɪ, æmɪn'diːvɪ/ former name of Indian island group ◊Lakshadweep.

lace a plain or decorative textile fabric of an openwork or network type. Needle-point or point laces were first evolved in Italy in the late 15th or early 16th centuries; the craft spread to France, Germany, and England. The other chief variety of lace is bobbin or pillow ('true') lace, which is made by twisting threads together in pairs or groups, according to a pattern marked out by pins set in a cushion, and is said to have been invented by Barbara Uttmann (born 1514) of Saxony. From 1589 various attempts were made at producing machine-made lace, and in 1809 John Heathcoat achieved success with a bobbin net machine: the principles of this system are kept in modern machines making plain net. The earliest machine for making true lace was the invention of another Englishman, John Leavers, in 1813; the principle involved is the same as in the modern machines at Nottingham, the great centre of machine-made lace. Early laces were principally made from linen thread, enriched with gold, silver, or silk: later materials included cotton, wool, rayon, nylon. Great centres of lace-making have been Venice, Alençon, and Argentan (point lace), and Mechlin, Valenciennes, and Honiton (bobbin lace); both types are made at Brussels.

La Ceiba /læ 'seɪbə/ chief Atlantic port of Honduras; population (1982) 69,000.

lacertid member of a class of radio-emitting star-like bodies, which show no lines in their optical spectra. They appear to be a variety of galaxy, and are in the process of ridding themselves of excess non-thermal energy.

lacewing insect of the families Hemerobiidae (the brown lacewings) and Chrysopidae (the green lacewings) of the order Neuroptera. Found throughout the world, they are so named because of the veining of their two pairs of semi-transparent wings, and have narrow bodies and long thin antennae. They are predators, especially on aphids.

Lachish /'leɪkɪʃ/ ancient city SW of Jerusalem, where inscribed potsherds have thrown light on the early development of the alphabet. It was identified by Albright in 1929 as having occupied the mound of Telled-Duweir some 40 km/25 mi SW of Jerusalem.

Lachlan /'læklən/ river in Australia which rises in the Blue Mountains, a tributary of the Murrumbidgee; length 1,485 km/920 mi.

Laclos /læ'kləʊ/ Pierre Choderlos de 1741–1803. French author. An army officer, he wrote a single novel in letter form, *Les Liaisons*

dangereuses/Dangerous Acquaintances 1782, an analysis of moral corruption.

lacquer the craft of painting wooden pots and furniture in coloured, often opaque varnish, often in several successive layers, developed in China around 1700 under the Shang dynasty.

lacrosse Canadian ball game, adopted from the American Indians, and named from a fancied resemblance of the lacrosse stick to a bishop's crozier. Thongs across its curved end form a pocket to carry the small rubber ball, and the pitch is approximately 100 m/110 yd long and a minimum 55 m/60 yd wide in the men's game, which is played ten a side; the women's pitch is larger, and they play 12 a side. The goals are just under 2 m/6 ft square, with loose nets.

World Championship first held in 1967 for men, 1969 for women

men
1967 United States
1974 United States
1978 Canada
1982 United States
1986 United States
women
1969 Great Britain
1974 United States
1978 Canada
1982 United States
1986 Australia

---

lactation the secretion of ◊milk from the mammary glands of mammals. In late pregnancy the cells lining the lobules inside the mammary glands undergo a change which makes them extract substances from the blood to produce milk. The supply of milk starts shortly after birth with the production of colostrum, a clear fluid consisting largely of water, protein, ◊antibodies and ◊vitamins. The milk becomes established in a few days, and will then continue practically as long as the infant continues to suck.

lactic acid *hydroxypropanoic acid* an organic acid $CH_3CH(OH)COOH$, a colourless, almost odourless syrup, which is produced by certain bacteria during fermentation, and occurs in yoghurt, buttermilk, sour cream, wine, and certain plant extracts; it is also present in muscles when they are exercised hard, and in the stomach. It is commercially used in food preservation, and the preparation of pharmaceuticals.

lactose a white, crystalline sugar, found in solution in milk; it forms 5% of cow's milk. It is commercially prepared from the whey obtained in cheese-making. Like table sugar (sucrose) it is a disaccharide, that is it consists of two basic sugar units (monosaccharides), in this case, glucose and galactose. Unlike sucrose, it is tasteless.

Ladakh /lə'dɑːk/ subsidiary range of the ◊Karakoram and district of NE Kashmir, India, on the border of Tibet. After China occupied Tibet in 1951, it made claims on the area.

Ladins /læ'diːnz/ ethnic community (about 16,000) in the Dolomites whose language (Ladin) derives directly from Latin; they descend from the Etruscans and other early

Italian tribes, and have links with the speakers of ◊Romansch.

Ladoga /'lædəgə/ largest lake in Europe, in the USSR, just NE of Leningrad; area 18,400 sq km/7,100 sq mi. It receives the waters of the Svir, which drains Lake Onega, and other rivers, and runs to the Gulf of Finland by the river Neva. Lake Ladoga forms a link in the White Sea–Baltic Canal.

lady in the UK, the formal title of the daughter of an earl, marquis, or duke; and of any woman whose husband is above the rank of baronet or knight, as well as (by courtesy only) the wives of these latter ranks.

ladybird beetle of the family Coccinellidae, generally red or yellow in colour, with black spots. There are many species which, with their larvae, feed upon aphids and scale-insect pests.

Lady Day Christian festival (25 Mar) of the Annunciation of the Virgin Mary; until 1752 it was the beginning of the legal year in England, and it is still a ◊quarter day.

Ladysmith /'leɪdɪsmɪθ/ town in Natal, South Africa, 185 km/115 mi NW of Durban, near the Klip. It was besieged by the Boers, 2 Nov 1899–28 Feb 1900, during the South African War. Ladysmith was named in honour of the wife of Sir Henry ◊Smith, a colonial administrator.

lady's smock an alternative name for the cuckoo flower *Cardamine pratensis*.

Lafayette /,læfaɪ'et/ Marie Joseph Gilbert de Motier, marquis de Lafayette 1757–1834. French soldier and statesman. He fought against Britain in the American War of Independence. During the French Revolution he sat in the National Assembly as a constitutional royalist, and in 1789 was given command of the National Guard. In 1792 he fled the country after attempting to restore the monarchy, and was imprisoned by the Austrians until 1797. He supported Napoleon during the Hundred Days, sat in the Chamber of Deputies as a Liberal from 1818, and assisted the revolution of 1830. He was a popular hero in the USA, and towns in Louisiana and Indiana are named after him.

Lafayette /,læfaɪ'et/ Marie-Madeleine, comtesse de Lafayette 1634–1693. French author. Her *Mémoires* of the French court are keenly observed, and her *La Princesse de Clèves* 1678 is the first French psychological novel and *roman à clef* (novel with a 'key') in that real-life characters (including ◊La Rochefoucauld, who was for many years her lover) are presented under fictitious names.

La Fontaine /,læ fɒn'teɪn/ Jean de 1621–1695. French poet. Born at Château-Thierry, from 1656 he lived largely in Paris, enjoying the friendship of Molière, Racine, and Boileau. His outstanding works are his *Fables* 1668–94, and his *Contes* 1665–74, a series of witty and bawdy tales in verse.

Laforgue /læ'fɔːg/ Jules 1860–1887. French poet, who pioneered ◊free verse and who greatly influenced later French and English writers.

Lagash /'lɑːgəʃ/ Sumerian city north of Shatra Iraq. Discovered 1877 and excavated by Earnest de Sarzec, then French consul in Basra, it was of great importance under independent and semi-independent rulers from c. 3000 to 2700 BC.

Lagerkvist /'lɑːgəkvɪst/ Pär 1891–1974. Swedish author of lyric poetry, dramas (*The Hangman* 1935), and novels (*Barabbas* 1950). He was awarded a Nobel prize in 1951.

Lagerlöf /'lɑːgələːf/ Selma 1858–1940. Swedish novelist. Originally a schoolteacher, she won fame in 1891 with a collection of stories of peasant life, *Gösta Berling's Saga*. She received a Nobel prize in 1909.

lagoon a coastal body of shallow salt water, usually with limited access to the sea. The term is normally used to describe the shallow sea area cut off by a ◊coral reef or shingle ridge.

Lagos /'leɪgɒs/ port in Nigeria, W Africa, chief commercial centre and until 1976 the capital; population (1975) 1,061,000. At the W end of an island in a lagoon, it is linked by bridges with the mainland via Iddo Island. University 1962; Onikan Museum has one of the world's richest collections of African art.

Lagrange /læ'grɒnʒ/ Joseph Louis 1736–1813. French mathematician who presided over the commission that introduced the metric system in 1793. His *Mécanique analytique* 1788 applied mathematical analysis, using principles established by Isaac Newton, to such problems as the movements of planets when affected by each others' gravitational force.

Lagrangian points five points in space where a small body can remain in a stable orbit with two much more massive bodies. Three of the points lie on a line joining the two bodies. The other two points, L4 and L5, which are the most stable, lie either side of the line. Their existence was predicted in 1772 by J L ◊Lagrange. The *Trojan asteroids* lie at Lagrangian points L4 and L5 in Jupiter's orbit around the Sun. Clouds of dust and debris may lie at the Lagrangian points of the Moon's orbit around the Earth.

Lagrangian points

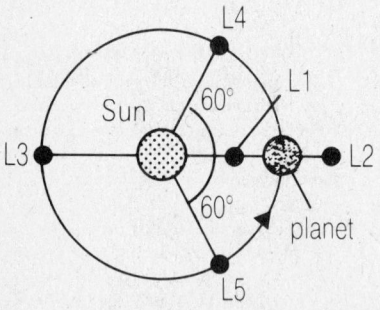

La Guardia /lə 'gwɑːdiə/ Fiorello Henrico 1882–1947. American politician. Elected mayor of New York in 1933 against the opposition of the powerful Tammany Hall machine, he cleaned up the administration, suppressed racketeering, and organized unemployment relief, slum-clearance schemes, and social services. Although nominally a Republican, he strongly supported Roosevelt's New Deal. La Guardia Airport, New York, is named after him.

La Hogue /lɑː 'ɔʊg/ a naval battle fought off the Normandy coast in 1692 in which the combined English and Dutch fleets defeated the French.

Lahore /lə'hɔː/ capital of the province of Punjab and second city of Pakistan; university (1882); industry (engineering, textiles, carpets, chemicals); population (1981) 2,900,000. Lahore has many associations with the Mogul rulers Akbar, Jahangir, and Aurangzeb, whose capital it was in the 16th–17th centuries.

Laibach /'laɪbæx/ German name of Ljubljana, city in Yugoslavia.

Laing /læŋ/ R(onald) D(avid) 1927– . Scottish psychoanalyst, originator of the 'social theory' of mental illness, for example that ◊schizophrenia is promoted by family pressure for its members to conform to standards alien to themselves. His books include *The Divided Self* 1960 and *The Politics of the Family* 1971.

laissez-faire the theory that the state should refrain from all intervention in economic affairs. The phrase originated with the 18th-century French economists, the Physiocrats, whose maxim was *laissez-faire et laissez-passer* (literally 'let go and let pass', in other words, leave the individual alone, and let commodities circulate freely). As capitalist enterprises developed in the 16th and 17th centuries, entrepreneurs shook off the control of the guilds and local authorities, and in Britain the revolution of 1640–60 weakened the hold of the state on economic life. By the 18th century this process was complete. See Adam ◊Smith.
The reaction against laissez-faire began in the mid-19th century, and found expression in the factory acts, and elsewhere. This reaction was inspired partly by humanitarian protests against the social conditions created by the Industrial Revolution, partly by the wish to counter the popular unrest of the 1830s and 1840s by removing some of its causes. In general the past century has shown an increasing degree of state intervention to promote social benefits, which after 1945 was extended into the field of nationalization of leading industries and services in the UK. However, under the Thatcher government since 1979, laissez-faire policies (for example privatization) were actively pursued.

lake body of still water lying in depressed ground without direct communication with the sea. Lakes are common in formerly glaciated regions, along the courses of slow rivers, and in low land near the sea. The main classifications are by origin as follows: *glacial lakes* such as in the Alps; *barrier lakes* formed by landslides, valley glaciers, and the like; *crater lakes*; *tectonic lakes* occurring in natural fissures. Most lakes are freshwater, such as the N American group including Superior, Michigan, and Huron, but in hot regions where evaporation is excessive they may be saltwater, for example the Dead Sea.
In the 20th century large artificial lakes have been created in connection with hydro-electric and other works. Some lakes have become polluted as a result of human activities and sometimes ◊eutrophication (a state of overnourishment) of lakes occurs.

Lake District area (1,800 sq km/700 sq mi) in Cumbria, embracing the principal English lakes separated by wild uplands rising to many peaks, including Scafell Pike 978 m/3,210 ft. Windermere, in the SE, is connected with Rydal Water and Grasmere. The westerly Scafell range extends S to the Old Man of Coniston overlooking Coniston Water, and N to Wastwater. Ullswater lies in the NE of the district, with Hawes Water and Thirlmere nearby. The river Derwent flows N through Borrowdale forming Derwentwater and Bassenthwaite.
The Lake District has associations with the writers Wordsworth, Coleridge, Southey, De Quincey, Ruskin, and Beatrix Potter, and was made a national park in 1951.

lake dwellings Stone Age villages built on piles driven into the bottom of a lake. Such villages are found in Europe, West Africa, South America, Borneo and New Guinea. British examples include a lake village of the 1st centuries BC and AD excavated near Glastonbury.

Lake Havasu City /'hævəsuː/ small town in Arizona, USA, which has been developed as a tourist resort. Old London Bridge was transported and reconstructed there in 1971.

lakh lac or lak; Indian term for 100,000.

Lakshadweep /læk'ʃædwiːp/ group of 14 coral islands, ten inhabited, in the Indian Ocean, 320 km/200 mi off the Malabar coast
area 28 sq km/11 sq mi
administrative headquarters Kavaratti Island
products coir, copra, fish
population (1981) 40,241
religion mainly Muslim
history the first Western visitor was Vasco da Gama in 1499. The islands were British from 1877 until Indian independence, and created a Union Territory of the Republic of India in 1956. Formerly known as the Laccadive, Minicoy and Amindivi Islands, they were renamed Lakshadweep in 1973.

Lakshmi /'lækʃmi/ Hindu goddess of wealth and prosperity, consort of Vishnu, whose festival (Diwali) in Oct/Nov is marked by the lighting of lamps and candles, feasting, and exchange of gifts.

Lalande /læ'lɒnd/ Michel 1657–1726. French organist and composer of church music for the court at Versailles.

La Línea /læ 'liniə/ town and port on the isthmus of Algeciras Bay, Spain, adjoining the frontier zone with Gibraltar; population (1970) 55,700.

Lalique /læ'liːk/ René 1860–1945. French designer of ◊Art Nouveau jewellery, glass, and house interiors.

Lallans /'lælənz/ a variant of 'lowlands' and a name for Lowland Scots, whether conceived as a language in its own right or as a northern dialect of English. Because of its rustic associations, Lallans has been known since the 18th century as 'the Doric', in contrast with the 'Attic' usage of Edinburgh ('the Athens of the North'). See ◊Scots language.

Lamaism the religion of ◊Tibet and Mongolia; a form of ◊Buddhism belonging to the Mahayana school. Buddhism was introduced into Tibet in 640, but the real founder of Lamaism was the Indian missionary Padma Sambhava who began his activity about 750. In the 15th century Tsongkhapa founded the sect of Geluk-Pa (virtuous), which has remained the most powerful organization in the country. The ◊Dalai Lama, residing at the palace of the Potala at Lhasa, exercised both spiritual and temporal authority as head of the Tibetan State until 1959, and is considered an incarnation of Bodhisattva Avalokitesvara. See also ◊Panchen Lama. On the death of the Dalai Lama great care is taken in finding the infant in whom he has been reincarnated.

Before Chinese Communist rule, it was estimated that one in four of Tibet's male population was a Lamaist monk, but now their numbers are greatly reduced.

La Mancha /læ 'mæntʃə/ former province of Spain (Arabic *al mansha*, the dry land), now part of the autonomous region of Castilla-La Mancha; see under ◊Castile. Cervantes' *Don Quijote de la Mancha* 1605 begins there.

Lamarck /læ'maːk/ Jean Baptiste de 1744–1829. French naturalist. Born at Bazentin, he was forced by ill-health to abandon a military career, and studied medicine and meteorology before turning to botany. His greatest works were his *Philosophie Zoologique/Zoological Philosophy* 1809 and the *Histoire naturelle des animaux sans vertèbres/Natural History of Invertebrate Animals* 1815–22. He proposed a theory of evolution based on the now discredited idea that ◊acquired characters are inherited: he argued that particular use of an organ or limb strengthens it, and that this development may be 'preserved by reproduction' – thus explaining why giraffes have come to have long necks.

Lamarckism a theory of ◊evolution advocated during the early 19th century by ◊Lamarck. It differed from the modern theory of evolution (formulated by ◊Darwin) in that it was based on the idea that ◊acquired characters were inherited.

Lamartine /ˌlæmaː'tiːn/ Alphonse de 1790–1869. French poet. Born at Maçon he achieved immediate success with his first volume of musically romantic poems, *Méditations* 1820. He entered the Chamber of Deputies in 1833, and by his *Histoire des Girondins/History of the Girondins* 1847 influenced the revolution of 1848.

Lamb /læm/ Charles 1775–1834. British essayist and critic. Born in London, he was educated at Christ's Hospital (a contemporary of ◊Coleridge, with whom he published some poetry in 1796). His sister Mary (1764–1847) stabbed their mother to death in 1796, and Charles cared for her between her periodic returns to an asylum. He and Mary collaborated in *Tales from Shakespeare* 1807. From 1820 he contributed essays under the pseudonym 'Elia' to the *London Magazine* which were collected in 1823 and 1833.

Lambert /'læmbət/ John 1619–1683. English general, a cavalry commander under Cromwell (at ◊Marston Moor, Preston, Dunbar, and Worcester). Lambert broke with him over the

Lamb The British essayist and critic Charles Lamb collaborated with his sister Mary in *Tales from Shakespeare*. His portrait is by fellow essayist William Hazlitt.

proposal to award Cromwell the royal title. After the Restoration he was imprisoned for life.

Lambeth /'læmbəθ/ borough of S central Greater London.
features Lambeth Palace (chief residence of the archbishop of Canterbury since 1197); Tradescant museum of gardening history; the ◊South Bank; the Oval (headquarters of Surrey County Cricket Club from 1846) at Kennington, where the first England–Australia test match was played in 1880
population (1981) 245,500.

Lambeth Conference see ◊Anglican Communion.

Lamburn /'læmbəːn/ Richmal Crompton. Full name of British writer Richmal ◊Crompton.

lamina in flowering plants (◊angiosperms), the blade of the ◊leaf on either side of the midrib. The lamina is generally thin and flattened, and is usually the primary organ of ◊photosynthesis. The term 'lamina' is also used more broadly to describe any thin, flat plant structure, such as the ◊thallus of many seaweeds.

Lammas medieval festival ('loaf-mass') of harvest, celebrated on 1 Aug. At one time it was an English ◊quarter day, and is still a quarter day in Scotland.

lammergeier bird of prey *Gypaetus barbatus*, also known as the bearded vulture, with a wing-span of 2.7 m/9 ft. It ranges over S Europe, N Africa and Asia, in wild mountainous areas.

Lammermuir Hills /'læməmjuə/ a range of hills dividing Lothian and Borders regions, Scotland, from Gala Water to St Abb's Head.

Lampedusa /ˌlæmpɪ'duːzə/ Giuseppe Tomasi di 1896–1957. Italian aristocrat, author of *The Leopard* 1958, a novel set in his native Sicily.

lamprey eel-shaped jawless fish belonging to the family Petromyzontidae. Lampreys feed on other fish by fixing themselves by the round mouth to their host and boring into the flesh with

their toothed tongue. The sea-lamprey is a food fish.

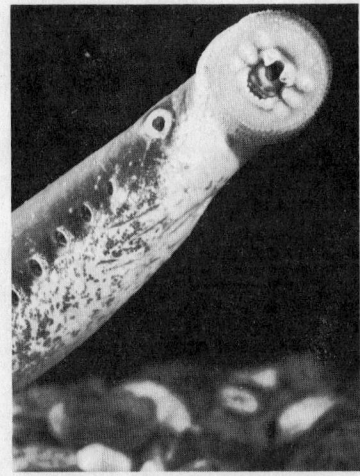

lamprey The river lamprey *Lampetra fluviatilis* showing the suctorial mouth and seven gill slits. Henry I is reputed to have died of a surfeit of this, his favourite fish.

Lamu /'laːmuː/ island off the E coast of Kenya.

Lanark /'lænək/ formerly county town of Lanarkshire, Scotland. William Wallace once lived here, and later returned to burn the town and kill the English sheriff. *New Lanark* to the S, founded in 1785 by Robert Owen, was a socialist 'ideal village' experiment.

Lanarkshire /'lænəkʃə/ a former S inland county of Scotland, merged in 1975 in the region of Strathclyde. The county town was Lanark.

Lancashire /'læŋkəʃə/ county in NW England
area 3,063 sq km/1,182 sq mi
towns administrative headquarters Preston, which forms part of Central Lancashire New Town (together with Fulwood, Bamber Bridge, Leyland, and Chorley), Lancaster, Accrington, Blackburn, Burnley; ports Fleetwood and Heysham; seaside resorts Blackpool, Morecambe, and Southport
features river Ribble; Pennines; Forest of Bowland (moors and farming valleys); Pendle Hill, traditional centre of witchcraft
products formerly the world centre of cotton manufacture but this has been replaced with newer varied industries
population (1981) 1,376,500
famous people Kathleen Ferrier, Gracie Fields, George Formby, Rex Harrison.

Lancaster /'læŋkəstə/ city in Lancashire, England, on the river Lune; population (1983) 126,400. Former county town of Lancashire (now Preston). University (1964); industry (textiles, floor coverings, furniture, plastics).

Lancaster /'læŋkəstə/ city in Pennsylvania, USA, 115 km/70 mi W of Philadelphia, producing textiles and electrical goods; population (1980) 54,700.

Lancaster, Duchy and County Palatine of /'læŋkəstə/ created in 1351, and attached to the

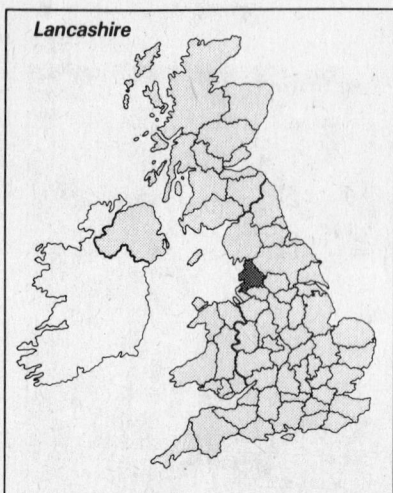

Lancashire

crown since 1399. The office of Chancellor of the Duchy is actually a 'sinecure', usually held by a member of the Cabinet with a special role outside that of the regular ministries, for example, Harold Lever as financial adviser to the Wilson-Callaghan governments from 1974.

Lancaster /'læŋkəstə/ Osbert 1908–1986. English cartoonist and writer. He first achieved notice as a book illustrator and muralist, and in the 1930s and 1940s produced several wittily debunking books on modern architecture (such as *Homes, Sweet Homes* 1939 and *Drayneflete Revisited* 1949). In 1939 he began producing his daily 'pocket cartoons' for the *Daily Express*. He was knighted in 1975.

Lancaster House Agreement accord reached at a conference in Sept 1979 at Lancaster House, London between Britain and representative groups of Rhodesia, including the Rhodesian government under Ian Smith, and black nationalist groups. The Agreement enabled a smooth transition to the independent state of ◊Zimbabwe in 1980.

lancelet marine animal, genus *Amphioxus* included in the ◊chordates. It has no skull, vertebral column, centralized brain, nor paired limbs, but there is a notochord (a supportive rod, precursor of the backbone) which runs from end to end of the body, a tail, and a number of gillslits. Found in all seas, it burrows in the sand but when disturbed swims freely.

Lancelot of the Lake /'lɑːnslɒt/ in British legend the most celebrated of King ◊Arthur's knights, the lover of Queen ◊Guinevere. Originally a folk-hero, he was introduced into the Arthurian cycle of tales in the 12th century.

Lanchow /ˌlænˈtʃaʊ/ former name of ◊Lanzhou, city in China.

Lancret /lɒŋˈkreɪ/ Nicholas 1690–1743. French artist. Born in Paris, he was a follower of ◊Watteau, painting graceful *fêtes galantes* (works depicting pastoral scenes) and illustrating the amorous *Contes de la Fontaine*.

Land federal unit (plural Länder) of West Germany.

Land /lænd/ Edwin 1909– . American inventor of the Polaroid camera 1947, which develops the film inside the camera.

Landes /lɒnd/ sandy, low-lying area in SW France, along the Bay of Biscay, about 12,950 sq km/5,000 sq mi in extent. It gives its name to a department, and extends into the departments of Gironde and Lot-et-Garonne. There is a testing range for rockets and missiles at Biscarosse, 72 km/45 mi SW of Bordeaux. For the oilfield in Landes department, see ◊Parentis-en-Born.

Land League Irish peasant organization, formed by Michael ◊Davitt in 1879 to fight against evictions. It forced Gladstone's government, by its skilful use of the boycott against any man who took a farm from which another had been evicted, to introduce a law in 1881 restricting rents and granting tenants security of tenure.

landlord and tenant in law, the relationship which exists when an owner of land or buildings (the landlord) gives to another (the tenant) the exclusive right of occupation for a definite limited period, whether it be a year, a term of years, a week or a month. When the terms of the contract are embodied in a deed they are said to be covenants, and the whole agreement is termed a lease.

In the UK there was traditionally freedom of contract between landlord and tenant, but wartime shortage of rented accommodation for lower income groups led to abuse by unscrupulous landlords and from 1914 acts were passed affording protection for tenants against eviction and rent increases. The shortage was aggravated by World War II and from 1939 Rent Acts were passed greatly increasing the range of dwellings so protected. Extensive decontrol under the 1957 Rent Act led to hardship, and further legislation followed, notably the Rent Act of 1974, under which tenants of furnished and unfurnished premises were given equal security of tenure. The Housing Act of 1980 attempted to make it more attractive to landlords to let property, while still safeguarding the tenant, notably by creating a new category of tenure – the protected shorthold.

Landor /'lændɔː/ Walter Savage 1775–1864. British poet and essayist. He lived much of his life abroad, dying in Florence, to which he had fled from a libel suit in 1858. His best-known works are the *Imaginary Conversations of Literary Men and Statesmen* 1824–29.

Land Registry, HM in the UK, state register of landowners voluntarily submitting titles to their land for examination and approval by the registrar on behalf of the State established in 1862. By the Land Registry Act of 1897 the principle of compulsory registration was introduced, which makes the future buying or selling of land much easier and cheaper, since absolute titles granted by the Land Registry (administered under the Lord Chancellor by the Chief Land Registrar) are guaranteed and lengthy examinations of title are unnecessary.

Landsat a series of satellites for the monitoring of earth resources. The first was launched in 1972.

Landseer /'lændsɪə/ Edwin Henry 1802–1873. British painter and sculptor. His sentimental studies of animals, have a counterbalance in studies of extreme cruelty or suffering. His best-known sculptures are the lions in Trafalgar Square, London. He was knighted in 1850.

Land's End /'lændz 'end/ promontory of W Cornwall, 15 km/9 mi WSW of Penzance, the most westerly point of England. An extension of Land's End is a group of dangerous rocks, the Longships, a mile out, marked by a lighthouse.

Landskrona /ˌlændzˈkruːnə/ town and port (shipyards, machinery, chemicals, sugar refining) in Sweden, on the Sound, 32 km/20 mi N of Malmö; population (1978) 36,500. Carl XI defeated the Danes off Landskrona in 1677.

landslide a sudden downward movement of a mass of soil or rocks from a cliff or steep slope. Landslides happen when a slope becomes unstable, usually because the base has been undercut or certain boundaries of materials within the mass have become wet and slippery. There are several types. A mudflow occurs when soil or loose material is soaked so that the material no longer adheres to the slope; it forms a tongue of mud that reaches downhill from a semicircular hollow. A slump occurs when the material stays together as a large mass, or several smaller masses, and these may form a tilted steplike structure as they slide. A landslip is formed when ◊beds of rock slide along a lower bed when they dip towards a cliff. Earthquakes may precipitate landslides.

Landsteiner /'lændstaɪnə/ Karl 1868–1943. Austrian immunologist, who was awarded the 1930 Nobel Prize for Physiology of Medicine for his discovery of the ABO ◊blood group system between 1900 and 1902, during his work at the Vienna Pathology Laboratory. While working at the Rockerfeller Institute for Medical Research in New York he was involved in the discovery of the MN blood groups in 1927 and the Rhesus blood factors in 1940. In 1936 he wrote *The Specificity of Serological Reactions* which helped establish the science of immunology. He also developed a test for syphilis and discovered the polio virus.

Landtag legislature of each of the *Länder* (states) that form the federal republics of Germany and Austria.

Lanfranc /'lænfræŋk/ c. 1010–1089. archbishop of Canterbury. Born at Pavia in Italy he entered the monastery of Bec, Normandy, in 1042, where he opened a school which achieved international fame; ◊Anselm was his pupil there. His skill in theological controversy did much to secure the Church's adoption of the doctrine of transubstantiation. Appointed archbishop of Canterbury in 1070, he rebuilt the cathedral, replaced English clergy by Normans, enforced clerical celibacy, and separated the ecclesiastical from the secular courts.

Lang /læŋ/ Andrew 1844–1912. Scottish historian and folklore scholar. His writings include historical works, anthropological essays, and novels, but he is best remembered for a series of children's books, beginning with the *Blue Fairy Tale Book* 1889.

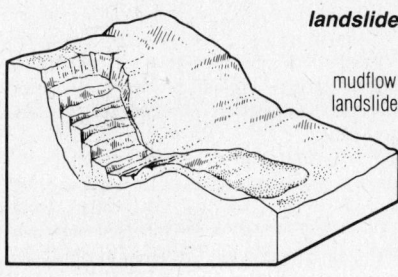

landslide

mudflow
landslide

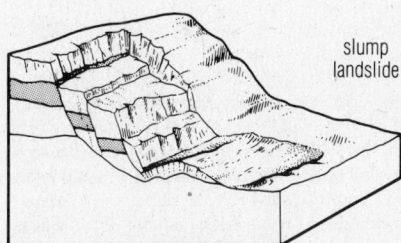

slump
landslide

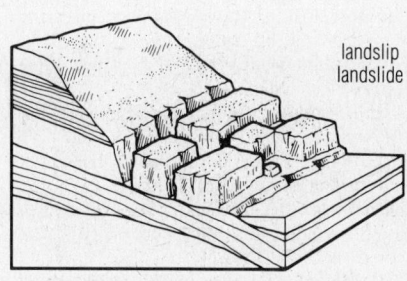

landslip
landslide

Lange Labour prime minister of New Zealand. Since his 1984 general election victory, David Lange has implemented a non-nuclear defence policy.

Lang /læŋ/ Fritz 1890–1976. American film producer. Born in Vienna, he caused a sensation in 1931 with *M*, in which Peter Lorre starred as a child-killer. Lang fled to Hollywood from Germany in 1936 after his anti-dictator *Dr Mabuse* 1933, and there made *Fury* 1936 with Spencer Tracy, and *You Only Live Once* 1937 with Henry Fonda, and other films with a strong sense of social realism.

Lange /'lɒŋi/ David Russell 1942– . New Zealand socialist politician, Labour Party leader from 1983, prime minister from 1984.
Lange was called to the New Zealand Bar and was elected to the House of Representatives in 1977, becoming party leader in 1983. Labour had a decisive win in the 1984 general election on a non-nuclear defence policy, which Lange immediately put into effect, despite criticism from other Western countries, particularly the USA. He introduced a free-market economic policy and he was re-elected 1987.

Langevin /lɒnʒ'væŋ/ Paul 1872–1946. French physicist who contributed to the studies of magnetism and X-ray emissions. During World War I he invented an apparatus for locating enemy submarines. The nuclear institute at ◊Grenoble is named after him.

Langland /'læŋlənd/ William c. 1332–c. 1400. English poet. Born in the W Midlands, he took minor orders, and in later life settled in London. His alliterative *Vision concerning Piers Plowman* appeared in three versions between about 1362 and 1398, but some critics believe he was only responsible for the first of these. The poem forms a series of allegorical visions, in which Piers develops from the typical poor peasant to a symbol of Christ, and condemns the social and moral evils of 14th-century England.

Langley /'læŋli/ Samuel Pierpont 1834–1906. American inventor. Professor of physics and astronomy at the Western University of Pennsylvania 1866–87, he did valuable research on the infra red portions of the solar spectrum. His steam-driven aeroplane flew for 90 seconds in 1896, making the first flight by an engine-equipped aircraft.

Langmuir /'læŋmjʊə/ Irving 1881–1957. American scientist, who invented the mercury vapour pump for producing a high vacuum and the atomic hydrogen welding process; he was also a pioneer of the thermionic valve. In 1932 he was awarded a Nobel prize for his work on surface chemistry.

Langobards alternative name for ◊Lombards.

Langton /'læŋtən/ Stephen c. 1150–1228. English priest. He studied in Paris, where he became chancellor of the university, and in 1206 was created a cardinal. When in 1207 Innocent III secured his election as archbishop of Canterbury King John refused to recognize him, and Langton was not allowed to enter England until 1213. He supported the barons in their struggle against John, and was mainly responsible for ◊Magna Carta.

Langtry /'læŋtri/ Lillie 1853–1929. British actress, known as the 'Jersey lily' from her birthplace, and an intimate friend of Edward VII.

language the general name for human communication through speech or writing, or both; 'a language' is any expression of language used by one or more communities for everyday purposes (the English language, the European languages, the Indo-European language family, the Japanese language, and so on). In addition, the term is broadly used to cover any system of communication with language-like qualities, for example *animal language* (ways in which animals at large communicate), *body language* (gestures, expressions and stance, used to express attitudes), *computer language* (the binary and other more complex systems of computer software, such as BASIC and COBOL), the language of love (how lovers express their feelings), and so on.
Natural human language has a neurological basis centred on the left hemisphere of the brain and expressed through two distinct mediums in most present-day societies: mouth and ear (the medium of sound, or *phonic medium*) and hand and eye (the medium of writing, or *graphic medium*). It appears to develop in every normal child under normal circumstances, either as a unilingual or multilingual skill, crucially between the ages of 1 to 5 as a necessary interplay of innate and environmental factors.
When forms of language are as distinct as Dutch and Arabic, it is easy to make such statements as 'Dutch and Arabic are different languages'. When, however, they are as close as Dutch and Flemish such a statement is harder to make, because these two forms are mutually intelligible. Rather than say that Dutch and Flemish are 'dialects' of a common Netherlandic language, Dutch and Flemish speakers may, for traditional reasons that include ethnic pride and political distinctness, prefer to talk about two distinct languages. To strengthen the differences among similar languages, groups may emphasize those differences (for example, the historical distancing of Portuguese from Castillian Spanish) or adopt different scripts (as in Urdu being written in Arabic script, Hindi in Devanagari script). From outside, Italian appears to be a single language; inside Italy, it is a standard variety resting on a base of many very distinct dialects. The terms 'language' and 'dialect' are not therefore easily defined and distinguished. English is today the dominant world language , but it has so many varieties (often mutually unintelligible) that scholars now talk about 'Englishes' and even 'the English languages' – all, however, united for international purposes by 'Standard English'.

Languedoc-Roussillon /,lɑ:ŋgə'dɒk ,ru:si:'jɒn/ region of S France; capital Montpellier; population (1982) 1,926,500.
In the Middle Ages dialects were spoken in the Languedoc area in which *oc* meant 'yes', whereas in N France *oui* meant 'yes', hence *langue d'oc*, also known as Provençal: see ◊Provence.

langur type of monkey found in S Asia. Tree-living, langurs feed on leaves and have specialized stomachs in which bacteria help to break down the food. They are related to the colobus monkeys of Africa.

Lanier /lə'nɪə/ Sidney 1842–1881. American poet. Born in Georgia, he served in the Civil War, and subsequently studied law, which he abandoned for music. His *Poems* 1877 contain some interesting metrical experiments, in accordance with the theories expounded in his *Science of English Verse* 1880.

lanolin a sticky, purified wax obtained from sheep's wool, and used in cosmetics, soap, preparing leather, and so on.

Lansbury /'lænzbəri/ George 1859–1940. British Labour leader. He sat on Poplar borough council in London from 1903, and went to prison with most of the councillors in 1921 rather than modify the council's policy of more generous unemployment relief. Leader of the Labour Party in the House 1931–35, he resigned (as a pacifist) in opposition to the party's policy in the ◊Ethiopian War.

Lansdowne /'lænzdaun/ Henry Charles, 5th Marquis of Lansdowne 1845–1927. British Conservative politician. He was governor-general of Canada 1883–88, viceroy of India 1888–93, war minister 1895–1900, and foreign secretary 1900–06; while at the Foreign Office he abandoned Britain's isolationist policy by forming alliances with Japan and France. His publication in 1917 of proposals for a compromise peace led to a violent controversy.

Lansing /'lænsɪŋ/ capital of Michigan, USA, at the confluence of the Grand and Red Cedar rivers; industry (motor vehicles, diesel engines, pumps, furniture); population (1980) 130,400.

lanthanides the 15 chemically related elements of the lanthanide series, from ◊lanthanum (atomic number 57) to lutetium (atomic number 71), in the ◊Periodic Table. They are: lanthanum, cerium, praseodymium, neodymium, promethium, samarium, enopium, gadolinium, terbium, dysprosium, holmium, erbium, thulium, ytterbium and lutetium. The name 'cave earth' is also used for them, although it strictly means the oxides of these elements.

lanthanum in chemistry, a rare metallic element, symbol La, atomic number 57, atomic weight 138.9. First element of the ◊lanthanide series.

Lanzhou /ˌlæn'dʒəu/ capital (formerly Lanchow) of Gansu province, China, on the Huang Ho river, 190 km/120 mi S of the Great Wall; industries (oil refining, chemicals, fertilizer, synthetic rubber); population (1982) 1,430,000.

Laois /liːʃ/ county in Leinster Province, Republic of Ireland
area 1,720 sq km/664 sq mi
county town Portlaoise
physical flat except for the Slieve Bloom mountains in the NW
products sugarbeets, dairy products, woollens, agricultural machinery
population (1981) 51,170.

Laon /lɒŋ/ capital of Aisne department, N France, 120 km/75 mi NE of Paris, noted for its 12th-century cathedral; population (1982) 29,100.

Laos /'laus/ landlocked country in SE Asia, bordered to the N by China, E by Vietnam, S by Kampuchea, and W by Thailand.
government Laos became a Republic in Dec 1975. when the monarchy was abolished. The indirectly elected, 264-member national

congress of people's representatives appointed Prince Souphanouvong (1909–) as executive head of state (president) to be served by a cabinet (council of ministers) led by a prime minister. A 45-member supreme people's assembly, chaired by the president, was established to frame a new constitution. The controlling force and only political party in Laos is the Communist Party (Lao People's Revolutionary Party), which is dominated by its 17-member Political Bureau and which heads the broader Lao Front for National Reconstruction.

history occupied from the 4th–5th centuries by immigrants from ◊China, Laos came under Indian influence and adopted ◊Buddhism during the 7th–11th centuries. As part of the ◊Khmer empire from the 11th–13th centuries, it experienced much artistic and architectural activity. From the 12th century, the country was invaded by the Lao from Thailand, who established small independent kingdoms and became Buddhists. Laos became an independent kingdom in the 14th century and was first visited by Europeans in the 17th century, becoming a French protectorate 1893–1945. After brief Japanese occupation, France re-established control in 1946 despite opposition from the Chinese-backed *Lao Issara* (Free Laos) nationalist movement. The country became semi-autonomous in 1950, when, under the constitutional monarchy of the king of ◊Luang Prabang, it became an Associated State of the French Union.

In 1954, after the Geneva Agreements, Laos gained full independence. Civil war broke out between two factions of former *Lao Issara* supporters: a moderate, royalist-neutralist group led by Prince Souvanna Phouma, which had supported the 1950 French compromise and was the recognized government for most of the country; and a more extreme Communist resistance group, the *Pathet Lao* led by ex-Prince Souphanouvong (the half-brother of Prince Souvanna) and supported by China and the Vietminh, which controlled much of N Laos.

A coalition government was established after the 1957 ◊Vientiane Agreement. This soon collapsed and in 1960 a third, right-wing, force emerged when Gen Phoumi Nosavan, backed by the royal army, overthrew Souvanna Phouma and set up a pro-Western government headed by Prince Boun Gum. A new Geneva Agreement in 1962 established a tripartite (right-left-neutral) government under Prince Souvanna Phouma. Fighting continued, however, between the N Vietnamese-backed *Pathet Lao*, and the US-backed neutralists and right-wing, until the 1973 Vientiane Agreeement established a cease-fire line dividing the country NW to SE, giving the Communists two-thirds of the country including the Plain of Jars and the Bolovens Plateau in the S, but giving the Souvanna Phouma government two-thirds of the population.

All foreign forces (N Vietnamese, Thai and American) were to be withdrawn, and both sides received equal representation in Souvanna Phouma's provisional government of 1974. In 1975 the Communist *Pathet Lao* (renamed the Lao People's Front) seized power. King Savang

Vatthana (1908–80), who had succeeded in 1959, abdicated and Laos became a People's Democratic Republic under the presidency of Prince Souphanouvong. Prince Souvanna Phouma remained as an 'adviser' to the government.

The new administration attempted to reorganize the country along socialist lines, nationalizing businesses and industries and collectivizing agriculture but, faced with the flight of more than 250,000 refugees to Thailand, modified its approach in 1979. Laos, which is now closely tied to the Soviet Union and N Vietnam (which has 40,000 troops stationed in Laos), still suffers from border skirmishes with rebels backed by Thailand in the S and China in the N. There have, however, been attempts to improve relations with Thailand and China for economic reasons.

Lao Zi /ˌlau'dziː/ ?604–531 BC. Chinese philosopher, commonly regarded as the founder of ◊Taoism. Many legends gathered round him, but nothing certain is known of his life, and he is variously said to have lived in the 6th and the 4th century BC. The *Tao Tè Ching*, the Taoist scripture, is attributed to him, but apparently dates from the 3rd century BC.

La Palma see under La ◊Palma, one of the Spanish Canary Islands.

La Pampa /læ 'pæmpə/ province in Argentina, see under ◊Pampas.

La Paz /læ 'pæz/ city in Bolivia, the seat of government since about 1900 (Sucre is the official capital); 3,800 m/12,400 ft above sea level; founded in 1548; university 1830; population (1985) 992,600.

lapis lazuli or *lazurite* deep blue mineral used in inlaying and ornamental work, and in the manufacture of pigment. Chemically, it consists of a sodium aluminium silicate with sodium sulphide, $3(NaAlSiO_4)Na_2S$. Lapis Lazuli occurs in metamorphic limestones, and is found in Afghanistan, Siberia, Chile, and Iran.

Laplace /læ'plæs/ Pierre Simon, marquis de Laplace 1749–1827. French mathematician and astronomer. Born in Normandy, he was appointed professor of mathematics at the Paris École Militaire in 1767. In 1796, he theorized that the ◊solar system was born from a cloud of gas, the nebular hypothesis. He studied the motion of the moon and planets, and published *Traité de méchanique céleste* 1799–1825.

Lapland /'læplænd/ region of Europe within the Arctic Circle in Norway, Sweden, Finland, and USSR, without political definition. Lapland has low temperatures, with three months' continuous daylight in summer and three months' continuous darkness in winter. There is summer agriculture, but the chief resources of Lapland are minerals (chromium, copper, iron), timber, hydroelectric power, and tourism. The Lapps were originally nomadic, of Mongolian descent. They now form only a small proportion of the population, numbering some 20,000. They live by hunting, fishing, reindeer herding, and handicrafts.

La Plata /læ 'plɑːtə/ capital of Buenos Aires province, Argentina, founded in 1882, 9 km/5.5 mi from its port Ensenada; industries (meat

Laos

LAO PEOPLE'S DEMOCRATIC REPUBLIC

AREA 235,700 sq km/91,000 sq mi
CAPITAL Vientiane
TOWNS Luang Prabang, the former royal capital
PHYSICAL high mountains in the E; Mekong river in the W; jungle
FEATURES hydroelectric power from the Mekong is exported to Thailand; Plain of Jars, where a prehistoric people carved stone jars large enough to hold a person; used to be known as the Land of a Million Elephants
HEAD OF STATE Prince Souphanouvong from 1975; Phoumi Vong Vichit acting president from 1987
HEAD OF GOVERNMENT Kaysone Phomvihane from 1975
GOVERNMENT one-party communist
EXPORTS tin, teak (worked by elephants)
CURRENCY kip (57.68 = £1 Sept 1987)
POPULATION 42,643,000 (1985); annual growth rate 2.6%
LANGUAGE Lao
RELIGION traditionally Theravada Buddhist
LITERACY 51% male/46% female (1980 est)
GNP $601 million (1983); $85 per head of population
CHRONOLOGY
1893–1945 Laos became a French protectorate.
1945 Temporarily occupied by Japan.
1946 Retaken by France.

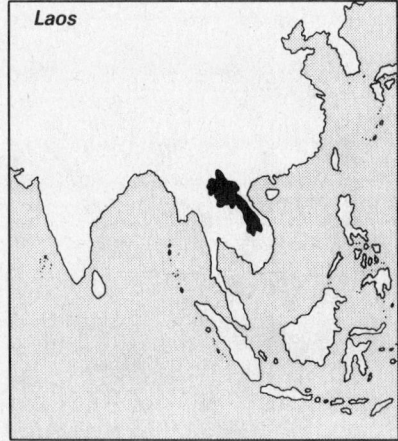
Laos

1950 Granted semi-autonomy in French Union.
1954 Full independence achieved.
1960 Right-wing government seized power.
1962 Coalition government established; civil war continued.
1973 Vientiane ceasefire agreement.
1975 Communist-dominated republic proclaimed with Prince Souphanouvong as head of state.
1987 Phoumi Vong Vichit became acting president.

Laplace Astronomer Pierre Simon Laplace was called 'the French Newton' for his work on planetary orbits.

packing, petroleum refining); university 1897; population (1980) 455,000.

La Plata, Río de /læ 'plɑːtə/ estuary in S America into which the rivers Paraná and Uruguay flow; length 320 km/200 mi and width up to 240 km/145 mi. The basin drains much of Argentina, Bolivia, Brazil, Uruguay, and Paraguay, and all five cooperate in its development. In English also called River Plate.

Laptev Sea /'læptev/ part of the Arctic Ocean off the N coast of the USSR between Taimyr Peninsula and New Siberian Island.

lapwing bird *Vanellus vanellus* of the plover family, also known as the green plover, and from its call, as the peewit. Bottle-green above and white below, with a long thin crest, and rounded wings, it is about 30 cm/1 ft long and inhabits moorland in Europe and Asia.

Laramie /'lærəmi/ town in Wyoming, USA, on the Laramie Plains, a plateau 2,300 m/7,500 ft above sea level, bounded to the N and E by the Laramie Mountains; population 24,400 (1980). The Laramie river, on which it stands, is linked with the Missouri via the Platte. Laramie features in Western legend.

larceny in the UK, formerly the name for stealing, the illegal deprivation of the lawful owner of his or her personal property, which is now included in the more comprehensive offence of ▷theft. Until 1827 larceny was divided into 'grand larceny', punishable by death or transportation for life, and 'petty larceny', when the stolen articles were valued at less than a shilling (5p). In the USA the usage and the distinction survive.

larch tree, genus *Larix*, of the family Pinaceae. The common larch (*Larix decidua*) was introduced to Britain in the 17th century and grows to 40 m/130 ft. It is one of the few ▷conifer trees to shed its leaves annually. Closely resembling it is the tamarack (*Larix laricina*), and both are timber trees. The golden larch (*Pseudolarix amabilis*), a native of China, turns golden in autumn.

lard edible fat high in saturated fatty acids prepared from pigs, used in margarine, soap, and ointment.

Lardner /'lɑːdnə/ Ring 1885–1933. American short-story writer. A sporting correspondent especially keen on baseball, he based his characters on the people he met professionally and his collected volumes of short stories include his first *You Know Me, Al* 1916, *Round Up* 1929, and *Ring Lardner's Best Short Stories* 1938, all in a lively argot.

Laredo /lə'reɪdəʊ/ industrial city (oil refining, meat processing) on the Rio Grande, Texas, USA; population (1980) 91,450. *Nuevo Laredo*, Mexico, on the opposite bank, is a textile centre; population (1980) 203,300. There is much cross-border trade.

Lares and Penates in Roman mythology, spirits of the farm and of the store cupboard, often identified with the family ancestors, whose shrine was the centre of family worship in Roman homes.

Largo Caballero /'lɑːgəʊ ˌkæbə'jeərəʊ/ Francisco 1869–1946. Spanish socialist and leader of the Spanish socialist party (PSOE). He became prime minister of the popular front government elected in Feb 1936 and remained in office for the first ten months of the civil war before being replaced by Juan Negrin in May 1937.

La Rioja /læ ri'ɒxə/ region of N Spain. See under ▷Castile.

Larisa /lə'rɪsə/ town in Thessaly, Greece, a centre of textile manufacture; population (1981) 103,000.

lark songbird of the family Alaudidae, mainly of the Old World. The northern *skylark Alauda arvensis* breeds in Britain. Light-brown, 18 cm/7 in long, it nests on the ground, and sings as it rises almost vertically in the air.

Larkin /'lɑːkɪn/ Philip 1922–1985. British poet. Born in Coventry, he was educated at Oxford, and from 1955 was librarian at Hull University. His verse includes *The North Ship* 1945, *The Whitsun Weddings* 1964, and *High Windows* 1974.

larkspur plant of genus ▷delphinium.

Larne /lɑːn/ seaport of County Antrim, N Ireland, on Lough Larne, terminus of sea routes to Stranraer, Liverpool, Dublin.

La Rochefoucauld /læ ˌrɒʃfuː'kəʊ/ François, duc de La Rochefoucauld 1613–1680. French writer. Born in Paris, he became a soldier, and took part in the ▷Fronde. His later years were divided between the court and literary society. His best-known work is his *Réflexions, ou sentences et maximes morales/Reflections, or Moral Maxims* 1665, a collection of brief, epigrammatic and cynical observations on life and society, with the epigraph 'Our virtues are mostly our vices in disguise'. He was a lover of Mme de ▷la Fayette.

La Rochelle /ˌlæ rɒˈʃel/ port in W France; population (1982) 78,231. A Huguenot stronghold, it was taken by Cardinal Richelieu in the siege of 1627–28.

Larousse /læˈruːs/ Pierre 1817–1875. French grammarian and lexicographer. His encyclopedic dictionary, the *Grand Dictionnaire universel du XIXᵉ siècle/Great Universal 19th-Century Dictionary* 1865–76, was an epoch-making achievement and continues in subsequent revisions.

larva the young of an animal, in species where the young has a different appearance and way of life from the adult. Larvae are typical of the ◊invertebrates, and some (for example, shrimps) have two or more distinct larval stages. (However, some invertebrates hatch as tiny replicas of their parents, while in others the young differ only slightly, for example, the ◊nymphs of certain insects.) Among ◊vertebrates, it is only the amphibians and some fish that have a larval stage. The process whereby the larva changes into another stage, such as a pupa (chrysalis) or adult, is known as ◊metamorphosis.

laryngitis inflammation of the lining membrane of the ◊larynx. The acute form is due to a cold, excessive use of the voice, inhalation of irritating smoke, and so on. The voice may be completely lost. With rest the inflammation usually subsides in a few days.

larynx a cavity at the upper end of the trachea (windpipe) of mammals containing the ◊vocal cords, by which sounds are produced. It is stiffened with ◊cartilage and lined with ◊mucous membrane. The larynx of amphibians and reptiles is a much simpler structure, with no vocal cords. In birds, a similar cavity is found lower down the trachea, where it branches to form the bronchi. This organ is known as the *syrinx*, and is very complex, with well developed vocal cords.

la Salle /lə ˈsæl/ René Robert Cavelier, Sieur de la Salle 1643–1687. French explorer, who made an epic voyage through North America exploring the Mississippi down to its mouth, and in 1682 founded Louisiana. Returning with colonists, he failed to find the river mouth again, and was eventually murdered by his mutinous men.

lascar /ˈlæskə/ E Indian seaman. The word derives from the Persian *lashkar*, 'army', 'camp', and lascars were originally a class of ◊sepoy.

Las Casas /læs ˈkɑːsəs/ Bartolomé de 1447–1566. Spanish missionary, historian, and colonial reformer, born in Seville. He was the first European to call for the abolition of Indian slavery. He sailed to Hispaniola in the West Indies in 1502, and was ordained priest there in 1512. After taking part in the conquest of Cuba, he returned to Spain in 1515 to plead for the Indian cause, winning the support of Charles V. He returned to what is now Venezuela but was unsuccessful in founding a settlement of free Indians. In 1530, shortly before the conquest of Peru, he persuaded the Spanish government to forbid slavery there. In 1542 he became bishop of Chiapas in Mexico; he returned finally to Spain in 1547. His most famous work, the *Historia de las Indias* (published 1875–76)

chronicles the European oppression of the Indians as he had witnessed it.

Las Casas Spanish priest and missionary to Latin America, the 'Apostle of the Indians'. He persuaded his government in 1530 to abolish slavery.

Lascaux /læsˈkəʊ/ cave system near Montignac in the Dordogne, SW France, discovered in 1940. It has rich paintings of buffalo, horses and deer of the Upper Palaeolithic, about 18,000 BC. The caves are now closed to the public, but there is an adjacent museum replica.

Lasdun /ˈlæzdən/ Denys 1914– . British architect. He designed the Royal College of Physicians, London, parts of the University of East Anglia, Norwich, and the National Theatre. He was knighted in 1976.

laser acronym for *Light Amplification by Stimulated Emission of Radiation*. Device for producing a narrow highly parallel beam of light, capable of travelling over vast distances without dispersion, and of being focused to give enormous power densities (10^8 watts per cm^2 for high-energy lasers) and operating on a principle similar to that of the ◊maser.
Many solid, liquid and gaseous substances have been used for laser materials including synthetic ruby crystal (used for the first extraction of laser light in 1960 and giving a high-power pulsed output) and a helium-neon gas mixture, capable of continuous operation, but at a lower power. In 1962 a laser was used to throw light at the Moon's surface, a reflection being detected 2½ seconds later (Massachusetts Institute of Technology). Uses of lasers include communications (a laser beam can carry much more information than radio waves), cutting, drilling, welding, satellite tracking, medical and biological research, surgery (as a 'laser scalpel' and in eye operations), and entertainment – theatre, concerts and light shows. In espionage, sound wave vibrations from the window glass of a room can be picked up by reflected laser beam, extracted by a receiver within horizon distance,

and amplified. See also ◊beam weapons and ◊bomb.

Lashio /ˈlæʃiəʊ/ town in the Shan state, Burma, about 200 km/125 mi NE of Mandalay; beginning of the Burma Road, constructed in 1938, to Kunming in China.

Laski /ˈlæski/ Harold 1893–1950. British political theorist. Professor of political science at the London School of Economics from 1926, he taught a modified Marxism, and published *A Grammar of Politics* 1925. He was chair of the Labour Party 1945–46.

Las Palmas /læs ˈpælməs/ tourist resort on the NW coast of Gran Canaria, Canary Islands; population (1981) 360,000. Its port is La Luz.

La Spezia /læ ˈspetsiə/ industrial port (shipbuilding, engineering, electrical goods, textiles) in NW Italy, chief Italian naval base; population (1984 est) 111,500. The poet Shelley drowned in the Gulf of Spezia.

lassa fever fever caused by a virus, first detected in 1969 and spread by a species of rat found only in W Africa. There is no known cure, the survival rate being less than 50 per cent.

Lassalle /læˈsæl/ Ferdinand 1825–1864. German socialist. He took part in the 1848 ◊revolution, during which he met Marx, and in 1863 founded the General Association of German Workers (later the Social-Democratic Party).

Lassus /ˈlæsəs/ Roland de Lassus c. 1532–1594. (Italian, Orlando di Lasso) Franco-Flemish composer of polyphonic sacred music, and of many songs and madrigals, including settings of poems by his friend ◊Ronsard.

Las Vegas /læs ˈveɪgəs/ city in Nevada, USA, known for its nightclubs and gambling casinos; population (1980) 164,675.

Latakia /ˌlætəˈkiːə/ port with tobacco industries in NW Syria; population (1981) 196,800.

latent heat in physics, ◊heat which changes the state (for example from solid to liquid) of a substance without changing its ◊temperature.

lateral line system a system of sense organs in fishes and larval amphibians (tadpoles) which detects water movement. It usually consists of a row of interconnected pores on either side of the body and head.

Lateran treaties a series of agreements that marked the reconciliation of the Italian state with the papacy in 1929. They were hailed as a propaganda victory for the Fascist regime. The treaties involved recognition of the sovereignty of the ◊Vatican City, the payment of an indemnity for papal possessions lost during unification in 1870, and agreement on the role of the Catholic Church within the Italian state in the form of a concordat between Pope Pius XI and Mussolini.

laterite a soft, friable, clay-like rock, produced by the weathering of basalts, granites and shales, and occurring in the tropics.

latex (Latin 'liquid') a lactiferous fluid of angiospermous plants, an emulsion of various substances. It circulates longitudinally in branched tubes conducting plastic substances and acting as a reservoir. Latex is exuded from the Para rubber tree and worked into rubber.

lateral line system

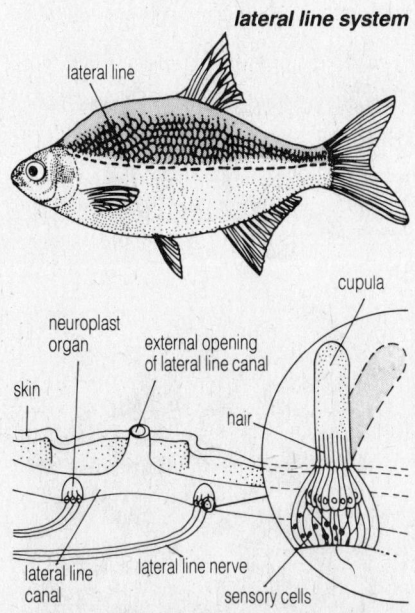

lateral line

neuroplast organ

skin

external opening of lateral line canal

cupula

hair

lateral line canal

lateral line nerve

sensory cells

lathe the most widely used ◊machine tool, development of the screw-cutting lathe of Henry Maudslay built in 1797. The lathe carries out a machinery operation called *turning*. The workpiece to be machined is held and rotated, while a variety of cutting tools are moved into it. Modern lathes are driven by electric motors.

Latimer /ˈlætɪmə/ Hugh 1490–1555. English Protestant reformer. After his conversion to ◊Protestantism in 1524 he was several times imprisoned, but was protected by ◊Wolsey and Henry VIII. He was appointed bishop of Worcester in 1535, but resigned in 1539. Under Edward VI his sermons denouncing social injustice won him great influence. He was arrested for heresy in 1553, and burned.

Latin /ˈlætɪn/ an Indo-European language of ancient Italy, named after the Latini, the inhabitants of Latium ('the broad plain'), the territory around the river Tiber and the city of Rome. Latin has passed through four influential phases: as the language of (1) Republican Rome, (2) the Roman Empire, (3) the Roman Catholic Church, and (4) W European culture, science, philosophy and law during the Middle Ages and the Renaissance. It is the parent form of the ◊Romance languages, noted for its highly inflected grammar and conciseness of expression; thus, one word *amabunt* expresses the three English words 'they will love', and *amabuntur* means 'they will be loved'. The direct influence of Latin in Europe has decreased since Renaissance times but is still considerable, and indirectly both the language and its classical literature still affect many modern languages and literatures. The insistence of Renaissance scholars upon an exact classical purity together with the rise of the European nation-states contributed to the decline of Latin as an international cultural medium. Latin vocabulary has entered English in two major waves: as religious vocabulary from Anglo-Saxon times until the Reformation, and

as the vocabulary of science, scholarship and the law from the Middle Ages onward. In the 17th century the makers of English dictionaries deliberately converted Latin words into English, enlarging the already powerful French component of English vocabulary into the language of education and refinement, placing *fraternity* alongside 'brotherhood', *comprehend* beside 'understand', *feline* beside 'cat-like', and so on. Many 'Latin tags' are in regular use in English: *habeas corpus* ('you may have the body'), *ipse dixit* ('he said it himself'), *non sequitur* ('it does not follow'), and so on. English which consists of many Latin elements is 'Latinate', and often has a grandiose and even pompous quality. Nowadays, with fewer students studying Latin in schools and universities, there is a tendency to make Latin words more conventionally English (for example, 'cactuses' rather than *cacti* as the plural of 'cactus'); this tendency has led to some uncertainty about usage, for example, whether words like 'data' and 'media' are singular or plural.

Latin America countries of ◊South and ◊Central America (also including Mexico) in which Spanish, Portuguese, and French are spoken. There are three economic organizations: Central American Common Market (1960); Andean Group (1969); and Latin America Integration Association (1980). The *Latin American Economic System* (SELA from its Spanish initial letters), established in 1975, also includes Caribbean members. It aims at integration and industrial cooperation, and coordination of existing organizations.

Latin literature only a few hymns and inscriptions survive from the earliest period of Latin literature before the 3rd century BC. Greek influence began with the work of Livius Andronics (c. 284–204 BC) who translated the *Odyssey* and Greek plays into Latin. Naevius and Ennius both attempted epics on patriotic themes; the former used the native 'Saturnian' metre, but the latter introduced the Greek hexameter. Plautus and Terence successfully adapted Greek comedy to the Latin stage. Lucilius (190–103 BC) founded Latin verse satire, while the writings of Cato were the first important works in Latin prose.

In the *De Rerum Natura* of Lucretius, and the passionate lyrics of Catullus, Latin verse reached maturity. Cicero set a standard for Latin prose, in his orations, philosophical essays, and letters. To the same period belong the histories of Caesar.

The Augustan age (43 BC – 17 AD) is usually regarded as the golden age of Latin literature. There is strong patriotic feeling in the work of the poets Virgil and Horace, and the historian Livy, who belonged to Augustus's court circle. Virgil produced the one great Latin epic, the *Aeneid* while Horace brought charm and polish to both the lyric and satire. Younger poets of the period were Ovid and the elegiac poets Tibullus and Propertius.

The 'silver age' of the Empire begins with the writers of Nero's reign: the Stoic philosopher Seneca, Lucan, author of the epic *Pharsalia*, the

satirist Persius and, by far the greatest, the realistic novelist Petronius. At the end of the 1st and beginning of the 2nd centuries came two major writers, the historian Tacitus and the satirist Juvenal; other writers of the period were the epigrammatist Martial, the scientist Pliny the Elder, the letter-writer Pliny the Younger, the critic Quintilian, the historian Suetonius, and the epic poet Statius.

The 2nd and 3rd centuries produced only one pagan writer of importance, the romancer Apuleius, but there were several able Christian writers, such as Tertullian, Cyprian, Arnobius (died 327), and Lactantius (died 325). In the 4th century there was something of a poetic revival, with Ausonius and Claudian, and the Christian poets Prudentius and St Ambrose. The Classical period ends, and the Middle Ages begin, with St Jerome's translation of the Bible, and St Augustine's *City of God*.

Throughout the Middle Ages Latin remained the language of the Church, and was normally employed for theology, philosophy, histories, and other learned works. Latin verse, adapted to rhyme and non-classical metres, was used both for hymns and the secular songs of the wandering scholars. Even after the Reformation, Latin retained its prestige as the international language of scholars, and was used as such by More, Bacon, Milton, and many others.

latitude and longitude *latitude* is the angular distance of any point from the ◊equator, measured N or S along the Earth's curved surface, equalling the angle between the respective horizontal planes. It is measured in degrees, minutes, and seconds, each minute equalling one sea-mile (1.85 km) in length. For map-making latitude is based on the supposition that the Earth is an oblate spheroid. The difference between this (the geographical) and astronomical latitude is the correction necessary for local deviation of plumb-line.

Longitude is the angle between the terrestrial meridian drawn from the pole, through a place, and a standard meridian now taken at Greenwich, England. All determinations of longitude are based on the Earth turning through 360° in 24 hours, or the Sun reaching 15° W each hour. At the equator one degree of longitude measures approximately 112 km/70 mi.

Latitudinarian in the Church of England, from the 17th century, a member of the group of clergymen, who were willing to accept modifications of forms of church government and worship to accommodate dissenters.

Latium /ˈleɪʃɪəm/ Latin name for ◊Lazio, a region of W central Italy.

La Tour /læˈtuə/ Georges de 1593–1652. French artist. His name was unknown until discovered by an art historian in 1863 and in the 20th century several pictures attributed to others were identified as his, although the authenticity of some has been questioned. He served as court painter to the king and to the duke of Lorraine.

La Trobe /lə ˈtrəub/ Charles Joseph 1801–1875. Australian administrator. He was superintendent of Port Phillip district 1839–51, and first lieutenant-governor of Victoria 1851–54. The *Latrobe River* is named after him,

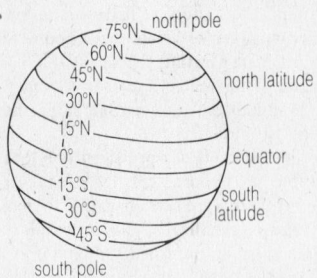

latitude and longitude

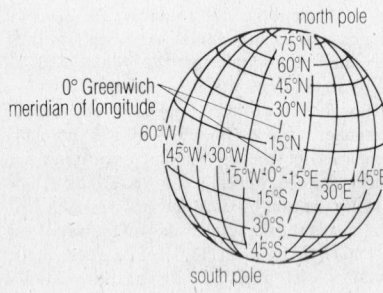

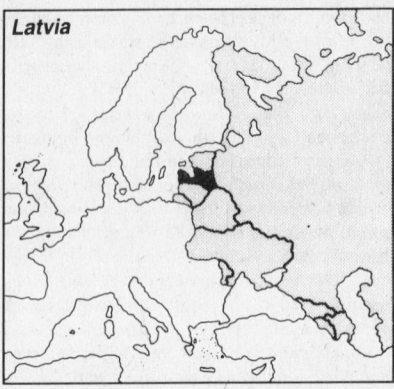

Latvia

and flows generally south east through Victoria to Lake Wellington, through one of the world's largest deposits of brown coal.

Latter-day Saint see ◊Mormon.

Latvia /ˈlætvɪə/ constituent republic of W USSR from 1940
area 63,700 sq km/24,600 sq mi
capital Riga
towns Daugavpils, Liepaja, Jelgava, Ventspils
physical lakes, marshes, and wooded lowland
products meat and dairy products; communications equipment; most of Soviet consumer durables, plus large share of motorcycles and locomotives
population (1984) 2,600,000; Letts 54%, Russian 33%
language Latvian
religion mostly Lutheran Protestant with a Roman Catholic minority
recent history formerly part of the Russian empire, Latvia became an independent republic in 1918 (recognized by Russia in 1920). In 1939 the USSR demanded military bases and in 1940 incorporated Latvia as a constituent republic. As in the other Baltic republics, there has been nationalist dissent since 1980, influenced by the Polish example and prompted by an influx of Russian workers and officials.

Latvian language the language of Latvia, one of the two surviving members of the Baltic branch of the Indo-European language family, the other being Lithuanian.

Laud /lɔːd/ William 1573–1645. English priest. As archbishop of Canterbury from 1633, his High Church policy, support for Charles I's unparliamentary rule, censorship of the press, and persecution of the Puritans, all aroused bitter opposition, while his strict enforcement of the statutes against enclosures and of laws

regulating wages and prices alienated the propertied classes. His attempt to impose the use of the Prayer Book on the Scots provoked a revolt which precipitated the English ◊Civil War. Impeached by Parliament in 1640 he was imprisoned in the Tower, condemned to death by a bill of ◊attainder, and beheaded.

Laud William Laud's attempts to impose the Prayer Book on the Scots provoked a revolt which precipitated the Civil War. He was beheaded in 1645. This portrait is after a painting by Van Dyck.

Lauderdale /ˈlɔːdədeɪl/ John Maitland, Duke of Lauderdale 1616–1682. Scottish politician. Formerly a zealous ◊Covenanter, he joined the Royalists in 1647, and as high commissioner for Scotland 1667–1679 persecuted the Covenanters. He was created duke of Lauderdale in 1672.

Laue /ˈlaʊə/ Max Theodor Felix 1879–1960. German physicist who was a pioneer in measuring the wavelength of X-rays by their diffraction through the closely spaced atoms in a crystal. His work led to the powerful technique now used to elucidate the structure of complex biological materials, for example, ◊DNA. He was awarded a Nobel prize 1914.

Laugharne /lɑːn/ village at the mouth of the river Towey, Dyfed, Wales. The home of the poet

Dylan Thomas, it features in his work as 'Milk Wood'.

laughing jackass another name for ◊kookaburra.

Laughton /ˈlɔːtn/ Charles 1899–1962. Anglo-American character actor, born in Scarborough. His larger-than-life film roles include the king in *The Private Life of Henry VIII* 1933 and Captain Bligh in *Mutiny on the Bounty* 1935.

Laughton An actor with a wide dramatic range, Charles Laughton won an Academy Award for his performance in the film *The Private Life of Henry VIII* 1933.

Launceston /ˈlɔːnstən/ town in Cornwall, UK, 34 km/21 mi NW of Plymouth, with ruins of a Norman castle, besieged in the Civil War.

Launceston /ˈlɔːnsəstən/ industrial port (woollen blankets, saw milling, engineering, furniture and pottery making, railway workshops) in NE Tasmania, Australia, on the Tamar river, founded 1805; population (1985) 60,500.

Laurasia /lɔːˈreɪʃə/ the old 'supercontinent' formed by the fusion of northern America, Greenland, Europe, and Asia that existed between 240 and 80 million years ago. It formed the northern half of the supercontinent ◊Pangaea; ◊Gondwanaland formed the southern half; between was the Tethys Sea. Laurasia broke up with the separation of N America from Europe in the Upper Cretaceous period.

laurel the true laurel tree *sweet bay* is *Laurus nobilis*, family Lauraceae, of which the aromatic leaves are used in cookery, and in classical times formed wreaths for athletes, symbolizing victory. The ornamental shrub laurels, for example, *cherry laurel Prunus laurocerasus*, family Rosaceae, are poisonous.

Laurel and Hardy /ˈlɒrəl, ˈhɑːdi/ Stan Laurel (1890–1965) and Oliver Hardy (1892–1957) American film comedians (Laurel was English-born). The most successful comedy team in the history of the screen, their unique partnership survived the transition from silent films to sound, and delighted audiences for decades. Their films were revived as a worldwide cult in the 1970s and include *Way Out West* 1937, and *A Chump at Oxford* 1940.

Laurel and Hardy The popular American comic duo Laurel and Hardy, one of the most successful comedy teams in cinema history.

Laurence /ˈlɒrəns/ Margaret 1926–1987. Canadian novelist, who in the 1960s inspired a generation of younger Canadian writers with a series of four novels, the Manawaka Quartet, set in the Canadian prairies. She also wrote short stories set in Africa, where she lived for a time.

Laurier /ˈlɔrieɪ/ Wilfrid 1841–1919. Canadian Liberal politician. As prime minister 1896–1911 – the first French-Canadian to hold the office – he supported imperial preference and the building of Canadian warships to co-operate with the British Navy, and sent Canadian troops to serve in the South African War.

laurustinus evergreen shrub *Vibernum tinus* in the family Caprifoliaceae. It has clusters of white flowers in the winter months, and is of Mediterranean origin.

Lausanne /lɒuˈzæn/ capital of Vaud canton, Switzerland, above the N shore of Lake Geneva, with a cathedral (1275) and university (1537); industries (chocolate, scientific instruments, publishing); population (1983) 127,000.

Lausanne, Treaty of peace settlement 1923 between Greece and Turkey after Turkey refused to accept the Treaty of Sèvres 1920. It involved the surrender by Greece of Smyrna to Turkey and the enforced exchange of the Greek population of Smyrna for the Turkish population of Greece.

lava the molten material exuded from a ◊volcano which cools to form extrusive ◊igneous rock. Lava differs from its parent ◊magma in that the fluid 'fractionates' on its way to the surface of the earth, that is certain heavy or high-temperature minerals settle out and the constituent gases form bubbles and boil away into the atmosphere. A lava high in silica is very stiff and does not flow far, while low-silica lava can flow for long distances.

Laval /ləˈvæl/ Pierre 1883–1945. French politician. Born near Vichy, he entered the Chamber of Deputies in 1914 as a Socialist, but after World War I moved towards the right. He was prime minister and foreign secretary 1931–32, and again 1935–36, his second period of office being marked by the Hoare-Laval agreement for concessions to Italy in Abyssinia. He joined Pétain's government as vice-premier in June 1940; dismissed in December, he was reinstated by Hitler's orders as head of the government and foreign minister in 1942. His share of in the deportation of French labour to Germany made him universally hated. On the Allied invasion he fled the country, but was arrested in Austria, tried for treason, and shot after trying to poison himself.

La Vallière /læ ˌvæliˈeə/ Louise de la Baume le Blance, Duchesse de la Vallière 1644–1710. Mistress of Louis XIV (by whom she had four children 1661–74), she retired to a convent on her supersession by Mme de Montespan.

La Vendée see ◊Vendée, La.

lavender sweet-smelling herb of the family Labiatae, genus *Lavandula*, a native of the western Mediterranean countries. The bush *Lavandula angustifolia* is low-growing with long, narrow, erect leaves of a silver-green colour. The flowers (borne on a terminal spike) vary in colour from lilac to deep purple, and are covered with small fragrant oil glands. The oil is extensively used in pharmacy and perfumes.

laver red seaweed *Porphyra umbicalis* growing on the shore and below, attached to rocks and stones but often where sand shifts over them. It forms thin flat irregularly rounded sheets of tissue up to about 20 cm/8 in across, of dark purplish red, almost black when dry. It is edible and in some places is considered a delicacy.

Lavery /ˈleɪvəri/ John 1856–1941. British portrait-painter of Edwardian society.

Lavoisier /læˈvwæzieɪ/ Antoine Laurent 1743–1794. French chemist, sometimes called the founder of modern chemistry. He proved that combustion needed only a part of 'air' which he called oxygen. He thereby destroyed the theory of phlogiston (an imaginary 'fire element' released during combustion). With ◊Laplace, he showed that water was a compound of oxygen and hydrogen. In this way he established the modern basic rules of chemical combination.

Lavoisier French chemist Antoine Lavoisier founded the classification of substances which is in use today. Eager for reforms, he held a government post, but it led him to the guillotine during the Reign of Terror.

Lavrentiev /læˈvrentief/ Mikhail 1900– . Soviet scientist. As director of the Institute for Precision Mechanics and Computer Engineering from 1950, he developed from 1957 the Akademgorodok ('Science City') in ◊Novosibirsk.

law the body of rules and principles under which justice is administered or order enforced in a state. In western Europe there are two main systems:

Roman law first codified in 450 BC and finalized under Justinian 528–34 AD, advanced to a system of international law (*jus gentium*), applied in disputes between Romans and foreigners or provincials, or between provincials of different states. Church influence led to the adoption of Roman law all over western continental Europe, and it was spread to E Europe and parts of Asia by the French *Code Napoléon* in the 19th century. Scotland and Quebec (because of their French links) and South Africa (because of its link with Holland) also have it as the base of their systems.

English law derives from Anglo-Saxon customs, which were too entrenched to be broken by the

Norman Conquest, and still form the basis of the ◊Common Law (that is, common to the whole country) which by 1250 had been systematized by the royal judges. Alongside it there grew up a system of ◊equity developed in the Court of Chancery, where the Lord Chancellor considered petitions, and the ordinary rules were mitigated where their application would operate harshly in particular cases. In the 19th century there was major reform of the law (for example, the abolition of many capital offences, in which juries would not in any case convict) and of the complex system of courts (see ◊law courts). Unique to ◊English law are the *judicial precedents* whereby the reported decisions of the courts form a binding source of law for future decisions. In modified form English law was adopted by countries throughout the world which came under English influence, including the USA.

Law /lɔː/ Andrew Bonar 1858–1923. British Conservative politician. Born in New Brunswick, he made a fortune in Scotland as a banker and iron-merchant, and entered Parliament in 1900. Elected leader of the opposition in 1911, he became colonial secretary in Asquith's coalition government 1915–16, and was chancellor of the exchequer 1916–19, and Lord Privy Seal 1919–21, in the Lloyd George coalition. He formed a Conservative cabinet in 1922, but resigned because of ill health in 1923.

Law /lɔː/ William 1686–1761. English cleric. His ◊Jacobite opinions caused him to lose his fellowship at Emmanuel College, Cambridge, in 1714. His most famous work is *A Serious Call to a Devout and Holy Life* 1728, which influenced the ◊Wesleys.

law courts the legal system of England and Wales. It is headed by the House of Lords, which hears appeals in both civil and criminal cases. Below it, under the Courts Act (1971) are the Supreme Court of Judicature as the Court of Appeal (civil and criminal) and the High Court of Justice (civil), comprising the Chancery, Queen's Bench and Family Divisions and the Crown Court. All more serious criminal work not covered by the Magistrates' Courts is handled by the Crown Courts (as are also certain civil cases), which are organized in six circuits. The towns of each circuit are first-tier (High Court and Circuit Judges dealing with both criminal and civil cases), second-tier (High Court and Circuit Judges dealing with criminal cases only), or third-tier (Circuit Judges dealing with criminal cases only). The former assizes and quarter sessions were abolished, but the ◊Central Criminal Court (the 'Old Bailey') continued to be the Crown Court for London. Cases are allotted according to gravity among High Court and Circuit Judges and Recorders (part-time judges with the same jurisdiction as Circuit Judges). Solicitors were allowed for the first time to appear in and conduct cases at the level of the Crown Courts, and solicitors as well as barristers of ten years' standing became eligible for appointments as Recorders, who after five years become eligible as Circuit Judges.

County Courts, dealing with minor civil cases, are served by Circuit Judges. Minor criminal cases are heard by two to seven lay Justices of the Peace, exercising summary jurisdiction, although in London and other large towns trained lawyers sit as Stipendiary ('paid') Magistrates. Juvenile Courts, held in separate buildings, are presided over by specially qualified justices. See also ◊Courts, Small Claims.

There are also special courts, such as the Restrictive Practices Courts, and Employment Appeal Tribunal. In Scotland, the Supreme civil court is the Court of Session, with appeal to the House of Lords; the highest criminal court is the High Court of Justiciary, with no appeal to the House of Lords.

In the USA the head of the federal judiciary is the Supreme Court which also hears appeals from the inferior federal courts and from the decisions of the highest courts of the states. The US Courts of Appeals – organized in circuits – deals with appeals from the US District Courts in which civil and criminal cases are heard. State Courts deal with civil and criminal cases involving state laws, the lowest being those of the justices of the peace.

Lawes /lɔːz/ Henry 1596–1662. British composer, whose works include music for Milton's masque *Comus* 1634. His brother *William* (1602–45) was also a composer.

Lawes /lɔːz/ John Bennet 1814–1900. British agriculturist, who in 1843 established the Rothamsted Experimental Station (Hertfordshire) at his birthplace; he patented the first artificial manure 'super-phosphate'.

Lawler /ˈlɔːlə/ Ray 1921– . Australian actor and playwright. He is best known for his play *The Summer of the Seventeenth Doll* 1955 about sugar-cane cutters, in which he played the lead role in the first production in Melbourne.

law lords in England, the ten Lords of Appeal in Ordinary who, together with the Lord Chancellor and other peers, make up the House of Lords in its judicial capacity.

Lawrence /ˈlɒrəns/ industrial town (textiles, clothing, paper, radio equipment) in Massachusetts, USA, established in 1845 to utilize power from the Merrimack Rapids on a site first settled in 1655; population (1980) 63,175.

Lawrence /ˈlɒrəns/ D(avid) H(erbert) 1885–1930. British novelist and poet, who in his work expressed his belief in emotion and the sexual impulse as creative and true to human nature. Son of a Nottinghamshire miner, he studied at Nottingham University, and became a teacher. He achieved fame with the semi-autobiographical *Sons and Lovers* 1913, which includes a portrayal of his mother (died 1911). In 1914 he married Frieda von Richthofen, ex-wife of his university professor, with whom he had run away in 1912, and who was the model for Ursula Brangwen in *The Rainbow* 1915, suppressed for obscenity, and its sequel *Women in Love* 1921. His travels in search of health (he suffered from tuberculosis, from which he eventually died near Nice) prompted books such as *Mornings in Mexico* 1927. Most famous of his novels is *Lady Chatterley's Lover* 1928, banned as obscene in the UK until 1960.

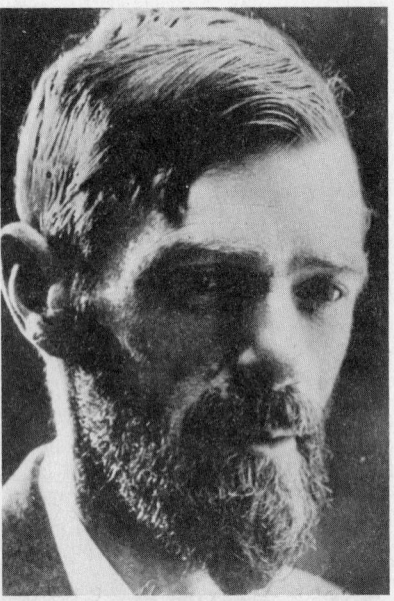
Lawrence Son of a Nottinghamshire miner, novelist and poet D H Lawrence achieved fame with *Sons and Lovers* 1913. His notorious *Lady Chatterley's Lover* was not published in an unexpurgated form in Britain until 1960.

Lawrence /ˈlɒrəns/ Ernest O(rlando) 1901–1958. American physicist. During his long period in California, he was professor of physics at the University of California, Berkeley, from 1930 and director of the Radiation Laboratory from 1936, which he built up into a large, brilliant school for research in nuclear physics. His invention of the cyclotron pioneered the production of artificial radioisotopes and led to many new fields of investigation. He was awarded a Nobel prize in 1939.

Lawrence /ˈlɒrəns/ Gertrude 1898–1952. English actress who established her reputation in both London and New York during the 1920s mainly as a dancer and later as leading role in revue and musical comedy revue and musical comedy. Her greatest success was *Private Lives* 1930–31, written specially for her by Noel Coward, with whom she co-starred.

Lawrence /ˈlɒrəns/ T(homas) E(dward) 1888–1935. British soldier, known as 'Lawrence of Arabia'. He was born in Wales; he studied at Oxford, and during 1910–14 took part in archaeological expeditions to Syria and Mesopotamia. Appointed to the military intelligence department in Cairo, he took part in negotiations for an Arab revolt against the Turks, and in 1916 attached himself to the emir Faisal. He showed himself a guerrilla leader of genius, combining raids on Turkish communications with the stirring up of revolt among the Arabs. He joined the Royal Air Force in 1922 as an aircraftman under the name Ross, transferring to the tank corps under the name T E Shaw in 1923 when his identity became known. He returned to the RAF in 1925, and adopted the name Shaw by deed poll in 1927. In 1935 he was killed in a motorcycle accident. His account of the Arab revolt, *Seven Pillars of Wisdom* 1935 (published privately 1926), has been described as the last great romantic war book.

Lawrence Known as Lawrence of Arabia, T E Lawrence led a campaign of guerrilla raids and pitched battles against the Turks culminating in the capture of Damascus 1918. He wrote an account in *Seven Pillars of Wisdom* 1935.

Lawrence /'lɒrəns/ Thomas 1769–1830. British portrait artist. Born at Bristol, son of an innkeeper, he succeeded ◊Reynolds as painter to George III in 1792. He painted portraits of many of his famous contemporaries including the series of Allied sovereigns and statesmen in Windsor Castle.

Lawrence, St /'lɒrəns/ Christian martyr. Probably born in Spain, he became a deacon of Rome under Pope Sixtus II, and when summoned to deliver the treasures of the Church displayed the beggars in his charge, for which he was broiled on a grid-iron. His feast day is 10 Aug.

lawrencium a synthetic radioactive element, symbol Lr, atomic number 103, atomic weight of isotope with longest half-life 260. It was first made in 1961 and named after E O ◊Lawrence.

Lawson /'lɔːsən/ Nigel 1932– . British Conservative politician. A former financial journalist, he was financial secretary to the Treasury 1979–81, secretary of state for energy 1981–83, and chancellor of the Exchequer from 1983.

laxative drug used to relieve constipation. Current medical opinion discourages their regular or prolonged use: a diet high in vegetable fibre is believed to be the best means of preventing and treating constipation.

Laxness /'læksnes/ Halldor 1902– . Icelandic novelist, writing about Icelandic life in the style of the early sagas. Nobel prize 1955.

Layamon /'laɪəmən/ English poet who lived about 1200. A priest of Arley Regis, Worcestershire, he wrote the *Brut*, a chronicle of about 30,000 alliterative lines on the history of

Britain from the legendary Brutus onwards, which gives the earliest version of the Arthurian story in English.

Layard /'leɪəd/ Austen Henry 1817–1894. British diplomat and archaeologist. Born in Paris, he travelled to the Middle East in 1839, conducted two expeditions to Nineveh and Babylon 1845–51, and sent to England the specimens forming the greater part of the Assyrian collection in the British Museum.

Lá Youn /lɑː 'juːn/ former name of ◊El Aaiún, capital of Western Sahara.

lay reader in the Church of England, a lay member of the church who is permitted to read the lessons, or under licence from the bishop of the diocese to conduct morning or evening prayer.

Lazarus /'læzərəs/ Emma 1849–1887. American poet, author of the poem on the base of the Statue of Liberty which includes the words: 'Give me your tired, your poor, / Your huddled masses yearning to breathe free'.

Lazio /'lætsiəu/ region (Roman *Latium*) of W central Italy; capital Rome; population (1981) 5,001,700. Home of the Latins from the 10th century BC, it was dominated by the Romans from the 4th century BC. It includes the low-lying Campagna, and the Pontine Marshes, which the Romans tried to drain, but which remained until Mussolini succeeded in 1926.

LCD abbreviation of ◊*l*iquid-*c*rystal *d*isplay.

Lea /liː/ river rising in Bedfordshire, England, which joins the Thames at Blackwall.

Leach /liːtʃ/ Bernard 1887–1979. British potter. His simple designs, influenced by a period of study in Japan, pioneered the modern revival of the art. He established the Leach Pottery at St Ives in 1920. His son David Leach is also a potter.

Leach Bernard Leach at work in his pottery in St Ives. His unmistakeable style owed much to his early studies in Japan.

Leacock /'liːkɒk/ Stephen Butler 1869–1944. Canadian humorist. Born in Hampshire, he lived in Canada from 1876, and

was head of the department of economics at McGill University, Montreal, 1908–36. He published works on politics and economics, studies of Mark Twain and Dickens, but is best known for his humorous writings, such as *Literary Lapses* 1910, *Nonsense Novels* 1911, and *Frenzied Fiction* 1918.

lead one of the four most-used metallic elements. Symbol Pb (Latin *plumbum*), atomic weight 207.21, atomic number 82. Known since prehistoric times (mentioned in Exodus), it is blueish-grey, and the heaviest, softest and weakest of the common metals; it lacks elasticity and is a poor conductor of electricity, but is resistant to corrosion by acids. Lead is used as a shield for radioactive sources, and in ammunition, batteries, glass, ceramics, and alloys such as pewter and solder. Lead is a cumulative poison within the body, and lead water pipes and lead-based paints are a health hazard, as is the use of lead in 'anti-knock' petrol additives.

lead-acid cell a type of ◊accumulator (storage battery).

lead ore lead is extracted from a number of minerals. The main primary ore is the sulphide galena, PbS. This is unstable and on prolonged exposure to the atmosphere it oxidizes into the minerals cerussite, $PbCO_3$, and anglesite, $PbSO_4$. Lead ores occur in a number of ways but most commercial deposits are in the form of veins, where hot fluids have leached the metal from cooling ◊igneous masses and deposited it in cracks in the surrounding country rock, and in thermal ◊metamorphic zones, where the heat of igneous intrusions has altered the minerals of the surrounding rocks. Lead ores are usually associated with other metals, particularly silver – which can be mined at the same time – and zinc, which can cause problems in the smelting. Lead is mined in over 40 countries, but half of the world's output comes from the USA, the USSR, Canada, and Australia.

leaf lateral outgrowth on the stem of a plant, and in most species the primary organ of ◊photosynthesis. Typically leaves are composed of three parts: the sheath or leaf-base, the petiole or stalk, and the ◊lamina or blade. The lamina has a network of veins through which water and nutrients are conducted. The chief leaf types are ◊cotyledons (seed leaves), ◊scale-leaves (on underground stems), foliage leaves, and ◊bracts (in the axil of which a flower is produced). A *simple leaf* is undivided, as in the beech or oak. A *compound leaf* is composed of several leaflets, as in the blackberry, horse-chestnut or ash tree (the latter being a ◊pinnate leaf). Leaves that fall in the autumn are termed *deciduous*, while evergreens are *persistent*.

Structurally the leaf is made up of ◊mesophyll cells surrounded by the epidermis and usually, in addition, a waxy layer, termed the ◊cuticle, which prevents excessive evaporation of water from the leaf tissues by ◊transpiration. The epidermis is interrupted by small pores, or ◊stomata through which gas exchange occurs.

leaf-hopper ◊bug of the family Cicadellidae. These small insects are numerous and are found

leaf (margins)

entire serrate dentate incised crenate sinuate scalloped undulate

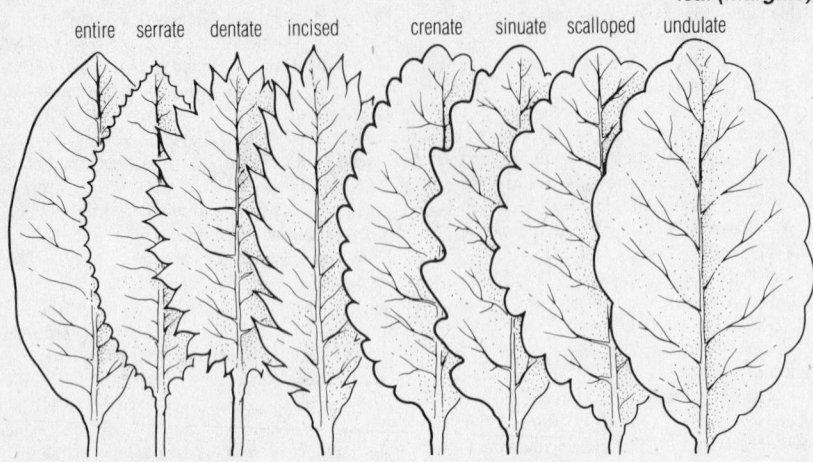

leaf

internal vein

xylem
phloem

midrib vein

upper epidermis
palisade cells

spongy cells

air space

guard cells of stoma

guard cells of stoma

lower epidermis

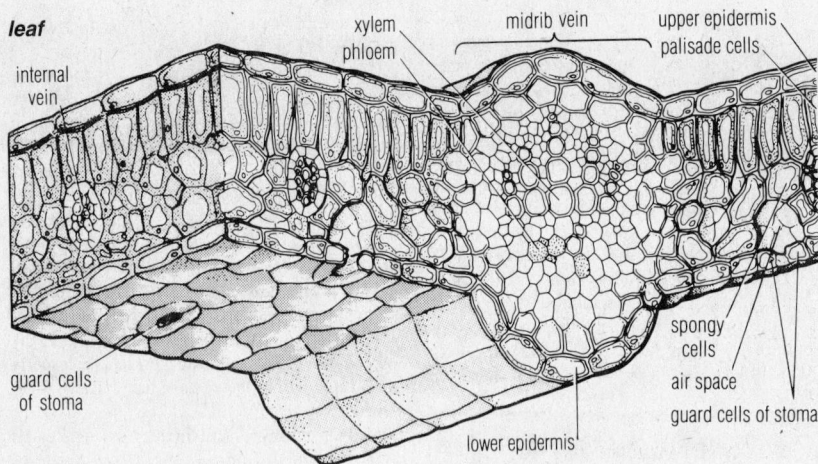

on leaves, where they suck the sap. Each species feeds on a limited range of plants.

leaf insect insect of the order Phasmida, with a depressed and leaf-like body, remarkable for closely resembling the foliage on which they live. They are most common in SE Asia.

League of Nations international organization suggested in President Woodrow Wilson's 'Fourteen Points' (1917) as part of the peace settlement for World War I. The League covenant was drawn up by the Paris Peace Conference in 1919 and incorporated into the Versailles and other peace treaties. Established in Geneva in 1920, the League included representatives from states throughout the world, but was severely weakened by the US decision not to become a member. The states which did become members undertook to preserve the territorial integrity of all, and to submit international disputes to the League or to arbitration. The League enjoyed a good deal of success in the humanitarian field (international action against epidemics, drug traffic and the slave trade) and also established a number of important subsidiary organizations, most notably:

leaf insect The leaf insect is almost invisible among leaves, and even its legs develop leaf-like forms.

International Labour Organization (ILO) based in Geneva and concerned primarily with working conditions and social welfare. Formed

in 1919, the ILO continued to exist as an affiliated body of the ◊United Nations.

High Commission for Refugees (Nansen Office) an organization created to assist refugees, primarily from Russia and eastern Europe. Built on the work of Norwegian explorer Fridtjof Nansen as first High Commissioner, the high commission declined in importance after his death and the entry of the USSR to the league. Formed the basis for post-1945 refugee work by the United Nations.

Permanent Court of Justice court created in the Hague in 1921 and based on ideas for some form of international court put forward at the Hague congress of 1907.

The League also achieved some success in organizing population exchanges after the Paris peace conferences had established new national boundaries, and in deferring arguments over disputed territories and former German colonies by mandating a League member to act as a caretaker of administration for a specified period of time, or until a permanent solution could be found. Mandates were created for Palestine (Britain), SW Africa (South Africa), and Danzig. In the political and diplomatic field, the League was permanently hampered by internal rivalries and the necessity for unanimity in the decision-making process. No action was taken against Japan's aggression in Manchuria (1931); attempts to impose sanctions against Italy for the invasion of Ethiopia (1935–36) collapsed; no actions were taken when Germany annexed Austria and Czechoslovakia, nor when Poland was invaded. Japan (1932) and Germany (1933) simply withdrew from the League and the expulsion of Russia in 1939 had no effect on the Russo-Finnish war.

Long before the outbreak of World War II, diplomacy had abandoned international security and reverted to a system of direct negotiation and individual alliances.

Leakey /'liːki/ Louis Seymour Bazett 1903–1972. British archaeologist. Born at Kabete, Kenya, he was curator of Coryndon Museum, Nairobi, 1945–61, and in 1958 discovered gigantic animal fossils at ◊Olduvai Gorge, as well as sharing with his wife Mary ◊Leakey in discovering many early remains of a human type.

Leakey /'liːki/ Mary 1913– . British archaeologist, wife of Louis ◊Leakey. She discovered in 1948, on Rusinga Island, Lake Victoria, East Africa, the prehistoric ape skull known as Proconsul, about 20 million years old; and human remains at Laetolil, to the south, about 3,750,000 years old.

Leakey /'liːki/ Richard 1944– . British archaeologist, son of Louis and Mary ◊Leakey. In 1972 he discovered at Lake Turkana, Kenya, an ape-form skull with some human characteristics, and a brain capacity of 800 cc, which was estimated to be about 2,900,000 years old. In 1984 his team found an almost complete skeleton of *Homo erectus* some 1.6 million years old.

Leamington /'lemɪŋtən/ officially *Royal Leamington Spa* town and health resort in the West Midlands, England, on the river Leam,

Leakey Richard Leakey holds the skull of *Australopithecus* in his right hand, and in his left the breakthrough '1470' skull of a hominid at least 2.6 million years old, which indicated that at least two types of early human co-existed.

adjoining Warwick; population (1985) 56,500. The Royal Pump Room offers modern spa treatment.

Lean /liːn/ David 1908– . British film director. Beginning as a camera assistant in 1928, he was assistant director of *Pygmalion* 1938. His films, noted for their atmospheric quality, include *Blithe Spirit* 1945, *Brief Encounter* 1946, *The Bridge on the River Kwai* 1957 (Academy Award), *Lawrence of Arabia* 1962 (Academy Award), and *A Passage to India* 1985. He was knighted in 1984.

Lear /lɪə/ Edward 1812–1888. British artist and humorist, best known for his *Book of Nonsense* 1846, which popularized the limerick. Born in Holloway, London, he first attracted attention by his paintings of birds, and later turned to landscapes. He travelled in Italy, Greece, Egypt and India, publishing books on his travels with his own illustrations, and spent most of his later life in Italy.

learning theory in psychology, a theory about how an organism acquires new behaviours. Two main theories are classical and operant ◊conditioning.

leasehold in law, land or property held for a specified period, usually at a rent. Houses and flats in the UK are often held on a 99-year lease, for which a lump sum is paid, plus an annual 'ground rent': the entire property reverts to the original owner at the end of the period. Under the Leasehold Reform Act of 1967, tenants were in many instances given the right to purchase the freehold or extend the lease of houses; and in the 1980s extension of the right to flats was under consideration, possibly in the form of *strata title*, a method used in Australia, where a building is subdivided (usually by voluntary agreement between landlord and tenants on payment of a capital sum) into 'strata', each comprising a standardized freehold (with specified rights, obligations, and rules of management).

lease-lend programme of mutual aid between Britain, the USA, and their Allies during World War II and begun under the USA's Lease-and-Lend Act of 1941–45, empowering the president

to sell, exchange, transfer, lease, or lend war materials to any country whose defence was considered essential to the defence of the USA. War supplies could thus be sent to Britain on a credit basis instead of the cash-and-carry system introduced by the Neutrality Act of 1939.

In Feb 1942, after the USA's entry into the war, an agreement between Britain and the USA provided for mutual lease-lend assistance, and for collaboration to deal with post-war economic problems.

least action principle (known also in biology as the *parsimony principle*) in science, principle that indicates that Nature 'chooses' the easiest path for moving objects, rays of light and so on.

leather material prepared, mainly from the hides and skins of domesticated animals, by tanning with vegetable tannins (from tree bark, and so on), and chromium salts. Plastic substitutes have made leather a 'luxury' item.

Leavis /'liːvɪs/ F(rank) R(aymond) 1895–1978. British literary critic and Cambridge academic. He edited the controversial review *Scrutiny* 1932–53, championed the work of D H Lawrence and James Joyce, and in 1962 attacked Snow's theory of 'Two Cultures'. *New Bearings in English Poetry* 1932 and *The Great Tradition* 1948 are important critical works.

Leavitt /'levɪt/ Henrietta Swan 1868–1921. US astronomer. Born in Lancaster, Massachusetts, she joined Harvard College Observatory in 1902 where in 1912 she discovered the *period-luminosity law* that links the brightness of a ◊Cepheid variable star to its period of variation. This law allows astronomers to use Cepheid variables as 'standard candles' for measuring distances in space.

Lebanon /'lebənən/ country in W Asia, bordered N and E by Syria, S by Israel, and W by the Mediterranean.

leather There are three main stages in the process of converting animal skin into leather – cleaning, tanning, and dressing. The picture shows leatherworkers in Bermondsey, London in 1862.

Leatherhead /'leðəhed/ town in Surrey, England, SW of London, on the river Mole at the foot of the N Downs; population (1985) 40,300. It has industrial research stations, the Thorndike Theatre (1968), and the Royal School for the Blind (1799).

leatherjacket the larva of the ◊crane-fly.

leaven element inducing fermentation; especially applied to the yeast added to dough in bread making. Hence it is used figuratively of any pervasive influence, usually in a good sense, although in the Old Testament it symbolized corruption, and unleavened bread was used in sacrifice.

government under the 1926 constitution, amended in 1927, 1929, 1943 and 1947, legislative power is held by the national assembly, whose 99 members are elected by universal adult suffrage, through a system of proportional representation, in order to give a fair reflection of all the country's religious groups. The assembly serves a four-year term. The president is elected by the assembly for a six-year term, and appoints a prime minister and cabinet who are collectively responsible to the assembly. Elections to the assembly were last held in 1972 and its life has been extended at least six times until 1988. There are several political parties but membership of the national assembly is more easily recognized in terms of religious groupings.

history the area now known as Lebanon was once occupied by ◊Phoenicia, an empire which flourished from the 5th century BC–1st century AD, when it came under Roman rule. ◊Christianity was introduced during the Roman occupation, and ◊Islam arrived with the Arabs in 635. Part of the Turkish ◊Ottoman Empire from the 16th century, Lebanon was administered by France, under a League of Nations mandate, from 1920–41. It was declared independent in 1941, became a republic in 1943, and achieved full autonomy in 1944.

Lebanon has a great variety of religions, including Christianity and many Islamic sects. For many years these co-existed peacefully, giving Lebanon a stability which enabled it, until the mid-1970s, to become a commercial and financial centre. Beirut's thriving business district was largely destroyed 1975–76 and Lebanon's role as an international trader has been greatly diminished.

After the establishment of ◊Israel in 1948, thousands of Palestinian refugees fled to Lebanon, and the ◊Palestine Liberation Organization (PLO) was founded in Beirut in 1964, moving its headquarters to Tunis in 1982. The PLO presence in Lebanon has been the main reason for Israeli invasions and much of the subsequent civil strife. Fighting has been largely between left-wing Muslims, led by Kamul Joumblatt of the Progressive Socialist Party, and conservative Christian groups, mainly members of the Phalangist Party. There have also been differences between pro-Iranian traditional Muslims, such as the ◊Shi'ites, and and Syrian-backed deviationist Muslims, such as the ◊Druze.

In 1975 the fighting developed into full-scale civil war. A cease-fire was agreed in 1976 but fighting began again in 1978, when Israeli forces invaded Lebanon in search of PLO guerrillas. The UN secured Israel's agreement to a withdrawal and set up an international peace-keeping force, but to little avail. In 1979 Major Saad Haddad, a right-wing Lebanese army officer, with Israeli encouragement, declared an area of about 700 square miles in S Lebanon an 'independent free Lebanon' and the following year Christian Phalangist soldiers took over an area N of Beirut. Throughout this turmoil the Lebanese government was virtually powerless. In 1982 Bachir Gemayel, youngest son of the founder of the Phalangist Party, became president. He was assassinated before he could assume office and his brother Amin took his place.

In 1983, after exhaustive talks between Lebanon and Israel, under US auspices, an agreement declared an end to hostilities and called for the withdrawal of all foreign forces from the country within three months. Syria refused to recognize the agreement and left about 40,000 troops, with about 7,000 PLO fighters, in N Lebanon. Israel responded by refusing to take its forces from the S. Meanwhile, a full-scale war began between Phalangist and Druze soldiers in the Chouf mountains, ending in a Christian defeat and the

creation of a Druze-controlled mini-state. The multinational force was drawn gradually but unwillingly into the conflict until it was withdrawn in the spring of 1984. Attempts were made in 1985 and 1986 to end the civil war but rifts within both Muslim and Christian groups have so far prevented it. Meanwhile Lebanon, and particularly Beirut, has seen its infrastructure and earlier prosperity virtually destroyed as it continues to be a battlefield for the rival factions.

Lebanon
REPUBLIC OF (*al-Jumhouria al-Lubnaniya*)

AREA 10,400 sq km/3,400 sq mi
CAPITAL and port Beirut
TOWNS ports Tripoli, Tyre, Sidon
PHYSICAL valley N—S between mountain ranges
FEATURES few of the celebrated cedars of Lebanon remain; Mount Hermon; Chouf Mountains; archaeological sites at Baalbeck, Byblos, Tyre; until the civil war, the financial centre of the Middle East
HEAD OF STATE AND OF GOVERNMENT Amin Gemayel from 1982
GOVERNMENT parliamentary democracy
EXPORTS citrus and other fruit; industrial products to Arab neighbours
CURRENCY Lebanese pound (452.77 = £1 Sept 87)
POPULATION (1985) 2,619,000 (including 350,000 Palestinian refugees, many driven out, killed in fighting or massacred 1982– 85); annual growth rate -0.2%
LANGUAGE Arabic (official); French and English
RELIGION Christian (Maronite and Orthodox) 40%, Muslim (Shi'ite 33%, Sunni 24%) 57%, Druze 3%
LITERACY 83% male/64% female (1980 est)
GNP $3 bn (1983); $1,150 per head of population
CHRONOLOGY
1944 Full independence achieved.
1964 Palestine Liberation Organization (PLO) founded in Beirut.

Lebanon

1975 Outbreak of civil war between Christians and Muslims.
1976 Ceasefire agreed.
1978 Israel invaded S Lebanon in search of PLO fighters. International peacekeeping force established. Fighting broke out again.
1979 Part of S Lebanon declared an 'independent free Lebanon'.
1982 Bachir Gemayel became president, but was assassinated before he could assume office. His brother Amin Gemayel became president.
1983 Agreement reached for the withdrawal of Syrian and Israeli troops, but not honoured.
1984 Most of international peacekeeping force withdrawn.
1985 Lebanon nearing chaos, with many foreigners being taken hostage.
1987 Syrian troops sent into Beirut.

In the Leblanc process, salt was first converted into sodium sulphate by the action of sulphuric acid, which was then roasted with chalk or limestone (calcium carbonate) and coal to produce a mixture of sodium carbonate and sulphide. The carbonate was leached out with water and the solution crystallized. Leblanc devised this cheap method of producing soda (for use in making glass, paper, soap and various other chemicals) in order to win a prize offered in 1775 by the French Academy of Sciences, but the

Lebda /ˈlebdə/ former name of ◊Homs, a city in Syria near the river Orontes.

Lebedev /ˈlebɪdjef/ Peter Nikolaievich 1866–1912. Russian physicist. While professor at Moscow university 1892–1911 he succeeded in proving experimentally, and then measuring, the minute pressure which light exerts upon a physical body; confirming ◊Clerk Maxwell's theoretical determination.

Lebensraum (German 'living space') slogan used by the Nazis to justify their annexation of neighbouring states and their demand for the return of the former German colonies, on the ground that Germany was overpopulated.

Leblanc /ləˈblɒŋ/ Nicolas 1742–1806. French chemist, best known for developing in 1790 a process for making sodium carbonate (soda ash) from sodium chloride (common salt).

Revolutionary government granted him only a patent (1791) which they seized along with his factory three years later. A broken man, Leblanc committed suicide.

Lebrun /ləˈbrɜːn/ Albert 1871–1950. French politician. He became president of the senate in 1931 and in 1932 was chosen as president of the republic. In 1940 he handed his powers over to Marshal Pétain.

Le Brun /ləˈbrɜːn/ Charles 1619–1690. French artist, who was appointed First Painter to Louis XIV in 1662. He helped to found the French Academy and was director of the ◊Gobelins Manufactory, which employed its members to produce the art, tapestries, and furnishings for Louis's new Palace of Versailles.

Le Carré /lə ˈkæreɪ/ John, pseudonym of British author David John Cornwell 1931– .

After teaching at Eton, he was a member of the Foreign Service 1960–64, and then turned to writing thrillers. His low-key realistic accounts of complex East-West espionage include *The Spy Who Came in from the Cold* 1963, *Tinker Tailor Soldier Spy* 1974, and *Smiley's People* 1980. He used the Middle East as a background in *The Little Drummer Girl* 1983. He also popularized the term 'mole' for someone working subversively within an organization.

Le Carré British thriller writer John Le Carré spent four years in the British Foreign Service and used his experiences in *The Spy Who Came in from the Cold* 1963 and other novels of international espionage.

Le Chatelier's principle (or *Le Chatelier-Braun principle*. In science, the principle that if a change in conditions is imposed on a system in equilibrium, the system will react so as to counteract that change and restore the equilibrium; it has many applications outside the field of chemistry, where it was first discovered in 1884 by French chemist Henri le Chatelier (1850–1936).

lecithin a type of lipid (fat), containing nitrogen and phosphorus, which forms a vital part of the cell membranes of plant and animal cells. The name is from the Greek, *lekithos* meaning 'egg yolk', eggs being an important source of lecithin.

Leclair /lə'kleə/ Jean-Marie 1697–1764. French violinist and composer. Originally a dancer and ballet-master, he composed ballet music, operas (*Scilla and Glaucus*), and violin concertos. He was murdered in a street crime.

Leclanché /lə'klɒnʃeɪ/ Georges 1839–1882. French engineer who in 1866 invented a primary electrical ◊cell which is still the basis of most dry batteries. In its simplest form, a Leclanché cell consists of a carbon rod (the ◊anode) dipping into a mixture of powdered carbon and manganese dioxide contained in a porous pot. The pot, in turn, sits in a glass jar containing an ◊electrolyte (conducting medium) of ammonium chloride

solution, into which dips a zinc ◊cathode. The cell produces a continuous current, the carbon mixture acting as a depolarizer, that is, preventing hydrogen bubbles from forming on the anode and increasing resistance. In a dry battery, the electrolyte is made in the form of a paste with starch, and a thin zinc can acts as both container and cathode.

Leclanché cell

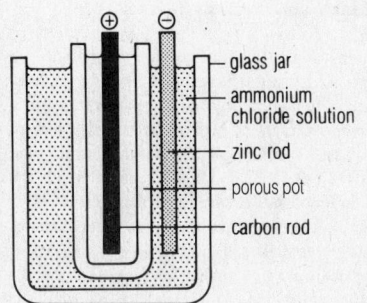

glass jar
ammonium chloride solution
zinc rod
porous pot
carbon rod

Leconte de Lisle /lə'kɒnt də 'liːl/ Charles Marie René 1818–1894. French poet. Born on Réunion, he settled in Paris in 1846 and headed Les ◊Parnassiens 1866–76. Distinguished by perfection of versification and form, his work drew inspiration from the ancient world, as in *Poèmes antiques/Antique Poems* 1852, *Poèmes barbares/Barbaric Poems* 1862, and *Poèmes tragiques/Tragic Poems* 1884.

Le Corbusier /lə ˌkɔː'bjuːzieɪ/ pseudonym of French architect Charles Edouard Jeanneret 1887–1965. Born in Switzerland, he was originally a painter and engraver, but turned his attention to the problems of modern industrial society. For Le Corbusier the house was a habitable machine which should be designed according to functional criteria. He won the contest for the Palace of the Nations at Geneva, devised town-planning schemes for Algiers, Barcelona, Buenos Aires, and Nemours (Algeria), and planned Cité Radieuse, Marseille and Chandigarh, India. *Le Modulor* 1948 explains his mathematical system for proportioning and relating the parts of buildings.

Lecouvreur /ləˌkuː'vrɜː/ Adrienne 1692–1730. French actress. She gained fame at the ◊Comédie Française, where she first appeared 1717, and her many admirers included Voltaire, and Maurice de Saxe; a rival mistress of the latter, the Duchesse de Bouillon, is thought to have poisoned her.

LED abbreviation for ◊light-emitting diode.

Leda /'liːdə/ in Greek mythology, wife of Tyndareus, by whom she was the mother of ◊Clytemnestra. By ◊Zeus, who came to her as a swan, she was the mother of ◊Helen of Troy, ◊Castor and ◊Pollux.

Le Duc Tho /'leɪ ˌdʊk 'təʊ/ 1911– . North Vietnamese diplomat, who was awarded (with ◊Kissinger) the Nobel Peace Prize in 1973, but indefinitely postponed receiving it.

Lee /liː/ Bruce, stage name of Lee Yuen Kam 1941–1973. American 'Chinese Western' film-actor, an expert in ◊kung fu, who popularized the oriental martial arts in the West.

Lee /liː/ Jennie, Baroness Lee 1904– . British socialist politician. She became a Member of Parliament for the ◊Independent Labour Party at the age of 24, and in 1934 married Aneurin ◊Bevan. On the left wing of the Labour Party, she was on its National Executive Committee 1958–70 and was minister of education 1967–70. She was made a baroness in 1970.

Lee /liː/ Kuan Yew 1923– . Singapore politician, prime minister from 1959.
Lee, trained as a barrister in London, founded the moderate, anti-communist Socialist People's Action Party in 1954 and entered the Singapore legislative assembly in 1955. He was elected the country's first prime minister in 1959 and has remained in power ever since. His son, Brigadier-General Lee Hsien Loong (1952–), already a minister, is viewed as a possible successor.

Lee /liː/ Laurie 1914– . British writer, born in Slad, near Stroud, Gloucestershire. His works include the autobiographical novel *Cider with Rosie* 1959, a classic evocation of childhood; nature poetry (*The Bloom of Candles* 1947) and travel writing (*A Rose for Winter* 1955).

Lee /liː/ Nathaniel 1653–1692. English dramatist. After an unsuccessful attempt to become an actor, he wrote from 1675 a number of extravagant tragedies, the best of which was *The Rival Queens* 1677.

Lee /liː/ Robert E(dward) 1807–1870. American general and military strategist. Born in Virginia, he was commissioned in 1829, served in the Mexican War, and in 1859 suppressed John Brown's raid on Harper's Ferry. On the outbreak of the Civil War he joined the Confederate army of the southern states, and became military adviser to Jefferson Davis. In 1862 he received the command of the army of North Virginia and won the Seven Days' Battle against McClellan. During 1862–63 he made several raids into Northern territory, winning victories at Fredericksburg and Chancellorsville, but after his defeat at Gettysburg was compelled to take the defensive. He surrendered in 1865 at Appomattox Court House.

leech worm in the class Hirudinea. Leeches inhabit fresh water and in tropical countries infest damp forests. As blood-sucking animals they are injurious to people and animals, to whom they attach themselves by means of a strong suctorial mouth. Formerly the medicinal leech *Hirudo medicinalis* was used extensively for 'bleeding' for a variety of ills. It still has some medicinal use, and is the source of the anti-coagulant hirudin.

Leech /liːtʃ/ John 1817–1864. British caricaturist. Born in London, he studied medicine before turning to art. He illustrated many books, including Charles Dickens' *Christmas Carol*, and during 1841–64 contributed about 3,000 humorous drawings and political cartoons to *Punch* magazine.

Leeds /liːdz/ industrial city (engineering, printing, chemicals, glass, woollens) in W Yorkshire, England, on the river Aire, a centre of communications where road, rail and canal (to Liverpool and Goole) meet; population (1984) 712,200. Noted buildings include the Town Hall designed by Cuthbert Brodrick, Leeds University 1904, the Art Gallery 1844, Temple Newsam (birthplace of Henry Darnley in 1545, now a museum), and the Cistercian Abbey of Kirkstall 1147.

leek plant of the family Liliaceae. The cultivated leek is a variety of the wild *Allium ampeloprasum* of the Mediterranean area and Atlantic islands. The lower leaf-parts (bulb) are eaten as a vegetable. It is the national emblem of Wales.

Leeuwarden /'leɪwɑːdn/ city in the Netherlands, capital of Friesland province; it is a marketing centre, and makes gold and silver ware; population (1984) 85,435. Noteworthy buildings include the palace of the stadholders of Friesland, and the church of St Jacob.

Leeuwenhoek /'leɪwənhuːk/ Anthony van 1632–1723. Dutch anatomist and pioneer microscopist. Born at Delft, he turned from business to microscopic research. With the simple (single-lens) microscopes he constructed he was able to observe cells and microorganisms for the first time, and he investigated a great many different subjects, including the structure of the red blood cells, the sperm cells of animals, and yeasts.

Leeward Islands /'liːwəd/ a general term for the N half of the Lesser Antilles in the West Indies. The British Leeward Islands comprise ◊Antigua, ◊Montserrat, ◊St Christopher/St Kitts-Nevis, and ◊Anguilla.
The Leeward Islands, together with the British ◊Virgin Islands, were until 1960 a single colony, and were members of the Federation of the West Indies 1958–62. The status of associated state was then granted to Antigua and to St Kitts-Nevis-Anguilla. Subsequently Anguilla claimed it was dominated by the St Kitts federal administration, and in 1969 declared itself a republic. After intervention by a small force from Britain, Anguilla was again, at its own request, under direct rule from Britain 1971–75. In 1976 Anguilla was granted internal autonomy while still formally part of the associated state. St Christopher-Nevis became fully independent in 1983.

Le Fanu /'lefənuː/ (Joseph) Sheridan 1814–1873. Irish writer. Born in Dublin, he wrote novels and short stories, such as *The House by the Churchyard* 1863, *Uncle Silas* 1864, and *In a Glass Darkly* 1872, which rank high among stories of the mysterious.

left-handedness in humans, use of the left hand for most actions. It occurs in about 16 per cent of the population, predominantly males, and is associated with a higher frequency of auto-immune diseases, conditions such as epilepsy, and learning difficulties (such as dyslexia, and stuttering). Right-handedness seems to have had an evolutionary advantage in that left-handed people are more sensitive to substances which act on the brain. Left-handedness may be caused by an excess of the male hormone, testosterone, while the child is still in the womb; this slows down development of the left-hand lobe of the brain, so that the right-hand lobe (which governs the left of the body) becomes dominant.

left wing in politics, a term used to describe the socialist or more progressive parties. It originated in the French National Assembly in 1789, where the nobles sat in the place of honour to the right of the president, and the third estate sat to the left; this arrangement has become customary in European parliaments, where the progressives sit on the left and the conservatives on the right. It is also usual to speak of the right, left, and centre, when referring to the different elements composing a single party.

legacy in law, a bequest of personal property made by a testator in a will and passing on the testator's death to the legatee. Specific legacies are definite named objects, for example, a piece of jewellery. General legacies are sums of money or items not specially identified, for example, 'one of my clocks'. A residuary legacy is all the remainder of the deceased's personal estate after his debts have been paid and the other legacies have been distributed.

legend term (from Latin *legere* 'to read') originally applied to the books of readings designed for use in Divine Service, and afterwards extended to the stories of saints read at matins and at mealtimes in monasteries. The best-known collection of such stories was the 13th-century *Legenda Aurea* by Jacobus de Voragine. The term has since extended its meaning to traditional or undocumented stories about famous people.

Léger /le'ʒeɪ/ Fernand 1881–1955. French artist, whose ◊Cubist works from 1911 especially favoured cylindrical and machine forms, reducing his human beings to robot-like figures. His works also include ballet settings, and murals.

Leghorn /'leghɔːn/ former English name for the Italian port ◊Livorno.

legionnaire's disease pneumonia-like disease, so called because it was first identified when it attacked a convention of American legionnaires (ex-servicemen) in 1976. It is caused by the bacterium *Legionella pneumophila* which breeds in warm water (for example in the cooling towers of air-conditioning systems). It is spread in minute water droplets, which are inhaled into the lung to spread the disease.

Legitimist the party in France which continued to support the claims of the house of ◊Bourbon after the revolution of 1830. When the direct line became extinct in 1883 the majority of the party transferred their allegiance to the house of Orléans.

Legnano, Battle of defeat of Holy Roman Emperor Frederick I (Barbarossa) by members of the Lombard League in 1176 at Legnano, NW of Milan. It was the greatest setback to the emperor's plans for imperial domination in Italy, and showed for the first time the power of infantry against feudal cavalry.

Le Guin /lə'gwɪn/ Ursula K(roeber) 1929– . American writer of science fiction and fantasy. Her novels include *The Left Hand of Darkness* 1969, which questions sex roles; the *Earthsea* trilogy 1968–72; and *The Dispossessed* 1974, which contrasts an anarchist and a capitalist society.

Lehár /leɪ'hɑː/ Franz 1870–1948. Hungarian composer. Born at Komárom, he studied at Prague Conservatoire, intending to become a violinist, but then became a conductor. He wrote many popular operettas, among them *The Merry Widow* 1905, *The Count of Luxembourg* 1909, *Gypsy Love* 1910 and *The Land of Smiles* 1929. He also composed songs, marches, and a violin concerto.

Le Havre /lə 'hɑːvrə/ industrial port (engineering, chemicals, oil refining) in NW France, on the Seine; population 264,500.

Lehmann /'leɪmən/ Lotte 1888–1976. German-born American soprano, who excelled in Wagnerian operas and was an outstanding Marschallin in Richard ◊Strauss's *Der Rosenkavalier*.

Lehmann /'leɪmən/ Rosamond Nina 1903– . British novelist; her books include *Dusty Answer* 1927, *Invitation to the Waltz* 1932, *The Weather in the Streets* 1936, *The Ballad and the Source* 1944, and *A Sea-Grape Tree* 1976. Her novels, at one time neglected as too romantic, have regained popularity in the 1980s because of their sensitive portrayal of girls' and women's experience. Her brother *John Lehmann* (1907–87) was a noted literary publisher and editor.

Leibniz /'laɪbnɪts/ Gottfried Wilhelm 1646–1716. German philosopher and mathematician. In his metaphysical works (such as *The Monadology*, 1714) he argued that the world (that is, the totality of everything there is) consisted of innumerable units – ◊'monads'. Each monad's properties determined its past, present, and future, and were selected by God so that monads, though independent of each other, interacted predictably; this meant that Christian faith and scientific reason need not be in conflict, and that 'this is the best of all possible worlds'.

Leicester /'lestə/ industrial city (food processing, hosiery, footwear, light and precision engineering, electronics, printing, plastics) and administrative headquarters of Leicestershire, England, on the river Soar, 156 km/97 mi NW of London; university 1957; population (1983) 282,300. The Roman Ratae Coritanorum founded 50 AD, it is one of the oldest towns in England. The guildhall dates from the 14th century and ruined Bradgate House was the home of Lady Jane Grey.

Leicester /'lestə/ Robert Dudley, Earl of Leicester c. 1532–1588. English courtier. Son of the duke of Northumberland, he was created Earl of Leicester in 1564. His good looks won him the favour of Queen Elizabeth I, who might have married him if he had not been previously married to Amy Robsart. When his wife died in 1560, by a fall downstairs, Dudley was suspected of murdering her. In 1576 he secretly married the widow of the Earl of Essex. Elizabeth gave him command of the army sent to the Netherlands in 1585–87, and of the one prepared to resist the threat of Spanish invasion in 1588.

Leicester and Holkham /'lestə, 'hɒlkəm/ Earl of Leicester and Holkham, title of Thomas William ◊Coke, British 19th-century agriculturist.

Leicestershire /'lestəʃə/ county in central England.

Leicester The controversial favourite of Elizabeth I, Robert Dudley, Earl of Leicester, commanded the army sent to the Netherlands and the one raised to resist the Spanish Armada in 1588.

area 2,553 sq km/986 sq mi
towns administrative headquarters Leicester; Loughborough, Melton Mowbray, Market Harborough
features Rutland district (formerly England's smallest county, with Oakham as its county town); Rutland Water, one of Europe's largest reservoirs; Charnwood Forest; Vale of Belvoir (under which are large coal deposits)
products horses, cattle, sheep, dairy products; coal
population (1986) 871,100
famous people C P Snow.

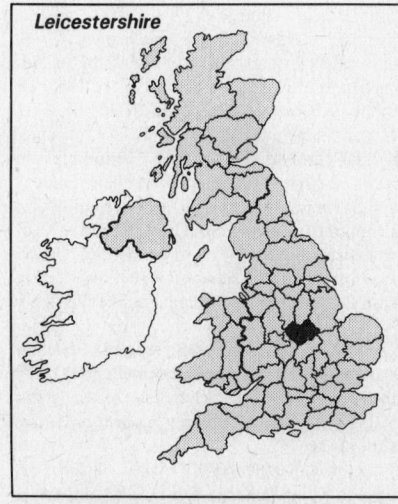

Leicestershire

Leichhardt /ˈlaɪkhɑːt/ Friedrich 1813–1848. Australian explorer, born in Prussia. In 1843 he walked 965 km/600 mi from Sydney to Moreton Bay, Queensland, and in 1844 went from Brisbane to Arnhem Land, but on a further expedition from Queensland in 1848 disappeared, never to be seen again. Patrick ◊White used the character of Leichhardt in *Voss* 1957.

Leiden /ˈlaɪdn/ industrial city (woollens, cigars; a printing centre ever since 1580) in S Holland province, Netherlands; linked by canal to Haarlem, Amsterdam, and Rotterdam; university 1575; population (1985) 104,670. The painters Rembrandt and Jan Steen were born here.

Leif Ericsson /ˈleɪf ˈerɪksən/ lived about 1000. Viking explorer, the son of ◊Eric the Red; he is said to have discovered 'Vinland', generally identified with ◊Nova Scotia.

Leigh /liː/ Mike 1943– . British playwright and director, who directs his own plays which evolve through improvisation before they are scripted, and include the comedies *Abigail's Party* 1977, and *Goose-Pimples* 1981. His work for television includes *Nuts in May* 1976, and *Home Sweet Home* 1982.

Leigh /liː/ Vivien 1913–1967. British actress, born Vivien Mary Hartley. Noted for her fragile beauty and vivacity, she excelled as Sabina in *The Skin of Our Teeth*. Her films include *Lady Hamilton* 1941, *Gone with the Wind* 1939 (Academy Award), and *A Streetcar Named Desire* 1951 (Academy Award). She was married to Laurence Olivier 1940–60, and starred with him in *Antony and Cleopatra* 1951.

Leigh British actress Vivien Leigh won an Academy Award for the role of Scarlett O'Hara in the Hollywood epic *Gone With the Wind* 1939. She and Laurence Olivier were married in 1940 in a blaze of publicity.

Leigh-Mallory /ˈliː ˈmæləri/ Trafford 1892–1944. British air chief marshal. As Air Officer Commanding No 12 Fighter Group 1937–40, he took part in the Battle of Britain, and was commander-in-chief of Allied air forces during the invasion of France. He was killed in an air crash.

Leighton /ˈleɪtn/ Frederick, Baron Leighton 1830–1896. British Victorian artist and sculptor. Born at Scarborough, he spent most of his early life abroad, and achieved fame in 1855 with his *Cimabue's Madonna Carried in Procession*. Most of his works represented historical, especially classical, subjects, for example *Captive Andromache* 1888, and *The Return of Persephone* 1891.

Leinster /ˈlenstə/ SE province of the Republic of Ireland, comprising the counties of Carlow, Dublin, Kildare, Kilkenny, Laoighis, Longford, Louth, Meath, Offaly, Westmeath, Wexford, Wicklow; area 19,635 sq km/7,581 sq mi; population (1981) 1,790,521.

Leipzig /ˈlaɪpzɪg/ capital of Leipzig district, East Germany, 145 km/90 mi SW of Berlin; its trade fairs are a centre of commerce for E and W Europe and have stimulated its industries (furs, leather goods, cloth, glass, cars, musical instruments); university 1409; population (1984) 1,384,050. The old town has narrow streets with 16th- and 17th-century houses, including the Rathaus 1558 and Auerbach's Hof about 1530. Leipzig was the scene of Napoleon's defeat in the Battle of the Nations 1813.

leishmaniasis parasitic disease caused by microscopic protozoans (*Leishmania*) identified by William Leishman (1865–1926) prevalent across the tropical countries of the world and transmitted by sandfly midges. Symptoms include ulcerative growths that eat away the nose, mouth and throat; anaemia; and liver and spleen enlargement.

Leith /liːθ/ Scottish port S of the Firth of Forth, incorporated in Edinburgh 1920. Leith was granted to Edinburgh as its port by Robert Bruce in 1329.

leitmotiv (German 'leading motive') in music, a recurring theme or motive used to indicate a character or idea – a technique used especially by Wagner in his operas.

Leitrim /ˈliːtrɪm/ county in Connacht province, Republic of Ireland, bounded on the NW by Donegal Bay
area 1,525 sq km/589 sq mi
county town Carrick-on-Shannon
physical the N is tableland; Lough Allen divides it into two
features rivers Shannon, Bonet, Drowes and Duff
products potatoes, linen, woollens, pottery, coal, iron, lead
population (1981) 27,600.

Leix /liːʃ/ spelling used 1922–35 of ◊Laois, county of Ireland.

lek the focus of a form of mating system, in which a closely spaced set of very small ◊territories (collectively called the lek) are each occupied by a single male. The lek is a traditional site, where both males and females congregate during the breeding season. The males display to passing females in the hope of attracting them to mate. Once mated, the females go elsewhere to lay their eggs or complete gestation. Leks are found in several birds (for example, ruff and grouse) and a few antelopes.

Leland /ˈliːlənd/ John 1506–1552. English antiquary, born in London. He became chaplain and librarian to Henry VIII, and during 1534–43 toured England collecting material for a history of English antiquities. The *Itinerary* was published in 1710. His manuscripts have proved a valuable source for scholars.

Lely /'liːli/ Peter 1618–1680. Adopted name of Pieter van der Faes, Anglo-German portrait artist. He worked for Charles I, Cromwell, and Charles II, who knighted him in 1679. His most famous paintings are the portraits of the fashionable women of Charles II's court, now at Hampton Court.

Lely German-born portrait artist Peter Lely succeeded Van Dyck as court painter. This self-portrait was painted in about 1660.

Lemaître /lə'meɪtrə/ Georges Edouard 1894–1966. Belgian cosmologist who put forward the ◊Big Bang theory for the origin of the Universe. Born in Charleroi, he was ordained a priest in 1922 before studying ◊astrophysics in England and the USA. In 1927, Lemaître predicted that the entire Universe was expanding, which ◊Hubble confirmed, and suggested that the expansion had been started by an initial explosion, the Big Bang, a theory that is now generally accepted.

Le Mans /lə 'mɒŋ/ town in France, site of an annual motor race; see ◊Mans, Le.

Lemberg /'lembeək/ German name of ◊Lvov, city in USSR.

lemming small rodent found in America, N Europe and Asia. The European lemming *Lemmus lemmus*, common in Norway, is 12 cm/5 in long and yellowish brown. Periodically, when their population exceeds the available food supply, lemmings undergo mass migrations.

Lemnos /'lemnɒs/ Greek island (Greek Límnos) in the N of the Aegean Sea
area 466 sq km/180 sq mi
towns Kastro, Mudros
physical of volcanic origin, rising to 430 m/1,411 ft
products mulberries and other fruit, tobacco, sheep
population (1971) 17,789.

lemon fruit of the lemon tree *Citrus limon*. It may have originated in NW India, and was introduced into Europe by the Spanish Moors in the 12th or 13th century. It is now grown largely in Italy, Spain, California, Florida, South Africa, and Australia.

lemur type of ◊primate inhabiting Madagascar and the Comoro Islands. They are arboreal animals, and some species are nocturnal. Many are threatened with extinction. They feed upon fruit, insects, and small animals. The ring-tailed lemur *Lemur catta* is often seen in zoos.

Lena /'liːnə , Russian 'ljenə/ longest river in Asiatic Russia, 4,800 km/3,000 mi, with numerous tributaries before flowing into the Arctic Ocean. It is ice-covered for half the year.

Le Nain /lə 'næŋ/ *Antoine* 1588–1648, *Louis* 1593–1648 and *Mathieu* 1607–1677. French painters. The three brothers were born at Laon, settled in Paris, and were among the original members of the French Academy. They painted portraits, but mainly devoted themselves to pictures of peasant life.

Lenclos /lɒŋ'kləu/ Ninon de 1615–1705. French courtesan. As the recognized leader of Parisian society, she was the mistress in turn of many highly placed men, including ◊Condé and ◊La Rochefoucauld.

Lenglen /lɒŋ'glɒŋ/ Suzanne 1899–1938. French tennis player, Wimbledon champion 1919–25, and introducer of modern sports clothes, designed by Jean ◊Patou.

Lenin /'lenɪn/ Vladimir Ilyich. Adopted name of Russian politician Vladimir Ilyich Ulyano 1870–1924. Born at Simbirsk (now renamed Ulyanovsk), he became a lawyer in St Petersburg (now Leningrad). Sent to Siberia for revolutionary Marxist propaganda 1895–1900, he then edited the Social Democratic paper *Iskra* ('The Spark') from abroad, and visited London several times (see ◊Tower Hamlets). In *What is to be done?* 1902, he advocated a professional core of party activists to spearhead the revolution in Russia, a suggestion accepted by the majority (*bolsheviki*) at the London party congress in 1903. Active in the 1905 Revolution, Lenin had again to leave Russia when it failed, settling in Switzerland in 1914, from where he attacked Socialist support for World War I as for an 'imperialist' struggle, and wrote *Imperialism* 1917. On the renewed outbreak of revolution in Mar 1917, he returned to Russia. With the overthrow of the provisional government, he became president of a Soviet government, concluded peace with Germany, and organized a successful resistance to 'White' (pro-Tsarist) uprisings and foreign intervention. Communism proving inadequate to put the country on its feet, he introduced a private enterprise New Economic Policy (NEP) from 1921 (reversed by Stalin in 1929). He had founded the Third (Communist) International in 1919, but his health declined following injuries in an assassination attempt in 1918. His embalmed body is a tourist attraction in a mausoleum in Red Square, Moscow. He married in 1898 *Nadezhda Konstantinova Krupskaya* (1869–1939), who shared his work, and wrote *Memories of Lenin*.

Leninakan /ˌlenɪnə'kɑːn/ industrial town (textiles, engineering) and railway junction in the Armenian Republic, USSR, 40 km/25 mi

Lenin Russian politician Vladimir Lenin photographed in 1922 with family and friends.

NW of Yerevan; population (1985) 223,000. It was founded in 1837 as a fortress called Alexandropol, and virtually destroyed by an earthquake in 1926.

Leningrad /'lenɪngræd/ capital of the Leningrad region and second city of the USSR, at the head of the Gulf of Finland; industries (shipbuilding, machinery and machine tools, chemicals, textiles, diesel motors, tyres, rubber boots); university 1819; population (1985) 4,867,000. It is split up by the mouths of the Neva, which connects it with Lake Lagoda. The site is low and swampy, and the climate severe.
history capital of the Russian Empire 1709–1918, it was founded as an outlet to the Baltic in 1703 by Peter the Great, who took up residence there in 1712. Originally called St Petersburg, it was renamed Petrograd in 1914, and Leningrad in 1924. Leningrad was the centre of all the main revolutionary movements from the Decembrist revolt of 1825 up to the 1917 revolution. During the German invasion in World War II the city withstood siege and bombardment from Sept 1941 to Jan 1944.
Leningrad is famous for its wide boulevards and the scale of its architecture. Most of its fine baroque and classical buildings of the 18th and early 19th centuries survived World War II. Museums include the Winter Palace, occupied by the tsars until 1917, the Hermitage, the Russian Museum (formerly Michael Palace), and St Isaac's Cathedral. The oldest building in Leningrad is the fortress of St Peter and St Paul, on an island in the Neva, now a political prison. Leningrad became a seaport when it was linked with the Baltic by a ship canal built 1875–93. It is also linked by canal and river with the Caspian and Black seas, and in 1975 a seaway connection was completed via lakes Onega and Ladoga with the White Sea near Belomorsk, so that naval forces can reach the Barents Sea free of NATO surveillance.

Leninsk-Kuznetsky /'lenɪnsk kuz'netski/ town in Kemerovo region, S USSR, on the Inya river, 320 km/200 mi SSE of Tomsk; population (1977) 131,000. It is a mining centre in the Kuzbas, with a large iron and steel works; coal, iron, manganese, and other metals, and precious stones occur in the neighbourhood. Formerly Kolchugino, the town was renamed Leninsk-Kuznetsky in 1925.

Le Nôtre /lə 'nəutrə/ André 1613–1700. French landscape gardener, creator of the gardens at Versailles and the Tuileries.

Lens /lɒns/ coalmining town in Pas-de-Calais department, France; population (1982) 38,300. During World War I it was in German occupation and close to the front line from Oct 1914 to Oct 1918, when the town and its mines were severely damaged. In World War II it was occupied by Germany from May 1940 to Sept 1944, but suffered less physical damage.

lens in optics, a piece of a transparent material such as glass with two polished surfaces – one concave or convex, and the other plane, concave or convex – to modify rays of light according to the type of lens they traverse. A convex lens converges the light and a concave lens diverges it. Lenses are essential to spectacles, microscopes, telescopes, cameras and almost all optical instruments. Compound lenses for special purposes are built up from two or more lenses made of glass (or other suitable material) of different refractive index.

The image formed by a single lens suffers from several defects or aberrations, notably spherical aberration in which a straight line becomes a curved image, and chromatic aberration in which an image in white light tends to have coloured edges. Aberrations are corrected by the use of compound lenses.

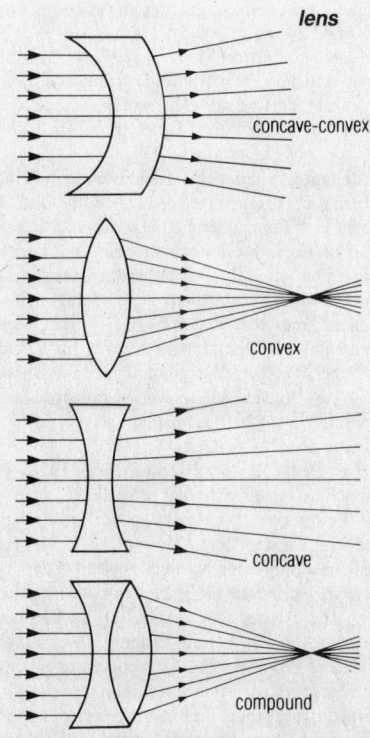

lens

concave-convex

convex

concave

compound

lens, gravitational In astronomy, object in space which by its gravitational field, bends light in a similar way to a spectacle lens. As a result of this, in 1979, observers on earth saw

two quasars which appeared physically almost identical. However, such twin effects are more likely to be due to double images of a single quasar produced by an intervening galaxy, itself faintly visible between the two images. A gravitational lens also produces a magnifying effect, and from a focal point some 300,000 million km out in space objects seen behind the sun would be magnified 20 million times: it has been suggested that this is the direction of astronomy in the future.

Lent in the Christian Church, the forty days' period of fasting which precedes Easter, beginning on Ash Wednesday, but omitting Sundays.

Lenthall /'lentɔːl/ William 1591–1662. English lawyer. Speaker of the House of Commons in the ◊Long Parliament of 1640–60, he took an active part in the Restoration.

lenticel a small pore on the stems of woody plants or the trunks of trees. Lenticels are means of gas exchange between the stem interior and the atmosphere. They consist of loosely-packed cells with many air spaces between them, and are easily seen on smooth-barked trees such as cherries, where they form horizontal lines on the trunk.

lentil annual plant of the Leguminosae family *Lens culinaris* of which the small seeds are widely used for food. The plant, which resembles the vetch, is probably native to the shores of the Mediterranean. It grows 15–45 cm/6–18 in high, and has white, blue, or purplish flowers. The pods are about 1.6 cm/0.6 in long, containing two seeds. The commonest varieties are the greyish French lentil and the red Egyptian lentil.

Lenya /'leɪnjə/ Lotte. Stage-name of Austrian actress and singer Karoline Blamauer 1905–1981. She married Kurt ◊Weill in 1926, and appeared in several of the Brecht-Weill operas, notably *The Threepenny Opera* 1928.

Lenz's law in physics, law stating that an induced current (generated by moving a magnet near a wire or a wire in a magnetic field) flows in the direction that tends to oppose the motion producing it. Named after the German physicist Heinrich Friedrich Lenz (1804–1865), who announced it in 1833. See ◊electromagnetic induction.

Leo /'liːəu/ constellation of the ◊zodiac, representing a lion, through which the sun passes from mid-Aug to mid-Sept. Its brightest star is first-magnitude Regulus, a blue-white star 85 light years away; Gamma Leonis is a striking double star for small telescopes.

Leo III /'liːəu/ the Isaurian c. 680–740. Byzantine emperor. A soldier who seized the throne in 717, he successfully defended Constantinople against the Saracens in 717–18, and attempted to suppress the use of images in church worship.

Leo /'liːəu/ name of thirteen popes, including:

Leo I /'liːəu/ St (the Great) c. 390–461. Pope from 440. One of the most important of the early popes for establishing the Christian liturgy, Leo summoned the Chalcedon Council where his famous 'Dogmatical Letter' was accepted as the voice of St Peter. Acting as ambassador to the emperor Valentinian III, Leo saved Rome from

devastation by ◊Attila the Hun, by buying off the city with large sums of money.

Leo III /'liːəu/ c. 750–816. Pope from 795. After the withdrawal of the Eastern emperors, the popes had become de facto rulers in Rome. Leo III was forced to flee following a conspiracy in Rome, and took refuge at the court of Charlemagne. He returned to Rome in 799, and crowned Charlemagne emperor on Christmas Day 800, thus establishing the temporal sovereignty of the pope over Rome under the suzerainty of the emperor.

Leo X /'liːəu/ (Giovanni de' Medici) 1475–1521. Pope from 1513. The son of Lorenzo the Magnificent, he was created a cardinal at 13. He bestowed on Henry VIII of England the title of 'Defender of the Faith', but later excommunicated him. Famous as a patron of the arts, he sponsored the rebuilding of St Peter's, Rome. He raised funds for this by selling indulgences, a sale which led ◊Luther to rebel against papal authority. He excommunicated Luther in 1513, and condemned him in the bull *Exsurge domine* 1520.

Leo XIII /'liːəu/ (Gioacchino Pecci) 1810–1903. Pope from 1878. After a successful career as a papal diplomat, Leo XIII established good relations between the papacy and European powers, USA, and Japan. He encouraged foreign missions and emphasized the duty of the Church in matters of social justice. His encyclical *Rerun novarum* 1891 pointed out the moral duties of employers towards workers. Leo remained intransigent in negotiations with the Italian government over the status of Rome, insisting that he keep control over part of it.

León /leɪ'ɒn/ industrial and university city in W Nicaragua, founded 1524; population (1981) 248,700.

León /leɪ'ɒn/ city in Castilla-León, Spain; population (1980) 131,135. It was the capital of the kingdom of León 10th century–1230, when it was merged with Castile.

León /leɪ'ɒn/ industrial city in central Mexico; population (1980) 655,800.

Leonard /'lenəd/ Elmore 1925– . American author of westerns and thrillers, marked by vivid dialogue, for example *Stick* 1983.

Leonardo da Vinci /ˌliːə'nɑːdəu də 'vɪntʃi/ 1452–1519. Italian painter, sculptor, architect, musician, engineer, and scientist, considered to be the embodiment of ◊Renaissance man. Born at Vinci in Tuscany, the illegitimate son of a lawyer, he studied under ◊Verrochio. From c. 1477 he worked under the patronage of ◊Lorenzo the Magnificent, then in 1482 became state engineer, court painter, and director of court festivities to Lodovico ◊Sforza in Milan. From 1500 he moved from place to place in Italy, including a spell in 1502 as architect and engineer to Cesare ◊Borgia, then in 1516 settled in France at the invitation of ◊Francis I at the Château Cloux, near Amboise, where he died. It is now a museum of his varied achievements, with many models made from his technical drawings. Leonardo's enquiring scientific mind led him to investigate many aspects of the natural world from anatomy to aerodynamics. His notebooks and drawings remain his finest legacy, but his experiments also revolutionized painting style. Instead of a white background, he used a dark one to allow the overlying colour a more three-dimensional existence. He invented 'aerial perspective' whereby the misty atmosphere (*sfumato*) blurs and changes the colours of the landscape as it dissolves into the distance. His principle of grouping figures within an imaginary pyramid, linked by their gestures and emotions, became a High Renaissance compositional rule. His two versions of the Madonna and child with St Anne, *Madonna on the Rocks* (Louvre, Paris, and National Gallery, London) exemplify all these ideas. Other chief works include *The Adoration of the Magi* 1481, in the Uffizi, Florence; *The Last Supper* (badly deteriorated, but under restoration in the 1980s) 1495–98, on the wall of the refectory of Santa Maria Delle Grazie, Milan; the *Mona Lisa* (wife of Zanoki del Giocondo, hence also known as *La Gioconda*) 1503, Louvre, Paris; and the *Battle of Anghiari* 1504–05, formerly in the Palazzo Vecchio, Florence.

Leonardo da Vinci Self-portrait of Italian artist Leonardo da Vinci. His enquiring scientific mind led him to investigate every aspect of the natural world from anatomy to aerodynamics, and to revolutionize methods and style in painting. Distinguished in many different fields, he is considered the embodiment of the Renaissance spirit.

Leoncavallo /ˌleɪɒnkəˈvæləʊ/ Ruggiero 1857–1919. Italian operatic composer. Born in Naples, he played in restaurants, composing in his spare time, until in 1892 *Pagliacci* was performed and immediately became popular. Of his other operas, only *La Bohème* 1897 (contemporary with Puccini's) and *Zaza* enjoyed some success.

Leonidas /liːˈɒnɪdæs/ died 480 BC. King of Sparta. He was killed while defending the pass of ◊Thermopylae with 300 Spartans, 700 Thespians, and 400 Thebans against a huge Persian army.

leopard member of the cat family *Panthera pardus*, also known as the panther, found over almost all Africa and Asia. The ground colour of the coat is golden and the spots form rosettes which differ according to the variety; black panthers are simply mutants and retain the patterning as a 'watered-silk' effect. The leopard varies in size from 1.5–2.5 m/5–8 ft, including the tail, which may measure 1 m/3 ft.

The snow leopard or ounce *Panthera uncia*, which has irregular rosettes of much larger black spots on a light cream or grey ground, is a native of mountains in central Asia. The clouded leopard *Neofelis nebulosa* is rather smaller, about 1.75 m/5.8 ft overall, with large blotchy markings rather than rosettes, and found in SE Asia.

Leopardi /ˌleɪəʊˈpɑːdi/ Giacomo, Count Leopardi 1798–1837. Italian romantic poet. Born at Recanati, of a noble family, he wrote many of his finest poems, including his great patriotic odes, before he was 21. His first collection, *Versi/Verses*, appeared in 1824, and was followed by his philosophical *Operette Morali/Minor Moral Works* 1827, in prose, and *Canti/Lyrics* 1831. After 1830 his life was divided between Florence, Rome, and Naples, where he died. Throughout life he was tormented by ill-health, by the consciousness of his deformity (he was hunch-backed), by loneliness and a succession of unhappy love-affairs, and by his 'cosmic pessimism' and failure to find consolation in any philosophy. He has nevertheless been called the greatest Italian lyric poet since Dante.

Leopardi 19th-century Italian poet Giacomo Leopardi was tormented by his deformity, ill-health and unhappy love affairs. His work is pessimistic, but of great lyrical beauty.

Leopold /ˈleɪəʊld/ three kings of the Belgians:

Leopold I /ˈleɪəpəʊld/ 1790–1865. King of

Belgium from 1831, having been elected to the throne on the creation of an independent Belgium. Through his marriage to Princess ◊Charlotte, he was the uncle of Queen ◊Victoria, and exercised considerable influence over her.

Leopold II /ˈleɪəpəʊld/ 1835–1909. King of Belgium from 1865, son of Leopold I. He financed ◊Stanley's explorations in Africa, which resulted in the foundation of the Congo Free State (now ◊Zaïre), from which he extracted a huge fortune by ruthless exploitation.

Leopold III /ˈleɪəpəʊld/ 1901–1983. King of Belgium from 1934, he surrendered to the Germans in 1940. Postwar charges against his conduct led to a regency by his brother Charles, and his eventual abdication in 1951 in favour of his son ◊Baudouin.

Leopold /ˈliːəpəʊld/ the name of two Holy Roman Emperors:

Leopold I /ˈliːəpəʊld/ 1640–1705. Holy Roman Emperor from 1657, in succession to his father ◊Ferdinand III. He warred against Louis XIV and the Turks.

Leopold II /ˈliːəpəʊld/ 1747–1792. Holy Roman Emperor in succession to his brother ◊Joseph II, he was the son of ◊Maria Theresa. His hostility to the French Revolution led to the outbreak of war a few weeks after his death.

Léopoldville /ˈliːəpəʊldvɪl/ former name of ◊Kinshasa, city in Zaïre.

Leonov /ljeˈɒnɑːf/ Aleskei Arkhipovich 1934– . Russian cosmonaut who became the first person to carry out mechanical tasks away from his base vehicle while serving as co-pilot of *Voskhod 2* 1965.

Leonov /ljeˈɒnɑːf/ Leonid 1899– . Russian novelist and playwright whose writing style owes much to ◊Dostoevsky. His works include the novel *The Badgers* 1924 and the drama *The Orchards of Polovchansk* 1938.

Lepanto /lɪˈpæntəʊ/ Italian name of the Greek port of Naupaktos, on the N of the Gulf of Corinth. A famous sea battle was fought in the Gulf of Corinth off Lepanto, then in Turkish possession, on 7 Oct 1571, between the Turks and Christian League forces from Spain, Venice, Genoa, and the Papal States which were commanded by Don ◊John of Austria. Instigated by Pope ◊Pius V, the League delivered a crushing blow to Muslim sea power. Cervantes was wounded in the battle, which is the subject of a stirring poem by G K Chesterton.

Le Pen /lə ˈpen/ Jean-Marie 1928– . French extreme right-wing politician.

Le Pen served as a paratrooper in French Indochina and ◊Algeria during the 1950s. He became a right-wing National Assembly deputy in 1956. During the 1960s, Le Pen was connected with the extremist ◊Organisation de l'Armée Secrète (OAS), before forming the French National Front in 1972. This party, supporting immigrant repatriation and capital punishment, gained 10 per cent of the national vote in the 1986 election. Le Pen, a powerful orator, was elected to the European Parliament in 1984.

Lepenski Vir the site of Europe's oldest urban settlement (6th millenium BC), now submerged by an artificial lake on the Danube.

lepidoptera an order of insects, including ◊butterflies and ◊moths; the order consists of some 165,000 species. Both butterflies and moths have overlapping scales on their wings.

leprosy also known as *Hansen's disease* a disease due to infection by the lepra bacillus. It is most common in hot, damp countries, especially Africa, but is found all over the world. In the nodular type the skin thickens, lumps appear all over it and break down into ulcers: the patient eventually dies of exhaustion, tuberculosis, or kidney disease. In the smooth type the microbe chiefly attacks the nerves of the skin, producing discoloured patches, loss of feeling, paralysis, and the death and shedding of fingers and toes. The bacillus may be transmitted by contact, or enter through stomach and lungs. It is curable with sulphone drugs and currently a vaccine is undergoing trials.

Leptis Magna /'leptɪs 'mægnə/ ruined city in Libya, 120 km/75 mi E of Tripoli. It was founded by the Phoenicians, then came under Carthage, and in 47 BC under Rome. Excavation in the 20th century brought to light remains of fine Roman buildings.

lepton a type of sub-atomic or elementary ◊particle.

leptospirosis infectious disease of domestic animals, especially cattle, causing abortion; transmitted to humans, it causes meningitis and jaundice.

Le Puy /lə'pwiː/ capital of Haute-Loire *département*, SE France, dramatically situated on a rocky plateau; it has a 12th-century cathedral.

Lérida /'leridə/ (Catalan 'Lleida') industrial city (leather, paper, glass, cloth), capital of Lérida province in N Spain, on the Segre, 132 km/82 mi W of Barcelona; population (1981) 107,000. Lérida was captured by Caesar in 49 BC. It has a palace of the kings of Aragon.

Lermontov /'leəmɒntɒf/ Mikhail Yurevich 1814–1841. Russian romantic poet and novelist. Born in Moscow, he received a commission in the Guards, but in 1837 was exiled to the Caucasus for a revolutionary poem on the death of ◊Pushkin, which criticized Court values. The romantic scenery of the Caucasus deeply influenced his poetry. After returning to St Petersburg in 1838 he published his psychological novel *A Hero of Our Times* 1840 and a volume of poems *October* 1940. He was again exiled to the Caucasus in the same year, and was killed in a duel while on leave in 1841.

Lerner /'lɜːnə/ Alan Jay 1918–1986. American lyricist, collaborator with Frederick ◊Loewe on musicals including *Brigadoon* 1947, *Paint Your Wagon* 1951, *My Fair Lady* 1956, *Gigi* 1958, and *Camelot* 1960.

Lerwick /'lɜːwɪk/ fishing and oil port, administrative headquarters of Shetland, Scotland; population (1985) 8,000. Hand-knitted shawls are a speciality. A Viking tradition survives in the Jan festival of Up-Helly-Aa when a copy of a longship is burned.

Le Sage /lə 'sɑːʒ/ Alan René 1668–1747. French novelist and dramatist. Born in Brittany, he abandoned law for literature. His novels include *Le Diable boîteux/The Devil upon Two*

Sticks 1707 and his picaresque masterpiece *Gil Blas* 1715–1735, much indebted to Spanish originals.

lesbianism ◊homosexual relationship between women, so-called from the Greek Island of Lesbos, home of ◊Sappho the poet.

Lesbos /'lezbɒs/ ancient name of ◊Lesvos, an island in the Aegean Sea. It was an Aeolian settlement, the home of the poets ◊Alcaeus and ◊Sappho.

Lesotho /lɪ'suːtuː/ landlocked country in southern Africa, an enclave within South Africa.
government Lesotho is an independent monarchy within the Commonwealth. Its 1966 constitution was suspended, reinstated, and then suspended again, and all executive and legislative powers are now vested in the hereditary king, assisted by a six-member military council and a council of ministers. The constitution provides for a 99-member, single-chamber elected national assembly. The last elections were in 1973, when the Basotho National Party (BNP) won a majority of the seats. Elections due in 1985 were cancelled by the king because no candidates opposed the BNP, all of whose nominees were deemed to have been returned unopposed.
history the area now known as Lesotho was originally inhabited by the San, or Bushmen. During the 18th–19th centuries they were superseded by the Sotho, who were being driven southwards by the *Mfecane* ('the shaking-up of peoples') caused by the rise of the ◊Zulu nation. Under the name of Basutoland, the Sotho nation was founded by Moshoeshoe I (1790–1870) from 1827, and at his request it became a British protectorate in 1868. It achieved internal self-government in 1965, with the paramount chief, Moshoeshoe II as king, and was given full independence, as Lesotho, in 1966.
The BNP, a conservative group favouring limited co-operation with South Africa, held power from independence until 1986. Its leader, Chief Leabua Jonathan, became prime minister in 1966 and after 1970, when the king's powers were severely curtailed, the country was effectively under the prime minister's control. Since 1975 an organization called the Lesotho Liberation Army (LLA) has carried out a number of attacks on BNP members, with alleged South African support. South Africa has denied complicity but at the same time has pointed out that Lesotho allows the banned South African nationalist movement the African National Congress (ANC), to use it as a base.
Economically, Lesotho is dependent on South Africa but has openly rejected the policy of ◊apartheid. In retaliation, South Africa has tightened its border controls, causing food shortages in Lesotho. It has been alleged that South Africa has encouraged BNP dissenters to form a new party, the Basotho Democratic Alliance (BDA), and plotted with the BDA to overthrow the Lesotho government. Lesotho has also been under pressure from South Africa to sign a non-aggression pact, similar to the ◊Nkomati Accord between South Africa and Mozambique, but the Lesotho government has refused to do so.

In 1986 South Africa imposed a border blockade, cutting off food and fuel supplies to Lesotho, and the government of Chief Jonathan was ousted and replaced in a coup led by Gen Justin Lekhanya. He announced that all executive and legislative powers would be vested in the king, ruling through a military council chaired by Gen Lekhanya, and a council of ministers. A week after the coup about 60 ANC members were deported to Zambia and on the same day the South African blockade was lifted. Although South Africa has denied playing any part in the coup, it is clear that it will find the new government more acceptable than the old.

Less Developed Country (LDC) any country late in developing an industrial base, and dependent on cash crops and unprocessed minerals. The 'Group of 77' was established in 1964 to pressurize developed countries into giving greater aid to LDCs.

Lesseps /'lesəps/ Ferdinand, Vicomte de Lesseps 1805–1894. French engineer, constructor of the ◊Suez Canal 1859–69; he began the ◊Panama Canal in 1879, but failed when he tried to construct it without locks.

Lessing /'lesɪŋ/ Doris (May) (born Taylor) 1919– . British novelist, born in Iran and brought up in Rhodesia. Much concerned with social and political themes, particularly the place of women in society, her work includes *The Grass is Singing* 1950, *The Golden Notebook* 1962, *The Good Terrorist* 1985, and the five-novel series *Children of Violence* 1952–69, tracing the growing up of its central character, Martha Quest, in a changing society. She has also written an 'inner space fiction' series *Canopus in Argus Archives* 1979–83, which chronicles events in a fictional universe, and, under the pseudonym 'Jane Somers', *The Diary of a Good Neighbour* 1981.

Lessing /'lesɪŋ/ Gotthold Ephraim 1729–1781. German dramatist and critic. Born at Kamenz in Saxony, he studied at Leipzig, and subsequently lived in Berlin, Leipzig, and Hamburg. His dramatic masterpieces include *Miss Sara Sampson* 1755, the first German tragedy of ordinary life; *Philotas* 1759 a one-act prose tragedy; the comedy *Minna von Barnhelm* 1767 with a Seven Years' War background; the domestic tragedy *Emilia Galotti* 1772; and the verse play *Nathan der Weise* 1779, which treats the theme of religious tolerance. As a critic he decisively influenced the course of German literature with *Laokoon* 1766 in which he analysed the functions of poetry and the plastic arts; and with the *Hamburgische Dramaturgie* 1767–68, in which he re-interpreted Aristotle and attacked the restrictive form of French classical drama in favour of the freer approach of Shakespeare. His many theological and philosophical writings include *Ernst und Falk* 1777–80, advocating tolerance and understanding in human affairs.

Les Six French name ('the six') given in 1920 to a group of six French composers – Georges ◊Auric, Louis Durey (1888–1979), Arthur ◊Honegger, Darius ◊Milhaud, Francis ◊Poulenc, and Germaine Tailleferre (1892–1983) – dedicated to producing works

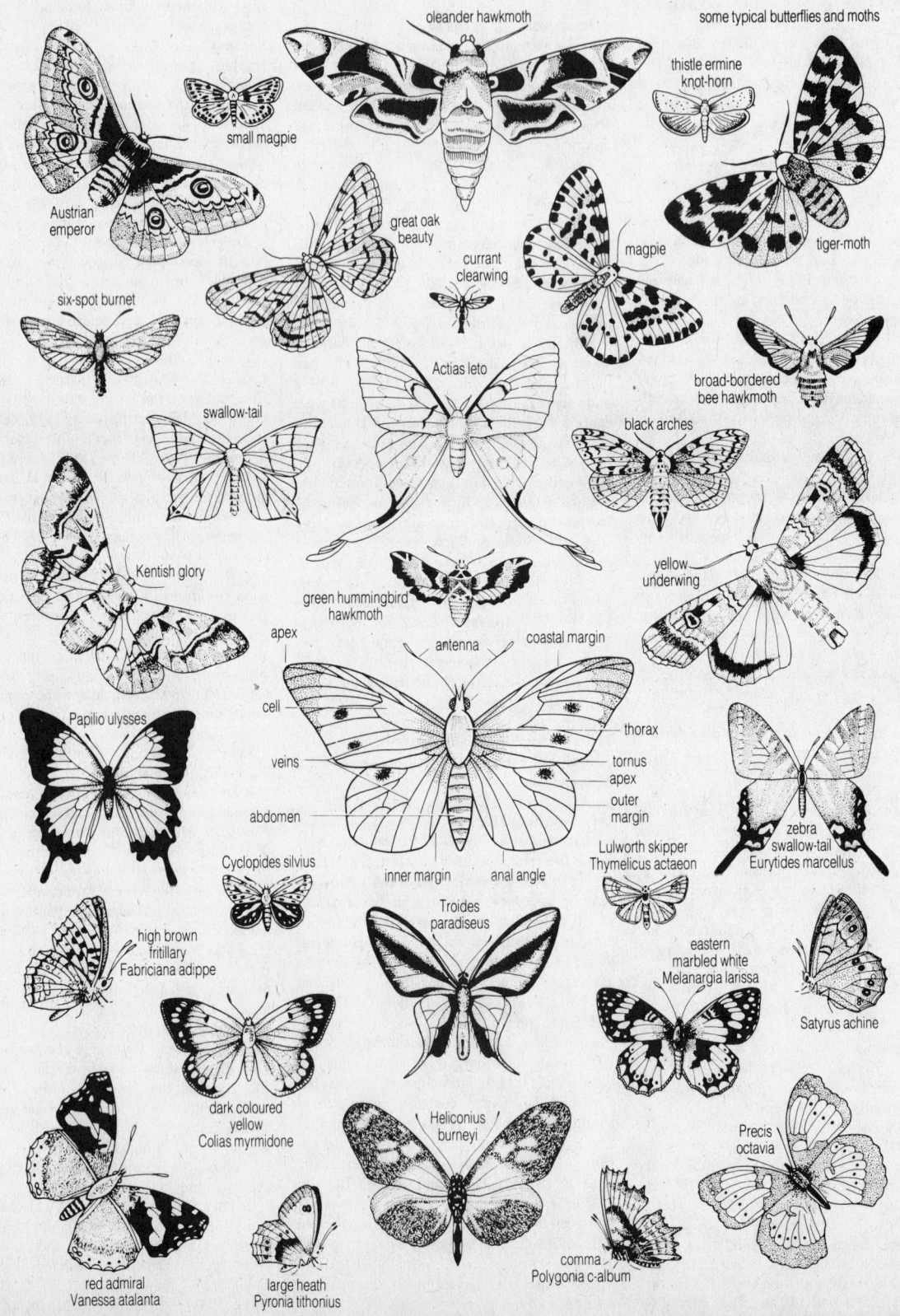

some typical butterflies and moths

oleander hawkmoth

small magpie

Austrian emperor

thistle ermine knot-horn

tiger-moth

great oak beauty

currant clearwing

magpie

six-spot burnet

Actias leto

broad-bordered bee hawkmoth

swallow-tail

black arches

Kentish glory

green hummingbird hawkmoth

yellow underwing

apex

antenna

coastal margin

cell

thorax

Papilio ulysses

veins

tornus
apex
outer margin

abdomen

zebra swallow-tail
Eurytides marcellus

Cyclopides silvius

inner margin

anal angle

Lulworth skipper
Thymelicus actaeon

high brown fritillary
Fabriciana adippe

Troides paradiseus

eastern marbled white
Melanargia larissa

Satyrus achine

dark coloured yellow
Colias myrmidone

Heliconius burneyi

Precis octavia

red admiral
Vanessa atalanta

large heath
Pyronia tithonius

comma
Polygonia c-album

Lesotho
KINGDOM OF

AREA 30,346 sq km/11,716 sq mi
CAPITAL Maseru
PHYSICAL mountainous
FEATURES Lesotho is an enclave within South Africa
HEAD OF STATE Moshoeshoe II from 1966
HEAD OF GOVERNMENT Justin Lekhanya from 1986
GOVERNMENT military
EXPORTS wool, mohair; diamonds
CURRENCY maloti (3.38 = £1 Sept 1987)
POPULATION 1,512,000 (1985); annual growth rate 2.6%
LANGUAGE Sesotho and English (official)
RELIGION Christian 70% (Roman Catholic 40%)
LITERACY 65% (1984)
GNP $678.2 million (1981); $355 per head of population
CHRONOLOGY
1966 Basutoland achieved full independence, within the Commonwealth, as the Kingdom of Lesotho, with Chief Leabua Jonathan as prime minister.

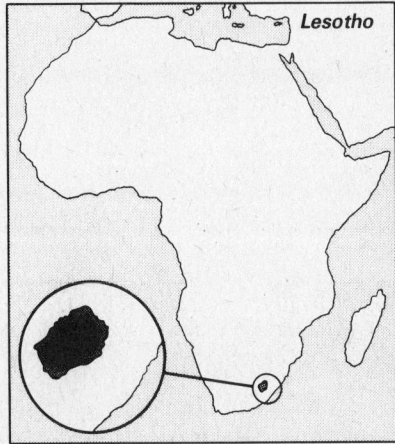

1975 Members of the ruling party attacked by guerrillas backed by South Africa.
1986 South Africa imposed a border blockade, forcing the deportation of 60 African National Congress members.
1987 Gen Lekhanya ousted Chief Jonathan in a coup.

Lessing British novelist Doris Lessing was brought up in Rhodesia. She wrote the autobiographical series *Children of Violence* and *The Golden Notebook*.

free from foreign influences and reflecting the modern world. The music was marked by its wit and irreverence. The group, although influential, quickly split up.

Lesvos /'lezvɒs/ Greek island in the Aegean Sea, near the coast of Turkey
area 1,749 sq km/675 sq mi
capital Mytilene
products olives, wine, grain
population (1981) 104,620
history its ancient name was ◊Lesbos. It was conquered by the Turks from Genoa in 1462, and annexed to Greece in 1913.

Letchworth /'letʃwəθ/ industrial town (clothing, furniture, scientific instruments, light metal goods, printing) in Hertfordshire, England, 56 km/35 mi NNW of London, founded in 1903 as the first British ◊garden city; population (1981) 31,835.

Lethaby /'leθəbi/ William Richard 1857–1931. English architect, and assistant to Richard Norman ◊Shaw. He embraced the principles of William ◊Morris and Philip ◊Webb and had a great influence in the ◊Arts and Crafts Movement, especially as first director of the Central School of Arts and Crafts (which he helped to found) from 1894. His most influential work was *Form in Civilization, 1922*.

Lethe /'liːθi/ in Greek mythology, a river of the underworld whose waters, when drunk, brought forgetfulness of the past.

Le Touquet /lə 'tuːkeɪ/ resort in N France, fashionable in the 1920s–30s.

letter a written or printed message, especially a personal communication. Letters are valuable as reflections of social conditions, literary, and political life. Ownership of a letter (as a document) passes to the recipient, but the copyright remains with the writer. Outstanding examples include:
ancient Cicero and Pliny the Younger, and St Paul;
medieval Abelard and Héloïse (12th-century France), the Paston letters (15th-century England);
16th century Erasmus, Luther, Melanchthon, Spenser, Sidney;
17th century Donne, Milton, Cromwell, Dorothy Osborne, Wotton; (France) Pascal, Mme de Sévigné;

18th century Pope, Walpole, Swift, Mary Wortley Montagu, Chesterfield, Cowper, Gray; (France) Bossuet, Voltaire, Rousseau;
19th century Byron, Lamb, Keats, Fitzgerald, Stevenson; (USA) Emerson, J R Lowell; (France) George Sand, Saint-Beuve, Goncourt brothers; (Germany) Schiller, Goethe; (Switzerland) Gottfried Keller;
20th century T E Lawrence, G B Shaw and Ellen Terry, Katherine Mansfield; (Germany) Rilke.

letterpress the method of printing from raised type, pioneered by Johannes Gutenberg in the 1450s. Compare ◊gravure, ◊offset-litho.

lettres de cachet /'letrə də 'kæʃeɪ/ French term for an order signed by the king and closed with his seal (*cachet*); especially an order under which persons might be imprisoned or banished without trial. They were used as a means of disposing of politically dangerous persons or criminals of high birth without the embarrassment of a trial. The system was abolished during the French Revolution.

lettuce annual plant *Lactuca sativa* belonging to the family Compositae, and believed to have been derived from the wild species, *Lactuca serriola*. There are two common forms, the cabbage lettuce, with round or loose heads, and the Cos lettuce, with long, upright heads. Other types include the cut-leaved lettuce, with deeply serrated leaves.

leucite a silicate mineral, $KAlSi_2O_6$, occurring frequently in volcanic rocks of recent origin, and other rocks low in silica content and rich in potash. It is dull white to grey, and usually opaque. It can be a useful source of potassium as fertilizer.

leucocyte a white blood cell. Human blood contains about 11,000 leucocytes to the cubic millimetre – about one to every 500 red cells. They are part of the body's defences and give ◊immunity against disease. There are several different types of leucocyte. Some (◊phagocytes or macrophages) engulf invading micro-organisms, others kill infected cells, while a third type, the ◊lymphocytes, produce more specific immune responses. Leucocyte numbers may be reduced (leucopenia) by starvation, pernicious anaemia, and certain infections, such as typhoid and malaria. An increase in the numbers (leucocytosis) is a reaction to normal events such as digestion, exertion and pregnancy, and to abnormal ones such as loss of blood, cancer and most infections.

leucotomy or *frontal lobotomy* in medicine, the surgical severing of nerves in the frontal lobes of the brain for treating certain mental disorders. It is now rarely used. See also ◊psychosurgery.

leukaemia form of cancer of the blood, marked by an increase in the white blood cells. Cure or control is by radiotherapy or drugs, especially successful in younger patients.

Levant /lɪ'vænt/ the E Mediterranean region, or more specifically, the coastal regions of Turkey-in-Asia, Syria, Lebanon, and Israel.

Le Vau /lə'vəu/ Louis 1612–1670. French architect, who drafted the plan of Versailles, and built the Louvre and Tuileries.

level a simple instrument for finding horizontal level, used in surveying and building construction. Often called a spirit, or bubble level, it consists of a coloured liquid in a glass tube, in which a bubble is trapped. When the tube is horizontal, the bubble moves to the centre.

Levellers the democratic party in the English Revolution. They found wide support among Cromwell's New Model Army and the yeoman farmers, artisans, and small traders, and during 1647–49 proved a powerful political force. Their programme included the establishment of a republic, government by a parliament of one house elected by male suffrage, religious toleration, and sweeping social reforms. Mutinies by the Levellers in the army were suppressed by Cromwell in 1649. They were led by John ◊Lilburne.

Leven, Loch /'liːvən/ loch in Tayside region, Scotland; area 16 sq km/6 sq mi. It is drained by the river Leven, and has seven islands; Mary Queen of Scots was imprisoned 1567–68 on Castle Island.

Leven /'liːvən/ Alexander Leslie, 1st Earl of Leven c. 1580–1661. Scottish general. After a distinguished career in the Swedish service, he led the ◊Covenanters' army which invaded England in 1640. He also commanded the Scottish army sent to aid the English Puritans in 1643–46, and shared in the victory of ◊Marston Moor. In 1641 he was created Earl of Leven.

lever /'liːvə/ a simple machine comprising a rigid rod pivoted at a fulcrum, used for shifting or raising a heavy load or applying force in a similar way. Levers are classified into orders according to where the effort is applied, and the load-moving force developed, in relation to the position of the fulcrum. In a first-order lever, the load and effort are on opposite sides of the fulcrum, for example, a see-saw, beam balance or pair of scissors. A second-order lever has the load and effort on the same side of the fulcrum, with the load nearer the fulcrum, for example, a wheelbarrow, a pair of nut crackers. In a third-order lever, the effort is nearer the fulcrum than is the load with both on the same side of it, for example, a pair of tweezers or tongs. The mechanical advantage of a lever is the ratio of load to effort, equal to the perpendicular distance of the effort's line of action from the fulcrum divided by the distance to the load's line of action. Thus tweezers, for instance, have a mechanical advantage of less than 1.

Lever /'liːvə/ Charles James 1806–1872. Irish novelist. Born in Dublin, he wrote novels of Irish and army life, such as *Harry Lorrequer* 1837, *Charles O'Malley* 1840, and *Tom Burke of Ours* 1844, which achieved huge popularity in their time.

Leverkusen /'leɪvəkuːzən/ river port in North Rhine-Westphalia, West Germany, 8 km/5 mi N of Cologne, with chemical industries; population (1984) 156,500.

Leverrier /lə,veri'eɪ/ Urbain Jean Joseph 1811–1877. French astronomer, who predicted the existence and position of ◊Neptune.

Lévesque /le'vek/ René 1922–1987. French-Canadian politician. A law student, he served as a war correspondent in World War II and Korea.

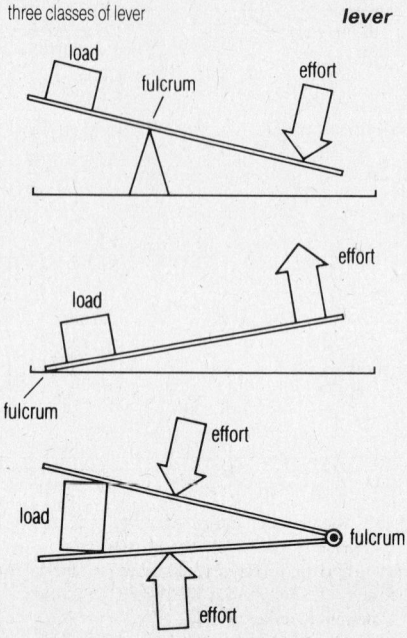

three classes of lever   *lever*

In 1968 he founded the Parti Québecois, with the aim of an independent Quebec, but a national referendum rejected the proposal in 1980. He was premier of Quebec 1976–85. In 1985 he resigned from the leadership of the party.

Levi /'levi/ Primo 1919–1987. Italian novelist, who joined the anti-Fascist resistance during World War II and was captured and sent to Auschwitz concentration camp. He wrote memorably of his experience as a Jewish survivor in *Se Questo e un uomo/If This is a Man* 1947.

leviathan in the Old Testament, a mythical evil sea monster identified by later commentators with the whale.

Lévi-Strauss /'levi 'straʊs/ Claude 1908– . French anthropologist. He sought to find a universal structure governing all societies, reflected in the way myths are created. His books include *Tristes Tropiques* 1955, and *Mythologiques/Mythologies* 1964–71.

levitation counteraction of gravitational forces on a body. As claimed by medieval mystics, and spiritualist mediums, it is unproven. In the laboratory it can be produced scientifically, for example, electrostatic force and acoustical waves have been used to suspend water drops for microscopic study. It is also used in technology, for example, in magnetic levitation as in 'maglev' trains (parts of the train and the track are made like the poles of a magnet, so that the carriage is suspended slightly above the track surface).

Levite in the Old Testament, a member of one of the 12 peoples of Israel. Descended from Levi, a son of ◊Jacob, the Levites performed the lesser services of the Temple; the priesthood was confined to the descendants of ◊Aaron.

Lewes /'luːɪs/ market town (administrative headquarters) in E Sussex, England; population (1981) 13,800. The Glyndebourne music festival is held nearby. Simon de Montfort defeated Henry III here in 1264; there is a house once

belonging to Anne of Cleves, and a castle. The town is known for its 5th Nov celebrations.

Lewes /'luːɪs/ George Henry 1817–1878. English philosopher and critic. From acting he turned to literature and philosophy; his works include a *Biographical History of Philosophy* 1845–46, and *Life and Works of Goethe* 1855. He married in 1840, but left his wife in 1854 to form a life-long union with the writer Mary Ann Evans (George ◊Eliot), whom he had first met in 1851.

Lewis /'luːɪs/ N part of Lewis-with-Harris in the Outer ◊Hebrides.

Lewis /'luːɪs/ Arthur 1915– . British economist, born on St Lucia, West Indies. He specialized in the economic problems of developing countries, as in *The Theory of Economic Growth* 1955, and shared a Nobel prize in 1979.

Lewis /'luːɪs/ Carl 1956– . American athlete. At the 1984 Olympics, he won four gold medals, in the 100 metres, 200 metres, sprint relay and long jump. He won three gold medals at the inaugural world championships in 1983. His sister, Carol Lewis, is also a world class long jumper.

Lewis /'luːɪs/ Cecil Day see ◊Day Lewis.

Lewis /'luːɪs/ C(live) S(taples) 1898–1963. British academic and writer. From 1954–63 he was professor of Medieval and Renaissance English at Cambridge, and his books include the medieval study *The Allegory of Love* 1936, and the space fiction *Out of the Silent Planet* 1938. He was a committed Christian and wrote essays in popular theology such as *The Screwtape Letters* 1942 and *Mere Christianity* 1952; the autobiographical *Surprised by Joy* 1955, and a series of books of Christian allegory for children, set in the magic land of Narnia. His house at Headington, Oxford, is a museum.

Lewis /'luːɪs/ (Harry) Sinclair 1885–1951. American novelist. Born in Minnesota, he stayed for a time at Upton Sinclair's socialist colony in New Jersey, then became a freelance journalist. He made a reputation with *Main Street* 1920, depicting American small-town life; *Babbitt* 1922, the story of a real-estate dealer of the midwest caught in the conventions of his milieu; and *Arrowsmith* 1925, a study of a scientist. His later books include *It Can't Happen Here* 1945, *Cass Timberlane* 1945, and *The God-Seeker* 1949. He received a Nobel prize in 1930.

Lewis /'luːɪs/ Jerry Lee 1935– . US country and rock-and-roll singer and pianist. His trademark was the 'pumping piano' style in hits which included 'Whole Lotta Shakin' Going On' and 'Great Balls of Fire' 1957 , and 'What Made Milwaukee Famous' 1968.

Lewis /'luːɪs/ Matthew Gregory 1775–1818. British writer, known as 'Monk' Lewis from his popular terror romance *The Monk* 1795.

Lewis /'luːɪs/ Meriwether 1774–1809. American explorer. Private secretary to President Jefferson, he was commissioned with William Clark 1770–1838 to find a land route to the Pacific. He followed the Missouri River to its source, crossed the Rocky Mountains, and followed the Columbia River to the Pacific, then returned overland to St Louis, 1804–06. He was rewarded with the governorship of the Louisiana Territory. His death, near Nashville, Tennessee, has been ascribed to suicide, but was more probably murder.

Lewis /'luːɪs/ (Percy) Wyndham 1884–1957. British writer and artist. Born off Maine, in his father's yacht, he was educated at the Slade art school and in Paris. On returning to England he pioneered the new spirit of art which his friend Ezra Pound called Vorticism: he also edited *Blast*, a literary and artistic magazine proclaiming its principles. His paintings are boldly hard and aggressive, like his literary style, his portraits being especially memorable, such as those of Edith Sitwell and T S Eliot. Among his novels are *Tarr 1918 and The Childermass* 1928, but he also wrote a number of theoretical books, including *Time and Western Man* 1927, and the autobiographical *Blasting and Bombardiering* 1937 and *Rude Assignment* 1950. Although he has been assessed by some as a leading spirit of the early 20th century, his support in the 1930s of Fascist principles and Hitler alienated most critics.

Lewisham /'luːɪʃəm/ borough of SE Greater London
features at Deptford shipbuilding yard (1512–1869), Drake was knighted and Peter the Great worked here; ◊Crystal Palace (re-erected at Sydenham in 1854) site now partly occupied by the National Sports Centre; the poet James Elroy Flecker was born here
population (1981) 233,225.

Lexington /'leksɪŋtən/ industrial town (printing, publishing) in Massachusetts, USA; population (1981) 29,500. The *Battle of Lexington and Concord* (1775) opened the ◊American War of Independence. See also Paul ◊Revere.

Lexington-Fayette /'leksɪŋtən 'feɪət/ town in Kentucky, USA, centre of the bluegrass country; population (1981) 204,160. Race horses are bred in the area, and races and shows are held. There is a tobacco market and the University of Kentucky and Transylvania (1780).

Leyden alternative form of ◊Leiden, city in the Netherlands.

Leyland /'leɪlənd/ industrial town (paint, vehicles) in Lancashire, England. The Rover Group (previously British Leyland), largest of British firms producing cars, buses, and lorries, has its headquarters here.

Lhasa /'lɑːsə/ (the 'Forbidden City') capital of the autonomous region of Tibet, China, at 5,000 m/16,400 ft; population (1982) 105,000. Potala, former home of the ◊Dalai Lama and now a museum, has 200,000 statues, 1,000 rooms, and 10,000 chapels.

Lhote /ləut/ André 1885–1962. French artist. Born in Bordeaux, he was very influential through his treatises on art in which he explored questions of technique and ultimate artistic aims. His *Rugby* in the Musée d'Art Moderne, Paris, is an example of his use of colour and geometric style.

Li Xiannian /liː ʃiˌæn niˈæn/ 1905– . Chinese politician, member of the Chinese Communist Party (CCP) Politburo from 1956, president from 1983.

Li, born into a poor peasant family in Hubei province, joined the CCP in 1927 and served as a political commissar during the Long March of 1934–36. During the 1950s and early 1960s Li was vice premier to the State Council and minister for finance and was inducted into the CCP Politburo and secretariat in 1956 and 1958 respectively. He fell out of favour during the 1966–69 Cultural Revolution, but was rehabilitated as finance minister by ◊Zhou Enlai in 1973, supporting cautious economic reform. Li was appointed state president by ◊Deng Xiaoping in Jun 1983. He retains his seat on the Politburo's standing committee.

liability in economics, a financial obligation. In accountancy liabilities are placed alongside assets on a balance sheet to show the current financial status.

liana a woody, perennial climbing plant with very long stems, that grows around trees up to the canopy, where there is more sunlight. Lianas are especially common in tropical rain forests, where individual stems may grow up to 70 m/255 ft long. They have an unusual stem structure which allows them to retain some flexibility, despite becoming woody.

Liao /liˈaʊ/ river in NE China, frozen Dec–Mar; the main headstream rises in the mountains of Inner Mongolia and flows E, then S to the Gulf of Liaodong; length 1,450 km/900 mi.

Liaoning /liˌaʊˈnɪŋ/ province of NE China
area 230,000 sq km/88,780 sq mi
capital Shenyang
towns Anshan
features it was developed by Japan 1905–45, including the *Liaodong Peninsula* whose ports had been conquered from the Russians (see ◊Lüda), and the province is one of China's most heavily industrialized areas
products cereals; coal and iron
population (1982) 35,721,693. See ◊Manchuria.

Liaoyang /liˈaʊ 'jæŋ/ industrial city (engineering, textiles) in Liaoning province; population (1970) 250,000. In 1904 Russia was defeated by Japan here.

Liaquat Ali Khan /'lɪəkwət 'æli 'kɑːn/ 1895–1951. Pakistani nationalist, prime minister of Pakistan from independence in 1947 to his death in 1951. The chief lieutenant of ◊Muhammad Jinnah, he was a leader of the Muslim League. He was assassinated in 1951.

Libau /'liːbaʊ/ German name of Latvian port ◊Liepaja.

Libby /'lɪbi/ Willard Frank 1908–1980. American chemist, whose development of ◊radiocarbon dating in 1947 won him a Nobel prize in 1960.

libel in law, defamation in permanent form, for example newspaper, book, or broadcast. In civil proceedings in England truth is usually a valid defence; in criminal libel (where the statement is so extreme as to tend to provoke the libelled person to a breach of the peace in retaliation), the statement needs also to be in the public interest. The latter became obsolete, but in the 1980s it was proposed to introduce a new offence of criminal libel to deal with 'character assassination' – the making of a statement which

the maker knew and believed to be untrue, the prosecution having to prove both the untruth and the maker's knowledge and belief that it was a lie. See also ◊slander. Certain statements, for example in the courts or parliament, are 'privileged' and not counted as libellous. Considerable latitude is allowed by the law to criticism of matters of general interest (including new books, plays and films, and all public sports and pastimes), but if facts are quoted they must be quoted with substantial accuracy, and the criticism must be reasonably temperate. The stringency of English libel law has been widely attacked as limiting freedom of the press; in the USA, for example, the position is much more elastic.

liberalism the political and social theory associated with the ◊Liberal Party in Britain, and similar parties elsewhere. Liberalism developed during the 17th–19th centuries, for example the ◊Democratic Party in the USA, as the distinctive theory of the industrial and commercial classes in their struggle against the power of the monarchy, the church, and the feudal landowners. In politics it stood for parliamentary government, freedom of the press, speech and worship, and the abolition of class privileges; economically it was associated with ◊laissez-faire, a minimum of state interference in economic life, and international free trade. In the late 19th and early 20th centuries these ideas were modified by the acceptance on the one hand of universal suffrage, hitherto opposed by most liberals, and on the other of a certain amount of state intervention, in order to ensure a minimum standard of living and to remove extremes of poverty and wealth. The classical statement of liberal principles is found in *On Liberty* and other works of J S ◊Mill.

Liberal Party in the UK, a political party, the successor to the ◊Whig Party. The term 'Liberal', used officially from about 1840 and unofficially from about 1815, marked the transfer of control from the aristocrats to the more radical industrialists, backed by the Benthamites, Nonconformists, and the middle classes. During the Liberals' first period of power 1830–41, they promoted parliamentary and municipal government reform and the abolition of slavery, but their ◊utilitarian and ◊laissez-faire theories led to the harsh Poor Law of 1834. Liberal pressure forced Peel to repeal the ◊Corn Laws in 1846, thereby splitting the Tory party, and except for two short periods the Liberals were in power 1846–66, but the one outstanding figure of the period, Palmerston, was very conservative and the only major change was the general adoption of ◊free trade.

Extended franchise in 1867 and ◊Gladstone's emergence as leader began a new phase, dominated by the Manchester school with a programme of 'peace, retrenchment, and reform'. Gladstone's 1868–74 government introduced many important reforms, including elementary education and vote by ballot. The party's left, mainly composed of working-class ◊Radicals led by ◊Bradlaugh and Joseph ◊Chamberlain, repudiated the laissez-faire ideology and inclined towards republicanism, but the Liberals were split over Home Rule in 1886 and many joined the Conservatives. Except for 1892–95, the Liberals remained out of power until 1906, when, reinforced by Labour and Irish support, they returned with a huge majority: old-age pensions, National Insurance, limitation of the powers of the Lords, and the Irish Home Rule Bill followed.

From 1914 the Liberal Party declined. ◊Lloyd George's alliance with the Conservatives 1916–22 divided them between him and ◊Asquith, and although reunited in 1923 the Liberals continued to lose votes. They briefly joined the National Government 1931–32, but after World War II were reduced to a handful of members of parliament. A revival began under the leadership 1956–67 of ◊Grimond, and continued under Jeremy ◊Thorpe, who resigned after a period of controversy within the party in 1976. After a caretaker return by Grimond, David ◊Steel became the first party leader in British politics to be elected by party members who were not also members of parliament. In 1977–78 Steel entered into an agreement to support Labour in any vote of confidence in return for consultation on measures undertaken. Steel joined forces with the ◊Social Democratic Party (SDP) for the 1983 and 1987 elections. In the 1987 election the ◊Alliance achieved 22 seats and 22.6 per cent of votes. Proportional representation is advocated by the Liberal Party. Following the 1987 defeat the SDP voted to merge with the Liberals.

Liberal Party, Australian political party established in 1944 by Robert Menzies, after a Labor landslide, and derived from the former United Australia Party. Remaining in power from 1949–83, with a brief Labor intermission 1972–75, it was led in succession by ◊Holt, ◊Gorton, Sir William McMahon (1908–), Sir Billy Snedden (1926–), and Malcolm ◊Fraser. It was defeated in 1983 by Labor under Bob Hawke.

liberation theology Western Christian intellectual theory of Christ's primary importance as the 'Liberator', personifying the poor and devoted to freeing them from oppression (Matthew xix 21, xxv 35, 40). Initiated by the Peruvian priest Gustavo Gutierrez in his *The Theology of Liberation* 1969, and enthusiastically adopted in South America, it embodies a Marxist interpretation of the class struggle, and has resulted in violence. One of its leaders is Leonardo Boff (1939–), a Brazilian Franciscan priest. Pope ◊John Paul II warned against involvement of priests in political activity, for example, the holding of government posts in Nicaragua, explicitly condemned in 1984, though also warning the rich against the inevitable consequences of their position.

Liberia /laɪˈbɪərɪə/ country in W Africa, bounded to the N and NE by Guinea, E by the Ivory Coast, S and SW by the Atlantic, and NW by Sierra Leone.
government from 1980–84 Liberia was under military rule by a People's Redemption Council (PRC). The PRC was then dissolved and its functions taken over by an interim national assembly of 58 members, (22 former PRC

members and 36 civilians appointed by the president), pending a new constitution which was later approved by referendum. This provides for a two-chamber national assembly consisting of a 26-member senate and a 64-member house of representatives, elected, like the president, by universal suffrage for a six-year term.
history the area now known as Liberia was bought by the American Colonization Society, a philanthropic organization active in the first half of the 19th century. The society's aim was to establish a settlement for liberated black slaves from the southern USA. The first settlers arrived in 1822, and Liberia was declared an independent republic in 1847. The new state suffered from financial difficulties, bankruptcy in 1909 bringing reorganization by US army officers. For almost 160 years the country's leaders were descended from the black American settlers, but the 1980 coup put Africans in power. William Tubman was president from 1944 until his death in 1971 and was succeeded by Vice-President William R Tolbert (1913–1980), who was re-elected in 1975. In 1980 Tolbert was assassinated in a coup led by Master Sgt Samuel Doe (1952–), who suspended the constitution, banned all political parties and ruled through the PRC. He proceeded to stamp out corruption in the public service, encountering considerable opposition and making enemies who were later to threaten his position.
A new draft constitution, providing for an elected two-chamber national assembly and an elected president, was approved by the PRC in 1983 and by national referendum in 1984. Political parties were again permitted, provided they registered with the Special Electoral Commission (SECOM). In 1984 Doe founded the National Democratic Party of Liberia (NDPL) and announced his intention to stand for the presidency. By 1985 there were 11 political parties, but they complained about the difficulties of the registration process and only three registered in time for the elections. Doe's party won clear majorities in both chambers, despite alleged election fraud, and he was pronounced president with 50.9% of the vote. In 1985 there was an unsuccessful attempt to unseat him. Doe alleged complicity by neighbouring Sierra Leone and dealt harshly with the coup leaders.

liberty, equality, fraternity (*liberté égalité fraternité*) motto of the French republic from 1793; it was briefly changed 1940–44 under the Vichy regime to 'work, family, fatherland'.

Li Bo /ˌliːˈbəʊ/ 705–762. Chinese poet. He wrote in traditional forms, but his exuberance, the boldness of his imagination, and the intensity of his feeling have won him recognition as perhaps the greatest of all Chinese poets. Although he was mostly concerned with higher themes, he is also noted for his celebration of the joys of drinking.

Libra faint constellation of the ◊zodiac, representing the scales of justice. The Sun passes through Libra during Nov.

libretto (Italian 'little book') the text of an opera or other dramatic vocal work, or the scenario of a ballet.

Libreville /ˈliːbrəviːl/ capital of Gabon, on the estuary of the river Gabon; population (1985) 350,000. Founded in 1848 as a refuge for freed slaves, Libreville developed into a port.

Libya /ˈlɪbɪə/ country in N Africa, bordered to the N by the Mediterranean, E by Egypt, SE by the Sudan, S by Chad and Niger, and W by Algeria and Tunisia.
government the 1977 constitution created an Islamic socialist state and the government is designed to allow the greatest possible popular involvement, through a large congress and smaller secretariats and committees. There is a General People's Congress (GPC), of 1,112 members, which elects a secretary-general who was intended to be head of state. The GPC is serviced by a general secretariat, which is Libya's nearest equivalent to a legislature. The executive organ of the state is the General People's Committee, which replaces the structure of ministries which operated before the 1969 revolution. The Arab Socialist Union (ASU) is the only political party and, despite Libya's elaborately democratic structure, ultimate power rests with the party and the Revolutionary Leader, Col Khaddhafi.
history the area now known as Libya was successively under the domination of ◊Phoenicia, ◊Greece, ◊Rome, the ◊Vandals and ◊Byzantium, and from the 16th century was part of the Turkish ◊Ottoman empire. In 1911 it was conquered by Italy, being known as Libya from 1934. After being the scene of much fighting during World War II, in 1942 it was divided into three provinces: Fezzan, which was placed under French control; Cyrenaica, and Tripolitania, which were placed under British control.
In 1951 it achieved independence as the United Kingdom of Libya, Muhammad Idris-as-Sanusi becoming King Idris. The country enjoyed internal and external stability until a bloodless revolution in 1969, led by young nationalist officers, deposed the king and proclaimed a Libyan Arab Republic. Power was vested in a Revolution Command Council (RCC), chaired by Col Moamer al-Khaddhafi, with the Arab Socialist Union (ASU) as the only political party. Khaddhafi soon began proposing schemes for Arab unity, none of which was permanently adopted. In 1972 he planned a federation of Libya, ◊Syria and ◊Egypt, and later that year a merger between Libya and Egypt. In 1980 he proposed a union with Syria and in 1981 with ◊Chad.
Khaddhafi tried to run the country on socialist-Islamic lines, with people's committees pledged to socialism and the teachings of the ◊Koran. The 1977 constitution made him secretary-general of the general secretariat of the GPC, but in 1979 he resigned the post in order to devote more time to 'preserving the revolution'. His attempts to establish himself as a leader of the Arab world have brought him into conflict with Western powers, particularly the USA. In the eyes of the US President, he has become a threat to world peace similar to Fidel ◊Castro of Cuba. In particular, the ◊Reagan administration has objected to Libya's presence in Chad and its attempts to unseat the French-US sponsored

Liberia
REPUBLIC OF

AREA 112,820 sq km/43,548 sq mi
CAPITAL Monrovia
PHYSICAL forested highlands; swampy coast where six rivers end
FEATURES nominally the world's largest merchant navy because minimal controls make Liberia's a flag of convenience
HEAD OF STATE AND OF GOVERNMENT Samuel Kanyon Doe from 1980
GOVERNMENT military
EXPORTS iron ore, rubber, diamonds; coffee, cocoa, palm oil
CURRENCY Liberian dollar (1.65 = £1 Sept 1987)
POPULATION (1985) 1,512,000 (95% belonging to the indigenous peoples); annual growth rate 3.4%
LANGUAGE English (official)
RELIGION Muslim 20%, Christian 15%, traditional 65%
LITERACY 24% (1984)
GNP $900 million (1983); $400 per head of population
CHRONOLOGY
1847 Founded as an independent republic.
1944 William Tubman elected president.
1971 Tubman died and was succeeded by William Tolbert.

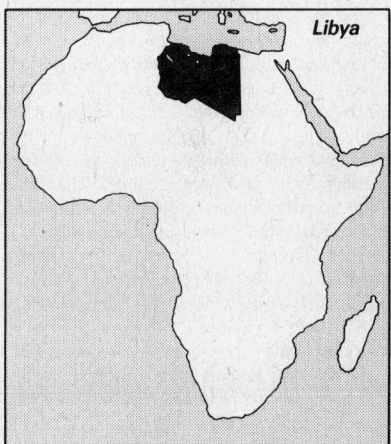

1980 Tolbert assassinated in a coup led by Samuel Doe, who suspended the constitution and ruled through a People's Redemption Council (PRC).
1984 New constitution approved. National Democratic Party of Liberia (NDPL) founded by Doe.
1985 NDPL won decisive victory in general election. Unsuccessful coup against Doe.

Liddell Hart /'lɪdl 'hɑːt/ Basil 1895–1970. British military scientist. Gassed during World War I, he had retired from the army by 1927, and was military correspondent to the *Daily Telegraph* 1925–35 and *The Times* 1935–39. He was an exponent of mechanized warfare, and his ideas were adopted in Germany in 1935 in creating the First Panzer Division, combining motorized infantry and tanks: from 1937 he advised the War Office on British Army reorganization. His books include biographies of Scipio, Foch and T E Lawrence.

Lidice /'liːdɪtseɪ/ Czech mining village, replacing one destroyed by the Nazis on 10 Jun 1942 as a reprisal for the assassination of ◊Heydrich. The men were shot, the women sent to concentration camps, and the children taken to Germany. The Sudeten German responsible was hanged at Prague in 1946.

Lie /liː/ Trygve Halvdan 1896–1968. Norwegian statesman. He became secretary of the Labour Party in 1926, was Foreign Minister in the exiled government 1941–46, when he helped keep the Norwegian fleet for the Allies, and first Secretary-General of the United Nations 1946–53. He resigned following Soviet opposition to his handling of the Korean War.

Liebig /'liːbɪg/ Justus, Baron von Liebig 1803–1873. German chemist, and a major contributor to agricultural chemistry. He introduced the theory of ◊radicals, and discovered chloroform and chloral.

Liebknecht /'liːpknext/ Karl 1871–1919. German socialist, son of Wilhelm ◊Liebknecht.

government of President Habré. The USA has linked Khaddhafi to worldwide terrorist activities, despite his denials of complicity, and the killing in 1986 of a US serviceman in a bomb attack in Berlin prompted a raid by US aircraft, some of them British-based, on Khaddhafi's personal headquarters.
Within the Arab world Khaddhafi is seen as somewhat unorthodox in his views, with Syria and the extreme wing of the ◊PLO as his only dependable allies.

licence document issued by some government or other recognized authority conveying permission to the holder to do something otherwise prohibited, and designed to facilitate accurate records, the maintenance of order, and collection of revenue. In Britain examples are licences required for marriage, for driving, for keeping a gun, and for sale of intoxicating liquor.

lichen organism of the group *Lichenes*, which consist of a fungus and an alga existing in a mutually beneficial relationship. They are found on trees, rocks, and other substrates and flourish under very adverse conditions. Some lichens have food value, for example reindeer moss and Iceland moss, others give dyes such as litmus, or are used in medicine. They are sensitive to atmospheric pollution – see ◊indicator species.

Lichfield /'lɪtʃfiːld/ town in the Trent Valley, Staffordshire, England; population (1985) 26,310. The cathedral, 13th–14th century, has three spires. Samuel ◊Johnson was born here.

Lichfield /'lɪtʃfiːld/ Patrick Anson, 5th Earl of Lichfield 1939– . British photographer, especially noted for portraits.

Libya
SOCIALIST PEOPLE'S LIBYAN ARAB STATE OF THE MASSES (*Al-Jamahiriyah Al-Arabiya Al-Libya Al-Shabiya Al-Ishtirakiya*)

AREA 1,780,000 sq km/680,000 sq mi
CAPITAL Tripoli
TOWNS ports Benghazi, Misurata
PHYSICAL desert; mountains in N and S
FEATURES Gulf of Sirte; rock paintings of c. 3000 BC in the Fezzan; Roman city sites of Leptis Magna, Sabratha among others; the plan to pump water from below the Sahara to the coast risks rapid exhaustion of a largely non-renewable supply
HEAD OF STATE AND OF GOVERNMENT Moamar Khaddhafi from 1969
GOVERNMENT Islamic one-party socialist
EXPORTS oil, natural gas
CURRENCY Libyan dinar (0.49 = £1 Sept 1987)
POPULATION (1985) 3,752,000 (including 500,000 foreign workers); annual growth rate 4.5%
LANGUAGE Arabic
RELIGION Sunni Muslim
LITERACY 60% (1985)
GDP $25 bn (1984); $7,000 per head of population
CHRONOLOGY
1951 Achieved independence as the United Kingdom of Libya, under King Idris.
1969 King deposed in a coup led by Col

Moamar Khaddhafi. Revolution Command Council set up and the Arab Socialist Union (ASU) proclaimed the only legal party.
1972 Proposed federation of Libya, Syria, and Egypt abandoned.
1980 Proposed merger with Syria abandoned. Libyan troops began fighting in Chad.
1981 Proposed merger with Chad abandoned.
1986 US bombing of Khaddhafi's headquarters, following allegations of his complicity in guerrilla activities.

A founder of the German Communist Party, originally known as the Spartacus League, he led an unsuccessful revolt in Berlin in 1919, and was murdered by army officers.

Liebknecht /'liːpknext/ Wilhelm 1826–1900. German socialist. A friend of ◊Marx, with whom he took part in the ◊revolution of 1848; he was imprisoned for opposition to the Franco-Prussian War. He was the father of Karl ◊Liebknecht.

Liechtenstein /'lɪktənstaɪn/ landlocked country in W central Europe, situated between Austria to the E, and Switzerland to the W.

government the 1921 constitution established a hereditary principality with a single-chamber parliament, the *Landtag*. The prince is formal and constitutional head of state. The *Landtag* has 15 members, nine from the Upper Country and six from the Lower Country, elected for a four-year term through a system of proportional representation. The *Landtag* elects five people to form the government for its duration.

history Liechtenstein's history as a sovereign state began in 1342, its boundaries being unchanged since 1434. It has been known by its present name since 1719. Because of its small population of less than 30,000, it has found it convenient to associate itself with larger nations in international matters. For example, since 1923 it has shared a customs union with Switzerland, which since 1919 represents it abroad. Before this Austria undertook its diplomatic representation.

Liechtenstein is one of the world's richest countries, with a per capita income greater than that of the USA, nearly twice that of the UK, and only slightly less than that of Switzerland. It has chosen not to be a full member of the UN but is represented in some UN specialist agencies. Prince Franz Josef II came to power in 1938, and although he has retained the title, he passed the duties of prince to his heir, Hans Adam, in 1984. Liechtenstein's political system is innately conservative in that women did not achieve the right to vote in national elections until 1984 and are still debarred from voting in local affairs.

Lied (German 'song') a musical setting of a poem, usually for solo voice and piano; a genre particularly associated with the Romantic songs of Schubert, Schumann, Brahms and Wolf. The plural is *Lieder*.

lie detector popular name for a ◊polygraph.

Liège /liˈeɪʒ/ industrial city (weapons, textiles, paper, chemicals), capital of Liège province in Belgium, SE of Brussels, on the Meuse; university (1817); population (1984) 650,000. It has a number of ancient churches, the oldest, St Martin's, dating from 692.

Liepaja /lɪˈpaɪə/ (German *Libau*) naval and industrial port (steel, engineering, textiles, chemicals) in the Republic of Latvia, USSR; population (1981) 108,000. The Knights of Livonia founded Liepaja in the 13th century.

Lifar /lɪˈfɑː/ Serge 1905–1986. Russian dancer and choreographer. Born in Kiev, he studied under ◊Nijinsky, joined the Diaghilev company in 1923 and was *maître de ballet* at the Paris Opéra 1930–44 and 1947–59. A noted experimenter, he produced his first ballet without

Liechtenstein
PRINCIPALITY OF

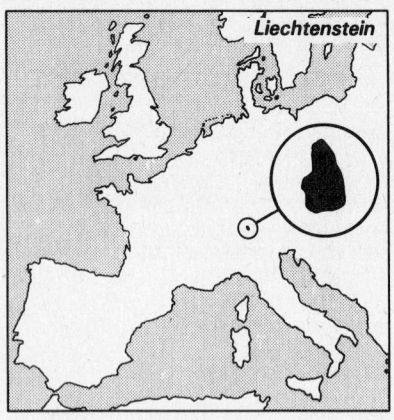
Liechtenstein

AREA 160 sq km/62 sq mi
CAPITAL Vaduz
PHYSICAL Alpine; includes part of Rhine Valley
FEATURES only country in the world to take its name from its reigning family; most highly industrialized country
HEAD OF STATE Franz Josef II from 1938
HEAD OF GOVERNMENT Hans Brunhart from 1978
GOVERNMENT constitutional monarchy
EXPORTS microchips, precision engineering, processed foods, postage stamps; easy tax laws make it an international haven for foreign companies and banks
CURRENCY Swiss franc (2.49 = £1 Sept 1987)
POPULATION (1985) 27,000 (33% foreign); annual growth rate 0.7%
LANGUAGE German
RELIGION Roman Catholic
LITERACY 100% (1986)
GDP 1 bn Swiss francs (1984); $16,440 per head of population
CHRONOLOGY
1938 Prince Franz Josef II came to power.
1984 Vote extended to women in national elections.

music, *Icare*, in 1935, and published the same year the controversial *Le Manifeste du choréographe*. He developed the importance of the male dancer in his *Prometheus* 1929 and *Romeo and Juliet* (Prokofiev) 1955.

life the ability to grow, stay in 'working order', reproduce, and respond to such stimuli as light, heat and sound. It is thought that life began about 4,000 million years ago, the earliest fossil evidence being thread-like chains of cells discovered in 1980 in deposits in the NW of Australia, that have been dated as 3,500 million years old.

It seems probable that the original atmosphere of earth consisted of carbon dioxide, nitrogen and water and that complex organic molecules such as ◊amino acids were created when the atmosphere was bombarded by ultra-violet radiation or by atmospheric lightning. Experiments in the laboratory have attempted to replicate these conditions and have successfully shown that amino acids, purine and pyrimidine ◊bases (which make up ◊DNA) and other vital molecules can be created in this way. The earliest forms of cellular life were very probably bacteria-like and from these developed the network of plant and animal life of today.

Although it has also been suggested that life could have been 'imported' to earth from elsewhere in the universe in the form of complex organic molecules present in meteors or comets, this is not really an alternative explanation because these primitive life-forms must then have been created elsewhere by much the same process. See also ◊biogenesis and ◊virus.

lifeboat small land-based vessel specially built for saving life at sea, or a boat carried aboard a larger ship in case of shipwreck. In Britain the Royal National Lifeboat Institution (RNLI), founded in 1824 at the instance of Sir William Hillary, provides a voluntarily manned and supported service. The US Coast Guard is part of the government service. A modern RNLI boat is about 16 m/52 ft long and self-righting, so that it is virtually unsinkable. Inflatables are used for inshore work, and helicopters play an increasing role.

life cycle in biology, the sequence of different stages through which members of a given species pass. Most vertebrates have a simple life cycle consisting of the production of sex cells or ◊gametes, ◊fertilization and a period of development as an ◊embryo, followed by a period of juvenile growth after hatching or birth, with a concluding phase of ◊sexual reproduction which terminates at death. Invertebrate life cycles are generally more complex and may involve major reconstitution of the individual's appearance (◊metamorphosis) and completely different styles of life. Thus, dragonflies live an aquatic life as larvae and an aerial life during the adult phase. In many other invertebrates and protozoa there are several different stages in the life cycle, and in parasites these often occur in different host organisms. Plants have a special type of life cycle with two distinct phases, known as an ◊alternation of generations.

life insurance an ◊insurance policy that pays money on the death of the holder.

life sciences term for the scientific study of the living world as a whole, a new synthesis of several traditional scientific disciplines including ◊biology, ◊zoology, and ◊botany, and newer, more specialized areas of study such as ◊biophysics and ◊sociobiology. This approach has led to many new ideas and discoveries, as well as to an emphasis on ◊ecology, the study of living organisms in their natural environment.

life table in ◊demography, a way of summarizing the probability that an individual will give birth or die during successive periods of life. From this the proportion of individuals who

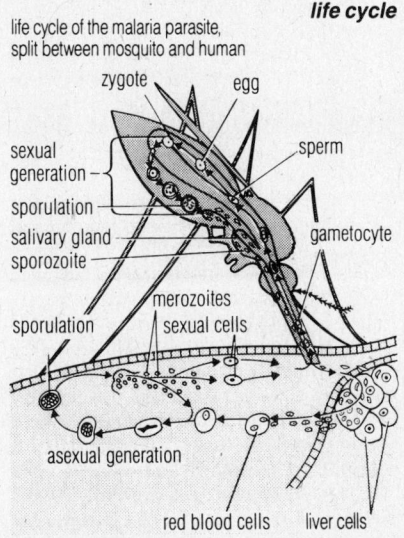

life cycle

life cycle of the malaria parasite,
split between mosquito and human

zygote
egg
sexual
generation
sperm
sporulation
salivary gland
sporozoite
gametocyte
sporulation
merozoites
sexual cells
asexual generation
red blood cells   liver cells

survive from birth to any given age (*survivorship*) and the mean number of offspring produced (*net reproductive rate*) can be determined. Insurance companies use life tables to estimate risks of death in order to set their premiums, while governments use them to determine future needs for education and health services.

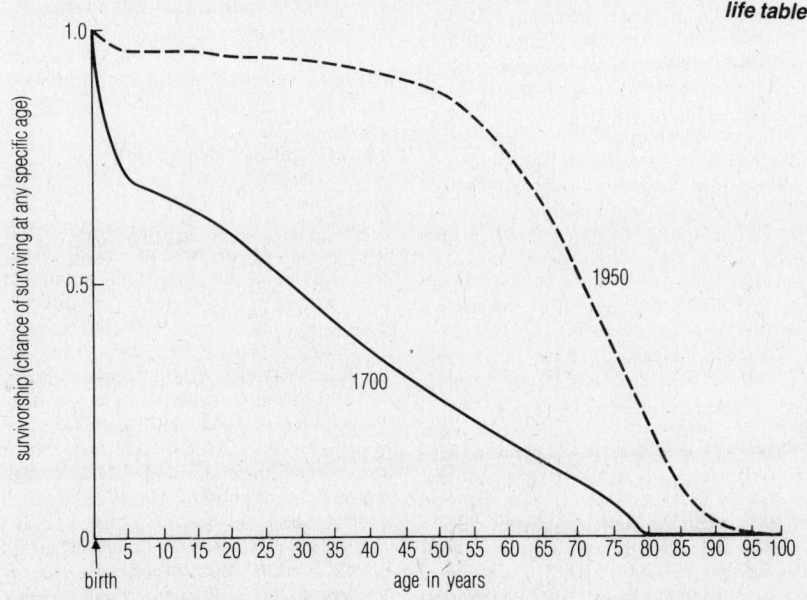

life table

survivorship (chance of surviving at any specific age)

1950

1700

1.0

0.5

0

birth   5 10 15 20 25 30 35 40 45 50 55 60 65 70 75 80 85 90 95 100
age in years

Liffey /'lɪfi/ river in E Ireland, flowing from the Wicklow mountains to Dublin Bay; length 80 km/50 mi.

lift also called the *elevator* (USA), a device for lifting passengers and goods vertically, usually between the floors of a building. American inventor Elisha Graves Otis developed the first passenger lift, installed in 1857. The invention of the lift allowed the development of the ◊skyscraper from the 1880s.

Ligachev /'lɪgətʃef/ Egor Kuzmich 1920– . Soviet politician. Ligachev joined the Communist Party of the Soviet Union in 1944, and has been a member of the Soviet ◊Politburo since 1985.

ligament a strong flexible connective tissue, made up of the protein collagen, which joins ◊bone to bone at moveable joints. Ligaments prevent bone dislocation (under normal circumstances) but permit joint flexion.

ligature 'thread' (nylon, gut, wire) tying a blood vessel, limb, or base of a tumour, chiefly to stop the flow of blood or other fluid through it.

Ligeti /'lɪgəti/ György (Sándor) 1923– . Austrian composer, born in Hungary. He taught at the Budapest Academy of Music before moving to the West in 1956 and coming into contact with avant-garde composers, including Stockhausen. He worked briefly at the electronic studio in Cologne, West Germany, and won international recognition in 1960 for his orchestral *Apparitions*. He developed a dense, highly chromatic, polyphonic style, in which melody and rhythm are sometimes lost in shifting blocks of sound. His works include *Aventures* 1962, *Requiem* 1965, an opera *Le Grand Macabre* 1978, and *Poème symphonique* 1962 for 100 metronomes.

light electromagnetic radiation in the visible range, that is, from about 400 nanometers in the extreme violet to about 770 nanometers in the extreme red (see ◊electromagnetic waves). Light is considered to exhibit both particle and wave properties and the fundamental particle or quantum of light is called the *photon*. The speed of light (and of all electromagnetic radiation) in a vacuum is approximately 300 million metres per second or 186,000 miles per second, and is a universal constant denoted by *c*. This is allegedly the fastest speed in nature, but in 1971 a jet from the galaxy 3C 273 was calculated as travelling at three times this speed, which should be impossible according to current theories. Newton was the first to discover, in 1666, that sunlight is composed of a mixture of light of all different colours in certain proportions and that it could be separated into its components by dispersion. Before his time it was supposed that dispersion of light produced colour instead of separating already existing colours.

light-emitting diode (LED) a means of displaying, usually figures, in electronic instruments and devices. The first digital watches and calculators had LED display, but for this use it has been superseded by ◊liquid-crystal display (LCD). An LED is made of ◊semiconductor material, such as gallium arsenide phosphide, which glows when electricity is passed through it.

Lighthill /'laɪthɪl/ James 1924– . British mathematician, Lucasian professor at Cambridge 1969–79, who specialized in the application of mathematics to high-speed aerodynamics and jet propulsion. He was knighted in 1971 and is provost of University College London (1979–).

lighthouse structure carrying a powerful light to aid marine or aerial navigation. Among early lighthouses were the Pharos of Alexandria (about 280 BC) and those built by the Romans at Ostia, Ravenna, Boulogne and Dover. In England beacons burning in church towers served as lighthouses until the 17th century, and in the earliest lighthouses such as the Eddystone, first built 1698, open fires or candles were used. Today dissolved acetylene or electricity is used, and the light of the burner or lamp is magnified and directed out to the horizon (or up to the zenith for aircraft) by a series of mirrors or prisms. For identification lights are individually varied, usually either flashing (the dark period exceeding the light) or occulting (the dark being equal or less): fixed lights are liable to confusion. Manned lightships replace lighthouses where reefs or sandbanks make erection of a lighthouse impossible. Where it is impossible to maintain keepers, unattended lightbuoys equipped for up to a year's service are used. In fog sound signals are made (horns, sirens, explosives), and in the case of lightbuoys, fog bells and whistles operated by the movement of the waves. In the UK there are three general lighthouse authorities – Trinity House, Commissioners of Northern Lighthouses, and Commissioners of Irish Lights: in the USA the supervisory authority is the Coast Guard.

lightning high-voltage electrical discharge between two charged rainclouds or between a cloud and the earth. Air in the path of lightning ionizes (and becomes conducting), and the accompanying noise is heard as thunder. Currents of 10,000 amps and temperatures of 30,000°C/50,000°F are common.

light pen in computing, an ◊input device resembling an ordinary pen, used to indicate or mark locations on a computer screen. At its tip, the pen has a photoreceptor which emits signals as light from the screen passes beneath it. From the timing of this signal and a gridlike representation of the screen in the computer's memory, a computer program can calculate the position of the light pen. With certain computer-aided design (CAD) programs, the light pen can be used to instruct the computer to change the shape, size, position and colours of sections of a screen image.

light year a measure in astronomy, the distance travelled by a beam of light in one year, 9.461×10^{12} km/5.88 million million mi.

lignin a naturally occuring substance, produced by plants, to strengthen their tissues. It is the essential ingredient of all ◊wood and is therefore of great commercial importance. Chemically it is made up of thousands of rings of carbon atoms joined together in a long chain. The way in which they are linked up varies all along the chain, and this irregularity makes it difficult for ◊enzymes to attack lignin, so that living organisms cannot digest wood, with the exception of a few specialized fungi and bacteria.

lignite a type of ◊coal that is brown, fibrous, with a relatively low carbon content. In Scandinavia it is used to generate power.

Likud alliance of right wing Israeli political parties which defeated the Labour Party coalition in the election of May 1977 and brought Menachim Begin to power. In 1987, Likud were part of an uneasy national coalition formed to solve Israel's economic crisis.

lilac flowering shrub *Syringa vulgaris*, of the family Oleaceae. The panicles of small white or purplish flowers are sweetly scented. The smaller Persian lilac is also popular in gardens.

Lilburne /'lɪlbɜːn/ John 1614–1657. English republican politician. He was imprisoned 1638–40 for circulating Puritan pamphlets, fought in the Parliamentary army in the Civil War, and by his advocacy of a democratic republic won the leadership of the ◊Levellers. He was twice tried for sedition and acquitted, and after his acquittal he was imprisoned 1653–55.

Lilienthal /'liːliəntɑːl/ Otto 1848–96. German aviation pioneer, who inspired the ◊Wright brothers. He made and successfully flew many gliders before he was killed in a glider crash.

Lilith /'lɪlɪθ/ in Old Testament, Assyrian female demon of the night. According to the ◊Talmud she was the wife of Adam before Eve's creation.

Lille /liːl/ industrial city (textiles, chemicals, engineering, distilling), capital of Nord-Pas-de-Calais, France; population (1983) 189,500. In the Middle Ages it was the capital of Flanders; there is a 17th-century fortress built by Vauban, a Pasteur Institute and university 1887; and the world's first entirely automatic underground system was opened in 1982.

Lilongwe /lɪ'lɒŋweɪ/ capital of Malawi; population (1985) 186,800. It has light industries (tobacco).

lily flower of the genus *Lilium*, of which there are some 80 species, most with showy flowers growing from bulbs. Also used of many lily-like plants of allied genera and families.

lily of the valley plant *Convallaria majalis* in the family Liliaceae, growing in woods in Europe, N Asia, and N America, and a common garden plant. The white flowers are scented.

lily G H Ehret's illustration of a Tiger Lily *Lilium tigrinum*, a true lily which comes from China. There are some 80 species of the genus *Lilium*, including hyacinths, tulips, asparagus and plants of the onion genus.

Lima /'liːmə/ capital of Peru, and industrial city (textiles, chemicals, glass, and cement), with its port at Callao; population (1983) 5,258,600. Founded by the conquistador Pizarro in 1535, it was rebuilt after destruction by an earthquake in 1746. Survivals of the colonial period are the university 1551, cathedral 1746, government palace (the rebuilt palace of the viceroys), and the senate house (once the Inquisition).

Liman von Sanders /'liːmæn fɒn 'saːndəz/ Otto 1855–1929. German general seconded to the Turkish army to become inspector-general and a Turkish field-marshall in Dec 1913. This link between the Turks and the Germans caused great suspicion on the part of the French and Russians.

Limassol /'lɪməsɒl/ port in Cyprus; population (1985) 120,000. Cigarettes are made and wine traded. Richard I married Berengaria of Navarre here in 1191.

limbo (dance) a West Indian dance in which the performer, his or her body being bent over backwards, passes under a pole, which is lowered closer to the ground at successive attempts.

limbo (Latin 'border' or 'edge'). In medieval theology, a region for the souls of those who were not admitted to the divine vision; the word was first used in this sense by Thomas Aquinas. *Limbus infantum* was a place where unbaptized infants enjoyed inferior blessedness; and *limbus patrum* was the place where the prophets and fathers of the Old Testament dwelt.

Limburg /'lɪmbɜːg/ former duchy of Lower Lorraine (until 1839), which is now divided into *Limbourg* a NE province of Belgium, capital Hasselt, and *Limburg* a SE province of the Netherlands, capital Maastricht.

lime calcium oxide CaO, or hydroxide, CaOH. Calcium oxide, also known as quicklime, is made commercially by heating calcium carbonate, $CaCO_3$, obtained from limestone or chalk. A white powdery substance, it is used to reduce soil acidity. Quicklime readily absorbs water to become calcium hydroxide, also known as slaked lime.

lime citrus fruit *Citrus aurantifolia*. It is a native of India and grows on small thorny bushes. The white flowers are succeeded by light green or yellow fruits resembling lemons but more globular in shape.

lime or *linden* genus of northern temperate deciduous trees *Tilia* family Tiliaceae. The *common lime* is *Tilia vulgaris* which has greenish yellow fragrant flowers, succeeded by small bobbly fruits, spread by an oval modified leaf or 'wing' on the base of the flower stalk.

limerick /'lɪmərɪk/ five-line nonsense verse, which first appeared in England about 1820, and was popularized by Edward ◊Lear. An example is:

There was a young lady of Riga,
Who rode with a smile on a tiger;
They returned from the ride
With the lady inside,
And the smile on the face of the tiger.

Limerick /'lɪmərɪk/ city and county town in Limerick, Republic of Ireland, on the Shannon estuary and chief port of W Ireland; population (1981) 60,736. It was unsuccessfully besieged by William III in 1691.

Limerick /'lɪmərɪk/ county in SW Republic of Ireland, in Munster province
area 2,686 sq km/1,037 sq mi
county town Limerick
physical fertile, with hills in the S
products dairy products
population (1981) 161,500.

limestone a sedimentary rock chiefly composed of calcium carbonate, $CaCO_3$, usually in the form of the calcareous remains of freshwater or marine organisms, for example, crustacea, mollusca, foraminifera. ◊Corals build up solid masses of limestone. Limestone may also be of chemical origin, having been precipitated out of colution in seawater by evaporation. Various types of limestone are used as building stones. Marble is metamorphosed limestone. It has undergone natural recrystallization at high temperature and pressure. It takes a high polish, and may be either beautifully coloured and patterned or pure white, for example, ◊Carrara marble. Certain so-called marbles, such as Purbeck 'marble' and Fosterley marble, are not marbles but fine-grained fossiliterous limestones that can take an attractive polish. See ◊cave, ◊karst, ◊stalagtite.

Limitation, Statutes of under English law, Acts of Parliament limiting the time within which certain classes of action may be inaugurated, for example in simple contracts and most civil wrongs an action must be started by the aggrieved party within six years. In principle US law is similar, but varies from state to state.

Limits, Territorial and Fishing see under ◊Maritime Law.

limnology study of ◊lakes and other bodies of open fresh water, in terms of their plant and animal biology and their physical properties.

Limoges /lɪˈməʊʒ/ industrial city (textiles, electrical equipment, metal goods), capital of Limousin, France; population (1982) 144,000. Fine enamels were made here in the medieval period, and it is the centre of the modern French porcelain industry. The city was sacked by the Black Prince in 1370.

limonite an ◊iron ore, hydrated iron oxide, $2Fe_2O_3 3H_2O$. The mineral, also known as brown iron ore, is found in bog deposits.

limpet type of mollusc. It has a conical shell, and adheres firmly to rocks by the disc-like foot. Limpets are marine animals, and the common limpet *Patella vulgata* remains in the intertidal area. They leave their fixed position only to graze on seaweeds, always returning to the same spot.

Limpopo /lɪmˈpəʊpəʊ/ river in SE Africa, rising in the Transvaal and reaching the Indian Ocean in Mozambique; length 1,600 km/1,000 mi.

Linacre /ˈlɪnəkə/ Thomas c. 1460–1524. English humanist, physician to Henry VIII from 1509, from whom he obtained a charter in 1518 to found the Royal College of Physicians, of which he was first president.

linar ('line' + 'star') in astronomy, point source discovered 1970 which emits with great energy at wavelengths characteristic of the spectral line of certain chemical compounds. Detectable in any weather, linars have potential value in navigation.

Lin Biao /ˌlɪnˈbjaʊ/ 1908–1971. Chinese soldier and politician. He joined the Communists in 1927, became a commander of ◊Mao Zedong's Red Army, and led the Northeast People's Liberation Army in 1945. He became defence minister in 1959, and in 1969, as vice-chairman of the party, he was expected to be Mao Zedong's successor.

Lincoln /ˈlɪŋkən/ industrial city (excavators, cranes, gas turbines, power units for oil platforms, cosmetics) in Lincolnshire, England; population (1981) 76,200. It was the flourishing Roman colony of Lindum, and had a big medieval wool trade. Paulinus built a church here in the 7th century, and the 11th–15th-century cathedral has the earliest Gothic work in Britain. The 12th-century High Bridge is the oldest in Britain still to have buildings on it.

Lincoln /ˈlɪŋkən/ industrial city (engineering, oil refining, food processing), capital of Nebraska, USA; population (1981) 172,000.

Lincoln /ˈlɪŋkən/ Abraham 1809–1865. 16th president of the USA 1861–65, born in Kentucky. Self-educated, he became a practising lawyer from 1837 at ◊Springfield, Illinois, joined the new Republican Party in 1856, and was elected in 1860 on a minority vote. His refusal to evacuate Fort Sumter, ◊Charleston, precipitated the American ◊Civil War, in which his chief concern was the preservation of the Union from which the Confederate (southern) slave states had seceded. In 1863 he proclaimed the freedom of the slaves with the Emancipation Proclamation, and made the ◊Gettysburg Address, declaring the war aims of preserving a 'nation conceived in liberty, and dedicated to the proposition that all men are created equal' and ensuring that 'government of the people, by the people, for the people, shall not perish from the earth'. Re-elected 1864, he advocated a reconciliatory policy towards the south 'with malice towards none, with charity for all', Five days after ◊Lee's surrender, he was assassinated by an actor, John Wilkes Booth.

Lincoln President of the USA Abraham Lincoln believed in equality for all and in preserving the Union. He planned to reconstruct the South devastated by the Civil War, but he was assassinated by John Wilkes Booth.

Lincolnshire /ˈlɪŋkənʃə/ county in E England
area 5,915 sq km/2,283 sq mi
towns administrative headquarters Lincoln; resort Skegness
physical Lincoln Wolds; marshy coastline; the Fens in the SE; rivers Witham and Welland
features 16th-century Burghley House; Belton House, a Restoration mansion
products cattle, sheep, horses; cereals; flower bulbs; oil at Nettleham
population (1986) 563,000
famous people Sir Isaac Newton, Alfred Tennyson, Margaret Thatcher.

Lind /lɪnd/ Jenny 1820–1887. Swedish soprano singer of remarkable range, the 'Swedish nightingale'.

Lindbergh /ˈlɪndbɜːg/ Charles Augustus 1902–74. American aviator, who made the first solo non-stop flight across the Atlantic (New York–Paris) in 1927 in the *Spirit of St Louis*. His baby son was kidnapped in 1932, and the kidnapper (B R Hauptmann) was executed for murder in 1936.

linden another name for ◊lime, genus of decidous trees.

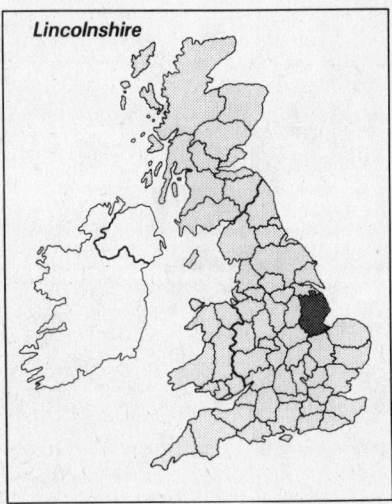

Lindisfarne /ˈlɪndɪsfɑːn/ site of monastery off the coast of Northumberland, England; see under ◊Holy Island.

Lindow Man name applied to the remains of an Iron Age man discovered in a peat bog at Lindow Moss in Cheshire, England, in 1984. The chemicals in the bog had resulted in the body being in an excellent state of preservation.

Lindsey /ˈlɪndzi/ *Parts of* former administrative county within Lincolnshire, England. The largest of the three administrative divisions (or 'parts') of the county with its headquarters at Lincoln. In 1974 Lindsey was divided between the new county of Humberside and a reduced Lincolnshire.

linear accelerator in physics, a machine in which charged ◊particles are accelerated to high speed in passing down a straight evacuated tube or waveguide. Acceleration of the particles is produced by ◊electromagnetic waves in the tube or by ◊electric fields. See also ◊accelerator.

linear equation in mathematics, an equation involving two variables, of the general form $y = mx + c$, where m and c are constants. In ◊coordinate geometry, such an equation plotted using ◊Cartesian coordinates gives a straight-line graph of slope m; c is the value of y where the line crosses the x-axis. Linear equations can be used to describe the behaviour of buildings, bridges, trusses, and other static structures.

linear motor type of ◊electric motor, an induction motor in which the stationary stator and moving armature are straight and parallel to each other (rather than being circular and one inside the other as in ordinary induction motor). Linear motors are used, for example, to power sliding doors. There is a magnetic force between the stator and armature, and this has been used to support a vehicle, as in the experimental 'maglev' linear motor train.

linear programming in mathematics and economics, a set of techniques for finding the maxima or minima of certain variables governed by ◊linear equations or inequalities. These maxima and minima are used to represent 'best'

Lindbergh American aviator Colonel Charles Lindbergh with his plane, *Spirit of St Louis*, in France in 1927, after he had made the first solo non-stop flight across the Atlantic. During World War II he flew combat missions in the Pacific.

themselves normally speak that language at home and cannot otherwise do business; for example English is a lingua franca used by Japanese doing business in Finland, or Swedes in Saudi Arabia. The term derives from Italian (*la lingua franca* = the Frankish tongue), referring to French as used around the Mediterranean shores in the Middle Ages. Many of the world's lingua francas are pidgin languages, for example Bazaar Hindi (Hindustani), Bazaar Malay, and Melanesian Pidgin English (also known as Tok Pisin), the official language of Papua New Guinea.

linguistics the scientific study of language, from its origins, to the changing way it is pronounced (phonetics), derivation of words through various languages (etymology), development of meanings (semantics), and the arrangement and modifications of words to convey a message (grammar).

linkage in ◊genetics, the association between two or more ◊genes, which tend to be inherited together because they are on the same ◊chromosome. The closer together they are on the chromosome, the less likely they are to be separated by crossing-over (one of the processes of ◊recombination) and they are then described as being 'tightly linked'.

Linköping /'lɪntʃɜːpɪŋ/ industrial town (hosiery, aircraft and engines, tobacco) in Sweden 172 km/107 mi SW of Stockholm; population (1984) 115,500. It has a 12th-century cathedral.

Linlithgow /lɪn'lɪθgəʊ/ John Adrian Louis Hope, 1st Marquess Linlithgow 1860–1908. British administrator, son of the 6th earl of Hopetoun. He was first governor-general of the Australian Commonwealth 1900–02. His son *Victor A J Hope* (1887–1952) was viceroy and governor-general of India 1936–43.

Linlithgowshire /lɪn'lɪθgəʊʃə/ former name of ◊West Lothian, now included in Lothian region, Scotland.

Linnaeus /lɪ'niːəs/ Carolus 1707–1778. Swedish naturalist and physician, born Carl von Linné, but more commonly known by the Latinized version of his name. He travelled extensively in Europe, collecting hundreds of new species, and wrote 14 botanical works, including *Systema Naturae* 1758. This contained his system for classifying plants and animals into groups depending on the number of stamens in their flowers, which provided a much-needed framework for identification. His other great achievement was the system he devised for naming plants and animals, using one Latin (or Latinized) word to represent the genus and a second to distinguish the species. Thus every organism has a unique and concise name that can be recognized throughout the world. For example, in the Latin name of the daisy, *Bellis perennis*, *Bellis* is the name of the genus to which the plant belongs, and *perennis* distinguishes the species from others of the same genus. By tradition the generic name always begins with a capital letter. The author who first described a particular species is often indicated after the name, for example, *Bellis perennis* Linnaeus,

solutions in terms of goals such as maximizing profit or minimizing cost.

Line Islands /laɪn/ Pacific coral-island group of which eight belong to Kiribati and two (Palmyra and Jarvis) are administered by the USA.

linen the yarn spun and the textile – one of the oldest known – woven from ◊flax. To get the longest possible fibres, flax is pulled not cut by hand or machine, just as the seed bolls are beginning to set. After preliminary drying, it is steeped in water so that the fibre can be more easily separated from the wood of the stem, then 'hackled' (combed), classified, drawn into continuous fibres, and spun. Bleaching, weaving, and finishing processes vary according to the final product, which ranges from sailcloth, canvas and sacking to cambric and lawn. Because of its length of fibre, linen yarn has twice the strength of cotton, and is superior in delicacy, so that it is

especially suitable for lace making. It mixes well with synthetics.

line of force in physics, a representation of a ◊magnetic field.

ling deepwater long-bodied fish *Molva molva* of the cod family found in the seas off NW Europe. It reaches 2 m/6 ft long and 20 kg/45 lb in weight.

ling or common heather, *Calluna vulgaris*, a low-growing carpet-forming shrub up to 60 cm/2 ft high which may dominate large areas of heath or moorland, and other areas with well-drained acid soil, up to about 750 m/2,400 ft above sea level. The pale pink-purple flowers are borne in spikes in late summer. It can be found over much of Europe.

lingam in Hinduism, phallic emblem of ◊Siva, the *yoni* being the female equivalent.

lingua franca any language that is used as a means of communication by groups who do not

showing that the author was Linnaeus. See also ◊binomial classification, ◊taxonomy.

linnet bird of the finch family *Acanthis cannabina* common in Europe. Mainly brown, the males have a crimson crown and breast in summer. It nests low in bushes and feeds on weed seeds and some insects. It is a noted songster.

linotype typesetting machine once universally used for newspaper work, which sets complete lines (slugs) of metal type. It was invented in the USA in 1884 by German-born Ottmar ◊Mergenthaler.

Lin Piao /'lɪn pi'aʊ/ alternative form of ◊Lin Biao.

linsang nocturnal arboreal mammal of the mongoose family. The *African linsang Poiana richardsoni* is a long, low and lithe spotted animal about 33 cm/1.1 ft long with a 38 cm/1.25 ft tail. The two species of oriental linsang genus *Prionodon* of Asia are slightly bigger.

linseed seeds of the flax plant *Linum usitatissimum*, from which linseed oil is expressed, the residue being used as feeding cake for cattle. The oil is used in paint and varnishes, and in the manufacture of linoleum.

Linz /lɪnts/ industrial port (iron and steel, metalworking) on the Danube in N Austria; population (1981) 198,000.

lion member of the cat family *Panthera leo*, found in Africa and NW India and formerly more widely. The coat is tawny, the young having darker spot markings which usually disappear in the adult, and the male has a heavy mane and a tuft at the end of the tail. Head and body measure about 2 m/6 ft, plus 1 m/3 ft of tail, the lioness being slightly smaller. Lions produce litters of two to six cubs, and often live in parties (prides) of several adult males and females with several young. Capable of short bursts of speed, they skilfully collaborate in stalking their prey which consists of the large herbivorous animals. Old lions whose teeth and strength are failing may resort to eating humans. In zoos, a *liger* is the offspring of a male lion and female tiger; a *tigon* of a male tiger and female lion. 'Mountain lion' is a name for the ◊puma.

Lipari /'lɪpəri/ or *Aeolian Islands* volcanic group of seven islands off NE Sicily, including Lipari (on which is the capital of the same name), Stromboli (active volcano 926 m/3,038 ft high) and Vulcano (also with an active volcano); area 114 sq km/44 sq mi. See ◊Aeolus.

Lipchitz /'lɪpʃɪts/ Jacques 1891–1973. Lithuanian sculptor, a US citizen from 1941. Outstanding in his ◊Cubist phase is *Femme assise* 1916. He often worked in bronze.

Li Peng /'liː 'peŋ/ 1928– . Chinese politician, born in Sichuan, premier of China from Jan 1988.
When Li Peng was three years old, his father, a communist, was executed by the Nationalists. He studied engineering at Moscow University, survived the Cultural revolution unscathed, and was elected to the Central Committee 1982. He became vice-premier 1983, and a member of the Politburo in 1985.

lipids a group of organic compounds soluble in solvents such as ethanol (alcohol), but not in

lion The lion, with its distinctive mane (in the male) and tufted tail, is found mainly in Africa and India.

water. They include oils, fats, waxes, steroids, carotenoids and other fatty substances.

Lippe /'lɪpə/ river of N West Germany flowing into the Rhine; also a former German state, now part of N Rhine-Westphalia.

Lippershey /'lɪpəʃaɪ/ Hans 1560–1619. Dutch spectacle maker, credited with inventing the first ◊telescope in about 1608.

Lippi /'lɪpi/ Filippino 1457–1504. Italian artist, son of Filippo ◊Lippi; he studied under ◊Botticelli. He produced frescoes and altarpieces, and possibly his best known painting is *The Vision of St Bernard* 1486.

Lippi /'lɪpi/ Filippo 1406–69. Italian Renaissance artist, called Fra (Brother) Filippo, born at Florence and patronized by the Medici. His works include frescoes at Prato Cathedral 1452–64, representing the lives of John the Baptist and St Stephen, and the Barbadori Altarpiece.

Lippizaner pure white horse, named after its place of origin in Yugoslavia, used in the Spanish Riding School in Vienna.

Lippmann /'lɪpmən/ Gabriel 1845–1921. French doctor, who invented the direct colour process in ◊photography. Nobel prize 1908.

liquid state of matter between a ◊solid and a ◊gas, in which a substance forms a level surface and beneath the surface assumes the shape of its container. Its atoms do not occupy fixed postions as in a crystalline solid, nor do they have freedom of movement as in a gas. Unlike a gas, a liquid is difficult to compress since pressure applied at one point is equally transmitted throughout (Pascal's principle). This property is made use of in ◊hydraulics.

liquid air air that has been cooled so much that it has liquefied. This happens at temperatures below about –196°C. From liquid air, the various constituent gases can be separated by the technique of fractional distillation, including nitrogen, oxygen, argon and neon. Air is liquefied by the *Linde process*, in which air is alternately compressed, cooled and expanded, the expansion resulting each time in a considerable reduction in temperature.

liquidation in economics, the termination of a company by converting all its ◊assets into money to pay off its ◊liabilities.

liquid crystal display (LCD) a display of numbers (for example in a calculator) or picture (on a pocket television screen) produced by molecules of an organic substance in a semi-liquid state. The display is a blank until the application of an electric field which 'twists' the molecules so that they reflect or transmit light falling on them. Compare ◊light-emitting diode.

liquid crystal display

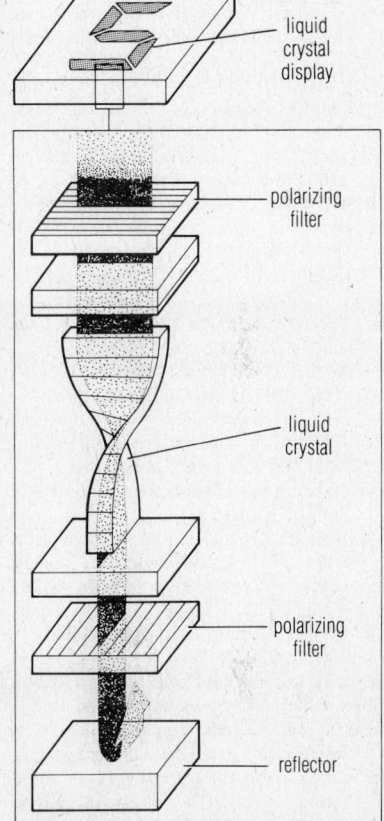

liquid crystal display

polarizing filter

liquid crystal

polarizing filter

reflector

liquidity in economics, the state of possessing sufficient money and/or ◊assets to be able to pay off all ◊liabilities.

liquorice perennial European herb *Glycyrrhiza glabra*, family ◊Leguminosae; the long sweet root yields an extract made into a hard black paste, used in confectionery, and in medicines.

lira the standard Italian currency unit.

Lisboa /liːʒ'bɔɪə/ Portuguese form of ◊Lisbon, capital of Portugal.

Lisbon /'lɪzbən/ (Portuguese *Lisboa*) industrial city (steel, textiles, chemicals, pottery, shipbuilding, fishing) and capital of Portugal from 1260; university 1911; population (1981) 817,627. It lies in the SW on the tidal lake and estuary formed by the ◊Tagus.
history Lisbon has been an important centre since Roman times. The fortress of São Jorge was taken from the Moors by Alfonso I in 1147, and

the city reached its peak of prosperity in the period of Portugal's overseas empire in the 16th century. In 1755 it was almost completely destroyed by an earthquake.

Points of interest include the cathedral, a Moorish citadel founded 1150, the nearby 15th-century Batalha Abbey, the palace of the National Assembly (formerly a Benedictine monastery), the Palacio das Necessidades (formerly the royal palace), the museums of ancient and contemporary art, and the English cemetery, where the novelist Henry Fielding is buried.

Lisburn /'lɪzbɜːn/ cathedral city and market town in Antrim, N Ireland, on the river Lagan, noted for linen and furniture; population (1985) 87,900.

Lisieux /liːz'jɜː/ town in Calvados *département*, France, to the SE of Caen; population (1982) 25,823. St Thérèse of Lisieux spent most of her life in the Carmelite convent here, and her tomb attracts pilgrims.

Lisp a computer-programming language for list processing used primarily in artificial-intelligence (AI) research. Developed in the 1960s, and until recently common only in university laboratories, Lisp is more popular in the USA than in Europe, where Prolog is often preferred for AI work.

Lister /'lɪstə/ Joseph, 1st Baron Lister 1827–1912. British surgeon. He was professor of surgery at Glasgow 1860–69, at Edinburgh 1869–77, and at King's College, London, 1877–92. The first to use antiseptic treatment for wounds, he introduced antiseptic surgery and the prevention of infection by the utmost cleanliness in the operating room. He was president of the Royal Society 1895–1900, and was created Baron Lister of Lyme Regis in 1897. In 1902 he received the Order of Merit.

Liszt /lɪst/ Franz 1811–1886. Hungarian pianist and composer. Born in Raiding, he was originally taught by his father, but after his first public performance when only nine he went to Vienna to study under Czerny and Salieri and at 11 claimed Beethoven among his many admirers. Becoming possibly the greatest virtuoso pianist of all time, he travelled widely in Europe, producing an opera *Don Sanche* in Paris at 14. In 1833 he began a ten-year affair with the comtesse d'Agoult, by whom he had three children and with whom he lived mainly in Switzerland. As musical director and conductor at Weimar 1848–59, where he lived with the Princess Caroline Sayn-Wittgenstein, he was a champion of the music of Berlioz and Wagner. Retiring to Rome, he turned again to his early love of religion and in 1865 became a secular priest (hence his adoption of the title Abbé), but continued to teach and give concert tours. Although born in Hungary, he never spoke Hungarian, and the majority of his letters are in French. He died at Bayreuth.

Liszt's music, expressive, rhetorical, and in later years highly chromatic, greatly influenced many younger musicians, including ◊Franck, ◊Smetana, and ◊Greig. Much of it is programmatic; he also originated the symphonic poem. His most notable compositions are his

Lister British surgeon Joseph Lister was the first to use antiseptic treatment for wounds as a consequence of Louis Pasteur's theories about bacteria.

lyrical, but often technically very difficult, piano works, including the popular *Liebesträume* and the *Hungarian Rhapsodies*, based on gipsy music. He also wrote a *Faust* and a *Dante Symphony*; masses and oratorios; songs; and piano arrangements of works by Beethoven, Schubert, and Wagner among others.

Liszt The Hungarian Franz Liszt, probably the world's greatest virtuoso pianist, composed the *Liebesträume* and *Hungarian Rhapsodies*. In his later years he became a secular Franciscan priest.

litany in the Christian Church, a form of prayer or supplication led by a priest with set responses by the congregation.

litchi or *lychee*, tree *Litchi chinensis* of the family Sapindaceae. The delicately flavoured ovate fruit is about the size of a walnut, and is

encased in a brownish rough outer skin and has a hard seed. The litchi is a native of S China, where it has been cultivated for 2,000 years.

literacy the ability to read and write at a level to enable an adult to function in the society in which he or she lives. The level at which functional literacy is set rises as society becomes more complex, and it becomes increasingly difficult for an illiterate person to find work and cope with the other demands of everyday life.

literary criticism the establishment of principles governing literary composition, and the assessment of literary works. The earliest systematic literary criticism was the *Poetics* of Aristotle; a later Greek critic was the author of the treatise *On the Sublime*, usually attributed to Longinus. Horace and Quintilian were influential Latin critics. The Italian Renaissance introduced humanist criticism, and the revival of classical scholarship exalted the authority of Aristotle and Horace. Like literature itself, European criticism then applied Neo-Classical, Romantic, and modern approaches. Contemporary criticism often applies insights to literary works from structuralism, semiotics, feminism, Marxism, and psychoanalysis, whereas earlier criticism tended to deal with moral or political ideas, or with a literary work as a formal object independent of its creator.

literature the great body of world literature consists of words set apart in some way from ordinary everyday communication. In the ancient oral traditions, before stories and poems were written down, literature had a mainly public function – mythic and religious. As literary works came to be preserved in writing, and then, eventually, printed, their role became more private, as a vehicle for the exploration and expression of emotion and of the human situation. Aesthetic criteria came increasingly to the fore; the English poet and critic Coleridge defined prose as words in their best order, and poetry as the 'best ' words in the best order. The distinction between ◊verse and ◊prose is not always clear cut, but in practice ◊poetry tends to be metrically formal (making it easier to memorize), whereas prose corresponds more closely to the patterns of ordinary speech. Poetry therefore had an early advantage over prose in the days before printing, which it has not relinquished until comparatively recently. Over the centuries poetry has taken on a wide range of forms, from the lengthy narrative such as the ◊epic to the lyric, expressing personal emotion in songlike form; from the ◊ballad, and the 14-line ◊sonnet, to the extreme conciseness of the 17-syllable Japanese ◊haiku. Prose came into its own in the West as a vehicle for imaginative literature with the rise of the modern ◊novel in the 18th century, and ◊fiction has since been divided into various genres such as the ◊historical novel, ◊detective fiction, ◊fantasy, and ◊science fiction. See also the literature of particular countries, under ◊English literature, ◊French literature, ◊Russian literature, ◊Spanish literature, and so on.

lithification the solidification of ◊sediments into sedimentary rock. An alternative term for ◊diagenesis.

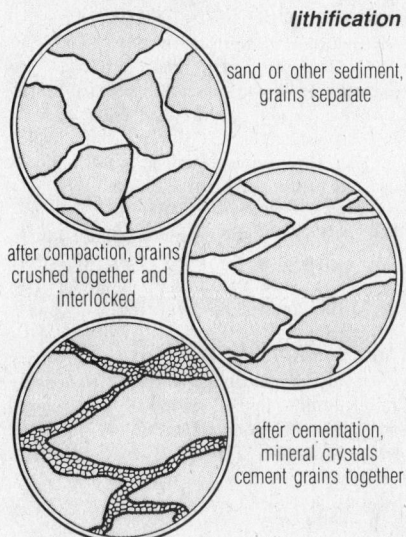

lithification

sand or other sediment, grains separate

after compaction, grains crushed together and interlocked

after cementation, mineral crystals cement grains together

lithium the lightest metallic element, symbol Li, atomic number 3, atomic weight 6.940. It was discovered by Arfvedson in 1817. Lithium has a silvery lustre and tarnishes rapidly in air, so it is kept under naphtha. It is soft and ductile, and burns in air at 200°C. Never occurring free in nature, it is nevertheless widely distributed, traces being found in nearly all ◊igneous rocks and many mineral springs. It is used as a reducing agent, in batteries, to harden alloys, and in producing ◊tritium. Lithium compounds are used in medicine to treat depression.

lithography in printing, graphic reproduction by a process originated by Aloys ◊Senefelder, in which a drawing is made with greasy ink on an absorbent stone, which is then washed with water. The water then repels any ink applied to the surface, and the grease attracts it, so that the drawing can be printed, and each print is an 'artist's original'. Modern lithographic printing is used in book production, and has developed this basic principle into complex processes.

lithosphere the topmost layer of the earth's structure, forming the plates that take part in the movements of ◊plate tectonics. The lithosphere comprises the ◊crust and the upper ◊mantle. It is regarded as being rigid and moves about on the less rigid ◊asthenosphere. The lithosphere is probably about 75 km/47 mi thick.

Lithuania /ˌlɪθjuːˈeɪnɪə/ constituent republic of the W USSR from 1940
area 65,200 sq km/25,300 sq mi
capital Vilnius
towns Kaunas, Klaipeda
physical river Niemen; 25% forested; lakes, marshes, and complex sandy coastline
products bacon, dairy products; cereals, potatoes; heavy engineering and electrical goods, cement
population (1984) 3.5 million, 80% Lithuanian
language Lithuanian, an Indo-European tongue which has retained many ancient features and is related to Latvian; it is written in a Latin alphabet

religion only Soviet republic that is predominantly Roman Catholic
famous people Jacques Lipchitz
recent history formerly part of the Russian Empire, Lithuania became an independent republic in 1918, recognized by the USSR in 1920. In 1939 the USSR demanded military bases and in 1940 incorporated it as a constituent republic. As in the other Baltic republics, there has been nationalist dissent since 1980, influenced by the Polish example and prompted by the influx of Russian workers and officials.

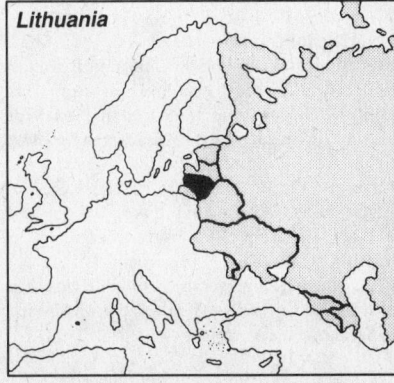

Lithuania

Lithuanian language an Indo-European language spoken by the people of Lithuania that through its geographical isolation has retained many ancient features of the Indo-European language family. It acquired a written form in the 16th century, using the Latin alphabet, and is currently spoken by some 3–4 million people.

litmus dye obtained from lichens, and used as an indicator to test the acidic or alkaline nature of aqueous solutions; it turns red in the presence of acid, and blue with alkali.

litre metric unit of volume, (l). The special name for the cubic decimetre. Formerly used to denote the volume occupied by 1 kg of pure water at 4°C at standard pressure. Equal to 1.76 pints.

Little Bighorn /ˈlɪtl ˈbɪghɔːn/ site in Montana, USA, of General George ◊Custer's defeat by the Sioux Indians 25 Jun 1876 under chiefs ◊Crazy Horse and ◊Sitting Bull, known as Custer's Last Stand.

Little Ice Age a time of particularly severe winters that gripped N Europe between the 13th and 17th (or 16th and 19th) centuries. Writings and paintings of the time show that Alpine glaciers were much more extensive than at present, and rivers such as the Thames, which do not ice over today, were so frozen that festivals could be held on them.

Little Rock /ˈlɪtl rɒk/ industrial city and capital of Arkansas, USA; population (1980) 158,461. Black/white integration of the schools caused riots here in 1957 and was enforced by federal troops.

Littlewood /ˈlɪtlwʊd/ Joan 1914– . British theatre director. After early experience with the Manchester Repertory Theatre, she founded Theatre Workshop in 1945, and gained her reputation with vigorous productions at the Theatre Royal, Stratford (London) 1953–75, for

example *A Taste of Honey* 1959, *The Hostage* 1959–60, *Fings ain't Wot They Used T'Be* 1960–61, and *Oh What a Lovely War* 1963. She also worked in France from 1975.

liturgy in the Christian Church, a term originally limited to the celebration of the ◊Eucharist, but now used of any or all services for public worship.

Litvinov /lɪtˈviːnɒf/ Maxim 1876–1951. Russian politician, commissioner for foreign affairs under Stalin from Jan 1931 until his removal from office in May 1939.

Liu /ˈljuː ʃaʊˈtʃɪ/ Shaoqi (formerly Liu Shao-chi) 1898–1969. Chinese communist politician, president 1960–67.
The son of a Hunan peasant farmer, Liu attended the same local school as ◊Mao Zedong. As a member of the Chinese Communist Party (CCP), he was sent to Moscow to study communism and returned to Shanghai in 1922 to work as a labour organizer. He emerged as a firm proponent of the Soviet line of development based around disciplined one-party control, the use of incentive gradings, and priority for industry over agriculture. This was opposed by Mao, but began to be implemented when Liu, as state president, gained control of the government 1960–65. In 1967, during the Cultural Revolution, Liu was forced to step down. He was stripped of his post and expelled from the CCP in Apr 1969 and banished to Kaifeng in Henan province, where he died in Nov 1969.

liver a large organ of vertebrates, which has many regulatory and storage functions. It is situated in the upper ◊abdomen and in humans weighs approximately 2 kg/4 lb. It receives the products of digestion, converting glucose to glycogen (a long-chain carbohydrate used for storage), and breaking down fats. It removes excess ◊amino acids from the blood, converting them to ◊urea, which is excreted by the ◊kidneys. The liver also synthesizes vitamins, produces ◊bile and blood clotting factors, and removes damaged red cells and toxins such as alcohol from the blood.

Livermore Valley /ˈlɪvəmɔː/ valley in California, USA, site of the Lawrence Livermore Laboratory (named after Ernest ◊Lawrence). Part of the University of California, it shares with Los Alamos Laboratory, New Mexico, all US military research into nuclear warheads and atomic explosives. It also conducts research into nuclear fusion, using high-integrity ◊lasers.

Liverpool /ˈlɪvəpuːl/ city and seaport (a ◊free port), administrative headquarters of Merseyside, NW England; population (1984) 497,300. Developing under Charles II as American and West Indian trade grew, it was the chief centre of the slave trade. In the 19th and early 20th century, it exported the textiles of Lancashire and Yorkshire, and is still Europe's chief Atlantic port with miles of specialized, mechanized quays on the Mersey. The Maritime Museum is devoted to this aspect of its history. However, such traditional industries as ship-repairing and engineering have declined. There are industrial estates at Aintree, Kirkby, and Speke. The Mersey Tunnel 1934 links Liverpool and Birkenhead, and a tunnel to Wallasey was opened in 1971.

Outstanding buildings are Speke Hall, the classical St George's Hall 1854, the university, the Dock Offices, Liver Building and Cunard Building on Pier Head; galleries include Walker Art Gallery 1877 and the Tate in the North in restored dockland buildings 1987. The Anglican Cathedral 1904–79, by Sir Giles Gilbert Scott, is the largest church in England; the Roman Catholic Metropolitan Cathedral of Christ the King 1967 is by ◊Gibberd. The International Garden Festival Hall 1984 was adapted as a sports complex. The ◊Beatles were born here, and a Beatles museum was opened in 1984.

Liverpool /'lɪvəpuːl/ Robert Banks Jenkinson, 2nd Earl Liverpool 1770–1825. British Tory politician. He entered Parliament in 1790, and was foreign secretary 1801–03, home secretary 1804–06 and 1807–09, war minister 1809–12, and prime minister 1812–27. His government conducted the Napoleonic Wars to a successful conclusion, but its ruthless suppression of freedom of speech and of the press aroused such opposition that during 1815–20 revolution frequently seemed imminent.

Liverpool Robert Banks Jenkinson, 2nd Earl of Liverpool. The portrait is by Sir Thomas Lawrence.

liverwort plant of the class Hepaticae, related to mosses. Usually small, liverworts live in damp places and the main sexual generation consists of a 'thallus', which may be flat, green and lobed, like a small leaf, or 'leafy' and moss-like. The spore-bearing generation is smaller, typically 'parasitic' on the thallus, and throws up a capsule from which spores are spread. About 290 species are found in Britain.

livery companies the ◊guilds of the City of London. Their role is now social rather than industrial, many administering valuable charities, especially educational.

Livia Drusilla /'lɪvɪə druː'sɪlə/ 58 BC–29 AD. Roman empress, wife of ◊Augustus from 39 BC, she was the mother by her first husband of ◊Tiberius, and intrigued to secure his succession to the imperial crown. She remained politically influential to the end of her life.

Livingston /'lɪvɪŋstən/ industrial new town (chemicals, brass and iron founding, ship repairing) in W Lothian, Scotland; population (1985) 40,000.

Livingstone /'lɪvɪŋstən/ town in Zambia; population (1984) 83,000. Founded in 1905, it was named after the explorer, and was capital of N Rhodesia 1907–35. Victoria Falls is nearby.

Livingstone /'lɪvɪŋstən/ David 1813–1873. Scottish missionary explorer. Born in Blantyre, Strathclyde, he took his medical degree at Glasgow University in 1840, and in 1844 went out to Africa. He reached Lake Ngami 1849; followed the Zambezi to its mouth and saw the Victoria Falls 1855; went to East and Central Africa 1858–64, reaching Lakes Shirwa and Malawi; and from 1866 disappeared to try to trace the source of the Nile, reaching Ujiji in Oct 1871, where ◊Stanley caught up with him. He died in Old Chitambo, Zambia, but was buried in Westminster Abbey.

Livingstone Scottish doctor and missionary David Livingstone was the first European to explore many parts of Central and East Africa. In 1866 he went to trace the source of the Nile and was rescued by H M Stanley in 1871.

Livingstone /'lɪvɪŋstən/ Ken(neth) 1945– . British Labour politician, leader of the Greater London Council (GLC) 1981–86.
Livingstone joined the Labour Party in 1968, and was active in London politics from 1971. As leader of the GLC until its abolition in 1986, he displayed outside GLC headquarters current unemployment figures so that they were clearly visible to MPs in the Palace of Westminster across the river Thames. He was elected to Parliament representing the London constituency of Brent East in 1987.

Livonia /lɪ'vəʊnɪə/ former region on the E of the Baltic Sea comprising most of ◊Latvia and ◊Estonia. Conquered and converted to Christianity in the early 13th century by the Livonian Knights, a crusading order, Livonia was independent until 1583, when it was divided between Poland and Sweden. In 1721 it was ceded to ◊Peter the Great of Russia.

Livorno /lɪ'vɔːnəʊ/ (English Leghorn) industrial port (distilling, motor vehicles) in W Italy; population (1984) 175,500. A fortress town since the 12th century, it was developed by the Medici family; it has a naval academy, and is also a resort.

Livy /'lɪvɪ/ Titus Livius 59 BC–17 AD. Roman historian, famous for his narrative *History of Rome*, from its foundation to 9 BC, based partly on legend. It was composed of 142 books, of which 35 survive, 1–10 and 21–45, covering the periods from the arrival of Aeneas in Italy to 293 BC and 218–167 BC.

lizard reptile of the suborder Lacertilia, belonging with the snakes in the order Squamata. Lizards are normally distinguishable from snakes by having four legs, movable eyelids, eardrums and a fleshy tongue, but some lizards are legless and very snakelike in appearance. There are about 3,000 species of lizard worldwide, and like other reptiles they are most abundant in the tropics, although the *common* or *viviparous lizard Lacerta vivipara*, about 15 cm/6 in long, lives in Europe as far north as the Arctic circle, where it hibernates through the long winter. Like many other species it can shed its tail as a defence, later regrowing it. There are some 20 families of lizards, including ◊geckos, ◊chameleons, ◊skinks, ◊monitors, ◊agamas and ◊iguanas. The *frilled lizard Chlamydosaurus kingi* of Australia has an erectile collar to frighten its enemies. For flying lizard see ◊*flying dragon*.

Ljubljana /luː'bljɑːnə/ (German *Laibach*) capital and industrial city (textiles, chemicals, paper, leather goods) of Slovenia, Yugoslavia; population (1981) 305,220. It has a nuclear research centre and is linked with S Austria by the Karawanken road tunnel under the Alps (1979–83). It has a medieval castle.

llama South American animal *Lama peruana*, used in Peru as a beast of burden. Llamas can be white, brown or dark, sometimes with spots or patches. They are very hardy, and require little food or water. They spit profusely when annoyed. The ◊alpaca is an allied species.

Llandaff /'lændəf/ town in S Glamorgan, Wales, 5 km/3 mi NW of Cardiff, of which it forms part. The 12th-century cathedral, heavily restored, contains Epstein's sculpture 'Christ in Majesty'.

Llandrindod Wells /ɬæn'drɪndɒd 'welz/ spa in Powys, Wales, administrative headquarters of the county; population (1981) 4,186.

Llanelli /ɬæn'eɬi/ (formerly Llanelly) industrial port (tinplate, copper smelting) in Dyfed, Wales; population (1981) 41,391.

Llewellyn /lʊ'welɪn/ Richard, pen name of Richard Vivian Llewellyn Lloyd 1907–1983. Welsh author and dramatist, best known for *How*

llama In Peru an Aymara Indian girl looks after a mixed herd of sheep and llamas. The llama is often used as beast of burden.

Green Was My Valley 1939, a novel about a S Wales mining family.

Llewelyn /lʊ'welɪn, Welsh ɬə'welɪn/ two kings of Wales:

Llewelyn I died 1240, King from 1194, who extended his rule to all Wales not in Norman hands.

Llewelyn II c. 1225–82, King from 1246, grandson of Llewelyn I, who was compelled by Edward I in 1277 to acknowledge him as overlord and to surrender S Wales. His death while leading a national uprising ended Welsh independence.

Lleyn /ɬiːn/ peninsula in Gwynedd, N Wales, between Cardigan Bay and Caernarvon Bay. It included the resort Pwllheli, and Bardsey Island at the tip of Peninsula Lleyn is the traditional burial place of 20,000 saints.

Lloyd /lɔɪd/ Harold 1893–1971. American film comedian, noted for his 'trademark' of spectacles with thick horn rims, who appeared from 1913 in silent and talking films.

Lloyd /lɔɪd/ John. 15th-century Welsh seaman, known as John Scolvus, 'the skilful', who carried on an illegal trade with Greenland and is claimed to have reached N America, sailing as far south as Maryland, in 1477 (15 years before the voyage of Columbus).

Lloyd /lɔɪd/ Marie, stage name of Matilda Alice Victoria Wood 1870–1922. British music-hall artist whose Cockney songs included 'Oh! Mr Porter' and embodied the music-hall traditions of 1890s comedy.

Lloyd /lɔɪd/ Selwyn. See ◊Selwyn Lloyd.

Lloyd George /'lɔɪd 'dʒɔːdʒ/ David, 1st Earl Lloyd George 1863–1945. Welsh Liberal politician. A pioneer of social reform, he was born in Manchester, became a solicitor, and was Member of Parliament for Caernarvon Boroughs from 1890. During the South African War, he was prominent as a pro-Boer. As chancellor of the exchequer 1908–15, he introduced old-age pensions in 1908 and health and unemployment insurance in 1911. His 1909 budget (with graduated direct taxes and taxing land values) provoked the Lords to reject it, and resulted in the Act of 1911 limiting their powers. He held ministerial posts during World War I until in 1916 there was an open breach between him and ◊Asquith, and he became prime minister

of a coalition government. Securing a unified Allied command, he enabled the Allies to withstand the last German offensive and achieve victory, and as one of the Big Three, with ◊Wilson and ◊Clemenceau, he had a major role in the ◊Versailles peace treaty.

In the 1918 elections, he achieved a huge majority over Labour and Asquith's followers, but high unemployment, intervention in the Russian Civil War, and use of the ◊black-and-tans in Ireland eroded his support. Creation of the Irish Free State in 1921, and his pro-Greek policy against the Turks, led to withdrawal of the Conservatives and collapse of the coalition in 1922. He had become largely distrusted within his own party, and never regained power.

Lloyd George David Lloyd George, Welsh Liberal politician, was prime minister at the time of the Allied victory in World War I.

Lloyd's Register of Shipping founded 1760, an international society for the survey and classification of merchant shipping which provides rules for the construction and maintenance of ships and their machinery. It is governed by a large committee representing ship-owners, ship-builders, marine engineers and underwriters. The register book, published annually, contains particulars of all known sea-going ships of 100 tonnes gross and over.

Lloyd Webber /'lɔɪd 'webə/ Andrew 1948– . British composer. His early musicals, with lyrics by Tim Rice, include *Jesus Christ Superstar* 1970, and *Evita* 1978, based on the life of Eva Perón. He also wrote *Cats* 1981 and *The Phantom of the Opera* 1986.

loach carp-like freshwater fish, family Cobitidae, with a long narrow body, and no teeth in the small downward pointing mouth, which is surrounded by barbels. Many species live in Asia, three in Europe, including the *stone loach Noemacheilus barbatulus*, with no scales and six barbels at the mouth.

Lobachevsky /ˌlɒbə'tʃefski/ Nikolai Ivanovich 1792–1856. Russian mathematician, who with the Hungarian Janos Bulyai (1802–1860), but independently of him, founded non-Euclidean geometry in 1829. Lobachevsky

published the first account of the subject in 1829, but his work went unrecognized until the German Riemann's system was published.

lobby individual or group which sets out to influence government action. The lobby is particularly prevalent in the USA, where the term originated in the 1830s from the practice of those wishing to influence state policy waiting for their electoral representative in the lobby of the Capitol. Under the UK lobby system, certain parliamentary journalists are given unofficial access to confidential news.

lobelia temperate and tropical genus of plants, family Lobeliaceae, named after French botanist Matthias de l'Obel, with flowers in white to mauve. They may grow to small trees.

Lobengula /ˌləʊbən'gjuːlə/ 1833–1894. King of ◊Matabeleland 1870–1893, when he rebelled, after accepting British protection in 1888. He was defeated near Bulawayo.

lobster marine member of the order ◊Decapoda. Lobsters are grouped with the freshwater ◊crayfish in the suborder Reptantia ('walking'), though both lobsters and crayfish can also swim, using their fanlike tails. All have eyes on stalks and long antennae, and are mainly nocturnal. They scavenge and eat dead or dying fish.

true lobsters family Homaridae, are distinguished by having very large 'claws' or pincers on their first pair of legs, and smaller ones on their second and third pairs. They include the edible *common lobster Homarus gammarus* found off Britain, which is blueish-black before cooking; the closely related *American lobster Homarus americanus*; and the *Norwegian lobster Nephrops norvegicus* a small orange species, taken by trawling and sold as 'scampi'.

spiny lobsters family Palinuridae, have no large pincers, including the *spiny lobster Palinurus vulgaris* found off Britain, of which only the 'tail' or small abdomen is eaten. They communicate by means of a serrated pad at the base of their antennae, the 'sound' being picked up by tufts of hair (not ears) on their fellow lobsters up to 60 m/180 ft away: it is 'conversational', that is, when it ceases, the rest look for shelter, and there is a warning call for overt danger.

local government that part of government dealing mainly with matters concerning the inhabitants of a particular district or place, together with those the administration of which has been delegated to local authorities.

history the system of local government in England developed haphazardly; in the 18th century it varied in the towns between democratic survivals of the ◊guild system and the narrow rule of small oligarchies. The Municipal Reform Act 1835 established the rule of elected councils, although their actual powers remained small. In country areas local government remained in the hands of the justices of the peace (JPs) assembled in Quarter Sessions, until the Local Government Act 1888 set up county councils. These were given a measure of control over the internal local authorities, except the major bodies, which were constituted as county boroughs. The Local Government Act 1894 set

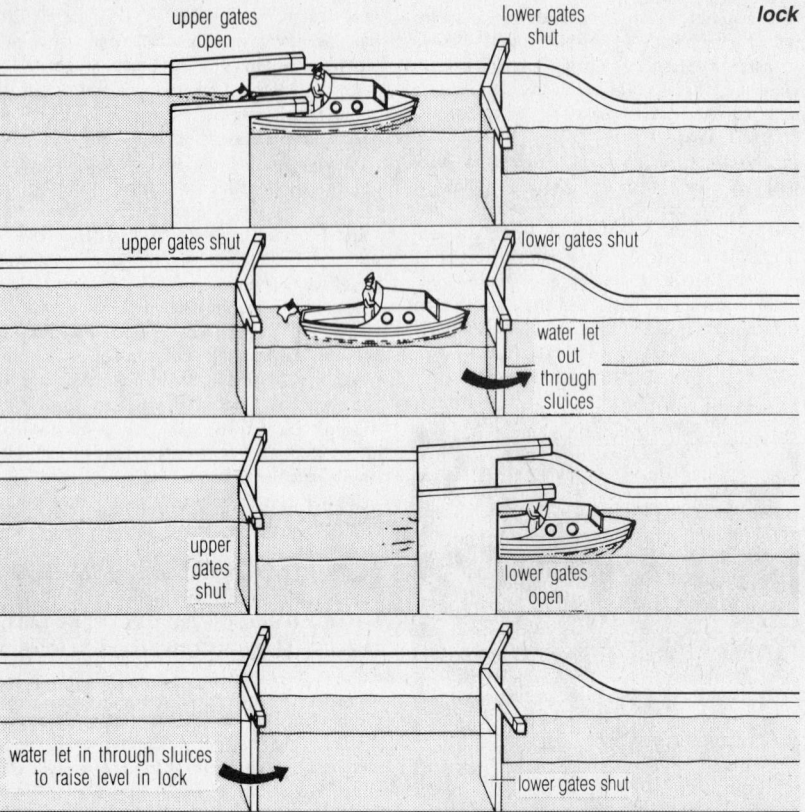

upper gates open

lower gates shut

lock

upper gates shut

lower gates shut

water let out through sluices

upper gates shut

lower gates open

water let in through sluices to raise level in lock

lower gates shut

up urban and rural district councils and, in the rural districts only, parish councils.

Under the Local Government Act 1972 the upper range of local government for England and Wales was established on a two-tier basis, with 46 counties in the former and eight in the latter. London and six other English cities were created metropolitan areas with metropolitan county councils (the latter councils were abolished in 1986, and their already limited functions redistributed to the metropolitan district councils), and the non-metropolitan 'shire' counties had county councils. The counties were subdivided into districts (of which there are 300, each with a district council, replacing the former county borough, borough, and urban and rural district councils) and then, in rural areas, into parishes and, in Wales, into 'communities' across the country, each again with its own council dealing with local matters.

County councils consist of councillors elected for four years, who then elect a chair from among their number. (The category of senior councillor known as ◊alderman was abolished in 1972.) The responsibilities of county councils include broad planning policy; highways; education, personal social services, and libraries; police, fire, and traffic control; and refuse disposal. District councils consist of councillors elected for four years. One-third retire at a time, district elections being held in three out of four years (county council elections take place in the fourth). They are headed by an annually elected chair or, in cases where the place has honorary borough or

city status, by a mayor or lord mayor. Their responsibilities cover housing; local planning and development; roads (excluding trunk and classified); bus services; environmental health; rating; museums and art galleries; parks and playing fields, swimming baths, and cemeteries. In the case of metropolitan district councils education, personal social services, and libraries are also included.

Under the Local Government Act 1974 a Commission for Local Administration for England and Wales was set up, creating an 'ombudsman' for complaints about local government. Under the Local Government (Scotland) Act 1973 Scotland was divided into regions (nine) and island areas, rather than counties; these are subdivided into districts, which may in turn have subsidiary community councils, but the latter are not statutory bodies with claims on public funds as of right. Northern Ireland has a single-tier system of 26 district councils. The activities of local government are financed largely by local property taxes known as ◊rates, subsidized by central government (see under ◊rate support grant). In the mid-1980s the Thatcher administration sought to remove many services from the aegis of local authorities and offer them for tender to private companies; thus in many areas school-meals provision was privatized, as was refuse collection, maintenance of council vehicles, street cleaning, and upkeep of parks and sports facilities. In 1987 a code of practice was issued to restrict the ability of local authorities to promote 'partisan' activities.

In other European countries, such as France, West Germany, and the USSR, local government has tended historically to be more centrally controlled than in Britain, although German cities have a tradition of independent action, as exemplified in Berlin, and France from 1969 moved towards regional decentralization. In the USA the emphasis is more on local autonomy, and the system shows evidence of the early type of settlement (for example in New England the town is the unit of local government, in the South the county, and in the N Central states the combined county and township). A complication is the tendency to delegate power to special authorities in such fields as education. In Australia, although an integrated system similar to the British was planned, the scattered nature of settlement, apart from the major towns, has prevented implementation of any uniform tiered arrangement.

Local Group in astronomy, a cluster of about three dozen ◊galaxies that includes our own. Its two largest galaxies are our own and ◊Andromeda; most of the others are small and faint. The local group is held together by the gravitational attraction between its members, and does not expand with the expanding ◊Universe.

local option the right granted by a government to the electors of each particular area to decide whether the sale of intoxicants shall be permitted. Such a system has been tried in certain states of the USA, in certain Canadian provinces, and in Norway and Sweden.

Locarno /lə'kɑːnəʊ/ health resort in the Ticino canton of Switzerland on the north of Lago Maggiore, west of Bellinzona. Formerly in the duchy of Milan, it was captured by the Swiss in 1803. Population (1978) 15,300.

Locarno /lə'kɑːnəʊ/ Pact of. A series of diplomatic documents initialled at Locarno on 16 Oct 1925, and formally signed in London on 1 Dec 1925. The Pact settled the question of the Rhineland, and the powers – Britain, France, Belgium, Italy, and Germany – guaranteed the existing frontiers between Germany and France, and Germany and Belgium. The prime mover in the Pact was Austen Chamberlain. Following the signing of the Pact, Germany was admitted to the League of Nations, but in 1936 the Nazis under Hitler formally denounced the pact and troops were sent into the Rhineland.

Lochner /'lɒxnə/ Stephan c. 1400–1451. German painter. He was born on the Upper Rhine, and all his principal works are in the cathedral and museums of Cologne, including the *Madonna in the Rose Garden*, *Adoration of the Kings*, and *Presentation in the Temple*.

Loch Ness /ˌlɒx 'nes/ very deep lake in Highland region, Scotland. There have been reports of a 'monster' since the 15th century.

lock a gated chamber installed in canals, rivers and seaways that allows boats to sail from one level to another. A lock has gates at each end. A boat sails in through one gate when the levels are the same outside and inside. Then water is allowed in (or out of) the lock until the water level rises (or falls) to the new level outside the other gate. In a 4 km/2.5 mi stretch of the Worcester

Locke English philosopher John Locke is best known for his *Treatise on Government and Essay Concerning Human Understanding*. The painting is by Dutch artist Herman Verelst (c. 1689).

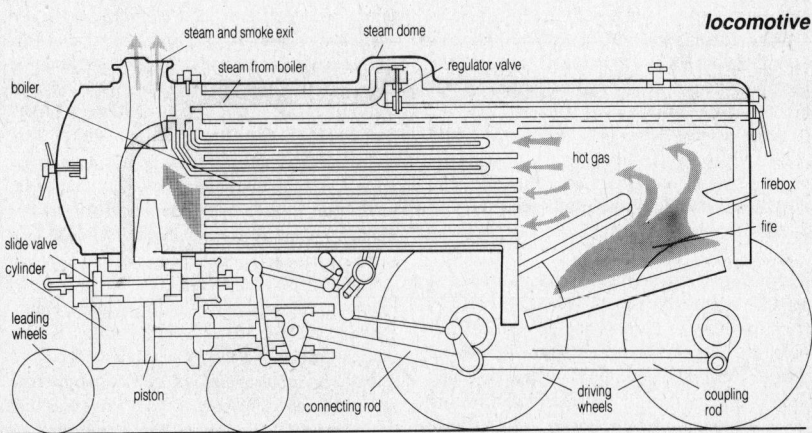

locomotive

and Birmingham Canal at Tardebigge there are 36 locks that drop the canal nearly 79 m/260 ft.

lock and key devices that provide security, usually fitted to a door of some kind. Locks originated in the Far East over 4,000 years ago. The Romans developed the warded lock, which contains obstacles (wards) that the key must pass to turn. In 1778 English locksmith Robert Barron made the forerunner of the modern mortise lock, which contains levers that the key must raise to an exact height before the bolt can be moved. The ◊Yale lock, a pin-tumbler design, was invented by Linus Yale Jr in 1865. More secure locks include combination locks, whose dial mechanism must be turned certain distances backwards and forwards to open, and time locks, which can be opened only at specific times.

Locke /lɒk/ John 1632–1704. English philosopher. Born in Somerset, he studied at Oxford, practised medicine, and in 1667 became secretary to the Earl of Shaftesbury. He consequently fell under suspicion as a Whig and in 1683 fled to Holland, where he lived until the 1688 revolution. In later life he published many works on philosophy, politics, theology and economics; these include, *Letters on Toleration 1689–92*, *Two Treatises on Government 1690*, *Essay concerning Human Understanding 1690*, and *Some Thoughts concerning Education 1693*. His *Treatises on Government* supply the classical statement of Whig theory, and enjoyed great influence in America and France. It supposed that governments derive their authority from popular consent (regarded as a 'contract'), so that a government may be rightly overthrown if it infringes such fundamental rights of the people as religious freedom. His *Essay concerning Human Understanding* deals with the nature, origin, and limits of human knowledge. It maintained that experience was the only source of knowledge (empiricism), and

that 'we can have knowlege no farther than we have ideas' prompted by such experience. This raised problems which dominated 18th-century philosophy until Kant.

lockjaw popular name for ◊tetanus.

locomotive a machine for hauling trains on the railways. Cornishman Richard Trevithick built the first locomotive in 1804; it was a steam engine on wheels. Locomotive design did not improve radically until George Stephenson built the *Rocket* 1829, which featured a multitube boiler and blastpipe, standard in all ***steam locomotives*** ever since. In a steam locomotive, fuel (usually coal, sometimes wood) is burned in a furnace. The hot gases and flames produced are drawn through tubes running through a huge water-filled boiler and heat up the water to steam. The steam is then fed to the cylinders, where it forces the pistons back and forth. Movement of the pistons is conveyed to the wheels by cranks and connecting rods.

Most locomotives these days, however, are diesel or electric. ***Diesel locomotives*** have a powerful ◊diesel engine, burning oil. The engine may drive a generator to produce electricity to power electric motors that turn the wheels, or the engine drives the wheels mechanically or through a hydraulic link. ***Electric locomotives*** are driven by electric motors. They pick up their current either from an overhead power line or a "third rail" alongside the ordinary track. A number of ***gas-turbine locomotives*** are in use, in which a turbine spun by hot gases provides the power to drive the wheels. See also ◊railways.

locus (Latin 'place') in mathematics, the path traced out by a moving point. For example, the locus of a point that moves so that it is always at the same distance from another fixed point is a circle; the locus of a point that is always at the same distance from two fixed points is a straight line that perpendicularly bisects the line joining them.

locust swarming grasshopper, with short antennae and auditory organs on the abdomen, in the family Acrididae. When the larvae ('hoppers') emerge from the eggs, which are laid in the ground, they form into bands. As winged adults, flying in swarms, they may be carried by

the wind hundreds of kilometres from their breeding grounds, and on alighting devour all vegetation. Locusts occur in nearly every continent, the migratory locust *Locusta migratoria* ranging from Europe across the Soviet Union to China, and even small swarms may cover several square kilometres and weigh thousands of tonnes. Control by spreading poisoned food amongst the bands is very effective, but it is cheapest to spray concentrated insecticide solutions from aircraft over the insects or the vegetation on which they feed. They eat the equivalent of their own weight in a day, and, flying at night on the desert wind, may cover some 500 km/300 mi.

locust tree alternative name for the ◊carob, small tree of the Mediterranean region.

Lodge /lɒdʒ/ David (John) 1935– . British novelist, short story writer, and critic. Much of his fiction takes as its central concern the question of what it means to be a Catholic in mid-20th-century England, exploring the situation in *The British Museum is Falling Down 1967*, and in *How Far Can You Go? 1980*.

Lodge /lɒdʒ/ Henry Cabot 1850–1924. American historian, Republican senator from 1893, who influenced the USA to stay out of the League of Nations 1920.

Lodge /lɒdʒ/ Henry Cabot, Jr 1902–1985. American statesman. Grandson of the elder Henry Cabot Lodge, he was Eisenhower's campaign manager, and US representative at the United Nations 1953–60. Ambassador to S Vietnam 1963–64, and 1965–67, he took over from Harriman as Nixon's negotiator in the Vietnam peace talks in 1969.

Lodge /lɒdʒ/ Oliver Joseph 1851–1940. British physicist. He developed a system of wireless communication in 1894, and his work was influential in the development of radio receivers. He was also greatly interested in psychic research, his son having been killed in 1915.

Lodge /lɒdʒ/ Thomas c. 1558–1625. English author, whose romance *Rosalynde 1590* was the basis of Shakespeare's *As You Like It*.

Lodi /ˈlɔːdi/ town in Italy, 30 km/18 mi SE of Milan, a market for agricultural produce;

fertilizers, agricultural machinery and textiles are made; population (1980) 46,000. Napoleon's defeat of Austria at the battle of Lodi in 1796 gave him control of Lombardy. Napoleon was first called Le Petit Caporal at Lodi.

Lódź /lɒdz, Polish wuːtʃ/ (Polish Łódź) industrial town (textiles, textile machinery, dyes) in Poland, capital of Lódź voivodship, 120 km/75 mi SW of Warsaw; university (1945); population (1984) 849,000.

loess a yellow loam, accumulated by wind in periglacial regions during the ice ages. It usually attains considerable depths, and the soil derived from it is very fertile and can be used to grow excellent crops. There are large deposits in central Europe, especially Hungary, in China and N America. It was first described in 1821 in the Rhine area, and takes its name from a village in Alsace.

Loewe /'ləʊi/ Frederick 1901–1988. American composer of musicals. Born in Austria, son of an operatic tenor, he studied music including the piano under Busoni, and in 1924 went with his father to the USA. In 1942 he joined forces with the lyricist Alan Jay ◊Lerner 1918–86, and their joint successes include *Brigadoon* 1947, *Paint Your Wagon* 1951, *My Fair Lady* 1956, *Gigi* 1958, and *Camelot* 1960.

Lofoten and Vesterålen /'ləʊfəʊtn, 'vestərɑːlən/ island group off NW Norway; area 4,530 sq km/1,750 sq mi. Hinnoy, in the Vesterålens, is Norway's largest island. The surrounding waters are rich in cod and herring. The *Maelström*, a hazardous whirlpool which gives its name to similar features elsewhere, occurs in one of the island channels.

Lofting /'lɒftɪŋ/ Hugh 1886–1947. Anglo-American writer and illustrator of children's books, especially the 'Dr Doolittle' series, in which the hero can talk to animals.

log an apparatus which measures the speed of a ship, originally a piece of weighted wood (log-chip) attached to a line with knots at equal intervals. This was cast from the rear of a ship, and the vessel's speed was estimated by timing the passage of the knots with a sand glass (like an egg-timer). Modern logs use electro-magnetism and sonar. The term 'log' has also come to be used for the daily record of events on board a ship or aircraft.

loganberry hybrid between ◊blackberry and ◊raspberry with large dull, but sweet, red fruit. It was first developed by US judge James H Logan in 1881.

logarithm mathematical function that makes the multiplication and division of large numbers simpler by substituting respectively the operations of addition and subtraction. The principle of logarithms is also the basis of the slide rule. With the general availability of the electronic pocket calculator, the need for logarithms has been reduced. More formally, a logarithm (or log) is the exponent or ◊index of a number to a specified base. For example, the log of 10 to the base 10 is 1; the log of 100 to the base 10 is 2, because $10^2 = 10 \times 10 = 100$. To multiply 100 by 100 (that is, $10^2 \times 10^2$), the indices are added, giving 10^4. For more difficult calculations,

tables of logarithms and antilogarithms are available (usually to the base 10) which show conversions of numbers into logarithms, and vice versa. For example, to multiply 6,560 x 980, one looks up the logarithms of the numbers – 3.8169 and 2.9912 – adds them together (6.8081), then looks up the antilogarithm of this to get the answer (6,428,000). Natural, or Naperian, logarithms are to the base *e*, an ◊irrational number equal to approximately 2.7183. Log tables were first published by the Scottish mathematician John Napier in 1614; base-10 logs were introduced by the Englishman Henry Briggs (1561–1631) and the Dutch mathematician Adriaen Vlacq (1600–1667).

logic a branch of philosophy which studies the structure and principles of valid reasoning and argument. It is also the study of those relations in virtue of which one thing may be said to follow from or be a consequence of another (deductive logic). ◊Aristotle's *Organon* is the founding work on logic, and Aristotelian methods as revived in the medieval church by ◊Abelard in the 12th century were used in the synthesis of ideas aimed at in ◊scholasticism. As befitted the spirit of the Renaissance, Bacon considered many of the general principles used as premisses by the scholastics to be groundless; he envisaged that in natural philosophy principles worthy of investigation would emerge by 'inductive' logic, which works backward from the accumulated facts to the principle which accounts for them. The modern contribution to logic has been its mathematical expression by philosophers such as ◊Boole, ◊Frege, and ◊Russell.

Logo a computer-programming language designed to teach mathematical concepts. Developed around 1970 at the Massachusetts Institute of Technology, it has recently become popular in schools and with home computer users because of its 'turtle graphics' feature. This allows the user to write programs that can create line drawings on a computer screen, or drive a small mobile robot (a 'turtle' or a 'buggy') around the floor. It encourages the use of languages in a logical and structured way, leading to 'microworlds' in which problems can be solved using a few standard solutions.

logos (Greek 'word') a term in Greek, Hebrew and Christian philosophy and theology. It was used by Greek philosophers as the embodiment of 'reason' in the Universe. Under Greek influence the Jews came to conceive of 'Wisdom' as an aspect of God's activity. The Jewish philosopher ◊Philo (1st century AD) attempted to reconcile Platonic, Stoic, and Hebrew philosophy by identifying the logos with the Jewish idea of 'Wisdom'. Several of the New Testament writers took over Philo's conception of the logos, which they identified with Christ, and hence the second person of the Trinity.

Lohengrin /'ləʊəngrɪn/ son of ◊Parsifal, hero of a late 13th-century legend, on which ◊Wagner based his German opera *Lohengrin* 1847. He married Princess Elsa, who broke his condition that she never ask his origin, and he returned to the temple of the ◊Grail.

Loir /lwɑː/ French river, rising N of Illiers in the *département* of Eure-et-Loir and flowing SE, then SW to join the Sarthe near Angers. It gives its name to the *départements* of Loir-et-Cher and Eure-et-Loir.

Loire /lwɑː/ the longest river in France, rising in the Cévennes at 1,350 m/4,430 ft and flowing for 1,050 km/625 mi first N then W till it reaches the Bay of Biscay at St Nazaire, passing Nevers, Orléans, Tours, and Nantes. It gives its name to the *départements* of Loire, Haute-Loire, Loire-Atlantique, Indre-et-Loire, Maine-et-Loire, and Saône-et-Loire. There are many chateaux and vineyards along its banks.

Loiret /lwɑːˈreɪ/ French river, 11 km/7 mi long. It rises near Olivet and joins the Loire 8 km/5 mi below Orléans. It gives its name to Loiret *département*.

Loki /'ləʊki/ in Norse mythology, one of the Aesir, but the cause of dissension among the gods, and the slayer of ◊Baldur. His children are the Midgard serpent Jörmungander which girdles the earth, the wolf Fenris, and Hela, goddess of death.

Lollard name, probably meaning 'mutterers', given to a follower of the English religious reformer John ◊Wycliffe in the 14th century. The Lollards condemned transubstantiation, advocated the diversion of ecclesiastical property to charitable uses, and denounced war and capital punishment. Propaganda began about 1377; after the passing of the statute *De Heretico Comburendo* (of the necessity of burning of the heretic) 1401 many Lollards were burned, and in 1414 they raised an unsuccessful revolt in London. Lollardy lingered on in London and East Anglia, and in the 16th century became absorbed into the Protestant movement.

Lombard or *Langobard* member of a Germanic people who invaded Italy in 568, and occupied Lombardy (named after them; see also ◊Monza) and central Italy. They were conquered by Charlemagne in 774.

Lombardy /'lɒmbədi/ region of N Italy (Italian *Lombardia*), including Lake Como, and the country's chief industrial area; capital Milan; population (1984) 8,885,000.

Lombok /'lɒmbɒk/ Indonesian island, E of Java, one of the Sunda Islands; chief town Mataram; area 4,730 sq km/1,826 sq mi; population (1973) 1,300,250. It comprises a fertile plain between N and S mountain ranges.

Lombroso /lɒmˈbrəʊsəʊ/ Cesare 1836–1909. Italian criminologist. He became a professor of mental diseases at Pavia in 1862. Subsequently he held chairs in forensic medicine, psychiatry, and criminal anthropology at Turin. His principal work is *L'uomo delinquente* 1889. He held the now discredited idea that there was a physically distinguishable criminal 'type'.

Lomé /'ləʊmeɪ/ capital and port of Togo; population 247,000. The *Lomé Convention* 1975 (renewed 1979, 1985) established economic cooperation between the EEC and African, Caribbean, and Pacific countries.

lomentum a type of ◊fruit, similar to a pod but constricted between the seeds. When ripe, it splits into one-seeded units, as seen, for example, in the fruit of sainfoin (*Onobrychis viciifolia*) and radish (*Raphanus raphanistrum*). It is a type of ◊schizocarp.

Lomond, Loch /'ləumənd/ largest freshwater Scottish lake, 37 km/23 mi long, area 70 sq km/25 sq mi, divided between Strathclyde and Central regions. It is overlooked by the mountain *Ben Lomond* 296.5 m/973 ft.

London /'lʌndən/ the capital of England, and the United Kingdom, on the river Thames
area 1,580 sq km/610 sq mi
population (1984) 6,756,000
It comprises:
City of London original nucleus of Greater London
area 274 ha/677 acres, known as the 'square mile'
population (resident) 5,300; daytime workers more than 500,000
features financial and commercial centre of the UK, with the Bank of England, the Royal Exchange, the Stock Exchange, the Baltic Exchange, Lloyd's, the head offices of the principal banks and insurance companies, the Bankers' Clearing House, and similar institutions; it also includes the Tower of London, built by William the Conqueror on a Roman site, which houses the crown jewels and the royal armouries; 15th-century Guildhall; Mansion House (residence of the lord mayor); the Monument (a column designed by Wren) marking the site in Pudding Lane where the Great Fire of 1666 began; ◊St Paul's Cathedral; Barbican arts and conference centre; Museum of London; Central Criminal Court (Old Bailey) and the Inner and Middle Temples; the headquarters of the Port of London Authority; and markets including Smithfield (meat) and Spitalfields (fruit and vegetables).
government by a corporation from the 12th century. Its structure and the electoral procedures for its common councillors and aldermen are medievally complex and it is headed by the lord mayor (who is, broadly speaking, nominated by the former and elected annually by the latter). After being sworn in at the Guildhall, he or she is presented the next day to the lord chief justice at the Royal Courts of Justice in Westminster, and the *Lord Mayor's Show* is a ceremonial procession there in Nov.
history Roman Londinium was established soon after the Roman invasion in 43 AD on a site probably not previously settled: this was the town burned by Boudicca in 61 AD; in the 2nd century London became a walled city, part of the wall surviving (for example at Cripplegate); timbers of the Roman London Bridge have also been found, remains of a Roman palace under Cannon Street station, and of a temple to Mithras. Chief city of England by the time of William the Conqueror, it gradually extended beyond the walls and linked with the originally separate City of Westminster. Proliferating suburbs steadily took in surrounding villages.
Greater London from 1965 comprises the City of London, which forms a self-governing enclave, and 32 boroughs: Barking and Dagenham, Barnet, Bexley, Brent, Bromley, Camden, Croydon, Ealing, Enfield, Greenwich, Hackney, Hammersmith and Fulham, Haringey, Harrow, Havering, Hillingdon, Hounslow, Islington, Kensington and Chelsea, Kingston upon Thames, Lambeth, Lewisham, Merton, Newham, Redbridge, Richmond upon Thames, Southwark, Sutton, Tower Hamlets, Waltham Forest, and Wandsworth. Certain powers were exercized over this whole area by the Greater London Council (GLC) until its abolition 1986.
architecture London contains specimens of all styles of English architecture since the 11th century. Examples include Norman: the White Tower, Tower of London; St Bartholomew's, Smithfield; the Temple Church. Gothic: Westminster Abbey; Westminster Hall; Lambeth Palace; Southwark Cathedral. Tudor: St James's Palace; Staple Inn, Holborn. 17th century: Banqueting Hall, Whitehall (Inigo Jones); St Paul's, Kensington Palace, and many City churches (Wren). 18th century: Somerset House (Chambers); St Martin-in-the-Fields; Buckingham Palace. 19th century: British Museum (Neoclassical); Houses of Parliament; Law Courts (Gothic); Westminster Cathedral (Byzantine). 20th century: Lloyd's of London.
commerce and industry important from Saxon times, the Port of London once dominated the Thames from Tower Bridge to Tilbury; its activity is now centred outside the metropolitan area, and downstream Tilbury has been extended to cope with container traffic. The prime economic importance of London is as a financial centre. There are various industries, mainly on the outskirts. There are also recording, broadcasting, television, and film studios; publishing companies, and the works and offices of the national press. Tourism is important.
education and entertainment among its museums are the British, Victoria and Albert, Natural History, and Science museums, the National and Tate galleries. London University is the largest in Britain, while the Inns of Court have been the training school for lawyers since the 13th century. London has been the main centre of English drama ever since its first theatre was built by Burbage in 1576.

London /'lʌndən/ city in S Ontario, Canada, on the river Thames, 160 km/100 mi SW of Toronto; population (1981) 283,500. The centre of a farming district, it has tanneries, breweries, and factories making hosiery, radio and electrical equipment, leather and shoes. It dates from 1826 and is the seat of the University of Western Ontario and of the Stratford Shakespeare festival.

London /'lʌndən/ Jack (John Griffith) 1876–1916. American novelist, born in San Francisco. He is best known for adventure stories, for example, *The Call of the Wild* 1903, *The Sea Wolf* 1904, and *White Fang* 1906, the story of a dog.

London County Council an administrative authority for London created 1888 by the Local Government Act; it incorporated parts of Kent, Surrey, and Middlesex in the metropolis. It was replaced by the Greater London Council 1964–86.

Londonderry /ˌlʌndən'deri/ or *Derry* county of N Ireland

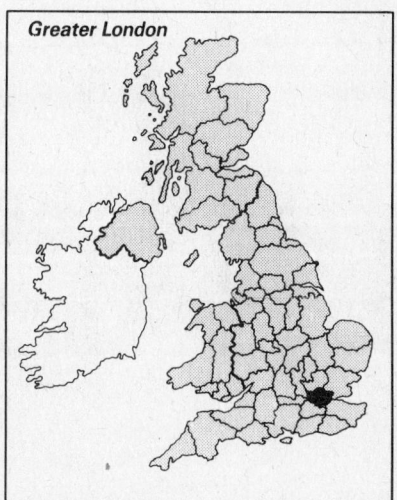
Greater London

area 2,082 sq km/804 sq mi
towns Derry (county town, formerly Londonderry), Coleraine
features rivers Foyle, Bann, and Roe; borders Lough Neagh
products mainly agricultural, but farming is hindered by the very heavy rainfall; flax, dairy products; food processing, textiles, light engineering
population (1971) 130,296
famous people Joyce Cary.

Long /lɒŋ/ Huey 1893–1935. US politician, nicknamed 'the Kingfish', governor of Alabama 1928–31, US senator 1930–35, legendary as a demagogue. He was popular with poor white voters for his programme of social and economic reform, which he called the 'Share the Wealth' programme; but his own extravagance, including the state capitol building at Baton Rouge built of bronze and marble, was widely criticized. He was assassinated.

Long Beach industrial city (oil refineries, aircraft), naval base, and pleasure resort in California, USA; population (1980) 361,334. Forms part of the ◊Los Angeles conurbation.

Longfellow /'lɒŋˌfeləu/ Henry Wadsworth 1807–1882. American poet, born in Portland, Maine. He was professor of modern languages at Harvard 1836–54. He is remembered for ballads ('Excelsior' and 'The Wreck of the Hesperus'), the narrative *Evangeline* 1847, and his metrically haunting *The Song of Hiawatha* 1855.

Longford /'lɒŋfəd/ county of Leinster province, Republic of Ireland
area 1,044 sq km/403 sq mi
county town Longford
features rivers Camlin and Inny; the Shannon marks the W boundary; several lakes
population (1981) 31,000.

Longford /'lɒŋfəd/ Elizabeth, Countess of Longford (born Harman) 1906– . English historical writer whose books include *Victoria RI* 1964. She is married to Lord ◊Longford; their eldest daughter is Lady Antonia ◊Fraser.

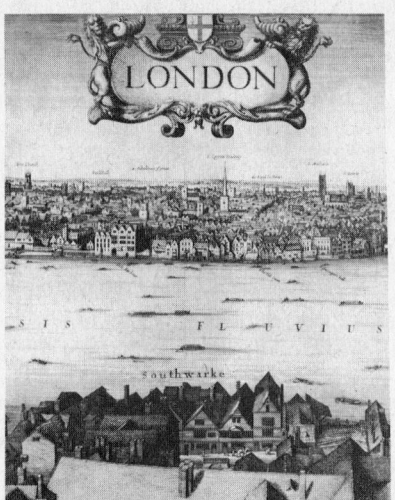

London Some of the docks in the East End of London, once the busiest in the world, have been sold to the Docklands Development Corporation, which has built new houses, factories and a railway.

An engraving of 17th-century London by Wenceslaus Hollar 1647.

in 1642, and the Presbyterian right were excluded in 1648, the remaining Rump ruled England until expelled by Cromwell in 1653. Reassembled 1659–60, the Long Parliament initiated the negotiations for the ◊Restoration.

Lonsdale /ˈlɒnzdeɪl/ Hugh Cecil Lowther, 5th Earl of Lonsdale 1857–1944. British sportsman. He was an expert huntsman, steeplechaser, boxer, and yachtsman, and as president of the National Sporting Club laid down the rules of boxing and presented the 'Lonsdale belts'.

loofah fruit of *Luffa cylindrica*, family Cucurbitaceae, of which the woody 'sponge skeleton' is used for washing.

loom a machine on which weaving is carried out. The first looms were in use at least 7,000 years ago, when wool from sheep was woven. Essentially the loom is a frame on which a set of lengthwise threads (warp) are strung. Then a second set of threads (weft) is inserted at right-angles over and under the warp. The weft threads are carried in a shuttle. In practice the warp threads are separated, up and down as appropriate, to create a gap, or shed, through

Longford /ˈlɒŋfəd/ Frank (Francis) Aungier Pakenham, 7th Earl of Longford 1905– . Anglo-Irish Labour politician. He was brought up in High Tory Protestant circles but is a leading Catholic layman; worked in the Conservative Party Economic Research Department 1930–32, yet became a prominent member of the Labour Party and held ministerial posts 1948–51 and 1964–68. 1965–66. He is a keen advocate of penal reform. He is married to Lady ◊Longford; their eldest daughter is Lady Antonia ◊Fraser.

Longinus /lɒnˈdʒaɪnəs/ Cassius 213–273. Greek philosopher. He taught in Athens for many years. Adviser to ◊Zenobia of Palmyra, he instigated her revolt against Rome, and was put to death when she was captured. He was formerly thought to be the author of *On the Sublime*.

Longinus /lɒnˈdʒaɪnəs/ Dionysius, lived 1st century AD. Greek critic, author of a treatise *On the Sublime* in literature which was influential

until the 18th century (for example, Dryden and Pope).

Long Island /ˈlɒŋ ˌaɪlənd/ island off the coast of Connecticut and New York, separated from the mainland by Long Island Sound. It includes two boroughs of New York City (Queens and Brooklyn), John F Kennedy airport, suburbs, and resorts; it also has Brookhaven National Laboratory for atomic research.

longitude see ◊latitude.

Long March, The the 10,000 km/6,000 mi trek undertaken by Mao Zedong and his troops from SE to NW China, under harassment from ◊Chiang Kai-shek, from 1934 to 1935. The *New Long March* is the plan to achieve world leadership for China in science and technology by the year 2000.

Long Parliament the period of English Parliament 1640–60, which carried through the English Civil War. After the Royalists withdrew

which the shuttle can be passed in a straight line. The warp threads are moved by means of a harness. The loom has another device, called a reed, which presses each new line of weave tight against the previous ones. All looms have similar features, but on the modern power loom weaving takes place automatically at great speed. Mechanization of weaving began in 1733 when John Kay invented the flying shuttle. A little over half a century later Edmund Cartwright introduced a steam-powered loom. Among the recent developments are shuttleless looms, which work at very high speed, passing the weft through the warp by means of 'rapiers', and jets of air or water.

Loos /ləʊs/ Adolf 1870–1933. Viennese architect. He rejected the ornamentation and curved lines of the Viennese Art Nouveau. His most important buildings are private houses on Lake Geneva 1904 and the Steiner House in

Vienna 1910. His main importance, however, is as a polemicist; his most famous and influential article was *Ornament and Crime*, published in 1908.

Loos /luːz/ Anita 1893–1981. American author of the humorous fictitious diary *Gentlemen Prefer Blondes* 1925.

loosestrife plant of the family Primulaceae such as the yellow loosestrife *Lysimachia vulgaris*, 1 m/3 ft high on river banks in Britain with spikes of yellow flowers; creeping jenny *Lysimachia nummularia*; also the striking purple loosestrife *Lythrum saclicaria* in the family Lythraceae.

Lope de Vega (Carpio) /'ləʊpeɪ də 'veɪgə/ Felix 1562–1635. Spanish poet and dramatist, one of the founders of modern Spanish drama. Born in Madrid, he served with the Armada in 1588, and in 1613 took orders. He wrote epics, pastorals, odes, sonnets, and novels, and over 1,500 plays, most of which are tragi-comedies. He set out his views on drama in *Arte nuevo de hacer comedias/The New Art of Writing Plays* c. 1609, while reaffirming the classical form. Possibly his best known play is *Fuenteovejuna* 1614, acclaimed in this century as the first proletarian drama.

López /'ləʊpes/ Carlos Antonio 1790–1862. Paraguayan dictator (in succession to his uncle José Francia) from 1840, who achieved some economic improvement, and was succeeded by his son Francisco ◊López.

López /'ləʊpes/ Francisco Solano 1827–1870. Paraguayan dictator in succession to his father Carlos ◊López. He involved the country in a war with Brazil, Uruguay and Argentina during which five-sixths of the population died.

Lop Nor /ˌlɒp 'nɔː/ series of shallow lakes (formerly Lop-Nor) with shifting boundaries in the Taklimakan Shamo (desert) in Xinjiang Uyghur, China. Marco Polo visited Lop-Nor, then a single lake of considerable extent, about 1273. The area is used for atomic tests.

loquat evergreen tree of the family Rosaceae, *Eriobotrya japonica*, native to China and Japan and known also as the Japan medlar. The golden pear-shaped fruit is of delicate sweet-sour taste.

Lorca /'lɔːkə/ Federico García 1899–1936. Spanish poet. Born in Granada, his *Romancero gitano/Gipsy Ballad-book* 1928 shows the influence of the Andalusian songs of the area. In 1929–30 Lorca visited New York, and his experiences are reflected in *Poeta en Nuevo York*. Returning to Spain, he founded a touring theatrical company and himself wrote plays such as *Bodas de sangre/Blood Wedding* 1933, and *La casa de Bernarda Alba/The House of Bernarda Alba* 1936. Possibly one of his finest poems is his *Lament* for the bullfighter Mejías. He was shot by the Falangists.

Lord in the UK, prefix used informally as alternative to the full title of a marquess, earl, or viscount; normally also in speaking of a baron, and as a courtesy title before the forename and surname of younger sons of dukes and marquesses. A bishop is formally addressed as the Lord Bishop of – .

Lord Advocate chief law officer of the Crown in Scotland.

Lord Howe Island dependency of New South Wales, Australia, 700 km/435 mi NE of Sydney; area 15 sq km/6 sq mi; population (1984) 300.

lord-lieutenant in the UK, the Sovereign's representative in a county, who recommends magistrates for appointment, and so on.

lord mayor in the UK, ◊mayor of a city.

Lord's headquarters of the Marylebone Cricket Club (MCC), regulating body of English cricket since 1788, and also the county ground of Middlesex. *Thomas Lord* (1757–1832) first opened a ground in Dorset Square in 1787, moving to the present site in St John's Wood in 1814.

Lords, House of see ◊parliament.

Lord's Supper another name for the ◊Eucharist.

Lorenz /'lɔːrənts/ Konrad 1903– . Austrian ethologist. Director of the Max Planck Institute for the Physiology of Behaviour in Bavaria 1961–73, he is known for his studies of animal behaviour, *King Solomon's Ring* 1952 and *On Aggression* 1966. In 1973 he shared a Nobel prize with N ◊Tinbergen and Karl von ◊Frisch, in recognition of their work in founding the science of ◊ethology.

Lorenz /'lɔːrənts/ Luwig Valentine 1829–1891. Danish mathematician and physicist who developed mathematical formulae to describe various phenomena, such as the relationship between refraction of light and the density of a pure transparent substance, and the relationship between a metal's electrical and thermal conductivity and temperature.

Loreto /lə'retəʊ/ town in central Italy, which allegedly contains the Virgin Mary's house, carried there by angels from Nazareth; hence Our Lady of Loreto is the patron saint of aviators.

Lorient /ˌlɔːri'ɒŋ/ commercial and naval port in NW France; population (1983) 70,000.

lorikeet type of small brightly-coloured parrot, found in SE Asia and Australasia.

loris small Asian primate. Lorises are arboreal and nocturnal. Arms and legs are a similar length, and the tail is a stump or absent. They climb without leaping, gripping branches tightly and moving on or hanging below them. The eyes are huge. The *slender loris Loris tardigradus* of S India and Sri Lanka is about 20 cm/8 in long. The tubbier *slow loris Nycticebus coucang* of SE Asia is 30 cm/1 ft. The angwantibo and potto are similar African forms.

Lorrain /lɒ'ræn/ Claude 1600–1682. French painter; see ◊Claude Lorrain.

Lorraine /lɒ'reɪn/ region of France; see ◊Alsace-Lorraine.

Lorraine, Cross of /lɒ'reɪn/ see under ◊Alsace-Lorraine.

lory type of Australasian, honey-eating ◊parrot which is brilliantly coloured.

Los Alamos /lɒs 'æləmɒs/ centre for atomic and space research from 1942, New Mexico, USA; population 12,000. In World War II the atom (nuclear fission) bomb was designed here, working on data from other research stations (see ◊Oppenheimer); and the ◊H-bomb developed.

Los Angeles /lɒs 'ændʒəliːz/ city and port (commercial, fishing, and naval) in S California, USA; population of urban area (1980) 9,447,926. It has aerospace, electronic, film, chemical, clothing, printing, and food-processing industries. It comprises ◊Long Beach, Redondo Beach, Venice, Santa Monica, Burbank, Hollywood (centre of the US film industry from 1911), Beverly Hills (with homes of film stars), Glendale, Pasadena, Pomona, and a number of other places. Features include the Hollywood Bowl concert arena; observatories at Mt Wilson and Mt Palomar; Disneyland; the Huntingdon Art Gallery and Library; and the Getty Museum, the richest in the world.

Los Angeles /lɒs 'æŋheles/ Victoria de 1923– . Spanish soprano, interpreter especially of Spanish songs, and the roles of Manon and Madame Butterfly in Puccini's operas.

Losey /'ləʊsi/ Joseph 1909–1984. American film director. Black-listed as a former Communist in the ◊McCarthy era, he settled in England, where his films included *The Servant* 1963 and *The Go-Between* 1971.

Losey Early in his career, American film director Joseph Losey was influenced by Brecht and worked with him. Black-listed as a former Communist in the McCarthy era, he moved to England.

Lot /ləʊ/ river in France; see under ◊Gironde.

Lot /lɒt/ in the Bible, Abraham's nephew, who escaped the destruction of Sodom, although his wife was turned into a pillar of salt.

Lothair /ləʊ'θeə/ 825–869. Son of Lothair I, King of Lotharingia (so-called after him, and later corrupted to ◊Lorraine) from 855, when he inherited from his father a district west of the Rhine, between the Jura mountains and the North Sea.

Lothair /ləʊ'θeə/ two Holy Roman Emperors:

Lothair I /ləʊ'θeə/ 795–855. Holy Roman Emperor from 817 in association with his father ◊Louis I. On the latter's death the Empire was divided between Lothair and his brothers; Lothair took North Italy and the valleys of the Rhône and Rhine.

Lothair II /ləʊˈθeə/ c. 1070–1137. Holy Roman Emperor 1133–37 and German king 1125–37. His election as Emperor, opposed by the ◊Hohenstaufens, was the start of the Guelph/◊Ghibelline feud.

Lothian /ˈləʊðiən/ region of Scotland
area 1,753 sq km/677 sq mi
towns administrative headquarters Edinburgh; Livingston
features Lammermuir, Moorfoot, and Pentland Hills; Bass Rock in the Firth of Forth, noted for sea birds
products bacon, vegetables, coal, whisky, engineering, electronics
population (1984) 744,500
famous people birthplace of R L Stevenson in Howard Place, Edinburgh.

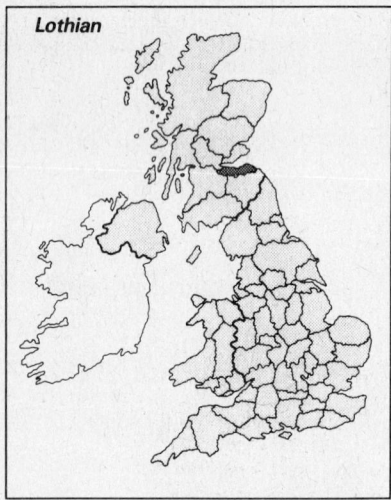

Lothian

lottery game of chance in which tickets sold may win a prize. In the UK lotteries are subject to tight restriction. The largest lottery is in effect the government-issued *Premium Savings Bonds* (from 1956), repayable at par without interest, but eligible for monthly prize-winning draws. In the USA state lotteries may bring a winner many millions, for example, in Illinois in 1984 one ticket brought a prize of $40 million.

Lotto /ˈlɒtəʊ/ Lorenzo 1480–1556. Italian painter, born in Venice, who worked there and in several other Italian cities. His intensely wrought works, in highly contrasting colours, are a very personal interpretation of the high Renaissance tradition of ◊Titian and ◊Bellini. His paintings include several fine portraits, for example *Andrea Odoni* (Hampton Court, England).

lotus genus of plants in the family Leguminosae; the bird's foot trefoil is *Lotus corniculatus*; also the shrub *Zizyphus lotus*, known to the ancient Greeks who used its fruit to make a type of bread and also a wine supposed to induce happy oblivion – hence lotus-eaters; and the water-lilies *Nymphaea lotus*, frequent in Egyptian art, and *Nelumbium nuciferum*, the sacred lotus of the Hindus which (unlike the Egyptian) does float but stands erect above the water.

loudspeaker an electromechanical device that converts electrical signals into sound waves, used in all sound-reproducing systems – radio, record-player, tape recorder, television, and so on. The common type is the moving-coil speaker. Electrical signals from, say, a radio are fed to a coil of fine wire wound around the top of a cone. The coil is surrounded by a magnet. When signals pass through it, the coil becomes an electromagnet, and so it moves, causing the cone to vibrate, which thus sets up sound waves. See ◊hi-fi, compare ◊microphone.

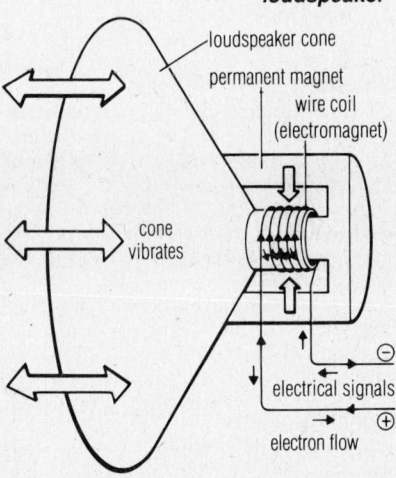

loudspeaker

loudspeaker cone
permanent magnet
wire coil (electromagnet)
cone vibrates
electrical signals
electron flow

Loughborough /ˈlʌfbərə/ industrial town (engineering, bell-founding, electrical goods, knitwear), with a university of technology from 1966, in Leicestershire, England; population (1981) 47,647.

Louis, Prince of Battenberg /ˈluːi/ 1854–1921. British admiral. A member of the Battenberg family, he took British nationality 1917. He was forced to resign as First Sea Lord (1912–14) because of anti-German sentiment. In 1917 he changed his name to ◊Mountbatten, and was made 1st Marquess of Milford Haven in 1917. He was admiral of the fleet from 1921.

Louis /ˈluːs/ Joe. Professional name of Joe Louis Barrow 1914–1981. American boxer, nicknamed 'the brown bomber'. Born in Alabama, he was world heavyweight champion 1937–49, the longest reigning heavyweight champion.

Louis /ˈluːi/ name of 18 kings of France, including:

Louis I /ˈluːi/ 788–840. Holy Roman Emperor, called 'the Pious', who succeeded his father ◊Charlemagne in 814, and counts as Louis I of France.

Louis V /ˈluːi/ 967–987. King of France from 986, last of the ◊Carolingians.

Louis VII /ˈluːi/ c. 1111–1180. King of France from 1137, who led the Second ◊Crusade.

Louis VIII /ˈluːi/ 1187–1226. King of France from 1223, who was invited to become King of England in place of ◊John by the English barons, and unsuccessfully invaded England 1215–17.

Louis IX /ˈluːi/ St 1214–1270. King of France from 1226, leader of the Seventh and Eighth ◊Crusades. He was defeated in the former by the Saracens, spending four years in captivity, and died at Tunis as he set out on the latter. Feast day, 25 Aug.

Louis XI /ˈluːi/ 1423–1483. King of France from 1461. He broke the power of the nobility (headed by ◊Charles the Bold) by intrigue and military power.

Louis XII /ˈluːi/ 1462–1515. Duke of Orléans until he succeeded his cousin ◊Charles VIII to the French throne in 1499. His reign was devoted to Italian wars.

Louis XIII /ˈluːi/ 1601–1643. King of France from 1610 (in succession to his father Henry IV), assuming royal power in 1617; he was under the political control of ◊Richelieu 1614–42.

Louis XIV /ˈluːi/ the 'Sun King' 1638–1715. King of France from 1643, though until 1661 France was ruled by ◊Mazarin. The policy of Louis as ruler was summed up in his saying *L'État c'est moi* ('I am the State'). Greatest of his ministers was ◊Colbert, whose work was undone by Louis's military adventures. Louis attempted 1667–68 to annex the Spanish Netherlands, but was frustrated by an alliance of Holland, England, and Sweden. Having detached England from the alliance, he invaded Holland in 1672, but the Dutch stood firm (led by ◊William of Orange) and despite the European alliance formed against France, achieved territorial gains at the Peace of Nijmegen in 1678. When war was renewed 1688–97 between Louis and the Grand Alliance (including England), formed by William of Orange, the French were everywhere victorious on land, but the French fleet was almost destroyed at La ◊Hogue in 1692. The acceptance by Louis of the Spanish throne in 1700 (for his grandson) precipitated the War of the ◊Spanish Succession, however, and the Peace of ◊Utrecht (1713) ended French supremacy in Europe. In 1660 Louis married the Infanta Maria Theresa of Spain, but he was greatly influenced by his mistresses, including Louise de ◊La Vallière, Mme de ◊Montespan, and Mme de ◊Maintenon.

Louis XV /ˈluːi/ 1710–1774. King of France, great-grandson of Louis XIV; king from 1715, with the Duke of Orléans as regent until 1723. Indolent and frivolous, Louis left government in the hands of his ministers, the Duke of Bourbon and Cardinal Fleury. On the latter's death in 1743, he attempted to rule alone, but became entirely dominated by his mistresses, Mme de ◊Pompadour and Mme du ◊Barry. His foreign policy led to Canada and India being lost to France.

Louis XVI /ˈluːi/ 1754–1793. Grandson of Louis XV; king of France from 1774. He was dominated by his queen, ◊Marie Antoinette, and the finances fell into such confusion that in 1789 the States General had to be summoned, and revolution began. Louis lost his personal popularity in Jun 1791, when he attempted to flee the country (the Flight to Varennes) and in Aug 1792 the Parisians stormed the ◊Tuileries and

Louis XIV The flamboyant 'Sun King' Louis XIV of France was renowned for his chaotic military adventures and extra-marital liaisons. This marble bust from the Palace of Versailles is by Italian sculptor Lorenzo Bernini.

took the royal family prisoner. Deposed in Sept, he was tried in Dec, sentenced for treason in Jan 1793, and guillotined.

Louis XVII /'luːi/ 1785–1795. Nominal king of France, the son of Louis XVI. He was imprisoned with his parents in 1792, and probably died there.

Louis XVIII /'luːi/ 1755–1824. Younger brother of Louis XVI; he assumed the title of king of France in 1795, having fled into exile in 1791, but became king only on the fall of Napoleon in Apr 1814. Expelled during Napoleon's brief return (the '100 Days') in 1815 he returned after ◊Waterloo, pursuing a policy of calculated liberalism until ultra-royalist pressure became dominant after 1820.

Louisiana /luːˌiːziˈænə/ southern state of the USA; Pelican State
area 125,675 sq km/48,523 sq mi
capital Baton Rouge
towns New Orleans, Shreveport
features Mississippi delta
products rice, cotton, sugar, maize; oil, natural gas, sulphur, salt; processed foods; petroleum products, lumber, paper
population (1980) 4,206,000, which includes the Cajuns, descendants of 18th-century religious exiles from Canada, who speak a French dialect
famous people Louis Armstrong, Pierre Beauregard, Huey Long
history explored by La Salle, it was named after Louis XIV and claimed for France in 1682; was Spanish 1762–1800, and passed to the USA under the ◊Louisiana Purchase in 1803.

Louisiana Purchase purchase in 1803 by the USA from France of an area covering about 2,144,000 sq km/828,000 sq mi, including the present-day states of Louisiana, Missouri, Arkansas, Iowa, Nebraska, N and S Dakota, and

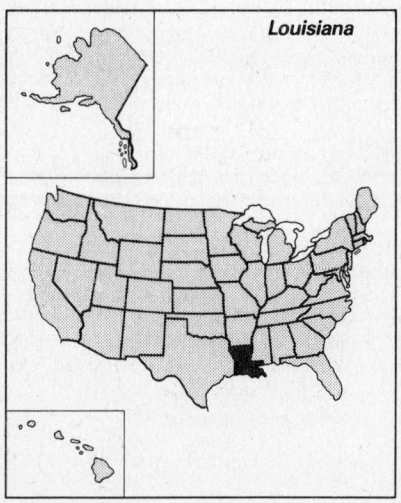

Louisiana

Oklahoma. The sale, which doubled the size of the USA, marked the end of Napoleon's plans for a colonial empire, and ensured free navigation on the Mississippi for the USA. The price was about US$27 million.

Louis Philippe /'luːi fɪ'liːp/ 1773–1850. King of France 1830–48. Son of the Duke of Orleans (he was known, like him, as *Philippe egalité*, from his early support of the 1792 Revolution). He fled into exile 1793–1814, but became king after the 1830 Revolution with the backing of the rich bourgeoisie. Corruption discredited his regime, and after his overthrow, he escaped to England and died there.

Louisville /'luːivɪl/ industrial city (electrical goods, agricultural machinery, motor vehicles, tobacco, baseball bats), and river port on the Ohio, Kentucky, USA; population (1980) 655,000. It is noted for its Kentucky Fair and Exposition Center, and the Kentucky Derby. See also ◊horseracing.

Lourdes /luəd/ town in SW France with a shrine to St ◊Bernadette which has a reputation for miraculous cures.

Lourenço Marques /lə'rensəʊ 'maːks/ former name of ◊Maputo, capital of Mozambique.

louse parasitic insect, order Anoplura, with a flat, segmented body without wings and a sucking tube attached to the head, with which it sucks the blood of mammals on which it lives. Some occur on man including the hair-louse *Pediculus capitis*, and the body-louse *Pediculus corporis*, a typhus carrier. Most mammals have their own varieties of lice. Biting-lice belong to a different order of insects, Mallophaga, and feed on skin, feathers or hair.

Louth /lauð/ smallest county (county town Dundalk) of the Republic of Ireland, province of ◊Leinster.

Louvain /luːˈvæŋ/ (Flemish *Leuven*) industrial town in central Belgium; population (1985) 85,000.

Louvre /'luːvrə/ former palace of the French kings, in Paris, converted by Napoleon to an art gallery in 1793. It contains the *Venus de Milo*, *Mona Lisa* by ◊Leonardo, and (in the Jeu de

Paumes in the gardens of the Tuileries) an Impressionist collection.

Lovat /'lʌvət/ Simon Fraser, 12th Baron Lovat c. 1667–1747. Scottish ◊Jacobite. Throughout a political career lasting 50 years he constantly intrigued with both Jacobites and Whigs, and was beheaded for supporting the 1745 rebellion.

love-bird a small bird of the ◊parrot family.

Lovecraft /'lʌvkrɑːft/ H(oward) P(hillips) 1890–1937. American writer of horror fiction, whose stories of hostile, supernatural forces, known collectively as the Cthulhu Mythos, have lent names and material to many other writers in the genre. Much of his work on this theme was collected in *The Outsider and Others* 1939.

love-in-a-mist perennial plant of S Europe *Nigella damascena*, family Ranunculaceae, with specialized fern-like leaves, and delicate blue or white flowers.

Lovelace /'lʌvleɪs/ Richard 1618–1658. English poet. Imprisoned in 1642 for petitioning for the restoration of royal rule, he wrote 'To Althea from Prison', and in a second spell of jail in 1648 revised his collection *Lucasta* 1649.

Lovell /'lʌvəl/ Bernard 1913– . British astronomer. During World War II he worked at the Telecommunications Research establishment (1939–45), and in 1951 became professor of radio astronomy at the University of Manchester and director of ◊Jodrell Bank Experimental Station (now Nuffield radio astronomy laboratories). His books include *Radio Astronomy* 1951 and *The Exploration of Outer Space* 1961. He was knighted in 1961.

Low /ləʊ/ David 1891–1963. New Zealand-born cartoonist, radical creator (in newspapers such as the *Evening Standard*, and the *Guardian*) of Colonel Blimp, the TUC carthorse, and others.

Low Countries the region of Europe which consists of ◊Belgium and the ◊Netherlands, and usually includes ◊Luxembourg.

Lowell /'ləʊəl/ industrial city (electronics) in Massachusetts, USA; population (1980) 92,500. Once a textile centre, it was designated a national park in 1978 as a birthplace of the US industrial revolution.

Lowell /'ləʊəl/ Amy (Lawrence) 1874–1925. American poet, who succeeded ◊Pound as leader of the ◊Imagists. Her works, in free verse, include *Sword-Blades and Poppy Seed* 1916.

Lowell /'ləʊəl/ J(ames) R(ussell) 1819–1891. American poet (*The Vision of Sir Launfal* 1848, and satirical, dialect poems *The Biglow Papers* 1848), critic and diplomat (ambassador in London 1880–85). He encouraged the growth of an American literary tradition.

Lowell /'ləʊəl/ Percival 1855–1916. American astronomer. Born in Boston, Massachusetts, in 1894 he founded the Lowell Observatory at Flagstaff, Arizona, where he reported seeing 'canals' on the surface of ◊Mars (now known to be an optical illusion). He started the search for a planet beyond Neptune, which led to the discovery of ◊Pluto.

Lowell /'ləʊəl/ Robert (Traill Spence) 1917–1977. American poet (*Lord Weary's Castle* 1946, *For the Union Dead* 1964). A

Roman Catholic convert from 1940, he was imprisoned in 1943 as a conscientious objector.

Lower California English name for ◊Baja California, Mexico.

Lower Saxony /'sæksəni/ (German Niedersachsen)*Land* of N West Germany
area 47,475 sq km/18,300 sq mi
capital Hanover
towns Brunswick, Göttingen, Oldenburg
features formed 1946 from Hanover, Oldenburg, Brunswick, and Schaumburg-Lippe; Lüneburg Heath; Harz mountains
products cereals; cars, machinery, electrical engineering
population (1984) 7,200,000
religion 75% Protestant, 20% Roman Catholic.

Lowestoft /'ləustɒft/ most easterly port in Britain, in Suffolk; population (1981) 55,000. The composer Benjamin Britten was born here.

Lowry /'lauri/ L(aurence) S(tephen) 1887–1976. British artist. Born in Manchester, he painted the industrial landscape of the 1930s, peopled with spindly human figures, for example, *The Pond* 1950.

a derivative of ◊ergot. Colourless, odourless, and easily synthesized, it is non-addictive, but its effects are unpredictable.

LSI (large-scale integration) the technology by which whole electrical circuits can be etched into a piece of semiconducting material just a few millimetres square. By the late 1960s a complete computer processor could be integrated on a single ◊silicon chip, and in 1971 the electronics company Intel produced the first commercially available ◊microprocessor (as such chips are called). LSI is the technology on which most of today's electronics industry is based. See also ◊VLSI.

Lualaba /ˌluːə'laːbə/ another name for the river ◊Zaïre in Africa, as it flows N through Zaïre from near the Zambia border.

Luanda /luːˈændə/ capital and industrial port (cotton, sugar, tobacco, timber, paper) of Angola, founded in 1575; population (1982) 700,000.

Luang Prabang /luːˈæŋ prɑːˈbæŋ/ Buddhist religious centre in Laos, on the Mekong at the head of river navigation; population (1984)

population (1984) 213,400. It has five Gothic churches and a cathedral from 1173. Once head of the powerful ◊Hanseatic League, it later lost much of its trade to Hamburg and Bremen, but improved canal and port facilities helped it to retain its position as a centre of Baltic trade. Lübeck was a free state of both the Empire and the Weimar Republic.

Lubitsch /'luːbɪtʃ/ Ernst 1892–1947. German-American film director, known for his stylish comedies, for example *Ninotchka* 1939, starring Greta ◊Garbo.

Lublin /'lublɪn/ industrial city (textiles, engineering, aircraft, electrical goods) in Poland, on the Bystrzyca river, 150 km/95 mi SE of Warsaw; population (1983) 320,000. A trading centre from the 10th century, it has an ancient citadel, 16th-century cathedral, and a university (1918). A council of workers and peasants proclaimed Poland's independence at Lublin in 1918; and a Russian-sponsored committee of national liberation, which proclaimed itself the provincial government of Poland at Lublin on 31 Dec 1944, was recognized by Russia five days later.

lubricant a substance insinuated between moving surfaces to reduce friction. A solid lubricant is graphite (plumbago), either flaked or emulsified (colloidal) in water (aquadag) or oil (oildag). Semi-solid and liquid lubricants are more important, consisting of animal, vegetable, and mineral oils. The lubricants most used are carbon-based (organic) lubricants, commonly called grease and oil, recovered from petroleum distillation.

Extensive research has been carried out on chemical additives to lubricants, which can reduce corrosive wear, prevent the accumulation of 'cold sludge' (often the result of stop-start driving in city traffic jams), keep pace with the higher working temperatures of aviation gas turbines, or provide radiation-resistant greases for nuclear power plants. Silicon-based spray-on lubricants are also used domestically; they tend to attract dust and dirt less than carbon-based ones.

Lubumbashi /ˌluːbum'bæʃɪ/ (formerly Elisabethville) chief commercial centre of the Shaba mining region, Zaïre; population (1982) 451,332.

Lucan /'luːkən/ Marcus Annaeus Lucanus 39–65 AD. Latin poet, born in Cordova, a nephew of ◊Seneca and favourite of ◊Nero until the emperor became jealous of his verse. He then joined a republican conspiracy and committed suicide on its failure. His epic *Pharsalia* deals with the civil wars of ◊Caesar and ◊Pompey.

Lucas /'luːkəs/ George 1944– . American director and producer, whose imagination was fired by the comic books in his father's shop. He is best known for his collaboration with Steven Spielberg on *Star Wars* 1977, *The Empire Strikes Back* 1980, and *Return of the Jedi* 1983.

Lucas /'luːkəs/ Robert 1937– . US economist, leader of the Chicago University school of 'new classical' macroeconomics which contends that wage and price adjustment is almost instantaneous and that the level of unemployment at any time must be the natural

Lowry *Old Property* by the English artist L S Lowry. He produced numerous pictures of industrial Lancashire of the 1930s and 1940s.

Loyalists the one-third of the American population remaining loyal to Britain in the American War of Independence. Many went to Canada after 1783.

Loyalists ◊Ulster protestants who oppose any kind of united Irish state.

Loyola /lɔɪˈəʊlə/ see ◊Ignatius Loyola.

Lozère /ləʊˈzɛə/ section of the Cévennes Mountains, S France. It rises in Finiels to 1,702 m/5,584 ft, and gives its name to a *département*.

LPG liquified petroleum gas.

LSD hallucinogen (*l*ysergic acid *d*iethylamide), a powerful mind-changing drug,

44,244. It was the capital of the kingdom of Luang Prabang, incorporated in Laos in 1946, and the royal capital of Laos 1946–75.

Lubbers /'lʌbəz/ Rudolph Frans Marie 1939– . Netherlands politician, prime minister from 1982.

Lubbers initially joined the family engineering business, Lubbers Hollandia. He became minister for economic affairs in 1973 and prime minister in 1982.

Lübeck /'luːbek/ seaport of Schleswig-Holstein, West Germany, on the Baltic Sea, 60 km/37 mi NE of Hamburg, founded in 1143;

rate (it cannot be reduced by government action except in the short term and at the cost of increasing inflation).

Lucas van Leyden /'luːkəs væn 'laɪdn/ c. 1494–1533. Dutch artist. Born at Leiden, he executed his first engravings when a boy, and was later influenced by Dürer, whom he met at Antwerp. He was himself an influence on ◊Rembrandt. His principal paintings include *The Chess Players* (Berlin) and *Virgin and Child* (Munich).

Lucca /'lʊkə/ city in NW Italy, an independent republic from 1160 until its absorption into Tuscany in 1847; population (1981) 91,246. The composer Puccini was born here.

Luce /luːs/ Clare Boothe. Married name of American writer Clare ◊Boothe.

Luce /luːs/ Henry Robinson 1898–1967. American publisher, founder of the magazine *Time* 1923, and of the pictorial weekly *Life* in 1936. He married the writer Clare ◊Boothe.

Lucerne /luːˈsɜːn/ (German *Luzern*) capital and tourist centre of Lucerne canton, Switzerland, on the Reuss where it flows out of Lake Lucerne; population (1984) 158,000. Grown up around the Benedictine monastery, established about 750, it owes its prosperity to its position on the St Gotthard road and railway. There is a 17th-century cathedral.

Lucerne, Lake /luːˈsɜːn/ (German *Luzern*) scenic lake in central Switzerland; area 114 sq km/44 sq mi.

lucerne /luːˈsɜːn/ another name for the plant ◊alfalfa.

Lucian /'luːsiən/ c. 125–c. 190. Greek writer. Born at Samosata in Syria, for a time he was an advocate at Antioch, but later travelled before settling in Athens c. 165. He died in Egypt, where he occupied an official post. Lucian is chiefly remembered for his satirical dialogues, in which he pours scorn on all religions.

Lucknow /'lʌknaʊ/ capital and industrial city (engineering, chemicals, textiles, many handicrafts) of the province of Uttar Pradesh, India; university (1921); population (1981) 1,007,604. During the Indian Mutiny, it was besieged (see Henry ◊Lawrence) 2 Jul–16 Nov 1857, when it was relieved by Colin Campbell (see ◊Clyde).

Lucretia /luːˈkriːʃiə/ (died c. 509 BC) a Roman woman, the wife of Collatinus, said to have committed suicide after being raped by Sextus, son of ◊Tarquinius Superbus. According to tradition, this incident led to the dethronement of Tarquinius and the establishment of the Roman republic in 509 BC.

Lucretius /luːˈkriːʃiəs/ (Titus Lucretius Carus) c. 99–55 BC. Roman poet and ◊Epicurean philosopher, whose *De Rerum Natura/On the Nature of Things* envisaged the whole universe as a combination of atoms, and had some concept of evolutionary theory: animals were complex but initially quite fortuitous clusters of atoms, only certain combinations surviving to reproduce.

Lucullus /luːˈkʌləs/ Lucius Licinius 110–56 BC. Roman general. As commander against ◊Mithridates of Pontus 74–66 he showed himself

one of Rome's ablest generals and administrators, until superseded by Pompey. He then retired from politics. Enormous wealth enabled him to indulge in well-bred luxury, and Lucullan feasts were famous.

Lüda /ˌluːˈdɑː/ (formerly Hüta) industrial port (engineering, chemicals, textiles, oil refining, shipbuilding, food processing) in Liaoning, China, on Liaodong Peninsula, facing the Yellow Sea; population 4,200,000. It comprises the naval base of Lüshun (known under 19th-century Russian occupation as Port Arthur) and the commercial port of Dalien (formerly Talien/Dairen). Both were leased to Russia (who needed an ice-free naval base) in 1898, but were ceded to Japan after the ◊Russo-Japanese War; Lüshun was under Japanese siege Jun 1904–Jan 1905. After World War II Lüshun was occupied by Russian airborne troops (returned to China in 1955) and Russia was granted shared facilities at Dalien (ended on the deterioration of Sino-Russian relations in 1955).

Luddite name given to a person taking part in the machine-wrecking riots in England of 1811–16. The main organizer of the Luddites, possibly an imaginary person, was referred to as General Ludd. The movement, which began in Nottinghamshire and spread to Lancashire, Cheshire, and Yorkshire, was primarily a revolt against the unemployment caused by the introduction of machines in the ◊Industrial Revolution. Many Luddites were hanged or transported.

Ludendorff /'luːdndɔːf/ Erich von 1865–1937. German general, Chief of Staff to ◊Hindenburg in World War I, and responsible for the eastern front victory at ◊Tannenberg in 1914. After Hindenburg's appointment as Chief of General Staff and that of himself as Quartermaster-General in 1916, he was also politically influential (see ◊Bethmann-Hollweg). Later he took part in the Nazi rising at Munich 1923, and sat in the Reichstag as a Nazi.

Ludlow /'lʌdləʊ/ market town in Shropshire, England, on the Teme, 42 km/26 mi S of Shrewsbury; at Ludlow Castle Milton's masque *Comus* was presented in 1634. Population (1983) 8,130.

Ludwig /'lʊdvɪg/ three kings of Bavaria:

Ludwig I /'lʊdvɪg/ 1786–1868. Succeeded his father Maximilian Joseph I as king of Bavaria in 1825. He made Munich an international cultural centre, but his association with the dancer Lola ◊Montez led to his abdication in 1848.

Ludwig II /'lʊdvɪg/ 1845–1886. Succeeded his father Maximilian II as king of Bavaria in 1864. He supported Austria during the Austro-Prussian War of 1866, but brought Bavaria into the Franco-Prussian War as Prussia's ally, and in 1871 offered the German crown to the king of Prussia. He was ◊Wagner's patron, and built the Bayreuth theatre for him. Declared insane in 1886, he drowned himself soon after.

Ludwig III /'lʊdvɪg/ 1845–1921. King of Bavaria from 1913; abdicated in 1918.

Ludwigshafen /'luːdvɪgz,hɑːfən/ industrial city (chemicals, dyes, fertilizers, plastics, textiles) and Rhine river port, Rhineland

Palatinate, West Germany; population (1984) 156,000.

Luftwaffe German air force in World War I and also, as reorganized by ◊Goering in 1933, in World War II, when it also covered anti-aircraft defence and launching of the ◊V1 and ◊V2.

Lugano /luːˈgɑːnəʊ/ town on Lake Lugano, Switzerland; population (1978) 28,600.

Lugano, Lake /luːˈgɑːnəʊ/ lake partly in Italy, between lakes Maggiore and Como, and partly in Switzerland; area 49 sq km/19 sq mi.

Lugansk /luːˈgænsk/ former name of ◊Voroshilovgrad, Ukrainian Republic, USSR.

Lugard /luːˈgɑːd/ Frederick John Dealtry, 1st Baron Lugard 1858–1945. British colonial administrator. He served in the army 1878–89 and then entered the service of the British East Africa Company, for whom he took possession of Uganda in 1890. He later became high commissioner for N Nigeria (1900–07); governor of Hong Kong (1907–12); and governor-general of Nigeria (1914–19). He received a barony in 1928. His *Dual Mandate* 1922 was an influential plea for development through the existing African system of chieftainship, rather than western democracy.

lugworm genus *Arenicola* of marine worms (also known as lobworms) common between tide-marks where their whereabouts are known by their castings. They are used by anglers as bait, but are useful – as are earthworms on land – for their cleansing and powdering of the sand.

Lu Hsün /'luː 'ʃuːn/ former name of Chinese writer ◊Lu Xun.

Luik /laɪk/ Flemish name of ◊Liège, town in Belgium.

Lukács /'luːkɑːtʃ/ Georg 1885–1971. Hungarian philosopher, generally considered to be the founder of the tradition of western Marxism, a philosophical current opposed to the Marxism of the official communist movement. In his book *History and Class Consciousness* 1923 he emphasized the Hegelian aspects of Marxism, arguing that the working class was both subject and object of history, and could therefore grasp society as a 'totality'. However, Lukács himself repudiated the book, and spent much of the rest of his life as an orthodox communist. He also made major contributions to Marxist aesthetics and literary theory.

Luke, St /luːk/ traditionally the compiler of the third Gospel and of the Acts of the Apostles in the New Testament. He appears to have been a physician and to have accompanied Paul after the ascension of Christ. Of his life little is known, although it is surmised that he was a non-Jewish native of Antioch and that he died in Bithynia at the age of 74.

Luleå /'luːliɔː/ port (exporting iron ore, and timber in ice-free months) in N Sweden, on the Gulf of Bothnia at the mouth of the river Luleå; population (1984) 67,000.

Lully /luːˈliː/ Jean-Baptiste 1632–1687. Adopted name of Giovanni Battista Lulli. Italian-born French composer, a French citizen from 1661. Court composer to Louis XIV, he composed music for Molière's plays, established French opera, for example *Alceste* 1674, and

Armide et Renaud 1686, and ballet (he was himself a dancer).

lumbago pain in the lower region of the back, usually due to muscle strain or spasm after unaccustomed exertion. Other causes include 'slipped disc' (displacement of one of the spinal vertebrae). Usually it arises suddenly, and treatment includes rest, application of heat, and skilled manipulation. If it becomes chronic, surgery may be needed.

Lumbini /lum'biːni/ birthplace of ◊Buddha in the foothills of the Himalayas near the Nepalese-Indian frontier. A Sacred Garden and shrine was established 1970 by the Nepalese government.

lumen ◊SI unit of luminous flux (lm). Defined as the flux emitted by a uniform point source of 1 candela in a solid angle of 1 steradian (the unit of solid angle). Equivalent to 0.001471 watts.

Lumière /ˌluːmiˈeə/ Auguste Marie (1862–1954) and Louis Jean (1864–1948). French brothers who pioneered cinematography. In 1895 they patented their cinematograph, a combined camera and projector which operated at 16 frames per second. They opened the world's first cinema in Paris to show their films.

luminescence emission of light from a body when its atoms are excited by means other than raising its temperature.

luminous paint a preparation containing a mixture of pigment, oil, and a phosphorescent sulphide, usually calcium or barium. After exposure to light it appears luminous in the dark. The luminous paint used on watch faces is slightly radioactive and does not require exposure to light.

Lumumba /luˈmumbə/ Patrice 1926–1961. Congolese statesman. Imprisoned by the Belgians, but released in time to attend the conference giving the Congo (now Zaïre) independence, he led the National Congolese Movement to victory in the subsequent general election and became prime minister in 1960. He was deposed in a coup d'état, and murdered by Congolese rivals while in custody in Katanga.

Lund /lund/ city in Sweden, 16 km/10 mi NE of Malmö; university 1666; population (1984) 81,000. It has an 11th-century Romanesque cathedral. The treaty of Lund was signed in 1676 after Carl XI had defeated the Danes.

Lundy /ˈlʌndi/ rocky island at the entrance to the Bristol Channel, 19 km/12 mi NW of Hartland Point, Devon, England; area 419 ha/1,047 acres; population (1975) 40. Formerly used by pirates and privateers for a lair, it is now a National Trust bird sanctuary and the first British marine reserve (1987).

Lüneburg /ˈluːnəbɜːg/ industrial town (chemicals, paper) in Lower Saxony, West Germany; population (1985) 61,000.

Lüneburg Heath site in Lower Saxony, West Germany, where more than a million German soldiers surrendered to Montgomery on 4 May 1945.

lung a large cavity of the body, used for gas exchange. A lung is found in some slugs and snails, particularly those that live on land. Some fish (lungfish) and most tetrapod vertebrates have a pair of lungs, which occupy the ◊thorax,

the upper part of the trunk. In mammals they fit exactly into this conical space, but do not meet in the middle, the ◊heart being between them. Their function is to remove carbon dioxide dissolved in the blood and supply oxygen which is carried by ◊haemoglobin in red blood cells. The blood is brought into contact with the air in the ◊air sacs or alveoli at the ends of the smallest divisions of the air tubes/ bronchi. The lung tissue, consisting of multitudes of air sacs and blood vessels, is very light and spongy. Air is drawn into the lungs through the ◊trachea and bronchi by the expansion of the ◊ribs and the contraction of the diaphragm. The expansion and contraction is partly controlled by the will, and partly involuntary. The principal diseases of the lungs are tuberculosis, pneumonia, bronchitis, and cancer.

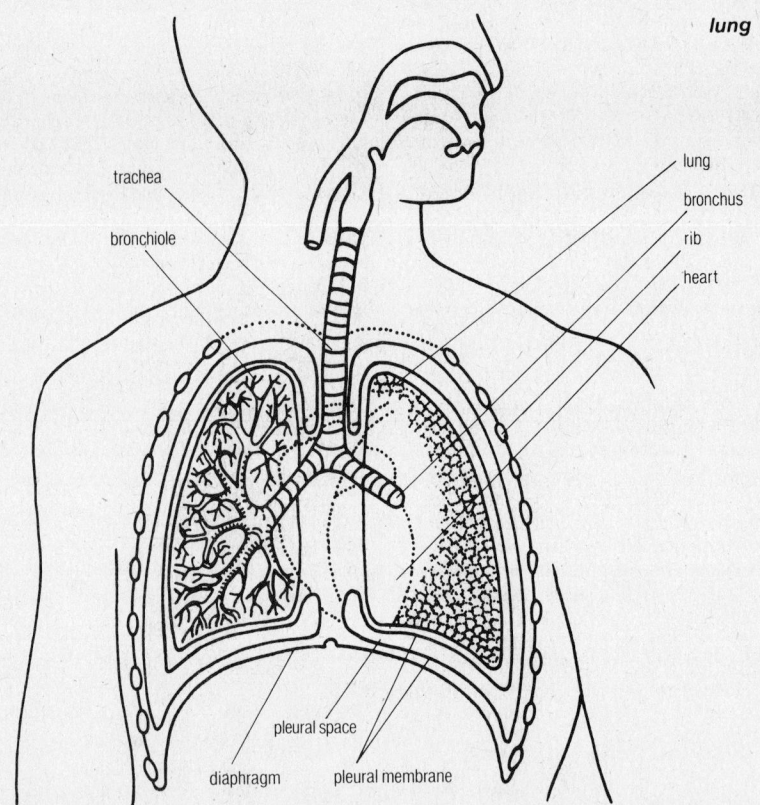

lung

lungfish type of fish, abundant 350 million years ago, now reduced to three genera of the order Dipnoi (related to the ◊coelacanth) found in Africa, South America, and Australia. They grow to about 2 m/6 ft, are eel shaped, long-lived, and (in addition to gills) have 'lungs' (modified swim bladders) with which they can breathe air in drought conditions.

Lunt /lʌnt/ Alfred 1893–1977. American actor. Born in Wisconsin, he went straight from school into the theatre, and in 1922 married Lynn ◊Fontanne. Known as 'the Lunts', they formed a sophisticated comedy duo, and the New York Lunt-Fontanne theatre was named after them. Their shows included *Design for Living* 1933,

There Shall Be No Night 1940–41, and *The Visit* 1960.

Luo Guan-zhong /ˈluːəu ˌgwænˈdʒɒŋ/ 14th-century Chinese novelist (formerly Luo Kuan-chung), who reworked popular tales into *The Romance of the Three Kingdoms* and *The Water Margin*, the latter a favourite of ◊Mao Zedong.

Luo Kuan-chung former form of ◊Luo Guan-zhong.

Luoyang /ˌluːəuˈjæŋ/ (formerly Loyang) industrial city and former capital of China in Henan province; population 1,114,000.

Lupercalia a Roman festival celebrated on 15 Feb. Goats and a dog were sacrificed, and the priests ran round the city carrying goatskin thongs, a blow from which was believed to cure sterility in women. The ritual probably combined fertility magic with charms conveying protection against wolves.

lupin in botany, plant of the genus *Lupinus*, which comprises about 300 species. They are native to Mediterranean regions and parts of N and S America, and some species are naturalized in Britain. The spikes of pea-like flowers may be white, yellow, blue or pink. *Lupinus albus* is cultivated in some places for cattle fodder, and for green manuring. The seeds contain toxic chemicals, which hinder their widespread use as human food, but non-toxic varieties are being bred.

lupus in medicine, tuberculosis of the skin (lupus vulgaris). The organism produces ulcers which spread and eat away the underlying tissues. Treatment is primarily with standard antituberculous drugs, such as streptomycin, but ultraviolet light may also be used. Lupus erythematosus is a chronic inflammation of the skin of the face, with red patches usually on the cheeks and across the nose, with or without scales. It is caused by the sufferer's own antibodies.

Lurçat /luə'saː/ Jean 1892–1966. French artist influenced by the ◊Cubists, who revived tapestry design, as in *Le Chant du Monde*.

Lurgan /'ləːgən/ see ◊Craigavon, town in Northern Ireland.

Luristan /ˌluərɪ'staːn/ mountainous district in SW Iran, inhabited by Lur tribes (estimated at 500,000) who live by their sheep and cattle. Excavation in the area has revealed a culture of the 8th–7th centuries BC with bronzes decorated with animal forms: its origins are uncertain.

Lusaka /luː'saːkə/ capital of Zambia from 1964 (of N Rhodesia 1935–64), 370 km/230 mi NE of Livingstone; commercial and agricultural centre (flour mills, tobacco factories, vehicle assembly, plastics and printing); University of Zambia 1966; population (1980) 538,469.

Lüshun-Dalien /ˌluː'ʃuːn ˌdɑː'lɪən/ see ◊Lüda, port in China.

Lusitania /ˌluːsɪ'teɪnɪə/ ◊Cunard liner sunk by German submarine on 7 May 1915 with the loss of some 1,200 lives, including some Americans; its destruction helped bring the USA into World War I.

Lusitanian member of an ancient people of the Iberian peninsula, inhabiting an area roughly equivalent to modern Portugal. Conquered by Rome in 139 BC, the province of Lusitania rebelled periodically until final conquest by Pompey 73–72 BC.

lusophone term referring to the countries in which the ◊Portuguese language is spoken, or which were formerly ruled by Portugal.

Lü-ta /ˌluː'tɑː/ former name of ◊Lüda, port in China.

lute family of stringed musical instruments of the 14th–18th centuries, which include the mandore, theorbo, and chitarrone. They are pear-shaped and plucked with the fingers. Members of the lute family were extremely popular both as solo instruments and for vocal accompaniment, and were often used as well as, or instead of, keyboard continuo instruments in larger ensembles and in opera. They have been revived in the 20th century.

lutetium silvery-white metallic element, symbol Lu, atomic number 71, atomic weight 174.97. Lutetium is the last of the ◊lanthanide series and is used in the 'cracking' or breakdown of petroleum, and in other chemical processes. A radioactive isotope is used to compare the age of meteorites with that of the earth.

Luther /'luːθə, German 'luːtə/ Martin 1483–1546. German reformer, usually regarded as the founder of Protestantism. Born at Eisleben, the son of a miner, he studied at the university of Erfurt, spent three years as a monk in the Augustinian convent there, and in 1507 was ordained priest. Shortly afterwards he attracted attention as a teacher and preacher in the university of Wittenberg; and in 1517, after returning from a visit to Rome, he attained nationwide celebrity for his denunciation of the Dominican monk Tetzel, who was one of those sent out by the Pope to sell ◊indulgences as a means of raising funds for the rebuilding of St Peter's at Rome. On 31 Oct 1517, he nailed on the church door at Wittenberg a statement of 95 theses on indulgences, and in the next year he was summoned to Rome to defend his action. His reply was to attack the papal system even more strongly, and in 1520 he publicly burnt in Wittenberg the papal bull that had been launched against him. Charles V summoned him to the Imperial Diet at Worms in 1521, where he refused to retract anything. On his way home he was taken into 'protective custody' by the elector of Saxony in the castle of the Wartburg. Later he became estranged from ◊Erasmus, who had formerly supported him in his attacks on papal authority, and engaged in violent controversies with political and religious opponents. In 1525 he married Catherina von Bora (1499–1552), an ex-nun. After the drawing up of the Augsburg Confession in 1530, he gradually retired from the Protestant leadership. His translation of the scriptures marks the emergence of modern German. Formerly condemned by Communism, he had by the 1980s been rehabilitated as a revolutionary socialist hero, and was claimed as patron saint by both East and West Germany.

Lutheranism a form of Protestantism derived from the life and teaching of Martin ◊Luther; it is sometimes called Evangelical to distinguish it from the other main branch of European Protestantism, the Reformed. It is the principal form of Protestantism in Germany, and is the national faith of Denmark, Norway, Sweden, Finland, and Iceland. The organization may be episcopal (Germany, Sweden) or synodal (the Netherlands and USA): the Lutheran World Federation has its headquarters in Geneva. The most generally accepted statement of Lutheranism is that of the Augsburg Confession 1530 but Luther's Shorter Catechism also carries great weight. Lutheranism is also very strong in the midwestern USA where several churches were originally founded by German and Scandinavian immigrants. It is the largest Protestant body, including some 80 million persons, of whom 40 million are in Germany, 19 million in Scandinavia, 8½ million in the USA and Canada, and most of the remainder in central Europe.

Luthuli /luː'tuːli/ Albert 1899–1967. South African leader. A Zulu tribal chief, he became president of the African National Congress in 1952, and preached non-violence and multiracialism. This prompted the formation of the rival militant Pan-Africanist Congress in 1958. Arrested in 1956, Luthuli was never actually tried for treason, although he suffered certain restrictions from 1959. He was under suspended sentence for burning his pass (an identity document required of non-white South Africans) when awarded the Nobel Peace Prize for 1960.

Lutine British bullion vessel lost off Holland 1799. Its bell, salvaged 1859, is at ◊Lloyd's. It is sounded once when a ship is missing and twice for good news.

Luton /'luːtn/ industrial town (cars, chemicals, electrical goods, ballbearings; traditional manufacture of hats) in Bedfordshire, England, 53 km/33 mi SW of Cambridge; Luton airport is a secondary one for London; population (1985) 165,000. Luton Hoo, a Robert Adam mansion, was built in 1762.

Lutosławski /ˌluːtəʊ'swæfski/ Witold 1913– . Polish composer, born in Warsaw. His early music, dissonant and powerful (*First Symphony* 1947), was criticized by the communist government, and he adopted a more popular style. With the lifting of artistic repression, his music once more became atonal, sometimes heavily contrapuntal. He has written chamber, vocal, and orchestral music, including three symphonies, *Livre pour orchestre* 1968 and *Mi-parti* 1976.

Lutyens /'lʌtjənz/ (Agnes) Elisabeth 1906–1983. British composer, daughter of Edwin ◊Lutyens. Her works, using the 12-tone system, are expressive and tightly organized, and include a substantial amount of chamber music, stage, and orchestral works. Choral and vocal works include a setting of ◊Wittgenstein's *Tractatus* and a cantata *The Tears of Night*.

Lutyens /'lʌtjənz/ Edwin Landseer 1869–1944. British architect, whose works include the government buildings in New Delhi, St Jude's church in Hampstead Garden Suburb, the Whitehall Cenotaph, London, the British embassy in Washington, Castle Drogo, Devon, and numerous country houses.

Lützen /'lutsən/ town in East Germany, SW of Leipzig, where in 1632 Gustavus Adolphus, king of Sweden, defeated the German commander Wallenstein in the Thirty Years' War; Gustavus was killed in the battle. Napoleon overcame the Russians and Prussians here in 1813.

lux ◊SI unit of illuminance (lx). Defined as the illumination produced by a luminous flux of 1 lumen distributed uniformly over an area of 1 m². Equivalent to 0.0929 ft candle.

Luxembourg, Palais du /'lʌksəmbɑːg, French ˌluksæm'buəg/ palace in Paris, France, in which the Senate sits. Built 1615 for Marie de' Medici by Salomon de Brosse, it was later enlarged; ◊Watteau used the gardens in his backgrounds.

Luxembourg /'lʌksəmbɑːg, French ˌluksæm'buəg/ capital of Luxembourg; population (1985) 76,000. It has the 16th-century Grand Ducal Palace, European Court of Justice, and European Parliament secretariat, but plenary sessions of the parliament are now held only in ◊Strasbourg.

Luxembourg /'lʌksəmbɑːg, French ˌluksæm'buəg/ landlocked country in W Europe, bordered N and W by Belgium, E by West Germany, and S by France.

government Luxembourg is a hereditary and constitutional monarchy. The 1868 constitution, revised 1919 and 1956, provides for a single-chamber legislature, the 64-member chamber of deputies, elected by universal suffrage through a system of proportional representation, for a five-year term. There is also an advisory body called the Council of State, whose 21 members are appointed by the grand duke for life. Any of its decisions can be overruled by the chamber of deputies. The grand duke also appoints a prime minister and council of ministers who are collectively responsible to the chamber. The four main political parties are the Christian Social Party, the Socialist Party, the Democratic Party – 'Liberals', and the Communist Party.

history formerly part of the ◊Holy Roman Empire, Luxembourg became a duchy in 1354. From 1482 it was under ◊Hapsburg control, and in 1797 was ceded, with Belgium, to France. The 1815 Treaty of Vienna made Luxembourg a grand duchy, ruled by the king of the Netherlands. In 1830 Belgium and Luxembourg revolted against Dutch rule, Belgium achieved independence in 1839 and most of Luxembourg became part of it, the rest becoming independent in its own right in 1848.

Although a small country, Luxembourg occupies an important position in W Europe, being a founder member of many international organizations, including The ◊European Coal and Steel Community (ECSC), the ◊European Atomic Energy Commission (EURATOM), and the ◊European Community (EC). It formed an economic union with Belgium and the Netherlands in 1948 (◊Benelux), which was the forerunner of wider European cooperation. Grand Duchess Charlotte abdicated in 1964, after a reign of 45 years, and was succeeded by her son, Prince Jean. She died in 1985, aged 89. Proportional representation has resulted in a series of coalition governments. The Christian Social Party headed most of these from 1945–74, when its dominance was challenged by the Socialists. It regained pre-eminence in 1979, and leads the current administration.

Luxembourg Accord French-initiated agreement in 1966 that a decision of the Council of Ministers of the European Community may be vetoed by a member whose national interests are at stake.

Luxemburg /'lʌksəmbɜːg, German 'luksəmbuək/ Rosa 1870–1919. Polish-born German Communist, collaborator with ◊Liebknecht in founding the ◊Spartacus League, and murdered with him in the 1919 Berlin Revolt. She wrote famous letters while in prison in World War I.

Luxor /'lʌksɔː/ village in Egypt near the ruins of ◊Thebes.

Lu Xun /'luː 'ʃuːn/ pseudonym of Chon Shu-jêu 1881–1936. Chinese short-story writer. In 1926 he became dean of the College of Arts at Sun Yat Sen University. His three volumes of satirically realistic stories, *Call to Arms*, *Wandering*, and *Old Tales Retold*, reveal the influence of Gogol. His supreme mastery of the form makes him one of the most popular of modern Chinese writers.

Luzern /luːtˈseən/ German name of ◊Lucerne, town and lake in Switzerland.

Luzon /luːˈzɒn/ largest island of the ◊Philippines, with US military bases.

Lvov /lvɒf/ (Ukrainian *Lviv*) capital and industrial city (textiles, engineering, metals) of

Luxembourg

GRAND DUCHY OF (*Grand-Duché de Luxembourg*)

AREA 2,586 sq km/999 sq mi
CAPITAL Luxembourg
PHYSICAL on the river Moselle; part of the Ardennes (Oesling) forest in the N
HEAD OF STATE Grand Duke Jean from 1964
HEAD OF GOVERNMENT Jacques Santer from 1984
GOVERNMENT constitutional monarchy
EXPORTS iron and steel, chemicals, synthetic textiles; banking is very important; Luxembourg is economically linked with Belgium
CURRENCY Luxembourg franc (61.95 = £1 Sept 1987)
POPULATION 366,000 (1985); annual growth rate -0.1%
LANGUAGE French (official); local Letzeburgesch; German
RELIGION Roman Catholic
LITERACY 100% (1983)
GDP $3.8 bn (1981); $10,444 per head of population

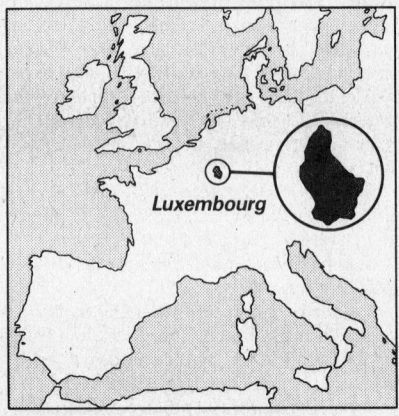

Luxembourg

CHRONOLOGY
1948 With Belgium and the Netherlands, formed the Benelux customs union.
1958 Benelux became economic union.
1961 Prince Jean became acting head of state on behalf of his mother, Grand Duchess Charlotte.
1964 Grand Duchess Charlotte abdicated and Prince Jean became grand duke.

Lvov region in the Ukrainian Republic, USSR; university 1661; population (1985) 742,000.
history Lvov, founded in the 13th century by a Galician prince (the name means city of Leo or Lev), was Polish 1340–1772, Austrian 1772–1919, Polish 1919–39, annexed by USSR in 1945.

Lwów /lvuːf/ Polish form of ◊Lvov, city in Ukraine, USSR.

lycanthropy folk belief in human transformation to a ◊werewolf; or, in psychology, a delusion involving this belief.

Lyceum an ancient Athenian gymnasium and garden, with covered walks, where ◊Aristotle taught. It was SE of the city, and named after the nearby temple of Apollo Lyceus.

Lyceum London theatre, situated in Wellington Street, near the Strand. It was opened in 1809 (rebuilt 1834) and under the management of Henry ◊Irving (1878–1902), saw many of Ellen ◊Terry's triumphs.

lychee alternative spelling of ◊litchi.

Lycurgus /laɪˈkɜːgəs/ (lived 9th century BC) Spartan lawgiver. He is said to have been a member of the royal house, who, while acting as regent, gave the Spartans their constitution and system of education. Many scholars believe him to be purely mythical.

Lydia /'lɪdiə/ ancient kingdom of Asia Minor (7th–6th centuries BC), with its capital at Sardis. The Lydians were the first Western people to use standard coinage. Their last king, ◊Croesus, was conquered by the Persians in 546 BC.

Lyell /'laɪəl/ Charles 1797–1875. Scottish geologist. He trained and practised as a lawyer, but, being from a rich family, he was able to retire from the law in 1827 and devote himself full-time to geology and writing. He wrote 46 books, the most important of which is *The Principles of*

Geology, Being an Attempt to Explain the Former Changes of the Earth's Surface, By Reference to Causes now in Operation 1830–33, in which he opposed ◊Cuvier's theory that the features of the earth were formed by a series of catastrophes, and asserted that the features we see today have been established through the work over millennia of the actual forces we see in operation today. This view is termed ◊uniformitarian. He thus implied that the earth was much older than the 6,000 years of prevalent contemporary theory. He provided the first detailed description of the ◊Tertiary period in geology, with divisions into Eocene, Miocene, and Pliocene epochs. Although he did not until late in his life accept that species had changed through evolution, he nevertheless provided ◊Darwin with a geological framework within which evolutionary theories could be placed. Darwin simply applied Lyell's geological method – explaining the past through what is observable in the present – to biology.

Lyly /'lɪli/ John c. 1553–1606. English playwright and author of the romance *Euphues, or the Anatomy of Wit* 1578. Its elaborate stylistic devices gave rise to the word 'euphuism' for an affected rhetorical style.

Lyme Regis /'laɪm 'riːdʒɪs/ seaport and resort in Dorset, England; the rebel duke of Monmouth landed here in 1685; and the Cobb (a massive stone pier) features in Jane Austen's *Persuasion* 1818 and John Fowles' *The French Lieutenant's Woman* 1969.

lymph the fluid found in the lymphatic system of vertebrates, which carries nutrients, oxygen and white blood cells (◊leucocytes) to the tissues, and waste matter away from them. It exudes from the finest blood vessels, (◊capillaries) into the tissue spaces between the cells and is made

Lyell Scottish geologist Charles Lyell helped win acceptance for Hutton's theory of uniformitarianism and Darwin's theory of evolution with his *Principles of Geology* 1830–33, which asserted that the earth's crust was gradually wrought through millennia of change.

up of ◊blood plasma, plus white cells. Lymph is drained from the tissues by lymph capillaries which empty into larger lymph vessels (lymphatics). These lead to lymph nodes, small round bodies chiefly situated in the neck, armpit, groin, thorax and abdomen. Their function is to process the ◊lymphocytes produced by the bone marrow and to filter out harmful substances and ◊bacteria. From the lymph nodes, vessels carry the lymph to the thoracic duct and the right lymphatic duct, which lead into the large veins in the neck. In some vertebrates (for example, amphibians) there is a lymph heart which pumps lymph through the lymph vessels.

lymph nodes small masses of lymphatic tissue in the body, which occur at various points along the major lymphatic vessels. Tonsils and adenoids are large lymph nodes. As the ◊lymph fluid passes through them it is filtered, and bacteria and other microorganisms are engulfed by cells known as macrophages. ◊Lymph nodes are sometimes mistakenly called 'lymph glands', and the term 'swollen glands' refers to swelling of the lymph nodes caused by infection.

lymphocyte a type of white ◊blood cell, or ◊leucocyte, with a large nucleus, produced in the bone marrow of vertebrates. Although most occur in the blood and ◊lymph, lymphocytes also wander around the body tissues. They are of two main types, B-lymphocytes and T-lymphocytes. The former are responsible for the production of ◊antibodies which bind to specific ◊antigens rendering them harmless. T-lymphocytes themselves bind to specific antigens and destroy infected cells; they also help to activate the B-lymphocytes. See also ◊thymus.

Lynch /lɪntʃ/ 'Jack' (John) 1917– . Irish politician, born in Cork. He became a noted Gaelic footballer and a barrister. In 1948 he

entered the parliament of the republic as a Fianna Fáil member, and was prime minister 1966–73 and 1977–79.

lynching the execution of an alleged offender by a summary court having no legal authority. In the USA the custom originated on the frontiers, where no regular courts existed and outlaws and cattle thieves abounded. Later examples mostly occurred in the southern states, where it was used by mobs after the Civil War against supposed black offenders. During 1882–1900 the annual figure for the USA varied between 96 and 231, but it is today an exceptional occurrence for black or white.

Lynn /lɪn/ Vera 1917– . British singer, the 'Forces' Sweetheart' of World War II with 'We'll Meet Again' and 'White Cliffs of Dover'. Dame of the British Empire 1975.

Lynn The British singer Vera Lynn captured the hearts of the troops in World War II through her renditions of songs such as 'White Cliffs of Dover'.

lynx cat *Felis lynx* found in rocky and forested regions of North America and Europe. Larger than a wild cat, it has a short tail, tufted ears, and the long, silky fur is reddish brown or grey with dark spots. The US bobcat or bay lynx *Felix rufus* is a smaller relative. See also ◊caracal.

Lyons /'liːɒŋ/ (French *Lyon*) industrial city (textiles, chemicals, machinery, printing) and capital of Rhône *département*, and second city of France, at the confluence of the Rhône and Saône, 275 km/170 mi NNW of Marseilles; law and university centre; population (1982) 1,221,000.

history formerly a chief fortress of France, it it was the ancient Lugdunum, taken by the Romans 43 BC.

Lyons /'laɪənz/ Joseph Aloysius 1879–1939. Australian politician. A native of Tasmania, he was elected to the Federal Parliament in 1929, and became Postmaster-General and Minister for Works. In 1931 he resigned from the cabinet and formed the United Australia Party. After

the general election in the following Dec, Lyons formed a coalition government with the Country Party, which was confirmed in office by the 1934 and 1937 general elections. He died in office in April 1939.

lyophilization freeze-drying process used for foods and drugs, and in the preservation of organic archaeological remains.

Lyra small but prominent constellation of the northern hemisphere, representing the lyre of Orpheus. Its brightest star is ◊Vega; Epsilon Lyrae, the 'double double', is a system of four linked stars; Beta Lyrae is an eclipsing binary. The Ring Nebula, M 57, is a famous planetary nebula – a shell of gas around a dying star.

lyre stringed instrument of great antiquity. It originated in Asia, and was used in Greece and Egypt. It consisted of a soundbox with two curved arms joined by a crosspiece. There were four to ten strings which were stretched from the crosspiece to a bridge near the bottom of the soundbox. It was played with a plectrum held with the right hand.

lyre-bird genus of Australian birds *Menura*. The male has a large lyre-shaped tail, brilliantly coloured. They nest on the ground, and feed on insects, worms, and snails.

Lysander /laɪ'sændə/ (died 395 BC) Spartan general. He brought the Peloponnesian War to a successful conclusion by capturing the Athenian fleet at Aegospotami in 405 BC, and by starving Athens into surrender in the following year. He then aspired to make Sparta supreme in Greece, and himself in Sparta; he set up puppet governments in Athens and her former allies, and intrigued to secure himself the Spartan Kingship, but was killed in battle with the Thebans.

Lysenko /lɪ'seŋkəʊ/ Trofim Denisovich 1898–1976. Soviet biologist, who believed in the inheritance of ◊acquired characters and used his position under Stalin to officially exclude ◊Mendel's theory of inheritance. He was removed from office after the fall of Khrushchev in 1964.

Lysippus /laɪ'sɪpəs/ 4th century BC. Greek sculptor at the court of Alexander. His naturalistic work included an athlete and portrait busts, then a new form of art.

lysis in biology, any process which destroys a ◊cell by rupturing its lysis membrane.

lysosome a structure or ◊organelle inside a ◊cell, principally found in animal cells. Lysosomes contain ◊enzymes that can break down proteins and other biological substances. They are bounded by a membrane that resists the attack of these enzymes and thus protects the cell from them. They play a part in digestion, and in the white blood cells known as ◊phagocytes the lysosome enzymes attack ingested bacteria.

Lyte /laɪt/ Henry Francis 1793–1847. British cleric, author of the hymns 'Abide with me' and 'Praise, my soul, the King of Heaven'.

Lytton /'lɪtn/ Edward George Earle Lytton Bulwer, 1st Baron Lytton of Knebworth 1803–1873. British author. Born in London, he wrote novels which successfully followed every turn of the public taste and include *Falkland* 1827, the Byronic *Pelham* 1828, *The Last Days of Pompeii* 1834, and *Rienzi* 1835.

M the 13th letter of the Roman alphabet. It corresponds to the Greek *mu* and the Semitic *mem*, and is almost always sounded as a voiced labial nasal. Finally, or before consonants, it disappears in French, Portuguese, and other languages, leaving a trace in nasalization of the preceding vowel. In Roman numerals M equals 1,000.

Maas /mɑːs/ Dutch or Flemish name for the river ◊Meuse.

Maastricht /'mɑːstrɪxt/ industrial city (metallurgy, textiles, pottery) and capital of the province of Limburg, the Netherlands, on the Maas, near the Dutch-Belgian frontier; population (1985) 158,000. Maastricht dates from Roman times.

Maazel /mɑːˈzel/ Lorin (Varencove) 1930– . American conductor. He was conductor of the Cleveland Orchestra 1972–82 and then director of the Vienna State Opera.

Mabuse /məˈbjuːz/ Jan c. 1472–c. 1534. Name adopted by Flemish artist Jan Gossaert, derived from his birthplace, Maubeuge. His journey to Italy in 1508 with Philip of Burgundy started a vogue for Italian journeys and the Italian style. His works include *The Adoration of the Magi* (National Gallery, London), and a number of portraits, in which the hands are used to convey character.

McAdam /məˈkædəm/ John Loudon 1756–1836. Scottish engineer. Born at Ayr, he was appointed general surveyor of roads in 1827. The word 'macadamizing' was coined for his system of constructing roads of broken granite.

macadamia edible nut from trees of the genus *Macadamia*, native to Queensland, in the family Proteaceae.

Macao /məˈkaʊ/ Portuguese possession on the S coast of China, about 65 km/40 mi W of Hong Kong, from which it is separated by the estuary of the Canton river; it comprises a peninsula and the islands of Taipa and Colôane.
area 15.5 sq km/6 sq mi
capital Macao, on the peninsula
features the peninsula is linked to Taipa by a bridge, and to Colôane by a causeway, both 2 km/1 mi long
currency pataca

Maazel American conductor Lorin Maazel made his debut as a conductor at the age of nine and as a violinist a few years later.

population (1986) 400,000.
language Cantonese; Portuguese (official)
religion Buddhist, with a 6% Catholic minority
government under the constitution ('organic statute') of 1976, Macao enjoys considerable political autonomy. The Portuguese president controls the colony's external affairs but appoints, in consultation with the local Legislative Assembly, a governor to exercise control over domestic matters. The governor works with a cabinet of five appointed secretaries and confers with a ten-member Consultative Council and a 17-member Legislative Council, both composed of a mixture of elected and nominated members. The Legislative Council frames internal legislation, but any bills passed by less than a two-thirds majority can be vetoed by the governor. A number of 'civic associations'

and interest groups function, sending representatives to the Legislative Council.
history Macao was first established as a Portuguese trading and missionary post in the Far East in 1537, being leased from China in 1557. It was annexed 1849 and recognized as a Portuguese colony by the Chinese government in a treaty of 1887. The port declined in prosperity during the late 19th and early 20th centuries, following the silting up of its harbour and the consequent diversion of international trade to Hong Kong and the new Treaty Ports. The colony thus concentrated instead on local 'country trade' and became a centre for gambling and, later, tourism.

In 1951 Macao became an overseas province of Portugal, sending an elected representative to the Lisbon parliament. After the Portuguese revolution of 1974, it became a 'special territory' and was granted considerable autonomy, power being exercised by a governor appointed by the Portuguese president.

In 1986 negotiations opened between the Portuguese and Chinese governments over the question of the return of Macao's sovereignty under similar 'one country, two systems' terms to those agreed by China and Britain for ◊Hong Kong. These negotiations proved successful and were concluded in Apr 1987 by the signing of the 'Macao Pact' under which Portugal agreed to hand over sovereignty to the People's Republic in Dec 1999, and China agreed in return to guarantee to maintain the port's capitalist economic and social system for at least 50 years.

macaque type of monkey of the genus *Macaca*. Various species of these medium sized monkeys live from the Far East to N Africa. They range from longtailed to tailless types. All climb, but many spend a high proportion of their time on the ground. They have well-developed cheek pouches to carry food. The ◊rhesus and the ◊Barbary ape are part of this group.

MacArthur /məˈkɑːθə/ Douglas 1880–1964. American general. As commander of US forces in the Far East he defended the Philippines against the Japanese 1941–42, escaped to Australia, and in Mar 1942 assumed command of the Allied forces in the SW Pacific. He was

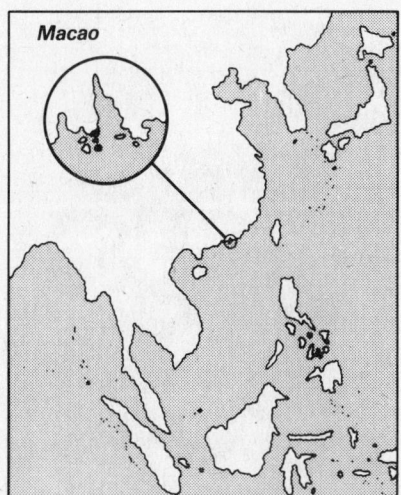

Macao

MacArthur US general Douglas MacArthur was commander of the Allied forces in the Pacific during World War II.

responsible for the reconquest of New Guinea in 1942–45 and of the Philippines in 1944–45, being appointed general of the Army in 1944. After the surrender of Japan he commanded the Allied occupation forces there. During 1950 he commanded the UN Forces in Korea, but in April 1951, after expressing views contrary to US and UN policy, he was relieved of all his commands by President Truman.

Macassar /mə'kæsə/ another name for ◊Ujung Pandang, port in Indonesia.

Macaulay /mə'kɔːli/ Rose 1881–1958. British novelist. The serious vein of her early novels changed to light satire in *Potterism* 1920 and *Keeping up Appearances* 1928. Her later books, very few of them novels, include *The*

Towers of Trebizond 1956. She was created Dame of the British Empire in 1958.

Macaulay /mə'kɔːli/ Thomas Babington, Baron Macaulay 1800–1859. British historian, essayist, poet, and politician. He entered Parliament as a liberal Whig in 1830, and advocated Parliamentary reform and the abolition of slavery. As a Member of the Supreme Council in India 1834–38, he was mainly responsible for the Indian penal code. He sat again in Parliament 1839–47 and 1852–56, and in 1857 accepted a peerage. His only volume of verse, *Lays of Ancient Rome*, appeared in 1842. The four volumes of his masterpiece, the *History of England* published 1848–61, written from a Whig viewpoint, treated the years up to 1702.

macaw large long-tailed tropical American ◊parrot.

Macbeth /mək'beθ/ king of Scotland from 1040, died 1058. The son of Findlaech, hereditary ruler of Moray, he was commander of the forces of Duncan, king of Scotia, whom he killed in battle in 1040. His reign was prosperous until Duncan's son ◊Malcolm led an invasion and killed him at Lumphanan. Shakespeare's tragedy *Macbeth* was based on ◊Holinshed's *Chronicle*.

McBride /mək'braɪd/ Willie John 1940– . Irish Rugby Union player. He was capped 63 times by Ireland, and won a record 17 British Lions caps. He went on five Lions tours, 1962, 1966, 1968, 1971 and in 1974 as captain, when they returned from South Africa undefeated.

Maccabees /'mækəbiːz/ Jewish family, sometimes known as the Hasmonaeans. It was founded by the priest Mattathias (died 166 BC) who with his sons led the struggle for Jewish independence against the Syrians in the 2nd century BC. Judas (died 161) reconquered Jerusalem in 165 BC, and Simon (died 135) established Jewish independence in 142 BC.

McCarthy /mə'kɑːθi/ Joseph Raymond (Joe) 1909–1957. American Republican politician. A lawyer, he became senator for his native Wisconsin in 1946, and in 1950 caused a sensation by claiming to hold a list of about 200 Communists working in the State Department. He continued a 'witch-hunting' campaign until the enquiries against these officials were halted in 1954, when it was shown that McCarthy and his aides had been falsifying evidence. By this time, however, many thousands of people in public life and the arts had been unofficially blacklisted as suspected Communists or communist sympathizers. He gave his name to the practice of McCarthyism (making unsupported accusations).

McCarthy /mə'kɑːθi/ Mary (Therese) 1912– . US novelist and critic. Much of her work looks probingly at US society, for example the novels *The Groves of Academe* 1952, which describes the anti-Communist witch-hunts of the ◊McCarthy era, and *The Group* 1963, her best known, which follows the post-college careers of eight women. Autobiographical works include *Memoirs of a Catholic Girlhood* 1957.

McClellan /mə'klelən/ George Brinton 1826–1885. American Civil War general,

McCarthy American senator Joe McCarthy exhibiting 'evidence' to the House of Representatives Un-American Activities committee.

commander-in-chief of the Union forces 1861–62.

McClintock /mə'klɪntɒk/ Barbara 1902– . American geneticist. She established that ◊genes changed their position on the chromosome from generation to generation in a random way. The existence of such transposable elements (TEs) would explain how originally identical cells are enabled to take on specialized functions as skin, muscle, bone, nerve, and also how evolution could give rise to the multiplicity of species.

McClure /mə'kluə/ Robert John 1807–1873. British explorer. While on an expedition 1850–54 searching for ◊Franklin, he was the first to pass through the North-West Passage.

McCormick /mə'kɔːmɪk/ Cyrus Hall 1809–1884. American inventor of a mechanical reaper in 1831.

McCowen /mə'kauən/ Alec 1925– . British actor. His many, varied roles include leading Shakespeare parts and solo performances.

MacCready /mə'kriːdi/ Paul 1925– . American designer of the *Gossamer Condor* aircraft which made the first controlled flight by human power alone in 1977. His *Solar Challenger* flew from Paris to London under solar power; and in 1985 he reconstructed a powered ◊pterodactyl.

McCullers /mə'kʌləz/ Carson (Smith) 1917–1967. US novelist. Most of her writing (including her best-known novels *The Heart is a Lonely Hunter* 1940 and *Reflections in a Golden Eye* 1941) is set in the Southern states, where she was born, and deals with spiritual isolation.

McDiarmid /mək'dɑːmɪd/ Hugh, pen name of Christopher Murray Grieve 1892–1978. Scottish nationalist and Marxist poet. His works include *A Drunk Man looks at the Thistle* and two *Hymns to Lenin*.

MacDonald /mək'dɒnld/ (James) Ramsay 1866–1937. British Labour politician. Born in Scotland, the son of a labourer, he joined the ◊Independent Labour Party in 1894, and helped to found and became first secretary of the ◊Labour Party in 1900. He was elected to Parliament in 1906, and led the party until 1914, when his opposition to World War I lost him the leadership. This he recovered in 1922, and in Jan–Oct 1924 governed with the support of the Liberal party. He returned to office in 1929, again as leader of a minority government, which collapsed in 1931 as a result of the economic crisis. MacDonald left the Labour Party to form a national government with backing from both Liberal and Conservative parties. He resigned the premiership in 1935, remaining Lord President of the Council.

Macdonald /mək'dɒnld/ Flora 1722–1790. Scottish heroine who rescued Prince Charles Edward, the Young Pretender, after the Battle of ◊Culloden in 1746. Disguising him as her maid, she escorted him from her home in the Hebrides to France. She was arrested, but released in 1747.

Macdonald /mək'dɒnld/ John Alexander 1815–1891. Canadian Conservative politician. He was born in Glasgow but taken to Ontario as a child. In 1857 he became prime minister of Upper Canada. He took the leading part in the movement for federation, and in 1867 became the first prime minister of Canada. Defeated in 1873, he returned to office in 1878, and retained it until his death.

Macdonnell Ranges /ˌmækdə'nel/ mountain range in central Australia, Northern Territory, with the town of Alice Springs; highest peak Mount Zeil 1,510 m/4,955 ft.

MacDowell /mək'dauəl/ Edward Alexander 1860–1908. American Romantic composer, influenced by ◊Liszt. His works include the *Indian Suite* 1896, and piano concertos and sonatas.

Macedonia /ˌmæsɪ'dəʊnɪə/ a federal republic of Yugoslavia
area 25,13 sq km/9925 sq mi
capital Skopje
features mountainous; chief rivers Struma and Vardar
population (1981) 1,909,000, including 1,279,000 Macedonians, 377,000 Albanians, and 87,000 Turks
language Macedonian, closely allied to Bulgarian, and written in Cyrillic
religion Macedonian Orthodox Christian
history Macedonia was an ancient country of SE Europe between Illyria, Thrace, and the Aegean Sea; settled by Slavs in the 6th century, conquered by Bulgars in the 7th century, by Byzantium 1014, by Serbia in the 14th century, and by the Ottoman Empire 1355; divided up between Serbia, Bulgaria, and Greece after the Balkan Wars of 1912–13.

Maceió /ˌmæseɪ'əʊ/ industrial town (sugar, tobacco, textile, timber industries) in NE Brazil, capital of Alagaos state with its port at Jaraguá; population (1980) 375,800.

McEwan /mə'kjuːən/ Ian 1948– . English novelist and short story writer. His tightly written works often have sinister or macabre undertones and contain elements of violence and bizarre sexuality, as in the short stories in *First Love, Last Rites* 1975. His novels include *The Comfort of Strangers* 1981 and *The Child in Time* 1987.

Macgillycuddy's Reeks /mə'gɪlɪˌkʌdiz 'riːks/ a range of mountains in SW Ireland lying W of Killarney, in County Kerry; includes Carrantuohill 1,041 m/3,414 ft, the highest peak in Ireland.

McGonagall /mə'gɒnəgəl/ William 1830–1902. Scottish poet, noted for the unintentionally humorous effect of his extremely bad serious verse, for example, his poem on the Tay Bridge disaster of 1879.

Mach /mɑːk, German mæx/ Ernst 1838–1916. Austrian philosopher and physicist. An empiricist, he laid down that science was a record of facts perceived by the senses, and that acceptance of a scientific law depended solely on its standing the practical test of use. He researched airflow, and ◊Mach numbers are named after him.

Machado /mə'tʃɑːdəʊ/ Antonio 1875–1939. Spanish poet and dramatist. Born in Seville, he was inspired by the Castilian countryside in his lyric verse, contained in *Campos de Castilla/Countryside of Castile* 1912.

Machault /mæ'ʃəʊ/ Guillame de 1300–1377. French poet and composer. Born in Champagne, he was in the service of John of Bohemia for 30 years, and later of King John the Good of France. He gave the forms of the *ballade* and *rondeau* a new individuality.

Machel /mæ'ʃel/ Samora 1933–1986. Mozambique ◊Frelimo leader, president 1975–86. Machel was active in the Mozambique liberation front Frelimo from its conception in 1962, fighting for independence from Portugal. In 1966 he became Frelimo leader, and Mozambique's first president from independence in 1975 until his death in a plane crash near the South African border in 1986.

Machiavelli /ˌmækɪə'veli/ Niccolò 1469–1527. Italian politician and author, whose name is now synonymous with cunning and cynical statecraft. Born in Florence, he became second chancellor to the republic 1498–1512. On the accession to power of the Medici in 1512, he was arrested and imprisoned on a charge of conspiracy, but in 1513 released to exile in the country. He completed his *Il Principe/The Prince* in 1513, a guide for the future prince of a unified Italian state, showing ways in which rulers can advance the interests of their states (and themselves) though an often amoral and opportunist manipulation of other people. The theories expressed in *Il Principe* and in his *Discorsi/Discourses* 1531 influenced political science. He also wrote the comedies *La Mandragola/The Mandrake* 1524, and *Clizia*.

machine code in computing, a binary (two-state) code in which computer programs are expressed as a prerequisite to being executed by the computer. (See also ◊binary number system.) Once, all computer programs had to be written in machine code. Later, ◊assembler (or assembly code) and, finally, high-level ◊programming

Machiavelli Italian diplomat and writer Niccolò Machiavelli's reputation rests largely on his work *The Prince*, based on his observations of Cesare Borgia.

languages were developed which are easier for people to use and can automatically be translated into machine code prior to execution.

machine gun a rapid firing automatic gun perfected in the USA by Gatling in 1860. A number of barrels were arranged about a central axis, and the breech containing the reloading, ejection and firing mechanism was rotated by hand; shots being fired through each barrel in turn. The Maxim (named after its inventor, US-born H S Maxim 1840–1916) of 1884 was recoil operated, but some later types have been gas-operated (Bren) or recoil assisted by gas (some versions of the Browning). The sub-machine gun, first exploited by Chicago gunmen in the 1920s, was widely used in World War II, for instance, the recoil-operated Sten. See ◊rocket, and ◊small arms.

machine politics term used to describe the organization of a local political party to ensure its own election by controlling the electorate, and then to retain power through control of key committees and offices. The idea of machine politics was epitomized in the US in the late 19th century, where it was used to control individual cities.

machine tool a power-driven machine for cutting and shaping metals. Machine tools must have powerful electric motors to force cutting tools into the metal. These tools are made from hardened steel containing heat-resistant metals such as tungsten and chromium. The use of precision machine tools is crucial to ◊mass-production assembly methods, for it ensures that all duplicate parts produced are virtually identical. Many machine tools now work automatically under computer control and are a key factor in factory ◊automation. The commonest machine tool is the ◊lathe, which shapes shafts and similar objects. A ◊milling machine cuts metal with a rotary toothed cutting wheel. Other machine tools cut, plane, grind, drill and polish.

Mach number ratio of the speed of a body to that of sound in the undisturbed medium through which the body travels. Mach 1 is reached when an aircraft has a velocity greater than that of sound ('passes the sound barrier'), namely 331 metres sec $^{-1}$/1,087 ft sec $^{-1}$ at sea level. Mach numbers are named after Ernst ◊Mach.

Machu Picchu /'mɑːtʃuː 'piːktʃuː/ a ruined Inca city in Peru, situated NW of Cuzco. It was discovered in 1911 by Hiram Bingham at the top of 300 m/1,000 ft high cliffs, containing well-preserved remains of houses and temples. It was built c. 1500 AD.

Machu Picchu The legendary Inca city that the Spanish conquistadors never found.

Macis Nguema /məˈsiːəs əŋˈgweɪmə/ former name (until 1979) of ◊Bioko, an island in the Bight of Bonny, West Africa.

MacInnes /məˈkɪnɪs/ Colin 1914–1976. English novelist, son of the novelist Angela Thirkell. He made a reputation with sharp depictions of London youth and subcultures of the 1950s, particularly in *City of Spades* 1957 and *Absolute Beginners* 1959.

Macintosh /'mækɪntɒʃ/ Charles 1766–1843. Scottish manufacturing chemist who invented a waterproof fabric lined with a rubber that was used for raincoats – hence 'mackintosh'. Other waterproofing processes have now largely superseded this method.

McKellen /məˈkelən/ Ian 1939– . British actor, whose stage roles include Richard II, Edward II and modern drama. His film roles include *Plenty* 1985.

Mackensen /'mækənzən/ August von 1849–1945. German field marshal. During World War I he accomplished the breakthrough at Gorlice and the conquest of Serbia 1915, and in 1916 had a big share in the overthrow of Romania.

Mackenzie, River /məˈkenzi/ river in the Northwest Territories, Canada, flowing from the Great Slave Lake to the Arctic Ocean; about 1,600 km/1,000 mi long. Discovered by the British explorer Alexander ◊Mackenzie in 1789.

Mackenzie /məˈkenzi/ Alexander c. 1755–1820. British explorer, discoverer of the ◊Mackenzie River in 1789.

Mackenzie /məˈkenzi/ Compton 1883–1972. Scottish author. The son of actor parents,

McKellen British actor Ian McKellen in the title role of the film *Walter*, the story of a mentally handicapped man at the mercy of society's attitudes.

he was educated at Oxford University, and published his first novel *The Passionate Elopement* in 1911. Works later were *Carnival* 1912, *Sinister Street* 1913–14 – an autobiographical novel; and the comic *Whisky Galore* 1947. Invalided from the army in 1915, he returned to serve as an intelligence officer for the remainder of World War I, and his *Greek Memories* led to a trial under the Official Secrets Act. He published his autobiography 1963–71.

Mackenzie /məˈkenzi/ William Lyon 1795–1861. Canadian politician, grandfather of W L Mackenzie ◊King. Born near Dundee, he emigrated to Canada in 1820, and in 1837 led a rising at Toronto against the oligarchic rule of 'establishment' families, the Family Compact. After its failure he lived in the USA until 1849, and 1851–58 sat in the Canadian legislature as a Radical.

mackerel food fish *Scomber scombrus*, found in the N Atlantic and Mediterranean. It is blue with irregular black bands down its sides, the latter and the under surface showing a metallic sheen. The chief mackerel fisheries of Britain are off the SW coast.

Mackerras /məˈkerəs/ Charles 1925– . Australian conductor. Noted for his advocacy of the music of ◊Janáček, whom he has helped to popularize, he was conductor of the English National Opera 1970–78, and was knighted in 1979.

McKinley, Mount /məˈkɪnli/ peak in Alaska, USA, the highest in N America, 6,194 m/20,320 ft; named after US president William McKinley. See ◊Rocky Mountains.

McKinley /məˈkɪnli/ William 1843–1901. 25th president of the USA. Born in Ohio, he was elected to Congress in 1876 as a Republican, becoming president in 1896 and again in 1900. His period of office was marked by America's adoption of an imperialist policy, as exemplified in the Spanish-American War of 1898 and the annexation of the Philippines. He was assassinated at Buffalo in 1901.

Mackintosh /'mækɪntɒʃ/ Charles Rennie 1868–1928. Scottish ◊Art Nouveau architect, designer and painter. His buildings include Glasgow School of Art 1896, and Hill House, Helensburgh 1903.

Mackmurdo /mæk'mɜːdəʊ/ Arthur H 1851–1942. English designer and architect. He founded the Century Guild in 1882, a group of architects, artists, and designers inspired by William ◊Morris and John ◊Ruskin. His book and textile designs are forerunners of ◊Art Nouveau.

MacLeish /məˈkliːʃ/ Archibald 1892–1982. American poet. Born in Illinois, he was assistant secretary of state in 1944–45 and helped to draft the constitution of UNESCO. He made his name with a poem *Conquistador* 1932, which describes Cortes' march to the Aztec capital, but his later plays in verse, *Panic* 1935 and *Air Raid* 1938, deal with contemporary problems.

Macleod /məˈklaʊd/ Iain Norman 1913–1970. British Conservative politician. As colonial secretary 1959–61, he forwarded the independence of former British territories in Africa; he died in office as chancellor of the Exchequer.

Maclise /məˈkliːs/ Daniel 1806–1870. Irish artist. Born at Cork, he moved to London in 1827 and painted portraits and historical pictures, including *The Meeting of Wellington and Blücher after Waterloo*, and *Death of Nelson* for the Westminster Palace.

McLuhan /məˈkluːən/ (Herbert) Marshall 1911–1981. Canadian theorist of communication, noted for his views on the effects of technology on modern society. He coined the phrase 'the medium is the message', meaning that the form rather than the content of information was crucial. His best-known works were *The Gutenberg Galaxy* 1962 (coining the phrase 'the global village' for the modern electronic society); *Understanding Media 1964*, and *The Medium is the Massage* (sic) 1967.

MacMahon /məˈkmɑːn/ Marie Edmé Patrice, Comte de MacMahon 1808–1893. Marshal of France. Captured at Sedan in 1870 during the ◊Franco-Prussian War, he suppressed the Paris ◊Commune after his release, and as president of the Republic 1873–79 worked for a royalist restoration until forced to resign.

Macmillan /məˈkmɪlən/ (Maurice) Harold, 1st Earl of Stockton 1894–1986. British Conservative politician. Member of a family of publishers, he entered Parliament as a Unionist 1924 and received his first ministerial post 1951; he became foreign secretary in 1955. As chancellor of the Exchequer 1955–57 he introduced Premium Savings Bonds. He took over as prime minister in 1957, on Eden's resignation after the Suez crisis, and led his party to victory in the 1959 elections on the slogan 'You've never had it so good'. (The phrase came from a speech at Bedford in 1957, in which he was actually warning of the coming danger of inflation.) His realization of the 'wind of change' in Africa advanced the independence of former colonies, but Britain's attempt to enter the Common Market in 1963 was blocked by de Gaulle. Macmillan resigned later that year. His nickname Supermac was coined by cartoonist Vicky. He was made an earl in 1984.

McMillan /mək'mɪlən/ Edwin Mattison 1907– . American physicist. He shared a Nobel prize in chemistry with ◊Seaborg in 1951. In 1963 he and I Veksler, director of the Russian Joint Institute for Nuclear Research, won an Atoms for Peace award for their independent arrival 20 years before at a method of overcoming the limitations of the cyclotron (see ◊accelerator).

MacMillan /mək'mɪlən/ Kenneth 1929– . Scottish choreographer. After studying at the Sadler's Wells Ballet School he was director of the Royal Ballet 1970–77 and then principal choreographer. He is particularly renowned for his work with the Canadian dancer Lynn Seymour such as *La Baiser de la Fée* 1960 and *Anastasia* 1967–71. Other works include *Elite Syncopations* 1974 and *Mayerling* 1978. He was knighted in 1983.

MacMillan /mək'mɪlən/ Kirkpatrick died 1878. Scottish blacksmith, who invented the bicycle in 1839. His invention consisted of a hobby-horse that was fitted with treadles and propelled by pedalling.

MacNeice /mək'niːs/ Louis 1907–1963. Anglo-Irish poet, born in Belfast. He made his debut with *Blind Fireworks* 1929 and developed a polished ease of expression, reflecting his classical training, as in *Autumn Journal* 1939. Unlike many of his contemporaries, he was politically uncommitted. Later works include radio plays and translations of Goethe's *Faust* and the Greek classics.

Mâcon /'mɑːkɒŋ/ capital of the French department of Saône-et-Loire, on the Saône, 72 km/45 mi N of Lyons; known for wine; population (1983) 39,000. Mâcon dates from ancient Gaul.

Macpherson /mək'fɜːsən/ James 1736–1796. Scottish author, born at Ruthven. In 1760 he published *Fragments of Ancient Poetry collected in the Highlands of Scotland*, followed by the epics *Fingal* 1761 and *Temora* 1763, which he claimed as the work of the 3rd-century bard ◊Ossian. When challenged by Dr Samuel Johnson, Macpherson failed to produce his originals and a committee decided in 1797 that he had combined fragmentary materials with oral tradition. Nevertheless, the works of 'Ossian' influenced the development of the ◊Romantic movement in Britain and in Europe.

Macquarie /mə'kwɒri/ Lachlan 1761–1834. Scottish administrator. He succeeded ◊Bligh as governor of New South Wales 1808–1821. Lachlan river and Macquarie river and island are named after him. *Macquarie Island* is a Tasmanian dependency, some 1,370 km/850 mi SE of Hobart, uninhabited except for an Australian government research station.

McQueen /mə'kwiːn/ Steve (Terrence Steven) 1930–1980. American actor. He was one of the most popular film stars of the 1960s and 1970s, admired for his portrayals of characters in the American tradition of the strong, silent loner. He starred in the television series *Wanted Dead or Alive* in the late 1950s, and became a film star with *The Magnificent Seven* 1960. In

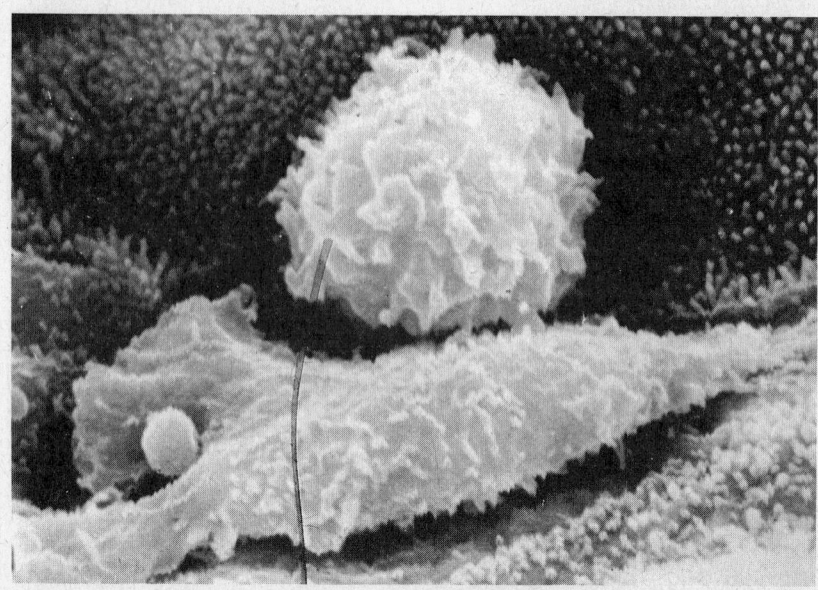

macrophage Scanning electron micrograph (SEM) of two macrophages on human lung tissue. The top one is the normal shape, covered with ruffles. The one below has elongated itself to engulf the particle at left. Macrophages are essential to clear the lung of dust and bacteria.

The Great Escape 1963 he performed all the stunts himself. His last film was *The Hunter* 1980.

McQueen A former US Marine, American actor Steve McQueen starred in Hollywood films of the 1960s and 1970s. In real life a racing enthusiast, he did his own stunt work, including the classic motorcycle chases in *The Great Escape* 1963 and *Bullitt* 1968.

macramé the art of making decorative fringes and lacework with knotted threads. The name comes from the Arabic word for 'striped cloth', which is often decorated in this way.

Macready /mə'kriːdi/ William Charles 1793–1873. British actor. In 1816 he made his debut at Covent Garden, London, and in the roles of Shakespeare's tragic heroes was only rivalled by Edmund ◊Kean. He was partly responsible for returning the theatre to the original texts of Shakespeare, after the earlier bowdlerized versions. His diary gives a vivid picture of life in the theatre in his day.

macro in computing, an instruction in a ◊programming language that is composed of a sequence of other instructions. Issuing a macro command causes the computer to obey the sequence of commands from which the macro was built. Macros allow a higher-level programming language to be created from the instructions of a lower-level language.

macrobiotics in Zen Buddhism, a diet system stressing organically grown wholefoods. It attempts to balance the principles of yin and yang.

macroeconomics the division of ◊economics concerned with the study of whole (aggregate) economies or systems, including such aspects as government income and expenditure, the ◊balance of payments, ◊fiscal policy, ◊inflation, and ◊unemployment. It seeks to understand the influence of all relevant economic factors on each other and thus to quantify and predict aggregate ◊national income.

Modern macroeconomics takes much of its inspiration from the work of ◊Keynes, whose *The General Theory of Employment, Interest and Money* 1936 proposed that governments could prevent financial crises and unemployment by adjusting demand through control of ◊credit and ◊currency. *Keynesian macroeconomics* thus analyses aggregate supply and demand and holds that markets, especially the labour market, do not continuously 'clear' (quickly attain equilibrium between supply and demand) and may require intervention if objectives such as full employment are thought desirable.

Keynesian macroeconomic formulations were generally accepted well into the post-war era and have been refined and extended by the *neo-Keynesian* school, which contends that in a recession the market will clear only very slowly and that full employment equilibrium may never return without significant demand management (by government). At the same time, however, *neo-classical* economics has experienced a recent resurgence, using tools from ▷microeconomics to challenge the central Keynesian assumption that resources may be under-employed and that full employment equilibrium requires state intervention.

Another important school is *new classical* economics, which seeks to show the futility of Keynesian demand management policies and stresses instead the importance of *supply-side economics*, believing that the principal factor influencing growth of national output is the efficient allocation and use of labour and ▷capital. A related school is that of the *Chicago monetarists* led by Milton ▷Friedman, who have revived the old idea that an increase in ▷money supply leads inevitably to an increase in prices rather than in output; however, whereas the new classical school contends that wage and price adjustment is almost instantaneous and so the level of employment at any time must be the natural rate, the Chicago monetarists (see ▷monetarism) are more gradualist, believing that such adjustment may take some years.

macromolecule in chemistry, a very large ▷molecule, generally of a ▷polymer.

macrophage a type of white blood cell or ▷leucocyte found in all vertebrate animals. Macrophages specialize in the removal of bacteria and other microorganisms, or of cell debris following injury. Like ▷phagocytes, they engulf foreign matter, but they are larger than phagocytes and have a longer life-span. They are found throughout the body, but especially in the lymph, connective tissues and lungs; here they can ingest dust, fibres and other inhaled particles, as well as microorganisms.

Madagascar /ˌmædəˈgæskə/ island in the Indian Ocean, off the coast of E Africa, about 400 km/280 mi from Mozambique.

government the 1975 constitution radically changed government structure and renamed the state the Democratic Republic of Madagascar. The constitution provides for a single-chamber national people's assembly of 137 members, elected by universal suffrage for a five-year term, and a president elected in the same way for a seven-year term. The president appoints and chairs a Supreme Revolutionary Council (SRC), which acts as 'the guardian of the Malagasy Socialist Revolution'. A third of its members are nominated by the assembly and the rest are chosen by the president, who is also secretary-general of the political organization which embraces all the various party factions, the National Front for the Defence of the Malagasy Socialist Revolution (FNDR). Power therefore ultimately lies with the president's party. For day-to-day administration, the president appoints a prime minister and council of ministers.

Madagascar

DEMOCRATIC REPUBLIC OF (*Repoblika Demokratika n'i Madagaskar*)

AREA 594,000 sq km/228,500 sq mi
CAPITAL Antananarivo
TOWNS chief port Toamasina
PHYSICAL central highlands; humid valleys and coastal plains
FEATURES one of the last places in the world to be inhabited, it evolved in isolation with unique animals, for example the lemur, now under threat from destruction of the forests
HEAD OF STATE AND OF GOVERNMENT Didier Ratsiraka from 1975
GOVERNMENT one-party socialist
EXPORTS coffee, sugar, spice, textiles
CURRENCY Malagasy franc (1,180 = £1 Sept 1987)
POPULATION 9,941,000 (1985); annual growth rate 2.8%
LANGUAGE Malagasy (of the Malayo-Polynesian family, official); French and English
RELIGION animist 50%, Christian 40%, Muslim 10%
LITERACY 68% male/55% female (1980 est)
GNP $2.7 bn (1983); $279 per head of population
CHRONOLOGY
1960 Achieved full independence, with Philibert Tsiranana as president.
1972 Army took control of the government.

1975 Martial law imposed under a national military directorate. New constitution proclaimed the Democratic Republic of Madagascar, with Didier Ratsiraka as president.
1976 Front-Line Revolutionary Organisation (AREMA) formed.
1977 National Front for the Defence of the Malagasy Socialist Revolution (FNDR) became the sole legal political organization.
1983 Ratsiraka re-elected, despite strong opposition from radical socialist National Movement for the Independence of Madagascar (MONIMA) under Monja Jaona.

history Madagascar was first colonized over 2,000 years ago by Africans and Indonesians. They were joined from the 12th century by Muslim traders, and from 1500, Europeans began to visit the island. Portuguese, Dutch, and English traders having given up, the French established a colony in the mid-17th century but fled after a massacre by local inhabitants. Madagascar was subsequently divided into small kingdoms until the late 18th century when, aided by traders and Christian missionaries, the Merina (the inhabitants of the highland area) united almost all the country under one ruler. In 1885 the country was made a French protectorate, though French control was not complete until 20 years later.

Madagascar remained loyal to Vichy France during World War II, but after being taken by British forces 1942–43, was handed over to the Free French. During the post-war period nationalist movements became active, and Madagascar became an autonomous state within the French community in 1958 and achieved full independence, as a republic, in 1960. Its history since independence has been greatly influenced by the competing interests of its two main ethnic groups, the coastal people, the 'cotiers', and the highland Merina.

The first president of the republic was Philibert Tsiranana, leader of the Social Democratic Party (PSD), which identified itself with the cotiers. In 1972 the army, representing the Merina, took

control of the government and pursued a more nationalistic line than Tsiranana. This caused resentment among the cotiers and, with rising unemployment, led to a government crisis in 1975 which resulted in the imposition of martial law under a national military directorate, and the banning of all political parties. Later that year a new, socialist constitution was approved and Lieut-Comdr Didier Ratsiraka, a cotier, was elected president of the Democratic Republic of Madagascar. Political parties were permitted again and in 1976 the Front-Line Revolutionary Organization (AREMA) was formed by Ratsiraka, as the nucleus of a single party for the state. By 1977 all political activity was concentrated in FNDR and all the candidates for the National People's Assembly were FNDR nominees.

In 1977 the National Movement for the Independence of Madagascar (MONIMA), a radical socialist party, withdrew from the FNDR and was declared illegal. MONIMA's leader, Monja Jaona, unsuccessfully challenged Ratsiraka for the presidency and, although his party did well in the capital, AREMA won 117 of the 137 assembly seats in the 1983 elections. Despite this overwhelming victory, social and political discontent has continued, particularly among the Merinas, who have openly demonstrated their opposition to the government.

Madeira /mə'dɪərə/ group of five Portuguese islands (Portuguese *Funchal*) off the NW coast of Africa, about 420 km/260 mi N of the Canary Islands
area 790 sq km/308 sq mi
capital Funchal on Madeira
features Madeira, the largest, and Porto Santo, are the only inhabited islands. Their mild climate makes them an all-year-round resort. Pico Ruivo on Madeira is the highest mountain at 1,846 m/6,056 ft
products madeira (a fortified wine), sugar cane, fruit, fish, handicrafts
population (1984) 265,000
history Portuguese from the 15th century, Madeira was occupied by Britain in 1801 and 1807–14. In 1980 Madeira gained partial autonomy but remains a Portuguese overseas territory.

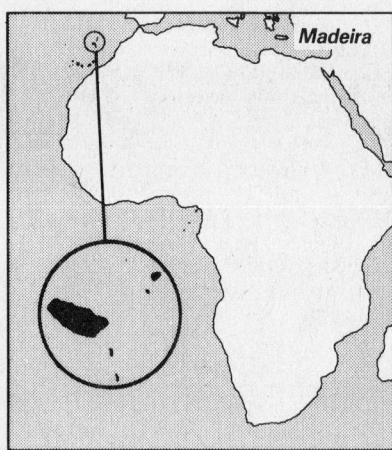

Madeira

Madhya Bharat /'mʌdjə 'baːrət/ state of India 1950–56. It was a union of 24 states of which Gwalior and ◊Indore were the most important. In 1956 Madhya Bharat was absorbed in ◊Madhya Pradesh.

Madhya Pradesh /'mʌdjə prə'deʃ/ central state of India
area 442,841 sq km/170,936 sq mi
capital Bhopal
towns Indore, Jabalpur, Ujjain, Gwalior
features it is the largest of the states
population (1981) 52,131,720
language Hindi
history formed 1950 from the former British province of Central Provinces and Berar and the princely states of Makrai and Chattisgarh. In 1956 it lost some SW districts, including ◊Nagpur, and absorbed Bhopal, Madhya Bharat, and Vindhya Pradesh.

Madison /'mædɪsən/ capital of Wisconsin, USA, 193 km/120 mi NW of Chicago, between lakes Mendota and Monona; state university. Population (1980) 323,545.

Madison /'mædɪsən/ James 1751–1836. 4th president of the USA 1809–17. In 1787 he became a member of the Philadelphia Constitutional Convention and took a leading part in drawing up the US constitution and the Bill of Rights. He became Secretary of State in

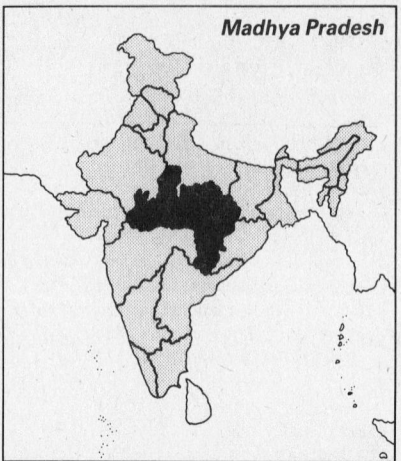

Madhya Pradesh

Jefferson's government 1801–09, in which his main achievement was the ◊Louisiana Purchase. He became president in 1809; and was re-elected in 1812. During his period of office the USA became involved in the ◊War of 1812 with Britain.

Madoc, Prince /'mædək/ legendary prince of Gwynned, Wales, supposed to have discovered America and been an ancestor of a group of light-skinned, Welsh-speaking Indians in the American West.

Madonna Italian name for the Virgin ◊Mary, meaning 'my lady'.

Madras /mə'draːs/ industrial port (cotton, cement, chemicals, iron and steel) and capital of Tamil Nadu, India, on the Bay of Bengal; university 1857; population (1981) 4,277,000. Fort St George 1639 remains from the East India Company. Madras was occupied by the French 1746–48, and shelled by the German ship *Emden* in 1914, the only place in India attacked in World War I.

Madras /mə'draːs/ former name of Tamil ◊Nadu, state of India.

Madrid /mə'drɪd/ industrial city (leather, chemicals, furniture, tobacco, paper) and capital of Spain and Madrid province; population (1981) 3,188,500. There is a university, the Real Academia de Bellas Artes 1752, the Prado Museum 1785, and the royal palace 1764.
history Madrid began as a Moorish citadel captured by Castile 1083. It became important in the times of Charles V and Philip II and was designated capital 1561. During the civil war Madrid was besieged by the Nationalists 7 Nov 1936–28 Mar 1939.

madrigal in music, a form of secular song in four or five parts, usually sung without instrumental accompaniment. It originated in Italy around the beginning of the 14th century, and was particularly popular in Elizabethan England. Madrigal composers include ◊Gabrieli, ◊Monteverdi, Thomas ◊Morley, and Orlando ◊Gibbons.

Madura /mə'dʊərə/ an island in Indonesia, off Surabaya; one of the Sunda Islands

area 4,564 sq km/1,762 sq mi; with offshore islands, more than 5,000 sq km/2,000 sq mi
capital Pamekasan
features central hills rising to 4,800 m/1,545 ft; forested
products rice, tobacco, salt, cattle, fish
population (1970) 2,447,000
history See ◊Java.

Madurai /'mædjʊraɪ/ city in Tamil Nadu, India; site of the great 16th–17th century Hindu temple of Sundareswara, known for its elaborate carving, and of Madurai University 1966; cotton industry; population (1981) 904,000.

Maeander /mi'ændə/ anglicized form of the ancient Greek name of the river ◊Menderes in Turkey.

Maecenas /maɪ'siːnəs/ Gaius Cilnius 69–8 BC. Roman patron of the arts. The friend and counsellor of Augustus, he encouraged the work of ◊Horace and ◊Virgil.

maelstrom /'meɪlstrɒm/ whirlpool off the ◊Lofoten Islands, also known as the Moskenstraumen, which gave its name to whirlpools in general.

maenad in Greek mythology, a woman participant in the orgiastic rites of ◊Dionysus.

Maestricht alternative form of ◊Maastricht, city in the Netherlands.

Maeterlinck /'meɪtəlɪŋk/ Maurice, Count Maeterlinck 1862–1949. Belgian poet and dramatist. He achieved international fame with his play *Pelléas et Mélisande* 1892, *L'Oiseau bleu/The Blue Bird* 1908, and *Le Bourgmestre de Stilmonde/The Burgomaster of Stilemonde* 1918, celebrating Belgian resistance in World War I – a theme which caused his exile to America in 1940. His philosophical essays include *Le Trésor des humbles/The Treasure of the Humble* 1896 and *La Vie des abeilles/The Life of the Bee* 1901. He was awarded the Nobel Prize for Literature in 1911.

Mafeking /'mæfɪkɪŋ/ former name of ◊Mafikeng, town in South Africa.

Mafia /'mæfiə/ originally a secret society of 15th century Sicily, hostile to the law and avenging wrongs by means of terror and vendetta. In the 19th century the Mafia was employed by absentee landlords to manage their *latifundia* (landed estates), and through intimidation soon became the unofficial ruling group of Sicily. In spite of loss of power on the *latifundia*, which were expropriated and divided among the peasants after World War II, the Mafia is still said to be powerful in Sicily, especially in the towns. The government has waged periodic campaigns of suppression, notably in 1927 and 1963–64. The Mafia has spread abroad, particularly to the USA, through immigration, where it is known as *Cosa Nostra*. Organization is in 'families', each with its own boss or *capo*, which are reputed to control organized crime such as gambling, loansharking, drug peddling, prostitution, and protection in the major US cities such as New York and Chicago. Intimidation of witnesses, combined with a code of loyalty and secrecy, makes it difficult even to prove the existence of the Mafia or to bring criminal charges against its alleged members.

The Mafia features frequently in fiction, for example in the film *The Godfather* 1972.

Mafikeng /'mæfɪkeŋ/ town (until 1980 Mafeking) in Bophuthatswana, South Africa; the British officer Baden-Powell held it under Boer siege 12 Oct 1899–17 May 1900.

Magadha /'mʌɡədə/ a kingdom of ancient India. Roughly corresponding to the middle and southern parts of modern ◊Bihar, it witnessed many incidents in the life of the Buddha, and was the seat of the Maurya dynasty, founded by ◊Chandragupta.

magazine a publication brought out periodically, typically containing articles, essays, reviews, illustrations, and so on.

history among the first magazines in Britain were the *Compleat Library* 1691 and the *Gentleman's*

Journal 1692, which contained articles and book reviews. Notable successors, mainly with a mixture of political and literary comment, included ◊Steele's *Tatler* 1709, ◊Addison's *Spectator* 1711, ◊Cave's *Gentleman's Magazine* 1731 (the first to use the word 'magazine' in this sense), ◊Wilkes's *North Briton* 1762, the *Edinburgh Review* 1802, *Quarterly Review* 1806, *Blackwood's Magazine* 1817, and *Contemporary Review* 1866. The earliest illustrations were wood engravings; the half-tone process was invented 1882 and photogravure was used commercially from 1895. ◊Printing and paper-manufacturing techniques made great progress during the 19th century, making larger print runs possible. Advertising began to appear in magazines around 1800, was a moderately

important factor by 1850 and crucial to most magazines' finances by 1880.

Specialist magazines for different interests and hobbies appeared in the 20th century. The 1930s saw the rise of the photojournalism magazines such as *Life* in the USA and the introduction of colour printing. The US pulp magazines of the 1930s and 1940s, which specialized in crime fiction and science fiction, were breeding grounds for writers such as ◊Chandler and ◊Asimov. The development of cheap offset litho printing made possible the flourishing of the underground press in the 1960s, of which the main survivors are the satirical *Private Eye* 1961 and the London listings guide *Time Out* 1968 in Britain and the rock-music paper *Rolling Stone* 1968 in the USA.

MAGAZINES
(circulation figures in thousands)

	founded	circulation		founded	circulation		founded	circulation
Australia			**India**			Electronics and Wireless		
Australasian Post	1946	280	Blitz News Magazine	1941	418	World	1911	45
TV Week	1957	850	Chandamama	1947	462	Homes and Gardens	1919	214
Woman's Day		560	Kumudam	1947	620	Illustrated London News	1842	59
Belgium			Rani Weekly	1962	384	The Lady	1885	76
Bonne Soirée	1922	300	**Italy**			The Lancet	1823	27
Kwik/Zondag Nieuws	1962	287	Domenica del Corriere	1899	800	The Listener	1929	35
Libelle/Rosita	1945	325	La Famiglia Cristiana	1931	1,202	My Weekly	1910	713
Brazil			Gente	1956	1,000	New Scientist	1956	77
Claudia	1962	254	Oggi	1945	743	New Statesman	1913	30
Manchete	1952	223	**Japan**			People's Friend	1869	666
Veja	1968	523	Ie-no-Hikari/Light of Home	1925	1,200	Private Eye	1961	200
Canada			Kaisha Shikiho	1936	600	Punch	1841	75
Chatelaine	1928	1,100	**Netherlands**			Radio Times	1923	3,296
Maclean's Canada's			Margriet		615	Reader's Digest	1939	1,500
Weekly Newsmagazine	1905	644	Kampioen		2,000	Spectator	1828	23
Perspectives	1959	598	Veronica	1971	650	Time Out	1968	76
Reader's Digest	1943	1,327	**New Zealand**			TV Times	1955	3,220
TV Guide	1976	845	New Zealand Listener	1979	350	Woman	1937	1,151
China *(People's Republic)*			New Zealand Woman's			Woman's Own	1932	1,186
Shichang Zhoubao/Market			Weekly	1932	250	Woman's Weekly	1911	1,389
Weekly	1979	1,000	Reader's Digest		165			
Tiyu Kexue/Sports Science	1950	1,200	**South Africa**			**USA**		
France			Huisgenoot	1916	450	Better Homes and Gardens	1922	8,003
Le Canard Enchaîné	1915	500	Rapport	1970	408	Cosmopolitan	1962	2,988
L'Express	1953	585	Reader's Digest		447	Family Circle	1932	7,004
Femmes d'Aujourd'hui	1933	1,600	**Spain**			Good Housekeeping	1885	5,297
Içi Paris	1941	700	¡Hola!	1944	468	Ladies' Home Journal	1883	5,120
Modes et Travaux	1919	1,500	Interviú		494	Life	1978	1,400
Nous Deux	1947	1,000	Pronto		822	McCall's Magazine	1876	6,224
Paris-Match	1949	912	TP Teleprograma		841	National Enquirer	1952	4,713
Sélection du Reader's Digest		1,300	**USSR**			National Geographic		
Télé-Poche	1966	2,150	Krokodil	1922		Magazine	1888	10,500
Télé 7 Jours	1960	3,000	Novy Mir	1925		Newsweek	1933	3,037
Germany *(West)*			Pionerskaya Pravda	1925	11,000	The New Yorker	1925	500
Burdamoden	1949	2,300	Rabotnitsa	1914	13,300	New York Review of Books	1963	120
Funk Uhr		2,150	Zdoroviye	1955	12,600	Penthouse	1969	3,771
Hörzu	1946	4,300	**UK**			Playboy	1953	4,202
Neue Post		1,995	Country Life	1897	48	Reader's Digest	1922	18,000
Der Spiegel	1947	915	The Economist	1843	264	Time	1923	3,600
Stern		1,525				TV Guide	1953	17,345
TV Hören + Sehen		2,600				Variety	1905	45
						Woman's Day		6,500

The US *Reader's Digest* 1922, with editions in many different countries and languages, is the world's best-selling magazine; in individual countries publications that give details of television schedules regularly achieve the highest sales.

In the UK distribution and sale of magazines is largely through newsagents' shops; in the USA postal subscriptions also account for a large percentage of sales.

women's magazines from the *Ladies' Mercury* 1693 until the first feminist publications of the late 1960s the content of mass-circulation women's magazines in Britain has been largely confined to the domestic sphere – housekeeping, recipes, beauty and fashion, advice columns, patterns – and gossip. In the late 18th century, women's magazines reflected society's temporary acceptance of women as intellectually equal to men, discussing public affairs and subjects of general interest, but by 1825 the trend had reversed. Throughout the 19th century the mildest expression of support for women's rights was enough to kill a magazine and often male editors saw their functions as instructing and improving women by moral teaching. Around 1900 publications for working women began to appear, lurid weekly novelettes known as penny dreadfuls. The first colour magazine for women in Britain, *Woman*, appeared in 1937.

comics are usually aimed at children, although in Japan millions of adults read them and artistically sophisticated adult comics are produced in several European countries, notably France. They developed from ◊comic strips in newspapers or, like those of Walt ◊Disney, as spinoffs from animated cartoon films. The first superhero, Superman, created 1938 by Jerome Siegel and Joseph Shuster, soon had his own periodical, and others followed; the Marvel Comics group, formed 1961, was selling 50 million copies a year worldwide by the end of the 1960s and found a cult readership among college students for titles such as *Spiderman* and *The Incredible Hulk*. British children's comics such as the *Beano* and *Dandy* are less sophisticated in style and content.

Magdeburg /'mægdəbɜg/ industrial city (vehicles, paper, textiles and machinery) in East Germany, capital of Magdeburg district; population 289,000. Magdeburg was a member of the Hanseatic League, and has a 13th-century Gothic cathedral.

Magellan, Strait of /mə'gelən/ channel between South America and Tierra del Fuego, named after the navigator. It is 595 km/370 mi long, and joins the Atlantic and Pacific.

Magellan /mə'gelən/ Ferdinand 1480–1521. Portuguese navigator. He was brought up at court and entered the royal service, but later transferred his services to Spain. His proposal to sail to the East Indies by a westerly route was accepted, and in 1519 he started from Seville. He sailed through the *Magellan Strait*, crossed the Pacific, to which he gave its name, and in 1521 reached the Philippines. Here he was killed in battle. His companions reached Seville in 1522, completing the return voyage under Del Cano, but Magellan and his Malay slave, Enrique de Malacca, were the first circumnavigators of the globe, since they had originally sailed from the Philippines to Europe.

Magellanic Clouds in astronomy, two small, irregular-shaped galaxies that are the closest neighbours to our own ◊Galaxy. They appear as detached parts of the ◊Milky Way, in the southern constellations Dorado and Tucana. The Large Magellanic Cloud is 160,000 light years away, and is about one-third the diameter of our Galaxy. The Small Magellanic Cloud, about 180,000 light years away, is one-fifth the diameter of our Galaxy.

Magenta /mə'dʒentə/ town in Lombardy, Italy, 24 km/15 mi W of Milan, where France and Sardinia defeated Austria in 1859 during the struggle for Italian independence.

Maggiore, Lago /mə'dʒɔːreɪ/ lake partly in Italy, partly in Swiss canton of Ticino, with Locarno on its N shore; 63 km/39 mi long and up to 9 km/5.5 mi wide (area 212 sq km/ 82 sq mi), with fine scenery.

maggot name of the footless larvae of insects, especially those of flies, a typical example being the larva of the blow-fly which is deposited as an egg on flesh.

Maghreb /'mʌgrəb/ name for NW Africa (Arabic 'west', 'sunset'). The Maghreb powers – Algeria, Libya, Morocco, Tunisia, and Western Sahara – agreed on economic coordination 1964–65, with Mauritania cooperating from 1970. Chad and Mali are sometimes included. See also ◊Mashraq.

magi /'meɪdʒaɪ/ priests of the Zoroastrian religion of ancient Persia. The term is used in the New Testament of the Latin Vulgate Bible where the Authorized Version gives 'wise men'. The three magi who came to visit the infant Christ with gifts of gold, frankincense, and myrrh were in later tradition described as 'kings'.

magic the art of controlling the forces of nature by supernatural means such as charms and ritual. A central idea is that like produces like; for instance, the ceremonial sprinkling of water will produce rain, a dance imitating a successful hunt will ensure success in hunting, to destroy the image of an enemy will cause his death. It is now generally accepted that most early religious practices and most early art are of magical origin. Under Christianity existing rites were either suppressed (though they survived in modified form in folk-custom and superstition) or replaced by those of the Church itself. Those still practising the ancient rites were persecuted as witches.

magic numbers in atomic physics the numbers of ◊neutrons or ◊protons (2, 8, 20, 28, 50, 82, 126) in the ◊nuclei of elements of outstanding stability such as lead and helium. It is accounted for by the neutrons and protons being arranged in completed 'layers' or 'shells'.

magic realism in art, term coined in the 1920s, originally in the field of painting, now more common in literature, to suggest a fantastic situation realistically treated, as in the works of many Latin American writers, such as Isabel Allende, ◊Borges, ◊García Márquez; pioneered in Europe by ◊Hoffman and ◊Hesse; and practised in the UK by, among others, Angela ◊Carter and Salman ◊Rushdie.

magic square in mathematics, a square array of different numbers in which the rows, columns, and diagonals add to the same total. A simple example employing the numbers 1 to 9, with a total of 15, is:

$$
\begin{array}{ccc}
6 & 7 & 2 \\
1 & 5 & 9 \\
8 & 3 & 4
\end{array}
$$

Maginot Line /'mæʒɪnəʊ/ French fortification system along the German frontier from Switzerland to Luxembourg. Built 1929–36 under the direction of the War Minister, André Maginot, it consisted of semi-underground forts armed with heavy guns, joined by underground passages, and protected by anti-tank defences.

maglev short for *magnetic levitation*, a method of supporting, for example, a train above the track by magnetic forces. See ◊levitation.

magma molten material beneath the Earth's surface from which ◊igneous rocks are formed. This may not be the same as ◊lava extruded at the surface, since as magma rises to form lava it may distil off some of its gaseous components, and some of its solids may crystallize before eruption.

Magna Carta (Latin 'great charter') in English history, the charter granted by King ◊John in 1215, traditionally seen as guaranteeing human rights against the excessive use of royal power.

As a reply to the king's demands for excessive feudal dues and attacks on the privileges of the Church, Archbishop Langton proposed to the barons the drawing up of a charter in 1213. John was forced to accept this at ◊Runnymede on 15 Jun 1215. Magna Carta begins by reaffirming the rights of the Church. Certain clauses guard against infringements of feudal custom, for example, the king was prevented from making excessive demands for money from his barons without their consent. Others are designed to check extortions by officials or maladministration of justice, for example, no freeman to be arrested, imprisoned or punished except by the judgment of his peers or the law of the land. The privileges of London and the cities were also guaranteed.

As feudalism declined Magna Carta lost its significance, and under the Tudors was almost forgotten. During the 17th century it was rediscovered and reinterpreted by the parliamentary party as a democratic document.

magnesia magnesium oxide, MgO, a white powder or colourless crystals, formed when magnesium is burned in air or oxygen. It is used to treat acidity of the stomach, and in some industrial processes.

magnesium a light, white, fairly tough metal, which tarnishes in air, symbol Mg, atomic weight 24.32 and atomic number 12. It was first found in Magnesia, a district in Thessaly, and is widely distributed in its silicate, carbonate and chloride forms. Recognized as an element by ◊Black in 1755, isolated by ◊Davy in 1808, and prepared in coherent form by Bussy in 1831, it is used in alloys, to strengthen aluminium for aircraft construction, and with uranium as a canning material in nuclear reactors. Its incendiary properties are used in flashlight photography, flares and fireworks.

magnet an object that forms a magnetic field. See ◊magnetism.

magnetic field in physics, a region around a permanent ◊magnet, or around a ◊conductor carrying an electric current, in which a force is extended on a moving charge or on a magnet placed in the field. The field can be represented by lines of force, which by conventions link north and south poles and are parallel to the directions of a small compass needle placed on them. Its magnitude and direction are given by the ◊magnetic flux density, expressed in ◊teslas.

the earth's magnetic field

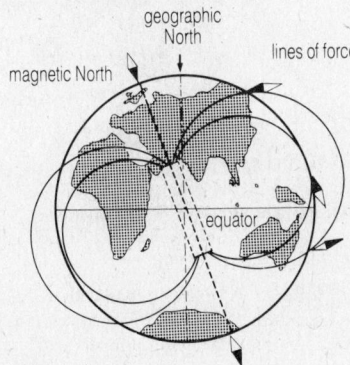

geographic North
lines of force
magnetic North
equator

magnetic flux phenomenon produced in the neighbourhood of electric currents and magnets. The amount of magnetic flux through an area equals the product of the area and the magnetic field strength at a point within that area. It is measured in ◊webers; one weber per square metre is equal to one ◊tesla.

magnetic storm in meteorology, a sudden magnetic disturbance in the earth, causing anomalous disturbances in radio transmissions and magnetic compasses. It is probably caused by ◊sunspot activity.

magnetic tape a narrow plastic ribbon coated with an easily magnetizable material, used in ◊sound recording, audiovisual systems (◊videotape), and computing.

In computing, to record data and programs, magnetic tape was first used in 1951 as part of the UNIVAC 1 system and was very popular as a storage medium for external ◊memory in the 1950s–60s. Since then it has largely been replaced by magnetic disks. Information is recorded on the tape in binary form, with two different strengths of signal representing 1 and 0. It is quite common for around 20,000 bits of information to be recorded on each centimetre of tape and the tape drives of a mini- or mainframe computer can be capable of reading 5 metres of tape each second. For mass storage on commercial mainframe computers, large reel-to-reel tapes are used, but for the smaller mini- and microcomputers, tape cassettes and cartridges are more usual.

magnetism branch of physics dealing with the properties of ◊magnets and ◊magnetic fields. Magnetic fields are produced by moving charged particles: in electromagnets electrons flow through a coil of wire connected to a battery; in magnets spinning electrons within the atoms generate the field. Only certain ferromagnetic materials can be made into magnets; this is because forces act between adjacent atoms so that large groups, forming regions or domains, produce fields which reinforce.

Substances differ in degree and kind in their ability to be magnetized (permeability). Those substances, such as iron, which have very high permeabilities, are said to be ferromagnetic. Apart from its universal application to ◊dynamos, ◊electric motors, switch-gear, and so forth, magnetism has become of considerable importance in modern science, including particle ◊accelerators for nuclear research, memory stores for ◊computers, tape recorders, ◊cryogenics and investigations of matter and space.

Experiments have confirmed that homing pigeons and some other animals rely on their perception of Earth's magnetic field for their sense of direction.

magnetite a black ◊iron ore, magnetic iron oxide, Fe_3O_4, found in igneous rocks. It may possess polarity (a lodestone) and was used as a compass as early as the first millennium BC.

magneto a simple electric generator, often used to provide the electricity for the ignition system of motor cycles. It consists of a rotating magnet, which sets up an electric current in a coil.

magnetohydrodynamics a method of producing electrical power using hot gases. See ◊MHD.

magnetosphere the volume of space in which the Earth's magnetic field forms a magnetic 'shell' around the planet. It extends 64,000 km/25,000 mi (10 times the Earth's radius) towards the Sun, but on the side away from the Sun it is drawn out into a longer *magnetotail*. The outer edge of the magnetosphere is the *magnetopause*. Beyond this is a turbulent region, the *magnetosheath*, where the ◊solar wind is deflected around the magnetosphere. Inside the magnetosphere, atomic particles follow the Earth's lines of magnetic force. It contains the ◊Van Allen belts. Other planets with magnetic fields also have magnetospheres, notably ◊Jupiter.

magnetron ◊thermionic valve (vacuum tube) for generating very high-frequency oscillations, used in radar, and to produce microwaves in a microwave oven.

magnification in optics, a measure of the enlargement or reduction of an object in forming an image (for example, by means of a ◊lens). Linear magnification is the ratio of size (height) of the image to the height of the object; it is equal to the distance of the image from the centre of the system divided by the distance of the object. Angular magnification is the ratio of the angle formed by the image to the angle subtended by the object when viewed directly.

Magnitogorsk /mæg'niːtəʊgɔːsk/ industrial town (steel, motor vehicles) in Chelyabinsk region, USSR, on the E slopes of the Ural Mountains; population (1985) 422,000. It was founded in 1931 to work the iron, manganese, bauxite, and other metals in the district.

magnitude in astronomy, measure of the brightness of a ◊star or other celestial object. Faint objects have larger magnitudes, sixth magnitude being the faintest visible to the naked eye under good conditions. The brightest objects have negative (minus) magnitudes, such as ◊Sirius, brightest star in the night sky, magnitude -1.46. A difference of five magnitudes is equal to a brightness difference of 100 times; each magnitude step is equal on this geometric scale to a brightness difference of 2.512 times. *Apparent magnitude* is the brightness that an object appears from Earth, *absolute magnitude* is the brightness at a standard distance of 10 parsecs (32.6 light years) from the star. The apparent magnitude of the Sun is -26.8, its absolute magnitude +4.8.

magnolia tree or shrub of the family Magnoliaceae, native to China, Japan, N America, and the Himalayas. They vary in height from 50 cm/2 ft to 30 m/150 ft. The large single flowers are white, rose, or purple in colour.

Magnox an early type of nuclear reactor used in Britain, for example, in Calder Hall, the world's first commercial nuclear power station. This type of reactor uses uranium fuel encased in tubes of magnesium alloy called Magnox. Carbon dioxide gas is used as a coolant to extract heat from the reactor core. See ◊nuclear energy.

magpie genus of birds *Pica* in the crow family. The common magpie *Pica pica* has black and white plumage, the long tail having a metallic gloss. It feeds on insects, snails, young birds and carrion, and is found in Europe, Asia, North Africa, and W North America.

Magritte /mə'griːt/ René 1898–1967. Belgian artist. A ◊Surrealist, he painted humorous couplings of illusion and reality.

Magyar member of a Hungarian people; the largest ethnic group in ◊Hungary.

Mahabharata /mə,haː'baːrətə/ Sanskrit epic 'great poem of the Bharatas'. Consisting of 18 books probably composed in its present form about 300 BC, it forms with the *Ramayana* the two great epics of the Hindus. It deals with the fortunes of the rival families of the Kauravas and the Pandavas, and contains the ◊Bhagavad-Gita, or *Song of the Blessed*, an episode in the sixth book. See also ◊Krishna.

Maharashtra /,maːhə'ræʃtrə/ state in W central India
area 307,762 sq km/118,717 sq mi
capital Bombay
towns Pune, Nagpur, Sholapur
features cave temples of Ajanta, containing 200 BC–7th century AD Buddhist murals and sculptures; Ellora cave temples 6–9th century with Buddhist, Hindu, and Jain sculptures
products cotton, rice, groundnuts
population (1981) 62,694,000
language Marathi 50%
religion Hindu 80%, Parsee, Jain, and Sikh minorities

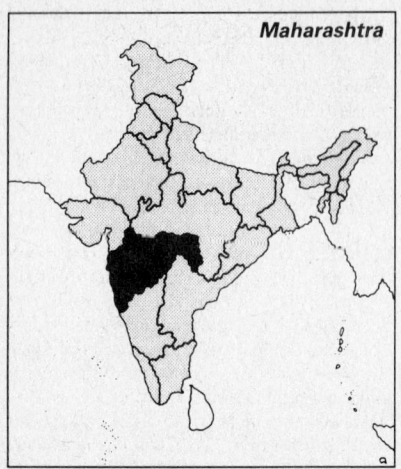
Maharashtra

Mahler Austrian composer and conductor Gustav Mahler wrote nine long Romantic symphonies, some of which include choruses and solo voices.

history formed in 1960 from the S part of the former Bombay state.

maharishi /ˌmɑːhəˈriːʃi/ Hindu guru, or spiritual leader (Sanskrit *maha* 'great', *rishi*, 'sage'). The Maharishi Mahesh Yogi influenced the ◊Beatles and other Westerners in the 1960s.

mahatma (Sanskrit 'great soul') title conferred on Mohandas K ◊Gandhi by his followers as the first great national Indian leader.

Mahayana /ˌmɑːhəˈjɑːnə/ (Sanskrit 'greater vehicle') one of the two major forms of ◊Buddhism, common in N Asia (China, Korea, Japan, and Tibet).

Mahdi /ˈmɑːdi/ in Islam, the title of a coming messiah who will establish the reign of justice on earth. Meaning 'he who is guided aright', it has been assumed by many Muslim leaders, notably the Sudanese sheik Mohammed Ahmed 1848–85, who headed a revolt in 1881 against Egypt and in 1885 captured Khartoum. His great-grandson *Sadiq el Mahdi* (1936–   ) leader of the Umma party in the Sudan, was prime minister 1966–67, and imprisoned 1969–74 for attempting to overthrow the military regime.

mah-jong originally an ancient Chinese card game, dating from the Song dynasty 960–1279. It is now usually played by four people with 144 small ivory tiles or 'dominoes', divided into six suits. The name means 'sparrows'.

Mahler /ˈmɑːlə/ Gustav 1860–1911. Austrian Romantic composer. Born in Bohemia (now Czechoslovakia), he studied at Vienna Conservatoire. He worked as a conductor throughout his life, notably with the Vienna Opera and the New York Philharmonic. His nine massive, richly textured symphonies, the moving *Das Lied von der Erde/Song of the Earth* 1909 and his song cycles display a synthesis of Romanticism and new uses of chromatic harmonies and musical forms.

mahogany timber obtained from several genera of trees found in America especially in Belize, and in Africa. It is a warm red colour, very durable, and takes a high polish. True mahogany comes from the *Swietenia* but other types come from the Spanish and Australian cedars, the Indian redwood, and other trees of the family Meliaceae, native to Africa and the E Indies.

Mahón /mɑːˈɒn/ capital and port of the Spanish island of Minorca, probably founded by the Carthaginians. It was in British occupation 1708–56 and 1762–82.

Mahrattas or *Marathas* people of ◊Maharashtra, India, speaking the Marathi language. In the 17th–18th centuries they formed a powerful military confederacy rivalling the Mogul emperors. The Afghan allies of the latter defeated them 1761, and, after a series of wars with the British 1779–1871, most of their territory was annexed.

Maiden Castle /ˈmeɪdn ˈkɑːsəl/ a prehistoric fort and successive later earthworks on Fordington Hill, near Dorchester, Dorset, England. A rampart, about 18 m/60 ft high, enclosed an area of 18 ha/45 acres. The site was inhabited from Neolithic times (c. 2000 BC) and was stormed by the Romans in 43 AD.

maidenhair fern *Adiantum capillus-veneris* with hair-like fronds terminating in small kidney-shaped pinnules bearing the spores. It is widely distributed in America, and is sometimes found in the W of the British Isles.

maidenhair tree another name for ◊ginkgo, an ornamental tree.

maid of honour in Britain, the closest attendant on a queen. They are chosen generally from the daughters and grand-daughters of peers, but in the absence of another title bear that of Honourable.

Maidstone /ˈmeɪdstəʊn/ industrial town in Kent, England, on the Medway, administrative headquarters of the county; population (1983) 71,800. Notable are the ruins of All Saints' College 1260 and Chillington Manor (Elizabethan).

Maiduguri /ˌmaɪduˈɡuəri/ city in NE Nigeria; population (1975) 189,000.

Maikop /maɪˈkɒp/ capital of Adyge autonomous region of the USSR on the river Bielaia, with timber mills, distilleries, tanneries, and tobacco and furniture factories; population (1981) 132,000. Oilfields, discovered in 1900, are linked by pipeline with Tapse on the Black Sea.

Mailer /ˈmeɪlə/ Norman 1923–   . American writer. He gained wide attention with his novel of World War II *The Naked and the Dead* 1949. Later works include the novel *An American Dream* 1964, and *The Executioner's Song* 1979 (Pulitzer prize), dealing with a convicted murderer.

Mailer The American novelist and journalist Norman Mailer, photographed in 1965 on the balcony of his Brooklyn Heights apartment. He has become a leading commentator on contemporary American society.

Maillol /maɪˈɒl/ Aristide Joseph Bonaventure 1861–1944. French sculptor. He was a noted painter and graphic artist before turning to sculpture in 1902. His work is bold and monumental, for example the figures *Fame* for the Cézanne monument at Aix-en-Provence, and *Flora* and *Pomona* at Winterthur.

Maimonides /maɪˈmɒnɪdiːz/ Moses (Moses Ben Maimon) 1135–1204. Jewish rabbi and philosopher, known as one of the greatest Hebrew scholars. Born at Cordova, he evolved a philosophy of religion of great significance. His codification of Jewish Law is known as the *Mishneh Torah/The Torah Reviewed* 1180, and his philosophical classic is *More nevukhim/The Guide to the Perplexed* 1176–91, which helped to introduce the theories of Aristotle into medieval philosophy.

Maine /meɪn/ old French province bounded on the N by Normandy, on the W by Brittany, and on the S by Anjou. The modern *départements* of Sarthe and Mayenne approximately correspond with it.

Maine /meɪn/ French river, 11 km/7 mi long, formed by the junction of the Mayenne and Sarthe; it enters the Loire below Angers, and gives its name to Maine-et-Loire *département*.

Maine /meɪn/ north-easternmost state of the USA, largest of the New England states; nicknamed Pine Tree State
area 86,027 sq km/33,215 sq mi
capital Augusta
towns Portland
features Appalachian Mountains; Acadia National Park; 80% of the state is forested
products dairy and market garden produce; paper, pulp and timber; textiles; tourism is important

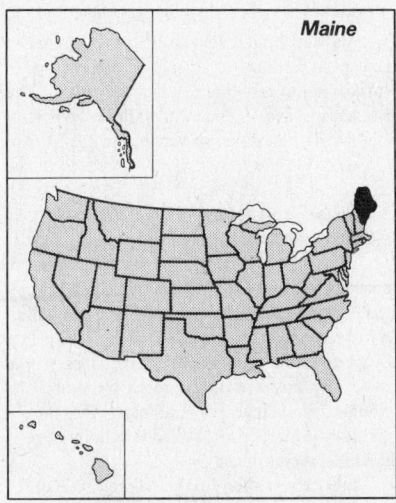

Maine

population (1983) 1,146,000
famous people Longfellow, Edna St Vincent Millay, Kate Douglas Wiggin
history settled from 1623, it became a state in 1820.

mainframe a large computer used for commercial data processing and other large-scale operations. The ◊supercomputer is more powerful than the mainframe.

main sequence in astronomy, the part of the ◊Hertzsprung-Russell diagram that contains stars in the prime of their lives, such as the ◊Sun. It runs diagonally from the top left to the lower right. The most massive (and hence brightest) stars are at the top left, with the least massive (and hence coolest) stars at the bottom right.

Maintenon /ˌmæntəˈnɒŋ/ ·Françoise d'Aubigné, Marquise de Maintenon 1653–1719. Second wife of ◊Louis XIV of France from 1684. Widow of the poet Scarron, she was governess to the children of Mme de ◊Montespan by Louis, and secretly married the king after the death of Queen Marie Thérèse in 1683. Her political influence was considerable, and, as a Catholic convert from Protestantism, her religious opinions were zealous.

Mainz /maɪnts/ capital of Rhineland-Palatinate, West Germany, on the Rhine, 37 km/23 mi WSW of Frankfurt-am-Main; population (1984) 187,000. In Roman times it was a fortified camp and became the capital of Germania Superior. Printing was invented about 1448 in Mainz by ◊Gutenberg.

maiolica or *majolica* a kind of enamelled ◊pottery, so-named from the Italian form of Majorca, where such ware was made. The term is especially applied to the richly decorated enamel pottery produced in Italy between the 15th and 18th centuries.

maize plant *Zea mays* of the grass family, cultivated by American Indians – hence its alternative name of Indian corn or in US usage 'corn' – and introduced to Europe by Columbus. It is now grown extensively in all subtropical and warm temperate regions, its range having been extended by hardy varieties in the 1960s to colder

zones, and is widely used as animal feed. Sweetcorn, a variety in which the sugar is not converted to starch, is a familiar vegetable as 'corn on the cob': other varieties are made into hominy, polenta, popcorn, and corn bread. Uses include fermenting into alcohol, corn oil, and from the stalks, paper and hardboard.

maize 'Corn on the cob' piled high as the crop is gathered, just outside Beijing, China.

Majorca /məˈjɔːkə/ (Spanish *Mallorca*) largest island of the ◊Balearics, belonging to Spain, in the W Mediterranean
area 3,639 sq km/1,405 sq mi
capital Palma
features the highest mountain is Puig Mayor 1,445 m/4,741 ft
products olives, figs, oranges, wine, brandy; tourism is the mainstay of the economy
population (1981) 534,500
history united with the kingdom of Aragon in the 14th century.

major-general one of the officers appointed by Oliver Cromwell in 1655 to oversee the 12 military districts into which England had been divided. Their powers were extensive and included organizing the militia, local government and the collection of some taxes.

Makalu /ˈmʌkəluː/ a mountain in the ◊Himalayas, in Nepál on the border with Tibet.

Makarios III /məˈkɑːrɪɒs/ 1913–1977. Cypriot Orthodox archbishop 1950–77. Exiled by the British to the Seychelles 1956–57 for supporting armed action to achieve union with Greece, he was president of the republic of Cyprus 1960–77 (briefly deposed by a Greek military coup Jul–Dec 1974).

Makarova /məˈkɑːrəvə/ Natalia 1940– . Russian ballerina. She danced with the Kirov Ballet 1959–70, then sought political asylum in

Makarios III Archbishop Makarios, president of Cyprus 1960–77.

the West. Her great roles include Giselle, and Aurora in *The Sleeping Beauty*.

Makeyevka /məˈkeɪəfkə/ industrial city (coal, iron and steel, chemicals) in the Donets Basin, SE Ukraine, USSR; population (1985) 451,000.

Makhachkala /məˌkætʃkəˈlɑː/ capital of Daghestan, USSR, on the Caspian Sea, ESE of Grozny, from which pipelines bring petroleum to Makhachkala's refineries; other industries (shipbuilding, meat packing, chemicals); population (1985) 301,000.

Malabar Coast /ˈmæləbɑː ˈkaʊst/ the coastal area of Karnataka and Kerala states, India, lying between the Arabian Sea and the Western Ghats; about 65 km/40 mi W to E, 725 km/450 mi N to S A fertile area with heavy rains, it produces food grains, coconuts, rubber, spices; teak, ebony, and other woods. Lagoons fringe the shore. A district of Tamil Nadu transferred in 1956 to Kerala was called Malabar Coast.

Malacca /məˈlækə/ state of W Malaysia, Federation of Malaysia
area 1,650 sq km/640 sq mi
capital Malacca
products rubber
population (1980) 453,000 (about 70% Chinese)
history the town originated in the 13th century as a fishing village frequented by pirates, and later developed into a trading port. Portuguese from 1511, then Dutch from 1641, it was ceded to Britain in 1824, becoming part of the Straits Settlements.

Malacca, Strait of /məˈlækə/ channel between Sumatra and the Malay Peninsula; length 965 km/600 mi; narrows to less than 38 km/24 mi wide. It carries all shipping between the ◊Indian Ocean and the ◊South China Sea.

malachite a common ◊copper ore.

Málaga /ˈmæləgə/ industrial seaport (sugar refining, distilling, brewing, olive-oil pressing, shipbuilding) and holiday resort in Andalusia, Spain; capital of Málaga province· on the Mediterranean; population (1981) 503,250.

history founded by the Phoenicians and taken by the Moors in 711, Málaga was capital of the Moorish kingdom of Malaga from the 13th century until captured in 1487 by Ferdinand and Isabella.

Malagasy Republic /ˌmæləˈgæsi/ former name (1958–75) of ◊Madagascar.

Malamud /ˈmæləmʌd/ Bernard 1914–1986. American novelist. He first attracted attention with *The Natural* 1952, taking a professional baseball player as his hero. Later works, often dealing with Jewish immigrant tradition, include *The Assistant* 1957, *The Fixer* 1966, *Dubin's Lives* 1979, and *God's Grace* 1982.

malapropism a form of expression similar to a slip of the tongue, arising from the confusion of similar-sounding words. The result can be amusing or ridiculous (for example, an allegory rather than an alligator in the Florida swamps). Linguistically, the expression derives from the French *mal à propos* ('inappropriate'); historically, it is associated with Mrs Malaprop, a character in Sheridan's play *The Rivals* (1775), who was the pineapple (= pinnacle) of perfection in such matters. As a literary device, however, malapropism dates back at least to Shakespeare.

malaria infectious disease, marked by periodic fever and an enlarged spleen, which affects some 200 million people a year. When a female mosquito of the *Anopheles* genus bites a human with malaria, it takes in with the human blood the malaria parasite (*Plasmodium*). This matures within the insect, and is then transferred when the mosquito bites a new victim. Inside the human body the parasite settles first in the liver, then multiplies to attack the red blood cells, when the symptoms of malaria become evident. Tests on a vaccine were begun in Nov 1986 in the USA.

Malawi, Lake /məˈlɑːwi/ lake which for the most part is included in the Republic of Malawi, and is formed in a section of the Great ◊Rift Valley. It is about 500 m/1,500 ft above sea level and 560 km/350 mi long, with an area of 37,000 sq km/14,200 sq mi. It is intermittently drained to the S by the Shiré into the Zambezi.

Malawi /məˈlɑːwi/ country in SE Africa, bordered N and NE by Tanzania, E, S and W by Mozambique, and W by Zambia.

government the 1966 constitution provides for a president elected for a five-year term, but was amended in 1971 to make Hastings ◊Banda president for life. Malawi is a one-party state, all adults being required to be members of the Malawi Congress Party (MCP). The single-chamber legislature, the national assembly, has 101 elected members, and the president may appoint any number of additional members. He also appoints a cabinet whose members are directly responsible to him. Hastings Banda's system of personal, paternalistic rule has not been seriously challenged in his 20 years of office. There are at least three opposition groups which operate from outside Malawi.

history during the 15th–19th centuries the Malawi empire occupied roughly the S part of the region which makes up present-day Malawi. In the 17th century the Portuguese were the first Europeans to visit the area, but Britain intervened to prevent them annexing it and thereby linking the Portuguese colonies of Angola and Mozambique. In 1891 Britain annexed the country, making it the British protectorate of Nyasaland from 1907. Between 1953–64 it was part of the Federation of Rhodesia and Nyasaland, which comprised the territory which is now Zimbabwe, Zambia and Malawi.

Dr Hastings Banda, through the Malawi Congress Party (MCP), led a campaign for independence and in 1963 the Federation was dissolved. Nyasaland became independent as Malawi in 1964, and two years later became a republic and a one-party state, with Dr Banda as its first president. He has governed his country in a very individual way, tolerating no opposition, and his foreign policies have at times been rather idiosyncratic. He astonished his black African colleagues in 1967 by officially recognizing the republic of South Africa, and in 1971 became the first African head of state to visit that country. In 1976, however, he also recognized the communist government in Angola.

Banda keeps a tight control over his government colleagues and, as yet, no successor has emerged. In 1977 he embarked upon a policy of what can best be described as cautious liberalism, releasing some political detainees and allowing greater press freedom. His external policies are based on a mixture of national self interest and practical reality and have enabled Malawi to live in reasonable harmony with its neighbours.

is the basis of both standard Malay in Malaysia and Bahasa Indonesia, the official language of Indonesia. Bazaar Malay is a widespread pidgin variety used for trading and shopping. The Malaysian and Indonesian varieties officially employ slightly different versions of the Roman alphabet but are also sometimes written in the Jawi form of Arabic script.

Malayo-Polynesian also known as Austronesian, a family of languages spoken from Malaysia through the Indonesian archipelago, parts of Indo-China, Taiwan, Madagascar, and the Melanesian islands to Polynesia (excluding Australia and most of New Guinea). The group contains some 500 distinct languages, some spoken by only a few hundred people, others the standard languages of millions. The family includes ◊Malay in Malaysia, Bahasa Indonesia, Fijian, Hawaiian, and Maori.

Malay Peninsula /məˈleɪ/ S projection of the continent of Asia lying between the Strait of Malacca, which divides it from Sumatra, and the China Sea. The N portion is partly in Burma, partly in Thailand; the S forms part of the Federation of ◊Malaysia. The island of Singapore lies off its S extremity.

Malaysia /məˈleɪziə/ country in SE Asia, comprising the Malay Peninsula, bordered to the N by Thailand, and surrounded E, S, and W by the South China Sea; and the states of Sabah and Sarawak, which occupy the N part of the island of Borneo, the S being part of Indonesia.

Malawi
REPUBLIC OF (*Malaŵi*)

AREA 117,000 sq km/47,950 sq mi
CAPITAL Lilongwe
TOWNS Blantyre-Limbe
PHYSICAL occupies the mountainous W side of Lake Malawi
FEATURES Livingstonia National Park on the Nyika Plateau in the N, rich in orchids, arthropods, elephants; Shiré Highlands, noted for tea and tobacco, and rising to 1,750 m/5,800 ft
HEAD OF STATE AND OF GOVERNMENT Hastings Kamusu Banda from 1966
GOVERNMENT one-party authoritarian
EXPORTS tea, tobacco, cotton, groundnuts, sugar
CURRENCY kwacha (3.68 = £1 Sept 1987)
POPULATION 7,056,000 (1985); annual growth rate 3.1%
LANGUAGE English (official); Chichewa
RELIGION Christian 50%; Muslim 30%
LITERACY 48% male/25% female (1980 est)
GNP $1.1 bn (1984); $200 per head of population
CHRONOLOGY
1964 Nyasaland achieved independence,

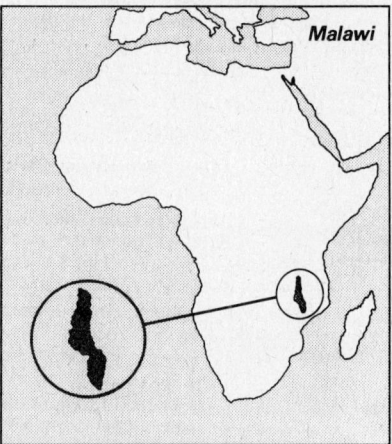

Malawi

within the Commonwealth, as Malawi.
1966 Became a one-party republic, with Hastings Banda as president.
1971 Banda was made president for life.
1977 Banda started a programme of moderate liberalization, releasing some political detainees and allowing greater freedom of the press.

Malay language a member of the Western or Indonesian branch of the ◊Malayo-Polynesian language family, used in the Malay peninsula and many of the islands of Malaysia and Indonesia. The dialect of the S Malay peninsula

government Malaysia is a federation of 13 states: Johore, Kedah, Kelantan, Malacca, Negri Sembilan, Pahang, Penang, Perak, Perlis, Sabah, Sarawak, Selangor, and Trengganu. Each has its own constitution, head of state, and

Malaysia

AREA 331,500 sq km/128,000 sq mi
CAPITAL Kuala Lumpur
TOWNS Kuching in Sarawak and Kota
Kinabalu in Sabah
PHYSICAL comprises W Malaysia (the nine
Malay states – Perlis, Kedah, Johore,
Selangor, Perak, Negri Sembilan, Kelantan,
Trengganu, Pahang – plus Penang and
Malacca); and E Malaysia (Sarawak and
Sabah); 75% of the area is covered in tropical
jungle; there is a central mountain range;
swamps in the E
HEAD OF STATE Tunku Mahmood Iskander
from 1984
HEAD OF GOVERNMENT Mahathir bin Mohamad
from 1981
GOVERNMENT federal, constitutional monarchy
EXPORTS pineapples, palm oil; rubber; timber;
petroleum (Sarawak), bauxite
CURRENCY ringgit (4.16 = £1 Sept 1987)
POPULATION (1985) 15,467,000 (Malaysian
47%, Chinese 34%, Indians, Pakistanis 9%,
and indigenous peoples – Dayaks, Ibans – of
E Malaysia 10%); annual growth rate 2.3%
LANGUAGE Malay (official, usually written in
Arabic characters); in Sarawak English is also
official
RELIGION Muslim (official)
LITERACY 79% male/61% female (1980 est)
GNP $29.7 bn (1983); $714 per head of
population

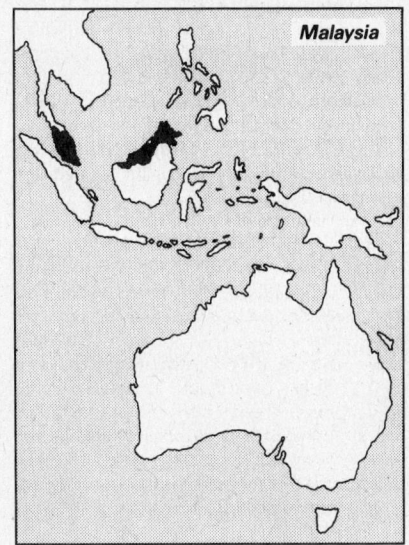

CHRONOLOGY
1963 Formation of federation of Malaysia.
1965 Secession of Singapore from federation.
1969 Anti-Chinese riots in Kuala Lumpur.
1971 Launch of Bumiputra 'new economic
policy'.
1981 Election of Dr Mahathir bin Mohamad as
prime minister.
1982 Mahathir bin Mohamad re-elected.
1986 Mahathir bin Mohamad re-elected.

elected assembly, led by a chief minister and
cabinet, and legislates on matters outside the
federal parliament's sphere.

Under the 1957 constitution, a monarch is
elected for five-year terms by and from among
the hereditary rulers of Johore, Kedah,
Kelantan, Negri ˌSembilang, Pahang, Perak,
Perlis, Selangor, and Trengganu. The
paramount ruler's powers are similar to those of
the British monarch, including discretion in the
appointment of a prime minister and in granting
a dissolution of parliament. Generally, the
monarch acts on the advice of the prime minister
and cabinet, who wield effective power.

The two-chamber federal legislature or
parliament is composed of a 58-member upper
house or senate, *Dewan Negara*, comprising 32
members appointed by the monarch and two
members elected by each of the 13 state
assemblies for six-year terms, and a house of
representatives *Dewan Rakyat*, whose 177
members are elected for five-year terms from
single-member constituencies by universal
suffrage. The Senate can only delay bills already
approved by the dominant House of
Representatives, whose majority party or
coalition provides the prime minister, who
governs with a cabinet selected from parliament.
Malaysia's principal party is the United Malays'
National Organization (UMNO), which is
orientated towards native Malays. It leads the
National Front coalition, which is composed of
12 other parties, most importantly the Chinese-

orientated Malaysian Chinese Association
(MCA), and Gerakan Party, and the Indian-
orientated Malaysian Indian Congress (MIC).
The principal opposition parties are the
moderate, mainly Chinese, Democratic Action
Party (DAP), and the radical Muslim Parti-Sa
Islam Malaysia (PAS). Smaller regional parties
operate at state level.

history the areas which comprise present-day
Malaysia were part of the Buddhist Sri Vijaya
empire between the 9th–14th centuries. This was
overthrown by Majapahit, Java's last Hindu
kingdom. Following this period of Indian
influence, there came the introduction of Islam,
and a powerful Muslim empire developed in the
area. Its growth was checked, however, by the
Portuguese conquest of Malacca in 1511. In 1641
the Dutch ousted the Portuguese, and the area
came under British control from 1786, with a
brief return to Dutch rule 1818–24. Britain
succeeded in unifying its protectorates in Borneo
and the Malay Peninsula after World War II,
making them a crown colony under the name of
the Federation of Malaya in 1948.

The Federation of Malaysia was formed 1963 by
the union of the 11 states of the Federation of
Malaya with the British crown colonies of N
Borneo (then renamed ◊Sabah) and ◊Sarawak,
and ◊Singapore, which seceded from the
federation in 1965. Since 1966 the 11 states on
the Malay Peninsula have been known as West
Malaysia, and Sabah and Sarawak as East
Malaysia. The two regions are separated by 400

miles of the S China Sea. The establishment of
the federation was opposed by guerrillas backed
by ◊Sukarno of ◊Indonesia 1963–66, while the
◊Philippines disputed the sovereignty of East
Malaysia in 1968.

Tunku Abdul ◊Rahman (1903–) was
Malaysia's first prime minister 1963–69, and his
multiracial style of government was successful
until anti-Chinese riots in Kuala Lumpur in 1969
forced the formation of an emergency
administration. These riots followed a fall in
support for UMNO in the federal election, and
were indicative of Malay resentment of the
economic success of the Chinese business
community. They prompted the resignation of
Tunku Abdul Rahman in 1970 and the creation
by his successor, Tun Abdul Razak, of a broader
National Front governing coalition, including
previous opposition parties in its ranks. In
addition, a major 'new economic policy' was
launched in 1971, with the aim of raising the
percentage of Malay-owned businesses from 4%
to 30% by 1990, and to extend the use of pro-
Malay 'affirmative action' quota systems for
university entrance and company employment.
During the 1970s Malaysia enjoyed economic
growth, but relations with the Chinese
community deteriorated as a result of the
government's refusal to welcome Vietnamese
refugees. Even more serious has been a revival in
fundamentalist Islam in the W and N.

Dr Mahathir bin ◊Mohamad (1925–) became
the new leader of the UMNO and prime minister
in 1981 and pursued a more narrowly Islamic and
Malay strategy than his predecessors. He also
launched an ambitious industrialization
programme, seeking to emulate Japan. He has
encountered opposition from his MCA coalition
partners, Christian-Muslim conflict in Sabah,
and slower economic growth as a result of the fall
in world tin, rubber, and palm oil prices.
Malaysia joined ◊ASEAN in 1967 and originally
adopted a pro-Western, anti-Communist
position, but relations with the communist
powers have since improved.

Malcolm III /'mælkəm/ called Canmore,
died 1093, king of Scotland from 1054, the son
of ◊Duncan I; he was killed at Alnwick while
invading Northumberland.

Maldives /'mɔːldiːvz/ group of 1,196 islands
in the N Indian Ocean, about 640 km/400 mi SW
of Sri Lanka, only 203 of which are inhabited.
government the 1968 constitution provides for a
single-chamber citizens' council (*Majilis*) of 48
members, and a president, nominated by the
Majilis and elected by referendum. They all
serve a five-year term. 40 of the *Majilis's*
members are elected by universal suffrage and
eight are appointed by the president, who
appoints and leads a cabinet which is responsible
to the *Majilis*. There are no political parties.
history the islands, under Muslim control from
the 12th century, came under Portuguese rule in
1518. A dependency of Ceylon from 1645–1948,
they were under British protection from
1887–1965 as the Maldive Islands, and became
a republic in 1953. The Sultan was restored in
1954 and then, three years after achieving full

independence as Maldives, the islands returned to republican status in 1968.

Maldives became fully independent as a sultanate outside the Commonwealth in 1965, with Ibrahim Nasir as prime minister. Nasir became president when the sultan was deposed for the second time, in 1968, and the country became a republic. It rejoined the Commonwealth in 1982. Britain had an air force staging post on the S island of Gan 1956–75, and its closure meant a substantial loss of income. The president nevertheless refused a Soviet offer in 1977 to lease the former base, saying that he did not want it used for military purposes again, nor leased to a superpower.

In 1978 Nasir announced that he would not stand for re-election and the *Majilis* nominated Maumoon Abdul Gayoom, a member of Nasir's cabinet, as his successor. Nasir went to Singapore but was called back to answer charges of misusing government funds. He denied the charges and attempts to extradite him failed.

Maldives
REPUBLIC OF (*Divehi Jumhuriya*)

AREA 298 sq km/115 sq mi

CAPITAL Malé

PHYSICAL comprises some 1,000 coral islands, largely flat, none bigger than 13 sq km/5 sq mi

FEATURES only about 200 of the islands are inhabited

HEAD OF STATE AND OF GOVERNMENT Maumoon Abdul Gayoom from 1978

GOVERNMENT authoritarian

EXPORTS coconuts and copra, and bonito (fish related to tunny); tourism is important

CURRENCY Maldivian rupee (11.54 = £1 Sept 1987)

POPULATION 182,000 (1985); annual growth rate 3.2%

LANGUAGE Divehi (related to Sinhalese)

RELIGION Sunni Muslim

LITERACY 82% male/82% female (1977)

GNP $56 million (1983); $470 per head of population

CHRONOLOGY

1953 Originally a sultanate, the Maldive Islands became a republic within the Commonwealth.

1954 Sultanate restored.

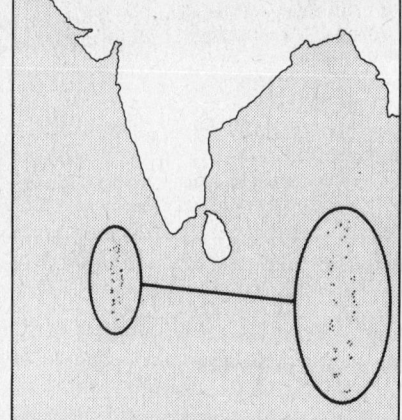
Maldives

1965 Achieved full independence outside the Commonwealth.

1968 Sultan deposed and a republic reinstated with Ibrahim Nasir as president.

1978 Nasir retired and was replaced by Maumoon Abdul Gayoom.

1982 Rejoined the Commonwealth.

1983 Gayoom re-elected.

Maldon /'mɔːldən/ English market town in Essex, at the mouth of the river Chelmer, the scene of a battle in which the East Saxons were defeated by the Danes in 991, commemorated in the Anglo-Saxon poem *The Battle of Maldon*.

Malebranche /mæl'brɒnʃ/ Nicolas 1638–1715. French philosopher. His *De la Recherche de la Vérité/Search after Truth* 1674–78 was inspired by Descartes: he maintained that exact ideas of external objects are obtainable only through God.

Malenkov /'mælənkɒf/ Georgi Maximilianovich 1901–1988. Soviet prime minister 1953–55, ousted by ⟡Khrushchev.

Malevich /'mælɪvɪtʃ/ Kasimir 1878–1935. Russian abstract painter, born in Kiev, whose *Black Square on White Ground* 1915 launched ⟡Suprematism.

Malherbe /mæ'leəb/ François de 1555–1628. French poet and grammarian. Court poet from about 1605 under Henry IV and Louis XIII, he advocated reform of language and versification and established the 12-syllable Alexandrine as the standard form of French verse.

Mali /'mɑːli/ landlocked country in NW Africa, bordered to the NE by Algeria, E by Niger, SE by Burkina Faso, S by the Ivory Coast, SW by Senegal and Guinea, and W and N by Mauritania.

government the 1974 constitution, amended in 1981 and 1985, provides for a one-party state, with a president elected by universal suffrage, and an 82-member national assembly, elected from a party list for a three-year term. The president serves for six years and may be re-elected any number of times. The party is the Malian People's Democratic Union (UDPM).

history in the 7th–11th centuries part of the ⟡Ghana empire, then of the Muslim ⟡Mali empire during the 7th–15th centuries, the area now known as Mali came under the rule of the ⟡Songhai empire during the 15th–16th centuries. In 1591 an invasion by Moroccan forces seeking to take over the W Sudanese gold trade destroyed the Songhai empire, and left the area divided into small kingdoms.

Because of its inland position, the region had little contact with Europeans, who were trading around the coast from the 16th century, and it

was not until the 19th century that France, by means of treaties with local rulers, established colonies throughout most of NW Africa. As French Sudan, Mali was part of French West Africa from 1893. In 1959, with Senegal, it formed the Federation of Mali. In 1960 Senegal left and Mali became a fully independent republic. Its first president, Modibo Keita, imposed an authoritarian socialist regime but his economic policies failed and he was removed in an army coup in 1968. The constitution was suspended, political activity was banned, and government was placed in the hands of a Military Committee for National Liberation (CMLN) with Lieut Moussa Traoré as president and head of state. In 1969 he became prime minister as well and in 1974 a new constitution made Mali a one-party state. A new party, the UDPM, was announced in 1976. Despite student opposition to a one-party state and army objections to civilian rule, Traoré successfully made the transition so that by 1979 Mali had a constitutional government, while ultimate power lay with the party and the military establishment.

In 1983 Mali and Guinea signed an agreement for eventual economic and political integration. In 1985 a border dispute with Burkina Faso resulted in a five-day conflict which was eventually settled by the intervention of the International Court of Justice.

Mali Women passing a mud-built mosque in Djenné, Mali.

malic acid an organic compound, $C_4H_6O_5$, that can be extracted from apples, plums, cherries, grapes and other fruits. It occurs in all living cells, though in smaller amounts, being one of the intermediates of ⟡Krebs's cycle.

Mali empire a ⟡Muslim empire which existed in NW Africa during the 7th–15th centuries. Thriving on its trade in gold, it reached its peak in the 14th century under Mansa Musa (reigned 1312–37), when it occupied the area which includes present-day Senegal, Gambia, Mali,

Mali

REPUBLIC OF (*République du Mali*)

AREA 1,204,000 sq km/465,000 sq mi
CAPITAL Bamako
PHYSICAL river Niger in S; savanna; part of the
Sahara in N
FEATURES the old town of Timbuktu
HEAD OF STATE AND OF GOVERNMENT Moussa
Traoré from 1968
GOVERNMENT one-party, partly military
EXPORTS cotton, groundnuts, livestock
CURRENCY CFA franc (replacing Mali Franc in
1984 (498.38 = £1 Sept 1987)
POPULATION 7,908,000 (1985); annual growth
rate 2.5%
LANGUAGE French (official), Bambara
RELIGION Sunni Muslim 65%, animist 35%
LITERACY 13% male/6% female (1976)
GNP $1.1 bn (1983); $140 per head of
population
CHRONOLOGY
1959 With Senegal, formed the Federation of
Mali.
1960 Became the independent Republic of
Mali, with Mobido Keita as president.
1968 Keita replaced in an army coup by Moussa
Traoré.

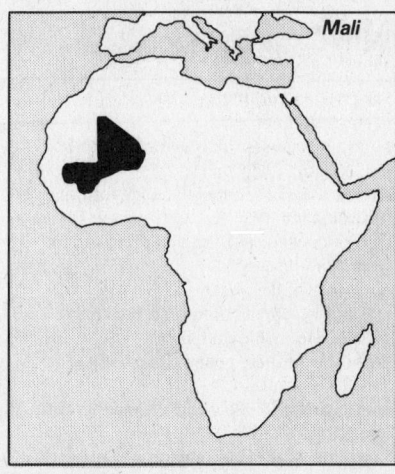
Mali

1974 New constitution made Mali a one-party
state.
1976 New national party, the Malian People's
Democratic Union, announced.
1983 Agreement between Mali and Guinea
for eventual political and economic integration
signed.

and S Mauritania. Mali's territory was similar
(though larger) to that previously ruled by the
◊Ghana empire, and gave way in turn to the
◊Songhai empire.

Malik /'mælɪk/ Yakob Alexandrovich
1906–1980. Soviet diplomat. He was permanent
representative at the United Nations 1948–53
and 1968–76, and it was his walk-out from the
Security Council in Jan 1950 which allowed the
authorization of UN intervention in Korea to
pass.

Malines /mæ'liːn/ French name for
◊Mechelen, city in Belgium.

Malinovsky /ˌmælɪ'nɒfski/ Rodion
Yakolevich 1898–1967. Russian soldier and
politician. In World War I he fought at
Stalingrad, commanded in the Ukraine, and led
the advance through the Balkans to capture
Budapest 1945. He was Minister of Defence
1957–67.

Malinowski /ˌmælɪ'nɒfski/ Bronislaw
1884–1942. Polish anthropologist, one of the
founders of the theory of ◊functionalism in the
social sciences. His study of the peoples of New
Guinea led him to see customs and practices in
terms of their function in creating and
maintaining social order.

Malipiero /ˌmælɪ'pjeərəʊ/ Gian Francesco
1882–1973. Italian composer, editor of
Monteverdi and Vivaldi. His own works include
operas based on Shakespeare's *Julius Caesar*
1934–35 and *Antony and Cleopatra* 1936–37 in
a Neo-Classical style.

mallard common wild ◊duck *Anas
platyrhynchos* found almost worldwide and from
which domestic ducks were bred.

Mallarmé /ˌmælɑ'meɪ/ Stéphane 1842–
1898. French poet, with Verlaine founder of the
◊Symbolist school. His belief that poetry should
be evocative and suggestive was reflected in
L'Après-midi d'un faune/Afternoon of a Faun
1876, which inspired Debussy. Later
publications are *Vers et prose/Verse and Prose*
1893, and the prose *Divagations/Digressions*
1897.

mallee mixture of dwarf eucalyptus trees with
many small stems and thick underground stems
retaining water, and more treelike forms. Before
irrigation farming it characterized the mallee
region of NW Victoria, Australia.

Mallorca Spanish form of ◊Majorca, an
island in the Mediterranean.

mallow flowering plant of family Malvaceae,
including European *common mallow Malva
sylvestris*; *tree mallow Lavatera arborea*; and
marsh mallow Althaea officinalis. See also
◊hollyhock. Most have pink or purple flowers.

Malmaison /ˌmælmer'zon/ chateau near
Paris formerly belonging to the empress
◊Josephine.

Malmö /'mælməʊ/ industrial port
(shipbuilding, textiles) in Sweden; population
(1985) 229,100.

Malory /'mæləri/ Thomas English author of
the prose romance *Morte d'Arthur*. It is a
translation from the French modified by material
from other sources, and deals with the exploits
of Arthur's knights of the Round Table and the
quest for the Grail. Malory's identity is
uncertain, but he is thought to have been the
Warwickshire landowner of that name who was
Member of Parliament for Warwick in 1445, and

in 1451 and 1452 was charged with rape, theft,
and attempted murder. If that is so, he must have
compiled *Morte d'Arthur* during his 20 years in
Newgate prison.

Malpighi /mæl'piːgi/ Marcello 1628–1694.
Italian physiologist, who made many discoveries
(still known by his name) in his microscope
studies of animal and plant tissues.

Malplaquet /ˌmælplæ'keɪ/ village in Nord
département, France, to the NW of Maubeuge,
where on 11 Sept 1709 the British, Dutch, and
Austrians, under Marlborough and Prince
Eugene of Savoy, defeated the French under
Villars during the War of ◊Spanish Succession.

Malraux /mæl'rəʊ/ André 1901–1976.
French novelist and scholar. He became involved
in the nationalist/communist revolution in
China in the 1920s, reflected in *La Condition
humaine/Man's Estate* 1933; *L'Espoir/Days of
Hope* 1937 is set in Civil War Spain, where he
was a bomber-pilot in the International Brigade.
In World War II he supported the Gaullist
Resistance, and was Minister of Cultural Affairs
1960–69.

malt in brewing, grain – barley, oats, wheat –
artificially germinated and then dried in a kiln.
Control of the rate and temperature of drying
produce amber, brown, black or pale malt. Malts
are fermented to make beers or lagers, and then
distilled to produce spirits such as whisky.

Malta, Knights of /'mɔːltə/ another name for
members of the military-religious order of the
Hospital of St John of Jerusalem.

Malta /'mɔːltə/ island in the Mediterranean,
S of Sicily, E of Tunisia, and N of Libya.
government the 1974 constitution provides for a
single-chamber legislature, the 65-member
House of Representatives, elected by universal
suffrage, through a system of proportional
representation, for a five-year term. As formal
head of state the president is elected by the House
for a five-year term, and appoints a prime
minister and cabinet, drawn from and
collectively responsible to the House, which may
be dissolved within its five-year term. The main
political parties are the Malta Labour Party
(MLP), and the Nationalist Party.
history Malta was occupied in turn by
◊Phoenicia, ◊Greece, ◊Carthage, and ◊Rome,
and fell to the Arabs in 870. In 1090 the ◊Norman
Count Roger of ◊Sicily conquered Malta, and it
remained under Sicilian rule until the 16th
century, when the ◊Holy Roman Emperor
◊Charles V handed it over to the Knights of ◊St
John of Jerusalem in 1530. After a Turkish
attack in 1565 the knights fortified the island,
and held it until 1798, when they surrendered to
◊Napoleon. After requesting British protection,
Malta was annexed by Britain in 1814, and
became an important naval base. A vital link in
World War II, Malta came under heavy attack
and was awarded the ◊George Cross decoration.
The island was made self-governing in 1947, and
in 1955 Dom Mintoff, leader of the MLP,
became prime minister. In 1956 the MLP's
proposal for integration with the UK was
approved by a referendum but opposed by the
conservative Nationalist Party, led by Dr
Giorgio Borg Olivier. In 1958 Mintoff rejected

the British proposals and resigned, causing a constitutional crisis. By 1961 both parties favoured independence, and talks began in 1962, with Borg Olivier as prime minister.

Malta became a fully independent state within the Commonwealth, and under the British crown, in 1964, having signed a ten-year defence and economic aid treaty with Britain. In 1971 Mintoff and the MLP returned to power with a policy of international non-alignment. He declared the 1964 treaty invalid and began to negotiate a new arrangement for leasing the Maltese NATO base and obtaining the maximum economic benefit from it for his country.

Eventually a seven-year agreement was signed in 1972. Malta became a republic in 1974 and in the 1976 general election the MLP was returned with a reduced majority. It again won a narrow majority in the House of Representatives in 1981, even though the Nationalists had a bigger share of the popular vote. As a result, Nationalist MPs refused to take up their seats for over a year. Relations between the two parties were also damaged by allegations of pro-government bias in the broadcasting service. At the end of 1984 Mintoff announced his retirement and Dr Mifsud Bonnici succeeded him as MLP leader and prime minister.

Malthus /'mælθəs/ Thomas Robert 1766–1834. British economist. His *Essay on the Principle of Population* 1798 and 1803 argued for population control (which influenced ◊Darwin), since people increase in geometric ratio, and food only in arithmetical ratio. He saw war, famine, and disease as necessary checks on population growth. Later editions of his work suggested that 'moral restraint' (delaying marriage and sexual abstinence before it) could also keep numbers from increasing too quickly, a statement seized on by later birth-control pioneers (the 'neo-Malthusians').

Maluku /mə'luːkuː/ or *Moluccas* group of Indonesian islands
area 83,675 sq km/32,300 sq mi
capital Ambon on Amboina
population (1980) 1,411,000
history as the Spice Islands, they were formerly part of the Netherlands E Indies, and the S Moluccas attempted secession from the newly created Indonesian Republic from 1949; exiles continue agitation in the Netherlands.

Malvern /'mɔːlvən/ English spa in Hereford and Worcester, on the E side of the *Malvern Hills*, which extend for about 16 km/10 mi, and have their high point in Worcester Beacon 425 m/1,395 ft; population (1981) 32,000. The *Malvern Festival* was revived in 1977.

Malvinas /mæl'viːnəs/ Argentine name for the ◊Falkland Islands.

mamba venomous snake of the cobra family found in Africa S of the Sahara. The *green mamba Dendroaspis angusticeps* is 1.5 m/5 ft long or more and lives in trees, feeding on birds and lizards. The *black mamba Dendroaspis polylepis* is the largest venomous snake in Africa, occasionally as much as 3.4 m/11 ft long, and spends more time on the ground.

Malta
REPUBLIC OF (*Repubblika Ta'Malta*)

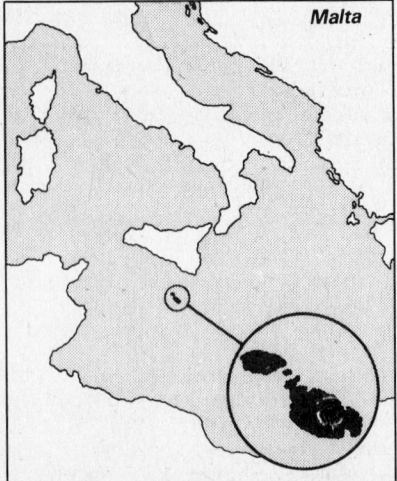

Malta

AREA 316 sq km/122 sq mi
CAPITAL Valletta
PHYSICAL includes the island of Gozo 67 sq km/26 sq mi and Comino 2.5 sq km/1 sq mi
FEATURES large commercial dock facilities
HEAD OF STATE Paul Xuereb from 1987
HEAD OF GOVERNMENT Eddie Fenech-Adami from 1987
GOVERNMENT democratic
EXPORTS vegetables; knitwear, handmade lace; plastics, electronic equipment
CURRENCY Maltese pound (0.56 = £1 Sept 1987)
POPULATION 355,000 (1985); annual growth rate 1.1%
LANGUAGE Maltese (related to Arabic, with Phoenician survivals and influenced by Italian)
RELIGION Roman Catholic
LITERACY 83% male/80% female (1980 est)
GNP $1.04 bn (1983); $2,036 per head of population
CHRONOLOGY
1942 Awarded the George Cross.
1955 Dom Mintoff of the Malta Labour Party (MLP) became prime minister.
1956 Referendum approved proposal for integration with the UK. Proposal opposed by the Nationalist Party.
1958 MLP rejected the integration proposal.
1962 Nationalists elected, with Borg Olivier as prime minister.
1964 Achieved full independence, within the Commonwealth. Ten-year defence and economic aid treaty with Britain signed.

1971 Mintoff re-elected. The 1964 treaty declared invalid and negotiations began for the leasing of the NATO base in Malta.
1972 Seven-year NATO agreement signed.
1974 Became a republic.
1984 Mintoff retired and was replaced by Mifsud Bonnici as prime minister and MLP leader.
1987 Eddie Fenech-Adami (Nationalist) became prime minister.

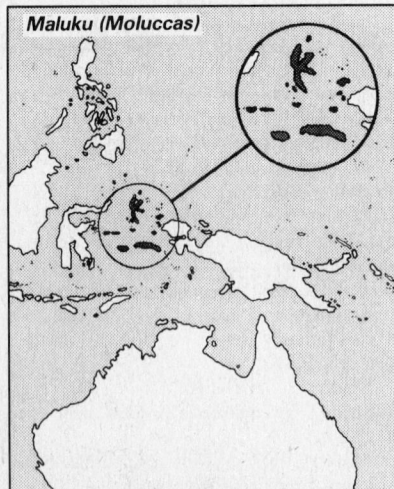

Maluku (Moluccas)

Mameluke /'mæməluːk/ member of a powerful political class who dominated Egypt. Descended from freed Turkish slaves, they formed the royal bodyguard in the 13th century, and in 1250 placed one of their own number on the throne. Mameluke sultans ruled Egypt until the Turkish conquest of 1517, and they remained the ruling class until 1811, when they were massacred by ◊Mehemet Ali.

mammal vertebrate which suckles its young and has hair, lungs and four-chambered heart. It maintains a constant body temperature in varied surroundings. Most mammals give birth to live young, but the platypus and echidna lay eggs. There are over 4,000 species, adapted to almost every conceivable way of life. The smallest shrew weighs only 2 g/0.07 oz, the largest whale up to 150 tonnes.

The orders of mammals are: ◊*Monotremata* echidna, platypus; ◊*Marsupialia* kangaroo, koala, opossum; ◊*Insectivora* shrew, hedgehog, mole; ◊*Chiroptera* bat; *Primates* lemur, monkey, ape, humans; ◊*Edentata* anteater, armadillo, sloth; ◊*Pholidota* pangolin; ◊*Dermoptera* flying lemur; ◊*Rodentia* rat, mouse, squirrel, porcupine; ◊*Lagomorpha* rabbit, hare; ◊*Cetacea* whale, dolphin, porpoise; ◊*Carnivora* cat, dog, weasel, bear; ◊*Pinnipedia* seal, walrus; ◊*Artiodactyla* pig, deer, camel, cattle, giraffe; ◊*Perissodactyla* horse, rhinoceros, tapir; ◊*Sirenia* dugong; *Tubulidentata* aardvark; *Hyracoidea* hyrax; *Proboscidea* elephant.

mammary gland ◊milk-producing gland derived from epithelial cells underlying the skin of mammals; it is only active in the female after the production of young. In all but ◊monotremes (egg-laying mammals), the mammary glands terminate in teats which aid infant suckling. The number of glands and their position varies between species. In humans there are two, in cows four and in pigs between ten and fourteen. See also ◊lactation.

mammography an X-ray procedure that detects breast cancer at an early stage.

mammoth genus *Mammuthus* of extinct elephants whose remains are found worldwide, some being half as tall again as modern species. The woolly mammoth *Elephas primigenius*, the size of an Indian elephant, had long fur, and huge inward-curving tusks. Mammoths were abundant in N Europe in Pleistocene times.

Mammoth Cave huge limestone cavern in Mammoth Cave National Park 1936, Kentucky, USA. The main cave is 6.5 km/4 mi long, and rises to a height of 38 m/125 ft; it is known for its stalactites and stalagmites. Indian councils were once held here.

management information system (MIS) in commercial organizations with computer support, a set of programs for abstracting and summarizing computer-held information for the purposes of management consumption. Such systems normally provide regular printed reports and allow requests for particular reports and statistical analyses.

Managua /mə'nɑːgwə/ capital and chief industrial city of Nicaragua, on the lake of the same name; population (1984) 650,000. It has twice been destroyed by earthquake and rebuilt, in 1931 and 1972.

manakin bird of the family Pipridae found in S and Central America. Manakins are sparrow-sized and often brightly coloured. They feed on berries and other small fruits.

Manama /mə'nɑːmə/ capital and oil port of Bahrain, on Bahrain Island; population (1981) 122,000.

manatee plant-eating aquatic mammal of the genus *Trichechus* belonging to the order Sirenia or sea-cows. Manatees are found on the eastern coasts of tropical N and S America, and also in W Africa. They occur in fresh and sea water. The forelimbs are flippers, the hindlimbs are absent, but there is a short rounded dorso-ventrally flattened tail which is used for propulsion. They have flat bristly muzzles.

Manaus /mə'naus/ capital of Amazonas, Brazil, on the Rio Negro, near its confluence with the Amazon; population (1980) 613,000. Although 1,600 km/1,000 mi from the Atlantic, it can be reached by sea-going vessels.

Manawatu /,mænə'wɑːtuː/ river in North Island, New Zealand, rising in the Ruahine Range.
Manawatu Plain is a rich farming area, specializing in dairying and fat lamb production.

Mancha /'mæntʃə/ see ◊La Mancha, former province of Spain.

Manche, La /mɒnʃ/ French name for the English ◊Channel. It gives its name to a French *département*.

Manchester /'mæntʃɪstə/ city in N England, on the river Irwell, 50 km/31 mi E of Liverpool. A centre for manufacture, commerce and finance, as well as a port (linked by Manchester Ship Canal 1894 to the river Mersey and the sea). Population (1985) 451,000.
features home of the Hallé Orchestra, the Northern College of Music, the Royal Exchange (built 1869, now a theatre), a town hall (by Alfred ◊Waterhouse), and a Cotton Exchange (now a leisure centre).
history originally a Roman camp, Manchester is mentioned in the Domesday Book, and already by the 13th century was a centre for the wool trade. Its damp climate made it ideal for cotton, introduced in the 16th century, and in the 19th century the Manchester area was a world centre of manufacture, using cotton imported from North America and India. After 1945 there was a sharp decline, and many disused mills were refurbished to provide alternative industrial uses.
Long a centre of ◊Radical thought, Manchester has always been a cultural and intellectual centre; it was the original home of the *Guardian* (founded as the *Manchester Guardian* 1821).

Manchester, Greater /'mæntʃɪstə/ former (1974–86) metropolitan county of NW England, replaced by residuary body in 1986 which covers some of its former functions.
area 1,287 sq km/497 sq mi
towns administrative headquarters Manchester; Altrincham, Bolton, Bury, Oldham, Rochdale, Salford, Stockport, and Wigan
features Manchester Ship Canal; Old Trafford cricket ground at Stretford, and the football ground of Manchester United
products industrial
population (1985) 2,597,800
famous people Anthony Burgess, John Dalton, David Lloyd George, James Joule, Emmeline Pankhurst.

Manchu dynasty ruling dynasty in China from 1644 until their overthrow in 1912. Originally a nomadic tribe from Manchuria, they established power through a series of successful invasions from the north.

Manchukuo /,mæntʃuː'kwəu/ former Japanese puppet state in ◊Manchuria.

Manchuria /mæn'tʃuəriə/ European name for the NE region of China (provinces of Heilongjiang, Jilin, and Liaoning). From the 17th century it was controlled by the Manchus, and a Manchu dynasty ruled China by conquest 1644–1912. Chinese colonization of Manchuria began in the 18th century (80% of the population by 1900), but as the Chinese Empire declined Japan and Russia were rivals for its control. The Japanese gained the advantage through the ◊Russo-Japanese War, although it was not until 1932 that Japan consolidated her position by creating a puppet state (Manchukuo) under Henry ◊Pu Yi (capital Hsinking, modern Chinese ◊Changchun), which disintegrated on

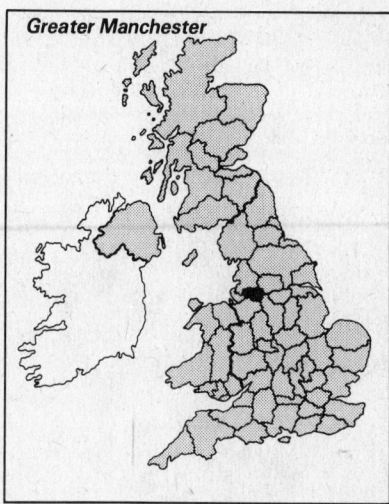

Greater Manchester

the defeat of Japan in World War II in 1945. Japanese settlers were expelled.

Mandaean a member of the only surviving Gnostic sect of Christianity (see under ◊Gnosticism). The Mandaeans live near the Euphrates, S Iraq, and their sacred book is the *Ginza*.

mandala a circular design in Hindu and Buddhist art which represents the Universe.

Mandalay /,mændə'leɪ/ chief town of Upper Burma, on the river Irrawaddy, about 495 km/370 mi N of Rangoon; population (1983) 533,000. Founded by King Mindon Min in 1857, it was capital of Burma 1857–85, and has many pagodas, temples, and monasteries.

mandarin Chinese imperial official. The word was adopted in the 16th century from the Portuguese, its ultimate origin being Sanskrit *mantrin*, 'counsellor'. In China the mandarins were chosen from the 7th century by competitive examination. The term Mandarin was also applied to the ◊Chinese language as spoken by the mandarins; the form of it spoken in Beijing has become the standard language of China, used by 70 per cent of the population.

mandarin variety of the tangerine orange *Citrus reticulata*.

mandate in general, any official command. In politics, the right (given by the electors) of an elected government to carry out its programme of policies. In particular, the term is used for the system, under the Treaty of Versailles, after World War I, whereby the administration of former German and Turkish possessions (including Iraq, Syria, Lebanon, and Palestine) was entrusted to Allied states by the ◊League of Nations. The latter was replaced as the responsible authority in 1945 by the United Nations, when mandates which had not achieved independence or self-government became known as ◊Trust Territories. ◊Namibia (SW Africa) is an exception in that the Republic of South Africa does not recognize United Nations authority in this.

Mandela /mæn'delə/ Nelson (Rolihlahla) 1918– . South African lawyer-politician. As organizer of the banned African National Congress (ANC), he was acquitted of treason in 1961 but was jailed for life in 1964 on charges of sabotage and plotting to overthrow the government.

Mandela Nelson Mandela, leader of the African National Congress, has been incarcerated since 1964.

Mandela /mæn'delə/ Winnie (Nomzamo) 1934– . Black activist for civil rights in South Africa. She was first arrested for her activities with the Women's League of the African National Congress in 1958, the year in which she married Nelson ◊Mandela. After his imprisonment in 1964 she became a leading spokesperson for the ANC. In 1966 she was jailed for a year, and subsequently she has been banned and put under house arrest several times.

Mandelshtam /'mændlʃtæm/ Osip Emilevich 1891–1938. Russian poet. Son of a Jewish merchant, he was sent to a concentration camp by the Communist authorities in the 1930s, where he died. His posthumously published work, saved by his widow, with its classic brevity, established his reputation as one of the greatest modern Russian poets.

Mandeville /'mændvɪl/ John. Supposed author of a 14th-century travel manual for pilgrims to the Holy Land, originally written in French and probably the work of Jean d'Outremeuse of Liège. As well as references to real marvels such as the pyramids, there are tales of headless people with eyes in their shoulders, and other such fantastic inventions.

mandolin musical instrument with eight/ten strings, descended from the ◊lute, and so called because it had an almond-shaped body (Italian *mandorla* 'almond').

mandragora genus of almost stemless plants with narcotic properties, also known as *mandrake*, family ◊Solanaceae. They have large leaves, pale blue or violet flowers, and globose

berries (devil's apples); the humanoid shape of the root started a superstition that it shrieks when pulled from the ground.

mandrake another name for the plant ◊mandragora.

mandrill large W African ground living monkey *Mandrillus sphinx*. The nose is bright red and the cheeks striped with blue. There are red callosities on the buttocks; the fur is brown, with a yellow beard. Males are much larger than females.

Manes /'mɑːneɪz/ in ancient Rome, the spirits of the dead, revered as lesser deities, or sometimes identified with the gods of the underworld.

Manet /'mæneɪ/ Édouard 1832–1883. French painter. Born in Paris, he came under the influence of ◊Velazquez and ◊Hals, and exhibited with ◊Monet, ◊Renoir and ◊Whistler at the *Salon des Refusés* in 1863. This exhibition marked the beginning of the ◊Impressionist movement, of which Manet was a leading spirit. He summed up his aims in the dictum, 'The principal person in a picture is the light'. Manet carried on ◊Courbet's scientific spirit of realism, making the eye the sole judge of reality. Stylistically, he gave up modelling forms in volume to suggest them by juxtaposed colours and gradations of tones, and the subject matter of his pictures was always modern life. His *Déjeuner sur l'herbe/Luncheon on the Grass* (Louvre) updated a Renaissance prototype to 1862. Other well known works include *Olympia* 1865 and *L'Absinthe/The Absinth Drinker* 1859.

Mangalore /ˌmæŋgə'lɔː/ industrial port (textiles, food-processing) in Karnataka, India; population (1981) 306,000.

manganese a silvery-white metallic element, symbol Mn, atomic number 25, atomic weight 54.9. Manganese is among the most common metals in the Earth's crust and is used to make certain steels, as well as bronze, brass, and nickel alloys.

manganese ore mineral from which ◊manganese is produced. The main ores are the oxides, such as hausmannite (Mn_3O_4), barunite (Mn_2O_3) and manganite (MnO(OH)). The carbonate, rhodochrosite ($MnCO_3$), and the sulphide, alabandite (MnS), are also important. Manganese ores may accumulate as ◊sedimentary deposits, particularly as nodules on the sea floor and in metamorphic rocks. The world's major producers are the USSR, S Africa, Brazil, Gabon and India.

mangel wurzel or *mangold* a variety of the common beet *Beta vulgaris* used chiefly as feed for cattle and sheep.

mango tree *Mangifera indica* native to India but now widely cultivated for its oval fruits in other tropical and subtropical areas, for example, West Indies.

mangold another name for ◊mangel wurzel.

mangrove tree mostly belonging to the family Rhizophoraceae, native to muddy swamps of tropical coasts and estuaries where, by sending down aerial roots from its branches, it rapidly forms close-growing mangrove swamps. Its timber is impervious to water and resists marine worms.

Manet One of French Impressionist painter Edouard Manet's best-known works is *Un bar aux Folies-Bergère/Bar at the Folies-Bergère*, painted in 1882.

mangabey type of African monkey genus *Cercocebus* with long limbs and tail living in tropical forests.

Manhattan /mæn'hætn/ an island 20 km/12.5 mi long and 4 km/2.5 mi wide, lying between the Hudson and East rivers and forming a borough of the city of ◊New York, USA; population (1980) 1,428,285.

Manhattan project code-name for the development of the atom bomb in the USA in World War II.

manic depression a mental disorder in which ◊depression alternates with overactivity.

Manichaeism religion founded by the prophet Mani (Latinized as Manichaeus, c. 216–276), who proclaimed his creed in 241 at the Persian court. Returning from missions to China and India, he was put to death at the instigation of the Zoroastrian priesthood. Despite persecution Manichaeism spread and flourished until about the 10th century. Its fundamental tenet was that the material world is an invasion of the realm of light by the powers of darkness: particles of goodness imprisoned in matter were to be rescued by messengers such as Jesus, and finally by Mani himself.

Manila /məˈnɪlə/ industrial port (textiles, tobacco, distilling, shipbuilding) and capital of the Philippines, on the island of Luzon; population (1980) 6 million.
history Manila was founded 1571 by Spain, captured by the USA in 1898, and in 1945 during World War II the old city to the S of the river Pasig was reduced to rubble in fighting between US and Japanese troops. It was replaced as capital by ◊Quezon City 1948–76.

manioc another name for the plant ◊cassava.

Manipur /ˌmʌnɪˈpʊə/ NE state of India
area 22,356 sq km/8,629 sq mi
capital Imphal
features Loktak Lake; original Indian home of polo
population (1981) 1,420,953
language Hindi
religion Hindu 70 per cent.

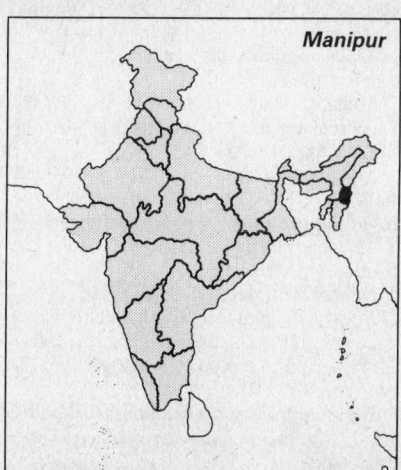

Manipur

Man, Isle of island in the Irish Sea, a dependency of the British crown, but not part of the UK
area 518 sq km/221 sq mi
capital Douglas
towns Ramsey, Peel, Castletown
features Snaefell 620 m/2034 ft; annual TT (Tourist Trophy) motorcycle races, gambling casinos, Britain's first free port, tax haven;

tailless Manx cat; tourism, banking, and insurance are important
exports light engineering products
currency the island produces its own coins and notes (including one for 50p) in British values
population (1981) 64,700
language English (Manx, nearer to Scottish than Irish Gaelic, has been almost extinct since the 1970s)
government crown-appointed lieutenant-governor, a legislative council, and the representative House of Keys, which together make up the Court of Tynwald, passing laws subject to the royal assent. Laws passed at Westminster only affect the island if specifically so provided
history Norwegian until 1266, when the island was ceded to Scotland, it came under crown administration in 1765.

Manitoba, Lake /ˌmænɪˈtəʊbə/ lake in Manitoba province, Canada, which drains into Lake Winnipeg to the NE through the river Dauphin; area 4,700 sq km/1,800 sq mi.

Manitoba /ˌmænɪˈtəʊbə/ western prairie province of Canada
area 650,088 sq km/251,000 sq mi
capital Winnipeg
features lakes Winnipeg, Winnipegosis, and Manitoba (area 4,700 sq km/1,800 sq mi); 50 per cent forested
exports grain, manufactured foods, and beverages; machinery; furs, fish, minerals (nickel, zinc, copper, and Manitoba has the world's largest caesium deposits)
population (1985) 1,070,500.

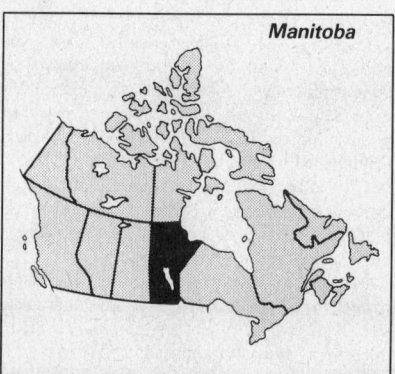

Manitoba

Manizales /ˌmænɪˈsɑːles/ city in the Central Cordillera in W Colombia 2,150 m/7,000 ft above sea level, centre of a coffee-growing area; population (1985) 328,000. It is linked with Mariquita by the world's longest overhead cable transport system 72 km/45 mi.

Manley /ˈmænli/ Michael 1924–. Jamaican politician, prime minister 1972–80. His father, *Norman Manley* (1893–1969) was founder of the Peoples National Party and prime minister 1959–62.

Mann /mæn/ Heinrich 1871–1950. German novelist, who fled to the USA with his brother Thomas ◊Mann. His books include *Professor Unrat/The Blue Angel* 1904, depicting the sensual downfall of a schoolmaster.

Mann /mæn/ Thomas 1875–1955. German novelist and critic, particularly concerned with the theme of the artist's relation to society. He worked in an insurance office in Munich and on the staff of the periodical *Simplicissimus*. His first novel *Buddenbrooks* 1900 portrays the decline of one of the great Hanseatic families in his native Lübeck; *Der Zauberberg/The Magic Mountain* 1924, is set in a Swiss sanatorium. His opposition to the Nazi regime forced him to live abroad and in 1940 he became a US citizen. Among his other works are the comic masterpiece *Die Bekenntnisse des Hochstaplers Felix Krull/Confessions of Felix Krull* 1954, and a number of short stories including *Tonio Kröger* 1903 and *Der Tod in Venedig/Death in Venice* 1913. He was awarded a Nobel prize in 1929.

manna a sweetish exudation obtained from many trees such as the ash and larch, and used in medicine. The manna of the Bible is thought to have been from the tamarisk tree.

Mannerheim /ˈmænəhaɪm/ Carl Gustav Emil von 1867–1951. Finnish general and politician. After the establishment of a Finnish socialist republic in 1917 he formed a 'white' army, crushed the socialists with German assistance, and 1918–19 acted as regent. He commanded the Finnish armies during the soviet wars of 1939–40 and 1941–44, and was president of Finland 1944–46.

Mannerism in painting and architecture, a term coined by ◊Vasari and used to describe the reaction away from the peak of ◊Renaissance classicism. It is characterized by a conscious breaking of the 'rules' of classical composition; thus, a typical Mannerist painting displays the human body in a distorted pose, often off-centre or in the corner of the picture, using harsh, non-blending colours. The effect is one of unsettling the viewer, who is expected to understand the norms which the Mannerist picture is deliberately violating. Strictly speaking, Mannerism is used to describe painters and architects in Italy (primarily Rome and Florence) during the years 1520 to 1575 beginning with, and largely derived from, the later works of ◊Michelangelo in painting and architecture, and including the works of the painters ◊Rosso and ◊Parmigianino, and the architect Giulio ◊Romano, but the term has been extended to cover similar ideas in other arts and in other countries.

Mannheim /ˈmænhaɪm/ industrial city (heavy machinery, glass, earthenware, chemicals) in Baden-Württemberg, West Germany; population (1984) 297,000. The modern symphony orchestra, with its balance of instruments and the important role of the conductor, originated at Mannheim in the 18th century when the elector palatine assembled the finest players of his day.

Mannheim /ˈmænhaɪm/ Karl 1893–1947. Hungarian sociologist, who settled in the UK in 1933. In *Ideology and Utopia* 1929 he argued that all knowledge except maths and physics is ideological, a reflection of class interests and values; there is no such thing as objective knowledge. Later works such as *Man and Society*

1940 analysed modern mass society in terms of its fragmentation and susceptibility to extremist ideas and totalitarian governments.

Manning /'mænɪŋ/ Henry Edward 1808–1892. British cleric. In 1851 he was converted to Roman Catholicism, founded in 1857 the congregation of the Oblates of St Charles Borromeo, and in 1865 succeeded Wiseman as archbishop of Westminster. He was created a cardinal in 1875, the year of his ardent dispute (*The Vatican Decrees*) with Gladstone on the question of papal infallibility.

Manning /'mænɪŋ/ Olivia 1911–1980. British novelist. Best-known of her books were the semi-autobiographical *The Great Fortune* 1960, *The Spoilt City* 1962, and *Friends and Heroes* 1965, forming 'the Balkan trilogy' set in World War II, and a later 'Levant trilogy'.

Manoel two kings of Portugal:

Manoel I /mən'wel/ 1469–1521. King of Portugal. He succeeded his uncle John II in 1495, and was known as 'the Fortunate', because his reign was distinguished by the discoveries made by Portuguese navigators and the expansion of the Portuguese Empire.

Manoel II /mən'wel/ 1889–1932. King of Portugal. He ascended the throne on the assassination of his father, Carlos I, in 1908, but was driven out by a revolution in 1910, and lived in England.

manometer instrument for measuring the pressure of liquids (including human blood pressure) or gases. In its basic form, it is a U-tube part-filled with coloured liquid; pressure of a gas entering at one side is measured by how far the liquid rises at the other.

manometer

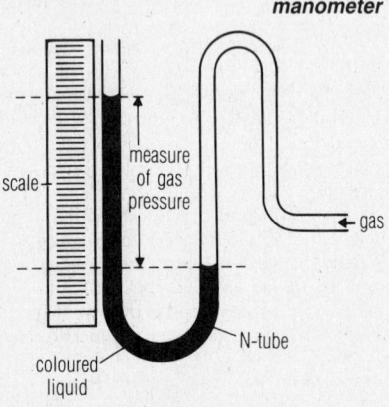

scale — measure of gas pressure — gas — N-tube — coloured liquid

manor basic economic unit in ◊feudalism in Europe, and systematically put into effect under the Norman conquest in England. It usually comprised the lord's demesne (land round the manor house cultivated for his own use), land held by the free tenants (usually at a rent), and that held by villeins (usually in return for heavy labour on the lord's land); common land (unenclosed, on which villagers might have specific rights to pasture cattle, and so on); woodland, and waste land. Here and there traces of the system survive in England – the common land may have become an area for public

recreation – but the documents sometimes sold at auction and entitling the owner to be called 'lord of the manor' seldom have any rights attached to them.

Manpower Services Commission (MSC) in the UK, official body appointed by the government to oversee training for employment. The training division runs the Youth Training Scheme (YTS) and training services for adults both in and out of work. The employment services division is responsible for Jobcentres, training advice, and publications. The MSC also has responsibility for schemes for technical and vocational education for 14 to 18-year-olds in schools and further education colleges, and for the funding of 25 per cent of vocational courses for the over-16s in further education. In 1987 the government announced the MSC would change its name to the Training Commission, and would work exclusively on training.

Mansart /mɒn'saː/ Jules-Hardouin 1646–1708. French architect of the palace of Versailles and Grand Trianon, and designer of the Place de Vendôme and the Place des Victoires, Paris.

Mansfield /'mænsfiːld/ industrial town (textiles, shoes, machinery, chemicals, coal) in Nottinghamshire, England; population (1981) 59,000.

Mansfield /'mænsfiːld/ Katherine, pen name of New Zealand writer Kathleen Beauchamp 1888–1923. Born near Wellington, New Zealand, she was educated in London, to which she returned after a two-year visit home. She wrote short stories, and her works include *In a German Pension* 1911, *Bliss* 1920 and *The Garden Party* 1923.

manslaughter under English law, an unlawful killing of a human being in circumstances not so culpable as murder; for example, when the killer suffers extreme provocation, or is in some way mentally sick (diminished responsibility); did not intend to kill but did so accidentally in the course of another crime or by behaving with criminal recklessness; or is the survivor of a genuine suicide pact which involved killing the other person.

Mans, Le /mɒn/ industrial town in Sarthe *département*, France, with a ◊motor racing circuit on which is held an annual 24-hour endurance race (established 1923) for GT (grand touring) and sports cars, and their prototypes. Population (1982) 150,330.

Mansûra /mæn'suərə/ industrial town (cotton) and capital of Dakahlia province, NE Egypt, on the Damietta branch of the Nile; population (1983) 310,900. Mansûra was founded about 1220; St Louis IX, king of France, was imprisoned in the fortress while on a Crusade, 1250.

manta large ray, ◊devilfish.

Mantegna /mæn'tenjə/ Andrea c. 1431–1506. Italian painter of the Paduan school. Born at Vicenza, he came under the influence of ◊Donatello, ◊Uccello, and Filippo ◊Lippi, and was the most important painter of the early Renaissance. Archaeologically minded, he painted figures which look like antique sculptures. His works include nine panels

depicting *The Triumph of Caesar* at Hampton Court, near London, and *The Madonna with John the Baptist and the Magdalen* and *The Agony in the Garden* (both in London).

mantis insect of the family Mantidae, related to cockroaches. The praying mantis *Mantis religiosa* of S Europe adopts an attitude characteristic of devotion while waiting for its prey – flies, grasshoppers, and caterpillars. The eggs are laid in September and hatch early in the following summer. There are about 2,000 species of mantis, mainly tropical.

mantle the section of the Earth's structure between the ◊crust and the ◊core. It is separated from the former by the ◊Mohorovičić discontinuity, and from the latter by the Gutenberg discontinuity. Mantle material is thought to consist of silicates such as ◊olivine and ◊spinel. The patterns of seismic waves passing through it show its lower layers to be solid. However, from 75 km to 250 km/45 to 155 mi in depth is a zone through which seismic waves pass more slowly (the 'low-velocity zone'). The inference is that materials in this zone are close to their melting points and they are partly molten. The low-velocity zone is probably the ◊asthenosphere on which the ◊lithosphere rides. The solid mantle and the crust above it constitute the rigid plates of the lithosphere.

mantra in Hindu or Buddhist belief, a word repeatedly intoned to assist concentration and develop spiritual power, for example *om*, which represents the names of Brahma, Vishnu, and Siva. Followers of a guru may receive their own individual mantra.

Mantua /'mæntjuə/ (Italian *Mantova*) capital of Mantua province, Lombardy, Italy, on an island of a lagoon of the river Mincio, SW of Verona; industry (chemicals); population (1981) 60,866. The poet Virgil was born near Mantua, which dates from Roman times; it has Gothic palaces and a cathedral founded in the 12th century.

Manu /'maːnuː/ in Hindu mythology, the founder of the human race, who was saved by Brahma from a deluge.

Manutius /mə'njuːʃiəs/ Aldus 1450–1515. Italian printer, established in Venice (which he made the publishing centre of Europe) from 1490; he introduced italic type and was the first to print Greek books.

Manx Gaelic see ◊Gaelic language.

Manzoni /mænd'zəuni/ Alessandro, Count Manzoni 1785–1873. Italian author, best-known for the historical romance *I promessi sposi/The Betrothed* 1825–27.

Maoism form of communism based on the ideas and teachings of Chinese communist leader ◊Mao Zedong. It involves an adaptation of Marxism to fit objective conditions in China and apportions a much greater role for agriculture and the peasantry in the building of socialism – thus effectively by-passing the capitalist (industrial) stage envisaged by Marx.

Maori /'maʊri/ a Polynesian people of New Zealand, who traditionally migrated there from Hawaii about 1350, overcoming and absorbing a related people already in the North Island. Numbering about 150,000 at the arrival of

Europeans, they had a neolithic civilization. They were agriculturists, skilled in working stone and wood, and in weaving patterned cloth. A tradition of song, dance, and story-telling was maintained, with myths of heroes and strange monsters, and a supreme god, Io.

In recent years there has been increased Maori consciousness, and a demand for official status for the Maori language and review of the Waitangi Treaty of 1840 (under which the Maoris surrendered their lands to British sovereignty). The *Maori Unity Movement/Kotahitanga* was founded in 1983 by Eva Rickard. In the 1980s Maoris made up about 10% of the New Zealand population or (1981) 279,000.

Maori language a member of the Polynesian branch of the Malayo-Polynesian language family, spoken by one-third of the Maori people of New Zealand. Efforts are being made to strengthen it after a long period of decline and official indifference. In Maori, New Zealand is *Aotearoa* ('land of the long white cloud') and European settlers are *Pakeha*, a term often used by white New Zealanders when constrasting themselves with the Maori.

Mao Zedong /ˈmaʊ dziˈdʌŋ/ 1893–1976 (former transcription *Mao Tse-tung*). Chinese political leader and theoretician. A founder of the Chinese Communist Party (CCP) in 1921, Mao soon emerged as its leader. He organized the Long March 1934–36 and the war of liberation 1937–49, and headed the CCP and government until his death. Mao adapted communism to Chinese conditions, as popularly set out in the *Little Red Book*.

Mao, son of a peasant farmer in Hunan province, was once library assistant at Beijing University and a headmaster at Changsha. He became chief of CCP propaganda under ◊Sun Zhong Shan (Sun Yat-sen) until sacked by ◊Chiang Kai-shek (Jiang Jie Shi). In 1931–34 he set up a communist republic at Jiangxi and, with ◊Zhu De, marshalled the Red Army in preparation for the Long March to Shaanxi. CCP chair from 1935, Mao secured an alliance with the ◊Guomindang (nationalists) 1936–45. He built up a people's republic at Yan'an 1936–47, where he married his third wife ◊Jiang Qing in 1939. During the liberation war and civil wars, he successfully employed mobile, rural-based guerrilla tactics.

Mao served as party chair until his death in Sept 1976 and as state president until 1959. His influence diminished with the failure of his 1958–60 Great Leap Forward, but emerged dominant again during the 1966–69 Cultural Revolution. Working with ◊Zhou Enlai, he oversaw a period of reconstruction from 1970 until deteriorating health weakened his political grip in the final years.

Mao's writings and thoughts dominated the functioning of the People's Republic 1949–76. He stressed the need for rural rather than urban-based revolutions in Asia, for reducing rural–urban differences, and for perpetual revolution to prevent the emergence of new elites. Overseas, Mao helped precipitate the Sino-Soviet split in 1960 and was a firm advocate of a ◊nonaligned Third World strategy.

Mao Zedong Chairman Mao with Lin Biao, the latter holding the 'Little Red Book' of Mao's thoughts.

map a diagrammatic representation of an area, for example, of part of the Earth's surface, or the distribution of the stars. Modern maps are made using aerial photography; a series of overlapping stereoscopic photographs are taken which can then be used to prepare a three-dimensional image. Laser beams, microwaves, and infrared equipment are also used for land surveying, and satellite pictures make a valuable contribution when large areas are under survey. Maps vary significantly in ◊projection (the means by which a three-dimensional body is shown in two dimensions).

MAPAI (Miphlegeth Poolei Israel). The Israeli Workers' Party or Labour Party. Founded in 1930, its leading figure until 1965 was David ◊Ben-Gurion. In 1968, the party allied with two other democratic socialist parties to form the Israeli Labour Party led initially by Levi Estikol and later Golda ◊Meir.

maple deciduous tree of the genus *Acer* with opposite, stalked, palmately lobed leaves and green flowers, followed by two-winged samaras. There are about 115 species, chiefly in north temperate regions. The only British species is *Acer campestre*; but *Acer pseudoplatanus*, the sycamore or great maple, is naturalized. The sugar maple, *Acer saccharum*, is a N American species, and source of maple syrup.

Maputo /məˈpuːtəʊ/ (former name to 1975 *Lourenço Marques*) industrial port (textiles, food processing, furniture) and capital of Mozambique, on Delagoa Bay; population (1982) 785,512. Linked by rail with Zimbabwe and South Africa, it is the second largest port in Africa.

maquis a type of vegetation common in many Mediterranean countries, comprising scrub woodland with many low-growing tangled bushes and shrubs, typically including species of broom, gorse, heathers, and rockroses. The name was also given by analogy to the French ◊Resistance movement that fought against German occupation during World War II.

mara rodent *Dolichotis patagona* of the guinea-pig family occurring in Argentina, with a body form like that of a hare and long back limbs. Active during the day, maras or 'Patagonian cavies' reach a head and body length of 75 cm/2.5 ft, with a very short tail.

marabou type of stork *Leptoptilos crumeniferus* found in Africa. It has a bald head and is a feeder on carrion, often seen in the company of vultures. It is largely dark grey and white and has an inflatable throat pouch.

Maracaibo /ˌmærəˈkaɪbəʊ/ oil-exporting port in Venezuela, on the channel connecting Lake Maracaibo with the Gulf of Venezuela; population (1980) 929,000. The university of Zulia dates from 1891.

Marat /ˈmærɑː/ Jean Paul 1743–1793. French revolutionary leader and journalist. He was a hero of the Paris revolutionary crowds, and was elected in 1792 to the National Convention, where he carried on a long struggle with the ◊Girondins, ending in their overthrow in May 1793. In Jul he was murdered by Charlotte ◊Corday.

Marathon, Battle of /ˈmærəθən/ 490 BC. Fought between the Greeks (under Miltiades) and invading Persians on the plain of Marathon, 40 km/25 mi NE of Athens. The news was taken to the city by Pheidippides, who fell dead on arrival. His feat is commemorated by the *Marathon race* of about 42 km/26 mi 385 yds, first included in the Olympic Games at Athens in 1896, and more recently by races open to application by all comers through city streets, for example London Marathon from 1981.

marble a ◊limestone that takes and retains a good polish, and is used in building and sculpture. In its pure form it is white, but mineral impurities give it various colours and patterns. Most marbles were originally limestones of ordinary character which have undergone recrystallization under the action of ◊metamorphism, for instance the Carrara marbles. An exception is Purbeck marble, which is clayey limestone containing remains of freshwater shellfish.

Marble Arch triumphal arch in London designed by John ◊Nash to commemorate Nelson's victories. It was intended as a ceremonial entry to Buckingham Palace; in 1851 it was moved to Hyde Park at the end of Oxford Street.

Marburg /ˈmɑːbɜːg/ manufacturing town in Hessen, West Germany, on the river Lahn, 80 km/50 mi N of Frankfurt-am-Main; university 1527 founded as a centre of Protestant teaching: Luther and Zwingli disputed on religion at Marburg in 1529; population (1984) 77,300.

Marburg disease viral disease of central Africa, first known in Europe in 1967 among research workers in Germany working with African green monkeys, hence its common name 'green monkey disease'. It is characterized by haemorrhage of the mucous membranes, fever, vomiting and diarrhoea; mortality is high.

Marc /mɑːk/ Franz 1880–1916. German ◊Expressionist painter, associated with ◊Kandinsky in founding the ◊Blaue Reiter movement.

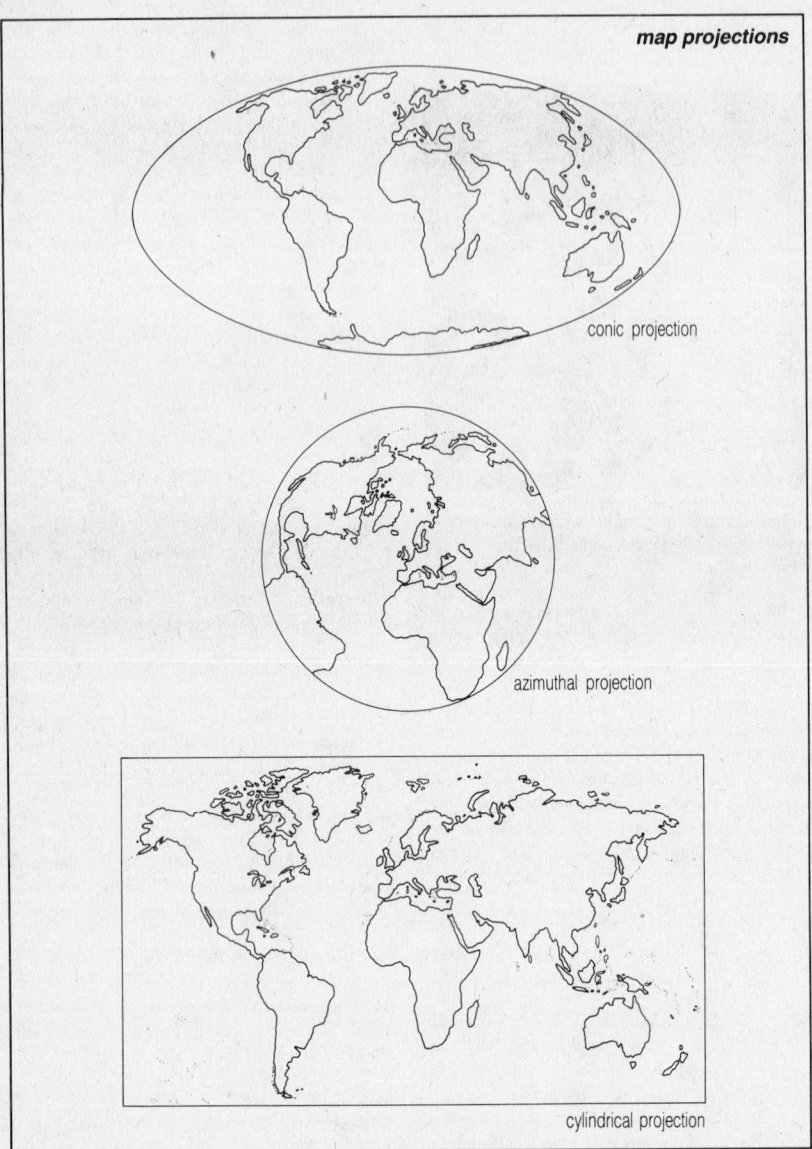

map projections

conic projection

azimuthal projection

cylindrical projection

1286–1330); of the Scottish marches, Patrick Dunbar (died 1285).

Marconi /mɑːˈkəʊni/ Guglielmo 1874–1937. Italian pioneer in the invention and development of wireless telegraphy. Born at Bologna, in 1895 he established wireless communication over more than a mile. In 1896 he went to England, and conducted successful experiments on the roof of the Post Office building in London, on Salisbury Plain, and across Bristol Channel. In 1897 he formed the company that became Marconi's Wireless Telegraph Company Ltd. The following year he successfully transmitted signals across the English Channel, and in 1901 established communication with St John's, Newfoundland, from Poldhu in Cornwall, and in 1918 with Australia. Marconi was an Italian delegate to the Peace Conference in 1919, and received the Nobel Prize for Physics in 1909.

Marcos /ˈmɑːkɒs/ Ferdinand 1919– . Filipino politician. He was convicted while a law student in 1939 of murdering a political opponent of his father, but eventually secured his own acquittal. In World War II he was a guerrilla fighter, survived prison camps of ◊Bataan, and became president in 1965. His regime, backed by the USA, became increasingly repressive, with the use of the secret marshals, anti-crime squads executing those only suspected of offences. He was overthrown and exiled in 1986 by a popular front led by Corazón ◊Aquino.

Marcus Aurelius Antoninus /ˈmɑːkəs ɔːˈriːliəs ˌæntəˈnaɪnəs/ 121–180. Roman emperor and Stoic philosopher. Born in Rome, he was adopted, at the same time as Lucius Aurelius Verus, by his uncle, the emperor Antoninus Pius, whom he succeeded in 161. He conceded an equal share in the rule to Lucius Verus (died 169). Marcus Aurelius spent much of his reign warring against the Germanic tribes, and died in Pannonia, where he had gone to drive back the invading Marcomanni. Although generally considered one of the best of the Roman emperors, he persecuted the Christians for political reasons. He also wrote philosophical *Meditations*.

Marcuse /mɑːˈkuːzə/ Herbert 1898–1979. American political philosopher, whose neo-Marxist theories combining Marxism and Freudianism greatly influenced radical thought in the 1960s. A refugee from Hitler's Germany from 1934, he wrote several books, including *One Dimensional Man* 1964. He preached the overthrow of the existing social order by using the system's very tolerance to ensure its defeat but was not an advocate of violent revolution.

Marduk /ˈmɑːdʊk/ chief god of ancient Babylonia. Originally an inferior spirit connected with water magic, he became associated with Babylon, and on the rise of that city to greatness, the priesthood gave him the qualities of a sun-god, recognizing him as creator of the earth and the human race.

mare (plural *maria*) dark lowland plain on the ◊Moon. The name comes from Latin, 'sea', because they were once wrongly thought to be areas of water.

Marengo, Battle of /məˈrɛŋɡəʊ/ defeat of the Austrians by Napoleon (14 Jun 1800) as part

Marceau /mɑːˈsəʊ/ Marcel 1923– . French mime artist. Born at Strasbourg, he is the creator of the clown-harlequin Bip.

Marchais /mɑːˈʃeɪ/ Georges 1920– . Leader of the French Communist Party (PCF) from 1972.

Marchais joined the PCF in 1947 and worked his way up through the party organization to become its general secretary. Under his leadership, the party committed itself to a 'transition to socialism' by democratic means and entered into a union of the left with the Socialist Party (PS). This was severed in 1977 and the PCF returned to a more orthodox pro-Moscow line. Marchais sanctioned the PCF's participation in the ◊Mitterrand government 1981–84. He remained leader of the PCF despite a fall in its national vote from 21% in 1973 to 10% in 1986.

Marchand /mɑːˈʃɒŋ/ Jean Baptiste 1863–1934. French general and explorer. In 1898 he headed an expedition from the French Congo which occupied Fashoda on the White Nile. The subsequent arrival of British troops under Kitchener resulted in a crisis which nearly led to war between Britain and France.

Marche, Le /ˈmɑːkeɪ/ (English *the Marches*) region of E central Italy comprising the provinces of Ancona, Ascoli, Piceno, Macerata, and Pesaro e Urbino; capital Ancona.

marches /ˈmɑːtʃɪz/ the boundary areas of England with Wales, and England with Scotland. In the Middle Ages these troubled frontier regions were held by lords of the marches, sometimes called *marchiones* and later Earls of March. The 1st Earl of March of the Welsh marches was Roger de Mortimer (c.

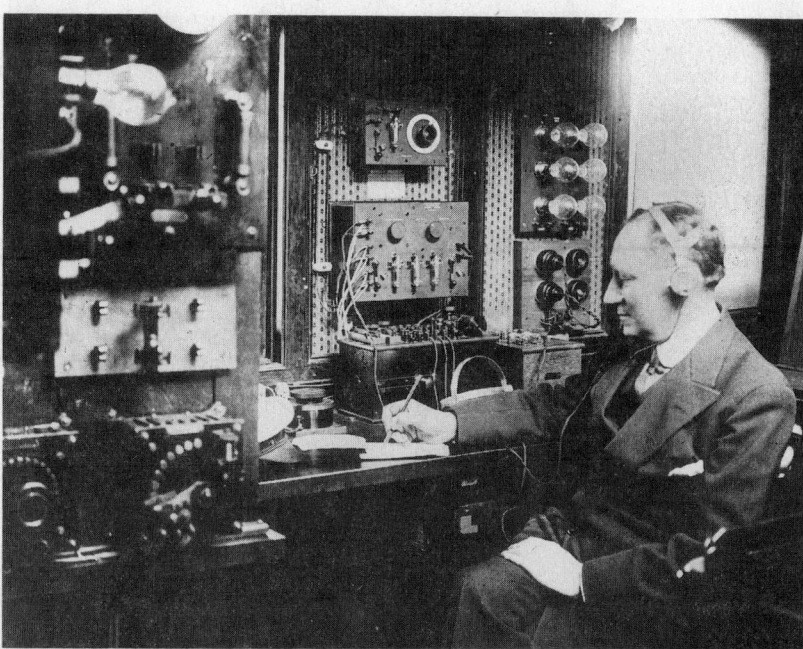

Marconi The Italian inventor Guglielmo Marconi, in the wireless room on his yacht, *Elettra*. He experimented with wireless telegraphy, and in 1895 he sent signals from his house to his garden. When the Italian government showed little interest, he went to England and sent a signal nine miles.

of his Italian campaign, named after the nearby village of Marengo in Piedmont, Italy.

Margaret /'mɑːgrət/ 1283–1290. Known as the 'Maid of Norway'. Margaret was the daughter of Eric II, King of Norway, and Princess Margaret of Scotland. On the death of her grandfather, Alexander III, she became Queen of Scotland, but died in the Orkneys on the voyage to her kingdom.

Margaret of Anjou /ɒn'ʒuː/ 1430–1482. Queen of England. The daughter of René of Anjou, she was married to Henry VI in 1445. After the outbreak of the Wars of the Roses in 1455, she acted as the leader of the Lancastrians, her one object being to secure the succession of her son, Edward (born 1453). She withdrew to France in 1463, but returned during the Lancastrian reaction of 1471, only to be defeated and captured at Tewkesbury, where her son was killed. After five years' imprisonment she was allowed in 1476 to return to France, where she died in poverty.

Margaret (Rose) /'mɑːgrət/ 1930– . Princess of the UK, younger daughter of George VI. In 1960 she married Anthony Armstrong-Jones, later created Lord Snowdon, but in 1976 they agreed to live apart, and were divorced in 1978. Their children are *David, Viscount Linley* (1961–), and *Lady Sarah Armstrong-Jones* (1964–).

Margaret, St /'mɑːgrət/ 1045–1093. Queen of Scotland. The grand-daughter of king Edmund Ironside of England, she went to Scotland after the Norman Conquest, and soon after married Malcolm III. Through her influence the Lowlands, until then purely Celtic, became largely anglicized. The marriage of her

daughter Matilda to Henry I united the Norman and English royal houses. She was canonized in 1251.

margarine a butter substitute, made from animal fats and vegetable oils. French chemist Hippolyte Mège-Mouries invented margarine in 1889. Margarines are often made with vegetable oils such as sunflower oil that are low in saturated fats.

Margate /'mɑːgeɪt/ town and seaside resort on the N coast of Kent, England; population (1981) 53,280. It has a fine promenade and sands.

margay small wild cat *Felis wiedi* found from S USA to S America in forested areas, where it hunts birds and small mammals. About 60 cm/2 ft long plus 40 cm/1.3 ft tail, the margay has a rather rounded head, and has black spots and blotches on a yellowish-brown coat.

margrave (German *Markgraf*) German title (equivalent of marquess) for the 'counts of the March', who guarded the frontier regions of the Holy Roman Empire from Charlemagne's time. Later the title was used by other territorial princes. The most important were the margraves of Austria and of Brandenburg.

Margrethe II /mɑː'greɪdə/ 1940– . Queen of Denmark. The eldest daughter of Frederik IX, she succeeded him in 1972. She married in 1967 French diplomat Count Henri de Laborde de Monpezat, who took the title Prince Hendrik. Her heir is Crown Prince Frederik (1968–).

marguerite popular name for *Leucanthemum vulgare* of the botanical family Compositae. It is a shrubby perennial bearing white ray-florets surrounding a yellow centre.

Marguerite d'Angoulême /ˌmɑːgə'riːt ˌdɒŋguː'leɪm/ 1492–1549. Queen of Navarre, French poet, and author of the *Heptaméron*, a collection of stories in imitation of Boccaccio's *Decameron*. The sister of Francis I, she was born in Angoulême, and married as her second husband Henri d'Albret, king of Navarre, in 1527.

Mari /'mɑːri/ republic of the USSR, E of Gorky and W of the Urals
area 23,200 sq km/8,900 sq mi
capital Yoshkar-Ola
features the Volga flows through the SW; 60% is forested
products timber, paper; grain, flax, potatoes, fruit
population (1985) 725,000; about 43% are ethnic Mari
history the Mari were conquered by Russia in 1552. Mari was made an autonomous region 1920, an autonomous republic 1936.

Marianas /ˌmæri'ɑːnəz/ archipelago in the NW Pacific, discovered by Magellan in 1521, and comprising:
Guam unincorporated territory of USA
area 535 sq km/206 sq mi
capital Agaña
towns port Apra
features largest of the Marianas; major US air and naval base, much used in the Vietnam War; tropical, with much rain
products sweet potatoes, fish; tourism is important
currency US dollar
population (1980) 106,000
language English, Chamorro (basically Malay-Polynesian)
religion Roman Catholic 96%
government popularly elected governor (Ricardo Bordallo from 1985) and single-chamber legislature
recent history Guam was ceded by Spain to USA in 1898, and occupied by Japan 1941–44. Granted full US citizenship and self-government from 1950
Northern Marianas commonwealth in union with USA
area 479 sq km/185 sq mi
capital Garapan on Saipan
features comprises 14 islands and atolls
products sugar, coconuts, coffee
currency US dollar
population 16,780, mainly Micronesian
language English
religion mainly Roman Catholic
government own constitutional elected government
history sold to Germany by Spain in 1899, the islands were mandated to Japan in 1918, and taken by US Marines 1944–45 in World War II. Under US trusteeship from 1947, they voted to become a commonwealth of the USA in 1978.

Mariana Trench or *Marianas* the lowest region on the Earth's surface; the deepest part of the sea floor. The trench is 2,500 km/1,500 mi long and is situated 300 km/200 mi E of the Mariana Islands, in the NW Pacific Ocean. Its deepest part is the gorge known as the Challenger

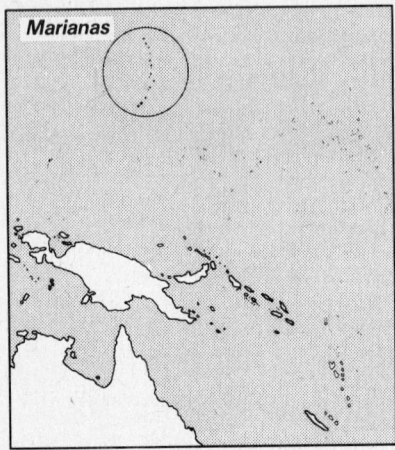

Marianas

Deep, which extends 11,034 m/36,201 ft below sea level.

Mariánské Lázně /ˈmæriænskeɪ ˈlɑːznieɪ/ spa town in Czechoslovakia, famous before World War II under its German name *Marienbad*; population (1981) 17,950. The water of its springs, which contains ◊Glauber salts, has been used medicinally since the 16th century.

Maria Theresa /məˈriːə təˈreɪzə/ 1717–1780. Austrian empress. The daughter of the Emperor Charles VI, she married her cousin Francis of Lorraine in 1736, and succeeded her father as Archduchess of Austria and Queen of Hungary and Bohemia in 1740. Her claim was challenged by Charles of Bavaria, who was elected emperor in 1742, while Frederick of Prussia occupied Silesia. The War of the Austrian Succession followed, in which Austria was allied with Britain, and Prussia with France; when it ended in 1748, Maria Theresa retained her heritage, except that Frederick kept Silesia, while her husband had succeeded Charles as emperor in 1745. Intent on recovering Silesia, she formed an alliance with France and Russia against Prussia; the Seven Years War of 1756–63, which resulted, exhausted Europe and left the territorial position as before. After 1763 she pursued a consistently peaceful policy, concentrating on internal reforms; although her methods were despotic, she fostered education, codified the laws, and abolished torture. She also expelled the Jesuits. In these measures she was assisted by her son, Joseph II, who became emperor in 1765, and succeeded her in the Hapsburg domains.

Maribor /ˈmæribɔː/ Yugoslav town and resort in Slovenia, on the river Drave, with a 12th-century cathedral and some industry; population (1981) 185,500. Maribor dates from Roman times.

Marie /məˈriː/ 1875–1938. Queen of Romania. The daughter of the Duke of Edinburgh, second son of Queen Victoria of the UK, she married Prince Ferdinand of Romania in 1893, who was king 1922–27. She wrote a number of literary works, notably *Story of My Life* 1934–35. Her son Carol became king of Romania, and her daughters, Elisabeth and

Marie, queens of Greece and Yugoslavia respectively.

Marie Antoinette /ˌæntwəˈnet/ 1755–1793. Queen of France. She was the daughter of ◊Maria Theresa, and married ◊Louis XVI of France in 1770. With a reputation for frivolity and extravagance, she meddled in politics in the Austrian interest, and influenced her husband to resist concessions in the revolution of 1789, for example, ◊Mirabeau's plan for a constitutional settlement. She instigated the disastrous flight to Varennes, which discredited the monarchy, and welcomed foreign intervention against the revolution, betraying French war strategy to the Austrians in 1792. She was tried for treason in Oct 1793 and guillotined.

Marie de France /də ˈfrɒns/ c. 1150–1215. French poet, thought to have been the illegitimate child of Geoffrey Plantagenet (second husband of ◊Matilda, queen of England), and to have become abbess of Shaftesbury 1181–1215. She wrote *Lais* (verse tales) and *Ysopet*, a collection of fables.

Marie de' Medici /deɪ ˈmedɪtʃi/ 1573–1642. Queen consort of ◊Henry IV of France from 1600, and regent (after his murder) for their son ◊Louis XIII. She left the government to her favourites, the Concinis, until in 1617 Louis XIII seized power and executed them. She was banished, but after she led a revolt in 1619, ◊Richelieu effected her reconciliation with her son, making it the stepping stone to his own power. When she attempted to oust him in 1630, she was again sent into exile.

Marie Louise /luˈiːz/ 1791–1847. Queen consort of Napoleon I from 1810 (after his divorce from ◊Josephine), she was the daughter of Francis I of Austria (see under Emperor ◊Francis II). She bore him a son (see ◊Napoleon II), and on his fall returned to Austria. In 1815 she was granted the duchy of Parma.

Marienbad /ˈmæriənbæd, German məˈriːənbɑːt/ German name of ◊Mariánské Lázně, spa town in Czechoslovakia.

marigold name for several members of the plant family Compositae, including *pot marigold Calendula officinalis*, whose orange petals are used in cooking for their flavour; and the tropical American *French marigold Tagetes patula*.

marijuana popular name for the dried leaves and flowers of the hemp plant ◊cannabis, used as a drug.

Mariner spacecraft series of US space probes that explored the planets from Mercury to Mars and achieved many 'firsts'.

marines a fighting force equally at home on land or sea, although the British *Corps of Royal Marines* established in 1664, is primarily a military force trained also for fighting at sea, and providing commando units, landing craft, crews, frogmen, and so on, whereas the *US Marine Corps*, 1775, is primarily a naval force trained for fighting on land.

Marinetti /ˌmærɪˈneti/ Filippo Tommaso 1876–1944. Italian author. Born at Alexandria, in 1909 he published the first manifesto of ◊Futurism, which called for a break with tradition in art, poetry, and the novel, and glorified the machine age. He illustrated his

theories in *Mafarka le futuriste/Mafarka the Futurist* 1910, plays, and a volume on theatrical practice 1916. He welcomed Mussolini with *Futurismo e fascismo/Futurism and Fascism* 1924.

Marini /məˈriːni/ Marino 1901–1980. Italian sculptor. Influenced by African sculpture, he was particularly well known for his bronze horses, riders, and dancers, and worked in an elongated, elegant style.

marionette type of ◊puppet, a jointed figure controlled from above by wires or strings. They early reached a high artistic level in Burma and Ceylon and at the courts of Italian princes in the 16th–18th centuries, and Haydn wrote an operetta *Dido* 1778 for the Esterhazy Marionette theatre. In the 20th century there was a revival, especially in television, and marionettes have reverted to being a popular rather than aristocratic entertainment.

Maritain /ˌmærɪˈtæn/ Jacques 1882–1973. French philosopher. Originally a disciple of ◊Bergson, for example *La philosophie bergsonienne/Bergsonian Philosophy* 1914, he later became the best-known of the Neo-Thomists applying the methods of Thomas ◊Aquinas to contemporary problems, for example *Introduction à la Philosophie/ Introduction to Philosophy* 1920.

maritime law that part of law dealing with fishing areas, ships, and navigation. Under the United Nations convention of 1982 there is a 19 km/12 mi territorial limit from a country's coast; a 320 km/200 mi exclusive economic zone (EEZ) increasingly adopted; and under special jurisdiction an International Seabed Authority would be established to exploit the deep seabed resources, but there was dispute as to the share allotted to developing countries of mining to be carried out by developed ones, and it has not yet been set up.

Maritsa /məˈrɪtsə/ river, rising in the Rhodope Mountains, Bulgaria, which forms the Greco-Turkish frontier before entering the Aegean Sea near Enez: length 440 km/275 mi.

Mariupol /ˌmæriˈuːpəl/ former name (until 1948) of the port of ◊Zhdanov in the USSR.

Marius /ˈmeəriəs/ Gaius 155–86 BC. Roman military commander and politician. Born near Arpinum, he served in Spain in 134 BC, and in the Jugurthine War 109–106 BC. He was elected consul seven times, the first time in 107 BC. He defeated the Cimbri and the Teutones (Germanic tribes attacking Gaul and Italy) 102–101 BC. Marius tried to deprive Sulla of the command in the East against Mithridates, and as a result civil war broke out in 88 BC. Sulla marched on Rome, and Marius fled to Africa, but later Cinna held Rome for Marius. Cinna and Marius created a reign of terror in Rome until the death of Marius.

Marivaux /ˌmærɪˈvəʊ/ Pierre Carlet de Chamblain de 1688–1763. French novelist and dramatist. He wrote for both of the major Paris theatre companies: the ◊Comédie Française and the Comédie Italienne, which specialized in ◊commedia dell'arte. His polished, sophisticated comedies include *Le Jeu de l'amour et du hasard/The Game of Love and Chance* 1730, and

Les Fausses Confidences/False Confidences 1737; his best novel, *Le Vie de Marianne/The Life of Marianne* 1731–41 has autobiographical elements. Marivaux gave the word *marivaudage* (over-subtle lovers' conversation) to the French language.

marjoram aromatic herb of the Labiatae family. Wild marjoram *Origanum vulgare* is found both in Europe and Asia and has become naturalized in America: the culinary sweet marjoram is *Origanum majorana*.

Mark /mɑːk/ in the New Testament, Christian apostle and evangelist, whose name is given to the second Gospel. His first name was John, and his mother, Mary, was one of the first Christians in Jerusalem. He was a cousin of Barnabas, and accompanied Barnabas and Paul on their first missionary journey. He was a fellow worker with Paul in Rome, and later became Peter's interpreter after Paul's death. According to tradition he was the founder of the Christian Church in Alexandria, and Jerome says that he died and was buried there. He is the patron saint of Venice; feast day, 25 Apr.
The Gospel according to St Mark was probably written 65–70 AD, and used by the authors of the first and third Gospels.

Mark Antony /ˈæntəni/ 83–30 BC. Roman politician and soldier. He served under Julius Caesar in the later campaign in Gaul. As tribune he defended Caesar's interests at Rome during the civil war, and when consul 44 BC tried to secure for Caesar the title of king. After Caesar's assassination, Antony with Octavius and Lepidus formed a triumvirate, and in 42 BC Antony assisted in the defeat of Brutus and Cassius at Philippi. During 41 BC Antony toured the eastern provinces, where he met Cleopatra, with whom he fell in love. When the three triumvirs divided the empire between them, Antony secured Egypt for his share. In 32 BC the Senate declared war on Cleopatra. Defeated by Octavius at the naval battle of Actium in 31, Antony committed suicide.

markhor large wild goat *Capra falconeri*, with spirally twisted horns and long shaggy coat. It is found in the Himalayas.

Markievicz /ˈmɑːkjɪvɪtʃ/ Constance Georgina, Countess Markievicz (born Gore Booth) 1868–1927. Irish nationalist, who married the Polish Count Markievicz in 1900. Her death sentence for taking part in the Easter Rebellion of 1916 was commuted, and after her release from prison in 1917 she was elected to the Westminster Parliament as a Sinn Féin candidate in 1918 (technically the first British woman Member of Parliament), but did not take her seat.

Markov /ˈmɑːkɒv/ Andrei 1856–1922. Russian mathematician, formulator of the ◊Markov chain.

Markova /mɑːˈkəʊvə/ Alicia, stage name of Lilian Alicia Marks 1910– . British ballet dancer. Trained by ◊Pavlova, she was ballerina with ◊Diaghilev's company 1925–29, was the first resident ballerina of the Vic-Wells Ballet 1933–35, partnered ◊Dolin in their own Markova-Dolin Company 1935–37, and danced with the Ballet Russe de Monte Carlo 1938–41

Mark Antony A great orator and soldier, Mark Antony committed suicide after his defeat at the battle of Actium in 31 BC.

and Ballet Theatre, USA, 1941–46. She was created Dame of the British Empire in 1963. She is associated with the great classical ballets, especially *Giselle*.

Markov chain in statistics, a chain of events in which the transition between each event is a matter only of established probability, uninfluenced by earlier links in the chain, such as the tossing of a coin.

Marks /mɑːks/ Simon, 1st Baron of Broughton 1888–1964. British chain-store magnate. The son of Polish immigrant Michael Marks, who started with Yorkshireman Tom Spencer a number of 'penny bazaars' in 1887, he entered the business in 1907 and built up a chain of more than 200 Marks and Spencer stores.

marl a sedimentary rock sometimes called a clayey limestone, and including various types of calcareous clays and argillaceous limestones. Marls are commonly laid down in freshwater lakes, and are usually soft, earthy and of a white, grey, or brownish colour. They are used in cement making and as a top dressing for farmland.

Marlborough /ˈmɔːlbrə/ John Churchill, 1st Duke of Marlborough 1650–1722. English soldier. In 1688 he deserted his patron, James II, for William of Orange, but in 1692 fell into disfavour for Jacobite intrigue. He had married Sarah Jennings (1660–1744), confidante of the future Queen Anne, who created him a duke on her accession. In the War of the ◊Spanish Succession, he saved Vienna from the French by his victory at the Battle of ◊Blenheim, and achieved victories at ◊Ramillies in 1706, ◊Oudenaarde in 1708, and ◊Malplaquet in 1709. However, the return of the Tories to power and his wife's quarrel with the queen led to his dismissal in 1711 and his flight to Holland to avoid charges of corruption. He returned in 1714. The Blenheim mansion in ◊Oxfordshire was

Marlborough The 1st Duke of Marlborough, a portrait after Kneller.

granted in recognition of his services. His London home was ◊Marlborough House.

Marlborough House mansion in Pall Mall, London. Designed by Wren, it was ◊Marlborough's London home; and from 1962 used for gatherings of Commonwealth members.

Marley /ˈmɑːli/ 'Bob' (Robert Nesta) 1945–1980. Jamaican reggae singer, a Rastafarian whose songs, many of which were topical and political, popularized reggae in the UK and the US in the 1970s. His best-known song is 'No Woman No Cry', and his albums include *Natty Dread* 1975 and *Exodus* 1977.

marlin or *spearfish* several genera of game fish, family Istiophoridae, order Perciformes. Some 2.5 m/7 ft long, they are found in warmer waters, and have elongated snouts, and high-standing dorsal fins.

Marlowe /ˈmɑːləʊ/ Christopher 1564–1593. English poet-dramatist. Born in Canterbury, he was educated at Cambridge, where he is thought to have become a government agent. In London from 1587, he wrote the blank verse plays *Tamburlaine* about 1587, *The Jew of Malta* about 1589, *Edward II* and *Dr Faustus*, both about 1592. Best known of his other works are his poem *Hero and Leander* and a 1598 version of Ovid's *Amores*. His life was turbulent, with a brief imprisonment in connection with a man's death in a brawl (of which he was cleared), and a charge of atheism (following statements by the playwright ◊Kyd under torture). He was murdered in a Deptford tavern, allegedly in a dispute over the bill, but it may have been a political killing. His work influenced Shakespeare and others.

Marmara /ˈmɑːmərə/ small inland sea separating Turkey in Europe from Turkey in

Asia, and connected through the Bosporus with the Black Sea, and through the Dardanelles with the Aegean; length 275 km/170 mi, breadth up to 80 km/50 mi.

Marmontel /ˌmaːmɒnˈtel/ Jean François 1723–1799. French novelist and dramatist. He wrote tragedies and libretti, and contributed to the *Encyclopédie* (see ◊encyclopaedia); in 1758 he obtained control of the journal *Le Mercure/The Mercury*, in which his *Contes Moraux/Moral Studies* 1761 appeared. Other works include *Bélisaire/ Belisarius* 1767, and *Les Incas/The Incas* 1777.

marmoset small monkey in the family Hapalidae found in South and Central America. Most species have characteristic tufted ears and handsome tail, and some are full-grown when the body is only 18 cm/7 in. Best-known is the common marmoset *Callithrix jacchus* of Brazil, often kept there as a pet.

marmot large burrowing rodent of the genus *Marmota*. They live from the Alps to the Himalayas, and also in North America. Some live high in mountains. *Marmota marmota* is the typical marmot of the Central European Alps. Marmots live in colonies, make burrows, one to each family, and hibernate. Some in North America are called woodchucks.

Marne /maːn/ river in France which rises in the plateau of Langres and joins the Seine at Charenton near Paris. It gives its name to the *départements* of Marne, Haute Marne, Seine-et-Marne and Val de Marne; and to two battles of ◊World War I.

Marne, Battles of the /maːn/ in World War I, two unsuccessful German offensives: *first battle* 6–9 Sept 1914, von Moltke's advance was halted by the ◊British Expeditionary Force and the French under Foch; *second battle* 15 Jul–4 Aug 1918, Ludendorff's advance was defeated by British, French, and US troops under Pétain, and German morale crumbled.

Maronite member of a Christian sect probably deriving mainly from refugee ◊Monothelites (Christian heretics) of the 7th century. They were subsequently united with the Roman Catholic Church, and number about 400,000 in the Lebanon and Syria with an equal number scattered overseas in southern Europe, and the Americas.

Maroon (from Spanish *cimarrón*, wild, untamed). Freed or escaped African slaves, organized and armed by the Spanish, in Jamaica in the late 17th century and early 18th century, who harried the British with guerrilla tactics.

Marquesas /maːˈkeɪsæs/ island group in ◊French Polynesia.

marquess or *marquis* title and rank of a nobleman who in the British peerage ranks below a duke and above an earl. The first English marquess was created in 1385, but the lords of the Scottish and Welsh 'marches' were known as *marchiones* before this date. The premier English marquessate is that of Winchester. The wife of a marquess is a marchioness.

Marquette /maːˈket/ Jacques 1637–1675. French Jesuit missionary and explorer. Going to Canada in 1666, he explored the upper lakes of the St Lawrence, and in 1673 made a remarkable voyage down the Mississippi.

Márquez Gabriel García see ◊García Márquez.

Marquis /ˈmaːkwɪs/ Don(ald Robert Perry) 1878–1937. American author, born in Illinois. He is chiefly known for *archy and mehitabel* 1927, the typewritten verse adventures of the cockroach archy to the cat mehitabel.

Marquises /maːˈkiːz/ French form of Marquesas, islands in ◊French Polynesia.

Marrakesh /ˌmærəˈkeʃ/ town in Morocco in the foothills of the Atlas mountains, about 210 km/130 mi S of Casablanca, with textile and food processing industries; population (1982) 482,500. Founded in 1062, it has a medieval palace and mosques, and was formerly the capital of Morocco.

marram grass coarse perennial grass *Ammophila arenaria* which flourishes on sandy patches and, because of its tough and creeping rootstocks, is largely employed to hold coast dunes in place, particularly in Holland.

Marrano one of the Spanish and Portuguese Jews converted by force to Christianity in the 14th and 15th centuries, many of whom secretly preserved their adherence to Judaism and carried out Jewish rites. Under the Spanish Inquisition thousands were burned at the stake.

marriage the legally or culturally sanctioned union of one man and one woman (monogamy); one man and two or more women (polygyny); one woman and two or more men (polyandry). The basis of marriage varies considerably in different societies (romantic love in the west; arranged marriages in some other societies), but most marriage ceremonies, contracts or customs involve a set of rights and duties such as care and protection, and there is generallly an expectation that children will be born of the union to continue the family line. In different cultures and communities there are various conventions and laws that limit the choice of a marriage partner. Restrictive factors include: age-limits, below which no marriage is valid (16 in the UK); degrees of consanguinity or other special relationships within which marriage is either forbidden or enjoined; economic factors such as ability to pay a required bride price or dowry; rank, caste or religious differences; medical requirements such as the blood tests of some states of the USA; the necessity of obtaining parental, family, or community consent; the negotiations of a marriage broker in some cultures, as in Japan or formerly among Jewish communities; or colour, for example, marriage was illegal until 1985 between 'European' and 'non-European' people in South Africa, and until 1967 was illegal between white and black people in some southern US states, and between white and oriental people in some western states. In Western cultures, social trends have led to increased legal equality for women within marriage: in England married women were not allowed to hold property in their own name until 1882; in California community property laws entail the equal division of all assets between the partners on divorce. Other legal changes have made ◊divorce easier, notably in the USA and increasingly in the UK, so that re-marriage is more and more frequent for both sexes within the lifetime of the original partner. In England marriages can be effected according to the rites of the Church of England or those of other faiths, or in a superintendent registrar's office. In most other European countries and in the USA civil registration of marriage, as well as (or instead of) a religious ceremony is obligatory. Common-law marriages (that is, cohabitation as man and wife without a legal ceremony) are recognized in, for example, Scotland, some states of the USA, and the USSR. As a step to international agreement on marriage law the United Nations in 1962 adopted a convention on consent to marriage, minimum age for marriage, and registration.

marriage The wedding of a prince and princess in the traditional ceremonial robes of ancient Japan.

marrow plant *Cucurbita pepo* family Cucurbitaceae, producing large pulpy fruits used as vegetables and in preserves; the young fruits of one variety are known as courgettes (USA zucchini).

Marryat /ˈmæriət/ Frederick 1792–1848. British naval officer and novelist, popularly known as 'Captain Marryat'. He wrote a number of popular adventure stories, including *Peter Simple* 1834, *Mr Midshipman Easy* 1836, and a series of children's books, such as *Masterman Ready* 1841, *Settlers in Canada* 1844, and *Children of the New Forest* 1847.

Mars /maːz/ in Roman mythology, the god of war, after whom the month of March is named.

Mars /maːz/ in astronomy, the fourth ◊planet in order of distance from the Sun. Its average distance from the Sun is 227,800,000 km/141,500,000 mi, and it may approach Earth to within 54,700,000 km/34,000,000 mi, so that it is then closer than any planet apart from ◊Venus; at such times it is very brilliant and recognisable by its red colour. It is, however, much smaller than Venus or Earth: diameter 6,790 km/4,200 mi, and mass only 0.11 that of Earth. It resembles Earth in having a rotation period of 24 hr 37 min, but its year is 687 Earth days. The first man-made object to orbit another planet was *Mariner 9* (USA 1971–72), and this and later spacecraft, including *Viking 1* and *2* with landers in 1976, provided much information. The planet is pear-shaped, with a low and level northern hemisphere, comparatively uncratered and geologically 'young', and a heavily cratered 'ancient' southern hemisphere: in this it resembles Earth before the break-up of ◊Pangaea by continental drift. The landscape is a dusty, red, eroded lava plain, resembling Arizona; red dust in the atmosphere accounts for the light pink sky; and winds of 200 kph/125 mph have been recorded. There are four enormous volcanoes near the equator, of which the largest is Olympus Mons 24 km/15 m high, with a base 600 km/375 mi across, and a crater 65 km/40 mi wide. To the E of these volcanoes lies a high plateau cut by a system of valleys some 4,000 km/2,500 mi long, up to 200 km/120 mi wide and 6 km/4 mi deep: these features are apparently caused by faulting and wind erosion. Mars has white polar caps composed of water ice and frozen carbon dioxide which advance and retreat with the seasons. Studies in 1985 showed that enough water might exist to sustain prolonged missions by space crews. The atmosphere is mainly carbon dioxide, but includes 3% nitrogen and 1.5% argon. Temperatures have been recorded from -100°C to -29°C. The atmospheric pressure is 7 millibars, equivalent to the pressure 35 km/22 mi above the Earth. No proof of life on Mars has been obtained. Mars has two satellites: ◊Phobos and Deimos.

marsala /mɑːˈsɑːlə/ a type of dessert wine produced in Sicily which has a dark amber colour and burnt sugar flavour. It is made with the addition of grape juice that has been cooked and reduced to one-third of its original volume.

Marsala /mɑːˈsɑːlə/ port in W Sicily, Italy, noted for export of sweet wine of the same name; population (1980) 85,000. The nationalist leader ◊Garibaldi landed here in 1860.

Marseillaise, La /ˌmɑːseɪˈeɪz/ French national anthem; both words and music were composed in 1792 by the army officer Rouget de Lisle.

Marseille /mɑːˈseɪ/ (English *Marseilles*) chief seaport of France, industrial centre (chemicals, oil refining, metallurgy, shipbuilding, food processing) and capital of the *département* of Bouches-du-Rhône, on the Golfe du Lion, Mediterranean Sea; university 1409; population (1982) 1,110,511. It is connected with the river Rhône by a canal, and there are several offshore islands including ◊If.
history Marseille was founded by mariners of Phocaea in Asia Minor in 600 BC. Under the Romans it was a free city, and then, after suffering successive waves of invaders, became in the 13th century an independent republic, until included in France in 1481. Much of the old quarter was destroyed by Germany in 1943.

Marsh /mɑːʃ/ Ngaio 1899–1982. New Zealand novelist, in England from 1928. Her first detective novel *A Man Lay Dead* 1934, in which she introduced Chief Inspector Roderick Alleyn, had many sequels. Created Dame Commander of the Order of the British Empire 1966.

marshal a title given in certain countries to a high officer of state, though originally it meant one who tends horses, in particular one who shoes them. The ◊Earl Marshal is a high officer of state in England who organizes state ceremonies; the office is hereditarily held by the dukes of Norfolk. The corresponding officer in Scotland was the Earl Marischal. The rank of a Marshal of the Royal Air Force corresponds to that of Admiral of the Fleet in the navy and ◊Field Marshal in the army. In the French Army the highest officers bear the designation of Marshal of France.

Marshall /ˈmɑːʃəl/ Alfred 1842–1924. British economist. A founder of neo-classical economics, he stressed the power of supply and demand to generate equilibrium prices in markets, introducing the concept of elasticity of demand relative to price. His *Principles of Economics* 1890 remains influential.

Marshall /ˈmɑːʃəl/ George Catlett 1880–1959. American soldier and politician. In 1939 he became chief of staff with the rank of general. On resigning in Nov 1945 he became ambassador to China, attempting to secure a coalition between the Nationalist and Communist forces against Japan. He was Secretary of State 1947–49, and as Secretary of Defence Sept 1950–Sept 1951 (a post never normally held by a soldier), backed Truman's recall of MacArthur from Korea. He initiated the ◊Marshall Plan.

Marshall /ˈmɑːʃəl/ John 1755–1835. American jurist. Born in Virginia, as chief justice of the Supreme Court 1801–35, he laid down interpretations of the US constitution in a series of important decisions, which have since become universally accepted.

Marshall /ˈmɑːʃəl/ John Ross 1912– . New Zealand National Party politician. Noted for his negotiations of a free-trade agreement with Australia. He was deputy to ◊Holyoake as prime minister and succeeded him Feb–Nov 1972.

Marshall Islands /ˈmɑːʃəl/ the Radak (13 islands) and Ralik (11 islands) chains in the W Pacific
area 158 sq km/61 sq mi
capital Majuro
features include two atolls used for US atom-bomb tests 1946–63, Eniwetok and Bikini (hence the name given to two-piece swimsuits which supposedly had an explosive impact) – radioactivity will last for 100 years, and the people have made claims for rehabilitation; and Kwajalein atoll (the largest) which has a US intercontinental missile range
products copra, phosphates, fish; tourism is important
currency US dollar
population (1984) 35,000
language English (official)
religion Christian and local faiths
government internally self-governing, with elected governments
recent history German 1906–19, they were then administered by Japan until 1946, when they passed to USA as part of the Pacific Islands Trust Territory in 1947. In 1986 a compact of Free Association with the USA was signed, under which the islands manage their own internal and external affairs but the USA controls military activities in exchange for financial support.

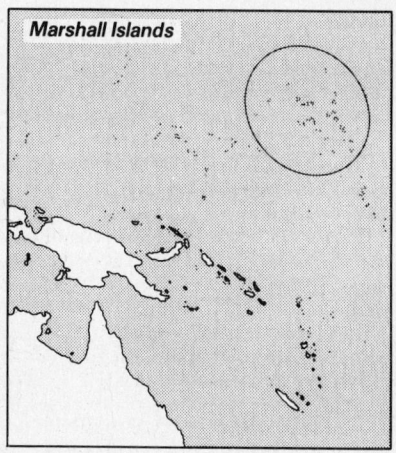

Marshall Islands

Marshall Plan a programme of US financial aid to Europe set up at the end of World War II. Officially known as the European Recovery Programme, it was initiated by George ◊Marshall in a speech at Harvard in Jun 1947, but was in fact the work of a State Department group led by Dean ◊Acheson. It involved the use of US funding to rebuild the economies of W Europe and totalled $17,000 million between 1948–52. It set the pattern for the large-scale foreign aid by the US which was subsequently widened in scope to cover the entire non-Communist world.

marsh gas a form of the gas ◊methane. It is produced in swamps and marshes by the action of bacteria.

marsh marigold plant *Caltha palustris* of the buttercup family Ranunculaceae, known as the kingcup in England and as the cowslip in the USA. The five-sepalled yellow flowers are brilliant in moist sheltered spots in Mar.

Marsilius of Padua /mɑːˈsiliəs/ 1270–1342. Italian scholar and jurist. Born at Padua, he studied and taught at Paris, and in 1324 collaborated with John of Jandun in writing the *Defensor pacis/Defender of the Peace*, a plea for the subordination of the ecclesiastical to the secular power. He played a part in the establishment of the Roman republic in 1328, and was made archbishop of Milan.

Marston Moor, Battle of /ˈmɑːstən ˈmʊə/ battle fought in the English Civil War on 2 Jul 1644 on Marston Moor, 11 km/7 mi W of York. The Royalists, under Prince Rupert and the duke of Newcastle, were completely defeated by the Parliamentarians and Scots, under Cromwell and Lord Leven. Lord Fairfax, on the right of the Parliamentarians, was routed, but Cromwell's cavalry charges were decisive.

marsupial (Greek *marsupion*, little purse or bag), mammal in which the female has a pouch in which she carries her young for some considerable time after birth. Marsupials include the ◊kangaroo, ◊wombat, ◊opossum, ◊Tasmanian wolf, ◊bandicoot, and ◊wallaby.

Martello tower any of a number of towers built along the English coast, especially in Sussex and Kent, in 1804, as a defence against the threatened French invasion. The name is derived from a tower on Cape Mortella, Corsica, which was captured by the British with great difficulty in 1794, and was taken as a model. They are round towers of solid masonry, sometimes moated, with a flat roof for mounted guns.

marten small carnivorous mammal belonging to the family Mustelidae, genus *Martes*. Martens live in North America, Europe and Asia. Some are hunted for their fur. The pine-marten *Martes martes* has long, brown fur, and is about 75 cm/2.5 ft long. It is found in Britain. The stone or beech marten *Martes foina* is lighter in colour. The sable *Martes zibellina* lives in E Siberia, and provides the most valued fur. The largest is the fisher *Martes pennanti*, with black fur and reaching 125 cm/4 ft, of North America.

Martens /'mɑːtəns/ Wilfried 1936– . Prime minister of Belgium from 1979, member of Social Christian Party. Martens was president of the Dutch-speaking CVP 1972–79 and as prime minister headed six coalition governments: 1979–81, 1981–85, and from 1985.

Martha's Vineyard /'mɑːθəz 'vɪnjəd/ island 32 km/20 mi long off the coast of Cape Cod, Massachusetts, USA, former home of whaling captains, and now a summer resort.

Martial /'mɑːʃəl/ (Marcus Valerius Martialis) 41–104. Latin epigrammatist. Born in Bilbilis, Spain, he settled in Rome in 64, where he lived by his literary and social gifts. His poetry, often bawdy, reflects contemporary Roman life, and is unrivalled in correctness of diction, versification, and form.

martial arts styles of armed and unarmed combat developed in the East, including:
aikido Japanese combination of judo and karate
judo modern sport in which an opponent is compelled to submit by the use of minimum force, a development of jujitsu; loose jackets are worn, and falls are broken by a mat
jujitsu Japanese method of unarmed self-defence developed by the ◊Samurai; the ancestor of judo
karate method of unarmed combat developed in 17th-century Okinawa (influenced by kung fu); it differs from judo in its emphasis on striking with the open hand or closed fist, and kicking
kendo Japanese fencing using bamboo replicas of ◊Samurai swords, and wearing masks and protective padding
kung fu Chinese unarmed combat originating in the sixth century, possibly under Indian influence in the Shaolin temple, Honan. It combines the principles of karate and judo.

martial law the replacement of civilian by military authorities in the maintenance of order. In Britain, the legal position as regards martial law is ill-defined, but in effect, when war or rebellion is in progress in an area, the military authorities are recognized as having powers to maintain order by summary means. In the USA martial law is usually proclaimed by the president or the government of a state in areas of the country where the civil authorities have been rendered unable to act, or to act with safety. Martial law, though neither in the constitution nor laid down in statutes, has frequently been used in the US, for example in Hawaii 1941–44 after the bombing of Pearl Harbor.

martin name of several genera of birds, allied to the swallow, in the family Hirundinidae. The European house martin *Delichon urbica*, a summer migrant from Africa, is blue-black above and white below, distinguished from the swallow by its shorter, less forked tail. The cup-like mud nest is usually constructed under the eaves of buildings. Best-known of other species are the brownish European sand martin *Riparia riparia*, which tunnels to make a nest in sandy banks, also a migrant from Africa, and the purple martin of North America *Progne subis*, a handsome steely-blue bird which often nests in hollow trees.

Martin /'mɑːtɪn/ Archer John Porter 1910– . British biochemist, Nobel prizewinner for chemistry in 1952 for work with Richard Synge on paper ◊chromatography in 1944.

Martin /'mɑːtɪn/ Violet Florence 1862–1915. Irish novelist under the pen name 'Martin Ross'. Born in Galway, she collaborated with her cousin Edith Somerville in tales of Anglo-Irish provincial life, for example *Some Experiences of an Irish RM* 1899.

Martin V /'mɑːtɪn/ 1368–1431. Pope from 1417. A member of the Roman family of Colonna, he was elected during the Council of Constance, and ended the Great Schism between the rival popes of Rome and Avignon.

Martin du Gard /mɑː'tæn dju: 'gɑː/ Roger 1881–1958. French novelist. Born at Neuilly, he realistically recorded the way of life of the bourgeoisie in the eight-volume *Les Thibault/The World of the Thibaults* 1922–40. He was awarded a Nobel prize in 1937.

Martineau /'mɑːtɪnəʊ/ Harriet 1802–1876. British moralist, journalist, economist, and novelist. She wrote popular works on political issues, as well as children's stories.

Martinet /,mɑːtɪ'neɪ/ Jean, died 1762. French inspector-general of infantry under Louis XIV, whose constant drilling brought the army to a high degree of efficiency – hence the use of his name to mean a strict disciplinarian.

Martínez Ruiz /mɑː'tiːneθ ru:'iːθ/ José Real name of ◊Azorin, Spanish author.

Martini /mɑː'tiːni/ Simone c. 1284–1344. Italian painter, greatest of the Sienese school, whose influence was widespread. Born in Siena, he was a pupil of ◊Duccio, but excelled his master in his development of line and colour. He painted a portrait of Laura for Petrarch and is commemorated by the poet in two sonnets. He died at Avignon.

Martinique /,mɑːtɪ'niːk/ French island in the West Indies (Lesser Antilles)
area 1,100 sq km/420 sq mi
capital Fort-de-France
features several active volcanoes; Napoleon's empress Josephine was born in Martinique, and her childhood home is a museum
products sugar, cocoa, rum
population (1984) 327,000
history Martinique was reached by Spanish navigators in 1493, became a French colony in 1635, and was a French overseas *département* 1947–72, when it became an overseas region.

Martineau English writer Harriet Martineau became a prominent and controversial literary figure for her writings on Unitarianism, political science, and the abolition of slavery.

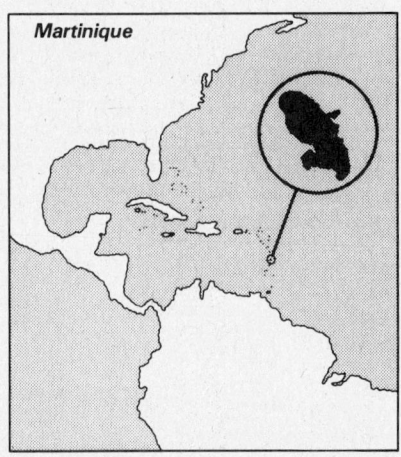

Martinique

Martinmas in the Christian calendar, the feast of St Martin, 11 Nov. Fairs were frequently held on this day, at which farm-workers were hired. In the Middle Ages it was also the day on which cattle were slaughtered and salted for winter consumption.

Martin, St /'mɑːtɪn/ 316–400. Bishop of Tours. Born in Pannonia, SE Europe, a soldier by profession, he was converted to Christianity, left the army, and lived for ten years as a recluse. As bishop of Tours from about 371, he worked for the extinction of idolatry and the extension of monasticism in France. He is usually represented as tearing his cloak to share it with a beggar.

Martin's Hundred /'mɑːtɪnz/ plantation town established in Virginia, USA, in 1619, and eliminated by an Indian massacre three years later. Its remains, the earliest extensive trace of

British colonization in America, were discovered in 1970.

Martinů /'mɑːtɪnuː/ Bohuslav (Jan) 1890–1959. Czech composer, born Polička, who studied in Paris. He left Czechoslovakia after the Nazi occupation of 1939. The standard of his music varies greatly, but at its best is richly expressive and has great vitality. Works include the operas *Julietta* 1937 and *The Greek Passion* 1959, symphonies, and much chamber music.

martyr in the Christian Church, one who voluntarily suffers death for refusing to renounce the Christian faith. The first recorded Christian martyr was St Stephen, who was killed in Jerusalem shortly after Christ's ascension. The word comes from the Greek for 'witness'.

Marvell /'mɑːvəl/ Andrew 1621–1678. English metaphysical poet and satirist, born in Winestead, Humberside. He was committed to the Parliamentary cause, being employed as tutor by Lord ◊Fairfax and ◊Cromwell, and as assistant to ◊Milton when the latter was Latin Secretary to the Council of State 1657–60. He was Member of Parliament for Hull from 1659. His poems include 'To His Coy Mistress' and 'Horatian Ode upon Cromwell's Return from Ireland'. He devoted his last years mainly to verse satire and controversial prose works.

Marx /mɑːks/ Karl Heinrich 1818–1883. German philosopher and social theorist. Born at Trèves, he studied at Bonn and Berlin, and during 1842–43 edited the *Rheinische Zeitung/Rhineland Newspaper* until its suppression. In 1844 began his life-long collaboration with ◊Engels, with whom he developed the Marxist philosophy, first formulated in their joint works, *Die heilige Familie/The Holy Family* 1844, and *Die deutsche Ideologie/German Ideology* 1846, and Marx's *Misère de la philosophie/Poverty of Philosophy* 1847. Both joined the Communist League, a German refugee organization, and in 1847–48 they prepared its programme, *'The Communist Manifesto'*. During the 1848 revolution Marx edited the *Neue Rheinische Zeitung/New Rhineland Newspaper*, until in 1849 he was expelled from Prussia.

He then settled in London, where he wrote *Die Klassenkämpfe in Frankreich/Class Struggles in France* 1849, *Die Achtzehnte Brumaire des Louis Bonaparte/The 18th Brumaire of Louis Bonaparte* 1852, *Zur Kritik der politischen Ökonomie/Critique of Political Economy* 1859, and his monumental work *Das Kapital/Capital* 1867. In 1864 the International Working Men's Association was formed, whose policy Marx, as a member of the general council, largely controlled. Although he showed extraordinary tact in holding together its diverse elements, it was disrupted by the intrigues of the anarchists, and in 1872 collapsed. The second and third volumes of *Das Kapital* were edited from his notes by Engels, and published posthumously. Marx was buried at Highgate, London.

His account of change through conflict is known as historical materialism. The theory demonstrates the material basis of all human activity: 'Life is not determined by consciousness, but consciousness by life'

(German Ideology). Marx also developed a powerful critique of capitalist society, which he saw as giving rise to alienation, and as ultimately a self-destructive system. See also ◊Marxism.

Marx Brothers team of American film comedians *Leonard 'Chico'* (from the 'chicks' – girls – he chased) 1891–1961; *Arthur 'Harpo'* (from the harp he played) 1893–1964; *Julius 'Groucho'* 1895–1977; *Milton 'Gummo'* (from his gumshoes or galoshes) 1901–77, and *Herbert 'Zeppo'* (born at the time of the first zeppelins) 1900–79. Their films include *Duck Soup* 1933 and *A Night at the Opera* 1935.

Marxism philosophical system, developed by ◊Marx and ◊Engels, also known as 'dialectical materialism', under which matter gives rise to mind (materialism) and all is subject to change (from dialectic; see ◊Hegel). As applied to history, it supposes that social and political institutions progressively change their nature as economic developments transform material conditions, so that the succession of feudalism, capitalism, socialism (called 'modes of production', the last seen as the ultimate rational system) is inevitable. The stubborn resistance of any existing system to change necessitates its complete overthrow in the 'class struggle', in the case of capitalism by the proletariat, not an attempt at gradual modification. The orthodox belief is that each successive form is 'higher' than the last; an ideal state being when perfect socialism is achieved, and the state is alleged to wither away. Marxism has proved one of the most powerful and controversial theories in modern history, inspiring both dedicated exponents and bitter opponents. See ◊communism, also ◊Plekhanov, ◊Lenin, ◊Trotsky, ◊Stalin, ◊Mao Zedong.

Mary /'meəri/ in the New Testament, the mother of Jesus Christ (Blessed Virgin Mary). Traditionally the child of Joachim and Anna in their old age, she married ◊Joseph and accompanied him to Bethlehem. Roman Catholic doctrine assumes that the brothers of Jesus were Joseph's sons by an earlier marriage, and that she remained a virgin. The Roman Catholic Church also maintains her ◊Immaculate Conception and bodily Assumption into Heaven, and venerates her as a mediator.

Mary /mə'riː/ town (ancient ◊Merv) in Turkmenistan, S USSR; population 72,000. It is at an oasis in the Kara Kum desert, where Alexander the Great founded a city.

Mary /'meəri/ Duchess of Burgundy 1457–1482. The daughter of Charles the Bold, she married Maximilian of Austria in 1477, thus bringing the Low Countries into the possession of the Hapsburgs, and ultimately of Spain.

Mary /'meəri/ Queen 1867–1953. Consort of ◊George V of the UK. The daughter of the Duke and Duchess of Teck, the latter a grand-daughter of George II, she became engaged in 1891 to the Duke of Clarence, eldest son of the Prince of Wales (later Edward VII). After his death in 1892, she married his brother George, Duke of York, in 1893, who succeeded to the throne in 1910.

Mary /'meəri/ Queen of Scots 1542–1587. Queen of Scotland from 1542. Also known as Mary Stuart, she was the daughter of James V and the French Mary of Guise. Born in Linlithgow, she was sent to France, where she married the dauphin, later Francis II. After his death she returned in 1561 to Scotland, which, during her absence, had accepted Protestantism. She married her cousin, the Earl of Darnley, in 1565, but they soon quarrelled, and Darnley took part in the murder of Mary's secretary, Rizzio. In 1567 he was assassinated as the result of a conspiracy formed by the Earl of Bothwell, possibly with Mary's connivance, and shortly after Bothwell married her. A rebellion followed; defeated at Carberry Hill, Mary abdicated and was imprisoned. She escaped in 1568, raised an army, and after its defeat at Langside fled to England. Elizabeth I held her a prisoner, while the Roman Catholics, who regarded Mary as rightful queen of England, formed many conspiracies to place her on the throne. The discovery that she was involved in Babington's plot led to her trial and execution at Fotheringay Castle in 1587.

Mary Mary Stuart, the half-French Queen of Scots, was next in line to the throne of England after Elizabeth I. Their rivalry, and her stormy political and personal life, ended with her execution in 1587.

Mary two queens of England:

Mary I /'meəri/ 1516–1558. Queen from 1553. The daughter of Henry VIII by Catherine of Aragon, she was born at Greenwich. When Edward VI died, she secured the crown without difficulty in spite of the conspiracy to substitute Lady Jane ◊Grey. In 1554 she married ◊Philip II of Spain, and as a devout Catholic obtained the restoration of papal supremacy. Although naturally humane, she sanctioned the persecution of Protestants which won her the nickname of Bloody Mary.

Mary II /'meəri/ 1662–1694. Queen from 1688. The elder daughter of ◊James II, she was married in 1677 to her cousin, ◊William of Orange. After the 1688 revolution she accepted the crown jointly with William. During his absences abroad she took charge of the government, and showed courage and resource when invasion seemed possible in 1690 and 1692.

Maryland /'meərilænd/ state of the USA; nicknamed Old Line or Free State

area 27,394 sq km/10,577 sq mi

capital Annapolis

towns Baltimore

features Chesapeake Bay, an inlet of the Atlantic; ◊horse racing, the Preakness Stakes at Baltimore; yacht racing at Annapolis; Fort Meade, a government electronic-listening centre

products fruit, cereals, tobacco; fish and oysters

population (1984) 4,349,000

famous people Francis Scott Key, Stephen Decatur, H L Mencken, Upton Sinclair

history one of the original ◊Thirteen Colonies, first settled in 1634; it became a state in 1788.

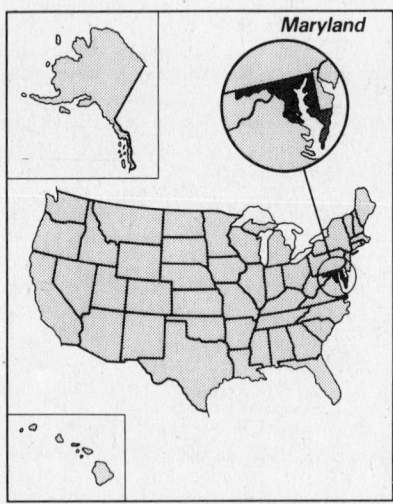

Maryland

Mary Magdalene /ˌmægdə'liːni/ woman who according to the New Testament was present at the Crucifixion and was the first to meet the risen Jesus. She is often identified with the woman of St Luke's gospel who anointed Christ's feet. Her feast day is 22 Jul.

Mary of Modena /'mɒdɪnə/ 1658–1718. Queen consort of England and Scotland. The daughter of the Duke of Modena, Italy, she married James, Duke of York, later ◊James II, in 1673. The birth of their son, James, 'the Old Pretender', popularly thought to have fraudulently arrived in a warming pan, was the signal for the revolution of 1688 which overthrew James II. Mary of Modena fled to France.

Mary Rose greatest warship of Henry VIII, which sank before his eyes off Southsea, Hampshire, on 19 Jul 1545. Located in 1971, the wreck was raised 1982 for preservation next to Nelson's flagship *Victory*.

Masaccio /mə'zætʃəʊ/ pseudonym of Tomaso di Giovanni di Simone Guidi 1401–1428. Florentine painter. With his teacher, Masolino di Panicale (c. 1384–1447), he decorated Santa Maria del Carmine, Florence. He was first painter to apply the scientific laws of perspective newly discovered by the architect ◊Brunelleschi.

Mary of Modena James II's consort, Mary of Modena, joined him in his refuge in France after the invasion of England by William of Orange. Her elegant portrait is by the Dutch painter William Wissing c. 1685.

Masada /mə'sɑːdə/ rock fortress 396 m/1,300 ft above the west shore of the Dead Sea, Israel. Besieged by the Romans 72 AD, its population of 953 committed mass suicide: the site was excavated 1963–65, including the palace of Herod.

Masai /'mɑːsaɪ/ African people who speak a Nilotic language. Originally warriors and nomadic breeders of humped zebu cattle, on which they relied for their diet of milk, meat, and blood, they are gradually adopting a more settled life. Their territory is divided between Tanzania and Kenya, and at the time of independence in 1963 they unsuccessfully demanded its total inclusion in either one country or the other.

Masaryk /'mæsərɪk/ Jan Garrigue 1886–1948. Czech politician, son of Thomas ◊Masaryk. Foreign minister from 1940, when the Czech government was exiled in London in World War II, he returned in 1945, retaining the post but as a result of communist political pressure committed suicide.

Masaryk /'mæsərɪk/ Thomas Garrigue 1850–1937. Czech politician. He directed the Czech revolutionary movement against the Austrian Empire, founding with Beneš and Stefanik the Czechoslovak National Council, and in 1918 was elected first president of the newly formed Czechoslovak Republic. Three times re-elected, he resigned in 1935 in favour of Beneš.

Mascagni /mæs'kɑːnji/ Pietro 1863–1945. Italian composer of the one-act opera *Cavalleria rusticana/Rustic Chivalry*, first produced in Rome in 1890.

Mascara /mæs'kɑːrə/ town and wine-trade centre, 96 km/60 mi SE of Oran, Algeria; the headquarters of Abd-el-Kader (c. 1807–83) who fought the French invasion of Algeria 1830–47, Mascara being captured 1841.

Masefield /'meɪsfiːld/ John 1878–1967. British poet. Born in Herefordshire, he went to

Masaryk The first president of Czechoslovakia, Thomas Garrigue Masaryk was also a scholar and philosopher.

sea, then joined the *Manchester Guardian* before settling in London. He attracted notice by such volumes of poetry as *Salt-Water Ballads* 1902 (which include 'Sea Fever'), but fame came with the verse narrative of a drunkard's conversion *The Everlasting Mercy* 1911, with its forcefully colloquial language. His novels include *Sard Harker* 1924 and *Badon Parchments* 1947 and for children *The Box of Delights* 1935. He was appointed Poet Laureate in 1930, and in 1935 was awarded the Order of Merit.

maser (microwave amplification by stimulated emission of radiation). In physics, a high-frequency amplifier or oscillator dependent on the quantum properties of electrons (see ◊quantum theory). By inverting the populations of a pair of electron spin energy levels (that is, by making the upper level more densely populated than the lower one) the resonance absorption at a frequency corresponding to the energy difference can be changed to emission; a maser results from suitable coupling of this ◊radiation to a microwave cavity or travelling-wave structure. The population inversion can be achieved by beam focusing, as in a two-level ammonia gas maser, first suggested in 1954 by C H Townes at Columbia University and independently the same year by Basov and Prokhorov in the USSR, or pumping at a different frequency between another pair of levels, as in a solid-state three-level maser, the most sensitive amplifier known, envisaged by Bloembergen in 1956 at Harvard. The principle has since been extended to other parts of the electromagnetic spectrum. (See ◊laser.) The ammonia maser is used as a frequency standard oscillator (see ◊clocks) and the three-level maser as a receiver for satellite communications and radioastronomy.

Maseru /mə'seəruː/ capital of Lesotho, South Africa, on the Caledon river; a trading centre; population (1986) 288,951.

Mashhad /mæʃˈhæd/ holy city of the Shi'ites (Muslims in NE Iran), also an industrial centre (carpets, textiles, leather goods), in NE Iran; population (1982) 1,120,000.

Mashonaland /məˈʃɒnəlænd/ eastern Zimbabwe, the land of the Shona people; Prime Minister Mugabe is a Shona. Granted to the British South Africa Company in 1889, it was included in Southern Rhodesia in 1923. The ◊Zimbabwe ruins are here.

Mashraq /mæʃˈrɑːk/ (Arabic 'east') the Arab countries of the E Mediterranean: Egypt, Sudan, Jordan, Syria, and Lebanon. The term is contrasted with ◊Maghreb, Arab countries of NW Africa.

Masirah Island /məˈsɪərə/ an island in the Arabian Sea, part of the sultanate of ◊Oman.

Maskelyne /ˈmæskəlɪn/ Nevil 1732–1811. British astronomer, fifth Astronomer Royal (1765–1811). He began publication of the *Nautical Almanac*, containing tables for navigators. In 1769 he accurately measured the distance from the Earth to the Sun by observing a transit of Venus across the Sun's face. In 1774 he measured the density of the Earth from the deflection of a plumbline near a large mountain.

masochism a desire to subject oneself to physical or mental pain, humiliation, or punishment, either for erotic pleasure, to alleviate guilt, or out of destructive impulses turned inwards. The term is derived from Leopold von ◊Sacher-Masoch.

Mason-Dixon Line in the USA, the boundary line between Maryland and Pennsylvania (latitude 39°,43 minutes,/26.3 seconds N), named after Mason and Dixon, English astronomers who surveyed it 1763–67. It was popularly seen as dividing the North from the South (slave-owning states).

masque a spectacular and essentially aristocratic 'entertainment' with a fantastic or mythological theme in which music, dance, and extravagant costumes and scenic design were more important than plot. Originating in Italy, it reached its height of popularity at the English court between 1600 and 1640, with the collaboration of Ben ◊Jonson as writer and Inigo ◊Jones as stage designer. The masque had great influence on the development of ballet and opera, and the elaborate frame in which it was performed developed into the proscenium arch.

mass in physics, the quantity of matter in a body. In the SI system, the base unit of mass is the kilogram. Mass determines the acceleration produced in a body by a given force acting on it, the acceleration being inversely proportional to the mass of the body. The mass also determines the force exerted on a body by the gravitational attraction of the Earth (see ◊gravity), although this attraction varies slightly from place to place. At a given place, however, equal masses experience equal gravitational forces, which are known as the weights of the bodies. Masses may, therefore, be compared by comparing the weights of bodies at the same place, as by using ◊balance. The standard unit of mass from which all other masses are compared is a platinum-iridium cylinder of 1 kg.

Mass in Christianity, the celebration of the ◊Eucharist.

Mass in music, the setting of the invariable parts of the Mass, that is *Kyrie*, *Gloria*, *Credo*, *Sanctus* with *Benedictus*, and *Agnus Dei*, such as Bach's *Mass in B Minor*.

Massachusetts /ˌmæsəˈtʃuːsɪts/ New England state of the USA; nicknamed Bay State or Old Colony
area 21,385 sq km/8257 sq mi
capital Boston
towns Worcester, Springfield, Nantucket
features the two large Atlantic islands of Nantucket and Martha's Vineyard, former whaling centres; rivers Merrimac and Connecticut; University of Harvard 1636; Massachusetts Institute of Technology (MIT) 1861; Woods Hole Oceanographic Institute; Massachusetts Biotechnology Research Park
products mainly industrial, especially electronic and communications equipment, shoes, textiles, machine tools; building stone; cod
population (1984) 5,741,000
famous people Samuel Adams, Louisa May Alcott, Emily Dickinson, Emerson, Hawthorne, Oliver Wendell Holmes, Winslow Homer, Morse, Poe, Revere, Thoreau, Whistler
history one of the original ◊Thirteen Colonies, it was first settled in 1620 by the Pilgrims at Plymouth, and became a state in 1788.

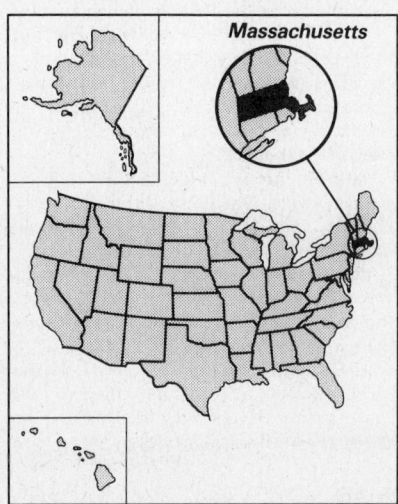

Massachusetts

massage manipulation of the tissues and muscles of the body for therapeutic effect. The basic movements are pétrissage (moulding or kneading), friction, effleurage (stroking), tapotement (patting), and vibration. It is considered particularly useful in the case of sporting injuries.

Massawa /məˈsɑːwə/ chief port and naval base of Ethiopia, in Eritrea, on the Red Sea, with salt production and pearl fishing; population (1980) 33,000. It is one of the hottest inhabited spots in the world, the temperature reaching 100°F/37.8°C in May. Massawa was an Italian possession 1885–1941.

Masséna /ˌmæseɪˈnɑː/ André 1756–1817. marshal of France. He served in the wars of the

Massawa Temperatures here may reach 46°C/115°F and water evaporates quickly. About 230,000 tonnes of salt are collected from these pans every year.

◊French Revolution, and under Napoleon was created a marshal of France in 1804, duke of Rivoli in 1808, and prince of Essling in 1809. He was in command in Spain 1810–11, and was defeated by Wellington.

mass-energy equation ◊Einstein's famous equation $E = mc^2$, denoting the equivalence of mass and energy, where E is the energy in ◊joules, m is the ◊mass in kg, and c is the speed of light in metres per second.

Massenet /ˌmæsəˈneɪ/ Jules Émile Frédéric 1842–1912. French composer of many operas, including *Hérodiade* 1881, *Manon* 1884, *Le Cid* 1885, and *Thaïs* 1894; and also ballets, oratorios and orchestral suites, including *Scènes pittoresques* 1874.

Massif Central /mæˈsiːf sɒnˈtrɑːl/ mountainous plateau region of S central France; area 93,000 sq km/36,000 sq mi, highest peak Puy de Sancy 1,886 m/6,188 ft. It is a source of hydroelectricity and includes the ◊Auvergne and ◊Cévennes.

Massine /mæˈsiːn/ Léonide 1895–1979. Russian choreographer and dancer. Important as a creator of comedy in ballet and also symphonic ballet using concert music, he succeeded ◊Fokine at the Ballets Russes and continued with the company after ◊Diaghilev's death, later working in both America and Europe. Among his best-known works are the first Cubist-inspired ballet *Parade* 1917, *La Boutique Fantasque* 1919 and *The Three-Cornered Hat* 1919.

Massinger /ˈmæsɪndʒə/ Philip 1583–1640. English dramatist, whose masterpiece is *A New Way to Pay Old Debts* c. 1625, noted for the usurer Sir Giles Overreach. He collaborated with ◊Fletcher and ◊Dekker, and has been credited with a share in Shakespeare's *Two Noble Kinsmen* and *Henry VIII*.

mass observation the study of the details of people's daily lives through observation and interview. A society of the name was founded in London in 1937 for the purpose, employing a panel of observers and a number of trained investigators, and publishing the results.

Massorah a collection of philological notes on the Hebrew text of the Old Testament. At first merely oral tradition, the Massorah was committed to writing in the Aramaic language at Tiberias in Palestine between the 6th and 9th centuries.

mass production the manufacture of goods on a large scale, a technique that aims for low unit cost and high sales at the expense of craft skill. In modern factories mass production is achieved by a variety of means. One is the division and specialization of labour. The job to be carried out is divided into a number of steps, so that no worker is involved in more than one stage of manufacture. ◊Mechanization speeds up production and allows the manufacture of interchangeable parts, which can then be assembled quickly into a finished product on an ◊assembly line. Many of the machines now used in factories work automatically under computer control. See also ◊robot.

mass spectrometer in physics, an apparatus in which positive ◊ions (charged particles) of a substance are separated by an electromagnetic system and which permits accurate measurement of the relative concentrations of the various ionic masses present, particularly ◊isotopes.

Master of the King's/Queen's Musick appointment to the British royal household, the holder composing appropriate music for state occasions. The first was Nicholas Lanier, appointed by Charles I in 1626; the composer Malcolm ◊Williamson was appointed in 1975.

Master of the Rolls title of an English judge ranking immediately below the Lord Chief Justice. He presides over the Court of Appeal, besides being Keeper of the Records and head of the Public Record Office.

Masters /'mɑːstəz/ Edgar Lee 1869–1950. American poet, born in Kansas. In his *Spoon River Anthology* 1915, the people of a small town tell of their frustrated lives.

mastiff British dog, usually fawn, which was originally bred for sporting purposes. It has a large head, wide-set eyes, and broad muzzle.

mastodon primitive elephant, whose fossil remains have been discovered in all the continents except Australia, particularly in deposits of Pleistocene Age in the USA and Canada. It resembled the modern elephant, but was lower and longer; its teeth suggest that it ate leaves in the primeval swamps and forests.

Masulipatnam /mə,suːlɪpət'næm/ Indian seaport (its name means fish town) in Andhra, at the mouth of the N branch of the river Kistna; population (1971) 112,650.

Masurian Lakes /mə'svərɪən/ lakes in Poland (former East Prussia) which in 1914–15 were the scene of battles in which the Germans defeated the Russian invaders.

Matabeleland /ˌmætə'biːlilænd/ the W portion of Zimbabwe, inhabited by the Ndebele people
area 181,605 sq km/70,118 sq mi
towns Bulawayo
features rich plains watered by tributaries of the Zambezi and Limpopo, with mineral resources
language Matabele
famous people Joshua Nkomo
history Matabeleland was granted to the British South Africa Company in 1889 and occupied in

1893 after attacks on white settlements in Mashonaland; in 1923 it was included in Southern Rhodesia.

Matadi /mə'tɑːdi/ chief port of Zaïre on the river Zaïre, 115 km/70 mi from its mouth, linked by oil pipelines with Kinshasa; population (1976) 143,600.

Mata Hari /'mɑːtə 'hɑːri/ ('Eye of the Day'), stage name of Margaretha Geertruida Zella 1876–1917. Dutch courtesan, 'oriental dancer', and probable spy. In World War I she appears to have been a double agent, in the pay of both France and Germany, but it was the French who finally shot her on espionage charges. She remained the archetypal exotic spy.

matamata S American freshwater turtle or terrapin *Chelys fimbriata* with a shell up to 40 cm/1.3 ft long. The head is flattened with a 'snorkel' nose, and the neck has many projections of skin. The movement of these in the water may attract prey which is taken in by opening the mouth suddenly to produce an inrush of water.

Matanzas /mə'tænsəs/ industrial port (tanning, textiles, sugar) in Cuba, founded 1693; population (1981) 99,000.

Matapan /ˌmætə'pæn/ southernmost cape of the mainland of Greece, off which, on 28 Mar 1941, during World War II, a British fleet under Admiral Cunningham sank an Italian squadron.

match a small strip of wood or paper, tipped with combustible material for producing fire. Friction matches containing phosphorus were first made by John Walker of Stockton-on-Tees about 1826. A 'safety' match is one in which the oxidizing agent and the combustible body are kept apart, the former being incorporated into the striking surface on the side of the box, the latter into the match.

maté dried leaves of the Brazilian holly *Ilex paraguensis*, an evergreen shrub akin to the common holly, that grows in Paraguay and Brazil. They are made into a tea.

materialism the philosophical theory that there is nothing in existence over and above matter. Such a theory excludes the possibility of deities. It sees mind as an attribute of the physical, not independent of body. Like most other philosophical ideas, materialism probably arose among the early Greek thinkers. The ◊Stoics and the ◊Epicureans were materialists, and so were the ancient Buddhists. Among modern materialists have been ◊Hobbes, Büchner, and ◊Haeckel.

mathematical induction see ◊induction.

mathematics the science of spatial and numerical relationships. *Pure mathematics* includes, as its main divisions, geometry, arithmetic, algebra, calculus, trigonometry, and so on; mechanics, the mathematical theories of astronomy, electricity, optics, thermodynamics and atomic studies come under the heading of *applied mathematics*.
Probably prehistoric human beings learned to count at least up to 10 on their fingers. The Chinese, Hindus, Babylonians and Egyptians all devised methods of counting and measuring. The first theoretical mathematician is held to be Thales of Melitus (active 580 BC), who is believed to have proposed the first theorems in plane

geometry. His disciple ◊Pythagoras established geometry as a recognized science among the Greeks. The later school of Alexandrian geometers (4th and 3rd centuries BC) included ◊Euclid and ◊Archimedes. Our present decimal numerals are based on a Hindu-Arabic system which reached Europe about AD 100 from Arab mathematicians of the Near East such as al-Khwarizmi. Western mathematics began to develop from the 15th century. Geometry was revitalized by the invention of coordinate geometry by Descartes in 1637; Pascal and Fermat developed probability theory, Napier invented logarithms, and Newton and Leibniz developed calculus. In Russia Lobachevsky rejected Euclid's parallelism and developed non-Euclidean geometry, a more developed form of which (by Riemann) was later utilized by ◊Einstein in his relativity theory.
Today higher mathematics has a powerful new tool in the high-speed electronic computer, which can create and manipulate mathematical 'models' of various systems in science, technology and commerce. Modern methods of teaching ◊arithmetic, involving ◊sets, are sometimes referred to as 'new maths'.

Matilda /mə'tɪldə/ 1102–1167. Queen of England 1141–1153. Recognized during the reign of her father ◊Henry I as his heir, she married first the Holy Roman Emperor ◊Henry V, and after his death Geoffrey Plantagenet, Count of Anjou. On her father's death in 1135, the barons elected her cousin Stephen to be king. In order to press her claim to the throne Matilda invaded England in 1139, and was crowned in 1141. Civil war ensued until in 1153 Stephen was finally recognized as king, with Henry II (Matilda's son) as his successor.

Matisse /mæ'tiːs/ Henri 1869–1954. French artist. Born at Le Cateau Nord, he was a member of the group known as *les ◊Fauves*. One of the leading modern French painters, he employed pure colour, distorted natural forms, and subordinated subject matter to pattern in a way which greatly influenced 20th century art and art theory. In 1947–51 he designed and decorated a chapel for the Dominicans of Vence, near Nice.

Matlock /'mætlɒk/ spa town with warm springs, administrative headquarters of Derbyshire, England; population (1981) 21,000.

Mato Grosso /'mætəʊ 'grɒsəʊ/ (Portuguese 'dense forest') area of SW Brazil, now forming two states, with their capitals at Cuiaba and Campo Grande. The forests, now depleted, supplied rubber and rare timbers; diamonds and silver are mined.

matriarchy a form of social organization in which women head the family, and descent and relationship are reckoned through the female line. Matriarchy, often associated with polyandry (one wife with several husbands), occurs in certain parts of India, in the South Pacific, Central Africa, and among some N American Indian peoples.

matrix in mathematics, a method of condensing information about mathematical systems as a square or rectangular array of numbers or quantities. Matrices can be used, for, among other things, solving simultaneous linear

MATHEMATICAL SYMBOLS

$a{\rightarrow}b$	a tending toward b
∞	infinity
lim	limiting value
$a{\sim}b$	a approximately equal to b
$a{\approx}b$	a very nearly equal to b
$a{=}b$	a equal to b
$a{\equiv}b$	a identical with b (for formulae only)
$a{>}b$	a greater than b
$a{<}b$	a smaller than b
$a{\gg}b$	a much greater than b
$a{\ll}b$	a much smaller than b
$a{\neq}b$	
$a{\gtrless}b$	a not equal to b
$b{<}a{<}c$	a greater than b and smaller than c
$a{\geqq}b$	a equal to or greater than b, that is, a at least as great as b
$a{\geq}b$	
$a{\leqq}b$	a equal to or smaller than b, that is, a at most as great as b
$a{\leqslant}b$	
$b{\leqq}a{\leqq}c$	a lying between b and c
$\lvert a \rvert$	absolute value of a; this is always positive, for example $\lvert{-}5\rvert=5$
$+$	addition sign, plus, positive
$-$	subtraction sign, minus, negative
$\times$ or $\odot$	multiplication sign, times
: or $\div$	division sign, divided by
$a{+}b{=}c$	$a{+}b$, read as 'a plus b', denotes the sum of a and b. The result of the addition, c, is also known as the sum.
$\int$	indefinite integral
$_a{\int}^b$	definite integral, or integral between $x{=}a$ and $x{=}b$
$a{-}b{=}c$	$a{-}b$, read as 'a minus b', denotes subtraction of b from a.
	$a{-}b$, or c, is the difference. Subtraction is the opposite of addition.
$a{\times}b{=}c$	
	$a{\times}b$, read as 'a times b', denotes multiplication of a by b. a and b are the multiplicands
$ab{=}c$	or factors; $a{\times}b$, or c, is the product.
$a{\cdot}b{=}c$	
$a{:}b{=}c$	$a{:}c$, read as 'a divided by b', denotes division. a is the dividend, b is the divisor; $a{:}b$, or c, is the quotient. Division is the opposite of multiplication and can also be represented by the fraction $\frac{a}{b}$ or a/b.
	In fractions, a is the numerator (= dividend), b the denominator (= divisor).
$a^b{=}c$	a^b, read as 'a to the power b'; a is the base, b the exponent.
$^b{\sqrt{a}}{=}c$	$^b\sqrt{a}$, is the bth root of a, b being known as the root exponent. In the special case of $\sqrt[2]{a}{=}c$, $\sqrt[2]{a}$ or c is known as the square root of a, and the root exponent. is usually omitted, that is, $\sqrt[2]{a}=\sqrt{a}$.
e	base of natural (napierian) logarithms = 2.7182818284.
π	ratio of the circumference of a circle to its diameter = 3.1415925535.

Matisse French artist-designer Henri Matisse simplified form and subordinated subject matter to pattern, as in this 1929 lithograph, *Odalisque*.

Matterhorn The ascent by Whymper's party in 1865 was a landmark in mountaineering . From the Swiss side the mountain appears to be an isolated peak, but it is actually the end of a ridge.

equations. Much early matrix theory was developed by the British mathematician Arthur Cayley, although the term was first coined by his contemporary James Sylvester (1814–97).

matrix in biology, usually refers to the ◊extracellular matrix.

Matsuyama /ˌmætsəˈjɑːmə/ largest city on Shikoku, Japan; population (1984) 418,000. There is a feudal fortress 1634.

Matsys /ˈmætsaɪs/ (also Massys or Metsys) Quentin 1466–1530. Flemish painter. Born at Louvain, he was influenced by the masters of the Italian Renaissance, and is famous for his sacred pictures, such as the triptych of the 'Pietà', in the Antwerp museum. He also painted portraits, including one of Erasmus, which he presented to Thomas More.

matter in physics, the 'stuff' out of which all objects outside the mind are considered to be composed. The history of science and philosophy is largely taken up with accounts of theories of matter, ranging from the hard atoms of Democritus to the 'waves' of modern quantum theory. See also ◊atom.

Matterhorn /ˈmætəhɔːn/ mountain peak in the Alps on the Swiss-Italian border (French *le Cervin*, Italian *il Cervino*): 4,478 m/14,690 ft. It was first climbed in 1865 by an English mountaineer Edward Whymper (1840–1911); four members of his party of seven were killed when the rope broke during the descent.

Matthews /ˈmæθjuːz/ Stanley 1915– . English footballer. He played soccer for Blackpool, Stoke City and England. He won the FA Cup Winner's medal in 1953 at 38. An outstanding right winger known as the 'wizard of the dribble', he made 701 league and 54 international appearances.

Matthew, St Christian apostle and evangelist, the traditional author of the first Gospel. He is usually identified with Levi, who was a tax-collector in the service of Herod Antipas, and was called by Jesus to be a disciple as he sat by the Lake of Galilee receiving customs dues. His feast day is 21 Sept.

Matthias Corvinus /mə'θaɪəs kɔː'vaɪnəs/ 1440–1490. Greatest of the kings of Hungary. The son of the great warrior, John Hunyadi, he was elected king in 1458. His aim of uniting Hungary, Austria, and Bohemia involved him in long wars with the emperor and the kings of Bohemia and Poland, during which, in 1485, he captured Vienna and made it his capital.

Maudling /'mɔːdlɪŋ/ Reginald 1917–1979. British Conservative politician, chancellor of the exchequer 1962–64, contender for the party leadership in 1965, and home secretary 1970–72. He resigned when referred to during the bankruptcy proceedings of architect John Poulsen, since (as home secretary) he would have been in charge of the Metropolitan Police investigating the case.

Maugham /mɔːm/ (William) Somerset 1874–1965. British writer. His novel *Of Human Bondage* 1915 was largely autobiographical, though its hero was lame (Maugham had a stammer). Other books include *The Moon and Sixpence* 1919, based on Gauguin's life. During World War I he was a secret agent in Russia, trying to prevent the outbreak of revolution, and his Ashenden spy stories have a genuine basis.

Maugham Somerset Maugham in 1931, a portrait by P Steegman.

Mau Mau name given by white settlers to a Kenyan terrorist secret society with nationalist aims 1952–60, an offshoot of the Kikuyu Central Association banned in World War II. Attacks on other Kikuyu (about 1,000 killed) were far more common than on whites (about 100 killed). The term was used as a verb by US radicals in the 1960s (meaning 'to terrorize').

Maundy Thursday in the Christian Church, the Thursday before Easter. The name has been derived from the Latin *mandatum*, the first word of the service chanted at the ceremony of washing the feet of pilgrims on that day, which was instituted in commemoration of Jesus' washing of the apostles' feet. The ceremony was observed in the Church from about the 4th century, and performed by the English sovereigns until the time of William III. The rite of foot-washing was abandoned in 1754, but the Maundy money (Maundy pennies) is still presented in Westminster Abbey (elsewhere in alternate years).

Maupassant /ˌməʊpæ'sɒŋ/ Guy de 1850–1893. French author, born in Normandy. A civil servant, he was encouraged as a writer by ◊Flaubert, and established a reputation with the short story 'Boule de Suif/Ball of Fat' 1880; his novels include *Une Vie/A Woman's Life* 1883 and *Bel-Ami* 1885.

Mauriac /ˌmɔːri'æk/ François 1885–1970. French novelist. Born in Bordeaux, he published his first important work *Le Baiser au lêpreux/A Kiss for the Leper* in 1922, which shows the conflict of an unhappy marriage. Similarly preoccupied with the irreconcilability of Christian practice and human nature are *Fleuve de feu/River of Fire* 1923, and *Le Désert de l'amour/The Desert of Love* 1925. He was awarded a Nobel prize in 1952.

Maurist one of a congregation of French Roman Catholic monks, belonging to the Benedictine order, established in 1621 at the Benedictine monastery of St Maur-sur-Loire. Subsequently its chief house was in Paris, and there the Maurist fathers carried on literary and historical work, while still maintaining the strict monastic discipline. In 1792 the congregation was suppressed.

Mauritania /ˌmɒri'teɪnɪə/ country in NW Africa, bordered to the NE by Algeria, E and S by Mali, SW by Senegal, W by the Atlantic Ocean, and NW by Western Sahara.
government the 1961 constitution was suspended in 1978 after a coup, and was replaced by a charter which gave executive and legislative power to a Military Committee for National Recovery (CMRN), which in 1979 became the Military Committee for National Salvation (CMSN). The chair of the CMSN is also president of the republic, prime minister, and minister of defence. The only political party, the Mauritanian People's Party (PPM), was banned in 1978 and some of its exiled supporters now operate from Paris, through the Alliance for a Democratic Mauritania (AMI), or from Dakar, in Senegal, through the Organization of Nationalist Mauritanians.
history Mauritania was the name of the Roman province of NW Africa, after the Mauri, a Berber people who inhabited it. ◊Berbers occupied the region during the 1st–3rd centuries AD, and it came under the control of the ◊Ghana empire between the 7th–11th centuries. The Berbers were converted to ◊Islam from the 8th century, and Islamic influence continued to dominate as the area was controlled by the ◊Almoravids and then the Arabs. French influence began in the 17th century, with the trade in gum arabic, and developed into colonization by the mid-18th century, when France gained control of S Mauritania.

Mauritania became a French colony, as part of French West Africa, in 1920. It achieved internal self-government within the French Community in 1958 and full independence in 1960. Moktar Ould Daddah, leader of the PPM, became president in 1961.
In 1975 Spain ceded the western part of Sahara to Mauritania and Morocco, leaving them to decide how to share it. Without consulting the Saharan people, Mauritania occupied the southern area, leaving the N to Morocco. A resistance movement developed against this occupation, the Popular Front for Liberation, or the Polisario Front, with Algerian backing, and Mauritania and Morocco found themselves engaged in a guerrilla war, forcing the two former rivals into a mutual defence pact. The conflict weakened Mauritania's economy and in 1978 President Daddah was deposed in a bloodless coup led by Col Mohamed Khouna Ould Haidalla. Peace with the Polisario was eventually agreed in Aug, allowing diplomatic relations with Algeria to be restored.
In Dec 1984, while Col Haidalla was attending a Franco-African summit meeting in Burundi, Col Moaouya Ould Sidi Ahmed Taya, a former prime minister, led a bloodless coup to overthrow him. Diplomatic relations with Morocco were broken in 1981 and the situation worsened in 1984 when Mauritania formally recognized the Polisario regime in Western Sahara. Normal relations were restored in 1985.

Mauritius /mə'rɪʃəs/ island in the Indian Ocean, E of Madagascar.
government Mauritius is an independent state within the Commonwealth, with a resident governor-general as head of state, representing the British monarch. Its 1968 constitution, amended in 1969, provides for a single-chamber legislative assembly of up to 71 members, 62 elected by universal adult suffrage, plus the speaker and up to eight of the most successful non-elected candidates, as 'additional' members. The governor-general appoints the prime minister and a council of ministers who are collectively responsible to the assembly. Of a number of political parties, the three most significant are the Mauritius Labour Party (MLP), the Mauritius Socialist Movement (MSM) and the Mauritius Militant Movement (MMM).
history uninhabited until the 16th century, the island was colonized on a small scale by the Dutch, who named it Mauricius after Prince Maurice of Nassau. They abandoned it in 1710, and in 1715 it was occupied by the French, who imported African slaves to work on their sugar cane plantations. Mauritius was seized by Britain in 1810, and was formally ceded by the Treaty of Paris in 1814. The abolition of slavery in 1833 brought about the importation of indentured labourers from India, whose descendants now make up about 70% of the island's population. In 1957 Mauritius was granted internal self-government, and full independence within the Commomwealth was achieved in 1968.
Seewoosagur Ramgoolam, leader of the MLP, who had led the country since 1959, became its

Mauritania

ISLAMIC REPUBLIC OF (*République Islamique de Mauritanie*)

AREA 1,030,000 sq km/419,000 sq mi
CAPITAL Nouakchott
PHYSICAL valley of river Senegal in S; the rest is arid
FEATURES includes part of the Sahara Desert
HEAD OF STATE AND OF GOVERNMENT Moaouya Ould Sidi Ahmed Taya from 1984
GOVERNMENT military
EXPORTS iron ore, fish
CURRENCY ouguiya (123.61 = £1 Sept 1987)
POPULATION (1985) 1,656,000 (30% Arab Berber, 30% black Africans, 30% Haratine – descendants of black slaves, who remained slaves till 1980); annual growth rate 2.9%
LANGUAGE Arabic (official), French
RELIGION Sunni Muslim
LITERACY 2.9%
GDP $614 million (1984); $466 per head of population
CHRONOLOGY
1960 Achieved full independence, with Moktar Ould Daddah, as president.
1975 Western Sahara ceded by Spain. Mauritania occupied the southern part and Morocco the rest. Polisario Front formed in Sahara to resist the occupation by Mauritania and Morocco.

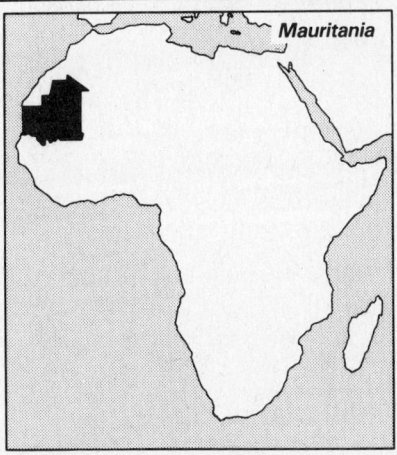
Mauritania

1978 Daddah deposed in bloodless coup and replaced by Mohamed Khouni Ould Haidalla. Peace agreed with Polisario Front.
1981 Diplomatic relations with Morocco broken.
1984 Haidalla overthrown by Moaouya Ould Sidi Ahmed Taya. Polisario regime formally recognized.
1985 Relations with Morocco restored.

include the semi-autobiographical *Bernard Quesnay* 1926, but he was best known for his fictionalized biographies, such as *Ariel* 1923, a life of Shelley, and for his essays on contemporary problems.

Mauroy /mɔːˈwɑː/ Pierre 1928– . French socialist politician, prime minister 1981–84. Mauroy worked for the FEN teachers' trade union and served as national secretary for the Young Socialists during the 1950s, rising in the ranks of the Socialist Party (PS) in the NE region. He entered the National Assembly in 1973 and was prime minister in the ◊Mitterrand government of 1981. Mauroy oversaw the introduction of a radical reflationary programme, but was replaced by ◊Fabius in Jul 1984.

Mawson /ˈmɔːsən/ Douglas 1882–1958. Australian (British-born) Antarctic explorer, who on Shackleton's expedition of 1907–09 discovered the South Magnetic Pole, and himself led expeditions 1911–14 and 1929–31; knighted 1914. Australia's first permanent Antarctic base was named after him.

Maximilian /ˌmæksɪˈmɪliən/ 1832–1867. Emperor of Mexico. Brother of the Emperor Franz Joseph of Austria. He was given command of the Austrian navy in 1854, and was governor of Lombardy and Venetia 1857–59. He married Princess Charlotte of Belgium in 1857. He was Emperor of Mexico 1864–67, accepting the title when ◊Napoleon III's troops occupied Mexico, but encountered resistance from ◊Juárez, and in 1866, after the French troops withdrew on the

first prime minister. During the 1970s he led a succession of coalition governments and even in 1976, when the MMM became the assembly's largest single party, Ramgoolam formed another fragile coalition. Dissatisfaction with the government's economic policies led to Ramgoolam's defeat and the formation in 1982 of an MMM-Mauritius Socialist Party (PSM) coalition government led by Aneerood Jugnauth. Strains developed within the alliance, 12 MMM ministers resigned in 1983, and the coalition was dissolved. Jugnauth then founded the MSM, and the PSM was incorporated in the new party. A general election later that year resulted in an MSM-MLP-Mauritius Social Democratic Party (PMSD) coalition, which won 37 assembly seats. Jugnauth became prime minister on the understanding that Sir Seewoosagur Ramgoolam would be president if Mauritius became a republic. When the constitutional change failed to get legislative approval, Sir Seewoosagur Ramgoolam was appointed governor-general in 1983. He died in 1985 and former finance minister, Sir Veersamy Ringadoo, replaced him. Recent economic policies have greatly cut inflation and unemployment, on the strength of which Aneerood Jugnauth was re-elected in an early general election in Aug 1987.

Maurois /mɔːˈwɑː/ André, pen name of French author Emile Herzog 1885–1967. In World War I he was attached to the British Army, and the essays *Les Silences du Colonel Bramble* 1918 give humorously sympathetic observations on the British character. His novels

Mauritius

STATE OF

AREA 1,865 sq km/720 sq mi; the island of Rodrigues is part of Mauritius and there are several small island dependencies
CAPITAL Port Louis
PHYSICAL a mountainous, volcanic island surrounded by coral reefs
FEATURES geologically part of Gondwanaland, it has unusual wildlife including flying fox and ostrich; it was the home of the dodo (extinct from about 1680)
HEAD OF STATE Elizabeth II representd by Veerasamy Ringadoo from 1986
HEAD OF GOVERNMENT Aneerood Jugnauth from 1982
GOVERNMENT parliamentary democracy
EXPORTS sugar; knitted goods; tourism is increasingly important
CURRENCY Mauritius rupee (21.5 = £1 Sept 1987)
POPULATION 1,024,900 (1985); annual growth rate 1.1%
LANGUAGE English (official); creole French
RELIGION Hindu 45%, Christian 30%, Muslim 15%
LITERACY 86% male/72% female (1980 est)
GNP $957 million (1984); $1,240 per head of population
CHRONOLOGY
1968 Achieved full independence within the

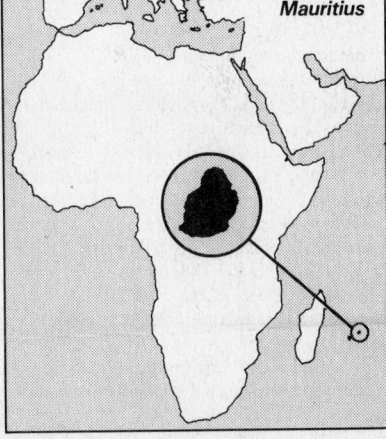
Mauritius

Commonwealth, with Seewoosagur Ramgoolam as prime minister.
1982 Aneerood Jugnauth prime minister.
1983 Jugnauth formed a new party, the Mauritius Socialist Movement, pledged to make Mauritius a republic within the Commonwealth, but Assembly refused. Ramgoolam appointed governor general. Jugnauth formed coalition government.
1985 Ramgoolam died, succeeded by Ringadoo.
1987 Jugnauth's coalition re-elected.

insistence the USA, Maximilian was captured by the republicans and shot in 1867.

Maximilian I /ˌmæksɪˈmɪliən/ 1459–1519. Son of Emperor Frederick III, and Holy Roman Emperor from 1493. He had acquired the Low Countries through his marriage with Mary of Burgundy in 1477; married his son ◊Philip the Handsome to the heiress to the Spanish throne, and undertook long wars with Italy and Hungary in attempts to extend Hapsburg power.

Maximilian I Holy Roman Emperor Maximilian I was a patron of the arts. This engraving is by Dürer, whom he supported.

maximum and minimum in mathematics, of a curve representing a ◊function in ◊coordinate geometry, the point at which the slope changes from positive to negative after reaching a turning point (maximum), or from negative to positive after reaching a turning point (minimum). A tangent to the curve at a maximum or minimum has zero gradient. Maxima and minima can be found by differentiating the function for the curve and setting the differential to zero (the value of the slope at the turning point). For example, differentiating the function for the ◊parabola $y = 2x^2 - 8x$ gives $dy/dx = 4x - 8$. Setting this equal to zero gives $x = 2$, so that $y = -8$ (found by substituting $x = 2$ into the parabola equation). Thus the function has a minimum at the point $(2, -8)$.

maxwell /ˈmækswəl/ former (◊cgs) unit of magnetic flux (Mx). Defined as the flux through 1 cm² perpendicular to a field of 1 gauss; replaced by the SI unit, the ◊weber.

Maxwell /ˈmækswəl/ James Clerk 1831–1879. British physicist. Born in Edinburgh, he was professor of natural philosophy at Aberdeen 1856–60, and then of physics and astronomy at London. In 1871 he became professor of experimental physics at Cambridge. Maxwell's short life was rich in contributions of the first order to every branch of physical science, particularly on gases, optics and colour sensation, and magnetism. His

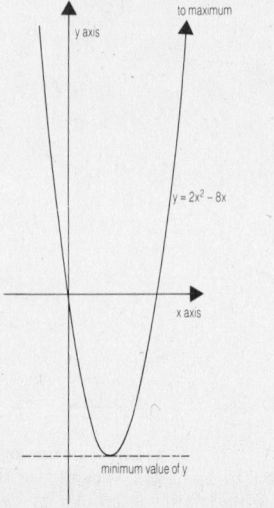

maximum and minimum

y axis

to maximum

$y = 2x^2 - 8x$

x axis

minimum value of y

theoretical work in the last sphere prepared the way for wireless telegraphy and telephony.

Maxwell-Boltzmann statistics basic equation concerning the distribution of velocities of the molecules of a gas. See ◊Boltzmann.

May /meɪ/ Thomas Erskine 1815–1886. English constitutional jurist. He wrote the standard *Treatise on the Law, Privileges, Proceedings, and Usage of Parliament* 1844.

maya (Sanskrit 'illusion') term applied frequently in Hindu philosophy, particularly in the Vedanta, to the cosmos which Isvara, the personal expression of Brahma or the Atman, has called into being. This is real, yet it also is illusion, since its reality is not everlasting.

Maya /ˈmaɪə/ American Indian civilization originating in the Yucatan Peninsula about 2600 BC, with later sites in Mexico, Guatemala, and Belize, and enjoying a classic period 325–925 AD, after which it declined. The Maya constructed stone buildings and 'stepped pyramids' without metal tools; used hieroglyphic writing in manuscripts of which only three survive; were skilled potters, weavers, and agriculturalists; and regulated their rituals and warfare by observations of the planet Venus. Mexican influence was strong until 1200, and their religion involved human sacrifices but on a smaller scale than those of the Aztecs.

Mayakovsky /ˌmaɪəˈkɒfski/ Vladimir 1893–1930. Russian futurist poet, who combined revolutionary propaganda with efforts to revolutionize poetic technique in his poems '150,000,000' 1920 and 'V I Lenin' 1924. However, his satiric play *The Bedbug* 1928 was taken in the West as an attack on philistinism in the USSR. He committed suicide.

May Day first day of May, traditionally the beginning of summer, still marked in England by pre-Christian magical rites, for example, the dance round the maypole (an ancient fertility symbol). In many countries it is a public holiday in honour of labour (in the UK the first Monday in May). See also ◊Labour Day.

Mayence /maɪˈɒns/ French name for the West German city of ◊Mainz.

Mayenne /maɪˈen/ *département* of W France in Pays-de-Loire region
area 5,212 sq km/2,033 sq mi
capital Laval
features river Mayenne
products iron, slate; paper
population (1982) 271,184.

Mayenne /maɪˈen/ river in W France which gives its name to the *département* of Mayenne; length 200 km/125 mi. It rises in Orne, flows in a generally S direction through Mayenne and Maine-et-Loire, and joins the river Sarthe just above Angers to form the Maine.

Mayer /ˈmaɪə/ Julius Robert von 1814–1878. German physicist who in 1842 anticipated ◊Joule in deriving the mechanical equivalent of heat and ◊Helmholtz in the principle of conservation of energy.

Mayflower the ship in which the ◊Pilgrims sailed from Plymouth to Massachusetts in 1620.

mayfly insect of the order Ephemeroptera (Greek *ephemeros* lasting for a day, an allusion to the very brief life of the adult), found in many parts of the world. The larval stage, which can last a year or more, is passed in water, the adult form developing gradually from the nymph through successive moults. The adult has transparent, net-veined wings, the hind pair being noticeably smaller, and three caudal filaments. Both nymphs and adults are important as food for fish, especially trout.

Maynard Smith /ˈmeɪnɑːd ˈsmɪθ/ John 1920– . British biologist, who worked initially as an aircraft designer before turning to the study of evolution. He applied ◊game theory to animal behaviour, and developed the concept of an ◊ESS (evolutionarily stable strategy) as a mathematical tool for studying the evolution of behaviour. His books include *The Theory of Evolution* and *Evolution and the Theory of Games*.

Mayo /ˈmeɪəʊ/ county in Connacht province of the Republic of Ireland
area 5,397 sq km/2,084 sq mi
towns administrative town Castlebar
features Lough Conn; wild Atlantic coast scenery; Achill Island; the village of Knock, where two women claimed a vision of the Virgin with two saints in 1897, now a site of pilgrimage
population (1981) 114,766.

mayor in England, Wales, and N Ireland, the principal officer of a district council which has been granted district-borough status under royal charter; in certain cases the chair of a city council may (under a similar grant by letters patent) have the right to be called **Lord Mayor** (a usage also followed by Australian cities). Parish councils which adopt the style of town councils have a chair known as the town mayor. In Scotland the equivalent officer is known as a ◊provost. In the USA a mayor is the elected head of a city or town. The office of mayor was revived (for the first time since 1871) in Paris for Jacques Chirac in 1977.

Mayotte /maɪˈɒt/ island of the Comoro group off the E coast of Africa, a *collectivité*

Maya Civilization

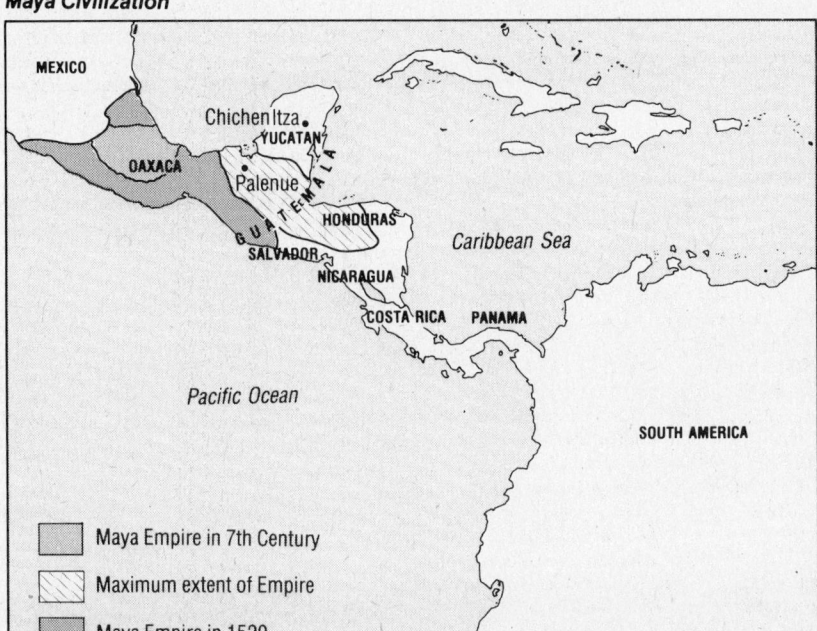

Maya Empire in 7th Century

Maximum extent of Empire

Maya Empire in 1520

particulière of France by its own wish: see ◊Comoros Republic
area 374 sq km/144 sq mi
capital Dzaoudzi
population (1984) 56,000.

mayweed name applied to several species of the daisy family. *Pineapple mayweed Matricaria matricarioides* is a low annual, much branched with leaves split into many short green threads. The flowers, borne in summer and autumn, have no ray florets and look like tall yellowish green buttons. The plant smells of pineapple. It has been introduced to many parts of the world, but is probably native to NE Asia. *Scentless mayweed Tripleurospermum inodorum* also has leaves with fine thread-like branches, but produces flowers with a yellow disc and many white ray florets. It has no smell, but like pineapple mayweed is a successful weed of arable and waste places.

Mazarin /ˌmæzəˈræŋ/ Jules 1602–1661. Italian-born French politician, born at Piscina. He passed from the Papal diplomatic service to that of ◊Richelieu in 1639, was created cardinal in 1641, and succeeded Richelieu as chief minister in 1642. His attack on the power of the nobility led to the ◊Fronde and his temporary exile, but his diplomacy achieved a successful conclusion to the ◊Thirty Years' War, and, in alliance with Cromwell, he gained victory over Spain.

mazurka a stirring national dance of Poland from the 16th century. In triple time, it is characterized by foot-stamping and heel-clicking, together with a turning movement.

Mazzini /mætˈsiːni/ Giuseppe 1805–1872. Italian nationalist. Born at Genoa, he studied law and later joined the revolutionary society, the ◊Carbonari. He was imprisoned in 1830, then went to France, where he founded the nationalist movement *Giovane Italia/Young Italy* in 1832. This was followed in 1834 by an international revolutionary organization, 'Young Europe'. For many years he lived in exile, but returned to Italy (after having been condemned to death in his absence by the Sardinian government) on the outbreak of the 1848 revolution. He headed a republican government established in Rome, but was forced into exile again on its overthrow. He acted as a focus for the concept of Italian unity.

Mboma another spelling of ◊Boma, port in Zaïre.

Mboya /əmˈbɔɪə/ Tom 1930–1969. Kenyan politician, a founder of the Kenya African National Union (KANU), and Minister of Economic Planning (opposed to nationalization) from 1964 until his assassination.

mead /miːd/ drink made from honey and water fermented with yeast, and used by the ancient Greeks, Britons, and so on.

Mead /miːd/ George Herbert 1863–1931. American philosopher and social psychologist, who helped to found the philosophy of pragmatism. He is regarded as the founder of ◊symbolic interactionism. His work on group interaction had a major influence on sociology, stimulating the development of ◊role theory, ◊phenomenology, and ◊ethnomethodology.

Mead /miːd/ Margaret 1901–1978. US anthropologist, who challenged the conventions of Western society with *Coming of Age in Samoa* 1928, but whose field work has since been questioned.

Meade /miːd/ James Edward 1907– . British Keynesian Cambridge economist (see ◊Keynes). He shared a Nobel prize in 1977 for his work on trade and ◊capital movements, and published a four-volume *Principles of Political Economy* 1965–76.

mean in mathematics, a specific related term intermediate between the first and last terms of a ◊progression. The simple *arithmetic mean* is the average value of the quantities, that is, the sum of the quantities divided by their number. The *weighted mean* takes into account the frequency of the terms that are summed; it is calculated by multiplying each term by the number of times it occurs, summing the results and dividing this total by the total number of occurrences. The *geometric mean* is the corresponding root of the product of the quantities.

meander a loop-shaped curve in a river flowing across flat country. As a river flows, any curve in its course is accentuated by the current. The current is fastest on the outside of the curve where it cuts into the bank; on the curve's inside the current is slow and deposits any transported material. In this way the river changes it course across the floodplain. A loop may become so accentuated that it becomes cut off and forms an ◊oxbow. The word comes from the river *Meander* (◊Mendres) in Turkey.

mean deviation in statistics, a measure of the spread of a sample population over a norm, usually taken to be the arithmetic ◊mean. Thus, if there are n observations with a mean of m, the mean deviation is the sum of the differences of the observation values from m, divided by n.

mean free path in physics, the average distance travelled by a ◊particle, ◊atom or ◊molecule between successive collisions. Of importance in the ◊kinetic theory of gases.

measles infectious virus disease (rubeola), traditionally a 'childhood disease'. Symptoms are severe catarrh, small spots inside the mouth, and a raised, blotchy red rash appearing after about a week's incubation. In the West it is not usually a serious disease, though serious complications may develop, but Third World children may suffer a high mortality. Prevention is by vaccination. It is different from ◊german measles.

meat flesh of animals taken as food, in Western countries chiefly from cattle, sheep and pigs, and poultry: major exporters include Argentina, Australia, New Zealand, Canada, USA, and Denmark (chiefly bacon). Meat is wasteful in production (the same area of grazing land would produce much greater food value in cereal crops), and modern research suggests that, in a healthy diet, meat (especially with a high fat content) should play a smaller part.

Meath /miːð/ county in the province of Leinster of the Republic of Ireland
area 2,338 sq km/903 sq mi
county town Trim
features Tara Hill, 155 m/507 ft high, was the site of a palace and coronation place of many kings of Ireland (abandoned in the 6th century) and St Patrick preached here.
population (1981) 95,420.

meat-packing the industry of preparing meat for consumption at a distance, particularly overseas. It depends on refrigeration, which was invented in 1861. Frozen beef was first sent to

Smithfield, London, from America in 1874. The first frozen meat was dispatched from Argentina in 1878 and from Australia in 1879. Chicago had the world's largest meat-packing plants, until the stockyards closed in 1971.

Mecca /'mekə/ city in Saudi Arabia and, as birthplace of Muhammad, the holiest city of the Islamic world; population (1974) 366,800. Most pilgrims come via the port of ◊Jidda. In the centre of Mecca is the Great Mosque, in whose courtyard is the ◊Kaaba; it also contains the well Zam-Zam, associated by tradition with the biblical characters Hagar and Ishmael.

mechanical equivalent of heat in physics, a constant factor relating the ◊calorie (an old unit of heat) to the ◊joule (the unit of mechanical ◊energy), equal to 4.1868 joules per calorie. It is redundant in the SI system of units, which measures heat and all forms of energy in joules (and so the mechanical equivalent of heat equals 1).

mechanics branch of applied mathematics dealing with the motions of bodies and the forces causing them, and also with the forces acting on bodies in ◊equilibrium. It is usually divided into ◊dynamics and ◊statics. *Quantum mechanics* is the system based on the ◊quantum theory which has superseded Newtonian mechanics in the interpretation of physical phenomena on the atomic scale.

mechanization use of machines as a substitute for manual labour or the use of animals. Until the 1700s there were few machines available to help people in the home, on the land and in industry. There were no factories, only cottage industry, in which people carried out work, such as weaving, in their own home for other people. In the 1700s came the first of a long series of inventions that ushered in a machine age and brought about the ◊Industrial Revolution. The inventions took place at first in the textile industry – they were made by John ◊Kay (flying shuttle, 1773), James ◊Hargreaves (spinning jenny, 1767), Richard ◊Arkwright (water frame, 1769) and others. Arkwright indeed pioneered the modern mechanized factory system by installing many of his ◊spinning machines in one building and employing people to work them. See also ◊automation and ◊mass production.

Mechelen /'mexələ/ industrial city (furniture, carpets, textiles) in Antwerp province, N Belgium, which gave its name to Mechlin lace; population (1985) 76,120.

Mecklenburg /'meklənbɜːg/ historic name of an area of the Baltic coast of Germany. Formerly the two grand duchies of Mecklenburg-Schwerin and Mecklenburg-Strelitz, which became free states of the Weimar Republic 1918–34, and were joined in 1946 (with part of Pomerania) to form a region of East Germany. In 1952 it was split into the districts of Rostock, Schwerin, and Neubrandenburg.

medals and decorations usually coin-like metal pieces. They are struck or cast to commemorate historic events; mark distinguished service, whether civil or military (in the latter case in connection with a particular battle, or for individual feats of courage, or for service over the period of a campaign); or as a badge of membership of an order of knighthood, society, or other special group. UK awards may be valid in other Commonwealth countries; or such countries may have their own systems, coexistent or exclusive. Famous medallists include Pisanello, Dürer, Cellini.

Armada medal issued by Elizabeth I following the defeat of the Armada; the first English commemorative medal
George Cross 1940 highest British civilian award for bravery, the medallion in the centre of the cross depicting St ◊George and the Dragon; the
George Medal 1940 is the second highest
Iron Cross German, see under ◊knighthood
King's Medal established in 1945; 1 King's Medal for courage in the cause of freedom, and 2 King's Medal for service in the cause of freedom designed for Allied or other foreign civilians who assisted Britain in World War II
Légion d'honneur French, see under ◊knighthood
Medal of Honor US highest award for the navy (1861) and army (1862) for gallantry in action; of differing design, both are bronze stars with the goddess Minerva encircled in their centres, equivalent of British Victoria Cross
Medal for Merit US civilian, 1942
Ordre National du Mérite French, civil and military, 1963, replacing earlier merit awards
Order of Merit British, see ◊Merit, Order of, ◊knighthood
Order of the Purple Heart US military, established by Washington in 1782, when it was of purple cloth (modern ones are of bronze and enamel); revived by Hoover in 1932, when it was issued to those wounded in action from World War I onward.
Pour le Mérite German, instituted by Frederick the Great, military in 1740, and since 1842 for science and art
Presidential Medal of Freedom USA, highest peacetime civilian award from 1963
USSR Gold Star Medal Soviet Union, civilian and military
Victoria Cross British military, 1856
Waterloo Medal British, established in 1816; until the 19th century medals were awarded only to officers; this was the first to be issued to all ranks.

Medawar /'medəwə/ Peter 1915–1987. British scientist, awarded a Nobel prize for medicine in 1960 (with Macfarlane Burnet) for work in immunology. They discovered that the body's resistance to grafted tissue is undeveloped in the new-born child, and studied the way it is acquired. Order of Merit in 1981.

Mede /miːd/ member of a people of NW Iran who first appear in the 9th century BC as tributaries to ◊Assyria, with their capital at Ecbatana (◊Hamadán). Allying themselves with Babylon, they destroyed the Assyrian capital of ◊Nineveh in 612, and extended their conquests into central Asia Minor. In 550 BC the Persians, till then subject to them under their own King ◊Cyrus, successfully revolted; Cyrus ruled both peoples, who rapidly merged.

Medea /mɪ'dɪə/ in Greek mythology, the sorceress daughter of the king of Colchis. When ◊Jason reached the court, she fell in love with him, helped him acquire the golden fleece, and fled with him. When Jason married Creusa, Medea killed his bride with the gift of a poisoned garment, and also killed her own two children by Jason.

Medellín /ˌmeðeɪ'iːn/ industrial town (textiles, steel) in the Central Cordillera, Colombia, 1,538 m/5,046 ft above sea level; three universities; population (1985) 2,069,000.

median in mathematics, the middle number of a group of numbers listed in ascending or descending order. If there is no middle number (because there is an even number of terms), the median is the ◊mean (average) of the two middle numbers. For example, the median of the group 2, 3, 7, 11, 12 is 7; that of 3, 4, 7, 9, 11, 13 is 8.

mediation a technical term in ◊Hegel's philosophy, and in Marxist philosophy influenced by Hegel, describing the way in which an entity is defined through its relations to other entities.

Medici /'meditʃi/ family founded in Florence by *Giovanni* 1360–1429, businessman and banker, politically influential as a supporter of the popular party. His eldest son *Cosimo* 1389–1464, regarded as the embodiment of ◊Macchiavelli's *Prince*, dominated the government from 1434, and was succeeded by his inept son *Piero* 1416–69, and grandson *Lorenzo the Magnificent* 1449–92, who was also a poet and, like his grandfather, a munificent patron of the arts. Lorenzo's son *Giovanni* 1475–1521, became Pope in 1513 as Leo X. Pope ◊Clement VII was also a member of the Medici family.

medicine the science of preventing, diagnosing, alleviating, or curing disease, both physical and mental; also any substance used in the treatment of disease. The basis of medicine is anatomy or the structure and form of the body, and physiology or the study of the body's functions. In the West, medicine increasingly relies on new drugs and sophisticated surgical techniques.

medicine, alternative forms of medical treatment which do not use synthetic drugs or surgery in response to the symptoms of a disease, but which aim to treat the patient as a whole (◊holism). There is stress on maintaining health (with diet and exercise) rather than waiting for the onset of illness; use of more natural herbal drugs; and techniques such as ◊acupuncture, ◊homeopathy, and ◊osteopathy. Some alternative treatments are increasingly accepted by orthodox medicine, but the absence of enforceable standards in some fields has led to the proliferation of eccentric or untrained practitioners.

medieval art the art of the Middle Ages in Europe, traditionally dated from the decline of the Roman Empire to the beginning of the Italian ◊Renaissance.

early Christian and Byzantine art 330–1453 AD. Churches were built, and artistic traditions adapted to the portrayal of the new Christian saints and symbols. Roman burial chests *(sarcophagi)* were adopted by the Christians and their imagery of pagan myths gradually changed into biblical themes.

MEDICINE: CHRONOLOGY

c.400 BC   Hippocrates recognized disease had natural causes.

c.200 AD   Galen, the authority of the Middle Ages, consolidated the work of the Alexandrian doctors.

1543   Andreas Versalius gave the first accurate account of the human body.

1628   William Harvey discovered the circulation of the blood.

1768   John Hunter began the foundation of experimental and surgical pathology.

1785   Digitalis used to treat heart disease; the active ingredient was isolated in 1904.

1798   Edward Jenner published his work on vaccination.

1882   Robert Koch isolated the tuberculosis bacillus.

1884   Edwin Klebs, German pathologist, isolated the diptheria bacillus.

1885   Louis Pasteur produced the rabies vaccine.

1890   Joseph Lister demonstrated antiseptic surgery.

1897   Martinus Beijerinck, Dutch botanist, discovered viruses.

1899   Felix Hoffman developed aspirin; Sigmund Freud founded psychiatry.

1910   Paul Ehrlich synthesized the first specific bacterial agent, salvarsan (cure for syphilis).

1922   Insulin was first used to treat diabetes.

1928   Alexander Fleming discovered the antibiotic penicillin.

1930s   Electro-convulsive therapy (ECT) was developed.

1932   Gerhard Domagk, German bacteriologist and pathologist, began work on the sulphonamide drugs, a kind of antibiotic.

1950s   Major development of antidepressant drugs and also beta blockers for heart disease; Medawar's work on the immune system.

1950–75   Manipulation of the molecules of synthetic chemicals, the main source of new drugs.

1954   Vaccine for polio developed by Jonas Salk.

1960s   Heart transplant surgery began with the work of Christiaan Barnard; new generation of minor tranquillizers called benzodiazepenes was developed.

1971   Viroids, disease causing organisms even smaller than viruses, isolated outside the living body.

1978   Birth of the first 'test-tube baby'. Louise Brown, on 25 July in England.

1980s   AIDS (Acquired Immune Deficiency Syndrome) first recognized in the USA.

1980   Smallpox declared eradicated by the World Health Organization.

1984   Vaccine for leprosy developed; discovery of the Human Immuno-deficiency Virus (HIV) responsible for AIDS, at the Institut Pasteur in Paris and in the USA.

1987   World's longest-surviving heart transplant patient died in France, 18 years after his operation.

Byzantine style developed in the East in Constantinople, which in 330 became the headquarters of the Roman Empire, and an Eastern Christian tradition was maintained there until 1453 when Constantinople was conquered by the Turks. The use of mosaic came to be associated with both Byzantine art and early Christian church decoration in the West. As Ravenna became the Western imperial capital in the 5th century, the ecclesiastical buildings there, built in the 5th and 6th centuries, are a glorious tribute to the art of mosaic, presenting powerful religious images on walls and vaults in brilliant, glittering colour. Byzantine art moved away from the natural portrayal of people and froze into stylization symbolizing the divine. Ornament flattened into intricate lacework patterns. Oriental, highly decorative and unchanging, the Byzantine style can be seen in the icons, often thought to be miracle-working, which have remained for centuries the main religious art of Greece and Russia.

art of the Dark Ages 252–900 AD. The 500 years between the fall of the Roman Empire and the establishment of Charlemagne's new Holy Roman Empire in 800 are known as the Dark Ages, and its art that of the **Migration Period**. Through a time of turmoil and invasion, with the northern 'barbarians' overrunning the old Mediterranean civilizations, the Christian church maintained its stability and the interchange of artistic traditions fostered creativity.

The art of the migrant peoples consisted mainly of portable objects, articles of personal use or adornment. They excelled in metalwork and jewellery, often in gold with garnet or enamel inlays and ornamented with highly stylized, animal-based interlace patterns. This type of ornament was translated into manuscript illumination such as the decorated pages of the *Lindisfarne Gospel* in the British Museum which dates from the 7th century, or the 8th century *Book of Kells* in Trinity College, Dublin. With Charlemagne's Christian Empire modelled on that of ancient Rome, a cultural renaissance ensued, drawing its inspiration from the late Classical artistic traditions of the early Christians. At Charlemagne's capital, Aachen, the human figure was re-introduced into art and continuous narrative was rediscovered in the *Tours Bibles* produced there. They in turn influenced the sculptured reliefs on the bronze doors at St Michael's Church, Hildesheim in Germany, dating from 1015, the first doors cast in one piece in the West since Roman times.

art of the Middle Ages 900–1300 AD. Under the unifying force of the Latin Church, a new civilization spread across Europe which during the 10th century produced a style in art called ◊Romanesque, and in England, ◊Norman. Chiefly evident in relief sculpture surrounding church portals, on capitals and corbels, it translated manuscript illuminations into stone, combining naturalistic elements from the antique Roman style with the fantastic, poetical, and pattern-loving Celtic and Germanic tradition. Imaginary beasts, monsters, saints and sinners mingle with humour and innocence in an enchanted world of biblical themes. Fine examples remain in Burgundy and southwest France, extending down into Spain on the pilgrimage route to Santiago de Compostela.

◊**Gothic art** During the late 12th and 13th centuries European cities began to raise great cathedrals, and the sculptural decoration became more monumental. The cathedrals of Chartres and Reims in France had such extensive sculptural programmes that many artists came from far afield to work and learn there. A new interest in the natural world is shown in such examples as the strikingly life-like founder figures of Naumberg Cathedral, East Germany, (c. 1245) or in the naturalistic foliage on the capitals at Southwell in England.

With the increased height of the cathedrals, stained glass windows became their new glory. Chartres, where an entire set of stained glass is preserved, awesomely illustrates the magical effect of coloured light seemingly suspended within its dark interior. Both windows and sculpture, by depicting the lives of the saints and texts from the bible, gave the faithful an encyclopedic view of the Christian history of the world.

Art patronage, although still mainly concerned with religious imagery, now burgeoned in the many small courts of Europe and under this influence art became more stylized, delicate and refined. Even the Virgin Mary was portrayed as an elegant young queen. In her most characteristic pose, holding the Christ child in her arms, her weight shifts gracefully onto one hip causing her body to form an S-curve and her drapery to fall into elegant folds. This figure stance, the 'Gothic sway', became a hallmark of the period. Court patronage produced exquisite small ivories, precious goldsmith's work, devotional books illustrated with miniatures, and tapestries which warmed cold castle walls, depicting romantic tales or the joys of springtime.

In Italy, the monumentality of the antique Roman past subdued the spread of northern Gothic ideas. A type of Gothic Classicism was developed by the sculptors Nicola and Giovanni ◊Pisano (working 1258–1314).

An innovative group of painters brought the art of ◊fresco painting, always important in Italy, to a new height. ◊Giotto's cycle of the lives of Mary and Christ in the Arena Chapel, Padua (c. 1300) set a new standard for figural naturalism, seen as proto-Renaissance, and in the Town Hall of Siena Ambrogio Lorenzetti illustrated the effects of *Good and Bad Government* (1337) in panoramic townscapes and landscapes.

Panel painting, in jewel-like colours on a gold background, developed from Byzantine models, and the Sienese painter ◊Duccio's *Maestà* for the High Altar of Siena Cathedral (1308–11) achieved a peak of expressive power of line and colour. Simone ◊Martini developed this into courtly refinement in both frescoes (for example Assisi, Siena) and panel paintings, and became a major influence on the *International Gothic* style which in the years around 1400 achieved the perfect mix of French courtliness and the Italian command of form, together with a delight in the observed details of nature. A magnificent example of this moment in art can be seen in the miniatures painted for the devotional book the *Très Riches Heures du Duc de Berry*, by the Flemish *Limbourg* brothers in about 1415.

Medina /me'di:nə/ city in Saudi Arabia, about 355 km/220 mi N of Mecca; the second holiest city in the Islamic world, containing the tombs of Muhammad and the caliphs or Muslim leaders ◊Abu Bekr, ◊Omar, and Fatima, Muhammad's daughter; it has a university. Population (1974) 198,000.

Mediterranean /ˌmedɪtə'reɪniən/ inland sea separating Europe from N Africa, with Asia to the E; extreme length 3,700 km/2,300 mi; area 2,966,000 sq km/1,145,000 sq mi. It is linked to the Atlantic (at the Strait of Gibraltar), Red Sea, and Indian Ocean (by the Suez Canal), Black Sea (at the Dardanelles and Sea of Marmara); and is subdivided into the Adriatic, Aegean, Ionian, and Tyrrhenian seas.

The Mediterranean is almost tideless, saltier and warmer than the Atlantic, and shallows from Sicily to Cape Bon (Africa) divide it into an E and W basin. It is endangered by human and industrial waste pollution: 100 million people live along the coast and it is regularly crossed by oil tankers. The Barcelona Convention 1976 to clean up the Mediterranean was signed by 17 countries and led to a ban on dumping of mercury, cadmium, persistent plastics, DDT, crude oil, and hydrocarbons.

Mediterranean climate a climate characterized by hot dry summers and warm wet winters. Rain is brought in winter by the ◊Westerlies; during the summer Mediterranean zones are under the influence of the ◊trade winds. They are situated in either hemisphere on the W side of continents, between latitudes of 30 and 60°. Countries bordering the Mediterranean Sea, California, central Chile, the Cape of Good

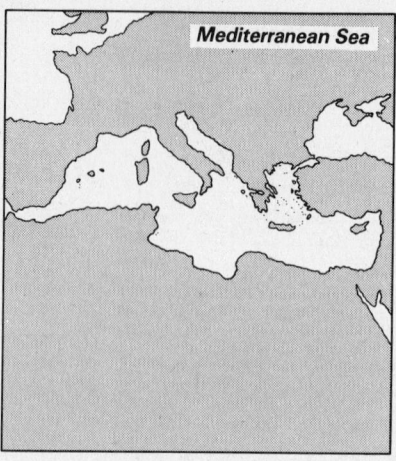
Mediterranean Sea

Hope, and parts of S Australia have such climates.

medlar small European fruit tree *Mespilus germanica* of the family Rosaceae, with fruits resembling a small brown-green apple. These are eaten when decay has set in and the taste is agreeably acid.

Médoc /meɪ'dɒk/ French district bordering the Gironde, N of Bordeaux, famed for its wines; Margaux and St Julien are two of the best-known varieties.

Medusa /mə'dju:zə/ in Greek mythology, a mortal woman who was transformed into a ◊Gorgon.

medusa jellyfish stage in Cnidarian (coelenterate) life cycle.

Medway /'medweɪ/ river of SE England, rising in Sussex and flowing through Kent and the *Medway towns* (Chatham, Gillingham, Rochester) to Sheerness, where it enters the Thames; about 96 km/60 mi long. In local tradition it divides the 'Men of Kent', who live to the E, from the 'Kentish Men', who live to the W.

Meegeren /'meɪgərən, Dutch 'meɪxərə/ Hans van 1889–1947. Unsuccessful Dutch artist who achieved fame as a technically brilliant forger, especially of Vermeer. He was arrested for collaboration when a 'Vermeer' sold to ◊Goering was traced back to him after World War II, and to prove his innocence on this charge he confessed to 14 fakes and painted another under observation in prison. Sentenced to a year's imprisonment, he died two months later.

meerschaum a soft white mineral, hydrated magnesium silicate, which floats on water and is used for making pipe bowls. The word is German for 'sea froth'.

Meerut /'mɪərət/ industrial city in Uttar Pradesh, India; population (1981) 538,000. The ◊Indian Mutiny began here in 1857.

megalith Greek 'great stone': prehistoric stone monuments, of the late Neolithic or early Bronze Age, and often of unknown purpose. They include single, large uprights (menhirs, for example, the Five Kings, Northumberland); rows (alignments, for example, ◊Carnac); circles, generally with a central 'altar stone' (such as ◊Stonehenge), and the remains of burial

chambers with the covering earth removed, looking like a 'hut' (dolmen, for example, Kits Koty House, Kent).

megamouth filter-feeding deep sea shark *Megachasma pelagios*, first discovered in 1976, which has a bulbous head with protruding jaws and blubbery lips, is 4.5 m/15 ft long, and weighs 750 kg/1,650 lb.

megapode large ground-living bird of the family Megapodidae, found mainly in Australia, but also in SE Asia. These birds lay their eggs in a pile of rotting vegetation, and the warmth from this, rather than a parent, provides the heat for incubation. The mound may be 4 m/13 ft across. The male bird feels the mound with his tongue and adjusts it to provide the correct temperature.

megatherium extinct giant ground sloth of America. Various species lived from about 7 million years ago until geologically recent times. They were plant-eaters, and some grew 6 m/20 ft long.

megaton one million (10^6) tons. Frequently used to indicate the explosive power of a nuclear weapon. Equivalent to one million tons of trinitrotoluene (TNT).

Meghalaya /ˌmegə'leɪə/ NE state of India
area 22,489 sq km/8,680 sq mi
capital Shillong
features mainly agricultural and hilly
population (1981) 1,328,000, mainly of the Khasi, Jaintia, and Garo ethnic groups
language various
religion Hindu 70%.

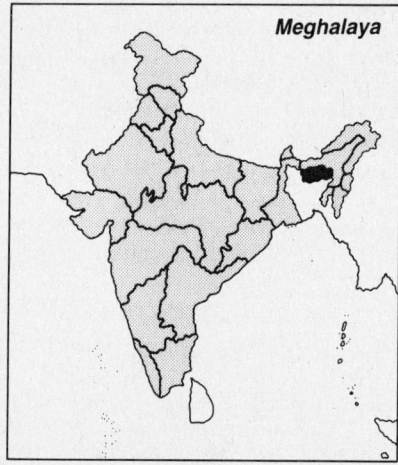
Meghalaya

Megiddo /mə'gɪdəʊ/ site of a fortress town in N Israel, where Thothmes III defeated the Canaanites in c. 1469 BC; the Old Testament figure ◊Josiah was killed in battle in c. 609 BC; and ◊Allenby broke the Turkish front in 1918.

Mehemet Ali /mɪ'hemɪt 'ɑːli/ 1769–1849. ◊Pasha of Egypt from 1805, and founder of the dynasty that ruled till 1953. An Albanian in the Turkish service, he had originally been sent to Egypt to fight the French. As pasha, he established a European-style army and navy, fought his Turkish overlord in 1831 and 1839, and conquered the Sudan.

Mehta /'meɪtə/ Zubin 1936– . Indian conductor, director of the Israel Philharmonic

Orchestra from 1968 (for life from 1981), and of the New York Philharmonic from 1978.

Meiji Tenno /'meɪdʒiː 'tenəu/ Japanese emperor. See ▷Mutsuhito.

meiosis in biology, a process of cell division in which the number of ▷chromosomes in the cell is halved. It only occurs in ▷eukaryotic cells, and is an important part of a life cycle that involves ▷sexual reproduction, because it allows the genes of two parents to be combined without the total number of chromosomes increasing. In many animals that are normally ▷diploid (having two sets of chromosomes per cell) meiosis occurs during formation of the ▷gametes (sex cells, sperm and egg), so that the gametes are ▷haploid (having only one set of chromosomes). When the gametes unite during ▷fertilization, the diploid condition is restored. In plants, meiosis occurs just before spore-formation. Thus the spores are haploid and develop into a haploid plant called a gametophyte which produces the gametes (see ▷alternation of generations). See also ▷mitosis.

meiosis

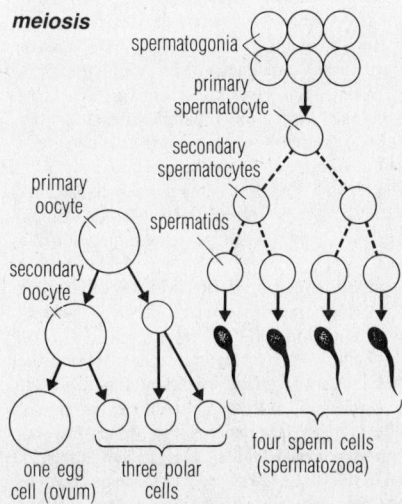

spermatogonia
primary spermatocyte
secondary spermatocytes
primary oocyte
spermatids
secondary oocyte
one egg cell (ovum)
three polar cells
four sperm cells (spermatozooa)

Meir /meɪˈɪə/ Golda 1898–1978. Israeli Labour (*Mapai*) politician, born in Russia. Foreign minister 1956–66, and prime minister 1969–74, she resigned following criticism of the Israeli's lack of preparation for the 1973 Arab-Israeli War.

Meissen /'maɪsən/ city in the Dresden district of East Germany, on the river Elbe; known for Meissen or Dresden porcelain from 1710; population (1983) 38,908.

Meistersinger (German 'master singer') one of a group of German lyric poets, singers, and musicians of the 14th–16th centuries, who formed guilds for the revival of minstrelsy at ▷Nuremberg and elsewhere. Hans ▷Sachs was a noted Meistersinger, and Richard Wagner's opera, *Die Meistersinger von Nüremberg* 1868 depicts the tradition.

Meitner /'maɪtnə/ Lise 1878–1968. Austrian physicist, who was the first to realise that ▷Hahn had inadvertently achieved the fission of uranium. Driven from Nazi Germany because of her Jewish origin, she later worked in Sweden. She refused to work on the atomic bomb.

Meir Israeli politician Golda Meir resigned after the Yom Kippur War. She was a fighter for peace in the Middle East.

Meknès /mek'nes/ city in N Morocco, known for carpetmaking; population (1982) 386,085.

Mekong /ˌmiːˈkɒŋ/ river rising in Tibet and flowing to the S China Sea; length 4,500 km/2,800 mi. It is being developed for irrigation and hydroelectricity by Kampuchea, Laos, Thailand, and Vietnam.

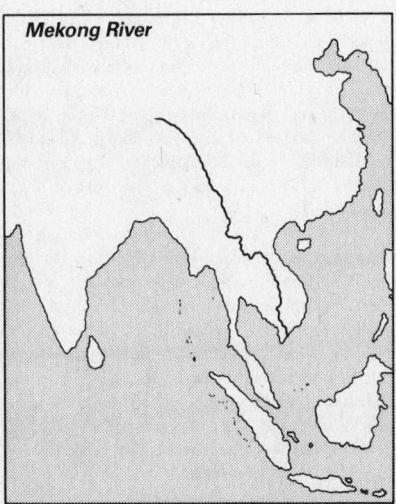

Mekong River

Melanchthon /məˈlæŋkθən/ Philip 1497–1560. German Protestant theologian (real name Schwarzerd), who helped ▷Luther in preparing his German translation of the New Testament. Professor of Greek at Wittenberg from 1518, in 1521 he issued the first systematic formulation of Protestant theology. He composed the ▷Augsburg Confession in 1530.

Melanesia /ˌmeləˈniːziə/ a division of the islands in the central and W Pacific between Micronesia to the N and Polynesia to the E, embracing all the islands from the New Britain archipelago to the Fiji Islands.

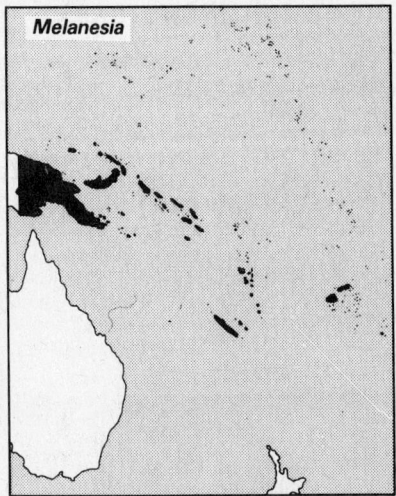

Melanesia

Melanesian languages see ▷Malayo-Polynesian languages.

Melanesian pidgin English see ▷pidgin English.

melanism black colouration of animal bodies caused by abnormally large amounts of the pigment melanin. In some species the production of melanic individuals only occurs as a result of ▷mutation. In others, individuals have the capacity to produce extra melanin in response to environmental changes. Dark individuals can be at an advantage to paler individuals for a variety of reasons. In industrial areas, they match sooty backgrounds and escape predation, but they are at a disadvantage in rural areas where they do not match their backgrounds. Thus melanic mutants become more common than the normal type in smoky areas. This phenomenon, known as industrial melanism, is most frequent in insects. Melanin is of significance in other insects, because melanic individuals warm more rapidly in sunshine than do pale individuals and can be more active in cool weather. A fall in temperature may stimulate such insects to produce more melanin.

melanoma skin cancer formed of dark-coloured cells. Sunspot activity appears to increase the ultraviolet quality of sunlight, making it brighter, and approximately two years later the skin cancer rate shows an increase. It is more common among light-skinned people in sunnier climates, such as Australia and the USA, than in Britain.

Melba /'melbə/ Nellie, stage name of Helen Mitchell 1861–1931. Australian soprano, born near Melbourne. Her roles included Donizetti's *Lucia*; Dame of the British Empire 1918, Dame Grand Cross of the British Empire 1927. *Peach melba* (half peach plus vanilla ice cream and melba sauce, made from sweetened, fresh raspberries) and *Melba toast* (crisp and thin) are named after her.

Melbourne /'melbən/ industrial city (engineering, food processing, clothing and textiles) and capital of Victoria, Australia, near the mouth of the river Yarra; the country's second largest city, with three universities; population (1984) 2,888,400.

history founded in 1835, it was named after Lord Melbourne in 1837, grew in the wake of the gold rushes, and was the seat of the Commonwealth government 1901–27.

Melbourne /'melbən/ William Lamb, 2nd Viscount 1779–1848. British Whig politician. He married Lady Caroline Ponsonby (novelist Lady Caroline Lamb) in 1805, but they separated in 1825. Home secretary 1830–34, he was briefly prime minister in 1834, and then again 1835–41. Accused in 1836 of seducing Caroline ◊Norton, he lost the favour of William IV, but was an adviser to the young Queen Victoria.

Melbourne The English politician Viscount Melbourne was friend and mentor to Queen Victoria on her accession.

Melilla /me'liljə/ port and military base on the NE coast of Morocco; captured by Spain in 1496, it is still under Spanish rule; population (1981) 58,450. Also administered from Melilla are three other Spanish possessions: Peñón ('rock') de Velez de la Gomera, Peñón d'Alhucemas, and the Chaffarine Islands.

melitin extract (Greek 'bee') of honey-bee poison, a powerful antibiotic.

melodrama although today often used as a derogatory term, it was first applied to plays accompanied by music, which became popular throughout Europe during the 19th century. The early melodramas used extravagant theatrical effects for artificially heightening the violent emotions and actions, and were frequently played against a Gothic background of mountains or ruined castles. Beginning with the early work of ◊Goethe and ◊Schiller, it was popularized in France by Pixérécourt and first introduced to England in an unauthorized translation by Thomas Holcroft, *A Tale of Mystery* in 1802.

melody in music, a sequence of notes forming a theme or tune.

melon twining plant of the family Cucurbitaceae. The musk melon *Cucumis melo* and the water melon *Citrullus vulgaris* are common edible varieties.

Melos /'miːlɒs/ (modern Greek *Milos*) Greek island in the Aegean, area 155 sq km/60 sq mi, one of the Cyclades, where the sculpture *Venus de Milo* was discovered in 1820 (now in the Louvre). The capital is Plaka.

Melpomene /mel'pɒməni/ in Greek mythology, the ◊Muse of tragedy.

Melrose /'melrəʊz/ town in Borders region, Scotland, with the ruins of Melrose Abbey 1136, commemorated in verse by Sir Walter Scott.

meltdown a very serious type of accident that can befall a nuclear reactor (see ◊nuclear energy). If the reactor's cooling system fails and a major part of the core reaches its melting point (about 2,900°C/5,200°F), the metal reactor vessel may also melt, burn through the concrete floor beneath and release radioactive material into the Earth and into the atmosphere (see ◊fallout). A meltdown was narrowly avoided at Three Mile Island in the United States in 1979, but occurred in a reactor at Chernobyl in the Soviet Union in 1986, spreading radioative fallout over a large area of northern Europe.

Melville /'melvɪl/ Henry Dundas, Viscount Melville 1742–1811. British Tory politician. Born in Edinburgh. He entered Parliament in 1774, and as home secretary 1791–94 persecuted the parliamentary reformers. He received a peerage 1802 and was First Lord of the Admiralty 1804–05. His impeachment for malversation (misconduct) in 1806 was the last in English history.

Melville /'melvɪl/ Herman 1819–1891. American author of *Moby-Dick* 1851, story of the symbolic conflict between Captain Ahab and the great white whale, which was inspired by his own whaling experiences in the South Seas. Melville worked in the New York Customs 1866–85. His other books include *Typee* 1846, *Omoo* 1847, several volumes of verse, and *Billy Budd* 1924.

membrane in living things, a continuous layer, made up principally of fat molecules, which encloses a ◊cell or a part of a cell (◊organelle). Certain small molecules can pass through the cell membrane, but most must enter or leave the cell via channels in the membrane made up of special proteins. In cell organelles, ◊enzymes may be attached to the membrane at specific positions, often alongside other enzymes involved in the same process, like workers at a conveyor belt. Thus membranes help to make cellular processes more efficient. The ◊Golgi body within the cell produces certain membranes.

Memel /'meɪməl/ German name for ◊Klaipeda, port in Lithuania, USSR.

Memlinc /'memlɪŋ, -lɪŋk/ (or Memling) Hans c. 1430–1494. Flemish artist, whose teachers are said to have included ◊Lochner and van der ◊Weyden. He was town painter in Bruges 1475–87, where some of his best work is in the Hospital of St John (*Adoration of the Magi* altar 1479, *Deposition* triptych 1480, and shrine of St Ursula 1489).

Memorial Day in the USA, a day of remembrance (formerly Decoration Day) instituted in 1868 for those fallen in the American Civil War. Now observed as a public holiday on the last Monday in May, in remembrance of all Americans killed on active service in subsequent wars.

memory in computing, any device, collection of devices, or components in a computer system used to store data and programs either permanently or temporarily. There are two main types: internal memory and external memory.

Internal memory is either read-only (stored in ◊ROM, ◊PROM and ◊EPROM chips) or it is read/write (stored in ◊RAM chips). Read-only memory stores information that must be constantly available or accessed very quickly, and that is unlikely to need to be changed. It is non-volatile, that is, it is not lost when the computer is switched off. Read/write memory is volatile; it stores programs and data temporarily only while the computer is switched on.

External memory is permanent, non-volatile memory employing storage devices which include magnetic ◊disks (such as floppy disks, hard disks), ◊magnetic tape (tape streamers, cassettes), laser disks including CD-ROM (compact discs) and ◊bubble memories. By rapidly swapping blocks of information in and out of internal memory from external memory, the limited size of a computer's memory may artificially be increased. To the user, this virtual memory, as it is called, gives the impression of a very large internal memory. All computer memory stores information in binary code (using the ◊binary number system). Memory capacity is measured in K (kilobytes).

Memphis /'memfɪs/ ruined city beside the Nile, 19 km/12 mi south of Cairo, Egypt. Centre of the worship of Ptah, it was the earliest capital of a united Egypt under King ◊Menes, but was superseded by ◊Thebes under the new empire in 1570 BC. It was later used as a stone quarry, but the 'cemetery city' of Sakkara survives, with the step-pyramid built for Zoser by ◊Imhotep, probably the world's oldest stone building.

Memphis /'memfɪs/ industrial port (pharmaceuticals, food processing, tobacco) and largest city in Tennessee, USA; population (1980) 646,356. Known for recording studios and record companies (Sun 1953–68, Stax 1960–75); Graceland, the home of Elvis Presley, is a museum.

Menai Strait /'menaɪ/ channel of the Irish Sea, dividing Anglesey from the Welsh mainland; about 22 km/14 mi long, up to 3 km/2 mi wide. Bridges crossing it include Telford's suspension bridge 1826 (reconstructed 1940) and Stephenson's tubular rail bridge 1850.

Menam /miː'næm/ another name for the ◊Chao Phraya river, Thailand.

Menander /me'nændə/ c. 342–291 BC. Greek comic dramatist, born in Athens, who influenced Shakespeare. Of his 105 plays only fragments (many used as papier-mâché for Egyptian mummy cases) and Latin adaptations were known till the discovery in 1957 of the *Dyscholos/The Bad-tempered Man*.

Mencius /'menʃiəs/ Latinized name of Mengzi c. 372–289 BC. Chinese philosopher and moralist. Born in Shantung (now Shandong) province, he was founder of a school in the tradition of Confucius (see ◊Kong Zi). After 20 years' unsuccessful search for a ruler to put into practice his enlightened political programme, based on people's innate goodness, he retired. His teachings are preserved as the *Book of Mengzi*.

Mencken /'meŋkən/ H(enry) L(ouis) 1880–1956. American essayist and critic, known from his birthplace as 'the sage of Baltimore'. His unconventionally phrased, satiric contributions to *Smart Set* and *American Mercury* (both of which periodicals he edited) roused great controversy. His best known book was *The American Language* 1918 and often revised.

Mendel /'mendl/ Gregor Johann 1822–1884. Austrian biologist, abbot of the Augustinian abbey at Brünn (now Brno) from 1868. His garden experiments with successive generations of peas gave the basis for his theory of organic inheritance (◊genetics), governed by dominant and recessive characters (genes). His results, published 1865–69, remained unrecognized until early this century.

mendelevium an artificially-made element, symbol Md, atomic number 101. One of the ◊actinide series, it is a radioactive element produced by bombardment of ◊einsteinium-253.

Mendeleyev /ˌmendə'leɪef/ Dmitri Ivanovich 1834–1907. Russian chemist, framer of the Periodic Law which states that the chemical properties of the elements are periodic functions of their atomic weights. This law is the basis of the ◊Periodic Table of the elements. See ◊chemistry.

Mendelism in ◊genetics, the theory of inheritance originally outlined by Gregor ◊Mendel. He suggested that, in sexually reproducing species, characters (such as hair colour) are inherited through indivisible *factors* (now equated with ◊genes) contributed by each parent to its offspring.

Mendelssohn (-Bartholdy) /'mendlsən (-baː'tɒldi)/ (Jakob Ludwig) Felix 1809–1847. German composer, born in Hamburg. He was also a pianist and conductor, the first director of the Leipzig Conservatoire in 1843, and made several visits to England. Using Classical forms, he was nevertheless an early Romantic in the subjective quality he brought to his music. His works include *A Midsummer Night's Dream* 1827; the *Fingal's Cave* overture 1832; chamber music (including string quartets); the Italian (1833) and Scottish (1842) symphonies; a violin concerto 1844; *Songs Without Words* 1832–45 for the piano, including the so-called 'Spring Song' and 'The Bees' Wedding'; and the oratorios *St Paul* 1836 and *Elijah* 1846.

Menderes /ˌmendə'res/ river in European Turkey (Turkish, Buyuk Menderes, Great Menderes). It rises near Afyonkarahisar and flows for about 400 km/250 mi by a very winding course into the Aegean: hence the word 'meander' which is derived from the ancient Greek name for the river.

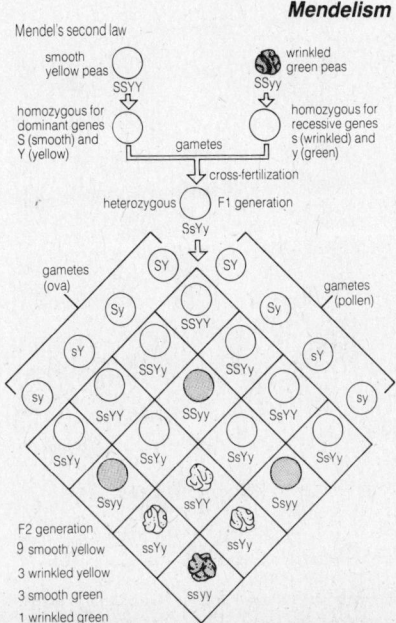

Mendelism

Mendel's second law

smooth yellow peas — SSYY — homozygous for dominant genes S (smooth) and Y (yellow)

wrinkled green peas — SSyy — homozygous for recessive genes s (wrinkled) and y (green)

gametes — cross-fertilization

heterozygous — F1 generation — SsYy

gametes (ova) — SY — SY — gametes (pollen)

SY   Sy   SY   Sy
Sy   SSYY SSYy Sy
sY   SSYy SSYY sY
sy   SsYY SsYy SsYY SsYy   sy
      SsYy Ssyy ssYY ssYy

F2 generation
9 smooth yellow   ssYy   ssYy
3 wrinkled yellow
3 smooth green
1 wrinkled green   ssyy

Mendelssohn Felix Mendelssohn began his musical career as a pianist at the age of 10. He produced most of his major works, including the overtures *A Midsummer Night's Dream, Fingal's Cave*, and *The Hebrides*, between the ages of 17 and 21.

Mendès-France /ˌmɒndes'frɒns/ Pierre 1907–1982. French prime minister and foreign minister 1954–55. He concluded the war in Indo-China, and granted Tunisian independence.

mendicancy in law, the solicitation of alms (begging). It is illegal in Britain; legislation began in the 14th century, and it is an offence to solicit alms on the public highway, to expose any sore or malformation to attract alms, or cause a child to beg, and begging letters containing false statements are also illegal. Begging is traditional and widespread in many countries and in the Middle East and Asia almsgiving is often considered a religious obligation. Stringent measures are taken against mendicancy in the USSR.

Mendicant Order in the Roman Catholic Church, one of the four orders of Mendicant Friars – Franciscans, Dominicans, Carmelites, and Augustinians – who are dependent on alms. Hinduism has similar orders.

Mendoza /men'dəusə/ capital of the Argentine province of the same name; population (1980) 597,000. It was founded in 1561 and developed owing to its position on the Trans-Andean railway.

Mendoza /men'dəusə/ Antonio de 1490–1552. First Spanish viceroy of New Spain (Mexico) 1535–51. His rule was enlightened, in that he aimed at developing agriculture and improving the conditions of the Indians, and the system he established lasted until the 19th century. He was subsequently viceroy of Peru 1551–52.

Menelik II /'menəlɪk/ 1844–1913. Negus (emperor) of Abyssinia (now Ethiopia) from 1889. He defeated the Italians in 1896, and retained the independence of his country.

Menes /'miːniːz/ traditionally, the first king of the first dynasty of ancient Egypt, about 3200 BC. He is said to have founded Memphis and organized worship of the gods.

menhir a standing stone. See under ◊megalith.

Menindee /mə'nɪndi/ village and sheep centre in New South Wales, Australia, on the Darling river, centre of a scheme for conserving the waters of the Darling in *Menindee Lake* (155 sq km/60 sq mi) and lakes nearby.

meningitis inflammation of the meninges, the lining membranes of the base of the brain and spinal cord. An acute attack can be caused by spread of infection from disease of the nose or ear, by other infections, such as influenza or typhoid fever, or by the organism of spotted fever (cerebro-spinal fever), so-called because it also often produces a rash. More chronic forms are due to tuberculosis or syphilis. Bacterial meningitis responds well to treatment by antibiotics, but is more dangerous to life in infancy or old age. It is epidemic and virulent in tropical Africa.

meniscus in physics, the curved shape of the surface of a liquid in a thin tube, caused by the cohesive effects of ◊surface tension. Most liquids adopt a concave curvature (viewed from above), although with highly viscous liquids (such as mercury) the meniscus is convex. Meniscus is also the name given to a concavo-convex or convex-concave lens (see ◊lens).

Mennonite member of a Christian sect rejecting infant baptism, originating in Zürich in 1523, whose members refuse to hold civil office or do military service, later named Mennonites after Menno Simons (1496–1559), leader of a group in Holland. When they came under persecution, some settled at Germantown, Pennsylvania. The Hutterian Brethren (named after Jacob Hutter who died in 1536) hold substantially the same beliefs, and Hutterian principles are the basis of the Bruderhof (Society

meniscus

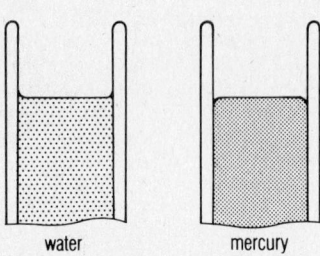

water   mercury

of Brothers) who live in groups of families (single persons being assigned to a family), marry only within the sect (divorce being disallowed), and retain a 'modest' dress for women (cap or headscarf, and long skirts). Originally established in Germany, there are Bruderhof communities in the USA, and at Robertsbridge, E Sussex; they support themselves by making children's toys.

menopause in women the cessation of reproductive ability, also known as the 'change of life'. The time of onset is usually about 45, but varies greatly. ◊Menstruation becomes irregular and ceases. The 'change' is natural and usually uneventful, but some women suffer from complications such as flushing, excessive bleeding, and nervous disorder. Since the 1950s hormone replacement therapy (HRT) has been developed to counteract such effects. It involves treatment with ◊oestrogen or an alternation of oestrogen and ◊progesterone.

Menorca /me'nɔːkə/ Spanish form of ◊Minorca, one of the Balearic Islands.

Menotti /me'nɒti/ Gian Carlo 1911– . American composer. Born in Italy, he moved to the USA in 1928. He has written orchestral and chamber music, and operas. Best-known are *The Medium* 1946, *The Telephone* 1947, *The Consul* 1950, *Amahl and the Night Visitors* 1951, and *The Saint of Bleecker Street* 1954.

Mensheviks the right wing of the Russian Social-Democratic Party. They were so called because they formed the minority (Russian *menshinstvo*) at the 1903 party congress, the left-wing majority being known as Bolsheviks. During the Russian revolution they succeeded in setting up a government in Georgia, but after its overthrow they disappeared.

menstrual cycle the cycle that occurs in female mammals of reproductive age, in which the body is prepared for ◊pregnancy. At the beginning of the cycle, immediately after ◊menstruation, a pulse of *follicle-stimulating hormone* (FSH) produced by the ◊pituitary gland stimulates the development of an egg follicle (Graafian follicle) in the ovary and the production of ◊oestrogen, which causes the inner wall of the uterus to develop into a soft spongy lining. Oestrogen inhibits FSH production and stimulates *luteinizing hormone* (LH) production. This causes the release of the egg from the ovary, and the production of ◊progesterone by the remains of the Graafian follicle, the corpus luteum. This hormone

Menotti The Italian composer Gian Carlo Menotti. *Amahl and the Night Visitors* was the first opera to be written for television.

vascularizes the uterine lining and stimulates *luteotrophic hormone* (LTH) production, which further increases progesterone production. If fertilization does not occur the corpus luteum degenerates, and progesterone production declines, causing the uterine lining to degenerate and to be shed. This is what causes the loss of blood that marks menstruation. The decline in progesterone production stimulates the production of FSH, and the cycle then begins again. If fertilization occurs, the corpus luteum persists and goes on producing progesterone, until this function is taken over by the ◊placenta; during pregnancy, progesterone prevents abortion and the further release of eggs.

menstruation the regular shedding of the lining of the ◊uterus of female mammals. In humans this occurs about every 28 days, from ◊puberty to the onset of the ◊menopause, and is part of the ◊menstrual cycle, which is under hormonal control.

mental handicap impairment of intelligence which can be very mild, but which in the more severe cases is associated with social problems and difficulties in living independently. Individuals may be born with mental handicap or may acquire it through brain damage. Mental handicap is also known as pervasive learning difficulty.

menthol peppermint camphor; an alcohol derivative of menthone. It occurs in peppermint and is responsible for the plant's odour.

Menton /mɒn'tɒŋ/ resort (Italian *Mentone*) on the French Riviera, close to the Italian frontier; population (1982) 22,234. It belonged to the princes of Monaco from the 14th century until briefly independent 1848–60, when the citizens voted to merge with France.

menu in computing, a list of options, displayed on screen, from which the user may choose in order to operate a program.

Menuhin /'menjuɪn/ Yehudi 1916– . American violinist, naturalized British in 1985. A child prodigy, he achieved great depth of interpretation, and was often accompanied on the piano by his sister Hephzibah (1921–81). In 1963 he founded a boarding school (named after him) at Stoke D'Abernon, Surrey, for training young musicians. Knighted 1965, Order of Merit 1987.

Menzies /'menzɪz/ Robert Gordon 1894–1978. Australian politician. A Melbourne lawyer, he entered politics in 1928, was attorney-general in the federal parliament 1934–39, and in 1939 succeeded Lyons as prime minister and leader of the United Australia Party (1939–41). Leading the Opposition from 1943, he initiated in 1944 the formation of a new party – the Australian Liberal Party – to unite all anti-Labour groups except the Country Party, and in 1949 became prime minister of a Liberal-Country Party coalition government, being re-elected 1951, 1954, 1955, 1958, 1961, and 1963. Knighted in 1963, he succeeded Churchill as Lord Warden of the Cinque Ports in 1965, and retired as prime minister 1966.

Mequines another name for ◊Meknés, a town in Morocco.

Mercalli scale the scale used to measure the *intensity* of an ◊earthquake. (It differs from the ◊Richter scale in that the latter measures *magnitude*.) Intensity is a subjective value, based on observed phenomena, and varies from place to place with the same earthquake. It was named after the Italian seismologist Giuseppe Mercalli (1850–1914).

mercantilism economic theory held 16th–18th centuries, that a nation's wealth (in the form of bullion or treasure) was the key to its prosperity. To this end, foreign trade should be regulated to obtain a surplus of exports over imports, and the state should intervene where necessary (for example subsidizing exports and taxing imports). The bullion theory of wealth was demolished by Adam ◊Smith in Book IV of *The Wealth of Nations* 1776.

Mercator /mɜː'keɪtə/ Gerardus 1512–1594. Latinized form of the name of the Flemish map-maker Gerhard Kremer, who devised *Mercator's projection* in which the parallels and meridians on maps are drawn uniformly at 90°. The true area of countries is increasingly distorted the further N and S they are from the equator. See ◊projection.

Mercer /'mɜːsə/ David 1928–1980. British dramatist, born in Yorkshire, who first became known for television plays. His works include *A Suitable Case for Treatment* (TV) 1962, and *After Haggerty* (stage) 1970.

Merchant /'mɜːtʃənt/ Ismael 1936– . Indian producer, who collaborated with James ◊Ivory on films including *Shakespeare Wallah* 1965, *The Europeans* 1979, *Heat and Dust* 1983, *Room with a View* 1986 and *Maurice* 1987.

merchant navy the passenger and cargo ships of a country, the majority owned by companies, but in the USSR and other Communist countries

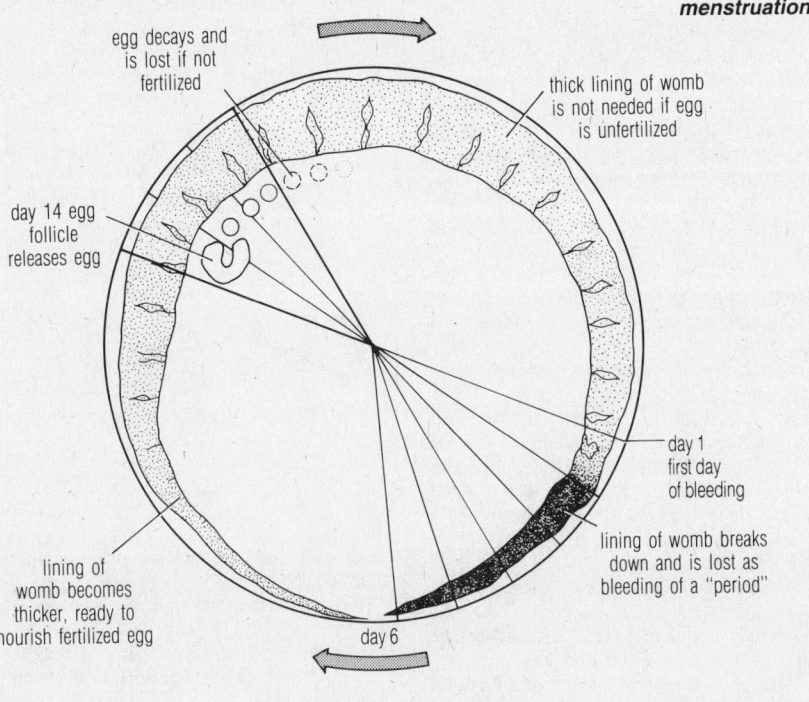

menstruation

egg decays and
is lost if not
fertilized

thick lining of womb
is not needed if egg
is unfertilized

day 14 egg
follicle
releases egg

day 1
first day
of bleeding

lining of womb breaks
down and is lost as
bleeding of a "period"

lining of
womb becomes
thicker, ready to
nourish fertilized egg

day 6

MERCALLI SCALE

Intensity value	Description
I	Only detected by instrument.
II	Felt by people resting.
III	Felt indoors; hanging objects swing; feels like passing traffic.
IV	Feels like passing heavy traffic; standing cars rock; windows, dishes, and doors rattle; wooden frames creak.
V	Felt outdoors; sleepers are woken; liquids spill; doors swing.
VI	Felt by everybody; people stagger; windows break; trees and bushes rustle; weak plaster cracks.
VII	Difficult to stand upright; noticed by vehicle drivers; plaster, loose bricks, tiles and chimneys fall; bells ring.
VIII	Car steering affected; some collapse of masonry; chimney stacks and towers fall; branches break from trees; cracks in wet ground.
IX	General panic; serious damage to buildings; underground pipes break; cracks and subsidence in ground.
X	Most buildings destroyed; landslides; water thrown out of canals.
XI	Rails bent; underground pipes totally destroyed.
XII	Damage nearly total; rocks displaced; objects thrown into air.

state-owned and closely associated with the navy. To avoid strict regulations on safety or union rules on crew wages, and so on, many ships are today registered under 'flags of convenience', that is, those of countries which do not have such rules. Types of ship include:
tramps either in home coastal trade, or carrying bulk cargoes worldwide;
tankers the largest ships afloat, up to about 500,000 tonnes and 380 m/1,245 ft long, and other vessels carrying specialized cargo;

cargo liners combining cargo and passenger traffic on short or world voyages. Most merchant ships are diesel-powered, but there have been attempts to revive sails (under automatic control) in combination with diesel to reduce costs, the first commercial venture being the Japanese *Aitoku Maru* 1980. Nuclear power was used in the *Savannah* 1959 (USA), but problems with host ports mean that only the USSR builds such ships for 'internal' use, for example, Arctic icebreakers and the 26,400 tonne N

Pacific/Arctic barge carrier *Sevmorput* 1985.

Merchants Adventurers trading company founded in 1407 and comprising guilds and traders in many northern European ports. In direct opposition to the Hanseatic League, it controlled most English overseas trade by 1550.

Mercia /'mɜːsiə/ an Anglo-Saxon kingdom which emerged in the 6th century, and by the 8th dominated all England south of the Humber, but from about 825 came under the power of ◊Wessex. See ◊Midlands, ◊Penda, and ◊Offa.

Merckx /meəks/ Eddie 1945– . Belgian cyclist, known as 'the Cannibal'. Turned professional 1966, and won his first classic, the Milan-San Remo. He won the Tour de France five times 1969–72 and 1974, and wore a record 96 leader's yellow jerseys. He was three times world road race champion.

Mercury /'mɜːkjʊri/ ancient Roman god, who has been identified with the Greek Hermes, and like him represented with winged sandals and a winged staff entwined with snakes. He was the messenger of the gods.

mercury liquid chemical element, the only common liquid metal at ordinary temperatures. Symbol Hg, atomic number 80, atomic weight 200.61. A dense, mobile silvery liquid, it is found free in nature and was known to the ancient Chinese and Hindus and is found in Egyptian tombs of c. 1500 BC. The chief source is the mineral cinnabar, HgS. Its alloys with other metals are called amalgams. It is used in drugs and chemicals, for mercury vapour lamps, arc rectifiers, power-control switches, barometers, and thermometers.

Mercury /'mɜːkjʊri/ the closest ◊planet to the Sun, at an average distance of 57,900,000 km/ 36,000,000 mi. Its diameter is 4,880 km/3,000 mi, and it orbits the Sun every 88 days. Radar measurements show that Mercury spins on its axis every 59 days. On its sunward side the surface temperature reaches over 400°C, but on the 'night' side it falls to -170°C. Mercury has virtually no atmosphere. The US space probe Mariner 10 in 1974 discovered that its surface is cratered by ◊meteorite impacts like the surface of the Moon. Mercury's largest known feature is the Caloris Basin, 1,400 km/870 mi wide. There are also cliffs hundreds of kilometres long and up to 4 km/2.5 mi high, thought to have been formed by shrinking of the planet. Inside is an iron core three-quarters of the planet's diameter, which produces a ◊magnetic field 1% the strength of the Earth's. Mercury has no moons.

mercury fulminate highly explosive compound used in detonators and percussion caps. It is a grey, sandy powder, and extremely poisonous.

Mercury project the US project to put a human in space in the one-seat Mercury spacecraft, on Redstone or Atlas rockets. The first two Mercury flights were simple hops to the edge of space and back, without going into orbit. The first US orbital flight was the third in the series, made by John ◊Glenn.

Meredith /'merədɪθ/ George 1828–1909. British novelist and poet. He published his first realistic psychological novel *The Ordeal of Richard Feverel* 1859. His later works include

The Egoist 1879, and *Diana of the Crossways* 1885. He was awarded the Order of Merit in 1905.

merganser type of diving duck with a saw-bill for catching fish. The goosander *Mergus merganser* is widely distributed in the N hemisphere.

Mergenthaler /ˈmɜːɡənˌtɑːlə/ Ottmar 1854–1899. German-American who invented a typesetting method. Born in Württemberg, where he served his apprenticeship as a watchmaker, he went to the USA in 1872 and there developed 1876–86 the first **linotype** machine (for casting metal type as lines of type – hence the name).

Mérida /ˈmerɪðə/ capital of Yucatán state, Mexico, a centre of the sisal industry; dating from 1542, it has a cathedral 1598 and university; population (1980) 424,500.

meridian half a ◊great circle drawn on the Earth's surface passing through both poles, and thus through all places with the same longitude. Terrestrial longitudes are usually measured from the Greenwich Meridian. An astronomical meridian is a great circle passing through the pole and the zenith. See also ◊latitude and longitude.

Mérimée /ˌmeriˈmeɪ/ Prosper 1803–1870. French author. Born in Paris, he entered the public service, and under Napoleon III was employed on unofficial diplomatic missions. Among his best works are the stories *Colomba* 1841, dealing with a Corsican feud, the Spanish *Carmen* 1846; and the witty and sceptical *Lettres à une inconnue/Letters to an Unknown Girl* 1873.

merino breed of sheep. Its close-set, silky wool is of extremely good quality, and the merino, now found all over the world, is the breed on which the Australian industry is built.

Merionethshire /ˌmeriˈɒnəθʃə/ former county of N Wales, UK, included in the new county of Gwynedd in 1974. Dolgellau was the administrative town.

meristem a region of plant tissue containing cells which are actively dividing to produce new tissues (or have the potential to do so). Meristems found in the tip of roots and stems, the apical meristems, are responsible for the growth in length of these organs. The ◊cambium is a lateral meristem which is responsible for increase in girth in perenial plants. Some plants also have intercalary meristems, as in the stems of grasses, for example. These are responsible for their continued growth after cutting or grazing has removed the apical meristems of the shoots. Meristem culture involves growing meristems taken from shoots on a nutrient-containing medium, and including hem to generate new plants. It is used to progagate infertile plants or hybrids which do not breed true from seed, and to generate virus-free stock, since viruses rarely infect apical meristems.

Merit, Order of British order of chivalry, founded on the lines of an order of ◊knighthood.

meritocracy a system of education, government, and so on, in which selection is by performance in competitive examinations, which therefore favours intelligence and ability rather than social position or wealth. The result is the creation of an elite group. The term was coined by Michael Young in his *The Rise of the Meritocracy* 1958.

Merleau-Ponty /meə,ləupɒnˈtiː/ Maurice 1908–1961. French philosopher, one of the most significant contributors to ◊phenomenology after ◊Husserl. He attempted to move beyond the notion of a pure experiencing consciousness, arguing in *The Phenomenology of Perception* 1945 that perception is intertwined with bodily awareness and with language. In his posthumous work, *The Visible and the Invisible* 1964 he argued that our experience is inherently ambiguous and elusive, and that the traditional concepts of philosophy are therefore inadequate to grasp it.

Merlin /ˈmɜːlɪn/ legendary magician and counsellor to King ◊Arthur; he was later alleged to have supported Vortigern in fighting ◊Hengist and the Saxons, and to have built Stonehenge. Welsh bardic literature has a cycle of poems attributed to him, and he may have been a real person. He is said to have been buried in a cave in the park of Dynevor Castle, Dyfed.

merlin small ◊falcon.

mermaid mythical sea creature (the male is a *merman*), having a human upper part, and the lower body a fishtail. The ◊dugong and ◊seal are among suggested origins for the idea.

Meroe /ˈmerəʊi/ ancient city of the Republic of the Sudan, on the Nile near Khartoum, capital of Nubia from about 600 BC to 350 AD. Tombs and inscriptions have been excavated, and iron smelting slag-heaps have been found.

Merovingian a Frankish dynasty, named after its founder, Merovech (5th century). His descendants ruled France from the time of Clovis (481–511) to 751.

Mersey beat a type of popular music of the mid-1960s which originated in the north of England (also called Liverpool sound in the UK and British Invasion in the US). The beat groups characteristically had a simple, guitar-dominated line-up, vocal harmonies, and catchy tunes; for example, the ◊Beatles, the Hollies (1962–), and the Zombies (1962–67).

Merseyside /ˈmɜːzisaɪd/ former (1974–86) metropolitan county of NW England, replaced by residuary body in 1986 which covers some of its former functions
area 652 sq km/252 sq mi
towns administrative headquarters Liverpool; Bootle, Birkenhead, St Helens, Wallasey, Southport
features river Mersey; Merseyside Innovation Centre (MIC), linked with Liverpool University and Polytechnic (◊science park); Prescot Museum of clock and watch making; Speke Hall (Tudor), and Croxteth Hall and Country Park (a working country estate open to the public)
products industrial
population (1983) 1,500,800
famous people the Beatles.

Mersin /meəˈsiːn/ industrial free port (chrome, copper, and oil refining) in Turkey; population (1980) 216,300.

Merthyr Tydfil /ˈmɜːθə ˈtɪdvɪl/ industrial town (light engineering, electrical goods) in Mid Glamorgan, Wales, UK; formerly a centre of the

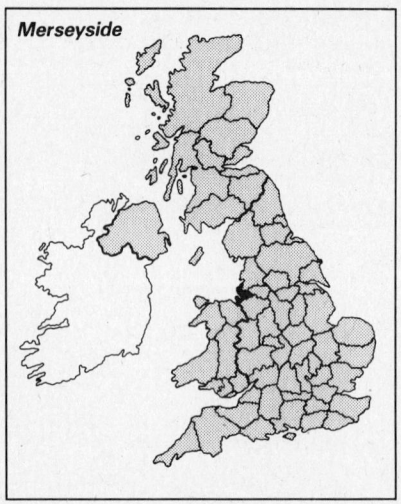

Merseyside

Welsh coal and steel industries; population (1982) 60,000.

Merton /ˈmɜːtn/ borough of SW Greater London
features part of Wimbledon Common (includes Caesar's Camp – an Iron Age fort); All England Tennis Club 1877
population (1982) 166,600.

Merv /meəf/ oasis in Russian Turkmenistan, a centre of civilization from at least 1200 BC, and site of a town founded by Alexander the Great. Old Merv was destroyed by the Emir of Bokhara 1787, and the modern town of ◊Mary, founded by the Russians in 1885, lies 29 km/18 mi west.

mesa a flat-topped mountain with steep cliff sides, particularly those found in the desert areas of the USA and Mexico. The word is Spanish for table.

Mesa Verde /ˈmeɪsə ˈvɜːdi/ (Spanish 'green table'), a wooded clifftop in Colorado, USA, with Pueblo dwellings, called the Cliff Palace, built into its side. Dating from about 1000 BC, with 200 rooms and 23 circular ceremonial chambers (kivas), it had an estimated population of about 400 people and was probably a regional centre.

mescalin drug derived from a turnip-shaped cactus (*Lophophora williamsii*) of Texas and N Mexico, known locally as ◊peyote. The tops, which scarcely appear above ground, are dried and chewed, or added to alcoholic drinks. Allegedly non-habit-forming and without after-effects, mescalin is said to heighten the perceptions and is used by the Navajos of California and Indians of other states in church ceremonial. It was used experimentally by Aldous ◊Huxley and others.

Meshed /meˈʃed/ a variant spelling of ◊Mashhad, a town in Iran.

Mesmer /ˈmesmə/ Friedrich Anton 1733–1815. Austrian physician, who claimed to reduce people to trance state by consciously exerted 'animal magnetism', their willpower being entirely subordinated to his. Expelled by the police from Vienna, he created a sensation in Paris in 1778, but was denounced as a charlatan in 1785. He seems to have been an early experimenter in ◊hypnosis, which was formerly (and popularly) called mesmerism after him.

mesmerism former term for ◊hypnosis, from Friedrich ◊Mesmer.

Mesolithic the Middle Stone Age period of ◊Prehistory.

meson unstable particle with mass intermediate between those of the electron and the proton, found in cosmic radiation and emitted by nuclei under bombardment by very high-energy particles. Its existence was predicted in 1935 by Japanese physicist Hideki ◊Yukawa.

mesophyll the tissue between the upper and lower epidermis of a leaf blade (◊lamina), consisting of parenchyma-like cells containing numerous ◊chloroplasts. In many plants mesophyll is differentiated into two distinct layers. The palisade mesophyll is usually just below the upper epidermis and is composed of regular layers of elongated cells. Lying below them is the spongy mesophyll, composed of loosely arranged cells of irregular shape. This layer contains fewer chloroplasts and has many intercellular spaces for the diffusion of gases (required for ◊respiration and ◊photosynthesis), linked to the outside by means of ◊stomata.

Mesopotamia /ˌmesəpəˈteɪmiə/ name derived from the Greek for 'middle' and 'river' given to the land between the Euphrates and the Tigris. Here the civilizations of Sumer and Babylon flourished, and some consider it the site of the earliest civilization. It is part of modern Iraq.

Mesozoic the era of geological time between 230 and 65 million years ago, when dinosaurs ruled the land and other giant reptiles dominated the sea and air; ferns, horsetails, and cycads were numerous plants. The era comprises the ◊Triassic, ◊Jurassic, and ◊Cretaceous periods.

Mesrine /mezˈriːn/ Jacques 1937–1979. French criminal. From a wealthy family, he became a burglar celebrated for his glib tongue, sadism, and bravado, and most of all for his escapes from the police and prison. Towards the end of his life he had links with left-wing guerrillas. Police cornered him in Paris and shot him with 21 bullets.

Messager /ˌmesɑːˈʒeɪ/ André Charles Prosper 1853–1929. French composer and conductor. He studied under ◊Saint-Saëns. Messager was successful with his light operas, such as *La Béarnaise* 1885 and *Véronique* 1898.

Messalina /ˌmesəˈliːnə/ Valeria c. 22–48 AD. Third wife of the Roman emperor ◊Claudius, whom she dominated. She was notorious for her immorality, forcing a noble to marry her in 48 AD, although still married to Claudius, who then had her executed.

Messerschmitt /ˈmesəʃmɪt/ Willy 1898–1978. German plane designer, whose ME-109 was a standard Luftwaffe fighter in World War II, and whose ME-262 (1942) was the first mass-produced jet fighter.

Messiaen /ˌmesiˈɒŋ/ Olivier 1908– . French composer and organist. Born in Avignon, he has spent most of his life in Paris, where he was appointed organist at La Trinité church in 1931. A devout Christian, he considers that his music has two predominant elements: religious faith and colour. An innovator both with tone and

rhythm, his teaching influenced contemporary composers including Boulez and Stockhausen. Among his better-known works are the *Quatuor pour la fin du temps* 1941, the large-scale *Turangalîla Symphony* 1949, and several organ pieces.

messiah word derived from the Hebrew for 'the anointed', the Greek equivalent of which is Christ. Jews from the time of the Old Testament exile in Babylon have looked forward to the coming of a messiah who will be a saviour or deliverer. Christians believe that the messiah came in the person of ◊Jesus Christ.

Messier /ˌmesiˈeɪ/ Charles 1730–1817. French astronomer, who discovered 15 comets and in 1781 published a famous list of 103 ◊star clusters and nebulae. Objects on this list are given M (for Messier) numbers which astronomers still use today, such as M1, the ◊Crab nebula, and M31, the ◊Andromeda galaxy.

Messina /meˈsiːnə/ city and port in NE Sicily; population (1984) 266,000. Originally an ancient Greek settlement, it was taken first by Carthage and then by Rome.

Messina, Strait of /meˈsiːnə/ channel in the central Mediterranean separating Sicily from mainland Italy; in Greek legend a monster (Charybdis), who devoured ships, lived in the whirlpool on the Sicilian side, and another (Scylla), who devoured sailors, in the rock on the Italian side. The classical hero Odysseus passed safely between them.

metabolism the chemical processes of living organisms, which comprise a constant alternation of building up (anabolism) and breaking down (catabolism). Among the most familiar are those by which green plants build up complex organic substances from water, carbon dioxide, and mineral salts (see ◊photosynthesis), and by which animals, by taking them in as food, break them down partially by digestion and subsequently resynthesize them in their own bodies.

metal a type of element with certain chemical characteristics and physical properties. Metals are good conductors of heat and electricity; opaque, but reflect light well; malleable, which enables them to be cold-worked and rolled into sheets; and ductile, which permits them to be drawn into thin wires. Generally hard, they are crystalline in their normal pure state, many of them mixing with one another to form alloys, whose properties depend on the proportions of their constituents. Their hardness, tensile strength, toughness, brittleness, and so on, may be varied by physical means such as heat-treatment, or work-hardening, but their physical properties, such as melting point, coefficient of thermal expansion, and density, are constant. Sixty to seventy metals are known, but only the following are widely used in commerce: (i) *precious metals*: gold, silver, mercury, platinum and the platinum metals, used principally in jewellery; (ii) *heavy metals*: iron, copper, zinc, tin and lead, the common metals of engineering; (iii) *rarer heavy metals*: nickel, cadmium, chromium, tungsten, molybdenum, manganese, cobalt, vanadium, antimony, and bismuth, used principally for alloying with the heavy metals;

(iv) *light metals*: aluminium and magnesium; (v) *alkali metals*: sodium, potassium and lithium; and (vi) *alkaline earth metals*: calcium, barium and strontium, used principally for chemical purposes.

Other metals have come to the fore because of special nuclear requirements, for example, technetium, produced in nuclear reactors, is corrosion-inhibiting; zirconium may replace aluminium and magnesium alloy in canning uranium in reactors. See also ◊metallic glass, ◊metalloid.

metal detector an electronic device for detecting metal, usually below ground. It developed from the wartime mine detector. In the head of the metal detector is a coil, which is part of an electronic circuit. The presence of metal causes the frequency of the signal in the circuit to change, setting up an audible note in the headphones worn by the person using it.

metal fatigue a condition in which metals fail or fracture under relatively light loads, when these loads are applied repeatedly. Structures that are subject to flexing, such as the airframes of aircraft, are prone to metal fatigue.

metallic glass a substance produced from metallic materials (non-corrosive alloys rather than simple metals) in a liquid state which, by very rapid cooling, are prevented from reverting to their regular metallic structure. Instead they take on the properties of glass, while retaining the metallic properties of malleability and relatively good electrical conductivity.

metallurgy the science or technique of working metals. Extractive or *process metallurgy* is concerned chiefly with the extraction of metals from their ◊ores, and refining and adapting them for use. *Physical metallurgy* is interested in their properties and application. The foundations of metallurgical art were laid about 3500 BC in Egypt, Mesopotamia, and India, where the art of ◊smelting metals from ores was discovered, starting with ◊bronze. Later, gold, silver, copper, lead, and tin were worked. The smelting of iron appears to have been discovered about 1500 BC. The Romans hardened and tempered steel, using ◊heat treatment. From then until about 1400 AD, advances in metallurgy were due to the Arabian chemists. ◊Cast iron began to be made in the 14th century (in a crude blast furnace). The demands of the Industrial Revolution led to an enormous increase in iron production, particularly of ◊wrought iron. The invention by Henry Bessemer of the ◊Bessemer process in 1856 made cheap ◊steel available for the first time, leading to its present widespread use.

Metals can be extracted from their ores in three main ways: (1) dry processes such as smelting, volatilization or amalgamation – treatment with mercury; (2) wet processes involving chemical reactions, and (3) electrolytic processes which work on the principle of ◊electrolysis.

metamorphic rock a rock altered in structure and composition by pressure and/or heat although it does not melt (in which case it is termed ◊igneous rock).

METAMORPHIC ROCKS

typical depth and temperature of formation	*shale with several minerals*	*sandstone with only quartz*	*limestone with only calcite*
	MAIN PRIMARY MATERIAL (BEFORE METAMORPHISM)		
15 km 300°C	slate	quartzite	marble
20 km 400°C	schist		
25 km 500°C	gneiss		
30 km 600°C	hornfels	quartzite	marble

metamorphism geological term referring to the changes that have occurred in the rocks of the Earth's crust (see also ◊metamorphic rock).

metamorphosis a period during the ◊life cycle of many invertebrates, most amphibians and some fish, during which the individual's body changes from one form to another through a major reconstitution of its tissues. Thus, adult frogs are produced by metamorphosis from tadpoles, while butterflies are produced from caterpillars following metamorphosis within a ◊pupa.

metaphor a ◊figure of speech whose name in Greek means 'transfer' and implies the use of an analogy or close comparison between two things that are not normally treated as if they had anything in common. Thus, if we call people cabbages or foxes, we are indicating that in our opinion they share certain qualities with those vegetables or animals: an inert quality in the case of cabbages, a cunning quality in the case of foxes, that may lead on to calling people 'foxy' and saying 'He really foxed them that time', meaning that he tricked them. Such usages are metaphorical, and metaphor is a common means of extending the uses and references of words; for example, if a scientist is doing research in the *field* of nuclear physics, the word 'field' results from comparison between scientists and farmers (who literally work in fields). See also ◊simile.

metaphysical in English literature, a term applied to a group of 17th-century poets, whose work is characterized by conciseness, ingenious, often highly intricate word-play, and striking imagery. Best-known representatives of this genre are ◊Donne, ◊Herbert and ◊Cowley.

metaphysics a branch of philosophy that deals with first principles, especially 'being' and 'knowing', and which is concerned with the ultimate nature of reality. It has been maintained that no certain knowledge of metaphysical questions is to be had. ◊Epistemology, or the study of how we know, lies at the threshold of the subject. Metaphysics is concerned with the nature and origin of matter and of mind, the interaction between them – that is, the 'mind-body problem'; the meaning of time and space, causation, determinism and free will, personality and the Self, arguments for belief in God, and human immortality. The foundations of metaphysics were laid by ◊Plato and ◊Aristotle. St Thomas ◊Aquinas, basing himself on Aristotle, produced a metaphysical structure that is accepted by the Catholic Church. The subject has been advanced by Descartes, Spinoza, Leibniz, Berkeley, Hume, Locke, Kant, Hegel, Schopenhauer, and Marx; and in modern times by Bergson, Bradley, Croce, McTaggart, Whitehead, and Wittgenstein.

Metastasio /ˌmetəˈstæziəu/ pseudonym of Pietro Trapassi 1698–1782. Italian poet and the leading librettist of his day, creating 18th-century Italian *opera seria* (serious opera).

Metaxas /ˌmetækˈsæs/ Joannis 1871–1941. Greek soldier and politician, born in Ithaca. He restored ◊George II as king of Greece, under whom he established a dictatorship as prime minister from 1936, and introduced several important reforms. He led resistance to the Italian invasion of Greece in 1941, refusing to abandon Greece's neutral position.

metazoa another name for animals. It reflects an earlier system of classification, in which there were two main divisions within the ◊animal kingdom, the multicellular animals, or metazoa, and the single-celled 'animals' or protozoa. The ◊protozoa are not now included in the animal kingdom, so only the metazoa remain.

metempsychosis another name for ◊reincarnation.

meteor in astronomy, a flash of light in the sky, popularly known as a ***shooting star***, caused by a particle of dust burning up in the atmosphere. Most meteors are smaller than grains of sand. They enter the atmosphere at speeds up to 70 km/45 mi per sec and burn up by friction at a height of around 100 km/60 mi. On any clear night, several ***sporadic*** meteors can be seen each hour. But several times each year the Earth encounters swarms of dust shed by ◊comets. which give rise to a ***meteor shower***. The meteors in a shower seem to radiate from one particular point in the sky, after which the shower is named, for example, the Perseid meteor shower in August each year appears to radiate from the constellation ◊Perseus. A brilliant meteor is termed a ***fireball***.

meteorite a piece of rock or metal from space that reaches the surface of the Earth, Moon or other body. Meteorites are thought to be fragments from ◊asteroids, although some may be pieces from the heads of ◊comets. Over 5,000 meteorites are estimated to hit the Earth each year. Most fall in the sea or in remote areas and are never recovered. Most meteorites are stony in composition, although some are made of iron and a few have a mixed rock–iron composition. The largest known meteorite is one composed of iron, weighing 60 tonnes, which lies where it fell in prehistoric times at Grootfontein, Namibia.

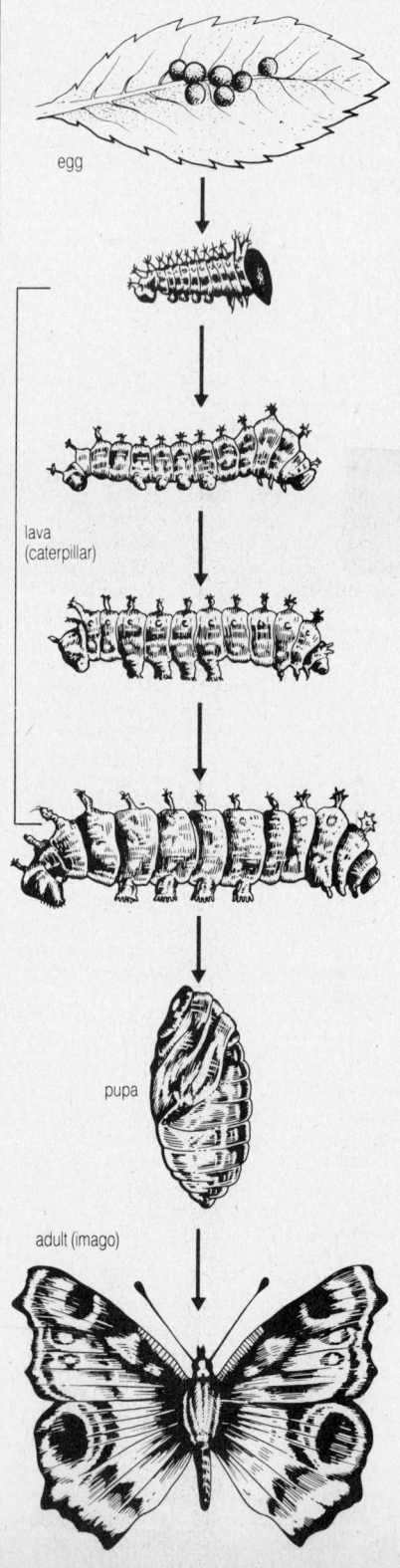

egg

larva (caterpillar)

pupa

adult (imago)

Meteorites are slowed down by the Earth's atmosphere, but if they are moving fast enough they can form a ◊crater on impact. Mrs Hewlett Hodges of Sylacauga, Alabama, was bruised on the hip by a meteorite that fell through the roof of her house on 30 Nov, 1954 – the only recorded case of human injury by a meteorite.

meteorite Crater left by a meteorite at Flagstaff, Arizona, USA.

meteorology the scientific observation and study of the ◊atmosphere, to enable weather to be accurately forecast. At meteorological stations readings are taken of the factors determining weather conditions: atmospheric pressure, temperature, humidity, wind (using the ◊Beaufort scale), cloud cover (measuring both type of cloud and coverage), and precipitation (rain, snow, hail, etc.) (measured at 12-hourly intervals). Data from these stations and from weather satellites is collated by computer at central agencies such as the Meteorological Office in London, and a forecast and ◊weather maps based on current readings are issued at regular intervals.

methane the simplest hydrocarbon, CH_4, of the paraffin series. Colourless, odourless, and lighter than air, it burns with a bluish flame, and explodes when mixed with air or oxygen. It is the chief constituent of *natural gas* and also occurs in the explosive ◊firedamp of coal mines, and in *marsh gas* formed from rotting vegetation, which results by spontaneous combustion in the pale flame seen over marshland, and known as *will-o'the-wisp* or *ignis fatuus*.

methanogenic bacteria one of a group of primitive bacteria (◊archaebacteria). They give off methane gas as a by-product of their metabolism, and are common in sewage treatment plants and hot springs, where the temperature is high and oxygen is absent.

methanol or *methyl alcohol* the simplest of the alcohols (CH_3OH). It can be made by the dry distillation of wood (hence it is also known as wood alcohol), but today is usually made from

coal or natural gas. When pure, it is a colourless, inflammable liquid with a pleasant odour, and is highly poisonous. It is used to produce formaldehyde (from which resins and plastics can be made); methyl-tert-butyl ether (a replacement for lead as an octane-booster in petrol); and vinyl acetate.

Method name given to the US adaptation of ◊Stanislavsky's teachings on acting and direction, in which importance is attached to the psychological building of a role rather than the technical side of its presentation. Emphasis is placed on improvisation, the result being, theoretically, a spontaneous and realistic style of acting. One of the principal exponents of the Method was the US actor and director Lee ◊Strasberg.

Methodism evangelical Christian movement founded by John ◊Wesley in 1739, within the Church of England, which became a separate body in 1795. Its doctrines are contained in Wesley's sermons and *Notes on the New Testament*. A series of doctrinal divisions in the early 19th century were healed by a conference in London in 1932 which brought Wesleyan methodists, Primitive methodists and United methodists into the Methodist Church. The church government is presbyterian in Britain (episcopal in USA), with supreme authority vested in the annual conference (50% ministers, 50% laymen); members are grouped under 'class leaders' and churches into 'circuits'.

Methuselah /mə'θju:zələ/ in the Old Testament, Hebrew patriarch who lived before the Flood; his supposed age of 969 years made him the archetype of longevity.

methyl alcohol another name for ◊methanol.

methylated spirit adulterated or 'denatured' alcohol, which has been rendered undrinkable, and is free of duty for industrial purposes. It is nevertheless drunk by some individuals, resulting eventually in death. One of the poisonous

substances in it is ◊methanol, or methyl alcohol, and this gives it its name. (The 'alcohol' of alcoholic drinks is ◊ethanol).

metonymy a ◊figure of speech whose Greek name suggests a transferred title. When people speak or write metonymically they work by association. Thus, they may refer to the theatrical profession as 'the stage', because of the close association of actors and stages, or call journalists 'the press', because of a long-standing association between such writers and the printing press. See also ◊synecdoche.

metre the ◊SI unit of length (m), defined as the length of the path travelled by light in a vacuum during a time interval of 1/299,792,458 of a second. This definition, agreed at the General Conference on Weights and Measures in Oct 1983, replaced one of 1967 based on the wavelength of a particular colour of radiation from a krypton lamp. It is equivalent to 1.094 yards.

metric system system of weights and measures developed in France in the 18th century and recognized by other countries including the UK in the 19th century. In 1960 an international conference on weights and measures recommended the universal adoption of a revised International System (Système International d'Unités, or SI), with seven prescribed 'base units', the metre 'm' for length, kilogram 'kg' for mass or weight, second 's' for time, ampere 'A' for electric current, kelvin 'K' for thermodynamic temperature, candela 'cd' for luminous intensity and mole 'mol' for quantity of matter. Two supplementary units are included in the system – the radian (rad) and steradian (sr) – used to measure plane and solid angles. In addition, there are recognized derived units which can be expressed as simple products or divisions of powers of the basic units, with no other integers appearing in the expression, for example the watt.

Some non-SI units, well established and internationally recognized, remain in use in conjunction with SI: minute, hour and day in measuring time; multiples or submultiples of base or derived units which have long-established names, such as tonne for mass, the litre for volume, and specialist measures such as the metric carat for gemstones. Prefixes used with metric units are tera (T) million million times (10^{12}); giga (G) billion (thousand million) times (10^9); mega (M) million times (10^6); kilo (k) thousand times (10^3); hecto (h) hundred times (10^2); deka (da) ten times (10); deci (d) tenth part (10^{-1}); centi (c) hundreth part (10^{-2}); milli (m) thousandth part (10^{-3}); micro (μ) millionth part (10^{-6}); nano (n) billionth part (10^{-9}); pico (p) trillionth part (10^{-12}); femto (f) quadrillionth part (10^{-15}); atto (a) quintillionth part (10^{-18}). The metric system was made legal for most purposes in the UK and USA in the 19th century. The UK government agreed to the adoption of SI as the primary system of weights and measures in 1965, but compulsion was abandoned in 1978, although further discussions will be needed in 1989 when Britain has to to conform to European Community regulations. A Metric Act was passed in the USA in 1975, but popular resistance to metrication has been widespread.

metropolitan (Greek 'mother-state, capital') generally, a bishop who has rule over other bishops (termed **suffragans**). In the Church of England, the archbishops of York and Canterbury are both metropolitans. In the Orthodox Church, a metropolitan has a rank between an archbishop and a ◊Patriarch.

metropolitan county in England, a group of six counties (1974–86) established under the Local Government Act 1972 in the major urban areas outside London: Tyne and Wear, South Yorkshire, Merseyside, West Midlands, Greater Manchester, and West Yorkshire. Their elected assemblies were abolished 1986 when their areas of responsibility reverted to county or district councils.

Metropolitan Opera Company foremost opera company in the USA, founded 1883 in New York. The Metropolitan Opera House (opened 1883) was demolished 1966, and the company transferred to the Lincoln Center.

Metsu /'metsju/ Gabriel 1630–1667. Dutch painter, known for anecdotal pictures, as in *The Duet* and *Music Lesson* (National Gallery, London).

Metternich /'metənɪk/ Klemens Wenzel Lothar, Prince von (family name Metternich-Winneburg) 1773–1859. Austrian foreign minister from 1809 until the 1848 revolution forced him to flee to England. At the Congress of Vienna of 1815 he advocated cooperation by the great powers to suppress democratic movements.

Metternich The architect of the 1815 Congress of Vienna, Austrian chancellor and foreign minister Prince von Metternich.

Metz /mets, French mes/ industrial city (shoes, metal goods, tobacco) in NE France; population (1982) 118,505. Part of the Holy Roman Empire 870–1552, it became one of the great frontier fortresses of France, and was German 1871–1918. The cathedral is largely 13th century. The poet Verlaine was born here.

Meurthe /mɜːt/ French river 163 km/102 mi long, which rises in the Vosges mountains and

flows in a generally NW direction to join the Moselle at Frouard, near Nancy. It gives its name to the *département* of Meurthe-et-Moselle.

Meuse /mɜːz/ (Dutch *Maas*) river flowing through France, Belgium, and the Netherlands; length 900 km/560 mi. It was a line of battle in both World Wars.

Mewar /me'wɑː/ another name for ◊Udaipur, a city in Rajasthan, India.

Mexicali /ˌmeksɪ'kæli/ city in NW Mexico; population (1984) 500,000. There are many US companies attracted by cheap labour (Hughes Aerospace, Rockwell International, and others).

Mexican Empire short-lived empire lasting only eight months 1822–23. When ◊Napoleon put his brother Joseph on the Spanish throne in 1808, links between Spain and its colonies weakened and an independence movement grew in Mexico. There were several unsuccessful uprisings until, in 1821, Augustin de Iturbide (1783–1824) published a plan promising independence, protection for the church, and the establishment of a monarchy. As no European came forward, in 1822 he proclaimed himself emperor. Forced to abdicate, he went into exile; on his return to Mexico he was shot by republican leaders Guadalupe Victoria and Santa Anna; the former became the first president of Mexico.

Mexican War war between the USA and Mexico 1846–48, begun when General Zachary Taylor invaded New Mexico. Mexico City was taken in 1847, and under the Treaty of Guadaloupe-Hidalgo, Mexico lost Texas, New Mexico, and California (half its territory) to the USA for $15 million compensation.

Mexico /'meksɪkəʊ/ country in Central America, bordered N by the USA, E by the Gulf of Mexico, SE by Belize and Guatemala, and SW and W by the Pacific Ocean.

government Mexico is a federal republic of 31 states and a federal district, based in Mexico City. The constitution dates (with minor amendments) from 1917. Legislative power rests with a two-chamber national congress of senate, chamber of deputies, and directly elected president, all serving a six-year term. The president chooses the cabinet. The Senate has 64 members, each state and the federal district being represented by two senators. The Chamber has 400 members, 300 representing single-member constituencies and 100 elected by proportional representation so as to give due weight to minority parties. Members of Congress are elected by universal suffrage. Each state has an elected governor and chamber of deputies, elected for a six-year term.

Political parties must register and meet certain criteria in order to operate. The main parties are the moderate, left-of-centre, Institutional Revolutionary Party (PRI), and the National Action Party (PAN).

history Mexico was the centre of the ◊Maya civilization, which existed in Central America from about 1500 BC until the Spanish conquest in the 16th century. Other inhabitants were the Toltecs and the Aztecs, who settled on the central plateau and whose last king, Montezuma II, was killed in 1520 during the Spanish invasion.

In 1535 Mexico became the viceroyalty of New Spain. Spanish culture and Catholicism were established, and the country's natural resources were exploited. Colonial rule became increasingly oppressive; the struggle for independence began 1810, and Spanish rule was ended 1821. See also ◊Mexican Empire.

Mexico's early history as an independent nation was marked by civil and foreign wars, and was dominated until 1855 by the dictator Antonio López de ◊Santa Anna. The US annexation of Texas in 1835 brought about the ◊Mexican War (1846–48), in the course of which Mexico suffered further losses, including New Mexico and California. Santa Anna was overthrown in 1855 by Benito Juárez, whose liberal reforms included many anti-clerical measures.

In 1861, enticed by the offer of 30% of the proceeds, France planned to intervene in the recovery of 79,000,000 francs owed to a Swiss banker by former Mexican president, Miramon, who was overthrown and exiled by Juárez in 1860. Seeking to regain power, in 1862 Miramon appealed to Empress ◊Eugénie, consort of ◊Napoleon III, saying that steps must be taken against Juárez and his anti-Christian policies. Eugénie proposed Maximilian, the brother of Emperor Franz-Josef of Austria. Napoleon agreed, since the plan suited his colonial ambitions, and in 1864 Maximilian accepted the crown offered him by conservative opponents of Juárez. Juárez and his supporters continued to fight against this new branch of the ◊Hapsburg empire, and in 1867 the monarchy collapsed and Maximilian was executed.

There followed a capitalist dictatorship under Gen Porfirio Diaz, who gave the country stability but whose handling of the economy made him unpopular. He was overthrown in 1910 by Madero, who re-established a liberal regime but was himself assassinated in 1913.

The 1910 revolution brought changes in land ownership, labour legislation, and reduction in the powers of the Roman Catholic Church. The broadly-based PRI has dominated Mexican politics since the 1920s, pursuing moderate, left-of-centre policies. Its popularity has been damaged in recent years by the country's poor economic performance and rising international debts. However, despite criticisms from vested interest groups such as the trade unions and the Church, the PRI scored a clear win over all other parties in the 1985 elections. The government's problems grew worse later that year when an earthquake in Mexico City caused thousands of deaths and made hundreds of thousands homeless.

Mexico's foreign policy has been influenced by its proximity to the US. At times the Mexican government has criticized US policy in Central America, and as a member, with Colombia, Panama and Venezuela, of the ◊Contadora Group, has argued for the withdrawal of all foreign advisers from the region.

Mexico City /'meksɪkəʊ/ capital and industrial and cultural centre of Mexico 2,255 m/7,400 ft above sea level on the S edge of the central plateau; population (1985) 15,667,000. Notable buildings include the 16th-century

Mexico
UNITED STATES OF (*Estados Unidos Mexicanos*)

AREA 1,979,650 sq km/763,944 sq mi
CAPITAL Mexico City
TOWNS Guadalajara, Monterrey; port
Veracruz
PHYSICAL partly arid central highlands flanked
by Sierra Madre mountain ranges E and W;
tropical coastal plains
FEATURES frontier of 2,000 miles with USA;
resorts Acapulco, Mexicali, Tijuana; Baja
California peninsula; volcanoes, for example
Popocatepetl; archaeological sites of pre-
Spanish period
HEAD OF STATE AND OF GOVERNMENT Miguel de
la Madrid Hurtado from 1982
GOVERNMENT federal democracy
EXPORTS silver, gold, lead, uranium; oil and
natural gas (to USA); traditional handicrafts;
fish and shellfish
CURRENCY peso (2,525 = £1 Sept 1987)
POPULATION (1985) 79,662,000 (a minority are
criollos of Spanish descent, 12% are American
Indian, and the majority are of mixed descent;
50% of the total are under 20 years of age);
annual growth rate 2.6%
LANGUAGE Spanish (official); Indian languages
include Nahuatl, Maya, and Mixtec
RELIGION Roman Catholic
LITERACY 74% (1983)
GNP $168 bn (1983); $ 1,800 per head of
population

Mexico

CHRONOLOGY
1821 Mexico achieved independence from
Spain.
1846–48 Mexico at war with USA.
1848 Maya Indian revolt suppressed.
1917 New constitution introduced, designed
to establish permanent democracy.
1983–84 Financial crisis.
1985 Institutional Revolutionary Party (PRI)
returned to power. Earthquake devastated
Mexico City.
1986 IMF loan agreement signed to keep the
country solvent until at least 1988.

cathedral, the national palace, national library,
Palace of Justice, and national university; the
Ministry of Education has murals 1923–27 by
Diego Rivera. The city is thought by many to be
the most polluted in the world.
history The city dates from about 1325, when
the Aztec capital Tenochtitlán was begun on an
island in Lake Texcoco. This city was levelled in
1521 by the Spaniards, who in 1522 founded a
new city on the site.

Meyerbeer /'maɪəbeə/ Giacomo. Adopted
name of German composer Jakob Liebmann
Beer 1791–1864. Born in Berlin, from 1826 he
lived mainly in Paris, apart from his work after
1842 as general musical director in Berlin. A
talented pianist, he became best known for his
spectacular operas, including *Robert le Diable*
1831 and *Les Huguenots* 1836.

Meynell /'menl/ Alice (born Thompson)
1847–1922. British poet. She published *Preludes*
1875 and her collected poems appeared in 1923.
She married the author and journalist Wilfrid
Meynell (1852–1948).

mezzanine architectural term (derived from
the diminutive of the Italian *mezzano*, middle)
for a storey with a lower ceiling placed between
two higher storeys, usually between the ground
and first floors of a building.

mezzogiorno /ˌmetsəu'dʒɔːnəu/ (Italian
'midday') the hot, impoverished regions of S
Italy.

mezzo-soprano female voice halfway
between soprano and contralto.

mezzotint a method of etching in tone, widely
practised during the 18th century. A copper or
steel plate for use in printing is roughened by
means of a rocking tool, which makes
indentations and raises a 'burr'. The burr is then
scraped away where lighter tones are wanted in
the design. See also ◊print.

Mfecane (Bantu 'shaking-up of peoples') a
series of disturbances among African
communities in what is today the eastern part
of South Africa. They arose when chief ◊Chaka
conquered the Nguni peoples between the
Tugela and Pongola rivers, then created by
conquest a centralized, militaristic Zulu
kingdom from several communities, resulting in
large-scale displacement of people. These had
repercussions as far north as modern Tanzania.

MHD *m*agneto*h*ydro*d*ynamics, a field of
science concerned with the behaviour of ionized
gases in a magnetic field. Schemes have been
developed that use MHD to generate electrical
power.

mho the ◊SI unit of electrical conductance,
now called the siemens. It is equivalent to a
reciprocal ohm.

Miami /maɪ'æmi/ city and port in Florida,
USA; population (1984) 383,000. An influx of
immigrants from Cuba, Haiti, Mexico, and S
America after 1959 has made it the financial and
trading capital of Latin America and the
Caribbean. It is also a centre for oceanographic
research, and a tourist resort for its beaches.

mica a group of minerals that split easily into
thin flakes along lines of weakness in their crystal
structure (perfect basal cleavage). They are
glossy and have a pearly lustre. Their chemical
composition is complicated, but they are silicates
with the silica arranged in Si_4O_{10} groups in
continuous sheets, so giving perfect cleavage.
They are found in schists, gneisses, and granites;
their good thermal and electrical insulation
quality makes them valuable in industry.

Micah /'maɪkə/ (lived 8th century BC) in the
Old Testament, a Hebrew prophet whose
writings denounce the oppressive ruling class of
Judah, and demand justice.

Michael /'maɪkəl/ in the Bible, an archangel,
referred to as the guardian angel of Israel. In the
New Testament Book of Revelation he leads the
hosts of heaven to battle against Satan. In
paintings he is depicted with a flaming sword.

Michael /'maɪkəl/ Mikhail Fyodorovich
Romanov 1596–1645. Tsar of Russia from 1613.
Elected tsar by a national assembly, at a time of
anarchy and foreign invasion, he was the first of
the house of Romanov, which ruled until 1917.

Michael /'maɪkəl/ 1921– . King of
Romania 1927-30 and 1940-47. The son of Carol
II, he succeeded his grandfather as king in 1927,
but was displaced when his father returned from
exile in 1930. In 1940 he was proclaimed king
again on his father's abdication, and in 1944
overthrew the dictatorship of Antonescu and
enabled Romania to share in the victory of the
Allies at the end of the World War II. He
abdicated and left Romania in 1947.

michaelmas daisy popular name for species
of ◊*Aster* of the family Compositae, and also for
the sea aster or starwort.

Michaelmas Day in church tradition, the
festival of St Michael and all Angels, observed
on 29 Sept, and one of the English ◊quarter days.

Michelangelo Buonarroti /ˌmaɪkəl
'ændʒələu ˌbwɒnə'rɒti/ (Michelangiolo di
Lodovico Buonarroti Simoni) 1475–1564.
Italian sculptor, painter, architect, and poet.
Born near Florence, he was a student of
Domenico ◊Ghirlandaio, and worked for
Lorenzo de' ◊Medici. His giant talent dominated
the High Renaissance, with no other artist able to
escape his influence. He said of his stone carvings,
such as the monumental *David* in Florence
1501–04 that he was simply revealing the figure
hidden within the block. His massive figure style
was translated into paint in the Sistine chapel
frescoes (Vatican, Rome) covering the ceiling
with human figures, mostly nude, all grandly
Classical, telling the Old Testament story from
Genesis to the Deluge 1508–11 and finishing on
the altar wall with a titanic *Last Judgement*
1541. Other works in Rome, where he mainly
worked 1496–1501 and 1508–64, include
sculptures (the *Pietà*, tomb of Pope Julius II with
Moses and the Slaves); and the dome of St
Peter's (where he was chief architect from 1547).
In Florence his works include the design of the
Medici sepulchral chapel, and the *Pietà* in
Florence cathedral in which Nicodemus is a self-
portrait. His friendship with Vittoria ◊Colonna
in his later years inspired many of his sonnets and
madrigals.

Michels /'maɪklz/ Robert 1876–1936. German social and political theorist. Originally a radical, he became a critic of socialism and Marxism, and in his last years supported Hitler and Mussolini. In *Political Parties* 1911 he propounded the *Iron Law of Oligarchy*, arguing that in any organization or society, even a democracy, there is a tendency towards rule by the few in the interests of the few, and that ideologies like socialism and communism were merely propaganda to control the masses.

Michelson /'maɪkəlsən/ Albert Abraham 1852–1931. German-born US physicist, the first American scientist to win a Nobel prize 1907. He invented the Michelson interferometer, made precise measurement of the speed of light, and from 1892 was professor of physics at the University at Chicago. In conjunction with Edward Morley he performed in 1887 the *Michelson-Morley experiment* to detect the motion of the Earth through the postulated ◊ether. The failure of the experiment indicated the non-existence of the ether (a medium believed to be necessary for the propagation of light) and led ◊Einstein to his theory of ◊relativity.

products chiefly industrial; cars, iron, cement, oil
population (1983) 9,069,000
famous people General Custer, Edna Ferber, Henry Ford
history explored by the French from 1618, it became British in 1763, and a state in 1837. In 1973, 97% of the population were contaminated by PBB (poly-brominated biphenyl), a flame-retardant chemical inadvertently mixed with livestock feed.

Michigan, Lake /'mɪʃɪgən/ the third largest of the ◊Great Lakes of N America, and the only one completely in the USA; area 57,441 sq km/22,178 sq mi.

Mickiewicz /,mɪtski'evɪtʃ/ Adam 1798–1855. Polish revolutionary poet, whose *Pan Tadeusz* 1832–34 is Poland's national epic.

micro prefix denoting one millionth part (10^{-6}), symbol μ, for example a micrometre, μm, one millionth of a metre.

microbe in biology, a microscopic organism, a germ, virus, microorganism, or bacterium, which has life and the ability to multiply. See ◊bacteria.

microbiological warfare use of harmful microbes as a weapon. See ◊biological and ◊chemical warfare.

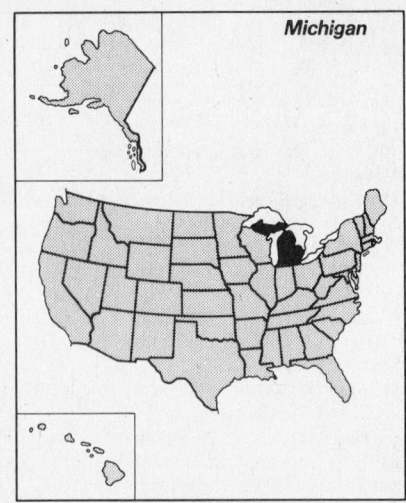

Michigan

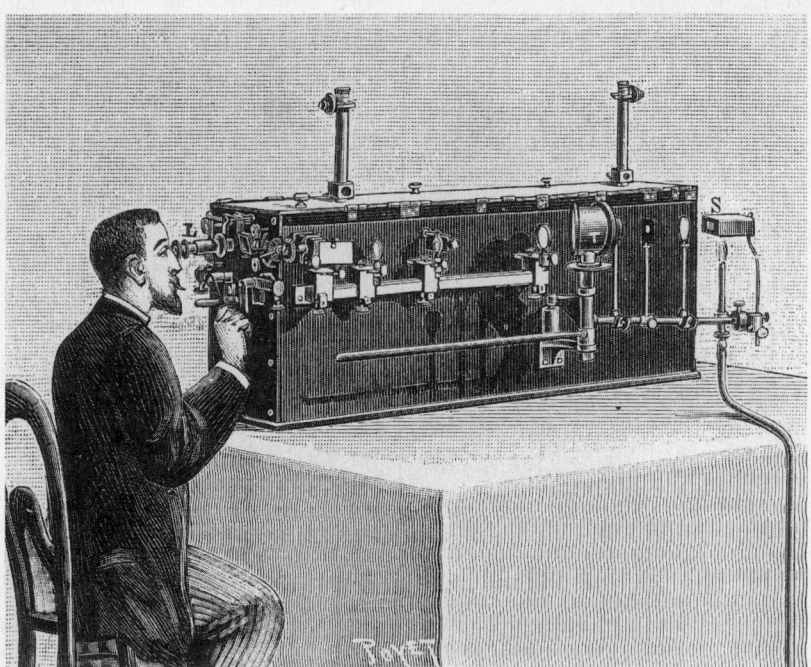

Michelson Albert Abraham Michelson's interferometer. The instrument was used to take measurements in the Michelson-Morley experiment designed to detect a difference in the velocities of light in directions parallel to and perpendicular to the motion of the earth.

Michigan /'mɪʃɪgən/ state of the USA; nicknamed Great Lake State or Wolverine State, bordered by the Great Lakes and Canada
area 150,777 sq km/58,216 sq mi, including inland water
capital Lansing
towns Detroit, Grand Rapids, Flint
features Lake Michigan; Porcupine Mountains; Muskegon, Grand, St Joseph, and Kalamazoo rivers; over 50% forested

microbiology the study of organisms that can only be seen under the ◊microscope, mostly single-celled organisms such as ◊viruses, ◊bacteria, ◊protozoa, and ◊yeasts. The practical applications of microbiology are concerned with medicine (since many ◊microorganisms cause disease); with brewing, baking, and so on, where the microorganisms carry out ◊fermentation; and with ◊genetic engineering, which is making microbiology an increasingly important field.

microchip popular name for the ◊silicon chip or ◊integrated circuit.

microcomputer or *micro* a small desktop or portable computer, typically built around a single ◊printed circuit board and including a ◊microprocessor chip. It normally comprises three 'boxes', two or more of which may be combined: a processor unit with built-in disk drives, a keyboard, and a ◊VDU (screen).

microeconomics the division of ◊economics concerned with the study of individual decision-making units within an economy: a consumer, firm, or industry. It looks at how individual markets work and how individual producers and consumers make their choices and with what consequences. This is done by analysing how relevant prices of goods are determined and the quantities that will be bought and sold.
The operation of the market is therefore a central concern of microeconomics. For simplicity, microeconomics begins by analysing a market in which there is *perfect competition*, a theoretical state which exists only when no individual producer or consumer can influence the market price. In the real world, there is always imperfect competition for various reasons (◊monopoly practices, barriers to trade, and so on), and microeconomics examines what effect these have on wages and prices.
Underlying these and other concerns of microeconomics is the concept of *optimality*, first advanced by Vilfredo ◊Pareto in the 19th century. Pareto's perception of the most efficient state of an economy, when there is no scope to reallocate resources without making someone worse off, has been extremely influential.

microform any of the media that reduce printed text to a size unreadable by the naked eye, especially 35-mm roll film, 16-mm film, and *microfiche*, a flat sheet of film generally 105 x 148 mm, including up to 420 pages of text.

microlight aircraft very light aircraft, with small engines, rather like powered hang-gliders. They are portable on a car roof-rack.

micrometer an instrument for making very small measurements with the greatest accuracy.

For astronomical use, it consists of two very fine wires, one fixed and the other movable, placed in the focal plane of a telescope; the movable wire is fixed on a sliding plate and can be moved parallel to the other until the object appears between the wires. The movement is then indicated by a scale on the adjusting screw. *Micrometer gauges* are measuring gauges having their adjustment effected by an extremely accurate fine-pitch screw (◊vernier); they are of great value in engineering.

and other well-known examples are those used with broadcasting and sound-film apparatus.

microprocessor a computer's central processing unit (◊CPU) contained on a single ◊integrated circuit (see also ◊silicon chip). The appearance of the first microprocessors in 1971 heralded the introduction of the ◊microcomputer. The pocket calculator is also a product of microprocessor technology. The microprocessor has led to a dramatic fall in the size of machines and cost of computing power.

acoustic which uses an acoustic wave travelling down a sapphire rod, an image being built up by scanning the specimen. This results in the object being 'seen' in a different way, which may reveal quite diffferent detail from that revealed by light or electrons, and also enables the inside of a microchip or a living cell to be made visible. The idea was suggested by D Y Sokolov (USSR) in the 1950s, and developed in the USA in 1973. Also under development are *X-ray* and *laser* microscopes.

micrometer

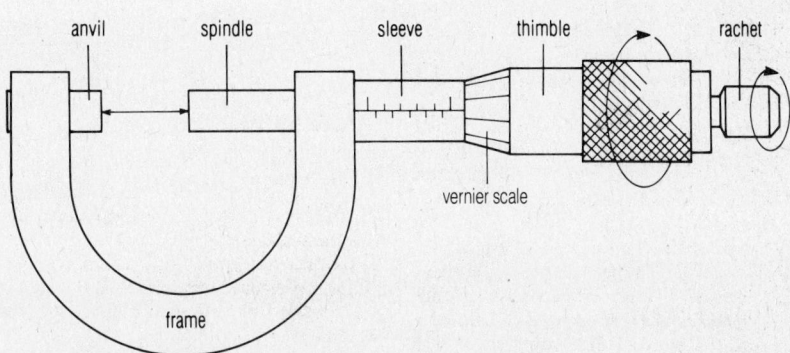

anvil   spindle   sleeve   thimble   rachet

vernier scale

frame

microscope

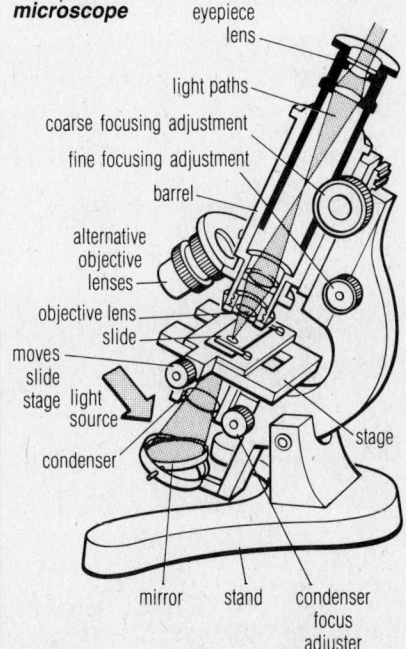

eyepiece lens

light paths

coarse focusing adjustment

fine focusing adjustment

barrel

alternative objective lenses

objective lens

slide

moves slide stage

light source

condenser

stage

mirror   stand   condenser focus adjuster

micrometre one millionth of a ◊metre.

microminiaturization the reduction in size and weight of electronic components and circuits to meet space, airborne, and military needs. The first size reduction in electronics was brought about by the introduction of the ◊transistor. This was followed by 'quantum leap' size reductions in ◊integrated circuits and in the ◊silicon chip.

micron obsolete name for the ◊micrometre.

Micronesia /ˌmaɪkrəʊˈniːzɪə/ in full *Federated States of Micronesia* a group of islands (Kosrae, Ponape, Truk, and Yap) in the W Pacific; population (1984) 88,500.

history purchased by Germany from Spain in 1898, they were occupied 1914 by Japan. They were captured by the USA in World War II, and became part of the US Trust Territory of the Pacific in 1947. Micronesia became internally self-governing from 1980, and in free association with the USA from 1985 (there is US control of military activities in return for economic aid).

Micronesia the part of the Pacific Ocean lying N of ◊Melanesia, including the Federated States of Micronesia, Belau, Kiribati, the Mariana and Marshall Islands, Nauru, and Tuvalu.

microorganism or *microbe* an organism invisible to the naked eye but visible under a ◊microscope. Most are single-celled; they include ◊bacteria, ◊protozoa, ◊yeasts, ◊viruses, and some ◊algae. The term has no taxonomic significance in biology. The study of microorganisms is known as ◊microbiology.

microphone the first component in a sound-reproducing system, whereby the mechanical energy of sound waves is converted into electrical energy. One of the simplest is the telephone receiver mouthpiece, invented by Bell in 1876,

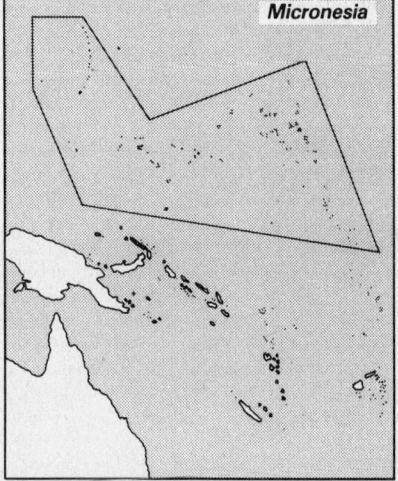

Micronesia

microscope instrument for magnification with high resolution for detail. The chief types are:

optical usually with two sets of glass lenses and an eyepiece, invented in 1609 by Dutchman Zacharias Janssen (1580–c. 1638).

electron (developed from 1932) which uses a beam of electrons instead of a beam of light, and, since these are not visible, replaces the eyepiece with a fluorescent screen or photographic plate; far higher magnification and resolution is possible than with the optical microscope. A *scanning electron microscope* (SEM), developed in the mid-1960s, probes the surface of a specimen and represents it three-dimensionally.

microwave an ◊electromagnetic wave with a wavelength in the range 0.1 to 3 cm (between radio waves and ◊infrared radiation). They are used in radar sets, as carrier waves in radio broadcasting, and in ◊microwave heating and cooking.

microwave heating heating by means of short radio waves, or ◊microwaves. In the home, microwave ovens use this form of heating for the rapid cooking and reheating of foods. Whereas in a normal oven food is heated by conduction from the outside, in a microwave oven heat is generated throughout the food simultaneously. Its use was patented in 1945 by Dr Percy Spencer, for popping corn. Industrially, microwave heating is used for destroying insects in grain and enzymes in processed food; pasteurizing and sterilizing liquids; and drying timber and paper.

Midas /ˈmaɪdæs/ in Greek legend, a King of Phrygia, who was granted the gift of converting all he touched to gold, and who, for preferring the music of Pan to that of Apollo, was given ass's ears by the latter.

MIDAS /ˈmaɪdæs/ acronym for *M*issile *D*efence *A*larm *S*ystem.

Mid-Atlantic Ridge the ◊ocean ridge that runs along the centre of the Atlantic Ocean, parallel to its edges, for some 14,000 km/8,800 mi almost from the Arctic to the Antarctic. It is central because the Atlantic Ocean has continually grown outwards from it at a steady rate during the past 200 million years. In Iceland it reaches the surface of the ocean. See ◊plate tectonics.

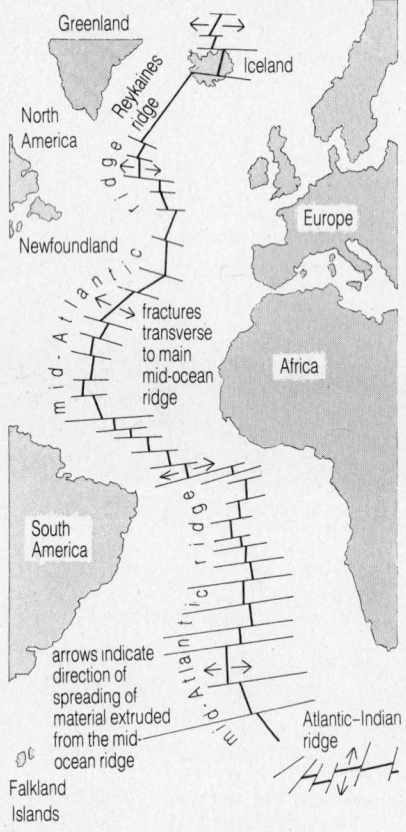

mid- Atlantic ridge

Greenland

Iceland

North America

Reykjanes ridge

Europe

Newfoundland

Africa

fractures transverse to main mid-ocean ridge

mid-Atlantic ridge

South America

mid-Atlantic ridge

arrows indicate direction of spreading of material extruded from the mid-ocean ridge

Atlantic–Indian ridge

Falkland Islands

Middelburg /'mɪdlbɜːg/ industrial town in SW Netherlands, capital of Zeeland and former ◊Hanseatic town; population (1985) 38,930.

Middle Ages a term used from the 17th century for the period of European history between the fall of the Roman Empire and the Renaissance. It is usually regarded as beginning in the 5th century and ending in the 15th. Among its distinctive features were the unity of Western Europe within the Roman Catholic Church; the feudal organization of political, social, and economic relations; and, in ◊medieval art, the use of painting and sculpture almost exclusively for Christian ends.

Middle East indeterminate area now usually taken to include the Balkan States, Egypt, and SW Asia. (Until the 1940s this area was generally called the Near East, and the term Middle East referred to the area from Iran to Burma.)

Middle English the period of the ◊English language from about 1050 to 1550.

Middle Kingdom *Egyptian* a period of Egyptian history extending from the late 11th to the 13th dynasty (roughly 2040–1670 BC);

Chinese Chinese name for China and its empire up to 1912, describing its central position in the Far East.

Middle Range or *Middleback range* mountain range in the NE of Eyre Peninsula, South Australia, about 65 km/40 mi long, parallel with the W coast of Spencer Gulf. Iron deposits are mined.

Middlesbrough /'mɪdlzbrə/ industrial town and port on the Tees, Cleveland, England, commercial and cultural centre of the urban area formed by Stockton-on-Tees, Redcar, Billingham, Thornaby, and Eston; population (1983) 148,400. Formerly a centre of heavy industry, it diversified its products in the 1960s.

Middlesex /'mɪdlseks/ former English county, absorbed by Greater London in 1965. Contained within the Thames basin, and providing good agricultural land before it was built over, it was settled in the 6th century, and its name comes from its position between the East and West Saxons. The name is still used, as in Middlesex County Cricket Club.

Middleton /'mɪdltən/ Thomas c. 1570–1627. English dramatist. Born in London, he produced numerous romantic plays and realistic comedies, both alone and in collaboration. Best-known are *A Fair Quarrel* and *The Changeling* 1622 with Rowley; *The Roaring Girl* with Dekker; and *Women Beware Women* 1621. His political satire *A Game of Chess* 1624 was concerned with the plots to unite the royal houses of England and Spain, and caused a furore with the authorities.

Middle West or *Midwest* a large area of N central USA. It is a loosely defined geographic region rather than a political entity, and is generally taken to comprise the states of Ohio, Indiana, Illinois, Michigan, Iowa, Wisconsin, Minnesota, and sometimes Nebraska. It tends to be conservative socially and politically, and isolationist. Traditionally its economy is divided between agriculture and heavy industry.

midge popular name for many ◊gnat-like insects, generally divided into biting midges (family Ceratopogonidae) that suck blood, and non-biting midges (family Chironomidae). The larvae of some midges are the 'bloodworms' of stagnant water.

Mid Glamorgan /'mɪd glə'mɔːgən/ county of S Wales, UK
area 1,019 sq km/393 sq mi
towns administrative headquarters Cardiff; resort Porthcawl; Aberdare, Merthyr Tydfil, Bridgend, Pontypridd
features Caerphilly Castle, with its water defences
products the N was formerly an important coal (Rhondda) and iron and steel area; agriculture in the S; Caerphilly noted for mild cheese
population (1983) 536,400, largest of the Welsh counties
language 8% Welsh-speaking.

Midi-Pyrénées /mɪ'diː ˌpɪrə'neɪ/ region of SW France; capital Toulouse; population (1984) 2,340,000.

Midlands /'mɪdləndz/ area of England corresponding roughly to the Anglo-Saxon kingdom of ◊Mercia

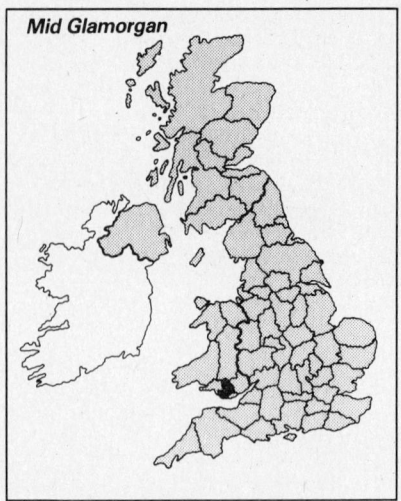

Mid Glamorgan

E Midlands Derbyshire, Leicestershire, Northamptonshire, Nottinghamshire
W Midlands the former metropolitan county of ◊West Midlands created from parts of Staffordshire, Warwickshire, and Worcestershire.
In World War II the E Midlands was worked for oil, and substantial finds were made in the 1980s; the oilbearing E Midlands Shelf extends into Yorkshire and Lincolnshire.

Midlothian /mɪd'ləʊðɪən/ former Scottish county S of the Firth of Forth, included in 1975 in the region of Lothian; Edinburgh was the administrative headquarters.

midnight sun appearance of the Sun (within the Arctic and Antarctic circles) above the horizon at midnight during the summer.

Midrash /'mɪdræʃ/ (Hebrew 'inquiry') the ancient Jewish commentaries on the Bible, in the form of sermons in which allegory and legendary illustration are used. They were mainly compiled in Palestine between 400–1200 AD.

midshipman trainee naval officer.

midsummer the summer ◊solstice, about 21 Jun, but Midsummer Day is 24 Jun – a quarter day and the festival of St John the Baptist.

Midway Islands /'mɪdweɪ/ two islands in the N Pacific; area 5.5 sq km/2.2 sq mi. Annexed by the USA in 1867, they are administered by the US Navy. The naval *Battle of Midway* 3–6 Jun 1942, between the USA and Japan, was the turning point in the Pacific in World War II.

midwifery the assistance of women in childbirth. As one of the principal divisions of the qualifying course for medical practitioners, it includes all sorts of treatment, medical and surgical, connected with birth, but the functions of a midwife are in most countries limited by law to the making of preparations and examinations, the giving of ordinary assistance and after-care, and the summoning of a doctor in an emergency.

Mies van der Rohe /'miːs ˌvæn də 'rəʊə/ Ludwig 1886–1969. German architect, who practised in the USA from 1937. Son of a stonemason, he was born in Aachen, and was director of the ◊Bauhaus 1929–33. He became professor at the Illinois Institute of Technology 1938–58, for which he designed new buildings from 1941. He also designed the bronze-and-glass Seagram building in New York 1956–59.

mignonette sweet-scented garden plant *Reseda odorata*, bearing usually yellowish-green flowers in racemes, with abundant foliage. A native of N Africa, it was brought to England about 1752. Related species are found wild.

migraine acute, sometimes incapacitating, headaches which recur, often with advance symptoms, such as flashing lights, and accompanied by nausea. No cure has been discovered, but drugs may reduce pain, and changes in diet may help prevent attacks.

migration the movement, either seasonal or as part of a single life cycle, of certain animals, especially birds and fish, to particular breeding or feeding grounds. Allied to it is the homing ability of pigeons, bees, and other creatures. Patterns of migration have been established by marking specimens recovered after death, or which pass through scientific stations en route, but the precise methods by which animals navigate and how they know where to go are still obscure. Birds have much sharper eyesight and better visual memory of ground clues than humans, but in long-distance flights appear to navigate by the Sun and stars, possibly in combination with an internal biological 'clock' which acts roughly in the same way as a marine chronometer, and with a 'reading' of the Earth's magnetic field through an inbuilt 'magnetic compass'. The last-named is a tiny mass of tissue between the eye and brain in birds, and similar cells occur in 'homing' honeybees, and in certain bacteria which use it to determine which way is 'down' (see ◊magnetism). Most striking, however, is the migration of young birds which have never flown a route before and are unaccompanied by adults. It is postulated that they may inherit as part of their genetic code an overall 'sky chart' of their journéy which is triggered into use when they become aware of how the local sky pattern above the place in which they hatch fits into it. Similar theories have been advanced in the case of fish, such as eels and salmon, with whom vision obviously plays a less important role, but for whom currents and changes in the composition and temperature of the sea in particular locations may play a part, for example in enabling salmon to return to the precise river in which they were spawned. Migrations also occurs with land animals, for example, the ◊lemming.

Mihailovich or *Mikhailovich* /mɪˈhaɪləvɪtʃ/ Draga 1893–1946. Yugoslav soldier, leader of the guerrilla 'Chetniks' of World War II against the German occupation. His feud with Tito's Communists led to the withdrawal of Allied support and that of his own exiled government from 1943. He turned for help to the Italians and Germans, and was eventually shot for treason.

mikado old title ('honorable palace gate') of the Japanese emperor, replaced in the late 19th century by *tenno* ('heavenly sovereign').

Milan /mɪˈlæn/ (Italian *Milano*) industrial city (aircraft, cars, locomotives, textiles), financial and cultural centre, capital of

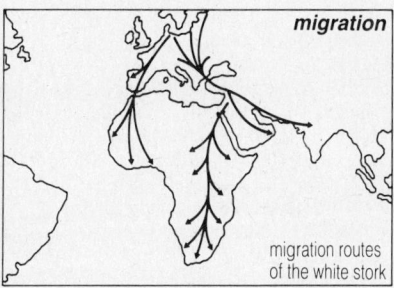

migration

migration routes of the white stork

Lombardy, Italy; population (1984) 1,534,000. *features* the Gothic cathedral c. 1450, crowned with pinnacles, can hold 40,000 worshippers; there are two universities, the Brera art gallery, the convent with Leonardo da Vinci's *Last Supper* 1495–97, and La Scala opera house (Italian *Teatro alla Scala*) 1778.

history settled by the Gauls in the 5th century BC, it was conquered by the Roman consul Marcellus in 222 BC to become the Roman city of *Mediolanum*. Under Diocletian, in 286 AD, Milan was capital of the Western empire. Destroyed by ◊Attila the Hun in 452, and again by the Goths in 539, the city regained its power through the political importance of its bishops. In 1045 it became an autonomous commune. In 1162 the city was taken by ◊Frederick I (Barbarossa); only in 1176 were his forces finally defeated, at the battle of Legnano. In the Guelph-Ghibelline struggle the Visconti family emerged at the head of the Ghibelline faction; they gained power in 1277, establishing a dynasty which lasted until 1450 when Francesco Sforza seized control. The Sforza court marked the highpoint of Milan as a cultural and artistic centre. In 1499 control of the city passed to Louis XII of France, and in 1540 it was annexed by Spain, beginning a long decline. In 1714 the city was ceded to Austria by the Treaty of ◊Utrecht, and in the 18th century began a period of intellectual enlightenment. In 1796 Milan was taken by ◊Napoleon, who made it the capital of the Cisalpine Republic in 1799, and in 1805 capital of the kingdom of Italy until 1814, when it reverted to the Austrians. In 1848, it rebelled unsuccessfully (the famous *Cinque Giornate*/Five Days), and in 1859 was joined to Piedmont.

Milankovitch hypothesis the combination of factors governing the occurrence of ◊ice ages proposed in 1930 by the Yugoslavian geophysicist of that name (1879–1958).

mildew name given to minute fungi, like a thin whitish coat, which appear as a destructive growth on plants, paper, leather, or wood, when exposed to damp.

mile a measure of length in the imperial system. A statute mile is equal to 1,760 yds/1.60934 km, and a nautical mile (used internationally) is equal to 6076.12 ft/1,852 m. It is derived from the Roman mile of 1,000 paces.

Mile End /ˈmaɪl ˈend/ area of the East End of London, in the district of Stepney, now part of the London borough of Tower Hamlets. Mile End Green (now Stepney Green) was the scene

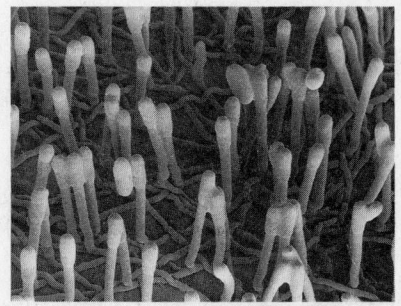

mildew Scanning electron micrograph of a harmful fungus *Erisyphe pisi*, the cause of powdery mildew. The infection begins with a short germ tube. It attaches to a surface with a pad which sends tubes into it. As shown here on the surface of a pea, *haustoria* (food gathering organs) may develop with a network of mycelia.

of Richard II's meeting with the rebel peasants in 1381, and in later centuries was the exercise ground of the London trained bands (see ◊militia).

Miles /maɪlz/ Bernard, Baron Miles 1907– . British actor and producer. He founded a trust which built the City of London's first theatre for 300 years, the Mermaid 1959, and was created a life peer in 1979.

Miletus /mɪˈliːtəs/ ancient Greek city in SW Asia Minor, with a port which eventually silted up. It carried on an important trade with Egypt and the Black Sea. The scientists Thales, Anaximander, and Anaximenes were born at Miletus.

milfoil another name for the herb ◊yarrow. Water milfoils are unrelated, plants of the genus *Miriophyllum*, with whorls of fine leaves.

Milford Haven, Marquess of /ˈmɪlfəd ˈheɪvən/ 1854–1921. title given in 1917 to Prince ◊Louis of Battenburg (1854–1921).

Milhaud /ˈmiːjəʊ/ Darius 1892–1974. French composer. A member of the group of composers ◊*Les Six*, he lived for a time in Brazil, and his treatment of the Latin-American folk song *Le Boeuf sur le toit* 1920 caused a sensation. His other most famous work was the jazz ballet *La Création du monde* 1923. He was associated with Paul ◊Claudel, with whom he collaborated in ballets. Much of his later work, which includes chamber, orchestral, and choral music, is polytonal.

miliaria itchy blisters formed in the skin condition ◊prickly heat.

Militant Tendency a faction within the British ◊Labour Party, aligned with the newspaper *Militant*. It became active in the 1970s, with radical socialist policies based on Trotskyism (see ◊Trotsky), and gained some success in local government, especially in inner city areas, for example in Liverpool. In the mid-1980s the Labour Party considered it to be an organization within the party and banned it. A number of senior Militants were expelled from the party in 1986, amid much legal conflict.

military law articles or regulations that apply to members of the armed services. See under ▷martial law.

militia a body of citizen soldiers, usually with some military training, who are on call in emergencies, distinct from professional soldiers. In England King Alfred established the first militia, or *fyrd*, in the 9th century in which every freeman was liable to serve. After the Conquest a feudal levy was established in which landowners were responsible for raising the men required. This in turn led to the increasing use of the general levy by English kings to combat the growing power of the barons. In the 16th century, under such threats as the Spanish Armada, plans for internal defence relied increasingly on the militia, or what came to be called 'trained bands', of the general levy. After the Restoration, the militia fell into neglect, but it was re-organized in 1757, and relied upon for home defence during the French wars; and in the 19th century it extended its activities abroad, serving in the Peninsular, Crimean, and South African wars. In 1852 it adopted a volunteer status, and in 1908 was merged with the ▷Territorial Army and the Special Reserve forces, to supplement the Regular Army, and ceased to exist as a separate force.

The principle of a militia was introduced into the USA with the first settlers. After an Act of 1792, it more or less replaced for a time the Regular Army, but was itself supplanted in the late 19th century by the volunteer ▷*National Guard* units of individual states, which are under federal orders in emergencies, and are now an integral part of the US Army. In Switzerland, the militia is the national defence force, and every able-bodied man is liable for service in it.

milk the secretion of the ▷mammary glands of female mammals, with which they suckle their young. The milk of cows, goats, or sheep is that most usually consumed by humans: over 85 per cent is water, the remainder comprising protein, fat, lactose (a sugar), calcium, phosphorus, a little iron, and vitamins. Milk composition varies between species, depending on the nutritional requirements of the young; human milk contains less protein and more lactose than that of cows. See also ▷lactation.

milking machine a machine that uses suction to milk cows. A suction milking machine was invented in the USA by L O Colvin in 1860. Later it was improved so that the suction was regularly released by a pulsating device, since it was found that continuous suction was bad for the cow. Modern milking machines also work by suction and pulsation.

Milky Way the faint band of light crossing the sky, consisting of countless stars in the plane of our ▷Galaxy, too distant to be seen individually by the naked eye. The name Milky Way is sometimes also used for our Galaxy. The densest parts lie in the constellation Sagittarius, towards the centre. In places, the Milky Way is interrupted by lanes of dark dust which obscure light from the stars beyond, such as the Coalsack Nebula in ▷Crux (the Southern Cross).

Mill /mɪl/ James 1773–1836. Scottish philosopher and political thinker. Born near Montrose, Mill moved to London 1802. Associated for most of his working life with the East India Company, he wrote a vast *History of British India* 1817–18. He was one of the founders of University College, London, together with his friend and fellow ▷Utilitarian Jeremy ▷Bentham. Mill is remembered for his political articles, and for the rigorous education he gave his son John Stuart Mill.

Mill /mɪl/ John Stuart 1806–1873. British philosopher and economist, celebrated for his work in logic, economics, political theory, and ethics. He was born in London, the son of James Mill (1773–1836), an eminent Utilitarian philosopher. In 1822 he entered the East India Company, where he remained until retiring in 1858. In 1826, as described in his *Autobiography* 1873, he passed through a mental crisis; he found his father's bleakly intellectual Utilitarianism emotionally unsatisfying, and abandoned it for a more human philosophy influenced by ▷Coleridge. In his social philosophy he gradually abandoned the Utilitarians' extreme individualism for an outlook akin to liberal socialism, while still laying great emphasis on the liberty of the individual; this change can be traced in the later editions of *Principles of Political Economy* 1848 and in his book *Utilitarianism* 1863, which puts forward the 'greatest happiness' principle. This states that actions are right if they bring about happiness and wrong if they bring about the reverse of happiness. He sat in Parliament as a Radical 1865–68, and introduced a motion for women's suffrage. His feminist views inspired his *On the Subjection of Women* 1869. His philosophical and political writings include *A System of Logic* 1843, *On Liberty* 1859, the classic philosophical defence of liberalism, and *Considerations on Representative Government* 1861.

Millais /'mɪleɪ/ John Everett 1829–1896. British artist. Born at Southampton, he joined Holman ▷Hunt and ▷Rossetti in 1848, founding the ▷Pre-Raphaelite Brotherhood, and his best works were painted in the Pre-Raphaelite manner, for example, *Ophelia* 1852, and *Autumn Leaves* 1856. In 1855 he married Effie Gray, Ruskin's divorced wife. His early work provoked fierce criticism, but he later achieved great popularity with his story-pictures, such as the *Boyhood of Raleigh* 1870, and *The Northwest Passage* 1874, sentimental child-studies, such as *Bubbles* 1886 (a poster for Pears soap), and portraits. He was created a baronet in 1885 and elected president of the Royal Academy in 1896.

Millay /mɪ'leɪ/ Edna St Vincent 1892–1950. American poet, born in Maine, who wrote emotional verse, including *Renascence* 1917 and *The Harp-Weaver* 1922.

millennium a period of 1,000 years. Some Christian sects believe that Christ will return to govern the Earth in person at the millennium, the 6001st year after the creation (the creation itself had been located by Archbishop Ussher at 4004 BC). This belief, *millenarianism*, also called Chiliasm (from the Greek for 1,000), was widespread in the early days of Christianity. As hopes were disappointed, belief in the Second

Mill Educated by his father, John Stuart Mill was reading Plato and Demosthenes with ease at the age of ten. His *Autobiography* gives a painful account of the teaching methods which turned him against Utilitarianism.

Coming tended to fade, but millenarian views have been expressed at periods of great religious excitement, such as the Reformation. The Fifth Monarchy Men were millenarians, as are Jehovah's Witnesses.

Miller /'mɪlə/ Arthur 1915– . American playwright. Deeply concerned with family relationships and contemporary American values, his plays include *All My Sons* 1947, *Death of a Salesman* 1949; and *The Crucible* 1953, which some saw as equating the Salem witch hunt with the anti-communist crusade of Joseph ▷McCarthy (Miller was convicted of contempt of Congress in 1957 for refusal to name those present at a meeting of Communist writers in 1947). He was married 1956–61 to Marilyn ▷Monroe, for whom he wrote the film *The Misfits* 1960, and with whom Maggie, in his play *After the Fall* 1964, has been identified.

Miller /'mɪlə/ Glenn 1904–1944. US trombonist and, as bandleader, creator of the big-band sound of the era, from 1938. He composed his signature tune 'Moonlight Serenade'. He disappeared without trace on a flight between England and France during World War II.

Miller /'mɪlə/ Henry 1891–1980. American writer, born in New York. Years spent in the Paris underworld underpin his novels *Tropic of Cancer* 1934 and *Tropic of Capricorn* 1938. They were so outspoken that the former was banned in England till 1963, and the latter was published in the USA only in 1961.

miller's thumb another name for ▷bullhead, a small fish.

millet /mɪ'leɪ/ type of grass, family Gramineae, cultivated in various countries, the grains as a cereal food and the stems as fodder. The most important are *Panicum miliaceum*, extensively cultivated in the warmer parts of Europe, and *Sorghum bicolor*, also known as ▷durra.

Millais The Pre-Raphaelite Brotherhood produced paintings with meticulously observed detail, usually with a serious, moralizing subject, such as Sir John Millais' *Christ in the House of his Parents* 1890.

Miller American playwright Arthur Miller.

Millet /miːˈleɪ/ Jean François 1814–1875. French painter. Born in Normandy of a peasant family, he went to Paris to study in 1837. He settled at ◊Barbizon, in the forest of Fontainebleau,in 1848, and there became the leader of a group of artists who concentrated on paintings of peasant life and rustic scenery. He is best known for his romantic studies of peasants, such as *The Reapers* 1854, *The Gleaners* 1857 and *The Angelus* 1859.

Millett /'mɪlɪt/ Kate 1934– . American radical feminist lecturer, writer and sculptor, whose book *Sexual Politics* 1970 was a landmark in feminist thinking. She was one of the earliest and most influential theorists of the Women's Movement and was a founding member of the *National Organization of Women* (NOW). Later books include *Flying* 1974.

millibar a unit of pressure, equal to one thousandth of a ◊bar.

Millikan /'mɪlɪkən/ Robert Andrews 1868–1953. American physicist, awarded a Nobel prize in physics in 1923 for his determination of the ◊electric charge on an ◊electron. In Millikan's famous oil-drop experiment (which took him five years up to 1913

Millet Jean François Millet's idealized view of peasant life is seen in *Peasants Going to Work* 1855.

to perfect), he observed oil droplets, charged by external ◊radiation, falling under ◊gravity between two horizontal metal plates connected to a high-voltage supply. By varying the voltage, he was able to make the electrostatic field between the plates balance the gravitational field so that some droplets became stationary and floated. If a droplet of weight W is held stationary between plates separated by a distance d and carrying a potential difference V, the charge on the drop, e is equal to Wd/V.

millilitre one thousandth of a litre (ml). Roughly equivalent to 1 cm³ (cc).

Millin /'mɪlɪn/ Sarah Gertrude (born Liebson) 1889–1968. South African novelist, an early opponent of racial discrimination, for example, *God's Step-Children* 1924.

milling a metal machining method which uses a rotating toothed cutting wheel to shape a surface.

millipede arthropod of worldwide distribution, of the class Diplopoda. It has a segmented body, each segment usually bearing two pairs of legs, and the distinct head bears a pair of short clubbed antennae. The class is divided into a number of orders; some species roll into a ball. Certain orders are provided with silk glands. Millipedes live in damp dark places, feeding mainly on rotting vegetation. Some species injure crops by feeding on tender roots, and some produce a poisonous secretion in defence. Most are a few cms long; a few in the tropics are 30 cm/12 in

Mills /mɪlz/ C Wright 1916–1962. US sociologist, whose concern for humanity, ethical values, and individual freedom led him to criticize the US Establishment. Originally in the liberal tradition, he later adopted Weberian and even Marxist ideas. He aroused considerable popular interest in sociology with such works as *White Collar* 1951, *The Power Elite* 1956, depicting the US as ruled by businessmen, military experts, and politicians. and *Listen, Yankee* 1960.

Mills /mɪlz/ John 1908– . British actor-director. Acting in films from 1933, he made a reputation in stiff-upper-lip wartime roles, as in *In Which we Serve*; later were *Scott of the Antarctic* 1949, and *Ryan's Daughter*, for which he received an Oscar as best supporting actor in 1971. He was knighted in 1976.

Mills Cross a type of ◊radio telescope consisting of two rows of aerials at right angles to each other, invented in 1953 by the Australian radio-astronomer Bernard Mills. The cross-shape produces a narrow beam useful for pin-pointing the positions of radio sources.

Milne /mɪln/ A(lan) A(lexander) 1882–1956. British author, best known for his children's books based on the teddy bear and other toys of his son Christopher Robin (*Winnie-the-Pooh* 1926 and *The House at Pooh Corner* 1928); volumes of children's verse (*When We Were Very Young* 1924 and *Now We Are Six* 1927); and his stage adaptation of Kenneth Grahame's *The Wind in the Willows* as *Toad of Toad Hall* 1929.

Milner /'mɪlnə/ Alfred, Viscount Milner 1854–1925. British colonial administrator. As governor of Cape Colony 1897–1901, he negotiated with ◊Kruger but failed to prevent the ◊South African War; and as governor of the Transvaal and Orange River colonies 1902–05 after their annexation, he reorganized their administration. He emphasized the 'organic union' of the Empire, rather than the need for independence for its members. In 1916 he became a member of Lloyd George's war cabinet, and as secretary for war 1918–19 was largely responsible for creating a unified Allied command under Foch.

Miłosz /'miːwɒʃ/ Czesław 1911– . Polish-American poet. Born in Lithuania, he became a diplomat before defecting and taking US nationality. He was awarded a Nobel prize in 1980, notably for his *Bells in Winter* 1980.

Milstein /'mɪlstaɪn/ César 1927– . British molecular biologist, who in 1984 shared a Nobel medicine prize (with George ◊Kohler and Niels ◊Jerne) for techniques used to produce ◊antibodies giving immunity against specific diseases.

Milton /'mɪltən/ John 1608–1674. English poet, author of the epic poem *Paradise Lost*. Born in London, the son of a scrivener, he was educated at Cambridge. His early poems include the pastoral style *L'allegro* and *Il penseroso* of 1632, the masque *Comus* 1633, and the elegy for a dead friend *Lycidas* 1637. His middle years were devoted to the Puritan cause and pamphleteering, including one advocating divorce, and another (*Areopagitica*) freedom of the press. From 1649 he was (Latin) secretary to the Council of State. His assistants (as his sight failed) included ◊Marvell. His first wife was Mary Powell, who was 17 when they married in 1643, and who left him, though three daughters were born after their reconciliation in 1645 (who were later his somewhat unwilling amanuenses). After Mary's death in 1652, the year of his total blindness, he married twice more, his second wife Catherine Woodcock dying in childbirth, while Elizabeth Minshull survived him for over half a century. The masterpieces of his old age in retirement are his epic poems *Paradise Lost* 1667, and *Paradise Regained* 1677, and the classic drama *Samson Agonistes* 1677.

Milton The 17th century English poet John Milton is best remembered for his epic poem in blank verse, *Paradise Lost*, in which he hoped 'to justify the ways of God to man'.

Milton Keynes /'mɪltən 'kiːnz/ industrial new town founded 1967 on a grid designed by Richard Llewelyn-Davies in ◊Buckinghamshire, England; the headquarters of the Open University; population (1983) 146,000.

Milwaukee /mɪl'wɔːki/ port (on Lake Michigan) and industrial city (meatpacking,

brewing, engineering, textiles) in Wisconsin, USA; population (1980) 1,207,000.

mime in modern usage, a term for acting in which gestures, movements and facial expression replace dialogue. In ancient Greece mime was a crude, realistic comedy with speech and exaggerated gesture. It is essential to the stage actor's repertory of expression, and plays an important role in ballet. It has also developed as a form of theatre in its own right, particularly in France, where Marcel ◊Marceau and Jean-Louis ◊Barrault have continued the traditions established in the 19th century by Deburau, and the practices of the ◊commedia dell'arte in Italy.

mimicry the imitation of one ◊species (or group of species) by another. The most common form is Batesian mimicry (named after H W ◊Bates) where the mimic resembles a model that is poisonous or unpleasant to eat and has ◊aposematic colouration: the mimic thus benefits from the fact that predators learn to avoid the model. Hoverflies which resemble bees or wasps are an example. In Mullerian mimicry, two or more equally poisonous or distasteful species have a similar colour pattern, thereby reinforcing the warning each gives to predators. In some cases, mimicry is not for protection, but allows the mimic to prey on, or parasitize, the model. And while appearance is usually the basis for mimicry, calls, songs, scents and other signals can also be mimicked.

mimicry

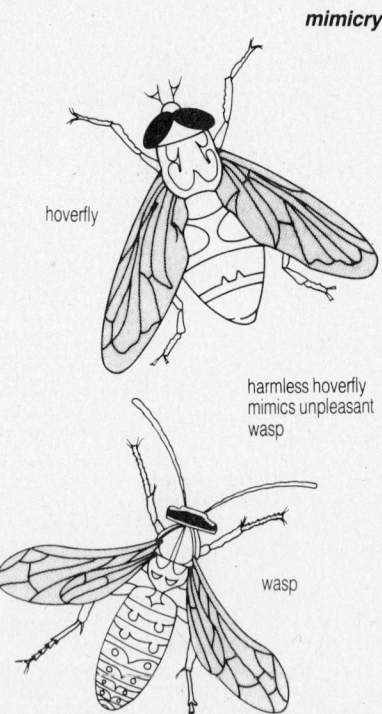

hoverfly

harmless hoverfly mimics unpleasant wasp

wasp

mimosa plant of the family Leguminosae found in tropical and subtropical regions and ranging from herbs to large trees. The flowers are small, fluffy, golden balls, tufts of stamens, and

the leaves are pinnate, divided into a multiplicity of small leaflets. Certain species, for example, the sensitive plant of Brazil *Mimosa pudica*, shrink momentarily on being touched.

minaret a slender turret or tower attached to a Muslim mosque. It has one or more balconies, from which the *muezzin* calls the people to prayer five times a day.

mind in philosophy, the presumed mental or physical being or faculty that enables a person to think, will, and feel; the seat of the intelligence and of memory; sometimes only the cognitive or intellectual powers as distinguished from the will and the emotions. It may be seen as synonymous with the merely random chemical reactions within the brain, or as a function of the brain as a whole, or (more traditionally) as existing independently of the physical brain, through which it expresses itself, or even as the only reality, matter being considered the creation of intelligence. The relation of mind to matter may be variously regarded. Traditionally, ◊Materialists identify the two: mental phenomena equally with physical are to be explained in terms of matter and motion. ◊Dualists hold that mind and matter exist independently side by side. ◊Idealists maintain that mind is the ultimate reality, and that matter is the creation of intelligence, and does not exist apart from it. See also ◊psychology.

Mindanao /,mɪndə'naʊ/ the second-largest island of the Philippines
area 94,227 sq km/36,381 sq mi
town Davao
features the mountainous rain forest was found in 1971 to harbour an isolated stone-age tribe, the Tasaday. The active volcano Apo reaches 2,855 m/9,369 ft, and Mindanao is subject to severe earthquakes. There is a Muslim guerrilla resistance movement
population (1980) 10,905,250.

Minden /'mɪndən/ industrial town of North Rhine-Westphalia, W Germany, on the river Weser; population (1985) 80,000. The French were defeated here in 1759 by an allied army from Britain, Hanover, and Brunswick, commanded by the duke of Brunswick.

Mindoro /mɪn'dɔːrəʊ/ island of the Philippine Republic, S of Luzon
area 10,347 sq km 3,995 sq mi
towns Calapan
features Mount Halcon 2,590 m/8,500 ft
population (1980) 500,000.

Mindszenty /'mɪndsenti/ József 1892–1975. Roman Catholic Primate of Hungary. Imprisoned by the Communists in 1949, he escaped in 1956 to take refuge in the US legation. Persuaded by the Pope to go into exile in Austria in 1971, he was 'retired' when Hungary's relations with the Vatican improved in 1974.

mine explosive charge on land or sea, or in the atmosphere, designed to be detonated by contact, vibration (for example from an enemy engine), by magnetic influence, or by a timing device. Counter-measures include metal detectors (useless for plastic types), specially equipped helicopters, and (at sea) *minesweepers*. These, in their most modern form, are small vessels of about 725 tonnes, built of reinforced plastic (immune to magnetic and acoustic mines), which, when they detect a mine on the sea bed by sonar, direct two remotely controlled miniature submarines to lay destructive charges alongside.

mineral a naturally formed inorganic substance with a particular chemical composition and usually a well-defined crystal structure. Either in their perfect crystalline form, or otherwise, minerals are the constituents of rocks. In more general usage a mineral is any substance economically valuable for mining (including coal and oil, despite their organic origin)

mineral dressing preparing a mineral ore for

Minerva /mɪˈnɜːvə/ in ancient Roman mythology, the goddess of intelligence, and of the handicrafts and arts, counterpart of the Greek ◊Athene. From the earliest times she had a temple on the Capitol in Rome.

minesweeper small vessel for locating and destroying mines at sea. See under ◊mine.

Mingus /ˈmɪŋgəs/ Charles 1922–1979. US bass player and composer. He was influential for his experimentation with atonality and dissonant effects, opening the way for the new style of free collective improvisation of the 1960s.

Minhow /ˌmɪnˈhaʊ/ name in use 1934–43 for Foochow, now ◊Fuzhou, a town in SE China.

market. See ◊bank rate.

mining extraction of minerals from under the land or sea for industrial or domestic use. Exhaustion of easily accessible resources has led to new techniques, for example extraction of oil from under the North Sea and from land shale reserves, which are more difficult. Technology is also under development for the exploitation of minerals from asteroids in space, and from entirely new undersea sources:

mud deposits laid down by hot springs about 350°C, that is, sea water penetrates beneath the ocean floor, and on its return carries copper, silver, and zinc with it. Such springs occur along the mid-ocean ridges of the Atlantic and Pacific, and in the geological rift between Africa and Arabia under the Red Sea.

mineral nodules which form on the ocean bed and contain manganese, cobalt, copper, molybdenum, nickel; they stand out on the surface, and 'grow' by only a few millimetres every 100,000 years. See also ◊bacteria and law of the ◊sea.

mink carnivorous mammal of the weasel family, usually found in or near water. There are two species, *Mustela vison*, the mink of North America (used in fur farms), and the Eurasian mink *lustela lutreola*. Up to 50 cm/1.7 ft, excluding their bushy tails which add 20 cm/8 in, they produce an annual litter of six in their riverbank burrows. The demand for their rich brown fur led to the establishment from the 1930s of mink ranches, and production of varying shades. 'Escapees' become destructive pests.

Minneapolis /ˌmɪniˈæpəlɪs/ industrial city in Minnesota, USA, forming with St ◊Paul the Twin Cities area; population (1980) 371,000. The world's most powerful computers (Cray 2 supercomputer 1985) are built here: used for long-range weather forecasting, spacecraft design, code-breaking. The city centre is glass-covered against the difficult climate; there is an arts institute, symphony orchestra, Minnesota University, and Tyrone ◊Guthrie theatre.

Minnesinger one of the German lyric poets of the 12th and 13th centuries, who in their songs dealt mainly with the theme of courtly love without revealing the identity of the object of their affections. Among the best-known Minnesingers were Dietmar von Aist, Friedrich von Hausen, Heinrich von Morungen, Reinmar, and especially Walther von der Vogelweide.

Minnesota /ˌmɪnɪˈsəʊtə/ Midwest state of the USA; North Star or Gopher State
area 217,735 sq km/84,068 sq mi
capital St Paul
towns Minneapolis, Duluth
features sources of the Red, St Lawrence, and Mississippi rivers; Minnehaha Falls at Minneapolis; Mayo Clinic at Rochester
products cereals, potatoes, livestock products; pulpwood; iron ore (60% of US output); farm and other machinery
population (1983) 4,145,500
famous people F Scott Fitzgerald, Sinclair Lewis, William and Charles Mayo
history the first Europeans to explore were French fur traders in the 17th century; part was ceded to Britain in 1763, and part passed to the

---

MINERALS
Major Economic Minerals and their Sources

Major Metals	Minor Metals	Fuels	Chemicals	Miscellaneous
Iron	Nickel	Coal	Sulphur	Talc
Hematite	*Pentlandite*	Oil	*Pyrites*	*Talc*
Magnetite	Chrome	Gas	*Anhydrite*	Mica
Limotite	*Chromite*		*Native Sulphur*	*Muscivite*
Aluminium	Tin		Salt	*Biotite*
Bauxite	*Cassiterite*		*Halite*	Asbestos
Copper	Tungsten		Potash	*Chrysotile*
Calcocite	*Wolframite*		*Sylvite*	Kaolin
Chalcopyrite	Titanium		Phosphate	*Kaolinite*
Zinc	*Rutile*		*Apatite*	Diamond
Sphalerite	*Ilmenite*			*Diamond*
Calamine	Silver		mineral = roman	
Lead	*Argenite*		source = *italic*	
Galena				

---

processing. Ore is seldom in a fit state to be processed when it is mined. It often contains much unwanted rock and dirt. So first it is usually crushed into a uniform size, and then separated from the dirt, or *gangue*. This may be done magnetically (with some iron ores), or by washing (with gold), by treatment with chemicals (copper ores), and by ◊flotation.

mineralogy the study of minerals. The classification of minerals is chiefly based on their chemical constitution: metallic, ionic, and molecular. In addition, their crystallographic and physical characters, their mode of formation and occurrence form part of the study. In the case of minerals of economic importance a knowledge of mining and metallurgy is also needed.

mineral oil oil obtained from mineral sources, for example coal, petroleum, as distinct from those obtained from vegetable or animal sources.

mineral water water with mineral constituents gathered from the rocks over which it flows and classified by these minerals into earthy, brine, and oil mineral waters. Many people believe that mineral waters have curative powers, the types of these medicinal waters being: alkaline (Vichy), bitter (Seidlitz), salt (Droitwich), earthy (Bath), sulphurous (Aachen), and special varieties, such as barium (Harrogate). The name mineral water is also applied to prepared drinks charged with carbon dioxide.

miniature painting the art of painting on a very small scale, which originated in the tiny illustrations in medieval manuscripts: Latin *miniare* 'to paint with minium' (a vermilion colour). It was practised in Persia and India in the medieval period. Modern miniatures, in the sense of small portraits, originated in the 16th century with ◊Holbein the Younger. The first English miniaturist was Nicholas ◊Hilliard. Later English artists include: Samuel Cooper, Isaac Oliver, Richard ◊Cosway, George ◊Engleheart; in France Jean (1486–1541) and François Clouet (c. 1522–72); in Spain ◊Goya, and in the USA C W ◊Peale.

minicomputer a computer whose size and processing power are between those of a ◊mainframe and a ◊microcomputer. Minicomputers are often found in medium-sized businesses, or university departments handling ◊database or other commercial programs, or running scientific or graphical applications that require lots of numerical computation.

minimalism term used in the arts from the 1960s to mean the reduction of creative self-expression to a minimum. In painting, using simple geometrical shapes and colours; in music, not being committed to anything beyond the particular note or interval of silence being experienced at the moment.

minimum lending rate rate of ◊interest at which the central bank lends to the money

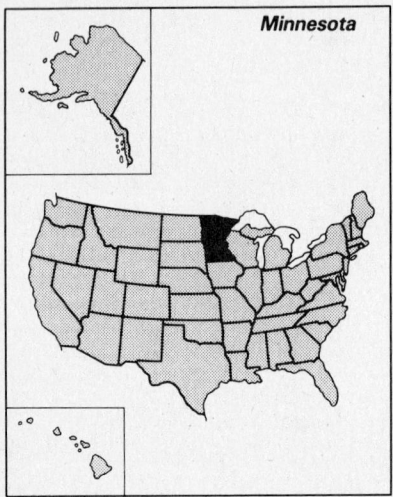

Minnesota

USA under the Louisiana Purchase in 1803; it became a state in 1858.

minnow abundant small fish *Phoxinus phoxinus* of the carp family found in steams and ponds in Europe and Asia. It is an important food for many predators.

Minoan civilization Bronze Age civilization on the Aegean island of Crete. The name is derived from Minos, reputed to be the son of the god Zeus, and the most famous of the legendary kings of Crete. No palaeolithic remains have yet been found in Crete, but in the Neolithic Age some centuries before 3000 BC the island was inhabited by people coming probably from SW Asia Minor, and akin to the early Bronze Age inhabitants of the Greek mainland. With the opening of the Bronze Age, c. 3000 BC, the Minoan culture proper begins. This is divided into three main periods: Early Minoan, c. 3000–2200 BC, Middle Minoan, c. 2200–1580 BC; and Late Minoan, c. 1580–1100 BC. Each period is marked by cultural advances in copper and bronze weapons, pottery of increasingly intricate design, fresco-painting, and the construction of palaces (notably at Knossos, Phaistos, and Mallia), and of fine houses. About 1400 BC, in the late Minoan Period, the civilization was suddenly destroyed by earthquake or war. A partial revival continued till about 1100. In religion the Minoans seem to have worshipped principally a great mother goddess with whom was associated a young male god. The tales of Greek mythology about Rhea, the mother of Zeus, and the birth of Zeus himself in a Cretan cave seem to be based on Minoan religion. The Minoan language was deciphered by Michael ◊Ventris from tablets written in Linear B script.

minor the legal term for those under the age of majority. Under the Family Law Reform Act (1969) for England and Wales the age of majority in civil law was reduced to 18 from 21, and those under age are described as minors instead of infants. The act legalized marriage without parental consent, and the making of a valid will after the age of 18 (both already possible in Scotland), and enabled anyone over

16 to give valid consent to personal medical treatment. In the USA and some European countries the age of majority is also 18.

Minorca /mɪˈnɔːkə/ second largest of the ◊Balearic Islands in the Mediterranean
area 702 sq k/271 sq mi
towns Mahon
population (1985) 55,500.

Minos /ˈmaɪnɒs/ in Greek mythology, a king of Crete (son of ◊Zeus and ◊Europa).

Minotaur /ˈmaɪnətɔː/ in Greek mythology, a monster, half man-half bull, offspring of Pasiphaë, wife of King Minos of Crete, and a bull. It lived in the labyrinth at ◊Knossos and its victims were seven girls and seven youths, sent in annual tribute by Athens, until ◊Theseus slew it, with the aid of Ariadne, the daughter of Minos.

Minsk /mɪnsk/ industrial city (machinery, textiles, leather; centre of the Soviet computer industry) and capital of the Byelorussian Republic, USSR; has Byelorussian state university; population (1985) 1,472,000.
history dating back to the 11th century and in turn held by Lithuania, Poland, Sweden, and Russia, Minsk was destroyed by Napoleon in 1812 and the Germans in 1944.

minster /ˈmɪnstə/ originally, a monastery, and in this sense often preserved in place names, such as Westminster; later the word was also applied to the church attached to a monastery, for example, York Minster.

mint in economics, place where money is coined by government authority. The Royal Mint is the government department which manufactures all British coins and also distinctive coinages, official medals and seals for the Commonwealth and foreign countries. For centuries in the Tower of London, the Royal Mint was housed in a building on Tower Hill from 1810 until the new Royal Mint was opened at Llantrisant, near Cardiff, Mid Glamorgan, 1968. The nominal head is the Master Worker and Warden, who is the Chancellor of the Exchequer, but the actual chief is the Deputy Master and Comptroller, a permanent civil servant. The equivalent in the USA is the Bureau of the Mint.

mint in botany, aromatic plant genus *Mentha* in the family Labiatae, widely distributed in temperate regions. The plants have square stems and creeping rootstocks, and the flowers grow in a terminal spike, usually pink or purplish. *Garden mint Mentha spicata* and *peppermint Mentha X piperita*) are the best-known.

Mintoff /ˈmɪntɒf/ Dom (Dominic) 1916– . Labour prime minister of Malta 1971–84, violently intolerant of opposition. He negotiated the removal of British and other foreign military bases 1971–79, and made treaties with Libya.

Minton /ˈmɪntən/ Thomas 1765–1836. British potter. He at first worked under Spode, but in 1789 established himself at Stoke-on-Trent as engraver of designs (he was the first to devise the 'willow pattern') and in 1793 founded a pottery there producing high quality bone china including much tableware.

minuet European courtly dance of the 17th century, later used with the trio as the third movement in a classical symphony.

minuteman a US three-stage inter-continental ballistic missile; originally the term was used for the armed citizens who agreed to act 'in a minute' before the American War of Independence. The name minutemen was also adopted in 1959 by a right-wing organization established by Robert DePugh, a Missouri manufacturer, in case of a Communist invasion or uprising. The New York police seized quantities of arms in 1966, and DePugh was imprisoned.

Miocene the fourth division of the ◊Tertiary period of geological time between 22.5 and 5 million years ago. The name means 'middle recent'. At this time the grasslands spread over much of the continents, and hoofed mammals became numerous.

Miquelon Islands /ˈmiːkəlɒn/ small group of islands off the S coast of Newfoundland which with St ◊Pierre form a French overseas *département*
area 216 sq km/83 sq mi
products cod; silver fox and mink are bred
population (with St Pierre, 1982) 6,045.

Mir (Russian 'peace') series of Soviet space stations, first launched on 20 Feb, 1986; an improved version of the earlier ◊Salyut. Mir contains six docking ports, so that smaller modules can be attached to it in orbit for scientific and technical experiments. Mir weighs about 20 tonnes, is approximately 13.5 m/49 ft long, and has a maximum diameter of 4.15 m/15 ft. In Dec 1987 it became the first permanently manned space station.

Mirabeau /ˈmɪrəbəʊ/ Honoré Gabriel Riqueti 1749–1791. French politician. From a noble Provençal family, he had a stormy career before the Revolution, during which he was three times imprisoned, and passed several years in exile. In 1789 he was elected to the States General as a representative of the third estate. His eloquence won him the leadership of the National Assembly; nevertheless, he was out of sympathy with the majority of the deputies, whom he regarded as mere theoreticians, his own aim being to establish a parliamentary monarchy on the English model. From May 1790 he secretly acted as political adviser to the king.

miracle an event which cannot be explained by the known laws of nature and which is therefore attributed to divine intervention.

miracle play medieval religious drama based on the Bible or saints' lives, which was performed on church festivals, and reached its hight in Europe in the 15th and 16th centuries. Separate episodes were performed by the various guilds of the towns on mobile stages, and in some instances, for example, the Wakefield, York, and Chester plays, almost complete cycles survive. See also ◊morality play.

Mirandola Italian 15th century philosopher. See ◊Pico della Mirandola.

Miró /mɪˈrəʊ/ Joan 1893–1983. Spanish painter, born at Barcelona. He was, with ◊Dali, a founder of ◊Surrealism. His pictures are characterized by spindly lines, blobs and primary colours, for example *Still Life with an Old Shoe* and *Dog Barking at the Moon*. He designed sets for the ballet director Diaghilev. A ceramic wall

Mirabeau As leader of the National Assembly, Honoré Gabriel Mirabeau sought to remodel rather than overthrow the French monarchy.

decoration by Miró is in the UNESCO building, Paris 1958.

Mirren /'mɪrən/ Helen 1946– . British actress, whose stage roles include Lady Macbeth; films include *The Long Good Friday* 1981.

mirror any polished surface that reflects light; often made from 'silvered' (in practice, a coating of mercury alloy) glass. A plane (flat) mirror produces a same-size, erect 'virtual' image located behind the mirror at the same distance from it as the object is in front of it; that is, the light rays appear to come from behind the mirror but do not actually do so. A spherical concave mirror produces a reduced, inverted real image (an image in which the rays of light pass through it) in front or an enlarged, erect virtual image behind it (as with a shaving mirror), depending on how close the object is to the mirror. A spherical convex mirror produces a reduced, erect virtual image behind it (as with a car's rear-view mirror). The ◊focal length *f* of a spherical mirror is half the radius of curvature; it is related to the image distance *v* and object distance *u* by the equation $1/v + 1/u = 1/f$.

Mirzapur /,mɪrzə'pʊə/ city of Uttar Pradesh, Republic of India, on the river Ganges; a grain and cotton market, with bathing sites and temples on the river; population (1981) 127,785.

miscarriage spontaneous expulsion of a foetus from the womb before it is capable of independent survival. See under ◊abortion.

misdemeanour in English law, an offence for which the penalties are greater than for a ◊felony, although the distinction is not always clear. In the USA, a misdemeanour is defined as an offence punishable only by a fine or short term in prison, while a felony carries a term of imprisonment of a year or more.

misericord or *miserere* in architecture, a bracket on the under-side of a hinged seat of the choir stalls in a church, used as a rest for a priest

when standing during long services. Misericords are often decorated with carvings.

Mishima /'mɪʃɪmə/ Yukio 1925–1970. Japanese novelist, whose work often deals with sexual desire and perversion, as in *Confessions of a Mask* 1949, and *The Temple of the Golden Pavilion* 1956. He committed hara-kiri (ritual suicide) as a demonstration against the corruption of the nation and the loss of the samurai warrior tradition.

Mishima Japanese novelist Yukio Mishima, holding the samurai sword with which he committed hara-kiri.

Mishna /'mɪʃnə/ a commentary on written Hebrew law, consisting of discussions between rabbis and handed down orally from their inception in 70 AD until about 200, when with the Gemara, the discussions in schools of Palestine and Babylon on law, it was committed to writing to form the Talmud.

Miskito /mɪ'kiːyəu/ American Indian people of Central America, living mainly in the area which is now ◊Nicaragua.

Miskolc /'mɪʃkɒlts/ industrial city (textiles, furniture, paper) in Hungary, 145 km/90 mi NE of Budapest; population (1985) 212,000.

Misr /'mɪsrə/ Egyptian name for ◊Egypt and for ◊Cairo.

misrelated participle see ◊participle.

missal in the Roman Catholic Church, a service-book containing the complete office of Mass for the entire year. A simplified missal in the vernacular was introduced 1969 (obligatory from 1971). It was the first major reform since 1570.

missile rocket-propelled weapon, which may be nuclear-armed (see ◊nuclear warfare). First wartime use of a long-range missile was against England in World War II, the jet-powered German V1 (*Vergeltungswaffe*, 'Revenge Weapon' 1 or Flying Bomb), a monoplane (wingspan about 6 m/18 ft, length about 8.5 m/26 ft); and the first rocket-propelled missile

(with a pre-set guidance system) the German V2; see ◊air raid. A longer range version of the latter, capable of reaching New York, was under preparation. After the war captured V2 material became the basis of the space race in both the USSR and USA (see von ◊Braun). In the ◊Falklands conflict non-nuclear *sea-skimming missiles* were used (the French *Exocet*) against British ships by the Argentines; more recent types have a 95 km/60 mi range, home on target by radar (a digital computer aboard allows attack beyond the radar horizon of the launching aircraft), and can select the 'prime target' among a group of ships despite electronic decoy counter measures.

mission an organized attempt to spread a particular religion. Throughout its history Christianity has been the most influential missionary religion. During its first three centuries, Christianity was spread throughout the Roman Empire by missionaries, of whom the best known was Paul, and later beyond the Empire, by men such as Gregory the Illuminator, Ulfilas, Chrysostom, Patrick, and Martin of Tours. In addition to the missionaries of medieval times, such as Columba, Aidan, Boniface and Cyril, there were the efforts of the Benedictine, Dominican and Franciscan orders. The explorations of the Renaissance opened new fields, and the foundation of the Jesuit order supplied such missionaries as Francis Xavier (1506–52). Gradually the Protestant churches also showed an interest in missions, the pioneer being the Society for Promoting Christian Knowledge (SPCK), founded in 1698, and after 1731 the continental Moravians. In the late 18th and early 19th centuries many Protestant missionary societies were founded, including the Baptist (1792), the London (1795), and the Church (1799). Efforts were maintained throughout the century, notably in the foundation of the China Inland Mission by J H Taylor (1865), but renewed impetus came from the career of David Livingstone, and since the World Missionary Conference at Edinburgh in 1910 there has been growing international co-operation. The 19th century also saw a growth of activity on the part of the Roman Catholic and Eastern Orthodox churches.

Islam has also traditionally had a missionary role. It became in the 20th century the second religion in Europe, and made increasing numbers of converts in Africa and the USA, particularly among blacks, as in the ◊Black Muslim movement.

Missionary activity, particularly in the Third World, has in recent years frequently been criticized for its political, economic, and cultural effects on indigenous peoples.

Mississippi /,mɪsɪ'sɪpi/ river in the USA; with the Missouri, considered by some the longest river in the world: length of Mississippi proper 3,779 km/2,348 mi; of the Missouri and the Lower Mississippi 5,863 km/3,643 mi. It is the main arm of the great river system draining the USA between the Appalachian and the Rocky mountains. The Mississippi rises in the lake region of N Minnesota, with St Anthony Falls at Minneapolis. Below the tributaries

Minnesota, Wisconsin, Des Moines, and Illinois, the confluence of the Missouri and Mississippi occurs at St Louis. The river turns at the Ohio junction, passing Memphis, and takes in the St Francis, Arkansas, Yazoo, and Red tributaries before reaching its delta on the Gulf of Mexico beyond New Orleans.

The Mississippi was first recorded in 1541 by the Spanish explorer Hernando de Soto, who reached a point near present-day Memphis.

Mississippi/Missouri Rivers

Mississippi /ˌmɪsɪ'sɪpi/ Southern state of the USA; nicknamed Magnolia State
area 123,584 sq km/47,716 sq mi
capital Jackson
towns Biloxi
features Mississippi river; Vicksburg National Military Park (Civil War site)
products cotton, sweet potatoes, sugar, rice; canned sea food at Biloxi; timber and pulp; oil and natural gas, chemicals
population (1983) 2,587,000
famous people William Faulkner, Elvis Presley, Eudora Welty
history De Soto was the first European to reach the Mississippi in 1540; the area was subsequently settled in turn by French, English, and Spanish until passing under American control in 1798; it became a state in 1870.

Mississippian American term for the Lower ◊Carboniferous period of geological time, named after the state of Mississippi.

Missolonghi /ˌmɪsə'lɒŋgi/ town in W Greece, on the N shore of the Gulf of Patras; several times under siege by the Turks in the wars of 1822–26, it was the place of the British poet Byron's death.

Missouri /mɪ'zuəri/ border state of the USA; nicknamed Show Me State
area 180,445 sq km/69,674 sq mi
capital Jefferson City
towns St Louis, Kansas City, Springfield, Independence
features Mississippi and Missouri rivers; Pony Express Museum at St Joseph; birthplace of Jesse James; Mark Twain State Park; Harry S Truman Library at Independence
products meat and other processed food; aerospace, transport equipment; lead, clay, coal
population (1982) 4,951,000
famous people T S Eliot, Joseph Pulitzer, Mark Twain

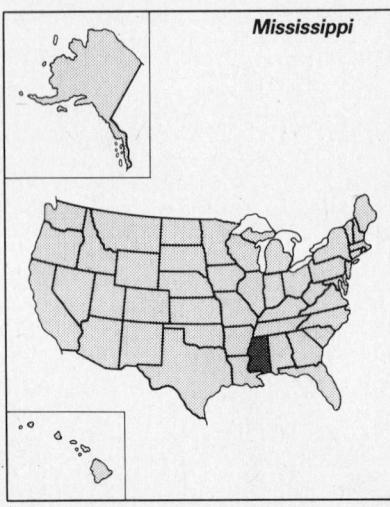

Mississippi

history explored by de Soto in 1541; acquired under the ◊Louisiana Purchase; became a state in 1821.

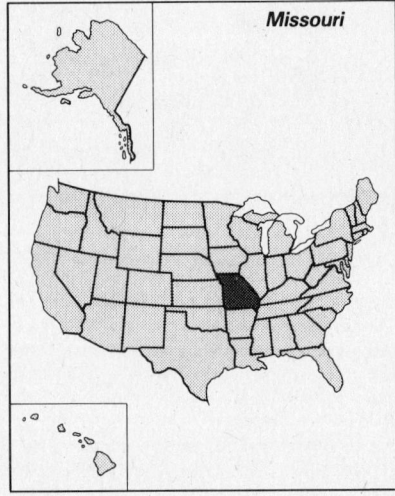

Missouri

Missouri River /mɪ'zuəri/ river in central USA, a tributary of the ◊Mississippi which it joins at St Louis.

Mistinguett /ˌmiːstæŋ'get/ stage name of Jeanne Bourgeois 1873–1956. French actress and dancer. A leading music-hall artist in Paris from 1899, she also appeared in revue at the Folies-Bergère, Casino de Paris, and Moulin Rouge. She was famous for the song 'Mon Homme' and her partnership with Maurice Chevalier.

mistletoe parasitic European evergreen unisexual plant *Viscum album* which occurs on trees as a branched bush, with translucent white berries, and is used as a Christmas decoration.

mistral /mɪs'trɑːl/ a cold, dry, northerly wind that occasionally blows during the winter on the Mediterranean coast of France. It has been known to reach a velocity of 145 kph/90 mph.

Mistral /mɪs'trɑːl/ Gabriela, pen name of Lucila Godoy Alcayaga 1889–1957. Chilean poet, best known for her *Sonnets of Death* 1915; Nobel Prize for Literature 1945.

Mitchell /'mɪtʃəl/ Juliet 1940– . British psychoanalyst and writer. She was one of the first to use Marxist theory to try to explain the reasons behind women's oppression, as in *Women's Estate* 1971 and *Psychoanalysis and Feminism* 1974.

Mitchell /'mɪtʃəl/ Margaret 1900–1949. American novelist, born in Atlanta, Georgia. Her one book *Gone With the Wind* 1936, a story of the American Civil War, was the first modern bestseller.

Mitchell /'mɪtʃəl/ Peter 1920– . British chemist. He received a Nobel prize in 1978 for work on the conservation of energy by plants during respiration and ◊photosynthesis.

Mitchell /'mɪtʃəl/ R(eginald) J(oseph) 1895–1937. British aircraft designer, whose Spitfire fighter was a major factor in winning the Battle of ◊Britain.

mite minute animal belonging to the Arachnida, allied to spiders. Mites may be free living scavengers or predators. Some are parasitic, such as the *itch mite Sarcoptes scabiei* which burrows in human skin, or the *red mite Dermanyssus gallinae* which sucks blood from poultry and other birds.

Mitford sisters the six daughters of Lord Redesdale, including:
Nancy (1904–73), author of the semi-autobiographical *The Pursuit of Love* 1945 and *Love in a Cold Climate* 1949, and editor and part author of *Noblesse Oblige* 1956 elucidating 'U' (upper-class) and 'Non-U' behaviour;
Jessica (1917–), author of the auto-biographical *Hons and Rebels* 1960 and *The American Way of Death* 1963;
Unity (1914–48), who became an admirer of Hitler; and
Diana (1910–) who married Oswald ◊Mosley.

Mithraism the ancient Persian worship of ◊Mithras.

Mithras /'mɪθræs/ in Persian mythology, the god of light.
Mithras represented the power of goodness, and promised his followers compensation for present evil after death. His cult was introduced into the Roman Empire in 68 BC, rapidly developed, particularly among soldiers, and by the 3rd century AD rivalled Christianity in strength. Mithras was said to have captured and killed the sacred bull, from whose blood all life sprang, and a bath in the blood of a sacrificed bull formed part of the initiation ceremeony.

Mithridates VI /ˌmɪθrɪ'deɪtiːz/ the Great 132–63 BC. King of Pontus (NE Asia Minor, on the Black Sea) from 120 BC. He massacred 80,000 Romans in over-running the rest of Asia Minor, and went on to invade Greece. He was successively defeated by ◊Sulla in the First Mithridatic War 88–84; by ◊Lucullus in the Second 83–81; and by ◊Pompey in the Third 74–64. He was killed by a soldier at his own order rather than surrender to captivity.

Mitilíni /ˌmɪti'liːni/ modern Greek name of ◊Mytilene, town on the island of Lesvos.

Mithras Wearing a Phrygian cap, this marble head was found in the excavation of London's temple of Mithras.

mitochondrion rod-like or spherical body within the ◊eukaryotic cell, containing enzymes which perform respiration (that is, they break up organic compounds to release energy). They are thought to be derived from free-living bacteria, which, at a very early stage in the history of life, invaded larger cells and took up a ◊symbiotic way of life there. Each still contains its own small loop of ◊DNA, and new mitochondria arise by division of existing mitochondria.

mitosis in biology, the process of cell division. The genetic material of ◊eukaryotic cells is carried on a number of ◊chromosomes, and a mechanism is needed to control their movements during cell division so that both new cells get a full set. This is provided by a system of protein tubules, known as the spindle, which organizes the chromosomes into position in the middle of the cell before they replicate. The spindle then controls the separation of the daughter chromosomes as the cell divides in two.

mitre in the Christian Church, the head-dress worn by bishops, cardinals, and mitred abbots at solemn services. There are mitres of many different shapes, but in the Western Church it usually takes the form of a tall cleft-capital. The mitre worn by the Pope is called a tiara.

Mitterrand /ˌmiːtəˈrɒn/ François 1916– . French socialist politician, founder of the French Socialist Party (PS) in 1971, president from 1981. Mitterrand studied law and politics in Paris. During World War II he was prominent in the Resistance. He entered the National Assembly as a centre-left deputy for Nièvre and held ministerial posts in 11 governments between 1947 and 1958. Opposed to ◊de Gaulle's creation of the Fifth Republic in 1958, he established the centre-left anti-Gaullist Federation of the Left in the 1960s. He became leader of the new Socialist Party in 1971. An electoral union with the Communist Party 1972–77 established PS as the most popular party in France.

Mitterrand was elected president in 1981. His programme of reform was hampered by deteriorating economic conditions after 1983 and in 1985 his introduction of proportional representation was allegedly to weaken the growing opposition from left and right. When the Socialists lost their majority in Mar 1986, Mitterrand was compelled to work with a right-wing prime minister, ◊Chirac.

Mitterrand After two unsuccessful attempts, François Mitterrand gained the French presidency in 1981.

Mitylene /ˌmɪtɪˈliːni/ alternative spelling of ◊Mytilene, Greek city on the island of Lesvos.

mixed ability teaching the practice of teaching children of all abilities in a single class. Mixed ability teaching is normal practice in British primary schools but most secondary schools begin to divide children according to ability, either in sets or, more rarely, streams, as they approach public examinations at 16.

Mizoram /ˌmaɪzəˈræm/ a state of India formed in 1972 from the Mizo Hill district of Assam; area 21,230 sq km/8,200 sq mi; population (1981) 493,755. Rebels carried on a

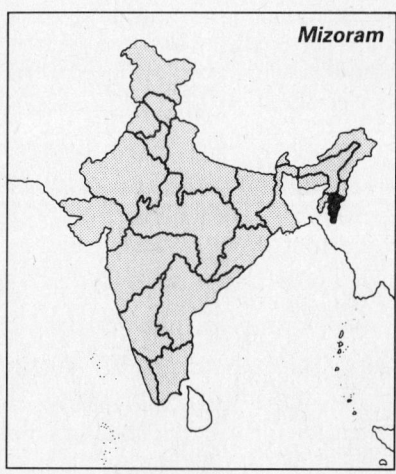

Mizoram

guerrilla war 1966–76, but in 1976 acknowledged Mizoram as an integral part of India.

MKS system system of units in which the base units metre, kilogram, second, replace the centimetre, gram, second of the ◊CGS system, which it now supersedes. Its adoption has been advocated since 1901, since it simplifies the incorporation of the electrical units into the metric system, and it was included in ◊SI. For application to electrical and magnetic phenomena the ampere is added, the reference then being to the MKSA system.

Mmabatho /məˈbɑːtəʊ/ capital of ◊Bophuthatswana, South Africa.

mmHg a unit of pressure. Defined as the pressure exerted under gravity by a height of 1 millimetre of mercury, or 133,322 pascals. It is used in meteorology and in the measurement of blood pressure.

moa type of extinct bird, once found in New Zealand. They varied from 0.5–3.5 m/2–12 ft, with strong limbs, a long neck, and no wings. They occurred as far back as the Pliocene age, and survived to the 1700s. The Maoris used them as food, but the use of European firearms enabled them to be killed in too large numbers.

Moab /ˈməʊæb/ an ancient country situated E of the S part of the river Jordan and the Dead Sea, in the area of modern Jordan. The region is hilly and in parts is very fertile; cereals and vines were formerly cultivated. The inhabitants were closely akin to the Hebrews in culture, language, and religion, but were often at war with them, as recorded in the Old Testament. Moab eventually fell to Arabian tribes. The Moabite Stone, discovered in 1868 at Dhiban, dates from the 9th century BC, and records the rising of Mesha, king of Moab, against Israel.

Mobile /məʊˈbiːl/ industrial city (meat-packing, paper, cement, clothing, chemicals) and only seaport in Alabama, USA; population (1980) 443,500. Founded 1702 by the French a little to the N of the present city, Mobile was capital of the French colony of Louisiana until 1763, then British until 1780, Spanish to 1813.

Mobutu /məˈbuːtuː/ Seso-Seko-Kuku-Ngbeandu-Wa-Za-Banga 1930– . Zaïrean general who assumed the presidency by coup in 1965, and created a unitary state under his centralized government. He abolished secret voting in elections in 1976 in favour of a system of acclamation at mass rallies.

Mobutu The harshness of some of President Mobutu's policies attracted widespread international criticism of Zaïre, but in 1983 amnesty was offered to all political exiles. Mobutu was re-elected for a third term in 1984.

Mobutu Sese Seko Lake /mə'buːtu: 'seseɪ 'sekəʊ/ lake on the border of Uganda and Zaïre in the Great ◊Rift Valley; area 4,275 sq km/1,650 sq mi. The first European to see it was the British explorer Sir Samuel ◊Baker, who named it Lake Albert after the Prince Consort. It was renamed in 1973 by Zaïre's president Mobutu after himself.

Moçambique /ˌmuːsəm'biːkə/ the Portuguese name for ◊Mozambique.

mocking bird American bird *Mimus polyglottos*, related to the thrushes, which has remarkable powers of mimicry; it is brownish grey, with white markings on the black wings and tail.

mock orange deciduous shrub of genus *Philadelphus*, family Philadelphaceae, especially *Philadelphus coronarius* which has white, strongly scented flowers, resembling those of the orange; it is sometimes referred to as ◊syringa.

mod a youth movement that originated in London and Brighton in the early 1960s around the French view of the English; revived in the late 1970s. Mods were fashion-conscious, speedy, and upwardly mobile; they favoured scooters and soul music.

Model Parliament English ◊parliament, set up 1295 by Edward I; it was the first to include representatives from outside the clergy and aristocracy, and was established because Edward needed the support of the whole country against his opponents: Wales, France, and Scotland. His sole aim was to raise money for defence, and the parliament did not pass any legislation.

The parliament comprised archbishops, bishops, abbots, earls, and barons (all summoned by special writ, and forming the basis of the modern House of Lords); also present were the lower clergy (heads of chapters, archdeacons, two clergymen from each diocese, and one from each cathedral) and representatives of the shires, cities, and boroughs (two knights from every shire, two representatives from each city, and two burghers from each borough).

modem (*mo*dulator-*dem*odulator) in computing, an electronic device for converting digital (discrete) signals from a computer into analogue (continuous) signals on a telecommunications network and vice versa.

Modena /'mɒdɪnə/ city in Emilia, Italy, capital of the province of Modena, 37 km/23 mi NW of Bologna; population (1984) 178,500. Fine buildings include the 12th-century cathedral, the 17th-century ducal palace, and the university 1683, noted for its medical and legal faculties.

Moderator in the Church of ◊Scotland, the minister chosen to act as president of the annual General Assembly.

moderator in a nuclear reactor, the material used to reduce the energy, and hence the speed, of fast neutrons, so far as possible without capturing them. Slow neutrons are much more likely to cause ◊fission in a uranium-235 nucleus than to be captured in a U-238 (non-fissile uranium) nucleus. By using a moderator, a reactor can thus be made to work with fuel containing only a small proportion of U-235.

Modernism a liberal church movement from about 1910, which attempts to reconsider Christian beliefs in the light of modern scientific theories and historical methods without abandoning the essential doctrines. Modernism was condemned by Pope Pius X in 1907.

modernism a general term used to describe various tendencies in the arts in the first three-quarters of the 20th century. It refers mainly to a conscious attempt to break away from the artistic traditions of the past, and especially of the 19th century, and also to a concern with form and the exploration of technique as opposed to content and narrative. In the visual arts, direct representationalism gave way to abstraction (see under ◊abstract art); in literature, writers experimented with alternatives to orthodox sequential story-telling, such as ◊stream-of-consciousness; in music, the traditional concept of key was challenged by ◊atonality; and in architecture, functionalism ousted decorativeness as a central objective. Critics of modernism have found in it an austerity that is seen as dehumanizing; modernism as a movement is followed by ◊post-modernism.

Modern Jazz Quartet, the US jazz group specializing in group improvisation, formed 1952, led by pianist John Lewis (1920–), with Milt Jackson (1923–) on vibraphone, bass player Percy Heath (1923–), and as drummer first Kenny Clarke and later Connie Kay; disbanded 1974 although reunited in the 1980s for touring. Noted for elegance and mastery of form, they were sometimes criticized for being too 'classical'.

Modigliani /ˌmɒdɪl'jɑːni/ Amedeo 1884–1920. Italian artist. Born in Livorno, he

settled in Paris in 1906, became interested in primitive art, and in 1909 began to produce sculptures showing the influence of African masks. His strangely elongated portraits have a mournful attraction.

modular course in education, a course, usually leading to a recognized qualification, which is divided into short and often optional units which are assessed as they are completed.

modulation in ◊radio, the intermittent change of frequency, or amplitude, of a radio carrier wave, in accordance with the audio-frequency speaking voice, music, or other signal being transmitted.

modulation in music, movement from one ◊key to another in harmony.

module in construction, a part which governs the form of the rest, for example Japanese room sizes are traditionally governed by multiples of standard tatami floor mats; modern prefabricated buildings are mass-produced in a similar way; and in space the components of a spacecraft are designed in co-ordination, for example for the Moon landings the craft comprised a command module (for working, eating, sleeping), service module (electricity generators, oxygen supplies, manoeuvring rocket), and lunar module (to land and return the astronauts).

module in computing, a small, self-contained part of a program. When designing a computer program, a programmer often divides the tasks the computer will be called upon to perform into small units, and writes and tests a program for each. When all these units, or modules, are free of mistakes (bugs), the programmer links them together to make the complete program.

modulus in mathematics, of a ◊real number, modulus is its positive value irrespective of its sign, indicated by a pair of vertical lines. Thus |3| is 3; and |5| is 5. For a ◊complex number, the modulus is its distance to the origin when it is plotted on an ◊Argand diagram, and can be calculated (without plotting) by applying ◊Pythagoras' theorem. In general, the modulus of the complex number $a + b$ is $+\sqrt{(a^2 + b^2)}$.

Mogadishu /ˌmɒɡə'dɪʃuː/ capital and chief port of Somalia; population (1983) 600,000. It has a cathedral built 1925–28 and mosques dating back to the 13th century.

Mogilev /ˌmɒɡɪl'jɒf/ industrial city (tractors, clothing, furniture) in the Byelorussian Republic, USSR, 193 km/120 mi E of Minsk; population (1985) 343,000. It was annexed by Russia from Sweden in 1772.

Mogul emperors North Indian dynasty. They were descendants of ◊Tamerlane, the 14th century Mongol leader, and ruled till the last Mogul emperor was dethroned and imprisoned by the British in 1857; they included ◊Akbar and ◊Shah-Jehan.

Mohács /'məʊhɑːtʃ/ river port and town on the Danube, Hungary, site of the two Battles of ◊Mohács.

Mohács, Battle of /'məʊhɑːtʃ/ Austro-Hungarian defeat of the Turks 1687 which effectively marked the end of Turkish expansion into Europe. Also the site of an earlier Turkish victory in 1526.

mohair hair of the Angora goat. Fine, white, and lustrous, the fibre is manufactured into fabric. Commercial mohair is now obtained from cross-bred animals, pure-bred supplies being insufficient.

Mohamad /mə'hæməd/ Mahathir bin 1925– . Prime minister of Malaysia from 1981 and leader of the United Malays' National Organization (UMNO). Mahathir bin Mohamad was elected to the House of Representatives in 1964 and gained the support of the dominant UMNO's radical youth wing as an advocate of economic help to *bumiputras* (ethnic Malays) and as a proponent of a more Islamic social policy. Dr Mahathir held a number of ministerial posts from 1974 before being appointed prime minister and UMNO leader in 1981. His 'look east' economic policy emulates Japanese industrialization.

Mohammed /məʊ'hæmɪd/ six sultans of Turkey, including: *Mohammed II* (1430–81), captured Constantinople in 1453 and conquered Greece. *Mohammed VI* (1861–1926), the last sultan, was deposed in 1922, and died in exile.

Mohammed /məʊ'hæmɪd/ alternative form of ▷Muhammad, founder of ▷Islam.

Mohammedanism another name for ▷Islam, the religion founded by ▷Muhammad.

Mohawk N American Indian nation, part of the ▷Iroquois confederation.

Mohenjo Daro /mə'hendʒəʊ 'dɑːrəʊ/ site of a city of about 2500–1600 BC, on the lower Indus, Pakistan, where excavations from the 1920s have revealed the ▷Indus Valley civilization.

Mohican and *Mohegan* two closely related N American Indian peoples, akin to the Algonquians, who formerly occupied Connecticut and the Hudson valley. James Fenimore ▷Cooper confused the two peoples.

Mohole US project for drilling a hole through the Earth's crust, so named from the ▷Mohorovičić discontinuity that marks the transition from crust to mantle. Initial tests were made in the Pacific in 1961, but the project was subsequently abandoned. The cores that were brought up illuminated the geological history of the Earth and aided the development of geophysics.

Moholy-Nagy /'məʊhɔɪ 'nɒdʒ/ Laszlo 1895–1946. American photographer. Through his illuminating theories and practical experiments in photography he had great influence on the photography of this century.

Mohorovičić /ˌmæʊhə'rəʊvɪtʃɪtʃ/ Andrija 1857–1936. Yugoslav discoverer in 1909 of the Mohorovičić discontinuity, or moho, which marks the transition from the Earth's ▷crust to the first inner layer or ▷mantle: the crust varies in thickness, from more than 50 km/30 mi to 5 km/3 mi, being thinnest beneath the oceans.

Mohs /məʊz/ Friedrich 1773–1839. German mineralogist, who in 1812 devised the scale (known by his name) of minerals classified in order of hardness.

Mohs scale scale of hardness for minerals (in ascending order of hardness): 1 talc; 2 gypsum; 3 calcite; 4 fluorite; 5 apatite; 6 feldspar; 7 quartz; 8 topaz; 9 corundum; 10 diamond. The scale is useful in mineral identification because any mineral will scratch any other mineral lower on the scale than itself, and similarly it will be scratched by any other mineral higher on the scale.

MOHS SCALE

Number	Defining mineral	Other substances compared
1	talc	
2	gypsum	2½ fingernail
3	calcite	3½ copper coin
4	fluorite	
5	apatite	5½ steel blade
6	orthoclase	5¾ glass
7	quartz	7 steel file
8	topaz	
9	corundum	
10	diamond	

The scale is not regular; diamond, at number 10, the hardest natural substance, is 90 times harder in absolute terms than corundum, number 9.

Moi /mɔɪ/ Daniel arap 1924– . Kenyan politician. A schoolmaster, he became minister of home affairs in 1964, vice-president in 1967, and in 1978 succeeded Kenyatta as president.

Moi Initially a teacher, the Kenyan politician Daniel arap Moi has been president since 1978.

Mojave Desert /məʊ'hɑːvi/ arid region in S California, USA, part of the Great Basin; area 38,500 sq km/15,000 sq mi.

Mokha /'məʊkə/ or *Mocha* seaport of N Yemen near the mouth of the Red Sea, once famed for its coffee exports. It has declined since the USSR built a new port near Hodeida. Population (1980) 8,000.

molasses the drainings from raw cane sugar; the term is commonly used as a synonym for treacle. Molasses from sugar cane produces rum in fermentation; that from beet sugar gives alcohol.

Mold /məʊld/ market town in ▷Clwyd, Wales; population 8,555 (1980). It is the administrative headquarters of Clwyd.

Moldavia /mɒl'deɪvɪən/ constituent republic of the Soviet Union from 1940
area 33,700 sq km/13,100 sq mi
capital Kishinev
features ▷Black Earth region
products wine, tobacco, canned goods
population 4 million, 65% Moldavians, a branch of the Romanian people, Ukrainian 14%, Russian 12%
language Moldavian, allied to Romanian
religion Russian Orthodox
recent history formed from part of the former Moldavian Republic of the USSR (within the Ukraine) and areas of Bessarabia ceded by Romania in 1940, except the area bordering the Black Sea (added to Ukraine SSR).

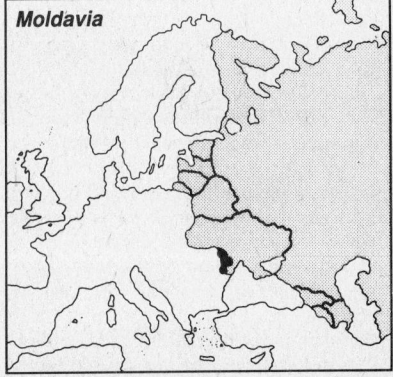

Moldavia

mole burrowing insectivorous mammal of the family Talpidae. The common mole of Europe *Talpa europaea* has a thick-set body about 18 cm/7 in with soft dark fur. Practically blind, it lives underground in circular grass-lined nests and excavates extensive tunnels in its search for worms and grubs, throwing up the earth at intervals in 'mole-hills'. The short muscular forelimbs and shovel-like feet are adapted for burrowing. Some members of the family are aquatic, such as the *Russian desman Desmana moschata*.

mole basic unit in the ▷SI system, unit symbol *mol*, indicating amount of substance. The mole is the amount of substance of a system which contains as many elementary entities as there are atoms in 0.012 kg of the ▷isotope carbon 12. The entities must be specified (whether atoms, molecules, ions, electrons, and so on).

mole a mechanical device for boring horizontal holes underground without the need for digging trenches. It is used for laying pipes and cables.

mole a person working subversively within an organization. The term, popularized in the novels of John Le Carré, originally meant a person who spends several years working for a government department or a company, establishing a reputation for trustworthiness, with the intention of ultimately betraying it by passing secret information to a rival or enemy. The term has come to be used more broadly for someone who gives out secret information in the public interest; in the UK, for example, it has been applied to Sarah Tisdall and Clive Ponting, civil servants who leaked government information to the press 1983–84.

molecular biology the study of the molecular basis of life, including the ◊biochemistry of molecules such as ◊DNA, ◊RNA and ◊proteins, and the structure and function of the various parts of living ◊cells.

molecular clock the use of rates of ◊mutation in genetic material to calculate the length of time since two related species diverged from each other during evolution. The method can be based on comparisons of the DNA itself, or comparisons of widely occurring proteins, such as haemoglobin. Since mutations are thought to occur at a constant rate, the length of time that must have elapsed in order to produce the difference between two species can be estimated. This information can be compared with the evidence obtained from ◊palaeontology to reconstruct evolutionary events.

molecule smallest particle of any substance that can exist free yet still exhibit all the chemical properties of the substance. Molecules are composed of ◊atoms ranging from one atom in, for example, a helium molecule to many thousands of atoms in the molecules of complex organic substances. The composition of the molecule is determined by the nature of the bonds, usually electric forces, which hold the atoms together.

According to the molecular or ◊kinetic theory of matter, molecules are in a state of constant motion, the extent of which depends on their temperature, and they exert forces on one another.

Molecules were inferrable from ◊Avogadro's hypothesis 1811, but only became generally accepted in 1860 when proposed by S Cannizzarro (1826–1910).

Molière /'mɒliɛə/ Pen name of French satiric playwright Jean Baptiste Poquelin 1622–1673. In 1643 he became one of the founders of the *Illustre Théâtre*, of which he was later the leading actor. He established his reputation with *Les Prêcieuses ridicules* 1659. This was followed by his satiric masterpieces, including *Tartuffe* 1664 (banned until 1697), *Le Misanthrope* 1666, *L'Avare* 1668, *Le Bourgeois gentilhomme* 1670, and *Le Malade imaginaire* 1673. Molière's comedies, based on the exposure of hypocrisy and cant in the church, medicine, and so on, exposed him to many attacks from his enemies (from which he was protected by Louis XIV) and mark a new departure in the French theatre away from reliance on classical Greek themes.

Molinos /məʊ'liːnɒs/ Miguel de 1640–1697. Spanish mystic. His doctrine, known as ◊quietism, puts particular emphasis on disinterested love and on the attainment of a state of spiritual repose as a means of approaching most closely to God.

molecule

covalent bonding

shared path of electron

proton proton

atoms of hydrogen sharing electrons

ionic bonding

7 electrons in outer ring   1 electron in outer ring

chlorine   sodium   chlorine   sodium

shared electron

Molière Molière died a day after performing the title role in his *Le Médecin malgré lui*.

Molise /mɒ'liːzeɪ/ region of S central Italy, chiefly agricultural; capital Campobasso; population (1984) 332,500.

mollusc invertebrate animal of the phylum Mollusca. The majority are marine animals, but some inhabit fresh water, and a few are terrestrial. They include shell-fish, snails, slugs, and cuttles. The body is soft, limbless, and cold-blooded. There is no internal skeleton, but most species have a hard shell covering the body. The shell takes a variety of forms, univalve (snail), bivalve (mussel), chambered (nautilus), and many other variations. In some cases, e.g. octopus and squid, the shell is internal. There is a fold of skin, the mantle, which covers the whole body or the back only, and which secretes the calcareous substance forming the shell. The lower ventral surface forms the locomotory organ, or foot. Molluscs vary in diet, the carnivorous species feeding chiefly upon other members of the class. Some are vegetarian. Reproduction is by means of eggs, and is sexual. Shell-fish (oysters, mussels, clams) are commercially valuable, especially when artificially bred and 'farmed'. The Romans, and in the 17th century, the Japanese, experimented with advanced methods, and raft culture of oysters is now widely practised. The cultivation of pearls, pioneered by Kokichi Mikimoto, began in the 1890s and became an important export industry after World War I.

mollusc This species of mollusc, the European cuttle, with ten 'arms' and tentacles neatly aligned in front of it, is the source of the pigment sepia, used by artists.

Molnár /'mɔʊlnɑː/ Ferenc 1878–1952. Hungarian novelist and playwright known for his play *Liliom* 1909, adapted as the musical *Carousel*.

MOLLUSCS: CLASSIFICATION

Phylum Mollusca

Class Monoplacophora	Primitive marine forms, including *Neopilina* (*2 species*)
Class Amphineura	(*1150 species*)
1 APLACOPHORA	Wormlike marine forms.
2 POLYPLACOPHORA	Chitons, coat-of-mail shells.
Class Gastropoda	Snail-like molluscs, with single or no shell (*90000 species*).
1 PROSOBRANCHIA	Limpets, winkles, whelks.
2 OPISTHOBRANCHIA	Seaslugs.
3 PULMONATA	Land and freshwater snails, slugs.
Class Scaphopoda	Tusk shells, marine burrowers (*350 species*).
Class Bivalvia	Molluscs with a double (two-valved) shell (*15,000 species*) Mussels, oysters, clams, cockles, scallops, tellins, razor shells, shipworms.
Class Cephalopoda	Molluscs with shell generally reduced, arms to capture prey and beak-like mouth. Body bilaterally symmetrical and nervous system well-developed (*750 species*). Squids, cuttlefish, octopuses, pearly nautilus, argonaut.

Moloch /'məʊlɒk/ or *Molech* in the Old Testament, a Phoenician deity worshipped at Jerusalem in the 7th century BC, to whom live children were sacrificed in fire.

Molokai /ˌməʊləˈkaɪ/ mountainous island of Hawaii state, USA, SE of Oahu
area 673 sq km/259 sq mi
features Kamakou 1,512 m/4,960 ft is the highest peak;
population (1980) 6,049.
history the island is famous as the site of a leper colony organized 1873–89 by Belgian missionary Joseph ◊De Veuster (Father Damien).

Molotov /'mɒlətɒf/ the former name (1940–62) for the port of ◊Perm in USSR.

Molotov /'mɒlətɒf/ Vyacheslav Mikhailovich. Assumed name of V M Skryabin 1890–1986. Soviet politician. He was chair of the Council of People's Commissars (prime minister) 1930–41. and foreign minister 1939–49, during which period he negotiated the non-aggression pact with Hitler, and again 1953–56. In 1957 he was one of the 'anti-party' group expelled from the government for Stalinist activities.

molotov cocktail home-made weapon consisting of a bottle of petrol fired by a wick. It was first used by resistance groups during World War II and was named after ◊Molotov.

Moltke /'mɒltkə/ Helmuth Carl Bernhard, Count von Moltke 1800–1891. Prussian general, was responsible for the Prussian strategy in the wars with Denmark 1863–64, Austria 1866, and France 1870–71. He was created a count in 1870 and a field marshal in 1871.

Moltke /'mɒltkə/ Helmuth Johannes Ludwig von Moltke 1848–1916. German general (nephew of Count von ◊Moltke), chief of the German general staff 1906–14. His use of General Schlieffen's Plan for a rapid victory on two fronts failed and he was superseded.

Moluccas /məʊ'lʌkəz/ another name for the ◊Maluku islands in Indonesia.

molybdenite molybdenum disulphide, MoS_2, the chief ore mineral of molybdenum. It possesses a hexagonal crystal structure, and has a metallic lustre resembling graphite.

molybdenum very brittle, malleable, white metallic element, an electric furnace product of ◊molybdenite and wulfenite, and one of many fission products from a nuclear reactor. Symbol Mo, atomic number 42, atomic weight 95.975. Discovered by Scheele in 1778, it has a melting point of 2,620°C, and is not found in the free state. Producing countries include the USA, Canada and Norway. Important in making specialized steels, it is also used for electrodes (since it is easily welded to soda and Pyrex glass, and to other metals), and for filaments (alloyed with tungsten) in thermionic valves. As an aid to lubrication, molybdenum disulphide (MoS_2) makes an outstanding reduction in surface friction between ferrous metals.

Mombasa /mɒm'bæsə/ industrial port (oil refining, cement) in Kenya (serving also Uganda and Tanzania), extending from Mombasa island to the mainland; population (1984) 481,000.

moment in physics and engineering, the product of a quantity and a distance. In particular the moment of a force about a point is the product of the force and the perpendicular distance from the point to the line of action of the force; it measures the turning effect or torque produced by the force.

moment of inertia in physics, of a rotating object, the sum of all the point masses that make up the object multiplied by the squares of their respective distances from the axis of rotation. It is analagous to the ◊mass of a stationary object or one moving in a straight line. In linear ◊dynamics, ◊Newton's second law of motion states that the force on a moving object F equals the products of its mass m and acceleration a ($F = ma$); the analogous equation in rotational dynamics is $T = I\alpha$, where T is the torque (the turning effect of a force) that causes an angular acceleration α and I is the moment of inertia. For a given object, I depends on its shape and the position of its axis of rotation.

momentum in physics, of a body, the product of its mass and its linear velocity; angular momentum (of a body in rotational motion) is the product of its ◊moment of inertia and its angular velocity. The momentum of a body does not change unless it is acted on by an external force. The law of conservation of momentum is one of the fundamental concepts of classical physics. It states that the total momentum of all bodies in a closed system is constant and unaffected by processes occurring within the system.

Mona /'məʊnə/ Latin name for ◊Anglesey island in Wales, UK.

Monaco /'mɒnəkəʊ/ enclave in southern France, with the Mediterranean to the S.
government under the 1911 constitution, largely rewritten 1962, Monaco is a hereditary principality. Legislative power is shared between the prince and a single-chamber national council, with 18 members elected by universal suffrage for a five-year term. Executive power is formally vested in the prince but in practice is exercised by a four-member council of government.
There are no political parties as such but the 1983 National Council elections were contested by the National and Democratic Union (UND), which supports Prince Rainier, and the Democratic and Socialist Union. The UND won all 18 seats and its rival organization has since become dormant.
history formerly part of the ◊Roman empire, Monaco became a Genoese possession in the 12th century, and has been ruled since 1297 by the Grimaldi family. It was a Spanish protectorate 1542–1641, then came under French protection and during the ◊French revolution was annexed by France. The ruling family were imprisoned (one was guillotined), but regained power after the 1814 Treaty of Paris. In 1815 Monaco became a protectorate of Sardinia but reverted to French protection in 1861. In 1940 it was occupied by Italy, and in 1943 by Germany, but was liberated in 1945.
Agreements between France and Monaco state that Monaco will be incorporated in France if the reigning prince dies without a male heir. France is closely involved in the government of Monaco, providing a civil servant, of the prince's choosing, to head its Council of Government.

monad a technical philosophical term deriving from the philosophy of ◊Leibniz, suggesting a soul or metaphysical unit which has a self-contained life. In Leibniz the monads were independent of each other, but were co-ordinated by a 'pre-established harmony'.

Monadnock /mə'nædnɒk/ a mountain in New Hampshire, USA: Mount Monadnock 1,063 m/3,186 ft. The term Monadnock is also used to mean any isolated hill or mountain.

Monaghan /'mɒnəhən/ county of the Republic of Ireland, province of Ulster
area 1,290, sq km/498 sq mi
towns county town Monaghan
features rivers Finn and Blackwater
products cereals, linen
population (1981) 6,177.

monasticism devotion to the religious life under vows of poverty, chastity, and obedience, known to Judaism (for example ◊Essenes), Buddhism, and other religions, before Christianity. The institution of Christian monasticism is ascribed to St ◊Anthony in 3rd-century Egypt, but the inauguration of communal life is attributed to his disciple, St ◊Pachomius. Possibly communities for women

Monaco
PRINCIPALITY OF

AREA 1.5 sq km/0.575 sq mi
CAPITAL Monaco-Ville
TOWN Monte Carlo, noted for its film festival, motor races, and casino
PHYSICAL steep slope
FEATURES surrounded landward by French territory, it is being expanded by filling in the sea; aquarium and oceanographic centre
HEAD OF STATE Rainier III from 1949
HEAD OF GOVERNMENT Jean Ausseil from 1986
GOVERNMENT constitutional monarchy under French protectorate
EXPORTS some light industry, but economy depends on tourism and gambling
CURRENCY French franc (9.97 = £1 Sept 1987)
POPULATION 28,000 (1985); annual growth rate -0.5%
LANGUAGE French
RELIGION Roman Catholic
LITERACY 99% (1985)

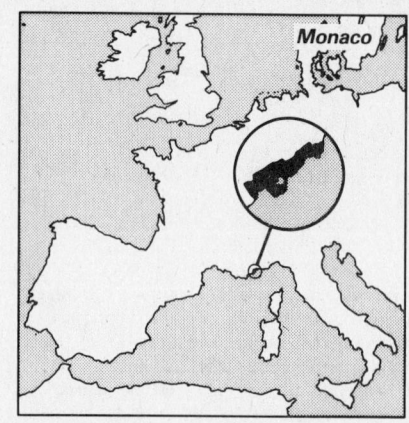
Monaco

CHRONOLOGY
1861 Became an independent state, under French protection.
1918 France given a veto over succession to the throne.
1949 Prince Rainier III ascended the throne.

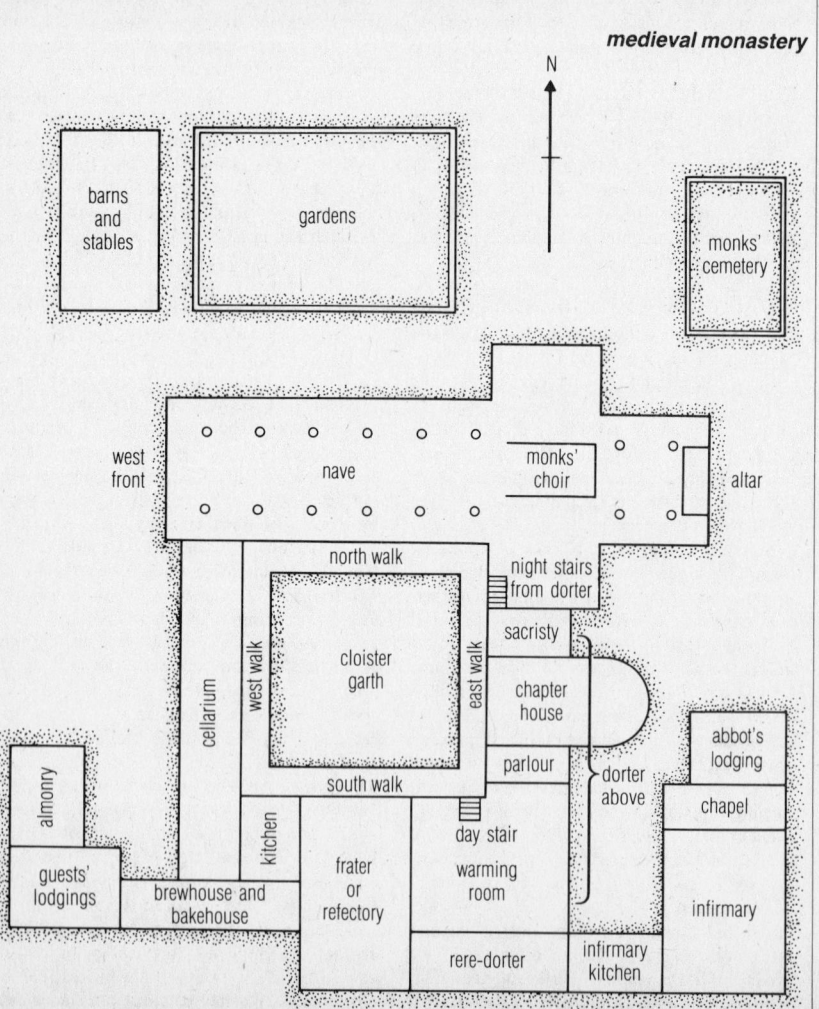
medieval monastery

N

barns and stables

gardens

monks' cemetery

west front

nave

monks' choir

altar

night stairs from dorter

north walk

sacristy

cloister garth

west walk

cellarium

east walk

chapter house

parlour

dorter above

abbot's lodging

south walk

day stair

chapel

almonry

kitchen

frater or refectory

warming room

infirmary

guests' lodgings

brewhouse and bakehouse

rere-dorter

infirmary kitchen

(nuns, from Latin *nonna* 'elderly woman') preceded those for men, and most male orders have their female counterpart. Full adaptation to conditions in W Europe was made by St ◊Benedict in the 6th century, his 'rule' being generally adopted. In 910 the foundation of ◊Cluny began the system of orders whereby each monastery was subordinated to a central institution. During the Middle Ages other forms of monasticism were established, including the hermit-like ◊Carthusians 1084, the ◊Augustinian Cannons, who were clerics organized under a monastic system (11th century); the military Knights ◊Templar and Knights Hospitallers of St ◊John (12th century); and in the early 13th the four mendicant orders of friars, ◊Franciscans, ◊Dominicans, ◊Carmelites and ◊Augustinians. Monasticism reached the height of its influence during the 13th century, declining during the 14th, and was severely affected by the Reformation. A revival came with the foundation of orders dedicated to particular missions, such as the great weapon of the Counter-Reformation, the Society of Jesus 1540 (commonly known as ◊Jesuits). The 20th-century trend in many orders is to modern dress, and involvement as 'workers' outside the monastery, despite disapproval by Pope John Paul II.

Monastir /ˌmɒnəˈstɪə/ Turkish name for the town of ◊Bitolj in S Yugoslavia.

monazite a mineral, (Ce, La, Y, Th)PO₄, yellow to red, valued as a source of ◊cerium and ◊thorium.

Mönchen-Gladbach /ˌmʌnʃənˈɡlædbæk/ industrial city (textiles, machinery, paper) in N Rhine-Westphalia, West Germany, near Düsseldorf; population (1984) 261,000. It is the NATO headquarters for N Europe.

Mond /mɒnd/ Ludwig 1839–1909. German chemist, who moved to England in 1862 and perfected a process for recovering sulphur during the manufacture of alkali. In 1867 he became a British subject, and in 1873 helped to found the firm of Brunner, Mond and Co., which pioneered the British chemical industry. Mond was also instrumental in developing the Canadian nickel industry . His son Alfred Mond, 1st Baron Melchett (1868–1930) was a founder of Imperial Chemical Industries (ICI).

Mondale /ˈmɒndeɪl/ Walter 'Fritz' 1928– . US Democrat politician, unsuccessful presidential candidate in the 1984 election. Mondale was a senator 1964–76 for his home state of Minnesota, and vice president to Jimmy ◊Carter 1977–80. After losing the 1984 presidential election to Reagan, Mondale retired from national politics to resume his law practice.

Monday the first day of the week. It replaced Sunday on the recommendation of the International Standardization Organization, ratified by Britain in 1971. The name derives from its having been considered sacred to the Moon (Old English *Mōnandaeg* and Latin *Lunae dies*).

Mondrian /ˈmɒndriɑːn/ Piet 1872–1944. Dutch abstract painter who tried to express the 'truths of the Universe' through pure aesthetics.

Using primary colours, black, white, and mid-grey, he painted parallel horizontal lines which intersected vertical ones. He founded in 1917 (with *Theo van Doesburg* 1883–1931) the review and movement known as ◊de Stijl (*The Style*). It advocated *Neoplasticism*, a combination of abstract geometrical design and simplified colour in painting, as well as in architecture and other forms of design, and influenced the ◊Bauhaus.

Monet /'mɒneɪ/ Claude 1840–1926. French ◊Impressionist painter. Born in Paris, he studied under Boudin. He became a prominent member of the French Impressionist group, which including◊Manet,◊Degas,◊Renoir, and◊Sisley. His painting *Impression, Sunrise* 1872 gave the movement its name. He was obsessed with the optical effects of light on colour and carried his original fragmented technique to the final extreme in series of paintings such as those on the facade of Rouen Cathedral 1894 or his famous water lilies, showing the changing colour effects at different times of day, which anticipated the abstract art of the 20th century. In 1980 the gardens at Giverny, which inspired many of his paintings, were restored.

monetarism economic policy, advocated by the economist Milton ◊Friedman and others, which proposes control of a country's ◊money supply to keep it in step with the country's ability to produce goods, with the aim of curbing ◊inflation. Cutting government spending is advocated, and the long-term aim is to return as much of the economy as possible to the private sector allegedly in the interests of efficiency. Additionally, ◊credit is restricted by high interest rates, and industry is not cushioned against internal market forces or overseas competition (with the aim of preventing 'over-manning', 'restrictive' union practices, 'excessive' wage demands, etc.) ◊Unemployment results, but, monetarists claim, less than eventually occurs if Keynesian methods (see ◊Keynes) are adopted. The theory was ineffectively applied by Edward ◊Heath in the UK in the early 1970s, and from 1979 the ◊Thatcher government attempted a more complete application of monetarism.

monetary policy an approach by governments which sees control of the ◊money supply and of liquidity as essential to the achievement of desired objectives and thus places less emphasis on tools such as ◊fiscal policy and ◊incomes policy. A monetary policy may not fully embrace all the doctrines of ◊monetarism, but use of it usually indicates that the practitioner gives a higher priority to price stability and ◊balance-of-payments equilibrium than to low ◊unemployment and consumption.

money any common medium of exchange, used by custom, convention, or law, in a community. Coinage is said to have been first used by the Lydians in the 7th century BC, and paper money was in use in China about AD 800, because bandits easily ran down the imperial messengers whose horses were laden with coin. From the earliest times both coin and notes have been issued as a government monopoly. Today coins – which are for the most part alloy tokens,

rather than of metal such as gold or silver of equivalent intrinsic value – and notes are supplemented by modern developments such as the ◊cheque and the ◊credit card.

International money the problems that faced nations after World War II were not dissimilar to those that existed after World War I. Disordered exchanges, depreciated monetary units, with the resulting interference with overseas trade, were the common experience. Various measures were tried, the suspension of the gold standard among them. Then in July 1944 a United Nations Monetary and Financial conference was held at ◊Bretton Woods, New Hampshire, USA, which led to the establishment of an International Bank for Reconstruction and Development (◊World Bank), and the opening of the ◊International Monetary Fund, in Washington, USA, replacing the ◊gold standard, without its rigidity. However, distorted ◊balance of payments positions were a marked feature of the late 1960s, for example, Britain struggled against an adverse balance and Germany in the reverse position.

recent developments in the 1970s the rise in demand for commodities, and especially for oil, led to more widespread imbalances, and worldwide ◊inflation. These years also saw a switch from fixed ◊exchange rates for the currencies of various countries to a 'floating rate', which limited speculation by those anticipating the ◊devaluation or revaluation of any particular currency, but tended in itself to add to the instability of the international monetary situation. Some attempts at an international currency are made by organizations such as the EEC, where official farm prices are expressed in units of account (u.a.) with an agreed value of so many grams of fine gold per unit. See also ◊European Monetary System, ◊money supply, ◊mint.

money supply term used to denote the amount of money present in an economy at a given moment. In Britain there are several definitions of money supply, none of them totally satisfactory, and often revised. M0 was defined as notes and coins in circulation, together with the operational balance of clearing banks with the Bank of England. The M1 definition encompasses M0 plus current account deposits; M2, now rarely used, covers the M1 items plus deposit accounts; M3 covers M2 items plus all other deposits held by UK citizens and companies in the UK banking sector. In May 1987 the Bank of England introduced new terms including M4 (M3 plus building society deposits) and M5 (M4 plus Treasury bills and local authority deposits). See also ◊monetarism, ◊monetary policy.

Mongolia, Inner /mɒŋ'gəʊlɪə/ autonomous region (Chinese *Nei Menggu*) of NE China from 1947
area 450,000 sq km/173,700 sq mi
capital Hohhot
features strategic frontier area with USSR
products cereals under irrigation; coal; reserves of rare earth oxides, europium, yttrium at Bayan Obo
population (1982) 19,274,279.

Mongolia /mɒŋ'gəʊlɪə/ country in E Central Asia, bounded N by the USSR and S by China.
government Mongolia is a socialist state with, under the 1960 constitution, a single-chamber legislature, the 370-deputy People's Great Assembly *Ardyn Ih Hural*, elected by universal suffrage for five-year terms. The assembly meets annually and elects a ten-member policy-making Presidium, whose chairman functions as state president, to take over its functions between sittings. It also appoints a council of ministers to carry out day-to-day executive administration, and a state procurator, who heads the judicial system. However, Mongolia's controlling force and sole political party is the Mongol People's Revolutionary Party, headed by Jambyn Batmunkh. This is organized on Communist lines and has a Congress, Central Committee, Secretariat and Politburo, all serving five-year terms.

history formerly inhabited by nomads from N Asia, the area was united under ◊Genghis Khan in 1206, and by the end of the 13th century was part of the vast ◊Mongol empire which stretched right across Asia. From 1691 it was part of ◊China.

After the revolution of 1911–12 Mongolia became autonomous under Jebsten Damba Khutukhtu (the Living Buddha). In 1924 it adopted the Soviet system of government and proclaimed itself a People's Republic. China recognized its independence in 1946, but relations deteriorated as Outer Mongolia took the Soviet side in the Sino-Soviet dispute. In 1966 Outer Mongolia signed a 20-year friendship, cooperation and mutual assistance pact with the USSR, and the thousands of Soviet troops based in the country caused China to see it as a Russian colony.

Isolated from the outside world during the 1970s, it underwent great economic change as new urban industries developed and settled agriculture on the collective system spread, with new areas being brought under cultivation. Since the accession to power in the USSR of Mikhail ◊Gorbachev, Outer Mongolia has been encouraged to broaden its outside contacts. Cultural exchanges with China have increased, diplomatic relations have been established with the US, and fewer Soviet troops are stationed in the country. A Mongolian nationalist revival has developed, with increasing study and use of the Mongolian script.

mongolism former name (now considered offensive) for ◊Down's syndrome.

Mongoloid a former racial classification, based on physical features, used to describe people of E Asian and N American origin; see ◊race.

mongoose carnivorous mammal of the family Viverridae. The Indian mongoose *Herpestes mungo* is greyish in colour, about 50 cm/1.5 ft, with a long tail. It may be tamed, and is often kept for its ability to kill snakes. The Egyptian mongoose or ichneumon is larger.

monism in philosophy, the theory that reality is made up of one, and only one, substance. This view is usually contrasted with ◊dualism, which divides reality into two substances, matter and

MONEY: WORLD CURRENCIES

country	unit	£ value Sept 87	country	unit	£ value Sept 87	country	unit	£ value Sept 87
Afghanistan	Afghani	99.25	Haiti	Gourde	8.2400	Puerto Rico	US $	1.6480
Albania	Lek	10.1411	Honduras	Lempira	3.3001			
Algeria	Dinar	7.7172	Hungary	Forint	78.4808	Qatar	Qatari Ryal	6.0180
Andorra	French Franc	9.9675						
	Spanish Peseta	199.96				Romania	Leu	16.32
Angola	Kwanza	49.923	Iceland	Icelandic Krona	64.18	Rwanda	Rwanda Franc	130.83
Antigua	E Caribbean $	4.46	India	Indian Rupee	21.30			
Argentina	Austral	4.1018	Indonesia	Rupiah	2726.99			
Australia	Australian $	2.2425	Iran	Rial	117.50	St Christopher	E Caribbean $	4.46
Austria	Schilling	21.01	Iraq	Iraqi Dinar	0.5109	St Lucia	E Caribbean $	4.46
			Irish Republic	Punt	1.1135	St Vincent	E Caribbean $	4.46
			Israel	Shekel	2.635	San Marino	Italian Lira	2159.54
Bahamas	Bahama $	1.6480	Italy	Lira	2159.54	São Tomé & Principe	Dobra	57.9226
Bahrain	Dinar	0.6230	Ivory Coast	CFA Franc	498.38	Saudi Arabia	Saudi Ryal	6.1938
Bangladesh	Taka	50.30				Senegal	CFA Franc	498.38
Barbados	Barbados $	3.3146				Seychelles	S Rupee	9.10
Belgium	Belgian Franc	62.40	Jamaica	Jamaican $	8.9050	Sierra Leone	Leone	(O)36.20
Belize	B $	3.2960	Japan	Yen	236.50	Singapore	Singapore $	3.4465
Benin	CFA Franc	498.38	Jordan	Jordanian Dinar	0.5660	Solomon Islands	Solomon Is $	3.4465
Bhutan	Ngultrum	21.30				Somali Republic	Somali Shilling	198.08
Bolivia	Boliviano	(O)3.4537				South Africa	Rand	(Cm)3.3790
Botswana	Pula	2.7800	Kenya	Kenya Shilling	27.45			(Fn)5.5100
Brazil	Cruzado	82.5150	Kiribati	Australian $	2.2425	Spain	Peseta	199.96
Brunei	Brunei $	3.4465	Korea (North)	Won	1.5491	Sri Lanka	SL Rupee	49.10
Bulgaria	Lev	1.3860	Korea (South)	Won	1335.38	Sudan Republic	Sudan £	4.1200
Burkina Faso	CFA Franc	498.38	Kuwait	Kuwaiti Dinar	0.4636	Surinam	S Guilder	2.9417
Burma	Kyat	10.8865				Swaziland	Lilangeni	3.3790
Burundi	Burundi Franc	204.75				Sweden	Swedish Krona	10.5025
			Laos	New Kip	57.680	Switzerland	Swiss Franc	2.4950
			Lebanon	Lebanese £	452.77	Syria	Syrian £	(O)6.4684
Cameroon	CFA Franc	498.38	Lesotho	Maluti	3.3790			
Canada	Canadian $	2.1670	Liberia	Liberian $	1.6480			
Cape Verde Islands	Cape V Escudo	147.11	Libya	Libyan Dinar	0.4915	Taiwan	New Taiwan $	49.74
Cent. Afr. Republic	CFA Franc	498.38	Liechtenstein	Swiss Franc	2.4950	Tanzania	Tan Shilling	113.90
Chad	CFA Franc	498.38	Luxembourg	Luxembourg	61.95	Thailand	Baht	41.70
Chile	Chilean Peso	369.92		Franc		Togo Republic	CFA Franc	498.38
China	Renminbi Yuan	6.1524				Tonga Islands	Palanga	2.2425
Colombia	Col. Peso	419.56	Malawi	Kwacha	3.6850	Trinidad & Tobago	Trinidad & Tob. $	5.9328
Comoro Islands	CFA Franc	498.38	Malaysia	Ringgit	4.1595	Tunisia	Tunisian Dinar	1.3921
Congo (Brazzaville)	CFA Franc	498.38	Maldive Islands	Ruflyra	11.5360	Turkey	Turkish Lira	1505.01
Costa Rica	Colon	105.31	Mali Republic	CFA Franc	498.38	Tuvalu	Australian $	2.2425
Cuba	Cuban Peso	1.2967	Malta	Maltese £	0.5655			
Cyprus	Cyprus £	0.7850	Mauritania	Qugulya	123.61			
Czechoslovakia	Koruma	15.51	Mauritius	Mauritian Rupee	21.50	Uganda	Uganda Shilling	98.00
			Mexico	Mexican Peso	2517.91	United States	US $	1.6480
			Monaco	French Franc	9.9675	Uruquay	Uruquay Peso	403.47
Denmark	Danish Kroner	11.4875	Mongolia	Tugrik	5.5299	United Arab Emirates	UAE Dirham	6.0658
Djibouti Republic of	Djibouti Franc	290.00	Montserrat	E Caribbean $	4.46	USSR	Rouble	1.0380
Dominica	E Caribbean $	4.46	Morocco	Dirham	13.60			
Dominican Republic	Dominican Peso	5.2715	Mozambique	Metical	667.61			
						Vanuatu	Vatu	174.50
						Vatican	Italian Lira	2159.54
Ecuador	Sucre	(O)263.84	Nauru Islands	Australian $	2.2425			
		(F)304.92	Nepal	Nepalese Rupee	34.70	Vietnam	Dong	(O)132.20
Egypt	Egyptian £	3.634	Netherlands	Guilder	3.3650			
El Salvador	Colon	8.2509	New Zealand	NZ $	2.5635			
Equatorial Guinea	CFA Franc	498.38	Nicaragua	Cordoba	3629.89	Western Samoa	Tala	(A)3.3400
Ethiopia	Ethiopian Birr	3.4113	Niger Republic	CFA Franc	498.38			
			Nigeria	Naira	6.9975	Yemen (North)	Ryal	(A)16.95
Fiji Islands	Fiji $	2.0925	Norway	Norwegian Krone	10.93	Yemen (South)	S Yemen Dinar	0.5668
Finland	Markka	7.2383				Yugoslavia	New Y Dinar	1345.00
France	Franc	9.9675						
			Oman Sultanate of	Rial Omani	0.6365			
						Zaïre Republic	Zaïre	192.04
Gabon	CFA Franc	498.38				Zambia	Kwacha	12.70
Gambia	Dalasi	12.2946	Pakistan	Pakistan Rupee	28.40	Zimbabwe	Zimbabwe $	2.7750
Germany (East)	Ostmark	2.9900	Panama	Balboa	1.6480			
Germany (West)	Deutsche Mark	2.9900	Papua New Guinea	Kina	1.4568			
Ghana	Cedi	282.5775	Paraguay	Guarani	523.04			
Greece	Drachma	228.52			1323.94			
Grenada	E Caribbean $	4.46			32.90			
Guatemala	Quetral	1.6480	Peru	Inti	47.83	(F) free rate		
		(F)4.4921			61.70	(Cm) commercial rate		
Guinea	Franc	561.85	Philippines	Philippine Peso	33.20	(Fn) financial rate		
Guinea-Bissau	Peso	1074.13	Poland	Zioty	476.79	(O) official rate		
Guyana	Guyanese $	14.85	Portugal	Escudo	235.08	(A) approximate rate		

Mongolia

MONGOLIAN PEOPLE'S REPUBLIC (*Bügd Nayramdakh Mongol Ard Uls*)

AREA 1,560,000 sq km/600,000 sq mi
CAPITAL Ulan Bator
TOWNS Darkhan, Choybalsan
PHYSICAL a high plateau with steppe (grasslands)
FEATURES Altai Mountains; salt lakes; part of Gobi Desert
HEAD OF STATE Jambyn Batmunkh from 1984
HEAD OF GOVERNMENT Dumagiin Sodnom from 1984
GOVERNMENT one-party communist
EXPORTS meat and butter; varied minerals; furs
CURRENCY tugrik (5.53 = £1 Sept 1987)
POPULATION 1,893,000 (1985); annual growth rate 2.7%
LANGUAGE Khalkha Mongolian (official), Chinese, Russian
RELIGION formerly Tibetan Buddhist Lamaist, suppressed in the 1930s
LITERACY 93% male/85% female (1980 est)
GNP $1.8 bn (1983); $750 per head of population
CHRONOLOGY
1911 Outer Mongolia gained autonomy from China.

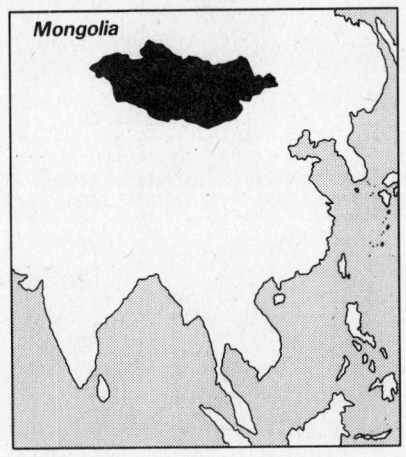
Mongolia

1924 People's Republic proclaimed.
1946 China recognized Outer Mongolia's independence.
1966 20-year friendship, cooperation, and mutual-assistance pact signed with USSR. Deterioration in relations with China.
1986 Soviet troop numbers reduced and Outer Mongolia's external contacts broadened.

mind. ◊Spinoza, the celebrated monist, saw the one substance as God or Nature.

monitor type of lizard of the family Varanidae. Monitors are generally large carnivorous lizards, with well-developed legs and claws, and a long powerful tail which can be swung in defence. They are found in Africa, S Asia and Australasia. Monitors include the ◊Komodo dragon, the largest of all lizards, and also the slimmer *Salvador's monitor Varanus salvadorii* which may reach 2.5 m/8 ft. Several other monitors such as the *lace monitor Varanus varius* and the *perentie Varanus giganteus* of Australia and the *Nile monitor Varanus niloticus* of Africa are up to 2 m/6 ft long.

Moniz /'mɒnɪz, Portuguese mu'niːʃ/ Antonio Egas 1874–1955. Portuguese neurologist, pioneer of prefrontal leucotomy (surgical separation of white fibres in the prefrontal lobe of the brain) to treat schizophrenia and paranoia; the treatment is today considered questionable. Nobel prize 1949.

Monk /mʌŋk/ or *Monck*, George, 1st Duke of Albemarle 1608–1669. English soldier. During the Civil War he fought for King Charles I, but after being captured changed sides and took command of the Parliamentary forces in Ireland. He served in Cromwell's Scottish campaign 1650, and at sea against the Netherlands 1652–53, and under the Commonwealth became commander in chief in Scotland. Leading his army into England in 1660 he brought about the restoration of Charles II, and was created duke of Albemarle.

Monk /mʌŋk/ Thelonious 1917–1982. US jazz pianist and composer. Working in Harlem during the Depression, he developed the jazz style known as *bebop* or *bop*. He became popular in the 1950s, and is remembered for numbers such as 'Round Midnight'.

monkey term for the smaller, mainly tree-dwelling primates, excluding humans and the anthropoid ◊apes. *Old World* monkeys, family Cercopithecidae, of tropical Africa and Asia are distinguished by their close-set nostrils and differentiated thumbs, some also having cheek pouches and behinds with bare patches (callosities) of hardened skin. They include ◊baboons, ◊langurs, ◊macaques and guenons. *New World* monkeys of Central and South America are characterized by wide-set nostrils, and some have highly sensitive prehensile tails. They comprise: (1) family Cebidae which includes the larger species: saki, ◊capuchin, squirrel, howler and spider monkeys; (2) the family Callithricidae which includes the very small species, notably the ◊marmosets and tamarins.

monkey-puzzle tree or *Chilean pine*. Evergreen tree *Araucaria araucana* native to Chile, first cultivated in Britain in 1796.

Monmouth /'mʌnməθ/ James Scott, Duke of Monmouth 1649–1685. Claimant to the English crown, leader of a rebellion against ◊James II. Born at Rotterdam, the natural son of Charles II and Lucy ◊Walter, he was created Duke of Monmouth in 1663. He married Anne Scott, Countess of Buccleuch (1651–1732), and adopted her surname. The Whig opposition attempted unsuccessfully to secure him the succession to the crown by the Exclusion Bill, and in 1684, having become implicated in a Whig conspiracy, he fled to Holland. After James II's accession in 1685, he landed at Lyme Regis,

Dorset, claimed the crown, and raised a rebellion, which was crushed at Sedgemoor in Somerset. Monmouth was captured and beheaded on Tower Hill, and 320 of his accomplices were condemned to death by Judge ◊Jeffreys.

Monmouthshire /'mʌnməθʃə/ former county of Wales, UK, which in 1974 became, less a small strip on the border with Mid Glamorgan, the new county of Gwent.

Monnet /'mɒneɪ/ Jean 1888–1979. French economist. The originator of Churchill's offer of union between the UK and France in 1940, he devised the French modernization programme of which he took charge under de Gaulle in 1945, and in 1950 produced the 'Shuman Plan' initiating the coordination of European coal and steel production in the European Coal and Steel Community (ECSC), which developed into the ◊Common Market (EEC).

monocarpic or *hapaxanthic* describing plants which flower and produce fruit only once during their lifecycle, after which they die. Most ◊annual and ◊biennial plants are monocarpic, but there are also a small number of monocarpic ◊perennials which flower just once, sometimes after as long as ninety years, dying shortly afterwards, for example, century plant (*Agave*) and some species of bamboo (*Bambusa*). See also ◊semel parity.

monocotyledon angiosperm (flowering plant) with a single cotyledon (seed-leaf) (as opposed to ◊dicotyledons, which have two). Monocotyledons usually have narrow leaves with parallel veins and smooth edges, and hollow or soft stems. Their flower parts are arranged in threes. Most are small plants such as orchids, grasses and lilies, but some are trees such as palms.

Monod /'mɒnəʊ/ Jacques 1910–1976. French biochemist who was awarded a Nobel prize in 1965 (with two colleagues) for research in genetics and microbiology.

monody in music, declamation by accompanied solo voice, used particularly at the turn of the 16th and 17th centuries.

monoecious having separate male and female flowers borne on the same plant. Maize (*Zea mays*), for example, has a tassel of male flowers at the top of the stalk and a group of female flowers (on the car, or 'cob') lower down. Monoecy is a way of avoiding self-fertilization. ◊Dioecious plants have male and female flowers on separate plants.

monogamy the state or practice of having only one husband or wife at a time. See under ◊marriage.

monopoly in the UK, originally a royal grant of the sole right to manufacture or sell a certain article. In modern commerce, the domination of a particular industry by a single company which is large enough to restrict competition against itself and keep prices high. In practice, a company can be said to be in a monopolistic situation when it controls a significant proportion of the market; in the UK the Fair Trading Act of 1973 defines a monopoly supplier as one having 'a quarter of the market', and the Monopolies and Mergers Commission controls any attempt to reach this position; in the USA 'antitrust laws' are similarly used. In communist countries the state itself has the overall monopoly; in capitalist ones some services such as transport or electricity supply may be state monopolies, but in the UK the Competition Act of 1980 covers both private monopolies and possible abuses in the public sector. A *monopsony* is a situation in which there is only one buyer, for example, most governments are the only legal purchasers of military equipment inside their countries. See also ◊oligopoly.

monorail a railway that runs on a single (mono) rail. It was originally invented in 1882 to carry light loads, and when run by electricity was called a telpher. The most successful monorail, the Wuppertal Schwebebahn, has been running in Germany since 1901. It is a suspension monorail, the passenger cars hanging from an arm fixed to a trolley that runs along the rail. Most modern monorails are of the straddle type, the passenger cars running on top of the rail. Straddle-type monorails are often used to transport passengers between terminals at airports, as at Birmingham, a monorail using the ◊maglev principle.

monosodium glutamate the sodium salt of glutamic acid (an ◊amino acid found widely in proteins which has an important role in the metabolism of plants and animals), formula $NaC_5H_8O_4$. It is used to enhance the flavour of many packaged and 'fast' foods and in many Chinese dishes. Ill-effects may arise from over consumption of this and some people are very sensitive to it, even in small amounts.

monotheism the belief or doctrine that there is only one God, the opposite of polytheism. See also ◊religion.

monotreme member of the order Monotremata, the only living egg-laying mammals. Native to the Australian region, they include the echidna and platypus.

Monroe /mən'rəʊ/ James 1758–1831. 5th president of the USA. Born in Virginia, he served in the War of Independence, was minister to France 1794–96, and during 1803 negotiated the Louisiana Purchase. He was secretary of state 1811–17, and was elected president in 1816, and again in 1820. His name is associated with the ◊Monroe doctrine.

Monroe /mən'rəʊ/ Marilyn. Stage-name of American film actress Norma Jean Mortenson 1926–1962. She became a star in such adroit comedies as *The Seven Year Itch* 1955, *Bus Stop* 1956, and *Some Like It Hot* 1959. Her second husband was baseball star Joe di Maggio, and her third Arthur ◊Miller.

Monroe doctrine the principle that the Americas should not be considered as subjects for colonization by any European power, and that any attempt to extend European colonies in the Americas will be regarded as dangerous to USA peace and safety. It was enunciated by James ◊Monroe in a message to Congress in 1823, when European intervention against rebel Spanish colonies in S America had been proposed.

Monrovia /mɒn'rəʊviə/ capital and port of Liberia, founded in 1821 and named after US president Monroe; population (1985) 500,000.

Monroe Marilyn Monroe dancing with Truman Capote in New York, 1955. She has become a legendary example of the 'sex symbol'.

Mons /mɒnz/ (Flemish *Bergen*) industrial city (coalmining, textiles, sugar) and capital of the province of Hainaut, Belgium; population (1985) 90,500. The military headquarters of NATO is at nearby Chièvres-Casteau.

monsoon (Old Dutch 'monçon') a type of ◊wind common in S Asia which blows towards the sea in winter and towards the land in summer, carrying much rain.

monstrance in the Roman Catholic Church, a vessel used from the 13th century to hold the Sacred Host when exposed at Benediction or in processions.

Montagnards (French 'the members of the mountain') a group in the Legislative Assembly and National Convention convened after the French Revolution of 1789. Supporting the more extreme aims of the revolution they were destroyed as a political force after the fall of Robespierre in 1795.

Montagu /'mɒntəgjuː/ Lady Mary Wortley (born Pierrepont) 1689–1762. British letter-writer. A society hostess, she had a famous quarrel with Alexander ◊Pope, her former friend and correspondent. She introduced inoculation against smallpox into Britain.

Montaigne /mɒn'teɪn/ Michel Eyquem de Montaigne 1533–1592. French writer, regarded as the creator of the essay form. Born at the Château de Montaigne, near Bordeaux, he studied law, and in 1554 became a counsellor of the Bordeaux *parlement*, and regularly visited the court of Francis II and Paris. In 1571 he retired to his estates, relinquishing his magistracy, and in 1580 published the first two volumes of his *Essais*. He toured Germany, Switzerland, and Italy 1580–81, returning on his election as mayor of Bordeaux, a post he held until 1585. The third volume of *Essais* appeared in 1588. In his essays, Montaigne deals with all aspects of life from the urbanely sceptical viewpoint, and through the translation of John Florio in 1603 influenced Shakespeare.

monsoon Moyna, a region to the west of Calcutta, India, in the aftermath of heavy rains. The monsoon rains may cause destructive flooding all over India and SE Asia from Apr to Sept. Thousands of people are rendered homeless each year.

monstera or *Swiss cheese plant* plant of the Arum family, Araceae, a native of tropical America. A striking feature is the drying up of areas between the veins of the leaves, which ultimately form holes and deep marginal notches. The fruits are edible.

Montana /mɒn'tænə/ mountain state of the USA on the Canadian border; Treasure State
area 381,085 sq km/147,138 sq mi
capital Helena
features Missouri and Yellowstone rivers; Glacier National Park; ◊Custer Battlefield

products wheat under irrigation; cattle, wool; copper, oil, and natural gas
population 817,000 (1983)
famous people Gary Cooper
history first settled in 1809, it became a state in 1889.

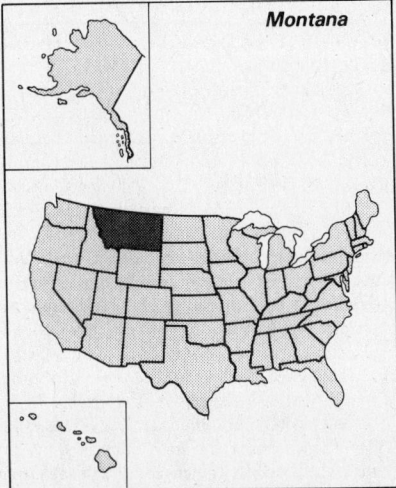

Montana

Montanism movement within the early Church which strove to return to the purity of primitive Christianity. Originating in Phrygia in about 156 with the teaching of a prophet named Montanus, it spread to Asia Minor, Rome, Carthage, and Gaul. The emperor ◊Tertullian was a noted Montanist.

Mont-aux-Sources /ˌmɒnt əu ˈsuəs/ highest mountain in the ◊Drakensberg range in South Africa; height 3,482 m/10,822 ft.

Mont Blanc /ˌmɒm ˈblɒŋ/ (Italian *Monte Bianco*) a mountain between France and Italy; the highest mountain in the ◊Alps. Height 4,807m/15,772 ft.

montbretia plant *Tritonia X crocosmiflora* in the family Iridaceae. The orange or reddish flowers are borne on long stems.

Montcalm /mɒntˈkɑːm/ Louis-Joseph de Montcalm-Grozon, Marquis de Montcalm 1712–1759. French general, commander of the troops in Canada from 1756. He won a succession of victories over the British, but was defeated by Wolfe at Quebec, where both he and Wolfe were killed.

Mont Cenis /ˌmɒn səˈniː/ pass in the Alps between Lyon in France and Turin in Italy at 2,082 m/6,831 ft.

Monte Bello Islands /ˈmɒnti ˈbeləu/ group of uninhabited islands in the S Pacific, off Western Australia; the largest is Barrow Island.

Monte Carlo /ˈmɒnti ˈkɑːləu/ a town and resort in ◊Monaco, famous for its gaming tables; population (1985) 12,000.

Monte Cristo /ˈmɒnti ˈkrɪstəu/ a small uninhabited island 40 km/25 mi to the S of Elba, in the Tyrrhenian Sea; its name supplied a title for Dumas' hero in *The Count of Monte Cristo*.

Montego Bay /mɒnˈtiːgəu ˈbeɪ/ port and resort in Jamaica; population (1980) 43,000.

Montélimar /mɒnˈteɪlɪmɑː/ town in Drôme district, France; noted for the nougat to which its name is given; population (1982) 30,213.

Montenegro /ˌmɒntɪˈniːgrəu/ constituent republic of Yugoslavia
area 13,812 sq km/4,226 sq mi
capital Titograd
town Cetinje
features smallest of the republics; very mountainous; Skadarsko Jezero (Lake Scutari) shared with Albania
population (1981) 584,000, including 38,000 Albanians
language Serbian variant of Serbo-Croat
religion Serbian Orthodox
history once part of ◊Serbia, it became independent in the 14th century and never submitted to Turkish rule, being recognized as a sovereign principality under the Treaty of Berlin of 1878. Prince Nicholas took the title of king in 1910. Overrun by Austria in World War I, it voted in 1918 after the deposition of King Nicholas to become part of the future Yugoslavia.

Monterey /ˌmɒntəˈreɪ/ fishing port on Monterey Bay in California, USA, once the state capital; it is the setting for Steinbeck's novels *Cannery Row* 1945 and *Tortilla Flat* 1935 dealing with migrant fruit workers; population (1980) 27,500.

Monterrey /ˌmɒntəˈreɪ/ industrial city (iron and steel, food processing) in NE Mexico; population (1980) 1,916,472. There is an 18th-century cathedral, a university, and institute of technology.

Montespan /ˌmɒntesˈpɒŋ/ Françoise-Athénais de Rochechouart, Marquise de Montespan 1641–1707. Mistress of Louis XIV from 1667, by whom she had seven children, for whom she was unwise enough to engage the future Mme de ◊Maintenon as governess. She retired to a convent in 1691.

Montesquieu /ˌmɒntesˈkjɜː/ Charles Louis de Secondat, baron de la Brède 1689–1755. French philosophical historian. Born near Bordeaux, he became adviser to the Bordeaux parliament in 1714. After the success of his *Lettres Persanes*/*Persian Letters* 1721, he adopted a literary career, writing *Considérations sur les Causes de la grandeur des Romains et de leur décadence* 1734. His great work *De l'Esprit des Lois*/*The Spirit of the Laws* 1748, a 31-volume philosophical disquisition on politics and sociology, as well as legal matters, was seminal in that his approval of the British constitution influenced the initial stages of the French Revolution.

Montessori /ˌmɒnteˈsɔːri/ Maria 1870–1952. Italian educationalist. Born near Ancona, she was the first woman to take a medical degree at Rome University in 1894, and from her experience with mentally handicapped children developed the *Montessori method*, an educational system for all children based on a more informal approach incorporating instructive play and allowing children to develop at their own pace.

Monteux /mɒnˈtɜː/ Pierre 1875–1964. French conductor. He established a reputation as conductor of ◊Diaghilev's Russian Ballet 1911–14 and 1917, and Ravel's *Daphnis and Chloe* and Stravinsky's *Rite of Spring* were first performed under his direction. For many years he conducted in America, notably with the San Francisco Symphony Orchestra 1935–52.

Monteverdi /ˌmɒntɪˈveədi/ Claudio (Giovanni Antonio) 1567–1643. Italian composer. Born in Cremona, he was in the service of the Duke of Mantua about 1591–1612, and was director of music at St Mark's, Venice, from 1613. The greatest 17th-century Italian composer and an exponent of monody and recitative as opposed to polyphony, Monteverdi holds an important place in European music. His operas *Orfeo* 1607 and *The Coronation of Poppea* 1642 are two early masterpieces in the form. He also wrote many madrigals, motets, and much sacred music, notably the *Vespers* 1610.

Monteverdi Claudio Monteverdi's first opera, *Orfeo*, was produced for the carnival at Mantua in 1607.

Montevideo /ˌmɒntɪvɪˈdeɪəu/ capital and chief port (grain, meat products, hides) of Uruguay, on Río de la Plata; population (1983) 1,362,000. Montevideo, founded 1726, has a cathedral and a university 1849.

Montez /ˈmɒntez/ Lola, stage-name of actress Maria Gilbert 1818–1861. Born in Ireland, she appeared on the stage as a Spanish dancer, and in 1847 became the mistress of King Ludwig I of Bavaria, whose policy she dictated for a year. Her liberal sympathies led to her banishment through Jesuit influence in 1848. She later acted in the USA and Australia, and danced in New York.

Montezuma II /ˌmɒntɪˈzuːmə/ 1466–1520. The last Aztec emperor 1502–19, when ◊Cortés invaded Mexico and imprisoned him. He was murdered, either by the Spaniards, or by his own subjects during the Aztec attack on Cortés' forces as they tried to leave Tenochtitlán.

Montfort /ˈmɒntfət/ Simon de Montfort, Earl of Leicester c. 1208–1265. English politician. Son of Simon de Montfort (c. 1160–1218) who led a crusade against the Albigenses. Born in Normandy, he arrived in England in 1230, married Henry III's sister and was granted the earldom of Leicester. From 1258 he led the baronial opposition to Henry III's misrule during the ◊Barons' War and in 1264 defeated and captured the king at Lewes. In 1265, as head of government, he summoned the first parliament in which the towns were represented, but was killed at the Battle of Evesham.

Montgolfier /mɒŋˈgɒlfieɪ/ Joseph Michel 1740–1810 and Étienne Jacques 1745–1799. French brothers whose balloon was used for the first successful human flight. They were papermakers of Annonay, near Lyon, where on 5 Jun 1783 they sent up a balloon filled with hot air. The first successful human flight was made in a Montgolfier balloon on 21 Nov 1783. The Montgolfier experiments greatly stimulated scientific interest in aviation.

Montgomery /mənt'gʌməri/ town in Alabama, USA, famous for 'Montgomery Bus Boycott' 1955, which began when a black passenger, Rosa Parks, refused to give up her seat to a white passenger. Led by Martin Luther King, it was a landmark in the civil-rights campaign. Alabama's bus-segregation laws were outlawed by the US Supreme Court 13 Nov 1956.

Montgomery /mənt'gʌməri/ Bernard Law, 1st Viscount Montgomery of Alamein 1887–1976. British field marshal. Son of an Ulster clergyman, he served in France during World War I. In World War II he commanded the third division, which formed part of the British Expeditionary Force in France 1939–40, and took part in the evacuation from ◊Dunkirk. In Aug 1942 he took command of the Eighth Army, then barring the German advance on Cairo; the victory of El ◊Alamein in Oct turned the tide in N Africa, and was followed by the expulsion of Field Marshal Rommel from Egypt and rapid advance into Tunisia. In Feb 1943 his forces came under Eisenhower's command, and took part in the conquest of Tunisia and Sicily and the invasion of Italy. He commanded the Allied armies during the opening phase of the invasion of France in Jun 1944, and from Aug the British and Imperial troops that liberated the Netherlands, overran N Germany, and entered Denmark. At his 21st Army Group headquarters on Lüneberg Heath, he received the German surrender on 3 May 1945.

He was in command of the British occupation force in Germany until Feb 1946, when he was appointed chief of the Imperial General Staff. He was promoted to field marshal in 1944, and in 1946 was created a viscount. In 1948 Montgomery became permanent military chair of the commanders-in-chief committee for W European defence, and 1951–58 was deputy supreme commander Europe.

Montgomeryshire /mənt'gʌmriʃə/ former county of N Wales, UK, included in Powys in 1974.

month a unit of time based on the motion of the Moon around the Earth. The time from one

Montgomery The British field marshal, Viscount Montgomery of Alamein, advances in the turret of a tank during the carefully planned attack on El Alamein, Oct 1942.

new or full Moon to the next (the *synodic month*) is 29.53 days. The time for the Moon to complete one orbit around the Earth relative to the stars (the *sidereal month*) is 27.32 days. The *calendar month* is a human invention consisting of a whole number of days, devised to fit the calendar year.

Montherlant /ˌmɒnteəˈlɒŋ/ Henri de Millon 1896–1972. French author. He was a Nazi sympathizer, and his novels are marked by an obsession with the physical. He wrote the play *Maître de Santiago/Master of Santiago* 1947. His most critically acclaimed work is *Le Chaos et la nuit/Chaos and Night* 1963.

Montoneros left-wing guerrillas in ◊Argentina.

Montpellier /mɒmˈpeliɛɪ/ industrial city, capital of ◊Languedoc-Roussillon, France; population (1982) 221,000. There is a 14th-century cathedral and a university 1229 noted for its medical school.

Montreal /ˌmɒntriˈɔːl/ capital, inland port, industrial city (aircraft, chemicals, oil and petrochemicals, meat packing) of Quebec, Canada, on Montreal island at the junction of the Ottawa and St Lawrence rivers
population (1981) 2,828,500
features Mont Réal (Mount Royal, 230 m/753 ft) overlooks the city; an artificial island in the St Lawrence (site of the international exhibition of 1967) three universities; except for Paris, the world's largest French-speaking city
history Jacques ◊Cartier reached the site in 1535, ◊Champlain established a trading post in 1611, and the original Ville Marie (later renamed Montreal) was founded in 1642 by Paul de Chomédy, Sieu de Maisonneuve (1612–1676). It was the last town surrendered by France to Britain in 1760. Nevertheless, when troops of the rebel Continental Congress occupied the city 1775–76, the citizens refused to be persuaded (even by a visit from Benjamin Franklin) to join the future USA in its revolt against Britain.

Montreux /mɒnˈtrɜː/ winter resort in W Switzerland on Lake Geneva, in which is the island rock fortress of Chillon, where the patriot François Bonward (commemorated by the poet Byron) was imprisoned 1530–36; population (1980) 21,000. At the annual television festival (first held in 1961), the premier award is the *Golden Rose of Montreux*.

Montreux, Convention of /mɒnˈtrɜː/ agreement 1936 allowing Turkey to remilitarize the ◊Dardenelles.

Montrose /mɒnˈtrəuz/ James Graham, 1st Marquess of Montrose 1612–1650. Scottish soldier. Son of the 4th earl of Montrose. He supported the ◊Covenanters in their struggle against Charles I, but after 1640 went over to the king's side. In 1644 Charles created him a marquess and lieutenant-general in Scotland, whereupon he rallied the Highlanders and won a succession of victories against the Covenanters. Defeated in 1645 at Philiphaugh, he escaped to Norway. Returning in 1650 to raise a revolt, he survived shipwreck only to have his weakened forces defeated, and (having been betrayed to the Covenanters) was hanged in Edinburgh.

Mont St Michel /'mɒn ˌsæm miˈʃel/ islet in NW France converted to a peninsula by an artificial causeway; noted for its Benedictine monastery, founded in 708.

Montserrat /'mɒntsəræt/ mountain in NE Spain, 1,240 m/4,070 ft, so called because its uneven outline resembles the edge of a saw (Spanish *monte serrado* serrated mountain).

Montserrat /'mɒntsəræt/ volcanic island in the West Indies, one of the Leeward group; capital Plymouth; area 101 sq km/39.5 sq mi; population (1980) 12,034. It produces cotton, cotton-seed, coconuts, citrus and other fruits, and vegetables. Its first European visitor was Christopher ◊Columbus 1493, who named it after a mountain in Spain. It was first colonized by the Irish 1632, became British in 1783 and is still a British colony.

Monument, the in London, England, a tower commemorating the Great Fire of London 1666. It was designed by ◊Wren and completed in 1677. It stands near the site of the house in Pudding Lane where the conflagration began.

Monza /'mɒnzə/ town in N Italy, known for its motor-racing circuit; population (1984) 122,500. Once the capital of the ◊Lombards, it preserves the Iron Crown of Lombardy in the 13th-century cathedral. Umberto I was assassinated here.

Moon, the /muːn/ the natural satellite of the Earth, 3,476 km/2,160 mi in diameter, with a mass $\frac{1}{81}$ that of the Earth. Its average distance from Earth is 384,400 km/238,850 mi, and it orbits Earth every 27.32 days (the *sidereal month*). The Moon spins on its axis so that it keeps one side permanently turned towards the Earth. The Moon is illuminated by sunlight, and goes through a cycle of phases from New (invisible) via First Quarter (half Moon) to Full and back again to New, every 29.53 days (the *synodic month*, also known as a *lunation*).
The Moon has no air or water. On its sunlit side temperatures reach 110°C, but during the two-week lunar night the surface temperature drops

to -170°C. Its composition is rocky, with a surface heavily scarred by ◊meteorite impacts that have formed ◊craters up to 240 km/150 mi across. The youngest craters are surrounded by bright rays of ejected rock. The largest scars have been filled by dark lava to produce the lowland plains known as seas or ◊*maria* (see ◊mare). These dark patches form the familiar 'man-in-the-Moon' pattern. Rocks brought back by ◊Apollo astronauts show the Moon is 4,600 million years old, the same age as the Earth. Unlike the Earth, most of the Moon's surface features were formed within the first 1,000 million years of its history when it was subjected to heavy bombardment by meteorites.

The origin of the Moon is open to debate. Theories suggest that it split from the Earth; that it was a separate body captured by Earth's gravity; or that it formed in orbit around the Earth. The latest idea suggests that the Moon was formed from debris thrown off when a body the size of Mars struck the Earth early in the Earth's history.

moon /muːn/ in astronomy, any small body that orbits a ◊planet. ◊Mercury and ◊Venus are the only planets that do not have moons.

Moon /muːn/ Sun Myung 1920– . Korean industrialist and founder of the ◊Unification Church 1954. From 1973 Moon launched a major mission in the USA. The church has been attacked for allegedly 'brainwashing' devotees (Moonies). Moon was convicted of tax fraud in the USA in 1982.

Moon /muːn/ William 1818–1894. British inventor of the Moon alphabet for the blind. Devised in 1847, it uses only nine symbols in different orientations. From 1983 it has been possible to write it with a miniature 'typewriter'.

Moonie /'muːni/ popular name for a follower of the ◊Unification Church, a religious sect founded by Sun Myung ◊Moon.

Moon probe the first space probe to hit the Moon was the Soviet Luna 2, on 13 Sept 1959 (Luna 1 had missed the Moon eight months earlier). In Oct 1959, Luna 3 sent back the first photographs of the Moon's far side. Luna 9 was the first probe to soft-land on the Moon, on 3 Feb 1966, transmitting photographs of the surface to Earth. Luna 16 was the first probe to return automatically to Earth carrying Moon samples, in Sept 1970, although by then Moon rocks had already been brought back by ◊Apollo astronauts. Luna 17 landed in Nov 1970 carrying a lunar rover, Lunokhod, which was driven over the Moon's surface by remote-control from Earth. The first successful US Moon probe was Ranger 7, which took close-up photographs before it hit the Moon on Jul 31, 1964. Surveyor 1 on Jun 2, 1966, was the first US probe to soft-land on the lunar surface. It took photographs, and later Surveyors analysed the surface rocks. Between 1966 and 1967 a series of five Lunar Orbiters photographed the entire Moon in detail, in preparation for the Apollo landings.

moonstone a translucent, pearly variety of potassium sodium ◊feldspar, found in Sri Lanka or Burma, and distinguished by a blue, silvery or red tint. It is valued as a gem.

Moor name (English form of Latin *Maurus*) originally applied to an inhabitant of the Roman province of Mauritania, in NW Africa. In current English usage the term is applied mainly to the Muslims who conquered Spain and occupied its southern part from 711 to 1492. They were of mixed Arab and Berber origin.

Moorcock /'muːkɒk/ Michael 1939– . British writer, associated with the 1960s new wave in science fiction. As editor of the magazine *New Worlds* 1964–69, he introduced mainstream and avant-garde literary methods and concepts into science fiction. He is noted for works featuring Elric (a sword-wielding fantasy hero) or Jerry Cornelius (unconventional time-traveller based in London), and the novels *The Condition of Muzak* 1977 and *Gloriana* 1978.

Moore /muːə/ (John) Jeremy 1928– . British Major-General Commando Forces, Royal Marines, 1979–82, he commanded the land forces in the ◊Falklands campaign. He was made Knight Commander of the Bath 1982.

Moore /muːə/ G(eorge) E(dward) 1873–1958. British philosopher. Educated at Trinity College, Cambridge University, he was professor of philosophy at the university 1925–39, and edited the journal *Mind*, to which he contributed 1921–47. His books include *Principia Ethica* 1903, in which he attempted to analyse the moral question 'what is good?', and *Some Main Problems of Philosophy* 1953, but his chief influence was as a teacher.

Moore /muːə/ George (Augustus) 1852–1933. Irish novelist. Born in County Mayo, he studied art in Paris 1870, and published two volumes of poetry there. His first novel, *A Modern Lover* 1883, was sexually frank for its time and banned in some quarters. It was followed by others, including his most successful *Esther Waters* 1894.

Moore /muːə/ Gerald 1899–1987. British pianist, renowned as an accompanist, particularly of singers, a role he raised from servitude to equal partnership.

Moore /muːə/ Henry 1898–1986. British sculptor. Born in Yorkshire, he studied at Leeds and the Royal College of Art. His forms became gradually more abstract and monumental as he refined the shapes of his series of *Reclining Woman*. Much of his work is designed to be exhibited outdoors, including the open air 'sculpture parks' at his former home at Perry Green, Hertfordshire. His popular reputation began with his drawings of London air-raid shelter scenes in World War II as an official artist. He was awarded the Order of Merit in 1963.

Moore /muːə/ John 1761–1809. British general. Born in Glasgow, he entered the army in 1776, serving in the American and French Revolutionary Wars and against the Irish rebellion of 1798. In 1808 he commanded the British army sent to Portugal in the ◊Peninsular War. After advancing into Spain he had to retreat to ◊Corunna, and was killed in the battle fought to cover the embarkation. Charles ◊Wolfe wrote a well known poem on his burial.

Moore /muːə/ Marianne 1887–1972. American poet. Born in Missouri, she edited the literary *Dial* 1925–29, and published volumes of witty and intellectual verse including *Observations* 1924, *What are Years* 1941, and *A Marianne Reader* 1961.

Moore /muːə/ Robert Frederick ('Bobby') 1941– . British footballer. Captain of West Ham United, he played for England 108 times, and headed the winning World Cup team in 1966. He managed Southend United football club 1983–86.

Moore /muːə/ Thomas 1779–1852. Irish poet, born in Dublin. Among his best-known works are the verse romance, *Lalla Rookh* 1817, and the *Irish Melodies* 1807–35. These were set to music by Sir John Stevenson, 1807–35, and include 'The Minstrel Boy' and 'The Last Rose of Summer'. He was a friend and biographer of ◊Byron, who gave him his manuscript *Memoirs* to assist him financially. However, Moore allowed their mutual publisher, John Murray, to burn it in 1824 on grounds of propriety.

moorhen bird *Gallinula chloropus* of the rail family, common in shoreside vegetation and water of swamps, lakes and ponds in Eurasia, Africa and N and S America. About 33 cm/1.1 ft long, it is mainly brown and grey, but has a red bill and forehead, and vivid white underside to the tail. The big feet are not webbed or lobed, but the moorhen can swim well.

moose largest deer. See ◊elk.

moot a legal and administrative assembly found in nearly every community in medieval England.

moped a lightweight motor cycle which has pedals. Early mopeds (like the autocycle) were like motorized bicycles, the pedals being used to start the bike and assist propulsion uphill. A few modern mopeds are like this, but many are hardly distinguishable from lightweight motorbikes, and their pedals have little function.

Moradabad /ˌmɔːrədə'bæd/ trading city in Uttar Pradesh, India, on the Ramganga river; produces textiles and engraved brassware; population (1981) 348,000. It was founded in the 17th century by Rustam Khan, and the Great Mosque dates from 1631.

moraine rocky debris carried along and deposited by a ◊glacier. Material eroded from the side of a glaciated valley and carried along the glacier's edge is called 'lateral moraine'; that worn from the valley floor and carried along the base of the glacier is called 'ground moraine'. When two glaciers converge their lateral moraines unite to form a 'medial moraine'. Debris that has fallen down crevasses and become embedded in the ice is termed 'englacial moraine'; when this is exposed at the surface due to partial melting it becomes 'ablation moraine'. Rubble dropped at the snout of a melting glacier is a 'terminal moraine'.

morality play didactic medieval verse drama, in part a development of the ◊miracle play, in which human characters are replaced by personified virtues and vices, the limited humorous elements being provided by the Devil. The morality play flourished in the 15th century, the most famous example being the *Everyman*. They exerted an important influence on the development of Elizabethan drama and comedy.

Moore British sculptor Henry Moore wanted his human figures to convey 'pent-up energy and life of their own', as in the abstract forms in this sketch.

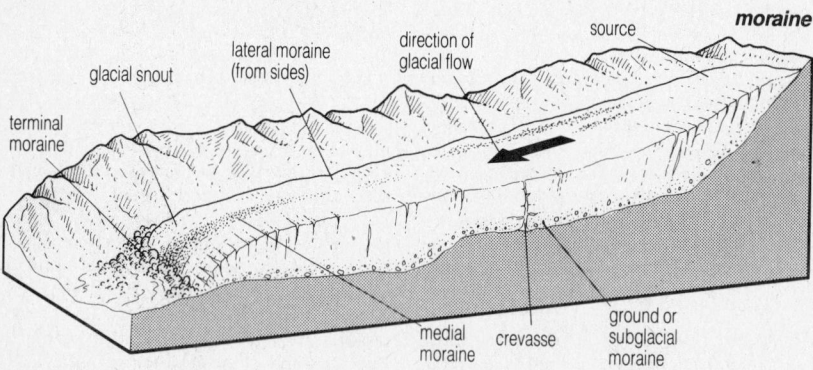

moraine

glacial snout
lateral moraine
(from sides)
direction of
glacial flow
source
terminal
moraine
medial
moraine
crevasse
ground or
subglacial
moraine

history by the end of the 6th century Slavs had settled in Moravia; they were converted to Christianity in the 9th century, when Moravia became part of the German Empire under Charlemagne. In 874 the kingdom of Great Moravia was founded by the Slavic prince Sviatopluk, who ruled until 894. The country was conquered by the Magyars in 906, but became part of the Holy Roman Empire in 958; in 1029 it was incorporated in Bohemia, in 1526 brought under the rule of the Hapsburgs, and in 1849 it became an Austrian crown land. It was incorporated in the new republic of Czechoslovakia in 1918, forming a province until 1949.

Moravia /mə'reɪvɪə/ Alberto, pseudonym of Italian novelist Alberto Pincherle 1907– . His criticism of Mussolini's regime led to a stifling of his work by the government until after World War II. Novels include *La romana/Woman of Rome* 1949, and *La ciociara/Two Women* 1958. He is noted for his bare and compelling narrative.

Moravia Italian writer, journalist and critic, Alberto Moravia is a leading figure in Italian intellectual and cultural life.

Moravian member of a Protestant sect, also known as the Moravian Brethren. An episcopal Church founded in Bohemia in 1457, as an offshoot of the Hussite movement (see John ▷Huss), its followers suffered much persecution after 1620, and were held together mainly by the leadership of their bishop, Comenius. Driven out in 1722 by further persecution, they spread over Germany and into England and North America. In 1732 missionary work was begun. There are about 63,000 Moravians in the USA, and small congregations in England and the rest of Europe.

Moray Earl of Moray see ▷Murray.

Moray Firth /'mʌri/ North Sea inlet in Scotland, between Burghead (Grampian) and Tarbat Ness (Highland region), 38 km/15 mi wide at its entrance.

Morayshire /'mʌriʃə/ former county of NE Scotland, divided 1975 between Highland region

Moral Rearmament a worldwide movement calling for moral and spiritual renewal. It was founded by F N D ▷Buchman in 1938.

Moravia /mə'reɪvɪə/ district of central Europe, from 1960 two regions of Czechoslovakia:
South Moravia
area 15,022 sq km/5,800 sq mi
capital Brno

population (1984) 2,053,500
North Moravia
area 11,060 sq km/4,270 sq mi
capital Ostrava
population (1984) 1,949,000.
features (N and S) river Morava; 25% forested
products maize, grapes, wine in the S; wheat, barley, rye, flax, sugarbeets in the N; coal and iron

(the SW section) and Grampian region (the NE); the county town was Elgin.

Morazán /ˌmɒrəˈθɑːn/ Francisco 1792–1842. Central American politician. Born in Honduras, he led the successful liberal-federalist revolt of 1827 in Honduras and in Salvador and Guatemala in 1828 and 1829. Elected president of the Central American Confederation in 1830, he was re-elected in 1834, but Honduras, Nicaragua, and Costa Rica seceded in 1838 and Guatemala in 1839. Attempting to hold the union together by force he was driven out by the Guatemalan dictator, Carrera, and a further attempt to revive union in 1842 ended in his capture and execution in Honduras. He now symbolizes the movement for Central American unity.

Morbihan, Gulf of /ˌmɔːbiˈɒŋ/ seawater lake in ◊Brittany, W France, linked by a channel with the Bay of Biscay; area 104 sq km/40 sq mi. Morbihan is a Breton word meaning 'little sea' and the gulf gives its name to a *département*.

Mordovia /mɔːˈdəʊviə/ another name for ◊Mordvinia, republic of the USSR.

Mordvinia /mɔːdˈvɪnɪən/ (or *Mordovia*) republic of central USSR
area 26,200 sq km/10,100 sq mi
capital Saransk
features river Sura on the E; forested in the W
products sugar beet, grains, potatoes; sheep and dairy farming; timber, furniture, and textiles
population (1985) 966,000
history Mordvinia was conquered by Russia during the 13th century. It was made an autonomous region in 1930, an Autonomous Soviet Socialist Republic 1934.

More /mɔː/ Thomas 1478–1535. British politician and author. Born in London, he studied under Linacre and Grocyn at Oxford, and was influenced in his religious beliefs by ◊Colet. In 1497 he first met ◊Erasmus, while studying law at Lincoln's Inn, and in 1504 entered Parliament. From 1509 he was favoured by Henry VIII and employed on foreign embassies, becoming a member of the privy council in 1518 and Speaker of the House of Commons in 1523. He was knighted in 1521, and on the fall of Wolsey became Lord Chancellor in 1529, but resigned in 1532 owing to his failure to agree with King Henry's ecclesiastical policy and his marriage with Anne Boleyn. In 1534 he refused as a devout Catholic to take the oath of Supremacy to Henry VIII as head of the Church, and after imprisonment in the Tower was executed. Among his writings are: in Latin, *Utopia* (1516), sketching an ideal commonwealth; in English, *Dialogue* (1528), directed against Tyndale, and a *History of Richard III*. More was canonized in 1935.

Moreau /mɔːˈrəʊ/ Gustave 1826–1898. French ◊Symbolist painter whose paintings of biblical and mythological subjects contain psychological overtones expressed through exotic settings, strange colours and eerie light.

Moreau /mɔːˈrəʊ/ Jean Victor Marie 1763–1813. French general who won a brilliant victory over the Austrians at Hohenlinden; as a republican he intrigued against Napoleon, and

More Initially favoured by Henry VIII, Thomas More was executed for refusing to take the oath of supremacy to the king as head of the Church. This portrait is after Holbein.

when banished, joined the Allies and was killed at the Battle of Dresden.

Morecambe Bay /ˈmɔːkəm ˈbeɪ/ inlet of the Irish Sea, between the Furness Peninsula (Cumbria) and Lancashire, England, with shallow sands. There are oil wells, and natural gas 50 km/30 mi offshore.

morel type of mushroom. The common morel, *Morchella esculenta*, grows abundantly in Europe and N America. A yellowish-brown, its edible cap is much wrinkled and about 2.5 cm/1 in long. It is used for seasoning gravies, soups, and sauces.

Moresby /ˈmɔːzbi/ John 1830–1922. British naval explorer and author. He is remembered as the first European to visit New Guinea's finest harbour, now ◊Port Moresby.

Morgan /ˈmɔːgən/ Henry c. 1635–1688. Welsh buccaneer in the Caribbean. He made war against Spain, capturing and sacking Panama in 1671. Knighted in 1674, he became lieutenant-governor of Jamaica.

Morgan /ˈmɔːgən/ Lewis Henry 1818–1881. US anthropologist. He studied American Indian culture, especially the role of property, and was adopted by the Iroquois.

Morgan /ˈmɔːgən/ Thomas Hunt 1866–1945. American geneticist, awarded a Nobel prize in 1933 for his pioneering studies in classical ◊genetics. He was the first to work on the fruit fly, *Drosophila*, which has since become a major part of genetic studies. He helped to establish that the ◊genes were located on the

◊chromosomes, discovered sex chromosomes and invented the techniques of genetic mapping.

morganatic marriage marriage (recognized by the Church and with legitimate issue) in which a wife of lower rank than the husband is not raised to his level, and whose children do not inherit their father's rank or lands. From medieval Latin *matrimonium ad morganaticum* 'marriage of the morning-gift', a token given by the husband to his wife on marrying her. George I of England was married in this way.

Morgenthau Plan a document named after Henry Morgenthau Junior (US Secretary of the Treasury) and related to the allied plans for Germany after World War II. It proposed the elimination of war industries in the Ruhr and Saar basins and the conversion of Germany 'into a country primarily agricultural and pastoral in character'. Although agreed in principle by the allies at the second Quebec conference in Sept 1944, the plan for the pastorialization of Germany had already been dropped by the time Churchill, Roosevelt and Stalin met at Yalta in Feb 1945 even though no alternative plan had been suggested.

Morisco one of the Spanish Muslims and their descendants who accepted Christian baptism. They were all expelled from Spain in 1609.

Morisot /ˌmɒriˈsəʊ/ Berthe 1841–1895. French ◊Impressionist artist. The grand-daughter of the artist ◊Fragonard, she specialized in paintings of women and children, and had an important influence on the work of ◊Manet.

Morland /ˈmɔːlənd/ George 1763–1804. British painter. Born in London, the son of the artist Henry Morland 1730–97, he first exhibited at the Royal Academy at the age of 10. He excelled at painting country subjects, showing gypsies, stable interiors, and so on.

Morley /ˈmɔːli/ John, 1st Viscount Morley of Blackburn 1838–1923. British Liberal politician and writer. He entered Parliament in 1883, and was secretary for Ireland in 1886 and 1892–95. As secretary for India 1905–10, he prepared the way for more representative government. He was Lord President of the Council 1910–14, but resigned in protest against the declaration of war in 1914. He published lives of Voltaire, Rousseau, Burke, and Gladstone. He received a peerage in 1908.

Morley /ˈmɔːli/ Malcolm 1931– . British painter. He has been called the first photo-realist, and his works include landscapes and animals from life combined with mythological motifs. He also paints abstracts. He won the inaugural Turner Prize for art in 1984.

Morley /ˈmɔːli/ Thomas 1557–1602. English composer. A student of ◊Byrd, he became organist at St Paul's Cathedral, London, obtaining a monopoly of music printing. He was the most influential composer of the English madrigal school, and also wrote a large amount of polyphonic sacred music, songs for Shakespeare's plays, and a musical textbook, *Plaine and Easie Introduction to Practicall Musicke* 1597.

Mormon or *Latter-day Saint* religious organization founded by Joseph Smith (1805–44). Born in Vermont, USA, Smith received his first religious call in 1820, and in 1827 claimed to have been granted the revelation of the *Book of Mormon* (an ancient prophet), inscribed on gold plates and concealed a thousand years before in a hill near Palmyra, New York state. Christ is said to have appeared to an early American people after his ascension to establish his church in the New World. The Mormon Church is claimed to be a re-establishment of this by divine intervention. The 'Church of Jesus Christ of Latter-day Saints' was founded at Fayette, New York, in 1830 and accepted the book as supplementing the Christian scriptures. Further settlements were rapidly established despite opposition, and Brigham Young and the Twelve Apostles undertook the first foreign Mormon mission in England, the earliest European converts reaching the USA in 1840. Their doctrines met with persecution, and Smith was killed in Illinois. To escape further persecution, Brigham ◊Young led a migration of most of the church's members to the Valley of the Great Salt Lake in 1847 and in 1850 Utah was created a territory with Young as governor 1851–58. Most of the Mormons who remained in the Middle West (headquarters Independence, Missouri) accepted the founder's son Joseph Smith (1832–1914) as leader, adopted the name *Reorganized Church of Jesus Christ of Latter-day Saints*, and now claim to be the true successor of the original church. They do not accept the non-Christian doctrines later proclaimed by Young in 1852, notably that of polygamy, which Young attributed to the original founder in 1843 although Smith is on record as condemning it. The doctrine was also formally repudiated by the Utah Mormons in 1890, and Utah was recognized as a State of the Union in 1896. The Mormons worldwide number about 6,000,000.

morning glory plant *Ipomoea purpurea* of the family Convolvulaceae, native to tropical America. It has dazzling blue flowers and small quantities of substances similar to ◊LSD are found in the seeds of one variety.

Moro /'mɔːrəʊ/ Aldo 1916–1978. Italian Christian Democrat politician. Prime minister 1963–68 and 1974–76, he was expected to become Italy's president, when he was kidnapped and shot by Red Brigade urban guerrillas.

Morocco /mə'rɒkəʊ/ country in N Africa, bordered N and NW by the Mediterranean, E and SE by Algeria, and S by Western Sahara.

government Morocco is an unusual constitutional monarchy in that the king, as well as being the formal head of state, presides over his appointed cabinet and has powers, under the 1972 constitution, to dismiss the prime minister and other ministers, as well as to dissolve the legislature. This consists of a 306-member chamber of representatives, serving a six-year term. 206 are directly elected by universal suffrage and 100 are chosen by an electoral college of local councillors and employers' and employees' representatives. There are a number of political parties, the most significant being the

Constitutional Union (UC), the National Rally of Independents (RNI), the Popular Movement (MP), Istiqlal, the Socialist Union of Popular Forces (USFP) and the National Democratic Party (PND).

history originally occupied by ◊Berber tribes, the coastal regions of the area now known as Morocco were under Phoenician rule during the 10th–3rd centuries BC, and it became a Roman colony in the 1st century AD. It was invaded in the 5th century by the ◊Vandals, in the 6th century by the ◊Visigoths, and in the 7th century began to be conquered by the Arabs. From the 11th century the region was united under the ◊Almoravids, who ruled a Muslim empire which included Spain, Morocco, and Algeria. They were followed by the ◊Almohads, another Muslim dynasty, whose empire included Libya and Tunisia.

In the 15th century Portugal occupied the Moroccan port of Ceuta, but was defeated in 1578. Further European influence began in the 19th century, and was more lasting, with Morocco being divided in 1912 into French and Spanish protectorates. It became fully independent as the Sultanate of Morocco in 1956, under Mohammed V (Sultan since 1927). The former Spanish protectorate joined the new state, with Tangier, which had previously been an international zone.

The Sultan was restyled King of Morocco in 1957. After his death in 1961 he was succeeded by King Hassan II, who has survived several attempted coups and assassinations. Between 1960–72 several constitutions were formulated in an attempt to balance personal royal rule with demands for greater democracy.

Hassan's reign has been dominated by the dispute over Western Sahara, a former Spanish colony seen as historically Moroccan. In 1975 Spain ceded it to Morocco and ◊Mauritania, leaving them to divide it . The inhabitants, who had not been consulted, reacted violently through an independence movement, the Polisario Front. Less than a year later, Morocco and Mauritania were involved in a guerrilla war. With Algerian support, Polisario set up a government-in-exile in Algiers, the Sahrahwi Arab Democratic Republic (SADR). This prompted Hassan to sever diplomatic relations with Algeria in 1976. In 1979 Mauritania agreed a peace treaty with Polisario, and Morocco annexed the part of Western Sahara which Mauritania had vacated. Polisario reacted by intensifying its operations. In 1983 the Organization of African Unity (OAU) proposed a cease-fire, direct negotiations between Morocco and Polisario, and a referendum in Western Sahara. Morocco agreed but refused to deal directly with Polisario.

Although the war was costly, it allowed Hassan to capitalize on the patriotism it generated in his country. In 1984 he unexpectedly signed an agreement with Col ◊Khaddhafi of Libya, who had been helping Polisario, for economic and political cooperation and mutual defence. Meanwhile, Morocco was becoming more isolated as SADR gained wider recognition.

Moroni /mə'rəʊni/ capital of the Comoros Republic on Grand Comore; population 16,000.

Morpheus /'mɔːfjuːs/ in Greek and Roman mythology, the god of dreams, son of Hypnos or Somnus, god of sleep.

morphine in medicine, the name generally applied to an alkaloid extracted from ◊opium, used to alleviate pain. In the UK it is a controlled drug. Its regular administration may lead to dependence.

morphology the study of the physical structure and form of organisms, in particular their soft tissues.

Morris /'mɒrɪs/ Henry 1889–1961. British educationalist. As chief education officer for Cambridgeshire 1922–54, he inspired and oversaw the introduction of the 'village college' and ◊community school.

Morris /'mɒrɪs/ William 1834–1896. British poet, socialist, and designer. He was educated at Oxford, where he formed a lasting friendship with ◊Burne-Jones and was influenced by ◊Ruskin and ◊Rossetti. He abandoned architecture to study painting, but had a considerable influence on such architects as ◊Lethaby and Philip ◊Webb. In 1858 published his first book of verse, *The Defence of Guenevere*. In 1862 he founded his own firm for the manufacture of furniture, wallpapers, church decorations, and the like, He also published several more volumes of verse-romances. A visit to Iceland in 1871 inspired his greatest poem, *Sigurd the Volsung* 1876, and his translations of the Sagas. He joined the Social Democratic Federation in 1883, but left it in 1884 because he found it too moderate, and set up the Socialist League. To this period belong the romances, *A Dream of John Ball* 1888 and *News from Nowhere* 1891, both of which reflect his socialist ideology: the critical and sociological studies, *Signs of Change* 1888 and *Hopes and Fears for Art* 1892; and the narrative poem, *The Pilgrims of Hope* 1885. He founded the Kelmscott Press at Hammersmith in 1890 to print beautifully decorated books.

Morris dance an English folk-dance. In earlier times it was usually performed by six men, one of whom wore girl's clothing, while another portrayed a horse. The others wore a costume decorated with bells. It probably originated in pre-Christian ritual dances.

Morrison /'mɒrɪsən/ Herbert Stanley, Baron Morrison of Lambeth 1888–1965. British Labour politician. On leaving school he became a shop assistant. He was appointed secretary of the London Labour Party 1915–45, and was a member of the ◊London County Council 1922–45. Entering Parliament in 1923, he was minister of transport 1929–31, home secretary 1940–45, and Lord President of the Council and leader of the House of Commons 1945–51, briefly succeeding Bevin as foreign secretary Mar–Oct 1951. In 1955 he was defeated by Gaitskell in the contest for party leadership.

Morse /mɔːs/ Samuel Finley Breese 1791–1872. American who invented the magnetic ◊telegraph. Born in Massachusetts, in 1836 he produced the first adequate electric telegraph, and in 1843 was granted $30,000 by

Morocco
KINGDOM OF (*Al-Mamlaka al-Maghrebia*)

AREA 458,730 sq km/166,000 sq mi
CAPITAL Rabat
TOWNS Marrakesh, Fez, Kenes; ports
Casablanca, Tangier
PHYSICAL mountain ranges NE–SW; plains in
W
FEATURES Atlas Mountains; the towns Ceuta
(from 1580), Melilla (from 1492), and three
small coastal settlements are held by Spain; a
tunnel across the Strait of Gibraltar to Spain
was proposed in 1985
HEAD OF STATE Hassan II from 1961
HEAD OF GOVERNMENT Mohamed Karim
Lamrani from 1984
GOVERNMENT constitutional monarch has real
power
EXPORTS dates, figs; cork, wood pulp; canned
fish; phosphates; tourism is important
CURRENCY dirham (13.6 = £1 Sept 1987)
POPULATION 23,117,000 (1985); annual growth
rate 3.3%
LANGUAGE Arabic (official); French, Spanish
RELIGION Sunni Muslim
LITERACY 41% male/18% female (1980 est)
GNP $15.6 bn (1983); $800 per head of
population
CHRONOLOGY
1956 Achieved independence from France as
the Sultanate of Morocco.
1957 Sultan restyled king of Morocco.
1961 Hassan II came to the throne.
1972 Major revision of the constitution.

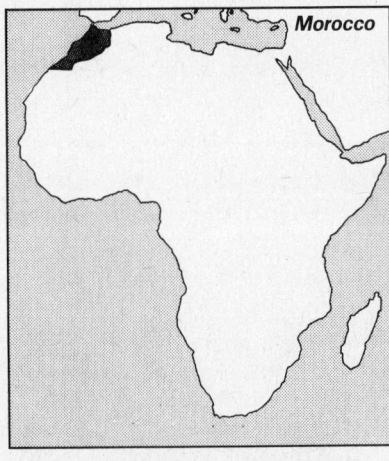
Morocco

1975 Western Sahara ceded by Spain to
Morocco and Mauritania.
1976 Guerrilla war in the Sahara by the
Polisario Front. Sahrawi Arab Democratic
Republic (SADR) established in Algiers.
Diplomatic relations between Morocco and
Algeria broken.
1979 Mauritania signed a peace treaty with
Polisario.
1983 Peace formula for the Sahara proposed
by the Organization of African Unity (OAU)
but not accepted by Morocco.
1984 Hassan signed an agreement for
cooperation and mutual defence with Libya.

Morris Best known for his design work and
association with the Arts and Crafts movement,
William Morris was a founder member of the
British socialist movement. The photograph is by
Abel Lewis (c. 1880).

Congress for an experimental line between
Washington and Baltimore. With his assistant
Alexander Bain he invented the ◊Morse code.

morse code

A	B	C	D	E	F
G	H	I	J	K	L
M	N	O	P	Q	R
S	T	U	V	W	X
		Y	Z		
	1	2	3	4	5
	6	7	8	9	0

Morse code international code for
transmitting messages by wire or radio using
signals of short (dots) and long (dashes)
duration, originated by Samuel ◊Morse for use
on his ◊telegraph. The letters SOS (3 short, 3
long, 3 short) form the international distress
signal, being distinctive and easily transmitted
(popularly *Save Our Souls*). By radio telephone

the distress call is 'Mayday', for similar reasons
(popularly alleged to drive from French *m'aidez*,
help me).

mortality rate in ◊demography, the
probability that an organism will die during any
given period of its life.

mortgage a transfer of property – usually a
house – as a security for repayment of a loan.
This is normally paid to a ◊bank or ◊building
society over a period of years. A mortgage is
made by a deed which conveys the full ownership
of the property to the mortgagee subject to the
mortgagor's right to recover it on payment of
both principal and interest.

Mortimer /'mɔːtɪmə/ John 1923– . British
barrister and writer. His works include the plays
The Dock Brief 1958, and *A Voyage Round My
Father* 1970, the novel *Paradise Postponed* 1985
and the television series *Rumpole of the Bailey*
from 1978, centred on a fictional barrister.

Mortimer /'mɔːtɪmə/ Roger de c. 1287–1330.
8th Baron of Wigmore and 1st Earl of March.
English nobleman. A rebel, he was imprisoned
by Edward II for two years before making his
escape from the Tower of London to France.
There he joined with the English queen, Isabella,
who was conducting negotiations at the French
Court and returned with her to England in 1326.
Edward fled when they landed with their
followers, and after securing Edward's
deposition by Parliament, Mortimer ruled
England as the Queen's lover. In 1328 he was
created Earl of March. He was popularly
supposed responsible for Edward II's murder,
and Edward III had him seized at Nottingham
Castle; he was hanged, drawn and quartered at
Tyburn.

Morton /'mɔːtn/ 'Jelly Roll' (Ferdinand
Joseph) 1885–1941. Pioneer US jazz pianist,
singer and composer, who achieved fame with
the Red Hot Peppers. Influenced by Scott Joplin,
he played a major part in the development of jazz
from ragtime to swing by means of improvisation
and imposing his own personality on the music.

Morton /'mɔːtn/ J(ohn) B(ingham) 1893–
1979. British journalist. Educated at Oxford, he
is best known for the humorous column he
contributed to the *Daily Express* 1924–76 under
the pseudonym of 'Beachcomber'.

mosaic a design or picture, usually for a floor
or wall, produced by inlay of small pieces of
marble, glass, or other materials. Mosaic was
commonly used by the Romans for their villas
(for example Hadrian's Villa at Tivoli), and by
the Byzantines. The art was revived by the
Italians during the 13th century, when it was
used chiefly for the decoration of churches (for
example San Vitale, ◊Ravenna).

Moscow /'mɒskəʊ/ (Russian *Moskva*),
capital of the USSR and of the Moskva region,
on the Moskva river 640 km/400 mi SE of
Leningrad
population (1985) 8,642,000
features the 12th-century Kremlin (Citadel), at
the centre of the city, is a walled enclosure
containing a number of historic buildings,
including three cathedrals, one of them the burial
place of the tsars; the Ivan Veliki tower 90 m/300
ft, a famine-relief work commissioned by Boris

Morse The American Samuel Morse invented the magnetic telegraph and the Morse code.

Godunov in 1600; various palaces, including the former imperial palace, museums, and the Tsar Kolokol, the world's largest bell (200 tonnes) 1735. The walls of the Kremlin are crowned by 18 towers and have five gates. Red Square, used for political demonstrations and processions, contains St Basil's Cathedral, the state department store GUM, and Lenin's tomb. The headquarters of the ◊KGB, with Lubyanka Prison behind it, is in Dzerzhinsky Square; the underground railway, opened in 1935, is a showpiece. Institutions include Moscow University 1755 and People's Friendship University (for foreign students) 1953; ◊Academy of Sciences, which moved from Leningrad in 1934; Tretyakov Gallery of Russian Art, 1856; Bolshoi Theatre 1780 for opera and ballet; Moscow Art Theatre 1898; Moscow State Circus. Moscow is the seat of the patriarch of the Russian Orthodox Church. On the city outskirts is Star City (Zvezdnoy Gorodok), the Soviet space centre

products machinery, electrical equipment, textiles, chemicals, and many food products; Moscow is the largest industrial centre of the USSR, linked with Stavropol by oil pipeline 480 km/300 mi 1957

history Moscow, founded in the 12th century, was the capital of Imperial Russia 14th century–1709 (see ◊Peter the Great). It was burned in 1571 by the khan of the Crimea, and

ravaged by fire in 1739, 1748, and 1753; in 1812 it was burned by its own citizens to save it from Napoleon's troops, or perhaps by accident. It became capital of the Russian Soviet Federated Social Republic (RSFSR) 1918, and of the Union of Soviet Socialist Republics (USSR) 1922. In World War II Hitler's troops were within 20 mi of Moscow on the NW by Nov 1941, but the stubborn Russian defence and severe winter weather forced their withdrawal in Dec.

Moseley /'məʊzli/ Henry Gwyn-Jeffreys 1887–1915. British physicist who did valuable work on atomic structure, and in 1913 devised the series of atomic numbers (see ◊periodic table).

Moselle /məʊ'zel/ a river in W Europe some 515 km/320 mi long; it rises in the Vosges, France, and is canalized from Thionville to its confluence with the ◊Rhine at Koblenz in Germany. It gives its name to the *départements* of Moselle and Meurthe-et-Moselle in France.

Moses /'məʊzɪz/ Hebrew lawgiver and judge who led the Israelites out of Egypt to the promised land of Canaan. According to the ◊Torah, Moses was hidden among the bulrushes on the banks of the Nile when the Pharoah commanded that all newborn male Hebrew children should be destroyed. He was found by a daughter of Pharoah, who reared him. Eventually he became the leader of the Israelites in their Exodus from Egypt, and their 40 years' wandering in the wilderness. On Mount Sinai he

received from Jehovah the Ten Commandments engraved on tablets of stone, and died at the age of 120, after having been allowed a glimpse of the Promised Land from Mount Pisgah.

Moses /'məʊzɪz/ Anna Mary 'Grandma' (born Robertson) 1860–1961. American painter. She began working as a serious artist only in about 1927 when she was 67, after a life as a farmer's wife. She achieved great popularity with her colourful and simple scenes.

Mosi-oa-tunya /'məʊsi 'əʊə 'tuːnjə/ the African name for the ◊Victoria Falls of the Zambezi river.

Moskva /mʌsk'vɑː/ the Russian name for ◊Moscow, capital of USSR.

Moslem alternative name for Muslim; a follower of ◊Islam.

Mosley /'məʊzli/ Oswald Ernald 1896–1980. British politician, founder of the British Union of Fascists (BUF). See ◊fascism. He held seats in Parliament as a Unionist 1918–22, Independent 1922–24, and Labour member 1924 and 1926–31, and then represented BUF in 1932. Interned during World War II, he was released on health grounds in 1943, and resumed fascist propaganda with his Union Movement, the revived BUF. His first marriage was to a daughter of the Conservative politician Lord ◊Curzon, his second to Diana Freeman-Mitford, one of the ◊Mitford sisters.

mosque in ◊Islam, a place of worship. The earliest mosques (Arabic *mesjid*) were based on the plan of Christian basilicas, although different influences contributed to their architectural development. Mosques vary a great deal in style in various parts of the world. Chief features are: the dome, the minaret, a balconied turret from which the faithful are called to prayer, the *mihrab*, or prayer niche, in one of the interior walls, showing the direction of ◊Mecca, and an open court surrounded by porticoes.

mosquito fly of the family Culicidae. In mosquitoes the female has needle-like mouthparts and sucks blood, needing a meal before egglaying. Males feed on plant juices. Some mosquitoes carry diseases such as malaria.

moss small non-flowering plant of the class Musci (10,000 species), forming with the ◊liverworts the order Bryophyta. Each plant comprises a stem, bearing rhizoids which anchor the plant, with leaves spirally arranged on its lower portion and producing sexual organs at its tip, but no true roots. Most mosses flourish best in damp conditions where other vegetation is thin. The peat or bog moss *Sphagnum* was formerly used for surgical dressings. Moss gardens are popular in Japan, the most famous being at the Moss Temple, near Kyoto.

Mossadeq /'mɒsədek/ Muhammad 1880–1967. Iranian prime minister 1951–53. He instigated the dispute with the Anglo-Iranian Oil Company over the control of Iran's oil production, and when he failed in his attempt to overthrow the Shah he was imprisoned. From 1956 he was under house arrest.

Mostaganem /mə,stægə'nem/ industrial port (metal and cement) in NW Algeria, linked by pipeline with the natural gas fields at Hassi

Messaoud; population (1974) 107,000. It was founded in the 11th century.

Mostar /'mɒstɑː/ industrial town (aluminium, tobacco) in Bosnia-Hercegovina, Yugoslavia, noted for its grapes and wines; population (1981) 110,377.

Mosul /'məusəl/ city and oil centre in Iraq, on the right bank of the Tigris, opposite the site of ancient ◊Nineveh; population (1970) 293,000. Once it manufactured the light cotton fabric *muslin*, which was named after it.

motet a form of sacred, polyphonic music for unaccompanied voices which originated in the 13th century.

moth one of the insects forming the greater part of the order Lepidoptera, normally distinguished from ◊butterflies by the absence of a knob on the end of the antennae. When at rest, moths commonly hold their wings flat or sloping over the body; butterflies close them vertically. The wings are covered with flat, microscopic scales, but in the bee hawk-moths and the clearwings the scales are confined to certain areas. The mouth-parts are formed into a sucking proboscis, but certain moths have no functional mouth-parts, and, being unable to feed, rely upon stores of fat and other reserves built up during the caterpillar stage. In many cases the males are smaller and more brightly coloured than the females, and have the antennae branched or comb-like. In other cases, including the vapourer and winter moths, the females have wings either absent or reduced to minute flaps. Moths vary greatly in size: thus the minute Nepticulidae sometimes have a wing-spread less than 3 mm, while the giant Noctuid or owlet moth, *Erebus agrippina*, measures about 280 mm/11 in across its extended wings. The largest British moths are the death's head and convolvulus hawk-moths, which have a wing-spread ranging from 114 mm/4.5 in to 133 mm/5.25 in. Moths feed chiefly on the nectar of flowers, on honeydew, and other fluid matter: some, like the hawk-moths, frequent flowers and feed while poised with rapidly vibrating wings. The larvae or caterpillars have a well-developed head, three thoracic and ten abdominal segments. Each thoracic segment bears a pair of short legs, ending in single claws; a pair of sucker-like abdominal feet is present on segments three to six and ten of the hind-body. In the family Geometridae the caterpillars bear the abdominal feet only on segments six and ten of the hind-body. They move by a characteristic looping gait and are known as 'loopers' or geometers. Projecting from the middle of the lower lip of a caterpillar is a minute tube or spinneret, through which silk is emitted to make a cocoon within which the change to the pupa or chrysalis occurs. Silk glands are especially large in the silkworm moth. Many caterpillars, including the geometers, which are sought by birds, are protected by their resemblance in both form and coloration to their immediate surroundings. Others, distasteful to their enemies, are brightly coloured or densely hairy. Moths are economically important, owing to the damage caused by the feeding caterpillars; the winter moth and the codling moth which attack fruit

trees; the Mediterranean flour moth, which infects flour mills; and the several species of clothes moth. At least 100,000 different species of moth are known.

mother of pearl the smooth lustrous lining in the shells of pearl-bearing molluscs. See under ◊pearl.

Motherwell and Wishaw /'mʌðəwəl, 'wɪʃɔː/ industrial town (Ravenscraig iron and steel works, coal mines) in Strathclyde, Scotland, SE of Glasgow; population (1981) 68,000. The two burghs were amalgamated in 1920.

motor a machine that provides mechanical power, particularly an ◊electric motor. Machines that burn fuel (petrol, diesel) are usually called engines.

motor boat small, water-borne craft powered by a petrol, diesel or gas turbine engine. For increased speed, especially in racing, motor boat hulls are designed to skim the water (aquaplane) and reduce frictional resistance. Plastics, steel, and light alloys are now used in construction as well as the traditional wood. In recent designs, drag is further reduced with hydrofins and ◊hydrofoils, which enable the hull to rise clear of the water, at normal speeds. Notable events in motor or 'power-boat' racing include the American Gold Cup 1947 over a 145 km/90 mi course, and the Round-Britain race 1969.

motor car a self-propelled vehicle for use on normal roads.
Although it is recorded that in 1479 one Gilles de Dom was paid 25 livres by the treasurer of Antwerp in the Low Countries, for supplying such a vehicle, the 'ancestor of the automobile' is generally agreed to be N Cugnot's cumbrous steam carriage 1769, still preserved in Paris.
Another Parisian, Etienne Lenoir, made the first gas engine in 1860, and in 1885 ◊Benz built and ran the first petrol-driven motor car; and Panhard 1890 (front radiator, engine under bonnet, sliding-pinion gearbox, wooden ladder-chassis) and Mercédès 1901 (honeycomb radiator, in-line four-cylinder engine, gate-change gearbox, pressed-steel chassis) set the pattern for the modern car. Emerging with Haynes and Duryea in the early 1890s, US demand was so fervent that 300 makers existed by 1895: many so ephemeral that there were only 109 left in 1900.
In the 19th century practical steam coaches by English pioneers Hancock and Goldsworthy Gurney were used for public transport, until stifled by punitive road tolls and legislation, particularly the notorious Red Flag Act 1831. F W Lanchester in 1896 produced a petrol-driven motor vehicle.
Among the motor cars of the early 1900s are: *De Dion Bouton*, with the first practical high-speed engines; Napier, the 24-hour record holder in 1907, unbeaten for 17 years; the *Silver Ghost* Rolls-Royce; the enduring *Model T* ◊Ford; and the many types of *Bugatti* and *Delage*.
After World War I popular motoring was inaugurated with cheap light (baby) cars made by Citroën, Peugeot and Renault (France); Austin 7, Morris, Clyno, and Swift (England); Fiat (Italy), and the cheap though bigger Ford, Chevrolet, and Dodge in the USA.

In Britain, the Ministry of Transport was established 1919, roads were improved, and various laws and safety precautions imposed to govern the ownership and use of cars.
A typical modern European medium-sized saloon car has a semi-monocoque construction in which the body panels, suitably reinforced, support the road loads through independent front and rear sprung suspension, with seats located within the wheelbase for comfort. It is powered by ◊petrol engine using a carburettor to mix petrol and air for feeding to the engine cylinders (typically four or six). The engine is usually water cooled. From the engine power is transmitted through a clutch to a 4-or 5-speed gearbox and thence, in a front-engine rear-drive car, through a drive (propeller) shaft to a ◊differential gear, which drives the rear wheels. In a front-engine front-wheel drive car, clutch, gearbox and final drive are incorporated with the engine unit. An increasing number of high-performance cars are being offered with four-wheel drive. This gives superior roadholding. From the 1950s automatic transmission for small cars, rubber suspension, transverse engine mounting, self-levelling ride, disc brakes and safer wet-weather tyres were introduced, and later the stratified-charge petrol engine, using a fuel injector to achieve 20 per cent improvement in petrol consumption; weight reduction in the body by the use of aluminium and plastics; and 'slippery' body designs with low air resistance, or drag. Microprocessors were developed to measure temperature, engine speed, pressure and oxygen content of exhaust gases, and readjust parts of the engine accordingly.

motor cycle a two-wheeled vehicle propelled by a ◊petrol engine. Gottlieb ◊Daimler, a German engineer, created the first motor cycle when he installed his lightweight petrol engine in a bicycle frame in 1885. Earlier (1868) Ernest and Pierre Michaux in France had experimented with a steam-powered bicycle, but the steam power unit was too heavy and cumbersome.
The first really successful two-wheel design was devised by Michael and Eugene Werner in France 1901. They adopted the classic motor cycle layout with the engine low down between the wheels. Harley Davidson in the USA and Triumph in the UK began manufacture 1903. Road races like the Isle of Man TT (Tourist Trophy), established in 1907, helped improve motor cycle design. Today Japanese motor cycles are predominant, particularly Honda, Suzuki, Yamaha and Kawasaki. They make a wide variety of machines, from ◊mopeds to 1,200 cc motorbikes.
The lightweight bikes are generally powered by a ◊two-stroke petrol engine, while bikes with an engine capacity of 250 cc upwards are generally ◊four-strokes. The two-strokes and most of the four-strokes are air cooled – their engines are surrounded by metal fins to offer a large surface area. A few large-engine bikes have a water-cooling system similar to that of a car. A few bikes have single-cylinder engines, though large machines can have as many as six. In the majority of bikes a chain carries the drive from the engine to the rear wheel, though some larger machines are fitted with shaft drive.

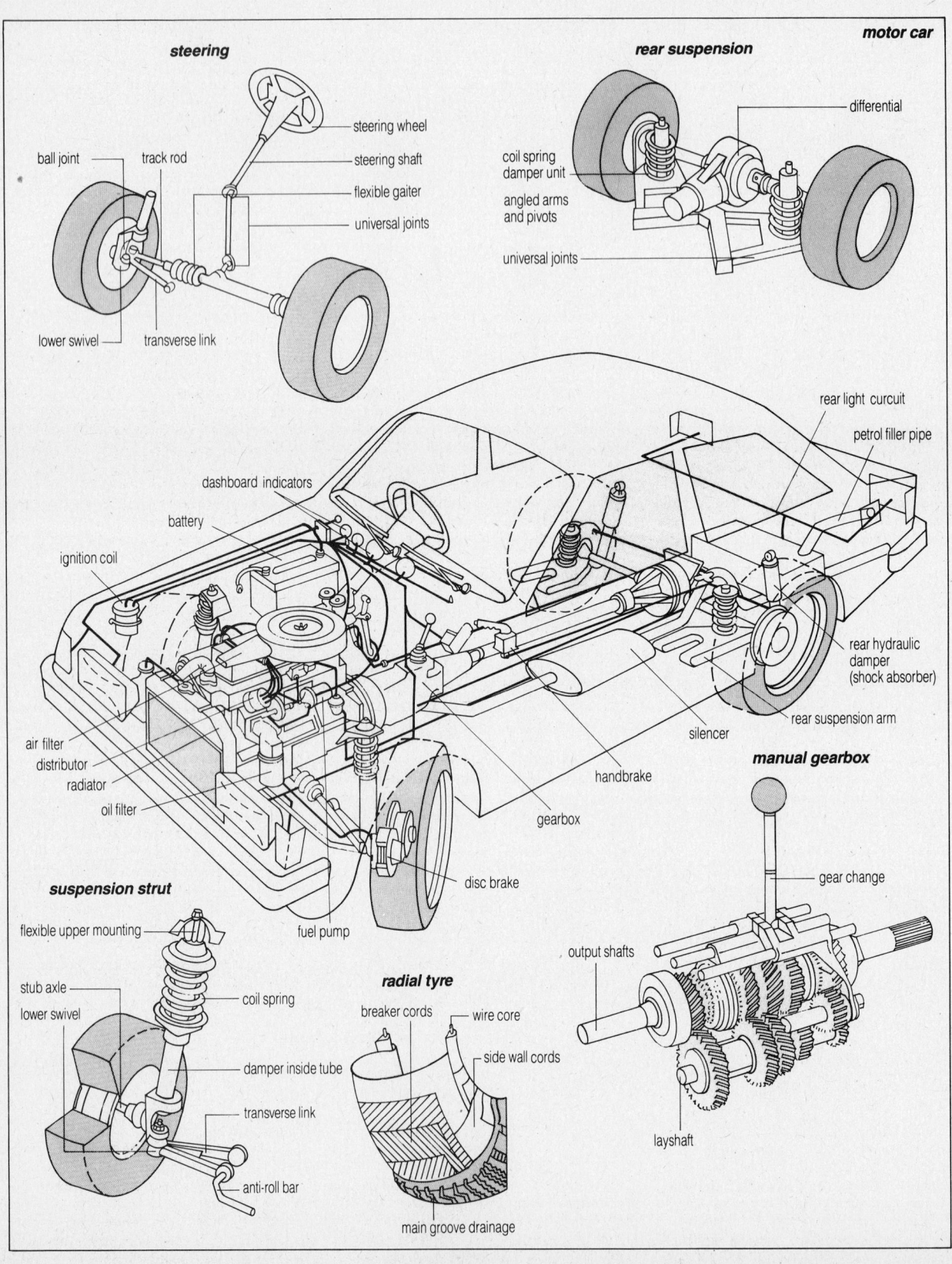

motor car

steering

- steering wheel
- steering shaft
- flexible gaiter
- universal joints
- ball joint
- track rod
- lower swivel
- transverse link

rear suspension

- differential
- coil spring damper unit
- angled arms and pivots
- universal joints

- rear light curcuit
- petrol filler pipe
- dashboard indicators
- battery
- ignition coil
- rear hydraulic damper (shock absorber)
- rear suspension arm
- air filter
- distributor
- radiator
- oil filter
- silencer
- handbrake
- gearbox
- disc brake
- fuel pump

manual gearbox

- gear change
- output shafts
- layshaft

suspension strut

- flexible upper mounting
- stub axle
- lower swivel
- coil spring
- damper inside tube
- transverse link
- anti-roll bar

radial tyre

- breaker cords
- wire core
- side wall cords
- main groove drainage

MOTOR CAR: CHRONOLOGY

1769	Nicholas-Joseph Cugnot in France built a steam tractor.
1801	Richard Trevithick built a steam coach.
1860	Jean Etienne Lenoir built a gas-fuelled internal combustion engine.
1831	The British government passed the 'Red Flag' Act, requiring a man to precede a 'horseless carriage' with a red flag.
1876	Nikolaus August Otto improved the gas engine, making it a practical power source.
1885	Gottlieb Daimler developed a lightweight petrol engine and fitted it to a bicycle to create the prototype of the modern motorbike; Karl Benz fitted his lightweight petrol engine to a three-wheeled carriage to pioneer the motor car.
1886	Gottlieb Daimler fitted his engine to a four-wheeled carriage to produce a four-wheeled motor car.
1891	René Panhard and Emile Levassor established the modern design of cars by putting the engine in front.
1896	Frederick Lancaster introduced epicyclic gearing, which foreshadowed automatic transmission.
1901	The first Mercedes took to the roads. It was the direct ancestor of the modern car; Ransome Olds in the USA introduced mass production on an assembly line.
1906	Rolls-Royce introduced the legendary Silver Ghost, which established their reputation for superlatively engineered cars.
1908	Henry Ford also used assembly-line production to manufacture his famous Model T, nicknamed the Tin Lizzie because it used lightweight steel sheet for the body, which looked 'tinny'.
1911	Cadillac introduced the electric starter and dynamo lighting.
1913	Ford introduced the moving conveyor belt to the assembly line, further accelerating production of the Model T.
1920	Duesenberg began fitting four-wheel hydraulic brakes.
1922	The Lancia Lambda featured unitary (all-in-one) construction and independent front suspension.
1928	Cadillac introduced the synchromesh gearbox, facilitating gear changing.
1934	Citroën pioneered front-wheel drive in their 7CV model.
1936	Fiat introduced their baby car, the Topolino, 500 cc.
1938	Germany produced their 'people's car', the Volkswagen 'beetle'.
1948	Jaguar launched the XK120 sports car; Michelin introduced the radial-ply tyre; Goodrich produced the tubeless tyre.
1950	Dunlop announced the disc brake.
1951	Buick and Chrysler introduced power steering.
1952	Rover's gas-turbine car set a speed record of 243 kph/152 mph.
1954	Bosch introduced fuel-injection for cars.
1955	Citroën produced the advanced DS-19 'shark-front' car with hydropneumatic suspension.
1957	Felix Wankel built his first rotary petrol engine.
1959	BMC (now Rover) introduced the Issigonis-designed Mini, with front-wheel drive, transverse engine and independent rubber suspension.
1966	California introduced legislation to reduce air pollution by cars.
1972	Dunlop introduced safety tyres, which sealed themselves after a burst.
1980s	Lean-burn engines were introduced to improve fuel consumption; electronic ignition and engine controls became widely available; on-board computers were introduced to monitor engine performance, speech synthesizers to issue audible warnings.

There are many forms of motor-cycle racing – road and track races, trials, motocross (once called scrambling) and speedway. Drag racing is a newer sport in which riders compete on very powerful, often multi-engined machines to cover a set distance in the shortest possible time.

motor nerves in anatomy nerves which transmit impulses from the ▷central nervous system to muscles or body organs. Motor nerves cause voluntary and involuntary ▷muscle contractions and stimulate ▷glands to secrete hormones.

motor racing competitive events, beginning with a timed trial from Paris to Rouen in 1894, important for manufacturers' prestige. Great road races have included the mountainous *Targa Florio* (Sicily), and *Mille Miglia* (Italy). The 24-hr race of Le Mans 1923 is the foremost proving ground for sports cars. Famous circuits include Brands Hatch, Brooklands (to 1939) and Silverstone, UK; Montlhéry, France; Nurburgring, Germany; and Indianapolis, USA. In Grand Prix motor racing (1906) individual events in numerous different countries, notably the Monaco Grand Prix, count towards the world championship, introduced 1950. Motor rallies are for mass-produced cars, the toughest being the E African Safari Rally 1953 run every Easter. The first six drivers in each race score points. The one with the most points at the end of the season is declared champion.

World Driver's Championship first held 1950
1977 Niki Lauda *(Austria)*
1978 Mario Andretti *(USA)*
1979 Jody Scheckter *(South Africa)*
1980 Alan Jones *(Australia)*
1981 Nelson Piquet *(Brazil)*
1982 Keke Rosberg *(Finland)*
1983 Nelson Piquet *(Brazil)*
1984 Niki Lauda *(Austria)*
1985 Alain Prost *(France)*
1986 Alain Prost *(France)*
1987 Nelson Piquet *(Brazil)*
Le Mans Grand Prix d'Endurance ('Le Mans 24-Hour Race') first held 1923
1977 Jacky Ickx *(Belgium)*/Jurgen Barth *(West Germany)*
1978 Didier Pironi *(France)*/Jean-Pierre Jassaud *(France)*
1979 Klaus Ludwig *(West Germany)*/Bill Whittington *(USA)*/Don Whittington *(USA)*
1980 Jean-Pierre Jassaud *(France)*/Jean Rondeau *(France)*
1981 Jacky lckx *(Belgium)*/Derek Bell *(UK)*
1982 Jacky Ickx *(Belgium)*/Derek Bell *(UK)*
1983 Vern Schuppan *(Austria)*/Al Holbert *(USA)*/Hurley Haywood *(USA)*
1984 Klaus Ludwig *(West Germany)*/Henri Pescarolo *(France)*
1985 Klaus Ludwig *(West Germany)*/'John Winter'*(West Germany)*/Paolo Barilla *(Italy)*
1986 Hans Stuck *(West Germany)*/Derek Bell *(Great Britain)*/Al Holbert *(USA)*
1987 Hans Stuck *(West Germany)* Derek Bell *(Great Britain)* Al Holbert *(USA)*
Indianapolis 500 first held 1911,
1977 A J Foyt *(USA)*
1978 Al Unser *(USA)*
1979 Rick Mears *(USA)*
1980 Johnny Rutherford *(USA)*
1981 Bobby Unser *(USA)*
1982 Gordon Johncock *(USA)*
1983 Tom Sneva *(USA)*
1984 Rick Mears *(USA)*
1985 Danny Sullivan *(USA)*
1986 Bobby Rahal *(USA)*
1987 Al Unser *(USA)*.

Motown the first black-owned US record company, founded in Detroit (*motor town*) 1959 by Berry Gordy Jr (1929–). Its distinctive sound, created by in-house producers and

motor racing The severe banking of the old Brooklands circuit at Weybridge, Surrey, is apparent as this 4.5 litre Bentley driven by Henry Birkin cornered at the top of the banking. This car was capable of speeds up to 217kph/135mph.

songwriters such as Marvin ◊Gaye, Smokey Robinson (1940–   ), and the team of Holland-Dozier-Holland, and performed by Stevie Wonder, the ◊Supremes, the Temptations, and many others, dominated 1960s pop music. Its influence faded after the company's move to Los Angeles 1971, but it still provided a breeding ground for singers such as Lionel Richie (1950–   ) and Michael Jackson (1958–   ).

Mott /mɒt/ Nevill 1905–   . British physicist noted for his research on the electronic properties of glass, and its use in computer materials. He shared a Nobel prize in 1977.

mouflon type of sheep *Ovis ammon* found wild in Corsica and Sardinia. It has woolly underfur in winter, but this is covered by the heavy guard hairs. The coat is brown, with white belly and rump. Males have strong curving horns. The mouflon lives in rough mountain areas.

mould mainly saprophytic ◊fungi living on food-stuffs and other organic matter, a few being parasitic on plants, animals, or each other. Many are of medical or industrial importance, such as penicillin.

moulding a common method of shaping plastics, clays, glass and other materials. In *injection moulding*, molten plastic, for example, is injected into a water-cooled mould and takes the shape of the mould when it solidifies. In *blow moulding*, air is blown into a blob of molten plastic inside a hollow mould. In *compression moulding*, synthetic resin powder is simultaneously heated and pressed into a mould. When metals are used, the process is called ◊casting.

Moulins /muːˈlæn/ capital of the *département* of Allier, France; population (1975) 26,900. Moulin was capital of the old province of Bourbonnais 1368–1527.

Moulmein /maʊlˈmeɪn/ port in Burma, on the Salween estuary; population (1983) 202,967.

moulting the periodic shedding of the hair or fur of mammals, feathers of birds, or skin of reptiles. In mammals and birds moulting is usually seasonal and is triggered by changes of daylength; see ◊photoperiodism. The term is also often applied to the shedding of the ◊exoskeleton of arthropods, but this is more correctly called ◊ecdysis.

Moundbuilder a member of various N American Indian peoples (see ◊Hopewell, ◊Natchez) who built earth mounds, linear and conical in shape for tombs, and 'platforms' for chiefs' houses, and temples from about 300 BC. They carried out group labour projects under the rule of an elite. A major site is Monk's Mound in Mississippi. They were in decline by the time of the Spanish invasion.

mountain ash or rowan. Flowering tree *Sorbus aucuparia* of the family Rosaceae. Growing to 50 ft/15 m it has pinnate leaves and large clusters of whitish flowers, followed by scarlet berries.

mountaineering the art and practice of mountain climbing. For major peaks of the Himalayas it was formerly thought necessary to have elaborate support from Sherpas, and fixed ropes and oxygen at high altitudes. However, in the 1980s the 'Alpine style' was introduced. This dispenses with these aids, and relies on human ability to adapt to high altitude. In 1854 *Wetterhorn*, Switzerland, was climbed by Alfred Wills, thereby founding the sport; 1865 *Matterhorn*, Switzerland-Italy, by ◊Whymper; 1897 *Aconcagua*, Argentina, by Zurbriggen; 1938 *Eiger*, Switzerland, (north face) by Heinrich Harrer; 1953 *Everest*, Nepál/Tibet, by ◊Hilary/◊Tenzing; 1981 *Kongur*, China by ◊Bonington.

mountain lion another name for ◊puma.

Mountbatten /maʊntˈbætn/ Louis, 1st Earl Mountbatten of Burma 1900–1979. British admiral. Son of Princess Victoria (a granddaughter of Queen Victoria), and Prince ◊Louis Alexander Mountbatten, marquess of Milford Haven, he entered the navy in 1913 and was present at the Battle of ◊Jutland. In World War II at the battle of Crete the ship he commanded, HMS *Kelly*, was sunk, and he was picked up from the sea. He became chief of combined operations in 1942, and was criticized for the heavy loss of allied lives in the ◊Dieppe raid. In 1943 he became commander in chief in SE Asia.
As last viceroy of India 1947 he oversaw the transition to independence, becoming first governor-general of India until 1948. He was First Sea Lord 1955–59, and chief of UK Defence Staff 1959–65. He was created an earl in 1947, and received the Order of Merit in 1965. He was killed by an Irish Republican Army bomb aboard his yacht at Mullaghmore, County Sligo.

Mount Isa /ˈaɪzə/ mining town (copper, lead, silver, zinc) in NW Queensland, Australia; population (1984) 25,000.

Mount Lofty Range /ˈlɒfti/ mountain range in SE South Australia; Mount Bryan 934 m/3,064 ft is the highest peak.

Mount Rushmore /ˈrʌʃmɔː/ mountain in the Black Hills, South Dakota, USA, 1890 m/3064 ft high; on its granite face are carved giant portrait heads of presidents Washington, Jefferson, Lincoln, and Theodore Roosevelt. The sculptor was Gutzon ◊Borglum.

Mount St Helens /seɪnt ˈhelənz/ volcanic mountain NE of Portland, Oregon, USA. When it erupted in 1980 after being quiescent for 450 years, its height was reduced from 2,945 m/9,667 ft to 2,560 m/8,400 ft.

Mount Vernon /ˈvɜːnən/ village in Virginia, USA, on the Potomac river, where George Washington lived 1752–99 and was buried on the family estate, now a national monument.

mouse name given to many small rodents, particularly those of the family Muridae. The house mouse *Mus musculus* is universally distributed; 75 mm/3 in long, with naked tail of equal length, with grey-brown body, it nests in paper and straw. Commonly found in Britain is the wood mouse *Apodemus sylvaticus*, richer in colour. The tiny harvest mouse *Micromys minutus*, 65–75 mm/2.5–3 in long, makes spherical nests of straw supported on grass stems. *Jumping mice*, family Zapodidae, with enlarged back legs, live across the N hemisphere, but are absent from Britain.

mouse in computing, an input device, used to control a pointer on a computer screen. Moving the mouse across a desktop produces corresponding movement in the pointer. A mouse normally has one or more controlling buttons to instruct the computer in a specific way when the pointer is superimposed on the screen.

mousebird bird of the order Coliiformes, including the single family (Coliidae) of small crested birds peculiar to Africa. They have hair-like feathers, long tails and mouse-like agility; largest is the *blue-naped mousebird Colius macrourus*, 35 cm/about 1 ft long.

Moustier, Le cave in the ◊Dordogne, SW France, giving the name *Mousterian* to the flint tool culture of Neanderthal peoples; the earliest ritual burials are linked with Mousterian settlements.

mouth the cavity forming the entrance of the digestive tract. In mammals it is also the entrance of the respiratory tract, and is enclosed by the ◊jaws, cheeks and ◊palate.

mouth organ another name for ◊harmonica, a musical instrument.

movement in music, a section of a large work, such as a symphony, which is often complete in itself.

Moyse /mwɑːz/ Marcel 1889–1984. French flautist. Trained at the Paris Conservatoire, he made many recordings and was an influential teacher.

Mozambique /ˌməʊzəmˈbiːk/ country in SE Africa, bordered to the N by Zambia, Malawi, and Tanzania, E by the Indian Ocean, S by South Africa, and E by Swaziland and Zimbabwe.
government The 1975 constitution, revised 1978, provides for a one-party, socialist state, based on the National Front for the Liberation of Mozambique (Frelimo), reconstituted in 1977 as a 'Marxist-Leninist vanguard party'. The president heads its political bureau and central committee secretariat. There is a 210-member People's Assembly, comprising 130 members of Frelimo's central committee plus 80 others from central and provincial governments, the armed forces and citizens' representatives. The Assembly is convened by the president and meets

twice a year. Its functions are performed in its absence by a 15-member inner group, called the Permanent Commission, also convened and presided over by the president.

history Mozambique's indigenous peoples are of Bantu origin. By the 10th century the Arabs had established themselves on the coast. The first European to reach Mozambique was Vasco da ◊Gama in 1498, and the country became a Portuguese colony in 1505. Portugal exploited Mozambique's resources of gold and ivory, and used it as a source of slave labour, both locally and overseas.

Guerrilla groups opposed Portuguese rule from the early 1960s. Frelimo was formed in 1962 by a merger of three nationalist parties, the Mozambique National Democratic Union, the Mozambique African Nationalist Union, and the African Union of Independent Mozambique. Its leader, Samora Machel, demanded complete independence, and in 1974 internal self-government was granted, with Joaquim Chissano, a member of Frelimo's Central Committee, as prime minister.

Becoming president of an independent Mozambique in 1975, Machel was faced with the emigration of hundreds of thousands of Portuguese settlers, leaving no trained replacements in key economic positions. Two activities had been the mainstay of Mozambique's economy: transit traffic from South Africa and Rhodesia and the export of labour to South African mines. Although Machel supported the African National Congress (ANC) in South Africa, and the Patriotic Front in Rhodesia, he knew he must co-exist and trade with his two white-governed neighbours. He put heavy pressure on the Patriotic Front for a settlement of the guerrilla war and this eventually bore fruit in the 1979 Lancaster House Agreement and the eventual election victory of Robert ◊Mugabe, a reliable friend of Mozambique.

From 1980 the country was faced with widespread drought, which affected most of southern Africa, and attacks by mercenaries, under the banner of the Mozambique National Resistance (Renamo, or the MNR), covertly backed by South Africa. The attacks concentrated on Mozambique's transport system.

Machel, showing considerable diplomatic skill, had by 1983 repaired relations with the US, undertaken a successful European tour, and established himself as a respected African leader. In 1984 he signed the ◊Nkomati Accord, under which South Africa agreed to deny facilities to the MNR, and Mozambique in return agreed not to provide bases for the banned ANC. Machel took steps to honour his side of the bargain but was doubtful about South Africa's good faith. In Oct 1986 he died in an air crash near the South African border. Despite the suspicious circumstances, an inquiry pronounced his death an accident.

The following month Frelimo's Central Committee elected former prime minister Joaquim Chissano as his successor. Chissano immediately pledged to carry on the policies of his predecessor. He has strengthened the ties forged by Machel with Zimbabwe and Britain and in 1987 attended as an observer the Commonwealth Heads of Government summit. Mozambique's economic problems were aggravated in 1987 by food shortages, after another year of drought.

Mozambique

PEOPLE'S REPUBLIC OF (*República Popular de Moçambique*)

AREA 784,960 sq km/303,070 sq mi
CAPITAL and chief port Maputo
TOWNS ports Beira, Nacala
PHYSICAL mostly flat; mountains in W
FEATURES rivers Zambezi, Limpopo
HEAD OF STATE AND OF GOVERNMENT Joaquim Chissano from 1986
GOVERNMENT one-party socialist
EXPORTS sugar, cashews, tea, cotton, copra, sisal
CURRENCY metical (replaced escudo 1980) (667.61 = £1 Sept 1987)
POPULATION (1985) 13,638,000 (mainly indigenous Bantu peoples; Portuguese 50,000); annual growth rate 3.2%
LANGUAGE Portuguese (official)
RELIGION animist 69%, Roman Catholic 21%, Muslim 10%
LITERACY 44% male/23% female (1980 est)
GDP $2.7 bn (1983); $220 per head of population
CHRONOLOGY
1962 Frelimo (liberation front) established.
1975 Full independence achieved as a socialist

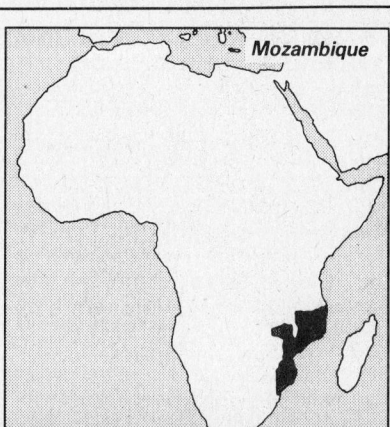

Mozambique

republic, with Samora Machel as president and Frelimo as the sole legal party.
1983 Re-establishment of good relations with Western powers.
1984 Nkomati Accord signed with South Africa.
1986 Machel killed in air crash, and succeeded by Joaquim Chissano.

Mozart /'məutsɑːt/ Wolfgang Amadeus 1756–1791. Austrian composer. Born in Salzburg, he showed astonishing precocity as a pianist and was trained by his father, Leopold Mozart (1719–87), also a professional musician and composer. With his sister, Maria Anna, he was taken on a number of tours 1762–79, visiting Vienna, the Rhineland, Holland, Paris, London, and Italy. Mozart not only gave public recitals, but had already begun to compose a considerable amount of music. In 1772–81 he was master of the archbishop of Salzburg's court band. From then on he lived mostly in Vienna. Strongly influenced by ◊Haydn, Mozart's music marks the height of the Classical age in its purity of melody and form.

He composed prolifically, his works including 25 piano concertos, 23 string quartets, 35 violin sonatas; some 50 symphonies, of which the best known are the E flat K543, G minor K550, and C major K551 ('Jupiter') symphonies, all composed 1788; a number of operas, including *Idomeneo* 1781, *Il seraglio/Die Entführung aus dem serail/The Abduction from the Seraglio* 1782, *Le Nozze di Figaro/The Marriage of Figaro* 1786, *Don Giovanni* 1787, *Così fan tutte/Thus Do All Women* 1790, and *Die Zauberflöte/The Magic Flute* 1791. His *Requiem* unfinished at his death, was completed by a pupil.

MPLA (Portuguese *Movimento Popular de Libertacão de Angola*, Popular Movement for the Liberation of Angola) socialist organization which was active to free Angola from Portuguese rule 1961–75 before being involved in the Civil War against its erstwhile allies UNITA (National Union for the Total Independence of Angola) and FNLA (National Front for the Liberation of Angola) 1975–76. The MPLA took control of the country with military aid from Cuba and arms from Eastern Europe, but UNITA guerrilla activities continue today, supported by South Africa.

Mubarak /muːˈbɑːræk/ Hosni 1928– . Egyptian politician. A technocrat, he commanded the Air Force 1972–5 (being responsible for the initial victories in the Egyptian campaign of 1973 against Israel), when he became an active vice-president to Sadat, and succeeded him on his assassination in 1981. He has continued to pursue Sadat's moderate policies, and has significantly increased the freedom of the press and of political association.

mucous membrane thin skin found on all internal body surfaces of animals (for example, eyelids, breathing and digestive passages, genital tract). It secretes mucus, a moistening, lubricating and protective fluid.

mudfish another name for ◊bowfin.

mudnesters Australian name for a group of birds making their nests from mud, and including the apostle bird *Struthidea cinerea* so-called from its appearance in little flocks of about twelve; the white-winged chough *Corcorax melanorhamphos* and the magpie lark *Grallina cyanoleuca*.

mudpuppy amphibian *Necturus maculosus* which remains permanently larval in form, with large external gills. It lives in streams in North America.

mudskipper type of fish, genus *Periophthalmus*, found in brackish water and shores in the tropics. It can walk or even climb, using its strong pectoral fins as legs, and has eyes set close together on top of the head.

muezzin Muslim official who calls the faithful to prayer from the minaret of a mosque.

mufti a Muslim legal expert (see Law under ◊Islam). In Turkey the *Grand Mufti* had supreme spiritual authority until the establishment of the republic in 1924.

Mugabe /muːˈɡɑːbi/ Robert Gabriel 1925– . Zimbabwe politician. He is a member of the Shona people, educated at Fort Hare University, South Africa. He was in detention in Rhodesia for nationalist activities 1964–74, then carried on guerrilla warfare from Mozambique. As leader of ◊ZANU, he was in alliance with Joshua ◊Nkomo of ◊ZAPU from 1976, and in 1980 became prime minister of independent Zimbabwe. In 1985 he postponed the introduction of a multi-party state for five years.

mugwump (Algonquian Indian 'chief') in US political history, a colloquial name for the Republicans who voted in the 1884 presidential election for Cleveland, the Democratic candidate, rather than for their Republican nominee, James G Blaine, hence the modern meaning: one who refuses to follow the official party line.

Muhammad /məˈhæməd/ or *Mohammed, Mahomet* c. 570–632. (Arabic 'praised'.) Founder of ◊Islam, born in ◊Mecca. Originally a shepherd and caravan conductor, he found leisure for meditation by his marriage with a wealthy widow in 595, and received his first revelation in 610. After some years of secret teaching, he openly declared himself the prophet of God in about 616, the Koran (revealed to him by God and later written down by his followers) being the basis of his teaching. Persecuted as the number of his followers increased, he fled to the town now known as ◊Medina in 622 (the flight, *Hegira*, marks the beginning of the Islamic era). After the battle of Badr in 623, he was continuously victorious, entering Mecca as the recognized prophet of Arabia 630. The succession was troubled.

Mujaheddin (Arabic *Mujahid*, 'fighters', from *jihad*, 'holy war') Islamic fundamentalist guerrillas of contemporary Afghanistan and Iran.

Mujibur /muːˈdʒiːbuə/ Rahman, Sheikh 1921–1975. ◊Bangladeshi politician. Several times arrested for campaigning for the autonomy of East Pakistan, he won the elections of 1970 as leader of the Awami League but was again arrested when negotiations with the Pakistan government broke down. After the civil war of 1971, he became prime minister of newly independent Bangladesh. He was presidential dictator Jan–Aug 1975, when he was assassinated.

Mukden /ˈmʊkdən/ former name of ◊Shenyang, city in China.

Mukden, Battle of /ˈmʊkdən/ the taking of Mukden from Russian occupation by the Japanese, 20 Feb–10 Mar 1905, during the ◊Russo-Japanese War.

Mukden Incident surprise attack on 18 Sept 1931 by the Japanese on the Chinese garrison at ◊Mukden, which marked the beginning of their invasion of China.

mulberry tree, genus *Morus*, of the family Moraceae, with a dozen species of which the best-known is black mulberry *Morus nigra*. Native to W Asia, it was introduced into Britain in the 16th century. It has heart shaped toothed leaves, and spikes of whitish flowers. The fruit resembles a raspberry in appearance, but is a cluster of small drupes. The leaves of the white mulberry *Morus alba* are those used in feeding silkworms.

Muldoon /mʌlˈduːn/ Robert David 1921– . New Zealand politician. A chartered accountant, he was minister of finance 1967–72, and in 1974 became leader of the National Party. He became prime minister in 1975 and pursued austere economic policies; abroad he supported the Western alliance, and at home he sought to introduce curbs on trade unions. He was defeated in the general election of 1984 by the Labour Party's David Lange.

mule hybrid animal usually the offspring of a male ass and a mare.

Mulhouse /mjuˈluːz/ (German *Mühlhausen*) industrial city (textiles, engineering, electrical goods) in Haut-Rhin department, E France; population (1982) 113,794.

Mull /mʌl/ second largest island of the Inner ◊Hebrides, Strathclyde, Scotland; area 950 sq km/367 sq mi. It is separated by the Sound of Mull from the mainland. There is only one town, Tobermory.

mullah (Arabic 'master') a teacher, scholar, or religious leader of ◊Islam. It is also a title of respect given to various other dignitaries who perform duties connected with the sacred law.

mullein plant of the genus *Verbascum* family Scrophulariaceae. Great mullein *Verbascum thapsus* produces lance-shaped leaves 12 in/30 cm or more in length covered in woolly down, and in the second year of growth a large spike of yellow flowers. Common in Britain, and found through Europe and Asia, it is naturalized in N America.

Muller /ˈmulə/ Hermann 1890–1967. American geneticist, who discovered the effect of radiation on genes by his work on fruit flies. He received a Nobel prize in 1946.

Müller /ˈmjuːlə/ Johannes Peter 1801–1858. German comparative anatomist whose studies of nerves and sense organs demonstrated the physical nature of sensory perception. His name is associated with a number of discoveries, including Müllerian ducts in the mammalian foetus and the lymph heart in frogs.

Muller /ˈmulə/ Paul 1899–1965. Swiss chemist awarded a Nobel prize in 1948 for his discovery of the first synthetic contact insecticide, ◊DDT in 1939.

mullet two types of fish. The *red mullet Mullus surmuletus* is found from the Mediterranean and warm Atlantic north to the English Channel. About 40 cm/1.3 ft long, it is prized as a food fish. It is red with yellow stripes, and has long barbels round the mouth. The *grey mullet Crenimugil labrosus* lives inshore and in estuaries. It is greyish above, with longitudinal dark stripes, and grows to 60 cm/2 ft.

Mulliken /ˈmʌlɪkən/ Robert Sanderson 1896– . American chemist and physicist, who received a Nobel chemistry prize in 1966 for his development of the molecular orbital theory.

Mullingar /ˌmʌlɪnˈɡɑː/ county town of Westmeath, Republic of Ireland; population (1983) 7,000.

Mulready /ˈmʌlredi/ William 1786–1863. Irish artist and illustrator. In 1840 he designed the first penny-postage envelope, known as the 'Mulready envelope'.

Mulroney /mʌlˈrəuni/ Brian 1939– . Canadian politician. A former labour lawyer, he replaced Joe Clark as Progressive Conservative Party leader in 1983, and achieved a landslide in the 1984 elections to become prime minister. He has sought to re-establish Canada's special relationship with the USA.

Multan /ˌmulˈtɑːn/ industrial city (textiles, precision instruments, chemicals, pottery, jewellery) in central Pakistan, on a site inhabited since the time of Alexander the Great, 205 km/190 mi SW of Lahore; population (1981) 732,000.

multi-cultural education in the UK, a term used to describe education aimed at preparing children to live in a multi-racial society by giving them an understanding and appreciation of the culture of different ethnic groups now living in the UK and their historical and geographical links. The initiative for multi-cultural teaching rose out of the Swann Report 1985 against ◊racism or ◊racial disadvantage in schools.

multinational corporation company or enterprise operating in several countries, sometimes defined as one which has 25 per cent or more of its output capacity located outside its country of origin. Such enterprises, many of them US-based, are seen in some quarters as posing a threat to individual national sovereignty and as exerting undue influence to secure favourable operating conditions.

multiple births in humans, the production of more than two babies (◊twins) from one pregnancy. Multiple births are rare, but can be due to more than two eggs being produced and fertilized during one ◊menstrual cycle, often as the result of hormone therapy to assist pregnancy. Alternatively a single fertilized egg can divide more than once before ◊implantation.

multiple sclerosis (MS) chronic disease of the central nervous system. The white fatty substance of the sheath of certain nerve fibres turns to hard scar tissue. It is usually progressive, causing weakness of the muscles, tremors, paralysis, and affecting all the senses, or it may in some cases disappear. It may be caused by the action of antibodies to viruses of childhood diseases, such as measles, entering the brain. Recent research has suggested that a diet rich in essential fatty acids may help to alleviate some of the symptoms.

multiplier in economics, the theoretical concept, formulated by J M ◊Keynes, of the effect on national income or employment by an adjustment in overall demand. Thus investment by a company in new plant will stimulate new income and expenditure, which will in turn generate new investment, and so on, so that the actual increase in national income may be several times greater than the original investment.

multi-stage rocket a rocket launch vehicle consisting of a number of rocket stages joined together, usually end to end. See ◊step rocket.

Mumford /'mʌmfəd/ Lewis 1895– . American sociologist. He was concerned with the effect of technology on modern society. His books include *Technics and Civilisation* 1934 and *The Culture of Cities* 1938.

mummers' play or *St George play* British folk-drama enacted in dumb show by masked performers, performed on Christmas Day to celebrate the death of the old year and rebirth of the new, usually through a duel between St George and an infidel knight, in which one of them is killed but later revived by a doctor.

mummy human or animal body preserved after death, either naturally or artificially (for example, by drying or freezing – the science of ◊cryonics). Examples are mammoths preserved in glacial ice from 25,000 years ago; shrunken heads preserved by the ◊Jivaro people in South America; the mummies of ancient Egypt; and the modern mummies such as Lenin and Eva Perón.

mumps virus infection marked by fever and swelling of the parotid salivary glands (under the ear). Usually minor in children, although meningitis is a possible complication, it may rarely affect the fertility of adult males.

Munch /muŋk/ Edvard 1863–1944. Norwegian artist. He studied in Paris and Berlin and was influenced by ◊van Gogh and ◊Gauguin. His severe mental illness in 1908 is foreshadowed in the agonized tension of *The Scream* 1893 and *The Kiss*. Many of his works also exist as engravings and woodcuts.

München /'munʃən/ German name of ◊Munich, city in West Germany.

Münchhausen /mun'tʃauzən/ Karl Friedrich, Freiherr (Baron) von 1720–1797. German soldier. Born in Hanover, he had served with the Russian Army against the Turks, and after his retirement in 1760 told exaggerated stories of his campaigning adventures. This idiosyncrasy was utilized by the German writer, Rudolph Erich Raspe (1737–94), in his extravagantly fictitious account of the *Adventures of Baron Münchhausen* 1785, compiled while he was taking refuge in London from a charge of theft in his own country.

Münchhausen's syndrome an emotional disorder in which a patient feigns or invents symptoms in order to secure medical treatment. In some cases the patient will secretly ingest substances to produce real symptoms. It was named after the exaggerated tales of Baron ◊Münchhausen.

Munich /'mjuːnɪk/ (German *München*) industrial city (brewing, printing, precision instruments) capital of Bavaria, West Germany, on the river Isar. The university, founded at Ingolstadt 1472, was transferred to Munich 1826; to the NE at Garching there is a nuclear research centre.

features Munich owes many of its buildings and art treasures to the kings ◊Ludwig I and ◊Maximilian II of Bavaria. The cathedral is late 15th century. The Alte Pinakothek contains paintings by old masters, the Neue Pinakothek, modern paintings; there is the Bavarian National Museum, the Bavarian State Library, and the Deutsches Museum (science and technology).

population (1984) 1,277,000

history dating from the 12th century, Munich became the residence of the dukes of Wittelsbach in the 13th century, and the capital of independent ◊Bavaria. It was the scene of the Nov revolution of 1918, the 'Soviet' republic of 1919, and the Hitler putsch of 1923. It became the centre of the Nazi movement, and the ◊Munich Agreement of 1938 was signed here.

Munich Agreement signed on 29 Sept 1938 by ◊Chamberlain (UK), ◊Daladier (France), ◊Hitler (Germany), and ◊Mussolini (Italy), under which Czechoslovakia was compelled to surrender its Sudeten-German districts (the Sudetenland) to Germany. Most districts were not given the option of a plebiscite. Despite signatory guarantees, Hitler seized the rest of the country in Mar 1939. After World War II the area was returned to Czechoslovakia, and over two million German-speaking people were expelled from the country. Characterized at the time by Chamberlain as an agreement which would guarantee 'peace in our time', its speedy abrogation by Hitler led to its becoming symbolic of gullible appeasement.

Munro /mən'rəu/ H(ugh) H(ector) British author who wrote under the pen name of ◊Saki.

Munster /'mʌnstə/ southern province of Republic of Ireland, comprising the counties of ◊Clare, ◊Cork, ◊Kerry, ◊Limerick, North and South ◊Tipperary, and ◊Waterford; area 24,128 sq km/9,319 sq mi; population (1981) 998,315. It was a kingdom until the 12th century, and was settled in plantations by the English from 1586.

Münster /'munstə/ industrial city (wire, cement, iron, brewing and distilling) in NW West Germany, formerly the capital of Westphalia; university 1773; population (1985) 273,000. The Treaty of Westphalia was signed simultaneously here and at Osnabrück in 1648, ending the Thirty Years' War. Badly damaged in World War II, its ancient buildings, including the 15th-century cathedral and town hall, have been restored or rebuilt.

Munternia /mʌn'tɜːniə/ Romanian name of ◊Wallachia, former province of Romania.

muntjac small deer, genus *Muntiacus*, found in SE Asia. The buck has short spiked antlers, and two sharp canine teeth forming tusks. Sometimes called 'barking deer' because of their voice, they mostly live in dense vegetation and do not form herds. Some have escaped from parks in central England and become established.

mural painting (Latin *murus*, wall). The decoration of walls, and, by extension, of vaults and ceilings, by means of ◊fresco, oil, ◊tempera, or ◊encaustic methods. Mural painters include ◊Cimabue, ◊Giotto, ◊Leonardo da Vinci, and Diego ◊Rivera.

Murasaki Shikibu /ˌmuərəˈsɑːki ˈʃikibuː/ pseudonym of an unknown Japanese writer c. 978–c. 1015. Her *Tale of Genji* is one of the classic works of Japanese literature, and has been described as the world's first novel.

Murat /mjuˈrɑː/ Joachim 1767–1815. King of Naples. The son of an innkeeper, he rose rapidly in the French Army through the friendship of Napoleon, and won the reputation of a dashing cavalry commander. He was made king of Naples by Napoleon in 1808, but deserted him in 1813 in the vain hope that the Allies would recognize him. In 1815 he attempted unsuccessfully to make himself king of all Italy, and when he landed in Calabria in an attempt to recover the throne he was captured and shot.

Murcia /'muəθiə/ industrial city (silk, metal, glass), capital of the Spanish province of Murcia, on the river Segura; population (1981) 288,631. Murcia was founded in 825 on the site of a Roman colony by Abd-ur-Rahman II, caliph of Cordoba. It has a university and 14th-century cathedral.

Murcia /'muəθiə/ autonomous region of SE Spain. It includes the cities Murcia and Cartagena. Population (1981) 957,900.

murder unlawful killing of one person by another, who is of sound mind, has reached years of discretion, and acts with malice afore thought, express or implied (as opposed to ◊manslaughter).

Murdoch /'mɜːdɒk/ Iris 1919– . British novelist, born in Dublin. Her novels combine philosophical speculation with tangled human relationships. They include *The Sandcastle* 1957, *A Severed Head* 1961, and *The Philosopher's Pupil* 1983. A lecturer in philosophy from 1948 at Oxford University, she published in 1953 *Sartre, Romantic Rationalist*.

Murdock /'mɜːdɒk/ William 1754–1839. Scottish inventor who first used coal gas for domestic lighting. He illuminated his house and offices in Redruth using coal gas in 1792, and in 1797 and 1798 he held public demonstrations of his invention.

Murger /mjuəˈʒeə/ Henri 1822–1861. French writer, author of *Scènes de la vie de bohème/Scenes of Bohemian Life* 1848 which formed the basis of Puccini's opera, *La Bohème*.

Murillo /mjuəˈrɪləu/ Bartolomé Estéban 1617–1682. Spanish painter. Born in Seville, he went to Madrid in 1642, where he was befriended by ◊Velázquez, then at the height of his fame. After his return to Seville in 1645 he received many important commissions, and founded the academy there 1660. One of the leading painters of the Spanish school, he is known for rather sentimental paintings of the Holy Family and for studies of street urchins.

Murmansk /muəˈmænsk/ seaport in NW USSR, on the Barents Sea; the USSR's most important fishing port, and base of the icebreakers that keep open the North East Passage; population (1985) 419,000. It is the world's most northern metropolis, the centre of Soviet Lapland, and the only port on the Arctic coast of the USSR that is ice-free at all times of

Murdoch Iris Murdoch has won numerous awards
including the Booker prize in 1978 for *The Sea,
The Sea* and was again shortlisted for the award
in 1987 for *The Book and the Brotherhood*.

the year. After the entry of the USSR into World
War II in 1941, supplies from Britain and later
from the USA were unloaded there. The Festival
of the North in Mar marks the end of the two-
month Arctic night.

Murnau /'muənau/ pseudonym of the
German film director Friedrich Wilhelm Plumpe
1889–1931. Murnau's 'subjective' use of a
moving camera to tell the story, through
expressive images and without subtitles, in the
silent *Der Letzte Mumm/The Last Laugh* 1924
made him famous. Other films include *Nosferatu*
1922, a version of the Dracula story.

Murray /'mʌri/ principal river of Australia,
2,575 km/1,600 mi long. It rises in the Australian
Alps near Mount Kosciusko and flows W,
forming the boundary between New South
Wales and Victoria, and reaches the sea at
Encounter Bay. Tributaries include the
◊Lachlan, the ◊Darling, and the
◊Murrumbidgee.

Murray /'mʌri/ Gilbert 1866–1957. British
scholar, best known for verse translations of the
Greek dramatists, especially Euripides. Order of
Merit 1941.

Murray /'mʌri/ James Augustus Henry
1837–1915. Scottish philologist. He was the first
editor of the *Oxford English Dictionary*
(originally the *New English Dictionary*) from
1878 until his death; the first volume was
published 1884.

Murray /'mʌri/ James Stuart, Earl of
Murray, or Moray 1531–1570. Regent of
Scotland from 1567. An illegitimate son of
◊James V. Murray was one of the leaders of the
Scottish Reformation, and after the deposition
of his half-sister, ◊Mary, Queen of Scots, became
regent. He was assassinated by one of her
supporters.

murray cod Australian freshwater fish
Maccullochella macquariensis which grows to
about 2 m/6 ft.

Murrumbidgee /,mʌrəm'bɪdʒi/ river of New
South Wales, Australia, 1,690 km/1,050 mi
long. It rises in the Australian Alps, flows N to
the Burrinjuck reservoir, and then W to meet the
◊Murray.

Murry /'mʌri/ John Middleton 1889–1957.
British writer. In 1913 he married Katherine
◊Mansfield, whose biography he wrote. He
produced studies of Dostoievsky, Keats, Blake,
and Shakespeare, poetry and an
autobiographical novel, *Still Life* 1916. He was
a friend of D H Lawrence.

Muscat /'mʌskæt/ capital of the sultanate of
Oman, adjoining the port of Mutrah, which has
a deepwater harbour from 1974, Port Qabus,
named after the sultan; combined population
(1982) 80,000.

Muscat and Oman the former name of
◊Oman, country in the Middle East.

muscle contractile animal tissue which
produces locomotion and maintains the
movement of substances within the body. Muscle
is made of long cells which can contract to
between one half and one third of their relaxed
length. Vertebrate muscle can be divided into
three types. *Striped* muscles are activated by
◊motor nerves under voluntary control; they are
attached to bones, except for those that form the
tongue. *Involuntary* or *smooth* muscle is
controlled by motor nerves of the ◊autonomic
nervous system, and located in the gut, blood
vessels, the ◊iris and ducts. *Cardiac* muscle,
which only occurs in the ◊heart, is likewise under
the control of the autonomic nervous system.

muscular dystrophy progressive muscular
weakness of genetic origin, resulting in
◊paralysis. The commonest form of the disease,
Duchenne dystrophy, is more usual in boys than
girls.

Muses in Greek mythology, the nine
daughters of ◊Zeus and Mnemosyne (goddess of
memory) and inspirers of creative arts:
Calliope epic poetry;
Clio history;
Erato love poetry;
Euterpe lyric poetry;
Melpomene tragedy;
Polyhymnia hymns;
Terpsichore dance;
Thalia comedy;
Urania astronomy.

Musgrave /'mʌzgreɪv/ Thea 1928– .
Scottish composer. Her works, which are
intellectually rigorous, but not avant-garde,
include concertos for horn, clarinet, and viola;
string quartets; and operas, including *Mary,
Queen of Scots* 1977.

Musgrave Ranges /'mʌzgreɪv/ Australian
mountain ranges on the border between South
Australia and the Northern Territory; the
highest peak is Mount Woodruffe 1,525 m/5,000
ft. The area is an Aboriginal reserve.

mushroom edible fungus with a cap, the
fruiting body, on a stalk, such as the field
mushroom *Agaricus campestris*. See also
◊toadstool.

music the art of combining sounds into a
unified whole, typically in accordance with fixed
patterns and for an aesthetic purpose. The Greek
word *mousikē* covered all the arts presided over
by the Muses. Of ancient Greek music only a few
fragments have survived. The various
civilizations of the ancient and modern world
developed their own musical systems. Eastern
music recognises many more subdivisions of an
interval than Western music, and also differs
from Western music in that the absence until
recently of written notation ruled out the
composition of major developed works and
fostered melodic and rhythmic patterns, freely
interpreted (as in the Indian *raga*).
The documented history of Western music since
Classical times begins with the liturgical music
of the medieval Catholic Church, derived from
Greek and Hebrew antecedents. The four scales,
or modes, to which the words of the liturgy were
chanted, were traditionally first set in order by St
Ambrose in 384 AD. St Gregory the Great added
four more to the original Ambrosian modes, and
this system forms the basis of Gregorian
plainsong still used in the Roman Catholic
Church. The organ was introduced in the 8th
century, and in the 9th century harmonized
music began to be used in churches with notation
developing towards its modern form. In the 11th
century counterpoint was introduced, notably at
the monastery of St Martial, Limoges, France,
and in the late 12th century at Nôtre Dame in
Paris by Léonin and Perotin the Great. In the late
Middle Ages the Provençal and French
◊troubadours and court composers such as
Machault developed secular music, derived from
church and folk music (see also ◊Minnesingers).
The 15th and 16th centuries in Europe saw the
growth of contrapuntal or polyphonic music. One
of the earliest composers was the English John
Dunstable, whose works influenced the French
composer Guillaume Dufay, founder of the
Flemish school; its members included Dufay's
pupil Joannes Okeghem and the Renaissance
composer Josquin Desprez. Other composers of
this era were the Italian Palestrina and the
Flemish Roland de Lassus, the Spanish Victoria
and the English Tallis and Byrd. The
Elizabethan age in England was notable for the
◊madrigal, written by such composers as Thomas
Morley and Orlando Gibbons.
The 17th century Florentine Academy, a group
of artists and writers, aimed to revive the
principles of Greek tragedy. This led to the
invention of dramatic recitative, and the
beginning of opera. An early operatic composer
was ◊Monteverdi; by the end of the century the
form had evolved further in the hands of
Alessandro Scarlatti in Italy and Lully in France.
In England the outstanding composer of the
period was Purcell.
The early 18th century is dominated by J S ◊Bach
and ◊Handel. Bach was a master of harmony and
counterpoint. Handel is noted for his dramatic
oratorios. Bach's sons, C P E ◊Bach and J C
◊Bach, reacted against contrapuntal forms and
developed sonata form, the basis of the Classical
sonata, quartet, and symphony. In these fields
mastery of style was reached by the Viennese

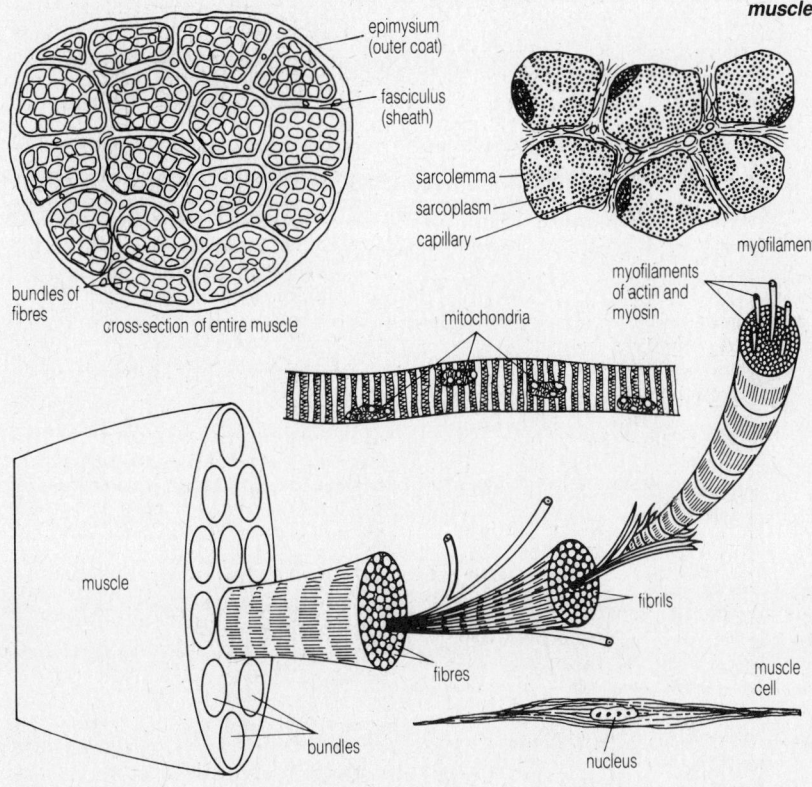

muscle

epimysium (outer coat)

fasciculus (sheath)

sarcolemma

sarcoplasm

capillary

myofilament

myofilaments of actin and myosin

bundles of fibres

cross-section of entire muscle

mitochondria

muscle

fibrils

fibres

muscle cell

bundles

nucleus

composers ◊Haydn and ◊Mozart. With ◊Beethoven, music assumed new dynamic and expressive functions.

Romantic music, represented in its early stages by Weber, Schubert, Schumann, Mendelssohn, and Chopin, tended to be subjectively emotional. The resources of orchestral colour were increasingly exploited – particularly by Berlioz – and harmony became more chromatic. Nationalism became prominent at this time, for example, the intense Polish nationalism of Chopin, and the exploitation of Hungarian music by Liszt, the Russians Rimsky-Korsakov, Borodin, Mussorgsky, and, less typically, Tchaikovsky, the Czechs Dvořák and Smetana, and the Norwegian Grieg. The most revolutionary changes were brought by Wagner in the field of opera, though traditional Italian lyricism continued with the line of Rossini, Verdi, and Puccini. Wagner's contemporary Brahms stood for Classical discipline of form combined with Romantic feeling. The Belgian César Franck, though increasingly chromatic, also renewed the tradition of polyphonic writing.

Around 1900 there was a reaction against Romanticism and a tendency to experiment, first apparent in the French Impressionists, including Debussy and Ravel. In Austria and Germany, Bruckner, Mahler, and Richard Strauss, the last Romantic composers, were succeeded by the intellectual atonality (and subsequent serialism) of Schoenberg, Webern, and Berg. Other experiments included the Neo-Classicism of Stravinsky, Bartók, and Hindemith, and the

work of the French ◊Les Six, including Francis Poulenc and Darius Milhaud. Notable also was the Finnish Romanticism of Sibelius.

A revival in British music begun by Sullivan, Stanford, and Parry was continued in the early 20th century by Elgar, Delius, and Holst. Among 20th century composers in Britain are Vaughan Williams, William Walton, Benjamin Britten, Michael Tippett, Harrison Birtwistle, Peter Maxwell Davies, and John Tavener; in the USA Charles Ives, Aaron Copland, Elliott Carter, George Gershwin, and John Cage; in the USSR Prokofiev and Shostakovich; in France Olivier Messiaen, Pierre Boulez; the Italians Luciano Berio and Bruno Maderna, and in Germany Hans Werner Henze and Karlheinz Stockhausen.

The second half of the 20th century has seen dramatic changes in the nature of composition and in the instruments used to create sounds. Use of recording and synthesizers has facilitated the development of *musique concrète/concrete music*, in which recorded natural sounds are combined; this has implied that works may be composed in their 'final form' without being replayed and interpreted by performers. *Electronic music* is the name given to musical sounds produced by audio frequency oscillations of signal generators, electro-magnetic instruments, and so on. Since the 1960s electronic music has been linked to computer composition, as in the work of Cage, Stockhausen, and Boulez (most notably in the IRCAM centre, Paris). The 20th century has

also seen the development of ◊jazz and ◊pop music and a revival of interest in ◊folk music.

musical recent form of popular dramatic musical performance, combining elements of song, dance, and the spoken word:

operetta a light-hearted entertainment, with extensive musical content: Offenbach, Johann Strauss, Franz Lehár, and Gilbert and Sullivan

musical comedy an anglicization of the French *opéra bouffe* of which the first was *A Gaiety Girl* 1893, mounted by George Edwardes (1852–1915) at the Gaiety Theatre, London

1920s typical were *Rose Marie* 1924 (Rudolf Friml 1879–1972), *The Student Prince* 1924 and *The Desert Song* 1926 (both Sigmund Romberg 1887–1951), and *No, No Nanette* 1925 (Vincent Youmans 1898–1946)

1930s–40s a sophisticated era, with many filmed examples and strong US presence (Irving Berlin, Jerome Kern, Cole Porter, and George Gershwin); and in England Noel Coward and the more romantic Ivor Novello

musical Rodgers and Hammerstein's *Oklahoma!* in 1943 brought with it a more integrated combination of plot and music, as in Lerner and Loewe's *My Fair Lady* 1956 and Bernstein's *West Side Story* 1957. Sandy Wilson's *The Boy Friend* 1953 revived the British musical, and was followed by hits such as Bart's *Oliver!* 1960. Musicals began to branch into religious and political themes with *Oh What a Lovely War!* 1963 produced by Joan Littlewood and Charles Chiltern, and the hugely successful Lloyd Webber musicals including *Jesus Christ Superstar* 1970, *Evita* 1978, and *The Phantom of the Opera* 1986. Another branch of the musical, which substitutes a theme for a conventional plot, is seen in works such as Stephen Sondheim's *Company* 1970, and Hamlisch and Kleban's *A Chorus Line* 1975.

music hall a theatre offering light entertainment consisting of 'turns', in which singers, dancers, comedians, acrobats, and so on, perform in turn. The heyday of the British music hall was at the beginning of the 20th century, with such artists as Albert Chevalier (1861–1923) ('My Old Dutch'), Marie ◊Lloyd, Harry ◊Lauder, and George ◊Formby. Later stars of music hall have included Sir George Robey and Gracie ◊Fields. With the onset of radio and television, music hall declined. The American equivalent is known as 'vaudeville'.

music theatre the staged performance of vocal music that avoids the grandiose style and large forces of traditional opera. It can be traced to the 1920s and 1930s, in plays with music like Kurt Weill's *Mahagonny-Songspiel*, but it came into its own in the 1960s. It includes not just opera (such as Alexander Goehr's *Naboth's Vineyard*) but also works such as Peter Maxwell Davies's *Eight Songs for a Mad King*, a song cycle acted out on stage.

Musil /'muːzɪl/ Robert 1880–1942. Austrian novelist. His reputation, largely posthumous, is based on *Der Mann ohne Eigenschaften/The Man without Qualities* (three volumes, 1930–43).

musk perennial plant *Mimulus moschatus* of the family Scrophulariaceae. The small oblong

MUSIC: GREAT COMPOSERS

Giovanni Palestrina	c.1525–1594	Italian	motets, masses
Claudio Monteverdi	1567–1643	Italian	operas, vocal music
Henry Purcell	1659–1695	English	vocal music, operas
Antonio Vivaldi	1678–1741	Italian	concertos, chamber music
Georg Frideric Handel	1685–1759	German	oratorios, operas, orchestral music
Johann Sebastian Bach	1685–1750	German	keyboard, choral music, concertos
Joseph Haydn	1732–1809	Austrian	symphonies, oratorios, chamber music
Wolfgang Amadeus Mozart	1756–1791	Austrian	symphonies, operas, chamber music
Ludwig van Beethoven	1770–1827	German	symphonies, chamber music, opera
Carl Maria von Weber	1786–1826	German	operas, concertos
Gioacchino Rossini	1792–1868	Italian	operas
Franz Schubert	1797–1828	Austrian	songs, symphonies, chamber music
Hector Berlioz	1803–1869	French	operas, symphonies
Felix Mendelssohn	1809–1847	German	symphonies, concertos
Frédéric Chopin	1810–1849	Polish	piano music
Robert Schumann	1810–1856	German	piano, vocal music, concertos
Franz Liszt	1811–1886	Hungarian	piano, orchestral music
Richard Wagner	1813–1883	German	operas
Giuseppe Verdi	1813–1901	Italian	operas
César Franck	1822–1890	Belgian	symphony, organ works
Bedrich Smetana	1824–1884	Czech	symphonies, operas
Anton Bruckner	1824–1896	Austrian	symphonies
Johann Strauss II	1825–1899	Austrian	waltzes, operettas
Johannes Brahms	1833–1897	German	symphonies, concertos
Camille Saint-Saëns	1835–1921	French	symphonies, concertos, operas
Modest Mussorgsky	1839–1881	Russian	operas, orchestral music
Peter Ilyich Tchaikovsky	1840–1893	Russian	ballet music, symphonies
Antonin Dvořák	1841–1904	Czech	symphonies, operas
Edvard Grieg	1843–1907	Norwegian	concertos, orchestra music
Nikolai Rimsky-Korsakov	1844–1908	Russian	opera, orchestral music
Leos Janáček	1854–1928	Czech	operas, chamber music
Edward Elgar	1857–1934	English	orchestral music
Giacomo Puccini	1858–1924	Italian	operas
Gustav Mahler	1860–1911	Czech	symphonies
Claude Debussy	1862–1918	French	operas, orchestral music
Richard Strauss	1864–1949	German	operas, orchestral music
Carl Nielsen	1865–1931	Danish	symphonies
Jean Sibelius	1865–1957	Finnish	symphonies, orchestral music
Sergei Rachmaninov	1873–1943	Russian	symphonies, concertos
Arnold Schoenberg	1874–1951	Austrian	operas, orchestral and chamber music
Maurice Ravel	1875–1937	French	piano, chamber music
Béla Bartók	1881–1945	Hungarian	operas, concertos
Igor Stravinsky	1882–1971	Russian	ballets, operas
Anton Webern	1883–1945	Austrian	chamber, vocal music
Alban Berg	1885–1935	Austrian	operas, chamber music
Sergei Prokofiev	1891–1953	Russian	symphonies, ballets
George Gershwin	1898–1937	American	musicals, operas
Dmitri Shostakovich	1906–1975	Russian	piano music
Olivier Messiaen	1908–	French	piano, organ, orchestral music
Benjamin Britten	1913–1976	English	vocal music, operas
Karlheinz Stockhausen	1928–	German	electronic, vocal music

leaves formerly exuded the musky scent which gave it its name, but at the beginning of the 20th century the scent disappeared. It has yellow flowers.

musk deer small deer *Moschus moschiferus* native to Asia. It has no antlers, does not travel in herds, and is hunted and farmed for the musk secreted by an abdominal gland, and used as a medicine or a perfume.

musk ox hoofed mammal *Ovibos moschatus* native to the Arctic regions of North America. It displays characteristics of both the sheep and the ox, is about the size of small domestic cattle, and has long brown hair. At certain seasons it exhales a musky odour. Its underwool (qiviut) is almost as fine as vicuna and musk ox farms have been established in Alaska, Quebec and Norway.

muskrat rodent *Ondatra zibethicus*. About 30 cm/1 ft long, its body is adapted to aquatic life, having webbed feet and a flattened tail. It builds up a store of food, plastering it over with mud, for winter consumption. The light brown fur, *musquash*, is highly valued.

Muslim or *Moslem* a follower of ◊Islam.

Muslim Brotherhood movement founded by members of the ◊Sunni branch of Islam in Egypt in 1928. It aims at the establishment of a theocratic Islamic state and is headed by a 'Supreme Guide'. It is also active in Jordan, Sudan, and Syria.

mussel popular name for a number of bivalve molluscs. Most notable of the sea mussels is the edible *Mytilus edulis*, which is found in clusters attached to rocks around the Atlantic coasts in the N hemisphere and the Mediterranean, and has a blue-black shell. The freshwater pearl mussels such as *Unio margaritiferus* are found in some N American and European rivers. The green-lipped mussel, found only off New Zealand, produces an extract which is used in the treatment of arthritis.

Musset /mjuː'seɪ/ Alfred de 1810–1857. French poet and playwright. In 1833 he accompanied the writer George Sand to Italy as her lover, and his *Confession d'un enfant du siècle/Confessions of a Child of the Century* 1835 recounts their broken relationship. Most typical of his work are the verse *Les Nuits/Nights* 1835–37 and the short plays *Comédies et proverbes/Comedies and Proverbs* 1840.

Mussolini /ˌmusəˈliːni/ Benito 1883–1945. Italian dictator. Born in the Romagna, the son of a blacksmith, he was expelled from the Socialist movement in 1914 for advocating Italian intervention in World War I. In 1919 he founded the Fascist Party (see ◊fascism), whose programme combined violent nationalism with demagogic republican and anti-capitalist slogans, and launched an intimidation campaign against the Socialists. This movement was backed by many landowners and industrialists, and by the heads of the army and police, and in Oct 1922 the king and the army leaders installed Mussolini as prime minister. Known as *Il Duce* 'the leader', in 1925 he assumed dictatorial powers, and in 1926 all opposition parties were suppressed. During the years that followed the entire political, legal and education system was remodelled on fascist lines.

In 1935–36 Mussolini embarked on a career of conquest, with his successful invasion of Ethiopia; this was followed by Italian intervention in the Spanish Civil War of 1936–39 in support of Franco, and the conquest of Albania in 1939. This policy drew Mussolini into close cooperation with Nazi Germany; indeed, his Blackshirt followers were the forerunners of Hitler's Brownshirts. In Jun 1940 Italy entered World War II supporting Hitler. Italian defeats in N Africa and Greece, the Allied invasion of Sicily, and discontent at home destroyed Mussolini's prestige, and in Jul 1943 he was compelled to resign by his own Fascist Grand Council. He was released from his imprisonment by German parachutists in Sept, and set up a 'Republican Fascist' government in Northern Italy. In Apr 1945 he and his mistress, Clara Petacci, were captured at Lake Como by partisans while trying to flee the country, and shot.

Mussorgsky /muˈsɔːgski/ Modest Petrovich 1839–1881. Russian composer. A member of the group of nationalist composers, the Five, he was influenced by both folk music and literature, and was largely self-taught. His opera *Boris Godunov* was completed in 1869, although not produced in St Petersburg until 1874. Other works include the orchestral *A Night on the Bare Mountain* 1867, the suite for piano *Pictures at an Exhibition* 1874, and many songs.

Mustafa Kemal /ˈmʊstəfə kəˈmɑːl/ Turkish leader, who assumed the name of ◊Atatürk.

mustard annual plant of the family Cruciferae. The seeds of black mustard *Brassica nigra*, and white mustard *Sinapis alba*, are used in the production of table mustard, and are cultivated in Europe, N America and England, where wild mustard or charlock *Sinapis arvensis* is also found. The seedlings of white mustard are used as a salad food. Mustard is frequently grown by farmers and ploughed in to enrich the soil.

Mustique /muˈstiːk/ an island in the Caribbean. See under ◊St Vincent and the Grenadines.

Mutare /muˈtɑːri/ (former name to 1982 *Umtali*) industrial town (vehicle assembly, engineering, textiles, paper) in E Zimbabwe; population (1982) 69,621.

mutation in biology, a change in the genes; more specifically, a change in the ◊DNA or RNA that makes up the hereditary material of all living organisms. Mutations are the raw material of ◊evolution. They occur due to mistakes during replication (copying) of DNA molecules. Common mutations include the omission or insertion of base (one of the chemical subunits of DNA), being known as *point mutations*. Larger-scale mutations include removal of a whole segment of DNA or its inversion within the DNA strand. Not all mutations affect the organism, because there is a certain amount of redundancy in the genetic information. If a mutation is 'translated' from DNA into the ◊protein that makes up the organism's structure, it may be in a non-functional part of the protein and thus have no detectable effect. This is known as a neutral mutation, and is important in ◊molecular clock studies because such mutations tend to accumulate gradually as time passes. Some mutations do affect functional parts of proteins, or genes that control protein production, and most of these are lethal to the organism. Only a few improve the organism's performance and are therefore favoured by ◊natural selection. Mutation rates are increased by certain chemicals, and by radiation.

Muti /ˈmuːti/ Riccardo 1941– . Italian conductor of the Philharmonia Orchestra, London, 1973–83, the Philadelphia Orchestra from 1980, and artistic director of La Scala, Milan, from 1986. He is known as a purist, devoted to carrying out a composer's intentions to the last detail.

Mutiny Act in Britain, an act of Parliament, passed 1689 and re-enacted annually since then (since 1882 as part of the Army Acts), for the establishment and payment of a standing army. The act is intended to prevent an army existing in peacetime without Parliament's consent.

Mutsuhito /ˌmuːtsuːˈhiːtəʊ/ 1852–1912. Emperor of Japan. He took the title Meiji Tenno ('enlightened peace') when he became emperor in 1867. During his reign Japan became a world military and naval power.

mutton bird or *short-tailed shearwater* bird *Puffinus tenuirostris* which breeds in burrows on islands off SE Australia. The young are very fat, and are killed for food.

mutual induction in physics, the production of an ◊electromotive force (e.m.f.) or voltage in an electric circuit caused by a changing ◊magnetic flux in a neighbouring circuit. The two circuits are often coils of wire, as in a transformer, and the size of the induced e.m.f. depends largely on the numbers of turns of wire in each of the coils. See also ◊electromagnetic induction.

mutualism or *symbiosis* an association between two organisms of different ◊species whereby both profit from the relationship.

Muybridge /ˈmaɪbrɪdʒ/ Eadweard 1830–1904. British photographer. He made a series of animal locomotion photographs in the USA in the 1870s which proved that, at speed, animals often do not touch the ground. He then explored motion in birds and humans.

Muzorewa /ˌmuːzəˈreɪwə/ Abel Tendekayi 1925– . Zimbabwean politician. Bishop Muzorewa was educated at Methodist colleges in Rhodesia and Nashville, Tennessee. He was president of the African National Council 1971–85, and was prime minister of Zimbabwe-Rhodesia 1979. He was detained for a year in 1983–84.

Muzorewa Former teacher, lawyer, and prime minister of Zimbabwe, Abel Musorewa, Bishop of the United Methodist Church, is now leader of the minority United Africa National Council.

MVD Russian Ministry of Internal Affairs. See under ◊KGB.

Mwiiny /mwiːˈiːni/ Ali Hassan 1925– . President of Tanzania, who succeeded ◊Nyerere in 1985. A devout Muslim and socialist, he had to begin a revival of private enterprise and control of state involvement and spending, to restore solvency.

myasthenia gravis muscular weakness caused by a defect in the body's immune system. Usually beginning in the muscles round the eye, it sometimes spreads and affects breathing.

mycelium an interwoven mass of thread-like filaments or ◊hyphae, forming the main body of most ◊fungi. The reproductive structures, or 'fruiting bodies', grow from this mycelium.

Mycenaean the civilization, also known as the *Aegean civilization*, which flourished in Crete, Cyprus, Greece, the Aegean Islands, and W Anatolia c. 4000–1000 BC. Originating in Crete, it spread into Greece c. 1600 BC, where it continued to thrive, with its centre at Mycenae, after the decline of Crete c. 1400. It was finally overthrown by the Dorian invasions, c. 1100. The system of government was by kings, who also monopolized priestly functions. The Mycenaeans have been identified with the ◊Achaeans of Homer, and were among the besiegers at ◊Troy. They may also have been the marauding ◊sea peoples of Egyptian records. They were magnificent architects, for example Mycenae on the plain of Argos (Lion Gate and beehive tombs), and used a form of Greek written in Linear B (deciphered by Michael ◊Ventris). Their palaces were large and luxurious, and contained efficient sanitary arrangements. Commercial relations were maintained with Egypt throughout. Pottery, fresco-painting, and metalwork reached a high artistic level. Excavated by ◊Schliemann at Troy, Mycenae, and Tiryns (a stronghold on the plain of Argolis) from 1870 onwards, and Arthur ◊Evans in Crete from 1899.

mycorrhiza a mutualistic association occurring between the plant roots and a soil fungus. An ectotrophic mycorrhiza occurs on many tree species, which usually grow much better as a result, especially in the seeding stage. Typically the roots become repeatedly branched and coral-like, penetrated by hyphae of a surrounding fungal ◊mycelium. Mycorrhizal roots take up nutrients more efficiently, and the fungus benefits by obtaining carbohydrates from the tree. In a endotrophic mycorrhiza, the growth of the fungus is mainly inside the root, as in orchids. Such plants do not usually grow properly, and may not even germinate, unless the appropriate fungus is present.

myelin sheath the insulating layer that surrounds ◊nerve cells in vertebrate animals. It acts to speed up the passage of nerve impulses. The myelin itself is made up of fats and proteins and is formed from up to a hundred layers of membrane, laid down by special cells, the Schwann cells.

My Lai massacre the killing of the civilian inhabitants of My Lai, a village in South Vietnam, by US troops in Mar 1968. The Americans mistakenly believed that it was occupied by Viet Cong troops. An investigation in 1969 led to to the conviction of Lt William Calley, commander of the platoon, in 1971 for the murder of at least 109 Vietnamese civilians. Sentenced to life imprisonment, he was later released on parole. His superior officer was acquitted but the trial revealed a US army policy of punitive tactics against civilians. News of the massacre contributed to domestic pressure for the USA to end its involvement in Vietnam.

mynah name given to a number of starling species of birds, especially of SE Asia. The glossy black *hill mynah Gracula religiosa* of India is a realistic mimic of sounds and human speech.

myoglobin a globular protein, closely related to ◊haemoglobin, which is located in vertebrate muscle. Oxygen binds to myoglobin and is released only when the blood haemoglobin can no longer supply adequate oxygen to ◊muscle cells.

myopia short sight, in which vision of distant objects is blurred. It is due to a defect in the structure of the eye, causing incoming light to be focused before it reaches the retina. Concave lenses are used to correct it; surgery (in the form of a series of small slits cut in the cornea of the eye) is controversial in its effectiveness as a cure.

Myrdal /'mɜːdɑːl/ Gunnar 1898–1987. Swedish economist, author of many works on development economics. He was awarded the Nobel prize in 1974.

myrmecophyte a plant that lives in association with a colony of ants, and possesses specialized organs in which the ants live. For example, *Myrmecodia*, an epiphytic plant from Malaysia, develops root tubers containing a network of cavities inhabited by ants. Several species of *Acacia* from tropical America have specialized hollow thorns for the same purpose. This is probably a mutualistic relationship, with the ants helping to protect the plant from other insect pests and in return receiving shelter.

Myron /'maɪrən/ c. 500–440 BC. Greek sculptor. His *Discus-Thrower* and *Marsyas*, described by ancient critics, are known through Roman copies.

myrrh gum resin produced by a small tree *Commiphora myrrha*, found in the Middle East. In ancient times it was used for incense and perfume, and in embalming.

myrtle genus *Myrtus* of evergreen shrubs in the family Myrtaceae. The common Mediterranean myrtle *Myrtus communis* has oval opposite leaves and white flowers followed by purple berries, all of which are fragrant.

Mysore /ˌmaɪˈsɔː/ industrial city (engineering, silk) in ◊Karnataka, some 130 km/80 mi SW of Bangalore, India; population (1981) 476,000.

mystery play another name for ◊*miracle play*.

mystery religion any of various cults of the ancient world, open only to the initiated, for example the cults of Demeter (see ◊Eleusis), ◊Dionysus, Cybele, ◊Isis, and ◊Mithraism. Underlying them is a primitive fertility ritual, in which a deity undergoes death and resurrection, and initiates feed on the flesh and blood to attain communion with the divine and ensure their own life beyond the grave. The influence of mystery religions on early Christianity was considerable.

mysticism religious belief based on personal spiritual experience, not necessarily involving an orthodox deity, though found in all the major religions. Mysticism was first introduced to Western Europe through ◊Neoplatonism which was largely affected by Oriental schools of thought, and in its turn influenced the rise of Christian mysticism. It flourishes in periods of social crisis, as in Germany in the 14th–16th centuries, when feudalism was breaking down. Christian mystics of this era were Thomas à ◊Kempis and Jacob ◊Boehme. Often mysticism assumed heretical forms, as with the ◊Anabaptists and early ◊Quakers, but the Counter-Reformation also produced mystics such as St Teresa and St John of the Cross. Mystical movements of the 17th century included those of the Quietists in France (see under ◊Quietism), and Henry ◊More and the Cambridge Platonists in England, while the 18th century produced two great English mystics in William ◊Law and William ◊Blake. In the 20th century mysticism is expressed in the works of W B ◊Yeats and Aldous ◊Huxley. The scientific study of mysticism was established by the work of William ◊James and others.

mythology the study and interpretation of the stories inherent in a given culture and how they relate to similar stories told in other cultures. These stories involve gods and other supernatural beings, with whom human beings may have relationships, devised to explain the operation of the universe and human history. Ancient mythologies, with the names of the chief gods of each, include those of Egypt (◊Osiris), Greece (◊Zeus), Rome (◊Jupiter), India (◊Brahma), and the Teutonic peoples (◊Odin/Woden).

Mytilene /ˌmɪtɪˈliːni/ (modern Greek *Mitilíni*) port, capital of the Greek island of Lesvos (to which the name Mytilene is sometimes applied) and a centre of sponge fishing; population (1981) 24,000.

myxoedema also known as *hypothyroidism* underactivity of the thyroid gland. It can affect memory and speech, and can be treated by giving thyroid preparation.

myxomatosis a contagious, usually fatal virus infection of rabbits which causes much suffering. It is sometimes deliberately introduced to reduce rabbit population.

N 14th letter of the Roman alphabet, representing when spoken an alveolar nasal sound. In several Romance languages it disappears, with nasalization of the preceding vowel. It is the symbol for the element nitrogen, and the newton, the ▷SI unit of force.

NAACP abbreviated name of US civil rights organization ▷National Association for the Advancement of Colored People.

NAAFI acronym for Navy, Army, and Air Force Institutes. Non-profit-making association, providing canteens for HM British Forces in the UK and abroad.

Nabis, Les (from Hebrew 'prophet') a group of late 19th-century artists, followers of ▷Gauguin, who used simple forms and flat colours as he did for emotional effect in a style called *synthetisme*. Painters included ▷Bonnard and ▷Vuillard.

Nablus /'nɑːbləs/ town on the West Bank of the river Jordan, N of Jerusalem, the largest Palestinian town, after E Jerusalem, in Israeli occupation, population (1971) 64,000. As Shechem, it was the ancient capital of ▷Samaria (see also ▷Samaritans). The British field marshal Allenby's defeat of the Turks here in 1918 completed the conquest of Palestine.

Nabokov /nə'bəʊkɒf/ Vladimir 1899–1977. Russian author. Born in St Petersburg, he settled in the USA in 1940, becoming a US citizen in 1945. He was professor of Russian literature at Cornell University 1948–59, producing a translation and commentary on *Eugene Onegin* in 1963. His books include *The Real Life of Sebastian Knight* 1945, *Pnin* 1957, *Pale Fire* 1962, and perhaps his best known, *Lolita* 1955, the story of the infatuation of the middle-aged Humbert Humbert for a precocious child of 12, which added the word 'nymphet' to the English language.

Nachingwea /nə'tʃɪŋweɪə/ military training base in Tanzania. About 360 km/225 mi south of Dar-es-Salaam and linked by rail with the port of Mtwara 145 km/90 mi to the east. It was used by ▷Frelimo (Mozambique) 1964–75, and by the African National Council (Zimbabwe) 1975–80.

Nabokov Born in Russia, Vladimir Nabokov was an exile for all his adult life. The theme of alienation runs throughout his work, and his best-known novel remains the controversial *Lolita* 1955.

Nadar /nə'dɑː/ pseudonym of Gaspard-Felix Tournachan 1820–1910. French writer, caricaturist, and photographer who took photographs in the Paris metro using lights.

Nader /'neɪdə/ Ralph 1934– . American lawyer. The 'scourge of corporate morality', he has led many major consumer campaigns. His book *Unsafe at Any Speed* 1965 led to US car safety legislation.

nadir in astronomy, the point of the sky that is vertically 'below' the observer, (that is, beneath the Earth) and hence is diametrically opposite to the ▷zenith.

Naemen /'nɑːmən/ Flemish form of ▷Namur, city in Belgium.

naevus a type of ▷birthmark, sometimes colloquially known as a 'port wine mark'. It is a bright red coloured area of the skin, consisting of a mass of small blood vessels. A naevus of moderate size is harmless, and such marks are usually disguised cosmetically unless they are extremely disfiguring, when they can sometimes be treated by cutting out, by burning with an electric needle, by freezing with carbon dioxide snow, or by argon laser treatment.

Nagaland /'nɑːgəlænd/ state of NE India, bordering Burma on the east
area 16,488 sq km/6,366 sq mi
capital Kohima
products rice, tea, coffee, paper, sugar
population (1981) 773,500
history formerly part of Assam, seized by Britain from Burma 1826. The British sent 18 expeditions against the Naga peoples in the north 1832–87. After India attained independence in 1947, there was Naga guerrilla activity against the Indian government; the state of Nagaland was established in 1963 in response to demands for self-government, but fighting continued sporadically.

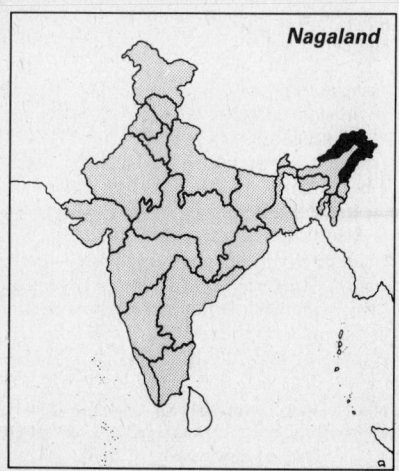

Nagaland

nagana animal sleeping sickness (see ▷tsetse).

Nagasaki /ˌnægə'sɑːki/ industrial port (coal, iron, shipbuilding) on Kyushu island, Japan; population (1984) 446,000.
history Nagasaki was the only Japanese port open to European trade from the 16th century

until other ports were opened in 1859. It was destroyed by an atom bomb during World War II on 9 Aug 1945, three days after ◊Hiroshima. Of its population of 212,000, 73,884 were killed, 76,796 injured, not counting the long-term victims of radiation.

Nagoya /nə'gɔɪə/ industrial seaport (cars, textiles, clocks) on Honshu island, Japan; population (1984) 2,066,000. It has a Shogun fortress (1610) and a noted Shinto shrine, Atsuta Jingu.

Nagpur /ˌnæg'puə/ industrial city (textiles, metals) in Maharashtra, India; university (1923); population (1981) 1,298,000.

Nagy /nɒdʒ/ Imre 1896–1958. Hungarian politician and leader of the revolt against Soviet domination in 1956, for which he was executed.

Naha /'nɑːhɑː/ chief port on Okinawa island, Japan; population (1984) 304,000.

Nahum /'neɪhəm/ (7th century BC) in the Old Testament, a Hebrew prophet, possibly born in Galilee, who forecast the destruction of Nineveh.

naiad in classical mythology, name for a water-nymph.

nail in biology, a hard, flat, flexible outgrowth of the digits of primates (humans, monkeys and apes). Nails are derived from the ◊claws of ancestral primates.

Naipaul /'naɪpɔːl/ V(idiadhar) S(urajprasad) 1932– . British writer. Born in Trinidad of Hindu parents, he is best known for his novels *A House for Mr Biswas* 1961, *Mr Stone and the Knights Companion* 1963, and *A Bend in the River* 1979. His brother *Shiva(dhar) Naipaul* 1940–85 was also a novelist (*Fireflies* 1970) and journalist.

Nairnshire /'neənʃə/ former county of Scotland, bounded on the north by the Moray Firth, included 1975 in the Highland region.

Nairobi /naɪ'rəubi/ industrial city (light industry, food processing), capital of Kenya, in the central highlands at 1,660 m/5,450 ft; University of Nairobi 1970; population (1985) 1,100,000. Nairobi, founded 1899, is the headquarters of the United Nations Environment Programme (UNEP).

Nakasone /ˌnækə'səuneɪ/ Yasuhiro 1917– . Japanese conservative politician, leader of the Liberal Democratic Party (LDP) and prime minister 1982–87.

Nakasone was educated at Tokyo University before entering politics. He held ministerial posts from 1967 and established his own faction within the conservative LDP. In 1982 he was elected president of the LDP and prime minister. Nakasone stepped up military spending, increased Japanese participation in international affairs, and encouraged a less paternalist approach to economic management. Although embarrassed by the conviction of one of his supporters in the 1983 Lockheed corruption scandal, he was re-elected in 1986 by a landslide, but retired from office in 1987.

Nakhodka /nə'xɒdkə/ pacific port in USSR. US-caught fish, especially pollock, is processed by Soviet factory ships in a joint venture.

Namaqualand /næ'mɑːkwələænd/ or Namaland near-desert area on the SW coast of Africa divided between Namibia and South Africa

Great Namaqualand is in Namibia, north of the Orange river, area 388,500 sq km/150,000 sq mi; sparsely populated by the Nama, a Hottentot people

Little Namaqualand is in Cape Province, South Africa, south of the Orange river, area 52,000 sq km/20,000 sq mi; copper and diamonds are mined here.

Namatjira /ˌnæmə'tʃɪərə/ Albert 1902–1959. Australian Aboriginal artist. Born in the Northern Territory, he painted watercolour landscapes of the Australian interior. Acclaimed after an exhibition in Melbourne in 1938, he eventually became an alcoholic and died destitute.

Namib Desert a coastal desert region in Namibia between the Kalahari and the Atlantic Ocean.

Namibia /nə'mɪbiə/ (South West Africa)
area 823,167 sq km/317,825 sq mi
capital Windhoek
towns ports Lüderitz, Walvis Bay
features Namib Desert on the coast; mountainous central plateau; part of Kalahari Desert
exports karakul lamb pelts; diamonds, vanadium, tin, copper; economy completely interlocked with, and dependent on, South Africa
currency South African rand
population (1982) 1,039,800; 51% Ovambo; the remainder including the pastoral Hereros, the Nama, and ◊Bushmen, as well as 75,600 whites
language Afrikaans, English, and indigenous languages
religion Christian and local
government a South African-appointed 'transitional government of national unity' was introduced in 1985, but rejected by the South West Africa People's Organization (◊SWAPO)
history annexed by Germany in 1884, it was occupied in World War I by South African forces under L ◊Botha, and was mandated to South Africa in 1920. South Africa did not accept the termination of the mandate by the United Nations in 1966, though accepting the principle of ultimate independence in 1976; in 1968 the United Nations renamed the territory Namibia. South Africa supports the Democratic Turnhalle Alliance, but the strong SWAPO guerrilla movement, led by Sam ◊Nujoma, is recognized by the United Nations as the sole representative of the people.

Namur /nə'mjuə/ (Flemish *Namen*) industrial city (cutlery, iron and steel), capital of the province of Namur, in S Belgium; population (1985) 102,000.

Nanaimo /næ'naɪməu/ coal-mining centre of British Columbia, Canada, on the E coast of Vancouver Island; population (1985) 50,500.

Nana Sahib /'nɑːni 'sɑːb/ 1820–c. 1859. name by which Dandhu Panth, an adopted son of the ex-peshwa (chief minister) of the ◊Mahrattas, was commonly known. He joined the rebels in the ◊Indian Mutiny, and was responsible for the massacre at ◊Kanpur. After the rebellion he took refuge in Nepal.

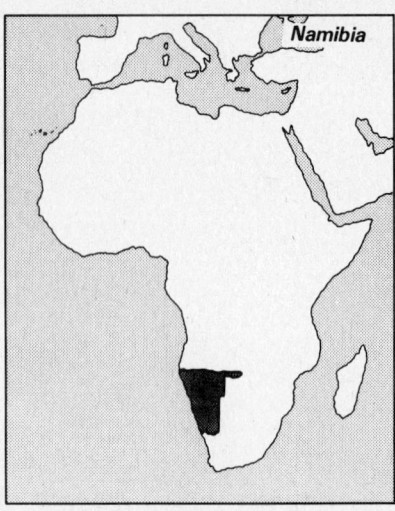

Namibia

Nancecuke /næns'kjːk/ site in Cornwall of a secret Ministry of Defence Establishment. A branch of the Chemical Defence Establishment at ◊Porton Down until 1978, it was closed when Britain gave up chemical and biological weapons.

Nanchang /ˌnæn'tʃæŋ/ industrial city (textiles, glass, porcelain, soap), capital of Jianqxi province, China, about 260 km/160 mi SE of Wuhan; road and rail junction; university; population (1982) 1,046,000.

history Nanchang was originally a walled city built in the 12th century. The first Chinese Communist rising took place here 1 Aug 1927.

Nancy /'nɒnsi/ capital of the *département* of Meurthe-et-Moselle and of the region of Lorraine, France, 280 km/175 mi E of Paris; university; population (1982) 307,000. Nancy dates from the 11th century and contains many fine buildings, including the Hôtel de Ville and the cathedral 1742.

Nanda Devi /'nʌndə 'diːvi/ peak in the Himalayas, Uttar Pradesh, India; 7,817 m/25,645 ft.

Nanga Parbat /'nʌŋgə 'pɑːbæt/ peak in the Himalayas, Azad ◊Kashmir; 8,126 m/26,660 ft.

Nanjing /ˌnæn'dʒɪŋ/ capital (formerly Nanking) of Jiangsu province, China, 270 km/165 mi NW of Shanghai; centre of industry, commerce, and communications; university 1888; population (1982) 2,130,000. The bridge 1968 over the Chang Jiang river is the longest in China at 6,705 m/22,000 ft.

history The city dates from the 2nd century BC, perhaps earlier. It received the name Nanjing ('southern capital') under the Ming dynasty (1368–1644), and was the capital of China 1368–1403, 1928–37, 1946–49.

Nanking /ˌnæn'kɪŋ/ former name of ◊Nanjing, city in China.

Nanning /ˌnæn'nɪŋ/ industrial river port, capital of Guangxi Zhuang region, China, on the river You Jiang; population (1982) 866,000.

nano prefix used in ◊SI units of measurement. It is equivalent to one thousand millionth part (10⁻⁹), for example, nanosecond.

Nansen /'nænsən/ Fridtjof 1861–1930. Norwegian explorer, scientist, and statesman. He made his first voyage to Greenland waters in a sealing-ship in 1882, and in 1888–89 attempted to cross the Greenland icefield. He sailed to the Arctic in 1893 in the *Fram*, which was deliberately allowed to drift with an iceflow. Later, Nansen left the *Fram* and, accompanied by F J Johansen, continued northwards on foot. They reached 86°,14' North, the highest latitude then attained. After World War I Nansen became League of Nations High Commissioner for refugees, and in 1923 received the Nobel peace prize for his work. The Nansen institute for humanist and social research was established at Oslo, Norway, in 1956.

Nanshan Islands /'næn 'ʃæn/ Chinese name for the ◊Spratly Islands.

Nantes /nɒnt/ port in W France on the Loire, capital of Pays de la Loire; population (1982) 465,000. It has a cathedral 1434–1884 and a castle founded 938.

Nantes, Edict of /nɒnt/ edict by which Henry IV of France granted religious freedom to the ◊Huguenots in 1598. It was revoked in 1685 by Louis XIV.

Nantucket /næn'tʌkɪt/ island and resort in Massachusetts, USA, S of Cape Cod, 120 sq km/46 sq mi; in the 18–19th centuries Nantucket was a whaling port.

napalm fuel used in flame-throwers and incendiary bombs. Produced from jellied petrol, it is named from *na*phthenic and *palm*itic acids. It was widely used by the US Army during the Vietnam War. Extensive burns are caused by napalm, because it sticks to the skin even when alight.

naphtha originally applied to naturally occurring liquid hydrocarbons, the term is now used for the mixtures of hydrocarbons obtained by destructive distillation of petroleum, coal-tar and shale oil. It is a major raw material for the petrochemicals and plastics industry.

naphthalene a solid, aromatic hydrocarbon, $C_{10}H_8$, obtained from coal-tar. A white, shiny, crystalline solid with a smell of moth-balls, it is used in making indigo and certain azo-dyes, and as a mild disinfectant and insecticide.

Napier /'neɪpɪə/ wool port of North Island, New Zealand; population (with Hastings) (1985) 117,000.

Napier /'neɪpɪə/ Charles James 1782–1853. British general. He conquered ◊Sind in India 1841–43 with a very small force and governed it till 1847. He was the first commander to mention men from the ranks in his dispatches.

Napier /'neɪpɪə/ John 1550–1617. Scottish mathematician who invented ◊logarithms in 1614, and 'Napier's bones', an early logarithmic calculating device for multiplication and division.

Napier /'neɪpɪə/ Robert Cornelis, 1st Baron Napier of Magdala 1810–1890. British field marshal. Knighted for his services at ◊Lucknow, and thanked by Parliament for his part in the Chinese War of 1855, he stormed Magdala in the Abyssinian campaign of 1868.

Naples /'neɪpɒlz/ (Italian *Napoli*) industrial port (shipbuilding, cars, textiles, paper, food processing) and capital of Campania, Italy, on the Tyrrhenian Sea; university 1224; population (1984) 1,207,000.

features Naples is the third largest city of Italy, and as a port second in importance only to Genoa. To the south is the Isle of Capri, and behind the city is Mount Vesuvius, with the ruins of Pompeii at its foot. Buildings include the royal palace, the San Carlo Opera House, and the Castel Nuovo.

history The city began as the Greek colony Neapolis in the 6th century BC and was taken over by Romans 326 BC; it became part of the Kingdom of the Two ◊Sicilies 1140 and capital of the Kingdom of ◊Naples from 1282.

Naples, Kingdom of /'neɪpɒlz/ the S part of Italy, alternately independent and united with ◊Sicily in the Kingdom of the Two Sicilies: with Sicily 1140–1282, first under Norman rule 1130–94, then Hohenstaufen 1194–1266, then Angevin from 1268; apart from Sicily, but continued Angevin rule to 1435; reunited with Sicily 1442–1503, under house of Aragon to 1501; a Spanish Hapsburg possession 1504–1707 and Austrian 1707–35; under Spanish Bourbon rule 1735–99. The *Neapolitan Republic* was established 1799 after Napoleon had left Italy for Egypt, but fell after five months to the forces of reaction under Cardinal Ruffo, with the British admiral Nelson blockading the city by sea; many prominent citizens were massacred after the capitulation. The Spanish Bourbons were restored 1799, 1802–05, and 1815–1860, when Naples joined the Kingdom of Italy.

Napoleon I /nə'pəʊlɪən/ Bonaparte 1769–1821. Emperor of the French. Born at Ajaccio, Corsica, he received a commission in the artillery in 1785 and first distinguished himself at the seige of Toulon in 1730. Having suppressed a royalist rising in Paris in 1795, he was given command against the Austrians (see ◊Revolutionary Wars) in Italy, and defeated them at Lodi, Arcole, and Rivoli in 1796–97. Egypt – seen as a halfway house to India – was overrun and Syria invaded, but his fleet was destroyed by ◊Nelson, at the Battle of the Nile. He returned to France to overthrow the government of the Directory (see under ◊French revolution) and establish his own dictatorship, nominally as First Consul. The Austrians were again defeated at Marengo in 1800, and the coalition against France shattered, a truce being declared in 1802. A plebiscite the same year made him consul for life. In 1804 a plebiscite made him Emperor. While retaining and extending the legal and educational reforms of the Jacobins, he replaced the democratic constitution established by Revolution with a centralized despotism, and by his Concordat conciliated the Church. War was renewed by Britain in 1803, aided by Austria and Russia from 1805, and Prussia from 1806 (see ◊Napoleonic Wars). Prevented by the Navy from invading England, he drove Austria out of the war by victories at Ulm and Austerlitz in 1805, and Prussia by the victory at Jena in 1806. Then he formed an alliance with Russia at Tilsit (1807). Napoleon now forbade entry of British goods to Europe, under the 'Continental System', occupied Portugal and in 1808 placed his brother Joseph on the Spanish throne. Both countries revolted, with British aid, and Austria attempted to re-enter the war, but was defeated at Wagram.

In 1796 Napoleon had married ◊Josephine de Beauharnais, but now, to assert his equality with the Hapsburgs, he divorced her to marry the Emperor's daughter, Marie ◊Louise. When Russia failed to enforce the Continental System, Napoleon occupied ◊Moscow, but his retreat in the bitter winter of 1812 encouraged Prussia and Austria to declare war again in 1813, and Napoleon was defeated at Leipzig and driven from Germany. After a brilliant campaign on French soil, he abdicated in 1814, and was banished to Elba. In March 1815 he reassumed power, but was defeated by the Allies at ◊Waterloo. Surrendering to the British, he again abdicated, and was exiled to St Helena. His body was brought back in 1840 for interment in the Hôtel des Invalides.

Napoleon I After surrendering to the British in 1815, Napoleon Bonaparte was exiled to St Helena.

Napoleon II /nə'pəʊlɪən/ 1811–1832. Title given by the Bonapartists to the son of Napoleon I and Marie Louise; until 1814 he was known as the king of Rome, and after 1818 as the duke of Reichstadt. After his father's abdication in 1814 he was taken to the Austrian court, where he spent the rest of his life. By Hitler's order his body was removed from Vienna in 1940 and reinterred in the Hôtel des Invalides, Paris.

Napoleon III /nə'pəʊlɪən/ 1808–1873. Emperor of the French. The son of Louis Bonaparte and Hortense de Beauharnais, brother and step-daughter respectively of Napoleon I, he led two unsuccessful revolts, at Strasbourg in 1836 and at Boulogne in 1840. After the latter he was imprisoned. Escaping in 1846, he lived in London until 1848. He was elected president of the republic in December, and set himself to secure a following by posing as the champion of order and religion against the revolutionary menace. He secured his re-election by a military coup d'état in 1851, and a year later was proclaimed emperor. Hoping to strengthen his regime by military triumphs, he joined in the Crimean War, waged war with Austria in 1859 winning the battle of Solferino, and attempted unsuccessfully to found a vassal empire in Mexico 1863–67. In so doing he aroused the mistrust of Europe and isolated France. At home, his regime was discredited by its notorious corruption; republican and socialist opposition grew, in spite of severe repression, and forced Napoleon, after 1860, to make concessions in the direction of parliamentary government. Manoeuvred by Bismarck in 1870 into war with Prussia, he was forced to surrender at Sedan, whereupon the empire collapsed. After the war he withdrew to England, where he died.

Napoleon III The versatility and political skill of Napoleon III had ensured his imperial status, but his imprudent acts and foolish boasts put France into war with Prussia, leading to his defeat and English exile.

Napoleonic Wars 1803–1815 a series of European wars which followed the ◊Revolutionary Wars.
1803 British renewed the war, following an appeal from the Maltese against Napoleon's seizure of the island
1805 Napoleon's planned invasion of Britain from Boulogne ended by Nelson's victory at Trafalgar; coalition formed by Britain, Austria, Russia, Sweden. Austria defeated at Ulm; Austria and Russia at Austerlitz
1806 Prussia, latest member of the coalition, defeated at Jena; Napoleon instituted an attempted blockade, the Continental System, to isolate Britain from Europe
1807 Russia defeated at Eylau and Friedland and on making peace with Napoleon under the Treaty of Tilsit changed sides, agreeing to attack Sweden, and was forced to retreat
1808 Napoleon's invasion of Portugal, and habit of installing his relatives as puppet kings, led to his defeat in the ◊Peninsular War
1809 revived Austrian opposition to Napoleon

was ended by defeat at Wagram
1812 the Continental System finally collapsed on its rejection by Russia, and Napoleon made the fatal decision to invade; he reached Moscow but was defeated by the Russian resistance, and by the bitter winter as he retreated through a countryside laid waste by the retreating Russians (380,000 French soldiers died)
1813 Britain, Prussia, Russia, Austria and Sweden formed a new coalition, defeated Napoleon at the Battle of the Nations and he abdicated and was exiled to Elba

Napoleon's European Empire 1803–1815

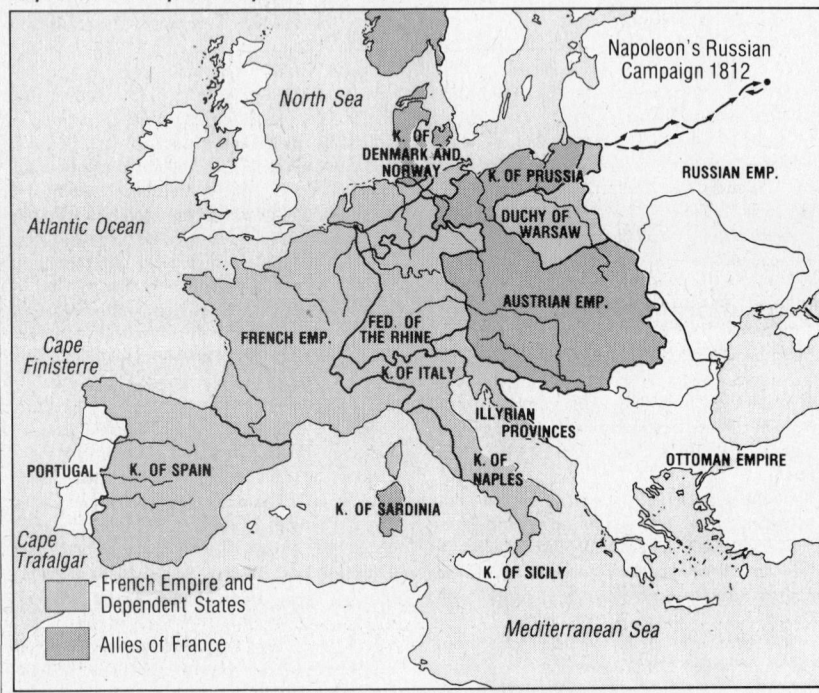

1814 Louis XVIII became king of France, and the Congress of Vienna met to conclude peace
1815 Napoleon returned to Paris. 16 Jun Wellington defeated Ney at Quatre Bras (in Belgium, SE of Brussels), and after a Hundred Days Napoleon was finally defeated at Waterloo S of Brussels, 18 Jun. The Congress resumed with Napoleon more securely incarcerated at St Helena.

Napoli /ˈnɑːpəli/ Italian form of ◊Naples, city in Italy.

Nara /ˈnɑːrə/ city in Japan, in the S of Honshu island, the capital of the country AD 710–94; population (1984) 316,000. It was the birthplace of Japanese art and literature.

Narbonne /ˌnɑːˈbɒn/ city in S France, the chief town of S Gaul in Roman times and a port in medieval times; population (1983) 39,246.

narcissism in psychology, an excessive valuation of the self and its attributes, an exaggeration of normal self-respect and pride in oneself into vanity and conceit, which may amount to mental disorder.

Narcissus /nɑːˈsɪsəs/ in Greek mythology, a beautiful youth, who rejected the love of the nymph ◊Echo, and as a punishment was

condemned to fall in love with his own reflection in a stream. He eventually pined away for love of himself, and in the place where he died a flower sprang up which was named after him.

narcissus genus of bulbous plants of the family Amaryllidaceae, of which the best-known are the daffodil, jonquil, and narcissus.

narcotic pain-relieving and sleep-inducing drug. The principal narcotics induce dependency and include opium and its derivatives and synthetic modifications (such as morphine and heroin); the alcohols (for example paraldehyde and ethyl alcohol); and the barbiturates.

Narodnik member of a secret Russian political movement active 1873–76 before its suppression by the Tsarist authorities. Composed largely of university students, their main purpose was to convert the peasantry to socialism.

Narragansett Bay /ˌnærəˈgænsɪt/ Atlantic inlet, Rhode Island, USA. It encloses a number of islands, running inland 45 km/28 mi.

Narses /ˈnɑːsiːz/ c. 478–c. 573. Byzantine statesman and general. Originally a eunuch slave, he later became an official in the imperial treasury. He was joint commander with Belisarius in Italy 538–39, and in 552 destroyed the Ostrogoths at Taginae.

Narvik /ˈnɑːvɪk/ seaport in Norway, on Ofot Fjord, exporting iron ore from Swedish mines; population (1980) 19,500. To secure this ore supply Germany seized Narvik in Apr 1940. British, French, Polish, and Norwegian forces recaptured the port but had to abandon it on 10 Jun to cope with the worsening Allied situation elsewhere in Europe.

narwhal small whale *Monodon monoceros*, found only in the Arctic Ocean. The male has a single spirally fluted tusk which may be up to 2.7 m/9 ft long.

NASA *N*ational *A*eronautics and *S*pace *A*dministration. The US government agency, founded in 1958, for non-military spaceflight and aeronautical research. Its headquarters are in Washington DC and its major installation is at ◊Cape Canaveral.

Naseby, Battle of /'neɪzbi/ decisive battle of the English Civil War 14 Jun 1645, when the Royalists led by Prince ◊Rupert were defeated by Cromwell and Fairfax. Named after the nearby village of Naseby, 20 km/12 mi NNW of Northampton.

Nash /næʃ/ John 1752–1835. British architect. He laid out Regent's Park, London, and designed many of the terraces nearby. Between 1813 and 1820 he planned Regent Street (later rebuilt), and repaired and enlarged Buckingham Palace for which he designed Marble Arch, intended as the entrance gateway. He also designed the flamboyant Pavilion, Brighton 1815.

Nash /næʃ/ John Northcote 1893–1977. British landscape artist and engraver. He was the brother of artist Paul ◊Nash.

Nash /næʃ/ Ogden 1902–1971. American poet. Born in Rye, New York, he published numerous volumes of humorous verse of quietly puncturing satire, with unorthodox rhymes, including *Hard Lines* 1931, *The Face is Familiar* 1941, and *Collected Verses* 1961.

Nash /næʃ/ Paul 1889–1946. British artist. Born in London, he became famous for his pictures of World War I, such as *The Menin Road*, in which he created strange patterns out of the scorched landscape of the Western Front. During World War II he was appointed official war artist to the Air Ministry. Two of his most celebrated pictures are *Totes Meer/Dead Sea* and *The Battle of Britain*.

Nash /næʃ/ Richard 1674–1762. British dandy, known as 'Beau Nash'. As master of ceremonies at Bath from 1705, he made it the most fashionable watering-place in England, and did much to introduce a more polished code of manners into general use.

Nash(e) /næʃ/ Thomas 1567–1601. English poet, dramatist and pamphleteer. Born at Lowestoft, he settled in London about 1588, where he was rapidly drawn into the Martin ◊Marprelate controversy. Among his later works are the satire *Pierce Pennilesse* 1592; the religious *Christes Teares over Jerusalem* 1593; the first English picaresque novel; and the comedy, *Summer's Last Will and Testament* 1592.

Nash /næʃ/ Walter 1882–1968. New Zealand Labour politician. Born in England, he emigrated to New Zealand in 1909. He was prime minister 1957–60, and leader of the Labour Party until 1963.

Nashville /'næʃvɪl/ port on the Cumberland river and capital of Tennessee, USA; it is a banking and commercial centre and has large printing, music-publishing and recording industries; population (1980) 455,651. It is the hub of the country-music business.

Nash Self-portrait of Paul Nash, the British war artist, dating from 1922–23.

history Nashville dates from 1778, and the Confederate army was defeated here in 1864 in the American Civil War.

Nasmyth /'neɪsmɪθ/ Alexander 1758–1840. Scottish portrait and landscape painter. Born in Edinburgh, he is best remembered for his portrait of the poet Robert Burns.

Nasmyth /'neɪsmɪθ/ James 1808–1890. Scottish engineer and machine-tool manufacturer, whose many inventions included the steel hammer in 1839. At his factory near Manchester, he developed the steam hammer for making large steel forgings (the first of which was the propeller shaft for ◊Brunel's steamship *Great Britain*).

Nassau /'næsɔː/ capital and port of the Bahamas, on New Providence island; population (1980) 135,437. It was founded in 1629.

Nasser /'næsə/ Gamal Abdel 1918–1970. Egyptian politician. Son of a postal clerk, he entered the army from Cairo Military Academy, and was wounded in the Palestine War of 1948–49. In 1952 he was the driving power behind the Neguib coup, which ended the monarchy. He became prime minister in 1954 and in 1956 president of Egypt (the United Arab Republic 1958–   ). His nationalization of the ◊Suez Canal and his ambitions for an Egyptian-led Arab union led to disquiet in the Middle East (and in the West).

Nasser Gamal Abdel Nasser was among the leaders of the 1952 coup to overthrow King Farouk. He went on to become president of Egypt and the United Arab Republic, which he formed in 1958.

nastic movement a plant movement that is caused by an external stimulus, such as light or temperature, but which is directionally independent of its source, unlike ◊tropisms. Nastic movements occur due to changes in water pressure within specialized cells, or as a result of differing rates of growth in part of the plant. Examples include the opening and closing of *Crocus* flowers following an increase or decrease in temperature (thermonasty), and the opening and closing of evening primrose (*Oenothera*) flowers on exposure to dark and light (photonasty). The leaf movements of Venus's fly trap following a tactile stimulus, and the rapid collapse of the sensitive plant's (*Mimosa pudica*) leaflets are examples of haptonasty. Sleep movements, where the leaves or flowers of some plants adopt a different position at night, are described as nyctinasty.

nasturtium genus of plants of the family Cruciferae, including *Nasturtium officinale*, watercress, a perennial aquatic plant of Europe and Asia, grown as a salad crop. The garden species, *Tropaeolum majus*, which has orange- or scarlet-coloured flowers, and *Tropaeolum minus*, which has smaller flowers, belong to the South American Tropaeolaceae. The leaves and buds are sometimes served in salads.

Natal /nəˈtæl/ province of South Africa, NE of Cape Province, bounded on the E by the Indian Ocean
area 86,965 sq km/33,578 sq mi
capital Pietermaritzburg
towns Durban
physical slopes from the Drakensberg to a fertile subtropical coastal plain
products sugar cane, black wattle (*Acacia mollissima*), maize, fruits, vegetables, tobacco, and coal
population (1980) 2,676,500
history called Natal because Vasco da Gama reached it on Christmas Day 1497. It was a part of the British Cape Colony 1843–56, when it was made into a separate colony. Zululand was annexed to Natal in 1897, and the districts of Vrijheid, Utrecht, and part of Wakkerstroom were transferred from the Transvaal to Natal in 1903. In 1910 the colony became a part of the Union of South Africa.

Natal /nəˈtæl/ industrial (textiles, salt refining) seaport in Brazil, capital of the state of Rio Grando do Norte; population (1980) 376,500.

Natchez /ˈnætʃɪz/ member of a North American Indian people of the Mississippi area, one of the ◊Moundbuilder group of peoples. They had a highly developed caste system, headed by a ruler priest (the 'Great Sun'), unusual in North America. This lasted until the near genocide of the Natchez by the French in 1731: only a few survive in Oklahoma.

Natchez /ˈnætʃɪz/ trading centre in Mississippi, USA, on the bluffs above the Mississippi river; important in the heyday of steamboat traffic; population (1980) 22,000.

national accounts the organization of a country's finances. In the UK the economy is divided into the public sector (central government, local authorities, and public corporations), the private sector (the personal and company sector), and the overseas sector (transactions between residents and non-residents of the UK). The ◊public sector borrowing requirement (PSBR), as the state took over a larger and larger share of the economy, became a crucial factor in budgets of the UK and other countries in the 1970s. It is the deficit between the amount the public sector receives, from ◊taxation and other sources, and the amount it needs to finance its activities. In the UK central government revenue and expenditure is channelled through the Consolidated Fund, which meets expenditure out of revenue arising largely from taxation, and the National Loans Fund which handles most of central government's domestic lending and borrowing.

national anthem a patriotic song for official occasions. In Britain 'God Save the ◊King/Queen' has been accepted as such since 1745, although both tune and words are of much earlier origin. 'Deutschland über Alles/Germany before everything' is sung to a tune by Haydn. In 1951 President Herss selected a new national anthem for the Federal Republic (Germany having been without one 1945–45) but this was unpopular and the old one was revived in 1952. The French national anthem, the ◊'Marseillaise', dates from the revolution of 1792, and the Belgian 'Brabançonne' from that of 1830. The ◊Internationale, adopted as the Russian national anthem in 1917, was replaced by the song 'Unbreakable Union of Freeborn Republics' in 1944. The American national anthem, 'The Star-spangled Banner', written during the war of 1812, was officially adopted in 1931. Countries within the Commonwealth retain 'God Save the King/Queen' as the 'royal anthem', adopting their own anthem as a mark of independence. These include 'Advance Australia Fair' 1974–76 and from 1984 and 'O Canada' from 1980. The anthem of united Europe is Schiller's 'Ode to Joy' as set by Beethoven in his Ninth Symphony.

National Army Museum official museum, established in 1960 in Chelsea, London, for the British forces 1485–1914. The Imperial War Museum deals with the period from 1914.

National Assistance in Britain, former term 1948–66 for ◊Supplementary Benefit.

National Association for the Advancement of Colored People (NAACP) US civil rights organization, dedicated to ending black inequality and segregation through nonviolent protest, founded 1910 by William Walling and Oswald Villiard. Its first aim was to eradicate lynching, which was largely achieved by the 1950s. The NAACP was noted particularly for its long campaign to end segregation in state schools; it funded test cases which eventually led to the Supreme Court decision 1954 outlawing school segregation. The organization has at times been criticized by militants and black separatists for its moderate stance and its commitment to integration.

National Book League former name of ◊Book Trust.

National Country Party former name for the Australian ◊National Party.

national debt debt incurred by the central government of a country, on which it pays interest. In Britain the national debt is managed by the ◊Bank of England, under the control of the Treasury. The first issue of government stock in Britain was made in 1693, to raise a loan of £1,000,000. Historically, the main cause of increase in the debt has always been wartime expenditure; thus, after the War of the Spanish Succession (1701–14), it reached £54,000,000. By 1900 it had been brought down to £610,000,000, but World War I forced it up, by 1920, to £7,828,000,000, and World War II, by 1945, to £21,870,221,651. Since then other factors have increased the national debt including nationalization expenditure and overseas borrowing to support the pound. However, as a proportion of ◊gross domestic product, the national debt has fallen since 1945 and stabilized at around 40–45 per cent. In the 1970s it stood at over £35,000 million. The US Public Debt $2,436,453,269 in 1870, was $1,132,357,095 in 1905, but had risen to $24,299,321,467 by 1920 and it has since risen almost continuously, reaching $1,823,103 million in 1985.

National Front in the UK, extreme right-wing political party founded in 1967. It was formed from a merger of the League of Empire Loyalists and the British National Party. In 1980 dissension arose and splinter groups formed. Electoral support in the 1983 general election was minimal. Some of its members had links with the National Socialist movement of the 1960s: see under ◊Nazi Party.

National Gallery London art gallery housing the British national collection of pictures by artists no longer living. It was founded in 1824, when Parliament voted £57,000 for the purchase of 38 pictures from the collection of John Julius, plus £3,000 for the maintenance of the building in Pall Mall, where they were housed. The present building in Trafalgar Square was designed by William Wilkins 1778–1839, and opened in 1838: there have been several extensions.

National Guard a ◊militia force recruited by each state of the USA.

National Heritage Memorial Fund government fund established in Britain in 1980 to save the countryside, historic houses, and works of art, as a memorial to those who gave their lives in World War II.

national income the total income of a state over a given period, usually a year, comprising both the wages of individuals and the profits of companies. It is equal to the value of the output of all goods and services during the same period. National income is equal to ◊Gross National Product minus an allowance for replacement of ageing capital stock.

national insurance in the UK, state insurance which provides payments to the unemployed, sick, and retired, and also covers medical treatment. It is paid for by weekly contributions from employees and employers.

nationalism in politics, general term for movements aiming to strengthen national feeling and tradition, and particularly to unify a nation or to liberate it from foreign rule. Stimulated by the French Revolution, strong movements arose in the 19th century in favour of national unification in Germany and Italy, and advancing national independence in Italy, Ireland, Belgium, Hungary, Bohemia, Poland, and the Balkan states. They remained a potent factor in European politics until 1918. Since 1900 nationalism has become a strong force in Asia and Africa. In recent years a strongly national literary and political movement has developed in Scotland and Wales.

nationalism in music, a movement which became evident in the 19th century when composers (such as Smetana and Grieg) showed particular concern for the folk material of their country, the local instruments and, above all, the national spirit and its expression in music.

nationalization policy of bringing a country's essential services and industries under public ownership. It was pursued by the UK Labour government 1945–51. Acts were passed nationalizing the Bank of England, coal, and most hospitals in 1946; transport and electricity in 1947; gas in 1948, and iron and steel in 1949. In 1953 the succeeding Conservative government provided for the return of road haulage to private enterprise and for decentralization of the railways. It also denationalized iron and steel in 1953 but it was renationalized by the next Labour government in 1967. In 1977 Callaghan's Labour government nationalized the aircraft and shipbuilding industries. In recent

years the trend towards nationalization has slowed and in some countries (Britain, France, and Japan) reversed (see also ◊privatization). The term is also used for the taking over of assets in the hands of foreign governments or companies, for example ◊Abadan, and ◊Suez Canal.

National Park area set aside and conserved for public enjoyment. In England and Wales under the National Park Act 1949 the Peak District, Lake District, Snowdonia, Dartmoor, Pembrokeshire coast, Yorkshire Dales, North Yorkshire Moors, Northumberland, Brecon Beacons, Exmoor, and other areas of great natural beauty were designated as National Parks. Port Hacking, New South Wales, near Sydney, Australia, is the chief National Park in Australia. National Parks in the USA include Crater Lake, Oregon; the Grand Canyon, Arizona; the Mammoth Cave, Kentucky; Mount McKinley, Alaska; Sequoia and Yosemite, California; and the Everglades, Florida. The Kruger and Natal National Park were pioneer African examples. The increasing use by the public of National Parks has partly defeated their purpose, and a modern innovation is the reservation of ◊'wilderness areas' with no motorized traffic, no overflying aircraft, no hotels, hostels, shops or cafés, no industry and the minimum of management. See also ◊nature reserve.

National Party, Australian Australian political party representing the interests of the farmers and people of the smaller towns. It developed from about 1860 as the National Country Party, and holds the power balance between Liberals and Labour. It has been in coalition with the Liberals since 1949. Its former leader, Douglas Anthony 1929– , was deputy prime minister in the Fraser government 1975–83. Its leader since 1984 has been Ian Sinclair 1929– .

National Physical Laboratory (NPL) research establishment, set up in 1900 at Teddington, England, under the control of the Department of Industry.

National Portrait Gallery art gallery in London, containing individual portraits of distinguished British men and women of the past. It was founded in 1856 and the present building in St Martin's Place, Trafalgar Square, opened in 1896. In addition to paintings, busts and photographs are displayed.

National Research Development Council UK corporation exploiting inventions derived from public or private sources, usually jointly with industrial firms. It was set up in 1967.

National Savings name applied to several government savings schemes in the UK, including the National Savings Bank (NSB), which operates through the Post Office; National Savings Certificates; and British Savings Bonds.

national security adviser office of adviser on foreign affairs to the US president and head of the National Security Council, created by President ◊Eisenhower in 1953. It was almost a clerical post at first, but took on greater stature when held by McGeorge Bundy 1961–66 and Walt Rostow 1966–69. With the appointment of

◊Kissinger 1969–75, it rivalled that of secretary of state, an office also held by Kissinger 1973–77. ◊Brzezinski, appointed 1977, exceeded Secretary of State ◊Vance in his influence on ◊Carter, and Vance resigned in 1980. President Reagan's adviser, Admiral John Poindexter, who succeeded Robert McFarlane (1937–) in 1985, was forced to resign in 1986 because of scandal surrounding his part in the sale of arms to Iran (see ◊Irangate). He was succeeded by Frank Carlucci (1930–) and he in turn by Lt-Gen Colin Powell.

National Security Agency agency handling US security communications worldwide. Known popularly as the Puzzle Palace, its headquarters are at Fort Meade, Maryland (with a major facility at Menwith Hill, England).

National Socialism official name for the ◊Nazi movement in ◊Germany; see ◊Hitler.

National Theatre British national theatre company established in 1963, and the theatre complex to house it on London's South Bank opened in 1976. Sir Peter ◊Hall succeeded Sir Laurence ◊Olivier as director from 1973.

National Trust British trust founded in 1895 for the preservation of land and buildings of historic interest or beauty, incorporated by Act of Parliament in 1907, it is the largest private landowner in Britain. The National Trust for Scotland was established in 1931.

National Westminster Tower building designed by Richard Seifert, located in the City of London. It is 183 m/600 ft high, and has 49 storeys. Completed in 1979, it cost £2 million.

native metal term used to describe a mineral consisting of the metal uncombined with any other element. Copper and silver can be found as native metals.

nativity a Christian festival celebrating a birth: 1 *Christmas* celebrated 25 Dec from 336 AD in memory of the birth of Jesus in Bethlehem; 2 *Nativity of the Virgin Mary* celebrated by the Catholic and Greek Churches, 8 Sept; 3 *Nativity of John the Baptist* celebrated by the Catholic, Greek and Anglican Churches, 24 Jun.

natural gas a mixture of flammable gases found in the Earth's crust, which is now one of our three main fossil fuels (with coal and oil). Natural gas is a mixture of ◊hydrocarbons, notably methane, ethane, butane and propane. Before the gas is piped to homes butane and propane are removed and liquefied to form 'bottled gas'.

Natural History Museum the British Museum (Natural History) in London, containing the departments of zoology, entomology, geology, mineralogy, palaeontology, and botany. The museum is in a building designed by Waterhouse and erected 1873–80 in South Kensington, and has no adminstrative connection with the ◊British Museum.

natural logarithms in mathematics, the exponent of a number expressed to base e, where e represents the ◊irrational number 2.72828. Natural ◊logarithms are also called Naperian logarithms, after their inventor, the Scottish mathematician John Napier.

natural selection the process whereby gene frequencies in a population change due to certain organisms producing more descendents than others, because they are better able to survive and reproduce. Natural selection results in the genetic constitution of the population, and ultimately the species, being altered in favour of the particular genes that successful individuals bear. The accumulated effect of natural selection is to produce ◊adaptations such as the thick coat of a polar bear or the spade-like forelimbs of a mole. It was recognized by ◊Darwin as the main process driving ◊evolution.

Nature Conservancy Council (NCC) UK government agency established in 1949 to oversee nature conservation. It is responsible for designating and managing National Nature Reserves and other conservation areas (for example, Sites of Special Scientific Interest, SSSIs) and for the enforcement of legislation that protects wildlife and habitats.

nature-nurture controversy a long-standing dispute among philosophers and psychologists over the relative importance of inheritance ('nature') and experience ('nurture'); more recently called the ◊environment-heredity controversy.

nature reserve area set aside to preserve its original scenic formation or vegetation, and often to provide a sanctuary and breeding ground for rare birds or animals. The ◊National Parks Act, 1949, gave powers to designate such areas in Britain.

Naukratis Nile delta city of Greek traders in ancient Egypt, rediscovered by ◊Petrie in 1884.

Nauru /nau'ru:/ island country in the SW Pacific, in ◊Polynesia, W of Kiribati.
government the constitution dates from independence in 1968. It provides for a single-chamber parliament of 18 members, elected by universal suffrage for a three-year term, and a president who is both head of state and head of government. The size of the country allows a very intimate style of government, with the president combining several portfolios in a cabinet of only five. Voting in parliamentary elections is compulsory. There are no political parties, and all members of parliament are elected as independents.
history the first Europeans, Britons, arrived 1798 and called it Pleasant Island. The German empire seized it 1888. Nauru was placed under Australian administration by the League of Nations in 1920, with the UK and New Zealand as co-trustees. Japan occupied Nauru 1942–45. In 1947 Nauru became a United Nations trust territory administered by Australia.
Internal self-government was granted 1966 and in 1968, on achieving full independence, Nauru became a 'special member' of the Commonwealth, which means that it does not have direct representation at meetings of heads of government. The head chief of Nauru, Hammer DeRoburt, was elected president in 1968 and re-elected until 1983 with one interruption, 1976–78, when Bernard Dowiyogo was president. The Dec 1986 elections resulted in a hung parliament and the need for fresh polls.

Nauru is attempting to sue its former trustees (New Zealand, the UK, and Australia) for removing nearly all the island's phosphate-rich soil 1922–65, leaving it barren. Nauru received $2,500,000 for phosphate worth $65 million and had to pay Australia $20 million to keep the remaining soil.

nautical mile the unit of distance used in navigation. It equals the average length of one minute of arc on a great circle of the Earth. In the UK it was formerly defined as 6,080 feet. The international nautical mile is now defined as 1,852 m.

nautilus /'nɔːtɪləs/ type of ◊cephalopod found in the Indo-Pacific Ocean. The *pearly nautilus Nautilus pompilius* has a chambered spiral shell about 20 cm/8 in in diameter. Its body occupies the outer chamber, and the animal has a large number of short grasping tentacles surrounding a sharp beak. The living nautilus is a representative of a group common 450 million years ago. Paper nautilus is an alternative name for the ◊argonaut, a type of octopus.

Navajo /'nævəhəu/ North American Indian people. Related to the ◊Apache, they were defeated by Kit ◊Carson and American troops in 1864, and were rounded up and exiled. Their reservation, created in 1868, is the largest in the USA (65,000 sq km/25,000 sq m), and is mostly in Arizona. They earn an income from uranium, natural gas, tourism, rugs and blankets, and silver and turquoise jewellery. They use ◊sand painting to make temporary altars.

Navarino, Battle of /ˌnævəˈriːnəu/ 20 Oct 1827, a decisive naval action off Pylos in the Greek war of liberation which was won by the combined fleets of the English, French, and Russians under ◊Codrington, over the Turkish and Egyptian fleets. Navarino is the Italian and

historic name of ◊Pylos Bay, Greece, on the W coast of the Peloponnese.

Navarre /nə'vɑː/ (Spanish *Navarra*) autonomous mountainous region of N Spain
area 10,600 sq km/4,090 sq mi
capital Pamplona
features Monte Adi 1,503 m/4,931 ft; rivers Ebro and its tributary the Arga
population (1981) 507,500
history part of the medieval kingdom of ◊Navarre. Estella, to the SW, where Don Carlos was proclaimed king in 1833, was a centre of agitation by the ◊Carlists.

Navarre, Kingdom of /nə'vɑː/ former kingdom comprising the Spanish province of ◊Navarre and part of the French *département* of Basses-Pyrénées. It resisted the ◊Moorish conquest, and was independent until it became French in 1284 on the marriage of Philip IV to the heiress of Navarre. In 1479 Ferdinand of Aragon annexed Spanish Navarre, with French Navarre going to Catherine of Foix, who kept the royal title. Her grandson became Henry IV of France, and Navarre was absorbed in the French crown lands in 1620.

nave in architecture, the central part of a church, between the choir and the entrance.

navel a small circular mark in the centre of the abdomen of mammals, the remains of the site of attachment of the ◊umbilical cord, which connected the foetus to the ◊placenta.

navigation, biological the ability of animals to find their way around, both in long distance ◊migrations, and over shorter distances when foraging (for example, the honey bee finding its way from the hive to a nectar site and back). Much animal navigation consists of following established routes around known territory. Birds may 'home' on features that can be seen from

---

Nauru
REPUBLIC OF

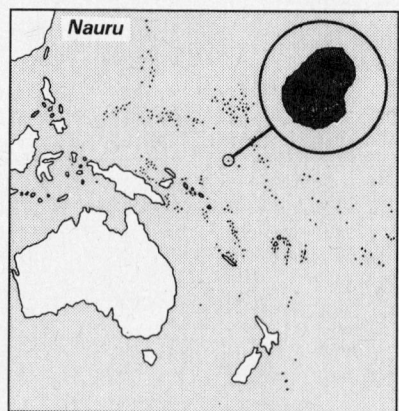

AREA 21 sq km/8 sq mi
CAPITAL Yaren
PHYSICAL island country in W Pacific
FEATURES plateau circled by coral cliffs and sandy beach
HEAD OF STATE AND OF GOVERNMENT Hammer DeRoburt from 1978
GOVERNMENT democratic
EXPORTS phosphates
CURRENCY Australian dollar
POPULATION (1985) 8,000 (mainly Polynesian; Chinese 8%, European 8%); annual growth rate 3.1%
LANGUAGE Nauruan (official), English
RELIGION Protestant 45%
LITERACY 99%
GDP $155 million (1981); $21,400 per head of population
CHRONOLOGY
1888 Annexed by Germany.
1920 Administered by Australia, New Zealand, and UK until independence, except

1942–45, when it was occupied by Japan.
1968 Full independence achieved, with 'special member' Commonwealth status. Hammer DeRoburt elected president.
1976 Bernard Dowiyogo elected president.
1978 DeRoburt returned to power.

very great distances (such as the cloud caps that often form above isolated mid-ocean islands), and even smells can act as a landmark. Aquatic species like salmon are believed to learn the characteristic taste of the river where they hatch and return to it, often many years later. However, many animals can navigate without such landmarks. Experiments have shown that some birds can find their way back to their nest site, having been removed several thousand miles, over unknown terrain. Equally striking is the navigation of young birds which have never flown a route before and are unaccompanied by adults. Such navigational feats may be based on compass information derived from the position of the sun, moon or stars (such as the Pole star) or on the characteristic patterns of the earth's magnetic field (probably using filaments of a magnetic substance found in the brains of vertebrates and the bodies of bees).

navigation the means of finding the position, course and distance travelled by a ship, plane, spacecraft, and so on. Traditional methods use a magnetic ◊compass and ◊sextant. Mostly today the gyrocompass is used, together with highly sophisticated electronic methods, such as *Decca*, *Loran* and *Omega*. These employ beacons that beam out radio signals. Satellite navigation employs ◊satellites that broadcast time and position signals. The United States Global Positioning System, when complete, will feature 18 *Navstar* satellites that will enable users (including eventually motorists and walkers) to triangulate their position (from any three satellites) to within 15 m/ 45 ft.

Navigation Acts a series of acts passed from 1381 to protect English shipping from foreign competition, and to ensure monopoly trading between Britain and its colonies. The last was repealed in 1849. The most important were:
1650 'Commonwealth Ordinance' forbade foreign ships to trade in English colonies.
1651 Forbade the importation of goods except in English vessels or in vessels of the country of origin of the goods. This Act led to the ◊Anglo-Dutch War 1652–54.
1660 All colonial produce was required to be exported in English vessels.
1663 Colonies were prohibited from receiving goods in foreign (rather than English) vessels.
The Navigation Acts were enormously influential in establishing England as a major sea power. They brought about the ruination of the Dutch merchant fleet in the 17th century, and were one of the causes of the ◊American War of Independence.

Navratilova /ˌnævrætɪˈləʊvə/ Martina 1956– . Lawn tennis player. Born in Prague, Czechoslovakia, she was naturalized American 1981. A dominant figure in women's tennis since 1978, she won the Wimbledon singles title seven times including six in succession 1982–87, and has won over US $10 million in prize money. Her total of 45 Grand Slam event titles is second only to Margaret Court's record of 66.

navy a nation's warships and the organization to maintain them. Naval power was an important factor in the struggle for supremacy in the Mediterranean in the 5th century BC, for example

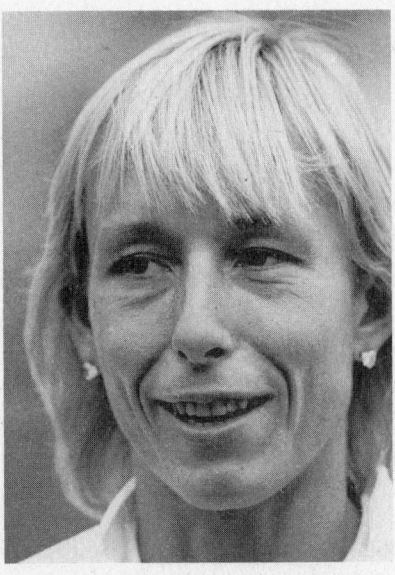

Navratilova Martina Navratilova confirmed her position at the top of women's tennis by winning her sixth Wimbledon title in 1987. She equalled the Wimbledon record of eight singles titles held by Helen Wills-Moody.

the defeat of Persia by Greece at Salamis, but the first permanent naval organization was established by the Roman Empire in 311 BC with the appointment of navy commissioners to safeguard trade routes from pirates and eliminate the threat of rival sea power. Next came Byzantine dominance until the Turkish invasions of the 12th century AD. During the Middle Ages the Italian city-states were influential. From Genoa came the admirals of the first French royal fleet, established by Louis IX in the 13th century. There was a great deal of cross-Channel raiding during the Hundred Years' War 1339–1453 on both sides. The English forces taking part had their origins in the fleet (a few king's ships, plus ships from the shires and some privileged coastal towns) with which Alfred the Great overcame the Danes in 878. Building on the beginnings made by his father Henry VII, Henry VIII raised a force which included a number of proper battleships such as the ◊*Mary Rose*, created the long-enduring administrative machinery of the Admiralty, and by mounting heavy guns low on a ship's side revolutionized strategy by the use of the 'broadside'. Elizabeth I encouraged Drake, Frobisher, Hawkins, Raleigh and others who were to set the seal on the decline of the great sea power of Spain, which had burgeoned through exploration and conquest in the early 16th century, by their defeat of the Armada. In the 17th century there was a remarkable development in naval power among the powers of northern Europe, for example in the Netherlands, which then founded an empire in the East; France, where a strong fleet was built up by Richelieu and Louis XIV which maintained the links with possessions in India and Canada; and England, comparatively briefly

under Cromwell. In the late 17th century the British overtook the Dutch as the leading naval power (◊Pepys was an efficient secretary to the Admiralty at this time); and, effectively reorganized by Pitt in time for the French revolutionary wars, the Royal Navy under Nelson won a victory over the French at Trafalgar in 1805 which ensured British naval supremacy for the rest of the 19th century.

The American navy owes its origin to the need for the more exposed provinces to protect their harbours at the outbreak of the War of Independence, and Washington's need to capture British war supplies. Late in 1775 Washington prepared five schooners and a sloop, manned with army personnel, and sent them to prey on inbound supply vessels. By the time of the Declaration of Independence in 1776 these were augmented by armed brigs and sloops from the various colonies: the hero of the period was John Paul ◊Jones. The fleet earned further distinction in actions against Tripoli 1803–05 and Britain 1812–14, and rapidly expanded during the Civil War and again for the Spanish War of 1898. In World War I Britain fought off Germany's bid for naval power, but in the inter-war years the American fleet was developed to protect US trade routes, and also with an eye to the renewed German threat and the danger from Japan, see ◊World War I and ◊World War II. After World War II the American fleet emerged as the world's most powerful, but the Cuban crisis (see under ◊Cuba), demonstrated the Soviet Union's impotence at sea and led to a striking development under Admiral Sergei Gorshkov 1910– . Today, the Soviet fleets (based in the Arctic, Baltic, Mediterranean and Pacific) are more powerful than the combined NATO force, and are completely coordinated in their operation with all other Soviet sea-going vessels. The USSR has one of the world's largest merchant fleets, and the world's largest fishing, hydrographic and oceanographic fleets, in which all ships have intelligence-gathering equipment. The pattern of the new navy reflects that of other modern fleets: over 400 submarines, many with Polaris-type missiles, and over 200 surface combat vessels (mostly of recent date) include helicopter carriers, cruisers, destroyers and escort vessels. The UK today has a force of small carriers, destroyers, frigates and submarines. The largest surface warships of the superpowers are still aircraft carriers, such as the US *Carl Vinson* 1982, 81,600 tonnes, and the USSR has large nuclear powered carriers under construction, the first of which may be operational by 1992, while the *Kirov* and *Frunze* battle cruisers are the largest combatant warships of any other type to be built since World War II. In any future major war nuclear-propelled and nuclear-armed submarines are considered the prime means of combat.

Naxalite member of an Indian extremist communist movement named for the town of Naxalbari, W Bengal, where a peasant rising was suppressed in 1967. The movement was founded by Charu Mazumdar (1915–72).

Naxos /ˈnæksɒs/ an island of Greece, the largest of the Cyclades, area 453 sq km/175 sq mi. Known since early times for its wine, it was a centre for the worship of Bacchus, who, according to Greek mythology, found the deserted Ariadne on its shore and married her.

Nazareth /'næzərəθ/ town in Galilee, N Israel, SE of Haifa; the boyhood home of Jesus according to the New Testament; population (1972) 33,300.

Nazarite a Hebrew under a vow, who in ancient times observed certain rules until it was fulfilled, for example not to cut his hair or to drink wine. ◊Samson and ◊Samuel were Nazarites for life.

Nazca /'næskə/ town S of Lima, Peru, near a plateau that has geometric linear markings interspersed with giant outlines of birds and animals. They were made by American Indians, possibly in the 6th century AD, and their function is thought to be ritual rather than astronomical. As the full effect is visible only from the air, it is possible the makers used hot-air balloons.

Naze, the /neɪz/ headland on the coast of Essex, England, S of the port of Harwich.

Nazi Party German political party. The name is derived from the first two syllables of the full name, *Nationalsozialistische Deutsche Arbeiterpartei (National Socialist German Workers' Party)*. It included the *Sturmabteilung* (SA, 'stormtroops' or Brownshirts, established in 1921), led by ◊Röhm, and the elite *Schutz-Staffel* (SS, 'protective squadron' or Blackshirts) which began as a bodyguard to Hitler in 1925 and was organized under ◊Himmler from 1928. It included both full-time and *Waffen-SS* ('armed' SS) who were elite combat troops. It carried out 'police' duties, the persecution of the Jews, and the brutalities of the concentration camps. See ◊Fascism and ◊Hitler. Movements related to the Nazis were founded in Britain by Sir Oswald ◊Mosley and Colin Jordan (National Socialist Movement 1962) and in 1967 the ◊National Front. In the USA the American Nazi Party was founded in 1958 by George Lincoln Rockwell. In contrast to the large neo-Fascist movement in Italy, prompted by fear of the large Communist party there, the Nazis survived in Germany chiefly as a fanatical remnant carrying out guerrilla outrages.

N'djamena /ˌəndʒɒ'meɪnə/ capital of Chad, central Africa; population (1979) 303,000. Former name (until 1973) Fort Lamy.

Neagh, Lough /neɪ/ lake in Northern Ireland, the largest in the British Isles, 396 sq km/153 sq mi.

Neagle /'niːgəl/ Anna 1908–1986. British actress, born in East London, whose films include *Nell Gwyn* 1934, *Victoria the Great* 1937, and *Odette* 1950.

Neale /niːl/ John Mason 1818–1866. Anglican cleric. He translated ancient and medieval hymns, including 'Jerusalem, the golden'.

Neanderthal hominid of the Palaeolithic period originating 120,000 years ago (named from a skeleton found in the Neanderthal valley in the Rhineland in 1857). Extinct from 30,000 years ago, they were replaced throughout Europe by (or possibly interbred with) modern *Homo sapiens sapiens*. See ◊primate.

Nazi Party The Olympic torch arrives at the 1936 Games in Berlin, which were exploited as an opportunity to demonstrate the supposed supremacy of the Aryan race. Hitler gave a public display of fury at the success of the black athletes and walked out as Jesse Owens won one of his four gold medals.

Near East term used until the 1940s to describe the area of the Balkan states, Egypt and SW Asia, now known as the ◊Middle East.

Neath /niːθ/ town in W Glamorgan, Wales, near the mouth of the river Neath; population (1984) 26,000. The Roman fort of Nidum was discovered nearby in 1949.

Nebraska /nə'bræskə/ prairie state of the USA; nicknamed Cornhusker State
area 200,036 sq km/77,227 sq mi
capital Lincoln
towns Omaha
features Rocky Mountain foothills; tributaries of the Missouri; Boys' Town for the homeless near Omaha; the ranch of Buffalo Bill
products cereals, livestock, processed foods; fertilizers, oil, natural gas
population (1984) 1,606,000
famous people Fred Astaire, Willa Cather, Henry Fonda, Gerald Ford, Harold Lloyd, Malcolm X
history part of the ◊Louisiana Purchase in 1803, and first settled in 1847, it became a state in 1867.

Nebuchadnezzar /ˌnebjukəd'nezə/ or **Nebuchadrezzar** king of ◊Babylonia, died 562 BC. Shortly before his accession in 604 BC he defeated the Egyptians at Carchemish and brought Palestine and Syria into his empire. Judah revolted, with Egyptian assistance, in 596 and 587–586 BC; on each occasion he captured Jerusalem and carried many Jews into captivity. He largely rebuilt ◊Babylon, and constructed the Hanging Gardens.

nebula in astronomy, a cloud of gas and dust in space. Nebulae are the birthplaces of ◊stars. One is the ◊Orion nebula, visible to the naked eye below the 'belt' of Orion. It is an *emission nebula*, glowing brightly because its gas is energized by stars that have formed within it. In another type

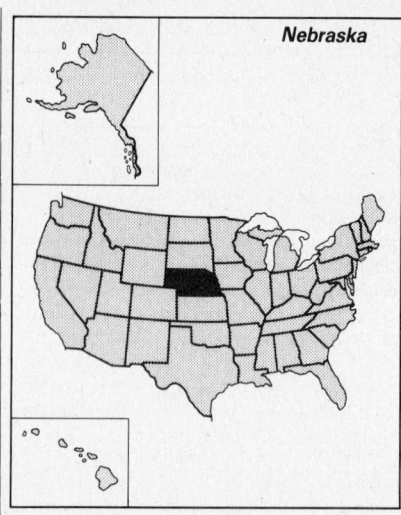

Nebraska

of bright nebula, a *reflection nebula*, light from stars is reflected off grains of dust in the nebula, as surrounds the stars of the ◊Pleiades cluster. A *dark nebula* appears as a dark patch silhouetted on a lighter background, such as the Coalsack nebula in ◊Crux (the Southern Cross). Some nebulae are produced by gas thrown off from dying stars; see ◊planetary nebula; ◊supernova.

nebula A dramatic planetary nebula in Aquarius, photographed with a 500 cm/200 in telescope.

neck the structures between the head and the trunk. Its bones are the upper seven (cervical) vertebrae, it comprises many powerful muscles which support and move the head, and in front it contains the pharynx and wind-pipe (trachea), and behind these the gullet (oesophagus). Within it are the large arteries (carotid, temporal, maxillary), and veins (jugular), which supply the brain and head.

Necker /'nekə/ Jacques 1732–1804. French politician. Finance minister 1776–81, he attempted reforms, and was dismissed through ◊Marie Antoinette's influence. Recalled in 1788, he persuaded Louis XVI to summon the ◊States-General, which earned him the hatred of the court, and in Jul 1789 he was banished. The storming of the Bastille forced his reinstatement, but in Sept 1790 he resigned.

nectar a sugary liquid secreted by some plants from a nectary, a specialized gland usually situated near the base of the flower. It attracts insects, birds, bats and other animals to the flower for ◊pollination, and is the raw material used by bees in the production of honey.

nectarine smooth-skinned peach, usually smaller than other peaches, with firmer flesh.

needlefish long thin-bodied fish of the ◊garfish type with needle teeth.

Needles, the /'niːdlz/ a group of rocks in the sea near the Isle of ◊Wight.

Nefertiti /ˌnefəˈtiːti/ or *Nofretète* 14th century BC, wife of ◊Ikhnaton, pharaoh of Egypt.

negative/positive term in photography for a reverse image, which when printed is again reversed, restoring the original scene. Invented by Fox ◊Talbot around 1834.

Negev /'negev/ desert in S Israel which tapers to the port of Eilat. It is fertile under irrigation and minerals include oil and copper.

negligence in law, negligence consists in doing some act which a 'prudent and reasonable' person would not do, or omitting to do some act which such a person would do. Negligence may arise in respect of a person's duty towards an individual or towards other people in general. In the first class are such duties as arise from parenthood, guardianship, trusteeship, or a contractual relationship. In the second are the duties owed to the community, such as care upon the public highway, and the maintenance of structures in a safe condition. Contributory negligence is a defence sometimes raised where the defendant to an action for negligence claims that the plaintiff by his own negligence contributed to the cause of the action.

Negro /'niːgrəʊ/ term used to refer to a member of the indigenous people of Africa south of the Sahara, today distributed around the world. The term generally preferred today is ◊black.

Nehemiah /ˌniːəˈmaɪə/ 5th century BC Jewish governor of Judaea under Persian rule, who rebuilt Jerusalem's walls, and made religious and social reforms.

Nehru /'neəruː/ Jawaharlal 1889–1964. Indian politician. Born at Allahabad, and educated at Harrow and Cambridge, he led the Socialist left wing of the Congress Party, and was second only in influence to M K ◊Gandhi. He was nine times imprisoned 1921–45 for his political activities. He was prime minister from the creation of the Dominion (later Republic) of India in Aug 1947, and originated the theory of non-alignment. His daughter was Indira ◊Gandhi.

Nejd region of central Arabia consisting chiefly of desert. It forms part of the kingdom of Saudi Arabia, and is inhabited by Bedouins. The capital is Riyadh. Area about 2,720,000 sq km/800,000 sq m.

Nekrasov /nɪˈkrɑːsɒf/ Nikolai Alekseevich 1821–1877. Russian poet and publisher. He espoused the cause of the freeing of the serfs and identified himself with the peasants in such

Nehru Pandit Jawaharlal Nehru (left) with Mohammed Ali Jinnah, the founder of Pakistan.

poems as 'Who Can Live Happy in Russia?' 1876.

Nelson /'nelsən/ Horatio, Viscount 1758–1805. British admiral. He was born at Burnham Thorpe, Norfolk, where his father was rector, and entered the navy in 1770. While serving in the West Indies he married Mrs Frances Nisbet. He was almost continuously on active service in the Mediterranean 1793–1800 and as a result of wounds he lost the sight of his right eye in 1794 and his right arm in 1797. His share in the victory off Cape St Vincent in 1797 made him a national hero, and was rewarded by promotion to rear-admiral.

In 1798 he tracked the French fleet to Aboukir Bay, and almost entirely destroyed it in the Battle of the Nile. He then lingered at Naples for a year, during which he helped to crush a democratic uprising, and fell completely under the influence of Lady ◊Hamilton. In 1800 he returned to England, and soon after separated from his wife. He was promoted to vice-admiral in 1801, and sent to the Baltic to operate against the Danes, nominally as second-in-command; in fact, it was Nelson who was responsible for the victory of Copenhagen, and for negotiation peace with Denmark. On his return to England he was created a viscount.

In 1803 he received the Mediterranean command, and for nearly two years blockaded Toulon. When in 1805 Villeneuve eluded him, Nelson pursued him to the West Indies and back, and on 21 Oct totally defeated the combined

French and Spanish fleets off Cape Trafalgar, 20 of the enemy ships being captured. Nelson himself was mortally wounded; his body was brought to England, and buried in St Paul's.

Nelson British admiral Horatio Nelson's long naval career ended at the Battle of Trafalgar in 1805; though victorious, he was mortally wonded.

nematode unsegmented worm, pointed at both ends, and with a tough smooth outer skin, of the phylum Aschelminthes. Nematodes include some soil and water forms, but a large number are parasites, such as the roundworms and pinworms that live in humans, or the eelworms that attack plant roots.

Nemesis in Greek mythology, the goddess of retribution, especially punishing hubris (Greek *hybris*), arrogant self-confidence.

Nennius /'neniəs/ (wrote about 800). Welsh chronicler, believed to be the author of a Latin *Historia Britonum*, which contains the earliest reference to King Arthur's wars against the Saxons.

Neo-Classicism revival and imitation of the ancient Greek and Roman style of art c. 1750–1850, following the excavation of Pompeii and Herculaneum, for example by Canova, Thorvaldsen (sculpture), David, Ingres (painting), Robert Adam (architecture), Flaxman (art).

Neo-Darwinism the modern theory of ◊evolution, built up since the 1930s by integrating ◊Darwin's theory of evolution through ◊natural selection with the theory of ◊genetic inheritance founded on the work of Gregor ◊Mendel.

Neo-Impressionism a late 19th-century French art movement characterized by the use of pure colours, without mixing. Artists include ◊Seurat and ◊Pissarro. See ◊pointillism.

Neolithic latest division of the ◊Stone Age. It lasted in SW Asia from about 9000–6000 BC, and in Europe from about 4000–2400 BC.

neon a chemically inert gaseous element discovered by Ramsay and Travers in 1898:

symbol Ne, atomic number 10, atomic weight 20.183. Present in the atmosphere in the proportion 18 parts-per-million (by volume), it is extracted by liquefaction and fractional distillation. It glows bright orange-red in a ◊discharge tube, and is used in lights such as advertisement signs. Neon is also used in ◊lasers.

neoprene a ◊synthetic rubber, developed in the USA in 1931. It is made from acetylene and hydrogen chloride. It is much more resistant to heat and petrol than ordinary rubber.

Neo-Realism in cinema, term used to describe a filmmaking movement that emerged in Italy in the 1940s. Neo-Realism was characterized by its naturalism: real-life problems such as poverty and deprivation were tackled and visual authenticity was achieved by shooting the films on location. Important exponents of the Italian Neo-Realist movement were ◊De Sica, ◊Visconti, and ◊Rossellini.

neoteny in biology, the retention of some juvenile characteristics in an animal that seems otherwise mature. An example is provided by the ◊axolotl, a salamander that can reproduce sexually although it retains its larval form. It has been suggested that new species could arise in this way, and that our own species evolved from its apelike ancestors by neoteny, on the grounds that facially we resemble a young ape.

NEP see ◊New Economic Policy.

Nepál /nɪˈpɔːl/ landlocked country in the Himalayan mountain range, bounded to the N by Tibet, to the E by Sikkim, and to the S and W by India.

government under the constitution of 1962, amended 1980, Nepál is ruled by a monarch. There is a tiered system of *panchayats* (councils) and a one-chamber legislature, the *Rashtriya Panchayat* (National Assembly), of whose members 112 are directly elected every five years and 28 are nominated by the monarch, who may veto its decisions. The Panchayat debates and passes bills and elects a prime minister, who heads and, with the monarch, selects the cabinet. Executive power is exercised by the sovereign and cabinet.

history from one of a group of small principalities, the Gurkhas emerged to unite Nepál under King Prithwi Narayan Shah in 1768. The country was recognized as fully independent by Britain in 1923. Between 1846 and 1951 Nepál was ruled by a hereditary prime minister of the Rana family. The Ranas were overthrown in a revolution led by the Nepáli congress, and the monarchy, in the person of King Tribhuvan, was restored to power.

In 1959 King Mahendra Bir Bikram Shah, who had succeeded his father in 1955, promulgated the nation's first constitution and held elections. The Nepáli Congress Party leader B P Koriala became prime minister and proceeded to clash with the king over policy. King Mahendra thus dissolved parliament in Dec 1960 and issued a ban on political parties in Jan 1961. In Dec 1962 he introduced the new constitution with an indirectly elected assembly.

King Mahendra died in 1972. His son Birendra (1945–), faced with mounting agitation for political reform led by B P Koriala, held a referendum on the constitution. As a result, it was amended and the first elections to the National Assembly were held in May 1981. They led to the defeat of a third of the pro-government candidates and returned a more independently minded National Assembly which in Jul 1983 unseated Prime Minister Surya Bahadur Thapa, despite his royal support, and installed in office Lokendra Bahadur Chand. Opposition to the banning of political parties has increased in recent years, with terrorist actions in Kathmandu in Jun 1985. In May 1986 new elections to the National Assembly returned a majority of members opposed to the partyless *panchayat* system and resulted in the replacement of Prime Minister Chand. Four opposition parties function unofficially: the Communist Party of Nepál, the Nepáli Congress Party, the United Liberation Torchbearers, and the Democratic Front.

In foreign affairs, Nepál has pursued a neutral, ◊nonaligned policy, seeking to create a 'zone of peace' in S Asia between India and China.

Nepál
(Sri Nepala Sarkar)

AREA 141,400 sq km/54,600 sq mi
CAPITAL Katmandu
PHYSICAL descends from the Himalaya mountain range in the N to the river Ganges plain in the S
FEATURES Mt Everest, Mt Kanchenjunga
HEAD OF STATE King Birendra Bir Bikram Shah Dev from 1972
HEAD OF GOVERNMENT Marich Man Singh Shrestha from 1986
GOVERNMENT constitutional monarchy
EXPORTS jute, rice, timber
CURRENCY Nepalese rupee (34.7 = £1 Sept 1987)
POPULATION (1985) 16,480,000 (mainly known by the name of the predominant clan, the Gurkhas; the Sherpas are a Buddhist minority of NE Nepál); annual growth rate 2.2%
LANGUAGE Nepali
RELIGION Hindu, with Buddhist minority
LITERACY 33% m/5% female (1975)
GNP $2.6 bn (1983); $140 per head of population
CHRONOLOGY
1768 Nepál emerged as unified kingdom.
1846–1951 Ruled by the Rana family.
1951 Monarchy restored.
1959 Constitution created elected legislature.

Nepál

1960–61 Parliament dissolved by king and political parties banned.
1980 Constitutional referendum held following popular agitation.
1981 Direct elections held to national assembly.
1983 Overthrow of monarch-supported prime minister.
1986 New assembly elections return a majority opposed to the partyless *panchayat* system.

neper a unit used in telecommunications to express a ratio of powers and currents which gives the attenuation of amplitudes as the natural logarithm of the ratio.

nephritis inflammation of the substance of the kidney; Bright's disease. It is sometimes due to cold or pregnancy, but more commonly to infection by a streptococcus, the colon bacillus, or tuberculosis. Symptoms include an accumulation of fluid under the skin, back pain, and fever. The degree of illness varies; it may be quickly fatal, or not very incapacitating. Usual treatment is drugs and/or ◊dialysis, possibly transplant in rare cases.

Neptune /ˈnɛptjuːn/ in Roman mythology god of the sea, the equivalent of the Greek ◊Poseidon.

Neptune /ˈnɛptjuːn/ in astronomy, the eighth planet in average distance from the Sun, discovered in 1846 by J G ◊Galle at Berlin after calculations by J C ◊Adams in England and U J J ◊Leverrier in France had predicted its existence. Neptune orbits the Sun every 164.8 years at an average distance of 4,497 million km/2,794 million mi. It is a giant gas planet with a diameter of 48,600 km/30,200 mi and a mass 17.2 times that of Earth. It is believed to have a central rocky core covered by a layer of ice and topped by a deep atmosphere composed mainly of hydrogen and helium, with methane clouds. Its rotation period is uncertain, but seems to be about 18 hours. Neptune has two moons, Nereid and Triton. Nereid orbits every 360 days on a highly elliptical path; Triton orbits every 5.9 days in an east-to-west *(retrograde)* direction and is thought to be similar in nature to the planet ◊Pluto. There is evidence of partial rings around Neptune. The planet is due to be surveyed by the Voyager 2 space probe in August 1989.

neptunium an artificially made element, symbol Np, atomic number 93. Neptunium is a member of the ◊actinide series produced in nuclear reactors by neutron bombardment of uranium. It is radioactive and chemically highly reactive.

Nereid in Greek mythology, a minor sea goddess who sometimes mated with mortals.

Nergal /'nɜːgæl/ Mesopotamian god of the sun, war, and pestilence, ruler of the underworld, symbolized by a winged lion.

Nero /'nɪərəʊ/ 37–68 AD. Roman emperor. Son of Domitius Ahenobarbus and Agrippina, he was adopted by his stepfather, ◊Claudius, and succeeded him as emperor in 54. He is said to have murdered Claudius's son, Britannicus, his own mother, his wives, Octavia and Poppaea, and many others. He was a poet and connoisseur of art, and performed publicly as an actor and singer. After the great fire of Rome in 64, he persecuted the Christians, who were suspected of causing it. Military revolt followed in 68; the senate condemned Nero to death, whereupon he committed suicide.

Neruda /ne'ruːdə/ Pablo, pen name of Chilean poet Ricardo Reyes 1904–1973. His work includes lyrics and the epic of the American continent *Canto General* 1950. He was awarded a Nobel prize in 1971.

Neruda As a poet, Pablo Neruda of Chile identified with the working class from which he came, voicing the dreams and sorrows of his people.

Nerva /'nɜːvə/ (Marcus Cocceius Nerva) c. 35–98 AD. Roman emperor. He was proclaimed emperor on Domitian's death in 96 AD, and introduced state loans for farmers, family allowances, and allotments of land to poor citizens.

Nerval /neə'væl/ Gérard de, pen name of French writer Gérard Labrunie 1808–1855. One of the first French symbolists and surrealists, he lived a wandering life, darkened by periodic insanity. His writings include short stories, including the collection *Les Filles du feu* 1854; poetry; a novel *Aurélia* 1855; and drama. He committed suicide.

nerve a strand of ◊nerve cells enclosed in a sheath of connective tissue connecting the ◊central nervous system with receptor and effector organs. A single nerve may contain both ◊motor and sensory nerve cells, but they act independently.

nerve cell an elongated cell (neuron) that transmits electrical impulses, forming part of the ◊nervous system. Impulses are received by the cell body and passed, as a pulse of electric charge along the elongated ◊axon. At the far end of the axon there are ◊synapses where the impulse triggers the release of the chemical ◊neurotransmitter which stimulates another nerve cell, or the action of an effector organ (for example, a muscle). Nerve impulses travel quickly, in humans as fast as 160 m/525 ft per second along a nerve cell.

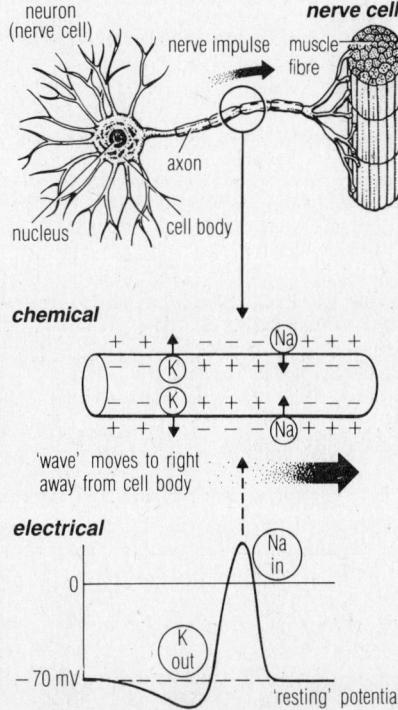

Nervi /'neəviː/ Pier Luigi 1891–1979. Italian architect, who used soft steel mesh within concrete to give it flowing form, for example Turin exhibition hall 1949 and UNESCO building in Paris 1952.

nervous system the system of interconnected ◊nerve cells of most invertebrates and all vertebrates. It may be as simple as the nerve net of coelenterates (for example, jellyfish) or as complex as the mammalian nervous system, with a ◊central nervous system comprising brain and spinal cord, and a peripheral nervous system connecting up with sensory organs, ◊muscles and ◊glands. See also ◊autonomic nervous system.

Nesbit /'nezbɪt/ E(dith) 1858–1924. British author of children's books, including *The Treasure-Seekers* 1899, and *The Railway Children* 1906.

Ness, Loch /nes/ see ◊Loch Ness.

Nestorianism doctrine held by the Syrian ecclesiastic Nestorius (died c. 457), patriarch of Constantinople 428–431, banished for maintaining that Mary was the mother of the man Jesus only, and therefore should not be called the 'Mother of God'. His followers survived as the Assyrian Church in Syria, Iraq,

Iran, and as the Christians of St Thomas in S India.

Netherlands, the /'neðələndz/ country in W Europe on the North Sea, bounded to the E by West Germany and to the S by Belgium.

government the Netherlands is a hereditary monarchy. Its constitution of 1983, based on that of 1814, provides for a two-chamber legislature called the States-General, consisting of a First Chamber of 75 and a Second Chamber of 150. Members of the First Chamber are indirectly elected by representatives of 11 provincial councils for a six-year term, half retiring every three years, and Second Chamber members are elected by universal adult suffrage, through a system of proportional representation, for a four-year term. Legislation is introduced and bills amended in the Second Chamber, while the First has the right to approve or reject.

The monarch appoints a prime minister as head of government, and the prime minister chooses the cabinet. Cabinet members are not permitted to be members of the legislature but they may attend its meetings and take part in debates, and they are collectively responsible to it. There is also a council of state, the government's oldest advisory body, whose members are intended to represent a broad cross-section of the country's life, and include former politicians, scholars, judges, and business people, all appointed for life. The sovereign is its formal president but appoints a vice president to chair it.

Although not a federal state, the Netherlands gives considerable autonomy to its 11 provinces, each of which has an appointed governor and an elected council.

history the land S of the Rhine, inhabited by ◊Celts and Germanic people, was brought under Roman rule by Julius Caesar as governor of ◊Gaul in 51 BC. The ◊Franks followed, and their kings subdued the ◊Frisians and Saxons N of the Rhine in the 7th–8th centuries and imposed Christianity on them. After the empire of ◊Charlemagne broke up, the local feudal lords, headed by the count of ◊Holland and the bishop of ◊Utrecht, became practically independent although they owed nominal allegiance to the ◊German or ◊Holy Roman Empire. Many Dutch towns during the Middle Ages became prosperous trading centres, usually ruled by small groups of merchants. In the 15th century the Netherlands or Low Countries (Holland, ◊Belgium, ◊Flanders) passed to the dukes of ◊Burgundy and thence in 1504 to the Spanish ◊Hapsburgs.

The Dutch aspired to political freedom and ◊Protestantism and rebelled from 1568 against the tyranny of the Catholic ◊Philip II of Spain. ◊William the Silent, Prince of Orange, and his sons Maurice (1567–1625) and Frederick Henry (1584–1647) were the leaders of the revolt and of a confederation established in the N, the United Provinces, which repudiated Spain 1581. The S (now Belgium and Luxembourg) was reconquered by Spain, but not the N, and in 1648 its independence as the Dutch Republic was finally recognized under the Treaty of Westphalia. A long struggle followed between the Orangist or popular party, which favoured centralization under the Prince of Orange as chief magistrate or *stadholder*, and the oligarchical or states' rights party. The latter, headed by John de ◊Witt, seized control 1650, but ◊William of Orange (William III of England) recovered the *stadholderate* with the French invasion of 1672.

Despite the long war of independence, during the early 17th century the Dutch led the world in trade, art, and science, and founded an empire in the E and W Indies. Commercial and colonial rivalries led to naval wars with England 1652–54, 1665–67, and 1672–74. Thereafter until 1713 Dutch history was dominated by a struggle with France under Louis XIV. These wars exhausted the Netherlands, which in the 18th century ceased to be a great power. The French revolutionary army was welcomed in 1795 and created the Batavian Republic. In 1806 Napoleon made his brother Louis king of Holland and 1810–13 annexed the country to France. The Congress of ◊Vienna united the N and S Netherlands under King ◊William I (son of Prince William V of Orange) but the S broke away 1830 to become independent Belgium.

Under ◊William I (reigned 1814–40), ◊William II (1840–49), ◊William III (1849–90), and Queen ◊Wilhelmina (1890–1948), the Netherlands followed a path of strict neutrality, but its brutal occupation by Germany 1940–45 persuaded it to adopt a policy of cooperation with its neighbours. It became a member of the Western European Union, the ◊North Atlantic Treaty Organization (NATO), the ◊Benelux customs union, the European Coal and Steel Community, the European Atomic Energy Community (Euratom), and the ◊European Community. In 1980 Queen ◊Juliana, who had reigned since 1948, abdicated in favour of her eldest daughter, ◊Beatrix.

The granting of independence to former colonies (◊Indonesia 1949; ◊Suriname 1975; see also ◊Netherlands Antilles) increased immigration and unemployment. All governments since 1945 have been coalitions, with the parties differing mainly over economic policies. The three most significant are the Christian Democratic Appeal (CDA, 54 seats in the Second Chamber 1986), the Labour Party (PvdA, 52 seats), and the liberal People's Party for Freedom and Democracy (VVD, 27 seats). Rodolph Lubbers currently heads a CDA-VVD coalition.

Netherlands Antilles /'neðələndz æn'tɪliːz/ overseas part of the Netherlands, with full internal autonomy, comprising the Caribbean islands of ◊Curaçao and Bonaire, together with St Eustatius, Saba, and the S part of St Maarten
area 797 sq km/308 sq mi
capital Willemstad on Curaçao
products oil from Venezuela is refined here
population (1983) 193,000.

Netherlands East Indies former name of ◊Indonesia (1798–1945).

netsuke toggle of ivory, wood, or other materials, made to secure a purse, or tobacco pouch, for men wearing Japanese traditional costume. Made especially in the Edo period in Japan 1601–1867, miniature sculptures are valued as works or art in their right.

Netherlands

KINGDOM OF THE (*Koninkrijk der Nederlanden*), popularly referred to as HOLLAND

AREA 34,000 sq km/13,020 sq mi
CAPITAL Amsterdam
TOWNS The Hague (seat of government); chief port Rotterdam
PHYSICAL almost completely flat; rivers Rhine, Schelde (*Scheldt*), Maas; Frisian Islands
TERRITORIES Aruba, Netherlands Antilles
FEATURES land reclamation has turned the former Zuider Zee inlet into the freshwater IJsselmeer
HEAD OF STATE Beatrix Wilhelmina Armgard from 1980
HEAD OF GOVERNMENT Rudolph Lubbers from 1982
GOVERNMENT parliamentary democracy
EXPORTS dairy products; flower bulbs, vegetables; petro-chemicals; electronics
CURRENCY guilder (3.36 = £1 Sept 1987)
POPULATION (1985) 14,481,000 (including 300,000 of Dutch-Indonesian origin absorbed 1949–64 from former colonial possessions); annual growth rate 0.5%
LANGUAGE Dutch
RELIGION Roman Catholic 35%, Protestant 28%
LITERACY 99% (1985)

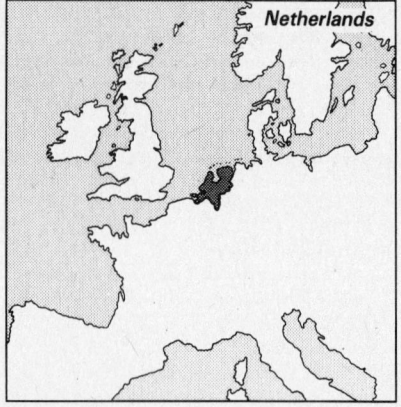
Netherlands

GNP $122.4 bn (1984); $9,175 per head of population
CHRONOLOGY
1940–45 Occupied by Germany.
1947 Joined Benelux Union.
1948 Queen Juliana succeeded Queen Wilhelmina to the throne.
1949 Founder member of NATO.
1958 Joined European Community.
1980 Queen Juliana abdicated in favour of her daughter Beatrix.
1981 Opposition to cruise missiles averted their being sited on Dutch soil.

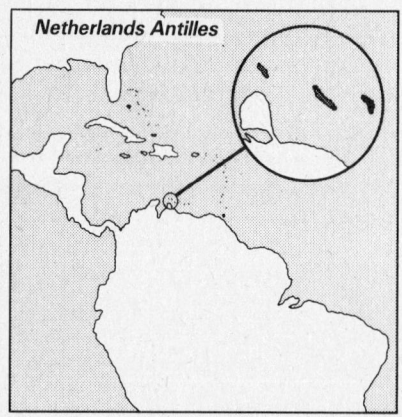
Netherlands Antilles

nettle genus of plants *Urtica*, family Urticaceae. Stinging hairs on the generally ovate leaves can penetrate the skin causing inflammation. The *common nettle Urtica dioica* grows on waste ground in Europe and is naturalized in N America.

nettle-rash popular name for the skin disorder ◊urticaria.

network in computing, a pattern of communication links between computers and their ◊peripheral (input and output) devices. The main types are classified by the pattern of the connections, for example, star or ring network; or by the degree of geographical spread allowed, for example, local area networks (LANs) for communication within a room or building, and wide area networks (WANs) for more remote systems.

Neuchâtel /ˌnɜːʃæˈtel/ capital of Neuchâtel canton in NW Switzerland; population (1980) 34,500.

Neumann /'nɔɪmæn/ Balthasar 1687–1753. German military engineer and Rococo architect, whose work includes the bishop's palace at Würzburg.

neuralgia a severe pain felt along the track of a nerve, especially one of the head or face.

neuritis nerve inflammation caused by injury, or its degeneration as a result of alcoholic, lead, or arsenical poisoning; or the toxins of diseases such as diphtheria, or sleeping sickness.

neuron another name for a ◊nerve cell.

neurosis in psychology, a general term referring to emotional disorders, such as ◊anxiety, ◊depression, and ◊obsessions. The main disturbance tends to be one of mood, whereas contact with reality is relatively unaffected, in contrast to ◊psychosis.

neuroticism a personality dimension described by ◊Eysenck. People with high neuroticism are worriers, emotional and moody. The opposite to neuroticism is emotional stability.

neurotoxin substance, such as lead and organo-lead compounds, organo-chlorines, manganese and mercury, which poisons the nervous system.

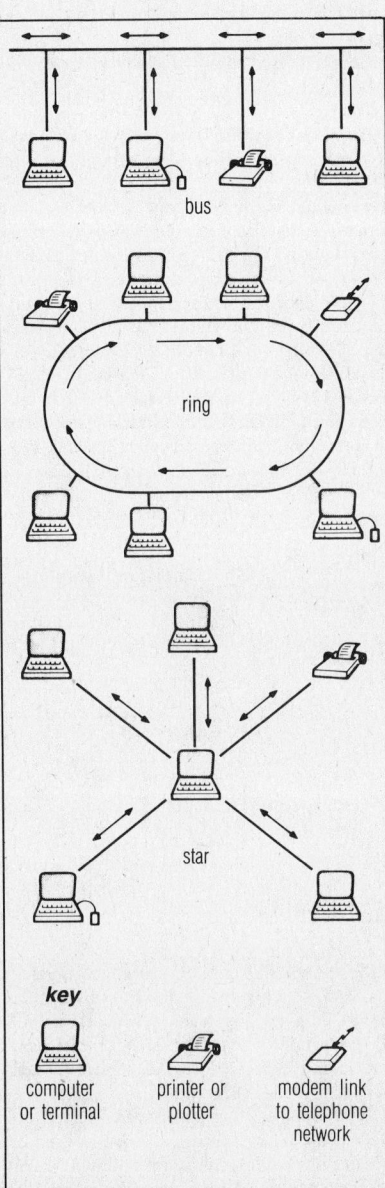

network

bus

ring

star

key

computer   printer or   modem link
or terminal   plotter   to telephone
                                      network

neurotransmitter a chemical which diffuses across a ◊synapse, and thus transmits nerve impulses between ◊nerve cells, or between nerve cells and effector organs (for example muscles). Common neurotransmitters are noradrenalin (norepinephrine) acetylcholine, the latter being most frequent at junctions between nerve and muscle. Some neurotransmitters also act as hormones, for example norepinephrine; see ◊adrenal gland.

Neutra /'nɔɪtrɑː/ Richard Joseph 1892–1970. Austro-American architect, a US citizen from 1929. His works include the Lovell Health House, Los Angeles.

neutrality the legal status of a country that decides not to take part in a war. Certain states,

notably Switzerland and Austria, have opted for permanent neutrality. Neutrality always has a legal connotation whereas the term 'nonalignment' is normally used in a political sense to signify non-membership of the major postwar alliance systems.

neutrino a very small uncharged ◊elementary particle of minute ◊mass, very difficult to detect and of great penetrating power, emitted in all radioactive disintegrations which give rise to ◊beta rays.

neutron one of the three chief subatomic ◊particles (the others being the ◊proton and the ◊electron). Neutrons have about the same ◊mass as protons but no ◊electric charge, and occur in the nuclei of all ◊atoms except hydrogen. They contribute to the mass of atoms but do not affect their chemistry, which depends on the proton or electron numbers. For instance, ◊isotopes of a single element (with different masses) differ only in the number of neutrons in their nuclei and have identical chemical properties. Outside a nucleus a neutron is radioactive, decaying with a ◊half-life of about 12 minutes to give a proton and an electron. The neutron was discovered in 1932 by the British chemist James ◊Chadwick.

neutron beam machine a nuclear reactor or accelerator producing a stream of neutrons, which can 'see' through metals, and is used in industry to check molecular changes in metal under stress, and so on.

neutron bomb small H-bomb that kills by radiation; see under ◊nuclear warfare.

neutron star a very small, dense ◊star composed mostly of ◊neutrons. These stars are thought to form when massive stars explode as ◊supernovae at the ends of their lives. In the explosion, the ◊protons and ◊electrons of the star's atoms merge to make neutrons. A neutron star may have the mass of the Sun, or more, compressed into a globe only 20 km/12 mi in diameter. Being so small, neutron stars can spin very quickly. The rapidly 'flashing' radio stars called ◊pulsars are believed to be neutron stars. A neutron star cannot have a mass of more than about three Suns, or its gravity will be so strong that it shrinks even further to become a ◊black hole.

Nevada /nɪ'vɑːdə/ mountain state of the USA; Sagebrush or Battleborn State
area 286,300 sq km/110,540 sq mi
capital Carson City
towns Las Vegas, Reno
features Mojave Desert; Lake Tahoe; Nuclear Rocket Development Station at Jackass Flats NW of Las Vegas: fallout from nuclear tests in the 1950s may have caused subsequent deaths, including that of John Wayne, who was filming there; legal gambling
products gold, copper, oil; gaming machines
population (1985) 970,000
history ceded to the USA after the Mexican War in 1848, and first settled 1851; it became a state in 1864.

Nevers /nə'veə/ industrial town in central France, capital of the former province of Nivernais; population (1982) 44,800.

New Amsterdam /nju: 'æmstədæm/ town in Guyana, on the Berbice, founded by the Dutch;

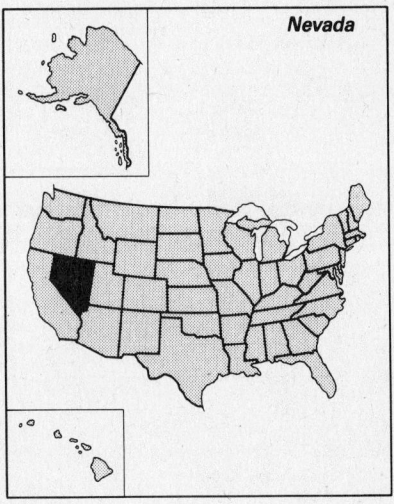

Nevada

population (1976) 19,200. Also a former name (1624–64) of ◊New York.

Newark /'njuːək/ largest city (industrial and commercial) of New Jersey, USA; population (1980) 1,963,000. Its main products are electrical equipment, machinery, fountain pens, chemicals, paints, canned meats.

Newark /'njuːək/ market town in Nottinghamshire, England; population (1981) 24,000; it has the ruins of a 12th-century castle in which King John died.

Newbolt /'njuːbəult/ Henry John 1862–1938. British poet and naval historian. He is best remembered for his *Songs of the Sea* 1904 and *Songs of the Fleet* 1910 which were set to music by Stanford.

New Britain /nju: 'brɪtn/ largest island in the ◊Bismarck Archipelago, part of Papua New Guinea; capital Rabaul; population (1985) 253,000.

New Brunswick /nju: 'brʌnzwɪk/ maritime province of E Canada
area 73,437 sq km/28,340 sq mi
capital Fredericton
towns Saint John, Moncton
features Grand Lake, St John river; Bay of Fundy
products cereals; wood, paper; fish; lead, zinc, copper, oil and natural gas
population (1981) 696,400 – 37 per cent French-speaking
history first reached by Europeans (Cartier) in 1534, it was explored by Champlain in 1604, remaining a French colony until, as part of Nova Scotia, it was ceded to England in 1713. It was separated from Nova Scotia in 1784, when many United Empire Loyalists settled there, and became a province.

Newbury /'njuːbəri/ market town in Berkshire, England, noted for its racecourse and training stables; nearby ◊Aldermaston and ◊Harwell; and by 1983 the main UK base for US cruise missiles at RAF ◊Greenham Common; population (1981) 26,000.

Newby /'njuːbi/ (George) Eric 1919– . British sailor and explorer. His books include *A*

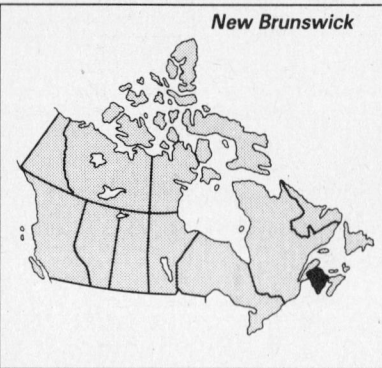

New Brunswick

Short Walk in the Hindu Kush 1958 and *Slowly Down the Ganges* 1966.

New Caledonia /'njuː ˌkælɪ'dəʊnɪə/ island in the S Pacific, between Australia and the Fiji Islands. It is a French overseas territory; capital Noumaéa; area 19,200 sq km/7,400 sq mi; population (1981) 142,500. Surrounded by a barrier reef, it is fertile and has nickel, chrome, and iron resources. New Caledonia was visited by Captain James ◊Cook 1774. It became French in 1853, and in a referendum Sept 1987 there was a clear majority in favour of remaining a French dependency.

Newcastle /'njuːkɑːsəl/ industrial port (iron, steel, ships) in New South Wales, Australia; university 1965; population (1985) 300,000.

Newcastle /'njuːkɑːsəl/ Thomas Pelham-Holles, Duke of Newcastle 1693–1768. British Whig politician. He was secretary of state 1724–54, and then prime minister during the ◊Seven Years' War, until 1762, although ◊Pitt was mainly responsible for the conduct of the war.

Newcastle-under-Lyme /'njuːkɑːsəl ʌndə 'laɪm/ industrial town (coal, bricks and tiles, clothing) in Staffordshire, England; population (1981) 120,100. Keele University is nearby.

Newcastle upon Tyne /'njuːkɑːsəl əpɒn 'taɪn, locally njuː'kæsəl-/ industrial port (coal mining, shipbuilding, marine and electrical engineering, chemicals, metal) in Tyne and Wear, England, administrative headquarters of Tyne and Wear and Northumberland, and the commercial and cultural centre of the NE; university 1962; population (1981) 277,829.

features parts are preserved of a castle built by Henry II 1172–77 on the site of an older castle; the cathedral is chiefly 14th-century; there is a 12th-century church, and the Guildhall 1658. Newcastle is connected with the neighbouring town of Gateshead by several bridges.

history chiefly known as a coaling centre, Newcastle first began to trade in coal in the 13th century. In 1826 ironworks were established by George ◊Stephenson, and the first engine used on the Stockton and Darlington railway was made at Newcastle.

Newcomen /'njuːkʌmən/ Thomas 1663–1729. British inventor of an early ◊steam engine. Born at Dartmouth, he patented his 'fire engine', in 1705, which was used for pumping water from mines until ◊Watt invented one with a separate condenser.

New Deal programme introduced in USA by F D Roosevelt from 1933 to counter the depression of 1929, including employment on public works such as the ◊Tennessee Valley Authority, farm loans at low rates, raising of agricultural prices by restriction of output. Combined with the programme were the introduction of old-age and unemployment insurance; prevention of child labour; protection of employees against unfair practices by employers; and loans to local authorities for slum clearance. Many of its provisions were declared unconstitutional by the Supreme Court in 1935–36, and full employment did not come until World War II.

New Delhi see ◊Delhi, capital of India.

New Democratic Party Canadian political party, moderately socialist, formed in 1961 by a merger of the Labour Congress and the Cooperative Commonwealth Federation; leader Edward Broadbent (1936–   ) from 1975.

New Economic Policy (NEP) economic policy of the USSR introduced by Lenin following a series of peasant uprisings, and the uprising at ◊Kronstadt in Mar 1921. Aimed at re-establishing an alliance with the peasantry, it began as an agricultural measure to act as an incentive for peasants to produce more food. Rather than requisitioning all produce above a stated subsistence allowance, the state requisitioned only a fixed proportion of the surplus; the rest could be traded freely by the peasant. The NEP thus reinstated a limited form of free market trading. The state retained complete control of major industries. The NEP was ended in Jan 1929 by Stalin's first ◊Five Year Plan which began the collectivization of agriculture.

New England region of NE USA, comprising the states of Maine, New Hampshire, Vermont, Massachusetts, Rhode Island, and Connecticut, originally settled by Pilgrims and Puritans from England. It is a geographic region rather than a political entity. The area is still heavily forested and the economy relies on tourism as well as industry.

New England district of N New South Wales, Australia, especially the tableland area of Glen Innes and Armidale.

New English Art Club British society founded 1886 to secure better representation for younger painters than was given by the Royal Academy. It included ◊Sargent, Augustus ◊John, Paul ◊Nash, ◊Rothenstein, and ◊Sickert.

New Forest ancient forest in S England: see under ◊Hampshire.

Newfoundland massive breed of dog, said to have originated in Newfoundland. It is gentle in temperament. The fur is dense, flat and dull black, brown, or white with black markings.

Newfoundland and Labrador /'njuːfənlənd, 'læbrədɔː/ province of E Canada

area 404,517 sq km/156,185 sq mi

capital St John's

physical Newfoundland island and the coast of Labrador on the other side of the Straits of Belle Isle; wild and rocky

features Grand Banks section of the continental shelf rich in cod; home of the Newfoundland and Labrador dogs

products newsprint, fish products, hydroelectric power, iron, copper, zinc, uranium, and oil offshore

population (1981) 567,681

history probably colonized by Vikings about AD 1000. The navigator John Cabot reached Newfoundland in 1497, and it was the first English colony, Sir Humphrey ◊Gilbert taking possession in 1583. France also made settlements and British sovereignty was not recognized until 1713. France did not surrender fishing rights until 1904, and still retained the offshore islands of St Pierre and Miquelon. Internal self-government was granted to the island in 1855, but in 1934, as Newfoundland had fallen into financial difficulties, administration was vested in a governor and a special commission. A 1948 referendum favoured federation with Canada, and in 1949 Newfoundland with ◊Labrador became the tenth province of Canada.

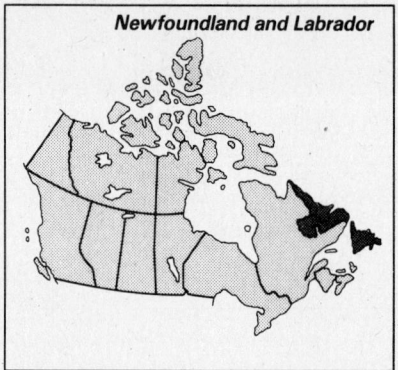

Newfoundland and Labrador

Newgate /'njuːgɪt/ a prison in London, England, which stood on the site of the ◊Old Bailey. Originally a gatehouse (hence the name), it was established in the 12th century, and demolished in 1903. Public executions were held outside it 1783–1868.

New Guinea /njuː 'gɪnɪ/ large island in the SW Pacific. The tropical rain forest, now under threat from logging companies and resettlement schemes, harbours birds of paradise and brilliant butterflies, and various mammals, such as the small kangaroos, show the island's Australian links. The chief rivers are the Fly, Sepik, Mamberano, and Digul. Its native peoples are Melanesian, some in the highlands being pygmies. The island is now divided into ◊*Papua New Guinea* and *West Irian* (*Irian Jaya*)

area 420,000 sq km/162,000 sq mi

capital Jayapura

population (1980) 1,174,000

history part of the Dutch East Indies from 1828, ceded by the UN to Indonesia in 1963.

Newham /'njuːəm/ borough of E Greater London

features former residents include Dick Turpin and Gerard Manley Hopkins; former Royal Victoria and Albert and King George V docks.

population (1984) 209,400.

New Hampshire /njuː ˈhæmpʃə/ New England state of the USA; Granite State
area 24,100 sq km/9,304 sq mi
capital Concord
towns Manchester, Nashua
features White Mountains; Mount ◊Monadnock 1,063 m/3,186 ft; the state's ◊primary elections: no president has ever come to office without succeeding here
products electrical machinery, sand and gravel, apples and maple syrup, and livestock
population (1983) 959,000
famous people Mary Baker Eddy, Robert Frost
history first settled in 1623, it was the first colony to declare its independence of Britain. It became a state in 1788, one of the original Thirteen States.

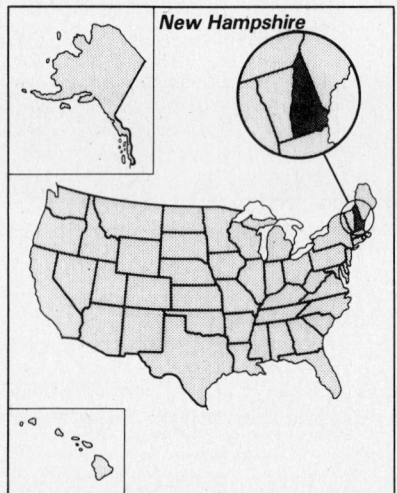
New Hampshire

Newhaven /njuː ˈheɪvən/ port in E Sussex, England, with cross-channel services to Dieppe; population (1985) 11,000.
New Haven /njuː ˈheɪvən/ town in Connecticut, USA; population (1980) 126,000. *Yale University*, third oldest in the USA, was founded here in 1701 and named after Elihu Yale (1648–1721), an early benefactor.
New Hebrides /njuː ˈhebrɪdiːz/ former name (until 1980) of ◊Vanuatu.
New Ireland Forum a meeting between politicians of the Irish Republic and Northern Ireland in May 1983. The Forum was the idea of John Hume, leader of the Northern Irish SDLP. It suggested three possibilities for a solution to the Northern Irish problem: unification under a nonsectarian constitution, a federation of North and South, or joint rule from London and Dublin. All three options were rejected by the UK government after talks between the British and Irish leaders in Nov 1984.
New Jersey /njuː ˈdʒɜːzi/ state of NE USA; nicknamed Garden State
area 20,295 sq km/7,836 sq mi
capital Trenton
towns Newark, Jersey City, Paterson, Elizabeth

features coastal resorts, including Atlantic City; Princeton University 1746; Walt Whitman's house in Camden
products asparagus, fruit, potatoes, tomatoes, poultry; chemicals, metal goods, electrical machinery; clothing
population (1984) 7,515,000
famous people Aaron Burr, James Fenimore Cooper, Stephen Crane, Thomas Edison, Alexander Hamilton, Thomas Paine, Paul Robeson, Frank Sinatra, Bruce Springsteen
history colonized in the 17th century by the Dutch, it was ceded to England in 1664, and became a state in 1787, one of the original Thirteen States.

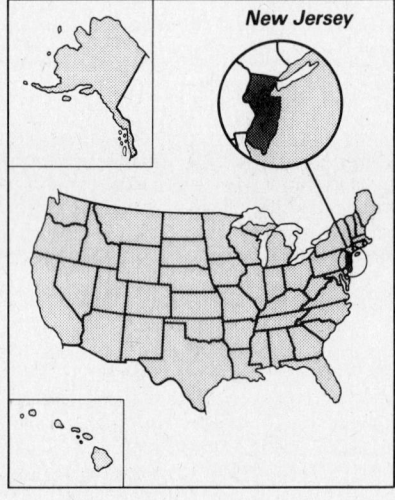
New Jersey

New London /njuː ˈlʌndən/ naval base and yachting centre of SE Connecticut, USA.
newly industrialized country (NIC) term used to denote a former less-developed country which has made a breakthrough into manufacturing and rapid export-led economic growth. The prime examples are South Korea, Singapore, Brazil and Mexico, which on average expanded their ◊gross domestic product (GDP) twice as fast as the older industrialized countries during the 1970s.
Newlyn /ˈnjuːlɪn/ seaport near Penzance, Cornwall, England, which gives its name to the Newlyn School of artists 1880–90, including Stanhope Forbes (1857–1947). The Ordnance Survey relates heights in the UK to mean sea level here.
Newman /ˈnjuːmən/ John Henry 1801–1890. British cardinal. Born in London, he was ordained in the Church of England in 1824, and in 1827 became vicar of St Mary's, Oxford. There he was influenced by R H Froude and ◊Keble, and in 1833 published the first of the *Tracts for the Times*, which gave their name to the 'Tractarian Movement', and culminated in *Tract 90* in 1841 which found the Thirty-nine Articles compatible with Roman Catholicism. He was received into the Roman Catholic Church in 1845, and finally settled as an oratorian at Edgbaston. Appointed rector of

Dublin University in 1854, he published lectures on *The Idea of a University* 1852, and in 1864 published his autobiography, *Apologia pro vita sua*, defending himself against Kingsley's attack on the Roman Catholic attitude to truth. His poem, *The Dream of Gerontius* (later set to music by ◊Elgar), appeared in 1866, and *The Grammar of Assent*, an analysis of the nature of belief, in 1870. In 1879 he was created a cardinal. His best-known hymn is 'Lead, kindly light'.
Newman /ˈnjuːmən/ Paul 1925– . American actor and director, born in Cleveland, Ohio. Hollywood's leading male star of the 1960s and 1970s. Films in which he has appeared include *The Hustler* 1962, *Butch Cassidy and the Sundance Kid* 1969, *The Sting* 1973, *Fort Apache, the Bronx* 1982, and *The Color of Money* 1986 (for which he won an Academy Award).
Newmarket /ˈnjuːmɑːkɪt/ town in Suffolk, England, centre for horse racing since James I's reign, notably the One Thousand and Two Thousand Guineas, the Cambridgeshire, the Jockey Club Stakes and the Cesarewitch. It is the headquarters of the Jockey Club, and a bookmaker who is 'warned off Newmarket Heath' is banned from all British racecourses.
New Mexico /njuː ˈmeksɪkəʊ/ state of the USA; Land of Enchantment
area 315,113 sq km/121,666 sq mi
capital Santa Fé
towns Albuquerque
physical more than 75 per cent is over 1,200 m/4,000 ft above sea level
features Great Plains and Rocky Mountains; Rio Grande; Carlsbad Caverns, the largest known; Los Alamos atomic and space research centre; White Sands Missile Range (also used by Space Shuttle); Kiowa Ranch, site of D H Lawrence's Utopian colony in the Sangre de Christos mountains
products uranium, oil, natural gas, cotton, cereals, vegetables
population (1984) 1,423,500
famous people Billy the Kid, Kit Carson
history explored by Spain in the 16th century; most of it was ceded to the USA by Mexico in 1848, and it became a state in 1912.
New Model Army army created in 1645 by Oliver Cromwell to support the cause of Parliament during the English Civil War. It was characterized by better organization and discipline, and Thomas Fairfax was appointed as its first commander.
New Orleans /njuː ˈɔːliənz/ commercial and industrial city (banking, oil refining, Saturn rockets for *Apollo* spacecraft) and Mississippi port in Louisiana, USA; population (1980) 557,500. Founded by the French in 1718, it still has a distinctive French Quarter and Mardi Gras celebrations. ◊Jazz was born here, and Dixieland exponents still play at Preservation Hall. The Superdome sports palace is among the world's largest enclosed stadiums.
New Plymouth /njuː ˈplɪməθ/ town in North Island, New Zealand; population (1983) 36,500.
Newport /ˈnjuːpɔːt/ river port, capital of the Isle of Wight, England; population (1981)

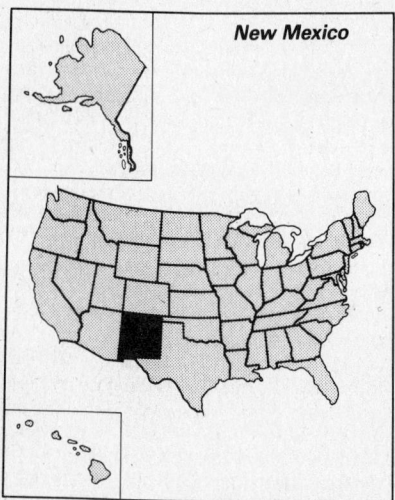

New Mexico

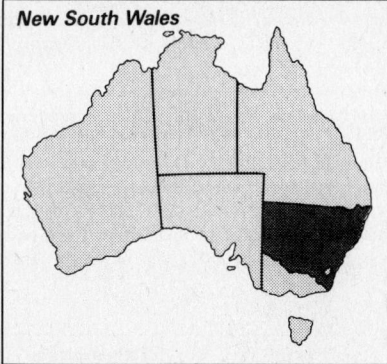

New South Wales

23,500. Charles I was imprisoned in nearby Carisbrooke Castle.

Newport /'njuːpɔːt/ seaport in Gwent (administrative headquarters), Wales; population (1983) 130,200. There is a steelworks at nearby Llanwern.

Newport News /'njuːpɔːt 'njuːz/ industrial city (engineering, shipbuilding) and port of Virginia, USA; population (1980) 144,903.

news agency agency handling news stories and photographs, the chief in the West being Associated Press and Reuters (see Julius ◊Reuter), which are then sold to newspapers and magazines. Third World countries dislike the dominance of the agencies, which are accused of 'Western bias', and have attempted to start their own system.

New South Wales /'njuː saʊθ 'weɪlz/ state of SE Australia
area 801,396 sq km/309,433 sq mi
capital Sydney
towns Newcastle, Wollongong, Broken Hill
physical Great Dividing Range (including Blue Mountains) and part of the Australian Alps (including Snowy Mountains and Mount Kosciusko); Murray, Darling, Murrumbidgee river system irrigating the Riverina district
features a major radio telescope at Parkes, and Siding Spring Mountain 859 m/2,817 ft, NW of Sydney, has telescopes that can observe the central sector of our galaxy. ◊Canberra forms an enclave within the state.
products cereals, fruit, sugar, tobacco; wool, meat, hides and skins; rich mineral deposits including gold, silver, copper, tin, zinc, and coal; hydroelectric power from the Snowy river
population (1985) 5,504,900 – 60 per cent living in Sydney
history called New Wales by Captain Cook, who put in at Botany Bay in 1770 and was struck by the resemblance of the coast to that of Wales. Used as a convict settlement 1788–1850, it was opened to free settlement by 1819, received self-government 1856, and in 1901 became a state of the Commonwealth of Australia. Since 1973 there has been decentralization to counteract the

pull of Sydney, and the New England and Riverina districts have separatist movements.

newspaper a daily or weekly publication in the form of folded sheets containing news and comment.
history One of the earliest newspapers, the Roman *Acta Diurna*, said to have been started by Julius Caesar, contained announcements of marriages, deaths, military appointments, and so on, and was posted up in public places. Newssheets as commercial undertakings followed the invention of printing and were introduced 1609 in Germany, 1616 in the Netherlands, and 1622 the first newspaper appeared in English, the *Weekly News* edited by Nicholas Bourne and Thomas Archer. By 1645 there were 14 news weeklies on sale in London. Parliament by various measures restricted the number of printers and publications 1649–94, when it abandoned the licensing system and a rapid expansion of newspapers and magazines followed. The first daily was the subsidized pro-government *Daily Courant* 1702. Arrests, seizure of papers, and prosecution for libel or breach of privilege were employed by the government against opposition publications, and taxes and restrictions were imposed 1700–1820 in direct relation to the growth of radical opinion. The last of these taxes, stamp duty, was abolished 1855. Improved ◊printing (steam printing 1814, the rotary press 1846 USA and 1857 UK), newsprint (paper made from woodpulp, used in the UK from the 1880s), and a higher literacy rate led to the growth of sensational Sunday papers, by 1900 read by 10 per cent of adults. A big breakthrough was the Linotype machine that cast whole lines of type, introduced in Britain 1896, and better train services made national breakfast-time circulation possible. There were nine evening papers in the London area at the end of the 19th century, and by 1920, 50 per cent of British adults read a daily paper; by 1947, just before the introduction of television, the average adult read 1.2 daily papers and 2.3 Sunday papers; in 1975 only 49 per cent of adults read a daily paper.
The first generation of press barons in the UK, ◊Beaverbrook, ◊Northcliffe, and ◊Rothermere, used their power to propagate their own political opinions. Newspaper proprietors now own papers that espouse conflicting viewpoints. Ownership and control of the means of

communication have narrowed and its organization is chiefly for profit. The same pattern of diminishing choice and increasing monopoly is repeated throughout Europe. Some countries, such as Sweden, have a system of government subsidies to encourage competition. Newspapers in the first half of the 20th century reinforced the traditional class model of British society, being aimed at upper, middle, or working-class readers respectively. During World War II and until 1958, newsprint rationing prevented market forces from killing off the weaker papers. Polarization into 'quality' and 'tabloid' newspapers followed. Sales of national newspapers that have closed, such as the *News Chronicle*, were over 1 million: they were popular with the public but not with advertisers. Papers with smaller circulation, such as *The Times* and the *Independent*, survive because their readership is comparatively well off so they can sell advertising space at higher rates, and because production costs have fallen considerably with the introduction of new technology. The *Guardian* is owned by a nonprofit trust. Colour supplements have proliferated since their introduction by some Sunday papers in the 1960s. The mass-circulation papers have huge sales boosted by lotteries and photographs of women in states of undress; their factual news content is small. Some of them claim not to be newspapers in the traditional sense: their editorial policy is to entertain rather than inform.
British newspapers cover a political spectrum from the moderate left to the far right. Investigative reporting is restricted by stringent laws of libel and contempt of court and by the Official Secrets Act. The ◊Press Council was established 1953 to foster 'integrity and a sense of responsibility to the public', but has no power to enforce its recommendations.

newt one of the tailed ◊amphibians of the genus *Triturus* occurring in Europe. The smooth newt *Triturus vulgaris* is about 5 cm/2 in long plus a 4 cm/1.6 in tail. It is olive, spotted in the breeding male, and the underside is orange with blotches. It eats small invertebrates and fish.

newton SI unit of force, being the amount of force required to accelerate a mass of 1 kg by 1 metre per sec. It is named after Isaac ◊Newton (unit symbol N).

Newton /'njuːtn/ Isaac 1642–1727. British mathematician, who laid the foundation of physics as a modern discipline. Born at Woolsthorpe, Lincolnshire, he was educated at Grantham grammar school and Trinity College, Cambridge, of which he became a Fellow in 1667. During 1665–66 he discovered the binomial theorem and the differential and integral ◊calculus, and began to investigate the phenomenon of universal gravitation (see ◊gravity). He was elected Fellow of the Royal Society in 1672, and soon afterwards published his *New Theory about Light and Colours. De Motu corporum in gyrum / On the motion of bodies in orbit* was written in 1684, and the next year his universal law of gravitation was completely expounded as follows: 'Every particle of matter in the universe attracts every other

NEWSPAPERS

British National Newspapers

Daily	Founded	Circulation in 000s
The Sun	1964	4,100
Daily Mirror	1903	3,000
Daily Express	1900	1,900
Daily Mail	1896	1,800
Star	1978	1,300
Daily Telegraph	1855	1,200
The Guardian	1821	487
The Times	1785	478
Today	1986	307
The Independent	1986	302
Financial Times	1888	233
Morning Star	1938	28

Evening (London)		
The Evening Standard	1827	507

Sunday		
News of the World	1843	5,100
Sunday Mirror	1915	3,000
Sunday People	1881	2,900
Sunday Express	1918	2,500
Mail on Sunday	1982	1,600
Sunday Times	1822	1,200
Observer	1791	736
Sunday Telegraph	1961	686

Other Leading Newspapers of the World

Argentina		
Clarín	1945	480
La Nación	1870	197

Australia		
Sun News-Pictorial	1922	551
Daily Mirror	1941	390
The Sun	1910	350
Daily Telegraph	1879	326
The Herald	1840	293
Sydney Morning Herald	1831	266
The Age	1854	236

Austria		
Neue Kronen-Zeitung	1900	857
Kurier	1954	429
Arbeiter-Zeitung	1889	68

Belgium		
Het Laatste Nieuws	1888	306
Le Soir	1887	220

Brazil		
Jornal da Tarde	1966	250
Fôlha de São Paulo	1921	230
O Día	1951	207

Canada		
Toronto Star	1892	498
The Globe & Mail	1844	320
Le Journal de Montréal	1964	308
Toronto Sun	1971	228

China (People's Republic)		
Jiefangjun Bao (Liberation Army Daily)	1955	100,000
Renmin Ribao (People's Daily)	1948	5,000

Czechoslovakia		
Rudé právo	1920	950

Egypt		
al-Ahram	1875	800

France		
France-Soir	1941	419
Le Monde	1944	360
Le Parisien Libéré	1944	352
Le Figaro	1828	332
L'Equipe	1946	327

Germany, Democratic Republic		
Neues Deutschland	1946	1,000

Germany, Federal Republic		
Bild Zeitung	1952	5,400
Die Zeit	1946	398
Frankfurter Allgemeine Zeitung	1949	350
Süddeutsche Zeitung	1945	350
Die Welt	1946	200

Greece		
Ethnos	1981	203
Ta Nea	1931	155

Hungary		
Népszabadság	1942	705

India		
Navbharat Times	1947	400
Hindustan Times	1923	260
Statesman	1875	202
Times of India	1838	194
Indian Express	1933	180

Ireland		
Irish Independent	1905	175

Israel		
Háareyz	1918	55
Davar	1925	39

Italy		
Corriere della Serra	1876	625
La Stampa	1867	523
La Repubblica	1976	520
Il Giorno	1965	180

Japan		
Yomiuri Shimbun	1874	5,500
Asahi Shimbun	1879	3,800

Netherlands		
De Telegraaf	1893	687
De Volkskrant	1920	263

New Zealand		
New Zealand Herald	1863	246

Pakistan		
Daily Jang	1937	648
Dawn	1947	70

Poland		
Trybuna Ludu	1948	700

South Africa		
The Star	1887	188

Spain		
El País	1976	347

Sweden		
Aftonbladet	1830	328
Svenska Dagbladet	1884	225

Switzerland		
Neue Zürcher Zeitung	1790	136
Journal de Genève	1826	21

USSR		
Pravda	1912	10,700
Izvestiya	1917	7,000

USA		
Los Angeles Times	1881	1,000
New York Times	1851	935
Chicago Tribune	1847	776
Wall Street Journal	1889	757
Washington Post	1877	736
Philadelphia Inquirer	1829	526
Baltimore Sun	1837	348

particle with a force whose direction is that of the line joining the two, and whose magnitude is directly as (proportional to) the product of the masses, and inversely as (proportional to) the square of their distance from each other.' His greatest work, *Philosophiae Naturalis Principia Mathematica*, was published in three volumes 1686–87, with the aid of ◊Halley. Newton resisted James II's attacks on the liberties of the universities, and sat in the parliaments of 1689 and 1701/1702 as a Whig. Appointed Warden of the Royal Mint in 1695, and Master in 1699,

he carried through a reform of the coinage. He was elected president of the Royal Society in 1703, published his *Optics* in 1704, and was knighted in 1705. Newton was buried in Westminster Abbey.

Newtonian physics ◊physics as based on the concepts of Isaac ◊Newton, before the formulation of ◊quantum theory or ◊relativity theory.

Newton's laws of motion in physics, the three laws that form the basis of Newtonian mechanics. They are: 1) Unless acted upon by a net force, a body at rest stays at rest and a moving body continues moving at the same speed in the same straight line. 2) A net force applied to a body gives it a rate of change of ◊momentum proportional to the force and in the direction of the force. 3) When a body A exerts a force on a body B, B exerts an equal and opposite force on A, that is, to every action there is an equal and opposite reaction.

Newton's ring in optics, ◊interference phenomenon seen (using white light) as concentric rings of spectral colours where light

Newton Isaac Newton is universally known for his law of gravity but also developed theories about other natural forces, motion and light.

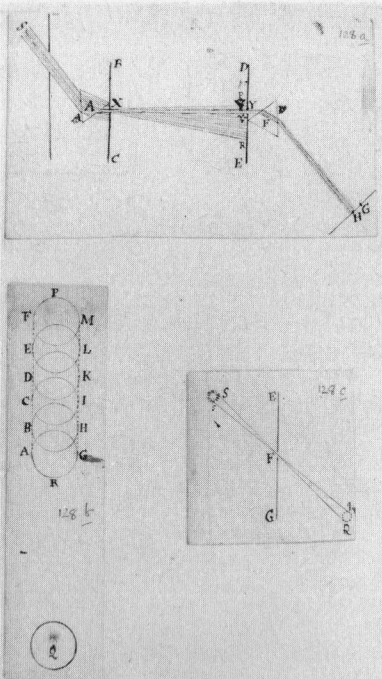

Newton In Newton's so-called 'crucial experiment', the sun's rays (S, top left) were split by a prism (A) into the colours of the spectrum. Shining one of the coloured bands through a second prism (F) did not split any further, showing that white light was a mixture of 'pure' colours.

passes through a thin film of transparent medium, such as the wedge of air between a large-radius convex lens and a flat glass plate. With monochromatic light (light of a single wavelength), the rings take the form of alternate light and dark bands. They are caused by interference (interaction) between light rays reflected from the plate and those reflected from the curved surface of the lens. They are named after Isaac ◊Newton.

new town in the UK, a town either newly established or greatly enlarged after World War II, when the population was rapidly expanding and city centres had either decayed or been destroyed. Fourteen were planned 1946–50, with population 25–60,000, among them Cwmbran and Peterlee, to stimulate employment in depressed areas, and eight near London to relieve congestion there. Fifteen more, with population up to 250,000, were established 1951–75, but by then a static population and cuts in government spending halted their creation.
By the later 1970s the policy, which had been criticized for disrupting family groupings and local communities, destroying small shops and specialist industries, and leading to the decay of city centres, was being reversed.

New Wave French literary movement of the 1950s, a cross-fertilization of the novel (Marguerite Duras, Alain Robbe-Grillet, Nathalie Sarraute) and film (directors Jean-Luc Godard, Alain Resnais and François Truffaut).

New World the Americas, so called by Europeans who reached them later than other continents. The term is used as an adjective to describe animals and plants that live in the western hemisphere.

New York /ˌnjuː ˈjɔːk/ state of the NE USA; nicknamed Empire State
area 128,400 sq km/49,576 sq mi
capital Albany
towns New York (City), Buffalo, Rochester, Yonkers, Syracuse
physical Adirondack and Catskill mountains, the former especially noted for scenery and sporting facilities and including Lake Placid; part of lakes Erie and Ontario; Hudson river; Niagara Falls; ◊Long Island
features West Point, site of the US Military Academy 1802; National Baseball Hall of Fame, Cooperstown; racing at Saratoga Springs; Washington Irving's home at Philipsburg Manor; Fenimore House (J F ◊Cooper), Cooperstown; home of F D Roosevelt at Hyde Park, and the Roosevelt Library; home of Theodore Roosevelt
products clothing, printing; Steuben glass; titanium concentrate; cereals, apples, maple syrup; poultry, meat and dairy products
population (1982) 17,659,000
famous people Henry and William James, Herman Melville, Walt Whitman
history first explored by Champlain and Hudson in 1609, colonized by the Dutch from 1614, and annexed by the English in 1664. The first constitution was adopted in 1777, when New York became one of the original Thirteen States.

New York /ˌnjuː ˈjɔːk/ largest city in USA, industrial port (printing, publishing, clothing), cultural and commercial centre in New York State, at the junction of the Hudson and East rivers; comprises the boroughs of the ◊Bronx, ◊Brooklyn, ◊Manhattan, Queens, and Richmond; population (1984) 7,165,000.
features The Statue of Liberty stands on Liberty Island (called Bedloe's Island until 1956) in the inner harbour. Skyscrapers include the World Trade Center (412 m/1,350 ft), the Empire State Building (381 m/1,250 ft), and the Art Deco Chrysler Building. St Patrick's Cathedral is 19th-century Gothic. There are a number of notable art galleries, among them the Frick Collection, the Metropolitan Museum of Art, the Museum of Modern Art, and the Guggenheim, designed by Frank Lloyd Wright. Columbia University 1754 is the best known of a number of institutions of higher education. Central Park is the largest park.

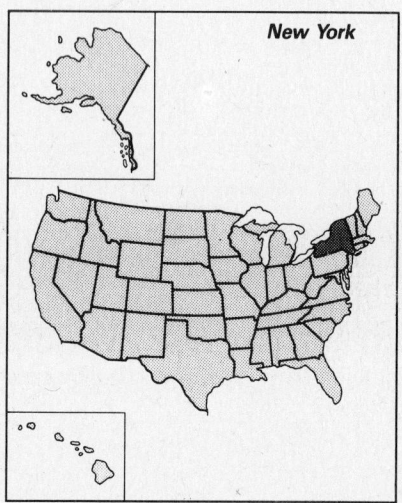

New York

history The Italian navigator Giovanni da Verrazano (? 1485–? 1528) reached New York Bay 1524, and Henry Hudson explored it 1609. The Dutch established a settlement on Manhattan 1613, named New Amsterdam from 1626; this was captured by the English in 1664 and renamed New York. During the War of Independence, British troops occupied New York 1776–84; it was the capital of the USA 1785–89.

New Zealand /ˌnjuː ˈziːlənd/ country in the S Pacific, SE of Australia.
government New Zealand is a constitutional monarchy. As in Britain, the constitution is the gradual product of legislation, much of it passed by Parliament in London. The governor-general represents the British monarch as formal head of state and appoints the prime minister, who chooses the cabinet. All ministers are drawn from and collectively responsible to the single-chamber legislature, the House of Representatives. This has 95 members, including four Maoris, elected by universal suffrage from single-member constituencies. It has a maximum life of three years and is subject to dissolution within that period.
history New Zealand was occupied by the ◊Polynesian ◊Maoris some time before the 14th century. ◊Tasman reached it 1642 but the Maoris would not let him land. ◊Cook explored the coasts in 1769, 1773, and 1777. British missionaries began to arrive from 1815. By the Treaty of Waitangi 1840 the Maoris accepted British sovereignty; colonization began, and

New Zealand

AREA 268,675 sq km/103,736 sq mi
CAPITAL Wellington
TOWNS Hamilton, Palmerston North,
Christchurch, Dunedin; ports Wellington,
Auckland
PHYSICAL comprises North and South islands,
Stewart and Chatham islands; mainly
mountainous
TERRITORIES overseas comprise Tokelau Island
(three atolls transferred 1926 from the former
Gilbert and Ellice Islands colony) and Niue
Island (one of the Cook Islands, but separately
administered from 1903: chief town Alafi).
The Cook Islands are internally self-
governing, but share common citizenship with
New Zealand. The Ross Dependency is in the
Antarctic
FEATURES on North Island are Ruapehu, at
2,797 m/9,175 ft the highest of three active
volcanoes, the geysers and hot springs of the
Rotorua district, Lake Taupo (616 sq km/238
sq mi), source of Waikato River, and NE of
the lake, Kaingaroa state forest, one of the
world's largest planted forests. On South
Island are the Southern Alps and Canterbury
Plains, noted for sheep
HEAD OF STATE Elizabeth II from 1952
represented by Sir Paul Reeves from 1985
HEAD OF GOVERNMENT David Lange from 1984
GOVERNMENT parliamentary democracy
EXPORTS lamb and beef, wool and leather,
dairy products and other processed foods; kiwi
fruit became a major export crop in the 1980s;
seeds and breeding stock; timber, paper, pulp;
light aircraft
CURRENCY New Zealand dollar (2.56 = £1
Sept 1987)
POPULATION (1985) 3,271,000 (including
270,000 Maoris and 60,000 other Polynesians;
the whites are chiefly of British descent);
annual growth rate 0.9%
LANGUAGE English (official); Maori (the Lange
government pledged to give it official status)

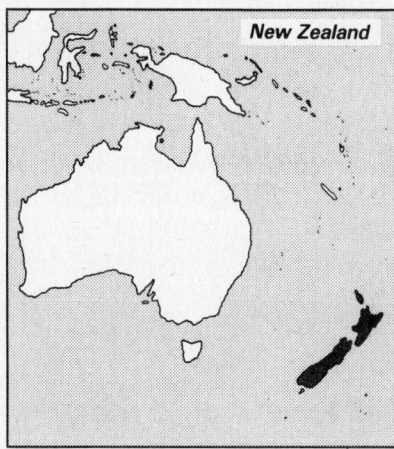

New Zealand

RELIGION Protestant 50%, Roman Catholic
15%
LITERACY 99% (1984)
GNP $21.4 bn (1984); $7,916 per head of
population
CHRONOLOGY
1947 Full independence within the
Commonwealth confirmed by the New
Zealand parliament.
1972 National Party government replaced
Labour Party, with Norman Kirk as prime
minister.
1974 Kirk died and was replaced by Wallace
Rowling.
1975 National Party returned, with Robert
Muldoon as prime minister.
1984 Labour Party returned under David
Lange.
1985 Non-nuclear defence policy created
disagreements with France and the USA.
1987 National Party declared support for the
Labour government's non-nuclear policy.
Lange re-elected. New Zealand officially
became a 'friendly' rather than 'allied' country
in the eyes of the USA, because of its non-
nuclear defence policy.

office, but growing inflation was aggravated by
the 1973–74 energy crisis which resulted in a
balance-of-payments deficit. The Labour
government's foreign-policy line was influenced
by Britain's decision to join the European
Community, which was likely to affect New
Zealand's future exports. It began a phased
withdrawal from some of the country's military
commitments in SE Asia. Norman Kirk died in
Aug 1974 and was succeeded by the finance
minister, Wallace Rowling. The state of the
economy worsened and in 1975 the National
Party, led by Robert ◊Muldoon, was returned to
power. However, the economy failed to revive
and in 1984 Muldoon introduced controversial
labour legislation. To renew his mandate, he
called an early election but was swept out of office
by the Labour Party, now led by David ◊Lange.
It had fought the election on a non-nuclear
defence policy, which Lange immediately put
into effect, forbidding any vessels carrying
nuclear weapons or powered by nuclear energy
from entering New Zealand's ports. This put a
great strain on relations with the USA. In 1985
the trawler *Rainbow Warrior*, the flagship of the
environmentalist pressure group, ◊Greenpeace,
which was monitoring nuclear tests in French
Polynesia, was mined in Auckland harbour by
French secret-service agents. The French prime
minister eventually admitted responsibility.

There are currently seven active political parties.
James McLay was leader of the National Party
1984–86, replaced by James Bolger. In the 1984
general election Labour won 56 seats in the
House and the National Party 37. In Jul 1987 the
National Party gave its support to the
government in a bi-partisan non-nuclear policy,
and as a result the USA re-classified New
Zealand as a 'friendly', rather than an 'allied'
country. In Aug Lange was re-elected.

New Zealand: prime ministers
J Ballance (Liberal) 1891
R J Seddon (Liberal) 1893
W Hall-Jones (Liberal) 1906
Joseph Ward (Liberal) 1906
T MacKenzie (Liberal) 1912
W F Massey (Reform) 1912
J G Coates (Reform) 1925
Joseph Ward (United) 1928
G W Forbes (United) 1930
M J Savage (Labour) 1935
P Fraser (Labour) 1940
S G Holland (National) 1949
K J Holyoake (National) 1957
Walter Nash (Labour) 1957
K J Holyoake (National) 1960
J Marshall (National) 1972
N Kirk (Labour) 1972
W Rowling (Labour) 1974
R Muldoon (National) 1975
D Lange (Labour) 1984

large-scale sheep farming was developed. The
colony was granted self-government 1853. The
Maoris resented the loss of their land and rose in
revolt 1845–47 and 1860–72, until concessions
were made, including representation in
parliament. Sir George Grey, governor 1845–53
and 1861–70 and Radical prime minister
1877–84, was largely responsible for the
conciliation of the Maoris and the introduction
of male suffrage.
The Conservatives held power 1879–90 and were
succeeded by a Liberal government which ruled
with trade-union support; this government
introduced women's suffrage 1893 and old-age
pensions 1898 and was a pioneer in labour
legislation. After 1912 the Reform (formerly
Conservative) Party regained power, and the

trade unions broke with the Liberals to form the
Labour Party. The Reform and Liberal parties
united to become the National Party 1931. New
Zealand became a dominion in the British
Empire 1907 and was granted full independence
in 1931. New Zealand troops had served in the
Boer War in South Africa, and more than
100,000 fought in World War I and II.
Independence was formally accepted by the New
Zealand legislature in 1947.
The country has a record of great political
stability, with the centrist National Party
holding office from the 1930s until it was replaced
by a Labour Party administration, led by
Norman Kirk, in 1972. During this period New
Zealand built up a good social-security system.
The economy was thriving at the time Kirk took

New Zealand literature earliest of the
popular poets was Thomas Bracken, author of
the New Zealand national song, followed by
native-born Jessie Mackay and W Pember
Reeves, though the latter is better known as the
author of the prose account of New Zealand *The*

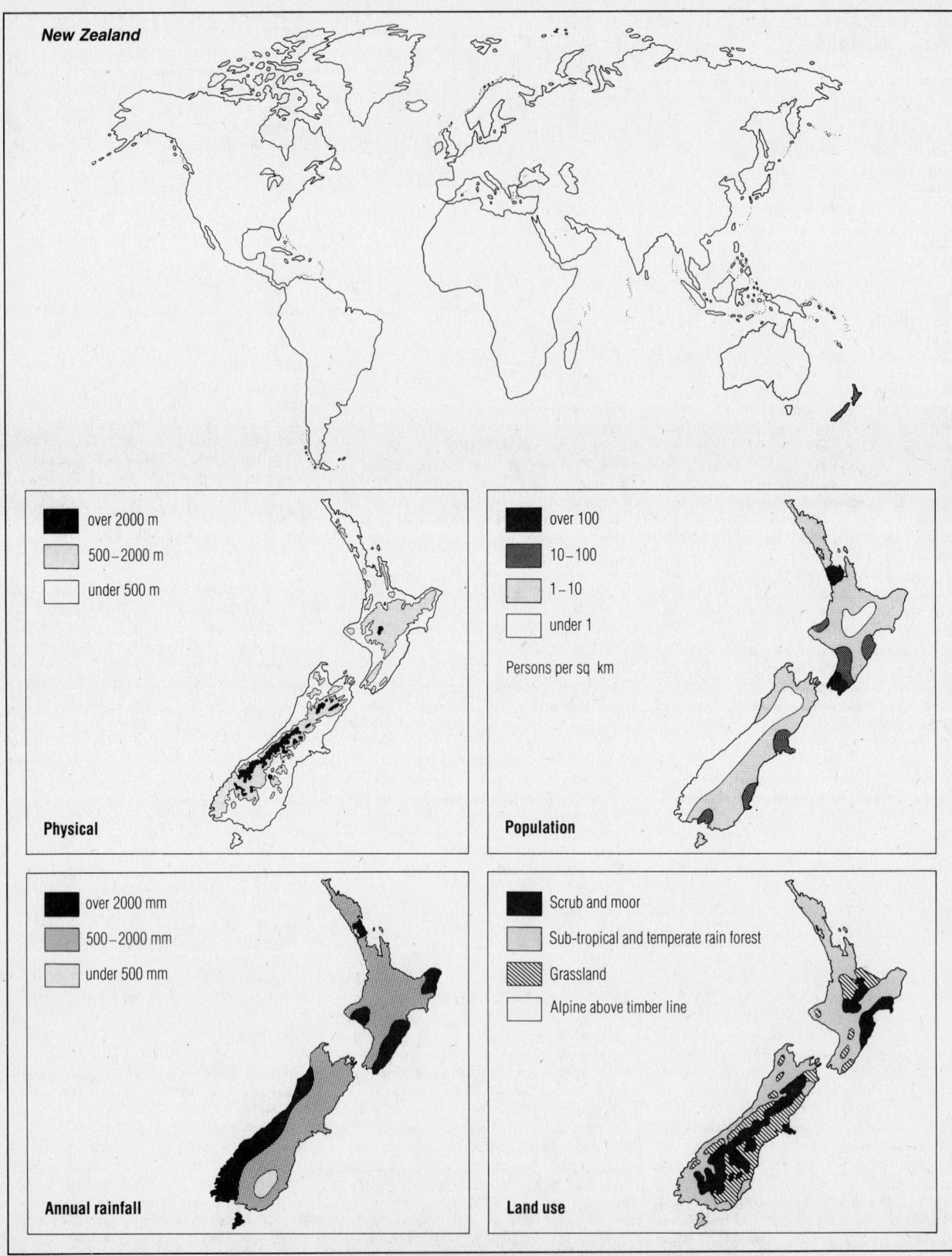

New Zealand

Physical

over 2000 m

500 – 2000 m

under 500 m

Population

over 100

10 – 100

1 – 10

under 1

Persons per sq km

Annual rainfall

over 2000 mm

500 – 2000 mm

under 500 mm

Land use

Scrub and moor

Sub-tropical and temperate rain forest

Grassland

Alpine above timber line

NEW ZEALAND

	Area in sq km
North Island	114,688
South Island	150,460
Stewart Island	1,735
Chatham Islands	963
Minor Islands	320
	268,675

Island Territories:

Niue Island	260
Tokelau Islands	10
Cook Islands	230
Ross Dependency	453,250

Long White Cloud. In the 20th century New Zealand literature gained an international appeal with the short stories of Katherine ◊Mansfield, produced an excellent exponent of detective fiction in Dame Ngaio ◊Marsh, and struck a specifically New Zealand note in *Tutira, the Story of a New Zealand Sheep Station* 1926, by W H Guthrie Smith (1861–1940). Poetry of a new quality was written by R A K Mason (1905–71) in the 1920s, and in the 1930s by a group of which A R D Fairburn (1904–57) with a witty conversational turn, and Allen Curnow (1911–), poet, critic, and anthologist, are the most striking. In fiction the 1930s were remarkable for the short stories of Frank Sargeson (1903–) and Roderick Finlayson (1904–), and the talent of John Mulgan (1911–45), who is remembered both for his novel *Man Alone*, and for his posthumous factual account of the war in which he died, *Report on Experience* 1947. More recently Kendrick Smithyman (1922–) has struck a metaphysical note in poetry, and Janet Frame (1924–) has a brooding depth of meaning in such novels as *The Rainbirds* 1968, and *Intensive Care* 1970. In 1985 Keri Hulme (1947–) won the Booker prize for her novel *The Bone People*.

Ney /neɪ/ Michael, Duke of Elchingen, Prince of Ney 1769–1815. Marshal of France. The son of a cooper, he joined the army in 1788, and rose from the ranks to marshal of France. He served throughout the Revolutionary and Napoleonic Wars, commanding the rearguard during the retreat from Moscow, and for his personal courage was called 'the bravest of the brave'. When Napoleon returned from Elba, Ney was sent to arrest him, but instead deserted to him and fought at Waterloo. He was subsequently shot for treason.

Niagara Falls /naɪˈægərə/ two waterfalls on the Niagara river, on the Canada–USA border, separated by Goat Island. The *American Fall* is 51 m/167 ft high, 330 m/1,080 ft wide; *Horseshoe Fall*, in Canada, is 49 m/160 ft high, 790 m/2,600 ft across.
On the Niagara river, below the falls, lie: on the W bank, *Niagara Falls*, a city in Ontario, Canada, with a large hydroelectric generating plant; population (1976) 69,400; on the E bank,

Niagara Falls, a city in New York State, USA; population (1980) 71,384.

Niamey /ˌnɪəˈmeɪ/ capital of ◊Niger; population (1983) 399,000.

Nibelungenlied anonymous 12th-century German epic poem, *Song of the Nibelungs*, derived from older sources. ◊Siegfried, possessor of the Nibelung treasure, marries Kriemhild (sister of Gunther of Worms) and wins Brunhild as a bride for Gunther. However, Gunther's vassal Hagen murders Siegfried, and Kriemhild achieves revenge by marrying Etzel (Attila) of the Huns, at whose court both Hagen and Gunther are killed. Richard ◊Wagner made use of the legends in his *Ring* cycle.

Nicaea /naɪˈsiːə/ ruined city (modern Iznik) in Turkey, site in 325 of the Council of ◊Nicaea.

Nicaea, Council of /naɪˈsiːə/ Christian church council held at Nicaea in 325, called by the Emperor Constantine, in which ◊Arianism was condemned as heretical and the doctrine of the ◊Trinity was established under ◊Athanasius as the ◊Nicene Creed.

Nicaragua /ˌnɪkəˈrægjuə, Spanish ˌnikaˈraːɡwa/ country in Central America, between the Pacific Ocean and the Caribbean, bounded N by Honduras and S by Costa Rica.
government The constitution dates from Jan 1987. The 96-member National Constituent Assembly is elected by universal suffrage through a system of proportional representation, and a president serves a six-year term, with the assistance of a vice president and an appointed cabinet. The two main parties are the Sandinista National Liberation Front (FSLN) and the Democratic Conservative Party (PCD).

Nicaragua
REPUBLIC OF (*República de Nicaragua*)

AREA 148,000 sq km/57,150 sq mi
CAPITAL Managua
TOWNS chief port Corinto
PHYSICAL volcanic mountain ranges; lakes Nicaragua and Managua
FEATURES largest state of Central America and most thinly populated
HEAD OF STATE AND OF GOVERNMENT Daniel Ortega Saavedra from 1985
GOVERNMENT democratic socialist
EXPORTS coffee, cotton, sugar
CURRENCY cordoba (3,630 = £1 Sept 1987)
POPULATION (1985) 2,232,000 (70% mestizo, 15% Spanish descent, 10% Indian or black); annual growth rate 3.7%
LANGUAGE Spanish (official)
RELIGION Roman Catholic
LITERACY 61% male/60% female (1980 est)
GDP $3.4 bn (1983); $804 per head of population
CHRONOLOGY
1838 Achieved full independence.
1962 Sandinista National Liberation Front (FSLN) formed to fight Somoza regime.
1979 Somoza government ousted by FSLN.

Nicaragua

1982 Subversive activity against the government promoted by the USA. State of emergency declared.
1985 Denunciation of Sandinista government by US president Reagan. FSLN won big victory in assembly elections.
1987 Central American peace agreement co-signed by Nicaraguan leaders.
1988 Peace agreement failed and Nicaragua held talks with Contra rebel leaders.

history For early history, see ◊American Indian. The first European to reach Nicaragua was Gil Gonzalez de Avila 1522, who brought it under Spanish rule. It remained Spanish until 1821 and was then briefly united with Mexico. Nicaragua achieved full independence in 1838.
In 1912, at the Nicaraguan government's request, the USA established military bases in the country. Their presence was opposed by a guerrilla group led by Augusto César Sandino. The USA withdrew its forces in 1933 but not before it had set up and trained a national guard, commanded by a trusted nominee, Gen Anastasio Somoza. Sandino was assassinated 1934, reputedly on Somoza's orders, but some of his followers continued their guerrilla activity on a small scale.
The Somoza family began a near-dictatorial rule which was to last for over 40 years. During this time they developed wide business interests and amassed a huge personal fortune. Gen Anastasio Somoza was elected president in 1936 and stayed in office until his assassination in 1956, when he was succeeded by his son Luis. The left-wing FSLN, named after the former guerrilla leader, was formed 1962 with the object of overthrowing the Somozas by revolution. Luis Somoza was followed by his brother Anastasio, who headed an even more notorious regime. In 1979, after considerable violence and loss of life, Somoza was ousted and fled the country. The FSLN established a provisional junta of national reconstruction led by Daniel Ortega Saavedra, published a guarantee of civil rights, and appointed a council of state, prior to an elected national assembly and a new constitution.

Nicaragua's relations with the USA deteriorated rapidly with the election of President Reagan. He froze the package of economic assistance arranged by his predecessor, Jimmy Carter, alleging that the Sandinista government was supporting attempts to overthrow the administration in San Salvador. In Mar 1982 the Nicaraguan government declared a state of emergency in the wake of attacks on bridges and petroleum installations. The Reagan administration embarked on a policy of destabilizing Nicaragua's government and economy by actively supporting the counter-revolutionary forces (the Contras), known to have executed prisoners, killed civilians, and engaged in forced conscription, and by covert ◊Central Intelligence Agency operations, including the mining of Nicaraguan harbours 1984. In Feb 1985 Reagan denounced Ortega's regime, saying that his objective was to 'remove it in the sense of its present structure'. In May 1986 the US Congress approved $100 million in overt military aid to the Contras.

Political parties are now operating again and a large number fought the 1984 election for the new national assembly. The FSLN won 61 seats and the PCD 14. In Aug 1987 a peace plan put forward by US President Reagan was rejected by Nicaragua and, instead, a Central American Peace Agreement, instigated by Costa Rican President Oscar Arias, was signed in Guatemala by leaders of Nicaragua, El Salvador, Guatemala, Honduras, and Costa Rica.

Nice /niːs/ resort on the French Riviera; population (1982) 449,500. There is an annual Battle of Flowers, and chocolate and perfume are made.

Nicene Creed one of the fundamental creeds of Christianity, promulgated by the Council of ◊Nicaea in 325. It gives the orthodox doctrine of the Trinity as against the Arian heresy (see ◊Arianism). The Nicene Creed was modified by the Council of Constantinople in 381, and the *filioque* clause was added during the 5th and 6th centuries in the Western Church.

niche in ◊ecology, the 'place' occupied by a species in its habitat, including its food requirements, the time of day at which it feeds, the parts of the habitat it uses (for example, trees or open grassland). Ecological theory holds that two species cannot occupy exactly the same niche and coexist; they will be in direct competition and one will eventually give way to the other.

Nicholas two Tsars of Russia:
Nicholas I /'nɪkələs/ 1796–1855. Tsar from 1825, his Balkan ambitions led to war with Turkey 1827–29, and the ◊Crimean War.

Nicholas II /'nɪkələs/ 1868–1918. Last Tsar, succeeding in 1894, he was dominated by his wife, Princess Alix of Hesse, who in turn was under the influence of ◊Rasputin. His mismanagement of the ◊Russo-Japanese War led to the revolution of 1905, which he ruthlessly suppressed. He took Russia into World War I in 1914, was forced to abdicate in 1917, and was shot with his family by the Bolsheviks at Ekaterinburg in Jul 1918. See also ◊Anastasia.

Nicholas of Cusa /'kjuːzə/ 1401–1464.

German philosopher, important in the transition from ◊scholasticism to the philosophy of the modern period. He argued that knowledge is learned ignorance (*docta ignorantia*), since God, the ultimate object of knowledge, stands above the opposites in terms of which human reason grasps the objects of nature. Nicholas also asserted that the universe is boundless and that it has no circumference, thereby breaking with the cosmology of the Middle Ages.

Nicholas, St /'nɪkələs/ Lived 4th century. In the Christian Church, patron saint of Russia, children, merchants and sailors, bishop of Myra (now in Turkey). His legendary gifts of dowries to poor girls led to the custom of giving gifts to children on the eve of his feast day, 6 Dec, still retained in some countries, such as Germany and the Netherlands, although elsewhere now transferred to Christmas Day – hence the association of his name, Santa Claus (corruption of San Nicolaas).

Nicholson /'nɪkəlsən/ Ben 1894–1982. British artist, born in Denham, Buckinghamshire, son of William ◊Nicholson. Developing an interest in abstract art, he became known for his geometrical reliefs and as an exponent of ◊Constructivism. Awarded Order of Merit 1968.

Nicholson /'nɪkəlsən/ William 1872–1949. British artist, noted for his development of the poster produced with his brother-in-law, James Pryde, as 'The Beggarstaff Brothers'. He was the father of Ben ◊Nicholson.

Nicholas II Tsar Nicholas II of Russia in his youth. His reign caused so much dissatisfaction, both over domestic and foreign policies, that it led to the outbreak of the Russian Revolution of 1917, overthrowing the monarchy and establishing the first communist state.

nickel a lustrous white metallic element discovered by Cronstedt in 1751, the name being an abbreviation of Swedish *kopparnickel* (false copper): symbol Ni, atomic weight 58.71, atomic number 28. It has a high melting point, low electrical and thermal conductivity, and can be magnetized. Nickel may be forged readily when hot, and is tough, malleable, and ductile when cold. Canada provides the most extensive deposits, which are usually extracted with copper. Smelting precedes separation, after which the nickel is purified. It is used in coinage; in the chemical and food industries because of its resistance to corrosion; in electronics and for ◊electroplating. The most important use, however, is in alloys with iron, steel, copper, and chromium, including nickel steel for armour plating and burglar-proof safes, Monel metal, invar, constantan, nichrome permalloy, perminvar, and other magnetic alloys and stainless steels, cupro-nickel, nickel-silver, and others. Finely divided nickel is used as a catalyst in the hydrogenation of vegetable oils.

Nicklaus /'nɪklaus/ Jack William 1940– . American golfer. Nicknamed 'The Golden Bear', he has won a record 20 major titles: US Amateur 1959, 1961; US Masters 1963, 1965–66, 1972, 1975, 1986; US Open 1962, 1967, 1972, 1980; US PGA 1963, 1971, 1973, 1975, 1980; British Open 1966, 1970, 1978. He was the oldest winner of the Masters in 1986. His son, Jack (Jnr), also plays professional golf.

Nicobars /'nɪkəbɑːz/ group of islands in the Bay of Bengal, a territory (with the ◊Andamans) of the Republic of India; population (1981) 30,500. The islands were occupied by Japan 1942–45.

Nicolson /'nɪkəlsən/ Harold 1886–1968. British diplomat and author. He served on the British delegation to the Paris Peace Conference of 1919. Briefly associated with ◊Mosley, he was a National Labour Member of Parliament 1935–45, and in 1947 joined the Labour Party. His biographies include *Curzon: the Last Phase* 1934 and *King George V* 1952. He also published studies such as *Monarchy* 1962, but he is chiefly remembered for his *Diaries and Letters* 1930–62. He married Victoria ◊Sackville-West in 1913.

Nicosia /ˌnɪkə'siːə/ capital of Cyprus, with leather, textile, and pottery industries; population (1984) 150,000.
history Nicosia was the residence of Lusignan kings of Cyprus 1192–1475. The Venetians, who took Cyprus in 1489, surrounded Nicosia with a high wall which still exists; it fell to the Turks 1571. It was again partly taken by the Turks in the invasion of 1974. The Greek and Turkish sectors are separated by the Green Line.

nicotine an ◊alkaloid obtained from the dried leaves of the tobacco plant (*Nicotiana tabacum*) and used as an insecticide. A colourless oil, soluble in water, it turns brown on exposure to the air. Nicotine in its pure form is one of the most powerful poisons known: it is named after a 16th-century French diplomat, Jacques Nicot, who introduced tobacco to France. It is the component of cigarette smoke that causes bodily addiction.

Niebuhr /'niːbʊə/ Barthold Georg 1776–1831. German historian. He wrote a history of Rome (1811–32), famous for the critical use of sources.

Niebuhr /'niːbʊə/ Reinhold 1892–1971. American Protestant theologian. His *Moral Man and Immoral Society* 1932 reflected liberalism for biblical theology, and attacked depersonalized industrial society.

Niedersachsen /'niːdə,sæksən/ German name for the region of ◊Lower Saxony in West Germany.

nielsbohrium alternative name for the element ◊unnilpentium.

Nielsen /'niːlsən/ Carl (August) 1865–1931. Danish composer. His works show an openness to new musical ideas and a reaction against Romanticism, and are notable for their progressive tonality, as in his opera *Saul and David* and six symphonies. His compositions also include concertos for violin, 1911, and clarinet, 1928, and chamber and piano works.

Niemeyer /'niːmaɪə/ Oscar 1907– . Brazilian architect, joint designer of the United Nations headquarters in New York, and of many buildings in ◊Brasilia.

Niemöller /'niːmɜːlə/ Martin 1892– . German pastor. A former U-boat commander, sent to a concentration camp for campaigning against Nazification of the German Church. In 1946 he proclaimed Germany's war guilt at the International Missionary Council in Geneva, and was first bishop of the newly formed Evangelical Church of Hesse-Nassau 1947–64, and president of the World Council of Churches 1961–68.

Niepce /njeps/ Joseph Nicéphore 1765–1833. French pioneer of ◊photography.

Nietzsche /'niːtʃə/ Friedrich Wilhelm 1844–1900. German philosopher. Born at Röcken, Saxony, he attended Bonn university and was professor of Greek at Basle 1869–80. He had abandoned theology for philology, and was influenced by the writings of ◊Schopenhauer and the music of ◊Wagner, of whom he became both friend and advocate. Both these attractions passed, however, and ill-health caused his resignation from the university. He spent his later years in N Italy, in the Engadine and in S France. During his mature years he published *Morgenröte* 1880 81, *Die fröhliche Wissenschaft* 1881–82, *Also sprach Zarathustra* 1883–85, *Jenseits von Gut und Böse* 1885–86, *Genealogie der Moral* 1887, and *Ecce Homo* 1888. He suffered a permanent breakdown in 1889 from overwork and loneliness.

The philosophy of Nietzsche is the rejection of the accepted absolute moral values and the 'slave morality' of Christianity, for he argued that 'God is dead', and that people are therefore free to create their own values. His ideal was the *Übermensch* or 'Superman' who would impose his will on the weak and worthless. Until this century, his beliefs remained ignored or opposed, by conservatives and socialists alike, but support for modern ◊totalitarianism has often been claimed in Nietzsche's writings, by the ◊Nazi movement, among others. Nietzsche claimed that knowledge is never objective, but always serves some interest or unconscious purpose. His insights into the relation between thought and language have had an important influence on contemporary philosophy.

Nietzsche Friedrich Nietzsche has exercised considerable influence on literature, philosophy, psychoanalysis, and religion, while his Superman has been considered a prototype for Hitler's ideal Aryan.

Nièvre /ni'eɪvrə/ river in central France, rising near Varzy and flowing 40 km/25 mi S to join the Loire at Nevers; it gives its name to a department.

Niger /'naɪdʒə/ third longest river in Africa, 4,185 km/2,600 mi, it rises 240 km/150 mi from the W coast, in the highlands bordering Sierra Leone and Guinea. Its flow has been badly affected by the expansion of the Sahara Desert; it is sluggish and frequently floods its banks.

Niger /niː'ʒeə/ landlocked country in W Africa, bounded to the N by Nigeria and Libya, to the E by Chad, to the S by Nigeria and Benin, and to the W by Burkina Faso and Mali.

government The 1960 constitution was suspended after a military coup in 1974 and Niger is now ruled by a supreme military council of army officers and a council of ministers appointed by the president, who is head of state as well as head of government. In a move towards greater democracy, the National Development Council, of 150 elected members, was reconstituted 1983 and given the task of drawing up a national charter. Since 1974 all political parties have been banned.

history Niger was part of ancient and medieval empires in ◊Africa. European explorers arrived in the late 18th century, and Tuareg people invaded the area from the N. France seized it from the Tuaregs 1904 and made it part of French West Africa, although fighting continued until 1922. It became a French overseas territory 1946 and an autonomous republic within the French Community 1958.

Niger achieved full independence in 1960, and Hamani Diori was elected president. Maintaining very close and cordial relations with France, Diori seemed to have established one of the most stable regimes in Africa, and the discovery of uranium deposits promised a sound economic future. However, a severe drought 1968–74 resulted in widespread civil disorder and in Apr 1974 Diori was ousted by the army led by the chief of staff, Lt-Col Seyni Kountché. Having suspended the constitution and established a military government with himself as president, he tried to restore the economy and negotiated a more equal relationship with France through a cooperation agreement 1977.

Still threatened by possible droughts and consequential unrest, Kountché has tried to widen his popular support by liberalizing his regime and releasing political prisoners, including former President Diori. More civilians have been introduced into the government with the prospect of an eventual return to constitutional rule. When Lietenant-Colonel Seyni Kountche died in 1987, the Supreme Military Council appointed Colonel Ali Seybou to acting president.

Nigeria /naɪ'dʒɪəriə/ country in W Africa on the Gulf of Guinea, bounded to the N by Niger, to the E by Chad and Cameroon, and to the W by Benin.

government The constitution is based on one of 1979, amended after military coups 1983 and 1985. The president is head of state, commander in chief of the armed forces, and chair of the 28-member Armed Forces Ruling Council (AFRC), composed of senior officers of the army and police force. The AFRC appoints the National Council of Ministers, which is also headed by the president.

Nigeria is a federal republic of 19 states. Each of the states has a military governor, appointed by the AFRC, who in turn appoints and leads a state executive council. There is also a coordinating federal body called the National Council of States, which includes the president and all the state governors. All political parties are now banned.

history Nigeria has been inhabited since at least 700 BC. In the 12th–14th centuries civilizations developed in the Yoruba area and in the Muslim N. Portuguese and British slave traders raided from the 15th century (see ◊slavery).

◊Lagos was supposedly bought from a chief by British traders in 1861; in 1886 it became the colony and protectorate of Lagos. The Niger river valley was developed by the National African Company (later the Royal Niger Company), which came to an end 1899, and in 1900 two protectorates were set up: N Nigeria and S Nigeria. Britain's largest African colony, Nigeria was united 1914.

Nigeria became a federation 1954 and achieved full independence, as a constitutional monarchy within the Commonwealth, in 1960. In 1963 it became a republic, based on a federal structure so as to accommodate the many different ethnic groups, which included the Ibo, the Yoruba, the Aro, the Angas, and the Hausa. Nigeria's first president was Dr Nnamdi Azikiwe, a banker and

Niger
REPUBLIC OF (*République du Niger*)

AREA 1,187,000 sq km/459,000 sq mi
CAPITAL Niamey
PHYSICAL mountains in centre; arid except in S (savanna) and SW (river Niger)
FEATURES part of the Sahara Desert and subject to Sahel droughts
HEAD OF STATE AND OF GOVERNMENT Ali Seybou from 1987
GOVERNMENT military
EXPORTS groundnuts; livestock; gum arabic; tin, uranium
CURRENCY CFA franc (498.38 = £1 Sept 1987)
POPULATION 6,491,000 (1985); annual growth rate 2.8%
LANGUAGE French (official), Hausa, Djerma
RELIGION Sunni Muslim 85%, animist 15%
LITERACY 14% male/6% female (1980 est)
GDP $2.3 bn (1982); $475 per head of population
CHRONOLOGY
1960 Achieved full independence from France with Hamani Diori elected president.
1974 Diori ousted in an army coup led by Seyni Kountché.
1977 Cooperation agreement signed with France.
1987 Kountché died and was replaced by the army commander-in-chief Ali Seybou.

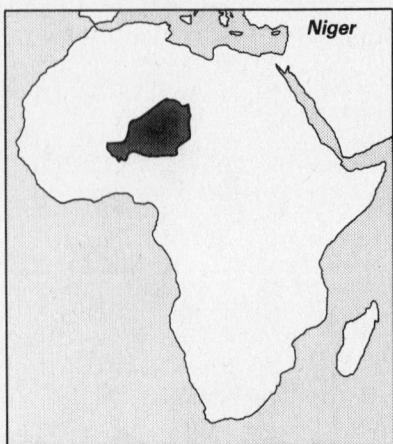

Nightingale A pencil drawing of Florence Nightingale by Sir George Scharf, made just after the end of the Crimean War in 1857.

proprietor of an influential newspaper group, who had played a leading part in the movement for independence. He came from the Ibo tribe. His chief rival was Abubakar ◊Tafawa Balewa, who was prime minister from 1957 until he was assassinated in a military coup in 1966. The coup had been led mainly by Ibo junior officers from the E region, which had become richer after the discovery of oil there in 1958. The offices of president and prime minister were suspended and it was announced that the state's federal structure would be abandoned. Before this could be done, the new military government was overturned in a counter-coup by a mostly Christian group from the N, led by Col Yakubu ◊Gowon. He re-established the federal system and appointed a military governor for each region. Soon afterwards tens of thousands of Ibos in the N were killed.

In 1967 a conflict developed between Gowon and the military governor of the E region, Col Chukwuemeka Odumegwu-Ojukwu, about the distribution of oil revenues, which resulted in Ojukwu's declaration of an independent Ibo state of Biafra. Gowon, after failing to pacify the Ibos, ordered federal troops into the E region and a civil war began, lasting until Jan 1970, when Biafra surrendered to the federal forces. It was the first modern war between black Africans and left the economy gravely weakened.

In 1975, while he was out of the country, Gowon was replaced in a bloodless coup led by Brig Murtala Mohammad, but he was killed within a month and replaced by Gen Olusegun Obasanjo. He announced a gradual return to civilian rule and in 1979 the leader of the National Party of Nigeria, Shehu Shagari, became president. In Dec 1983, with the economy suffering from falling oil prices, Shagari's civilian government

was deposed in another bloodless coup, led by Maj-Gen Muhammadu Buhari. In 1985 another peaceful coup replaced Buhari with a new military government, led by Maj-Gen Ibrahim Babangida, the army Chief of Staff. At the end of the year an attempted coup by rival officers was thwarted.

Babangida has promised a return to a democratic civilian government in 1992.

nightingale songbird *Luscinia megarhynchos* of the thrush family with a song of great beauty and variety, heard at night as well as in the day, celebrated in poetry and song. About 16.5 cm/6.5 in long, it is dull brown, lighter below, with a reddish-brown tail. It feeds on insects and small animals. It is a summer visitor to Europe and winters in Africa.

Nightingale /ˈnaɪtɪŋgeɪl/ Florence 1820–1910. British hospital reformer, born in Florence. She took a team of nurses to Scutari in 1854 and reduced the ◊Crimean War hospital death rate from 42 per cent to 2 per cent. An invalid in retirement for the rest of her life, she still worked to raise the status of nursing. She received the Order of Merit in 1907.

nightjar nocturnal bird *Caprimulgus europaeus* that catches insects on the wing. About 28 cm/11 in long, it is patterned in shades of brown, and well camouflaged. It is a summer visitor to Europe and winters in tropical Africa.

nightshade common name for several plants in the family Solanaceae: best-known are the black nightshade *Solanum nigrum*, bittersweet or woody nightshade *Solanum dulcamara*, and deadly nightshade or ◊belladonna.

Nihilist member of a group of Russian revolutionaries of the reign of Alexander II 1855–81. The name, popularized by Turgenev, means one who approves of nothing (Latin *nihil*)

belonging to the existing order. From 1878 the Nihilists launched a guerrilla campaign which culminated in the murder of the tsar in 1881.

Niigata /ˈniːɡɑːtə/ industrial port (textiles, metals, oil refining and chemicals) on Honshu island, Japan; population (1984) 459,000.

Nijinsky /nɪˈdʒɪnski/ Vaslav 1888–1950. Russian dancer and choreographer. A legendary member of ◊Diaghilev's Ballets Russes, for whom he choreographed ◊Debussy's *L'Aprèsmidi d'un faune* 1912 and *Jeux* 1913 and ◊Stravinsky's *The Rite of Spring* 1913, he also took lead roles in ballets such as *Le Spectre de la rose* and *Petrushka* 1911.

Nijmegen /ˈnaɪmeɪgən/ industrial city (brewery, leather, tobacco) in E Netherlands; population (1985) 146,500. The Roman Noviomagus, Nijmegen was a free city of the Holy Roman Empire and a member of the Hanseatic League.

Nijmegen /ˈnaɪmeɪgən/ Treaties of Netherlands, Spain and the Holy Roman Empire, ending the Third Dutch War.

Nike /ˈnaɪkiː/ in Greek mythology, goddess of victory, represented as 'winged', as in the statue from Samothrace in the Louvre. One of the most beautiful architectural monuments of Athens was the temple of Nike Apteros.

Nikolayev /ˌnɪkəˈlaɪev/ port (with shipyards) and naval base on the Black Sea, in Ukraine, USSR; population (1985) 486,000.

Nile /naɪl/ river in Africa, the world's longest, 6,695 km/4,160 mi. Its remotest headstream is the Luvironza (rising in Burundi).

Nigeria
FEDERAL REPUBLIC OF

AREA 924,000 sq km/357,000 sq mi
CAPITAL and chief port Lagos
TOWNS administrative headquarters Abuja;
Ibadan, Ogbomosho, Kano; ports Port
Harcourt, Warri, Calabar
PHYSICAL the arid N becomes savanna and
farther S tropical rain forest, with mangrove
swamps along the coast; river Niger
FEATURES harmattan (a dry wind from the
Sahara); rich artistic heritage, for example
Benin bronzes
HEAD OF STATE AND OF GOVERNMENT Ibrahim
Babangida from 1985
GOVERNMENT military
EXPORTS petroleum (richest African country
in oil resources); cocoa, groundnuts, palm oil,
cotton, rubber; tin
CURRENCY naira (7 = £1 Sept 1987)
POPULATION (1985) 102,783,000 (of three
main ethnic groups, Yoruba in the W, Ibo in
the E, and Hausa-Fulani in the N); annual
growth rate 3.4%
LANGUAGE English (official), Hausa, Ibo,
Yoruba
RELIGION Sunni Muslim in the N, Christian in
the S
LITERACY 46% male/23% female (1980 est)
GDP $65 bn (1983); $750 per head of
population
CHRONOLOGY
1960 Achieved full independence within the
Commonwealth.
1963 Became a republic, with Nnamdi
Azikiwe as president.

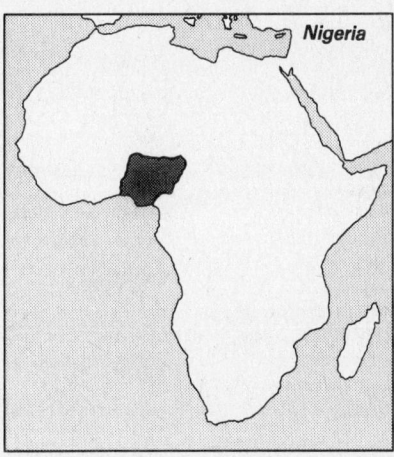

1966 Military coup, followed by a counter-coup led by Gen. Yakubu Gowon. Slaughter of thousands of members of the Ibo tribe in the N.
1967 Conflict about oil revenues leads to declaration of an independent state of Biafra and outbreak of civil war.
1970 Surrender of Biafra and end of civil war.
1975 Gowon ousted in military coup; a second coup puts Gen Obasanjo in power.
1979 Shehu Shagari becomes civilian president.
1983 Shagari's government overthrown in coup by Maj-Gen Buhari.
1985 Buhari replaced in a bloodless coup led by Maj-Gen Ibrahim Babangida.

Nijinsky The great Russian dancer and choreographer Vaslav Nijinsky as 'Le Dieu Bleu' in 1912. Noted for his powerful but graceful technique, he rejected the conventional forms of classical ballet in favour of free expression.

Nin /nɪn/ Anais 1903–1977. American novelist and diarist. Born in Paris, she emigrated to the USA in 1940, becoming a prominent member of the Greenwich Village literary society in New York. Her extensive and impressionistic diaries, published 1966–76, reflect her interest in dreams, which along with psychoanalysis form recurring themes of her gently erotic novels (such as *House of Incest* 1936 and *A Spy in the House of Love* 1954).

nineteen propositions demands presented by the English parliament to Charles I in 1642. They were designed to limit the powers of the crown and their rejection represented the final breakdown of peaceful negotiations and the effective beginning of the English Civil War.

Nineveh /'nɪnɪvə/ capital of the Assyrian Empire from the 8th century BC until its destruction by the Medes under Cyaxares in 612 BC. It was situated on the Tigris opposite the modern town of ◊Mosul, and was adorned with splendid palaces. Excavations from 1842 onwards by ◊Layard brought to light the ruins of Nineveh under the mounds, or tells, of Kuyunjik and Nebi Yunus.

Ningbo /ˌnɪŋ'bəʊ/ port (formerly Ningpo) in Zhejiang province, China; population (1973) 400,000. Already a centre of foreign trade under the Tang dynasty (618–907), it was one of the original treaty ports in 1842.

Ningxia Hui /'nɪŋʃiɑː 'huːi/ autonomous region (formerly Ninghsia-Hui) of NW China.
area 170,000 sq km/65,600 sq mi
capital Yinchuan
features desert plateau with nomad herdsmen
products cereals and rice under irrigation; coal

The Nile proper begins on leaving Lake Victoria above ◊Owen Falls. From Lake Victoria it flows over rocky country, and there are many cataracts and rapids, including the Murchison Falls, until it enters Lake Mobutu (Albert). From here it flows across flat country and in places spreads out to form lakes. At Lake No it is joined by the Bahr el Ghazal, and from this point to Khartoum it is called the White Nile. At Khartoum it is joined by the Blue Nile, which rises in the Ethiopian highlands, and 320 km/200 mi below Khartoum it is joined by the Atbara. From Khartoum to ◊Aswan there are six cataracts. The Nile is navigable to the second cataract, a distance of 1,545 km/960 mi. The delta of the Nile is 190 km/120 mi wide. From 1982 Nile water has been piped beneath the Suez Canal to irrigate ◊Sinai.

Nile, Battle of the /naɪl/ 1798. Alternative name for Battle of ◊Aboukir Bay, in which Nelson defeated Napoleon's fleet.

nilgai large antelope *Boselaphus tragocamelus* found in India. The bull has short conical horns and is bluish-grey. The female is brown.

Nîmes /niːm/ city in the S of France; population (1982) 132,500. Roman remains include an amphitheatre dating from the 2nd

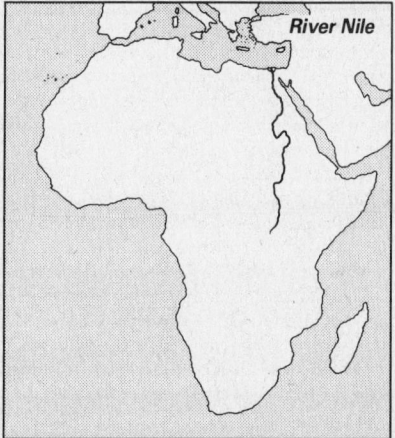

century AD and the Pont du Gard (aqueduct).

Nimitz /'nɪmɪts/ Chester William 1885–1966. American admiral. During World War II, he reconquered the Solomons in 1942–43, Gilbert Islands in 1943, and Marianas and Marshalls in 1944, and signed the Japanese surrender as the US representative.

population (1982) 3,895,578, including many Muslims.

Niobe /'naɪəbɪ/ in Greek mythology, the daughter of Tantalus and wife of Amphion, the king of Thebes. Contemptuous of the mere two children of the goddess Leto, Apollo and Artemis, her own twelve offspring were killed by them in revenge. She died of grief, and was changed to stone by Zeus.

niobium light-grey metal closely allied to ◊tantalum, and formerly known in the USA as columbium, which was first prepared by Blomstrand in 1864, though discovered in an ore by Hatchett in 1801. Symbol Nb, atomic weight 92.91, atomic number 41. Occurring in a number of rare minerals, it is generally obtained from an African ore, and is a valuable addition to stainless steels. It is also used for canning high-temperature nuclear fuel elements, for example in fast breeder-reactors, espicially when liquid sodium is the coolant.

Nippon /'nɪpɒn/ English transliteration of the Japanese name for ◊Japan.

Nirvana in ◊Buddhism, the attainment of perfect serenity by the eradication of all desires. To some Buddhists it means complete annihilation, to others it means the absorption of the self in the infinite.

Nithsdale /'nɪθsdeɪl/ William Maxwell, 5th Earl of Nithsdale 1676–1744. Jacobite leader who was captured at Preston and condemned to death on 9 Feb 1716. With his wife's assistance he escaped from the Tower of London in woman's dress, and fled to Rome.

nitrate any salt of nitric acid, containing the NO_3- ion. Nitrates are widely used in explosives, in the chemical and drugs industries, and as fertilizers, and run-off from fields results in nitrates polluting rivers and reservoirs.

nitre or *saltpetre*, potassium nitrate, KNO_3, a mineral found on the ground and in the soil near the surface of the ground at Bihar, India, Iran and Cape Province, S Africa. The native salt was formerly used for the manufacture of gunpowder, but the supply of nitre for explosives is nowadays largely met by making the salt from nitratine (Chile saltpetre, $NaNO_3$).

nitric acid an acid, HNO_3, also called *aqua fortis*, obtained by the oxidation of ammonia, or the action of sulphuric acid on potassium nitrate. It is a strong oxidizing agent, dissolves most metals, and is used for nitration and esterification of organic substances, for explosives, plastics and dyes and in making sulphuric acid and nitrates. Nitrous acid, HNO_2, is a weak acid which, in solution with water, decomposes quickly to form nitric acid and nitrogen dioxide.

nitrite any salt or ester of nitrous acid containing the nitrite ion (NO_2-). Nitrites are used as a preservative (for example to prevent the growth of botulism spores) and colouring in cured meats, such as bacon and sausages.

nitrocellulose a series of esters with 2–6 nitrate (NO_3) groups per molecule, made by the action of concentrated nitric acid on cellulose (for example cotton waste) in the presence of concentrated sulphuric acid. Those with 5 or more nitrate groups are explosive (gun cotton), but those with less were once used in lacquers,

rayon and plastics, especially coloured and photographic film, until replaced by non-inflammable cellulose acetate.

nitrogen a colourless, odourless, inert gas isolated by Daniel Rutherford (1749–1819) in 1772. Each molecule of nitrogen consists of two atoms of this element, symbol N, atomic weight 14.008, atomic number 7. There are an estimated 4,000 billion tonnes of nitrogen in the atmosphere, or about 78 per cent by volume. Many nitrogen compounds, for example nitric acid, nitrates, ammonia and the oxides, are of importance in foods, drugs, fertilizers, dyes and explosives. Nitrogen is a constituent of many organic substances, particularly ◊proteins. It is obtained for use in industry by liquefaction and fractional distillation of air. Nitrogen is used in the ◊Haber process to make ammonia, NH_3, and to provide an inert atmosphere for certain chemical reactions. In nature atmospheric nitrogen is 'fixed' by certain soil bacteria, see ◊nitrogen fixation.

nitrogen cycle in ◊ecology, the process whereby ◊nitrogen is passed through the ◊ecosystem. Nitrogen in the form of inorganic compounds (such as nitrates) in the soil is absorbed by plants and turned into organic compounds (such as proteins) in plant tissue. A proportion of this nitrogen is consumed by ◊herbivores and used for their own biological processes, with some of this in turn being passed on to the ◊carnivores. The nitrogen is finally returned to the soil, either as excreta or when the organisms die, to be returned to inorganic form by bacterial ◊decomposers. Although the atmosphere contains a great deal of free nitrogen, this cannot be used by most organisms. However, certain bacteria and cyanobacteria are capable of ◊nitrogen fixation, that is they can extract nitrogen directly from the atmosphere and convert it to compounds such as nitrates which other organisms can use. Some nitrogen-fixing bacteria live in a ◊mutualistic association with leguminous plants (peas and beans) or other plants (for example, alder) where they form characteristic nodules on the roots. The presence of such plants greatly increases the nitrate content, and hence the fertility, of the soil.

nitrogen fixation the process in which nitrogen in the atmosphere is converted into nitrogenous compounds either by lightning, or by the action of microorganisms, such as cyanobacteria and bacteria; see ◊nitrogen cycle.

nitroglycerine a substance produced by the action of nitric and sulphuric acids on ◊glycerol. It is very poisonous and explodes with great violence if heated in a confined space. It is used in the preparation of dynamite, cordite, and other high explosives.

Niue /'njuːeɪ/ island in the S Pacific, W of the Cook Islands; overseas territory of New Zealand
area 260 sq km/100 sq mi
towns port Alofi
products coconuts, passion fruit, honey
population (1984) 3,000
history annexed by New Zealand 1901; attained self-government in free association with New Zealand in 1974.

Nixon /'nɪksən/ Richard Milhous 1913–   . US Republican president 1968–74. After rising to prominence as a right-wing Republican as vice-president to Eisenhower during the 1950s, Nixon lost the 1960 presidential election to J F ◊Kennedy, but was successful at the second attempt in 1968. As president he was responsible for US withdrawal from Vietnam, and forged new links with China, but at home his willingness to use illegal methods to ensure re-election in 1972 led to his resigning in 1974 after being threatened with ◊impeachment.

Of Quaker family, Nixon grew up in Whittier, California; he became a lawyer, entered Congress in 1947, and in 1948 attracted attention as a member of the Un-American Activities Committee when he pressed for the investigation of Alger ◊Hiss. He was senator for California from 1951 until elected vice-president of the US under Eisenhower 1952–60. He failed to defeat J F Kennedy in the presidential elections of 1960, but in a 'law and order' campaign defeated Vice-President Humphrey in 1968 in one of the most closely contested elections in US history.

In 1969 he formulated the ◊Nixon Doctrine which resulted in the ending of the American commitment in Vietnam in 1973. Re-elected 1972 in a landslide victory, he resigned in 1974 – the first US president to do so – following ◊Watergate and the threat of impeachment on 3 counts: obstruction of the administration of justice in the investigation of Watergate; violation of constitutional rights of citizens, for example attempting to use the CIA as a weapon against political opponents; failing to produce 'papers and things' as ordered by the Judiciary committee. He was granted a free pardon in 1974 by President Ford.

Nixon Doctrine formulated in 1969 at Guam by President ◊Nixon, it abandoned policies of close involvement with Asian countries to avoid further situations such as the ◊Vietnam War.

Nixon The first US president to resign from office, Nixon was involved in illegalities during the 1972 election campaign which were revealed during the Watergate hearings in 1974, together with his subsequent attempts to 'cover up'.

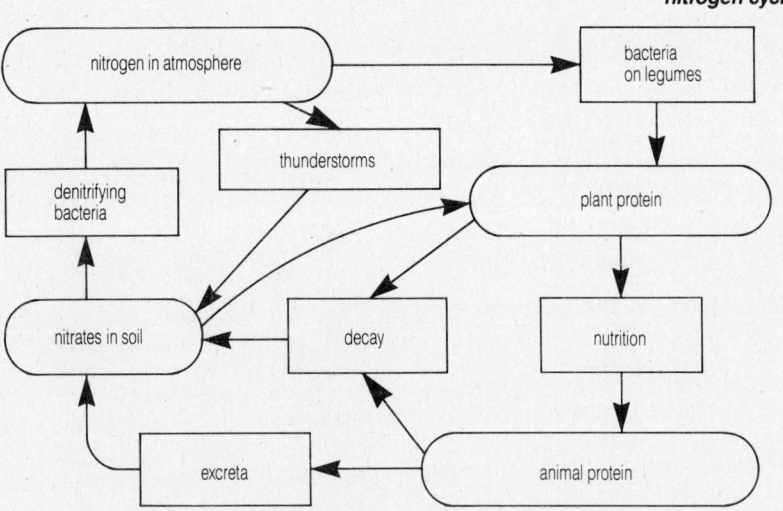

nitrogen cycle

Nizhni-Novgorod /'nɪʒni 'nɒvgərɒd/ former name (until 1932) of the city of ◊Gorky in central USSR.

Nkomati accord a non-aggression treaty between South Africa and Mozambique concluded in 1984. Under the agreement both sides bound themselves not to give material aid to opposition movements in each other's countries, which in effect meant that South Africa pledged itself not to support the Mozambique National Resistance (Renamo), while Mozambique was committed not to help the outlawed African National Congress (ANC). Mozambique was forced to enter into the accord because of the state of its economy, and it proved to be a largely one-sided arrangement, with South Africa barely honouring its obligations.

Nkomo /əŋ'kəʊməʊ/ Joshua 1917– . Zimbabwean politician, president of ZAPU (Zimbabwe African People's Union) from 1961, and a member of Robert ◊Mugabe's cabinet 1980–82 and 1987– .

Joshua Nkomo was a welfare officer on Rhodesian Railways and later organizing secretary of the Rhodesian African Railway Workers' Union. He moved into politics in 1950 and rose to become president of the ZAPU. He was soon arrested, and spent the next eleven years (1963–74) in various forms of detention. After his release he joined forces with Robert Mugabe as a joint leader of the Patriotic Front in 1976, opposing the white-dominated Smith regime. Nkomo took part in the Lancaster House Conference which led to Rhodesia's independence as the new state of Zimbabwe and was a member of Mugabe's cabinet from 1980 to 1982, and later 1987– .

Nkrumah /əŋ'kruːmə/ Kwame ·1909–1972. Ghanaian politician. Originally a schoolmaster, he studied later in both Britain and the USA, and following his return to Africa, formed the Convention People's Party in 1949 with the aim of immediate self-government. He was imprisoned in 1950 for incitement of illegal strikes, but was released the same year, becoming prime minister of the Gold Coast 1952–57, of Ghana 1957–60, and first president of the republic from 1960 until he was deposed while on a visit to Peking in 1966. He remained in exile until his death, but in 1973 was posthumously 'rehabilitated'.

Nkrumah Educated in America and England, the first president of Ghana, Kwame Nkrumah, was deposed by a military coup while visiting China. He sought exile in Guinea, where he was made a co-head of state.

NKVD (Russian 'People's Commissariat of Internal Affairs') name of the Soviet secret police 1934–38, which superseded the ◊CHEKA and was in turn replaced by the ◊KGB. The NKVD was reponsible for the infamous ◊purges of Stalin carried out during the 1930s.

Noah /'nəʊə/ in the Old Testament, the son of Lamech and father of Shem, Ham, and Japheth, who built an ark so that he and his family and specimens of all existing animals might survive the ◊Flood.

Nobel /nəʊ'bel/ Alfred Bernhard 1833–1896. Swedish chemist. Born at Stockholm, he invented dynamite in 1867, and ballistite, a smokeless gunpower, in 1889. He amassed a large fortune from the manufacture of explosives and the exploitation of the Baku oilfields, the bulk of which by his will he left in trust for the endowment of five ◊Nobel prizes.

nobelium metallic, radioactive element of the ◊actinide series, symbol No, atomic number 102. It is obtained by bombarding curium, and was first produced 1958. It is named after Alfred ◊Nobel.

Nobel prize annual prize, first awarded 1901, for achievement in chemistry, physics, medicine, literature and the promotion of peace; a sixth for economics, financed by the Swedish National Bank, was first awarded 1969.

nocturne in music, a lyrical, dreamy piece, often for piano, introduced by John Field (1782–1837) and adopted by ◊Chopin.

nodule in geology, a lump of mineral or other matter found within rocks or formed on the seabed surface; see ◊mining.

Noel-Baker /'nəʊəl 'beɪkə/ Philip John 1889–1982. British Labour politician. An ardent supporter of the League of Nations and United Nations, he published *The Arms Race* 1958, and he was in 1959 awarded the Nobel Peace Prize.

Nofretete alternative name for ◊Nefertiti, wife of Iknaton, pharaoh of Egypt.

Noguchi /nəʊ'guːtʃi/ Hideyo 1876–1928. Japanese bacteriologist, who researched into syphilitic diseases, and discovered the parasite of yellow fever, a disease from which he died while working in British W Africa.

noise unwanted sound, seen as an increasing problem in industrialized societies. Permanent, incurable loss of hearing can be caused by prolonged exposure to high noise levels (above 85 decibels in an octave). If the noise is in a narrow frequency band, temporary loss can occur even though the level is below 85 decibels or exposure is only for short periods. Roadside meter tests, introduced by the Ministry of Transport in Britain in 1968, allowed 87 decibels as the permitted limit for cars and 92 for lorries.

Nolan /'nəʊlən/ Sidney 1917– . Australian artist, born in Melbourne, and noted for his interpretation of the outback, for example the 1960s series on Ned ◊Kelly.

Nolde /'nɒldə/ Emil. Pseudonym of German ◊Expressionist artist Emil Hansen 1867–1956. Working both in watercolour and oil, he is noted for vividly coloured seascapes and such mystic religious works as *The Last Supper* and *Joseph tells his Dream*.

Nollekens /'nɒlɪkənz/ Joseph 1737–1823. British sculptor. Born in Soho, London, he worked in Rome 1760–70. On his return to London he enjoyed great success, executing busts of George III, the Prince of Wales (later George IV), Pitt, Fox, Garrick, Sterne, and others.

Nom Chinese-style characters used in writing the Vietnamese language. Nom characters were used from the 13th century for ◊Vietnamese literature, but were replaced in the 19th century by a romanized script known as Quoc Ngu.

nominalism one of the two main trends in the medieval philosophy of ◊scholasticism. In opposition to the ◊Realists, who maintained that universals (the distinctive qualities which enable us to group objects into classes) have a real existence, the Nominalists taught that they are mere names invented to describe the qualities of real things; that is, classes of things have no independent reality. William of ◊Occam was a leading medieval exponent of nominalism.

non-aligned movement strategic and political theory of neutrality ('non-alignment') towards major powers, specifically the USA and USSR. The term was originally used by ◊Nehru and adopted in 1961 at an international conference in Belgrade by ◊Tito, in general opposition to colonialism, neo-colonialism, and imperialism, and to the dominance of dangerously conflicting E and W alliances. However, many members were in receipt of aid from either E or W or both, and some went to war with one another (Vietnam–Kampuchea, Ethiopia–Somalia). Although originally used by poorer states, the non-aligned position came later to be adopted by oil-producing nations as well.

Nonconformist in religion, a term originally applied to the Puritan section of the Church of England clergy who, in the Elizabethan age, refused to conform to certain practices of the Church, for example kneeling to receive Holy Communion. After 1662 the term was confined to those who left the Church rather than conform to the Act of Uniformity requiring the use of the Prayer Book. It is now applied mainly to members of the Free Churches.

Nonjurors priests of the Church of England who after the Revolution of 1688 refused to take the oaths of allegiance to William and Mary. They continued to exist as a rival church for over a century, and consecrated their own bishops, the last of whom died in 1805. Notable Nonjurors were Thomas Ken (1637–1711), Jeremy ◊Collier, and William ◊Law.

Nordenskjöld /'nɔːdnʃəʊld/ Nils Adolf Erik, Baron Nordenskjöld 1832–1901. Swedish explorer. He made voyages to the Arctic with the geologist Torell, and in 1878–79 discovered the North-East Passage.

Nordic racial designation formerly used to describe the Germanic peoples mainly of Scandinavia.

Nord-Pas-de-Calais /'nɔː ˌpɑː də kæ'leɪ/ region of N France; capital Lille; population (1984) 3,941,500. *Pas-de-Calais* is the French term for the Straits of Dover.

Nore, the /nɔː/ sandbank at the mouth of the river Thames, England; site of the first lightship 1732.

Nore mutiny /nɔː/ British naval mutiny in 1797, caused by low pay and bad conditions.

Norfolk /'nɔːfək/ county on E coast of England
area 5,368 sq km/2,072sq mi
towns administrative headquarters Norwich; King's Lynn, and resorts Great Yarmouth, Cromer, and Hunstanton

features rivers Ouse, Yare, Bure, Waveney; the ◊Broads; Halvergate Marshes wildlife area; traditional reed thatching; Grime's Graves (Neolithic flint mines); shrine of Our Lady of Walsingham, a medieval and modern centre of pilgrimage; Blickling Hall (Jacobean); residence of Elizabeth II at Sandringham (built 1869–71)
products cereals, turnips, sugar beet; turkeys and geese; offshore natural gas
population (1986) 719,100
famous people Fanny Burney, John Sell Cotman, John Crome ('Old Crome'), Rider Haggard.

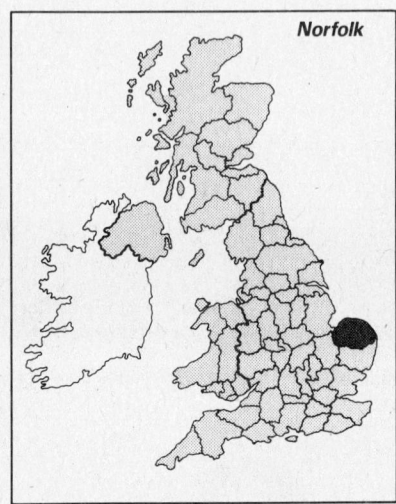

Norfolk

Norfolk /'nɔːfək/ seaport in Virginia, USA, headquarters of the US Atlantic fleet; population (1980) 267,000.

Norfolk /'nɔːfək/ Miles Fitzalan-Howard, 17th Duke of Norfolk 1915– . Earl Marshal of England, and premier duke and earl. As Earl Marshal, he is responsible for the organization of ceremonial on major state occasions. He succeeded his cousin Bernard Fitzalan-Howard, 16th Duke of Norfolk (1908–75), who organized the coronations of George VI and Elizabeth II.

Norfolk Island /'nɔːfək/ Pacific island territory of Australia, S of New Caledonia
area 34 sq km/13 sq mi
products citrus fruit, bananas; tourism is important
population (1982) 1,800
history reached by Cook in 1774, settled in 1856 by descendants of the mutineers of the *Bounty* (see ◊Bligh) from ◊Pitcairn Island; Australian territory from 1914, largely self-governing from 1979.

Norilsk /nə'rɪlsk/ world's most northerly industrial city (most of the USSR's nickel, cobalt, platinum; also selenium, tellurium, gold and silver), Siberia, USSR; population (1985) 180,000. The permafrost is 30 m/1,000 ft deep, and the winter temperature may be – 55°C.

Norman /'nɔːmən/ the ◊Norsemen to whom Normandy was granted by the king of France 911, and who adopted French language and culture. In the 11th–12th centuries they conquered England (under ◊William the Conqueror), parts of Wales and Ireland, S Italy,

Sicily, and Malta, settled in Scotland, and took a prominent part in the Crusades. They ceased to exist as a distinct people after the 13th century.

Norman /'nɔːmən/ Jessye 1945– . American soprano. Born in Augusta, Georgia, Jessye Norman made her operatic debut at the Deutsche Oper, Berlin, in 1969. She is noted for her interpretation of *Lieder*, as well as operatic roles, and for her powerful voice.

Norman American soprano Jessye Norman is noted for her powerful voice in opera and solo performances.

Norman /'nɔːmən/ Montagu, 1st Baron Norman 1871–1950. British banker. Governor of the Bank of England 1920–44, he handled German reparations after World War I, and by his advocacy of a return to the ◊gold standard in 1925 and other policies, was held by many to have contributed to the economic depression of the 1930s.

Norman architecture /'nɔːmən/ English term for ◊Romanesque, the style of architecture used in England from the time of Edward the Confessor until the end of the 12th century. Norman buildings are massive, using the semi-circular arch, buttresses are of slight projection, and vaults are barrel-roofed. Examples in England include the Keep of the Tower of London, and parts of the cathedrals of Chichester, Gloucester, and Ely.

Normandy /'nɔːməndi/ two regions of N France:
Haute-Normandie
capital Rouen
population (1984) 1,672,000
Basse-Normandie
capital Caen
population (1984) 1,361,000
towns Alençon, Bayeux, Dieppe, Deauville, Lisieux, Le Havre, Cherbourg
features the painter Monet's restored home and garden at Giverny; Mont St Michel; Château Miromesnil, birthplace of de Maupassant;

Victor Hugo's house at Villequier; the invasion beaches of World War II in 1944.

Norman French the form of French used by the Normans in Normandy from the 10th century, and by the Norman ruling class in England after the Conquest. Although generally replaced by English in the 14th century, it remained the language of the court until the 15th century, the official language of the law courts until the 17th century, and is still used in the Channel Islands. There is a considerable literature, including the 12th century chronicles of Gaimar and Wace, and the fables of ◊Marie de France.

Norris /'nɒrɪs/ Frank 1870–1902. American novelist, born in Chicago. He completed only two parts of a projected trilogy, the *Epic of Wheat: Octopus* 1901, dealing with the growing of wheat, and *The Pit* 1903, describing the gamble of the Chicago wheat exchange.

Norseman early inhabitant of Norway. The term Norsemen is also applied to Scandinavian ◊Vikings who during the 8th–11th centuries raided and settled in Britain, Ireland, France, Russia, Iceland, and Greenland. The Norse religion (banned in 1000) was recognized by the Icelandic government in 1973.

North /nɔːθ/ Frederick, 8th Lord North 1732–1792. British politician. He was prime minister in a government of Tories and 'king's friends' from 1770. His hard line against the American colonies was supported by George III, but in 1782 he was forced to resign by the failure of his policy. In 1783 he returned to office in a coalition with ◊Fox, and after its defeat retired from politics.

North The policies of Lord North, largely dictated by George III and an influential circle of 'king's friends', precipitated the American Revolution.

North /nɔːθ/ Thomas 1535–1601. English translator, whose version of ◊Plutarch's *Lives* 1579 was the source for Shakespeare's Roman plays.

Northallerton /nɔː'θælətən/ market town, administrative headquarters of N Yorkshire, England, with tanning and flour milling industries; population (1985) 13,800.

BC
c. 35000   American Indians entered N America from Asia.
9000   Marmes man, earliest human remains.
300   earliest Moundbuilder sites.
AD
c. 1000   Leif Ericsson traditionally reached N America.
12th–14th   height of the Moundbuilder and Pueblo cultures.
centuries
1492   Columbus first sighted land in the Caribbean.
1565   first Spanish settlements in Florida.
1607   first permanent English settlement, Jamestown, Virginia.

North America third largest of the continents (including Central America), and over twice the size of Europe
area 24,000,000 sq km/9,500,000 sq mi
largest cities (population over 1 million) Mexico City, New York, Chicago, Toronto, Los Angeles, Montreal, Guadalajara, Monterrey, Philadelphia, Houston, Guatemala City, Vancouver, Detroit
physical mountain belts to the E (Appalachians) and W (see ◊Cordilleras), the latter including the Rocky Mountains and the Sierra Madre; coastal plain on the Gulf of Mexico, into which the Mississippi river system drains from the central Great Plains; the St Lawrence and the Great Lakes form a rough crescent (with the Great Bear and Great Slave lakes, and lakes Athabasca and Winnipeg) around the exposed rock of the great Canadian/Laurentian Shield, into which Hudson Bay breaks from the N
features climatic range is wide from arctic in Alaska and N Canada (only above freezing Jun–Sept) to the tropical in Central America, and much of the W of USA is arid. There are also great extremes within the range, owing to the vast size of the land mass
exports the immensity of the US home market makes it less dependent on exports, and its industrial and technological strength automatically tend to exert a pull on the economies N and S of it. The continent is unique in being dominated in this way by a single power, which also exerts great influence over the general world economy
population (1981) 345 million; the aboriginal American Indian, Inuit, and Aleut peoples are now a minority within a population predominantly of European immigrant origin. Many Africans were brought in as part of the slave trade.
language predominantly English, Spanish, French
religion predominantly Christian, Jewish.

Northampton /nɔː'θæmptən/ town in Northamptonshire, England; population (1984) 163,000. Boots and shoes (of which there is a museum) are still made, but engineering has superseded them as the chief industry.

Northamptonshire /nɔː'θæmptənʃə/ county in central England
area 2,367 sq km/914 sq mi
towns administrative headquarters Northampton, Kettering

features river Nene; Canons Ashby, Tudor house, home of the Drydens for 400 years; churches with broached spires
products cereals, cattle
population (1986) 546,100
famous people John Dryden.

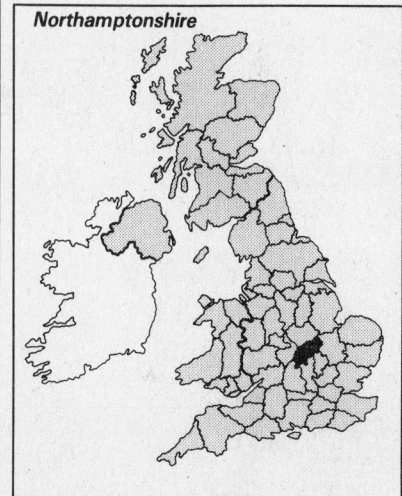

Northamptonshire

North Atlantic Drift the warm ocean ◊current in the N Atlantic Ocean, moving NE along the East coast of N America as the Gulf Stream and crossing the Atlantic Ocean to bathe the coasts of the British Isles and Scandinavia. It has mellowing effect on the climate of coastal Europe.

North Atlantic Treaty signed 4 Apr 1949 by Belgium, Canada, Denmark, France, Iceland, Italy, Luxembourg, Netherlands, Norway, Portugal, UK, USA; later accessions Greece, Turkey in 1952; West Germany in 1955; Spain in 1982. They agreed that 'an armed attack against one or more of them in Europe or N America shall be considered an attack against them all'.

North Atlantic Treaty Organization (NATO) association set up under the ◊North Atlantic Treaty 1949 to provide for the collective defence of the major W European and N American states against the perceived threat from the USSR. Its chief body is the Council of Foreign Ministers, and there is an international secretariat in Brussels, where there is also the

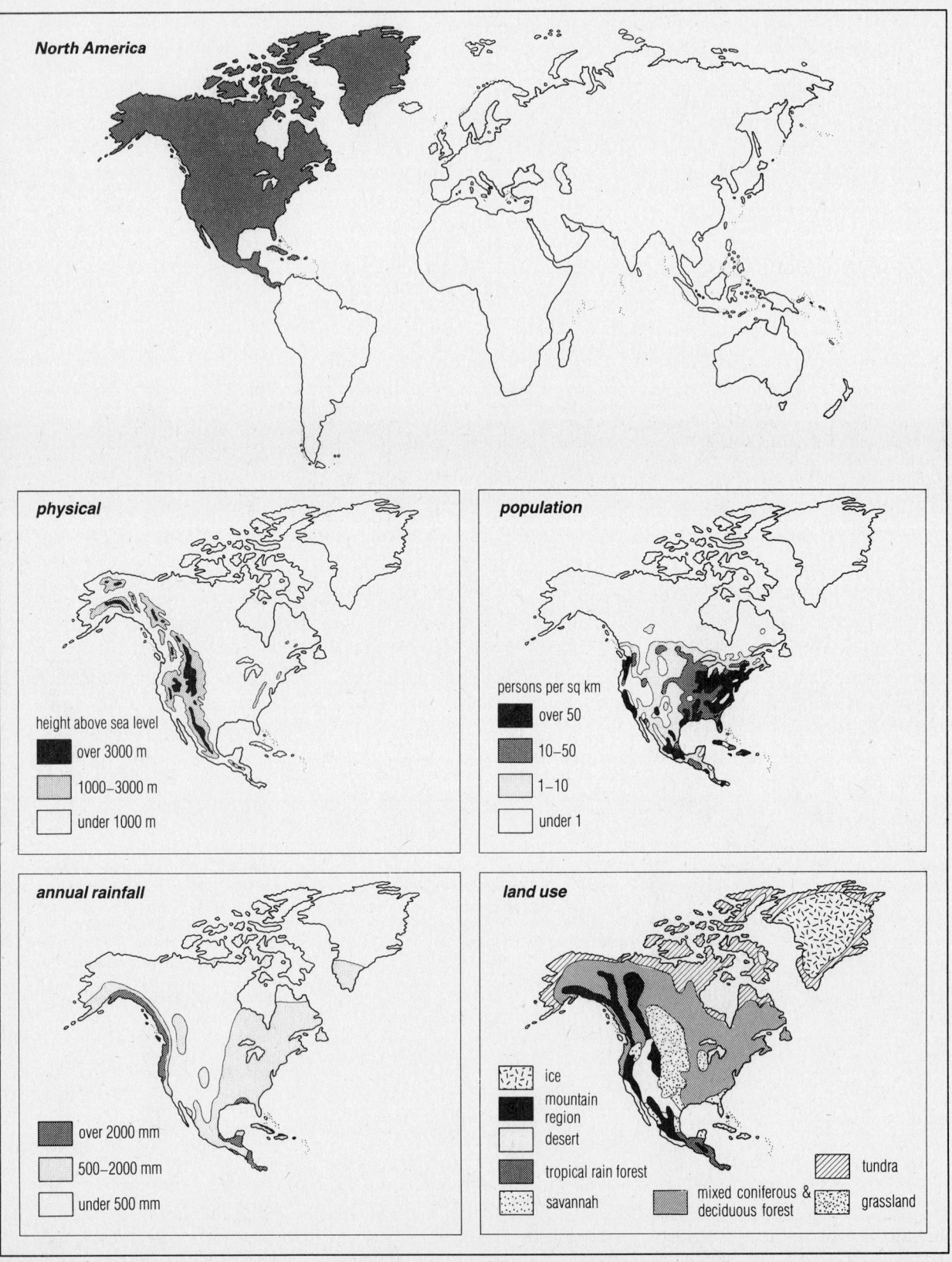

North America

physical

height above sea level

- over 3000 m
- 1000–3000 m
- under 1000 m

population

persons per sq km

- over 50
- 10–50
- 1–10
- under 1

annual rainfall

- over 2000 mm
- 500–2000 mm
- under 500 mm

land use

- ice
- mountain region
- desert
- tropical rain forest
- savannah
- mixed coniferous & deciduous forest
- tundra
- grassland

Military Committee consisting of the Chiefs of Staff. The military headquarters SHAPE (Supreme Headquarters Allied Powers, Europe) is at Chièvres, near Mons. Both the Supreme Allied Commanders (Europe and Atlantic) are American, but there is also an Allied Commander, Channel (a British admiral). In 1960 a permanent multinational *Allied Mobile Force* (AMF) was established to move immediately to any NATO country under threat of attack; headquarters ◊Heidelberg.

France withdrew from the organization (not the alliance) in 1966; Greece withdrew politically, but not militarily 1974. In 1980 Turkey was opposed to Greek re-entry because of differences over operational rights in the Aegean Sea. NATO has encountered numerous problems since its inception over such issues as the hegemonial position of the USA, the presence in Europe of US nuclear weapons, burden sharing, and standardization of weapons. See also ◊Warsaw Pact.

North Carolina /ˈnɔːθ ˌkærəˈlaɪnə/ state of the USA
area 136,523 sq km/52,712 sq mi
capital Raleigh
towns Charlotte, Greensboro, Winston-Salem
features Appalachian Mountains (including Blue Ridge and Great Smoky Mountains); site of Fort Raleigh on Roanoke Island (see under history below); Wright Brothers National Memorial at Kitty Hawk
products tobacco, maize, soybeans; livestock, poultry and dairy products; textiles and clothing, furniture, computers; mica, feldspar, bricks
population (1983) 6,082,000
famous people Billy Graham, O Henry
history Sir Walter ◊Raleigh sent out 108 colonists from Plymouth in 1585 under his cousin Sir Richard Grenville, who established the first English settlement in the New World on Roanoke Island; the survivors were taken home by Drake in 1586. Further attempts failed there, the settlers having disappeared without trace by 1590. The first permanent settlement in the state was made in 1663. It became one of the original Thirteen States in 1789.

Northcliffe /ˈnɔːθklɪf/ Alfred Charles William Harmsworth, 1st Viscount Northcliffe 1865–1922. British newspaper proprietor. Founding the *Daily Mail* 1896, he revolutionized popular journalism, and with the *Daily Mirror* 1903 originated the picture paper: in 1908 he also obtained control of *The Times*. His brother Harold Sidney Harmsworth, 1st Viscount Rothermere (1868–1940), was associated with him in many of his newspaper projects.

North Dakota /ˈnɔːθ dəˈkəʊtə/ prairie state of the USA; Sioux or Flickertail State
area 183,020 sq km/70,665 sq mi
capital Bismark
towns Fargo, Grand Forks
features fertile Red River Valley, Missouri Plateau; Bad Lands, so called because the pioneers had great difficulty in crossing them
products cereals, meat products; farm equipment
population (1984) 686,000
famous people Maxwell Anderson

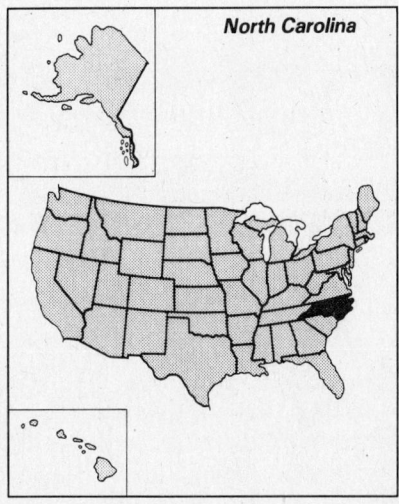

North Carolina

history acquired by the USA partly in the ◊Louisiana Purchase 1803, and partly by treaty with Britain in 1813; it became a state in 1889.

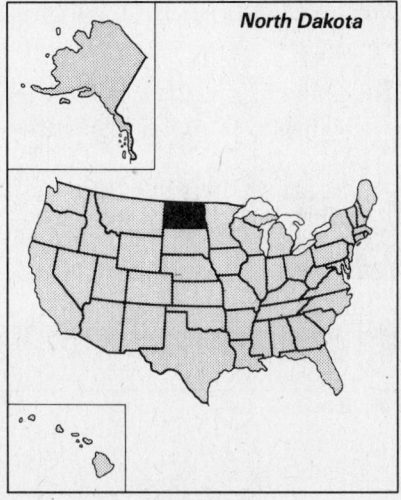

North Dakota

North-East Frontier Agency former name (until 1972) for ◊Arunachal Pradesh, India.

North-East India area of India (Meghalaya, Assam, Mizoram, Tripura, Manipur, and Nagaland, and the union territory of Arunachal Pradesh) linked with the rest of India only by a narrow corridor. There is opposition to immigration from Bangladesh and the rest of India, and demand for secession.

North-East Passage sea route from the N Atlantic, around Asia, to the N Pacific, pioneered by ◊Nordenskjöld 1878–79, and developed by the USSR in settling N Siberia from 1935. The USSR owns offshore islands, and claims it as an internal waterway; the USA claims that it is international.

Northern Areas districts N of Azad Kashmir, directly administered by Pakistan but not merged with it. India and Azad Kashmir each claim them as part of disputed Kashmir. They

include Baltistan, Gilgit and Skardu, and Hunza (an independent principality for 900 years until 1974).

Northern Rhodesia /ˈnɔːðən rəʊˈdiːʃə/ former name (until 1964) of ◊Zambia.

Northern Territory territory of Australia
area 1,356,165 sq km/523,620 sq mi
capital Darwin
towns chief port Darwin; Alice Springs
features mainly within the tropics, though with wide range of temperature; very low rainfall, but artesian bores are used; Macdonnell Ranges (Mt Zeil 1,510 m/4,955 ft); ◊Cocos and ◊Christmas Islands were included in the territory in 1984
exports beef cattle; prawns; bauxite (Gove), gold and copper (Tennant Creek), uranium (Ranger)
population (1984) 139,000 including Aborigines
government there is an administrator and legislative assembly, and the territory is also represented in the federal parliament
history originally part of New South Wales, it was annexed in 1863 to South Australia, but 1911–78 (when self-government was granted) was under the control of the Commonwealth of Australia government. Mineral discoveries on land occupied by Aborigines led to a royalty agreement 1979.

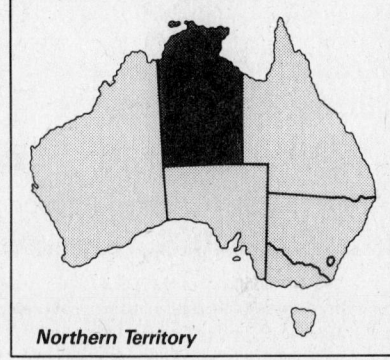

Northern Territory

North Korea see ◊Korea, North.

North Ossetian /ˈnɔːθ ɒˈsiːʃən/ area of the Caucasus, USSR; see also ◊Ossetia.

North Pole the north point of penetration of the earth's surface by the axis about which it revolves; see also ◊Poles and ◊Arctic.

North Rhine–Westphalia /ˈnɔːθ ˈraɪn westˈfeɪlɪə/ administrative *Land* of West Germany
area 34,150 sq km/13,110 sq mi
capital Düsseldorf
towns Cologne, Essen, Dortmund, Duisberg, Wuppertal
features valley of the Rhine; Ruhr industrial district
products iron and steel, coal and lignite, electrical goods, fertilizers, synthetic textiles
population (1984) 16,704,000
religion Roman Catholic 53 per cent, Protestant 42 per cent
history see ◊Westphalia.

North Sea sea to the E of Britain and bounded by the coasts of Belgium, the Netherlands, Germany, Denmark, and Norway; area 523,000 sq km/202,000 sq mi; average depth 55 m/180 ft, greatest depth 660 m/2165 ft. There are fisheries, among them Dogger Bank, and oil and gas.

North Sea The discovery of North Sea oil has provided the UK economy with a unexpected boost over the years. Fixed oil production platforms, comprising drilling towers, cranes, helipads, flares, communications equipment, and lifeboats, are used to bring oil to the surface.

North Uist /'juːɪst/ an island of the Outer ◊Hebrides, Scotland.

Northumberland /nɔːˈθʌmbələnd/ county in N England

area 5,032 sq km/1,942 sq mi

towns administrative headquarters Morpeth; Berwick-upon-Tweed, Hexham

features Cheviot Hills, rivers Tweed and upper Tyne of Northumberland National Park in the W; ◊Holy Island; ◊Farne Islands; part of Hadrian's Wall and Housestead's Fort; Alnwick and Bamburgh castles; Thomas ◊Bewick museum

products sheep

population (1986) 300,700

famous people Bobby Charlton.

Northumberland /nɔːˈθʌmbələnd/ John Dudley, Duke of Northumberland c. 1502–1553. English politician, son of the privy councillor Edmund Dudley (beheaded 1510), raised to a dukedom in 1551, and chief minister until Edward VI's death 1553. He then tried to place his daughter-in-law Lady Jane ◊Grey on the throne, and was executed on Mary's accession. His son was the influential Earl of Leicester.

Northumbria /nɔːˈθʌmbriə/ Anglo-Saxon kingdom which covered NE England and SE Scotland, comprising the 6th-century kingdoms

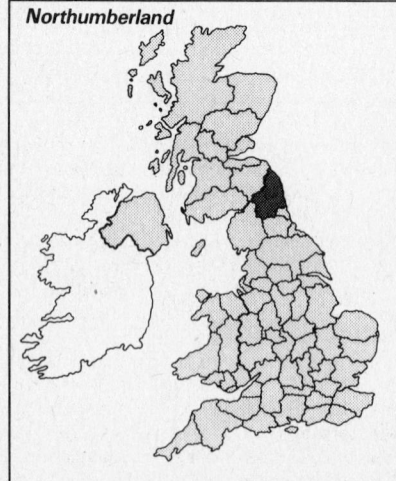

Northumberland

of Bernicia (Forth–Tees) and Deira (Tees–Humber), united in the 7th century. Influenced by Irish missionaries, it was a cultural

and religious centre until the 8th century with priests such as Bede, Cuthbert, and Wilfrid. It accepted the supremacy of Wessex in 827, and was conquered by the Danes in the later 9th century.

North-West Frontier Province province of Pakistan; capital Peshawar. In the 1980s it has had to accommodate a stream of refugees from neighbouring Afghanistan. It was a province of British India 1901–47. It includes the strategic Khyber Pass, the site of constant struggle between the British Raj and the ◊Pathan warriors.

North-West Passage Atlantic-Pacific sea route around the north of Canada. Early explorers included ◊Frobisher and ◊Franklin, whose failure to return in 1847 led to the organization of 39 expeditions in the next ten years. R McClune explored the passage 1850–53 though he did not cover the whole route by sea: ◊Amundsen was the first European to sail through. Canada, which owns offshore islands, claims it as an internal waterway; the USA insists that it is an international waterway, and to demonstrate its claim sent an icebreaker through without permission 1985.

Northwest Territories /'nɔːθwest 'terɪtəriz/ territory of Canada

area 3,379,689 sq km/1,304,903 sq mi

capital Yellowknife

physical extends to the North Pole, to Hudson's Bay in the E, and in the W to the edge of the Canadian Shield

features Mackenzie river; Great Slave Lake and Great Bear Lake; Dawson City; the Klondike region

products oil and natural gas, zinc, lead, gold, tungsten, silver

population (1984) 50,500, over 50 per cent native American peoples (Indian, Inuit)

history the area was the northern part of Rupert's Land, bought by the Canadian government from the Hudson's Bay Company in 1869. An Act of 1952 placed the Northwest Territories under a commissioner acting at Ottawa.

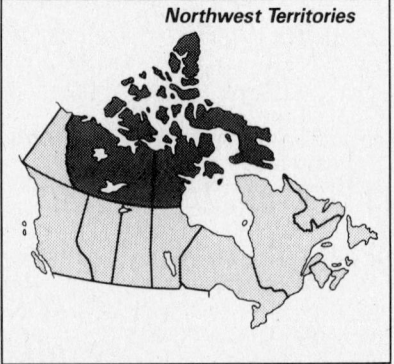

Northwest Territories

North Yorkshire /'jɔːkʃə/ county in NE England

area 8,309 sq km/3,207 sq mi

towns administrative headquarters Northallerton; York, and the resorts of Harrogate, Scarborough, and Whitby *features* England's largest county; including part of the Pennines, the Vale of York, and the Cleveland Hills and North Yorkshire Moors, which form a national park (within the park are Fylingdales radar station to give early warning of nuclear attack, and Rievaulx abbey); Yorkshire Dales National Park; rivers Derwent and Ouse; Fountains Abbey near Rippon; Castle Howard; York Minster

products cereals; wool and meat from sheep; dairy products; coal (Selby)

population (1986) 691,100

famous people Alcuin, W H Auden.

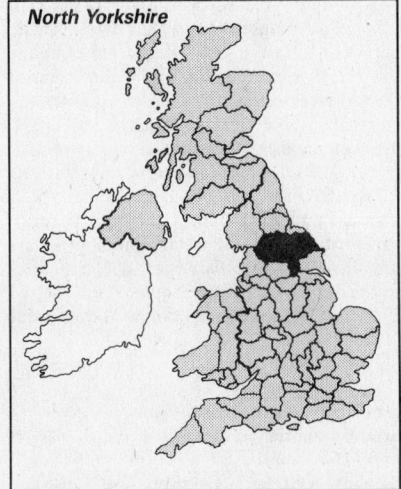

North Yorkshire

Norton /'nɔ:tn/ Caroline 1808–1877. British writer, granddaughter of R B ◊Sheridan. In 1836 her alcoholic husband the Hon George North (1800–75), falsely accused Lord Melbourne of seducing her, obtained custody of their children, and tried to obtain the profits from her books. Public reaction to this helped forward changes in the law of infant custody, and married women's property rights. Her works include *Undying One* 1830, and *Voice from the Factories* 1836, attacking child labour.

Norway /'nɔ:weɪ/ the world's largest passenger liner ever, measuring 316 m/1035 ft long and with a gross tonnage of over 70,200 tonnes. The *Norway* was launched originally as the *France* in 1979, and renamed in 1981 after purchase by Knut Kloster of Norway. It can carry 2,400 passengers.

Norway /'nɔ:weɪ/ country in NW Europe, on the Scandinavian peninsula, bounded E by Sweden and NE by Finland and the USSR.

government Norway's constitution dates from 1814. The hereditary monarch is the formal head of state and the legislature consists of a single-chamber parliament, the *Storting*. The monarch appoints a prime minister and state council on the basis of support in the *Storting*, to which they are all responsible.

The *Storting* has 157 members, elected for a four-year term by universal suffrage through a system of proportional representation. Once elected, it divides itself into two parts, a quarter of the members being chosen to form an upper

house, the *Lagting*, and the remainder a lower house, the *Odelsting*. All legislation must be first introduced in the *Odelsting* and then passed to the *Lagting* for approval, amendment, or rejection. Once a bill has had parliamentary approval it must receive the royal assent.

history Norway was originally inhabited by Lapps and other nomads, and gradually invaded by ◊Goths. It was under local chieftains until unified by Harald Fairhair (reigned 872–933) as a feudal country. Norway's ◊Vikings raided and settled in many parts of Europe in the 8th–11th centuries. Christianity was introduced by ◊Olaf II in the 11th century; he was defeated 1030 by rebel chiefs backed by ◊Canute, but his son Magnus I regained the throne 1035. Haakon IV (1217–63) established the authority of the crown over the nobles and the church and made the monarchy hereditary.

◊Denmark and Norway were united by marriage in 1380, and in 1397 Norway, Denmark, and Sweden became united under one sovereign. Sweden broke away 1523 but Norway remained under Danish rule until 1814, when it was ceded to Sweden. Norway rebelled, Sweden invaded, and a compromise was reached whereby Norway kept its own parliament but was united with Sweden under a common monarch.

Conflict between the Norwegian parliament and the Swedish crown continued until 1905, when the parliament declared Norway completely independent. Prince Carl of Denmark was elected king as Haakon VII. He ruled for 52 years until his death in 1957. His son ◊Olav V is the reigning monarch.

The experience of German occupation 1940–45 persuaded the Norwegians to abandon their traditional neutral stance and join NATO 1949, the Nordic Council 1952, and the European Free Trade Area (EFTA) 1960. Norway was accepted into membership of the European Community in 1972 but a referendum held that year rejected the proposal and the application was withdrawn. Its exploitation of North Sea oil and gas resources have given it a higher income per head of population than most of its European neighbours, and it has succeeded in maintaining good relations with the USSR without damaging its commitments in the West.

Norway has enjoyed stability under a series of coalition governments. The four most significant political parties are the Labour Party, led by the prime minister (71 seats in the 1985 elections), the Conservative Party (50 seats), the Christian Democratic Party (16 seats), and the Centre Party (12 seats).

Norwegian literature Norway and Iceland originated the tradition of the ◊saga; in modern times, a revival of the literary tradition came through the work of the great folklorists and under the influence of vernacular writers such as Aasmund Vinje (1818–70) and Arne Garborg (1851–1924) who adopted Ivar ◊Aasen's *Landsmål*. The great figure of the later 19th century was Henrik ◊Ibsen, and the novelists Jonas ◊Lie and Alexander Kielland (1849–1906). To the earlier 20th century belong the novelists Knut Hamsun (1859–1952) and Sigrid ◊Undset. Later prominent figures are

Helge Krog (1889–1962), dramatist and critic; the poets Arnulf Overland (1889–1968) and Olaf Bull (1887–1933); the novelists Cora Sandel (1880–1974), and Sigurd Hoel (1890–1960); and the poet, playwright, and novelist Nordahl Grieg (1902–1943).

Norwegian Sea /nɔ:'wiːdʒən 'siː/ part of the ◊Arctic Ocean.

Norwich /'nɒrɪdʒ/ industrial city (shoes, clothing, chemicals, confectionery, engineering, printing) in Norfolk, England; population (1981) 122,500. It has a university, a cathedral (founded 1096) and Norman castle, with a collection of paintings by the Norwich school (◊Cotman, ◊Crome); 15th-century Guildhall, medieval churches, Tudor houses, Georgian Assembly House. The Sainsbury Laboratory 1987, in association with the John Innes Institute, was founded to study the molecular foundations of pathogenicity.

Norwich /'nɒrɪdʒ/ 1st Viscount Norwich title of (Alfred) Duff ◊Cooper.

nose in humans, the upper orifice of the respiratory tract; the organ of the sense of smell. It is divided down the middle by a septum of ◊cartilage. The ◊nostrils or outer portion contain plates of cartilage which can be moved by muscles and have a growth of stiff hairs at the margin to prevent foreign bodies from entering. The whole nasal cavity is lined with ◊mucous membrane which warms and moistens the air and ejects dirt.

Nostradamus /ˌnɒstrə'dɑːməs/ 1503–1566. Latinized name of Michel de Notredame, French physician and astrologer. He was consulted by Catherine de' Medici and was physician-in-ordinary to Charles IX. His book of prophesies in rhyme, *Centuries*, written in 1555, has had a number of interpretations.

nostril in vertebrates, the opening of the nasal cavity, in which cells sensitive to smell are located. In humans, and most other mammals, the nostrils are located on a ◊nose.

notation in music, the use of symbols to represent individual sounds (such as the notes of the chromatic scale) so that they can be accurately interpreted and reproduced.

In dance, notation is the recording of dances by symbols. There are several dance notation systems, prominent among which is ◊labanotation.

notochord the stiff but flexible rod that lies between the gut and nerve cord of all embryonic and larval chordates, including the ◊vertebrates. It forms the supporting structure of the adult amphioxus (small eel-like creature), but in vertebrates it is replaced by the vertebral column, or ◊spine, during embryonic development.

Nott /nɒt/ John 1932– . British Conservative politician, minister for defence 1981–83 during the ◊Falklands campaign.

Nottingham /'nɒtɪŋəm/ industrial city (engineering, coalmining, textiles, pharmaceuticals, tobacco, lace, electronics) and administrative headquarters of Nottinghamshire, England; university 1881; Playhouse (opened 1963) and the recently refurbished Theatre Royal. Population (1981)

Norway

KINGDOM OF (*Kongeriget Norge*)

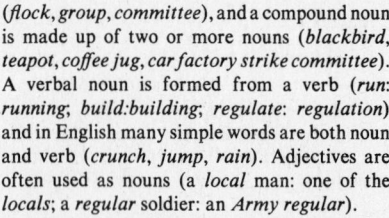

AREA 324,220 sq km/125,065 sq mi
CAPITAL Oslo
TOWNS Bergen, Trondheim
PHYSICAL mountainous; forests cover 25%; extends N of Arctic Circle
TERRITORIES dependencies in the Arctic (Svalbard and Jan Mayen) and in the Antarctic (Bouvet and Peter I Island, and Queen Maud Land)
FEATURES beautiful fjords, including Hardanger and Sogne, the longest 185 km/115 mi and deepest 1,245 m/4,080 ft; glaciers in N; midnight sun and northern lights; great resources of hydroelectric power
HEAD OF STATE Olav V from 1957
HEAD OF GOVERNMENT Gro Harlem Brundtland from 1986
GOVERNMENT parliamentary democracy
EXPORTS petrochemicals from North Sea oil and gas; paper, wood pulp, furniture; iron ore and other minerals; high-tech goods, for example gas turbines, TV sets; sports goods; fish
CURRENCY krone (10.93 = £1 Sept 1987)
POPULATION 4,152,000 (1985); annual growth rate 0.3%
LANGUAGE Riksmal (formal Dano-Norwegian) and Landsmal (based on the local dialects of Norway)
RELIGION Evangelical Lutheran (endowed by state)
LITERACY 100% (1984)

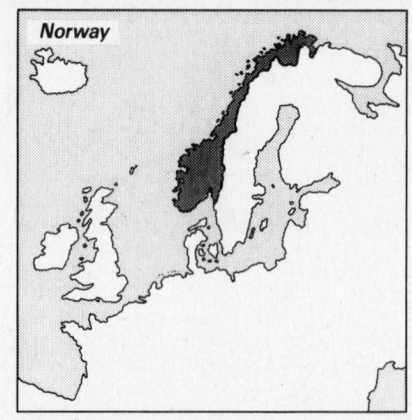

GNP $56 bn (1982); $12,432 per head of population
CHRONOLOGY
1814 Independent from Denmark.
1905 Links with Sweden ended.
1940–45 Occupied by Germany.
1949 Joined NATO.
1952 Joined Nordic Council.
1957 King Haakon VII succeeded by his son, Olav V.
1960 Joined EFTA.
1972 Accepted into membership of the European Community but application withdrawn after a referendum.

217,080. Nearby are Newstead Abbey, home of Byron, and D H Lawrence's home at Eastwood.

Nottinghamshire /ˈnɒtɪŋəmʃə/ county in central England
area 2,164 sq km/836 sq mi
towns administrative headquarters Nottingham; Mansfield, Worksop
features river Trent; the remaining areas of Sherwood Forest (home of ◊Robin Hood), formerly a royal hunting ground, are included in the 'Dukeries'
products cereals, cattle, sheep; light engineering, footwear; ironstone and oil
population (1986) 1,005,900
famous people D H Lawrence, Alan Sillitoe.

Nouakchott /ˌnuːækˈʃɒt/ capital of Mauritania; population (1976) 135,000.

noun the grammatical ◊part of speech that names (or stands for) such classes of words as persons (*child*, *John*), animals (*cat*, *Rover*), places (*hill*, *London*), things (*hat*, *thunder*, *Fascism*), qualities (*love*, *yellowness*), actions (*arrest*, *jumping*, *improvement*, *amelioration*), ideas and abstractions (*idea*, *abstraction*, *reality*, *Communism*, *Roman Catholicism*), and so on. A common noun does not begin with a capital letter (*child*, *cat*), while a proper noun does, because it is the name of a particular person, animal, or place (*John*, *Rover*, *London*). A concrete noun refers to things which can be sensed (*dog*, *box*), while an abstract noun relates

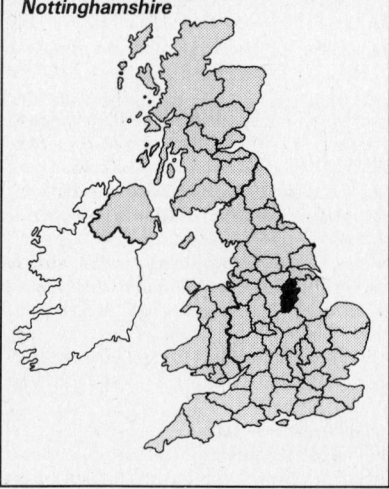

to generalizations 'abstracted' from life as we observe it (*love*, *condition*, *illness*). A countable noun can have a plural form (*book*: *books*), while an uncountable noun or mass noun cannot (*dough*). Many English nouns can be used both countably and uncountably (*wine*: 'Have some wine; it's one of our best wines'). A collective noun is singular in form but refers to a group

(*flock*, *group*, *committee*), and a compound noun is made up of two or more nouns (*blackbird*, *teapot*, *coffee jug*, *car factory strike committee*). A verbal noun is formed from a verb (*run*: *running*; *build*:*building*; *regulate*: *regulation*) and in English many simple words are both noun and verb (*crunch*, *jump*, *rain*). Adjectives are often used as nouns (a *local* man: one of the *locals*; a *regular* soldier: an *Army regular*).

nova in astronomy, a faint ◊star that suddenly erupts in brightness, becoming visible in binoculars or to the naked eye. The name comes from the Latin meaning 'new', although novae are not new stars at all. They occur in close ◊double-star systems, where gas from one star flows on to a neighbouring ◊white dwarf (small, hot star in its last stages). The gas ignites, and is thrown off in an explosion. During the outburst, the star increases in brightness by 10,000 times or more. Unlike a ◊supernova, the star is not disrupted by the outburst. After a few weeks or months the star subsides to its previous state.

Novalis /nəʊˈvɑːlɪs/ pen name of Freiherr von Hardenburg 1772–1801. Pioneer German Romantic poet, best known for his *Hymnen an die Nacht/Hymns to the Night* 1800, prompted by the death of his fiancée Sophie von Kühn.

Nova Lisboa /ˈnəʊvə lɪzˈbəʊə/ former name (1928–73) for ◊Huambo, in Angola.

Nova Scotia /ˈnəʊvə ˈskəʊʃə/ province of E Canada
area 54,558 sq km/21,065 sq mi
capital and chief port Halifax
towns Dartmouth
features Alexander Graham Bell Museum, Fortress Louisbourg; Strait of Canso Superport is the largest deepwater harbour on the Atlantic coast of the continent
products coal, gypsum; dairy products, poultry, fruit; forest products; fish products, including scallop and lobster
population (1985) 881,300
history Nova Scotia was visited by Cabot in 1497. A French settlement was established 1604, but expelled 1613 by English colonists from Virginia. The name of the colony was changed from Acadia to Nova Scotia 1621. England and France contended for possession of the territory until in 1713 Nova Scotia was ceded to Britain; Cape Breton Island remained French until 1763. Nova Scotia was one of the four original provinces of the dominion of ◊Canada.

Novaya Zemlya /ˈnəʊvɪə ˈzemlɪə/ Arctic island group off the north east of the USSR; population, a few Samoyed. It is rich in birds, seals, and walrus.

novel an extended fictitious prose narrative, often including some sense of the psychological development of the central characters and of their relationship with a broader world. The European novel is often said to have originated in Greece in the 2nd century BC. Best-known of the Greek examples is the *Daphnis and Chloë* of Longus, and almost the only surviving Latin example which could be called a novel is the *Golden Ass* of Apuleius, based on a Greek model. There is a similar, but until the 19th century independent, tradition of prose narrative including psychological development in the Far

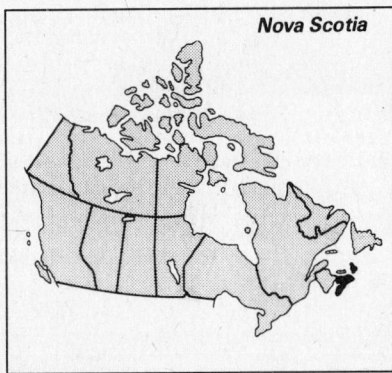

Nova Scotia

East, notably in Japan, with *The Tale of Genji* by the woman writer Murasaki Shikibu (978–c. 1015). But the modern novel took its name and inspiration from the Italian *novella*, the short tale of varied character which became popular in the late 13th century. Probably the best known of these Italian writers were Boccaccio and Bandello, whose works were translated into English in such collections as Painter's *Palace of Pleasure* 1566–67, and inspired the Elizabethan novelists, including Lyly, Sidney, Greene, Nash, and Lodge. In Spain, Cervantes's *Don Quixote* 1604 contributed to the development of the novel through its translation into other European languages , but the 17th century was largely dominated by the French romances of La Calprenède and Mlle de Scudéry, although Congreve and Aphra Behn continued the English tradition.

In the 18th century the realistic novel was established in England in the work of Defoe, Richardson, Fielding, Sterne, and Smollett. Walpole, and later Mary Shelley, developed the Gothic novel; in the early 19th century Sir Walter Scott developed the historical novel, and Jane Austen perfected the novel of manners. Novelists of the Victorian Age in Britain are Dickens, Thackeray, the Brontës, George Eliot, Trollope, and Stevenson. The 19th century was also a great period for the novel in Europe, with Hugo, Balzac, the two Dumas, George Sand, and Zola in France; Goethe and Jean Paul in Germany; in Russia with Gogol, Turgenev, Dostoievsky and Tolstoy; and in the USA with Cooper, Melville, Hawthorne, and Twain.

The transition period from Victorian times to the 20th century in England includes Meredith, Butler, Hardy, Gissing, Henry James, Kipling, Conrad, and George Moore, Wells, Bennett, and Galsworthy. Slightly later are W Somerset Maugham, E M Forster, James Joyce, D H Lawrence, Ivy Compton-Burnett, and Virginia Woolf – the last three being particularly influential in the development of novel technique. Among those who began writing in the 1920s are J B Priestley, Richard Hughes, Aldous Huxley, Christopher Isherwood, Graham Greene, V S Pritchett, and Evelyn Waugh; and the women writers Elizabeth Bowen, Rose Macaulay, and Rosamund Lehmann. The 1930s produced Nigel Balchin, Joyce Cary, Lawrence Durrell, and

George Orwell, and more recent British writers include Anthony Powell, John Fowles, Kingsley Amis, Anthony Burgess, Iris Murdoch, Angela Carter, Doris Lessing, Salman Rushdie, and Martin Amis. 20th-century European novelists include (German) Lion Feuchtwanger, Thomas Mann, Franz Kafka, Stefan Zweig, Heinrich Böll, and Gunter Grass; (French) André Gide, Marcel Proust, Jules Romains, François Mauriac, and Alain Robbe-Grillet; (Italian) Gabriele d'Annunzio, Alberto Moravia, Italo Calvino, and Primo Levi; (Russian) Maxim Gorky, Mikhail Sholokhov, Aleksei Tolstoi, Boris Pasternak, and Alexander Solzhenitsyn; (Spanish) Arturo Baréa and Ramón Pérez de Ayala. In the Americas contemporary novelists include (Latin-American) Mario Vargas Llosa and Gabriel García Márquez; (Canadian) Robertson Davies and Margaret Atwood; and (US) Ernest Hemingway, William Faulkner, Bernard Malamud, Eudora Welty, Vladimir Nabokov, and Saul Bellow.

As the main form of narrative fiction in the 20th century, the novel is frequently classified according to genres and sub-genres such as the ◊historical novel, ◊detective fiction, ◊fantasy, and ◊science fiction.

Novello /nə'veləʊ/ Ivor 1893–1951. Stage-name of British composer and actor manager I(vor) N(ovello) Davies. Born in Cardiff, son of the singer Clara Novello Davies, he made his name as a writer of popular songs, such as 'Keep the Home Fires Burning', in World War I, but is best remembered for the musical play spectaculars in which he often appeared as the romantic lead, including *Glamorous Night* 1925, *The Dancing Years* 1939, *Perchance to Dream* 1945–47, *King's Rhapsody* 1949 and *Gay's the Word* 1951.

November criminals name given by right-wing nationalists in post-1918 Germany to the socialist politicians who had taken over the government after the abdication of Kaiser Wilhelm II and had signed the armistice with the Western Allies in November 1918.

Noverre /nɒ'veə/ Jean-Georges 1727–1810. French choreographer, writer and ballet reformer. In his efforts to promote ◊ballet *d'action* and simple, free movement in dance, he elevated ballet to an art form, and is often considered the creator of modern classical ballet. *Les Petits Riens* 1778 was one of his most successful works.

Novgorod /'nɒvgərɒd/ industrial (chemicals, engineering, clothing, brewing) city in the NW USSR; population (1985) 220,000. It was the original capital of the Russian state, founded there at the invitation of the people of the city by the Viking (Varangian) chieftain Rurik in 862, and was an important and prosperous city from the 12th century until destroyed by ◊Ivan the Terrible in 1570.

Novi Sad /'nɒvi 'saːd/ industrial and commercial (pottery and cotton) city, capital of the autonomous province of Vojvodina, Yugoslavia; population (1981) 257,500.

Novocaine trade name for *procaine hydrochloride*, a synthetic drug widely used as a local anaesthetic. It is as effective as cocaine

Novgorod Inside the Novgorod kremlin, showing the theatre, the monument to the thousandth anniversary of the foundation of the Russian state (1862), and the cathedral of St Sophia (11th century).

when injected, but only one-third as toxic and not habit-forming. It is, however, not nearly so effective when used as a surface anaesthetic. It is always used with adrenaline.

Novokuznetsk /ˌnɒvəkʊz'netsk/ industrial city (steel, aluminium, chemicals) in the Kuzbas, S central USSR; population (1985) 577,000. It was called Stalinsk 1932–61.

Novorossiisk /ˌnɒvərɒ'siːsk/ USSR Black Sea port and industrial (cement, metallurgy, food processing) city; population (1985) 175,000.

Novosibirsk /ˌnɒvəsɪ'bɪəsk/ industrial (engineering, textiles, food processing) city in W Siberia, USSR; population (1985) 1,393,000. Winter lasts eight months here. At Akademgorodok 'Science City', population 25,000, advanced research is carried on into Siberia's local problems.

Noyes /nɔɪz/ Alfred 1880–1958. British poet. He is best remembered for poems about the sea, and anthology favourites, 'The Highwayman' and 'Go down to Kew in lilac-time...'.

NTP (*n*ormal *t*emperature and *p*ressure) a former name for ◊STP (*s*tandard *t*emperature and *p*ressure).

Nubia /'njuːbiə/ former African country now divided between Egypt and Sudan; it gives its name to the *Nubian Desert* S of Lake Nasser. Ancient Egypt, which was briefly ruled by Nubian kings in the 8th–7th century BC, knew the N as Wawat and the S as Kush, with the dividing line roughly at Dongola. Egyptian building work in the area included ◊Abu Simbel, Philae, and a defensive chain of forts which established the lines of development of medieval fortification. Nubia's capital c. 600 BC–350 AD was Meroe, near Khartoum. About 250–550 AD most of Nubia was occupied by the *x-group people*, of whom little is known; their royal mound tombs (mistaken by earlier investigations for natural mounds created by wind erosion) were excavated by W B ◊Emery, and many horses and attendants were found to have been slaughtered to accompany the richly jewelled dead.

nuclear arms verification the process of checking the number and types of nuclear weapons held by a country (see also ◊disarmament), the chief means are:

reconnaissance satellites which detect submarines or weapon silos, using angled cameras to give 3-D pictures of installations; penetrating camouflage by means of scanners; and partially seeing through cloud and darkness by infra-red devices

telemetry (radio transmission of instrument readings) *interception* to get information on performance of weapons under test, and *radar tracking* of missiles in flight

seismic monitoring of underground tests, in the same way as with earthquakes; this is not accurate and on-site inspection is needed. Tests in the atmosphere, space, or the oceans are forbidden, and the ban is accepted because explosions are not only dangerous to all, but immediately detectable.

nuclear energy energy from the inner core or ◊nucleus of the ◊atom, as opposed to energy released in chemical processes, which is derived from the electrons surrounding the nucleus.

nuclear fission, as in an atom bomb, is achieved by allowing a neutron to strike the nucleus of an atom of uranium-235, which then splits apart to relase perhaps two to three other neutrons. If the material is pure uranium-235, a chain reaction is set up when these neutrons in turn strike other nuclei. This happens with great rapidity, resulting in the tremendous burst of energy we associate with the atom bomb. However, the process can be controlled by absorbing excess neutrons in 'control rods' (which may be made of steel alloyed with boron), and slowing down the speed of those neutrons allowed to act. This is what is done inside a nuclear power plant.

nuclear fusion the process (release of thermo-nuclear energy by the conversion of hydrogen nuclei to helium nuclei) which occurs in the hydrogen bomb and, as a continuing reaction, in the sun and other stars. It avoids the loss of much of the energy produced which occurs in the original atom bomb, so that it is correspondingly more powerful. Attempts to harness it for commercial power production have so far not succeeded.

nuclear reactors there are various types of (fission) reactor in commercial use. In a gas-cooled reactor, a circulating gas under pressure (such as carbon dioxide) removes heat from the core of the reactor, which usually contains natural uranium and has neutron-absorbing control rods made of boron. The Calder Hall reactor is of this type. An advanced gas-cooled reactor (AGR) generally has enriched uranium oxide as its fuel. A water-cooled reactor, such as the steam-generating heavy-water reactor at Winfrith, Dorset, has water circulating through the hot core. The water is converted to steam which drives turbo-alternators for generating electricity. In a pressurized water reactor (PWR) the coolant consists of a sealed system of pressurized water (deuterium oxide), which heats water to form steam in heat exchangers in

an external circuit. The spent fuel from either type of reactor contains some plutonium, which can be extracted and used as a fuel for the so-called fast breeder reactor (such as the one at Dounreay, Scotland). This produces more plutonium than it consumes by converting uranium placed in a blanket round the main core. The usual coolant is liquid sodium, a substance that is difficult to handle. A major danger with any type of reactor is the possibility of ◊meltdown, which can result in the release of radioactive material. Problems can also arise over the reprocessing of nuclear fuel and disposal of nuclear waste.

nuclear accidents the most serious have been: *Apr 1986* at Chernobyl (USSR): a leak from a non-pressurized boiling-water reactor, one of the largest in the Soviet Union, caused by overheating. The resulting clouds of radioactive isotopes were traced as far away as Sweden, and hundreds of people and thousands of kilometres of land were contaminated. *1979* at ◊Three Mile Island, Harrisburg, USA: a PWR leaked radioactive matter, a leak caused by a combination of mechanical and electrical failure, as well as operator error. In this type of reactor the heat formed by the fission of the uranium is carried away a sealed and pressurized loop of irradiated water (chiefly ◊'heavy' water) to steam generators. *1957* at Windscale (now ◊Sellafield), England: fire destroyed the core of a reactor, releasing large quantities of lethal radioactive fumes into the atmosphere.

atom bomb the original weapon relied on use of a chemical explosion to trigger a 'chain reaction'. The first test explosion was at Alamogordo, New Mexico, 16 Jul 1945; the first use in war was 6 Aug over ◊Hiroshima and three days later at ◊Nagasaki.

hydrogen bomb a much more powerful weapon, relies on the release of thermo-nuclear energy by the condensation of hydrogen nuclei to helium nuclei (as happens in the sun). The first detonation on earth was at Eniwetok Atoll 1952 by the USA, through the triggering of tritium (hydrogen isotope of atomic weight 3.0170) by an ordinary atom bomb.

neutron bomb or enhanced radiation weapon (ERW) is a very small hydrogen bomb which has relatively high radiation, but relatively low blast, designed to kill (in up to six days) by a brief neutron radiation which leaves buildings and weaponry intact.

nuclear methods of attack now include aircraft bombs, rocket-propelled ◊missiles with nuclear warheads (long or short range, surface-to-surface, and surface to air), depth charges, and high-powered landmines ('atomic demolition munitions' to blast craters in the path of an advancing enemy army). The major subjects of Soviet–US negotiation are:

intercontinental ballistic missiles (ICBMs) which have from 1968 been equipped with clusters of warheads (which can be directed to individual targets) and are known as multiple independently targetable reentry vehicles

nuclear energy British Nuclear Fuels' Sellafield site in Cumbria, showing part of the Calder Hall plant which houses the plutonium and electricity production reactors and two of its four cooling towers.

nuclear physics the study of the properties of the nucleus of the ◊atom.

nuclear warfare war involving the use of nuclear weapons. Nuclear weapons derive their explosive force from ◊nuclear energy. Research was carried on in Britain from 1940, but transferred to USA after America entered the war (Manhattan Project, directed by ◊Oppenheimer at ◊Los Alamos).

(MIRVs). The latest US design is the MX (Peacekeeper) with up to ten warheads in each of about 100 missiles to be permanently placed in land silos. Britain retained an independent nuclear deterrent in 1980 by agreeing to buy submarine-launched Trident missiles from the USA: each warhead has eight independently targetable re-entry vehicles (each nuclear-armed); range about 6400 km/4000 mi to eight

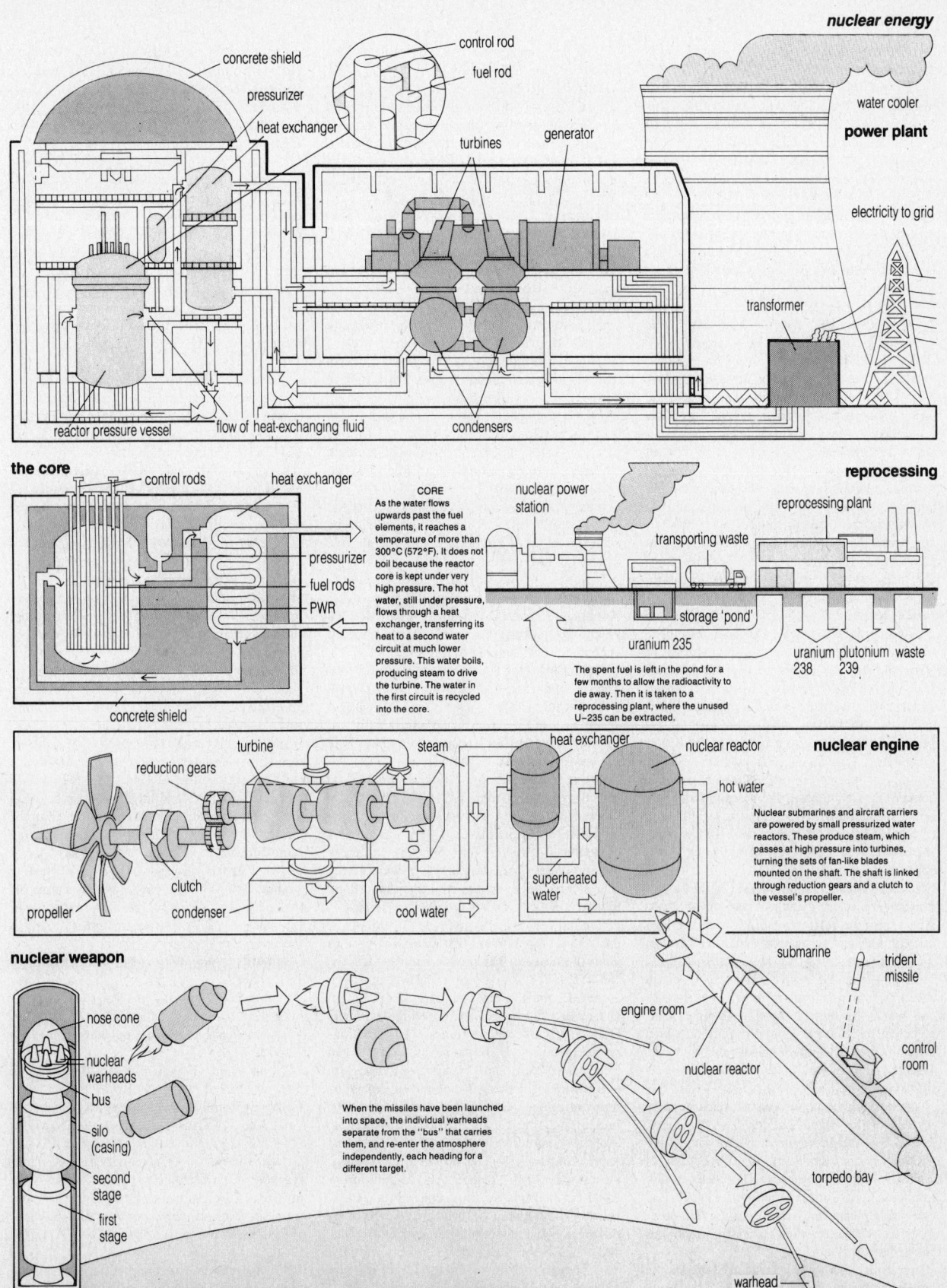

nuclear energy

- concrete shield
- pressurizer
- heat exchanger
- control rod
- fuel rod
- turbines
- generator
- water cooler

power plant

- electricity to grid
- transformer
- reactor pressure vessel
- flow of heat-exchanging fluid
- condensers

the core

- control rods
- heat exchanger
- pressurizer
- fuel rods
- PWR
- concrete shield

CORE
As the water flows upwards past the fuel elements, it reaches a temperature of more than 300°C (572°F). It does not boil because the reactor core is kept under very high pressure. The hot water, still under pressure, flows through a heat exchanger, transferring its heat to a second water circuit at much lower pressure. This water boils, producing steam to drive the turbine. The water in the first circuit is recycled into the core.

reprocessing

- nuclear power station
- transporting waste
- reprocessing plant
- storage 'pond'
- uranium 235
- uranium 238
- plutonium 239
- waste

The spent fuel is left in the pond for a few months to allow the radioactivity to die away. Then it is taken to a reprocessing plant, where the unused U–235 can be extracted.

nuclear engine

- turbine
- steam
- heat exchanger
- nuclear reactor
- reduction gears
- hot water
- propeller
- clutch
- condenser
- cool water
- superheated water

Nuclear submarines and aircraft carriers are powered by small pressurized water reactors. These produce steam, which passes at high pressure into turbines, turning the sets of fan-like blades mounted on the shaft. The shaft is linked through reduction gears and a clutch to the vessel's propeller.

nuclear weapon

- nose cone
- nuclear warheads
- bus
- silo (casing)
- second stage
- first stage

When the missiles have been launched into space, the individual warheads separate from the "bus" that carries them, and re-enter the atmosphere independently, each heading for a different target.

- submarine
- trident missile
- engine room
- control room
- nuclear reactor
- torpedo bay
- warhead

separate targets within about 240 km/150 mi of the central aiming point.

cruise missiles developed 1976, which are nuclear-armed pilotless planes 6 m/19 ft long, with a range of some 3000 km/2000 mi, launched by land, sea or air, and computer-programmed to change direction to confuse defences; they have already been deployed among NATO allies in Europe (see ▷Newbury).

methods of defence include: *anti-ballistic missile* (ABM) earth-based systems, with two types of missile, one short range with high acceleration, and one comparatively long-range for interception above the atmosphere

Strategic Defence Initiative (announced by the USA 1983 to be operative from 2000, and popularly known as the 'Star Wars' programme). 'Directed energy weapons' firing laser beams would be mounted on space-based battle stations, and by burning holes in incoming missiles would either collapse them or detonate their fuel tanks

nuclear waste is produced in three forms:
gas still in small enough quantity to be released into the atmosphere;
solid irradiated fuel element cans and other equipment. When of low activity, this is packaged for sea disposal, but this is controversial. High activity waste may be combustible (plutonium being recovered from the incinerator), or may be buried, the latter being also controversial;
liquid high activity liquid wastes pose the greatest problems of all. Storage has been proposed in salt mines, granite formations, or 'clay basins'; or on or under the seabed. Controversy is greatest on this form of waste, because no container can be guaranteed against decay, volcanic action, and so on, for 100,000 years. The most hopeful proposed method is by vitrification into solid glass cylinders, which would be placed in titanium-cobalt alloy containers and deposited on dead planets in space. Beneath the sea the containers would start to corrode after 1,000 years, and the cylinders themselves would dissolve within the next 1,000 years.

nuclear winter contamination of the earth's atmosphere after a nuclear war or accident. Apart from the destruction of life and cities in a nuclear war, and subsequent radiation hazards, it has been calculated that the atmosphere would be so contaminated by dust, smoke, soot and ash resulting from firestorms in target areas that the sun would be blotted out for about a year, sufficient to eradicate most plant life on which other life depends, and the cold would be intense. Insects and grass would have the best prospects of survival.

nucleic acids complex organic acids made up of long chains of nucleotides. The two types, known as ▷DNA (deoxyribonucleic acid) and ▷RNA (ribonucleic acid), form the basis of heredity in living organisms. The neucleotides are made up of a sugar, a phosphate group, and one of four purine or pyrimidine bases. The order of the bases along the nucleic acid strand contains the genetic 'message'.

nucleolus in biology, a structure found in the nucleus of ▷eukaryotic cells. It produces the

▷RNA that makes up the ▷ribosomes, from instructions in the ▷DNA.

nucleus in physics, the positively charged central part of an ▷atom. Some of the most complex natural nuclei, for example those of uranium and radium, are radioactive, that is, they spontaneously disintegrate with the emission of a fragment containing 2 neutrons and 2 protons, a alpha particle. If a large number of atoms of say uranium–238 are considered, about half of them will have disintegrated after about 4,000 million years; so the half-life of uranium-238 is 4,000 million years. See also ▷molecule, and ▷periodic table of elements.

nucleus in biology, the central part of a ▷eukaryotic cell, containing the ▷chromosomes.

Nuffield /'nʌfiːld/ William Richard Morris, Viscount Nuffield 1877–1963. British manufacturer and philanthropist. Starting with a small cycle-repairing business, he designed (in 1910) a car to run at low cost for people with ordinary incomes, and built up Morris Motors Ltd at Cowley, Oxford. He endowed Nuffield College, Oxford, in 1937 and the Nuffield Foundation in 1943.

nugget a piece of gold found as a lump of the ▷native ore. Nuggets occur in ▷alluvial deposits where river-borne particles of the metal have adhered to one another.

Nujoma /nuː'dʒəʊmə/ Sam 1929– . Namibian politician, exiled in 1960, after founding ▷SWAPO (South West African People's Organization) in 1959, and controller of guerrillas from Angolan bases.

Nukua'lofa /ˌnuːkuə'laʊfə/ capital and port of Tonga on Tongatapu; population (1984) 21,716.

Nullarbor Plain /'nʌləbɔː/ (Latin *nullus arbor*, 'no tree') arid coastal plateau area divided between Western and Southern Australia; there is a network of caves beneath it.

Numa Pompilius /'njuːmə pɒm'pɪliəs/ legendary king of Rome c. 716–c. 679 BC, who succeeded Romulus, and was credited with the introduction of religious rites.

numbat Australian banded anteater *Myrmecobius fasciatus*. It is brown, boldly striped with white on the back and has a long tubular tongue to gather termites and ants.

number a symbol used in counting or measuring. In mathematics, there are various kinds of numbers. The ordinary numerals, 0, 1, 2, 3, 4, 5, 6, 7, 8, 9, give a counting system which, in the ▷decimal system, continues 10, 11, 12, 13, and so on. These are whole decimal numbers (also called cardinals or integers), with fractions represented as ¼, ½, ¾ and so on, or as decimal fractions (0.25, 0.5, 0.75 and so on). They are also ▷rational numbers. Numbers that cannot be represented as fractions and require symbols, such as →2, π and e are irrational: they can be expressed numerically only as the (inexact) approximations 1.414, 3.142 and 2.728 (to three places of decimals) respectively. In addition, π and e are examples of transcendental numbers, because they (unlike →2) cannot be derived by solving a ▷polynomial equation (an equation with one ▷variable quantity) with rational ▷coefficients (multiplying factors). Rational and irrational numbers together make up the ▷real

number system. ▷Complex numbers include both real and ▷imaginary numbers. They take the general form $a + bi$, where $i = \text{—}\cdot1$ (that is, $i^2 = -1$) and a is the real part and b is the imaginary part. Number systems can also be devised with bases other than 10. For example, numbers to base two (binary numbers), using only the 0 and 1, produce a series which starts 0, 1, 10, 11, 100, 101, 110, 111. They are commonly used in digital computers to represent the two-state 'on' or 'off' pulses of electricity. The ancient Egyptians, Greeks, Romans, and Babylonians all evolved number systems although none had a zero, which was introduced from India by way of Arab mathematicians in about the 6th century AD to complete the ▷decimal system. ▷Binary numbers were developed by Gottfried Leibniz in the late 17th century.

Numidia /njuː'mɪdiə/ Roman N African territory ('nomads land'), modern E Algeria.

numismatics the study of coins and medals. The invention of coinage is attributed to the Chinese in the 2nd millennium BC, the earliest types being small-scale bronze reproductions of barter objects, such as knives and spades. In the W coinage of stamped, guaranteed weight originated with the Lydians of Asia Minor (early 7th century BC) who used electrum, a local natural mixture of gold and silver: the first to issue gold and silver coins was Croesus of Lydia in the 6th century BC. In modern times the right to make and issue coins is a state monopoly and the great majority are tokens, in that their face value is greater than that of the metal of which they consist. A milled edge, originally used on gold and silver coins to avoid fraudulent 'clipping' of the edges, is retained in some modern token coinage. See also ▷money.

nun (Latin *nonna*, an elderly woman). A woman belonging to a religious order devoted to the Christian service of God under the vows of poverty, chastity, and obedience, and living under a particular rule. It is possible that the institution of communities for nuns preceded the establishment of monasteries, and the majority of the male orders have their female counterparts. The convent is ruled by a superior (often elected), who is subject to the authority of the bishop of the diocese or sometimes directly to the Pope. See also ▷monasticism.

nunatak a mountain peak protruding through an ice sheet.

Nuneaton /nʌn'iːtn/ market town making industrial ceramics, tiles and bricks, in Warwickshire, England; population (1984) 72,000.

Nunn /nʌn/ Trevor 1940– . British stage director, linked with the Royal Shakespeare Company from 1968, who received a Tony award (with John Caird) for his production of *Nicholas Nickleby* 1982, and for *Les Miserables* 1987.

Nuremberg /'njʊərəmbɜːg/ (German *Nürnberg*). Industrial city (electrical and other machinery, precision instruments, textiles, and toys, for which an annual fair is held) in Bavaria, West Germany; population (1984) 471,500. Created an imperial city 1219, it has an 11th–16th century fortress and many medieval buildings, including the home of Hans ▷Sachs, where the ◊Meistersingers met. The artist Dürer was born here. From 1933 the ◊Nuremberg rallies were held here: and in 1945 the ◊Nuremberg Trials.

Nuremberg rallies name given to the annual meetings (1933–38) of the Nazi Party. They were characterized by extensive marches in party formations and mass rallies addressed by Nazi leaders such as ◊Hitler and ◊Goebbels.

Nuremberg Trials the trials of the 24 chief ◊Nazi war criminals Nov 1945–Oct 1946. The International Military Tribunal consisted of four judges and four prosecutors; one of each from UK, USA, USSR and France. The main charges in the indictment were: (1) conspiracy to wage wars of aggression; (2) crimes against peace; (3) war crimes, for example, murder and ill-treatment of civilians and prisoners of war and killing of hostages; (4) crimes against humanity, for example, mass-murder of the Jews and other peoples, and murder and ill-treatment of political opponents. An appendix accused the German Cabinet, General Staff, and High Command, Nazi leadership corps, ◊SS, ◊SA, and ◊Gestapo of criminal responsibility. Of the accused, Krupp was too ill to be tried; Ley committed suicide during the trial, and ◊Bormann, who had fled, was sentenced to death in his absence. Fritsche, Schacht, and ◊Papen were acquitted. The other 18 were found guilty on one or more counts. ◊Hess, Funk and ◊Raeder were sentenced to life imprisonment, Shirach and Speer to 20 years, Neurath to 15 years, and Doenitz to 10 years. The remaining 11 men, sentenced to death by hanging, were ◊Göring (who committed suicide before he could be executed), ◊Ribbentrop, ◊Kaltenbrunner, ◊Rosenberg, Frank, Frick, Sauckel, Seyss-Inquart, Streicher, ◊Keitel, and ◊Jodl. The leadership corps, SS, and Gestapo were declared criminal organizations.

Nureyev /nju'reɪef/ Rudolf 1938– . Russian dancer and choreographer. He defected to the West in 1961 and was Margot ◊Fonteyn's principal partner.

nursery rhyme jingle current among children. Usually limited to a couplet or quatrain with strongly marked rhythm and rhymes, nursery rhymes have often been handed down by oral tradition in forms differing from those in adult collections. Some of the oldest nursery rhymes are connected with a traditional tune and accompanied the ancient ring games, for example, 'Here we go round the mulberry bush', which were part of the May Day festivities.

nursing supervision of health as well as care of the sick, very young, very old and the disabled. In ancient times very limited care was associated with some temples, and in Christian times became associated with the religious orders until the Reformation brought it into secular hands in Protestant countries. Organized training first originated in 1836 in Germany, and was developed in Britain by the work of Florence ◊Nightingale who during the Crimean War established standards of scientific, humanitarian care in military hospitals. Many varied qualifications are now available, standards being maintained by the National Boards (England, Scotland, Wales and N Ireland) for Nursing,

Midwifery and Health Visiting, and the Royal College of Nursing (1916) is the professional body. In the US, although registration is the responsibility of individual states, an almost uniform standard has been established by the National League for Nursing (1952).

Nusa Tenggara /'nuːsə teŋˈgɑːrə/ volcanic archipelago in Indonesia, also known as the *Lesser Sunda Islands*, including ◊Bali, ◊Lombok, and ◊Timor; area 73,144 sq km/28,241 sq mi. The islands form two provinces of Indonesia: *Nusu Tenggara Barat*, population (1980) 2,724,500; and *Nusu Tenggara Timur*, population (1980) 2,737,000.

nut a dry, single-seeded ◊fruit that does not split open to release the seed. It is formed from more than one carpel, but only one seed becomes fully formed, the remainder aborting. The wall of the fruit, the ◊pericarp, becomes hard and woody, forming the outer shell. Examples of nuts are the acorn, hazelnut and sweet chestnut. The term is also popularly used to describe various hard-shelled fruits and seeds, including almonds and walnuts, which are really the stones of ◊drupes, and Brazil nuts and shelled peanuts, which are both seeds.

nut and bolt a common method of fastening pieces of metal together. They came into use at the turn of the 19th century, following Henry Maudslay's invention of a precision screw-cutting ◊lathe a few years earlier.

nutation in astronomy, a slight 'nodding' of the Earth in space, caused by the varying gravitational pulls of the ◊Sun and ◊Moon. Nutation changes the angle of the Earth's axial tilt (average 23.5°) by about 9 seconds of arc.

nutation in biology, the spiral movement exhibited by the tips of certain stems during growth: it enables a climbing plant to find a suitable support. The direction of the movements is usually characteristic for particular species. Nutation sometimes also occurs in tendrils and flower stalks.

nutcracker bird *Nucifraga caryocatactes* of the crow family found in mountainous forest areas in Asia and Europe. About 33 cm/1.1 ft long, it has a speckled plumage and powerful beak. It feeds particularly on conifer seeds.

nuthatch European bird *Sitta europaea* about the size of a sparrow, having a blue-grey back and buff breast. It is a climber and feeds chiefly upon nuts. The nest is placed in a hole in a tree, and five to eight white eggs with reddish-brown spots are laid in early summer.

nutmeg kernel of the seed of the evergreen tree *Myristica fragrans*, native to the Moluccas. Both the nutmeg and its secondary covering known as mace are used as a spice in cookery.

nutrition the science of food, and its effect on human life and health (for example, the diseases caused by lack of vitamins and protein in the Third World and those caused by high cholesterol and sugar content in the diet of wealthy countries). It also deals with animals, notably the food requirements of poultry and livestock reared for human consumption.

Nuuk /nuːk/ Greenlandic for ◊Godthaab, capital of Greenland.

nyala antelope *Tragelaphus angasi* found in

SE Africa. About 1 m/3 ft at the shoulder, it is greyish-brown with thin vertical white stripes. Males have horns up to 80 cm/2.6 ft long. Nyala live in thick bush.

Nyasa /niˈæsə/ another name for Lake ◊Malawi.

Nyasaland /niˈæsəlænd/ former name (until 1964) for ◊Malawi.

Nyerere /njəˈreəri/ Julius Kambarage 1922– . Tanzanian politician. A Christian and dedicated socialist, he became a schoolmaster until devoting himself in 1954 to the formation of the Tanganyika African National Union and subsequent campaigning for independence. He was prime minister of Tanganyika 1961–62, president of the newly formed Tanganyika Republic 1964–85, president of Tanzania 1964–85, and head of the Organization of African Unity 1984.

Nyerere President of Tanzania from 1964 to 1985, Dr Julius Nyerere founded the Tanganyika African National Union in 1954, and believed Tanzanian economic development should be based on self-help.

nylon group of synthetic fibre-forming plastics, which are similar in chemical structure to proteins and were developed in the USA by W H ◊Carothers and his associates. Nylon is used in the manufacture of toilet articles, textiles, medical sutures, and so on. Nylon fibres are stronger and more elastic than silk, and relatively insensitive to moisture and mildew. Nylon is particularly suitable for hosiery and woven goods, simulating other materials such as silks and furs; it is also used in carpets.

nymph in Greek mythology, a guardian spirit of nature; hamadryads or dryads guarded trees; naiads, springs and pools; oreads, hills and rocks; nereids, the sea.

nymph in entomology, the immature form of insects which do not have a pupal stage, for example, grasshoppers and dragonflies. Nymphs generally resemble the adult (unlike ◊larvae), but do not possess fully formed reproductive organs or wings.

O 15th letter of the Roman alphabet, whose form was derived from the Semitic alphabet. In modern English it represents a wide range of sounds, from the diphthong ō (*so*) to the open sounds in *or*, and *on*, and the oo-sound in *wolf*.

Oahu /əʊˈɑːhuː/ island of Hawaii, USA, in the N Pacific
area 1,525 sq km/589 sq mi
towns state capital Honolulu
physical formed by two extinct volcanoes
features Waikiki beach; Pearl Harbor naval base
products sugar, pineapples; tourism is important
population (1980) 762,000.

oak genus of trees and shrubs *Quercus* in the beech family Fagaceae. Widely distributed in temperate zones, over 300 species are known. They are valuable for their timber, the wood being durable and straight grained, but *oak wilt*, the result of a symbiotic partnership between a beetle and a fungus, resembles Dutch ◊elm disease and is equally virulent. The English oak *Quercus robur*, also found in Europe, grows to 36 m/120 ft and girth of 15 m/50 ft. Other European varieties are the evergreen oak *Quercus ilex*, the Turkey oak *Quercus cerris*, and the cork oak *Quercus suber*, of the W Mediterranean region; valuable American timber oaks are the white oak *Quercus alba* and the evergreen live oak *Quercus virginiana*. Their fruits are called acorns.

Oakley /ˈəʊkli/ Annie (Phoebe Annie Oakley Mozee) 1860–1926. American sharpshooter, member of Buffalo Bill's Wild West Show, noted for her expert gun shooting.

Oak Ridge /ˈəʊk ˈrɪdʒ/ town in Tennessee, USA, noted for the Oak Ridge National Laboratory 1943 which manufactures ◊plutonium for nuclear weapons; population (1970) 28,300.

Oaks horse-race, run at ◊Epsom racecourse, England, by fillies of three years old, usually on the Friday of Derby Week.

oarfish oceanic fish *Regalecus glesne*, also called *ribbon-fish*, with greatly elongated body which is flattened from side to side. It can grow to at least 7 m/23 ft.

oarweed name for the large brown seaweeds (algae) found on the lower shore and below, also known as *kelps* or *tangles*, in particular *Laminaria digitata*. This species has fronds 1 to 2 m/3 to 6ft long. A branched holdfast attaches it to a rock, there is a thick stalk, then the frond divides into a flat 'fingers'.

OAS abbreviation for ◊Organization of American States.

oasis an area of land made fertile by the presence of water in an otherwise arid region. The occurrence of oases dictates the distribution of plants, animals, and people in the desert regions of the world.

Oastler /ˈəʊstlə/ Richard 1789–1861. British social reformer, born in Leeds. He opposed child labour and the ◊Poor Law of 1834, winning the nickname of 'the Factory King', and was largely responsible for securing the Factory Act of 1833 and the Ten Hours Act of 1847.

Oates /əʊts/ Joyce Carol 1938– . American author. Her novels, often tinged with surrealism and violence, include *A Garden of Earthly Delights* 1967 and *A Bloodsmoor Romance* 1982.

Oates /əʊts/ Laurence Edward Grace 1880–1912. British Antarctic explorer, who accompanied ◊Scott on his second expedition to the South Pole. On the return journey, suffering from frostbite, he went out alone into the blizzard to die rather than delay the others.

Oates /əʊts/ Titus 1649–1705. British conspirator. A Jesuit priest, he announced he had discovered a 'popish plot' to murder Charles II and re-establish Catholicism. Although this story was almost entirely false, many innocent Roman Catholics were executed during 1678–80 on Oates's evidence. In 1685 he was flogged, pilloried, and imprisoned for perjury. He was pardoned and granted a pension after the revolution of 1688.

oath a solemn promise to tell the truth or perform some duty, combined with an appeal to a deity or something held sacred. In English courts witnesses normally swear to tell the truth holding a ◊New Testament in their right hand; in the USA witnesses raise their right hand in taking the oath. People who object to the taking of oaths, such as ◊Quakers and atheists, give a solemn promise to tell the truth. A Jew swears holding

Oates The fictitious 'popish plot' concocted by Titus Oates was supposed to involve the murder of the king, the burning of London, and slaughter of Protestants. Oates was later flogged, pilloried and imprisoned for perjury, but many Roman Catholics had lost their lives on his evidence.

the Pentateuch, with his head covered. Muslims and Hindus swear by their respective sacred books; a Chinese witness breaks a saucer before giving evidence.

oats genus of plants *Avena*, a type of grass; an important cereal food. The plant has long, narrow leaves, and a stiff straw stem; the panicles of flowers, and later of grain, hang downwards. The cultivated oat *Avena sativa* is produced for human food and for feeding horses and domestic animals and birds.

OAU abbreviation for ◊Organization of African Unity.

Ob /ɒb/ river in Asiatic USSR, flowing 3,380 km/2,100 mi from the Altai mountains through the W Siberian Plain to the Gulf of Ob in the Arctic Ocean.

Oban /'əubən/ seaport and resort in W Scotland, population (1981) 8,000.

OBE Order of the British Empire, a British order of knighthood. See also ◊medal.

Obeid, El /'əubeɪd/ see ◊El Obeid, city in Sudan.

Oberammergau /ˌəubər'æməgau/ village in Bavaria, West Germany, famed for the performance of a Passion play, performed every ten years (except during the world wars) since 1634 to commemorate the ending of the plague.

Oberhausen /'əubə,hauzən/ industrial city in the Ruhr valley, North Rhine-Westphalia, West Germany; population (1984) 224,000.

Oberon /'əubərɒn/ king of the elves or fairies, and, according to a 13th-century French romance *Huon of Bordeaux*, an illegitimate son of Julius Caesar. Shakespeare adopted him for *A Midsummer Night's Dream*

obesity condition of being overweight (generally, 20% or more above the desirable weight for your sex and height). Obesity increases susceptibility to disease and strains the vital organs, and lessens life expectancy; it is remedied by healthy diet and exercise.

obi a form of witchcraft practised in the West Indies. It combines elements of Christianity and African religion such as snake-worship.

objectivity in science, the belief that scientific method, properly understood and applied, can in principle avoid the influence of cultural and social values so as to build up a picture of a reality independent of the observer. Improved techniques and mechanical devices, which apparently improve the reliability of measurements, might seem to support this view; however the realization that observations of sub-atomic particles actually influence their behaviour has critically undermined the view that objectivity is possible in science (see ◊uncertainty principle).

oboe a musical instrument of the ◊woodwind family. Played vertically, it is a wooden tube with a bell, is double-reeded, and has a yearning, poignant tone. The range is almost three octaves. There are oboe concertos by ◊Vivaldi, ◊Albinoni, Richard ◊Strauss, and others.

Obote /əu'bəuti/ (Apollo) Milton 1924– . Ugandan politician who led the independence movement from 1961. He became prime minister 1962, and was president 1966–71 and 1980–85, being overthrown by ◊Amin and ◊Okello.

Obraztsov /ˌɒbrɒst'sɒf/ Sergei 1901– . Russian puppeteer. Born in Moscow, where he runs the State Central Puppet Theatre, the world's largest puppet theatre (staff 300), he has a repertoire built up since 1923.

Obrenovich /ɒ'brenəvɪtʃ/ name of a Serbian dynasty which ruled 1816–42 and 1859–1903. The dynasty engaged in a feud with the rival house of Karageorgevich, which obtained the throne by the murder of the last Obrenovich in 1903.

observation in science, the perception of a phenomenon – examining the Moon through a telescope, watching mice to discover their mating habits, or seeing how a plant grows. Traditionally observation was seen as entirely separate from theory, free from preconceptions and therefore important to the belief in ◊objectivity. However, as the examples show, observations are ordered according to a pre-existing theory; for instance, one cannot observe mating behaviour without having decided what mating behaviour might look like. In addition many observations actually affect the behaviour of the observed (for instance, of mating mice). The discovery that sub-atomic particles are affected by observation lends further support to the belief that science actively constructs a world view that is based only partly on external reality.

observatory a site or facility for observation of natural phenomena, especially astronomical. The earliest recorded observatory was at Alexandria, built by Ptolemy Soter, c. 300 BC. The erection of observatories was revived in W Asia c. 1000 AD, and extended to Europe. The one built on Hveen island, Denmark, in 1576, for Tycho ◊Brahe, was elaborate, but survived only to 1597. It was followed by those at Paris 1667, Greenwich 1675, and Kew 1769. Among the most famous modern observatories are the Hale at Mount Palomar, California; Kitt Peak in Arizona; La Palma in the Canary Islands; and Mount Semirodniki in the Caucasus, which have the most powerful optical ◊telescopes covering the sky from the northern hemisphere. Famous ◊radio astronomy observatories include ◊Jodrell Bank, the Mullard at Cambridge, England, ◊Arecibo in Puerto Rico, Effelsberg in W Germany, and ◊Parkes in Australia. Until recently the skies of the southern hemisphere were comparatively neglected, but in the 1970s important optical telescopes were established at Cerro Tololo, Chile; La Silla, Chile; and Siding Spring, Australia. Observatories can now also be set up in orbit, above the Earth's atmosphere, as satellites, in space stations, and in the ◊Space Shuttle.

obsession repetitive unwanted thought that is often recognized by the sufferer as being irrational, but which nevertheless causes distress. It can be associated with a compulsion where the individual feels an irresistible urge to carry out a repetitive series of actions. For example, a person excessively troubled by fears of contamination by dirt or disease may engage in continuous hand-washing.

obsidian a glassy volcanic rock, chemically similar to ◊granite, but formed by cooling rapidly on the Earth's surface at low pressure. The glassy texture is the result of this rapid cooling, which inhibited the growth of crystals. Obsidian was greatly valued by early peoples for making sharp-edged tools.

O'Casey /əu'keɪsi/ Sean 1884–1964. Irish dramatist. Born in Dublin, he worked as a labourer in early life, and was largely self-educated. His first plays, *The Shadow of a Gunman* 1922, and *Juno and the Paycock* 1925, created a sensation by their realistic picture of Dublin slum life during the 'troubles'; they were followed by *The Plough and the Stars* 1926, an unromantic depiction of the Easter Rebellion, which led to riots when first produced. All three plays are tragi-comedies, blending realism with symbolism and the vernacular with a poetic diction. His later plays include *The Silver Tassie* 1929, *Within the Gates* 1934, *The Star Turns Red* 1940, *Red Roses for Me* 1943, *Oak Leaves and Lavender* 1946 and *The Drums of Father Ned* 1960.

Occam /'ɒkəm/ or Ockham, William of c. 1300–1349. English philosopher, known as the Invincible Doctor. Born in Ockham, Surrey, he became a Franciscan monk, defended the doctrine of evangelical poverty against Pope John XXII, and was imprisoned at Avignon on charges of heresy in 1328. He escaped to Munich, where he died. In philosophy, he revived the fundamentals of Nominalism. The principles of reducing assumptions to the absolute minimum is known as 'Occam's Razor'.

Occitanie /ˌɒksɪtæ'niː/ area of S France; see ◊Languedoc.

occultation in astronomy, the obscuring of a star by the Moon or a ◊planet. Occultations are used to track slight changes in the Moon's orbit and they can provide information about the structure of objects in space, such as radio sources, as the Moon passes in front of them. The exact shapes and sizes of planets and ◊asteroids can be found when they occult stars. The rings of ◊Uranus were discovered when that planet occulted a star in 1977.

occupational psychology the study of human behaviour at work. It includes dealing with problems in organizations, advising on management difficulties, and investigating the relationship between humans and machines (as in the design of aircraft controls). Another important area is the use of ◊psychometric assessment to assist in selection of personnel.

ocean great mass of salt water. There are strictly three oceans – ◊Atlantic, ◊Indian, and ◊Pacific – to which the Arctic is usually added.
area approximately 70 per cent of the total surface area of the Earth: 363,000,000 sq km/140,000,000 sq mi
depth (average) 3,660 m/12,000 ft, but shallow ledges 180 m/600 ft run out from the continents, and the continental slope reaches down to the abyssal zone, the largest area, at 1,800–5,500m/6,000–18,000 ft. Only a small area lies deeper, the deepest recorded being 11,000 m/36,200 ft (by the *Vityaz* , USSR) in the Mariana Trench in the W Pacific 1957
features deep trenches (especially off E and SE Asia, and western S America), volcanic belts (especially in the W Pacific and E Indian Ocean), and ocean ridges (in the mid-Atlantic, E Pacific, and Indian Ocean)
temperature varies on the surface with latitude (-2° to +29°); decreases rapidly to 370 m/1,200 ft, then more slowly to 2,200 m/7,200 ft; and hardly at all beyond that
water contents salinity averages about 3 per cent; minerals commercially extracted include bromine, magnesium, potassium, salt; those potentially recoverable include aluminium, calcium, copper, gold, manganese, silver.

oceanarium large display tank in which aquatic animals and plants live together much as they would in their natural environment. First created by the explorer and naturalist W Douglas Burden in 1938 in Florida, USA.

oceanarium A grouper being hand fed, while dolphins hover in the background. Aquatic animals and plants live together in an oceanarium much as they would in the ocean itself.

Oceania /ˌəʊʃiˈɑːniə/ the islands of the S Pacific (◊Micronesia, ◊Melanesia, ◊Polynesia). The term is sometimes taken to include ◊Australasia and the ◊Malay archipelago, in which case it is considered as one of the seven continents.

Ocean Island /ˈəʊʃən/ another name for ◊Banaba, island in Kiribati.

ocean ridge topographical feature of the seabed indicating the presence of a constructive plate margin (see ◊plate tectonics). It can rise many thousands of metres above the surrounding abyssal plain. Ocean ridges usually have a ◊rift valley along their crests, indicating where the flanks are being pulled apart by the growth of the lithospheric plates beneath. The crests are usually free of sediment; increasing depths of sediment are found with increasing distance down the flanks. A curved ocean ridge is formed by several straight sections, each section being slightly offset along ◊faults, for example the ◊Mid-Atlantic Ridge.

ocean trench topographical feature of the seabed indicating the presence of a destructive plate margin (see ◊plate tectonics). The subduction or dragging downwards of one lithospheric plate beneath another means that the bed of the ocean is pulled down. Ocean trenches are found around the edge of the Pacific Ocean and the NE Indian Ocean; minor ones occur in the Caribbean and near the Falkland Islands. Ocean trenches represent the deepest parts of the ocean floor, the deepest being the ◊Mariana Trench which has a depth of 11,000 m/36,200 ft.

Oceanus /əʊˈsɪənəs/ in Greek mythology, the god (one of the ◊Titans) of a river supposed to encircle the earth. He was the progenitor of other river gods, and the nymphs of the seas and rivers.

ocelot wild ◊cat of Central and South America, about 1 m/3 ft long plus 45 cm/1.5 ft tail, with a pale yellowish coat marked with longitudinal stripes and blotches.

O'Connell /əʊˈkɒnl/ Daniel 1775–1847. Irish politician, called 'the Liberator'. Although ineligible as a Roman Catholic to take his seat, he was elected MP for County Clare in 1828, and so forced the government to grant Catholic emancipation. In Parliament he cooperated with the Whigs in the hope of obtaining concessions until 1841, when he launched his campaign for repeal of the union. His reserved and vacillating leadership and conservative outlook on social questions alienated his most active supporters, who broke away and formed the 'Young Ireland' movement.

O'Connor /əʊˈkɒnə/ Feargus 1794–1855. Irish parliamentary follower of ◊O'Connell. He sat in parliament 1832–35 and as editor of the *Northern Star* became the most influential figure of the Chartist movement (see ◊Chartism).

OCR (**optical character recognition**) the technology for transforming written material directly into computer-readable codes. OCR typically involves reflecting a scanning light beam from the text onto photoreceptors which convert it into electrical signals. Once, OCR required specially designed characters such as the OCRA-B lettering which appears on cheques, but current devices will recognize most standard typefaces.

Octans ◊constellation containing the southern celestial pole. It represents the octant, a navigational instrument that was a forerunner of the sextant.

Octavian /ɒkˈteɪviən/ original name of ◊Augustus, the first Roman emperor.

October Revolution the second Russian revolution of 1917 which brought Lenin and the Bolsheviks to power after a *coup d'état*.

Octobrists a group of Russian liberal constitutional politicians who accepted the reforming October Manifesto instituted by Tsar Nicholas II after the 1905 Revolution and rejected more radical reforms.

octopus type of ◊cephalopod having a round or oval body, and eight arms with rows of suckers on each. Occurring in all temperate and tropical seas, where they feed on crabs and other small animals, they can vary their coloration according to their background and may either swim with their arms or proceed through a type of jet propulsion by means of their funnel. The common octopus *Octopus vulgaris*, relished as a delicacy in S Europe, may reach 2 m/6 ft and is sometimes found off Britain. Generally speaking the perils of octopus attack are exaggerated, but off the Pacific coast the giant *Octopus apollyon* may span more than 8 m/26 ft.

ode lyric poem of complex form and charged emotion, originally chanted in ancient Greece to a musical accompaniment. Exponents include Sappho, Pindar, Horace and Catullus, and among British poets: Spenser, Milton, Dryden, Gray, Collins, Coleridge, Wordsworth, Shelley, Keats, Tennyson and Swinburne.

Odense /ˈəʊdənsə/ industrial port (shipbuilding, electrical goods, glass, textiles) on the island of Fyn, Denmark; population (1985) 171,500.

Oder /ˈəʊdə/ European river flowing from Czechoslovakia to the Baltic (the ◊Neisse is a tributary); length 885 km/550 mi.

Oder-Neisse Line /ˌəʊdəˈnaɪsə/ border between Poland and East Germany which has run along these two rivers since 1945.

Odessa /əˈdesə/ seaport in the Ukraine, USSR, on the Black Sea, capital of Odessa region; university; population (1985) 1,126,000. *history* Odessa was founded by Catherine II in 1795 near the site of an ancient Greek settlement. Occupied by Germany 1941–44, Odessa suffered severe damage under the Soviet scorched-earth policy and from German destruction.

Odets /əʊˈdets/ Clifford 1906–1963. American playwright, most famous for his play about a taxi-drivers' strike *Waiting for Lefty* 1935.

Odin /ˈəʊdɪn/ chief god of Scandinavian mythology, the ◊Woden or Wotan of the Germanic peoples. A sky god, he is resident in Asgard, at the top of the world-tree, and receives the souls of heroic slain warriors from the Valkyries, the 'divine maidens', feasting with them in his great hall, Valhalla. At Ragnarök (doomsday) the warriors were envisaged as fighting a final battle in support of Odin against the evil giants, a new order arising from the ensuing general destruction. The wife of Odin is ◊Frigga or Freyja, and ◊Thor is their son. Wednesday is named after him.

Odoacer /ˌɒdəʊˈeɪsə/ 433–493. King of Italy from 476, when he deposed ◊Romulus Augustulus. He was overthrown and treacherously killed by ◊Theodoric the Great.

Odoyevsky /ˌɒdəˈjefski/ Vladimir 1804–1869. Russian writer who wrote works in many different genres, including tales of the supernatural and science fiction.

Odysseus /əˈdɪsjuːs/ the chief character of the *Odyssey* (see ◊Homer), mentioned also in the *Iliad* as one of the most prominent leaders of the Greek forces at the siege of Troy. He is said to have been the ruler of the island of Ithaca, and to have met the lotus-eaters, Circe, Scylla and Charybdis, and the Sirens. Among the Greek heroes Odysseus was distinguished for his sagacity.

OECD abbreviation for ◊Organization for Economic Cooperation and Development.

oedema a general accumulation of ◊lymph in the body tissues or cavities, caused by failure of the heart, kidneys, liver, and so on, and treated with drugs to induce greater flow of urine.

Oedipus /ˈiːdɪpəs/ in Greek legend, king of Thebes. He was exposed and left to die at birth because his father Laius had been warned by an oracle that his son would kill him. Saved and brought up by the King of Corinth, Oedipus killed Laius in a quarrel (without recognizing him) and, because he saved Thebes from the Sphinx, was granted the Theban kingdom and Jocasta (wife of Laius and mother of Oedipus) as his wife. After four children had been born, the truth was discovered; Jocasta hanged herself, Oedipus blinded himself, and as an exiled wanderer was guided by his daughter, Antigone. ◊Sophocles used the story in two tragedies.

Oedipus complex in psychology, term coined by ◊Freud for the unconscious antagonism of a son to his father, whom he sees as a rival for his mother's affection. For a girl antagonistic to her mother for the same reason, the term is Electra complex. Freud saw this as a universal part of childhood development, which in most children is resolved during late childhood. Contemporary theory places less importance on the Oedipus complex than did Freud and his followers.

oersted the ◊c.g.s. unit of magnetic field strength (Oe). Defined as the field strength that would exert a force of 1 dyne on a unit magnetic pole in a vacuum, it is = ¼π × 10³ amperes per metre (SI system).

Oersted /'ɜːsted/ Hans Christian 1777–1851. Danish physicist who founded the science of ◊electromagnetism. He discovered the ◊magnetic field associated with an electric current in 1820.

oesophagus gullet; the passage by which food travels from mouth to stomach. In a human it is about 23 cm/9 in long, and its upper end is at the bottom of the ◊pharynx, immediately behind the windpipe.

oestrogen the general term for a group of hormones produced by the ◊ovaries of vertebrates, and for various synthetic hormones which mimic their effects. The principal oestrogen in mammals is oestradiol. Oestrogens promote the development of female secondary sexual characteristics in mammals, stimulate egg production, and prepare the lining of the ◊uterus for pregnancy. See also ◊menstrual cycle.

oestrus in mammals, the period during a female's reproductive cycle (also known as the oestrus cycle or ◊menstrual cycle) when mating is particularly likely to occur. It usually coincides with ◊ovulation.

Offa /'ɒfə/ king of Mercia from 757; died 796. He conquered Essex, Kent, Sussex, and Surrey, defeated the Welsh and the W Saxons, and established Mercian supremacy over all England S of the Humber.

Offaly /'ɒfəli/ county of the Republic of Ireland, in the province of Leinster, between Galway on the W and Kildare on the E
area 1,997 sq km/771 sq mi
towns county town Tullamore
features rivers Shannon (along the W boundary), Brosna, Clodagh, and Broughill; Slieve Bloom mountains in the SE
population (1981) 58,300.

Offa's Dyke /'ɒfəz/ a defensive earthwork along the Welsh border, of which there are remains from the mouth of the river Dee to that of the river Severn. It represents the boundary secured by ◊Offa's wars with Wales.

Offenbach /'ɒfənbɑːk/ Jacques 1819–1880. French composer. He wrote light opera, initially for presentation at the Bouffes-Parisiens, of which he held the lease. His most widely known works are *Orphée aux enfers/Orpheus in the Underworld* 1858, *La Belle Hélène* 1864, and *Les Contes d'Hoffmann/The Tales of Hoffmann* 1881.

office automation the introduction of computers and other electronic equipment to support an office routine. Increasingly, over the past decade, computers have been used to support administrative tasks such as document processing, filing, mail, and diary management; project planning and management accounting have also been computerized. The trend is now towards increased integration of all these functions, resulting in the 'paperless office'.

Official Secrets Act UK act of Parliament of 1911, which superseded that of 1889 and introduced new sections making it an offence for anyone who had ever served the crown to communicate to any person information acquired in that service, whether it is harmful to the state or not. In the 1980s there were demands that it should be replaced by a Freedom of Information Act (on US lines) which would differentiate between what was considered essential to be kept secret for the security of the state, and what it was merely inconvenient to the government or the civil service to have made public knowledge.

offset litho now the most common method of ◊printing, which uses smooth printing plates. It works on the principle of ◊lithography, that grease and water repel one another. The printing plate is prepared using a photographic technique, resulting in a type image which attracts greasy printing ink. On the printing press the plate is wrapped around a cylinder and wetted and inked in turn. The ink adheres only to the type area. This image is then transferred via an intermediate blanket cylinder to the paper.

O'Flaherty /əʊ'flɑːhəti/ Liam 1897–1984. Irish author whose novels of ◊Fenian activities in county Mayo include *The Neighbour's Wife* 1923 and *Land* 1946.

Ogaden /ˌɒgə'den/ region in Harar province, SE Ethiopia, which juts into and is claimed by Somalia. It is a desert plateau, rising to 1,000 m/3,000 ft; arid farming is practised by nomads. Intermittent guerrilla fighting continues despite the 1986 meeting between the Somalian and Ethiopian leaders. Civilian rule was returned to Ethiopia in Sept 1987.

Ogbomosho /ˌɒgbə'məʊʃəʊ/ city and commercial centre in Nigeria, 80 km/50 mi NE of Ibadan; population (1975) 432,000.

Ogden /'ɒgdən/ C(harles) K(ay) 1889–1957. British writer and scholar. With I A ◊Richards he developed the simplified form of English known as ◊Basic English.

Ogdon /'ɒgdən/ John 1937– . British pianist. He created a sensation in Moscow in 1962 when he shared the Tchaikovsky award with Ashkenazy. He is noted for his interpretation of Chopin, Liszt, and Busoni.

Ogilvy /'əʊgəlvi/ Angus James Bruce 1928– . British entrepreneur. Second son of the earl of Airlie, he married Princess ◊Alexandra.

Oglethorpe /'əʊgəlθɔːp/ James Edward 1696–1785. English soldier. He joined the Guards, and in 1732 obtained a charter for the colony of Georgia, intended as a refuge for debtors and for European Protestants.

OGPU former name of the Soviet secret police, the ◊KGB.

O'Higgins /əʊ'hɪgɪnz/ Bernardo 1776–1842. Chilean revolutionary, of Irish descent. He was a leader of the struggle for independence from Spanish rule 1810–17, and head of the first permanent national government 1817–23.

Ohio /əʊ'haɪəʊ/ river in the USA, 1,580 km/980 mi long; it is formed by the union of the Allegheny and Monongahela at Pittsburgh, Pennsylvania, and flows SW until it joins the Mississippi at Cairo, Illinois.

Ohio /əʊ'haɪəʊ/ Midwest state of the USA; nicknamed Buckeye State
area 106,714 sq km/41,222 sq mi
capital Columbus
towns Cleveland, Cincinnati, Toledo, Akron, Dayton, Youngstown
features Ohio river; Serpent Mound, a 1.3 m/4 ft embankment, 405 m/1,330 ft long, and about 6 m/18 ft across (built by ◊Hopewell Indians around 1st–2nd century BC).
products coal, cereals, livestock; machinery
population (1980) 10,797,420
famous people Thomas Edison, John Glenn, Paul Newman, General Sherman, Orville Wright; six presidents (Garfield, Grant, Harding, Harrison, Hayes and McKinley)
history ceded to Britain by France in 1763, and first settled by Europeans 1788, it became a state in 1803.

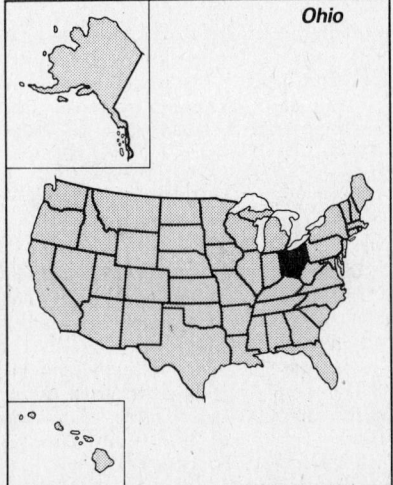

Ohio

Ohm /əʊm/ Georg Simon 1787–1854. German physicist who promulgated what is known as Ohm's law 1827. It states: the steady current in a metallic circuit is directly proportional to the constant total ◊electromotive force in the circuit. If a current I flows between two points in a ◊conductor across which the ◊potential difference (voltage) is E, then E/I is a constant (which is known as the ◊resistance between the two points). Hence $E/I = R$. Equations relating E, I, and R are often quoted as Ohm's law, but the term resistance did not enter into the law as originally stated.

oil inflammable substance, usually insoluble in water, and chiefly composed of carbon and hydrogen. Oils may be solids (fats) at ordinary temperatures, or liquids. There are three main types:

essential oils volatile liquids which have the odour of their plant source and are used in perfumes and flavouring essences.

fixed oils mixtures of ◊esters of fatty acids, of varying consistency, found in both animals (for example, fish oils) and plants (in nuts and seeds). They are used as food; in soaps, paints and varnishes; and for lubrication.

mineral oils which are obtained chiefly from ◊petroleum.

oil palm type of ◊palm tree *Elaeis guineensis*, whose fruit yields valuable oils which can be used as food or processed into margarine, soaps and livestock feeds.

Oise /waːz/ European river which rises in the Ardennes, Belgium, and flows through France in a generally SW direction for 300 km/186 mi to join the Seine about 65 km/40 mi below Paris.

Oistrakh /'ɔɪstrɑːk/ David Fyodorovich 1908–1974. Russian violinist. Born at Odessa, he became famous for his performances of both the standard and contemporary Russian repertoire. ◊Shostakovich wrote both his violin concertos for him.

okapi animal *Okapia johnstoni* of the giraffe family, though with much shorter legs and neck, found in the tropical rain forests of central Africa. Purplish brown, with creamy face and black and white stripes on the legs, it is excellently camouflaged. Unknown to Europeans until 1901, only a few hundred are thought to survive.

Okayama /ˌɒkə'jɑːmə/ industrial port (textiles) in W Honshu, Japan; population (1984) 555,000. Noted for three Buddhist temples.

Okeechobee /ˌəuki'tʃəubi/ lake in the N Everglades, Florida, USA; 65 km/40 mi long and 40 km/25 mi wide.

Okefenokee /ˌəukɪfɪ'nəuki/ swamp in SE Georgia, USA, rich in alligators, bears, deer and birds. Much of its 1700 sq km/660 sq mi forms a Natural Wildlife Refuge.

Okeghem /'ɒkəgem/ Johannes (Jean d') c. 1420–1497. Flemish composer, noted for his church music, particularly masses and motets. He was court composer to Charles VII, Louis XI, and Charles VIII of France.

Okhotsk, Sea of /əu'xɒtsk/ arm of the N Pacific between the Kamchatka Peninsula and Sakhalin, and bordered southward by the Kurile Island. Free of ice only in summer, it is often fogbound. Area 937,000 sq km/582,000 sq mi.

Okinawa /ˌɒkɪ'nɑːwə/ largest of the Japanese ◊Ryukyu Islands in the W Pacific
area 1,176 sq km/454 sq mi
capital Naha
population (1983) 1,146,000
history captured by the USA in the ***Battle of Okinawa*** 1 Apr–21 Jun 1945 with 47,000 US casualties (12,000 dead) and 60,000 Japanese (only a few hundred survived as prisoners). Returned to Japan 1972.

Oklahoma /ˌəuklə'həumə/ SW state of the USA; nicknamed Sooner State
area 181,088 sq km/69,919 sq mi
capital Oklahoma City

towns Tulsa
features Arkansas, Red, and Canadian rivers; Wichita and Ozark ranges; the Oklahoma panhandle is part of the Dust Bowl
products cereals, peanuts; livestock; oil, natural gas, helium; machinery and other metal products
population (1984) 3,298,000
famous people Woody Guthrie, Will Rogers
history the region was acquired with the ◊Louisiana Purchase in 1803. Part of the present state formed the Territory of Oklahoma from 1890, and was thrown open to settlers with lotteries and other hurried distribution of land. Together with what remained of Indian Territory, it became a state in 1907.

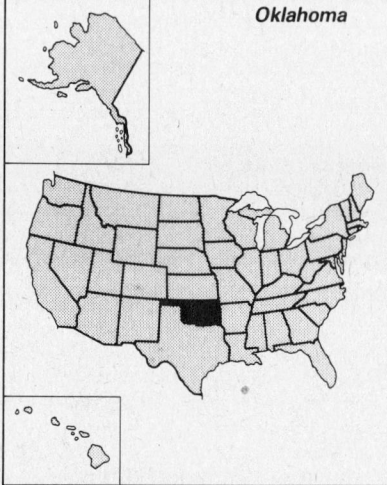

Oklahoma

Oklahoma City /ˌəuklə'həumə/ industrial city (oil refining, oil-related machinery, aircraft, telephone equipment), capital of Oklahoma, USA, on the Canadian river; population (1984) 443,500.

Okovango Swamp /ˌɒkə'væŋgəu/ marshy area in NW ◊Botswana.

okra type of ◊hibiscus plant, with edible fruit (*bhindi* or ladies' fingers).

Olaf /'əuləf/ name of five kings of Norway, including: *Olaf I* Tryggvesson (969–1000), elected king in 995, began the conversion of Norway to Christianity, and was killed in a sea battle against the Danes and Swedes. *Olaf II* Haraldsson (995–1030), king from 1015, offended his subjects by his centralizing policy and zeal for Christianity, and was killed in battle by Norwegian rebel chiefs backed by ◊Canute of Denmark. He was declared the patron saint of Norway in 1164. *Olaf V* (1903–) succeeded his father ◊Haakon VII in 1957.

Olbers paradox a question put forward in 1826 by the German astronomer Heinrich Olbers 1758–1840, who asked: if the Universe is infinite in extent and filled with stars, why is the sky dark at night? The answer is that the stars do not live infinitely long, so there is not enough starlight to fill the Universe. A wrong answer is frequently given: that the expansion of the Universe weakens the starlight.

Olbrich /'ɒlbrɪʃ/ Joseph Maria 1867–1908. Viennese architect who worked under Otto ◊Wagner and was opposed to the lush over-ornamentation of Art Nouveau. His most important buildings, however, remain Art Nouveau in spirit: the Vienna Secession 1897–98, the Hochzeitsturm 1907 and the Tietz department store, both in Düsseldorf.

old age the later years of life. The causes of progressive degeneration of bodily and mental processes associated with it are still not precisely known (see ◊ageing), but every one of the phenomena can occur at almost any age, and the process does not take place throughout the body at an equal speed. Normally, however, ageing begins after about 30. The arteries start to lose their elasticity, so that a greater strain is thrown upon the heart. The resulting gradual impairment of the blood supply is responsible for many of the changes, but, between 30 and 60 there is a period of maturity in which, if life is lived sensibly, ageing makes little progress. Research into the process of old age (gerontology) includes study of dietary factors, and the mechanisms behind structural changes in arteries and bones. Geriatrics is the branch of medicine dealing with old age and its diseases.

Old Bailey properly the name of a street in the City of London, England, leading off Ludgate Hill. More usually it is applied to the ◊Central Criminal Court in London.

Old Catholic one of various breakaway groups from Roman Catholicism, especially those in Austria, Czechoslovakia, Germany, and Switzerland, who rejected the proclamation of ◊papal infallibility of 1870. Their clergy are not celibate, and they have much in common with the Eastern Orthodox Churches.

Oldenburg /'əuldənbɜːg/ city in Lower Saxony, West Germany; population (1984) 138,500.

Old English another term for ◊Anglo-Saxon; see also ◊English language.

Oldham /'əuldəm/ industrial city (textiles and textile machinery, plastics, electrical goods, electronic equipment) in Greater Manchester, England; population (1981) 95,470.

Old Moore's Almanac annual publication in Britain containing 'prophecies' of the events of the following year. It was first published in 1700, under the title *Vox Stellarum/Voices of the Stars*, by Francis Moore (1657–c. 1715).

Old Pretender nickname of ◊James Edward Stuart, the son of James II of England.

Old Sarum /'seərəm/ Iron Age hill-fort site near ◊Salisbury, England.

Old Stone Age art see under ◊Ancient art.

Old Style a qualification, often abbreviated as 'O S', applied to dates before the year 1752 in England as quoted in later writers. In that year the calendar in use in England was reformed by the omission of 11 days, in order to bring it into line with the more exact Gregorian system, and the beginning of the year was put back from 25 Mar to 1 Jan. See ◊calendar.

Old Testament Christian term for the Hebrew ◊Bible, which is the first part of the Christian Bible.

Olduvai Gorge /'ɒlduvaɪ 'gɔːdʒ/ deep cleft in the Serengeti steppe, Tanzania, where the ◊Leakeys found stone tools in the 1930s. Later, they discovered 1958–59 Pleistocene remains of prehumans and gigantic animals. These included sheep the size of a carthorse, pigs as big as a rhinoceros, and a gorilla-sized baboon. The skull of an early hominid (1.75 million years old) *Australopithecus boisei* (its huge teeth earned it the nickname 'Nutcracker Man'), was also found here, as well as remains of *Homo habilis* and primitive types of *Homo erectus*. The gorge has given its name to the **Olduvai culture**, a simple stone-tool culture of prehistoric hominids, dating from 2–0.5 million years ago.

Old Vic /'əʊld 'vɪk/ theatre S of the river Thames in London, founded in 1818 as the Coburg. Taken over by Emma Cons in 1880, when it was known as the Royal Victoria Hall, it became a popular centre for opera and drama, and was affectionately dubbed the Old Vic. In 1898 Lilian Baylis, niece of Emma Cons, assumed the management, and in 1914 began a celebrated series of Shakespeare productions. It was badly damaged in 1940 air raids, but reopened 1950–81, acting as temporary home of the National Theatre 1963–76, and in 1985 was completely refurbished.

Old World the continents of the eastern hemisphere, so called because they were familiar to Europeans before the Americas. Used as an adjective to describe animals and plants that live in the eastern hemisphere.

oleander or *rose bay* an evergreen Mediterranean shrub *Nerium oleander* family Apocynaceae, with pink or white flowers, and leaves secreting the poison oleandrin.

O Level, General Certificate of Education in the UK, the examination usually taken at 16 plus by the most able children and superseded by the ◊GCSE in 1988.

Olga, St /'ɒlgə/ died 969. The wife of Igor, the Scandinavian Prince of Kiev. Her baptism around 955 was an important step in the Christianization of Russia.

Oligocene the third division of the ◊Tertiary period of geological time between 38 and 22.5 million years ago. The name, from Greek, means 'a little recent', referring to the presence of some of the modern types of animals at that time.

oligopoly in economics, a situation in which a small group of companies controls a large proportion of a particular market and concerts its actions to perpetuate such control. This will usually include agreements on prices, with prices fixed at well above costs. See ◊cartel.

Oliphant /'ɒlɪfənt/ Margaret 1828–1897. Scottish writer, author of over 100 novels, biographies, and numerous articles and essays. Her best-known work is the series *The Chronicles of Carlingford* 1863–66, including *The Perpetual Curate* and *Hester*.

Olivares /ˌɒlɪ'vɑːres/ Count-Duke of (born Gaspar de Guzmán) 1587–1645. Spanish prime minister and favourite of King ◊Philip IV. As prime minister 1621–43 he overstretched Spain in foreign affairs, and unsuccessfully attempted domestic reform. He committed Spain to recapturing Holland and to major involvement in the ◊Thirty Years' War 1618–48, and his efforts to centralize power led to revolts in Catalonia and Portugal, which brought about his downfall.

olive evergreen tree *Olea europaea* of the family Oleaceae. It grows up to 15 m/50 ft high, has opposite, lance-shaped leaves. The white flowers are followed by bluish-black oval fruits, from which olive oil is pressed: pale yellow, it is chiefly composed of glycerides and, besides being edible, is used in soaps and ointments, and as a lubricant. It is native to Mediterranean regions, but is now widely distributed in warm climates.

olivenite hydrated copper arsenate, $Cu_3As_2O_2.Cu(OH)_2$, occurring as a mineral in olive-green prisms.

Oliver /'ɒlɪvə/ Isaac c. 1556–1617. British miniaturist, originally a Huguenot refugee, who studied under ◊Hilliard, and portrayed John Donne and members of the court of James I.

Oliver The British miniaturist Isaac Oliver, a popular figure at the court of James I. The miniature is a self-portrait, c. 1590.

Olives, Mount of /'ɒlɪvz/ a range of hills E of Jerusalem. Gethsemane was at its foot, while a chapel (now a mosque), marks the traditional site of the Ascension (see ◊Ascension Day).

Olivier /ə'lɪvɪeɪ/ Laurence Kerr, Baron Olivier 1907– . British actor-director, born in Dorking, Surrey. Knighted in 1947, life peer 1970 and Order of Merit 1981, he was for many years associated with the Old Vic, was director of the National Theatre company 1962–73, and the Olivier Theatre (part of the National Theatre on the South Bank) was named after him. Famous early films include *Wuthering Heights* and *Rebecca* and his major stage roles include Henry V, Hamlet, Richard III and Archie Rice in *The Entertainer*. His acting and direction of filmed versions of Shakespeare's plays have received outstanding critical acclaim, for example *Henry V* 1944, *Hamlet* 1948 (both of which earned him Academy Awards), and *Richard III* 1955.

olivine a greenish mineral, magnesium iron silicate, $(Mg, Fe)_2SiO_4$. It is an important rock-forming mineral in such rocks as ◊gabbro and ◊basalt. Olivine is known as *peridot* when pale green and transparent, and used in jewellery.

olm cave-dwelling aquatic salamander *Proteus anguinus* found along the E Adriatic seaboard in Italy and Yugoslavia. About 25 cm/10 in long the 'adult' is permanently larval in form, with external gills. See ◊neoteny.

Olney /'əʊlni/ small town in Buckinghamshire, England, where every Shrove Tuesday local women run a pancake race. The poet William Cowper spent the end of his life here.

Olomouc /'ɒləmaʊts/ industrial city (sugar refining, brewing, metal goods) in Czechoslovakia, at the confluence of the Bystrice and Morava; population (1984) 104,000.

Olsztyn /'ɒlʃtɪn/ industrial town in NE Poland; population (1980) 132,000. Founded 1334 and formerly in E Prussia, it was known as Allenstein.

Olympia /ə'lɪmpiə/ sanctuary in the W Peloponnese, Ancient Greece, with a temple of Zeus, and the stadium (for foot races, boxing, wrestling) and hippodrome (for chariot and horse races), where the original ◊Olympic games were held.

Olympic Games sporting contests originally held in Olympia, Ancient Greece, every four years during a sacred truce; records were kept from 776 BC. Women were forbidden to be present, and the male contestants were naked. The games were abolished 394 AD.
The revival of the modern Olympic Games was initiated by the French Baron Pierre de Coubertin (1863–1937) in 1894; an International Olympic Committee organized the meetings which it was intended should be held each four years, but they were interrupted by both world wars. The Olympic emblem of five interlaced circles represents the five continents. The first modern Olympic Games (1896) were held in Athens. The modern Olympic Games cover a much wider range of events, for example, swimming, skating, equestrian events, football, rowing.

Olympus /ə'lɪmpəs/ several mountains in Greece and elsewhere, the most famous being: *Mount Olympus* in N Thessaly, Greece, a group of hills in which the high point is 2,918 m/9,570 ft. It was identified as the abode of the gods. *Mount Olympus* on Mars, about 24,000 m/80,000 ft.

OM abbreviation for ◊Order of Merit.

Omagh /'əʊmə/ county town of Tyrone, Northern Ireland, on the river Strule, 48 km/30 mi S of Londonderry; population (1981) 14,625.

Omaha /'əʊməhɑː/ city in E Nebraska, USA, on the Missouri; livestock-market centre, with food-processing and meat-packing industries; population (1980) 314,000.

Oman /əʊ'mɑːn/ country on the Arabian peninsula, bounded to the W by the United Arab Emirates, Saudia Arabia, and South Yemen.
government Oman has no written constitution and the sultan has absolute power, ruling by decree. There is no legislature. The sultan takes

Olympic Games Britain's relay team after their victory at the Berlin Olympics 1936, left to right: Brown, Wolfe, Rampling and Roberts.

advice from an appointed cabinet. There is also a consultative assembly of 55 nominated members. There are no political parties.

history for early history, see ◊Arabia. The city of ◊Muscat has long been an important trading post. The country was in Portugal's possession 1508–1658, and was then ruled by Persia until 1744. By the early 19th century, the state of Muscat and Oman was the most powerful in Arabia: it ruled Zanzibar until 1861 and also coastal parts of Persia and Pakistan.

In 1951 it became the independent sultanate of Muscat and Oman and signed a treaty of friendship with Britain. Said bin Taimur, who had been sultan since 1932, was overthrown by his son, Qaboos bin Said, in a bloodless coup in 1970, and the country was renamed Oman. Qaboos embarked on a more liberal and expansionist policy than his father. The Popular Front for the Liberation of Oman has been fighting to overthrow the sultanate since 1965. Oman's wealth is based on a few oil fields. Conflicts in neighbouring countries, such as the Yemen, Iran, Iraq, and Afghanistan, have not only emphasized the country's strategic importance but put its own security at risk. The sultan has tried to follow a path of nonalignment, maintaining close ties with the USA and other NATO countries but also keeping good relations with the USSR.

Omar /ˈəʊmɑː/ 581–644. Adviser of ◊Muhammad, who in 634 succeeded Abu ◊Bekr as caliph, and conquered Syria, Palestine, Egypt, and Persia. He was assassinated by a slave. The Mosque of Omar in Jerusalem is attributed to him.

Omar Khayyam /ˈəʊmɑː kaɪˈæm/ c. 1050–1123. Persian astronomer and poet. He founded a school of astronomical research and assisted in reforming the calendar. The result of his observations was the *Jalālī* era, begun in 1079. In the West, Omar Khayyam is chiefly known as a poet through ◊Fitzgerald's version of the *The Rubaiyat of Omar Khayyam* 1859.

Omayyads /əʊˈmaɪædz/ Arab dynasty which held the caliphate 661–750. They were overthrown by Abbasids, but a member of the family escaped to Spain, and in 756 assumed the title of emir of Cordova. His dynasty, which took the title of caliph in 929, ruled at Cordova until the early 11th century.

ombudsman person appointed to safeguard citizens' rights against encroachment by the government or its employees. The post is of Scandinavian origin: it was introduced in Sweden 1809, Denmark 1954, and Norway 1962. The ombudsman investigates complaints of injustice that would otherwise have no hope of redress. The first Commonwealth country to appoint an ombudsman was New Zealand 1962;

the UK followed 1966 with a parliamentary commissioner; and Hawaii was the first US state to appoint an ombudsman, 1967. The UK Local Government Act 1974 set up a local ombudsman, or commissioner for local administration, to investigate maladministration by local councils, police, health or water authorities.

Omdurman /ˌɒmdəˈmɑːn/ city in the republic of Sudan, on the White Nile, opposite Khartoum; population (1983) 526,500. It was the residence of the Mahdi 1884–98, and is an important trading centre. The Battle of Omdurman 1898 was a victory for British troops under Kitchener over the forces of the Mahdi.

omnibus a road conveyance for several passengers. See ◊bus.

omnivore an animal which feeds on both plant and animal material. Omnivores have digestive adaptations intermediate between those of ◊herbivores and ◊carnivores, with relatively unspecialized digestive systems and gut micro-organisms which can digest a variety of foodstuffs.

Omsk /ɒmsk/ industrial city (agricultural and other machinery, food processing, sawmills, oil refining) in the USSR, capital of Omsk region; population (1985) 1,108,000. The refineries are linked with Tuimazy in Bashkiria by a 1,600 km/1,000 mi pipeline.

onager type of wild ass *Equus hemionus* found in W Asia.

Onassis /əʊˈnæsɪs/ Aristotle (Socrates) 1906–1975. Turkish-born Greek shipowner. During the 1950s he was one of the first shipbuilders to build supertankers. In 1968 he married Jacqueline Kennedy, widow of John F ◊Kennedy.

onchocerciasis disease found in tropical Africa and Latin America. It is transmitted by bloodsucking blackflies, which infect the victim with parasitic worms producing skin disorders and blindness.

Onega, Lake /əʊˈneɪgə/ second largest lake in Europe, NE of Leningrad, partly in Karelia, USSR; area 8,030 sq km/3,820 sq mi. The *Onega canal*, along its S shore, is part of the Mariinsk system linking Leningrad with the river Volga.

Oneida /əʊˈnaɪdə/ small town in New York State, USA, named after the Oneida people (a nation of the ◊Iroquois confederacy). It became known from 1848 for the *Oneida Community*, a religious sect which practised a form of 'complex marriage' until its dissolution 1879.

O'Neill /əʊˈniːl/ Eugene (Gladstone) 1888–1953. American playwright, widely regarded as the leading US dramatist between World Wars I and II. Born in New York City, he had varied experience as gold prospector, sailor, and actor. His best plays are characterized by a down-to-earth quality, even when he experimented with expressionism, symbolism, or stream of consciousness, and include *Beyond the Horizon* 1920, *Anna Christie* 1922, *Desire under the Elms* 1924 (which provoked the censor), *Mourning Becomes Electra* 1931 (a trilogy on the theme of ◊Orestes), *A Moon for the Misbegotten* 1947 (written 1943), and the posthumously produced autobiographical drama *Long Day's Journey into Night* 1956

Oman
SULTANATE OF

AREA 212,000 sq km/82,000 sq mi
CAPITAL Muscat
TOWNS Salalah
PHYSICAL mountains and a high arid plateau; fertile coastal strip
FEATURES Jebel Akhdar highlands; Kuria Muria islands; Masirah Island is used in aerial reconnaissance of the Arabian Sea and Indian Ocean
HEAD OF STATE AND OF GOVERNMENT Qaboos bin Said from 1970
GOVERNMENT absolute monarchy
EXPORTS oil, dates, silverware
CURRENCY Omani rial (0.64 = £1 Sept 1987)
POPULATION 1,228,000 (1985); annual growth rate 4.8%
LANGUAGE Arabic
RELIGION Sunni Muslim
LITERACY 20% (1983)
GNP $7 bn (1983); $2,400 per head of population
CHRONOLOGY
1951 The Sultanate of Muscat and Oman achieved full independence. Treaty of

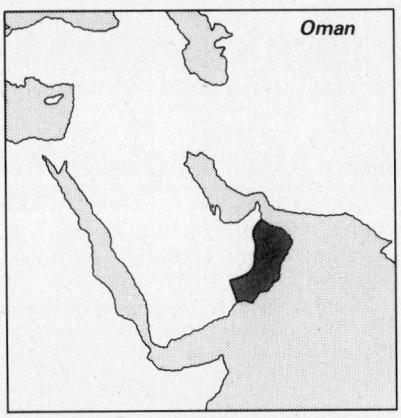

Oman

friendship with Britain signed.
1970 After 38 years' rule, Sultan Said bin Taimur replaced in coup by his son Qaboos bin Said. Name changed to Sultanate of Oman.
1975 Left-wing rebels in the S defeated.
1982 Memorandum of Understanding with the UK signed, providing for consultation on international issues.

towns Hamilton, Ottawa (federal capital), London, Windsor, Kitchener, Sudbury
features Black Creek Pioneer Village, ◊Niagara Falls; richest, chief manufacturing, most thickly populated, and leading cultural province of English-speaking Canada
products nickel, iron, gold; forest products; motor vehicles, iron and steel, paper, chemicals
population (1981) 8,625,100
history first explored by the French in the 17th century, it came under British control in 1763 (Treaty of Paris). An attempt in 1841 to form a merged province with French-speaking Quebec failed, and Ontario became a separate province of Canada in 1867.

Ontario

(written 1940). He was awarded a Nobel prize in 1936.

O'Neill Previously a sailor, gold prospector, actor and reporter, the American playwright Eugene O'Neill was awarded the Nobel prize for literature in 1936.

O'Neill /əʊ'niːl/ Terence, Baron O'Neill of the Maine 1914– . Northern Irish Unionist politician. He was prime minister of Ulster 1963–69. He resigned when opposed by his party on measures to extend rights to Roman Catholics, including a universal franchise. He was made a life peer 1970.

onion bulbous plant *Allium cepa* of the family Liliaceae. Cultivated from ancient times, it may have originated in Asia. The edible part is the bulb, containing an acrid volatile oil, giving a strong flavour. The onion is a biennial, the common species producing a bulb in the first season and seeds in the second.

online system in computing, a system that allows the computer to work interactively with its users, responding to each instruction as it is given and prompting users for information when necessary. Since the fall in the cost of computers in the 1970s, online operation has become increasingly attractive commercially. See also ◊batch system.

onomatopoeia a ◊figure of speech whose Greek name means 'name-making', on the principle of copying natural sounds. Thus, the word or name 'cuckoo' arises out of imitating the sound that the cuckoo makes. Such words as *bang, crash, ripple, smash, splash* and *thump* are often said to be onomatopoeic. However, onomatopoeia works differently in different languages, the English *bowwow* for a sound made by dogs being paralleled by the French *oua, oua*. Onomatopoeia may be built into prose or verse, as in 'a sudden sizzling sound', the 's' and 'z' sounds used to suggest frying.

Onsager /'ɒnsɑːgə/ Lars 1903–1976. Norwegian-American physicist, whose discovery of the 'reciprocity relations of Onsager' in 1931 was vital to the production of nuclear energy. He was awarded a Nobel prize in 1968.

Ontario /ɒn'teəriəʊ/ central province of Canada
area 1,068,587 sq km/412,582 sq mi
capital Toronto

Ontario, Lake /ɒn'teəriəʊ/ smallest of the ◊Great Lakes.

ontogeny the process of development of a living organism, including that part of development that takes place after hatching or birth. The idea that 'ontogeny recapitulates phylogeny', proposed by ◊Haeckel, is now discredited.

ontology that branch of philosophy concerned with the study of being as such. In the 20th century, ◊Heidegger distinguished between an 'ontological' enquiry (an enquiry into *Being*) and an 'ontic' enquiry (an enquiry into a specific kind of entity).

onyx a semi-precious variety of the mineral ◊silica in which the crystals are too fine to be detected microscopically (cryptocrystalline). It has straight parallel bands of different colours: milk-white, black and red. Sardonyx has layers of sand or red carnelian alternating with lighter layers of onyx. It can be used for cutting cameos.

oolite a calcareous rock formed of small grains of carbonate of lime, resembling the hard roe of a fish. The structure may arise from the accretion of carbonate of lime around grains of sand or particles of shell in moving water. It may also be formed from calcareous algae deposited in hot springs. The term is also used to indicate the middle and upper layers of the ◊Jurassic system. The name is derived from the Greek for 'egg' and 'stone'.

Oort /ɔːt/ Jan Hendrik 1900– . Dutch astronomer, who in 1927 calculated the mass and size of our galaxy, and the Sun's distance from its centre, from the observed movements of stars around the galaxy's centre. In 1944 Oort's student Hendrik van de Hulst calculated that hydrogen in space would emit radio waves at 21 cm wavelength, and in the 1950s Oort's team mapped the spiral structure of the galaxy from the radio waves given out by interstellar hydrogen. In 1950 Oort proposed that ◊comets exist in a vast swarm, now called the *Oort Cloud*, at the edge of the solar system.

oosphere another name for the female gamete or ◊ovum of certain plants such as algae.

Oostende /əʊst'endə/ Flemish form, meaning 'east end', of ◊Ostend.

ooze a ◊sediment of fine texture consisting mainly of organic matter found on the ocean floor at depths greater than 2,000 m/6,700ft. Several kinds of ooze exist, each named after its constituents: siliceous ooze is composed of the ◊silica shells of tiny marine plants, diatoms; calcareous ooze is formed from the ◊calcite shells of microscopic animals, foraminifera.

opal a non-crystalline form of ◊silica, occurring in stalactites in volcanic rocks. The common opal is opaque, milk-white, yellow, red, blue, or green, and lustrous. The precious opal is colourless, having innumerable cracks from which emanate brilliant colours produced by minute crystals of cristobalite. Opals are found in Hungary, New South Wales (black opals were first discovered there in 1905) and Mexico.

Op Art form of art, especially popular in the early 1960s. Op Art is based on the creative use of scientifically-based optical illusions, confusing the spectator's eye with coloured lines and dots that appear to jump, blend, and waver, as in the work of Jeffrey Steele and Bridget ◊Riley.

OPEC abbreviation for ◊Organization of the Petroleum Exporting Countries.

opencast mining also called open-pit mining, it is mining at the surface rather than underground. Coal, iron ore, and phosphates are often extracted by opencast mining. Often the mineral deposit is covered by soil, which must first be stripped off, usually by huge ◊excavators, such as walking draglines and bucketwheel excavators. Then the ◊ore deposit is broken up by explosives. One of the largest excavations in the world has been made by opencast mining at the Bingham Canyon copper mine in Utah, USA, measuring 790 m/2590 ft deep and 3.7 km/2.3 mi across.

Open College in the UK, an ◊open learning initiative launched by the ◊Manpower Services Commission to enable people to gain and update technical and vocational skills by means of distance teaching, such as correspondence, radio, and television.

open door policy economic philosophy suggested by US secretary of state John Jay in Sep 1899 to allow all nations free access to trade with China. Its significance lies in the rejection of a sphere of influence agreement for Chinese trade, and the term is now used to describe any policy based on equal access to markets.

open-hearth furnace once the most important method of steelmaking, now largely superseded by the ◊basic-oxygen process. The open-hearth furnace was developed in England by German-born William and Friedrich Siemens and improved by Pierre and Emile Martin in

1864. In the furnace molten pig iron and scrap are packed into a shallow hearth and heated by overhead gas burners using preheated air.

open learning teaching which is available to students without pre-qualifications by means of flexible attendance at an institution and very often including teaching by correspondence, radio, television, or tape, for example the ◊Open University and ◊Open College.

open shop factory or other business employing men and women not belonging to trade unions, as opposed to the 'closed ◊shop', which employs trade unionists only.

Open University an institution established in the UK in 1969 to enable mature students without qualifications to study to degree level without regular attendance. Open University teaching is based on a mixture of correspondence courses, TV and radio lectures and demonstrations, personal tuition organized on a regional basis, and summer schools.

opera dramatic work in which singing takes the place of speech. Opera originated in late 16th-century Florence when a number of young poets and musicians attempted to reproduce in modern form the musical declamation, lyrical monologues, and choruses of classical Greek drama. One of the earliest composers was Jacopo Peri (1561–1633), whose *Euridice* influenced Monteverdi. At first solely a court entertainment, opera soon became popular and in 1637 the first public opera house opened in Venice. In the later 17th century the elaborately conventional aria, designed to display the virtuosity of the singer, became predominant over the dramatic element. Composers of this type of opera included Cavalli, Cesti, and Alessandro Scarlatti. In France opera was developed by Lully and Rameau, and in England by Purcell, but the Italian style retained its ascendance, as in the career of Handel. Comic opera (*opera buffa*) was developed in Italy by such composers as Pergolesi, while in England *The Beggar's Opera* 1728 of John Gay started the vogue of the ballad opera, using popular tunes and spoken dialogue, of which *Singspiel* was the German equivalent (although here the music was newly composed). A lessening of artificiality began with Gluck, who insisted on the pre-eminence of the dramatic over the purely vocal element. Mozart learned much from Gluck in his serious operas, but his greatest triumphs were won in the field of Italian *opera buffa* and in those works, such as *The Magic Flute* in which, taking the *Singspiel* as a basis, he laid the foundations of a purely German opera. This line was continued by Beethoven in *Fidelio* and in the work of Weber, in which the Romantic style appears for the first time in opera. The Italian tradition, which placed the main stress on vocal display and melodic suavity, continued unbroken into the 19th century in the operas of Rossini, Donizetti, and Bellini. It is in the Romantic operas of Weber and Meyerbeer that the work of Wagner has its roots. Dominating the contemporary operatic scene, Wagner attempted to create, in his 'music-dramas', a new art-form, and completely transformed the 19th-century conception of opera. In Italy, Verdi

succeeded in assimilating, in his mature work, much of the Wagnerian technique, without sacrificing the Italian virtues of vocal clarity and melody, and this tradition was continued by Puccini. In French opera in the mid-19th century, represented by such composers as Delibes, Gounod, Saint-Saëns, and Massenet, the drama was subservient to the music. More serious artistic ideals were put into practice by Berlioz in *The Trojans*, but the merits of his work were largely neglected in his own time. Bizet's *Carmen* began a fashion for 'realism' in opera; his lead was followed in Italy by Mascagni, Leoncavallo, and Puccini. Debussy's *Pelléas and Mélisande* represented a reaction against the over-emphatic emotionalism of Wagnerian operas. National operatic styles were developed in Russia by Glinka, Rimsky-Korsakov, Mussorgsky, Borodin and Tchaikovsky, and in Bohemia by Smetana, and several notable composers of light opera emerged, including Sullivan, Lehár, Offenbach, and Johann Strauss. In the 20th century the Viennese school produced an outstanding opera in Berg's *Wozzeck*, and the Romanticism of Wagner was revived by Richard Strauss, in for example, *Der Rosenkavalier*.

Modern composers of opera include in Britain, Tippett and Britten; in Germany Hans Werner Henze; in Italy Petrassi; in the USA, Gershwin, Menotti, Weill, and Stravinsky; and in the USSR, Prokofiev and Shostakovich.

opera buffa (Italian 'comic opera') a type of humorous opera, with characters taken from everyday life; it is contrasted with ◊opera seria. The form began as a musical intermezzo in the 18th century, which was then adopted in Italy and France for complete operas. An example is Rossini's *The Barber of Seville*.

opéra–comique (French 'comic opera') opera which includes text to be spoken, not sung; thus, Bizet's *Carmen* is an example. The distinction was important since of the two Paris opera houses in the 18th–19th centuries, the *Opéra* (which aimed at setting a grand style) allowed no spoken dialogue, unlike the *Opéra–Comique*.

opera seria (Italian 'serious opera') a type of opera distinct from ◊opera buffa, or humorous opera. Common in the 17th-18th centuries, it tended to formality and frigidity. Examples include many of ◊Handel's operas.

operating system (OS) in computing, a program that controls the routine operations of a ◊computer. Sometimes called DOS (disk operating system) when the program also controls the disk. The operating system looks after the computer's filing system and handles the input and output of data and programs between the processor unit, external memory devices (such as disk drives), and input and output devices (such as keyboard and screen). Many makes of computer have their own operating system, but some are accepted standards. These include CP/M (by Digital Research) and MS-DOS (by Microsoft) for microcomputers, and Unix (by Bell Laboratories) for minicomputers.

operetta a light opera, which may use spoken dialogue.

MAJOR OPERAS AND THEIR FIRST PERFORMANCES

Date	Opera	Composer	Librettist	Place
1607	Orfeo	Monteverdi	Striggio	Mantua
1642	The Coronation of Poppea	Monteverdi	Busenello	Venice
1689	Dido and Aeneas	Purcell	Tate	London
1724	Julius Caesar in Egypt	Handel	Haym	London
1762	Orpheus and Eurydice	Gluck	Calzabigi	Vienna
1786	The Marriage of Figaro	Mozart	Da Ponte	Vienna
1787	Don Giovanni	Mozart	Da Ponte	Prague
1790	Così fan tutte	Mozart	Da Ponte	Vienna
1791	The Magic Flute	Mozart	Schikaneder	Vienna
1805	Fidelio	Beethoven	Sonnleithner	Vienna
1816	The Barber of Seville	Rossini	Sterbini	Rome
1821	Der Freischütz	Weber	Kind	Berlin
1831	Norma	Bellini	Romani	Milan
1835	Lucia di Lammermoor	Donizetti	Cammarano	Naples
1836	Les Huguenots	Meyerbeer	Scribe	Paris
1842	Russlan and Ludmilla	Glinka	Shirkov/Bakhturin	St Petersburg
1850	Lohengrin	Wagner	Wagner	Weimar
1851	Rigoletto	Verdi	Piave	Venice
1853	Il Trovatore	Verdi	Cammarano	Rome
1853	La Traviata	Verdi	Piave	Venice
1859	Faust	Gounod	Barbier/Carré	Paris
1865	Tristan and Isolde	Wagner	Wagner	Munich
1866	The Bartered Bride	Smetana	Sabina	Prague
1868	Die Meistersinger von Nürnberg	Wagner	Wagner	Munich
1871	Aida	Verdi	Ghislanzoni	Cairo
1874	Boris Godunov	Mussorgsky	Mussorgsky	St Petersburg
1874	Die Fledermaus	Johann Strauss II	Haffner/Genée	Vienna
1875	Carmen	Bizet	Meilhac/Halévy	Paris
1876	The Ring of the Nibelung	Wagner	Wagner	Bayreuth
1879	Eugene Onegin	Tchaikovsky	Tchaikovsky/Shilovsky	Moscow
1881	The Tales of Hoffman	Offenbach	Barbier	Paris
1882	Parsifal	Wagner	Wagner	Bayreuth
1885	The Mikado	Sullivan	Gilbert	London
1887	Otello	Verdi	Bioto	Milan
1890	Cavalleria Rusticana	Mascagni	Menasci/Targioni-Tozzetti	Rome
1890	Prince Igor	Borodin	Borodin	St Petersburg
1892	Pagliacci	Leoncavallo	Leoncavallo	Milan
1892	Werther	Massenet	Blau/Milliet/Hartmann	Vienna
1896	La Bohème	Puccini	Giacosa/Illica	Turin
1900	Tosca	Puccini	Giacosa/Illica	Rome
1902	Pelléas et Mélisande	Debussy	Maeterlinck	Paris
1904	Jenůfa	Janáček	Janáček	Brno
1904	Madame Butterfly	Puccini	Giacosa/illica	Milan
1905	Salome	Richard Strauss	Wilde/Lachmann	Dresden
1909	The Golden Cockerel	Rimsky-Korsakov	Byelsky	Moscow
1911	Der Rosenkavalier	Richard Strauss	Hofmannsthal	Dresden
1918	Duke Bluebeard's Castle	Bartók	Balázs	Budapest
1925	Wozzeck	Berg	Berg	Berlin
1935	Porgy and Bess	Gershwin	Ira Gershwin/Heyward	Boston
1937	Lulu	Berg	Berg	Zürich
1945	Peter Grimes	Britten	Slater	London
1946	War and Peace	Prokofiev	Prokofiev/Mendelson	Leningrad
1951	The Rake's Progress	Stravinsky	Auden/Kallman	Venice
1978	Paradise Lost	Penderecki	Fry	Chicago
1986	The Mask of Orpheus	Birtwistle	Zinovieff	London

operon a group of ◊genes which are found next to each other on a ◊chromosome, and are turned on and off as an integrated unit. They usually produce enzymes which control different steps in the same biochemical pathway. Operons were discovered (by ◊Jacob and ◊Monod) in bacteria; they are less common in higher organisms where the control of metabolism is a more complex process.

Ophiuchus large ◊constellation of the equatorial region of the sky, representing Asclepius, the Greek god of medicine. The Sun passes through Ophiuchus each Dec, although the constellation is not part of the ◊zodiac. Ophiuchus contains the second-closest star to the Sun, ◊Barnard's Star.

ophthalmia inflammation of the eye. Ophthalmia neonatorum (newborn) is an acute inflammation of a baby's eyes at birth with the organism of gonorrhoea caught from the mother. Sympathetic ophthalmia is the diffuse inflammation of the sound eye which is apt to follow septic inflammation of the other.

opiates, endogenous naturally-produced chemicals in the body which have effects similar to morphine and other opiate drugs. See ◊endorphins and ◊enkephalins.

Opie /ˈəʊpi/ John 1761–1807. British artist. Born in St Agnes, Cornwall, he became famous as a portrait painter in London from 1780, later painting historical pictures such as *The Murder of Rizzio*.

Opie /ˈəʊpi/ Peter Mason 1918–1982 and Iona Margaret Balfour (born Archibald) 1923– . Husband-and-wife team of folklorists who specialized in the myths and literature of childhood. They wrote many books together, including *The Lore and Language of Schoolchildren* 1959.

opinion poll public attempt to measure public opinion as a whole by taking a survey of the views of a small, representative sample of the electorate. The first accurately sampled opinion poll was carried out by George ◊Gallup during the US presidential election 1936.
Opinion polls have encountered criticism on the grounds that they may influence the outcome of an election rather than simply predicting it, for example, by making the lead of one party seem so great that its supporters feel they need not bother to vote.

opium drug extracted from the unripe seeds of the opium poppy *Papaver somniferum* of SW Asia. An addictive narcotic, it includes the alkaloids *morphine*, one of the most powerful natural painkillers and addictive narcotics known; *heroin*, a synthetic derivative of morphine, is even more powerful; *codeine* a milder painkiller; and *thebaine* highly poisonous. When dissolved in alcohol, opium is known as *laudanum*.

Opium Wars wars waged against China to enforce the opening of Chinese ports to trade, especially the opium traffic. Opium from British India paid for Britain's imports from China, such as porcelain and silks, but above all tea, then only obtainable in bulk from China. The *First Opium War* 1840–42, between Britain and China, resulted in the cession of Hong Kong to Britain and the opening of five 'treaty ports'. A *Second Opium War* 1857–60 followed between Britain and France in alliance against China, when there was further Chinese resistance, notably in Canton, one of the treaty ports. At its close the Summer Palace in Peking was set fire to.

Opole /ɒˈpəʊleɪ/ industrial town (textiles, chemicals, cement) and agricultural market centre in Poland, on the Oder; population (1982) 119,342.

Oporto /əʊˈpɔːtəʊ/ (Portuguese *Porto*) industrial city (textiles, leather, pottery) in Portugal, on the Douro, 5 km/3 mi from its mouth; known for the export of port; population (1984) 327,500. It is the second largest city in Portugal, and has a 12th-century cathedral.

opossum marsupial of the family Didelphidae. Opossums are small arboreal animals, with prehensile tails, and hands and feet well adapted for grasping. The cat-sized common opossum *Didelphis marsupialis*, with yellowish-grey fur, has spread its range into North America. Most true opossums are confined to central and South America, but the name is popularly applied to some of the somewhat similar phalangers found in Australia.

Oppenheimer /'ɒpən,haɪmə/ Robert 1904–1967. American physicist, who developed the first atomic bomb. The son of a German immigrant, he worked with ◊Rutherford at Cambridge. As director of the Los Alamos Science Laboratory 1943–45, he was in charge of the development of the atomic bomb. Objecting to the development of the H-bomb, he was declared a security risk in 1953 by the US Atomic Energy Commission but was rehabilitated in 1963 when the Commission granted him the ◊Fermi Award.

Oppenheimer After his objections to US construction of the H-bomb, Robert Oppenheimer, who had previously been head of the laboratory which produced the first atom bomb, was declared a security risk by the Atomic Energy Commission.

Opposition, Leader of His/Her Majesty's in Britain, official title (from 1937) of the leader of the largest opposition party in the ◊Commons.

optical aberration see ◊aberration, optical.

optical computer a computer in which both light and electrical signals are used in the CPU (central processing unit). The technology is still not fully developed, but a computer that uses pulses of light promises to be faster and less vulnerable to outside electrical interference than one that relies solely on electricity.

optical contouring computerized monitoring of a light pattern projected onto a patient to detect discrepancies in breathing movements.

optical fibre very fine optically pure glass fibre through which light can be reflected to transmit an image or information from one end to the other. Bundles of such fibres are used in ◊endoscopes to inspect otherwise inaccessible parts of machines or of the living body. Optical fibres are increasingly being used to replace copper wire in telephone cables, the messages being coded as pulses of light rather than a fluctuating electric current (see ◊digital).

optical illusion a scene or picture that fools the eye. An example is that the moon appears bigger when it is on the horizon than it does when it is high in the sky, this being due to the ◊refraction of light rays by the Earth's atmosphere.

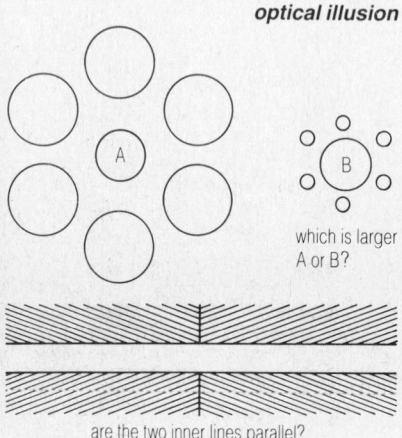

optical illusion

which is larger A or B?

are the two inner lines parallel?

optics scientific study of light and vision, for example shadows cast by opaque objects, images formed in mirrors, and lenses, microscopes, telescopes, cameras, etc. Light rays travel for all practical purposes in straight lines, although ◊Einstein has demonstrated that they may be 'bent' by a gravitational field. On striking a surface they are reflected or refracted with some attendant absorption of energy, and the study of these facts is the subject of geometrical optics.

opto-electronics a branch of ◊electronics concerned with the development of devices (based on the semiconductor gallium arsenide) which respond to ◊photons.

opuntia genus of the ◊prickly pear.

opus (Latin 'work') in music, a term used to indicate the numbering of a composer's works, usually in chronological order.

Opus Dei /'əupəs 'deɪiː/ (Latin 'God's work') a Roman Catholic secular institution aiming at the dissemination of the ideals of Christian perfection, particularly in intellectual and influential circles. Founded in Madrid in 1928, it is now international. Its members may be of either sex, and lay or clerical.

Oracle the ◊teletext system operated in Britain by Independent Television, introduced in 1973. See also ◊Ceefax.

oracle Greek sacred site where answers (also called oracles) were given by a deity to inquirers about future events; these were usually ambivalent, so that the deity was proved right whatever happened. The earliest was probably at Dodona (in ◊Epirus), where priests interpreted the sounds made by the sacred oaks of ◊Zeus, but the most celebrated was that of Apollo at ◊Delphi where the priestesses are thought to have inhaled volcanic vapours to induce the ecstasy productive of the best results.

Oradea /ɒˈrɑːdiə/ industrial city (agricultural machinery, chemicals, non-ferrous metallurgy, leather goods, printing, glass, textiles, clothing, brewing) in Romania; population (1983) 198,000.

oral literature stories which are or have been transmitted in spoken form, such as public recitation, rather than through writing or printing. Most preliterate societies seem to have had a tradition of oral literature, including short 'folk tales', legends, proverbs, and riddles as well as longer narrative works; and most of the ancient epics – such as the Greek *Odyssey* and the Mesopotamian *Gilgamesh* – seem to have been composed and added to over many centuries before they were committed to writing. Some ancient stories from oral traditions have only been written down as literary works relatively recently, such as the Finnish *Kalevala* (1822); many *fairy tales*, such as those collected in Germany in the early 19th century by the Grimm brothers, also come into this category. The extent to which this sort of *folk literature* has been consciously embellished and altered, particularly in Europe in the 19th century for nationalistic purposes, is controversial.

Oran /ɔːˈrɑːn/ seaport in Algeria; university 1967; population (1984) 663,500.
history part of the Ottoman Empire except 1509–1708 and 1732–91 under Spanish rule. Oran was occupied by France in 1831.

Orange /'ɒrɪndʒ/ town in France, N of Avignon, with the remains of a Roman theatre and arch; population (1975) 26,470. It was a medieval principality from which came the royal house of ◊Orange.

Orange /'ɒrɪndʒ/ town in New South Wales, Australia, 200 km/125 mi NW of Sydney; population (1984) 32,000. There is a woollen-textile industry, and fruit is grown.

Orange /'ɒrɪndʒ/ river in South Africa, rising on the Mont aux Sources in Lesotho and flowing W to the Atlantic; length 2,100 km/1,300 mi. It runs along the S boundary of the Orange Free State, and was named 1779 after William of Orange. Water from the Orange is diverted via the Orange–Fish River Tunnel 1975 to irrigate the semi-arid E Cape Province.

Orange, House of /'ɒrɪndʒ/ the royal family of the Netherlands. The title is derived from the small principality of Orange, in S France, held by the family from the 8th century to 1713. They held considerable possessions in the Netherlands, to which, after 1530, was added the German county of Nassau. From the time of William the Silent the family dominated Dutch history, bearing the title of stadholder for the greater part of the 17th and 18th centuries. The son of the Stadholder William V was made King William I by the Allies in 1815.

Orange, Project /'ɒrɪndʒ/ plan 1980 for a white South African 'homeland' (Projek Oranje) to be established on the border between Orange Free State and the Northern Cape. No black would be allowed to live or work there.

orange evergreen tree *Citrus sinesis*, remarkable for bearing blossom and fruit at the same time. They are commercially cultivated in Spain, Israel, Brazil, S Africa, USA, and elsewhere, but seem to have originated in SE Asia. Among the principal types are the Jaffa, blood, and navel. Tangerines and mandarins belong to a related species *Citrus reticulata*. Sevilles, *Citrus aurantium*, are the bitter oranges used in making marmalade.

Orange County /'ɒrɪndʒ/ metropolitan area of S California, USA, adjoining Los Angeles County, with aerospace and electronics industry; population (1976) 1,706,000. Oranges and strawberries are grown, Disneyland is here, and Santa Ana is the chief town.

Orange Free State /'ɒrɪndʒ ˌfriː 'steɪt/ province of the Republic of South Africa
area 129,152 sq km/49,866 sq mi
capital Bloemfontein
features plain of the High Veld; Lesotho forms an enclave on the Natal–Cape Province border
products grain, cattle; gold, oil from coal
population (1985) 1,775,500 (1,445,000 ethnic Africans)
history original settlements from 1810 were complemented by the Great Trek, and it was recognized by Britain as independent in 1854. Following the South African or Boer War of 1899–1902, it was annexed by Britain until it entered the union as a province in 1910.

Orangeman member of the Ulster Protestant Orange Society established 1795 in opposition to the ◊United Irishmen and the Catholic secret societies. It was a revival of the Orange Institution 1688, formed in support of ◊William (III) of Orange, the anniversary of whose victory at the Battle of the ◊Boyne 1690 is commemorated by Protestants in parades on 12 Jul.

orang-utan anthropoid ape *Pongo pygmaeus*, found solely in Borneo and Sumatra. Up to 1.65 m/5.5 ft in height, it is covered with long red-brown hair, and lives mainly a solitary arboreal life, feeding chiefly on fruit. It is slow-moving and has been hunted by local people for food, as well as by animal collectors. Now an endangered species, it is officially protected, and is threatened mainly by habitat destruction (logging, forest clearance for farming). It is sometimes considered the most intelligent of the apes: the name means 'man of the forest'.

Orasul Stalin /'ɔːrəsuːl 'staːlɪn/ name 1948–56 of the Romanian town ◊Braşov.

Oratorian a member of the Roman Catholic order of secular priests, called in full Congregation of the Oratory of St Philip Neri, formally constituted by St Philip Neri in 1575 at Rome, and characterized by the degree of freedom allowed to individual communities. It was first established in England by Cardinal Newman in 1848, and in 1884 Brompton Oratory in London was opened. The churches of the Oratorians are famed for their music.

oratorio musical setting of religious texts, scored for orchestra, chorus, and solo voices, on a scale more dramatic and larger than a cantata. The term derives from St Philip Neri's Oratory in Rome, where settings of the *Laudi spirituali* were performed in the 16th century. The definitive form of oratorio began in the 17th

century with Cavalieri, ◊Carissimi, Alessandro ◊Scarlatti, and ◊Schütz, and reached perfection in such works as J S ◊Bach's *Christmas Oratorio* and *St Matthew Passion*, and ◊Handel's *Messiah*. Other famous examples of oratorios are ◊Haydn's *The Creation*, ◊Mendelssohn's *Elijah*, and ◊Elgar's *The Dream of Gerontius*.

orbit the path of one body in space around another, such as the orbit of the Earth around the Sun, or the Moon around the Earth. When the two bodies are similar in mass, as in a ◊double star, both bodies move around their common centre of mass. The movement of objects in orbit follows ◊Kepler's laws, which apply to artificial satellites as well as to natural bodies. As stated by the laws, the orbit of one body around another is an ellipse. The ellipse can be highly elongated, as in the case of ◊comet orbits around the Sun, or it may be almost circular, as in ◊planets and some artificial satellites. The closest point of a planet's orbit to the Sun is called *perihelion*; the most distant point is *aphelion*. (For a body orbiting the Earth, the closest and furthest points of the orbit are called *perigee* and *apogee*.)

orchestra a group of musicians playing together, usually on a variety of different instruments. The term was originally used in Greek theatre for the semicircular space in front of the stage, and was adopted in 17th-century France to refer first to the space in front of the stage where musicians sat, and later to the musicians themselves.

In contemporary Western music, the term orchestra is commonly applied to an ensemble containing bowed string instruments with more than one player to a part, which may also include wind, brass, and percussion instruments.

The string section is commonly divided into two groups of violins (first and second), violas, cellos, and double basses. The woodwind section became standardized by the end of the 18th century, when it consisted of two each of flutes, oboes, clarinets, and bassoons, to which were later added piccolo, cor anglais, bass clarinet, and double bassoon. At that time, two timpani and two horns were also standard, and two trumpets were occasionally added. During the 19th century, the brass section was gradually expanded to include four horns, three trumpets, three trombones, and tuba. From Turkey came the bass drum, side drum, cymbals, and triangle. One or more harps became common, and to maintain balance the number of string instruments to a part also increased. Other instruments sometimes used in the orchestra include xylophone, celesta, piano, and organ.

The term is sometimes also applied to non-western ensembles, such as the Indonesian gamelan orchestra consisting solely of percussion instruments, mainly tuned gongs and bells.

orchestration the scoring of a composition for orchestra.

orchid plant of the family Orchidaceae containing some 18,000 species, distributed throughout the world except in the coldest areas, and most numerous in damp equatorial regions. The flowers have three sepals and three petals. The lowest petal, the labellum, is usually large, and may be spurred, fringed, pouched, or crested.

The flowers are sometimes solitary, but more usually are borne in spikes, racemes or panicles, either erect or drooping. Many tropical orchids are epiphytes attached to trees, although non-parasitic, but temperate orchids commonly grow on the ground, such as the spotted orchis *Dactylorhiza maculata* and other British species. Orchids are cultivated for the luxury flower trade, and among private collectors, some specimens commanding huge prices.

Orczy /'ɔːtsi/ Baroness Emmusca 1865–1947. Hungarian-born novelist, daughter of Baron Felix Orczy, who married the Englishman, Montague Barstow. Going to London in 1881 to study art, Orczy began to write in 1900, and is best remembered as the author of *The Scarlet Pimpernel* 1905.

ordeal in medieval times, method of testing guilt of an accused person based on a belief in heaven's protection of the innocent. Examples of such ordeals are walking barefoot over glowing ploughshares, dipping the hand into boiling water, and swallowing consecrated bread.

order in classical architecture, the ◊column (including capital, shaft, and base) and the entablature, considered as an architectural whole. The five orders are Doric, Ionic, Corinthian, Tuscan, and Composite.

order in biological classification, a group of related ◊families. Thus the horse, rhinoceros, and tapir families are grouped in the order Perissodactyla, the odd-toed ungulates, because they all have either one or three toes on each foot. The names of orders are not shown in italic (unlike genus and species names) and by convention they all have the ending -formes (birds and fish), -a (mammals, amphibians, reptiles, and other animals), or -ales (fungi and plants). Related orders are grouped in a ◊class.

Order in Council in Britain, an order issued by the sovereign with the advice of the Privy Council; in practice it is issued only on the advice of the cabinet. Acts of parliament often provide for the issue of Orders in Council to regulate the detailed administration of their provisions or they may be used to introduce wartime emergency legislation.

Order of Merit British order of chivalry founded in 1902 by Edward VII and limited in number to 24. Though not a knighthood, it is highly regarded.

ordinal number in mathematics, one of the series first, second, third, fourth... Ordinal numbers relate to order, whereas ◊cardinal numbers (1, 2, 3, 4...) relate to quantity.

Ordnance Survey official department for the mapping of Britain, established 1791; revision is continuous.

Ordovician the period of geological time between 500 and 435 million years ago. Animal life was confined to the sea, and fish were beginning to evolve. The period is named after the Ordovices, an ancient Welsh people, because the system of rocks formed in the Ordovician was first studied in Wales.

ore a deposit of ◊sediments or a body of ◊rock worth mining because of the economically valuable minerals it contains.

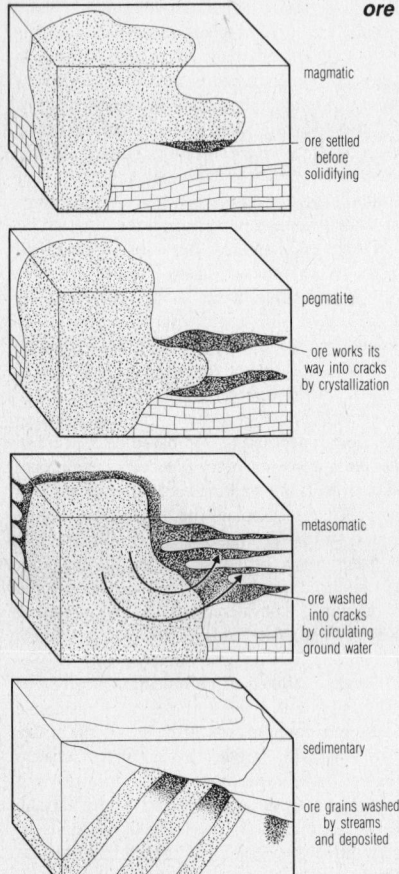

ore

magmatic

ore settled
before
solidifying

pegmatite

ore works its
way into cracks
by crystallization

metasomatic

ore washed
into cracks
by circulating
ground water

sedimentary

ore grains washed
by streams
and deposited

Oregon /ˈɒrɪgən/ Pacific state of the USA; nickname Beaver State
area 251,180 sq km/96,981 sq mi
capital Salem
towns Portland, Eugene
features fertile Willamette river valley; Columbia and Snake rivers; Crater Lake, deepest in the USA (589 m/1,932 ft); Coast and Cascade mountain ranges, the latter including ◊Mount St Helens
products wheat, livestock; timber; gold, silver, nickel
population (1983) 2,662,000
famous people Linus Pauling
history the Oregon Trail (3,200 km/2,000 mi from Independence, Missouri, to the Columbia river) was the pioneer route across the USA 1841–60. Settled 1811 by the Pacific Fur Company, Oregon Territory included Washington until 1853; it became a state in 1859.

Orel /ˌɔːriˈɒl/ industrial city (engineering), rail centre, and grain market in the USSR, capital of Orel region, on the Oka 320 km/200 mi SSW of Moscow; population (1985) 328,000.

Orenburg /ˈɒrənbɜːg/ city in S central USSR, trading and mining centre and capital of Orenburg region, on the right bank of the Ural river; population (1985) 519,000. It dates from

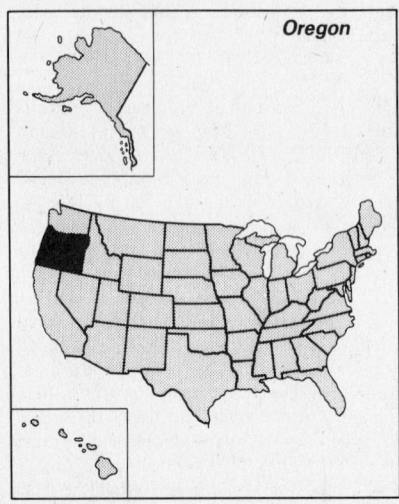

Oregon

the early 18th century and was called Chkalov 1938–57 in honour of a long-distance flyer.

Orense /ɒˈrenseɪ/ town in NW Galicia, Spain; population (1981) 96,000.

Orestes /ɒˈriːstiːz/ in Greek legend, the son of Agamemnon and ◊Clytemnestra.

Öresund /ˌɜːrəˈsʊnd/ strait between Sweden and Denmark; in English called the ◊Sound.

orfe fish *Leuciscus idus* of the carp family. Up to 45 cm/1.5 ft, it lives in fresh water and feeds on small animals. Generally greyish-black, an ornamental variety is orange. It comes from E Europe and was introduced to Britain.

Orff /ɔːf/ Carl 1895–1982. German composer. An individual stylist, using sharp dissonances and percussion, he is best remembered for his cantata *Carmina Burana* 1937, and his operas, including *Antigone* 1949.

Orford, 1st Earl of /ˈɔːfəd/ title of the British politician Robert ◊Walpole.

organ musical wind instrument of ancient origin. It developed from the Pan-pipe and hydraulus, and is mentioned as early as the 3rd century BC. Organs were imported to France from Byzantium in the 8th and 9th centuries, after which their manufacture in Europe began. The superseding of the old drawslides by the key system dates from the 11th–13th century, the first chromatic keyboard from 1361. The more recent designs date from the 1809 composition pedal.

The modern organ produces sound from varying-sized pipes under applied pressure. One note only is sounded by each pipe, but these are grouped into stops, which are ranks or scales of pipes prepared to 'speak' by a knob. These, in turn, form part of a sectional organ, one of the tonal divisions comprising the whole organ. These separate manuals are the great, swell, choir, solo, echo, and pedal organs, controlled by the player's hands and feet. By this grouping and sub-division extremes of tone and volume are obtained. Apart from its continued use in churches, the organ has been adapted for entertainment. The electrically controlled organ substitutes electrical impulses and relays for some of the air-pressure controls.

Those, such as the Hammond organs, built during the 1930s for the large cinemas of the period, include many special sound effects as well as colour displays.

organ in biology, part of a living body, such as the liver or brain, that has a distinctive function or set of functions. An organ is composed of various ◊tissues.

Organ /ˈɔːgən/ (Harold) Bryan 1935– . British portraitist, born in Leicester, whose subjects include Macmillan, Tippett, Elton John, and the Prince and Princess of Wales.

organelle a discrete and specialized structure in a living cell; organelles include ◊mitochrondia, ◊chloroplasts, ◊lysosomes, ◊ribosomes, and the ◊nucleus.

organic chemistry the chemistry of ◊carbon compounds, particularly the more complex carbon compounds. Many of these are made only by living organisms (for example proteins, carbohydrates), and it was once believed organic compounds could not be made by any other means. This was disproved when ◊Wöhler synthesized urea, but the name 'organic' (that is 'living') chemistry has remained in use. Many organic compounds are derived from oil, which represents the chemical remains of millions of microscopic marine organisms. The basis of organic chemistry is the ability of carbon to form long chains of atoms, branching chains, rings, and other complex structures. In a typical organic compound, each carbon atom forms a bond with each of its neighbouring carbon atoms in the chain or ring, and two more with hydrogen atoms (carbon has a valency of four). Other atoms that may be involved in organic molecules include oxygen and nitrogen. Compounds containing only carbon and hydrogen are known as hydrocarbons. Organic chemistry is largely the chemistry of a great variety of homologous series, in which the molecular formulae, when arranged in ascending order, form an arithmetical progression. The physical properties undergo a gradual change from one member to the next.

The chain of carbon atoms forming the backbone of an organic molecule may be built up from beginning to end without branching; or it may throw off branches at one or more points. This division of organic compounds is known as the *open-chain* or *aliphatic* compounds. Sometimes, however, the ropes of carbon atoms curl round and form rings. These constitute the second division of organic compounds, known as *closed-chain, ring,* or *cyclic* compounds. Upon the capacity of carbon atoms to form molecular rings and chains depends the infinite variety of organic nature.

In inorganic chemistry a specific formula usually represents one substance only, but in organic chemistry it is exceptional for a molecular formula to represent only one substance. Substances having the same molecular formula are called *isomers*, and the relationship is known as *isomerism*. Where substances have the same molecular formula, but differ in their structural formulae, they are called *structural isomers*. *Spatial isomers*, or *stereo-isomers*, have the same molecular formula, and also the same structural formula, the difference lying in their spatial dispositions. The study of spatial isomers is known as *stereochemistry*.

Hydrocarbons form one of the most prolific of the many organic types; fuel oils are largely made up of hydrocarbons. Typical groups containing only carbon, hydrogen, and oxygen are alcohols, aldehydes, ketones, ethers, esters, carbohydrates, and so on. Among groups containing nitrogen are amides, amines, nitro-compounds, amino-acids, proteins, purines, alkaloids, and many others, both natural and artificial. Other organic types contain sulphur, phosphorus, or halogen elements.

The most fundamental of all natural processes are oxidation, reduction, hydrolysis, condensation, polymerization, and molecular rearrangement. In nature, such changes are often brought about through the agency of promoters known as *enzymes*, which act as catalytic agents in promoting specific reactions. The most fundamental of all natural processes is *synthesis*, or building up. In living plant and animal organisms the energy stored in carbohydrate molecules, is released by slow oxidation and utilized by the organisms. The complex carbohydrates thereby revert to carbon dioxide and water, from whence they were built up with absorption of energy. Thus, a so-called carbon food cycle exists in nature. In a corresponding nitrogen food cycle, complex proteins are synthesized in nature from carbon dioxide, water, soil nitrates, and ammonium salts, and these proteins ultimately revert to the elementary raw materials from which they sprung, with the discharge of their energy of chemical combination.

organic farming see ◊agriculture.

Organisation de l'Armée Secrète (OAS) guerrilla organization formed 1961 by French settlers devoted to perpetuating their own rule in Algeria. It collapsed on the imprisonment 1962–68 of its leader General Raoul ◊Salan.

Organization for Economic Co-operation and Development (OECD) Paris-based intergovernmental organization of 24 industrialized countries active in co-ordinating member states' economic policy strategies. It superseded the Organization for European Economic Co-operation (established 1948 to promote European recovery under the ◊Marshall Plan) in 1961, when the USA and Canada became members and its scope was extended to include development aid.

Organization of African Unity (OAU) established 1963 to eradicate colonialism, and improve economic, cultural, and political cooperation in Africa; headquarters Addis Ababa. The French-speaking *Joint African and Mauritian Organization (Organisation Commune Africaine et Mauritienne: OCAM)* 1962, works within the framework of the OAU; headquarters Yaoundé, Cameroon.

Organization of American States (OAS) association established originally in 1890 to encourage friendly relations between countries of N and S America, and known as the International Union of American Republics 1890–1910 and Pan-American Union

COMMON ORGANIC MOLECULE GROUPINGS

Formula	Name	Atomic bonding
CH_3	Methyl	
CH_2CH_3	Ethyl	
CC	Double bond	
CHO	Aldehyde	
CH_2OH	Alcohol	
CO	Ketone	
COOH	Acid	
CH_2NH_2	Amine	
C_6H_6	Benzene ring	

1910–1948; it became in 1948 the central and permanent organ of the more comprehensive Organization of American States. It is now largely concerned with the social and economic development of Latin America. Its central offices are in Washington.

Organization of Central American States (*Organizacion de Estados Centro Americanos: ODECA*) International organization promoting common economic, political, educational, and defence aims in Central America. The first organization of this name, established in 1951, was superseded by a new one in 1962; membership: Costa Rica, El Salvador, Guatemala, Honduras, and Nicaragua. The permanent headquarters is in Guatemala City.

Organization of the Petroleum Exporting Countries (OPEC) 13-nation body established in 1960 to co-ordinate the price and supply policies of oil-producing states. Its concerted action in raising crude oil prices sharply in the 1970s triggered worldwide recession, and generated huge revenues for OPEC members,

some of these sums being donated or recycled to poorer developing countries. In the 1980s OPEC's dominant position was undermined by reduced demand for oil in industrialized countries and by rising non-OPEC production, notably from the ◊North Sea. These factors and others caused a sharp fall in world oil prices, forcing OPEC to institute production cutbacks.

organizer in embryology, part of the embryo that causes changes to occur in another part, through ◊induction, thus 'organizing' development and ◊differentiation.

orienteering sport of pedestrian route-finding invented in Sweden 1918. Competitors start at one-minute intervals, and have their control cards stamped at points (approximately 0.8 km/0.5 mi apart) marked on a map. World championships have been held since 1966.

origami art of folding paper into forms such as dolls and birds, originating in Japan in the 10th century.

Origen /'ɒrɪdʒen/ c. 185–c. 254. Christian theologian, born at Alexandria, who produced a fancifully allegorical interpretation of the Bible.

original sin Christian doctrine that Adam's fall rendered humankind able to achieve salvation only through divine grace.

Orinoco /ˌɒrɪ'nəʊkəʊ/ river in N South America, flowing for about 2,400 km/1,500 mi through Venezuela and forming for about 320 km/200 mi the boundary with Colombia, in which rise a number of tributaries including the Guaviare, Meta, Apure, Ventuari, Caura, and Caroni. The Orinoco is navigable by large steamers for 1,125 km/700 mi from its Atlantic delta; rapids obstruct the upper river.

oriole name given to birds, often brightly coloured, of two families. In Africa and Eurasia, orioles belong to the family Oriolidae, such as the *golden oriole Oriolus oriolus* an occasional visitor to Britain; in the Americas to the Icteridae, such as the ◊bobolink.

Orion in Greek mythology, a giant of ◊Boeotia, famed as a hunter.

Orion in astronomy, major ◊constellation in the equatorial region of the sky, representing the hunter of Greek mythology. It contains the bright stars ◊Betelgeuse and ◊Rigel, as well as a distinctive row of three stars that make up Orion's belt. Beneath the belt, marking the sword of Orion, is the ◊Orion nebula.

Orion nebula a luminous cloud of gas and dust 1,500 light years away, in the constellation Orion, from which ◊stars are forming. The nebula is about 15 light years in diameter and contains enough gas to make thousands of stars. At the nebula's centre is a group of hot young stars, called the *Trapezium*, which make the surrounding gas glow. It is visible to the naked eye as a misty patch below the belt of ◊Orion.

Orissa /ɒ'rɪsə/ state of NE India
area 155,782 sq km/60,132 sq mi
capital Bhubaneswar
towns Cuttack, Rourkela
features mainly agricultural; Chilka lake with fisheries and game; temple of Jangannath or Juggernaut at ◊Puri
population (1981) 26,370,500
language Oriya (official)

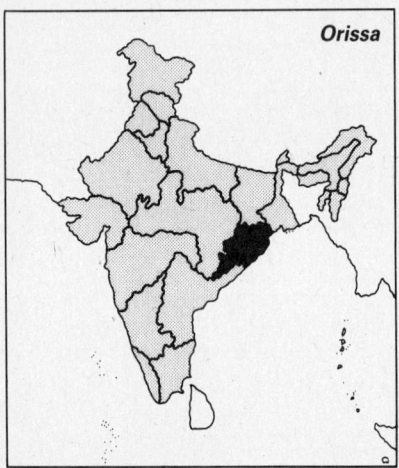

Orissa

religion Hindu 90 per cent.

Orizaba /ˌɒrɪˈsɑːbə/ industrial city (brewing, paper, textiles) and resort in Veracruz state, Mexico; population (1980) 115,000.

Orizaba /ˌɒrɪˈsɑːbə/ Spanish name for ◊Citlaltepec, mountain in Mexico.

Orkney Causeway construction put up in World War I, completed in 1943 during World War II, joining four of the Orkney islands, built to protect the British fleet from intrusion through the eastern entrances to Scapa Flow.

Orkney islands /ˈɔːkni/ area of Scotland
area 984 sq km/380 sq mi
towns administrative headquarters Kirkwall, on Mainland (Pomona)
features comprises about 90 islands and islets; population, long falling, has in recent years risen as their remoteness from the modern world attracts new settlers, for example, Peter Maxwell ◊Davies on Hoy; mild climate owing to the Gulf Stream; Skara Brae, a remarkably well-preserved Neolithic village on Mainland; Scapa Flow, between Mainland and Hoy, was a naval base in both world wars, and the German fleet scuttled itself here 21 Jun 1919
products fishing and farming, wind power (Burgar Hill has the world's most productive wind generator; blades 60 m/197 ft diameter)
population (1981) 18,900
history ◊Harold I (Fairhair) of Norway conquered the islands in 876; they were pledged to James III of Scotland 1468 for the dowry of Margaret of Denmark, and annexed by Scotland (the dowry unpaid) in 1472.

Orkneys, South /ˈɔːkniz/ islands in the British Antarctic Territory; see ◊South Orkneys.

Orlando /ɔːˈlændəʊ/ industrial city in Florida, USA, near Kennedy Space Center and Disney World; population (1984) 137,000.

Orlando /ɔːˈlændəʊ/ Vittorio Emanuele 1860–1952. Italian politician, prime minister 1917–19. He attended the Paris Peace Conference, but dissatisfaction with his handling of the Adriatic settlement led to his resignation in 1919.

Orleanists French monarchist group which supported the Orleans branch of the royal family in opposition to the Bourbon Legitimists. Both

Orkney islands The houses of the Neolithic village of Skara Brae are of drystone construction.

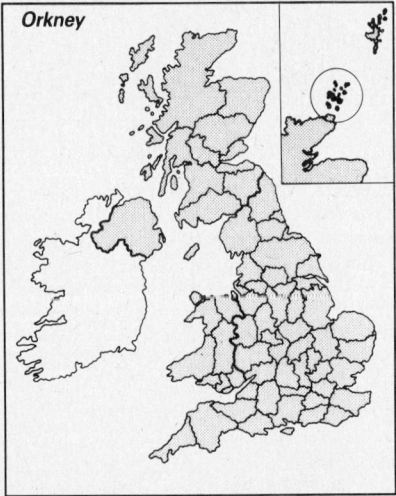

Orkney

groups were united in 1883 when the Bourbon line died out.

Orléans /ɔːˈlɪənz, French ˌɔːleɪˈɒŋ/ industrial city (engineering, food processing), capital of Loiret *département*, France, on the Loire, 115 km/70 mi SW of Paris; population (1982) 220,500. Orléans, of pre-Roman origin and formerly the capital of the old province of Orléanais, is associated with Joan of Arc, who liberated it from English rule in 1429.

Ormandy /ˈɔːməndi/ Eugene 1899–1985. Hungarian-American conductor, originally a violin virtuoso. He championed ◊Rachmaninov and ◊Shostakovich, and was music director of the Philadelphia Orchestra 1936–80.

ormolu an alloy of copper, zinc, and sometimes tin, used for furniture decoration. The name derives from the French – *or moulu* meaning 'ground gold'.

Ormonde /ˈɔːmənd/ James Butler, Duke of Ormonde 1610–1688. Irish general. He commanded the Royalist troops in Ireland 1641–50 during the Irish rebellion and the English revolution, and was lord lieutenant 1644–47, 1661–69, and 1677–84.

His grandson, *James*, 2nd duke (1665–1745), succeeded Marlborough as commander in chief in 1711, but was impeached in 1715 for Jacobite intrigues, and exiled.

Ormuzd /ˈɔːmuzd/ another name for ◊Ahura Mazda, the good god of ◊Zoroastrianism.

Orne /ɔːn/ French river rising E of Sées and flowing NW, then NE to the English Channel below Caen; 152 km/94 mi long. It gives its name to a *département;* population (1982) 295,500.

ornithology section of zoology concerned with the study of ◊birds. It covers not only scientific aspects relating to the structure and classification of birds, but also the activities of the many people in all countries interested in the natural beauty of birds, their habits, song, flight, or in their value to agriculture as destroyers of insect pests. This interest has led to the formation of societies for their protection (developing into their study), of which the Society for the Protection of Birds 1889 in Britain was the first; it received a royal charter in 1904. The Audubon Society 1905 in the USA has similar aims. There is an International Council for Bird Preservation with its headquarters at the Natural History Museum. The headquarters of the British Trust for Ornithology is in Hertfordshire. Migration, age, pollution effects, and so on, are monitored by ringing (trained government-licensed operators fit numbered metal rings to captured specimens with a return address). Legislation in various countries to protect wild birds dates from a British Act of 1880.

ornithophily the ◊pollination of flowers by birds. Ornithophilous flowers are typically brightly coloured, often red or orange. They produce copious quantities of thin, watery nectar, and are scentless because most birds do not respond well to smell. They are mostly found in tropical areas, with hummingbirds being the most important pollinators in N and S America, and the sunbirds in Africa and Asia.

orogeny the formation of mountains, by such processes as folding, faulting, and upthrusting (see ◊plate tectonics).

Orontes /ɒˈrɒntiːz/ river flowing through Lebanon, Syria, and Turkey to the Mediterranean, and used mainly for irrigation; length 400 km/250 mi.

Orpen /ˈɔːpən/ William Newenham Montague 1878–1931. Irish artist. He became famous as a portraitist and genre artist, and was knighted in 1918

Orpheus /ˈɔːfjuːs/ mythical Greek poet and musician. He was the son of Apollo and a muse, and married Eurydice, who died from the bite of a snake. Orpheus went down to Hades to bring her back, relying on his sweet singing to charm the nether gods. Her return to life was granted on condition that he walked ahead of her without looking back. Orpheus broke this condition, and Eurydice was irretrievably lost. In his grief, he despised the Maenad women of Thrace, and was torn in pieces by them.

Orphism ancient Greek mystery cult, of which the Orphic hymns formed part of the secret rites which, accompanied by an ascetic regime, were aimed at securing eventual immortality. It became popular in Rome, and remains of an Orphic temple were found at Hungerford, Berkshire, in 1980.

orrery a mechanical device for demonstrating the motions of the heavenly bodies. Invented in about 1710 by George Graham, it was named after his patron, the 4th Earl of Orrery. It is the forerunner of the modern ◊planetarium.

orris root the underground stem of species of iris grown in S Europe. Violet-scented, it is used in perfumery.

Orsini /ɔːˈsiːni/ Felice 1819–1858. Italian political activist, a member of the *Carbonari* secret political group, who attempted unsuccessfully to assassinate Napoleon III in Paris in Jan 1858. He was subsequently executed, but the Orsini affair awakened Napoleon's interest in Italy and led to a secret alliance with Piedmont at Pilombières in 1858, directed against Italy.

Orsk /ɔːsk/ industrial city (oil refining, locomotives, aluminium) in the USSR, at the junction of the Or and Ural rivers; population (1985) 266,000. Its refineries are fed by a pipeline from Guriev.

Ortega (Saavedra) /ɔːˈteɪɡə/ Daniel 1945– . Nicaraguan politician, a member of the Sandinista Liberation Front (FSLN) which overthrew the regime of Anastasion Somoza in 1979, and leader from 1981.

Active in underground activities against the Somoza regime from an early age, Ortega was imprisoned and tortured several times. He became a member of the National Directorate of the FSLN and fought in the campaign which overthrew Somoza in 1979, when he became a member of the Junta of National reconstruction, and then its coordinator two years later.

Ortega y Gasset /ɔːˈteɪɡə iː ɡæˈset/ José 1883–1955. Spanish philosopher and critic. He considered Communism and Fascism the cause of the downfall of western civilization. His *Toward a Philosophy of History* 1941 contains philosophical reflections on the State, and an interpretation of the meaning of human history.

orthochromatic a photographic film or paper of decreased sensitivity, which can be processed with a red safe-light. Blue objects appear lighter and red ones darker because of increased blue sensitivity.

orthodontics branch of ◊dentistry, mainly dealing with correction of problems such as irregularity of teeth.

orthopaedics correction of bodily injuries, diseased parts, and malformations, particularly of muscle, cartilage, and bone. Among its most important techniques are the treatment of fractures, bone and nerve grafting, the restoration of function after paralysis, the reconstruction of joints, and especially

rehabilitation, in which patients recveive the appropriate therapies from surgery, medicine, psychology, physical training and occupational therapy. Increasing use is made of electronics to stimulate residual powers of movement.

ortolan bird *Emberiza hortulana* of the bunting family, common in Europe and W Asia. Migrating S or returning, it is netted, then fed and killed for the table. It is brownish, with a grey head.

Orton /ˈɔːtn/ Joe 1933–1967. British dramatist, noted for bizarre black comedies in which surreal and violent action takes place in genteel and unlikely settings. Plays include *Entertaining Mr Sloane* 1964, *Loot* 1966, and *What the Butler Saw* 1968. His diaries, and autobiography, *Prick Up Your Ears*, deal frankly with his personal life. He was murdered by his flatmate Kenneth Halliwell.

Orvieto /ˌɔːviˈetəʊ/ town in Umbria, Italy, NE of Lake Bolsena, population (1977) 25,500. Built on the site of Volsinii, an Etruscan town destroyed by the Romans 280 BC, Orvieto has many Etruscan remains.

Orwell /ˈɔːwel/ George, pen name of British author Eric Arthur Blair 1903–1950. Born in India, he was educated at Eton, and for five years served in the Burmese police force, an experience reflected in the novel *Burmese Days* 1935. Adventures as dishwasher, schoolmaster, and bookshop assistant were related in *Down and Out in Paris and London* 1933 and service for the Republican cause in the Spanish Civil War in *Homage to Catalonia* 1938. His best-known books are the satire *Animal Farm* 1945 which included such sayings as 'All animals are equal, but some are more equal than others', and the prophetic *1984* 1949, portraying state control of existence carried to the ultimate extent.

oryx large African desert antelope. The Arabian oryx *Oryx leucoryx* was extinct in the wild but bred in captivity and has been successfully reintroduced into the wild. The scimitar-horned oryx of the Sahara is also rare. Beisa oryx in East Africa and gemsbok in the Kalahari are more common. In profile the two long horns appear as one, which may have given rise to the legend of the unicorn.

Osaka /əʊˈsɑːkə/ industrial port (iron, steel, shipbuilding, chemicals, textiles), the second largest city in Japan, on Honshu island; university 1931; population (1984) 2,534,000. Lying on a plain sheltered by hills and opening on to Osaka bay, Osaka is honeycombed with waterways. It is a tourist centre for Kyoto and the Seto Inland Sea, and linked with Tokyo by fast electric train 200 kph/124 mph.

history oldest city of Japan, Osaka was at times the seat of government in the 4th–8th centuries. It was a mercantile centre in the 18th century, and in the 20th century set the pace for Japan's revolution based on light industries.

Osborne /ˈɒzbɔːn/ Dorothy 1627–1695. English letter-writer. In 1655 she married Sir William Temple (1628–99), to whom she wrote her letters 1652–54, first published in 1888.

Osborne /ˈɒzbɔːn/ John (James) 1929– . English dramatist and actor. He became well known as an 'angry young man' when his first

Orwell During a period of poverty, Eton-educated George Orwell worked as a dishwasher and lived as a tramp. A gifted literary critic as well as a novelist, he is best known for the political allegories *Animal Farm* and *1984*.

Osaka Osaka Castle, completed in 1586, but destroyed several times, took 40,000 workmen three years to construct. The donjon, above, was rebuilt in 1931.

play, *Look Back in Anger* 1956, in which the hero rebels against middle-class life, was produced. His later plays include *The Entertainer* 1957,

Luther 1960, *West of Suez* 1971, and *Watch it Come Down* 1976.

Osborne House favourite residence of Queen Victoria, for whom it was built in 1845, 1.6 km/1 mi SE of Cowes in the Isle of Wight, England. It was presented to the nation by Edward VII.

Oscar in cinema, popular name for ◊Academy Award.

Oscar two kings of Sweden and Norway:

Oscar I /ˈɒskə/ 1799–1859. Succeeded his father, ◊Charles XIV, in 1844.

Oscar II /ˈɒskə/ 1829–1907. Younger son of ◊Oscar I, he came to the throne in 1872. He abandoned the title of king of Norway on the separation of the two kingdoms in 1905.

oscillator generator producing a desired oscillation (vibration); an essential part of a radio transmitter, generating the high-frequency carrier signal necessary for radio communication. There are many types of oscillator involving various arrangements of valves or components such as ◊transistors, ◊inductors, ◊capacitors, and ◊resistors. The ◊frequency is often controlled by the vibrations set up in a ◊crystal, for example, quartz.

oscillograph instrument for recording oscillations, electrical or mechanical; an *oscilloscope* shows variations in electrical ◊potential on the screen of a ◊cathode-ray tube, by means of deflection of a beam of ◊electrons.

Oshogbo /ɒˈʃɒgbəʊ/ city and trading centre in W Nigeria, 200 km/125 mi NE of Lagos, with cotton industry; population (1986) 405,000.

osier tree or shrub of the willow genus *Salix*, cultivated for basket making, especially *Salix viminalis*.

Osijek /ˈɒsiek/ industrial river port (textiles) in Croatia, Yugoslavia, on the Drava; population (1981) 158,800.

Osiris /əʊˈsaɪrɪs/ ancient Egyptian god (who wears a tall curved hat with a plume each side), embodiment of goodness, who went to rule the underworld, after being killed by *Set*, the god of night, the desert, and evil (portrayed as a grotesque animal). The sister-wife of Osiris was the sky and fertility goddess ◊*Isis/Hathor* (who wears a cow's horns, with a sun-disc between them). Her rites were mysterious, as were those of ◊Demeter, with whom she was identified by the Greeks. The son of Osiris and Isis was *Horus* (falcon-headed, or shown as a boy, representing the youthful sun), the pharaohs were thought to be his incarnation. Horus captured his father's murderer Set. Under ◊Ptolemy I's Graeco-Egyptian empire Osiris was developed (as a means of uniting his Greek and Egyptian subjects) into *Serapis* (Osiris+Apis, the latter being the bull-god of Memphis who carried the dead to the tomb), elements of the cults of Zeus and Hades being included, which did not please the Egyptians; the greatest temple of Serapis was the Serapeum at Alexandria. The cult of Osiris, and that of Isis, later spread to Rome.

Oslo /ˈɒzləʊ/ capital and industrial port (textiles, engineering) of Norway; population (1985) 447,500. Built at the head of Oslo fjord, which is kept open in winter by icebreakers. There is a viking museum, 13th-century Akershus Castle, and a 17th-century cathedral.

history The first recorded settlement was made by Harald III (Hardrada: see under ◊Harold II), but after a fire in 1624, it was entirely replanned by Christian IV and renamed Christiania 1624–1924.

Osman I /ˈɒzmən/ or *Othman I* 1259–1326. Turkish sultan. He began his career in the service of the Seljuk Turks, but in 1299 he set up a kingdom of his own in Bithynia and assumed the title of sultan. He conquered a great part of Asia Minor, so founding the Turkish Empire. His successors were known as 'sons of Osman', from which the term ◊Ottoman Empire is derived.

osmium a bluish-white, hard, crystalline metallic element, very heavy and infusible; Symbol Os, atomic number 76, atomic weight 190.2. Discovered in 1803 by Tennant in residue left when crude platinum was dissolved in aqua regis (concentrated nitric and hydrochloric acids). It is found in platinum-bearing river sands and with iridium in osmiridium. Heated in air it gives off a pungently irritating poisonous vapour. It is used for lamp filaments, with iridium to form a very hard alloy suitable for pen-nibs and fine machine bearings, and as a catalyst.

osmoregulation the process whereby the water content of living organisms is maintained at a constant level. If the water balance is disrupted, the concentration of salts will be too high or too low and vital functions, such as nerve conduction, will be affected. In mammals, loss of water by evaporation is counteracted by increased intake, and by mechanisms in the kidneys that enhance the rate at which water is resorbed before ◊urine production. Both these responses are mediated by ◊hormones, especially those of the ◊adrenal cortex.

osmosis movement of solvent (liquid) through a semipermeable membrane separating solutions of different concentrations. The solvent passes from the diluter side to the more concentrated side until the two concentrations are equal. Applying external pressure to the solution on the more concentrated side arrests osmosis, and is a measure of the osmotic pressure of the solution. Many cell membranes behave as semipermeable membranes, and osmosis is an important mechanism in the transport of fluids in living organisms, for example in the transport of water from the roots up the stems of plants. Fish have protective mechanisms to counteract osmosis, which would otherwise cause fluid transport between the body of the animal and the surrounding water (outwards in saltwater fish, inwards in freshwater ones).

Osnabrück /ˌɒznəˈbruk/ industrial city (engineering, iron and steel, textiles and clothing, paper, food processing) in West Germany, 115 km/70 mi W of Hanover; population (1984) 154,500. Before World War II, it had fine examples of Gothic and Renaissance architecture.

history Osnabrück bishopric was founded by Charlemagne 783. The Treaty of Westphalia was signed at Osnabrück and Münster in 1648, ending the Thirty Years' War.

osprey bird of prey *Pandion haliaetus*, known in America from its diet as the fish hawk. Once extinct in Britain, it is now breeding again in

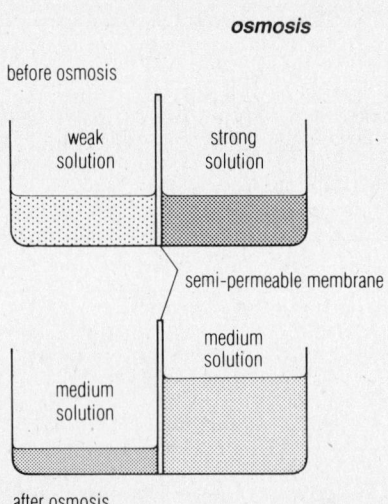

osmosis

before osmosis

weak solution — strong solution

semi-permeable membrane

medium solution — medium solution

after osmosis

Scotland. Dark brown above and a striking white below, it measures 0.6 m/2 ft with a 2 m/6 ft wingspread.

Ossa /ˈɒsə/ mountain in Thessaly, Greece; height 1,978 m/6,490 ft. Two of Poseidon's giant sons were said to have tried to dislodge the gods from Olympus by piling nearby Mount Pelion on top of Ossa to scale the great mountain.

Ossetia /ɒˈsiːʃə/ area of the Caucasus, home of the Ossets, who speak the Iranian language Ossetic, and who were conquered by the Russians in 1802. Some live in the *North Ossetian* Republic of the SW USSR; area 8,000 sq km/3,088 sq mi; population (1985) 613,000; capital Ordzhonikidze. The rest live in the *South Ossetian* autonomous region of the Georgian Republic, population (1984) 98,000; capital Tshkinvali.

Ossian /ˈɒsɪən/ Irish hero and poet, in Celtic called *Oisin*. He is represented as the son of Finn Mac Cumhaill, c. 250, and as having lived to tell the tales of Finn and the Ulster heroes to St Patrick, about 400. The publication, from 1760 onwards, of the 'Ossianic' poems of J ◊Macpherson made Ossian's name familiar throughout Europe.

ossification the process whereby ◊bone is formed in vertebrate animals by special cells (osteoblasts) that secrete layers of ◊extracellular matrix on the surface of the existing ◊cartilage. This is then converted to bone by the deposition of calcium phosphate crystals.

Ossory /ˈɒsəri/ ancient kingdom, lasting until 1110, in Leinster, Ireland; the name is preserved in existent Church of Ireland and Roman Catholic bishoprics.

Ostade /ɒsˈtɑːdə/ Adriaen van 1610–1685. Dutch painter and engraver. Famous for his pictures of tavern scenes, and village fairs, Ostade studied under Frans ◊Hals. His brother, *Isaac van Ostade* (1621–49), excelled in winter landscapes, and roadside and farmyard scenes.

Östberg /ˈɜːstbæg/ Ragnar 1866–1945. Swedish architect, famous for his design of the City Hall, Stockholm, Sweden (1911–23).

Ostend /ɒs'tend/ seaport and pleasure resort in W Flanders, Belgium, Flanders, 108 km/67 mi NW of Brussels; population (1985) 69,000. There are large docks, and the Belgian fishing fleet has its headquarters here.

osteoarthritis degenerative disease of the joints in later life, sometimes resulting in disabling stiffness and wasting of muscles. Formerly thought to be due to wear and tear, it has been shown to be less common in the physically active. It appears to be linked with calcium phosphate deposits in cartilage, a discovery which suggests hope of eventual prevention.

osteology part of the science of ◊anatomy, dealing with bones and their uses.

osteomyelitis infection of bone, often linked with a knock or fall. The symptoms are high fever, severe illness, and pain over the limb. If the infection is at the surface of the bone it may quickly form an abscess; if it is deep in the bone marrow it may spread into the circulation and lead to blood poisoning. Most cases can be treated with antibiotics, but sometimes surgery is needed.

osteopathy system of alternative medical practice which relies on physical manipulation to treat mechanical stress and claims to relieve not only postural problems and muscle pain, but asthma and other disorders.

osteoporosis bone demineralization, rendering fractures more likely, which occurs in women after the menopause, and also in young women runners. Suggested prevention is by hormone replacement therapy. A well-balanced diet with plenty of calcium-rich foods and regular exercise will keep bones healthy so that at the menopause they are in good condition, but calcium cannot prevent the disease developing.

Ostia /'ɒstiə/ ancient Italian town and harbour near the mouth of the Tiber. Dating from about 330 BC, it was the port of Rome and at one time had a population of about 100,000; in modern times a seaside resort, *Ostia Mare*, has been established nearby.

Ostpolitik German 'eastern policy': West German Chancellor ◊Brandt's policy of rapprochement with the Communist bloc from 1971, pursued to a modified extent also by ◊Schmidt and ◊Kohl.

ostracism ancient Athenian political device to preserve public order. Votes on pieces of broken pot (Greek *ostrakon*) were used to exile unpopular politicians for ten years.

Ostrava /'ɒstrəvə/ industrial city (iron works and furnaces) in Czechoslovakia, capital of N Moravian region, NE of Brno, in a coalmining district; population (1984) 324,000.

ostrich flightless bird *Struthio camelus* found in Africa and Arabia. The male may be about 2.5 m/8 ft tall and weigh 135 kg/300 lb, and is the largest of extant birds. Living in family groups of one cock with several hens, the ostrich has exceptionally strong legs and feet (two-toed) which enable it to run at high speed and are also used in defence. The beautiful tail feathers have commercial value and ostriches are bred in farms, especially in South Africa.

ostrich A two-week-old ostrich surveying its shell. Ostriches develop strong legs which enable them to run at high speed.

Ostrogoths branch of the E Germanic people, the ◊Goths.

Ostwald /'ɒstvælt/ Wilhelm 1853–1932. German chemist, whose work on catalysts laid the foundations of the petrochemical and other industries. He received a Nobel prize in 1909.

Oswald, St /'ɒzwəld/ c. 605–642. King of Northumbria from 634, who had become a Christian convert during his exile in Iona. With the help of St Aidan he furthered the spread of Christianity until he was defeated and killed by King Penda of Mercia.

Oswestry /'ɒzwəstri/ market town, also making agricultural machinery and plastics, in Shropshire, England, population (1981) 12,400, with a church dedicated to St ◊Oswald.

Oswiecim town in S Poland (German ◊Auschwitz).

Otaru /əʊ'tɑːruː/ fishing port on W coast of Hokkaido, Japan, with paper mills; processes fish and makes sake; population (1984) 179,000.

Othman /ɒθ'mɑːn/ c. 574–656. Arabian caliph. A son-in-law of Muhammad, he was elected caliph in 644. Under his rule the Arabs became a naval power and captured Cyprus, but his personal weaknesses led to his assassination. He was responsible for the final editing of the ◊Koran.

Othman I another name for the Turkish sultan ◊Osman.

Otho I /'əʊθəʊ/ 1815–1867. King of Greece. The 17-year-old son of King ◊Ludwig I of Bavaria, he was selected by the European powers as the first king of independent Greece in 1832. His long reign (to 1862) was ended when he was overthrown by a popular revolt.

Otis /'əʊtɪs/ Elisha Graves 1811–1861. American engineer, who developed a lift with a safety device, making it acceptable for passenger use in the first skyscrapers. The safety device, invented in 1852, consisted of rachets on the sides of the lift shaft into which spring-loaded catches would engage and 'lock' the lift in position in the event of cable failure.

Otranto /ɒ'træntəʊ/ seaport in Apulia, Italy, on the *Strait of Otranto*, with Greek and Roman remains; population (1971) 4,151. The ruined castle inspired Horace Walpole's novel *The Castle of Otranto* 1764.

Ottawa /'ɒtəwə/ capital of Canada, in the province of Ontario, on the hills overlooking the river Ottawa, and divided by the Rideau Canal into the Upper (western) and Lower (eastern) Town; it is also an industrial city (timber, pulp and paper, engineering, food processing, publishing); population (1981) 718,000.
features National Museum, National Art Gallery, Observatory, Rideau Hall (the governor-general's residence), and the National Arts Centre 1969
history Founded 1826–32 as Bytown (in honour of John By whose army engineers were building the Rideau Canal), it was renamed 1854 after the Outaouac Indians, and in 1858 was chosen by Queen Victoria as the country's capital.

Ottawa agreements the trade agreements concluded at the Imperial Economic Conference, held at Ottawa in 1932, between Britain and the Dominions (except the Irish Free State), India, and S Rhodesia. The Dominions agreed to lower their preferential tariffs on British manufactures, while Britain admitted almost all Dominion produce free of duty, granted preferences to the rest, and increased duties on foreign imports competing with Dominion produce. The agreements marked the abandonment by Britain of her traditional ◊free-trade policy.

otter aquatic carnivore of the weasel family. The otter of Europe and Asia *Lutra lutra* has a broad head, elongated body covered by grey-brown fur, short legs, and webbed feet: including a 45 cm/1.5 ft tail, it measures over 1 m/3.5 ft. It lives on fish. There are a number of American species, such as the commercially valuable fur-bearing sea otter *Enhydra lutris* of the North Pacific.

Otto /'ɒtəʊ/ four Holy Roman emperors including:
Otto I 912–73 who succeeded in 936, restored the power of the empire, asserted his authority over the Pope and the nobles, ended the Magyar menace by his victory at the Lechfeld in 955, and refounded the East Mark, or Austria, as a barrier against them.
Otto IV about 1182–1218, who was elected emperor in 1198, engaged in controversy with Innocent III, and was defeated by the Pope's ally, Philip of France, at Bouvines in 1214.

Otto /'ɒtəʊ/ Nikolaus August 1832–1891. German engineer, who in 1876 patented an effective internal combustion engine.

Otto cycle the correct name for the ◊four-stroke engine cycle, introduced by the German engineer Nikolaus ◊Otto in 1876. It improved upon existing engine cycles by compressing the fuel mixture before it was ignited.

Ottoman Empire /'ɒtəmən/ the successor of the ◊Seljuk Empire 1300–1920, founded by ◊Osman I and reaching its height with ◊Suleiman. At its greatest extent its bounds were Europe as far as Hungary, part of South Russia, Iran, the Palestinian coastline, Egypt, and North Africa. In decline from the 17th century, there was an attempted revival and reform under the Young Turk party (led by ◊Enver Pasha) in 1908, but the regime crumbled when Turkey took the German side in World War I. The sultanate was abolished by ◊Atatürk in 1922.

Expansion of the Ottoman Empire 1453–1680

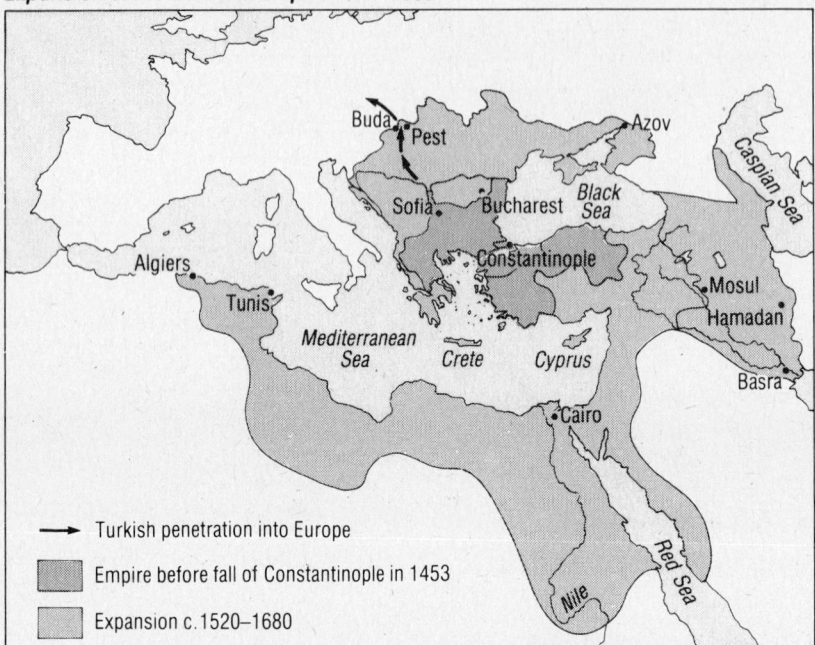

→ Turkish penetration into Europe

Empire before fall of Constantinople in 1453

Expansion c. 1520–1680

Otway /ˈɒtweɪ/ Thomas 1652–1685. British dramatist. Born near Midhurst, Sussex, he wrote for the stage from 1675, his chief plays being *Don Carlos* 1676, *The Orphan* 1680, and *Venice Preserv'd* 1682. He died destitute in London.

Ouagadougou /ˌwæɡəˈduːɡuː/ capital and industrial and commercial centre of Burkina Faso; population (1985) 375,000.

Oudenaarde /ˈuːdənɑːd/ small town of E Flanders, Belgium, on the Scheldt, 28 km/18 mi SSW of Ghent. Oudenaarde was the site of the victory by the British, Dutch, and Austrians over the French in 1708 during the War of Spanish Succession.

Oudh /aʊd/ region of N India, now part of Uttar Pradesh. An independent kingdom before it fell under Mogul rule, Oudh regained independence 1732–1856, when it was annexed by Britain. Its capital was Lucknow, centre of the ◊Indian Mutiny 1857–58. In 1877 it was joined with Agra, from 1902 as the United Provinces of Agra and Oudh, renamed Uttar Pradesh 1950.

Ouessant /ˈwesɒn/ French form of ◊Ushant, an island W of Brittany.

Oughtred /ˈuːtrɪd/ William 1575–1660. English mathematician. A priest, Oughtred was the vicar of Albury, Surrey. In his spare time he wrote his major work *Clavis mathematicae/The Key to Mathematics* 1631, which introduced the '×' symbol for multiplication, as well as the symbols for *sin, cos,* and *tan.* He is also credited as the inventor of the slide rule.

Ouida /ˈwiːdə/ pen name of Marie Louise de

la Ramée 1839–1908. British romantic novelist whose novels included *Under Two Flags* 1867 and *Moths* 1880.

Oughtred William Oughtred is an example of the learning and intellectual achievement of the clergy of his time: his *Clavis mathematicae* was a survey of the entire body of mathematical knowledge of his day.

Oujda /uːʒˈdɑː/ industrial city (lead and coalmining) in N Morocco, near the border with Algeria; population (1982) 479,000.

Oulu /ˈəʊluː/ industrial port (saw mills, tanneries, shipyards) in Finland (Swedish *Uleåborg*) on the Gulf of Bothnia; university 1958; population (1984) 96,000.

ounce snow leopard. See ◊leopard.

ounce unit of weight, the 12th part of a pound troy = 480 grains; in avoirdupois, the 16th part of a pound = 437.5 grains; in metric, 28.3 grams. The fluid ounce is a measure of capacity, in the UK equivalent to an avoirdupois ounce of distilled water at 62 C.

Ouse /uːz/ name of several British rivers: The *Great Ouse* rises in Northamptonshire, and after winding about 250 km/160 mi it enters the Wash north of King's Lynn. A huge sluice across the Great Ouse, near King's Lynn, was built as part of extensive flood-control works 1959. The Yorkshire *Ouse* is formed by the junction of the Ure and Swale near Boroughbridge, and joins the Trent to form the Humber. The Sussex *Ouse* rises between Horsham and Cuckfield, and flows through the S Downs to enter the English Channel at Newhaven.

ousel or ouzel ancient name of the blackbird. The ring ouzel *Turdus torquatus* is similar to a blackbird, but has a white band across the breast. It is found in Europe in rocky country. Water ouzel is another name for the ◊dipper.

Ouspensky /uːˈspenski/ Peter 1878–1947. Russian mystic. Originally a scientist, he became a disciple of ◊Gurdjieff, and expanded his ideas in terms of other dimensions of space and time, for example, *Tertium Organum* 1912.

outback the inland region of Australia.

outlawry in medieval England, a declaration that a criminal was outside the protection of the law, with his or her lands and goods forfeited to the Crown, and all civil rights being set aside. It was a lucrative royal 'privilege'; ◊Magna Carta restricted its use and under Edward III it was further modified. Some outlaws became popular heroes, for example, ◊Robin Hood.

output device in computing, any device for displaying, in a form intelligible to the user, the results of processing done by a computer. The most common output devices are the ◊VDU (visual display unit, or screen) and the ◊printer.

Outram /ˈuːtrəm/ James 1803–1863. British general. He served in the Afghan and Sikh wars, and commanded in the Persian campaign of 1857. On the outbreak of the ◊Indian Mutiny he cooperated with Havelock to raise the siege of Lucknow.

Oval, the /ˈəʊvəl/ a cricket ground, dating from 1846, the headquarters of the Surrey County Cricket Club, at Kennington, London, England. The first test match between England and Australia was played here in 1880.

ovary an organ found in female animals, which generates the ◊ova, or ◊eggs. In humans the ovaries are two whitish rounded bodies about 25 mm/1 in by 35 mm/1.5 in located in the abdomen near the ends of the ◊Fallopian tubes. They secrete the hormones responsible for the secondary sexual characteristics of the female, such as smooth, hairless skin and enlarged breasts.

In botany, an ovary is the expanded basal portion of the ◊carpel of flowering plants, containing one or more ◊ovules. It is hollow with a thick wall to protect the ovules. Following fertilization of the ovum, it develops into the ◊fruit wall or pericarp. The relative position of the ovary to the other floral parts is often an important character in classification: it may be either inferior or superior, depending on whether the petals and sepals are inserted above or below.

Ovens river /ˈʌvənz/ river in Victoria, Australia, a tributary of the Murray.

Overijssel /ˌəʊvərˈaɪsəl/ province of the E central Netherlands
area 3,800 sq km/1,470 sq mi
capital Zwolle
features generally flat; rivers Ijssel and Vecht
products sheep, cattle, dairy products
population (1985) 1,045,000.

overlanders Australian drovers who in the 19th century opened up new territory by driving their cattle to new stations, or to market, before the establishment of regular stock routes.

overland telegraph the cable erected 1870–72 linking Port Augusta in S Australia and Darwin in Northern Territory, and the latter by undersea cable to Java: it ended the communications isolation of the Australian continent.

Overlord name given to the Allied invasion of Normany on 6 June 1944 in World War II.

overture a piece of instrumental music, usually preceding an opera. There are also overtures to suites, plays, and so on, and 'concert' overtures such as Elgar's *Cockaigne*. The use of an overture in opera came into being during the 17th century, the 'Italian' overture consisting of two quick movements interspersed with a slow one, and the 'French' of a quick movement between two in slower tempo.

Ovid /ˈɒvɪd/ 43 BC–17 AD. Roman poet whose full name was Publius Ovidius Naso. Born at Sulmo, he studied rhetoric in Rome in preparation for a legal career, but soon turned to literature. In 8 AD he was banished by Augustus to Tomi, on the Black Sea, where he died: this punishment was supposedly for his immoral *Ars amatoria*, but was probably because of some connection with Julia, the profligate daughter of Augustus. Among his works are the youthful *Amores*; the *Metamorphoses*, mythical stories of miraculous transformations; the *Fasti*, forming an incomplete poetic calendar; and the fruits of his exile, the elegiac *Tristia* and *Epistulae ex Ponto*.

Oviedo /ˌɒviˈeɪdəʊ/ industrial city (textiles, matches, chocolate, sugar), capital of Asturias region, Spain, 25 km/16 mi S of the Bay of Biscay; university 1604; population (1981) 184,500.

ovipary a method of animal reproduction in which eggs are laid by the female and develop outside her body. It is the most common form of reproduction. See also ◊ovovivipary, ◊vivipary.

ovovivipary a method of animal reproduction in which fertilized ◊eggs develop within the female, but the embryo gains no nutritional substances from the female, unlike true ◊vivipary. It occurs in some invertebrates, fish and reptiles. See also ◊ovipary.

ovule a structure found in seed plants which develops into a seed after fertilization. It consists of an ◊embryo sac containing the female gamete (◊ovum or egg cell), surrounded by nutritive tissue, the nucellus. Outside this there are one or two integuments which provide protection, developing into the testa or seed coat following fertilization. In flowering plants (◊angiosperms) the ovule is within an ◊ovary, and is attached to the ovary wall by a short stalk or funicle. In ◊gymnosperms (conifers and their allies) the ovules are borne on the surface of an ovuliferous scale, usually within a ◊cone, and are not enclosed by an ovary.

ovum the female ◊gamete (sex-cell) before ◊fertilization. In animals, it is called an ◊egg, and is produced in the ◊ovaries. In plants, where it is also known as an egg-cell or oosphere, the ovum is produced in an ◊ovule. The ovum is non-motile. It must be fertilized by a male gamete before it can develop further, except in cases of ◊parthenogenesis.

Owen /ˈəʊɪn/ David 1938– . British politician. Originally a doctor, he entered parliament in 1966, and was Labour Foreign Secretary 1977–79. In 1981 he was associated with Shirley Williams, William Rodgers, and Roy Jenkins in the ◊Limehouse Declaration founding the ◊Social Democratic Party, and in 1983 succeeded Jenkins as its leader. He stood down from this post in 1987 following the party's decision to merge with the Liberals.

Owen /ˈəʊɪn/ Robert 1771–1858. British socialist. Born in Wales. He became manager in 1800 of a mill at New Lanark, Scotland, where by improving working and housing conditions and providing schools he created a model community. From 1817 he proposed that 'villages of cooperation', self-supporting communities run on socialist lines, should be founded; these, he believed, would ultimately replace private ownership. He organized the Grand National Consolidated Trades Union in 1833, in order that the unions might take over industry and run it cooperatively. Although this scheme collapsed in 1834, Owen's ideas did much to stimulate the ◊cooperative movement.

Owen /ˈəʊɪn/ Wilfred 1893–1918. British poet of World War I. Born at Plas Wilmot, Oswestry, in 1913 he went to France as a tutor, returning to England to enlist in 1915, and was killed in action a week before the Armistice. His poetry expresses his hatred of war, for example *Anthem for Doomed Youth*, published after his death 1921.

Owen Falls /ˈəʊɪn/ waterfall in Uganda on the White Nile, 4 km/2.5 mi below the point at which the river leaves Lake Victoria. A dam provides hydroelectricity for Uganda and Kenya, and helps to control the flood waters.

Owens /ˈəʊɪnz/ James 'Jesse' 1913–1980. American athlete. He excelled in running on the flat and over hurdles, and in the long jump. At the Olympics in Berlin in 1936 he won four gold medals. Newsreels of the event were shown around the world, demonstrating the ludicrousness of the Nazi myth of Aryan superiority. Hitler is said to have stormed out of the stadium in disgust at the black man's triumph.

owl bird of the order Strigiformes. These are mainly nocturnal birds of prey, with mobile heads, soundless flight, acute hearing, and forward-facing eyes. All species lay white eggs, and begin incubation as soon as the first is laid.

Owen In *A New View of Society*, the philanthropist Robert Owen claimed that personal character is wholly determined by environment. He had earlier abolished child employment, established sickness and old-age insurance, and opened educational and recreational facilities at his cotton mills in the north of England.

Owens The American track and field athlete Jesse Owens gives an exhibition of the long jump at White City, 1936. His long jump of 8.13 m/26 ft 8 ins was not equalled for another 25 years.

They disgorge indigestible remains of their prey in pellets (castings). They comprise two families: *typical owls* family Strigidae, including *tawny owl Strix aluco* a brown-flecked species of Europe and the Middle East; *little owl Athene noctua* Greek symbol of wisdom and bird of ◊Athena, found widely near human homes, and naturalized in Britain; *snowy owl Nyctea scandiaca* of the Arctic; and the largest of the owls, the *eagle owl Bubo bubo* of Eurasia, and *powerful owl Ninox strenua* of Australia, both up to 0.75 m/2.25 ft long. *Barn owls* family

Tytonidae, including the world-wide **barn owl** *Tyto alba* the world's most cosmopolitan bird, formerly common in Britain, but now diminished by pesticides and loss of habitat.

ox the castrated male of domestic species of ◊cattle, used in Third World countries for ploughing and other agricultural purposes, also the extinct wild ox or aurochs of Europe, and extant wild species.

oxalic acid one of the oldest known organic acids, $(COOH)_2.2H_2O$. It is a white, crystalline, poisonous solid, soluble in water, alcohol, and ether. Oxalic acid is found in rhubarb, and its salts (oxalates) occur in wood sorrel and other plants. It is used in the leather and textile industries, in dyeing and bleaching, ink manufacture, metal polishes, and for removing rust and ink stains.

oxbow a curved lake found on the floodplain of a river. Oxbows are caused by the loops of ◊meanders being cut off at times of flood and the river subsequently adopting the shorter course. The US term is ◊bayou.

Oxbridge generic term for Oxford and Cambridge universities, the two oldest foundations in the UK and still distinctive because of their ancient collegiate structure and their separate entrance procedures.

Oxenstjerna /'ùksən,∫eənə/ Axel Gustafsson, Count Oxenstjerna 1583–1654. Swedish statesman. As chancellor from 1612, he ably seconded Gustavus Adolphus's foreign policy by his organizing and diplomatic ability. He acted as regent for Queen Christina, and conducted the Thirty Years' War to a successful conclusion.

OXFAM (*Ox*ford Committee for *Fam*ine Relief) established 1942 by Canon Theodore Richard Milford (1896–1987), initially to assist the starving people of Greece, and subsequently to relieve poverty and famine worldwide, and fund long-term aid projects.

Oxford /'ɒksfəd/ Edward de Vere, 17th Earl of Oxford 1550–1604. English lyric poet, sometimes suggested as the real author of Shakespeare's works

Oxford and Asquith Earl of Oxford and Asquith, title of British politician Herbert ◊Asquith.

Oxford English see ◊English language.

Oxford Group an early name for the Moral Rearmament movement founded by Frank ◊Buchman.

Oxford Movement known also as the Tractarian Movement and Catholic Revival, a movement which attempted to revive Catholic religion in the Church of England. Newman dated the movement from Keble's sermon at Oxford in 1833. The Oxford Movement by the turn of the century had transformed the face of the Anglican communion, and is represented today by Anglo-Catholicism.

Oxfordshire /'ɒksfədʃə/ county in S central England
area 2,608 sq km/1,006 sq mi
towns administrative headquarters Oxford; Abingdon, Banbury, Henley-on-Thames, Witney, Woodstock
features river Thames and tributaries; Cotswolds and Chiltern Hills; Vale of the White Horse

(chalk hill figure 114 m/374 ft long); Oxford University; Europe's major fusion project JET (Joint European Torus) is being built at the UK Atomic Energy Authority's fusion laboratories at Culham
products cereals; cars, paper, bricks, cement
population (1986) 562,900
famous people Flora Thompson.

Oxfordshire Blenheim Palace was built to the designs of Hawksmoor and Vanbrugh. It retains the landscaped grounds laid out by 'Capability' Brown, as well as the formalized patterns typical of the 18th century in the gardens close to the house.

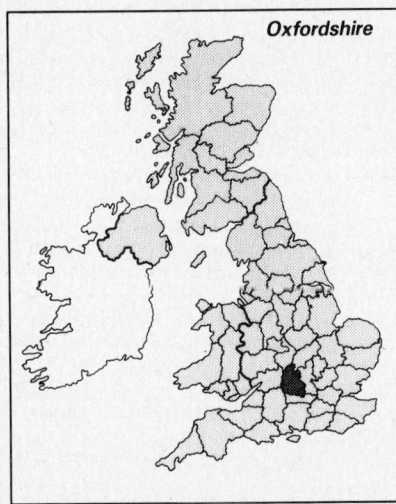

Oxfordshire

Oxford University oldest of the British universities, established during the 12th century, the earliest existing college being founded in 1249. After suffering from land confiscation during the Reformation, it was reorganized by Elizabeth I in 1571. Besides the colleges, notable academic buildings are the Bodleian Library with the New Bodleian, opened in 1946, the Divinity School, and the Sheldonian Theatre. The university is governed by the Congregation of the University; Convocation, composed of Masters and Doctors, has a delaying power. Normal business is conducted by the

Hebdomadal Council. In 1985 there were 9,000 undergraduates, and 3,000 post-graduates.

oxide a binary compound of oxygen and another element, for example nitrous oxide, N_2O ('laughing gas'). The three main classes are: acidic oxides, which combine with basic oxides to form salts; basic oxides, reacting with acids to form salts; and neutral oxides, with neither acid nor basic properties.

oxlip see under ◊cowslip.

oxpecker African bird, genus *Buphagus*, of the starling family that clambers about the bodies of large mammals feeding on ticks and other parasites.

Oxus /'ɒksəs/ ancient name of ◊Amu Darya, river in USSR.

oxyacetylene torch a gas torch that burns acetylene in pure oxygen, producing a high-temperature (3000°C) flame. It is widely used in welding to fuse metals. In the cutting torch, a jet of oxygen burns through metal already melted by the oxyacetylene flame.

oxygen a colourless, odourless, tasteless gaseous element, slightly soluble in water; symbol O, atomic number 8, atomic weight 16.00. Discovered by ◊Priestley in 1774 by heating mercuric oxide using the Sun's rays and a burning glass, and independently in the same year by Scheele. It is the most abundant element on the Earth's surface, and both free and combined makes up nearly one-half of the total material on the surface of the Earth -21 per cent by volume of the atmosphere, nearly 50 per cent by weight of the rocks, and 89 per cent by weight of the water. The only gas able to support ◊respiration, it is just as essential for almost all combustion, and is used in high-temperature welding and improving blast-furnace working. Liquefied oxygen is pale blue and magnetic and is used as a rocket fuel. Oxygen is obtained by fractional distillation of liquid air, by electrolysis of water, or by heating manganese dioxide with potassium chlorate. It is very reactive, and combines with all other elements except the inert gases and fluorine, in the process of oxidation.

oxymoron a ◊figure of speech, whose Greek name means 'sharply dull' or 'pointedly foolish'. It is the bringing together of two words or phrases that are normally kept apart as opposites, in order to startle. 'Bittersweet' is an oxymoron, as are 'cruel to be kind' and 'beloved enemy'.

oyster bivalve mollusc with the upper valve flat, the lower concave, hinged by an elastic ligament. The mantle, lying against the shell, protects the inner body, which includes respirative, digestive and reproductive organs. Oysters are distinguished by their change of sex, which may alternate annually or more frequently, and by the number of their eggs – a female may discharge up to a million eggs during a spawning period. Among the species commercially exploited for food are the European oyster *Ostrea edulis* – there are famous beds at Whitstable, Kent, and Colchester – and the American *Ostrea virginica* of the Atlantic coast. Oyster farming is increasingly practised, the beds being specially cleansed for the easy setting of the free-swimming larva (which then as a miniature oyster is known as 'spat'), and the oysters later properly spaced for growth and fattened. ◊Pearls are not obtained from members of the true oyster family.

oyster catcher wading bird allied to the plovers. The common oyster catcher of European coasts, *Haemotopus ostralegus*, is black and white, with a long red beak to open shellfish.

ozalid process a copying process used, for example, to produce printing proofs from film images. The film is placed on top of chemically treated paper, and then exposed to ultraviolet light. The image is developed using ammonia.

Ozark Mountains /ˈəʊzɑːk/ varied scenic area in USA (shared by Arkansas, Illinois, Kansas, Mississippi, Oklahoma) of ridges, valleys and streams, highest point only 645 m/2,300 ft; area 130,000 sq km/50,000 sq mi.

ozone a highly reactive blue gas, O_3, comprising three atoms of oxygen. It is formed when the molecule of the stable form of oxygen (O_2) is split by ultraviolet radiation or electrical discharge. It forms a layer in the upper atmosphere, and protects life on Earth from ultraviolet rays, a cause of skin cancer. There is concern over damage to the ozone layer, caused by chlorofluorocarbons, chemicals which are used in refrigerators and as propellants in some aerosols, and which liberate chlorine into the upper atmosphere, thus destroying ozone. There is a growing hole in the ozone layer over Antarctica. Alternatives to chlorofluorocarbons are available, whose use in aerosols has now been banned in some countries. At ground level, ozone is less beneficial, and can cause asthma attacks, stunted growth in plants and corrosion of certain materials. It is produced by the action of sunlight on car exhaust fumes, and is a major air pollutant. Ozone is a powerful oxidizing agent and is used industrially in bleaching and air-conditioning.

Ozu /ˈəʊzuː/ Yasujiro 1903–1963. Japanese film director, who became known in the West only in his last years. *Tokyo Monogatari/Tokyo Story* 1953 illustrates his typical low camera angles, and his theme of middle-class family life.

P 16th letter of the Roman alphabet. In Semitic languages, in Greek, and in Latin *p* had much of the same sound as it normally has today in English when final, or when following *s* at the beginning of a word, the sound of an unvoiced labial stop. In other positions in English, and especially when initial, *p* is aspirated.

P2 Italian masonic lodge implicated in a number of political and financial scandals during the 1980s.

paca nocturnal, burrowing ◊rodent of Central and S America, about 60 cm/2 ft long.

Pacaraima /ˌpækəˈraɪmə/ Sierra mountain range along the Brazil–Venezuela frontier, extending into Guyana; length 620 km/385 mi. Highest point *Mount Roraima* a plateau about 50 sq km/20 sq mi, 2,629 m/8,625 ft above sea level, surrounded by 300 m/1,000 ft cliffs. Formed 300 million years ago, it has a largely unique fauna and flora, consisting only of grasses, bushes, flowers, insects, and small amphibians.

pacemaker a medical device implanted in patients whose hearts beat irregularly. It delivers minute electric shocks to stimulate the heart muscles at the correct time. The latest ones are powered by radioactive ◊isotopes for long life.

Pachomius, St /pəˈkəumiəs/ 292–346. Egyptian Christian, the founder of the first Christian monastery near Dendera on the river Nile. Originally for Copts, the monastic movement soon spread to include Greeks.

Pacific Islands /pəˈsɪfɪk ˈaɪləndz/ United Nations trust territory in the W Pacific comprising over 2,000 islands and atolls, under Japanese mandate 1919–47 and administered by the USA 1947–80, when all its members, the ◊Carolines, ◊Marianas (except ◊Guam), and ◊Marshalls, had achieved independence.

Pacific Ocean world's largest ocean, extending from Antarctica to the Bering Strait; area 166,242,500 sq km/64,186,300 sq mi; average depth 4188 m/13,739 ft; greatest depth of any ocean 11,000 m/36,200 ft in the ◊Mariana Trench.

Pacific Security Treaty former collective security organization; see ◊Anzus.

Pacific War 1879–83 war conducted by Bolivia and Peru in alliance against Chile, in which Chile seized Antofagasta and the coast between the mouths of the rivers Loa and Paposo, thus rendering Bolivia landlocked. Peru lost much of its southern coastline – from Arica to the river Loa. Bolivia has since tried to regain Pacific access, either by a corridor across Antofagasta or by a twin port with Arica at the end of the rail link from La Paz. Brazil supports Bolivian claims, which would facilitate its own transcontinental traffic. See ◊Peru.

pacifism complete renunciation of violence, even in self-defence, in settling disputes, as by some Christians (such as the ◊Society of Friends and ◊Jehovah's Witnesses), and some Hindus (such as ◊Gandhi).

pact of steel the military alliance 1939 between Nazi Germany and Mussolini's Italy.

Padang /ˈpɑːdæŋ/ port on the W coast of Sumatra, Indonesia; university 1951; population (1980) 480,000.

Paderborn /ˌpɑːdəˈbɔːn/ market town, manufacturing leather goods and precision instruments, in North Rhine-Westphalia, West Germany; population (1984) 109,500.

Paderewski /ˌpædəˈrefski/ Ignacy Jan 1860–1941. Polish pianist, composer, and politician, son of a Polish patriot. He became noted in Europe and America as an exponent of Chopin. During World War I he helped to organize the Polish army in France; in 1919 as prime minister he represented the newly independent Poland, but he was forced to resign the same year.

Padua /ˈpædjuə/ (Italian *Padova*) city in N Italy, 45 km/25 mi W of Venice, known for its university 1222, where the astronomer Galileo taught, its 13th-century Palazzo della Ragione, the basilica of S Antonio, and the botanical garden 1545; population (1984) 229,000.

paediatrics or *pediatrics* branch of medicine which studies children and their diseases.

paedomorphosis an alternative term for ◊neoteny.

Paestum /ˈpiːstəm/ ancient Greek city, near Salerno in S Italy, founded about 600 BC.

Pagalu /pəˈɡɑːluː/ name of an island in ◊Equatorial Guinea.

Pagan village in Burma close to the ruins of the former capital (founded 847, taken by Kublai Khan 1287). These include magnificent Buddhist temples with wall-paintings of the great period of Burmese art 11th–13th centuries.

Paganini /ˌpægəˈniːni/ Niccolò 1782–1840. Italian violinist, a soloist from the age of nine. His appearance, wild amours, and virtuosity (especially on a single string) fostered a rumour of his being in league with the devil. He composed works for the violin notable for their ingenious exploitation of every potential of the instrument.

Paganini A drawing by Ingres of the Italian violinist and composer Paganini.

Page /peɪdʒ/ Earle (Christmas Grafton) 1880–1961. Australian leader of the Country Party 1920–39, and briefly prime minister in Apr 1939. He represented Australia in the British War Cabinet 1941–42, and as minister of health 1949–55 introduced Australia's health scheme in 1953.

Page /peɪdʒ/ Frederick Handley 1885–1962. British aircraft engineer, founder of an early manufacturing company in 1909, and designer of long-range civil aircraft and multi-engined bombers in both world wars, for example, the Halifax in World War II.

pageant originally the wagon on which medieval ◊mystery plays were performed; the term was later applied to the moving, spectacular procession of songs, dances and tableaux which became fashionable during the 1920s and which exists today in forms such as the Lord Mayor's Show in London.

Pago Pago /ˈpɑːŋɡəʊ ˈpɑːŋɡəʊ/ capital of American Samoa; a harbour in the island of Tutuila. Population (1980) 3,060.

Pahang /pəˈhʌŋ/ state of Malaysia
area 35,930 sq km/13,873 sq mi
capital Kuantan
towns port Tanjung Gelang
features mountainous and forested
government ruled by a sultan
products rubber, tin, gold
population (1980) 770,650.

Pahlavi dynasty Iranian dynasty founded by Riza Khan 1877–1944, an army officer who seized control of the government in 1921 and was proclaimed shah in 1925. During World War II Britain and the USSR were nervous of his German sympathies, and, compelling him to abdicate in favour of his son, occupied Iran 1941–46. His son Mohammed Riza Shah Pahlavi (1919–80) encountered strong political opposition. In 1953 he attempted the arrest of ◊Mossadeq, the prime minister, but was himself forced to flee the country and returned only with CIA assistance. Given massive aid by the USA, he made Iran a major military and industrial power. He used Savak, the secret police he founded in 1957, to suppress opponents. In Jan 1979 he went into exile; he died in Egypt. His heir is Crown Prince Riza 1960, his son by his third wife, Farah Diba.

Pahsien /ˌpɑːˈʃjen/ another name for ◊Chòngqing, port in SW China.

pain sensation of hurt or discomfort caused by a message to the brain which travels along the nerves as electrical impulses. When these reach the gap between one nerve and another, chemicals govern whether this gap is bridged, and may also either increase or lessen the attention the message receives, or modify its intensity in either direction. The main type of transmitter is known simply by an initial as 'substance P', a neuropeptide (SP), which is concentrated in a certain area of the spinal cord. Substance P has been found in fish, and there is also evidence that the same substances that cause pain in humans, for example, bee venom, cause a similar reaction in invertebrates such as spiders.

Paine /peɪn/ Thomas 1737–1809. British author. Born at Thetford, Norfolk, he went to America in 1774, where he fought for the colonists in the War of Independence. In 1787 Paine returned to England, and in 1791 he published *The Rights of Man*, an answer to Burke's *Reflections on the Revolution in France*. In 1792 he was indicted for treason but escaped to France. Narrowly escaping the guillotine, he regained his seat after the fall of Robespierre. In 1793 he published *The Age of Reason*, opposing deism to Christianity and atheism. He returned to America in 1802, and died in New York.

Paine British political writer Thomas Paine wrote *The Rights of Man*, in his reply to Burke's treatise on the French Revolution, which he accuses Burke of 'rancour, prejudice and ignorance'. Shortly after its publication in 1792, Paine was forced to flee the country to avoid indictment for treason.

paint material used to give surfaces a protective and decorative finish. Paints consist of a pigment suspended in a vehicle which dries and hardens to form an adhesive film.

Lacquers consist of a synthetic resin (such as an acrylic resin or cellulose acetate) dissolved in a volatile organic solvent, which evaporates rapidly to give a quick-drying paint. A typical oil-based paint has a vehicle of a natural drying oil (such as linseed oil) or a synthetic alkyl resin, containing a prime pigment of iron, lead, titanium, or zinc oxide, to which coloured pigments may be added. The finish – gloss, semi-matt or matt – depends on the amount of inert pigment (such as clay or silicates). *Oil-based paints* can be thinned, and brushes cleaned, in petroleum product. *Emulsion paints* consist of pigments dispersed in a water-based emulsion of a polymer (such as polyvinyl chloride [PVC], or acrylic resin) and can be thinned with water.

painting the application of paint to an object. The chief methods of painting are:
tempera emulsion painting, with a gelatinous (for example egg yolk) rather than oil base; as in ancient Egypt, and many early Italian works.
fresco watercolour painting on plaster walls before they dry, for example palace of ◊Knossos, Crete.
oil ground pigments in linseed oil, developed by the ◊Van Eycks.
watercolour pigments combined with gum arabic and glycerine, diluted with water; the method was developed in the 15th–17th centuries from wash drawings, and reached its height with ◊Turner.
acrylic (see ◊acrylic acid) the colours are very hard and brilliant.

For the history of painting see under ◊Ancient art; ◊Medieval art; ◊Greek and ◊Chinese art, and so on.

Pakhtoonistan /pɑːkˌtuːnɪˈstɑːn/ independent state desired by the ◊Pathan people.

Pakistan /ˌpɑːkɪˈstɑːn/ country in S Asia, stretching from the Himalayas to the Arabian Sea, bounded to the W by Iran, to the NW by Afghanistan, to the NE by China, and to the E by India.

government The 1973 constitution, suspended 1977, has been restored in part and amended 1985 to make the president the dominant political figure. Primary power resides with the central government, headed by an executive president who is elected for five-year terms by a joint sitting of the federal legislature. Day-to-day administration is performed by a prime minister (drawn from the National Assembly) and cabinet appointed by the president.

Pakistan is a federal republic comprising four provinces: Sind, Punjab, NW Frontier Province, and Baluchistan, administered by appointed governors and local governments drawn from elected provincial assemblies, and tribal areas which are administered by the centre. The federal legislature (*Majlis i-Shura*) comprises two chambers, a lower house (National Assembly) composed of 207 members directly elected for five-year terms by universal suffrage as well as 20 women and 10 minority group appointees, and an upper chamber (Senate) composed of 87 members elected, a third at a time, for six-year terms by provincial assemblies and tribal areas following a quota system. The National Assembly is the most powerful chamber, enjoying sole jurisdiction over financial affairs.

history For history before 1947, see ◊India. The name Pakistan for a Muslim division of British India was put forward in 1930; it was made up by Choudhary Rahmat Ali (1897–1951) from the names of the predominantly Muslim parts of the subcontinent: *P*unjab, the *A*fghan NW Frontier, *K*ashmir, *S*ind, and Baluchi*stan*. *Pak* means 'pure' in Urdu and *stan* means 'land'. Fear of domination by the Hindu majority in India led in 1940 to a serious demand for a separate Muslim state, which delayed for some years India's independence. In 1947 British India was divided into two dominions, India and Pakistan.

Pakistan, after the death of its leader ◊Jinnah in 1948, remained as a dominion with the British monarch as head of state until being declared a republic in Mar 1956. Its new constitution was abrogated in Oct 1958 and military rule imposed through a coup by Gen Muhammad Ayub Khan. The country experienced rapid economic growth during the 1960s but regional tension mounted between demographically dominant East Pakistan and West Pakistan, where political and military power was concentrated.

After serious strikes and riots in Mar 1969, Gen Ayub Khan was replaced by the commander-in-chief, Gen Agha Muhammad Yahya Khan. Pakistan's first elections with universal suffrage were held in Dec 1970 to elect an assembly to frame a new constitution. Sheikh ◊Mujib ur-Rahman's Awami League, which proposed autonomy, gained a majority of seats in E Pakistan and the Pakistan People's Party in the W. E Pakistan declared its independence from the W in Mar 1971, precipitating a civil war. India intervened on E Pakistan's side in Dec 1971, and the independent republic of ◊Bangladesh emerged.

Gen Yahya Khan resigned, passing power in (W) Pakistan to the People's Party leader Zulfiqar Ali ◊Bhutto, who introduced a new constitution (Apr 1973) and a socialist economic programme of land reform and nationalization. From the mid-1970s the Sind-based Bhutto faced deteriorating economic conditions and growing regional opposition, particularly from Baluchistan and from ◊Pathans campaigning for an independent Pakhtoonistan. Bhutto won a majority in the Mar 1977 Assembly elections, but was accused of ballot-rigging by the Pakistan National Alliance opposition. Riots ensued and after four months of unrest, the Punjabi Muslim army Chief of Staff, Gen ◊Zia ul-Haq, seized power in a bloodless coup in Jul 1977. Martial law was imposed, Bhutto was imprisoned for alleged murder and hanged in Apr 1979.

After the Dec 1979 Soviet invasion of ◊Afghanistan, over 2 million refugees poured into Pakistan, which became the recipient of US aid. The economy also relied on remittances from workers in the Middle East. Between 1979 and 1981 Gen Zia imposed severe restrictions on political activity. He introduced a broad Islamization programme aimed at deepening his support base and appeasing Islamic fundamentalists. This was opposed by middle-class professionals and by the Shi'ite minority. In Mar 1981, nine banned opposition parties, including the People's Party of Pakistan, formed the Movement for the Restoration of Democracy. The military government responded by arresting several hundred opposition politicians. From 1982, however, Gen Zia slowly began enlarging the civilian element in his government and in Dec 1984 he held a successful referendum on the Islamization process, which was taken to legitimize his continuing as president for a further five-year term. In Feb 1985, direct elections were held, a new civilian cabinet was formed and an amended constitution adopted.

In Dec 1985, martial law and the ban on political parties were lifted, military courts were abolished and military administrators stepped down in favour of civilians. The present governing party is the Pagaro faction of the Pakistan Muslim League led by Mohammad Khan Junejo, which supports Gen Zia. Opposition parties still operate under tight restrictions. Benazir ◊Bhutto (1953–), the daughter of Zulfiqar Ali Bhutto, returned from self-exile in London in Apr 1986 to lead the People's Party and demand immediate open elections. Riots erupted in Lahore, Karachi and rural Sind, where troops were sent in, and People's Party leaders arrested.

In foreign affairs, Pakistan's relations with India have been strained since independence, with border wars over Kashmir in 1965 and East Pakistan in 1971. It left the Commonwealth in

1972, when the new state of Bangladesh was accepted. As a result of shared hostility to India, Pakistan has been allied with China since the 1950s; and in recent years it has developed close relations with the USA, at the same time joining the ◊nonaligned movement (1979) and drawing closer to the Islamic states of the Middle East and Africa.

Pakistan
ISLAMIC REPUBLIC OF

AREA 803,900 sq km/310,400 sq mi; one-third of Kashmir is under Pakistani control
CAPITAL Islamabad
TOWNS Karachi (largest city and port), Lahore
PHYSICAL fertile plains; Indus river; Himalaya mountains in the N
FEATURES the 'five rivers' (Indus, Jhelum, Chenab, Ravi and Sutlej) feed one of the world's largest irrigation systems; K2; Khyber Pass; sites of the Indus Valley civilization
HEAD OF STATE Mohammad Zia ul-Haq from 1978
HEAD OF GOVERNMENT Mohammad Khan Junejo from 1985
GOVERNMENT military
EXPORTS cotton textiles; rice; leather, carpets
CURRENCY Pakistan rupee (28.4 = £1 Sept 1987)
POPULATION (1985) 99,199,000 (66% Punjabi, 13% Sindhi); annual growth rate 3.1%
LANGUAGE Urdu and English (official); Punjabi
RELIGION Sunni Muslim 75%, Shi'ite Muslim 20%, Hindu 4%
LITERACY 39% male/18% female (1980 est)
GDP $35 bn (1983); $280 per head of population
CHRONOLOGY
1947 Pakistan formed following partition of India.
1956 Proclaimed a republic.
1958 Military rule imposed by Gen Ayub Khan.
1969 Power transferred to Gen Yahya Khan

Pakistan

1971 Secession of East Pakistan (Bangladesh). After civil war, power was transferred to Zulfiqar Ali Bhutto.
1977 Bhutto overthrown in military coup by Gen Zia ul-haq. Martial law imposed.
1979 Bhutto executed.
1981 Opposition Movement for Restoration of Democracy formed. Islamization process pushed forward.
1985 Non-party elections held, amended constitution adopted, martial law and ban on political parties lifted.
1986 Agitation for free elections launched by Benazir Bhutto.

zenith, and amphibians were the first vertebrates to walk on land.

Palamas /'pæləməs/ Kostes 1859–1943. Greek poet. He enriched the Greek vernacular as a literary language by his use of it, particularly in his poetry, such as *Songs of my Fatherland* 1886 and *The Flute of the King* 1910, which expresses his vivid awareness of Greek history.

Palaeocene the first division of the ◊Tertiary period of geological time, between 65 and 54 million years ago. It is characterized by the rapid spread of many types of mammals after the disappearance of dinosaurs and other great reptiles of the Mesozoic.

Palaeolithic earliest division of the Stone Age; see ◊prehistory.

palaeontology the study of ancient life. The science encompasses the structure of ancient organisms, their environment, evolution, and ecology as revealed by their ◊fossils. The practical aspects of palaeontology lie in using the presence of different fossils to date particular ◊rock strata and to identify rocks that were laid down under particular conditions.

Palaeozoic the era of geological time between 570 and 230 million years ago. It comprises the ◊Cambrian, ◊Ordovician, ◊Silurian, ◊Devonian, ◊Carboniferous, and ◊Permian periods. Plants and invertebrates such as insects invaded the land. Fish reached their

palate in mammals, the ceiling of the mouth. The bony front part is the hard palate, the muscular rear part the soft palate. Incomplete fusion of the palate causes interference with speech.

Palatinate /pə'lætɪneɪt/ a historic division of W Germany, ruled by a county palatine (hence the name). When it was attached to Bavaria in 1815 it consisted of Rhenish (or Lower) Palatinate on the Rhine (capital Heidelberg), and Upper Palatinate (capital Amberg on the Vils) 210 km/130 mi to the E. In 1946 Rhenish Palatinate became an administrative division of the Land of Rhineland-Palatinate (capital at Neustadt); Upper Palatinate remained an administrative division of Bavaria (capital Regensburg).

Palau /pə'laʊ/ former name (until 1981) of the island of the Carolines, Republic of ◊Belau.

Paldiski /'pɑːldɪski/ small, ice-free port in Estonia, a Soviet naval base 40 km/25 mi W of Tallinn at the entrance to the Gulf of Finland.

Palembang /pə'lembæŋ/ oil-refining city in Indonesia, capital of S Sumatra province, population (1980) 786,000. Palembang was the capital of a sultanate when the Dutch established a trading station there in 1616. The large mosque dates from 1740.

Palermo /pə'leəməu/ capital and seaport of Sicily; university 1805; population (1984) 716,000. Palermo, founded by the Phoenicians in the 8th century BC, has the Capella Palatina built by King Roger II in the 12th century.

Palestine /'pælɪstaɪn/ the area (also called the *Holy Land* because of its links with Judaism, Christianity, and Islam) between the Mediterranean and the river Jordan, with Lebanon to the N and Sinai to the S. It was in ancient time dominated in turn by Egypt, Assyria, Babylonia, Persia, Macedonia, the Ptolemies, the Seleucids, and the Roman and Byzantine empires.
AD *636* conquest by the Muslim Arabs, which made it a target for the ◊Crusades (see also ◊Jerusalem)
1516 conquest by the Turks
1917–18 Turks driven out by ◊Allenby in World War I
1922 Britain received Palestine as a League of Nations mandate (incorporating the ◊Balfour Declaration) to administer both historic Palestine and lands across the river Jordan which were recognized in 1923 as the Hashimite Kingdom of ◊Jordan
1929 and *1936–38* Arab revolts fuelled by Jewish immigration (300,000 during 1920–39)
1939–45 both Arab and Jewish Palestinians served in the Allied forces in World War II
1947 following Jewish guerrilla activities, prompted by restriction of Jewish immigration, Britain put the question before the United Nations, which proposed partition: neither side agreed
1948 15 May (eight hours before Britain's renunciation of the mandate was due) a Jewish state of ◊Israel was proclaimed. A series of ◊Arab-Israeli Wars resulted in the total loss of the Palestinian state, and Palestinian guerrilla war followed
1974 the ◊Palestine Liberation Organization became the first nongovernmental delegation to be admitted to a plenary session of the United Nations General Assembly
The name Palestine derives from the ◊Philistines, but the Palestinian people (about 500,000 in the West Bank, E Jerusalem, and the Gaza Strip; 1,200,000 in Jordan; 1,200,000 in Israel; thousands in camps in Lebanon and Syria; and 100,000 in USA) are descendants of the ◊Canaanites. Archaeological evidence, hotly contested, suggests that their origins and those of the Israelis are closely linked.

Palestine Liberation Organization (PLO) Palestinian organization founded in 1964 to bring about an independent state of Palestine. It is formed of several distinct groupings, the chief of which is ◊al-Fatah, led by Yassir ◊Arafat, president of the PLO since 1969. To achieve its ends it has pursued diplomatic initiatives, but also operates as a guerilla army. In 1974 it

became the first non-government delegation admitted to a session of the United Nations General Assembly. In the 1980s the growth of factions within it reduced its effectiveness. When Israel invaded the Lebanon in 1982 it had to abandon its headquarters there; it moved on to Tunis and in 1986 to Baghdad. PLO members who remained in the Lebanon after the expulsion were drawn into the internal conflict; see ◊Arab-Israel Wars. In 1986 Jordan suspended 'political coordination' with the PLO and expelled Arafat's deputy, dealing instead directly with Palestinians in Israeli-occupied territories.

Palestrina /ˌpælɪ'striːnə/ Giovanni Pierluigi da 1525–1594. Italian composer. Born at Palestrina, he became choirmaster at the Vatican in 1551. He wrote much secular and sacred choral music, his religious work gaining him a reputation as the master of polyphonic vocal music. Apart from motets and madrigals, his greatest achievement is considered to be his 105 masses, which include the outstanding *Missa Papae Marcelli*.

Pali /'pɑːli/ an ancient Indo-European language of N India, related to Sanskrit and a classical language of Buddhism.

Palissy /ˌpælɪ'siː/ Bernard 1510–1589. French potter, noted for his richly coloured rustic pottery. He was favoured by Catherine de' Medici but was imprisoned in the ◊Bastille as a Huguenot in 1588.

Palladio /pə'lɑːdiəu/ Andrea 1518–1580. Italian architect, whose country houses (for example, Malcontenta, and the Villa Rotonda near Vicenza) were designed from 1540 for patrician families of the Venetian Republic. These buildings influenced neo-classical architecture, such as Washington's home at Mount Vernon, USA, the palace of Tsarskoe Selo in Russia, and in England, Holkham, Prior Park, and Stowe.

palladium in Greek mythology, an image of Pallas ◊Athena, supposed to be a gift from Zeus to the city of Troy, which could not be captured while the image remained. It was stolen by Odysseus and Diomedes, and was later alleged to have been taken to Rome by Aeneas.

palladium in chemistry, a white metal of the platinum family, discovered in 1803 by Wollaston, and found in platinum ore in Brazil, California and the Urals, and in nickel ores of Canada: symbol Pd, atomic weight 106.4, atomic number 46. It is also a non-radioactive product of a slow-neutron nuclear reactor. Palladium does not tarnish in air, and when finely divided absorbs up to 3000 times its volume of hydrogen and is used as a catalyst.

pallium a pure wool vestment worn by the pope and by Catholic metropolitans, primates, and archbishops. It is in the shape of a Y, falling across the shoulders back and front.

palm plant of the family Palme, characterized by a single tall stem carrying a thick cluster of large palmate or pinnate leaves at the top. The majority of the some 3,500 species are tropical or subtropical. Some, such as the coconut, date, sago, and oil *Elaeis guineensis* palms, have products of great economic importance.

Palma /'pælmə/ (Spanish *Palma de Mallorca*) industrial port (textiles, cement, paper, pottery), resort, and capital of the Balearic Islands, Spain, on Majorca; population (1981) 304,500. Palma was founded 276 BC as a Roman colony, and has a Gothic cathedral begun in 1229.

Palma, La /'pælmə/ one of the ◊Canary Islands, Spain
area 728 sq km/281 sq mi
capital Santa Cruz de la Palma
features forested
products wine, fruit, honey, silk; tourism is important
population (1981) 76,500.

Palmas, Las /'pælməs/ see under ◊Las Palmas, port in the Spanish Canary Islands.

Palm Beach /'pɑːm 'biːtʃ/ winter resort in Florida, USA, on an island between Lake Worth and the Atlantic; population (1980) 9,730.

Palmerston During his life-long career at the forefront of British politics as foreign secretary, home secretary, and prime minister, Palmerston was popular with the people but incurred the displeasure of Queen Victoria with his imperious attitude.

Palmerston /'pɑːməstən/ Henry John Temple, 3rd Viscount Palmerston 1784–1865. British Whig politician. He succeeded to an Irish peerage 1802 and became a Tory Member of Parliament 1807, secretary-at-war 1809–28. He broke with the Tories 1830 and sat in the Whig cabinets of 1830–34, 1835–41, and 1846–51 as foreign secretary. His foreign policy was marked by distrust of France and Russia, against whose designs he backed the independence of Belgium and Turkey. He was home secretary 1852 and prime minister 1855–58 (when he rectified Aberdeen's mismanagement of the Crimean War, suppressed the Indian Mutiny, and carried through the Second Opium War) and 1859–65. He was popular with the people, and made good use of the press, but his high-handed attitude annoyed Queen Victoria and other ministers.

Palmerston North /'pɑːməstən 'nɔːθ/ town on

North Island, New Zealand, population (1985) 95,500. Massey University 1963 is known for its agricultural college.

Palm Sunday in the Christian calendar, the Sunday before Easter, and first day of Holy Week, which commemorates Christ's entry into Jerusalem, when the crowd strewed palm leaves in his path.

Palmyra /pæl'maɪrə/ ancient city and oasis in the desert of Syria, about 240 km/150 mi NE of Damascus. Palmyra, the Biblical Tadmor, was flourishing by about 300 BC, but was destroyed in 272 AD after Queen Zenobia had led a revolt against the Romans. Extensive temple ruins exist, and on the site is a village called Tadmur in Arabic.

Palmyra /pæl'maɪrə/ coral atoll 1,600 km/1,000 mi SW of Hawaii, in the Pacific, purchased by the USA from a Hawaiian family in 1979 for the storage of highly radioactive nuclear waste from 1986.

Palomar, Mount /'pæləmɑː/ the location of an ◊observatory, 80 km/50 mi NE of San Diego, USA, with a 5 m/200 in diameter reflector.

Pamirs /pə'mɪəz/ central Asian plateau mainly in the USSR, but extending into China and Afghanistan, traversed by mountain ranges. Mount Communism (Kommunizma Pik 9,495

Palomar, Mount The 200-inch Halte telescope shown pointing north at the Hale Observatory, Mount Palomar, California.

m/24,590 ft) in the Akademiya Nauk range is the highest mountain in the USSR.

Pampas /'pæmpəz/ flat treeless Argentine plains, lying between the Andes and the Atlantic. In the E Pampas are the great cattle ranches and the flax-and grain-growing area of Argentina; to the W the Pampas are arid and unproductive.

pampas grass genus of South American grasses (*Cortaderia*). *Cortaderia argentea* is

grown in gardens and has tall leaves and large panicles of white flowers.

Pamplona /pæm'plɔʊnə/ industrial city (wine, leather, shoes, textiles) in Navarre, Spain; known for an annual running of bulls through the streets in Jul; population (1981) 183,220.

history A pre-Roman town, it was rebuilt by Pompey in 68 BC, sacked by Charlemagne in 778, captured by the Visigoths 476, became the capital of Navarre, and was taken by Wellington in the Peninsular War 1813.

Pan /pæn/ in Greek mythology, god (Roman Sylvanus) of flocks and herds, shown as a man with the horns, ears and hoofs of a goat, and playing a shepherd's pipe.

Pan-Africanist Congress (PAC) militant black nationalist group, which broke away from the larger ◊African National Congress in 1959. More radical than the latter, the Pan-Africanist Congress has a black-only policy for Africa, as well as a military wing, Poqo ('we alone'). In Mar 1960, the PAC organized a campaign of protest against South African pass laws, resulting in the ◊Sharpeville massacre; the following month, the PAC was declared an illegal organization by the South African government. It has since continued guerrilla activities against South Africa from bases in Botswana.

Panama /ˌpænə'mɑː/ country in Central America, on a narrow isthmus between the Caribbean and the Pacific Ocean, bounded to the W by Costa Rica and to the E by Colombia.

government The constitution was revised in 1983, when a new, single-chamber legislative assembly of 67 members, elected by universal suffrage for a five-year term, was created. The president, elected in the same way for a similar period of office, is assisted by two elected vice presidents and an appointed cabinet.

Panama is divided into nine provinces, each with its own governor, appointed by the president. There are also three Indian reservations, which enjoy a high degree of self-government.

history For early history, see ◊American Indian. Panama was visited by Christopher ◊Columbus 1502. Vasco Núñez de ◊Balboa 'discovered' the Pacific from the ◊Darien isthmus 1513. Spanish settlements were sacked by Francis ◊Drake 1572–95 and Henry ◊Morgan 1668–71. Remains of Fort St Andrews, built by Scottish settlers 1698–1701, were discovered in 1976. Panama remained part of the viceroyalties of Peru and New Granada until 1821, when it gained independence from Spain and joined Gran Colombia.

Panama achieved full independence in 1903 with US support, which at the same time bought the rights to build the ◊Panama Canal and was given control of a ten-mile-wide strip of territory, known as the Canal Zone, in perpetuity. Panama was guaranteed US protection and an annuity. In 1939 Panama's protectorate status was ended by mutual agreement, and in 1977 two treaties were signed by Panama's president (1968–78), Gen Omar Torrijos Herara, and US President Carter. One transferred ownership of the canal to Panama and the other guaranteed its subsequent neutrality, with the conditions that only Panamanian forces would be stationed in the zone, and that the USA would have the right to use force to keep the canal open if it became obstructed.

The 1980s saw a deterioration in the state of Panama's economy, with opposition to the austerity measures that the government introduced to try to halt the decline. There are a large number of political organizations, the most significant being represented in the assembly by two coalitions, the centre-right National Democratic Union (Unade), which won 40 seats in the 1984 general election, and the centre-left Democratic Opposition Alliance (ADO), which won 27 seats. After a very close result, Dr Nicolas Ardito Barletta, the Democratic Revolutionary Party (PRD) candidate, was declared president, but in 1985 he resigned, amid speculation that he had been forced to do so by the commander of the National Guard. Relations between Panama and the USA deteriorated with the departure of President Barletta, and the Reagan administration cut and later suspended its financial aid.

Barletta was succeeded by Eric Arturo del Valle, but the country has since 1983 effectively been ruled by the army commander in chief, Gen Manuel Noriega. In 1987 he was accused of corruption, election rigging, involvement in the cocaine trade, and the murder of a political opponent. Political parties, labour and student unions, and business groups united as the National Civic Crusade to campaign for his removal; demonstrations were suppressed by riot police. In Jul 1987 President Noriega successfully resisted calls for his removal, despite the suspension of US military and economic aid.

Panama
REPUBLIC OF (*República de Panamá*)

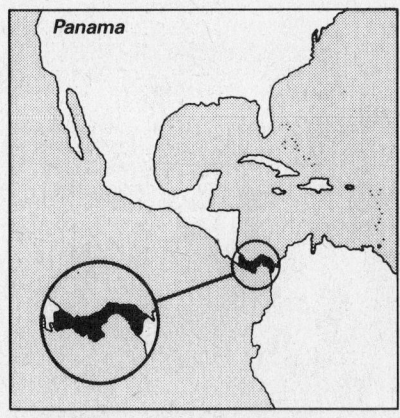
Panama

AREA 76,614 sq km/31,293 sq mi
CAPITAL Panama City
TOWNS Cristóbal, Balboa, Colón
PHYSICAL mountain ranges; tropical rain forest
FEATURES Panama Canal; Barro Colorado Island in Gatun Lake (the reservoir which supplies the canal), a tropical forest reserve since 1923; Smithsonian Tropical Research Institute
HEAD OF ARMED FORCES Manuel Antonio Noriega in power from 1981
HEAD OF STATE AND OF GOVERNMENT Eric Arturo del Valle from 1985
GOVERNMENT military
EXPORTS bananas; petroleum products; copper from one of the world's largest deposits; shrimps
CURRENCY balboa (1.65 = £1 Sept 1987)
POPULATION 2,180,000 (1985); annual growth rate 2.2%
LANGUAGE Spanish
RELIGION Roman Catholic
LITERACY 87% male/87% female (1980)
GDP $4.1 bn (1983); $1,116 per head of population
CHRONOLOGY
1903 Became independent from Colombia.
1974 Agreement to negotiate a full transfer of the Panama Canal from the USA to Panama.
1977 US-Panama treaties transfer the canal to Panama, with the USA guaranteeing its protection and an annual payment.
1984 Nicolas Ardito Barletta elected president.
1985 Barletta resigned to be replaced by Eric Arturo del Valle.
1987 Gen Noriega successfully resisted calls for his removal, despite the suspension of US military and economic aid.

Panama Canal /ˌpænəˈmɑː/ canal across the Panama isthmus in Central America, connecting the Pacific and Atlantic oceans; length 80 km/50 mi. The original construction company, headed by the French engineer Ferdinand de Lesseps, began construction in 1879, but collapsed in 1889 because of financial scandals. The work was taken over by the USA in 1904, and the canal was opened 1914, formally 1920. The Panama Canal runs SE from Cristóbal on the Atlantic to Balboa on the Pacific, and has 12 locks.
The *Panama Canal Zone* was acquired 'in perpetuity' by the USA in 1903, and comprised land extending for about 5 km/3 mi on either side of the canal. It was designed to ensure free passage to international shipping in a turbulent area, but in the 1960s was the focus of US strategy in South America as a training for special forces devised by President Kennedy to fight irregular wars. Nationalist feeling in Panama led to anti-US riots in 1964, and under the treaty of 1978 negotiated by President Carter, the Zone passed to Panama in 1979. The USA retains control of the management and defence of the canal itself until 1999, and the use of about 25 per cent of the former land area of the Zone for these purposes.

Panama City /ˌpænəˈmɑː/ capital of the Republic of Panama, near the Pacific end of the Panama Canal; population (1980) 388,650. Panama has its port at Balboa in the Canal Zone. An earlier Panama, to the NE, founded 1519, was destroyed 1671 by the Welsh buccaneer Morgan, and the city was founded on the present site 1673.

Pan-American Highway road linking the USA with Central and South America; length 25,300 km/15,700 mi; built 1923–60. Starting from Nuevo Laredo, Texas, it runs through Mexico City to Panama City, then down the W side of South America to Valparaiso, Chile, where it crosses the Andes and goes to Buenos Aires, Argentina.

Pan-American Union former name of the ◊Organization of American States.

Panay /pæˈnaɪ/ one of the Philippine islands, lying between Mindoro and Negros
area 11,515 sq km/4,446 sq mi
capital Iloilo
features mountainous, 2,215 m/7,265 ft in Madiaás
products rice, sugar, pineapples, bananas, copra; copper
history seized by Spain 1569; occupied by Japan 1942–45.

Panchen Lama /ˈpɑːntʃən ˈlɑːmə/ 10th Incarnation 1935– . Tibetan spiritual leader, second in importance to the Dalai ◊Lama. A protégé of the Chinese since childhood, he is not indisputably recognized. On the flight of the Dalai Lama in 1959, he was deputed by the Chinese to take over, but stripped of power for subversion 1964, and said to have been deported to China 1965.

panchromatic in photography, a highly sensitive black and white film made to render all visible spectral colours in correct grey tones. It is always developed in total darkness.

pancreas a gland in vertebrates between the spleen and duodenum. When stimulated by ◊secretin it secretes enzymes into the duodenum which digest starch, proteins and fats. In humans it is about 18 cm/7 in long and lies behind and below the stomach. It also contains groups of cells called the islets of Langerhans, which secrete the hormones insulin and glucagon which regulate the blood sugar level.

panda mammal of NW China (◊Sichuan) and Tibet. The *giant panda Ailuropoda melanoleuca* 1.5 m/4.5 ft long, has black and white fur with black eye patches and feeds on bamboo shoots; its DNA shows it to be a highly specialized bear. It is the symbol of the World Wildlife Fund and the focus of conservation efforts. The *lesser panda Ailurus fulgens*, 50 cm/1.5 ft long, is black and chestnut, with a long tail, and has links with the ◊raccoons.

Pandora /pænˈdɔːrə/ in Greek mythology, the first woman. ◊Zeus sent her to earth with a box of evils (to counteract the blessings brought to mortals by ◊Prometheus' gift of fire); she opened it, and they all flew out. Only hope was left inside as a consolation.

Pangaea or *Pangea* /pænˈdʒiːə/ the supercontinent that existed between 250 and 200 million years ago. It was formed by the conjunction of all the continental masses and can be regarded as a combination of ◊Gondwanaland and ◊Laurasia. The rest of the Earth was covered by the ◊Panthalassa ocean.

pangolin or *scaly anteater* Afro-Asian toothless, long-tailed mammal, order Pholidota, up to 1 m/3 ft long. The upper part of the body is covered with horny plates for defence. Nocturnal in habit, pangolins are found in Africa and S Asia.

Panipat /ˈpɑːnɪpət/ town in Punjab, India; scene of three decisive battles: 1526, when Baber (1483–1530), great-grandson of Tamerlane, defeated the emperor of Delhi and founded the ◊Mogul Empire; 1556, won by his descendant ◊Akbar; 1761, when the ◊Mahrattas were defeated by ◊Ahmad Shah of Afghanistan.

Pankhurst /ˈpæŋkhɜːst/ Emmeline (born Goulden) 1858–1928. British suffragette. Founder of the Women's Social and Political Union in 1903, she launched in 1906 the militant suffragette campaign, and was several times imprisoned and then released after hunger strikes. In 1926 she turned her attention to politics and joined the Conservative Party. She became the prospective parliamentary candidate for the Whitechapel district of London. She was supported by her daughters Christabel Pankhurst (1880–1958), the political leader of the movement, and Sylvia Pankhurst (1882–1960) who was imprisoned nine times under the 'Cat and Mouse Act' was a pacifist in World War I and a staunch supporter of the Ethiopian cause against Italy.

pansy perennial garden flower, also known as *heartsease*, derived from the European wild pansy *Viola tricolor*. There are many highly developed varieties bred for size, colour, or special markings.

Mav.21.1914

Pankhurst The suffragette Emmeline Pankhurst being carried off after demonstrating outside the gates of Buckingham Palace 1914, as part of her militant campaign to gain equal voting rights for women.

Pantelleria /ˌpæntelə'rɪə/ volcanic island in the Mediterranean, 100 km/62 mi SW of Sicily and part of that region of Italy
area 115 sq km/45 sq mi
town Pantelleria
population (1971) 11,000
history Pantelleria has drystone dwellings dating from prehistoric times. The Romans called it *Cossyra* and sent people into exile there. Because of its strategic position the island has been much fought over. It was strongly fortified by Mussolini in World War II, and surrendered to the Allies 11 Jun 1943.

Panthalassa the ocean that covered the surface of the globe not occupied by the supercontinent ◊Pangaea between 250 and 200 million years ago.

pantheism (Greek *pan*, all; *theos*, God). A mode of thought which regards God as a pervading presence immanent in the universe. It is expressed in Egyptian religion and Brahmanism; Stoicism, Neo-Platonism, Judaism, Christianity, and Islam can be interpreted in pantheistic terms. Pantheistic philosophers have included Bruno, Spinoza, Fichte, Schelling, and Hegel.

pantheon originally a temple for worshipping all the gods, such as that in ancient Rome, rebuilt by ◊Hadrian and still used as a church. In more recent times, as in the Panthéon, Paris, a building where famous people are buried.

panther another name for ◊leopard.

pantomime in British theatre, a traditional Christmas entertainment with its origins in the harlequin spectacle of the 18th century and burlesque of the 19th century, which gave rise to the tradition of the principal boy being played by an actress and the dame by an actor. The role of the harlequin diminished altogether as themes developed on folktales such as *The Sleeping Beauty* and *Cinderella*, and with the introduction of additional material such as popular songs, topical comedy, and audience participation.

The term 'pantomime' was also applied to Roman dumbshow performed by a masked actor, to 18th-century ballets with mythical themes, and, in 19th-century France, to the wordless Pierrot plays from which modern ◊mime developed.

panzer German ('armour') mechanized divisions and regiments in World War II, used in connection with armoured vehicles.

papacy the office of the ◊pope or bishop of Rome, as head of the Roman Catholic Church.

papal infallibility doctrine formulated by the Roman Catholic Vatican Council of Jul 1870 which stated that the pope, when speaking officially on certain doctrinal or moral matters, was protected from error by God and such rulings, therefore, could not be challenged.

Papal States area of central Italy in which the pope was temporal ruler 756 AD–1870, when Italy became a single united state.

Papandreou /ˌpæpæn'dreɪu:/ Andreas George 1919– . Greek socialist politician, founder of the Pan-Hellenic Socialist Movement (PASOK), and prime minister from 1981.

Son of a former prime minister, he studied law in Athens and at Harvard. He was director of the Centre for Economic Research in Athens 1961–64, and economic adviser to the Bank of Greece. For his political activities he was imprisoned Apr–Dec 1967, after which he founded PASOK. After another spell in overseas universities, Papandreou returned to Greece in 1974 and threw himself into national politics. He was leader of the opposition 1977–81, and then became Greece's first socialist prime minister, re-elected 1985. He favours a single-party quasi-Marxist regime, and opposed the re-election of ◊Karamanlis as president 1985.

Papeete /ˌpɑːpi'eɪti/ capital and port of French Polynesia on Tahiti; population (1983) 79,000.

Papen /'pɑːpən/ Franz von 1879–1969. German chancellor in 1932, when he negotiated the Nazi-Conservative alliance which put Hitler in the chancellorship in 1933.

paper a sheet of vegetable fibre. The name comes from ◊papyrus, made from water reed, used in ancient Egypt. The invention of true paper, originally made of pulped fishing nets and rags, is credited to Tsai Lun, Chinese minister of agriculture in 105 AD. Its use gradually spread from the 8th century and the first English paper mill was established at Stevenage in the 15th century.

Louis Robert invented in 1799 a machine to produce paper on a continuous reel. Today most paper is made from ◊woodpulp on a ◊Foudrinier machine. Recycling avoids some of the enormous waste of trees.

Paphos /ˈpæfɒs/ legendary birthplace of ◊Aphrodite, where she rose from the sea foam, in SW Cyprus.

pappus a modified ◊calyx comprising a ring of fine, silky hairs, or sometimes scales or small teeth, which persists after fertilization. Pappi are found in members of the daisy family, (Compositae) such as the dandelions (*Taraxacum*), where they form a parachute-like structure which aids dispersal of the fruit.

Papua /ˈpɑːpuə/ original name of the island of New Guinea, but latterly its SE section, now part of ◊Papua New Guinea.

Papua New Guinea /ˈpɑːpuə ˌnjuː ˈɡɪni/ country in the SW Pacific, comprising the E part of the island of New Guinea, the New Guinea islands, the Admiralty islands, and part of the Solomon islands.
government The British monarch is the formal head of state, represented by a resident governor-general. The governor-general appoints the prime minister and cabinet, who are drawn from and responsible to the parliament.
The constitution from 1975 provides for a single-chamber legislature, the National Parliament, consisting of 109 members elected by universal suffrage for a five-year term, 89 drawn from the whole country and 20 representing particular localities. Although Papua New Guinea is not a federal state, it has 20 provincial governments with a fair degree of autonomy. Out of about six political parties, the Pangu Party, People's Progress Party, National Party and United Party are the most significant.
history New Guinea has been inhabited for at least 10,000 years, probably by Asians arriving from Indonesia. It was visited by the Portuguese explorer Jorge de Menezes about 1526 and by Dutch traders in the 17th century. The Dutch East India Company took control of the W half

of the island and in 1828 it became part of the Netherlands East Indies. In 1884 the SE was claimed by Britain, the N by Germany; the British part, Papua, was transferred to Australia 1905 and the German part after World War I, when Australia was granted a League of Nations mandate and then a trusteeship over the area.
Once freed from Japanese occupation in 1945, the two territories were jointly administered by Australia and, after achieving internal self-government as Papua New Guinea, became fully independent, within the Commonwealth, in 1975. The first prime minister after independence was Michael Somare who held office until 1980, when Sir Julius Chan, leader of the People's Progress Party, succeeded him. Somare returned to power in 1982, but in 1985 he was replaced by Paias Wingti, who headed a new, five-party coalition, with former prime minister Chan as his deputy. In Aug 1987 Prime Minister Wingti returned to power with a slender majority of three votes. He announced a more independent foreign policy of good relations with the USSR, USA, Japan, and China.

Papua New Guinea

AREA 462,000 sq km/178,260 sq mi
CAPITAL Port Moresby
PHYSICAL mountains in centre; thickly forested
FEATURES wholly within the tropics, with annual rainfall 1,000 mm; rare birds of paradise, the world's largest butterfly, orchids
HEAD OF STATE Elizabeth II from 1975 represented by Kingsford Dibela
HEAD OF GOVERNMENT Paias Wingti from 1985
GOVERNMENT parliamentary democracy
EXPORTS copra, coconut oil, palm oil, tea; copper
CURRENCY kina (1.46 = £1 Sept 1987)
POPULATION (1985) 3,326,000 (including Papuans, Melanesians, Pygmies, and various minorities); annual growth rate 4.7%
LANGUAGE English (official); pidgin English
RELIGION Protestant 33%, Roman Catholic 18%, local faiths
LITERACY 48% male/30% female (1980 est)
GNP $2.5 bn (1983); $480 per head of population
CHRONOLOGY
1883 Annexed by Queensland, and soon became known as the Australian Territory of Papua.
1884 NE New Guinea annexed by Germany; SE claimed by Britain.
1914 NE New Guinea occupied by Australia.

1921–42 Held as a League of Nations mandate.
1942–45 Occupied by Japan.
1975 Achieved full independence, within the Commonwealth, with Michael Somare as prime minister.
1980 Sir Julius Chan became prime minister.
1982 Somare returned to power.
1985 Somare challenged by deputy prime minister, Paias Wingti, who later formed a new, five-party coalition government.

defined as a path traced out by a point that moves in such a way that it is always the same distance from a fixed point (focus) and a fixed straight line (directrix); it thus has an ◊eccentricity of 1. The trajectories of missiles within the Earth's gravitational field approximate closely to parabolas (ignoring the effect of air resistance). The corresponding solid figure, the paraboloid, is formed by rotating a parabola about its axis. It is a common shape for headlamp reflectors, dish-shaped microwave and radar aerials, and for radiotelescopes, since a source of radiation placed at the focus of a paraboloidal reflector is propagated as a parallel beam.

Paracels /ˌpærəˈselz/ group of about 130 small islands in the S China Sea (Chinese *Xisha*/Vietnamese *Hoang Sa*). Situated in an oil-bearing area, they were occupied by China following a skirmish with Vietnam 1974.

Paracelsus /ˌpærəˈselsəs/ original name Theophrastus Bombastus von Hohenheim 1493–1541. Swiss physician, who lectured at Basel on the need for observational experience rather than traditional lore in medicine: he made

papyrus type of paper made by the ancient Egyptians from the stem of the papyrus or paper reed *Cyperus papyrus* family Cyperaceae.

Pará /pəˈrɑː/ alternative name of the Brazilian port ◊Belém.

parabola in mathematics, a curve formed by cutting a right circular cone with a plane parallel to the sloping side of the cone; one of the family of curves known as ◊conic sections. Can also be

a public bonfire of the works of ◊Avicenna and ◊Galen.

parachute umbrella-shaped device, made of some two dozen panels of nylon with shroud lines to a harness. It is used to slow down the descent of a human being, or supplies, from a plane or missile to a safe speed for landing, or to aid (through braking) the landing of a plane or missile itself. Modern designs enable the

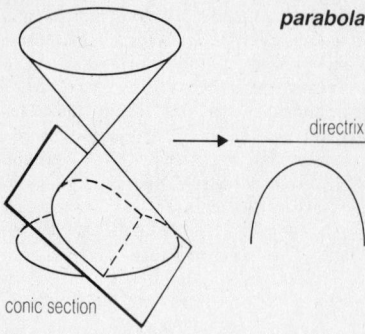

parabola

directrix

conic section

parachutist to exercise considerable control of direction, as in ▷skydiving. See ▷freefalling. The first descent, from a balloon, was made in 1797 by Garnerin, and from an aircraft, by Berry in 1912.

paradigm a term used by the American historian of science T S ▷Kuhn to describe all those factors, both scientific and otherwise, which influence the research of the scientist. The term has subsequently spread to the areas of social studies and politics.

Paradise (Persian 'pleasure garden') in various religions, a place or state of happiness. Examples are the Garden of Eden, the Messianic kingdom, or the heaven of after life; the Islamic Paradise of the Koran is a place of sensual pleasure.

paraffin a general term for hydrocarbons of the paraffin series, general formula C_nH_{2n+2}. The lower members are gases, for example methane (marsh or natural gas). The middle ones (mainly liquid) form the basis of petrol (gasolene), kerosene and lubricating oils, while the higher ones (paraffin waxes) are used in ointment and cosmetic bases.

Paraguay /ˌpærəˈgwaɪ/ landlocked country in S America, bounded to the NE by Brazil, to the S by Argentina, and to the NW by Bolivia.

government The 1967 constitution provides for a president and a two-chamber legislature, the National Congress, consisting of the Senate and Chamber of Deputies, all elected by universal suffrage for a five-year term. The president appoints and leads the cabinet, which is called the Council of Ministers.

The Senate has 30 members and the Chamber 60, and the party winning the largest number of votes in the congressional elections is allocated two-thirds of the seats in each chamber. A law passed in 1981 prescribes that a political party must have a minimum of 10,000 members, and must contest at least a third of the constituencies before it can operate.

history For early history, see ▷American Indian. The Guarani Indians had a settled agricultural civilization before the arrival of Europeans: Sebastian ▷Cabot 1526–30, followed by Spanish colonists, who founded the city of Asunción 1537. From about 1600–1767, when they were expelled, ▷Jesuit missionaries administered much of the country. It became a province subordinate to the Spanish viceroyalty of Peru, then from 1776 part of the viceroyalty of Buenos

Aires, and in 1811 Paraguay declared its independence.

The first president was J G R Francia ruled (1816–40), a despot; he was followed by his nephew C A López and he in turn (1862) by his son F S López, who involved Paraguay in a war with Brazil, Argentina, and Uruguay. Paraguay was invaded and López killed at Aquidaban 1870. When the war was finally over the population consisted mainly of women and children. Recovery was slow with many revolutions. Continuing disputes with Bolivia over the frontier in the torrid Chaco zone of the N flared up into war 1932–35; arbitration by the USA and five S American republics reached a peace settlement 1938.

Since 1940 Paraguay has been mostly under the control of military governments led by strong, autocratic leaders. Gen Morinigo was president 1940–47 and Gen Alfredo Stroessner has been in control since 1954. During the US presidency of Jimmy Carter the Stroessner regime came under strong criticism for its violation of human rights and this resulted in some tempering of the general's ruthless rule. Criticism by the Reagan administration has been less noticeable. Stroessner has maintained his supremacy by ensuring that the armed forces and business community have shared in the spoils of office, and by preventing opposition groups from coalescing into a credible challenge. In the 1983 Congress elections the National Republican Party, led by the president, with the largest number of votes, automatically secured 20 Senate and 40 Chamber seats. The Radical Liberal Party came second.

Since 1984 there has been speculation about the eventual succession. Within the government party, a militant faction favours Stroessner seeking an eighth term, with his son Gustavo succeeding him, while the traditionalists believe that he should retire in 1988. The general is reported to favour staying on.

parakeet small ▷parrot.

paraldehyde a colourless liquid formed from acetaldehyde $(CH_3CHO)_3$. It is soluble in water.

parallax the change in the apparent position of an object against its background when viewed from two different positions. In astronomy, nearby ▷stars show a shift due to parallax when viewed from different positions on the Earth's orbit around the Sun. A star's parallax is used to deduce its distance. Nearer bodies such as the Moon, Sun and ▷planets also show a parallax due to the observer's position on the Earth. *Diurnal parallax* is caused by the Earth's rotation.

parallel computing or *parallel processing* an emerging computer technology that allows more than one computation at the same time. Currently, this means having a few computer processors working in parallel, but in future the number could run to thousands or millions of processors. The technique, which involves breaking down computations into small parts and performing thousands of them simultaneously rather than in a linear sequence, offers the prospect of a vast improvement in the speed at which computers work.

parallel lines and parallel planes in mathematics, lines or planes that always remains the same distance from one another no matter how far they are extended. This is a principle of Euclidean geometry and has been important in everyday consequences as well as for mathematics and science. Some non-Euclidean geometries, such as elliptical and hyperbolic geometry, however, reject Euclid's parallel axiom.

parallelogram in mathematics, a quadrilateral (four-sided plane figure) with opposite pairs of sides equal in length and parallel. In the special cases when all four sides are equal in length, the parallelogram is known as a rhombus, and when the internal angles are right angles, it is a rectangle or square. The diagonals of a parallelogram bisect each other and angles diagonally opposite each other are equal. Its area is the product of the length and the height (the perpendicular distance between the longer pair of sides).

parallelogram of forces in physics and applied mathematics, a method of calculating the resultant (combined effect) of two different forces acting together on an object. Because a force has both magnitude and direction it is a ▷vector quantity and can be represented by a straight line. A second force acting at the same point in a different direction is represented by another line drawn at an angle to the first. By completing the parallelogram (of which the two lines are sides) a diagonal may be drawn from the original angle to the opposite corner to represent the resultant force vector. Other vector quantities, such as velocity, can be resolved in a similar way.

paralysis failure of muscle action, after injury (for example a wound) or infection (▷poliomyelitis) of the nerves supplying it. Other forms are caused by cerebral haemorrhage, multiple sclerosis, muscular dystrophy, myasthenia gravis. Damage to one side of the brain may cause *hemiplegia* (paralysis of one side of the body only); damage to the spinal cord may result in paralysis of the legs only (*paraplegia*) or of both arms and legs (*quadriplegia*), according to the site of the injury.

Paramaribo /ˌpærəˈmærɪbəʊ/ port and capital of Suriname, 24 km/15 mi from the sea on the Suriname river, an important trading and commercial centre; population (1980) 68,000.

Paraná /ˌpærəˈnɑː/ river in South America, formed by the confluence of the Rio Grande and Paranaiba; the Paraguay joins it at Corrientes, and it flows into the Rio de la Plata with the Uruguay; length 4,000 km/2,500 mi. It is used for ▷hydroelectric power by Argentina, Brazil, and Paraguay.

paranoia mental disorder marked by a single-channelled delusion, for example, that the patient is someone of great importance, the subject of a conspiracy, etc. This dominates the whole way of life, sometimes to the danger of the patient or others.

parapsychology study of phenomena, for example, extra-sensory perception, which are not within the range explicable by established

Paraguay
REPUBLIC OF (*República del Paraguay*)

AREA 406,752 sq km/157,042 sq mi
CAPITAL Asunción
TOWN port Concepción
PHYSICAL mostly flat; divided by river
Paraguay; river Paraná in S
FEATURES Itaipú dam on border with Brazil;
Gran Chaco plain with huge swamps
HEAD OF STATE AND OF GOVERNMENT Alfredo
Stroessner Mattiauda from 1954
GOVERNMENT right-wing authoritarian
EXPORTS cotton, soya beans, timber, tung oil,
maté
CURRENCY guaraní (1,324 = £1 Sept
1987)
POPULATION (1985) 3,989,000 (95% of mixed
Guaraní Indian-Spanish descent); annual
growth rate 3.1%
LANGUAGE Spanish (official), spoken by 4%;
Guaraní 50%; remainder bilingual
RELIGION Roman Catholic
LITERACY 89% male/83% female (1980 est)
GDP $5.6 bn (1983); $1,614 per head of
population
CHRONOLOGY
1811 Independent from Spain.
1865–70 At war with Argentina, Brazil and
Uruguay. Much territory lost.
1932–35 Much territory won from Bolivia
during the Chaco War.

Paraguay

1940–48 Gen Higino Morinigo president.
1948–54 Political instability with six different
presidents.
1954 Gen Alfredo Stroessner in power. He
has since been re-elected six times, despite
increasing opposition and accusations of
human-rights violations.
1984–87 Speculation increased about
Stroessner's successor. He will be 76 in 1988
but is likely to stay on for an eighth term.

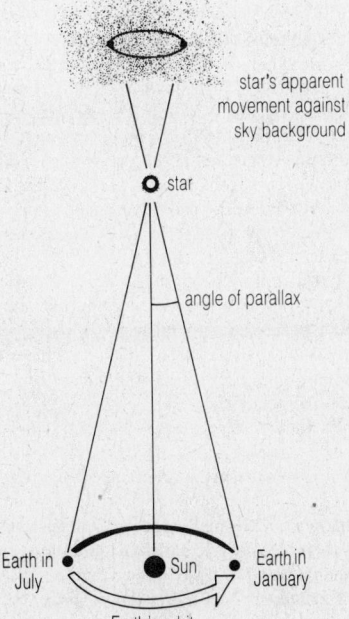

parallax

star's apparent
movement against
sky background

star

angle of parallax

Earth in
July

Sun

Earth in
January

Earth's orbit

science. The faculty allegedly responsible for
them, and common to humans and other animals,
is known as *psi* (23rd letter of the Greek

alphabet). They include: *mediumship* supposed
contact with the spirits of the dead, usually via
an intermediate 'guide'; *precognition*,
foreknowledge of events, as by 'second sight';
telekinesis, movement of objects from one
position to another by human mental
concentration; *telepathy*, term coined by ◊Myers
for 'communication of impressions of any kind
from one mind to another, independently of the
recognized channels of sense'. The majority of
scientists are sceptical, but a chair of
parapsychology was endowed by Arthur
◊Koestler in 1984 at Edinburgh University.

paraquat a non-selective herbicide (l-
dimethyl-4, 4-bipyridium). Although quickly
degraded by soil microorganisms, it results in
irreversible lung damage to human beings if
ingested.

parasite an organism which lives on or in
another organism (called the 'host'), feeding on
the host without immediately killing it, and
dependent on it to some degree. Parasites that
live inside the host, such as liver flukes and
tapeworms, are called *endoparasites*; those that
live on the outside, such as fleas and lice, are
called *ectoparasites*.

parathyroid a small ◊endocrine gland. There
is a pair of parathyroid glands located behind the
◊thyroid gland of most vertebrates. They secrete
parathyroid hormone, which regulates the
amount of calcium in the blood.

paratyphoid fever an infective fever like
typhoid but milder and less dangerous.

parenchyma a plant tissue composed of
loosely packed, more or less spherical cells, with
thin cellulose walls.

parent governor the 1980 ◊Education Act in
the UK made it mandatory for all maintained
schools to include elected parent representatives
on their governing bodies, in line with the existing
practice of some local education authorities. The
1986 Education Act increased parental
representation.

parent teacher association (PTA) group
attached to a school consisting of parents and
teachers who support the school by fund raising
and educational activities amongst the parent
body. In the UK, PTAs are organized into a
national federation which increasingly acts as a
pressure group for maintained schools.

Pareto /pəˈreɪtəʊ/ Vilfredo 1848–1923.
Italian economist and political philosopher, born
in Paris. A founder of welfare economics, he put
forward a concept of 'optimality' which contends
that optimum conditions exist in an economic
system if no-one can be made better off without
at least one other person becoming worse off. A
vigorous opponent of socialism and liberalism,
Pareto justified inequality of income on the
grounds of his empirical observation (Pareto's
law) that income distribution remained constant
whatever efforts were made to change it.

Paris /ˈpærɪs, French pæˈriː/ port and capital
of France at the confluence of rivers Marne and
Seine; university about 1150. The City of Paris
(*Ville de Paris*) forms a *département* in the Île
de France region
area 105 sq km/40.5 sq mi
features central Paris was replanned in the 19th
century by Baron ◊Haussmann. The Seine is
spanned by 32 bridges, the oldest being the Pont
Neuf 1578. Churches include Nôtre-Dame
cathedral, 1163–1250; the Invalides, with the
tomb of Napoleon; the Gothic Saint-Chapelle;
and the 19th-century basilica of Sacré-Coeur,
125 m/410 ft high. Among notable buildings are
the Palais de Justice, the Hôtel de Ville, the
Luxembourg Palace and Gardens; the former
palace of the Louvre is now one of the world's
most important art galleries, and the Orsay
Museum 1986 (19th-century and Impressionist
paintings). Other landmarks are the Tuileries
gardens, the Place de la Concorde, the Champs-
Elysées leading to the Arc de Triomphe, with the
tomb of the Unknown Warrior under it; the Eiffel
Tower, and the Jardin des Plantes. To the W is
the Bois de Boulogne; ◊Montmartre is in the N
of the city
products metal goods, chemicals, leather goods,
glass, tobacco, food products, luxury goods
population (1982, metropolitan area) 8,707,000
history Paris, the Roman *Lutetia*, capital of the
Parisii, a Gaulish tribe, was occupied by Julius
Caesar 53 BC. The Merovingian king Clovis made
it his capital in about 508, but it attained
importance only under the Capetian kings
987–1328. Paris was occupied by the English
1420–36, and was besieged by Henry IV,
1590–94. The Bourbon kings did much to
beautify the city. Napoleon adorned it with new
boulevards, bridges, and triumphal arches, as did
Napoleon III. Paris was the centre of the

revolutions of 1789–94, 1830, and 1848. It was besieged by Prussia 1870–71, and by government troops under the Commune, and during World War I suffered from air raids and bombardment. In World War II it was occupied by Germany Jun 1940–Aug 1944.

Paris, Treaty of any of various peace treaties signed in Paris; they include

1763 ending the ◊Seven Years War

1783 recognizing ◊American Independence

1814 and *1815* following the abdication and final defeat of ◊Napoleon

1856 ending the ◊Crimean War

1898 ending ◊Spanish-American War

1919–20 the conference preparing the *Treaty of Versailles* at the end of World War I was held in Paris

1946 after World War II the peace treaties between the ◊Allies and Italy, Romania, Hungary, Bulgaria, and Finland.

Paris /'pæris, French pæ'ri:/ in Greek legend, a prince of Troy whose abduction of Helen, wife of King Menelaus of Sparta, caused the Trojan war.

Paris /'pæris/ Henri d'Orléans, Comte de Paris 1909– . Head of the house of ◊Bourbon.

Paris /'pæris/ Matthew. English chronicler. He entered St Albans Abbey in 1217, and wrote a valuable history of England up to 1259.

Paris Club an international forum dating from the 1950s for the rescheduling of debts granted or guaranteed by official bilateral creditors; it has no fixed membership nor an institutional structure. In the 1980s it has been closely involved in seeking solutions to the serious debt crisis affecting many developing countries.

Paris Commune a provisional government of socialists and left-wing Republicans, elected in Mar 1871 after an attempt by the right-wing National Assembly at Versailles to disarm the Paris National Guard. It held power until May, when the Versailles troops captured Paris and massacred at least 20,000 people. It is famous as the first socialist government in history.

parish council system of local government in England and Wales, based on church parishes, established by the Local Government Act 1894. They provide and maintain monuments, playing fields, footpaths, and churchyards, administer local charities, may impose a limited local rate, are elected every four years and function in parishes of 200 or more electors. In Wales they are commonly called community councils. Most of the legal powers of a parish council were abolished by the 1972 Local Government Act.

Park /pɑːk/ Mungo 1771–1806. Scottish explorer. He traced the course of the Niger 1795–97, and died during a second expedition in 1805–06. He published *Travels in the Interior of Africa* 1799.

Park Chung Hee /'pɑːk ˌtʃʊŋ 'hiː/ 1917–1979. president of South Korea 1963–79. Under his rule South Korea had the world's fastest-growing economy and the wealth was widely distributed, but recession and his increasing authoritarianism led to his assassination in 1979.

Parker /'pɑːkə/ 'Charlie', 'Bird', 'Yardbird' (Charles Christopher) 1920–1955. US alto

Paris Commune Scenes of destruction under the provisional socialist government. This statue of Napoleon had been on top of the Column Vendôme.

saxophonist and composer, closely associated with the trumpeter Dizzy Gillespie in developing the be-bop style. His mastery of improvisation influenced performers on all jazz instruments.

Parker A virtuoso on the alto saxophone, Charlie Parker was able to improvise on any theme from traditional ballads and lullabies to the rhythmic blues numbers he made famous, such as *Now's the Time*, *Chi Chi*, and *Parker's Mood*.

Parker /'pɑːkə/ Dorothy (born Rothschild) 1893–1967. American poet and wit. She reviewed for the magazines *Vanity Fair* and the *New Yorker*, and is best remembered for her verses, including the collection *Not So Deep As A Well* 1940, and for short stories.

Parker /'pɑːkə/ Matthew 1504–1575. English cleric, born in Norwich. He was converted to Protestantism at Cambridge. He received preferment under Henry VIII and

Edward VI, and, as archbishop of Canterbury from 1559 was largely responsible for the formal establishment of the Church of England.

Parkes /pɑːks/ the site in New South Wales of the Australian National Radio Astronomy Observatory, featuring a radio telescope of 64 m/210 ft aperture, run by the Commonwealth Scientific and Industrial Research Organization.

Parkes /pɑːks/ Henry 1815–1896. Australian politician who did much to promote education and the cause of federation, and suggested the name Commonwealth. He was five times premier of New South Wales 1872–91. ◊Parkes in New South Wales is named after him.

Parkinson /'pɑːkɪnsən/ Cecil Edward 1931– . British Conservative politician. As chair of the party 1981–83, he masterminded the electoral victory of 1983, and was created minister for trade and industry, but resigned in Oct 1984 following disclosure of an affair with his secretary. In 1987 he rejoined the cabinet as secretary of state for energy.

Parkinson /'pɑːkɪnsən/ Cyril Northcote 1909– . British historian, celebrated for his study of public and business administration *Parkinson's Law* 1958, which included the dictum: 'work expands to fill the time available for its completion'.

Parkinson /'pɑːkɪnsən/ James 1755–1824. British neurologist, who first described *Parkinson's disease*, a progressive deterioration of the small region of the brain that produces dopamine, a chemical used in the transmission of nerve signals. The patient's ability to walk is impaired and he or she suffers from tremor.

Parliament the legislative body of a country. In the UK it is the supreme legislature and comprises the Sovereign, the House of Lords and the House of Commons at the Palace of Westminster. Parliament originated under the Norman kings as the Great Council of royal tenants-in-chief, to which in the 13th century representatives of the shires were sometimes summoned. De Montfort's parliament 1265 set a precedent by including representatives of the boroughs as well as the shires, which was followed by Edward I from 1275 onwards. Under Edward III the burgesses and knights of the shires began to meet separately from the barons, thus forming the House of Commons. By the 15th century Parliament had acquired the right to legislate, vote and appropriate supplies, examine public accounts, and impeach royal ministers. The powers of Parliament were much diminished under the Yorkists and Tudors, but under Elizabeth I a new spirit of independence appeared. The revolutions of 1640 and 1688 established parliamentary control over the executive and the judiciary, and finally abolished all royal claim to tax or legislate without parliamentary consent. During these struggles the two great parties (Whig and Tory) emerged, and after 1688 it became customary for the king to choose his ministers from the party dominant in the Commons. The English parliament was united with the Scottish in 1707, and with the Irish during 1801–1922. The franchise was extended to the middle classes in 1832, to the urban working classes in 1867, to agricultural labourers in 1884, and to women in 1918 and 1928. Payment of members was introduced in 1911.

The duration of parliaments was fixed at three years in 1694, at seven in 1716, and at five in 1911, but any parliament may extend its own life, as happened during both world wars. Constituencies are kept under continuous review by the Parliamentary Boundary Commissions 1944. There are 650 MPs each representing a geographical constituency. The House of Lords comprises the temporal peers, that is all hereditary peers of England created to 1707, all hereditary peers of Great Britain created 1707–1800, and all hereditary peers of the UK 1801 onward; all hereditary Scottish peers (under the Peerage Act 1963); all peeresses in their own right (under the same act); all life peers (both the law lords and those created under the Life Peerages Act of 1958); and the spiritual peers – the two archbishops and 24 of the bishops (London, Durham and Winchester by right, and the rest by seniority). The Lords are presided over by the Lord Chancellor, and the Commons by the Speaker.

A public bill is given a preliminary first reading and discussed in detail at the second reading; it is then referred to a select or standing committee, after which it is considered by a committee of the whole house. After the third reading it is sent to the Lords, whose procedure is similar. If it passes both houses, it receives the royal assent and so becomes law.

parliamentary paper an official document, such as a White Paper or report of a select committee, which is prepared for the information of Members of Parliament.

Parliament, European governing body of the ◊European Economic Community (EEC). Originally merely consultative, it became directly elected 1979, and assumed increased powers. Though still not a true legislative body,

it can dismiss the Commission en bloc, and reject the Community budget in its entirety. Full sittings are in Strasbourg; most committees meet in Brussels, and the seat of the secretariat is in Luxembourg. The socialists currently form the largest single group, but are outnumbered by the aggregate strength of the centre and right.

Parliament, Houses of the building where the British legislative assembly meets. The present Houses of Parliament in London were designed by Charles ◊Barry and A.W. ◊Pugin and built in 1840–60, the previous building having been burned down in 1834. It incorporates portions of the medieval Palace of Westminster. The Commons debating chamber was destroyed by incendiary bombs in 1941: the rebuilt chamber (opened 1950) is the work of Gilbert ◊Scott and preserves its former character.

Parma /'pɑːmə/ city in Emilia-Romagna, N Italy, with industry (food processing, textiles, engineering); 12th-century cathedral; university 1502; population (1984) 177,000. It has given its name to Parmesan cheese

history founded by the Etruscans; capital of the duchy of Parma 1545–1860.

Parmenides /pɑːˈmenɪdiːz/ c. 510–450 BC. Greek philosopher, head of the Eleatic school (so called after Elea in S Italy). Against ◊Heraclitus' doctrine of Becoming, Parmenides presented the world in a state of Being.

Parnassiens, Les /ˌpɑːnæsˈjæŋ/ school of French poets including Leconte de Lisle, Mallarmé, and Verlaine, which flourished 1866–76. Named from the review *Parnasse Contemporain*, it advocated 'art for art's sake' in opposition to the ideas of the Romantics.

Parnassus /pɑːˈnæsəs/ mountain in Greece; height 2,457 m/8,062 ft, the abode of Apollo and the Muses. Delphi lies on its S flank.

Parnell /pɑːˈnel/ Charles Stewart 1846–1891. Irish politician, born in County Wicklow. He was elected Member of Parliament for Meath in 1875. Parnell supported a policy of obstruction and violence, and became the president of the Nationalist Party in 1877. In 1879 he approved the Land League, and his attitude led to his imprisonment in 1881. He welcomed Gladstone's Home Rule Bill, and continued his agitation after its defeat in 1886. In 1887 his reputation suffered from an unfounded accusation by *The Times* of his complicity in the murder of Lord Frederick ◊Cavendish. He was finally ruined by being cited as correspondent in a divorce case. For fear of losing the support of Gladstone, his party deposed him in 1890.

parody in literature and the other arts, a work that imitates the style of another work, usually with mocking or comic intent.

Parr /pɑː/ Catherine 1512–1548. Sixth wife of Henry VIII of England. She had already lost two husbands when in 1543 she married Henry VIII. She survived him, and in 1547 married Lord Seymour of Sudeley (1508–49).

Parramatta /ˌpærəˈmætə/ river, W arm of Port Jackson, New South Wales, Australia. It is 24 km/15 mi long and is lined with industrial suburbs of Sydney: Balmain, Drummoyne,

Parnell As chair of the Home Rule party and militant campaigner for Irish self-government, Parnell earned the nickname of 'uncrowned king of Ireland'.

Concord, Parramatta, Ermington and Rydalmere, Ryde, and Hunter's Hill.

parrot bird of the order Psittaciformes, abundant in the tropics, especially in Australia and South America: the smaller species are commonly referred to as parakeets. They are vegetarian, except for the New Zealand ◊kea. The plumage is colourful, although the call is a harsh screech: the talent for imitating human speech is most marked in the grey parrot *Psittacus erithacus* of Africa.

Parry /'pæri/ Charles Hubert Hastings 1848–1918. British composer, born in Bournemouth. His works include songs, motets, and the setting of Milton's 'Blest Pair of Sirens' and Blake's 'Jerusalem'.

Parry /'pæri/ William Edward 1790–1855. British admiral and Arctic explorer. He made detailed charts during explorations of the North-West Passage 1819–20, 1821–23, and 1824–25, and an attempt to reach the Pole in 1827. The *Parry Islands*, off Canada, are named after him.

parsec in astronomy, a unit of distance applied to stars and galaxies. One parsec is equal to 3.2616 light years. It is the distance at which a star would have a ◊parallax (apparent displacement) of one second of arc, taking the baseline as the Earth's distance from the Sun.

Parseeism the religion of the followers of ◊Zoroaster who fled from Persia after its conquest by the Arabs, and settled in India in the 8th century AD. About 100,000 now live mainly in Bombay state, maintaining their rituals of the sacred fire and the exposure of their dead.

Parsifal in Germanic legend, the father of ◊Lohengrin and one of the knights who sought the Holy Grail.

parsley biennial herb *Petroselinum crispum*, cultivated for flavouring; 45 cm/1.5 ft high; it has pinnate, aromatic leaves and yellow umbelliferous flowers.

parsnip temperate Eurasian biennial *Pastinaca sativa* family Umbelliferae, with a fleshy edible root.

Parsons /'pɑːsənz/ Charles Algernon 1854–1931. British engineer, who invented the Parsons steam ◊turbine 1884, a landmark in marine engineering and later universally used in electricity generation (to drive an alternator). Knighted in 1911, Order of Merit in 1927.

Parsons /'pɑːsənz/ Talcott 1902–1979. American sociologist, professor of sociology at Harvard University from 1931 until his death, and author of over 150 books and articles. His theory of structural functionalism dominated American sociology in the 1940s, 1950s and 1960s, and as an attempt to explain social order and individual behaviour it was a major step in establishing sociology as an academic and scientific discipline.

parthenocarpy the formation of fruits without seeds. This phenomenon, of no obvious benefit to the plant, occurs naturally in some plants, such as bananas. It can also be induced in some fruit crops, either by breeding or by applying certain plant hormones.

parthenogenesis the development of an ovum (egg) without any genetic contribution from a male. In most cases, there is no ◊fertilization at all, but in a few the stimulus of being fertilized by a sperm is needed to initiate development, although the male's chromosomes are not absorbed into the nucleus of the ovum. Parthenogenesis is the normal means of reproduction in some plants (for example, dandelions) and animals (for example, certain fish and rotifers). Certain sexually reproducing species, such as aphids, show parthenogenesis at some stage in their life cycle, and it can be artificially induced in many animals (such as rabbits) by cooling, pricking or applying acid to an egg.

Parthenon /'pɑːθənən/ temple of Athena Parthenos ('the Virgin') on the Acropolis at Athens; built 447–438 BC under the supervision of Phidias, and the most perfect example of Doric architecture (by Callicrates and Ictinus). In turn a Christian church and Turkish mosque, it was then used as a gunpowder magazine, and reduced to ruins when the Venetians bombarded the Acropolis in 1687. Greek sculptures from the Parthenon were removed by Lord Elgin in the early 19th century; see ◊Elgin marbles.

Parthia /'pɑːθiə/ ancient name for a country in W Asia in what is now NE Iran. Originating about 248 BC, it reached the peak of its power under Mithridates I in the 2nd century BC. Ctesiphon was the capital of Parthia, which was annexed to Persia in 226 AD. Their horsemen feigned retreat, and shot their arrows unexpectedly backwards, hence 'Parthian shot'.

participle a form of the verb, in English either a *present participle* ending in *-ing* (for example, 'work*ing*' in 'They were working', 'working men', and 'a hard-working team') or a *past participle* ending in *-ed* in regular verbs (for example, 'train*ed*' in 'They have been trained well', 'trained soldiers', and 'a well-trained team'). In irregular verbs the past participle has a special form (for example, drive/*driven*; light/*lit*,

burn/*burned, burnt*). The participle is also used to open such constructions as 'Coming down the stairs, she paused and...' and 'Angered by the news, he...'. Such constructions, however, are not always logically formed, with amusing or ambiguous results. 'Driving along a country road, a stone broke my windscreen' suggests that the stone was driving along the road. This illogical usage is a *misrelated participle*; a *dangling* or *hanging participle* has nothing at all to relate to: 'While driving along a country road there was a loud noise under the car.' Such sentences need to be completely re-expressed.

particle, subatomic any of the subdivisions of the ◊atom. They are frequently classified in groups of ◊elementary particles: baryons, which include the massive particles (proton, neutron, antiproton, antineutron); mesons, which include the intermediate-mass particles (pion); leptons, which include the light particles (electron, positron, neutrino); and the ultra-elementary particles, ◊quarks.

partisan member of an armed group that operates behind enemy lines or in occupied territories during wars. The name 'partisans' was first given to armed bands of Russians who operated against Napoleon's army in Russia during 1812 but has since been used to describe Russian and Polish ◊Resistance groups against the Germans during World War II. In Yugoslavia the communist partisans under ◊Tito played a major role in defeating the Germans.

partnership in English law, two or more persons carrying on a common business for shared profit (for instance, accountants, bankers, and solicitors). It differs from an ordinary company in that the individuals remain separate in identity and are not protected by limited liability, so that absolute mutual trust is essential.

part of speech a category of words, as described in the ◊grammar of the Western languages which has described Greek and Latin over the centuries since classical times. The 'part of speech' of a word is its grammatical function. The four major parts of speech are the ◊noun, ◊verb, ◊adjective, and ◊adverb; the minor parts of speech vary according to schools of grammatical theory, but include the ◊article, ◊conjunction, ◊preposition, and ◊pronoun.

partridge game bird, two species of which are found in the UK. The grey partridge *Perdix perdix* is mottled brown above, with grey speckled breast, and patches of chestnut barred on the sides. The French partridge *Alectoris rufa* is distinguished from the grey partridge by red legs, bill, and eyelids. The back is plain brown, with a white throat edged with black. The sides are barred chestnut and black.

Partridge /'pɑːtrɪdʒ/ Eric 1894–1979. New Zealand lexicographer. He studied at Oxford University after serving in World War I and settled in England to write a number of dictionaries including *A Dictionary of Slang and Unconventional English* 1934 and 1970, and *Dictionary of the Underworld, British and American* 1950.

Pasadena /ˌpæsə'diːnə/ city in California, USA, part of the ◊Los Angeles conurbation. On

1 Jan the East–West football game is held here in the 85,000-seat Rose Bowl. The California Institute of Technology (Caltech) owns the Hale Observatories (which include the Mount Palomar telescope) and is linked with the Jet Propulsion Laboratories. Pasadena began as a Spanish settlement.

Pascal /'pæskæl/ a high-level computer-programming language. Designed by Niklaus Wirth (1934–) in the 1960s as an aid to teaching programming, it is still widely used as such in universities, but is also recognized as a good general-purpose programming language.

Pascal /'pæskæl/ Blaise 1623–1662. French philosopher and mathematical physicist. Author of *Pensées* 1670. He contributed to the development of hydraulics, calculus, and ◊probability theory.

After a mystical experience 1654, Pascal took refuge in the ◊Jansenist Catholic monastery of Port Royal and defended the Jansenists against the Jesuits in his *Lettres provinciales* 1656. His influential *Pensées* was part of an unfinished defence of the Christian religion. His description of man as 'a thinking reed' is often quoted.

In mathematics Pascal is best known for his work on conic sections and (with Pierre de Fermat) probability theory. *Pascal's triangle* is an array of numbers in which each is the sum of the pair of numbers above it. Plotted at equal distances along a horizontal axis, the numbers in the rows approximate to the normal (bell-shaped) probability distribution curve which describes the incidence of many natural phenomena. In physics, Pascal's chief work concerned fluid pressure and hydraulics. Pascal's principle states that the pressure everywhere in a fluid is the same, so that pressure applied at one point is transmitted equally to all parts of the container. This is the principle of the hydraulic press and jack.

PASCAL'S TRIANGLE

```
                 1
               1   1
             1   2   1
           1   3   3   1
         1   4   6   4   1
       1   5  10  10   5   1
     1   6  15  20  15   6   1
   1   7  21  35  35  21   7   1
```

Pas-de-Calais /ˌpɑːdə'kæleɪ/ French name for the ◊Strait of Dover and of the French *département* bordering it, of which Arras is the capital and Calais the chief port. See also ◊Nord-Pas de Calais.

pas de deux a dance for two performers. A *grand pas de deux* is danced by the prima ballerina and the premier danseur.

Pashto or **Pushtu** an Indo-European language, officially that of Afghanistan, and also spoken in another dialect in N Pakistan.

Pasmore /'pɑːsmɔː/ Victor 1908– . British artist noted for abstract compositions and as an exponent of the 'classic' tendency in British art. He became a Companion of Honour 1981.

Parthenon The temple of Athena Parthenos, on the Acropolis at Athens, is being extensively restored to the ruin left after the Venetian bombardment of 1687.

Pasolini /ˌpæsəˈliːni/ Pier Paolo 1922–1975. Italian poet, novelist, and film director, an influential figure of the post-war years. His writings (making much use of Roman dialect) include volumes of poetry, and the novels *Ragazzi di vita/The Ragazzi* 1955 and *Una vita violenta/A Violent Life* 1959. Films include *Il vangelo secondo Mateo/The Gospel According to St Matthew* 1964, *Il decamerone/The Decameron* 1971, and *I racconti de Canterbury/The Canterbury Tales* 1972.

pasque flower *Pulsatilla vulgaris* of the buttercup family. A low-growing hairy perennial with feathery leaves, it has large purple bell-shaped flowers which start erect then droop. The anthers are bright yellow and the purple bell is made up of sepals. It blooms in spring. Found in Europe and Asia, it is characteristic of grassland on lime soils and in Britain is found mainly in the SE.

Passau /ˈpæsaʊ/ town in Bavaria, West Germany, at the junction of the Inn and Ilz with the Danube. The *Treaty of Passau* 1552 between Maurice, elector of Saxony, and the future emperor Ferdinand I allowed the Lutherans full religious liberty, and prepared the way for the Peace of Augsburg: see ▷Reformation.

Passchendaele /ˈpæʃəndeɪl/ village in W Flanders, Belgium, near Ypres: the Passchendaele ridge before Ypres was the object of a costly, but unsuccessful, British offensive in World War I, Jul–Nov 1917; British casualties numbered nearly 400,000.

passion flower tropical American genus of climbing plants *Passiflora* family Passifloraceae. Parts of the flower resemble symbols of the crucifixion, such as a crown of thorns.

passion play play representing the death and resurrection of a god, as of Osiris, Dionysus, and Christ. With its origins in medieval ▷mystery plays, the most famous takes place every ten years at ▷Oberammergau, West Germany.

Passover Jewish spring festival, dating from ancient times, which commemorates the exodus from Egypt. See ▷Judaism.

passport document issued by the foreign office of any country authorizing the bearer to go abroad and guaranteeing the bearer the state's protection. Some countries require an intending visitor to obtain a special endorsement or *visa*.

Pasternak /ˈpæstənæk/ Boris Leonidovich 1890–1960. Russian poet and novelist. Born in Moscow, he remained in Russia when his father, the artist Leonid Pasternak (1862–1945), emigrated. His volumes of lyric poems include *A Twin Cloud* 1914, and *On Early Trains* 1943, and he translated Shakespeare's tragedies. His novel *Dr Zhivago* 1958, dealing with a scientist's disillusion with the Russian revolution, was followed by a Nobel prize (which he declined), and was banned in the USSR as 'a hostile act'.

Pasteur /ˈpæstɜː/ Louis 1822–1895. French chemist, whose discovery that fermentation was caused by microorganisms led to the science of microbiology (the study of microbial infection, prevention, and immunology). He inspired his pupil Lister's work in antiseptic surgery. He later researched into silkworm disease, ▷anthrax, and especially ▷rabies, for which his development of a vaccine led to the foundation of the Institut Pasteur in Paris 1888. See ▷pasteurization.

PARTICLE: MAJOR FUNDAMENTAL (SUBATOMIC) PARTICLES

Name	Symbol	Category	Mass (electron = 1)	Charge	Spin	Parity
electron	e	lepton	1	−1	1/2	
graviton	g	quantum	0	0	2	
K meson (kaon)	K	meson	998	−1,0,+1	0	−1
lambda particle	Λ	baryon	2231	0	1/2	+1
muon	μ	lepton	211	−1	1/2	
neutrino	ν	lepton	0	0	1/2	
neutron	n	baryon	1880	0	1/2	+1
omega particle	Ω	baryon	3345	−1	3/2	+1
photon	∝	quantum	0	0	1	−1
pion	π	meson	280	−1,0,+1	0	−1
proton	p	baryon	1876	+1	1/2	+1
sigma particle	Σ	baryon	2380	−1,0,+1	1/2	+1
xi particle	Ξ	baryon	2644	−1,0	1/2	+1

More than one charge in the Charge *column indicates that there is more than one particle of that type, which differ in charge (there may also be slight differences in mass). Certain particles with a single charge have antiparticles of opposite charge. Thus the positron resembles the electron in every respect except that its charge is +1; similarly, the antiproton has a charge of −1.*

Lambda, omega, sigma, and xi particles are known collectively as hyperons.

Baryons and mesons together make up the type termed hadrons.

Pasteur Although a chemist by training, Louis Pasteur was the most important medical scientist of the 19th century. It was not until the end of his career that he turned to human disease and pioneered effective treatments against anthrax and rabies.

pastiche a term applied in the arts to a work which imitates another's style, or a medley composed of fragments from an original. The intention is normally homage, rather than ridicule as in parody.

Patagonia /ˌpætəˈɡəʊnɪə/ geographic area of South America, south of latitude 40° S, with sheep farming and coal and oil resources. Sighted by Magellan 1520, it was divided between Argentina and Chile in 1881.

patchouli oriental soft-wooded shrub *Pogostemon heyneanus* family Labiateae, source of the perfume patchouli.

paten flat dish of gold or silver used for holding the consecrated bread at the ◊Eucharist.

patent letters patent, more usually known as a patent, are documents conferring the exclusive right to make, use, and sell an invention (ideas are not eligible, neither is anything not new) for a limited period. There is a London Patent Office, and a central office (established in Munich, with a branch at The Hague, 1977) grants patents for 20 years in 16 European countries, also covering designs and trade marks; in the USA the period of patent is only 17 years. In 1987 the USA began issuing patents for new animal forms created by gene splitting. See also ◊Frankenstein law.

Pater /ˈpeɪtə/ Walter Horatio 1839–1894. British critic, born in London. A noted stylist and supporter of 'art for art's sake', he published *Studies in the History of the Renaissance* 1873, *Marius the Epicurean* 1885, *Imaginary Portraits* 1887, and other works.

Paternoster /ˌpætəˈnɒstə/ (Latin 'Our father') name for the Lord's Prayer, from the opening words of the Latin version.

Pathan /pəˈtɑːn/ Muslim people of NW Pakistan and Afghanistan. Formerly a constant threat to the British Raj, the Pakistani Pathans now claim independence, with the Afghani Pathans, in their own state of Pakhtoonistan.

Patiala /ˌpʌtiˈɑːlə/ city in E Punjab, India, with textile and metalwork industries; Punjabi

University 1962; population (1981) 206,254.

Patinir /ˌpɑːtɪˈnɪə/ (also Patenier, Patinier) Joachim c. 1485–c. 1524. Flemish artist, noted for its landscape backgrounds to his depictions of the saints, which blend fantasy with naturalistic detail.

Patmore /ˈpætmɔː/ Coventry 1823–1896. British poet and critic. He was a librarian at the British Museum 1846–66, and as one of the Pre-Raphaelites achieved fame with the poem *The Angel in the House* 1854–63 and the collection of odes *The Unknown Eros* 1877.

Patmos /ˈpætmɒs/ Greek island in the Aegean, one of the Dodecanese. St John is said to have written the New Testament Book of Revelation while in exile here.

Patna /ˈpætnə/ capital of Bihar state, India, on the Ganges; university 1917; population (1981) 916,000. It has remains of a hall built by the emperor Asoka in the 3rd century BC.

Paton /ˈpeɪtn/ Alan 1903– . South African writer, born in Pietermaritzburg. He became first a schoolmaster and in 1935 principal of a reformatory near Johannesburg, which he ran on enlightened lines. His novel *Cry, the Beloved Country* 1948 touched the heart of South Africa's problems: later books include the study *Land and People of South Africa* 1956, *The Long View* 1968, and his autobiography *Towards the Mountain* 1980.

Patou /pæˈtuː/ Jean 1880–1936. French designer of sporting clothes (as worn by Suzanne ◊Lenglen) from 1922 and bias-cut white satin evening dresses 1929; and creator of the perfume Joy 1926.

Patras /ˈpætrəs/ (Greek *Patrai*) industrial city (hydroelectric installations; textiles and paper) in the NW Peloponnese, Greece, on the Gulf of Patras; population (1981) 141,500. The ancient *Patrae*, it is the only one of the 12 cities of ◊Achaea to survive.

patriarch (Greek 'ruler of a family') in the Old Testament, one of the ancestors of the human race, and especially those of the Jews from Adam to the sons of Jacob. In the ◊Orthodox Church, the term refers to the leader of a national church.

patricians /pəˈtrɪʃənz/ privileged class in ancient Rome, descended from the original citizens. After the 4th century BC the rights formerly exercised by the patricians alone were thrown open to the plebeians, and patrician descent became only a matter of prestige.

Patrick, St /ˈpætrɪk/ 389–461 or 493. The patron saint of Ireland. Born in Britain, probably in S Wales, he was carried off by pirates to six years' slavery in Antrim before escaping either to Britain or Gaul – his poor Latin suggests the former – to train as a missionary. He is variously said to have landed again in Ireland in 432 or 456, and is credited with founding the diocese of Armagh, of which he was bishop, though this was probably the work of a 'lost apostle' (Palladius or Secundinus). His work was a vital factor in the spread of Irish Christian influence. Of his writings only his *Confessio* and an *Epistola* survive. His feast day is 17 Mar.

patronage the right of appointment to an office or position in politics and the church. In Britain, where it was nicknamed 'Old Corruption', patronage existed in the 16th century, but was most common from the restoration of 1660 to the 19th century, when it was used to manage elections and ensure party support.

Ecclesiastical patronage was the right of selecting a person to a living or benefice, termed an advowson. *Salaried patronage* was the nomination to a salaried post: at court, in government, the Church of England, the Civil Service, the armed services, or to the East India Company. The Northcote-Trevelyan report on the Civil Service 1854 advised the replacement of patronage in the Civil Service by open competitive examination, although its recommendations were carried out only later in the century. Commissions in the British army were bought and sold openly until the practice was abolished in 1871. Church livings were bought and sold as late as 1874.

Patronage survives today in the political honours system (awards granted to party supporters) and the appointment of university professors, leaders of national corporations and government bodies, and so on, which is often by invitation rather than by formal application. Selection on the grounds of justice rather than solely on the basis of ability lives on today with the practice of positive ◊discrimination.

In the arts, patronage takes the form of sponsorship or support, formerly by individuals (often royal or noble) or by the church. In this century, patrons have tended to be the state and (increasingly) private industry.

Patti /'pæti/ Adelina 1843–1919. Anglo-Italian soprano opera singer, noted for her performance of Lucia in *Lucia di Lammermoor* and Amina in *La sonnambula*.

Patton /'pætn/ George Smith 1885–1945. American general, known for his fiery daring as 'Blood and Guts' Patton. He commanded the 2nd Armoured Division in 1940, and in 1942 led the Western Task Force which landed at Casablanca. After commanding the 7th Army, he led the 3rd Army in France, Belgium, and Germany, and in 1945 took over the 15th Army.

Pau /pəʊ/ industrial city (electrochemical and metallurgical) and resort, capital of Pyrénées-Atlantiques *département* in SW France, near the Spanish border; population (1982) 131,500. It is the centre of the ◊Basque area of France, and there has been guerrilla activity.

Paul /pɔːl/ name of six popes, including Paul VI (Giovanni Battista Montini) (1897–1978), born near Brescia, Italy. He spent more than 25 years in the Secretariat of State under Pius XI and Pius XII before becoming archbishop of Milan in 1954. In 1958 he was created a cardinal by Pope John, and in 1963 he succeeded him as pope and was crowned in St Peter's Square, taking the name of Paul as symbolic of ecumenical unity. His encyclical *Humanae Vitae/Of Human Life* 1968 reaffirmed the Church's traditional teaching on birth control, thus following the minority report of the

Patton An accomplished fencer, sailor, airplane pilot, and athlete, the US general Patton demanded rigorous standards of individual fitness and unit training of his troops during World War II.

commission originally appointed by Pope John, rather than the majority view.

Paul, St /pɔːl/ c. 3–c. 64 or 68 ad. One of the ◊Apostles. The Jewish form of his name is Saul. He was born in Tarsus, son of well-to-do ◊Pharisees, and had Roman citizenship. Opposed to Christianity, he took part in the stoning of ◊Stephen, but was converted by a vision on the road to Damascus. He made great missionary journeys, for example to ◊Philippi, ◊Ephesus, hence becoming known as the 'Apostle of the ◊Gentiles' (non-Jews). On his return to Jerusalem, he was arrested, appealed to Caesar, and (as a citizen) was sent to Rome for trial about 57 or 59. After two years in prison, he may have been released before his final arrest and execution under ◊Nero. 13 epistles in the New Testament are attributed to him. His theology was rigorous on such questions as sin and atonement, and his views on the role of women became those of the Church generally. His feast day is 29 Jun.

Paul /pɔːl/ 1901–1964. King of the Hellenes. The son of King Constantine, he served in the navy for some years and in 1947 he succeeded his brother George II. He married in 1938 Princess Frederika 1917– , daughter of the Duke of Brunswick, whose political role brought her under attack. He was succeeded by his son Constantine II.

Paul I /pɔːl/ 1754–1801. Tsar of Russia from 1796, in succession to his mother ◊Catherine II. Already mentally unstable, he pursued an erratic foreign policy, and was assassinated.

Pauli /'paʊli/ Wolfgang 1900–1958. Austrian-American physicist, a Nobel prizewinner 1945 for his work on atomic

structure. He originated *Pauli's exclusion principle*: in a given system no two ◊electrons, ◊protons, ◊neutrons or other particles of half-integrated spin can be characterized by the same set of ◊quantum numbers. He also predicted the existence of neutrinos.

Pauling /'pɔːlɪŋ/ Linus Carl 1901– . American chemist, noted for his fundamental work on the nature of the chemical bond and on the discovery of the helical structure of many proteins. He was awarded the Nobel prize for chemistry in 1954. An outspoken opponent of nuclear testing, he received the Nobel peace prize in 1962.

Paulinus /pɔːˈlaɪnəs/ Roman missionary who joined ◊Augustine in Kent in 601, converted the Northumbrians in 625, and became the first archbishop of York. Excavations 1978 revealed a church he built in ◊Lincoln. He died in 644.

Paulus /'paʊlus/ Friedrich von 1890–1957. German field marshal, commander of the forces that besieged Stalingrad (now Volgograd) in USSR 1942–43; he was captured and gave evidence at the Nuremberg trials before settling in East Germany.

Pausanias /pɔːˈseɪnɪæs/ 2nd century BC. Greek geographer, author of a valuably accurate description of Greece from his own travels.

Pavarotti /ˌpævəˈrɒti/ Luciano 1935– . Italian operatic tenor, whose roles include Rodolfo in *La Bohème*, Cavaradossi in *Tosca*, the Duke of Mantua in *Rigoletto*, and Nemorino in *L'Elisir d'amore*.

Pavia, Battle of /pəˈviːə/ 1525. The Hapsburg emperor ◊Charles V defeated and captured ◊Francis I of France; it signified the onset of Hapsburg dominance in Italy.

Pavlov /'pævlɒv/ Ivan Petrovich 1849–1936. Russian physiologist who studied conditioned reflexes in animals. His work greatly influenced ◊behavioural and ◊learning theory. See also ◊conditioning.

Pavlova /'pævləvə/ Anna 1881–1931. Russian dancer. Prima ballerina of the Imperial Ballet from 1906, she left Russia in 1913, going on to become the world's most famous classical ballerina. With London as her home, she toured extensively with her own company, influencing dancers worldwide with roles such as ◊Fokine's *The Dying Swan* solo 1905.

pawnbroker one who lends money on the security of goods held. The traditional sign of the premises is three gold balls, the symbol used in front of the houses of the medieval Lombard merchants.

pawpaw or *papaya* tropical tree *Carica papaya*, originating in South America and grown in many tropical countries. The edible fruits resemble a melon, with orange-coloured flesh and numerous blackish seeds in the central cavity, and may weigh 9 kg/20 lb. The fruit juice or the tree sap are often used to tenderize meat. In the USA the name 'pawpaw' is given to *Asimina triloba*, which has an unpleasant odour but carries edible oval berries 75 mm/3 in long.

Pax Roman goddess of peace; Greek counterpart ◊Irene.

Paxton /'pækstən/ Joseph 1801–1865. British architect, garden superintendent to the

Duke of Devonshire from 1826 and designer of the Great Exhibition building of 1851 (◊Crystal Palace), revolutionary in its structural use of glass and iron.

PAYE (Pay As You Earn) in the UK, a system whereby a proportional amount of ◊income tax is deducted by the employer and transferred to the Inland Revenue before wages are paid, reliefs due being notified to the employer by a code number for each employee. Introduced in Britain in 1944, it was devised by the British economist Sir Paul ◊Chambers. Other countries have similar systems; in the USA it is called withholding tax.

paymaster-general head of the Paymaster-General's Office, the British government department (established 1835) which acts as paying agent for most other departments.

Paysandú /ˌpaɪsænˈduː/ third largest city of Uruguay, capital of Paysandú department, on the river Uruguay; tinned meat is the main product; population (1980) 80,000. It dates from 1772, and is linked by bridge 1976 with Puerto Colón in Argentina.

Pays de la Loire /peɪˈiː də lɑː ˈlwɑː/ agricultural region of W France; capital Nantes.

Paz /pɑːs/ Octavio 1914– . Mexican poet, whose *Sun Stone* 1957 is a personal statement based on the ◊Aztec Calendar Stone.

pea climbing plant *Pisum sativum* family Leguminosae, with pods of edible seeds; the *sweet pea Lathyrus odoratus* is grown for its scented flowers.

Peace /piːs/ river formed in British Columbia, Canada, by the union at Finlay Forks of the Finlay and Parsnip rivers and flowing through the Rockies and across Alberta to join the river Slave just N of Lake Athabasca; length 1,600 km/1,000 mi.

Peace Corps a body of trained men and women, established in the USA by President Kennedy in 1961, providing skilled workers for the developing countries, especially in the fields of teaching, agriculture, and health. Living among the country's inhabitants, volunteers are paid only a small allowance to cover their basic needs and maintain health. The Peace Corps was inspired by Voluntary Service Overseas (see ◊British Volunteer Programme).

peace movement the peace movements of the 1980s can trace their origins to the pacifists of the 19th century, conscientious objectors during World War I, and peace campaigners during the interwar years. The campaign since has concentrated on opposing the spread, and even the existence, of nuclear weapons and has attracted not only pacifists but also those opposed to all uses of nuclear power.

peach tree *Prunus persica* in the family Rosaceae. It has ovate leaves and small, usually pink flowers. The yellowish edible fruits have thick velvety skins; the nectarine is a smooth-skinned variety.

Peacock /ˈpiːkɒk/ Thomas Love 1785–1866. British satiric novelist and official of the East India Company. His works include *Headlong Hall* 1816, and *Crotchet Castle* 1831.

peafowl bird of the pheasant family, native to India and Sri Lanka. The common peacock *Pavo cristatus* is rather larger than a pheasant and has a large fan-shaped tail, brightly coloured with blue, green, and purple 'eyes' on a chestnut ground. The peahen is brown with a small tail.

Peak District /piːk/ tableland of the S Pennines in NW Derbyshire. England. It is a tourist region and a national park. The highest point is Kinder Scout 636 m/2,088 ft.

Peake /piːk/ Mervyn (Lawrence) 1911–1968. British writer and illustrator, best known for the grotesque fantasy trilogy *Titus Groan* 1946, *Gormenghast* 1950, and *Titus Alone* 1959, which deals with the inhabitants of a great isolated house.

Peale /piːl/ Charles Wilson 1741–1827. American artist, noted for portraits of leading figures in the War of Independence, including the earliest known portrait of Washington 1722.

peanut another name for ◊groundnut.

pear Eurasian temperate tree *Pyrus communis* family Rosaceae, with a succulent edible fruit, less hardy than the apple.

pearl calcareous substance (nacre) secreted by many molluscs, which when deposited in thin layers on the inside of the shell forms the mother-of-pearl used in ornamental and inlay work, and when deposited round some irritant body forms pearls. Although commercially valuable pearls are obtained from freshwater mussels and oysters, the precious pearl comes from the various species of *Margaritifera* found in tropical waters off N and W Australia, the Californian coast, and in the Indian Ocean. Artificial pearls were first cultivated in Japan in 1893. A tiny bead of shell from a clam, plus a small piece of membrane from another pearl oyster's mantle (to stimulate the secretion of nacre) is inserted in oysters kept in cages in the sea for three years, and then the pearls are harvested.

Pearl Harbor /ˈpɜːl ˈhɑːbə/ US Pacific naval base in Oahu, chief of the islands forming Hawaii State, USA, the scene of a Japanese attack on 7 Dec 1941, which brought America into World War II. It took place while Japanese envoys were holding so-called peace talks in Washington. The local commanders Admiral Kummel and Lt-Gen Short were relieved of their posts and held responsible for the fact that the base, despite warnings, was totally unprepared at the time of the attack.

Pears /pɪəz/ Peter 1910–1986. British tenor. A co-founder with ◊Britten of the Aldeburgh Festival, he was closely associated with the composer's work and played the title role in *Peter Grimes*: he was also often the first performer of works by Tippett and Berkeley. Knighted in 1978.

Pearse /pɪəs/ Patrick Henry 1879–1916. Irish poet prominent in the Gaelic revival, and leader of the Easter Rebellion of 1916. Proclaimed president of the provisional government, he was court-martialled and shot after its suppression.

Pearson /ˈpɪəsən/ Lester Bowles 1897–1972. Canadian Liberal politician. Appointed foreign minister by St Laurent 1948–57, he effectively represented Canada at the United Nations and only Soviet opposition prevented his becoming secretary-general: in 1957 he was awarded a Nobel peace prize, principally because of his role in the creation of the United Nations Emergency Force. Leader of the Liberal Party from 1958, he was prime minister 1963–68.

Peary /ˈpɪəri/ Robert Edwin 1856–1920. US Polar explorer. At his seventh attempt he was the first person to reach the North Pole, on 6 Apr 1909. He sailed to Cape Sheridan in the *Roosevelt*, and then made a sledge journey to the Pole.

Peasants' Revolt the rising of the English peasantry in Jun 1381. Led by Wat ◊Tyler and John ◊Ball, the rebels occupied London and forced Richard II to abolish serfdom, but after Tyler's murder the rebels were forced to withdraw. The movement was suppressed, and the king's concessions revoked.

peat fibrous organic substance found in ◊bogs and formed by the incomplete decomposition of plants such as sphagnum moss. The USSR, Canada, Finland, Ireland, and other places have large deposits, which have been dried and used as fuel from ancient times. Peat can also be used as a soil additive.

pecan nut-producing tree *Carya pecan*, native to southern USA and N Mexico, and now widely cultivated. The tree grows to over 45 m/150 ft, and the edible nuts are smooth-shelled, the kernel resembling a smoothly ovate walnut.

peccary American genus of piglike animals *Tayassu*, having a gland in the middle of the back which secretes a strong-smelling substance. Blackish in colour, they are covered with bristles, and the skins make a useful leather.

Pechenga /ˈpetʃɪŋgə/ ice-free fishing port in Murmansk, USSR, on the Barents Sea, more familiar under its Finnish name *Petsamo*. Russia ceded Pechenga to Finland in 1920 but recovered it under the 1947 peace treaty.

Pechora /pɪˈtʃɔːrə/ river in the USSR, rising in the N Urals; it carries coal, timber, and furs (Jun–Sept) to the Barents Sea 1,800 km/1,125 mi to the N.

Pecs /peɪtʃ/ city in SW Hungary, with metallurgical industries; the centre of a coalmining area on the Yugoslavia frontier; university; population (1985) 175,000
history the town dates from Roman times. It was under Turkish rule 1543–1686.

pedicel the stalk of an individual flower, attaching it to the main floral axis, and often developing in the axil of a bract.

pediment in architecture, the triangular part crowning the fronts of buildings in classic styles. The pediment was a distinctive feature of Greek temples.

pedometer small instrument that gives an approximate distance covered by a pedestrian; each step moves a swinging weight, which in turn causes the mechanism to rotate, so moving a pointer round the face of a dial.

Pedro /ˈpedrəʊ/ name of two emperors of Brazil:

Pedro I 1798–1834. Emperor of Brazil 1822–31. The son of John VI of Portugal, he escaped to Brazil on Napoleon's invasion, and was appointed regent in 1821. He proclaimed Brazil independent in 1822 and was crowned emperor, but abdicated in 1831 and returned to Portugal.

Pedro II 1825–1891. Emperor of Brazil 1831–89. He proved an enlightened ruler, but his anti-slavery measures alienated the landowners, who in 1889 compelled him to abdicate.

Peeblesshire /'piːbəlzʃə/ former county of S Scotland, included from 1975 in Borders region. Peebles was the county town.

Peel /piːl/ fishing port in the Isle of Man, 19 km/12 mi NW of Douglas.

Peel /piːl/ Robert 1788–1850. British Conservative politician. Born in Lancashire. He entered Parliament as a Tory in 1809. As home secretary 1822–27 and 1828–30, he founded the modern police force and in 1829 introduced Roman Catholic emancipation. After the passing of the Reform Bill 1832, which he had resisted, he reformed the Tories under the name of Conservative Party, on a basis of accepting necessary reforms and seeking middle-class support. He was prime minister 1834–35 and 1841–46; he fell from office owing to his repeal of the ◊Corn Laws 1846 which was opposed by the majority of his party. He and his followers then formed a third party standing between the Liberals and Conservatives; the majority of the Peelites, including Gladstone, subsequently joined the Liberals.

Peel A portrait of Robert Peel, founder of the police force, by H. W. Pickersgill.

Peele /piːl/ George 1558–1597. English dramatist. Born in London, he wrote a pastoral, *The Arraignment of Paris* 1584; a fantastic comedy, *The Old Wives' Tale* 1595; and a tragedy, *David and Bethsabe* 1599.

Peenemünde /ˌpeɪnəˈmʊndə/ fishing village in East Germany, used from 1937 by the Germans to develop the V1 and V2 rockets used in World War II.

peepul an Indian tree. See under ◊fig and ◊bo-tree.

peerage in the UK, holders of the hereditary temporal dignities of duke, marquess, earl, viscount, and baron, certain of which may be held by a woman in default of a male heir. In the later 19th century they were augmented by the Lords of Appeal in Ordinary (life peers), and from 1958 by a number of specially created life peers of either sex (usually long-standing members of the Commons). Since 1963 peers have been able to disclaim their titles (for example Lord ◊Home and Tony ◊Benn), usually to allow them to sit in the Commons.

peer group in the social sciences, a term used to refer to people who have a common identity based on such characteristics as similar social status, interests, age, or ethnic group. The concept has proved useful in analysing the power and influence of workmates, school friends, and ethnic and religious groups in socialization and social behaviour.

Pegasus /'pegəsəs/ in astronomy, large ◊constellation of the northern hemisphere, representing the winged horse of Greek mythology. It is the seventh-largest constellation in the sky, and its main feature is a square outlined by four stars, one of which is actually part of the adjoining constellation ◊Andromeda.

Pegasus /'pegəsəs/ in Greek mythology, the winged horse which sprang from the blood of Medusa. Hippocrene, the spring of the Muses on Mount Helicon, is said to have sprung from a blow of his hoof. He was transformed to a constellation.

pegmatite a coase-grained ◊igneous rock found in veins usually associated with large granite masses.

Pegu /pe'guː/ city in Burma, on the river Pegu, NE of Rangoon; population (1983) 254,761. It was founded AD 573 and is noted for the Shwemawdaw pagoda.

Péguy /peɪ'giː/ Charles 1873–1914. French Catholic socialist, who established a socialist publishing house in Paris. From 1900 he published on political topics *Les Cahiers de la Quinzaine/Fortnightly Notebooks* and poetry, including *Le Mystère de la charité de Jeanne d'Arc/The Mystery of the Charity of Joan of Arc* 1897.

Pei /'peɪ/ Ieoh Ming 1917– . Chinese-born American modernist/high tech architect. His best known buildings include the John Hancock tower, Boston; the National Airlines terminal at Kennedy Airport, New York; and the extension to the National Gallery, Washington DC. Projects during the 1980s include renovations to the Louvre Museum, Paris.

Peiping /ˌpeɪ'pɪŋ/ name, meaning 'northern peace', 1928–49 of ◊Peking in China.

Peipus, Lake /'paɪpəs/ lake on the Estonian border in the USSR; in Estonian *Peipsi* and in Russian *Chudskoye*. Alexander Nevski defeated the Teutonic Knights 1242 on its frozen surface.

Peirce /pɪəs/ Charles Sanders 1839–1914. US philosopher, founder of ◊pragmatism, who argued that genuine conceptual distinctions must be correlated with some difference of practical effect. He wrote extensively on the logic of scientific enquiry, suggesting that truth could be conceived of as the object of an ultimate consensus.

pekan or *fishea* North American ◊marten.

Peking /ˌpiː'kɪŋ/ (Pinyin *Beijing*) capital of China

features Tian Anmen Gate (Gate of Heavenly Peace) and Tian Anmen Square; the Forbidden City, built 1406–20 as Gu Gong (Imperial Palace) of the Ming emperors, when there were 9,000 ladies in waiting and 10,000 eunuchs in service (it is now the seat of the modern government); the Great Hall of the People 1959 (used for official banquets); museums of Chinese history and of the Chinese revolution; Chairman Mao Memorial Hall 1977 (shared from 1983 with Zhou En Lai, Zhu De, and Liu Shaoqi); the Summer Palace, built by the dowager empress Zi Xi (damaged by the European powers 1900, but restored 1903); Temple of Heaven (Tiantan); Ming tombs 50 km/30 mi to the NW
population (1982) 9,230,500

history founded 3,000 years ago, it was the 13th-century capital of ◊Kublai Khan, called by the Mongols Khanbaligh, Marco Polo's Cambaluc. Later replaced by Nanking, it was again capital from 1421, except 1928–49, when it was renamed Peiping, and was held by Japan 1937–45.

pekingese toy dog first bred at the Chinese court as the 'Imperial Lion Dog'. The first specimens were brought to Britain during the Opium Wars when the Summer Palace in Peking was looted in 1860.

Peking man early type of human, *homo erectus*. A skull found near Peking 1927 was sent to the USA 1941 and disappeared; others have since been found. Dating varies from 500,000 to 1,500,000 years old.

Pelagius /pe'leɪdʒɪəs/ 360–420. British theologian. He went to Rome about 400, and there taught that every man possesses free will, denying Augustine's doctrines of predestination and original sin. Cleared of heresy by a synod at Jerusalem in 415, he was later condemned by the pope and the emperor.

pelargonium flowering plant of genus *Pelargonium*, grown extensively in gardens, where it is familiarly known as 'geranium'. It is related to the true geraniums. Ancestors of the garden hybrids came from S Africa.

Pelée, Mont /pə'leɪ/ volcano (1,258 m/4,428 ft) on Martinique, which destroyed the town of St Pierre during its eruption 1902.

Pelham /'peləm/ Henry 1696–1754. British Whig politician. He held a succession of offices in Walpole's cabinet 1721–42, and was prime minister 1743–54.

pelican type of water bird remarkable for the pouch beneath the bill used as a fishing net and temporary store for its catches of fish, and including the pinkish common pelican *Pelicanus onocrotalus* of Europe, Asia, and Africa; the Australian black-backed pelican *Pelicanus conspicillatus*; and the American brown pelican *Pelicanus occidentalis*, which is marine, and dives for its food.

pellagra a disease of subtropical countries in which the staple food is maize, due to deficiency of nicotinic acid (one of the B vitamins), which is contained in protein foods and yeast.

pellitory-of-the-wall plant *Parietaria judaica* of the nettle family, found growing particularly in cracks in walls and rocks and also on banks, in W and S Europe. It is much branched, softly hairy, and up to 1 m/3 ft high.

The stems are reddish, the leaves lance-shaped, and the greenish male and female flowers are separate but on the same plant.

Peloponnese /ˌpeləpə'niːs/ peninsula forming the S part of Greece; area 21,549 sq km/8,320 sq mi; population (1981) 1,012,500. It is joined to the mainland by the narrow isthmus of Corinth, and is divided into the nomes of Argolis, Arcadia, Achaea (Akhaia), Elis, Corinth, Lakonia, and Messenia, representing its seven ancient states.

Peloponnesian War conflict between Athens and Sparta and their allies, 431–404 BC, originating in suspicions of 'empire-building' ambitions of Pericles. It was ended by ◊Lysander's destruction of the political power of Athens.

pelota very fast ball game (the name means 'ball') of Basque derivation, also known as *jai alai* (pronounced /'haɪ 'laɪ/, 'merry festival'), popular in Latin-American countries. It is played in a walled court or cancha, and resembles squash, but the players use a long, curved wickerwork basket or cesta, strapped to the hand, to hurl the ball (about the size of a baseball) against the walls.

Peltier effect in physics, a change in temperature at the junction of two different metals produced when an electric current flows through them. The extent of the change depends on what the conducting metals are, and the nature of change (rise or fall in temperature) depends on the direction of current flow. It is the reverse of the ◊Seebeck effect. Named after the French physicist Jean Charles Peltier (1785–1845) who discovered it in 1834.

Pemba /'pembə/ coral island in the Indian Ocean, 48 km/30 mi NE of Zanzibar, and forming with it part of Tanzania
area 984 sq km/380 sq mi
products cloves, copra
population (1985) 257,000.

Pembroke /'pembrʊk/ seaport and engineering centre in Dyfed, Wales; Henry VII was born in Pembroke Castle, begun 1200; population (1981) 15,600.

Pembrokeshire /'pembrʊkʃə/ former extreme SW county of Wales, which became part of Dyfed in 1974. The county town was Haverfordwest.

pemmican preparation of dried fatless beef or venison pressed into cubes, used as a food by Arctic explorers and N American Indians.

PEN literary association established in 1921 by C A Dawson Scott, to promote international understanding between writers. The initials stand for Poets, Playwrights, Editors, Essayists, Novelists.

penance in theology, a Roman Catholic sacrament, involving ◊confession of sins and the reception of absolution; and works performed or punishment self-inflicted in atonement for sin. Penance is worked out now in terms of good deeds rather than routine repetition of prayers.

Penang /pɪ'næŋ/ state in W Malaysia, formed of Penang Island, Province Wellesley, and the Dindings on the mainland
area 1,034 sq km/400 sq mi
capital Georgetown, with port Penang
population (1980) 911,500

history Penang Island was bought by Britain from the ruler of Kedah 1785; Province Wellesley was acquired 1800.

penates /pe'nɑːteɪz/ the household gods of a Roman family. See ◊lares and penates.

Penda /'pendə/ king of Mercia from about 633. He raised Mercia to a powerful kingdom, and defeated and killed two Northumbrian kings, Edwin and ◊Oswald. He was killed in battle with Northumbria.

Penderecki /ˌpendə'retski/ Krzystof 1933– . Polish composer in his own notation system, including *Threnody for the Victims of Hiroshima* 1961 and *St Luke Passion* 1966.

Penelope /pə'neləpi/ in Greek legend, wife of ◊Odysseus. During his absence after the siege of Troy she kept her many suitors at bay by asking them to wait until she had woven a shroud for her father-in-law, but undid her work nightly. When Odysseus returned, he killed her suitors.

penetration technology the development of missiles which have low radar, infrared and optical signatures, and can penetrate an enemy's defences undetected. In 1980 the USA announced that it had developed such piloted aircraft, known as *Stealth*.

penguin flightless, marine diving bird found in the S hemisphere. It fills the ecological niche held by the ◊auks in the N hemisphere. Penguins congregate in 'rookeries' to breed. Largest is the *emperor penguin Aptenodytes forsteri* 1.2 m/over 3 ft tall, whose single annual egg is brooded by the male in the warmth of a flap of his body skin, so that it rests on his feet. Among the small species is the *jackass penguin Spheniscus demerss*, which lays two eggs in a scraped hollow in the ground.

penicillin an organic acid formed during the growth of the common mould, *Penicillium notatum*. Even in very weak dilutions it prevents the growth of certain bacteria, many of which are harmful to humans, including some of the staphylococci and streptococci, and the organisms of pneumonia, gonorrhoea, anthrax and tetanus. It was discovered by Sir Alexander Fleming, and its practical use was developed by Sir Howard Florey and E B Chain at Oxford.

peninsula a tongue of land surrounded on three sides by water but still attached to a larger landmass. Florida, USA, is an example.

Peninsular War the war of 1808–14 caused by Napoleon's invasion of Portugal and Spain. Portugal was occupied by the French in 1807, and in 1808 Napoleon placed his brother Joseph on the Spanish throne. Armed revolts followed all over Spain and Portugal. A British force under Sir Arthur Wellesley was sent to Portugal and defeated the French at Vimeiro; Wellesley was then superseded, and the French were allowed to withdraw. Wellesley took a new army to Portugal in 1809, and advanced on Madrid, but after defeating the French at Talavera had to retreat. During 1810–11 Wellesley (now Viscount Wellington) stood on the defensive; in 1812 he won another victory at Salamanca, occupied Madrid, and forced the French to evacuate S Spain. The victory at Vittoria (1813) drove the French from Spain, and in 1814

Wellington invaded S France. The war was ended by Napoleon's abdication.

penis male reproductive organ, used for internal ◊fertilization; it transfers ◊sperm to the female reproductive tract. In mammals, the penis is erected by vessels which fill with blood, and in most mammals (but not men) is stiffened by a bone. It also contains the urethra, through which urine is passed when not erect. Sometimes the term penis is used exclusively for mammals, but usually it is applied to other erectile male organs as well. These are seen in almost all reptiles, snakes and lizards having two penes, other reptiles only one. A few birds, mainly ducks and geese, also have a type of penis, as do snails, barnacles, and some other invertebrates. Many insects have a rigid, non-erectile male organ, usually referred to as an intromittent organ.

Penn /pen/ Irving 1917– . US fashion, advertising, portrait, editorial, and fine art photographer. He began in 1948 a series of journeys to Africa and the Far East, resulting in a series of portrait photographs of local people, avoiding sophisticated technique. He has been associated with *Vogue* magazine in the USA throughout his long career.

Penn /pen/ William 1644–1718. British Quaker. Born in London, son of Admiral Sir William Penn 1621–70. He joined the Quakers in 1667. In 1681 he obtained a grant of land in America, in settlement of a debt owed by the king to his father, on which he established the colony of Pennsylvania as a refuge for the persecuted Quakers.

Penney /'peni/ William, Baron Penney 1909– . British scientist. He worked at Los ◊Alamos 1944–45, and for his design of the first British atomic bomb was knighted in 1952. He developed the advanced gas-cooled nuclear reactor used in some power stations, such as at Dungeness. Director of the Atomic Weapons Research Establishment 1953–59, he was chair of the UK Atomic Energy Authority 1964–67: created life peer 1967, Order of Merit 1969.

Pennines /'penaɪnz/ mountain system, 'the backbone of England', broken by a gap through which the river Aire flows to the E and the Ribble to the W; length (Scottish border to the Peaks in Derbyshire) 400 km/250 mi. Britain's first long-distance footpath was the *Pennine Way* 1965.

Pennsylvania /ˌpensɪl'veɪniə/ state of NE USA; nickname Keystone State
area 117,412 sq km/45,333 sq mi
capital Harrisburg
towns Philadelphia, Pittsburgh, Erie, Scranton
features Allegheny mountains; Ohio, Susquehanna and Delaware rivers; University of Pennsylvania is one of the leading research campuses in the USA
products mushrooms, fruit, flowers, cereals, tobacco; meat, poultry, dairy products; anthracite
population (1984) 11,901,000
famous people Marian Anderson, Maxwell Anderson, Stephen Foster, Benjamin Franklin, George C Marshall, Robert E Peary, Gertrude Stein, John Updike
history founded and named by William ◊Penn in 1682, following a land grant by Charles II. It was

one of the original Thirteen States. There was a breakdown at the Three Mile Island nuclear reactor plant in Harrisburg 1979.

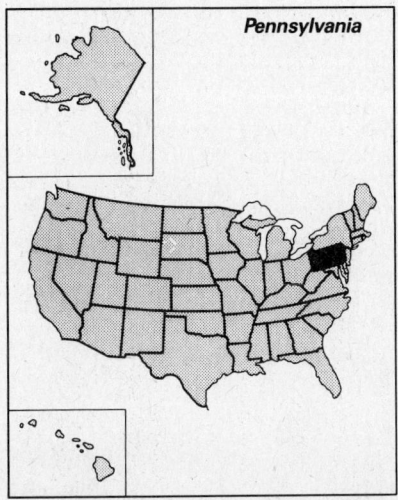

Pennsylvania

Pennsylvanian the American term for the upper ◊Carboniferous period of geological time, named after the US state.

pennyroyal perennial plant *Mentha pulegium*. It has oblong leaves, whorls of purplish flowers, and the characteristic scent of mint. It is found in wet places on sandy soil.

Pensacola /ˌpensəˈkəʊlə/ port in Florida, USA, on the Gulf of Mexico, with a large naval air-training station; population (1984) 60,500. Pensacola was founded by the Spanish in 1696.

Pentagon the headquarters of the American Department of Defense, Washington. One of the world's largest office buildings, it is constructed in five rings with a pentagonal central court. The *Pentagon Papers* were classified documents published by the US press in 1971 on US involvement in Vietnam.

Pentateuch Greek (and Christian) name for the first five books of the ◊Bible, ascribed to Moses, and called the *Torah* by Jews.

Pentecost Jewish festival (50th day after ◊Passover) celebrating the end of the Palestinian grain harvest; in the Christian Church, day on which the Holy Spirit descended, and commemorated on ◊Whit Sunday.

Pentecostal Movement Christian revivalist movement inspired by the baptism in the Holy Spirit with 'speaking in tongues' experienced by the Apostles at the time of the Jewish Feast of Pentecost, or Feast of Harvest (Acts 2). Hence it is sometimes also known as the Tongues movement.

The modern Pentecostal Movement dates from 4 Apr 1906 when members of the black congregation of the Azusa Street Mission in Los Angeles met, under their minister W J Seymour, in a private house and experienced 'baptism in the Spirit'. The movement spread, and was brought to the UK by Thomas Barratt, a Cornish-born Methodist minister. It was well-received in revivalist areas of Wales and N England, but was less successful there than in Scandinavia, South America (especially Brazil and Chile), and South Africa. In the USA, the largest grouping is the Assemblies of God. Worldwide membership is more than 10 million, so that it has been spoken of as the 'third force' in Christendom. The Pentecostal Movement represents a reaction against rigid theology and formal worship, the services being informal and gospel hymns sung with insistent refrains and exclamations of 'Hallelujah'. There is belief in the literal word of the Bible, and a moral code which disapproves of alcohol, tobacco, dancing, the theatre, and so on. It is a missionary faith, and recruitment has been rapid since the 1960s.

Pentland Firth /ˈpentlənd ˈfɜːθ/ the channel separating the Orkney Islands from N Scotland.

Penza /ˈpenzə/ industrial city (sawmills, bicycles, watches, calculating machines, textiles) in the USSR, capital of Penza region, 560 km/350 mi SE of Moscow, at the junction of the Penza and Sura rivers; population (1985) 527,000. Founded as a fort in 1663.

Penzance /penˈzæns/ English seaport for the Scilly Isles and resort in Cornwall, on Mount's Bay, the most westerly town in England; population (1981) 19,500. Humphrey ◊Davy was born here.

peony perennial plant in the family Paeoniaceae, remarkable for showy flowers. Most popular are the common peony *Paeonia officinalis* and the white peony *Paeonia lactiflora*.

Peoria /piˈɔːriə/ city in Illinois, USA, on the river Illinois, a transport, mining, and agricultural centre; Bradley University 1897; population (1980) 124,000. Fort Crève Coeur was built here by the French explorer La Salle in 1680 and became a trading centre; the first American settlers arrived in 1818. In US comedy, Peoria is the epitome of a small town.

Pepin /ˈpepɪn/ King of the Franks. The son of Charles Martel, he acted as mayor of the palace to the last Merovingian king, Childeric III, until in 751 he deposed him and assumed the royal title himself, founding the Carolingian line.

pepper climbing plant *Piper nigrum* native to the E Indies. When gathered green, the berries are crushed to produce the seeds for condiment black pepper; when the berries are ripening and turning red, the seeds are removed and soaked to remove the outer skin to produce white pepper. Sweet pepper is the ◊capsicum.

peppermint perennial herb *Mentha piperita*, with ovate aromatic leaves, and purple flowers. The oil is used in medicine and in confectionery.

peptide a molecule comprising two or more ◊amino acids joined by peptide bonds. A peptide is generally a much smaller molecule than a ◊protein, but there is no clear dividing line between them. The term 'peptide' is applied to the breakdown products of proteins, to the precursors of proteins, and to hormones such as vasopressin and oxytocin (nine amino acids each). The term 'polypeptide' is used interchangeably with 'peptide' although it generally implies a longer-chain molecule.

Pepys /piːps/ Samuel 1633–1703. British diarist. Born in London, he entered the navy office 1660, just after beginning his diary, written 1659–69 (when his sight failed) in shorthand. A unique record of both the daily life of the period and the intimate feelings of the man, it was not deciphered till 1825. He was secretary to the Admiralty 1672–79, when he was imprisoned in the Tower on suspicion of being connected with the ◊Popish Plot; and was then reinstated in 1684 and finally deprived, after the 1688 ◊Revolution, for suspected disaffection.

Pepys Samuel Pepys wrote his diaries in a private shorthand; they were not deciphered until 1825.

Perak /ˈpeərə/ state of Malaysia
area 20,668 sq km/7,980 sq mi
capital Ipoh
towns Taiping
government sultanate
products tin, rubber
population (1980) 1,762,300.

percentage a way of representing a number as a ◊fraction of 100. Thus 45 per cent (or 45%) equals 45/100, and 45% of 20 is 20 x 45/100 = 9. In general, if a quantity x changes to y, the percentage change is $100(x - y)/x$. Thus, if the number of people in a room changes from 40 to 50, the percentage increase is $(100 \times 10)/40 = 25\%$. To express a fraction as a percentage, its denominator must first be converted to 100, for example, $1/8 = 12.5/100 = 12.5\%$. The use of percentages makes it easier to compare fractions without a common denominator.

Perceval /ˈpɜːsɪvəl/ Spencer 1762–1812. British Tory politician, son of the earl of Egmont. He became chancellor of the Exchequer in 1807, and prime minister in 1809. He was shot in the lobby of the House of Commons in 1812.

perch freshwater fish *Perca fluviatilis*, found in Europe and N Asia. It is olive green or yellowish in colour, with dark vertical bands. It can be 50 cm/1.6 ft long but is usually less. It is a predator found in still water and rivers.
Perch-like fishes form the largest order of bony fishes, the Perciformes, with some 8,000 species. This order includes the sea breams, cichlids, damselfishes, mullets, barracudas, wrasses, gobies and many others.

percussion instrument musical instrument played by being struck with the hand or stick. Percussion instruments can be divided into those which can be tuned to produce a sound of definite pitch, and those without pitch. Examples of tuned percussion instruments include:
kettledrum a hemisperical bowl of metal with a membrane stretched across the top
tubular bells suspended on a frame
glockenspiel (German *'bell play'*) using a set of steel bars
xylophone similar to a glockenspiel, but with wooden rather than metal bars.
Instruments without definite pitch include:
snare drum, which has a membrane across both ends, and a 'snare' which rattles when the drum is beaten
bass drum, which produces the lowest sound in the orchestra
tambourine a wooden hoop with a membrane stretched across it and with metal plates inserted in the sides
triangle a triangular-shaped steel bar, played by striking it with a separate bar of steel. The sound produced remains distinctive even when played alongside a full orchestra
cymbals two brass plates struck together
castanets two round-shaped pieces of wood struck together
gong a heavy circular piece of metal struck with a soft hammer.

Percy /'pɜːsi/ Henry 'Hotspur' 1364–1403. English soldier, son of the 1st Earl of Northumberland. He defeated the Scots at Homildon Hill 1402, and was killed at Shrewsbury while in revolt against Henry IV.

Percy /'pɜːsi/ Thomas 1729–1811. British scholar and bishop of Dromore from 1782. He discovered a manuscript collection of songs, ballads, and romances, from which he published a selection as *Reliques of Ancient English Poetry* 1765, largely influential in the Romantic revival.

Perelman /'perəlmən/ S(idney) J(oseph) 1904–1979. American humorist, born in New York. He wrote for the magazine the *New Yorker* and film scripts for the ◊Marx Brothers; he shared the Academy Award for the film script *Around the World in 80 Days*.

perennating organ in plants, that part of a ◊biennial or herbaceous ◊perennial that allows it to survive the winter, usually a root, tuber, rhizome, bulb, or corm.

perennial plant a plant that lives for more than two years. There are two main types. Herbaceous perennials have aerial stems and leaves which die each autumn, and they survive the winter by means of an underground storage (◊perennating) organ, such as a bulb or rhizome. The trees and shrubs, or woody perennials, have stems which persist above ground throughout the year, and may be either ◊deciduous or ◊evergreen. *See also* ◊annual, ◊biennial.

Peres /'peres/ Shimon 1923– . Israeli socialist politician, Labour Party leader from 1977, prime minister 1984–86. Peres emigrated from Poland to Palestine in 1934, but was educated in the USA. In 1959 he was elected to the Knesset (parliament). He became leader of the opposition in 1977. Under a power-sharing

percussion instruments

bass drum

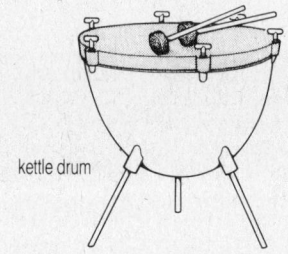
kettle drum

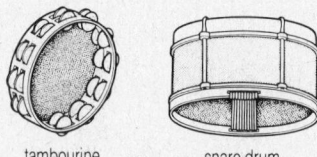
tambourine   snare drum

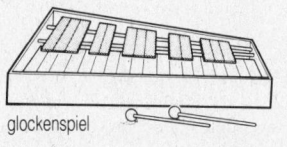
glockenspiel

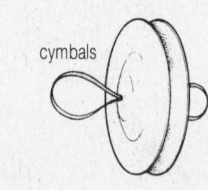
cymbals

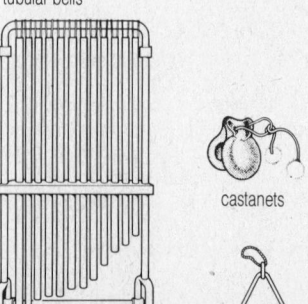
tubular bells   castanets   triangle

agreement with Itzhak ◊Shamir, Peres was prime minister from 1984 to 1986.

perestroika (Russian 'restructuring') term used by Soviet leader ◊Gorbachev for the wide-ranging economic and government reforms initiated during his leadership of the Soviet state and its institutions. It is also the title of book by Gorbachev (1987).

Pérez de Cuellar /'peres də 'kweɪjɑː/ Javier 1920– . Peruvian diplomat. A delegate to the first United Nations General Assembly 1946–47, he held several ambassadorial posts and was appointed secretary general of the UN in 1982.

Pérez de Cuellar Formerly ambassador to the USSR and to Venezuela, the Peruvian diplomat Javier Pérez de Cuellar was appointed secretary general of the United Nations in 1982.

Pérez Galdós /'peres gæl'dɒs/ Benito 1843–1920. Spanish novelist, born in the Canary Islands. His works include the 46 historical novels in the cycle *Episodios nacionales* and the 21-novel cycle *Novelas españolas contemporáneos*, which includes *Doña Perfecta* 1876 and the epic *Fortunata y Jacinta* 1886–87, his masterpiece. In scale he has been compared to Balzac and Dickens.

perfume fragrant essence in which more than 100 natural aromatic materials may be blended from a range of 60,000 flowers, leaves, fruits, seeds, woods, barks, resins, and roots, linked by natural animal fixatives and various synthetics, the latter increasingly used even in expensive products. Favoured ingredients include ◊balsam, ◊civet, ◊hyacinth, ◊jasmine, lily of the ◊valley, ◊musk, ◊orange blossom, ◊rose, and ◊tuberose. Culture of cells of such plants on membranes which are constantly bathed in a solution to carry the essential oils away for separation is now being adopted to reduce costs.

Perga /'pɜːgə/ ruined city of Pamphylia, 16 km/10 mi NE of Adalia, Turkey, noted for its local cult of Artemis. It was visited by St Paul.

Pergamum /'pɜːgəməm/ ancient Greek city in W Asia Minor, which became the capital of an independent kingdom in 283 BC. As the ally of Rome it achieved great political importance in the 2nd century BC, and became a famous centre of art and culture. On its site is the Turkish town of Bergama.

peri in Persian myth, a beautiful, harmless being, ranking between angels and evil spirits. Peris were ruled by Eblis, the greatest of the evil spirits.

Peri /'peəri/ Jacopo 1561–1633. Italian composer, who served the ◊Medici, and whose experimental melodic opera *Euridice* 1600 established the opera form and influenced ◊Monteverdi.

perianth a collective term for the outer whorls of the ◊flower which protect the reproductive parts during development. In most ◊dicotyledons the perianth is composed of two distinct whorls, the calyx of ◊sepals and the corolla of ◊petals, whereas in many ◊monocotyledons they are indistinguishable and the segments of the perianth are then known individually as tepals.

pericarp the wall of a ◊fruit. It encloses the seeds and is derived from the ◊ovary wall. In fruits such as the acorn, the pericarp becomes dry and hardened, forming a shell around the seed. In fleshy fruits the pericarp is typically made up of three distinct layers. The *epicarp* or *exocarp* forms the tough outer skin of the fruits, while the *mesocarp* is often fleshy and forms the middle layers. The innermost layer or *endocarp*, which surrounds the seeds, may be membranous, or it may be thickened and hard, as in the ◊drupe (stone) of cherries, plums, and apricots.

Pericles /'perikliːz/ c. 490–429 bc. Athenian politician, who dominated the city's affairs from 461 BC (as leader of the democratic party), and under whom Greek culture reached its climax. He created a confederation of cities under the leadership of Athens, but the disasters of the ◊Peloponnesian War led to his overthrow 430 BC. Although quickly reinstated, he died soon after.

peridot a gem variety of the mineral ◊olivine. Perdotite is a rock that consists almost entirely of olivine.

Périgueux /ˌperiˈgɜː/ capital of Dordogne *département*, 127 km/79 mi ENE of Bordeaux; trades in wine and truffles; population (1982) 35,392. The Byzantine cathedral dates from 984.

Perim /'perim/ island in the strait of Bab-el-Mandeb, the S entrance to the Red Sea; part of South Yemen; area 13 sq km/5 sq mi.

period a punctuation mark (.). The term 'period' is universally understood in English, and is the preferred usage in N America; the term 'full stop' is the preferred form in Great Britain. Traditionally, the period has two functions: to mark the end of a properly formed sentence, and to indicate abbreviation. In practice these functions continue, but in fictional dialogue and advertising periods often follow incomplete sentences, in order to represent speech more faithfully or for purposes of emphasis. In addition, acronyms are unlikely to have periods (NATO rather than N.A.T.O.) and contractions may or may not have periods (for instance, 'Mr Greene' or 'Mr. Greene', as preferred).

period another name for ◊menstruation.

periodic table of the elements a classification of the elements, first devised by ◊Mendeleyev in 1869, in which they are arranged, in order of their

Pericles Bust of Pericles found near Tivoli, Italy, 1781. Under his rule, Greek culture reached its finest expression.

atomic number (originally, their atomic weight, but this gives some anomalies), in tabular form. There are striking similarities in the chemical properties of the elements in each of the main vertical groups, and a gradation of properties along the horizontal periods. These are dependent on the electronic and nuclear structure of atoms of the elements. The table has been used to predict the existence of ◊transuranic elements.

periodontal disease (formerly known as *pyorrhoea*) disease of the supporting tissues of the teeth caused by the accumulation of plaque; the gums recede, the teeth become loose and eventually drop out.

peripheral device in computing, any item of equipment attached to and controlled by a computer. Peripherals are typically for input from and output to the user (for example, ◊keyboard, ◊printer), storing data (for example, ◊disk drive), communications (for example, ◊modem) or for performing physical tasks (for example, ◊robot).

periscope optical instrument designed for observation from a concealed position. Basically it consists of a tube with parallel mirrors at each end inclined at 45° to its axis. It attained prominence in naval (especially in submarines) and military operations of World War I.

peristalsis contractions that pass along tubular organs, such as the intestines, in waves produced by the contraction of smooth ◊muscle. Also, the wave-like motion of earthworms and some other invertebrates, in which part of the body contracts as another part elongates.

peritoneum the tissue lining the abdominal cavity and digestive organs of vertebrates. Puncturing the external body wall or rupturing of

the digestive tract, as for example in appendicitis, results in ◊peritonitis.

peritonitis inflammation within the ◊peritoneum. It can be variously caused, for example by a wound to the abdomen, or appendicitis.

periwinkle in zoology, snail-like marine mollusc found on the shore. The common edible species of winkle *Littorina littorea*, abundant in Britain, has spread to the US Atlantic coast.

periwinkle in botany, genus *Vinca* of trailing blue-flowered evergreen plants, family Apocynaceae. The related *Madagascar periwinkle Catharanthus roseus* produces chemicals which inhibit the division of cells and are used to treat leukaemia.

perjury the offence of deliberately making a false statement on oath when appearing as a witness in legal proceedings, on a point material to the question at issue. In Britain it is punishable by a fine, imprisonment up to seven years, or both.

Perkin /'pɜːkin/ William Henry 1838–1907. British chemist. In 1856 he discovered the mauve dye which originated the aniline dye industry.

Perkins Gilman /'pɜːkinz 'gilmən/ Charlotte 1860–1935. US feminist socialist poet, novelist, and historian. She is best known as the author of *Women and Economics*, proposing the ending of the division between 'men's work' and 'women's work' by abolishing housework. She wrote and published a magazine *The Forerunner* in which her feminist Utopian novel *Herland* 1915 was serialized.

Perlis /'pɜːlis/ most northerly state of Peninsular Malaysia, Malaysia
area 803 sq km/310 sq mi
capital Kangar
government ruled by a raja
products rubber, rice, coconuts, tin
population (1980) 147,750
history transferred by Siam to Britain in 1909.

Perm /pɜːm/ industrial city (shipbuilding, aircraft, chemicals, sawmills), capital of Perm region, USSR, on the Kama near the Ural mountains; population (1985) 1,056,000. It was called Molotov 1940–57.

permafrost a condition in which a deep layer of ◊soil does not thaw out during the summer but remains at below 0°C/–32°F for at least two years, despite thawing of the soil above. Permafrost gives rise to a poorly drained summer landscape typical of N Canada and Siberia, known as ◊tundra. It is claimed that 26 per cent of the world's land surface is permafrost.

Permian the period of geological time between 280 and 230 million years ago. It is the last period of the ◊Palaeozoic era and its end was marked by a significant change in marine life, including the extinction of many corals and trilobites. Gymnosperms (cone-bearing plants) came to prominence, while amphibians and theropods (mammal-like reptiles) were the most important land animals.

permutation in mathematics, specified arrangement of a group of objects. In general, the number of permutations of *a* items taken *b* at a time is given by $a!/(a-b)!$, where the symbol ! stands for ◊factorial (the product of all the integers (whole numbers) up to and including the number). For example, the number of permutations of four letters taken from any group of six different letters is $6!/2! = (1 \times 2 \times 3 \times 4 \times 5 \times 6)/(1 \times 2) = 360$. The theoretical number of four-letter 'words' that can be made from an alphabet of 26 letters is $26!/22! = 358,800$.

Pernambuco /ˌpɜːnæmˈbuːkəʊ/ state of NE Brazil, on the Atlantic
area 98,281 sq km/37,946 sq mi
capital Recife (former name Pernambuco)
features highlands; the coast is low and humid
population (1985) 6,776,000.

Perón /peˈrɒn/ Eva ('Evita') Maria 1922–1952. Argentinian populist leader, born in Buenos Aires. A successful actress, in 1945 she married Juan ◊Perón. When he was ousted from power and arrested she roused the trade unions to fight for his release and election as president. She gained great power and popularity, particularly among the *descamisados*, 'shirtless ones', and in 1951 stood for the post of vice-president, but was opposed by the army and withdrew; she died soon afterwards.

Perón /peˈrɒn/ Juan Domingo 1895–1974. Argentine politician. He took part in the military pro-fascist coup of 1943, was elected president in 1946. He lost popularity after the death of his second wife Eva ◊Perón, and was deposed in 1955, but returned from exile to the presidency in 1973. He was succeeded by his third wife *Maria Estela* 'Isabel(ita)' (1930–) until her overthrow and subsequent detention in 1976.

Perpendicular name given to a period of English Gothic architecture lasting from the end of the 14th to the middle of the 16th century. The main characteristics of the style are: window tracery consisting chiefly of vertical members; arches that consist either of four arcs ('four centred') or of two arcs forming a blunt point; vaults that are lavishly decorated; and wall surfaces covered with traceried panels. Good examples of the style are the choir and cloister of Gloucester Cathedral, and King's College Chapel, Cambridge.

perpetual motion idea that a machine can be designed and constructed in such a way that, once started, it will continue in motion indefinitely without requiring any further input of energy (motive power). Such a device is scientifically impossible and contradicts the two laws of thermodynamics that state that (a) energy can neither be created nor destroyed (the law of conservation of energy) and (b) heat cannot by itself flow from a hot object to a cooler object. As a result, all practical (real) machines require a continuous supply of energy, and no heat engine is able to convert all the heat into useful work. Probably the closest thing to perpetual motion is the motion of a satellite in orbit, where there is no air friction to slow it down.

Perpignan /ˌpɜːpiːnˈjɒn/ capital of the Pyrénées-Orientales *département* of France, just off the Mediterranean coast, near the Spanish border; population (1982) 138,000. Overlooking Perpignan is the castle of the counts of Roussillon; the cathedral was founded in 1324.

Perrault /peˈrəʊ/ Charles 1628–1703. French author of the fairy tales *Contes de ma*

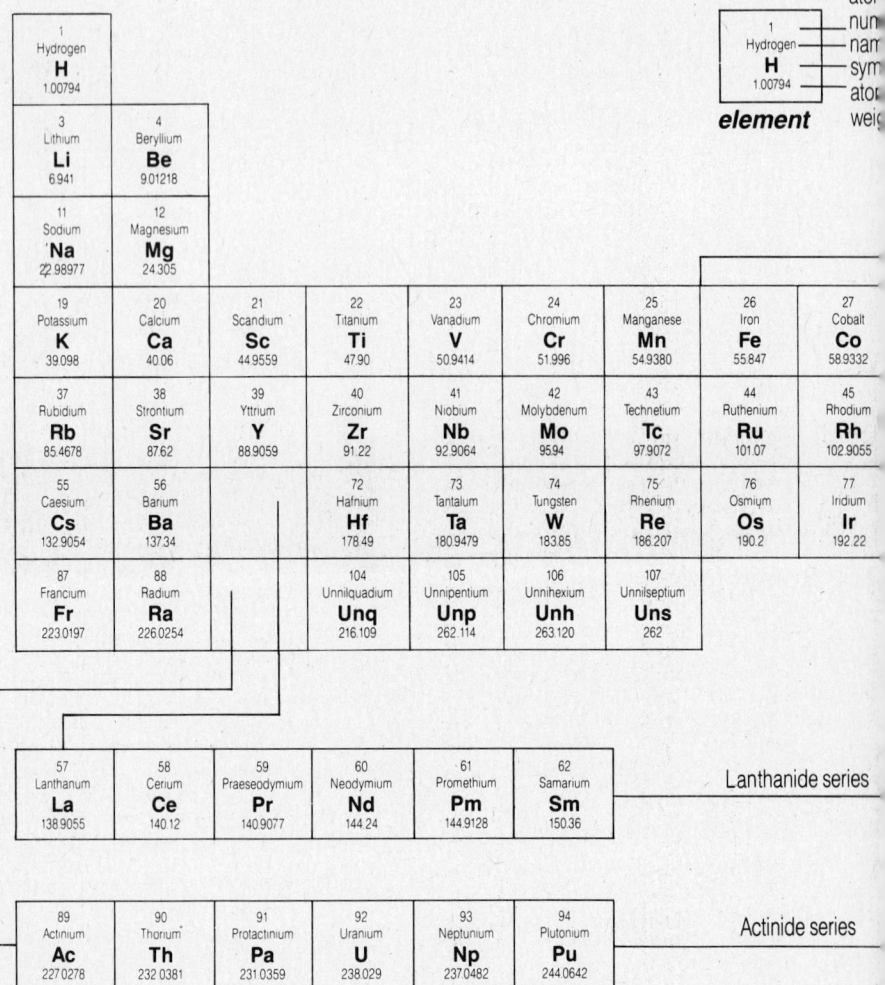

mère l'oye/ Mother Goose's Fairy Tales 1697, including the classics 'Sleeping Beauty', 'Red Riding Hood', 'Blue Beard', 'Puss in Boots', and 'Cinderella'.

perry alcoholic liquor made from pears, produced mainly in Normandy and the English West Country.

Perry /ˈperi/ Matthew Calbraith 1794–1858. US naval officer, commander of the 1853 expedition which reopened communication between Japan and the outside world after 250 years' isolation. He negotiated the treaty of 1854 giving the USA trading rights with Japan.

Perse /pɜːs/ Saint-John, pseudonym of Alexis Saint-Léger 1887–1975. French poet. His first book of verse *Éloges* 1911 reflects the ambience of the West Indies, where he was born and raised. He emigrated permanently to the USA. His later works include *Anabase* 1924, an epic poem translated by T S Eliot in 1930. He was awarded a Nobel prize in 1960.

Persephone /pɜːˈsefəni/ Greek goddess, the daughter of Zeus and Demeter. She was carried off to the underworld by Pluto, who later agreed that she should spend six months of the year with her mother. The myth was interpreted by later commentators as symbolizing the growth and decay of vegetation.

Persepolis /pɜːˈsepəlɪs/ ancient capital of the Persian Empire, 65 km/40 mi NE of Shiraz. It was burned down after its capture in 331 BC by Alexander the Great.

Perseus /ˈpɜːsjuːs/ in Greek mythology, son of ◊Zeus and ◊Danae. He slew ◊Medusa, the Gorgon; rescued ◊Andromeda; and became king of ◊Tiryns.

Perseus /ˈpɜːsjuːs/ in astronomy, a ◊constellation of the N hemisphere. The eye of the decapitated Gorgon is represented by the variable star ◊Algol. Perseus lies in the ◊Milky Way and contains the Double Cluster of stars. Every Aug the Perseid meteor shower radiates from its northern part.

Persia, Ancient the early Persians were a nomadic Aryan people (the modern name ◊Iran derives from Aryan), including the Persians and

periodic table of the elements

																	2 Helium **He** 4.00260
											5 Boron **B** 10.81	6 Carbon **C** 12.011	7 Nitrogen **N** 14.0067	8 Oxygen **O** 15.9994	9 Fluorine **F** 18.99840	10 Neon **Ne** 20.179
											13 Aluminium **Al** 26.98154	14 Silicon **Si** 28.086	15 Phosphorus **P** 30.97376P	16 Sulphur **S** 32.06	17 Chlorine **Cl** 35.453	18 Argon **Ar** 39.948
28 Nickel **Ni** 58.70	29 Copper **Cu** 63.546	30 Zinc **Zn** 65.38	31 Gallium **Ga** 69.72	32 Germanium **Ge** 72.59	33 Arsenic **As** 74.9216	34 Selenium **Se** 78.96	35 Bromine **Br** 79.904	36 Krypton **Kr** 83.80
46 Palladium **Pd** 106.4	47 Silver **Ag** 107.868	48 Cadmium **Cd** 112.40	49 Indium **In** 114.82	50 Tin **Sn** 118.69	51 Antimony **Sb** 121.75	52 Tellurium **Te** 127.75	53 Iodine **I** 126.9045	54 Xenon **Xe** 131.30
78 Platinum **Pt** 195.09	79 Gold **Au** 196.9665	80 Mercury **Hg** 200.59	81 Thallium **Tl** 204.37	82 Lead **Pb** 207.37	83 Bismuth **Bi** 207.2	84 Polonium **Po** 210	85 Astatine **At** 211	86 Radon **Rn** 222.0176

63 Europium **Eu** 151.96	64 Gadolinium **Gd** 157.25	65 Terbium **Tb** 158.9254	66 Dysprosium **Dy** 162.50	67 Holmium **Ho** 164.9304	68 Erbium **Er** 167.26	69 Thulium **Tm** 168.9342	70 Ytterbium **Yb** 173.04	71 Lutetium **Lu** 174.97

95 Americium **Am** 243.0614	96 Curium **Cm** 247.0703	97 Berkelium **Bk** 247.0703	98 Californium **Cf** 251.0786	99 Einsteinium **Es** 252.0828	100 Fermium **Fm** 257.0951	101 Mendelvium **Md** 258.0986	012 Nobelium **No** 259.1009	103 Lawrencium **Lr** 260.1054

the Medes, that migrated through the Caucasus to the Iranian plateau. By the 7th century BC they were established in the present region of Fars, which then belonged to the Assyrians.

◊Cyrus the Great was founder of the Persian Empire, and king of the Persians, originally as vassal to the ◊Medes, whose empire he overthrew in 550 BC. He conquered all Asia Minor, adding Babylonia (including Syria and Palestine) to his empire in 539 BC.

In 529 ◊Darius I became king of Persia. He organized an efficient centralized system of administration and extended Persian rule east into modern Afghanistan and NW India and as far north as the Danube, but the empire was weakened by internal dynastic struggles.

The *Persian Wars*, 499–449, were the revolt of the Greek city-states against the Persian empire under Darius; in 490 Darius was defeated by the Greeks at Marathon; the Greeks were defeated at Thermopylae 480 by Xerxes I but won the battles of Salamis and Plataea 479, driving the Persians from the country; this defeat was a turning point in the Persian domination of the ancient world and marked the beginning of Greek greatness (see ◊Greece, Ancient).

In 331 BC ◊Alexander the Great drove the Persians under Darius III (died 330 BC) into retreat at Arbella on the Tigris, marking the end of the Persian Empire and the beginning of the Hellenistic period under the Seleucids.

A new Persian empire was established in about 226 AD under the Sassanids, which flourished until 637, when Arabs took the capital, Ctesiphon, and introduced Islam in place of Zoroastrianism.

For modern history see ◊Iran.

Persian art see under ◊Ancient art: art of early civilizations.

Persian Gulf shallow bay, area 233,000 sq km/90,000 sq mi, linked by the Strait of Hormus and the Gulf of Oman to the Arabian Sea. Important oilfields lie on its shores.

Persian language a member of the Indo-Iranian branch of the Indo-European language family and the official language of the state once known as Persia but now officially called Iran. Persian is known to its own speakers as *Farsi*, the language of the province of Fars (Persia proper). It is written in the Arabic script, from right to left, and has a large admixture of Arabic religious, philosophical, and technical vocabulary.

Persian literature before the Arab conquest is represented by the sacred books of ◊Zoroastrianism known as the Avesta and later translated into Pahlavi, in which language there also appeared various secular writings. After the conquest the use of Arabic became widespread. The Persian language was revived during the 9th century and the following centuries saw a succession of brilliant poets including the epic writer ◊Firdawsi, the didactic S'adi 1184–1291, the mystic Rumi 1207–73, the lyrical ◊Hafiz, and Jami who combined the gifts of his predecessors and is considered the last of the classical poets. Omar ◊Khayyam, well known outside Persia, is less considered there. In the 16th and 17th centuries many of the best writers worked in India, still using classical forms and themes, and it was not until the revolutionary movements and contact with the West in the 20th century that Persian literature developed further.

Persian Wars a series of conflicts between the Greeks and the Persians 499–449 BC.
499 Revolt of the Ionian Greeks against Persian rule
490 Darius I defeated at Marathon
480 Xerxes I victorious at Thermopylae (narrow pass from Thessaly to Locris, which Leonidas, king of Sparta, and 1,000 men defended to the death against the Persians); Athens was captured, but the Greek navy was victorious at ◊Salamis
479 Greeks under Spartan general Pausanias (died about 470) victorious at Plataea, driving the Persians from the country.

persicaria plant *Polygonum persicaria* of the dock family growing in waste places and arable land, often near water. Sprawling, with lance-shaped leaves with black spots, its shoots end in spikes of pink flowers. *Pale persicaria Polygonum lapathifolium* is slightly larger, with pale dots on the leaves, and usually has heads of white flowers. Both are found through much of the N hemisphere.

persimmon or Virginian date plum. Tree *Diospyros virginiana* of the family Ebenaceae, native to N America. Some 12 m/40 ft high, the persimmon has alternate oval leaves, and yellow-green unisexual flowers. The small sweet orange fruits are edible. The Japanese persimmon *Diospyros kaki* has larger fruits and is widely cultivated.

personality an individual's characteristic way of behaving across a wide range of situations. Two broad dimensions of personality are ◊extraversion and ◊neuroticism. A number of more specific personal traits have also been described, including ◊psychopathy.

personification a ◊figure of speech in which animals, plants, objects, and ideas are treated as if they were human or alive ('Clouds chased each other across the face of the moon'; 'The future beckoned eagerly to them').

Perón Former stage and radio actress Eva (Evita) Perón used her talents as a broadcaster and speaker to gain support for her husband Juan Perón, the Argentinian leader.

Perspex trade name for a clear tough plastic widely used for watch glasses, motorboat windscreens, and protective shields, first produced in 1930. Its chemical name is polymethylmethacrylate (PMMA). In the USA it is called Plexiglas.

perspiration the excretion of water and dissolved substances from the ◊sweat glands of the skin of mammals. Perspiration has two main functions: body cooling by the evaporation of water from the skin surface, and excretion, that is, the removal of waste products such as salts.

Perth /pɜːθ/ industrial town in Tayside, E Scotland; population (1981) 42,000. Capital of Scotland from the 12th century until James I of Scotland was assassinated here 1437.

Perth /pɜːθ/ capital of Western Australia, with its port at nearby Fremantle on the Swan river; population (1984) 983,500. It is the commercial and cultural centre of the state, and headquarters of the Royal Perth Yacht Club, from which the America's Cup challenge was staged 1987.

Perthshire /ˈpɜːθʃə/ former inland county of central Scotland, of which the major part was included in 1975 in Tayside, the SW being included in Central region.

Peru /pəˈruː/ country in S America, on the Pacific, bounded to the N by Ecuador and Colombia, to the E by Brazil and Bolivia, and to the S by Chile.

government The 1980 constitution provides for a president who is head of both state and government, elected by universal suffrage for a five-year term, and governing with an appointed council of ministers.

The two-chamber legislature, the National Congress, comprises a 60-member Senate and a 180-member Chamber of Deputies, also popularly elected for five years. Senators are elected on a national basis but members of the Chamber are elected, through a system of proportional representation, from local constituencies. The two main political parties are the democratic left-wing American Popular Revolutionary Alliance (APRA), and the alliance of six left-wing parties, the Unified Left (IU).

history For early history, see ◊American Indian. The ◊Chimu culture flourished from about 1200 and was gradually superseded by the ◊Inca empire, building on 800 years of Andean civilization and covering a large part of S America. Civil war had weakened the Incas when

the conquistador ◊Pizarro arrived from Spain 1532, raiding, looting, and enslaving the people. He executed the last of the Inca emperors, Atahualpa, 1533. Before Pizarro's assassination in 1541, Spanish rule was firmly established.

An Indian revolt by ◊Tupac Amaru in 1780 failed, and during the successful rebellions by the European settlers in other Spanish possessions in S America 1810–22, Peru remained the Spanish government's headquarters; it was the last to achieve independence, 1824. It attempted union with Bolivia 1836–39, engaged in a naval war against Spain 1864–66 and in the ◊Pacific War against Chile 1879–83 over the nitrate fields of the Atacama Desert, in which Peru was defeated and lost three provinces (one, Tacna, was returned in 1929). Other boundary disputes were settled by arbitration in 1902 with Bolivia, 1927 with Colombia, and 1942 with Ecuador.

Peru was ruled by right-wing dictatorships from the mid-1920s until 1945 when free elections returned. Although Peru's oldest political organization, APRA, was the largest party in Congress, it was constantly thwarted by smaller, conservative groups, anxious to protect their business interests. APRA was founded in the 1920s to fight imperialism throughout S America but Peru was the only country where it became established.

In 1948 a group of army officers led by Gen Manuel Odría ousted the elected government, temporarily banned APRA and installed a military junta. Odría became president in 1950 and remained in power until 1956. In 1963 military rule ended and Fernando Belaunde, the joint candidate of the Popular Action (AP) and Christian Democrats (PDC) parties, won the presidency, while APRA took the largest share of the Chamber of Deputies seats.

After economic problems and industrial unrest, Belaunde was deposed in a bloodless coup in 1968 and the army returned to government led by Gen Velasco. Velasco introduced land reform, with private estates being turned into cooperative farms, but he failed to return any land to Indian peasant communities, and the Maoist guerrillas of Sendero Luminoso became increasingly active in the Indian region of S Peru.

Another bloodless coup, 1975, brought in Gen Morales Bermúdez. He called elections for the presidency and both chambers of Congress in May 1980 and Belaunde was re-elected. Belaunde began a programme of agrarian and industrial reform but at the end of his presidency, in 1985, the country was again in a state of economic and social crisis. His constitutionally elected successor was the young Social Democrat, Alan García Pérez, who embarked on cleansing the army and police of the old guard. By Feb 1986 about 1,400 had elected to retire. After trying to expand the economy with price and exchange controls, in Jul 1987 he announced his intention to nationalize the banks and insurance companies, but delayed the move in Aug, after a vigorous campaign against the proposal.

García Pérez has declared his support for the Sandinista government in Nicaragua and criticised US policy throughout Latin America.

Peru
REPUBLIC OF (*República del Perú*)

AREA 1,332,000 sq km/514,060 sq mi
CAPITAL Lima, including port of Callao
TOWNS Arequipa, Iquitos, Chiclayo
PHYSICAL Andes mountains N–S cover 27%; Amazon river-basin jungle in NE
FEATURES Lake Titicaca; Peru Current; Atacama Desert; monuments of the Chimu and Inca civilizations
HEAD OF STATE AND OF GOVERNMENT Alan García Perez from 1985
GOVERNMENT parliamentary democracy
EXPORTS coffee; alpaca, llama and vicuna wool; fish meal; lead, copper, iron, oil
CURRENCY sol (official rate 26.28 = £1 Sept 1987)
POPULATION (1984) 19,698,000 (46% American Indian, mainly Quechua and Aymara; 43% of mixed Spanish-American Indian descent); annual growth rate 2.6%
LANGUAGE Spanish, Quechua (both official)
RELIGION Roman Catholic
LITERACY 89% male/72% female (1980 est)
GNP $18.6 bn (1983); $655 per head of population
CHRONOLOGY
1824 Achieved independence from Spain, the last South American country to do so.
1902 Boundary dispute with Bolivia settled.
1927 Boundary dispute with Colombia settled.
1942 Boundary dispute with Ecuador settled.
1948 Army coup, led by Gen Manuel Odria, installed a military government.
1963 Return to civilian rule, with Fernando Belaunde as president.

Peru

1968 Return of military government in a bloodless coup by Gen Juan Velasco.
1975 Velasco replaced, in a bloodless coup, by Gen Morales Bermudez.
1980 Return to civilian rule, with Fernando Belaunde as president.
1981 Boundary dispute with Ecuador renewed.
1985 Belaunde succeeded by Social Democrat Alan García Perez.
1987 President García delayed the nationalization of Peru's banks after a vigorous campaign against the proposal.

Peru Current or *Humboldt Current* cold ocean current flowing N from the Antarctic along the W coast of South America to S Ecuador, then W. It reduces the temperature of the coasts past which it flows, making the W slopes of the Andes arid because winds are already chilled when they cross the coast.

Perugia /pə'ruːdʒə/ city in Umbria, Italy, 520 m/1,700 ft above the Tiber, about 137 km 85 mi N of Rome, with industries including textiles, liqueurs, chocolate; university 1276; population (1984) 145,000. There is a 15th-century cathedral, a palace begun in 1281, and other fine buildings with many art treasures. One of the 12 cities of Etruria, it surrendered to Rome 309 BC.

Perugino /ˌperuˈdʒiːnəʊ/ Pietro. Real name Pietro Vannucci 1446–1524. Italian artist who worked chiefly in Perugia, but also helped to decorate the Sistine Chapel, Rome. ◊Raphael was his pupil.

Pescadores /ˌpeskəˈdɔːrɪz/ (Chinese *Penghu*) group of about 60 islands off Taiwan, of which they form a dependency; area 130 sq km/50 sq mi.

Pescara /pesˈkɑːrə/ town in Abruzzi e Molise, Italy, at the mouth of the Pescara river, on the Adriatic; population (1984) 132,000. Hydroelectric installations supply Rome with electricity.

peseta the standard currency of Spain.

Peshawar /pəˈʃaʊə/ capital of North-West Frontier Province, Pakistan, 18 km/11 mi E of the Khyber Pass; population (1981) 555,000. Strategically placed, it was taken by Britain in 1849.

Pestalozzi /ˌpestəˈlɒtsi/ Johann Heinrich 1746–1827. Swiss educationalist on ◊Rousseau's 'natural' principles, as described in *Wie Gertrude ihre Kinder lehrt/How Gertrude Teaches her Children* 1801. He stressed the importance of mother and home in a child's education.

pesticide chemical used mainly in farming and gardening to combat pests and diseases. Pesticides are of three main types – insecticides (insects), fungicides (fungal diseases), and herbicides (weeds). The safest pesticides are those made from plants, such as the insecticides pyrethrum and derris. More potent are synthetic products, particularly chlorinated hydrocarbons. These products, including DDT and dieldrin, are highly toxic to wildlife and human beings (see ◊pollution), so their use is now declining. Safer pesticides such as malathion are based on organic phosphorus compounds.

Pétain /peˈtæn/ Henri Philippe 1856–1951. French general and politician. His defence of Verdun in 1916 during World War I made him a national hero, and in 1917 he was created French commander-in-chief, although he became subordinate to Foch in 1918. He suppressed a rebellion in Morocco in 1925–26. As a member of the Higher Council of National Defence he advocated a purely defensive military policy, and was strongly conservative in politics. He became prime minister Jun 1940, following the disastrous Battle of France, and signed an armistice with Germany. Removing the seat of government to Vichy, he established a repressive regime on the fascist model. On the Allied invasion he was taken to Germany, but returned in 1945 and was sentenced to death for treason, the sentence being commuted to life imprisonment.

petal part of a flower whose function is to attract pollinators such as insects or birds. They are frequently large and brightly coloured, and may also be scented. Some have a nectary at the base and markings on the petal surface, known as ◊honey guides, to direct pollinators to the source of the nectar. In wind-pollinated plants, however, the petals are usually small and insignificant, and sometimes absent altogether. Some insect-pollinated plants also have inconspicuous petals, with large colourful ◊bracts or ◊sepals taking over their role, or strong scents that attract pollinators such as flies unaided. Petals are derived from modified leaves, and collectively they are known as a ◊corolla.

Peter /'piːtə/ several tsars of Russia:

Peter I /'piːtə/ 1672–1725. Tsar of Russia, called the Great. He succeeded to the throne in 1682 on the death of his brother Tsar Feodor, and assumed control of the government in 1689. After a successful campaign against the Turks in 1696, he visited Holland and England to study Western techniques, and worked in Dutch and English shipyards. On his return to Russia he set out to reorganize the country on Western lines; the army was modernized, a fleet was built, the administrative and legal systems were remodelled, education was encouraged, and the church was brought under state control. In order to secure an outlet to the Baltic, Peter undertook a war with Sweden 1700–21, which resulted in the acquisition of Estonia and part of Latvia and Finland. On the Baltic coast Peter built his new capital, St Petersburg. A war with Persia 1722–23 added Baku to Russia.

Peter II /'piːtə/ 1715–1730. Tsar of Russia from 1727. Son of Peter the Great, he had been passed over in favour of Catherine I in 1725, but succeeded her in 1727. He died of smallpox.

Peter III /'piːtə/ 1728–1762. Tsar of Russia 1762. Weak-minded son of Peter I's eldest daughter, Anne, he was adopted 1741 by his aunt ◊Elizabeth, and at her command married the future Catherine II in 1745. He was deposed in favour of his wife, and probably murdered by her lover Alexius Orlov.

Peter I /'piːtə/ 1844–1921. King of Serbia. He was the son of Prince Alexander Karageorgevich, and was elected king when the last Obrenovich king was murdered in 1903. He took part in the retreat of the Serbian army in 1915, and in 1918 was proclaimed first king of the Serbs, Croats, and Slovenes.

Peter I A portrait engraved from a painting by I Kupetsky in 1737. One of the boats built by Peter the Great is still preserved in the Maritime Museum in London.

Peter II /'piːtə/ 1923–1970. King of Yugoslavia. He succeeded his father, King Alexander, in 1934, and assumed the royal power after the overthrow of the regency in 1941. He escaped to England following the German invasion, and married Princess Alexandra of Greece in 1944. He was dethroned in 1945.

Peterborough /'piːtəbərə/ city with varied industries in Cambridgeshire, England, noted for its 12th-century cathedral; population (1981) 115,400. It was designated a new town 1967. Six miles of the river Nene run through the city as a park; the Nene Valley has a steam railway. Nearby Flag Fen disclosed in 1985 a well-preserved Bronze Age settlement of 660 BC.

Peterhead /,piːtə'hed/ industrial seaport (fishing – largest white-fish port in Europe – shipbuilding, light engineering, whisky distilling, woollens) in Grampian, Scotland, 54 km/33 mi NE of Aberdeen; population (1981) 17,015. The Old Pretender landed here in 1715. The harbour is used by service industries for North Sea oil.

Peter I Island /'piːtə/ uninhabited island in the Bellingshausen Sea, Antarctica, belonging to Norway; area 180 sq km/69 sq mi.

Peterlee /,piːtə'liː/ new town in County Durham, England, established 1948; population (1981) 22,750. It was named after Peter Lee, first Labour chair of a county council.

Peter Lombard /'piːtə 'lɒmbaːd/ 1100–1160. Italian theologian whose *Sententiarum libri* influenced Catholic doctrine.

Peterloo massacre name given, in analogy with Waterloo, to the events in St Peter's Fields, Manchester, England, on 16 Aug 1819, when an open-air meeting in support of parliamentary reform was charged by yeomanry and hussars: 11 people were killed and 500 wounded.

Peter, Saint leader of the ◊Apostles, named Simon, but nicknamed Cephas ('Peter', from the Greek for 'rock') by Jesus, as being the rock on which he founded his Church. Originally a fisherman of Capernaum, he may have been a follower of ◊John the Baptist, and was the first to acknowledge Jesus as the Messiah. Tradition has it that he later settled in Rome, being regarded as the first bishop of Rome, whose mantle the pope inherits. He is said to have been crucified under Nero in 64 AD. Bones excavated from under the Basilica of St ◊Peter's 1968 were accepted as those of the Apostle by Pope Paul. Two New Testament letters are attributed to him. Feast day 29 Jun.

Peter's Pence voluntary annual contribution to papal administrative costs; during 10th–16th-centuries it was a compulsory levy of one penny per household.

Peter the Hermit /'piːtə/ 1050–1115. French priest whose eloquent preaching of the First ◊Crusade sent thousands of peasants marching against the Turks, who massacred them in Asia Minor. Peter escaped and accompanied the main body of crusaders to Jerusalem.

petiole the stalk attaching the leaf blade, or ◊lamina, to the stem. Typically it is continuous with the midrib of the leaf and attached to the base of the lamina, but occasionally it is attached to lower suface of the lamina (a peltate leaf), as in the nasturtium. Petioles that are flattened and leaf-like are termed phyllodes. Leaves that lack a petiole are said to be ◊sessile.

Petipa /pə,tiː'paː/ Marius 1818–1910. French choreographer. A major figure in 19th-century ballet, from 1862 to 1903. He worked as ballet master with the Imperial Ballet in Russia, creating masterpieces such as *La Bayadère* 1877 *The Sleeping Beauty* 1890, *Swan Lake* 1895 (with Ivanov) and *Raymonda* 1898, which are still performed.

Petition of Right in British law, the procedure whereby, before the passing of the Crown Proceedings Act 1947, a subject petitioned for legal relief against the crown, whether for money due under a contract, or for property of which the crown had taken possession. Also the petition of Parliament accepted by Charles I in 1628, declaring illegal taxation without parliamentary consent, imprisonment without trial, billeting of soldiers on private persons, and use of martial law.

Petöfi /'petəːfi/ Sándor 1823–1849. Hungarian nationalist poet. He published his first volume of poems in 1844. He expressed his revolutionary ideas in the semi-autobiographical poem 'The Apostle', and fell fighting the Austrians in the battle of Segesvár.

Petra /'petrə/ (Arabic *Wadi Musa*) ruined city carved out of the red rock at a site in modern Jordan, on the E slopes of the Wadi el Araba, 90 km/56 mi S of the Dead Sea. An Edomite stronghold, capital of the Nabataeans in the 2nd century, it was captured by Trajan in 106 AD and wrecked by the Saracens in the 7th century. It was lost to knowledge until rediscovered in 1812 by the Swiss traveller J L Burckhardt.

Petrarch /'petraːk/ (Italian *Petrarca*) Francesco 1304–1374. Italian poet, born in Arezzo, a devotee of the classical tradition. His *Il Canzoniere* were sonnets in praise of his idealized love 'Laura' (see ◊Martini), whom he first saw in 1327 (a married woman, she refused to become his mistress) and who died of plague 1348. From 1337 he often stayed in secluded study at his home at Vaucluse, near Avignon, and, eager to restore the glories of Rome, wanted to return the papacy there from Avignon. He was a friend of ◊Boccaccio, and supported ◊Rienzi's republic in 1347.

petrel two families of seabirds (Procellariidae and Hydrobatidae) so called from their skimming the water surface as St Peter did. Most familiar is the storm-petrel of the N Atlantic *Hydrobates pelagicus*, also known as Mother Carey's chicken. Seldom coming to land except to breed, they lay a single egg in holes among the rocks. They are sooty-black with a white patch on the tail.

Petrie /'piːtri/ William Matthew Flinders 1853–1942. British archaeologist. Grandson of Matthew ◊Flinders, he is remembered for his work in Egypt (Tanis, the Pyramids, Tell el Amarna, Abydos) 1880–1926.

Petrograd /'petrəgræd/ name 1914–24 of ◊Leningrad, city in the USSR.

petrol engine the prime power source for cars and motorcycles, introduced by the German engineers Gottlieb ◊Daimler and Karl ◊Benz in 1885. The petrol engine is a complex piece of machinery made up of about 150 moving parts. It is a reciprocating ◊piston engine, in which a number of pistons move up and down in cylinders. A mixture of petrol and air is introduced to the space above the pistons and ignited. The gases produced force the pistons down, generating power. The engine-operating cycle is repeated every four strokes (upward or downward movement) of the piston, this being known as the ◊four-stroke cycle. The motion of the pistons drive round a ◊crankshaft, at the end of which is a heavy ◊flywheel. From the flywheel the power is transferred to the car's driving wheels via the transmission system of ◊clutch, gearbox, and final drive.

The numerous parts of the petrol engine can be subdivided into a number of systems, which each play a part in making the engine run. The *fuel system* pumps fuel from the petrol tank into (usually) the carburettor. There it mixes with air and is sucked into the engine cylinders. The *ignition system* supplies the sparks to ignite the fuel mixture in the cylinders. By means of an ignition ◊coil and contact breaker, it boosts the 12-volt battery voltage to pulses of 18,000 volts or more. These go via a ◊distributor to the ◊spark plugs in the cylinders, where they create the sparks. Ignition of the fuel in the cylinders produces temperatures of 700°C or more, and the engine must be cooled to prevent overheating. Most engines have a *water-cooling system*, in which water circulates through channels in the cylinder block and extracts the heat. It flows through pipes in a radiator, which are cooled by air. A few cars and most motorbikes are air-cooled, the cylinders being surrounded by many fins to present a large surface area to the air. The *lubrication system* also removes some heat, but its main job is to lubricate the moving parts with oil. Throughout the system oil is pumped under pressure to the camshaft, crankshaft, and valve-operating gear. See ◊diesel engine.

petroleum mineral oil, a thick greenish-brown liquid found underground in permeable rocks. Petroleum consists of hydrocarbons mixed with oxygen, sulphur, and so on, in varying proportions. It is often found in association with natural gas (mainly methane). It occurs in anticlines and other traps below impervious rock layers. Flowing wells are due to gas pressure from above or water pressure from below the oil, which causes it to rise up the borehole; many wells require artificial aids to bring the oil to the surface. The origin of petroleum is uncertain; it is thought to be derived from organic material which has been converted by bacterial action, followed by the effects of heat and pressure, but its origin may be chemical rather than biological. From the crude petroleum or rock oil various products are made by distillation and other processes, for example, fuel oil, gasoline (petrol), kerosene, diesel or gas oil, lubricating oil, paraffin wax, and petroleum jelly. Aviation spirit is a very volatile form of petrol.

The occurrence of mineral oil was known in ancient times, but the exploitation of oil-fields began with the first commercial well in Pennsylvania in 1859. In the early years the USA held the lead, but in the 1960s the Middle East became dominant, huge reserves leading to worldwide dependence on cheap oil for transport and industry. In 1961 the Organization of Petroleum Exporting Countries (OPEC) was established to avoid exploitation of member countries; the International Energy Agency (IEA) was established in 1974 to protect the interests of oil-consuming countries.
Research is being carried out into energy sources that might be not only cheaper but freer from pollutants than oil. Pollution is a risk also in the transport of oil to the consumer, for example, the *Torrey Canyon* (1967) tanker lost off Cornwall, which led to agreement by the international oil companies in 1968 to pay compensation for massive shore pollution.
Petroleum products and chemicals serve as raw materials for widely different industries and are used in large quantities in the manufacture of detergents, artificial fibres, plastics, insecticides, fertilizers, pharmaceuticals, toilet requisites, and synthetic rubber. A new kind of bacterium was developed in the USA, capable of 'eating' oil, as a means of countering spillage. Its creation gave rise to the so-called ◊Frankenstein law.

petrology the branch of ◊geology that deals with the study of rocks, their mineral compositions and their origins.

Petronius /pə'trəʊnɪəs/ Gaius, known as Petronius Arbiter. Roman author of a licentious romance *Satyricon*. Supervisor of the pleasures of the emperor Nero, he committed suicide.

Petropavlovsk /ˌpetrəʊpæv'lɒvsk/ industrial city (flour, agricultural machinery, leather) in the Kazakh Republic, USSR, on the Ishim river, the Trans-Siberian railway, and the

petroleum

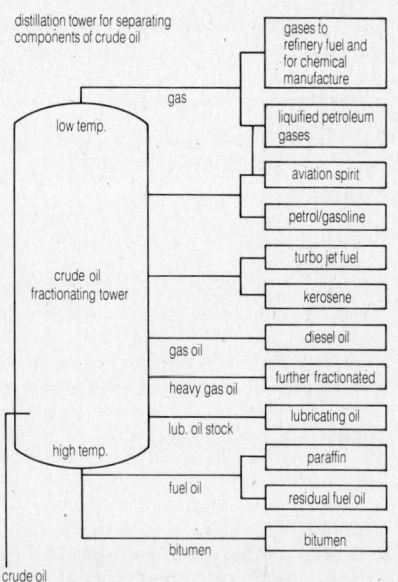

distillation tower for separating components of crude oil

gas — low temp. — gases to refinery fuel and for chemical manufacture / liquified petroleum gases / aviation spirit / petrol/gasoline

crude oil fractionating tower — turbo jet fuel / kerosene

gas oil — diesel oil

heavy gas oil — further fractionated

lub. oil stock — lubricating oil

high temp. — paraffin

fuel oil — residual fuel oil

bitumen — bitumen

crude oil

Transkazakh line, opened 1953; population (1985) 226,000. A former caravan station, it was founded as a Russian fortress 1782.

Petropavlovsk-Kamchatski /-kæm'tʃætski/ port and naval base on the Kamchatka peninsula, USSR; population (1985) 245,000.

Petrópolis /pe'trɒpəlɪs/ hill resort in SE Brazil, founded by Pedro II; population (1980) 149,427.

Petrovsk /pɪ'trɒvsk/ former name (until 1921) of the Soviet port ◊Makhachkala.

Petrozavodsk /ˌpetrəʊzə'vɒdsk/ industrial city (metal goods, cement, prefabricated houses; sawmills), capital of Karelia Republic, USSR, on the W shore of Lake Onega; population (1985) 255,000. Peter the Great established the township in 1703 as an ironworking centre; it was named Petrozavodsk in 1777.

Petsamo /'petsəməʊ/ Finnish name of the Murmansk port ◊Pechenga.

Pevensey /'pevənsi/ English village in Sussex, 8 km/5 mi NE of Eastbourne, the site of William the Conqueror's landing in 1066. The walls remain of the Roman fortress of Anderida, later a Norman castle, and prepared against German invasion in World War II.

Pevsner /'pevznə/ Nikolaus 1902–1983. Anglo-German art historian. Born in Leipzig, he fled to England from the Nazis. In his series *Buildings of England* 1951–74, he achieved a first-hand report on every notable building in the country.

pewter an ◊alloy of tin and lead, known for centuries, once widely used for domestic utensils but now used mainly for ornamental ware.

peyote cactus *Lophopora williamsii* of Mexico and southern USA, which produces the hallucinogen *mescalin* used by the Indians in religious ceremonies.

Pfalz /pfælts/ German name of the historic division of Germany, the ◊Palatinate.

Pforzheim /'pfɔːtshaɪm/ city of Baden-Württemberg, West Germany, 26 km/16 mi SE of Karlsruhe, with goldsmith industries; population (1984) 104,500. It was a Roman settlement, and the residence of margraves of Baden 1300–1565.

pH a scale for measuring acidity or alkalinity. A pH of 7.0 indicates neutrality, below 7 is acid, while above 7 is alkaline. The scale runs from 0 to 14 and properly defined is the Briggs logarithm of the reciprocal of the hydrogen ion (H$^+$) concentration. Strong acids, as used in car batteries, have a pH of about 2; acidic fruits such as citrus fruits are about pH 4. Fertile soils have a pH of about 6.5 to 7.0, while weak alkalis such as soap are 9 to 10. Corrosive alkalis such as lye are pH 13.

Phaethon /'feɪəθən/ in Greek mythology, the son of ◊Helios, who was allowed for one day to drive the chariot of the sun. Losing control of the horses, he almost set the earth on fire, and was killed by Zeus with a thunderbolt.

phage another name for a ◊bacteriophage.

phagocyte a type of white blood cell, or ◊leucocyte, which can engulf a bacterium or other invading microorganism. They are found in blood, ◊lymph and other body tissues, where they also ingest foreign matter or dead tissue.

Phalaris /'fælərɪs/ 570–554 bc. Tyrant of Agrigentum, Sicily. He is said to have built a brazen bull in which victims were roasted alive. He was killed in a popular revolt. The letters attributed to him were proved by the scholar Richard ◊Bentley to be a later forgery.

phalarope genus of seabirds related to plovers. Of the three species the red-necked *Phalaropus ilobatus* and grey *Phalaropus fulicarius* visit Britain from the Arctic and *Phalaropus tricolor* is exclusively American. The male is courted by the female and hatches the eggs. The female is larger and more colourful.

phallus (Hindu *lingam*) a model of the male sexual organ, used in fertility rituals in ancient Greece and Asia Minor, in India, and in many other parts of the world.

phanerogam an obsolete name, once applied to plants which bore flowers or cones and reproduced by means of seeds, that is, ◊angiosperms and ◊gymnosperms, or ◊seed plants. Plants such as mosses, fungi, and ferns, were known as *cryptogams*.

Pharaoh /'feərəʊ/ Hebrew form of the Egyptian royal title Per-'o. This term, meaning 'great house', was originally applied to the royal household, and after about 950 BC to the king.

Pharisee member of a Jewish sect which arose in the 2nd century BC, in protest against all compromise with Hellenistic culture. The main emphasis was on strict observance of the law, rather than on ritual; hence the Pharisees came into conflict with the priestly caste, or ◊Sadducees. Although they believed in a coming Messiah, they rejected political action, and in the 1st century AD the left wing of their followers, the Zealots, broke away to pursue a revolutionary nationalist policy. After the fall of Jerusalem, Pharisee ideas became the basis of orthodox Judaism.

pharmacology study of the origin, application, and effect of chemical substances on animals and humans. These products of the pharmaceutical industry range from aspirin to anti-cancer agents, and about 3 per cent of gross sales in the UK are devoted to research; 10,000 new substances may have to be synthesized to find one or two useful products. Well-proven formulations are listed in the official pharmacopoeia.

pharynx the interior of the throat, the cavity at the back of the mouth. Its walls are made of ◊muscle strengthened with a fibrous layer and lined with ◊mucous membrane. It has an opening into the back of each nostril (choanae) and downwards into the gullet and (through the epiglottis) into the windpipe. On each side the Eustachian tube leads from it to the middle ear. The upper part (naso-pharynx) is an airway, but the remainder is a passage for food. Inflammation of the pharynx is named pharyngitis.

phase in physics, a physical state of matter: for example, ice and liquid water are different phases of water; a mixture of the two is termed a two-phase system. Also, a stage in an oscillatory motion, such as a wave motion: two waves are in phase when their peaks and their troughs coincide. Otherwise, there is a phase difference, which has important consequences in ◊interference phenomena and ◊alternating current electricity. See also change of state.

pheasant bird of the family Phasianidae, which also includes quail and peafowl. The common pheasant *Phasianus colchicus* was introduced from Asia to Europe, according to legend by the Argonauts who brought it from the banks of the river Phasis. The plumage of the male is richly tinted with brownish-green and yellow and red markings, but the female is a camouflaged brownish colour; the nest is made in the ground, and the male is polygamous.
In Britain pheasants are semi-domesticated and the shooting season is 1st Oct to 31 Jan. The pheasant is also naturalized in North America.

phenol *carbolic acid* an aromatic compound, extracted from coal tar; pure phenol consists of colourless, needle-shaped crystals which readily take up moisture from the atmosphere. Phenol has a strong and characteristic smell and was once used as an antiseptic. It is, however, toxic by absorption through the skin. Phenol is very important industrially, being used to make dyes, drugs, nylon, and various plastics.

phenomena in philosophy, a technical term used in ◊Kant's philosophy, describing things as they appear to us, rather than as they are in themselves.

phenomenalism a philosophical position which argues that statements about objects can be reduced to statements about what is perceived or perceivable. Thus, J S ◊Mill defined material objects as 'permanent possibilities of sensation'. Phenomenalism is closely connected with certain forms of ◊empiricism.

phenomenology ◊Husserl's philosophical perspective, which in the social sciences concentrates on phenomena as objects of perception (rather than as facts or occurrences which exist independently) in attempting to examine the ways people think about and interpret the world around them. In contrast to positivism or 'scientific' philosophy, phenomenology sees reality as essentially relative and subjective, and uses such tools as ethnomethodology and symbolic interactionism to focus on the structure of everyday life. It has been practised by ◊Heidegger, ◊Sartre, and ◊Merleau-Ponty.

phenotype in ◊genetics, the traits actually displayed by an organism. The phenotype is not a direct reflection of the ◊genotype because some alleles are masked by the presence of other ◊dominant alleles. Furthermore, the phenotype is modified by the effects of the environment (for example, poor food stunting growth).

phenylketonuria condition arising from genetic causes, in which the liver of a child cannot control the level of phenyldanine (found in protein foods) in the bloodstream in the normal way by excretion in the urine. It is controlled by special diet.

pheromone chemical signal that is emitted (like an odour) by one animal and affects the behaviour of others. Pheromones are used by many animal species to attract mates.

Phidias /'fidiæs/ Greek sculptor. Born at Athens about 500 BC, he was a friend of Pericles, who made him superintendent of public works. He constructed the Propylaea and the Parthenon, and executed the colossal statue of Zeus at Olympia, which was one of the seven wonders of the world.

Philadelphia /ˌfilə'delfiə/ industrial city and port on the Delaware river in Pennsylvania, USA
features Independence Hall 1732–59 (in which the Declaration of Independence was adopted and which contains the Liberty Bell), City Hall 1872 (surmounted by statue of Penn), the US Mint 1792, and the grave of Benjamin Franklin. The Philadelphia Science Centre is linked with the University of Pennsylvania and the Franklin Institute for Applied Science 1824. The symphony orchestra is famous, and there are notable art collections
products refined oil, chemicals, textiles, processed food, printing and publishing
population (1980) 1,688,200
history founded by William ◊Penn 1682 as the 'city of brotherly love', it was the first capital of the USA 1790–1800.

Philae /'faili:/ island in the Nile, Egypt, above the first rapids, famed for the beauty of its temple of Isis (founded about 350 BC and in use until the 6th century AD), set among palm trees. In 1977 the temple was re-erected on the nearby island of Agilkia above the flooding caused by the Aswan Dam.

philately the collection and study of postage stamps. Originating in France about 1860, it became popular throughout the world. The world's largest collection is in the British Museum, London, the second largest in the Smithsonian Institution, Washington; probably the world's finest private collection is that of Queen Elizabeth II.

Philby /'filbi/ 'Kim' (Harold) 1912– . Son of Harry ◊Philby. British intelligence officer from 1940 (already a Soviet agent from 1933), who was liaison officer in Washington 1949–51, when he was asked to resign. Named in 1963 as having warned Guy Burgess (1911–63) and Donald Maclean (1913–83) (similarly double agents) that their activities were known, he fled to the USSR, and became a Soviet citizen and general in the ◊KGB. A fourth member of the ring was Anthony ◊Blunt; Sir Roger Hollis (1905–73), head of MI5 1956–65, was alleged without confirmation to be a fifth.

Philby /'filbi/ Harry St John Bridger 1885–1960. British explorer. As chief of the British political mission to central Arabia, 1917–18, he carried out extensive exploration and was the first European to visit the southern provinces of Najd; and in 1932 crossed the Rub 'al Khali desert. He wrote *The Empty Quarter* 1933, and *Forty Years in the Wilderness* 1957.

Philharmonic Society a group of people organized for the advancement of music; the term is derived from Greek 'love of harmony'. The Royal Philharmonic Society was founded in London in 1813 by the pianist Johann Baptist Cramer (1771–1858) for the purpose of improving musical standards by means of orchestral concerts organized on a subscription basis. Another Philharmonic Society was founded in New York in 1842.

Philip /'filip/ 1921– . Prince of the UK. A grandson of George I of Greece and a great-great-grandson of Queen Victoria, he was born in Corfu but raised in England and educated at Gordonstoun and Dartmouth Naval College. During World War II he served in the Mediterranean, taking part in the battle of Matapan, and in the Pacific. A naturalized British subject, taking the surname Mountbatten in Mar 1947, he married Princess Elizabeth (from 1952 Elizabeth II) in Westminster Abbey on 20 Nov 1947, having the previous day received the title Duke of Edinburgh. In 1956 he founded the Duke of Edinburgh's Award Scheme to encourage creative achievement among young people, and is also greatly interested in the Commonwealth. He was created a prince of the UK in 1957; Order of Merit 1968.

Philip the Good /'filip/ 1396–1467. Duke of Burgundy from 1419. He engaged in the Hundred Years' War as an ally of England and made the Netherlands a centre of art and learning.

Philip /'filip/ six kings of France, including:
Philip **II** /'filip/ (Philip-Augustus) 1165–1223. King of France from 1180. He waged war in turn against the English kings Henry II, Richard I (with whom he also went on the First Crusade), and John (against whom he won the final battle of Bouvines 1214) to evict them from their French possessions, and establish a strong monarchy.

Philip IV /'filip/ the Fair 1268–1314. King of France from 1285. He engaged in a feud with Pope Boniface VIII, whom in 1303 he made a prisoner. Clement V, elected pope through Philip's influence, moved to Avignon, and collaborated with Philip to suppress the Templars. Philip allied with the Scots against England, and invaded Flanders.

Philip VI /'fɪlɪp/ 1293–1350. King of France 1328, first of the house of Valois, elected by the barons on the death of his cousin, Charles IV. His claim was challenged by Edward III of England, who in 1346 defeated him at Crécy.

Philip II of Macedon /'fɪlɪp/ 382–336 bc. King of ◊Macedonia from 359 BC. He seized the throne from his nephew, for whom he was regent, conquered the Greek city states and formed them into a league whose forces could be united against Persia. He was assassinated just as he was planning this expedition, and was succeeded by his son ◊Alexander the Great. His tomb was discovered at Vergina, N Greece, in 1978.

Philip /'fɪlɪp/ five kings of Spain, including:

Philip I the Handsome 1478–1506. Son of Maximilian I, and king of Castile from 1504, through his marriage 1496 to Joanna the Mad (1479–1555).

Philip II 1527–1598. King of Spain from 1556. Son of the Hapsburg emperor Charles V, he was born at Valladolid, and in 1554 married Queen Mary of England. On his father's abdication in 1556 he inherited Spain, the Netherlands, and the Spanish possessions in Italy and America, and in 1580 he annexed Portugal. His intolerance and lack of understanding of the Netherlanders drove them into revolt. Political and religious reasons combined to involve him in war with England, and after 1589 with France. The defeat of the ◊Armada marked the beginning of the decline of Spanish power.

Philip II After the death of Queen Mary of England, Philip II of Spain, her husband, wished to marry Elizabeth I. Instead, for political and religious reasons, he became involved in a continuing war with England during her reign, culminating in the defeat of his Armada in 1588.

Philip V 1683–1746. First Bourbon king of Spain from 1700, a grandson of Louis XIV of France. He was not recognized by the major European powers until 1713.

Philip Neri, St /'nɪəri/ 1515–1595. Italian priest who organized the Congregation of the Oratory, and built the oratory over the church of

Philippines
REPUBLIC OF THE (*Republika ng Pilipinas*)

AREA 300,000 sq km/115,700 sq mi
CAPITAL Manila (on Luzon)
TOWNS Quezon City
PORTS Cebu, Davao (on Mindanao) and Iloilu
PHYSICAL comprises over 7,000 islands, with volcanic mountain ranges traversing the main chain N–S, and 50% of the area still forested. The largest islands are *Luzon* 108,172 sq km/41,765 sq mi and *Mindanao* 94,227 sq km/36,381 sq mi; others include Samar, Negros, Palawan, Panay, Mindoro, Leyte, Cebu and the Sulu group
FEATURES Luzon, the scene of fierce fighting in World War II at Bataan and Corregidor, is the site of Clark Field, US air base used as a logistical base in the Vietnam War, and Subic Bay, US naval base; Mindanao has the active volcano Apo (2,855 m/9,369 ft) and mountainous rain forest, in which the Stone Age people of the Tasaday were first encountered in 1971
HEAD OF STATE AND OF GOVERNMENT Corazón Aquino from 1986
GOVERNMENT parliamentary democracy
EXPORTS sugar, copra and coconut oil; timber; iron ore and copper concentrates
CURRENCY peso (33.2 = £1 Sept 1987)
POPULATION (1985) 56,808,000 (93% Malaysian); annual growth rate 2.6%
LANGUAGE Filipino (based on the Malay dialect Tagalog), but English and Spanish are in common use
RELIGION Roman Catholic 84%, Protestant 9%, Muslim 5%

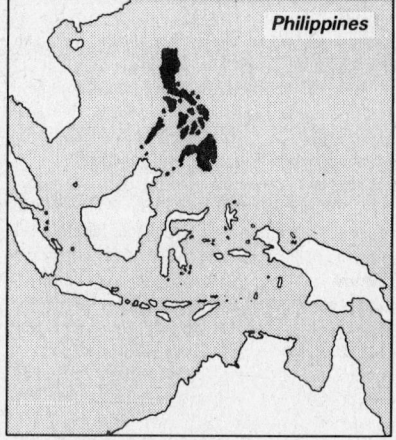

Philippines

LITERACY 90% male/88% female (1980 est)
GNP $16 bn (1984); $772 per head of population
CHRONOLOGY
1542 Named the Philippines by Spanish explorers.
1565 Conquered by Spain.
1898 Ceded to the USA.
1935 Grant of internal self-government.
1942–45 Japanese occupation.
1946 Independence granted.
1965 Ferdinand Marcos elected president.
1983 Murder of Benigno Aquino.
1986 Overthrow of Marcos by Corazón Aquino's 'people's power' movement.
1987 Attempted right-wing coups suppressed. Communist guerrillas active.

St Jerome, Rome, where prayer meetings were held, and scenes from the Bible were performed with music – hence *oratorio*; canonized 1622.

Philippeville /'fɪlɪpvɪl/ former name of Algerian port of ◊Skikda.

Philippi /fɪ'lɪpaɪ/ ancient city of Macedonia founded by Philip of Macedon, 358 BC. Near Philippi, Antony and Octavius defeated Brutus and Cassius in 42 BC. It was the first European town where St Paul preached (about 53 AD), founding the congregation to which he addressed the Epistle to the Philippians.

Philippines /'fɪlɪpiːnz/ country on an archipelago between the Pacific Ocean to the E and the South China Sea to the W.

government The constitution was approved by plebiscite in Feb 1987. It provides for an executive president and a two-chamber legislature composed of 24 senators and 250 representatives.

history The people of the Philippine islands probably came from the ◊Malay Peninsula. They were semi-nomadic hunters and fishermen when the first European arrived, ◊Magellan, 1521, followed by conquering Spanish forces in 1565. Roman Catholicism was introduced during the reign of ◊Philip II (after whom the islands were named), replacing Islam, which had been spread

by Arab traders and missionaries.

During the 19th century there were a series of armed nationalist revolts. These continued after the islands were ceded by Spain to the USA in 1898, and increasing self-government was granted in 1916 and 1935. The Philippines were occupied by Japan 1942–45, before becoming a fully independent republic in 1946. A succession of presidents drawn from the islands' wealthy estate-owning elite followed, who did little to improve the lot of the ordinary peasant.

In 1965 President Diosdado Macapagal was defeated by Ferdinand ◊Marcos, the leader of the Nationalist Party. Marcos initiated rapid economic development and some land reform. He was re-elected in 1969, but encountered growing opposition from communist insurgents and Muslim separatists in the S. A high rate of population growth aggravated poverty and unemployment. Some months before his second term had been completed, Marcos declared martial law, suspended the constitution and began to rule by decree. Intermittent referenda allowed him to retain power. Marcos's authoritarian leadership was criticized for corruption and in 1977 the opposition leader, Benigno Aquino, was jailed under sentence of death for alleged subversion. In 1978 martial law was relaxed, the 1972 ban on political parties was lifted and elections for an interim National Assembly were held, resulting in an overwhelming victory for Marcos.

In Jan 1981 martial law was lifted completely and hundreds of political prisoners released. Marcos then won approval, by referendum, for a partial return to democratic government with himself as president, working with a prime minister and executive council. Political and economic conditions deteriorated, communist guerrilla insurgency escalated, unemployment climbed to over 30% and the national debt increased. In 1983 Benigno Aquino, allowed to travel to the USA for medical treatment, was shot dead on his arrival at Manila airport. A commission of inquiry reported that Aquino had been killed by the military guard escorting him as part of a broader conspiracy.

National Assembly elections were held in May 1984, amid violence and widespread claims of corruption, and although the government party stayed in power, the opposition registered significant gains. Then early in 1986 the main anti-Marcos movement, United Nationalist Democratic Organization (UNIDO), chose Corazón ◊Aquino, Benigno's widow, despite her political inexperience, to contest new elections for the presidency which Marcos had been persuaded to hold as a means of maintaining vital US economic and diplomatic support.

The campaign resulted in over 100 deaths, and large-scale electoral fraud was witnessed by international observers. On 16 Feb 1986 the National Assembly declared Marcos the winner, a result disputed by an independent electoral watchdog, the National Citizens' Movement for Free Elections (Namfrel). Corazón Aquino began a non-violent protest, termed 'people's power', which gathered massive popular support, backed by the Roman Catholic church, and President Marcos came under strong international pressure, particularly from the USA, to stand down. On 22 Feb 1986 the army, led by Chief of Staff Lt-Gen Fidel Ramos and defence minister Juan Enrile, declared its support for Aquino and on 25 Feb Marcos left for exile in Hawaii.

On assuming the presidency, Corazón Aquino dissolved the pro-Marcos National Assembly. She proceeded to govern in a conciliatory fashion, working with a coalition cabinet team comprising opposition politicians and senior military figures. She freed 500 political prisoners and granted an amnesty to the New People's Army communist guerrillas in an effort to end the 17-year-old insurgency, and introduced a major rural-employment economic programme, with land reforms opposed by property owners.

The new administration endured a series of attempted coups by pro-Marcos supporters and faced serious opposition from Juan Enrile, dismissed in Nov 1986. The communist National Democratic Front remains officially banned. The most significant party groupings are the centre-right UNIDO, led by Vice President Salvador Laurel, the liberal-left Convenors' Group, led by Aquino, and PDP-Laban Party, led by her brother José Cojuangco, and the right-wing pro-

Marcos New Society Movement and Nationalist Party, led by Enrile.

President Aquino secured the firm backing of the Philippines' close ally, the USA, which has had major military bases at Subic Bay and Clark Field on ◊Luzon Island since 1947.

Philip, St in the Bible, one of the 12 Apostles. He was an inhabitant of Bethsaida, and is said to have worked as a missionary in Asia Minor. Feast day 11 May.

Philistine /ˈfɪlɪstaɪn/ member of a people of non-Semitic origin (possibly from Asia Minor, but see ◊Sea Peoples) who founded city states on the Palestinian coastal plain in the 12th century BC, adopting a ◊Semitic language and religion. They were at war with the Israelites in the 11th–10th centuries BC (hence the pejorative use of their name for anyone uncivilized in intellectual and artistic terms), were temporarily subdued by the Hebrew king David, and later came under Assyrian rule.

Phillip /ˈfɪlɪp/ Arthur 1738–1814. British vice-admiral, founder and governor of the convict settlement at Sydney, Australia.

philology a Greek term, originally meaning 'love of learning and literature'. It is sometimes used in the sense of ◊linguistics, the systematic study of language, but more often defines the critical study of the literary remains of the past, especially of Greek and Roman antiquity. In this sense the scholars of Alexandria, who edited Homer, were philologists. The Renaissance gave great impetus to this kind of study. Dutch scholars took the lead in the 17th century and Richard ◊Bentley made significant contributions in England. From the study of Sanskrit there arose at the beginning of the 19th century, under Bopp's leadership, what is called comparative philology, originally mainly concerned with the ◊Indo-European family of languages, while the Romantic movement greatly inspired the establishment of national philology.

philosophy (Greek 'love of knowledge'). The field of theoretical studies which includes metaphysics (the nature of existence), epistemology (theory of knowledge), ethics and aesthetics. Some branches of philosophy have acquired their own status or separate discipline: mathematics, physics, chemistry, biology, and (until this century) psychology were formerly included in philosophy, and logic is in the process of separation.

Philosophy is concerned with fundamental problems, including the nature of mind and matter, perception, self, free will, causation, time and space, the existence of moral judgements, which cannot be resolved by a specific method. Contemporary philosophers are inclined to think of philosophy as an investigation of the fundamental assumptions that govern our ways of understanding and acting in the world.

Oldest of all philosophical systems is the Vedic system of about 2,500 BC, but like many other Eastern systems it rests on a primarily mystic basis. The first scientific system originated in Greece in the 6th century BC with the Milesian school (◊Thales, Anaximander, and

Anaximenes). Both they and later pre-Socratics (◊Pythagoras, ◊Xenophon, ◊Parmenides, ◊Zeno of Elea, ◊Empedocles, Anaxagoras, ◊Heraclitus and ◊Democritus) were lively theorists, and ideas such as atomism, developed by Democritus, occur in later schemes of thought. In the 5th century ◊Socrates, foremost among the teachers known as the ◊Sophists, laid the foundation of ethics; ◊Plato evolved a system of universal ideas; ◊Aristotle developed logic. Later schools include ◊Epicureanism (◊Epicurus), ◊Stoicism (◊Zeno) and ◊Scepticism (◊Pyrrhon); the eclectics – not a school, they selected what appealed to them from various systems (◊Cicero and ◊Seneca) – and the neo-Platonists, infusing a mystic element into the system of Plato (Philo, Plotinus and, as disciple, Julian the Apostate).

The close of the Athenian schools of philosophy by Justinian in 529 AD marks the end of ancient philosophy, though many of its teachers moved eastwards and Greek thought emerges in Muslim philosophers such as ◊Avicenna and ◊Averroes, and the Jewish ◊Maimonides. For the West the work of Aristotle was transmitted through ◊Boethius, and an enumeration of medieval scholastic philosophers, mainly concerned with the reconciliation of ancient philosophy with Christian belief, begins in the 9th century with John Scotus ◊Erigena and includes ◊Anselm, ◊Abelard, ◊Albertus Magnus, Thomas ◊Aquinas (greatest of them all), his opponent ◊Duns Scotus, and William of ◊Occam.

In the 17th century ◊Descartes, with his rationalist determination to doubt, and faith in mathematical proof, marks the beginning of modern philosophy, and was followed by ◊Spinoza, ◊Leibniz, and ◊Hobbes; but the ◊empiricists, principally an 18th-century English school (◊Locke, ◊Berkeley, and ◊Hume), turned rather to physics as indicating what can be known and how, and led up to the transcendental criticism of ◊Kant. In the early 19th century classical German idealism (◊Fichte, ◊Schelling, ◊Hegel) repudiated Kant's limitation of human knowledge; and in France ◊Comte developed the positivist thought which attracted ◊Mill and ◊Spencer. Notable also in the 19th century are the pessimistic atheism of ◊Schopenhauer; the dialectical materialism of ◊Marx and ◊Engels; the work of ◊Nietzsche and ◊Kierkegaard, which led towards 20th-century ◊existentialism; and the pragmatism of William ◊James and ◊Dewey.

Among 20th-century movements are the logical positivism of the Vienna circle (◊Carnap, ◊Popper, ◊Ayer); the creative evolution of ◊Bergson; neo-Thomism, the revival of the medieval philosophy of Aquinas (◊Maritain); existentialism (◊Heidegger, ◊Jaspers, ◊Sartre); the phenomenology of ◊Husserl, who influenced ◊Ryle; and realism (◊Russell, ◊Moore, and ◊Wittgenstein). 20th-century philosophers have been especially interested in the nature and limits of language.

Phiz /fɪz/ pseudonym of Hablot Knight Browne 1815–1882. British artist who illustrated the greater part of the *Pickwick Papers* and other works by Dickens.

PHILOSOPHY: GREAT PHILOSOPHERS

name	dates	nationality	representative work
Heraclitus	c.544–483 BC	Greek	*On Nature* (fragments)
Parmenides	c.510–c.450 BC	Greek	fragments
Socrates	469–399 BC	Greek	———
Plato	428–347 BC	Greek	*Republic; Phaedo*
Aristotle	384–322 BC	Greek	*Nicomachean Ethics; Metaphysics*
Epicurus	341–270 BC	Greek	fragments
Lucretius	c.99–55 BC	Roman	*On the Nature of Things*
Plotinus	205–270 AD	Greek	*Enneads*
Augustine	354–430	N African	*Confessions; City of God*
Aquinas	c.1225–1274	Italian	*Summa Theologica*
Duns Scotus	c.1266–1308	Scottish	*Opus Oxoniense*
William of Occam	c.1285–1349	English	*Commentary of the Sentences*
Nicholas of Cusa	1401–1464	German	*De Docta Ignorantia*
Giordano Bruno	1548–1600	Italian	*De la Causa, Principio e Uno*
Bacon	1561–1626	English	*Novum Organum; The Advancement of Learning*
Hobbes	1588–1679	English	*Leviathan*
Descartes	1596–1650	French	*Discourse on Method; Meditations on the First Philosophy*
Pascal	1623–1662	French	*Pensées*
Spinoza	1632–1677	Dutch	*Ethics*
Locke	1632–1704	English	*Essay Concerning Human Understanding*
Leibniz	1646–1716	German	*The Monadology*
Vico	1668–1744	Italian	*The New Science*
Berkeley	1685–1753	Irish	*A Treatise Concerning the Principles of Human Knowledge*
Hume	1711–1776	Scottish	*A Treatise of Human Nature*
Rousseau	1712–1778	French	*The Social Contract*
Diderot	1713–1784	French	*D'Alembert's Dream*
Kant	1724–1804	German	*The Critique of Pure Reason*
Fichte	1762–1814	German	*The Science of Knowledge*
Hegel	1770–1831	German	*The Phenomenology of Spirit*
Schelling	1775–1854	German	*System of Transcendental Idealism*
Schopenhauer	1788–1860	German	*The World as Will and Idea*
Comte	1798–1857	French	*Cours de philosophie positive*
Mill	1806–1873	English	*Utilitarianism*
Kierkegaard	1813–1855	Danish	*Concept of Dread*
Marx	1818–1883	German	*Economic and Philosophical Manuscripts*
Dilthey	1833–1911	German	*The Rise of Hermeneutics*
Peirce	1839–1914	American	*How to Make our Ideas Clear*
Nietzsche	1844–1900	German	*Thus Spake Zarathustra*
Bergson	1859–1941	French	*Creative Evolution*
Husserl	1859–1938	German	*Logical Investigations*
Russell	1872–1970	English	*Principia Mathematica*
Lukács	1885–1971	Hungarian	*History and Class Consciousness*
Wittgenstein	1889–1951	Austrian	*Tractatus Logico–Philosophicus; Philosophical Investigations*
Heidegger	1889–1976	German	*Being and Time*
Gadamer	1900–	German	*Truth and Method*
Sartre	1905–1980	French	*Being and Nothingness*
Merleau-Ponty	1908–1961	French	*The Phenomenology of Perception*
Quine	1908–	American	*Word and Object*
Foucault	1926–1984	French	*The Order of Things*

phlebitis inflammation of the lining of a vein. It causes the blood in the area to clot (thrombosis). Simple or non-infective phlebitis may be caused by an injury or pressure, and was common in the main thigh veins of women after childbirth. The blood clots and obstructs the circulation (white leg). Septic phlebitis is caused by infection, for example in the lateral sinus and the jugular vein by infection from the middle ear.

phloem a tissue found in vascular plants whose main function is to conduct sugars and other food materials from the leaves, where they are produced, to all other parts of the plant. Phloem is mainly composed of sieve elements and their associated companion cells, together with some ◊sclerenchyma and ◊parenchyma cell types. Sieve elements are long, thin-walled cells joined end to end forming sieve tubes; large pores in the end walls allow the continuous passage of nutrients. Phloem is usually found in association with ◊xylem, the water-conducting tissue, but unlike the latter it is a living tissue.

phlogiston term invented by G Stahl (1660–1734) to describe a hypothetical substance produced when something burns. The phlogiston theory has now been replaced by a corresponding theory of oxygen gain/loss.

phlox plant native to Siberia and N America. The British varieties are half-hardy annuals cultivated from *Phlox drummondii*. They have lanceolate, opposite leaves, and flowers, borne in panicles.

Phnom Penh /'nɒm 'pen/ capital of Kampuchea, on the Mekong, 210 km/130 mi NW of Saigon; an important trade centre with textile and food-processing industries; population (1981) 400,000.

phobia an excessive irrational fear, for example, agoraphobia (fear of open spaces and crowded places), acrophobia (fear of heights), claustrophobia (fear of enclosed places). ◊Behaviour therapy is one form of treatment.

Phobos and Deimos the two small moons of the planet ◊Mars, discovered in 1877 by the American astronomer Asaph Hall at the US Naval Observatory, Washington DC. Both are irregularly shaped lumps of rock, cratered by ◊meteorite impacts. Phobos is 27×19 km/17×12 mi across, and orbits Mars every 0.32 days. Deimos measures 15×11 km/9×7 mi and orbits every 1.26 days. They are thought to be ◊asteroids captured by the gravity of Mars.

Phoenicia /fə'nɪʃɪə/ ancient Greek name for the seaboard of Lebanon and Syria, N of Mount Carmel, inhabited in ancient times by a people who called themselves Canaanites (see ◊Canaan). They were seafaring traders and artisans, who visited the Scillies (and possibly Cornwall) and are said to have circumnavigated Africa, and their cities (Tyre and Sidon being the chief) were independent states ruled by hereditary kings, but dominated by merchant oligarchies. Documents found at ◊Ugarit in 1929 give much information on their civilization, and their deities include El, Baal, Anat, Astarte or Ashtaroth, and Melkart or Moloch. Their colonies were established in Cyprus, N Africa (for example, Carthage), Malta, Sicily, and Spain, and competition from these combined with the attacks of the Sea Peoples, the Assyrians and Greeks, on the cities in Phoenicia led to their ultimate decline: the fall of Tyre to Alexander the Great in 332 BC ended the separate history of Phoenicia.

Phoenix /'fiːnɪks/ capital of Arizona, USA; industrial city (steel, aluminium, electrical and electronic goods, food processing) and tourist centre; population (1984) 866,500.

phoenix mythical Egyptian bird that burned itself to death on a pyre every 500 years, and rose rejuvenated from the ashes.

Phoenix Islands /'fiːnɪks/ group of eight islands in the South Pacific, included in Kiribati; total land area 18 sq km/11 sq mi. Drought has rendered them all uninhabitable.

phon unit of loudness equal to the intensity in decibels of a sound with a frequency of 1,000 hertz and a sound pressure of 20×10^{-6} pascals that seems equally loud to the human ear.

phonetics the identification, description, and classification of sounds used in articulate speech. These sounds are codified in the International Phonetic Alphabet (a highly modifed version of the Roman alphabet). A *phoneme* is the range of sound which can be substituted without change of meaning in the words of a particular language, for example, 'r' and 'l' form a single phoneme in Japanese, but are two in English.

phoney war term used to describe the period in World War II between Oct 1939 when the Germans had defeated Poland, and Apr 1940 when Denmark and Norway were invaded. There were few signs of hostilities in Western Europe, indeed Hitler made attempts to arrange a peace settlement with Britain and France.

phonograph the name Thomas ◊Edison gave to his sound-recording apparatus, which developed into the modern ◊record player.

phosphate any salt of phosphorous oxy-acids, including hypophosphorous acid (H_3PO_2), phosphorous acid (H_3PO_3), hypophosphoric acid ($H_4P_2O_6$) and orthophosphoric acid (H_3PO_4). Phosphates are used as fertilizers.

phosphor a substance that gives out visible light when it is illuminated by a beam of electrons or ◊ultraviolet light. The television screen is coated on the inside with phosphors which glow when beams of electrons strike them. Fluorescent lamp tubes are also phosphor-coated.

phosphorescence in physics, the emission of light by certain substances after they have absorbed energy, whether from visible light, other electromagnetic radiation such as ultraviolet rays or X-rays, or ◊cathode rays (a beam of electrons). When the stimulating energy is removed phosphorescence ceases, although it may persist for a short time after (unlike ◊fluorescence, which stops immediately). The most common uses of phosphorescent substances, called phosphors, are as light-emitting coatings on the inside of television screens, in so-called fluorescent lamps and tubes, in day-glo paints and as optical brighteners in detergents.

When exposed to an external energy source, the outer electrons in atoms of a phosphorescent substance absorb energy and are stimulated to occupy atomic orbitals at a higher energy level. When these electrons 'jump' back to their former level they emit their excess energy in the form of light. The term phosphorescence as applied to the emission of light by certain living organisms is more properly called ◊bioluminescence.

phosphorus an element that is essential to life, discovered by the German alchemist Hennig Brand in 1669: symbol P, atomic number 15, atomic weight 30.975. It occurs in several forms, the commonest being white phosphorus (a waxy solid emitting a greenish glow in air, burning spontaneously to phosphorus pentoxide, and very poisonous) and red phosphorus (neither igniting spontaneously nor poisonous). Production of phosphorus and its compounds has greatly increased since World War II, for example, the use of ◊phosphates as fertilizers, in matches in

the prevention of scale and corrosion in pipes and boiler tubes, and in certain organic chemicals.

photocell or *photoelectric cell* device for measuring or detecting light, or other electromagnetic radiation. In a *photoemissive* cell the radiation causes electrons to be emitted and a current to flow (see ◊photoelectric effect); a *photovoltaic* cell causes an ◊electromotive force to be generated in the presence of light across the boundary of two substances. A *photoconductive* cell, which is semiconductor-based, increases its conductivity when exposed to electromagnetic radiation. They are used for photographers' exposure meters, burglar and fire alarms, automatic doors, and in solar arrays.

photocopier machine that uses some form of photographic process to produce copies of documents. The most common modern type, pioneered by the American Xerox Corporation, uses electrostatic photocopying, or xerography ('dry writing'). It employs a drum coated with a light-sensitive material such as selenium, which holds a pattern of static electricity charges corresponding to the dark areas of an image projected on to the drum by a lens. Finely divided pigment (called toner) of opposite electric charge sticks to the charged areas of the drum, and is then transferred to a sheet of paper which is heated briefly to melt the toner and make it stick to the paper. Additional facilities include enlargement and reduction, copying on both sides of the sheet of paper, and copying in colour.

photoelectric effect in physics, the emission of ◊electrons from a metallic surface when it is struck by ◊photons (quanta of electromagnetic radiation), usually those of visible light or ◊ultraviolet radiation. The energy of the emitted electrons depends on the frequency of the incident radiation (which must exceed a characteristic threshold frequency); the higher the frequency, the greater the energy of its photons. The number of electrons emitted depends on the radiation's intensity (rate of transfer of energy per unit area). The theory of the photoelectric effect, a ◊quantum theory of radiation, was formulated in 1905, by ◊Einstein.

photofit system aiding the identification of wanted criminals. Witnesses select photographs of a single feature (hair, eyes, nose, mouth), their choices resulting in a composite likeness, then re-photographed and circulated. It is a sophisticated development by Jacques Penry in 1970 for Scotland Yard of the identikit system evolved by an American, Hugh C McDonald (1913–).

photogram a picture produced on photographic material by means of exposing it to light, but without using a camera.

photography a process for producing images on sensitized materials by various forms of radiant energy, for example, visible light, ultraviolet, infrared, X-rays; radioactive radiation; electron beam.

photometer an instrument that measures luminous intensity. Bunsen's early greasespot photometer compares the intensity of a light source with a known source by each illuminating half of a translucent area. Modern photometers

use ◊photocells, as in a photographer's exposure meter; a ◊photomultiplier can also be used.

photomultiplier an instrument that detects low levels of electromagnetic radiation (usually visible ◊light or ◊infrared radiation) and amplifies it to produce a detectable signal. One type resembles a ◊photocell with an additional series of coated ◊electrodes (called dynodes) between the ◊cathode and ◊anode. Radiation striking the cathode releases electrons (primary emission) which hit the first dynode, producing yet more electrons by ◊secondary emission which go on to strike the second dynode and so on. The result is a cascade effect, with a measurable signal up to 100 million times larger than the original signal eventually leaving the anode. Similar devices, more properly called image intensifiers, are used in television camera tubes that 'see' in the dark.

photon in physics, the smallest 'package', 'particle', or quantum of energy in which ◊light, or any other form of electromagnetic radiation, is emitted.

photoperiodism a biological mechanism which controls the timing of certain activities by responding to changes in day length. The flowering of many plants is initiated in this way, in autumn-flowering species by days that are shorter than a critical length (for example, chrysanthemum and soybean), in spring-flowering ones by days that are longer than a given length (such as radish and lettuce). Photoperiodism in plants is regulated by a light-sensitive pigment, phytochrome. The breeding seasons of many temperate animals are also triggered by changing day length: in autumn-breeding mammals such as goats and deer by declining day length, in spring-breeding birds by increasing day length. See also ◊biorhythms.

photosphere the visible surface of the Sun, which emits the light and heat we receive on Earth. About 300 km/200 mi deep, it consists of incandescent gas at a temperature of 5,800 K or about 5,500°C. Rising cells of hot gas produce a mottling of the photosphere known as *granulation*, each granule being about the size of the British Isles. The photosphere is often marked by large, dark patches called ◊sunspots.

photosynthesis the process by which green plants and photosynthetic bacteria and cyanobacteria utilize light energy from the sun to produce food molecules (◊carbohydrates) from carbon dioxide and water. There are two distinct stages within the process. During the *light reaction* sunlight is used to split water (H_2O) into oxygen (O_2), protons (hydrogen ions, H^+) and electrons. Oxygen is given off as a by-product during the light reaction. The protons and electrons are then used to convert carbon dioxide (CO_2) into carbohydrates (CH_2O) constituting the *dark reaction*, for which sunlight is not required. Photosynthesis is dependent on the ability of ◊chlorophyll to capture the energy of sunlight and use it to split water molecules. Other pigments, such as ◊carotenoids, are also involved in capturing light energy and passing it on to chlorophyll. Photosynthesis by cyanobacteria was responsible for the appearance of oxygen in the Earth's atmosphere 2,500 million years ago,

PHOTOGRAPHY: CHRONOLOGY

1515 Leonardo da Vinci described the camera obscura.

1750 The painter Canaletto used a camera obscura as an aid to his painting in Venice.

1790 Thomas Wedgewood in England made photograms – placing objects on leather, sensitized using silver nitrate.

1826 Nicephore Niépce (1765–1833), a French doctor, produced the world's first photograph from nature on pewter plates with a camera obscura and an eight-hour exposure.

1835 Niépce and L J M Daguerre produced the first daguerreotype camera photograph.

1839 Daguerre was awarded an annuity by the French government and his process given to the world.

1841 Fox Talbot's calotype process was patented – the first multi-copy method of photography using a negative/positive process, sensitized with silver iodide.

1843 Hill and Adamson began to use calotypes for portraits in Edinburgh.

1844 Fox Talbot published the first photographic book, *The Pencil of Nature*.

1851 Fox Talbot used a one-thousandth of a second exposure to demonstrate high-speed photography.

1855 Roger Fenton made documentary photographs of the Crimean War from a specially constructed caravan with a portable darkroom.

1859 Under the pseudonym Nadar, Gaspard-Felix Tournachan (1820–1910), French writer, caricaturist and photographer, made photographs underground in Paris using battery-powered arc lights.

1860 Queen Victoria was photographed by Mayall. Abraham Lincoln was photographed by Matthew Brady for political campaigning.

1861 The single lens reflex plate camera was patented by Thomas Sutton.

1862 Nadar took aerial photographs over Paris.

1870 Julia Margaret Cameron used long lenses for her distinctive portraits.

1878 In the USA Eadweard Muybridge analysed the movements of animals through sequential photographs, using a series of cameras.

1880 A silver bromide emulsion was fixed with hypo. Photographs were first reproduced in newspapers in New York using the half-tone engraving process. The first twin-lens reflex camera was produced in London.

1889 Eastman Company in the USA produced the Kodak No. 1 camera and roll film, facilitating universal, hand-held snapshots.

1902 In Germany Deckel invented a prototype leaf shutter and Zeiss introduced the Tessar lens.

1904 The autochrome colour process was patented by the Lumière brothers.

1905 Alfred Steiglitz opened the gallery '291' in New York promoting photography. Lewis Hine used photography to expose the exploitation of children in American factories, causing protective laws to be passed.

1907 The autochrome process began to be factory-produced.

1914 Oskar Barnack designed a prototype Leica camera for Leitz in Germany.

1924 Leitz launched the first 35 mm camera, the Leica, delayed because of World War I. It became very popular with photo-journalists because it was quiet, small, dependable and had a range of lenses and accessories.

1929 Rolleiflex produced a twin-lens reflex camera in Germany.

1935 In the USA, Mannes and Godowsky invented Kodachrome transparency film, which has great sharpness and rich colour quality. Electronic flash was invented in the USA. Social documentary photography received wide attention through the photographs of Dorothea Lange, Margaret Bourke-White, Arthur Rothstein, Walker Evans, and others taken for the US government's Farm Security Administration of the plight of the poor tenant farmers in the mid-West.

1936 *Life* magazine, noted for photo-journalism, was first published in the USA.

1938 *Picture Post* magazine was introduced in the UK.

1940 Multigrade enlarging paper by Ilford was made available in the UK.

1945 The Zone System of exposure estimation was explained in the book *Exposure Record* by Ansel Adams.

1947 Polaroid black and white instant process film was invented by Dr Edwin Land, who set up the Polaroid corporation in Boston, Massachusetts. The principles of holography were demonstrated in England by Dennis Gabor.

1955 Kodak introduced Tri-X, a black and white 200 ASA film.

1959 The zoom lens was invented in Germany by Voigtlander.

1960 Laser was invented in the USA, making holography possible. Polacolor, a self-processing colour film, was introduced by Polaroid, using a 60-second colour film and dye diffusion technique.

1963 Cibachrome, paper and chemicals for printing directly from transparencies, was made available by Ciba-Geigy of Switzerland. One of the most permanent processes, it is marketed by Ilford in the UK.

1969 Photographs were taken on the Moon by US astronauts.

1972 SX70 system, a single lens reflex camera with instant prints, was produced by Polaroid.

1980 Ansel Adams sold an original print *Moonrise: Hernandez* for $45,000, a record price, in the USA. Voyager 1 sent photographs of Saturn back to Earth across space.

1985 Minolta Corporation in Japan introduced the world's first body-integral autofocus single lens reflex camera.

---

and photosynthesis by plants maintains the oxygen level today.

phrase structure grammar a theory of language structure which proposes that a given language has several different potential sentence patterns, consisting of various sorts of phrase, which can be expanded in various ways. For example, the sentence 'the girl opened the door' contains a noun phrase 'the girl', and a verb phrase 'opened the door'.

phrenology theory, now discredited, of the Viennese physician Dr Franz Josef Gall (1758–1828) that the skull shape revealed psychological and intellectual features.

Phrygia /ˈfrɪdʒɪə/ former kingdom of western Asia covering the Anatolian tableland. Inhabited in ancient times by an Indo-European people; it achieved great prosperity in the 8th century BC under a line of kings bearing in turn the names Gordius and Midas, but then fell under Lydian rule. From Phyrigia the cult of Cybele was introduced into Greece and Rome.

Phryne /ˈfraɪnɪ/ Athenian courtesan famous for her beauty.

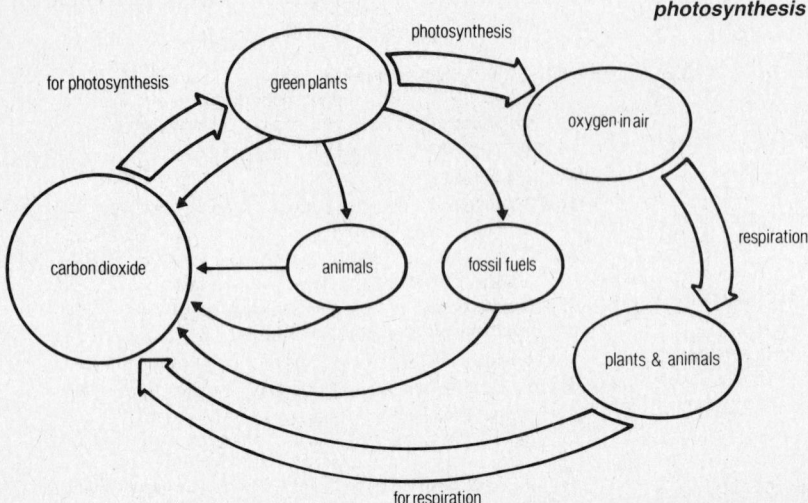

photosynthesis

photosynthesis

green plants

for photosynthesis

oxygen in air

respiration

carbon dioxide

animals

fossil fuels

plants & animals

for respiration

phyllite a ◊metamorphic rock produced by pressure in which mica crystals are aligned so that the rock splits along their plane of orientation, the resulting break being shiny and smooth. It is intermediate between ◊shale and ◊schist.

phyllotaxis the arrangement of leaves on a plant stem. Leaves are nearly always arranged in a regular pattern and in the majority of plants they are inserted singly, either in a *spiral* arrangement up the stem, or on *alternate* sides. Other principal forms are opposite leaves, where two arise from the same node, and whorled, where three or more arise from the same node.

phylloxera aphid-like insect. The species *Phylloxera vitifolia*, a native of North America, attacks grape vines, laying its eggs under the bark. European vines are especially susceptible and many French vineyards suffered terribly on the arrival of the pest in Europe in the 19th century; most European vines are now grafted on to root stock of the American vine, which is not as susceptible to the disease. The phylloxera bug (hemipteran) may be destroyed by spraying with carbon disulphide or petroleum.

phylogeny the historical sequence of changes that occurs in a given ◊species during the course of evolution. See also ◊ontogeny.

phylum a major grouping in biological classification (plural *phyla*). Mammals, birds, reptiles, amphibians, and fish belong to the phylum Chordata; the phylum Mollusca consists of snails, slugs, mussels and clams, squid and octopuses; the phylum Porifera contains sponges, and the phylum Echinodermata includes starfish, sea urchins, and sea cucumbers. Among plants there are between four and nine phyla depending on the classification used; all flowering plants belong to a single phylum, Angiospermata, and all conifers to another, Gymnospermata. Related phyla are grouped together in a ◊kingdom; phyla are subdivided into ◊classes.

physics (formerly also called 'natural philosophy') a branch of science concerned with

the ultimate laws that govern the structure of the universe, and forms of matter and energy and their interactions. For convenience, physics is often divided into branches such as nuclear physics, solid and liquid state physics, ◊electricity, ◊electronics and ◊magnetism, ◊optics, ◊acoustics, heat and ◊thermodynamics.

physiological psychology an aspect of ◊experimental psychology.

physiology that branch of biology which deals with the functioning of living animals. See also ◊anatomy.

physiotherapy use of external means such as heat (infrared lamps, hot water), electrical stimulation (low-voltage currents), massage, and exercise to treat patients suffering from a number of conditions, including rheumatism and lung complaints; most common now are sports injuries.

Piacenza /ˌpiːə'tʃentsə/ industrial city (agricultural machinery, textiles, pottery) in Emilia-Romagna, Italy, on the Po, 65 km/40 mi SE of Milan; population (1984) 107,000. The Roman *Placentia*, Piacenza dates from 218 BC and has a 12th-century cathedral.

Piaf /'piːæf/ Edith. Stage name of Edith Gassion 1915–1963. French Parisian singer and songwriter. Her defiant song 'Je ne regrette rien/I Regret Nothing' reflected an emotionally full life that ended in drink and drugs.

Piaget /pi'æʒeɪ/ Jean 1896–1980. Swiss psychologist known for his studies of the development of thought, concepts of space and movement, logic and reasoning in children.

pianoforte (**piano**) a stringed musical instrument, whose keyed hammers make it percussive and capable of soft (piano) or strong (forte) tones – hence its name. The ◊clavichord and the 16th-century ◊virginal were forerunners of the design evolved in 1709 by Bartolommeo Cristofori, a Paduan harpsichord-maker. Subsequent improvement has been closely linked with the names of famous pianoforte makers, such as Broadwood and Stodart, Pleyel, Erard, Collard, Steinway, Blüthner, and Bechstein. The

practice of building the strings vertically has prevailed in the upright pianoforte. The horizontally strung grand piano is recognized as superior in tone and is used for concert performance. In modern times there has been a revival of manufacture of earlier keyboard instruments such as the ◊harpsichord to recreate baroque and early classical music on the instruments for which it was composed.

Piazzi /pi'ætsi/ Giuseppe 1746–1826. Italian astronomer, director of Palermo Observatory. In 1801 he discovered the first asteroid, which he named ◊Ceres.

Picabia /pɪ'kɑːbiə/ Francis 1879–1953. French artist of Spanish origin. Constantly in search of new ideas he anticipated many developments of American art in the 1960s.

Picardy /'pɪkədi/ (French *Picardie*) region of N France, including Aisne, Oise, and Somme *départements*.

picaresque (Spanish *picaro* 'rogue') in literature, a genre of novels which take for their heroes rogues and villains, telling their story in a series of loosely linked episodes. Examples include Defoe's *Moll Flanders*, Smollett's *Roderick Random*, and Fielding's *Tom Jones*.

Picasso /pɪ'kæsəʊ/ Pablo 1881–1973. Spanish artist. Born in Málaga, son of an art teacher, José Ruiz Blasco, and an Andalusian mother, Maria Picasso López; he discontinued use of the name Ruiz in 1898. He was a mature artist at ten, and at 16 was holding his first exhibition. In 1900 he made an initial visit to Paris, where he was to settle, and during his Blue Period 1901–04 painted mystic distorted figures in blue tones; a brief, more supple, Rose Period 1905–06 followed, but in 1907 he completed the revolutionary *Les Demoiselles d'Avignon* by which ◊Cubism was fully launched. Picasso has also been regarded as the founder of ◊Surrealism, but his subsequent development included by turns Classicism, Romanticism, ◊Realism, ◊Expressionism, ◊Abstractionism, and ◊Naturalism, and ranged through ceramics, sculpture, sets for ballet (for example *Parade* in 1917 for Diaghilev), book illustrations, and portraits (Stravinsky, Valéry, and others). By the 1930s his work took on a more serious foreboding and anguished aspect, culminating in *Guernica* 1936, where all his expressive innovations are used to show the universal horror felt in the civilized world by Franco's bombing of a Basque town in the ◊Spanish Civil War. He continued to paint into his 80s.

Piccard /pɪ'kɑː/ August 1884–1962. Swiss scientist, who carried out aerial and undersea research. Born in Basel, he became professor of physics at the University of Brussels in 1922. In 1931–32 he and his twin brother Jean Félix made ascents to 16,800 m/55,000 ft in a balloon of his own design, resulting in important discoveries concerning such stratospheric phenomena as ◊cosmic rays. Subsequently he built and used bathyscaphes for research under the sea.

piccolo a musical instrument of the ◊flute family.

Pickford /'pɪkfəd/ Mary (born Gladys Smith) 1893–1979. American actress. She and

PHYSICS: LANDMARKS

c.400 BC	The first 'atomic' theory was put forward by Democritus.
c.250 BC	Archimedes' principle of buoyancy was established.
1600 AD	Magnetism was described by English physicist and physician William Gilbert (1544–1603).
c.1610	The principle of falling bodies descending to Earth at the same speed was established by Galileo.
1642	The principles of hydraulics were put forward by French mathematician, physicist, and philosopher Blaise Pascal (1623–62).
1643	The mercury barometer was invented by Italian physicist Evangelista Torricelli (1608–47).
1656	The pendulum clock was invented by Dutch physicist and astronomer Christiaan Huygens (1629–95).
c.1665	Newton put forward the law of gravity, stating that the Earth exerts a constant force on falling bodies.
1677	The simple microscope was invented by Dutch microscopist Antoni van Leeuwenhoek (1632–1723).
1690	The wave theory of light was propounded by Huygens.
1704	The corpuscular theory of light was put forward by Newton.
1714	The mercury thermometer was invented by German physicist (Gabriel) Daniel Fahrenheit.
1771	The link between nerve action and electricity was discovered by Italian anatomist and pysiologist Luigi Galvani (1737–98).
1795	The metric system was adopted in France.
1798	The link between heat and friction was discovered by American-British physicist Count Benjamin Thomson Rumford (1753–1814).
1800	Volta invented the Voltaic cell.
1808	The 'modern' atomic theory was propounded by British physicist and chemist John Dalton (1766–1844).
1811	Avogadro's hypothesis relating volumes and numbers of molecules of gases was proposed by Italian physicist and chemist Amedeo Avogadro (1776–1856).
1815	Refraction of light was explained by French physicist Augustin Fresnel (1788–1827).
1819	The discovery of electromagnetism was made by Danish physicist Hans Oersted (1777–1851).
1821	The dynamo principle was described by British physicist and chemist Michael Faraday (1791–1867); the thermocouple was discovered by German physicist Thomas Seebeck (1770–1831).
1827	*Ohm's law* was established by German physicist G.S. Ohm; Brownian motion resulting from molecular vibrations was observed by British botanist Robert Brown (1773–1858).
1831	Electromagnetic induction was discovered by Faraday.
1842	The principle of conservation of energy was observed by German physician and physicist Julius von Mayer (1814–78).
c.1847	The mechanical equivalent of heat was described by Joule.
1849	A measurement of speed of light was put forward by French physicist Armand Fizeau (1819–96).
1851	The rotation of the Earth was demonstrated by Foucault.
1859	Spectrographic analysis was made by German chemist Robert Bunsen (1811–99) and German physicist Gustav Kirchhoff (1824–87).
1861	Osmosis was discovered.
1873	Light was conceived as electromagnetic radiation by British physicist James Clerk Maxwell.
1877	A theory of sound as vibrations in an elastic medium was propounded by British physicist John Rayleigh (1842–1919).
1887	The existence of radio waves was predicted by Hertz.
1895	X-rays were discovered by German physicist Wilhelm Röntgen (1845–1923).
1896	The discovery of radioactivity was made by French physicist Antoine Becquerel (1852–1908).
1897	The electron was discovered by J J Thomson.
1899	Rutherford discovered alpha and beta rays.
1900	Quantum theory was propounded by Planck; the discovery of gamma rays was made by French physicist Paul-Ulrich Villard (1860–1934).
1902	Heaviside discovered the ionosphere.
1904	The theory of radioactivity was put forward by Rutherford and British chemist Frederick Soddy (1877–1966).
1905	Einstein propounded his *special theory of relativity*.
1911	The discovery of the atomic nucleus was made by Rutherford.
1915	Einstein put forward his *general theory of relativity*; X-ray crystallography was discovered by William and Lawrence Bragg.
1922	The orbiting electron atomic theory was propounded by Bohr.
1924	Appleton made his study of the Heaviside layer.
1927	The uncertainty principle of atomic physics was established by German physicist Werner Heisenberg (1901–76).
1928	Wave mechanics was introduced by Schrödinger.
1931	The cyclotron was developed by American physicist Ernest Lawrence (1901–58).
1932	The discovery of the neutron was made by Chadwick; the electron microscope was developed by Soviet-American physicist Vladimir Zworykin (1889–1982).
1933	The positron, the antiparticle of the electron, was discovered by Millikan.
1934	Artificial radioactivity was developed by Frédéric and Irène Joliot-Curie.
1939	The discovery of nuclear fission was made by Hahn and German chemist Fritz Strassman (1902–).
1942	The first controlled nuclear chain reaction was achieved by Fermi.
1956	The neutrino, a fundamental particle, was discovered.
1960	The Mössbauer effect of atom emissions was discovered by German physicist Rudolf Mössbauer (1929–); the first maser was developed by American physicist Theodore Maiman (1927–).
1963	Maiman developed the first laser (a term for *l*ight *a*mplification by *s*timulated *e*mission of *r*adiation).

Picasso Widely regarded as the artistic giant of the 20th century, Picasso continued to work until he was well into his 80s.

her second husband (from 1920), Douglas ◊Fairbanks senior, were known as 'the world's sweethearts'.

Pico della Mirandola /'piːkəʊ ˌdelə mɪˈræn dələ/ Count Giovanni 1463–1494. Italian mystic philosopher. He studied Hebrew, Chaldean, and Arabic, showing particular interest in the Jewish and theosophical system, the ◊Kabbala. His attempt to reconcile the religious base of Christianity, Islam, and the ancient world displeased Pope Alexander VI.

picric acid a yellow crystalline solid $C_6H_2(NO_2)_3OH$, 2,4,6-trinitrophenol. It is a strong acid, which is used to dye wool and silks yellow, for the treatment of burns, and in the manufacture of explosives.

Pict Roman term for a member of the peoples of N Scotland, possibly meaning 'painted' (tattooed). Probably of pre-Celtic origin, and speaking a non-Celtic language, the Picts were united with the Celtic Scots under the rule of Kenneth MacAlpin in 844.

Picton /'pɪktən/ small port at the NE extremity of South Island, New Zealand, with a ferry to Wellington in North Island.

pidgin English /'pɪdʒɪn 'ɪŋglɪʃ/ commonly and loosely used to mean any kind of 'broken' or 'native' version of the English language, pidgin English proper began as a trade jargon or contact language between the British and the Chinese in the 19th century. It combined words of English with a rough-and-ready Chinese grammatical

structure, while Melanesian pidgin English (also known as *Tok Pisin*) tends to combine English and the syntax of local Melanesian languages. Thus, instead of the English pronoun 'we', Melanesian pidgin English has both *yumi* (you and me, speaking to each other) and *mifela* (me and fellow, excluding you). See also ◊Creole languages.

pidgin languages trade jargons, contact languages, or lingua francas arising in ports and markets where people of different linguistic backgrounds meet. Generally, a pidgin comes into existence to answer short-term needs, for example Korean Bamboo English as used during the Korean War. Unless there is a reason for extending the life of such a hybrid form it will fade away when the need passes. Usually a blend of the vocabulary of one language with the syntax or grammar of one or more other groups. ◊Pidgin English in various parts of the world, *francais petit negre*, and bazaar Hindi or Hindustani are examples of pidgins which have served long-term purposes, to the extent of being acquired by children as one of their everyday languages.

Pieck /piːk/ Wilhelm 1876–1960. German communist politician. He was a leader of the 1919 Spartacist revolt and a founder of the Socialist Unity Party in 1946, and from 1949 was president of the German Democratic Republic: the office was abolished on his death.

Piedmont /'piːdmɒnt/ (Italian *Piemonte*)a region of N Italy, bordering Switzerland on the N and France on the W and surrounded, except on the E, by the Alps and the Apennines
area 25,399 sq km/9,804 sq mi
capital Turin
towns Alessandria, Asti, Vercelli, Novara
features fertile Po river valley
products agricultural; cars
population (1984) 4,412,000
history from Piedmont, under the house of Savoy, the movement for the unification of Italy started in the 19th century.

Piero della Francesca /pi'eərəʊ ˌdelə fræn 'tʃeskə/ c. 1418–1492. Italian Renaissance artist, born in San Sepolcro, Tuscany. A member of the Umbrian school, he was one of the earliest painters in oils and wrote a treatise on perspective. His mastery of geometry, proportion, form, and colour is breathtakingly evident in his series of frescoes of the *Legend of the True Cross* in the church of San Francesco, Arezzo, 1452–66.

Piero di Cosimo /pi'eərəʊ diː 'kɒzɪməʊ/ c. 1462–c. 1521. Italian artist, much influenced by ◊Signorelli and ◊Leonardo da Vinci, and noted for mythical subjects.

Pietermaritzburg /ˌpiːtəˈmærɪtsbɜːg/ industrial city (footware, furniture, brewing), capital from 1842 of Natal, South Africa; population (1980) 179,000. Founded 1838 by Boer trekkers, it was named after their leaders, Piet Retief and Gert Maritz, killed by the Zulus.

Pietism movement within ◊Lutheranism in the 17th century which emphasized spiritual and devotional Christianity.

Pietro /pi'etrəʊ/ Berrettini da Cortona 1596–1669. Italian painter and architect and one

of the initiators of the Roman High ◊Baroque style. He painted huge frescoes, for example the *Allegory of Divine Providence* 1629–37 in the Barberini Palace, Rome, glorifying the pope and his family. Hundreds of figures are drawn upwards towards God's golden light in which swarm bees, the Barberini family emblem.

piezoelectric effect property of some ◊crystals, for example, ◊quartz, of developing an electromotive force or voltage across opposite faces when subjected to a mechanical strain, and, conversely, of altering in size when subjected to an electromotive force. Piezoelectric crystal ◊oscillators are used as frequency standards, for example, replacing balance wheels in watches.

pig hoofed mammal of family Suidae. The European *wild boar Sus scrofa* is the ancestor of domesticated breeds; it is 1.5 m/4.5 ft long and 1 m/3 ft high, with formidable tusks, but not naturally aggressive. Other wild pigs include the ◊babirusa, and the ◊warthog. Of the domestic pigs, the Tamworth is a survival from the Iron Age; modern breeders aim at a heavy carcass and lean meat, for example by a hybrid of the Landrace, Saddleback, and Large White.

Pigalu /ˌpiːgəˈluː/ island (formerly Annobon) in Equatorial Guinea; area 17 sq km/7 sq mi; its inhabitants are descended from slaves of the Portuguese and still speak a form of that language.

pigeon general term for members of the family Columbidae, sometimes also called doves, distinguished by their large crops which, becoming glandular in the breeding season, secrete a milky fluid ('pigeon's milk') which aids digestion of food for the young. There are many species, one of the most important being the rock dove *Columba livia* from which the domesticated varieties derive (pouter, fantail, homer). Similar is the stock-dove *Columba oenas*, but the wood-pigeon *Columba palumbus* is much larger and has white patches on the neck. The American species include the passenger-pigeon, *Ectopistes migratorius*, once millions strong but extinct from 1914, and the mourning-doves, which (like the European turtle-doves) live much on the ground. The fruit pigeons of Australasia and the Malay regions are beautifully coloured.

pigeon racing sport of transporting domesticated pigeons to a given location, from where they fly back to their home lofts, and their arrival is timed; in Britain the National Homing Union dates from 1896 and Elizabeth II has a racing pigeon manager.

Piggott /'pɪgət/ Lester 1935– . British jockey. He was many times champion, and had nine Derby wins. He retired in 1985, and took up training horses. In 1987 he was imprisoned for tax evasion.

Pigou /'pɪguː/ Arthur Cecil 1877–1959. British economist, whose notion of the 'real balance effect' (the 'Pigou effect') contended that employment was stimulated by a fall in prices, because the latter increased liquid wealth and thus demand for goods and services.

Pigs, Bay of inlet on the S coast of Cuba about 145 km/90 mi SW of Havana: the site of an unsuccessful invasion attempt by 1,500 anti-

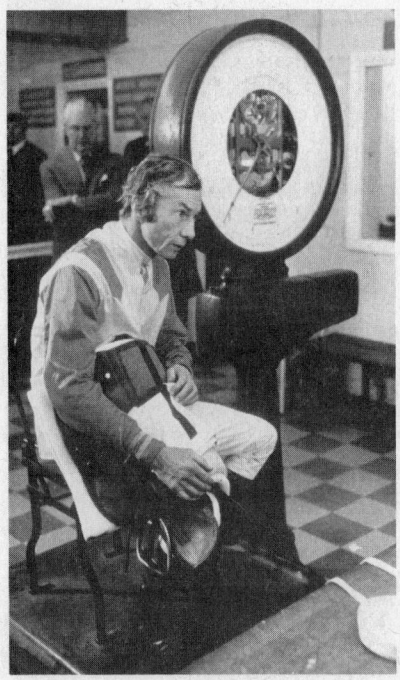

Piggott Last weigh-in for champion jockey Lester Piggott after the final Handicap Stakes, Nottingham, 29 Oct 1985. He rode more than 4,000 winners, many of them in the classic races in Britain, France, and the USA.

Castro Cuban exiles 17–20 Apr 1961. 1,173 were taken prisoner. The anti-revolutionary force was created by the CIA authorized by the Eisenhower administration and the project was executed under that of J F Kennedy. In 1962 most of the Cuban prisoners were ransomed for $53 million in food and medicine.

pika also known as *mouse-hare*, small mammal of the family Ochotonidae belonging with rabbits and hares in the order Lagomorpha. Pikas have short rounded ears and most species are about 20 cm/8 in long, with greyish-brown fur and no visible tail. They live from SE USSR across N Asia and also in the Rocky Mountains of N America. The warning call is a sharp whistle. They are vegetarian and in late summer cut grasses and other plants and place them in piles to dry as hay, which is then stored for the winter.

pike freshwater sporting fish *Esox lucius* family Esocidae, of Europe and N America; it is a voracious feeder and may reach 1.5 m/5 ft.

pike-perch freshwater fish *Stizostedion lucioperca*, related to the perch. The European pike-perch has been introduced to Britain: it reaches over 1 m/3 ft, is voracious, and of some value as a food fish.

Pikes Peak /ˈpaɪks ˈpiːk/ mountain in the Rampart range of the Rocky Mountains, Colorado, USA; 4,300 m/14,110 ft. It was discovered by Lt Zebulon M Pike 1806.

Pilate /ˈpaɪlət/ Pontius Roman procurator of Judaea 26–36 AD. Unsympathetic to the Jews, his actions several times provoked riots, and in

36 AD he was recalled to Rome to account for disorder in Samaria. The gospels describe his reluctant ordering of Christ's crucifixion. The Greek historian ◊Eusebius says he committed suicide.

pilchard fish *Sardina pilchardus* of the herring family. Bluish-green above and silvery beneath, it grows to 25 cm/10 in long. The chief pilchard fisheries are off Spain and Portugal.

pilgrimage journey to sacred places inspired by religious devotion. For Hindus the holy places include Benares and the purifying Ganges; for Buddhists the places connected with the crises of Buddha's career; for the ancient Greeks the shrines at Delphi, Ephesus, among others; for the Jews, the sanctuary at Jerusalem; and for Muslims, Mecca. Among Christians, pilgrimages were common by the 2nd century, and as a direct result of the established necessity of making pilgrimages there arose numerous hospices catering for pilgrims, the religious orders of knighthood, and the Crusades. The great centres of Christian pilgrimages have been, or are, Jerusalem, Rome, the tomb of St James of Compostela in Spain, the shrine of Becket at Canterbury, and the holy places at La Salette and Lourdes in France.

pilgrimage Hindu pilgrims bathe in the Ganges from the ghats at Varanesi in the ritual purification.

Pilgrimage of Grace a rebellion against Henry VIII of England 1536–37, originating in Yorkshire and Lincolnshire. The rising, headed by Robert Aske (died 1537), was directed against the policies of the monarch, particularly the dissolution of the monasteries and the effects of ◊enclosure. At its peak, the rebels controlled York and included the archbishop there among their number. A truce was arranged in Dec and the insurrection dispersed, but the rebels' demands were not met, and a further revolt broke out in 1537, which was suppressed with severity, with the execution of over 200 of the rebels.

Pilgrims name given to the emigrants who sailed from Plymouth in the *Mayflower* on 16 Sept 1620 to found the first colony in New England at New Plymouth, Massachusetts. Of the 102 passengers less than a quarter were Puritan refugees. They originally set sail in the *Mayflower* and *Speedwell* from Southampton on

5 Aug 1620, but had to put into Dartmouth when the latter needed repair. Bad weather then drove them into Plymouth Sound where the *Speedwell* was abandoned.

Pilgrims' Way track running from Winchester to Canterbury, England, which was the route of medieval pilgrims visiting the shrine of Thomas à Becket. Some 195 km/120 mi long, the Pilgrims' Way can still be traced for more than half its length.

pillory instrument of punishment consisting of a wooden frame set on a post, with holes in which the prisoner's head and hands were secured, bystanders threw whatever was available at the miscreant. Its use was abolished in England in 1837.

pilotfish small sea fish *Naucrates ductor*, which keeps station below sharks, turtles, or boats, using the shade as a base from which to prey on smaller fish. It is found in all warm oceans and grows to about 36 cm/1.2 ft.

Pilsen /ˈpɪlzən/ German form of Czechoslovakian town of ◊Plzeň.

Pilsudski /pɪlˈsʊdski/ Joseph 1867–1935. Polish politician. Born in Russian Poland, he founded the Polish Socialist Party in 1892, and was twice imprisoned for anti-Russian activities. During World War I he commanded a Polish force to fight for Germany, but fell under suspicion of intriguing with the Allies, and in 1917–18 was imprisoned by the Germans. When Poland became independent he was elected chief of state, and led the unsuccessful Polish attack on the USSR in 1920. He retired in 1923, but in 1926 led a military coup which established his dictatorship until his death.

Piltdown man /ˈpɪltdaʊn/ fossilized skull fragments 'discovered' by Charles Dawson (died 1916) at Piltdown, E Sussex in 1913; believed to be the earliest European human remains until proved a hoax 1953 (the jaw was that of an orang-utan). The most likely perpetrator was Samuel Woodhead, a lawyer friend of Dawson, who was an amateur palaeontologist.

pimento tree found in tropical America. The dried fruits of the species *Pimenta dioica* are used as a spice known as allspice.

pimpernel plant, genus *Anagallis* in the family Primulaceae. The scarlet pimpernel *A. arvensis* grows in cornfields and is easy to overlook, since the flowers open only in full sunshine. It is naturalized in N America.

Pincus /ˈpɪŋkəs/ Gregory 1903–1967. American biologist. Specializing in reproductive biology, he played a major role in the development of oral contraceptives.

Pindar /ˈpɪndə/ c. 552–442 BC. Greek poet, born near Thebes. He was noted for choral lyrics, 'Pindaric odes'.

Pindling /ˈpɪndlɪŋ/ (Lynden) Oscar 1930– . Bahamian politician. After studying law in London, he returned to the island to join the newly formed Progressive Liberal Party, and then became the first black prime minister of the Bahamas in 1967.

Pindus Mountains /ˈpɪndəs/ range in N central Greece, between Epirus and Thessaly: highest point Smolikas 2,637 m/8,652 ft.

pine evergreen coniferous tree genus *Pinus* with some 70–100 species, of which the Scots pine *Pinus sylvestris* is grown commercially for soft timber (deal) and its yield of turpentine, tar, and pitch. The oldest living thing is probably the bristlecone pine *Pinus aristata*, native to California, of which some specimens are said to be 4,600 years old.

pineal gland an outgrowth of the vertebrate ◊brain. In some lower vertebrates, this develops a lens and retina, which show it to be derived from an eye, or pair or eyes, situated on the top of the head in ancestral vertebrates. The pineal still detects light (through the skull) in some fish, lizards and birds. In fish that can change colour to match the background, it is the pineal that perceives the light level and controls the colour change by releasing ◊hormones which affect pigment distribution in the skin. In birds, the pineal detects changes in daylight and stimulates breeding behaviour as spring approaches (see ◊biorhythms). Mammals also have a pineal gland, but it is located within the brain. It secretes a hormone-like substance, melatonin, which may influence rhythms of activity (see ◊biological clock).

pineapple plant *Ananas comosus* native to S and Central America, now cultivated in many other tropical areas, such as Queensland, Australia. The mauvish flowers are produced midway in the second year, and subsequently consolidate with their bracts into a fleshy fruit.

pine-marten type of ◊marten, a small mammal.

Pinero /pɪˈnɪərəʊ/ Arthur Wing 1855–1934. British dramatist, a leading exponent of the 'well-made' play, author of *The Second Mrs Tanqueray* 1893, and the comedies *Trelawny of the 'Wells'* 1898, and *The Gay Lord Quex* 1899.

pink perennial plant of the genus *Dianthus* such as the maiden pink *Dianthus deltoides* found in dry grassy places. For garden forms see ◊carnation.

Pinkerton /ˈpɪŋkətən/ Allan 1819–1884. American detective, born in Glasgow. He founded 1852 Pinkerton's National Detective Agency, and the federal secret service from the system he developed during the ◊Civil War.

Pink Floyd British psychedelic rock group, which emerged from London's hippie scene in the late 1960s. It is perhaps best known for its albums *The Dark Side of the Moon* 1973 and *The Wall* 1979.

Pinkie, Battle of /ˈpɪŋki/ battle on 10 Sept 1547 near Musselburgh, Lothian, Scotland, in which the Scots were defeated by the English under the duke of Somerset.

pinna the primary division of a ◊pinnate leaf. In mammals, the external part of the ear.

pinnate leaf a leaf that is divided up into many small leaflets, arranged in rows along either side of a midrib, as in ash tres (*Fraxinus*). It is a type of compound ◊leaf. Each leaflet is known as a *pinna*, and where the pinnae are themselves divided, the secondary divisions are known as pinnules.

Pinochet Ugarte /ˈpiːnəʊʃeɪ uːˈɡɑːteɪ/ Augusto 1915– . Military ruler of Chile from 1973.

Pinochet began his army career in 1933 and reached the rank of full general in 1973, when he was made commander-in-chief; in the same year he led a CIA-backed coup that ousted and killed the Marxist president Dr Salvador Allende. Pinochet ruled ruthlessly, crushing all opposition. In 1986, despite widespread opposition to his harsh regime, he announced that he was considering remaining in office for another eight years.

pint liquid measure of capacity (0.6 litre), ½ of a quart, ⅛ of a gallon: equivalent to 20 fluid oz in imperial measure UK, and 16 fluid oz in USA.

Pinter /ˈpɪntə/ Harold 1930– . British dramatist and poet, born in E London, originally an actor. He specializes in the tragicomedy of the breakdown of communication, broadly in the tradition of the theatre of the ◊absurd, for example, *The Birthday Party* 1958 and *The Caretaker* 1960, and his favourite themes are unexplained threats and fears, mental disorders, sexual fantasy, and family quarrels. His many later successes include *The Homecoming* 1965, *Old Times* 1971, and *Betrayal* 1978. He writes for radio and television, and his screenplays include *The Go-Between* 1969 and *The French Lieutenant's Woman* 1982.

Pinturicchio /ˌpɪntuˈrɪkiəʊ/ (or Pintoricchio) pseudonym of Bernardino di Betti c. 1454–1513. Italian artist who assisted ◊Perugino in decorating the Sistine Chapel, Rome.

pinworm ◊nematode worm *Enterobius vermicularis*, an intestinal parasite of humans.

Pinyin the Chinese phonetic alphabet approved in 1956, and used from 1979 in transcribing all names of people and places from the Chinese language into foreign languages using the Roman alphabet. For example, Chou En-lai becomes Zhou Enlai, Hua Kuo-feng becomes Hua Guofeng, Teng Hsiao-ping becomes Deng Xiaoping, Peking becomes Beijing.

Pioneer probes a series of US space probes. The first Pioneers, launched 1958–1959, were intended Moon probes, but all failed to reach their target. Pioneer 5, launched in 1960, was the first of a series to study the ◊solar wind between the planets. Pioneer 10, launched in Mar 1972, was the first probe to reach ◊Jupiter, in Dec 1973; In 1983 it became the first probe to leave the solar system. Pioneer 11, launched in Apr 1973, passed Jupiter in Dec 1974 and then became the first probe to reach ◊Saturn in Sept 1979 before also heading out of the solar system. Pioneers 10 and 11 both carry plaques containing messages from Earth in case they are found by other civilizations among the stars. In May and Aug 1978 two Pioneer-Venus probes were launched. One went into orbit around ◊Venus, the other delivered instruments into the atmosphere of Venus.

Piozzi /piˈɒtsi/ Hester Lynch (born Salusbury) 1741–1821. British writer, best remembered for her friendship with Dr ◊Johnson. She published *Anecdotes of the late Samuel Johnson* 1786, and their correspondence 1788. Johnson had been a constant visitor to her house when she was married to her first husband, Henry Thrale, but after Thrale's death Johnson was alienated by her marriage to the musician Gabriel Piozzi.

pipefish fish related to seahorses but long and thin like a length of pipe. The **great pipefish** *Syngnathus acus* grows up to 50 cm/1.6 ft, and the male has a brood pouch for eggs and developing young.

pipeline a pipe for carrying water, oil, gas, or other material over long distances. They are widely used in water-supply and oil-and gas-distribution schemes. The USA has over 300,000 km/200,000 mi of oil pipelines alone. One of the longest is the ◊Trans-Alaskan Pipeline in Alaska.

Piper /ˈpaɪpə/ John 1903– . British artist. From early landscapes of southern England, he went on in the 1930s to two-dimensional abstracts; to pictures of air-raid destruction in World War II; then to architectural compositions against romantic backgrounds; theatre sets; and stained glass windows.

pipit name for several birds in the family Motacillidae allied to the wagtails. The European meadow pipit *Anthus pratensis* is about the size of a sparrow and streaky brown, but has a slender bill. It lives in open country and feeds on the ground.

piracy the taking of a ship, or any of its contents, from lawful ownership while on the high seas, punishable under international law by the court of any country where the pirate may be found or taken. Algiers (see ◊corsairs), the West Indies (see ◊buccaneers), the coast of Trucial Oman (the Pirate Coast), Chinese and Malay waters, and such hideouts as Lundy Island were long pirate haunts, but modern communications and the complexities of supplying and servicing modern vessels tend to eliminate piracy. The contemporary equivalent is ◊hijacking.

Piraeus /paɪˈriːəs/ port of both ancient and modern ◊Athens and main port of Greece, on the Gulf of Aegina. Constructed as the port of Athens about 493 BC, it was linked with that city by the Long Walls about 460 BC. After the destruction of Athens by Sulla in 86 BC, Piraeus declined. Modern Piraeus is an industrial suburb of Athens.

Pirandello /ˌpɪrənˈdeləʊ/ Luigi 1867–1936. Italian writer. Born in Sicily, he settled as a teacher in Rome, and won fame with the novel *Il fu Mattia Pascal/The Late Mattia Pascal* 1904 and with his many highly acclaimed short stories. His first venture in the field of drama was *La Morsa/The Vice* 1912, which was followed by *Sei personaggi in cerca d'autore/Six Characters in Search of an Author* 1921, *Enrico IV/Henry IV* 1922, and others. The theme and treatment of his plays anticipated the work of ◊Brecht, ◊O'Neill, ◊Anouilh, and ◊Genet. In 1934 he received the Nobel Prize for Literature.

Piranesi /ˌpɪrəˈneɪzi/ Giovanni Battista 1720–1778. Italian architect and artist, noted for his powerful etchings of Roman antiquities, and as a theorist of architecture, advocating imaginative use of Roman models.

piranha South American freshwater fish, genus *Serrusalmus*. About 30 cm/1 ft long with razor-edge teeth, some species rapidly devour animals, especially if attracted by blood.

Piranesi The 18th-century Italian architect Giambattista Piranesi engraved Roman antiquities on copper and worked in Rome on a great series of etchings of the city of his day and in ancient times. This etching is one of the *Carceri d'Invenzione*.

Pisa The famous leaning tower is some 54 m/179 ft high, and has foundations only about 3 m/10 ft deep. Galileo did not make experiments, as legend claims, from the top of the tower.

Piran, St lived c. 500. Missionary sent to Cornwall by St ◊Patrick. There are remains of his oratory at Perranzabuloe, and he is the patron saint of Cornwall and its nationalist movement; feast day 5 Mar.

pirouette a complete turn of the body on one leg with the other raised.

Pisa /'piːzə/ city in Tuscany, Italy, noted for its 11th–12th-century cathedral (see Giovanni ◊Pisano); university 1338; population (1984) 104,000. The Leaning Tower is some 54 m/179 ft high and has foundations only about 3 m/10 ft deep.

Pisanello /ˌpiːzə'neləʊ/ pseudonym of Antonio Pisano c. 1395–1455/6. Italian artist from Verona, noted for his medals and his frescoes. Those in the Palazzo Ducale in Mantua were rediscovered after World War II.

Pisano /piː'saːnəʊ/ Nicola (c. 1220/5–c. 1284) and his son Giovanni c. 1245–c. 1314. Italian sculptors, whose four great pulpits carved in relief at Siena, Pisa, and Pistoia show the influence of antique sarcophagi but also that of French Gothic in the dramatic expressiveness of their figures.

Pisces faint constellation of the ◊zodiac, represented by two fishes tied together by their tails, through which the Sun passes from mid-Mar to late Apr. Pisces contains the **vernal** ◊**equinox**, the point at which the Sun's path around the sky (the ◊**ecliptic**) crosses the celestial equator. The Sun reaches this point around Mar 21 each year.

Pisistratus /paɪ'sɪstrətəs/ c. 605–527 BC. Athenian politician who assumed the leadership of the peasant party, and seized power in 561 BC.

He was twice expelled, but recovered power from 541 BC till his death. Ruling as a dictator under constitutional forms, he was the first to have the Homeric poems written down, and founded Greek drama by introducing the Dionysiac peasant festivals into Athens.

Pissarro /pɪ'saːrəʊ/ Camille 1831–1903. French painter, born in the West Indies. He studied under ◊Corot and became a leader of the ◊Impressionist movement. He is noted mainly for his ◊landscapes in a varity of media – oils, pastel, gouache, and so on. His son **Lucien Pissarro** (1863–1944), a landscape painter and engraver, came to England in 1890 and influenced book illustration and printing.

pistachio deciduous Eurasian tree *Pistacia vera* family Anacardiaceae, with edible green nuts, eaten salted or used to flavour foods.

pistil a general term describing the female part of a flower, either referring to one single ◊carpel or a group of several fused carpels.

Pistoia /pɪ'stɔɪə/ city in Tuscany, Italy, 16 km/10 mi NW of Florence, producing steel, small arms, paper, pasta, and olive oil; it is surrounded by walls (1302) and has a 12th-century cathedral; population (1982) 92,500. Pistoia was the site of the Roman rebel Catiline's defeat 62 BC.

pistol small ◊firearm designed for one-hand use. Pistols were in use from the early 15th century and their evolution closely parallels that of the corresponding shoulder arm. The problem of firing more than once without reloading was tackled by using many combinations of multiple barrels, both stationary and revolving. A breech-loading, multi-chambered revolver of as early as 1650 still survives; the first practical solution, however, was Samuel Colt's six-gun 1847. Behind a single barrel, a short six-chambered cylinder was rotated by cocking the hammer, and a fresh round brought into place. The automatic pistol, operated by gas or recoil, was introduced in Germany in the 1890s. Both revolvers and automatics are in widespread military use.

piston /'pɪstən/ a barrel-shaped device used to harness power in reciprocating engines (◊steam, ◊petrol, ◊diesel). Pistons are driven up and down in cylinders by expanding steam or hot gases. They pass on their motion via a connecting rod and crank to a ◊crankshaft.

Piston /'pɪstən/ Walter 1894–1976. US composer. After studying in Paris with Nadia ◊Boulanger, he became a lecturer and later professor at Harvard, and wrote a number of influential textbooks, including *Harmony* 1941. His music includes eight symphonies.

Pitcairn Islands /'pɪtkeən/ British colony in Polynesia, 5,300 km/3,300 mi NE of New Zealand
area 5 sq km/2 sq mi
capital Adamstown
features in the group are the uninhabited Henderson Islands 31 sq km/12 sq mi, an unspoiled coral atoll with a rare ecology, and tiny Ducie and Oeno, annexed by Britain in 1902
exports fruit and souvenirs to passing ships
population (1982) 54
language English
government the governor is the British high commissioner in New Zealand
history discovered by British admiral Philip Carteret 1767. They were first settled by nine mutineers from the ◊*Bounty* together with some Tahitians, their occupation remaining unknown until 1808.

pitch a black substance, hard when cold, but liquid when hot, used as a sealant on roofs. It is made by the destructive distillation of wood or coal tar.

pitch the position of a note in the musical scale, dependent on the frequency of the predominant sound wave. In *standard pitch* A above middle C has a frequency of 440 Hz. *perfect pitch* is an ability to name or reproduce any note heard or asked for; it does not necessarily imply high musical ability.

pitchblende an ore consisting mainly of uranium oxide U_3O_8, but also containing radioactive salt of radium $RaBr_2$, first separated by Marie and Pierre ◊Curie in 1898 from pitchblende from N Bohemia, in which it occurs in about 1 part in 3 million.

pitcher plant insectivorous plant of the genus *Nepenthes*, in which leaves shaped like a pitcher are filled with fluid and trap insects.

Pitman /'pɪtmən/ Isaac 1813–1897. British inventor of Pitman's shorthand. A teacher, he studied Samuel Taylor's scheme for shorthand writing and published in 1837 his own system, *Stenographic Soundhand*, speedy and accurate, and adapted for use in many languages. A

simplified *Pitman Script*, combining letters and signs, was devised 1971 by Emily D Smith. His grandson *Sir (Isaac) James Pitman* (1901–85) devised the 44-letter Initial Teaching Alphabet in the 1960s to help children to read.

Pitot tube an instrument that measures fluid (gas and liquid) flow. Invented in the 1730s by Henri Pitot (1695–1771) in France. It is used to measure the airspeed of aircraft. It works by sensing pressure differences in different directions in the airstream.

Pitt /pɪt/ William, the Elder, 1st Earl of Chatham 1708–1778. British Whig politician, 'the Great Commoner'. He served effectively as prime minister 1756–61 and 1766–68.
Entering Parliament in 1735, Pitt led the Patriot faction opposed to the Whig prime minister Walpole and attacked Walpole's successor, Carteret, for his conduct of the War of the Austrian Succession. As paymaster of the forces 1746–55, he broke with tradition by refusing to enrich himself; he was dismissed for attacking Newcastle, the prime minister. Recalled by popular demand to form a government on the outbreak of the Seven Years' War 1756, he was in 1757 forced to form a coalition with Newcastle. A 'year of victories' ensued in 1759, and the French were expelled from India and Canada. Forced to resign in 1761 by George III, Pitt was again recalled to form an all-party government in 1766. He championed the Americans against the king, though rejecting independence.

Pitt The politician and orator, William Pitt the Elder, Lord Chatham, championed the rights of the American colonists, although he stopped short of supporting independence.

Pitt /pɪt/ William, the Younger 1759–1806. British ◊Tory politician, prime minister 1783–1801 and 1804–06. He carried out fiscal reforms and union with Ireland; he attempted to keep Britain at peace but became embroiled in wars with France from 1793.
Son of William ◊Pitt the Elder, 1st Earl of Chatham, he entered Parliament in 1781. He was

the Whig Shelburne's chancellor of the Exchequer 1782–83, and with the support of the Tories and king's friends became England's youngest prime minister 1783. He reorganized the country's finances and negotiated reciprocal tariff reduction with France. In 1793, however, the new French republic declared war and England fared badly. Pitt failed to understand the significance of the French Revolution, which only reinforced his opposition to political reform. His policy in Ireland led to the 1798 revolt, and he tried to solve the Irish question by the Act of Union in 1800, but George III rejected the Catholic emancipation Pitt had promised as a condition, and Pitt resigned in 1801.
On his return to office in 1804, he organized an alliance with Austria and Russia against Napoleon, which was shattered at Austerlitz. In declining health, he died on hearing the news, saying: 'Oh, my country! How I leave my country!' He was buried in Westminster Abbey.

Pitt William Pitt the Younger entered Parliament at the age of 22 and two years later became England's youngest prime minister.

pitta bird of the genus *Pitta*. Some 20 or more species can be found in the forests of the Old World and Australian tropics. They have round bodies and big heads and are often beautifully coloured. They live on the ground and in low undergrowth, and can run from danger.

Pitt-Rivers /'pɪt 'rɪvəz/ Augustus Henry 1827–1900. British general and archaeologist. He made a series of model archaeological excavations in Wiltshire, being among the first to recognize the value of everyday objects as well as art treasures. The Pitt-Rivers Museum, Oxford, contains the best of his collection.

Pittsburgh /'pɪtsbɜːg/ industrial city (iron and steel) and inland port, where the Allegheny and Monongahela join to form the Ohio river in Pennsylvania, USA; population (1980) 423,940. The Carnegie Institute of Technology is here.

pituitary gland the most important of the ◊endocrine glands of vertebrates. It is attached to the base of the brain, and is divided into two distinct lobes. From the anterior lobe ▷hormones are secreted, some of which control the activities of other glands (▷thyroid, gonads, and ▷adrenal cortex); others are direct-acting hormones affecting ▷milk secretion, and controlling growth. Secretions of the posterior lobe regulate body water balance, contraction of the ▷uterus, etc. The anterior pituitary is regulated by the ▷hypothalamus, part of the brain, and thus links the nervous and hormonal systems.

Pius /'paɪəs/ name of 12 popes, including:

Pius IV 1499–1565. Pope from 1559, one of the ▷Medici. He reassembled the Council of Trent (see Counter-Reformation under ▷Reformation) and completed its work in 1563.

Pius V 1504–1572. Pope from 1566, who excommunicated Elizabeth I of England, and organized the expedition against the Turks which won the victory of ▷Lepanto.

Pius VI 1717–1799. Pope from 1775, strongly opposed the French Revolution, and died a prisoner in French hands.

Pius VII 1740–1823. Pope from 1800, who concluded a ▷Concordat with France in 1801, and took part in Napoleon's coronation, but was a prisoner 1809–14. After his return to Rome in 1814 he revived the ▷Jesuit order.

Pius IX 1792–1878. Pope from 1846. He never accepted the incorporation of the Papal States and of Rome in the kingdom of Italy, and proclaimed the dogmas of the Immaculate Conception of the Virgin 1854 and papal infallibility 1870; his pontificate was the longest in history.

Pius X 1835–1914. Pope from 1903, canonized 1954, who condemned Modernism (see under ▷Christianity) in a manifesto of 1907.

Pius XI 1857–1939. Pope from 1922, he signed the ▷Concordat with Mussolini 1929.

Pius XII 1876–1958. (Eugenio Pacelli) Pope from 1939. He proclaimed the dogma of the bodily assumption of the Virgin Mary 1950 and in 1951 restated the doctrine (strongly criticized by Protestants) that the life of an infant must not be sacrificed to save a mother in labour.

pixel (contraction of 'picture cell') on a computer screen (VDU), any one of the points in the matrix of points from which displayed images are constructed and illuminated (sometimes in colour) under the control of a computer. A matrix of as few as 400 × 200 pixels is often used for displaying text but screens with over 1000 × 1000 pixels are now quite common for graphical (pictorial) displays.

Pizarro /pɪ'zɑːrəʊ/ c. 1475–1541. Spanish conquistador who took part in the expeditions of Balboa and others. In 1526–27 he explored the NW coast of South America, and conquered Peru in 1530 with 180 followers. The Inca king (Atahualpa) was treacherously seized and murdered. In 1535 Pizarro founded Lima. A feud now began between the Spanish leaders, and Pizarro was assassinated.

pizzicato (Italian 'pinched') in music, an instruction to pluck a bowed stringed instrument (such as the violin) with the fingers.

Plaatje /'plɑːtʃi/ Sol 1876–1932. Pioneer South African nationalist who was the first

secretary-general and founder (1912) of the ▷African National Congress.

Place /pleɪs/ Francis 1771–1854. British Radical. He showed great powers as a political organizer and made Westminster a centre of Radicalism. He secured the repeal of the anti-union Combination Acts in 1824.

Place A tailor by trade, Francis Place was largely responsible for repealing the Combination Acts which had made trade unionism illegal.

placenta

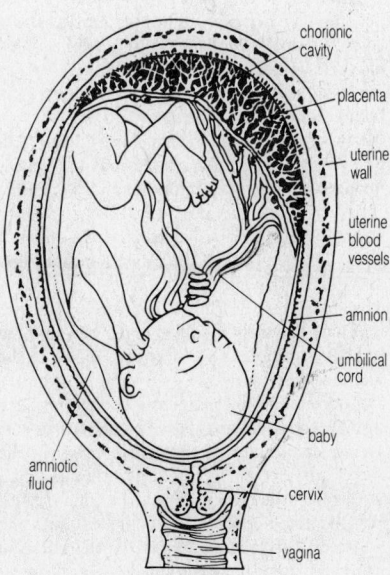

chorionic cavity

placenta

uterine wall

uterine blood vessels

amnion

umbilical cord

baby

amniotic fluid

cervix

vagina

placenta the organ composed of maternal and embryonic tissue which attaches the developing ▷embryo, or ▷foetus, of placental mammals to the maternal ▷uterus. Oxygen, nutrients and waste products are exchanged between maternal and foetal blood over the placental membrane, but the two blood systems are not in direct contact. The placenta also produces ▷hormones which regulate the progress of pregnancy. It is shed as part of the afterbirth.

plague disease transmitted by fleas (carried by the black ▷rat) which infect the sufferer with the bacillus *Pasturella pestis*. An early symptom is swelling of lymph nodes, usually in the armpit and groin; such swellings are called 'buboes', hence 'bubonic' plague. It causes virulent blood poisoning and the death rate is high. Notable epidemics include the ▷Black Death and the Great Plague of London 1665. Other forms are septicaemic and pneumonic, the latter being invariably fatal before the introduction of sulpha drugs and antibiotics.

plaice food-fish *Pleuronectes platessa* belonging to the flat-fish group, abundant in N European waters. It is white beneath and brownish with orange spots on the 'eyed' side.

Plaid Cymru /'plaʊd 'kʌmri/ (Welsh 'Party of Wales'). Welsh political party established 1925, dedicated to an independent ▷Wales.

Plains Indian any of the N American Indians of the High Plains, which run over 3,000 km/2,000 mi from Alberta to Texas. The various groups shared a warrior-horserider culture; many lived in skin tents or *tipis* and wore war paint, buffalo robes, and eagle-feather war bonnets, characteristics latterly adopted by many tribes who never originally had them. In war some groups would cut off the scalps of their victims. Their myths include that of the *thunderbird* creator of the storms of the great plains. Their chief ritual was the *sundance* at summer solstice, when a warrior was tied to a sacred pole by ropes ending in wooden skewers thrust through the flesh, and danced until the flesh gave way, receiving in return supernatural assistance. The main tribes were ▷Blackfoot, Cheyenne, Comanche, Pawnee, and the Dakota or ▷Sioux.

Gen George ▷Custer attacked a Sioux camp at Little Bighorn, Montana (under chiefs Crazy Horse and ▷Sitting Bull) and was killed with his troops in *Custer's Last Stand* 25 Jun 1876. Congress then abrogated the Fort Laramie Treaty of 1868 (granting the Indians a large area in Dakota's Black Hills, where gold had by now been found, and where today uranium, coal, oil, and natural gas are worked). The last confrontation of the Sioux and US Army was at *Wounded Knee*, South Dakota, after Chief Sitting Bull had been killed on 15 Dec 1890, allegedly resisting arrest. On 29 Dec 1890 Indians who were associated with him in the *Ghost Dance Movement* (aimed at recovering control of N America with the aid of spirits of dead braves) were surrounded and 153 killed.

In 1973 the American Indian Movement held hostages in a siege of Wounded Knee 27 Feb–8 May, demanding investigation of the treaty question, and in 1980 the Sioux, who survive in South Dakota and Nebraska, received $160 million compensation.

plainsong ancient chant of the Christian Church first codified by Ambrose, bishop of

Milan, and then by Pope Gregory in the 6th century. See ◊Gregorian chant.

Planck /plæŋk/ Max 1858–1947. German physicist who framed the quantum theory 1900. Born in Kiel, he was appointed to the chair of physics at Kiel in 1885 and at Berlin in 1889, and 1930–37 was president of the Kaiser Wilhelm Institute. He was awarded the Nobel Prize for Physics in 1918, and became a Fellow of the Royal Society in 1926.

Planck One of the founders of 20th-century physics and formulator of the quantum theory, Max Planck was professor of theoretical physics at Berlin University. Much of his early work was in thermodynamics.

plane tree, genus *Platanus*. Species include the oriental plane *Platanus orientalis*, a favourite plantation tree of the Greeks and Romans; the hybrid London plane *Platanus x hispanica*, with palmate, usually five-lobed leaves, which throws off city smog by the smoothness of its foliage and shedding its bark annually in large flakes; and the American plane or buttonwood *Platanus occidentalis*. All have pendulous burr-like fruits and are capable of growth to 30 m/100 ft high.

planet a body in ◊orbit around a ◊star. Planets do not give out light of their own, but reflect the light of the central star. Planets can be made of rock, metal or gas. There are nine planets in the ◊solar system. The inner four, called the *terrestrial planets*, are small and rocky, and include our planet Earth. The outer planets are large balls of liquid and gas; the largest is ◊Jupiter, which contains more than twice as much mass as all the solar-system planets combined. There is no good evidence for any unknown planets beyond ◊Pluto.

planetarium optical projection device by means of which the motions of the stars and planets are reproduced for educational purposes on a domed ceiling representing the sky as it appears from Earth.

planetary nebula a shell of gas thrown off by a ◊star at the end of its life. (Planetary nebulae

PLANETS

planet	main constituents	atmosphere	distance from Sun in millions of km	time for one orbit in Earth-years	diameter in thousands of km	average density if density of water is 1 unit
Mercury	rocky, ferrous	–	5.8	0.24	4.9	5.4
Venus	rocky, ferrous	carbon dioxide	108	0.61	12.1	5.2
Earth	rocky, ferrous	nitrogen, oxygen	150	1.00	12.8	5.5
Mars	rocky	carbon dioxide	228	1.88	6.8	3.9
Jupiter	liquid hydrogen, helium	–	778	11.86	142.8	1.3
Saturn	hydrogen, helium	–	1427	29.50	120.0	0.7
Uranus	icy, hydrogen, helium	hydrogen, helium	2875	84.00	51.1	1.2
Neptune	icy, hydrogen, helium	hydrogen, helium	4496	164.80	49.5	1.7
Pluto	icy, rocky	methane	5900	248.40	4.0	about 1

have nothing to do with planets. They were named by William ◊Herschel, who thought their rounded shape resembled the disk of a planet as seen through a telescope.) After a star such as the Sun has expanded to become a ◊red giant, its outer layers are ejected into space to form a planetary nebula, leaving the core of the former giant star as a ◊white dwarf at the centre.

planimeter a simple integrating instrument for measuring the area of a plane surface. It consists of two hinged arms; one is kept fixed and the other is traced round the boundary of the area. This actuates a small graduated wheel and the area is found from its change in position.

plankton small, often microscopic, forms of plant and animal life that drift in fresh or salt water, and are a source of food for larger animals.

plant an organism that carries out ◊photosynthesis, has ◊cellulose cell walls and complex ◊eukaryotic cells and is immobile. A few parasitic plants have lost the ability to photosynthesize, but are still considered as plants. See under ◊plant classification. Many of the lower plants (the ◊algae and bryophytes) consist of a simple body or ◊thallus upon which the organs of reproduction are borne. Simplest of all are the threadlike algae, for example *Spirogyra*, which consist of a chain of cells. The seaweeds (algae) and mosses and liverworts (bryophytes) represent a further development, with simple, multicellular bodies that have specially modified areas in which the reproductive organs are carried. Higher in the morphological scale are the ferns, clubmosses and horsetails (◊pteridophytes). Ferns produce leaflike fronds bearing sporangia on their under-surface in which the spores are carried. The spores are freed and germinate to produce small independent bodies carrying the sexual organs; thus the fern, like other pteridophytes, and some seaweeds, has two quite separate generations in its life cycle, see ◊alternation of generations. The pteridophytes have special supportive water-conducting tissues, which identify them as ◊vascular plants. This group includes all seed plants, that is the ◊gymnosperms (conifers, yews, cycads and ginkgo) and the ◊angiosperms (flowering plants).

The seed plants are the largest group, and structurally the most complex. They are usually divided into three parts, ◊root, ◊stem, and ◊leaves. Stems grow above or below ground. Their cellular structure is designed to carry water and salts from the roots to the leaves in the ◊xylem, and sugars from the leaves to the roots in the ◊phloem. The leaves manufacture the food of the plant by means of ◊photosynthesis, which occurs in the ◊chloroplasts which they contain. ◊Flowers and ◊cones are modified leaves arranged in groups and enclosing the reproductive organs from which the ◊fruits and ◊seeds result.

Plants are ◊autotrophs, that is they make carbohydrates from water and carbon dioxide, and are the primary producers in all ◊food chains, so that all animal life is directly or indirectly dependent on them. They play a vital part in the ◊carbon cycle, removing carbon dioxide from the atmosphere and generating oxygen. The study of plants is known as ◊botany.

Plantagenet English royal house, reigning 1154–1399, whose name comes from the nickname of Geoffrey, Count of Anjou (father of ◊Henry II) who often wore a sprig of broom 'planta genista' in his hat; ◊Richard, Duke of York, revived it as a surname to emphasize his superior claim to the throne over ◊Henry VI.

plantain genus of plants *Plantago*. The great plantain *Plantago major* has oval leaves, grooved stalks and a spike of green flowers with purple anthers followed by seeds liked by cage-birds. The name plantain is also given to various types of ◊banana.

plant classification the taxonomy or ◊classification of plants. Originally the plant ◊kingdom included bacteria, diatoms, dinoflagellates, fungi and slime moulds, but these are not now thought of as plants. The unicellular algae, such as *Chlamydomonas*, are often now put with the protists instead of the plants, and some classification schemes even classify the multicellular algae (seaweeds and freshwater weeds) in a new kingdom, the Protoctista, along with the protists. The groups that are always classified as plants are the ◊bryophytes (mosses and liverworts), ◊pteridophytes (ferns,

plant

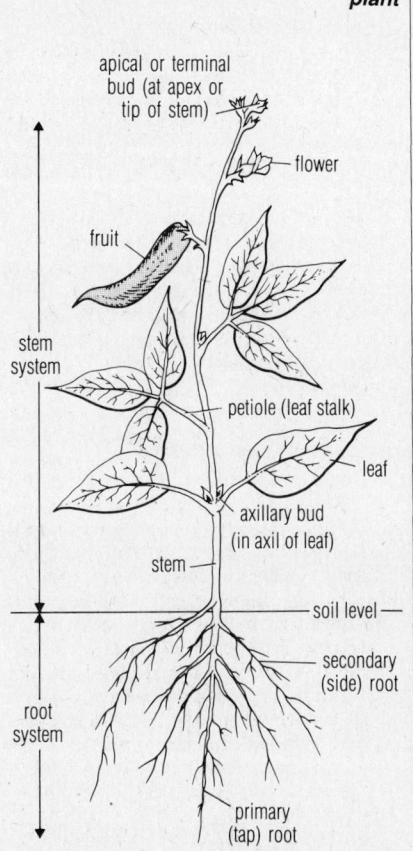

apical or terminal
bud (at apex or
tip of stem)

flower

fruit

stem
system

petiole (leaf stalk)

leaf

axillary bud
(in axil of leaf)

stem

soil level

secondary
(side) root

root
system

primary
(tap) root

plant classification
taxonomic (classification) levels

- 1 Kingdom
- 2 sub-kingdom
- 3 division
- 4 class

Plant Kingdom

Cryptograms

Thallophyta

Algae

Lichens

Bryophyta

Liverworts

Mosses

Pteridophyta

Clubmosses

Horsetails

Ferns

Phanerograms

Gymnosperms

Ginkos

Cycads

Gnetals

Conifers

Angiosperms

Monocotyledons

Dicotyledons

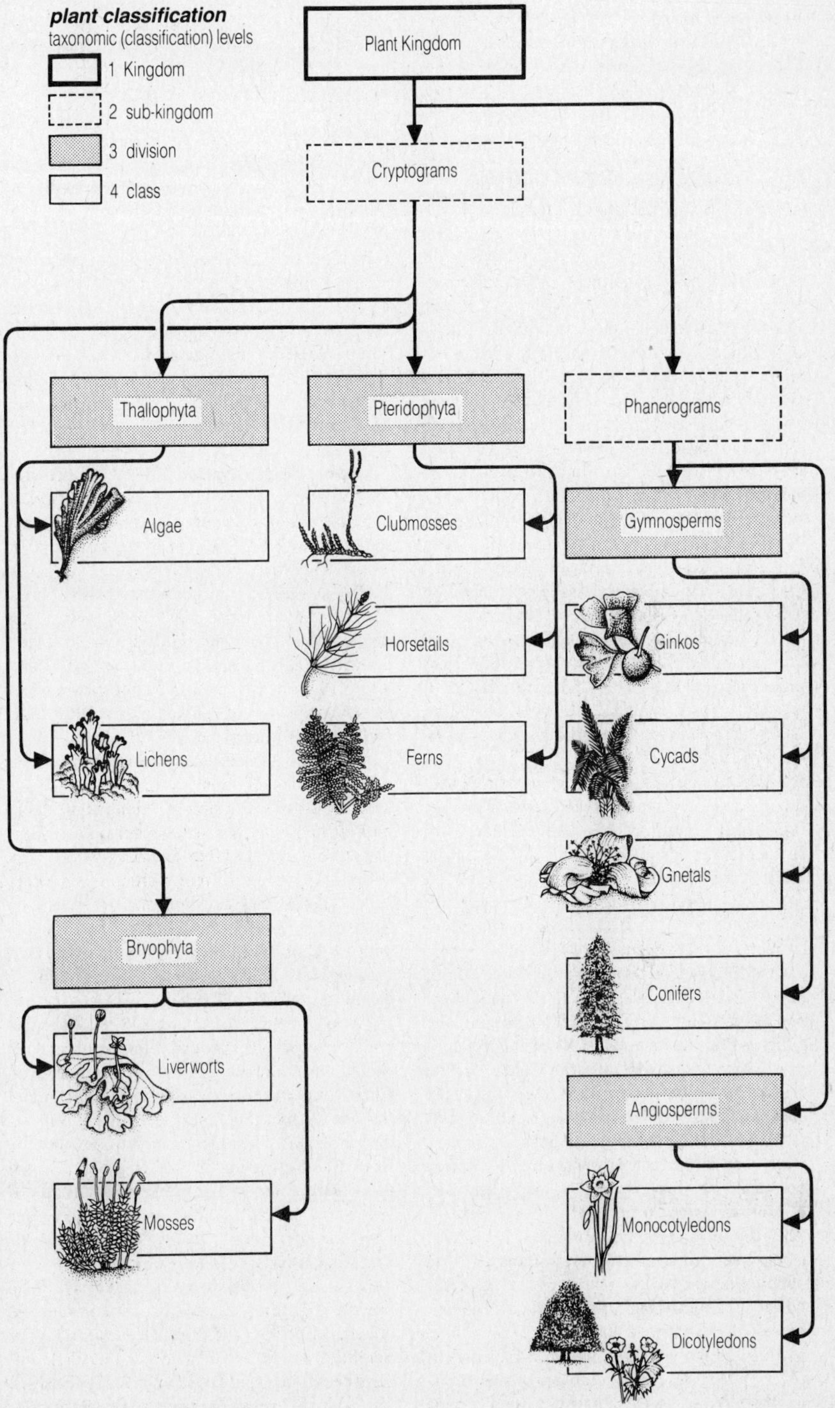

horsetails, and clubmosses), ◊gymnosperms (conifers, yews, cycads, and ginkgos) and ◊angiosperms (flowering plants). The angiosperms are split into the ◊monocotyledons (for example, orchids, grasses, lilies) and the ◊dicotyledons (for example, oak, buttercup, geranium, and daisy).

The basis of plant classification was established by ◊Linnaeus. Among the angiosperms, it is largely based on the number and arrangement of the flower parts.

plant hormone a substance produced by a plant which has a marked effect on its growth, flowering, leaf-fall (◊abscission), fruit-ripening, or some other process. Examples include ◊auxin, ◊gibberellins, ◊ethylene, and ◊cytokinins. Unlike animal ◊hormones, these substances are not produced by a particular area of the plant body (see ◊gland) and they may be less specific in their effects. It has therefore been suggested that they should not be described as hormones at all.

plasma in biology, the liquid part of the ◊blood.

plasma in physics, an ionized gas produced at extremely high temperatures, as in the Sun and other stars, and which contains positive and negative charges in approximately equal numbers, is affected by a magnetic field, and is a good electrical conductor.

plasmapheresis in medicine, the removal from the body of large quantities of whole blood and its fractionization by centrifugal force in a

continuous flow cell separator. Once separated, the elements of the blood (such as plasma corpuscles, and platelets) are isolated and available for specific treatment, or even replacement from donor blood. Restored blood is then returned to the venous system of the patient.

Plassey, Battle of /'plæsi/ a victory 1757 for the British under Clive over Suraj-ud-Dowlah near a village in West Bengal, India, on the

Bhagirathi river, 50 km/31 mi NNW of Krishnagar.

plaster of Paris a form of ◊gypsum, mixed with water for making casts and moulds.

plastic any of the stable synthetic materials which are fluid at some stage in their manufacture, when they can be shaped and which later set to rigid or semi-rigid solids. Plastics today are chiefly derived from

◊petroleum. Most are polymers, that is, they are made up of long chains of identical molecules. Processed by extrusion, injection-moulding, vacuum-forming and compression, they emerge in consistencies ranging from hard and inflexible to soft and rubbery.

Thermoplastics soften when warmed, then re-harden as they cool, for example polystyrene, a clear plastic used in kitchen utensils or (when expanded into a 'foam' by gas injection) in insulation and ceiling tiles; polyethylene or polythene, used for containers and wrapping; and polyvinyl chloride (PVC), used for drainpipes, floor tiles, audio discs, shoes, and handbags.

Thermosets remain rigid once set, and do not soften when warmed. They include bakelite, used in electrical insulation and telephone receivers; epoxy resins, used in paints and varnishes, to laminate wood, and as adhesives; polyesters, used in synthetic textile fibres and, with glassfibre reinforcement, in car bodies and boat hulls; and polyurethane, prepared in liquid form as a paint or varnish, and in foam form for upholstery and in lining materials (where it may be a fire hazard). One group of plastics, the silicones, is based on a chain of oxygen and silicon atoms, the latter having organic groups attached to them. They are chemically inert, have good electrical properties, and repel water. Silicones find use in silicone rubber, paints, electrical insulation materials, laminates, waterproofing for walls and stain-resistant textiles.

Biodegradable plastics are being developed; other plastics cannot be broken down by micro-organisms, so cannot easily be disposed of. Incineration leads to the release of toxic fumes, unless carried out at very high temperatures.

plastic surgery the surgical repair of seriously damaged tissues, or operations to effect cosmetic change. See under ◊surgery.

plastid a general name for a cell ◊organelle of plants that is enclosed by a double membrane and contains a series of internal membranes and vesicles. Plastids contain DNA and are produced by division of existing plastids. They can be classified into two main groups, the chromoplasts, which contain pigments such as ◊carotenes and ◊chlorophyll, and the leucoplasts, which are colourless; however, the distinction between the two is not always clear-cut. ◊Chloroplasts are the major type of chromoplast. They contain chlorophyll, are responsible for the green colouration of most plants, and perform ◊photosynthesis. Other chromoplasts give the flower petals or the fruits their distinctive colour. Leucoplasts are important food-storage bodies and include amyloplasts, found in the roots of plants, which store large amounts of starch.

Plate, River /pleɪt/ English name of Río de ◊la Plata, estuary in S America.

plate tectonics the concept that attributes ◊continental drift and ◊seafloor spreading to the continual formation and destruction of the outermost layer of the Earth. This layer is seen as consisting of major and minor plates, curved to the planet's spherical shape and with a jigsaw fit to each other. Convection currents within the Earth's ◊mantle produce upwellings of new material along joint lines at the surface. These lines are the ◊ocean ridges. The new material extends the plates at the surface and these move away from the ocean ridges. At the point of contact of two plates, one overrides the other and the lower is absorbed back into the mantle. These 'subduction zones' occur in the ◊ocean trenches. The moving plates consist of ocean crust and the topmost solid layer of mantle, together called the ◊lithosphere. The plates move on a mobile layer of a mantle called the ◊asthenosphere. The continents take little part in the generation and destruction of the plate material. Because they are made of a lighter substance they are carried along passively on the moving plates.

The concept of continental drift was first put forward by the German ◊Wegener; plate tectonics was formulated in the mid-1960s, and has gained widespread acceptance among earth scientists.

Plath /plæθ/ Sylvia 1932–1963. US poet and novelist, born in Boston, Massachusetts. She married the poet Ted Hughes 1956; they separated in 1962. She committed suicide while living in London.

Plath's powerful, highly personal poems, often expressing a sense of desolation, are distinguished by their intensity and sharp imagery. Collections include *The Colossus* 1960, *Ariel* 1965, published after her death. Her autobiographical novel, *The Bell Jar* 1961, deals with a young woman's emotional breakdown.

platinum a metallic element, symbol Pt, atomic number 78, atomic weight 195.09. It is a greyish-white, ductile and malleable metal, untarnishable in air and very resistant to heat and strong acids. Platinum occurs as the metal, and alloyed with iridium, osmium and other similar metals, and with gold and iron, especially in the Urals (USSR), and in S Africa, Canada and the USA. Both pure and as an alloy, it is used extensively in jewellery, dentistry, and the chemical industry.

Plato /'pleɪtəʊ/ c. 428–c. 348 BC. Athenian philosopher whose profound thinking survived in written form and has exerted wide influence on Christianity and European culture, directly and through ◊Augustine, the Florentine Platonists during the ◊Renaissance, and countless others. Born of noble family, he entered politics on the aristocratic side, and in philosophy became a follower of ◊Socrates. He travelled widely after Socrates' death in about 387, and founded his Academy in order to train a new ruling class.

Of his work, some 30 dialogues survive. The principal figure in these ethical and philosophical debates is Socrates and the early ones employ the Socratic method, in which he asks questions and traps the students into contradicting themselves, for example, *Iron*, on poetry. Other famous dialogues include the *Symposium*, on love, *Phaedo*, on immortality, and *Apology and Crito*, on Socrates' trial and death. It is impossible to say whether Plato's Socrates is a faithful representative of the real man. Plato's philosophy rejects scientific rationalism (that is, establishing facts through experiment) in favour of arguments, because mind, not matter, is fundamental, and material objects are merely imperfect copies of abstract and eternal 'ideas'.

His political philosophy is expounded in two treatises, *The Republic* and *The Laws*, both of which describe ideal states (see also under ◊Utopia). Platonic love is inspired by a person's best qualities and seeks their development; Plato conceived such love as homosexual, but during the Renaissance the term was applied to heterosexual relationships which excluded physical desires.

platypus monotreme mammal *Ornithorhynchus anatinus*, found in Tasmania and E Australia. Semi-aquatic, it has naked jaws resembling a duck's beak, small eyes and no trace of an external ear. It lives in long burrows in banks of rivers, where it lays eggs in a rough nest. It feeds on water worms and insects, and when full-grown is 45 cm/18 in long.

Plautus /'plɔːtəs/ Roman dramatist. Born in Umbria, he settled in Rome and worked in a bakery before achieving success as a dramatist. He wrote at least 56 comedies, freely adapted from Greek originals, of which 20 survive. Shakespeare based *The Comedy of Errors* on his *Menoechmi*.

playgroup a voluntary, usually part-time pre-school group, run by parents or sometimes by charitable organizations. Playgroups sprang up in the 1960s in the UK in response to a national shortage of places in maintained nursery education. By the 1980s they were catering for 450,000 children annually, with training and services organized nationally by the Pre-School Playgroups Association.

Pleasance The mild demeanour of Donald Pleasance reveals little of his sinister acting career. Dr Crippen and Count Dracula are but two of the evil characters he has portrayed.

Pleasance /'plezəns/ Donald 1919– . British actor. He has been especially successful as Leone Gola in Pirandello's *The Rules of the Game*, Davies in Pinter's *The Caretaker*, and in the title role of the film *Dr Crippen* 1962, conveying the sinister aspect of the outcast from society.

plebeians the unprivileged class in ancient Rome, composed of aliens and freed slaves, and

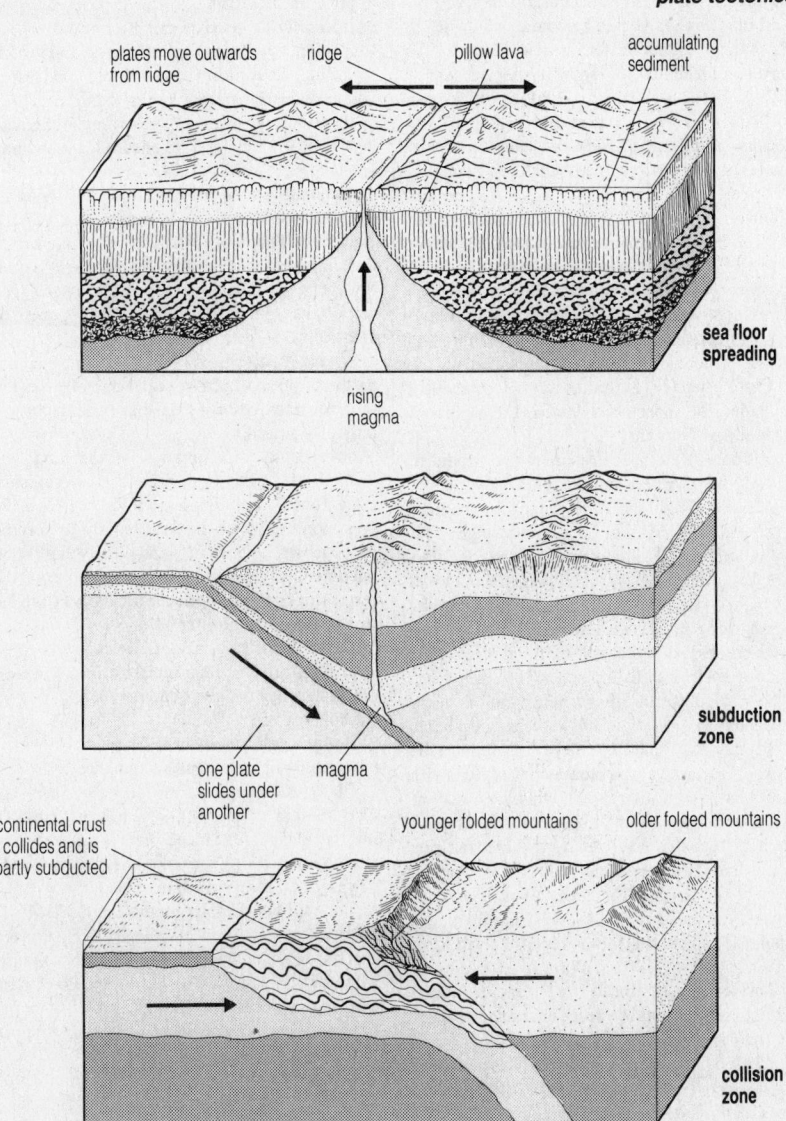

plate tectonics

plates move outwards from ridge — ridge — pillow lava — accumulating sediment

sea floor spreading

rising magma

subduction zone

one plate slides under another — magma

continental crust collides and is partly subducted — younger folded mountains — older folded mountains

collision zone

satellites since 1966, many of them for military purposes.

pleurisy inflammation of the pleura – a membrane which covers the lungs and also lines the space in which they rest; the two surfaces move easily on one another, being lubricated by small quantities of fluid. When it is inflamed the surfaces may dry up or stick together, making breathing difficult and painful. A large volume of fluid may collect in the pleural cavity, the space between the two surfaces. Pus in the pleural cavity is called empyema. Pleurisy occurs in pneumonia and tuberculosis, but may also be a consequence of scarlet fever or rheumatism.

Pleven /ˈplevən/ industrial town (textiles, machinery, ceramics) in N Bulgaria; population (1983) 140,500. In the Russo-Turkish War of 1877 Pleven surrendered to the Russians after a siege of five months.

Plimsoll /ˈplɪmsəl/ Samuel 1824–1898. British social reformer, born in Bristol. He sat in Parliament as a Radical 1868–80, and through his efforts the Merchant Shipping Act was passed in 1876, providing for Board of Trade inspection of ships, and the compulsory painting of a ◊Plimsoll line.

Plimsoll line a loading marking painted on the hull of ships, first suggested by Samuel ◊Plimsoll. It shows the safe levels to which the hull can sink in various waters at various times.

Plimsoll line

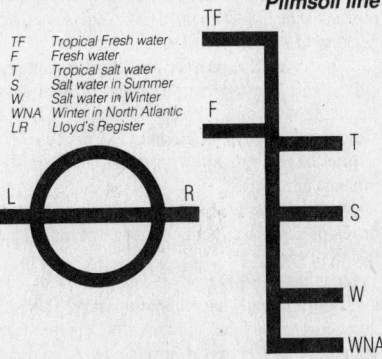

TF	Tropical Fresh water
F	Fresh water
T	Tropical salt water
S	Salt water in Summer
W	Salt water in Winter
WNA	Winter in North Atlantic
LR	Lloyd's Register

Pliny /ˈplɪni/ Gaius Plinius Caecilius Secundus c. 61–113. The Younger. Roman administrator, nephew of ◊Pliny the Elder, whose correspondence is of great interest. Among his surviving letters are those describing the eruption of Vesuvius, his uncle's death, and his correspondence with the emperor ◊Trajan.

Pliny /ˈplɪni/ Gaius Plinius Secundus c. 23–79 ad. The Elder. Roman scientist and historian; only his works on astronomy, geography, and natural history survive. He was killed in an eruption of Vesuvius.

Plisetskaya /plɪˈsetskiə/ Maya 1925– . Russian ballerina and actress. Educated at the Moscow Bolshoi Ballet School, she succeeded ◊Ulanova as prima ballerina of the Bolshoi Ballet.

Ploești /plɔɪˈeʃt/ city in SE Romania; oil centre; population (1983) 215,500.

plotter an ◊output device that draws pictures under computer control. *Flatbed plotters* move a pen up and down across a flat drawing surface,

their descendants. During the 5th–4th centuries BC they waged a long struggle with the patricians.

plebiscite ◊referendum or direct vote by all the electors of a country or district on a specific question. Since the 18th century it has been employed on many occasions to decide to what country a particular area should belong, for example, in Upper Silesia and elsewhere after World War I, and in the Saar in 1935.

Pléiade, La /pleɪˈɑːd/ group of seven poets in 16th-century France led by Ronsard, who were inspired by classical models to the improvement of French verse. They were so called from the seven stars of the Pleiades group.

Pleiades /ˈplaɪədiːz/ in astronomy, a star cluster about 400 light years away in the constellation ◊Taurus, representing the Seven Sisters of Greek mythology. Its brightest stars are visible to the naked eye, while binoculars and

telescopes show hundreds of fainter ones. The brightest are highly luminous ◊blue giants only a few million years old, very young as stars go. The stars of Pleiades are still surrounded by traces of the ◊nebula from which they formed, visible on long-exposure photographs.

Pleiades /ˈplaɪədiːz/ in Greek mythology, seven daughters of ◊Atlas, who asked to be changed to stars to escape the pursuit of ◊Orion.

pleiotropy a process whereby a given ◊gene influences several different observed characteristics of an organism.

Plenty, Bay of /ˈplenti/ broad inlet on the NE coast of North Island, New Zealand, with the port of Tauranga. One of the first canoes bringing Maori immigrants landed here about 1350.

Plesetsk /plɪˈsetsk/ a rocket-launching site in the USSR, 170 km/105 mi S of Archangel. From here the USSR has launched unpiloted

while *roller plotters* roll the drawing paper past the pen as it moves from side to side.

Plough, the in astronomy, a popular name for the most prominent part of the constellation ◊Ursa Major.

plough the most important agricultural implement, used for tilling the soil. The plough dates from about 3500 BC, when oxen were used to pull a wooden blade. In about 500 BC the iron blade, or share, came into use.

By about 1000 AD horses as well as oxen were used to pull wheeled ploughs. Steam ploughs came into use in the 1860s, superseded half a century later by tractor-drawn ploughs. The modern plough consists of many 'bottoms', each comprising a curved ploughshare and angled mouldboard. The bottom is so designed that it slices into the ground and turns the soil over.

Plovdiv /'plɒvdɪv/ industrial city (textiles, chemicals, leather, tobacco) in Bulgaria, on the Maritsa; population (1983) 373,500. Conquered by Philip of Macedon in the 4th century BC, it was known as Philippopolis (Philip's city). It was capital of Roman Thrace.

plover wading bird of the family Charadriidae with a short bill. The European *golden plover Pluviatilis apricaria* of heathland and sea coast is about 28 cm/11 in long. The ringed plover *Charadrius hiaticula*, with a black and white face, and black band on the throat, is found on British shores, but largest of the ringed plovers is the US *Charadrius vociferus*, so called because of its cry.

plum tree *Prunus domestica*, bearing an edible fruit. There are many varieties, including the greengage, and the sloe (*Prunus spinosa*) is closely related. The dried plum is a prune.

plumbago an alternative name for the mineral ◊graphite.

plumule the part of a seed embryo which develops into the shoot, bearing the first true leaves of the plant.

pluralism in political science, the view that decision-making in contemporary liberal democracies is the outcome of competition among several interest groups in a political system characterized by free elections, representative institutions, and open access to the organs of power. It is opposed by corporatist and other approaches that perceive power to be centralized in the state and its principal elites.

pluralism in philosophy, the belief that reality consists of several different elements, not just two – matter and mind – as in ◊dualism.

Plutarch /'pluːtɑːk/ c. 46–120 BC. Greek biographer. Born at Chaeronea, he lectured on philosophy at Rome, and was appointed procurator of Greece by Hadrian. His *Parallel Lives* consist of pairs of biographies of Greek and Roman soldiers and politicians followed by comparisons between the two. North's 1579 translation inspired Shakespeare's Roman plays.

Pluto /'pluːtəʊ/ in astronomy, the outermost planet of the ◊solar system, orbiting the Sun every 248 years at an average distance of 5,900 million km/3,600 million mi. Its orbit is more elliptical than that of any other planet, and at its nearest to the Sun it can cross the orbit of ◊Neptune, as between 1979 and 1999. Pluto was

discovered in 1930 at Lowell Observatory, Arizona, by Clyde ◊Tombaugh during a photographic search for a new planet. The smallest planet in the solar system, it has a diameter of about 3,000 km/2,000 mi and a mass 450 times less than that of Earth. It is of low density, composed of rock and ice with frozen methane on its surface, and is probably irregularly shaped. In 1978 a moon of Pluto was discovered, called Charon. This is about 40 per cent of Pluto's diameter and orbits the planet every 6.39 days, the same time that Pluto takes to spin on its axis, so that Charon remains permanently above the same place on Pluto. Some astronomers have suggested that Pluto was a former moon of Neptune that escaped.

Pluto /'pluːtəʊ/ in Roman mythology, the lord of Hades, the underworld. He was the brother of Jupiter and Neptune.

plutonium a synthetic element first produced in 1940 by ◊Seaborg and his co-workers at the University of California by bombarding uranium with deuterons: symbol Pu, atomic weight 242, atomic number 94. Its most stable isotope, Pu-239 (discovered 1941), has a ◊half-life of 24,000 years, is fissile, and usually made in reactors by bombarding U-238 with neutrons. It is used in atom bombs, as a fissionable material in reactors, and for enriching the abundant U-238, but has awkward physical properties, and is very poisonous to animals, being absorbed into bone.

Plymouth /'plɪməθ/ city and seaport in Devon, England, at the mouth of the Plym, with dockyard, barracks, and naval base at Devonport; population (1981) 244,000. The city rises N from the Hoe headland where tradition has it that ◊Drake played bowls before leaving to fight the Spanish Armada. John ◊Hawkins, Drake, and the *Mayflower* sailed from Plymouth Sound. The city centre was reconstructed after heavy bombing in World War II.

Plymouth Brethren a fundamentalist Christian Protestant sect characterized by extreme simplicity of belief, founded in Dublin c. 1827 by the Reverend John Nelson Darby (1800–82). The movement gained strength and an assembly was held in Plymouth in 1831 to celebrate its arrival in England, but by 1848 the movement had split into 'Open' and 'Close' Brethren. The latter refuse communion with all those not of their persuasion. The Plymouth Brethren are found mainly in the fishing villages of NE Scotland; membership 80,000.

Plynlimon /plɪn'lɪmən/ mountain in Powys, Wales, with three summits, the highest 752 m/2,468 ft.

plywood a manufactured wood made up of thin sheets, or plies, of wood. They are stuck together so that the grain of one sheet is at right-angles to the grain of the plies on either side, which gives plywood equal strength in every direction.

Plzeň /'pɪlzən/ (German *Pilsen*) industrial city (heavy machinery, cars; Skoda armaments works; known for its lager beer) in W Czechoslovakia, at the confluence of the Radbuza and Mze rivers, 84 km/52 mi SW of Prague; population (1984) 174,000.

pneumatic drill a drill operated by compressed air, used in mining and tunnelling for drilling shot-holes (for explosives) and in road mending. It contains an air-operated piston which delivers hammer blows to the drill ◊bit many times a second. The French engineer Germain Sommeiller developed it for tunnelling in the Alps in 1861.

pneumatophore an erect root that rises up above the soil or water and promotes gaseous exchange. They are formed by certain swamp-dwelling trees, such as mangroves, since there is little oxygen available to the roots in waterlogged conditions. They have numerous pores or ◊lenticels over their surface.

pneumoconiosis disease of the lungs caused by dust, especially from coal, which causes the lung to become fibrous, so that the patient has difficulty breathing.

pneumonia inflammation of the lung, the result of infection by microorganisms. Pneumonias are divided into the specific pneumonias, which are caused by a specific pathogenic organism; and the aspiration pneumonias, in which some abnormality of the respiratory system allows the lung to be attacked by non-specific bacteria of low virulence. Treatment is usually by antibiotics.

pneumothorax presence of air in the pleural cavity between the lungs and the thorax, causing the collapse of the former.

Pnom Penh /'nɒm 'pen/ alternative form of ◊Phnom Penh, capital of Kampuchea.

Po /pəʊ/ longest river in Italy, from the Cottian Alps to the Adriatic; length 668 km/415 mi. Its valley is fertile and there is natural gas.

Pobeda, Pik /pɒb'jedə/ mountain in the ◊Tyan-Shan range in China.

Pocahontas /ˌpɒkə'hɒntəs/ c. 1595–1617. American Indian princess alleged to have saved the life of John ◊Smith, the English colonist, when he was captured by her father Powhatan. She married an Englishman, and has many modern American descendants. She died in Gravesend, Kent.

pochard type of diving duck. The common pochard *Aythya ferina*, in which the male has a rich red head, black breast, and whitish body and wings with black markings, is about 45 cm/1.5 ft long. The canvas-back *Aythya valisineria*, a related species, is especially prized in America as food.

pod in botany, a type of ◊fruit that is characteristic of plants, such as peas and beans, belonging to the Leguminosae family. It develops from a single carpel and splits down both sides when ripe to release the seeds. In certain species the seeds may be ejected explosively due to uneven drying of the fruit wall, which sets up tensions within the fruit.

Podgorica /'pɒdgərɪtsə/ former name of ◊Titograd, city in Yugoslavia.

Podolsk /pə'dɒlsk/ industrial city (oil refining, machinery, cables, cement, ceramics) in the USSR, 40 km/25 mi SW of Moscow; population (1985) 208,000.

Poe /pəʊ/ Edgar Allan 1809–1849. American author, born in Boston. He was orphaned 1811, and joined the army but he was court-martialled for neglect of duty. He failed to earn a living by writing, became addicted to alcohol, and in 1847 lost his wife (commemorated in his poem *Annabel Lee*). His verse, of haunting lyric beauty, influenced the French ◊Symbolists (for example, *Ulalume* and *The Bells*). His popular reputation rests on his short stories, unrivalled in the creation of horrific atmosphere (such as 'The Fall of the House of Usher' 1839) and acute reasoning (for example, 'The Gold Bug' 1843 and 'The Murders in the Rue Morgue' 1841), in which the investigators Legrand and Dupin anticipated ◊Conan Doyle's Sherlock Holmes.

Poe Daguerreotype of American writer Edgar Allan Poe. Although his horror stories such as *The Fall of the House of Usher*, and *The Murders in the Rue Morgue* are some of the most popular short stories ever written, Poe failed to make a living from his writing and died an alcoholic and penniless at the age of 40.

Poet Laureate poet of the British royal household, so called because of the laurel wreath awarded to eminent poets in the Graeco-Roman world. Early poets with unofficial status were ◊Chaucer, ◊Skelton, ◊Spenser, ◊Daniel, and ◊Jonson; the first official title-holder was ◊Dryden. There is a stipend of £70 per annum, plus £27 in lieu of a traditional butt of sack.

Poets Laureate
1638 Sir William Davenant
1668 John Dryden
1689 Thomas Shadwell
1692 Nahum Tate
1715 Nicholas Rowe
1718 Laurence Eusden
1730 Colley Cibber
1757 William Whitehead
1785 Thomas Warton
1790 Henry Pye
1813 Robert Southey
1843 William Wordsworth
1850 Alfred, Lord Tennyson
1896 Alfred Austin
1913 Robert Bridges
1930 John Masefield
1968 Cecil Day Lewis
1972 Sir John Betjeman
1984 Ted Hughes

poetry the imaginative expression of emotion, thought, or narrative, often in metrical form, and often in figurative language. Poetry has traditionally been distinguished from prose (ordinary written language) by rhyme or rhythmical arrangement of words, although the distinction is not always clear cut. Poetry is often described as lyric, or songlike (sonnet, ode, elegy, pastoral), and narrative, or story-telling (ballad, lay, epic). Poetic form has also been used as a vehicle for satire, parody, and expositions of philosophical, religious, and practical subjects.

pogrom Russian term, literally meaning 'devastation', applied to unprovoked attacks on the Jews, especially those carried out with official connivance. The Russian pogroms began in 1881, and were common throughout the country down to the Revolution. Also applied to anti-Jewish actions elsewhere in E Europe and Germany.

poikilothermy the condition in which an animal's body temperature is largely dependent on the temperature of the air or water in which it lives. It is characteristic of all animals except birds and mammals, which, being ◊homeothermic, are able to generate heat metabolically and thus maintain a constant body temperature. Poikilotherms are often referred to as 'cold-blooded animals', but this is not really correct: their blood may be as warm as their surroundings, which means it may be warmer than the blood of birds and mammals, for example, in very hot climates. Poikilotherms have some means of warming themselves up, above the air temperature, such as basking in the sun, or shivering, and can cool themselves down by sheltering from the sun under a rock or by bathing in water.

Poincaré /'pwæŋkæreɪ/ Jules Henri 1854–1912. French mathematician, who developed the theory of differential equations and was a pioneer in ◊relativity theory.

Poincaré /'pwæŋkæreɪ/ Raymond Nicolas Landry 1860–1934. French politician, a cousin of Jules Henri ◊Poincaré. He was prime minister 1912–13, president 1913–20, and again prime minister 1922–24 (when he carried out the occupation of the Ruhr, Germany) and 1926–29.

poinsettia winter flowering shrub *Euphorbia pulcherrima*, also known as Mexican flame-leaf and Christmas-flower, with large red leaves encircling small greenish-yellow flowers. Named after its discoverer, J R Poinsett, in 1836. It is widely associated with Christmas and in Mexico it is known as the Flower of the Holy Night.

pointe the tip of the toe. A dancer *sur les pointes* is dancing on her toes in blocked shoes, as first popularized by Marie ◊Taglioni in 1832.

Pointe-Noire /'pwænt 'nwɑː/ chief port of the Congo, with shipbuilding yards, formerly (1950–58) the capital; population (1980) 185,105.

pointer breed of dog developed to indicate the position of game which it has scented by standing nose pointed towards it, often with one foot raised, in silence. They are often liver and white, about 60 cm/2 ft tall.

pointillism technique in oil painting in which dabs of pure colour are applied to the canvas, and arranged in such a way that when viewed from a distance they blend into harmonious tones. Green grass, for instance, is made up of closely packed points of blue and yellow. This technique, also known as Neo-Impressionism, was adopted by ◊Seurat, ◊Signac, and others.

poise ◊c.g.s. unit of viscosity (P). Defined as the viscosity of a fluid in which a tangential force of 1 dyne/cm^2 maintains a difference of velocity of 1 cm/s between two parallel planes 1 m apart.

Poiseuille's formula in physics, a relationship describing the rate of flow of a fluid through a narrow tube. For a capillary (very narrow) tube of length l and radius r with a pressure difference p between its ends, and a liquid of ◊viscosity ϵ, the velocity of flow expressed as the volume per second is $\pi pr^4/8l\epsilon$. The formula was devised in 1843 by the French physicist Jean Louis Poiseuille (1799–1869).

poison a chemical substance which when introduced into or applied to the body is capable of injuring health or destroying life. The majority of poisons may be divided into *corrosives*, for example, sulphuric, nitric, hydrochloric acids, caustic soda, and· corrosive sublimate, which burn and destroy the parts with which they come into contact; *irritants* such as arsenic, copper sulphate, zinc chloride, silver nitrate, and green vitriol, which have an irritating effect on the stomach and bowels; *narcotics*, for example, opium, prussic acid, potassium cyanide, chloroform, carbon monoxide, which affect the brain and spinal cord, inducing a stupor; *narcotico-irritants* which combine intense irritations and finally act as narcotics, for example, carbolic acid, foxglove, henbane, deadly nightshade (belladonna), tobacco, and many other substances of plant origin.

In non-corrosive poisoning every effort is made to remove the poison from the system as soon as possible, for example, usually by vomiting induced by an emetic. For some corrosive and irritant poisons there are chemical antidotes, but for recently developed poisons in a new category, for example, ◊paraquat, which produce proliferative changes in the system, there is no antidote.

In most countries the sale of poison is carefully controlled by law, and, in general, only qualified and registered pharmacists and medical practitioners may dispense them.

Poitiers /'pwætieɪ/ capital of Poitou-Charentes, France; cathedral begun 1162; university 1431; population (1982) 103,000. The Merovingian king Clovis defeated the Visigoths under Alaric here 507; ◊Charles Martel stemmed the Saracen advance 732, and ◊Edward the Black Prince defeated the French 1356.

Poitou-Charentes /pwɑː'tuː ʃæ'rɒnt/ region of W central France; capital Poitiers; population (1984) 1,575,500.

poker card game of US origin, in which two to eight people play (usually for stakes), and try to obtain a hand of five cards ranking higher than those of their opponents. The one with the best scoring hand wins the central pool.

Poland /'pəʊlənd/ country in E Europe, bounded to the E by the USSR, to the S by Czechoslovakia, and to the W by East Germany.
government Under the constitution of 1952, Poland has a single-chamber, 460-member parliament (*Sejm*) which is the supreme organ of state power. Since 1985, 410 of its members have been elected for four-year terms by universal suffrage from constituencies in which there is a choice of two candidates. The remaining 50 members are elected unopposed from a national list of conspicuous public figures. The *Sejm* elects a 17-member council of state, headed by a president, to function as its permanent policy-making organ, and a council of ministers, headed by the prime minister, as its executive organ, effecting day-to-day government administration. The Supreme Board of Control supervises the work of both bodies.
The dominant force in Poland is the Polish United Workers' Party (PUWP), organized on traditional Communist lines. It leads the broader Patriotic Movement for National Rebirth (which includes two minor parties) in presenting an approved list of election candidates. At the local level, there are elected people's councils in each of the country's 49 provinces (*voivodships*).
history In the 10th century the Polish tribes were first united under one Christian ruler, Mieczyslaw. Mongols devastated the country in 1241, and thereafter German and Jewish refugees settled among the◊Slav population. The first parliament met in 1331, and Casimir the Great (1333–70) raised the country to a high level of prosperity. Under the Jagellion dynasty (1386–1572) Poland became a great power, the largest country in Europe when it was united with Lithuania (1569–1776). Elected kings followed the death of the last Jagellion, a reactionary nobility wielded much power, and Poland's strength declined. But Stephen Bathory defeated Ivan the Terrible of Russia 1581 and in 1683 John III Sobieski forced the Turks to raise their siege of Vienna. In the mid-17th century a war against Russia, Sweden, and Brandenburg ended in the complete defeat of Poland, from which it never recovered.
Wars with the Ottoman Empire, dissension among the nobles, quarrels at the election of every king, the continuance of serfdom, and the persecution of Protestants and Greek Orthodox Catholics, laid the country open to interference by Austria, Russia, and Prussia, ending with partition 1772, and again in 1793, when Prussia and Russia seized further areas. A patriotic rising led by Tadeusz Kosciuszko was defeated and Russia and Prussia occupied the rest of the country 1795. The Congress of Vienna rearranged the division in 1815 and reconstituted the Russian portion as a kingdom under the tsar. Risings in 1830 and 1863 led to intensified

repression and an increased attempt to Russianize the population.
Poland was revived as an independent republic in 1918, under the leadership of Jósef Pilsudski, taking advantage of Russia's internal upheaval to advance into Lithuania and the Ukraine before the Polish troops were driven back by the Red Army. Russia and Poland then agreed on a frontier E of the ◊Curzon Line, and Pilsudski effectively ruled Poland until his death in 1935. In Apr 1939 Britain and France concluded a pact with Poland to render military aid if it was attacked, and at the beginning of Sept Germany invaded (see ◊World War II).
A treaty between Russia and Poland in Aug 1945 (ratified 1946) established Poland's eastern frontier at the Curzon Line. Poland lost 70,000 sq mi in the E to Russia but gained 39,000 sq mi in the W from Germany. After elections, a 'people's republic' was established in Feb 1947 and Poland joined ◊Comecon (1949) and the ◊Warsaw Pact (1955), remaining under close Soviet supervision, with the Soviet marshal ◊Rokossovsky serving as minister for war 1949–56. A harsh, Stalinist form of rule was instituted under the leadership of Boleslaw Bierut (1892–1956), involving rural collectivization, the persecution of Catholic church opposition and the arrest, in 1953, of Cardinal Stefan Wyszynski. In Jun 1956, serious strikes and riots, leading to 53 deaths, broke out in Poznan in opposition to Soviet 'exploitation' and food shortages. The more pragmatic Wladyslaw ◊Gomulka took over as PUWP leader, reintroduced private farming and released Cardinal Wyszynski.
A further outbreak of strikes and rioting in Gdansk, Gdynia, and Szczecin in Dec 1970 followed sudden food-price rises. This led to Gomulka's replacement as PUWP leader by the Silesia party boss Edward ◊Gierek, whose programme aimed at raising living standards and consumer-goods production. The country's foreign debt grew and food prices again triggered strikes and demonstrations in Jun 1976. Opposition to the Gierek regime, which was accused of corruption, mounted in 1979 after a visit to his homeland by the recently elected pope ◊John Paul II. Strikes in Warsaw in 1980, following a poor harvest and meat-price rises, rapidly spread across the country. The government attempted to appease workers by entering into pay negotiations with unofficial strike committees, but at the Gdansk shipyards demands emerged for permission to form free, independent trade unions. The government conceded the right to strike, and in Aug 1980 in Gdansk the Solidarity (Solidarność) union was formed under the leadership of Lech ◊Walesa.
In Sept 1980, the ailing Gierek was replaced as PUWP leader by Stanislaw Kania, but unrest continued as the 10-million member Solidarity campaigned for a five-day working week and established a rural section. With food shortages mounting and PUWP control slipping, Kania was replaced as PUWP leader by the prime minister, Gen Wojciech ◊Jaruzelski, in Oct 1981; the Soviet army was active on Poland's borders; and martial law was imposed on 13 Dec

1981. Trade-union activity was banned, the leaders of Solidarity arrested, a night curfew imposed, and the Military Council of National Salvation established, headed by Gen Jaruzelski. Five months of severe repression ensued, resulting in 15 deaths and 10,000 arrests. The USA imposed economic sanctions.
In Jun 1982, curfew restrictions were eased, prompting further serious rioting in Aug. In Nov Walesa was released and in Dec 1982 martial law was suspended (lifted 1983). Pope John Paul II visited Poland 1983 and called for conciliation. The authorities responded by dissolving the Military Council and granting an amnesty to political prisoners and activists. In 1984, 35,000 prisoners and detainees were released on the 40th anniversary of the People's Republic, and the USA relaxed its economic sanctions.
The Jaruzelski administration pursued pragmatic reform, including liberalization of the electoral system. Conditions remained tense, however, strained by the murder of Father Jerzy Popieluszko, a pro-Solidarity priest, by security-force members in 1984; by the continued ban on Solidarity; and by a threat (withdrawn 1986) to try Lech Walesa for slandering state electoral officials. Economic conditions and farm output slowly improved, but Poland's foreign debt remained huge. In Sept 1986, with the release of further prominent dissidents and the establishment of the broad new Consultative Council, the Jaruzelski administration sought to regain the public's trust. Strong opposition persists in the form of Catholic Intelligentsia clubs and the underground Temporary Advisory Council and Peace and Freedom human-rights monitoring groups.

Polanski /pə'lænski/ Roman 1933– . French-born film director. He suffered a traumatic childhood in Nazi-occupied Poland, and later his wife, actress Sharon Tate, was the victim of a particularly brutal murder. His tragic personal life is reflected in a fascination with horror and violence in his work. His films include *Repulsion* 1965, *Cul de Sac* 1966, *Rosemary's Baby* 1968, and *Tess* 1979.

polar coordinates in mathematics, a way of defining the position of a point in terms of its distance r from fixed point (the origin) and its angle τ to a fixed line or axis. The coordinates of the point are (r, τ). Often the angle is measured in ◊radians, rather than degrees. The system is useful for defining positions on a plane in programming the operations of computer-controlled cloth-and metal-cutting machines.

Polaris the bright ◊star closest to the north celestial pole (see ◊celestial sphere), and the brightest star in the constellation ◊Ursa Minor; also known as Alpha Ursae Minoris or the Pole Star. Polaris is a yellow supergiant about 700 light years away, its position indicated by the 'pointers' in ◊Ursa Major. It currently lies within 1 degree of the north celestial pole. ◊Precession (Earth's axial wobble) will bring Polaris closest to the celestial pole (less than half a degree away) about 2100 AD.

polarized light ordinary light can be regarded as electromagnetic vibrations at right angles to the line of propagation but in different

Poland

PEOPLE'S REPUBLIC OF (*Polska Rzeczpospolita Ludowa*)

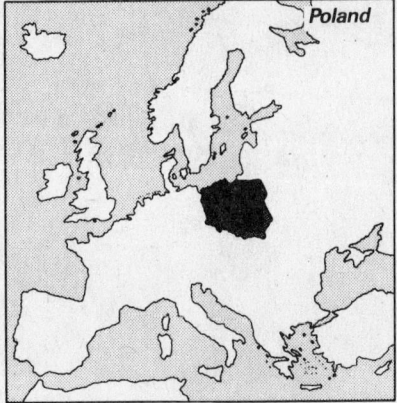

Poland

AREA 312,600 sq km/120,600 sq mi
CAPITAL Warsaw
TOWNS Lódź, Kraków, Wroclaw, Poznań, Katowice, Bydgoszcz; Lublin; ports Gdánsk, Szczecin, Gdynia
PHYSICAL comprises part of the great plain of Europe; Vistula, Oder, and Neisse rivers; Sudeten, Tatra, and Carpathian mountains
FEATURES Black Madonna at Czestochowa
HEAD OF STATE Wojciech Jaruzelski from 1985
HEAD OF GOVERNMENT Zbigniew Messner from 1985
GOVERNMENT communist
EXPORTS coal, softwood timber, chemicals, machinery, ships
CURRENCY zloty (467.79 = £1 Sept 1987)
POPULATION (1985) 37,160,000
LANGUAGE Polish, a member of the western branch of the Slavonic family
RELIGION Roman Catholic 93%
LITERACY 99.3% male/98.3% female (1978)
GNP $110 bn (1984); $2,750 per head of population
CHRONOLOGY
1918 Poland revived as independent republic.
1939 German invasion and occupation.
1944 Germans driven out by Soviet force.
1945 Polish boundaries redrawn at Potsdam Conference.
1947 Communist people's republic proclaimed.
1956 Poznań riots. Gomulka installed as Polish United Workers' Party (PUWP) leader.
1970 Gomulka replaced by Gierek after Gdansk riots.
1980 Emergence of Solidarity free trade union following Gdansk disturbances.
1981 Imposition of martial law by General Jaruzelski.
1983 Ending of martial law.
1984 Amnesty for political prisoners.
1987 Referendum on economic reform rejected.

planes. Light is said to be polarized when the vibrations take place in one particular plane. Ordinary light may be plane polarized by reflection from a polished surface or by passing it through a Nicol prism or a synthetic polarizing film such as Polaroid. Polarized light is used to test the strength of sugar solutions, to measure stresses in transparent materials, and to prevent glare, among other applications.

Polaroid camera an instant-picture camera, invented by Edwin Land in the USA in 1947. The original camera produced black-and-white prints in about one minute. Modern cameras can produce black-and-white prints in a few seconds and colour prints in less than a minute. An advanced model has automatic focusing and exposure. The film consists of layers of emulsion and colour dyes together with a pod of chemical developer. When the film is ejected, the pod bursts and processing begins, in the light.

polar reversal the changeover in polarity of the Earth's magnetic poles. Studies of the magnetism of rocks have shown that in the past the Earth's N magnetic pole was the S one, and vice versa. Polar reversal seems to be relatively frequent, taking place three or four times every million years. The last occasion was 700,000 years ago, and it is calculated that in about 1,200 years' time the N magnetic pole will become the S magnetic pole. Movements of the Earth's molten core are thought to be responsible for both the Earth's magnetic field and its reversal.

Pole /poul/ Reginald 1500–1558. English cardinal from 1536, who returned from Rome to England on the accession of Mary as papal legatee to readmit England to the Catholic church, and succeeded ◊Cranmer as archbishop of Canterbury 1556.

polecat species of weasel *Mustela putorius* with a brown back and dark belly. The body is about 45 cm/18 in long and it has a strong smell. The ancestor of the domestic ferret.

poles the geographic N and S points of penetration of the Earth's surface by the axis about which it rotates. The magnetic poles are the points towards which a freely suspended magnetic needle will point, and they vary continually; in 1985 the magnetic N pole was some 350 km/218 mi NW of Resolute Bay in the Northwest Territories. It moves northwards about 10 km/6 mi each year, although it can vary in a day about 80 km/50 mi from its average position. It is relocated every decade in order to update navigational charts. Periodic changes within the Earth's core cause a reversal of the magnetic poles (see ◊polar reversal). Many animals, including migrating birds and fish, are thought to orientate themselves partly using the Earth's magnetic field. There is a permanent inhabited scientific base at the South Pole.

Pole Star see ◊Polaris, the northern pole star.

police civil law-and-order force. In the UK it is under the Home Office, with 56 autonomous police forces, generally speaking organized on a county basis; mutual aid is given in circumstances such as mass picketing in the 1984–85 miners' strike, but there is no national police force or police riot unit (such as the French CRS riot squad). The predecessors of these forces were the ineffective medieval watch and London's Bow Street runners, introduced 1749 by Henry ◊Fielding, which formed a model for the London police force established by ◊Peel's government 1829 (hence 'peelers' or 'bobbies'); the system was introduced throughout the country from 1856.

Landmarks include: *Criminal Investigation Department* detective branch of the London Metropolitan Police (New Scotland Yard) 1878, recruited from the uniformed branch (such departments now exist in all UK forces); women police 1919; motorcycle patrols 1921; two-way radio cars 1927; personal radio on the beat 1965; and *Special Patrol Groups* (SPG) 1970, squads of experienced men concentrating on a specific problem (New York has the similar Tactical Patrol Force). Unlike most other police forces, the British are armed only on special occasions, but arms issues grow more frequent.

Foreign police forces include the Garda Síochána in the Republic of Ireland, Carabinieri in Italy, Guardia Civil in Spain, Police Nationale (under the Ministry of the Interior) for the cities and Gendarmerie (part of the army) elsewhere in France.

polio (poliomyelitis) viral inflammation of the anterior horn cells of the spinal cord (governing muscle action), causing paralysis, especially in children. It has been practically eliminated by the use of vaccines, the first developed by ◊Salk.

Polish Corridor strip of land, designated under the Treaty of ◊Versailles 1919 to give Poland access to the Baltic, and which cut off East Prussia from the rest of Germany. It was absorbed when Poland took over the southern part of East Prussia in 1945.

Polish language a member of the Slavonic branch of the Indo-European language family, spoken mainly in Poland. Polish is written in the Roman and not the Cyrillic alphabet and its standard form is based on the dialect of Poznań in W Poland.

Politburo contraction of 'political bureau', a subcommittee (known as the Praesidium 1952–66) of the Central Committee of the Communist Party in the USSR and some other communist states, which lays down party policy.

political action committee (PAC) an organization in the USA which raises funds for political candidates and in return commits them to a particular policy. It also spends money on changing public opinion. There were 3,500 PACs in 1984, and they controlled 25 per cent of all funds spent in ◊Congress elections.

Polk /pauk/ James Knox 1795–1849. 11th president of the USA, born in North Carolina. He was elected president as a Democrat in 1844, admitted Texas to the Union, and forced the war on Mexico which resulted in the annexation of California and New Mexico.

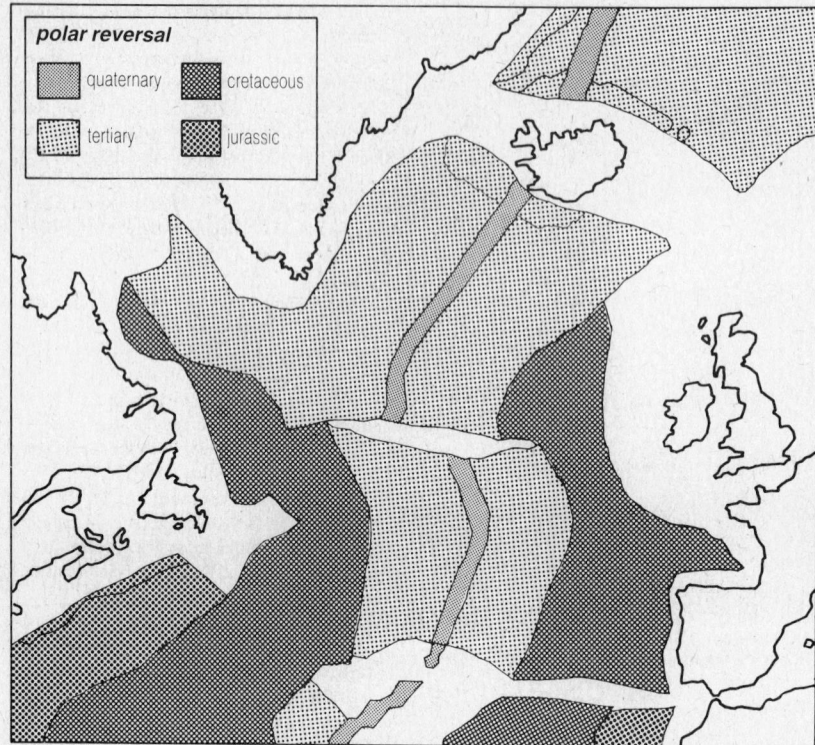

polar reversal

- quaternary
- cretaceous
- tertiary
- jurassic

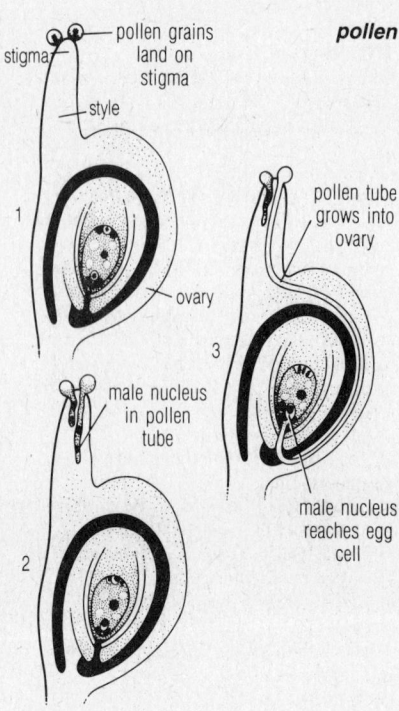

pollen

pollen grains land on stigma

stigma

style

1

ovary

pollen tube grows into ovary

3

male nucleus in pollen tube

male nucleus reaches egg cell

2

polka folk dance in lively two-four time originating in Bohemia. From about 1830 it became fashionable in European society.

pollack marine fish *Pollachius pollachius* of the cod family, growing to 75 cm/2.5 ft, and found inshore where it is caught by anglers.

Pollaiuolo /pɒˌlaɪuˈʊuləu/ Antonio 1429–1498. Italian sculptor and engraver, who worked with ◊Ghiberti on the doors of the ◊Baptistery, Florence. He is also noted for his study of the body in action, shown in paintings such as the *Martyrdom of St Sebastian* 1475 (National Gallery, London).

pollarding a type of pruning whereby the young branches of a tree are severely cut back, about 6–12 ft/2–4 m above the ground, to produce a stump-like trunk with a rounded, bushy head of thin new branches. It is often practised on willows, where the new branches or 'poles' are cut at intervals of a year or more, and used for fencing and firewood.

pollen the grains formed by seed plants that contain the male gametes. In ◊angiosperms pollen is produced within ◊anthers, and in most ◊gymnosperms it is produced in male ◊cones. A pollen grain is typically yellow and, when mature, has a hard outer wall. On germination a pollen tube grows out through one of the pores in the pollen grain wall and the nuclei migrate into this tube on their journey to the female reproductive organs. Pollen of insect-pollinated plants (see ◊pollination) is often sticky and spiny, and larger than the smooth, light grains produced by wind-pollinated species. The outer wall of both is often elaborately sculptured with ridges or spines, so distinctive that individual species or genera of plants can be recognized from their pollen. Since pollen grains are extremely resistant to decay, much important information on the vegetation of earlier times can be gained from the study of fossil pollen. The study of pollen grains is known as palynology.

pollen tube an outgrowth from a ◊pollen grain that grows towards the ◊ovule, following germination of the grain on the stigma. In angiosperms the pollen tube reaches the ovule by growing down through the ◊style, carrying the male gametes inside. The gametes are discharged into the ovule and one fertilizes the egg cell.

pollination the process by which ◊fertilization occurs in the sexual reproduction of higher plants. In flowering plants there are two main types: self-pollination occurs when ◊pollen is transferred to a stigma of the same flower, or to another flower on the same plant; cross-pollination occurs when pollen is transferred to another plant. The latter involves external pollen-carrying agents, such as wind (see ◊anemophily), water, insects, birds (see ◊ornithophily), bats or other small mammals. Animal pollinators carry the pollen on their bodies and are attracted to the flower by scent, or by the sight of the ◊petals. Most flowers are adapted for pollination by one particular agent only. Those that rely on animals generally produce nectar, a sugary liquid, or surplus pollen, or both, on which the pollinator feeds. Thus the relationship between pollinator and plant is an example of ◊mutualism, in which both benefit. However in some plants, the pollinator receives no benefit (as in ◊pseudocopulation), while in others, nectar may be removed by animals that do not effect pollination.

Pollination of flowering plants also leads to the formation of the ◊endosperm, for whch a second male gamete is needed; the process is known as *double fertilization*.

pollinium a group of pollen grains which is transported as a single unit during pollination. Pollinia are especially common in orchids.

Pollock /ˈpɒlək/ Jackson 1912–56. US artist. From the 1940s he became the leading exponent of ◊action painting. By putting his canvas on the floor and swirling paint on it he created a web of multicoloured trails which the spectator could retrace with his eyes, thereby reliving the artist's dynamic act of creation.

poll tax or *community tax* tax levied on every individual, without reference to their income or property. Being simple to administer, it was among the earliest sorts of tax (introduced in England 1377), but because of its indiscriminate nature it has often proved unpopular: it led to the ◊Peasants' Revolt in 1381 and was abolished in England in 1698, while in the USA it was declared unconstitutional because of its frequent abuse as a tool for disenfranchising blacks. In 1987 the British government proposed its reintroduction as a replacement for property-based local taxation (◊rates).

pollution the harmful effect on the environment of the by-products of any human activity, principally industrial and agricultural processes, for example, noise, smoke, gases, chemical effluents in seas and rivers, indestructible pesticides, sewage, and household waste. Natural disasters may also cause pollution: volcanic eruptions, for example, cause ash to be ejected into the atmosphere and deposited on the land surface. Pollution control involves higher production costs for the industries concerned, but failure to implement adequate controls results in damage to the environment, and an increase in the incidence of diseases such as cancer. Heavily polluted areas may eventually become uninhabitable.

polo game played between two teams of four on horseback, which originated in Iran, spread to India and was first played in England 1869, where the rules were evolved by Hurlingham Club 1875. A game lasts about an hour, divided into 'chukkas' of 7½ minutes. The small ball is struck with the side of a mallet through goals at each end of the ground.

Polo /'pəʊləʊ/ Marco 1254–1324. Venetian traveller. He allegedly travelled overland to China 1271–75, where he claimed to have been a favourite of ◊Kublai Khan, whom he served until he returned to Europe by sea 1292–95. He was then captured while fighting for Venice against Genoa, and in prison wrote an account of his travels. Modern scholars suspect that he may never have reached China, and that the reliable and valuable material in his narrative derives from conversations with merchants who had been there.

polonaise a Polish dance, in stately three-four time, which dates from the 16th century. Chopin developed the polonaise as a musical form.

polonium the first radioactive element discovered by Marie and Pierre ◊Curie in 1898 (in pitchblende residues) and named after Marie Curie's native Poland: symbol Po, atomic number 84, atomic weight 210. Polonium occurs naturally, but only in minute quantities. It has the largest number of isotopes of any element. One potential use for polonium is as a lightweight power source in satellites.

Poltava /pɒl'tɑːvə/ city in the Ukrainian Republic, USSR, capital of Poltava region, on the river Vorskla; population (1985) 302,000. Peter the Great defeated ◊Charles XII of Sweden here in 1709.

poltergeist (German 'noisy ghost') unexplained phenomenon that invisibly moves objects or hurls them about, start fires, or causes other mischief; often linked to adolescents.

polyandry system whereby a woman has more than one husband at the same time. It is found in many parts of the world, for example, in Madagascar, Malaya, and certain Pacific isles, and among certain Inuit and South American Indian groups. In Tibet and certain parts of India polyandry takes the form of the marriage of one woman to several brothers.

polyanthus garden variety of ◊primrose, with multiple flowers on one stalk.

Polycarp, Saint /'pɒlɪkɑːp/ c. 69–c. 155. Christian martyr allegedly converted by St John. As bishop of ◊Smyrna, Asia Minor, for over 40 years he carried on a vigorous struggle against various heresies, and was burned alive at a public festival; feast day 26 Jan.

polychlorinated biphenyls (PCBs) a group of dangerous industrial chemicals, valuable for their fire-resisting qualities, but an environmental hazard because of persistent toxicity. Since 1973 their use has been limited by international agreement.

polyester a type of thermosetting ◊plastic, used in making synthetic fibres, such as Dacron and Terylene, resins, and constructional plastics. With glass fibre added as reinforcement, polyesters are used in, for example, car bodies and boat hulls.

polyethylene a polymer of the gas ethylene, (now called ethene, C_2H_4), best known under the tradename Polythene. It is a thermoplastic (see plastic) and was first made by the German chemist ◊Ziegler.

polygamy the practice of a man having more than one wife at the same time. It is found among many peoples, especially in Africa. Normally it is confined to chiefs and nobles, as in Ancient Egypt and among the primitive Teutons, Irish, and Slavs. Among the Hebrews a man could have any number of wives, but Islam limits a man's legal wives to four. Certain Christian sects, for example, the Anabaptists of Münster, Germany, and the Mormons, have practised polygamy.

polygon in geometry, a plane (two-dimensional) figure with three or more sides. Common polygons have their own names, which define the number of sides (for example, triangle, quadrilateral, pentagon). These are all convex polygons, having no interior angle greater than 180°. In general, the more sides a polygon has, the larger the sum of its internal angles and, in the case of a convex polygon, the more closely it approximates to a circle.

POLYGON

Polygon	number of sides	sum of interior angles (degrees)
triangle	3	180
quadrilateral	4	360
pentagon	5	540
hexagon	6	720
heptagon	7	900
octagon	8	1,080
decagon	10	1,440
duodecagon	12	1,800
icosagon	20	3,240

polygraph also called a *polygram*: an instrument that records graphically certain body activities, such as thoracic and abdominal respiration, blood pressure, pulse rate, and galvanic skin response. Changes in these activities when a person answers a question may indicate that the person is lying.

polyhedron in geometry, a solid figure with four or more plane faces. Common polyhedra have their own names (for example, pyramid, tetrahedron, cube, cuboid, prism). There are only five types of regular polyhedra (with all faces the same size and shape), as was deduced by early Greek mathematicians; they are the tetrahedron (four equilateral triangular faces), cube (six square faces), octahedron (eight equilateral triangles), dodecahedron (12 regular pentagons) and icosahedron (20 equilateral triangles). The more faces there are on a polyhedron, the more closely it approximates to a sphere. Knowledge of the properties of polyhedra is important in crystallography and

stereochemistry in determining the shapes of crystals and molecules.

Polyhymnia in Greek mythology, the ◊Muse of singing, mime, and sacred dance.

polymer a compound made up of large molecules composed of many repeated simple units or *monomers*, for example starch, nylon, Perspex. In *addition polymerization*, the monomers are simply concatenated (chained together); in *condensation polymerization*, the reaction involves the formation of a small molecule such as water or alcohol.

polymerization the chemical union of two or more (usually small) molecules of the same kind to form a new compound. There are three types: addition polymerization, simple multiples of the same compound; condensation polymerization, in which molecules are joined together by the elimination of water; and co-polymerization, in which the polymer is built up from two or more different types of molecules. There are many important polymers, both natural (for example cellulose, chitin, lignin) and synthetic, (for example, polyethylene and nylon); see ◊plastics.

polymorphism in ◊genetics, the coexistence of several distinctly different types in a ◊population. Examples include the different ◊blood groups in humans, and different colour forms in some butterflies.

Polynesia /ˌpɒlɪ'niːziə/ those islands of ◊Oceania E of 170° E latitude, including ◊Hawaii, ◊Kiribati, ◊Tuvalu, ◊Fiji, ◊Tonga, ◊Tokelau, ◊Samoa, ◊Cook Islands, and ◊French Polynesia.
Polynesians, who include the ◊Maori of New Zealand, are probably of Asiatic origin, and are distinct from the Melanesians, with whom there has been a degree of mixture.

Polynesia

Polynesia /ˌpɒlɪ'niːziə/ French islands in the South Pacific; see under ◊French Polynesia.

Polynesian languages see ◊Malayo-Polynesian languages.

polynomial in mathematics, algebraic expression that has only one ◊variable (denoted by a letter). A polynomial whose highest ◊power of x is 1, as in $2x + 1$, is called a linear polynomial;

$3x^2 + 2x + 1$ is quadratic; $4x^3 + 3x^2 + 2x + 1$ is cubic, and so on. The general expression for a polynomial in which n is the highest power is given by $ax^n + bx^{n-1} + cx^{n-2} +$ where a, b and c are arbitrary ◊constants.

polypeptide a long-chain ◊peptide.

polyphony music combining two or more 'voices' or parts, each with an individual melody.

polyploid in genetics, possessing three or more sets of ◊chromosomes in cases where the normal complement is two sets (◊diploid). Polyploidy arises spontaneously and is common in plants (especially among the angiosperms), but rare in animals. Matings between polyploid individuals and normal diploid ones are invariably sterile. Hence, an individual which develops polyploidy through a genetic aberration can initially only reproduce vegetatively, ◊parthenogenetically or by self-fertilization (modes of reproduction that are common only among plants). Once a polyploid population is established, however, they can reproduce sexually. Many crop plants are natural polyploids, including wheat, which has four sets of chromosomes per cell (durum wheat) or six sets (bread wheat). Plant breeders can induce the formation of polyploids by treatment with a chemical, colchicine.

polypus small 'stalked' benign tumour, most usually found on mucous membrane of the nose and bowel. They are usually removed to avoid their later becoming cancerous.

polysaccharide long-chain carbohydrate made up of hundreds or thousands of linked simple sugars (monosaccharides) such as glucose. The polysaccharides are natural polymers. They either act as energy-rich food stores in plants (starch) and animals (glycogen), or have structural roles in the plant cell wall (cellulose) or the tough outer skeleton of insects and similar creatures (chitin).

polysaccharide

glucose molecules linked to form polysaccharide glycogen (animal starch)

oxygen | CH₂OH | OH | CH₂OH | OH
carbon | hydrogen | OH | CH₂OH | OH | CH₂OH

polystyrene a type of ◊plastic.

polytechnic in the UK, an institution for further education offering courses mainly at degree level and concentrating on full-time vocational courses, although many polytechnics provide a wide range of part-time courses at advanced levels. Polytechnic financing is largely by local authorities and academic validation of courses is carried out by the CNAA. In 1981 there were 127,000 full-time students at 30 polytechnics. Best known is the Central London Polytechnic (originally the Regent Street Polytechnic), founded by Sir George Cayley in 1838 and reconstituted by Quintin Hogg in 1882.

polytheism the worship of many gods, as opposed to monotheism (belief in one god). Examples are the religions of ancient Egypt, Babylon, Greece and Rome, Mexico, and modern Hinduism.

Polythene trade name for a variety of ◊polyethylene.

polytonality in music, the simultaneous use of more than one ◊key. A combination of two keys is bitonality.

polyunsaturate a type of animal or vegetable fat whose molecules consist of long carbon chains with many double bonds. Polyunsaturated fats are considered healthier than saturated fats (such as butter), and are widely used in margarines and cooking oils. See also ◊fatty acids.

polyurethane a type of ◊plastic.

polyvinyl chloride (PVC) a type of ◊plastic.

pome a type of ◊pseudocarp or false fruit typical of certain plants belonging to the Rosaceae family. The outer skin and fleshy tissues are developed from the receptacle after fertilization and the five carpels (the true ◊fruit) form the 'core' of the pome which surrounds the seeds. Examples of pomes are apples, pears, and quinces.

pomegranate fruit of a deciduous shrub or small tree *Punica granatum* native to SW Asia and cultivated elsewhere. The edible seeds of the reddish-yellow fruit can be made into wine.

Pomerania /ˌpɒməˈreɪnɪə/ (Polish *Pomorze*, German *Pommern*) region along the S shore of the Baltic Sea, including the island of Rügen, forming part of Poland and (W of the Oder-Neisse line) East Germany from 1945; formerly a province of Germany.

pomeranian small breed of dog resembling a small chow. It has long straight hair with a neck frill, and the tail is carried over the back.

Pomfret /ˈpʌmfrɪt/ an old form of ◊Pontefract, a town in Yorkshire, England.

Pommern /ˈpɒmən/ German form of ◊Pomerania, former province of Germany.

Pomorze /pɒˈmɔʒeɪ/ Polish form of ◊Pomerania, region of N Europe, now largely in Poland.

Pompadour /ˈpɒmpədʊə/ Jeanne Antoinette Poisson, Marquise de Pompadour 1721–1764. Mistress of ◊Louis XV. Born in Paris, she became the king's mistress in 1744, and largely dictated the government's ill-fated switch to anti-Austrian, rather than anti-Prussian policy. She acted as the patron of ◊Voltaire, ◊Diderot, and the *philosophes*.

Pompeii /pɒmˈpeɪiː/ ancient city in Italy, near ◊Vesuvius, 21 km/13 mi SE of Naples. In 63 AD an earthquake destroyed much of the city which had been a Roman port and pleasure resort; it was completely buried beneath lava when Vesuvius erupted in 79 AD. Over 2,000 people were killed. Pompeii was rediscovered in 1748 and the systematic excavation begun in 1763 still continues.

Pompey /ˈpɒmpi/ the Great (Gnaeus Pompeius Magnus) 106–48 bc. Roman soldier and politician. Originally a supporter of ◊Sulla and the aristocratic party, he joined the democrats when he became consul with ◊Crassus in 70 BC. He conquered ◊Mithridates of Pontus, and annexed Syria and Palestine. In 60 BC he formed the First Triumvirate with ◊Caesar (whose daughter ◊Julia he married) and ◊Crassus, and when it broke down after 53 BC he returned to the aristocratic party. On the outbreak of civil war in 49 BC he withdrew to Greece, was defeated by Caesar at Pharsalia in 48 BC, and was murdered in Egypt.

Pompidou /ˌpɒmpɪˈduː/ Georges 1911–1974. French politician and scholar. An adviser on de Gaulle's staff 1944–46, he held administrative posts until he became director-general of the French House of Rothschild in 1954, and even then continued in close association with de Gaulle. In 1962 he became prime minister, but resigned after the Gaullist victory in the elections of 1968, and was elected to the presidency in 1969 on de Gaulle's resignation.

Ponce /ˈpɒnseɪ/ industrial port (textiles, sugar, rum) in S Puerto Rico, USA, named after ◊Ponce de León; population (1980) 189,000.

Ponce de León /ˈpɒnseɪ deɪ leɪˈɒn/ Juan c. 1460–1521. Spanish soldier and explorer, the first European to reach Florida (1513). He is believed to have sailed with Columbus in 1493, and served 1502–04 in *Hispaniola*. In 1508 he conquered Puerto Rico, and was made governor in 1509. He returned to Spain in 1514 to report his 'discovery' of Florida (which he thought was an island), and was given permission by King Ferdinand to colonize it. In the attempt, he received an arrow wound of which he died in Cuba.

Pondicherry /ˌpɒndɪˈtʃeri/ union territory of SE India

area 479 sq km/186 sq mi

capital Pondicherry

products rice, groundnuts, cotton, sugar

language French, English, Tamil, Telegu, Malayalam

population (1981) 604,500

history Pondicherry was founded by France in 1674 and changed hands several times between French, Dutch, and British before being returned to France in 1814 at the close of the Napoleonic wars. With Karikal, Yanam, and Mahé (on the Malabar Coast) it formed a French colony until 1954 when all were transferred to the government of India. Since 1962 they have formed the union territory of Pondicherry.

pond-skater water ◊bug that rows itself across the surface using its middle legs. Found on the surface film of still waters, the common pond skater *Gerris lacustris* feeds on smaller insects.

pondweed aquatic plant genus *Potamogeton* either floating or submerged. The leaves often have two forms, with the floating leaves broad and leathery, and submerged leaves which are narrower and translucent; the flowers grow in green spikes.

Ponta Delgada /'pɒntə del'gɑːdə/ port, resort, and chief commercial centre of the Portuguese ◊Azores, on São Miguel; population (1981) 22,200.

Pontefract /'pɒntɪfrækt/ town in W Yorkshire, England, 34 km/21 mi SW of York, with remains of the Norman castle where Richard II died; population (1981) 33,000. Pontefract cakes are a type of liquorice sweet.

Pontiac /'pɒntiæk/ c. 1720–1769. American Indian, chief of the Ottawa from 1755. He led in 1763–64 the 'Conspiracy of Pontiac' in an attempt to stop British encroachment on Indian lands. He achieved remarkable success against overwhelming odds, but eventually signed a peace treaty in 1766, and was murdered by an Illinois Indian at the instigation of a British trader.

Pontine Marshes /'pɒntaɪn/ formerly malarial marshes in Latium Italy, near the coast some 40 km/25 mi SE of Rome. They defied the attempts of the Romans to drain them, and it was not until 1926 that they were brought into cultivation under Mussolini's administration: cereals, fruit and vines, and sugar beet.

Pontus /'pɒntəs/ kingdom of NE Asia Minor on the Black Sea from about 300–65 BC when its greatest ruler, ◊Mithridates VI was defeated by ◊Pompey.

Pontypool /ˌpɒntə'puːl/ industrial town (coalmining, iron and steel goods, tinplate glass, synthetic textiles) in Gwent, Wales, 15 km/9 mi N of Newport; population (1981) 36,761.

Pontypridd /ˌpɒntə'priːð/ industrial town (chain and cable works, light industry on the Treforest trading estate) in Mid Glamorgan, Wales; population (1981) 33,134.

pony small horse under 14.2 hands, that is, 1.47 m/58 in shoulder height. Although of Celtic origin, all the pony breeds have been crossed with thoroughbred and Arab stock, except for the smallest – the hardy Shetland – less than 105 cm/42 in. Other British breeds, including the small Exmoor and Dartmoor, the slightly larger New Forest, and the large Welsh cob, are found elsewhere in Europe and the East. They are often ridden by adults, for example, in polo, or used to pull carts. In 1929 the Pony Club was established in the UK for children.

poodle a breed of dog, including the standard (above 38 cm/15 in at shoulder); miniature (below 38 cm/15 in) and toy (below 28 cm/11 in) types. The poodle probably originated in Russia, was naturalized in Germany, where it was used as a sporting dog and gained its name (from the German *pudeln*, to splash), and became a luxury dog. Their long curly coats, usually cut into elaborate styles, are mostly either black or white (the only colours acceptable in France), although greys and browns are also bred.

pool game derived from billiards, and played with balls of various colours. See ◊snooker.

Poole /puːl/ industrial town (chemicals, engineering, boatbuilding, confectionery; pottery from local clay) and yachting centre on Poole harbour, Dorset, England, 8 km/5 mi W of Bournemouth; population (1984) 123,000. The first Boy Scout camp was held in 1907 on Brownsea Island in the harbour.

Pool Malebo /'puːl mə'liːbəʊ/ lake on the border between the Congo and Zaïre, formed by a widening of the Zaïre river, 560 km/350 mi from its mouth.

Poona /'puːnə/ former spelling of ◊Pune, city in India.

poor law system in England from 1572 of raising money by means of a parish rate (local tax) for the building of poorhouses, relief of the destitute and the aged, and apprenticing pauper children. From 1834 it was reorganized, with boards of guardians elected by the ratepayers. Relief of the able-bodied, except within a workhouse (where conditions were deliberately made repellent), was forbidden, and the basis of administration continued until the Ministry of Health, operating through county and county-borough councils, took over in 1929. After World War II a series of administrative reorganizations ended in 1968 with the creation of the Department of Health and ◊Social Security.

pop art art movement developed by a group of artists in the 1950s, reacting against what they saw as the elitism of abstract art. Pop art used popular imagery such as soup tins, comic strips, or movie-star faces. It was a mischievous, cheerful art called by one of its British initiators, Richard Hamilton (1922–), 'low-cost, mass-produced, young and Big Business'. Other artists include ◊Hockney, ◊Warhol, and ◊Lichtenstein.

Pope /pəʊp/ the Bishop of Rome as head of the Catholic Church, which claims him as the spiritual descendant of St ◊Peter. This primacy was never universally acknowledged, as for example in the breakaway of ◊Constantinople 1054. Through the medieval period the papacy developed its temporal power, reaching its height in the 11th–13th centuries (◊Gregory VII and ◊Innocent III), but came under French control (headquarters Avignon rather than Rome) 1309–78, 'the Babylonian Captivity'. The 'Great Schism' followed, with rival popes at Avignon and Rome 1378–1417; papal political power further declined with the withdrawal of allegiance by the Protestant states at the ◊Reformation, and by 1929 the Lateran Treaty recognized papal territorial sovereignty even in Italy only within the Vatican City (see ◊Papal States). However, the 16th–17th century Counter-Reformation revived papal spiritual influence and at the Vatican Council 1870 the doctrine of papal infallibility was proclaimed. Elected by the Sacred College of Cardinals, a pope dates his pontificate from his coronation with the tiara, or triple crown, at St Peter's, Rome, and has (since the Second Vatican Council 1962–66) an episcopal synod of 200 bishops elected by local hierarchies to collaborate in the government of the Church. Under ◊John Paul II, however, power has been more centralized, and bishops and cardinals have been chosen from the more traditionally minded clerics, and from the Third World. In 1982 a commission of the Catholic and Anglican churches agreed that in any union between them, the pope would be 'universal primate'.

Pope /pəʊp/ Alexander 1688–1744. British poet and satirist, noted for his biting wit, which he expressed in the form of heroic couplets. As a Catholic, he was subject to discrimination, and his life was embittered by a deformity of the spine. He established his reputation with the precocious *Pastorals* 1709 and *Essay on Criticism* 1711, which were followed by a parody of the heroic epic *The Rape of the Lock* 1712–14 and 'Eloisa to Abelard' 1717. The success of a highly Neo-Classical translation of ◊Homer's *Iliad* and *Odyssey* 1715–26 made it possible for him to settle in Twickenham from 1719, but his edition of Shakespeare attracted scholarly ridicule, for which he revenged himself by a satire on scholarly dullness, the *Dunciad* 1728. A venture into philosophy, in his *An Essay on Man* 1733–34 and *Moral Essays* 1731–35, was influenced by ◊Bolingbroke. His finest mature productions are his *Imitations of the Satires of Horace* 1733–38, and his personal letters. Among his friends were the writers ◊Swift, ◊Arbuthnot, and ◊Gay. His line 'A little learning is a dangerous thing' is often misquoted.

Pope English poet and satirist Alexander Pope was also a keen landscape gardener, who devoted much of his time to cultivating a garden and grotto on his estate in Twickenham. The painting is by Hoare c. 1739.

Popish Plot a supposed plot to murder Charles II; see under Titus ◊Oates.

poplar deciduous tree genus *Populus*, with broad leaves. The white poplar *Populus alba* has a smooth grey trunk and the leaves are white below. Other varieties are the aspen *Populus tremula*, and grey poplar *Populus canescens*.

pop music short for popular music, umbrella term for all modern music not classifiable as jazz or classical.

Pop music became distinct from ◊folk music with the advent of sound-recording techniques, which gave a wider audience and more lasting influence to ◊blues and ◊country-and-western musicians, among others. In the 1940s, electronic amplification led to more vigorous, aggressive styles (see ◊rhythm and blues), and the 1950s saw the rise of ◊rock and roll. Rock music, based on electric guitar and drums but incorporating technological advances with alacrity, has diversified into a profusion of styles: doo-wop, folk rock, surf music, ◊Mersey beat, ◊psychedelic rock, ◊heavy metal, ◊punk, hardcore, and so on. The traditional format is a song of roughly three minutes with verse, chorus, and middle eight. There is no clear divide between rock and pop, although pop can be said to be concerned more with entertainment than with art and to encompass dance music (◊disco, ◊hip-hop, go-go, house, and so on), novelty records, and acts aimed at children and young teenagers. Lyrics range from trivial and crass to sophisticated and emotionally powerful, and may reflect attitudes of protest or social concern. New sounds are drawn from a variety of sources, in the 1980s especially ◊roots music, and there is constant cross-fertilization between styles.

Popocatépetl /ˌpɒpəˌkætəˈpetl/ (Aztec 'smoking mountain') volcano in Mexico, SE of Mexico City; 5,340 m/17,520 ft.

Popov /ˈpɒpɒv/ Alexander 1859–1905. Russian physicist who devised the first ◊aerial in advance of ◊Marconi (but did not use it for radio communication) and a detector for radio waves.

Popper /ˈpɒpə/ Karl (Raimund) 1902– . Austrian-born British philosopher of science. Born and educated in Vienna, he was naturalized British in 1945 and was professor of logic and scientific method at the London School of Economics 1949–69. A critic of Marxism and other dogmas, he has had a great impact on the social sciences as well as the natural sciences, particularly with his theory of ◊falsification, the idea that scientific discovery is a process of falsification rather than verification – that ideas and theories can only be proved false, not correct. There is no such thing as absolute truth or objective knowledge, and good science involves a process of conjecture and refutation (trial and error) whereby ideas are developed, tested, and in most cases rejected. His view of scientific practice has been criticized by T S ◊Kuhn and other writers. Main works include *The Logic of Scientific Discovery* 1934, *Conjectures and Refutations* 1963, and *Objective Knowledge* 1972.

poppy plant, genus *Papaver*, having a milky sap, and including the crimson field *Papaver rhoeas* and ◊opium poppies, found in Europe and Asia. Closely related are the Californian poppy *Eschscholzia californica* and the yellow horned or sea poppy *Glaucium flavum*.

popular front a political alliance of liberals, socialists, communists, and other centre and left-wing parties against fascism. This policy was proposed by the Communist International in 1935, and was adopted in France and Spain, where popular-front governments were elected in 1936; that in France was overthrown in 1938, and in Spain in 1939. In Britain a popular-front policy was advocated by Sir Stafford Cripps and others, but rejected by the Labour Party. The resistance movements in the occupied countries during World War II represented a revival of the popular-front idea, and in postwar politics the term tends to recur whenever a strong right-wing party can be counterbalanced only by an alliance of those on the left.

population in biology and ecology, a group of animals of one species, living in a certain area and able to interbreed; the members of a given species in a ◊community of living things.

population cycle in biology, the regular fluctuations in the size of a population as seen in lemmings, for example. Such cycles are often caused by density-dependent mortality: high mortality due to overcrowding causes a sudden decline in the population, which then gradually builds up again. Population cycles may also result from an interaction between a predator and its prey.

population genetics the branch of genetics which studies the way in which the frequencies of different ◊alleles in populations of organisms change, as a result of ◊natural selection and other processes, to give rise to evolution.

porcelain translucent ceramic ware, made with kaolin (china clay). See under ◊pottery.

porcupine ◊rodent with sharp quills on its body. Porcupines of the family Hystricidae are terrestrial in habit. They are characterized by long spines in the coat. The colouring is brown with black and white quills. American porcupines constitute the family Erethizontidae and differ from the Old World varieties in being arboreal, having a prehensile tail, and much shorter spines.

porcupine fish another name for ◊globefish.

Pori /ˈpɔːri/ ice-free industrial port (nickel and copper refining, sawmills, paper, textiles) in SW Finland; population (1985) 79,000.

pornography literature, pictures, photos, films, and so on, intended to arouse sexual desire. Standards are subjective as to what is offensive, hence the difficulty in agreement on lines of censorship.

porphyria rare hereditary metabolic disorder, known as the 'royal disease' because sufferers included ◊Mary Queen of Scots, ◊James I, and (controversially) ◊George III, which may cause mental confusion. Other symptoms, for example, excessive growth of hair, contraction of muscles to reveal the teeth, sensitivity to sunlight, and a need for blood infusions, have been suggested as the basis for vampirism and werewolf legends.

porphyry any rock composed of large crystals in a purplish matrix.

porpoise small, squat dolphin without a 'beak', among the smallest of the whale group. The *common porpoise Phocoena phocoena*, is black above, white below and up to 1.8 m/5 ft long. It feeds on fish.

Porsche /pɔːʃ/ Ferdinand 1875–1951. German car designer, for example, the Volkswagen (People's Car) marketed after World War II, and Porsche sports cars.

port sweet, fortified (with brandy) dessert wine (red, tawny, or white), from grapes grown in the Douro basin of Portugal and exported from Oporto, hence the name.

Port Adelaide /ˈpɔːt ˈædɪleɪd/ industrial port (cement, chemicals) in South Australia, on Gulf St Vincent, 11 km/7 mi NW of Adelaide; population (1985) 37,000.

Port Arthur /ˈɑːθə/ industrial deepwater port (oil refining, shipbuilding, brass, chemicals) in Texas, USA, 24 km/15 mi SE of Beaumont; population (1980) 61,000. Founded 1895, it rose to importance with the discovery of petroleum near Beaumont in 1901.

Port Augusta /ɔːˈɡʌstə/ port in South Australia, at the head of Spencer Gulf; population (1985) 17,000.

Port-au-Prince /ˌpɔːtəuˈprɪns/ capital and industrial port (sugar, rum, textiles, plastics) of Haiti; population (1982) 763,000.

Port Darwin /ˌpɔːt ˈdɑːwɪn/ port serving ◊Darwin, capital of Northern Territory, Australia.

Port Elizabeth /ɪˈlɪzəbəθ/ industrial port (boots, flour, jam) in Cape province, S Africa, about 710 km/440 mi E of Cape Town on Algoa Bay; university 1964; population (1980) 492,140. It was founded in 1820 by British settlers and named after the wife of Rufane Donkin (1773–1841), then governor of the Cape of Good Hope.

Porter /ˈpɔːtə/ Cole (Albert) 1891–1964. American composer and lyricist of musical comedies. His shows include *Gay Divorce* 1932 and *Kiss Me Kate* 1948.

Porter /ˈpɔːtə/ Eric 1928– . English actor. His numerous classical roles include title parts in *Uncle Vanya*, *Volpone*, *Macbeth*, and *King Lear*; on television he appeared in *The Forsyte Saga*, *Anna Karenina*, and *The Jewel in the Crown*.

Porter /ˈpɔːtə/ Katherine Anne 1890–1980. US writer, born in Texas. She published three volume of short stories between 1930 and 1944, and the allegorical novel *Ship of Fools* 1962.

Porter /ˈpɔːtə/ Rodney Robert 1917–1985. British biochemist and Nobel prizewinner (with G M ◊Edelmann) in 1972 for pioneering work on the chemical structure of ◊antibodies.

Port Harcourt /ˈhɑːkɔːt/ industrial port in E Nigeria, on the river Bonny in the Niger delta; population (1983) 296,200.

Port Klang /klæŋ/ Malaysian rubber port (Port Swettenham until 1971) on the Strait of Malacca, 40 km/25 mi SW of Kuala Lumpur. Population (1980) 192,080.

Portland /ˈpɔːtlənd/ industrial port (aluminium, paper, timber, lumber machinery, electronics) and largest city in Oregon, USA, on the Columbia river, 173 km/108 mi from the sea, at its confluence with the Willamette river; population (1980) 1,237,000. Ocean-going vessels can reach Portland harbour.

Portland /ˈpɔːtlənd/ industrial port (shipbuilding) and largest city of Maine, USA, on Casco Bay; population (1980) 61,500.

Portland /ˈpɔːtlənd/ William Henry Cavendish Bentinck, 3rd Duke of Portland

population

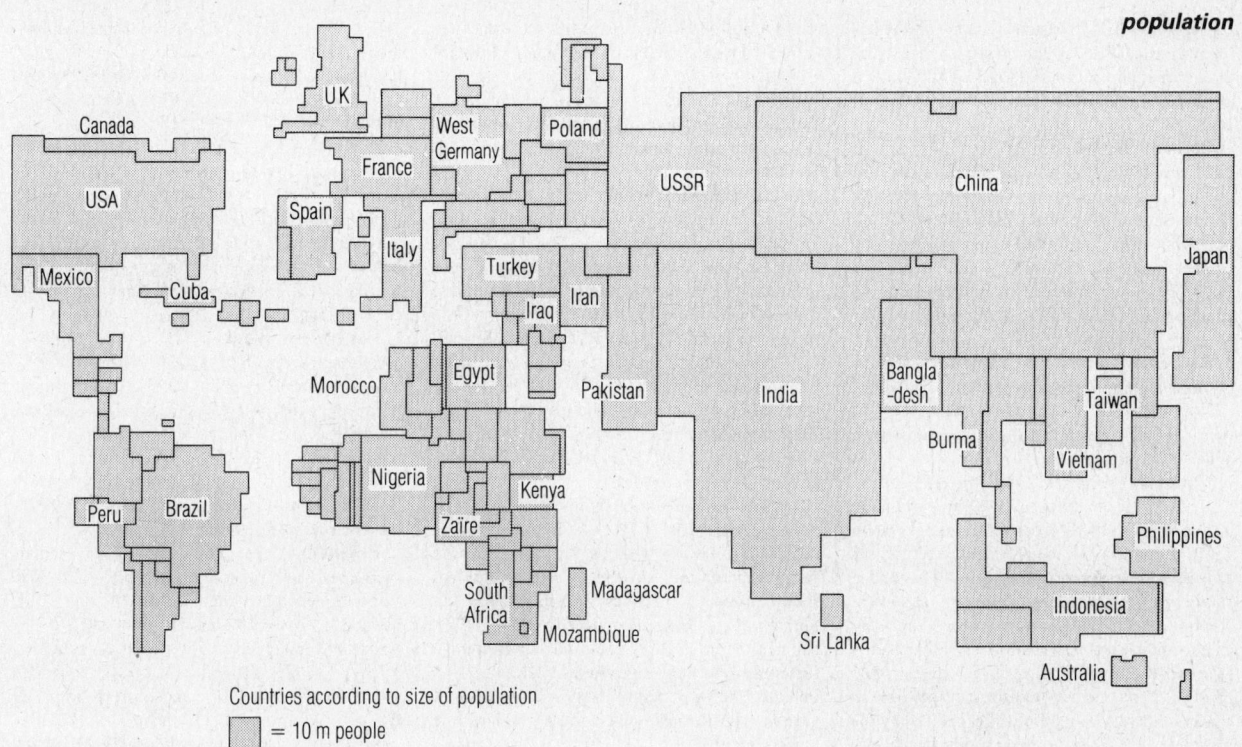

Countries according to size of population

▨ = 10 m people

population cycle

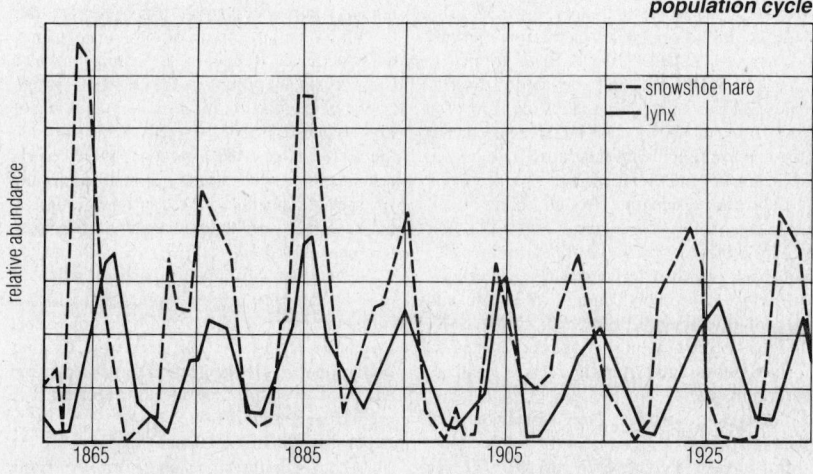

1738–1809. British politician, originally a Whig, who in 1783 became nominal prime minister in the Fox-North coalition government. During the French Revolution he joined the Tories, and was prime minister 1807–09.

Portland, Isle of /'pɔːtlənd/ rocky peninsula off Dorset, England, joined to the mainland by the ◊Chesil Bank. Portland Castle was built by Henry VIII 1520; building stone is still quarried.

Port Mahon /'pɔːt mɑː'ɒn/ port serving ◊Mahon on the Spanish island of Minorca.

Portmeirion /pɔːt'meəriən/ holiday resort in Gwynedd, Wales, built by the architect Clough Williams-Ellis in Italianate fantasy style; setting of the cult television series *The Prisoner*.

Port Moresby /'mɔːzbi/ capital and port of Papua New Guinea; University of Papua New Guinea 1965; population (1980) 123,625.

Port-of-Spain /'pɔːt əv 'speɪn/ port and capital of Trinidad and Tobago, on Trinidad; population (1980) 56,000.

Porton Down /'pɔːtn 'daʊn/ site of the British Microbiological Research Establishment of the Ministry of Defence in Wiltshire, SW England; as a 'germ warfare' centre it came under political attack in the 1960s.

Porto Novo /'pɔːtəʊ 'nəʊvəʊ/ capital of ◊Benin W Africa; population (1982) 208,258.

Porto Rico /'pɔːtəʊ 'riːkəʊ/ name until 1932 of ◊Puerto Rico, US island in the Caribbean.

Port Phillip Bay /'fɪlɪp/ inlet off Bass Strait, Victoria, Australia, on which Melbourne stands.

Port Pirie /'pɪri/ industrial port (smelting of ores from the Broken Hill mines, and chemicals) in South Australia; population (1985) 16,030.

Port Rashid /ræ'ʃiːd/ port serving ◊Dubai in the United Arab Emirates.

Port Royal /,pɔːt 'rɔɪəl/ former capital of ◊Jamaica.

Port Royal /,pɔːt 'rɔɪəl/ former Cistercian convent, SW of Paris, founded in 1204. In 1626 the buildings were taken over by a male community which became a centre of ◊Jansenist teaching. During the second half of the 17th century it was subject to periodic persecutions and finally in 1709 was dispersed; the following year the buildings were destroyed by order of Louis XIV.

Port Said /saɪd/ port in Egypt, on reclaimed land at the N end of the ◊Suez Canal; population (1983) 364,000. It was founded 1859 when the canal was begun. In 1967 in the Arab-Israel war the city was damaged and the canal was blocked; Port Said was evacuated by 1969, but by 1975 had been largely reconstructed.

Portsmouth /'pɔːtsməθ/ city and naval port in Hampshire, England, opposite the Isle of Wight; population (1981) 179,500. It was already a port in the days of King Alfred; the Tudor warship ◊*Mary Rose* and Nelson's flagship, HMS *Victory*, are exhibited here.

Portsmouth /'pɔːtsməθ/ port in New Hampshire, USA, on the estuary of the river Piscataqua; population (1980) 26,000. Founded in 1623, Portsmouth was the state capital 1679–1775.

Portsmouth /'pɔːtsməθ/ port in Virginia, USA, on Elizabeth river, seat of a US navy yard and training centre; population (1980) 104,577. It also makes textiles and raises oysters.

Portsmouth /'pɔːtsməθ/ Louise de Kéroualle, Duchess of Portsmouth 1649–1734. Mistress of ◊Charles II, a Frenchwoman who came to England as ◊Louis XIV's agent 1670, and was hated by the public.

Port Swettenham /'swetnəm/ former name of ◊Port Klang, Malaysian port.

Port Talbot /'tɔːlbət/ industrial port (tinplate and steel strip mill) in W Glamorgan, Wales; population (1981) 47,500.

Portugal /'pɔːtjugəl/ country in SW Europe, on the Atlantic, bounded to the N and E by Spain.
government The 1976 constitution, revised in 1982, provides for a president, elected by universal suffrage for a five-year term, and a single-chamber, 250-member assembly, similarly elected and serving a four-year term. The president, an active politician rather than a figurehead, appoints a prime minister who chooses the council of ministers, responsible to the assembly. A council of state, chaired by the president, acts as a supreme national advisory body.
history Portugal originated in the 11th century as a country subject to ◊León, while the S was ruled by the ◊Moors. It became an independent monarchy in the reign of Alfonso I (1128–85), who captured Lisbon 1147. Alfonso III (1248–79) expelled the Moors. During the 13th century the *Cortes*, an assembly representing nobles, clergy, and cities, began to meet and secured control of taxation. A commercial treaty with England was signed 1294 and an alliance established 1373. During the 15th century Portuguese mariners explored the African coast, opened the sea route to India, and reached Brazil, and colonists followed in the 16th century.
In 1580 ◊Philip II of Spain seized the crown. The Portuguese rebelled against Spanish rule in 1640, placed the house of Braganza on the throne, and after a long war forced Spain to recognize their independence 1668. Portugal fought as the ally of Britain in the War of the ◊Spanish Succession. France invaded Portugal 1807–11 (see ◊Peninsular War). A strong democratic movement developed and after a civil war 1828–34, constitutional government was established. ◊Carlos I was assassinated in 1908; his son ◊Manuel II driven from the country by revolution in 1910 and a republic proclaimed.
Portugal remained economically weak and corrupt until the start of the dictatorship of Dr Antonio de Oliveira ◊Salazar, prime minister from 1928. Social conditions were improved at the cost of personal liberties.
Salazar was succeeded as prime minister in 1968 by Dr Marcello Caetano, who proved unable to liberalize the political system or deal with the costly wars in Portugal's colonies of Angola and Mozambique. Criticisms of his administration led to a military coup in Apr 1974 to 'save the nation from government'. The Junta of National Salvation was set up, headed by Gen Antonio Ribeiro de Spinola. He became president a month later, with a military colleague replacing the civilian prime minister.
The new president promised liberal reforms, but after disagreements within the Junta, Spinola resigned in Sept and was replaced by Gen Francisco da Costa Gomes. In 1975 there was a swing to the left among the military and President Gomes narrowly avoided a communist coup by collaborating with the leader of the moderate Socialist Party (PS), Mario ◊Soares. In 1976 Portugal's first free assembly elections in 50 years were held. The PS won 36% of the vote and Soares formed a minority government. The army chief, Gen Antonio Ramalho ◊Eanes, won the presidency, with the support of centre and left-of-centre parties.
After surviving precariously for over two years, Soares resigned in 1978. A period of political instability followed, with five prime ministers in two and a half years, until, in Dec 1980, President Eanes invited Dr Francisco Balsemão, a co-founder of the Social Democratic Party (PSD), to form a centre-party coalition. Dr Balsemão survived many challenges to his leadership, and in Aug 1982 the assembly approved his draft of a new constitution, which would reduce the powers of the president and move the country to a fully civilian government. In 1983 Soares entered a coalition with the PSD, whose leader was now the former finance minister, Professor Aníbal Cavaco Silva. In Jun 1985 the PS-PSD coalition broke up and a premature general election was called. Cavaco Silva formed a minority government, and was able to form a majority government after a landslide victory for the PSD in Jul 1987. He has increased economic growth and raised living standards, and favours a free market and privatization.
In the 1986 presidential election Soares won a surprising victory to become Portugal's first civilian president for 60 years. He promised a more open and cooperative presidency. Portugal entered the ◊European Community in 1986, and is a committed member of ◊NATO. In Jul 1987 the PSD won an absolute majority in parliament.

Portuguese East Africa former name of ◊Mozambique.

Portuguese Guinea /'gɪni/ former name of ◊Guinea-Bissau.

Portuguese language a member of the Romance branch of the Indo-European language family, the national language of Portugal, closely related to Spanish and strongly influenced by Arabic. It is also spoken in Brazil, Angola, Mozambique, and other former Portuguese overseas possessions.

Portuguese literature under Provençal influence, medieval Portuguese literature produced popular ballads and troubadour songs, and the Renaissance stimulated the outstanding work of the dramatist Gil Vicente, and the lyric and epic poet ◊Camöens. In the 17th and 18th centuries there was a decline to formality, but the *Letters of a Portuguese Nun*, supposed to have been written by Marianna ◊Alcoforado, were a poignant exception, and found echoes in the modern revolutionary period. No single figure has achieved international acclaim among the varied writers of the 19th and 20th centuries, although there is a lively tradition of writing in Brazil, and Angola developed its own school of Portuguese-African poetry.

Portuguese man-of-war colonial coelenterate with the appearance of a large jellyfish. There is a gas-filled float on the surface, below which hang feeding, stinging and reproductive individuals. The float can be 30 cm/1 ft long.

Portuguese West Africa former name of ◊Angola.

pos (short for 'point of sale') of business premises, point where a sale is transacted, for example, a supermarket checkout. In conjunction with ◊EFT (electronic funds transfer), pos is part of the terminology of 'cashless shopping', enabling buyers to transfer funds directly from their bank accounts.

Poseidon /pɒ'saɪdn/ Greek god (Roman Neptune), the brother of ◊Zeus and ◊Pluto. The brothers dethroned their father, ◊Cronos, and divided his realm, Poseidon taking the sea; he was also worshipped as god of earthquakes (see ◊Troy). See also ◊Triton.

Posen /'pəuzən/ German form of ◊Poznań, city in Poland.

positivism the philosophical system of Auguste ◊Comte, which confines genuine knowledge within the bounds of science and observation. The theory is especially hostile to theology and metaphysics, which overstep this boundary. On the basis of positivism Comte constructed his 'Religion of Humanity', in which the object of adoration was the Great Being, that is, the personification of humanity as a whole. *Logical positivism* or ◊empiricism developed in the 1920s: it rejected any metaphysical world beyond everyday science and common sense, and confined statements to those of formal logic or mathematics. Leading exponents were ◊Carnap, ◊Mach, and A J ◊Ayer.

positron an ◊elementary particle, produced in some radioactive ◊decay processes, which is similar in every respect to an ◊electron except that it carries a positive ◊electric charge. It is thus the ◊antiparticle to the electron. When a positron and electron collide they anihilate each other to produce gamma radiation.

possum Australian name for many of the smaller marsupials found in Australia (shortened form of opossum). The tiny *honey possum Tarsipes spencerae* has a long tongue to take nectar from flowers. The big *gliding possum Schoinobates volans* can glide 100 m/300ft or more on the huge membrane stretched between front and back limbs. The *brush possum Trichosurus vulpecula* has become very common in New Zealand after being introduced.

postal service the system for delivering mail. In Britain regular permanent systems were not created until the emergence of modern nation state. Henry VIII in 1516 appointed Sir Brian Tuke as Master of the Posts, to maintain a regular service on the main roads from London. Postmasters (usually innkeepers) passed the

Portugal

REPUBLIC OF (*República Portuguesa*)

AREA 91,631 sq km/34,861 sq mi (including Azores and Madeira)
CAPITAL Lisbon
TOWNS Coimbra, ports Oporto, Setúbal
PHYSICAL mountainous in the N, plains in the S
FEATURES rivers Minho, Douro, Tagus, Guadiana; Serra da Estréla
HEAD OF STATE Mario Alberto Nobre Lopes Soares from 1986
HEAD OF GOVERNMENT Cavaco Silva from 1985
GOVERNMENT parliamentary democracy
EXPORTS port wine, olive oil, resin, cork, sardines, textiles, pottery, pulpwood
CURRENCY escudo (235 = £1 Sept 1987)
POPULATION 10,046,000 (1985); annual growth rate 0.7%
LANGUAGE Portuguese, one of the Romance languages, ultimately derived from Latin, but considerably influenced later by Arabic
RELIGION Roman Catholic
LITERACY 85% male/76% female (1980 est)
GDP $19.4 bn (1984); $1,930 per head of population
CHRONOLOGY
1928–68 Military dictatorship under Antonio de Oliveira Salazar.
1968 Salazar succeeded by Marcello Caetano.
1974 Caetano removed in a military coup led by Gen Antonio Ribeiro de Spinola. Spinola was then replaced by Gen Fransisco da Costa Gomes.
1975 Independence granted to African colonies.

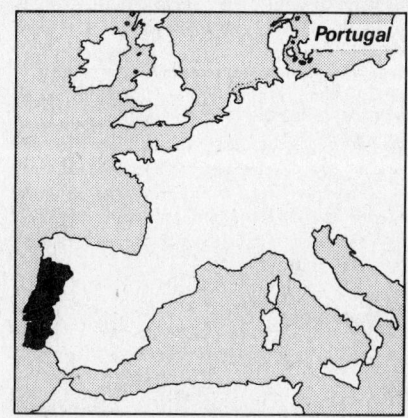
Portugal

1976 New constitution, providing for a gradual return to civilian rule, adopted. Minority government appointed, led by the Socialist Party leader Mario Soares.
1978 Soares resigned.
1980 Francisco Balsemão formed a centre-party coalition after two and a half years of political instability.
1982 Draft of new constitution approved, reducing the powers of the presidency.
1983 Centre-left coalition government formed.
1985 Cavaco Silva became prime minister.
1986 Mario Soares elected first civilian president for 60 years. Portugal joined European Community.
1987 Soares re-elected with large majority.

PORTUGAL: FORMER COLONIES

Name	Colonized	Independent
Brazil	1532	1822
Uruguay	1533	1828
Mozambique	1505	1975
Angola	1491	1975

mail to the next post, and supplied horses for the royal couriers; private people wishing to send letters or to travel themselves 'post haste' were permitted to use the service. Private services were discouraged to avoid losing revenue for the state service and assisting treasonable activities, the latter point being stressed by the act establishing the Post Office, passed under ◊Cromwell in 1657. Mail coaches first ran in 1784, and in 1840 Rowland Hill's prepaid penny postage stamp, for any distance within the United Kingdom, led to a massive increase in use. Services were extended to registered post 1841; post boxes 1855 (see Anthony ◊Trollope); savings bank 1861; postcards 1870; postal orders 1881, parcel post 1883, air mail 1911, telephone 1912, data processing by computer 1967, and giro 1968. In 1969 the original General Post Office ceased to be a government department, and was split into two, the Post Office and ◊British Telecom. International cooperation is through the Universal Postal Union, 1875, at Berne.

poster advertising announcement for public display, often illustrated, first produced in France from the mid-19th century, when colour lithography came into its own, with the work of Jules Chéret 1836–1932. Later artists include ◊Millais, the Austrian Secessionist artist Koloman ◊Moser; ◊Toulouse-Lautrec, Edward McKnight ◊Kauffer, the Beggarstaff Brothers (see Sir William ◊Nicholson), and Charles Dana ◊Gibson. Poster art flourished in the 1960s (see ◊hippie), with artists such as Michael English and Martin Sharp in the UK and Rick Griffin, Peter Max, and Stanley Mouse in the USA.

Post-Impressionism term applied to various styles of painting which followed ◊Impressionism, and first used by Roger Fry to describe the works of ◊Cézanne, ◊van Gogh, and ◊Gauguin in 1911. Post-Impressionists moved away from the spontaneous vision of the Impressionists to infuse their work with a greater degree of permanence.

Postmodernism late 20th-century movement in the arts against the preoccupation of ◊modernism with form and technique rather than content. In the visual arts, and particularly in architecture, it uses an amalgam of styles from the past, whose slightly off-key familiarity has a more immediate appeal than the austerities of modernism.

potash general name for any ◊potassium-containing mineral, most often applied to potassium carbonate (K_2CO_3). The potassium content of soils and fertilizers is also commonly expressed as potash, although it is usually potassium oxide (K_2O). Potash, originally made by roasting plants to ashes in earthenware pots, is commercially produced from the mineral sylvite (potassium chloride, KCl) used in artificial fertilizers, glass and soap.

potassium metallic element of the alkali group, symbol K, atomic number 19, atomic weight 39.1. Discovered in 1807 by Sir Humphry Davy by electrolysis of caustic potash (KOH) the first instance of a metal being isolated by an electric current. It is a soft, silvery-bright, metal which reacts violently with water, forming potassium hydroxide and hydrogen which ignites and burns spontaneously with a violet flame. The element is therefore kept under kerosene or naphtha.
Widely distributed in nature in combination with other elements, it is found in salt deposits (carnallite and kainite) and minerals (feldspar, greensand, alunite, leucite), and forms 2.9 per cent of the Earth's solid crust. The salts are important, especially as essential constituents of fertilizers. Alloyed with sodium, it may be used as a coolant in nuclear reactors.

potato perennial *Solanum tuberosum* family Solanaceae, with edible tuberous roots, used by the Andean Indians for at least 2,000 years.
It was introduced to Europe by the mid-16th century, and reputedly to England by Sir Walter ◊Raleigh. The Irish *potato famine* of 1845, caused by a parasitic fungus, led to large-scale emigration to the USA. See also *sweet potato* under ◊convolvulus.

poteen Irish alcoholic liquor illicitly made from potatoes, or barley and yeast.

Potemkin /pɒˈtemkɪn/ Grigory Aleksandrovich, Prince 1739–1791. Russian politician. He entered the army and attracted the notice of ◊Catherine II, maintaining her friendship throughout his life. He was an active and able adminstrator who reformed the army, built the Black Sea Fleet, conquered the Crimea, developed S Russia, and founded the ◊Kherson arsenal.

potential, electric the relative electrical state of an object. A charged ◊conductor, for example, has a higher potential than the earth, whose potential is taken by convention to be zero. An electric ◊cell has a potential in terms to e.m.f. (◊electromotive force) which can make current flow in an external circuit. The difference in potential between two points -the potential difference -is expressed in ◊volts; that is, a 12V battery has a potential difference of 12 volts between its negative and positive terminals.

potential energy ◊energy possessed by an object by virtue of its position or state. It is contrasted with ◊kinetic energy.

potentiometer in physics, an electrical ◊resistor that can be divided so as to compare or measure voltages. A simple type consists of a length of uniform resistance wire (about 1 m/3 ft long) carrying a constant current provided by a cell connected across the ends of the wire. The source of ◊potential difference (voltage) to be measured is connected (to oppose the cell) between one end of the wire, through a ◊galvanometer (instrument for measuring small currents), to a contact free to slide along the wire. The sliding contact is moved until the galvanometer shows no deflection. In radio circuits, any rotary variable resistance (such as volume control) may be referred to as a potentiometer.

Potomac /pə'təumək/ river of the USA, rising in the Allegheny mountains, and flowing SE through Washington, DC, into Chesapeake Bay. It is formed by the junction of the N Potomac and S Potomac and is 459 km/285 mi long.

Potosí /ˌpotəu'siː/ town in SW Bolivia, known for its tin and silver mines; population (1982) 103,000. Standing on the Cerro de Potosí slopes at 4,020 m/13,189 ft, it is among the highest towns in the world.

pot pourri mixture of dried flowers and leaves, for example, rose petals, lavender, and verbena, used to scent the air.

Potsdam /'potsdæm/ capital of Potsdam district, East Germany; population (1984) 137,500. The New Palace 1763–70 and ◊Sans Souci were both built by ◊Frederick the Great, and Hitler's Third Reich was proclaimed in the garrison church 21 Mar 1933.

Potsdam Conference conference held at Potsdam in July 1945 between Britain, USSR and USA. It established the political and economic principles governing the treatment of Germany in the initial period of Allied control at the end of World War II, and sent the ultimatum to Japan demanding unconditional surrender on pain of utter destruction.

Potter /'potə/ Beatrix 1866–1943. British writer and illustrator of children's books, beginning with *Peter Rabbit* 1900; her code diaries were published 1966. Her Lake District home is a museum.

Potter /'potə/ Paul 1625–1654. Dutch animal painter, son of the landscape painter *Pieter Potter.*

Potteries, the /'potəriz/ the centre of the china and earthenware industry in England, lying in the upper Trent basin of N Staffordshire. ◊Wedgwood and ◊Minton are famous names associated with the Potteries, which covers the area around Stoke-on-Trent, and includes the formerly separate towns of Burslem, Hanley, Longton, Fenton, and Tunstall.

pottery and porcelain ◊ceramics in domestic and ornamental use including:
earthenware made of porous clay and fired, whether unglazed (when it remains porous, for example, flowerpots, winecoolers) or glazed (most tableware).

stoneware made of non-porous clay with a high silica content, fired at high temperature, which is very hard.

bone china (softpaste) semi-porcelain made of 5 per cent bone ash and china clay (◊kaolin); made in the West in imitation of Chinese porcelain.

porcelain (hardpaste) characterized by its ringing sound when struck, translucence, and shining finish, like that of a cowrie shell (Italian *porcellana*); made of kaolin and petuntse (fusible feldspar consisting chiefly of quartz, and reduced to a fine, white powder).

Potter Beatrix Potter's *Peter Rabbit* books began life as a series of letters to the children of a former governess.

pottery and porcelain history of BC *10,000* earliest known pottery in Japan
c. 5000 potter's wheel developed by the Egyptians
c. 600–450 black and red figured vases from Greece
AD *6th century* fine quality stoneware developed in China, as the forerunner of porcelain
7–10th century Tang porcelain in China
10–13th century Song porcelain in China
14–17th century Ming porcelain in China; Hispano-Moresque ware
16th century Majolica Italian tin-glazed earthenware with painted decoration, especially large dishes with figures;
faience (from ◊Faenza) name applied both to this and delftware
17th century Chinese porcelain first imported to the West; it was soon brought in large quantities as a ballast in tea clippers;
delftware tin-glazed earthenware brought to perfection in ◊Delft, especially the white with blue decoration, also copied in England
18th century Dresden in 1710 the first European hardpaste porcelain was made in Dresden by Böttger 1682–1719; the factory later transferred to Meissen;
Sèvres from 1769 hardpaste porcelain as well as softpaste made in ◊Sèvres, France, remarkable for its ground colours;

Wedgwood c. 1760 cream-coloured earthenware perfected by ◊Wedgwood, who also devised stoneware, with white decoration in Neo-Classical designs on a blue ground, still among the wares made in Barlaston, Staffordshire, England;
English softpaste made c. 1745–1810, first in Chelsea, later in Bow, Derby, and Worcester.
English hardpaste first made in Plymouth 1768–70, and Bristol 1770–81, when the stock was removed to New Hall in Staffordshire;
Bone China c. 1789 first produced by Josiah Spode (1754–1827); Coalport, near Shrewsbury, and ◊Minton (both 1796) similar, and from 1815 all English tableware of this type
19th century large-scale production of fine wares, in Britain notably Royal Worcester from 1862, and Royal (Crown) Derby from 1876
20th century revival in the craft of the individual potter, for example, ◊Leach, Lucie ◊Rie, ◊Coper.

potto small arboreal African mammal *Perodicticus potto* belonging to the loris family of primates. It climbs slowly through the lower branches of trees, gripping tightly with its hands, and feeds on small animals and some fruit.

poujadists an extreme right wing political movement in France led by Pierre Poujade which was prominent in French politics 1954–1958.

Poulenc /'puːlæŋk/ Francis (Jean Marcel) 1899–1963. French composer and pianist, born in Paris. A self-taught composer of witty and irreverent music, he was a member of the group of French composers known as ◊Les Six. In later years the deliberately disconcerting humour of his work gave way to music of grace and melodic charm, often achieved by the simplest of means. His works include the operas *Les Mamelles de Tirésias* 1947, and *Les Dialogues des Carmèlites* 1957, the ballet *Les Biches* 1923, orchestral music such as the Concerto for Organ, timpani, and strings 1938, and choral and chamber music.

Poulsen /'pəulsən/ Valdemar 1869–1942. Danish engineer who in 1900 was the first to demonstrate that sound could be recorded magnetically – originally on a moving steel wire or tape.

poultry term applied to domestic birds such as ducks, geese, turkeys and chickens. Good egg-laying breeds of chicken are Leghorns, Minorcas, and Anconas; varieties most suitable for the table are Dorkings and Indian Game; those useful for both purposes are Orpingtons, Rhode Island Reds, Wyandottes, and Plymouth Rocks. Nowadays most farm poultry are hybrids, selectively bred for useful characteristics.
Since World War II the development of battery-produced eggs and intensive breeding of broiler fowls and turkeys for the table, introduced from the US, has roused a public outcry against these 'animal factories'.

pound pre-metric *standard unit of weight* avoirdupois (UK, USA, and Canada), 0.45 of a kilogram.

pound the *British standard monetary unit* issued as a gold sovereign before 1914, as a note 1914–83, and as a circular yellow metal alloy coin from 1983. The edge inscriptions are 1983 *Decus et tutamen* 'An ornament and a safeguard'; 1984 (Scottish) *Nemo me impune* *lacessit* 'No one injures me with impunity' (see Thistle under ◊knighthood); 1985 (Welsh) *Pleidiol wyf i'm gwlad* ('True am I to my country', from the national anthem). The **green pound** is the ◊European Community exchange rate for conversion of EEC farm prices to sterling. The pound is also the unit of currency in Egypt, the Falkland Islands, Gibraltar, the Lebanon, Malta, St Helena, the Sudan, and Syria.

Pound /paʊnd/ (Alfred) Dudley Pickman Rogers 1877–1943. British admiral of the fleet. As First Sea Lord and Chief of the British Naval Staff 1939–43, he was responsible for the effective measures taken against the U-boats.

Pound /paʊnd/ Ezra 1885–1972. American poet, who lived in London from 1907, influencing T S ◊Eliot, ◊Yeats, and ◊Joyce, and who, by his verse *Personae* and *Exultations* 1909, established the principles of the ◊Imagist movement. In Paris 1921–25, he was the friend of Gertrude ◊Stein and ◊Hemingway, and then settled in Rapallo. His anti-Semitism and sympathy with ◊Mussolini led him to broadcast from Italy in World War II, and he was arrested by US troops 1945. Found unfit to plead, he was confined in a mental hospital until 1958. His first completely 'modern' poem was *Hugh Selwyn Mauberley* 1920, but his largest 'modern' work was the series of *Cantos* 1925–1969 (intended to number 100), which gave a selective view of history. He also wrote versions of Old English, Provençal, Chinese, and ancient Egyptian.

poundal the f.p.s. unit of force (pdl), defined as the force required to give a mass of pound an acceleration of 1 ft/s². Equivalent to 0.1382 newton or 1.382×10^4 dynes.

Poussin /puːˈsæn/ Nicolas 1594–1665. French artist. Born at Les Andelys, he went to Rome in 1624, spending the rest of his life there apart from a brief period as court painter to Louis XIII 1640–43. Influenced by the romantic Classical past, he composed his landscapes with mathematical precision and peopled them with noble, heroic figures. In his *Last Supper* 1647 Christ and the disciples lounge on couches as if at a Roman banquet. Other important works include the historical *Rape of the Sabines* and *The Worship of the Golden Calf* c. 1635.

Poverty Bay /ˈpɒvəti ˈbeɪ/ inlet on the E coast of North Island, New Zealand, on which the port of Gisborne stands. Captain ◊Cook made his first landing here 1769.

powder metallurgy a method of shaping heat-resistant metals such as tungsten. Metal powder is pressed into a mould and then sintered, or heated to very high temperatures.

Powell /ˈpaʊəl/ (John) Enoch 1912– . British politician. He was professor of Greek 1937–39; Conservative Member of Parliament for Wolverhampton 1950, minister of health 1960–63, and contested the party leadership 1965. Always controversial, he made a speech against immigration at Birmingham 1968 which led to his dismissal from the shadow cabinet. Declining to stand in the Feb 1974 election, he attacked the ◊Heath government and resigned from the party. From 1974 to 1987 he was Official Unionist Party member for S Down. He is an eloquent speaker.

Powell /ˈpaʊəl/ Anthony (Dymoke) 1905– . British novelist, whose chief work is the monumental series of 12 volumes *A Dance to the Music of Time* 1951–75, which begins shortly after World War I, and chronicles a period of 50 years in the lives of Nicholas Jenkins and his circle of upper-class friends.

Powell /ˈpaʊəl/ Cecil Frank 1903–1969. British physicist, awarded a Nobel prize 1950 for his use of photographic emulsion as a method of tracking charged nuclear particles.

Powell /ˈpaʊəl/ Michael 1905– . English director, best known for his collaboration with screenwriter Emeric Pressburger. Their work, often criticized for extravagance, shows an extraordinary imagination and originality. Films include *A Matter of Life and Death* 1946, and *Black Narcissus* 1947.

power in physics, the rate of doing work or consuming energy; measured in watts or other units of work per unit time.

power in mathematics, power, also called an index or exponent, is denoted by a superior small numeral. A number or symbol raised to the power 2 is said to be squared (for example, 3^2, x^2) and something raised to the power three is said to be cubed (for example, 2^3, y^3).

power boat a ◊motorboat used for racing.

power of attorney legal authority to act on behalf of another, for specific transaction, for a particular period, or indefinitely if a person no longer feels competent to handle their affairs.

Powys /ˈpaʊɪs/ central county of Wales
area 5077 sq km/1960 sq mi
towns administrative headquarters Llandrindod Wells
features Brecon Beacons National Park, Black mountains, rivers Wye and Severn, which both rise on Plynlimon (see ◊Dyfed); Lake Vyrnwy, artificial reservoir supplying Liverpool and Birmingham, and same size as Lake ◊Bala; alternative technology centre near Machynlleth
products mainly agricultural, dairy cattle, sheep
population (1980) 100,600
language 20% Welsh-speaking.

Poynter /ˈpɔɪntə/ Sir Edward John 1836–1919. British artist, first head of the Slade School, London, 1871–75, and president of the Royal Academy in succession to ◊Millais. He produced decorous nudes, mosaic panels for Westminster Palace 1870.

Poznań /ˈpɒznæn/ (German *Posen*) industrial city (locomotives, farm machinery, precision instruments, aircraft, bicycles, beer) in W Poland; population (1984) 571,000. Settled by German immigrants 1253, it passed to Prussia 1793, but was restored to Poland 1919. ◊Hindenburg was born here.

Pozzuoli /ˌpɒtsuːˈəʊli/ port in S Italy, shaken by some 25 earthquakes a day. Some 60 per cent of its buildings are uninhabitable, and an eventual major eruption, as in the case of ◊Pompeii, seems inevitable.

Prado /ˈprɑːdəʊ/ a throughfare of Madrid, Spain, which gave its name to the picture gallery Réal Museo de Pintura del Prado/Royal Picture

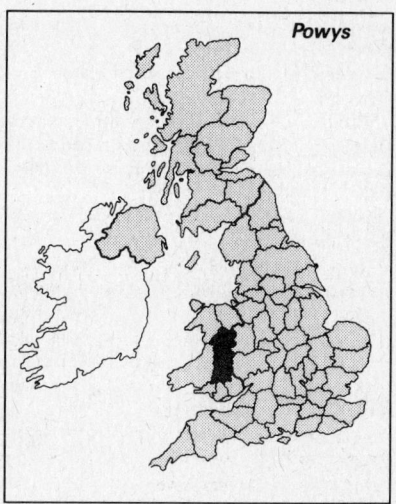
Powys

Gallery of the Prado, containing the national collection, founded by Charles III in 1785.

praesidium the name given to the executive committee of the Supreme Soviet in the USSR, and 1952–66 to the ◊Politburo.

praetor a Roman magistrate, elected annually, who assisted the ◊consuls and presided over the civil courts. The number of praetors was finally increased to eight.

pragmatism a philosophical tradition which interprets truth in terms of the practical effects of what is believed, and in particular the usefulness of these effects. ◊Peirce is often accounted the founder of pragmatism; it was further advanced by William ◊James.

Prague /prɑːg/ (Czech *Praha*) industrial city (cars and aircraft, chemicals, paper and printing, clothing, brewing and food processing), capital of Czechoslovakia; population (1983) 1,185,693. It is a beautiful city on the river Vltava, with fine palaces, bridges and churches, and a university founded by Emperor ◊Charles IV in 1438. Since the time of the Austro-Hungarian Empire, it has been the venue quinquennially of the Spartakiada, a physical education spectacle at the Strahov stadium in which 250,000 take part. It was occupied by Germany 1939–45, and the Nazi official Heydrich was assassinated here. The reform programme introduced in Jan 1968 by Dubček and ended in Aug by Soviet army invasion was known as the Prague Spring from an annual music festival.

prairie the central N American plains, formerly grass-covered, extending over most of the region between the Rockies on the W and the Great Lakes and Ohio river on the E, and northward into Canada.

prairie dog a kind of ◊marmot.

Prakrit /ˈprɑːkrɪt/ (Sanskrit 'natural') a general name for the ancient Indo-European dialects of N India, contrasted with the sacred classical language Sanskrit. The Prakrits are considered to be the ancestors of the languages Hindi, Punjabi, and Bengali.

praseodymium a silver-white metallic element, symbol Pr, atomic number 59 atomic weight 140.098. It is a member of the lanthanide series of elements and occurs naturally in monazite and bastnasite. It is used in carbon-arc lights and as a pigment in glass.

Prato /'prɑːtəʊ/ industrial town in central Italy; population (1984) 162,500. The 12th-century cathedral has works of art by Donatello, Filippo Lippi, and Andrea della Robbia.

prawn member, together with the shrimp, of the suborder Natantia 'swimming', order ◊Decapoda, as contrasted with the lobsters and crayfish, which are able to 'walk'. The edible *common prawn Leander serratus* of temperate seas has a long saw-edged spike or rostrum just in front of its eyes, and antennae much longer than its body-length. It is distinguished from the shrimp not only by its larger size, but by having pincers on its second pair of legs. The larger *Norway lobster* or *Dublin Bay prawn Nephrops norwegicus* are sold as 'scampi'.

Praxiteles /præk'sɪtəliːz/ Greek sculptor who lived in Athens during the 4th century BC. The works credited to him include the statue of Hermes carrying Dionysus and the bas-relief of Aphrodite of Cnidus.

prayer address to divine power, ranging from a magical formula to attain a desired end, to selfless communication in meditation. Within Christianity the Catholic and Orthodox churches sanction prayer to the Virgin, angels, and saints as intercessors, whereas Protestantism limits prayer to God alone, and does not provide for prayer for the dead.

preadaptation in biology, the fortuitous possession of a character that allows an organism to exploit a new situation. In many cases, the character evolves to solve a particular problem that a species encounters in its preferred habitat, but once evolved may allow the organisms to exploit an entirely different situation.

precession a slow wobble of the Earth on its axis, like that of a spinning top. The gravitational pulls of the Sun and Moon on the Earth's equatorial bulge cause the Earth's axis to trace out a circle on the sky every 25,800 years. Hence the position of the celestial pole is constantly changing due to precession, as are the positions of the ◊equinoxes (the points at which the celestial equator intersects the Sun's path around the sky). The *precession of the equinoxes* means that there is a slow but steady drift in the coordinates of objects on the ◊celestial sphere.

precipitation the meteorological term for water that falls to earth from the atmosphere. It includes ◊rain, ◊snow, sleet, ◊hail, ◊dew, and hoar frost.

predestination in Christian theology, the doctrine which asserts that God has determined all events beforehand, including the ultimate salvation or damnation of the individual human soul. The theory of predestination was elucidated in the controversy between ◊Augustine, who claimed the absolute determination of choice by God, and ◊Pelagius, who upheld the doctrine of freewill. ◊Luther and ◊Calvin adopted the Augustinian view at the Reformation, although in differing degrees, but ◊Arminius adopted the Pelagian standpoint.

prefect French government official who, under the centralized Napoleonic system 1800–1984, was responsible for enforcing government policy in each *département* and *région*.

pregnancy in humans the condition in which a child is growing within the womb or ◊uterus. It begins at conception and ends at birth, and the normal length is 40 weeks, though abortion or premature birth may occur at any time, and the period may be exceeded. ◊Menstruation usually stops on conception. After the second month the breasts become tense and tender, and the area round the nipple becomes darker. Enlargement of the uterus can be felt at about the end of the third month, and thereafter the abdomen enlarges progressively.

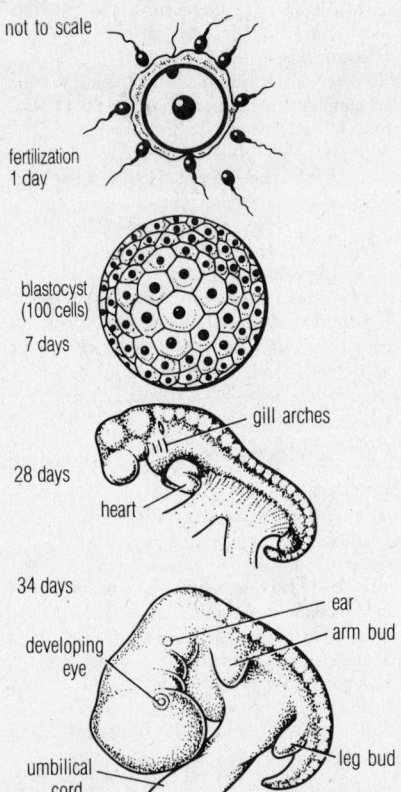

not to scale

fertilization 1 day

blastocyst (100 cells) 7 days

gill arches

28 days

heart

34 days

developing eye

umbilical cord

ear

arm bud

leg bud

prehistoric art see under ◊Ancient art.

prehistory the classification of cultures before the use of writing, based on the materials used by early humans for tools and weapons.
Stone Age in which flint was predominant, divided into:
Old Stone Age (Palaeolithic), ranging from 3,500,000 BC – 5,000 BC in which the tools were chipped into shape, and which includes ◊Neanderthal and Cromagnon people. Outstanding cave paintings were produced 20,000–8,000 years ago, notably at ◊Altamira and ◊Lascaux.
Middle Stone Age (Mesolithic) and *New Stone Age* (Neolithic) when tools were ground and polished, and agriculture and domestication of cattle and sheep were practised.

Bronze Age period of bronze tools and weapons beginning approximately 6,000 BC in the Far East, and continuing in the Middle East until about 1,200 BC; in Britain it lasted about 2,000–500 BC, and in Africa the transition from stone tools to iron was direct.
Iron Age period when iron was hardened by the addition of carbon, so that it superseded bronze for tools and weapons; in the Old World generally, the period from about 1,000 BC.

prelude in music, a composition intended as the preface to further music, as in Wagner's *Lohengrin*; as used by ◊Chopin, a short piano work.

Preminger /'premɪŋgə/ Otto (Ludwig) 1906–1986. American film producer-director. His films show a highly developed technique of

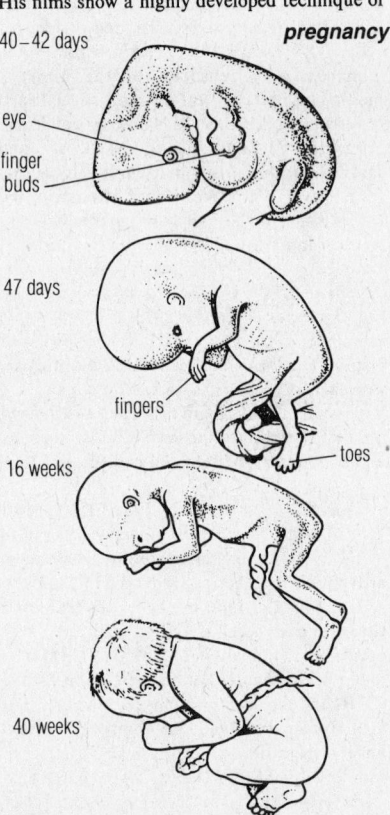

pregnancy

40–42 days

eye

finger buds

47 days

fingers

16 weeks

toes

40 weeks

story-telling, which clearly presents the issues, without judging them; they include *Margin for Error* 1942, *Anatomy of a Murder* 1959, and *Rosebud* 1974.

Premonstratensian a Roman Catholic monastic order founded by St Norbert at Prémontré, France, in 1120. Members were known as White Canons.

Prempeh I /'prempeɪ/ Chief of the Ashanti people in West Africa. He became king in 1888, and later opposed British attempts to take over the region. He was deported and in 1900 the Ashanti were defeated. Converted to Christianity, he returned to Kumasi in 1924.

preparatory school (prep school) a fee-paying independent school; in the UK a junior school which prepares children for entry to a senior school at about age 13; in the USA a school which prepares students for university entrance at about age 18.

preposition a grammatical ◊part of speech coming before a noun or pronoun in order to show a location ('in', 'on'), time ('during'), or some other relationship (for example figurative relationships in phrases like 'by heart' or 'on time'). In the sentence 'Put the book on the table' *on* is a preposition governing the noun 'table' and relates the verb 'put' to the phrase 'the table', indicating where the book should go.

Pre-Raphaelite Brotherhood a group of Victorian artists who abandoned the rules of art developed under Raphael, and painted biblical and literary subjects in the clear, detailed style they saw in painters earlier than Raphael. The Brotherhood, founded in 1848, had only three members – Dante Gabriel ◊Rossetti, John Everett ◊Millais, and Holman ◊Hunt – though

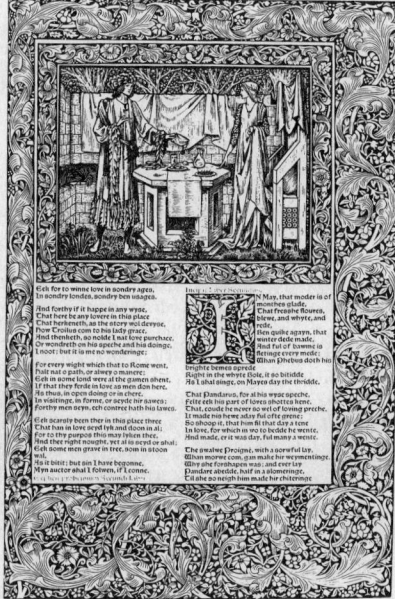

Pre-Raphaelite Brotherhood The Gothic revival idealized medieval life and chivalry. Literary or religious symbolism also characterized the work of the Pre-Raphaelites, combined with intricate and decorative detail, as in this edition by William Morris of Chaucer's *Troilus and Criseyde*.

many other artists came under their influence, notably Ford Madox ◊Brown, ◊Burne-Jones, Frederick Sandys, and William ◊Morris. The Brotherhood broke up in 1853 when Millais left to become an Associate of the Royal Academy.

Presbyterianism system of church government expounded by John ◊Calvin which gives its name to the established church of Scotland, and is also practised in England, Ireland, Switzerland, the USA, and elsewhere. There is no compulsory form of worship and each congregation is governed by presbyters or elders (clerical or lay), who are of equal rank, and congregations are grouped in presbyteries, ◊synods, and general assemblies.

prescription in law, the legal acquisition of title or right by uninterrupted use or possession from time immemorial.

prescription in medicine, an order written in a recognized form by a practitioner of medicine, dentistry, or veterinary surgery to a pharmacist for a preparation of drugs to be used in treatment. By tradition it is written in Latin, except for the directions addressed to the patient.

president the usual title of the head of state in a republic; the office may range from the equivalent of a constitutional monarch to the actual head of the government. For presidents of the USA, see ◊United States of America.

presidential medal of freedom highest peacetime civilian award in the USA, instituted in 1963, conferred annually on Independence Day by the president on those making significant contributions to the 'quality of American life'. It replaced the Medal of Freedom (1945) awarded for acts and service aiding US security.

Presley /'prezli/ Elvis (Aaron) 1935–1977. US singer and guitarist, born in Tupelo, Mississippi, probably the most influential performer of the rock-and-roll era. With his recordings for Sun Records in Memphis, Tennessee, 1954–55, and early hits such as 'Heartbreak Hotel' 1956, 'Hound Dog' 1956, and 'Love Me Tender' 1956, he created an individual vocal style, influenced by Southern blues and gospel music, country music, and rhythm and blues.

press the news media. See under ◊newspaper.

Pressburg /'presbʊək/ German name of ◊Bratislava, city in Czechoslovakia.

Press Council in the UK, organization (established 1953) that aims to preserve the freedom of the press, to maintain standards, consider complaints, and report on monopoly developments.

press gang method used to recruit soldiers and sailors into the British armed forces in the 18th and early 19th centuries. In effect it was a form of kidnapping carried out by the services or their agents, often with the aid of armed men.

pressure in physics, force per unit area. In a fluid (liquid or gas) pressure increases with depth. At the edge of earth's atmosphere, pressure is zero whereas at ground level it is about 1013.25 millibars (or 1 atmosphere). Pressure at a depth h in a fluid of density d is equal to hdg, where g is the acceleration due to ◊gravity. The SI unit of pressure is the ◊pascal (◊newton per square metre), equal to 0.01 millibars. Pressure has also been measured using a mercury column (see ◊Torricelli); 1 atmosphere equals 760 mm of mercury.

pressure cooker a closed pot in which food is cooked in water under pressure which boils at a higher temperature than normal boiling point (100°C/212°F), and therefore cooks food quicker. The French scientist Denis Papin invented the pressure cooker in England in 1679.

pressure group (also called *interest group* or *lobby*) group that puts pressure on parties or governments to ensure laws and treatment favourable to its own interest. Pressure groups have played an increasingly prominent role in contemporary Western democracies. In general they fall into two types: groups concerned with a single issue, such as nuclear disarmament, and groups attempting to promote their own interest, such as oil producers.

Prestel the ◊viewdata service provided by British Telecom (1975), which provides information on the television screen via the telephone network.

Prester John /'prestə 'dʒɒn/ legendary Christian prince who in the 12th–13th centuries was believed to rule a powerful empire in Asia. In the 14th–16th centuries Prester John was identified with the king of Ethiopia.

Preston /'prestən/ industrial seaport (textiles, chemicals, electrical goods, aircraft and shipbuilding), adminstrative headquarters of Lancashire, England, on the river Ribble 34 km/21 mi S of Lancaster; population (1983) 125,000. Cromwell defeated the Royalists at Preston in 1648.

Prestonpans, Battle of /ˌprestən'pænz/ Prince ◊Charles Edward's Jacobite forces defeated the English in 1745 at Prestonpans, a town in Lothian region, Scotland.

Prestwick /'prestwɪk/ town in Strathclyde, Scotland; population (1985) 13,532. There is a golf course and an international airport, linked with a ◊free port.

Pretoria /prɪ'tɔːrɪə/ administrative capital of the Republic of South Africa from 1910 and capital of Transvaal province from 1860; industries (engineering, iron and steel); two universities; population (1985) 741,300. Founded 1855, it was named after Boer leader Andries Pretorius (1799–1853).

Previn /'prevɪn/ André (George) 1929– . American conductor and composer. Born in Berlin, he became a US citizen in 1943. After a period working as a composer and arranger in the American film industry, he concentrated on conducting. He was principal conductor of the London Symphony Orchestra 1968–79. In 1985 he was appointed music director of the Royal Philharmonic Orchestra (a post he relinquished the following year, staying on as principal conductor), and of the Los Angeles Philharmonic from 1986. He has done much to popularize classical music.

Prévost d'Exiles /preˈvəʊ degˈziːl/ Antoine François 1697–1763. French novelist, known as Abbé Prévost. His *Manon Lescaut* 1731 inspired operas by Massenet and Puccini.

Priapus /praɪˈeɪpəs/ Greek god of garden fertility, son of ◊Dionysus and ◊Aphrodite, represented as grotesquely ugly, with an exaggerated phallus.

Pribilof Islands /ˈprɪbɪlɒf/ group of four islands in the Bering Sea, of volcanic origin, 320 km/200 mi SW of Bristol Bay, Alaska, USA. Named after Gerasim Pribilof who reached them in 1786, they were sold by Russia to the USA in 1867 with Alaska, of which they form part. They were made a fur-seal reservation in 1868.

prickly heat inflammation of the sweat glands; a disorder caused by excessive sweating. Small itchy blisters (or miliaria) are formed but quickly dry up and heal.

prickly pear cactus genus *Opuntia* native to America, especially Mexico and Chile, but naturalized in southern Europe, northern Africa, and Australia, where it is a pest. The common prickly pear *Opuntia vulgaris* is low-growing, with bright yellow flowers, and has pleasant-tasting oval fruit.

Pride's purge expulsion of 140 members from the English House of Commons by a detachment of soldiers led by Col Thomas Pride in 1648. They were accused of negotiating with King Charles I and were seen as unreliable by the army. The remaining members were termed the Rump and voted in favour of the king's trial. Pride acted as one of the judges at the trial and signed the king's death warrant.

Priestley /ˈpriːstli/ J(ohn) B(oynton) 1894–1984. British novelist and playwright. His first success was a novel about travelling theatre, *The Good Companions* 1929. He followed it with a realist novel about London life, *Angel Pavement* 1930; later books include *Lost Empires* 1965 and *The Image Men* 1968. As a playwright he was often preoccupied with theories of time, as in *An Inspector Calls* 1945. He was also noted for his wartime broadcasts, and his literary criticism, as in *Literature and Western Man* 1960. Order of Merit 1977.

Priestley /ˈpriːstli/ Joseph 1733–1804. British chemist and Unitarian minister. He discovered oxygen in about 1774 and was elected Fellow of the Royal Society in 1766. In 1791 his chapel and house in Birmingham were sacked by a mob because of his support for the French Revolution. In 1794 he emigrated to America.

priest's hole hiding place in private homes for Catholic priests in the 16th–17th centuries when there were penal laws against them in Britain. Many still exist, for example at Speke Hall, near Liverpool.

primary in presidential election campaigns in the USA, an election to decide the candidates for the major parties. Held in some 35 states, primaries begin with New Hampshire in Feb and

Priestley Best known for discovering oxygen, Joseph Priestley was a Presbyterian minister and a political radical who supported the French Revolution.

continue until Jun, and operate under varying complex rules. Generally speaking, the number of votes received by a candidate governs the number of delegates who will vote for that person at the national conventions in Jul/Aug, when the final choice of candidate for both Democratic and Republican parties is made.

primary education the education of children between the ages of 5 and 11 in the maintained school system in England and Wales, and up to 12 in Scotland.

primate in zoology, member of the order of mammals that includes monkeys, apes, and humans, as well as lemurs, bushbabies, lorises, and tarsiers. Generally they have forward-directed eyes, gripping hands and feet, and opposable thumbs and big toes, and tend to have nails rather than claws.

primate in the Christian Church, the official title of metropolitans. The archbishop of Canterbury is the Primate of All England, and the archbishop of York the Primate of England.

prime minister or *premier* head of a parliamentary government, usually the leader of the largest party. The first in Britain is usually considered to have been Robert ◊Walpole, but the office was not officially recognized until 1905. In some countries, such as Australia, a distinction is drawn between the prime minister of the whole country, and the premier of an individual state. In countries with an executive president, such as France, the prime minister is of lesser standing.

prime number a number that can be divided only by 1 or itself, that is, having no other factors. There is an infinite number of primes, the first ten of which are 2, 3, 5, 7, 11, 13, 17, 19, 23 and 29. The number 2 is the only even prime (because all other even numbers have 2 as a factor). Over the centuries mathematicians have sought general methods (algorithms) for calculating primes, from Eratosthenes' sieve to modern programs on powerful computers. Eratosthenes'

methods (dating from about 200 BC) is to write in sequence all numbers from 2, then, starting with 2, underline every second number, thus eliminating numbers that can be divided by 2. Next, starting with 3, cross out every third number (whether or not they are underlined), thus eliminating numbers divisible by 3. Continue the process for 5, 7, and so on. Numbers that remain are primes.

Primitivism influence on modern art (◊Kirchner, ◊Modigliani, ◊Picasso, and others) of aboriginal cultures of Africa, Australia, the Americas, and also of Western folk art.

Primo de Rivera /ˈpriːməʊ deɪ rɪˈveərə/ Miguel 1870–1930. Spanish soldier and politician. He was captain-general of Catalonia when, in 1923, he led a coup against the ineffective monarchy and became virtual dictator of Spain with the support of Alfonso XIII. Premier from 1925, he resigned 1930.

primrose woodland plant *primula vulgaris*, common to Britain and Europe, bearing pale yellow flowers in spring. Related to it is the cowslip, and the false oxlip is a hybrid of the two.

prince a royal or noble title. In Rome and medieval Italy it was used as the title of certain officials, for example, *princeps senatus* (Latin 'leader of the Senate'). The title was granted to the king's sons in 15th century France, and in England from Henry VII's time. The British sovereign's eldest son is normally created Prince of Wales.

Prince /prɪns/ Harold 1928– . American director, noted for his stylish productions of musicals such as *Cabaret* 1968 and *Follies* 1971 on Broadway, and *Evita* 1978 and *Sweeney Todd* 1980 in London's West End.

Prince /prɪns/ stage name of Prince Rogers Nelson 1960– . US rock star from Minneapolis, who composes, arranges, and produces his own records and usually plays all the instruments. His hits include 'Little Red Corvette' from the album *1999* 1982, 'Kiss' from *Parade* 1986, and 'Sign O' The Times' 1987.

Prince Edward Island /ˈedwəd/ province of Canada
area 5,657 sq km/2184 sq mi
capital Charlottetown
features named after Prince Edward of Kent, father of Queen Victoria; PEI National Park; Summerside Lobster Carnival
products potatoes, dairy products; lobsters and oysters; farm vehicles
population (1981) 124,200.

Prince Imperial title of Eugène, son of Emperor ◊Napoleon III of France.

Prince Rupert /ˈruːpət/ fishing port at the mouth of the Skeena river in British Columbia, Canada, on Kaien Island, W side of Tsimpsean peninsula; population (1983) 16,786.

princess royal title often conferred on the British sovereign's eldest daughter; currently held by Princess Anne.

Princeton /ˈprɪnstən/ borough in New Jersey, USA, 80 km/50 mi SW of New York, the seat of Princeton University founded in 1746 at Elizabethtown and moved to Princeton 1756; population (1983) 12,035.

PRIME MINISTERS OF BRITAIN

Sir Robert Walpole	(Whig)	1721
Earl of Wilmington	(Whig)	1742
Henry Pelham	(Whig)	1743
Duke of Newcastle	(Whig)	1754
Duke of Devonshire	(Whig)	1756
Duke of Newcastle	(Whig)	1757
Earl of Bute	(Tory)	1762
George Grenville	(Whig)	1763
Marquess of Rockingham	(Whig)	1765
Duke of Grafton	(Whig)	1766
Lord North	(Tory)	1770
Marquess of Rockingham	(Whig)	1782
Earl of Shelburne	(Whig)	1782
Duke of Portland	(Coalition)	1783
William Pitt	(Tory)	1783
Henry Addington	(Tory)	1801
William Pitt	(Tory)	1804
Lord Grenville	(Whig)	1806
Duke of Portland	(Tory)	1807
Spencer Perceval	(Tory)	1809
Earl of Liverpool	(Tory)	1812
George Canning	(Tory)	1827
Viscount Goderich	(Tory)	1827
Duke of Wellington	(Tory)	1828
Earl Grey	(Whig)	1830
Viscount Melbourne	(Whig)	1834
Sir Robert Peel	(Conservative)	1834
Viscount Melbourne	(Whig)	1835
Sir Robert Peel	(Conservative)	1841
Lord J Russell	(Liberal)	1846
Earl of Derby	(Conservative)	1852
Lord Aberdeen	(Peelite)	1852
Viscount Palmerston	(Liberal)	1855
Earl of Derby	(Conservative)	1858
Viscount Palmerston	(Liberal)	1859
Lord J Russell	(Liberal)	1865
Earl of Derby	(Conservative)	1866
Benjamin Disraeli	(Conservative)	1868
W E Gladstone	(Liberal)	1886
Benjamin Disraeli	(Conservative)	1874
W E Gladstone	(Liberal)	1880
Marquess of Salisbury	Conservative)	1885
W E Gladstone	(Liberal)	1886
Marquess of Salisbury	(Conservative)	1886
W E Gladstone	(Liberal)	1892
Earl of Rosebery	(Liberal)	1894
Marquess of Salisbury	(Conservative)	1895
A J Balfour	(Conservative)	1902
Sir H Campbell-Bannerman	(Liberal)	1905
H H Asquith	(Liberal)	1908
H H Asquith	(Coalition)	1915
D Lloyd George	(Coalition)	1916
A Bonar Law	(Conservative)	1922
Stanley Baldwin	(Conservative)	1923
Ramsay MacDonald	(Labour)	1924
Stanley Baldwin	(Conservative)	1924
Ramsay MacDonald	(Labour)	1929
Ramsay MacDonald	(National)	1931
Stanley Baldwin	(National)	1935
N Chamberlain	(National)	1937
Sir Winston Churchill	(Coalition)	1940
Clement Attlee	(Labour)	1945
Sir Winston Churchill	(Conservative)	1951
Sir Anthony Eden	(Conservative)	1955
Harold Macmillan	(Conservative)	1957
Sir Alec Douglas-Home	(Conservative)	1963
Harold Wilson	(Labour)	1964
Edward Heath	(Conservative)	1970
Harold Wilson	(Labour)	1974
James Callaghan	(Labour)	1976
Margaret Thatcher	(Conservative)	1979

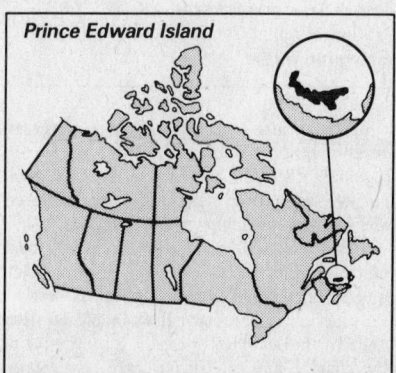

Prince Edward Island

Princetown /'prɪnstaʊn/ English village on the W of Dartmoor, Devon, containing Dartmoor prison, opened 1809.

print a picture that is printed. In art there are three types:

wood-cuts and *wood-engraving* in which the areas and lines of the design are left in relief (Thomas ◊Bewick, Eric ◊Gill);

intaglio prints made by engraving, using a burin (engraver's tool) with pushing action, and etching (using corrosive acid on a design drawn through a wax coating on metal) (◊Dürer, ◊Van Dyck, ◊Hollar, ◊Rembrandt, ◊Whistler, ◊Brangwyn, ◊Sickert). An *aquatint* is a tone etching that gives a water-colour effect (◊Goya, ◊Picasso, John ◊Piper); *dry-point* uses no acid, but makes a burr in incising the plate which gives the lines a velvety quality (◊Dürer, ◊Rembrandt, and J M ◊Whistler). In *mezzotint* a copper or steel plate is roughened with a rocking tool, and the resultant burr is then scraped away where lighter tones are wanted (the process was used to reproduce the works of ◊Turner, ◊Reynolds, ◊Constable, ◊Romney and ◊Lawrence);

surface prints, made by means of lithography (Greek *lithos* stone), so called because originally made with greasy ink on absorbent stone (now aluminium sheeting), which was then washed with water. The water having repelled the printing ink, the design was printed from the greasy area. Artists include ◊Bonington, ◊Delacroix, ◊Daumier, ◊Toulouse-Lautrec, ◊Whistler.

printed circuit board (PCB) an electrical circuit created by laying (printing) 'tracks' of a conductor such as copper onto one or both sides of an insulating board. Components such as integrated circuits (chips), resistors, and capacitors can be soldered to the surface of the board (surface-mounted) or, more commonly, attached by inserting their connecting pins or wires into holes drilled in the board. The PCB was invented in 1936 by the Austrian scientist Paul Eisler. PCBs were first used on a large scale in 1948.

printed circuit board

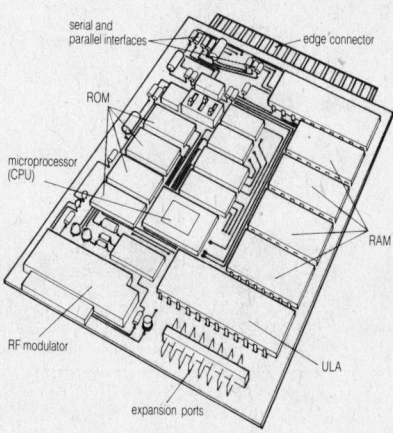

printer in computing, an output device for producing printed copy of textual, numeric, and graphical data. Types include the *daisywheel*, which produces good-quality text but no graphics; the *dot matrix*, which creates character patterns from a matrix of small dots, producing text and graphics; and the *laser printer*, which produces high-quality text and graphics.

printing the reproduction of text or illustrative material on paper, as in books and newspapers, or on an increasing variety of materials, for example on tins and plastic containers. In China the art of printing from a single wooden block was known in the 6th century AD, and moveable type was being used by the 11th century. In Europe it was only in the 15th century that moveable type was re-invented, traditionally by Johannes ◊Gutenberg in Germany. William ◊Caxton introduced printing to England. In the 19th century, steam power replaced hand operation of the presses, making possible long 'runs', and hand composition of type (each tiny metal letter was taken from the case and placed in the narrow stick which carried one line of text) was replaced by machines operated by a keyboard. The *Linotype*, used in newspapers (it produced a line of type in a solid slug) was invented by Ottmar Mergenthaler in 1886, and the *Monotype*, used in bookwork (it produced a series of individual characters, which could be hand corrected) by Tolbert Lanston in 1889. The printing process still involved pressing inked raised type onto paper, a method called ◊letterpress. In the 1960s came ◊offset litho, a method that prints from an inked flat surface, while high-circulation magazines were printed by the ◊gravure method, which uses recessed plates.

Electronic photo-typesetting machines allowed the entire process of setting and correction to be done in the same way as a copy-typist operates, and leaving only the making of plates and the running of the presses to be done traditionally. By the 1970s the final steps were taken to plateless printing, using various processes, such as a computer-controlled laser beam, or continuous jets of ink acoustically broken up into tiny equal-sized drops which are electrostatically charged under computer control. See also ◊four-colour process.

printing

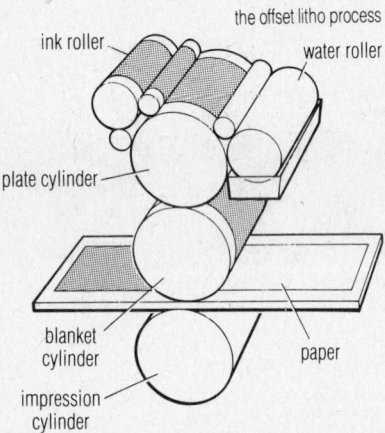

the offset litho process

ink roller

water roller

plate cylinder

blanket cylinder

paper

impression cylinder

prion a microorganism, a hundred times smaller than a ◊virus, claimed to have been discovered at the University of California in 1982. Composed of ◊protein, and mysteriously without any detectable amount of ◊nucleic acid (genetic material), it is thought to cause diseases such as scrapie in sheep, and some degenerative diseases of the nervous system in humans.

prior, prioress in a religious community, either the deputy of an abbot or abbess, responsible for discipline, or in certain Roman Catholic orders the principal of a monastery or convent.

Prior /'praɪə/ Matthew 1664–1721. British poet and diplomat. He was associated under the Whigs with the negotiation of the treaty of Ryswick 1697 ending the war with France and under the Tories with that of Utrecht 1714 ('Matt's Peace') ending the war of the Spanish succession, but on the return of the Whigs to power he was imprisoned by Walpole 1715–17. His gift as a poet was for light occasional verses.

Pripet /'priːpɪt/ river in W Russia, a tributary of the Dnieper, which it joins 80 km/50 mi above Kiev, in the Ukraine, after a course about 800 km/500 mi. The *Pripet marshes* near Pinsk were of strategic importance in both world wars.

prism in mathematics, a solid figure (◊polyhedron) with two equal polygonal faces (bases) in parallel planes, the other faces being parallelograms, of the same number as there are sides to one of the bases. If these faces are rectangles, the figure is a right prism.

prism in optics, a triangular block of transparent material (plastic, glass or silica) commonly used to 'bend' a ray of light or split a

beam into its spectral colours (see ◊spectrum). Prisms are used rather like mirrors to define the optical path in binoculars, camera viewfinders, and periscopes. The dispersive property of prisms is used in the ◊spectroscope.

prison place of confinement for those contravening the laws of the state. Until the late 18th century criminals were commonly sentenced to death, mutilation, or transportation rather than imprisonment, so that the growth of criminal prisons as opposed to places of detention for those awaiting trial, confined for political reasons, was a late development. One of the greatest reformers in Britain was John ◊Howard, whose Prison Act of 1778 established the principle of separate confinement combined with work in an attempt at reform (it was eventually carried out when Pentonville prison was built in 1842). Another noted campaigner against the appalling conditions in early 19th-century prisons was Elizabeth ◊Fry. Penal servitude was introduced in 1857, after the refusal of the colonies to accept convicts, but this and hard labour were abolished in Britain by the Criminal Justice Act of 1948, so that there is only one form of prison sentence, namely imprisonment.

Under the Criminal Justice Act of 1967 courts may suspend prison sentences of two years or less, and, unless the offender has previously been in prison or ◊borstal, will normally do so; that is, the sentence comes into effect only if another offence is committed. After serving one-third of their sentence (minimum 12 months), selected prisoners may be released on parole.

The Criminal Justice Act 1972 required the courts to consider information about an offender before sentencing them to prison for the first time, and introduced the concept of ◊community service to replace prison for non-violent offenders, and of day training centres for the social education under intensive supervision of those who could not integrate well into society. Most countries aim at rehabilitation and in the USSR, for example, stress is laid on constructive work and the return of the prisoner to a normal life. Notable experiments have also been made in Britain and elsewhere in 'open prisons' without bars, release of prisoners to work in ordinary jobs outside the prison in the final stages of their sentence, and after-care on release. Attempts to deal with the increasing number of young offenders include from 1982 accommodation in community homes in the case of minor offences, with (in more serious cases) 'short, sharp shock' treatment in the modern version of ◊borstal (although the latter was subsequently found to have little effect on reconviction rates).

Pritchett /'prɪtʃɪt/ V(ictor) S(awdon) 1900– . British novelist and critic. Noted for the witty and satirical style of his short stories. His critical works include *The Living Novel* 1946 and a biography of the French novelist Balzac. He was knighted in 1975.

privacy the right of the individual to be free from secret surveillance (by scientific devices or other means), and from the disclosure to unauthorized persons of personal data, as accumulated in computer data banks. Always an issue complicated by considerations of state

security, public welfare (in the case of criminal activity), and other factors, it has been rendered more complex by modern technology.

All Western countries now have computerized-data protection. In the USA the Privacy Act 1974 requires that there should be no secret databanks and that agencies handling data must ensure their reliability and prevent misuse (information gained for one purpose must not be used for another). The public must be able to find out what is recorded and how it is used, and be able to correct it. In Britain under the Data Protection Act 1984 a register is kept of all businesses or organizations that store and process personal information, and they are subject to a code of practice set out in the act.

private enterprise system whereby economic activities are in private hands and are carried on for private profit, as opposed to national, municipal, or cooperative ownership.

private school alternative name for a fee-paying ◊independent school in the USA and UK.

privatization the selling or transfer into private hands of state-owned or public assets and services (notably nationalized industries). Privatization of services takes place by the contracting out to private firms of the rendering of services previously supplied by public authorities. The policy has been pursued by several governments in recent years, particularly the post-1979 Conservative administrations in Britain, as well as in France, Japan, and Italy.

Industries in Britain privatized since 1979:
British Telecom
British Gas Corporation
British National Oil Corporation
British Airways
British Airports Authority
British Aerospace
British Shipbuilders
British Transport Docks Board
National Freight Company
Enterprise Oil

---

privet genus *Ligustrum* of semi-evergreen shrubs, family Oleaceae, with dark green leaves, including the wild *common privet Ligustrum vulgare*, with white flowers and black berries, and *hedge privet Ligustrum ovalifolium*.

Privy Council originally the chief royal officials of the ◊Norman kings in Britain, which under the ◊Tudors and early ◊Stuarts became the chief governing body. It was replaced from 1688 by the ◊cabinet, originally a committee of the council, and the council itself now retains only formal powers, in issuing royal proclamations and orders-in-council. Cabinet ministers are automatically members, and it is presided over by the Lord President of the Council. The *Judicial Committee of the Privy Council*, once a final court of appeal for members of the Commonwealth, is almost obsolete.

privy purse the personal expenditure of the British sovereign, which derives from his/her own resources (as distinct from the ◊civil list which now finances only expenses incurred in pursuance of official functions and duties). The office that deals with this expenditure is also known as the Privy Purse.

Privy Seal, Lord until 1884, the officer of state in charge of the royal seal to prevent its misuse; the honorary title is now held by a senior cabinet minister who has special nondepartmental duties.

Prix Goncourt French literary prize for fiction, given by the Académie ◊Goncourt from 1903.

probability the likelihood or ◊chance that something will happen, often expressed as odds or, in mathematics, numerically as a fraction or decimal. In tossing an unbiased coin, the chance that it will land heads is the same as the chance that it will land tails, that is, 1 to 1 or even; mathematically this probability is expressed as ½ or 0.5. The odds against any chosen number coming up on the roll of an unbiased die are 6 to 1; the probability is $\frac{1}{6}$ or 0.1666... If two dice are rolled there are 6 x 6 = 36 different possible combinations. The chance that a double (two numbers the same) will come up is only one of these combinations; thus the probability is $\frac{1}{36}$ or 0.02777... In general, the probability that n particular events will happen out of a total of m possible events is n/m. A certainty has a probability of 1; an impossibility has a probability of 0.

Probability theory was first developed by the French mathematicians Pascal and Fermat in the 17th century. Today probability plays a major part in the mathematics of atomic theory and in insurance and statistical studies in general.

probate formal proof of a will. In the UK, if its validity is unquestioned, it is proved in 'common form'; the executor, in the absence of other interested parties, obtains at a probate registry a grant upon their own oath. Otherwise, it must be proved in 'solemn form': its validity established at a probate court (in the chancery division of the high court), those concerned being made parties to the action.

probation in the UK and USA, the placing of offenders under supervision in the community, as an alternative to prison. The *probation service* also assists the families of those imprisoned, and gives the prisoner supervisory aftercare on release, as well as assisting in preventive measures to avoid family breakdown, which may lead to crime. Juveniles are no longer placed on probation, but under a 'supervision' order.

procedure a part of a computer program describing the processing required to achieve a particular result. Most programming languages have a special notation to encourage the splitting of programs into small parts (procedures and ◊functions), each of which, like a miniprogram, carries out a small part of the overall computation (see ◊structured programming).

processing cycle in computing, the sequence of steps performed repeatedly by a computer in the execution of a program. The computer's ◊CPU (central processing unit) continuously works through a loop of fetching a program instruction from the ◊memory, fetching any data it needs, operating on the data and storing the

result in the memory, before it fetches another program instruction, and so on.

proconsul Roman ◊consul who went on to govern a province when his term ended.

Proconsul the name of the prehistoric ape whose skull was found on Rusinga Island in Lake Victoria, E Africa, by Mary ◊Leakey. It is believed to be 20 million years old.

Procrustes /prəʊˈkrʌstiːz/ (Greek 'the stretcher') in Greek mythology, a robber who tied his victims to a bed; if they were too tall for it, he cut off the ends of their legs, and if they were too short he stretched them.

procurator-fiscal officer of a Scottish sheriff's court who (combining the role of public prosecutor and coroner) inquires into suspicious deaths and carries out the preliminary questioning of witnesses to crime.

Procyon the eighth-brightest ◊star in the sky, and the brightest in the constellation ◊Canis Minor. Procyon is a white star 11.3 light years away, with a mass of 1.7 Suns. A white dwarf companion star orbits it every 40 years.

productivity, biological in an ◊ecosystem, the amount of material produced by the primary producers – plants – in the ◊food chain, that is available for consumption by animals. Plants turn carbon dioxide gas into sugars and other complex carbon compounds by means of ◊photosynthesis. Their net productivity is defined as the quantity of carbon compounds formed, less the quantity used up by the plants' own respiration. See also ◊autotroph.

profit-sharing a system whereby an employer pays the workers a fixed share of the profits. It originated in France in the early 19th century, and was widely practised for a time within the cooperative movement.

Profumo /prəˈfjuːməʊ/ John Dennis 1915– . British Conservative politician, secretary of state for war 1960–Jun 1963, when he resigned on the disclosure of his involvement with Christine Keeler, mistress also of a Soviet naval attaché.

progesterone a ◊hormone which occurs in vertebrates. In mammals, it regulates the ◊menstrual cycle and ◊pregnancy.

programme music term for music that tells a story, depicts a scene or painting, or illustrates a literary or philosophical idea, such as Richard Strauss's *Don Juan*.

programming in computing, writing statements in a ◊programming language for the control of a computer. Applications programming is for end-user programs, such as accounts programs or word-processing packages. Systems programming is for operating systems and the like, which are concerned more with the internal workings of the computer. There are several programming styles:

Procedural programming, in which programs are written as lists of instructions which the computer obeys in sequence, is by far the most popular. It is the 'natural' style, closely matching the computer's own sequential operation. Procedural programming languages, such as BASIC and COBOL, all support three basic constructs: sequence (executing statements in the list in strict order); iteration (looping through

parts of the list); and selection (jumping to different parts of the list when different conditions are met).

Declarative programming, such as in the programming language Prolog, does not describe how to solve a problem, but rather describes the logical structure of the problem. Running such a program is more like proving an assertion than following a procedure.

Functional programming is a style based largely on the definition of ◊functions. There are very few functional programming languages, Hope and ML being the most widely used, though many more conventional languages (for example C) make extensive use of functions.

Object-oriented programming, the most recently developed style, involves viewing a program as a collection of objects which behave in certain ways when they are passed certain 'messages', for example an object might be defined to represent a table of figures which will be displayed on screen when a 'display' message is received.

Today most programming is done at a computer terminal using special-purpose program-editing software, rather like word processing. In the past, the process was more laborious, with programs having to be coded as holes punched into cards or paper tape.

programming language in computing, a special notation in which instructions for controlling a computer are written. They are designed to be easy for users to write and read but must be capable of being mechanically translated (by a ◊compiler or ◊interpreter) into the ◊machine code that the computer can execute.

progression sequence of numbers each formed by a specific relationship to its predecessor: an *arithmetical progression* (see ◊arithmetic sequence) has numbers which increase or decrease by a common sum or difference (for example 2, 4, 6, 8); a *geometric progression* (see ◊geometric series) has numbers each bearing a fixed ratio to its predecessor (for example 3, 6, 12, 24), and a *harmonic progression* is a sequence with numbers whose ◊reciprocals are in arithmetical progression, for example 1, ½, ⅓, ¼.

progressive education a generic term for teaching methods which take as their starting point children's own aptitudes and interests and encourage them to follow their own investigations and lines of enquiry.

prohibition law forbidding the sale of intoxicating liquor, as in USA when a prohibition amendment to the US constitution (known as the Volstead Act, after the congressman who introduced it) became operative in 1920. The federal government lost revenue and it led to bootlegging (the illegal distribution of liquor, often illicitly distilled), to the financial advantage of gangsters such as Al ◊Capone, and public opinion insisted on repeal 1933. Prohibition on religious grounds is enforced with varying degrees of severity in Islamic countries.

projection in cartography, the means of depicting the spherical surface of the earth on a flat piece of paper. The theory is that, if a light were placed at the centre of a transparent earth, the surface features could be thrown as shadows on a piece of paper placed close to the surface. This paper may be flat and placed on a pole (azimuthal or zenithal), or may be rolled cylindrically around the equator (cylindrical), or may be in the form of a tall cone resting on the equator (conical). The resulting maps differ from one another, distorting either area or direction, and each is suitable for a particular purpose. For example, projections distorting area the least are used for distribution maps, and those with least distortion of direction are used for navigation charts. ◊Mercator's projection dates from 1569.

projector an apparatus that projects a picture onto a screen. In a *slide projector*, a lamp shines a light through the photographic slide and a projection ◊lens throws an enlarged image of the slide onto the screen. A *ciné projector* has similar optics, but incorporates a mechanism that holds the film still while light is shone through each frame (picture). A shutter covers the film when it moves between frames.

prokaryote in biology, an organism whose cells lack ◊organelles such as nuclei, mitochondria and chloroplasts. The prokaryotes comprise the ◊bacteria and ◊cyanobacteria; all other organisms are ◊eukaryotes. Prokaryote DNA is not arranged in chromosomes but forms a simple loop.

Prokofiev /prə'kɒfief/ Sergey (Sergeyevich) 1891–1953. Russian composer. Born near Ekaterinoslav, he studied at St Petersburg under ◊Rimsky-Korsakov and achieved fame as a pianist. For some time he lived in the USA and in Paris, but returned to Moscow in 1933. He was essentially a classicist in his use of form, but his varied output demonstrates great lyricism, humour, and skill. His music includes operas such as *The Love of Three Oranges* 1921; ballets for ◊Diaghilev, including *Romeo and Juliet* 1935; seven symphonies including the *Classical Symphony* 1916–17; music for films; pianoforte and violin concertos; songs and cantatas; and *Peter and the Wolf* 1936.

Prokopyevsk /prə'kɒpjefsk/ coalmining city of the Kuzbas, Siberia, USSR; population (1985) 274,000.

proletariat in Marxist theory, those classes in society which possess no property, and therefore depend upon the sale of their labour-power or expertise, as opposed to the capitalists or bourgeoisie, who own the means of production, and the petty bourgeoisie, or working small property-owners. The term is derived from the Latin *proletarii*, the class possessing no property, whose contribution to the state was considered to be their offspring *(proles)*.

Prolog in computing, a ◊programming language based on logic. Invented in 1971 at the University of Marseilles, it is used mainly for ◊artificial-intelligence programming.

PROM (*p*rogrammable *r*ead-*o*nly *m*emory) in computing, a memory device in the form of a silicon chip that can be programmed to hold information permanently.

promenade concert originally a concert in which the audience walked about, now in the UK the name of any one of an annual BBC series

(the Proms) at the Royal Albert Hall, London, at which part of the audience stands. Their originator was Sir Henry ◊Wood in 1895.

Prometheus /prə'miːθjuːs/ in Greek mythology, a ◊Titan who stole fire from heaven for the human race. In revenge, ◊Zeus had him chained to a rock with an eagle preying on his liver, until he was rescued by ◊Hercules.

promethium an element of the ◊rare earth group, of which the existence in nature is unconfirmed: symbol Pm, atomic number 61, atomic weight uncertain (probably 147). Several isotopes have been reported, obtained by fission of uranium or by neutron bombardment of neodymium.

prominence a bright cloud of gas projecting above the surface of the ◊Sun. Prominences can extend into space for 100,000 km/60,000 mi or more. *Quiescent prominences* last for months, and are held in place by ◊magnetic fields in the Sun's corona. *Surge prominences* shoot gas off into space at speeds of 1,000 km/600 mi per sec. *Loop prominences* are gases falling back to the Sun's surface after a solar ◊flare.

promissory note a written promise to pay on demand, or at a fixed future time, a specific sum of money to a named person or bearer. Like a cheque, it may be negotiated by endorsement by the payee. A commercial paper is a form of promissory note that can be bought and sold. These forms of payment are usually issued by large corporations at times when credit is otherwise difficult to obtain.

pronghorn hoofed mammal *Antilocapra americana* of the N American plains, only surviving member of family Antilocapridae, between deer and cattle. It is 1 m/3 ft high, sheds its horns annually, and is a swift runner.

pronoun a grammatical ◊part of speech that is used in place of a noun, usually to save repetition of the noun (for example 'The people arrived around nine o'clock. *They* behaved as though we were expecting *them*'). Words like 'they', 'them', 'he', and 'she', are *personal pronouns* (because they represent people), words like 'this/these', and 'that/those' are *demonstrative pronouns* (because they demonstrate or point to something : this book and not that book. and so on), words like 'that' and 'who' can be *relative pronouns* in sentences like 'She said that she was coming' and 'Tell me who did it' (because they relate one clause to another), and words like 'myself' and 'himself' are *reflexive pronouns* (because they reflect back to a person, as in 'He did it himself').

pronunciation the way in which words are rendered into human speech sounds; either a language as a whole or a particular word or name. The pronunciation of languages forms the academic subject of ◊phonetics. A particular speaker's pronunciation of his or her language or other languages is termed an *accent*. The pronunciation of individual words in English is a matter of convention rather than absolute correctness; notoriously, it cannot be predicted from the spelling. The pronunciations of foreign words shown in the *Hutchinson Encyclopedia* are established English versions, where these exist; otherwise, they are acceptable renderings

of the foreign-language pronunciation into English sounds.

propaganda literally the spreading of information, used particularly with reference to the promotion of a religious or political doctrine. This century the word has acquired pejorative connotations because of its association with the use of propaganda by Nazi Germany.

propane a gaseous hydrocarbon (C_3H_8), found in petroleum and used as fuel.

propellant the substance burned in a rocket for propulsion. Two propellants are used – fuel and oxidizer are stored in separate tanks and pumped independently into the combustion chamber. Liquid oxygen (oxidizer) and liquid hydrogen (fuel) are common propellants, used for example in the space-shuttle main engines; Russia's Soyuz launch vehicles use kerosene (paraffin) and liquid oxygen as propellants.

propeller a screw-like device used to propel ships and some aeroplanes. A propeller has a number of curved blades, and accelerates fluid (liquid or gas) backwards when it rotates. ◊Reaction to this backward movement of fluid sets up a propulsive thrust forwards. The marine screw propeller was developed by Francis Pettit Smith in Britain and Swedish-born John Ericsson in the USA.

proper motion the gradual change in the position of a star that results from its motion in ◊orbit around the ◊galaxy. Proper motions are slight, undetectable to naked eye, but can be accurately measured on photographs through telescopes taken many years apart. ◊Barnard's Star is the star with the largest proper motion, 10.3 arc seconds per year.

Propertius /prə'pɜːʃəs/ Sextus c. 47–15 BC. Roman elegiac poet, a member of ◊Maecenas' circle, who wrote of his love for his mistress 'Cynthia'.

property the right to control the use of a thing (such as land, a building, a work of art, or a computer program, which is 'owned' by copyright). In English law, a distinction is made between *real property*, which involves a degree of geographical fixity, and *personal property*, which does not. Property is never absolute, since any society places limits on an individual's property (such as the right to transfer that property to another). Different societies have held widely varying interpretations of the nature of property and the extent of the rights of the owner of that property. Major writers on property include Plato, Locke, and Marx.

prophet a person thought to speak from divine inspiration or who foretells the future. In the Bible, one of the succession of Hebrew saints and seers who preached and prophesied in the Hebrew kingdoms in Palestine from the 8th century BC until the suppression of Jewish independence in 586 BC, and possibly later. The chief prophets were ◊Elijah, ◊Amos, Hosea, and ◊Isaiah. The prophetic books of the Old Testament constitute a division of the Hebrew Bible.

proportional representation (PR) electoral system in which distribution of party seats corresponds to their proportion of the total votes cast, and minority votes are not wasted, (as opposed to a simple majority, or 'first past the post', system). Forms include:

party list or additional member system (AMS). As recommended by the Hansard Society 1976 for introduction in Britain, three-quarters of the members would be elected in single-member constituencies on the traditional majority-vote system, and the remaining seats be allocated according to the overall number of votes cast for each party (a variant of this is used in West Germany). In France in 1985 it was proposed to introduce a system under which, after ruling out parties with less than a 5 per cent poll in each department, the votes for the rest would be divided by the number of seats to obtain an electoral quotient (for example, if the quotient were 15,000 votes, party A with 30,000 votes would win two seats, and party B with 12,000 would win none); unallocated seats would be distributed in a second round when each party's poll would be divided by the number of seats it had already won, plus one (that is, party A would now be credited with only 10,000 votes; party B, having won no seat so far, would be credited with its original 12,000, and so gain a seat).

single transferable vote (STV), in which candidates are numbered in order of preference by the voter, and any votes surplus to the minimum required for a candidate to win are transferred to second preferences, as are second-preference votes from the successive candidates at the bottom of the poll until the required number of elected candidates is achieved (this is in use in the Republic of Ireland).

The chief arguments against proportional representation are its tendency to produce unstable coalitions, and the delay in getting results. See also under ◊vote.

prop root a modified root that grows from the lower part of a stem or trunk down to the ground, providing a plant with extra support. Prop roots, also sometimes known as stilt roots, are common on some woody plants, such as mangroves, and also occur on a few herbaceous plants, such as maize. Buttress roots are a type of prop root found at the base of tree trunks, extended and flattened along the upper edge to form massive triangular buttresses.

propyl alcohol usually a mixture of two isomeric compounds, normal propyl alcohol and isopropyl alcohol ($CH_3CHOHCH_3$). The former is also known as 1-propanol, and the latter as 2-propanol. It is a colourless liquid and can be mixed with water. It is used in perfumery.

propylene second member of the alkene series of hydrocarbons (C_3H_6). A gas, it is widely used by industry to make organic chemicals, including polypropylene plastics.

prose spoken or written language without metrical regularity; in literature, prose corresponds more closely to the patterns of everyday speech than ◊poetry. In modern literature, however, the distinction between verse and prose is not always clear-cut. In Western literature prose was traditionally used for what today is usually called non-fiction; that is, history, biography, essays, and so on, while verse was used for imaginative literature. Prose came

into its own as a vehicle for ◊fiction with the rise of the modern ◊novel in the 18th century.

Prosecution Service, Crown body proposed under a bill of 1984, to be headed by the director of public prosecutions (DPP), and so bring England and Wales in line with Scotland (see ◊procurator fiscal) in having a prosecution service independent of the police. In most cases the decision to prosecute would be made on the basis of evidence presented by the police to local crown prosecutors in each of 43 police authority areas. The DPP had previously taken action (under the guidance of the attorney general), only in cases of special difficulty or importance.

Proserpina Roman equivalent of ◊Persephone, goddess of the underworld.

prostaglandin a complex ◊fatty acid that acts as a messenger substance between cells. There are several different prostaglandins in vertebrates. Some stimulate the contraction of smooth muscle, of the womb during birth for example; they are used to induce labour in humans and domestic animals. Others regulate the production of stomach acid. In excess, prostaglandins may produce inflammatory disorders such as arthritis.

prostate gland a gland surrounding, and opening into, the urethra at the base of the ◊penis of male mammals. The prostate gland produces an alkaline fluid which is released during ejaculation; this fluid activates ◊sperm and prevents their clumping together.

prosthesis replacement of a body part with an artificial substitute. Prostheses in the form of ◊artificial limbs, such as metal hooks for hands and wooden legs, have been used for centuries. Modern artificial limbs are more natural-looking and comfortable to wear. The latest myoelectric, or bionic, arms are electronically operated and are worked by minute electrical impulses from body muscles. Other protheses include such things as hearing aids, false teeth and eyes, heart ◊pacemaker and internally, plastic heart valves and blood vessels.

prostitution receipt of money by a man or woman for satisfying the sexual wishes of others. In the UK a compromise system makes it legal to be a prostitute, but not to solicit for custom publicly; keeping a brothel, living on 'immoral earnings', and 'procuring' (arranging to make someone into a prostitute) are illegal. The English Collective of Prostitutes is an organization that represents the interests of prostitutes.

protactinium a rare element, symbol Pa, atomic number 91, atomic weight 231.04. One of the actinide series of elements, it is present in very small quantities in pitchblende, as a member of the uraniun decay series.

protandry in a flower, the state where the male reproductive organs reach maturity before those of the female. This is a common method of avoiding self-fertilization. See also ◊protogyny.

protectionism in economics, the imposition of heavy duties or import quotas by a government as a means of discouraging the import of foreign goods likely to compete with domestic products. The opposite practice is ◊free trade.

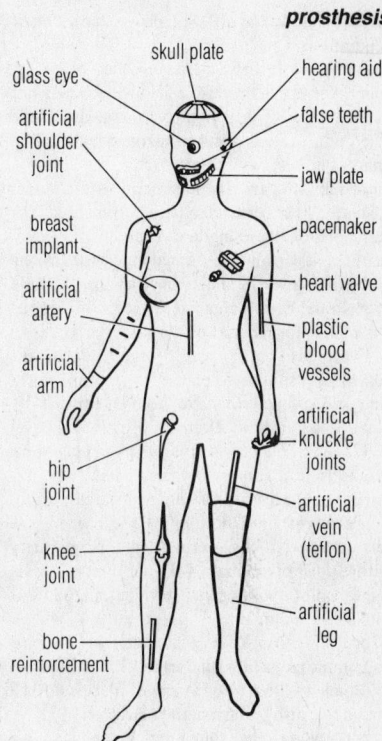

prosthesis

skull plate — glass eye — hearing aid — artificial shoulder joint — false teeth — jaw plate — breast implant — pacemaker — artificial artery — heart valve — artificial arm — plastic blood vessels — artificial knuckle joints — hip joint — artificial vein (teflon) — knee joint — bone reinforcement — artificial leg

protectorate formerly in international law, a small state under the direct or indirect control of a larger one. The modern equivalent is a ◊trust territory. In English history the rule of Oliver and Richard ◊Cromwell 1653–59 is referred to as the Protectorate.

protein a long chain molecule made up of ◊amino acids, joined together by peptide bonds. Proteins are essential to all living organisms. As ◊enzymes they regulate all aspects of ◊metabolism. Structural proteins such as keratin and collagen make up the skin, claws, bones, tendons, and ligaments, while ◊muscle proteins produce movement, ◊haemoglobin transports oxygen, and membrane proteins regulate the movement of substances into and out of cells. For humans, protein is an essential part of the diet, and is found in greatest quantity in meat, eggs, cheese, soya beans and other grain legumes, although most foods contain some protein. See also ◊peptide.

Protestantism one of the main divisions of ◊Christianity, consisting of many separate sects; it emerged from Roman Catholicism at the ◊Reformation.

Proteus in Greek mythology an old man, the warden of the sea beasts of Poseidon, who possessed the gift of prophecy, but could transform himself to evade questioning.

prothallus the short-lived gametophyte of many ferns and other ◊pteridophytes. It bears either the male or female sex organs, or both. Typically it is a small, green flattened structure which is anchored in the soil by several ◊rhizoids and needs damp comditions to survive. The reproductive organs are borne on the lower surface close to the soil. See also ◊alternation of generations.

protist in biology, a single-celled organism which has a ◊eukaryotic cell, but which is not member of the plant, fungal or animal kingdoms. The main protists are ◊protozoa. Single-celled ◊photosynthetic organisms, such as diatoms and dinoflagellates, are classified as protists or algae. Recently the term has also been used for members of the kingdom Protoctista, which features in certain five-◊kingdom classifications of the living world. This kingdom may include slime moulds, all algae (seaweeds as well as unicellular forms) and protozoa.

Protocols of Zion forged document containing supposed plans for Jewish world conquest alleged to have been submitted by ◊Herzl to the first Zionist Congress at Basel 1897, and published in Russia 1905. They were proved to be a forgery by *The Times* 1921, but were used by Hitler in his anti-Semitic campaign.

protogyny in a flower, the state where the female reproductive organs reach maturity before those of the male. Like ◊protandry, this is a method of avoiding self-fertilization, but it is much less common.

proton (Greek 'first') positively charged subatomic particle, a fundamental constituent of all ◊nuclei, which live on average for at least $10x^{32}$ years. See also ◊neutron and ◊electron.

protonema the young ◊gametophyte of a moss, which develops from a germinating spore, see ◊alternation of generations. Typically it is a green, branched, thread-like structure which grows over the soil surface bearing several buds that develop into the characteristic adult moss plants.

Proton rocket a Soviet space rocket introduced in 1965, used to launch heavy satellites, space probes and the Salyut and Mir space stations. Proton consists of up to four stages as necessary. It has never been used to launch people into space.

protoplasm the contents of a living ◊cell. Strictly speaking it includes all the discrete structures in a cell (◊organelles), but it is often used simply to mean the jelly-like material in which these float. See also ◊cytoplasm.

prototype in technology, term used for the first few machines of a new design. Prototypes are tested for performance, reliability, economy, and safety; then the main design can be modified before full-scale production begins.

protozoa a group of single-celled ◊eukaryotic organisms without rigid cell walls. Some, such as amoeba, ingest other cells, but most are ◊saprotrophs or ◊parasites. A few of the euglenoids contain chlorophyll and are ◊photosynthetic. The group is polyphyletic, that is, it contains organisms which have different evolutionary origins.

Proudhon /pruː'dɒŋ/ Pierre Joseph 1809–1865. French anarchist, born in Besançon. He sat in the Constituent Assembly of 1848, was imprisoned for three years, and had to go into exile in Brussels. He published *Qu'est-ce que la propriété/What is Property?* 1840 and *Philosophie de la misère/Philosophy of Poverty* 1846. His most noted dictum is 'property is theft'.

prototype The first prototype of Edgeley Aircraft's Optica. A revolutionary design for low-speed reconnaissance such as traffic surveys and air searches, it was devised as a cheaper alternative to the helicopter. The Optica project was blighted by the fatal crash of a prototype in 1985.

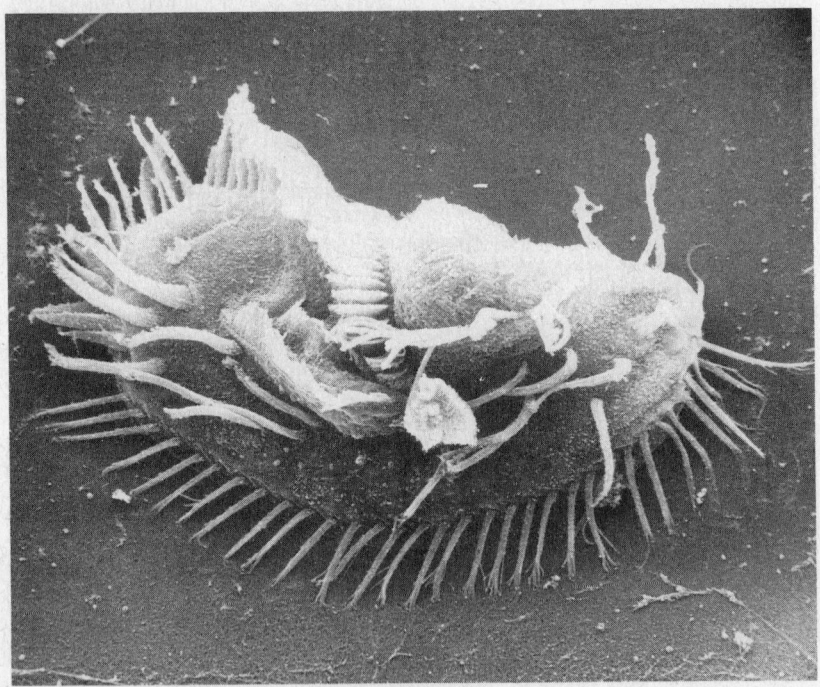

protozoa Scanning electron micrograph (SEM) of ciliate protozoa *Oxtricha*. They are microscopic, unicellular and free-living; they are highly evolved and contain two kinds of nucleus. The cilia which decorate the bodies help in locomotion and feeding.

Proust /pruːst/ Joseph Louis 1754–1826. French chemist. He was the first to state the principle of constant composition of compounds – that compounds consist of the same proportions of elements wherever found.

Proust /pruːst/ Marcel 1871–1922. French novelist and critic, born at Auteuil. He was a delicate, asthmatic child, and although he moved in fashionable Parisian society in his youth, he shut himself away after the death of his parents 1904–05 in a cork-lined room in his Paris flat. He dedicated himself to his mammoth auto-biographical novel, *À la recherche du temps perdu/Remembrance of Things Past* 1913–37, the expression of his childhood memories coaxed from his subconscious, which is also a precise reflection of life in provincial France at the end of the 19th century.

Provençal language a member of the Romance branch of the Indo-European language family, spoken in and around Provence in SE France. It is now regarded as a dialect or patois

Proust During the 1890s, around the time this photograph was taken, Marcel Proust moved in the most fashionable Parisian circles, but shortly afterwards he became a virtual recluse, dedicating his time to his autobiographical novel, *A la recherche du temps perdu*.

but during the Middle Ages was in competition with French, was the language of the troubadours, and had a strong literary influence on such neighbouring languages as Italian, Spanish and Portuguese. Since the 19th century attempts have been made to revive it as a literary language.

Provençal literature Provençal literature originated in the 10th century, and flowered in the 12th century with the work of the ◊troubadours, particularly Bernart de Ventadorn, Arnaut Daniel, Giroud de Borneil, Gilet de Sauvetage, Raimbaut d'Orrange, and Bertran de Born. After the decline of the troubadours in the 13th century, Provençal disappeared as a literary medium from the 14th until the 19th century, when Jacques Jasmin (1798–1864) and others paved the way for the Félibrige group of poets, of whom the greatest are Joseph Roumanille (1818–91), Frédéric Mistral (1830–1914), and Félix Gras (1844–1901).

Provence-Côte d'Azur /prə'vɒns ˌkəʊt dæ 'zjʊə/ region of SE France; capital Marseille; population (1982) 3,965,200. Provence was an independent kingdom in the 10th century, and the area still has its own language, ◊Provençal; the *Côte d'Azur*, the Mediterranean coast Menton–St Tropez, is a tourist centre.

Proverbs a book of the Hebrew Bible (and Christian Old Testament), traditionally ascribed to ◊Solomon. The Proverbs form a series of maxims on moral and ethical matters.

Providence /'prɒvɪdəns/ industrial port (jewellery, silverware, textiles and textile machinery, watches, chemicals, meat packing), capital of Rhode Island, USA, on the Providence river, 43 km/27 mi from the Atlantic; Brown University 1764; Population (1980) 919,000.

Providence was settled by Roger ◊Williams in 1636.

provost chief magistrate of a Scottish burgh, approximate equivalent of an English mayor.

Proxima Centauri the closest ◊star to the Sun, 4.2 light years away. It is a faint red dwarf, visible only with a telescope, and is a member of the ◊Alpha Centauri triple-star system. It is called Proxima because it is about 0.1 light years closer to us than its two partners.

proxy in law, a person authorized to stand in another's place; also the instrument of conferment thereof. The term usually refers to voting at meetings, but there may be marriages by proxy.

Prudhoe Bay /'prʌdəʊ 'beɪ/ bay in ◊Alaska.

Prunus genus of trees of the northern hemisphere, family Rosaceae, producing fruit with a fleshy, edible pericarp; including plums, peaches, apricots, almonds, and cherries.

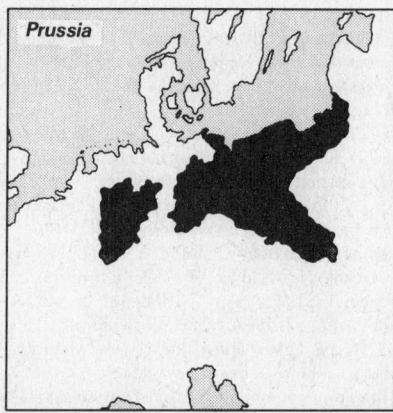

Prussia

Prussia /'prʌʃə/ former N German state formed 1618 by the union of ◊Brandenburg and the duchy of Prussia. Its military power was founded by ◊Frederick William, the 'Great Elector', and it became a kingdom under ◊Frederick I in 1701. Military and economic expansion took place under ◊Frederick William. During the reign of his son Frederick the Great 1740–86 Silesia, East Frisia, and West Prussia were annexed. The reign of Frederick William III 1797–1840 was marked by the defeat at Jena by Napoleon 1806; his possessions were reduced, but after the Congress of Vienna 1815 Prussia regained its lost territories and also acquired lands in the Rhineland and Saxony. The year 1848 was marked by revolutionary outbreaks. In 1864 war with Denmark resulted in the acquisition of Schleswig and Holstein, while after the defeat of Austria in 1866 Hanover, Nassau, Frankfurt-am-Main, and Hesse-Cassel were annexed to Prussia, which became the head of the North German Confederation. Converted to a republic after World War I, Prussia lost its local independence in Hitler's Germany in 1933, and the ◊Allies abolished the state altogether in 1946, its territories being divided among East and West Germany, Poland, and the USSR.

prussic acid an old name for ◊hydrocyanic acid.

Prynne /prɪn/ William 1600–1669. English Puritan. He published in 1632 *Histriomastix* , a work attacking stage plays; it contained aspersions on the queen for which he was pilloried and lost his ears. In 1637 he was again pilloried and branded for an attack on the bishops. He opposed the execution of Charles I, and actively supported the Restoration.

Przemyśl /'pʃemɪsu:/ industrial city (timber, ceramics, flour milling, tanning, distilling, food processing) in SE Poland; population (1981) 62,000.

history Founded in the 8th century, it belonged alternately to Poland and Kiev in the 10th–14th centuries. An Austrian territory 1722–1919, it was a frontier fortress besieged by Soviet troops Sept 1914–Mar 1915, and was occupied by the Germans Jun 1941–Jul 1944.

psalm a sacred poem or song of praise. The best-known collection is the Book of Psalms in the Hebrew Bible (Christian Old Testament), which is divided into five books containing 150 psalms. They are ascribed to ◊David.

PSBR abbreviation for ◊public sector borrowing requirement.

pseudocarp a ◊fruit-like structure which incorporates tissue that is not derived from the ovary wall. The additional tissues may be derived from floral parts such as the ◊receptacle and ◊calyx. For example, the coloured, fleshy part of a strawberry develops from the receptacle and the true fruits are small achenes – the 'pips' embedded in its outer surface. Rose hips are a type of pseudocarp that consists of a hollow, fleshy receptacle containing a number of achenes within. A coenocarpium is a fleshy, multiple pseudocarp derived from an ◊inflorescence rather than a single flower. An example is the pineapple, which has a thickened central axis surrounded by fleshy tissues derived from the receptacles and floral parts of many flowers. A fig is a type of pseudocarp termed a syconium, formed from a hollow receptacle with small flowers attached to the inner wall. After fertilization the ovaries of the female flowers develop into one-seeded achenes. Apples and pears are ◊pomes, another type of pseudocarp.

pseudocopulation the attempted copulation by a male insect with a flower. It results in ◊pollination of the flower and is common in the orchid family, where the flowers of many species resemble a particular species of female bee. When a male bee attempts to mate with a flower, the ◊pollinia stick to its body. They are then transferred to the stigma of another flower, when the insect attempts copulation again.

PSFD abbreviation for public sector financial deficit. See under ◊public sector borrowing requirement.

psi in parapsychology, a hypothetical facility common to humans and other animals said to be responsible for extra-sensory perception (ESP) and telekinesis.

Psilocybe genus of mushroom with hallucinogenic properties. The Mexican sacred mushroom *Psilocybe mexicana* contains compounds with effects similar to LSD.

pseudocopulation

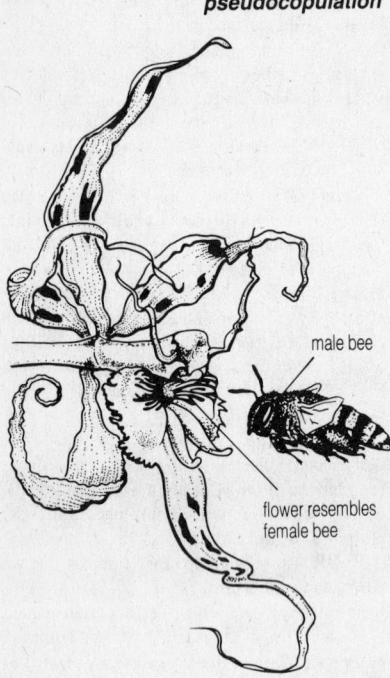

male bee

flower resembles
female bee

psittacosis virus disease, contracted by humans from birds (especially parrots), which may result in pneumonia.

Pskov /pskɒf/ industrial city (food processing, leather) in USSR; population (1985) 194,000. Dating from 965, it was independent 1348–1510, when it became Russian. It was under German occupation 1941–44 during World War II.

psoriasis chronic skin inflammation resulting in raised red patches, especially on the arms and legs, covered with whitish scales. The first attack usually takes place in childhood and attacks recur at regular intervals. Ultraviolet light and steroid creams provide some relief.

Psyche /'saɪki/ late Greek personification of the soul as a winged girl. The love story of Eros and Psyche is told by the Roman writer Apuleius. The goddess Aphrodite was so jealous of Psyche's beauty that she ordered her son Eros, the god of love, to make her fall in love with the worst of men, but he fell in love with her himself.

psychedelic rock also called *acid rock*, a type of pop music, with advanced electronic equipment for light and sound, which began about 1966 (see ◊hippie), leading by the 1980s to stadium performances with lasers and other special effects.

psychiatry the branch of medicine dealing with the diagnosis and treatment of mental disorder. In practice there is considerable overlap between psychiatry and ◊clinical psychology, the fundamental difference being that psychiatrists are trained medical doctors (holding an MD degree) and may therefore prescribe drugs, whereas psychologists may hold a PhD but do not need a medical qualification to practise.

psychic a person allegedly possessed of parapsychological, or paranormal, powers.

psychoanalysis a theory and treatment method for neuroses, developed by ◊Freud. It emphasizes the impact of early childhood sexuality and experiences which are stored in the unconscious and can lead to the development of adult emotional problems. The main treatment method involves the free association of ideas, and interpretation. Treatment typically is expensive and prolonged and there is controversy about its effectiveness. Modern approaches, drawing from Freud's ideas, tend to be briefer and problem-focused.

psychology the systematic study of human and animal behaviour. The first psychology laboratory was founded 1879 by Wilhelm ◊Wundt at Leipzig.

The subject includes diverse areas of study and application, among them the roles of instinct, heredity, environment and culture; the processes of sensation, perception, learning and memory; the bases of motivation and emotion; and the functioning of thought, intelligence and language. ◊Experimental psychology emphasizes the application of rigorous and objective scientific methods to the study of a wide range of mental processes and behaviour, whereas social psychology concerns the study of individuals within their social environment; for example, within groups and organizations. This has led to the development of related fields such as ◊occupational psychology, which studies human behaviour at work, and ◊educational psychology. ◊Clinical psychology concerns the understanding and treatment of health problems, particularly mental disorders, such as ◊anxiety, ◊phobias, or ◊depression; treatment may include ◊behaviour therapy, ◊cognitive therapy, ◊counselling, ◊psychoanalysis, or some combination of these.

Influential psychologists have included Gustav ◊Fechner (founder of psychophysics); Wolfgang Köhler 1887–1967, one of the ◊gestalt or 'whole' psychologists; Sigmund ◊Freud and his associates ◊Jung, ◊Adler, and ◊Rorschach; William ◊James, Jean ◊Piaget; Carl ◊Rogers; Hans ◊Eysenck; J B ◊Watson, and B F ◊Skinner. Modern studies have been diverse, for example the psychological causes of obesity; the nature of religious experience; and the underachievement of women seen as resulting from social pressures. Other related subjects are the nature of ◊sleep and ◊dreams, and possible extensions of the senses, which leads to the more controversial ground of ◊parapsychology.

psychometrics the measurement of mental processes. This includes intelligence and aptitude testing to help in job selection and in the clinical assessment of cognitive deficiencies resulting from brain damage.

psychopathy a general term, less used now than formerly, for a personality disorder characterized by chronic antisocial behaviour (violating the rights of others) and an absence of feelings of guilt about the behaviour.

psychosis or psychotic disorder. A general term for a serious ◊mental disorder where the individual commonly loses contact with reality and may experience hallucinations (seeing or hearing things that do not exist) or delusions

(fixed false beliefs). For example, in a paranoid psychosis, an individual may believe that others are plotting against him or her. A major type of psychosis is ◊schizophrenia.

psychosomatic medicine study of the interaction between mind and body in illness. It covers particular illnesses assumed to be triggered by psychological factors; for example, emotional stress may be accompanied by skin disease. More broadly, many practitioners (as in ◊holism) now believe that mental and physical well-being are interrelated in all cases.

psychosurgery operation to achieve some mental effect, for example *leucotomy*/(US) *lobotomy* the separation of the white fibres in the prefrontal lobe of the brain, as a means of relieving a deep state of anxiety. It is irreversible, the degree of personality change is not predictable, and its justification is controversial.

psychotherapy treatment approaches for mental problems which involve talking rather than surgery or drugs. Examples of such approaches include ◊behaviour therapy, ◊cognitive therapy, and ◊psychoanalysis.

psychotic disorder another name for ◊psychosis.

Ptah Egyptian god, the divine potter, a personification of the creative force. He was worshipped especially at ◊Memphis, and often portrayed as a mummified man. He was the father of ◊Imhotep.

ptarmigan a type of ◊grouse *Lagopus mutus* found in the Arctic and mountains of N Britain and Europe. About 36 cm/1.2 ft long, it has a white coat in winter.

pteridophyte a simple type of ◊vascular plant. The pteridophytes include four classes: the Psilosida, comprising the most primitive vascular plants, found mainly in the tropics; the Lycopsida, including the clubmosses and *Selaginella*; the Sphenopsida, including the horsetails; and the Pteropsida, including the ferns. They are mainly terrestrial, non-flowering plants characterized by the presence of a vascular system, the possession of true stems, roots and leaves, and by a marked ◊alternation of generations, with the sporophyte forming the dominant generation in the life-cycle. They differ from other vascular plants (◊angiosperms and ◊gymnosperms) in not producing seeds. The pteridophytes formed a large and dominant flora during the Carboniferous period, but many are now known only from fossils.

pterodactyl extinct flying reptile of the order Pterosauria, existing in the Mesozoic age. Pterosaurs were formerly assumed to be smooth-skinned gliders, but recent discoveries show that at least some were furry, probably warm-blooded, and may have had strong flapping flight. They ranged from starling size to the largest with 17 m/50 ft wingspan.

PTFE poly*tetra*fluoroethylene, a tough, waxlike and heat-resistant plastic, also known by the tradename Teflon, much used for the coating on non-stick kitchenware.

Ptolemy /'tɒləmi/ (Claudius Ptolemaeus) c. 100–178 ad. astronomer and geographer. A native of Egypt, he carried out observations in Alexandria, and published a *Geography* which

PSYCHOLOGY

1897 Wilhelm Wundt founded the first psychological laboratory, in Leipzig.

1890 William James published the first comprehensive psychology text, *Principles of Psychology*.

1895 Freud's first book on psychoanalysis was published.

1896 The first clinical psychology clinic was founded by Witner at the University of Pennsylvania.

1903 Pavlov reported his early studies on conditioned reflexes in animals.

1905 Binet and Simon developed the first effective intelligence test.

1908 A first textbook of social psychology was published by William McDougall.

1913 J B Watson published his influential work *Behaviourism*.

1926 Jean Piaget presented his first book on child development.

1947 Eysenck published *Dimensions of Personality*, a large scale study of neuroticism and extraversion.

1953 Skinner's *Science of Human Behaviour*, a text of operant conditioning, was published.

1957 Chomsky's *Syntactic Structures*, which stimulated the development of psycho-linguistics, the study of language processes, was published.

1963 Milgram's studies of compliance with authority indicated conditions under which individuals behave cruelly to others when instructed to do so.

1967 Neisser's *Cognitive Psychology* marked renewed interest in the study of cognition after years in which behaviourism had been dominant.

1972 Newell and Simon simulated human problem solving abilities by computer, an example of artificial intelligence.

---

was a standard source of information until the 16th century. His greatest work was known as the *Almagest*, in which he developed the theory of ◊Aristotle that the Earth is the centre of the universe, with the Sun, Moon, and stars revolving around it. Not until 1543 was the *Ptolemaic system* superseded by the theory of ◊Copernicus.

Ptolemy /'tɒləmi/ dynasty of ◊Macedonian kings who ruled Egypt over a period of 300 years; they included:

Ptolemy I King of Egypt from 304 BC. He was one of ◊Alexander the Great's generals, and possibly his half-brother (see also ◊Thaïs). He established the library at ◊Alexandria.

Ptolemy XIII 63–47 BC. Ruler of Egypt with his sister-wife Cleopatra; she put him to death.

ptomaine group of extremely toxic chemical substances produced as a result of putrefaction, but not the relevant factor in 'food poisoning', which is usually caused by bacteria of the *Salmonella* genus.

puberty stage in human development when the individual becomes sexually mature. It may occur from the age of ten upwards. The sexual organs take on their adult form and pubic hair grows.

pubes the lowest part of the front of the trunk, where the external generative organs are situated. The underlying bony structure, the pubic arch, is formed by the union in the midline of the two pubic bones, which are the front portions of the hip bones. In women it is more prominent to allow more room for the passage of the child's head at birth, and carries a pad of fat and connective tissue, the mons veneris (mountain of Venus), for its protection.

public house in Britain a house licensed for consumption of intoxicating liquor, and either 'free' (when the licensee has free choice of suppliers), or 'tied' to a company owning the house.

public lending right (PLR) method of rectifying the anomaly that, although performance of a play or piece of music involves payment of a royalty, authors did not profit when books were borrowed from libraries. Payment to the copyright holder was introduced in Australia in 1974 and in the UK in 1984.

public order in the UK public order is governed by the Public Order Act 1986, which created a range of statutory offences: ◊riot, violent disorder (similar to riot but requiring only three people and no common purpose), affray (fights), threatening behaviour (shouting abuse), and disorderly conduct (minor acts of hooliganism). It extends police powers to control marches and demonstrations by rerouting them or restricting their size and duration.

public school in the UK a fee-paying ◊independent school (mainly for boys 12–18). Some (for example ◊Eton, ◊Harrow, ◊Rugby, ◊Winchester) are ancient foundations, usually originally intended for poor scholars; others developed in the 18–19th centuries. Among those for girls, Roedean is best known, and some boys' schools take girls in the sixth form. Some discipline (less than formerly) is in the hands of senior boys/girls (prefects), and the stress on classical subjects and sports has been modified. In Scotland, the USA, and many other English-speaking countries, a 'public' school is a state-maintained school, and independent schools are generally known as 'private' schools.

public sector borrowing requirement (PSBR) amount of money needed by a national economy to cover the deficit in sums needed by the central government to finance its own activities and loans to local authorities and public corporations, and the funds raised by local authorities and public corporations from other sources. The PSBR is financed chiefly by sales of debt to the public outside the banking system, (◊gilt-edged stocks, national savings, and local authority ◊stocks and bonds), by external transactions with other countries, and by borrowing from the banking system. After the 1986 budget this measure was changed to the *Public Sector Financial Deficit (PSFD)*, which is the net of the asset sales thought to distort the PSBR.

publishing the production of books for sale. The publisher arranges for the printing, binding, and distribution to booksellers or bookclubs. The publisher may commission books, and edits them. Although all rights in a book may be purchased by the publisher for a single outright fee, it is more usual and generally fairer to publisher and author if a fixed royalty is paid on every copy sold, in return for the exclusive right to publish in an agreed territory.

Puccini /puˈtʃiːni/ Giacomo (Antonio Domenico Michele Secondo Maria) 1858–1924. Italian opera composer, whose music shows a strong gift for melody and dramatic effect. His realist works include *Manon Lescaut* 1893, *La Bohème* 1896, *Tosca* 1900, *Madame Butterfly* 1904, and the unfinished *Turandot* 1926.

Giacomo Puccini

Puccini Striving for perfection in the drama of his operas as much as in the scores, Puccini drove his librettists Giacosa and Illica to produce 'a libretto that would move the world'. The libretti of his masterpieces *Madame Butterfly* and *Tosca* are models of their kind.

Pudovkin /puˈdɒfkɪn/ Vsevolod 1893–1953. Russian film director, whose greatest films were silent, for example *Mother* 1926 (based on ◊Gorky's novel) *The End of St Petersburg* 1927, and *Storm over Asia* 1928. He also wrote *Film Technique* and *Film Acting*.

Puebla (de Zaragoza) /'pweblə deɪ ˌsæ rə'ɡɒsə/ industrial city (textiles, sugar refining, metallurgy, and hand-crafted pottery and tiles) in S Mexico; population (1980) 836,000. First founded 1535 as Pueblo de los Angeles, it was later renamed after Gen de Zaragoza, who defeated the French here 1862.

Pueblo /'pweɪbləʊ/ generic name for North American Indians of SW North America (from Spanish *pueblos* villages), of whom the best-known are the ◊Hopi (famous for their biennial Snake Dance), who build multistorey communal villages of mud-brick or stone. The *Mesa Verde* ('green table') cliff dwelling in Colorado, constructed about 1000 AD, has some 200 rooms.

puerperal fever infection of the genital tract of the mother after childbirth which formerly often resulted in fatal blood poisoning, but which is now usually treated by antibiotics.

Puerto Rico /'pweətəʊ 'riːkəʊ/ the Comonwealth of
area 8,891 sq km/3,435 sq miles
capital San Juan
towns ports Mayagüez, Ponce
features highest per capita income in Latin America
exports sugar, tobacco, rum, pineapples; textiles, plastics, chemicals, processed foods
currency US dollar
population (1980) 3,196,520, 62% urban
language Spanish and English (official)
religion Roman Catholic
government under the constitution of 1952, similar to that of the USA, with a governor elected for four years, and a legislative assembly with a senate and house of representatives
history visited in 1493 by Columbus, it was annexed by Spain 1509, ceded to the USA after the ◊Spanish American War in 1898, and in 1952 achieved Commonwealth status with local self-government. This was confirmed in preference to independence by a referendum 1967, but there is an independence movement, and another wishing incorporation as a state of the USA.

puff adder see ◊adder.

puffball globulous fruiting body of certain ◊fungi which cracks with maturity, releasing the enclosed spores, for example *common puffball Lycoperdon perlatum*.

puffer fish fish of the family Tetraodontidae that can inflate its body with air or water as a means of defence. Puffer fish are mainly found in warm waters, in sea, brackish, and fresh water. Also known as globefish.

puffin bird *Fratercula arctica* of the ◊auk family, found in the NE Atlantic, and coming to land to nest in burrows, otherwise far out to sea. About 30 cm/1 ft long, it has a large deep bill, very brightly coloured in summer.

pug breed of small dog with short wrinkled face, chunky body, and tail curled over the hip.

Pugin /'pjuːdʒɪn/ Augustus Welby Northmore 1812–1852. British Neo-Gothic architect, collaborator with ◊Barry in the detailed design of the Houses of Parliament.

Puglia /'puːljə/ Italian form of ◊Apulia, region of Italy.

Pula /'puːlə/ commercial and naval port in Croatia, Yugoslavia; population (1981) 77,278. A Roman naval base, *Colonia Pietas Julia*, it was seized by Venice in 1148, passed to Austria 1815, to Italy 1919, and Yugoslavia 1947. It has a Roman theatre, and a castle and cathedral constructed under Venetian rule.

Pulitzer /'pulɪtsə/ Joseph 1847–1911. American newspaper proprietor, born in Hungary. He acquired the *New York World* 1883 and founded 1903 the school of journalism at Columbia University, which awards the annual Pulitzer prizes in journalism and letters.

Pulitzer Prize for fiction
1982 John Updike *Rabbit is Rich*
1983 Alice Walker *The Color Purple*
1984 William Kennedy *Ironweed*
1985 Alison Lurie *Foreign Affairs*
1986 Larry McMurtry *Lonesome Dove*
1987 Peter Taylor *A Summons to Memphis*

---

pulley a simple machine consisting of a grooved wheel round which rope or chain can be run. A simple pulley serves only to change the direction of the applied effort (as in a simple hoist for raising loads). The use of more than one pulley results in a mechanical advantage, so that a given effort can raise a heavier load. How great the mechanical advantage is depends on the arrangement of the pulleys.

pulsar a celestial source that emits pulses of energy at very regular intervals, ranging from a few seconds to small fractions of a second. Pulsars were discovered in 1967 at the Mullard Radio Astronomy Observatory, Cambridge, England, by a team under Antony ◊Hewish. Over 300 radio pulsars are now known in our ◊galaxy, although a million may exist. They are thought to be rapidly rotating ◊neutron stars, which flash at radio and other wavelengths like a lighthouse as they spin. Two pulsars, the one in the ◊Crab Nebula and one in the constellation ◊Vela, give out flashes of visible light. Pulsars gradually slow down as they get older, and eventually the flashes fade. *X-ray pulsars* are a related class of object caused by hot gas falling on to a spinning neutron star in a ◊binary system.

pulse the impulse transmitted by the heartbeat throughout the arterial system of vertebrates. When the heart muscle contracts it forces blood into the ◊aorta. Because the ◊arteries are elastic, the sudden rise of pressure causes a throb or sudden swelling through them all. It can be felt where the artery is near the surface, as in the wrist. The actual flow of the blood continues more or less uniformly at about 60 cm/2 ft a second in humans. The pulse rate is generally about 70 per minute.

puma large wild cat found in N and S America, also called cougar or mountain lion. Tawny-coated, it is 1.5 m/4.5 ft long plus 90 cm/3 ft tail, and feeds mainly on deer.

pumice a light volcanic rock, with the texture of a hard sponge, used as an abrasive both commercially and for personal toilet.

pump a device for moving liquids and gases, or compressing gases. Gas pumps are often called ◊compressors (as in ◊jet engines) or fans. Some

pulley

20N

20N

simple pulley (above)
pulley system used for
heavy weights (below)

5N

20N

pumps work by a reciprocating (up-and-down) action, as in the traditional *lift-pump* used to raise water from wells. It uses a piston with a one-way valve moving in a cylinder with a one-way valve. Movement of the piston creates a partial vacuum in the cylinder, which sucks up water into it. *Gear pumps*, used to pump oil in a car's lubrication system, have two meshing gears which rotate inside a housing. The oil is moved by the teeth. *Rotary pumps* contain a rotor with vanes projecting from it inside a casing. The vanes sweep the oil round as they move. Special pumps, such as mercury diffusion pumps, are used to create a high vacuum.

pumped storage a type of hydroelectric plant which uses surplus electricity to pump water back into a high-level reservoir. In normal working the water flows from this reservoir through the ◊turbines to generate power for feeding into the national grid. At times of low power demand, electricity is taken from the grid to turn the turbines into pumps which then pump water back again.

pumpkin type of marrow, *Cucurbita pepo* family Cucurbitaceae, with a large spherical fruit having a thick, orange rind, pulpy flesh, and many seeds.

pun a ◊figure of speech, a play on words or double meaning that is technically known as *paronomasia* (Greek: 'adapted meaning'); they may be intended as jokes or as clever and compact remarks. Puns may depend on either the sound or the look of a word, or may require some modification of the words in question to produce their effect (for example, a political meeting described as 'coming apart at the themes', echoing 'seams').

Punch (shortened form of the name Punchinello) the hero of the ◊puppet play *Punch and Judy*, in which he overcomes or outwits all opponents. Punch has a hooked nose, hunched back, and a squeaky voice. The play is performed by means of glove puppets, manipulated by a single operator concealed in a portable canvas stage frame. Punch originated in Italy, and was probably introduced to England at the time of the Restoration.

punch drink of Indian origin, made of spirits, fruit juice, sugar, spice, and hot water.

punctuated equilibrium model an evolutionary theory which claims that periods of rapid change alternate with periods of relative stability (stasis), and that the appearance of new lineages is a separate process from the gradual evolution of adaptive changes within a species. The idea was developed in 1972 by Niles Eldridge and Steven J Gould to explain discontinuities in the fossil record. The pattern of stasis and more rapid change is now widely accepted, but the second part of the theory remains unsubstantiated.

punctuation the system of conventional signs (*punctuation marks*) and spaces by means of which written and printed language is organized so as to be as readable, clear, and logical as possible. It contributes to the effective layout of visual language: if a work is not adequately punctuated there may be problems of ambiguity and unclear association among words. However, there are preferred styles in the punctuation of a language like English, and conventions of punctuation also differ from language to language. The standard punctuation marks and conventions are the ◊period (full stop or point), ◊comma, ◊colon, ◊semicolon, ◊exclamation mark (or point), ◊question mark, ◊apostrophe, ◊asterisk, ◊hyphen, and ◊parenthesis (including dashes, brackets, and the use of parenthetical commas).

Pune /'puːnə/ (formerly *Poona*) industrial city (chemicals; rice, sugar, cotton and paper mills; jewellery) in Maharashtra, India; university 1948; population (1981) 1,202,848. There is the Armed Forces Medical College, and, at nearby Khadakvasla, the National Defence Academy.

Punic Wars three wars between ◊Rome and ◊Carthage:
First 264–241 BC, resulted in the defeat of the Carthaginians under ◊Hamilcar Barca and the cession of Sicily to Rome
Second 218–201 BC, Hannibal invaded Italy, defeated the Romans under ◊Fabius Maximus at

◊Cannae, but was finally defeated by ◊Scipio at Zama (now in Algeria)
Third 149–146 BC ended in the destruction of Carthage, and its possessions becoming the Roman province of Africa.
In 1985 Rome and modern Carthage signed a symbolic peace treaty.

Punjab /ˌpʌn'dʒɑːb/ name meaning 'five rivers' (the Indus tributaries: Jhelum, Chenab, Ravi, Beas and Sutlej), for a former NW state of British India. See also ◊Punjab (Pakistan) and ◊Punjab (India).

Punjab /ˌpʌn'dʒɑːb/ state of NW India
area 50,362 sq km/19,440 sq miles
capital Chandigarh
towns Amritsar, Sikh holy city
features mainly agricultural, crops chiefly under irrigation; longest life expectancy rates in India (59 for women, 64 for men); Harappa, see Indus ◊Valley civilization
population (1981) 16,669,755
language Punjabi
religion Sikhism 60%, Hinduism 30%; there is friction between the two groups.

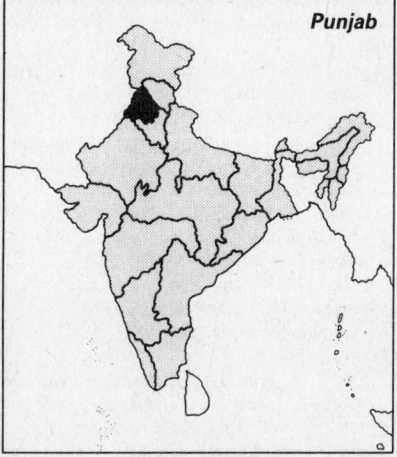

Punjab

Punjab /ˌpʌn'dʒɑːb/ state of Pakistan, the former W section of a state of British India formed after annexation by Britain in 1849 after the Sikh Wars 1845–46 and 1848–49
area 181,761 sq km/70,178 sq mi
capital Lahore
features wheat cultivations (by irrigation)
population (1981) 47,292,000
language Punjabi, Urdu
religion Muslim.

Punjabi language a member of the Indo-Iranian branch of the Indo-European language family, spoken in the Punjab provinces of India and Pakistan. It is considered by some to be a variety of Hindi, by others to be a distinct language.

punk a movement of disaffected youth of the late 1970s, manifesting itself, especially in Britain, in fashions and music designed to shock or intimidate. Punk rock stressed aggressive performance within a three-chord, three-minute format, for example, the Sex Pistols 1975–78 and the Slits 1977–82.

Punta Arenas /'puntə ə'reinəs/ seaport in Chile, capital of Magallanes province, on Magellan Strait, most southerly town on the American mainland; population (1982) 99,000. The name means 'sandy point' in Spanish.

pupa the non-feeding, largely immobile stage of some insect lifecycles, in which larval tissues are broken down and adult tissues and structures are formed. In many insects it is exarate, with the appendages (legs, antennae, wings) visible outside the pupal case, but in butterflies and moths it is obtect, with the appendages developing inside the pupal (chrysalis) case.

puppet figure manipulated on a small stage, usually by an unseen operator. Known from the 10th century BC in China, the types include *finger* or *glove puppets*, of which the most famous is ◊Punch; *string marionettes* (which reached a high artistic level in ancient Burma and Sri Lanka and in Italian princely courts 16–18th centuries, and for which ◊Haydn wrote his operetta *Dido* 1778 for performance in the Esterhazy theatre); *shadow silhouettes* (operated by rods and seen on a lit screen, as in Java); and *bunraku* (devised in ◊Osaka, Japan), in which three or four black-clad operators on stage may combine to work each puppet about 1 m/3 ft high.
During the 16th and 17th century puppet shows became popular with the aristocracy and puppets were extensively used as vehicles for caricature and satire until the 19th century. There has been a revival of interest in puppet theatre in the 20th century, stimulated by the influence of the Joruri tradition in Japan, with its large, intricate puppets, and by leading exponents such as ◊Obraztsov and his Moscow Puppet Theatre, and, most recently in Britain, Fluck and Law, whose satirical 'Spitting Image' puppets caricature famous people on television.

Purana any of a set of religious Sanskrit epics dealing with the mythology of the Hindus dating probably from the 8th century AD. See also ◊Hinduism.

Purbeck, Isle of /'pɜːbek/ a peninsula in the county of ◊Dorset, England. Purbeck marble and china clay are obtained from the 'isle' which includes Corfe Castle and Swanage.

Purcell /'pɜːsəl/ Henry 1659–1695. English composer. Born at Westminster, he became a chorister at the Chapel Royal, and subsequently was a pupil of Dr John ◊Blow. In 1677 he was appointed composer to the Chapel Royal, and in 1679 organist at Westminster Abbey. As composer to the king, Purcell set to music odes or anthems. His work marks the high point of Baroque music in England, and shows an ability to express deep emotion. *Dido and Aeneas* 1689 was a landmark in the history of opera. Purcell wrote music for Dryden's *King Arthur* 1691 and for *The Fairy Queen* 1692.

Purchas /'pɜːtʃɪs/ Samuel 1577–1626. English compiler of travel books, rector of St Martin's Ludgate, 1614–26. His collection *Purchas, his Pilgrimage* 1613, was followed by another in 1619, and in 1625 by *Hakluytus Posthumus or Purchas his Pilgrimes*, largely based on papers left by Hakluyt.

vehicle (hence the word 'juggernaut'). Devotees formerly threw themselves beneath its wheels.

Puritan from 1564, a member of the Church of England who wished to eliminate Roman Catholic survivals in ritual or substitute a ◊presbyterian for an episcopal form of church government. The term is used to cover also the Separatists who withdrew from the Church altogether. The Puritans were identified with the parliamentary opposition under ◊James I and ◊Charles I, and after the ◊Restoration were driven from the Church, and more usually known as ◊Dissenters or Nonconformists.

Purple Heart, order of the the earliest American military award for distinguished service beyond the call of duty, established by Washington in 1782, when it was the equivalent of the modern Congressional Medal of Honour. Of purple cloth bound at the edges, it was worn on the facings over the left breast. After the American Revolution it lapsed until revived by President Hoover in 1932, when it was issued to those wounded in World War II and subsequently.

purpura spontaneous bleeding beneath the skin localized in spots. It may be harmless, as sometimes with the elderly, or linked with disease.

pus yellowish liquid which forms in the body as a result of bacterial attack; it includes white blood cells (leucocytes) 'killed in battle' with the bacteria, plasma, and broken-down tissue cells. Pus is formed wherever infection exists, and an enclosed collection of pus is an abscess.

Pusan /ˌpuːˈsæn/ chief industrial port of South Korea (textiles, rubber, salt, fishing, and, at nearby Pohang, iron and steel); population (1984) 3,495,500. Invaded by the Japanese in 1592, opened to foreign trade in 1883. It was a United Nations supply port during the Korean War of 1950–52.

Pusey /'pjuːzi/ Edward Bouverie 1800–1882. British cleric and Regius professor of Hebrew at Oxford University. In 1835 he joined J H ◊Newman in issuing the *Tracts for the Times*. After Newman's conversion to Catholicism, Pusey became leader of the High Church Party or Puseyites, striving until his death to keep them from conversion.

Pushkin /'pʊʃkɪn/ town NW of Leningrad, USSR; population 80,000. Founded by ◊Peter the Great as Tsarskoe Selo (tsar's village) 1708, it has a number of imperial summer palaces, restored after the Germans devastated the town 1941–44. In the 1920s it was renamed Detskoe Selo (children's village) but since 1937 it has been named after the poet.

Pushkin /'pʊʃkɪn/ Aleksandr 1799–1837. Russian lyrical poet, born in Moscow. He was exiled in 1820 for his political verse, and in 1824 was in trouble for his atheistic opinions. He wrote ballads such as *The Gypsies* 1827, and the novel in verse *Eugene Onegin* 1833. Other works include the tragic drama *Boris Godunov* 1825 and the prose pieces *The Captain's Daughter* 1836 and *The Queen of Spades* 1834. Pushkin's range was enormous, and his willingness to experiment freed later Russian writers from many of the archaic conventions of the literature

of his time. He was mortally wounded in a duel with his brother-in-law.

Pushkin Portrait of the founder of modern Russian literature, Aleksandr Pushkin, by Vasily Tropinin, dated 1827.

Pushtu /'pʌʃtuː/ another name for the ◊Pashto language.

putrefaction decomposition of organic matter by microorganisms.

putsch German term used to describe a military, paramilitary, or civilian coup d'état, such as Hitler and Ludendorff's abortive beer-hall putsch of Nov 1923, which attempted to overthrow the Bavarian government.

putting the shot or *shot put*. Sport of hurling (from the shoulder) a round weight or 'shot' 7.26 kg/16 lb for men, and 4 kg/8.8 lb for women from a circle 5.42 m/7 ft boarded 10 cm/4 in high.

Puttnam /'pʌtnəm/ David Terence 1941– . British film producer, largely influential in reviving the British film industry internationally. Notable successes include *Chariots of Fire* 1981 and *The Killing Fields* 1984.

Puvis de Chavannes /pjuːˈviːs də ʃæ'væn/ Pierre Cécile 1824–1898. French decorative artist, born in Lyons. He attempted to recreate something of the Italian fresco style using oil on canvas in pastel colours for murals in public buildings, for example the ◊Panthéon. He influenced ◊Gauguin.

Pu Yi /'puː 'jiː/ Henry 1906–1967. Last emperor of China (as Hsuan Tung) from 1908 until his deposition 1912; he was restored for a week in 1917. He was president 1932–34 and emperor 1934–45 of the Japanese puppet state of ◊Manchukuo; captured by the Russians, he was freed by Mao Zedong when the Russians handed

Purcell Henry Purcell, whose work marks the high point of Baroque music in England. He wrote more than 500 works, ranging from secular operas and incidental music for plays to cantatas and church music.

purchasing-power parity a system for comparing standards of living between different countries. Comparing the ◊gross domestic product of different countries involves first converting them to a common currency (usually US dollars or sterling), a conversion which is subject to large fluctuations with variations in exchange rates. Purchasing power parity aims to overcome this by measuring how much money in the currency of those countries is required to buy the comparable ranges of goods and services.

purdah Persian and Hindu 'curtain', hence a symbol of the seclusion of upper-class women practised by some Islamic and Hindu peoples. It had begun to disappear with the adoption of Western culture, but the fundamentalism of the 1980s revived it, for example, the wearing of the *chador*, a black mantle, in Iran. This originated in the period of ◊Cyrus the Great in ancient Persia, and was adopted by the Arab conquerors of the ◊Byzantines. The ◊Koran actually requests only 'modesty' in dress.

purgative or *laxative*, drug to ease or acclerate the emptying of the bowels, such as ◊Epsom salts, ◊senna, castor ◊oil.

purgatory in Roman Catholic belief, a purificatory state or place for the souls of those who have died in a state of grace to expiate their venial sins.

purge term usually applied to the removal of suspected opponents, especially by Joseph Stalin in the USSR during the 1930s. The purges were carried out by the secret police against political opponents, minorities, civil servants, and large sections of the armed forces' officer corps. Some 7 million people were executed or deported to labour camps 1934–38.

Puri /'pʊəri/ town in Orissa, India, with a statue of Jagganath or Vishnu, one of the three gods of ◊Hinduism, dating from about 318, which is annually taken in procession on a large

Master PYM
HISSPEECH
In Parliament, on Wednesday, the
fifth of January, 1641,
Concerning the Vote of the House of Commons,
for his discharge upon the Accusation of High
Treason, exhibited against himselfe, and the
Lord Kimbolton Mr. Iohn Hampden, Sr.
Arthur Haslerig, Mr. Strowd,
M. Hollis, by his Majesty.

London Printed for I. W. 1641.

Pym English politician John Pym, painted in 1641, on the eve of the Civil War. Pym played a leading role in the impeachment of ministers Strafford and Laud and of King Charles I, all of whom were eventually beheaded.

him over in 1949, he became a deputy in the Chinese parliament 1964.

Puy, Le see ◊Le Puy, town in France.

PVC polyvinylchloride, a type of ◊plastic.

Pwllheli /puɬˈheli/ resort in Gwynedd, Wales; the Welsh National Party, Plaid Cymru, was founded here 1925.

PWR pressurized *water reactor*, a nuclear reactor design extensively used in nuclear power stations in many countries, and in nuclear-powered submarines. In the PWR water under pressure is the coolant and ◊moderator. It circulates through a steam generator, where its heat boils water to provide steam to drive power ◊turbines.

pyelitis inflammation of the renal pelvis, the central part of the kidney where urine accumulates before discharge.

Pygmalion /pɪgˈmeɪliən/ in Greek legend, a king of Cyprus who fell in love with an ivory statue he had carved, and when ◊Aphrodite brought it to life as Galatea, he married her.

Pygmy /ˈpɪgmi/ small-statured peoples of equatorial Africa (Negrillos) and SE Asia and Melanesia (Negritos). They are noted for their mastery of forest lore.

Pyke /paɪk/ Margaret 1893–1966. British birth-control campaigner. Originally a teacher, she became in the early 1930s secretary of the National Birth Control Association (later the Family Planning Association), and campaigned vigorously to get local councils to set up clinics. She became chair of the FPA in 1954.

Pylos /ˈpaɪlɒs/ port in SW Greece where the battle of ◊Navarino was fought.

Pym /pɪm/ Barbara 1913–1980. British novelist, born in Shropshire. She wrote a number of novels of manners, including *Some Tame Gazelle* 1950, treating a circumscribed life with

comic irony and attention to detail. Her later books were *The Sweet Dove Died* 1978 and *A Few Green Leaves* 1980.

Pym /pɪm/ John 1584–1643. English parliamentarian, largely responsible for the ◊Petition of Right in 1628. As leader of the Puritan opposition in the ◊Long Parliament, he moved the impeachment of Charles I's advisers Strafford and Laud, drew up the ◊Grand Remonstrance, and was the chief of the five Members of Parliament whom Charles I failed to arrest in 1642. Just before his death he negotiated the alliance between Parliament and the Scots.

Pynchon /ˈpɪntʃən/ Thomas 1937– . American novelist, whose works include *V* 1963 and *Gravity's Rainbow* 1973.

Pyongyang /ˌpjɒŋˈjæŋ/ capital and industrial city (coal, iron and steel, textiles, chemicals) of North Korea; population 1,280,000 (1981).

pyorrhoea former name for gum disease, now known as ◊periodontal disease.

pyramid in geometry, a solid figure with triangular side-faces meeting at a common vertex (point) and with a ◊polygon as its base. A pyramid with a triangular base is called a tetrahedron; the Egyptian pyramids have square bases. The volume of a pyramid, no matter how many faces it has, is equal to the area of the base multiplied by one-third of the perpendicular height. A pyramid with its pointed top cut off by a plane parallel to the base is a type of ◊frustum.

pyramid

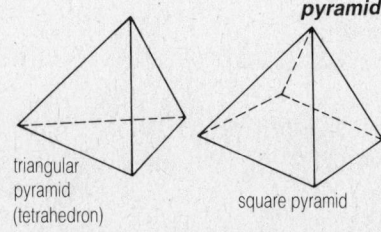

triangular pyramid (tetrahedron)

square pyramid

pyramid pyramidal building used in ancient Egypt to enclose a royal tomb, for example the Great Pyramid of Khufu/Cheops at Gizeh, near Cairo; 230 m/755 ft square and 147 m/481 ft high. In ◊Babylon and ◊Assyria broadly stepped pyramids (ziggurats) were used as the base for a shrine to a god: the Tower of Babel (see also ◊Babylon) was probably one of these. Pyramidal temple mounds were also built by the ◊Aztecs and ◊Mayas, for example at ◊Chichen Itza and Cholula, near Mexico City, which is the world's largest in ground area (300 m/990 ft base, 60 m/195 ft high).

Pyramus and Thisbe /ˈpɪrəməs, ˈθɪzbi/ legendary Babylonian lovers whose story was retold by ◊Ovid. Pursued by a lioness, Thisbe lost her veil, and when Pyramus arrived at their meeting-place, he found it bloodstained. Assuming Thisbe was dead, he stabbed himself, and she, on finding his body, killed herself. Shakespeare used the story in *A Midsummer Night's Dream*.

Pyrénées /ˌpɪrəˈniːz/ mountain range in SW Europe between France and the Iberian

peninsula; length about 435 km/270 mi; highest peak Aneto (French *Néthon*) 3,404 m/11,168 ft. The Basque country is on the French-Spanish frontier, and Andorra is entirely within the range. Hydroelectric power has encouraged industrial development in the foothills.

pyrethrum popular name for some flowers of the genus *Chrysanthemum* in the family Compositae. The ornamental species *Chrysanthemum coccineum*, and hybrids derived from it, is commonly grown in gardens. Pyrethrum powder is a powerful contact herbicide for aphids and mosquitoes.

pyridine a heterocyclic compound C_5H_5N (see ◊cyclic compounds). It is a liquid with a sickly smell, and occurs in coal tar. It is soluble in water, acts as a strong base, and is used as a solvent in the manufacture of plastics.

pyrites a common ◊iron ore, FeS. Its metallic lustre gives it its common name 'fool's gold'.

pyrogallol trihydroxybenzene, a derivative of benzene $C_6H_3OH_3$, prepared from gallic acid, and used in gas analysis for the measurement of oxygen, because its alkaline solution turns black as it rapidly absorbs oxygen. It is also used in photograph development.

pyrometer instrument for measuring high temperatures. See under ◊thermometer.

pyroxenes a group of minerals, silicates of calcium, iron, and magnesium, found in ◊igneous and ◊metamorphic rocks. Jadeite, $NaAlSi_2O_6$, from which one of the forms of ◊jade comes, is a pyroxene.

Pyrrho /ˈpɪrəʊ/ c. 360–c. 270 BC. Greek philosopher, founder of the ◊Sceptic school, who maintained that since certainty was impossible, peace of mind lay in renouncing all claims to knowledge.

Pyrrhus /ˈpɪrəs/ c. 318–c. 272 BC. King of ◊Epirus from 307, who invaded Italy in 280, as an ally of the ◊Tarentines against Rome. He twice defeated the Romans, but with such heavy losses that a 'Pyrrhic victory' is a byword for one not worth winning, and he returned to Greece in 275 after his defeat at Beneventum.

Pythagoras
for right-angled triangles

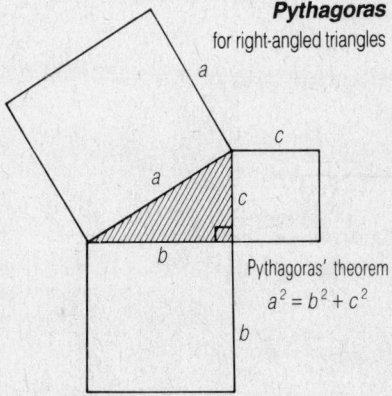

Pythagoras' theorem
$$a^2 = b^2 + c^2$$

Pythagoras /paɪˈθægərəs/ c. 580–500 BC. Greek mathematician and philosopher.
He was the founder of a politically influential religious brotherhood in Croton, S Italy (suppressed in the 5th century). Its tenets included immortality of the soul and

◊transmigration.

Much of Pythagoras' work concerned numbers, to which he assigned mystical properties. For example, he classified numbers into triangular ones (1, 3, 6, 10,...) which can be represented as a triangular array, and square ones (1, 4, 9, 16,...) which form squares. He also observed that any two adjacent triangular numbers add to a square number (for example, 1 + 3 = 4, 3 + 6 = 9, 6 + 10 = 16,...).

In geometry, *Pythagoras' theorem* states that in a right-angled triangle, the square of the hypotenuse (the longest side) is equal to the sum of the squares of the lengths of the other two sides. If the hypotenuse is h units long and the lengths of the other sides are a and b, then $h^2 = a^2 + b^2$. This provides a way of calculating the length of any side of such a triangle if the lengths of the other two sides are known. The theorem is also true for any regular polygons constructed on the sides of a right-angled triangle (not merely for squares).

Pythagorus of Rhegium Greek sculptor of the 5th century BC. Born at Samos, he settled in Rhegium, Italy, and established a reputation for his statues of athletes.

Pytheas /'pɪθɪəs/ 4th century BC. Greek navigator from Marseille who explored the coast of W Europe at least as far as Denmark, sailed round Britain, and reached ◊Thule (probably the Shetlands).

Pythian Games /'pɪθɪən/ ancient Greek festival in honour of ◊Apollo, celebrated near Delphi every four years.

Pythias /'pɪθɪæs/ in Greek legend, a Pythagorean whose friend Damon offered his own life as security when Pythias was condemned to death by a tyrant.

python type of constricting snake found in the tropics of Africa, Asia, and Australia, allied to the boas but laying eggs rather than producing living young. Some species are small, but others grow 6 m/20 ft long or more. The reticulated python of SE Asia can grow to 10 m/33 ft.

pyx (Latin 'box') the container used in the Catholic Church for the reservation of the wafers of the sacrament. The *Trial of the Pyx* is the test of coinage by a goldsmith, at the hall of the Goldsmiths' Company, London, and is so called because of the box in which specimens of coinage are stored.

Q 17th letter of the alphabet, representing *koppa* of the earliest Greek alphabet. In Latin, as in English, it is always followed by *u: qu*, pronounced *kw*.

Qaddafi alternative form of ▷Khaddhafi, Libyan leader.

Qadsiyah, Battle of battle fought in S Iraq in 637. A Muslim Arab force defeated a larger ▷Zoroastrian Persian army and ended the ▷Sassanian Empire. The defeat is still resented in Iran, where modern Muslim Arab nationalism threatens the break-up of the Iranian state.

qat shrub *Catha edulis* related to coffee; the leaves are chewed as a mild narcotic in some Arab countries; banned in ▷Somalia 1983.

Qatar /ˈkætɑː/ country in the Middle East, occupying Qatar peninsula in the Arabian Gulf, bounded to the SW by Saudi Arabia and to the S by United Arab Emirates.

government A provisional constitution adopted in 1970 confirmed Qatar as an absolute monarchy, with the emir holding all executive and legislative powers. The emir appoints and heads a council of ministers. An advisory council was established in 1972, with limited powers to question ministers. There are no political parties.

history For early history, see ▷Arabia. Qatar, which used to be under ▷Bahrain's control, has had a treaty with Britain since 1868. It was part of the ▷Ottoman Empire from 1872 until World War I. The British government gave formal recognition in 1916 to Sheikh Abdullah al-Thani as Qatar's ruler, guaranteeing protection in return for an influence over the country's external affairs.

In 1968 Britain announced its intention of withdrawing its forces from the Persian Gulf area by 1981, and Qatar, having failed in an attempt to form an association with other Gulf states, became fully independent on 1 Sept 1971. A new treaty of friendship with Britain replaced the former arrangements.

In 1972, while the emir, Sheik Ahmad, was out of the country, his cousin, the crown prince, Sheik Khalifa, led a bloodless coup; already prime minister, he declared himself also emir. He embarked on an ambitious programme of social and economic reform, curbing the extravagances

of the royal family. Qatar has good relations with most of its neighbours and is regarded as one of the more stable and moderate Arab states.

Qatar
STATE OF (*Dawlat Qatar*)

AREA 11,437 sq km/4,250 sq mi
CAPITAL and chief port Doha
TOWNS Dukhan, centre of oil production
PHYSICAL mostly flat desert
FEATURES negligible rain and surface water, so that only 3% is fertile, but irrigation allows self-sufficiency in fruit and vegetables; rich oil discoveries since World War II
HEAD OF STATE AND OF GOVERNMENT Sheik Khalifa bin Hamad al-Thani from 1972
GOVERNMENT absolute monarchy
EXPORTS oil and natural gas, petrochemicals, fertilizers, iron and steel
CURRENCY Qatar riyal (6.02 = £1 Sept 1987)
POPULATION (1985) 301,000 (mainly in Doha); annual growth rate 4.3%
LANGUAGE Arabic
RELIGION Sunni Muslim
LITERACY 60% (1985)
GNP $5.9 bn (1983); $35,000 per head of population

area 721,000 sq km/278,000 sq mi
capital Xining
features mainly desert, with nomadic herders

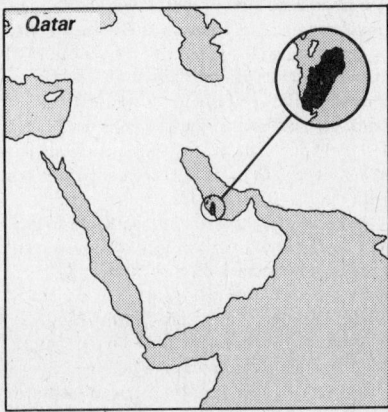

CHRONOLOGY
1970 Constitution adopted, confirming the emirate as an absolute monarchy.
1971 Achieved full independence. New treaty of friendship with Britain signed.
1972 Emir Sheik Ahmad replaced in a bloodless coup, by his cousin, Crown Prince Sheik Khalifa.

Qattara Depression /kəˈtɑːrə/ tract of the Western Desert, Egypt, up to 125 m/400 ft below sea level. Its very soft sand makes it virtually impassable to vehicles, and it protected the left flank of the Allied armies before and during the battle of ▷Alamein 1942. Area 20,000 sq km/7,500 sq mi.

Qin /tʃɪn/ Chinese dynasty 221–206 BC. ▷Shi Huangdi was its most noted emperor.

Qingdao /ˌtʃɪŋˈdaʊ/ (formerly Tsingtao) industrial port and summer resort in Shandong province, China; population (1982) 1,180,000. It is noted for its beer.

Qinghai /ˌtʃɪŋˈhaɪ/ (formerly Tsinghai) province of NW China

products oil
population (1982) 3,895,700, including many Tibetans and other minorities. Criminals may be deported here as a labour force.

Qisarya /kiːˈsɑːriə/ Mediterranean port N of Tel Aviv–Jaffa, Israel; there are underwater remains of Herod the Great's port of Caesarea.

quadrathon a sports event in which the competitors must swim two miles, walk 30 miles, cycle 100 miles, and run 26.2 miles (a marathon) within 22 hours.

quadratic equation in mathematics, a ▷polynomial ▷equation of second degree (that is, an equation containing as its highest power the square of a single unknown variable, such as x^2).

The general formula of such equations is $ax^2 + bx + c = 0$, in which a, b, and c are ◊constants and only the ◊coefficient a cannot equal 0. A quadratic equation may have as its solution values of x, two identical values of x, or no real values of x (that is, the ◊solutions are ◊complex numbers), depending on the value of $b^2 - 4ac$. Some quadratic equations can be solved by factorization, or the values of x can be found by using the formula for the general solution

$$x = \frac{-b \pm \sqrt{(b^2-4ac)}}{2a}$$

In ◊coordinate geometry, a quadratic function represents a ◊parabola.

quadrille a square dance for four or more couples, or the music for the dance, which alternates between two and four beats in a bar.

Quadruple Alliance name of two alliances, the first formed in 1718 by Britain, Austria, the United Provinces (Netherlands), and France to prevent Spain from taking Sardinia and Sicily, and the second formed in 1813 by Britain, Austria, Russia, and Prussia aimed at defeating Napoleon; renewed 1815 and 1818.

quaestor a Roman magistrate whose duties were mainly concerned with public finances. The quaestors originated as assistants to the consuls.

quagga extinct species of S African wild horse; it resembled a partially striped zebra.

Quai d'Orsay /'keı dɔː'seı/ part of the left bank of the Seine in Paris, where the French Foreign Office and other government buildings are situated. The name has become synonymous with the Foreign Office itself.

quail smallest species of the partridge family. The common quail *Coturnix coturnix* is reddish-brown, and is found in Europe, Asia, and Africa. They are highly valued as food, and are netted while migrating to and from North Africa.

Quaker popular name, originally derogatory, for a member of the Society of ◊Friends.

quango British term coined as an acronym from *q*uasi-*a*utonomous *n*on-governmental *o*rganization, for example the Equal Opportunities Commission (1975). They are nominally independent, but rely on government funding. Many (such as the Location of Offices Bureau) were abolished by the Thatcher government from 1979.

Quant /kwɒnt/ Mary 1934– . British fashion designer. Her Chelsea boutique, Bazaar, achieved a practical off-beat revolution in women's clothing and make-up, which epitomized 'swinging London' of the 1960s.

quantity theory of money theory dating originally from the 17th century and elaborated by the US economist Irving Fisher (1867–1947) to show, in essence, that an increase in the amount of money in circulation will cause a proportionate increase in prices. Supported and developed by Milton ◊Friedman, it forms the theoretical basis of modern ◊monetarism.

Quantrill /'kwɒntrıl/ William Clarke 1837–1865. American bandit, who became leader of a guerrilla unit on the ◊Confederate side in the ◊Civil War which went in for robbery and murder. Jesse and Frank ◊James were among his aides, and all appear in ballad legend.

quantum number in physics, one of a set of four numbers that uniquely characterize an ◊electron and its state in an ◊atom. The principal quantum number n (= 1, 2, 3 etc.) defines the electron's main energy level, corresponding to shells (energy levels) also known by their spectroscopic designations K, L, M, and so on). The orbital quantum number l,(= $n-1$, $n-2$, and so on to 0) relates to angular momentum, giving rise to a series of subshells designated s, p, d, f, and so on, of slightly different energy levels. The magnetic quantum number m (= l, $l-1$, $l-2$ and so on to 0 and then on to ... – $(l-2)$, – $(l-1)$ and -l) describes the energies of electrons in a magnetic field, allowing further subdivision of the subshells (making three subdivisions p_x, p_y and p_z in the p subshell, for example, of the same energy level). Finally the spin quantum number m_s (= $+\frac{1}{2}$ or $-\frac{1}{2}$) gives the spin direction of the electron. No two electrons in an atom can have the same set of quantum numbers (the ◊Pauli exclusion principle).

quantum theory in physics, theory that many quantities, such as ◊energy, cannot have continuous range of values but only a number of discrete (particular) ones, because they are packaged in 'quanta of energy'. The theory began with the work of Max ◊Planck in 1900 on radiated energy, and was extended by ◊Einstein to electromagnetic radiation generally (see ◊electromagnetic waves), including ◊light. Niels ◊Bohr used it to explain the ◊spectrum of light emitted by excited hydrogen atoms. Later work by ◊Schrödinger, ◊Heisenberg, ◊Dirac and others elaborated the theory to what is called quantum mechanics (or wave mechanics). Just as the earlier theory has shown how light, generally seen as a wave motion, could also in some ways be seen as composed of discrete particles (◊photons), so quantum mechanics shows how atomic particles like electrons may also be seen as having wave-like properties. Quantum mechanics is the basis of ◊particle physics, modern theoretical chemistry and the solid-state physics which describes the behaviour of the ◊silicon chips used in modern computers.

quarantine term (from French *quarantaine* 40 days) applied to any period for which people, animals, or vessels may be detained in isolation when suspected of carrying contagious disease. In the UK (to prevent the spread of rabies) immigrant dogs and cats must be kept in quarantine kennels for six months.

quart imperial capacity measure, equal to 2 pints or 1.2 litres.

quarter day in the financial year, any of the four dates on which such payments as ground rents become due: in England 25 Mar (Lady Day), 24 Jun (Midsummer Day), 29 Sept (Michaelmas), and 25 Dec (Christmas Day).

quarter session former local criminal court in England, replaced in 1972 by crown courts (see under ◊law courts).

quartz one of the commonest minerals of the Earth's crust, it is a crystalline form of ◊silica, SiO_2. When impurities, such as ◊oxides, occur in the crystals, they produce such gem varieties as cairngorm, ◊amethyst, and ◊tourmaline. Quartz is used in jewellery and ornamental work, and its

reaction to electricity makes it valuable in electronic instruments (see ◊piezoelectric effect). Quartz crystals that would take 3 million years to form can now be 'grown' in pressure vessels to a standard that allows them to be used in scientific instruments, and in electronics, such as quartz wristwatches.

quartzite a ◊metamorphic rock consisting of pure quartz sandstone that has recrystallized under pressure.

quasar an object that appears star-like but that lies far off in the universe, named for its *quasi*-stellar appearance. Light from quasars shows large ◊red shifts, which places them far off in the universe, the most distant lying 10,000 million light years or more away. Although quasars are small, with diameters of less than a light year, they give out as much energy as hundreds of ◊galaxies. Quasars are thought to be the brilliant centres of distant galaxies, caused by stars and gas falling towards an immense ◊black hole at the galaxy's centre. Some quasars emit radio waves (see ◊radio astronomy), which is how they were first identified in 1963, but most are radio-quiet. About 3,000 are now known. They are important in studies of the early history of the ◊universe.

Quasimodo /ˌkwɑːzɪ'mɔʊdoʊ/ Salvatore 1901–1968. Italian poet. He first became known with *Acque e terre/Waters and Land* 1930, and his later books, such as *Il falso e vero verde/The False and True Green* 1956, reflect a growing preoccupation with contemporary political and social problems. He won a Nobel prize in 1959.

quassia trees of S America which have a bitter bark and wood, for example, *Quassia amara* family Simaroubaceae. An infusion was formerly used as a tonic, and quassia is now used in insecticides.

Quatre Bras, Battle of /'kætrə 'brɑː/ battle fought 16 Jun 1815, in which Wellington defeated French forces under Marshall ◊Ney (see under ◊Napoleonic Wars). Named after a hamlet in Brabant, Belgium, 32 km/20 mi SE of Brussels.

Quayle /kweıl/ Anthony 1913– . English actor and director. 1948–56 he directed at the Shakespeare Memorial Theatre and appeared as Falstaff in *Henry IV*, Petruchio in *The Taming of the Shrew*, and *Othello*.

Québec /kwı'bek/ capital and industrial port (textiles and leather; timber, pulp, paper; printing and publishing) of Québec province, Canada; population (1984) 164,000. Québec is a centre of French culture, and there are two universities, Laval 1663 and Quebec 1969. Founded 1608 by the French explorer ◊Champlain, its picturesque old town survives below the citadel about 110 m/360 ft above the St Lawrence river. The British, under Gen ◊Wolfe, captured Quebec 1759; both Wolfe and the French commander (◊Montcalm) were killed.

Quebec/Québec /kwı'bek/ province of E Canada
area 1,540,676 sq km/594,860 sq mi
capital Québec
towns Montreal, Laval, Sherbrooke, Verdun, Hull, Trois-Rivières

features immense water-power resources, for example the James Bay project

products iron, copper, gold, zinc; cereals, potatoes; forest products, including paper; textiles; fish

population (1984) 6,553,500

language French is the only official language since 1974, though the legislation was modified by Quebec court rulings 1984–85

history see under ◊Canadian history. In the 1960s nationalist feeling (despite existing safeguards for Quebec's French-derived civil law, customs, religion, and language) led to the foundation of the Parti Québecois by René ◊Lévesque in 1968. Premier is Pierre Marc Johnson, who succeeded Lévesque in 1985.

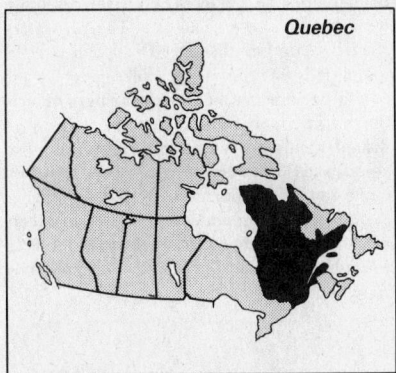
Quebec

Quebec Conference conference in the city of Quebec 1943, at which ◊Roosevelt, ◊Churchill, Mackenzie ◊King, and Tse-ven ◊Soong approved ◊Mountbatten as supreme Allied commander SE Asia and made plans for the invasion of France, for which ◊Eisenhower was to be supreme commander.

quebracho /keɪˈbrɑːtʃəʊ/ several S American trees with very hard wood, especially the *red quebracho Schinopsis lorentzii* family Anacardiaceae used in tanning.

Quechua /ˈketʃwə/ (also Quichua, or Kechua) S American Indians of the Andean regions, whose ancestors include the Inca. The Quechua language is the second official language of Peru, and is also spoken in Ecuador.

Queen Anne style style of furniture popular in England 1700–1720, characterized by restrained curves and the use of walnut veneer.

Queen Charlotte Islands /ˈʃɑːlət/ archipelago about 160 km/100 mi off ◊British Columbia, Canada, of which it forms part; area 9,790 sq km/3,780 sq mi; population 2,500. Graham and Moresby are the largest islands. There are timber and fishing industries

Queen's Award British award established in 1965 as the Queen's Award to Industry, and replaced from 1976 by two separate awards, for export achievement and for technological achievement. Made to organizations who may display a special emblem for five years, awards are made annually on the birthday of Queen Elizabeth II (21 Apr).

Queensberry /ˈkwiːnzbəri/ John Sholto Douglas, 8th Marquess of Queensberry 1844–1900. British patron of boxing, who in 1867 drew up the *Queensberry rules* which underlie modern regulations. He was the father of Lord Alfred ◊Douglas.

Queen's Counsel or *QC* in England, a barrister appointed to senior rank by the Lord Chancellor. A QC wears a silk gown, and takes precedence over a junior member of the Bar. When the monarch is a king the term is King's Counsel.

Queen's County former name of ◊Laoighis, county in the Republic of Ireland.

Queensland /ˈkwiːnzlænd/ state of Australia
area 1,736,524 sq km/670,500 sq mi
capital Brisbane
towns Gold Coast, Townsville, Toowoomba, Rockhampton
features Great Dividing Range, including Mount Bartle Frere 1,657 m/5,438 ft; Great Barrier Reef (collection of coral reefs and islands about 2,000 km/1,250 mi long off the E coast, rich in wildlife); City of Gold Coast holiday area in the south, population 120,000; Mount Isa mining area
exports sugar, pineapples; beef; cotton and wool; tobacco; copper, gold, silver, lead, zinc, coal, nickel, bauxite, uranium, natural gas
population (1985) 2,546,440
history part of New South Wales until 1859, it then became self-governing.

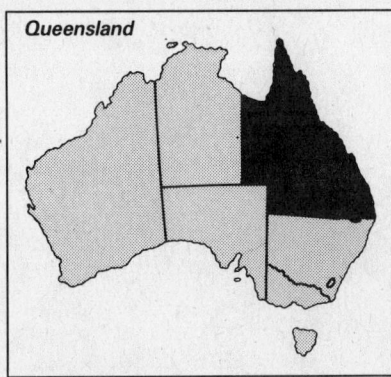
Queensland

Queen's Proctor in England, the official representing the crown in matrimonial cases. Their chief function is to intervene in divorce proceedings to stop a decree nisi being made absolute if it is discovered that material facts have been concealed from the court or that there has been collusion, or adultery by the petitioner since the decree, or any other cause against the dissolution of the marriage. When the monarch is a king the term is King's Proctor.

Queenstown /ˈkwiːnztaʊn/ former name of ◊Cóbh, port in the Republic of Ireland.

Quemoy /keˈmɔɪ/ island off the SE coast of China, and administered (with ◊Matsu) by Taiwan; area 130 sq km/50 sq mi; population (1982) 57,847. When the islands were shelled from the mainland in 1960, the USA declared they would be defended if attacked.

quenching a kind of ◊heat treatment used to harden metals, which are heated to a certain temperature and then quickly plunged into cold water or oil.

Quennell /kwɪˈnel/ Peter 1905– . British biographer and critic. He edited the journal *History Today* 1951–79, and wrote biographies of Byron 1935, Ruskin 1949, Pope 1968, and Dr Johnson 1972.

question mark a punctuation mark (?), used to indicate enquiry or doubt. When indicating enquiry, it is placed at the end of a *direct question* ('Who is coming?') but never at the end of an *indirect question* (He asked us who was coming). When indicating doubt, it usually appears between brackets, to show that a writer is puzzled or uncertain about a statement.

Quetta /ˈkwetə/ town and summer resort in Baluchistan, Pakistan; population (1981) 281,000. There is a military staff college and a university.

quetzal long-tailed brightly coloured Central American bird. See under ◊trogon.

Quetzalcoatl /ˌketsəlkəʊˈætl/ feathered serpent god of air and water in the pre-Columbian ◊Aztec and ◊Toltec cultures of Central America. In legendary human form, he was said to have been fair-skinned and bearded, and to have reigned on earth during a golden age. He disappeared across the sea, with a promise to return; ◊Cortes exploited the coincidence of description when he invaded. Ruins of one of his temples survive at Teotihuacán in Mexico.

Quevedo y Villegas /keˈveɪdəʊ iː viːˈjeɪɡəs/ Francisco Gómez de 1580–1645. Spanish novelist and satirist. His picaresque novel *La Vida del Buscón/The Life of a Scoundrel* 1626 follows the tradition of the roguish hero who has a series of episodic adventures. *Sueños/Visions* 1627 are a brilliant series of satirical portraits of contemporary society.

Quezon City /ˈkeɪsɒn ˈsɪti/ capital of the Philippines 1948–76; population (1980) 1,165,865. Laid out from 1940 in a NE suburb of Manila, it was named after the first president of the republic, Manual Quezon (1878–1944).

Qufu /ˌtʃuːˈfuː/ (formerly Chufu) town in Jinan province, China; population 27,000. It is the birthplace of Kong Fuzi (formerly ◊Confucius) and has the Great Temple of Confucius.

Quiberon /ˌkiːbəˈrɒn/ peninsula and coastal town in Brittany, France; in 1759 the British admiral ◊Hawke defeated a French fleet (under ◊Conflans) in Quiberon Bay.

quicksilver former name for the element ◊mercury.

quietism a religious attitude, displayed periodically in the history of Christianity, consisting of meditation to achieve union with God. The founder of modern quietism was the Spanish priest ◊Molinos in his *Guida Spirituale/Spiritual Guide* 1675.

Quiller-Couch /ˈkwɪlə ˈkuːtʃ/ Arthur Thomas 1863–1944. British scholar and writer who edited *The Oxford Book of English Verse* 1900 and wrote a number of critical studies.

Quilter /ˈkwɪltə/ Roger 1877–1953. British composer, known for song settings of ◊Tennyson and ◊Shakespeare, including 'Now Sleeps the Crimson Petal' 1904 and 'To Daisies' 1906, and for his *Children's Overture* 1920.

Quimper /kæm'peə/ town in Brittany, France; population (1982) 60,162. There is a fine 15th-century Gothic cathedral, and a decorative pottery industry.

quince W Asian tree *Cydonia oblonga* family Rosaceae; the bitter, yellow pear-shaped fruit is used in preserves.

Quine /kwaɪn/ Willard Van Orman 1908– . US philosopher and logician. In his paper 'Two Dogmas of Empiricism' 1951, Quine argued against the ◊analytic/◊synthetic distinction. In *Word and Object* 1960, he put forward the thesis of radical untranslatability, the view that a sentence can always be regarded as referring to many different things.

Quinquagesima (Latin 'fiftieth') in the Christian Church calendar, the Sunday before Lent and 50 days before Easter.

Quintana Roo /kɪn'tɑːnə 'rəʊəʊ/ isolated area of the ◊Yucatan peninsula, constituting a state of Mexico. There are ◊Maya remains.

Quintero /kɪn'teərəʊ/ Serafin Alvarez 1871–1938 and Joaquin Alvarez 1873–1945. Spanish dramatists. These brothers, born near Seville, always worked together and from 1897 they produced some 200 successful plays, principally dealing with Andalusia. Among them are *Papá Juan: Centenario* 1909 and *Los Mosquitos* 1928.

Quintilian /kwɪn'tɪliən/ (Marcus Fabius Quintilianus) c. 35–95 AD. Roman rhetorician. Born at Calgurris, Spain, he taught rhetoric in Rome from 68 AD and wrote the *Institutio Oratorio/The Education of an Orator*, advocating a simple and sincere style of public speaking.

quipu (Quechua 'knot') a device used by the ◊Incas of ancient Peru to record numerical information, consisting of a set of knotted cords of one or several colours.

Quirinal /'kwɪrɪnəl/ one of the seven hills on which ancient Rome was built. Its summit is occupied by a palace built in 1574 as a summer residence for the pope and occupied 1870–1946 by the kings of Italy. **Quirinus** was the local god of the ◊Sabines, hence the name.

Quisling /'kwɪzlɪŋ/ Vidkun 1887–1945. Norwegian politician. Leader from 1933 of the Norwegian ◊Fascist Party, he aided the ◊Nazi invasion in 1940 by delaying mobilization and urging non-resistance. Made premier by Hitler in 1942, he was arrested and shot as a traitor by the Norwegians in 1945. His name became generic for a traitor who aids an occupying force.

Quito /'kiːtəʊ/ capital and industrial city (textiles, chemicals, leather, gold and silverware) of Ecuador, about 3,000 m/9,350 ft above sea level in the ◊Cordillera so that it has a temperate climate all year round; two universities; population (1982) 1,110,250. An ancient settlement, it was taken by the ◊Incas about 1470 and by the Spanish 1534.

Quixote, Don novel by the Spanish writer ◊Cervantes, with a hero of the same name.

Qum /kum/ holy city of the ◊Shi'ite Muslims in central Iran, 145 km/90 mi S of Tehran; population (1982) 4,240,050. The Islamic academy of Madresseh Faizieh (1920) became the headquarters of Ayatollah ◊Khomeini.

Qumran or /'kumrɑːn/ *Khirbet Qumran* ruined site, excavated from 1951, in the foothills on NW shores of the Dead Sea in Jordan. Originally an Iron Age fort (6th century BC) it was occupied in the 2nd century BC by a monastic community, the ◊Essenes, until the buildings were burned down in 68 AD. The monastery library comprises the the ◊Dead Sea Scrolls, discovered 1947 hidden for safekeeping.

quoits game in which a rubber ring or quoit is thrown at a hob from a point 16.5 m/18 yd distant. Landing over the hob, a 'ringer' gains two points, and that landing nearest the hob, within a circle 1 m/3 ft in diameter, one point.

quorum a minimum number of members required to be present for the proceedings of an assembly to be valid. The actual number required for a quorum may vary.

R 18th letter of the alphabet, corresponding to the Semitic *resh* and Greek *rho*. A liquid, pronounced with the tip of the tongue on the palate, it is sometimes 'trilled' by vibration of the tongue, especially in Scotland, but in S England r is often weak when used medially and silent finally.

Rabat /rə'bɑːt/ capital of Morocco, industrial port (cotton textiles, carpets, leather goods) on the Atlantic coast, 177 km/110 mi W of Fez; university 1957; population (1982) 893,042. There is a 12th-century mosque.

Rabaul /rɑː'baʊl/ largest port of Papua New Guinea, on the volcanic island of New Britain; population (1980) 14,954.

rabbi the chief religious minister of a synagogue; the spiritual leader of a Jewish congregation; see under ◊Judaism.

rabbit greyish-brown, long-eared mammal *Oryctolagus cuniculus* of Europe and N Africa (introduced to Australia and elsewhere), which reveals the white underside of its brief tail in its hopping run. It produces several large litters in a year, and is destructive to crops. Living in groups of interconnected underground burrows, 'warrens', rabbits are especially subject to the virus disease *myxomatosis*, which has led to some degree to an above-ground life style. Rabbits are bred for food and fur, the pelts usually being treated to resemble more costly furs. The North American equivalent of the species is the woodland *cottontail Silvilagus floridanus* in the group Lagomorpha (with hares and pikas).

Rabelais /'ræbəleɪ/ François 1495–1553. French satirist, monk, and physician, whose name has become synonymous with bawdy humour. He was the author of satirical allegories, *La Vie inestimable de Gargantua/The Inestimable Life of Gargantua* 1535 and *Faits et dits hèroïques du grand Pantagruel/Deeds and Sayings of the Great Pantagruel* 1533, the story of two giants (father and son) Gargantua and Pantagruel.

rabies or *hydrophobia* 'aversion to water'. Virus disease with a high mortality rate, which runs a painful course ending in spasms of the throat brought on by drinking, or by the sight of water (hence the name). It is contracted by a bite from an affected animal (usually a dog or fox). Louis ◊Pasteur was the first to produce an effective vaccine, and the Pasteur Institute was founded to treat the disease. As a control measure for foxes and other wild animals oral vaccination (by bait) is recommended, rather than destruction.

Rabin /ræ'biːn/ Itzhak 1922– . Israeli prime minister who succeeded Golda Meir 1974–77.

raccoon or *racoon* omnivorous nocturnal mammal of North and Central America *Procyon lotor*. About 60 cm/2 ft long, it has grey-brown body fur and a black and white ringed tail.

race in ◊anthropology, term sometimes applied to a physically distinctive group of people, on the basis of difference from other groups in skin colour, head shape, hair type, and physique.
Formerly anthropologists divided the human race into three hypothetical racial groups – the Caucasoid, Mongoloid, and Negroid – on the basis of these characteristics. Between five and 32 such races have been recognized at different times by different authorities. However, scientific studies have failed to indicate any absolute confirmation of genetic racial divisions. Different characteristics reflect changes in gene frequencies within populations, due to accident (genetic 'drift') and adaptation to local climatic conditions, but they are all highly variable. Beyond the superficial differences, such as skin colour, there are no major distinctions between humans. They do not differ in intellectual abilities, and the fact that they can all interbreed to produce fertile offspring shows that they all belong to the same genetic ◊species. The attempt to categorize human types, as in South Africa for the purposes of segregation, is inevitably doomed by the absence of any straightforward distinction. Many anthropologists today thus completely reject the concept of race, and social scientists tend to prefer the term ethnic group (see ◊ethnicity) to refer to people's sense of cultural identity, which may or may not include skin colour or common descent.

raceme a type of ◊inflorescence.

Rachel /'reɪtʃəl/ in the Old Testament, the favourite wife of ◊Jacob, and mother of ◊Joseph and Benjamin.

Rachel /ræ'ʃel/ stage name of Elizabeth Félix 1821–1858. French tragedienne who excelled in Racine's *Phèdre*.

Rachmaninov /ræk'mænɪnɒf/ Sergei (Vasilevich) 1873–1943. Russian composer and pianist. He studied at the St Petersburg and Moscow conservatoires. After the 1917 Revolution he went to the USA. His dramatically emotional music has a strong melodic basis and includes operas, for example, *Francesca da Rimini* 1906, three symphonies, four piano concertos, piano pieces, and songs. Among his most familiar works are the *Prelude in C Minor* and *Rhapsody on a Theme of Paganini* for piano and orchestra.

racial disadvantage term used to describe a condition in which children from ethnic minority groups perform less well than they should. There is evidence that this is the case in British schools. The Swann Report 1986 recommended methods of combating racial disadvantage in schools, and local authorities are increasingly adopting anti-racist policies and attempting to give their curricula a ◊multi-cultural dimension.

Racine /ræ'siːn/ Jean 1639–1699. French dramatist and greatest exponent of the classical tragedy in French drama. Most of his tragedies have women in the title role, for example *Andromaque* 1667, *Iphigénie* 1674, and *Phèdre* 1677. After the contemporary failure of the latter he no longer wrote for the secular stage, but influenced by Madame de ◊Maintenon wrote two religious dramas, *Esther* 1689 and *Athalie* 1691, which achieved considerable posthumous success.

racism or *racialism* a belief in, or set of implicit assumptions about, the superiority of one's own ◊race or ethnic group, often accompanied by prejudice against members of an ethnic group different from one's own. Racism may be active, and used to justify the practice of ◊discrimination, verbal or physical abuse, or even genocide, as in Nazi Germany. However, many social scientists believe that even where there is no overt discrimination, racism exists as an

Racine The tragedies of Racine are part of the great flowering of dramatic and poetic writing in 17th-century France. His subjects came from Greek mythology and he observed the rules of classical Greek drama.

unconscious attitude in many individuals and societies, based on a ◊stereotype or preconceived idea about different ethnic groups, which is damaging to individuals (both perpetrators and victims) and to society as a whole. In fact, many anthropologists today reject the concept of race itself as racist. See also ◊ethnicity.

rackets or *racquets*. Game played in an enclosed court usually 18.3 m/60 ft long by 9.1 m/30 ft wide, by two or four persons each with a racket about 75 cm/2.5 ft long, weighing 255 grammes/9 oz. The ball is 25 mm/1 in diameter and weighs 28 grammes/1 oz. Play begins from a service box, one of which is marked at each side of mid-court, and the ball must hit above a 2.75 m/9 ft line on the endwall. After service it may be played anywhere above a 68.5 cm/27 in high line on the endwall, the general rules of tennis applying thereafter. See also ◊squash.

rack railway a railway used in mountainous regions, which uses a toothed pinion running in a toothed rack to provide traction. The rack runs usually between the rails. Ordinary wheels lose their grip even on quite shallow gradients, but rack railways, like that on Mount Pilatus in Switzerland, can climb slopes as steep as 1 in 2.1.

radar (from *radio direction and ranging*) a means of locating an object in space, direction finding, and navigation using high-frequency radio waves. Direction of an object is ascertained by transmitting a beam of short-wavelength (1 cm–100 cm) short-pulse radio waves, and picking up the reflected beam; and distance by timing the journey of the radio waves (travelling at the speed of light) there and back (see ◊Appleton and ◊Watson-Watt). Essential to navigation in darkness, cloud and fog, it can be thwarted in warfare by aircraft and missiles with a modified shape which reduces their radar cross-section; radar-absorbent paints; and electronic jamming. A countermeasure in pinpointing small targets is the use of ◊laser 'radar' instead

of ◊microwaves. Chains of ground radar stations are used to warn of enemy attack, for example, North Warning System 1985, consisting of 52 stations across the Canadian Arctic and N Alaska. It is also used in ◊meteorology and ◊astronomy: radar reflections from the Moon were first detected during World War II, and the timed delay in receiving echoes from the Sun and planets has improved the calculation of their distances from Earth.

radar astronomy the bouncing of radio waves off objects in the solar system, such as planets, moons and asteroids, and reception and analysis of the 'echoes'. Radar contact with the Moon was first made in 1945 and with Venus in 1961. The travel time for radio reflections allows the exact distances of objects to be determined. Also, analysis of the reflected beam reveals the rotation period and allows the object's surface to be mapped. The rotation periods of Venus and Mercury were first determined by radar, and the first maps of Venus were made by radar.

Radcliffe /'rædklɪf/ Anne (born Ward) 1764–1823. British novelist, a chief exponent of the ◊Gothic novel or 'romance of terror', for example, *The Mysteries of Udolpho* 1794.

radian in mathematics, an alternative unit to the ◊degree for measuring angles. It is defined as the angle subtended at the centre of a circle by an arc (length of circumference) equal in length to the radius of the circle. There are 2π (approximately 6.284) radians in a full circle or 360°; 1 radian is approximately 57°, and 1° is $\pi/180$ or approximately 0.0175 radians. Radians are commonly used to specify angles in ◊polar coordinates.

radiation in physics, the emission of radiant ◊energy as ◊particles, waves, sound, and so on.

radiation biology the study of how living things are affected by ◊radioactive (ionizing) emissions, and by ◊electromagnetic (non-ionizing) radiation. The former is more harmful. Exposure to high levels produces radiation burns and ◊radiation sickness, plus genetic damage (resulting in birth defects) and cancers in the longer term. Exposure to low-level ionizing radiation can also cause genetic damage and cancers, particularly leukaemia. Electromagnetic radiation is usually harmful only if exposure is to high-energy emissions, for example close to powerful radio transmitters or near radar-wave sources. Such exposure can cause organ damage, cataracts, loss of hearing, leukaemia, and other cancers, or premature ageing. It may also affect the nervous system and brain, distorting their electrical nerve signals and leading to depression, disorientation, headaches, and other symptoms. Individual sensitivity varies and some people are affected by electrical equipment such as televisions, computers, and refrigerators. Radiation, both ionizing and non-ionizing, can be used therapeutically, for example to treat cancer, when the radiation dose is very carefully controlled (*radio therapy* or *X-ray therapy*).

radiation sickness sickness resulting from overlong exposure to radiation, including X-rays, gamma-rays, neutrons and other nuclear radiation. Such radiation ionizes atoms in the

body and causes nausea, vomiting, diarrhoea, and other symptoms. The body cells themselves may be damaged, even by relatively small doses, causing ◊leukaemia. Genetic changes may also be induced.

radiation units units of measurement that express the activity of a radionuclide and the dose of ionizing radiation. Their temporary use has been approved while the derived SI units become familiar. 1 curie = 3.7×10^{10} becquerel (activity); 1 rad = 10^{-2} gray (absorbed dose); 1 rem = 10^{-2} sievert (dose equivalent); 1 roentgen = 2.58×10^{-4} coulomb/kg (exposure to ionizing radiation).

Radić /'rɑːdɪtʃ/ Stjepan 1871–1928. Yugoslav politician. Born near Fiume, he led the Croat national movement within the Austro-Hungarian Empire, and supported union with Serbia in 1919. His opposition to Serbian supremacy within Yugoslavia led to his murder in the parliament house.

Radical supporter of parliamentary reform in Britain before the ◊Reform Bill of 1832. As a group the Radicals later became the advanced wing of the ◊Liberal Party. During the 1860s (led by ◊Cobden, ◊Bright, and J S ◊Mill) they campaigned for extension of the franchise, free trade, and ◊*laissez-faire*, but after 1870, under the leadership of J ◊Chamberlain and ◊Dilke, they adopted a republican and semi-socialist programme. With the growth of ◊socialism in the later 19th century, Radicalism ceased to exist as an organized movement. In the USA a radical is anyone of left-wing opinions.

radical in chemistry, a group of ◊atoms (for example the methyl radical, CH_3) forming part of a ◊molecule which takes part in chemical reactions without disintegration, yet often cannot exist alone.

radicle the part of a plant embryo that develops into the primary root. Usually it emerges from the seed before the embryonic shoot, or ◊plumule, its tip protected by a root cap, or calyptra, as it pushes through the soil. The radicle may form the basis of the entire root system, or it may be replaced by adventitious roots.

radio the transmission and reception of radio waves. The theory of ◊electromagnetic waves was first developed by James Clerk ◊Maxwell 1864, given practical confirmation in the laboratory 1888 by Heinrich ◊Hertz, and put to practical use by ◊Marconi, who in 1901 achieved reception of a signal in Newfoundland transmitted from ◊Poldhu in Cornwall.

In radio transmission a microphone converts ◊sound waves (pressure variations in the air) into an audiofrequency electrical signal. An ◊oscillator produces a carrier wave of high frequency; different stations are allocated different transmitting carrier frequencies. A modulator superimposes the audiofrequency signal on the carrier (see ◊modulation). There are two main ways of doing this: amplitude modulation (AM), used for long- and medium-wave broadcasts, in which the strength of the carrier is made to fluctuate in time with the audio signal; and frequency modulation (FM), as used for VHF broadcasts, in which the frequency of the carrier is made to fluctuate. The transmitting aerial emits the modulated electromagnetic waves which travel outwards from it.

In radio reception a receiving aerial picks up minute voltages in response to the waves sent out by a transmitter. A tuned circuit selects a particular frequency, usually by means of variable ◊capacitor connected across a coil of wire (see ◊inductance). A demodulator disentangles the audio signal from the carrier, which is now discarded, having served its purpose (see ◊demodulation). An amplifier boosts the audio signal for feeding to the loudspeaker which reproduces sound waves.

original nucleotide is known as the parent substance, and the product is a daughter nucleotide (which may or may not be radioactive).

radioactive tracer the radioactive isotope used in a ◊labelled compound.

radioactive waste any waste that emits radiation in excess of the background level. It comprises various types of nuclear waste including that from mining, from nuclear reactors, and from scientific experiments using labelled compounds. Tailings contaminate a site where uranium is mined or milled for use, and may have an active life of several thousand years.

energy highly penetrating protons. Beta and gamma radiation are both damaging to body tissues, but are especially dangerous if a radioactive substance is ingested or inhaled. See also ◊particle physics, ◊half-life.

radio astronomy the study of radio waves emitted naturally by objects in space. Radio emission comes from hot gas (*thermal radiation*), electrons spiralling in magnetic fields (*synchroton radiation*), and specific wavelengths (*lines*) emitted by atoms and molecules in space, such as the 21-cm line emitted by hydrogen gas. Radio astronomy began in 1832 when Karl ◊Jansky detected radio waves from the centre of our ◊galaxy, but the subject did not develop until after World War II. Astronomers have mapped the spiral structure of our galaxy from the radio waves given out by interstellar gas, and they have detected many individual radio sources within our galaxy and beyond.

Among the radio sources in our galaxy are the remains of ◊supernova explosions, such as the ◊Crab Nebula and ◊pulsars. Short-wavelength radio waves have been detected from complex molecules in dense clouds of gas where stars are forming. Searches have been undertaken for signals from other civilizations in the galaxy, so far without success.

Strong sources of radio waves beyond our galaxy include ◊radio galaxies, and ◊quasars. Their existence far off in the Universe demonstrates how the Universe has evolved with time. Radio astronomers have also detected weak *background radiation* thought to be from the ◊Big Bang explosion that marked the birth of the universe. Radio astronomy has greatly improved our understanding of the evolution of stars, the structure of galaxies, and the origin of the universe.

radio beacon a radio transmitter in a fixed location, used in marine and aerial navigation. Ships and aircraft pinpoint their position by reference to the signals given out by two or more beacons.

radiocarbon dating a method of dating organic materials (for example bone, wood) found by archaeologists. It depends on the fact that plants take up carbon dioxide gas from the atmosphere and incorporate it into their tissues. Some of that carbon dioxide contains the radioactive isotope of carbon, carbon-14. On death, the plant ceases to take up carbon-14 from the atmosphere and that already taken up decays at a known rate, allowing the time which has elapsed since the tree was felled to be measured. Animals that eat the plant tissues take the carbon-14 into their own bodies and so their remains can be similarly dated. See W F ◊Libby, also ◊radiometric dating. After 120,000 years so little carbon-14 is left that it is difficult to get accurate results.

radio, cellular the use of a series of short-range transmitters at the centre of adjacent cells (each about 4 km/2.5 mi in diameter), using the same frequencies over and over again throughout the area covered. It is used for personal communication among subscribers via car phones, portable units, and such.

radio

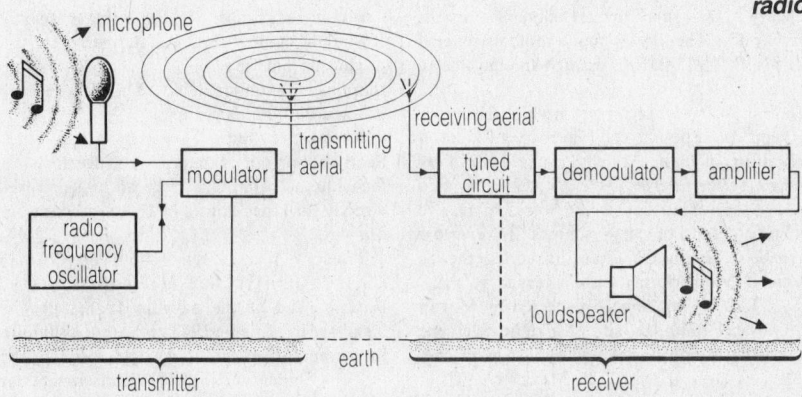

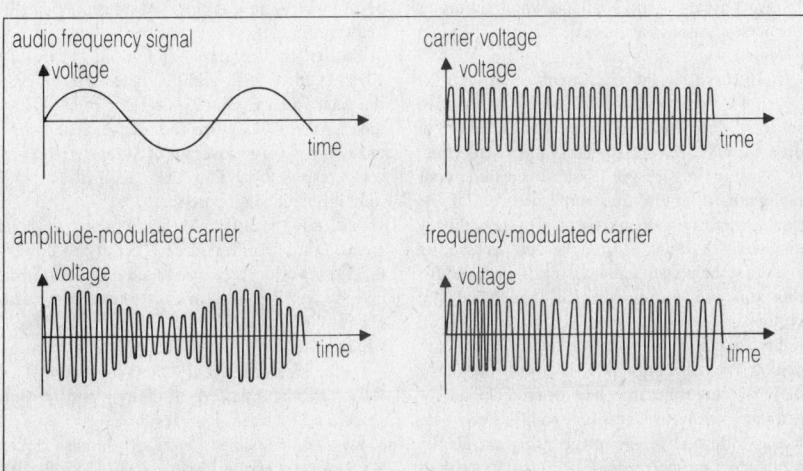

radioactive cobalt-60 (half-life 5.3 years) substance produced by neutron radiation in heavy-water reactors, and used in large sources for gamma rays in cancer therapy, substituting for the much more costly radium.

radioactive decay the process of continuous disintegration undergone by the nuclei of radioactive elements, such as radium and various isotopes of uranium and the transuranic elements. Certain lighter artificially created isotopes also undergo radioactive decay. The associated radiation consists of alpha rays, beta rays, or gamma rays (or a combination of these) and it takes place with a characteristic half-life, which is the time taken for half of any mass of a radioactive isotope to decay completely. The

Reactor waste is of three types: high-level spent fuel, or the residue when nuclear fuel has been removed from a reactor and reprocessed to extract uranium and plutonium; intermediate, which may be long-or short-lived; and low-level, but bulky, waste from reactors, which has only short-lived radioactivity. Disposal, by burial on land or at sea, raises problems of safety, environmental pollution, and security.

radioactivity the spontaneous emission of radiation from the nuclei of atoms of certain substances, termed radioactive. The radiation is of three main types: *alpha rays*, fast-moving particles containing two protons and two neutrons, equivalent to helium nuclei, *beta rays*, fast-moving electrons, and *gamma rays*, high-

radiochemistry the chemical study of radioactive isotopes and their compounds (whether produced from naturally radioactive or irradiated materials) and their use in the study of other chemical processes. When such isotopes are used in labelled compounds, they enable the biochemical functioning of different parts of the living body to be observed, and can help in the testing of new drugs, showing where the drug goes in the body and how long it stays there; they are also important in diagnosis, for example cancer, foetal abnormalities, and heart disease.

radio frequencies and wavelengths classification of. In order to name them it is convenient to group frequencies and wavelengths together in bands, each band referring to waves having similar propagation characteristics, and for which similar techniques are used in the radio terminal equipment. For the internationally agreed radio frequency spectrum, see ◊electromagnetic waves.

radio galaxy a ◊galaxy that is a strong source of electromagnetic waves of radio wavelengths. All galaxies, including our own, emit some radio waves, but radio galaxies are up to a million times more powerful. In many cases the strongest radio emission comes not from the visible galaxy but from two clouds, invisible in an optical telescope, that can extend for millions of light years either side of the galaxy. This double structure at radio wavelengths is also shown by some quasars, suggesting a close relationship between the two types of object. In both cases, the source of energy is thought to be a massive black hole at the centre. Some radio galaxies are thought to result from two galaxies in collision or recently merged. See also ◊radio telescope.

radiography a branch of science concerned with the use of radiation (particularly ◊X-rays) to produce images on photographic film or fluorescent screens. X-rays penetrate matter according to its nature, density, and thickness. In doing so they can cast shadows on photographic film, producing a radiograph. Radiography is widely used in medicine for examining bones and tissues and in industry to check welded seams in pipelines, for example. See also ◊tomography.

radioisotope (radioactive ◊isotope). In physics, a radioactive form of an element. Most natural isotopes of mass below 208 are not radioactive. Most radioisotopes are made by bombarding an ordinary inactive material with neutrons in the core of a nuclear reactor. The radiations given off are easy to detect (hence their use as ◊tracers), can in some instances penetrate substantial thicknesses of materials, and may have profound effects on living matter.

radiometric dating a method of dating rock by assessing the degree of ◊radioactive decay of naturally occurring ◊isotopes. The dating of rocks often uses the gradual decay of uranium into lead. The ratio of the amounts of 'parent' to 'daughter' isotopes in a sample gives a measure of the time it has been decaying, that is, of its age. Once-living matter can often be dated by ◊radiocarbon dating.

radiosonde a balloon carrying a radio transmitter, used to 'sound' or measure conditions in the atmosphere. It carries instruments to measure temperature, pressure, and humidity. A radar target is often attached, allowing it to be tracked.

radio telescope an instrument for detecting radio waves from the ◊Universe. Radio telescopes usually consist of a metal bowl, which collects and focuses radio waves the way a concave mirror collects and focuses light waves. Other radio telescopes are shaped like long troughs, while some consist of simple rod-shaped aerials. Radio telescopes are much larger than optical telescopes, because the wavelengths they are detecting are much longer than the wavelength of light. Even a large dish such as that at ◊Jodrell Bank can see the ◊radio sky less clearly than a small optical telescope sees the visible sky. The largest single radio astronomy dish is 305 m/1,000 ft across, at ◊Arecibo, Puerto Rico.

Interferometry is a technique in which the output from two dishes is combined to give better resolution of detail than with a single dish. *Very long baseline interferometry* (VBLI) uses radio telescopes spread across the world to resolve minute details of radio sources. In *aperture synthesis*, several dishes are linked together to simulate the performance of a very large single dish. This technique was pioneered by Martin ◊Ryle at Cambridge, site of a radio telescope consisting of eight dishes in a line 5 km/3 mi long. The very large array in New Mexico consists of 27 dishes arranged in a Y-shape, which simulates the performance of a single dish 27 km/17 mi in diameter.

radiotherapy the treatment of disease by ◊radiation from X-ray machines or radioactive sources. Radiation reduces the activity of dividing cells and is of especial value for its effect on certain malignant tissues, certain non-malignant tumours, and some diseases of the skin. Generally speaking, the rays of the ordinary diagnostic X-ray machine are not penetrating enough to be very efficient in treatment, and for this purpose more powerful machines are required, operating from 10,000 to over 30 million volts. The lower-voltage machines are similar to conventional X-ray machines; the higher-voltage ones may be of special design, for example, linear accelerators and betatrons.

Much radiation is now given using artificially produced ◊radio isotopes. Radioactive cobalt (symbol Co) is the most useful, as this produces gamma rays (very penetrating), and machines with sources of this material are used instead of very high-energy X-ray machines. Similarly certain radioactive substances may be used by actual administration to patients, for example, radioactive iodine for thyroid disease. In the past much use was made of radium, but this has now been largely supplanted by artificially produced radioactive substances, which are more easily obtainable. Small sources may actually be implanted into the tissue being treated, in an attempt to localize the irradiation.

radish annual herb *Raphanus sativus* family Cruciferae, grown for its fleshy, pungent, edible root, usually reddish, but sometimes white or black.

radium white, luminescent metallic element: symbol Rd, atomic number 88, atomic weight 226.02. It is found in pitchblende in small quantities and in other uranium ores. Radium is used to treat cancer in radiotherapy, and in luminous paints.

Radnorshire /'rædnəʃə/ former border county of Wales, merged with Powys 1974. Presteign was the county town.

Radom /'rɑːdɒm/ industrial city (flour-milling, brewing, tobacco, leather, bicycles, machinery; iron works) in Poland, 96 km/60 mi S of Warsaw; population (1984) 199,000. Radom became Austrian 1795, Russian 1825, and was returned to Poland 1919.

radon radioactive gaseous element: symbol Rn, atomic number 86. One of the inert gases, it is produced from the radioactive decay of radium, thorium and actinium. It is used in ◊radiotherapy as a source of alpha particles.

Raeburn /'reɪbɜːn/ Henry 1756–1823. Scottish portrait painter, who developed a technique of painting with broad brush strokes directly on the canvas without preparatory drawings.

Raeder /'reɪdə/ Erich 1876–1960. German admiral. Chief of Staff in World War I, he became head of the navy in 1928, but was dismissed by Hitler in 1943 because of his failure to prevent Allied Arctic convoys reaching the USSR. Sentenced to life imprisonment at ◊Nuremberg, he was released on grounds of ill health in 1955.

Raffles /'ræfəlz/ Thomas Stamford 1781–1826. British administrator. He entered the East India Company's service in early life, took part in the capture of Java from the Dutch in 1811, and while governor of Sumatra 1818–23 was responsible for the acquisition and foundation of Singapore in 1819.

rafflesia parasitic Malayan plant without stems, family Rafflesiaceae. The largest flowers in the world are produced by *Rafflesia arnoldiana*. About 1 m/3 ft across, they also exude a powerful smell, that of rotting flesh, which attracts the flies which pollinate them.

raga (Sanskrit *rāga* 'tone' or 'colour') in Indian music, a pattern of melody and rhythm associated with religious devotion.

Raglan /'ræglən/ FitzRoy James Henry Somerset, 1st Baron Raglan 1788–1855. British general. In the Peninsular War under Wellington, he was foremost in the storming of ◊Badajoz, and at ◊Waterloo lost his right arm. He commanded the British forces in the ◊Crimea. The *raglan sleeve*, with no shoulder seam but cut right up to the neckline, is named after him.

ragnarök in Norse mythology, the ultimate cataclysmic battle between gods and forces of evil from which a new order will come.

ragtime syncopated music ('ragged time') in two-four rhythm, developed among black American musicians in the late 19th century; it was influenced by folk tradition, the minstrel shows, and the marching bands, and later merged into jazz. Scott ◊Joplin was a leading writer of ragtime pieces, called rags.

Ragusa /rə'guːzə/ town in Sicily, 54 km/34 mi SW of Syracuse; textile industries; population (1981) 64,492. It stands over 450 m/1,500 ft above the river Ragusa, and there are ancient tombs in caves nearby.

Ragusa Italian name (to 1918) for the Yugoslavian town of ◊Dubrovnik. Its English name was *Arrogosa*, from which the word 'argosy' is derived, because of the town's fame for its trading fleets while under Turkish rule in the 16th century.

ragwort perennial plant *Senecio jacobaea*, family ◊Compositae, prolific on waste ground; it has bright yellow flowers and is poisonous.

Rahere /'reɪhɪə/ died 1144. Minstrel and favourite of Henry I of England. In 1123 he founded St Bartholomew's priory and St Bartholomew's hospital in London.

Rahman /'rɑːmən/ Tunku Abdul 1903– . Malaysian politician, the first prime minister of independent Malaya 1957 and of Malaysia 1963–70.
Born at Kuala Keda, the son of the sultan and his sixth wife, a Thai princess, the Tunku studied law at Cambridge University and became a barrister in London. After returning to Malaysia he founded the Alliance party in 1952. The party was successful in the 1955 elections, and the Tunku became prime minister of Malaya on gaining independence in 1957, continuing when Malaya became part of Malaysia in 1963. His principal achievement was an ability to bring together the Malay, Chinese, and Indian peoples within the Alliance party, but in the 1960s he was accused of showing bias towards the Malays. After serious ethnic riots in Kuala Lumpur, the Tunku retired in Jan 1970.

Raikes /reɪks/ Robert 1735–1811. British printer, who started the first ◊Sunday school in Gloucester in 1780, and stimulated weekday voluntary 'ragged schools' for poor children.

rail general name for birds of the family Rallidae, including the ◊corncrake, coots, moorhens, and gallinules.

railway method of transport in which trains convey passengers and goods along a twin rail track. Rails reduce friction, and iron rails were utilized at collieries before the 18th century. The work of the English steam pioneers, ◊Newcomen, ◊Watt, and others, led to the realization of self-propelled steam rail vehicles by ◊Trevithick 1804, Hedley 1813, and ◊Stephenson. Stephenson built the first public steam railway, from Stockton to Darlington, in 1825. Four years later he built the first steam passenger railway, the Liverpool and Manchester line, inaugurating it with his locomotive Rocket, which achieved a speed of 50 kph/30 mph.
The railway building that followed resulted in 250 separate companies in Britain, which resolved into four systems in 1921 and became the nationalized British Railways in 1948, known as British Rail from 1965.
European railways developed quickly during the 19th century, and in the USA and Canada the growth of railways made full exploitation of the central and western territories possible as well as enabling the North to win the American Civil War.

The supremacy of railways in freight and passenger transport was rapidly destroyed after World War II by the growth of car ownership and air services, which took away passenger traffic, and by road haulage, favoured by government policies, which took over in freight. Steam was replaced by electricity and diesel engines. Rising costs meant higher fares and fewer passengers, and declining freight traffic. By 1980 many train services in the UK were under threat of extinction. The *railbus* was developed, consisting of a single-decker bus, longer than a normal bus, but shorter than a railway carriage, and fitted with railway wheels; and the diesel high-speed train (HST) was introduced.
Elsewhere in the world super-fast trains running on specially-built tracks such as the ◊Shinkausen (Japan) and ◊TGV (France) networks offer a superior service. See also ◊maglev and ◊monorail.

rain precipitation in the form of separate drops of water that fall to the Earth's surface from clouds. The drops are formed by the accumulation of droplets that condense from water vapour in the air. The condensation is usually brought about by cooling when the air rises over a mountain range or a cooler air mass.

rainbow colourful arch formed in the sky by the dispersion of light into a ◊spectrum by the action of rain drops. Its cause was discovered by Theodoric of Freiburg in the 14th century. See under ◊meteorology.

rainbow alliance term applied from the mid-1980s to a political grouping of disparate elements who come together to further certain causes they have in common. It is typically used with reference to left-of-centre groups, and often encompasses sections of society that traditionally are politically underrepresented, such as nonwhite ethnic groups. It is a direct translation of French *Arc-en-Ciel*, a name applied in 1984 to an alliance of 20 Euro-MPs from various countries who supported Green environmental policies.

Raine /reɪn/ Kathleen 1908– . British poet. Her volumes of poetry include *Stone and Flower* 1943 and *The Lost Country* 1971 and reflect both the Northumberland landscape of her upbringing and the religious feeling which led

---

RAILWAYS: CHRONOLOGY

1500s Tramways — wooden tracks along which trolleys ran — were in use in mines.

1804 Richard Trevithick in England built the first steam locomotive and ran it on the track at the Pen-y-darren ironworks in South Wales.

1825 George Stephenson built the first public railway to carry steam trains — the Stockton and Darlington line.

1829 Stephenson designed his locomotive *Rocket*, which trounced its rivals at the Rainhill trials.

1830 Stephenson completed the Liverpool and Manchester Railway, the first steam passenger line; the first American-built locomotive, *Best Friend of Charleston*, went into service on the South Carolina Railroad.

1835 Germany pioneered steam railways in Europe, using *Der Adler*, a locomotive built by Stephenson.

1863 The Scotsman Robert Fairlie patented a locomotive with pivoting driving bogies, allowing tight curves in the track (this was later applied particularly in the Garratt locomotives); London opened the world's first underground railway.

1869 The first US transcontinental railway was completed at Promontory, Utah, when the Union Pacific and the Central Pacific Railroads met; George Westinghouse (USA) invented the compressed-air brake.

1879 Werner von Siemens demonstrated an electric train in Germany; Volk's Electric Railway along the Brighton seafront was the world's first public electric railway.

1883 Charles Lartique built the first monorail, in Ireland.

1885 The trans-Canada continental railway was completed, from Montreal in the east to Port Moody in British Columbia in the west.

1890 The first electric underground railway opened in London.

1901 The world's most successful monorail, the Wuppertal Schwebebahn, went into service.

1912 The first diesel locomotive took to the rails in Germany.

1926 The British steam locomotive *Mallard* set a steam rail speed record of 201 kph/125 mph.

1941 Swiss Federal Railways introduced a gas-turbine locomotive.

1964 Japan National Railways inaugurated the 512 km/320 mi New Tokaido line between Osaka and Tokyo, on which ran the 210 kph/130 mph 'bullet' trains.

1973 British Rail's High Speed Train (HST) set a diesel rail speed record of 229 kph/143 mph.

1979 Japan National Railways' maglev test vehicle ML-500 attained a speed of 517 kph/321 mph.

1981 France's TGV superfast trains began operation between Paris and Lyons, regularly attaining a peak speed of 270 kph/168 mph.

Railway (Top left) 2ft 6in gauge Baldwin 4-6-0 No 38, built 1911, at Sao Joao, Brazil. (Above left) 3ft 6in gauge Baldwin 2-8-0 No 53, built in 1953, at Sibambe on the Guayaquil & Quito Railway, Ecuador. (Top right) Modern Chinese steam power: QJ 2-10-2 No 1397 at Tangshan. (Above right) General Motors diesel at Lima, Peru. (Below left) Two views of the Japanese Shinkansen trains which operate the Tokaido line. (Below right) The French TGV which since 1981 has revolutionized services from Paris to Lyons and Geneva.

her to the Roman Catholic Church in 1944. She has written volumes of autobiography.

Rainier /rə'nɪə/ mountain in the ◊Cascade Range, Washington State, USA; 4,392 m/14,408 ft, crowned by 14 glaciers and carrying dense forests on its slopes. It is a quiescent volcano. Mount Rainier national park was dedicated 1899.

Rainier III /'reɪnɪeɪ/ 1923– . Prince of ◊Monaco from 1949.

Rais /reɪ/ Gilles de 1404–1440. French marshal who fought alongside ◊Joan of Arc. In 1440 he was hanged for the torture and murder of 140 children, but the court proceedings were irregular. He is the historical basis of the ◊Bluebeard character.

raisin a dried grape; the chief kinds are the common raisin, the sultana or seedless raisin, and the currant. They are produced in the Mediterranean area, California, and Australia.

Rajasthan /ˌrɑːdʒə'stɑːn/ state of NW India
area 342,214 sq km/131,995 sq mi
capital Jaipur
features includes the larger part of the ◊Thar Desert, where India's first nuclear test was carried out
population (1981) 34,262,000
language Rajasthani, Hindi
religion Hindu 90%, Muslim 3%
history formed 1948, enlarged 1956.

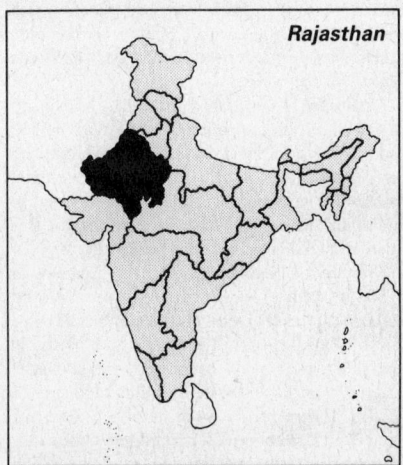

Rajasthan

Rajneesh meditation a form of meditation based on the teachings of Bhagwan Shree Rajneesh, who established an ashram or religious community in Poona, NW India, in the early 1970s. In 1981 the Bhagwan moved his ashram to Oregon, USA. Followers of the Bhagwan wear red or orange and are not expected to observe any specific prohibitions. They are encouraged to live in large groups.

Rajput /'rɑːdʒpʊt/ high-caste Hindus of India, predominantly soldiers and landowners. They are widespread over N India. The Rajput states of W India are now merged in Rajasthan. The Rana family (ruling aristocracy of Nepál until 1951) is also Rajput.

Raleigh /'rɔːli/ industrial city (food processing, electrical machinery, textiles),

capital of North Carolina, USA; population (1980) 148,000.

Raleigh /'rɔːli/ or *Ralegh* Walter c. 1552–1618. English adventurer, born in Devon. A favourite of ◊Elizabeth I, he was knighted in 1584, and made several attempts 1584–87 to establish a colony in 'Virginia' (now ◊North Carolina). In 1595 he led an expedition to South America (described in his *Discovery of Guiana*) and distinguished himself in expeditions against the Spaniards in ◊Cadiz in 1596 and the ◊Azores in 1597. After ◊James I's accession in 1603 he was condemned to death on a charge of conspiracy, but was reprieved and imprisoned in the Tower of London, where he wrote his unfinished *History of the World*. Released in 1616 to lead a gold-seeking expedition to the ◊Orinoco, which failed disastrously, he was beheaded on his return under his former sentence.

Raleigh, Fort /'rɔːli/ site of the first English settlement in America, at the N end of Roanoke Island, North Carolina, USA, to which in 1585 Sir Walter ◊Raleigh sent 108 colonists from Plymouth, England, under his cousin Sir Richard ◊Grenville. In 1586 Sir Francis ◊Drake took the dissatisfied survivors back to England.

RAM (random-access memory) an electronic ◊memory device that can be written to and erased by a computer; a computer's internal memory. RAM comes in the form of ◊integrated circuits (chips), usually with an information-handling system in multiples of 256 kilobits representing 32,000 or so characters. The size of RAM defines a computer's internal memory capacity. A modern microcomputer will have up to 4 Mb (megabytes, or million bytes) of RAM. Unlike ROM (read-only memory), RAM is volatile; it is erased when the machine is switched off.

Rama incarnation of ◊Vishnu, the supreme spirit of Hinduism.

Ramadan the ninth month of the Muslim year. Throughout Ramadan a strict fast is observed during the hours of daylight.

Raman /'rɑːmən/ Venkata 1888–1970. Indian physicist who in 1928 discovered what became known as the Raman effect: the scattering of monochromatic light when passed through a transparent substance. He was awarded a Nobel prize in 1930.

Ramat Gan /'rɑːmɑːt gɑːn/ industrial city (textiles, food processing) in W Israel, NE of Tel Aviv; population (1983) 117,000.

Ramayana /rɑː'maɪənə/ Sanskrit epic c. 300 BC, in which Rama, an incarnation of the god ◊Vishnu and his friend Hanuman (the monkey chieftain) strive to recover Rama's wife, Sita, abducted by demon king Ravana.

Rambert /'rɒmbeə/ Marie (born Cyvia Rambam) 1888–1982. British (from 1918) ballet dancer and teacher, born in Warsaw. She was with the Diaghilev ballet 1912–13, opened the Rambert School in 1920, and in 1926 founded the *Ballet Rambert* which she directed (renamed Rambert Dance Company 1987). She was created Dame Commander of the Order of the British Empire 1962.

Rambert As teacher and promoter to many leading dancers, choreographers, and stage designers, Marie Rambert was one of modern ballet's most influential figures.

Ramblers' Association society founded in Britain in 1935 to conserve the countryside and ensure that footpaths remained open. From 1985 it also campaigned for access to areas beyond the footpath network, for example, many moors and woods.

Rambouillet /ˌrɒmbu:'jeɪ/ town in the S of the forest of Rambouillet, SW of Paris, France; population (1985) 22,500. The former royal château is now the presidential summer residence. A breed of fine-woolled sheep is named after the town.

Rambouillet /ˌrɒmbu:'jeɪ/ Catherine de Vivonne, Marquise de 1588–1665. French society woman, whose salon at the Hôtel de Rambouillet in Paris included Descartes, La Rochefoucauld, and Mme de Sévigné.

Rameau /ræ'məʊ/ Jean-Philippe 1683–1764. French organist and composer. He wrote an influential *Treatise on Harmony* 1722 and his works include keyboard and vocal music and many operas, such as *Castor and Pollux* 1737.

Rameses /'ræmɪsiːz/ eleven kings of ancient Egypt, including:

Rameses II /'ræmɪsiːz/ king of Egypt c. 1300–1225 BC. The son of ◊Seti I, he campaigned successfully against the ◊Hittites, and built two rock temples at ◊Abu Simbel in Upper Egypt (the larger commemorates himself and the other his wife ◊Nefertari).

Rameses III /'ræmɪsiːz/ king of Egypt c. 1200–1168 BC. He won a naval victory over the ◊Philistines and other peoples, and asserted his suzerainty over ◊Palestine.

Ramillies /'ræmɪliz/ scene of ◊Marlborough's victory over the French on 23 May 1706, during the War of the ◊Spanish Succession, at a village in Brabant, Belgium.

ram jet a simple kind of ◊jet engine used in some guided missiles. It only comes into operation at high speeds. Then air is 'rammed'

Rameses II The entrance to the temple of Rameses II at Abu Simbel, before its removal to safety (in sections) above the flood waters of the Aswan Dam. The four colossi represent the king wearing the double crown of Egypt. Beneath the king's knees are figures of Queen Nefertari and some of the royal children.

into the combustion chamber, into which fuel is sprayed and ignited.

Ram Mohun Roy /'rɑːm 'məuhʊn 'rɔɪ/ 1774–1833. Indian religious reformer, founder 1830 of ◊Brahma Samaj, Indian mystic cult.

Ramphal /'ræmfɑːl/ Shridath Surendranath ('Sonny') 1928– . Guyanese politician. He studied at the University of London and Harvard Law School, and was minister of foreign affairs and justice in Guyana 1972–75. He became secretary-general of the Commonwealth in 1975.

Ramsay /'ræmzi/ Allan 1686–1758. Scottish poet, born in Lanarkshire. He became a wig-maker and then a bookseller in Edinburgh. He published *The Tea-Table Miscellany* 1724–37, and *The Evergreen* 1724, collections of ancient and modern Scottish song including revivals of the work of such poets as ◊Dunbar and ◊Henryson.

Ramsay /'ræmzi/ Allan 1713–1784. Scottish portrait painter, son of the poet Allan ◊Ramsay. A successful portraitist in London, noted for his studies of women, he became painter to King George III in 1760.

Ramsay /'ræmzi/ William 1852–1916. British chemist who together with Lord ◊Rayleigh discovered argon in 1894. In 1895 Ramsay manufactured helium, and in 1898, in cooperation with Morris Travers, identified neon, krypton, and xenon. With Frederick ◊Soddy he noted the transmutation of radium into helium in 1903, which led to the discovery of the density and atomic weight of radium. He received a Nobel prize in 1904.

Ramsgate /'ræmzgeɪt/ seaside resort and cross-Channel port in the Isle of Thanet, Kent, England; population (1981) 39,642. There is a maritime museum. The architect ◊Pugin built a home there.

Rance /rɑːns/ river in Brittany, France, flowing into the English Channel between Dinard and St Malo, where a dam built 1960–67

Ramsay After returning from study in Italy, the Scottish artist Allan Ramsay became a favourite of George III, and a member of Dr Johnson's circle. In his later years, he gave up painting for writing. The picture is a self-portrait, c. 1739.

(with a lock for ships) uses the 13 m/44 ft tides to feed a tidal power station.

Rand /rænd/ an abbreviation for the Witwatersrand, a gold-bearing ridge in Transvaal, South Africa, extending for about 65 km/40 mi W and E of Johannesburg. Gold was first found there in 1854.

rand the basic unit of South Africa's decimal currency from 1961.

Rand /rænd/ Ayn, adopted name of Alice Rosenbaum 1905–1982. US novelist of Russian origin. Her best-known novel, *The Fountainhead* 1943, displays her influential blend of virulent anti-communism and fervent belief in individual enterprise.

Rangoon /ˌrænˈguːn/ capital and chief port of Burma, on the Rangoon river, 32 km/20 mi from the Indian Ocean; university 1920; population (1983) 2,500,000. The golden Shwe Dagon pagoda, according to tradition built 585 BC, is a centre of pilgrimage for Burmese Buddhists.
history A city called Dagon was founded on the site 746 AD; it was given the name Rangoon (meaning 'end of conflict') by King Alaungpaya when he made it his capital, 1755. The ◊East India Company set up a factory 1790 in Rangoon, and the city was captured by the British 1852. It was occupied by Japan in World War II.

Ranjit Singh /'rændʒɪt 'sɪŋ/ 1780–1839. Indian maharajah. He succeeded his father as a minor Sikh leader in 1792, and created a Sikh army which conquered Kashmir and the Punjab. In alliance with the British, he established himself as 'Lion of the Punjab', ruler of the strongest of the native Indian states.

Ransom /'rænsəm/ John Crowe 1888–1974. American poet. His volumes of romantic but anti-rhetorical verse include *Poems about God* 1919, and *Two Gentlemen in Bonds* 1926.

Ransome /'rænsəm/ Arthur 1884–1967. British writer. Once a journalist – he was correspondent in Russia for the *Daily News* during World War I and the Revolution – he is best known for his adventure stories for children, such as *Swallows and Amazons* 1930.

Rao /rau/ Raja 1909– . Indian writer. He studied in France. He wrote about Indian independence from the perspective of a village in S India in *Kanthapura* 1938 and later, in *The Serpent and the Rope* 1960, about a young cosmopolitan intellectual seeking enlightenment.

Rapallo /rəˈpæləu/ port and winter resort in NW Italy, 24 km/15 mi SE of Genoa on the Gulf of Rapallo; population (1971) 27,000. Treaties were signed here 1920 (settling the common frontiers of Italy and Yugoslavia) and 1922 (cancelling German and Russian counter-claims for indemnities for World War I).

Rapa Nui /'rɑːpə 'nuːi/ another name for ◊Easter Island, an island in the Pacific.

rape sexual intercourse with a woman without her consent. From 1976 in Britain the victim's name may not be published, her sex history should not be in question, and her 'absence of consent' rather than (as previously required) proof of her 'resistance to violence' is the criterion of the crime. The anonymity of the accused is also preserved unless he is convicted.

rape two plant species, *Brassica rapa* and *Brassica napus*, grown for their seeds, which yield the pungent mustard rape oil. The common turnip is a variety of the former, and the swede turnip of the latter.

Raphael Sanzio /'ræfeɪəl 'sænziəu/ 1483–1520. Italian painter. Born at Urbino, the son of Giovanni Santi, a court painter, he studied under his father, and in 1499 went to Perugia, where he entered the studio of Perugino. In 1504–08 he was in Florence. Paintings of this period include the *St Catherine* and the *Ansidei Madonna* in the National Gallery, London. In 1508 he went to Rome where he was employed by Pope Julius II to redecorate a number of rooms in the Vatican. From then on he and his studio painted a great many works – frescoes and easel pictures. Perhaps less highly valued today than in the 19th century, when he was praised for achieving perfection of form and colour, he ranks nonetheless as one of the greatest High Renaissance masters, whose work influenced a whole generation of succeeding painters.

Rapid Deployment Force a military strike force established by the USA in 1979; headquarters Fort McDill, Tampa, Florida. From 1983, as the US Central Command, its potential operation area covers: Afghanistan, Arabia, Egypt, Ethiopia, Iran, Iraq, Jordan, Kenya, Pakistan, Somalia, Sudan, and the Red Sea and Arabian Gulf.

rap music a rapid, rhythmic chant performed over a prerecorded backing track. See also ◊hip-hop.

rare earth oxide of elements of the lanthanide series. They are found only in certain rare minerals. Sometimes also used for the lanthanide elements themselves.

rare gas another name for inert gas.

Raphael Sanzio The *Madonna della Sedia/Virgin of the Armchair* (Florence, Pitti Palace) by Raphael.

Ras al Khaimah /'ræs æl 'xaɪmə/ an emirate on the Persian Gulf, a member of the ◊United Arab Emirates.

raspberry prickly cane-plant *Rubus idaeus* of the Rosaceae family with white flowers followed by red or white fruits. These are used for jam and wine.

Rasputin /ræs'pjuːtɪn/ Gregory Efimovich 1871–1916. Siberian wandering 'holy man', the illiterate son of a poor peasant. He acquired great influence over the tsarina, wife of ◊Nicholas II, because of her faith in his power to cure her son the tsarevitch of his ◊haemophilia. The control he exercised through the tsarina over political and ecclesiastical appointments, and his notorious debauchery (the nickname Rasputin means 'dissolute') created a scandal which did much to discredit the monarchy. He was murdered by a group of nobles, who (when poison had no effect) dumped him in the river Neva after shooting him.

Rastafarianism religion originating in the West Indies, based on the ideas of Marcus ◊Garvey, who preached that the only way for black people to escape their poverty and oppression was to return to Africa. When Haile Selassie (Ras Tafari, the Lion of Judah) was crowned emperor of Ethiopia in 1930, this was seen as a fulfilment of prophecy, and Rastafarians acknowledged him as the Messiah, the incarnation of God (Jah). Rastafarians

identify themselves with the Chosen People, the Israelites, of the Bible: Ethiopia is seen as the promised land, while all countries outside Africa, and their cultures and institutions, are 'Babylon', the place of exile. Rastafarians use a distinct language, in particular using the term 'I and I' for 'we' to stress unity. Many Rastafarians do not cut their hair, because of Biblical injunctions against this, but wear their hair in long dreadlocks, often covered in woollen hats in the Rastafarian colours of red, green, and gold. Food laws are very strict: for example, no pork or shellfish, no salt, milk, or coffee. The term 'I-tal' is used for food as close as possible to its natural state. Medicines should be made from natural herbs, and the use of ganja (marijuana) is seen as a sacrament. There are no churches, but meetings are held regularly for prayer, discussion, and celebration, and at intervals there is a very large meeting or Nyabingi. There are currently about one million Rastafarians.

Rastatt, Treaty of (1714). See Treaty of ◊Utrecht.

rat name given to various large rodents, particularly the large members of the family Muridae. The brown rat *Rattus norvegicus* is about 200 mm/8 in with a tail of almost equal length. It frequents sewers, docks, and warehouses, and in the country hedges, ricks, granaries, and other food stores. Brown rats also infest ships, by which they have been spread over

the world. The black rat *Rattus rattus* is smaller than the brown rat, by which it has largely been replaced in Britain. Some black rats are still found in docks and on ships. They do not interbreed with the brown rats. See ◊plague.

rates in the UK, tax levied on residential, industrial, and commercial property by local authorities to cover their expenditure. (See ◊county council, ◊local government.) Rebates are given to ratepayers whose income falls below a certain level. The Thatcher government limited the level of rate that could be levied (*ratecapping*), and plans by 1990 to replace the rate with a *community charge* or ◊poll tax on each individual.

rate support grant an amount of money made available annually by central government in Britain to supplement rates as a source of income for local government. Already in the 19th century the government was giving such help – by 1888 grants accounted for 14 per cent of local revenue – and in 1929 the system was formalized, a block grant replacing various specific grants. This was slightly modified in 1948 (exchequer equalization grant) and 1958 (rate deficiency grant), and in 1967 the rate support grant was introduced, consisting of (1) a resources element, giving help to local authorities with small resources; (2) a needs element, based on population size; and (3) a domestic element, to reimburse local authorities for rate reductions for domestic ratepayers. Under the Conservative government 1979– the system has been used as a method of curbing local-authority spending by reducing or withholding the grant.

Rathenau /'rɑːtənau/ Emil 1867–1922. German politician. A leading industrialist, he was appointed economic director during World War I and developed a system of economic planning in combination with capitalism. After the war he founded the Democratic Party, and became foreign minister 1922. He signed the Rapallo Treaty of friendship with Russia in 1922, and soon after was murdered by right-wing fanatics.

Rathlin /'ræθlɪn/ island off the N Irish coast, in Antrim. St ◊Columba founded a church there in the 6th century, and in 1306 Robert ◊Bruce hid there after his defeat by the English at Methven.

rationalism in theology, the belief that human reason rather than divine revelation is the correct means of ascertaining truth and regulating behaviour. In philosophy, rationalism takes the view that self-evident propositions deduced by reason are the sole basis of all knowledge (disregarding experience of the senses). The Rationalist movement arose in Germany in the 18th century (see ◊Leibniz) following on from ◊Descartes and ◊Spinoza and others and had an impact all over Europe in the 18th and 19th centuries, extending to the USA. It is frequently contrasted with ◊empiricism.

rationalized units units for which the defining equations conform to the geometry of the system. Equations involving circular symmetry contain the factor 2ρ, those involving spherical symmety 4ρ. ◊SI units are rationalized, ◊c.g.s. units are not.

rational number in mathematics, any ◊number that can be expressed as an exact fraction (with a denominator not equal to 0) or decimal fraction (including recurring ones). For example 2, 3.3, 4, and ¼ are all rational numbers, whereas π (= 3.141592...) is not. Numbers such as π are called ◊irrational numbers.

Ratisbon /'rætɪzbɒn/ English name for the West German city of ◊Regensburg.

ratite bird with a breastbone without the keel to which flight muscles are attached, for example, ostrich, rhea, emu, cassowary, and kiwi. See ◊running birds.

rat-tail type of bony fish, also known as *grenadier*, of the family Macrouridae. They have stout heads and bodies and long tapering tails, and are common living on the sea floor in deep water on the continental slopes. Many have a light-emitting organ in front of the anus. Also known as rat-tails are some of the ◊chimaeras.

Rattigan /'rætɪgən/ Terence 1911–1977. British naturalistic playwright of the middle classes. His work ranged from the comedy *French Without Tears* 1936 to *The Browning Version* 1948 (dealing with a failed schoolmaster and a failed marriage). Knighted 1971.

Rattle /'rætl/ Simon 1955– . British conductor, principal conductor of the City of Birmingham Symphony Orchestra from 1980, noted for interpretations of Mahler and Sibelius.

Rattle British conductor Simon Rattle listens to the sound of the Birmingham Symphony Orchestra.

rattlesnake snake of the North American genus *Crotalus*, and related genera, distinguished by the horny flat rings of the tail, which rattle when vibrated. The venom injected by some rattlesnakes can be fatal.

Rau /rau/ Johannes 1931– . West German socialist politician, member of the Social Democratic Party (SPD).
The son of a Protestant pastor, Rau began work as a salesman for a church publishing company before joining the SPD. He became state premier of North Rhine–Westphalia in 1978.

Raunkiaer system of classification a scheme devised by the Danish ecologist Christen Raunkiaer (1860–1938) whereby plants are divided into groups according to the position of their ◊perennating buds in relation to the soil surface. For example, plants growing in cold areas, such as the tundra, generally have their buds protected below ground, whereas in hot, tropical areas they are above ground and freely exposed. This method of plant classification is useful for comparing vegetation types in different parts of the world. The main divisions are phanerophytes with buds situated well above the ground, chamaephytes with buds borne within 25 cm/10 in of the soil surface, hemicryptophytes with buds at or immediately below the soil surface, and cryptophytes with their buds either beneath the soil (*geophyte*) or below water (*hydrophyte*).

Ravel /ræ'vel/ (Joseph) Maurice 1875–1937. French composer. His work is noted for its sensuousness, unresolved dissonances, and 'tone colour', as in the piano pieces *Pavane pour une infante défunte* 1899 and *Jeux d'eau* 1901, and the ballets *Daphnis et Chloë* 1912 and *Boléro* 1928.

raven bird *Corvus corax* of the crow family. About 60 cm/2 ft long, the raven has black and lustrous plumage. Found only in the northern hemisphere, it is rare in Britain, breeding chiefly in N Scotland.

Ravenna /rə'venə/ historical city and industrial port (petrochemical works) in Emilia-Romagna, Italy; population (1981) 138,034. It lies in a marshy plain and is known for its Byzantine churches with superb mosaics.
history Ravenna was a Roman port and naval station, and capital of the W Roman emperors 404–93; of ◊Theodoric 493–526; and later of the Byzantine exarchs (bishops) 539–750.

Ravi /'rɑːvi/ river in the Indian subcontinent, a tributary of the ◊Indus. It rises in India, forms the boundary between India and Pakistan for some 95 km/70 mi, and enters Pakistan above Lahore, the chief town on its 725 km/450 mi course.

Rawalpindi /rɔːl'pɪndi/ city in Pakistan, in the foothills of the Himalayas; population (1981) 928,400. It was capital of Pakistan 1959–67, pending the construction of ◊Islamabad to the NW.

Rawlinson /'rɔːlɪnsən/ Henry Creswicke 1810–1895. British orientalist, political agent in Baghdad from 1844. He deciphered the Babylonian and Old Persian scripts of ◊Darius's trilingual inscription at Behistun, continued the excavation work of ◊Layard, and published a *History of Assyria* 1852.

Rawls /rɔːlz/ John 1921– . American philosopher, who revived in his *A Theory of Justice* 1971 the concept of the '◊social contract', and its enforcement by civil disobedience.

Rawsthorne /'rɔːsθɔːn/ Alan 1905–1971. British composer. He first became known for his *Theme and Variations* for two violins 1938, followed by other tersely energetic works.

ray cartilaginous fish with a flattened body, wing-like pectoral fins, and a tail like a whip, for example the stingrays, which have a serrate, poisonous spine on the tail, and the ◊torpedo fish.

Ray /reɪ/ John 1627–1705. British naturalist who devised a classification system accounting for nearly 18,000 plant species. It was the first to divide flowering plants into ◊monocotyledons and ◊dicotyledons, with additional divisions made on the basis of leaf and flower characters and fruit types.

Ray /reɪ/ Satyajit 1921– . Indian film director, noted for his trilogy of life in his native Bengal: *Pather Panchali, Unvanquished*, and *The World of Apu* 1955–59. Later films include *The Chess Players* 1977.

Rayleigh /'reɪli/ John W Strutt, 3rd Baron Rayleigh 1842–1919. British physicist who wrote the standard *Treatise on Sound*, experimented in optics and microscopy, and, with Sir William Ramsay, discovered argon.
He was awarded the Order of Merit, and became chancellor of Cambridge University. In 1904 he received a Nobel prize.

rayon artificial silk made from ◊cellulose. The most common type is ◊viscose.

razorbill resident British seabird *Alca torda*, of the auk family, which breeds on cliffs. It has a curved beak, and is black above and white below.

razorshell or *razor-fish*. Genera *Ensis* and *Solen* of bivalve molluscs, with narrow elongated shells, resembling an old-fashioned razor handle and delicately coloured. They are found in sand among rocks.

reaction principle principle first stated by ◊Newton as his third law of motion: to every action, there is an equal and opposite reaction. This means that a force acting in one direction is always accompanied by an equal force acting in the opposite direction. This explains how ◊jet and rocket propulsion works, and why a gun recoils after firing.

Reade /riːd/ Charles 1814–1884. British writer, best known for his historical novel *The Cloister and the Hearth* 1861.

Reading /'redɪŋ/ industrial town (biscuits, electronics) on the river Thames, administrative headquarters of Berkshire, England; university 1892; population (1985) 138,000. Oscar ◊Wilde spent two years in Reading jail.

Reading /'redɪŋ/ industrial city (textiles, special steels) in Pennsylvania, USA; population (1980) 78,686.

Reagan /'reɪgən/ Ronald 1911– . US Republican president from 1981. A former actor, Reagan was governor of California 1966–74. As president, Reagan has reduced state intervention, introduced deregulation of domestic markets, increased spending on defence, and maintained a firm foreign policy.
Reagan was born in Illinois, the son of an Irish immigrant shoe salesman who was bankrupted during the Depression. He became a Hollywood actor in 1937 and appeared in 50 films, including *Bedtime for Bonzo* 1951 and *The Killers* 1964. As president of the Screen Actors' Guild 1947–52, he became a conservative. He joined the Republican Party in 1962 and was governor of California 1966–74, a term marked by battles against insurgent students.
Having lost the Republican presidential nomination in 1968 and 1976 to Nixon and Ford, Reagan won it in 1980 and defeated President

Carter. He reduced taxes and social services, and increased the national budget deficit to record levels. He was wounded in an assassination attempt in 1981. The invasion of Grenada 1983 generated a revival of national patriotism, and Reagan was re-elected by a landslide in 1984. His insistence on militarizing space through the ◊Strategic Defense Initiative, popularly called Star Wars, prevented a disarmament agreement when he met the Soviet leader ◊Gorbachev in 1985 and 1986, but a 4 per cent reduction in nuclear weapons was agreed 1987. The extent of Reagan's interventionist policy in Central America was not revealed until in 1987 he was implicated in swapping guns for hostages with Iran and using the profits surreptitiously to fund Contra guerrilla forces in ◊Nicaragua (see ◊Irangate).

realism in medieval philosophy known as ◊scholasticism, the theory that the only truly real things are 'universals'; it is thus opposed to ◊nominalism. In modern philosophy the term stands for the doctrine that there is an intuitively appreciated reality apart from what is presented to the consciousness, that what is experienced through the senses has an independent existence. As such it is opposed to ◊idealism. Modern realists include C D ◊Broad and (although their views were later modified) ◊Russell and G E ◊Moore; ◊Wittgenstein has been an important later influence. In the arts, realism refers to a style of depicting life as we know it in everyday experience, as opposed to romanticism (an idealized portrayal), or to abstract or formalized representation.

real number in mathematics, any ◊rational or ◊irrational number. Real numbers exclude ◊imaginary numbers, found in ◊complex numbers of the general form $a + bi$ where $i = -1$, although these do include a real component a.

Realpolitik (German 'politics of realism') term coined in 1853 to describe ◊Bismarck's policies during the 1848 revolutions: the pragmatic pursuit of self-interest and power, backed up by force when necessary.

real presence the belief that there are present in the properly consecrated Eucharist the body and blood of Jesus Christ. It is held by Roman Catholics, and in some sense by Anglo-Catholics.

real-time system in computing and information technology, a program that responds to events in the world as they happen, as, for example, an automatic pilot program in an aircraft must respond instantly to correct course deviations. Programs in process control, robotics, airline reservation, games, and many military applications are all dependent on a real-time system.

recall a process by which voters can demand the dismissal from office of elected officials, as in some states of the USA.

Récamier /ˌreɪkæm'jeɪ/ Jeanne Françoise 1777–1849. French socialite, born in Lyons. She married at 15 Jacques Récamier, an elderly banker. She held a salon of literary and political celebrities.

received pronunciation (RP) see ◊English language.

receptacle the enlarged end of a flower stalk to which the floral parts are attached. Normally the receptacle is rounded but in some plants it is flattened or cup-shaped. The term is also used for the region on the thallus of some seaweeds that becomes swollen at certain times of the year and bears the reproductive organs.

recession in economics, a depression in business activity and consequently in prosperity.

recessivity in genetics, in a ◊diploid organism, a recessive ◊allele is one that can only produce a detectable effect on the ◊phenotype of the organism bearing it when both chromosomes carry it, that is, when the same allele has been inherited from both parents, and the individual is ◊homozygous for it. In ◊heterozygous individuals, its effects will be masked by a dominant allele; see ◊dominance.

Recife /re'siːfə/ industrial seaport (cotton textiles, sugar refining, fruit canning, flour milling) and naval base in Brazil, capital of Pernambuco state, at the mouth of the river Capibaribe; university 1946; population (1980) 1,184,215. It was founded 1504.

reciprocal in mathematics, of a quantity, that quantity divided into 1. Thus the reciprocal of 2 is $1/2 (= 0.5)$; of 150 is $1/150 (= 0.00666666...)$; of x^2 is $1/x^2$ or x^{-2}.

recitative speech-like declamation of narrative episodes in opera.

Recklinghausen /ˈreklɪŋˌhauzən/ industrial town (coal, iron, chemicals, textiles, engineering) in North Rhine–Westphalia, West Germany, 24 km/15 mi NW of Dortmund; population (1984) 118,500. It is said to have been founded by Charlemagne.

recombination in genetics, any process which recombines or 'shuffles' the genetic material, so increasing genetic variation in the offspring. The two main processes of recombination are ◊crossing over (in which chromosome pairs exchange segments), and the random reassortment of the chromosomes that occurs during ◊meiosis, when each gamete (sperm or egg) receives only one of each chromosome pair.

reconstruction in US history, term used for the period (1865–77) after the ◊Civil War during which the nation was reunited under the federal government after the defeat of the Southern Confederacy. Reconstruction acts, giving blacks civil rights, were enforced by federal troops under the Republican Party.

record in computing, an item of data stored in a ◊file of information.

recorder in the English legal system, a part-time judge who may sit alone or, in specified circumstances, with justices of the peace, to exercise jurisdiction in the crown courts in less serious cases. They are chosen from barristers of standing and also, since the Courts Act of 1971, from solicitors. Recorders may eventually become circuit judges.

recorder in music, an instrument of the ◊woodwind family, blown through one end, in which different notes are obtained by covering the holes in the instrument. It was a concert instrument until about the 18th century, when it was largely replaced by the flute, although it has

been revived in the 20th century for teaching children and for performing early music.

Record Office, Public a government office containing the English national records since the Norman Conquest, brought together from courts of law and government departments, including the Domesday Book, the Gunpowder Plot papers, and the log of HMS *Victory* at Trafalgar. It was established in 1838 in Chancery Lane, London; modern records from the 18th century on have been housed at Kew from 1976.

record player device for reproducing sound recorded, usually in a spiral groove on a disc or record. A motor-driven turntable rotates the record at a constant speed, and a stylus or needle on the head of a pick-up is made to vibrate by the undulations in the record groove. These vibrations are then converted to electrical signals by a ◊transducer in the head (often a ◊piezoelectric crystal). After amplification, the signals pass to one or more loudspeakers which convert them into sound.

The pioneers of the record player were ◊Edison, with his ◊phonograph, and Emile ◊Berliner, who invented the disc record 1896. More recent developments are stereophonic sound and digital recording on compact disc. In digital recording the signals picked up by the microphone are converted into precise numerical values by computer. These values, which represent the original sound wave form exactly, are recorded on compact disc. When it is played back by ◊laser, the exact values are retrieved. When fed via an amplifier to a loudspeaker, sound waves exactly like the original ones are recreated. See also ◊hi-fi.

rectangle a quadrilateral (four-sided figure) with opposite sides equal and parallel, and with right angles (90°) as the internal angles. A rectangle is a special case of a ◊parallelogram. The diagonals of a rectangle bisect each other. Its area A is the product of the length l and breadth b; that is, $A = l \times b$. A rectangle with all four sides equal is a ◊square.

rectifier device for obtaining one-directional current from an alternating source of supply, either by inversion of or suppression of alternate half-waves. Rectifiers are necessary in the conversion of AC (◊alternating current) supply to DC (direct current). The many different types (such as plate rectifiers, thermionic ◊diodes, and ◊semiconductor diodes) depend on being able to pass current in one direction but not in the reverse direction.

rector Anglican priest, formerly entitled to the whole of the ◊tithes levied in the parish, as against a *vicar* (Latin 'deputy') who was only entitled to part.

rectum the lowest part of the digestive tract of animals, which stores faeces prior to elimination (defecation).

recycling the reclamation of potentially useful material from household and industrial waste, thus reducing pollution, saving expenditure on scarce raw materials, and slowing down the depletion of non-renewable resources. Also, the investment by oil-producing nations of surplus funds in the industries of oil-importing

recycling At Winterhaven, Florida, USA, the landscape is covered with scrap motor cars, stockpiled before being stripped down, crushed, and recycled.

nations, so rectifying the shortfall in their profit-and-loss accounts.

red informal term for a leftist, revolutionary, or communist, which originated in the 19th century in the form 'red republican', meaning a republican who favoured a social as well as a political revolution, generally by armed violence. Red is the colour adopted by socialist parties throughout the world for flags and symbols.

Red Army former title of the army of the USSR. It developed from the Red Guards, volunteers who carried out the Bolshevik revolution, and received its name because it fought under the ◊red flag. Officially renamed the Soviet Army in 1946. The Chinese revolutionary army was also called the Red Army.

Redbridge /'redbrɪdʒ/ borough of NE Greater London, including Ilford, Wanstead, and Woodford, and parts of Chigwell and Dagenham
features part of ◊Epping Forest; ◊Hainault Forest
population (1981) 225,300.

red brigades extreme left-wing guerrilla groups active in Italy during the 1970s and early 1980s. They were implicated in many kidnappings and killings, including that of Christian Democrat leader Aldo Moro in 1978.

Red Cross, the international agency founded to assist wounded and prisoners in war. Prompted by war horrors described by the Swiss Henri ◊Dunant, the Geneva Convention of 1864 laid down the principles ensuring the safety of ambulances, hospitals, stores, and personnel distinguished by the emblem of the red Geneva Cross on a white ground. The British Red Cross Society was founded in 1870, and incorporated in 1908. In addition to dealing with associated problems of war, such as refugees and the care of the disabled, the Red Cross is increasingly concerned with the disasters of peace – epidemics, floods, earthquakes, and accidents. The American National Red Cross was founded 1881. The Moslem equivalent is the Red Crescent.

Redding /'redɪŋ/ Otis 1941–1967. US soul singer and songwriter. He had a number of hits in the mid-1960s, but his biggest hit, 'Dock of the Bay' 1968, was released after his death in a plane crash.

Redditch /'redɪtʃ/ industrial town (needles, fishing tackle, car and aircraft components, cycles, motorcycles, electrical equipment) in Hereford and Worcester, England; population (1981) 66,854. Developed from 1965 as a new town to take Birmingham's overspill.

Red Duster colloquial name for the Red Ensign, flag of the British merchant navy. First used in 1674, it was shared with the Royal Navy until 1864, when it became the exclusive symbol of merchant ships. See under ◊flag.

red dwarf a small, cool, faint ◊star. A typical red dwarf has a mass and diameter about one-tenth that of the Sun. Although red dwarfs are small, they are the longest-lived of all stars, because they burn very slowly. They have estimated lifetimes of 100,000 million years. Red dwarfs may be the most abundant type of star, but they are difficult to see because they are so faint. Two of the closest stars to the Sun, ◊Proxima Centauri and ◊Barnard's Star, are red dwarfs.

red flag the international symbol of socialism. In France it was used as a revolutionary emblem from 1792 onward, and was adopted officially as its flag by the Paris Commune of 1871. Since the revolution of Nov 1917, it has been the national flag of the USSR; as such it bears a golden hammer and sickle crossed, symbolizing the unity of the industrial workers and peasants, under a gold-rimmed five-pointed star, signifying peace between the five continents. The British Labour Party anthem, called 'The Red Flag', was written by Jim ◊Connell in 1889.

red giant a large and bright ◊star, with a cool surface. Red giants are thought to represent a late stage in the evolution of a star like the Sun, as it runs out of hydrogen fuel at its centre. Red giants have temperatures about 10 and 100 times that of the Sun. They are very bright because they are so large, although their surface temperature is lower than that of the Sun, about 2,000 to 3,000 K.

Redgrave /'redgreɪv/ Michael 1908–1985. British actor, who played leading Shakespearean roles on the stage; knighted 1959.

Redgrave /'redgreɪv/ Vanessa 1937– . British actress, daughter of Michael ◊Redgrave, whose roles include Shakespeare's Lady Macbeth 1974 and Cleopatra 1973 and 1986, and the title-part in the film *Julia* 1976 (Academy Award). She has also been active in left-wing politics.

Red Guards armed workers who took part in the ◊Bolshevik Revolution of 1917. The name was also given to the school and college students, wearing red armbands, active in the Cultural Revolution in ◊China 1966–68.

red-hot poker African plant *Kniphofia uvaria*, and related species of the family ◊Liliaceae, with a flame-red spike of flowers.

Redmond /'redmənd/ John Edward 1856–1918. Irish politician, Parnell's successor as leader of the Nationalist Party 1890–1916.

The 1910 elections saw him holding the balance of power in the House of Commons, and he secured the introduction of a ◊Home Rule bill, hotly opposed by Protestant Ulster. He supported the British cause on the outbreak of World War I, and the bill was passed, but its operation suspended till the war's end. The growth of the nationalist Sinn Féin and the 1916 Easter Rising ended his hopes and his power.

Redouté /,redu:'teɪ/ Pierre Joseph 1759–1840. French flower painter. His volumes of paintings (for example *Les Roses* 1817–24) reveal a sound knowledge of plant structure.

red pepper red fruit of the ◊capsicum.

Red River western tributary of the ◊Mississippi, USA, so called because of the reddish soil sediment it carries.

Red River river in North Vietnam, 500 km/310 mi long, which flows into the Gulf of Tonkin. Its extensive delta is a main centre of population.

Red Sea submerged section of the ◊Great Rift Valley (2,000 km/1,200 mi long and up to 320 km/200 mi wide). Egypt, Sudan, and Ethiopia (in Africa) and Saudi Arabia (Asia) are on its shores. The sludge of its floor is mineral-rich, and the split in the earth's crust running down it suggests that the Red Sea will eventually become an ocean. In the Old Testament the Israelites escaped from the pursuing Egyptians when its waters parted temporarily to let them pass.

redshank wading bird *Tringa totanus* of N Europe and Asia, where it nests in swampy areas, although most winter farther south. Named from its long red legs, it is greyish and speckled black.

red shift in astronomy, the lengthening of the wavelengths of light from an object, as a result of the object's motion away from us. It is an example of the ◊Doppler effect. Lengthening the wavelengths causes them to move or shift towards the red end of the ◊spectrum, hence the name. The amount of red shift can be measured by the displacement of lines in an object's spectrum. By measuring the amount of red shift in light from stars and galaxies, astronomers can tell how quickly these objects are moving away from us. The red shift in light from galaxies is evidence for the ◊expanding universe. A strong gravitational field (see ◊gravity) can also produce a red shift in light; this is termed *gravitational red shift*.

Red Spot a prominent feature in the atmosphere of the planet ◊Jupiter.

redstart bird *Phoenicurus phoenicurus* of the thrush family which winters in Africa and spends the summer in Europe. Named from its red tail, the male has a dark grey head (with white mark on the forehead and black face) and back, and brown wings with lighter underparts. The American redstart *Setophaga ruticilla* belongs to a different family.

Redstone rocket a short-range US military missile, modified for use as a space launcher. Redstone rockets launched the first two Mercury astronauts on suborbital flights (see ◊Mercury project). A modified Redstone, called Juno 1, launched the first US satellite, Explorer 1.

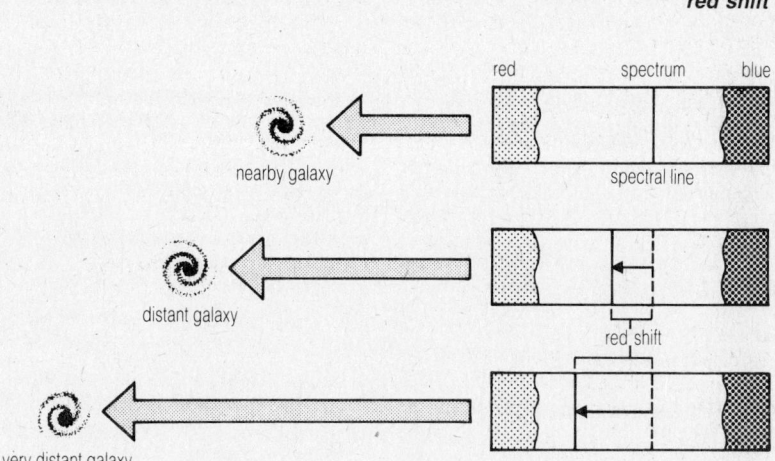

red shift

red   spectrum   blue

spectral line

nearby galaxy

distant galaxy

red shift

very distant galaxy

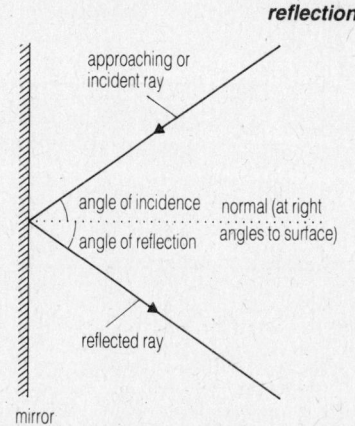

reflection

approaching or
incident ray

angle of incidence   normal (at right
angle of reflection   angles to surface)

reflected ray

mirror

red tape a derogatory term for bureaucratic methods, derived from the fastening for departmental bundles of documents in Britain.

red terror term used by opponents to describe the Bolshevik seizure and retention of power in Russia after Oct 1917.

redwing type of thrush *Turdus iliacus*, rather smaller than the song thrush, and with reddish wing and body markings. It breeds in the north of Europe and Asia, moving south in winter.

redwood giant coniferous tree. See ◊sequoia.

reed perennial aquatic grass. The common reed *Phragmites australis* attains 3 m/10 ft, having stiff erect leaves, and straight stems bearing a plume of purplish flowers.

Reed /riːd/ Carol 1906–1976. British film producer and director, an influential figure in the British film industry of the 1940s. His films include *The Third Man* 1950, written for him by Graham Greene.

Reed /riːd/ Lou 1942– . US rock singer, songwriter, and guitarist, the best-known former member (1965–70) of the seminal New York garage band the Velvet Underground. His solo work includes the albums *Berlin* 1973 and *Street Hassle* 1978, which deal with urban alienation and angst.

Reeves /riːvz/ William Pember 1857–1932. New Zealand politician and writer. He was minister of education 1891–96. He wrote the classic description of New Zealand, *Long White Cloud* 1898.

referee an arbitrator. The term is most commonly used of the official in charge of a game, such as football, but may also be applied in law to members of the court of referees appointed by the House of Commons to give judgment on petitions against private bills, and to the three official referees to whom cases before the high court may be submitted.

referendum the procedure whereby a decision on proposed legislation is referred to the electorate for settlement by direct vote of all the people. It is most frequently employed in Switzerland, but has also been used in Canada, Australia, New Zealand, and certain states of the USA. It was used in the UK for the first time in 1975 on the Common Market issue.

refining a process that purifies or converts something into a more useful form. Metals usually need refining after they have been extracted from their ores by such processes as ◊smelting. Electrolytic refining methods use the principle of ◊electrolysis to purify metals. Petroleum, or crude oil, needs refining before it can be used. The process of refining in this case involves first fractionation – splitting up the petroleum into separate fractions, or substances with similar boiling point. Subsequent refinery processes serve to convert the heavier fractions into more useful lighter products. The most important of these is ◊cracking. Other processes include ◊polymerization, hydrogenation, and reforming.

reflection deflection of waves, such as ◊light or ◊sound waves, when they hit a surface. The *law of reflection* states that the angle of incidence (the angle between the ray and a perpendicular line drawn to the surface) is equal to the angle of reflection (the angle between the reflected ray and a perpendicular to the surface). Thus, rays are reflected at the same angle at which they strike.

reflex an automatic response to a particular stimulus, controlled by the ◊nervous system. The receptor (for example, a sense organ) and the effector (such as a muscle) are linked directly (via the spinal ganglia or the lower brain, in vertebrates), making responses to stimuli very rapid. In animals with well developed ◊central nervous systems, reflex actions can often be modified by other nerves that are under voluntary control. For example, humans learn to control the reflex that leads the bladder to be emptied as soon as it becomes full. Reflex actions are more common in simple animals.

reflex camera a camera that uses a mirror and prisms to reflect light passing through the lens into the viewfinder, so showing the photographer exactly what scene he or she is shooting. When the shutter button is released the mirror springs out of the way, allowing light to reach the film. The commonest type is the single-lens reflex (SLR) camera, which usually takes 35 mm film. The twin-lens reflex (TLR) camera has two lenses – one has a mirror for viewing, the other is used for exposing the film.

Reformation movement in ◊Christianity (anticipated from the 12th century by the ◊Waldenses, ◊Lollards, and ◊Hussites) to reform the Catholic Church, which became effective in the 16th century when the new, centralized, absolute monarchies gave it support by challenging the political power of the ◊papacy and confiscated church wealth. It began in Europe with ◊Luther's protest against the sale of ◊indulgences in 1517, the name 'Protestants' being in general use by 1529, and ended the religious unity of W Europe; see ◊Zwingli, ◊Calvin, ◊Henry VIII, and John ◊Knox. The *Counter-Reformation* initiated by the Catholic Church at the *Council of Trent* 1545–1563 aimed at reforming abuses and regaining the lost ground by using moral persuasion and an extension of the Spanish ◊Inquisition to other countries. By the mid-17th century the present European alignment had been reached, with the separation of the Catholic and Protestant churches.

refraction in physics, the bending of ◊light when it passes from one medium to another, such as from air to glass. Since light travels more slowly in glass than in air, the light bends towards the normal, that is perpendicular, in going from air to glass, but away from the normal when going from glass to air.

refractive index in physics, a measure of the extent to which a ray of light is bent as it passes from one transparent medium to another. If the angle of incidence is i and the angle of refraction is r, the refractive index $n = \sin i/\sin r$ (Snell's law). It is also equal to the speed of light in the first medium divided by the speed of light in the second, and it varies with the wavelength of the light. See also ◊refraction.

refractory in technology, a material that resists high temperature. Mostly they are ◊ceramic materials made from clay, minerals or other earthy materials. Furnaces are lined with silica and dolomite. Alumina (aluminium oxide) is an excellent refractory, used for example for the body of spark plugs. Titanium and tungsten

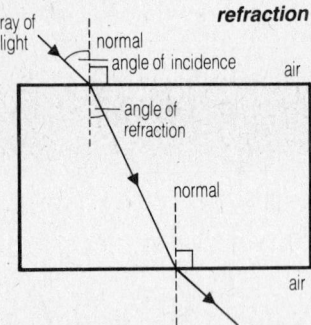

refraction

ray of light
normal
angle of incidence
air
angle of refraction
normal
air

are often called refractory metals because they are temperature resistant. ◊Cermets are refractory materials made up of ceramics and metals.

refrigeration the process of absorbing heat at a low temperature and rejecting it at a higher temperature. *Refrigerators* are used in the food industry for preserving foodstuffs by chilling or freezing. Refrigeration is also used in industrial processes and in air-conditioning. See also ◊deep freezing.

The refrigeration process may be effected by gas expansion, by absorption cycles, or most commonly by a vapour-compression cycle. This is based on the fact that a fluid will absorb heat in changing from the liquid to the gaseous state, and reject heat in changing from gaseous to liquid state: absorption can take place at a low temperature and heat rejection can take place at a higher temperature. Fluids used as refrigerants in the vapour-compression cycle include carbon dioxide (used on ships), ammonia (in industrial and marine equipment), and halogenated hydrocarbons, such as Freon-12, dichlorodifluoromethane (in domestic plants, shops and markets). See also ◊vacuum.

refrigerator

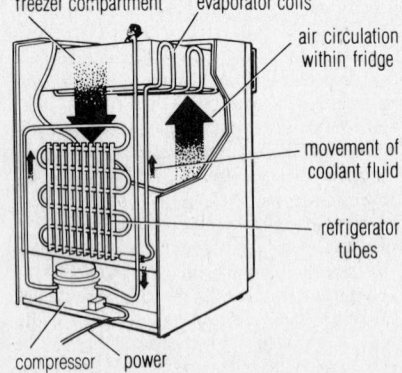

freezer compartment
evaporator coils
air circulation within fridge
movement of coolant fluid
refrigerator tubes
compressor
power

refugee someone fleeing from war or political persecution; see ◊displaced persons.

regalia or *crown jewels* symbols of royal authority. The British set (except for the Ampulla and the Anointing Spoon) were broken up at the time of Cromwellian rule in the mid-17th century, and now date from the ◊Restoration. In 1671 Captain Blood attempted to steal them, but was pardoned and pensioned by ◊Charles II. They are kept in the Tower of London in the Crown Jewel House (1967), and major items include St Edward's Crown; the Imperial State Crown; the jewelled Sword of State used only at the Coronation; the Sword of State used at the opening of Parliament and on other state occasions; the Curtana (Sword of Mercy); the Swords of Temporal and Spiritual Justice; the Orb; the Royal Sceptre or Sceptre with the Cross (containing the great Star of Africa, cut from the Cullinan diamond); the Rod with the Dove; St Edward's Staff; the Spurs; the Coronation Ring (the 'Wedding Ring of England'); the Armills (gold bracelets, given by the Commonwealth countries in 1953 for the coronation of Elizabeth II); the Ampulla (which contains the holy oil for the anointing); and the Anointing Spoon.

Regan /ˈriːgən/ Donald 1918– . US Republican politician. A believer in the unfettered forces of the market place, he was secretary of the Treasury 1981–85, and was chief of ◊Reagan's White House staff 1985–87, when he was forced to resign because of complicity in ◊Irangate.

regelation phenomenon in which water re-freezes to ice after it has been melted by pressure, at a temperature below the freezing point of water. Pressure makes an ice skate, for example, form a film of water which re-forms ice after the skater has passed.

Regency in Britain, the years 1811–20 during which ◊George IV, when Prince of Wales, acted as regent for his father ◊George III.

Regency style style of architecture which prevailed in England during the latter part of the 18th century and the early part of the 19th century. The style is characterized by its restrained simplicity, and its imitation of ancient classical architecture, especially Greek. The best-known architects of the period were Henry Holland (1746–1806), who designed many domestic buildings, John ◊Nash, and Decimus Burton (1800–81), who designed the screen at Hyde Park Corner, London.

regeneration in biology, the regrowth of a new organ or ◊tissue after the loss or removal of the original. It is very common in plants, where a new individual can often be produced from a 'cutting' of the original, a property exploited by gardeners. In animals, regeneration of major organs is limited to lower organisms: certain lizards can regrow their tails if these are lost, while in flatworms a whole new individual can grow from a tiny fragment. In mammals, regeneration is limited to repair of tissue in wound-healing and the regrowth of peripheral nerves following damage.

Regensburg /ˈreɪɡənsbʊək/ city in Bavaria, West Germany, on the Danube at its confluence with the Regen, 100 km/63 mi NE of Munich; population (1984) 128,000. It has many fine medieval buildings, including a Gothic cathedral 1275–1530.

history Regensburg stands on the site of a Celtic settlement dating from 500 BC; became the Roman *Castra Regina* 179 AD; capital of the Eastern Frankish Empire; a free city 1245; and

seat of the German *Diet* (parliament) 16th century–1806. It was included in Bavaria 1810.

regent person discharging the royal functions during a sovereign's minority or incapacity, or during a lengthy absence from the country.

Reger /ˈreɪɡə/ (Johann Baptist Joseph) Max(imilian) 1873–1916. German composer and pianist. He was conductor of the Meiningen ducal orchestra 1911–14. He composed prolifically, but alcoholic excess led to his early death. His works include fine organ and piano music, chamber music, and songs.

reggae the predominant form of West Indian popular music of the 1970s and 1980s, characterized by a heavily accented onbeat. The lyrics often refer to ◊Rastafarianism. Noted musicians include Bob ◊Marley, Lee 'Scratch' Perry (1940–) (performer and producer), and the group Black Uhuru 1974– .

Reggio di Calabria /ˈredʒəʊ diː kəˈlæbriə/ industrial town (farm machinery, olive oil, perfume), capital of Calabria, S Italy; population (1981) 173,486. It was founded by Greeks about 720 BC.

Regina /rəˈdʒaɪnə/ industrial city (oil refining, cement, steel, farm machinery, fertilizers), capital of Saskatchewan, Canada; population (1981) 164,500. It was founded 1882 as *Pile O'Bones*, and renamed in honour of Queen Victoria of England.

Regional Crime Squad in the UK, a local police force that deals with serious crime; see under New ◊Scotland Yard.

register in computing, a location for storing data, program instructions, and intermediate results in a computer's central processing unit (CPU). A microcomputer will typically have only a few registers, a mainframe computer many thousands.

Reich German 'empire'; the First Reich was identified with the ◊Holy Roman Empire; the Second Reich with the German Empire 1871–1918; and the Third Reich was ◊Hitler's Germany.

Reich /raɪk/ Steve 1936– . American composer, a pupil of Luciano Berio and Darius Milhaud. His work is characterized by extreme rhythmic and tonal regularity that is constantly being modifed by minute alterations. He does not allow his compositions to be performed unless he himself participates in the performance.

Reich /raɪk/ Wilhelm 1897–1957. Austrian doctor, who combined ◊Marxism and ◊psychoanalysis to advocate sexual freedom, for example in his controversial *Die Funktion des Orgasmus/The Function of the Orgasm* 1948. He emigrated to the USA in 1939.

Reichstadt, Duke of /ˈraɪkʃtæt/ another name of ◊Napoleon II, son of Napoleon I.

Reichstag /ˈraɪkstɑːg/ German parliament building and lower legislative house during the German Empire 1871–1918 and Weimar Republic 1919–33.

Reichstag Fire the burning of the German parliament building on 27 Feb 1933, less than a month after Hitler had become chancellor. The fire was used as a justification for the suspension of many constitutional guarantees, and also as an excuse to attack the communists. Although three

Bulgarians – ◊Dimitrov, Popov, and Tanev – and a German, Torgler, were all indicted for the crime and tried at Leipzig, only a Dutch communist, Marinus van der Lubbe, was convicted after being found at the scene of the crime and confessing. There is still some debate over Nazi involvement in the crime, not least because they were the main beneficiaries.

Reid /riːd/ Thomas 1710–1796. Scottish mathematician, Presbyterian minister, and philosopher. His *Enquiry into the Human Mind on the Principles of Common Sense* 1764 attempted to counter the sceptical conclusions of ◊Hume.

Reigate /'raɪgɪt/ town in Surrey, England, at the foot of the North Downs; population (1981) 52,554. With Redhill it forms a residential suburb of London.

Reign of Terror the period of the ◊French Revolution when the Jacobins were in power (1793–94) under Robespierre and instituted mass persecution of their opponents. About 1,400 were executed.

Reims /riːmz, French ræns/ (English *Rheims*) capital of Champagne-Ardenne region, France; population (1983) 178,000. It is the centre of the champagne industry, and has textile industries.

history Known in Roman times as *Durocorturum*; from 987 all but six French kings were crowned here. Ceded to England 1420, under the Treaty of Troyes, it was retaken by ◊Joan of Arc, who had ◊Charles VII consecrated in the 13th-century cathedral.

reincarnation the doctrine that the human soul or the spirit of a plant or animal after death may enter another human body or that of an animal. It is part of the teachings of many religions and philosophies, for example, Egyptian religion, Greek philosophy, Buddhism, Hinduism, Jainism, the philosophies of Pythagoras and Plato, certain Christian heresies (for example, ◊Cathars), and theosophy. It is also referred to as transmigration or metempsychosis.

reindeer deer *Rangifer tarandus* of the Arctic and sub-Arctic, common to both eastern and western hemispheres. About 120 cm/4 ft at the shoulder, it has a thick, brownish coat and broad hoofs well adapted to travel over snow. It is the only deer in which antlers are also present in the female: up to 150 cm/5 ft long, they are shed in winter. The Scandinavian form has been domesticated by the Lapps for centuries, and has been introduced to Alaska and the Canadian Arctic. The American form, known as caribou, occurs in two races – the large woodland caribou of the more southerly region and the barren-ground caribou of the north. Reindeer migrate southward in winter, moving in large herds, and in Dec–Mar the Lapps round them up for sorting by their owners. A frilly greyish lichen, *Cladonia rangiferina*, popularly known as reindeer moss, is their main food.

Reinhardt /'raɪnhɑːt/ 'Django' (Jean Baptiste) 1910–1953. Gypsy guitarist of German origin, born in Belgium. He was most famous for his haunting, melodic improvisation at a slow tempo, and was the first European jazz artist to influence American jazz musicians.

Reinhardt /'raɪnhɑːt/ Max 1873–1943. Austrian-American theatrical producer. In 1920 he founded the Salzburg Festival.

relative atomic mass or atomic weight the ratio of the average mass of 1 atom of the naturally occuring form of an element to one twelfth of the mass of a carbon-12 atom – a dimensionless number not an absolute weight. Within the ◊periodic table of elements, atoms are arranged by increasing relative atomic mass.

relative density in physics, also called specific gravity, the density (at 20°C) of a solid or liquid relative to (divided by) the maximum density of water (at 4°C). The relative density of a gas is its density divided by the density of hydrogen (or sometimes dry air) at the same temperature and pressure.

relative humidity in physics, the concentration of water vapour in the air; expressed as a percentage of its moisture content to the moisture content of the air if it were saturated with water at the same temperature and pressure. Relative humidity increases with temperature. See also ◊dew point and ◊hygrometer.

relativism a philosophical position which denies the possibility of objective truth, independent of some specific social or historical context or conceptual framework.

relativity two theories propounded by Albert ◊Einstein concerning the nature of space and time, and with far-reaching implications in physics.

The *special theory* 1905 was devised to simplify the theory of ◊electromagnetism. Starting with the premises that (1) the laws of nature are the same for all observers in unaccelerated motion; and (2) the speed of light is independent of the motion of its source, Einstein showed, for example, that the time interval between two events was longer for an observer in whose frame of reference the events occur in different places than for the observer for whom they occur at the same place. Such 'time dilation' has been confirmed by experiment and gives a degree of academic respectability to the notion of (forward) time-travel. Einstein's ideas were shown by Minkowski to imply that time was in many respects like an extra dimension to space, so physicists now talk of four-dimensional 'space–time'. Einstein showed that for consistency with premises (1) and (2) the principles of dynamics as established by ◊Newton needed modification; the most celebrated new result being the equation $E = mc^2$, which expresses an equivalence between mass (m) and ◊energy (E), c being the speed of light in vacuum.

The *general theory of relativity* 1915 involved a new twist to the concept of space–time; its geometrical properties were to be conceived as modified locally by the presence of a body with mass. A planet's orbit around the Sun (as observed in three-dimensional space) arises from its natural trajectory in modified space–time; there is no need to invoke, as Newton did, a force of ◊gravity coming from the Sun and acting on the planet. Einstein's theory predicted almost the same orbits for the planets as Newton's theory, but there were slight differences which should be observable in the cases of ◊Mercury; such indeed was the case. Again, according to the new theory light rays should be seen bending when they pass by a massive object, owing to its effect on local space–time. Physicists eagerly awaited the eclipse of the Sun in 1919, when light from distant stars passing close to the Sun would not be masked by sunlight. The predicted bending of starlight was observed.

Although since modified in detail, general relativity remains central to modern ◊astrophysics and ◊cosmology; it predicts, for example, the possibility of ◊black holes. General relativity theory was inspired by the simple idea that it is impossible in a small region to distinguish between acceleration and gravitation effects (as in a lift one feels heavier when the lift accelerates upwards), but the mathematical development of the idea is formidable. Such is not the case for the special theory, which a non-expert can follow up to $E = mc^2$ and beyond.

relay in physics, an electromagnetic switch. A small current passing through a coil of wire wound round an iron core attracts an ◊armature whose movement closes a pair of sprung contacts to complete a secondary circuit, which can be carrying a large current. The solid-state equivalent is a thyristor switching device.

relic a part of some divine or saintly person, or something closely associated with them. Examples include the arm of St ◊Teresa of Avila, the blood of St ◊Januarius, and the shroud of ◊Turin. In medieval times they were fiercely fought for. The cult was condemned by Protestant reformers, but upheld by the Council of ◊Trent. A non-religious relic is the preserved body of Lenin in Moscow.

relief in architecture, a term applied to carved figures and other forms which project from the background. The Italian terms *basso-rilievo* (low relief), *mezzo-rilievo* (middle relief), and *alto-rilievo* (high relief) are used according to the extent to which the sculpture projects. The French term *bas-relief* is commonly used for low relief.

religion code of belief and behaviour maintained independently of reason (that is, by faith), which often involves the worship of a ◊god or gods (Latin *religare*, to bind; perhaps humans to god). Belief in a supernatural power is not essential (absent in, for example, ◊Buddhism, ◊Confucianism) but faithful adherence is usually considered to be rewarded, for example by escape from human existence (◊Buddhism), by a future existence (◊Christianity, ◊Islam), or by worldly benefit (Soka Gakkai Buddhism). Among the chief religions are: *ancient and pantheist* religions of ◊Babylonia, ◊Assyria, ◊Egypt, ◊Greece, ◊Rome; *oriental* ◊Hinduism, ◊Buddhism, ◊Jainism, ◊Parseeism, ◊Confucianism, ◊Taoism, ◊Shinto; *'religions of a book'* ◊Judaism, ◊Christianity (the principal divisions are Roman Catholic, Eastern Orthodox and Protestant), ◊Islam (Muhammadanism); *combined derivation* for example, the ◊Bahai faith, ◊Moonies, ◊Mormons.

Comparative religion studies the various faiths impartially, but often with the hope of finding common ground, to solve the practical problems of competing claims of unique truth or inspiration. The earliest known attempt at a philosophy of religious beliefs is contained in fragments written by Xenophones in Greece in the 6th century BC, and later ◊Herodotus and ◊Aristotle contributed to the study. Serious work in comparative study began again with some Jesuit theologians in 17th-century China and comparisons between the Christian Bible and the sacred books of India carried out by English missionary scholars in Calcutta towards the end of the 18th century. The work of Charles ◊Darwin and the growth of anthropology stimulated the investigation of religious beliefs, notably by the Sanskrit scholar, Max Müller, Sir James ◊Frazer, Andrew ◊Lang, and R C Zaehner.

religious education (RE) the formal teaching of religion in schools. In England, RE is the only compulsory subject. In voluntary aided church schools, RE syllabuses are permitted to follow the specific teachings of the church concerned; in other maintained schools the syllabus is agreed between representatives of the local churches and the education authority. The law allows parents to withdraw their children from RE on conscientious grounds.

In the USA, religious education within the doctrines of a particular church is prohibited in public (state-maintained) schools, because of the separation of church and state guaranteed under the first amendment to the constitution; however, the study of comparative religion is permitted.

Remarque /rə'mɑːk/ Erich Maria 1898– . German novelist, a soldier in World War I, whose anti-war *All Quiet on the Western Front* 1929 led to his being deprived of German nationality. He later became a US citizen.

Rembrandt /'rembrænt/ Harmensz van Rijn 1606–1669. Dutch painter and etcher. Born in Leyden, the son of a wealthy miller, he studied under Swanenburgh, an architectural painter of Leyden, and for a short time under Pieter Lastman (1583–1633) in Amsterdam. Rembrandt is regarded as the greatest painter of the Dutch school. In his portraits and biblical scenes he saw light as a spiritual mystery which momentarily allows his characters to loom out of the surrounding shadows. His self-portraits (nearly 100) trace the drama of his own passage through life and even the large group portrait *The Night Watch* 1642 becomes a suspense story. His earliest pictures – for example, *St Paul in Prison* 1627 – were painted in Leyden, but most of his work was executed in Amsterdam, where he settled in 1631. He is said to have visited England about 1661–62. In 1656 he was declared bankrupt, and a collection of his etchings and drawings were sold for a fraction of their value. His later work shows greater emotional depths, for example the *Jewish Merchant* about 1650. Other famous works include *Presentation in the Temple* 1631, the *Anatomy Lesson* 1632, and *The Good Samaritan* 1632. He was also a skilled drawer and printmaker; over 1,000 drawings still survive.

remedial education special classes, or teaching strategies, which aim to help children

RELIGION – FESTIVALS

month	festival	religion	commemorating
Jan 6th	Epiphany	Western Christian	coming of the Magi
6th-7th	Christmas	Orthodox Christian	birth of Christ
18th-19th	Epiphany	Orthodox Christian	coming of the Magi
Jan-Feb	New Year	Chinese	Return of Kitchen God to heaven
Feb-Mar	Shrove Tuesday	Christian	day before Lent
	Ash Wednesday	Christian	first day of Lent
	Purim	Jewish	story of Esther
	Mahashivaratri	Hindu	Siva
Mar-Apr	Palm Sunday	Western Christian	first day of Holy Week
	Good Friday	Western Christian	Crucifixion of Christ
	Easter	Western Christian	Resurrection of Christ
	Passover	Jewish	escape from slavery in Egypt
	Holi	Hindu	Krishna
	Holi Mohalla	Sikh	(coincides with Holi)
	Rama Naumi	Hindu	birth of Rama
	Ching Ming	Chinese	remembrance of dead
Apr 13th	Baisakhi	Sikh	founding of the Khalsa
Apr-May	Easter	Orthodox Christian	Resurrection of Christ
May-Jun	Shavuot	Jewish	giving of Ten Commandments to Moses
	Whitsun	Western Christian	filling of Jesus's followers with Holy Spirit
	Wesak	Buddhist	day of Buddha's birth, enlightenment and death
	Martyrdom of Guru Arjan	Sikh	death of fifth guru of Sikhism
Jun	Dragon Boat Festival	Chinese	Chinese martyr
	Whitsun Orthodox Christian		
Jul	Dhammacakka	Buddhist	preaching of Buddha's first sermon
Aug	Raksha Bandhan	Hindu	family
Aug-Sept	Janmashtami	Hindu	birthday of Krishna
Sept	Moon Festival	Chinese	Chinese hero
Sept-Oct	Rosh Hashana	Jewish	start of Jewish New Year
	Yom Kippur	Jewish	day of fasting
	Succot	Jewish	Israelites' time in the wilderness
Oct	Dusshera	Hindu	goddess Devi
Oct-Nov	Divali	Hindu	goddess Lakshmi
	Divali	Sikh	release of Guru Hargobind from prison
Nov	Guru Nanak's Birthday	Sikh	founder of Sikhism
	Advent	Western Christian	preparation for Christmas
Nov-Dec	Bodhi Day	Buddhist (Mahayana)	Buddha's enlightenment
Dec	Hanukkah	Jewish	recapture of Temple of Jerusalem
	Winter Festival	Chinese	time of feasting
25th	Christmas	Western Christian	birth of Christ
Dec-Jan	Birthday of Guru Gobind Singh	Sikh	last (tenth) human guru of Sikhism
	Martyrdom of Guru Tegh Bahadur	Sikh	ninth guru of Sikhism

Rembrandt Dutch painter and etcher Rembrandt created nearly 100 self-portraits, most of which express his inner dramas. This etching was produced in 1639.

with learning difficulties to catch up with children within the normal range of achievement.

Remembrance Sunday (known until 1945 as Armistice Day) national day of remembrance for those killed in both world wars and later conflicts. In the UK it is observed by a two-minute silence at the time of the signature of the armistice with Germany on 11 Nov 1918, although since 1956 the day of commemoration has been the second Sunday of Nov. There are ceremonies at the Cenotaph in Whitehall, London, and elsewhere. 'Flanders poppies', symbolic of the blood shed, are sold in aid of war invalids and their dependants.

Remington /'remɪŋtən/ Philo 1816–1889. American inventor, best known for the breech-loading rifle and typewriter that bear his name. He began manufacturing typewriters in 1873, using the patent of Christopher Sholes (1819–90), and made improvements that resulted five years later in the first machine with a shift key, thus providing lower-case letters as well as capital letters. The Remington rifle and carbine, which had a falling block breech and a tubular magazine, were developed in collaboration with his father.

remora fish *Remora remora*, and related species, which have an adhesive disc on the head, by which they attach themselves to sharks and turtles, which provide them with shelter, transport, and possibly food in the form of parasites on the host's skin.

remote sensing gathering and recording information about things from a distance. This field of study has grown as a result of space technology. Space probes have sent back photographs and data about all the planets as distant as Uranus. Satellites such as *Landsat* have surveyed all of the Earth's surface from orbit. Computer processing of the data obtained by their scanning instruments and the application of false-colours have made it possible to reveal surface features invisible in ordinary light. (See ◊false-colour imagery.) This has proved valuable in agriculture, forestry, and urban planning, and has led to the discovery of new deposits of minerals.

REM sleep rapid-eye-movement ◊sleep, a phase of sleep which recurs several times nightly in humans and is associated with dreaming. The eyes flicker quickly beneath closed lids.

Renaissance (French 'rebirth') name given to the period and intellectual movement that in European history is traditionally seen as bringing an end to the Middle Ages and beginning modern times. It was seen as a revival of classical culture, which had supposedly been dormant since the fall of the Roman Empire.
The Renaissance started in Italy in the 14th and 15th centuries and spread all over western Europe in the 16th century. Among its characteristics were the belief in the individual and in the power of education to produce the 'complete human being', conversant with the

humanities, mathematics and science (including their application in war), the arts and crafts, and athletics and sport; the desire to enlarge the bounds of learning and geographical knowledge; the growth of scepticism and free-thought; and the study and imitation of Greek and Latin literature and art.
The beginning of the Italian Renaissance is usually dated in the 14th century with the work of ◊Dante, ◊Petrarch, and ◊Boccaccio. The invention of printing and the geographical discoveries gave a further impetus to the new spirit. Biblical criticism of ◊Erasmus and others contributed to the Reformation, and Counter-Reformation almost extinguished the movement in 16th-century Italy. Typical figures of the Renaissance were ◊Machiavelli, ◊Ariosto, ◊Leonardo da Vinci, ◊Michelangelo, ◊Tasso, ◊Bruno, ◊Galileo , ◊Cellini, ◊Campanella, and ◊Raphael in Italy; Rabelais and Montaigne in France; Cervantes in Spain; Camoens in Portugal; Copernicus in Poland; Dürer in Germany; and ◊More, ◊Sidney, ◊Marlowe, ◊Shakespeare and Bacon in England.
Especially in Italy, where the ideals of the Renaissance were considered to have been fulfilled by the great masters, the period 1490–1520 is known as the High Renaissance.

Renault /'renəu/ Mary, pen name of Mary Challans 1905–1983. British historical novelist.

Rendell /'rendl/ Ruth 1930– . British crime novelist, author of a detective series featuring Chief Inspector Wexford. She also writes psychological crime novels.

Renfrew /'renfru:/ town on the Clyde, in Strathclyde, 8 km/5 mi NW of Glasgow, Scotland; population (1981) 21,396. It was formerly the county town of Renfrewshire.

Renfrewshire /'renfru:ʃə/ former county of W central Scotland, bordering the Firth of Clyde. It was merged with the region of Strathclyde in 1975. The county town was Renfrew.

Reni /'reɪni/ Guido 1575–1642. Italian painter, influenced by ◊Caravaggio, who founded a school at Bologna. A painter in the classical tradition, he often succumbed to a popular taste for sentimental religiosity. His best known work is the fresco *Phoebus and the Hours preceded by Aurora* 1613 in Rome.

Rennes /ren/ capital of Ille-et-Vilaine *département*, W France, at the confluence of the Ille and Vilaine, 56 km/35 mi SE of St Malo; population (1983) 195,785. It was the old capital of Britanny, and its university specializes in Breton culture.

Rennie /'reni/ John 1761–1821. Scottish engineer who built the old Waterloo Bridge and old London Bridge.

Reno /'ri:nəu/ city in Nevada, USA, known for gambling and easy divorces; it has a branch of the University of Nevada. Population (1984) 112,000.

Renoir /'renwɑ:/ (Pierre) Auguste 1841–1919. French painter, one of the leading painters of the French ◊Impressionist movement. His paintings show contemporary life of great gaiety and colour; he is particularly noted for his voluptuous female nudes. Among his best-known works are *Les Parapluies/Umbrellas* 1883, *The Bathers* 1884–87, and *La Loge/The Theatre Box* 1874.

Renoir /'renwɑ:/ Jean 1894–1979. French film director, son of the painter Auguste ◊Renoir, and noted for his sensitive and subtle portrayal of social realism and his use of powerful visual imagery. His films include *La Grande Illusion/Grand Illusion* 1937, and *Règle du Jeu/The Rules of the Game* 1939. In 1975 he received an honorary Academy Award for his life's work.

Renoir Portrait of the French film director Jean Renoir by Cartier Bresson. He won the Croix de Guerre in World War I, and his films include the anti-war masterpiece *La Grande Illusion* 1937.

Rentenmark currency introduced in Germany at the end of 1923 by the president of the Reichsbank, Hjalmar Schacht (1877–1970), to replace old Reichsmarks which had been rendered worthless by inflation. As Germany had no appreciable gold reserves, the currency was guaranteed against the assets of the country, namely the land and railways.

reparation indemnity paid by countries defeated in war.

Repin /rɪ'pi:n/ Ilya Yefimovich 1844–1930. Russian artist. His work includes *Barge Haulers on the Volga* 1873 and portraits, including Tolstoy and Mussorgsky.

replication in biology, the production of copies of the genetic material, ◊DNA; it occurs during cell division (◊mitosis and ◊meiosis). See also ◊base pair.

repression in psychology, the unconscious process said to protect a person from ideas, impulses, or memories that would threaten emotional stability were they to become conscious.

reprieve the legal temporary suspension of the execution of a sentence pronounced after conviction of a capital offence. It is usually associated with the death penalty. In Britain it used to be made by the crown on the advice of the home secretary, and in the USA it is the prerogative of state governors; the president has this power in the case of federal offences, for example, treason.

reproduction the process by which a living organism produces other organisms similar to itself. Reproduction may be ◊asexual or ◊sexual.

reproduction rate in ecology, the rate at which a population or species reproduces itself; see ◊fecundity and ◊fertility.

reptile class of vertebrates (Reptilia) including the snakes, lizards, crocodiles, turtles and tortoises. They breathe by means of lungs; this distinguishes them from the ◊Amphibia, the larvae of which breathe through gills. They are cold-blooded, produced from eggs, and the skin is usually covered with scales. The metabolism is slow, and in some cases (some large snakes) intervals between meals may be months. Reptiles have a long history dating back over 300 million years. Many extinct forms are known, including the orders Pterosauria, Rhynchocephalia (containing one living form, the tuatara lizard), Plesiosauria, Ichthyosauria, and Dinosauria. The chief living orders are the Chelonia (tortoises and turtles), Crocodilia (alligators and crocodiles), and Squamata, divided into three sub-orders: Lacertilia (lizards), Rhiptoglossa (chameleons); Ophidia (snakes).

Repton /'reptən/ Humphrey 1752–1818. English landscape gardener, who coined the term 'landscape gardening'. He belonged to the generation after Lancelot ◊Brown, and worked for some years in partnership with John ◊Nash. Repton preferred more formal landscaping than Brown, and was responsible for the landscaping of some 200 gardens and parks.

republic a country where the head of state is not a monarch, either hereditary or elected, but usually a president whose role may or may not include political functions.

Republican Party one of America's two leading political parties, formed in 1854 by a coalition of opponents to ◊slavery, who elected their first president, Abraham ◊Lincoln, in 1860. In the early years, the Republican Party supported protective tariffs and favoured genuine settlers (homesteaders) over land speculators. Conservative tendencies and an antagonism of the legislature to the executive came to the fore after Lincoln's assassination. In the bitter period following the Civil War the party was divided into those who considered the South a beaten nation and those who wished to reintegrate the South into the country as a whole, but President Grant carried through a liberal reconstruction policy in the South.

Towards the end of the century the Republican Party was identified with US imperialism and industrial expansion. It became divided during President Theodore ◊Roosevelt's attempts at regulation and control of big business, and in forming the short-lived Progressive Party in 1912 Roosevelt effectively removed the liberal influence from the Republican Party until the 1940s.

With few intermissions, the Republican Party controlled the legislature from the 1860s until defeated by the New Deal Democrats in 1932. The Republican Party remained in eclipse until the election of ◊Eisenhower in 1952, rather a personal triumph than that of the party, whose control of Congress was soon lost and not regained by the next Republican president, Richard ◊Nixon, in 1968. After an isolationist period before World War II, the Republican Party adopted an active foreign policy under Nixon and ◊Ford, but the latter struggled under the aftermath of ◊Watergate, and was defeated when he stood for election in 1976. The party enjoyed landslide presidential victories for ◊Reagan and 1980–86 also carried the Senate.

requiem the mass for the dead in the Roman Catholic Church. Notable musical settings include those by Mozart and Berlioz.

reredos ornamental screen or wall-facing, behind a church altar.

research the primary activity in science, research is a combination of theory and experimentation directed towards finding scientific explanations of natural phenomena. It is commonly classified into two types. Pure research is the more basic, involving theories. Applied research is more immediate, looking for answers to problems for instance in medicine and engineering. The theories that develop from pure research may eventually be found to be of great value to society. Scientific research is expensive; most funding comes from government and industry and so a nation's wealth and priorities are likely to have a strong influence on the kind of work undertaken.

reserpine tranquillizer derived from the SE Asian plant *serpent wood Rauwolfia serpentina* which can lead to suicidal depression; it is also used to treat ◊hypertension.

reserve in economics, a country's holding of internationally acceptable means of payment (major foreign currencies or gold); central banks also hold the ultimate reserve of money for their domestic banking sector. On the asset side of company balance sheets, undistributed profits are listed as reserves.

resin substance exuded from pines, firs, and other trees in gummy drops which harden in air. Varnishes are the commonest products of the hard resins, and ointments those of the soft resins. Rosin is the solid residue of distilled turpentine, a soft resin. The name 'resin' is also given to many synthetic products, used in adhesives, plastics, and varnishes, with similar characteristics, but they are manufactured by polymerization.

resistance in physics, that property of a substance which restricts the flow of electricity through it, associated with conversion of electrical energy to heat; also the magnitude of this property. A *resistor* is an element whose principal characteristic is resistance, which depends on many factors which may include any or all of the following: the nature of the material, its temperature, dimensions, and thermal properties; degree of impurity, the nature and state of illumination of the surface and the frequency and magnitude of the current. The practical unit of resistance is the ◊ohm.

Resistance movement an opposition movement in a country occupied by an enemy or colonial power.

In E Europe during World War II resistance took the form of guerrilla warfare, for example in Yugoslavia (led by ◊Tito), in Greece and Poland, and by the partisan bands behind the German lines in the USSR. In more industrialized countries, such as France (where the underground movement was called the ◊maquis), Belgium, and Czechoslovakia, sabotage in factories and on the railways, propaganda, and the assassination of Germans and collaborators, were more important.

After World War II the same methods were used in, for example, ◊Palestine, South America, and European colonial possessions in Africa and Asia, to unsettle established regimes.

resistor in physics, any component in an electrical circuit that has a resistance to a current. For electronics purposes, resistors are often made from wire-wound coils or pieces of carbon. A variable resistor is a ◊rheostat or ◊potentiometer.

Resnais /re'neɪ/ Alain 1922– . French film director whose work is characterized by a preoccupation with memory and non-conventional concepts of time, as in *L'Année Dernière à Marienbad/Last Year at Marienbad* 1961, generally regarded as his masterpiece.

resources general term for things that can be used to provide the means to satisfy human wants. Because human wants are very diverse, and extend from basic physical requirements, such as food and shelter, through to ill-defined aesthetic needs, resources encompass a vast range of items. The intellectual resources of a society – its ideas and technologies – determine which aspects of the environment meet that society's needs, and therefore become resources. For example, in the 19th century uranium was used only in the manufacture of coloured glass. Today, with the advent of nuclear technology, it is a military and energy resource.

Resources are often categorized into *human resources*, such as labour supplies and skills, and *natural resources*, such as climate, fossil fuels, and water. Natural resources are divided into those which are non-renewable and those which can be replenished (renewable). Non renewable resources are things like coal, copper ores, and diamonds, which exist in strictly limited quantities. Once consumed they will not be replenished within the timespan of human history. In contrast, water supplies, timber, food crops, and similar resources can, if managed properly, provide a steady yield virtually for ever; they are therefore replenishable or renewable resources. Inappropriate use of renewable resources can lead to their destruction, as for example the cutting-down of rain forests. Some renewable resources, such as wind or solar energy, are continuous: supply is largely independent of people's actions.

Many people feel that the present and future demands of industrial societies cannot be sustained for more than a century or two, and that at the expense of the Third World and the environment. Other authorities believe that new technologies will emerge, enabling materials which are currently of little importance to become valuable resources when others are exhausted.

Respighi /res'piːgi/ Ottorino 1879–1936. Italian composer, a student of ◊Rimsky-Korsakov, whose works include the symphonic poems *The Fountains of Rome* 1917 and *The Pines of Rome* 1924, operas, and chamber music.

respiration the biochemical process whereby food molecules are progressively broken down to release energy in the form of ◊ATP. In most organisms this is an ◊aerobic process, so oxygen is required. In all higher organisms, respiration occurs in the ◊mitochondria. Respiration is also used to mean the process by which an organism exchanges gases with the atmosphere, although this is more accurately described as ◊gas exchange. See also ◊breathing.

rest mass in physics, the mass of a particle at rest or moving at only a low velocity compared with that of light. At very high velocities, there is a relativistic effect which increases the mass of a particle (see ◊relativity).

Restoration term used to describe the period in English history after the fall of the ◊Protectorate in 1660 and the re-establishment of the monarchy in the person of Charles II.

Restoration comedy period in English theatrical history, which witnessed the first appearance of women on the English stage, most notably in the 'breeches part', specially created in order to costume the actress in male attire, thus revealing her figure at its best advantage. The genre is popular and naturalistic, placing much emphasis on sexual candour. Examples include Wycherley's *The Country Wife* 1675, Congreve's *The Way of the World* 1700, and Farquhar's *The Beaux' Strategem* 1707.

retail price index an indicator of movement in the ◊cost of living.

retriever gundog used for retrieving game. The commonest breeds are the Labrador retriever, large, smooth-coated, and usually black or yellow; and the golden retriever – always golden – with either flat or wavy coat.

retrovirus a type of ◊virus containing the genetic material ◊RNA rather than the more usual ◊DNA. For the virus to express itself and multiply within an infected cell, its RNA must be converted to DNA. It does this using a built-in enzyme known as reverse transcriptase (since the transfer of genetic information from DNA to RNA is known as transcription, and retroviruses do the reverse of this). Retroviruses include those causing ◊AIDS and other infections of the ◊immune system.

Retz /res/ Jean François Paul de Gondi, Cardinal de Retz 1614–1679. French politician. He was behind the insurrection of the ◊Fronde. After a period of imprisonment and exile he was restored to favour in 1662 and created abbot of St Denis. His *Memoirs* are of great historical interest.

Réunion /ˌreɪuːnˈjɒŋ/ French island in the Indian Ocean, 915 km/570 mi E of Madagascar
area 2,500 sq km/970 sq mi
capital St Denis
physical forested, rising in Piton de Neiges to 3,069 m/10,068 ft
features administers five uninhabited islands also claimed by Madagascar
products sugar, maize, vanilla, tobacco, rum
population (1985) 543,000
history the island's first European visitors were the Portuguese 1513; it was annexed by Louis XIII of France 1642. It became an overseas *département* of France 1946, and an overseas region 1972.

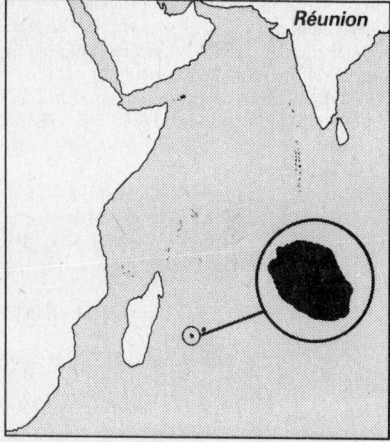
Réunion

Reuter /'rɔɪtə/ Paul Julius, Baron de Reuter 1816–1899. Founder of Reuters international news agency. Born in Cassel, Germany. He began a continental pigeon post in 1849, and in 1851 he set up a news agency in London. In 1858 he persuaded the press to use his news telegrams, and the service became worldwide. Reuters became a private trust in 1916, and was taken over by the Newspaper Proprietors' Association 1926–41. It became a public company in 1984.

Reval /'reɪvæl/ former name of the Soviet port of ◊Tallin.

Revere /rə'vɪə/ Paul 1735–1818. American patriot, a Boston silversmith, who carried the news of the approach of British troops to Lexington and Concord (see ◊American War of Independence) on the night of 18 Apr 1775.

revisionism a political theory derived from Marxism which moderates one or more of the basic tenets of Marx, and which is hence condemned by orthodox Marxists. The first noted Marxist revisionist was Eduard ◊Bernstein, who in Germany in the 1890s questioned the inevitability of a breakdown in capitalism. After World War II the term became widely used by established Communist parties, both in Eastern Europe and Asia, to condemn movements (whether more or less radical) which threaten the official party policy.

revolution any rapid, far-reaching or violent change in the political, social, or economic structure of society. It has usually been applied to different forms of political change: the American Revolution (War of Independence), where colonists broke free from their colonial ties and established a sovereign, independent state; the French Revolution, where an absolute monarchy was overthrown by opposition from inside the country and a popular rising; and the Russian Revolution, where a repressive monarchy was overthrown by those seeking social and economic changes in line with a socialist model. While political revolutions are often associated with violence, there are other types of change which often have just as much impact on society. Most notable is the Industrial Revolution, which imposed massive changes on economies and societies from the mid-18th century. In the 1980s, a silicon revolution can be identified, involving the increasing use of computers.

Revolutionary Wars a series of wars between France and the combined armies of England, Austria, Prussia, and others

1791 Emperor ◊Leopold II and Frederick ◊William II of Prussia issued the *Declaration of Pillnitz* inviting the European powers to restore ◊Louis XVI to power

1792 France declared war on Austria, who formed a coalition with Prussia, Sardinia, and (from 1793), Britain, Spain, and the Netherlands; victories for France at Valmy and Jemappes

1793 French reverses until the reorganization by ◊Carnot

1795 Prussia, the Netherlands, and Spain made peace

1796 Sardinia forced to make peace by ◊Napoleon's Italian campaign

1797 Austria compelled to peace under the Treaty of Campo-Formio

1798 Napoleon's fleet, after its capture of Malta, defeated by ◊Nelson in Egypt at the Battle of the Nile (Aboukir Bay), and he had to return to France without his army; William ◊Pitt organized a new coalition with Russia, Austria, Naples, Portugal, and Turkey

1798–99 Coalition mounted its major campaign in Italy (see ◊Suvorov), but dissension led to the withdrawal of Russia

1799 Napoleon, on his return from Egypt, reorganized the French army

1800 14 Jun Austrians defeated by Napoleon at Marengo in NW Italy, and again on 3 Dec (by ◊Moreau) at Hohenlinden near Munich

1801 Austria made peace under the Treaty of Lunéville; Sir Ralph Abercromby defeated the French by land in Egypt at the Battle of Alexandria, but was himself killed

1802 Peace of Amiens truce between France and Britain, followed by the ◊Napoleonic Wars.

revolutions of 1848 a series of revolts in various parts of Europe against monarchial rule. While some of the revolutionaries had republican ideas, many more were motivated by economic grievances. The revolution began in France and then spread to Italy, the Austrian Empire, and to Germany, where the short-lived Frankfurt Parliament put forward ideas about Germany political unity. None of the revolutions enjoyed any lasting success, and most were violently suppressed within a few months.

revolver a small hand gun that has a revolving chamber that holds the bullets. See ◊pistol.

revue a stage presentation involving short satirical and topical items in the form of songs, sketches, and monologues. In Britain the first

revue seems to have been *Under the Clock* 1893 by Seymour Hicks (1871–1949) and Charles Brookfield. The 1920s revues were spectacular entertainments, but the 'intimate revue' (such as *Sweet and Low* 1943) became increasingly popular under ◊Cochran, who employed writers such as Noel ◊Coward. During the 1960s the satirical revue took off with the Cambridge Footlights' production *Beyond the Fringe*, firmly establishing the revue tradition among the young and at fringe theatrical events.

Reykjavik /'reɪkjəviːk/ capital and chief port on the SW coast of Iceland; university 1911; population (1984) 88,500. Many of the houses are made of wood. Reykjavik is heated by underground mains fed by volcanic springs.

Reynaud /reɪ'nəʊ/ Paul 1878–1966. French prime minister, who succeeded ◊Daladier in Mar 1940, but resigned in Jun after the German breakthrough. He was imprisoned by the Germans until 1945.

Reynolds /'renldz/ Joshua 1723–1792. British artist. Born near Plymouth, he went to London at the age of 17, and was apprenticed to portrait painter Thomas Hudson (1701–79). From 1743 he was active as a portrait painter in London and Plymouth, and in 1749 went abroad to complete his studies in Rome and Venice. After his return to London in 1752 he became the most famous portraitist of his day and the first president of the Royal Academy. He was knighted in the same year (1768).

He was a life-long friend of Dr Johnson, and at Reynolds's suggestion the Literary Club was founded in 1764. He painted portraits of Johnson, Goldsmith, Garrick, and other in a modernized classical style. His artistic theories appear in his *Discourses* 1769–91.

Reynolds /'renldz/ Osborne 1842–1912. British physicist and engineer who did important work on ◊fluid flow and devised the Reynolds number, which relates to turbulance in flowing fluids.

rhapsody in music, an instrumental fantasia, often based on folk melodies, such as ◊Lizst's *Hungarian Rhapsodies*.

rhe unit of fluidity equal to the reciprocal of the ◊poise.

rhea type of bird, family Rheidae, found only in South America. They are incapable of flight, and differ from the ostrich in having a feathered neck and head and three-toed feet, and in their smaller size. There are two species *Rhea americana* and the smaller *Pterocnemia pennata*.

Rhee /riː/ Syngman 1875–1965. Korean politician. A rebel under Chinese and Japanese rule, he became president of the Korean Republic from 1948 until riots forced him to resign and leave the country in 1960. He established a repressive dictatorship and was an embarrassing ally for the USA.

rhenium metallic element: symbol Re, atomic number 75, atomic weight 186.22. Discovered in 1925 by Noddack, Tacke and Berg in the minerals columbite, tantalite and wolframite, it is a hard grey metal, used in thermocouples, and as a catalyst.

rheostat in physics, a variable ◊resistor (to an electric current), usually consisting of a high-resistance wire-wound coil with a sliding contact. The circular type in electronics (which can be used, for example, as the volume control of an amplifier) is also known as a ◊potentiometer.

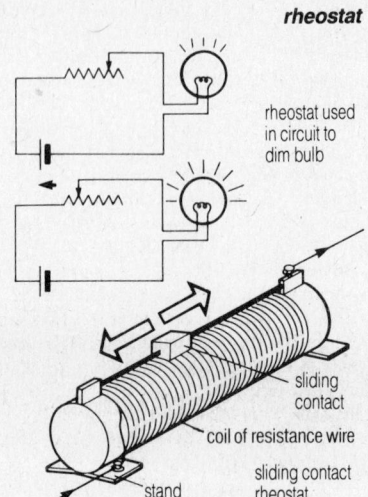

rheostat

rheostat used in circuit to dim bulb

sliding contact

coil of resistance wire

sliding contact rheostat

stand

rhesus macaque monkey *Macaca mulatta*, also known as the bandar, found in N India and N Indo-China. It has long, straight brown-grey hair, pinkish face, and red buttocks.

rhesus factor a ◊protein on the surface of red blood cells of humans, which is involved in the rhesus ◊blood-group system. Most individuals possess the main rhesus factor (Rh+), but those without (Rh-) will produce ◊antibodies if they come into contact with it. If an Rh-mother carries an Rh+ foetus, she may produce antibodies if foetal blood crosses the ◊placenta. This is not normally a problem with the first infant because antibodies are only produced slowly. However, the antibodies continue to build up after birth, and a second Rh+ child may be attacked by antibodies passing from mother to foetus. In such cases the blood of the infant has to be changed for Rh-blood. Alternatively, the problem can be alleviated by giving the mother anti-Rh globulin just after the first pregnancy, preventing the formation of antibodies. The name comes from rhesus monkeys, in whose blood the rhesus factors were first found.

rhetoric traditionally, the art of the orator (in Greek, *rhetor*) or of public speaking and debate. Accomplished rhetoricians are not necessarily sincere in what they say, and 'rhetoric' is often a pejorative term.

rhetorical question a question, often used by public speakers and debaters, which either does not require an answer or for which the speaker intends to provide his or her own answer ('Where else in the world can we find such brave young men as these?').

rheumatism a term loosely applied to a large variety of ailments associated with inflammation of the joints and muscles. Acute rheumatism, or *Rheumatic fever* is caused by a streptococcal throat infection which appears to trigger the formation of antibodies which attack the patient's own tissues. It is rare, especially in temperate zones, and most usual between 15 and 30, and is marked by a high temperature and inflammed swelling of the joints, which passes rapidly from one to another. It lasts about two weeks, and the chief danger is of possible damage to the heart muscle. See also ◊arthritis, ◊fibrositis.

Rhine /raɪn/ European river rising in Switzerland and reaching the North Sea via West Germany and the Netherlands; length 1,320 km/820 mi. Tributaries include the Moselle and the Ruhr. The Rhine is linked with the Mediterranean by the Rhine-Rhône Waterway, and with the Black Sea by the Rhine-Main-Danube Waterway.

The *Lorelei* is a rock in the river in Rhineland-Palatinate, West Germany, with a remarkable echo; the German poet Brentano gave currency to the legend of a siren who lured sailors to death with her song, also subject of a poem by Heine.

River Rhine

Rhine /raɪn/ Joseph Banks 1895–1980. American ◊parapsychologist. His work at Duke University, North Carolina, involving controlled laboratory experiments in telepathy, clairvoyance, precognition and psychokinesis, described in *Extra-Sensory Perception* 1934 made ESP a household word.

Rhineland-Palatinate /'raɪnlænd pə'lætɪnət/ administrative region (German *Land*) of West Germany
area 19,400 sq km/7,500 sq mi
capital Mainz
towns Koblenz, Trier, Ludwigshafen, Worms
features much wooded mountain country; river valleys of Rhine and Moselle
products wine (75% of German output), tobacco; chemicals, machinery, leather goods, pottery
population (1984) 3,628,000
religion Roman Catholic 56%, Protestant 41%
history formed 1946 of the Rhenish ◊Palatinate and parts of Hessen, Rhine province, and Hessen-Nassau.

rhinoceros hoofed mammal of the family Rhinocerotidae. Best-known are the one-horned Indian rhinoceros *Rhinoceros unicornis*, up to 2

m/6 ft at the shoulder and with a tubercled skin, folded into shield-like pieces; the African black rhinoceros *Diceros bicornis*, 1.5 m/5 ft high, with a prehensile upper lip for feeding on shrubs; and the broad-lipped or 'white' rhinoceros *Ceratotherium simum*, actually slaty-grey and with a squarish mouth for browsing grass. Both the latter are smooth-skinned and two-horned. An extinct species, *Baluchitherium*, reached 5.5 m/15 ft.

rhizoid a hair-like outgrowth found on the ◊gametophyte generation of ferns, mosses and liverworts. Rhizoids serve to anchor the plant to the substrate, and can absorb water and nutrients. They may be composed of many cells, as in mosses, where they are usually brownish, or unicellular as in liverworts, where they are usually colourless. Rhizoids fulfill the same basic functions as the ◊roots of higher plants but are simpler in construction.

rhizome a horizontal underground plant stem. It serves as a perennating organ in some species, where it is generally thick and fleshy, while in other species it is mainly a means of ◊vegetative reproduction, and is therefore long and slender, with buds all along it that send up new plants. The potato is a rhizome which has two distinct parts, the tuber being the swollen end of a long, cord-like rhizome. See also ◊rootstock.

Rhode Island /rəʊd 'aɪlənd/ smallest state of the USA, in New England; nicknamed Little Rhody or the Ocean State
area 3,144 sq km/1,214 sq mi
capital Providence
features ◊Narragansett Bay
products apples, potatoes, poultry (especially Rhode Island Reds), dairy products; jewellery (30% of the workforce), textiles, silverware, machinery, rubber, and plastics
population (1985) 968,000
history founded 1636 by Roger ◊Williams, exiled from Massachusetts Bay colony for religious dissent, Rhode Island was one of the original ◊Thirteen States.

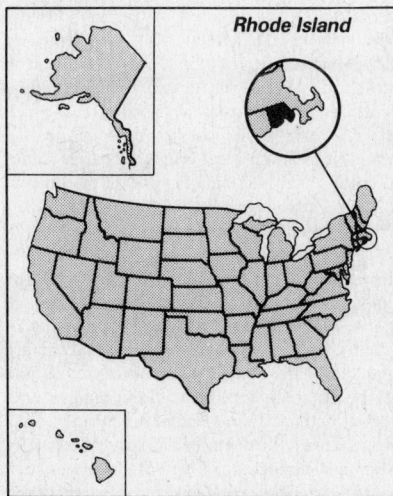

Rhode Island

Rhodes /rəʊdz/ Greek island, largest of the Dodecanese, in the E Aegean Sea

area 1,412 sq km/545 sq mi
capital Rhodes
products grapes, olives
population (1981) 40,500
history Rhodes was first settled by Greeks about 1000 BC. The ◊Colossus of Rhodes (fell 224 BC) was one of the ◊Seven Wonders of the World. Rhodes was held by the Knights Hospitallers of ◊St John 1306–1522, taken from Turkish rule by the Italian occupation 1912, and ceded to Greece 1947.

Rhodes /rəʊdz/ Cecil John 1853–1902. South African politician. Born in England, he went to Natal in 1870. As head of De Beers Consolidated Mines and Goldfields of South Africa Ltd, he amassed a large fortune. He entered the Cape legislature in 1881, and became prime minister in 1890. Aiming at the formation of a South African federation and of a block of British territory from the Cape to Cairo, he was largely responsible for the annexation of Bechuanaland in 1885, and formed the British South Africa Company in 1889, which occupied Mashonaland and Matabeleland, thus forming Rhodesia. The discovery of his complicity in the Jameson Raid forced him to resign the premiership in 1896. The Rhodes scholarships were founded at Oxford under his will, for students from the Commonwealth, USA, and Germany. Advocating Anglo-Afrikaner cooperation, he was less alive to the rights of black Africans, despite the final 1898 wording of his dictum: 'Equal rights for every civilized man south of the Zambezi'.

Rhodes /rəʊdz/ Zandra 1940– . British fashion designer, best known for the extravagant fantasy and luxury of her dress creations.

Rhodesia /rəʊ'diːʃə/ former name of ◊Zambia (North Rhodesia) and ◊Zimbabwe (South Rhodesia).

rhodium a silvery-white metal of the platinum family; symbol Rh, atomic number 45, atomic weight 102.91. Discovered in 1803 by the British chemist William Wollaston (1766–1828). Its salts form red solutions, and it is found native with platinum in river sands in the Urals and N and S America. Used in thermocouples and in electroplating, it gives a corrosion-free highly polished surface, superior to that of chromium. The name is derived from the Greek *rhodon*, rose.

rhododendron evergreen and deciduous shrub Rhododendron, family Ericaceae. The leaves are often dark and leathery, and the large racemes of flowers occur in all colours except blue.

rhombus a diamond-shaped plane figure, a parallelogram with four equal sides (opposite sides are equal in length and parallel) and no internal angle which is a right angle (otherwise it is a square). Its diagonals bisect each other at right angles. The area of a rhombus is equal to the length of a side multiplied by its height (the perpendicular distance between opposite sides).

Rhondda /'rɒnðə/ industrial town in Mid Glamorgan, Wales; population (1981) 81,725. Light industries have replaced coalmining, formerly the main source of employment.

Rhodes Cecil Rhodes bestrides the Cape and Cairo in this caricature, which refers to his achievement of a telegraphic link between them in 1892.

Rhône /rəʊn/ large river of S Europe. It rises in Switzerland and flows through the Lake of Geneva to Lyons in France, where at its confluence with the Saône the upper limit of navigation is reached. The river turns due S, passes Vienne and Avignon through a major wine-producing area, and takes in the Isère and other tributaries. Near Arles it divides into the *Grand* and *Petit Rhône*, flowing respectively SE and SW into the Mediterranean W of Marseille and forming a two-armed delta; the area between the tributaries is the ◊Camargue, a marsh.

rhubarb perennial plant *Rheum rhaponticum*, family Polygonaceae, grown for its red edible leaf stalks. The leaves are poisonous.

rhyme identity of sound, usually in the endings of lines of verse, such as 'wing' and 'sing'. Avoided as a blemish in Japanese, it is a common literary device in other modern Asian and European languages. Rhyme first appeared in western Europe in late Latin poetry, but was not used in classical Greek and Latin.

rhyolite an ◊igneous rock, the fine-grained volcanic equivalent of granite.

Rhys /riːs/ Jean 1894–1979. British novelist, born in Dominica, best known for *Wide Sargasso Sea* 1966, her recreation of the life of Rochester's mad wife in *Jane Eyre* by Charlotte Brontë.

rhythm and blues (R & B) a term covering all black US popular music of the 1940s–60s: it replaced the appellation 'race music'. The music drew on ◊swing and jump-jazz rhythms and ◊blues vocals and was a progenitor of ◊rock and roll. It diversified into ◊soul, ◊funk, and other styles. Singers include Bo Diddley (1928–   ), who wrote many classic numbers, Jackie Wilson (1934–84), and Etta James (c. 1938–   ).

ria a long narrow sea inlet, usually branching and surrounded by hills. A ria is deeper and wider towards its mouth, unlike a ◊fjord. It is formed by the flooding of a river valley due to either a rise in sea level or a lowering of a landmass.

rib a long, often curved bone that extends laterally from the ◊spine in vertebrates. Fish and some reptiles have ribs along most of the spine, but in mammals they are found in the ◊thorax (chest) only. In humans, there are 12 pairs of ribs. At the rear each pair is joined to one of the vertebrae of the spine. The upper seven are 'true' ribs, because they are joined by ◊cartilage directly to the breast bone/sternum; the eighth, ninth, and tenth are each joined by cartilage to the rib above; the 11th and 12th ('floating ribs') are not attached in front at all. The ribs protect the ◊lungs and ◊heart and at the same time allow the chest to expand and contract easily.

Ribbentrop /'rɪbəntrɒp/ Joachim von 1893–1946. German Nazi leader. He joined the Nazi Party in 1932, acted as Hitler's adviser on foreign affairs, and was German ambassador to Britain 1936–38 and foreign minister 1938–45. He was tried at Nuremberg as a war criminal in 1946, and hanged.

Ribera /rɪˈbɪərə/ José (Jusepe) 1591–1656. Spanish painter and etcher. Born near Valencia, he went to Italy where he was known as *Spagnoletto* ('Little Spaniard'). He carried a Caravaggesque style to brutal extremes to shock people into identifying with the sufferings inherent in Christian history, for example *Martyrdom of St Bartholomew* 1624.

riboflavin a ◊vitamin of the B complex whose absence in the diet causes stunted growth.

ribonucleic acid the full name of ◊RNA.

ribosome in biology, the protein-making machinery of the cell. Ribosomes are made of proteins and a special type of ◊RNA, ribosomal RNA. They receive messenger RNA (copied from the DNA) and ◊amino acids, and 'translate' the messenger RNA by using its chemically coded instructions to link amino acids in a specific order, to make a strand of a particular ◊protein.

Ricardo /rɪˈkɑːdəʊ/ David 1772–1823. British economist, widely regarded as the greatest of the classical economists after Adam ◊Smith. After making a fortune on the London ◊Stock Exchange, he published in 1817 *Principles of Political Economy*, in which 'laws' of rent, value, and wages, long generally accepted, were clearly enunciated, including the important concept of ◊comparative advantage (that countries can benefit by specializing in goods they produce most efficiently and trading internationally to buy others). Ricardo was one of the first to state the law of diminishing returns – that continued increments of capital and labour applied to a given quantity of land will eventually show a declining rate of increase in output.

rice principal cereal of the wet regions of the tropics; the yield is very large, and rice is said to be the staple food of one-third of the world population. It is derived from grass of the genus *Oryza sativa* probably native to India and SE Asia. It has been cultivated since prehistoric days in the East, and has now been introduced into suitable lands in other parts of the world. It takes 150–200 days to mature in warm, very wet conditions. During its growing period it needs to be flooded either by the heavy monsoon rains or by adequate irrigation. This restricts the cultivation of swamp rice, the usual kind, to level land and terraces. A poorer variety, known as hill rice, is grown on hillsides. Brown, or unhusked, rice has valuable vitamins which are lost in husking or polishing, but it is only in the polished state that most rice enters into European trade. Outside Asia there is some rice production in the Po valley of Italy, and in the United States in Louisiana, Carolina, and in California. Varieties with increased protein content have been developed by gamma radiation for commercial cultivation and yields are much higher.
Rice husks when burned provide a silica ash which, mixed with lime, produces an acid resistant cement.

Rice /raɪs/ Elmer 1892–1967. American playwright. His *Street Scene* 1929, was made into an opera by Kurt Weill.

Rich /rɪtʃ/ Adrienne 1929–   . American radical feminist poet and writer. In 1974, when given the National Book Award, she declined to accept it as an individual but with Alice Walker and Audrey Rich accepted it on behalf of all women. In 1976 she published *Of Woman Born*, on motherhood as a personal experience rather than as a institution, and *On Lies, Secrets and Silence*.

Richard three kings of England:

Richard I /'rɪtʃəd/ 1157–1199. Known as *the Lionheart*, French *Coeur-de-Lion*. King of England from 1189. He was the third son of Henry II, against whom he twice rebelled. In the third ◊Crusade 1191–92 he showed courage and generalship, although he failed to recover Jerusalem. While returning overland he was captured by the duke of Austria, who handed him over to the emperor Henry VI, and he was held prisoner until a large ransom was raised. His later years were spent in warfare in France, and he was killed while besieging Châlus. Himself a poet, he became a hero of romances after his death.

Richard II /'rɪtʃəd/ 1367–1400. King of England from 1377. Son of ◊Edward the Black Prince, he was born in Bordeaux. He succeeded his grandfather Edward III when only ten, the government being in the hands of a council of regency. His fondness for favourites resulted in conflicts with Parliament, and in 1388 the baronial party headed by the duke of Gloucester had many of his friends executed. Richard recovered control in 1389, and ruled moderately until 1397, when he had Gloucester murdered and his other leading opponents executed or banished, and made himself absolute. In 1399 his cousin Henry Bolingbroke, duke of Hereford (later Henry IV), returned from exile to lead a revolt; Richard II was deposed by Parliament and imprisoned in Pontefract Castle, where he died mysteriously.

Richard III /'rɪtʃəd/ 1452–1485. King of England from 1483. The son of Richard, duke of

York, he was created duke of Gloucester by his brother Edward IV, and distinguished himself in the Wars of the Roses. On Edward's death in 1483 he was created protector to his nephew Edward V, and soon secured the crown on the plea that Edward IV's sons were illegitimate. He proved a capable ruler, but the suspicion that he had murdered Edward V and his brother undermined his popularity. In 1485 Henry, earl of Richmond, raised a rebellion, and Richard III was defeated and killed at Bosworth. Modern scholars tend to minimize the evidence for his crimes as Tudor propaganda.

Richards /'rɪtʃədz/ Frank, pen name of British writer Charles Hamilton 1875–1961. Writing for the children's papers *Magnet* and *Gem*, he invented Greyfriars public school and the fat boy Billy Bunter.

Richards /'rɪtʃədz/ Gordon 1905–1986. British jockey. First riding in 1920, he had 21,834 mounts and 4,870 winners before his retirement in 1954. He was 26 times champion jockey, and was knighted in 1953, the year he won the Derby on Pinza.

Richardson /'rɪtʃədsən/ Harry Hobson 1838–1886. American architect, who built a great deal in a Romanesque style derived from that of N Spain.

Richardson /'rɪtʃədsən/ Henry Handel. Pseudonym of Australian novelist Ethel Henrietta Richardson 1880–1946. She was born in Melbourne, but left Australia when only 18; her best work *The Fortunes of Richard Mahony* 1917–29 reflects her father's life.

Richardson /'rɪtʃədsən/ Owen Williams 1879–1959. British physicist. At Cambridge he studied the emission of electricity from hot bodies, giving the name ◊thermionics to the subject. He received a Nobel prize in 1928.

Richardson /'rɪtʃədsən/ Ralph (David) 1902–1983. British actor, who played leading roles in drama from Shakespeare to Pinter. Knighted 1947.

Richardson /'rɪtʃədsən/ Samuel 1689–1761. British novelist, regarded as one of the founders of the modern novel. Born in Derbyshire, he was brought up in London and apprenticed to a printer. He set up his own business in London in 1719, becoming printer to the House of Commons. All his six young children died, followed by his wife in 1731, which permanently affected his health. His *Pamela* 1740–41, written in the form of a series of letters, and containing much dramatic conversation, achieved a sensational vogue throughout Europe, and was followed by *Clarissa* 1747–48, and *Sir Charles Grandison* 1753–54.

Richardson /'rɪtʃədsən/ Tony 1928– . British director and producer. With George Devine he established the English Stage Company in 1955 at the Royal Court Theatre, where his productions included *Look Back in Anger* 1956. His films include *Saturday Night and Sunday Morning* 1960, *A Taste of Honey* 1961, and *Dead Cert* 1974.

Richelieu /'riːʃljɜː/ Armand Jean du Plessis de 1585–1642. French cardinal and politician. Born in Paris of a noble family, he entered the church, and was created bishop of Luçon in 1606

and a cardinal in 1622. Through the influence of ◊Marie de' Medici he became ◊Louis XIII's chief minister in 1624, a position he retained until his death. At home he aimed to make the monarchy absolute; he ruthlessly crushed opposition by the nobility, and destroyed the political power of the ◊Huguenots, while leaving them religious freedom. Abroad he sought to establish French supremacy by breaking the power of the Hapsburgs; he therefore supported the Swedish king Gustavus Adolphus and the German Protestant princes against Austria, and in 1635 brought France into the Thirty Years' War. His secretary Père ◊Joseph was the original Grey Eminence.

Richelieu A triple portrait of Cardinal Richelieu by Philippe de Champaigne. An inscription on the back says that it was painted for the use of the sculptor Franchesco Mochi in Rome and the right-hand profile is marked as 'the better of the two'.

Richler /'rɪtʃlə/ Mordecai 1931– . Canadian novelist, born in Montreal. His novels, written in a witty, acerbic style, include *The Apprenticeship of Duddy Kravitz* 1959.

Richmond /'rɪtʃmənd/ capital of Virginia, USA; population (1980) 219,250. It is the centre of the Virginian tobacco trade. It was the ◊Confederate capital 1861–65, and a museum commemorates the writer Edgar Allan Poe, who grew up here.

Richmond upon Thames /'rɪtʃmənd əpɒn 'temz/ borough of SW Greater London
features Hampton Garrick Villa; Old Court House (the architect Wren's last home), Faraday House; ◊Hampton Court Palace and Bushy Park;
Kew outhoused departments of the Public Record Office; Kew Palace (former royal residence), within the ◊Royal Botanic Gardens.
Richmond gatehouse of former Richmond Palace (see ◊Henry VIII and ◊Elizabeth I), Richmond Hill and Richmond Park (including White Lodge, home of the Royal Ballet School); Ham House (17th century);
Teddington highest tidal point of the Thames; National Physical Laboratory;
Twickenham Kneller Hall (Royal Military School of Music); Marble Hill House (Palladian home of the Duchess of Suffolk, mistress of ◊George II); Strawberry Hill (home of Horace

◊Walpole); Twickenham Rugby Ground; *population* (1981) 157,867.

Richter /'rɪktə/ Charles Francis 1900–1985. US seismologist, deviser of the ◊Richter scale for measuring the strength of the waves from earthquakes.

Richter /'rɪʃtə/ Johann Paul Friedrich 1763–1825. German author, commonly known as Jean Paul. Born in Bavaria, he created a series of comic eccentrics rivalled only by those of Dickens. His books include *Die Flegeljahre/The Awkward Age* 1804–05.

Richter /'rɪxtə/ Sviatoslav (Teofilovich) 1915–1985. Russian pianist, an outstanding interpreter of romantic composers.

Richter scale a scale measuring the magnitude of an ◊earthquake. The magnitude is a function of the total amount of energy released, and each point on the Richter scale represents a tenfold increase in energy over the previous point. The magnitude of an earthquake differs from the intensity, measured by the ◊Mercalli scale, which is subjective and varies from place to place for the same earthquake. The Richter scale is named after the US seismologist who developed it.

Richthofen /'rɪʃthəʊfən/ Manfred, Freiherr von 1892–1918. German aeroplane pilot. He commanded in World War I a crack fighter squadron and shot down 80 aircraft before being killed in action behind British lines.

ricin poison obtained from the seeds of the ◊castor-oil plant.

rickets a vitamin D deficiency disease of young children, marked by soft, poorly developed bones, resulting in bow legs. Sunlight acts on fats in the skin to produce vitamin D necessary to enable calcium to be deposited in the bones, so hardening them; lack of sunlight can therefore cause the disease.

Ridgeway, the grassy track dating from prehistoric times which runs along the Berkshire Downs in S England from White Horse Hill to near Streatley.

Riding /'raɪdɪŋ/ Laura 1901– . American poet. A member of the Fugitive Group of poets, which flourished in the Southern US 1915–28, she went to England in 1926 and worked with Robert Graves. She published her *Collected Poems* in 1938. Thereafter she wrote no more verse.

Ridley /'rɪdli/ Nicholas c. 1500–1555. English Protestant bishop. He became chaplain to Henry VIII in 1541, and bishop of London in 1550. He took an active part in the Reformation and supported Lady Jane Grey's claim to the throne. After Mary's accession he was arrested and burned as a heretic.

Riefenstahl /'riːfənʃtɑːl/ Leni 1902– . German filmmaker. *Das blaue Licht/The Blue Light* 1932, which she directed, led Hitler to invite her to film the Nazi rallies at Nuremberg (*Triumph des Willens/Triumph of the Will* 1934). She made a two-part documentary of the 1936 Berlin Olympics. Under a cloud after World War II because of her apparent involvement with the Nazis, she was unable to pursue her film career, and instead published volumes of photographs of Africa.

RICHTER SCALE

Magnitude value	Relative amount of energy released	Notable examples
1		
2		
3		
4	1	Carlisle, 1979 (*a significant one for Britain*)
5	30	San Francisco
6	100	San Fernando, 1971
7	30,000	Chimbote
8	1,000,000	Tangsham, 1976 San Francisco, 1906 Lisbon, 1755 Alaska, 1964

Richthofen The German pilot Baron von Richthofen during World War I with his 11th Chasing Squadron, 'Richthofen's Flying Circus'; left to right are Festner, Schafer, Baron von Richthofen, Lother von Richthofen, Kurt Wolff.

Riel /ri'el/ Louis 1844–1885. French-Canadian rebel, a champion of the Métis (an Indian-French people), he established a provisional government in Winnipeg in an unsuccessful revolt 1869–70, and was hung for treason after leading a further rising in Saskatchewan 1884–85.

Riemann /'ri:mæn/ Georg Friedrich Bernhard 1826–1866. German mathematician whose system of non-Euclidean geometry, thought at the time to be a mere mathematical curiosity, was used by Einstein to develop his General Theory of ◊Relativity.

Rienzi /ri'enzi/ Cola di c. 1313–1354. Italian political reformer, who in 1347 tried to re-establish the forms of an ancient Roman republic. His second attempt seven years later ended with his assassination.

Riesman /'ri:smən/ David 1909– . American sociologist, author of *The Lonely Crowd: A Study of the Changing American Character* 1950.

Rietvelt /'ri:tfelt/ Gerrit Thomas 1888–1964. Dutch architect, an exponent of De ◊Stijl. His best-known building is the Schroeder House at Utrecht 1924; he is also well known for a colourful, minimalist chair design.

Rif, Er /rɪf/ mountain range about 290 km/180 mi long on the Mediterranean seaboard of Morocco.

Riff ◊Berber people of N Morocco, who under ◊Abd el-Krim long resisted the Spaniards and French.

rifle a ◊firearm that has spiral grooves (rifling) in its barrel. When a bullet is fired, the rifling makes it spin, which helps keep it travelling in a straight line. Rifled guns came into use in the 1500s.

rift valley a valley formed by the subsidence of a block of the Earth's ◊crust between two or more parallel ◊faults. Rift valleys are usually steep-sided and form where the crust is being pulled apart, as at ◊ocean ridges, or in the Great ◊Rift Valley.

Rift Valley, Great /rɪft/ volcanic valley formed 10–20 million years ago by a crack in the Earth's crust, and running from the ◊Jordan valley to Mozambique. The ◊Red Sea forms part of it, and also the series of lakes, including Lake Rudolf, which provided early humans with a helpful environment and preserved their stratified remains. At some points it is merely a depression, but elsewhere has two vertical fault lines with an infill of volcanic material.

Rift Valley fever virus disease originating S of the Sahara. Hosted by sheep and cattle, it is spread by mosquitoes.

Riga /'ri:gə/ capital and port of Latvian Republic, USSR; population (1985) 883,000.

history A member of the ◊Hanseatic League from 1282, Riga has belonged in turn to Poland from 1582, Sweden from 1621, and Russia from 1710; it was the capital of independent Latvia 1918–40, and was occupied by Germany 1941–44, before becoming part of the USSR.

Rigel the seventh-brightest ◊star in the sky, and the brightest in the constellation ◊Orion. Rigel lies 900 light years away; it is a blue-white supergiant 50,000 times more luminous than our Sun, and has an estimated diameter of over 50 Suns.

Rigg /rɪg/ Diana 1938– . British actress, whose television roles include Emma Peel in *The Avengers* 1965–67 and Lady Deadlock in *Bleak House* 1985.

right-angled triangle a triangle in which one of the angles is a right angle (90°). It is the basic form of triangle for defining trigonometrical ratios (for example, sine, cosine and tangent) and for which ◊Pythagoras' theorem holds true. The longest side of a right-angled triangle is called the hypotenuse; its area is equal to half the product of the lengths of the other two sides. A triangle constructed on the diameter of a circle with its opposite vertex (corner) on the circumference is a right-angled triangle. This is a fundamental theorem in geometry, first credited to the Greek mathematician Thales (in the 580s BC).

right ascension in astronomy, the coordinate on the ◊celestial sphere that it equivalent to longitude on Earth. Right ascension is measured in hours, minutes, and seconds eastwards from the point where the Sun's path, the ecliptic,

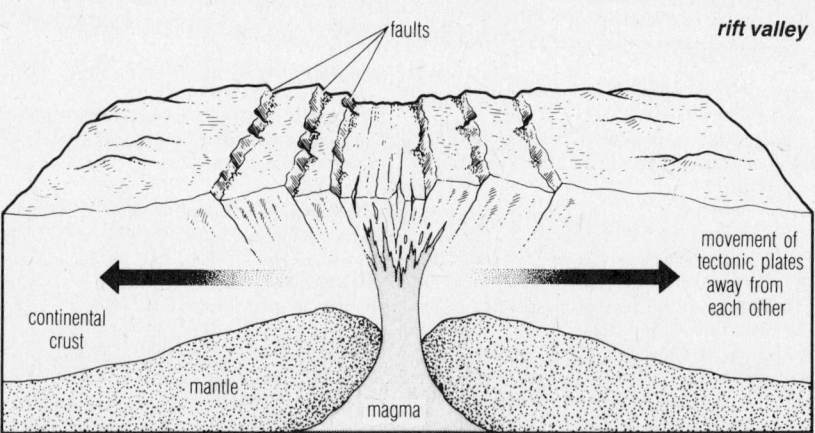

rift valley

(labels: faults, continental crust, mantle, magma, movement of tectonic plates away from each other)

intersects the celestial equator; this point is called the *vernal equinox*.

right of way right of a person to pass over land, for example a road (dedicated to public use) or footpath, in such use from time immemorial.

rights of man and the citizen declaration of according to the statement of the French National Assembly in 1789: representation in the legislature, equality before the law, equality of opportunity, freedom from arbitrary imprisonment, freedom of speech and religion, taxation in proportion to ability to pay, security of property. In 1946 were added: equal rights for women; right to work, join a union, and strike; leisure, social security, and support in old age;

and free education. Similar rights are enshrined in the ◊Bill of Rights of the US constitution.

right wing term applied to the more conservative or reactionary section of a political party or spectrum. It originated in the French national assembly in 1789, where the nobles sat in the place of honour on the president's right, whereas the commons were on his left (see under ◊left wing).

Rigi /'riːgi/ mountain in central Switzerland, between Lakes Lauerz, Lucerne, and Zug; height 1,800 m/5,908 ft.

Rijeka /ri'ekə/ industrial port (oil refining, distilling, paper, tobacco, chemicals) in NW Yugoslavia; population (1983) 193,044.
history It has changed hands many times, and after being seized by Gabriele ◊d'Annunzio 1919, was annexed by Italy 1924 (Italian *Fiume*). It was ceded back to Yugoslavia 1949.

Riley /'raɪli/ Bridget (Louise) 1931– British artist. A leading exponent of ◊Op Art in black-and-white and colour. Other works include two-colour silk-screen prints on Plexiglass.

Rilke /'rɪlkə/ Rainer Maria 1875–1926. Austrian lyric poet, born in Prague. He travelled widely, especially in Russia, and was for a time the sculptor Rodin's secretary. His prose works include the semi-autobiographical *Die Aufzeichnungen des Malte Laurids Brigge/Notebook of Malte Laurids Brigge* 1910, and his poetical works *Die Sonnette an Orpheus/Sonnets to Orpheus* 1923. His verse is characterized by a form of mystic pantheism.

Rimbaud /ræm'bəʊ/ (Jean Nicolas) Arthur 1854–1891. French poet who was an important influence on the ◊Symbolist movement. From 1871 he lived with ◊Verlaine. Although the association ended after Verlaine attempted to shoot him, it was Verlaine's analysis of Rimbaud's work in 1884 which first brought him fame. His verse was chiefly written before the age of 20 and includes *Les Illuminations* published in 1886.

Rimet /riː'meɪ/ Jules 1873–1956. French football administrator, founder of FIFA, the international federation of association football, and promoter of the World Cup competition, the original trophy being named after him.

Rimini /'rɪmɪni/ industrial port (pasta, footwear, textiles, furniture) and holiday resort in Emilia-Romagna, Italy; population (1981) 127,850.
history Its name in Roman times was *Ariminum*, and it was the terminus of the Flaminian Way from Rome. In World War II it formed the E strongpoint of the German 'Gothic' defence line, and was badly damaged in the severe fighting of Sept 1944, when it was taken by the Allies.

Rimsky-Korsakov /'rɪmski 'kɔːsəkɒf/ Nikolay Andreyevich 1844–1908. Russian composer. He made great use of Russian folk idiom and rhythms, and excelled in orchestration. His operas include *The Maid of Pskov* 1873, *The Snow Maiden* 1882, *Mozart and Salieri* 1898 and *The Golden Cockerel*, a satirical attack on despotism, banned till 1909. Other works include the symphonic poem *Sadko* 1867, the programme symphony *Antar* 1869, and the symphonic suite *Scheherazade* 1888. He also

(rather controversially) completed works by other composers, for example, ◊Mussorgsky's *Boris Godunov*.

rinderpest viral form of cattle diarrhoea which can be fatal. Almost eliminated in the 1960s, it revived in Africa in the 1980s.

ring ouzel see ◊ousel.

ringworm or *tinea* infestation by one of a group of parasitic microscopic fungi. On the scalp the fungus produces round patches of slight inflammation from which the hair falls out or breaks off.
Athlete's foot is a form beginning between the toes and spreading over the skin to produce a weeping eczema and an intolerable itch. Treatment is by antifungal drugs.

Rintelen /'rɪntələn/ Fritz von German spy. He led a spy ring in USA during World War I, sabotaging the shipment of Allied munitions until captured in 1915. He later settled in England and published reminiscences, *Dark Invader*.

Río de Janeiro /'riːəʊ də ʒə'nɪərəʊ/ port, naval base, and resort in Brazil; population (1980) 5,093,232. The name commemorates the arrival of Portuguese explorers 1 Jan 1502, but there is in fact no river. Sugar Loaf Mountain stands at the entrance to the harbour. It was the capital of Brazil 1822–1960, when it was replaced by ◊Brasilia. Some colonial churches and other buildings survive. Copacabana is a luxurious beachside suburb.

Rio Grande /'riːəʊ 'grænd, 'grændi/ river rising in the Rockies in S Colorado, USA, and flowing S to the Gulf of Mexico, where it is reduced to a trickle by irrigation demands on its upper reaches; length 2,800 km/1,800 mi. Its last 2,400 km/1,500 mi form the US-Mexican border.

Rio Grande do Norte /'riːəʊ 'grʌndi duː 'nɔːti/ state of NE Brazil; capital Natal; area 53,000 sq km/20,460 sq mi; population (1980) 1,900,750.

Riom /ri'ɒn/ town in of central France, the scene Feb–Apr 1942 of the 'war guilt' trials of several prominent Frenchmen, including ◊Blum, ◊Daladier, and ◊Gamelin, by the ◊Vichy government. At Hitler's instigation, the court was dissolved. The defendants remained in prison until released by the Allies in 1945.

Río Muni /'riːəʊ 'muːni/ the mainland portion of ◊Equatorial Guinea.

Río Negro /'riːəʊ 'neɪgrəʊ/ river in S America, rising in E Colombia and joining the Amazon at Manáus, Brazil; length 2,250 km/1,400 mi.

riot a disturbance caused by a potentially violent mob. In Britain, riots were formerly suppressed under the ◊Riot Act. Major riots in Britain include the Spitalfields weavers' riots 1736, the ◊Gordon riots 1780, the Newport riots 1839, and riots over the Reform Bill in Hyde Park, London, 1866; in the 1980s inner-city riots in Toxteth, Liverpool; St Paul's, Bristol; and Broadwater Farm, Tottenham, London, 1985. Modern methods of riot control include plastic bullets, stun bags (soft canvas pouches filled with buckshot which spread out in flight), water cannon, and CS gas (tear gas). Under the UK ◊Public Order Act 1986 a person is guilty of riot if in a crowd of 12 or more, threatening violence;

the maximum sentence is ten years' imprisonment.

Riot Act in the UK, an act passed in 1714 to suppress the ◊Jacobite disorders. If three or more persons assembled unlawfully to the disturbance of the public peace, a magistrate could read a proclamation ordering them to disperse (thus the expression 'reading the Riot Act'); if the rioters continued after the reading of the proclamation, they might be dispersed by force. Superseded by the 1986 ◊Public Order Act. See also ◊riot.

Ripon /'rɪpən/ city and market town in N Yorkshire, England; population (1981) 11,952. There is a cathedral 1154–1520; and the nearby 12th-century ruins of Fountains Abbey are among the finest monastic ruins in Europe.

ripple tank in physics, a shallow water-filled tray used for experiments that demonstrate various properties of waves, such as ◊reflection and ◊interference.

RISC (*reduced instruction-set chip*) in computing, a kind of ◊processor on a single ◊silicon chip. Computers based on RISC chips became commercially available in the late 1980s and considerably outperform their predecessors. (See ◊CPU and ◊ALU.)

Risorgimento (Italian 'resurrection') movement for Italian national unity and independence from 1815. Risings failed 1848–49, but the ◊Austrian War of 1859 was followed by the foundation of the Italian kingdom in 1861 (see ◊Piedmont). Unification was finally completed with the addition of Venezia in 1866 and the Papal States in 1870. Three leading fugures in the movement were ◊Cavour, ◊Mazzini, and ◊Garibaldi.

ritualization in ◊ethology, a term coined by Julian ◊Huxley for the stereotype that occurs in certain behaviour patterns when these are incorporated into displays. Thus, the exaggerated head toss of the goldeneye drake during courtship is derived by ritualization from the bathing movement used to wet the feathers. In courtship, its performance is exaggerated and stylized (to the point where it no longer wets the plumage) and its duration and form have become fixed. Ritualization may serve to make displays clearly recognizable and unambiguous, so helping to ensure that individuals mate only with members of their own species.

Riva del Garda /'riːvə del 'gɑːdə/ town on Lake Garda, Italy, where the Prix Italia broadcasting festival has been held since 1948.

river a body of water, larger than a stream, that flows downwards along a particular course. It originates at a point called its *source*, and enters the sea or a lake at its *mouth*. Along its length it may be joined by smaller rivers called *tributaries*. A river and its tributaries form a *river system*.

Rivera /rɪ'veərə/ Diego 1886–1957. Mexican artist. A committed communist, he expressed his ideas in the vast and vivid fresco murals he executed in Mexico and the USA, making this form widely popular.

Rivera /rɪ'veərə/ Primo de. Spanish politician. See ◊Primo de Rivera.

river blindness or *onchocerciasis* type of blindness (caused by a parasitic worm) prevalent in Third World countries.

Riverina /ˌrɪvəˈriːnə/ district of New South Wales, Australia, between the Lachlan and Murray rivers, through which runs the Murrumbidgee. On fertile land, artificially irrigated from the three rivers, wool, wheat, and fruit are produced.

Riverside /ˈrɪvəsaɪd/ city in California, USA, on the Santa Ana river E of Los Angeles; population (1980) 170,500. Founded 1870. It is the centre of a citrus-growing district and has a citrus research station: the seedless orange was developed at Riverside in 1873.

riveting a method of joining metal plates. A metal pin called a rivet, which has a head at one end, is inserted into matching holes in two overlapping plates and then the other end is struck and formed into another head, holding the plates tight. Riveting is used in building construction for erecting steel girders, in boilermaking and in shipbuilding, although it has largely been replaced in the latter by ◊welding.

Riviera /ˌrɪviˈeərə/ the Mediterranean coast of France and Italy from Marseille to La Spezia, the rest of the French Mediterranean coast being merely 'the south of France'. The most exclusive section, with the finest climate, is the ◊Côte d'Azur, Menton–St Tropez, which includes Monaco. It has the highest property prices in the world.

Riyadh /ˈriːæd/ capital of Saudi Arabia and of the Central Province, formerly the sultanate of Nejd, in an oasis, connected by rail with Damman on the Arabian Gulf; population (1984) 1 million. It is surrounded by a high wall with six fortified gates, outside which are date gardens irrigated from deep wells. There is a large royal palace.

Rizzio /ˈrɪtsɪəʊ/ David 1533–1566. Italian adventurer at the court of ◊Mary, Queen of Scots. After her marriage to ◊Darnley, Rizzio's influence over her incited her husband's jealousy, and he was murdered by Darnley and his noble friends.

RNA (*ribonucleic acid*) a ◊nucleic acid involved in the construction of ◊proteins from ◊DNA, the genetic material. It is usually single-stranded, unlike DNA, and consists of a large number of nucleotides strung together, each of which comprises the sugar ribose and one of four bases (uracil, cytosine, adenine, or guanine). RNA is copied from DNA by the formation of ◊base pairs, with uracil taking the place of thymine. RNA occurs in three major forms, each with a different function in the synthesis of protein molecules. *Messenger RNA* (mRNA) acts as the template for protein synthesis. Each ◊codon (a set of three bases) on the RNA molecule is matched up with the corresponding ◊amino acid, in accordance with the ◊genetic code. This process (translation) takes place in the ◊ribosomes, which are made up of proteins and *ribosomal RNA* (rRNA). *Transfer RNA* (tRNA) is responsible for combining with specific amino acids, and then matching up a special 'anticodon' sequence of its own with a codon on the mRNA. This is how the genetic code is translated.

Although RNA is normally associated only with the process of protein synthesis, it may be the hereditary material itself in some ◊viruses.

roach freshwater fish *Rutilus rutilus* of N Europe, dark green above, whitish below, and with reddish lower fins. It grows to 35 cm/1.2 ft.

roadrunner American bird *Geococcyx californianus* of the ◊cuckoo family that spends much time on the ground and is a fast runner.

Roanoke /ˈrəʊənəʊk/ industrial city (railway repairs, chemicals, steel goods, furniture, textiles) in Virginia, USA, on the Roanoke river; population (1980) 100,500. Founded in 1834 as Big Lick, it was a small village until 1881 when the repair shops of the Virginia Railway were set up here, after which it developed rapidly. The name is American Indian and means 'shell money'.

Robbe-Grillet /ˈrɒb griːˈjeɪ/ Alain 1922– . French writer. He worked in Africa and the West Indies as a research biologist before turning to writing. He is the leading theorist of *le nouveau roman/the new novel*, for example his own *Les Gommes/The Erasers* 1953, *La Jalousie/Jealousy* 1957, and *Dans le labyrinthe/In the Labyrinth* 1959, which concentrates on detailed description of physical objects. Other members of the school include ◊Butor and ◊Sarraute. He also wrote the script for the film *L'Année dernière à Marienbad/Last Year in Marienbad* 1961.

robbery in English law, a variety of theft: stealing from the person, with force used to intimidate the victim. The maximum penalty is life imprisonment.

Robbia, della /ˈrɒbɪə/ family of architects and sculptors from Florence, Italy. *Luca della Robbia* (1400–82) executed a number of works in Florence, particularly the cantoria in the cathedral, and produced beautiful pieces in terracotta, now known as della Robbia ware. *Andrea della Robbia* (1435–1525) the nephew and pupil of Luca, also produced enamelled reliefs. Five of Andrea's sons carried on the family tradition; the best known were *Giovanni della Robbia* (1469–1529), and *Girolamo della Robbia* (1488–1566) who produced terracottas for Fontainebleau in France.

Robbins /ˈrɒbɪnz/ Jerome 1918– . American dancer and choreographer. Soloist with the newly formed American Ballet Theatre 1941–46, he became in 1949 associate artistic director of the New York City Ballet and was ballet master 1969–83. Among his ballets are *Fancy Free* 1944 (with Leonard Bernstein) and *Facsimile* 1946. He also choreographed the musicals *The King and I* 1951, *West Side Story* 1957, and *Fiddler on the Roof* 1964.

Robert two dukes of Normandy:

Robert I /ˈrɒbət/ the 'Devil' Duke of Normandy from 1028. He was the father of ◊William the Conqueror, and is the hero of several romances; he was legendary for his cruelty.

Robert II /ˈrɒbət/ c. 1054–1134. The eldest son of William the Conqueror, succeeding him as duke of Normandy (but not on the English throne) in 1087. He took part in the First ◊Crusade, and was deposed by his brother, ◊Henry I in 1106, remaining a prisoner in England till his death.

Robert /ˈrɒbət/ three kings of Scotland:

Robert I 1274–1329. King of Scotland from 1306, known as Robert the Bruce. Grandson of Robert de ◊Bruce, he shared in the national rising led by William Wallace, and soon after Wallace's execution in 1305 Robert rose once more against Edward I and was crowned at Scone 1306. He defeated Edward II at Bannockburn 1314. In 1328 the treaty of Northampton recognized Scotland's independence and Robert as king.

Robert II 1316–1390. King of Scotland from 1371. He was the son of Walter (1293–1326), steward of Scotland, who married Marjory, daughter of Robert I. He was the first king of the house of Stuart.

Robert III c. 1340–1406. King of Scotland from 1390. Son of Robert II. He was unable to control the nobles, and the government fell largely into the hands of his brother, Robert, Duke of Albany.

Roberts /ˈrɒbəts/ Bartholomew 1682–1722. British merchant-navy captain who joined his captors when taken by pirates in 1718, and became richest of all the sea rovers until surprised and killed in battle by the British navy.

Roberts /ˈrɒbəts/ David 1796–1864. Scottish painter, who progressed from interior decorator to scene painter at Drury Lane Theatre, London, while making a name for himself with picturesque views of London and French cathedrals. He is remembered for his oriental paintings, the result of several trips to the Middle East; his best works convey a sense of mystery and grandeur.

Roberts /ˈrɒbəts/ Frederick Sleigh, 1st Earl Roberts 1832–1914. British field marshal, known as 'Bobs'. Born in India, he joined the Bengal Artillery in 1851, and served through the Indian Mutiny, receiving the VC, and the Abyssinian campaign of 1867–68. During the Afghan War of 1878–80 he occupied Kabul, and subsequently made a victorious march to Kandahar. After serving as commander in chief in India 1885–93 and Ireland 1895–99, he received the command in South Africa during the ◊Boer War, and by his occupation of Bloemfontein and Pretoria made possible the annexation of the Transvaal and Orange Free State. On returning to England he received an earldom, and was commander in chief 1900–05. Early in World War I he died while visiting the trenches.

Roberts /ˈrɒbəts/ Thomas William 'Tom' 1856–1931. Australian artist, who introduced plein-air Impressionism to Australia. Born in England, he arrived in Australia in 1869, returning to Europe to study in 1881. He painted the official picture of the opening of the first Australian federal parliament.

Robertson /ˈrɒbətsən/ Thomas William 1829–1871. British dramatist, at first an actor *David Garrick* 1864 set a new, realistic trend in English drama.

Robeson /'rəubsən/ Paul 1898–1976. American bass singer. He graduated at Columbia University as a lawyer, but limited opportunities for blacks led him instead to the stage in, for example, *The Emperor Jones* 1924. His films include *Sanders of the River* and *King Solomon's Mines*. An ardent advocate of black rights, he had his passport withdrawn 1950–58 because of his association with left-wing movements.

Robeson US singer and actor Paul Robeson is remembered for his singing of 'Ol' Man River' from *Showboat* 1928 and playing the title role in *Othello* 1930. His outspoken political stance brought him before the Un-American Activities Committee in 1950.

Robespierre /'rəubzpjeə/ Maximilien François Marie Isidore de 1758–1794. French politician. A lawyer, he was elected to the National Assembly of 1789–91. His defence of democratic principles made him widely popular in Paris, while his disinterestedness won him the nickname of 'the Incorruptible'. As leader of the ◊Jacobins in the National Convention he supported the execution of Louis XVI and the overthrow of the ◊Girondins, and in July 1793 was elected to the Committee of Public Safety. His zeal for social reform and his attacks on the excesses of the extremists made him enemies on both right and left; a conspiracy was formed against him, and in Jul 1794 he was overthrown and guillotined.

robin song-bird *Erithacus rubecula* of the thrush family. It is found in Europe, W Asia, Africa, and the Azores. Both sexes are olive brown, with a red breast. The nest is constructed in a sheltered place, and from five to seven white freckled eggs are laid. The much larger North American robin belongs to the same family. In Australia members of several unrelated genera have been given the familiar name, and may have white, yellowish, or red breasts.

Robin Hood legendary English outlaw and folk hero, who appears in ballads from the 13th century. He is said to have lived in the reign of Richard I. He feuded with the sheriff of Nottingham, and lived in Sherwood Forest with Maid Marian and a band of followers, his 'merry men'. They robbed the rich and gave to the poor.

Robinson /'rɒbɪnsən/ Edward G. Stage-name of American film actor Emanuel Goldenberg 1893–1973. Born in Romania, he emigrated with his family to the USA in 1903. He was noted for his gangster roles, such as *Little Caesar* 1930.

Robinson /'rɒbɪnsən/ Edwin Arlington 1869–1935. American poet. He dealt mainly with psychological themes in a narrative style. Among his publications are *The Children of the Night* 1897, which established his reputation, and *The Man Who Died Twice* 1924.

Robinson /'rɒbɪnsən/ Henry Crabb 1775–1867. British writer, whose diaries, journals, and letters are a valuable source of information on his friends ◊Lamb, ◊Coleridge, ◊Wordsworth, and ◊Southey.

Robinson /'rɒbɪnsən/ John Arthur Thomas 1919–1983. British Anglican cleric, Bishop of Woolwich 1959–69. A left-wing ◊Modernist, he wrote the controversial *Honest to God* 1963, interpreted as denying a personal God.

Robinson /'rɒbɪnsən/ Robert 1886–1975. British chemist, Nobel prizewinner in 1947 for his research on the structure of many natural products, for example alkaloids. He formulated the electronic theory now used in organic chemistry.

Robinson /'rɒbɪnsən/ W(illiam) Heath 1872–1944. British artist, known for his humorous drawings of fantastically complex machinery for performing simple operations, such as raising one's hat.

Robinson W Heath Robinson's illustration of Professor Branestawm's invention for peeling potatoes.

robot any machine that can be taught or programmed to do work. Records of mechanical people and animals go back more than 2,000 years, bolstered by the creations of popular myth. The word was coined in 1921 by the Czech writer Karel Čapek. Since the advent of the computer, robots have proliferated. The most common types are mechanical 'arms'. Fixed to the floor or a workbench, they perform usually routine, repetitive functions such as paint spraying or assembling parts in factories. Others include computer-controlled vehicles for carrying materials, and a miscellany of devices from cruise missiles, deep-sea and space-exploration craft to robotic toys.

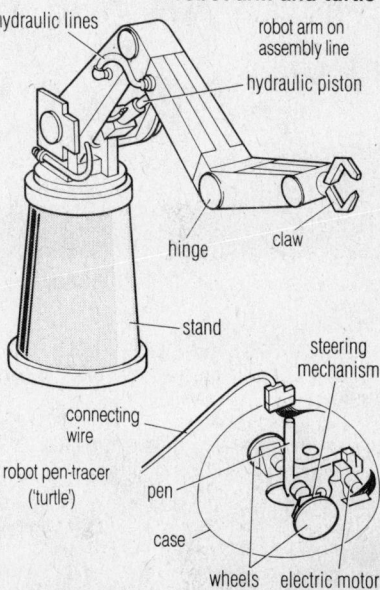

robot arm and turtle

hydraulic lines
robot arm on assembly line
hydraulic piston
hinge
claw
stand
connecting wire
robot pen-tracer ('turtle')
steering mechanism
pen
case
wheels   electric motor

Rob Roy /'rɒb 'rɔɪ/ nickname of Robert Macgregor 1671–1734. Scottish Highland ◊Jacobite outlaw. He lived by cattle theft and extortion. Pardoned in 1727.

Robsart /'rɒbsɑːt/ Amy c. 1532–1560. Wife of Robert Dudley, the Earl of ◊Leicester.

Robson /'rɒbsən/ Flora 1902–1984. British actress. She was created Dame of the British Empire in 1960.

Rochdale /'rɒtʃdeɪl/ industrial town (textiles, machinery, asbestos) in Greater Manchester, England, on the river Roch 16 km/10 mi NE of Manchester; population (1981) 92,704. The so-called Rochdale Pioneers founded the first Co-operative Society in England, in Toad Lane, Rochdale, 1844. The popular singer Gracie Fields was born here.

Rochelle, La /rɒ'ʃel/ see ◊La Rochelle, port in W France.

Rochester /'rɒtʃɪstə/ industrial city (flour, Kodak films and cameras) in New York State, USA, on the Genesee river S of Lake Ontario; university 1850; population (1980) 241,500.

Rochester /'rɒtʃɪstə/ commercial centre with dairy and food-processing industries in Minnesota, USA; population (1980) 57,890. The Mayo Clinic is here.

Rochester /'rɒtʃɪstə/ John Wilmot, 2nd Earl of Rochester 1647–1680. British poet. He fought gallantly at sea against the Dutch, but chiefly led

robot robots weld LeBaron cars at Chrysler's plant in Missouri, USA.

a debauched life at the court of Charles II. He wrote graceful lyrics, and *A Satire against Mankind* that rivals Swift.

Rochester The poet John Wilmot, 2nd Earl of Rochester, was patron to John Dryden and is remembered for his wit and sexual frankness.

Rochester upon Medway /ˈrɒtʃistə, ˈmedweɪ/ city in Kent, England; population (1983, with Chatham and Strood) 146,200. There is a 12th-century Norman castle keep, a 12th–15th-century cathedral, and many timbered buildings. A Dickens centre 1982 commemorates the town's many links with the novelist. The first borstal was near Rochester.

rochet a vestment worn mainly by Roman Catholic and Anglican bishops and abbots. The Roman Catholic type reaches to the knee, while the Anglican is nearly to the feet.

rock the constituent of the Earth's crust, either in its unconsolidated form as clay, mud, or sand, or consolidated into a hard mass as:

◊igneous rock, made from molten ◊lava or ◊magma solidifying on or beneath the Earth's surface (for example ◊basalt, ◊dolerite, ◊granite, ◊obsidian);

◊sedimentary rock, formed by deposition and compression at low temperatures and pressures, such as sandstone from sand particles, limestone from the remains of sea creatures or coal from those of plants; and

◊metamorphic rocks, formed by changes in existing igneous or sedimentary rocks under high pressure or heat, or chemical action, for example limestone to ◊marble.

rock Cliffs at Hunstanton, Norfolk, showing three distinct layers of rock.

Rockall /ˈrɒkɔːl/ British islet in the Atlantic, 24 m/80 ft across and 22 m/65 ft high, part of the Hatton-Rockall bank, and 370 km/230 mi W of N Uist in the Hebrides. The bank is part of a fragment of Greenland that broke away 60

million years ago. It is in a potentially rich oil/gas area. A party of British marines landed in 1955 formally to annex Rockall, but Denmark, Iceland, and Ireland challenge Britain's claims for mineral, oil, and fishing rights. The *Rockall Trough* between Rockall and Ireland, 250 km/155 mi wide and up to 3,000 m/10,000 ft deep, forms an ideal marine laboratory.

rock and roll a term popularized by the US disc jockey Alan Freed from 1951 for music based on a fusion of ◊rhythm and blues and ◊country and western which in the mid-1950s, with the advent of Elvis ◊Presley, became the main form of ◊pop music in the Western world. Based on electric guitar and drums, it found perhaps its purest form in late-1950s *rockabilly*; the blanket term 'rock' later came to comprise a multitude of styles. Among the most influential rock-and-roll singers and songwriters of the 1950s were Chuck ◊Berry, Buddy ◊Holly, and Gene Vincent (1935–71).

Rockefeller /ˈrɒkəˌfelə/ John D(avison) 1839–1937. American millionaire, founder of Standard Oil in 1870 (which achieved control of 90 per cent of US refineries), and of the philanthropic *Rockefeller Foundation* 1913 to which his son John D(avison) Rockefeller Jr (1874–1960) devoted his life. His grandson *Nelson (Aldrich) Rockefeller* 1908–79 was governor of New York 1958–74 and Ford's vice-president 1974–76. *Rockefeller Centre* in Manhattan, New York (which includes Radio City Music Hall), is the world's largest privately owned business and entertainment centre.

rocket projectile driven by the reaction of gases produced by a fast-burning fuel. Unlike the ◊jet engine, which is also a reaction engine, the rocket carries its own oxygen supply to burn its fuel and is totally independent of any surrounding atmosphere. Rockets have been valued as fireworks over the last seven centuries, but their intensive development as a means of propulsion to high altitudes – carrying payloads – started only in the inter-war years with the state-supported work in Germany (see ◊von Braun) and of Professor R H Goddard (1882–1945) in the USA. The only form of propulsion available which can function in a vacuum, rockets are essential to the exploration of outer space.

Two main kinds of rockets are used: one burns liquid propellants, the other solid propellants. The fireworks rocket uses gunpowder as a solid propellant. The ◊space shuttle's solid rocket boosters use a mixture of powdered aluminium in a synthetic rubber binder. Most rockets, however, have liquid propellants, which are more powerful and easier to control. Liquid hydrogen and kerosene are common fuels, while liquid oxygen is the most common oxygen-provider, or oxidizer. For space exploration, multi-stage, or ◊step rockets have to be used, which consist of a number of rockets joined together. One of the biggest rockets ever built, the *Saturn V* moon rocket, was a three-stage design, standing 111 m/365 ft high; it weighed more than 2,700 tonnes on the launch pad, and developed a take-off thrust of some 3.4 million kg/7.5 million lb.

In warfare the head of the rocket carries an explosive device. Such weapons were first used by the Chinese about AD 1100, and were encountered in India in the 18th century by the British forces. The rocket missile was then reinvented by Sir William Congreve (1772–1828) in England around 1805, and remained in use by various armies in the 19th century.

In World War II rockets were effectively used by aircraft, and by the Germans in their ◊V2 attacks on the London area in 1944–45: the V2 (15 m/50 ft long and carrying 1 tonne of high explosive in its warhead) was the first long-range ballistic missile.

Since World War II, the devastating combination of refined, precise guidance systems with atomic warheads has produced rocket missiles, which are the key to international power politics. They may be for surface-to-surface, air-to-surface, or surface-to-air use.

Rockets are also used to supplement conventional artillery, for instance in the US multiple-launch rocket system (MLRS). Armed with two pods of six rockets, which can be fired individually or otherwise, it has the advantage over guns in firepower, mobility, and cost, but is restricted to long range.

Rockhampton /ˌrɒkˈhæmptən/ port in E Queensland, Australia; population (1984) 56,500.

Rockingham /ˈrɒkɪŋəm/ Charles Watson Wentworth, 2nd Marquess of Rockingham 1730–1782. British Whig politician, prime minister 1765–66 and 1782 (when he died in office); he supported the Americans' claim to independence.

rock opera popular form of modern musical using rock and jazz elements, as in Andrew ◊Lloyd Webber's *Jesus Christ Superstar* 1970.

Rockwell /ˈrɒkwel/ Norman 1894–1978. American artist, noted for his magazine covers.

Rocky Mountains /ˈrɒki/ chief N American mountain system. They extend from the junction with the Mexican plateau, northward through the W central states of the USA, through Canada to the Alaskan border. Many large rivers rise in the Rocky Mountains, including the Missouri. The Rocky Mountain National Park 1915 in Colorado has more than 100 peaks over 3,350 m/11,000 ft; Mount Logan on the Canadian-Alaskan border is 6,050 m/19,850 ft.

Rococo stylistic term describing the late ◊Baroque period in European art and architecture during the 18th century. The Rococo is characterized by light, deft patterns with much ornamentation; it is found especially in France, Spain, S Germany, and Austria. It was followed in the mid-18th century by ◊Neo-Classicism.

rodent mammal of the worldwide order Rodentia. Besides ordinary 'cheek teeth', they have a single front pair of incisor teeth in both upper and lower jaw, which continue to grow as they are worn down. They are subdivided into three suborders, Myomorpha, Sciuromorpha, and Hystricomorpha, of which the rat, squirrel, and porcupine respectively are the typical members.

rodeo originally a practical round-up of cattle on American ranges, it is now usually a commercial show in the USA, Australia, and

Canada, in which calves are roped, near-wild horses ridden bareback, steers thrown, and so on. In the USA it remains a highly competitive sport. Considerable cruelty may be involved. One of the most famous is in ◊Calgary, Canada.

Rodgers /ˈrɒdʒəz/ Richard (Charles) 1902–1979. American composer. He collaborated with librettist Lorenz Hart (1895–1943) in songs such as 'Blue Moon' 1934 and the pioneer realistic musical with a squalid hero *Pal Joey* 1940; and with Oscar Hammerstein II (1895–1960) in the musicals *Oklahoma!* 1943, *South Pacific* 1949, *The King and I* 1951, and *The Sound of Music* 1959.

Rodin /rəʊˈdæ̃/ Auguste 1840–1917. French sculptor. Born in Paris, he studied under Barye and Carrier-Belleuse, and visited Italy in 1875, where he studied the works of ◊Donatello and ◊Michelangelo. In 1877 he made a tour of the French cathedrals, and was much influenced by Gothic sculpture. In the 1880s he was granted a studio in Paris by the state. Public recognition was world-wide after an exhibition in 1900.

Rodin's work shows an extraordinary technical facility and a deep understanding of the human form, and includes *Le Penseur/The Thinker* 1880, *Le Baiser/The Kiss* 1886, *Les Bourgeois de Calais/The Burghers of Calais* 1886 (copy in Embankment Gardens at Westminster, London), and his controversial masterpiece, the *Balzac* monument 1897. The Musée Rodin in Paris houses many examples of his work and their preparatory drawings.

Rodney /ˈrɒdni/ George Brydges Rodney, Baron Rodney 1718–1792. British admiral. In 1762 he captured Martinique, St Lucia, and Grenada from the French, and received a baronetcy in 1764. In 1780 he relieved Gibraltar by defeating a Spanish squadron off Cape St Vincent. In 1782 he crushed the French fleet under count de ◊Grasse off Dominica, for which he was raised to the peerage.

roebuck the male of the roe ◊deer.

Roeg /rəʊg/ Nicolas 1928– . British film director. His work is noted for its stylish visual appeal and imaginative, often off-beat, treatment of subjects. His films include *Walkabout* 1971, *Don't Look Now* 1973, and *Castaway* 1986.

Roeselare /ˈruːsəlɑːrə/ (French *Roulers*) textile town in West Flanders province, NW Belgium; population (1985) 52,000. It was a major German base in World War I.

Roethke /ˈretki/ Theodore 1908–1963. US poet, born in Michigan. His father owned a large nursery business, and the greenhouses and plants of his childhood provide the detail and imagery of much of his lyrical, personal, and visionary poetry. Collections include *Open House* 1941, *The Waking* 1953 (Pulitzer Prize), and the posthumous *Collected Poems* 1968.

Rogation Day one of the three days before ◊Ascension Day in the Christian calendar, which used to be marked by processions round the parish boundaries ('beating the bounds') and blessing of crops; now only rarely observed.

Rogers /ˈrɒdʒəz/ Carl 1902–1987. US psychologist who developed the client-centred approach to counselling and psychotherapy. This

stressed the importance of clients making their own decisions and developing their own potential (self-actualization).

Rogers /ˈrɒdʒəz/ Richard 1933– . British architect whose works include the Pompidou Centre in Paris 1977 (jointly with Renzo Piano) and the Lloyd's building in London 1986.

Roget /ˈrəʊʒeɪ/ Peter Mark 1779–1869. British physician, one of the founders of the University of London, and author of a *Thesaurus of English Words and Phrases* 1852.

Röhm /rɜːm/ Ernst 1887–1934. German leader of the Nazi 'Brown Shirts', the SA (◊Sturm Abteilung). On the pretext of an intended SA *Putsch* (uprising) some hundred of them, including Röhm, were killed 29–30 Jun 1934, sometimes referred to as 'the Night of the Long Knives'.

Rohmer /ˈrəʊmə/ Sax, pseudonym of British crime writer Arthur Sarsfield Ward 1886–1959. Creator of the sinister Chinese character Dr Fu Manchu 1913.

Roland /ˈrəʊlənd/ died 778. French soldier, killed, with his friend Oliver and the twelve peers of France, at Roncesvalles (in the Pyrenees) by the ◊Basques. He had headed the rearguard during ◊Charlemagne's retreat from his invasion of Spain. He is the hero of many romances, including the 11th-century *Chanson de Roland* and Ariosto's *Orlando Furioso*.

Roland de la Platière /rəʊˈlɒŋ də lɑː ˌplætiˈeə/ Jeanne Manon (born Philipon) 1754–1793. French intellectual politician, whose salon from 1789 was a focus of democratic discussion. Her ideas were influential after her husband Jean Marie Roland de la Platière (1734–93) was minister of the interior in 1792. As a supporter of the ◊Girondin party, opposed to Robespierre and Danton, she was condemned to the guillotine in 1793, without being allowed to speak in her own defence. Her last words were 'O liberty! What crimes are committed in thy name!'.

role in the social sciences, a term used to mean the part a person plays in society, either in helping the social system to work or in fulfilling social responsibilities towards others. Sociologists distinguish between formal roles, such as those of a doctor or politician, and informal roles, such as those of mother or husband, which are based on personal relationships. Social roles involve mutual expectations: a doctor can fulfil that role only if the patients play their part; a father requires the support of his children. *Role play* refers to the way children learn adult roles by acting them out in play (mothers and fathers, cops and robbers). Everyone has a number of roles to play in a society: a woman may be a mother, a wife, and an employee at the same time, for example. *Role conflict* arises where two or more of a person's roles are seen as incompatible.

Rolfe /rəʊf/ Frederick 1860–1913. British writer, who called himself Baron Corvo. A Roman Catholic convert, frustrated in his desire to enter the priesthood, he wrote the novel *Hadrian the Seventh* 1904, in which the character of the title rose from being a poor writer to become pope.

Rolle de Hampole /ˈrəʊl də ˈhæmpəʊl/ Richard c. 1300–1349. English hermit and

rocket Cape Canaveral, Florida, is the rocket launching pad for America's space programme.

author of English and Latin works including the mystic *Meditation of the Passion*.

roller bird of the family Coraciidae, somewhat resembling crows but related to kingfishers. They are found in the Old World, and the species *Coracias garrulus*, blue with a reddish-brown back, is an occasional British visitor. The name is derived from their habit of rolling over in flight.

rolling a common method of shaping metal. Rolling is carried out by giant mangles, consisting of several sets, or stands, of heavy rollers positioned one above the other. Red-hot metal slabs are rolled into sheet and also (using shaped rollers) girders and rails. Metal sheets are often cold-rolled finally to impart a harder surface.

Rolling Stones, the English rock band formed 1963. Original members were Mick Jagger, Keith Richards, Brian Jones, Bill Wyman, Charlie Watts, and the pianist Ian Stewart. Their earthy sound was influenced by ◊rhythm and blues, and their rebel image was contrasted with the early Beatles, whom they rivalled in popularity by the end of the 1960s. By the 1980s they had become a rock-and-roll institution. Classic early hits included

'Satisfaction' 1965, 'Paint It Black' 1966, 'Jumpin' Jack Flash' 1968, and 'Honky Tonk Women' 1969.

Rollins /'rɒlɪnz/ 'Sonny' Theodore Walter 1930– . US tenor saxophonist and jazz composer. A leader of the 'hard bop' school, he is known for the intensity and bravado of his music, and for his skilful improvisation.

Rollo /'rɒləʊ/ 1st Duke of Normandy c. 860–932. Duke from 912 until his retirement to a monastery in 927. He was a ◊Viking leader who was granted the province of Normandy by Charles III of France.

Rolls-Royce /'rəʊlz 'rɔɪs/ industrial company manufacturing cars and aeroplane engines, founded by Frederick William ◊Royce and Charles Stewart Rolls (1877–1910).

ROM (*read-only memory*) in computing, an electronic ◊memory device; a computer's permanent repository of important information or programs. ROM holds data or programs that will never need to be changed but must always be readily available, for example, a computer's operating system. It is an ◊integrated circuit (chip) and its capacity is measured in kilobytes (thousands of characters). ROM chips are filled during manufacture with the relevant data and

programs, which are not lost when the computer is switched off, as they are in RAM.

Romagna /rəʊ'mɑːnjə/ area of Italy on the Adriatic coast, under papal rule 1278–1860, and now part of the region of ◊Emilia-Romagna.

Romains /rəʊ'mæ̃/ Jules, pseudonym of Louis Farigoule 1885–1972. French novelist, playwright, philosopher, and poet. He developed the theory of Unanimism; this states that every group has a communal existence greater than that of the individual, which intensifies their perceptions and emotions. Of his plays, the farce *Knock, ou le triomphe de la médecine/Dr Knock* 1923 is best known.

Roman art 753 BC–410 AD. During the 8th century BC the Etruscans appeared as the first native Italian civilization, N and W of the river Tiber. Their art shows influences of archaic Greece and the Near East. Their coffins (*sarcophagi*) are carved with reliefs and topped with portraits of the dead, reclining on one elbow as if at an eternal banquet.

Under Julius Caesar's successor Augustus (27 BC–14 AD) the Roman Empire was established. Art and architecture played an important role in unifying the European nations under Roman rule. The Romans greatly admired Greek art and

rocket

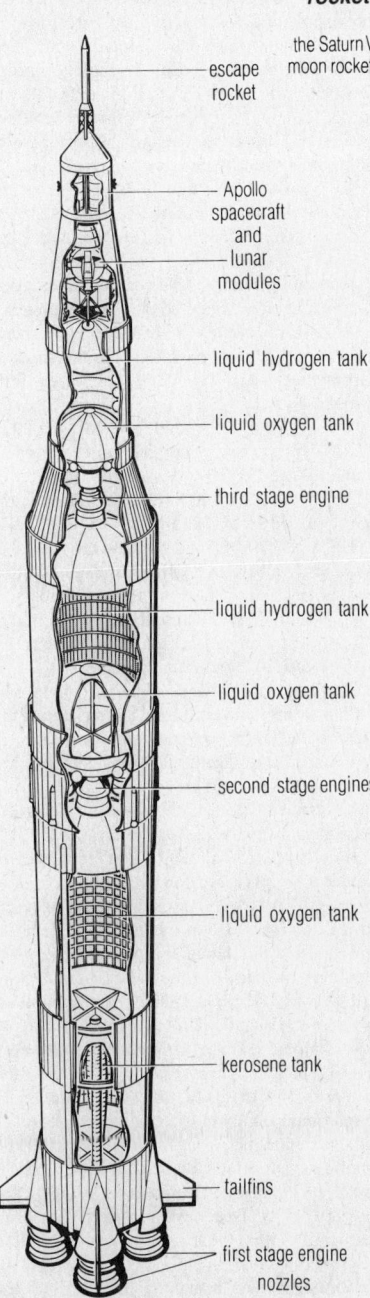

the Saturn V
moon rocket

escape rocket

Apollo spacecraft and lunar modules

liquid hydrogen tank

liquid oxygen tank

third stage engine

liquid hydrogen tank

liquid oxygen tank

second stage engines

liquid oxygen tank

kerosene tank

tailfins

first stage engine nozzles

Rocky Mountains The dramatically broken splendour of the Rockies in their Canadian section.

Rogers A characteristic of the work of British architect Richard Rogers is to give prominence to the parts of a building that are usually concealed. At Lloyd's of London, the external pipes and stairways are integral not only to the functions of the building, but also to its design.

These appeared on monumental altars, triumphal arches, and giant columns such as *Trajan's Column* 106–113 AD which records his historic battles like a strip cartoon, winding its way around the column for 656 ft. Strict realism in portraiture gave way to a certain amount of Greek-style idealization in the propaganda statues of the emperors, befitting their semi-divine status. Gods and allegorical figures feature with Rome's heroes on such narrative relief sculptures as those on Augustus's giant altar to peace, the *Ara Pacis* 13–9 BC.

Very little *Roman painting* has survived, and much of what has is because of the volcanic eruption of Mount Vesuvius in AD 79 which buried the S Italian seaside towns of Pompeii and Herculaneum under ash, thus preserving the lively and impressionistic wall paintings which publicly the glorious victories of their heroes.

became the first collectors, importing vast quantities of marbles and bronzes, and even Greek artisans to make copies. Realistic portrait sculpture was an important original development by the Romans. In public places official statues were erected of generals, rulers, and philosophers. The portrait bust developed as a new art form from about 75 BC; these were serious, factual portraits of a rugged race of patriarchs.

Narrative relief sculpture also flourished in Rome, again linked to the need to commemorate decorated the holiday villas of an art-loving elite.

Favourite motifs were illusionistic and still-life. A type of interior decoration known as *Grotesque*, rediscovered in Rome during the Renaissance, combined swirling plant motifs, strange animals, and tiny fanciful scenes. Grotesque was much used in later decorative schemes whenever it was fashionable to quote the Classical period.

The art of *mosaic* was universally popular throughout the Roman Empire. It was introduced from Greece and used for floors as well as walls and vaults, in *trompe l'oeil* effects, geometric patterns and scenes from daily life and mythology.

Roman Britain Roman relations with Britain began with Caesar's invasions of 55 and 54 BC, but the conquest was not begun until 43 AD. England was rapidly Romanized, but N of York fewer remains of Roman civilization have been found. After several unsuccessful attempts to conquer Scotland the N frontier was fixed at ◊Hadrian's Wall. During the 4th century Britain suffered from raids by the Saxons, Picts, and Scots. The Roman armies were withdrawn in 407 but there were partial re-occupations 417–c. 427 and c. 450. Roman towns include London, York, Chester, Caerleon, St Albans, Colchester, Lincoln, Gloucester, and Bath. The most permanent remains of the occupation were the system of military roads radiating from London.

Roman Catholicism one of the main divisions of ◊Christianity.

romance in literature, the term was first used for tales of love and adventure, in verse or prose, which became popular in France about 1200 and spread throughout Europe. There were Arthurian romances about the legendary King Arthur and his knights, and romances based on the adventures of Charlemagne and on classical themes. The term gradually came to mean any fiction remote from the conditions and concerns of everyday life. In this sense, romance is a broad term which can include or overlap with such genres as the ◊historical novel or ◊fantasy.

Romance languages the branch of Indo-European languages descended from the Latin of the Roman Empire ('popular' or 'vulgar' as opposed to 'classical' Latin). The present-day Romance languages with national status are French, Italian, Portuguese, Romanian, and Spanish. Romansh (or Rhaeto-Romanic) is a minority language of Switzerland which is nevertheless one of the four official languages of the country, while Catalan and Gallego (or Galician) in Spain, Provençal in France and Friulian and Sardinian in Italy are recognized as distinct languages with strong regional and/or literary traditions of their own.

Romanesque style of W European ◊architecture of the 8th to 12th centuries, marked by rounded arches, solid volumes, and emphasis on perpendicular elements. In England the style was called ◊Norman.

Romania /rəʊˈmeɪnɪə/ country in SE Europe, on the Black Sea, bounded to the N and E by the USSR, to the S by Bulgaria, to the SW by Yugoslavia, and to the NW by Hungary.

government Under the 1965 constitution, the supreme body of state power and sole legislative organ in Romania is the 369-member Grand National Assembly (*Marea Adunare Nationala*). The Assembly is elected every five years by universal suffrage. It meets for two working sessions each year and elects a subordinate 21-member state council to sit in permanent session and a Council of Ministers, headed by a prime minister, to assume charge of day-to-day executive administration. Since 1974 a president has also been elected by the Grand National Assembly to combine the duties of head of state, president of the State Council, supreme commander of the armed forces, and president of the Defence Council.

The controlling force and sole permitted political party in Romania is the Romanian Communist Party (RCP), which is prescribed a 'leading role' by the constitution and leads the broader Socialist Democracy and Unity Front (SDUF) in presenting approved candidate lists for all state elections. The RCP holds congresses every five years (most recently in 1984) to debate and adopt policy programmes and to elect a general secretary and a central committee, which in turn elects an executive political committee and secretariat to run the day-to-day affairs of the party.

history The earliest known inhabitants merged with invaders from ◊Thrace. Ancient ◊Rome made it the province of Dacia; the poet Ovid was one of the settlers, and the people and language were Romanized. After the withdrawal of the Romans in 275 AD, Romania was occupied by ◊Goths, and during the 6th–12th centuries was overrun by ◊Huns, Bulgars, ◊Slavs, and other invaders. The principalities of Wallachia in the S, and Moldavia in the E, dating from the 14th century, fell to the ◊Ottoman Empire in the 15th and 16th centuries.

Turkish rule was exchanged for Russian protection 1829–56. In 1859 Moldavia and Wallachia elected Prince Alexander Cuza, under whom they were united as Romania from 1861. He was deposed 1866 and Prince Charles of ◊Hohenzollern-Sigmaringen elected. After the Russo-Turkish war 1877–78, in which Romania sided with Russia, the great powers recognized Romania's independence, and in 1881 Prince Charles became King Carol I.

Romania fought against Bulgaria in the Second ◊Balkan War (1913) and annexed S ◊Dobruja. It entered World War I on the Allied side in 1916, was occupied by the Germans 1917–18, but received ◊Bessarabia from Russia and ◊Bukhovina and ◊Transylvania from the dismembered Hapsburg empire under the 1918 peace settlement, thus emerging as the largest state in the ◊Balkans. During the late 1930s, to counter the growing popularity of the fascist ◊Iron Guard movement, ◊Carol II abolished the democratic constitution of 1923 and established his own dictatorship. In 1940 he was forced to surrender Bessarabia, N Transylvania, and S Dobruja to the USSR, Hungary, and Bulgaria respectively and abdicated when Romania was occupied by Germany in Aug. Power was assumed by Gen Ion ◊Antonescu (ruling in the

name of Carol's son King ◊Michael), who signed the ◊Axis Pact in Nov 1940 and declared war on the USSR in Jun 1941. In Aug 1944, with the Red Army on Romania's borders, King Michael supported the ousting of the Antonescu government. Romania subsequently joined the war against Germany and in the Paris peace treaties of 1947 recovered Transylvania, but lost N Bukhovina to the USSR.

In the elections of 1946 a Communist-led coalition achieved a majority and proceeded to force King Michael to abdicate. The new Romanian People's Republic was proclaimed in Dec 1947 and dominated by the Romanian Communist Party, then termed the Romanian Workers' Party (RWP). Soviet-style constitutions were adopted in 1949 and 1952; Romania joined ◊Comecon 1949 and co-signed the ◊Warsaw Pact 1955; and a programme of nationalization was launched. After a rapid purge of opposition leaders, the RWP became firmly established in power, enabling Soviet occupation forces to leave the country in 1958.

The dominant political personality between 1945 and 1965 was RWP leader and state president Gheorghe Gheorghiu-Dej. He was succeeded by Nicolae ◊Ceausescu, who placed greater emphasis on national autonomy and proclaimed Romania a socialist republic. Under Ceausescu, Romania has adopted a foreign-policy line independent of the USSR, condemning the 1968 invasion of Czechoslovakia and refusing to participate directly in Warsaw Pact manoeuvres or allow Russian troops to enter the country. Ceausescu has called for multilateral nuclear disarmament and the creation of a Balkan nuclear-weapons-free zone and has maintained warm relations with China.

At home the RCP has sought broader participation in policy making, but a tight rein has been kept on dissident activities. Economic difficulties have mounted. There were widespread power cuts in the winters of 1985 and 1986 and the military occupied power plants. After a referendum in 1986 defence spending was cut by 5 per cent. Ceausescu was re-elected general secretary of the RCP and chair of the SDUF in Nov 1984 and state president in Mar 1985. Many members of his family hold prominent posts in the party and state executives.

Romanian language a member of the Romance branch of the Indo-European language family, spoken in Romania, Macedonia, Albania, and parts of N Greece. It has been strongly influenced by the Slavonic languages and by Greek. The Cyrillic alphabet was used until the 19th century, when a variant of the Roman alphabet was adopted.

Roman law one of the two main European legal systems, English law being the other. It originated under the republic, was developed under the empire, and continued in use in the Byzantine Empire until 1453. The first codification was that of the 12 Tables (450BC), of which only fragments survive. Roman law assumed its final form in the codification of Justinian (528–34AD). An outstanding feature of Roman law was its system of international law (*jus gentium*), applied in disputes between

Romans and foreigners or provincials, or between provincials of different states. During the Middle Ages Roman law was adopted, with local modifications, all over Europe, mainly through the Church's influence; its later diffusion was largely due to the influence of the French *Code Napoléon*, based on Roman law, which was adopted in the 19th century by several states of E Europe and Asia, and in Egypt. Inside the Commonwealth, Roman law forms the basis of the legal systems of Scotland, Quebec, and South Africa.

Roman numerals an old number system using different symbols from today's Arabic numerals (the ordinary numbers 1, 2, 3, 4, 5, and so on). The seven key symbols in Roman numerals as represented today (originally they were a little different) are I (= 1), V (= 5), X (= 10), L (= 50), C (= 100), D (= 500) and M (= 1,000). There is no zero. The first fifteen Roman numerals are I, II, III, IV (or IIII), V, VI, VII, VIII, IX, X, XI, XII, XIII, XIV and XV; the multiples of 10 from 20 to 90 are XX, XXX, XL, L, LX, LXX, LXXX and XC; and the year 1988 becomes MCMLXXXVIII. Although addition and subtraction are fairly straightforward using Roman numerals, the absence of a zero makes other arithmetic calculations (such as multiplication) clumsy and difficult.

Romano /rəu'mɑːnəu/ Giulio c. 1499–1546. Italian painter and architect. He was one of the creators of ◊Mannerism. An assistant to ◊Raphael, he exaggerated Raphael's style into an individual one of his own.

Romanov /'rəumənɒf/ dynasty which ruled Russia from 1613 to the revolution of Mar 1917.

Roman religion a religion that retained early elements of reverence to stones and trees, and totemism (see ◊Romulus and Remus), and had a strong domestic base in the ◊lares and penates, and the cult of ◊Janus and ◊Vesta. The main pantheon included ◊Jupiter and ◊Juno, ◊Mars and ◊Venus, ◊Minerva, ◊Diana, and ◊Ceres, all of whom had their Greek counterparts, and many lesser deities. The deification of dead emperors served a political purpose, and also retained the idea of family, that is that those who had served the national family in life continued to care, as did one's ancestors, after their death. Under the empire the educated classes tended to ◊Stoicism or ◊Scepticism, but there was a following for mystery cults (see ◊Isis), and ◊Mithraism (especially within the army) was a strong rival to ◊Christianity.

Romansh /rəu'mænʃ/ a member of the Romance branch of the Indo-European language family, spoken by some 50,000 people in the E cantons of Switzerland and accorded in 1937 official status alongside French, German, and Italian. It is also known among scholars as Rhaeto-Romanic.

Romanticism movement in the arts in Europe during the late 18th and early 19th century in which emotion and experience were given imaginative expression in a free form. Inspired by social change and revolution (American, French) and reacting against the classical restraint of the Augustan age and ◊Enlightenment, the Romantics asserted the

Romania

SOCIALIST REPUBLIC OF (*Republica Socialistă România*)

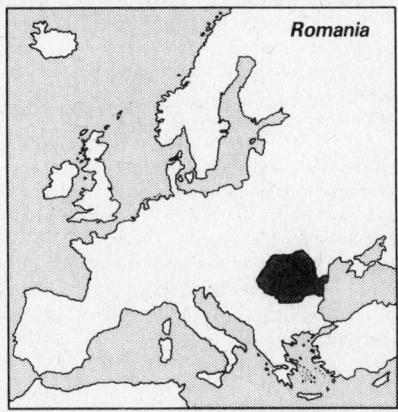

AREA 237,500 sq km/91,699 sq mi
CAPITAL Bucharest
TOWNS Brasov, Timisoara, Cluj, Iasi; ports Galati, Constanta, Sulina
PHYSICAL mountains surrounding a plateau, with river plains S and E
FEATURES Carpathian Mountains, Transylvanian Alps; river Danube; Black Sea coast; rich in mineral springs
HEAD OF STATE Nicolae Ceauşescu from 1974
HEAD OF GOVERNMENT Constantin Dascalescu from 1982
GOVERNMENT one-party communist
EXPORTS petroleum products and oilfield equipment, electrical goods, cars (largely to communist countries)
CURRENCY leu (noncommercial rate 16.32 = £1 Sept 1987)
POPULATION (1985) 22,734,000 (including 400,000 Germans); annual growth rate 0.8%
LANGUAGE Romanian, a Romance language descended from that of Roman settlers, though later modified by Slav influences
RELIGION Romanian Orthodox (linked with Greek Orthodox)
LITERACY 97% male/94% female (1980 est)
GNP $45 bn (1984); $5,250 per head of population
CHRONOLOGY
1944 Pro-Nazi Antonescu government overthrown.
1945 Communist-dominated government appointed.
1947 Boundaries redrawn. King Michael abdicated and People's Republic proclaimed.
1949 New constitution adopted. Joined Comecon.
1952 New Soviet-style constitution.
1955 Romania joined Warsaw Pact.
1958 Soviet occupation forces removed.
1965 New constitution adopted.
1974 Ceauşescu created president.
1985–86 Winters of austerity and power cuts.
1987 Workers demonstrations against austerity programme.

Romanticism A blending of French and English romantic feeling in Gustav Doré's interpretation of the Arthurian legend in his illustrations of Tennyson's *Idylls* – 'The Ride to Camelot'.

importance of how the individual feels about the world, natural and supernatural. The Romantics had, or claimed, heightened sensibilities, and pursued the ideals of freedom and beauty; they sacrificed all to their art. They often led tempestuous lives. Wandering about, sometimes in abject poverty, some became bitterly disillusioned, some died young. Their lives became as famous as their creative output. Many of the second wave of Romantics became caught up in nationalist fervour, for example Pushkin, Wagner, Verdi, Chopin.
literature 18th-century forerunners, for example Thomas Gray, William Collins, Rousseau, and Schiller; 19th century Coleridge, Wordsworth, Byron, Shelley, Keats, Walter Scott, Goethe, Brentano, Novalis, Eichendorff, Tieck, Chateaubriand, Lamartine, Musset, de Vigny, Hugo, Manzoni
music Schubert, Weber, Schumann, Berlioz, Wagner, Chopin, Liszt, Brahms
art Delacroix, Géricault.

Romany /'rɒmənɪ/ a nomadic people, also called *gypsy* in English; that term is a corruption of 'Egyptian', since they were erroneously thought to come from Egypt. In the 14th century they settled in the Balkan peninsula. During the next century they spread over Germany, Italy, and France, and they arrived in England about 1500. A long period of persecution followed, including accusations of cannibalism and child-stealing. They are traditionally associated with music, various crafts, fortune-telling, and skills with horses. Attempts have been made to encourage them to settle, and to provide those still nomadic with official camp sites and educational facilities.

Their language, also known as Romany, has relations with the Indo-European group, and some of its words correspond with words in Hindustani. All the countries through which the Romany people have passed have added to their word stock, but especially Greek and Slavonic.

Rome /rəum/ (Italian *Roma*) capital of Italy and ◊Lazio, on the Tiber, 27 km/17 mi from the Tyrrhenian Sea; population (1984) 2,827,000. Rome has few industries but is an important cultural, road, and rail centre; university; a large section of the population finds employment in government offices. E of the river are the seven hills on which it was originally built (Quirinal, Aventine, Caelian, Esquiline, Viminal, Palatine, and Capitol), to the W the popular quarter of Trastevere, the more modern residential quarters of the Prati, and the ◊Vatican.
features remains of the ancient city include the Forum, Colosseum, Pantheon, Castel Sant' Angelo (the mausoleum of the emperor ◊Hadrian), and baths of Caracalla; Renaissance palaces include the Lateran, Quirinal (with the Trevi fountain nearby), Colonna, Borghese, Barberini, and Farnese. There are a number of churches of different periods; San Paolo was founded by the emperor Constantine on St Paul's grave. The Piazza di Spagna is known for the Spanish Steps.

history for early history see ◊Rome, Ancient. After the deposition of the last emperor Romulus Augustus in 476, the papacy became the real ruler of Rome, and from the 8th century was recognized as such, although attempts were made, for example by Arnold of Brescia 1143–55 and Rienzi 1347–54, to revive the republic. As a result of the French Revolution Rome temporarily became a republic in 1798–99, and was annexed to the French Empire 1808–14, until the pope returned on Napoleon's fall. During the 1848–49 revolution, a republic was established under Mazzini's leadership, but in spite of Garibaldi's defence was overthrown by French troops. In 1870 Rome became the capital of Italy, the pope retiring into the Vatican until 1929 when the Vatican City was recognized as a sovereign state. The occupation of Rome by the Fascists in 1922 marked the beginning of Mussolini's rule. After his fall in 1943 Rome was occupied by Germany, but was captured by the Allies in 1944.

Rome, Ancient civilization around the Mediterranean Sea, based in Rome, which lasted for some 800 years. Traditionally founded in 753 BC, Rome became a self-ruling republic (and free of ◊Etruscan rule) only in 510 BC. From then, the history of Rome is one of continual expansion, interrupted only by civil wars in the period 133–27 BC, until the murder of Julius ◊Caesar and foundation of the empire under ◊Augustus and his successors. At its peak under ◊Trajan, the Roman Empire stretched from Britain to

Mesopotamia and the Caspian Sea. A long train of emperors ruling by virtue of military, rather than civil, power marked the beginning of Rome's long decline; under ◊Diocletian, the empire was divided into two parts although temporarily reunited under ◊Constantine, the first emperor formally to adopt Christianity. The end of the Roman Empire is generally dated by the sack of Rome by the Goths in 410, or by the deposition of the last emperor in the West in 476. The Eastern Empire continued until 1453 at ◊Constantinople.

The civilization of Ancient Rome had an incalculable influence on the whole of Western Europe throughout the Middle Ages, the Renaissance, and beyond, especially in the fields of art and architecture, literature, law, and engineering. See also ◊Latin.

Rome, Ancient Roman kitchen (above) reconstructed at the Museum of London; a Roman bust (below) of Julius Caesar.

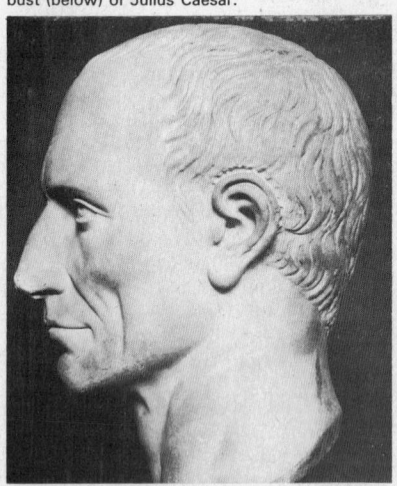

Rome, Sack of 410 AD. The invasion and capture of the city of Rome by the Goths. Generally accepted as marking the effective end of the Roman Empire.

Rome, Treaties of treaties establishing and regulating the ◊European Community.

Rommel /'rɒməl/ Erwin 1891–1944. German field marshal. He served in World War I, later joining the Nazi party. He played an important part in the invasions of central Europe and France, and was commander of the N African offensive from 1941 until defeated in the

Battles of ◊Alamein. He was commander in chief for a short time against the Allies in Europe in 1944 but (as a sympathizer with the ◊Stauffenberg plot) was forced to commit suicide.

Romney /'rʌmni/ George 1734–1802. British artist. Born near Dalton-in-Furness, Lancashire, the son of a carpenter and cabinet-maker, he was practically self-taught. He set up as a portrait painter in 1757, and deserting his family in 1762 he went to London. There he became, with Gainsborough and Reynolds, one of the most successful portrait painters of the late 18th century, although artistically inferior to both. His most famous sitter was Lady Hamilton, whom he painted several times.

Romney A portrait of Lady Hamilton by George Romney.

Romney Marsh /'rɒmni 'mɑːʃ/ a stretch of drained marshland on the Kent coast, England, between Hythe and Rye, used for sheep pasture. The seaward point is Dungeness. Romney Marsh was reclaimed in Roman times, and is known for its churches.
New Romney, formed by the amalgamation of Romney, one of the ◊Cinque Ports, with Littlestone and Greatstone, is now more than a mile from the sea; population (1981) 4,563.

Romsey /'rʌmzi/ market town in Hampshire, England; population (1984) 13,150. The fine Norman church of Romsey Abbey (founded by Edward the Elder) survives, as does King John's Hunting Box of about 1206 (now a

museum); nearby Broadlands was the seat of Earl Mountbatten and Lord Palmerston.

Romulus /'rɒmjʊləs/ in Roman mythology, the legendary founder and first king of Rome, the son of ◊Mars by Rhea Silvia. He and his twin brother Remus were exposed by their great-uncle Amulius, but were suckled by a she-wolf and rescued by a shepherd. On reaching manhood they killed Amulius and founded Rome. Having murdered Remus, Romulus reigned alone until he disappeared in a storm, and thereafter was worshipped as a god under the name of Quirinus.

Romulus Augustus /ɔː'gʌstəs/ c. 461–?. Last Roman emperor in the West. When about 14 he was made emperor by his soldier father Orestes in 475, but compelled to abdicate in 476 by Odoacer, leader of the barbarian mercenaries, who nicknamed him Augustulus. Orestes was executed and Romulus Augustus confined to a Neapolitan villa where he died.

Roncesvalles /'rɒnsəvælz, Spanish rɒnθez'væljes/ village of N Spain, in the Pyrenees 8 km/5 mi S of the French frontier, known as the scene of the defeat of the rearguard of Charlemagne's army under ◊Roland, who with the 12 peers of France was killed 778.

rondo a form of instrumental music where the principal section is repeated several times. Rondo form is often used for the last movement of a sonata or concerto.

Ronsard /rɒn'sɑː/ Pierre de 1524–1585. French poet, leader of the ◊Pléiade group of poets. He was a page at the French court and spent some years in Britain. Cut off by deafness from his intended diplomatic career, he came under the patronage of ◊Charles IX, and published verse in a lightly sensitive style, including odes and love sonnets, for example, *Les Amours/Lovers* 1552–53, and the 'Marie' cycle, *Continuation des amours/Lovers Continued* 1555–56. He was opposed by the supporters of ◊Marot.

Röntgen /'rʌntgən/ Wilhelm Konrad 1845–1923. German physicist who discovered X-rays in 1895. While investigating the passage of electricity through gases, he noticed the ◊fluorescence of a barium platinocyanide screen. This radiation Röntgen found would pass through some substances opaque to light, and affect a photographic plate. He received a Nobel prize in 1901. The unit of electromagnetic radiation (X-ray) is named after him, and $1 r = 2.58 \times 10^{-4}$ coulomb/kg.

rood alternative name for the cross of Christ, especially applied to the large crucifix which was placed above the rood screen in medieval churches.

Roodepoort-Maraisburg /'ruːdəpʊət mə'reisbɜːg/ goldmining town in Transvaal, South Africa, 15 km/9 mi W of Johannesburg, at an altitude of 1,745 m/5,725 ft; population (1980) 165,315. Leander Starr ◊Jameson and his followers surrendered here in 1896.

rook bird *Corvus frugilegus* of the crow family. The plumage is black and lustrous, and the face bare. Rooks live in colonies at the tops of trees.

Roon /rəʊn/ Albrecht Theodor Emil, Count von Roon 1803–1879. Prussian field marshal. As war minister from 1859, he reorganized the army and made possible the victories of 1866 and 1870–71 in the ◊Franco-Prussian war.

Roosevelt /'rəuzəvelt/ (Anna) Eleanor 1884–1962. US social worker, writer, and political activist, cousin and wife from 1905 of F D ◊Roosevelt. She chaired the UN commission on human rights 1946–51, and was a prominent ◊civil rights campaigner.

Roosevelt /'rəuzəvelt/ Franklin Delano 1882–1945. 32nd president of the USA. Born at Hyde Park, New York, of a wealthy family, he was educated in Europe and at Harvard and Columbia universities, and became a lawyer. In 1910 he was elected to the state senate as a Democrat. He was assistant secretary of the navy in Wilson's governments 1913–21, and increased the efficiency of the navy during World War I. He served as governor of New York 1929–33.

Elected president in 1932, he took office in 1933 amid the ◊Depression. Surrounding himself by a 'brains trust' of experts, he launched a reform programme. Banks were reopened; federal credit was restored, and when the ◊New Deal got under way, the gold standard was abandoned, and the dollar devalued. In 1935 Roosevelt introduced the Utilities Act, directed against abuses in the large holding companies, and the ◊Social Security Act, providing for unemployment and old-age insurance. He inculcated a new spirit of hope by his skilful 'fireside chats' on the radio and his inaugural address statement: 'The only thing we have to fear is fear itself.' The presidential election of 1936 was won entirely on the record of the New Deal. During 1935–36 Roosevelt was involved in a long conflict with the Supreme Court.

In his foreign policy Roosevelt endeavoured to use his influence to restrain Axis aggression, and to establish 'good neighbour' relations with other countries on the American continent. Soon after the outbreak of war he launched a vast rearmament programme and introduced conscription. In spite of strong isolationist opposition, and breaking a long-standing precedent in standing for a third term, he was re-elected in 1940. He then introduced his 'lease-lend' plan for the supply of war materials to the Allies, announced that the US would become the 'arsenal of democracy', and in 1941 drew up with the British prime minister Churchill the Atlantic Charter as a statement of Allied war aims. In that year he defined the '◊Four Freedoms'. From the Japanese attack on Pearl Harbor in Dec 1941, he devoted himself solely to the conduct of the war. He participated in the ◊Washington 1942 and ◊Casablanca conferences 1943, to plan the Mediterranean assault, and in those at ◊Quebec, ◊Cairo, ◊Tehran 1943, and ◊Yalta 1945, at which the final preparations were made for the Allied victory. He was re-elected for a fourth term in 1944, but died 1945.

Roosevelt /'rəuzəvelt/ Theodore 1858–1919. 26th president of the USA. Born in New York, he was elected to the state legislature as a Republican in 1881. He was assistant secretary of the Navy 1897–98, and during the ◊Spanish War of 1898 commanded a volunteer force of

Roosevelt Franklin Roosevelt's success in attacking the Depression was matched by his leadership in times of war.

'rough riders'. After serving as governor of New York 1898–1900 he was elected Republican vice-president in 1900 to McKinley, whom he succeeded as president on his assassination in 1901, and was elected in 1904. In office he campaigned against the great ◊trusts (combines that reduce competition), and initiated measures for the conservation of national resources, while carrying on a jingoist foreign policy designed to enforce US supremacy over Latin America.

Alienated after his retirement in 1909 by the conservatism of his successor ◊Taft, Roosevelt formed the Progressive or 'Bull Moose' Party, as whose candidate he unsuccessfully ran for the presidency in 1912 against Taft and Wilson. During World War I he strongly advocated American intervention.

He wrote historical and other works, including *The Winning of the West* 1889–96. A big-game hunter, he refused in 1902 to shoot a bear cub, and Teddy bears are named after him.

root the part of the plant that is usually underground, and whose primary functions are anchorage and the absorption of water and dissolved mineral salts. Roots are usually positively geotropic and hydrotropic (see ◊tropism), so they grow downwards and towards water. Their absorptive area is greatly increased by the numerous, slender ◊root hairs formed near the tips. A calyptra, or root cap, protects the tip of the root from abrasion as it grows through the soil.

Certain plants, such as epiphytic orchids that grow above ground, produce aerial roots which absorb moisture from the atmosphere. Others, such as ivy, have climbing roots arising from the stems that serve to attach the plant to trees and walls. Symbiotic associations occur between the roots of certain plants, such as clover, and various bacteria that fix nitrogen from the air (see ◊nitrogen fixation). Other modifications of roots include ◊contractile roots, ◊pneumatophores, ◊tap roots, and ◊prop roots.

root hair a tubular outgrowth from a cell on the surface of a plant root. It is a delicate structure which survives for a few days only, and

Roosevelt Theodore Roosevelt, the 26th US president, won the Nobel Peace Prize for his part in ending the Russo-Japanese war.

does not develop into a root. New root hairs are continually being formed near the root tip to replace the ones that are lost. The majority of land plants possess root hairs, which serve to greatly increase the surface area available for the absorption of water and mineral salts from the soil. The layer of the root's epidermis producing root hairs is known as the piliferous layer.

root-mean-square (rms). Value obtained by taking the square root of the mean (average) of the squares of a set of values; for example the rms value of four quantities a, b, c and d is

$$\sqrt{\frac{(a^2 + b^2 + c^2 + d^2)}{4}}$$

For an alternating current (AC), the rms value is equal to the peak value divided by the square root of 2.

roots music term originally denoting ◊reggae, later encompassing any music indigenous to a particular culture; also called *world music*. Examples are W African *mbalax*, E African *soukous*, S African *mbaqanga*, French Antillean *zouk*, Javanese gamelan, Latin American ◊salsa, ◊Cajun music, and European ◊folk music.

rootstock an underground stem that grows vertically (rather than horizontally, as in a ◊rhizome). It is seen in primrose (*Primula vulgaris*), plantains (*Plantago*), and certain ferns.

rope stout cordage over 2.5 cm/1 in circumference. It is made similarly to thread or twine, by twisting yarns together to form strands, which are then in turn twisted round each other in the direction opposite to that of the yarns. Although hemp is still the commonest material used to make rope, nylon is increasingly used.

Roquefort-sur-Soulzon /rɒk'fɔː sjuəsuːl'zɒŋ/ village in Aveyron *département*, France, giving its name to a strong cheese made of sheep's and goats' milk and matured in caves; population (1982) 880.

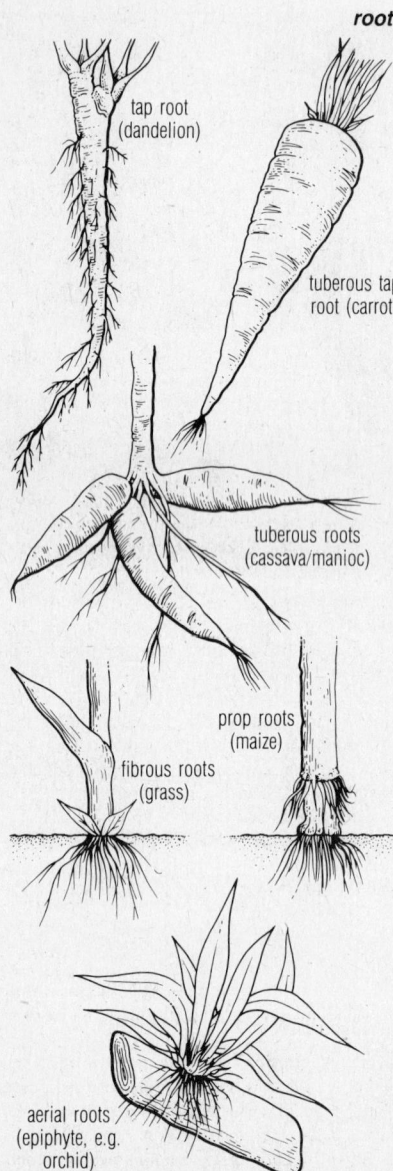

root

tap root (dandelion)

tuberous tap root (carrot)

tuberous roots (cassava/manioc)

prop roots (maize)

fibrous roots (grass)

aerial roots (epiphyte, e.g. orchid)

Roraima, Mount /rɔːˈraɪmə/ plateau in the ◊Pacaraima range in S America.

rorqual whale of the genus *Balaenoptera* – large, long, fin whales with pleated throats. The blue whale *Balaenoptera musculus* is the largest of all animals, measuring 30 m/100 ft and more. The common rorqual or fin whale *Balaenoptera physalus* is slate-coloured and not quite so long.

Rorschach test method of diagnosis involving the use of ink-blot patterns which subjects are asked to interpret, to help indicate personality type, degree of intelligence, and emotional stability. Invented by the Swiss psychiatrist Hermann Rorschach (1884–1922).

Rosa /ˈrəʊzə/ Salvator 1615–1673. Italian painter. Born near Naples, he spent much of his time when a youth travelling in S Italy, where he copied from nature. He went to Rome in 1635, and established a great reputation as a painter of

wild, romantic, and sometimes macabre landscapes. He also wrote verse satires.

Rosario /rəʊˈsɑːriəʊ/ industrial river port (sugar refining, meat packing, maté processing) in Argentina, 280 km/175 mi NW of Buenos Aires, on the Paraná; population (1980) 935,500. It was founded 1725.

rosary form of prayer used by Catholics, consisting of 150 ◊Ave Marias and 15 ◊Paternosters and Glorias. It is linked with the cult of the Virgin ◊Mary. The term is also used for a string of 165 beads for keeping count of the prayers.

Roscellinus /ˌrɒsəˈlaɪnəs/ Johannes c. 1050–c. 1122. Medieval philosopher; regarded as the founder of ◊scholasticism because of his defence of ◊nominalism (the idea that classes of things are simply names and have no objective reality) against ◊Anselm.

Roscius Gallus /ˈrɒskiəs ˈgæləs/ Quintus c. 126–62 BC. Roman actor, originally a slave, so gifted that his name became proverbial for a great actor.

Roscommon /rɒsˈkɒmən/ county of the Republic of Ireland in the province of ◊Connacht
area 2,463 sq km/951 sq mi
towns county town Roscommon
features bounded on the E by the river Shannon; lakes Gara, Key, Allen; rich pastures; remains of a castle put up in the 13th century by English settlers. The name, originally Ros-Comain, means 'wood around a monastery'
population (1981) 54,543.

rose genus of flowering plants, family Rosaceae. Many cultivated forms have been derived from the sweet briar *Rosa rubiginosa* and the dog-rose *Rosa canina*. There are many climbing varieties, but the more cultivated forms are bush roses and standards. These are cultivated roses grafted on to a briar stem. By a Royal National Rose Society ruling in 1979, as received by the World Federation of Rose Societies, the hybrid tea (so called from its scent since the early 19th century) was renamed the larger flowered rose, and the floribunda became the cluster-flower rose. Individual names, such as Peace, were unchanged.

Roseau /rəʊˈzəʊ/ capital of ◊Dominica, in the West Indies; population (1981) 20,000.

Rosebery /ˈrəʊzbəri/ Archibald Philip Primrose, 5th Earl of Rosebery 1847–1929. British Liberal politician, prime minister 1894. Rosebery was foreign secretary 1886 and 1892–94. He succeeded Gladstone as prime minister, but his government survived less than a year. After 1896 his imperialist views gradually estranged him from the Liberal Party.

rosemary evergreen shrub *Rosemarinus officinalis* bearing small scented leaves, used as a culinary herb. An aromatic oil is extracted from the clusters of pale purple flowers.

Rosenburg /ˈrəʊzənbɜːg/ Alfred 1893–1946. German politician. He became the chief Nazi ideologist, supervised the training of the party, and 1941–44 was Reich minister for eastern occupied territories. He was tried at Nuremberg in 1946 as a war criminal and hanged.

Rosenberg /ˈrəʊzənbɜːg/ Isaac 1890–1918. English poet of World War I, killed on the

Somme. Rosenberg wrote about the horror of life on the front line, as in 'Break of Day in the Trenches'. His work is now ranked with the best of the World War I poems, although he was largely unpublished during his lifetime.

Rosenberg /ˈrəʊzənbɜːg/ Julius 1918–53 and Ethel 1915–1953. American married couple, accused of being leaders of a nuclear espionage ring passing information to the USSR; both were executed.

Roses, Wars of the civil wars in England 1455–85 between the houses of ◊Lancaster (badge, red rose) and ◊York (badge, white rose):
1455 opened with battle of St Albans on 22 May, a Yorkist victory (◊Henry VI made prisoner)
1459–61 war renewed until ◊Edward IV, having become king, confirmed his position by a victory at Towton on 29 Mar 1461
1470 ◊Warwick (who had helped Edward to the throne), allied instead with Henry VI's widow, Queen Margaret, but was defeated by Edward at Barnet on 14 Apr and by Margaret at Tewkesbury on 4 May
1485 Yorkist regime ended with the defeat of ◊Richard III by the future ◊Henry VII at Bosworth (W of Leicester) 22 Aug.

Rosetta Stone a slab of basalt with a trilingual inscription found near the town of Rosetta, Egypt, in 1799 by one of Napoleon's officers, captured by the British in 1801, and in 1802 placed in the British Museum. It contains inscriptions dating from the 2nd century BC which were crucial in the decipherment of ◊hieroglyphics.

Rosh Hashana the two-day holiday which marks the start of the Jewish New Year (first new moon after the autumn equinox).

Rosicrucians a group of early 17th-century philosophers, who claimed occult powers and employed the terminology of ◊alchemy to expound their mystical doctrines (said to derive from ◊Paracelsus). The name comes from certain books published in 1614 and 1615, attributed to Christian Rosenkreutz ('rosy cross'), most probably a pen-name, but allegedly a writer living around 1460. Several societies have been founded which claim to be their successors, such as the Rosicrucian Fraternity (1614 in Germany, 1861 in USA).

Roskilde /ˈrɒskɪlə/ port and capital of Denmark from the 10th century till 1443; population (1981) 39,659. The 13th-century cathedral has tombs of Danish kings.

Ross /rɒs/ James 1800–1862. British explorer, associated with ◊Parry and his uncle Sir John Ross in Arctic exploration; he discovered the magnetic North Pole in 1831. He later went to the Antarctic; and Ross Island, Ross Sea, and Ross Dependency are named after him.

Ross /rɒs/ John 1777–1856. Scottish rear-admiral and explorer. He served in the wars with France and made voyages of Arctic exploration in 1818, 1829–33 and 1850.

Ross /rɒs/ Martin. Pen name of Violet Florence ◊Martin, Irish novelist.

Ross /rɒs/ Ronald 1857–1932. British physician and bacteriologist, born in India. He identified the malaria parasite 1895–98 and studied its life-history. Nobel prize 1902.

Ross and Cromarty /ˈkrɒməti/ former county of Scotland. In 1975 Lewis, in the Outer ◊Hebrides, became part of the ◊Western Isles, and the mainland area was included in ◊Highland region. Dingwall was the administrative headquarters.

Ross Dependency all the Antarctic islands and territories between 160° E and 150° W longitude and south of 60° S latitude; it includes Edward VII Land, Ross Sea and its islands, and parts of Victoria Land. It was placed under New Zealand in 1923. There are a few scientific bases with about 250 staff. Area 453,000 sq km/175,000 sq mi. The *Ross Ice Shelf* or Barrier is a permanent layer of ice across the Ross Sea about 425 m/1400 ft thick. It is probable that marine organisms beneath it had been undisturbed from the Pleistocene period until drillings were made in 1976.

Rossellini /ˌrɒsəˈliːni/ Roberto 1906–1977. Italian film director, regarded as the leader of Italian ◊Neo-Realism in films. His World War II theme trilogy of films, *Roma Città aperta/Rome, Open City* 1945, *Paisà/Paisan* 1946, and *Germania Anno Zero/Germany Year Zero* 1947, are seen as landmarks in postwar European cinema.

Rossetti /rəˈzeti/ Christina (Georgina) 1830–1894. British poet, sister of Dante ◊Rossetti, and a devout High Anglican (see ◊Oxford movement). Her verse includes *Goblin Market and Other Poems* 1862 and expresses unfulfilled spiritual yearning and frustrated love. She was a skilful technician and made use of irregular rhyme and line length.

Rossetti /rəˈzeti/ Dante Gabriel, abbreviated name of Gabriel Charles Dante Rossetti 1828–1882. British poet and artist, son of an exiled Italian, who founded the ◊Pre-Raphaelite Brotherhood with ◊Millais and ◊Hunt in 1848. His verse includes *The Blessed Damozel* 1850, and the *Poems* 1870, recovered from the grave of his wife Elizabeth Siddal (whom he had married in 1860, and who died in 1862), which were attacked as of 'the fleshly school of poetry'. He was a friend of ◊Ruskin, who helped establish his reputation as a painter, and of William ◊Morris and his wife, Jane, who became Rossetti's mistress and the subject of much of his work. His paintings include *Beata Beatrix*, *Monna Vanna*, and *Dante's Dream*. His sister was Christina ◊Rossetti.

Rossini /rɒˈsiːni/ Gioachino (Antonio) 1792–1868. Italian composer. His first success was the opera *Tancredi* 1813. In 1816 his 'opera buffa' *Il Barbiere di Siviglia/The Barber of Seville* was produced in Rome, initially a failure. During his fertile composition period, 1815–23, he produced 20 operas, and created (with ◊Donizetti and ◊Bellini) the 19th-century Italian operatic style. After *Guillaume Tell/William Tell* 1829 he gave up writing opera and his later years were spent in Bologna and Paris. Among the works of this period are the *Stabat Mater* 1842, and the piano music arranged for ballet by ◊Respighi as *La Boutique fantasque/The Fantastic Toyshop* 1919.

Ross Island /rɒs/ name of two islands in Antarctica:

Rossetti Dante Gabriel Rossetti was a central figure in the romantic Pre-Raphaelite movement. Many of his portraits feature his wife Elizabeth Siddal, who died two years after their marriage. He buried the manuscripts of his poems in her coffin but exhumed them seven years later.

Ross Island in Weddell Sea, discovered 1903 by the Swedish explorer Nordenskjöld, area about 3,885 sq km/1,500 sq mi;

Ross Island in Ross Sea, discovered 1841 by the British explorer James Ross, area about 6,475 sq km/2,500 sq mi, with the research stations Roos (New Zealand) and McMurdo (USA), and Mount Erebus 3,794 m/12,520 ft, the world's southernmost active volcano. Its lake of molten lava may provide a window on the ◊magma beneath the earth's crust which fuels volcanoes.

Ross Island A historic photograph taken by members of Scott's Antarctic expedition in 1911. Mount Erebus, seen here from the ship *Terra Nova*, was first climbed by Sir Douglas Mawson with two companions on Shackleton's Antarctic expedition of 1908.

Rosslare /ˌrɒsˈleə/ port in County Wexford, Republic of Ireland, 15 km/9 mi SE of Wexford; the Irish terminus of the steamer route from Fishguard from 1906. It was founded by the English in 1210.

Ross Sea /rɒs/ Antarctic inlet of the S Pacific. See also ◊Ross Dependency and ◊Ross Island.

Rostand /rɒsˈtɒŋ/ Edmond 1869–1918. French dramatist, remembered for *Cyrano de Bergerac* 1897, and *L'Aiglon* 1900, based on the life of Napoleon III, in which the celebrated actress Sarah Bernhardt played.

Rostock /ˈrɒstɒk/ port in East Germany, on the river Warnow, 13 km/8 mi S of the Baltic; university 1419; population (1984) 242,000. Founded in 1189 on a long-inhabited site, it became in the 14th century a powerful member of the Hanseatic League.

Rostov-on-Don /ˈrɒstɒv ɒn ˈdɒn/ industrial port (shipbuilding, tobacco, cars, locomotives, textiles) in SW USSR, capital of Rostov region, on the river Don, 23 km/14 mi E of the Sea of Azov; population (1985) 986,000. Rostov dates from 1761, and is linked by river and canal with Volgograd on the Volga.

Rostropovich /ˌrɒstrəˈpəʊvɪtʃ/ Mstislav 1927– . Russian cellist and conductor, deprived of Soviet citizenship in 1978. Honorary KBE 1987.

Rotary Club philanthropic society of business and professional people; founded by Paul Harris, an American lawyer (1878–1947) in 1905, it is now international, with some 750,000 members.

Roth /rɒθ/ Philip 1933– . American novelist, author of *Goodbye Columbus* 1959, *Portnoy's Complaint* 1969, and novels about the writer Nathan Zuckerman, including *The Ghost Writer* 1979, and *The Counterlife* 1987.

Rothenstein /ˈrəʊθənstaɪn/ William 1872–1945. British artist. His work includes decorations for St Stephen's Hall, Westminster, London, and portrait drawings. He was principal of the Royal College of Art 1920–35. His elder son *John Rothenstein* (1901–) was director of the Tate Gallery, London, 1938–64.

Rotherham /ˈrɒðərəm/ industrial town (pottery, glass, coal) in South Yorkshire, England; population (1981) 81,988.

Rothermere /ˈrɒðəmɪə/ Viscount 1868–1940. British newspaper proprietor, brother of Viscount ◊Northcliffe.

Rothko /ˈrɒθkəʊ/ Mark 1903–1970. Russian-born American artist, pioneer of ◊Abstract Expressionism. His large, simple canvases, in strong-toned colours, are designed for spiritual contemplation.

Rothschild /ˈrɒθstʃaɪld/ a European family, noted for its activity in the financial world for two centuries. Mayer Anselm (1744–1812) set up as a moneylender in Frankfurt-am-Main, Germany, and important business houses were established throughout Europe by his ten children. Nathan Mayer (1777–1836) settled in England, and his grandson Nathaniel (1840–1915) was created a baron in 1885. Lionel Walter (1868–1937) succeeded his father as 2nd baron Rothschild and was a noted naturalist. The 2nd baron's nephew, Nathaniel (1910–), 3rd baron Rothschild, is a scientist. He was head of the central policy-review staff in the Cabinet Office – the 'think tank' set up by Edward Heath – 1970–74. Of the French branch, Baron Eric de

Rothschild (1940–) owns Château Lafite and Baron Philippe de Rothschild (1902–88) owns Château Mouton-Rothschild, both leading claret-producing properties in Pauillac, SW France.

rotifer any of the tiny invertebrates, also called 'wheel animalcules' of the phylum Aschelminthes. Mainly freshwater, some marine, rotifers have a ring of cilia which carries food to the mouth, and also provides propulsion. Smallest of multicellular animals, few reach 0.05 cm/0.02 in.

Rotorua /ˌrəʊtəˈruːə/ town with medicinal hot springs and active volcanoes in North Island, New Zealand, near Lake Rotorua; population (1985) 52,000.

rotten borough an English parliamentary constituency before the Great Reform Act of 1832 which returned members to Parliament in spite of having small numbers of electors. Thus they could be easily manipulated by those with sufficient money or influence.

Rotterdam /ˈrɒtədæm/ industrial port (brewing, distilling, shipbuilding, sugar and petroleum refining) in the Netherlands, in the Rhine-Maas delta, linked by canal 1866–90 with the North Sea; university 1973; population (1985) 1,021,000. Rotterdam dates from the 12th century or earlier but the centre, now rebuilt, was destroyed by German air attack in 1940; its notable art collections were saved. The philosopher Erasmus was born here.

Rouault /ruːˈəʊ/ Georges 1871–1958. French artist. Born in Paris, he was apprenticed to a stained-glass maker – the influence of this craft is obvious in his later paintings – and studied under Gustave ◊Moreau. Early in his career he was associated with the ◊Fauvists. He used heavy dark colours for his moral themes of sad Messiah-like clowns, prostitutes, and evil lawyers.

Roubaix /ruːˈbeɪ/ town in N France, adjacent to Lille, important centre of French woollen textile production; population (1982) 102,000.

Roubillac /ˌruːbɪˈjæk/ or Roubiliac, Louis François c. 1695–1762. French sculptor who fled religious persecution to settle in England. He became the most popular sculptor of the day, his principal works including statues of ◊Handel, ◊Newton, and ◊George I, and portrait busts of ◊Pope and ◊Chesterfield.

Rouen /ruːˈɒŋ/ industrial port (cotton textiles, electronics, distilling, oil refining) on the Seine, capital of Haute-Normandie, France; population (1982) 380,000. It has a 13–16th-century cathedral.

history Rouen was capital of ◊Normandy from 912. Lost by King ◊John 1204, it returned briefly to English possession 1419–49; Joan of Arc was burned in the square in 1431. The novelist Flaubert was born here.

Rouget de Lisle /ruːˈʒeɪ də ˈliːl/ Claude-Joseph 1760–1836. French army officer, who composed, while at Strasbourg in 1792, the 'Marseillaise', the French national anthem and the song of the revolution.

Roulers /ruːˈleɪ/ French name of ◊Roeselare, town in Belgium.

roulette gambling game in which the players bet on the numbered division (0–36), coloured black or red, of a turning wheel into which an ivory ball will fall. The table, on which bets are laid, is designed in three columns of numbers corresponding to those of the wheel, and many methods of betting exist, with the odds appropriate to the chances against the number appearing. The play is under the control of a croupier.

Roundheads a member of the Parliamentary party during the English Civil War of 1640–60, opposing the royalist Cavaliers. The term referred to the short hair then worn only by the lower classes.

roup contagious respiratory disease of poultry and game. Caused by unhealthy conditions, it is characterized by swelling of the head and purulent catarrh.

Rousseau /ruːˈsəʊ/ Henri 1844–1910. French artist. He exhibited at the Salon des Indépendants from 1886 to 1910 and was associated with the group led by Apollinaire and ◊Picasso. An 'urban primitive', he painted poetic, sharply delineated fantasies in simplistic but atmospherically disturbing style, such as *The Sleeping Gypsy* 1897 and *The Snake Charmer* 1907. He was nicknamed 'Douanier' (customs official), although in fact he had been a toll collector.

Rousseau /ruːˈsəʊ/ Jean Jacques 1712–1778. French philosopher, born in Geneva. He published an examination of the *Origin and Foundations of Inequality Amongst Men* 1754 and *Émile* 1762, outlining a new theory of education to elicit the unspoiled nature and abilities of children. His revolutionary *Social Contract* 1762, which saw governments as given authority by the people, who could also withdraw it, was immensely influential.

Rousseau /ruːˈsəʊ/ Pierre Étienne Théodore 1812–1867. French landscape painter of the ◊Barbizon School. Born in Paris, he and settled in Barbizon in 1848. He became one of the pioneers of ◊Romanticism.

rowan another name for the ◊mountain ash tree.

Rowbotham /ˈrəʊbɒtəm/ Sheila 1943– . British socialist feminist, historian, lecturer, and writer. Her pamphlet *Women's Liberation and the New Politics* 1970 laid down the fundamental approaches and demands of the emerging British women's movement. Other publications include *Hidden from History* 1973; *Women's Consciousness, Man's World* 1973 and *Beyond the Fragments* 1979.

Rowe /rəʊ/ Nicholas 1674–1718. English dramatist and poet. His best-known dramas are *The Fair Penitent* 1702 and *Jane Shore* 1714, in which Mrs Siddons played. He edited Shakespeare, and was Poet Laureate from 1715.

rowing propulsion of a boat by oars, either by one rower with two oars (sculling) or by crews (two, four, or eight persons) with one oar each, often with a coxswain (steering). *Doggett's Coat and Badge* 1715, begun for Thames watermen, and the first English race, still survives; rowing as a sport began with the English Leander Club, 1817, followed by the Castle Garden boat club, USA, 1834. Chief annual races in the UK are the ◊Boat Race; Thames head of the river race; and

Rousseau The philosophical writings of Jean-Jacques Rousseau, his 'noble savage' concept and attacks on private property, caused much offence; his *Confessions*, a frank exposure of his personal faults and weaknesses, has had lasting influence on the nature of autobiography.

the events of ◊Henley royal regatta, also a major international event; in the USA the Harvard-Yale boat race is held on the Thames at New London, and the Poughkeepsie regatta is a premier event.

World Championship first held 1962 for men, 1974 for women
men – single sculls
1977 Joachim Dreifke *(East Germany)*
1978 Peter-Michael Kolbe *(West Germany)*
1979 Pertti Karppinen *(Finland)*
1981 Peter-Michael Kolbe *(West Germany)*
1982 Rudiger Reiche *(East Germany)*
1983 Peter-Michael Kolbe *(West Germany)*
1985 Pertti Karppinen *(Finland)*
1986 Peter-Michael Kolbe *(West Germany)*
women – single sculls
1977 Christine Scheiblich *(East Germany)*
1978 Christine Scheiblich-Hann *(East Germany)*
1979 Sanda Toma *(Romania)*
1981 Sanda Toma *(Romania)*
1982 Irina Fetisova *(USSR)*
1983 Jutta Hampe *(East Germany)*
1985 Cornelia Linse *(East Germany)*
1986 Jutta Hampe *(East Germany)*
The Boat Race first held 1829, rowed annually between Putney and Mortlake by crews from the Oxford and Cambridge University rowing clubs
1977–85 Oxford
1986 Cambridge
1987 Oxford
wins Cambridge 69 Oxford 63
Doggett's Coat and Badge first held 1715, the oldest continuous sporting trophy still regularly contested
1977 J C Dwan
1978 A McPherson
1979 F K Bearwood

1980 W R Woodward-Fisher
1981 W Hickman
1982 G Anness
1983 P Hickman
1984 S McCarthy
1985 R B Spencer
1986 C Woodward-Fisher

Rowlandson /ˈrəʊləndsən/ Thomas 1756–1827. British caricaturist of the social life of his times. Born in London, he studied at the Royal Academy schools and in Paris. Impoverished by gambling, he turned from portrait painting to caricature. His *Tour of Dr Syntax in Search of the Picturesque* 1809 and its two sequels 1812–21 proved very popular. Other works include *The Dance of Death* 1815–16 and illustrations for works by Smollett, Goldsmith, and Sterne.

Rowlandson This vigorous watercolour by the English artist Thomas Rowlandson is a typical example of his Dr Syntax series. The drawing is from the first series which appeared in 1809, *Tour of Dr Syntax in Search of the Picturesque,* for which William Combe wrote accompanying verses. It was a parody of popular picturesque travels of the day, especially William Gilpin.

Rowley /ˈrəʊli/ William c. 1585–c. 1642. English actor and dramatist, collaborator with ◊Middleton in *The Changeling* 1621 and with ◊Dekker and ◊Ford in *The Witch of Edmonton* 1658.

Rowling /ˈrəʊlɪŋ/ Wallace 'Bill' 1927– . New Zealand Labour politician, party leader 1969–75, prime minister 1974–75.

Roxburgh /ˈrɒksbərə/ former border county of Scotland, included in 1975 in Borders region. Jedburgh was the county town.

Royal Academy of Arts British society founded by George III in London in 1768 to encourage painting, sculpture, and architecture; its first president was Sir Joshua ◊Reynolds. It is now housed in Old Burlington House, Piccadilly. There is an annual summer exhibition for contemporary artists, and tuition is provided for students at Royal Academy schools.

Royal Academy of Dramatic Art (RADA) British college founded by Herbert Beerbohm ◊Tree in 1904 to train young actors. Its headquarters have been in Gower Street,

London, since 1905, and a royal charter was granted in 1920.

Royal Academy of Music. British senior music school in London, founded in 1822, which provides a full-time complete musical education.

Royal Aeronautical Society the oldest British aviation body, formed in 1866. Its members discussed and explored the possibilities of flight long before its successful achievement.

Royal Air Force (RAF) the ◊air force of Britain. The RAF was formed in 1918 by the merger of the Royal Naval Air Service and the Royal Flying Corps.

Royal Ballet title under which the Sadler's Wells Ballet (at Covent Garden), Sadler's Wells Theatre Ballet and the Sadler's Wells Ballet School (Richmond, Surrey) were incorporated in 1956.

Royal Botanic Gardens, Kew a botanic garden, located in Richmond, Surrey. It was founded in 1759 by the mother of George III as a small garden and passed to the nation by Queen Victoria in 1840. By then it was almost at its present size of 149 hectares and since 1841 has been open daily to the public. It contains a collection of more than 25,000 living plant species and many fine buildings, among them the majestic Palm House 1848, designed by Decimus Burton, the Temperate House 1899, and the Chinese Pagoda, some 50 m/165 ft tall, designed by William Chambers in 1761. More recently, two additions have been made to the glasshouses, the Alpine House 1981 and the Princess of Wales Conservatory, a futuristic building for plants from ten different climatic zones, 1987. The Herbarium is the biggest in the world with over 5 million dried plant specimens. Kew also has a vast botanical library, the Jodrell Laboratory, and three museums.

Much of its collection of trees was destroyed by

a gale in 1987. Since 1964 there have been additional grounds at Wakehurst Place, Ardingly, W Sussex (the seeds of 5,000 species are preserved there in the seed physiology department, 2 per cent of those known to exist, many of which are fast disappearing).

Royal Canadian Mounted Police Canadian police force known as the Mounties, with uniform of red jacket and broad-brimmed hat. Their Security Service (SS), established 1950, was disbanded in 1981 for exceeding its powers, and was replaced by the independent Security Intelligence Agency.

Royal College of Music British college providing full-time complete musical education. Founded in 1883, it is in Kensington, W London.

royal commission in Britain, a group of people appointed by the sovereign, on the advice of the government, to investigate a matter of public concern and make recommendations on any actions to be taken in connection with it, including changes in the law. Royal commissions are usually chaired by someone eminent in public life, and consist of experts in the field of inquiry. In cases where agreement on recommendations cannot be reached, a minority report can be submitted by dissenters. In recent years the system has fallen into disrepute because suggested law changes put forward by royal commissions have so often been ignored by governments, and since its election in 1979 the Thatcher administration has not set up any.

Royal Greenwich Observatory the national astronomical observatory of the UK, founded in 1675 at Greenwich, E London, by King Charles II to provide navigational information for seamen. The eminence of the observatory's work meant that, in 1884, Greenwich Time and the Greenwich Meridian were adopted as international standards of reference. After World War II the observatory was moved to Herstmonceux Castle in Sussex. The observatory also operates telescopes on La Palma in the Canary Islands, including the 4.2 m/165 in William Herschel Telescope from 1987.

Royal Horticultural Society British society established in 1804 for the improvement of horticulture. Flower shows are held at Vincent Square, London, with an annual show at Chelsea which is also a social event. There are gardens, orchards, and trial grounds at Wisley, Surrey, and the Lindley Library has one of the world's finest horticultural collections.

royal household the personal staff of a sovereign. In Britain the chief officers are the Lord Chamberlain, the Lord Steward, and the Master of the Horse. The other principal members of the royal family also maintain their own households.

Royal Institution of Great Britain organization for the 'promotion, diffusion, and extension of science and useful knowledge', founded in London in 1799 by Count ◊Rumford. ◊Faraday and ◊Davy were its most famous directors.

Royal Marines British military force trained for amphibious warfare. See under ◊Marines.

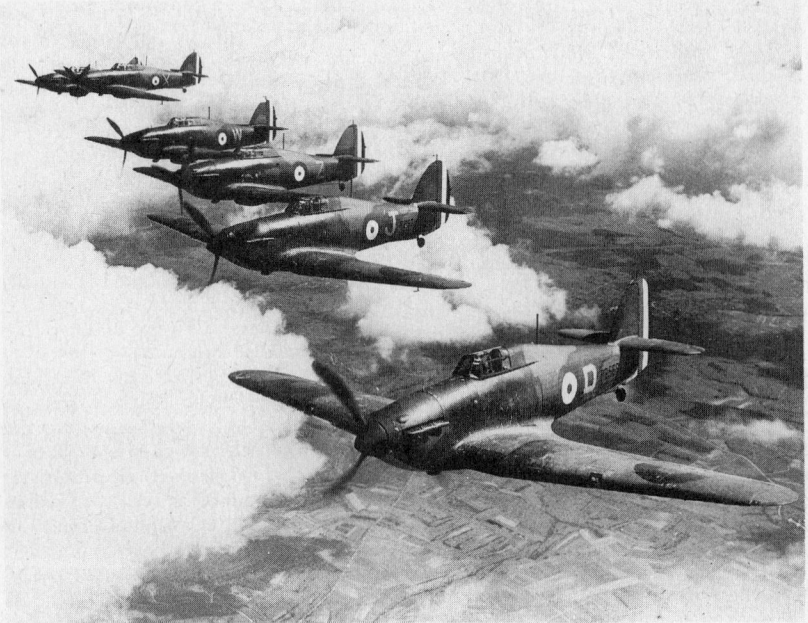

Royal Air Force Hawker Hurricanes Mark I, flying in formation over France, 1940.

Royal Military Academy British military training college, in Sandhurst, Berkshire; it is popularly known as Sandhurst.

Royal Opera House the leading British opera house, Covent Garden, London; the original theatre opened in 1732 and the present building dates from 1858.

Royal Shakespeare Company (RSC) British professional theatre company that performs Shakespeare and other serious drama. It was founded in 1961 from the company at the Shakespeare Memorial Theatre 1932 (now the Royal Shakespeare Theatre) at Stratford-upon-Avon, Warwickshire. It first director was Peter Hall. It initially presented mainly Shakespeare at Stratford, but these productions were usually transferred to London, where at the Aldwych theatre it also performed modern plays and non-Shakespeare classics. A second large theatre in Stratford, the Swan, opened in 1986 with an auditorium similar to theatres of Shakespeare's days. In 1968 Trevor Nunn replaced Peter Hall as artistic director, and continued to build up the RSC's international reputation for wide-ranging repertoire, good ensemble playing, and touring both in Britain and abroad. In 1982 it moved into a permanent London headquarters at the Barbican, and in 1986 in Trevor Nunn was succeeded by Terry Hands.

Royal Society the oldest and premier scientific society of Britain, originating in 1645 and chartered in 1660; Christopher ◊Wren and Isaac ◊Newton were prominent early members. Its headquarters is at Carlton House Terrace, London; its Scottish equivalent is the Royal Society of Edinburgh, 1783, in George Street.

Royal Society for the Prevention of Cruelty to Animals (RSPCA) British organization formed in 1824 to safeguard the welfare of animals; it promotes legislation, has an inspectorate to secure enforcement of existing laws, and runs clinics.

Royce /rɔɪs/ Frederick Henry 1863–1933. British engineer who so impressed the wealthy *Charles Stewart Rolls* 1877–1910 by the car he built for his own personal use in 1904 that in 1906 Rolls-Royce Ltd was formed to produce cars and engines. Royce's most famous car was the Phantom II Continental, but his greatest achievement was the Rolls-type engine which powered the Schneider Trophy-winning seaplane in 1929 and 1931, and was later developed into the Merlin engine for the Royal Air Force ◊Spitfires in World War II.

Ruahine /ˌruːə'hiːni/ mountain range in North Island, New Zealand.

Ruanda alternative spelling of ◊Rwanda, county in central Africa.

Ruapehu /ˌruːə'peɪhuː/ volcano in New Zealand, SW of Lake Taupo; it is the highest peak in North Island, 2,797 m/9,175 ft.

Rub' al Khali /'rʊb æl 'kɑːli/ vast sandy desert (Arabic 'empty quarter') in S Saudi Arabia; area 650,000 sq km/250,000 sq mi. The British explorer Bertram Thomas (1892–1950) was the first European to cross it in 1930–31.

rubato a musical term, from *tempo rubato* (Italian 'robbed time'): a slight flexibility in the tempo for extra expressive effect.

rubber coagulated latex of a great range of plants, mainly from the New World. Most important is Para rubber, so called from its original place of export, which derives from the tree *Hevea brasiliensis*. It was introduced from Brazil to SE Asia, where most of the world supply is now produced, the chief exporters being Malaysia, Indonesia, Sri Lanka, Cambodia, Thailand, Sarawak, and Brunei. At about seven years the tree, which may grow to 20 m/60 ft, is ready for 'tapping', small incisions being made in the trunk and the latex dropped into collecting cups. Other sources of rubber are: *Manihot glaziovii*, another Brazilian tree, which supplies Ceara rubber, and *Taraxacum Koksagyz*, or Russian dandelion, which grows in temperate climates and can yield about 45 kg/100 lb of rubber per tonne of roots, and guayule *Parthenium argentatum* which grows in SW USA and Mexico.

In the 20th century world production of rubber has increased a hundredfold, and World War II stimulated the production of synthetic rubber to replace the supplies from Malayan sources overrun by the Japanese. There are an infinite variety of synthetic rubbers adapted to special purposes, but overwhelmingly the most important economically is SBR (styrene-butadene rubber). Cheaper than natural rubber, it is preferable for some purposes, for example, car-tyre treads, where its higher abrasion-resistance is useful, and is either blended with natural rubber or used alone for industrial moulding and extrusions, shoe soles, hosepipes, latex foam, and other things.

rubber plant Asiatic tree *Ficus elastica*, family Moraceae, producing latex in its stem. Young plants are grown in the West as pot plants for their shiny, leathery, oval leaves.

Rubbra /'rʌbrə/ Edmund 1901–1986. British composer. He studied under ◊Holst and was a master of contrapuntal writing, as exemplified in his study *Counterpoint* 1960. His compositions include 11 symphonies, chamber music, and songs.

Rubens /'ruːbɪnz/ Peter Paul 1577–1640. Flemish painter. Born in Siegen, Westphalia, he was taken to Antwerp in 1587, and, after studying under Verhaecht, Adam van Noort, and Otto van Veen (1556–1629), went to Italy in 1600. In 1605 he visited Spain, and in Madrid painted many portraits of the Spanish nobility. He settled in Antwerp in 1609, and became court painter to the archduke Albert and his wife Isabella. His masterpiece, the *Descent from the Cross*, in the Antwerp cathedral, was painted in 1611–14. In 1620 he went to France at the invitation of ◊Marie de' Medici, where he was commissioned to produce the cycle of 21 enormous canvases allegorizing her life (Louvre, Paris). In 1628 he again went to Madrid, where he met Velazquez. In 1629–30 he was in London as envoy to Charles I, and painted a portrait of the king and his queen, and the *War and Peace*, now in the National Gallery, London.

Rubens brought the sensual exuberance of the Italian Baroque to the Netherlands. A many-sided genius, artist, scholar, and diplomat, he used his powerful pictorial imagination to create, with an army of assistants, innumerable religious and allegorical paintings for the churches and palaces of Catholic Europe. His sheer delight in life can be seen in his magnificent colours, opulent nudes, and expansive landscapes.

Rubicon /'ruːbɪkən/ ancient name of the small river flowing into the Adriatic which, under the Roman republic, marked the boundary between Italy proper and Cisalpine Gaul. When

Rubens A portrait by the Flemish artist Peter Paul Rubens. He delighted in rendering flesh tones and textures, whether his subjects were religious, secular, or mythical. Susanna Lunder models here for a painting entitled *Le Chapeau de Paille*.

◊Caesar led his army across it in 49 BC he therefore declared war on the republic; hence to 'cross the Rubicon' means to take an irrevocable step. Its identity is not certain, but the Fiumicino is officially recognized as the Rubicon; it rises in the Etruscan Apennines 16 km/10 mi WNW of San Marino and enters the Adriatic 16 km/10 mi NW of Rimini.

rubidium metallic element of the alkali group, symbol Rb, atomic number 27, atomic weight 85.48. It is a soft white metal which tarnishes instantly in air and ignites spontaneously. Discovered spectroscopically by Bunsen and Kirchoff in the mineral lepidolite, it is slightly radioactive, and is used as a photosensor.

Rubik /'ruːbɪk/ Erno 1944– . Hungarian architect, who invented the ***Rubik cube***, a multicoloured puzzle which can be manipulated and rearranged in only one correct way, but around 43 trillion wrong ones. Intended to help his students understand three-dimensional design, it became a world craze.

Rubinstein /'ruːbɪnstaɪn/ Artur 1887–1982. Polish-American pianist. He studied in Warsaw and Berlin, and appeared with the world's major symphony orchestras, specializing in the music of Chopin, Debussy, and the Spanish composers.

ruby the red transparent gem variety of the mineral ◊corundum, Al_2O_3, crystallizing in the hexagonal system; it is without true cleavage. The true ruby is found mainly in Burma, but rubies have been produced artificially and are widely used in ◊lasers.

Ruda Śląska /'ruːdə 'ʃlɒnskə/ town in Silesia, Poland, with metallurgical industries, created 1959 by a merger of Ruda and Nowy Butom; population (1984) 163,000.

rudd freshwater fish *Scardinius erythrophthalmus*, common in lakes and slow rivers of England and N Europe. Brownish green with red fins and golden eyes, it reaches a length of 30 cm/1 ft.

Rudolf /'ruːdɒlf/ former name of Lake ◊Turkana in E Africa.

Rudolph two Holy Roman Emperors:

Rudolph I /'ruːdɒlf/ 1218–1291. Holy Roman Emperor from 1273. Originally count of Hapsburg, he was the first Hapsburg emperor, and expanded his dynasty by investing his sons with the duchies of Austria and Styria.

Rudolph II /'ruːdɒlf/ 1552–1612. Holy Roman Emperor from 1576, when he succeeded his father Maximilian II. His intolerant policy led to unrest in Hungary and Bohemia, which compelled Rudolph to surrender Hungary to his brother Matthias in 1608, and to grant the Bohemians religious freedom.

Rudolph /'ruːdɒlf/ Crown Prince of Austria 1858–1889. Only son of the emperor ◊Franz Joseph. From an early age he showed progressive views which brought him into conflict with his father. In 1889 he and his mistress, Marie Vetsera, were found shot in his hunting lodge at Mayerling. The official verdict was suicide.

rue bitter-tasting shrubby perennial herb *Ruta graveolens*, of the family Rutaceae, native to S Europe and temperate Asia, used for flavourings and perfumes.

ruff bird *Philomachus pugnax* of the snipe family. The name is taken from the frill of erectile feathers developed in breeding-time round the neck of the male. The ruff is found across N Europe and Asia, more rarely in Britain, and migrates south in winter.

Rugby /'rʌgbi/ market town and railway junction in Warwickshire, England; population (1981) 59,500.

Rugby School 1567 established its reputation under Thomas ◊Arnold; rugby football originated there.

Rugby football originated at Rugby 'public school' in 1823, when a boy, William Webb Ellis, ran with the ball for the first time. There are 15 players a side, an oval ball, and the goal is high (above a crossbar). 'Tries' may also be scored, by 'touching down' the ball beyond the goal-line. Its most characteristic feature is the 'scrum-(mage)', a kind of heads-down free-for-all which restarts the game after some infringements of the rules. The Rugby Football Union was founded in 1871.

Rugby Union
International championship instituted 1884, it is now a tournament between England, France, Ireland, Scotland, and Wales
1977 France
1978 Wales
1979 Wales
1980 England
1981 France
1982 Ireland
1983 France and Ireland
1984 Scotland
1985 Ireland
1986 France
1987 France

County championship inaugurated 1889
1977 Lancashire
1978 East Midlands
1980 Lancashire
1981 Northumberland
1982 Lancashire
1983 Gloucestershire
1984 Gloucestershire
1985 Middlesex
1986 Warwickshire
1987 Yorkshire
John Player Special Cup the English club knockout tournament, first held 1971–72
1977 Gosforth
1978 Gloucester
1979 Leicester
1980 Leicester
1981 Leicester
1982 Gloucester and Moseley
1983 Bristol
1984 Bath
1985 Bath
1986 Bath
1987 Bath

Rugby League the Rugby League was founded in 1895 as the Northern Union, when northern clubs broke away from the Rugby Football Union who refused players 'broken time' payments for loss of earnings when playing on Saturdays. 21 clubs from Lancashire and Yorkshire were present at the first meeting in Huddersfield. The number of players was reduced from 15 (as in Rugby Union) to 13 in 1906. The scrum plays a less important role than in Rugby Union as rule changes over the years have tended to make it a more open and fast-moving game.

Challenge Cup final first held 1897, and at Wembley Stadium since 1929
1977 Leeds
1978 Leeds
1979 Widnes
1980 Hull Kingston Rovers
1981 Widnes
1982 Hull
1983 Featherstone Rovers
1984 Widnes
1985 Wigan
1986 Castleford
1987 Halifax
Premiership Trophy introduced at the end of the 1974–75 season; a knockout competition involving the top eight clubs in the first division
1977 St Helens
1978 Bradford Northern
1979 Leeds
1980 Widnes
1981 Hull Kingston Rovers
1982 Hull
1983 Widnes
1984 Hull Kingston Rovers
1985 St Helens
1986 Warrington
1987 Wigan

Rügen /'ruːgən/ island in the Baltic, part of Rostock district of East Germany; it is a holiday centre, linked by causeway to the mainland; chief town Bergen.

Ruhr /ruə/ river in West Germany; it rises in the Rothaargebirge and flows W to join the Rhine at Duisburg.

The *Ruhr valley* (228 km/142 mi), a metropolitan industrial area (petrochemicals, cars; iron and steel at Duisburg and Dortmund) was formerly a great coalmining and iron and steel centre. The area was occupied by French and Belgian troops 1923–25 in an unsuccessful attempt to force Germany to pay reparations laid down in the Treaty of Versailles. During World War II the Ruhr district was severely bombed. Allied control of the area from 1945 came to an end with the setting-up of the European Coal and Steel Community in 1952.

rule of law the doctrine that no individual, however powerful, is above the law. The principle had a significant influence on attempts to restrain the arbitrary use of power by rulers and on the growth of legally enforceable human rights in many Western countries. It is often used as a justification for separating legislative from judicial power.

rule of the road convention or law which governs the side of the road on which traffic drives. In Britain, this states that vehicles should be kept to the left of the road or be liable for any ensuing damage. The reverse applies nearly everywhere else in the world, all traffic keeping to the right. This latter is the rule at sea, and for two ships crossing, the one having the other on its starboard must give way.

Rum /rʌm/ island of the Inner Hebrides, Highland region, Scotland, area 109 sq km/42 sq mi, a nature reserve from 1957. Haskeval is 741 m/2,659 ft high.

rum spirit fermented and distilled from sugar cane. Scummings from the sugar-pans produce the best rum, molasses the lowest grade.

Rumania /ruːˈmeɪnɪə/ alternative spelling of ◊Romania.

Rumford /ˈrʌmfəd/ Benjamin Thompson, Count Rumford 1753–1814. Anglo-American physicist. On the British side in the War of American Independence, he travelled in Europe, and was created a count of the Holy Roman Empire for services to the elector of Bavaria in 1791. In 1798 he published his theory that heat is a mode of motion, not a substance. He founded the ◊Royal Institute in London in 1799.

ruminant general name for an even-toed hoofed mammal with a rumen, the 'first stomach' of the complex digestive system, in which plant food is stored and fermented before being brought back to the mouth for chewing (chewing the cud) before being swallowed to the next stomach. Ruminants include cattle, antelopes, goats, deer, and giraffes.

rummy card game in which the players try to obtain either cards of the same denomination, or in sequence in the same suit, to score. It probably derives from ◊mahjong.

Runcie /ˈrʌnsɪ/ Robert Alexander Kennedy 1921– . British cleric, archbishop of Canterbury from 1979, the first to be appointed on the suggestion of the church Crown Appointments Commission (formed in 1977) rather than by political consultation. He favours ecclesiastical remarriage for the divorced and the eventual introduction of the ordination of women.

Runciman /ˈrʌnsɪmən/ Walter, 1st Viscount 1870–1949. British Liberal politician. He entered Parliament in 1899 and held various ministerial offices between 1908 and 1939. In 1938 he undertook a mission to Czechoslovakia to persuade the Czech government to make concessions to Germany.

Runcorn /ˈrʌŋkɔːn/ industrial town (chemicals) in Cheshire, England, 24 km/15 mi up the Mersey estuary from Liverpool; population (1983) 64,600. As a new town it has received Merseyside overspill from 1964.

Rundstedt /ˈrʊndstet/ Karl Rudolf Gerd von 1875–1953. German field marshal in World War II. Largely responsible for the German breakthrough in France in 1940, he was defeated on the Ukrainian front in 1941. As commander in chief in France in 1942, he stubbornly resisted the Allied invasion of 1944, and in Dec launched the temporarily successful ◊Ardennes offensive. He was captured, but in 1949 war-crime charges were dropped owing to his ill-health.

rune a character in the oldest Germanic script, chiefly adapted from the Latin alphabet, the earliest examples being from the 3rd century found in Denmark. Runes were scratched on wood, metal, stone, or bone, and examples in England include those on the Bewcastle and Ruthwell crosses. Several 11th-century ◊Norse runestones are claimed to have been found in the USA.

runner a type of ◊stolon.

Runnymede /ˈrʌnimiːd/ a meadow on the S bank of the Thames near Egham, Surrey, England, where on 15 Jun 1215 King John put his seal to ◊Magna Carta.

Runyon /ˈrʌnjən/ Damon 1884–1946. American sports and crime reporter in New York, whose short stories *Guys and Dolls* 1932 deal wryly with the seamier side of the city's life in his own specially invented argot.

Rupert /ˈruːpət/ Prince 1619–1682. English Royalist general, admiral, and scientist. Born in Prague, son of the Elector Palatine Frederick V (1596–1632) and James I's daughter Elizabeth. Defeated by Cromwell at ◊Marston Moor and ◊Naseby, he commanded a privateering fleet 1649–52, until routed by Robert ◊Blake, and, returning after the Restoration, was a distinguished admiral in the Dutch Wars. He founded the ◊Hudson's Bay Company.

Rupert's Land area of N Canada, of which Prince ◊Rupert was the first governor. Granted to the ◊Hudson's Bay Company in 1670, it was later split among Quebec, Ontario, Manitoba, and the Northwest Territories.

rupture another term for ◊hernia.

Ruse /ˈruːseɪ/ (Anglicized name *Rustchuk*) Danube port in Bulgaria, linked by rail and road bridge with Giurgiu in Romania; population (1984) 299,000.

rush genus of plants *Juncus* of the family ◊Juncaceae, found in wet places in cold and temperate regions. The common rush has hollow stems which have been used for mat-making and basket work since ancient times.

Rupert Prince Rupert, Royalist general and admiral. His portrait is from the studio of Lely, c. 1670.

Rusk /rʌsk/ Dean 1909– . US Democratic politician. As assistant secretary of state for Far Eastern affairs he was prominent in ◊Korean War negotiations. He was secretary of state to presidents Kennedy and Johnson 1961–69, when he became unpopular through his involvement with the ◊Vietnam War.

Ruskin /ˈrʌskɪn/ John 1819–1900. British art critic and social critic. Born in London, only child of a prosperous wine-merchant, he was able to travel widely and was educated at Oxford. The first volume of his *Modern Painters* appeared in 1843. Many works followed, including *The Seven Lamps of Architecture* 1849 in which he stated his philosophy of art, and *The Stones of Venice* 1851–53, in which moral lessons are drawn from architectural history. His writings hastened the appreciation of painters considered unorthodox at the time, such as ◊Turner and the ◊Pre-Raphaelites. In 1848 he married Euphemia 'Effie' Chalmers Gray, but the marriage proved a failure because of his impotence; six years later she secured a decree of nullity and later married the painter Millais.

The fifth and final volume of *Modern Painters* appeared in 1860, and the remaining years of Ruskin's life were vigorously devoted to social and economic problems, in which he adopted an individual and radical outlook exalting the 'craftsman'. He became increasingly isolated in his views. To this period belong a huge series of lectures and pamphlets. From 1869 to 1879 Ruskin was Slade professor of art at Oxford, and he made a number of social experiments, such as St George's Guild, for the establishment of an industry on socialist lines. His last years were spent at Brantwood, Cumbria.

Ruskin College was founded in Oxford in 1899 by an American, Walter Vrooman, to provide education in the social sciences for working people. It is supported by trade unions and other organizations.

Ruskin John Ruskin is credited with establishing the Neo-Gothic style of architecture and laying the foundations for the Arts and Crafts Movement.

Russ /rʌs/ Joanna 1937– . American writer, best known for her strongly feminist science fiction, exemplified by the novel *The Female Man* 1975. Her short stories have been collected in *The Zanzibar Cat* 1983.

Russell /'rʌsəl/ Bertrand (Arthur William), 3rd Earl 1872–1970. British philosopher and mathematician. He was educated at Trinity College, Cambridge, where he specialized in mathematics and became a lecturer. Russell's pacifist attitude in World War I lost him the lectureship, and he served six months' imprisonment for an article he wrote in a pacifist journal. His *Introduction to Mathematical Philosophy* 1919 was written in prison. After visits to the USSR and China, he went to the USA in 1938 and taught at many universities. He later returned to England, and was a Fellow of Trinity College, Cambridge. He succeeded his brother in the earldom in 1931, and was awarded the OM in 1949 and the Nobel literary prize 1950. From 1949 he advocated nuclear disarmament and until 1963 was on the Committee of 100, an offshoot of the Campaign for Nuclear Disarmament.
Russell contributed greatly to the development of modern mathematical logic and was also significant in the early 20th-century revival of British ◊empiricism. Among his most important works are *Principles of Mathematics* 1903, *Principia Mathematica* 1910 (with A Whitehead), *Problems of Philosophy* 1911, *Principles of Social Reconstruction* 1917, *Marriage and Morals* 1929, *An Enquiry into Meaning and Truth* 1940, *History of Western Philosophy* 1946, and *New Hopes for a Changing World* 1951.

Russell /'rʌsəl/ Charles Taze 1852–1916. Founder of the ◊Jehovah's Witnesses.

Russell /'rʌsəl/ Dora (Winifred) (born Black) 1894–1986. English feminist. Educated at Girton College, Cambridge, of which she became a Fellow, she moved in radical socialist circles, and in 1921 married Bertrand ◊Russell. The 'openness' of their marriage (she subsequently had children by another man) was a matter of some contemporary controversy. In 1927 the Russells founded the progressive Beacon Hill School in Hampshire. She was a founder member of the National Council for Civil Liberties, and after World War II she actively supported the Campaign for Nuclear Disarmament. She wrote extensively on feminist topics.

Russell /'rʌsəl/ George William 1867–1935. Irish poet and essayist. An ardent nationalist, he helped found the Irish national theatre, and his poetry, published under the pseudonym 'AE', includes *Gods of War* 1915 and reflects his interest in mysticism and theosophy.

Russell /'rʌsəl/ John 1795–1883. British 'sporting parson', who developed the short-legged, smooth-coated Jack Russell terrier. They do not breed true and so are not recognized by the Kennel Club.

Russell /'rʌsəl/ John Peter 1858–1931. Australian artist. Having met Tom ◊Roberts while sailing to England, he became a member of the French ◊Post-Impressionist group.

Russell /'rʌsəl/ John, 1st Earl Russell 1792–1878. British Liberal politician, known as Lord John Russell. Prime minister 1846–52 and 1865–66.
Son of the 6th duke of Bedford. He entered the House of Commons in 1813, and supported Catholic Emancipation and the Reform Bill. He held cabinet posts 1830–41 and became prime minister 1846. As foreign secretary in Aberdeen's cabinet 1852 and in Palmerston's second government of 1859–65 he gave valuable assistance to Italy's struggle for unity, although his policies on Poland, Denmark, and the American Civil War provoked much criticism. He succeeded Palmerston as prime minister, but on the defeat of his Reform Bill in 1866 retired. He received an earldom in 1861.

Russell /'rʌsəl/ Ken 1927– . British film director. A flamboyant filmmaker, he is often criticized for self-indulgence in his work, which is full of vitality, imagination, and extravagance. His films include *Women in Love* 1969, *The Music Lovers* 1971, and *Gothic* 1986.

Russell /'rʌsəl/ Lord William 1639–1683. British Whig politician. Son of the 1st duke of Bedford, he was among the founders of the Whig Party, and actively supported attempts to exclude the Roman Catholic James II from suceeding to the throne. In 1683 he was accused, on dubious evidence, of complicity in the ◊Rye House Plot to murder Charles II, and was executed.

Russell /'rʌsəl/ William Howard 1821–1907. British journalist, born in Ireland. He acted as *The Times*'s correspondent during the ◊Crimean War, and created a sensation by his exposure of the mismanagement of the campaign. He was knighted in 1895.

Russell of Liverpool /'rʌsəl, 'lɪvəpuːl/ Edward Frederick Langley Russell, 2nd Baron 1895–1981. British barrister. As deputy judge advocate-general, British Army of the Rhine 1946–47 and 1948–51, he was responsible for all war-crime trials in the British Zone of Germany 1946–50, and published *The Scourge of the Swastika* 1954, *The Trial of Adolf Eichmann* 1962, and other books.

Russia /'rʌʃə/ originally the name of the pre-revolutionary Russian Empire (until 1917), and now accurately restricted to the ◊Russian Soviet Federal Socialist Republic only, but popularly used for the whole of the present ◊Union of Soviet Socialist Republics.

Russian art painting and other products of the visual arts made in Russia and later in the USSR.
From the 10th century, when Russia was organized as an independent state, until the time of ◊Peter the Great, Russian architecture and painting followed the ◊Byzantine style, and was dominated by the Greek Orthodox Church. Sculpture did not flourish because it was not allowed in churches. Instead, Russians' artistic and religious impulses found expression in icon-painting; a master of this art was Andrea Rublyov (1370–1430). In the 17th century Peter the Great introduced Western ideals into Russia, and foreign architects were employed to build his new capital of St Petersburg. For two centuries the art of Russia reflected tendencies in Italy, France, Germany, and Britain.
In the USSR art has been enlisted in the service of the state. Extreme forms of modern art are not officially encouraged, though they were in the early days of the Soviet regime, when the Russians sought to free art from all traditional slavery, and replaced the Imperial Academy by a Free College of Art. Early Russian modernism 1910–30 is increasingly recognized in the West as having anticipated later Western trends by half a century. Artists include Kasimir Malevich (1873–1943) and ◊Kandinsky, Natalya Goncharova (1881–1962), and Mikhail Larimov (1881–1964). The work of those who remained in Russia was suppressed by Stalin, and remains unseen in the USSR, though exhibited abroad by the Soviet government as in Paris in 1979. Unofficial recent artists include Oscar Rabin and Edward Zelenin, and Ivan Glazunov created a sensation with *The Return of the Prodigal Son* 1978 in which a blue-jeaned youth sought forgiveness of a Christ figure for the blood and carnage of modern times.

Russian history the southern steppes of Russia were originally inhabited by nomadic peoples, and the northern forests by Slavonic peoples, who slowly spread southward. Viking chieftains in the 9th–10th centuries established their own rule in Novgorod, Kiev, and other cities, and in the 10th–12th Kiev temporarily united the Russian peoples into an empire. Christianity was introduced from Constantinople in 988. In the 13th century the Mongols (the Golden Horde) overran the southern steppes, compelling the Russian princes to pay tribute, while in the 14th Byelorussia and the Ukraine came under Polish rule. Ivan III, prince of Moscow (1462–1505), threw off the Mongol yoke and united the NW, while Ivan IV (1547–84) assumed the title of tsar and conquered Kazan and Astrakhan. During his reign the colonization of Siberia began, and by

1700 it had reached the Pacific. A period of anarchy succeeded Ivan's death, until the first Romanov tsar was elected in 1613. Following a Cossack revolt, the E Ukraine was reunited with Russia in 1667.

Peter I (1682–1725) modernized the administration and army, founded a navy, introduced Western education, and wrested the Baltic seaboard from Sweden. Catherine II (1762–96) annexed the Crimea and part of Poland, and recovered the W Ukraine and White Russia. Russia intervened in the Revolutionary and Napoleonic Wars (1798–1801, 1805–07), and after repelling Napoleon's invasion took part in his overthrow (1812–14).

During the 19th century revolutionary ideas steadily spread, in spite of harsh repression. A rapid development of industry followed the abolition of serfdom 1861; a working-class movement developed, and in 1898 the Social Democratic Party was founded. A revolution in 1905, although suppressed, compelled the tsar to accept a parliament with limited powers.

Abroad, Russian attempts to dominate the Balkans led to wars with Turkey in 1827–29, 1853–56, and 1877–78, and provoked the hostility of Britain, France, and Austria. Russian expansion in central Asia also aroused British suspicions, while in the Far East the treaties of Aigun 1858 and Peking 1860 were imposed on China, annexing territories N of the Amur and E of the Ussuri rivers, and the occupation of Manchuria resulted in war with Japan in 1904–05. Russo-German rivalries in the Balkans nevertheless brought Russia into an alliance with France 1895 and Britain 1907, and were a main cause of World War I in 1914.

A revolution in Mar 1917 established a republic, but the provisional government's failure to make peace rallied popular support to the Bolsheviks, led by Lenin, who in Nov of the same year seized power.

For subsequent history, see ◊USSR.

Russian language a member of the Slavonic branch of the Indo-European language family. The people of Russia proper refer to it as 'Great Russian', in contrast with Ukrainian (which they call 'Little Russian') and the language of Byelorussia ('White Russian'). It is written in the Cyrillic alphabet and is the standard means of communication throughout the USSR. Words in English that derive from Russian include *apparatchik, commissar, cosmonaut, czar/tsar, pogrom, samovar,* and *vodka.*

Russian literature literary works produced in Russia and later in the USSR. The earliest productions of Russian literature are the sermons and chronicles and the unique prose poem 'Tale of the Armament of Igor', belonging to the period in the 11th and 12th centuries when the centre of literary culture was Kiev. By the close of the 14th century leadership had passed to Moscow, which was completely isolated from developments in the West until the 18th century: most noteworthy in this period are the political letters of ◊Ivan the Terrible, the religious writings of the priest Avvakum (1620–81), who was the first to use vernacular Slavonic (rather than the elaborate Church Slavonic language)

RUSSIAN TSARS/TSARINA (EMPERORS/EMPRESSES) 1721–1917

Ivan IV ('the Terrible')	1547–84
Fyodor (Theodore) I	1584–98
(Regent: Boris Gudunov 1584–98)	
Irina (widow of Fyodor I)	1598
Boris Gudunov	1598–1605
Fyodor (Theodore) II	1605
Dmitri (Dimitri) III	1605–6
Vasily (Basil) IV	1606–10
Mikhail (Michael) Romanov	1613–45
Aleksei (Alexis)	1645–76
Fyodor (Theodore) III	1676–82
Pyotr I ('Peter the Great')	1682–96
Ivan V (brothers)	
(Regent: Sophia Aleksevna 1682–89)	
Pyotr I ('Peter the Great'), Tsar	1689–1721
Emperor	1721–25
Ekaterina (Catherine) I,	1725–27
(widow of Pyotr I)	
Pyotr (Peter) II	1727–30
Anna Ivanovna	1730–40
Ivan VI	1740–41
(Regents: Ernst Biron 1740; Anna Leopoldovna 1740–41)	
Elisaveta (Elizabeth)	1741–62
Pyotr (Peter) III	1762
Ekaterina II ('Catherine the Great'),	1762–96
(widow of Pyotr III)	
Pavel (Paul) I	1796–1801
Aleksandr (Alexander) I	1801–25
Nikolai (Nicholas) I	1825–55
Aleksandr (Alexander) II	1855–81
Aleksandr (Alexander) III	1881–94
Nikolai (Nicholas) II	1894–1917

---

in literature, and the traditional oral folk-poems dealing with legendary and historical heroes which were collected in the 18th and 19th centuries.

Modern Russian literature begins with Mikhail Lomonosov (1711–65), who fused elements of Church Slavonic with colloquial Russian to create an effective written medium. Greatest of these earlier writers, working directly under French influence, were the fabulist Ivan Krylov (1768–1844) and the historian Nikolai Karamzin (1765–1826). Poetry reached its greatest height with Alexander ◊Pushkin and the tempestuously Byronic Mikhail ◊Lermontov, while prose was dominated by Nikolai ◊Gogol. Typical of the intellectual unrest of the mid-19th century is the prose writer Alexander ◊Herzen, known for his memoirs.

The golden age of the 19th-century Russian novel produced works by giants such as Ivan ◊Turgenev, Ivan ◊Goncharov, Fyodor ◊Dostoievsky, and Leo ◊Tolstoy. In their wake came the humorous Nikolai Leskov (1831–95), the morbid Vsevolod Garshin (1855–88), and Vladimir Korolenko (1853–1921), and in drama the innovative genius of Anton ◊Chekhov. Maxim ◊Gorky rose above the pervasive

---

pessimism of the 1880s and he had followers in Alexander Kuprin (1870–1938) and Ivan ◊Bunin; in contrast are the depressingly negative Leonid ◊Andreyev and Mikhail Artsybashev. To the more mystic school of thought belong the novelist Dmitri Merezhkovsky (1865–1941) and the poet philosopher Vladimir Soloviev (1853–1900), who moulded the thought of the greatest of the ◊Symbolist poets, Alexander ◊Blok. Many writers left the country at the Revolution, but in the 1920s two groups emerged: the militantly socialist LEF (Left Front of the Arts) led by the Futurist ◊Mayakovsky, and the fellow-travellers of NEP (New Economic Policy) including Boris Pilnyak (1894–1938), ◊Pasternak, Alexei ◊Tolstoy, and ◊Ehrenburg. Literary standards sank to a very low ebb during the first five-year plan (1928–32), when facts were compulsorily falsified to present a rosy view of contemporary life in the effort to fortify socialism, but the novelist ◊Sholokhov and poets ◊Mandelshtam, ◊Akhmatova, and Nikolai Tikhonov (1896–) were notable. More freedom was allowed by the subsequent Realism, for example ◊Simonov and the work of the poet Alexander Tvardovsky (1910–71).

During World War II censorship was again severe until the thaw after Stalin's death, when Vladimir ◊Dudintsev published his *Not by Bread Alone* 1956, but was then soon renewed. Landmarks were the controversy over the award of a Nobel prize to Pasternak, the public statements by the poet ◊Yevtushenko, and the imprisonment in 1966 of the novelists Andrei Sinyavsky (1926–) and Yuli Daniel (1926–) for smuggling their works abroad for publication. Others fled the country, such as Anatoly Kuznetsov (1929–), whose novel *The Fire* 1969 obliquely criticized the regime, and ◊Solzhenitsyn, who found a different kind of disillusion in the West. To evade censorship there has also been a resort to allegory, for example Vasili Aksyonov's *The Steel Bird* 1979 grotesquely satirizing dictatorship. Among those apart from all politics was the popular nonsense-verse writer Kornei ◊Chukovsky.

Russian Revolution the name given to the two revolutions of Mar and Nov 1917 which began with the overthrow of the Romanov imperial dynasty and ended with the establishment of a state run by Lenin and the Bolsheviks. The revolution of Mar 1917 arose in part from the repressive nature of tsarist government but primarily from the mismanagement of the war after 1914. Riots in St Petersburg led to the abdication of Tsar Nicholas II and the formation of a provisional government under Kerensky. The provisional government ruled until Oct 1917 but found its power increasingly undermined by the soldiers' and workers' soviets in Petrograd (St Petersburg) and Moscow. During this period, the Bolsheviks under Lenin's guidance had concentrated on gaining control of the soviets and advocating an end to the war and land reform. Under the slogan 'All power to the Soviets' they staged a coup on the night of 6–7 Nov which overthrew the government. The second All-Russian Congress of Soviets, which met the following day, proclaimed itself the new government of Russia. The Bolshevik seizure of power led to peace with Germany through the Treaty of Brest-Litovsk, but also to civil war as anti-Bolshevik elements within the army attempted to seize power. The war lasted until 1920, when the Red Army, organized by Trotsky, finally overcame 'white' opposition.

Russian Soviet Federal Socialist Republic (RSFSR) constituent republic of the USSR
area 17,076,000 sq km/6,590,000 sq mi
capital Moscow
features largest of the Soviet republics, it occupies about three-quarters of the USSR, and includes the fertile ◊Black Earth district; extensive forests; the ◊Urals, with large mineral resources; the heavily industrialized area around Moscow; and Siberia; it includes 16 autonomous republics (see list below)
products three-quarters of the agricultural and industrial output of the USSR
population (1985) 276,300,000, 83 per cent Russian
language Great Russian
religion traditionally Russian Orthodox
recent history see ◊USSR
Autonomous Soviet Socialist Republics: Bashkir *capital* Ufa; Buriat *capital* Ulan-Udé; Checheno-Ingush *capital* Grozny; Chuvash *capital* Cheboksary; Dagestan *capital* Makhachkala; Kabardino-Balkar *capital* Nalchik; Kalmyk *capital* Elista; Karelia *capital* Petrozavodsk; Komi *capital* Syktyvkar; Mari *capital* Yoshkar-Ola; Mordovia *capital* Saransk; North Ossetia *capital* Ordzhonikidze; Tatar *capital* Kazan; Tuva *capital* Kizyl; Udmurt *capital* Izhevsk; Yakut *capital* Yakutsk.

RUSSIAN SOVIET FEDERAL SOCIALIST REPUBLIC

Autonomous Soviet Socialist Republics	Capital	Area in sq km
Bashkir	Ufa	143,600
*Buriat	Ulan Ude	351,300
Chechen-Ingush	Grozny	19,300
Chuvash	Cheboksary	18,300
Daghestan	Makhachkala	50,300
Kabardino-Balkar	Nalchik	12,500
Kalmuck	Elista	75,900
Karelian	Petrozavodsk	172,400
Komi	Syktyvkar	415,900
Mari	Yoshkar-Ola	23,200
Mordvinian	Saransk	26,200
N. Ossetian	Ordzhonikidze	8,000
Tatar	Kazan	68,000
*Tuva	Kyzyl	170,500
Udmurt	Izhevsk	42,100
*Yakut	Yakutsk	3,103,000

Autonomous Regions:		
Adyge	Maikop	7,600
Karachai-Cherkess	Cherkesk	14,100
Gorno-Altai	Gorno-Altaisk	92,600
*Jewish	Birobidjan	36,000
*Khakass	Abakan	61,900

*In Asia

Russian Soviet Federal Socialist Republic

Russo-Japanese War war between Russia and Japan 1904–05, which arose from conflicting ambitions in Korea and ◊Manchuria, especially the Russian occupation of Port Arthur (modern ◊Lüda) in 1896 and of the Amur province in 1900.
1904–05 successful Japanese siege of Port Arthur May–Jan
1905 Japanese took Mukden 29 Feb–10 Mar; total defeat 27 May of Russian Baltic fleet which had sailed half round the world to Tsushima

Straits; peace signed at Portsmouth, USA, on 23 Aug. Russia surrendered her lease on Port Arthur, ceded S Sakhalin to Japan, evacuated Manchuria, and recognized Japan's interests in Korea.

russula type of fungus of the genus *Russula* of which there are many species. They are medium to large toadstools with a flattened cap, and many are brightly coloured. *Russula emetica* is a common species found in damp places under conifers. Up to 9 cm/3.5 in across,

the cap is scarlet, fading to cherry, and the gills are white. This toadstool tastes acrid and causes vomiting eaten raw, but some russulas are edible.

rust in chemistry, a reddish-brown oxide of iron (hydrated ferric oxide, $Fe_2O_3 . H_2O$) formed by the action of moisture and oxygen on the metal. Paints which penetrate beneath any moisture, and plastic compounds which combine with existing rust to form a protective coating, are used to avoid rusting.

rust in botany, common name for the minute parasitic fungi of the order Uredinales, which appear on the leaves of their hosts as orange-red spots, later becoming darker. The best-known is the wheat rust *Puccinia graminis*.

Ruth /ruːθ/ in the Old Testament, ◊Moabite ancestress of ◊David (King of Israel) by her second marriage to Boaz. When her first husband had died, she preferred to stay with her mother-in-law, Naomi, rather than return to her own people.

Ruth /ruːθ/ George Herman 'Babe' 1895–1948. American baseball player. Born at Baltimore, he joined the Boston Braves in 1914, becoming one of the best batters of all time, and in 1920 was sold to the New York Yankees. He returned to Boston in 1934 but left the team the same year. A baseball idol, he played in ten world series and made 714 home runs (60 in one season in 1927), a long-standing record.

Ruthenia /ruːˈθiːniə/ region of central Europe, home of the Ruthenes or Russniaks. Before World War I it was within Austria-Hungary; divided among Czechoslovakia, Poland, and Romania in 1918, and from 1945–47 all incorporated into the Ukrainian Republic, USSR.

ruthenium metallic element, symbol Ru, atomic number 44, atomic weight 101.06. It is a hard blue-white metal, a member of the platinum group, and used to harden platinum and palladium for use in electrical contracts. It is also a versatile catalyst.

Rutherford /ˈrʌðəfəd/ Ernest 1871–1937. New Zealand physicist, director of the Cavendish Laboratory, Cambridge, 1919–37. A pioneer of modern atomic science, his main researches were in the field of radioactivity, and he was the first to recognize the nuclear nature of the atom. In 1911 he showed that the scattering of alpha particles (see ◊radioactivity) by a thin foil implied that atoms of the foil — and by extension all atoms — had almost all their mass concentrated in a very small central positively charged nucleus, around which the electrons moved. He was awarded the Nobel prize in 1908 and in 1931 was created Baron Rutherford of Nelson, New Zealand.

Rutherford /ˈrʌðəfəd/ Margaret 1892–1972. British actress, specializing in formidable yet jovially eccentric roles. Among her most notable characterizations were Madame Arcati in *Blithe Spirit* by Noel Coward 1941, and the imposing Lady Bracknell in Oscar Wilde's *The Importance of Being Earnest* 1947.

rutherfordium artificially made element, symbol Rf, atomic number 104, named after Ernest Rutherford, but known in the USSR as kurchatovium (after scientist Igor Kurchatov).

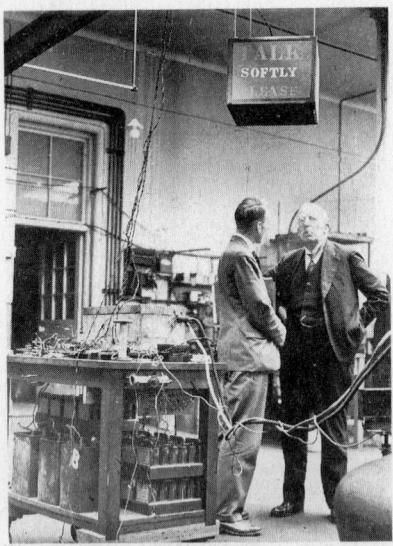

Rutherford The British physicist Ernest Rutherford (right) with J Ratcliffe in Cambridge, 1935. He discovered the three kinds of radiation, alpha, beta, and gamma rays, and the core of the atom, which he called the nucleus.

It is radioactive, with a very short half-life, only 70 seconds for the most stable of the isotopes. It is now renamed unnilquadium.

rutile naturally occurring crystalline form of titanium dioxide, TiO_2, from which titanium is extracted. It is also used as a pigment which gives a brilliant white to paint, paper, and plastics. The coastal sands of E and W Australia are a major source.

Ruysdael /'raɪzdɑːl/ Jacob c. 1628–1682. Dutch landscape painter. Born in Haarlem, he painted rural scenes near his native town and in Germany, and excelled with trees. The figures in his pictures were painted by other artists. His works are noted for their poetic feeling.

Ruyter /'raɪtə/ Michael Adrianszoon de 1607–1676. Dutch admiral who led his country's fleet with conspicuous success in the wars against England in the mid-17th century. On 1–4 Jun 1666 he forced the English fleet under Rupert and Albemarle to retire into the Thames, but on 25 Jul was heavily defeated off the North ◊Foreland. In 1667 he sailed up the Medway to burn three men-of-war at Chatham, and captured others. He was mortally wounded in an action against the French fleet off Messina, and died at Syracuse.

Rwanda /ruː'ændə/ landlocked country in central Africa, bounded to the N by Uganda, to the E by Tanzania, to the S by Burundi, and to the W by Zaïre.

government The 1978 constitution provides for a president and a single-chamber legislature, the National Development Council, all elected by universal adult suffrage for a five-year term. The president appoints and leads a council of ministers.

Rwanda is a one-party state, the sole legal party being the National Revolutionary Development

Movement (MRND), whose leader is the president.

history For early history, see ◊Africa. The population comprises two ethnic groups: the agrarian Hutu, over 80 per cent, were dominated by the pastoral Tutsi; there are also a few Pygmies.

Rwanda used to be linked to the neigbouring state of Burundi, 1891–1919 within the empire of German East Africa and then under Belgian administration as a League of Nations mandate, then as a United Nations trust territory.

In 1961 the monarchy was abolished and Ruanda, as it was then called, became a republic. It achieved full independence in 1962 as Rwanda, with Gregoire Kayibanda as its first president. Fighting broke out in 1959 between the Hutu and the Tutsi, resulting in the loss of some 20,000 lives before an uneasy peace was agreed in 1965. By the end of 1972 the civil warfare had restarted and in 1973 the head of the National Guard, Major-Gen Juvenal Habyarimana, led a bloodless coup, ousting Kayibanda and establishing a military government. Meetings of the legislature were suspended and the MRND was formed as the only legally permitted political organization. A referendum held at the end of 1978 approved a new constitution. Rwanda's great population density has led to soil erosion and cultivation of all arable land, and dependence on foreign aid.

Rwanda
REPUBLIC OF (*Republika y'u Rwanda*)

AREA 26,338 sq km/10,169 sq mi
CAPITAL Kigali
PHYSICAL high savanna and hills, with volcanic mountains in NW
FEATURES part of lake Kivu; highest peak Mount Karisimbi 4,507 m/14,786 ft; Kagera river (whose headwaters are the source of the Nile) and National Park
HEAD OF STATE AND OF GOVERNMENT Juvenal Habyarimana from 1973
GOVERNMENT one-party authoritarian
EXPORTS coffee, tea; pyrethrum; tin, tungsten
CURRENCY Rwanda franc (130.83 = £1 Sept 1987)
POPULATION (1984) 5,650,000 (Hutu 90%, Tutsi 9%); annual growth rate 3.4%
LANGUAGE Kinyarwanda (a Bantu language), French
RELIGION Christian (mainly Catholic) 54%, animist 45%, Muslim 1%
LITERACY 61% male/39% female (1980 est)
GNP $1.7 bn (1984); $270 per head of population
CHRONOLOGY
1962 Rwanda achieved full independence as

the Republic of Rwanda, with Gregoire Kayibanda as president.
1962–65 Tribal warfare between the Hutu and the Tutsi.
1972 Renewal of tribal fighting.
1973 Kayibanda ousted in a military coup led by Maj-Gen Juvenal Habyarimana.
1978 New constitution approved.

Rye /raɪ/ town in East Sussex, England, noted for its literary associations; population (1985) 4,490. It was formerly a flourishing port (and one of the ◊Cinque Ports), but silt washed down by the river Rother has left it 3 km/2 mi inland. The novelist Henry James lived here; another writer, E F Benson (who was mayor of Rye 1934–37), later lived in James's house.

rye a grain cereal *Secale cereale*, grown extensively in N Europe. The flour is used to make black bread, but in Britain rye is grown only as a forage crop.

rye-grass perennial, rather wiry, grass *Lolium perenne*, growing to about 60 cm/2ft high and flowering in midsummer. It is common in pastures and waste places. It sends up abundant leaves and is nutritious, so is useful for cattle. It is a Eurasian species but has been introduced to Australia and N America.

Rye House Plot alleged conspiracy by the Whigs in 1683 to murder Charles II and his brother James, Duke of York, while they passed the night at Rye House, Hertfordshire. It was said to involve the Duke of ◊Monmouth, and Lord ◊Russell and Algernon Sidney (1622–83) were executed for complicity.

Ryle /raɪl/ Gilbert 1900–1976. British philosopher, cousin of Martin ◊Ryle. His *The Concept of Mind* 1949 set out to show that the distinction between an inner and outer world in philosophy and psychology cannot be sustained.

Ryazan /rɪ'zæn/ industrial city (agricultural machinery, leather, shoes) dating from the 13th century, capital of Ryazan region, USSR, on the river Oka near Moscow; population (1985) 494,000.

Rybinsk /'rɪbɪnsk/ former name (until 1984) of ◊Andropov, city in the USSR.

He ridiculed the mind-body dualism of ◊Descartes as the doctrine of 'the Ghost in the Machine'.

Ryle /raɪl/ Martin 1918–1984. British radioastronomer, Astronomer Royal 1972–82. At the Mullard Radio Astronomy Observatory, Cambridge, he developed the technique of sky-mapping using 'aperture synthesis', combining smaller dish aerials to give the characteristics of one large one. His work on the distribution of radio sources in the universe brought confirmation of the ◊Big Bang theory. Nobel prize with Antony ◊Hewish 1974.

Rysbrack /ˈrɪzbræk/ John Michael 1694–1770. British sculptor, born in Antwerp, Netherlands. Settling in England in 1720, he produced portrait busts in Westminster Abbey and the equestrian statue of ◊William III, Bristol.

Ryukyu Islands /riˈuːkjuː/ southernmost island group of Japan, stretching towards Taiwan and including Okinawa, Miyako, and Ishigaki
area 2,200 sq km/848 sq mi
capital Naha on Okinawa
features 73 islands, some uninhabited; subject to typhoons
products sugar, pineapples, fish
population (1970) 945,000
history originally an independent kingdom; ruled by China from the late 14th century until seized by Japan 1874; taken by USA 1945 (see under ◊Okinawa). The northernmost group, Oshima, was restored to Japan 1953, the rest 1972.

S 19th letter in the English alphabet, and its principal sibilant. It represents an alveolar fricative, either voiceless (*sing*) or voiced (*roses*).

Saar /sɑː/ river in W Europe (French *Sarre*); it rises in the Vosges mountains, in France, and flows 240 km/149 mi N to join the Moselle river in West Germany. Its valley is noted for vineyards.

Saarbrücken /zɑːˈbrʊkən/ city on the Saar, West Germany; population (1980) 193,500, the capital of Saarland since 1919. It is situated on a large coalfield, and is a industrial centre.

Saarinen /ˈsɑːrɪnən/ Eero 1910–1961. Finnish-born American architect. The son of the architect and town planner Eliel ◊Saarinen, he was taken to the USA by his father in 1923 (becoming naturalized in 1940) and collaborated with him on a number of projects. His works include the US embassy, London, and Dulles Airport, Washington.

Saarinen /ˈsɑːrɪnən/ Eliel 1873–1950. Finnish architect and town planner, founder of the Finnish Romantic school. In 1923 he emigrated to the USA, where he contributed to US skyscraper design by his work in Chicago, and later turned to functionalism.

Saarland /ˈsɑːlænd, German ˈzɑːlænt/ *Land* (state) of West Germany, and crossed NW–S by the river Saar.

area 2,695 sq km/1,040 sq mi.

capital Saarbrücken.

features after World War I, the Saar district was under French administration until a plebiscite returned it to Germany 1935. Hitler gave it the name Saarbrücken. After World War II it was occupied by France, but a referendum in 1955 returned it to Germany; it is the smallest and poorest of the West German *Länder*.

products former flourishing coal and steel industries survive only by government subsidy. About half its area is cultivated for wheat, rye, oats, potatoes, and other crops; cattle, pigs, and poultry are reared, and one-third is forested.

population (1981) 1,064,400.

religion Roman Catholic 74%, Protestant 24%.

Sabah /ˈsɑːbə/ state of the federation of Malaysia, occupying NE Borneo, forming (with Sarawak) East Malaysia.

area 80,500 sq km/29,400 sq mi.

capital Kota Kinabalu.

features chiefly mountainous (highest peak Mount Kinabalu 4,098 m/3,445 ft) and forested.

exports hardwoods (quarter of the world's supplies), rubber, fish, cocoa, palm oil, copper, copra, hemp.

population (1980) 1,002,608, of which the Kadazans form the largest ethnic group at 30 per cent; also included are 250,000 immigrants from Indonesia and the Philippines.

language Malay (official); English.

religion Sunni Muslim 60 per cent; Christian 30 per cent (the Kadazans, among whom there is unrest at increasing Muslim dominance).

government constitutional head of state; chief minister, cabinet and legislative assembly.

recent history in 1877–78 the Sultan of Sulu made concessions to the North Borneo Company, which was eventually consolidated with Labuan as a British colony in 1946, and became the state of Sabah within Malaysia in 1963. The Philippines have advanced territorial claims on Sabah 1962 and 1968 on the grounds that the original cession by the Sultan was illegal, Spain having then been sovereign in the area.

Sabatini /ˌsæbəˈtiːni/ Rafael 1875–1950. British novelist, author of *Scaramouche* 1921.

Sabbath (Hebrew *shābath*, 'to rest') the seventh day of the week, regarded as a sacred day of rest; in Judaism, from sunset Friday to sunset Saturday; in Christianity, Sunday (or, in some sects, Saturday).

Sabine a member of a people of ancient Italy from the mountains beyond the Tiber; conquered by the Romans and amalgamated with them in the 3rd century BC. The rape of the Sabine women, who eventually reconciled the two tribes, is frequently depicted in art.

sable a small mammal, a type of ◊marten.

saccharin intensely sweet, white crystalline solid, ortho-sulpho benzimide, $C_7H_5NO_3S$, which is substituted for sugar as a slimming aid. In massive quantities it causes cancer in rats, but investigations following proposals to ban it in the USA led to no conclusive findings on its effect in humans.

Sacco-Vanzetti case /ˈsækəʊ, vænˈzeti/ murder trial in Massachusetts, USA 1920–27. Italian anarchist immigrants Nicola Sacco and Bartolomeo Vanzetti were convicted of murder during an alleged robbery, and executed in 1927, but in 1977 the verdict was declared unjust because of prejudice against the accused's anarchist views.

Sacco-Vanzetti case The Italian-American anarchists, Sacco and Vanzetti, entering a Massachusetts court house during their trial for murder, 1920–27.

Sacher-Masoch /ˈzæxə ˈmɑːzɒx/ Leopold von 1836–1895. Austrian novelist. His books dealt with the sexual pleasures to be obtained by having pain inflicted on oneself – hence ◊masochism.

Sachs /zæks/ Hans 1494–1576. German poet and composer who worked as a master shoemaker in Nuremberg. He composed 4,275 *Meisterlieder/mastersongs*, and figures prominently in ◊Wagner's opera *Die Meistersinger/The Mastersingers*.

Sachsen /ˈzæksən/ German form of ◊Saxony, former kingdom and state of Germany.

sackbut musical instrument of the ◊brass family, a form of trombone, common from the 14th century.

Sackville /'sækvɪl/ Thomas, first Earl of Dorset 1536–1608. English poet, collaborator with Thomas Norton in *Gorboduc* 1561, written in blank verse and one of the earliest English tragedies. He was Lord Treasurer from 1599, and created Earl of Dorset 1604.

Sackville-West /'sækvɪl 'west/ Victoria ('Vita') 1892–1962. British poet and novelist, born at Knole, Kent, wife of Sir Harold Nicolson from 1913. Her novels include *The Edwardians* 1930 and *All Passion Spent* 1931. She also wrote the pastoral poem *The Land*. She created fine gardens at Sissinghurst, Kent.

sacrament in Christian usage, observances forming the visible sign of inward grace. In the Roman Catholic Church there are seven sacraments: baptism, Holy Communion (Eucharist or mass), confirmation, rite of reconciliation (confession and penance), holy orders, matrimony, and the anointing of the sick; only the first two are held to be essential by the Church of England.

Sacramento /ˌsækrəˈmentəʊ/ industrial port in California, USA, 130 km/80 mi NE of San Francisco, state capital from 1854; population (1980) 274,105. It stands on the Sacramento river, which flows 615 km/382 mi through Sacramento Valley to San Francisco Bay. Industries include the manufacture of detergents and jet aircraft, and food processing, especially almonds, peaches, and pears. Founded as Fort Sutter in 1839, its old town has been restored.

Sacramento The State capitol, where the legislature meets, in California's capital city. Built 1860–69 in fine classical style, it stands in parkland.

Sadat /səˈdæt/ Anwar 1918–1981. Egyptian statesman. Succeeding ◊Nasser as president in 1970, he restored morale by his handling of the Egyptian campaign in the 1973 war against Israel. In 1974 his plan for economic, social, and political reform to transform Egypt was unanimously adopted in a referendum. In 1977 he visited Israel to reconcile the two countries, and shared the Nobel Peace Prize with Israeli Prime Minister Menachem Begin 1978. He was assassinated by Islamic fundamentalists.

Sadducee a member of an ancient Jewish sect opposed to the ◊Pharisees. Sadducees denied the

Sadat President Anwar Sadat of Egypt. A former newspaper editor, he became president in 1970 and with Prime Minister Begin of Israel was the architect of peace negotiations between the two countries.

immortality of the soul and maintained the religious law in all its strictness.

Sade /sɑːd/ Marquis de 1740–1814. French soldier and author. Born in Paris, he was imprisoned for sexual offences before finally being committed to an asylum. He wrote plays and novels dealing explicitly with a variety of sexual practices, especially ◊sadism.

S'adi or Saadi /sɑːˈdiː/ pseudonym of Sheikh Moslih Addin c. 1184–c. 1291. Persian poet. Born at Shiraz, he travelled widely before settling there finally about 1256. *Bustan/Tree-garden* and *Gulistan/Flower-garden* are the most celebrated of his works.

sadism a tendency to derive pleasure (usually sexual) from inflicting physical or mental pain on others. The term is derived from the Marquis de ◊Sade, who used the theme in his works.

Sadler's Wells /'sædləz 'welz/ a theatre in Islington, N London, England. The original theatre was a music hall. Lilian Baylis developed a later theatre on the site in 1931 as a northern annexe to the ◊Old Vic. For many years it was the home of the Sadler's Wells Opera Company, which moved to the London Coliseum in 1969 (renamed English National Opera Company in 1974), and of the Sadler's Wells Ballet, which later became the ◊Royal Ballet.

Sadowa, Battle of (also known as the Battle of Königgrätz) in which the Prussians defeated the Austrians 13 km/8 mi NW of Hradec Kralove (German Königgrätz) 3 Jul 1866, thus ending the ◊Seven Weeks' War. Named after the nearby village of Sadowa (Czech *Sadová*) in Czechoslovakia.

safety glass glass that does not splinter into sharp pieces when smashed. It is used, for example, in cars and other vehicles. There are two basic types: *Toughened glass* is made by

heating a glass sheet and then rapidly cooling it with a blast of cold air. It shatters into rounded pieces when smashed. *Laminated glass* is a 'sandwich' of a clear plastic film between two glass sheets. When this is struck, it simply cracks, the plastic holding the glass in place.

safety lamp a portable lamp designed for use in places where flammable gases such as ◊firedamp (methane) may be encountered, for example in coal mines. The electric head lamp used as a miner's working light has the bulb and contacts in specially protected enclosures. The flame safety lamp, now used primarily for gas detection, has the wick enclosed within a strong glass cylinder surmounted by wire gauzes. Sir Humphrey ◊Davy in 1815 and George ◊Stephenson each invented flame safety lamps.

safflower Asian plant *Carthamus tinctorius*, family Compositae, resembling a thistle with reddish-orange flowers. It is widely grown for the oil from its seeds (for cooking, making margarine, and also paints and varnishes); the seed residue is used as cattle feed.

saffron plant (*Crocus sativus*) probably native to Asia Minor. Similar to a purple crocus, saffron flowers in late autumn and was formerly widely cultivated in Europe. Its dried ◊stigmas are used for orange colouring and flavouring.

Safi /sæˈfiː/ Atlantic port of Morocco; population (1982) 706,500. It exports phosphates and has fertilizer plants, sardine factories, and boat building yards.

saga prose narrative written down in the 11th–13th centuries in Norway and Iceland. The sagas range from family chronicles, such as the *Landnamabok* of Ari (1067–1148), the *Heimskringla* of Snorri ◊Sturluson celebrating Norwegian kings 1178–1241, and the *Sturlunga* of Sturla Thordsson (1214–84), to the legendary and anonymous *Njala*, *Laxdaela*, and *Grettla* sagas.

Sagamihara /səˌgɑːmiˈhɑːrə/ town on the island of Honshu, Japan, with a large silkworm industry; population (1985) 477,000.

Sagan /'seɪgən/ Carl 1934– . American physicist and astronomer who became known as a populariser. His books include *The Cosmic Connection* 1973, and *Broca's Brain* 1979; he also presented the television series *Cosmos* 1980.

Sagan /sæˈgɒn/ Françoise 1935– . French novelist. Her studies of love relationships include *Bonjour Tristesse/Hello Sadness* 1954, *Un certain sourire/A Certain Smile* 1956, and *Aimez-vous Brahms?/Do You Like Brahms?* 1959. She has also written plays, including *L'Excès contraire/Opposite Extremes* 1987.

sage perennial herb (*Salvia officinalis*). The grey-green aromatic leaves are used as a seasoning. It grows up to 50 cm/1.6 ft high, and has bluish-lilac or pink flowers.

Sagittarius constellation of the ◊zodiac representing a centaur aiming a bow and arrow at neighbouring ◊Scorpius. The Sun passes through Sagittarius from mid-Dec to mid-Jan, including the winter solstice, when it is farthest south of the equator. The constellation contains the dense ◊Milky Way star fields towards the centre of our galaxy. The exact centre of the galaxy is marked by the radio source Sagittarius A.

sago the starchy material obtained from the pith of the sago palm, which forms a nutritious food, and is used for manufacturing glucose.

Saguenay /ˌsæɡəˈneɪ/ river in Quebec, Canada, used for hydroelectric power as it flows SE to the St Lawrence estuary; length 765 km/474 mi.

Sahara /səˈhɑːrə/ the largest desert in the world, occupying 5,500,000 sq km/3,500,000 sq mi of N Africa from the Atlantic to the Nile, covering southern Morocco, Algeria, Tunisia and Libya; western Egypt, much of Mauritania, Mali, Niger, and Chad; and part of W Sudan. Small areas in Algeria and Tunisia are below sea level, but it is mainly a plateau with a central mountain system, including the Ahaggar Mountains in Algeria, the Aïr Massif in Niger and the Tibesti Massif in Chad, of which the highest peak is Emi Koussi 3,415 m/11,204 ft. Oases punctuate the caravan routes, now modern roads. Resources include oil and gas in the north. Satellite observations have established a pattern of dried-up rivers below the surface, which existed some two million years ago. Cave paintings confirm that even 4,000 years ago there were running rivers and rich animal life. The area of the Sahara has expanded by 650,000 sq km/250,965 sq mi in the last half century, and reafforestation is being attempted, for example in Tunisia.

Sahara /səˈhɑːrə/ Western, a region of NW Africa, formerly called *Spanish Sahara*.
area 266,000 sq km/102,000 sq mi.
capital La'Youn (El Aaiún); phosphate mining town of Bou Craa.
features defensive fortified *Sahara Wall* enclosing the phosphate area.
exports phosphates.
currency dirham.
population (1979) 165,000.
language Arabic.
religion Sunni Muslim.
government at present in a state of war; within the Sahara Wall Morocco rules, and outside, Polisario (Popular Front for the Liberation of Saguia al Hamra and Rio de Oro).
recent history a Spanish possession until 1976, two-thirds was taken over by Morocco, and one-third by Mauritania (which withdrew in 1979 and was replaced by Morocco). Polisario proclaimed the *Sahrawi (Saharan) Arab Democratic Republic* (SADR) in 1976, and is supported by Algeria and Libya. By the end of 1985, 64 countries had granted diplomatic recognition to the SADR.

Sahel /ˈsɑːhel/ marginal area to the south of the Sahara, from Senegal to Somalia, where the desert has extended because of a population explosion, poor agricultural practice, destruction of scrub, and climatic change.

Saida /ˈsaɪdə/ port in Lebanon (ancient *Sidon*); population (1980) 24,740. It stands at the end of the Trans-Arabian oil pipeline from Saudi Arabia.
history Sidon was the chief city of ◊Phoenicia, a bitter rival of Tyre c. 1400–701 BC, when it was conquered by ◊Sennacherib. Later a Roman city, it was taken by the Arabs 637 AD, and fought over during the Crusades.

saiga antelope *Saiga tartarica* from the steppes of E Europe and W Asia. Buff-coloured, whitish in winter, it stands 75 cm/2.5 ft at the shoulder, with a body about 1.5 m/5 ft long, and only the male has horns. The nose is large and swollen, and greatly developed inside with complicated bones and membranes. This may help warm and moisten the air inhaled and keeps out the desert dust. The saiga can run at 80 kph/50 mph. Once a vanishing species, protection has allowed it to return in abundance to some areas, and herds of thousands migrate with the changing seasons.

Saigon /ˌsaɪˈɡɒn/ former name of ◊Ho Chi-minh City, Vietnam.

Saigon, Battle of /ˌsaɪˈɡɒn/ during the ◊Vietnam War, battle lasting from 29 Jan–23 Feb 1968. Five thousand infiltrating Vietcong were expelled by South Vietnamese and US forces, but the city was taken by North Vietnamese forces on 30 Apr 1975, following South Vietnamese withdrawal from the central highlands.

saint person eminently pious, especially one certified so in the Catholic Church by ◊canonization. The lives of thousands of saints have been collected by the ◊Bollandists (Belgian Jesuits). In 1970 Pope Paul VI revised the calendar of saints' days: excluded were Barbara, Catherine, Christopher, and Ursula (as probably non-existent); optional veneration might be given to George, Januarius, Nicholas (Santa Claus) and Vitus; insertions for obligatory veneration include St Thomas ◊More and the ◊Uganda Martyrs. For individual saints, see under Christian name, for example, ◊Paul, St.

St Albans /sənt ˈɔːlbənz/ city in Hertfordshire, England; population (1981) 51,000. The cathedral was founded 793 in honour of St ◊Alban; nearby are the ruins of the Roman city of Verulamium on Watling Street.

St Albans, Battle of /sənt ˈɔːlbənz/ Battle of 1455. See under Wars of the ◊Roses.

St Augustine /seɪnt ˈɔːɡəstiːn/ port and holiday resort in Florida, USA. Founded by the Spanish in 1565, it was burned by ◊Drake in 1586, and ceded to the USA in 1821. It includes the oldest house (late 16th century) in the USA.

St Austell /sənt ˈɔːstəl/ market town in Cornwall, England, 22 km/14 mi NE of Truro; population (1981) 36,500 (with Fowey, with which it is administered). It is the centre of the China clay area which supplies the Staffordshire potteries.

St Bartholomew, Massacre of /bɑːˈθɒləmjuː/ religious persecution of ◊Huguenots in Paris, 1572.

St Bernard /ˈbɜːnəd/ type of large dog named after the monks of St Bernard, who kept them for finding lost travellers in the Alps and to act as guides. The dogs are squarely built, with pendulous ears and lips, and large feet.

St Bernard Passes the *Great* and *Little St Bernard Passes* are passes through the ◊Alps.

St Christopher-Nevis /sənt ˈkrɪstəfə, ˈniːvɪs/ country in the West Indies, in the Leeward Islands.
government The islands of St Christopher and Nevis form a federal state within the Commonwealth. The constitution dates from independence in 1983. The governor-general is the formal head of state, representing the British monarch, and appoints the prime minister and cabinet, who are drawn from and responsible to the assembly.
There is a single-chamber national assembly of 14 members, 11 elected by universal suffrage and three appointed by the governor-general, two on the advice of the prime minister and one on the advice of the leader of the opposition. There are three main political parties, the People's Action Movement (PAM), the Nevis Reformation Party (NRP), and the Labour Party.
Nevis Island has its own assembly of five elected and three nominated members, a prime minister and cabinet and a deputy governor-general. It has the option to secede in certain conditions.
history The original ◊American Indian inhabitants were Caribs. St Christopher (then called Liamuiga) and Nevis were named by Christopher ◊Columbus in 1493. St Christopher became Britain's first West Indian colony 1623, and Nevis was settled soon afterwards. France also claimed ownership until 1713. Sugar plantations were worked by slaves.
The islands were part of the Leeward Islands Federation 1871–1956, and a single colony with the British Virgin Islands until 1960. In 1967 St Christopher (often called St Kitts), Nevis and Anguilla attained internal self-government within the Commonwealth as associated states and Robert Bradshaw, leader of the Labour Party, became the first prime minister. In 1970 the NRP was formed, calling for separation for Nevis, and the following year Anguilla, disagreeing with the government in St Christopher, chose to return to being a British dependency.
Bradshaw died in 1978 and was succeeded by his deputy, Paul Southwell. He died the following year to be replaced by Lee L Moore. The 1980 general election produced a hung assembly and, although Labour won more than 50% of the popular vote, a PAM-NRP coalition government was formed, with the PAM leader, Dr Kennedy A Simmonds, as prime minister.
On 1 Sept 1983 St Christopher and Nevis became independent. In the 1984 general election the PAM-NRP coalition was decisively returned to office.

St-Cloud /sæŋˈkluː/ town in the Ile de France region, France; population (1970) 30,000. It is the site of the ◊Sèvres porcelain factory.

St David's /sənt ˈdeɪvɪdz/ 'village' city (Welsh *Tyddewi*) in Dyfed, Wales. Its cathedral, founded by St ◊David, was rebuilt 1180–1522.

St-Denis /ˌsæn dəˈniː/ industrial town, a suburb of Paris, France; population (1983) 96,000. ◊Abelard was a monk at the famous 12th-century Gothic abbey, which contains many tombs of French kings.

Sainte-Beuve /sænt'bɜːv/ Charles Augustin 1804–69. French critic. Born at Boulogne-sur-Mer, he contributed to the *Revue des deux mondes/Review of the Two Worlds* from 1831. In 1840 he was appointed keeper of the Mazarin library, and was elected to the French Academy in 1844.

St Christopher (St Kitts)–Nevis

AREA 261 sq km/100 sq mi
CAPITAL Basseterre (on St Kitts)
TOWNS Nevis (chief town of Nevis)
PHYSICAL two islands in the Lesser Antilles
FEATURES St Kitts was the first of the British West Indian islands to be colonized
HEAD OF STATE Elizabeth II from 1983 represented by Clement Athelston Arrindell
HEAD OF GOVERNMENT Kennedy Alphonse Simmonds from 1980
GOVERNMENT federal democracy
EXPORTS sugar and molasses, cotton; tourism is important
CURRENCY East Caribbean dollar (4.46 = £1 Sept 1987)
POPULATION 47,000 (1985); annual growth rate 2.27%
LANGUAGE English
RELIGION Christian
LITERACY 90% (1984)
GNP $40 million (1983);
CHRONOLOGY
1967 St Christopher, Nevis and Anguilla were granted internal self-government, within the Commonwealth, with Robert Bradshaw, Labour Party leader, as prime minister.

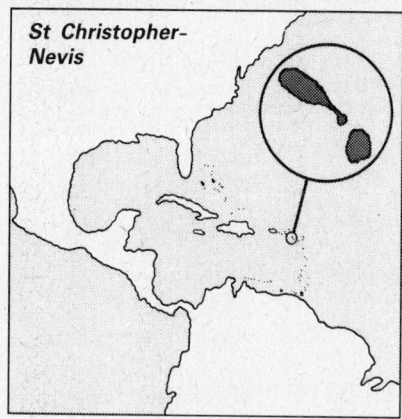

St Christopher–Nevis

1971 Anguilla left the federation.
1978 Bradshaw died and was succeeded by Paul Southwell.
1979 Southwell died and was succeeded by Lee L Moore.
1980 Coalition government led by Kennedy Simmonds.
1983 St Christopher–Nevis achieved full independence within the Commonwealth.
1984 Colition government re-elected.

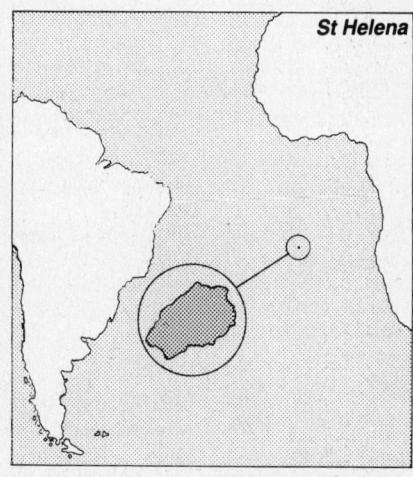

St Helena

and has shipbuilding, timber, fish processing, and textiles industries. Founded by the French as Saint-Jean in 1635, it was taken by the British in 1758.

St John, Order of *Knights Hospitallers of St John of Jerusalem* oldest order of Christian chivalry, named from the hospital at Jerusalem founded c. 1048 by merchants of Amalfi for pilgrims, whose travel routes the knights defended from the ◊Saracens. On being forced to leave Palestine, the knights went to Cyprus in 1291, to Rhodes in 1309, and to Malta (granted to them by Emperor Charles V) in 1530. Expelled by Napoleon (on his way to Egypt) in 1798, they established their headquarters in Rome (Palazzo di Malta). Today there are about 8,000 knights (male and female).

St John's /seɪnt ˈdʒɒnz/ capital and chief port of Newfoundland, Canada; population (1981) 83,750. The main industry is cod fish processing. It was founded by Humphrey ◊Gilbert in 1582.

Saint-Just /sæn ˈʒuːst/ Louis Antoine Léon Florelle de 1767–1794. French revolutionary. A close associate of ◊Robespierre, he became a member of the Committee of Public Safety in 1793, and was guillotined with Robespierre.

St Kilda /sənt ˈkɪldə/ an island of the Outer ◊Hebrides.

St Kitts-Nevis /sənt ˈkɪts ˈniːs/ contracted form of ◊St Christopher-Nevis.

Saint-Laurent /ˌsæn ləʊˈrɒŋ/ Yves (Henri Donat Mathieu) 1936– . French couturier, partner to ◊Dior from 1954 and his successor in 1957, who opened his own fashion house in 1962.

St Lawrence /seɪnt ˈlɒrəns/ river in N America. From ports on the ◊Great Lakes, it forms, with linking canals (which also give great hydroelectric capacity to the river), the *St Lawrence Seaway* for ocean-going ships, ending in the *Gulf of St Lawrence*; length 1046 km/650 mi, ice-bound for four months annually.

St Leger /sənt ˈledʒə/ famous flat race run at Doncaster, England; see ◊horse racing.

St Leonards /sənt ˈlenədz/ seaside town near ◊Hastings, England.

St Lô /sæn ˈləʊ/ town in Normandy, France. In World War II it was destroyed 10–18 Jul 1944, when US forces captured it from the Germans.

St Elias Mountains /ˌseɪnt ɪˈlaɪəs/ mountain range on Alaska-Canada border; Mount Logan 4,200 m/13,780 ft, Canada's highest mountain, is its highest peak.

St Elmo's fire harmless, flame-like electrical discharge, which occurs above ships' masts or about an aircraft in stormy weather. St Elmo (or St Erasmus) was a patron of sailors.

St Etienne /ˌsænt etˈjen/ city in S central France; population (1983) 219,850. Industries include the manufacture of aircraft engines, and chemicals, and it is the site of a school of mining, established 1816.

Saint-Exupéry /ˌsænt ek,sjuːpəˈriː/ Antoine de 1900–44. French author and pioneer aviator, who disappeared in World War II on a mission over occupied France. He wrote the autobiographical *Vol de nuit*/*Night Flight* 1931 and *Terre des hommes*/*Wind, Sand and Stars* 1939. His *Le petit prince*/*The Little Prince* 1943, a children's book, is also an adult allegory.

St Gall /sæn ˈɡæl/ town in NE Switzerland (German *Sankt Gallen*); population (1983) 82,000. Industries include natural and synthetic textiles. It was founded in the 7th century by the Irish missionary St Gall, and the Benedictine abbey library has many medieval manuscripts.

St George's /sənt ˈdʒɔːdʒɪz/ port and capital of ◊Grenada; population (1980) 7,500.

St George's Channel stretch of water between SW Wales and SE Ireland, linking the Irish Sea with the Atlantic. It is 160 km/100 mi long, and 80–150 km/50–90 mi wide.

St Germain-en-Laye, Treaty of /ˌsæn ʒeəˈmæŋ ɒn ˈleɪ/ treaty (1919) condemning the war between Austria and the Allies, signed at St Germain-en-Laye, a town 21 km/13 mi W of Paris. Representatives of the USA (an associated power) signed it, but after the US Senate failed to ratify the Treaty of Versailles, the Treaty of St Germain was not submitted to it. The USA made a separate peace with Austria in 1921.

St Gotthard Pass /sənt ˈɡɒtəd/ a pass through the ◊Alps.

St Helena /ˌsent ɪˈliːnə/ island in the S Atlantic, 1,900 km/1,200 mi W of Africa, capital Jamestown; area 122 sq km/47 sq mi; population (1981) 5,268. Ascension and Tristan da Cunha are dependencies. St Helena became a British possession in 1673. Napoleon died in exile here in 1821.

St Helens /sənt ˈhelənz/ town in Merseyside, England, 19 km/12 mi NE of Liverpool, and connected to the Mersey by canal; population (1981) 99,000. It is an important centre for the manufacture of sheet glass.

St Helier /sənt ˈheliə/ resort and capital of Jersey, Channel Islands; population (1971) 28,000. The 'States of Jersey', the island legislature, sits here in the *salle des états*.

St Ives /sənt aɪvz/ fishing port and resort in Cornwall. Its artists' colony, founded by ◊Sickert and ◊Whistler, later included Naum ◊Gabo, Barbara ◊Hepworth (a museum and sculpture gardens commemorate her), and Ben ◊Nicholson.

St James's Palace /sənt ˈdʒeɪmzɪz/ a palace in Pall Mall, London; it was a royal residence 1698–1837.

St John /seɪnt ˈdʒɒn/ largest city of New Brunswick, Canada, on the St John river; population (1985) 86,000. It is a fishing port,

St Louis /seɪnt 'luːɪs/ chief city of Missouri, USA, on the Mississippi river; population (1980) 450,000. It is an industrial river port, exporting aerospace equipment, aircraft, vehicles, chemicals, electrical goods, and steel. Founded as a French trading post in 1764, it passed to the USA in 1803 under the ◊Louisiana Purchase.

Saint Lucia /sənt 'luːʃə/ country in the West Indies, one of the Windward Islands.

government The constitution dates from independence in 1979. The governor-general is the formal head of state, representing the British monarch. The governor-general appoints a prime minister and cabinet, drawn from and responsible to the House of Assembly.

There is a two-chamber parliament comprising the Senate, of 11 appointed members, and the House of Assembly, of 17 members, elected from single-member constituencies by universal suffrage. Six senators are appointed by the governor-general on the advice of the prime minister, three on the advice of the leader of the opposition, and two after wider consultation. Parliament has a life of five years.

There are three active political parties, the United Workers' Party (UWP), the St Lucia Labour Party (SLP) and the Progressive Labour Party (PLP).

history The early inhabitants were Carib Indians. ◊Columbus arrived 1502. The island was settled by the French 1635, who introduced ◊slavery, and ceded to Britain 1803.

Saint Lucia was a colony within the Windward Islands federal system until 1960. and acquired internal self-government 1967 as a West Indies associated state. The leader of the UWP, John Compton, became prime minister. In 1975 the associated states agreed to seek independence separately and in Feb 1979, after prolonged negotiations, St Lucia achieved full independence within the Commonwealth, with Compton as prime minister.

The SLP came to power in 1979 led by Allan Louisy, but a split developed within the party and in 1981 Louisy was forced to resign, being replaced by the attorney general, Winston Cenac. Soon afterwards George Odlum, who had been Louisy's deputy, left with two other SLP members to form a new party, the PLP. For the next year the Cenac government had to fight off calls for a change of government which culminated in a general strike. Cenac eventually resigned and in the general election 1982 the UWP won a decisive victory, enabling John Compton to return as prime minister. In new elections in Apr 1987, Compton's UWP was only narrowly returned by a 9:8 majority over the SLP.

St-Malo /ˌsæm mɑː'ləʊ/ seaport and resort in the Ille-et-Vilaine *département*, W France, on the Rance estuary; population (1985) 47,500. It took its name from a Welshman, Maclou (late 6th century–c. 640) who was bishop there.

St Michael and St George British orders of ◊Knighthood.

St Michael's Mount /sənt 'maɪkəlz/ island in Mount's Bay, Cornwall, England, linked to the mainland by a causeway at low tide.

St Lucia

AREA 616 sq km/238 sq mi
CAPITAL Castries
PHYSICAL mountainous; mainly tropical forest
FEATURES volcanic in origin; second largest of the Windward group
HEAD OF STATE Elizabeth II from 1979 represented by Sir Vincent Floissac from 1987.
HEAD OF GOVERNMENT John G M Compton from 1982
GOVERNMENT parliamentary democracy
EXPORTS bananas, cocoa, copra; tourism is important
CURRENCY East Caribbean dollar (4.46 = £1 Sept 1987)
POPULATION 122,000 (1985); annual growth rate 1.2%
LANGUAGE English
RELIGION Roman Catholic 90%
LITERACY 78% (1984)
GNP $133 million (1982); $698 per head of population
CHRONOLOGY
1967 Granted internal self-government as a West Indies associated state.
1979 Achieved full independence within the Commonwealth, with John Compton, leader

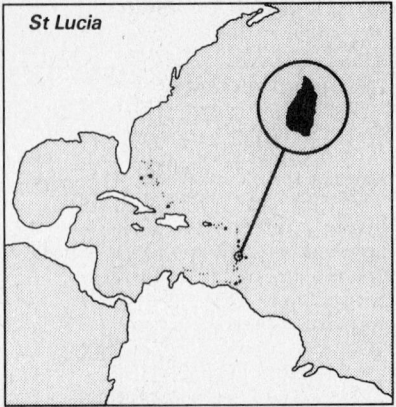

St Lucia

of the United Workers' Party (UWP), as prime minister. Allan Louisy, leader of the Saint Lucia Labour Party (SLP), replaced Compton as prime minister.
1981 Louisy resigned and was replaced by Winston Cenac.
1982 Compton returned to power at the head of a UWP government.

St Moritz /ˌsæm mɒ'rɪts/ winter sports centre (including from 1885 the Cresta Run for toboggans) in SE Switzerland.

St-Nazaire /ˌsæn næ'zɑː/ port in Brittany, France; population (1983) 69,800. It stands at the mouth of the river Loire, and in World War II was used as a German submarine base.

St-Omer /ˌsænt əʊ'meə/ town in Pas-de-Calais *département*, France, 42 km/26 mi SE of Calais; population (1985) 15,500. From 1914–16 the site of British general headquarters in World War I.

St Paul /seɪnt 'pɔːl/ capital and industrial city of Minnesota, USA, adjacent to ◊Minneapolis; population (1980) 270,000. Industries include electronics, publishing and printing, petrochemicals, cosmetics, and meat-packing.

St Paul's Cathedral cathedral church of the City of London, and the largest Protestant church in England. A Norman building, which had replaced the original Saxon church, was burnt down in the Great Fire of 1666; the present cathedral, built by ◊Wren, was built 1675–1710.

St Peter Port /sənt 'piːtə 'pɔːt/ only town of Guernsey, Channel Islands; population 16,000.

St Petersburg /'piːtəzbɜːg/ former name of the city of ◊Leningrad, USSR.

St Petersburg /'piːtəzbɜːg/ seaside resort and industrial city (space technology), Florida, USA; population (1980) 238,500.

St Pierre and Miquelon /ˌsæm piˈeə, ˈmiːkəlɒŋ/ overseas *département* of France, off the S coast of Newfoundland
area St Pierre 26 sq km/10 sq mi; Miquelon-Langlade 216 sq km/83 sq mi
capital St Pierre

St Paul's Cathedral The crowning glory of London's churches and symbol of Sir Christopher Wren's architectural achievement.

features comprises eight rocky islands in two small groups; the last surviving remnant of former French N American empire
currency French franc
population (1982) 6,100
language French
religion Roman Catholic
government commissioner and local council; and one representative in the National Assembly in France

history settled in the 17th century, the islands were a French territory 1816–76, when they became an overseas *département*.

St Quentin /ˌsæn kɒn'tæŋ/ town on the river Somme, N France; population (1985) 69,000. It was the site of a Prussian defeat of the French in 1871, and was almost obliterated in World War I.

Saint-Saëns /sæn'sɒns/ (Charles) Camille 1835–1921. French composer, pianist, and organist. Born in Paris, he studied at the Conservatoire. In 1857 he became organist at the Church of the Madeleine in Paris. His music is in the classical tradition, and can be colourful and expressive. His works include the symphonic poem *Danse macabre* 1875; the opera *Samson et Dalila* 1877; the orchestral *Carnaval des animaux/Carnival of the Animals* 1886; five symphonies, including the Organ Symphony 1886; five piano concertos; three violin concertos; and many pieces for organ.

Saint-Simon /ˌsænsiː'mɒŋ/ Claude Henri, Comte de 1760–1825. French socialist. Born in Paris, he fought in the American War of Independence and was imprisoned during the French Revolution. He advocated an atheist society ruled by technicians in *Du Système industrielle/The Industrial System* 1821.

Saint-Simon Ahead of his time, the Comte de Saint-Simon advocated a 'meritocracy', the equality of women, and a plan to link the Atlantic and Pacific by canal.

Saint-Simon /ˌsænsiː'mɒŋ/ Louis de Rouvroy, Duc de 1675–1755. French soldier, courtier and politician, whose *Mémoires* 1691–1723 are unrivalled as a description of the French court.

St Tropez /ˌsæntrəʊ'peɪ/ fishing port on the French Côte d'Azur; population (1985) 6,250. It became popular as a resort in the 1960s.

St Vincent /sənt 'vɪnsənt/ one of the Windward Islands, West Indies. Area 388 sq km/150 sq mi; capital Kingstown; population (1980) 116,000. It became a British possession in 1783 and independent as ◊St Vincent and the Grenadines in 1979.

St Vincent /sənt 'vɪnsənt/ John ◊Jervis, Earl of St Vincent, British admiral.

St Vincent /sənt 'vɪnsənt/ cape of the Portuguese coast off which England defeated the French and Spanish fleets 1797.

Saint Vincent and the Grenadines /sənt 'vɪnsənt, ˌgrenə'diːnz/ country in the Windward Islands, West Indies.

government The constitution dates from independence in 1979. The head of state is a resident governor-general representing the British monarch. The governor-general appoints a prime minister and cabinet, drawn from and responsible to the Assembly.

There is a single-chamber legislature, the House of Assembly, with 19 members, of which 13 are elected by universal suffrage, four appointed by the governor-general on the advice of the prime minister and two on the advice of the leader of the opposition. The Assembly has a life of five years.

There are a number of political parties, the most significant being the moderately left-of-centre New Democratic Party (NDP) and the St Vincent Labour Party (SVLP).

history The original inhabitants were Carib Indians. ◊Columbus landed on St Vincent 1498. Claimed and settled by Britain and France, with African labour (see ◊slavery), the islands were ceded to Britain in 1783.

Collectively known as St Vincent, the islands were part of the West Indies Federation until 1962 and acquired internal self-government in 1969 as an associated state. They achieved full independence, within the Commonwealth, as St Vincent and the Grenadines, in Oct 1979.

Until the 1980s two parties dominated politics in the islands, the SVLP and the People's Political Party (PPP). Milton Cato, SVLP leader, was prime minister at independence but his leadership was challenged in 1981 when a decline in the economy and his attempts to introduce new industrial-relations legislation resulted in a general strike. Cato survived mainly because of divisions in the opposition parties, and in 1984 the centrist NDP, led by an SVLP defector and former prime minister, James Mitchell, won a surprising victory.

Saint Vincent Gulf /sənt 'vɪnsənt/ inlet of the Southern Ocean, S Australia, on which Adelaide stands.

St Vitus's dance former name for the disease ◊chorea; St Vitus, traditionally martyred under Diocletian, was the patron saint of dancers.

Sakai /sɑː'kaɪ/ city on the island of Honshu, Japan; population (1980) 810,000. Industries include engineering, aluminium, and chemicals.

Sakhalin /ˌsæxə'liːn/ island in the Pacific, 965 km/600 mi long from N–S, lying N of Japan,

which since 1947 forms with the ◊Kurils a region of the USSR.

area 76,400 sq km/29,500 sq mi.

capital Yuzhno-Sakhalinsk (Japanese *Toyohara*).

features of military importance, with a missile base. Two parallel mountain ranges, rising to over 1,525 m/5,000 ft, extend throughout its length.

products agricultural (dairy farming, leguminous crops, oats, barley, sugar beet). In the milder south, also timber, rice, wheat, fish, and some oil and coal.

population (1981) 650,000, including aboriginal ◊Ainu and Gilyaks.

history the island was settled by both Russians and Japanese from the 17th century. In 1875 the S (Japanese *Karafuto*) was ceded by Japan to Russia, but Japan regained it in 1905, only to cede it again in 1945.

Sakharov /'sækərɒv/ Andrei Dmitrievich 1921– . Soviet physicist who is known both as the 'father of the Russian H-bomb' and as an outspoken civil rights campaigner. He protested against Soviet nuclear tests and was a founder of the Soviet Human Rights Committee. He was awarded the Nobel Peace Prize in 1975. In 1980 he was arrested and sent to internal exile in Gorky, following his criticism of Soviet action in Afghanistan. At the end of 1986 he was freed from exile and allowed to return to Moscow and resume his place in the Soviet Academy of Sciences.

Saki /'sɑːki/ pseudonym of Hugh Hector Munro 1870–1916. British author. Born in Burma, where he served with the Military Police, he was foreign correspondent of the *Morning Post* 1902–08, and was killed in action on the Western Front in World War I He produced a number of ingeniously witty short stories set in the Edwardian fashionable world.

Sakkara /sə'kɑːrə/ a village of Egypt, 16 km/10 mi S of Cairo, with 20 pyramids, of which the oldest (Third dynasty) is the 'Step Pyramid' designed by ◊Imhotep, whose own tomb here was the nucleus of the Aesklepieion, a centre of healing in the ancient world.

Sakti the female principle in ◊Hinduism.

Saladin /'sælədɪn/ or *Sala-ud-din* 1138–93. Sultan of Egypt from 1175, in succession to the Atabeg of Mosul on whose behalf he had conquered Egypt 1164–74. A Kurd (see under ◊Kurdistan), he conquered Syria 1174–87, and by his recovery of Jerusalem from the Christians in 1187, precipitated the third ◊Crusade. Renowned for knightly courtesy, Saladin made peace with Richard I of England in 1192.

Salado /sə'lɑːdəʊ/ two rivers of Argentina, both rising in the Andes, and about 1,600 km/1,000 mi long. *Salado del Norte* or *Juramento* flows from the Andes to join the Paraná; the *Salado del Sud* or *Desaguadero* joins the Colorado and flows into the Atlantic S of Bahía Blanca.

Salam /sə'lɑːm/ Abdus 1926– . Pakistani physicist known for his work on ◊forces. In 1979 he was the first from his country to receive a Nobel prize.

St Vincent and the Grenadines

AREA 389 sq km/150 sq mi, including N Grenadines 44 sq km/17 sq mi
CAPITAL Kingstown
PHYSICAL volcanic mountains, thickly forested
FEATURES Mustique, one of the Grenadines, is an exclusive holiday resort
HEAD OF STATE Elizabeth II from 1979 represented by Joseph Lambert Eustace from 1985.
HEAD OF GOVERNMENT James Mitchell from 1984
GOVERNMENT parliamentary democracy
EXPORTS bananas, arrowroot, copra
CURRENCY Eastern Caribbean dollar (4.46 = £1 Sept 1987)
POPULATION 102,000 (1985); annual growth rate -4%
LANGUAGE English
RELIGION Christian (Methodist, Anglican, Roman Catholic)
LITERACY 85% (1981)
GNP $90 million (1983); $250 per head of population

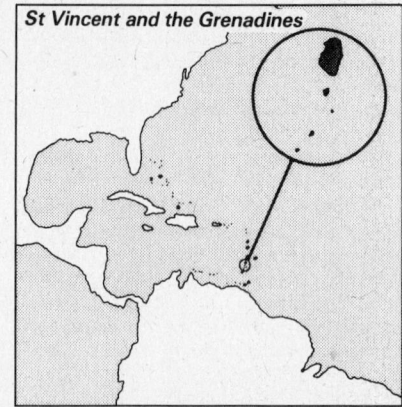
St Vincent and the Grenadines

CHRONOLOGY
1969 Granted internal self-government.
1979 Achieved full independence within the Commonwealth, with Milton Cato as prime minister.
1984 James Mitchell replaced Cato as prime minister.

Salamanca /ˌsælə'mæŋkə/ city in Castilla–León, W Spain, on the river Tormes, 260 km/160 mi NW of Madrid; population (1981) 153,981. Noted for its university (founded c. 1230), and superbly designed square, the Plaza Mayor.

Salamanca, Battle of /ˌsælə'mæŋkə/ ◊Wellington's most famous victory over the French in the ◊Peninsular War, 22 Jul 1812.

salamander general name for a tailed amphibian of the order Caudata. The typical salamanders of the family Salamandridae live in the northern hemisphere. The European *spotted* or *fire salamander, Salamandra salamandra,* is black with bright yellow, orange, or red markings, and up to about 20 cm/8 in long. It was falsely believed in medieval times to be immune to fire. Other types include the *giant salamander* of Japan *Andrias japonicus,* 1.60 m/5 ft, and the *Mexican salamander Ambystoma mexicanum,* or ◊*axolotl.*

Salamis /'sæləmɪs/ island off Piraeus, the port of ◊Athens, Greece; area 101 sq km/39 sq mi; population (1981) 19,000. The town of Salamis, on the W coast, is a naval station.

Salamis ancient city on the E coast of Cyprus, the capital under the early Ptolemies until its harbour silted up about 200 BC, when it was succeeded by ◊Paphos.

Salamis, Battle of /'sæləmɪs/ naval battle off the coast of the island of Salamis in which the Greeks defeated the Persians in 480 BC.

sal ammoniac an old name for ammonium chloride, NH_4Cl. A volatile salt, it forms white crystals round volcanic craters, and is prepared synthetically for use in 'dry-cell' batteries.

Salazar /ˌsælə'zɑː/ Antonio de Oliveira 1889–1970. Portuguese dictator. He was prime minister 1932–68, exercising a virtual dictatorship. A corporative constitution on the

Salamis The early Byzantine gymnasium at Salamis. Once the chief city of ancient Cyprus, Salamis had a Christian community founded by Paul and Barnabas.

Italian model was introduced in 1933, and until 1945 Salazar's National Union, founded 1930, remained the only legal party. Salazar was also foreign minister 1936–47, and during World War II maintained Portuguese neutrality.

Sale /seɪl/ residential suburb of Manchester, England; population (1981) 57,824.

Sale /seɪl/ town in Victoria, Australia, linked by canal via the Gippsland Lake to Bass Strait; population (1981) 13,000. It has benefited from the Strait deposits of oil and natural gas, and the brown coal to the south.

Salem /'seɪləm/ industrial city (iron mining, and textiles) in Tamil Nadu, India; population (1981) 361,394.

Salem /'seɪləm/ city and manufacturing centre in Massachusetts, USA, 24 km/15 mi NE of Boston; population (1980) 89,233. It was the site of witch trials, 1692, which ended in the execution of 19 people.

Salem /'seɪləm/ city in Oregon, USA, settled about 1840 and made state capital 1860; population (1980) 58,220.

Salerno /sə'leənəu/ port in Campania, SW Italy, 48 km/30 mi SE of Naples; population (1981) 157,400.

history Founded by the Romans c. 194 BC. It was destroyed by Charlemagne, and sacked by the Emperor Henry VI in 1194. The temple ruins of the ancient Greek city of ◊*Paestum,* with some of the earliest Greek paintings known, are nearby. The university (1150–1817, revived 1944) and Salerno's medical school have been famous since medieval times.

Salford /'sɔːlfəd/ industrial city in Greater Manchester, England on the river Irwell; population (1981) 98,000. Industries include engineering, electrical goods, textiles, and chemicals. Salford University (1966) was founded 1896 as the Royal Technical Institute.

Salic Law a law (mistakenly so-called from the Salian or northern division of the ◊Franks supposed to practise it) adopted in the Middle Ages by several European royal houses; it excluded women from succession to the throne. In Sweden in 1980 such a provision was abrogated to allow Princess Victoria to become Crown Princess.

salicylic acid the active chemical constituent of aspirin. The acid and its salts (salicylates) occur naturally in many plants; concentrated sources include willow bark and oil of wintergreen. When purified, salicylic acid is a white solid, $C_6H_4(OH)(COOH)$, which crystallizes into prismatic needles at 159°C. It is used as an antiseptic, in food preparation, dyestuffs, and in the preparation of aspirin.

Salieri /ˌsæli'eəri/ Antonio 1750–1825. Italian composer, who taught ◊Beethoven, ◊Schubert, and ◊Liszt, and was the rival of ◊Mozart, whom it has been suggested, without proof, he poisoned.

Salinger /'sælɪndʒə/ J(erome) D(avid) 1919– . American writer, born in New York. He contributed to the *New Yorker* magazine, and is best-known for the novel of adolescence *The Catcher in the Rye* 1951, and his stories of the Jewish Glass family, including *Franny and Zooey* 1961. His key characters are often children and his adults psychologically complex.

Salisbury /'sɔːlzbəri/ town in Wiltshire, England, 135 km/84 mi SW of London; population (1981) 35,355. The cathedral of St

Mary, built 1220–66, is a fine specimen of Early English architecture; its decorated spire 123 m/404 ft is the highest in England. Another name for Salisbury is New Sarum, Sarum being a medieval Latin corruption of the ancient Romano-British name Sorbiodonum. Old Sarum, on a 90 m/300 ft hill to the N, was deserted when New Sarum was founded in 1220.

Salisbury /'sɔːlzbəri/ former name of ◊Harare, capital of Zimbabwe. Rhodesia was the former name of Zimbabwe.

Salisbury /'sɔːlzbəri/ Robert Arthur James Gascoyne-Cecil, 5th Marquess of Salisbury 1893–1972. British Conservative politician. He was Dominions Secretary 1940–42 and 1943–45, Colonial Secretary 1942, Lord Privy Seal 1942–43 and 1951–52, and Lord President of the Council 1952–57. As an 'elder statesman' he was called upon by Elizabeth II when Eden resigned in 1957 to assist in ascertaining party views as to a successor; ◊Macmillan was preferred to ◊Butler.

Salisbury /'sɔːlzbəri/ Robert Arthur Talbot Gascoyne-Cecil, 3rd Marquess of Salisbury 1830–1903. British Conservative statesman. Born in Hatfield, he entered the Commons in 1853 and succeeded to the title in 1868. As foreign secretary 1878–80, he took part in the Congress of Berlin, and as prime minister 1885–86, 1886–92, and 1895–1902 gave his main attention to foreign policy and for most of the time was also foreign secretary.

Salisbury /'sɔːlzbəri/ Robert Cecil, 1st Earl of Salisbury. title conferred on Robert ◊Cecil, Secretary of State to Elizabeth I of England.

Salisbury Plain a 775 sq km/300 sq mi area of open downland between Salisbury and Devizes in Wiltshire, England. It rises to 235 m/770 ft in Westbury Down, and includes ◊Stonehenge. For many years it has been a military training area.

saliva a secretion which aids the swallowing and digestion of food. In some animals it contains the ◊enzyme ptyalin which digests starch, and in bloodsucking animals contains ◊anticoagulants.

Salk /sɔːlk/ Jonas Edward 1914– . American physician, born and educated in New York. A specialist in ◊polio, in 1954 he developed the original vaccine which led to virtual eradication of the disease in developed countries.

Sallust /'sæləst/ Gaius Sallustius Crispus 86–?34 BC. Roman historian, a supporter of Julius ◊Caesar. He wrote accounts of Catiline's conspiracy and the Jugurthine War in an epigrammatic style.

salmon fish of the family Salmonidae, especially the Atlantic salmon *Salmo salar*. The normal colour is silvery, blue-grey above with a few dark spots, but the colour changes at the spawning season. Salmon spawn up rivers in fresh water where the eggs hatch, but most of their life is spent in the sea. The spawning season is between Sept and Jan, although they occasionally spawn at other times. The orange eggs, about 6 mm/0.25 in in diameter, are laid on the river bed, fertilized by the male, and then covered with gravel by the female. The incubation period is from five weeks to five months. On hatching from the egg the young fish are known as *alevins*, and when they begin feeding they are called *parr*. At about two years

old the coat becomes silvery, and the young parr are then *smolts*. When the young fish return to the river to spawn between three and three and a half years of age they are *grilse*. They are noted for their jumps over river obstacles on their way to the spawning grounds (guided to their home stream by its scent). They are also 'farmed' in cages, and 'ranched' (selectively bred, hatched, and fed before release to the sea). Stocking rivers indiscriminately with hatchery fish may destroy the precision of their homing instinct by interbreeding between those originating in different rivers.

Salonika /ˌsælə'naɪkə, sə'lɒnɪkə/ English name for ◊Thessaloniki, a port in Greece.

Salop /'sæləp/ abbreviation and former official name for ◊Shropshire, county in England.

salsa a Latin big-band dance music popularized by Puerto Ricans in New York in the 1980s.

salsify hardy biennial *Tragopogon porrifolius*, family Compositae, often called 'vegetable oyster'; its white fleshy roots and spring shoots are eaten as a vegetable.

salt sodium chloride (NaCl), found in sea water, as rock salt, in brine deposits and so on. In chemistry salts are compounds comprising an acid and a base united in definite proportions, for example, hydrochloric acid and caustic soda unite to form the salt sodium chloride, and water. *Common salt* was widely used as a preservative before refrigeration. Excess salt, largely from processed food, is blamed by some medical authorities for high blood pressure, and increased risk of heart attacks.

saltation the idea that an abrupt genetic change can occur in an individual, which then gives rise to a new species. The idea has now been largely discredited, although the appearance of ◊polyploid individuals can be considered an example.

Salt Lake City /'sɔːlt 'leɪk 'sɪti/ capital of Utah, USA, on the river Jordan, 18 km/11 mi SE of the Great Salt Lake; population (1982) 164,000. Laid out in 1847 by Brigham ◊Young, it is the capital of the ◊Mormon Church, with a great granite temple 1853–93,

Salton Sea /'sɔːltən/ brine lake in SE California, USA, area 650 sq km/250 sq mi, accidentally created in the early 20th century during irrigation works from the Colorado river. It is used to generate electricity; see ◊solar ponds.

saltpetre an old name for sodium nitrate, NaNO₃. It is used in curing bacon and ham.

saluki breed of dog, also called the gazelle hound, descended from the hound of the Bedouins of the African deserts. As bred today it resembles the greyhound, is about 65 cm/26 in high, and has a silky coat, which can be almost any colour but is usually fawn, cream, or white.

Salvador /ˌsælvə'dɔː/ port and naval base in Brazil on the inner side of a peninsula separating Todos Santos Bay from the Atlantic; population (1980) 1,496,276. Industries include the processing of flour, sugar, and tobacco. Founded 1510, it was the capital of Brazil 1549–1763.

Salvador, El /el 'sælvədɔː/ republic in Central America; see ◊El Salvador.

Salt Lake City The Mormon temple was dedicated in 1893 and took forty years to build.

salvage saving for re-use, either as a whole or in part, of any property threatened with destruction, especially at sea. The term is also used more specifically for compensation payable to those who by voluntary effort have saved a ship and/or its cargo and passengers from complete loss through shipwreck, fire, or enemy action.

salvarsan organic compound, the first specific anti-bacterial agent, discovered by Paul Ehrlich in 1909. Because of its destructive effect on *Spirochaeta pallida*, it was widely used in the treatment of syphilis, prior to the development of modern antibiotics.

Salvation Army Christian evangelical, social service, and social reform organization, originating 1865 in London, England, with the work of William ◊Booth. Originally called the Christian Revival Association, it was renamed the East London Christian Mission in 1870 and from 1878 it has been known as the Salvation Army, now a worldwide organization. It has military titles for its officials and its weekly journal is the *War Cry*; it is renowned for its brass bands.

sal volatile smelling salts (a mixture of ammonium carbonate, bicarbonate, and carbamate). It is a strong reflex stimulant and helps restore consciousness after a fainting attack or narcotic poisoning.

Salween /'sælwiːn/ river rising in E Tibet and flowing 2,800 km/1,750 mi through Burma to the Andaman Sea; it has many rapids.

Salyut a series of seven ◊space stations launched by the USSR between 1971 and 1982. Salyut was cylindrical in shape, 15 m/50 ft long, and weighed 19 tonnes. It housed two or three cosmonauts at a time, for missions lasting up to eight months. Crews observed Earth and the sky, and carried out processing of materials in weightlessness.

Salzburg /'sæltsbɜːg/ city on the river Salzach, in W Austria; population (1981) 442,000; dominated by the Hohensalzburg fortress. It is the seat of an archbishopric founded about 700, and has a 17th-century cathedral. Mozart's birthplace is a museum, and since 1920 an annual music festival has been held.

samara a fruit, a type of ◊achene.

Samara /səˈmɑːrə/ name until 1935 of ◊Kuibyshev, a port in the USSR.

Samaria /səˈmeəriə/ hilly region of ancient Israel. The town of Samaria (modern Sebastiyeh) on the West Bank of the river Jordan, was the capital of Israel 10th–8th centuries BC, renamed Sebarte by Herod the Great. Extensive remains have been excavated.

Samaritan descendant of the colonists settled by the Assyrians in Samaria, after the destruction of the Israelite kingdom in 722 BC. Samaritans adopted Judaism, but rejected all sacred books except the Pentateuch, and regarded their temple on Mount Gerizim (not that at Jerusalem) as the true sanctuary. A very small community remains at Nablus.

Samaritans /səˈmærɪtənz/ voluntary organization aiding those tempted to suicide or despair, established in 1953 at St Stephen's Church, Walbrook, London, England by the Rector *Chad Varah* (1911–). Groups of lay people often consulting with psychiatrists, psychotherapists and doctors, offer friendship and counselling to those using their emergency telephone numbers, day or night. They are inspired by the story of the 'good Samaritan' of the New Testament, who aided the injured traveller who had been attacked and robbed, instead of 'walking by on the other side of the road'.

Samarkand /ˌsæmɑːˈkænd/ city in Uzbek Republic, USSR, capital of Samarkand region, near the river Zerafshan, 217 km/135 mi E of Bukhara; population (1981) 481,000. It was the capital of the empire of ◊Tamerlane, who is buried here, and the splendours of his city have been restored. Once an important city on the ◊Silk Road, it was occupied by the Russians in 1868. It remained a centre of Muslim culture until the Russian Revolution. Industries include cotton-ginning and silk manufacture.

Samarra /səˈmærə/ ancient town in Iraq, on the river Tigris, 105 km/65 mi NW of Baghdad; population (1970) 62,000. Founded in 836 by the Abbasid Caliph Motassim, it was the Abbasid capital until 876, and is a place of pilgrimage for ◊Shi'ite Muslims.

Samizdat (Russian 'self-published') material circulated underground to evade censorship, for example reviews of Solzhenitsyn's banned novel *August, 1914* 1972.

Samoa /səˈməuə/ volcanic island chain in the SW Pacific. It is divided into Western ◊Samoa and American ◊Samoa.

Samoa, American /səˈməuə/ group of islands 2,600 miles S of Hawaii
area 199 sq km/77 sq mi
capital Fagatogo on Tutuila
features five volcanic islands, including Tutuila, Tau, and Swain's Island, and two coral atolls
exports canned tuna, handicrafts
currency US dollar
population (1981) 33,000
language Samoan and English
religion Christian
government as a non-self-governing territory of the USA, under Governor A P Lutali, it is administered by the US Department of the Interior

history The islands were acquired by the United States in Dec 1899 by agreement with Britain and Germany under the Treaty of Berlin. A constitution was adopted 1960 and revised 1967.

Samoa, Western /səˈməuə/ country in the SW Pacific, in ◊Polynesia, NE of Fiji.
government Western Samoa is an independent state within the Commonwealth. The 1962 constitution provides for a parliamentary system of government, with a constitutional head of state, a single-chamber legislative assembly, and a prime minister and cabinet drawn from and responsible to the assembly. The head of state is normally elected by the assembly for a five-year term but the present holder of the office has been elected for life. The head of state appoints the prime minister and cabinet on the basis of assembly support.
The assembly has 47 members, who include 45 Samoans, representing 41 territorial constituencies, and two, usually European, members, all elected by universal suffrage. The assembly has a life of three years.
history the first Europeans to reach the island group of Samoa, 1722, were Dutch. In the 19th century Germany, the UK and the USA had conflicting interests in the islands, sometimes called the Navigators' Islands, and administered them jointly 1889–99, when they were divided into American ◊Samoa and Western Samoa. Western Samoa was a German colony until World War I, and from 1920 was administered by New Zealand, first as a League of Nations mandate and from 1946 as a United Nations trust territory.
Western Samoa was granted internal self-government gradually until it achieved full independence, within the Commonwealth, on 1 Jan 1962. The office of head of state was held jointly by two traditional rulers, but on the death of one of them, the other, Malietoa Tanumafili II, became the sole head of state for life. The prime minister at the time of independence was Fiame Mata Afa Mulinu'u. He lost power 1970 but regained it 1973 until his death 1975. In 1976 the first prime minister who was not of royal blood was elected, Tupuola Taisi Efi.
In 1974 the previously unorganized opposition politicians came together to form the Human Rights Protection Party (HRPP) and it won the 1982 election, Va'ai Kolone becoming prime minister. Later that year he was removed because of alleged voting malpractices and replaced by Tupuola Efi. Efi resigned a few months later when his budget was not approved, and was replaced by the new HRPP leader, Tofilau Eti Alesana. The HRPP won a decisive victory in the 1985 elections, with 31 of the assembly seats against the Christian Democratic Party with the remaining 16 seats. and Tofilau Eti continued as prime minister. At the end of the year, however, he resigned because of opposition to his budget proposals. The head of state refused to call another election and Va'ai Kolone returned to lead the government.

Samos /ˈseɪmɒs/ Greek island in the Aegean Sea, about 1.5 km/1 mi off the W coast of Turkey; area 466 sq km/180 sq mi; capital Limén Vathéos; population (1981) 40,519.

Mountainous but fertile, it produces wine and olive oil. The mathematician ◊Pythagoras was born here. The modern town of Teganion is on the site of the ancient city of Samos, which was destroyed by ◊Darius.

samoyed breed of dog, originating in Siberia; similar to a chow, but with a more pointed face and a white coat.

samphire perennial plant (*Crithmum maritimum*) found on sea cliffs of Europe. The aromatic leaves are fleshy and sharply pointed; the flowers grow in yellow-green umbels. It is used in salads, or pickled.

Samson /ˈsæmsən/ in the Old Testament, a hero of Israel. His exploits of strength against the Philistines, which ended when ◊Delilah cut off his hair, are told in the Old Testament book of Judges.

Samuel /ˈsæmjuəl/ in the Old Testament, the last of the judges who ruled the ancient Israelites before their adoption of a monarchy, and the first of the prophets; the two books bearing his name cover the story of Samuel and the reigns of ◊Saul and ◊David.

Samuelson /ˈsæmjuəlsən/ Paul 1915– . American economist. He was awarded a Nobel prize 1970 for his application of scientific analysis to economic theory. His books include *Economics* 1948, a classic textbook.

Samurai feudal military caste which held power in Japan from the 12th century until the fall of the Tokugawa shogunate in the 19th century, in which they had assisted. They obeyed the *bushido* code of bravery, honour, and service.

San'a /sæˈnɑː/ capital of North Yemen, SW Arabia, 320 km/200 mi N of Aden; population (1981) 278,000. A walled city, with fine mosques and traditional architecture, it is rapidly being modernized.

San Antonio /ænˈtəuniəu/ city in Texas, USA; population (1980) 786,000. It is a commercial and financial centre, and has aircraft maintenance, oil refining, and meat packing industries. Founded in 1718, it grew up round the site of the ◊Alamo fort.

San Bernadino /ˌbɜːnəˈdiːnəu/ city in California, USA, 80 km/50 mi E of Los Angeles; population (1980) 117,490. It was founded 1851 by ◊Mormons.

San Cristóbal /krɪsˈtəubæl/ city in Venezuela, near the Colombian border; population (1976) 249,000; founded by the Spanish in 1561. It stands on the ◊Pan-American Highway.

sanction measure used to enforce international law, such as the attempted economic boycott of Italy during the Abyssinian War by the League of Nations; of Rhodesia, after its unilateral declaration of independence, by the United Nations; and the call for measures against South Africa on human rights grounds by the United Nations and other organizations from 1985.

sand loose grains of rock, sized between 0.02–2.00 mm in diameter, consisting chiefly of quartz, but owing their varying colour to mixtures of other minerals. Used in cement-making, as abrasives, and for other purposes. Sands are classified into marine, freshwater,

Samoa, Western
(*Samoa i Sisifo*)

AREA 2,842 sq km/1,097 sq mi
CAPITAL Apia on Upolu
PHYSICAL comprises islands of Savai'i and
Upolu, with two smaller islands and islets;
mountain ranges on the main islands
FEATURES huge lava flows on Savai'i have cut
down the area available for agriculture
HEAD OF STATE King Malietoa Tanumafili II
from 1962
HEAD OF GOVERNMENT Va'ai Kolone from 1986
GOVERNMENT parliamentary democracy
EXPORTS copra, bananas, cocoa; tourism is
important
CURRENCY tala (3.34 = £1 Sept 1987)
POPULATION 160,000 (1985); annual growth
rate 1.1%
LANGUAGE English and Samoan (official)
RELIGION Christian
LITERACY 90% (1983)
GDP $65 million (1978); $400 per head of
population
CHRONOLOGY
1959 Local government elected.
1961 Referendum favours independence.
1962 Achieved full independence within the
Commonwealth, with Fiame Mata'afa
Mulinu'u as prime minister.
1975 Mata'afa died and was succeeded by
Tupuola Taisi Efi, the first non-royal prime
minister.
1982 Va'ai Kolone became prime minister, but

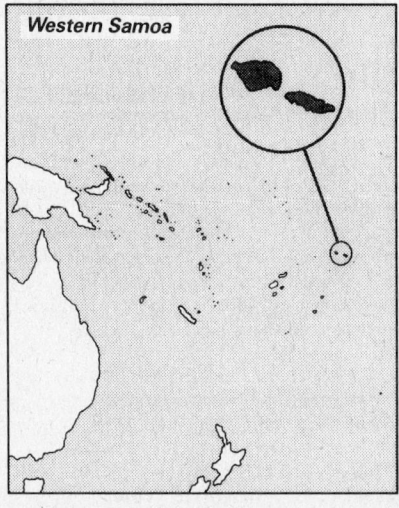
Western Samoa

was replaced the same year by Tupuola Efi.
Tupuola Efi then resigned when the assembly
failed to approve his budget and was replaced
by Tufilau Eti Alesana.
1985 At the end of the year Tufilau Eti resigned
over his budget proposals and the head of state
refused to call a general election, iniviting Va'ai
Kolombe to return to lead the government.

San'a A view of the old city. A majority of the inhabitants still live within the city walls.

glacial, and terrestrial. Some 'light' soils contain up to 50 per cent sand. Sands may eventually consolidate into ◊sandstone.

Sand /sɒnd/ George, pseudonym of French author Amandine Aurore Lucie Dupin 1804–1876. After nine years of marriage, she left her husband in 1831, and, while living in Paris as a writer, had love affairs with Alfred de ◊Musset, ◊Chopin, and others. She is best known for such novels as *La mare au diable/The Devil's Pool* 1846 and *La petite Fadette/The Little Fairy* 1848; her writing is often autobiographical.

sandbar a ridge of sand lying in the water across the mouth of a river or a bay, caused by a check on the current carrying sand. A sandbar stretching out from a headland is a *sand spit*.

Sandburg /'sændbɜːg/ Carl August 1878–1967. American poet, born in Illinois. He worked as a farm labourer, and a bricklayer, and his poetry celebrates ordinary American life, as in *Chicago Poems* 1916, and *The People, Yes* 1936. *Always the Young Strangers* 1953 is an autobiography.

sandgrouse bird of the family Pteroclidae allied to the pigeons. They are birds of dry country found in the Old World. They may travel long distances to water to drink. Some carry water back to their young by soaking the breast feathers.

sandhopper crustacean *Talitrus saltator* about 1.6 cm/0.6 in long, found hopping on rotting seaweed on the tide line on the upper shore. Also used of some other amphipod crustaceans.

Sandhurst /'sændhɜːst/ small town in Berkshire, England. The Royal Military Academy is nearby.

San Diego /ˌsæn diˈeɪgəʊ/ city and military and naval base in California, USA; population (1980) 875,538. Industries include bio-medical technology, aircraft missiles, and fish canning. There is a notable zoo. ◊Tijuana adjoins San Diego across the Mexican border.

sand painting picture in which coloured sands are laid on an adhesive ground, produced in Japan at least from the 18th century, and also by European artists. Striking sand paintings are also used in ◊Navajo Indian healing ceremonies: the patient sits in the middle of the design (measuring about 1 sq m/10 sq ft) while prayers are said.

sandpiper type of bird belonging to the snipe family Scolopacidae. The common sandpiper *Tringa hypoleucos* is a small graceful bird with long slender bill and short tail, drab above and white below. In summer it breeds near water in Britain and most of the rest of Europe, and winters far south.

Sandringham House private residence of the British sovereign, built by the Prince of Wales (afterwards Edward VII) 1869–71 on the estate which he had bought in Norfolk, NE of Kings Lynn, in 1863. It is named after the nearby village of Sandringham.

Sand George Sand, the pseudonym of French novelist Amandine Aurore Lucie Dupin. Her affairs with a succession of artists and poets including Alfred de Musset and Chopin provided the inspiration for much of her work. Her novels include *La mare au diable* 1846.

sandstone rocks formed from the consolidation of former sands. The principal component is quartz, and sandstones are classified according to the materials that cement together the grains of quartz, for example, ferriginous, siliceous, calcareous, barytic, gypseous and pyritic.

Sandwich /'sændwɪtʃ/ resort and market town in Kent, England; population (1981) 4,184. It has many medieval buildings, and was one of the ◊Cinque ports, but recession of the sea has left the harbour useless since the 16th century.

Sandwich /'sændwɪtʃ/ John Montagu, 4th Earl of Sandwich 1718–1792. British politician. He was an inept First Lord of the Admiralty 1771–82 during the American War of Independence, his corrupt practices being held to blame for the British navy's inadequacies. The Sandwich Islands were named after him, as are sandwiches, which he invented so that he could eat without leaving the gaming table.

Sandwich Islands a former name of ◊Hawaii, a group of islands in the Pacific.

Sandys /sændz/ Duncan Edwin 1908–1987. Original name of British politician Baron ◊Duncan-Sandys.

San Francisco /'sæn fræn'sɪskəʊ/ chief Pacific port of the USA, California; population (1982) 691,637. The city stands on a peninsula, south of the *Golden Gate*, the strait giving access to *San Francisco Bay*, which is crossed by the world's second longest single-span bridge, 1,280 m/4,200 ft (1937). ◊*Alcatraz Island* in the bay has a former military prison. Industries include meat-packing, fruit canning, printing and publishing.

history San Francisco was occupied in 1846 during the war with Mexico, and in 1906 was almost destroyed by an earthquake which killed 452 people (see ◊San Andreas Fault). It was the site of the drawing up of the United Nations Charter in 1945.

Sanger /'sæŋə/ Frederick 1918– . British biochemist; the first to win a Nobel Prize for Chemistry twice, the first for his elucidation of the structure of ◊insulin in 1958, and the second, which he shared with two American scientists for his work on the chemical structure of genes, and the decoding of DNA, in 1980.

Sanhedrin supreme Jewish court at Jerusalem (2nd century BC–1st century AD) headed by the high priest.

San José /'sæn həʊ'zeɪ/ capital of Costa Rica; population (1984) 245,370. The main trade is in coffee, cocoa, and sugar cane. The university of Costa Rica 1843 is nearby.

San José /'sæn həʊ'zeɪ/ city in Santa Clara Valley, California, USA; population (1980) 629,442. Industries include aerospace research and development, flowers, fruit canning, and wine making.

San Juan /'sæn 'wɑːn/ capital of Puerto Rico; population (1980) 434,850. It is a port and industrial city, and produces sugar, rum, and cigars.

San Luis Potosí /'sæn luː'iːs ˌpɒtəʊ'siː/ silver-mining city in central Mexico; population (1979) 327,333. Founded 1586, it has fine colonial buildings.

San Marino /'sæn mə'riːnəʊ/ landlocked country within N central Italy.

government San Marino has no formal constitution. The single-chamber Great and General Council has 60 members, elected by universal suffrage for a five-year term. The council elects two of its members, one representing the capital and one the country, to serve a six-month period as captains regent. Together they share the duties of head of state and head of government. They preside over a cabinet of ten, elected by the Council for a five-year term, called the Congress of State.

The country is divided into nine 'castles', which correspond to the original nine parishes of the republic. Each castle is governed by a castle captain and an auxiliary council, both serving a one-year term.

history San Marino claims to be the world's oldest republic, founded by St Marinus in the 4th century; it is the only city state to remain after the unification of Italy in the 19th century. It has had a treaty of friendship with Italy since 1862. Women had no vote until 1960.

San Marino's multi-party system mirrors that of the larger country that surrounds it. For the past 40 years it has been governed by a series of left-wing coalitions, the current one comprising the Communists (PCS), Socialists (PSS), and United Socialists (PSU). The San Marino Christian Democrat Party (PDCS) won 26 seats in the 1983 council elections and the PCS 15 seats.

km/30 mi from the Pacific, at the foot of San Salvador volcano 2,548 m/8,360 ft; population (1978) 408,811. Industries include food processing and textiles. Since San Salvador was founded in 1552, it has suffered from several earthquakes.

sansculotte (French 'without knee breeches') in the French Revolution, a member of the working classes, who wore trousers, as opposed to the aristocracy and bourgeoisie, who wore knee breeches.

San Sebastián /'sæn sɪ'bæstɪən/ port and resort in the Basque Country, Spain; population (1981) 175,580. It was formerly the summer residence of the Spanish court.

Sanskrit /'sænskrɪt/ the dominant classical language of the Indian subcontinent, a member of the Indo-Iranian group of the Indo-European language family, and the sacred language of Hinduism. The oldest form of Sanskrit is *Vedic*, the variety used in the Vedas and Upanishads (c. 1500–700 BC). *Classical Sanskrit* was systematized by Panini and other grammarians in the latter part of the 1st millennium BC and became fixed as the spoken and written language of culture, philosophy, mathematics, law, and medicine. It is written in devanagari script and is the language of the two great Hindu epics, the *Mahabharata* and the *Ramayana*, as well as many other classical and later works. Sanskrit vocabulary has not only influenced the languages of India, Thailand and Indonesia, but has also enriched several European languages, including

San Marino

MOST SERENE REPUBLIC OF (*Repubblica di San Marino*)

AREA 58 sq km/22.5 sq mi
CAPITAL San Marino
PHYSICAL on the slope of Mount Titano
FEATURES completely surrounded by Italian territory; one of the world's smallest states
HEAD OF STATE AND OF GOVERNMENT two captains-regent, elected for a six-month period
GOVERNMENT direct democracy
EXPORTS wine; ceramics, paint
CURRENCY Italian lira (2,160 = £1 Sept 1987)
POPULATION 22,300 (1985); annual growth rate 3%
LANGUAGE Italian
RELIGION Roman Catholic
LITERACY 97% (1985)
CHRONOLOGY
1862 Treaty with Italy signed, recognizing its independence and providing for its protection.

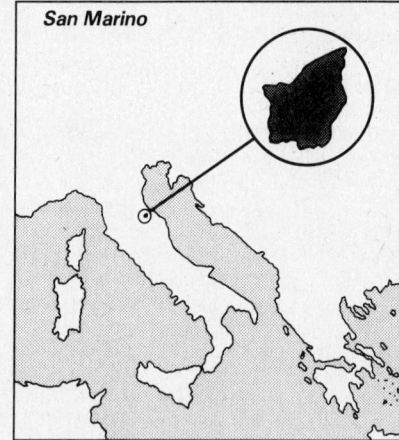
San Marino

1947–78 Governed by a series of left-wing coalitions.

San Martín /'sæn mɑː'tiːn/ José de San Martín 1778–1850. South American nationalist. Born in Argentina, he served in the Spanish army during the Peninsular War, but after 1812 he devoted himself to the South American struggle for independence, playing a large part in the liberation of Argentina, Chile, and Peru from Spanish rule.

San Salvador /'sæn 'sælvədɔː/ capital of the republic of El Salvador in Central America, 48

English, with such words as *bhakti*, *guru*, *karma*, *kundalini*, *mahatma*, *pundit*, *swami*, and *yoga*, all relating to Hindu religion and philosophy.

Santa Ana /'sæntə 'ænə/ periodic warm California ◊wind.

Santa Anna /'sæntə 'ænə/ Antonio Lopez de Santa Anna 1795–1876. Mexican revolutionary. A leader in achieving independence from Spain in 1821, he pursued a chequered career of victory and defeat and was in and out of office as president or dictator for the rest of his life; he led the attack on the ◊Alamo.

Santa Barbara /'bɑːbərə/ town in S California, USA; population (1980) 74,414. It is the site of a campus of the University of California.

Santa Claus /klɔːz/ another name for Father Christmas; see under Saint ◊Nicholas.

Santa Cruz de la Sierra /'kruːz ˌdelə si'erə/ capital of Santa Cruz department in E Bolivia; population (1981) 376,914. Sugar cane and cattle were the chief base of local industry until newly discovered oil and natural gas led to phenomenal growth.

Santa Cruz de Tenerife /'kruːz də ˌtenə'riːf/ capital of Tenerife and of the Canary Islands; population (1981) 185,899. It is a fuelling port and cable centre. Santa Cruz was bombarded by Blake in 1657, and by Nelson in 1797 – the action in which he lost his arm.

Santa Fé /feɪ/ capital of New Mexico, USA, on the river Santa Fé, 65 km/40 mi W of Las Vegas; population (1980) 48,935, many Spanish-speaking. A number of buildings date from the Spanish period, including a palace 1609–10; the cathedral 1869 is on the site of a monastery built 1622.

Santa Fé /feɪ/ capital of Santa Fé province, Argentina, on the Salado river 153 km/95 mi N of Rosario; population (1980) 287,000.

Santa Fé Trail US trade route 1821–80 from Independence, Missouri, to Santa Fé, New Mexico.

Santander /ˌsæntæn'deə/ port on the Bay of Biscay, Cantabria, Spain; population (1981) 180,350. Industries include vehicles and shipyards. It was sacked by ◊Soult in 1808, and was largely rebuilt after a fire in 1941.

Santayana /ˌsænti'ænə/ George 1863–1952. American philosopher. Born in Spain, he graduated at Harvard, where he taught the history of philosophy, 1889–1911. His books include *The Life of Reason* 1905–06, *The Realm of Truth* 1937, *Background of My Life* 1945.

Sant'Elia /sænt 'eliə/ Antonio 1888–1916. Italian architect. Although he died young, his drawings, conveying a Futurist vision of a metropolis with skyscrapers, traffic lanes, and streamlined factories, were influential.

Santiago /ˌsænti'ɑːgəʊ/ capital of Chile; population (1982) 4,039,287. Industries include textiles, chemicals, and food processing. It was founded in 1541, and is famous for its broad avenues.

Santiago de Compostela /deɪ ˌkɒmpɒs'telə/ city in Galicia, Spain; population (1981) 93,695. The 11th-century cathedral was reputedly built over the grave of Sant Iago el Mayor (St ◊James the Great), patron saint of Spain, and was one of the most popular places for medieval pilgrimage.

Santiago de Cuba /deɪ 'kuːbə/ port on the S coast of Cuba; population (1981) 345,289. Industries include sugar, rum, and cigars.

Santiago de los Caballeros /lɒs ˌkæbæl 'jeɒrɒs/ city in N Dominican Republic; population (1980) 278,638.

Santo Domingo /'sæntəʊ də'mɪŋgəʊ/ capital and chief sea port of the Dominican Republic, also formerly called Santo Domingo; population

(1981) 1,550,739. Founded in 1496 by Bartolomeo, brother of Christopher Columbus; it is the oldest city in the Americas.

Santos /'sæntɒs/ coffee-exporting port in Brazil, 72 km/45 mi SE of São Paulo; population (1980) 411,000.

San Yu /'sæn 'juː/ 1919– . Burmese politician. A member of the Revolutionary Council which came to power in 1962, he became president in 1981 and was re-elected in 1985.

Saône /səʊn/ river in E France, rising in the Vosges mountains and flowing 480 km/300 mi to join the Rhône at Lyon.

São Paulo /saʊm 'paʊləʊ/ city in Brazil 900 m/3,000 ft above sea level, 2° S of the Tropic of Capricorn and 72 km/45 mi NW of its port ◊Santos; population (1980) 7,033,529. It originated as a Jesuit mission in 1554, and is the centre of Brazil's coffee trade.

São Tomé e Principe /'saʊn tu'meɪ, 'prɪnsɪpə/ country in the Gulf of Guinea, off the coast of W Africa.

government The 1982 constitution describes the Movement for the Liberation of São Tomé e Principe (MLSTP) as the leading political force in the nation and the National People's Assembly as the supreme organ of the state. It has 40 members, all MLSTP nominees, elected by people's district assemblies for a five-year term. The president is also nominated by the MLSTP and elected for a five-year term by the national assembly.

history The islands were uninhabited until the arrival of the Portuguese in 1471, who brought convicts and exiled Jews to work on sugar plantations. Later on ◊slavery became the main trade, and in the 19th century forced labour was used on coffee and cocoa plantations.

As a Portuguese colony, São Tomé e Principe was given internal self-government in 1973. After the military coup in Portugal in 1974, the new government in Lisbon formally recognized the liberation movement, MLSTP, led by Dr Manuel Pinto da Costa, as the sole representative of the people of the islands and granted independence in Jul 1975. Dr da Costa became the first president and a National People's Assembly was elected. During the first years of his presidency there were several attempts to depose him and small opposition groups still operate from outside the country.

With a worsening economy, da Costa began to reassess his country's international links, which had made it too dependent on the Eastern bloc and, in consequence, isolated from the West. In 1984 he proclaimed that in future São Tomé e Principe would be a ◊non-aligned state, and the number of Angolan, Cuban, and Soviet advisers in the country was sharply reduced. Gradually São Tomé e Principe has turned more towards nearby African states such as Gabon, Cameroon, and Equatorial Guinea, as well as maintaining its links with Lisbon.

sap milky fluid exuded by certain plants, such as the rubber tree, and opium poppy, which contains alkaloids, protein, and starch.

Sapper /'sæpə/ pseudonym of Cyril McNeile 1888–1937. British author of *Bulldog Drummond* 1920 and its sequels.

sapphire the blue transparent gem variety of the mineral ◊corundum. The term can be applied to any colour of gem variety of corundum except red, for example yellow sapphire.

Sappho /'sæfəʊ/ c. 612–580 BC. Greek lyric poet, friend of the poet ◊Alcaeus, and leader of a female literary coterie at Mytilene (modern *Lesvos*, hence ◊lesbianism); legend says she committed suicide when her love for the boatman Phaon was unrequited. Only fragments of her poems have survived.

Sapporo /sə'pɒrəʊ/ capital of ◊Hokkaido, Japan; population (1983) 1,451,000. Industries include rubber and food processing. It is a winter sports centre, and was the site of the 1972 winter Olympics. Giant figures are sculpted in ice at the annual snow festival.

saprophyte an obsolete term for a ◊saprotroph.

saprotroph (formerly *saprophyte*) an organism that feeds on the products (such as excreta) or dead bodies of others. They include most fungi (the rest being ◊parasites), many bacteria and other single-celled organisms, animals such as dung beetles and vultures, and a few unusual plants, including several orchids. Saprotrophs cannot make food for themselves, so they are a type of ◊heterotroph. They are useful scavengers, and in sewage farms and refuse dumps break down organic matter into nutrients easily assimilable by green plants.

Saracen Greek and Roman term for an Arab, used in the Middle Ages by Europeans for all Muslims. The equivalent term used in Spain was Moor.

Saragossa /ˌsærə'gɒsə/ industrial city (Spanish *Zaragoza*) in Aragon, Spain; population (1980) 590,750. The medieval city walls and bridges over the Ebro survive, and there are Romanesque-Gothic and Baroque cathedrals, and a 15th-century university.

history Founded as Salduba in pre-Roman days, it took its present name from Roman conqueror Caesar Augustus; later it was captured by Visigoths and Moors, and was taken in 1118 by Alfonso the Warrior, King of Navarre and Aragon. It remained capital of Aragon until the end of the 15th century. In Jun 1808–Feb 1809, in the Peninsular War, it resisted a French siege. Maria Augustin, known as the 'Maid of Saragossa' who died 1859, became a national hero for her part in the defence: her story is told in Byron's *Childe Harold* 1812–18.

Sarajevo /ˌsærə'jeɪvəʊ/ capital of Bosnia-Hercegovina, Yugoslavia; population (1982) 448,500. Industries include carpets and ceramics. A Bosnian, Gavrilo Princip, assassinated Archduke ◊Francis Ferdinand here in 1914, thereby precipitating World War I.

Saratoga Springs /ˌsærə'təʊgə/ city and spa in New York State, USA, population (1980) 23,906. In 1777 the British general John ◊Burgoyne was defeated in two engagements nearby during the War of American Independence.

sard or *sardony* or *sardonyx* a yellow or red-brown variety of ◊onyx.

sardine name for several small fish in the herring family, though legally restricted in the

São Tomé e Principé
DEMOCRATIC REPUBLIC OF

AREA 964 sq km/372 sq mi
CAPITAL São Tomé
PHYSICAL comprises the two main islands and several smaller ones, all of volcanic origin; thickly forested and fertile
HEAD OF STATE AND OF GOVERNMENT Manuel Pinto da Costa from 1975
GOVERNMENT one-party socialist
EXPORTS cocoa, copra
CURRENCY dobra (57.92 = £1 Sept 1987)
POPULATION 105,000 (1985); annual growth rate 2.5%
LANGUAGE Portuguese
RELIGION Roman Catholic
LITERACY 73% male/42% female (1981)
GNP $31 million (1983); $261 per head of population
CHRONOLOGY
1973 Granted internal self-government.
1975 Achieved full independence, with Manuel Pinto da Costa as president.

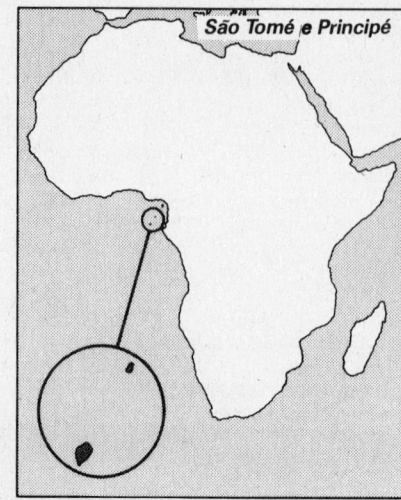

1984 Formally declared itself a nonaligned state.

Sapporo An example of the vivid demons and castles carved in solid ice for the annual snow festival; the figures may be as high as 12 m/40 ft.

UK, following a court ruling of 1915 in favour of an application by a French firm, to the young of the pilchard, caught off Sardinia (hence the name) and Brittany. In 1980 there were attempts to change this ruling which adversely affects packers of other small fish in the group which are indistinguishable in taste, and which are now marketed as sild or brisling.

Sardinia /saː'dɪnɪə/ mountainous island (Italian *Sardegna*), special autonomous region of Italy.
area 14,964 sq km/9,298 sq mi
capital Cagliari
features second largest Mediterranean island; Costa Smeralda (Emerald Coast) tourist area in NE; *nuraghi* (fortified Bronze Age dwellings)
exports cork, petrochemicals
population (1981) 1,594,175
recent history after centuries of foreign rule, it became linked in 1720 with Piedmont, and this dual kingdom became the basis of a united Italy in 1861.

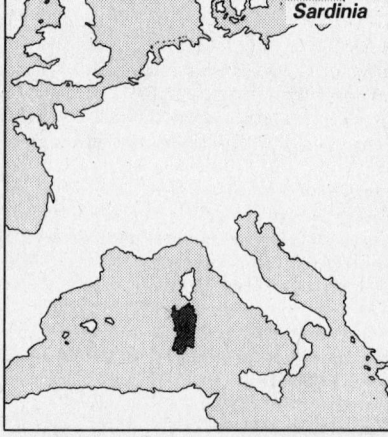

Sardou /saː'duː/ Victorien 1831–1908. French dramatist whose plays include *Fédora* 1882, *Madame Sans-Gêne* 1893, and *La Tosca* 1887 (the basis for the opera by ◊Puccini). Bernard ◊Shaw coined the expression 'Sardoodledom' to express his disgust with the contrivances of the 'well-made' play – a genre of which Sardou was the leading exponent.

Sargasso Sea /saː'gæsəu/ part of the N Atlantic (between 40° and 80° W and 25° and 30° N) left static by circling ocean currents, and covered with floating weed *Sargassum natans*.

Sargent /'saːdʒənt/ (Harold) Malcolm (Watts) 1895–1967. British conductor. He was chief conductor of the BBC Symphony Orchestra 1950–57, and then continued as conductor-in-chief of the Henry Wood ◊promenade concerts. He had an easy, polished style.

Sargent /'saːdʒənt/ John Singer 1856–1925. American artist, noted for portraits. Born in Florence of American parents, he studied there and in Paris. He settled in London, and was elected to the Royal Academy in 1897. His output was prolific and highly fashionable in its day with its technical skill, and superficial brilliance.

Sargeson /'saːdʒsən/ Frank 1903–1982. New Zealand writer of short stories and novels including *The Hangover* 1967 and *Man of England Now* 1972.

Sargon /'saːgɒn/ two Mesopotamian kings: *Sargon I* King of Akkad c. 2370–2230 BC, and founder of the first Babylonian empire. His story resembles that of Moses in that he was said to have been found floating in a cradle on the ◊Euphrates.
Sargon II died 705 BC. King of Assyria from 722 BC, who assumed the name of his famous predecessor. To keep conquered peoples from rising against him, he had whole populations moved from their homelands, including the Israelites from Samaria.

Sark /saːk/ one of the ◊Channel Islands, 10 km/6 mi E of Guernsey; area 5 sq km/2 sq mi; there is no town or village. It is divided into Great and Little Sark, linked by an isthmus. The Seigneurie of Sark was established by Elizabeth I, the ruler being known as Seigneur/Dame, and has its own parliament, the Chief Pleas. There is no income tax and cars are forbidden.

Sarmatian a member of an Indo-European nomadic people who slowly ousted the ◊Scythians from what is now S European USSR from the mid-3rd century BC and in turn gave way to the ◊Goths by the 3rd century AD.

Sarney /'saːneɪ/ José 1930– . President of Brazil from 1985, member of Brazilian Democratic Movement (PMDB).
Sarney was elected vice president in 1985 and within months, on the death of President Neves, became head of state. Despite earlier involvement with the repressive military regime, he and his party won a convincing victory in the 1986 general election.

Saroyan /sə'rɔɪən/ William 1908–1981. American author, whose *The Bicycle Rider in Beverly Hills* 1950 tells of his childhood in California. He is best known for short stories, such as *The Daring Young Man on the Flying Trapeze* 1934, idealizing the hopes and sentiments of the 'little man'. His plays include *The Time of Your Life* 1939.

Sarraute /sæ'rəut/ Nathalie 1920– . Russian-born French novelist whose books include *Portrait d'un inconnu/Portrait of a Man Unknown* 1948, *Les Fruits d'or/The Golden Fruits* 1964, and *Vous les entendez?/Do You Hear Them?* 1972. An exponent of the ◊nouveau roman, Sarraute bypasses plot, character, and style for the half-conscious interaction of minds.

sarsaparilla drink prepared from the long twisted roots of plants in the genus *Smilax*, native to Central and South America.

Sartre /'saːtrə/ Jean-Paul 1905–1980. French author and philosopher, one of the leading proponents of ◊Existentialism. Born in Paris, he published his first novel *La*

Nausée/Nausea in 1937. In World War II he was a prisoner for nine months, but on his return from Germany joined the Resistance. As a founder of Existentialism, he edited its journal *Les Temps modernes/Modern Times*, and expressed its tenets in his novels, for example, the trilogy *Les Chemins de la liberté/Roads to Freedom* 1944–45, and in his plays, including *Huis clos/In Camera* 1944 where two women and one man are confined in the hell they make for each other. In *Crime Passionel* 1948 he attacked aspects of communism while retaining a general sympathy. *L'Etre et le néant/Being and Nothingness* 1943, his first major work, is important for the radical doctrine of human freedom it propounds. According to Sartre, people's awareness of their own freedom takes the form of anxiety, and they attempt to flee from this awareness into what he terms *mauvaise foi/bad faith*. In his later work Sartre became more sensitive to the social constraints on people's actions, and in *Critique de la raison dialectique/Critique of Dialectical Reason* 1960 he attempted a synthesis of Existentialism and ◊Marxism. He refused the Nobel Prize for Literature in 1964 for 'personal reasons'.

Sarum /'seərəm/ former settlement from which the modern city of ◊Salisbury, Wiltshire developed.

Sary-Shagan /'saːri ʃə'gaːn/ weapons-testing area in Kazakhstan, USSR, near the Chinese border. In 1980 beam weapons were detected on trial there.

Sasebo /'saːsəbəu/ seaport and naval base on the W coast of Kyushu, Japan; population (1983) 252,000.

Saskatchewan /sæs'kætʃiwən/ province of W Canada.
area 651,901 sq km/251,700 sq mi
capital Regina
towns Saskatoon
features prairies in the S; to the N forests, lakes and subarctic tundra
exports produces more than 60% Canada's wheat; oil, natural gas, uranium, zinc, potash (world's largest reserves), copper, and helium
population (1983) 1,006,200.

Saskatchewan

Saskatoon /ˌsæskə'tuːn/ city in Saskatchewan, Canada; population (1985) 176,000. Industries include cement, oil refining, chemicals. It has a university (1907).

Sassanian Empire /sə'seiniən/ empire founded 224 AD by Ardashir, a chieftain in the area of modern Fars in Iran, who had taken over the ◊Parthian Empire; it was so-named from his grandfather, Sasan. The capital was Ctesiphon, near modern ◊Baghdad. After a rapid period of expansion, when it contested supremacy with Rome, it was destroyed in 637 by the Muslim Arabs at the Battle of ◊Qadisiyah.

Sassoon /sə'suːn/ Siegfried 1886–1967. British poet. In World War I he served in France and Palestine. His *War Poems* 1919 express the disillusion of his generation. As a prose writer he is known for his *Memoirs of a Foxhunting Man* 1928.

satellite any small body that orbits a larger one, either natural or artificial. Natural satellites that orbit planets are called ◊moons. The first *artificial satellite*, Sputnik 1, was launched into orbit around the Earth by the USSR in 1957. Artificial satellites are used for scientific purposes, communications, weather forecasting, and military purposes. At any time there are several thousand artificial satellites orbiting the Earth, including active satellites, those that have ended their working lives, and discarded sections of rockets. The largest artificial satellites can be seen by the naked eye. Artificial satellites eventually re-enter the Earth's atmosphere. Usually they burn up by friction, but sometimes debris falls to the Earth's surface, as with ◊Skylab.

satellite town new town planned and built to serve a particular local industry, or as a dormitory or overspill town for people who work in a (usually overcrowded) nearby metropolis. Early new towns in Britain were Letchworth (Hertfordshire), established in 1903, and Port Sunlight near Birkenhead (Cheshire), built to house workers at Lever Brothers soap factories. More recent examples include Basildon (1949), Corby (1950), Cumbernauld (1955), Harlow (1947), Milton Keynes (1967), and Welwyn Garden City (1948), whose populations will range from 50,000 (Welwyn) to 250,000 (Milton Keynes) by the end of the century. Such towns – there are 31 in all the UK – are planned by a government-financed corporation, in co-operation with the local authority.

Satie /sæ'tiː/ Erik (Alfred Leslie) 1866–1925. French composer. He was noted for his piano pieces, such as *Gymnopédies* 1888, which combine wit and melancholy. His orchestral works include *Parade* 1917, amongst whose bizarre sound effects is a typewriter. He was the mentor of the group of composers known as ◊*Les Six*, although not a member.

satire a work, in poetry or prose, which uses wit, humour, or irony, often through allegory or extended metaphor, to ridicule human pretensions or expose social evils. The Roman poets Juvenal and Horace wrote *Satires*, and the form became particularly popular in Europe in the 17th and 18th centuries, used by Voltaire in France and by Pope and Swift in England. Satire is related to *parody* in its intention to mock, but satire tends to be more subtle and to mock an attitude or a belief, whereas parody tends to mock a particular work such as a poem by imitating its style, often with purely comic intent rather than to make a moral point. Both satire and parody appeal to the intellect rather than the emotions; and both, to be effective, require a knowledge of the original attitude, person, or work being mocked (although much satire, such as *Gulliver's Travels* by Swift, can also be enjoyed simply on a literal level).

Sato /'saːtəu/ Eisaku 1901–1975. Japanese politician. Son of a brewer of *sake*; he opposed the policies of Hayato Ikeda (1899–1965) in the Liberal-Democratic Party, and succeeded him as prime minister 1964–72, pledged to a more independent foreign policy. He shared a Nobel Peace Prize in 1974 for his rejection of nuclear weapons. His brother *Nobosuke Kishi* (1896–1987) was prime minister of Japan 1957–60.

satrap title of a provincial governor in Ancient Persia. The Persian Empire was divided into some 20 of these under ◊Darius. Later the term was used to describe any local ruler, often in a derogatory way.

saturated solution in physics, a solution obtained when a solvent (liquid) can dissolve no more of a solute (usually a solid) at a particular temperature. Normally, a slight fall in temperature causes some of the solute to crystallize out of solution. If this does not happen, the phenomenon is called supercooling, and the solution supersaturated.

Saturn the second largest planet in the solar system, sixth outwards from the Sun, encircled by bright rings. Viewed through a telescope it is white, but appears lemon-coloured at closer range. Saturn orbits the Sun every 29.5 years at an average distance of 1,427 million km/886.7 million mi. Its equatorial diameter is 120,000 km/74,600 mi, but its polar diameter is 12,000 km smaller, a result of its fast rotation and low density. Saturn spins on its axis every 10 hr 14 min at its equator, slowing to 10 hr 40 min at high latitudes. Its mass is 95 times that of the Earth, and its magnetic field 1,000 times stronger, but it has an average density of only 70 per cent that of water, the lowest of any planet. Saturn is believed to have a small core of rock and iron, encased in ice and topped by a deep layer of liquid hydrogen.

Like Jupiter, Saturn's visible surface consists of swirling clouds, probably made of frozen ammonia at a temperature of -170°C, although the markings in the clouds are not as prominent as Jupiter's. The space probes Voyager 1 and 2 found winds reaching 1,800 kph/1,100 mph.

From Earth, Saturn's rings appear to be divided into three main sections. Ring A, the outermost, is separated from ring B, the brightest, by the Cassini division (named after its discoverer ◊Cassini), 3,000 km/2,000 mi wide; the inner, transparent ring C is also called the Crepe Ring. The visible rings span 275,000 km/170,000 mi from rim to rim, but they are only 100 m/300 ft thick, so they disappear when viewed edge-on. The ◊Voyager probes showed that the rings consist of thousands of closely spaced ringlets, looking like the grooves in a gramophone record. Each ringlet is made of a swarm of particles of ice and rock, a few centimetres to a few metres in diameter. Outside the A ring is the narrow and faint F ring, which the Voyagers showed to be twisted or braided. The rings of Saturn could be the remains of a shattered moon, or they may always have existed in their present form.

The Voyagers photographed numerous small moons orbiting Saturn, taking the total to over 20, more than for any other planet. The largest moon, Titan, has a dense atmosphere. Saturn's major satellites, in order of mean distance from the planet, include:

Mimas mean distance from its planet 186,000 km/115,000 mi, diameter 350 km/220 mi;

Enceladus mean distance from its planet 238,000 km/147,800 mi, diameter 350 km/220 mi;

Tethys mean distance from its planet 295,000 km/183,200 mi, diameter 1,020 km/635 mi;

Dione mean distance from its planet 370,000 km/234,117 mi, diameter 1,000 km/685 mi;

Titan mean distance from its planet 1,222,000 km/759,000 mi, diameter 5,150 km/3,199 mi;

Hyperion mean distance from its planet 1,483,000 km/920,940 mi, diameter 1,500 km/930 mi;

Phoebe mean distance from its planet 12,950,000 km/8,043,000 mi, diameter 160 km/100 mi.

Saturn in Roman mythology, the god of agriculture (Greek *Kronos*), whose period of rule was the ancient Golden Age. He was dethroned by his sons Jupiter, Neptune, and Pluto. At his festival, the saturnalia in Dec, gifts were exchanged, and slaves were briefly treated as their masters' equals.

Saturn rocket a family of large US rockets, developed by Werner ◊von Braun for the ◊Apollo programme. The two-stage Saturn IB was used for launching Apollo spacecraft into orbit around the Earth. The three-stage Saturn V sent Apollo spacecraft to the Moon, and launched the ◊Skylab space station. The lift-off thrust of a Saturn V was 3,500 tonnes. After Apollo and Skylab, the Saturn rockets were retired in favour of the ◊space shuttle.

satyagraha (Sanskrit 'grasping the truth') term applied in India to non-violent resistance, specifically to British rule. It was first employed by Gandhi in 1918, and the idea owes much to Tolstoy.

satyr in Greek mythology, a woodland being characterized by pointed ears, two horns on the forehead, and a tail, who attended Dionysus. Roman writers confused satyrs with the goat-footed fauns.

Saudi Arabia /'saʊdi ə'reɪbiə/ country on the Arabian peninsula, stretching from the Red Sea to the Arabian Gulf, bounded to the N by Jordan, Iraq, and Kuwait, to the E by Qatar and United Arab Emirates, to the SE by Oman, and to the S by North and South Yemen.

government Saudi Arabia is an absolute monarchy with no written constitution, no legislature and no political parties. The king rules, in accordance with Islamic law, by decree. He appoints and heads a council of ministers, whose decisions are the result of a majority vote but always subject to the sanction of the king.

history For early history, see ◊Arabia. The sultanate of Nejd in the interior came under Turkish rule in the 18th century. Present-day

Saudi Arabia is almost entirely the creation of King Ibn Saud who, after the dissolution of the ◊Ottoman Empire in 1918, fought rival Arab rulers until, in 1926, he had established himself as the undisputed king of the Hejaz and sultan of Nejd. In 1932 Nejd and Hejaz became the United Kingdom of Saudi Arabia.

Oil was discovered in the 1930s and commercially exploited from the 1940s and became the basis of the country's great prosperity. Ibn Saud died 1953 and was succeeded by his eldest son, Saud. During King Saud's reign relations between Saudi Arabia and Egypt became strained and criticisms of the king within the royal family grew until in 1964 he abdicated in favour of his brother Faisal. Under King Faisal, Saudi Arabia became a leader among Arab oil producers.

In 1975 Faisal was assassinated by one of his nephews, and his half-brother Khalid succeeded him. Khalid was in failing health and increasingly relied on his brother Fahd to perform the duties of government. King Khalid died of a heart attack in 1982 and was succeeded by Fahd.

Saudi Arabia has given financial support to Iraq in its war with Iran. The Gulf War has also prompted it to buy advanced missiles from the USA. Islamic fundamentalists have staged demonstrations in ◊Mecca in 1979 and 1987, leading to worsening relations with Iran.

Saudi Arabia

KINGDOM OF (*al-Mamaka al-'Arabiya as-Sa'udiya*)

AREA 2,400,000 sq km/927,000 sq mi
CAPITAL Riyadh
TOWNS Mecca, Medina; ports Jidda, Dammam
PHYSICAL desert, sloping to the Persian Gulf from a height of 2,750 m/9,000 ft in the W
FEATURES Nafud desert in the N, and the Rub' al Khali (Empty Quarter) in the S, area 650,000 sq km/ 250,000 sq mi
HEAD OF STATE AND OF GOVERNMENT King Fahd Ibn Abdul Aziz from 1982
GOVERNMENT absolute monarchy
EXPORTS oil
CURRENCY rial (6.19 = £1 Sept 1987)
POPULATION 11,152,000 (1985); annual growth rate 4.1%
LANGUAGE Arabic
RELIGION Sunni Muslim, with a Shi'ite minority in the E under the influence of Ayatollah Khomeini
LITERACY 34% male/12% female (1980 est)
GDP $110.5 bn (1983); $11,500 per head of population
CHRONOLOGY
1926–32 Territories united and kingdom established.

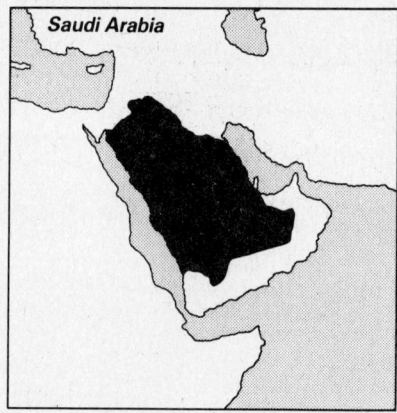
Saudi Arabia

1953 King ibn-Saud died and was succeeded by his eldest son, Saud.
1964 King Saud forced to abdicate and was succeeded by his brother Faisal.
1975 King Faisal assassinated by a nephew and succeeded by his half-brother Khalid.
1982 King Khalid died suddenly of a heart attack and was succeeded by his brother Crown Prince Fahd, who had effectively been ruling the country for some years because of King Khalid's ill health.

Sault Ste Marie /'suː seɪnt məˈriː/ twin industrial ports on the Canadian/US frontier, one in Ontario and one in Michigan; population (1981) 82,902 and (1980) 14,448 respectively. They stand at the falls (French *sault*) in St Mary's river, which links lakes Superior and Huron. The falls are bypassed by canals.

Saumur /səʊˈmjʊə/ town in Maine-et-Loire *département*, France, on the river Loire; population (1985) 34,000. The area is famous for its sparkling wines. The cavalry school (1768), has since 1942 also been a training school for the French armoured forces.

sauna a heat bath consisting of a small room or cabinet in which the temperature is raised to about 90°C/200°F, popular in health clubs, and sports centres. The occupant typically stays in it for only a few minutes and then follows it with a cold shower. It derives from a traditional Finnish heat bath in which steam is produced by throwing cold water over hot stones; this is traditionally followed by beating with birch twigs to stimulate the circulation, and often by a plunge into the snow outdoors.

Saunders /'sɔːndəz/ Clarence 1881–1953. American retailer, who opened the first self-service supermarket in Memphis, Tennessee, in 1919.

Sauternes /səʊˈtɜːn/ a sweet white table wine produced in the Gironde department, SW

Saul /sɔːl/ died c. 1010 BC. In the Old Testament, the first king of Israel, who was anointed by ◊Samuel and warred successfully against the ◊Ammonites and ◊Philistines. He turned against Samuel and committed suicide as his mind became unbalanced.

France. It takes its name from the village of Sauternes.

Savage /'sævɪdʒ/ Michael Joseph 1872–1940. New Zealand Labour politician. As prime minister 1935–40, he introduced much social-security legislation.

Savannah /sə'vænə/ city and port of Georgia, USA, 29 km/18 mi from the mouth of the Savannah river; population (1980) 141,390. Founded in 1733, Savannah was the first city in the USA to be laid out in geometrically regular blocks. It exports cotton, and produces cottonseed oil, fertilizers, and machinery. The *Savannah*, the first steam-powered ship to cross the Atlantic, was built at Savannah; most of the 25-day journey, in 1819, was made under sail. The first nuclear-powered merchant ship, launched by the USA in 1959, was given the same name.

savannah name originally given by the Spaniards to the treeless plains of the tropical American prairies; now denoting any extensive tropical grassland.

Savery /'seɪvəri/ Thomas c. 1650–1715. British engineer who invented the steam-driven water pump, precursor of the steam engine. The machine, built in 1696 for use in mines, and patented two years later, used a boiler to raise steam which was condensed (in a separate condenser) by an external spray of cold water. The partial vacuum created sucked water up a pipe from the mine shaft; steam pressure was then used to force the water away, after which the cycle was repeated.

savings unspent income, after deduction of tax. In economics a distinction is made between investment, involving the purchase of ◊capital goods, such as buying a house, and saving (where capital goods are not directly purchased, for example, buying ◊shares).

Savonarola /ˌsævənə'rəʊlə/ Girolamo 1452–1498. Italian reformer, a Dominican friar whose eloquent preaching won him popular influence. In 1494 he led a revolt in Florence which expelled the ◊Medicis and established a republic. However, his denunciations of Pope ◊Alexander VI led to his excommunication in 1497, and in 1498 he was arrested, tortured, hanged, and burned for heresy.

Savoy /sə'vɔɪ/ area of France between the Alps, the Lake of Geneva, and the river Rhône. It was formed into the *départements* of Savoie and Haute-Savoie, in Rhône-Alpes region. *history* Savoy was a medieval duchy and in 1720 became a province of the kingdom of Sardinia which, with Nice, was ceded to France in 1860 by Victor Emmanuel II (king of Italy from 1861) in return for French assistance in driving the Austrians from Italy.

sawfish fish of the ◊ray order. The *common sawfish Pristis pectinatus*, family Pristidae, is more than 6 m/19 ft long. It resembles a shark and has some 24 teeth along an elongated snout (2 m/6 ft) which can be used as a weapon.

sawfly type of insect of the order Hymenoptera, related to bees, wasps and ants, but lacking a 'waist' on the body. The egg-laying tube (ovipositor) of the female has a saw edge which she uses to make a slit in a plant stem to lay her eggs. Some species have sharp ovipositors which can drill into wood, as the large black and yellow European '*wood wasp*' *Uroceras gigas* about 4 cm/1.5 in long which bores into conifers.

Saxe /sæks/ French form of ◊Saxony.

Savonarola Savonarola's crusade against political and religious corruption led to the overthrow of the Medici rule in Florence and the establishment of a republic. His portrait is by Fra Bartolomeo.

Saxe /sæks/ Maurice, Comte de 1696–1750. Soldier, illegitimate son of the Elector of Saxony, who served under ◊Marlborough and ◊Eugène, and was created Marshal of France in 1743 for his exploits in the War of the ◊Austrian Succession.

Saxe-Coburg-Gotha /'sæks 'kəʊbɜːg 'gəʊtə/ Saxon duchy. Albert, the Prince Consort of Queen ◊Victoria of England, was a son of the first Duke (Ernest I 1784–1844), who was succeeded by Albert's elder brother, Ernest II (1818–93). It remained the name of the British royal house until 1917, when it was changed to Windsor.

saxhorn a type of ◊brass musical instrument with valves, invented by Adolphe Sax in 1845.

saxifrage plant of the family Saxifragaceae. They occur in rocky, mountainous, and alpine situations. London Pride (*Saxifraga umbrosa x spathularis*) is a familiar example.

Saxon belonging to a Teutonic people who invaded Britain in the early Middle Ages; see under ◊Anglo-Saxon.

Saxony /'sæksəni/ English form of *Sachsen*, a former kingdom of Germany, which is now the modern region of Leipzig, Dresden, and Karl-Marx-Stadt, East Germany. Saxony lay between Prussia, Bavaria, and Bohemia; Dresden was the capital. The name is derived from its Saxon inhabitants whose territories originally reached as far W as the Rhine, covering most of the *Land* of Germany formed in 1946 and named ◊Lower Saxony. Saxony was conquered by Charlemagne, but when his empire broke up after his death in 814, it became a dukedom. The area subsequently underwent many changes in territory and status: in the 13th century it became an electorate (that is, ruled by an Elector), and later a kingdom. Saxony supported Napoleon I and half the kingdom was given to Prussia by the Congress of Vienna, 1815, becoming the Prussian province of Saxony. The remaining kingdom joined the German Empire, founded 1871. At the end of World War I the king abdicated and Saxony became one of the federal states of the German Republic. After World War II, Saxony was made a new *Land* of East Germany as ◊Saxony-Anhalt.

Saxony-Anhalt /'sæksəni 'ænhælt/ former *Land* of East Germany, 1946–52. It consisted of Anhalt, a former duchy and state, and most of the former Prussian province of Saxony.

saxophone a woodwind musical instrument made of metal. It was invented by the Belgian Adolphe Sax (1814–94) in about 1840. Several varieties exist, all having a conical brass tube; commonly used in jazz music.

Sayan Mountains /saɪ'æn/ range in the south-eastern USSR, on the Mongolian border; the highest peak is Munku Sardik 3,489 m/11,447 ft. The mountains have coal, gold, and lead resources.

Sayers /'seɪəz/ Dorothy L(eigh) 1893–1957. English writer of crime novels featuring detective Lord Peter Wimsey including *Strong Poison* 1930, *The Nine Tailors* 1934, and *Gaudy Night* 1935.

Say's Law in economics, the 'law of markets' enunciated by Jean-Baptiste Say (1767–1832) to the effect that supply creates its own demand and that resources can never be under-used. Widely accepted by classical economists, the 'law' was regarded as erroneous by J M ◊Keynes in his analysis of the depression in Britain during the 1920s and 1930s.

SBS the Special Boat Service. The British Navy's equivalent of the ◊Special Air Service.

scabies contagious infection of the skin caused by the mite *Sarcoptes scaboi*. Treatment is by anti-parasitic creams and lotions.

scabious Mediterranean plant, family Dipsacaceae, with many small flowers, often blue, borne in a single head; the *small scabious Scabiosa columbaria* is common in Britain, as also is the *field scabious Knautia arvensis*.

Scafell Pike /ˌskɔː'fel/ highest mountain in England 978 m/3,210 ft. It is in Cumbria in the Lake District and is separated from Scafell 964 m/3,162 ft by a ridge called Mickledore.

scalar quantity in mathematics, any quantity that has magnitude but no direction.

scalawag or *scallywag* in US history, a derogatory term for white Southerners who during and after the Civil War of 1861–65 supported the Republican Party and black emancipation.

scale in general, a series of marks (such as degrees, inches) indicating the standard of measurement, enabling theoretical examination by reduction or enlargement. In music, progression of notes which varies according to the musical system being used, for example, the seven notes of the ◊diatonic scale, the 12 notes of the ◊chromatic scale. Major and minor scales derive from the Ionian and Aeolian modes respectively, two of the 12 modes or scales of ancient music.

scale insect small ◊bug, superfamily Cocceidea, that feeds on plants. Some species are major pests, for example the citrus mealy bug, which attacks citrus fruits in America. The female is often wingless and legless, attached to a plant by the head and with the body covered with a waxy scale. The rare males are winged.

scallop marine ◊mollusc of the family Pectinidae, with a bivalve fan-shaped shell, including the *edible scallop Chlamys opercularis* and *St James's shell Pecten jacobaeus* used as a badge by medieval pilgrims to ◊Santiago de Compostela. Scallops use 'jet propulsion' to move through the water to escape enemies such as starfish.

scampi (Italian 'shrimps') small lobster *Nephrops norwegicus* up to 15 cm/6 in long, ideal for processing and freezing.

Scandinavia /ˌskændɪˈneɪvɪə/ peninsula in NW Europe, comprising Norway and Sweden; politically and culturally it also includes Denmark and Finland.

scandium a scarce metallic element, symbol Sc, atomic number 21, atomic weight 44.96. It is one of the lanthanide series of elements and was discovered in 1879 in the Scandinavian mineral euxenite.

scanner a device, usually electronic, used to sense and reproduce an image. In medicine scanners are used in diagnosis (see ◊scanning) to provide images of internal organs; see also ◊X-rays and ◊tomography.

scanning non-invasive examination of body organs to detect abnormalities of structure or functioning. Detectable waves, for example ultrasound, magnetic, or X-rays, are passed through the part to be scanned. Their absorption pattern is recorded, analysed by computer, and displayed on a screen or as a photograph.

Scapa Flow /ˈskɑːpə ˈfləʊ/ expanse of sea in the Orkney Islands, Scotland, until 1957 a base of the Royal Navy. The main base of the Grand Fleet during World War I, in 1919 it was the scene of the scuttling of 71 surrendered German warships.

scapolite a group of white or greyish minerals, essentially silicates of aluminium, calcium, and sodium, which probably come from deep earth and may act as underground storehouses for gases such as carbon dioxide and sulphur dioxide.

scarab name for the dung-beetles of the family Scarabeidae, of which *Scarabeus sacer* was revered by the ancient Egyptians as the symbol of resurrection.

Scarborough /ˈskɑːbərə/ holiday resort in N Yorkshire, England; population (1985) 50,000.

Scarlatti /skɑːˈlæti/ (Giuseppe) Domenico 1685–1757. Italian composer, eldest son of Alessandro ◊Scarlatti. After working in Naples (his birthplace), Venice, and Rome, he lived for most of his life in Portugal and Spain in the service of the Queen of Spain. He is remembered for his highly original harpsichord sonatas.

Scarlatti /skɑːˈlæti/ (Pietro) Alessandro (Gaspare) 1660–1725. Italian Baroque composer, Master of the Chapel at the court of Naples, who developed the opera form (arias interspersed with recitative), writing more than 100 operas, such as *Tigrane* 1715, as well as much church music, including oratorios. His son Domenico ◊Scarlatti was also a composer.

scarlet fever more correctly *scarlatina*, an infectious disease caused by the bacterium *Streptococcus scarlatinae*, marked by fever, and a bright red rash spreading from the upper to the lower part of the body. The rash is followed by the skin peeling in flakes. It is treated by antibiotics.

scarp and dip in geomorphology, the two slopes formed when a sedimentary bed outcrops as a landscape feature. The scarp is the slope that cuts across the bedding plane; the dip is the opposite slope which follows the bedding plane. The scarp is usually steep, the dip is a gentle slope.

scent gland a ◊gland that opens at the skin surface of animals, producing odorous compounds which are used in communication. See also ◊pheromone.

Scepticism an ancient philosophical view that absolute knowledge of things is ultimately unobtainable, and that hence the only proper attitude is to suspend judgement. Its origins lay in the teachings of the Greek philosopher ◊Pyrrhon, who maintained that peace of mind lay in renouncing all claims to knowledge. It was taken up in a less extreme form by the Greek ◊Academy in the 3rd and 2nd centuries BC. Academic sceptics claimed that although truth is finally unknowable, a balance of probabilities can be used for coming to decisions. The most radical form of scepticism is known as ◊solipsism, which maintains that the self is the only thing that can be known to exist.

Schaffhausen /ˈʃæfˌhaʊzən/ town in N Switzerland; population (1980) 34,250. The Rhine falls here in a series of cascades some 60 m/180 ft high.

Scheer /ʃeə/ Reinhard 1863–1928. German admiral, commander of the High Sea Fleet in 1916 at the Battle of ◊Jutland.

Scheldt /skelt/ river (Dutch and Flemish *Schelde*, French *Escaut*) rising in France and flowing 400 km/250 mi to join the North Sea south of Walcheren, in the Netherlands; ◊Antwerp is the chief town on the Scheldt.

Schelling /ˈʃelɪŋ/ Friedrich Wilhelm Joseph 1775–1854. German philosopher, who began as a follower of ◊Fichte, but moved away from subjective ◊idealism towards a 'philosophy of identity' (*Identitätsphilosophie*), in which subject and object are seen as united in the absolute. His early philosophy influenced ◊Hegel, but in his later work he became one of the first critics of Hegel, arguing that being necessarily precedes thought.

scheltopusik another name for the ◊glass snake.

scherzo (Italian 'joke') in music, a lively piece, usually in rapid triple time, often the third movement of a symphony or sonata.

Scheveningen /ˈsxeɪfənɪŋə/ seaside resort near The ◊Hague, Netherlands.

Schiaparelli /skiˌæpəˈreli/ Elsa 1896–1973. Italian couturier. Born in Rome, she emigrated to the USA and in the early 1920s went to Paris, where her modernistic knitwear designs made a great impact. She became known for her innovative and often (at the time) outrageous fashion ideas, such as padded shoulders, sophisticated colours ('shocking pink') and the pioneering of zips and synthetic fabrics.

Schick test injection of a small quantity of ◊diphtheria toxin to ascertain whether a person is immune to the disease or not: in the latter case a local inflammation appears.

Schiele /ˈʃiːlə/ Egon 1890–1918. Austrian ◊Expressionist artist. Originally a landscape painter, he later painted dynamically distorted pictures, many of them erotic, such as the nudes in *Liebespaar I*.

Schiller /ˈʃɪlə/ Johann Christoph Friedrich von 1759–1805. German Romantic poet and playwright. A qualified surgeon, after the success of the play *Die Räuber/The Robbers* 1791, he devoted himself to literature and completed his tragedies *Fiesko/Fiasco* and *Kabale und Liebe/Love and Intrigue* 1783. Moving to Weimar in 1787 he wrote his more mature blank verse drama *Don Carlos* and the hymn 'An die Freude/Hymn to Joy', later used by ◊Beethoven in his ninth symphony. During his time as professor of history at Jena he developed a close friendship with ◊Goethe. To this period belong his essays on aesthetics and the famous piece of literary criticism *Über naive und sentimentalische/Naive and Sentimental Poetry*. A leading exponent of the ◊Sturm und Drang (storm and stress) movement, Schiller became the foremost German dramatist with his classic dramas *Wallenstein* (a trilogy) 1798–99, *Maria Stuart* 1800, *Die Jungfrau von Orleans/The Maid of Orleans* 1801, and *Wilhelm Tell/William Tell* 1804.

Schinkel /ˈʃɪŋkəl/ Karl Friedrich 1781–1841. Prussian architect of the Neo-Classical style, the greatest German architect of the 19th century. Works include the Old Museum, Berlin 1823–30, the War Memorial on the Kreuzbert 1818, the Nikolaikirche at Potsdam 1830–37, the Charlottenhof 1826 and the Roman Bath 1833 in the park of Potsdam.

schipperke /ˈʃɪpəki/ (Dutch 'little boatman' from its use on canal barges), tailless watchdog, bred in Belgium. It has black fur and erect ears, and is about 30 cm/1 ft high.

schist a foliated ◊metamorphic rock presenting layers of various minerals, for example, mica, which easily split off into thin plates. Schist is formed by great pressure applied from one direction.

schistosomiasis or *bilharzia* disease contracted by bathing in water containing the snails which act as host to the first larval stage of flukes of the genus *Schistosoma*; when these larvae leave the snail in their second stage of development, they are able to pass through human skin, become sexually mature, and produce quantities of eggs which pass to the intestine or bladder. The human host eventually dies, but before then numerous eggs have passed from the body in urine or faeces to continue the cycle. Some 300 million people are thought to suffer from this disease in the tropics. Treatment is by means of drugs, usually containing antimony, to kill the parasites.

schizocarp a type of dry ◊fruit that develops from two or more carpels, and which splits, when mature, to form separate one-seeded units known as mericarps. The mericarps may be dehiscent, splitting open to release the seed when ripe, as in

Geranium, or indehiscent, as in mallow (*Malva*) and plants of the Umbelliferae family, such as the carrot (*Daucus carota*) and parsnip (*Pastinaca sativa*).

schizophrenia a mental disorder, a psychosis of unknown origin. It may develop in early adulthood and can lead to profound changes in personality and behaviour. Modern treatment approaches use drugs, and can include family therapy, stress reduction, and rehabilitation.

Schlegel /ˈʃleɪgəl/ August Wilhelm von 1767–1845. German Romantic author, translator of Shakespeare, whose *Über dramatische Kunst und Literatur/Lectures on Dramatic Art and Literature* 1809–11 broke down the formalism of the old classical criteria of literary composition. Friedrich von ◊Schlegel was his brother.

Schlegel /ˈʃleɪgəl/ Friedrich von 1772–1829. German critic, who (with his brother August) was a founder of the Romantic movement, and a pioneer in the comparative study of languages. He studied Greek and Sanskrit literature and wrote extensively on literary history.

Schleswig-Holstein /ˈʃlezwɪg ˈhɒlstaɪn/ *Land* (state) of West Germany.
area 15,785 sq km/6,095 sq mi
capital Kiel
towns Lübeck, Flensburg, Schleswig
features river Elbe, Kiel Canal, Heligoland
products shipbuilding, mechanical and electrical engineering, food processing
population (1983) 2,616,598
religion Protestant 87%; Roman Catholic 6%
history Schleswig (Danish *Slesvig*) and Holstein were two duchies held by the kings of Denmark from 1460, but were not part of the kingdom; a number of the inhabitants were German, and Holstein was a member of the German Confederation formed in 1815. Possession of the duchies had long been disputed by Prussia, and when Frederick VII of Denmark died without an heir in 1863, Prussia, supported by Austria, fought and defeated the Danes in 1864 (see ◊Seven Weeks' War), and in 1866 annexed the two duchies. A plebiscite held in 1920 gave the N part of Schleswig to Denmark, which made it the province of Haderslev and Aabenraa; the rest, with Holstein, remained part of Germany.

Schlieffen Plan military plan produced by Chief of the German General Staff, General Count Alfred von Schlieffen (1833–1913) in Dec 1905 which formed the basis of German military planning before World War I It involved a simultaneous attack on Russia and France, the object being to defeat France quickly and then deploy all available resources against the Russians. A modified version of the plan was implemented in 1914 and it also inspired Hitler's plans in World War II.

Schliemann /ˈʃliːmən/ Heinrich 1822–90. German archaeologist. Fascinated from an early age by the Homeric epics, he in 1871 began excavating at Hissarlik, which he established as the site of Troy, although the 'palace and treasure of Priam' which he discovered belong to an earlier settlement on the site than the one which Homer describes. His most important later excavations were at Mycenae, where he thought

he had discovered the grave of Agamemnon, though again the find was of an earlier period.

Schmidt /ʃmɪt/ Helmut 1918– . West German socialist politician, member of the Social Democratic Party (SPD), chancellor 1974–83.
Schmidt was interior minister 1961–65, defence minister 1969–72, and finance minister 1972–74. He became chancellor (prime minister) on Willy ◊Brandt's resignation in 1974.
As chancellor, Schmidt introduced social reforms and continued Brandt's policy of ◊Ostpolitik. With the French president Giscard d'Estaing, Schmidt introduced annual world and European economic summits. He was a firm supporter of ◊NATO and of the deployment of US nuclear missiles in West Germany during the early 1980s. Re-elected 1980, he was defeated in the *Bundestag* in 1982 following the switch of allegiance by the SPD's coalition allies, the Free Democratic Party.

Schnabel /ˈʃnaːbəl/ Artur 1882–1951. Austrian pianist. Born in Lipnik, he taught music at the Berlin State Academy 1925–30, but settled in the USA in 1939. He excelled in playing Beethoven.

Schnabel Austrian pianist Artur Schnabel made his debut at the age of eight. With the arrival of the Nazi regime he emigrated to the USA where he became known for his interpretation of the German classics.

Schneider Trophy an aviation trophy presented by Jacques Schneider in 1913 for competition between seaplanes of any nation. From the first holder, M Prévost in 1913, who averaged 73.62 kph/45.75 mph, the trophy changed hands several times before being won outright by Britain, after victories in 1927, 1929 and 1931, the last creating a world record of 547.30 kph/340.08 mph.

Schoenberg /ˈʃɜːnbɜːg/ Arnold (Franz Walter) 1874–1951. Austrian composer, born Vienna. After lushly romantic early works in the idiom of Wagner (such as *Gurrelieder/Songs of Gurra* 1900–11) he flirted briefly with

◊atonality, producing such works as *Pierrot Lunaire* 1912, for chamber ensemble and voice (which is spoken or declaimed rather than sung, a technique he called *Sprechstimme*, 'speech-song') before developing the system for which he is best-known, the *12-note system*, providing a rigorous framework outside conventional tonality; his pupils ◊Berg and ◊Webern developed the technique further. After World War I he wrote several neo-classical works for chamber ensembles. He taught at the Berlin State Academy 1925–33. Driven from Germany by the Nazis, he settled in the USA in 1933. Later works include the opera *Moses and Aaron* 1932–51.

Schoenberg Arnold Schoenberg teaching at the University of California. A revolutionary composer, he developed the 12-note system of composition .

Scholasticism the theological and philosophical system of Christian Europe in the Middle Ages as studied in the schools or universities. It sought to integrate Christian teaching with Platonic and Aristolelean philosophy. John Scotus (Erigena) is sometimes regarded as the founder, but the succession of 'Schoolmen', as scholastic philosophers were called, definitely opened with Roscellinus at the end of the 11th century, when in his advocacy of Nominalism he was countered by Anselm, the champion of Realism. The controversy over 'Universals' thus begun continued for several centuries. William of Champeaux, Abélard, Alexander of Hales, Albertus Magnus, and Peter Lombard played prominent parts, but the greatest names are those of Thomas Aquinas, whose writings became the classical textbooks of Catholic doctrine, and the Franciscan Duns Scotus. The last of the Schoolmen is usually reckoned to have been William of Occam, who, in the first half of the 14th century, restated Nominalism.

school see ◊education.

Schopenhauer /ˈʃəʊpən,haʊə/ Arthur 1788–1860. German philosopher, whose chief work *The World as Will and Idea* 1818 expounded an atheistic, pessimistic theory akin to Buddhism. The driving force of irrational will in human beings results in an ever-frustrated cycle of desire, from which the only escape is a contemplative existence inspired by the arts, and eventual absorption into nothingness.

Schreiner /'ʃraɪnə/ Olive 1862–1920. South African novelist and supporter of women's rights. Her best-known work is *The Story of an African Farm* 1883, describing life on the South African veld.

Schrödinger /'ʃrɜːdɪŋə/ Erwin 1887–1961. Austrian physicist who greatly advanced the study of wave mechanics (see ◊quantum theory). He shared (with ◊Dirac) a Nobel prize in 1933.

Schubert /'ʃuːbət/ Franz (Peter) 1797–1828. Austrian composer, born in Vienna. In 1816 he gave up teaching to compose, and in 1818 was appointed music teacher to the Esterházy family on their estate in W Hungary. Very shortly he was back in Vienna, where he composed prolifically and lived a Bohemian existence. He was only 31 when he died, but his musical output was prodigious. Greatest of the ten published symphonies are the incomplete eighth in B minor (the 'Unfinished') and the 'Great' in C major 1829. He wrote chamber and piano music, including sonatas and fantasias, but he is best loved for his *Lieder* (songs), of which he wrote over 600, combining the romantic expression of emotion with pure melody. They include the cycles *Die schöne Müllerin/The Beautiful Maid of the Mill* 1823 and *Die Winterreise/The Winter Journey* 1827.

Schubert Franz Schubert is best known for his songs, including 'An die Musik/To music'.

Schumacher /'ʃuːmæxə/ Ernst 1911–1977. German writer and economist, who after a distinguished career as economic advisor to the UK National Coal Board 1950–70, wrote the book *Small is Beautiful* 1973. In it, he argued for small-scale economic growth without great capital expenditure, and which is adapted to the country for which it is intended.

Schuman /'ʃuːmɒŋ/ Robert 1886–1963. French politician. He was prime minister 1947–48, and as foreign minister 1948–53 created the Coal and Steel Community (the Schuman Plan treaty of 1951 and prepared the basis of the ◊European Community.

Schumann /'ʃuːmən/ Clara (Josephine) (born Wieck) 1819–1896. German pianist. Born in Leipzig, she married Robert ◊Schumann in 1840 (her father had been his piano teacher). After Schumann's death she devoted her life to popularizing his work, appearing frequently in London 1856–88.

Schumann /'ʃuːmən/ Robert Alexander 1810–1856. German composer. Born at Zwickau, Saxony, he taught at Leipzig Conservatoire and was musical director at Düsseldorf 1850–53. He was an influential member of the Romantic movement, and many of his works, particularly his songs and short piano pieces, show an ability to portray mood and emotion, sometimes with the simplest of material. His works include four symphonies, a piano concerto Opus 54, 1841, and sonatas Opuses 11 and 22 and a song cycle *Dichterliebe/Poet's Love* 1840. He also wrote much chamber music. His music criticism was published in his *Neue Zeitschrift für Musik/New Musical Journal* 1835–44. After a suicide attempt in 1854, he was sent to an asylum near Bonn, where he died.

Schumpeter /'ʃumpeɪtə/ Joseph A(lois) 1883–1950. Vienna-born US economist and sociologist. In *Capitalism, Socialism and Democracy* 1942 he contended that Western capitalism, impelled by its very success, was evolving into a form of socialism because firms would become increasingly large and their managements increasingly divorced from ownership, while social trends were undermining the traditional motives for entrepreneurial accumulation of wealth.

Schuschnigg /'ʃuʃnɪg/ Kurt von 1897–1977. Austrian Chancellor 1934, in succession to ◊Dollfuss. In Feb 1938 he was forced to accept a Nazi Minister of the Interior, and a month later Austria was occupied and annexed by Germany. He was imprisoned in Germany until 1945, when he went to the USA.

Schütz /ʃuts/ Heinrich 1585–1672. German composer, music director to the Elector of Saxony from 1614. He was influenced by ◊Monteverdi; his works include *The Seven Last Words* c. 1645, and the *Deutsch Magnificat/German Magnificat* 1671.

Schwarzkopf /'ʃvɑːtskɒpf/ Elisabeth 1915– . German soprano, noted for dramatic interpretation of operatic roles, such as the Marschallin in *Der Rosenkavalier*, as well as songs.

Schwarzwald /'ʃvɑːtsvælt/ German name for the ◊Black Forest, coniferous forest in West Germany.

Schweitzer /'ʃvaɪtsə/ Albert 1875–1965. French theologian, organist, and missionary surgeon. He founded the hospital at Lambaréné in Gabon in 1913, giving organ recitals to support his work there. He wrote a life of Bach and *Von reimarus zu Wrede/The Quest for the Historical Jesus* 1906, and was awarded the Nobel Peace Prize in 1952 for his teaching of 'reverence for life'.

Schwerin /ʃveˈriːn/ capital of Schwerin district, East Germany; population (1982)

124,975. Formerly the capital of ◊Mecklenburg and earlier of Mecklenburg-Schwerin.

Schwitters /'ʃvɪtəz/ Kurt 1887–1948. German artist influenced by the ◊Dadaists, who from 1918 developed ◊collage, using discarded rubbish such as buttons and bus tickets to create pictures and structures.

Schwyz /ʃviːts/ capital of Schwyz canton, Switzerland; population (1978) 12,100. Schwyz was one of the three original cantons of the Swiss Confederation (see ◊Switzerland) in 1291, which gave its name to the whole country from about 1450.

Sciascia /'ʃæʃə/ Leonardo 1921– . Sicilian novelist, who uses the detective novel to explore the hidden workings of Sicilian life, for example in *Il giorno della civetta/Mafia Vendetta* 1961.

sciatica persistent pain along the sciatic nerve which runs from the hip, down the back of the thigh, and, in its branches, to the toes. Causes of sciatica include inflammation of the nerve itself, or pressure on or inflammation of a nerve leading out of the lower spine, for example as a result of a slipped (intervertebral) disc.

science from Latin *scientia*, 'knowledge', a broad term which can be applied to any systematic field of study or body of knowledge. In particular, it is used to refer to the systematic study of the material and physical world. The word scientist (rather than philosopher) was first used in 1840 by William Whewell to designate students of the knowledge of the material world. The common aim of all the disciplines called sciences is to produce reliable explanations. Modern science is usually divided into separate areas of study, such as astronomy, biology, chemistry, mathematics, and physics, although more recently attempts have been made to synthesize traditionally separate disciplines under such headings as ◊life sciences and ◊earth sciences. All these areas are sometimes referred to as the natural sciences. The application of science for practical purposes is called *technology*. *Social science* refers to the systematic study of human behaviour, and includes such areas as anthropology, economics, psychology, and sociology. One area of contemporary debate is whether these disciplines are actually sciences; that is, whether the study of human beings is capable of scientific precision or prediction in the same way as natural science is seen to be. For example, in 1982 the British Government challenged the name of the Social Science Research Council, arguing instead for the term 'social studies'.

Activities such as healing, star-watching, and engineering have been practised in many societies since ancient times. Pure science, especially physics (formerly called 'natural philosophy'), had traditionally been the main area of study for philosophers. The European scientific revolution between about 1650 and 1800 replaced speculative philosophy with a new combination of observation, experimentation, and rationality.

The modern method of scientific research includes an interaction between tradition, experiment and observation, and deduction. The *philosophy of science* investigates this interaction, in particular the extent of its ability to gain access to the truth about the material world. It has long been recognized that induction from observation cannot give explanations based on logic. In this century Popper has described scientific method as a rigorous experimental testing of a scientist's ideas or hypotheses (see ◊hypothesis). The origin and role of these ideas, and their interdependence with observation, has been examined, for example by Kuhn, who places them in a historical and sociological setting. The *sociology of science* investigates how scientific theories and laws are produced, and questions the possibility of objectivity in any scientific endeavour. One controversial aspect is the undermining of scientific realism and its replacement by scientific relativism, as described by Feyerabend.

science fiction genre of writing sometimes known as *SF* or *Sci-Fi*. The genre often takes its ideas and concerns from current ideas in science and the social sciences. SF works are often set in the future and deal with such matters as travel through space and time, robots, aliens, utopias and dystopias (often satiric), and psychic powers. The genre is sometimes held to have its roots in the works of Mary Shelley, notably *Frankenstein* 1818; early practitioners were Jules Verne and H G Wells. In the 20th century the American pulp-magazine tradition of SF produced writers such as Arthur C Clarke, Isaac Asimov, and Frank Herbert; a consensus of 'pure storytelling' and traditional values was disrupted by writers associated with the British magazine *New Worlds* – Brian Aldiss, Michael Moorcock, J G Ballard – and by younger US writers – Joanna Russ, Ursula Le Guin, Thomas Disch, Gene Wolfe – who used the form for serious literary purposes and for political and sexual radicalism.

Science Museum British museum of science and technology in South Kensington, London. Founded in 1853 as the National Museum of Science and Industry, it houses exhibits from all areas of science except the life sciences. It includes from 1980–81 the Wellcome Museum of Medical Science.

science park site on which high-technology industrial businesses are housed near a university, so that they can benefit from the research expertise of the university's scientists. Science parks originated in the USA in the 1950s. By 1985 the UK had 13, beginning with Heriot-Watt (Edinburgh).

scientific law in science, those principles which are taken to be universally applicable. Laws (for instance ◊Boyle's Law, ◊Newton's laws of motion) form the basic theoretical structure of the physical sciences, so that the rejection of a law by the scientific community is an almost inconceivable event. On occasion however a law might be modified, as was the case when Einstein showed that Newton's laws of motion do not apply to objects travelling at speeds close to that of light.

Scientology an 'applied religious philosophy', its name derived from Latin *scire* 'to know' and Greek *logos* 'branch of learning', founded in California in 1954 by L Ron ◊Hubbard as the *Church of Scientology*, its

headquarters from 1959 being at Saint Hill Manor, East Grinstead, Sussex. It claims to 'increase spiritual awareness', but its methods of recruiting and retaining converts have been criticized.

scilla bulbous plant of the family ◊Liliaceae bearing blue, pink, or white flowers, including the spring squill *Scilla verna*.

Scilly Islands /'sɪli/ group of 140 islands and islets lying 40 km/25 mi SW of Land's End, England; administered by the Duchy of Cornwall. Area 16 sq km/6.3 sq mi. The five inhabited islands are *St Mary's*, the largest, on which is Hugh Town, capital of the Scillies; *Tresco*, the second largest, with sub-tropical gardens; *St Martin's*, third largest, noted for beautiful shells; *St Agnes*, and *Bryher*.
A mild climate and rich soil enable early vegetables and flowers to be produced, and tourism is important. The islands have remains of Bronze Age settlements.

scintillation counter an instrument for measuring very low levels of ◊radiation. The radiation strikes a scintillator, whose small light output is 'amplified' by a ◊photomultipier; its output current pulses, in turn are counted or summed by a scaler.

Scipio /'skɪpiəu/ Publius Cornelius died 211 BC. Roman general. Elected consul in 218, during the 2nd Punic War, he was defeated by Hannibal at Ticinus and killed by the Carthaginians in Spain.

Scipio Africanus Major /'skɪpiəu ˌæfrɪ'kaːnəs/ 237–c. 183 BC. Roman general also known as *Publius Cornelius Scipio*. He defeated the Carthaginians 210–206 BC, invaded Africa 204 BC, and defeated Hannibal 202 BC.

Scipio Africanus Minor /'skɪpiəu ˌæfrɪ'kaːnəs/ c. 185–129 BC. Roman general, the adopted grandson of Scipio Africanus Major, also known as *Scipio Aemilianus* and *Publius Cornelius Scipio*. He destroyed Carthage 146 BC, and subdued Spain 134 BC. He was opposed to the Gracchi (see ◊Gracchus), and his wife is thought to have shared in his murder.

SCLC abbreviated name of US civil rights organization ◊Southern Christian Leadership Conference.

sclerenchyma a plant tissue whose function is to strengthen and support. It is composed of thick-walled cells that are heavily lignified (see ◊lignin). When mature the cell within dies, and only the cell walls remain. Sclerenchyma may be made up of one or two types of cells: *Sclereids* can occur singly or in small clusters, and are often found in the hard shells of fruits, in seed coats, bark, and the stem cortex. They are more compact than the *fibres*, which are elongated cells, often with pointed ends, particularly associated with the vascular tissue (◊xylem and ◊phloem) of the plant. They are frequently grouped in bundles and some provide useful materials, such as flax from *Linum usitatissimum* and hemp from *Cannabis sativa*.

sclerosis disease of the nervous system; see under ◊multiple sclerosis.

Scofield /'skəufiːld/ Paul 1922– . English actor. He is best known for his portrayal of Sir

Thomas More in both stage and film versions of *A Man for All Seasons*.

scoliosis curvature of the ◊spine. Correction by operations to insert bone grafts (thus creating only a rigid spine) has been replaced by insertion of an electronic stimulative device in the lower back to contract the muscles.

Scone /skuːn/ village in Tayside, Scotland, N of Perth. Most of the Scottish kings were crowned in its former ancient palace on the Stone of Destiny (now in the Coronation Chair at Westminster).

scopolamine another name for ◊hyoscine, a sedative drug.

scorpion member of the order Scorpiones, class ◊Arachnida. Common in the tropics and sub-tropics, the scorpion has a segmented body with a long tail ending in a poisonous sting, though the venom is not usually fatal to a healthy adult. Some species reach 15 cm/6 in. They mate after a courtship dance, produce live young rather than eggs, and hunt chiefly by night.

scorpion fly insect of the order Mecoptera, an ancient group with relatively few living representatives. They have a characteristic downturned beak with jaws at the tip, and many males have a turned-up tail, giving them their common name. Most feed on insects or carrion.

Scorpius constellation of the ◊zodiac, representing a scorpion. The Sun passes briefly through Scorpius in the last week of Nov. The heart of the scorpion is marked by the red supergiant star ◊Antares. Scorpius contains rich ◊Milky Way star fields, plus the strongest ◊X-ray source in the sky, Scorpius X-1.

Scorsese /skɔː'seɪzi/ Martin 1942– . American director whose films concentrate on urban life. His work includes *Mean Streets* 1973, *Taxi Driver* 1976, *Raging Bull* 1979, *The Color of Money* 1986, and *After Hours* 1987.

SCOTLAND: REGIONS

Regions:	administrative headquarters	area in sq km
Borders	Newtown St Boswells	4,662
Central	Stirling	2,590
Dumfries and Galloway	Dumfries	6,475
Fife	Glenrothes	1,308
Grampian	Aberdeen	8,550
Highland	Inverness	26,136
Lothian	Edinburgh	1,756
Strathclyde	Glasgow	13,856
Tayside	Dundee	7,668
Island Authorities:		
Orkney	Kirkwall	974
Shetland	Berwick	1,427
Western Islands	Stornoway	2,901
		78,303

Scotland /'skɒtlənd/ country in N Europe, part of the British Isles
area 78,762 sq km/30,422 sq mi
capital Edinburgh
towns Glasgow, Dundee, Aberdeen

features the Highlands in the N (see ◊Grampian Mountains); central Lowlands, including valleys of the Clyde and Forth, with most of the country's population and industries; Southern Uplands (including the ◊Lammermuir Hills); and islands of the Orkneys, Shetlands, and Western Isles
exports electronics, aero and marine engines, oil and natural gas, chemicals, textiles and clothing, printing and paper; tourism
currency pound sterling
population (1981) 5,130,735
language English, but Scots, a northern (lowland, hence known as ◊Lallans) dialect of Anglo-Saxon existing from the 7th century is enjoying a revival (after near extinction in the 18th century), as is ◊Erse, the Scottish form of Gaelic spoken by 1.3 per cent, mainly in the Highlands
religion Presbyterian (the Church of ◊Scotland), Roman Catholic
famous people Robert the Bruce, Scott, Burns, Robert Louis Stevenson, Adam Smith
government Scotland sends members to the UK parliament at Westminster in proportion to its population. Local government is on similar lines to that of England (see under ◊Provost), but there is a differing legal system (see ◊Scots Law).

Scotland Yard, New headquarters of the Criminal Investigation Department (CID) of the London Metropolitan Police, established in 1878. Originally in Scotland Yard off Whitehall, it moved to the Embankment in 1890, and in 1967 to Broadway, Westminster. It houses the *Central Office* dealing with international crime and serious offences throughout the country, and controlling the Flying Squad, a rapid-deployment force for investigating serious robberies, etc; the *Fingerprint Department* which holds some two million prints of convicted criminals; the *Criminal Record Office* which also publishes the *Police Gazette*, and the *Special Branch* dealing with crimes against the state. There is also a national co-ordinator for the *Regional Crime Squads* established in London in 1954 and extended across the country in 1965. These have detectives drawn from local forces to deal with major crime.

Scots language the form of the English language as traditionally spoken and written in Scotland, regarded by some scholars as a distinct language. It is also known as *Inglis* (now archaic, and a variant of 'English'), ◊*Lallans* ('Lowlands'), *Lowland Scots* (in contrast with the Gaelic of the Highlands and Islands), and '*the Doric*' (as a rustic language in contrast with the 'Attic' or 'Athenian' language of Edinburgh's literati, especially in the 18th century). It is also often referred to as 'Broad Scots' in contrast to the anglicized language of the middle classes. Scots derives from the Northumbrian dialect of

SCOTLAND: KINGS AND QUEENS

(From the unification of Scotland to the union of the crowns of Scotland and England.)

Celtic Kings

Malcolm II	1005
Duncan I	1034
Macbeth	1040
Malcolm III Canmore	1057
Donald Ban	1093
Duncan II	1094
Donald Ban (restored)	1095
Edgar	1097
Alexander I	1107
David I	1124
Malcolm IV	1153
William the Lion	1165
Alexander II	1214
Alexander III	1249
Margaret of Norway	1286–90

English Domination

John Balliol	1292–96
Annexed to England	1296–1306

House of Bruce

Robert I Bruce	1306
David II	1329

House of Stuart

Robert II	1371
Robert III	1390
James I	1406
James II	1437
James III	1460
James IV	1488
James V	1513
Mary	1542
James VI	1567
Union of Crowns	1603

SCOTLAND: HISTORY

1st cent.	Romans prevented by Picts from penetrating far into Scotland.
5th–6th cent.	Christianity introduced from Ireland.
9th cent.	Kenneth MacAlpin united kingdoms of Scotland.
946	Malcolm I conquered Strathclyde.
1015	Malcolm II conquered Lothian.
1263	Defeat of Haakon, king of Norway at Battle of Largs.
1266	Scotland gained Hebrides from Norway at Treaty of Perth.
1292	Scottish throne granted by Edward I (attempting to annex Scotland) by John Baliol.
1297	Defeat of England at Stirling Bridge by Wallace.
1314	Robert Bruce defeated English at Bannocknurn.
1328	Scottish independence recognized by England.
1371	First Stuart king, Robert II.
1513	James IV killed at Battle of Flodden.
1540s–50s	Knox introduced Calvinism to Scotland.
1565	Mary Queen of Scots married Darnley.
1567	Darnley murdered.
1568	Mary fled to England.
1578	James VI took over government.
1587	Mary beheaded.
1592	Presbyterianism established.
1603	James VI became James I of England.
1638	Scottish rebellion against England.
1643	Solemn League and Covenant.
1651–60	Cromwell conquered Scotland.
1679	Covenanters defeated at Bothwell Brig.
1689	Jacobites defeated at Killiecrankie.
1692	Massacre of Glencoe.
1707	Act of Union with England.
1715, 1745	Failed Jacobite risings against England.
1945	First Scottish nationalist member of parliament elected.
1979	Referendum on Scottish directly elected asssembly fails.

Anglo-Saxon or Old English, and has been spoken in SE Scotland since the 7th century. During the Middle Ages it spread from the Central Lowlands NE to Aberdeenshire and the far north, where it blended with the Norn dialects of Orkney and Shetland (once distinct varieties of Norse). Scots has been a literary language since the 14th century, with a wide range of poetry, ballads and prose records, including two national epic poems, Barbour's *Bruce* and Blind Harry's *Wallace*. With the transfer of the court to England upon the Union of the Crowns in 1603 and the dissemination of the King James Bible, Scots ceased to be a national and court language in the 17th century, but has retained its vitality among the general population and in various literary and linguistic revivals. Words originating in Scots that are now widely used in English include *bonnie* (= good-looking), *glamour*, *raid* and *wee* (= small). In Scotland a wide range of traditional Scots usage intermixes with standard English.

Scots law the legal system of Scotland. Owing to modifications from the 16th century, Scotland has a system differing from the rest of the UK by incorporating elements derived from Roman law (see under ◊law). In recent years there has been some adoption in England of features already existing in Scots law, for example majority jury verdicts, and the replacement of police prosecution by a system of public prosecution (see under ◊procurator-fiscal). There is no separate system of ◊equity. The supreme civil court is the House of Lords, below which comes the Court of Session, and then the Sheriff Court (in some respects similar to the English county court, but with criminal as well as civil jurisdiction). The supreme criminal court is the High Court of Justiciary (with no appeal to the Lords). Juries have 15 members, and a verdict of 'not proven' can be given. There is no coroner, enquiries into deaths being undertaken by the ◊procurator fiscal.

Scott /skɒt/ (George) Gilbert 1811–1878. British architect, largely responsible for the mid-19th-century Gothic revival in England; his restoration work had debatable results, but his Albert Memorial, Foreign Office, and St Pancras Station, London, won praise.

Scott /skɒt/ Giles Gilbert 1880–1960. British architect, grandson of Sir George Gilbert ◊Scott. He designed Liverpool Anglican Cathedral, Cambridge University Library, and Waterloo Bridge 1945, and supervised the rebuilding of the House of Commons after World War II.

Scott /skɒt/ Paul (Mark) 1920–1978. British novelist, noted for *The Raj Quartet* comprising *The Jewel in the Crown* 1966, *The Day of the Scorpion* 1968, *The Towers of Silence* 1972 and *A Division of the Spoils* 1975, dealing with the British Raj in India.

Scott /skɒt/ Peter (Markham) 1909– . British naturalist, artist and explorer, son of Robert Falcon ◊Scott. He has published many books on birds.

Scott /skɒt/ Robert Falcon 1868–1912. British Antarctic explorer, commonly known as Captain Scott. Born at Devonport, he entered the navy in 1882. He commanded two Antarctic expeditions, in the *Discovery*, 1901–04, and in the *Terra Nova*, 1910–12. On 18 Jan 1912 he reached the South Pole, shortly after ◊Amundsen, but on the return journey he and his companions, Wilson, Oates, Bowers, and Evans, died. His journal was recovered and published in 1913.

Scott /skɒt/ Walter 1771–1832. Scottish novelist and poet, born in Edinburgh. His *Minstrelsy of the Scottish Border* appeared in 1802, and henceforth he combined the practice of literature with his legal profession. *The Lay of the Last Minstrel* 1805 was an immediate success, and so too were *Marmion* 1808, *The Lady of the Lake* 1810, and *Lord of the Isles* 1815. Out of the proceeds he purchased and rebuilt the house of Abbotsford on the Tweed, but Byron had to some extent now captured the lead with a newer style of verse romance, and Scott turned to prose fiction. *Waverley* was issued in 1814, and gave its name to a long series of historical novels, including *Guy Mannering* 1815, *The Antiquary* 1816, *Old Mortality* 1816, *Rob Roy* 1817, *The Heart of Midlothian* 1818 and *The Bride of Lammermoor* 1819. *Ivanhoe* 1819 transferred the scene to England; *Kenilworth* 1821, *The Talisman* 1825, and *The*

Scott Robert Falcon Scott seen writing his journal during his second, fateful expedition to the Antarctic 1910–12. Scott and his companions reached the South Pole but perished on the return journey. The diary was found and published posthumously.

Fair Maid of Perth 1828 followed. In 1820 Scott was created a baronet, but in 1826 he was involved in financial ruin through the bankruptcy of Constable, his chief publisher, with whom fell Ballantyne & Co, the firm of printers and publishers in which Scott had been for many years a sleeping partner. Refusing to accept bankruptcy, he set himself to pay off the combined debts of over £120,000 by writing. Continuous overwork ended in a nervous breakdown. He died at Abbotsford on 21 Sept 1832.

Scottish Gaelic language see ◊Gaelic language.

Scottish Gaelic literature the earliest examples of Scottish Gaelic prose belong to the period 1000–1150, but the most important early original composition is the history of the MacDonalds in the Red and Black Books at Clanranald. The first printed book in Scottish Gaelic was a translation of Knox's Prayer Book in 1567. Prose Gaelic is at its best in the folk-tales, proverbs, and essays by writers such as Norman MacLeod in the 19th century and Donald Lamont in the 20th. Scottish Gaelic poetry falls into two main categories. The older syllabic verse was composed by professional bards. The chief sources of our knowledge of this are the Book of the Dean of Lismore (16th century), which is also the main early source for the Ossianic ballads; the panegyrics in the Books of Clanranald; and the Fernaig manuscript. Modern Scottish Gaelic stressed poetry began in the 17th century but reached its zenith during the Jacobite period with Alexander MacDonald, Duncan Macintyre, Rob Donn, and Dugald Buchanan. Only William Livingstone (1808–70) kept alive the old nationalistic spirit in the 19th century. During

Scott Despite the success of his *Waverley novels*, Sir Walter Scott's last years were marred by frantic literary efforts to pay off his creditors after the bankruptcy of his publishing company in 1826.

and after World War II a new school emerged, including Somhairle MacGilleathain, George Campbell-Hay, and Ruaraidh MacThómais.

scout member of a non-military and non-political youth organization originating (as the Boy Scouts) with an experimental camp held in 1907 for 24 boys from throughout society by ◊Baden-Powell on Brownsea Island, Poole Harbour, Dorset, England. Baden-Powell's book *Scouting for Boys* 1908 led to the incorporation of the Boy Scout Association by royal charter in 1912, and the movement has spread throughout the Commonwealth and other countries. There are three branches, Cub Scouts (aged 8–11), Scouts (11–16), and Venture Scouts (16–29). The corresponding organization for girls is the Girl ◊Guides, incorporated by royal charter in 1922. The scheme was introduced to the USA by William D Boyce in 1910: a similar organization for girls, the Girl Scouts of the USA, was founded in 1912. Worldwide membership is now 16,000,000.

Scrabble board game for two to four players, based on the crossword puzzle, in which 'letter' counters of varying point values are used to form words. International competitions are now held.

scrambling circuit in radio-telephony, a transmitting circuit which renders signals unintelligible unless received by the corresponding unscrambling circuit.

Scranton /'skræntən/ industrial city on the Lackawanna river, Pennsylvania, USA; population (1980) 88,117. Anthracite is mined nearby.

scraper an earth-moving machine used in road construction. Self-propelled or hauled by ◊bulldozer, a scraper consists of an open bowl, with a cutting blade at the lower front edge. When moving, the blade bites into the soil, which is forced into the bowl.

scrapie fatal disease of sheep and goats, which attacks the central nervous system, causing deterioration of the brain cells. It is caused by a submicroscopic organism known as a ◊prion.

screamer South American bird of the family Anhimidae, of which there are just three species. The *horned screamer Anhima cornuta* is about 80 cm/2.6 ft long, a large-bodied bird with a short curved beak, and spurs on the front of the wings. It wades in wet forests and marshes, but the feet are scarcely webbed. Screamers are related to ducks and are placed in the same order of birds, the Anseriformes.

screening testing large numbers of apparently healthy people to detect early symptoms of disease.

screw thread cylindrical or tapering piece of metal (or formerly wood) with a helical groove cut into it. Each turn of a screw moves it forward or backwards by a distance equal to the pitch (the spacing between neighbouring threads). It can be thought of as an inclined plane (wedge) wrapped round a cylinder or cone. Its mechanical advantage equals $2 r/\rho$, where ρ is the pitch and r is the radius of the thread. Thus the mechanical advantage of a tapering wood screw, for example, increases as it is rotated into the wood.

Scriabin /skri'æbɪn/ alternative spelling of the name of the Russian composer ◊Skryabin.

Scribe member of an ancient Jewish group, both priests and laymen, who studied the law of Moses, and sat in the ◊Sanhedrin (supreme court). In the New Testament they are associated with the ◊Pharisees.

Scribe /skri:b/ Augustin Eugène 1791–1861. French dramatist. Born in Paris, he achieved fame with *Une Nuit de la garde nationale/Night of the National Guard* 1815, and with numerous assistants produced many plays of technical merit but little profundity, including *Le Verre d'eau/A Glass of Water* 1842, *Adrienne Lecouvreur* 1849, and *Bertrand et Raton/The School for Politicians* 1833.

scrofula ◊tuberculosis of the lymph glands.

scrub bird Australian bird, genus *Atrichornis*, of which there are two species. About 18 cm/7 in long, rather wren-like but longtailed, scrub birds are good mimics. *The noisy scrub bird Atrichornis clamosus* was feared to be extinct, but was rediscovered, although numbers are still low.

Scullin /'skʌlɪn/ James Henry 1876–1953. Australian Labour politician. He was leader of the Federal Parliamentary Labour Party 1928–35, and prime minister and minister of industry in the Depression years 1929–31.

sculpture the artistic shaping in relief or in the round of materials such as wood, stone, metal and, more recently, plastic and other synthetics. All ancient civilizations, including the Assyrian, Egyptian, Indian, Chinese, Maya, have left examples of sculpture, for the most part by unknown artists, and even in the case of the more recent masterpieces of European Gothic the craftsmen are unnamed. Traditional European sculpture descends through that of Greece, Rome, and Renaissance Italy, but particularly influential in the development of modern sculpture has been the indigenous tradition of sculpture in Africa (see ◊African art), South

America, and the Caribbean. In the 20th century Alexander ◊Calder invented the *mobile*, in which the suspended components move spontaneously with the currents of air. An extension is the *structure vivante*, in which a mechanism produces a pre-arranged pattern produced by magnets, lenses, bubbles, and so on, accompanied by sound.
World-famous sculptors include:
Ancient Greek Phidias, Praxiteles
Renaissance Donatello, Verrochio, della Robbia, Michelangelo
Baroque Grinling Gibbons, Bernini, Falconet, Houdon
Neo-Classical Canova, Flaxman
20th-century American Lipchitz, Calder
20th-century British Epstein, Henry Moore, Hepworth, Reg Butler, Caro
20th-century European Arp, Gaudier-Brzeska, Rodin, Maillol, Picasso, Mestrovic, Brancusi, Marini, Giacometti, Gabo, and Neizvestny.

Scunthorpe /'skʌnθɔːp/ industrial town in Humberside, England, 39 km/24 mi W of Grimsby; population (1981) 66,047. It has one of Europe's largest iron and steel works.

scurvy a disease caused by lack of vitamin C which is contained in fresh vegetables, fruit, and milk. The symptoms are bleeding into the skin, swelling of the gums, and drying up of the skin and hair. Treatment is by giving the vitamin.

scurvy-grass plant *Cochlearia officinalis* of the cabbage family, not a grass. Shoots may grow low, or more erect up to 50 cm/2.6 ft, and it has rather fleshy heart-shaped leaves. Flowers are white and four-petalled. It grows on salt marshes and banks by the sea. It is edible, with sharp tasting leaves which are a good source of vitamin C. It was formerly taken by sailors as a cure for scurvy.

Scylla and Charybdis /'sɪlə, kə'rɪbdɪs/ in classical mythology, a sea-monster and a whirlpool, between which Odysseus had to sail. Later writers located them in the Straits of Messina, between Sicily and Italy.

Scythia /'sɪðɪə/ region north of the Black Sea varying in extent from time to time, and situated between the Carpathians and the river Don, inhabited by the Scythians from the 7th–1st centuries BC. *Darius I* made an unsuccessful attempt to conquer the Scythians in the 6th century BC; from the middle of the 4th century BC they were slowly superseded by the Sarmatians.

SDI strategic *d*efence *i*nitiative, popularly known as ◊Star Wars.

sea anemone invertebrate sea-dwelling animal of the class Cnidaria with a tube-like body attached by the base to a rock or shell. The other end has an open 'mouth' surrounded by stinging tentacles, which capture crustaceans and other small organisms. Sea anemones occur in many beautiful colours, especially in tropical waters.

Seaborg /'si:bɔːg/ Glenn Theodore 1912– . American nuclear chemist. He was awarded a Nobel prize in 1951 for his discoveries of transuranic elements, and for production of the radio-isotope uranium 233.

sea-cucumber echinoderm of the class Holothuroidea with a cylindrical body which is tough-skinned, knobbed, or spiny. The body may

be several feet in length, and dried sea cucumbers from N Australia and the Pacific seaboard of the USA are esteemed as a delicacy (*trepang*) by the Chinese. Sea cucumbers are sometimes called 'cotton-spinners' from the sticky filaments they eject from the anus in self-defence.

seafloor spreading the growth of the ocean ◊crust outwards (sideways) from ◊ocean ridges. It was first detected by the British geophysicists F Vine and D Matthews in 1963, when they noted that the floor of the Atlantic Ocean was made of rocks that were arranged in strips, each strip being magnetized either normally or reversely (due to changes in the earth's polarity when the North Pole becomes the South Pole and vice versa, termed magnetic reversal). These strips were parallel to one another and to the ocean ridge. The inference was that each strip was formed at some stage in geological time when the magnetic field was polarized in a certain way (see ◊poles). Confirmation came when sediments were discovered to be deeper further away from the oceanic ridge, because they had been in existence longer and had more time to accumulate sediment. Nowadays the concept of seafloor spreading has been combined with that of continental drift and incorporated into ◊plate tectonics.

seagull see ◊gull.

sea-horse fish of one of several genera, of which *Hippocampus* is typical. They range from the Atlantic through the Mediterranean to Australia. The body is small and compressed and covered with bony plates raised into tubercles or spines. The tail is prehensile, and the tubular mouth sucks in small animals as food.

seakale perennial plant *Crambe maritima* of the family Cruciferae cultivated in Europe as a vegetable. The young shoots are forced and blanched.

seal marine mammal of the family Phocidae, found mainly in the cold seas of the world. Streamlined in body shape, they have thick blubber for insulation, no external earflaps and small front flippers. The hind flippers point backwards and are swung from side to side to provide the thrust for swimming, but they cannot be brought under the body for walking on land. They feed on fish, squid, or crustaceans. True seals include the *grey seal Halichoerus grypus*, whose main population is around British coasts, and grows to 2.7 m/9 ft, and also the shorter-nosed *common seal Phoca vitulina* found in coastal regions over much of the N hemisphere. The largest seal is the *Southern elephant seal Mirounga leonina* which can be 6 m/20 ft long and weighs 4 tonnes; the smallest is the *Baikal seal Pusa sibirica* only 1.2 m/4 ft long, and the only seal to live entirely in fresh water. See also ◊sealion.

sea law laws dealing with fishing areas, ships, and navigation. See under ◊maritime law.

sea-lily deep-water echinoderm of the class Crinoidea. The rayed, cup-like body is borne on a stalk, and has feathery arms in multiples of five.

sealion marine mammal of the family Otariidae which also includes the fur seals. Streamlined, the animal has large fore flippers which it uses to row itself through the water. The hind flippers can be turned beneath the body to walk on land. A small earflap is present. There are two species of sealion in the N hemisphere, three in the S They feed on fish, squid, and crustaceans. *Steller's sealion Eumetopias jubatus* lives in the N Pacific, large numbers breeding on the Aleutian Islands. Males may be up to 3.4 m/11 ft long, with a thick neck with the characteristic mane, and weigh up to one tonne. Females are one-third the weight. The *Californian sealion Zalophus californianus* only reaches 2.3 m/7 ft and is the species most often seen in zoos and as a 'performing seal'.

Sealyham breed of terrier dog, named after the place in Pembrokeshire where it originated as a cross of the Welsh and Jack Russell terriers.

sea-mouse marine bristle worm *Aphrodite aculeata*, up to 20 cm/8 in long, with an oval body, flattened beneath and covered above with a mat of grey bristles, with iridescent bristles showing at the edges. It is usually found on soft sea beds.

Sea Peoples unidentified seafaring warriors who may have been ◊Achaeans, ◊Etruscans, or ◊Philistines, who ravaged and settled the Mediterranean coasts in the 12th–13th centuries BC. They were defeated in 1191 by Rameses III of Egypt.

seaplane an aeroplane capable of taking off from, and alighting on, water. There are two major types, float-planes and flying-boats. The float-plane is similar to an ordinary aeroplane but has floats in place of wheels; the flying-boat has a broad hull shaped like a boat, and may also have floats attached to the wing tips. Although seaplanes need no airfield, they depend on smooth water for a good landing and since World War II few have been built.

sea-potato yellow-brown sea-urchin *Echinocardium cordatum* covered in short spines, and found burrowing in sand from the lower shore downwards.

Searle /sɜːl/ Ronald 1920– . British artist. A skilled draughtsman and cartoonist, he is well known for his sketches of places and people, *Paris Sketch Book* 1950, *Rake's Progress* 1955; for the creation of the schoolgirls of St Trinian's in 1941; and for his cartoons of cats.

Sears Tower skyscraper in Chicago, USA, rising 110 storeys to a height of 443 m/1,454 ft. 'Topped out' in 1973, it was then the world's tallest building. It is the headquarters of Sears, Roebuck & Co, and provides office accommodation for more than 16,000 people.

sea-slug marine gastropod mollusc in which the shell is reduced or absent. Nudibranch sea-slugs include some very colourful forms, especially in the tropics. Tentacles on the back help take in oxygen. They are largely carnivorous, feeding on hydroids and sponges. British species include the shore-living **common grey sea-slug** *Aeolidia papillosa* up to 8 cm/3 in and the yellow **sea-lemon** *Archidoris pseudoargus*.

season a particular climatic type, at any place, associated with a particular time of the year. The change in seasons is mainly due to the change in attitude of the Earth's axis in relation to the Sun, and hence the position of the Sun in the sky at a particular place.

In temperate latitudes four seasons are recognized: spring, summer, autumn (fall), and winter. The northern temperate latitudes have summer when the southern temperate latitudes have winter, and vice versa. During winter the Sun is low in the sky and has less heating effect because of the oblique angle of incidence and because the sunlight has further to travel through the atmosphere. The differences between the seasons are more marked inland than near the coast, where the sea has a moderating effect on temperatures.

In polar regions the change between summer and winter is abrupt; spring and autumn are hardly recognizable.

Tropical regions have two seasons – the wet and the dry. The belt of rain associated with the convergence of the ◊trade winds moves N and S with the Sun, as do the dry conditions associated with the belts of high pressure near the tropics. Monsoon areas around the Indian Ocean have three seasons – the cold, the hot, and the rainy – because of the influence of the oceanic water body surrounded at its N end by Asia.

brittle stars, but united to form a globular, heart-shaped, or shield-shaped and flattened body, enclosed with plates of lime and covered with spines. Sometimes the spines are holding-organs, and they also assist in locomotion. Sea-urchins feed on seaweed and the animals frequenting them, and some are edible.

seaweed general name for a vast collection of lower plant-forms belonging to the ◊Algae. They grow from about high-water mark to depths of 100–200 m/300–600 ft, and are green, blue-green, red, or brown. Many have traditionally been gathered for food, such as purple laver (*Porphyra umbilicalis*), green laver (*Ulva lactuca*), and carragheen moss (*Chondrus crispus*). From the 1960s–70s, however, seaweeds have been farmed, and the alginates extracted are used in convenience foods, ice-cream, and animal feed, as well as in toothpaste, soap, and the manufacture of iodine and glass.

Seawise Giant the biggest ship ever built (1979), a huge oil tanker of 564,739 tonnes deadweight with a length of 458.5 m/1,504 ft, a beam (width) of 68.9 m/226 ft, and a draught of 24.6 m/80 ft.

seasons
how the Earth's tilt and its orbit around the Sun cause the seasons

vernal equinox

summer solstice

sun

N

winter solstice

autumnal equinox

Season, London the period May–Jul when it was considered fashionable to take up residence in London. Young women made their social debut (hence debutantes) by being presented to their sovereign at court in a special white dress and headress – a custom abandoned in 1959.

sea-squirt ◊chordate of the class Ascidiacea. The adult is a pouch-shaped animal attached to a rock or other base, and drawing in food-carrying water through one siphon, and expelling it through another after straining through the gills. The young are free-swimming tadpole-shaped organisms.

SEATO acronym for ◊South-East Asia Treaty Organization.

Seattle /siˈætl/ port of the state of Washington, USA, situated between Puget Sound and Lake Washington; population (1980) 493,846. It is a centre for the manufacture of jet aircraft (Boeing), and also has shipbuilding, timber, and paper industries. There are two universities, Washington (1861) and Seattle (1891). First settled in 1851, as the nearest port for Alaska, Seattle grew in the late 19th century under the impetus of the Gold Rush.

sea-urchin name for a type of Echinoderm in which the rays are not free as in star fishes and

Sebastiano del Piombo /sɪˌbæstiˈɑːnəʊ del piˈɒmbəʊ/ 1485–1547. Italian painter. One of the Venetian painters of the High Renaissance, he was a pupil of ◊Giorgione before moving to Rome 1511, where his friendship with Michelangelo (and rivalry with ◊Raphael) inspired him to his greatest works, such as the *Flagellation* (San Pietro in Montorio, Rome).

Sebastian, St /sɪˈbæstiən/ died c. 288. Roman soldier, traditionally a member of the Emperor ◊Diocletian's bodyguard until his Christian faith was discovered. He was martyred by being shot with arrows; feast day 20 Jan.

Sebastopol /sɪˈbæstəpɒl/ alternative spelling of ◊Sevastopol, port in the USSR.

secant in trigonometry, of an angle in a ◊right-angled triangle, the length of the hypotenuse (the longest side) divided by the length of the side adjacent to the angle. It is the ◊reciprocal of the cosine (sec = 1/cos).

secession (Latin *secessio*) in politics, the withdrawal from a federation of states by one or more of its members, as in the secession of the Confederate states from the Northern states in 1860.

second basic ◊SI unit of time, one-sixtieth of a minute: defined as the duration of 9,192,631,770

Sebastiano del Piombo *The Flagellation of Christ* by Sebastiano del Piombo, San Pietro in Montorio, Rome, based on a drawing by Michelangelo

periods of the radiation corresponding to the transition between two hyperfine levels of the ground state of the ◊caesium 133 isotope.

secondary education in the UK, education from the age of 11 (12 in Scotland) until school-leaving at 16 or later.

secondary emission in physics, an emission of electrons that takes place at the surface of certain substances when they are struck by electrons or other particles from an external source. See also ◊photomultiplier.

secondary growth or *secondary thickening* the increase in diameter of the roots and stems of certain plants (notably shrubs and trees) that results from the production of new cells by the ◊cambium. It provides the plant with additional mechanical support and new conducting cells, the secondary ◊xylem and ◊phloem. Secondary growth is generally confined to ◊gymnosperms and, among the ◊angiosperms, to the dicotyledons. With just a few exceptions, the monocotyledons (grasses, lilies) exhibit only primary growth, resulting from cell division at the apical ◊meristems.

secondary modern school the secondary school which normally takes children who have failed to gain a ◊grammar school place, in those few areas of the UK which retain academic selection at 11 or 12.

secondary sexual character in biology, an external feature of an organism which is characteristic of its gender (male or female), but not the genitalia themselves. They include facial hair in men and breasts in women, combs in cockerels, brightly coloured plumage in many male birds, and manes in male lions. In many cases, they are involved in displays and contests for mates and have evolved by ◊sexual selection. Their development is stimulated by sex ◊hormones.

secretary bird long-legged, mainly grey-plumaged bird of prey *Sagittarius serpentarius*, about 1.2 m/4 ft tall. The only member of its family Sagittaridae, order Falconiformes, it has an erectile head crest looking like a pen behind a clerk's ear.

Secretary of State originally the title given under Elizabeth I of England to each of two officials conducting the royal correspondence. It is now a title held in the UK by a number of the more important ministers, for example, the Secretary of State for Foreign and Commonwealth Affairs. In the USA the Secretary of State deals with foreign affairs.

secretin a ◊hormone produced by the small intestine of vertebrates which stimulates the production of digestive secretions by the ◊pancreas and ◊liver.

secretion in biology, any substance (normally a fluid) produced by a cell or specialized ◊gland, for example, sweat, saliva, enzymes, and hormones. The process whereby the substance is discharged from the cell is also known as secretion.

Secret Service government ◊intelligence organization.

secret society society with membership by invitation only, often involving initiation rites, secret rituals, and dire punishments for those who break the 'code'. Originally often founded for religious reasons or mutual benefit, they can become the province of corrupt politicians or gangsters. They include the ◊Mafia, ◊Ku Klux Klan, ◊Opus Dei, ◊Freemasonry, and the ◊Triad.

sect a small ideological group, usually religious in nature, aspiring to personal perfection and claiming a monopoly of access to truth or salvation. Sects are usually highly exclusive. They demand strict conformity, total commitment to their code of behaviour, and complete personal involvement, sometimes to the point of rejecting mainstream society altogether in terms of attachments, names, possessions and family. Most sects are short-lived, either because their appeal dies out and their members return to mainstream society, or because their appeal spreads and they become part of mainstream society (for example, Christianity).

secularization the process through which religious thinking, practice, and institutions lose their social significance. The concept is based on the theory, held by some sociologists, that as societies become industrialized their religious morals, values, and institutions give way to secular ones.

Secunderabad /sə'kʌndərəbæd/ northern suburb of Hyderabad city, Andhra Pradesh, India; population (1981) 144,287. Formerly a separate town, it was founded as a British army cantonment, with a parade ground where 7,000 troops could be exercised. It was by experiments at Secunderabad that Sir Ronald ◊Ross established that malaria is carried by the anopheles mosquito.

Securities and Exchange Commission (SEC) official US agency created in 1934 to ensure full disclosure to the investing public and protection against malpractice in the securities (◊stocks and shares) and financial markets (such as ◊insider trading).

Securities and Investment Board UK body with the overall responsibility for policing financial dealings in the City of London. Introduced in 1987 following the deregulation process of the so-called ◊big bang, it acts as an umbrella organization to such self-regulating bodies as the ◊Stock Exchange.

Sedan /sɪ'dæn/ town on the river Meuse, in Ardennes *département*, NE France; population (1982) 24,535. In 1870 Sedan was the scene of Napoleon III's surrender to Germany during the ◊Franco-Prussian War. Industries include textiles and dyestuffs; the town's prosperity dates from the 16th–17th centuries, when it was a ◊Huguenot centre. It was the focal point of the German advance into France in 1940.

sedan chair an enclosed chair for one passenger carried on poles by two bearers, said to have been invented at Sedan, France. Introduced to England by James I, by the 18th century it was the equivalent of a one-person taxi.

sedative drug (minor tranquillizer) with a calming effect. Employed to treat anxiety and, in larger doses, as sleeping drugs. Sedatives can cause dependence and should not be taken for long periods.

Seddon /'sedn/ Richard John 1845–1906. New Zealand Liberal politician, prime minister 1893–1906.

sedge genus *Carex* of perennial grass-like plants, family Cyperaceae, with three-cornered solid stems, common in wet ground and marshes.

Sedgemoor, Battle of /'sedʒmʊə/ battle which took place on 6 Jul 1685, on a tract of marshy land 5 km/3 mi SE of Bridgwater, Somerset, England, in which ◊Monmouth's rebellion was crushed by James II of England.

sediment any loose material that has 'settled' – deposited from suspension in water or by wind, generally as the water or wind speed decreases. Typical sediments are, in order of increasing coarseness, clay, mud, silt, sand, gravel, pebbles, cobbles, and boulders. Organic materials, such as peat and coral debris, are also sediments. Sediments differ from ◊sedimentary rocks in which the grains are fused together in a solid mass of rock.

sedimentary rock a rock formed by the accumulation and cementation of particles.

sedition in the UK, the offence of inciting unlawful opposition to the Crown and Government. It includes attempting to bring into contempt or hatred the person of the reigning monarch, the lawfully established Government, or either house of Parliament; inciting a change of government by other than lawful means; and raising discontent between different sections of the sovereign's subjects. Unlike ◊treason, sedition does not carry the death penalty.

Seebeck effect in physics, the generation of a voltage in a circuit containing two different metals, or semiconductors, by keeping the junctions between them at different temperatures. Also called the thermoelectric effect. Discovered by the German physicist Thomas Seebeck (1770–1831), it is the opposite of the ◊Peltier effect (in which current flow causes a temperature difference between junctions of different metals). It is also the basis of the ◊thermocouple.

seed the reproductive structure of higher plants (◊angiosperms and ◊gymnosperms). It develops from a fertilized ovule and consists of an embryo and a food store, surrounded and protected by an outer seed coat, called the testa. The food store is contained either in a specialized nutritive tissue, the ▷endosperm, or in the ▷cotyledons of the embryo itself. In angiosperms the seed is enclosed within a ▷fruit, whereas in gymnosperms it is usually naked and unprotected, once shed from the female cone. Following ▷germination the seed develops into a new plant but there may be a delay in germination to ensure growth occurs under favourable conditions (see ▷after-ripening, ▷dormancy).

Seeds may be dispersed from the parent plant in a number of different ways. Agents of dispersal include animals, as with ▷burrs and fleshy edible fruits, or wind, where the seed or fruit may be winged or plumed. Water can disperse seeds or fruits that float, and various mechanical devices may eject seeds from the fruit, as in some pods or ▷legumes.

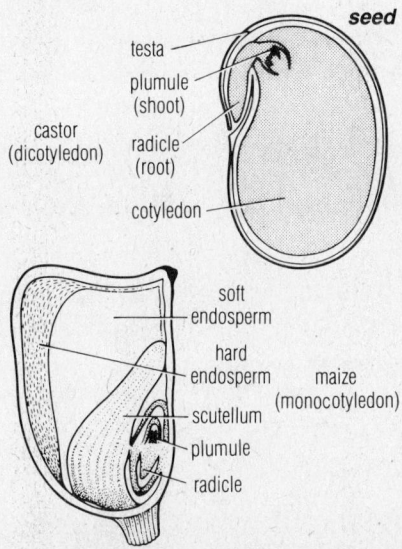

seed

testa
plumule (shoot)
castor (dicotyledon)
radicle (root)
cotyledon

soft endosperm
hard endosperm   maize (monocotyledon)
scutellum
plumule
radicle

seed drill a machine for sowing cereals and other seeds, developed by Jethro ▷Tull in England in 1701. The seed is stored in a hopper and delivered by tubes into furrows made in the ground by a set of blades called coulters attached in front. A ▷harrow is drawn behind the drill to cover up the seeds.

seed plant any ▷seed-bearing plant; also known as a spermatophyte. The seed plants are subdivided into two classes, the ▷angiosperms, or flowering plants, and the ▷gymnosperms, principally the ▷cycads and ▷conifers. Together, they comprise the major types of vegetation found on land. Gymnosperms differ from angiosperms in their ovules which are borne unprotected (not within an ▷ovary) on the scales of their cones. The arrangement of the reproductive organs, and their more simplified internal tissue structure also distinguishes them from the flowering plants. Angiosperms are the largest, most advanced, and most sucessful group of plants at the present time, occupying a highly diverse range of habitats. There are estimated to be about 250,000 different species. In contrast to the gymnosperms, the ovules of angiosperms are enclosed within an ovary and many species have developed highly specialized reproductive structures, associated with ▷pollination by insects, birds, or bats.

Seeger /'siːgə/ Pete 1919– . American folk singer and songwriter, particularly noted for 1960s anti-war protest songs such as 'Where have all the Flowers Gone?' 1961, and 'If I had a Hammer'1962.

Seeland /'zeɪlænt/ German form of ▷Sjælland, the main island of Denmark.

Seferis /sə'feərɪs/ George, pseudonym of Greek poet-diplomat Georgios Seferiades 1900–1971. Ambassador to the Lebanon 1953–57 and then to the UK 1957–62, he did much to help resolve the Cyprus crisis. He published his first volume of lyrics in 1931 and his *Collected Poems* in 1950, his work having a deep feeling for the Hellenic world and showing the influence of the French symbolists and of T S Eliot.

Segovia /sɪ'gəʊvɪə/ town in Castilla-León, central Spain; population (1981) 50,760. It has a Roman aqueduct with 118 arches in current use, and the Moorish ▷alcázar was the palace of the monarchs of Castile. Isabella of Castile was crowned here in 1474.

Segovia /sɪ'gəʊvɪə/ Andrés 1893–1987. Spanish virtuoso guitarist, for whom works were composed by De ▷Falla, ▷Villa-Lobos, and others.

Seifert /'siːfət/ Jaroslav 1901– . Czech poet, who became an original member of the Charter 77 human rights movement. Works include *Mozart in Prague* 1970. He was awarded a Nobel prize in 1984.

Seine /seɪn/ river rising on the Langres plateau NW of Dijon, France and flowing 674 km/481 mi in a NW direction to join the English Channel near Le Havre, passing through Paris and Rouen.

seismology the study of earthquakes and how their shock waves travel through the Earth. By examining the global pattern of waves produced by an earthquake, seismologists can deduce the nature of the materials through which they have passed. This leads to an understanding of the Earth's internal structure. On a smaller scale artificial earthquake waves, generated by explosions or mechanical vibrators, can be used to search for subsurface features in, for example, oil or mineral exploration.

Sekhmet /'sekmet/ Egyptian goddess of heat and fire. She was represented with the head of a lioness, and worshipped at Memphis as the wife of Ptah.

Selangor /sə'læŋə/ state of the Federation of Malaysia; area 8,202 sq km/3,167 sq mi; population (1980) 1,467,441. It was under British protection from 1874, and was a Federated State 1895–1946. The capital was transferred to Shah Alam from Kuala Lumpur in 1973. Klang is the seat of the Sultan and a centre for rubber-growing and tin-mining, and Port Klang (formerly Port Swettenham) exports tin.

Selbourne /'selbɔːn/ village in Hampshire, England, 8 km/5 mi SE of Alton, made famous by *The Natural History of Selbourne* 1789 of Gilbert ▷White 1720–93, who was born here. The Selbourne Society (founded 1885) promotes the study of wildlife.

Selby /'selbi/ town on the river Ouse, North Yorkshire, England; population (1981) 10,726. The nearby Selby coalfield, discovered in 1967, consists of 2,000,000,000 tonnes of pure coal.

Selden /'seldən/ John 1584–1654. English antiquarian and opponent of Charles I's claim to ▷divine right, for which he was twice imprisoned. His *Table Talk* 1689 consists of short essays on political and religious questions.

select committee name for several long-standing committees of the UK House of Commons. The former Estimates Committee, called the Expenditure Committee from 1970, was replaced in 1979 by 14 separate committees, each with a more specialized function, such as the Environment Committee, and the Treasury and Civil Service Committee. These were intended to restore parliamentary control of the executive, improve the quality of legislation, and scrutinize public spending and the work of government departments. Departmental ministers attend to answer questions, and if information is withheld on a matter of wide concern, a debate of the whole House may be called. Select comittees represent the major parliamentary reform of the 20th century, and a possible means – through their all-party membership – of avoiding the automatic repeal of one government's measures by its successor.

Selene /sɪ'liːni/ in Greek mythology, the goddess of the moon; in later times identified with ▷Artemis.

selenium an element discovered in 1817 by Berzelius, associated with telurium and the sulphur family. It exists in several allotropic forms, the grey being a conductor of electricity when illuminated and its conductivity increasing markedly with the brightness of the incident light. Symbol Se, atomic number 34, atomic weight 78.96. It occurs as selenides and in many sulphide ores, and is used in making red glasses and enamels. As a semiconductor it is used extensively in photocells and rectifiers.

self-induction or self-inductance. In physics, the creation of a back e.m.f. (▷electromotive force; voltage) in a coil because of variations in the ▷magnetic field surrounding it caused by fluctuations in the current flowing through it. See ▷inductance.

Selfridge /'selfrɪdʒ/ Harry Gordon 1857–1947. American businessman. Born in Wisconsin, USA, he founded in 1909 the Selfridge Store in London, the first large department store in Britain.

Seljuk Empire empire of the Turkish people, converted to Islam from the 7th century, under the leadership of the invading Tatars or Seljuk Turks. The Seljuk Empire 1055–1243 included all Asia Minor and most of Syria. It was succeeded by the ▷Ottoman Empire.

Selkirk /'selkɜːk/ Alexander 1676–1721. Scottish sailor. Serving as a privateer under ▷Dampier, he was marooned 1704–09 in the ▷Juan Fernández group of islands. His story inspired ▷Defoe to write *Robinson Crusoe*.

Selkirkshire /ˈselkɜːkʃə/ the former inland county of Scotland, included in 1975 in the Borders region. The area is mainly hilly, suitable for sheep grazing, and industries include wool and tanning. The chief rivers are the Tweed, Yarrow, and Ettrick. The adminstrative headquarters was Selkirk.

Sellers /ˈseləz/ Peter 1925–1980. British comedian and film actor, noted for his ability as a mimic, which often allowed him to take several parts. He first made his name in the zany radio *Goon Show* 1949–60. His films include *I'm All Right Jack* 1960, *Dr Strangelove* 1964, *The Pink Panther* 1963, (as the bumbling Inspector Clouseau), and *Being There* 1980.

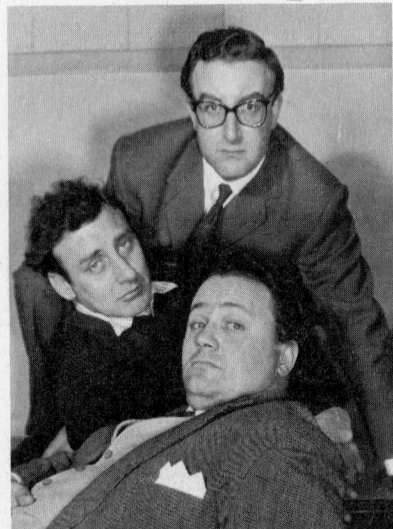

Sellers Comedians Peter Sellers (top centre), Spike Milligan (left) and Harry Secombe (bottom right), three members of the Goon Show which was first broadcast on radio from 1949–60.

Selous /səˈluː/ Frederick Courtney 1851–1917. British hunter-explorer. His pioneer journey in modern Zambia/Zimbabwe opened up the country to Europeans, and he fought in the first Matabele War (1893) and was killed in the East African campaign in World War I The *Selous Scouts* were were a multi-ethnic counter-insurgency force in Rhodesia in 1973–80. When it was disbanded many white scouts went to South Africa.

selvas equatorial rainforest, especially that in the Amazon basin in South America.

Selwyn Lloyd /ˈselwɪn ˈlɔɪd/ (John) Selwyn Lloyd, Baron 1904–1978. British Conservative politician. He was foreign secretary 1955–60, during the Suez crisis, and became Chancellor of the Exchequer in 1960, responsible for the creation of the National Economic Development Council, but the unpopularity of his policy of wage restraint in an attempt to defeat inflation forced his resignation 1962. He was Speaker of the House of Commons 1971–76.

Selznick /ˈselznɪk/ David O(liver) 1902–1965. American film producer. His independent company Selznick International was responsible for many influential films of the 1930s and 1940s, including *King Kong* 1932, and *Gone With the Wind* 1939.

semantics branch of ◊linguistics dealing with the meaning of words.

semaphore a visual signalling system in which the relative positions of two movable pointers or hand-held flags stand for different letters or numbers.

semaphore flags are red and yellow

A B C D E F G H I J K L M N O P Q R S T U V W X Y Z attention numerals follow error front

Semarang /səˈmɑːræŋ/ port in N Java, Indonesia; population (1980) 1,024,000. There is a shipbuilding industry and exports include coffee, teak, sugar, tobacco, kapok, and petroleum from nearby oilfields.

Semele /ˈsemɪli/ in Greek mythology, mother of ◊Dionysus by ◊Zeus. At ◊Hera's suggestion she demanded that Zeus should appear to her in all his glory, but when he did so she was consumed by lightning.

semelparity in biology, the occurrence of a single act of reproduction during an organism's lifetime. Most semelparous species produce very large numbers of offspring when they do reproduce, and normally die soon afterwards. Examples include the Pacific salmon and the pine looper moth. Many plants are semelparous or ◊monocarpic. See also ◊iteroparity.

semicolon a punctuation mark (;) with a function halfway between the separation of sentence from sentence by means of a full stop or period (.) and the gentler separation provided by a comma (,). Although not as often used as formerly, semicolons provide a useful half-way stage between commas and full stops. Rather than the abrupt *We saw John last night. It was good to see him again*, and the casual (and often condemned) *We saw John last night, it was good to see him again*, the semicolon both reflects the link between the two parts of the statement and is traditionally considered good style: *We saw John last night; it was good to see him again*.

semiconductor a crystalline material with an electrical conductivity between that of metals (good) and insulators (poor), and increasing with temperature, for example germanium, silicon, and gallium arsenide. By introducing carefully controlled quantities of specific 'impure' atoms into adjacent regions of the same semiconductor crystal, the flow of current can be regulated and channelled, allowing important electronic devices, such as diodes and transistors to be made. The simplest is the diode, which lets current pass through it in one direction only – useful for converting alternating to direct current. Light-emitting diodes (LEDs) need less current than filament lamps; their red or green glow is often seen on instrument panels. Transistors are capable of amplifying electrical signals. Circuits containing hundreds or even thousands of transistors together with ancillary components and connections are now formed on single 'chips' of silicon (see ◊computer).

semiology, or semiotics the study of the function of signs and symbols in human communication, both in language and by various non-linguistic means. Its starting point was the notion of the Swiss linguist Ferdinand de Saussure (1857–1913), that no word or other sign (*signifier*) is intrinsically linked with its meaning (*signified*), and it was developed as a scientific discipline especially by ◊Lévi-Strauss and ◊Barthes. See also ◊structuralism.

Semipalatinsk /ˌsemɪpəˈlætɪnsk/ town in Kazakh Republic, USSR; population (1985) 317,000. It was founded in 1718 as a Russian frontier post. Industries include meat-packing, tanning, and flour-milling, and the region produces nickel and chromium. The Kvzyl Kum atomic weapon testing ground is nearby.

Semiramis /seˈmɪrəmɪs/ Assyrian queen, c. 800 BC, who was later identified with the chief Assyrian goddess ◊Ishtar.

Semite a member of one of the ancient peoples of the Near and Middle East, who spoke Semitic languages (see ◊Hamito-Semitic languages). They are traditionally said to be descended from Shem, a son of Noah in the Bible.

Ancient Semitic peoples were the Israelites, Ammonites, Moabites, and Edomites, and the Babylonians, Assyrians, Chaldaeans, Carthaginians, Phoenicians, and Canaanites. Their descendants in the modern include many Jews, Arabs, and other Near and Middle Eastern people.

The Semitic peoples founded the religions of ◊Judaism, ◊Christianity, and ◊Islam.

Semitic languages /sɪˈmɪtɪk/ a branch of the ◊Hamito-Semitic family of languages.

Senanayake /ˌsenəˈnaɪəkə/ Don Stephen 1884–1952. First prime minister of independent Sri Lanka (formerly Ceylon) 1947–52.

Senanayake /ˌsenəˈnaɪəkə/ Dudley 1911–1973. Prime minister of independent Sri Lanka (formerly Ceylon) 1952–53, 1960, and 1965–70; son of Don ◊Senanayake.

senate the Roman 'council of elders'. Originally consisting of the heads of patrician families, it was recruited from ex-magistrates and persons who had rendered notable public service, but was periodically purged by the censors. Although nominally advisory, it controlled finance and foreign policy.

The *US Senate* consists of 100 members, two from each state, elected for a six-year term. The Italian upper chamber is also known as the senate, as is that of France under the Fifth Republic. The name is also given to the governing bodies in some universities.

Sendai /senˈdaɪ/ city in NE Honshu, Japan; population (1983) 657,000. Industries include metal goods (a Metal Museum was established 1975), textiles, pottery, and food processing.

Sendak /ˈsendæk/ Maurice 1928– . American book illustrator, born New York. He became known for his deliberately archaic children's book illustrations. His best known books include *Where the Wild Things Are* 1963, *In the Night Kitchen* 1970, and *Outside Over There* 1981 (all of which he also wrote).

Senegal /ˌseniˈɡɔːl/ country in W Africa, on the Atlantic, bounded to the N by Mauritania, to the E by Mali, to the S by Guinea and Guinea-Bissau, and enclosing Gambia on three sides.

government The constitution of 1963, amended, provides for a single-chamber legislature, the 120 member National Assembly, and a president who is head of state and head of government. The assembly and president are elected at the same time by universal suffrage to serve a five-year term. The president appoints and leads a council of ministers. The Senegalese Socialist Party (PS) is dominant.

Senegal's ten regions enjoy a high degree of autonomy, each having its own appointed governor and elected assembly and controlling a separate budget.

history For early history, see ◊Africa. Portuguese explorers arrived in the 15th century,

Sendak Condemned as disturbing by some parents and teachers, the strange creatures portrayed in *Where the Wild Things Are* by Maurice Sendak nonetheless convey extremely well the dreams and imaginings of childhood.

Seneca /ˈsenɪkə/ Lucius Annaeus c. 4 BC–65 AD. Roman Stoic philosopher-playwright, author of essays and nine tragedies. Born at Cordova, Spain, he was ◊Nero's tutor, but lost favour after his accession and was ordered to commit suicide. His tragedies were accepted as classical models by 16th-century dramatists.

Senefelder /ˈzeɪnəˌfeldə/ Alois 1771–1834. German engraver. Born at Prague, he is famous for his discovery in 1796 of the art of ◊lithography.

Senegal /ˌseniˈɡɔːl/ river in W Africa, formed by the confluence of the Bafing and the Bakhoy and flowing 1,125 km/700 mi NW and W to join the Atlantic near St Louis, Senegal. In 1968 the Organization of Riparian States of the River Senegal (Guinea, Mali, Mauretania, and Senegal) was formed to develop the river valley, including a dam for hydroelectric power and irrigation at Joina Falls in Mali: its headquarters is in Dakar.

and French settlers in the 17th. Senegal had a French governor from 1854, became part of French West Africa 1895, and a territory 1946. Senegal became an independent republic in Sept 1960, with Leopold Sedar Senghor, leader of the Senegalese Progresssive Union (UPS), as its first president. Senghor was also prime minister 1962–70. UPS was the only legal party from 1966 until in Dec 1976 it was reconstituted as PS and two opposition parties were legally registered. In 1978 Senghor was decisively re-elected.

Senghor retired at the end of 1980 and was succeeded by Abdou Diouf, who declared an amnesty for political offenders and permitted more parties to register. In the 1983 elections PS won 111 of the assembly seats and the main opposition, the Senegalese Democratic Party (PDS), eight seats. Later that year Diouf tightened control of his party and the government, abolishing the post of prime minister. This met open opposition, sometimes violent, but he and the PS remained firmly in power.

In 1980 Senegal sent troops to the Gambia to protect it against a suspected Libyan invasion, and it intervened again in 1981 to thwart an attempted coup. As the two countries came closer together, they agreed on an eventual merger and the confederation of Senegambia came into being in Feb 1982.

Senegal

REPUBLIC OF (*République du Sénégal*)

AREA 197,000 sq km/76,000 sq mi
CAPITAL and chief port Dakar
TOWNS Thies, Kaolack
PHYSICAL plains; swamp and tropical forest in SW
FEATURES river Senegal; The Gambia forms an enclave within Senegal
HEAD OF STATE AND OF GOVERNMENT Abdou Diouf from 1981
GOVERNMENT socialist democracy
EXPORTS groundnuts, cotton; fish; phosphates
CURRENCY CFA franc (498.38 = £1 Sept 1987)
POPULATION 6,485,000 (1985); annual growth rate 2.7%
LANGUAGE French (official)
RELIGION Muslim 80%, Christian 10% (chiefly Roman Catholic), animist 10%
LITERACY 31% male/14% female (1980 est)
GNP $2.7 bn (1983); $342 per head of population
CHRONOLOGY
1960 Achieved full independence, with Léopold Sedar Senghor, leader of the Sengalese Progressive Union (UPS), as president.
1966 UPS declared the only legal party.

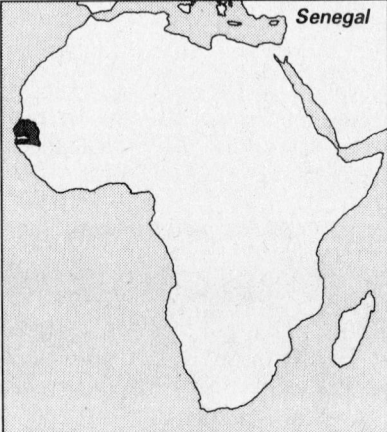

Senegal

1976 UPS reconstituted as the Sengalese Socialist Party (PS). Abdou Diouf nominated as Senghor's successor.
1980 Senghor retired and was succeeded by Diouf. Troops sent to defend The Gambia.
1981 Military help again sent to The Gambia.
1982 Confederation of Senegambia came into effect.
1983 Diouf re-elected. Post of prime minister abolished.

the capital of ◊Korea 1392–1910, and has a 14th-century palace, and four universities.

sepal part of a flower, usually green, which surrounds and protects the flower in bud. The sepals are derived from modified leaves, and collectively known as the ◊calyx. In some plants, such as the marsh marigold (*Caltha palustris*), where the true ◊petals are absent, they are brightly coloured and petal-like, taking over the role of attracting insect pollinators to the flower.

sequoia two species of conifer in the family Taxodiaceae, native to California, and named after Sequoya c. 1760–1843, the Cherokee Indian who gave his people an 'alphabet' for their language. The redwood (*Sequoia sempervivens*) is a valuable long-lived timber tree, and the Howard Libbey redwood is the world's tallest tree 110 m/362 ft, with a circumference of 13.4 m/44 ft. The big tree (*Sequoiadendron giganteum*) is the largest of living trees, having enormous bulk, up to some 30 m/100 ft at the base, as well as being almost as tall as the redwood. It is also, except for the bristlecone pine, the oldest, some specimens being known to have lived more than 3,000 years.

Serang /səˈræŋ/ alternative form of ◊Ceram, an Indonesian island.

seraph (plural *seraphim*) an ◊angel of the highest order. They were mentioned in the book of Isaiah in the Old Testament.

Serapis /ˈserəpɪs/ Graeco-Egyptian god, a combination of Hades and Osiris, invented by the Ptolemies; his finest temple was the Serapeum at Alexandria.

Serbia /ˈsɜːbɪə/ constituent republic of Yugoslavia
area 88,267 sq km/34,080 sq mi
capital Belgrade
features includes the autonomous provinces of *Kosovo*, capital Priština, of which the predominantly Albanian population demands unification with Albania; and *Vojvodina*, capital Novi Sad, largest town Subotica, with a predominantly Serbian population. Serbia has the fertile Danube plains in the north and is mountainous in the south
population (1981) 9,313,700
language the Serbian variant of Serbo-Croat, sometimes written in Cyrillic script
religion Serbian Orthodox
history the Serbs settled in the Balkans in the 7th century, and accepted Christianity in the 9th. They were united as one kingdom around 1169, and under Stephen Dushan (1331–55) founded an empire covering most of the Balkans. After their defeat at Kosovo in 1389 they came under the domination of the Turks, who in 1459 annexed Serbia. Uprisings 1804–16, led by Kara George and Milosh Obrenovich, forced the Turks to recognize Serbia as an autonomous prinicipality under Milosh. The assassination of Kara George on Obrenovich's orders gave rise to a long feud between the two houses. After a war with Turkey 1876–78, Serbia became an independent kingdom. On the assassination of the last Obrenovich in 1903 the Karageorgevich dynasty came to the throne. The two Balkan Wars of 1912–13 greatly enlarged Serbia's territory at the expense of Turkey and Bulgaria. Serbia's designs on Bosnia and Hercegovina, backed by Russia, led to friction with Austria, culminating in the outbreak of war in 1914. Serbia was completely overrun in 1915–16, and was occupied until 1918, when it became the nucleus of the new kingdom of the Serbs, Croats and Slovenes, later ◊Yugoslavia.

sere a type of plant ◊succession developing in a particular habitat. A lithosere, for example, is a succession starting on the surface of bare rock.

---

senescence in biology, the deterioration in physical and reproductive capacities associated with old age. See ◊ageing.

Senghor /sɒŋˈgɔː/ Leopold 1906– . President of Senegal 1960–80.

senile dementia see ◊dementia.

Sennacherib /sɪˈnækərɪb/ died 681 BC. King of Assyria from 704. Son of Sargon II, he rebuilt the city of ◊Nineveh, sacked Babylon in 689, and crushed ◊Hezekiah, King of Judah, though failing to take Jerusalem. He was assassinated by his sons. His son ◊Esarhaddon succeeded him.

Sens /sɒns/ town in Burgundy, France; population (1982) 26,961. Its 12th–16th-century cathedral is one of the earliest in the Gothic style in France.

Senussi /sɪˈnuːsi/ Sidi Mohammed ben Ali es c. 1796–1860. Moslem religious reformer. Born in Algeria, he preached a return to the puritanism of early Islam and met with much success in Libya, where he made Jaghbub his centre and founded the sect called after him.

Seoul /səʊl/ capital of South Korea, near the Han river, and with its chief port at Inchon; population (1983) 9,204,344. Industries include engineering, textiles, and food processing. It was

separation of powers an approach to limiting the powers of government by separating governmental functions into the executive, legislative, and judiciary. The concept has its fullest practical expression in the constitution of the USA.

Sephardim /sɪˈfɑːdɪm/ Jews descended from those expelled from Spain and Portugal in the 15th century, or from those forcibly converted to Christianity (Marranos) at that time. Many settled in North Africa, and some in other Mediterranean countries or in England.

sepoy a term used for an Indian soldier in the service of the British or Indian Army in the days of British rule in India. The ◊Indian Mutiny of 1857–58 was also known as the Sepoy Mutiny or Rebellion.

septicaemia technical term for ◊blood poisoning.

Septuagesima in the Christian church calendar, the third Sunday before Lent; the 70th day before Easter.

Septuagint (Latin *septuagint*, seventy) the oldest Greek version of the Old Testament, traditionally made by 70 scholars, hence the name.

A hydrosere is a succession in shallow freshwater, beginning with planktonic vegetation and the growth of pondweeds and other aquatic plants, and ending with the development of swamp. A plagiosere is the sequence of communities that develops following the clearing of the existing vegetation.

serenade in music, a piece for chamber orchestra or wind instruments in several movements, originally intended for evening entertainment, such as Mozart's *Eine kleine Nachtmusik/A Little Night Music.*

serfdom the legal and economic status of peasants under ◊feudalism. Serfs were normally bound to the soil, and while they could not be sold like slaves, they were not free to leave their lord's estate. They had to work without pay on their lord's land for a number of days every week, in addition to extra labour at harvest time and other busy seasons. They also had to pay tribute in kind; in return they were allowed to cultivate a portion of the estate for their own benefit. In England serfdom died out between the 14th and 17th centuries.

Sergius, St /'sɜːdʒiəs/ of Radonezh 1314–1392. patron saint of Russia. In 1334 he founded the monastery of the Blessed Trinity near Moscow. Mediator among Russian feudal princes, he inspired the victory of Dmitri, Grand Duke of Moscow, over the Tatar khan Mamai at Kulikovo, on the upper Don, in 1380.

serialism in music, another name for the ◊twelve-note system of composition.

Seringapatam /sə,rɪŋɡəpə'tæm/ town in Karnataka, India, on an island in the Cauvery. It was the capital of Mysore State 1610–1799, when it was taken from the Sultan of Mysore, Tipu Sahib, by the British general Cornwallis.

Serlio /'sɛəliəʊ/ Sebastiano 1475–1554. Italian painter, architect, and architectural theorist. He was most important as the author of *L'Architettura*, 1537–51, which spread the Neo-Classical style throughout Europe.

Serpens ◊constellation of the equatorial region of the sky, representing a serpent coiled around the body of Ophiuchus. It is the only constellation divided into two halves, Serpens Caput, the head (on one side of ◊Ophiuchus), and Serpens Cauda, the tail (on the other side).

serpentine a greenish to black mineral hydrated magnesium silicate, $Mg_3Si_2O_5.2H_2O$, occurring in soft rocks.

Serpent Mound embankment built by Hopewell Indians in 1st–2nd centuries BC in Ohio, USA. It is 405 m/1,330 ft long, 1.3 m/4 ft high, and about 6 m/18 ft across.

serum a clear fluid produced by clotted ◊blood. It is, in effect, blood plasma with the proteins that produce clotting removed, and can be made in the laboratory. It contains ◊antibodies and other proteins, as well as the fats and sugars of the blood. Medically, serum containing antibodies can be used to protect against disease.

serval African wildcat *Felis serval.* Slender, long-limbed cat with a yellowish-brown, black-spotted coat. It hunts rodents by sound, using its large ears. It is just under 1 m/3 ft long.

Servan-Schreiber /seə'vɒn ʃraɪ'beə/ Jean Jacques 1924– . French Radical politician, and founder of the magazine *L'Express* 1953. He created a furore with *Le Défi americain* 1967, maintaining that US economic and technological dominance would be challenged only by a united left-wing Europe. He was president of the Radical Party 1971–75 and 1977–79.

Servetus /sɜː'viːtəs/ Michael 1511–1553. Spanish theologian and Anabaptist. He was burned alive by ◊Calvin at Geneva for his unitarian views. As a physician, he was a pioneer in the study of the circulation of the blood.

service industry commercial activity that provides and charges for various services to customers (as opposed to manufacturing or supplying goods), such as take-away food outlets, restaurants, the tourist industry, hotels, and the retail trade (shops and supermarkets). With the decline in the manufacturing sector in many Western countries, such as Britain, service industries have gained importance.

services, armed the air, sea, and land forces of a country. In the UK the history of the Army and Navy can be traced back to the locally raised forces which prevented ◊Alfred's ◊Wessex being overrun by the ◊Danes. All three armed services are professionals, with no conscript element. The *Royal Navy* is known as the Senior Service, because of its formal origin under Henry VIII, whereas no permanent standing *Army* was raised until the time of Charles II (see also ◊Royal Marines). The ◊Territorial Army is a back-up force of volunteers. The *Royal Air Force* was formed in 1918 by the merger of the already existing Royal Naval Air Service and the Royal Flying Corps.

service tree deciduous Eurasian tree *Sorbus domestica*, family Rosaceae, with alternate leaves, white flowers, and small oval fruit. The wild service tree *Sorbus torminalis* is native to Britain.

servo system an automatic control system used in aircraft, motor cars, and other complex machines. A specific input, such as moving a lever or joystick, causes a specific output, such as feeding current to an electric motor that moves, for example, the rudder of the aircraft. At the same time the position of the rudder is detected and fed back to the central control, so that small adjustments can continually be made to maintain the desired course.

sesame annual plant (*Sesamum indicum*) of the family Pedaliaceas, probably native of SE Asia. It produces oily seeds used for food and soap making.

sessile in botany, a leaf, flower or fruit that lacks a stalk and sits directly on the stem, as with the acorns of sessile oak (*Quercus petraea*). In zoology, an animal that normally stays in the same place, such as a barnacle or mussel. The term is also applied to the eyes of crustaceans when these lack stalks and sit directly on the head.

Session, Court of one of the civil courts in Scotland. See ◊Scots law.

Sessions /'seʃənz/ Roger (Huntingdon) 1896–1985. American composer. Influenced by ◊Stravinsky and ◊Schoenberg, his dense and dissonant works include *The Black Maskers* incidental music, 1923, eight symphonies, and *Concerto for Orchestra* 1971.

Set in Egyptian mythology, the god of night, the desert, and of all evils. He was the murderer of ◊Osiris, and is portrayed as a grotesque animal.

set in mathematics, any collection of defined things, usually denoted by a capital letter and indicated by curly brackets (braces). For example $L = \{$ letters of the alphabet $\}$ represents the set that consists of all the letters of the alphabet. The symbol ϵ stands for 'is a member of'; thus $p\epsilon L$ means that p belongs to the set consisting of all letters, and $4\epsilon L$ means that 4 does not belong to the set consisting of all letters. Types of set include: an *infinite set*, which has an unlimited number of members, such as $\{$ all whole numbers $\}$; a *finite set* has a limited number of members, such as $\{$ letters of the alphabet $\}$; an *empty* or *null set* has no members, such as the number of people who have swum across the Atlantic Ocean, written as $\{\}$. A *single-element set* has only one member, such as days of the week beginning with M, written as $\{$ Monday $\}$; *equivalent sets* have the same number of members, for example, if $W = \{$ days of the week $\}$ and $R = \{$ colours of the rainbow $\}$, their equivalence is written $W+la+raR$; *equal sets* have the same members, for example if $W = \{$ days of the week $\}$ and $S = \{$ Sunday, Monday, Tuesday, Wednesday, Thursday, Friday, Saturday $\}$, their equality is written $W = S$. Sets with the same number of members are *equivalent sets*; sets with some members in common are *overlapping sets*; sets with no members in common are *disjoint sets*; sets contained within others are *subsets*. These types are often illustrated by a ◊Venn diagram.

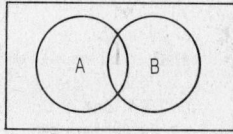
A and B are overlapping sets

set

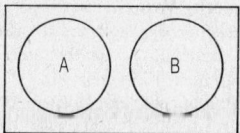
A and B are disjoint sets

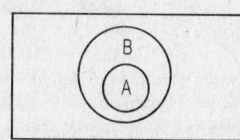
A is the subset of B

Sète /seɪt/ town on the Mediterranean coast of France, in Hérault *département*, SW of Montpellier; population (1982) 40,466. It is a seaport, and handles fish, wine, brandy, and chemicals.

Seton /'siːtn/ Ernest Thompson 1860–1946. British author and naturalist. His name was originally Ernest Seton Thompson. Born in

England, he was brought up in Canada, and became noted for illustrating his own books with drawings of animals.

Seto Naikai /'setəʊ 'naɪkaɪ/ ('Inland Sea') a narrow body of water almost enclosed by the islands of Homshu, Shikoku, and Kyushu, Japan. It is both a transport artery and a national park, with some 3,000 islands.

setter breed of dog, so called because they are trained in crouching or 'setting' on the sight of game to be pursued. The English setter may be white with black, tan, or liver markings and the Irish setter is usually a rich red.

Settlement, Act of law passed by Parliament in 1701 that confined the succession to the throne of England to Protestants and (after William III and Anne) to the house of Hanover.

Seurat /'sɜːrɑː/ Georges 1859–1891. French artist. Born in Paris, he introduced with the artist ◊Signac the oil-painting technique of ◊Pointillism. He departed from the Impressionists in evolving a more formal type of composition with a static quality, rather than capturing a fleeting moment of light or movement. An outstanding example of his work is *La Baignade/The Bathers at Asnières* 1884, (National Gallery, London).

Sevastopol /sɪ'væstəpəl/ port, resort, and fortress in the Crimea, Ukraine Republic, USSR; population (1985) 341,000. It is the base of the Russian Black Sea fleet, and also has shipyards and a wine-making industry. Founded by Catherine II in 1784, it was successfully besieged by the English and French in the Crimean War (Oct 1854–Sept 1855), and in World War II by the Germans (Nov 1941–4 Jul 1942), but was retaken by the Russians in 1944.

Sevenoaks /'sevənəʊks/ town in Kent, England. It lies 32 km/20 mi SE of London, population (1980) 19,000. Nearby are the 17th-century houses of Knole and ◊Chevening.

Seventh Day Adventist a member of the Protestant religious sect of the same name. It has its main following in the USA, and distinctive tenets are that Saturday is the Sabbath and that Christ's second coming is imminent.

Seven Weeks' War war between Austria and Prussia in 1866. It was engineered by ◊Bismarck, and was nominally about the possession of ◊Schleswig-Holstein (under the Treaty of ◊Prague, Prussia took both Holstein, previously seized by Austria, and Schleswig), but it was actually to confirm Prussia's supersession of Austria as the leading German state. The Battle of ◊Sadowa was the culmination of the Prussian General von Moltke's victories.

Seven Wonders of the World in antiquity, these were the pyramids of Egypt; the hanging gardens at Babylon; the temple of Artemis at Ephesus; the statue of Zeus at Olympia; the mausoleum at Halicarnassus; the Colossus of Rhodes; and the Pharos (lighthouse) at Alexandria.

Seven Years' War the war of 1756–63 between Britain and Prussia on the one hand, and France, Austria, and Russia on the other. Its military interest centres on the successful struggle of ◊Frederick II of Prussia against great odds. Britain's part in the war, under the

direction of ◊Chatham, was mainly confined to operations at sea, notably the victory of ◊Quiberon Bay 1759, and in the colonies. The victories of ◊Wolfe and ◊Clive in the colonies resulted in the conquest of Canada and the foundation of the Indian empire.

severe combined immune deficiency (SCID) rare condition in which a baby is born without the body's normal defences against infection. The child must be kept within a transparent plastic tent until a matched donor can provide a bone-marrow transplant.

Severn /'sevən/ river of Wales and England, rising on the NE side of Plynlimmon, N Wales, and flowing some 338 km/210 mi through Shrewsbury, Worcester, and Gloucester to the Bristol Channel. It is famous for the Severn bore (up to 2 m/6 ft tidal wave). S England and S Wales are linked near Chepstow by a rail tunnel 1873–85, and road bridge 1966. A barrage has been proposed (seaward of Cardiff and Weston-super-Mare) which would provide electric power, and improve dock developments in Cardiff and Bristol.

Severus /sɪ'vɪərəs/ Lucius Septimius 146–211 AD. Roman emperor. Born in North Africa, he held a command on the Danube when in 193 the emperor Pertinax was murdered. Proclaimed emperor by his troops, Severus proved an able administrator. The only African to become emperor, he died at York while campaigning against the Caledonians.

Seveso /sɪ'veɪsəʊ/ town in Lombardy, Italy, site of a factory manufacturing the herbicide hexachlorophene. In 1976 one of the by-products escaped in a cloud which contaminated the area, resulting in severe chlorance and deformed births.

Sévigné /,seɪviːn'jeɪ/ Marie de Rabutin-Chantal, Marquise de Sévigné 1626–1696. French writer, born in Paris. In her letters to her daughter, the Comtesse de Grignan, she gives a vivid picture of contemporary customs.

Seville /sɪ'vɪl/ city (Spanish *Sevilla*), in Andalusia, Spain, on the Guadalquivir river 96 km/60 mi N of Cadiz, population (1982) 653,800. Industries include machinery, spirits, porcelain, silk, and tobacco. Formerly the centre of a Moorish kingdom, it is famous for the 12th century Alcázar palace; the Gothic 15th–16th century cathedral; the church of La Caridad; the university, established 1502; the museum; and Holy Week Festival.

Sèvre /'seɪvrə/ name of two French rivers from which the *département* of Deux Sèvres takes its name. The *Sèvre Nantaise* joins the Loire at Nantes; the *Sèvre Niortaise* flows into the Bay of Biscay.

Sèvres /'seɪvrə/ town in the Ile de France region of France; now a Paris suburb, population about 21,000. The state porcelain factory was established in the park of ◊St Cloud in 1756, and it is also the site of a national museum of ceramics.

Sèvres /'seɪvrə/ fine porcelain produced at a factory in ◊Sèvres since 1756. One of its main characteristics is the use of intensely coloured backgrounds (in pink, royal blue, and so on)

against which flowers are painted in elaborately embellished frames.

sewage disposal the disposal of human excreta and other water-borne waste products from houses, factories, and streets. It is conveyed through sewers and treated before being discharged into rivers or the sea. Sewage works are the responsibility of local authorities. The sludge may be spread over fields attached to the works, or it may be processed and sold as a fertilizer. In places near the coast, raw sewage is sometimes dumped into the sea. A 1983 European Commission report identified a significant proportion of bathing beaches in the UK as having unacceptably high bacterial content, largely as a result of untreated sewage being discharged into the sea. The use of raw sewage as a fertilizer, (as long practised in China) has the drawback that disease-causing micro-organisms may survive in the soil and be taken into the body by consumption of subsequent crops.

Sewell /'sjuːəl/ Anna 1820–1878. British author. She is known for her single published work telling the life story of a horse, *Black Beauty* 1877. Although now regarded as a children's book, it was written to encourage sympathetic treatment of horses by adults.

sewing machine apparatus for the mechanical sewing of cloth, leather, and other materials by a needle, powered by hand, treadle, or belted electric motor. Among early inventors was the Englishman Thomas Saint in 1790. The popular modern lockstitch machine, using a double thread, was invented independently in America by both Walter Hunt (1834) and Elias Howe (1846). Howe's machine was the basis of the machine patented in 1851 by the American Isaac Singer (1811–75). In the latest ◊microprocessor-controlled sewing machines, as many as 25 different stitching patterns can be selected by pushbutton.

sex determination the process by which the sex of an organism is determined, in species with distinct sexes. In many species, the sex of an individual is dictated by the two sex ◊chromosomes (the ◊X and ◊Y chromosomes) it receives from its parents. In mammals, some plants and a few insects, males are XY, and females XX, but in birds, reptiles, some amphibians, and butterflies the reverse is the case. In bees and wasps, males are produced from unfertilized eggs, whereas females are produced from fertilized eggs. Most fish have a much more flexible system of sex determination, which can be affected by external factors. For example, in wrasse all individuals develop into females, but the largest individual in each area or school changes sex to become the local breeding male. Environmental factors can also affect some reptiles, such as turtles.

sexism belief in (or set of implicit assumptions about) the superiority of one's own sex, often accompanied by a ◊stereotype or preconceived idea about the opposite sex. Sexism may also be accompanied by ◊discrimination on the basis of sex, generally as practised by men against women. The term, coined by analogy with ◊racism, was first used in the 1960s by

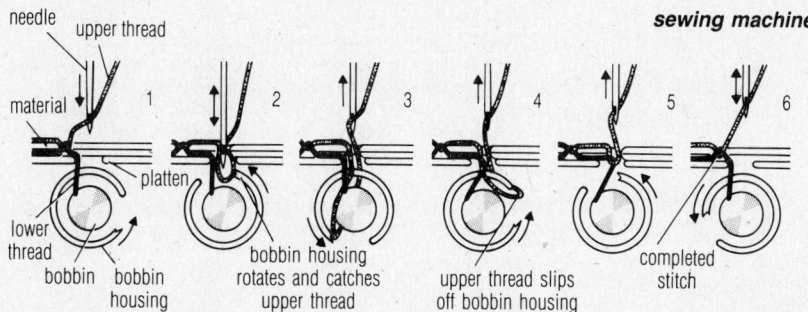

sewing machine

needle
upper thread
material
1 2 3 4 5 6
platten
lower thread
bobbin   bobbin housing
bobbin housing rotates and catches upper thread
upper thread slips off bobbin housing
completed stitch

feminist writers to describe language or behaviour which implied women's inferiority. Examples include the contentious use of male pronouns to describe both men and women, and the assumption that some jobs are typically performed only by one sex.

sex linkage in ◊genetics, the tendency for certain characteristics to occur exclusively, or predominantly, in one sex only. Human examples include red-green colour blindness and ◊haemophilia, both found predominantly in males. In both cases, these characteristics are ◊recessive and are determined by ◊genes on the ◊X chromosome: since females possess two X chromosomes, any such recessive ◊allele on one of them is likely to be masked by the corresponding allele on the other. In males (who have only one X chromosome paired with an inert ◊Y chromosome) any gene on the X chromosome will automatically be expressed. Colour blindness and haemophilia can appear in females, but only if they are ◊homozygous for these traits, due to inbreeding for example.

sextant navigational instrument for determining latitude by measuring the angle between some heavenly body and the horizon; it can only be used in clear weather. It was invented by John Hadley in 1730. When the horizon is viewed through the right-hand side *horizon glass*, which is partly clear and partly mirrored, the light from a star can be seen at the same time in the mirrored left-hand side by adjusting an *index mirror*. The angle of the star to the horizon can then be read on a calibrated scale.

sexual reproduction a reproductive process in living creatures which requires the union or ◊fertilization, of the ◊gametes (except in ◊fungi). These are generally produced by two different individuals, although self-fertilization can occur in ◊hermaphrodites. Most organisms other than bacteria and cyanobacteria show some sort of sexual process. Except in some lower organisms, gametes are of two types, called eggs and sperm. The organisms producing the eggs are called females, and those producing the sperm, males. The fusion of a male and female gamete produces a zygote from which a new individual develops.

sexual selection the process first noted by ◊Darwin, whereby competition between males to mate with females leads to the evolution of particular characteristics in the males. Examples include the antlers of male deer (used in combat for females) and the bright plumage of many male birds (used to attract females and warn off

sextant

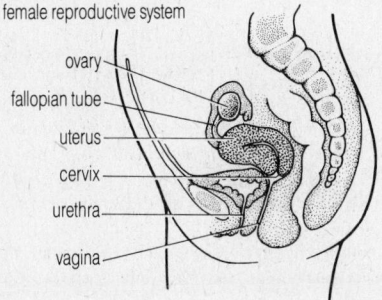

simplified diagram of a sextant

light from star
angle A
index mirror
pivot
angle A
horizon glass
telescope
light from horizon
angle scale
position of index arm when A = 0
index arm (fixed relative to telescope) calibrated to give angle A

sexual reproduction

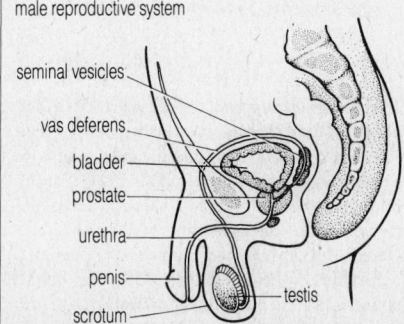

female reproductive system

ovary
fallopian tube
uterus
cervix
urethra
vagina

male reproductive system

seminal vesicles
vas deferens
bladder
prostate
urethra
penis
scrotum
testis

rival males). In some species, it is the females that compete for mates, and sexual selection then operates on the females.

Seychelles /seɪˈʃelz/ country in the Indian Ocean, off E Africa, N of Madagascar.
government Seychelles is a republic within the Commonwealth. The constitution of 1979 makes Seychelles a one-party state, the party being the Seychelles People's Progresssive Front (SPPF). The president, who is both head of state and head of government, and the single-chamber legislature, the National Assembly, both serve a five-year term. The president and 23 of the 25 assembly members are elected by universal suffrage, and two are appointed by the president.
history For early history, see ◊Africa. The islands were probably visited by the Portuguese about 1500 and became a French colony 1744. Seychelles was ceded to Britain by France in 1814 and was ruled as part of ◊Mauritius until it became a Crown Colony in 1903.
In the 1960s several political parties were formed, campaigning for independence, the most significant being the Seychelles Democratic Party (SDP), led by James Mancham, and the Seychelles People's United Party (SPUP), led by Albert René. René demanded complete independence while Mancham favoured integration with Britain. In 1975 internal self-government was agreed. The two parties then formed a coalition government with Mancham as prime minister. In Jun 1976 Seychelles became an independent republic within the Commonwealth, with Mancham as president and René as prime minister.
The following year René staged an armed coup while Mancham was attending a Commonwealth conference in London, and declared himself president. After a brief suspension of the constitution, a new one was adopted, creating a one-party state, with the SPUP being renamed the Seychelles People's Progressive Front. René, as the only candidate, was formally elected president in 1979 and then re-elected in 1984. There have been several unsuccessful attempts to overthrow him.
René has followed a policy of ◊non-alignment and has forbidden the use of port facilities to vessels carrying nuclear weapons. He has maintained close links with Tanzania.

Seyfert galaxy a type of ◊galaxy with a small, bright centre named after discoverer Carl Seyfert (1911–60). Almost all Seyferts are spiral galaxies. Their bright centres are caused by hot gas moving at high speed around a highly massive central object, possibly a ◊black hole. Seyferts seem to be closely related to ◊quasars, but about 100 times fainter.

Seymour /ˈsiːmɔː/ Jane c. 1509–1537. Third wife of Henry VIII, whom she married in 1536. She died soon after the birth of her son (Edward VI).

Sezession (German 'secession') various groups of German and Austrian artists who 'seceded' from official academic art institutions in order to found more modern schools of painting. The first was in Munich, 1892, and the most important that of Vienna, 1897, with which the paintings of Gustav ◊Klimt are linked.

Seychelles

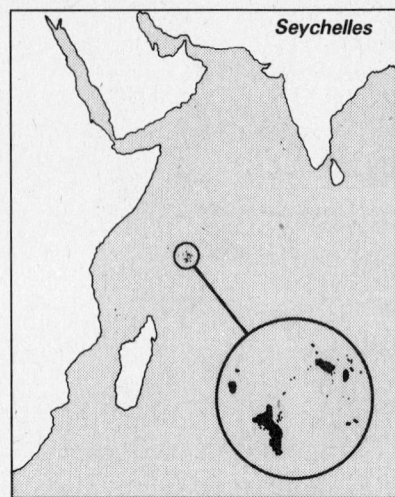

Seychelles

AREA 404 sq km/156 sq mi
CAPITAL Victoria on Mahé
PHYSICAL comprises two distinct island groups, one concentrated, the other widely scattered, totalling well over 100 islands and islets
FEATURES the unique 'double coconut'
HEAD OF STATE AND OF GOVERNMENT France-Albert René from 1977
GOVERNMENT one-party authoritarian
EXPORTS copra, cinnamon; tourism is important
CURRENCY Seychelles rupee (9.10 = £1 Sept 1987)
POPULATION 66,000 (1985); annual growth rate 0.6%
LANGUAGE creole, spoken by 95%, English and French (all official)
RELIGION Christian (Roman Catholic 90%)
LITERACY 60% (1983)
GDP $143 million (1982); $1,030 per head of population
CHRONOLOGY
1970 Constitutional conference in London on future status of Seychelles. James Mancham, leader of the Seychelles Democratic Party (SDP), argued for full independence, while France-Albert René, leader of the Seychelles People's United Party (SPUP), favoured full integration with the UK.
1975 Internal self-government granted.
1976 Full independence achieved as a republic within the Commonwealth, with Mancham as president.
1977 René ousted Mancham in an armed coup and took over the presidency.
1979 New constitution adopted, making the SPUP, restyled the Seychelles People's Progressive Front (SPPF), the only legal party.
1981 Attempted coup by South African mercenaries thwarted.
1984 René re-elected.

analyst's relationship with a boy obsessed with horses, and *Amadeus* 1979.

Shaftesbury /'ʃɑːftsbəri/ market town and agricultural centre in Dorset, England, 30 km/19 mi SW of Salisbury; population (1985) 6,000. King Alfred is said to have founded an abbey on the site in 880; Canute died at Shaftesbury in 1035.

Shaftesbury Miniature of Anthony Ashley Cooper, 1st Earl of Shaftesbury, by Samuel Cooper. Denounced by Charles II as 'the wickedest dog in England', Shaftesbury led the movement to exclude the future James II from the succession.

Shaftesbury /'ʃɑːftsbəri/ Anthony Ashley Cooper, 1st Earl of Shaftesbury 1621–1683. English politician, a supporter of the Restoration of the monarchy. He became lord chancellor in 1672, but went into opposition in 1673 and began to organize the ◊Whig Party. He headed the demand for the exclusion of the future James II from the succession, secured the passing of the Habeas Corpus Act in 1679 and, when accused of treason in 1681, fled to Holland.

Shaftesbury /'ʃɑːftsbəri/ Anthony Ashley Cooper, 7th Earl of Shaftesbury 1801–1885. British Tory politician. A strong supporter of the Ten Hours Act of 1847 and other factory legislation, he was largely responsible for the 1842 act forbidding the employment of women and children underground in mines. He was also associated with the movement for the establishment of ragged schools (providing free education) for the poor.

Shaftesbury /'ʃɑːftsbəri/ Anthony Ashley Cooper, 3rd Earl of Shaftesbury 1671–1713. English philosopher, author of *Characteristics* 1711 and other ethical speculations.

shag type of small ◊cormorant, *Phalacrocorax aristotelis*.

Shah /ʃɑː/ or, more formally *Shahanshah* 'king of kings', traditional title of ancient Persian

---

Sfax /sfæks/ port in Tunisia, N Africa; population (1980) 500,000. It is the capital of Sfax district, on the Gulf of Gabès, and lies about 240 km/150 mi SE of Tunis. Industries include leather, soap, and carpets; there are also salt works and phosphate workings nearby. Exports include phosphates, olive oil, dates, almonds, esparto grass, and sponges. Sfax was occupied by the French in 1881.

Sforza /'sfɔːtsə/ Italian family which ruled the duchy of Milan 1450–99 and 1522–35. Their court was a centre of Renaissance culture, *Ludovico Sforza* (1451–1508) being famous as the patron of ◊Leonardo da Vinci.

's Gravenhage /s,xrɑːvən'hɑːxə/ Dutch name for The ◊Hague.

Shaanxi /,ʃɑːn'ʃiː/ province (formerly *Shensi*) of NW China.
area 195,800 sq km/75,580 sq mi
capital Zian
features mountains; Huang He valley, one of the earliest settled areas of China
products iron and steel
population (1982) 28,904,400, including many Muslims.

Shaba /'ʃɑːbə/ formerly Katanga, a province of ◊Zaïre.

Shache /,ʃɑːtʃeɪ/ alternative name for ◊Yarkand, a city in China.

Shackleton /'ʃækəltən/ Ernest 1874–1922. British Antarctic explorer. Born in County Kildare, Republic of Ireland, he was a member of ◊Scott's Antarctic expedition of 1901–04. In 1907–09 he commanded an expedition which reached 88°,23' S latitude, located the south magnetic pole and climbed Mount ◊Erebus. He next commanded the expedition of 1914–16, when he had to abandon his ship, the *Endurance*, in the ice of the Weddell Sea. He died on board the *Quest* on another expedition 1921–22 to the Antarctic.

shad marine fish of the herring family. *Alosa alosa*, the allis, and *Alosa fallax*, the twaite, are NE Atlantic species; they enter rivers to breed.

Shadow Cabinet the chief members of the British parliamentary opposition. By commenting on the policies and performance of government ministries, they effectively form a parallel or 'shadow' cabinet.

Shadwell /'ʃædwəl/ Thomas 1642–1692. English dramatist and poet. His plays include *Epsom-Wells* 1672 and *Bury-Fair* 1689. He was involved in a violent feud with the poet ◊Dryden whom he attacked in 'The Medal of John Bayes' 1682, and succeeded as Poet Laureate.

SHAEF (*S*upreme *H*eadquarters *A*llied *E*xpeditionary *F*orce) established on 15 Feb 1944, at Norfolk House, St James's Square, London. It was transferred in Mar 1944 to Bushy Park, near Kingston-upon-Thames, where final plans for the Allied invasion of Europe (under US general ◊Eisenhower) were worked out.

Shaffer /'ʃæfə/ Peter 1926– . British playwright. His plays include *The Royal Hunt of the Sun* 1964, *Equus* 1973, which portrays an

Shackleton The British explorer Sir Ernest Shackleton led the Antarctic expedition of 1914–16 in the *Endurance*, seen here, crushed in the ice.

rulers, and also of those of the recent ◊Pahlavi dynasty in Iran.

Shah-Jehan /'ʃɑː dʒə'hɑːn/ 1592–1666. ◊Mogul emperor of India from 1627, when he succeeded his father Jehangir. He conquered the ◊Deccan, but was not so fortunate in his campaigns against the Persians. From 1658 he was a prisoner of his son ◊Aurungzebe. He built the Taj Mahal (◊Agra).

Shahn /ʃɑːn/ Ben 1898–1969. American artist. Born in Lithuania, he was taken to the USA as a child. His work shows a concern for social issues, for example his series on ◊Dreyfus, ◊Sacco and Vanzetti, and ◊Prohibition.

Shaka /'ʃɑːgə/ 1787–1828. Zulu leader, responsible for the formation of the Zulu nation. The illegitimate son of a minor Zulu chief, he seized power from his half brother 1816, and then embarked on a campaign to unite the Nguni (the area which today forms the South African province of Natal), initiating the period of warfare known as the ◊Mfecane; his success was the result of almost permanent mobilization and constant fighting. Extremely ambitious, he later became autocratic; he was murdered by his half-brothers.

Shaker popular name for a member of the Christian sect of the United Society of Believers in Christ's Second Appearing. This was founded by James and Jane Wardley in England about 1747, and taken to North America in 1774 by Ann Lee (1736–84), the wife of a Manchester blacksmith. The name was applied because of their ecstatic shakings in worship. They anticipated modern spiritualist beliefs, but their doctrine of celibacy led to their virtual extinction.

Shakespeare /'ʃeɪkspɪə/ William 1564–1616. English dramatist and poet,

Shakespeare The title page engraving by M Droeshout for the First Folio of Shakespeare's plays. Published in 1623, seven years after his death, it is one of only two images of Shakespeare with any strong claim to authenticity.

considered the greatest English playwright. Born at Stratford-on-Avon, the son of a wool-dealer, he was educated at the grammar school, and in 1582 married Anne ◊Hathaway. They had a daughter, Susanna, in 1583, and twins Hamnet (died 1596) and Judith in 1595. Having joined a company of players, he was by 1589 established in London as an actor and a playwright. Early plays, written around 1589–93, were the tragedy *Titus Andronicus*; the comedies *The Comedy of Errors*, *The Taming of the Shrew*, and *Two Gentlemen of Verona*; the three parts of *Henry VI*; and *Richard III*. About 1593 he came under

the patronage of the Earl of ◊Southampton, to whom he dedicated his long poems *Venus and Adonis* 1593 and *The Rape of Lucrece* 1594; he also wrote for him the comedy *Love's Labour's Lost*, satirizing ◊Raleigh's circle, and seems to have dedicated to him his sonnets written around 1593–96, in which the mysterious 'Dark Lady' appears. From 1594 Shakespeare was a member of the Chamberlain's (later the King's) company of players, and had no rival as a dramatist, for example, the lyric plays *Romeo and Juliet*, *Midsummer Night's Dream*, and *Richard II* 1594–95, followed by *King John* and *The Merchant of Venice* in 1596. The Falstaff plays of 1597–99: *Henry IV* (parts I and II), *Henry V*, and *The Merry Wives of Windsor* (said to have been written at the request of Elizabeth I), brought his fame to its height. About the same time he wrote *Julius Caesar* 1599. The period ended with the lyrically witty *Much Ado about Nothing*, *As You Like It*, and *Twelfth Night* about 1598–1601. With *Hamlet* begins the period of the great tragedies, 1601–08: *Othello*, *Macbeth*, *King Lear*, *Timon of Athens*, *Antony and Cleopatra*, and *Coriolanus*. This 'darker' period is also reflected in the comedies *Troilus and Cressida*, *All's Well that Ends Well*, and *Measure for Measure* around 1601–04. It is thought that Shakespeare was only part author of *Pericles*, which with the other plays of around 1608–11, *Cymbeline*, *The Winter's Tale*, and *The Tempest*, form the mature romance or 'reconciliation' plays of the end of his career. During 1613 it is thought that Shakespeare collaborated with Fletcher in *Henry VIII* and *Two Noble Kinsmen*. He had already retired to Stratford in about 1610, where he died on 23 Apr 1616. For the first 200 years after his death, Shakespeare's plays were frequently performed in cut or revised form (Nahum Tate's *King Lear* was given a happy ending), and it was not until the 19th century, with the critical assessment of ◊Coleridge and ◊Hazlitt, that the original texts were restored.

Shakhty /'ʃæxti/ town in the Russian Soviet Federal Socialist Republic, 80 km/50 mi NE of Rostov; population (1981) 214,000. Industries include anthracite mining, stone quarrying, textiles, leather, and metal goods.

shale a fine-grained black ◊sedimentary rock which splits into thin beds. It can be thought of as consolidated mud, and differs from mudstone in that the latter splits into flakes rather than thin beds.

shallot type of onion *Allium cepa* in which bulbs multiply freely, used for cooking and in pickles.

Shalmaneser /ˌʃælmə'niːzə/ five Assyrian kings including: *Shalmaneser III*, reigned 859–824 BC, who pursued an aggressive policy, and brought Babylon and Israel under the domination of Assyria.

Shamanism name (possibly derived from the Hindustani *shaman*, an idolater) applied to the religious beliefs and practices of the aboriginal tribes of northern Asia, and by extension other similar systems, especially among the North American Indians. The outstanding figure is the *shaman*, or medicine-man, a seer and sorcerer,

SHAKESPEARE: THE PLAYS

Title	Well known characters	Written	Performed	Printed/ First Authority*
Early Plays				
Henry VI Part I	Hal, Talbot, Joan	1594	1589–92	1623 *ff*
Henry VI Part II	Hal, Margaret	1590–91	1589–92	1623 *ff*
Henry VI Part III	Hal, Margaret	1590–91	1589–92	1623 *ff*
The Comedy of Errors	Adriana, Dromio, Antipholus	1591	1592–93	1623 *ff*
Titus Andronicus	Titus Andronicus, Aaron, Lavinia	1589	1593–94	1594 *fq*
The Two Gentlemen of Verona	Proteus, Julia	1590	1594–95	1623 *ff*
The Taming of the Shrew	Petruchio, Katharina, Sly	1590	1593–94	1623 *ff*
Love's Labour's Lost	Armado, Berowne	1588	1594–95	1598 *fq*
Romeo and Juliet	Romeo & Juliet, Mercutio, the Nurse	1591–96	1594–95	1599 *sq*
Histories				
Richard III	Richard, Margaret	1592–93	1592–93	1597 *fq*
Richard II	Richard, Bolingbroke	1597	1593–96	1597 *fq*
Henry IV Part I	Falstaff, Hotspur, Hal	1596	1597–98	1598 *fq*
Henry IV Part II	Falstaff, Hotspur, Hal	1597	1597–98	1600 *fq*
King John	King John, the Bastard, Constance	1590–91	1596–97	1623 *ff*
Henry V	Henry V (*formerly Hal*), Pistol, Nym	1599	1599	1623 *ff*
Roman Plays				
Julius Caesar	Caesar, Brutus, Antony	1599	1599–1600	1599 *ff*
Antony and Cleopatra	Antony, Cleopatra, Enobarbus	1607–08	1607–08	1623 *ff*
Coriolanus	Coriolanus, Volumnia	1607–08	1607–08	1623 *ff*
The 'Great' or 'Middle' Comedies				
The Merry Wives of Windsor	Falstaff, Mistress Quickly	1597	1600–01	1623 *ff*
Much Ado About Nothing	Claudio, Hero, Dogberry, Verges	1598	1598–99	1600 *fq*
The Merchant of Venice	Shylock, Portia	1596–98	1596–97	1600 *fq*
As You Like It	Rosalind, Orlando, Touchstone	1599	1599–1600	1600 *fq*
Twelfth Night	Orsino, Viola, Feste, Sir Andrew Aguecheek	1600–02	1601–02	1623 *ff*
A Midsummer Night's Dream	Puck, Bottom, Titania, Oberon	1595	1595–96	1600 *fq*
The Great Tragedies				
Hamlet	Hamlet, Ophelia, Rosencrantz & Guildenstern, Polonius	1600–01	1600–01	1604 *sq*
Othello	Othello, Desdemona, Iago	1604	1604–05	1622 *fq*
King Lear	Lear, the Fool, Cordelia, Edgar/Poor Tom, Kent	1605–06	1605–06	1608 *fq*
Macbeth	Macbeth & Lady Macbeth, Banquo & his ghost, the three witches	1605–06	1605–06	1623 *ff*
Timon of Athens	Timon of Athens	1605–09	1607–08	1623 *ff*
The 'Dark' Comedies				
Troilus and Cressida	Troilus, Cressida	1601–02	1601–02	1609 *ff*
All's Well That Ends Well	Parolles, Helena, Bertram	1602–03	1602–03	1602–03 *ff*
Measure For Measure	Isabella, Angelo, Vincentio	?	1604–05	1604 *ff*
Late Plays				
Pericles	Pericles, Marina	1607–08	1608–09	1609 *fq*
Cymbeline	Imogen, Iachimo	1609–10	1609–10	1623 *ff*
The Winter's Tale	Perdita, Florizel, Autolycus	1610–11	1610–11	1623 *ff*
The Tempest	Prospero, Miranda, Ferdinand, Caliban	1611	1611–12	1623 *ff*
Henry VIII	Henry VIII, Katherine, Wolsey	1613	1612–13	1623 *ff*

* *ff* = *First Folio*   *fq* = *First Quarto*   *sq* = *Second Quarto*

who is believed to make contact with spirits of good and evil.

Shamir /ʃæ'mɪə/ Yitzhak 1915– . Polish-born Israeli statesman. A leader of the ◊Stern Gang terrorists during the British Mandate in Palestine, he was foreign minister under Prime Minister Menachem ◊Begin 1980–83, prime minister 1983–84, and again foreign minister in the ◊Peres unity government from 1984. In Oct 1986, he and Peres exchanged positions, Shamir

becoming prime minister and Peres taking over as foreign minister.

shamrock name given to several trifoliate plants of family Leguminosae. One is said to have been used by St Patrick to illustrate the doctrine of the Holy Trinity, and it was made the national badge of Ireland.

Shamyl /ʃə'mɪl/ c. 1797–1871. Caucasian soldier. He led the tribesmen of ◊Dagestan in a fight for independence from Russia from 1834

until he was taken in 1859, when the Russians were able to deploy greater forces after the Crimean War.

Shan a member of a people of the mountainous borderlands between Thailand, Burma, and China. The Shans are akin to the Laos and the Thais.

The 41 **Shan States** in N Burma, area 149,740 sq km/57,815 sq mi, were annexed by Britain in 1885, and are now part of the Burmese Union.

Shandong /ˌʃæn'dʌŋ/ province (formerly *Shantung*) of NE China.
area 153,300 sq km/59,170 sq mi
capital Jinan
towns ports Yantai, Weihai, Qingdao, Shigiusuo
features crossed by the Huang He river and the ◊Grand Canal; Shandong Peninsula
products cereals, cotton; wild silk; varied minerals
population (1982) 74,419,000.

Shanghai /ˌʃæn'haɪ/ port on the Huang-pu river, Jiangsu province, China, 24 km/15 mi from the Chang Jiang estuary; area 5,800 km/2,240 sq mi; population (1982) 11,859,748; the largest city in China. Industries include textiles, paper, chemicals, steel, agricultural machinery, precision instruments; shipbuilding, flour and vegetable-oil milling, and oil refining. It handles about 50 per cent of China's imports and exports. Famous buildings include the Jade Buddha Temple 1882; the former home of the revolutionary ◊Sun Yat-sen; the house where the First National Congress of the Communist Party of China met secretly in 1921; and the house, museum, and tomb of the writer ◊Lu Xun.
history A city from 1360, it became important only after 1842, when the treaty of Nanking opened it to foreign trade. The international settlement then developed, which remained the commercial centre of the city after the departure of European interests 1943–46.

Shankar /'ʃæŋkɑː/ Ravi 1920– . Indian composer and musician. A virtuoso of the ◊sitar, he has composed film music and founded music schools in Bombay and Los Angeles.

Shannon /'ʃænən/ longest river in Ireland, rising in County Cavan and flowing 260 km/161 mi through Loughs Allen and Ree and past Athlone, to reach the Atlantic through a wide estuary below Limerick. It is famous for salmon, and is also the major source of electric power in the republic, with hydroelectric installations at and above Ardnacrusha, 5 km/3 mi N of Limerick.

Shansi /ˌʃæn'siː/ former name for the Chinese province of ◊Shanxi.

Shantou /ˌʃæn'taʊ/ port and industrial city (formerly *Swatow*) in SE China, population (1970) 400,000. It was opened as a special foreign trade area in 1979.

Shantung /ˌʃæn'tʌŋ/ former name for the Chinese province of ◊Shandong.

Shanxi /ˌʃæn'ʃiː/ province (formerly *Shansi*) of NE China.
area 157,100 sq km/60,640 sq mi
capital Taiyuan
features a drought-ridden plateau, partly surrounded by the ◊Great Wall; the province saw the outbreak of the Boxer Rising
products coal and iron
population (1982) 25,291,400.

Shaoshan /ˌʃaʊ'ʃæn/ the birthplace in the Chinese province of ◊Hunan of former Chinese Communist leader ◊Mao Zedong.

SHAPE acronym for Supreme Headquarters Allied Powers in Europe, the headquarters of ◊NATO. Originally at Fontainebleau, it was moved to its present home in Brussels in 1966.

Shapiro /ʃə'pɪərəʊ/ Karl 1913– . American poet. He was born in Baltimore, and his work includes the striking *V Letter* 1945, written after service in World War II.

Shapley /'ʃæpli/ Harlow 1885–1972. US astronomer, who measured the size of our ◊galaxy and defined the Sun's place in it. Born in Nashville, Tennessee, Shapley joined the Mount Wilson Observatory, California in 1914 where he studied ◊globular clusters of stars. He found that these were arranged in a halo around our galaxy, but that the Sun was not at the centre, as was then assumed. Instead, the Sun was shown to be about two-thirds of the way to the galaxy's rim.

share in finance, that part of the capital of a company held by a member (shareholder). Shares may be numbered and are issued as units of definite face value; shareholders are not always called on to pay the full face value of their shares, though they bind themselves to do so. Preference shares carry a fixed rate of dividend and have first claim on the profits of the company; ordinary shares have second claim, and if profits have been good may attract a higher dividend than the preference shares; deferred shares rank for dividend only after the rights of preference and ordinary shareholders have been satisfied. Fully paid-up shares can be converted by the company into ◊stock.

Shari'a the law of ◊Islam.

Sharjah /'ʃɑːdʒə/ one of the ◊United Arab Emirates; situated on the Arabian Gulf NE of Dubai; population (1980) 184,000. Since 1952 it has included the small state of Kalba. In 1974 oil was discovered offshore.

shark name given to the bigger members of the Pleurotremata, a large group of marine fish with cartilaginous skeletons. Worldwide in distribution, they include the 'maneater' *white shark Carcharodon carcharias* of tropical waters, which reaches about 12 m/40 ft, the *basking shark Cetorhinus maximus* of temperate seas, found off Britain, which reaches a similar size, but eats only marine organisms, and the equally harmless *whale shark Rhinocodon typus* which at 18 m/60 ft is the largest living fish. Superbly designed as hunters, sharks have high-speed manoeuvrability. Their eyes, though lacking acuity of vision or sense of colour, are highly sensitive to light; sounds or movements made by their prey are picked up at long distances; their sense of smell is so acute that one-third of the brain is given up to interpreting its signals and the slightest trace of blood in water will attract them. Relatively few attacks on humans are pursued to a fatal conclusion, and research suggests that they are not in search of food, but attempting to repel 'rivals' from their territory. Game fishing for 'sport', the eradication of sharks in swimming and recreation areas, and their industrial exploitation as a source of leather, oil and protein have reduced their numbers.

Sharon /'ʃeərən/ coastal plain in ◊Israel.

Sharp /ʃɑːp/ Cecil (James) 1859–1924. British collector and compiler of folk dance and song. Born in London, he travelled the country to record and save from extinction the folk-song tradition, for example *English Folk Song* 1907 (two volumes). When in the USA he tracked down survivals of English song in the Appalachian Mountains and elsewhere. Cecil Sharp House, the headquarters in London of the English Folk Dance and Song Society, commemorates his work.

Sharp /ʃɑːp/ Granville 1735–1813. British philanthropist, born in Durham. He was prominent in the anti-slavery movement, and in 1772 secured a legal decision 'that as soon as any slave sets foot on English territory he becomes free'.

Sharpeville /'ʃɑːpvɪl/ black township, 65 km/40 mi S of Johannesburg and N of Vereeniging, ◊South Africa. During a campaign launched by the Pan Africanist Congress against the ◊pass laws, 69 black people were killed when police fired on a crowd of between 5,000 and 20,000 demonstrators on 21 Mar 1960. On the anniversary in 1985, during funerals of black protesters against unemployment who had been killed, some 19 black people were shot by the police at Langa near Port Elizabeth.

Shastri /'ʃæstri/ Lal Bahadur 1904–1966. Indian politician. Several times imprisoned for civil disobedience before independence, he later held various ministerial posts, and in 1964 succeeded ◊Nehru as prime minister. He died of a heart attack in Tashkent after the signing of a peace agreement with Pakistan. Small of stature, he was known as 'the Sparrow'.

Shatt-al-Arab /'ʃæt æl 'ærəb/ 'river of Arabia', the waterway formed by the confluence of the ◊Euphrates and ◊Tigris; length 190 km/120 mi to the Arabian Gulf. Basra, Khorramshar and Abadan stand on it, and its lower reaches form a border of disputed demarcation between Iran and Iraq. In 1975 the two countries agreed on the deepest water line as the frontier, but Iraq repudiated this in 1980; the continuing dispute is a major factor in the ◊Iran-Iraq war.

Shaw /ʃɔː/ George Bernard 1856–1950. Irish dramatist. Born in Dublin, the son of a civil servant, he came to London in 1876, where he became a brilliant debater among the ◊Fabians. He worked as a music and drama critic, and wrote five unsuccessful novels. His support of the new realism in the theatre was illustrated by his *Quintessence of Ibsenism* 1891, and in 1892 his first play *Widowers' Houses* was produced. Attacking slum landlords, it showed his alliance with a new, essentially political and polemical movement in the theatre, aiming to engage the intellect rather than the emotions of his audience. *Widowers' Houses* was the first of the *Plays: Pleasant and Unpleasant* 1898, which included *The Philanderer*; *Mrs Warren's Profession*, dealing with prostitution and banned until 1902; and *Arms and the Man* – about war, *Candida*, *You Never Can Tell*, and *Man of Destiny*, a Napoleonic incident. The *Three Plays for Puritans* of 1901 contained the witty *Devil's*

Disciple; *Caesar and Cleopatra* (a companion piece to the play by Shakespeare, with whom he pursued a semi-comic rivalry); and *Captain Brassbound's Conversion*. The epic *Man and Superman* 1903, expanding his theme of Creative Evolution, was followed by *John Bull's Other Island* 1904, and *Major Barbara* 1905. *The Doctor's Dilemma* was published 1911. *Androcles and the Lion* was published in 1916 with the comedy *Pygmalion*, written for the actress Mrs Patrick ◊Campbell (converted to a musical as *My Fair Lady*). *Heartbreak House* 1917 deals with World War I and symbolizes the breakdown of European civilization, and in *Back to Methuselah* 1921 Shaw once more faced the problems of social evolution. Latest of his great dramas is *St Joan* 1924.

Shaw's theories were further elucidated in the voluminous prefaces to the plays, and in books such as *The Intelligent Woman's Guide to Socialism and Capitalism* 1928, and *Sixty Years of Fabianism* 1947.

Shaw /ʃɔː/ (Richard) Norman 1831–1912. British architect. His style was eclectic, using elements from vernacular and Georgian architecture rather than the Gothic and Tudor then popular. Major buildings include Swan House, Chelsea 1876.

Shchedrin /ʃtʃɪˈdriːn/ N. Pseudonym of Russian writer Mikhail Evgrafovich Saltykov 1826–1889. A uniquely pessimistic writer, he is remembered for his *Fables* 1884–85, in which Saltykov depicts misplaced 'good intentions', and for his novel *The Golovlevs* 1880, a family saga containing the famous character of the hypocrite Porfiry.

shearwater sea bird related to the petrels. The Manx shearwater *Puffinus puffinus* is the only species which breeds in Britain.

Sheba /ˈʃiːbə/ ancient name for modern South ◊Yemen (Sha'abijah). It was once famous for gold and spices. According to the Old Testament, its queen visited Solomon; the former Ethiopian royal house traced its descent from their union.

Shechem /ˈʃiːkem/ ancient town of Palestine, near Samaria. In the Old Testament, it is the traditional burial place of Joseph; nearby is Jacob's well. Shechem was destroyed about 67 AD by the Roman emperor Vespasian; on its site stands ◊Nablus (a corruption of Neapolis, built by Hadrian).

sheep genus *Ovis* of ruminant hoofed mammals of the family Bovidae. Wild species survive in the uplands of central Asia, and their domesticated descendants are reared worldwide for meat, wool, milk, and cheese (such as Parmesan and Roquefort), and for rotation on arable land to maintain its fertility. Among famous breeds are the Merino (thick, soft wool), Southdown (excellent for mutton), and Welsh mountain, a very agile, hardy breed.

sheepdog rough-coated, tailless breed of dog, formerly much used by shepherds, farmers, and drovers in southern England and in Wales. The Old English sheepdog is now mainly a show dog. In colour it is grey or blue-grey, with white markings, and it stands 56 cm/1.8 ft or more high.

Shaw A dramatist of ideas , George Bernard Shaw merged didacticism with entertainment in plays such as *Widowers' Houses* 1892 which attacks slum landlords, and *Mrs Warren's Profession* 1893 which deals with prostitution. His caricature is by Bernard Partridge, dated 1925.

Sheerness /ˌʃɪəˈnes/ seaport and resort on the Isle of ◊Sheppey, ◊Kent, England; population (1981) 11,250. Situated at the confluence of the Thames and Medway, it was originally a fortress in 1660, and was briefly held by the Dutch admiral de Ruyter in 1667. It was a royal dockyard until 1960.

Sheffield /ˈʃefiːld/ industrial city in South Yorkshire, England, 29 km/18 mi SW of Doncaster; population (1986) 538,700. From the 12th century, iron smelting was the chief industry, and by the 14th century Sheffield cutlery, silverware, and plate were famous. During the Industrial Revolution the iron and steel industries developed rapidly. It now produces alloys and special steels, cutlery of all kinds, permanent magnets, drills, and precision tools. The parish church of St Peter and St Paul (14th–15th centuries) is the cathedral of Sheffield bishopric established 1914. There are two art galleries; a theatre, The Crucible, 1971; there is also a university 1905, and a polytechnic 1969.

sheikh (Arabic 'old man') term used to describe the leader or chief of an Arab family or village.

Shelburne /ˈʃelbən/ William Petty FitzMaurice, 2nd Earl of Shelburne 1737–1805. British Whig politician. He was an opponent of George III's American policy. As prime minister in 1783, he concluded peace with the USA. He was created Marquess of Lansdowne in 1784.

shelduck duck *Tadorna tadorna* with dark green head and red bill and the rest of the plumage strikingly marked in black, white, and chestnut. Of widespread distribution in the Old World, it lays its eggs in rabbit burrows in sandy coasts, and is usually seen on estuary mudflats.

shelf sea the relatively shallow sea, usually no deeper than 200 m/650 ft, overlying the continental shelf around the coastlines. Most fishing and marine mineral exploitations are carried out in shelf seas.

shellac a resin derived from the ◊lac insect.

Shelley /ˈʃeli/ Mary Wollstonecraft 1797–1851. British writer, the daughter of Mary ◊Wollstonecraft and William ◊Godwin. She eloped in 1814 with the poet Percy Bysshe ◊Shelley, whom she married in 1816. In 1818 she published *Frankenstein*, a story of a scientist who created a man-monster and gave it life. She wrote other novels and edited her husband's works.

Shelley /ˈʃeli/ Percy Bysshe 1792–1822. British lyric poet, a leading figure in the ◊Romantic movement. Born in Sussex, he was educated at Eton and University College, Oxford, where his collaboration in a pamphlet *The Necessity of Atheism* 1811 caused his expulsion. While living in London he fell in love with 16-year-old Harriet Westbrook, whom he married in 1811. He visited Ireland and Wales writing pamphlets defending vegetarianism and political freedom, and in 1813 published privately *Queen Mab*, a poem with political freedom as its theme. Meanwhile he had become estranged from his wife and in 1814 left England with Mary Wollstonecraft Godwin, whom he married in 1816 after Harriet had drowned herself. *Alastor*, written in 1815, was followed by the epic *The Revolt of Islam*, and by 1818 Shelley was living in Italy. Here he produced the tragedy *The Cenci*; the satire on Wordsworth, *Peter Bell the Third* 1819; and the lyric drama *Prometheus Unbound* 1820. Other works of the period are 'Ode to the West Wind' 1819, 'The Cloud', and 'The Skylark', both 1820; 'The Sensitive Plant' and 'The Witch of Atlas'; 'Epipsychidion' and, on the death of the poet Keats, 'Adonais' 1821; the lyric drama *Hellas* 1822; and the prose *Defence of Poetry* 1821. In Jul 1822 Shelley was drowned while sailing near La Spezia, and his ashes were buried in Rome.

shellfish popular name for edible molluscs and crustaceans, including the whelk and periwinkle, mussel, oyster, lobster, crab, and shrimp.

shell-shock an obsolete name for various forms of mental disorder, also called combat neurosis, first identified in World War I soldiers exposed to heavy explosions or extreme ◊stress.

Shenandoah /ˌʃenənˈdəʊə/ river in ◊Virginia, USA, a tributary of the Potomac, which it joins

Shelley Expelled from Oxford at 19, Percy Bysshe Shelley eloped to Switzerland with Mary Wollstonecraft Godwin, and died by drowning before he was 30.

at Harper's Ferry. P H ▷Sheridan laid waste the Shenandoah valley in the American Civil War.

Shensi /ˌʃenˈsiː/ former name for the Chinese province of ▷Shaanxi.

Shenstone /ˈʃenstən/ William 1714–1763. British poet and essayist. His works include *Poems upon Various Occasions* 1737, the Spenserian *Schoolmistress* 1742, elegies, odes, songs, ballads, and levities.

Shenyang /ˌʃenˈjæŋ/ industrial city and capital of Liaoning province, China; population (1981) 2,905,000. It was the capital of the Manchu emperors 1644–1912, and their tombs are nearby. Historically known as Mukden, it was taken from Russian occupation by the Japanese in the Battle of Mukden 20 Feb–10 Mar 1905, and was again taken by the Japanese in 1931.

Shepard /ˈʃepəd/ E(rnest) (H)oward 1879–1976. British book illustrator, celebrated for his illustrations to books by A A ▷Milne (*Winnie-the-Pooh* 1926) and Kenneth ▷Grahame (*The Wind in the Willows* 1908).

Shepard /ˈʃepəd/ Sam 1943– . American dramatist and actor. His work is characterized by striking visual imagery and includes *The Tooth of Crime* 1972 about an ageing rock star, *Buried Child* 1978, for which he won the Pulitzer prize, *Seduced* 1979, based on the life of the recluse Howard Hughes, and *True West* 1980.

shepherd's purse annual plant *Capsella bursa-pastoris* of the Cruciferae family, interesting for its worldwide distribution in the temperate zones. It is a persistent weed with white flowers followed by heart-shaped seed pouches from which the name derives.

Sheppard /ˈʃepəd/ Jack 1702–1724. British criminal. Born in Stepney, he was an apprentice

Shepard Winnie-the-Pooh and Piglet in search of the Woozle; one of E H Shepard's illustrations to *Winnie-the-Pooh* 1926.

carpenter, but turned to theft and became a popular hero by four escapes from prison. He was finally caught and hanged.

Sheppey /ˈʃepi/ island off the N coast of ▷Kent, England; area 80 sq km/30 sq mi; population about 27,000. Situated at the mouth of the river Medway, it is linked with the mainland by Kingsferry road and rail bridge over the Swale, completed 1960. The resort and port of ▷Sheerness is on the Isle of Sheppey.

Sheraton /ˈʃerətən/ Thomas c. 1751–1806. English designer of elegant inlaid furniture, as in his *Cabinet-maker's and Upholsterer's Drawing Book* 1791. He was influenced by his predecessors ▷Hepplewhite and ▷Chippendale.

Sheridan /ˈʃerɪdən/ Philip Henry 1831–1888. American general of the ▷American Civil War. General (later President) ▷Grant gave him command of his cavalry in 1864, and soon after of the army of the Shenandoah Valley, which he cleared of Confederates and laid waste. In the final stage of the war, Sheridan forced General Lee's retreat to Appomattox, where he surrendered to Grant. See also ▷United States of America.

Sheridan /ˈʃerɪdən/ Richard Brinsley 1751–1816. Anglo-Irish dramatist. Born in Dublin, he was educated at Harrow School, and married Elizabeth Linley in 1773. He wrote his first social comedy *The Rivals*, celebrated for the character of Mrs Malaprop, in 1775, and in 1776 became lessee of the Drury Lane Theatre, where he produced *The School for Scandal* 1777 and *The Critic* 1779. In 1780 he entered Parliament as an adherent of ▷Fox, was a noted orator, directed the impeachment of the former governor-general of India, Warren Hastings, and was treasurer to the Navy 1806–07. His last years were clouded by financial ruin and mental breakdown.

sheriff (Old English *scīr* 'shire' + *gerēfa* 'reeve') in England and Wales, the Crown's chief executive officer in a county for ceremonial purposes. In Scotland, the equivalent of the English county court judge; and in the USA the popularly elected head law-enforcement officer of a county, combining judicial authority with administrative duties. In England, the office (elective until Edward II) dates from before the Norman Conquest. The sheriff, who is appointed annually by royal patent, and is chosen from the leading landowners, acts as returning officer for parliamentary elections, and attends the judges on circuit. The duties of keeping prisoners in safe custody, preparing panels of jurors for assizes, and executing writs, are supervised by the under-sheriff.

Sherman /ˈʃɜːmən/ William Tecumseh 1820–1891. American Union general. Born in Ohio, he received a command in the Federal army on the Mississippi front early in the American ▷Civil War, and collaborated with General ▷Grant in the Vicksburg campaign. In 1864 he captured Atlanta, from where he marched to the sea, laying Georgia waste, and then drove the Confederates northwards.

Sherpa /ˈʃɜːpə/ member of a people in NE Nepal of Mongolian origin, famous for their ▷mountaineering skill and traditionally employed as porters on Himalayan expeditions. A Sherpa, Norgay Tensing, was one of the two men to conquer Mount Everest for the first time.

Sherriff /ˈʃerɪf/ R(obert) C(edric) 1896–1975. British dramatist, remembered for his anti-heroic war play *Journey's End* 1929. Later plays include *Badger's Green* 1930, and *Home at Seven* 1950.

Sherrington /ˈʃerɪŋtən/ Charles Scott 1857–1952. British physiologist. His *The Integrative Action of the Nervous System* 1906 formulated the principles of reflex action. He received the Order of Merit 1924, and a Nobel prize (with ▷Adrian) 1932.

's Hertogenbosch /seəˌtɔːxənˈbɒs/ (French *Bois-le-Duc*) capital of North Brabant, Netherlands, on the river Meuse, 45 km/28 mi SE of Utrecht; population (1985) 89,600. It has a Gothic cathedral, and was the birthplace of painter Hieronymus Bosch.

Sherwood /ˈʃɜːwʊd/ Robert 1896–1955. American dramatist. His plays include *The Petrified Forest* 1934 (Humphrey ▷Bogart starred in the film), *Idiot's Delight* 1936, *Abe Lincoln in Illinois* 1938 and *There Shall Be No Night* 1940.

Sherwood Forest /ˈʃɜːwʊd/ a hilly stretch of parkland in W Nottinghamshire, England, area about 520 sq km/200 sq mi. Formerly a royal forest, it is associated with the legendary ▷Robin Hood.

Shetland /ˈʃetlənd/ islands off N coast of Scotland.
area 1,429 sq km/552 sq mi
towns administrative headquarters Lerwick, on Mainland, largest of 19 inhabited islands
features comprise over 100 islands; Muckle Flugga (60°,51'N latitude) is the most northerly of the British Isles

products Europe's largest oil port is Sullom Voe, Mainland; processed fish, handknits from Fair Isle and Unst; miniature ponies

population (1981) 27,300; the dialect is derived from Norse, the islands having been under Scandinavian rule 875–1468.

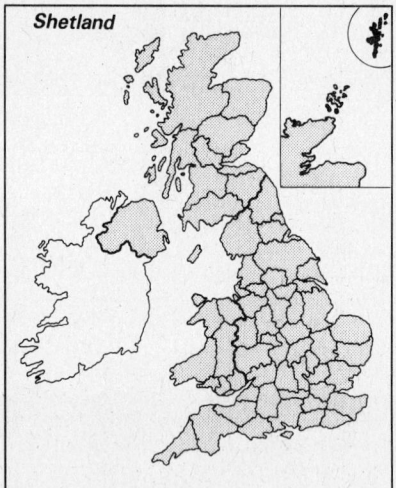

Shetland

Shevardnadze /ˌʃevəd'nɑːdzə/ Edvard 1928– . Soviet politician. A supporter of ◊Gorbachev, he was first secretary of the Georgian Communist Party from 1972, and an advocate of economic reform. He was Foreign minister from 1985.

Shiah/Shi'ite one of the two main sects of ◊Islam. See ◊Shi'ite.

shield in geology, another name for ◊craton, the ancient core of a continent.

shield any material used to reduce the amount of radiation (electrostatic, electromagnetic, heat, nuclear) reaching from one region of space to another, or any material used as a protection against falling debris, as in ◊tunnelling. Electrical conductors are used for electrostatic shields, soft iron for electromagnetic shields, and poor conductors of heat for heat shields. Heavy materials such as lead and concrete are used for protection against X-ray and nuclear radiation. See also ◊biological shield, ◊heat shield.

Shihchiachuang former name for the city of ◊Shijiazhuang in China.

Shih Huang Ti former name for the Chinese emperor ◊Shi Huangdi.

Shi Huangdi /'ʃiː ˌhwæŋ'diː/ 259–210 BC emperor of China. He succeeded to the throne of the state of Qin in 246 BC, and reunited the country as an empire by 228 BC. He burnt almost all existing books in 213 BC to destroy ties with the past; built the ◊Great Wall; and was buried in a magnificent tomb complex guarded by 10,000 individualized, life-size pottery warriors (still being excavated in the 1980s). He had so overextended his power that the dynasty and the empire collapsed at the death of his feeble successor in 207 BC.

Shi'ite /'ʃiːaɪt/ member of a Muslim sect prominent in Iran and the Lebanon who are doctrinally opposed to the Sunni Muslims or the successors of Muhammad; see ◊Islam.

Shijiazhuang /ˌʃiːˌdʒɪə'dʒwæŋ/ city (formerly *Shihchiachuang*), in Hebei province, China; population (1975) 960,000. Industries include textiles, chemicals, and light engineering.

Shikoku /ʃiː'kɒkuː/ one of the four main islands of Japan, S of Honshu, E of Kyushu; area 17,790 sq km/6,869 sq mi; population (1973) 4,750,000; chief town Matsuyama. It has a mild climate and annual rainfall in the S can reach 266 cm/105 in. The highest point is Mount Ishizuchi (1,980 m/6,497 ft). There are forests, and crops include rice, wheat, soya, sugar cane, and orchard fruits. Salt and copper are mined. A suspension bridge links Shikoku to Awajishima Island over the Naruto whirlpool in the ◊Seto Naikai (Inland Sea).

Shillelagh /ʃɪ'leɪlə/ village in county Wicklow, Republic of Ireland, which gave its name to a rough cudgel of oak or blackthorn.

Shillong /ʃɪ'lɒŋ/ capital of Meghalaya state, India; population (1981) 109,244.

Shimonoseki /ˌʃɪmənəʊ'seki/ seaport in the extreme SW of Honshu, Japan; population (1980) 269,000. It was opened to foreign trade in 1890. The first of the ◊Sino-Japanese Wars ended with a treaty signed at Shimonoseki in 1895.

shingles a virus disease of the ◊herpes group.

Shinkansen or 'New Trunk Line'; the superfast railway network operated by Japanese National Railways, on which the famous bullet trains run. The network, opened in 1964, uses specially built straight and level track, on which average speeds of 160 kph/100 mph are attained.

Shinto the Chinese transliteration of the Japanese Kami-no-Michi, the Way or Doctrine of the Gods, the indigenous religion of Japan. This mingles an empathetic oneness with natural forces and loyalty to the reigning dynasty as descendants of the Sun-goddess, Amaterasu-Omikami. State Shinto was the national faith of Japan; its holiest shrine is at Ise, near ◊Kyoto, where in the temple of the Sun-goddess is preserved the mirror that she is supposed to have given to Jimmu, the first emperor, in the 7th century BC. Sectarian Shinto consists of 130 sects, each founded by a historical character; the sects are officially recognized, but are not state-supported, as was State Shinto until its disestablishment by General ◊MacArthur's decree after World War II. Unquestioning obedience and devotion to the emperor is inculcated, but there is also an exemplary ethic. However, an aggressive nationalistic aspect was developed by the Meiji rulers. This was symbolized by the *Yasukuni* shrine, near Tokyo, since 1945 a purely religious memorial to 2.5 million war dead.

shinty a winter game popular in the Scottish Highlands. Played between teams of 12 players with sticks and a ball, it resembles hockey.

ship sea-going vessel of considerable size. The Greeks and Phoenicians built wooden ships, propelled by oar or sail. The Romans and Carthaginians fought in galleys equipped with rams and rowed by tiers of oarsmen. The oaken ships of the Norsemen were built for rough seas and propelled by oars and sail. The fleet of Richard Coeur de Lion was largely of sail. The invention of the compass in the 14th century led to a great age of exploration by sailing ship, resulting in the discovery of 'new worlds'. The 15th century saw the beginnings of Britain's Royal Navy; Henry VIII built the *Great Harry*, the first double-decked English warship. In the 16th century ships were short and high-sterned, and despite Pett's three-decker in the 17th century, English ships did not bear comparison with the Spanish and Dutch until the era of Sir Robert Seppings, a shipbuilding pioneer in the early 19th century. In the 1840s iron began replacing wood in shipbuilding, ◊Brunel's *Great Britain* 1845 being the pioneering vessel. The ultimate in sailing ships appeared at much the same time. These were the fast tea clippers. America and Britain experimented with steam propulsion as the 19th century opened. The paddle-wheel propelled *Comet* appeared in 1812, the Canadian *Royal William* crossed the Atlantic in 1833, and the English *Great Western* steamed from Bristol to New York in 1838. Pettit Smith applied the screw to the *Archimedes* in 1839, and after 1850 the paddle-wheel became obsolete. The introduction of the compound engine and turbine, the latter in 1902, completed the revolution in propulsion until the advent of nuclear-powered vessels after World War II, chiefly submarines. More recently ◊hovercraft and ◊hydrofoil boats have been developed for specialized purposes, particularly for short-distance ferries.

ship money tax for support of the navy, levied on the coastal districts of England in the Middle Ages. Charles I's attempts to levy it on the whole country in 1634–36, without parliamentary consent and in time of peace, aroused strong opposition from the MP J Hampden and others, who refused to pay. Ship money was declared illegal by Parliament in 1641.

Shiraz /ʃɪə'ræz/ ancient walled city of S Iran, the capital of Fars province; population (1982) 300,000. It is noted for wines, carpets, and silverwork, and for its many beautiful mosques.

Shiré Highlands /'ʃɪəreɪ/ an upland area of ◊Malawi.

Shizuoka /ˌʃiːzu'əʊkə/ town on Honshu, Japan; population (1983) 461,000. Industries include metal and food processing, and especially tea.

Shkodër /'ʃkəʊdə/ town (Italian *Scutari*) on the Bojana, Albania; SE of Lake Shkodër, 19 km/12 mi from the Adriatic; population (1980) 66,500. Industries include woollens and cement.

shock circulatory failure or sudden fall of blood pressure, resulting in pallor, sweating, faster (but weak) pulse rate, and possibly complete collapse, caused by a heart attack, burns, loss of blood, intense fear, and so on. Also the results of injury from electric shock. The blood-vessels dilate and the pressure falls below that necessary to supply the tissues of the body, especially the vital nerve-centres of the brain. Treatment is by drugs, rest, and, in the case of blood loss, by restoration of the normal circulating volume.

shock absorber the popular, though incorrect name for a ◊damper.

Shockley /'ʃɒkli/ William 1910– . American physicist who worked with ▷Bardeen and ▷Brattain on the invention of the ▷transistor. He was jointly awarded a Nobel prize with them in 1956.

shoebill or **whale-headed stork**, African bird *Balaeniceps rex* living in the papyrus swamps of the Sudan. Grey, up to 3.3 m/4 ft tall, it has a large wide beak 20 cm/8 in long, with which it scoops large fish out of the mud.

shogun formerly, the hereditary commander-in-chief of the Japanese army. Though nominally subject to the emperor, he was the real ruler of Japan from 1192 to 1867, when the emperor reassumed power.

Sholapur /ˌʃəʊləˈpʊə/ town in Maharashtra state, India; population (1981) 514,860. Industries include textiles, leather goods, and chemicals.

Sholokhov /'ʃɒləkɒf, Russian 'ʃɒləxɒf/ Mikhail Aleksandrovich 1905–1984. Russian novelist. His *And Quiet Flows the Don* 1926–40, telling of the Don Cossacks, is alleged by the Russian writer ▷Solzhenitsyn to have been written by Fyodor Kryukov (1870–1920), whose manuscript was appropriated.

shoot in botany, a general term for parts of a vascular plant growing above ground, comprising a stem bearing leaves, buds, and flowers. The shoot develops from the ▷plumule of the embryo.

shop a building for the retail sale of goods. Until the later 19th century, shop development had been almost static since ancient times, but with the growth of manufactured goods and the concentration of population in big towns came the development of the department store, in effect a number of small specialist shops under one roof, and of the chain store. This took the form of many shops scattered in different towns or counties, able to buy wholesale in such quantities that prices could be lowered below those of smaller competitors. As a development of wholesale purchase came direct links with factories producing goods, often under the same ownership, which further cut costs, and even the elimination of the shop itself by direct mail or mail ▷order.

Self-service, originated many years earlier in the USA by Clarence ▷Saunders, developed rapidly after World War II as a result of staff shortages, and in particular in supermarkets for groceries and hypermarkets outside towns with a very wide range of goods. In the 1970s there developed in the USA the 'controlled shopping environment' of an air-conditioned enclosed mall of up to 250 shops in carpeted arcades, often on several levels, with music, free parking, cinemas, restaurants, and childcare facilities, for example, Woodfield Mall, Chicago. The idea was adopted in the UK and elsewhere.

Gradually being introduced are direct debit from a customer's bank account by use of a plastic card inserted in a computer terminal at the point of sale, and laser check-outs, which automatically 'read' a line-pattern on the packaging of the goods and deliver an itemized bill to the customer, as well as recording for the store the deduction of the item from shelf stock.

Shostakovich Russian composer Dmitry Shostakovich pictured in his study in 1954. Despite his commitment to the ideology of Soviet society and use of political themes in much of his music, he had a turbulent relationship with officialdom throughout his career.

shop steward trade union representative in a 'shop' or department of a factory, who recruits for the union, inspects contribution cards, and reports grievances to the district committee. This form of organization originated in the engineering industry and has spread to all large industrial undertakings.

shorthand any system of rapid writing, such as the abbreviations practised by the Greeks and Romans. The earliest shorthand system to be based on the alphabet was that of John Willis published 1603. Later alphabetic systems were devised by Thomas Shelton in 1630 (used by the diarist ▷Pepys) and Thomas Burney in 1750, used by Charles ▷Dickens as a reporter. The first perfecter of an entirely phonetic system was Isaac ▷Pitman, by which system speeds of about 300 words a minute are said to be attainable. *Stenotype machines*, using selective keyboards enabling several word contractions to be printed at a time, are equally speedy and accurate. The abbreviations used can be transferred by the operator to a television screen, where they enable the deaf to follow the spoken word.

Short Parliament an English parliament that met briefly in 1640. Charles I summoned it on Apr 13 to raise funds for his war against the Scots, but when it became clear that the parliament was opposed to the war and would not grant him any money, he dissolved it on May 5. It was succeeded later in the year by the even more intransigent ▷Long Parliament.

short story a short work of prose fiction, which in general either sets up and resolves a single narrative point or sets up and leaves hanging a mood or an atmosphere. Various lengths of short narrative fiction were used before, and as alternatives to, the novel, and many writers of the 19th century wrote occasional short stories, but the form achieved real significance in the hands of Chekhov, Kipling, de Maupassant, and Katherine Mansfield.

Shostakovich /ˌʃɒstəˈkəʊvɪtʃ/ Dmitry (Dmitriyevich) 1906–1975. Russian composer, born in Leningrad (formerly St Petersburg). His music is tonal and expressive, and sometimes highly dramatic. It has not always been to official Soviet taste; of his 15 symphonies, the fifth is subtitled *'A Soviet Artist's Reply to Just Criticism'* 1937, while the patriotic seventh or *Leningrad* 1942 marked a temporary return to favour. He also wrote chamber music, ballets and operas, the latter including *Lady Macbeth of Mtsensk* 1934, suppressed as 'too divorced from the proletariat', but revived in 1963 as *Katerina Izmaylova*.

shot a ▷throwing event in athletics. See ▷putting the shot.

shoveler fresh-water duck *Anas clypeata*, so named from its long and broad flattened beak. The male has a green head and white and brown body plumage, the female is speckled brown. Spending the summer in northern Europe or America, it winters further south.

Shovell /'ʃʌvəl/ Cloudesley c. 1650–1707. English admiral. He took part (with ▷Rooke) in the capture of Gibraltar in 1704. In 1707 his flagship *Association* and four other ships of his home-bound fleet were lost off the Isles of Scilly. He was strangled for his rings by an islander when he came ashore.

show trial public and well-reported trials of people usually accused of crimes against the state. The most famous examples are of the Show Trials carried out during the 1930s and 1940s in the USSR by Stalin against economic saboteurs, communist party members, army officers and even members of the Bolshevik leadership.

Shrapnel /ˈʃræpnəl/ Henry 1761–1842. British army officer who invented shells containing bullets, to increase the spread of casualties, first used 1804. The word shrapnel remains in use for shell fragments.

Shreveport /ˈʃriːvpɔːt/ river port in Louisiana, USA; population (1980) 205,800. Industries include oil and natural gas, steel, telephone equipment, glass, and timber. It was founded 1836, and named after Henry Shreeve, a riverboat captain who cleared a giant log jam.

shrew insectivorous mammal of the family Soricidae, mouse-like but with a long nose and pointed teeth, and renowned for its insatiable appetite. The *common shrew Sorex araneus* is about 7.5 cm/3 in long. The *pigmy shrew Sorex minutus* is only about 50 cm/2 in long.

Shrewsbury, Earl of /ˈʃrəʊzbəri/ title in the peerage of England, held by the family of Talbot since 1442. It is the premier earldom of England.

Shrewsbury /ˈʃrəʊzbəri/ city on the river Severn, Shropshire, England; population (1985) 87,300. It is the administrative headquarters of the county. To the E is the site of the Roman city of Uriconium (larger than Pompeii). In the 5th century, as Pengwern, Shrewsbury was capital of the kingdom of Powis, which later became part of Mercia. In the battle of Shrewsbury 1403, Henry IV defeated the rebels led by Hotspur (Sir Henry ◊Percy).

shrike 'butcher-bird' of the family Laniidae, of which there are some 70 species, most African. A European species is the *great grey shrike Lanius excubitor*, which impales its prey (mainly insects, but also frogs, small mammals and reptiles) on thorns to form a 'larder'.

shrimp a small crustacean related to the ◊prawn. In Europe the *common shrimp Crangon vulgaris* is commercially valuable; it is greenish, semi-transparent, has its first pair of legs ending in pincers, possesses no rostrum (the beaklike structure which extends forward from the head in some crustaceans), and has comparatively shorter antennae than the prawn.

Shropshire /ˈʃrɒpʃə/ county in W England
area 3,490 sq km/1,348 sq mi
towns administrative headquarters Shrewsbury
features on the Welsh border, it is bisected NW to SE by the Severn; the name is sometimes abbreviated to *Salop*, and was officially so known from 1974 until local protest reversed the decision; the Clee Hills rise to about 610 m/1,800 ft in the SW; Ironbridge Gorge open-air museum of industrial archaeology includes the Iron Bridge 1779.
products chiefly agricultural, sheep and cattle being reared
population (1986) 390,000.

Shrove Tuesday the day before Ash Wednesday, the beginning of Lent in the Christian calendar, from *shrive* ('to confess one's

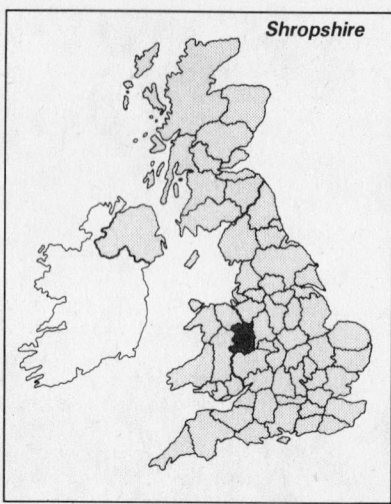

Shropshire

sins') that is, the time for confession before ◊Lent. It is also known as *Mardi Gras* and, in England, *Pancake Tuesday*, for the custom of eating up of rich things before the Lenten fast.

shrub a perennial, woody plant that typically produces several separate stems, at or near ground level, rather than the single trunk of most trees. A shrub is usually smaller than a tree, but there is no sharp division between large shrubs and small trees.

Shultz /ʃʊlts/ George P 1920– . US Republican politician, secretary of state from 1982.
Shultz taught as a labour economist at the University of Chicago before serving in the 1968–74 ◊Nixon administration. He was economics adviser to President ◊Reagan 1980–82, and was then appointed state department secretary, in charge of the formulation of US foreign policy. He was pragmatic and moderate, against the opposition of Defence Secretary Caspar ◊Weinberger (1917–   ).

Shute /ʃuːt/ Nevil, pen name of British novelist Nevil Shute Norway 1899–1960. Born in Ealing, he settled in Australia in 1950, writing popular novels including *A Town Like Alice* 1949 and *On the Beach* 1957.

shuttle diplomacy a form of international diplomacy prominent in the 1970s where an independent mediator would travel between belligerent parties in order to try and achieve a compromise solution. The best known exponent was Henry ◊Kissinger.

sial in geochemistry and geophysics, a term denoting the substance of the Earth's continental ◊crust, as distinct from the ◊sima of the ocean crust. The name is derived from *si*lica and *al*umina, its two main chemical constituents.

Sialkot /siˈælkɒt/ city in Pakistan; population (1981) 302,000. Industries include the manufacture of surgical and sports goods, metal ware, carpets, textiles, and leather goods.

siamang type of ◊gibbon *Symphalangus syndactylus* from Malaya and Sumatra. Black-haired, more heavily built and larger than other

gibbons, with head and body about 60 cm/2 ft long, and very long arms, siamangs have a large throat pouch to amplify the voice.

Sian /ˌsiːˈæn/ former name of ◊Xian, China.

Sibelius /sɪˈbeɪliəs/ Jean (Christian) 1865–1957. Finnish composer. He studied the violin and composition at Helsinki and went on to Berlin and Vienna. From the age of 32 he was supported as a composer by the State, though he stopped composing in his sixties. His works include strongly nationalistic symphonic poems such as *En Saga* 1893, *Finlandia* 1900, *Tapiola* 1926, the Violin Concerto 1904, and seven symphonies.

Sibelius The Finnish composer (right) receives a visit from Sir Thomas Beecham, a pioneer of his work in Britain.

Siberia /saɪˈbɪəriə/ region of the USSR, extending from the Urals to the Pacific.
area 12,050,000 sq km/4,650,000 sq mi.
towns Novosibirsk, Omsk, Krasnoyarsk, and Irkutsk.
features long and extremely cold winters; hydroelectric power from rivers Lena, Ob, and Yenisei; forestry; huge mineral resources, including gold, diamonds, oil and natural gas, iron, copper, nickel, cobalt.
history Overrun by Russia in the 17th century, it was used from the 18th to exile political and criminal prisoners. The first *Trans-Siberian Railway* 1892–1905 from Leningrad (via Omsk, Novosibirsk, Irkutsk and Khabarovsk) to Vladivostok, approximately 8,700 km/5,400 mi, began to open it up,

Sibley /ˈsɪbli/ Antoinette 1939–   . British dancer. Joining the ◊Royal Ballet in 1956, she became senior soloist in 1960. Her roles include Odette/Odile, Giselle, the betrayed girl in *The Rake's Progress*, and in 1964 she appeared in the premiere of ◊Ashton's *The Dream*.

Sibyl /ˈsɪbɪl/ in Roman mythology, priestess of Apollo, especially the Cumaean Sibyl living in a cave near Naples, Italy. She offered to sell ◊Tarquinius nine collections of prophecies, the *Sibylline Books*, but the price was too high. When she had destroyed all but three, he bought those for the identical price, and these were kept for consultation in emergency at Rome.

Sichuan /ˌsɪtʃ'wɑːn/ province (formerly *Szechwan*) of China.
area 569,000 sq km/219,634 sq mi
capital Chengdu
towns Chongqing
features surrounded by mountains, it was the headquarters of the Nationalist government 1937–45, and China's nuclear research centres are here; it is China's most populous administrative area
products rice; coal, oil and natural gas
population (1982) 99,713,310.

Sicily /'sɪsɪli/ largest Mediterranean island (Italian *Sicilia*).
area 25,709 sq km/9,976 sq mi
capital Palermo
towns ports Catania, Messina, Syracuse, Marsala
features forms (with the islands of ◊Lipari, Egadi, Ustica, and ◊Pantelleria), an autonomous region of Italy; Etna, at 3,323 m/10,902 ft the highest volcano in Europe, last major eruption 1971
exports Marsala wine, olives, citrus; refined oil and petrochemicals, pharmaceuticals
population (1981) 4,906,878
history conquered by most of the major powers of the ancient world, it flourished under the Greeks who colonized it during the 8th–5th centuries BC. It was invaded by Carthage, and became part of the Roman empire 241 BC–476 AD. In the Middle Ages it was ruled successively by the Arabs; by the Normans 1059–1194, who established the *Kingdom of the Two Sicilies* (that is, Sicily and the southern part of Italy); by the German emperors; and then by the Angevins, until the popular revolt known as the *Sicilian Vespers* in 1282. Spanish rule was invited and continued in varying forms, with a temporary displacement of the Spanish Bourbons by Napoleon, until ◊Garibaldi's invasion in 1860 resulted in the two Sicilies being united with Italy in 1861.

Sickert /'sɪkət/ Walter Richard 1860–1942. British artist, born in Munich. The son of a Danish painter, he was taken to London and studied at the Slade School and under ◊Whistler. His impressionist cityscapes of London and Venice, portraits, and domestic interiors capture subtleties of tone and light, often with a humorous touch. His works include *Mamma Mia Poareta*, *The Area Steps*, *The Evening Primrose*, and *Bath*.

sickle cell anaemia form of ◊anaemia common in African peoples and their descendants elsewhere. In those with two genes producing such distorted-shape red blood cells, serious illness results; in those with one healthy gene and one that is abnormal, there may be no sign of illness, rather the reverse, since this form gives resistance to malarial infection.

Siddons /'sɪdnz/ Sarah 1755–1831. British actress, born in Brecon, Wales. She toured the provinces with the company of Roger Kemble, her father, until she appeared in London to immediate acclaim. Her first success in ◊Otway's *Venice Preserv'd* in 1774 led to her engagement in 1775 to appear with ◊Garrick at Drury Lane. Her majestic presence made her most suited to tragic and heroic roles such as Lady Macbeth,

Zara in ◊Congreve's *The Mourning Bride* and Constance in *King John*. She appeared with acclaim until her retirement in 1812.

sidewinder type of North American rattlesnake *Crotalus cerastes* which lives in the deserts of the SW, and moves by throwing its coils into a sideways 'jump' across the sand. It is usually about 45 cm/1.5 ft long.

Sidi Barrâni /'sɪdi bɔ'rɑːni/ coastal settlement in Egypt, about 370 km/230 mi W of Alexandria, the scene of much fighting 1940–42 during World War II.

Sidi-Bel-Abbès /'sɪdi 'bel æ'bes/ trading city in Algeria; population (1983) 146,653. Because of its strategic position, it was the headquarters of the French Foreign Legion until 1962.

Siding Spring Mountain site 400 km/250 mi NW of Sydney, New South Wales, of an Anglo-Australian telescope (1974), which enabled the central sector of the galaxy to be adequately observed for the first time. Since these central regions exert a considerable controlling influence, the 3.81 m/150 in telescope is expected to throw light on cosmic origins.

Sidney /'sɪdni/ Philip 1554–1586. English poet and soldier, born in Penshurst, Kent. He entered Parliament in 1581, and in 1583 was knighted. In 1585 he was made governor of Flushing in the Netherlands, and died at Zutphen, fighting the Spaniards. Among his works are the sonnet sequence *Astrophel and Stella* 1591; *Arcadia* 1590, considered by many to be the finest of the Elizabethan romances; and the *Apologie for Poetrie* 1595, the earliest work of English literary criticism.

Sidney The perfect Renaissance hero, Sir Philip Sidney was a soldier, poet, and courtier.

Sidon /'saɪdn/ former name for ◊Saida, Lebanon.

Siegfried /'siːgfriːd, German 'ziːkfriːt/ legendary Germanic hero after whom the ◊Siegfried line was named. It is uncertain whether his story has a historical basis, but it was current about 700 AD. In the poems of the Norse

Elder Edda and in the prose Völsunga Saga, Siegfried appears under the name of Sigurd. The best-known version is in the German *Nibelungenlied*.

Siegfried line originally the defensive line established in 1918 by the Germans in France in World War I; in World War II the name given by the Allies to the West Wall, the German defensive line established along its western frontier, from the Netherlands to Switzerland.

Siemens /'siːmənz/ family of four brothers, creators of a vast industrial empire. Most famous were the eldest, Ernst Werner von Siemens (1812–92), who founded in 1847 the original electrical firm of *Siemens und Halske* and made many advances in telegraphy; and Wilhelm (1823–83), who became a British subject in 1859 and was knighted in 1883 as Sir William Siemens. He was manager of the firm Siemens Brothers, and perfected the open-hearth production of ◊steel (now superseded).

siemens /'siːmənz/ the ◊SI unit of electrical conductance (S). Defined as the conductance of a circuit or element with a resistance of 1 ohm. Formerly called the mho or reciprocal ohm. Named after Sir William ◊Siemens.

Siena /si'enə/ city in Tuscany, Italy; population (1985) 60,670. Founded by the Etruscans, it has fine medieval architecture by ◊Pisano and ◊Donatello, including a 13th-century Gothic cathedral, and many impressive examples of the Sienese school of painting which flourished from the 13th–16th century. The *Palio* ('banner', in reference to the prize) is a horse race in the main square, held annually since the Middle Ages.

Sienkiewicz /ˌʃeŋki'eɪvɪtʃ/ Henryk 1846–1916. Polish author. His books include the 17th-century historical trilogy *With Fire and Sword*, *The Deluge* and *Pan Michael* 1890–93; *Quo Vadis?* 1895, set in Rome in the time of Nero; and *Without Dogma* 1891.

Sierra Leone /si'erə li'əʊn/ country in W Africa, on the Atlantic, bounded to the N and E by Guinea and to the SE by Liberia.
government The 1978 constitution makes Sierra Leone a one-party state, the party being the All People's Congress (APC). The constitution also provides for a president, who is both head of state and head of government, and a single-chamber legislature, the House of Representatives. The House has 104 members, 85 elected for five years by universal suffrage, 12 paramount chiefs, one for each district, and seven additional members appointed by the president. The president, who is also leader and secretary general of the APC, is endorsed by the party as the sole candidate and then popularly elected for a seven-year term. The president appoints a cabinet and two vice presidents.
history For early history, see ◊Africa. Freetown, the capital, was founded by Britain 1787 for homeless Africans rescued from ◊slavery. Sierra Leone became a British colony 1808.
Sierra Leone achieved full independence, as a constitutional monarchy within the Commonwealth, in 1962, with Sir Milton Margai, leader of the Sierra Leone People's Party (SLPP), as prime minister. He died in 1964

and was succeeded by his half-brother, Dr Albert Margai. The 1967 general election was won by the APC, led by Dr Siaka Stevens, but the result was disputed by the army, which assumed control and temporarily forced the governor-general to leave the country. In 1968 another army revolt brought back Stevens as prime minister and in 1971, after the constitution had been changed to make Sierra Leone a republic, he became president. He was re-elected in 1976 and the APC, having won the 1977 general election by a big margin, began to demand the creation of a one-party state. To this end, a new constitution was approved by referendum in 1978, and Stevens was sworn in as president.

Stevens, who was now 80, did not run in 1985 and the APC endorsed the commander of the army, Maj-Gen Joseph Momoh, as the sole candidate for the party leadership and presidency. Momoh appointed a civilian cabinet and dissociated himself from the policies of his predecessor, who had been criticized for failing to prevent corruption within his administration. The last elections for the House of Representatives were held in May 1982 but annulled because of alleged irregularities:

Sierra Nevada /si'erə nɪ'vɑːdə/ mountain range of S Spain; highest point Mulhacén 3,481 m/11,421 ft.

Sierra Nevada /si'erə nɪ'vɑːdə/ mountain range in E California, USA; highest point Mount Whitney 4,418 m/14,495 ft. It includes the King's Canyon, Sequoia, and Yosemite Valley national parks.

sievert the ◊SI unit of dose equivalent (Sv). Defined as the absorbed dose of ionizing radiation (with certain dimensionless factors to account for different types of radiation causing different effects in biological tissue) of 1 joule/kg.

Signac /siːn'ʒæk/ Paul 1863–1935. French artist. Parisian-born, he was influenced by ◊Monet, and in 1884 joined with ◊Seurat in founding the Société des Artistes Indépendants and the technique of ◊pointillism. He expanded his brilliant watercolours made on the spot into large canvases imbued with colour and light.

signal a sign, gesture, sound, or action which conveys information. Examples include the use of flags (◊semaphore), light (as in traffic and railway signals), radio telephony, radio telegraphy (◊Morse code), electricity (as in

(1944). ◊Computers generally communicate using the ◊ASCII codes.

signal processing the use of computers for the analysis of complex signals, for example, satellite pictures or ultrasound scans. Signal processing allows the enhancement of images that might otherwise be indecipherable because of noise, that is, spurious, random variations in the signal. The procedure may involve the use of statistical techniques and may include the enhancement of images by the addition of colour.

Signorelli /ˌsiːnjə'reli/ Luca c. 1450–1523. Italian Renaissance artist of the Umbrian school, painter of large-scale frescoes, including those in Orvieto cathedral.

Sigurd in Norse mythology, a hero who appears in both the ◊Nibelunglied (under his German name of ◊Siegfried) and the ◊Edda.

Sihanouk /ˌsiːə'nuːk/ Norodom 1922– . Kampuchean socialist politician, king 1941–55, prime minister 1955–70 and 1975–76. Educated in Vietnam and Paris, he was elected king of Cambodia in 1941. He abdicated in 1955 in favour of his father, founded the Popular Socialist Community and governed as prime minister 1955–70.

Sihanouk was deposed by a right-wing military coup led by Lt-Gen Lon Nol in 1970. He established a government in exile in Beijing and formed a joint resistance front with ◊Pol Pot. This movement succeeded in overthrowing Lon Nol in Apr 1975 and Sihanouk was reappointed head of state, but in Apr 1976 he was forced to resign by the communist Khmer Rouge leadership. Now living in North Korea, he became the recognized leader of the Democratic Kampuchea government in exile in 1982.

Sikhism the religion professed by some ten million Indians living for the most part in the Punjab. It was founded by Nanak (1469–c. 1539). Its basis is the Unity of God and the Brotherhood of Man; Sikhism is strongly opposed to caste divisions. On Nanak's death he was followed as *Guru* (teacher) by a succession of leaders who converted the Sikhs (the word means disciple) into a military confraternity which established itself as a political power. Guru Gobind Singh (1666–1708) instituted the Khanda-di-Pahul, the Baptism of the Sword, and established the *Khalsa* ('the pure'), the Brotherhood of the faithful, the Singhs. The Singhs wear the five Ks: *kes*, long hair; *kangha*, a comb; *kirpan*, a sword; *kachh*, short trousers; and *kara*, a steel bracelet. The last of the Gurus, Gobind Singh, was assassinated by a Muslim in 1708, and since then the Granth Sahib, the holy book of the Sikhs, has taken the place of a leader. On the partition of India many Sikhs migrated from W to E Punjab, and in 1966 the efforts of Sant Fateh Singh (c. 1911–72) led to the creation of a separate Sikh state by partition of ◊Punjab. However, the Akali separatist movement agitates for a completely independent Sikh state, Khalistan, and a revival of fundamentalist belief was headed from 1978 by Sant Jarnail Singh Bhindranwale (1947–84), killed in the siege of the Golden Temple, Amritsar. In retaliation for this, the Indian prime minister, Indira Gandhi, was assassinated in Oct of the same year by her

Sierra Leone
REPUBLIC OF

AREA 73,325 sq km/27,925 sq mi
CAPITAL Freetown
TOWNS Bo, Kenema, Makeni
PHYSICAL mountains in E; hills and forest; coastal mangrove swamps
FEATURES hot and humid climate (3,500 mm/138 in rainfall annually)
HEAD OF STATE AND OF GOVERNMENT Joseph Saidu Momoh from 1985
GOVERNMENT one-party authoritarian
EXPORTS palm kernels, cocoa, coffee, ginger; diamonds, bauxite, rutile
CURRENCY leone (official rate 36.2 = £1 Sept 1987)
POPULATION 3,883,000 (1985); annual growth rate 1.8%
LANGUAGE English (official); local languages
RELIGION Muslim 60%, animist 30%
LITERACY 31% male/16% female (1980 est)
GNP $1.2 bn (1983); $176 per head of population
CHRONOLOGY
1962 Achieved full independence as a constitutional monarchy within the Commonwealth, with Sir Milton Margai, leader of the Sierra Leone People's Party (SLPP), as prime minister.
1964 Sir Milton succeeded by his half-brother Albert Margai.
1967 General election results disputed by the

Sierra Leone

army who set up a National Reformation Council and forced the governor general to leave.
1968 Another army revolt made Siaka Stevens, leader of the All-People's Congress (APC), prime minister.
1971 New constitution adopted, making Sierra Leone a republic, with Stevens as president.
1978 APC declared the only legal party. Stevens sworn in for another seven-year term.
1985 Stevens retired at the age of 80 and was succeeded by Maj-Gen Joseph Momoh.

Sierra Madre /si'erə 'mɑːdreɪ/ chief mountain system of Mexico, consisting of three ranges, enclosing the central plateau of the country; highest point Pico de Orizaba 5,700 m/18,700 ft. The Sierra Madre del Sur ('of the south') runs along the SW Pacific coast.

telecommunications and computer networks). The International Code of Signals used by shipping was drawn up by an international committee and published in 1931. The codes and abbreviations used by aircraft are dealt with by the International Civil Aviation Organization

Sikh bodyguard. Heavy rioting followed, in which 1,000 Sikhs were killed. Mrs Gandhi's successor, Rajiv Ghandi, reached an agreement for the election of a popular government in the Punjab and for state representatives to the Indian parliament with the moderate Sikh leader Sant Harchand Singh Longowal, who was himself killed in 1985 by Sikh extremists.

Sikh Wars two wars in India between the Sikhs and the British:

First 1845–46 following an invasion of British India by Punjabi Sikhs. The Sikhs were defeated and part of their territory annexed.

Second 1848–49 arising from a Sikh revolt of Multan. They were defeated and the British annexed the Punjab.

Si-Kiang /'ʃiː kiˈæŋ/ former name of ◊Xi Jiang, Chinese river.

Sikkim /'sɪkɪm/ NE state of India: formerly a protected state, it was absorbed by India in 1975, the monarchy being abolished. China does not recognize India's sovereignty.

area 7,298 sq km/2,817 sq mi

capital Gangtok

features Mount Kanchenjunga; rich wildlife including birds, butterflies, and orchids

population (1981) 315,000

language English, Bhutia, Lepcha, Khaskura (Nepali) (all official)

religion Mahayana Buddhism, Hinduism.

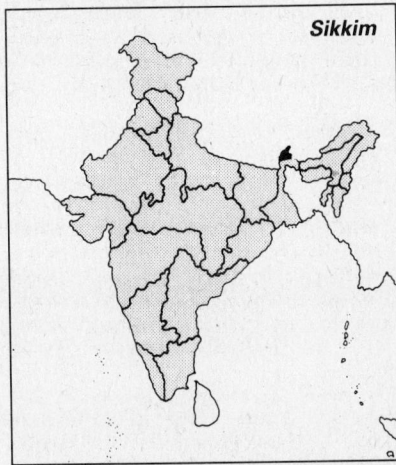

Sikkim

Sikorski /sɪˈkɔːski/ Wladyslaw 1881–1943. Polish general and politician, born in Galicia. He formed in 1909 the nationalist military organization which during World War I fought for the central powers. He served in the Russian war of 1920, and was prime minister 1922–23 and war minister 1923–25. In Sept 1939 he became prime minister of the exiled Polish government, which transferred to London in 1940. He was killed in an air crash. The intransigence of his government was a cause of Anglo-Russian friction, but allegations that his death was not accidental are unsubstantiated.

Sikorsky /sɪˈkɔːski/ Igor 1889–1972. Ukrainian-born American engineer who built the first successful helicopter. Born in Kiev, he emigrated to the USA in 1918 where he first constructed multi-engined flying boats. His first helicopter (the VS300) flew in 1939 and a commercial version (the R3) went into production in 1943.

silage fodder preserved in a ◊silo, an airtight structure for pressing green crops. It is now extended to refer to stacked crops which may be preserved indefinitely.

Silbury Hill /'sɪlbəri/ steep, rounded artificial mound (40 m/130 ft high) of the Bronze Age 2660 BC, in Wiltshire, near ◊Avebury, England; it was long thought to be a ◊barrow, but excavation has shown it not to be sepulchral.

Silchester /'sɪltʃɪstə/ archaeological site in ◊Hampshire, England, 10 km/6 mi N of Basingstoke. It was one of the most important towns in Roman Britain.

silencer also called muffler (US); a device in the exhaust system of cars and motorbikes which reduces the noise of the exhaust gases leaving the engine. Gases leave the engine at supersonic speeds. The exhaust system and silencer are designed to slow them down, which also silences them. Some silencers use baffle plates (plates with holes, which disrupt the airflow), others perforated tubes and an expansion box (a large chamber which slows down airflow and reduces noise).

Silenus /saɪˈliːnəs/ in Greek mythology, the son of Hermes, or Pan, and companion of ◊Dionysus. He is portrayed as a jovial old man, usually drunk.

Silesia /saɪˈliːziə/ long-disputed region of Europe, Austrian 1675–1745; Prussian/German 1745–1919 (having been seized by Frederick II of Prussia); and in 1919 divided among newly-formed Czechoslovakia, revived Poland, and Germany, which retained the major part. In 1945 all German Silesia east of the Oder-Neisse line was transferred to Polish administration: about ten million inhabitants of German origin, both here and in Czechoslovak Silesia, were expelled. The chief towns (with their German names) are: Wroclaw (Breslau), Katowice (Kattowitz), Zabrze (Hindenburg), Chorzow (Königshütte), Gliwice (Gleiwitz), and Bytom (Beuthen) in Poland, and Opava (Troppau) in Czechoslovakia.

silhouette a profile or shadow portrait filled in with black or a dark colour, named after Etienne de Silhouette (1709–67), a French finance minister whose economy led to his name being applied to cheap things.

silica silicon dioxide, SiO_2, the commonest mineral, of which the most familiar form is quartz. Chalcedony is a semi-precious form, which includes the banded ◊agate, ◊onyx, and sardonyx (which lend themselves to the making of cameos, and are often used in other jewellery); red carnelian; brownish jasper and flint. See ◊opal.

silicon a non-metallic element, symbol Si, atomic number 14, atomic weight 78.09. It is used in glass-making, as a hardener in steel alloys, in ◊silicon chips for microcomputers, and so on. *Silicones* are synthetic polymers based on a chain of oxygen and silicon atoms; see ◊plastic.

silicon chip popular term for an ◊integrated circuit with microscopically small electrical components on a piece of silicon crystal only a few millimetres square. This tiny circuit, often with upwards of a million components, is mounted in a rectangular plastic package and linked via gold wires to metal pins down the long sides of the package so that it can be connected to a printed circuit board for inclusion in electronic devices such as computers, calculators, televisions, car dashboards, and domestic appliances.

Silicon Valley nickname given to Santa Clara county, California, since the 1950s, the site of many high-technology electronic firms, whose prosperity is based on the silicon chip.

silicosis disease of miners and stone cutters who inhale flint dust, which makes lung tissue fibrous, less capable of aerating the blood and less resistant to tuberculosis.

silk fine soft thread produced by the larva of the ◊silkworm moth, and used in the manufacture of textiles. The introduction of synthetics originally harmed the silk industry, but rising standards of living have produced an increased demand for real silk. Japan produces over half the world's silk.

Silk Road ancient route by which silk was brought from China to Europe in return for trade goods; it ran via Transylvania, Mount Ararat, Samarkand, and the Gobi Desert. It has been revived as a tourist rail route.

silk-screen printing a method of printing using treated silk as a kind of stencil. It can be used to print to more or less any surface, from paper and plastic to cloth and wood. In the printing process, the silk is treated with a kind of varnish so that ink can only pass through where the image is required.

silkworm usually the larva of the *common silkworm moth Bombyx mori*, which after hatching from the egg and maturing on the leaves of white mulberry trees (or a synthetic substitute) 'spins' a protective cocoon of fine silk thread (275 m/300 yd). It is killed before emergence as a moth to keep the thread intact, and several threads are combined to form the commercial silk thread woven into textiles. Other moths produce different types, such as *tussah* from *Antheraea mylitta*.

Sillitoe /'sɪlɪtəʊ/ Alan 1928– . English novelist. Brought up in Nottingham, he set his first book there, *Saturday Night and Sunday Morning* 1958, dealing with a working-class hero, Arthur Seaton. *The Loneliness of the Long Distance Runner* 1959 was followed by many novels.

Sills /sɪlz/ Beverly 1929– . American operatic soprano. She was one of the world's most dramatically gifted singers, as in *Lucia di Lammermoor* and *La traviata*. In 1979 she became director of New York City Opera.

silo in farming, an airtight tower in which ◊silage is made by the fermentation of freshly cut grass and other forage crops. In military technology, a silo is an underground chamber for housing and launching a ballistic missile.

Silone /sɪˈləʊneɪ/ Ignazio, pseudonym of Italian novelist Secondo Tranquilli 1900–1978. His best-known novel, *Fontamara* 1933, deals with the hopes and disillusionment of a peasant village. Other works include *Una manciata di more/A Handful of Blackberries* 1952.

Silurian the period of geological time between 435 and 395 million years ago. Silurian sediments are mostly marine and consist of shales and limestone. Although most life was marine, the first land plants began to evolve during this period.

Silvanus /sɪl'veɪnəs/ a Roman woodland deity identified in later times with ◊Pan.

silver lustrous metal, extremely malleable and ductile: symbol Ag (Latin *argentum*), atomic number 47, atomic weight 107.873. Known since prehistoric times, silver occurs native in Peru, but the chief ores are sulphides, from which the metal is extracted by smelting with lead. It is one of the best metallic conductors of both heat and electricity, and its most important compounds are the chloride and bromide which darken on exposure to light, the basis of photographic emulsions. Silver is used for tableware, jewellery, coinage, electrical contacts and electroplating, and as a solder it makes good metallic joints at 720°C. The world's greatest producer of silver is Mexico (approximately 40,000,000 troy ounces per annum).

silver age period of Latin literature after the death of ◊Augustus, with writing rather too florid and rhetorical for modern taste; authors included Seneca, Juvenal, and Suetonius.

silverfish wingless insect, a type of ◊bristletail.

sima in geochemistry and geophysics a term denoting the substance of the Earth's ocean ◊crust, as distinct from the ◊sial of the continent crust. The name is derived from *si*lica and *ma*gnesia, its two main chemical constituents.

Simberg /'sɪmbeəg/ Hugo 1873–1917. Finnish artist, noted for his wistfully sympathetic etchings of devils, and for his landscapes.

Simenon /'siːmənɒŋ/ Georges 1903– . Belgian crime writer, born in Liège. Initially a pulp fiction writer, in 1930 he created Inspector Maigret of the Paris Sûreté who appeared in a series of detective novels. His other novels include *La Neige était sale/The Stain on the Snow* 1948.

Simeon Stylites, St /'sɪmiən staɪ'laɪtiːz/ c. 390–459. Syrian Christian ascetic, who practised self-denial by living for 37 years on a pillar.

Simferopol /ˌsɪmfə'rəʊpɒl/ town in the Crimea, Ukrainian Soviet Socialist Republic; population (1985) 331,000. Industries include the manufacture of soap and tobacco. It is on the site of the Tatar town of Ak-Mechet, conquered by the Russians 1783 and renamed.

simile a ◊figure of speech whose Latin name means 'likeness' and which in English uses the conjunctions 'like' and 'as' to express imaginative comparisons ('run like the devil'; 'as blind as a bat'). However, not every comparison that uses these words is a simile; for example, 'The city of Bristol is like Bordeaux' simply and literally compares two ports. In 'The city of Bristol is like a fine old ship' a more imaginative comparison (not city with city, but city with ship) creates an analogical link between less obvious contexts, and is a simile. See also ◊metaphor.

Simla /'sɪmlə/ capital of Himachal Pradesh state, India, 2,300 m/7,500 ft above sea level,

Simenon Georges Simenon, the novelist of the world of crime for whom the human element is the most important in the mystery equation.

population (1980) 70,604; it was the summer administrative capital of British India 1864–1947.

Simon /siː'mɒŋ/ Claude 1913– . French novelist, an exponent of the ◊nouveau roman. Originally an artist, he abandoned the 'time structure' in such difficult novels as *La Route de Flandres/The Flanders Road* 1960. His later novels include *Les Géorgiques* 1981.

Simon /'saɪmən/ Herbert 1916– . American social scientist. Researching decision-making in business corporations, he discovered that maximum profit was seldom the chief motive. He was awarded the Nobel Prize for Economics in 1978.

Simon /'saɪmən/ John Allsebrook, Viscount Simon 1873–1954. British Liberal politician. Home Secretary 1915–16, he resigned on the issue of conscription. He was foreign secretary 1931–35; Home Secretary again 1935–37; Chancellor of the Exchequer 1937–40, and Lord Chancellor 1940–45.

Simon /'saɪmən/ Neil 1927– . American playwright, whose wryly comic plays include *Barefoot in the Park* 1963, *The Odd Couple* 1965, and *The Sunshine Boys* 1972; and the more serious, autobiographical *Brighton Beach Memoirs* 1983. He also wrote the musicals *Sweet Charity* 1966, *Promises, Promises* 1968, and *They're Playing Our Song* 1978.

Simon /'saɪmən/ Paul 1942– . US pop singer and songwriter. In a folk-rock duo with Art Garfunkel (1942–), he rose to fame with hits like *'Mrs Robinson'* 1968 and *'Bridge Over Troubled Water'* 1970. His solo work includes the album *Graceland* 1986.

Simon Commission a commission set up by the British Government 1927–30, chaired by John ◊Simon, to recommend changes to the 1919 Indian constitution. The commission was boycotted by the Indian National Congress but nonetheless reported in 1930, recommending indirect elections and further responsible government. The commission had little practical result.

Simonstown /'saɪmənztaʊn/ naval base established in 1814 on False Bay, 37 km/23 mi S of Cape Town, South Africa.

simony name given to the buying and selling of church preferments, now usually regarded as a sin, derived from *Simon Magus* (Acts viii) who offered money to the Apostles for the power of the Holy Ghost.

simple harmonic motion (SHM), oscillatory or vibrational motion in which an object (or point) moves so that its acceleration towards a central point is proportional to its distance from it. A simple example is a pendulum, which also demonstrates another feature of SHM, that the maximum deflection is the same on each side of the central point. A graph of the varying distance with respect to time is a sine curve, a characteristic of the oscillating current or voltage of an alternating current (AC), which is another example of SHM.

Simplon /'sæmplɒn/ Alpine pass Switzerland–Italy; the road was built by Napoleon 1800–05, and the Simplon Tunnel, 19.8 km/12.3 mi, is one of the world's longest.

Simpson /'sɪmpsən/ (Cedric) Keith 1907–1985. British forensic scientist, head of department at Guy's Hospital, London, 1962–72. He sent John Haig (the acid bath murderer) and Neville Heath to the gallows, and in 1965 identified the first 'battered baby' murder in England.

Simpson /'sɪmpsən/ James Young 1811–1870. British physician. He qualified as a Doctor of Medicine at Edinburgh in 1832, became president of the Royal Medical Society 1835, and professor of midwifery 1839. He was largely instrumental in the introduction of chloroform as an anaesthetic in 1847.

Simpson /'sɪmpsən/ N(orman) F(rederick) 1919– . British dramatist. A lecturer in history and English for adult education, his plays *A Resounding Tinkle* 1957, *The Hole* 1958, and *One Way Pendulum* 1959 show the logical development of an abnormal situation, and belong to the 'Theatre of the ◊Absurd'. He also wrote a novel, *Harry Bleachbaker* 1976.

Simpson Desert desert area in Australia, chiefly in Northern Territory; area 145,000 sq km/56,000 sq mi. It was named after a president of the South Australian Geographical Society who financed its exploration.

simultaneous equation in mathematics, one of two or more algebraic equations that contain two or more unknown quantities and are simultaneously true. In the simplest case, that of two linear equations with two unknown variables, for example (i) $x + 3y = 6$ and (ii) $3y - 2x = 4$, the solution will be those unique values of x and y that are valid for both equations. One method of solution is first to eliminate one of the variables, whether by substitution, for example, in this case substituting for x in equation (ii) the value $6 - 3y$ obtained by rearranging equation (i); or by multiplying equation (i) by 2 (to give $2x + 6y = 12$) and adding this new equation to equation (ii) to give $9y = 16$, which is easily solved. Another method is by plotting the equations on a graph, because the two equations represent straight lines in ◊coordinate geometry and the coordinates of their point of intersection are the values of x and y that are true for both of them. Linear simultaneous equations can also be solved using ◊matrices.

Sinai /'saɪnaɪ/ peninsula in Egypt, at the head of the Red Sea; area 65,000 sq km/25,000 sq mi. Resources include oil, natural gas, manganese, and coal; irrigation water from the Nile is carried under the Suez Canal. Sinai was occupied by Israel 1967–82. After the Battle of ◊Sinai 1973, Israel began a gradual withdrawal from the area, under the disengagement agreement of 1975, and the Camp David peace treaty of 1979, and restored the whole of Sinai to Egyptian control by Apr 1982. Egypt established a religious complex (Jewish-Muslim-Christian) at Mount Sinai in 1979.

Sinai, Mount /'saɪnaɪ/ mountain near the tip of the Sinai Peninsula (Gebel Mûsa, 2,285 m/7,497 ft), allegedly the place where ◊Moses received the Ten Commandments from Jehovah.

Sinai, Battle of /'saɪnaɪ/ battle 14–19 Oct 1973 between Egypt and Israel; more tanks were used than at ◊Alamein. See ◊Arab–Israeli Wars.

Sinatra /sɪ'nɑːtrə/ Frank (Francis Albert) 1915– . US popular singer and film actor, born in Hoboken, New Jersey, the son of a former prizefighter. He achieved fame as a heart-throb singer with songs such as 'Night and Day' and 'You'd Be So Nice To Come Home To', and then established himself as an actor, as in *From Here to Eternity* 1953 which won him an Academy Award. Greatest of his later song successes is 'My Way'.

Sinclair /'sɪŋkleə/ Clive 1940– . British electronics engineer, the first to produce a widely available pocket calculator, pocket and wristwatch televisions, as well as a series of popular home computers. His inventive genius was overshadowed by a lack of business acumen, and his 'C5' personal transport (a three-wheeled device powered by a washing-machine motor) was a financial disaster. Knighted 1983.

Sinclair /'sɪŋkleə/ Upton 1878–1968. American novelist, born in Baltimore. His concern for social reforms is reflected in *The Jungle* 1906, dealing with the horrors of the Chicago stockyards, *Boston* 1928, and his Lanny Budd series 1940–53, including *Dragon's Teeth* 1942, which won a ◊Pulitzer prize.

Sind /sɪnd/ province of Pakistan, mainly in the Indus delta; area 122,000 sq km/47,000 sq mi; population (1981) 18,966,000. Annexed in 1843, it became a province of British India, and

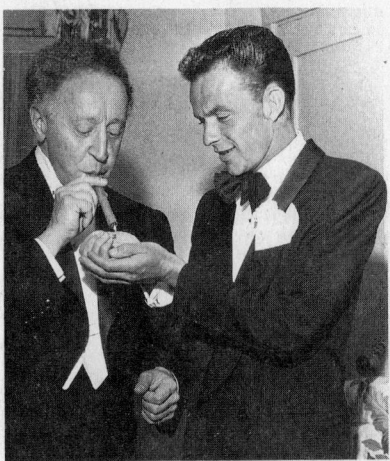

Sinatra The American singer and film actor Frank Sinatra lights the cigar of pianist Arthur Rubinstein.

part of Pakistan on independence. There is agitation for its creation as a separate state, Sindhudesh.

Sinden /'sɪndən/ Donald 1923– . English actor, noted for his resonant voice and versatility; his roles ranging from such classics as *Henry VI* and *Richard III* to light modern comedies such as *There's a Girl in My Soup*, *Present Laughter*, and the television series *Two's Company*.

Sinding /'sɪndɪŋ/ Christian (August) 1856–1941. Norwegian composer. His works include four symphonies, piano pieces (including *Rustle of Spring*), and songs. His brothers Otto (1842–1909) and Stephan (1846–1922), were painter and sculptor respectively.

sine in trigonometry, of an angle in a ◊right-angled triangle, the ratio of the length of the side opposite the angle to the length of the hypotenuse (the longest side). Various properties in physics vary sinusoidally, that is, they can be represented diagramatically by a sine wave (a graph obtained by plotting values of angles against the values of their sines). Examples include ◊simple harmonic motion, such as the way alternating current (AC) electricity varies with time.

sinfonietta an orchestral work which is of a shorter, lighter nature than a ◊symphony.

Singapore /ˌsɪŋə'pɔː/ country in SE Asia, off the tip of the Malay Peninsula

government Singapore has a single-tier system of government. The constitution of 1965 has provided for a one-chamber parliament, whose 70 members are elected for five-year terms by universal suffrage from single-member constituencies on a first-past-the-post basis. Parliament debates and votes on legislation and elects, for a four-year term, a ceremonial head of state (president). Executive power is held by a prime minister and cabinet drawn from the majority party within parliament. The dominant party in Singapore since independence has been the conservative People's Action Party.

history For early history, see ◊Malay Peninsula. Singapore was leased as a trading post in 1819 from the sultan of Johore by the British East India Company, on the advice of Sir Stamford

◊Raffles, at a time when it was a swampy jungle. It passed to the crown in 1858 and formed part of the ◊Straits Settlements 1867–1942.

During World War II, Singapore functioned as a vital British military base in the Far East. Designed to be invulnerable to naval attack, it was invaded by land and occupied by Japan Feb 1942–Sept 1945. Singapore became a separate British crown colony in 1946 and fully self-governing, with ◊Lee Kuan Yew as prime minister, from 1959. It joined the Federation of ◊Malaysia in 1963, but seceded in 1965, alleging discrimination against the federation's Chinese members. A new independent republic of Singapore was thus formed in Sept 1965, which remained within the Commonwealth.

The new republic's internal political affairs were dominated by Prime Minister Lee Kuan Yew's People's Action Party, which gained a monopoly of all parliamentary seats in the elections between 1968 and 1980. Under Lee's stewardship, Singapore has developed rapidly as a commercial and financial entrepot and as a centre for new export industries. Today its inhabitants enjoy the highest standard of living in Asia outside Japan.

Singapore allied itself closely with the USA 1965–74. Since the mid-1970s, however, it has pursued a neutralist foreign policy and improved its relations with China. It is a member of ◊ASEAN.

Singer /'sɪŋə/ Isaac Bashevis 1904– . US novelist and short story writer. Born in Poland, he became a US citizen in 1942. His works, written in ◊Yiddish, often portray traditional Jewish life in Poland, and the loneliness of old age. They include *Gimpel the Fool* 1957, *The Slave* 1960, *Shosha* 1978, *Old Love* 1979. He won the Nobel Prize for Literature in 1978.

Singer Famous for his novels and short stories portraying Jewish life in Poland during different periods in its history, the author Isaac Bashevis Singer won the Nobel Prize for Literature in 1978. He writes in Yiddish, keeping alive a long European tradition.

Singapore
REPUBLIC OF

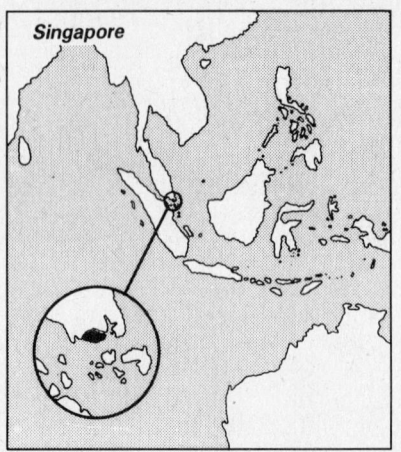

Singapore

AREA 581.5 sq km/225.6 sq mi

CAPITAL Singapore City in the S of the island, a major world port and financial centre, founded by Stamford Raffles

PHYSICAL comprises Singapore Island, which is low and flat, and 54 small islands

FEATURES Singapore Island is joined to the mainland by a causeway across the Strait of Johore; temperature ranges only 24°–31°C/76°–87°F

HEAD OF STATE Wee Kim Wee from 1985

HEAD OF GOVERNMENT Lee Kuan Yew from 1959

GOVERNMENT right-wing authoritarian

EXPORTS electronics, petroleum products, rubber, machinery, vehicles

CURRENCY Singapore dollar (3.45 = £1 Sept 1987)

POPULATION (1985) 2,556,000 (Chinese 75%, Malay 14%, Tamil 7%); annual growth rate 1.2%

LANGUAGE Malay, Chinese, Tamil, and English (all official)

RELIGION Buddhist, Taoist, Muslim, Hindu, Christian

LITERACY 92% male/74% female (1980)

GNP $17.9 bn (1984); $6,526 per head of population

CHRONOLOGY

1819 Singapore leased to British East India Company.
1858 Placed under crown rule.
1942 Invaded and occupied by Japan.
1945 Japanese removed by British forces.
1959 Independence granted from Britain: Lee Kuan Yew became prime minister.
1963 Joined new Federation of Malaya.
1965 Left federation to become independent republic.
1984 Opposition made advances in parliamentary elections.

Singer /'sɪŋə/ Isaac Merit 1811–1875. American inventor of domestic and industrial sewing machines. Within a few years of opening his first factory in 1851, he became the world's largest manufacturer (despite charges of patent infringement by Elias ◊Howe), and by the late 1860s more than 100,000 Singer sewing machines were in use in the USA alone.

single sideband transmission ◊radio wave transmission using either the frequency band above the carrier wave frequency, or below.

Sing Sing /'sɪŋ sɪŋ/ name until 1901 of the village of Ossining, New York, with a state prison of that name from 1825 (rebuilt 1930).

Sining /ˌʃiː'nɪŋ/ former name of the city of ◊Xining, Tsinghai province, W central China.

sinking fund money set aside for the repayment of debt. For a company, a sinking fund is used to allow annually for ◊depreciation; in the case of a nation, a sinking fund pays off a part of the national debt.

Sinn Féin /'ʃɪn 'feɪn/ Irish nationalist party ('We ourselves'), founded by Arthur Griffith (1872–1922) in 1905; in 1917 ◊de Valera became its president. It is the political wing of the Irish Republican Army, and is similarly split between comparative moderates and extremists. In 1985 it gained representation in 17 out of 26 district councils in Northern Ireland.

Sino–Japanese Wars wars waged by Japan against China to secure expansion on the mainland.
First Sino–Japanese War 1894–95. Under the treaty of Shimonoseki, Japan secured the 'independence' of Korea; cession of Taiwan and the ◊Pescadores, and of the Liaodong peninsula (for a naval base). France, Germany, and Russia pressurized Japan into returning the last-named, which Russia occupied in 1896 to establish Port Arthur (see ◊Russo–Japanese War and ◊Luda).
Second Sino–Japanese War 1931–45, the prelude in the Pacific to World War II.
1931–32 the Japanese occupied Manchuria, which they formed into the puppet state of ◊Manchukuo. They also attacked Shanghai, and moved into NE China.
1937 Chiang Kai-shek and ◊Mao Zedong were now in alliance to fight the Japanese; full-scale war was renewed as the Japanese overran NE China and seized Shanghai and Nanjing.
1938 Japanese capture of Wuhan and Guangzhou was followed by the transfer of the Chinese capital to ◊Chongqing; a period of stalemate followed.
1941 Japanese attack on Britain and the USA (see ◊Pearl Harbor) led to the extension of lease-lend aid to China.
1944 a Japanese offensive seriously threatened Chongqing.
1945 the Chinese shared in the final offensive and received the Japanese surrender at Nanjing in Sept.

Sioux /suː/ principal group of the Dakota family of N American ◊Plains Indians, now confined to South Dakota and Nebraska. Gen George Custer was killed with 250 men when he moved against a Sioux camp at Little Bighorn, Montana (under chiefs Crazy Horse and ◊Sitting Bull): the site of 'Custer's Last Stand' is a national monument. Following this Sioux revolt, Congress abrogated the Fort Laramie treaty of 1868 which had made over to the Indians a large area in the Black Hills of Dakota where gold was to be found. Today uranium, coal, oil and natural gas are also found there, and the Sioux were awarded $160 million compensation in 1980.

Sioux Falls /'suːˈfɔːlz/ largest city in South Dakota, USA; population (1980) 81,343. Its industry (electrical goods and agricultural machinery) is powered by the Big Sioux river over the Sioux Falls 30 m/100 ft.

siphon a tube in the form of an inverted U with unequal arms. When it is filled with liquid and the shorter arm is placed in a tank or reservoir, liquid flows out of the longer arm provided that its exit is below the level of the surface of the liquid in the tank. It works on the principle that the ◊pressure at the liquid surface is atmospheric pressure, whereas at the lower end of the longer arm it is less than atmospheric pressure, causing flow to occur.

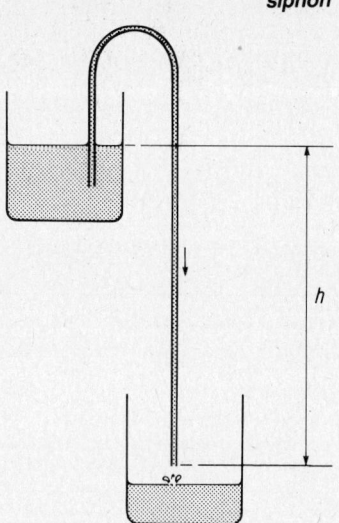

siphon

siren in Greek mythology, a sea nymph who lured sailors on to rocks by her singing. ◊Odysseus, in order to hear the sirens safely, tied himself to the mast and stuffed his crews' ears with wax; the Argonauts escaped them because the singing of Orpheus surpassed that of the sirens.

Sirius the brightest ◊star in the sky, lying 8.7 light years away in the constellation ◊Canis Major. Sirius is a white star with a mass of 2.3 suns, diameter 1.8 times that of the Sun, and a luminosity of 20 Suns. It is orbited every 50 years by a white dwarf, Sirius B.

Sirk /sɜːk/ Douglas, pseudonym of German film director Claus Detlef Sierck 1900–1987. Born in Hamburg, he became known for stage and film productions of classic dramas before leaving Germany in 1937. In the USA during the 1950s he made a series of lurid melodramas about capitalist America which have subsequently been highly praised by critics. His best films are *All that Heaven Allows* 1956 and *Written on the Wind* 1957.

sirocco a hot, normally dry and dust-laden wind that blows from the highland of Africa to N Africa, Malta, Sicily, and Italy. It occurs mainly in the spring. The name sirocco has been applied to southerly winds in the east of the USA.

Sirte, Gulf of /'sɜːti/ gulf on the Mediterranean coast of Libya, on which Benghazi stands.

sisal strong fibre made from various species of ◊agave, such as *Agave sisalina*.

siskin bird *Carduelis spinus* in the finch family Fringillidae, found in the Old World from Britain to Japan.

Sisley /'sɪzli/ Alfred 1839–1899. French artist, born in Paris, of English parents. He studied under Gleyre, and was influenced by ◊Monet and ◊Renoir. He met with little success in his lifetime, but he is now regarded as among the best of the Impressionists. Almost exclusively a landscape painter, his landscapes show the effect of light at different times of the day.

Sistine Chapel a chapel in the Vatican, Rome, begun under Pope Sixtus IV in 1473 by Giovanni del Dolci. Built to the proportions of Solomon's temple in the Old Testament (its height one-half, and its width one-third of its length), it houses the conclave which meets to select a new pope, and has frescoes on the walls (emphasizing the authority and legality of the papacy) by ◊Botticelli, ◊Ghirlandaio, and on the altar wall and ceiling by ◊Michelangelo.

Sisyphus /'sɪsɪfəs/ in Greek mythology, king of Corinth who, after his evil life, was condemned in the underworld to roll a huge stone uphill, which always fell back before he could reach the top.

sitar Indian instrument, similar to a ◊lute, with seven metal strings, a gourd body, and long neck with movable frets. Its characteristic 'singing' notes are produced by manipulation of the strings.

sitatunga African antelope *Tragelaphus spekei* found in several swamp regions in Central Africa. The hooves are long and splayed to help progress on soft surfaces. Males are dark greyish-brown, females and young are chestnut, all with whitish markings on the rather shaggy fur. Up to about 1 m/3 ft at the shoulder, only the males have the thick horns up to 90 cm/3 ft long.

Sitting Bull /'sɪtɪŋ 'bul/ *c.* 1834–1893. American Indian chief, who led the ◊Sioux onslaught against 'Custer's Last Stand'.

Sitwell /'sɪtwəl/ Edith 1887–1964. British poet, sister of Osbert and Sacheverell ◊Sitwell, with whom she enjoyed scandalizing 'the Establishment'. She is remembered for her series of poems *Façade*.

Sitwell /'sɪtwəl/ Osbert 1892–1969. British poet and author, elder brother of Edith and Sacheverell ◊Sitwell. Born in London, and son of Sir George Sitwell (1860–1943), he went to Eton, and served in the Grenadier Guards 1912–19. He published his *Selected Poems* in 1943, and wrote art criticism; novels, including *A Place of One's Own* 1941; and a series of autobiographical volumes 1945–62.

Sitwell /'sɪtwəl/ Sacheverell 1897– . British poet and art critic. Born in Scarborough, he has published art criticism, for example, *Southern Baroque Art* 1924 and *British Architects and Craftsmen* 1945; poetry; and prose miscellanies such as *Of Sacred and Profane Love* 1940 and *Splendour and Miseries* 1943.

SI units *Système International d'Unités*: system of scientific units originally proposed in 1960, based on seven basic units: the metre (m) for length, kilogram (kg) for weight, second (s) for time, ampere (A) for electrical current, kelvin (K) for temperature, mole (mol) for amount of substance, and candela (cd) for luminosity. It replaces the ◊mks, ◊cgs, and ◊fps systems, and is the accepted standard system used by scientists worldwide.

Siva /'ʃiːvə/ or *Shiva* (Sanskrit 'propitious') the third person in the Hindu triad. As Mahadeva (great lord), he is the creator, symbolized by the phallic *lingam*, who restores what as Mahakala he destroys. He is often sculptured as Nataraja, performing his fruitful cosmic dance. His consort or female principle (*sakti*), is Parvati, otherwise known as Durga or Kali.

Siva *Nataraja*: Siva as Lord of the Dance. A bronze statue from Madras State, probably Tanjore-Pudukottai region. It is of the Chola dynasty which ruled in the tenth century AD.

Six, The term used to describe the original six signatory countries to the Treaty of Rome which created the ◊European Community.

Six Articles an act introduced by Henry VIII in England in 1539, to settle disputes over dogma in the English Church: the articles affirmed belief in transubstantion, communion in one kind only, auricular confession, monastic vows, celibacy of the clergy, and private masses; those who rejected transubstantiation were to be burned at the stake. The act was repealed in 1547, replaced by 42 articles in 1551, and by an act of ◊Thirty-Nine Articles in 1571.

Six Counties the six counties which form Northern Ireland, namely Antrim, Armagh, Down, Fermanagh, Londonderry and Tyrone.

Six, Les a group of French 20th-century composers; see ◊Les Six.

sixth-form in UK education, an inclusive term used for pupils staying on for one or two years of study beyond school-leaving age in order to gain ◊A Level or other post-15 qualifications. In some areas, sixth-form education is concentrated in sixth-form colleges.

Sixtus /'sɪkstəs/ title of five popes, including: *Sixtus IV* 1414–84, pope from 1471, who built the Sistine Chapel, which is named after him. *Sixtus V* 1521–90, pope from 1585, who supported the Spanish Armada against Britain and the Catholic League against Henry IV of France.

Sjaelland /'ʃelənd/ the main island of ◊Denmark., on which Copenhagen is situated; area 7,000 sq km/2,700 sq mi; population (1970) 2,130,000. It is low-lying with an irregular coastline. The chief industry is dairy farming.

Skagerrak /'skægəræk/ arm of the North Sea between the S coast of Norway and the N coast of Denmark. In May 1916 it was the scene of the Battle of ◊Jutland.

Skåne /'skɔːnə/ province of S Sweden. It is a fertile agricultural region, comprising the counties of Malmöhus and Kristianstad. Malmö and Hälsingborg are important centres. It was under Danish rule until ceded to Sweden in 1658.

Skara Brae /'skærə 'breɪ/ remarkably preserved Neolithic village to the north of Stromness, on Pomona, ◊Orkney Island.

skate the name of several species of flatfish of the ray group. The *common skate Raja batis* is up to 1.8 m/6 ft, greyish, with black specks. An edible fish, it is found off the British coasts. The egg-cases ('mermaids' purses') are often washed ashore by the tide.

skateboard single flexible board mounted on wheels, and steerable by weight positioning. As a land alternative for surfing, skateboards developed in California in the 1960s and became a worldwide craze in the 1970s.

skating self-propulsion on ice by means of bladed skates, or on other surfaces by skates with four small rollers. Ice-skating became possible as a world sport from the opening of the first artificial ice-rink in London in 1876, and the chief competitive events are figure skating, for singles or pairs, which includes both compulsory figures and freestyle combinations to music; ice-dancing, which is increasingly a choreographed combination of ballet and popular dance movements welded to an artistic whole; and simple speed skating. The modern roller skate was the invention of James L Plympton, who opened the first rink at Newport, Rhode Island, USA, in 1866; events are as for ice-skating.

World Championships first world figure skating championships held 1896
men
1983 Scott Hamilton *(United States)*
1984 Scott Hamilton *(United States)*
1985 Alexsander Fadeev *(USSR)*

1986 Brian Boitano (*United States*)
1987 Brian Orser (*Canada*)
women
1983 Rosalynn Sumners (*United States*)
1984 Katerina Witt (*East Germany*)
1985 Katerina Witt (*East Germany*)
1986 Debi Thomas (*United States*)
1987 Katerina Witt (*East Germany*)
pairs
1983 Oleg Vasiliev and Yelena Valova (*USSR*)
1984 Paul Martini and Barbara Underhill (*Canada*)
1985 Oleg Vasiliev and Yelena Valova (*USSR*)
1986 Sergei Grinkov and Ekaterina Gordeeva (*USSR*)
1987 Sergei Grinkov and Ekaterina Gordeeva (*USSR*)
ice dance
1983 Christopher Dean and Jayne Torvill (*Great Britain*)
1984 Christopher Dean and Jayne Torvill (*Great Britain*)
1985 Andrei Bukin and Natalia Bestemianova (*USSR*)
1986 Andrei Bukin and Natalia Bestemianova (*USSR*)
1987 Andrei Bukin and Natalia Bestemianova (*USSR*)

Skegness /ˌskeg'nes/ holiday resort on the coast of Lincolnshire, England; population (1985) 14,553. It was the site of the first ◊Butlin holiday camp.

skeleton the rigid or semi-rigid framework found in all vertebrate animals and some invertebrates. It is composed of ◊bone, ◊cartilage, ◊chitin, and calcium carbonate or silica, and it supports the animal's body, as well as protecting the internal organs and providing anchorage points for the muscles. It may be internal, forming an ◊endoskeleton, or external, forming an ◊exoskeleton. Another type of skeleton, found in invertebrates such as earthworms, is the *hydrostatic skeleton*. This gains partial rigidity from fluid enclosed within a body cavity. Because the fluid cannot be compressed, contraction of one part of the body results in extension of another part, giving ◊peristaltic motion.

Skelmersdale /'skelmәzdeıl/ town W of Wigan, Lancashire, England; population (1985) 41,800. It was developed as a 'new town' from 1962, with many light industries.

Skelton /'skelton/ John c. 1460–1529. English poet, who was tutor to the future Henry VIII. His satirical poetry includes the rumbustious *The Tunnyng of Elynor Rummynge* 1516, and political attacks on Wolsey, such as *Collyn Cloute* 1522.

Skiddaw /'skıdɔ:/ mountain (930 m/3,053 ft) in Cumbria, England; in the Lake district, N of Keswick.

skiffle a style of popular music, introduced by Lonnie Donnegan in 1956, characterized by improvised percussion instruments such as tea chests and washboards.

skiing self-propulsion on snow by means of elongated runners for the feet, slightly bent upward at the tip, known from about 3000 BC, but developed for the modern sport only from 1896 when it became possible to manoeuvre more accurately. Events include downhill (with speeds up to 80 km/50 mi per hour); slalom, in which a series of turns between flags have to be negotiated; cross-country racing; and ski jumping, when jumps of over 150 m/400 ft are achieved from ramps up to 90 m/295 ft high. The *Fédération Internationale des Skieurs* (1924) is linked with the Ski Club of Great Britain (1924), the Canadian Amateur Ski Association (1920), and the National Ski Association of America (1904).

Alpine World Cup first held 1967
men – overall
1983 Phil Mahre (*United States*)
1984 Pirmin Zurbriggen (*Switzerland*)
1985 Marc Girardelli (*Luxembourg*)
1986 Marc Girardelli (*Luxembourg*)
1987 Pirmin Zurbriggen (*Switzerland*)
women
1983 Tamara McKinney (*United States*)
1984 Erika Hess (*Switzerland*)
1985 Michela Figini (*Switzerland*)
1986 Maria Walliser (*Switzerland*)
1987 Maria Walliser (*Switzerland*)

Skikda /'skıkdɑ:/ trading port in Algeria; population (1980) 547,347. Products include wine, citrus, and vegetables. Formerly Philippeville, it was founded by the French in 1838, and renamed after independence.

skin the covering of the body of ◊vertebrates. In mammals its outer layer, the epidermis, is insensitive and protective, and the cells of this are constantly being rubbed away and replaced from below. The lower layer, the true skin or dermis, is full of blood-vessels and ◊nerves of sensation, touch, and temperature control. It contains the ◊hair roots, and the ◊sweat and sebaceous glands, and is supported by a network of fibrous and elastic cells. *Skin-grafting* is the repair of injured skin by placing pieces of skin taken from elsewhere on the body so that the cells may multiply and cover it.

skink lizard of the family Scincidae, a large family of about 700 species found throughout the tropics and subtropics. There is a range of body form but in many there is a tendency for the body to be long and the legs reduced. Some are actually legless and rather snake-like. Many are good burrowers or can 'swim' through sand like the '*sandfish*' genus *Scincus* of N Africa. Some skinks lay eggs, others bear live young. Skinks include the tiny limbed *three-toed skink Chalcides chalcides* of S Europe and NW Africa, up to 40 cm/1.3 ft long, of which half is tail, and the *stump-tailed skink Tiligua rugosus* of Australia, which stores fat in its triangular tail and looks the same at either end, and feeds on fruit as well as small animals.

Skinner /'skınә/ B(urrhus) F(rederic) 1903– . American psychologist, a behaviourist, who rejects mental concepts, seeing the organism as a 'black box' (internal processes are not important in predicting behaviour). He studied operant conditioning and stressed that behaviour is shaped and maintained by its consequences.

His radical approach rejected almost all previous psychology; his text *Science and Human Behaviour* 1953 contains no references and no bibliography.

skittles game (also known as ninepins) in which nine wooden pins, arranged with the aid of a diamond-shaped frame at one end of an alley, are knocked down by a ball thrown from the other. Either two players or two teams compete. The game resembles ◊tenpin bowling.

Skopje /'skɒpjeı/ capital and industrial city of Macedonia, Yugoslavia; population (1981) 506,547. Industries include iron, steel, chromium mining, and food processing. It stands on the site of an ancient town destroyed by earthquake in the 5th century, and was taken in the 13th century by the Serbian king Milutin, who made it his capital. Again destroyed by earthquake 1963, Skopje was rebuilt on a safer nearby site. It is an Islamic centre.

Skryabin /skrı'æbin/ Alexander (Nikolayevich) 1872–1915. Russian composer and pianist born in Moscow, whose powerfully emotional tone poems, such as *Prometheus* 1911, and symphonies, such as *Divine Poem* 1903, employed a revolutionary system of harmony to express his mystical feelings.

skua dark-coloured gull-like seabird of which the largest species is the *great skua Stercorarius skua* of the N Atlantic, 60 cm/2 ft long and dark brown on the upper parts. Very aggressive, skuas seldom fish for themselves but force gulls to disgorge their catch.

skull in ◊vertebrates, the collection of flat and irregularly shaped bones (or pieces of cartilage) which enclose and protect the brain, forming the head. In mammals, the brain case/cranium consists of 22 plates of bone joined by sutures. The bones of the face carry the upper teeth, enclose some air spaces/sinuses and form the framework for the eyes, nose, and mouth. The lower ◊jaw is hinged to the middle of the cranium at its lower edge. Inside, the cranium is hollowed into various shallow cavities into which fit different parts of the ◊brain; the plate corresponding to the back of the head (occipital) is jointed at its lower edge with the upper section of the ◊spine (atlas and axis). The floor of the skull is pierced by a large hole for the spinal cord and a number of smaller apertures through which other nerves and blood vessels pass.

skunk North American mammal of the weasel family. The *common skunk Mephitis mephitis* has a long, arched body, short legs, a bushy tail, and black fur with white streaks on the back. In self-defence it discharges a foul-smelling fluid.

skydiving freefalling from an aircraft at up to 3,650 m/12,000 ft, performing aerobatics, and then opening a parachute 600 m/2,000 ft from the ground.

Skye /skaı/ largest island of the Inner ◊Hebrides, Scotland; area 1,665 sq km/643 sq mi; population (1971) 7,372. It is separated from the mainland by the Sound of Sleat. The chief port is Portree.

Skylab US space station, made from the adapted upper stage of a Saturn V rocket. At 75 tonnes, it was the heaviest object ever put into

skeleton

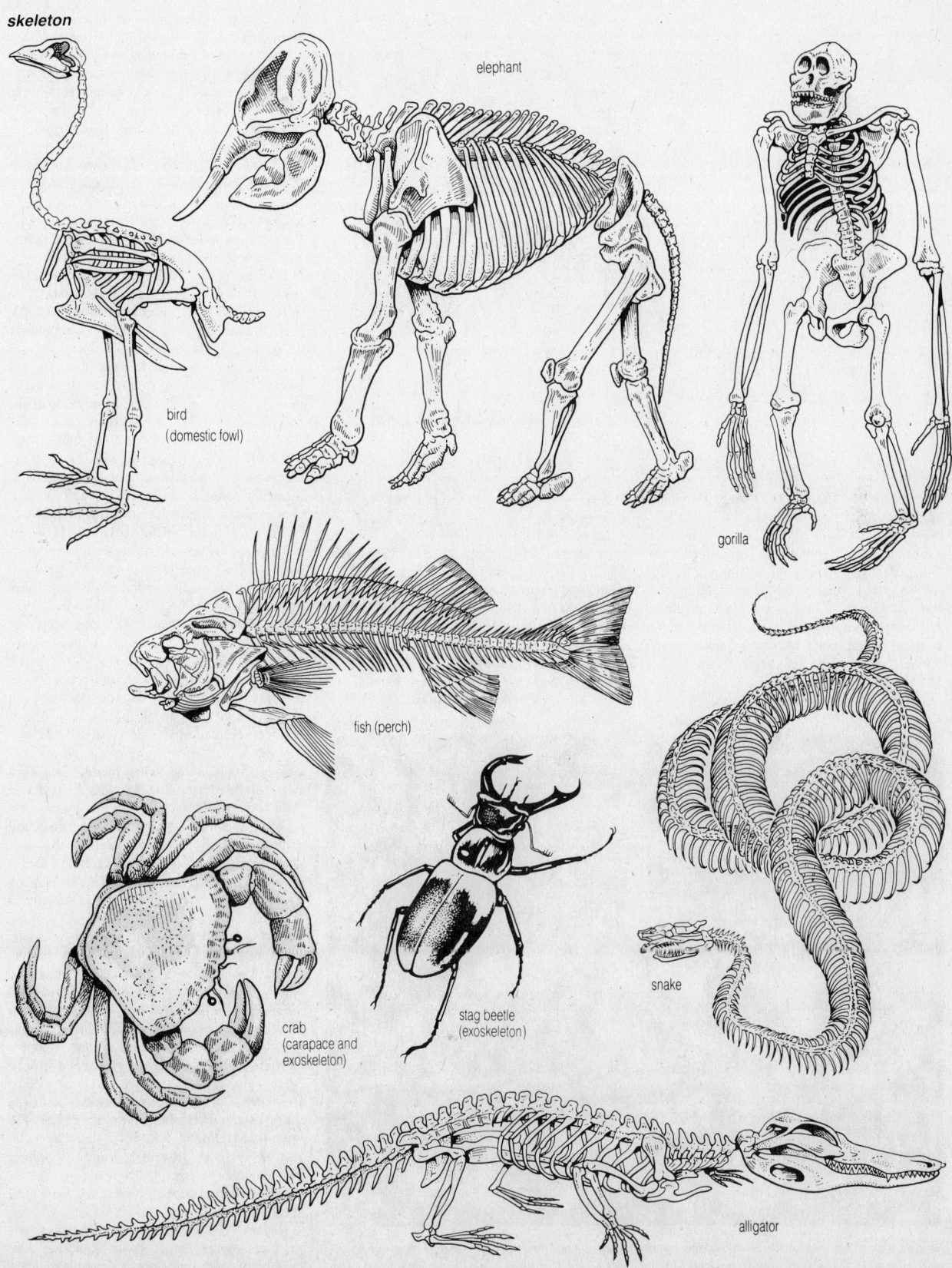

bird
(domestic fowl)

elephant

gorilla

fish (perch)

snake

crab
(carapace and
exoskeleton)

stag beetle
(exoskeleton)

alligator

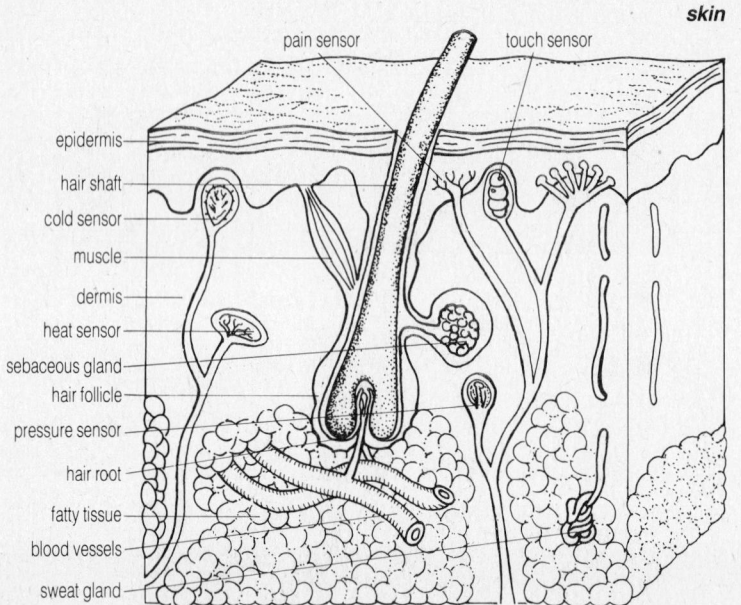

skin

Labels (top to bottom, left side): epidermis, hair shaft, cold sensor, muscle, dermis, heat sensor, sebaceous gland, hair follicle, pressure sensor, hair root, fatty tissue, blood vessels, sweat gland

Labels (top): pain sensor, touch sensor

space, and was 25.6 m/84 ft long. Damaged during launch, it had to be repaired by the first crew of ◊astronauts. Skylab contained a workshop for carrying out experiments in ◊weightlessness, an ◊observatory for monitoring the Sun, and cameras for photographing the Earth's surface. Three crews, each of three astronauts, occupied Skylab for periods of up to 84 days, at that time a record for human space-flight. Skylab finally fell to Earth on 11 Jul 1979.

skylark a type of ◊lark.

Skyros /'skaɪrɒs/ Greek island, see ◊Sporades.

skyscraper a building so tall that it appears to 'scrape the sky', first developed in 1868 in New York, USA, where land prices were high and the geology adapted to such methods of construction. In Manhattan, New York, are the famous Empire State Building (1931), 102 storeys and 381 m/1,250 ft high, and the twin towers of the World Trade Center 415 m/1,361 ft, but these are surpassed by the ◊Sears Tower 443 m/1,454 ft in Chicago. Chicago was also the home of the first modern skyscraper, the Home Insurance Building (1885), which was built ten storeys high with an iron and steel frame. A rigid steel frame is the key to skyscraper construction, taking all the building loads. The walls simply 'hang' from the frame (curtain walling), and they can thus be made from relatively flimsy materials such as glass and aluminium.

Slade /sleɪd/ Felix 1790–1868. British art collector, born in London. He bequeathed most of his art collection to the British Museum and endowed Slade art professorships at Oxford, Cambridge, and University College, London. The Slade School is a branch of the latter.

slander spoken defamatory statement (as opposed to ◊libel), although if broadcast on radio or television it constitutes libel. Some slanders, such as imputing that a person is incapable in his or her profession, are actionable in the UK without the need to prove that pecuniary loss has been suffered. As in the case of libel, the slander must be made to some person other than the person defamed for it to be actionable.

slang extremely informal language usage which often serves to promote a feeling of group membership. Slang is not usually accepted in serious, formal speech or writing, and includes expressions that may be impolite or taboo in conventional terms. Such forms of slang as army slang or Cockney rhyming slang are often extended into more general use because social conditions make them fashionable or people have grown accustomed to using them. Some types of slang are highly transient; others may last across generations, and gain currency in the standard language. Because slang is often vivid, suggestive, and linked with subjects such as defecation, urination, sex, blasphemy, and getting drunk, many people find it offensive. It is, however, pervasive in its influence and effects.

slate a fine-grained, bluish-purple ◊meta-morphic rock which splits readily into thin slabs suitable for roofing. Its cleavage is due to the alignment of platy minerals such as ◊mica. It is highly resistant to atmospheric conditions, and can also be used for writing upon with chalk. Quarrying slate takes such skill and time that it is now seldom used for roofing except in restoring historic buildings, elsewhere tiles or substitutes are used.

Slav a member of an Indo-European people, speaking ◊Slavonic languages, whose ancestors included the ◊Sarmatians and ◊Scythians, and who spread outward from the Carpathian mountains. By the 7th century AD they were the predominant population of E and SE Europe. During the 9th century they adopted Christianity, and in the course of the Middle Ages were expelled from what is now East Germany. After the 16th century they settled in Siberia on an increasingly large scale. They fall into three groups:
eastern Russians, Belorussians, and Ukrainians;
western Poles, Czechs, and Slovaks;
southern Serbs, Croats, Slovenes, Macedonians, and Bulgars.

slavery the involuntary servitude of one person to another, or one group to another. This usually involves outright ownership of the

Skylab A close-up view of the Skylab space station cluster, taken from the command module during the 'fly-around' inspection, prior to docking.

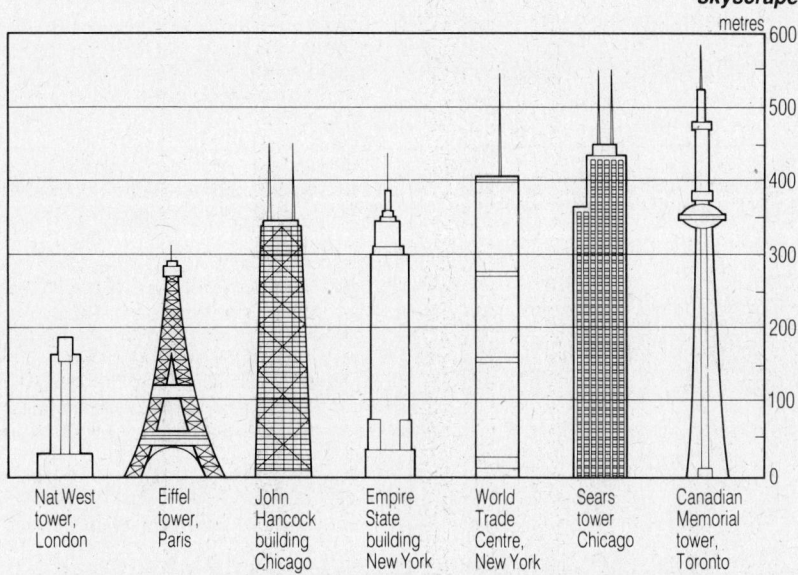

skyscraper
metres 600

500

400

300

200

100

0

Nat West tower, London | Eiffel tower, Paris | John Hancock building Chicago | Empire State building New York | World Trade Centre, New York | Sears tower Chicago | Canadian Memorial tower, Toronto

(chattel-) slave by a master, but there are other forms of partial slavery where an individual is tied to the land, or to another person, by legal obligations as in serfdom or villeinage. As a social and economic institution slavery originated in the times when humans adopted sedentary farming methods of subsistence rather than more mobile forms of hunting and gathering. Slave labour became commonplace during the Greek and Roman periods, when it was used to cultivate large estates and to meet the demand for personal servants in the towns. Slaves were created through the capture of enemies, through birth to slave parents, through sale into slavery by free parents, and as a means of punishment.

Slavery declined after the fall of the Roman Empire, but persisted in Muslim lands and in central Europe where many Slavonic peoples were captured and taken as slaves to Germany. (Hence the derivation of the word.) Slavery also persisted in Spain and Portugal where the reconquest of the peninsula from the Moors in the 15th century created an acute shortage of labour. Captured Muslims became the first victims of the increased use of slavery, but they were soon followed by slaves from Africa, imported by the Portuguese king Henry the Navigator after 1444. Slaves were used for a wide range of tasks, and a regular trade in slaves was established between the Guinea Coast and the slave markets of the Iberian peninsula.

Slavery became of major economic importance after the 16th century with the European conquest of South and Central America. Needing a labour force but finding the indigenous inhabitants unwilling to cooperate, the Spanish and Portuguese conquerors used ever increasing numbers of slaves drawn from Africa. Although used for a variety of tasks, the slaves had the greatest impact on the sugar and coffee plantations. An enormously lucrative 'triangular' trade was established with alcohol, firearms and textiles being shipped from Europe

to be traded for slaves in Africa. The slaves would then be shipped to South or Central America where they would be traded for staples such as molasses and later raw cotton. The profits from these ventures were enormous and became a major element in the British economy and the West Indian trade in general. It has been estimated that the British slave trade alone shipped 2 million slaves from Africa to the West Indies between 1680 and 1786. Other statistics show that the total slave trade to the Americas in the year 1790 may have exceeded 70,000.

Anti-slavery movements and changes in the political and economic structure of Europe helped to bring about the aboliton of slavery in most of Europe during the later 18th and early 19th century, followed by abolition in overseas territories somewhat later. The slave trade was outlawed in the British Empire in 1807 and slavery itself in 1833. Only in the southern states of the USA did slavery persist as a major, if not essential, component of the economy – providing the labour force for the cotton plantations. While the northern states abolished slavery in the 1787–1804 period, the southern states insisted on protecting the institution. Slavery became an issue in the economic struggles between southern plantation owners and northern industrialists in the first half of the 19th century, a struggle which culminated in the secession of the southern states from the Union (see ◊Confederacy) and the outbreak of the American ◊Civil War.

Although the war was not fought on the slavery issue, Abraham Lincoln saw the advantages of promising freedom for southern slaves and the Emancipation Proclamation was enacted in 1863. This was reinforced after the war by the 13th, 14th, and 15th amendments to the US ◊constitution (1865, 1868, and 1870), which abolished slavery altogether and guaranteed citizenship and civil rights to former slaves. Apart from the moral issues at stake in discussing slavery in the US, there has also been a good deal

of debate on the economic efficiency of slavery as a system of production. It has been argued that plantation owners might have been better off in employing labour, although the effect of emancipating vast numbers of slaves could, and did, have enormous political and social repercussions in the US after 1865 (see ◊Reconstruction).

Although outlawed in most countries of the world, various forms of slavery continue to exist – as evidenced by the steps taken by international organizations such as the League of Nations between the wars and the United Nations since 1945 to curb such practices. Most notable in this respect is the 1926 League of Nations Slavery Convention, which was adopted by the United Nations in 1953. Slavery was officially abolished in Saudi Arabia in 1963, and in Mauritania not until 1980.

Slavkov /ˈslæfkɒf/ Czech name of ◊Austerlitz.

Slavonic or Slavic languages a branch of the Indo-European language family spoken in Central and Eastern Europe, the Balkans, and parts of N Asia. The family divides into three groups: the *southern group* (Serbo-Croat, Slovene and Macedonian in Yugoslavia, and Bulgarian in Bulgaria); the *western group* (Czech and Slovak in Czechoslovakia, Sorbian in East Germany, and Polish and its related dialects); and the *eastern group* (Russian, Ukrainian and Byelorussian, in the Soviet Union). There is such a high degree of uniformity among the Slavonic languages that scholars speak of a 'dialect continuum' in which the users of one variety understand tolerably well much of what is said in other varieties. Some Slavonic languages, like Polish, are written in the Roman alphabet while others, like Russian, use the Cyrillic alphabet.

Slavophile intellectual and political group in 19th-century Russia which promoted the idea of an eastern orientation for the empire in opposition to those who wanted the country to adopt western methods and ideas of development.

sleep a state of reduced awareness and activity that occurs at regular intervals in many animal species. Sleep differs from ◊hibernation in occurring daily rather than seasonally, and involving less drastic reductions in metabolism. Most mammals and birds sleep, though there is considerable variation in the amount of time spent sleeping. The function of sleep is unclear. In some species it may serve to make animals inconspicuous at times when they might be vulnerable to predators; in humans it is linked with hormone levels and specific brain electrical activity, including delta waves, quite different from the brain's waking activity. People deprived of sleep become irritable, uncoordinated, forgetful, hallucinatory, and even psychotic. 'REM' (rapid eye movement) phases, associated with dreams, occur at regular intervals during sleep, when the eyes move rapidly below closed lids.

sleeping pill drug which promotes calmness and sleep. The two main groups are barbiturates and the anti-anxiety drugs, such as Benzodiazepine. The latter type are the most

Slavery: The Triangular Trade

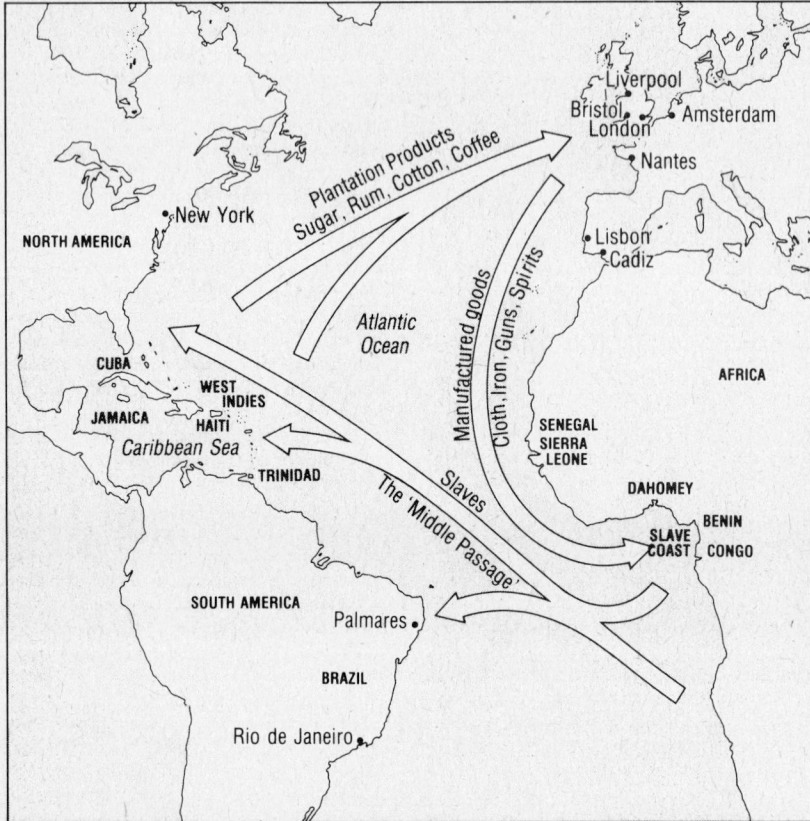

fur is greyish-brown, and the diet vegetarian. The chief species are the **three-toed sloth** or **ai** *Bradypus tridactylus*, and the **two-toed sloth** *Choloepus didactylus* of northern S America.

Slough /slau/ industrial town in Berkshire, England, near Windsor; population (1981) 97,000.

Slovakia /sləu'vɑːkiə/ region in the east of Czechoslovakia settled in the 5th–6th centuries by Slavs; occupied by the Magyars in the 10th century; part of the kingdom of Hungary until 1918, when it became a province of ◊Czechoslovakia. Slovakia was a puppet state under German domination 1939–45, and was abolished as an administrative division in 1949. Its capital and chief town was Bratislava.

Slovene a member of the Slav people of ◊Slovenia, and parts of the Austrian Alpine provinces of Styria and Carinthia; their language resembles Serbo-Croat.

Slovenia /sləu'viːniə/ constituent republic of NW Yugoslavia.
area 20,251 sq km/7,819 sq mi
capital Ljubljana
features mountainous; rivers Sava and Drava
population (1981) 1,891,864, of whom over 1,700,000 are Slovene
language Slovene, resembling Serbo-Croat, written in Roman characters
religion Roman Catholic
history settled by the ◊Slovenes in the 6th century, until 1918 Slovenia was the Austrian province of Carniola, and in 1946 was made an autonomous republic of Yugoslavia.

slow-worm harmless species of lizard *Anguis fragilis*, common in Europe and Britain. Superficially resembling a snake, it is distinguished by its small mouth and movable eyelids.

SLR camera a single-lens ◊reflex camera, in which the image is seen in the taking lens. This type of camera is the most widely used today, and usually comes in ◊thirty-five mm format.

slug air-breathing gastropod related to snails, but with absent or much-reduced shell. The **grey field slug** *Deroceras reticulatum* is the commonest British species, and a pest to crops and garden plants.

Sluter /'sluːtə/ Claus c. 1380–1406. Dutch sculptor, whose works mark a departure from the Gothic style towards a new realism.

small arms one of the two main divisions of ◊firearms, small arms came into use in the late 14th century as portable hand-guns, supported on the ground and ignited by hand. The matchlock, evolved during the 15th century, used a match of tow and saltpetre gripped by an S-shaped lever which was rocked towards the touch hole with one finger, enabling the gun to be held, aimed and fired in much the same way as today. Front and back sights, followed by a curved stock which could be held against the shoulder (in the hackbut or Hookgun), gave increased precision. The difficulty of keeping a match alight in wet weather was overcome by the introduction of the wheel lock, in about 1515, in which a shower of sparks was produced by a spring-drawn steel wheel struck by iron pyrites. This cumbrous and expensive mechanism evolved into the simpler

widely used, because they are safer, and have less marked side-effects. However, both groups can cause dependence and should be taken for short periods only.

sleeping sickness acute disease (trypanosomiasis) caused by blood parasites (*Trypariosma gambiense*) carried by the tsetse fly. Symptoms are fever, rash, sensitivity of the bones to blows, and drowsiness ending in death unless treated.

slide rule a mathematical instrument having pairs of sliding scales, used for multiplication, division, and the extraction of square roots, based on ◊logarithms. Formerly popular with draughtsmen and engineers, it has been largely superseded by the electronic calculator.

Sligo /'slaɪgəu/ county in ◊Connacht, Republic of Ireland. It is situated on the Atlantic coast of NW Ireland; area 1,795 sq km/693 sq mi; population (1981) 55,500; county town Sligo. The chief industry is livestock and dairy farming.

Slim /slɪm/ William Joseph, 1st Viscount Slim 1891–1970. British field marshal. A veteran of ◊Gallipoli, he commanded the 14th 'forgotten' army 1943–45, stemming the Japanese invasion of India at Imphal and Kohima, and then recovered Burma. He was governor-general of Australia 1953–60.

slime mould an extraordinary organism which shows some features of ◊fungi and some of ◊protozoa. They fall into two main types, the **cellular slime moulds** and the **plasmodial slime**

moulds. The former go through a phase of living as single cells, looking very like ◊amoebae, and feed by engulfing the bacteria found in rotting wood, dung, or damp soil. When a food supply is exhausted, up to 100,000 of these amoebae form into a colony resembling a single slug-like animal and migrate to a fresh source of bacteria. The colony then takes on the aspect of a fungus, and forms long-stalked fruiting bodies which release spores. These germinate to release amoebae, which repeat the life cycle. The plasmodial slime moulds are similar in many ways, but have a more complex lifestyle involving sexual reproduction. They form a slimy mass of protoplasm with no internal cell walls, which slowly spreads over the bark or fallen branches of trees.

Sloane /sləun/ Hans 1660–1753. British physician, born in County Down, Ireland. He settled in London, and in 1721 founded the Chelsea Physic Garden. He was president of the Royal College of Physicians 1719–35, and in 1727 succeeded Newton as president of the Royal Society. His library, which he bequeathed to the nation, formed the nucleus of the British Museum.

sloe another name for (the fruit of) the ◊blackthorn.

sloth mammal of the order Edentata, confined to South America. Sloths have small rounded heads, rudimentary tails, and prolonged forelimbs: each foot has long curved claws adapted to clinging upside down from trees. The

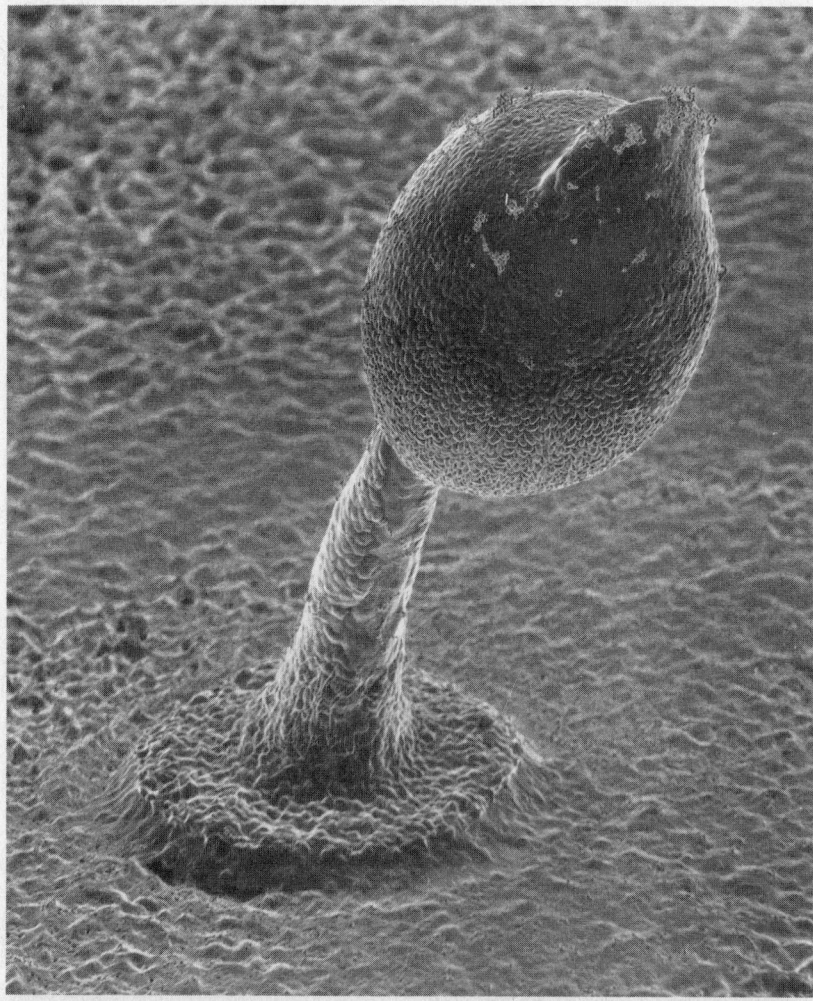

slime mould Electron micrograph showing the underside of a spore tower of slime mould. A curious organism displaying both animal and plant characteristics, slime mould reproduces itself by spores released form the spore tower.

flintlock in about 1625, operated by flint striking steel and in general use for 200 years until a dramatic advance, the 'percussion cap', invented in 1810 by a sport-loving Scottish clergyman, Alexander Forsyth, removed the need for external igniters. Henceforth, weapons were fired by a small explosive detonator placed behind or within the base of the bullet, struck by a built-in hammer.

The principles of rifling, breech loading, and the repeater, although known since the 16th century, were not successfully exploited until the 19th century. It was known that imparting a spin made the bullet's flight truer, but the difficulty of making the bullet bite the grooves had until then prevented the use of rifling. The Baker rifle, issued to the Rifle Brigade in 1800, was loaded from the front of the barrel (muzzle), and had a mallet for hammering the bullets into the grooves.

The first breech loader was Von Dreyse's 'needle gun', issued to the Prussian army in 1842, in which the detonator was incorporated with the cartridge. By 1870 breech loading was in general use, being quicker, and sweeping the barrel out after each firing. An early rifle with bolt action was the Lee-Metford 1888, followed by the Lee-Enfield, both having a 'magazine' beneath the breech, containing a number of cartridges. With modifications this model is still used by the British army. US developments favoured the repeater (such as the Winchester) in which the fired case was extracted and ejected, the hammer cocked, and a new charge inserted into the chamber, all by one reciprocation of a finger lever. In the semi-automatic, part of the explosion energy performs the same operations: the Garand, used by the US army, is of this type. Completely automatic weapons were increasingly adopted during World War II. From 1954 the British army standardized upon the Belgian FN 30, which is gas operated and can fire shots singly or automatically at 650–700 rounds per minute. See ♢machine gun.

Small Claims Court lowest level of law court in England and Wales, where small claims of £500 or less (for example, in respect of inferior goods) can be settled quickly and informally before a lawyer.

smallpox contagious viral disease, marked by fever and skin eruptions leaving pitted scars. It was endemic in Europe until the development of vaccination, and remained so in Asia, where the virulent form of the disease (variola major) entailed a fatality rate of 30 per cent, until the worldwide World Health Organization campaign from 1967 which resulted in its eradication by 1980. The virus now survives only in storage in various research institutes.

Smart /smɑːt/ Christopher 1722–1771. British poet. He became a fellow of Pembroke College, Cambridge, but settled in London as a hack writer. He was confined in 1756 to an asylum, where he wrote his greatest poems, 'A Song to David' and 'Jubilate Agno/Rejoice in the Lamb'.

smelling salts a mixture of ammonium carbonate, bicarbonate, and carbamate. They were once used to arouse people who had fainted, their strong and unpleasant smell having a marked stimulant effect.

smelt small inshore marine fish. The most common European smelt is the *sparling Osmerus eperlanus*, which is noted for its delicate flavour; related species occur on the coasts of the USA.

smelting processing a metallic ♢ore in a ♢furnace to produce the metal. Oxide ores such as iron ore are smelted with coke (carbon), which reduces the ore into metal and also provides fuel for the process. A substance such as limestone is often added during smelting to facilitate the melting process and to form a slag which dissolves many of the impurities present.

Smersh formerly the main administration of counter-intelligence in the USSR, established 1942. It was a subsection of the ♢KGB.

Smetana /'smetənə/ Bedřich 1824–1884. Czech composer, conductor at the National Theatre of Prague 1866–74. His music has a distinct national character, for example, the operas *The Bartered Bride* 1866, *Dalibor* 1868, and the symphonic suite *My Country* 1875–80. Deaf from 1874, he became insane in 1883.

Smiles /smaɪlz/ Samuel 1812–1904. Scottish author, remembered for the extremely popular Victorian didactic work *Self Help* 1859.

Smirke /smɜːk/ Robert 1780–1867. leading Greek Revival architect in Britain; designer of the British Museum.

Smith /smɪθ/ Adam 1723–1790. Scottish economist and philosopher, born in Kirkcaldy, and regarded as the founder of modern political economy. He was professor of moral philosophy at Glasgow 1752–63, publishing his *Theory of Moral Sentiments* in 1759. In *The Wealth of Nations* 1776 he defined national wealth in terms of labour, as the only real measure of value, which is expressed in terms of wages. The cause of wealth is explained by the division of labour – dividing a production process into several repetitive operations, each carried out by different workers. Smith advocated the free working of individual enterprise, and especially the necessity of 'free trade' rather than the ◊protectionism of the mercantile system.

Smith Adam Smith, Scottish economist and author of *The Wealth of Nations*.

Smith /smɪθ/ Bessie 1894–1937. US jazz and blues singer, born in Chattanooga, Tennessee. She established herself in the 1920s, recording with Louis Armstrong and Benny Goodman. She died after a car crash when she was refused admission to a whites-only hospital. She was known as the 'Empress of the Blues'.

Smith /smɪθ/ David 1906–1965. American sculptor and painter. His art evolved gradually from his long apprenticeship in using steel and acetylene welding in a car factory. His best-known pieces are enormous monumental accumulations of burnished steel cubes.

Smith /smɪθ/ Henry George Wakelyn 1787–1860. British general. He served in the Peninsular War. Subsequently he fought in South Africa and India, and was governor of Cape Colony 1847–52.

Smith /smɪθ/ Ian Douglas 1919– . Rhodesian politician. In 1948 he became a member of the South Rhodesia legislative assembly, was a founder of the Rhodesian Front 1962 and became prime minister 1964. In 1965 he made a unilateral declaration of Rhodesia's independence, and despite United Nations ◊sanctions and various other pressures, internal and external, maintained his regime with remarkable tenacity. In 1979 he was succeeded as prime minister by Bishop Abel Muzorewa, when the country was renamed Zimbabwe-Rhodesia. He was suspended from the Zimbabwe parliament in Apr 1987 and resigned in May as head of the white opposition party.

Smith /smɪθ/ John 1580–1631. English colonist. President of the colony of Virginia 1608–09. During an expedition among the American Indians his life is said to have been saved by ◊Pocahontas, whom he married. He explored New England in 1614.

Smith /smɪθ/ Joseph 1805–1844. US founder of the ◊Mormons.

Smith /smɪθ/ Maggie (Margaret Natalie) 1934– . British actress, whose roles include the title part (winning an Oscar) in the film *The Prime of Miss Jean Brodie* 1969. Other films include *A Private Function* 1984, and *A Room with a View* 1986.

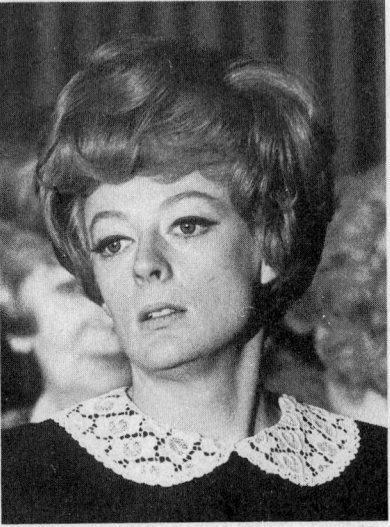

Smith British actress Maggie Smith portraying the title role in *The Prime of Miss Jean Brodie* 1969.

Smith /smɪθ/ Matthew 1879–1960. British artist, known for his exuberant treatment of nudes, luscious fruits and flowers, and landscapes.

Smith /smɪθ/ Ross Macpherson 1892–1922 and Keith Macpherson Smith 1890–1955. Australian airmen. Brothers, they made the first England to Australia flight 1919, and for this exploit were knighted.

Smith /smɪθ/ 'Stevie' (Florence Margaret) 1902–1971. British poet, noted for eccentrically direct verse, whose books include *Novel on Yellow Paper* 1936, and the poems *A Good Time was had by All* 1937, and *Not Waving but Drowning* 1957.

Smith /smɪθ/ William 1769–1839. British canal engineer. While supervising excavations he noted that different beds of rock could be identified by their fossils, and so established the basis of ◊stratigraphy.

Smithfield /'smɪθfiːld/ site of a meat market (1868) and poultry and provision market (1889), in the City of London, England. It was the scene of the execution of many Protestant martyrs in the 16th century, and of the murder of Wat ◊Tyler in 1381, while the annual Bartholomew Fair was held here 1614–1855.

Smithson /'smɪθsən/ James 1765–1829. British chemist. The Smithsonian Institution in Washington DC was established in 1846, following his bequest of $100,000 for this purpose, and includes a museum, art gallery, zoo park, and astrophysical observatory.

smoker a vent on the ocean floor, associated with an ◊ocean ridge, through which hot, mineral-rich groundwater erupts into the sea. Seawater percolating through the sediments and

crust is heated in the active area beneath and dissolves minerals from the hot rocks. As the charged water is returned to the ocean, the sudden cooling causes these minerals to precipitate from solution, forming thick clouds of suspension. The clouds may be dark or light, depending on the mineral content, thus producing 'white smokers' or 'black smokers'.

smoking inhaling the fumes from burning tobacco leaves, generally in the form of ◊cigarettes or ◊cigars. The practice can be habit-forming, and is dangerous to health. A direct link between lung cancer and smoking was established in 1950; there is also a link between smoking and bronchitis and chest and heart diseases. Manufacturers have attempted to filter harmful substances and to use milder tobaccos, and governments have carried out extensive anti-smoking advertising campaigns. In the UK and the USA all cigarette packets sold must carry a government health warning, and television advertising of cigarettes is forbidden.

Smolensk /smə'lensk/ city on the river Dnieper, W USSR; population (1985) 331,000. Industries include textiles and distilling.
history Founded 882, Smolensk was captured by Napoleon 1812. The Germans took the city in 1941, and it was liberated by the Russians in 1943. In nearby *Katyn Forest*, 4,500 Polish officer prisoners of war were shot in 1940, 10,000 others being killed elsewhere after the German-Soviet partition of Poland; the Germans and Russians blame each other, but the balance of the evidence is against the Russians.

Smollett /'mɒlɪt/ Tobias George 1721–1771. Scottish novelist, who made his name with the picaresque novels *Roderick Random* 1748, *Peregrine Pickle* 1751, *Ferdinand Count Fathom* 1753, *Sir Lancelot Greaves* 1760–62, and *Humphrey Clinker* 1771. His methods and vivid characterization greatly influenced ◊Dickens. Among his other works are a *History of England* 1757; a translation of *Don Quixote* 1755; and the satire *Adventures of an Atom* 1769. He died near Livorno, Italy.

smuggling the illegal import or export of prohibited goods, or the evasion of customs duties on dutiable goods. Restrictions on imports, originally a means of preventing debasement of coinage (for example, in 14th-century England), were later used for raising revenue, mainly on luxury goods, and led to a flourishing period of smuggling during the 18th century, in goods such as wines, brandy, tea, tobacco, and lace. Modern smuggling, on both the national and international scale, is concerned with such items as watches, diamonds, gold, and narcotics; it is punishable by fines, and in some cases by imprisonment.

smut parasitic ◊fungus, which infects flowering plants, especially cereals.

Smuts /smʌts/ Jan Christian 1870–1950. South African politician, born in Cape Colony. He studied at Cambridge, and was admitted to the Bar. Having settled in the Transvaal, he was appointed state attorney in 1898, and during the ◊South African War commanded the Boer forces in Cape Colony. He subsequently worked for reconciliation between Boers and the British and became minister of the interior 1910–12 and defence minister 1910–20, on the establishment of the Union. He commanded the South African forces in East Africa 1916–17, and entered the imperial war cabinet in 1917. He was prime minister 1919–24, and minister of justice 1933–39, and on the outbreak of war succeeded Gen Hertzog as premier, supporting the Allied Cause in both World Wars. He held office until defeated at the general election in 1948. He was created a field marshal in 1941 and received the Order of Merit in 1947. Although much more of an internationalist than his contemporaries such as Hertzog, Smuts nonetheless remained a segregationalist, voting in favour of legislation which took away black rights and land ownership.

Smyrna /ˈsmɜːnə/ former name of the Turkish port of ◊Izmir.

Smyth /smaɪθ/ Dame Ethel (Mary) 1858–1944. British composer. Born in Kent, she studied in Leipzig. Her works include the Mass in D 1893, and operas *The Wreckers* 1906, *The Boatswain's Mate* 1916. She was imprisoned as an advocate of women's suffrage, and wrote the autobiographical *Female Pipings in Eden* 1933 and *What Happened Next* 1940.

Snaefell /ˌsneɪˈfel/ highest mountain in the Isle of ◊Man, 620 m/2,034 ft.

snail any species of air-breathing gastropod mollusc, with a spiral shell. The typical snails of the genus *Helix* have two species in Europe. The ***common garden snail Helix aspersa***, is very destructive to plants; the ***Roman snail Helix pomatia*** is 'corralled' for the gourmet market. Over-collection has depleted the population.

Snake /sneɪk/ tributary of the Columbia river, NW USA; length 1,670 km/1,038 mi.

snake reptile of the suborder Serpentes of the order Squamata (which also includes lizards). Snakes are characterized by an elongated limbless body possibly evolved because of subterranean ancestors. One of the most striking internal modifications is the absence or greatly reduced size of the left lung. There are some 3,000 species found in the tropic and temperate zones, but none in New Zealand, Ireland, Iceland, and near the poles. The skin is covered in scales which are markedly wider underneath where they form, in all except a few species, an essential aid to locomotion. A snake is helpless on glass where these scales can effect no 'grip' on the surface: progression may be undulant, 'concertina', or creeping, or a combination of these. Detailed vision is limited at a distance, though movement is immediately seen; hearing is restricted to ground vibrations (sound waves are not perceived); the sense of touch is acute; besides the sense of smell through the nasal passages, the flickering tongue picks up airborne particles which are then passed to special organs in the mouth for investigation; and some (rattlesnakes) have a cavity between eye and nostril which is sensitive to infra-red rays (useful in locating warm-blooded prey in the dark). All snakes are carnivorous, and often camouflaged for better concealment in hunting as well as their own protection. Some are oviparous and others ovoviviparous, that is the eggs are retained in the

oviducts until development is complete; in both cases the young are immediately self-sufficient. The majority of snakes belong to the Colubridae, chiefly harmless, such as the common grass snake of Europe, but including the deadly African boomslang *Dispholidus typus*. The venomous families include the Elapidae comprising the true ◊cobras, the New World coral snakes, and the Australian taipan, copper-head and death adder; the Viperidae (see ◊viper), and the Hydrophiidae, aquatic sea-snakes. Anti-sera against snake-bite (made from the venom) are expensive to prepare and store, and specific to one snake species, so that experiments have been made with more widely valid treatment, for example, trypsin, a powerful protein-degrading enzyme, effective against the cobra/mamba group. Among the more primitive snakes are the Boidae, which still show links with the lizards and include the boa constrictor, anaconda, and python: these kill by constriction but their victims are usually comparatively small animals.

snake A king brown snake being 'milked'. The venom – the clear fluid at the bottom of the container – is used in making anti-sera.

snapdragon perennial herbaceous plant, genus *Antirrhinum*, family Scrophulariaceae, with spikes of bright-coloured two-lipped flowers. Some garden species have been bred so large that bees have difficulty in depressing the lower lip to enter and pollinate them.

snipe marsh bird of the family Scolopacidae, order Charadriiformes; species include ***common snipe Gallinago gallinago***, of Europe, and the rare ***great snipe Gallinago media***, of which the males hold spring gatherings to show their prowess. It is related to the ◊woodcock.

snooker game derived (via pool) from ◊billiards, played with 22 balls: 15 reds (value 1 point); the single 'pool' balls, black (value 7 points), pink (6), blue (5), brown (4), green (3), yellow (2), and the white 'cue ball'. The object is to pocket a red ball and a 'pool' ball alternately, each time returning the 'pool' ball (but not the red) to the table until all the reds are pocketed, when the 'pool' balls are then potted in order of numerical value. The maximum possible 'break' (score at one turn) is 147 (fouls excluded). The

advent of television, enabling large audiences to view the game has increased its popularity.

World Professional Championship first held 1927
1983 Steve Davis *(England)*
1984 Steve Davis *(England)*
1985 Dennis Taylor *(Northern Ireland)*
1986 Joe Johnson *(England)*
1987 Steve Davis *(England)*

---

snoring a loud noise during sleep made by vibration of the soft ◊palate caused by streams of air entering the nose and mouth at the same time. It is most common when the nose is blocked.

Snow /snəʊ/ C(harles) P(ercy), Baron Snow 1905–1980. British novelist, born in Leicester. He was chief of scientific personnel at the Ministry of Labour in World War II and parliamentary secretary to the Ministry of Technology 1964–66. His sequence of novels *Strangers and Brothers* ranges the British social scale from the 1920s. It includes *Corridors of Power* 1964. His Rede lecture at Cambridge in 1959, 'The Two Cultures and the Scientific Revolution', discussed the absence of communication between literary and scientific intellectuals in the West.

Snowden /ˈsnəʊdn/ Philip, 1st Viscount Snowden 1864–1937. British right-wing Labour politician, chancellor of the Exchequer 1924 and 1929–31. He entered the coalition National Government in 1931 as Lord Privy Seal, but resigned in 1932.

Snowdon /ˈsnəʊdn/ highest mountain in Wales, 1,085 m/3,560 ft above sea level. It consists of a cluster of five peaks. At the foot of Snowdon are the Llanberis, Aberglaslyn, and Rhyd-ddu passes. A rack railway ascends to the summit from Llanberis. Snowdonia, the surrounding mountain system, was made a National Park 1951.

Snowdon /ˈsnəʊdn/ Anthony Armstrong-Jones, Earl of Snowdon 1930– . British photographer specializing in portraits, who married Princess ◊Margaret 1960 (peerage 1961); divorced 1978.

snowdrop bulbous plant *Galanthus nivalis*, family Amaryllidaceae, with white bell-shaped flowers, touched with green, in spring.

snow leopard a type of ◊leopard.

Snowy Mountains /ˈsnəʊi/ range in the Australian Alps, chiefly in New South Wales, near which the Snowy river rises; both river and mountains are known for a hydroelectric and irrigation system.

snuff finely powdered ◊tobacco for sniffing up the nostrils as a stimulant or sedative. It was common in 17th-century England, and became universal in the 18th century.

Soames /səʊmz/ Christopher, Baron Soames 1920–1987. British Conservative politician. He was vice president of the Commission of the European Communities 1973–77 and governor of (Southern) Rhodesia during its transition to independence as Zimbabwe, Dec 1979–Apr 1980. He was created a life peer in 1978.

Soane /səʊn/ John 1753–1837. British architect, whose individual Neo-Classical style resulted in works curiously presaging modern taste. Little remains of his extensive work at the Bank of England, London. Other buildings include his own house in Lincoln's Inn Fields, London, now the Soane Museum.

soap a chemical compound used in washing; a mixture of the sodium salts of various fatty acids: palmitic, stearic, or oleic acid. It is made by the action of caustic soda or caustic potash (originally obtained from wood ash) on fats of animal or vegetable origin. Soap makes grease and dirt disperse in water through the same mode of action as a ◊detergent.

soap opera a television series or radio melodrama, named because it originated in the USA as a series of daytime programmes sponsored largely by washing-powder manufacturers. Notable television soap operas include:
Coronation Street (UK, 1960–)
Crossroads (UK, 1964–88)
Dallas (USA, 1978–)
Dynasty (USA, 1981–)
EastEnders (UK, 1985–).

soapstone a type of rock from which talc is derived.

Soares /ˈswɑːres/ Mario 1924– . Portuguese politician. Exiled in 1970, he returned to Portugal in 1974, and as leader of the Portuguese Socialist Party (PSP) was prime minister 1976–78. He resigned as party leader in 1980, but in 1986 was elected Portugal's first socialist president.

Sobers /ˈsəʊbəz/ Garfield St Aubrun (Gary) 1936– . West Indian cricketer, born in Barbados. He scored 8,032 test runs and took 235 wickets in his career. He holds the record for the highest individual test innings, 365 not out against Pakistan 1957–58. He hit a record six sixes off one over for Nottinghamshire against Glamorgan at Swansea 1968. Knighted 1975.

Sobieski /sɒbˈjeski/ John 1642–1696. alternative name for ◊John III, king of Poland.

soca Latin Caribbean music, a mixture of ◊soul and ◊calypso.

Sochi /ˈsɒtʃi/ seaside resort in the USSR, on the Black Sea; population (1985) 310,000. In 1976 it became the world's first 'no smoking' city.

social behaviour in zoology, behaviour concerned with altering the behaviour of other individuals of the same species. Thus, ◊courtship displays allow individuals to choose appropriate mates and form the bonds necesary for successful reproduction. Social behaviour also allows animals to live in groups, and form alliances within their group against other members (for example, subordinate animals can group together to prevent dominant individuals from monopolizing food). Social behaviour may be aggressive in character, or submissive, or designed to establish bonds (such as social grooming or preening). The social behaviour of mammals and birds is generally more complex than that of lower organisms, and involves relationships with individually recognized animals. By contrast, in the apparently complex social systems of bees, wasps, ants, and termites, an individual's status and relationships with others is largely determined by its biological

form, as a member of a caste of workers, soldiers or reproductives; see ◊eusociality.

social contract the idea that government authority derives originally from an agreement between ruler and ruled in which the former agrees to provide ◊order in return for obedience from the latter. It has been used to support either absolutism (◊Hobbes) or democracy (◊Locke, ◊Rousseau, and ◊Rawls).
The term was revived in the UK in 1974 when a head-on clash between the Conservative government and the trade unions resulted in a general election which enabled a Labour government to take power. It now denotes an unofficial agreement (hence also called 'social compact') between a government and organized labour that, in return for control of prices, rents, and so on, the unions would refrain from economically disruptive wage demands.

social credit theory, put forward by C H Douglas (1879–1952), that economic crises are caused by bank control of money, which leads to shortage of purchasing power. His remedy was payment of a 'social dividend'. There have been provincial social credit governments in Canada, but the central government has always vetoed the plan.

social democracy a political ideology of belief in the gradual evolution of a democratic ◊socialism within existing political structures. The earliest was the German *Sozial-demokratische Partei* (SPD), today one of the two major West German parties, created in 1875 from August Bebel's earlier German Social Democratic Workers' Party, itself founded 1869. The British Labour Party is in the social democratic tradition.

Social Democratic Labour Party (SDLP) Northern Irish left-wing political party, formed in 1970. It aims at Irish unification, but distances itself from the violent tactics of the Irish Republican Army (IRA), adopting a constitutional, conciliatory role. The SDLP, led by John Hume (1937–), was responsible for the setting-up of the ◊New Ireland Forum in 1983.

Social Democratic Party (SDP) British political party formed 1981 by Labour members of parliament Roy ◊Jenkins (its first leader), David ◊Owen (leader 1983–87), Shirley ◊Williams, and William Rodgers, who resigned from the Labour Party and took a more centrist position. The 1983 and 1987 general elections were fought in alliance with the ◊Liberal Party as the *Liberal/SDP Alliance* (1983 six seats, 11.6% of the vote; 1987 five seats, 9.8% of the vote). A merger of the two parties was voted for by the SDP in 1987, after which David Owen resigned the leadership and was replaced by Robert Maclennan.

socialism movement aiming to establish a classless society by substituting public for private ownership of the means of production, distribution, and exchange. The term has been used to describe positions as widely apart as anarchism and social democracy. Socialist ideas appeared in classical times; in early Christianity; among later Christian sects such as the ◊Anabaptists and ◊Diggers; and, in the ferment

of the revolutionary period at the end of the 18th and early 19th centuries, were put forward as systematized political aims by ◊Rousseau, ◊Saint Simon, ◊Fourier, and ◊Owen, among others. ◊Marx (*Communist Manifesto* 1848) and ◊Engels, in an age when faith in religion was being replaced among the newly literate by a faith in science, gave the movement wider appeal by promoting it on a pseudo-scientific basis as representing a stage in an inevitable historical succession (see ◊communism), the inevitability to be hastened by the 'class struggle' of the workers against the bourgeoisie (capitalists). In its perfected form, each citizen would give 'according to his abilities' and 'receive according to his need', and the state would wither away.
In the later 19th century socialist parties arose in most European countries, for example, in Britain the ◊Independent Labour Party. This period witnessed a reaction against Marxism, typified by the ◊Fabian Society in Britain and the German Revisionists, at the time when in Russia the Bolsheviks were reviving the original revolutionary significance of Marx's teachings. Weakened by these divisions, the second ◊International (founded in 1889) collapsed in 1914, right-wing socialists in all countries supporting participation in World War I while the left opposed it. The Russian Revolution removed socialism from the sphere of theory to that of practice, and was followed in 1919 by the foundation of the Third International, which completed the division between right and left. This lack of unity, in spite of the temporary successes of the popular fronts in France and Spain in 1936–38, facilitated the rise of fascism and National Socialism (◊Nazism) which appealed to popular nationalism and solved economic problems by similar means of state control of the economy, but in the general interests of private capital.
After World War II socialist and communist parties tended to formal union in Eastern Europe, although the rigid communist control that ensued was later modified in some respects in, for example, Poland, Romania, and Yugoslavia. Subsequent tendencies to broader communism were suppressed in Hungary (1956) and Czechoslovakia (1968). In Western Europe, however, a communist take-over of the Portuguese revolution failed 1975–76, and elsewhere, as in France under ◊Mitterrand, attempts at socialist–communist cooperation petered out. Most countries in Western Europe have a strong socialist party, for example, in West Germany the Social Democratic Party and in Britain the ◊Labour Party.

socialist realism artistic doctrine set up by the Soviet Union during the 1930s setting out the optimistic, socialist terms in which society should be portrayed in works of art (including music and painting as well as prose fiction). The policy was used as a form of censorship of artists whose work, it was felt, did not follow the approved Stalinist party line, or which were too 'modern'. The policy was relaxed after Stalin's death, but still remains in force. Artists whose work was censured in this way include the composer

◊Shostakovich, and the writers ◊Solzhenitsyn and ◊Sholokov.

socialization the process, beginning in childhood, by which a person learns how to become a member of a particular society, learning its norms, customs, laws, and ways of living. The main agents of socialization are the family, school, peer groups, work, religion, and the mass media. The main methods of socialization are direct instruction, rewards and punishment, imitation, experimentation, role play, and interaction.

social science the group of academic disciplines which investigate how and why people behave the way they do, as individuals and in groups. Western thought about society has been particularly influenced by the ideas and insights of such great theorists as Plato and Aristotle, Machiavelli, Rousseau, Hobbes, and Locke. The modern study of society, however, can be traced to the great intellectual period of the 18th century called the Enlightenment, and to the industrial and political revolutions of the 18th and 19th centuries, to the moral philosophy or ◊positivism. The French thinker Auguste ◊Comte, using the term 'social science', attempted to establish the study of society as a scientific discipline, capable of precision and prediction in the same way as natural science. The modern academic social sciences are generally listed as ◊sociology, ◊economics, ◊anthropology, ◊political science, and ◊psychology, but their area of study overlaps extensively with such subject areas as history, geography, law, philosophy, and even biology. And although some thinkers – such as Marx – have attempted to synthesize the study of society within one theory, none has yet achieved what Einstein has done for physics or Darwin for biology. A current debate is whether the study of people can or should be a science.

social security state provision of financial aid to alleviate poverty. The concept of such payments developed in the later 19th century in Europe, for example compulsory social insurance in Germany from 1883; non-contributory old-age pensions in Britain from 1909; and compulsory health and unemployment insurance in Britain from 1911.

The term 'social security' was first applied officially in the USA, in the Social Security Act 1935, passed to enable the federal government to cope with the effects of the Depression of 1929. It was first used officially in Britain in 1944, and following the ◊Beveridge Report in 1942 a series of acts was passed from 1945 to widen the scope of social security. Basic entitlements of those paying National Insurance contributions in Britain have included an old-age pension, unemployment benefit, widow's pension, and payment during a period of sickness in one's working life. In addition, people over 16 who are not at school, at work, or on strike and whose income is below a certain level are entitled to claim benefits and exemptions from certain charges; the scheme, known originally as National Assistance, was called Supplementary Benefit from 1966. Other benefits have included Family Income Supplement, Child Benefit

(known until 1977 as Family Allowance), and Attendance Allowance for those looking after sick or disabled people. Entitlements under National Insurance, such as Unemployment Benefit, have been paid at flat rates regardless of need; other benefits, such as Supplementary Benefit, have been 'means-tested', that is, claimants' income must be below a certain level. Most payments, with the exception of Unemployment Benefit, are made by the Department of Health and Social Security.

In 1987–88 further changes in the social security system included Income Support replacing Supplementary Benefit and Family Credit replacing Family Income Supplement; the abolition of death and maternity grants, to be replaced by means-tested payments from a new Social Fund; and the replacement of maternity allowances by Statutory Maternity Pay, paid by employers, not the DHSS.

In the USA the term 'social security' usually refers specifically to old-age pensions, which have a contributory element, in contrast to 'welfare'. The federal government is responsible for social security (medicare, retirement, survivors', and disability insurance) ; unemployment insurance is covered by a joint federal-state system for industrial workers, but few in agriculture are covered; and welfare benefits are the responsibility of individual states, with some federal assistance.

society the organization of people into groups. ◊Social science, in particular ◊sociology, is the study of human behaviour in a social context. Various aspects of society are discussed under ◊class, ◊community, ◊culture, ◊kinship, ◊norms, ◊role, ◊socialization, and ◊status.

Society Islands /sə'saɪəti/ an archipelago in ◊French Polynesia.

Socinianism form of 17th-century Christian belief which rejects such traditional doctrines as the Trinity and original sin, named after Socinus, the Latinized name of Lelio Francesco Maria Sozzini (1525–62), Italian Protestant theologian. His views on the nature of Christ were developed by his nephew, Fausto Paolo Sozzini (1539–1604), who also taught pacifist and anarchist doctrines akin to Tolstoy's. Socinianism denies the divinity of Jesus but emphasizes his virtues, and is an early form of ◊Unitarianism.

sociobiology the study of the biological basis of all social behaviour, including the application of ◊population genetics to the evolution of behaviour. It builds on W D ◊Hamilton's concept of ◊inclusive fitness to emphasize that the evolutionary function of behaviour is to allow an organism to contribute as many of its own ◊alleles as it can to future generations (an idea encapsulated in ◊Dawkins' notion of the 'selfish gene'). Contrary to some popular interpretations, it does not assume that all behaviour is genetically determined. The use of ◊game theory is an important aspect of sociobiology.

sociology the systematic study of society, in particular of social order and social change, social conflict and social problems. It studies social institutions, such as the family, law, and

the Church, as well as social concepts such as norm, role, and culture. See ◊social science.

Socotra /sɒ'kəʊtrə/ Yemeni island in the Indian Ocean; capital Tamridah; area 540 sq km/1,400sq mi. Under British protection from 1886, it became part of South Yemen 1967, and is used as a military base by the USSR.

Socrates /'sɒkrətiːz/ c. 469–399 BC. Athenian philosopher, said to have been a sculptor and soldier. He wrote nothing but was immortalized in the dialogues of his pupil, ◊Plato. In his desire to combat the scepticism of the ◊sophists, Socrates asserted the possibility of true knowledge. In the sphere of morality he put forward the view that the good person never knowingly does wrong. True knowledge emerges through dialogue and an abandoning of uncritical claims to knowledge. The effect of Socrates' teaching was disruptive since he opposed tyranny. Accused in 399 on charges of impiety and corruption of youth, he was condemned by the Athenian authorities to die by drinking hemlock.

Socratic method way of teaching used by ◊Socrates, in which he aimed to guide pupils to clear thinking on ethics and politics by asking questions and then exposing their inconsistencies in cross-examination.

Soddy /'sɒdi/ Frederick 1877–1956. British physical chemist, a pioneer of research into atomic disintegration – he coined the term 'isotope'. He wrote a classic work on radioactivity *Chemistry of the Radio-Elements* 1912–14, and was awarded a Nobel prize in 1921.

sodium a metallic element, symbol Na (Latin: *natrium*), atomic number 11, atomic weight 22.991. A soft, bright, silvery, reactive metal tarnishing quickly on exposure to air and reacting violently with water to form sodium hydroxide. First isolated by Sir Humphry ◊Davy in 1807, it is found abundantly in combination, the commonest form being sodium chloride (NaCl – common salt). Sodium metal is used to a limited extent as a spectroscopic reference, in discharge lamps, and alloyed with potassium as a heat-transfer medium in nuclear reactors. Sodium compounds are of the widest industrial importance and thousands of tonnes are manufactured annually. Among the more important are common salt, sodium carbonate (Na_2CO_3 – washing soda), and bicarbonate ($NaHCO_3$ – baking powder), sodium hydroxide or caustic soda (NaOH), sodium nitrate or Chile saltpetre ($NaNO_3$ – fertilizer), sodium thiosulphate or hypo ($Na_2S_2O_3$ – photographic fixer). An artificial isotope of sodium is used as a tracer in the human body.

Sodom and Gomorrah /'sɒdəm, gə'mɒrə/ two ancient cities in the Dead Sea area, recorded in the Old Testament (Genesis) as destroyed by fire and brimstone for their wickedness.

Sofia /'səʊfiə/ capital of Bulgaria since 1878; population (1980) 1,052,433. Industries include textiles, rubber, machinery, electrical equipment. It lies at the foot of the Vitosha Mountains, and is chiefly modern.

software in computing, any kind of program or programs (as opposed to hardware, that is, the mechanical and electrical components of a computer). A computer can do nothing without software. Computer programs tell the machine what to do, step by step and in minute detail. Even to execute a program a computer first needs another program to guide it. This may be built into the hardware or may need to be loaded on ◊disk (see ◊operating system). Getting started in this way is known as 'booting' or 'bootstrapping' the system.

software project lifecycle in computing, the various stages of development in the writing of a major program (◊software), from the identification of a requirement to the installation and support of the finished program. The most common pattern for the project lifecycle is the 'waterfall' model. See also ◊systems analysis and ◊systems design.

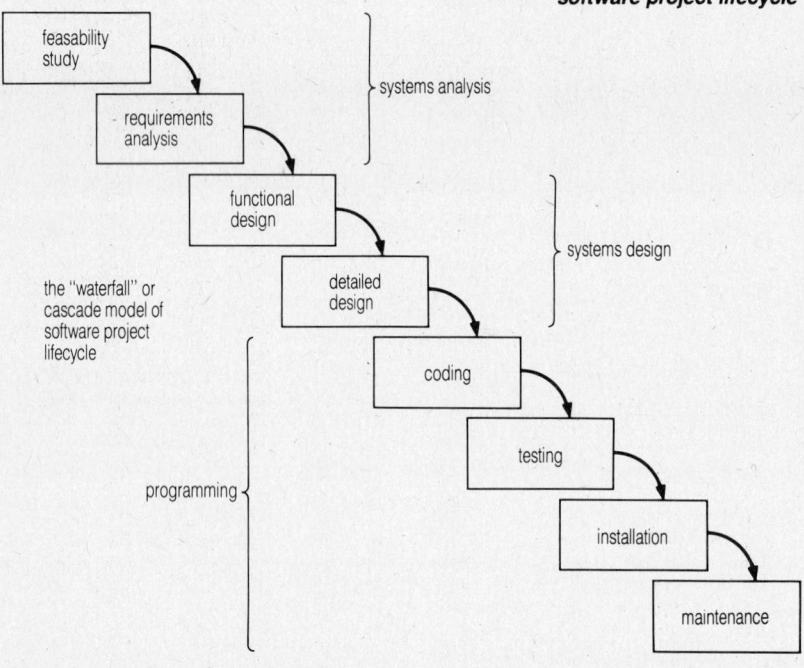

software project lifecycle

the "waterfall" or cascade model of software project lifecycle

systems analysis

systems design

programming

feasability study

requirements analysis

functional design

detailed design

coding

testing

installation

maintenance

softwood a coniferous tree, or the wood from it, which in general is softer and easier to work, but in some cases less durable, than wood from ◊deciduous trees.

Sogne Fjord /ˈsɒŋnəˈfiːɔːd/ longest and deepst fjord in ◊Norway, 185 km/115 mi long and 1,245 m/4,080 ft deep.

Soho /ˈsəʊhəʊ/ district of W London, England, which houses the offices of film and recording companies; restaurants, and nightclubs.

soil the loose covering of broken rocky material and decaying organic matter overlying the rocks of the Earth's surface. Various types of soil develop under different conditions: deep soils form in hot wet climates and in valleys and shallow soils form in cool dry areas and on slopes. The organic content of soil is widely variable, ranging from zero in some desert soils to almost 100 per cent in peats. Pedology, the study of soil, is significant because of the relative importance of different soil types to agriculture.

soil creep the gradual movement of soil down a slope. As each soil particle is dislodged by a raindrop it moves slightly further downhill. This eventually results in a mass downward movement of soil on the slope. Manifestations of this phenomenon are the formation of terracettes (steplike ridges along the hillside), leaning walls and telegraph poles, and trees that grow in a curve to counteract the progressive leaning.

soil mechanics a branch of engineering that studies the nature and properties of the soil. Soil is investigated during construction work to ensure that it has the mechanical properties necessary to support the foundations of dams, bridges, roads, and so on.

Soissons /ˈswæsɒŋ/ town in Picardy, N France; population (1982) 32,236. The chief industry is metallurgy. In 486 ◊Clovis defeated the Gallo-Romans here, ending their rule in France.

Sokol Czech educational and athletic organization founded in 1862, which plays an important part in public life. It also flourishes in Poland, Bulgaria, Yugoslavia, and other Slav countries. Until 1948 it was non-political.

Sokoto /ˈsəʊkətəʊ/ trading centre in NW Nigeria; population (1975) 118,000. It was the capital of a ◊Fula sultanate from the 16th century until occupied by the British in 1903.

Sokoto /ˈsəʊkətəʊ/ largest state in Nigeria, established 1976; capital Sokoto; area 149,050 sq km/57,500 sq mi; population (1983) 7,421,000.

solan goose another name for the ◊gannet.

solar energy energy derived from the Sun's radiation. A solar furnace, such as that built in 1970 at Odeillo in the French Pyrenees, has thousands of mirrors to focus the Sun's rays; it produces uncontaminated intensive heat for industrial and scientific or experimental purposes. Other solar heaters produce less energy and may have industrial or domestic uses. They usually consist of a black (heat-absorbing) panel containing pipes through which air or water is circulated, either by thermal ◊convection or by a pump. Solar energy may also be harnessed indirectly using solar cells made up of panels of ◊semiconductor material (usually silicon) which generate electricity when illuminated by sunlight. Despite their low running costs, their high installation cost and low power output have meant that solar cells have found few applications outside space probes and artificial satellites.

solar pond natural or artificial 'pond', such as the Dead or Salton seas, in which salt becomes more soluble in the Sun's heat. Water at the bottom becomes more salty and hotter, and is insulated by the less salty water layer at the top. Temperatures at the bottom reach about 100°C/200°F and can be used to generate electricity.

solar system the ◊Sun and all the other bodies in orbit around it: the nine ◊planets, their ◊moons, ◊asteroids and ◊comets. The solar system is thought to have formed from a cloud of gas and dust in space 4,600 million years ago. The Sun contains 99 per cent of the mass of the solar system. The edge of the solar system is not clearly defined; it is marked only by the limit of the Sun's gravitational influence, which extends about 1.5 light years, almost halfway to the nearest ◊star.

solar wind a stream of atomic particles, mostly ◊protons and ◊electrons, from the ◊Sun's corona flowing outwards through the ◊solar system at speeds from 300 km/200 mi to 1,000 km/60 mi per second. The fastest streams come from 'holes' in the Sun's corona that lie over areas where there is no surface activity. The solar wind pushes the gas of comets' tails away from the Sun, and 'gusts' in the solar wind cause geomagnetic disturbances and ◊aurorae on Earth.

solder alloy used for joining such as copper, its common alloys (brass and bronze) and tin-plated steel are used for making food cans. Soft solders (usually alloys of tin and lead, sometimes with added antimony) melt at low temperatures (about 200° C); it is used widely in the electrical industry for joining copper wires. Hard solders, such as silver solder (an alloy of copper, silver and zinc), melt at much higher temperatures, and form a much stronger joint (see also ◊brazing). A necessary preliminary to making any solder joint is cleaning of the surfaces of the metal to be joined (to remove oxide) and the use of a flux (to prevent the heat applied to melt the solder from re-oxidizing the metal).

sole flatfish *Solea solea*, also called Dover sole, found in the southern seas of NW Europe. Up to 50 cm/1.6 ft it is a prized food fish, as is the sand or French sole *Pegusa lascaris* further south.

solenodon rare mammal, genus *Solenodon*, of the insectivore order, looking like a slow-moving overgrown shrew. There are two species, one on Cuba and one on Hispaniola and they are threatened by introduced predators. They can

solar energy Solar energy panels on the roof of a hotel in Morocco. After its installation, solar energy is a non-polluting energy source.

solar system

central part
magnified

Sun

Mercury
Venus
Earth
Mars

Pluto

Neptune

Uranus

Saturn

Jupiter

Mars

Sun

asteroids

root in the ground with their long noses. About 30 cm/1 ft long plus 25 cm/10 in tail, they produce venomous saliva.

Solent, The /'səʊlənt/ channel between Hampshire, England, and the Isle of ◊Wight.

sol-fa short for tonic sol-fa, a method of teaching music, especially singing, systematized by John ◊Curwen.

Solferino /ˌsɒlfə'riːnəʊ/ village in Verona, N Italy, 8 km/5 mi S of Lake Garda, site of the battle in which ◊Napoleon III defeated the Austrians in 1859.

solicitor in the UK, a member of one of the two branches of the English legal profession, the other being a ◊barrister. A solicitor is a lawyer who provides all-round legal services (making wills and winding up estates, conveyancing of property, divorce, litigation defence of those accused of crime). In both civil and criminal cases above Crown Court level, a solicitor may not appear, but must brief a barrister on behalf of his client, and in the most serious cases (for example, murder), a ◊Kings Counsel/◊Queens Counsel as well. Solicitors may become circuit judges and recorders. In the USA the general term is lawyer or attorney, but the term solicitor may be used for practitioners in the court of equity, and, as in England, some public offices have special solicitors. See also ◊law courts.

Solicitor General in the UK, a law officer of the Crown, deputy to the ◊Attorney-General, a political appointee with ministerial rank.

solid in physics, a state of matter which holds its own shape (as opposed to a ◊liquid, which takes up the shape of its container, or a ◊gas, which totally fills its container). According to ◊kinetic theory, the ◊atoms or ◊molecules in a solid are not free to move but merely vibrate about fixed positions – such as those in crystal lattice.

Solidarity the national confederation of Independent Trade Unions in Poland, which was formed under the leadership of Lech Walesa in Sept 1980. It emerged from a summer of industrial disputes caused by the Polish government's attempts to raise food prices. The strikers created a trade union movement independent of the Communist Party. Protracted negotiations with the government led to recognition of Solidarity in exchange for an acceptance of the leading role of the Communist Party in Poland.

Continuing unrest and divisions in Solidarity's leadership led to the government attempting to ban the movement in 1981; but the movement still plays a major role in Polish political life.

solid-state circuit formerly an electronic circuit was always made by joining separate electronic components with wires. In a solid-state circuit all the components (resistors, capacitors, transistors and diodes) and interconnections are made at the same time, and by the same processes, in or on one piece of single crystal silicon. The small size of this construction accounts for its use in electronics for space vehicles and aircraft. See also ◊integrated circuit and ◊silicon chip.

Solingen /'zəʊlɪŋən/ city in N Rhine-Westphalia, West Germany; population (1984)

159,200. Once famous for swords, it now produces steel for razor blades and cutlery.

solipsism in philosophy, a view which maintains that the self is the only thing that can be known to exist. It is an extreme form of ◊scepticism. The solipsist sees himself or herself as the only individual in existence, assuming other people to be a reflection of his or her own consciousness.

soliton non-linear wave, so-named from a 'solitary' wave seen on a canal by British engineer John Scott Russell in the 19th century, who raced after it on his horse. Before he lost it, it had moved on for over a mile as a smooth, raised and rounded form, rather than widening and dispersing in the normal way. Such behaviour is characteristic of the waves of ◊energy which constitute the particles of atomic physics, so that the mathematical equations which sum up the behaviour of solitons are being used to further research in nuclear ◊fusion, ◊superconductivity, and so on.

Solomon, King of Israel /ˈsɒləmən/ c. 974–c. 937 BC. In the Old Testament, the son of ◊David by Bathsheba, who built the temple at Jerusalem with the aid of heavy taxation and forced labour. He was famed for his wisdom, the much later biblical *Proverbs*, *Ecclesiastes*, and *Song of Songs* being attributed to him.

Solomon Islands /ˈsɒləmən/ country in the W Pacific, E of New Guinea.

government the constitution dates from 1978 and creates a constitutional monarchy within the Commonwealth, with a resident governor-general representing the British monarch as head of state. There is a single-chamber legislature, the National Parliament, with 38 members elected by universal suffrage for a four-year term. The governor-general appoints a prime minister and cabinet drawn from and collectively responsible to the parliament.

The two main political parties are the Solomon Islands United Party (SIUP) and the People's Alliance Party (PAP).

history the islands, inhabited by Melanesians, were sighted by a 1568 expedition from Peru led by the Spanish navigator Álvaro de Mendaña. They became a British protectorate in the 1890s. The Solomon Islands were given internal self-government in 1976, with Peter Kenilorea, leader of the SIUP, as chief minister. He became prime minister when they achieved full independence, within the Commonwealth, in 1978. In 1981 he was replaced by Solomon Mamaloni of the People's Progressive Party. Kenilorea had been unable to devolve power to the regions while preserving the unity of the state, but Mamaloni created five ministerial posts specifically for provincial affairs.

In the 1984 general election SIUPA won 13 seats and the opposition, now PAP, 12. Sir Peter Kenilorea, as he had become, was put back into office at the head of a coalition government. He immediately abolished the five provincial ministries.

Solomon's seal wild plant *Polygonatum multiflorum*, family Liliaceae. It has bell-like white flowers drooping from arching leafy stems, followed by blue-black berries.

Solomon Islands

AREA 29,785 sq km/11,500 sq mi
CAPITAL Honiara on Guadalcanal
PHYSICAL comprises all but the northernmost islands (which belong to Papua New Guinea) of a Melanesian archipelago that stretches nearly 1,500 km/900 mi. The largest is Guadalcanal (area 4,000 sq km/2,500 sq mi); others are Malaita, San Cristobal, New Georgia, Santa Isabel, Choiseul; mainly mountainous and forested
FEATURES rivers ideal for hydroelectric power
HEAD OF STATE Elizabeth II from 1978 represented by Baddeley Devisi
HEAD OF GOVERNMENT Sir Peter Kenilorea from 1984
GOVERNMENT parliamentary democracy
EXPORTS palm oil, copra, rice, timber
CURRENCY Solomon Island dollar (3.45 = £1 Sept 1987)
POPULATION (1985) 267,000 (the majority Melanesian); annual growth rate 3.9%
LANGUAGE English (official)
RELIGION Christian
LITERACY 13% (1980)
GDP $160 million (1983); $628 per head of population

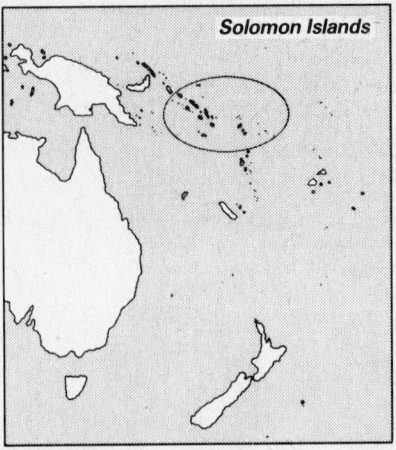

Solomon Islands

CHRONOLOGY
1978 Achieved full independence, within the Commonwealth, with Peter Kenilorea as prime minister.
1981 Solomon Mamaloni replaced Kenilora as prime minister.
1984 Kenilora returned to power, heading a coalition government.

Solon /ˈsəʊlɒn/ c. 638–558 BC. Athenian statesman. As one of the chief magistrates c. 594 BC he carried out the revision of the constitution which laid the foundations of Athenian democracy.

Soloviev /ˌsɒləˈjɒf/ Vladimir Sergeyevich 1853–1900. Russian philosopher and poet, whose blending of neo-Platonism and Christian mysticism attempted to link all aspects of human experience in a doctrine of divine wisdom.

solstice either of the points at which the Sun is farthest north or south of the celestial equator (see ◊celestial sphere) each year. The Sun reaches the *summer solstice*, its farthest north, around Jun 21 each year; and it reaches the *winter solstice*, its farthest south, around Dec 22.

Solti /ˈʃɒlti/ Georg 1912– . British conductor, born in Budapest. He was music director at Covent Garden 1961–71, and of the Chicago Symphony Orchestra from 1969. He was also principal conductor of the London Philharmonic Orchestra 1979–83.

solubility in physics, the maximum amount of solute (usually a solid or gas) that will dissolve in a given amount of solvent (usually a liquid) at a particular temperature. Solubility may be expressed as grams of solute per 100 grams of solvent or, for a gas, in parts per million of solvent. In ordinary terms, each is a way of expressing maximum possible concentration.

Solway Firth /ˈsɒlweɪ/ inlet of the Irish Sea, formed by the estuary of the Esk, at the W end of the border between England and Scotland.

Solyman I alternative form of ◊Suleiman.

Solzhenitsyn /ˌsɒlʒəˈnɪtsɪn/ Alexander 1918– . Russian novelist. After distinguished military service, he revolted against Stalinism and was in prison and exile 1945–57. However, ◊Khrushchev ensured publication of *One Day in the Life of Ivan Denisovich* 1962, dealing with the labour camps under Stalin. More basic criticism of the system in the novels *The First Circle* and *Cancer Ward* both 1968, and the exposé of the whole Russian camp network in *The Gulag Archipelago* 1973, led to his expulsion from the USSR 1974. He has adopted a Christian position, and his criticism of Western materialism is also stringent. He was awarded a Nobel prize in 1970. He became a US citizen in 1974.

soma Indian intoxicating drink made from the fermented sap of the Asclepias acida plant. It was sacrificed to the Hindu god ◊Indra.

Somalia /səˈmɑːlɪə/ country in the Horn of Africa, on the Indian Ocean.

government the 1979 constitution defines Somalia as a socialist state with power in the hands of the Somali Revolutionary Socialist Party (SRSP). As in most socialist states, the party and the state system operate alongside each other, with the president bestriding both. The president is chosen by the party as head of state and government and is secretary general of the party and president of its politburo. Party policy is formulated by the 51-member central committee, operating through 13 bureaux and sanctioned by the politburo. A council of ministers, appointed by the president, implements these policies. In the 177-member People's Assembly, six are presidential nominees and 171 elected by secret ballot for a five-year term from a single list of candidates approved by the party.

history for early history, see ◊Africa. Somalia developed around Arab trading posts which grew

Somalia

DEMOCRATIC REPUBLIC OF (*Jamhuriyadda Dimugradiga Somaliya*)

AREA 700,000 sq km/270,000 sq mi
CAPITAL Mogadishu
TOWNS Hargeisa, Kismayu, port Berbera
PHYSICAL mainly flat, with hills in the N
FEATURES many of the people are nomadic raisers of livestock
HEAD OF STATE AND OF GOVERNMENT Mohamed Siad Barre from 1969
GOVERNMENT one-party socialist
EXPORTS livestock, skins, hides; bananas
CURRENCY Somali shilling (198 = £1 Sept 1987)
POPULATION (1985) 7,595,000 (including 1 million refugees from W Somalia); annual growth rate 4.1%
LANGUAGE Somali (national language), Arabic (also official), Italian, English
RELIGION Sunni Muslim
LITERACY 11% male/3% female (1980 est)
GNP $1.2 bn (1983); less than $500 per head of population
CHRONOLOGY
1960 Achieved full independence.
1963 Border dispute with Kenya, diplomatic relations with the UK broken.
1968 Diplomatic relations with the UK restored.

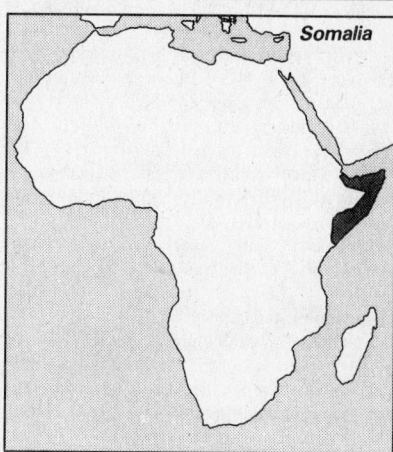

1969 Following the assassination of the president, the army seized power. Maj-Gen Mohamed Siad Barre suspended the constitution and set up a Supreme Revolutionary Council.
1978 Defeated in eight-month war with Ethiopia.
1979 New constitution for a socialist one-party state adopted.
1987 Barre re-elected.

into sultanates. A British protectorate of Somaliland was established 1884–87 and Somalia, an Italian protectorate, 1889. The latter was a colony from 1927 and incorporated into Italian East Africa 1936; it came under British military rule 1941–50, when as a UN trusteeship it was again administered by Italy. Somalia became a fully independent republic in 1960 through a merger of the two former colonial territories. Since then Somalia has been involved in disputes with its neighbours because of its insistence on the right of all Somalis to self-determination, wherever they have settled. This has applied particularly to those living in the Ogaden district of Ethiopia and in NE Kenya. A dispute over the border with Kenya resulted in a break in diplomatic relations with Britain 1963–68. The dispute with Ethiopia led to an eight-month war in 1978, in which Somalia was defeated by Ethiopian troops assisted by Soviet and Cuban weapons and advisers. Some 1.5 million refugees entered Somalia, and guerrilla fighting continues in Ogaden. There was a rapprochement with Kenya in 1984 and, in 1986, the first meeting for ten years between the Somalian and Ethiopian leaders.
The first president of Somalia was Aden Abdullah Osman, and he was succeeded in 1967 by Dr Abdirashid Ali Shermarke of the Somali Youth League (SYL), which had become the dominant political party. In Oct 1969 President Shermarke was assassinated and the army seized power under the commander in chief, Maj-Gen Mohamed Siad Barre. He suspended the 1960 constitution, dissolved the national assembly,

banned all political parties. and formed a military government. In 1970 he declared Somalia a socialist state.
In 1976 the junta transferred power to the newly created SRSP and three years later the constitution for a one-party state was adopted. Some unofficial opposition groups operate outside the country, from Ethiopia and London. Over the next few years Barre consolidated his position by increasing the influence of his own clan and reducing that of his northern rival, despite often violent opposition. He was re-elected in Jan 1987.

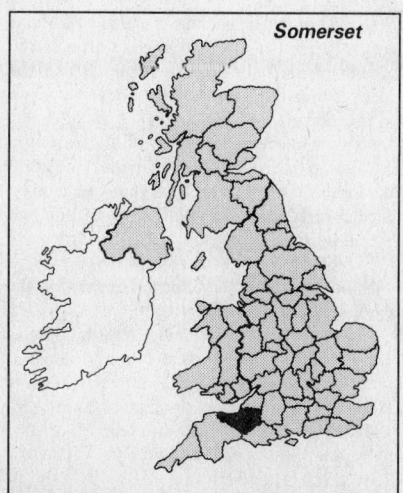

Somaliland /sə'mɑːlilænd/ region of Somali-speaking peoples in E Africa including British Somaliland Protectorate (established 1887), Italian Somaliland (made a colony 1927, conquered by Britain 1941 and administered by Britain until 1950), which both became independent as the ◊Somali Democratic Republic in 1960; and French Somaliland (1892–1967, when it became known as the Territory of the Afars and Issas until independence as ◊Djibouti 1977).

Somerset /'sʌməset/ county in SW England
area 3,451 sq km/1,365 sq mi
towns administrative headquarters Taunton; Wells, Bridgwater, Glastonbury, Yeovil
features rivers Avon, Parret, and Exe; marshy coastline on the Bristol Channel; Mendip Hills (including Cheddar Gorge and Wookey Hole, a series of limestone caves where Old Stone Age flint implements and bones of extinct animals have been found); Quantock Hills; ◊Exmoor
products dairy products, and cider
population (1986) 450,800
famous people Henry Fielding.

Somerset /'sʌməset/ Edward Seymour, 1st Duke of Somerset c. 1506–1552. English politician. Created Earl of Hertford, after Henry VIII's marriage to his sister Jane, he became Duke of Somerset and Protector (regent) for Edward VI in 1547. His attempt to check ◊enclosure offended landowners and his moderation in religion the Protestants, so that he was beheaded on a fake treason charge in 1549.

Somerset As protector of England from 1547, Edward Seymour, Duke of Somerset, instigated the First Book of Common Prayer.

Somerset House government office in the Strand, London, built in 1775. It is used by the Inland Revenue, Principal Probate Registry, and King's College. The river facade was designed by Sir William ◊Chambers. The General Register Office (births, marriages, and deaths), formerly at Somerset House, was merged with the Government Social Survey Department as the Office of Population Censuses and Surveys in 1970, and transferred to St Catherine's House, also in the Strand. Somerset House is the new home of the ◊Courtauld Gallery.

Somerville /ˈsʌməvɪl/ Edith Oenone 1861–1949. Irish novelist, best known for her stories of Irish life written jointly with her cousin, Violet ◊Martin.

Somerville /ˈsʌməvɪl/ Mary Fairfax 1780–1872. Scottish scientific writer. Despite having only a single year of formal education, her uncle supported her studies and, soon after moving to London in 1816 with her second husband she was publishing research papers for the Royal Society. She translated a work on astronomy by ◊Laplace (*Mechanism of the Heavens* 1831) and wrote several best-selling science textbooks, including *Physical Sciences* 1834, and *Physical Geography* 1848. Somerville College, Oxford, was named after her.

Somerville Scottish scientific writer Mary Somerville by James Swinton.

Somme /sɒm/ river in N France, on which Amiens and Abbeville stand; length 240 km/150 mi.

Somme, Battle of the /sɒm/ Allied offensive in World War I Jul–Nov 1916 at Beaumont-Hamel–Chaulnes, during which tanks were first used (see ◊Cambrai). The German offensive around St Quentin Mar–Apr 1918 is sometimes called the 'Second Battle of the Somme'.

sonar or echo-sounder. A method of locating underwater objects by the reflection of ultrasonic waves. In World War I an Allied Submarine Detection Investigation Committee was set up and an apparatus for detecting the presence of enemy U-boats beneath the sea surface by the use of ultrasonic echoes was perfected around 1920. It was named ASDIC, from its initials of the body responsible for it. In 1963 the name was changed, to accord with NATO practice, to sonar (from sound navigation and ◊ranging). The process is similar to that used in radar. The time taken for an acoustic beam in the audible or supersonic range to travel to the underwater object, whose distance is required, and back to the source, enables the distance to be found since the velocity of sound in water is known.

sonata (Italian 'sounded') term originally used to describe a composition for instruments, as opposed to the cantata, which is a composition for voices. The sonata is usually written for one or two instruments, one of which is normally a keyboard instrument (usually piano), and consists of a series of related movements.

sonata form in music, term coined in the 19th century to describe the structure of a movement, typically involving division into exposition, development, and recapitulation sections. Sonata form is the framework for much of classical music, including ◊sonatas, ◊symphonies, and ◊concertos.

Sondheim /ˈsɒndhaɪm/ Stephen (Joshua) 1930– . American composer and lyricist. His early interest in the American ◊musical was encouraged by Hammerstein, and he achieved success first as a witty and sophisticated lyricist of Bernstein's *West Side Story* 1957, and later as a composer of musicals, including *Company* 1970, *A Little Night Music* 1973, *Pacific Overtures* 1976, and *Sweeney Todd* 1979.

son et lumière French 'sound and light', the night-time dramatization of the history of a famous building, town, and so on, using theatrical lighting, sound effects, and narration.

song composition for one or more singers, often with instrumental accompaniment. Most of the great composers in Western ◊music have written songs, including ◊madrigals, and ◊chansons. Popular forms include folk song (see ◊folk music), and ◊ballad. The term song is usually used for secular music, whereas ◊motet, ◊cantata, and so on tend to be sacred forms.

Songhai Empire /ˌsɒŋˈgaɪ/ a former kingdom of NW Africa, founded in the 8th century, which developed into a powerful ◊Muslim empire under the rule of Sonni Ali (reigned 1464–92). It superseded the ◊Mali empire and extended its territory beyond that of its predecessor, occupying an area which includes present-day Senegal, Gambia, Mali, and parts of Mauretania, Niger, and Nigeria. In 1591 it was invaded by Morocco, seeking to take over the Saharan gold trade. The Songhai Empire was overthrown and the area was broken up into smaller kingdoms.

sonic boom a noise like a thunderclap that occurs when an aircraft passes through the ◊sound barrier, or begins to travel faster than the speed of sound. It is caused by shock waves set up by the aircraft.

sonnet fourteen-line poem of Italian origin introduced to England by Sir Thomas ◊Wyatt in the form used by Petrarch (rhyming abba abba cdcdcd or cdecde), as followed by Milton and Wordsworth; Shakespeare used the form abab cdcd efef gg.

Soochow /ˌsuːˈtʃaʊ/ former name for the Chinese city of ◊Suzhou.

Soper /ˈsəupə/ Donald, Baron Soper 1903– . British Methodist minister, superintendent of the West London Mission, Kingsway Hall, 1936–78. His books include *All his Grace* 1957. In 1965 he became a life peer.

Sophia /səˈfaɪə/ Electress of ◊Hanover 1630–1714. Daughter of the Elector Palatine and Elizabeth, daughter of James I of England, she married the Elector of Hanover. She was recognized as in succession to the English throne 1701, and her son George I founded the Hanoverian dynasty.

sophist Greek 'wise man', one of a group of 5th century BC lecturers on culture, rhetoric and politics, whom ◊Plato regarded as dishonest, hence 'sophistry' meaning fallacious reasoning.

Sophocles /ˈsɒfəkliːz/ 495–406 BC. Athenian dramatist and tragic poet. He produced his first plays in 468 BC, when he won the prize in competition with Aeschylus, and wrote over 120 plays in total, of which only seven survive. These are *Ajax*, *Electra*, *The Trachinian Maidens*, *Philoctetes*, and the Theban tragedies *Antigone*, *Oedipus Tyrannus*, and *Oedipus at Colonus*. He modified the form of tragedy by the introduction of a third actor and speeded the action by lessening the role of the chorus. Whereas he said of Euripides 'He paints men as they are', he said of himself 'I paint men as they ought to be' and is noted for his noble grandeur and preservation of traditional values.

soprano in music, the highest range of female voice.

Sopwith /ˈsɒpwɪθ/ Thomas Octave Murdoch 1888– . British designer of the Sopwith Camel biplane used in World War I, and joint developer of the Hurricane in World War II.

sorbic acid a tasteless acid found in the fruit of the rowan or mountain ash, widely used in the preservation of food, for example cider, wine, soft drinks, animal feedstuffs, bread and cheese.

Sorbonne /sɔːˈbɒn/ alternative name for the University of Paris. The Sorbonne was founded in 1253 by Robert de Sorbon, chaplain to Louis IX, as an institution for theological studies. Richelieu reconstructed the buildings in 1626, which were again rebuilt in 1885. In 1808 the Sorbonne became the seat of the Académie of Paris and of the University of Paris.

Sorbus genus of deciduous trees and shrubs of the northern hemisphere, family ◊Rosaceae, generally with white flowers, including ◊mountain ash, ◊whitebeam, ◊service tree.

Sorel /sɒˈrel/ Georges 1847–1922. French philosopher, born in Cherbourg. He believed that socialism could only come about through a general strike; his theory of the need for a 'myth' to sway the body of the people, was used by ◊Fascism.

sorghum type of cereal grass – also called great millet or guinea-corn – grown in Africa, India, China, USA, and S Europe.

sorority a club or society for university women in the USA; the men's equivalent is the ◊fraternity.

sorrel species of plants in genus *Rumex*, family Polygonaceae, especially *Rumex acetosa* grown for its bitter salad leaves.

Sorrento /sɒˈrentəu/ town on the Gulf of Naples, SW Italy; population (1981) 17,301. It has been a resort since Roman times.

sorus in ferns, a group of sporangia, the reproductive structures that produce spores. They occur on the lower surface of fern fronds.

SOS internationally recognized distress signal; forming part of the ◊Morse code.

soul music a ◊gospel-influenced style of ◊rhythm and blues, sung by, among others, Sam ◊Cooke and Aretha Franklin (1942–).

Soult /suːlt/ Nicolas Jean de Dieu 1769–1851. Marshal of France. He held commands in Spain in the Peninsular War (see ◊Santander), and was chief of staff at ◊Waterloo.

sound physiological sensation received by the ear, originating in a vibration (pressure variation in the air), which communicates itself to the air, and travels in every direction, spreading out as an expanding sphere. All sound waves in air travel with a speed which depends on the temperature of the atmosphere; under ordinary conditions this is about 340 m/1,120 ft per second. The pitch of the sound depends on the number of vibrations imposed on the air per second, but the speed is unaffected. The loudness of a sound is dependent primarily on the extent (amplitude) of the to-and-fro vibration of the air. The lowest note audible to a human being has a frequency of about 26 ◊hertz (vibrations per second), and the highest one of about 18,000 Hz: the lower limit of this range varies little with age, but the upper range falls steadily from adolescence onwards.

Sound, the /saund/ strait dividing SW Sweden from Denmark and linking the ◊Kattegat and the Baltic; length 113 km/70 mi; width 5–60 km/3–37 mi.

sound barrier the idea that the speed of sound, or sonic speed, (about 1,220 kph/760 mph at sea level) constitutes a speed limit to flight through the atmosphere. It was once thought this might be the case, since an ill-designed aircraft suffers severe buffeting at near sonic speed due to the formation of shock waves. But Charles (Chuck) E Yeager flew through the 'barrier' in 1947 in a Bell X-1 rocket plane. Now, by careful design, aircraft can fly supersonically (at faster than sonic speed) with ease, though they create in their wake a ◊sonic boom. See also ◊Concorde and ◊supersonic speed.

sound synthesis the generation of sound (usually music) by electronic means. The use of electrical ◊oscillators to drive loudspeakers can be coupled with the information processing power of a computer to generate all kinds of sounds from pure tones to human speech.

sound track a band at one side of a cine film on which the accompanying sound is recorded. Usually it takes the form of an optical track, a pattern of light and shade. The pattern is produced on the film when signals from the recording microphone are made to vary the intensity of a light beam. During playback, a light is shone through the track onto a photocell which converts the pattern of light falling on it into appropriate electrical signals. These signals are then fed to loudspeakers to recreate the original sounds.

Souphanouvong /ˌsuːfænuːˈvɒŋ/ Prince 1912– . Laotian politician. After an abortive revolt against French rule in 1945, he led the guerrilla Pathet Lao, and in 1975 became first president of the Republic of Laos.

Sousa /ˈsuːzə/ John Philip 1854–1932. American composer of marches, such as 'The Stars and Stripes Forever!' 1897.

South, the historically, in the USA, the states south of the ◊Mason and Dixon line, with an agrarian economy based on plantations worked by slaves, which seceded from the Union at the beginning of the US Civil War (see ◊Confederacy). The term is now loosely applied in a geographic and cultural sense, with Texas often regarded as part of the Southwest rather than the South.

South Africa

REPUBLIC OF (Afrikaans *Republiek van Suid-Africa*)

AREA 1,223,181 sq km/433,678 sq mi
CAPITAL Cape Town (legislative), Pretoria (administrative)
TOWNS Johannesburg, Bloemfontein; ports Cape Town, Durban, Port Elizabeth, East London
PHYSICAL a plateau
TERRITORIES Prince Edward Island in the Antarctic
FEATURES Drakensberg Mountains, Table Mountain; Limpopo and Orange rivers; the Veld and the Karroo; part of Kalahari Desert; Kruger National Park, largest in the world
HEAD OF STATE AND OF GOVERNMENT Pieter W Botha from 1984
GOVERNMENT right-wing authoritarian and racist
EXPORTS maize, sugar, fruit; wool; gold, platinum (world's largest producer), diamonds
CURRENCY rand (commercial rate 3.38 = £1 Sept 1987)
POPULATION (1985) 42,465,000 (68% black, of whom the largest nations are the Zulu, Xhosa, Sotho, and Tswana, 18% white, 10% of mixed ancestry, and 3% Asiatic); annual growth rate 2.5%
LANGUAGE Afrikaans and English (both official); various Bantu languages
RELIGION Christian; largest denomination is the Nederduits Gereformeerde Kerk/Dutch Reformed Church. Congregations are segregated
LITERACY 81% male/81% female (1980 est), ranging from 98% whites to 50% blacks
GNP $76.8 bn (1983); $1,296 per head of population
CHRONOLOGY
1910 Union of South Africa formed from two British colonies and two Boer republics.
1912 African National Congress (ANG) formed.
1948 Apartheid system of racial discrimination initiated by Daniel Malan.
1955 Freedom Charter adopted by ANC.
1958 Malan succeeded as prime minister by Hendrik Verwoerd.

South Africa

of Europeans, termed Whites in the context of ◊apartheid. There is only conditional participation in government for non-Whites, in the form of Coloureds, or persons of mixed European and African descent, and Asians. Black Africans are still completely unrepresented at national level.

The three-chamber parliament consists of the House of Assembly, for Whites, the House of

1960 ANC banned.
1961 South Africa withdrew from the Commonwealth and became a republic.
1962 ANC leader Nelson Mandela jailed.
1964 Mandela, Walter Sisulu, Govan Mbeki, and five other ANC leaders sentenced to life imprisonment.
1966 Verwoerd assassinated and succeeded by B J Vorster.
1976 Soweto uprising.
1977 Death in custody of Pan African Congress activist Steve Biko.
1978 Vorster resigned and was replaced by Pieter W Botha.
1981 Military operations launched against Angola and Mozambique.
1984 New constitution adopted, giving segregated representation to coloureds and Asians. Nonaggression pact with Mozambique.
1985 Growth of violence in black townships.
1986 Commonwealth agreed on limited sanctions. US Congress voted to impose sanctions. Some major multinational companies announced that they were closing down their South African operations.
1987 The government formally acknowledged the presence of its military forces in Angola.

South Africa /sauθ ˈæfrɪkə/ country on the S tip of Africa, bounded to the N by Namibia, Botswana, and Zimbabwe, and to the NE by Swaziland and Mozambique.
government the 1984 constitution is based on racial discrimination. The legislature and government are dominated by the descendants

Representatives, for Coloureds, and the House of Delegates, for Indians. The House of Assembly has 178 members, 166 elected by universal White suffrage, four nominated by the president on the basis of one for each province, and eight elected by the 166. The House of Representatives has 85 members, 80 elected by universal Coloured suffrage, two nominated by the president and three elected by the 80. The House of Delegates has 45 members, 40 elected by universal Indian suffrage, two nominated by the president, and three elected by the 40 directly elected members. Each house is responsible for its 'own affairs', meaning matters affecting only Whites, Coloureds, or Indians, as the case may be. General legislation applying to all races, including Black Africans, has to be approved by all three houses and the president. Members of all three houses serve a five-year term.

The state president, who combines the roles of head of state and head of government, is elected for the duration of Parliament by an 88-member electoral college: 50 from the House of Assembly, 25 from the House of Representatives and 13 from the House of Delegates. The president appoints and presides over a cabinet dominated by Whites, and is advised by an appointed council of 60 members: 20 from the House of Assembly, ten from the House of Representatives, five from the House of Delegates, and 25 chosen by the president. There are also three advisory ministers' councils: one for the whole country, one for the Coloured community, and one for the Indians.

Each of South Africa's four provinces has an adminstrator, appointed by the president, and an elected provincial council.

All Black political parties are banned. The main White parties are the National Party (NP) and the opposition Progressive Federal Party (PFP). *history* for early history, see ◊Africa. The area was originally inhabited by Bushmen and Hottentots. Bantus, including Sotho, Swazi, Xhosa, and Zulu, settled there before the 17th century. The ◊Cape of Good Hope was rounded by Bartolomeu ◊Diaz in 1488; the coast of Natal was sighted by Vasco da ◊Gama in 1497. The Dutch East India Company founded Cape Town 1652 as a port of call on the way to the Indies. Occupied by Britain in 1795 and 1806, Cape Town and the hinterland were purchased by Britain in 1814 for £6 million. Britons also settled in ◊Natal, on the coast near ◊Durban, 1824. In 1836 some 10,000 Dutch, wishing to escape from British rule, set out N on the Great Trek and founded the republic of ◊Transvaal and the ◊Orange Free State; they also settled in N Natal, which became part of Cape Colony 1844 and a separate colony 1856. The Orange Free State was annexed by Britain 1848 but became independent in 1854.

The discovery in 1867 of diamonds at Kimberley, in Cape Colony, and in 1886 of gold in Transvaal, attracted prospectors, who came in conflict with the Dutch farmers, the ◊Boers. Britain attempted to occupy Transvaal 1877–81 but withdrew after a severe defeat at Majuba (see ◊South African Wars). Denial of citizenship rights to the migrant miners (*uitlanders*) in Transvaal, and the imperialist ambitions of Cecil ◊Rhodes and others, led to the Jameson Raid (see L S ◊Jameson) and the Boer War 1899–1902 (see ◊South African Wars), won by Britain.

In 1910 the Union of South Africa was formed, comprising the provinces of Cape of Good Hope, Natal, Orange Free State, and Transvaal. A Boer rebellion on the outbreak of ◊World War I was speedily crushed by ◊Smuts. South Africa occupied German SW Africa (see ◊Namibia). Between the wars the union was alternately governed by the republican nationalists under ◊Hertzog and the South African Party under Smuts, who supported the Commonwealth connection. Hertzog wanted South Africa to be neutral in ◊World War II, but Smuts took over as premier and South African troops fought with the Allies.

The NP came to power in 1948 and has ruled South Africa ever since. Its leader, Daniel Malan, initiated the policy of apartheid, attempting to justify it as 'separate but equal' development. In fact, all but the White minority is denied a voice in the nation's affairs. In the 1950s the ◊African National Congress (ANC) led a campaign of civil disobedience until it and other similar movements were, in 1960, declared illegal, and in 1964 the ANC leader Nelson Mandela was sentenced to life imprisonment for alleged sabotage. He has become a symbol of Black opposition to the apartheid regime.

Malan was succeeded in 1958 by Hendrik ◊Verwoerd, who withdrew from the Commonwealth rather than abandon apartheid, and the Union became the Republic of South Africa 1961. Verwoerd was assassinated in 1966 but his successor, B J ◊Vorster, pursued the same policy. Pass laws restricting the movement of Blacks within the country had been introduced, causing international outrage, and ten 'homelands' (Bantustans; see ◊Black national state) were established to contain particular ethnic groups. By the 1980s thousands of the apartheid regime's opponents had been imprisoned without trial and more than 3,000,000 people had been forcibly resettled in Black townships. International condemnation of police brutality followed the news of the death in detention of the Black community leader Steve Biko in 1977. Despite all this, the NP continued to increase its majority at each election, with the White opposition parties failing to make any significant impact. The Progressive Federal Party is the main opposition party, calling for a federal constitution based on regional rather than race differences, and led by Colin Eglin; and the New Republic Party favours racial power sharing.

In 1978 Vorster resigned and was succeeded by Pieter W ◊Botha. He embarked on constitutional reform to involve Coloureds and Asians, but not Blacks, in the governmental process. This led to a clash within the NP and in Mar 1982 Dr Adries Treurnicht, leader of the hardline (*verkrampte*) wing, and 15 other extremists were expelled. They later formed a new party, the Conservative Party of South Africa (CPSA). Although there were considerable doubts about Botha's proposals in the Coloured and Indian communities as well as among the Whites, they were approved by 66 per cent of the voters in an all-White referendum and came into effect in Sept 1984. In 1985 a number of apartheid laws were amended or repealed, including the ban on sexual relations or marriage between people of different races and the ban on mixed racial membership of political parties, but the underlying inequalities in the system remained and dissatisfaction of the Black community grew. In the 1986 cabinet of 21, including Botha, there were 19 Whites, one Coloured, and one Indian. The main Coloured parties are the Labour Party of South Africa, led by the Rev Allan Hendrickse, and the People's Congress Party. The main Indian parties are the National People's Party, led by Amichand Rajbani, and the Solidarity Party, led by Dr J N Reddy.

In May 1986 South Africa attacked what it claimed to be guerrilla strongholds in Botswana, Zambia, and Zimbabwe. The exiled ANC leader Oliver ◊Tambo was receiving increasing moral support in meetings with politicians throughout the world, and Winnie ◊Mandela, during her husband's continuing imprisonment, was not afraid to condemn the system publicly. Non-violent resistance was advocated by Bishop ◊Tutu, the ◊Inkatha movement, and others. A state of emergency was declared in Jun 1986, a few days before the tenth anniversary of the first ◊Soweto uprising, marked by a strike in which millions of Blacks participated. Serious rioting broke out in the townships and was met with police violence, causing hundreds of deaths.

Abroad, calls for economic ◊sanctions against South Africa grew during 1985 and 1986. At the Heads of Commonwealth conference in 1985 the Eminent Persons' Group (EPG) of Commonwealth politicians was conceived to investigate the likelihood of change in South Africa without sanctions. The EPG reported in Jul 1986 that there were no signs of genuine liberalization. Reluctantly, Britain's prime minister, Margaret Thatcher, agreed to limited measures. Some Commonwealth countries, noticeably Australia and Canada, took additional independent action. The US Congress eventually forced President Reagan to move in the same direction. The decisions by individual multinational companies to close down their South African operations (see ◊disinvestment) may, in the long term, have the greatest effect. In Sept 1987 the government formally acknowledged the presence of its military forces in Angola.

SOUTH AFRICA: TERRITORIAL DIVISIONS

Provinces and Capital	Area in sq km
Cape of Good Hope *Cape Town*	721,000
Natal *Pietermaritzburg*	86,965
Transvaal *Pretoria*	286,064
Orange Free State *Bloemfontein*	129,152
	1,223,181
Administered territory	
SW Africa (Namibia) *Windhoek*	823,167
Walvis Bay	1,124
	2,047,472

South African literature the founder of South African literature in English was Thomas Pringle (1789–1834), who published lyric poetry and the prose *Narrative of a Residence in South*

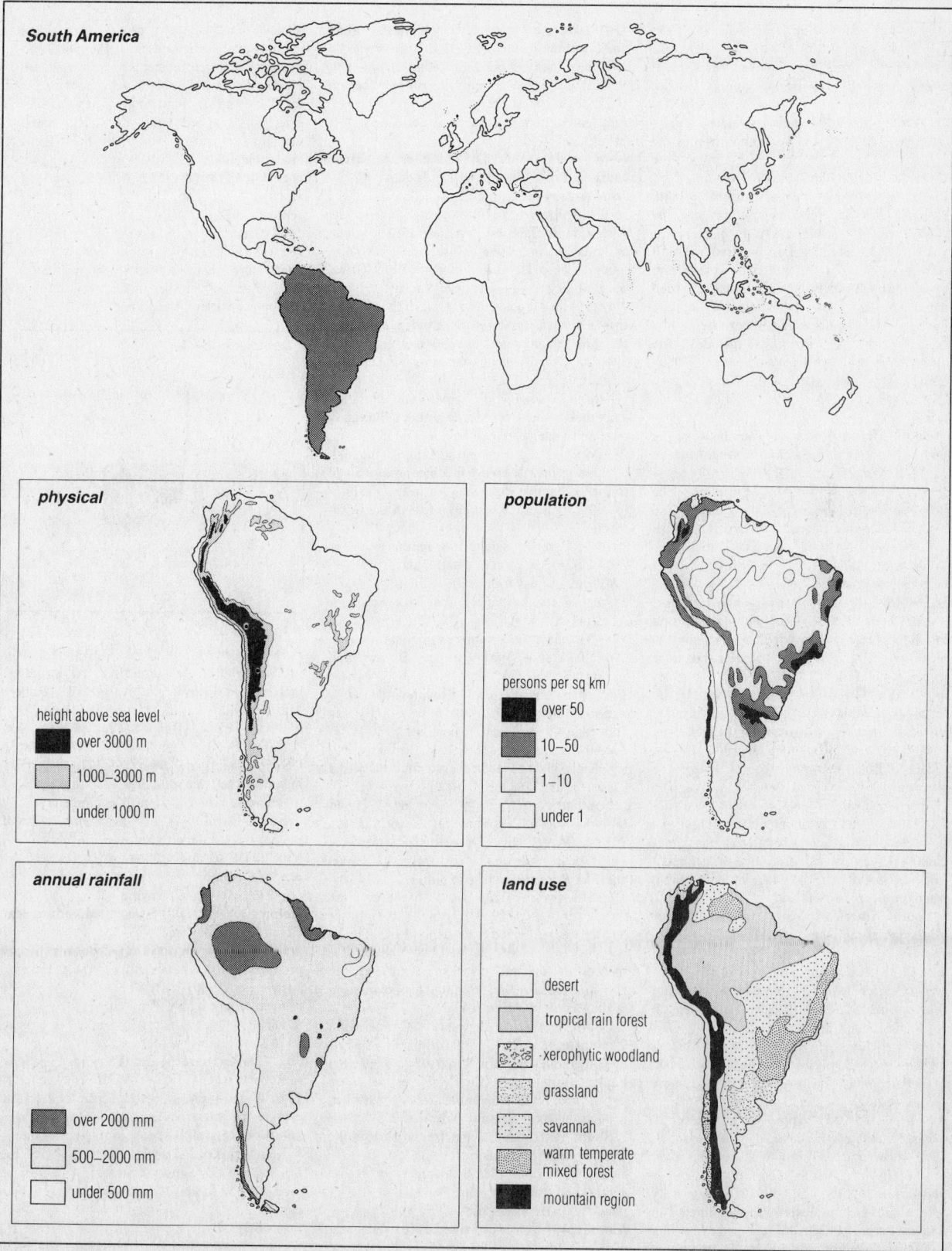

South America

physical

height above sea level
- over 3000 m
- 1000–3000 m
- under 1000 m

population

persons per sq km
- over 50
- 10–50
- 1–10
- under 1

annual rainfall

- over 2000 mm
- 500–2000 mm
- under 500 mm

land use

- desert
- tropical rain forest
- xerophytic woodland
- grassland
- savannah
- warm temperate mixed forest
- mountain region

Africa. The first work of South African fiction to achieve fame outside the country was Olive ◊Schreiner's *Story of an African Farm* 1833; later writers in English include Laurens ◊van der Post, Alan ◊Paton, and Nadine ◊Gordimer.

Original writing in ◊Afrikaans developed rapidly after the South African War, and includes the lyricists C L Leipoldt, and J F E Celliers; the satirical sketch and story writer C J Langenhoven, and the student of wildlife 'Sangiro' (A A Peinhar), author of *The Adventures of a Lion Family*. In more recent years the intellectual barriers imposed by South Africa's isolation have prevented its writers from becoming more widely known, but there has been much spirited work, including that of the novelists André P Brink and Etienne Leroux.

Notable black writings include the autobiographical *Down Second Avenue* 1959, by Ezekiel Mphahlele (1919–); and the drama *The Rhythm of Violence* 1964, by Lewis Nkosi (1936–).

South African Wars two wars between the Boers and the British; essentially fought for the gold and diamonds of the Transvaal:

War of 1881 was triggered by the attempt of the Boers of the ◊Transvaal to reassert the independence surrendered in return for British aid against native tribesmen. The British were defeated at Majuba, and the Transvaal again became independent.

War of 1899–1902, also known as the *Boer War,* was preceded by the armed Jameson Raid into the Boer Transvaal, inspired by ◊Rhodes to precipitate a revolt against ◊Kruger, the Boer leader, which failed. The *Uitlanders* (non-Boer immigrants) were still not given the vote by the Boers, negotiations failed, and the Boers invaded British territory, besieging ◊Ladysmith, ◊Mafeking, and ◊Kimberley. In 1900 Roberts succeeded Buller in command of the British, and was himself succeeded late that year by ◊Kitchener, who countered Boer guerrilla warfare by putting the non-combatants who supported them into concentration camps (about 26,000 women and children died of sickness). The war ended with the Peace of Vereeniging when the Boers surrendered.

South America /ˈsaʊθ əˈmerɪkə/ fourth largest of the continents, nearly twice as large as Europe

area 17,854,000 sq km/6,891,644 sq mi

largest cities (over 3.5 million inhabitants) Buenos Aires, São Paulo, Rio de Janeiro, Bogotá, Santiago, Lima, Caracas

features Andes in the W, Brazilian and Guiana highlands; central plains from the Orinoco basin to Patagonia; Parana-Paraguay-Uruguay system forming the La Plata estuary; Amazon river basin, with its remaining great forests

exports coffee, cocoa, sugar, bananas, oranges, wine; meat and fish products; cotton, wool; handicrafts; oil, silver, iron ore, copper

population (1985) 263,300,000, originally ◊American Indians, who survive chiefly in Bolivia, Peru, and Ecuador, and are increasing in number; in addition there are many mestizo (people of mixed Spanish or Portuguese and Indian ancestry) elsewhere; many people originally from Europe, largely Spanish, Italian and Portuguese; and many of African descent

language many American Indian languages; Spanish is the chief common language, except in Brazil (Portuguese)

religion Roman Catholic; American Indian beliefs

history for the archaic and later American Indian cultures, see ◊American Indian

16th century arrival of Europeans, with the Spanish (◊Pizarro) and Portuguese conquest; the American Indians were mainly either killed, assimilated, or, where unsuitable for slave labour, replaced by slaves imported from Africa.

18th century revolt of ◊Tupac Amaru

19th century Napoleon's toppling of the Spanish throne opened the way for the independence of the Spanish colonies; see ◊Bolivar and San ◊Martín; Brazil became peacefully independent; large-scale European immigration took place (Hispanic, Italian, and German) and interstate wars took a heavy toll, for example, ◊Paraguay War and ◊Pacific War.

20th century rapid industrialization, and high population growth. Heavy indebtedness incurred to fund economic expansion led in the 1980s to inability to meet interest payments in the world slump.

1946–55 Perón president in Argentina.

1954 US intervention in Guatamala.

1959 Cuban revolution led by Castro.

1970–73 Elected socialist regime under Salvador Allende in Chile.

1979 Takeover by Sandinistas in Nicaragua.

1982 Falklands War between Britain and Argentina.

1985 Overthrow of Duvalier regime in Haiti.

Southampton /saʊθˈhæmptən/ city in Hampshire, England; population (1981) 204,604. Industries include engineering, chemicals, plastics, and tobacco; and it is also a passenger and container port (a ◊freeport).

Southampton /saʊθˈhæmptən/ Henry Wriothesley, 3rd Earl of Southampton 1573–1624. English courtier, patron of Shakespeare, who dedicated *Venus and Adonis* and *The Rape of Lucrece* to him.

South Arabia /ˈsaʊθ əˈreɪbiə/ federation of. Former grouping (1959–67) of Arab emirates and sheikdoms, joined by ◊Aden in 1963. The W part of the area was claimed by ◊Yemen, and sporadic fighting and terrorism from 1964 led to British withdrawal in 1967 and the proclamation of the Republic of South Yemen.

South Asia Regional Cooperation Committee (SARC) organization established 1983 by India, Pakistan, Bangladesh, Nepál, Sri Lanka, Bhutan and the Maldives to cover agriculture, telecommunications, health, population, sport, art, and culture.

South Australia /ˈsaʊθ ɒsˈtreɪliə/ state of the Commonwealth of Australia

area 984,341 sq km/380,054 sq mi

capital and chief port Adelaide

towns Whyalla, Port Pirie

features Murray Valley irrigated area, including wine-growing Barossa Valley; Lakes ◊Eyre and ◊Torrens; Mount Lofty; Musgrave and Flinders Ranges; part of the ◊Nullarbor Plain; Great Victoria and Simpson deserts; experimental rocket range in the arid N at Woomera; and at Maralinga British nuclear tests were made 1963.

products meat and wool (80 per cent of land used for cattle and sheep grazing); wines and spirits; dried and canned fruit; iron; coal, copper, uranium; oil and natural gas in the NE; lead, zinc, iron; opals

population (1985) 1,362,880

history possibly known to the Dutch in the 16th century

1644 ◊Tasman surveyed the area.

1834 The first European settlement was founded.

1836 South Australia became a province.

1901 South Australia made a state of the Commonwealth of Australia.

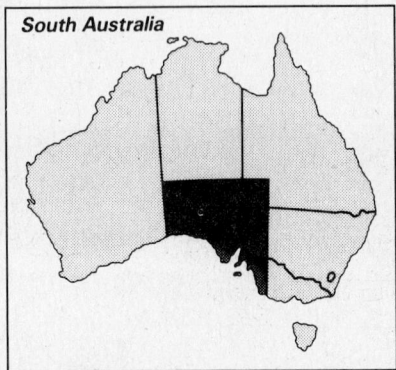

South Australia

South Bank an area of London south of the river Thames, the site of the Festival of Britain in 1951, and now a cultural centre. Buildings include the Royal Festival Hall (Robert Matthew and Leslie Martin, 1951) and the National Theatre (Denys Lasdun 1976).

South Bend /ˈsaʊθ ˈbend/ city in Indiana, USA; population (1980) 109,727. Industries include the manufacture of agricultural machinery, cars, and aircraft equipment.

South Carolina /ˈsaʊθ ˌkærəˈlaɪnə/ state of the SE USA; Palmetto State.

area 80,432 sq km/31,055 sq mi

capital Columbia

towns Charleston, Greenville

features large areas of woodland; subtropical climate in coastal areas

products tobacco, cotton, soybeans; meat products; textiles, paper and woodpulp, bricks

population (1980) 3,121,820

famous people John C Calhoun

history

1526 First Spanish settlers.

1629 Charles I gave the area (known as Carolina) to Robert Heath (1575–1649), attorney general.

1776 Declaration of independence; one of the original ◊Thirteen States of the USA.

1860 South Carolina's secession from the Union.

South Dakota /ˈsaʊθ dəˈkəʊtə/ state of USA; Coyote or Sunshine State.

area 199,550 sq km/77,047 sq mi

capital Pierre

towns Sioux Falls

features Great Plains; Black Hills (which include granite Mount Rushmore, on whose face giant relief portrait heads of former presidents

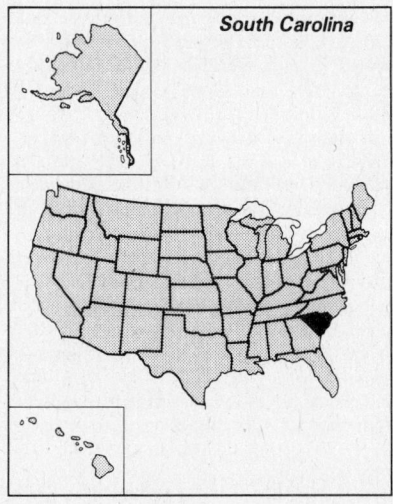

South Carolina

◊Washington, ◊Jefferson, ◊Lincoln and Theodore ◊Roosevelt are carved); Badlands
products cereals; livestock; gold
population (1980) 690,768
famous people Crazy Horse, Sitting Bull.
history
18th century The French claimed South Dakota.
1794 First settlement by Americans.
1889 South Dakota established as a state.

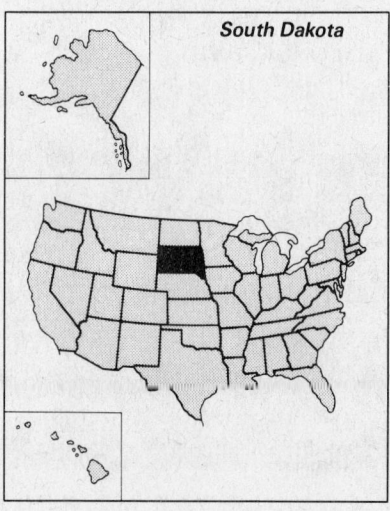

South Dakota

South-East Asia Treaty Organization (SEATO) collective defence system analogous to NATO established 1954 (Australia, France, New Zealand, Pakistan, the Philippines, Thailand, UK and USA. After the Vietnam War it was phased out by 1977, and its non-military aspects assumed by ◊ASEAN (see also ◊ANZUS Treaty).

South East Cape most southerly point of Australia, in Tasmania.

Southend-on-Sea /ˌsauθˈend ɒn ˈsiː/ resort in Essex, England; population (1981) 157,100. The shallow water of the Thames estuary enabled the building of a pier 2 km/1.25 mi long.

Southern and Antarctic Territories French overseas territory created 1955. It comprises the islands of *St Paul* and *Amsterdam* (67 sq km/28 sq mi); the *Kerguelen* and *Crozet* Islands (7,515 sq km/2,902 sq mi); and *Adélie Land* on Antarctica itself (432,000 sq km/166,800 sq mi). All are uninhabited, except for research stations.

Southern Christian Leadership Conference (SCLC) US civil rights organization founded 1957 by Martin Luther ◊King, and led by him until his assassination 1968. It advocated nonviolence and passive resistance.

Southern Cross popular name for the constellation ◊Crux.

Southey /ˈsauði/ Robert 1774–1843. British poet and author, friend of Coleridge and Wordsworth. Born in Bristol, he settled at Keswick, to be near Coleridge. He abandoned his early revolutionary views, and from 1808 contributed regularly to the Tory *Quarterly Review*. In 1813 he became Poet Laureate.

South Georgia /ˈsauθ ˈdʒɔːdʒə/ island 1,300 km/800 mi SE of the Falkland Islands, of which it is a dependency; area 3,775 sq km/1,450 sq mi. It was discovered by Captain ◊Cook in 1775.

South Glamorgan /ˈsauθ gləˈmɔːgən/ county of S Wales
area 416 sq km/161 sq mi
towns administrative headquarters Cardiff; Barry, Penarth
features fertile Vale of Glamorgan; Welsh Folk Museum at St Fagans, near Cardiff
products dairy farming
population (1986) 394,800
language 6 per cent Welsh-speaking; English.

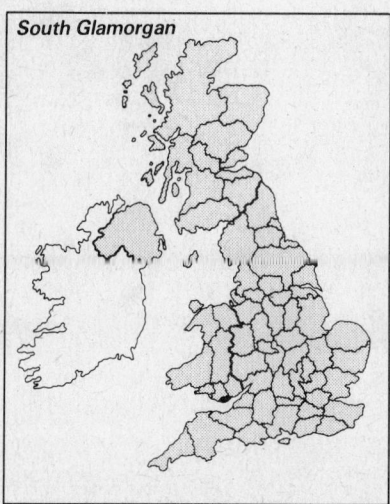

South Glamorgan

South Korea see ◊Korea, South.

Southland Plain /ˈsauθlænd/ plain in the south of South Island, New Zealand, on which Invercargill stands. It is an agricultural area.

South Orkney Islands group of islands in ◊British Antarctic Territory; area 620 sq km/240 sq mi. They are barren and uninhabited.

South Sandwich Islands actively volcanic uninhabited British group 750 km/470 mi SE of ◊South Georgia, administered from the ◊Falkland Islands; area 337 sq km/130 sq mi.

South Sea Bubble a financial crisis in Britain in 1720. The South Sea Company, founded 1711, which had a monopoly of trade with South America, offered in 1719 to take over more than half the national debt in return for further concessions. Its £100 shares rapidly rose to £1,000, and an orgy of speculation followed. When the 'bubble' burst, thousands were ruined. The discovery that cabinet ministers had been guity of corruption led to a political crisis.

South Shetlands /ˈsauθ ˈʃetləndz/ archipelago of 12 uninhabited islands in the South Atlantic, forming part of ◊British Antarctic Territory; area 337 sq km/130 sq mi.

South Shields /ˈsauθ ˈʃiːldz/ manufacturing port in Tyne and Wear on the Tyne estuary, England; population (1981) 87,125.

South Uist /ˈsauθ ˈjuːɪst/ an island in the Outer ◊Hebrides.

Southwark /ˈsʌðək/ borough of S central Greater London.
features site of Globe Theatre (built by Burbage, Shakespeare and others in 1599 on Bankside, and burned down 1613); 12th-century Southwark Cathedral; George Inn (last galleried inn in London); Imperial War Museum; Dulwich College and Picture Gallery, and the ◊Horniman Museum
population (1986) 215,400.

South West Africa /ˈsauθ ˌwest ˈæfrɪkə/ former name (until 1968) of ◊Namibia.

South Yorkshire /ˈsauθ ˈjɔːkʃə/ former metropolitan county of England 1976–86, replaced by residuary body 1986 which covers some of its former functions.
area 1,560 sq km/603 sq mi
towns administrative headquarters Barnsley; Sheffield, Doncaster
features River Don; part of Peak District National Park
products all the chief towns are metal-working centres; coal; dairy, sheep, and arable farming
population (1983) 1,310,500.

Soutine /suːˈtiːn/ Chaim 1894–1943. Lithuanian-born artist, who lived in Paris. He was one of the leaders of French ◊Expressionism, and his pictures have a distorted, frenzied form.

sovereign British gold coin, introduced by Henry VII, which became the standard monetary unit in 1817. Minting ceased for currency purposes in the UK in 1914, but it is still struck for use as 'unofficial' currency in the Middle East. The value is notionally £1, but the actual value is that of the weight of the gold at current rates.

sovereignty absolute authority within a given territory. The possession of sovereignty is taken to be the distinguishing feature of the state, as against other forms of community. The term has an internal aspect, in that it refers to the ultimate source of authority within a state such as a parliament or monarch, and an external aspect, where it denotes the independence of the state from any outside authority.

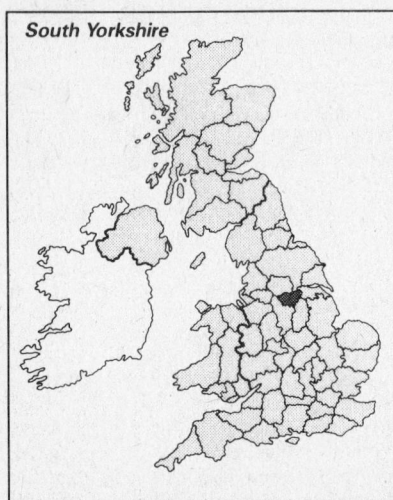

South Yorkshire

Sovetsk /sɒv'jetsk/ town in Kaliningrad region, USSR. In 1807 Napoleon signed peace treaties with Prussia and Russia here. Until 1945 it was known as Tilsit, part of East Prussia.

soviet (Russian 'council') the original soviets were strike committees elected by Russian workers in the 1905 revolution, and in 1917 were set up by peasants, soldiers, and factory workers. These sent delegates to the All-Russian Congress of Soviets to represent their opinions to a future government; taken over by the ◊Bolsheviks, they have ever since been mainly used to send party instructions in the reverse direction.

Soviet Central Asia formerly Russian Turkestan, an area consisting of the ◊Kazakh, ◊Uzbek, ◊Tadzhik, ◊Turkmen and ◊Kirghiz Republics of the USSR. These were subdued by Russia as recently as 1866–73, and even under Soviet rule nationalist sentiment persists, leading to shortfalls in agricultural production, and the establishment in 1962 of a Central Asian Bureau to strengthen centralized control by the Party Praesidium in Moscow.

Soviet Far East geographical, not administrative, division of Asiatic USSR, on the Pacific coast. It includes the Amur, Lower Amur, Kamchatka, and Sakhalin regions, and Khabarovsk and Maritime territories.

Soviet Union /'səuvɪət 'juːnɪən/ alternative name for ◊Union of Soviet Socialist Republics (USSR).

sovkhoz name given to a state-owned farm in the Soviet Union where the workers are state employed. The sovkhoz can be contrasted with the ◊kolkhoz where the farm is run by a collective.

Soweto /sə'weɪtəʊ/ (*South West Township*), city SW of Johannesburg, South Africa; population (1983) 915,872. It began as a shanty town in the 1930s, and is now the largest black city in South Africa, but until 1976 its population could have status only as temporary residents, serving as a workforce for Johannesburg. There were riots in 1976, sparked by a ruling that ◊Afrikaans be used in African schools there. Reforms followed but riots flared up again in 1985.

soya bean leguminous plant (*Glycine max*), native to E Asia, particularly to Japan and China. Originally grown as a forage crop, it is increasingly used for human consumption in cooking oils and margarine, as a flour, or processed and extruded as textured vegetable protein (TVP).

Soyer /swaː'jeɪ/ Alexis Benoît 1809–1858. French chef who worked in England. He was chef at the Reform Club, London, and visited the Crimea to advise on nutrition for the British army.

Soyinka /ʃɔɪ'ɪŋkə/ Wole 1934– . Nigerian author, a political prisoner in Nigeria 1967–69 (prison memoirs *The Man Died* 1972). His works include the play *The Lion and the Jewel* 1963, and *Akê, The Years of Childhood*, an autobiography. He was the first African to receive the Nobel Prize for Literature, in 1986.

Soyuz (Russian 'union') Soviet spacecraft, capable of carrying up to three ◊cosmonauts. On its first flight in April 1967 it crashed, killing the lone pilot, Vladimir Komarov. Soyuz consists of three parts: a rear section containing engines; the central crew compartment; and a forward compartment that gives additional room for working and living space. Soyuz spacecraft are used for ferrying crews up to ◊space stations.

can continue to move at high speed without extra energy. The space between the planets is not entirely empty but is filled with the tenuous gas of the ◊solar wind as well as dust specks. The space between ◊stars is also filled with thin gas and dust. There is even evidence of highly rarefied gas in the space between ◊galaxies, particularly between clusters of galaxies.

Spacelab a small space station built by the ◊European Space Agency to be carried in the cargo bay of the ◊Space Shuttle. It remains captive in the cargo bay throughout each flight and returns to Earth with the Shuttle. Spacelab consists of two parts: a pressurized module in which ◊astronauts can work, and a series of *pallets* open to the vacuum of space, on which equipment is mounted. Spacelab is used for ◊astronomy, Earth observation, and experiments utilizing the conditions of ◊weightlessness and vacuum in orbit. The pressurized module can be flown with or without pallets, or the pallets can be flown on their own, in which case the astronauts remain in the Shuttle's own crew compartment. All the sections of Spacelab can be reused many times. The first Spacelab mission, consisting of a pressurized module and pallets, lasted ten days in Nov–Dec 1983.

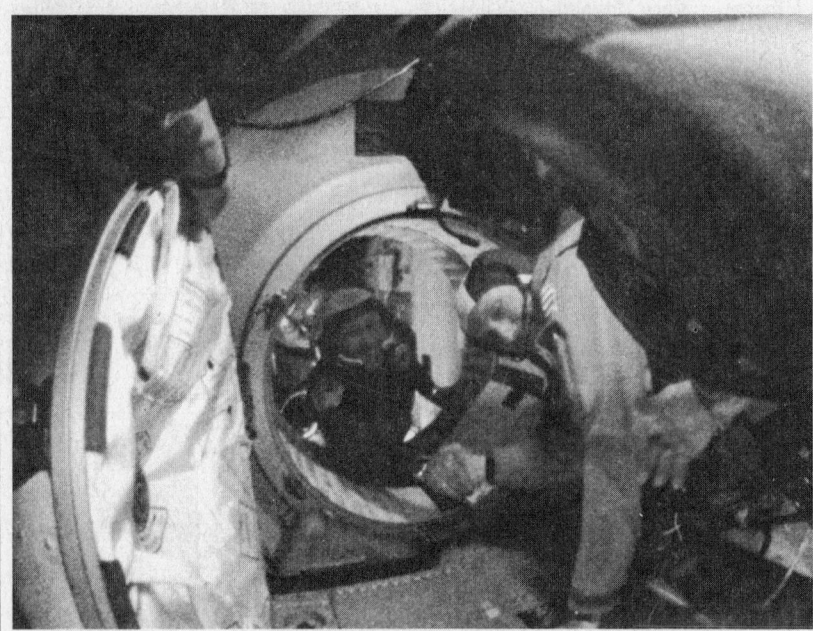

Soyuz The Soviet Soyuz space vehicle was launched in Jul 1975 from a cosmodrome in Kazakhstan to begin the joint US/USSR Apollo-Soyuz Test Project. They were joined in space for 47 hours and the two astronauts Stafford (foreground) and Leonov shake hands in earth orbit.

Spa /spaː/ town in Liège province, Belgium; population (1982) 9,600. Famous since the 14th century for its mineral springs, it has given its name to similar centres elsewhere.

Spaak /spaːk/ Paul-Henri 1899–1972. Belgian socialist politician. From 1936 to 1966 he held office almost continuously as foreign minister or prime minister.

space the void that exists above Earth's ◊atmosphere. Above 120 km/75 mi from the surface very little atmosphere remains, so objects

space probe any instrumented object sent beyond Earth, to other parts of the ◊solar system and on into deep space. The first probe was the Soviet Luna 1 which flew past the Moon in 1959. The first successful planetary probe was the US ◊Mariner 2 which passed Venus in 1962. In 1976 the US ◊Viking probes landed on Mars. Detailed views of the outer planets of the solar system were obtained by the US ◊Voyager probes. The first space probe to leave the solar system was the US ◊Pioneer 10.

SPACE RESEARCH CHRONOLOGY

1903   Tsiolkovsky published the first practical paper on astronautics.

1926   Goddard launched the first liquid fuel rocket.

1937–45 Werner von Braun developed the V2 rocket.

1957   Sputnik 1 (Russian 'fellow-traveller': USSR), the first space satellite, orbited Earth at a height of 229–898 km/142–558 mi in 96.2 min on 4 Oct; Sputnik 2 (USSR), was launched 3 Nov carrying a live dog 'Laika' (died on board 10 Nov).

1958   Explorer 1 (USA), the first US satellite, 31 Jan discovered Van Allen radiation belts.

1961   Vostok 1 (USSR), first manned spaceship (Yuri Gagarin), was recovered on 12 Apr after a single orbit at a height of 175–142 km/109–88 mi in 89.1 min.

1962   Friendship 7 (USA); John Glenn was the first American in orbit round the Earth on 20 Feb; Telstar (USA), a communications satellite, sent the first live television transmission between USA and Europe.

1963   Vostok 6 (USSR); Valentina Tereshkova was the first woman in space 16–19 Jun.

1966   Venera 3 (USSR), space probe, launched Nov 1965, crash-landed on Venus 1 Mar, the first man-made object to reach another planet.

1967   Soyuz 1 (USSR); Vladimir Komarov was the first man to be killed in space research when his ship crash-landed on Earth on 24 Apr.

1969   Apollo–Saturn 11 (USA) was launched 16–24 Jul; Neil Armstrong was the first man to walk on the moon.

1970   Luna 17 (USSR) was launched 10 Nov; its unmanned lunar vehicle, *Lunokhod*, took photos and made soil analyses on the Moon.

1971   Salyut 1 (USSR), the first orbital space station, was established 19 Apr; it was visited by the Soyuz 11 manned spacecraft.

1971–2 Mariner 9 (USA) was the first space probe to orbit another planet, when it circled Mars.

1972   Pioneer 10 (USA), Earth's first starship, was launched 3 Mar; it reached Jupiter 1973; in 1983 it made its first passage of the asteroid belt, reached Neptune, and passed on into the first voyage beyond the solar system. Apollo 17 (USA) was launched Dec.

1973   Skylab 2 (USA), the first US orbital space station, was established.

1975   Apollo 18 (USA), 15–24 Jul, made a joint flight with Soyuz 19 (USSR), in a link-up in space.

1976   Viking 1 (USA), unmanned spacecraft, was launched 20 Aug 1975; it reached Mars, the spacecraft lander touching down on 20 Jul 1976; Viking 2 (USA) was launched 9 Sept 1975, its lander touching down on Mars 3 Sept 1976.

1977   Voyager 1 (USA), launched 5 Sept 1977, and Voyager 2 (USA), launched 20 Aug, both unmanned spacecraft, reached Jupiter Jan/Jul 1979, Uranus 1986, and are expected to reach Neptune 1989.

1979   Ariane (European Space Agency satellite launcher) was launched.

1981   Space Shuttle (USA), first re-usable manned spacecraft, was launched 12 Apr.

1982   Venera 13 and 14 (USSR) landed on Venus; soil samples indicated that the surface is similar to earth's volcanic rock.

1986   Space Shuttle (USA) exploded shortly after launch killing all seven crew members. The space probe *Giotto* showed Halley's comet to be one of the darkest objects ever detected in the solar system, with an irregular nucleus 14.5 km/9 mi × 3km/2 mi. Voyager 2 reached Uranus and found it to have six more moons than was previously thought, making 12 known moons in all.

space shuttle reusable US manned spacecraft. The space shuttle is launched vertically like a conventional rocket, but glides back to land on a runway. Its maiden flight was on 12 Apr 1981. The space shuttle orbiter, the part that actually goes into space, is 37.2 m/122 ft long and weighs 68 tonnes empty. Two to eight crew members occupy the orbiter's nose section, and missions last up to ten days. In its cargo bay the orbiter carries up to 29 tonnes of satellites, scientific equipment, ◊Spacelab and military payloads. At launch, the shuttle's three main engines are fed with liquid fuel from a cylindrical tank attached to the orbiter; this tank is discarded shortly before the shuttle reaches orbit. Two additional solid-fuel boosters provide added thrust for launch, but are jettisoned after two minutes. Four orbiters were built: Columbia, Challenger, Discovery, and Atlantis. Challenger was destroyed in a mid-air explosion two minutes into its tenth launch on 28 Jan 1986, after which flights were postponed for many months.

space shuttle The first space shuttle with launcher at the Kennedy Space Center in Florida, USA, in 1981. The shuttle *Challenger* exploded shortly after launching in 1986, killing all seven crew members.

space sickness a feeling of nausea, sometimes accompanied by vomiting, experienced by about 40 per cent of all ◊astronauts during their first few days in space. It is akin to travel sickness, and is thought to be due to confusion of the body's balancing mechanism, located in the inner ear, caused by ◊weightlessness.

space station any large structure designed for human occupation in space for extended periods of time. Space stations are used for carrying out astronomical observations and surveys of Earth, as well as for biological studies and the processing of materials in ◊weightlessness.

The first space station was ◊Salyut 1, launched by the USSR on 19 Apr 1971. It was occupied for 23 days in Jun 1971 by a crew of three, who died during their return to Earth when their ◊Soyuz ferry craft depressurized. Salyut 2, in 1973, broke up in orbit before occupation. The first fully successful Salyut mission was a 14-day visit to Salyut 3 in Jul 1974. By then, US astronauts had spent up to 84 days aboard their ◊Skylab space station. In 1986, the Salyut series was superseded by ◊Mir, an improved design capable of being enlarged by additional modules sent up from Earth. A small space station called ◊Spacelab, built by the ◊European Space Agency, is carried in the cargo bay of the ◊Space Shuttle on some missions. The USA plans to build a large space station in orbit during the 1990s.

space suit a protective suit, worn by ◊astronauts in space. It provides an insulated, air-conditioned cocoon in which astronauts can live and work for hours at a time while outside the spacecraft. Inside the suit, the astronaut wears a cooling garment to keep the body at a comfortable temperature even during vigorous work. The suit provides air to breathe, and removes exhaled carbon dioxide and moisture. The suit's outer layers insulate the occupant from the extremes of hot and cold in space ($-150°C$ in the shade to $180°C$ in sunlight), and from the impact of small ◊meteorites. Some space suits have a jet-propelled backpack.

spadix a type of inflorescence consisting of a long fleshy axis bearing many small, stalkless flowers. It is partially enclosed by a large bract or ◊spathe. A spadix is characteristic of plants belonging to the family Araceae, including lords-and-ladies (*Arum maculatum*).

Spain /speɪn/ country in SW Europe, on the Iberian Peninsula between the Atlantic and the Mediterranean, bounded to the N by France and to the W by Portugal.

government the 1978 constitution puts a hereditary monarch as formal head of state. The monarch appoints a prime minister, called president of government, and a council of ministers, all responsible to the national assembly, *las Cortes Generales*. The *Cortes* consists of two chambers, the Chamber of Deputies, with 350 members, and the Senate, with 208. Deputies are elected by universal suffrage through a system of proportional representation, and 208 of the senators are directly elected to represent the whole country and 49 to represent the regions. All serve a four-year term. The main political parties are the Socialist Workers' Party (PSOE) and the Popular Coalition.

Spain has developed a regional self-government, whereby each of the 50 provinces has its own council (*Diputación Provincial*) and civil governor. The devolution process was extended in 1979 when 17 autonomous communities were approved, each with a parliament elected for a four-year term.

history Pre-Roman Spain was inhabited by Iberians, ◊Basques, ◊Celts, and Celtiberians. ◊Greece and ◊Phoenicia established colonies on the coast from the 7th century BC; ◊Carthage dominated from the 5th century, trying to found an empire in the SE. This was conquered by Ancient ◊Rome about 200 BC and after a long struggle all Spain was absorbed into the Roman Empire. At the invitation of Rome the Visigoths (see ◊Goths) set up a kingdom in Spain from the beginning of the 5th century AD until the invasion by the ◊Moors in 711. Christian resistance held out in the N and by 1250 they had reconquered all Spain except ◊Granada. During this struggle a number of small kingdoms were formed, all of which by the 13th century had been absorbed by ◊Castile and ◊Aragon. The marriage of ◊Ferdinand of Aragon to Isabella of Castile (1469) united their domains on their accession in

1479. The conquest of Granada in 1492 completed the unification of Spain.

Under Ferdinand and Isabella, Charles I (see ◊Charles V of the ◊Holy Roman Empire), and ◊Philip II, Spain became one of the greatest powers in the world. The discoveries of ◊Columbus made on behalf of Spain were followed by the conquest of most of Central and S America. Naples and Sicily were annexed 1503, Milan 1535, Portugal 1580, and Charles I inherited the Netherlands. But with the revolt in the Netherlands and the defeat of the Armada (1588), Spain's power began to decline. The loss of civil and religious freedom, constant wars, inflation, a corrupt bureaucracy, and the expulsion of the ◊Jews and Moors undermined the economy. By the peace of Utrecht that concluded the War of the ◊Spanish Succession 1713, Spain lost Naples, Sicily, Milan, Gibraltar, and its last possessions in the Netherlands.

The 18th century saw reforms and economic progress, but Spain became involved in the ◊Revolutionary and ◊Napoleonic wars, first as the ally, then as the opponent of France. France occupied Spain 1808 and was expelled with British assistance 1814. Throughout the 19th century conflict raged between monarchists and liberals; revolutions and civil wars took place in 1820–23, 1833–39, and 1868, besides many minor revolts, and a republic was temporarily established in 1873–74.

Spain lost its American colonies between 1810 and 1830 and after the ◊Spanish-American War 1898 ceded Cuba and the Philippines to the USA. Republicanism, socialism, and anarchism grew after 1900; ◊Primo de Rivera's dictatorship 1923–30 failed to preserve the monarchy under ◊Alfonso XIII, and in 1931 a republic was established. In 1936 the Popular Front, a centre-left alliance, took office and introduced agrarian and other reforms that aroused the opposition of the landlords and the Catholic church and led to the Spanish ◊Civil War 1936–39. The victorious Gen ◊Franco established a fascist dictatorship, which was nominally neutral in World War II. In 1947 Franco allowed the revival of a legislature with limited powers, and announced that after his death the monarchy would be restored, naming the grandson of the last monarch, Prince Juan Carlos de Bourbon, as his successor. Franco died in 1975 and King Juan Carlos became head of state. There followed a slow but steady progress to democratic government, with the new constitution endorsed by referendum in 1978.

Spain faced two main internal problems, the demands for independence by regional extremists and the possibility of a right-wing military coup. The aims of the ruling Democratic Centre Party (UCD), led by Adolfo Suárez, included a devolution of power to the regions (Basque, Catalonia, and eventually Andalucia), entry into NATO, and membership of the European Community. In 1981 Suárez suddenly resigned and was succeeded by his deputy, Calvo Sotelo. He was immediately confronted with an attempted army coup in Madrid, while at the same time the military commander of Valencia declared a state of emergency there and sent

tanks out on the streets. Both uprisings failed, and the two leaders were tried and imprisoned. Sotelo's decision to take Spain into NATO was widely criticized and, after defections from the party, he was forced to call a general election in Oct 1982. The result was a sweeping victory for the PSOE, led by Felipe Gonzalez.

The Basque separatist organization, ETA, had stepped up its campaign for independence with widespread terrorist activity, spreading in 1985 to the Mediterranean holiday resorts and threatening Spain's lucrative tourist industry. Unemployment in 1985 reached 22 per cent.

The PSOE had fought the election on a policy of taking Spain out of NATO and carrying out extensive nationalization. Once in office, however, Gonzalez showed himself to be a pragmatist. His nationalization programme was highly selective and he left the decision on NATO to a referendum. In Jan 1986 Spain became a full member of the European Community and in Mar the referendum showed popular support for remaining in NATO. In the Jul 1986 election the PSOE won 184 seats in the Chamber of Deputies and Gonzalez returned for another term as prime minister.

Spalato /ˈspaːlətəu/ Italian name for ◊Split, a port in Yugoslavia.

Spalding /ˈspɔːldɪŋ/ market town in Lincolnshire, England; population (1981) 18,250. The bulb farms are famous.

Spandau /ˈʃpændau/ suburb of W Berlin. The chief war criminals condemned at ◊Nuremberg in 1946 were imprisoned in the fortress here. The last of them was Rudolf ◊Hess.

spaniel type of dog, characterized by large, drooping ears and a long, silky coat. The heavy Clumber spaniel takes its name from the estate of the duke of Newcastle, who imported them from France; it is lemon and white, and very silent when hunting. The Sussex spaniel, believed to be the oldest variety, is a golden liver colour. The cocker is a small spaniel in various colours.

Spanish-American War war 1898 by Cuban revolutionaries (with US backing) against Spanish rule. The Treaty of Paris ceded Cuba, the Philippines, Guam and Puerto Rico to the USA.

Spanish architecture the architecture of Spain has been influenced by both the Classical and Islámic traditions. Styles include *Roman* (3rd–5th century, the period of Roman rule); *Asturian* (9th century), which takes its name from the district in NW Spain which was unconquered by the Moors; *Mozarabic* (9th–11th century), a style of Spanish Christian architecture, which shows the influence of Islamic architecture; *Romanesque* (11th and 12th centuries); *Gothic* (13th–16th century); *Renaissance* (15th–17th century), which is based on Italian models; *Baroque* (17th–18th century), a style which reached its peak in the fantastic designs of Churriguera and his followers; *Neo-Classic* (18th and 19th centuries); *Modern* Oscar Niemeyer and Antonio ◊Gaudi.

Spanish Armada the fleet sent by ◊Philip II of Spain against England in 1588. Consisting of 130 ships, it sailed from Lisbon, and carried on a

Spain
(*España*)

AREA 504,879 sq km/194,883 sq mi
CAPITAL Madrid
TOWNS Bilbao, Valencia, Saragossa, Murcia;
ports Barcelona, Seville, Málaga
PHYSICAL a central plateau with mountain
ranges; lowlands in the S
FEATURES includes Balearic and Canary
Islands, and Ceuta and Melilla; rivers Ebro,
Douro, Tagus, Guadiana, Guadalquivir;
Iberian Plateau (Meseta); Pyrenees,
Cantabrian Mountains, Andalusian
Mountains, Sierra Nevada
HEAD OF STATE Juan Carlos I from 1975
HEAD OF GOVERNMENT Felipe González
Marquez from 1982
GOVERNMENT parliamentary democracy
EXPORTS citrus, grapes, pomegranates,
vegetables, wine (especially sherry), olive oil,
tinned fruit and fish; iron ore, cork; cars and
other vehicles; leather goods; ceramics
CURRENCY peseta (199.96 = £1 Sept 1987)
POPULATION 38,829,000 (1985); annual growth
rate 0.8%
LANGUAGE Spanish (Castilian, official), but
regional languages are recognized within their
own boundaries (Basque, Catalan, Galician,
Valencian, and Majorcan are the chief
examples)
RELIGION Roman Catholic (there are
restrictions on the practice of Protestantism)
LITERACY 96% male/90% female (1981)
GDP $160.4 bn (1984); $5,500 per head of
population
CHRONOLOGY
1947 Gen Franco announced a return to the

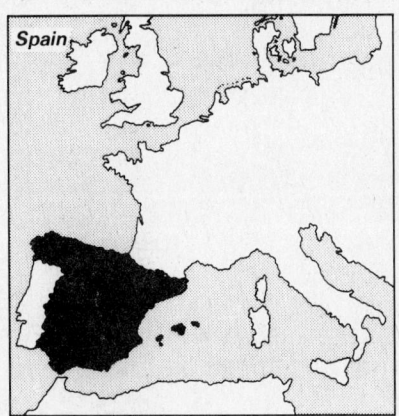

monarchy after his death, with Prince Juan
Carlos as his successor.
1975 Franco died and was succeeded by King
Juan Carlos I as head of state.
1978 New constitution adopted with Adolfo
Suárez, leader of the Democratic Centre
Party, as prime minister.
1981 Suárez resigned and was succeeded by
his deputy, Calvo-Sotelo. Attempted military
coup thwarted.
1982 Socialist Workers' Party (PSOE), led by
Felipe González, won a sweeping electoral
victory. Basque separatist organization (ETA)
stepped up its guerrilla campaign.
1985 ETA's campaign spread to holiday
resorts.
1986 Referendum confirmed NATO
membership. Spain joined the European
Community.

SPAIN: TERRITORIAL DIVISIONS

	Area in sq km
Andalusia	
Almería, Cádiz, Córdoba, Granada, Huelva, Jaén, Málaga, Sevilla	87,268
Aragón	
Huesca, Teruel, Zaragoza	47,669
Asturias	
Oviedo	10,565
Basque	
Álava, Guipúzcoa, Vizcaya *Navarra	17,682
Castilla la Nueva	
Ciudad Real, Cuenca, Guadalajara, Madrid, Toledo	72,363
Castilla la Vieja	
Avila, Burgos, Logroño, Santander, Segovia, Soria	49,976
Catalonia	
Barcelona, Gerona, Lérida, Tarragona	31,930
Extremadura	
Badajoz, Cáceres	41,602
Galicia	
La Coruña, Lugo, Orense, Pontevedra	29,434
Murcia	
Albacete, Murcia	26,175
Léon	
Léon, Palencia, Salamanca, Valladolid, Zamora	54,594
Valencia	
Alicante, Castellón, Valencia	23,305
Balearic Islands	
Baleares	5,014
Canary Islands	
Santa Cruz de la Tenerife, Las Palmas	7,273
	504,750

Option to join Basque region

---

running fight up-Channel with the English fleet
of 197 small ships under ◊Howard of Effingham
and ◊Drake. The Armada anchored off Calais,
but was forced to put to sea by fireships, and
a general action followed off Gravelines. What
remained of the Armada escaped round the N of
Scotland and W of Ireland, suffering many losses
by storm and shipwreck on the way. Only about
half the original fleet returned to Spain.

Spanish art *Painting*. Italian and Flemish
influences contributed to Spanish Renaissance
painting, and the great masters of this period
(end of 15th–16th century) including Bartolomé
Bermejo about (1440–95), Alonzo Sánchez
Coello (1515–90), Luis de Vargas (1502–68),
Francisco de Herrera the Elder, Juan de Juanes
(1523–79), Juan Navarrette (1526–79), Luis de
Morales (1509–86), and the greatest of all, ◊El
Greco. The greatest Spanish artist of the 18th
century is generally considered to be ◊Goya, who
exerted a great influence on European art of the
following century. Painters of the 20th century
include the cubist Juan Gris (1887–1927), the
surrealists Joan ◊Miró and Salvador ◊Dali, the
Impressionist Joaquín Sorolla y Bastida
(1863–1923) and, most notably, Pablo ◊Picasso,

widely regarded as the most innovative painter
of the 20th century.
Sculpture. The most outstanding sculptors
include Borgoña (died c. 1543), Berruguete (c.
1486–1561), Gregorio Fernandez (1566–1636),
Montañes (1564–1649), and Alonso de los Rios.

Spanish Civil War 1936–39. See ◊Civil War,
Spanish.

Spanish fly another name for blister ◊beetle.

Spanish Guinea /'spænɪʃ 'gɪnɪ/ former name
of the Republic of ◊Equatorial Guinea.

Spanish language a member of the Romance
branch of the Indo-European language family,
traditionally known as Castilian and originally
spoken only in NE Spain, in the kingdoms of
Castile and Aragon. As the language of the court
it has been the standard and literary language of
the Spanish state since the 13th century, but has
never succeeded in supplanting such regional
languages as Basque, Gallego or Galician, and
Catalan. Because of the long Muslim dominance
of the S Iberian peninsula, Spanish has been
strongly influenced by Arabic. Spanish is now a
world language, spoken in all South and Central
American countries (except Brazil, Guyana,
Suriname and French Guiana), as well as in

Mexico and the Philippines. Words in English of
Spanish origin include *bronco, cargo, galleon,
mosquito, ranch* and *sherry*.

Spanish literature of the classical epics, the
12th-century *El cantar de Mio Cid* is the only
complete example. The founder of Castilian
prose was King Alfonso X, El Sabio (the Wise),
who also wrote lyric poetry in the Galician
dialect. The first true poet was the 14th-century
satirist, Juan Ruiz (c. 1283–1350), archpriest of
Hita. To the 15th century belong the Marquis
of Santillana (Iñigo López de Mendoza), poet,
critic, and collector of proverbs; the chivalric
romances, for example, the *Amadis de Gaula*;
the ballads dealing with the struggle against the
Moors; and the *Celestina*, a novel in dramatic
form. The flowering of the verse drama began
with Lope de Rueda (died 1565), and reached its

SPAIN: FORMER COLONIES

Current Name	Colonial Names and History	Colonized	Independent
Paraguay	Viceroyalty of Buenos Aires	1537	1811
Argentina	Viceroyalty of Buenos Aires	16th cent.	1816
Chile		1541	1818
Costa Rica		1563	1821
Mexico	Viceroyalty of New Spain	16th cent.	1821
Peru		1541	1824
Bolivia		16th cent.	1825
Ecuador	Greater Colombia 1822–30	16th cent.	1830
Venezuela	Captaincy-General of Caracas to 1822; Greater Colombia 1822–30	16th cent.	1830
Honduras	Federation of Central America 1821–38	1523	1838
El Salvador	Federation of Central America 1821–39	16th cent.	1839
Guatemala	Federation of Central America 1821–39	16th cent.	1839
Dominican Republic	Hispaniola to 1821; ruled by Haiti to 1844	16th cent.	1844
Cuba		1512	1898
Colombia	Viceroyalty of New Granada to 1819; Greater Colombia to 1830	16th cent.	1903
Panama	Part of Colombia to 1903	16th cent.	1903
Philippines	Spain 1565–1898; US 1898–1946	1565	1946

height with Lope de ◊Vega and ◊Calderón de la Barca. In poetry the Golden Age of the 15th–16th centuries produced the lyrical Garcilaso de la Vega; the patriotic Fernando de Herrera (1534–97); the mystics Santa Teresa and Luis de León; the elaborate style of Luis de Góngora (1561–1627), who popularized the decadent 'gongorism'; and the biting satire of Francisco de Quevedo. In fiction there developed the pastoral romance, for example, Jorge de Montemayor's *Diana*; the picaresque novel, established by the anonymous *Lazarillo de Tormes*; and the work of ◊Cervantes. In the 18th century the Benedictine Benito J Feijoo introduced scientific thought to Spain, and French influence emerged in the comedies of Leandro F de Moratín (1760–1828) and others. Typical of the romantic era were the poet-dramatists Angel de Saavedra (Duque de Rivas) (1791–1865), and José Zorilla (1817–93); and the lyricist José de Espronceda (1810–42). Among 19th-century novelists are Pedro de Alarcón (1833–91), Emilia, condesa de Pardo Bazán (1852–1921), and Vicente Blasco Ibáñez (1867–1928); a 19th-century dramatist is José Echegaray (1832–1916).

The 'Generation of 1898' included the philosophers Miguel de Unamuno (1864–1936) and José Ortega y Gasset (1883–1955); the novelist Pío Baroja (1872–1956); the prose-writer Azorín (José Martínez Ruiz, 1874–1967); and the Nobel prizewinning poet Juan Ramón Jiménez (1881–1958). The next generation included novelist Camilo José Cela (1916–); the poets Antonio Machado (1875–1939), Rafael Alberti (1902–), Luis Cernuda (1902–63), and the Nobel prizewinner Vincente Aleixandre (1898–); and the dramatists Jacinto Benavente (1866–1954), the brothers ◊Quintero, and – the most striking – F García ◊Lorca. The Civil War and the strict censorship of the Franco government disrupted mid-20th century literary life, but later names include the novelists Rafael Sánchez Ferlosio (1927–), and Juan Goytisolo (1931–); and the poets Blas de Otero (1916–), and José Hierro (1922–).

Spanish Main term often used to describe the Caribbean in the 16th and 17th centuries, but more properly the S American mainland between the river Orinoco and Panama.

Spanish Sahara /ˈspænɪʃ səˈhɑːrə/ Spanish colony established in the late 15th century; independent since 1976 as ◊Western Sahara.

Spanish Succession, War of the a war of 1701–14 between Britain, Austria, the Netherlands, Portugal, and Denmark on the one side, and France, Spain, and Bavaria on the other. It was caused by Louis XIV's acceptance of the Spanish throne on behalf of his grandson, Philip, in defiance of the Partition Treaty of 1700, under which it would have passed to Archduke Charles of Austria. The war produced a series of notable battles:

1704 the French marched on Vienna to try to end the war, but were defeated at *Blenheim* by ◊Marlborough and ◊Eugène of Savoy

1705 the Allies invaded Spain, twice occupying Madrid but failing to hold it

1706 Marlborough was victorious over the French (under Villeroi) at *Ramillies* 23 May, in Brabant, Belgium

1708 Marlborough and Eugène were victorious over the French (under Duke of Burgundy and Vendôme) at *Oudenaarde* (near Ghent, Belgium) 30 Jun–11 Jul

1709 Marlborough was victorious with ◊Eugène over the French (under Villars) at *Malplaquet* 11 Sept

1713 Treaties of Utrecht and *1714* Rastat under which the Allies recognized Philip as King of Spain, but Gibraltar, Minorca, and Nova Scotia were ceded to Britain, and Belgium, Milan and Naples to Austria.

Spanish Town town in Jamaica; population (1971) 41,600. Founded by Diego Columbus about 1525, it was the capital of Jamaica 1535–1871.

Spark /spɑːk/ Muriel 1918– . Scottish novelist. She is a Catholic convert, and her works have an enigmatic satire: *The Ballad of Peckham Rye* 1960, *The Prime of Miss Jean Brodie* 1961, and *The Only Problem* 1984.

spark chamber electronic device for recording tracks of atomic ◊particles. In combination with a stack of photographic plates, a spark chamber enables the precise point, within a cubic centimetre, where an interaction has taken place to be located. At its simplest, it consists of two smooth thread-like ◊electrodes which are positioned 1–2 cm apart, the space between being filled by gas. See ◊charm.

spark plug a plug that produces an electric spark in the cylinder of a ◊petrol engine to ignite the fuel mixture. It consists essentially of two ◊electrodes insulated from one another. High-voltage (18,000 V) electricity is fed to a central electrode via the ◊distributor. At the base of the electrode, inside the cylinder, the electricity jumps to another electrode earthed to the engine body, and creates a spark. See also ◊coil ignition.

sparrow term for many small birds, of which the Eurasian *house sparrow Passer domesticus*, family Ploceidae, of the order Passeriformes, is common in Britain and has spread almost worldwide. With brown-black marked plumage and black chest and eye-stripe in the male, it is inconspicuous, intelligent and adaptable, with a cheery chirp and untidy nesting habits. For hedge sparrow see ◊dunnock.

sparrow-hawk bird of prey *Accipiter nisus* found mainly in wooded country across Eurasia.

Sparta /ˈspɑːtə/ ancient Greek city state (near the modern town of Sparte, founded 1934) in the S Peloponnese. The Dorians formed the ruling race, the original inhabitants being divided into *perioeci*, tributaries without political rights, and *helots* or serfs. The state was ruled by two hereditary kings, and under the constitution attributed to Lycurgus all citizens were trained for war from boyhood; hence the Spartans became proverbial for their indifference to pain or death, their contempt for luxury and the arts, and their harsh treatment of the helots. They distinguished themselves in the ◊Persian and ◊Peloponnesian wars, but in the 2nd century BC sank into insignificance.

Spartacist name given to left-wing radicals in Germany at the end of World War I, founders of the *Spartacus League*, which became the German Communist party in 1919. Spartacist

Week, a week of agitation by the Spartacists, ended with the murder of their leaders Karl ◊Liebknecht and Rosa ◊Luxemburg.

Spartacus /'spɑːtəkəs/ died 71 BC. Thracian gladiator who in 73 BC led a popular revolt of gladiators and slaves at ◊Crassus.

Spartakiad quadrennial games in the USSR (so-named from ancient Sparta's stress on physical fitness for state service), in which about 10,000 Soviet athletes compete (foreigners were admitted from 1979).

spastic a person affected by ◊cerebral palsy.

spathe the single large bract surrounding the type of inflorescence known as a ◊spadix. It is sometimes brightly coloured and petal-like, as in the brilliant scarlet spathe of the flamingo plant (*Anthurium andreanum*) from S America; this serves to attract insects.

speakeasy illegal bars which sold alcohol during the ◊Prohibition period in the United States.

Speaker the title applied to the presiding officer charged with the preservation of order in the legislatures of various countries. In the UK the Speaker in the House of Lords is the Lord Chancellor; in the House of Commons the Speaker is elected for each parliament, usually on an agreed basis among the parties, but often holds the office for many years. The original appointment dates from 1377.

Spear /spɪə/ Ruskin 1911– . British artist, whose portraits include Laurence Olivier (as Macbeth), Francis Bacon, and satirical representations of Margaret Thatcher.

spearmint garden mint *Mentha spicata*.

Special Air Service (SAS) specialist British regiment recruited mainly from parachute regiment volunteers. It was founded by Colonel David Stirling in North Africa 1942–45 and revived from 1952. Its headquarters is at Bradbury Lines near Hereford on the Welsh border. Members are anonymous. Their motto is 'Who dares wins' under a winged dagger.

Special Branch section of the British police established 1883 to deal with Irish 'Fenian' terrorists. All 42 police forces in Britain now have their own Special Branches. They act as the executive arm of MI5 (see ◊intelligence) in its duty of preventing or investigating espionage, subversion and sabotage; carry out duties at air and sea ports in respect of naturalization and immigration, and provide armed bodyguards for public figures.

special drawing right (SDR) the right of a member state of the ◊International Monetary Fund (IMF) to apply for money to finance its ◊balance of payments deficit. Originally, the SDR was linked to gold and the US dollar. After 1974 SDRs were defined in terms of a 'basket' of the 16 currencies of countries doing 1% or more of the world's trade. In 1981 the SDR was simplified to a weighted average of US dollars, French francs, German marks, Japanese yen and UK sterling.

special education education, often in separate 'special schools', for children with specific problems or disabilities: that is, the blind, deaf, or maladjusted. In the UK the 1981 ◊Education Act encouraged local authorities to integrate as many children with special needs into mainstream schools as was practicable but did not recommend the complete closure of special schools.

speciation the emergence of a new ◊species during evolutionary history. One cause of speciation is the geographical separation of ◊populations of the parent species, followed by their reproductive isolation, so that they no longer produce viable offspring if they interbreed. Other less common causes of speciation are ◊assortative mating, and the appearance of ◊polyploidy.

species in biology, a distinguishable group of organisms, which resemble each other or consist of a few distinctive types (as in ◊polymorphism), and which can all interbreed (actually or potentially) to produce fertile offspring. Species are the lowest level in the system of biological ◊classification. Examples include lions, Douglas firs, cabbage white butterflies, and sperm whales. All living human beings belong to the same species because they can all interbreed, even though they may differ considerably in such features as skin colour, height, head shape, and so on.

Related species are grouped together in a ◊genus. Within a species there are usually two or more separate ◊populations, which may become distinctive enough in time, to be designated sub-species or varieties, and could eventually give rise to new species, through ◊speciation.

specific gravity alternative term for ◊relative density.

specific heat capacity in physics, quantity of heat requires to raise unit mass (1 kg) of a substance by one degree ◊kelvin (1°C). The unit of specific heat capacity is the ◊joule per kilogram kelvin (J kg $^{-1}$ K $^{-1}$).

spectacles a pair of lenses fitted in a frame and worn in front of the eyes to correct or assist defective vision. They are said to have been invented in the 13th century by a Florentine monk. Few people found the need for spectacles until printing was invented, when the demand for them increased rapidly. It is not known when spectacles were introduced into England, but in 1629 Charles I granted a charter to the Spectacle Makers' Guild. Common defects of the eye corrected by spectacle lenses are short sight, or myopia by using concave (spherical) lenses, long sight, or hypermetropia by using convex (spherical) lenses, and astigmatism by cylindrical lenses, the direction of the axes of the cylinders being specified. Spherical and cylindrical lenses may be combined in one lens. For convenience bi-focal spectacles provide for correction both at a distance and for reading by combining two lenses of different curvatures in one piece of glass. Using photosensitive glass, lenses are produced which darken in glare and return to normal in ordinary light conditions. See also ◊contact lens.

Spector /'spektə/ Phil 1940– . US record producer, known for the Wall of Sound, created in mono with a large orchestra, distinguishing his work in the early 1960s with vocal groups such as the Crystals and the Ronettes.

spectroscopy in physics, the study of spectra associated with ◊atoms or ◊molecules in solid, liquid or gaseous phase. Emission spectroscopy is the study of the characteristic series of sharp lines in the spectrum produced when an ◊element is heated. Thus an unknown mixture can be analysed for its component elements. Related is absorption spectroscopy, dealing with atoms and molecules as they absorb energy in a characteristic way. Again, those dark lines are characteristic of the element or molecule present and can be used for analysis. More detailed structural information can be obtained using infrared spectroscopy (concerned with molecular vibrations) or nuclear magnetic resonance (NMR) spectroscopy (concerned with interactions between adjacent atomic nuclei). Spectroscopy can be used to identify unknown compounds and is an invaluable tool to scientists, industry (especially pharmaceuticals for purity checks), and medical workers.

spectrum in physics, an arrangement in order of magnitude of radiated frequencies of ◊electromagnetic waves, or of the energies of atomic particles. The visible spectrum was first studied by ◊Newton who showed in 1672 that a ray of white light (sunlight) passing through a glass prism could be broken into a band of coloured light, ranging from violet through indigo, blue, green, yellow, and orange to red. Visible light is part of the ◊electromagnetic spectrum and most sources emit waves of a range of wavelengths which can be broken up or 'dispersed' by suitable means, such as by a spectroscope (using a collimator to produce a parallel beam), a ◊prism or ◊diffraction grating, and a ◊telescope, into a succession of individual waves arranged in order of wavelength.

There are many types of spectra, both emission and absorption, for radiation and particles. Common examples include an incandescent body giving rise to a continuous spectrum where the dispersed radiation is distributed uninterruptedly over a range of wavelengths. An element gives a *line spectrum* – one or more bright discrete lines at characteristic wavelengths. Molecular gases give *band spectra* in which there are groups of close-packed lines shaded in one direction of wavelength. In an *absorption spectrum* dark lines or spaces replace the characteristic bright lines of the absorbing medium. The *mass spectrum* of an element is obtained from a mass spectrograph and shows the relative proportions of its constituent ◊isotopes. See also ◊spectroscopy.

Spee /ʃpeɪ/ Maximilian, Count von Spee 1861–1914. German admiral. Born in Copenhagen, he held North Sea and Far Eastern commands before World War I. He went down with his flagship in the 1914 battle of the Falkland Islands, and the *Graf Spee* battleship was named after him.

speech recognition a computer-based technology for analysing and recognizing speech. The three types, in increasing order of difficulty, are: *separate word recognition* for distinguishing up to several hundred separately spoken words; *connected speech recognition*, for speech where there is a short pause between words; and *continuous speech recognition*, for normal but carefully articulated speech. Speech 'recognizers' must be 'trained' for particular users, as speaker-independent speech recognition is not yet possible.

speech synthesis a computer-based technology for the generation of speech sounds. A speech synthesizer is controlled by a computer which supplies strings of codes representing basic speech sounds (phonemes) and these together make up words. Speech-synthesis applications include anything from children's toys to car and aircraft warning systems.

speedometer instrument attached to the gear-box of a vehicle by a flexible drive, which indicates the speed of the vehicle in miles or kilometres per hour on a dial easily visible to the driver.

speedway the sport of motorcycle racing on a dirt track. The first organized races were in Australia in 1923 and the first track in Britain was at Droylsden, near Manchester, in 1927. Four riders compete in each heat over four laps. A series of heats make up a match or competition. In Britain there are two Leagues, the British League and the National League. World championships exist for individuals, pairs, four-man teams, long-track racing, and ice speedway.

speedwell flowering plant, genus *Veronica*, of the figwort family. There are many wild species, most being low-growing plants with small bluish flowers. *Common speedwell Veronica officinalis* is a low creeping plant and grows in dry grassy places, heathland and open woods throughout Europe. It has oval leaves and spikes of lilac flowers with four joined petals. Exotic species of speedwell are also popular as garden plants.

Speenhamland system method of poor relief in England started by Berkshire magistrates in 1795, whereby wages were supplemented from the poor-rates. However, it encouraged the payment of low wages and was superseded by the 1834 ◊Poor Law. The concept of negative income tax is a more sophisticated equivalent.

Speke /spiːk/ John Hanning 1827–1864. British explorer, born in Somerset. He joined ◊Burton in an African expedition in which they reached Lake Tanganyika 1858, and Speke went on (after Burton was taken ill) to be the first European to see Lake ◊Victoria 1858; his claim that it was the source of the Nile was disputed by Burton, even after Speke and Grant made a second confirmatory expedition 1860–63. Speke accidentally shot himself out shooting in England, the day before he was due to debate the matter publicly with Burton.

speleology the scientific study of caves, their origin, development, physical structure, flora, fauna, folklore, exploration, surveying, photography, cave-diving, rescue work, and so on. It first developed in France in the late 19th century, where the Société de Spéléologie was founded in 1895, and in the form of potholing – which involves following the course of underground rivers or streams – has in the 20th century become a popular sport.

Spence /spens/ Basil 1907–1976. British architect. He was professor of architecture at the Royal Academy, London, 1961–68, and his controversial works include Coventry Cathedral, Sussex University, the British embassy in Rome, the Home Office and Knightsbridge Barracks. He was knighted in 1960 and awarded the Order of Merit in 1962.

Spencer /'spensə/ Herbert 1820–1903. British philosopher. Born at Derby, he was an engineer before entering journalism. While sub-editor on *The Economist*, he wrote *Social Statics* 1851, expounding his *laissez-faire* views on social and political problems, and in 1855 *Principles of Psychology* appeared, followed by *Education* in 1861. In 1862 he began his ten-volume *System of Synthetic Philosophy*, in which he extended ◊Darwin's theory of evolution to the entire field of human knowledge.

Spencer Largely self-taught, Herbert Spencer was a railway engineer before turning to philosophy.

Spencer /'spensə/ Stanley 1891–1959. British artist who was born and lived at Cookham-on-Thames, where a gallery of his work was opened 1962. He interpreted the Christian faith in terms of village life, for example *Christ Carrying the Cross* and *Resurrection*, both in the Tate Gallery, London, and murals of army life for the oratory of All Souls' at Burghclere in Berkshire.

Spender /'spendə/ Stephen (Harold) 1909–1985. British poet and critic. Educated at University College, Oxford, he founded with Cyril Connolly the magazine *Horizon* (of which he was co-editor 1939–41) and 1953–67 was co-editor of *Encounter*. His earlier poetry has a left-wing political content, as in *Twenty Poems* 1930, *Vienna* 1934, *The Still Centre* 1939, and *Poems of Dedication* 1946. Other works include the verse drama *Trial of a Judge* 1938, and the autobiography *World within World* 1951, and many translations.

Spengler /'ʃpenglə/ Oswald 1880–1936. German philosopher, whose *Decline of the West* 1918 argued that civilizations go through natural cycles of growth and decay. He was admired by the ◊Nazis.

Spenser /'spensə/ Edmund 1552–1599. English poet, born in London and educated at Cambridge. He has been called the 'poet's poet' because of his rich imagery and command of versification. He published *The Shepheard's Calendar* in 1579 with the Earl of ◊Leicester as his patron. In 1580 he became secretary to the Lord Deputy in Ireland, and at Kilcolman Castle completed the first three books of the great moral allegory *The Faerie Queene* 1590 (Elizabeth I being the 'Faerie Queene'). In 1598 Kilcolman Castle was burnt down by rebels, and Spenser with his family narrowly escaped. Three further books of *The Faerie Queene* were published in 1596, but the remaining six were probably lost in the fire. He died in London, and was buried in Westminster Abbey. Spenser's other works including the elegy on Sidney, *Astrophel* 1586; the love sonnets or *Amoretti* and the *Epithalamion* 1595.

sperm in biology, the male ◊gamete of animals, but the name is also sometimes applied to the motile male gametes, or ◊antherozoids, of lower plants. In most animals, the sperm are motile, and are propelled by a long ◊flagellum, but in some (such as crabs and lobsters) they are non-motile. Each sperm cell looks rather like a tadpole, with a head capsule containing a nucleus, a middle portion containing ◊mitochondria (which provide energy) and the long tail or flagellum behind.

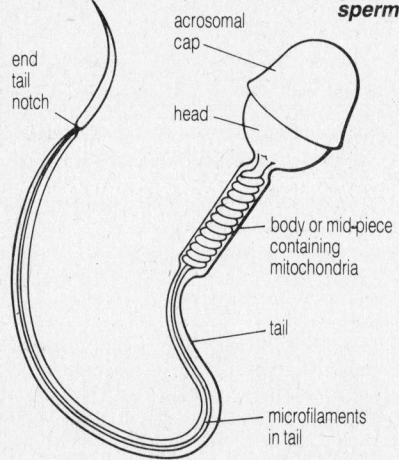

sperm

acrosomal cap

head

end tail notch

body or mid-piece containing mitochondria

tail

microfilaments in tail

spermaceti glistening wax-like substance, not a true oil, contained in the cells of the huge, almost rectangular 'case' in the head of the sperm whale, and amounting to about 2.5 tonnes. It rapidly changes in density according to temperature. Before the introduction of whaling restrictions it was much used in lubricants and cosmetics. In 1980 a blend of fatty acids and esters from tallow and coconut oil was developed as a substitute in cosmetics.

spermatophyte another name for a ◊seed plant.

Sperry /'speri/ Elmer Ambrose 1860–1930. American engineer who developed various devices using ◊gyroscopes, such as gyrostabilizers (for ships and torpedoes) and gyro-controlled autopilots. The first gyrostabilizers dated from 1912. During World War I Sperry designed a pilotless aircraft that could carry up to 450 kg/990 lb of explosives a distance of 160 km/100 miles (the first flying bomb) under gyroscopic control. By the mid-1930s Sperry autopilots were standard equipment on most large ships.

Spey /speɪ/ river in Highland region, Scotland, rising SE of Fort Augustus, and flowing 172 km/107 mi to the Moray Firth between Lossiemouth and Buckie.

Speyer /'ʃpaɪə/ (English name *Spires*) ancient city on the Rhine, in Rhineland-Palatinate, West Germany, 26 km/16 mi S of Mannheim; population (1972) 50,000. It was at the *Diet of Spires* 1529 that ◊Protestantism received its name.

sphere in mathematics, a circular solid figure with all points on its surface the same distance from the centre. For a sphere of radius r, the volume $V = \frac{4}{3}\pi r^3$ and the surface area $A = 4\pi r^2$.

Sphinx a mythological creature, represented in Egyptian, Assyrian and Greek art as a lion with a human head. The Great Sphinx at Gizeh, Egypt, 58 m/189 ft long, was built about 2900–2750 BC. In Greek myth the Sphinx was female, and killed travellers who failed to answer a riddle; she killed herself when ◊Oedipus gave the right answer.

sphygmomanometer instrument for measuring blood pressure, particularly of the arteries.

spice any aromatic vegetable substance used as a condiment and for flavouring food. Spices are obtained from tropical plants, and include pepper, cayenne pepper, nutmeg, ginger, and cinnamon.

Spice Islands /spaɪs/ former name of the ◊Moluccas, a group of islands in the Malay Archipelago.

spider jointed-legged animal of the class Arachnida in which (unlike insects) the head and breast are merged to form the cephalothorax, connected to the abdomen by a characteristic narrow waist. There are eight legs, and up to eight eyes. On the under-surface of the abdomen are the spinnerets from which a viscid fluid is exuded which hardens on exposure to the air to form silky threads, used to spin webs – in which the spider nests and catches its prey – and as a safeguard against falling. Their fangs inject substances to subdue and digest prey, the juices of which are then sucked in by the spider. Species of particular interest include the *common garden spider Araneus diadematus* which spins webs of remarkable beauty; the *zebra spider Salticus scenicus*, a longer-sighted species which stalks its prey and has pads on its feet which enable it to walk even on glass; the poisonous ◊*tarantula* and ◊*black widow*; the *water spider Argyroneta aquatica* which fills a 'diving bell' home with air trapped on the hairs of the body; and the largest members of the group, the *bird-eating spider* of South America *Mygale*, with a body some 5 cm/2 in long and a leg-span of 30 cm/1 ft.

Spielberg /'spiːlbɜːg/ Steven 1947– . American director, whose hugely successful films, including *Jaws* 1975, *Close Encounters of the Third Kind* 1977, *Raiders of the Lost Ark*

1981, and *ET* 1982 have given popular cinema a new 'respectable' appeal.

spikelet one of the units of a grass ◊inflorescence. It comprises a slender axis on which one or more flowers are borne. Each individual flower or floret has a pair of scale-like bracts, the glumes, and is enclosed by a membranous lemma and a thin, narrow palea, which may be extended into a long, slender bristle, or *awn*. See also ◊flower.

spikenard Himalayan plant *Nardostachys jatamansi*, family Valerianaceae; its underground stems give a perfume used in Eastern aromatic oils.

Spillane /spɪ'leɪn/ Mickey (Frank Morrison) 1918– . American novelist. Born in New York, he began by writing for pulp magazines and became known for violent crime novels, for example, *Vengeance is Mine* and *The Long Wait*.

spina bifida birth defect, a failure of the developing spinal canal to close completely (bifida means 'divided into two parts'). The nerves supplying the legs, arms and bladder are often involved. Modern treatment has increased survival prospects, but often at the cost of a heavily handicapped life.

spinach annual plant *Spinacia oleracea* in the family Chenopodiaceae. A native of Asia, it is cultivated as a vegetable.

spinal cord a major component of the ◊central nervous system in vertebrates. It is enclosed by the bones of the ◊spine and links the peripheral nervous system to the brain.

spine the backbone of vertebrates. In most mammals it contains 26 small bones called vertebrae. Each one has a thick, rounded, semi-circular body at the front to take weight, a bony ring behind creating a circular opening through which passes the ◊spinal cord, and three projections of bone (processes), one on each side and one to the rear. The lowest part of the spine is the sacrum. In humans this is a broad triangular structure consisting of five rudimentary vertebrae fused together, joined to the hip bones and ending in the tail bone (coccyx), which consists of four fused vertebrae. The spine in humans has four curves (front to rear), which allow for the increased size of the chest and pelvic cavities, and permit springing, to minimize jolting of the internal organs.

spinel a group of minerals possessing cubic symmetry and consisting chiefly of magnesia and alumina, for example, $MgAl_2O_4$ and $FeAl_2O_4$.

spinet a keyboard instrument, similar to a harpsichord but smaller, and having only one string for each note.

spinning the art of drawing out and twisting fibres into threads, by hand or machine. Synthetic fibres are extruded as a liquid through the holes of a spinneret.

spinning machine machine for spinning – drawing out fibres and twisting them into a long thread, or yarn. Originally, some 9,000 years ago, spinning was done by hand using a distaff (a cleft stick holding a bundle of fibres) and a weighted spindle, which was spun to twist the thread. In the 1300s the spinning wheel appeared in Europe, though it had been used earlier in the East. It provided a way of turning the spindle

mechanically. By the next century, the wheel was both spinning and winding the yarn onto a bobbin. In about 1767 James ◊Hargreaves in England built a machine that could spin eight, then 16 bobbins at once. It was called the spinning jenny. Later came Richard ◊Arkwright's water frame (1769) and Samuel ◊Crompton's spinning mule (1779). The latter, which has a moving carriage carrying the spindles, is still used. The other main spinning machine, the ring-spinning frame, was introduced in the USA in 1828. Sets of rollers moving at different speeds draw out finer and finer thread, which is twisted and wound onto rotating bobbins through travelling clips.

Spinoza /spɪ'nəuzə/ Benedict or Baruch 1632–1677. Dutch philosopher who abandoned Judaism for a rationalistic ◊pantheism that owed much to ◊Descartes. He taught that all that we know, mind and matter, is a manifestation of the all-embracing substance that is God, good and evil being relative. His *Ethics* 1677 is his chief work.

Spinoza The Dutch philosopher Benedict Spinoza is famous for his philosophy of rational pantheism.

spiracle in insects the opening of a ◊trachea, through which oxygen enters the body and carbon dioxide is expelled. In cartilaginous fish the same name is given to a circular opening that marks the remains of the first ◊gill slit. In tetrapod vertebrates, this spiracle has evolved into the Eustachian tube, which connects the middle ear cavity with the pharynx (throat).

spiraea herbaceous plant genus *Spiraea* and shrubs in the family Rosaceae which includes many cultivated species with ornamental panicles of flowers.

spiral a common curve such as that traced by a flat coil of rope or the groove in a gramophone record. Various kinds of spiral can be generated mathematically, such as an equiangular or logarithmic spiral (in which a tangent at any point on the curve always makes the same angle with it) and an ◊involute. They also occur in nature as a normal consequence of accelerating growth, such as the spiral shape of the shells of snails and some other molluscs.

Spires /spɪə or 'spaɪəz/ English name for the German city of ◊Speyer.

spirits of salts an old name for ◊hydrochloric acid.

spiritualism a belief in the survival of the human personality and in communication between the living and those who have 'passed on'. The spiritualist movement originated in the USA in 1848. In England the Society for Psychical Research was founded in 1882 by W H Myers and Henry Sidgwick to investigate the claims of spiritualism. Famous spiritualists include D D Home, William Crookes, Oliver Lodge, Arthur Conan Doyle, and Lord Dowding.

spit a ◊sandbar (sand ridge) projecting into a body of water and growing out from land, formed by a current carrying material from one direction to another across the mouth of an inlet.

Spitalfields /'spɪtlfiːldz/ district in the Greater London borough of ◊Tower Hamlets. It was once the home of ◊Huguenot silk weavers.

Spithead /,spɪt'hed/ a roadstead between the mainland of England and the Isle of ◊Wight. The name is often applied to the whole of the E area of the ◊Solent.

Spitsbergen /'spɪts,bɜːgən/ the main island in the Norwegian archipelago of ◊Svalbard.

Spitz /spɪts/ Mark Andrew 1950– American swimmer. At the 1968 Olympics he won two golds, silver and bronze medals and at the 1972 Olympics a record seven gold medals (all in world record-breaking times) making a total of 11 medals. He set 26 world records 1967–72.

spleen a organ found in vertebrates, situated behind the stomach. It is part of the lymphatic system, and helps to process the white blood cells known as ◊lymphocytes. The spleen also regulates the number of red ◊blood cells in circulation, destroys old red blood cells, and acts as a reservoir of iron.

Split /splɪt/ (Italian name *Spalato*), port in Yugoslavia, on the Adriatic; population (1981) 236,000. Industries include engineering, cement, and textiles, and it is also a tourist resort. The Roman emperor Diocletian retired here in 305.

Spock /spɒk/ Benjamin McLane 1903– . American paediatrician and writer on child care. His influential *Common Sense Book of Baby and Child Care* 1946 advocated less rigidity in bringing up children than had been advocated by previous generations of writers on the subject, but was popularly misunderstood as advocating complete permissiveness. In his later work he stressed that his 'common-sense' approach had not implied rejecting all discipline, but that his main aim was to give parents the confidence to trust their own judgement.

Spode /spəʊd/ Josiah 1754–1827. British potter, son of Josiah Spode the elder (an apprentice of Thomas Whieldon who started his own works at Stoke-on-Trent 1770), and his successor in the new firm in 1797. He developed bone porcelain (bone ash, china stone, and china clay) c. 1800, which was produced at all English factories in the 19th century, and became potter

to King George III in 1806.

spoils system in the USA, the granting of offices and favours among the supporters of a party in office. The spoils system, a type of ◊patronage, was used by Jefferson, and was enlarged in scope by the 1820 Tenure of Office Act which gave the President and Senate the power to reappoint posts which were the gift of the government after each four-yearly election. The system reached a peak under the presidency of Ulysses S Grant (1869–77).

The practice remained common in this century in US local government, particularly in large cities (New York, Chicago, Philadelphia), where civil service posts were often filled on the recommendation of newly elected political leaders. The system was epitomized by the Democratic Party 'machine' of Richard Daley (1902–76), mayor of Chicago 1955–76.

Spokane /spəʊ'kæn/ city in E Washington, USA; population (1980) 171,300. It is situated in the mining, timber, and rich agricultural area.

Spoleto /spə'leɪtəʊ/ town in Umbria, central Italy; population (1985) 37,000. There is an annual opera and drama festival established by Gian Carlo ◊Menotti. It was a papal possession 1220–1860.

sponge very simple animal of the phylum Porifera, usually marine. A sponge has a hollow body, its cavity lined by cells bearing flagellae, whose whip-like movements keep water circulating, bringing a stream of food particles. The body walls are strengthened with protein (as in the bath-sponge) or little spikes of silica.

spontaneous generation the erroneous belief that living organisms can arise spontaneously from non-living matter, which survived until the mid-19th century, when Louis ◊Pasteur demonstrated that a nutrient broth would not generate microorganisms if it was adequately sterilized. The theory of ◊biogenesis holds that spontaneous generation cannot occur.

spoonbill type of bird, of the family Threskiornithidae, characterized by a long, flat bill, dilated at the tip in the shape of a spoon. The *Eurasian spoonbill Platalea leucorodia* is found in shallow open water which it sifts for food.

Spoonerism a form of expression not unlike a slip of the tongue, arising from the exchange of elements in a flow of words. The result can often be amusing and even ridiculous (for example 'a troop of Boy Scouts' becoming *a scoop of Boy Trouts*). Dr William Spooner (1844–1930), Warden of New College, Oxford, from 1903 to 1924, gave his name to the phenomenon.

Sporades /'spɒrədiːz/ island group in the Aegean Sea. The chief island of the *Northern Sporades* is *Skyros* on which Rupert ◊Brooke is buried; area 207 sq km/79 sq mi. The *Southern Sporades* are more usually referred to as the ◊Dodecanese.

sporangium a structure in which ◊spores are produced.

spore a small reproductive or resting body, usually consisting of just one cell. Unlike a ◊gamete, it does not need to fuse with another cell in order to develop into a new organism. Spores are produced by the lower plants, most fungi, some bacteria, and certain protozoa. They

spore The earthstar (*Geastrum triplex*), is so called because the outer covering splits into a star shape. A water droplet has just landed on top of the fungus inducing it to expel a spore cloud.

are generally light and easily dispersed by wind movements. Plant spores are haploid and are produced by the sporophyte, following meiosis; see ◊alternation of generations.

sporophyte the diploid spore-producing generation in the life cycle of a plant that undergoes ◊alternation of generations.

sport many sports can be traced to ancient Egyptian or Greek times. Coursing was believed to have taken place in Egypt in 3000 BC, using Saluki dogs. Wrestling certainly took place in Egypt more than 4,000 years ago, and the Greeks participated in boxing around 1500 BC.

The real development of the majority of today's sport as competitions, rather than pastimes, was in the 18th and 19th centuries, when sports such as ◊cricket, ◊football, ◊rugby, ◊golf, ◊tennis, and many more became increasingly popular.

spreadsheet in computing, a program displaying a matrix of numbers with row and column headings, allowing complex numerical analyses. The users can 'program' each cell of the matrix to define how it is derived from other cells; for example, the last cell in a column may be defined as the sum of the cells above it. Spreadsheets are used primarily for financial calculations and forecasting analyses (changing values to see what effect this might have).

spring a device, usually a metal coil, which returns to its original shape when stretched or compressed. Springs are used in some machines (such as clocks) to store energy, which can be released at a controlled rate. In other machines (such as engines) they are used to close valves. In

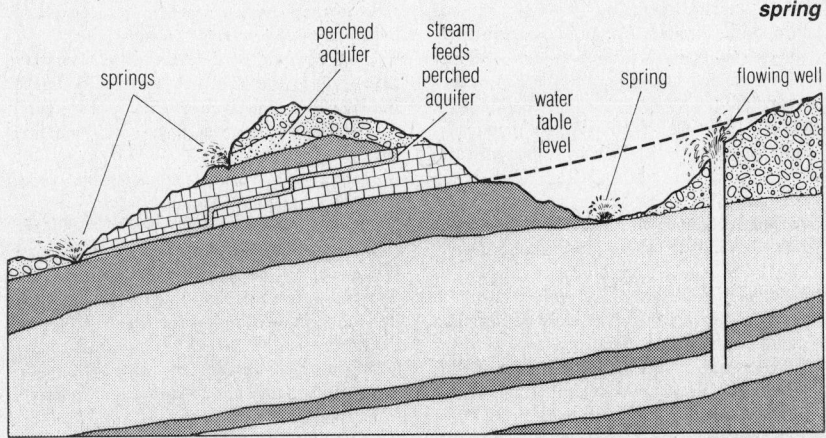

spring

springs / perched aquifer / stream feeds perched aquifer / water table level / spring / flowing well

vehicle suspension systems springs are used to cushion passengers from road shocks. These springs are used in conjunction with ▷dampers, which limit their amount of travel.

spring in geology a natural flow of water from the ground, formed at the point of intersection of the water table and the ground's surface. It may be continuous or intermittent and depends on the position of the water table and the topography (surface features). The source of water is rain that has fallen on the overlying rocks and percolated through. During its passage the water may have dissolved mineral substances which may then be precipitated at the spring.

Spring /sprɪŋ/ Richard 1950– . Irish Labour Party leader from 1982, who entered into coalition with ▷FitzGerald's Fine Gael 1982 as deputy prime minister (and minister for energy from 1983).

springbok S African antelope *Antidorcas marsupialis* about 80 cm/2.6 ft at the shoulder, with head and body 1.3 m/4 ft long, once migrating in herds of over a million, but now found only in small numbers where protected. They may leap 3 m/10 ft or more in the air when startled or playing (hence springbuck) and have a fold of skin along the middle of the back which is raised to a crest in alarm.

Springfield /'sprɪŋfi:ld/ capital and agricultural and mining centre of Illinois, USA; population (1980) 99,650. Abraham ▷Lincoln was born and is buried here.

Springfield /'sprɪŋfi:ld/ city in Massachusetts, USA; population (1980) 153,500. It was the site (1794–1968) of the US arsenal and armoury, famous for the Springfield rifle.

Springfield /'sprɪŋfi:ld/ city and agricultural centre in Missouri, USA; population (1980) 133,000. Industries include engineering and textiles.

Springs /sprɪŋz/ city in Transvaal, South Africa; population (1980) 154,000. It is a mining centre, producing gold, coal, and uranium.

Springsteen /'sprɪŋsti:n/ Bruce 1949– . US rock singer, and guitarist, born in New Jersey. His traditionalist songs of working-class life became hugely popular in the early 1980s.

spruce coniferous tree of the genus *Picea*, found over most of the N hemisphere. Pyramidal in shape, spruces have harsh needles and drooping leathery cones. Some are important forestry trees, such as the *Sitka spruce Picea sitchensis* originally from W North America, and the *Norway spruce* or 'Christmas tree' *Picea abies*.

Spurs, Battle of the a victory 1513 over the French, at Guinegate, NW France, by Henry VII of England; the name emphasizes the speed of the French retreat.

Sputnik (Russian 'fellow traveller') a series of ten Soviet Earth-orbiting ▷satellites. Sputnik 1 was the first artificial satellite, it carried only a simple radio transmitter which allowed scientists to track it as it orbited Earth. It was followed a month later by the larger Sputnik 2, carrying the dog Laika, the first living creature in space. Later Sputniks were unmanned test flights of the ▷Vostok spacecraft. They were superseded by the Cosmos series of launches, which continues.

Spycatcher the memoirs (published 1987) of former intelligence officer Peter ▷Wright.

square in geometry, a quadrilateral (four-sided plane figure) with all sides equal and at right-angles to each other. Its diagonals also bisect each other at right-angles. The area A of a square is the length l of one side multiplied by itself; $A = l^2$. Similarly, any quantity multiplied by itself, is also a square represented by an index (power) of 2; for example, $4^2 = 16$ and $6.8^2 = 46.24$. An algebraic expression is squared by doubling its index, and squaring its coefficient if it has one, for example, $(x^2)^3 = x^4$ and $(6y^3)^2 = 36y^6$. A number which has a whole number as its ▷square root is known as a perfect square; for example, 25, 144 and 54,756 are perfect squares (with roots of 5, 12 and 234, respectively).

square root in mathematics, of a number, another number which when squared (multiplied by itself) equals the given number. For example, the square root of 25 (written $\sqrt{25}$) is 5, because $5 \times 5 = 25$; the square root of 152.2756 is 12.34. As an ▷index, a square root is represented by ½; for example, $16^{½} = 4$. Strictly speaking, 16 (and all other numbers greater than zero) has two square roots: $+4$ and -4, because $(-4)^2$ also equals 16. Thus the square root of 16 is written ± 4. Negative numbers (less than 0) do not have square roots that are ▷real numbers. Their roots are represented by ▷complex numbers, in which the square root of -1 is given the symbol i (that is, $i^2 = -1$). Thus the square root of -4 is $+2i$.

squash game played in an enclosed court 9.75 m/32 ft long and 6.40 m/21 ft wide, usually by two persons, with rackets and a small 'squashy' synthetic rubber ball. The ball must hit the far (front) wall of the court (away from both players) above the 1.83 m/6 ft line when served, and on rebounding may be played almost anywhere within the boundary of the court in order to prevent the other player being able to return it.

World Open championship first held 1975
men
1982 Jahangir Khan (Pakistan)
1983 Jahangir Khan (Pakistan)
1984 Jahangir Khan (Pakistan)
1985 Jahangir Khan (Pakistan)
1986 Ross Norman (New Zealand)
women
1976 Heather McKay (Australia)
1979 Heather McKay (Australia)
1981 Rhonda Thorne (Australia)
1983 Vicky Cardwell (Australia)
1985 Sue Devoy (New Zealand)

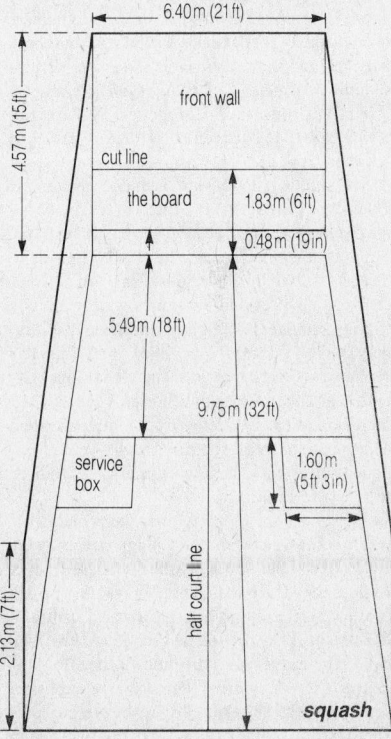

6.40 m (21 ft) / front wall / 4.57 m (15 ft) / cut line / the board / 1.83 m (6 ft) / 0.48 m (19 in) / 5.49 m (18 ft) / 9.75 m (32 ft) / service box / 1.60 m (5 ft 3 in) / half court line / 2.13 m (7 ft)

squash

squatter person illegally settling on land. By the mid-19th century, however, this term was used in Australia and New Zealand as synonymous with pastoralist or grazier, without an illegal imputation. Those who survived droughts and held on to their wealth established a politically powerful 'squattocracy', and built elegant mansions. As closer agricultural settlement spread at the close of the century, their influence waned. In the UK during the 1970s the word was applied to those taking over publicly or privately owned houses and other premises, either on grounds of homelessness or as a political manoeuvre, and special legislation was enacted to deal with the problem.

squill bulb-forming perennial plant, genus *Scilla* of the lily family. The *Spring squill Scilla verna* has narrow grass-like leaves, sometimes curled, which appear before the flowers. The violet-blue six-petalled flowers appear in early summer, two to twelve on a dense spike. Squill are found in dry places near the sea in W Europe. The *autumn squill Scilla autumnalis* is somewhat similar, but flowers in autumn prior to the emergence of leaves.

squirrel rodent of the family Sciuridae. Many are bushy-tailed tree-dwellers, but some are ground dwellers. The *red squirrel Sciurus vulgaris* is found throughout Europe and N Asia. About 23 cm/9 in long (plus 18 cm/7 in tail), the fur is red and the tail bushy. It rears its young in stick nests or 'dreys'. Although it is less active in winter, it does not hibernate, burying nuts as a winter store. In Britain the red squirrel has been replaced in most areas by the introduced *grey squirrel Sciurus carolinensis* from N America. Other squirrels include ground squirrels or *gophers* which make networks of tunnels in more open ground, and carry their food in cheek pouches, and the *prairie dogs* and *marmots*; also a number of genera of *flying squirrels*, mostly Asian, but some in E Europe and N America, which can glide between trees on skin stretched between front and back limbs.

Sri Lanka /sriː ˈlæŋkə/ island in the Indian Ocean, off the SE coast of India.

government under the 1978 constitution, the head of state and chief executive is the president, directly elected by universal suffrage for six-year terms. The president appoints and dismisses cabinet ministers, including the prime minister, may hold selected portfolios and dissolve parliament. Parliament is a single-chamber body with supreme legislative authority. There are 169 members, directly elected by a complex system of proportional representation for six-year terms. A two-thirds parliamentary majority is required to alter the constitution.

history the aboriginal people, the Veddas (of whom a few may remain in jungle areas), were conquered about 550 BC by the Sinhalese from N India under their first king, Vijaya. In the 3rd century BC the island became a world centre of Buddhism. The spice trade brought Arabs, who called the island Serendip, and Europeans, who called it Ceylon. Portugal established settlements 1505, taken over by the Netherlands 1658 and by Britain 1796. Ceylon was ceded to Britain 1802 and became a crown colony.

Under British rule Tamils from S India, Hindus who had been settled in the N and E for centuries, took up English education and progressed rapidly in administrative careers. Many more Tamils immigrated to work on the tea and rubber plantations developed in central Sri Lanka near Kandy. Conflicts between the Sinhalese majority and the Tamils surfaced during the 1920s as

nationalist politics developed. In 1931, universal suffrage was introduced for an elected legislature and executive council in which power was shared with the British, and in Feb 1948 independence was achieved.

Between 1948 and 1972, Sri Lanka remained a dominion within the British Commonwealth with a titular governor-general. The United National Party (UNP), led consecutively by Don and Dudley ◊Senanayake, held power until 1956, when the radical socialist and more narrowly Sinhalese Sri Lanka Freedom Party (SLFP), led by Solomon ◊Bandaranaike, gained electoral victory and established Sinhalese rather than English as the official language to be used for entrance to universities and the civil service. This precipitated Tamil riots, culminating in the prime minister's assassination by a Buddhist monk in Sept 1959. Bandaranaike's widow, Sirimavo, became prime minister and held office until 1977, except for UNP interludes in 1960 and 1965–70. She implemented a radical economic programme of nationalization and land reform, a pro-Sinhalese educational and employment policy, and an independent nonaligned defence policy.

In 1972 the Senate upper chamber was abolished and the new national name Sri Lanka 'Resplendent Island' adopted. Economic conditions deteriorated, spawning a serious wave of strikes in 1976, while Tamil complaints of discrimination bred a separatist movement calling for the creation of an independent Tamil state (Eelam) in the N and E. The Tamil United Liberation Front (TULF) coalition was formed in 1976 to campaign for this goal and emerged as the second-largest party in parliament from the elections of Jul 1977, easily won by the UNP led by Junius Jayawardene. The new government remodelled the 1972 constitution and introduced a new freer-market economic programme, which recorded initial success. In Oct 1980 Sirimavo Bandaranaike was deprived of her civil rights for six years for alleged abuses of power. The guerrilla activities of the Liberation Tigers of Tamil Eelam in the N and E provoked the frequent imposition of a state of emergency. In 1982 Jayawardene was re-elected president and the life of parliament was prolonged by referendum.

The violence escalated in 1983, causing the deaths of over 400 people, mainly Tamils in the Jaffna area. This prompted legislation outlawing separatist organizations, including the TULF. The near civil war has cost thousands of lives and blighted the country's economy; the tourist industry has collapsed, foreign investment dried up, and aid donors have become reluctant to prop up a government seemingly bent on imposing a military solution. All-party talks with Indian mediation repeatedly failed to solve the Tamil dispute, but in Jul 1987, amid protest riots, with several demonstrators killed by police, President Jayawardene and the Indian prime minister Rajiv ◊Gandhi signed a peace pact. It proposed to make Tamil and English official languages, create a semi-autonomous homeland for the Tamils in the N and E, recognize the Tigers as their representatives, and hold a referendum in

1988 in the E province, which has pockets of Sinhalese and 32 per cent Muslims.

The UNP is still headed by the octogenarian Jayawardene, the SLFP once more by Sirimavo Bandaranaike, the TULF is led by Appapillai Amirthalingam, and the Tigers by Velupillai Prakhakaran. There are in addition a number of smaller far-left parties, including the Lanka Sama Samaja (Equal Society) Party.

Sri Lanka remains a member of the ◊Commonwealth and ◊non-aligned movement and joined the ◊South Asian Association for Regional Cooperation in 1985. Its relations with India deteriorated during the early 1980s over the Tamil issue, but in the 1987 agreement Rajiv Gandhi pledged to enforce the peace with Indian troops if necessary and to stop Tamil militants from using S India as a base.

Srinagar /srɪˈnʌgə/ summer capital of the state of ◊Jammu and Kashmir, India; population (1981) 520,000. It is a beautiful resort, intersected by waterways, and has carpet, papier mâché, and leather industries.

SS Nazi elite corps (German *Schutz-Staffel* 'protective squadron') established 1925. Under ◊Himmler its 500,000 membership included the full-time *Waffen-SS* (armed SS), which fought in World War II, and spare-time members. The SS performed police duties, and was brutal in its treatment of the Jews and others in the concentration camps and occupied territories; it was condemned at the ◊Nuremberg trials.

stabilizer one of a pair of fins fitted to the sides of a ship and governed automatically by ◊gyroscope mechanism, designed to reduce side-to-side rolling of the ship in rough weather.

stadholder or *stadtholder* (Dutch *stadhouder*) the leader of the United Provinces of the Netherlands from the 15th–18th centuries. Originally a provincial leader appointed by the central government, stadholders were subsequently elected in the newly-independent Dutch republic. For much of their existence they completed with the ◊States General for control of the country. The stadholders later became dominated by the House of Orange-Nassau; in 1747 the office became hereditary, and was abolished 1795.

Staël /staːl/ Anne Louise Germaine Necker, Madame de Staël 1766–1817. French author, daughter of the financier ◊Necker. Banished from Paris by Napoleon 1803, because of her advocacy of political freedom, she gathered round her at Coppet, on Lake Geneva, men such as ◊Schlegel and ◊Byron. She wrote semi-autobiographical novels such as *Delphine* 1802 and *Corinne* 1807, and the critical work *De l'Allemagne* 1810, on German literature.

Staffa /ˈstæfə/ an uninhabited island in the ◊Hebrides, site of ◊Fingal's Cave.

Staffordshire /ˈstæfədʃə/ county in W central England
area 2,716 sq km/1,054 sq mi
towns administrative headquarters Stafford; Stoke-on-Trent
features largely flat, comprising the Vale of Trent and its tributaries; Cannock Chase
products coal in N; china and earthenware in the upper Trent basin; chinaware in the Potteries

Sri Lanka

DEMOCRATIC SOCIALIST REPUBLIC OF (former name Ceylon)

AREA 65,000 sq km/25,332 sq mi
CAPITAL and chief port Colombo
TOWNS Kandy; ports Jaffna, Galle, Negombo, Trincomalee
PHYSICAL flat in the N and around the coast; hills and mountains in the S
FEATURES Adam's Peak; ruined cities of Anuradhapura, Polonnaruwa
HEAD OF STATE Junius Richard Jayawardene from 1978
HEAD OF GOVERNMENT Ranasinghe Premadasa from 1978
GOVERNMENT parliamentary democracy
EXPORTS tea, rubber, coconut products; plumbago, sapphires, rubies, precious stones
CURRENCY Sri Lanka rupee (49.1 = £1 Sept 1987)
POPULATION (1985) 16,344,000 (including 2,500,000 Tamils); annual growth rate 1.4%
LANGUAGE Sinhalese (official, but English and Tamil are national languages)
RELIGION Buddhist 67% (official), Hindu 18%
LITERACY 91% male/81% female (1981)
GNP $5.3 bn (1984); $340 per head of population
CHRONOLOGY
1948 Independence from Britain achieved (as Ceylon).

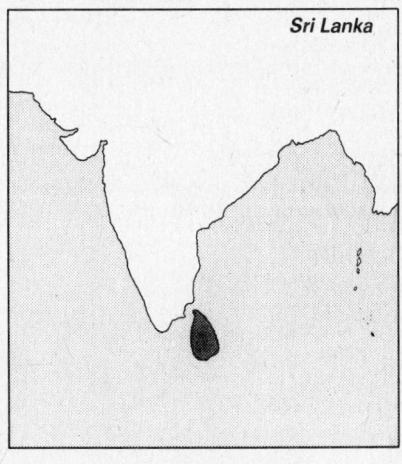

Sri Lanka

1956 Sinhalese established as official language.
1959 Assassination of Prime Minister Solomon Bandaranaike.
1972 Socialist Republic of Sri Lanka proclaimed.
1978 Presidential constitution adopted by new Jayawardene government.
1983 Tamil guerrilla violence escalated.
1987 Violence continued despite ceasefire policed by Indian troops.

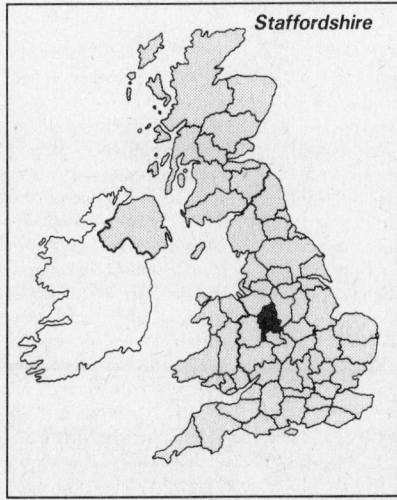

Staffordshire

population (1986) 1,022,300
famous people Peter ◊de Wint.

stagflation the economic condition (experienced in Britain in the 1970s) in which rapid inflation is accompanied by stagnating, even declining, output and by increasing unemployment. Its cause is often sharp increases in costs of raw materials and/or labour.

Stahlhelm German para-military and ex-servicemen's organization prominent in the 1920s and 1930s and associated with the German National People's Party (DNVP) and German People's Party (DVP).

stained glass term applied to the coloured transparent glass which is cut into various shapes and joined by lead strips to form a pictorial window design. The art is said to have originated in the Near East. At first it was usual for only one monumental figure to be represented on each window, but by the middle of the 12th century incidents in the life of Christ or of one of the saints were commonly depicted. Some of the most beautiful examples of medieval stained glass are to be found in the cathedrals of Canterbury, Lincoln, Chartres, Cologne, and Rouen. More recent designers include ◊Morris, ◊Burne-Jones, and ◊Chagall.

Stainer /'steɪnə/ John 1840–1901. British organist and composer. Most notable among his religious choral works are *The Crucifixion* 1887, an oratorio.

stainless steel a widely used ◊alloy that resists rusting. It is an alloy of iron, chromium and nickel.

Stakhanov /stə'kɑːnɒf/ Aleksei 1906–1977. Soviet miner in the ◊Donbas who consistently exceeded production norms, and who gave his name to the Stakhanovite movement of the 1930s, when workers were encouraged to initiate simplification and reorganization of work processes in order to increase production.

stalactite and stalagmite cave structures formed by the deposition of calcite dissolved in groundwater.

stalactites grow downwards from the roofs or walls and can be icicle-shaped, straw-shaped, curtain-shaped, or formed as terraces. They are formed when groundwater, hanging as a drip, loses a proportion of its carbon dioxide into the air of the cave. This reduces the amount of calcite that can be held in solution, and a small trace of calcite is deposited. Successive drips build up the stalactite over many years.

stalagmites grow upwards from the cave floor and can be conical, fir-cone-shaped, or resemble a stack of saucers. In stalagmite formation the calcite comes out of the solution because of agitation – the shock of a drop of water hitting the floor is sufficient to remove some calcite from the drop. The different shapes result from the splashing of the falling water.

Stalin Russian leader Stalin taking the salute during a march past of workers in Red Square, Moscow in May 1932.

Stalin /'stɑːlɪn/ adopted name (Russian 'steel') of Russian politician Joseph Vissarionovich Djugashvili 1879–1953. He was born near Tiflis, the son of a Georgian shoemaker; educated for the priesthood, he was expelled from his seminary for carrying on Marxist propaganda. He joined the Social Democratic Party in 1898, and was exiled to Siberia five times 1903–12, but on each occasion escaped and resumed his revolutionary activities. By 1913 he was editing *Pravda* and directing the ◊Bolshevik group in the Duma, when his book, *The National and Colonial Question*, attracted ◊Lenin's attention. From 1913 until the revolution of Mar 1917 he was an exile in Siberia. He then became a member of the Communist Party's ◊Politburo, and sat on the committee that directed the October Revolution. Appointed Commissar for Nationalities in the Soviet government he was responsible for the decree granting equal rights to all peoples of the Russian Empire. During the civil wars he held various himself by his defence of Tsaritsin (now Volgograd) against the 'Whites'.

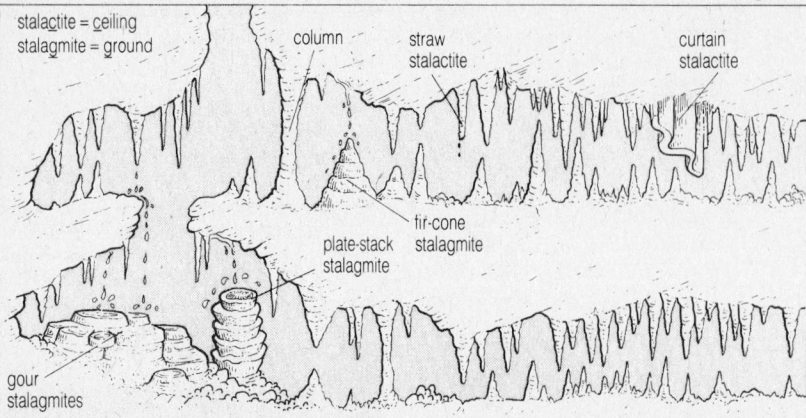

stalactite/stalagmite

stalactite = ceiling
stalagmite = ground

column

straw stalactite

curtain stalactite

fir-cone stalagmite

plate-stack stalagmite

gour stalagmites

Lenin, alarmed by Stalin's rapid consolidation of a powerful following (including ◊Molotov), died before being able to remove him from the general-secretaryship of the Communist Party (an appointment he received in 1922). Stalin, who wanted to create 'socialism in one country', now clashed with ◊Trotsky, who denied the possibility of socialism inside Russia until revolution had occurred in W Europe. Stalin won this ideological struggle by 1927, and a series of five-year plans was launched to collectivize industry and agriculture from 1928. All opposition was eliminated by the Great Purge 1936–38 (supposedly triggered by the assassination of ◊Kirov) by which Stalin disposed of all real and fancied enemies. During World War II, Stalin intervened in the military campaigns against Nazi Germany. He met Churchill and Roosevelt at Tehran in 1943 and at Yalta in 1945, and took part in the Potsdam conference.

After the war, Stalin maintained a one-man rule of single-minded intensity. His role was denounced after his death by ◊Khruschev.

Stalingrad /'stɑːlɪngræd/ name (1925–1961) of the Russian city of ◊Volgograd.

Stalinsk /'stɑːlɪnsk/ former name (1932–61) of ◊Novokuzentsk, city in USSR.

Stalker affair an inquiry begun 1984 by John Stalker, Deputy Chief Constable in Manchester, into the killing of six unarmed men in 1982 by Royal Ulster Constabulary (RUC) special units in Northern Ireland. The inquiry was halted and Stalker suspended from duty in 1986. Although he was later reinstated, the inquiry did not reopen, and no reason for his suspension was given.

Stamboul /ˌstæm'buːl/ the old part of the Turkish city of ◊Istanbul,

stamen the male reproductive organ of a flower. The stamens are collectively referred to as the ◊androecium. A typical stamen consists of a stalk, or *filament* with an *anther*, the pollen-bearing organ, at its apex, but in some primitive plants, such as *Magnolia*, the stamen may not be markedly differentiated. The number and position of the stamens are important characters in the classification of flowering plants. Generally the more advanced plant families have

fewer stamens, but they are often positioned more effectively so that the likelihood of successful pollination is not reduced.

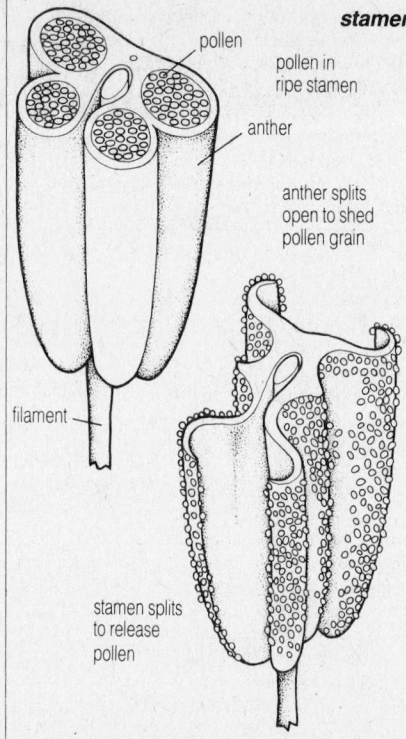

stamen

pollen

pollen in ripe stamen

anther

anther splits open to shed pollen grain

filament

stamen splits to release pollen

stamp act an Act of Parliament in 1765 which taxed (by requiring an official stamp) all publications and legal documents published in British colonies. The act provoked vandalism and looting in the American colonies, and the *Stamp Act Congress* in Oct of that year (the first truly inter-colonial congress) declared the act unconstitutional, with the slogan 'No taxation without representation', because the colonies were not represented in the UK parliament. A blockade of British merchant shipping proved so effective that the act was repealed the following year, under the new ministry of ◊Rockingham. The stamp act affair marked the first stage of the

American revolution (see ◊American Independence, war of).

standard deviation in statistics, a way of indicating the spread of items of data from their ◊mean (average) values. For example, to find the standard deviation of eight items of data (say the ages of a group of people in a room) the mean is first found (in this case by adding all the ages together and dividing the total by 8), and the deviations (differences) between all the individual ages and the mean calculated. The square of all these deviations is then found and their mean value calculated. The standard deviation is the square root of this mean (that is, the root mean square deviation). To work through the example, if the ages of the eight people are 14, 14½, 15, 15½, 16, 17, 19 and 21, the mean age is $132 \div 8 = 16.5$. The deviations between the individual ages and this mean age are $-2.5, -2, -1.5, -1, -0.5, +0.5, +2.5$ and $+4.5$, which square to 6.25, 4, 2.25, 1, 0.25, 6.25 and 20.25 with a mean value of $40.5 \div 8 = 5.0625$. The square root of this figure = 2.25, the standard deviation in years.

standing committee a committee of the UK House of Commons which examines parliamentary bills (proposed acts of parliament) for detailed correction and amendment. Several standing committees may be in existence at any time, each usually created for a particular bill (and thus not 'standing' at all). The committee comprises members of parliament from the main political parties, with a majority usually held by the government.

standing crop in ◊ecology, the total number of individuals of a given ◊species alive in a particular area at any moment. It is sometimes measured as the weight (or ◊biomass) of a given species.

Stanford /'stænfəd/ Charles Villiers 1852–1924. British composer, born in Ireland. He was a leading figure in the late-19th-century renaissance of British music, producing a large body of works in all forms, including operas such as *Shamus O'Brien* 1896, seven symphonies, chamber music, and church music.

Stanislavsky /ˌstænɪ'slævski/ Konstantin Sergeivich 1863–1938. Russian actor, director, and teacher of acting. He founded the Moscow Art Theatre in 1918 and achieved his greatest success as a director with his productions of Chekhov and Gorky. He was the originator of '◊Method' acting, which he described in *My Life in Art* 1924 and other works, and which had great influence on acting techniques in Europe and the USA (see also ◊Actor's Studio). He rejected the declamatory style of acting in favour of a more realistic approach concentrating on the psychological development of character.

Stanley /'stænli/ family name of Earls of ◊Derby.

Stanley /'stænli/ town on E Falkland, capital of the ◊Falkland Islands; population (1980) about 1,000.

Stanley /'stænli/ Henry Morton 1841–1904. British explorer-journalist, working for the *New York Herald* from 1867, who in 1871 was sent by James Gordon Bennett to find ◊Livingstone. They met at Ujiji, and explored Lake

Tanganyika together. He traced the course of the Zaïre (Congo) to the sea 1874–77; on a third expedition 1879–84, financed by ◊Leopold II, he established the Congo Free State (see ◊Zaïre) and made a fourth 1887–89.

Stanley Falls former name of ◊Boyoma Falls, on the Zaïre river.

Stanley Pool former name of ◊Pool Malebo, on the Zaïre river.

Stanleyville /'stænlɪvɪl/ former name of the Zaïrean port of ◊Kisangani.

Stansted /'stænstɪd/ site of London's third airport, in ◊Essex, England.

Stanton /'stæntən/ Elizabeth Cady 1815–1902. American feminist, who founded and led the first women's movement in the USA and who worked for the abolition of slavery. With Susan B ◊Anthony, she founded the National Woman Suffrage Association in 1869, and was its first president. Also with Anthony she wrote the *History of Women's Suffrage* from 1881–86 and organized the International Council of Women in Washington DC.

staple a medieval term used to describe the chief exports of England and also the towns permitted to market them. Thus the wool staple was established by the English crown in Dordrecht in 1294 before being moved to other contintental ports and then to English ports. This system of monopoly trading was finally abandoned in 1617.

star a luminous globe of gas, producing its own heat and light by nuclear reactions. The ◊Sun is an average star. Stars consist mostly of hydrogen and helium gas. They are born from large clouds of gas in space (see ◊nebula). Surface temperatures range from above 30,000°C down to 2,000°C, and the corresponding colours from blue-white to red. The brightest stars have masses 100 times that of the Sun, and emit as much light as millions of Suns. They live for less than a million years before exploding as ◊supernovae. The faintest stars are the ◊red dwarfs, less than one-thousandth the brightness of the Sun. The smallest mass possible for a star is about 8 per cent that of the Sun (80 times the mass of the planet ◊Jupiter), otherwise nuclear reactions do not take place. Objects with less than this critical mass shine only dimly, and are termed *brown dwarfs*. There is no firm distinction between a small brown dwarf and a large planet.

For most of a star's life, energy is produced by the ◊fusion of hydrogen into helium at its centre. Towards the end of its life, a star like the Sun swells up into a ◊red giant, before losing its outer layers as a ◊planetary nebula, and finally shrinking to become a ◊white dwarf. See also ◊binary star; ◊Hertzsprung-Russell diagram; ◊variable star.

starch a widely distributed long-chain carbohydrate (or polysaccharide), produced by plants as a food store. It occurs in granular form in cereals, pulses, and various tubers, including potatoes. Purified starch is a white powder used to stiffen textiles and paper, and to make various chemicals.

Star Chamber a civil and criminal court in England, so-named because of the star-shaped ceiling decoration of the room in the Palace of Westminster, London, where its first meetings were held. Created in 1487 by Henry VII, the Star Chamber comprised some 20 or 30 judges; it became notorious under Charles I for judgements favourable to the king and to Archbishop ◊Laud (for example, the branding on both cheeks of William ◊Prynne in 1637 for seditious libel). It was abolished 1641 by the ◊Long Parliament.

star cluster a group of related stars, usually held together by gravity. Members of a star cluster are thought to form together from one large cloud of gas in space. *Open clusters* such as the Pleiades contain from a dozen to many hundreds of young stars, loosely scattered over several light years. ◊Globular clusters are larger and much more densely packed, containing perhaps 100,000 old stars.

starfish echinoderm with arms radiating from a central body. Usually there are five arms, but some species have more. They are covered with spines and small pincer-like organs. There are also a number of small tubular processes on the skin surface which assist in respiration, and small tube-feet sometimes with suckers at the end. Starfish are predators, some species using their suckered tube-feet to pull open the shells of bivalve molluscs, then everting the stomach to surround and digest the animal inside. The poisonous and predatory 'crown of thorns' of the Pacific is very destructive to coral.

starling bird *Sturnus vulgaris* common in N Europe and Asia and naturalized in North America from the late 19th century. The black, speckled plumage is glossed with green and purple. Its own call is a bright whistle, but it mimics the songs of other birds. Strikingly gregarious in feeding, flight, and roosting, it often becomes a pest in large cities. More than 100 species of starling, family Sturnidae, are found in the Old World.

START acronym for the Strategic Arms Reduction Talks, held between the United States and the Soviet Union, first held in Jun 1982, but broken off in 1983 by ◊Andropov.

Star Wars popular term for the ◊Strategic Defence Initiative (SDI) announced by US President Reagan in 1983.

state the classic definition of a state is given by R M MacIver (*The Modern State* 1926): 'An association which, acting through law as promulgated by a government endowed to this end with coercive power, maintains within a community territorially demarcated the universal external conditions of social order'. There are four essential elements in this definition: the fact that people have formed an association to create and preserve social order; the fact that the community comprising the state is clearly defined in territorial terms; the fact that the government representing the people acts according to promulgated laws; and the fact that it has power to enforce these laws. Today, without exception, the state is seen as the nation state so that any community that has absolute sovereignty over a specific area is a state. Thus the so-called states of the USA, which are to some degree subject to the will of the federal government, are not states in international terms, nor are colonial or similar possessions which, too, are subject to an overriding authority.

Although most states are members of the United Nations Organization, this is not a completely reliable criterion: some are not members by choice, like Switzerland; some have been deliberately excluded, like Taiwan; and some are members but do not enjoy complete national sovereignty, like Byelorussia and the Ukraine, which both form part of the USSR.

It can be argued that with the growth of regional international bodies such as the European Community, states no longer enjoy absolute sovereignty.

State Department (Department of State) US government department responsible for ◊foreign relations.

Staten Island /'stætn/ island in New York harbour, part of New York (city) USA, constituting the borough of Richmond; area 155 sq km/60 sq mi; population (1980) 352,500.

States General the former French parliament which consisted of three estates – nobility, clergy, and commons. First summoned in 1302, it declined in importance as the power of the Crown grew. It was not called at all between 1614 and 1789 when the Crown needed to institute fiscal reforms to avoid financial collapse. Once called, the demands made by the States General formed the first phase in the ◊French Revolution. The term States General is also the name of the Dutch parliament.

static electricity ◊electric charge acquired by a body by means of electrostatic induction or friction. Its effects are due to the electrostatic ◊forces produced by the charge. Separation of electric charge is often brought about in everyday life by rubbing different materials together, and this is rendered visible by the sparks produced on combing one's hair in the dark or removing a nylon shirt. Static electricity has consequences in many industries, for example, in printing works where measures have to be taken to discharge the static electricity to prevent papers sticking together. In other processes static electricity is useful, as in paint spraying where the parts to be sprayed are charged with electricity of opposite polarity to that on the paint droplets, and in ◊xerography.

statics branch of mechanics concerned with the behaviour of bodies at rest and forces in equilibrium, and distinguished from ◊dynamics.

Stationery Office, His/Her Majesty's (HMSO) office established in 1786 to supply books and stationery to British government departments, and to superintend the printing of government reports and other papers, and books and pamphlets on subjects ranging from national works of art to industrial and agricultural processes. The corresponding establishment in the USA is the Government Printing Office.

Stations of the Cross in the Christian church, a series of 14 crosses, usually each with a picture or image, depicting the 14 stages in Christ's journey to the crucifixion.

statistical mechanics branch of physics in which the properties of large collections of ◊particles are predicted by considering the motions of the constituent particles and making various statistical assumptions.

statistics the branch of mathematics concerned with the collection and interpretation of data. For meaningful interpretations, there should be a large amount of data to analyse. For example, faced with the task of determining the ◊mean (average) age of the children in a school, an exact mean could be obtained by averaging the ages of every pupil in the school. A statistically acceptable answer might be obtained by calculating the average based on the ages of a representative sample, consisting say of a random tenth of the pupils from each class. ◊Probability is the branch of statistics dealing with predictions of events. The science has many applications in government, business, industry, and commerce.

status in the social sciences, term used for an individual's social position, or the esteem in which he or she is held by others in society. These two forms of social prestige may be separate or interlinked. Formal social status is attached to a particular social position, occupation, role, or office. Informal social status is based on an individual's own personal talents, skills, or personality. Both within and between most occupations or social positions there is a status hierarchy. Accompanying high status are usually *status symbols* , such as insignia of office or an expensive car. Sociologists distinguish between *ascribed status*, which is bestowed by birth, and *achieved status*, the result of one's own efforts. Max ◊Weber analysed social stratification in terms of three separate but interlinked dimensions: class, status, and power.

Staudinger /'ʃtaudɪŋə/ Hermann 1881–1965. German organic chemist, founder of macro-molecular chemistry, who did pioneering research into the structure of albumen and cellulose. He was awarded a Nobel prize in 1953.

Stauffenberg /'ʃtaufənbeək/ Claus von 1907–1944. German colonel, who planted a bomb in Hitler's headquarters conference room in the Wolf's Lair at Rastenburg, E Prussia, 20 Jul 1944. Hitler was injured, and Stauffenberg and some 200 others were executed.

Stavanger /stə'væŋə/ port in SW Norway, population (1980) 91,000. It has fish-canning, oil, and shipbuilding industries.

Stavropol /'stævrəpol/ town SE of Rostov, in the N Caucasus, USSR; known 1935–43 as Voroshilovsk; population (1981) 271,000. It is a market centre for an agricultural area, and makes agricultural machinery, textiles, and food products.

Stead /sted/ Christina 1902–1983. Australian writer. Her first stories were published in 1934; novels include *The Man Who Loved Children* 1940, *Cotter's England* 1966, and *I'm Dying Laughing* 1987.

steady-state theory theory that the Universe is in a steady state, that is, it appears the same wherever (and whenever) viewed. It seems to be refuted by the existence of cosmic background radiation. Held by ◊Lyell, among others, the theory was revived in the 20th century by Bondi and ◊Hoyle.

steam in chemistry, a dry, invisible gas formed by vaporizing water. The visible cloud which normally forms in the air when water is vaporized is due to minute suspended water particles. In this state it is called wet steam. The 'saturation temperature' is the temperature at which droplets begin to form from water vapour. Steam is widely used in industrial processes and for the generation of power.

stearic acid a saturated long-chain fatty acid, $(CH_3(CH_2)_{16}COOH)$ soluble in alcohol and ether but not in water. It is found in many fats and oils and used to make soap and candles, and as a lubricant. The salts of stearic acid are called stearates.

stearin name given to a mixture of stearic and palmitic acids, used to make soap.

Stębark /'stembɑːk/ Polish name for the village of ◊Tannenberg, formerly in E Prussia, now part of Poland.

Steed /stiːd/ Henry Wickham 1871–1956. British journalist. Foreign correspondent for *The Times* in Vienna 1902–13, he was then foreign editor 1914–19 and editor 1919–22.

Steel /stiːl/ David 1938– . British politician, leader of the Liberal Party from 1976. He entered into a compact with the Labour government 1977–78, and into an alliance with the Social Democratic Party 1983. He was a firm supporter of his party's decision to merge with the SDP in 1987.

steel band type of musical ensemble popular in the West Indies, especially Trinidad, consisting mostly of percussion instruments made from oil drums.

Steele /stiːl/ Richard 1672–1729. Irish essayist. Born in Dublin, he entered the guards, and then settled in London, and founded the journal *The Tatler* 1709–11, in which ◊Addison collaborated. They continued their joint work in *The Spectator*, also founded by Steele, 1711–12, and *The Guardian* 1713. He also wrote plays, for example, *The Conscious Lovers* 1722.

Steen /steɪn/ Jan 1626–1679. Dutch painter. Born in Leiden, he painted genre pictures from all walks of life, for example, *The Music Master*, and *Tavern Company*.

Steer /stɪə/ Philip Wilson 1860–1942. British artist. Born at Birkenhead, he studied in Paris, and was influenced by the French Impressionists, becoming a leader (with ◊Sickert) of the English movement and founder member of the ◊New English Art Club. His landscapes include *The Beach at Walberswick* (Tate Gallery, London). In 1931 he was awarded the Order of Merit.

Steichen /'staɪkən/ Edward 1897–1973. American photographer in both world wars, and also a fashion and portrait photographer.

Steiglitz /'staɪɡlɪts/ Alfred 1864–1946. American photographer. After forming the Photo Secession group in 1903, he began the magazine *Camera Work*. Through exhibitions at his gallery '291' in New York he established photography as an art form.

Stein /staɪn/ Gertrude 1874–1946. American author. Born in Pennsylvania, she studied medicine, and in 1904 went to Paris, where she became acquainted with Picasso. In her work she influenced writers such as

Steele As founder of *The Tatler* in 1709, Richard Steele aimed to raise moral and Christian standards as well as to amuse.

◊Hemingway and Scott ◊Fitzgerald by her cinematic technique, use of repetition and absence of punctuation; devices to convey immediacy and realism. Her works include the self-portrait *The Autobiography of Alice B Toklas* 1933.

Steinbeck /'staɪnbek/ John Ernst 1902–1968. American novelist. Born in California, he first achieved success with *Tortilla Flat* 1935, a humorous study of the lives of Monterey *paisanos*, following this with *In Dubious Battle* 1936, dealing with the brutal development of a strike by migrant fruit pickers, *Of Mice and Men* 1937, a compassionate vignette of two migrant farm labourers, and *The Grapes of Wrath* 1939, the saga of a farming family, refugees from the Oklahoma 'dust bowl', who struggle vainly against the inequitable conditions of the California they once regarded as their 'Promised Land'. In 1962 Steinbeck was awarded a Nobel prize.

Steinem /'staɪnəm/ Gloria 1934– . American journalist and feminist who emerged as a leading figure in the American women's movement in the late 1960s. She was also involved in other radical protest campaigns against racism and the Vietnam War. She co-founded the Women's Action Alliance in 1970.

Steiner /'ʃtaɪnə/ Rudolf 1861–1925. Austrian philosopher, originally a ◊theosophist, who developed his own mystic and spiritual teaching, anthroposophy, designed to develop the whole human being. His method of teaching is followed by a number of schools named after him.

Stellenbosch /ˌsteləm'bɒs/ town in Cape Province, South Africa; population (1985) 43,000. Next to Cape Town, it is the oldest European settlement in South Africa, founded 1679.

stem the main supporting axis of a ◊vascular plant that bears the leaves, buds, and reproductive structures; it may be simple or branched. The plant stem usually grows above ground, although some grow underground, including ◊rhizomes, ◊corms, ◊rootstocks, and ◊tubers. Stems contain a continuous vascular system that conducts water and food to and from all parts of the plant. The point on a stem from which a leaf or leaves arise is called a node, and the space between two successive nodes is the internode. In some plants, the stem is highly modified; for example, it may form a leaf-like ◊cladode or it may be twining, as in many clmbing plants, or fleshy and swollen to store water, as in cacti and other succulents. In plants exhibiting ◊secondary growth the stem may become woody, forming a main trunk, or a number of branches from ground level.

Stendhal /stæn'dæl/ pen name of French novelist Marie Henri Beyle 1783–1842. Born in Grenoble, he served in Napoleon's armies, taking part in the ill-fated Russian campaign, and, failing in his hopes of becoming a prefect, lived in Italy from 1814 until suspicion of espionage drove him back to Paris in 1821, where he lived by literary hackwork. The reputation of his novels *Le Rouge et le Noir/Red and black* 1830 and *La Chartreuse de Parme/The Charterhouse of Parme* 1839, pioneering in their treatment of disguise and hypocrisy, began with a review of the latter by ◊Balzac in 1840.

Stephen /'stiːvən/ c. 1097–1154. King of England from 1135. A grandson of William I, he was elected king in 1135, although he had previously recognized Henry I's daughter ◊Matilda as heiress to the throne. Matilda landed in England 1139, and civil war disrupted the country until 1153, when Stephen acknowledged Matilda's son, Henry, as his own heir.

Stephen /'stiːvən/ Leslie 1832–1904. English critic, first editor of the *Dictionary of National Biography* and father of novelist Virginia ◊Woolf.

Stephen I /'stiːvən/ St 975–1038. Hungarian king. He succeeded his father in 997, completed the conversion of Hungary to Christianity, and was canonized in 1803.

Stephens /'stiːvənz/ John Lloyd 1805–1852. American explorer in Central America, with Frederick ◊Catherwood. He recorded his findings among the ruined Maya cities in his two volumes of *Incidents of Travel* 1841–43.

Stephen, St died c. 35 AD, the first Christian martyr. Feast day 26 Dec.

Stephenson /'stiːvənsən/ George 1781–1848. British engineer who built the first successful steam locomotive. Born near Newcastle, he built his first locomotive in 1814. He also invented a safety lamp in 1815. He was appointed engineer of the Stockton and Darlington Railway, the world's first public railway, in 1821, and of the Liverpool and Manchester Railway in 1826. In 1829 he won a £500 prize with his famous *Rocket*. His son, *Robert Stephenson* (1803–59), achieved distinction as a civil engineer, constructing railway bridges, notably the high-level bridge at Newcastle, and the Menai and Conway tubular bridges in North Wales.

stem

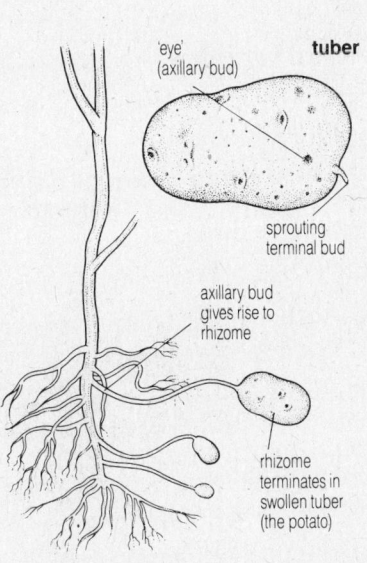

tuber

'eye' (axillary bud)

sprouting terminal bud

axillary bud gives rise to rhizome

rhizome terminates in swollen tuber (the potato)

corm

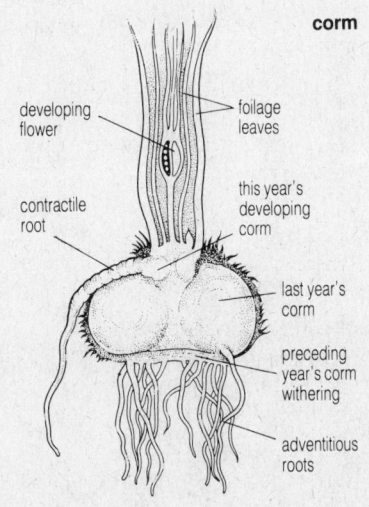

developing flower

foilage leaves

contractile root

this year's developing corm

last year's corm

preceding year's corm withering

adventitious roots

runner

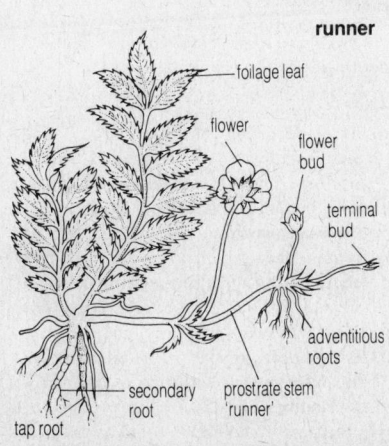

foilage leaf

flower

flower bud

terminal bud

adventitious roots

secondary root

prostrate stem 'runner'

tap root

Stepney /'stepni/ district now part of the London borough of ◊Tower Hamlets, N of the Thames, and E of the City of London.

steppe the temperate grassland of Europe and Asia. Sometimes the term is extended to other temperate grasslands, and it is also applied to semi-arid desert edges.

step rocket also called multi-stage ◊rocket; a rocket launch vehicle made up of several rocket stages (often three) joined end to end. The bottom stage fires first, boosting the vehicle to high speed, then it falls away. The next stage fires, thrusting the now lighter vehicle even faster. The remaining stages fire and fall away in turn, boosting the vehicle's payload to an orbital speed that can reach 28,000 kph/17,500 mph.

stereophonic sound a system of sound reproduction using two loudspeakers, which give a more natural 'depth' to the sound. See ◊hi-fi.

stereotype (Greek 'fixed impression') a one-sided, exaggerated, and preconceived idea about a particular group or society. It is based on prejudice rather than fact, but by repetition stereotypes become fixed in people's minds, resistant to change or to factual evidence to the contrary. The term, originally used for a method of duplicate printing, was adopted in a social sense by the American journalist Walter Lippman in 1922.

sterilization destruction of the power of reproduction. A man may be sterilized by ◊castration or by vasectomy, that is, tying off or cutting the tubes carrying sperm from the testicles to the seminal vesicles; a woman by cutting or tying the Fallopian tubes, or by hysterectomy (removing the womb). The word sterilization is also applied to the killing of bacteria by heat (asepsis) or disinfectants.

sterling silver an ◊alloy containing 925 parts of silver and 75 parts of copper. The copper hardens the metal, making it more useful for jewellery.

Stern /ʃtɜːn/ Otto 1888–1969. German physicist. The son of a wealthy merchant, Stern studied with Einstein in Prague and Zurich, where he became a lecturer in 1914. After World War I he demonstrated by means of the Stern-Gerlach apparatus that elementary particles have wave-like properties, as well as the properties of matter that had been demonstrated. He left Germany for the USA in 1933, and was awarded a Nobel prize in 1943.

Sterne /stɜːn/ Laurence 1713–1768. Irish writer, creator of the comic anti-hero Tristram Shandy. Born at Clonmel, Ireland, he took orders in 1737 and became vicar of Sutton-in-the-Forest, Yorkshire, in the next year. In 1741 he married Elizabeth Lumley, an unhappy union largely because of his infidelity. He had a sentimental love affair with Eliza Draper, of which the *Letters of Yorick to Eliza* 1775 is a record. His chief work is *The Life and Opinions of Tristram Shandy, Gent* 1760–67. Also very popular was his *A Sentimental Journey through France and Italy* 1768, the result of his travels in search of a cure for his tuberculosis.

Stern Gang (formal name 'Fighters for the Freedom of Israel') a Zionist terrorist group founded 1940 by Abraham Stern (1907–42).

Stephenson English engineer George Stephenson's locomotive *Rocket* winning the competition at Rainhill Bridge, near Manchester, 14 October, 1829. The prize was for the engine to be used on the Liverpool and Manchester Railway.

The group carried out anti-British attacks in Palestine, both on individuals and on strategic targets. Stern was killed by British forces in 1942, but the group survived until 1948, when it was outlawed with the creation of the independent state of Israel. Some of its members were subsequently assimilated into the Israeli army.

steroid in chemistry and/or medicine, a substance having a certain chemical formula; as a drug, an anti-inflammatory or immuno-suppressive agent. See also ◊hormone.

steroid in biology, a type of lipid (fat), derived from ◊sterols, with a complex molecular structure consisting of four carbon rings. Steroids include the sex ◊hormones, such as ◊testosterone, and the corticosteroid hormones produced by the ◊adrenal gland, which regulate the use of carbohydrates, proteins and fats, and the water and salt balance of the body. ◊Cholesterol, an important constituent of cell membranes, is also a steroid, as are the ◊bile salts, which aid the digestion of fatty food.

sterol one of a group of organic alcohols, with a complex structure, consisting of four carbon rings. ◊Steroids are derived from sterols, and have the same ring structure, but with various other chemical groups attached. They are physiologically very active.

stethoscope instrument used to ascertain the condition of the heart and lungs by listening to their action. It was invented by R T Laënnec (1781–1826), in 1819, and as now used consists of a small plate to be placed against the body and connected by flexible tubes with two ear-pieces.

Stettin /ʃteˈtiːn/ German name for the Polish city of ◊Szczecin.

Stevenage /ˈstiːvənɪdʒ/ town in Hertford-shire, England; population (1981) 74,300. Dating from medieval times, in 1946 Stevenage was the first place chosen for development as a ◊new town.

Stevens /ˈstiːvənz/ Wallace 1879–1955. American poet. Born in Reading, Pennsylvania, and educated at Harvard and the New York Law School. His volumes of poems include *Harmonium* 1923, *The Man with the Blue Guitar* 1937, and *Transport to Summer* 1947. *The Necessary Angel* 1951 is a collection of essays. Elegant and philosophical, his *Collected Poems* 1954 won a Pulitzer prize.

Stevenson /ˈstiːvənsən/ Adlai 1900–1965. American politician. Born in Los Angeles, he was educated at Princeton, and from Northwestern University Law School went on to be admitted to the Bar in 1926. As governor of Illinois 1949–53 he campaigned vigorously against corruption in public life, and as Democratic candidate for the presidency in 1952 and 1956 was twice defeated by ◊Eisenhower. In 1945 he was chief US delegate at the founding conference of the UN.

Stevenson /ˈstiːvənsən/ Robert 1772–1850. Scottish engineer, born in Glasgow, who built many lighthouses, including the Bell Rock lighthouse, 1807–11.

Stevenson /ˈstiːvənsən/ Robert Louis 1850–1894. Scottish novelist and poet. Born in Edinburgh, he studied at the university, and qualified as an advocate, but never practised. He travelled in Europe to improve his health, as recounted in *An Inland Voyage* 1878, and *Travels with a Donkey* 1879. In 1879 he went to the USA, married Mrs Osbourne, and, returning to Britain in 1880, published the volume of stories, *The New Arabian Nights* 1882. Fame came to him with *Treasure Island* 1883, *Kidnapped* 1886; (with its sequel *Catriona* in 1893), *The Black Arrow* 1888, *The Master of Ballantrae* 1889, *Dr Jekyll and Mr Hyde* 1886; and the incomplete *Weir of Hermiston* 1896 and *St Ives* 1897. His *A Child's Garden of Verses* appeared in 1885, and his *Letters* in 1899. In 1890 he settled at Vailima, in Samoa, where he sought a cure for the tuberculosis of which he died.

Stewart /ˈstjuːət/ James 1908– . American actor. Gangling and speaking with a soft drawl, he appeared in many films including *Mr Smith Goes to Washington* 1939, *The Philadelphia Story* 1940 (Academy award), *The Man from Laramie* 1955, *The FBI Story* 1959.

Stewart Island /ˈstjuːət/ volcanic island divided from South Island, New Zealand, by the Foveaux Strait; area 1,735 sq km/670 sq mi; population (1981) 600.

Stewart Famous for his roles as the stubbornly honest, upright American, actor James Stewart is seen here portraying a dedicated FBI investigator in the film *The FBI Story*.

stick insect insect of the order Phasmida, closely resembling a stick or twig. Many species are wingless.

stickleback fish of the family Gasterosteidae. Sticklebacks are widely distributed in the northern hemisphere, and the popular name is derived from the spines which take the place of the first dorsal fin. The common three-spined stickleback, *Gasterosteus aculeatus*, up to 10 cm/4 in, is found in most freshwater habitats and also on coasts.

stigma in a flower, the receptive surface at the tip of a ◊carpel which receives the ◊pollen. It often has short outgrowths, flaps, or hairs to trap pollen, and may produce a sticky secretion to which the grains adhere.

stigmata impressions or marks corresponding to the five wounds Christ received at his crucifixion, which are said to have been received by St Francis and other saints.

Stijl, De (the style) a group of 20th-century Dutch artists and architects led by ◊Mondrian from 1917. They believed in the concept of the 'designer', that all life, work, and leisure should be surrounded by art. Everything functional should be aesthetic as well. The group had a strong influence on the ◊Bauhaus.

Stilicho /'stılıkəʊ/ Flavius 359–408 AD. Roman general, of ◊Vandal origin, who campaigned successfully against the Visigoths and Ostrogoths. He virtually ruled the western empire as guardian of Honorius (son of ◊Theodosius I), but was executed on the orders of Honorius when he was suspected of wanting to make his own son successor to another son of Theodosius in the eastern empire.

Stilton /'stıltən/ village in Cambridgeshire, England, 10 km/6 mi SW of Peterborough. It

gives its name to a cheese brought here in coaching days for transport to London, and still made at and around ◊Melton Mowbray.

Stilwell /'stılwel/ Joseph Warren 1883–1946. US general, nicknamed 'Vinegar Joe'. In 1942 he became US military representative in China, when he commanded the Chinese forces cooperating with the British (with whom he quarrelled) in Burma; he later commanded all US forces in the Chinese, Burmese, and Indian theatres until recalled to the USA in 1944 after differences with ◊Chiang Kai-shek. Subsequently he commanded the US 10th Army on Okinawa.

Stimson /'stımsən/ Henry Lewis 1867–1950. US politician. He was war secretary in Taft's cabinet 1911–13, Hoover's secretary of state 1929–33, and war secretary 1940–45.

stinkhorn species of fungus (*Phallus impudicus*). It first appears as a white ball.

stinkwood term used for many 'smelly' trees, for example the S African tree *Ocotea bullata*, family Lauraceae, with offensive-smelling wood when newly felled, but fine, durable timber used for furniture. Another is *Gustavia augusta* from tropical America.

stipule an outgrowth arising from the base of a leaf or leaf stalk in certain plants. Stipules usually occur in pairs, or fused into a single semicircular structure. They may have a leaf-like appearance, as in goosegrass (*Galium aparine*), be spiny, as in false acacia (*Robina*), or look like small scales. In some species they are large, and contribute significantly to the photosynthetic area, as in the garden pea (*Pisum sativum*).

Stirling /'stɜːlıŋ/ town in central Scotland; population (1981) 38,600. It is the administrative headquarters of the Central region, and has a university.

history the castle predates the 12th century, and was long a Scottish royal residence. Wallace won a victory at Stirling bridge in 1297. In 1314 Edward II of England (in raising a Scottish siege of the town) went into battle at ◊Bannockburn.

Stirling /'stɜːlıŋ/ James 1926– . British architect, whose works include the engineering building at Leicester University, the Florey Building at Queen's College, Oxford, and the Clore Gallery (the extension to house the Tate's ◊Turner collection) at the Tate Gallery, London.

Stirling engine a hot-air engine invented by Scottish priest Robert Stirling in 1876. It is a ◊piston engine that uses hot air as a working fluid.

Stirlingshire /'stɜːlıŋʃə/ former county of Scotland. In 1975 most of it was merged with Central region, but a SW section, including Kilsyth, went to Strathclyde. The area lay between the Firth of Forth and Loch Lomond, and included the Lennox hills and the fringe of the Highlands. The county town was Stirling.

stoat carnivorous mammal *Mustela erminea* of the weasel family, about 25 cm/10 in long, plus an 11 cm/4.5 in black-tipped tail. Males are larger than females. The upper parts and tail are red-brown, the underparts white. Feeding on animals up to the size of a rabbit or hare, stoats live in Europe and N Asia. In the colder regions the coat turns white (ermine) in winter, still keeping a black-tipped tail.

stock in economics, in UK usage, the fully paid-up ◊capital of a company. It is bought and sold by subscribers not in units or shares (see ◊share), but in terms of its current cash value. See also ◊stocks and shares.

stock in botany, a popular garden flower, whose varieties have been derived from the wild *Matthiola incana*. The chief varieties are simple-stemmed, queen's, and ten-week; night-scented stock is *Matthiola bicornis*.

Stock Exchange institution for the buying and selling of ◊stocks and shares (securities). London's is the oldest stock exchange in the world, opened 1801. The former division between brokers (who bought shares from jobbers to sell to the public) and jobbers (who sold them only to brokers on commission, the 'jobbers' turn') was abolished in 1986; see ◊Big Bang. The major stock exchanges are London, New York (Wall Street), and Tokyo.

Stockhausen /'ʃtɒk,haʊzən/ Karlheinz 1928– . German composer. A student of ◊Messiaen, he moved from 12-note music to electronic composition, for example, *Kontakte* 1960. One of the most influential avant-garde composers, he has continued to explore new musical sounds and compositional techniques since the 1950s. His major works include *Klavierstücke* 1952–85, *Momente* 1961–64, revised 1972, *Mikrophonie I* 1964, and *Mikrophonie II* 1965. In recent years he has concentrated on a cycle of seven musical ceremonies, starting with *Donnerstag aus Licht* 1977–80.

Stockholm /'stɒkhəʊm/ capital, port and industrial city of Sweden; population (1980) 647,200. It is built on a number of islands; a network of bridges links them and the mainland; an underground railway was completed 1957. Industries include engineering, brewing, electrical goods, paper, textiles, and pottery. The 18th-century royal palace stands on the site of the 13th-century fortress defending the trading settlements of Lake Mälar, round which the town first developed. The old town is well preserved and has a church 1264. The town hall was designed by Ragnar Østberg 1923. Most of Sweden's educational institutions are in Stockholm (including the ◊Nobel Institute).

Stockport /'stɒkpɔːt/ town in Greater Manchester, England; population (1981) 136,500. Industries include chemicals, engineering, and still some cotton textiles.

stocks wooden device used until the 19th century to confine the legs or arms of minor offenders, and expose them to ignominy.

stocks and shares broadly, investment holdings (securities) in private or public undertakings. Although distinctions have become blurred, in Britain stock usually means fixed-interest securities, especially those issued by central and local government, while shares represent a stake in the ownership of a trading company and, if they are ordinary shares, yield to the owner dividends reflecting the success or otherwise of the company. In the USA the term stock generally signifies what in Britain are ordinary shares.

Stirling The Staatsgalerie, Stuttgart, by Stirling and Wilford. British architect James Stirling has a long association with collegiate and museum architecture.

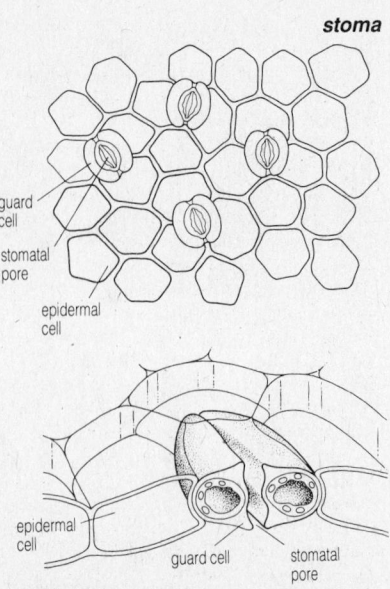

stoma

Stockton /ˈstɒktən/ industrial river port on the San Joaquin in California, USA; population (1980) 149,779.

Stockton-on-Tees /ˈstɒktən ɒn ˈtiːz/ town and port on the river Tees, Cleveland, England; population (1981) 154,600. There are shipbuilding, steel and chemical industries, and it is famous as having been the starting point for the world's first passenger railway.

stoic an advocate of *stoicism*, a Greek school of philosophy, founded in about 300 BC by ◊Zeno of Citium; it derived its name from the Stoa, or porch, at Athens in which he taught. The stoics were ◊pantheistic materialists who believed that happiness lies in accepting the law of the universe. In ethics they emphasized human brotherhood; their outlook was internationalist, and they denounced slavery. In the 3rd and 2nd centuries BC stoics took a prominent part in Greek and Roman revolutionary movements. After the 1st century BC stoicism became the philosophy of the Roman ruling class, and lost its revolutionary significance; outstanding stoics of this period were Seneca, Epictetus, and Marcus Aurelius.

Stoke-on-Trent /ˈstəʊk ɒn ˈtrent/ city in Staffordshire, England, population (1981) 252,400. It was formed 1910 from Burslem, Hanley, Longton, Stoke-upon-Trent, Fenton, and Tunstall, the heart of the Potteries, and is a major ceramic centre.

Stoke Poges /ˈstəʊk ˈpəʊdʒɪz/ village in Berkshire, England, which inspired Thomas ◊Gray to write his 'Elegy in a Country Churchyard'; the poet is buried here.

Stoker /ˈstəʊkə/ Bram (Abraham) 1847–1912. Irish novelist, actor, and theatre manager. He is best remembered for the novel ◊*Dracula* 1897, which crystallized most aspects of the traditional vampire legend and became the source for all subsequent popular fiction and films on the subject.

Stokes /stəʊks/ George Gabriel 1819–1903. British physicist who during the late 1940s studied the ◊viscosity (resistance to relative motions) of fluids. This culminated in Stoke's law, which applies to a sphere falling under gravity through a liquid. It states that if a sphere of radius r falls with a velocity v through a liquid of viscosity ϵ, the force acting on it $F = 6\pi\epsilon rv$.

Stokowski /stəˈkɒfski/ Leopold 1882–1977. US conductor, born in London. An outstanding experimentalist, he introduced modern music, for example, Mahler's Eighth Symphony, to the USA in 1916; appeared in several films; and conducted the music for Walt Disney's *Fantasia* 1940.

STOL (short take-off and landing) type of aircraft. STOL craft are fitted with special devices on the wings (such as sucking flaps), which increase aerodynamic lift at low speeds.

stolon a long aerial stem that grows horizontally, or arches over and bends to the ground, and which may form a new plant where a node lies on the soil surface. The daughter plants develop from axillary buds on the stem. Plants forming stolons include flowering currants (*Ribes*) and blackberries (*Rubus*). The horticultural technique of layering is a method of propagation by which ordinary shoots are pegged into the soil and induced to root like stolons. Runners, as seen in the strawberry plant, are a type of stolon; they generally creep over the soil surface, producing a new plantlet from the tip. When the daughter plant is firmly established the runner dies.

stoma a pore in the epidermis of a plant; plural ◊stomata.

stomach the first cavity in the digestive system of animals; it comes after the ◊mouth, ◊oesophagus, and ◊crop. In mammals, it is a bag of muscle situated just below the diaphragm. Food enters it from the gullet (oesophagus), is digested by the acid and ◊enzymes secreted by the stomach lining, and then passes into the duodenum. Some ◊herbivorous mammals have multi-chambered stomachs, which harbour bacteria in one of the chambers to assist in the digestion of ◊cellulose. See also ◊gizzard.

stomata pores in the epidermis of a plant; each stoma is surrounded by a pair of guard cells, that are crescent shaped when the stoma is open, but can collapse to an oval shape, thus closing off the opening between them. Stomata occur in large numbers on the aerial parts of a plant, especially on the undersurface of leaves, where there may be as many as 45,000 per square centimetre. They allow the exchange of carbon dioxide and oxygen (needed for ◊photosynthesis and ◊respiration) between the internal tissues of the plant and the outside atmosphere. They are also the main route by which water is lost from the plant, and they can be closed, to conserve water, the movements being controlled by changes in turgidity of the guard cells.

stone British unit of weight used to express bodyweight (st); 14 lbs comprise 1 stone. Equivalent to 6.35 kgs.

Stone /stəʊn/ (John) Richard 1913– . British economist, a statistics expert, whose system of 'national income accounting' has been adopted in many countries. Nobel prize 1984.

Stone /stəʊn/ Lucy 1818–1893. American feminist orator and editor, born in Massachusetts. She attended Oberlin College and gave public lectures from 1847 against black slavery and for women's rights. Married to the radical Henry Blackwell 1855, after a mutual declaration rejecting the legal superiority of the man in marriage, she gained wide publicity when she chose to retain her own surname despite her marriage. The epithet 'Lucy Stoner' was coined to mean a woman who advocated doing so. In the 1860s she helped to establish the American Woman Suffrage Association and founded and edited the Boston *Woman's Journal*, a suffragist paper which was later edited by her daughter, Alice Stone Blackwell (1857–1950).

Stone Age the period in prehistory before the discovery of the use of metals, that is, when tools and weapons were made chiefly of flint. It is divided into the Old Stone Age or Palaeolithic and the New Stone Age or Neolithic; in the latter the flint implements were more finely chipped. Sometimes an Eolithic or Dawn Stone Age is distinguished. The people of the Old Stone Age were hunters, and their few remains have been found in the deposits of caves, and river gravel. The period is divided into Upper, Middle, and Lower, each of which is subdivided into stages whose names are usually derived from the sites where the characteristic implements were first discovered; *Upper*: Magdalenian, Solutrean, and Aurignacian; *Middle*: Mousterian; *Lower*: Acheulean and Chellean. European Palaeolithic people lived in caves, and the most striking survivals of their culture are their wall paintings, for example, at Altamira and Lascaux. In Europe they were contemporary with the mammoth, woolly rhinoceros, reindeer, and cave bear, and lived before and during the ice ages. Neolithic people lived in a milder climate, and made the first steps in agriculture, domestication of animals, weaving, and pottery making. In Europe the Stone Age merged into the Bronze Age in about 2000 BC.

stonechat small bird *Saxicola torquata* of the thrush family (Turdidae) frequently found in Europe and Asia on open land with bushes. The male has a black head and throat, tawny breast, and dark back; the female is browner.

stonecrop name for many different species of the genus *Sedum* of the family Crassulaceae. Most have succulent leaves and star-like flowers. They are characteristic of dry rocky places. *Biting stonecrop* (*Sedum acre*) is low-growing, an evergreen with short fleshy leaves. The bright yellow flowers appear in early summer. It lives in Europe, N Asia and N Africa.

stonefish fish *Synanceia verrucosa* of the Indian and Pacific oceans, about 35 cm/14 in long and camouflaged to resemble encrusted rock. Its envenomed spines inflict such a painful sting that bathers may drown, even in shallow water.

stonefly insect of the order Plecoptera, long-tailed winged insects, living near water, and with aquatic larvae living mainly in streams with stony bottoms. They are used as anglers' bait.

Stonehenge /ˌstəʊnˈhendʒ/ megalithic monument (dating from about 2000 BC) on Salisbury Plain, Wiltshire, England, where it is one of a number of structures including about 400 round ◊barrows, Durrington Walls (once an ◊Avebury-style structure), Woodhenge (a 'henge' or 'enclosure' once consisting of great wooden posts), and The Cursus (a pair of banked ditches, about 100 m/300 ft apart, which run

straight for some 3 km/2 mi; dated 4th millenium BC). The purpose of none of these is known, although it is certain that they greatly antedate the ◊Druids. It seems they could have had a ritual purpose. Stonehenge's main feature consisted originally of a circle of 30 upright stones, their tops linked by lintelstones to form a continuous circle about 30 m/100 ft across. Within the circle was a horseshoe arrangement of five trilithons (each of two uprights plus a lintel, but set as separate entities), so-called 'altar-stone' – an upright pillar – on the axis of the horseshoe at the open, north-east end, which approximately faces the rising sun. It has been suggested that it served as an observatory.

Stonehenge The local sandstone, or 'sarsen', was used for the uprights, which measure 5.5 by 2m/18 by 7ft, and each weigh some 26 tonnes. A secondary circle and horseshoe within the sarsens was built of bluestones, originally brought from Pembrokeshire.

stoolball an ancient game, considered the ancestor of cricket, the main differences being that in stoolball bowling is underarm, and the ball is soft.

Stopes /stəʊps/ Marie Carmichael 1880–1958. British birth control campaigner. Founder in 1921 of a controversial London birth control clinic. She wrote plays and verse as well as the best-selling manual *Married Love* 1918.

Stoppard /ˈstɒpɑːd/ Tom 1937– . British (Czechoslovakian-born) playwright who first attracted attention with *Rosencrantz and Guildenstern are Dead* 1967. This was followed by comedies including *The Real Inspector Hound* 1968, a parody on the conventions of the stage thriller, *Jumpers* 1972, *Travesties* 1974, *Dirty Linen* 1976, a satire on politics, and *The Real Thing* 1982.

Storey /ˈstɔːri/ David Malcolm 1933– . British dramatist, son of a Yorkshire miner. His plays include *In Celebration* 1969, and *Early Days* 1980.

stork bird of family of carnivorous wading birds, typical of the mainly tropical order Ciconiiformes, with a long beak, slender body, and long thin neck and legs. It includes the *white stork* (*Ciconia ciconia*), which is encouraged to build on rooftops in Europe as a luck and fertility symbol; and the *jabiru* (*Jabiru mycteria*) of the

Stopes Chiefly remembered for her pioneering advocacy of birth control, Marie Stopes was also the first female science lecturer at Manchester University (specializing in fossils and coalmining).

Americas. Up to 1.5 m/5 ft high, it is white with a black and red head.

Stork An adult stork watches over young in a rooftop nest.

Stornoway /ˈstɔːnəweɪ/ port on the island of Lewis in the Outer ◊Hebrides, population (1981) 8,660. It is the administrative centre for the Western Isles.

Storting name given to the Norwegian parliament, which consists of 150 representatives, elected every four years.

Stoss /ʃtəus/ Veit c. 1440–1533. German wood carver also known as *Wit Stwosz*, because of the many years he lived in Poland. His works include the Krakow altarpiece, a complicated design with numerous figures.

Stourbridge /'stauəbrɪdʒ/ market town in West Midlands, England; population (1981) 54,500. Industries include glass and bricks.

Stowe /stəu/ Harriet Beecher 1811–1896. American suffragist, abolitionist, and author of of the anti-slavery novel *Uncle Tom's Cabin*, first published as a serial 1851–52. Her book was radical in its time and did much to spread anti-slavery sentiment, but in the 20th century the heroically loyal slave 'Uncle Tom' has become a byword for black subservience.

STP (standard temperature and pressure) in physics, a standard for comparing the properties of gases equal to a temperature of 273.15°K/0°C and a pressure of 101,325 pascals (760 mm of mercury). Formerly called normal temperature and pressure, or NTP.

Strabo /'streibəu/ c. 63 BC–24 AD. Greek geographer and historian, who travelled widely to collect first-hand material for his *Geography*.

Strachey /'streitʃi/ (Giles) Lytton 1880–1932. British critic and biographer. Educated at Trinity College, Oxford, he wrote *Landmarks in French Literature* 1912, but won fame and set a vogue by his wittily mocking treatment in *Eminent Victorians* 1918 of Cardinal Manning, Florence Nightingale, Thomas Arnold, and General Gordon.

Stradivari /ˌstrædɪ'vɑːri/ Antonio 1644–1737. Italian violin maker, generally considered the greatest of all violin makers. He was born in Cremona, and studied with Nicolo ◊Amati.

Strafford /'stræfəd/ Thomas Wentworth, 1st Earl of Strafford 1593–1641. English politician, originally an opponent of Charles I, but from 1628 on the Royalist side. He ruled despotically as Lord Deputy of Ireland 1632–39, when he returned to England as Charles's chief adviser and received an earldom. He was impeached in 1640 by Parliament, abandoned by Charles as a scapegoat, and beheaded.

Straits Settlements /'streits 'setlmənts/ former province of the ◊East India Company 1826–58, and British Crown colony 1867–1946: it comprised Singapore, Malacca, Penang, Cocos Islands, Christmas Island, and ◊Labuan.

Strand /strænd/ Paul 1890–1976. American photographer, who used large format cameras for his strong, clear, close-up photographs of natural objects.

Stranraer /ˌstræn'rɑː/ port in Dumfries and Galloway region, Scotland; population (1981) 10,800. There is a ferry service to Larne in Northern Ireland.

Strasberg /'stræzbɜːg/ Lee 1902–1982. American actor and director of ◊Actors Studio from 1948, who developed 'method' acting from ◊Stanislavsky's system.

Strasbourg /'stræzbuəg/ city in Bas-Rhin *département*, capital of ◊Alsace, France; population (1983) 252,300. Industries include car manufacture, tobacco, printing and publishing. There is a 13th-century cathedral. The ◊Council of Europe meets here, and sessions

Strafford Thomas Wentworth, the Earl of Strafford, aimed to make Charles I 'the most absolute prince in Christendom', but after his failure to quell rebellion in Scotland, the king was forced to assent to his execution.

of the European Parliament alternate between Strasbourg and Luxembourg. Seized by France 1681, it was surrendered to Germany 1870–1919 and 1940–44.

strata layers or ◊beds of ◊sedimentary rock. (Singular: stratum).

Strategic Arms Limitation (SALT) talks suggested by US President Johnson in 1967 for the mutual limitation and eventual reduction of strategic nuclear weapons. They were delayed by the Soviet invasion of Czechoslovakia but began in 1969. SALT I operated from 1972 to 1977. SALT II was mainly negotiated by Ford before 1976 and signed by Brezhnev and Carter at Vienna in 1979, but the Soviet invasion of Afganistan prevented ratification.

US–Soviet Summits
1969 SALT talks began in Helsinki
1972 Nixon and Brezhnev sign SALT I accord
1973 Brezhnev meets Nixon in Washington
1974 (Jun) Nixon meets Brezhnev in Moscow
1974 (Nov) Ford meets Brezhnev in Vladivostok
1975 Ford and Brezhnev at 35-nation meeting in Helsinki
1979 Carter and Brezhnev sign SALT II accord in Vienna
1983 Strategic Arms Reduction Talks (START) in Geneva
1986 Reagan and Gorbachev meet in Iceland
1987 ◊Intermediate Nuclear Forces treaty signed in Washington

---

Strategic Defense Initiative (SDI) also called 'Star Wars'. An attempt by the USA to develop a defence system against foreign nuclear missiles based in part outside the earth's atmosphere. Announced by President Reagan in Mar 1983, it was still being evaluated in 1987. The essence of the SDI is to attack enemy missiles at several different stages of their trajectory, so increasing the chances of disabling them, using

advanced laser and particle-beam technology. In 1987 Gorbachev acknowledged that the USSR was developing a similar defence system.

strategic islands islands (Azores, Canary Islands, Cyprus, Iceland, Madeira, and Malta) of great political and military significance likely to affect their stability; they held their first international conference in 1979.

Stratford /'strætfəd/ port and town in Ontario, Canada; population (1981) 26,000.

Stratford-upon-Avon /'strætfəd əpɒn 'eɪvən/ market town in Warwickshire, England; population (1981) 21,000. It is the birthplace of William ◊Shakespeare, whose grave is in the parish church. The Royal Shakespeare Theatre 1932 replaced an earlier building 1877–79 which burned down in 1926. Shakespeare's birthplace contains relics of his life and times. Anne ◊Hathaway's cottage is nearby.

Strathclyde /ˌstræθ'klaɪd/ region of Scotland
area 13,727 sq km/5,300 sq mi
towns administrative headquarters Glasgow; Paisley, Greenock, Kilmarnock, Clydebank, Hamilton, Coatbridge, Prestwick
features include some of Inner ◊Hebrides; river ◊Clyde; part of Loch ◊Lomond; Glencoe; Breadalbane; the islands of Arran, Bute, and Mull
products dairy, pig and poultry products; shipbuilding and engineering; coal
population (1981) 2,400,000, half the population of Scotland
famous people David Livingstone, William Burrell.

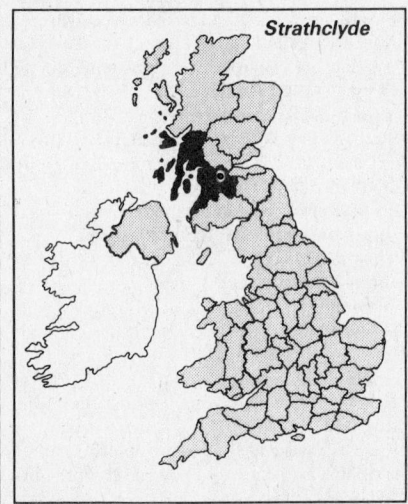

Strathclyde

stratigraphy the branch of ◊geology that deals with the sequence of formation of ◊sedimentary rocks and the conditions under which they were formed. Its basis was developed by William ◊Smith, a British canal engineer. It involves the investigation of sedimentary structures to determine ancient geographies and environments, and the study of fossils for identifying and dating particular beds of rock.

stratosphere that part of the atmosphere beyond 10 km/6 mi from Earth, wherein the temperature is constant. After the minimum

−55°C/−67°F is reached, there is even a slight rise up to 40 km/25 mi in the extremely rarefied air.

Straus /straus/ Oscar 1870–1954. Austrian composer. He is best remembered for the operetta *The Chocolate Soldier* 1909.

Strauss /straus/ Franz-Josef 1915– . West German conservative politician, leader of the Bavarian Christian Social Union (CSU) party from 1961.

Born and educated in Munich, Strauss, after military service 1939–45, joined the CSU and was elected to the *Bundestag* (parliament) in 1949. He held ministerial posts during the 1950s and 1960s and became leader of the CSU in 1961. In the 1970s, Strauss opposed ◊Ostpolitik. He left the *Bundestag* to become premier of Bavaria in 1978, and was heavily defeated in 1980 as chancellor candidate. Strauss has since 1982 sought to force changes in economic and foreign policy of the coalition under Chancellor ◊Kohl.

Strauss /straus/ Johann (Baptist) 1825–1899. Austrian composer. Born in Vienna, he was the son of Johann Strauss, (1804–49), a composer of waltz music. In 1872 he gave up conducting to compose, and wrote operettas, such as *Die Fledermaus* 1874 and numerous waltzes, such as 'The Blue Danube' and 'Tales from the Vienna Woods'.

Strauss /straus/ Richard (Georg) 1864–1949. German composer, born in Munich. A prominent conductor, he was influenced by the German Romantic heritage but had a strongly personal style, particularly in his use of bold, colourful orchestration. He first established his reputation with tone poems such as *Don Juan* 1889, *Till Eulenspiegel's Merry Pranks* 1895, and *Also sprach Zarathustra* 1896. He then moved on to operatic success with *Salome* 1905, and *Elektra* 1909, both of which have elements of polytonality, followed by a reversion to a more traditional style with *Der Rosenkavalier* 1911. He was made president (without being consulted) of the Nazi *Reichsmusikkammer* 1933, but resigned in 1935 when his opera *Die Schweigsame Frau* was boycotted because the libretto was by S ◊Zweig, a Jew.

Stravinsky /strə'vɪnski/ Igor 1882–1971. Russian composer. Born near St Petersburg, he studied under ◊Rimsky-Korsakov and wrote the music for the ◊Diaghilev ballets *The Firebird* 1910, *Petrushka* 1911, and *The Rite of Spring* 1913 (controversial at the time for their unorthodox rhythms and harmony). Having lived in Paris from 1920, he went to the USA in 1939 and in 1945 took US citizenship. His versatility is evident in the varied nature of his works: the Neo-Classicism of his ballet *Pulcinella* 1920, the choral-orchestral *Symphony of Psalms* 1930, and his later use of serial techniques in works such as the *Canticum Sacrum* 1955 and the ballet *Agon* 1953–57. His works also include symphonies, concertos (for violin and piano), chamber music, and operas.

strawberry genus of plants *Fragaria*, family Rosaceae, producing under cultivation red fruit rich in vitamin C and multiplying by runners; the wild strawberry *Fragaria vesca* found in Britain has small delicate fruit.

streaming in UK education, the practice of dividing pupils for all classes according to an estimate of their overall ability, with arrangements for 'promotion' and 'demotion' at the end of each academic year. Rigid streaming is unusual in secondary education in the 1980s and has disappeared from primary education.

streamlining shaping a body so that it offers the least resistance when travelling through an element, usually air or water. Aircraft, for example, must be carefully streamlined to reduce air resistance, or ◊drag. They must have very smooth surfaces and a suitable shape. High-speed aircraft must have swept-back wings, supersonic craft a sharp nose and narrow body.

stream of consciousness narrative technique in which a writer presents directly the uninterrupted flow of a character's thoughts, impressions, and feelings, without the conventional devices of dialogue and description. It first came to be widely used in the early 20th century, and leading exponents have included Virginia ◊Woolf and James ◊Joyce (whose 'Molly Bloom's soliloquy,' in *Ulysses*, is a major example of the genre). The term 'stream of consciousness' was introduced by the philosopher William ◊James in 1890.

Streep /striːp/ Meryl 1949– . American actress noted for her strong character roles. Her films include *The Deer Hunter* 1978, *Kramer vs Kramer* 1979, and *Out of Africa* 1985.

Streeton /'striːtn/ Arthur 1867–1943. Australian artist, who pioneered impressionistic renderings of Australia's landscape.

streptomycin ◊antibiotic discovered in 1944 and used to treat tuberculosis, influenzal meningitis, and other infections, some of which were unaffected by ◊penicillin.

stress in psychology, a wide range of situations or events which can tax the individual's physical or mental ability to cope. Examples of stress include excessive noise, marital conflict, and overwork. Individual reactions to stress are varied, including irritability, fatigue, anxiety or physical health problems, such as stomach ulcers, and high blood pressure.

stress and strain in the science of materials, measures of the deforming force applied to a body and of the resulting change in its shape. For a perfectly elastic material, stress is proportional to strain (◊Hooke's law).

Stretford /'stretfəd/ town in Greater ◊Manchester, England; population (1981) 47,600. Old Trafford, one of England's most famous cricket grounds, is here.

stridulatory organ a sound-producing organ of insects. These organs are most common in the crickets and grasshoppers and consist of two parts, which rub against each other to produce sound. In crickets the wings are rubbed together, but in grasshoppers the hind-leg is rubbed against the wing. Stridulation usually brings the sexes together, but may also be used in territorial behaviour.

strike and lockout a *strike* is a stoppage of work by employees, often as members of a ◊trade union, to obtain or resist change in wages, hours, or conditions. *Lockout* is a weapon of an employer to enforce such change by preventing employees working. Strikes may be 'official' (union-authorized) or 'wildcat' (undertaken spontaneously), and may be accompanied by a *sit-in* or *work-in*, the one being worker occupation of a factory and the other continuation of work in a plant the employer wishes to close. Another measure is *work to rule*, when production is virtually brought to a halt by strict observance of union rules. In a 'sympathetic' strike, action is in support of other workers on strike elsewhere, possibly in a different industry.

In the UK, under the Thatcher government, various measures to curb trade-union power to strike were introduced, for example, the act of 1984 which provided for loss of immunity from legal action if a secret ballot of members is not held before a strike. See also ◊industrial relations.

Strindberg /'strɪndbɜːg/ August 1849–1912. Swedish playwright. Born in Stockholm, he lived mainly abroad after 1883. His plays, influential in the development of dramatic technique, are in a variety of styles including historical plays, symbolic dramas (the two-part *The Dance of Death* 1901) and 'chamber plays' such as *the Ghost (or Spook) Sonata* 1907. His two best known plays, *The Father* 1887 and *Miss Julie* 1888, are both powerful studies of human frailty and hostility between the sexes.

Strindberg Drawing of Swedish dramatist August Strindberg by his friend Carl Larson. A confirmed misogynist, who had three broken marriages, Strindberg showed women emerging as the dominant force in his two most famous plays, *The Father* and *Miss Julie*.

stringed instrument musical instrument which produces a sound by making a stretched string vibrate. Types include:
bowed ◊violin family, ◊viol family;
plucked ◊guitar, ◊ukelele, ◊lute, ◊sitar, ◊harp, ◊banjo, ◊lyre;
plucked mechanically ◊harpsichord

struck mechanically ◊piano, ◊clavichord; ***hammered*** ◊dulcimer. See also ◊percussion, ◊brass, and ◊woodwind instruments.

strobilus a reproductive structure found in most ◊gymnosperms and some pteridophytes, notably the ◊clubmosses. In conifers the strobilus is commonly known as a ◊cone.

stroboscope instrument for studying continuous periodic motion using light flashing at the same frequency as that of the motion; for example, rotating machinery can be 'stopped' by illuminating it with a stroboscope flashing at the exact rate of rotation. Strobe lighting, flashing in time to the beat of music, is used in many discotheques, but continued for any length of time, especially at a critical frequency, it may cause hallucinatory fits (photic epilepsy).

stroke common name for a CVA (Cerebro-Vascular Accident) or ◊cerebral haemorrhage.

Stromboli /'strɒmbəli/ Italian island in the Tyrrhenian Sea, one of the ◊Lipari Islands; area 12.2 sq km/4.7 sq mi. It is famous for its active volcano, 926 m/3,038 ft high.

strontium metallic element, symbol SR, atomic number 38, atomic weight 87.63. Isolated electrolytically by ◊Davy in 1808, it is widely distributed in small quantities in the form of sulphate and carbonate. The silver-white ductile metal, which is used in electronics, resembles calcium. Its salts give a brilliant red colour to a flame and are used for fireworks.

Strophanthus genus of tropical plants of Afro-Asia, family Apocynaceae. Seeds of the handsome climber *Strophanthus gratus* yield a poison, used on arrows in hunting, and in medicine as a heart stimulant.

structuralism a 20th-century philosophical movement which has been influential in such areas as linguistics, anthropology, and literary criticism. Inspired by the work of the Swiss linguist Ferdinand de Saussure (1857–1913), structuralists believe that objects should be analysed as systems of relations, rather than as positive entities.

Saussure proposed that language is a system of arbitrary signs; since no word (signifier) is intrinsically linked with its meaning (signified), any given word can be defined only by its relationship with other words in a language. His ideas were taken further by Roman Jakobson (1896–) and the Prague school of linguistics, and were first elaborated into a general methodology by the anthropologist ◊Levi-Strauss.

The French writer ◊Barthes took the lead in applying structuralism to literary criticism: the 'New Criticism' he pioneered argued that a work of literature can be judged only on its own terms, not by reference to any criteria beyond itself (such as its author's life story). This approach has been taken further in the critical 'deconstruction' method based on the work of the French philosopher Jacques Derrida (1930–), which views a work of literature as having no ultimately definable meaning independent of the interpretation a reader brings to it.

structured programming the process of writing a computer program in such a way as to encourage its division into small, independent parts. This allows a more easily controlled program development and the individual design and testing of the component parts. Structured programs are built up from units called modules which normally correspond to single ◊procedures or ◊functions. Many programming languages are designed to support a structured programming style. ◊Pascal was the forerunner of today's structured programming languages such as Modula 2 and ◊Ada.

strychnine bitter-tasting poisonous alkaloid ($C_{21}H_{22}O_2N_2$), usually obtained from plants of the genus *Strychnos*, for example *Strychnos nux vomica*; curare is a related drug.

Stuart /'stjuːət/ John McDougall 1815–1866. Scottish-born Australian explorer. He went with ◊Sturt on his 1844 expedition, and in 1860, after two unsuccessful attempts, succeeded in crossing from Adelaide to the coast of Arnhem Land.

Stuart, House of /'stjuːət/ or *Stewart* royal family who inherited the Scottish throne in 1371 and the English in 1603.

Stuart Highway first Australian all-weather route north to south across the continent (Darwin-Alice Springs 1943, extended to Adelaide 1985); it was named after the explorer John Stuart, as was Mount Stuart on the route.

Stuart Highway The Stuart Highway was completed during World War II as part of Australia's aids to military defence.

Stubbs /stʌbz/ George 1724–1806. British artist. Born in Liverpool, he was originally a portrait painter, but in 1758 carried out a long series of dissections which resulted in his book of engravings *The Anatomy of the Horse* 1766.

Stud, National British establishment founded 1915, and since 1964 located at Newmarket, where stallions are kept for visiting mares. It is now maintained by the Horserace Betting Levy Board.

sturgeon fish of sub-class Chondrostei, especially the *beluga* (*Huso huso*) of the Caspian, length 8 m/25 ft and weight 1,500 kg/3,300 lb, whose roe forms the best caviare; and *common sturgeon* (*Acipenser sturio*) of the Atlantic and Mediterranean, length 3.5 m/12 ft.

Sturluson /'stuələsɒn/ Snorri 1179–1241. Icelandic author of the Old Norse poems called ◊Eddas, and the *Heimskringla*, a ◊saga chronicle of Norwegian kings until 1177.

Sturm Abteilung (SA) (German 'storm section') terrorist ◊militia, also known as Brown Shirts, of the ◊Nazi Party, in charge of physical training and political indoctrination.

Sturm und Drang (German 'storm and stress') German early Romantic movement in literature and music, from about 1775, concerned with depiction of extravagant passions. Writers associated includer ◊Herder, ◊Goethe, and ◊Schiller. The name is taken from a play by Friedrich von Klinger 1776.

Sturt /stɜːt/ Charles 1795–1869. Australian explorer. Born in India, he served in the army, and in 1827 discovered with ◊Hume the river ◊Darling. In 1828 he sailed down the Murrumbidgee to the estuary of the Murray in circumstances of great hardship, charting the entire river system of the region. Drawn by his concept of a great inland sea, he set out for the interior in 1844, crossing the Sturt Desert, but failing to penetrate the Simpson Desert.

Stuttgart /'ʃtutgɑːt/ capital of Baden-Württemberg, West Germany; population (1980) 580,400. Industries include publishing, vehicles, and electrical goods.

style in flowers, the part of the ◊carpel bearing the ◊stigma at its tip. In some flowers it is very short or completely lacking, while in others it may be long and slender, positioning the stigma in the most effective place to receive the pollen. Usually the style withers after fertilization but in certain species, such as traveller's joy (*Clematis vitalba*), it develops into a long feathery plume which aids dispersal of the fruit.

Style, Old and New see ◊calendar.

Styria /'stɪrɪə/ alpine province of SE Austria; capital Graz. An independent state from 1056 until it passed to the ◊Hapsburgs in the 13th century, it was annexed by Hitler in 1938. See ◊Slovene.

Styx /stɪks/ in Greek mythology, the river surrounding the underworld.

Suárez González /'swɑːreθ gɒn'θɑːleθ/ Adolfo 1933– . Spanish politician. A personal friend of King Juan Carlos, he worked in the National Movement for 18 years, but in 1975 became president of the newly-established Unión del Pueblo Español (UPE). He took office as prime minister in 1976, at the request of the king, to speed the reform programme. He was re-elected in 1977 and 1979.

subatomic particle see ◊particle, subatomic.

subliminal message a message delivered beneath the level of human consciousness. It may be visual (words or images flashed between the frames of a cinema or TV film), or aural (a radio message broadcast 9,000 times an hour at very

Stubbs Three plates from George Stubbs' *The Anatomy of the Horse*, first published 1766.

low volume). The aim may be commercial (to sell a product) or psychological (to wean a patient from alcohol or smoking). Subliminal advertising is illegal in Britain.

submarine an underwater ship, especially a warship. An early venture was an underwater boat constructed for King James I, by the Dutchman Cornelius van Drebbel in 1620. A century and a half later, David Bushness in the USA designed a submarine called *Turtle* for attacking British ships. Robert Fulton designed a submarine called *Nautilus* for Napoleon, for the same purpose in 1800. The first naval submarine, or submersible torpedo boat, the *Gymnote*, was launched by France in 1888. John P Holland, an Irish emigrant to the USA, designed a submarine in about 1875, which was adopted by both the US and British navies at the turn of the century. In both World Wars submarines, from the ocean-going to the midget type, played a vital role. The German U-boats were particularly feared. The conventional submarine of this period was driven by dicsel engine on the surface and by battery-powered electric motors underwater. The diesel engine also drove a generator that produced electricity to charge the batteries.

In 1954 the USA launched the first nuclear-powered submarine, the *Nautilus* (see ◊Arctic). The modern nuclear submarine *Ohio*, USA, in service from 1981, is 170 m/560 ft long, displacement about 18,700 tonnes, and carries 24 Trident missiles, each with a dozen independently targetable nuclear warheads with a range that is being extended to 11,000 km/6.750 mi. Operating depth is usually up to 300 m/1,000 ft, and nuclear power speeds of 30 knots (55 kph/34 mph) are reached. As in all nuclear submarines, propulsion is by steam ◊turbine driving a propellor. The steam is raised using the heat given off by the nuclear ◊reactor. In ◊oceanography, salvage, and pipe-laying, smaller submarines called submersibles are used. The Royal Navy's surface diving ship *Challenger* (1980) not only supports divers operating at 300 m/1,000 ft, but acts as mother ship for deep-diving submersibles which are hauled up a stern ramp. It also has a 'moon' pool, or cylindrical vertical internal shaft, down which a three-person ◊diving bell can be lowered. Depths of 6,000 m/20,000 ft are reached.

submersible a small submarine used by engineers and research scientists and as a ferry craft to support diving operations. The most advanced submersibles are the so-called lock-out type, which have two compartments – one for the pilot, the other to carry divers. The diving compartment is pressurized and provides access to the sea. They are used to ferry 'saturation' divers between compression chambers on a support ship and their place of work on the sea bed. The divers remain under compression for days at a time, avoiding the long decompression periods needed after every deep dive they make.

Subotica /'subətɪtsə/ largest town in Vojvodina, Serbia; population (1981) 154,600. It has chemical, electrical machinery, and other industries.

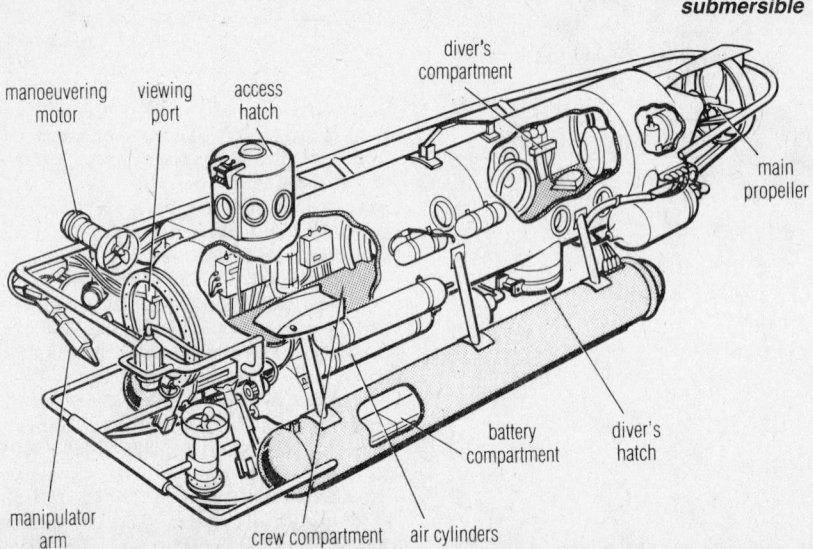

submersible

manoeuvering motor

viewing port

access hatch

diver's compartment

main propeller

manipulator arm

crew compartment

air cylinders

battery compartment

diver's hatch

subpoena in law, a writ (Latin 'under penalty'), requiring someone (who, it is presumed, would not come forward of his or her own volition) to give evidence before a court or judicial official at a specific time and place.

subway American term for underground railway; see ◊underground.

succession in ◊ecology, the change that occurs in the structure and composition of the vegetation in a given area from the time it is first colonized, or after it has been disturbed (for example, by fire, flood, or clearance). If allowed to proceed undisturbed, succession leads naturally to a ◊climax community (for example, oak forest or *savannah* grassland) that is determined by the climate and soil characteristics of the area.

succubus a female spirit; see ◊incubus.

succulent plant a thick, fleshy plant that stores water in its tissues, for example cacti and stonecrops (*Sedum*). Succulents either live in areas where water is very scarce, or in places where it is not easily obtainable due to the high concentrations of salts in the soil, as in salt marshes. See also ◊xerophyte.

Suceava /ˌsuːtʃiˈɑːvə/ town in N Romania; population (1980) 74,500. Industries include textiles and lumber.

sucker fish another name for ◊remora.

Suckling /ˈsʌklɪŋ/ John 1609–1642. English poet. Born in Whitton, he was an ardent Royalist who tried to effect ◊Strafford's escape from the Tower of London. On his failure, he fled to France and may have committed suicide. His chief lyrics appeared in *Fragmenta Aurea*.

Sucre /ˈsuːkreɪ/ capital of Bolivia; population (1982) 80,000. (◊La Paz is the seat of government.) It stands on the central plateau at an altitude of 2,840 m/9,330 ft. Founded 1538, its cathedral dates from 1553, and the university of San Francisco Xavier 1624 is probably the oldest in S America. The first revolt against Spanish rule in S America began here 25 May 1809.

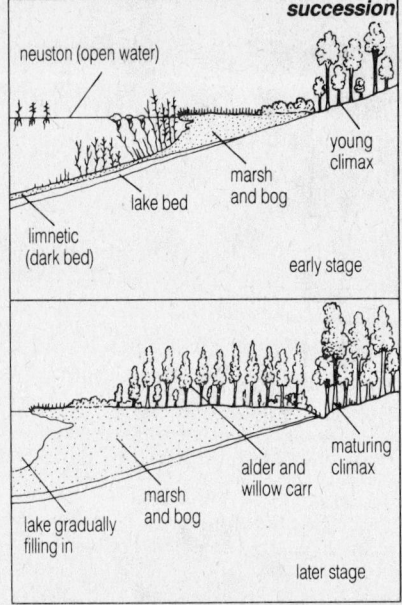

succession

neuston (open water)

young climax

marsh and bog

lake bed

limnetic (dark bed)

early stage

maturing climax

alder and willow carr

marsh and bog

lake gradually filling in

later stage

Sucre /ˈsuːkreɪ/ Antonio José de 1795–1830. Bolivian revolutionary leader. As the chief lieutenant of Simon ◊Bolivar, he took a leading part in freeing the colonies of South America from Spanish rule, winning several notable battles, and in 1826 became the first president of the new republic of Bolivia. After a mutiny by the army and ivasion by Peru, he resigned in 1828 and left the country to join Bolivar. While crossing the Andes he was killed by thieves.

Sudan /suːˈdɑːn/ country in NE Africa, S of Egypt, with a Red Sea coast; it is the largest country in Africa.

government after a military coup in Apr 1985 a transitional constitution was introduced, providing for a 264-member legislative assembly, a supreme council under a president, and a council of ministers led by a prime minister. The assembly is charged with the task of producing a new constitution and, after a further transitional period, of declaring itself a parliament, subject to election every four years.

history the region was once known as ◊Nubia and settled by Egypt. The people were converted to Coptic Christianity in the 6th century and to Islam in the 15th century when Arabs invaded. Sudan was again ruled by Egypt from 1820. A revolt began 1881, led by a sheik who took the title of ◊Mahdi and captured ◊Khartoum 1885. It was subdued by an Anglo-Egyptian army under ◊Kitchener 1896–98 and administered as an Anglo-Egyptian condominium from 1899.

The Sudan, as it was then called, achieved independence as a republic in 1956. Two years later a coup ousted the civil administration and a military government was set up, which in 1964 was itself overthrown and civilian rule was reinstated, but five years later the army returned in a coup led by Col Gaafar Mohammed Nimeri. All political bodies were abolished, the Revolutionary Command Council (RCC) set up and the country's name changed to the Democratic Republic of the Sudan. Close links were soon established with Egypt and in 1970 an agreement in principle was reached for eventual union. In 1972 this should have become, with the addition of Syria, the Federation of Arab Republics, but internal opposition blocked both developments. In 1971 a new constitution was adopted, Nimeri confirmed as president and the Sudanese Socialist Union (SSU) declared to be the only party.

The most serious problem confronting Nimeri was open aggression between the Muslim N and the chiefly Christian S, which had started as long ago as 1955. At a conference in Addis Ababa 1972 he granted the three southern provinces a considerable degree of autonomy, but fighting continued. Nimeri had come to power in a left-wing revolution but soon turned to the West, and particularly the USA, for support. By 1974 he had established a national assembly, but his position still relied on army backing. In 1983 he was re-elected for a third term but his regional problems persisted. By sending more troops S against the Sudan People's Liberation Army he alienated the N and then caused considerable resentment in the S by replacing the penal code with strict Islamic law. His economic policies contributed to the widespread unrest.

In Mar 1985 a general strike was provoked by a sharp devaluation of the Sudanese pound and an increase in bread prices. Nimeri was in the USA when army mutiny threatened. One of his supporters, Gen Swar al-Dahab, took over in a bloodless coup. He set up a transitional military council, and held elections for a legislative assembly in Apr 1986, contested by more than 40 parties, the three most significant being the New National Umma Party (NNUP), which won 99 seats, the Democratic Unionist Party (DUP), 63 seats, and the National Islamic Front, 51 seats. A coalition government was formed, with Ahmed Ali El-Mirghani (DUP) as president of the Supreme Council and Oxford-educated Sadiq Al-Mahdi (NNUP) as prime minister. Strikes and shortages persisted, with inflation running at about 100% and the highest national debt in Africa, and in Jul 1987 a state of emergency was declared. In Oct 1987 the prime minister announced the break-up of the government of national unity and the formation of a new coalition.

Sudan

DEMOCRATIC REPUBLIC OF (*Jamhuryat es-Sudan*)

AREA 2,500,000 sq km/967,500 sq mi
CAPITAL Khartoum
TOWNS Omdurman, Juba; chief port Port Sudan
PHYSICAL fertile valley of the river Nile separates Libyan Desert in W from high rocky Nubian Desert in E
FEATURES Sudd swamp; largest country in Africa
HEAD OF STATE Ahmed Ali El-Mirghani from 1986
HEAD OF GOVERNMENT Sadiq Al-Mahdi from 1986
GOVERNMENT transitional
EXPORTS cotton, gum arabic, sesame, groundnuts, durra
CURRENCY Sudanese pound (4.12 = £1 Sept 1987)
POPULATION (1985) 22,972,000 (Arab-speaking and Muslim, 70%, in the N, and speakers of African languages in the S); annual growth rate 2.9%
LANGUAGE Arabic (official), English
RELIGION Sunni Muslim in the N, animist in the S, with a Christian minority
LITERACY 38% male/14% female (1980 est)
GNP $27.3 bn (1983); $361 per head of population
CHRONOLOGY
1955 Civil war betwen the Muslim N and non-Muslim S broke out.
1956 The Sudan achieved independence as a republic.
1958 Military coup replaced the civilian government with a Supreme Council of the Armed Forces.
1964 Civilian rule reinstated.
1969 Coup led by Col Gaafar Mohammed Nimeri established a Revolutionary Command Council (RCC) and the country's

Suez Canal /'suːz/ artificial waterway from Port Said to Suez, linking the Mediterranean and Red seas, separating Africa from Asia, and providing the shortest sea route from Europe to the East, to Australasia, and to Africa's E coast. The French Suez Canal Company was formed

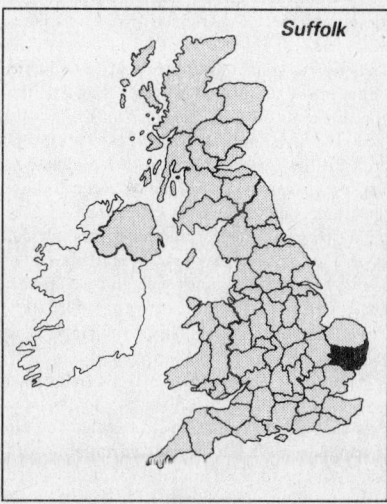

name was changed to the Democratic Republic of the Sudan.
1970 Agreement in principle on union with Egypt.
1971 New constitution adopted, Nimeri confirmed as president, and the Sudanese Socialist Union (SSU) declared to be the only legal party.
1972 Proposed Federation of Arab Republics, comprising Sudan, Egypt, and Syria, abandoned. Addis Ababa conference proposed autonomy for southern provinces.
1974 National assembly established.
1983 Nimeri re-elected amid growing opposition to his social, economic, and religious policies.
1985 Nimeri deposed in a bloodless coup led by Gen Swar al-Dahab, who set up a transitional military council.
1986 More than 40 political parties fought the general election and a coalition government was formed.

reassert international control of the canal, the British, French, and Israelis devised a plan whereby Israel would launch an attack towards the canal, after which the British and French would send in a force to keep the peace. Anglo-French landings were duly made, but were met with widespread international censure (the Soviet Union protested, the USA offered no support, and there was considerable opposition to the action within Britain itself), and the troops were soon withdrawn. The failure of the plan led ultimately to the resignation of the British prime minister ◊Eden.

Suffolk /'sʌfək/ county of eastern England.
area 3,797 sq km/1,466 sq mi
towns administrative headquarters Ipswich; Bury St Edmunds, Lowestoft, Sudbury, Aldeburgh
features low undulating surface and flat coastline; rivers Waveney, Alde, Deben, Orwell, Stour; part of the Broads; Minsmere marshland bird reserve, near Aldeburgh; site of ◊Sutton Hoo (7th-century ship-burial); site of 'Sizewell B', planned as the first of Britain's controversial pressurized-water reactor (PWR) plants.
products cereals, sugar beet; working horses (Suffolk punches); fertilizers, agricultural machinery
population (1986) 642,200
famous people Constable, Gainsborough, Elizabeth Garrett Anderson, Benjamin Britten.

Suffolk

Sudbury /'sʌdbəri/ town in Ontario, Canada; population (1981) 92,000. The chief industry is the mining of nickel (90% of world production), which comes from a buried ◊meteorite.

Sudetenland /suː'deɪtnlænd/ mountainous region of Czechoslovakia; see under ◊Munich Agreement.

Suetonius /ˌsuːɪ'təʊnɪəs/ (Gaius Suetonius Tranquillius) c. 69–140 AD. Roman historian, author of detailed *Lives of the Caesars*.

Suez /'suːz/ port at the Red Sea terminus of the ◊Suez Canal; population (1976) 194,000. Industries include oil refining and the manufacture of fertilizers. It was reconstructed after the ◊Arab-Israeli Wars.

1858 to execute the scheme of Ferdinand de Lesseps. The canal was opened 1869, and in 1875 British prime minister ◊Disraeli acquired a major shareholding for Britain from the khedive of Egypt. The 1888 Convention of Constantinople opened it to all nations. The Suez Canal was admininstered by a company with offices in Paris controlled by a council of 33 (ten of them British) until 1956 when it was forcibly nationalized by President ◊Nasser of Egypt. It was blocked by Egypt during the Arab-Israeli war 1967 and not re-opened until 1975.

Suez Crisis incident in Oct-Dec 1956 following the nationalization of the Suez Canal by President ◊Nasser of Egypt. In an attempt to

suffragan (Latin *suffragor* 'vote for, support') an assistant bishop, appointed to work in a part of the diocese.

suffragette a woman fighting for the right to vote, especially in Britain before 1914; in the USA, the preferred term was *suffragist*. Women's suffrage bills were repeatedly introduced and defeated in Parliament between 1886 and 1911. A militant campaign was launched in 1906 by Emmeline ◊Pankhurst and her daughters. Suffragettes (the term was coined by a *Daily Mail* reporter) chained themselves to railings, heckled political meetings, refused to pay taxes, and in 1913 bombed the home of Lloyd George, then chancellor of the Exchequer. One woman, Emily Davison, threw herself under the king's horse at the Derby in 1913 and was killed. Many suffragettes were imprisoned and were force-fed when they went on hunger strike; under the notorious 'Cat and Mouse Act' (1913) they could be repeatedly released to regain their health and then rearrested. The struggle was called off on the outbreak of World War I in 1914.

Public opinion changed during the war in the UK and in 1918 women were granted limited franchise; in 1928 it was extended to all women over 21. In the USA the 19th amendment to the constitution (1920) gave women the vote in state and national elections.

Sufism a mystical movement of ◊Islam. Sufis believe that deep intuition is the only real guide to knowledge.

sugar sweet, soluble carbohydrate, either a monosaccharide or disaccharide. Monosaccharides are the simplest of sugars; examples include fructose and glucose, both obtained from fruit and honey. Disaccharides are sugars which when hydrolysed by dilute acids give two of either the same or different simple sugars, that is, monosaccharides, an example is sucrose from sugar-cane. Polysaccharides for example, starch and cellulose, hydrolyse to many simple sugars. Commercially, sugar sucrose is produced from *sugar cane*, one of the ◊grasses, by crushing the stem. *Molasses* is the uncrystallized syrup drained from the sugar (fermented, it forms rum) and is then refined by stages to 'pure' whiteness.

Treacle and *golden syrup* are successive liquid stages in the refining of molasses. Bagasse, the fibrous residue, is used for paper-making, cattle feed, and fuel, and new types of cane are being bred for low sugar, and high fuel production. Sugar is also produced from *sugar* ◊*beet* of which remaining pulp is used as cattle feed. Highly refined forms of sugar include cube, granulated, caster, and icing. In all forms, sugar is a major source of energy; athletes suck glucose tablets, but it can also contribute to caries or tooth decay.

sugar maple North American maple tree *Acer saccharum.*

Suharto /suːˈhɑːtəʊ/ 1921–. Indonesian general. He ousted ◊Sukarno to become president in 1967, and was re-elected for the fourth time in 1983. He ended confrontation with Malaysia, invaded E Timor in 1975, and reached a cooperation agreement with Papua New Guinea 1979.

Suhl /suːl/ district in East Germany; capital Suhl; population (1982) 549,000.

suicide self-murder. Until 1960 it was a criminal offence in English law, if committed while of sound mind, and was in earlier times punished by the confiscation of the suicide's possessions. Even until 1823 burial was at night, without burial service, and with a stake through the heart; hence the frequency with which coroners' juries still find that the act was committed while the person was insane or give an open verdict. To aid and abet another's suicide is an offence, and euthanasia or mercy killing may amount to aiding in this context. In Japan ◊hara-kiri is considered honourable.

Suharto General Suharto, president of Indonesia. An army general, he assumed emergency execution powers after ousting Sukarno in 1967 and ended the confrontation with Malaysia.

suite in music, formerly a grouping of old dance forms. The term has more recently been used to describe a set of instrumental pieces, sometimes assembled from a stage work, such as Tchaikovsky's *Nutcracker Suite.*

Sukarno /suːˈkɑːnəʊ/ Achmed 1901–1970. Indonesian nationalist, who cooperated during World War II in the local administration set up by the Japanese, replacing Dutch rule. In 1945 he became president of the new Indonesian Republic, assuming the presidency for life 1966; he was ousted by ◊Suharto 1967.

Sukkur /suˈkuə/ port on the Indus, Pakistan; population (1981) 191,000. The Sukkur-Lloyd Barrage 1923–32 lies to the W.

Sulawesi /ˌsuːləˈweɪsɪ/ (formerly Celebes), island in E Indonesia, one of the ◊Sunda Islands. Area (with dependent islands) 190,000 sq km/73,000 sq mi; population (1980) 10,400,500.

Suleiman /ˌsuːlɪˈmɑːn/ or *Solyman* 1494–1566. Ottoman sultan, known as 'the Magnificent'. It was under his rule from 1520 that the Ottoman Empire reached its zenith. He captured Belgrade in 1521, Rhodes in 1523, defeated the Hungarians at Mohacs in 1526, and was only halted in his advance into Europe by his failure to take Vienna after a siege Sept–Oct 1529. In 1534 he turned more successfully against Persia, and then in campaigns against the Arab world took almost all North Africa and even Aden. Only the Knights of Malta inflicted severe defeat on both his army and fleet when he tried to take Valetta in 1565.

Sulla /ˈsʌlə/ Lucius Cornelius 138–78 BC. Roman soldier-politician, a leader of the senatorial party. Forcibly suppressing the democrats in 88 BC, he departed for a successful campaign against ◊Mithradates of Pontus. The democrats seized power in his absence, but on his return Sulla captured Rome and massacred all

opponents. As dictator, his reforms, which strengthened the senate, were backward-looking and shortlived. He retired in 79 BC.

Sullivan /ˈsʌlɪvən/ Arthur (Seymour) 1842–1900. British composer. Born in London, he studied at Leipzig. He composed oratorios, but became famous for the light operas written in collaboration with Sir William ◊Gilbert. These included *HMS Pinafore* 1878, *The Pirates of Penzance* 1879, *Patience* (which ridiculed the ◊Aesthetic movement) 1881, *The Mikado* 1885, *The Yeomen of the Guard* 1888, and *The Gondoliers* 1889. He also wrote various serious works for example, the opera *Ivanhoe* 1890, which he valued more highly than the operettas.

Sullivan /ˈsʌlɪvən/ Jim 1903–1977. Welsh Rugby League player. Born in Cardiff, he played Rugby Union for his home town team. He joined Wigan RLFC 1921. He established himself as the sport's greatest goal-kicker, achieving 2,859 goals in his 25-year career.

Sullivan /ˈsʌlɪvən/ Louis Henry 1856–1924. American architect, influenced by Harry Richardson. He worked in Chicago and designed early skyscrapers such as the Wainwright Building, St Louis 1890 and the Guaranty Building, Buffalo 1894.

Sully /sjuːˈliː/ Maximilien de Béthune, Duc de Sully 1560–1641. French politician, who served with the Huguenots in the Wars of ◊Religion, and, as Henry IV's superintendent of finances 1598–1611, aided French recovery.

sulphonamide drug any of a group of compounds containing the chemical group sulphonamide SO_2NH_2, or its derivatives, which were and still are in places used to treat bacterial diseases, for example wound infection, pneumonia.

sulphur non-metallic element: symbol S atomic number 16, atomic weight 32.066. Known from ancient times, it is a pale yellow, odourless, brittle solid; insoluble in water, but soluble in carbon disulphide, it is a good electrical insulator. Widely distributed as the element in volcanic regions, and as sulphides of many metals. There are two crystalline forms and an allotropic plastic form. It is essential to life, resembles oxygen chemically and can replace this element to form innumerable organic and inorganic compounds. It is widely used in the manufacture of sulphuric acid and in chemicals, explosives, matches, fireworks, dyes, fungicides, drugs, and in vulcanizing rubber.

sulphuric acid oil of vitriol, a dense, oily, colourless liquid (H_2SO_4) which gives out much heat when added to water. It is used extensively in the chemical industry, petrol refining, and in manufacturing fertilizers, detergents, explosives and dyes.

Sulu Archipelago /ˈsuːluː ˌɑːkɪˈpeləgəʊ/ group of about 870 islands off SW Mindanao in the Philippines, between the Celebes and Sulu seas; area 2,815 sq km/1,087 sq mi; population (1970) 425,600. The capital is Jolo, on the island (the largest) of the same name. Until 1940 the islands were an autonomous sultanate.

Sumatra /suˈmɑːtrə/ second largest island of Indonesia, one of the Sunda Islands; chief towns Palembang, Padang and Benkuelen; area

427,350 sq km/165,000 sq mi; population (1980) 28,000,000. E of a longitudinal volcanic mountain range is a wide plain; both are heavily forested. Products include rubber, rice, tobacco, tea, timber, tin, and petroleum. Northern Sumatra is rapidly being industrialized, and the Asakan river (rising in Lake Toba) has been dammed for power 1974.

history a Hindu empire was found in the 8th century, but Islam was introduced by Arab traders from the 13th century, and by the 16th century was adopted throughout the island.

Sumer /'suːmə/ area of S ◊Iraq where the ◊Sumerian civilization was established from about 5000 BC. The Sumerians may have been related to the ◊Dravidians.

Sumerian civilization the world's earliest civilization, situated in lower ◊Mesopotamia (modern Iraq), which arose about 3400 BC; it is known to have had a city state, with priests as secular rulers, and a common culture. Cities include ◊Lagash, ◊Eridu, and most famous of all, ◊Ur.

summer time practice (introduced in the UK 1916) whereby legal time from spring to autumn is an hour in advance of Greenwich mean time. Continental Europe 'puts the clock back' a month earlier than the UK in autumn. British summer time was permanently in force Feb 1940–Oct 1945 and Feb 1968–Oct 1971. Double summer time (2 hours in advance), was in force 1941–45 and 1947.

summons in law, a citation (order) officially delivered, requiring someone (who is one of the people involved in an action) to appear in court on a certain date, to answer a claim made by the plaintiff.

sumptuary law (Latin *sumptum* 'acquired, spent') a law restraining excessive individual consumption, such as expenditure on dress, or attempting to control religious or moral conduct. The Romans had several sumptuary laws; the *lex Orchia* for example in 181 BC limited the number of dishes at a feast. In England sumptuary laws were introduced by Edward III and Henry VII.

Sun the ◊star at the centre of the ◊solar system, around which Earth and other planets orbit. Its diameter is 1,392,000 km/865,000 mi, and it lies 149 million km/93 million mi from Earth. The Sun is composed of about 70 per cent hydrogen and 30 per cent helium, with other elements making up less than 1 per cent. The temperature at its centre is probably 15 million°C. Like all stars, the Sun generates energy by nuclear ◊fusion reactions that turn hydrogen into helium at its centre. The Sun is about 4,700 million years old, nearly halfway through its total predicted lifetime of 10,000 million years.

The Sun spins on its axis every 25 days near its equator, but more slowly towards the poles. Its rotation can be followed by watching the passage of dark ◊sunspots across its disc. Sometimes bright eruptions called ◊flares occur near sunspots. Above the Sun's photosphere lies a layer of thinner gas called the ◊chromosphere, visible only in special instruments or at ◊eclipses. Tongues of gas called ◊prominences extend from the chromosphere into the ◊corona, a halo of hot,

tenuous gas surrounding the Sun. Gas boiling from the corona streams outwards through the solar system, forming the ◊solar wind. Activity on the Sun, including sunspots, flares, and prominences, waxes and wanes during the *solar cycle* which peaks every 11 years or so.

Sunbelt popular name given to a region of the USA, S of Washington DC, between the Pacific and Atlantic coasts, because of its climate.

Sunda Islands /'sʌndə/ islands W of the Moluccas, in the Malay Archipelago, so called because they lie largely on the Indonesian extension of the Sunda continental shelf. They are divided into:

Greater Sundas, including: *Borneo* the third largest island in the world, comprising *Sabah* and *Sarawak* (Malaysia); *Brunei*; and, occupying by far the larger part, *Kalimantan* (Indonesia); *Java* chief island of Indonesia (including the small island of *Madura*); *Sumatra*; *Sulawesi* (Indonesia); *Billiton* between Borneo and Sumatra.

Lesser Sundas (Indonesian *Nusa Tenggara*), all Indonesian, including: *Bali*; *Lombok*; *Timor*.

sundance a North American Indian ceremony; see ◊Plains Indians.

Sunday seventh day of the week (see ◊Monday), which in the Christian religion is set aside for divine worship in commemoration of Christ's resurrection (replacing the Jewish ◊sabbath). In the UK activities such as shopping and the drinking of alcohol have been restricted since medieval times on this day; in 1969 curbs on sports, theatres, and dancing were lifted. A bill to enable Sunday trading was defeated in Apr 1986.

Sunderland /'sʌndələnd/ port in Tyne and Wear, England; population (1981) 196,150. Industries were formerly only coalmining and shipbuilding, but have now diversified to electronics, glass, and furniture.

Sunderland /'sʌndələnd/ Robert Spencer, 2nd Earl of Sunderland 1640–1702. English politician, a sceptical intriguer who converted to Roman Catholicism to secure his place under James II, and then reverted with the political tide. In 1688 he fled to Holland (disguised as a woman), where he made himself invaluable to the future William III. Now a Whig, he advised the new king to adopt the system, which still prevails, of choosing the government from the dominant party in the Commons.

sundew insectivorous plant, genus *Drosera*, with viscid hairs on the leaves to catch prey.

sundial instrument measuring time by means of a shadow cast by the Sun. Almost completely outdated by the invention of clocks, it survives ornamentally in gardens. The dial is marked with the hours at graduated distances, and a style or gnomon (parallel to Earth's axis and pointing to the N) casts the shadow.

Sundsvall /'sʊndsvæl/ port in E Sweden; population (1981) 95,000. It has timber and wood-pulp industries.

sunfish marine fish *Mola mola* with disc-shaped body 3 m/10 ft long found in the oceans. Also used of fish of the North American freshwater Centrarchidae family which have

compressed, almost circular bodies. The latter are nestbuilders and avid predators.

sunflower plant, genus *Helianthus* in the family Compositae. The *common sunflower Helianthus annuus* probably native of Mexico, grows to 4.5 m/15 ft in favourable conditions, and is commercially cultivated in central Europe and the USSR for the oil-bearing seeds which follow the yellow-petalled flowers.

Sungari /'sʊŋgəri/ river in NE China (◊Manchuria), which joins the Amur on the Siberian frontier; length 1,300 km/800 mi.

Sunni a member of the larger of the two main sects of ◊Islam. The name derives from the *Sunna*, a book of rules.

Sunningdale Agreement an agreement reached by the UK and Irish governments, together with the Northern Ireland executive, in Dec 1973, at the Civil Service College in Sunningdale, England. The agreement included provisions for a power-sharing executive in Northern Ireland. However, the executive lasted only five weeks before the UK government was defeated in a general election, and a subsequent general strike in May 1974 brought down the Northern Ireland government.

sunspot a dark patch on the surface of the ◊Sun, actually an area of cooler gas. Sunspots consist of a dark central *umbra* with a temperature about 4,000°C, and a lighter surrounding *penumbra* at about 5,500°C. Individual sunspots last from several days to a month or more, ranging in size from 2,000 km to groups stretching for over 100,000 km. The number of sunspots visible at a given time varies from none to over 100 in a cycle averaging 11 years. They are thought to be caused by strong ◊magnetic fields that block the outward flow of heat to the Sun's surface.

sunstroke an alternative name for ◊heat stroke.

Sun Yat-sen The founder of the Nationalist Guomindang party and guiding force behind the Chinese Revolution in 1911.

Sun Yat-sen /'sʌn ˌjæt'sen/ or *Sun Zhong Shan* 1867–1925. Chinese politician. The son of a Christian farmer, he founded the ◊Guomindang in 1894. After many years in exile he returned to China during the 1911 revolution which overthrew the Manchu dynasty and was

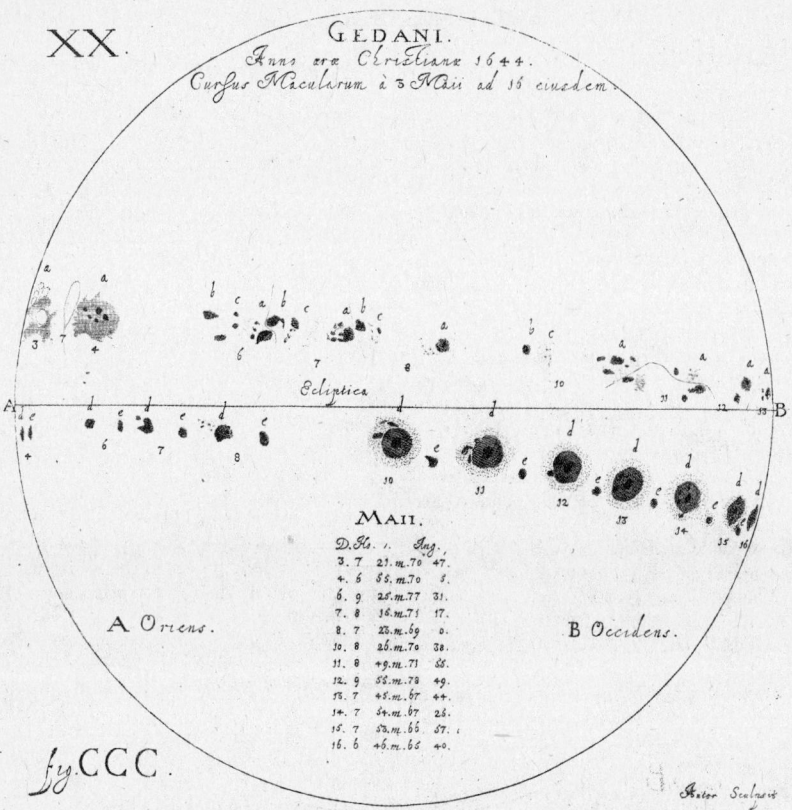

sunspot A line drawing by Hevelius of sunspots observed as long ago as May 1644. Usually occurring in groups, sunspots may influence the Earth's climate.

provisional president of the republic in 1912. When the reactionaries obtained control he established an independent republican government at Canton in 1921, in which he was proclaimed president. He was criticized for lack of organizational ability, but his 'three people's principles' of nationalism, democracy, and social reform are accepted by both the Guomindang and the Chinese Communists. His widow *Soong Ching-ling* (1890–), educated in the USA, remained influential in Chinese politics, being vice-chairman of the Republic from 1959, but came under attack in 1967 in the Cultural Revolution. After the death of Chu Teh, she served as acting head of state.

Sun Zhong Shan /ˈsʌnˌdʒɒŋˈʃɑːn/ Pinyin transliteration of Sun Yat-sen.

supercomputer the fastest, most powerful type of computer, capable of performing its basic operations in picoseconds (thousand-billionths of a second), rather than nanoseconds (billionths of a second) which is typical of most other computers. Supercomputers use several processors working together and other techniques (such as cooling processors down to nearly absolute zero temperature so that their components conduct electricity many times faster than normal) to achieve this enormous increase in speed.

superconductivity in physics, increase in electrical conductivity at low temperatures. The phenomenon, discovered by Kamerlingh Onnes in 1911, is exhibited by some metals and metallic compounds whose resistance decreases uniformly with decreasing temperature until at a critical temperature (the superconducting point), within a few degrees of absolute zero (0°K/–273°C), the resistance suddenly falls to zero. In this superconducting state an electric current induced by a magnetic field (see electromagnetic induction) in a closed circuit or ring of the material will continue after the magnetic field has been removed, provided that the material remains below the superconducting point. Superconductivity has been produced in a synthetic organic conductor which would operate at much higher temperatures, thus cutting costs. See ◊cryogenics.

supercooling in physics, the lowering in temperature of a ◊saturated solution without crystallization taking place, forming a supersaturated solution. Usually crystallization rapidly follows the introduction of a small (seed) crystal or agitation of the supercooled solution.

superego in Freudian psychology, the element of the human mind concerned with the ideal, responsible for ethics and self-imposed standards of behaviour. It is popularly characterized as a form of conscience, restraining the ◊ego, and responsible for feelings of guilt when the moral code is broken.

Superior, Lake /suːˈpɪərɪə/ largest of the ◊Great Lakes of North America.

supermarket a large self-service ◊shop selling food and household goods. The first was introduced by US retailer Clarence Saunders in Memphis, Tennessee, in 1919. *Hypermarkets* are supermarkets with an area greater than 2,500 sq m/25,000 sq ft.

supernova the explosive death of a ◊star. In a supernova outburst, the star temporarily attains a brightness of 100 million Suns or more, so that it can shine as brilliantly as a small ◊galaxy for a few days or weeks. The last supernova seen in our galaxy was in 1604, but they are seen in other galaxies. In 1987 a supernova visible to the unaided eye occurred in the Large ◊Magellanic Cloud, a neighbour galaxy to our ◊Milky Way. *Type I* supernovae are thought to occur in ◊double-star systems in which gas from one star falls on to a white dwarf, causing it to explode. *Type II* supernovae are caused by the explosion of a star ten times or more the Sun's mass. At the end of its life, such a massive star suffers runaway internal nuclear reactions, which lead to the explosion. Type II supernovae are thought to leave behind ◊neutron stars and ◊black holes. Gas ejected by the explosion causes an expanding radio source, such as the ◊Crab Nebula. Supernovae are thought to be the main source of elements heavier than hydrogen and helium in the Universe.

superpower term used to describe the USA and the USSR from the end of World War II.

supersonic speed speed greater than that at which sound travels: at sea level about 1,220 kph/760 mph, but decreasing with altitude until at 12,000 m/40,000 ft it is only 1,060 kph, remaining constant above that height. Squadron Leader John Derry (UK) was the first to achieve supersonic flight, in a De Havilland 108 research aircraft, 6 Sept 1948. See ◊Mach number. When an aircraft passes the ◊sound barrier, shock waves are built up which give rise to ◊sonic boom, often heard at ground level.

Supplementary Benefit (formerly called National Assistance 1948–66) in Britain, weekly payment made by the government to individuals whose income is considered to be lower than a legally-determined minimum and who do not qualify for contributory benefits such as Unemployment Benefit or earnings-related pensions. It is to be replaced by Income Support in 1988. Until 1983 it included housing subsidies.

supply and demand one of the fundamental approaches to ◊economics, which examines the supply of a good and compares it with the demand for that good (usually in the form of supply and demand curves, a graph of supply and demand plotted against price). For a typical good, the supply curve is upward sloping (the higher the price, the more the manufacturer is willing to sell), while the demand curve is downward-sloping (the cheaper the good, the more demand there is for it). The point where the curves intersect is the equilibrium at which supply equals demand.

support environment in computing, a collection of programs (◊software) used to help people to design and write other programs. At its simplest, this includes an editor (word-processing software) and a ◊compiler for translating programs into executable form; but can also include interactive debuggers for locating faults, data dictionaries for keeping track of the data used, and rapid prototyping tools for producing quick, experimental mock-ups of programs.

suprarenal gland another name for the ◊adrenal gland.

Supremacy, Acts of two Acts of the English Parliament in 1534 and in 1559, which established Henry VIII and Elizabeth I respectively as head of the English Church in place of the pope.

Suprematism Russian art movement developed by ◊Malevich from ideas of the ◊Futurism and ◊Cubist movements, which exploited only purely geometrical shapes (rectangles, triangles, circles). The aims of the movement were expressed by Malevich as 'the supremacy of pure feeling or perception in the pictorial arts – the expression of non-objectivity'. From the first of Malevich's works in 1913, each one became simpler until there was only a white square on a black background and finally a white square on a white background.

Supreme Court highest US judicial tribunal, composed of a chief justice and eight associate justices. Vacancies are filled by the president, and members can be removed only by impeachment. See ◊Law Courts.

Supremes, The US vocal group, pioneers of the ◊Motown sound, formed 1959 in Detroit, from 1962 a trio with Diana Ross, Mary Wilson, and Florence Ballard. The most successful female group of the 1960s, they combined pop with soul in a string of hits beginning with 'Where Did Our Love Go' 1964 and 'Baby Love' 1964.

Sur /suə/ Arabic name for the Lebanese port of ◊Tyre.

Surabaya /ˌsuərə'baɪə/ port on the island of ◊Java, Indonesia; population (1980) 2,028,000. It has oil refineries and shipyards, and is an important naval and military base.

Suraj-ud-Dowlah /su'rɑːdʒ ud 'daulə/ 1728–1757. Nawab of Bengal, see ◊Calcutta and ◊Plassey. He was killed at his capital, Murshidabad.

Surat /su'rɑːt/ city in Gujarat, India; population (1981) 775,700. The chief industry is textiles. The first East India Company 'factory' (trading post) in India was established here 1612.

surd term for the mathematical root of a quantity that can never be exactly written because it is an ◊irrational number, for example, √3(1.73205..).

Sûreté the criminal investigation department of the French police.

surface tension in physics, the property that causes the surface of a liquid to behave rather as if it were covered with a weak elastic skin – this is why one can, with care, float a needle on water. It is caused by cohesive forces between water ◊molecules; allied phenomena include the formation of droplets and the ◊capillary action by which water soaks into a sponge. See ◊cohesion.

surfing sport of riding on the crest of large waves while standing on a narrow, keeled

Suriname
REPUBLIC OF

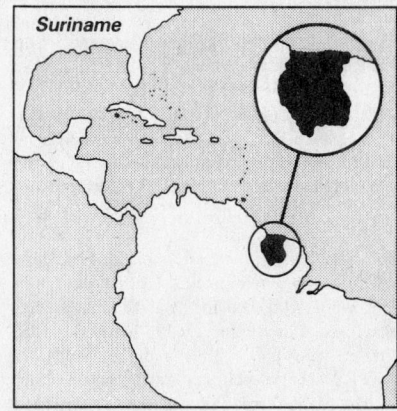
Suriname

AREA 163,265 sq km/63,250 sq mi
CAPITAL Paramaribo
PHYSICAL hilly and forested, with flat coast
FEATURES river Surinam
HEAD OF STATE Ramsewak Shankar from 1988 (president), Desi Bouterse from 1982 (military ruler)
HEAD OF GOVERNMENT Wym Udenhout from 1984
GOVERNMENT military transitional
EXPORTS bauxite; rice, citrus; timber
CURRENCY Surinam guilder (2.94 = £1 Sept 1987)
POPULATION (1985) 395,000 (Creole, Chinese, Hindu, and Indonesian peoples); annual growth rate 0%
LANGUAGE Dutch, English (both official)
RELIGION Christian 35%, Hindu 25%, Muslim 17%
LITERACY 65% (1984)
GNP $1.2 bn (1983); $2,600 per head of population
CHRONOLOGY
1954 Granted internal self-government as Dutch Guiana.
1975 Achieved full independence with Dr Johan Ferrier as president and Henck Arron as prime minister. About 40% of the population, especially those of East Indian origin, emigrated to the Netherlands.
1980 Arron's government overthrown in an army coup but President Ferrier refused to recognize the military regime and appointed Dr Henk Chin A Sen to lead a civilian administration. Army replaced Ferrier with Dr Chin A Sen.
1982 Army, led by Lt-Col Desi Bouterse, seized power, setting up a Revolutionary People's Front.
1985 Ban on political activities lifted.
1987 New constitution approved.
1988 Ramsewak Shankar elected president.

surfboard, usually of light synthetic material, about 1.8 m/5 ft long. See also ◊windsurfing.

surgeon fish fish of the tropical marine family Acanthuridae, which has a sharp moveable spine on each side of the tail which can be used as a weapon.

surgery in medicine, originally the removal of diseased parts or foreign substances from the body. The surgeon now uses not only the scalpel and electric cautery, but beamed high-energy ultrasonic waves, binocular magnifiers for microsurgery, and the intense light energy of the laser. There are many specialized fields, including cardiac (heart), orthopaedic (bones and joints), ophthalmic (eye), neuro (brain and nerves), thoracic (chest), and renal (kidney) surgery. Modern extensions of the field of surgery include:
microsurgery for which the surgeon uses a binocular microscope, magnifying 25 times, for example in rejoining a severed limb. Sewing of the nerves and blood vessels is done with a nylon thread so fine that it is only just visible to the naked eye. Restoration of movement and sensation may be comparatively limited;
plastic surgery repair of damaged tissue (for example skin grafts for burns) and restructuring of damaged or deformed parts of the body; also
cosmetic surgery for serious aesthetic reasons, when the patient is psychologically damaged by injury or deformity, and for reasons of vanity;
transplant surgery the transfer of an embryo, genetic material, an organ, tissue, and so on, from one part of the body to another, or to another body. Under the UK transplant code of 1979 covering the use of material from a donor, two doctors (being both independent of the tranplant team and clinically independent of each other) must certify the brain death of the donor.

Suriname /ˌsuərɪ'næm/ country in the N of S America, on the Atlantic coast, between Guyana and French Guiana.
government the constitution was suspended in 1980 and in 1982 an interim president took office as head of state, with ultimate power held by the army through its commander-in-chief who is also chairman of the Supreme Council, the country's controlling group. A nominated 31-member national assembly was established in January 1985, consisting of 14 military, 11 trade union, and six business nominees. It was given 27 months in which to prepare a new constitution.
history for early history, see ◊American Indian, ◊South America. Founded as a colony by the English 1650, Suriname became Dutch in 1667. In 1954, as Dutch Guiana, it was made an equal member of the Kingdom of the Netherlands, with internal self-government. Full independence was achieved in 1975, with Dr Johan Ferrier as president and Henck Arron, leader of the mainly Creole Suriname National Party (NPS), as prime minister. In 1980 Arron's government was overthrown in an army coup but President Ferrier refused to recognize the military regime and appointed Dr Henk Chin A Sen, of the Nationalist Republican Party, to head a civilian administration. Five months later the army staged another coup and President Ferrier was replaced by Dr Chin A Sen. The new president announced details of a draft constitution which

would reduce the army's role in government, whereupon the army, led by Lt-Col Desi Bouterse, dismissed Dr Chin A Sen and set up the Revolutionary People's Front.

There followed months of confusion in which a state of siege and then martial law were imposed. In the period Feb 1980–Jan 1983 there were no fewer than six attempted coups by different army groups. Because of the chaos, Netherlands and US aid was stopped and Bouterse turned to Libya and Cuba for assistance. The partnership between the army, the trade unions, and business, which had operated since 1981, broke up in 1985 and Bouterse turned to the traditional parties that had operated before the 1980 coup: the NPS, the left-wing Indian VHP and the Indonesian KTPI. The ban on political activity was lifted and leaders of the three main parties were invited to take seats on the Supreme Council, with Wym Udenhout as prime minister. In Sept 1987 a new constitution was approved prior to an election in Nov.

Surrealism movement in literature, painting, commercial art, photography, film, and stage design, which was developed from ◊Dadaism by André ◊Breton. Influenced by the Freudian theory of the unconscious, it sought to embody in art and poetry the irrational forces of dreams and the subconscious mind. Those linked with it include artists ◊Arp, ◊Chirico, ◊Dali, ◊Ernst, ◊Magritte, ◊Miro, ◊Picasso; poets ◊Aragon, ◊Eluard; film-maker ◊Buñuel.

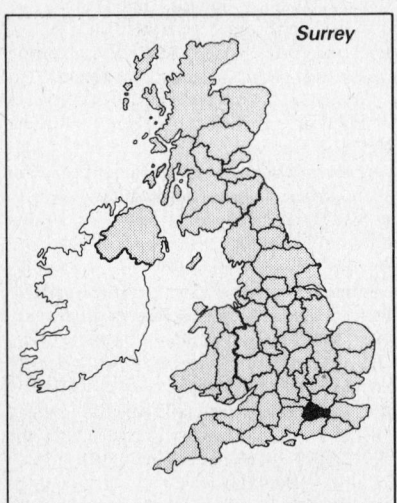

Surrey

Surrey /ˈsʌri/ county in S England
area 1,679 sq km/648 sq mi
towns administrative headquarters Kingston-upon-Thames; Guildford, Woking
features rivers Thames, Mole, and Wey; Box and Leith Hills; North Downs; Runnymede, Thameside site of the signing of ◊Magna Carta; Kew Palace and Royal Botanic Gardens.
products market garden vegetables, and general agricultural products
population (1986) 1,013,700

famous people John Galsworthy.

Surrey /ˈsʌri/ Henry Howard, Earl of Surrey c. 1517–1547. English soldier-poet, executed on a poorly-based charge of high treason. With ◊Wyatt, he introduced the sonnet to England, and was a pioneer of blank verse.

surrogacy popular term for the practice whereby a woman becomes pregnant with the intention of the resultant child being handed over to a couple (of whom the man may be the natural father, usually by artificial insemination), usually in return for payment. Such commercial surrogacy is practised in some European countries and in the USA, but is illegal (from 1985) in the UK. See also ◊embryo research.

Surtees /ˈsɜːtiːz/ R(obert) S(mith) 1803–1864. British novelist. He created Jorrocks, a sporting grocer, and in 1838 published *Jorrocks's Jaunts and Jollities*.

surveying the accurate measurements of the Earth's crust, or of land features or buildings. It is used to establish boundaries, and to evaluate the topography for engineering work. The measurements used are both linear and angular, and geometry and trigonometry are applied in the calculations.

Surya /ˈsuəriə/ in Hindu mythology, the sun-god, son of the sky-god Indra. His daughter, also named Surya, is a personification of the Sun.

Susa /ˈsuːzə/ (French *Sousse*) port and commercial centre in NE Tunisia ; population (1984) 83,500. It was founded by the Phoenicians, and has Roman remains.

suslik type of ground ◊squirrel.

suspension in physics, a colloidal state consisting of a solid dispersed in a liquid (a sol) or gas (an aerosol such as a smoke). See ◊colloid.

Susquehanna /ˌsʌskwɪˈhænə/ river rising in central New York state, USA, and flowing 715 km/444 mi to Chesapeake Bay. It is used for hydroelectric power. On the strength of its musical name, Samuel ◊Coleridge planned to establish a Pantisocratic (communal) settlement here with ◊Southey.

Sussex /ˈsʌsɪks/ former county of England, on the S coast, now divided into ◊East Sussex and ◊West Sussex. According to tradition, a Saxon chief, Ella, landed here 477, and founded the kingdom of the South Saxons which was absorbed by Wessex in 825.

sustained yield cropping in ◊ecology, the removal of surplus individuals from a ◊population of organisms such that the population maintains a constant size. This usually requires selective removal of animals of all ages and both sexes to ensure a balanced population structure. Excessive cropping of young females, for example, may lead to fewer births in following years, and a fall in population size. The appropriate cropping frequencies can be determined from an analysis of a ◊life table.

Sutcliff /ˈsʌtklɪf/ Rosemary 1920– . British historical novelist, who writes both for adults and children. Her books include *The Eagle of the Ninth* 1954, *Tristan and Iseult* 1971, and *The Road to Camlann* 1981.

Sutherland /ˈsʌðələnd/ Earl Wilbur 1915–1974. American physiologist, discoverer

Sussex The 'Long Man', a hill figure of human form, at Wilmington, East Sussex. Its original date is unknown, and one suggestion is that it represents Pol, god of the underworld, who stands at its gate. This is derived from a neighbouring place-name, Polegate.

of a chemical 'messenger' made by a special enzyme in the wall of cells. Many hormones operate by means of this messenger. He was awarded a Nobel prize in 1971.

Sutherland /ˈsʌðələnd/ Graham Vivian 1903–1980. British artist, whose early work was influenced by ◊Blake and the ◊Surrealists. His portraits, for example, Maugham, Beaverbrook, Helena Rubinstein, were popular, but his study of Churchill in 1954 was disliked by its subject and eventually burnt on the instructions of Lady Churchill. He was awarded the Order of Merit in 1960.

Sutherland /ˈsʌðələnd/ Joan 1926– . Australian soprano. She went to England in 1951, where she made her debut the next year in *The Magic Flute*; later roles include *Lucia di Lammermoor*, Donna Anna in *Don Giovanni*, and Desdemona in *Otello*. She was made a Dame of the British Empire in 1979.

Sutherlandshire /ˈsʌðələndʃə/ former county of Scotland, with deep sea lochs and mountains in the W, Ben More Assynt rising to 999 m/3,278 ft. In 1975 it was merged with Highland Region. Dornoch was the administrative headquarters.

Sutlej /ˈsʌtlɪdʒ/ river in Pakistan, a tributary of the river ◊Indus.

suttee Hindu custom whereby a widow committed suicide on her husband's funeral pyre, often under public and family pressure. It became illegal under British rule 1829. In modern India it has sporadically been illegally revived.

Sutton /ˈsʌtn/ borough of S Greater London.
features site of Nonsuch Palace built by Henry VIII, demolished in 17th century
population (1981) 168,000.

Sutton Coldfield /ˈsʌtn ˈkəʊldfiːld/ a residential part of the W Midlands conurbation around ◊Birmingham.

Sutton Hoo /ˈsʌtn ˈhuː/ village near Woodbridge, Suffolk, England, where in 1939 a Saxon ship burial was excavated. It is the funeral monument of Raedwald, king of the East Angles, who died c. 624/625. The jewellery, armour and weapons discovered were placed in the British Museum, London.

Sutton-in-Ashfield /'sʌtn ɪn 'æʃfiːld/ town in Nottinghamshire, England; population (1981) 41,250. Industries include coal and plastics.

Suva /'suːvə/ capital and industrial port of Fiji, on Viti Levu; population (1981) 68,255. It produces soap and coconut oil.

Suvorov /suːˈvɔːrɒv/ Aleksandr Vasilyevich 1729–1800. Russian field marshal, victorious against the Turks 1787–91, the Poles 1794, and the ◊Directory's French army in Italy 1798–99. See ◊Revolutionary Wars.

Suzhou /ˌsuːˈdʒəʊ/ city (formerly Soochow, and also known as Wuhsien 1912–49) in Jiangsu province, China; population (1983) 670,000. It stands on the ◊Grand Canal. It has embroidery and jade-carving traditions, and exquisite gardens, including Shizilin and Zhuozheng. The city dates from about 1000 BC.

Suzuki /suˈzuːki/ Zenko 1911– . Japanese politician. Originally a socialist member of the Diet in 1947, he became a conservative (Liberal Democrat) in 1949, and was prime minister 1980–82.

Svalbard /'svɑːlbɑː/ Norwegian archipelago in the Arctic Ocean; area 62,000 sq km/24,000 sq mi; population (1982) 4,000, including 1,450 Norwegians and 2,500 Russians. Under the *Svalbard Treaty* 1925, Norway has sovereignty, but allows free scientific and economic access to others. The chief settlement is Long Year City on the main island, *Spitzbergen*; other islands include *North East Land*, *Edge Island*, *Barents Island*, and *Prince Charles Foreland*. Coal is mined by Russia and Norway, and there are weather and research stations. Wildlife includes walrus and polar bear.

Sverdlovsk /svɪədˈlɒvsk/ industrial town in western USSR; population (1981) 1,240,000. Industries include the mining of copper, iron and platinum; engineering, and chemicals. Known as *Ekaterinburg* until 1924, it was here that ◊Nicholas II and his family were murdered 1918.

Svevo /'sveɪvəʊ/ Italo, pen name of Italian novelist Ettore Schmitz 1861–1928. His books include *As a Man Grows Older* 1898 and *Confessions of Zeno* 1923.

Swabia /'sweɪbɪə/ (German *Schwaben*) historic region of SW Germany, an independent duchy in the Middle Ages. It includes Augsburg and Ulm, and forms part of the modern *Länder* (states) of Baden-Württemberg, Bavaria, and Hessen.

Swahili language a language of Bantu origin and strongly influenced by Arabic, a widespread ◊lingua franca of E Africa and the national language of Tanzania (1967) and Kenya (1973).

swallow insect-eating bird of the family Hirundinidae, including the *common swallow Hirundo rustica* which winters in Africa and visits Europe April–Sept. Steel-blue above and creamy white beneath, it has a red-brown throat and deeply forked tail. It feeds in flight. Two broods a year are reared in nests of mud and straw shaped like a half-saucer and built on ledges.

swamp a low-lying, permanently water-logged tract of land, often associated with tree growth.

swamp cypress species of tree of the genus ◊*Taxodium*.

swan large long-necked bird of the duck family. The *mute swan Cygnus olor* is up to 150 cm/5 ft long, has white plumage, an orange bill with a black knob surmounting it, and black legs; the voice is a harsh hiss. Pairing is generally for life and the young (cygnets) are at first grey, later brownish. On the Thames, at the annual swan-upping, the cygnets are still marked on the beak as either the property of the Crown or of the two privileged City companies, the Dyers and Vintners. Other species include the *whooper Cygnus cygnus* of N Europe and Asia, and *Bewick's swan Cygnus bewicki*, both rare in Britain; the *black swan* of Australia, *Cygnus atratus*; and North American *trumpeter swan Cygnus buccinator*.

swan A flotilla of black swans at Williamstown on Port Phillip Bay, Victoria, Australia.

Swan /swɒn/ Joseph Wilson 1828–1914. British inventor of the incandescent filament electric lamp, and of bromide paper for use in photography.

Swanage /'swɒnɪdʒ/ town on the Isle of Purbeck, ◊Dorset, England.

Swansea /'swɒnzi/ port and administrative headquarters of W Glamorgan, S Wales; population (1981) 167,800. It has oil refineries and metallurgical industries.

Swapo *South West African People's Organization* organization formed in South West Africa (now commonly known as ◊Namibia) to oppose South African rule. Swapo guerrillas began attacking with support from Angola. Swapo is recognized by the United Nations as the legitimate goverment of Namibia.

swastika cross in which the bars are extended at right angles, all in the same clockwise or anti-clockwise direction. An Aryan and Buddhist mystic symbol, it was adopted by Hitler, first as the emblem of the Nazi Party, and then incorporated in the German national flag 1935–45.

Swatow /ˌswɑːˈtaʊ/ another name for the Chinese port of ◊Shantou.

Swazi kingdom African kingdom, established by Sobhuza (died about 1840) as a result of the ◊Mfecane disturbances, and named after his successor Mswati (ruled 1840–75).

Swaziland /'swɑːzilænd/ country in SE Africa, bounded by Mozambique and the Transvaal province of South Africa.

government Swaziland is a monarchy within the Commonwealth. Under the 1978 constitution the monarch is head of both state and of government, and chooses the prime minister and cabinet. There is a two-chamber legislature, the *Libandla*, consisting of a 20-member senate and a 50-member house of assembly. Ten senators are appointed by the sovereign and ten elected by and from an 80-member electoral college, made up of two representatives from each of the country's 40 chieftancies (*Tinkhundla*). 40 of the House of Assembly deputies are also elected by the electoral college, with the remaining ten appointed by the monarch.

The constitution makes the Imbokodvo National Movement (INM) the only legal political party, although there are at least three opposition groups based outside Swaziland.

history for early history, see ◊African history, ◊South Africa. Its original autonomy guaranteed by Britain and the Transvaal, Swaziland became a special High Commission territory in 1903. The South African government repeatedly asked for Swaziland to be placed under its jurisdiction but this call was resisted by the British government as well as the people of Swaziland. In 1967 the country was granted internal self-government and 1968 full independence within the Commonwealth, with King Sobhuza II as head of state. In 1973 the king suspended the constitution and assumed absolute powers. In 1978 the new constitution was announced.

King Sobhuza died in 1982 and the role of head of state passed to the queen mother, Dzeliwe, until the king's heir, Prince Makhosetive, should reach the age of 21 in 1989, but a power struggle developed within the royal family. Queen Dzeliwe was ousted by another of King Sobhuza's wives, Ntombi, who became queen regent in Oct 1983, and in Apr 1986 the crown prince was formally invested as King Mswati III. He has a supreme advisory body, the *Liqoqo*, all of whose 11 members are appointed by him. By Jun 1987 a power struggle had developed between the *Liqoqo* and Queen Ntombi over the accession of her son, Mswati III.

Swaziland needs to maintain good relations with South Africa as well as with other African states, and this has often been difficult, since the banned African National Congress (ANC) has tried to use it as a base.

sweat gland a ◊gland within the skin of mammals which produces sweat, or ◊perspiration, on the skin surface. In primates these glands are distributed over the whole body, but in most other mammals they are more localized. Those of cats and dogs are normally restricted to the feet and around the face.

swede see under ◊turnip.

Sweden /'swiːdn/ country in N Europe on the Baltic Sea, bounded to the W by Norway and to the NE by Finland.

Swaziland
KINGDOM OF

AREA 17,400 sq km/6,704 sq mi
CAPITAL Mbabane
PHYSICAL central valley; mountains in W
FEATURES landlocked enclave between South
Africa and Mozambique
HEAD OF STATE AND OF GOVERNMENT King
Mswati III from 1986
GOVERNMENT constitutional one-party
monarchy
EXPORTS sugar, citrus; timber, asbestos, iron
ore
CURRENCY lilangeni (3.38 = £1 Sept 1987)
POPULATION 636,000 (1985); annual growth
rate 4.3%
LANGUAGE Swazi 90%, English (both official)
RELIGION Christian, both Protestant and
Catholic; animist
LITERACY 64% male/58% female (1980 est)
GNP $610 million (1983); $790 per head of
population
CHRONOLOGY
1967 Granted internal self-government.
1968 Achieved full independence from
Britain, within the Commonwealth, as the
Kingdom of Swaziland, with King Sobhuza II
as head of state.
1973 The king suspended the constitution and
assumed absolute powers.
1978 New constitution adopted.
1982 King Sobhuza died and his place was
taken by one of his wives, Dzeliewe, until his

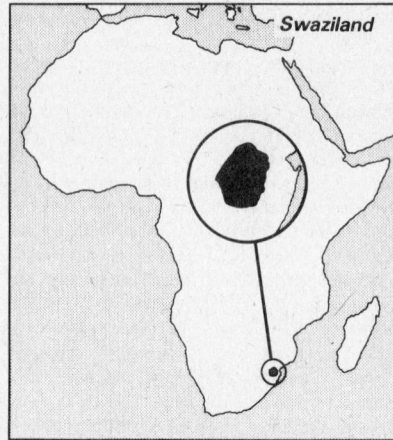

son, Prince Makhosetive, reached the age of
21.
1983 Queen Dzeliewe ousted by another wife,
Ntombi.
1984 After a royal power struggle, it was
announced that the crown prince would
become king at the age of 18.
1986 Crown prince formally invested as King
Mswati III.
1987 A power struggle developed between the
advisory council Liqoqo and Queen Ntombi
over the accession of the king.

government Sweden has a hereditary monarch
as formal head of state and a popularly elected
government. The constitution from 1809, several
times amended, is based on four fundamental
laws: the Instrument of Government Act, the Act
of Succession, the Freedom of the Press Act, and
the Riksdag Act. The *Riksdag* is a single-
chamber parliament of 349 members, elected by
universal suffrage, through a system of
proportional representation, for a three-year
term.

The prime minister is nominated by the Speaker
of the *Riksdag* and confirmed by a vote of the
whole house. The prime minister chooses a
cabinet and all are then responsible to the
Riksdag. The king or queen now has a purely
formal role; the normal duties of a constitutional
monarch, such as dissolving parliament and
deciding who should be asked to form an
administration, are undertaken by the Speaker.
history S Sweden has been inhabited since about
6000 BC. The Swedish Vikings in 800–1060 AD
sailed mainly E and founded the principality of
◊Novgorod. In the mid-12th century the Swedes
in the N were united with the Goths in the S and
accepted Christianity. A series of crusades in the
12th–14th centuries brought Finland under
Swedish rule. Sweden, Norway, and Denmark
were united under a Danish dynasty 1397–1520.
◊Gustavus Vasa was subsequently elected king
of Sweden; he established Lutheranism as the
state religion 1527. The Vasa line ruled until

1818, when the French marshal Bernadotte
established the present dynasty.
Sweden's territorial ambitions led to warfare in
Europe in the 16th–18th centuries (see
◊Gustavus Adolphus, ◊Thirty Years' War,
◊Charles X, ◊Charles XII) which left the country
impoverished. Science and culture flourished
under Gustavus III 1771–91. Sweden lost
Finland to Russia 1809 but seized Norway 1814,
a union dissolved 1905.
Sweden has a long tradition of neutrality and
political stability, and a highly developed social
welfare system. The office of ombudsman is a
Swedish invention and Sweden was one of the
first countries to adopt a system of open
government.
The Social Democratic Labour Party was
continuously in power 1951–76, usually in
coalition. In 1969 the leadership of the party
changed hands and Olof Palme became prime
minister. He carried out two major reforms of
the constitution, reducing the chambers in
parliament from two to one 1971, and 1975
removing the last of the monarch's constitutional
powers. In 1976 the general election was fought
on the issue of the level of taxation needed to
fund the welfare system and Palme was defeated.
Thorbjorn Fälldin, leader of the Centre Party,
formed a centre-right coalition government. The
Fälldin administration fell 1978 over its wish to
follow a non-nuclear energy policy and it was
replaced by a minority Liberal government led

by Ola Ullsten. Fälldin returned 1979, heading
another coalition, and in a referendum the
following year there was a narrow majority in
favour of continuing with a limited nuclear-
energy programme. Fälldin remained in power
until 1982, when the Social Democrats, with Olof
Palme, returned with a minority government.
Palme was soon faced with deteriorating
relations with the USSR, arising from suspected
violation of Swedish territorial waters. The
situation had improved substantially by 1985.
After the general election in that year, Palme's
party had 159 *Riksdag* seats and he was able to
continue with Communist support. The
Moderate Party won In Feb 1986 Olof Palme
was murdered by an unknown assailant in the
centre of Stockholm. His deputy, Ingvar
Carlsson, took over as prime minister and leader
of the Social Democratic Labour Party.

Swedenborg /ˈswiːdnbɔːg/ Emanuel
1688–1772. Swedish scientist and philosopher.
From 1747 he concentrated on scriptural study,
and in his *Divine Love and Wisdom* concluded
that the Last Judgment had taken place in 1757,
and that the **New Church**, of which he was the
prophet, had now been inaugurated. His writings
are the scriptures of the sect popularly known as
Swedenborgians.

Swedish art the rise of Sweden in the 17th
century ushered in a great cultural era. Around
Stockholm are the royal residences of Ulriksdal
1660, Karlsborg 1696–1718, and
Drottningsholm. Renaissance churches of
Stockholm include Maria Magdalen 1650, St
Catherina 1725, and the church of Adolphus
Frederick 1751–71. Towards the end of the 18th
century French influence is apparent. From 1830
to 1880 Swedish architecture reflected various
tendencies in fashion in Germany and Denmark,
but from 1890 the teachings of William ◊Morris
were influential on Swedish arts and crafts, and
in the 20th century Sweden became a world
leader in industrial art, and produced a notable
sculptor in Carl Milles 1875–1955.

Swedish language a member of the Germanic
branch of the Indo-European language family,
spoken in Sweden and Finland and closely
related to Danish and Norwegian. Words in
English of Swedish origin include *ombudsman*,
smorgasbord, and *tungsten*.

Swedish literature by the 14th century there
were a number of rhymed chronicles, ballads and
folk songs, but modern literature begins in the
17th century with the epic poet Georg
Stjernhjelm (1598–1672). In the 18th century
the names of Linnaeus, Celsius, and Swedenborg
typify the country's intellectual ferment, and the
poet-historian Olof von Dalin was an outstanding
literary figure. The period 1771–1809, covering
the reigns of Gustavus III (himself a playwright)
and Gustavus IV, saw much literary activity, for
example, the song lyrics of Carl Michael Bellman
(1740–95), and the dramas of Gudmund Jöran
Adlerbeth (1751–1818) and Henrik Kellgren
(1751–95), who assisted the king in the royal
theatre. Outstanding names of the Romantic era
are those of poet-playwright Per Daniel
Amadeus Atterbom (1790–1855), the poets
Esaias Tegnér and Eric G Geier (1783–1847)

Sweden

KINGDOM OF (*Konungariket Sverige*)

AREA 449,700 sq km/173,629 sq mi
CAPITAL Stockholm
TOWNS Göteborg, Malmö, Uppsala, Norrköping, Västerås
PHYSICAL mountains in the NW; plains in the S; much of the land is forested
FEATURES many lakes, for example Väner, Vätter, Mälar, Hjälmar; islands of Öland and Gotland; large herds of wild elk
HEAD OF STATE Carl XVI Gustav from 1973 (figurehead)
HEAD OF GOVERNMENT Ingvar Carlsson from 1986
GOVERNMENT parliamentary democracy
EXPORTS aircraft, cars, domestic equipment, ballbearings, drills, missiles, electronics; petro-chemicals; textiles; furnishings, ornamental glass
CURRENCY krona (10.5 = £1 Sept 1987)
POPULATION (1985) 8,348,000 (including 1,200,000 postwar immigrants from Finland, Turkey, Yugoslavia, Greece); annual growth rate 0.1%
LANGUAGE Swedish, one of the Scandinavian division of Germanic languages
RELIGION Christian (Evangelical Lutheran)
LITERACY 99% (1984)
GNP $88 bn (1983); $14,821 per head of population
CHRONOLOGY
12th century United as an independent nation.
1397–1520 Under Danish rule.
1914–45 Neutral in both world wars.
1951–76 Social Democratic Labour Party in power.

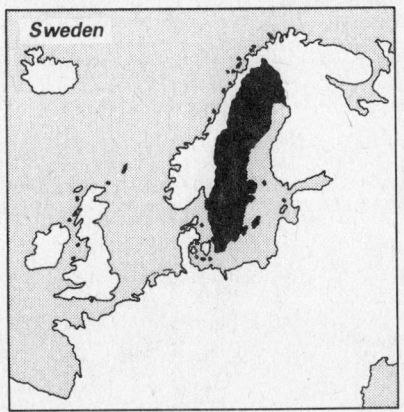

Sweden

1969 Olof Palme became Social Democratic Labour Party leader and prime minister.
1971 Constitution amended, creating a single-chamber parliament.
1975 Monarch's constitutional powers reduced.
1976 Thorbjörn Fälldin, leader of the Centre Party, became prime minister, heading centre-right coalition.
1982 Social Democrats, led by Palme, returned to power.
1985 Social Democrats won the largest number of seats in parliament and formed a minority government, with communist support.
1986 Olof Palme murdered in Stockholm. Ingvar Carlsson became prime minister and leader of the Social Democratic Labour Party.

and obtained the deanery of St Patrick in 1713. His *Journal to Stella* is a series of letters, 1710–13, in which he described his life in London. His works include *The Tale of a Tub* 1704, attacking corruption in religion and learning; brilliant contributions to the Tory paper *The Examiner*, which he edited 1710–11; the scarifying *Modest Proposal for Preventing the Children of Poor People from being a Burden to their Parents or the Country* 1729 (the satiric solution being to fatten and eat them), and the masterpiece of disguised satire, *Gulliver's Travels* 1726, a fantasy book of travel to lands inhabited by giants, miniature people, and intelligent horses. From about 1738 his mind began to fail, and he died insane.

Swift Nearly all Jonathan Swift's works were published anonymously, and with the exception of *Gulliver's Travels*, he received no payment for his work.

who sought inspiration in the legendary heroic past, and Afzelius, editor of national folk songs. To the period of romantic transition belong the novelist and poet Viktor Rydberg, the classic poet Carl Snoilsky (1841–1903), and the Finnish epic poet Johan Ludwig Runeberg (1804–77), but realism emerged in the novels of Carl Almqvist and Frederika Bremer (1801–65), and broke through in the work of ◊Strindberg. A new romantic idealism followed, for example, the poets Gustaf Fröding (1860–1911), Erik Axel Karlfeldt and Verner von Heidenstam (1859–1940), and the novelist Selma ◊Lagerlöf – the last three all Nobel prizewinners. Among more recent writers, also Nobel prizewinners, are Harry Martinson (1904–78), author of *The Road*, and *Aniara*; and Pär ◊Lagerkvist, lyricist, novelist (*Barabbas*), and playwright.

Sweet /swiːt/ Henry 1845–1912. British philologist, author of works on Old and Middle English, who took to England German scientific techniques of language study.

sweet cicely S European plant *Myrrhis odorata*, family Umbelliferae; the root is eaten as a vegetable.

sweet pea see ◊pea.

sweet potato tropical American plant *Ipomoea batatas*, family Convolvulaceae; the

white/orange tuberous root is used as a source of starch and alcohol, and eaten as a vegetable.

sweet william perennial S European plant, the *bearded pink Dianthus barbatus*, family Caryophyllaceae, introduced to England about 1575, and grown for its fragrant flowers.

Sweyn I /sweɪn/ died 1014. King of Denmark from c. 986, nicknamed 'Forkbeard'. He raided England, finally conquering it in 1013.

swift fast-flying, short-legged bird of the family Apodidae, found largely in the tropics. The *swift Apus apus*, about 16.5 cm/6.5 in long, dark brown with long swept-back wings, migrates to Europe in summer from Africa. It catches insects on the wing, and rarely perches except at the nest, even sleeping on the wing high in the air. Swifts often make colonies of nests on buildings, sticking the nest material together with saliva. The nests of the *grey-rumped swiftlet Collocalia francica* of Borneo are almost entirely solidified saliva, and are harvested for birds' nest soup.

Swift /swɪft/ Jonathan 1667–1745. Irish satirist and Anglican cleric, best known as the author of *Gulliver's Travels*. Born in Dublin, he was ordained in the English Church 1694, and in 1699 was made a prebendary of St Patrick's, Dublin. In 1710 he became a Tory pamphleteer,

swim bladder a thin-walled air-filled sac found in teleost fishes, between the gut and the spine. Air enters the bladder from the gut or from surrounding blood ◊capillaries, and changes of air pressure within the bladder maintain neutral bouyancy whatever the water depth, removing the necessity to swim to maintain that depth.

swimming self-propulsion of the body through water. The competition strokes are: breaststroke (developed from the 16th century); the front crawl (developed by the Australians from a South Sea Island method in the early 20th century, and still the fastest stroke); the backstroke (developed in the 1920s, which enables the swimmer to breathe very freely); and the butterfly (developed from the breaststroke in the USA in the 1930s, and the second fastest of the strokes). In competition the swimmers enter the water with a 'racing plunge' (except in the backstroke when they start in the water), or dive. Diving events are divided into springboard and the higher firm-board events. Underwater swimming, developed with the invention of frogman equipment (foot flippers, breathing apparatus, and individual motor propulsion), has techniques of its own.

Swinburne /'swɪnbɜːn/ Algernon Charles 1837–1909. British poet. Born in London, he was educated at Eton and Balliol College, Oxford, and attracted attention with the choruses of his Greek-style tragedy *Atalanta in Calydon* 1865, and the eroticism of poems such as 'Laus Veneris'/'In Praise of Love', 'Dolores', and 'A Litany' in *Poems and Ballads* 1866. However, he and ◊Rossetti were attacked in 1871 as leaders of 'the fleshly school of poetry', and the revolutionary politics of *Songs before Sunrise* 1871 alienated others.

Swindon /'swɪndən/ town in Wiltshire, 124 km/77 mi W of London, England; population (1981) 91,000. Since 1841 the site of the British Rail Engineering Works.

swine fever virus disease (hog cholera) of pigs, almost eradicated in the UK from 1963 by a slaughter policy;
swine flu is a virulent form of influenza, closely resembling that in humans;
swine vesicular disease is a virus disease (porcine enterovirus) closely resembling ◊foot and mouth and communicable to humans. Known in Italy and Hong Kong, it first occurred in Britain in 1972, and a slaughter policy was pursued.

swing music jazz style popular in the 1930s–1940s, with a simple harmonic base (of varying tempo) from the rhythm section (percussion, guitar, piano), and superimposed solo melodic line, for example, from trumpet, clarinet or saxophone. Exponents included Benny ◊Goodman, Duke ◊Ellington, and Glenn ◊Miller.

swing-wing correctly called a variable-geometry wing; an aircraft wing that can be moved during flight. The British engineer Barnes ◊Wallis developed the idea, now used in several aircraft, including the European *Tornado* and the American *F-111*. These craft have their wings projecting nearly at right-angles for take-off and landing and low-speed flight, but swing them back for high-speed flight.

Swinton /'swɪntən/ Ernest 1868–1951. British soldier and historian. He served in South Africa and World War I, rising to the rank of major-general, and was the inventor of the tank in 1916. Knighted in 1923, he was Chichele professor of military history at Oxford, 1925–39.

Swiss cheese plant popular name for a plant of the genus ◊*Monstera*.

Swithun, St /'swɪðən/ died 862. English cleric, chancellor of King Ethelwolf and Bishop of ◊Winchester 852–62. He is buried in the cathedral, and, according to legend, the weather on his feast day (15 Jul) is said to continue as either wet or fine for 40 days.

Switzerland /'swɪtsələnd/ landlocked country in W Europe, bounded to the N by West Germany, to the E by Austria, to the S by Italy, and to the NW by France.
government Switzerland is a federation of 20 cantons and six half-cantons (canton is the name for a political division, derived from Old French). The constitution dates from 1874 and provides for a two-chamber federal assembly, consisting of the National Council and the Council of States. The National Council has 200 members, elected by universal suffrage, through a system

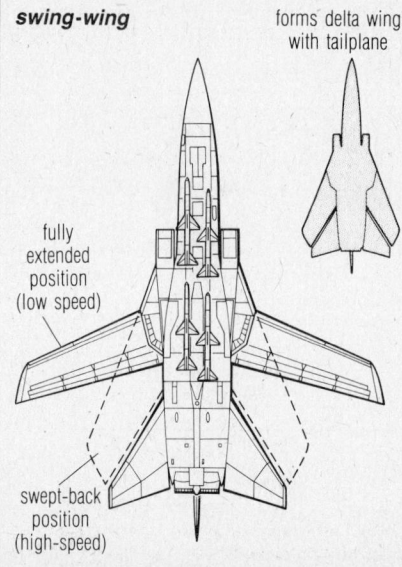

swing-wing

forms delta wing with tailplane

fully extended position (low speed)

swept-back position (high-speed)

of proportional representation, for a four-year term. The Council of States has 46 members, each canton electing two representatives and each half-canton one. Members of the Council of States are elected for three or four years, depending on the constitutions of the individual cantons.
The federal government is in the hands of the Federal Council, consisting of seven members elected for a four-year term by the assembly, each heading a particular federal department. The federal assembly also appoints one member to act as federal head of state and head of government for a year, the term of office beginning on 1 Jan. The federal government is allocated specific powers by the constitution and the residue is left with the cantons, each having has its own constitution, assembly, and government. At a level below the cantons are more than 3,000 communes, whose populations range from fewer than 20 to 350,000. Direct democracy is encouraged through communal assemblies and referenda.
history in 1291 the cantons of Schwyz, Uri, and Lower Unterwalden formed the Everlasting League to defend their liberties against their ◊Hapsburg overlords. More towns and districts joined them, and there were 13 cantons by 1513. The Reformation was accepted during 1523–29 by Zürich, Berne, and Basel, but the rural cantons remained Catholic. Switzerland gradually won more freedom from Hapsburg control until its complete independence was recognized by the Treaty of Westphalia 1648. A peasant uprising in 1653 was suppressed. A French invasion 1798 established the Helvetic Republic with a centralized government; this was modified by Napoleon's Act of Mediation 1803, which made Switzerland a democratic federation. The Congress of Vienna 1815 guaranteed Swiss neutrality, and Switzerland received Geneva and other territories, increasing the number of cantons to 22. After a civil war between the *Sonderbund* (a union of the Catholic

cantons Lucerne, Zug, Freiburg, and Valais) and the Liberals, a revised federal constitution, giving the central government wide powers, was introduced in 1848; a further revision in 1874 increased its powers and introduced the principle of the referendum.
Switzerland, for centuries a neutral country, has been the base for many international organizations and the host of many international peace conferences. A referendum in 1986 rejected the advice of the government and came out overwhelmingly against membership of the United Nations. Its domestic politics have been characterized by coalition governments and a stability that has enabled it to become one of the world's richest countries (per person).
Of several political parties, the most significant are the Radical Democratic Party, the Social Democratic Party, the Christian Democratic Party, the People's Party, and the Liberal Party. Women were not allowed to vote in federal elections until 1971. The first female cabinet minister was appointed in 1984. After the Oct 1987 election, the four-party coalition continued in power, although there was a significant increase in the number of seats held by the Green Party.

sword-fish fish of the family Xiphiidae, characterized by the long sword-like beak protruding from the upper jaw. The common swordfish *Xiphias gladius* sometimes reaches Britain. The sail-fishes and spear-fishes are of the closely related family Istiophoridae.

sycamore species of tree *Acer pseudo-platanus*. The leaves are five-lobed, and the hanging racemes of flowers are followed by winged fruits. The timber is used for furniture.

Sydney /'sɪdni/ capital and port of New South Wales, Australia; population (1981) 3,205,000. Industries include engineering, and the manufacture of scientific equipment, chemicals, clothing, and furniture. It is a financial centre, and has three universities.
history Originally a British penal colony 1788, rapid development followed the discovery of gold in the surrounding area. The main streets still follow the lines of the original wagon tracks, and the Regency Bligh House survives. Modern landmarks are the harbour bridge (single span 503.5 m/1,652 ft) 1923–32; Opera House 1959–73; Centre Point Tower 1980.

syenite a grey, crystalline, plutonic ◊igneous rock, made of ◊feldspar and ◊hornblende, distinguished from ◊granite by the absence of ◊quartz.

Syktyvkar /ˌsɪktɪf'kɑː/ capital of Komi Republic, USSR; population (1981) 180,000. Industries include timber, paper, and tanning. It was founded 1740 as a Russian colony.

Sylhet /sɪl'het/ town in NE Bangladesh; population (1981) 168,371. It is a tea-growing centre, and also produces rice, jute, and sugar.
history The former capital of a Hindu kingdom, it was conquered by Islam in the 14th century. In the 1971 civil war, which led to the establishment of Bangladesh, it was the scene of heavy fighting.

syllogism a set of philosophical statements devised by ◊Aristotle in his pioneering work on ◊logic. The purpose of the syllogism is to establish

Switzerland

SWISS CONFEDERATION (German *Schweiz*, French *Suisse*)

AREA 41,288 sq km/15,941 sq mi
CAPITAL Bern
TOWNS Zürich, Geneva, Lausanne; river port Basel
PHYSICAL most mountainous country in Europe (Alps and Jura Mountains)
FEATURES winter sports area of the upper valley of the river Inn (Engadine); lakes Maggiore, Lucerne, Geneva, Constance
HEAD OF STATE AND OF GOVERNMENT Pierre Aubert from 1987
GOVERNMENT federal democracy
EXPORTS electrical goods; chemicals and pharmaceuticals; watches, precision instruments; confectionery; banking, insurance, and tourism are important
CURRENCY Swiss franc (2.49 = £1 Sept 1987)
POPULATION 6,457,000 (1985); annual growth rate 0.2%
LANGUAGE German 69%, French 20%, Italian 10% (all official); Romansch 1%
RELIGION Roman Catholic 50%, Protestant 48%
LITERACY 99% (1985)
GNP $93.7 bn (1984); $14,408 per head of population

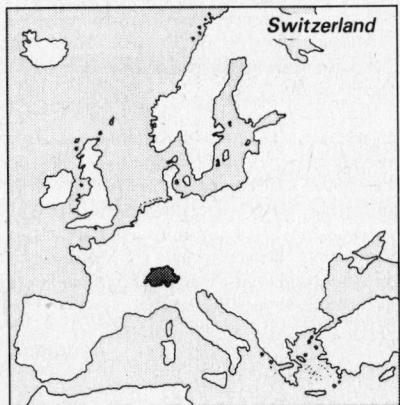
Switzerland

CHRONOLOGY
1648 Became independent of the Holy Roman Empire.
1798–1815 Helvetic Republic established by French Revolutionary armies.
1847 Civil war resulted in greater centralization.
1971 Women given the vote in federal elections.
1984 First female cabinet minister appointed.
1986 Referendum rejected a proposal for membership of United Nations.

sword-fish The sword-fish has a high reputation as a 'game' fish, and is greatly sought after by anglers who wear out its strength in contests from motor-boats.

the conditions under which a valid conclusion follows or does not follow by deduction from given premises. The following is an example of a valid syllogism: 'All men are mortal, Socrates is a man, therefore Socrates is mortal'.

Sylvanus in Roman mythology, the equivalent of ◊Pan, the god of shepherds.

symbiosis a biological term with two different meanings. It is commonly used for any close relationship between two organisms of different species, where both partners benefit from the association. A well-known example is the pollination relationship between insects and flowers, where the insects feed on nectar and carry pollen from one flower to another. Some biologists use the term '*mutualism*' for this sort of relationship, and use symbiosis in a broader sense to mean any close relationship between two organisms of different species, including ◊mutualism, ◊commensalism and ◊parasitism.

symbol in general, something that stands for something else. A symbol may be an aesthetic device, or a sign used to convey information visually, thus saving time, eliminating language barriers, or overcoming illiteracy. Symbols are used in art and literature; for practical use in science and medicine; for road signs; and as warnings.

symbolic interactionism sociological method, founded by G H ◊Mead, that studies the behaviour of individuals and small groups through observation and description, viewing people's appearance, gestures, and language as symbols they use to interact with others in social situations. In contrast to theories such as Marxism or functionalism which attempt to analyse society as a whole, through economic or political systems, it takes a perspective of society from within, as created by people themselves.

symbolic processor a computer purpose-built to run so-called symbol-manipulation programs rather than programs involving a great deal of numerical computation. Mostly, they exist for the ◊artificial-intelligence language ◊Lisp, although some have also been built to run ◊Prolog.

symbolism in the arts, the use of symbols as a device for concentrating or intensifying meaning. In particular, the term is used for a late 19th-century movement in French poetry, associated with ◊Verlaine, ◊Mallarmé, and ◊Rimbaud, who used words for their symbolic rather than concrete meaning.

Symington /'sɪmɪŋtən/ William 1763–1831. Scottish engineer who built the first successful steamboat. Born in Lanarkshire, he invented the steam road locomotive (1787) and a steamboat engine (1788).

Symonds /'sɪməndz/ John Addington 1840–1893. British critic, who spent much of his life in Italy and Switzerland, and campaigned for homosexual rights. He was author of *The Renaissance in Italy* 1875–86.

Symons /'sɪmənz/ Arthur 1865–1945. Welsh critic, follower of ◊Pater, and friend of Toulouse-Lautrec, Mallarmé, Beardsley, Yeats, and Conrad. He wrote *The Symbolist Movement in Literature* 1900.

symphonic poem in music, a term originated by ◊Liszt for his 13 one-movement orchestral works which interpret a story from literature or history, and used by many other composers. Richard ◊Strauss preferred the title *tone poem*.

symphony a musical composition for orchestra, traditionally in four contrasted but closely related movements. It developed from the smaller ◊sonata form, the Italian overture, and the dance suite of the 18th century. ◊Haydn established the mature form of symphony, written in slow, minuet, and allegro movements. Mozart and Beethoven (who replaced the minuet with the scherzo) expanded the classical form, which has been developed further by composers such as ◊Brahms, ◊Tchaikovsky, ◊Brückner, ◊Dvořák, ◊Mahler, ◊Sibelius, ◊Vaughan Williams, ◊Piston, ◊Prokofiev, ◊Nielsen, ◊Shostakovich, ◊Stravinsky, and ◊Copland.

synagogue a Jewish place of worship, also (particularly in the USA) called a temple. As an institution it dates from the destruction of the ◊temple in Jerusalem in 70 AD, though it had been in course of development from the time of the Exile. See under ◊Judaism.

synapse the 'junction' between two ◊nerve cells of an animal, or between a nerve cell and a muscle. The two cells involved are not in direct contact, being separated by a narrow gap called the synaptic cleft. Across this gap flow chemical ◊neurotransmitters, which have a specific effect on the receiving cell when they bind to special receptors on its surface. The response may be a nervous impulse in a nerve cell, contraction in a muscle cell, and so on.

synapsida mammal-like reptiles living 315–195 million years ago, whose fossil record is largely complete, and who were for a long time the dominant land animals.

syncline geological term for a fold in the rocks of the Earth's crust in which the layers or ◊beds dip inwards, thus forming a trough-like structure with a sag in the middle. The opposite, with the beds arching upwards, is an ◊anticline.

syncopation in music, the deliberate upsetting of rhythm by shifting the accent to a beat that is normally unaccented.

syndicalism (French *syndicat*, trade union) political movement that rejected parliamentary activity in favour of direct action, culminating in a revolutionary general strike to secure worker ownership and control of industry. The idea originated under Robert ◊Owen's influence in the 1830s, acquired its name and its more violent aspects in France (see ◊Sorel), and also reached the USA (Industrial Workers of the World). After 1918 it was absorbed in communism, although it continued to have an independent existence in Spain until the late 1930s.

synecdoche a ◊figure of speech whose Greek name means 'accepted together' and which uses (1) the part to represent the whole ('There were some new faces at the meeting', rather than *new people*), or (2) the whole to stand for the part ('The West Indies beat England at cricket', rather than naming the national teams in question).

synergy (Greek 'combined action') in medicine, the 'co-operative' action of two or more drugs, muscle or organs; in architecture, the augmented strength of systems, where the strength of a wall is greater than the added total of its individual units, for example, the stone walls of early South American civilizations, not held together by cement or mortar.

Synge /sɪŋ/ J(ohn) M(illington) 1871–1909. Irish playwright, a leading figure in the Irish dramatic revival of the early 20th century. His six plays are classics of Irish drama. They include *In the Shadow of the Glen* 1903, *Riders to the Sea* 1904, and his masterpiece, *The Playboy of the Western World* 1907.

synonymy near or identical meaning between or among words. There are, however, very few strict synonyms in any language, although there may be many near-synonyms, depending upon the contexts in which the words are used. Thus, 'brotherly' and 'fraternal' are synonyms in English, but a 'brotherhood' is not exactly the same as a 'fraternity'; people talk about the brotherhood of man but seldom if ever about the 'fraternity of man'. *Brotherhood* and *fraternity* are not therefore strictly synonymous.

synovial fluid a viscous yellow fluid which bathes movable joints between the bones of vertebrates. It nourishes and lubricates the ◊cartilage at the end of each bone.

synovitis inflammation of the lining of a joint, caused by injury or infection.

Syntax, Doctor a fictional clergyman invented by William Combe (1741–1823), who appeared in a series of verse satires, with drawings by Thomas ◊Rowlandson.

synthesizer device which uses electrical components to produce sounds, either such as conventional musical instruments produce physically, or in free creativity. In *pre-set synthesisers*, the sound of the various instruments is produced by a built-in computer-type memory, which triggers all the control settings required to produce the sound of a trumpet or violin. For example, the 'sawtooth' type sound wave produced by a violin is artificially produced by an electrical tone generator, or oscillator, and then fed into an electrical filter which is set to have the resonances characteristic of a violin-body. In *programmable synthesizers* any number of new instrumental or other sounds may be produced at the will of the

performer. See ◊electronics. *Speech synthesizers* can break down speech into 128 basic elements (allophones), which are then combined into words and sentences, as in the voice of electronic teaching aids.

synthetic an artificial material made from chemicals. Many of the materials used in everyday life are artificial including plastics (polythene, polystyrene), ◊synthetic fibres (nylon, acrylics, polyesters), synthetic resins and synthetic rubber. Plastics are made mainly from petroleum chemicals by the process of ◊polymerization, in which small molecules are joined to make very big ones.

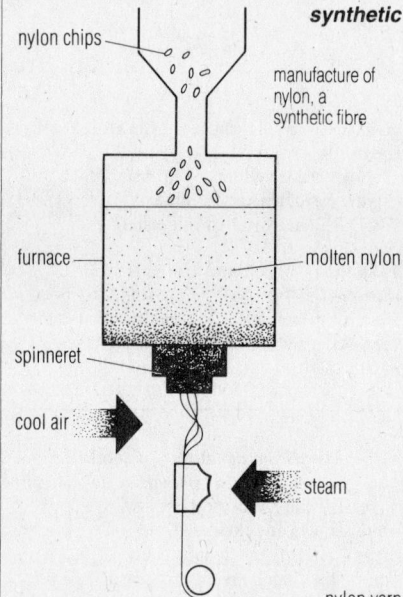

synthetic

nylon chips — manufacture of nylon, a synthetic fibre

furnace — molten nylon

spinneret

cool air — steam

— nylon yarn

synthetic in philosophy, a term employed in ◊Kant, and subsequently others, to describe a judgement in which the predicate is not contained within the subject, for example: 'The flower is blue' (this is synthetic, since every flower is not blue). It is the converse of ◊analytic.

synthetic fibre an artificial fibre, unknown in nature. There are two kinds of artificial fibre; one is made from natural materials that have been chemically processed in some way. ◊Rayon, for example, is made by processing the cellulose in woodpulp. The other type is the true synthetic fibre, made entirely from chemicals. ◊Nylon was the original, and is still one of the most important synthetic fibres. Like most other synthetic fibres, it is made from chemicals obtained from petroleum (crude oil). Fibres are drawn out into long threads or filaments, usually by so-called 'spinning' methods, melting or dissolving the parent material and then forcing it through the holes of a perforated plate, or spinneret.

syphilis venereal disease caused by the bacterium *Treponema pallidum*. In the initial stage an ulcerated sore develops, followed some weeks afterwards by a rash, and in the final stage (after some years) by swellings under the skin and in the internal organs, and destruction of the surrounding tissues and bones. The brain may

also be affected, causing **locomotor ataxia** or **tabes dorsalis**, affecting sight, co-ordination of movement, and general paralysis, in which the mind deteriorates and there is progressive paralysis. Initially, the discovery of ◊antibiotics revolutionized treatment, making it quick and easy, but resistant strains of the bacterium developed.

Syracuse /'saɪrəkjuːz/ industrial port in E Sicily; population (1981) 117,500. Industries include the production of chemicals and salt. It has a cathedral and remains of temples, aqueducts, catacombs, and an amphitheatre.
history founded 734 BC by the Corinthians, it became a centre of Greek culture, especially under the elder and younger ◊Dionysius. After a three-year siege it was taken by Rome 212 BC. In 878 it was destroyed by the Arabs, and the rebuilt town came under Norman rule in the 11th century.

Syracuse /'sɪrəkjuːz/ industrial city on Lake Onondaga, in New York State, USA; population (1980) 170,300. There are canal links with the ◊Great Lakes, the Hudson, and the St Lawrence. Syracuse was founded 1805 on the site of an ◊Iroquois Indian capital.

Syria /'sɪriə/ country in W Asia, on the Mediterranean, bounded to the N by Turkey, to the E by Iraq, to the S by Jordan, and to the SW by Israel and Lebanon.
government the 1973 constitution provides for a president elected by universal suffrage for a seven-year term, who appoints and governs with the help of a prime minister and a council of ministers. There is a single-chamber legislature, *Majlis al-Sha'ab*, also elected by universal suffrage.
history Syria was originally divided between various small kingdoms which fought against Israel and were subdued by the Assyrians. It was subsequently occupied by Babylonia, Persia, and Macedonia, but gained importance under Seleucus Nicator, founder of ◊Antioch 300 BC, and ◊Antiochus the Great. After forming part of the Roman and Byzantine empires, it was conquered by the Saracens in 636. During the Middle Ages it was the scene of many of the Crusaders' exploits.
Syria was part of the ◊Ottoman Empire 1516–1918. It was occupied by British and French troops 1918–19 and in 1920 placed under French mandate. Syria became independent in 1946 and three years later came under military rule.
In 1958 Syria merged with Egypt, to become the United Arab Republic (UAR), but after an army coup in 1961 Syria seceded and the independent Syrian Arab Republic was established. In 1963 a government was formed, mainly from members of the Arab Socialist Renaissance (Ba'ath) Party, but three years later the army removed it. In 1970 the moderate wing of the Ba'ath Party, led by Lt-Gen Hafiz al-Assad, secured power in a bloodless coup and in the following year Assad was elected president.
Since then President Assad has remained in office without any serious challenges to his leadership. He is head of state, head of government, secretary-general of the Ba'ath Arab Socialist

Party, and president of the National Progressive Front (NPF), an umbrella organization for the five main, socialist, parties. Syria is therefore in reality, if not in a strictly legal sense, a one-party state. Since 1983 Assad's health has suffered but no obvious successor has emerged. In the 1986 elections the NPF won 151 of the 195 seats.

Externally Syria has, under President Assad, played a leading role in Middle East affairs. In the Six-Day War of 1967 it lost territory to Israel and after the Yom Kippur War of 1973 Israel formally annexed the Golan Heights, which had previously been part of Syria. During 1976 Assad progressively intervened in the civil war in Lebanon, eventually committing some 50,000 troops to the operations. Relations between Syria and Egypt cooled after President Sadat's Israel peace initiative in 1977 and the subsequent Camp David agreement. Assad has consistently opposed US-sponsored peace moves in Lebanon, arguing that they infringed Lebanese sovereignty. He has also questioned Yasser Arafat's leadership of the Palestine Liberation Organization (PLO) and supported opposition to him.

In 1984 President Assad and the Lebanese president Amin Gemayel approved plans for a government of national unity in Lebanon, which would give equal representation to Muslims and Christians, and secured the reluctant agreement of Nabih Berri of the Shi'ite Amal Militia and Walid Joumblatt, leader of the ◊Druze. Fighting still continued, and Assad's credibility suffered. But in 1985 his authority proved sufficient to secure the release of 39 US hostages from an aircraft hijacked by the extremist Shi'ite group Hezbollah (Party of God). In Nov 1986 Britain broke off diplomatic relations after claiming to have proof of Syrian involvement in international terrorism, when someone attempted to blow up an Israeli plane at Heathrow, London. In Jul 1987 Syria instigated a crackdown on the pro-Iranian Hezbollah party. Syria has been leaning to the W, its policies in Lebanon in direct conflict with Iran's dream of an Islamic republic, and its crumbling economy has been promised Arab aid if Damascus switches allegiance. In Jun 1987, following a private visit by former US president Jimmy ◊Carter, Syria's relations with the USA began to improve, and efforts were made to arrange the release of Western hostages in Lebanon.

Syriac language an ancient Semitic language, originally the Aramaic dialect spoken in and around Edessa (now in Turkey) and widely used in W Asia from around 700 BC to 700 AD. From the 3rd to 7th centuries it was an important Christian liturgical and literary language.

Syria

SYRAIN ARAB REPUBLIC (*al-Jamhouriya al Arabia as-Souriya*)

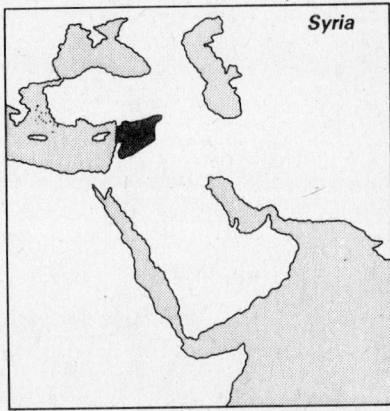

Syria

AREA 186,000 sq km/72,000 sq mi
CAPITAL Damascus
TOWNS Aleppo, Homs, Hama; chief port Lattakia
PHYSICAL mountains alternate with fertile plains and desert areas; river Euphrates
FEATURES Mount Hermon, Golan Heights; crusader castles (Krak des Chevaliers); Phoenician city sites (Ugarit)
HEAD OF STATE AND OF GOVERNMENT Hafiz al-Assad from 1971
GOVERNMENT Islamic socialist
EXPORTS cotton; cereals; oil, phosphates
CURRENCY Syrian pound (official rate 6.47 = £1 Sept 1987)
POPULATION 10,535,000 (1985); annual growth rate 3.4%
LANGUAGE Arabic (official)
RELIGION Sunni Muslim, but the ruling minority is Alawite, an Islamic sect; also Druze, again an Islamic sect
LITERACY 72% male/35% female (1980 est)
GNP $16.5 bn (1983); $702 per head of population
CHRONOLOGY
1946 Achieved full independence from France.
1958 Merged with Egypt to form the United Arab Republic (UAR).
1961 UAR disintegrated.
1967 Six-Day War resulted in the loss of territory to Israel.
1970–71 Syria supported Palestinian guerrillas against Jordanian troops.
1971 Following a bloodless coup, Hafiz al-Assad became president.
1973 Israel consolidated its control of the Golan Heights after the Yom Kippur War.
1976 Substantial numbers of troops committed to the civil war in Lebanon.
1981–82 Further military engagements in Lebanon.
1982 Islamic militant uprising suppressed; 5,000 dead.
1984 Presidents Assad and Gemayel approved a plan for government of national unity in Lebanon.
1985 Assad secured the release of US hostages held in an aircraft hijacked by an extremist Shi'ite group.
1987 Improved relations with USA and attempts to secure the release of western hostages in Lebanon.

syringa genus of shrubs. Lilac *Syringa vulgaris* is the best-known. The name is also given to the ◊mock orange.

Système International d'Unité see under ◊SI unit.

systems analysis in computing, an early stage in the process of constructing software, concerned with the analysis of the problem that the program is intended to solve. It involves an attempt to develop a formalized model of the problem using diagrams and formal languages (see ◊software project lifecycle). Systems currently in use include Yourdon, SSADM, and Soft Systems Methodology.

systems design in computing, a stage in the development of a program, concerned with its detailed design. It typically involves the use of diagramming conventions (such as ◊flow charts) and formalized language (pseudocode) to express the logic of the design. See also ◊software project lifestyle and ◊systems analysis.

Szczecin /'ʃtʃetʃiːn/ port in NW Poland; population (1980) 387,660. A ◊Hanseatic port from 1278, it was Swedish 1648–1720, when it was taken by Prussia, and (as *Stettin*) was Germany's chief Baltic port.

Szechwan /ˌseɪ'tʃwaːn/ alternative spelling for the central Chinese province of ◊Sichuan.

Szeged /'seged/ city in S Hungary; population (1980) 171,500. The chief industry is textiles.

Szymanowski /ˌʃɪmə'nɒfski/ Karol (Maliej) 1882–1937. Ukrainian-born Polish composer of orchestral works, operas, piano music, and violin concertos. He was director of the Conservatoire in Warsaw from 1926.

T the 20th letter of the alphabet, whose sound is usually a voiceless alveolar plosive. The earliest form was X, which the Phoenicians called *tau*, a cross or sign, but in the Greek alphabet its form was T.

Tabah /ˈtɑːbə/ area of disputed territory, 1 km/0.75 mi long, between Eilat (Israel) and the Sinai Desert (Egypt) on the Red Sea. Under an Anglo-Egyptian-Turkish agreement 1906, the border ran through Tabah; under a British survey of 1915 headed by T E ◊Lawrence (who made 'adjustments' allegedly under British government orders) it runs to the east.

Table Bay /ˈteɪbəl ˈbeɪ/ inlet on the SW coast of the Cape of Good Hope, South Africa, on which Cape Town stands. It is overlooked by Table Mountain (highest point Maclear's Beacon 1,087 m/3,567 ft), the cloud often above it being known as the 'tablecloth'.

table tennis game developed in Britain in about 1880 from real tennis, popularly known as 'ping pong'. The two or four players use solid-headed bats and plastic balls on a rectangular table 2.74 m/9 ft by 1.52 m/5 ft, over a net 15.25 cm/6 in high. Points are scored if the opponent makes a fault (fails to return a ball, strikes into the net, and so on), and 21 points make a game, a match normally being two out of three games.

Tabligh post-1945 missionary ('revival') movement in Islam, which feeds the militant organizations for the 'true Islamic state'; there is an annual gathering at Tongi, near Dacca.

taboo from Polynesian *tabu*, 'forbidden', applied to magical and religious objects. In psychology and the social sciences the term is used for practices which are generally prohibited because of religious or social pressures.

Tabora /təˈbɔːrə/ trading centre in W Tanzania; population (1978) 67,400. It was founded about 1820 by Arab traders in slaves and ivory.

Tabriz /tæˈbriːz/ city in NW Iran; population (1976) 599,000. Industries include metal casting, carpets, cotton and silk textiles.

tachograph combined speedometer and clock which records a vehicle's speed on a small card disc, magnetic disk or tape, and also the length of time it is moving or stationary; used especially to monitor a lorry-driver's working practice.

Tacna /ˈtækmə/ city in S Peru; population (1983) 46,250. It is undergoing industrial development. In 1880 Chile defeated a combined Peruvian-Bolivian army nearby, and occupied Tacna until 1929.

Tacoma /təˈkəʊmə/ port in Washington state, USA, on Puget Sound; population (1980) 158,500. Founded 1868, it developed after being chosen as the terminus of the North Pacific Railroad 1873.

Tadzhikistan /tæˌdʒiːkɪˈstɑːn/ constituent republic of the S central USSR from 1929, part of Soviet Central Asia
area 143,100 sq km/55,250 sq mi
capital Dushanbe
features few areas are below 3,500 m/11,000 ft; includes ◊Communism Peak; health resorts and mineral springs
products fruit; cereals, cotton; cattle and sheep; silks and carpets
population (1984) 4,400,000, 56% Tadzhik, 23% Uzbek, 13% Russian or Ukrainian
language Tadzhik, similar to Farsi (Persian)
religion Sunni Muslim
recent history formed 1924 from the Tadzhik areas of Bokhara and Turkestan.

taekwondo Korean ◊martial art similar to ◊karate, which includes punching and kicking.

Tafawa Balewa /təˈfɑːwə bəˈleɪwə/ Alhaji Abubakar 1912–1966. Nigerian politician. Entering the House of Representatives in 1952, he was minister of works 1952–54 and of transport 1954–57. In 1957 he became prime minister of the Federation of Nigeria, but was assassinated in the *coup d'état* of Jan 1966.

taffeta (Persian 'spun') light plainly woven silk fabric with a high lustre.

Taft /tæft/ Robert Alphonso 1889–1953. US Republican senator from 1939, and a candidate for the presidential nomination in 1940, 1944, 1948, and 1952. He sponsored the Taft-Hartley Labor Act 1947, restricting union power. He was the son of W H ◊Taft.

Taft /tæft/ William Howard 1857–1930. 27th president of the USA. Born at Cincinnati, he was secretary of war 1904–08, and was elected president in 1908 as a Republican. He was defeated in the election of 1912, and served as chief justice of the Supreme Court, 1921–30. His son was Robert ◊Taft.

Taganrog /ˌtæɡənˈrɒɡ/ port on the Sea of Azov, S USSR; population (1985) 289,000. Industries include iron, steel, metal goods, aircraft, machinery, and shoes. A museum commemorates the playwright ◊Chekhov, who was born here.

Taglioni /tælˈjəʊni/ Marie 1804–1884. Italian dancer. The most important ballerina of the Romantic era, acclaimed for her ethereal style and exceptional lightness, she was the first to use ◊pointe work, or dancing on the toes, as an expressive part of ballet rather than technique. She created many roles, the most famous being the title role in her father's ballet *La Sylphide* 1832, first performed at the Paris Opéra.

Tagore /təˈɡɔː/ Rabindranath 1861–1941. Indian writer in Bengali. One of the most influential Indian authors of the 20th century, he translated into English his own verse *Gitanjali* ('song offerings') 1912 and his verse play *Chitra* 1896. He was awarded a Nobel prize in 1913.

Tagus /ˈteɪɡəs/ river (Spanish *Tajo*, Portuguese *Tejo*) rising in Spain and reaching the Atlantic at Lisbon, Portugal; length 910 km/566 mi. At Lisbon it is crossed by the April 25 (formerly Salazar) Bridge, so named in honour of the 1974 revolution. The *Tagus-Segura* irrigation scheme serves the rainless Murcia/Alicante region for early fruit and vegetable growing.

Tahiti /təˈhiːti/ largest of the Society Islands, part of ◊French Polynesia; capital Papeete; area 1,040 sq km/402 sq mi; population (1983) 116,000.
history Tahiti was visited by Capt James ◊Cook 1769 and by Bligh of the *Bounty* 1788. It came under French protection 1843, becoming a colony 1880.

Tai Chi series of 108 complex slow-motion movements, each named (for example, The Eye of the Tiger, The White Crane Spreads its Wings) and designed to ensure effective circulation of the 'chi' or intrinsic energy of the Universe through the mind and body. It derives

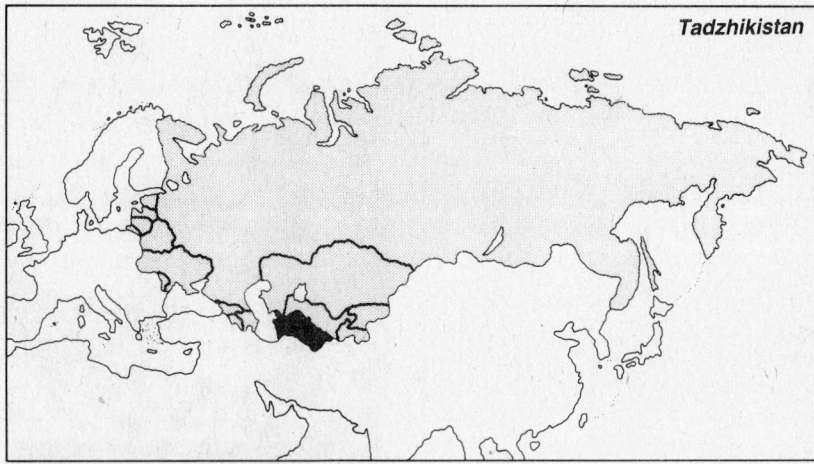

Tadzhikistan

Tagore Nobel prize-winning Indian writer Rabindranath Tagore photographed in 1920. One of this century's most influential Indian authors, he was an ardent nationalist and urged social reform. He resigned his knighthood as a gesture of protest against British repression.

partly from the Shaolin ▷martial arts of China, and partly from ▷Taoism.

taiga /'taɪgə/ Russian name for the heavily forested territory, some of it in the permafrost zone, in ▷Siberia. There is rich and varied fauna and flora, in delicate balance because the conditions of life are so precarious; this ecology is threatened by railway construction, mining, and forestry. The name is also applied to similar regions elsewhere.

Taine /teɪn/ Hippolyte Adolphe 1828–1893. French critic and historian. He was appointed professor at the Ecole des Beaux Arts in 1864. He analysed literary works as products of period and environment, for example in *Histoire de la littérature anglaise/History of English Literature* 1863 and *Philosophie de*

l'art/Philosophy of Art 1865–69. He also published *Les Origines de la France contemporaine/Origins of Contemporary France* 1876–99.

taipan Australia's deadliest snake *Oxyuranus scutellatus*, also found in New Guinea. Some 3 m/10 ft long, it is brown with yellow spots beneath.

Taipei /ˌtaɪ'peɪ/ capital (mainland spelling Taibei) and commercial centre of Taiwan; population (1985) 2,500,000. The National Palace Museum 1965 houses the world's greatest collection of Chinese art, taken there from the mainland 1948.

Taiwan /ˌtaɪ'wɑːn/ country in SE Asia, officially the Republic of China, occupying the island of Taiwan between the E China Sea and the S China Sea.

government the 1,020-member National Assembly (Kuo-Min Ta-Hui) elects the president and vice-president and has power to amend the constitution of 1947. Its members, originally elected from mainland China, have retained their seats ever since their constituencies fell under Communist Chinese control in 1949, and are termed 'life members'. Fresh elections have only been held for seats vacated by deceased deputies.

Taiwan's president, elected for a six-year term, is head of state, commander-in-chief of the armed forces, and promulgates laws. The president works with a cabinet, the Executive *Yuan*, headed by a prime minister (Yu Kuo-hua from 1984), responsible to a single-chamber legislature, the Legislative *Yuan*. The Legislative *Yuan* comprises 348 members, some of them presidential appointees but the majority 'life members' from former mainland seats. Since 1972, 70 vacated seats have, on average, been subject to fresh elections at three-yearly intervals. Three Control, Judicial and Examination *Yuans* also exist, with the tasks of investigating the work of the executive, interpreting the constitution, and overseeing entrance examinations for public offices.

The dominant political force and sole political party is the Nationalist Party of China

(Kuomintang), which is still staffed at its senior levels by pre-1949 mainlanders. Opposition candidates have been permitted to stand in elections under the banner of *dangwai* ('outside the party').

history Taiwan, then known as Formosa ('The Beautiful'), was settled by ▷China from the 15th century, briefly occupied by the Dutch during the mid-17th century, and annexed by the Manchu dynasty in 1683. It was ceded to Japan under the terms of the Treaty of Shimonoseki after the 1895 Sino-Japanese war and not regained by China until the Japanese surrender in Aug 1945. In Dec 1949 Taiwan became the refuge for the Chinese Nationalist government forces of ▷Chiang Kai-shek which were compelled to evacuate the mainland after their defeat by the Communist troops of ▷Mao Zedong. Chiang and his Nationalist followers, though only a 15 per cent minority, dominated the island and maintained an army of 600,000 in the hope of reconquering the mainland, over which they still claimed sovereignty. They continued to be recognized by the USA as the legitimate government of China, and occupied China's United Nations and Security Council seats until Oct 1971 when they were expelled and replaced by the People's Republic.

Taiwan was protected by American naval forces during the Korean War 1950–53 and signed a mutual defence treaty with the USA 1954. Benefiting from such security, the country enjoyed a period of rapid economic growth during the 1950s and 1960s, emerging as an export-orientated newly industrializing country. Political power during these years was concentrated in the hands of the Kuomintang and the armed forces led by President Chiang Kai-shek, with martial law imposed and opposition activity outlawed. During the 1970s the Taiwanese government was forced to adjust to rapid external changes as the USA adopted a new policy of détente towards Communist China. This culminated in Jan 1979 in the full normalization of Sino-American relations, the severing of American-Taiwanese diplomatic contacts, and the annulment of the USA's 1954 security pact. Other Western nations followed suit in ending diplomatic relations with Taiwan during the 1970s and early 1980s.

These developments, coupled with generational change within the Kuomintang, have prompted a slow review of Taiwanese policies, both domestic and external. Chiang Kai-shek died in Apr 1975 and his son Chiang Ching-kuo (1910–) became president. In the Dec 1986 elections a formal opposition party, the Democratic Progress Party, led by Chiang Peng-chien, was tolerated and captured 22 per cent of the vote to the Kuomintang's 69 per cent. Native Taiwanese have been progressively inducted into the Kuomintang, and martial law was replaced by a national security law in Jul 1987. Many political prisoners were released, parliamentary reform and liberalization promised.

In its external relations the Kuomintang government has remained firm in its claims to legitimate rule over mainland China. This policy is rejected by the native Taiwanese minority, who

Taiwan
REPUBLIC OF CHINA

AREA 36,000 sq km/14,000 sq mi
CAPITAL Taipei
TOWNS ports Keelung, Kaohsiung
PHYSICAL island (formerly Formosa) off the coast of the People's Republic of China; mountainous, with lowlands in the W
FEATURES Penghu (Pescadores), Jinmen (Quemoy), and Mazu (Matsu) islands
HEAD OF STATE Lee Teng Lui from 1988
HEAD OF GOVERNMENT Yu Kuo-hua from 1984
GOVERNMENT conservative democracy
EXPORTS with US aid, Taiwan is highly industrialized: textiles, petrochemicals, steel, plastics, electronics
CURRENCY Taiwan dollar (49.74 = £1 Sept 1987)
POPULATION (1985) 19,117,322 (89% Taiwanese, 11% mainlanders whose dominance causes resentment); annual growth rate 1.4%
LANGUAGE Mandarin Chinese
RELIGION officially atheist, but traditional religions are Taoist, Confucian, and Buddhist
LITERACY 89% (1983)
GNP $56.6 bn (1984); $3,000 per head of population
CHRONOLOGY
1683 Taiwan (Formosa) annexed by China.
1895 Ceded to Japan.
1945 Recovered by China.

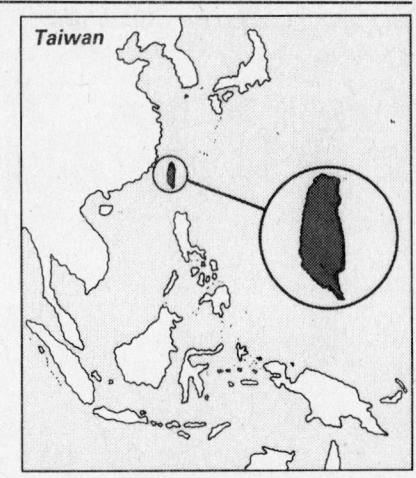

Taiwan

1949 Flight of Nationalist government to Taiwan after Chinese revolution.
1954 US-Taiwanese mutual defence treaty.
1971 Expulsion from United Nations.
1972 Commencement of legislature elections.
1975 President Chiang Kai-shek died and was succeeded by Yen Chia-kan.
1979 USA severed diplomatic relations and annulled security pact.
1986 Formation of first opposition party to the Nationalist Kuomintang.

Talbot Daguerrotype of William Henry Fox Talbot, who invented new techniques in photography, including the photographic negative from which copies could be made on paper.

seek self-determination and the creation of an independent Taiwan.

Taiyuan /ˌtaɪjuˈɑːn/ capital of Shanxi province, NE China; population (1982) 1,750,000. Industries include iron, steel, agricultural machinery, and textiles. It is a walled city, founded in the 5th century AD, on the river Fen He, and is the seat of Shanxi university.

Taizé /teɪˈzeɪ/ Protestant religious community based in the village of that name in SE France. Founded in 1940 by Swiss theologian Roger Schutz (1915–), it became in the 1960s an ecumenical centre for young people interested in the 'struggle and contemplation' combined in communal Christianity.

Taj Mahal /ˈtɑːdʒ məˈhɑːl/ a white marble mausoleum in ◊Agra, central India; built by ◊Shah Jehan.

Tajo /ˈtɑːxəʊ/ Spanish name for the river ◊Tagus.

takahe bird *Notornis mantelli* of the rail family and native to New Zealand. A heavy flightless species, with blue and green plumage and a red beak, the takahe was thought to have become extinct at the end of the 19th century, but in 1948 small numbers were rediscovered in a mountain valley on South Island.

Takao /tæˈkaʊ/ Japanese name for ◊Kaohsiung, a city on the W coast of Taiwan.

Takeshita /ˌtækeˈʃiːtə/ Noboru 1924– . Japanese politician, finance minister from 1982, leader of the Liberal Democratic Party (LDP) from 1987, and prime minister from Nov 1987.

Noboru Takeshita began his career as a schoolteacher before being elected to parliament as a member of the LDP in 1958. He gained a cabinet post in 1971, and was appointed finance minister in 1982. Originally allied to the powerful ◊Tanaka faction within the LDP, Takeshita later broke away to form his own large grouping. In Oct 1987 he became leader (president) of the LDP, and became Japan's new prime minister the following month. A more cautious figure than his predecessor, Yasuhiro ◊Nakasone, he enjoys only limited experience of foreign affairs.

Takoradi /ˌtɑːkəˈrɑːdi/ port in Ghana, administered with ◊Sekondi.

Talavera de la Reina /ˌtæləˈveərə delə ˈreɪnə/ town in Spain, on the ◊Tagus, 120 km/75 mi SW of Madrid; population (1970) 46,412. Spanish and British forces (under ◊Wellesley) defeated the French here in the ◊Peninsular War 1809.

Talbot /ˈtɔːlbət/ William Henry Fox 1800–1877. British pioneer of photography. He invented the ◊calotype process, the first ◊negative/positive method, and had made ◊photograms several years before Daguerre's invention was announced. *The Pencil of Nature* by Talbot was the first book of photographs published; he also made instantaneous photographs 1851 and photo engravings 1852. He lived at Lacock Abbey, Wiltshire, 1833–77, where a museum of his work was opened in 1975.

talc a mineral, magnesium silicate, $Mg_3Si_4O_{11} \cdot H_2O$, occurring in crystals, but the

massive form, known as steatite or soapstone, is more common. French chalk and potstone are varieties of talc. It is used in cosmetics, for lubricants and as a filler in paper manufacture. Soapstone has a 'greasy' feel to it, and is used in carving ornaments.

Talcahuano /ˌtælkəˈwɑːnəʊ/ port and chief naval base in Chile; population (1982) 208,941. Industries include oil refining and timber.

Talien /ˈtælien/ part of the port of ◊Lüda, China.

Taliesin /tælˈjesɪn/ lived c. 550. Legendary Welsh poet, a bard at the court of the king of Rheged in S Scotland, who allegedly died at Taliesin (named after him) in Dyfed.

Tallahassee /ˌtæləˈhæsi/ capital of Florida, USA (Cree Indian 'old town'); population (1980) 81,548. It is an agricultural and lumbering centre. The explorer ◊De Soto found an Indian settlement here 1539. It has many pre-Civil War mansions.

Talleyrand /ˈtælɪrænd/ Charles Maurice de Talleyrand-Périgord 1754–1838. French politician, bishop of Autun 1789–91. A supporter of moderate reform, he fled to the USA during the Terror (persecution of anti-revolutionaries), but became foreign minister under the Directory 1797–99, and under Napoleon 1799–1807. He represented France at the Congress of Vienna 1814–15, and was ambassador to London 1830–34.

Tallinn /ˈtælɪn/ port and capital of Estonian Republic (German name *Reval*), north-west USSR; population (1985) 464,000. Industries include electrical and oil drilling machinery, textiles, and paper. Founded 1219, it was a ◊Hanseatic port, passed to Sweden 1561, and to Russia 1750. Vyshgorod castle (13th century) and other medieval buildings remain.

Tallis /ˈtælɪs/ Thomas c. 1505–1585. English composer. He was organist at Waltham Abbey until 1540 and joint organist (with his pupil ◊Byrd) of the Chapel Royal from 1572. A master

Talleyrand The French politician Talleyrand-Périgord served France during a turbulent period of its history. As the Bishop of Autun, he pressed for moderate reform but was thwarted by the violent extremes of the French Revolution. He returned from exile in America to become France's foreign minister.

of the polyphonic style, he wrote masses, anthems, and other church music, including a setting for five voices of the *Lamentations of Jeremiah*, and for 40 of *Spem in alium*.

Tall Ships Race race for sailing ships from Bermuda to Halifax, Nova Scotia.

Talmud chief work of Jewish post-Biblical literature, providing a compilation of ancient Jewish law and tradition, based on the ◊*Mishnah*. To this was added the *Gemara*, discussions centring on its texts, during the 3rd and 4th centuries AD.

Tamale /tə'mɑːli/ town in NE Ghana; population (1970) 120,000. It is a commercial centre, dealing in rice, cotton, and peanuts.

tamandua tree-living anteater *Tamandua tetradactyla* found in tropical forests and tree savannah from S Mexico to Brazil. About 56 cm/1.8 ft long plus a prehensile tail of equal length, it has strong foreclaws with which it can break into nests of tree ants and termites, which it licks up with its narrow tongue; it has no teeth.

Tamar /'teɪmɑː/ in the Old Testament, the sister of ◊Absalom. She was raped by her half-brother Amnon, who was then killed by Absalom.

Tamar /'teɪmə/ river rising in N Cornwall, England, and flowing to Plymouth Sound; for most of its 97 km/60 mi length it forms the Devon-Cornwall border.

Tamar /'teɪmɑː/ river flowing into Bass Strait, Tasmania, formed by the union of the N and S Esk; length 65 km/40 mi.

tamarack coniferous tree *Larix laricina*, a type of larch native to northern N America where it is used for timber.

tamarind tropical tree *Tamarindus indica* of the family Leguminosae. An evergreen, it has pinnate leaves, and reddish-yellow flowers, followed by pods. The pulp surrounding the seeds is used medicinally.

tamarisk shrub, genus *Tamarix*, which flourishes in warm, salty, desert regions where no other vegetation is found. The *common tamarisk Tamarix gallica* has scale-like leaves and spikes of very small, pink flowers.

Tamatave /ˌtæmə'tɑːv/ former name (until 1979) for ◊Toamasina, the chief port of Madagascar.

Tambo /'tæmbəʊ/ Oliver 1917– . South African politician, in exile from 1960, president of the ◊African National Congress (ANC) from 1977. Tambo was expelled from teacher training for organizing a student protest, and joined the ANC 1944. He set up a law practice with Nelson ◊Mandela in Johannesburg in 1952. In 1956 he, with other ANC members, was arrested on charges of treason; he was released the following year. When the ANC was banned in 1960, Tambo left South Africa to set up an external wing. He became acting ANC president in 1967 and president in 1977, during Mandela's imprisonment.

tambourine musical percussion instrument of ancient origin, almost unchanged since Roman times, consisting of a shallow drum with a single skin and loosely set jingles in the rim which increase its effect.

Tambov /tæm'bɒv/ city in W central USSR; population (1985) 296,000. Industries include engineering, flour milling, and the manufacture of rubber and synthetic chemicals.

Tamerlane /'tæmələɪn/ or Timur i Leng 1336–1405. Mongol ruler of ◊Samarkand from 1369, who conquered Persia, Azerbaijan, Armenia, Georgia; defeated the ◊Golden Horde 1395; sacked Delhi 1398; invaded Syria and Asia Minor, and captured the sultan at Ankara 1402; and died invading China. He is the subject of ◊Marlowe's play *Tamburlaine the Great*.

Tamil language a Dravidian language of SE India, spoken principally in the state of Tamil Nadu (formerly, Madras state) and also in N Sri Lanka. It is written in its own distinctive script. Words in English of Tamil origin include *catamaran*, *cheroot*, *mulligatawny*, and *pariah*.

Tamil Nadu /nɑː'duː/ state of SE India
area 130,069 sq km/50,207 sq mi
capital Madras
features mainly industrial (cotton, textiles, silk, electrical machinery, tractors, rubber, sugar refining)
population (1981) 48,408,077
language Tamil
history until 1968 Tamil Nadu was called Madras. It comprises part of the former British Madras presidency (later province) formed from areas taken from France and ◊Tipu Sahib in the 18th century, which became a state of the Republic of India 1950. The NE was detached to form Andhra Pradesh 1953; other areas went to Kerala and Mysore (now Karnataka) 1956, and the Laccadive Islands (now Lakshadweep) became a separate Union Territory.

Tammany Hall ◊Democratic Party organization in New York. It originated in 1789 as the Society of St Tammany, named after an American Indian chief. It was dominant from

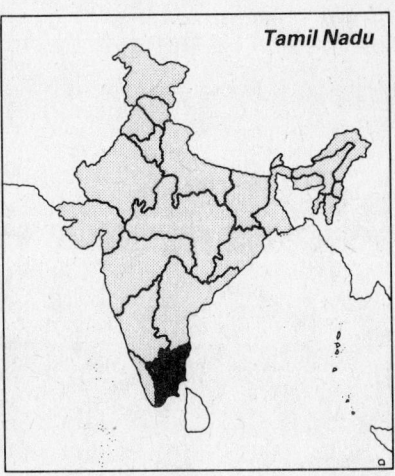

Tamil Nadu

1800 until the 1930s and gained a reputation for gangsterism; its domination was broken by Mayor ◊La Guardia.

Tammuz /'tæmuːz/ in Sumerian legend, a vegetation god, who died at midsummer and was brought back from the underworld in spring by his lover Ishtar. His cult spread over Babylonia, Syria, Phoenicia, and Palestine. In Greek mythology Tammuz appears as ◊Adonis.

Tampa /'tæmpə/ port and resort in Florida, USA; population (1980) 271,550. Industries include fruit and vegetable canning, shipbuilding, and the manufacture of fertilizers, clothing, and cigars.

Tampere /'tæmpəreɪ/ city in Finland; population (1985) 167,500. Industries include textiles, paper, footwear, and turbines.

Tampico /tæm'piːkəʊ/ port on the Rio Pánuco, 10 km/6 mi from the Gulf of Mexico, in Mexico; population (1980) 267,957. Industries include oil refining and fishing.

Tamworth /'tæmwɜːθ/ town in Staffordshire, England; population (1981) 64,315. Industries include engineering, paper, and clothing.

Tamworth /'tæmwɜːθ/ dairying centre with furniture industry in New South Wales, Australia; population (1984) 34,000.

Tana /'tɑːnə/ lake in Ethiopia, 1,800 m/6,000 ft above sea level; area 3,625 sq km/1,400 sq mi. It is the source of the Blue Nile.

Tanabata Japanese 'star festival' celebrated annually on 7 Jul, introduced from China in the 8th century and dedicated to Altair and Vega, stars in the constellation Aquila, which are united once yearly in the Milky Way. According to legend they represent two star-crossed lovers allowed by the gods to meet on that night.

tanager bird of the family Emberizidae, related to buntings. There are about 230 species in Central and South America, all with brilliant plumage.

Tanagra /'tænəgrə/ ancient Greek city in ◊Boeotia. Sparta defeated Athens here 457 BC, and it is also noted for terracotta statuettes excavated here in the 19th century.

Tananarive /tə,nænə'riːv/ former name for ◊Antananarivo, the capital of Madagascar.

Tanga /'tæŋgə/ port in NE Tanzania, on the

Empire of Tamerlane

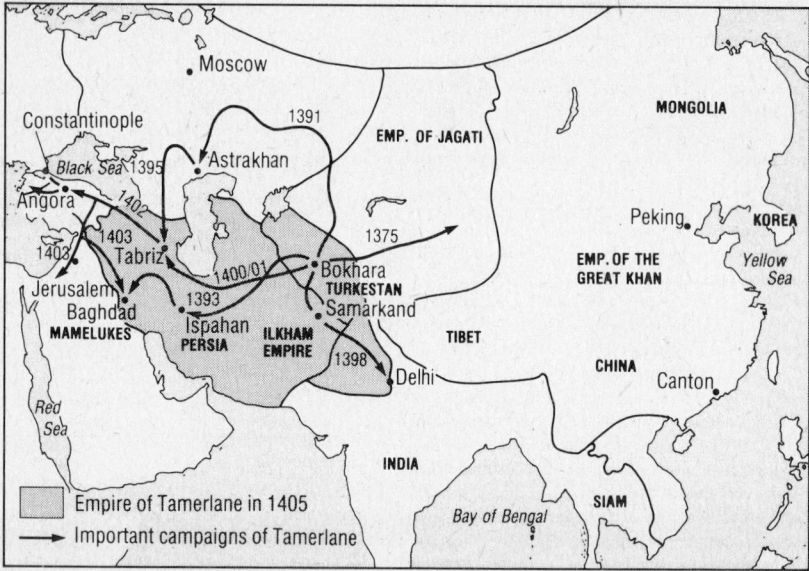

Empire of Tamerlane in 1405
→ Important campaigns of Tamerlane

Indian Ocean; population (1978) 103,409.

Tanganyika /ˌtæŋgən'jiːkə/ lake 772 m/2,534 ft above sea level in the Great Rift Valley, E Africa, between Zaïre to the W and Tanzania and Burundi to the E. It is about 645 km/400 mi long; area 31,000 sq km/12,700 sq mi, and is the deepest lake in Africa (1,435 m/4,708 ft); the mountains round its shores rise to some 2,700 m/9,000 ft. The chief ports are Bujumbura (Burundi), Kigoma (Tanzania), and Kalé mié (Zaïre).

Tanganyika /ˌtæŋgən'jiːkə/ former British colony in E Africa, which now forms the mainland of ◊Tanzania.

Tange /'tæŋgeɪ/ Kenzo 1913– . Japanese architect, whose works include the National Gymnasium, Tokyo, for the 1964 Olympics, and the city-plan of ◊Abuja, the capital of Nigeria.

tangent in trigonometry, of an angle in a right-angled ◊triangle, the ratio of the length of the side opposite the angle (not the right angle) to the length of the side adjacent to it; a way of expressing the slope of a line. In geometry, a tangent is a straight line that touches a curve and has the same slope as the curve at the point of contact. At a ◊maximum or minimum, the tangent to a curve has zero slope.

tangerine type of small orange, *Citrus reticulata.*

Tangier /tæn'dʒɪə/ city in Morocco, on the Strait of Gibraltar; population (1982) 436,227. *history* the city was a Phoenician trading centre in the 15th century BC. Captured by the Portuguese 1471, it passed to England 1662 as part of the dowry of ◊Catherine of Braganza, but was abandoned 1684 and later became a lair of ◊Barbary pirates. Under a convention effective 1925, Tangier and a small surrounding enclave became an international zone, which was administered by Spain 1940–45. In 1956 it was transferred to independent Morocco, and became a free port 1962.

tango slow dance in two-four time of partly African origin which came to Europe via South America, where it had blended with Spanish elements (such as the ◊habanera).

Tangshan /ˌtæŋ'ʃæn/ industrial city in Hebei province, China; population (1975) 1,086,000. Almost destroyed by an earthquake 1976, with 200,000 killed, it was rebuilt on a new site, coal seams being opened up under the old city.

Tanizaki /ˌtænɪ'zɑːki/ Jun-ichirō 1886–1965. Japanese novelist. Born in Tokyo, son of a family of printers, he was educated at Tokyo university. His work matured when he moved from Tokyo after the earthquake of 1923 to the Kyoto-Osaka region where ancient tradition is stronger. His works include a modern version of ◊Murasaki's *The Tale of Genji* 1939–41, *The Makioka Sisters* , published in three volumes, 1943–48, and *The Key* 1956.

tank an armoured fighting vehicle that runs on tracks. The term was originally a code name given to the first successful tracked armoured fighting vehicle used in the battle of the Somme in 1916, invented by Ernest Swinton. A tank consists of a body or hull of thick steel, on which are mounted machine guns and a larger gun. The hull contains the crew (usually consisting of a commander, driver, and two or three men), engine, radio, fuel tanks, and ammunition. The tank travels on endless bands, or 'caterpillar tracks', to enable it to cross rough ground.

tanker ship with tanks for carrying mineral oil, liquefied gas, and molasses in bulk. Currently the biggest oil tanker, and indeed the biggest ship of any kind, is the *Seawise Giant*, 458.5 m/1,504 ft long and nearly 565,000 tonnes deadweight.

Tannenberg, Battle of /'tænənbɜːg/ two battles, named after a village in N Poland:
(1) in 1410 the Poles and Lithuanians defeated the ◊Teutonic Knights, establishing Poland as a major power;

(2) in 1914, during World War I, when Tannenberg was part of East Prussia, ◊Hindenburg defeated the Russians here.

Tanner /'tænə/ Beatrice Stella. Unmarried name of actress Mrs Patrick ◊Campbell.

tannic acid a stringent substance, also called tannin. It occurs in tree bark, roots, fruits and galls. It precipitates gelatin to give an insoluble compound, used in the manufacture of leather from hides (◊tanning).

tanning treating animal skins to preserve them and make them into leather. This may be done by soaking the prepared skins in tannin, a substance obtained from the bark, wood and galls (growths) on certain trees, particularly the oak. This is called vegetable tanning. Chrome tanning, which is much quicker, is done using solutions of chromium salts instead.

Tannu-Tuva /'tænuː 'tuːvə/ former independent republic in NE Asia; see ◊Tuva.

tansy European perennial *Tanacetum vulgare*, family Compositae; the yellow flower heads grow in clusters and the leaves are used in cookery, and formerly in medicines.

tantalum a metallic element, symbol Ta, atomic number 73, atomic weight 180.95. It is a bluish-white metal, ductile and malleable, and resembling platinum when polished . Discovered in 1802 by Ekeberg, it occurs chiefly in the mineral tantalite. Tantalum can be drawn into wire with a very high melting point and great tenacity (useful for filament lamps subject to vibration). It is also used in alloys, for corrosion-resistant laboratory apparatus and chemical equipment, as a catalyst in the manufacture of synthetic rubber, in tools and instruments, and in rectifiers and capacitors. Tantalum carbide is an important abrasive.

Tantalus /'tæntələs/ in Greek mythology, a king whose crimes were punished in ◊Tartarus by food and drink he could not reach, hence the name *tantulus* for a lockable container for wine bottles, which leaves the drink still visible.

Tanzania /ˌtænzə'niːə/ country in E Africa, on the Indian Ocean, bounded to the N by Uganda and Kenya, to the S by Mozambique, Malawi, and Zambia, and to the W by Zaïre, Burundi, and Rwanda.
government the 1977 constitution made Tanzania a one-party state, the party being the Revolutionary Party of Tanzania (CCM). A president is chosen by the party to serve a maximum of two five-year terms. The president appoints two vice presidents from members of the National Assembly and if the president comes from the mainland, the first vice president must come from Zanzibar. The second vice president is termed prime minister. The president also appoints and presides over a cabinet.
The single-chamber National Assembly has up to 231 members: 101 are elected by universal suffrage for the mainland, up to 55 for the islands of Zanzibar and Pemba, five by the Zanzibar House of Representatives; 15 are allocated specifically for women, 15 represent party organizations, 15 are nominated by the president, and 25 are regional commissioners. Zanzibar has its own constitution, providing for a president elected by universal adult suffrage for

a five-year term, and its 45–55-member House of Representatives is similarly elected.

history for early history, see ◊Africa. Zanzibar was under Portuguese control during the 16th–17th centuries. In 1822 it was united with the nearby island of Pemba. It was a British protectorate 1890–1963, when it became an independent sultanate; an uprising followed and the sultan was overthrown 1964.

Tanganyika was a German colony 1884–1914, until conquered by Britain during World War I; it was a British League of Nations mandate 1920–46 and came under United Nations (UN) trusteeship 1946–62. It achieved full independence, within the Commonwealth, in 1961, with Julius ◊Nyerere as prime minister. He gave up the post some six weeks after independence to devote himself to the development of the Tanganyika African National Union (TANU) but in Dec 1962, when Tanganyika became a republic, he returned to become the nation's first president.

Tanzania was founded by the union of Tanganyika and Zanzibar in Apr 1964. Nyerere became president of the new United Republic of Tanzania and dominated the nation's politics for the next 20 years, being re-elected in 1965, 1970, 1975, and 1980. Known throughout Tanzania as Mwalimu (teacher), he established himself as a genuine Christian socialist who attempted to put into practice a philosophy that he fervently believed would secure his country's future. He committed himself in the Arusha Declaration of 1967 (the name comes from the N Tanzanian town where he made his historic statement) to building a socialist state for the millions of poor peasants through a series of village co-operatives (*Ujamas*). Nyerere became one of Africa's most respected politicians. In the final years of his presidency economic pressures, domestic and international, forced him to compromise his ideals and accept a more capitalistic society than he would have wished, but his achievements have included the best public health service on the African continent, according to UN officials, and a universal primary school system.

Relations between Tanzania and its neighbours have been variable. The East African Community (EAC) of Tanzania, Kenya, and Uganda, formed in 1967, broke up in 1977, and relations between Tanzania and the more capitalistic Kenya became uneasy. In 1979 Nyerere sent troops to support the Uganda National Liberation Front in its bid to overthrow President Idi Amin. This enhanced Nyerere's reputation but damaged his country's economy. Tanzania also supported the liberation movements in Mozambique and Rhodesia.

In 1977 TANU and the Afro-Shirazi Party of Zanzibar merged to become the Revolutionary Party of Tanzania (CCM) and this was made the only legal political organization. In Mar 1984 Nyerere announced his impending retirement and it was widely expected that he would be succeeded by the prime minister, Edward Sokoine, but he was killed in a road accident in the same year. The president of Zanzibar, Ali Hassan Mwinyi, was adopted as the sole presidential candidate by the CCM congress in

Dec 1985. Until the retirement of Julius Nyerere in 1985, the offices of state president and chair of CCM were held by the same person. Now, although Nyerere has given up the presidency, he is still party chair, and in Oct 1987 was renominated for another term.

Tanzania
UNITED REPUBLIC OF

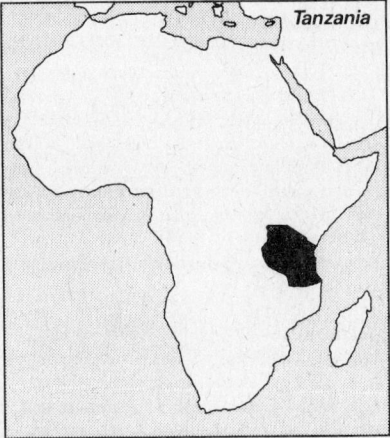
Tanzania

AREA 942,580 sq km/373,700 sq mi
CAPITAL Dodoma
TOWNS chief port Dar es Salaam
PHYSICAL a central plateau with lakes in the W and coastal plains
FEATURES comprises the islands of Zanzibar, and nearby Pemba; Mount Kilimanjaro, called 'shining mountain', because of the snow and glaciers which crown it (Kibo, an extinct volcano and its highest peak, is the highest mountain in Africa 5,895 m/19,340 ft); parts of Lakes Victoria and Tanganyika; Serengeti National Park, and the Olduvai Gorge; Ngorongoro Crater 14.5 km/9 mi across and 762 m/2,500 ft deep
HEAD OF STATE AND OF GOVERNMENT Ali Hassan Mwinyi from 1985
GOVERNMENT one-party authoritarian
EXPORTS coffee, cotton, sisal, cloves from Zanzibar, tea, tobacco
CURRENCY Tanzanian shilling (113.9 = £1 Sept 1987)
POPULATION 21,701,000 (1985); 3.2%
LANGUAGE Kiswahili, English (both official)
RELIGION Muslim 35%, Christian 35%, traditional 30%
LITERACY 78% male/70% female (1978)
GNP 4.9 bn (1983); $240 per head of population
CHRONOLOGY
1961 Tanganyika achieved full independence, within the Commonwealth, with Julius Nyerere as prime minister.
1962 Tanganyika became a republic with Nyerere as president.
1964 Tanganyika and Zanzibar became the United Republic of Tanzania with Nyerere as president.
1967 East African Community (EAC) formed. Arusha Declaration.
1977 Revolutionary Party of Tanzania (CCM) proclaimed the only legal party. EAC dissolved.
1979 Tanzanian troops sent to Uganda to help overthrow the president, Idi Amin.
1984 Nyerere announced his retirement but stayed on as CCM leader. Prime Minister Edward Sokoine killed in a road accident.
1985 Ali Hassan Mwinyi elected president.

Taoiseach /'tiːʃəx/ Gaelic name for the prime minister of the Irish Republic.

Taoism Chinese philosophical system, traditionally founded by ◊Lao-zi in the 6th century BC, though the scriptures, *Tao Te Ching* were apparently compiled in the 3rd century BC. The 'tao' or 'way' denotes the hidden Principle of the Universe, and less stress is laid on good deeds than on harmonious interaction with the environment, which automatically ensures right behaviour. The second important work is that of Zhuangzi c. 389–286 BC, *The Way of Zhuangzi*. The later magical side of Taoism is illustrated by the *I Ching* or *Book of Changes*, a book of divination.

Taormina /ˌtaːɔː'miːnə/ coastal resort in E Sicily, at the foot of Mount Etna; population (1985) 9,000. It has an ancient Greek theatre.

tap dancing derived from clog dancing, its main characteristic is the tapping of toes and heels. It was made particularly popular in ◊vaudeville and in films by dancers such as Fred ◊Astaire and Ginger Rogers.

tape recording, magnetic method of recording electric signals on a layer of iron oxide, or other magnetic material, coating a thin plastic tape. The electrical impulses are fed to the electromagnetic recording head, which magnetizes the tape in accordance with the ◊frequency and amplitude of the original signal, and may be audio (for sound recording), video (for television), or data (for computer).

For playback, the tape is passed over the same or another head to convert magnetic into electrical impulses, which are then amplified for reproduction. The higher the frequency to be recorded the faster the tape must be passed over the heads. Tapes are easily demagnetized (erased) for re-use, and come in cassette, cartridge, or reel form.

tapestry ornamental woven textile used for wall-hangings, furniture, and curtains. The tapestry design is threaded into the warp, and various shades of wool are used. Many ancient peoples made tapestries, and during the Middle Ages the art was practised in the monasteries. European tapestries of the 13th century were frequently ornamented with oriental designs brought back by the Crusaders. The great European centres of tapestry weaving were at Arras, Brussels, Aubusson, Beauvais, and Mortlake. The ◊Gobelin tapestry factory of Paris was made a royal establishment in the 17th century. In England, William ◊Morris established the Merton Abbey looms in 1877. Many fine tapestries are still made in France, for example, the tapestry designed by Graham Sutherland for Coventry cathedral, which was made at Felletin, where tapestries have been woven since the 15th century. Other designers have included ◊Raphael, ◊Rubens, and ◊Burne-Jones. The famous ◊Bayeux Tapestry is in fact an embroidery rather than a true tapestry.

tapeworm flat parasitic worm in the class Cestoda, of the phylum Platyhelminthes (flatworms) with no digestive organs. Tapeworms have a complicated life-history, and usually reach humans in imperfectly cooked meat or fish, causing anaemia and intestinal disorders.

tapioca a starch used in cooking, produced from the ◊cassava root.

tapir mammal of the ancient family Tapiridae, related to the ◊rhinoceros, and slightly more distantly to the horse. Their black skin is thick and hairy, and they have a short tail, no horns, and a short trunk. They are vegetarian, harmless, shy inhabitants of the forests of Central and South America, and also Malaysia. The Malaysian tapir *Tapirus indicus* is black with a large white patch on the back and hindquarters. The South American species are brown.

tap-root a single, robust, main ◊root which is derived from the embryonic root, or ◊radicle, and grows vertically downwards, often for some considerable depth. Tap-roots are often modified for food storage and are particularly common in biennial plants such as the carrot (*Daucus carota*), where they act as ◊perennating organs.

tar a dark brown or black viscous liquid, obtained by the destructive distillation of coal, shale, and wood. Tars consist of a mixture of hydrocarbons, acids and bases. Creosote and paraffin are produced from wood tar. See also ◊coal tar.

Tara Hill /'tɑːrə/ ancient religious and political centre in County Meath, S Ireland. The site of a palace and coronation place of many Irish kings, abandoned in the 6th century. St ◊Patrick preached here.

Taranaki /ˌtærəˈnæki/ peninsula in North Island, New Zealand, dominated by Mount ◊Egmont; volcanic soil makes it a rich dairy farming area, noted for cheese.

tarantella a peasant dance from Southern Italy, which gives its name to a piece of music composed for or in the rhythm of this dance in fast six-eight time.

Taranto /təˈræntəʊ/ naval base and port, capital of Apulia, SE Italy; population (1981) 244,000. Its steelworks is part of the new industrial complex of S Italy.
history the site of the ancient Greek *Tarentum* founded in the 8th century BC by ◊Sparta, it was captured by the Romans 272 BC.

tarantula poisonous spider *Lycosa tarantula* with a 2.5 cm/1 in body, so named from its occurrence near Taranto in Apulia, Italy. It spins no web, relying on its speed in hunting to catch its prey. In the Middle Ages its bite was thought

to cause hysterical ailments for which dancing was the cure, hence the dance named tarantella. Sometimes also used as a name for the large 'bird-eating' spiders of the tropics.

Tarbes /tɑːb/ capital of Hautes-Pyrénées *département*, SW France, a tourist centre for the Pyrenees; population (1983) 54,850. It belonged to England 1360–1406. Théophile ◊Gautier and Marshal ◊Foch were born here.

tare another name for ◊vetch.

Taree /ˌtɑːˈriː/ town in a dairying area of New South Wales, Australia; population (1981) 16,000.

tariff a tax on imports or exports from a country. Tariffs have generally been used by governments to protect home industries from low-priced foreign goods, and have been opposed by supporters of ◊free trade. For a tariff to be successful, it must not provoke retaliatory tariffs from other countries. Organizations such as the ◊European Community, ◊EFTA, and the General Agreement on Tariffs and Trade (GATT) 1948, have worked towards mutual lowering of tariffs between countries.

Tarim Basin /ˌtɑːˈriːm/ internal drainage area in Xinjiang Uygur province, NW China, between the Tyan Shan and Kunlun Mountains; area about 900,000 sq km/350,000 sq mi. It is crossed by the Tarim He river, and includes the lake of Lop Nur.

Tarkington /'tɑːkɪŋtən/ Booth 1869–1946. American novelist, born in Indiana. He is known for *Monsieur Beaucaire* 1900, and novels of the Middle West, for example *The Magnificent Ambersons* 1918.

Tarkovsky /tɑːˈkɒfski/ Andrei 1932–1986. Soviet film director, whose work is characterized by unorthodox cinematic techniques and visual beauty. His films include the science fiction epic *Solaris* 1972 (a philosophical science fiction story from a novel by Stanislaw ◊Lem), *Mirror* 1975, and *The Sacrifice* 1986.

Tarn /tɑːn/ river in SW France, rising in the Cévennes and flowing 350 km/220 mi to the Garonne.

taro, cocco or *eddo* names given to a plant *Colocasia esculenta* of the family Araceae, native to tropical Asia: the tubers are eaten.

tarpon marine game fish *Tarpon atlanticus*; it reaches 2 m/6 ft, and may weigh 135 kg/300 lb.

Tarquinius Superbus /tɑːˈkwɪniəs suːˈpɜːbəs/ legendary last king of Rome 534–510 BC. He was deposed when his son Sextus violated ◊Lucretia.

tarragon perennial bushy herb *Artemisia dracunculus* of the daisy family, growing to 1.5 m/5 ft, with narrow leaves and small green-white flowerheads arranged in groups. Tarragon contains a very aromatic oil and its leaves are used to flavour salads, pickles, and sauce tartare.

Tarragona /ˌtærəˈɡəʊnə/ port in Catalonia, Spain; population (1981) 111,689. Industries include petrochemicals, pharmaceuticals, and electrical goods. It has a cathedral and Roman remains, including an aqueduct.

Tarrasa /təˈrɑːsə/ town in Catalonia, NE Spain; population (1981) 155,360. Industries include textiles and fertilizers.

Tarshish /'tɑːʃɪʃ/ a city mentioned in the Old Testament, probably the Phoenician settlement of Tartessus in Spain.

tarsier small primate *Tarsius spectrum* intermediate on the evolutionary scale between lemurs and anthropoids. About the size of a rat, it has thick, light brown fur, very large eyes, and long feet and hands. Nocturnal and arboreal, it moves by leaping. It is found in Malaysia.

Tarsus /'tɑːsəs/ city in SE Turkey; population (1980) 121,033. Formerly the capital of the Roman province of Cilicia, and the birthplace of St ◊Paul.

tartan woollen cloth woven in specific chequered patterns individual to Scottish clans, with stripes of different widths and colours criss-crossing, and used in making plaids, kilts, and trousers. Developed in the 17th century, tartan was banned after the 1745 ◊Jacobite rebellion, and not legalized again until 1782.

Tartar a variant spelling of ◊Tatar, member of a Turkic people living mainly in the USSR.

tartaric acid colourless or white crystalline acid (COOH(CHOH)$_2$COOH). Present in fruit juices in the form of salts of potassium, calcium and magnesium, it is used in fizzy drinks, and baking powders.

Tartarus /'tɑːtərəs/ in Greek mythology, a part of ◊Hades, the underworld, where the wicked were punished.

Tartu /'tɑːtuː/ city in Estonian Republic, USSR; population (1981) 107,000. Industries include engineering and food processing. Once a stronghold of the ◊Teutonic Knights, it was taken by Russia 1558, and then held by Sweden and Poland, but has been under Russian control since 1704. It has a university founded by Gustavus Adolphus of Sweden.

Tasaday a people of the rain forests of Mindanao in the the the ◊Philippines.

Tashkent /ˌtæʃˈkent/ capital of Uzbek Republic, S central USSR; population (1985) 2,030,000. Industries include the manufacture of mining machinery, textiles, and leather goods. Founded in the 7th century, it became Russian 1865. A temporary truce between Pakistan and India over ◊Kashmir was established at the Declaration of Tashkent 1966.

Tasman /'tæzmən/ Abel Janszoon 1603–1659. Dutch navigator, first European to discover Tasmania (in 1642; he called it Van Diemen's Land in honour of the governor general of the Netherlands Indies, but it was renamed Tasmania in his honour in 1856). He also made the first European sighting of New Zealand, Tonga, and Fiji.

Tasmania /tæzˈmeɪnɪə/ island off the S coast of Australia, a state of the Commonwealth of Australia
area 68,331 sq km/26,383 sq mi
capital Hobart
towns chief port Launceston
features an island state (including small islands in the Bass Strait, and Macquarie Island); Franklin river, a wilderness area saved from a hydroelectric scheme 1983, which also has a prehistoric site; unique fauna include ◊Tasmanian devil, ◊Tasmanian 'tiger'

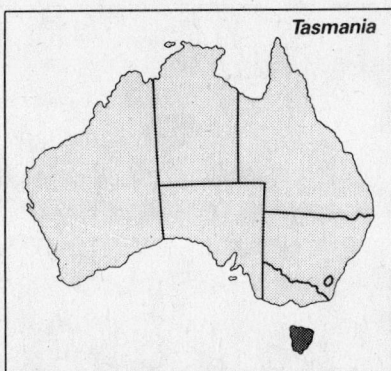
Tasmania

products wool, dairy products, apples and other fruit; timber; iron, tin, coal, copper, silver
population (1985) 442,111
history the first European to visit Tasmania was Abel ◊Tasman 1642; it joined the Australian Commonwealth as a state 1901. The last of the Tasmanian aboriginals died in 1876.

Tasmanian devil marsupial *Sarcophilus harrisii* found in Tasmania. Like a small bear in build, with a large head, it is blackish with white patches on the chest and hind parts, and is nocturnal and carnivorous.

Tasmanian devil This marsupial is peculiar to Tasmania although fossil remains have been found on the mainland of Australia.

Tasmanian tiger/wolf carnivorous marsupial *Thylacinus cynocephalus* also called thylacine; it is dog-like in appearance and can be nearly 2 m/6 ft from nose to tail tip. It was hunted to probable extinction in the 1930s, but there are still occasional but unconfirmed reports of sightings.

Tasman Sea /'tæzmən/ the part of the ◊Pacific Ocean between SE Australia and NW New Zealand.

Tass /tæs/ Soviet news agency: *T*elegrafnoye *A*gentstvo *S*ovyetskovo *S*oyuza.

Tasso /'tæsəʊ/ Torquato 1544–1595. Italian poet. At first a law student at Padua, he overcame his father's opposition to a literary career by the success of his romantic poem *Rinaldo* 1562, dedicated to Cardinal Luigi d'Este, who took him to Paris, where he met the members of the

◊Pléiade. Later he was under the patronage of the cardinal's brother, Duke Alfonso d'Este of Ferrara, for whose court theatre he wrote his pastoral play *Aminta* in 1573. His greatest work is his romantic epic of the First Crusade *La Gerusalemme Liberata/Jerusalem Delivered* 1574, followed by the *Gerusalemme Conquistata/Jerusalem Conquered*, written during the period from 1576 when he was mentally unstable.

Tatar Autonomous Soviet Socialist Republic republic of W central USSR, capital Kazan; area 68,000 sq km/26,250 sq mi; population (1984) 3,453,000. It was conquered by Russia 1552.

Tatar /'tɑːtə/ member of a Turkic, mainly Muslim people, the descendants of the followers of ◊Genghis Khan, called the Golden Horde because of their wealth. They now live mainly in the ◊Tatar and the ◊Uzbek Republics (where they were deported from the ◊Crimea in 1944) and SW Siberia, USSR.

Tate /teɪt/ Jeffrey 1943– . British conductor, born in Salisbury, Wiltshire. He qualified as a doctor before turning to a career in music, and worked with Boulez in Bayreuth 1976–80. He has conducted opera in Paris, in Geneva, and at the Metropolitan, New York. He was appointed principal conductor of the English Chamber Orchestra in 1985, and principal conductor of the Royal Opera House, Covent Garden, in 1986.

Tate British conductor Jeffrey Tate gave up a career in medicine for music and now has an international reputation and a post as conductor at the Royal Opera House, London.

Tate /teɪt/ Nahum 1652–1715. Irish poet. Born in Dublin, he wrote an adaptation of Shakespeare's *King Lear*, with a happy ending, a version of the psalms, and hymns; his best-known poem is 'While shepherds watched'. He became Poet Laureate in 1692.

Tate /teɪt/ Phyllis (Margaret) 1911–1987. British composer. Her principal works include

Concerto for Saxophone and Strings 1944, the opera *The Lodger* 1960, based on the story of Jack the Ripper, and *Serenade to Christmas* for soprano, chorus and orchestra 1972.

Tate Gallery art gallery (British paintings from late 16th century, and international from 1810) at Millbank, London. Endowed by sugar-merchant Henry Tate (1819–99), it was opened 1897; enlarged by Sir J Duveen and his son Lord Duveen of Millbank; later extensions include the Clore Gallery for Turner paintings, opened in 1987. The Liverpool branch of the Tate Gallery is scheduled to open in 1988.

Tati /tæˈtiː/ Jacques, stage-name of Jacques Tatischeff 1908–1982. French actor-film director. A brilliant comic mime, he is remembered for his portrayal of Monsieur Hulot (for example in *Les Vacances de M Hulot/Monsieur Hulot's Holiday* 1953), a character embodying polite opposition to modern mechanization.

Tatra Mountains /'tɑːtrə/ range in central Europe, extending for about 65 km/40 mi along the Polish-Czechoslovakian border; the highest part of the central ◊Carpathians.

Tattersall's /'tætəsɔːlz/ auctioneers of racehorses established at Knightsbridge Green, SW London, since 1864. It is named after Richard Tattersall (1724–95), who founded Tattersall's at Hyde Park Corner in 1766.

tatting lace-work in cotton, made from medieval times by knotting, with the aid of a small shuttle.

Tatum /'teɪtəm/ Art(hur) 1910–1956. American jazz pianist, who first achieved fame in the 1930s. He improvised with guitarist Tiny Grimes in a trio from 1943, and maintained his superb artistry in solo performances.

Tatum /'teɪtəm/ Edward Lawrie 1909–1975. American microbiologist. He shared a Nobel prize in 1958 for his work on biochemical genetics with George Wells ◊Beadle.

Taube /'tɔːbi/ Henry 1915– . US chemist, who established the basis of modern inorganic chemistry by his study of the loss or gain of electrons by atoms during chemical reactions. He was awarded a Nobel prize in 1983.

Taunton /'tɔːntən/ market town and administrative headquarters of Somerset, England; population (1985) 55,600. The Elizabethan hall survives, in which Judge ◊Jeffreys held the Bloody Assizes 1685 after the Duke of Monmouth's rebellion.

Taunus Mountains /'taʊnəs/ mountain range in ◊Hessen, West Germany.

Taupo /'taʊpəʊ/ largest lake in New Zealand, in a volcanic area of hot springs; area 616 sq km/238 sq mi. It is the source of the Waikato river.

Tauranga /taʊˈræŋə/ port in North Island, New Zealand; population (1981) 36,300. It exports citrus fruit, dairy produce, and timber.

Taurus /'tɔːrəs/ constellation of the ◊zodiac representing a bull. The Sun passes through Taurus from mid-May to late June; its brightest star is ◊Aldebaran, representing the bull's red eye. Taurus contains the ◊Hyades and ◊Pleiades star clusters, and the ◊Crab Nebula.

Taurus Mountains /'tɔːrəs/ mountain range in S ◊Turkey, forming the S edge of the Anatolian plateau, and rising to over 3,650 m/12,000 ft.

Tavener /'tævənə/ John (Kenneth) 1944– . British composer, whose works are individual and sometimes abrasive in style. They include the dramatic cantata *The Whale* 1968; the opera *Thérèse* 1979; and much music linked with the Russian Orthodox church.

Taverner /'tævənə/ John 1495–1545. English organist and composer. He was imprisoned in 1528 for heresy, and, as an agent of Thomas ◊Cromwell, assisted in the dissolution of the monasteries. He wrote masses and motets in polyphonic style, showing great contrapuntal skill, but as a Protestant renounced his art.

Tavistock /'tævɪstɒk/ market town in Devon, England; population (1981) 9,271.

taxation the raising of money from individuals and organizations by the state in order to pay for the goods and services it provides. Taxation can be *direct* (a deduction from income), or *indirect* (added to the purchase price of goods or services, that is, a tax on consumption). ◊*Income tax* is the most common form of direct taxation. The proportions of direct and indirect taxation in the total tax revenue vary widely from country to country; the USA, for example, has a high proportion of indirect taxation, while the UK has a higher proportion of direct taxation. By varying the effect of a tax on the richer and poorer members of society, a government can attempt to redistribute wealth from the richer to the poorer, both by taxing the rich more severely, and by returning some of the collected wealth in the form of *benefits*. A *progressive* tax is one which falls proportionally more on the rich; most income taxes, for example, have higher rates for those with higher incomes. A *regressive* tax, on the other hand, affects the poor proportionally more than the rich. In Britain, income tax is collected by the Inland Revenue, as are the other direct taxes, namely *corporation tax* on company profits; *capital gains tax*, introduced to prevent the use of capital as untaxed income in 1961; and *inheritance tax* (which replaced capital transfer tax).

Value-added tax (VAT) is the standard form of indirect taxation in the ◊EEC; it is based on the French TVA (*Taxe sur la Valeur Ajoutée*), and was introduced in the UK 1973. It is paid on the value added to any goods or services at each particular stage of the process of production or distribution, and although collected from traders at each stage, it is in effect a tax on consumers' expenditure. In some states of the USA a similar result is achieved by a *sales tax* deducted by the retailer at the point of sale. In the UK, ◊*rates* have been the form of taxation which pays for local government (in other countries, including the USA, the equivalents are local property taxes or a local income tax). However, rates are in the process of being replaced by a poll tax, or community charge, levied on each person of voting age. In Britain taxes are also levied on tobacco, wine, beer, and petrol (see ◊Customs and Excise).

The UK tax system has been criticized in many respects; alternatives include an *expenditure tax*, which would be imposed only on income spent, and the *tax-credit system* under which all are guaranteed an income bolstered as necessary by social security benefits, taxation beginning only above that level, hence eliminating the 'poverty trap', by which the unemployed receiving state benefits may have a net loss in income if they take employment at a low wage.

taxis or *tactic movement* the movement of a single cell, such as a bacterium, protozoan, single-celled alga or gamete, in response to an external stimulus; the plural is 'taxes'. A movement directed towards the stimulus is described as positive taxis, and away from it as negative taxis. The alga *Chlamydomonas*, for example, demonstrates positive phototaxis by swimming towards a light source to increase the rate of photosynthesis. Chemotaxis is a response to a chemical stimulus, as seen in many bacteria that move towards higher concentrations of nutrients.

Taxodium tree genus of the family Taxodiaceae. The American deciduous swamp cypress, *Taxodium distichum*, grows in or near water, and is a timber tree.

taxonomy another name for the ◊classification of living organisms.

Taylor /'teɪlə/ A(lan) J(ohn) P(ercivale) 1906– . British historian and television lecturer. International history lecturer at Oxford 1953–63, and author of *From Napoleon to Stalin* and *The Origins of World War II* 1961.

Taylor /'teɪlə/ Elizabeth 1932– . English-born American actress, whose films include *A Place in The Sun* 1950, *Butterfield 8* 1960 (Academy award), *Cleopatra* 1963, and *Who's Afraid of Virginia Woolf?* 1966. Her eight husbands have included the actors Michael Wilding and Richard ◊Burton (twice).

Taylor /'teɪlə/ Frederick Winslow 1856–1915. American engineer and management consultant, the founder of scientific management, which aims at improving working efficiency and industrial discipline. His ideas, published in *Principles of Scientific Management* 1911, were based on the breakdown of work to the simplest tasks, the separation of planning from execution of tasks, and the introduction of time and motion studies. His methods were most clearly expressed in 'assembly line' factories, but his ideas have been severely criticized for degrading and alienating workers and producing managerial dictatorship.

Tay-Sachs disease rare disorder of the body's ◊lipid metabolism caused by a defective gene, which occurs mainly in Jews of Eastern European descent, and often causes death of affected children by the age of five. They become blind, deaf and mentally retarded and lack muscular control. There is no treatment, but the disease can be detected in a foetus.

Tayside /'teɪsaɪd/ region of Scotland
area 7,511 sq km/2,899 sq mi
towns administrative headquarters Dundee; Perth, Arbroath, Forfar

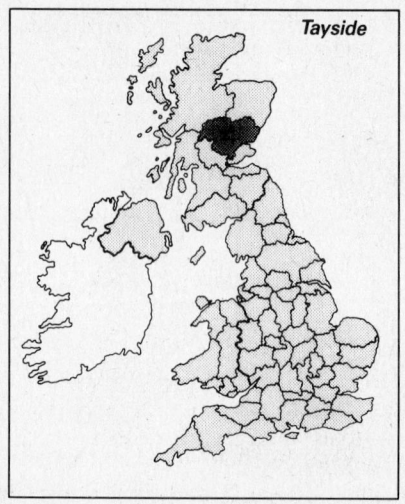
Tayside

features river Tay; ◊Grampian Mountains; Lochs Tay and Rannoch; Ochil and Sidlaw Hills; vales of the N and S Esk
products beef and dairy products; soft fruit from the fertile Carse of Gowrie
population (1981) 391,530
famous people James Barrie.

Tbilisi /dbɪ'liːsi/ capital (formerly *Tiflis*) of the Georgian Republic, USSR; population (1985) 1,158,000. Industries include textiles, machinery, ceramics, and tobacco. Dating from the 5th century AD, it is a centre of Georgian culture, with fine medieval churches and the Georgian Academy of Sciences.

Tchaikovsky /tʃaɪ'kɒfski/ Pyotr Ilyich 1840–1893. Russian composer. Born in Kamsko-Votinsk, he became a professor of harmony at Moscow in 1865, and later met ◊Balakirev, becoming involved with the nationalist movement in music. His marriage in 1877 was a complete failure (he was a homosexual), and was followed by a nervous breakdown. He was the first Russian composer to establish a reputation with Western audiences. His strong sense of melody, personal expression and brilliant orchestration are clear throughout his large output, which includes six symphonies; three piano concertos and a violin concerto; operas (for example *Eugene Onegin* 1879 and *The Queen of Spades* 1890); ballets (*Swan Lake* 1877, *The Sleeping Beauty* 1890, and *The Nutcracker* 1892); and orchestral fantasies (*Romeo and Juliet* 1870, *Francesca da Rimini* 1877, and *Hamlet 1888*); and chamber and vocal music.

tea plant *Camellia sinensis* from the leaves of which the beverage of the same name is made. Left to itself it reaches 12 m/40 ft, but is restricted in cultivation to bushes 1.5 m/4 ft high from which at five years the young shoots and leaves are picked. After 24 hrs spread on shelves in the 'withering' lofts, the leaves are broken up by rolling machines, which release the essential oils, and allowed to ferment. This process is then halted by passing the leaves through ovens where moisture is removed and the blackish-brown 'black' tea emerges ready for sifting into the

Taylor English-born actress Elizabeth Taylor with co-star Montgomery Clift in a scene from *Raintree County* 1957.

various grades. 'Green' tea is steamed and quickly dried before fermentation, remaining partly green in colour. Known in China as early as 2737 BC, tea was first brought to Europe in 1610 AD, but was not in use in England until 1657. It rapidly became a fashionable drink but remained expensive because cargoes had to be brought from China in the specially fast tea clippers. In 1823, however, tea was found growing wild in northern India, and some ten years later plantations were established in Assam and then in Sri Lanka: other modern producers include Africa, South America, Russia, Indonesia and Iran. Methods of consumption vary: in Japan special tea houses and an elaborate tea ceremony have evolved; in England 'afternoon' tea had its own ritual; and in Tibet hard slabs of compressed tea are used as money before being finally brewed.

teacher training in the UK teachers are trained by means of the four-year Bachelor of Education degree, which integrates professional training and the study of academic subjects, or by means of the one year post graduate Certificate of Education which offers one year of professional training to follow a normal degree course in a specialist subject.

teak tropical Asian timber tree *Tectona grandis*, family Verbenaceae, used in furniture and shipbuilding.

teal small duck *Anas crecca*. The drake has a reddish-brown head with green and buff

Tchaikovsky Although his works include opera, chamber and orchestral music, Tchaikovsky is probably best-loved for his ballet scores, including *Swan Lake* 1877 and *The Nutcracker* 1892.

markings on either side, and a black and white line on the wing. The female is buff and brown.

Teapot Dome Scandal US scandal which revealed the corruption of the ◊Harding administration. It centred on the leasing of naval oil reserves in 1921 at Teapot Dome, Wyoming, without competitive bidding as a result of bribing the Secretary of the Interior Albert B Fall. Fall was tried and imprisoned in 1929.

tear gas lacrimatory and irritant vapour used as a riot control agent. The gas is delivered in pressurized, liquid-filled canisters or grenades, thrown by hand or launched from a specially adapted rifle. Gases such as Mace cause violent coughing and blinding tears, which pass when the victim breathes fresh air, and there are no lasting effects. Blister gases (such as mustard gas) and nerve gases are much more harmful and may cause permanent injury or death.

teasel erect, prickly biennial Eurasian plant *Dipsacus fullonum*, family Dipsacaceae; the dry seed heads were once used industrially to 'tease' (raise the nap of) cloth.

Tebaldi /te'bældi/ Renata 1922– . Italian dramatic soprano, remarkable for the controlled purity of her voice and renowned for her roles in ◊Puccini operas.

Tebbit /'tebɪt/ Norman 1931– . British Conservative politician. He was minister for employment 1981–83, for trade and industry 1983–85, chancellor of the Duchy of Lancaster 1985–87, and chair of the party 1985–87.

technetium the first artificially made element (Greek *technetos*, artificial), symbol Tc, atomic number 43. Originally produced by Perrier and Segré in 1937 by bombarding molybdenum with deuterons or neutrons, it was later isolated in large amounts from the fission products of uranium. It is used as a hardener in steel alloys.

Technicolor trade name for a film colour process invented by Daniel F Comstock and Herbert T Kalmus 1922. Originally, Technicolor was a two-colour process in which superimposed red and green images were thrown on to the screen by a special projector. This proved expensive and imperfect and it was not until the improved three-colour process (producing separate negatives of blue, green and red images) was introduced in 1932 that the system came to be widely adopted, culminating in its use in *Gone with the Wind* 1939. Despite increasing competition, Technicolor has remained an important factor in colour cinematography.

technocracy term for a society controlled by technical experts such as scientists and engineers. The term was invented by Californian engineer W H Smyth in 1919 to describe his proposed 'rule by technicians', and was popularized by James Burham (1903–) in *Managerial Revolution* 1941.

technology the practical application of the arts and sciences in industry and commerce. Britain's industrial revolution preceded that of Europe by half a century, and its prosperity stimulated countries to encourage technological education. France established the École Polytechnique, the first technological university, in 1794, and Germany founded the remarkable series of Technische Hochschulen with one in Berlin in 1799. In Britain education in technology was catered for by the mechanics institutes, notably the University of Manchester Institute of Science and Technology (founded 1824, created university 1966) which, together with the Imperial College of Science and Technology (established 1907), still form the focus of technological work.

The USA was quick to grasp the importance of technology, most universities having schools of engineering and technology, and also established a number of institutes on European lines of which the most famous are the Massachusetts 1861 and the Rensselaer Polytechnic Institute (founded at Troy, New York, 1824). Intensive training of technologists, exceeding the pace of both western Europe and the USA, has been concentrated upon by the Soviet Union and China.

tectonics in geology, the study of the movements of rocks. On a small scale tectonics involves the formation of ◊folds and ◊faults, but on a large scale ◊plate tectonics deals with the movement of the Earth's entire surface.

Tecumseh /tɪˈkʌmsə/ 1768–1813. North American Indian chief of the Shawnee. He attempted to unite the Indian peoples against white settlers, and was killed in battle. The belief that he was backed by the British from Canada was a factor in the outbreak of the War of 1812 (see ◊United States of America: history).

Tedder /ˈtedə/ Arthur William, 1st Baron Tedder 1890–1967. Marshal of the Royal Air Force. He was Air Officer Commanding RAF Far East 1936–38 and Middle East 1941–43. As Deputy Supreme Commander under Eisenhower 1943–45, he was largely responsible for the initial success of the 1944 Normandy landings.

Teddington /ˈtedɪŋtən/ part of Twickenham, in the Greater London borough of ◊Richmond upon Thames; site of the National Physical Laboratory, established 1900.

Tees /tiːz/ river flowing from the Pennines in Cumbria, England, to the North Sea via Tees Bay in ◊Cleveland; length 130 km/80 mi.

Teeside /ˈtiːzsaɪd/ industrial area at the mouth of the river Tees, Cleveland, England. The traditional industries of shipbuilding and heavy engineering have made way for high technology, capital intensive steelmaking (Redcar has Europe's largest steel complex, 1979); Europe's biggest chemical site (ICI); an oil fuel terminal at Seal Sands; and the main North Sea natural gas terminal. ◊Middlesbrough is a major port.

Teflon a trade name for the plastic ◊PTFE.

Tegucigalpa /teɪˌɡuːsɪˈɡælpə/ capital of Honduras, population (1983) 532,600. It is a commercial city, with textile and food processing industries.

Tehran /ˌteəˈrɑːn/ city in Iran; population (1976) 4,496,000. Industries include textiles, chemicals, engineering, and tobacco. It became the capital 1788, and is the site of the Gulistan Palace (the former royal residence), and several universities.

Tehran Conference conference held in Tehran in 1943; the first meeting of World War II allies Stalin, Roosevelt, and Churchill.

Teignmouth /ˈtɪnməθ/ port and resort in S Devon, England; population (1985) 13,500.

Teilhard de Chardin /teɪˈɑː də ʃɑːˈdæn/ Pierre 1881–1955. French Jesuit mystic. Born in the Puy-de-Dôme, he entered the Society of Jesus in 1899, was ordained in 1911, and during World War I was a stretcher bearer, taking his final vows in 1918. Publication of his *Le Phénomène humain/The Phenomenon of Man* 1955 was delayed until after his death by the embargo of his superiors. He saw humanity as eventually in charge of its own evolution, and developed the concept of the *noosphere*, the unconscious union of thought among human beings.

Tejo /ˈtʌʒuː/ Portuguese name for the river ◊Tagus.

Te Kanawa /teɪˈkɑːnəwə/ Kiri 1944– . New Zealand opera singer, born in Gisborne. Her reputation was established by her performance as the Countess in Mozart's *The Marriage of Figaro* at Covent Garden in 1971. Dame of the British Empire 1982.

tektite small, rounded glassy stone (from Greek *tektos* 'molten'), found in certain regions of the Earth, especially Australasia. They are thought to be the scattered drops of molten rock thrown out by the impact of a large ◊meteorite or ◊comet, or possibly launched by a volcanic explosion on the Moon.

Tel Aviv-Jaffa /ˌtel əˈviːv ˈdʒæfə/ city in Israel, with its port at Ashdod; population (1979) 336,300. Industries include textiles, chemicals, sugar, printing, and publishing.

history Tel Aviv was founded 1919 as a Jewish residential area in the Arab town of Jaffa, with which it was combined 1949; their ports were superseded by Ashdod 1965.

telecommunications communications over a distance. For centuries bonfires have been used as a method of conveying a simple message, such as 'The Armada is coming' (1588). The first mechanical telecommunications systems were the ◊semaphore and heliograph (which used flashes of sunlight). But the forerunner of the modern telecommunications age was the electric telegraph (see ◊telegraphy). The earliest practicable instrument was invented by Cooke and ◊Wheatstone in Britain in 1837, and used by railway companies, the first public line being laid between Paddington and Slough in 1843. In the US ◊Morse invented a signalling code, ◊Morse code, which is still used, and a recording telegraph, first used commercially between England and France in 1851. As a result of ◊Hertz's discoveries using electromagnetic waves, ◊Marconi pioneered a 'wireless' telegraph, ancestor of the ◊radio. He established wireless communication between England and France 1899 and across the Atlantic 1901. The modern telegraph uses teleprinters to send coded messages along telecommunications lines. They are keyboard-operated machines which transmit a five-unit Baudot code. The receiving teleprinter automatically prints the received message.

Long-distance voice communication was pioneered in 1876 by Alexander Graham Bell, when he invented the ◊telephone as a result of Faraday's discovery of electromagnetism. Today it is possible to communicate with most countries by telephone cable, or by satellite or microwave link, with several hundred simultaneous conversations being carried. However, the chief method of relaying long-distance calls on land is microwave radio transmission. The drawback to this is that the transmissions follow a straight line from tower to tower, so that over the sea the system becomes impracticable.

A solution was put forward in 1945 by Arthur C ◊Clarke in *Wireless World*, when he proposed a system of communications satellites in an orbit 35,900 km/27,300 mi above the Equator, where they would circle the Earth in exactly 24 hours, and thus appear fixed in the sky. Such a system is now in operation internationally, by ◊Intelsat. The satellites are called ◊geostationary satellites, or synchronous satellites (syncoms). The first to be successfully launched, by *Delta* rocket from Cape Canaveral, was *Syncom 2* in Jul 1963. Numbers of such satellites are now in use, concentrated over heavy traffic areas such as the Atlantic, Indian and Pacific Oceans. Telegraphy, telephony and television transmissions are carried simultaneously by high-frequency radio waves. They are beamed to the satellites from large dish antennae or Earth stations, which connect with international networks. In Britain ◊Goonhilly and Madley are the main Earth stations.

In 1980 the Post Office opened its first System X (all electronic, digital) telephone exchange in London, a method already adopted in the USA. Other recent advances include the use of ◊fibre-optic cables consisting of fine glass fibres for telephone lines instead of the usual copper cables. The telecommunications signals are transmitted along the fibres on pulses of ◊laser light.

Procedures, technical standards, and frequencies in telecommunications are controlled by the International Telecommunications Union (ITU). See also ◊facsimile transmission.

Telecom Tower Britain's tallest building, in London, 189 m/620 ft high. Completed in 1966, and formerly known as the Post Office Tower, it is a microwave relay tower capable of handling up to 150,000 simultaneous telephone conversations and over 40 television channels.

telegraphy the transmission of coded messages along wires by means of electrical signals. The first modern form of telecommunication, it now uses printers for the transmission and receipt of messages. Telex is an international telegraphy network.

Telemann /ˈteɪləmæn/ Georg Philipp 1681–1767. German Baroque composer, organist and conductor at the Johanneum, Hamburg, from 1721. He produced operas, over 600 church cantatas, and other vocal and instrumental works.

telemetry measurement at a distance, particularly the systems by which information is obtained and sent back by instruments on board a spacecraft. See ◊remote sensing.

telepathy 'the communication of impressions of any kind from one mind to another, independently of the recognized channels of sense', as defined by F W H Myers who coined the term. The card-guessing experiments of Professor ◊J B Rhine of Duke university, N Carolina, in the 1930s, considered to have proved

telecommunications

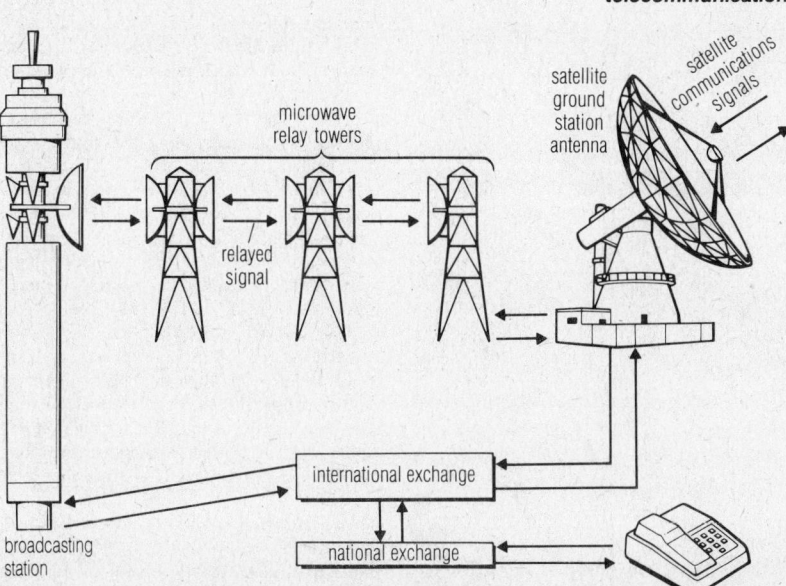

microwave relay towers

relayed signal

satellite ground station antenna

satellite communications signals

international exchange

national exchange

broadcasting station

TELECOMMUNICATIONS CHRONOLOGY

1794	Claude Chappe in France built a long-distance signalling system using semaphore.
1839	Charles Wheatstone and William Cooke devised an electric telegraph in England.
1843	Morse transmitted the first message along a telegraph line in the USA.
1858	The first transatlantic telegraph cable was laid.
1876	American Alexander Graham Bell invented the telephone.
1877	Edison invented the carbon transmitter for the telephone.
1894	Marconi pioneered wireless telegraphy in Italy, later moving to England.
1900	Fessenden in the USA first broadcast voice by radio.
1901	Marconi transmitted the first radio signals across the Atlantic.
1904	Fleming invented the thermionic valve.
1907	American Charles Krumm introduced the forerunner of the teleprinter.
1920	Stations in Detroit and Pittsburgh began regular radio broadcasts.
1922	The BBC began its first radio transmissions, for the London station 2LO.
1932	The Post Office introduced the Telex in Britain.
1956	The first transatlantic telephone cable was laid.
1962	Telstar pioneers transatlantic satellite communications, transmitting live TV pictures.
1966	Charles Kao advanced the idea of using optical fibres for telecommunications.
1969	Live TV pictures were sent from astronauts on the moon back to Earth.
1975	The Post Office announced Prestel, the world's first viewdata system.
1986	Voyager 2 transmitted images of Uranus some 3,000 million km/2,000 million mi, the signals taking 2 hours 45 minutes to reach Earth.

---

the phenomenon, were under suspicion in the 1980s.

telephone an instrument for communicating by voice over long distances, invented by Alexander Graham ◊Bell in 1876. The standard instrument has a handset, which houses the transmitter (mouthpiece) and receiver (earpiece) resting on a base, which has a dial or push-button mechanism for dialling a telephone number. The transmitter consists of a carbon microphone. It has a diaphragm that vibrates when a person speaks into it. The diaphragm vibrations compress grains of carbon to a greater or lesser extent, altering their resistance to an electric current passing through them. This sets up variable electrical signals, which travel along the telephone lines to the receiver of the person being called. There they cause the magnetism of an electromagnet to vary. This causes a diaphragm above the electromagnet to vibrate and give out sound waves, which mirror those that entered the mouthpiece originally.

A cordless telephone uses a unit, which is connected to a base unit, not by wires but by radio. It can be used at distances up to about 100 m/330 ft from the base unit. See also ◊telecommunications.

   telephone tapping method of listening in on a telephone conversation; in the UK a criminal offence if done without a warrant or the consent of the person concerned. Warrants are issued by the foreign secretary and home secretary (and those for Northern Ireland and Scotland), chiefly for the collection of ◊intelligence, defence of national security, and detection of crime.

   telephoto lens a photographic lens of longer focal length than normal, taking a very narrow view, and giving a large image through a combination of telescopic and ordinary photographic lenses.

   teleprinter or teletypewriter; a transmitting and receiving device used in ◊telecommunications to handle coded messages. Teleprinters are like automatic typewriters. They convert typed words into electrical signals (using a 5-unit baudot code) at the transmitting end, and signals into typed words at the receiving end.

   telescope a device for collecting and focusing light and other forms of ◊electromagnetic radiation (see also ◊radio telescope). A telescope makes objects seem nearer, and it shows objects too faint to be seen by the eye alone. A telescope with a large *aperture*, or opening, can distinguish finer detail and fainter objects than one with a small aperture.

There are two main types of optical telescope: the *refracting telescope*, which uses lenses, and the *reflecting telescope*, which uses mirrors. A third type, the *catadioptic telescope*, has a combination of lenses and mirrors. In a refractor, light is collected by a ◊lens called the *object glass* or *objective* which focuses light down a tube, forming an image magnified by an *eyepiece*. Invention of the refractor is attributed to a Dutch optician, Hans ◊Lippershey, in 1608. The largest refracting telescope in the world, at ◊Yerkes Observatory, Wisconsin, USA has an aperture of 102 cm/40 in.

In a reflector, light is collected and focused by a concave ◊mirror. The first reflector was built in 1668 by Isaac ◊Newton. Large mirrors are cheaper to make and easier to mount than large lenses, so all the largest telescopes are reflectors. The largest reflector, with a 6 m/236 in mirror, is at Zelenchukskaya, USSR. Telescopes with larger apertures are planned, but they will be composed of numerous smaller mirrors. The first such *multiple-mirror telescope* was installed on Mount Hopkins, Arizona, in 1979. It consists of six mirrors of 1.8 m/72 in aperture, which perform like a single 4.5 m/176 in mirror. *Schmidt telescopes* are used for taking wide-field

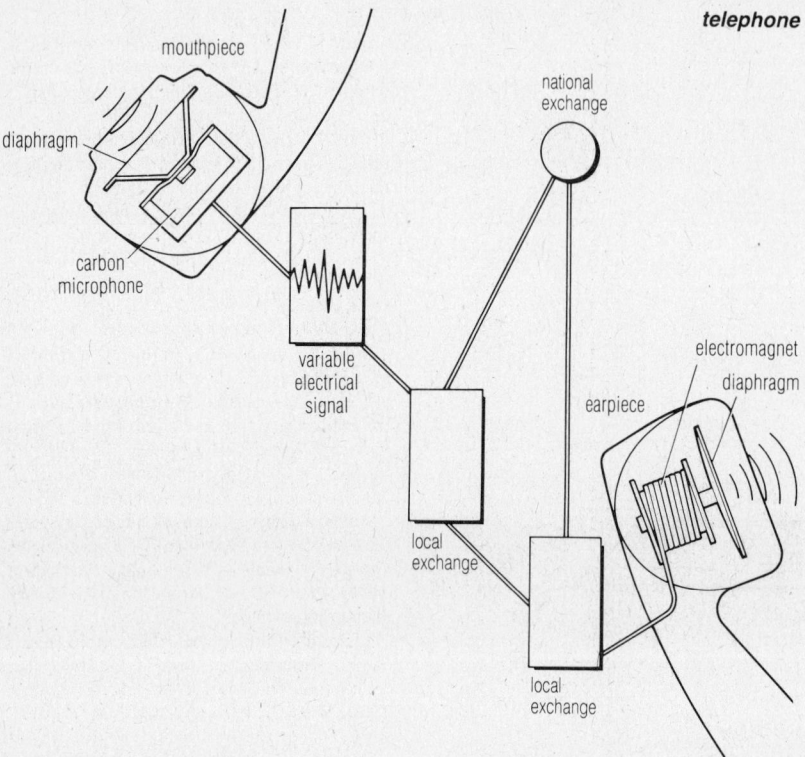

telephone

mouthpiece

diaphragm

carbon microphone

variable electrical signal

national exchange

earpiece

electromagnet

diaphragm

local exchange

local exchange

by-line by a beam of electrons from an electron gun, resulting in variable electrical signals that represent the visual picture. These vision signals are combined with a radio ◊carrier wave and broadcast. The TV aerial picks up the wave and feeds it to the receiver (TV set). This separates out the vision signals, which pass to the picture tube, which is a cathode-ray tube. The broad end of the tube, upon which the scene is to appear, has its inside surface coated with a fluorescent material. The vision signals control the strength of a beam of electrons from an ◊electron gun, aimed at the screen and making it glow more or less brightly. At the same time the beam is made to scan across the screen line-by-line, mirroring the action of the gun in the TV camera. The result is a recreation, spot-by-spot, line-by-line, of the pattern of light that entered the camera. Twenty-five pictures (30 in the US) are built up each second with interlaced scanning, with a total of 625 lines (in Europe, but 525 lines in the US and Japan).

colour television Baird gave a demonstration of colour television in London in 1928, but it was not until Dec 1953 that the first successful system was adopted for broadcasting, in the USA. This is called the NTSC system, since it was developed by the National Television System Committee, and variations of it have been developed in Europe, for example SECAM (sequential and memory) system in France and the PAL (phase alternation by line) in West Germany. The three differ only in the way colour signals are prepared for transmission. Agreement on a universal European system failing in 1964, the UK in 1967 adopted PAL (as did West Germany, the Netherlands and Switzerland) while France and the USSR adopted SECAM.

The method of colour reproduction in television is related to that used in colour photography and printing. It uses the principle that any colours can be made by mixing the primary colours red, green, and blue in appropriate proportions. In colour television the receiver reproduces only three basic colours: red, green and blue. The effect of yellow, for example, is reproduced by combining equal amounts of red and green light, while white is formed by a mixture of all three basic colours. It is thus possible to specify the colour which is required by sending signals which indicate the amounts of red, green and blue light which are to be generated at the receiver.

To transmit each of these three signals in the same way as the single brightness signal in black and white television would need three times the normal bandwidth, and reduce the number of possible stations and programmes to one-third of that possible with monochrome television. The three signals are therefore coded into one complex signal which is transmitted as a more or less normal black and white signal, and which produces a satisfactory – or compatible – picture on black and white receivers. A fraction of each primary red, green and blue signal is added together to produce the normal brightness, or luminance signal. The minimum of extra colouring information is then sent by a special subcarrier signal which is superimposed on the brightness signal. This extra colouring

photographs of the sky. They have a main mirror, plus a thin lens at the front of the tube to increase the field of view.

Large telescopes can now be placed in ◊orbit, above the distorting effects of the Earth's atmosphere. Telescopes in space have been used to study ◊infrared, ◊ultraviolet and X-rays that do not penetrate the atmosphere, but which carry much information about the births, lives and deaths of ◊stars and ◊galaxies.

teletext broadcast system of displaying information on television screens (entertainment, sport, finance) which is constantly updated. It is a form of ◊videotext, pioneered in Britain by the British Broadcasting Corporation with ◊Ceefax and by Independent Television with ◊Oracle.

television the reproduction of visual images at a distance by ◊radio waves.

history in 1873 it was realized that since the electrical properties of the non-metallic element selenium vary according to the amount of light to which it is exposed, light could be converted into electrical impulses, making it possible to transmit such impulses over a distance and then re-convert them into light. The chief difficulty was seen to be the 'splitting of the picture' so that the infinite variety of light and shade values might be transmitted and reproduced.

In 1908 Campbell-Swinton pointed out that the transmission and reception would be better done by the use of ◊cathode-ray tubes. Mechanical devices were used at the first practical demonstration of actual television, given by J L Baird in London on 27 Jan 1926, and cathode-

telescope

refractory telescope

objective lens

eyepiece

secondary mirror

reflecting telescope (Newtonian design)

eyepiece

main mirror

Schmidt telescope

focus

corrector lens

main mirror

ray tubes were used experimentally by the BBC from 1934. The world's first public television service was started from the BBC station at the Alexandra Palace, in N London, on 2 Nov 1936.

technology for transmission, a television camera converts the pattern of light it takes in into a pattern of electrical charges. This is scanned line-

television transmitter (essentials)   *television*

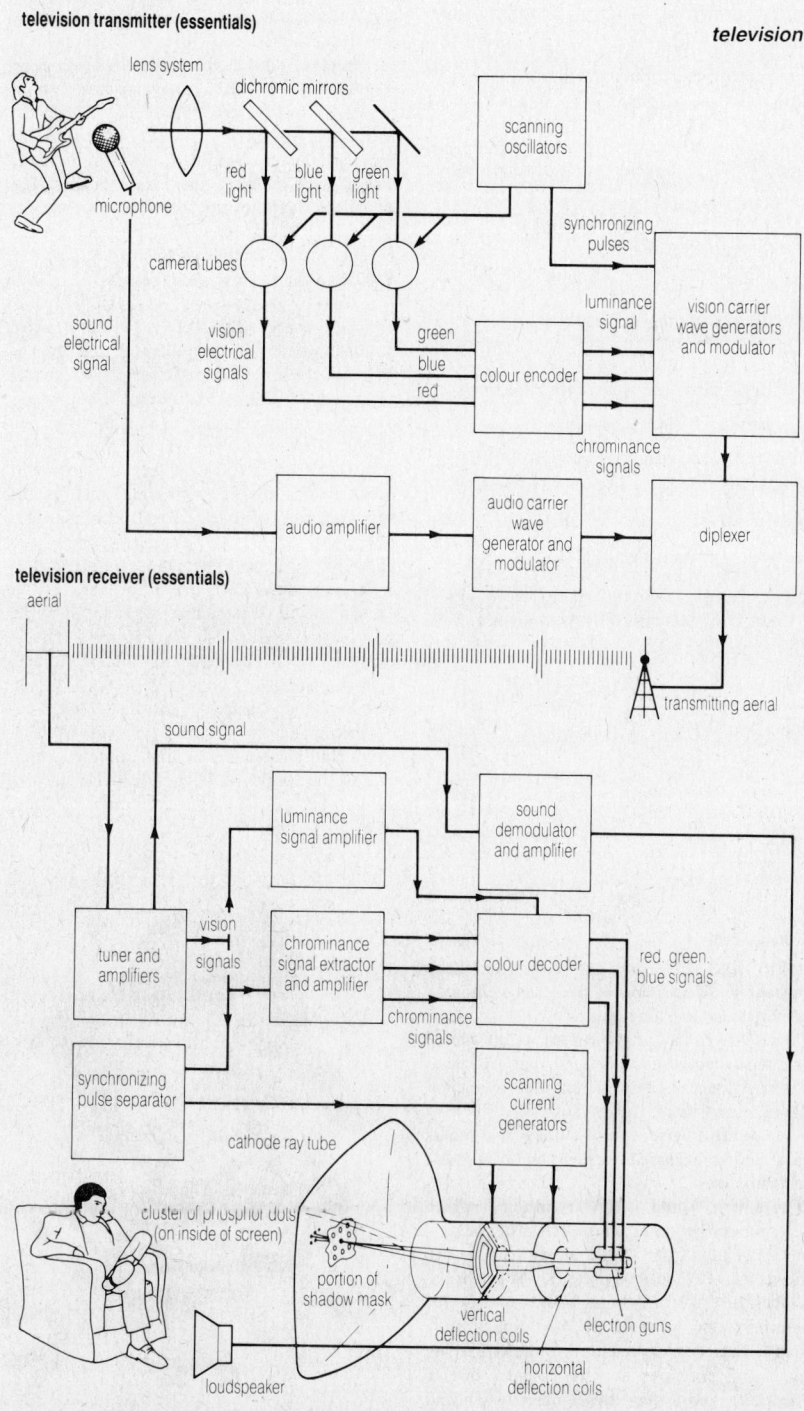

television receiver (essentials)

---

on similar electronic principles to the black and white television picture tube, but the screen is composed of a fine mosaic of over one million dots. One-third of the dots glow red when bombarded by electrons, one-third glow green and one-third blue. There are three sources of electrons (guns), respectively modulated by the red, green and blue signals. The tube is so arranged that the shadow mask allows only the red signals to hit red dots, the green signals to hit green dots, and the blue signals to hit blue dots. The glowing dots are so small that from a normal viewing distance the colours merge into one another and a picture with a full range of colours is seen.

television channels in addition to transmissions received by all viewers, the 1970s and 1980s saw the growth of *pay television*, which is received only by special subscribers, and of devices, such as those used in the Qube system (USA), which allow the viewers' opinion to be transmitted instantaneously to the studio via a response button. The number of programme channels continues to increase, following the introduction of satellite television. Further use of the television set has been brought about by ▷videotext and the use of ▷video recorders to record programmes or to play pre-recorded videocassettes.

television awards see under ▷film and television awards.

telex an international ▷telecommunications network that handles telegraph messages in the form of coded signals. It uses ▷teleprinters for transmitting and receiving, and makes use of land lines (cables), radio and satellite links to make connections between subscribers. The world Telex is an acronym for '*tel*etypewriter *ex*change service'.

Telford /ˈtelfəd/ Thomas 1757–1834. Scottish civil engineer who opened up N Scotland by building roads and waterways. He constructed many aqueducts and canals including the Caledonian (1802–23), and erected the Menai road bridge (1819–26) on the suspension principle, scarcely tried previously in England.

Tell /tel/ William. Legendary Swiss archer, said to have refused at Altdorf, on Lake Lucerne, to salute the Hapsburg badge. Sentenced to shoot an apple from his son's head, he did so, then shot the tyrannical Austrian ruler.

Tell el Amarna /ˈtel el əˈmɑːnə/ site of the ancient Egyptian capital ▷Akhetaton. The ▷Amarna tablets were found there.

tellurium a semi-metallic element of the sulphur group, symbol Te, atomic number 52, atomic weight 127.61. Discovered by Müller von Richtenstein in 1782 and named by Klaproth in 1798 (from Latin *tellus*, earth). It is used in colouring glass (blue to brown), in the electrolytic refining of zinc, and in opto electronic materials. Its strength and hardness are greatly increased by addition of 0.1 per cent lead, when it is used for pipes and cable sheaths. It is also used as a catalyst in petroleum refining.

Telstar US communications satellite, launched 10 Jul 1962, which relayed the first live television transmissions between the US and

---

information corresponds to the hue and saturation of the transmitted ▷colour, but without any of the fine detail of the picture. The impression of sharpness is conveyed only by the brightness signal, the colouring being added as a broad colour wash. The various colour systems differ only in the way in which the colouring signals are sent on the subcarrier signal.

The colour receiver has to amplify the complex signal and decode it back to the basic red, green and blue signals; these primary signals are then applied to a colour cathode-ray tube. The colour display tube is the heart of any colour receiver. Many designs of colour picture tube have been invented and the most successful of these is known as the 'shadow mask tube'. It operates

TELEVISION CHRONOLOGY

1878 William Crookes in England invented the Crookes tube, producing cathode rays.

1884 Paul Nipkow in Germany built a mechanical scanning device, the Nipkow disc, a rotating disc with a spiral pattern of holes in it.

1897 Karl Ferdinand Braun, also in Germany, modified the Crookes tube to produce the ancestor of the modern TV receiver picture tube.

1906 Boris Rosing in Russia began experimenting with the Nipkow disc and cathode-ray tube, eventually succeeding in transmitting some crude TV pictures.

1923 Zworykin in the USA invented the first electronic camera tube, the iconoscope.

1926 Baird demonstrated a TV system, using mechanical scanning by Nipkow disc.

1928 Baird demonstrated colour TV.

1929 The BBC began broadcasting experimental TV programmes using Baird's system.

1936 The BBC began regular broadcasting from Alexandra Palace, London.

1940 Experimental colour TV transmission began in the USA, using the modern system.

1953 Successful colour TV transmissions began in the USA.

1956 The first videotape recorder was produced in California by the Ampex Corporation.

1962 TV signals were transmitted across the Atlantic via the Telstar satellite.

1970 The first videodisc system was announced by Decca in Britain and AEG-Telefunken in Germany. It was perfected in the 1980s, when laser scanning was used for playback.

1975 Sony introduced a videocassette tape recorder system, Betamax, for home use; the British Post Office (now British Telecom) announced their Prestel viewdata system.

1973 The BBC and Independent Television introduced the world's first teletext systems, Ceefax and Oracle, respectively.

1979 Matsushita in Japan developed a pocket-sized flat-screen TV set, using a liquid-crystal display (LCD).

---

certain temperature and then cooling it suddenly in a water or oil bath.

Templars /'templəz/ a religious order, founded in 1119, of knights who took vows of poverty, chastity, and obedience and devoted themselves to the recovery of Palestine from the Saracens. They played a distinguished part in the Crusades of the 12th and 13th centuries. The enormous wealth of the order aroused the envy of Philip IV of France, who arranged for charges of heresy to be brought against its members in 1307, and the order was suppressed.

temple generally, a place of religious worship; specifically, the centre of Jewish national worship at Jerusalem. Three temples occupied the site: Solomon's Temple, which was destroyed by Nebuchadrezzar; Zerubbabel's Temple, built after the return from Babylon; and Herod's Temple, which was destroyed by the Romans in AD 70. The Mosque of Omar now occupies the site. The Wailing Wall is the surviving part of the western wall of the platform of the enclosure of the Temple of Herod, so-called by tourists because of the oriental chanting style of the Jews in their prayers there. Under Jordanian rule Jews had no access to the place, but took this part of the city in the 1967 campaign. In US usage, temple is another name for synagogue.

Temple /'tempəl/ Shirley 1928– . American actress. Born in Santa Monica, California, she became the most successful child star of the 1930s. As Shirley T Black, she was active in the Republican party, and was US Chief of Protocol 1976–77.

Telford Portrait of the Scottish engineer Thomas Telford by W Raddon, 1831. Telford made his name with two bridges over the Severn and the Ellesmere Canal (1793–1805) and in Scotland he constructed over 1,000 miles of road and 1,200 bridges, churches and harbours.

Europe. Telstar orbited the Earth every 158 minutes and so had to be tracked by ground stations, unlike the geostationary satellites of today.

Tema /'tiːmə/ port in Ghana; population (1970) 58,800. It has the largest artificial harbour in Africa, opened 1962, as well as oil refineries and a fishing industry.

tempera a painting medium for powdered pigments, consisting usually of egg yolk and water. A form of tempera was used in ancient Egypt and by many Italian masters.

temperature the state of hotness or coldness of a body, measured in degrees ◊centigrade (officially from 1948 called ◊Celsius), Kelvin or ◊Fahrenheit, and the condition which determines whether or not it will transfer heat to, or receive heat from, another body according to the laws of ◊thermodynamics. The normal temperature of the human body taken in the mouth is 36.86°C/98.436°F. Variation by more than a degree or so indicates ill-health, a rise signifying excessive activity (usually due to infection), and a decrease signifying deficient heat production (usually due to lessened vitality). To convert °C to °F multiply by $\frac{9}{5}$ and add 32 (below 32°F subtract 32); °F to °C subtract 32 then multiply by $\frac{5}{9}$. A useful quick approximation for converting °C to °F is to double the centigrade and add 30, for example 12°C = 24 + 30 = 54°F.

tempering a kind of ◊heat treatment used for improving the properties of metals, particularly steel alloys. It involves heating the metal to a

Temple Child actress Shirley Temple salutes and wins the hearts of cinema-goers and critics in *Bright Eyes* 1934, for which she received an Oscar. She went on to become prominent in US politics in the 1970s.

Temple Bar former western gateway of the City of London, between Fleet Street and the Strand (site marked by griffin); the heads of traitors were formerly displayed above it on spikes. Rebuilt by Wren 1672, it was at

Theobald's Park, Hertfordshire from 1878 until 1985, when it was placed near St Paul's Cathedral.

tempo (Italian 'time') in music, the speed at which a piece is played.

tench freshwater fish *Tinca tinca*. A member of the carp family, it is about 45 cm/18 in long, olive-green above and grey beneath.

tendon a type of ◊connective tissue which joins ◊muscle to ◊bone in vertebrates. Tendons are largely composed of the protein collagen, and because of their inelasticity are efficient at transforming muscle power into movement.

tendril a slender, thread-like structure that supports a climbing plant by coiling around suitable supports, such as the stems and branches of other plants. It may be a modified stem, leaf, leaflet, flower, or leaf stalk, and may be simple or branched. The tendrils of Virginia creeper (*Parthenocissus quinquefolia*) are modified flower-heads with pads at the end that stick to walls, while those of the grapevine (*Vitis*) grow away from the light and thus enter dark crevices where they expand to anchor the plant firmly.

tendrils

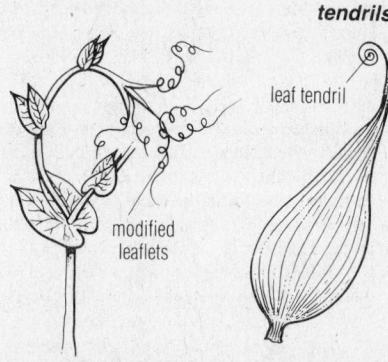

leaf tendril

modified leaflets

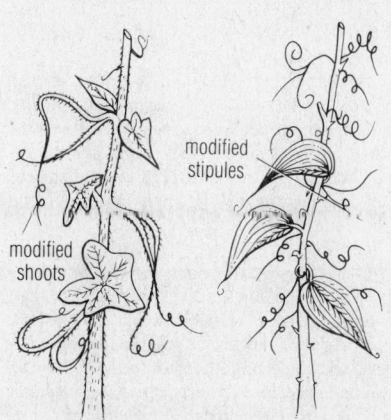

modified stipules

modified shoots

Tenerife /ˌtenəˈriːf/ largest of the ◊Canary Islands, Spain; area 2,060 sq km/795 sq mi; population (1981) 557,000.

Teng Hsiao-ping /ˈteŋ ˌʃaʊˈpɪŋ/ another spelling for ◊Deng Xiaoping, Chinese politician.

Teniers /ˈteniəz/ David, the Elder 1582–1649. Flemish painter, born in Antwerp and a student of Rubens and Elsheimer, who painted scenes of everyday life.

Teniers /ˈteniəz/ David, the Younger 1610–1690. Finest of the Flemish genre painters, and son of the elder Teniers. He was influenced by ◊Rubens and ◊Brouwer, and was court painter to Archduke Leopold William.

Tennessee /ˌtenəˈsiː/ state of the E central USA; Volunteer State
area 109,412 sq km/42,224 sq mi
capital Nashville
towns Memphis, Jackson, Knoxville, Chattanooga
features Tennessee Valley Authority; Great Smoky Mountains National Park
products cereals, cotton, tobacco; timber; coal, zinc, pyrites, phosphates; iron and steel and chemicals.
population (1980) 4,591,120
famous people Davy Crockett, David Farragut, Sam Houston, and the musician William C Handy, the first person to transcribe ◊Blues music on paper
history first settled 1757, it became a state 1796.

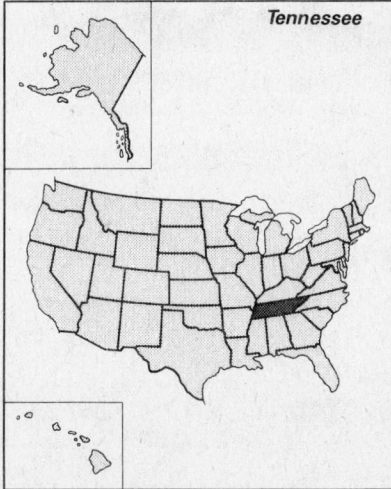

Tennessee

Tennessee Valley Authority (TVA) US government corporation founded 1933 to develop the Tennessee River basin (an area of some 104,000 sq km/40,000 sq mi). It was one of the most famous of President ◊Roosevelt's 'New Deal' measures, promoting economic growth by government investment.

Tenniel /ˈtenjəl/ John 1820–1914. British cartoonist and illustrator. Born in London, he joined *Punch* in 1850, and for over 50 years he was a leading cartoonist on that magazine. He illustrated Lewis ◊Carroll's *Alice in Wonderland* and other books.

tennis a racket and ball game invented in England in the late 19th century, and referred to as 'lawn tennis' whether played on a grass or composition court; some features (the hitting of a cloth ball over a central net) derive from ◊real tennis, which originated in France in the 12th century, as does the method of scoring. The aim of the two or four players is to strike the ball into the prescribed area of the court, with oval-headed rackets (strung with gut or nylon), in such a way that it cannot be returned. The game is won by those first winning four points (called 15, 30, 40, game), unless both sides reach 40 (deuce) when two consecutive points are needed to win. A set is won by winning six games with a margin of two over opponents, though a tie-break system operates, that is at six games to each side (or in some cases eight) excepting in the final set. Major events include the *Davis Cup* 1900 for international men's competition, and *Wightman Cup* 1923 for US and UK women's teams, and the annual All England Tennis Club championships (originating 1877), an open event for players of both sexes at Wimbledon. Winner of six successive women's titles is Martina Navratilova 1982–87; of the men Bjorn Borg has won five successive titles 1976–80 and William Renshaw won six between 1881–86; the youngest male winner was 17-year-old West German Boris Becker, 1985.

Wimbledon Championships first held 1877
men's singles
1983 John McEnroe (*USA*)
1984 John McEnroe (*USA*)
1985 Boris Becker (*West Germany*)
1986 Boris Becker (*West Germany*)
1987 Pat Cash (*Australia*)
women's singles
1983 Martina Navratilova (*USA*)
1984 Martina Navratilova (*USA*)
1985 Martina Navratilova (*USA*)
1986 Martina Navratilova (*USA*)
1987 Martina Navratilova (*USA*)
United States Open first held 1881 *men's singles*
1982 Jimmy Connors (*USA*)
1983 Jimmy Connors (*USA*)
1984 John McEnroe (*USA*)
1985 Ivan Lendl (*Czechoslovakia*)
1986 Ivan Lendl (*Czechoslovakia*)
women's singles
1982 Chris Evert-Lloyd (*USA*)
1983 Martina Navratilova (*USA*)
1984 Martina Navratilova (*USA*)
1985 Hana Mandlikova (*Czechoslovakia*)
1986 Martina Navratilova (*USA*)
Davis Cup first contested 1900
1982 USA
1983 Australia
1984 Sweden
1985 Sweden
1986 Australia.

---

tennis, real racket and ball game played in France from about 12th century over a central net in an indoor court, but with a sloping roof let into each end and one side of the court, against which the ball may be hit. The term real in this sense means 'royal', not 'genuine'. Basic scoring is as for 'lawn' ◊tennis, but with various modifications. The oldest court still in use is at Hampton Court, where it was installed by Henry VIII. It is also called Royal, Court, or Lord's tennis.

Tennyson /ˈtenɪsən/ Alfred, 1st Baron Tennyson 1809–1892. British poet, born at Somersby, Lincolnshire. His *Poems* 1832 include 'The Lady of Shalott' and 'The Lotus Eaters', and were admired for their majestic, musical language. The death of A H Hallam (a

Tenniel The Mad Hatter's tea party, from Lewis Carroll's *Alice in Wonderland*, illustrated by John Tenniel.

tennis Steffi Graff (West Germany) illustrates the perfect position for the backhand shot.

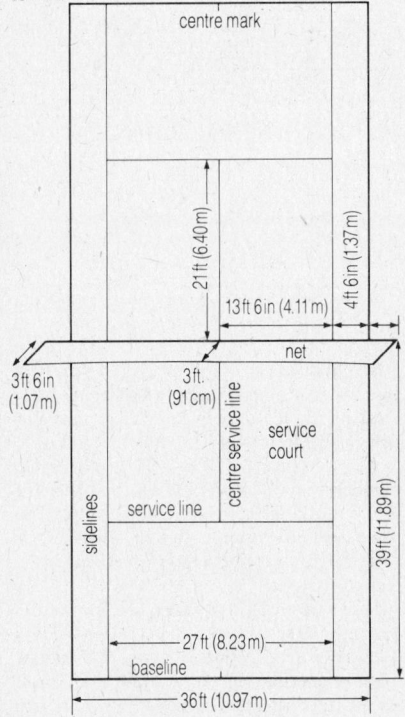

tennis

centre mark

21 ft (6.40 m)

13 ft 6 in (4.11 m)

4 ft 6 in (1.37 m)

net

3 ft 6 in (1.07 m)

3 ft. (91 cm)

service court

service line

centre service line

sidelines

39 ft (11.89 m)

27 ft (8.23 m)

baseline

36 ft (10.97 m)

close friend during his years at Trinity College, Cambridge) in 1833 prompted the elegiac *In Memoriam* unpublished till 1850, the year in which he succeeded Wordsworth as Poet Laureate and married. A long series of poems on the Arthurian legends, *The Idylls of the King* 1857–85, was a Victorian treatment of the medieval legends. Other poems include 'Ulysses', 'Break, Break, Break', 'The Brook', 'The Charge of the Light Brigade', and the longer narratives *Locksley Hall* 1832, *The Princess* 1847 and *Maud* 1855. Created a peer 1884.

tenor in music, the highest range of adult male voice not using ▷falsetto.

tenpin bowling game involving knocking down a set of 'pins' by rolling a ball at them. It is

of very early origin, said to have been taken to the USA by Dutch settlers in the 17th century. Modern bowling lanes measure 18.30 m/60 ft to the nearest pin and have an extra 4.57 m/15 ft approach area; they are 1 m/3 ft 6 in wide. Balls weighing up to 7.25 kg/16 lb are made of rubber composition and drilled with holes for thumb and two fingers. Pins made of maple are 38.1 cm/1 ft 3 in high. The game is usually between two players or teams of three, four, or five players a side. A game of ten pins is made up of ten 'frames'. The frame is the bowler's turn to play and in each frame he or she may bowl twice. One point is scored for each pin knocked down, with bonus points for knocking all ten pins down in either one ball or two. The player or team making the greater score wins. The US National Bowling Association was formed in 1875, and from the 1960s the game has become popular in Britain.

Tenzing /'tensɪŋ/ Norgay, popularly known as *Sherpa Tenzing* 1914–1986. Tibetan mountaineer. With Edmund ▷Hillary, the first to reach the summit of Mount Everest in 1953. He was awarded the George Medal.

Teotihuacan /ˌteɪəʊˌtiːwaˈkɑːn/ ancient city in central Mexico. Capital and religious centre of the ▷Toltec civilization.

Teplice /'teplɪtseɪ/ industrial city and spa in Czechoslovakia; population (1970) 53,500. Industries include peat- and lignite-mining, glass, porcelain, cement, and paper.

tequila Mexican alcoholic drink made from the agave plant (see ▷Amaryllidaceae).

terbium a metallic element, symbol Tb, atomic number 65, atomic weight 158.93. Used in lasers, semiconductors and television tubes, it is one of the lanthanide series.

Terence /'terəns/ Publius Terentius Afer 190–159 BC. Latin dramatist, born at Carthage, and brought as a slave to Rome where he was freed and came under ▷Scipio's patronage. His surviving six, subtly characterized comedies (including *The Eunuch* 161 BC) are based on Greek models.

Teresa, St /təˈriːzə/ 1515–1582. Spanish mystic. Born at Avila, she became a Carmelite nun, and in 1562 founded a new and stricter order. She was subject to fainting fits, during which she saw visions. In 1622 she was canonized, and became the first woman Doctor of the Church in 1970.

Tereshkova /ˌterɪʃˈkəʊvə/ Valentina 1937– . Soviet cosmonaut, the first woman to fly in space. In Jun 1963 she made a three-day flight in Vostok 6, orbiting the Earth 48 times.

term in architecture, a pillar in the form of a pedestal supporting the bust of a human or animal figure. Such objects derive from Roman boundary-marks sacred to *Terminus*, the god of boundaries, whose feast day was Feb 23.

terminal in computing, a keyboard and ▷VDU (screen) for communicating with a computer. Originally, 'terminal' or 'terminal equipment' was any input or output device connected to a computer, but today the word ▷peripheral is used instead in this wider sense.

termite soft-bodied social insect, of the tropical order Isoptera, living in large colonies, comprising one or more queens (of relatively enormous size and producing an egg every two seconds), much smaller kings, and still smaller soldiers, workers and immature forms. Termites build galleried nests of soil particles which are centrally heated and air-conditioned, and may be 6 m/20 ft high. The Macrotermitinae construct fungus gardens from their own faeces, which are then infected with a special fungus which digests the faeces and renders them once more edible so that they can be recycled. Termites may dispose of a quarter of the vegetation litter of an area, and their fondness for wood (as in houses and other buildings) brings them into conflict with human beings. The wood is broken down in their stomachs by numerous species of microorganism, living in ◊symbiosis with their hosts.

termite The mounds of magnetic termites in northern Australia reach some 5 m / 16 ft, and are aligned N–S. In this way they are spared the burning heat of the midday sun, but the broad sides of the nest catch the warmth in early morning and evening.

tern lightly built gull-like seabird, characterized by long wings and a forked tail. In the common tern *Sterna hirundo* the underparts are white, the upper wing grey and the crown of the head black.

Terpsichore in Greek mythology, the muse of dance and choral song.

terracotta a form of brownish-red baked clay used in building, sculpture, and pottery. It was first used in ancient times in countries where there was no stone available. Excavations at Xian, China, have revealed life-size terracotta figures of the army of the Emperor Qin c. 3rd century.

terrapin name commonly given to fresh-water members of the tortoise order. The diamond-back terrapin, a North American coastal species, is considered a delicacy.

Terre Haute /'terə 'həʊt/ city in Indiana, USA; population (1980) 61,125. Plastics, chemicals, and glass are manufactured.

terrier type of dog formerly used in hunting rabbits and following quarry such as foxes down into burrows. Mostly small and active, they are highly intelligent. They include the bull, cairn, fox, Irish, Scottish, Sealyham, Skye, and Yorkshire terriers.

Territorial Army British force of volunteer soldiers, created from volunteer regiments (incorporated 1872) as the *Territorial Force* 1908. It was raised and administered by County Associations, and intended primarily for home defence. It was renamed Territorial Army 1922. Merged with the Regular Army in World War II, it was revived 1947, and replaced by a smaller, more highly trained Territorial and Army Volunteer Reserve, again renamed Territorial Army 1979.

territorial behaviour in biology, the active defence of a ◊territory. It may involve aggressively driving out intruders, marking the boundary (with dung piles or deposits from special scent glands), conspicuous visual displays or characteristic songs or loud calls. In general, the territory-owner repels only individuals of its own species.

territory in ◊animal behaviour, an area that is actively defended by an individual or group. Animals may hold territories for many different reasons, for example, to provide a constant food supply, to monopolize potential mates, or to ensure access to refuges or nest sites. The size of a territory depends in part on its function, often being only a few square metres for some nesting and mating territories, but as much as hundreds of square kilometres for feeding territories.

terrorism systematic violence in the furtherance of political aims, especially by small ◊guerrilla groups.

Terry /'teri/ (John) Quinlan 1937– . British Neo-Classical architect whose work includes many country houses, for example Merks Hall, Great Dunmow, Essex 1982, and the larger scale Richmond riverside project commissioned 1984.

Terry /'teri/ Ellen 1847–1928. British actress, leading lady to Henry ◊Irving from 1878, and excelling in Shakespearean roles, such as Ophelia. She married the painter G F ◊Watts, but separation and divorce followed. She had a celebrated correspondence with G B Shaw.

Tertiary the period of geological time between 65 and 1.8 million years ago. It is divided into epochs: ◊Palaeocene, ◊Eocene, ◊Oligocene, ◊Miocene, and ◊Pliocene. During the Tertiary the mammals became the important land animals.

tertiary in the Roman Catholic church, a member of a 'third order' (see under ◊Holy Orders), that is a layman who, while marrying and following a normal employment, attempts to live in accordance with a modified version of the rule of one of the religious orders. The first such order was founded by St ◊Francis 1221.

tertiary college in the UK, term for a college for students over 16 which combines the work of a ◊sixth form and a ◊further education college.

Tertullian /tɜː'tʌliən/ Quintus Septimius Florens 155–222 AD. Latin name Tertullianus. Carthaginian Father of the Church, the first important Christian writer in Latin; he became a ◊Montanist in 213.

Terylene trade name for a polyester ◊synthetic fibre produced by ICI. It is made by polymerizing ethylene glycol and terephthalic acid. Cloth made from Terylene keeps its shape well and is hard-wearing.

terza rima in poetry, Italian metre used in ◊Dante's *Divine Comedy*, consisting of three-line stanzas in which the second line rhymes with the first and third of the following stanza. The best-known English example is ◊Shelley's 'Ode to the West Wind'.

tesla the derived SI unit (symbol T) of magnetic flux density, equal to 1 weber of magnetic flux per square metre, $Wb\,m^{-2}$. Named after Nikola ◊Tesla.

Tesla /'teslə/ Nikola 1856–1943. American electrical engineer, born in Croatia. He developed the ◊alternating current (AC) electrical supply system, and invented fluorescent lighting.

Test Act act passed in England in 1673 requiring all holders of public office to renounce the doctrine of ◊transubstantiation and take the sacrament in an Anglican church, thus excluding Catholics, Nonconformists, and non-Christians from office. Its clauses were repealed in 1828–29. The University Test Act 1871 abolished the theological test required for the MA degree and for Oxford University and College offices.

Test Ban Treaty a treaty signed by the USA, USSR, and Britain on 5 Aug 1963 which agreed to stop the testing of nuclear weapons, with the exception of underground tests. In the following two years 90 other nations signed the treaty, the only major non-signatories being France and the People's Republic of China who continued underwater and ground-level tests.

testis the organ that produces ◊sperm in male (and hermaphrodite) animals. In most animals it is internal, but in mammals (other than marine mammals) the paired testes descend from the body cavity during development, to hang outside the abdomen in a scrotal sac.

testosterone a ◊hormone secreted chiefly by the ◊testes of vertebrates. It promotes the development of the secondary sexual characters in males. In animals with a breeding season, the onset of breeding behaviour is accompanied by a rise in the level of testosterone in the blood. Synthetic or animal testosterone is used to treat inadequate development of male characteristics or (illegally) to give athletes additional energy. Like other sex hormones, testosterone is a ◊steroid.

tetanus or *lockjaw* an acute infectious disease caused by a bacterium, *Clostridium tetani*, entering a wound. The bacterium is chiefly found in richly manured soil. Untreated, tetanus produces muscular spasm, convulsions, and death. There is a vaccine.

Tethys in Greek mythology, one of the ◊Titans, the wife of the god ◊Oceanus.

Tethys Sea /'tiːθɪs/ sea which once separated ◊Laurasia from ◊Gondwanaland; roughly corresponding to the present-day Mediterranean.

Tet Offensive major offensive mounted by the Vietcong against Saigon in Jan and Feb 1968 during the ◊Vietnam War. Although the communist Vietcong were forced to withdraw, the attack on the South Vietnamese capital brought into question the ability of the South Vietnamese and their US allies to win the war.

tetra a brightly coloured tropical fish of the family Characidae.

tetrahedron in geometry, a solid figure (◊polyhedron) with four triangular faces; that is, a ◊pyramid on a triangular base. A regular tetrahedron has equilateral triangles as its faces; it can be constructed by joining four points that are equidistant from each other on the surface of a sphere. Tetrahedra are important in chemistry and crystallography in describing the shapes of molecules and crystals; for example, the carbon atoms in a crystal of diamond are arranged in space as a set of interconnected regular tetrahedra.

tetrahedron

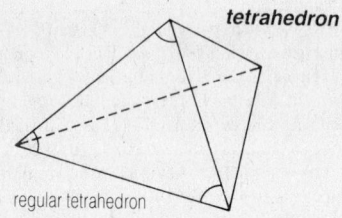

regular tetrahedron

tetrapod a type of ◊vertebrate (animal with backbone or spine). The group includes the mammals, birds, reptiles and amphibians. Although the name tetrapod means 'four-legged', birds are included because they evolved from four-legged ancestors, the forelimbs having become modified to form wings.

Tetuán /te'twɑːn/ town in NE Morocco, near the Mediterranean coast, 64 km/40 mi SE of Tangier; population (1975) 800,000.

Teutonic Knights German Christian military order, founded 1190, which crusaded against the pagan Prussians and Lithuanians from 1228. They ruled Prussia until the 15th century.

Texas /'teksəs/ state of the SW USA; Lone Star State
area 692,407 sq km/267,339 sq mi
capital Austin
towns Houston, Dallas, San Antonio, Fort Worth, El Paso
features Rio Grande del Norte and Red rivers; arid Staked Plains, reclaimed by irrigation; the Great Plains
products rice, cotton, sorghum, peanuts, pecans, vegetables, fruit; meat products; oil (a third of the needs of the USA), natural gas, asphalt, graphite, sulphur, salt, helium; chemicals, oil products, processed food, machinery, transport equipment
population (1980) 14,229,191
famous people James Bowie, Buddy Holly, Sam Houston, Howard Hughes, Lyndon Johnson, Katharine Ann Porter
history first settled by the Spanish 1682, the area (then part of Mexico) won independence in 1821, and American immigration followed with

resultant friction. ◊Santa Anna massacred the Alamo garrison 1836, but was defeated by Sam Houston at San Jacinto the same year. Houston then became president of the Texas Republic 1836–45. Texas became a state of the USA (the only one to have previously been an independent republic) 1845.

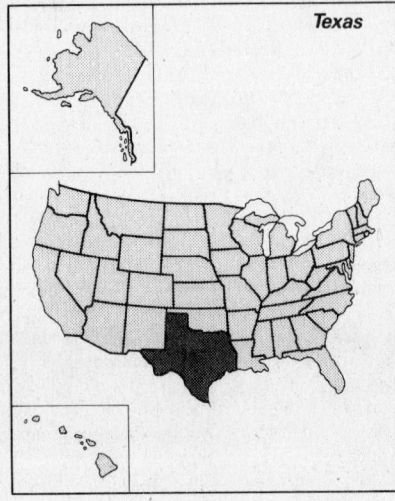

Texas

Texel /'tesəl/ largest and most westerly of the ◊Frisian Islands.

textile formerly only a material woven (Latin *texere* to weave) from natural spun thread, now loosely extended to machine-knits and spun-bonded fabrics (in which a web of fibre is created and then fuse-bonded by passing it through controlled heat).
natural textiles include cotton, linen, silk, wool (including angora, llama, and many others). For particular qualities, such as flame resistance, or water and stain repellence, these may be combined with synthetic fibres or treated with various chemicals.
synthetic the first commercial synthetic thread was 'artificial silk' or rayon (see ◊Chardonnet), with filaments made from modified cellulose (wood pulp) and known according to later methods of manufacture as *viscose* (using caustic soda and carbon disulphide) or *acetate* (using acetic acid). The first fully synthetic textile fibre was ◊*nylon* 1937; and this with the *acrylics* used in knitwear, for example Orlon; the *polyesters*, such as Terylene; and the *spandex* or *elastomeric fibres*, for example Lycra, form the base of most of today's industry.
geotextiles textiles made from plastic and synthetic fibres, and either felted for use as filters or stabilizing grids, or woven for strength. They form part of drainage systems, road foundations, and barriers to sea and river defences against erosion.

textured vegetable protein a manufactured foodstuff, see ◊TVP.

Teyte /teɪt/ Maggie 1888–1976. British lyric soprano. She studied under Jean de Reszke in Paris, and is remembered for her Mozartian roles, such as Cherubino in *The Marriage of Figaro*, and was coached as Mélisande in *Pelléas*

et Mélisande by the opera's composer Debussy. In 1958 she was created Dame of the British Empire.

TGV *train à grande vitesse*, a superfast French train that operates the world's fastest rail service between Paris and Lyon. Introduced in 1981 and electrically powered, the TGV covers the 425 km/264 mile journey in just two hours.

Thackeray /'θækərɪ/ William Makepeace 1811–1863. British novelist, author of *Vanity Fair*. Son of an East India Company official, he was born in Calcutta, and educated at Charterhouse and Trinity College, Cambridge. He studied law in the Middle Temple, and then art in Paris, before ultimately settling to journalism in London. For *Fraser's Magazine* he wrote 'The Yellowplush Correspondence' 1837–38, and 'The Great Hoggarty Diamond' 1841, and for *Punch* 'Mr Punch's Prize Novelists' 1847 and 'The Snobs of England' 1847, using such pseudonyms as Michael Angelo Titmarsh. He wrote the fairy tale *The Rose and the Ring* 1855 for his two daughters. His first novel was *Vanity Fair* 1847–48, creating the strong-willed heroine Becky Sharp; later novels are *Pendennis* 1848, *The History of Henry Esmond* 1852 (with a sequel *The Virginians* 1857–59), and *The Newcomers* 1853–55, in which Thackeray's tendency to sentimentality is most marked.

Thailand /'taɪlænd/ country in SE Asia on the Gulf of Siam, bounded to the E by Laos and Kampuchea, to the S by Malaysia, and to the W by Burma.
government under the constitution of 1978, Thailand is ruled by a hereditary monarch working with a two-chamber legislature, the National Assembly. The monarch is head of state and head of the armed forces and appoints a prime minister on the advice of the National Assembly. The prime minister and a selected cabinet formulate policy and are in charge of day-to-day government administration. These ministers may speak but not vote at National Assembly meetings; they must not be serving military officers.
The upper house of the National Assembly, the Senate, comprises 243 members who are appointed for six-year terms by the monarch on the recommendation of the prime minister. Senators must not be members of any political party. The lower house, the House of Representatives, comprises 347 members who are elected from single-member constituencies by universal suffrage for four-year terms. Far-left parties, such as the Communist Party, are outlawed, as are parties that field candidates in fewer than half the nation's constituencies. Effective political power in Thailand remains ultimately with the army leadership.
history Thailand has an ancient civilization, with Bronze Age artefacts from as early as 4000 BC. Siam, as it was called until 1939 (and 1945–49), has been united as a kingdom since 1350; the present dynasty dates from 1782. It was reached by Portuguese traders in 1511, followed by the British East India Company and the Dutch in the 17th century. Treaties of friendship and trade 1826 and 1855 established Britain as the

paramount power in the region and opened Siam to foreign commerce. Anglo-French diplomatic agreements of 1896 and 1904 established Siam as a neutral buffer kingdom between British Burma and French Indochina.

After World War I, a movement for national renaissance developed, which culminated in a coup against the absolute monarch King Prajadhipok and the establishment instead of a constitutional monarchy and an elected, representative system of government 1932. The name of Muang Thai (Land of the Free) was adopted 1939. Thailand was occupied by Japan 1941–44. The government collaborated, but there was a guerrilla resistance movement. A period of instability followed the Japanese withdrawal, King Ananda Mahidol was assassinated 1946, and the army assumed power in a coup 1947 led by Field Marshal Pibul Songgram.

The army retained control during the next two decades, with the leader of the military junta periodically changed by a series of bloodless coups: Field Marshal Pibul Songgram 1947–57, Field Marshal Sarit Thanarat 1958–63, and Gen Thanom Kittikachorn 1964–73. The monarch, King ◊Bhumibol Adulyadej, was only a figurehead, and experiments with elected assemblies were undertaken 1957–58 and 1968–71. During this era of junta rule, Thailand allied itself with the USA and encountered serious Communist guerrilla insurgency along its borders with ◊Laos, ◊Kampuchea and ◊Malaysia. Despite achievements in the economic sphere, the junta was overthrown by violent student riots in Oct 1973. A democratic constitution was adopted a year later, and free elections were held in 1975 and 1976. A series of coalition governments lacked stability and the military assumed power again 1976–77, annulling the 1974 constitution.

The army supreme commander, Gen Kriangsak Chomanan, held power 1977–80 and promulgated a new constitution in Dec 1978. This established a mixed civilian and military form of government under the monarch's direction. Having deposed Gen Kriangsak in Oct 1980, Gen Prem Tinsulanonda (1920–) formally relinquished his army office and headed the civilian coalition governments that were formed after the parliamentary elections of Apr 1983 and Jul 1986. Attempted coups in Apr 1981 and Sept 1985 (the latter involving Gen Kriangsak) were easily crushed by Prime Minister Prem, who has ruled in a cautious apolitical manner and has retained the confidence of the army leadership and the public. Sixteen political parties competed in the Jul 1986 election. The three most important were the conservative Chart Thai (Thai Nation, led by former general Chatichai Choonhavan), the Social Action Party (led by Siddhi Savetsila), and the more liberal Democrat Party (led by Bhichai Rattakul); these form the nucleus of the present government.

The continuing civil war in Kampuchea and Laos, which has resulted in the flight of more than 500,000 refugees to Thailand since 1975, has provided justification for continued quasi-military rule and the maintenance of martial law. Thailand has drawn closer to its ◊ASEAN allies, who jointly support the Kampuchean guerrilla movement, and its relations with Communist China have seen a thaw.

Thailand
KINGDOM OF (*Prathes Thai*)

AREA 514,000 sq km/198,247 sq mi
CAPITAL and chief port Bangkok
TOWNS Chiangmai
PHYSICAL central valley flanked by highlands; tropical rain forest
FEATURES rivers Chao Phraya, Mekong, Salween; tools and weapons from the Bronze Age
HEAD OF STATE King Bhumibol Adulyadej from 1946
HEAD OF GOVERNMENT Prem Tinsulanonda from 1980
GOVERNMENT constitutional monarchy
EXPORTS rice, sugar; rubber, teak; tin (fifth largest producer), rubies, sapphires
CURRENCY baht (41.7 = £1 Sept 1987)
POPULATION (1985) 51,546,000 (Thai 75%, Chinese 14%); annual growth rate 2.1%
LANGUAGE Thai and Chinese (both official)
RELIGION Buddhist
LITERACY 92% male/83% female (1980 est)
GNP $42 bn (1985); $823 per head of population
CHRONOLOGY
1782 Siam absolutist dynasty commenced.
1896 Anglo-French agreement recognized Siam as independent buffer state.
1932 Constitutional monarchy established.

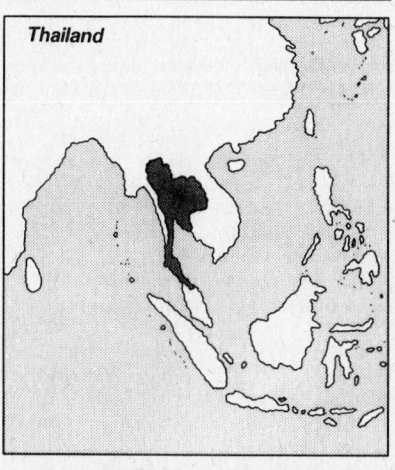
Thailand

1939 Name of Thailand adopted.
1941–44 Japanese occupation.
1947 Military seized power in coup.
1972 Withdrawal of Thai troops from S Vietnam.
1973 Military government overthrown.
1976 Military reassumed control.
1980 General Prem Tinsulandonda assumed power.
1983 Civilian government formed but martial law maintained.

Thaïs /'θeɪɪs/ 4th century BC. Greek courtesan, mistress of ◊Alexander the Great and later wife of ◊Ptolemy I, king of Egypt. She allegedly instigated the burning of ◊Persepolis.

thalassaemia form of ◊anaemia in which an abnormal haemoglobin molecule results in distortion of the red blood cells, and untreated children die in infancy. It is one of the world's most common genetic diseases.

Thales /'θeɪliːz/ 640–546 BC. Greek philosopher and scientist who lived at Miletus in Asia Minor. He made advances in geometry, predicted the sun's eclipse in 585, and as a materialist in philosophy, theorized that water was the first principle of all things, that the earth floated on water, and so proposed an explanation for earthquakes.

Thalia /θə'laɪə/ in Greek mythology, the Muse of comedy and pastoral poetry.

thalidomide tranquillizer developed in Germany 1957, and sold in Europe 1957–61. When taken by pregnant women it caused malformation of the foetus (in over 5,000 known cases) and the drug was withdrawn 1961.

thallium a metallic element symbol Tl, atomic number 81, atomic weight 204.39. It is a bluish-grey metal which tarnishes in air, is soft like lead, malleable but of low tenacity. Discovered spectroscopically and isolated by Crookes in 1861 (by Lamy 1862), it is a poor conductor of electricity and its compounds are poisonous, being used as rat poison and insecticide. Other compounds are used in optical and infared glass making, and in photoelectric cells.

thallus any plant body that is not divided into true leaves, stems and roots. It is often thin and flattened, as in the body of a seaweed, lichen or liverwort and the gametophyte generation (◊prothallus) of a fern. Some flowering plants (angiosperm) that are adapted to an aquatic way of life may have a very simple plant body which is described as a thallus (for example duckweed, *Lemna*).

Thames /temz/ river in SE England; length 338 km/210 mi. Its headstreams rise in the Cotswolds above Cirencester, and unite at Lechlade; tributaries from the N are the Windrush, Evenlode, Cherwell, Thame, Colne, Lea, and Roding; and from the S, Kennet, Loddon, Wey, Mole, Darent, and Medway. Above Oxford it is sometimes poetically called *Isis*; it is tidal as far as Teddington; and below London there is protection from flooding by means of the ◊Thames barrier.

Thames, Firth of /temz/ inlet between Auckland and the Coromandel Peninsula, New Zealand.

Thames barrier a moveable barrier built across the River Thames at Woolwich, London, as part of that city's flood defences. Completed in 1982, the barrier comprises curved flood gates which are rotated 90° into position from beneath the water to form a barrier when exceptionally high tides are expected.

Thanet, Isle of /'θænɪt/ NE corner of Kent, England, bounded by the North Sea and the river Stour. It was an island until the 16th century, and includes the coastal resorts of Broadstairs, Margate, and Ramsgate.

Thanksgiving (Day) national holiday in the USA (fourth Thursday in Nov) and Canada (second Monday in Oct), first celebrated by the Pilgrims on their first harvest 1621.

Thant /θænt/ U 1909–1974. Burmese diplomat, Secretary-General of the United Nations 1962–71. He helped to resolve the US-Soviet crisis over the Soviet installation of missiles in Cuba, and he made the controversial decision to withdraw the United Nations peacekeeping force from the Egypt-Israel border 1967 (◊Arab-Israeli Wars).

Thar Desert /tɑː/ or **Indian Desert** desert on the ◊Rajasthan-Pakistan border; area about 250,000 sq km/96,500 sq mi.

Thatcher /'θætʃə/ Margaret Hilda (born Roberts) 1925– . British Conservative politician. Her father, a grocer, was later mayor of ◊Grantham. She was educated at Oxford, qualified as a research chemist and barrister, and married in 1951 Denis Thatcher, a director of Burmah Oil. She entered Parliament in 1959. As minister of education 1970–74, she caused controversy when she abolished free milk for schoolchildren. She defeated Heath for the Conservative leadership in 1975, and became prime minister in 1979. She was re-elected 1983 and 1987, the first British prime minister to be elected for a third term since Lord ◊Liverpool. Landmarks of the Thatcher government include the independence of ◊Zimbabwe, the ◊Falklands conflict; the 1984–85 miners' strike; reduction of inflation; large-scale ◊privatization; the Public Order Act; the Anglo-Irish Agreement of 1985; and a large rise in unemployment.

thaumatrope in photography, a disc with two different pictures at opposite ends of its surface which combine into one when rapidly rotated because of the persistence of visual impressions.

theatre broad term applied to a performance by actors for an audience, which may include ◊drama, dancing, music, and so on. The term is also used for the place or building in which dramatic performances are given.
The first European theatres were in Greece and were originally open spaces round the altar of ◊Dionysus. The great stone theatre at Athens was begun about 500 BC, and its semicircular plan provided for an audience of 20,000 or 30,000 people sitting in tiers on the surrounding slopes; it served as a model for the theatres that were erected in all the important cities of the Graeco-Roman world. Extant Roman theatres are at, for example, Orange, France, and near St Albans, England, but after the collapse of the Roman Empire the theatres were deserted. In medieval times, several temporary stages of wood and canvas, one for each scene, were set up side by side in fairgrounds and market squares for the performance of mimes and ◊miracle plays. Small enclosed theatres were built in the 16th century, for example at Vicenza, built by Palladio 1518–80. The first London theatre was the 'theatre' in Shoreditch built in 1576 by James

Burbage, who also opened the first covered theatre in London, the Blackfriars (1596). His son was responsible for building the ◊Globe Theatre, the venue for Shakespeare's plays. Famous London theatres include the Haymarket (1720, rebuilt 1821), Drury Lane (1663), and Her Majesty's (1705), both several times rebuilt. In the USA the centre of the commercial theatre is New York City, with numerous theatres on Broadway and in that area, although Williamsburg, Virginia (1716), and Philadelphia (1766) were the first known American theatres. The 'little theatres' off Broadway developed to present wider, less commercial productions, often giving a dramatist's first production, and of these the first was the Theater Guild (1919); off-off Broadway then developed as ◊fringe or alternative theatre. In Britain the English Stage company was established at the Royal Court Theatre in 1956 to provide a platform for new works.
The ◊Comédie Française, Paris (founded by Louis XIV in 1690 and with a permanent home from 1792) was the first national theatre. In Britain the ◊National Theatre complex opened in 1976 on London's South Bank became the home of the National Theatre company established in 1963.

Theatre Museum museum in London opened in ◊Covent Garden on 23 Apr 1987, Shakespeare's birthday, which houses one of the largest collections of memorabilia from the world of the theatre, opera, ballet, dance, circus, puppetry, pop, and rock and roll.

thebaine highly poisonous extract of ◊opium.

Thebes /'θiːbz/ capital of Boeotia in ancient Greece. In the Peloponnesian War it was allied with Sparta against Athens, and for a short time after 371 BC it was the most powerful state in Greece. Alexander the Great destroyed it in 336 BC and although it was restored it was never again important. The poet Pindar lived at Thebes.

Thebes /'θiːbz/ Greek name of an ancient city (Niut-Ammon) in Upper Egypt, on the Nile, probably founded under the first dynasty, centre of the worship of ◊Ammon, and the Egyptian capital under the New Kingdom about 1600 BC. Magnificent temple ruins survive, near the modern villages of Karnak and Luxor, and in the nearby **Valley of the Kings** the 18th–20th dynasty kings, including ◊Tutankhamen and ◊Amenhotep, are buried.

theft in Britain, under the Theft Act 1968, the dishonest appropriation of another's property with the intention of depriving him/her of it permanently: maximum penalty ten years imprisonment. The act placed under a single head forms of theft which had formerly been dealt with individually, for example burglary and larceny.

theism belief in the existence of gods, but more especially in that of a single personal God, made known to the world in a special revelation.

theme in music, a basic melody or musical figure, which often occurs with variations.

Themis /'θemɪs/ in Greek mythology, the personification of law and order. She was one of the ◊Titans, the daughter of Uranus and Gaia.

Themistocles /θə'mɪstəkliːz/ 525–460 BC. Greek soldier. Largely responsible for the ostracizing of ◊Aristides in 483 BC, he held almost supreme power in Athens for ten years, created its navy and strengthened its walls, and fought with distinction in the Battle of ◊Salamis 480 BC during the Persian War. Banished by Spartan influence about 470 BC, he fled to Asia, where Artaxerxes, the Persian king, received him with favour, and he lived at Magnesia.

Theocritus /θi'ɒkrɪtəs/ fl. c. 270 BC–. Greek poet. Probably born at Syracuse, he spent much of his life at Alexandria. His **Idylls** became models for later pastoral poetry.

theodolite instrument used in surveying for the measurement of horizontal and vertical angles. It consists of a small telescope mounted so as to move on two graduate circles, one horizontal and the other vertical, while its axes pass through the centre of the circles. See also ◊triangulation.

Theodora /,θiːə'dɔːrə/ 508–548. Byzantine empress, originally a courtesan, the mistress of ◊Justinian, and his consort from about 523. She earned a reputation for charity and courage.

Theodorakis /,θiːədə'rɑːkɪs/ Mikis 1925– . Greek composer, imprisoned 1967–70 for attempting to overthrow the military regime.

Theodoric I /θi'ɒdərɪk/ King of the Visigoths 418–51AD, a grandson of ◊Alaric. After successful campaigns against the Romans, he united with them to fight the Huns (under ◊Attila), and was killed at ◊Châlons.

Theodoric /θi'ɒdərɪk/ the Great 455–526. King, in succession to his father, of the Ostrogoths from 474. He invaded Italy 488, overthrew ◊Odoacer (whom he murdered) and established his own Ostrogothic kingdom there (with its capital at Ravenna), ruling in the old tradition of the Roman emperors. He had no strong successor, and his kingdom eventually became part of the Byzantine Empire of ◊Justinian.

Theodoric of Freiburg /'fraɪbɜːg/ c. 1250–1310. German friar and scientist. He studied in Paris 1275–77. In his work **De Iride/On the Rainbow** he describes how he used a water-filled sphere to simulate a raindrop, and determined that colours are formed in the raindrops and that light is reflected within the drop and can be reflected again, which explains secondary rainbows.

Theodosius I /,θiːə'dəusɪəs/ the Great c. 346–c. 395. Roman Emperor in the East from 379 (the colleague of ◊Gratian, emperor of the West); sole emperor from 394. Born in Spain, he served under his father, a Roman general, in Britain and the Balkans. As emperor he subdued the Goths, allowing them autonomy as allies under the peace of 382. He instituted Christianity as the state religion, but blotted his reign by massacring 7,000 citizens of Thessaloniki in 390 after a riot in the circus there (St ◊Ambrose made him do penance).

Theodosius II /,θiːə'dəusɪəs/ 401–450. Byzantine emperor from 408, who defeated the Persians 421 and 441, and from 441 bought off Attila's Huns with tribute.

theology the study of God or gods, either by reasoned deduction from the natural world, or through revelation, as in the scriptures of Christianity, Islam, or other religions.

theorbo a form of ◊lute.

theosophy any religious or philosophical system based on intuitive insight into the nature of the divine, but especially that of the Theosophical Society founded in New York in 1875 by Madame ◊Blavatsky and Colonel H S Olcott, based on Hindu ideas of ◊karma and ◊reincarnation, with ◊nirvana as the eventual aim.

Theravāda one of the two major forms of ◊Buddhism, common in S Asia (Sri Lanka, Thailand, Kampuchea, and Burma); the other is the later ◊Mahāyāna.

Theresa /təˈreɪzə/ Mother, born Agnes Bojaxhiu 1910– . Indian Roman Catholic nun. She was born in Skopje, Albania and at 18 entered a Calcutta convent and became a teacher. In 1948 she became an Indian citizen, and founded the Missionaries of Charity, an order for men and women based in Calcutta, which especially helps abandoned children and the dying. She was awarded the Nobel Peace Prize 1979, and an honorary Order of Merit 1983.

Thérèse of Lisieux /təˈreɪz, liːˈsjɜː/ 1873–1897. French saint. Born at Alençon, she entered a Carmelite convent at Lisieux at 15, where her holy life induced her superior to ask her to write her spiritual autobiography. She advocated the Little Way of Goodness in small things in everyday life, and is known as Little Flower of Jesus. She died of tuberculosis and was canonized in 1925.

therm unit of energy defined as 10^5 British thermal units. Equivalent to 1.055×10^8 joules. It is no longer in scientific use.

thermal conductivity in physics, the ability of a substance to conduct heat. Good thermal conductors, like good electrical conductors, are generally materials with many free ◊electrons (such as metals). For a block of material of cross-sectional area a and length l, with temperatures T_1 and T_2 at its end faces, the thermal conductivity λ equals $Hl/at(T_2-T_1)$, where H is the amount of heat transferred in time t. Thermal conductivity is expressed in units of ◊joules per second per metre per degree ◊Kelvin $(Js^{-1}m^{-1}K^{-1})$.

thermal expansion also called expansivity. In physics, expansion that is due to a rise in temperature. It can be expressed in terms of linear, area or volume expansion. The coefficient of linear expansion α is the increase in unit length per degree temperature rise; area, or superficial, expansion β is the increase in unit area per degree; and volume, or cubic, expansion γ is the increase in unit volume per degree. To a good approximation, $\beta = 2\alpha$ and $\gamma = 3\alpha$.

thermic lance cutting tool consisting of a tube of mild steel, enclosing tightly-packed small steel rods and fed with oxygen. On ignition temperatures above 3000°C are produced and the thermic lance becomes its own sustaining fuel. It rapidly penetrates walls and a 23 cm/9 in steel door can be cut through in less than 30 seconds.

Thermidor eleventh month of the French revolutionary calendar which gave its name to the period after the fall of the Jacobins and the proscripton of Robespierre by the National Convention on 9 Thermidor 1794.

thermionics branch of science that deals with the emission of electrons from matter under the influence of heat. A thermionic valve, used in telegraphy and telephony and in radio and radar, is a device using space conduction by thermionically emitted electrons. Classification is into diode, triode, and multi-electrode valves, but in many applications valves have been replaced by ◊transistors. See O W ◊Richardson.

thermite process a process used in incendiary devices and welding operations. It uses a powdered mixture of aluminium and (usually) iron oxide, which, when ignited, gives out enormous heat. The oxide is reduced to iron, which is molten at the high temperatures produced. This can be used to make a weld. The process was discovered by German chemist Hans Goldschmidt in 1895.

thermocouple electric temperature-measuring device consisting of a circuit having two wires made of different metals welded together at their ends. A current flows in the circuit when the two junctions are maintained at different temperatures (◊Seebeck effect). The ◊electromotive force generated – measured by a millivoltmeter – is proportional to the temperature difference.

thermodynamics branch of physics dealing with the transforming of heat into other forms of energy, on which is based the study of the efficient working of engines, such as the steam and internal combustion engines. The three laws of thermodynamics are: (1) energy can be neither created nor destroyed, heat and mechanical work being mutually convertible; (2) it is impossible for an unaided self-acting machine to convey heat from one body to another at a higher temperature; (3) it is impossible by any procedure, no matter how idealized, to reduce any system to the ◊absolute zero of temperature (0°K/–273°C) in a finite number of operations. Put into mathematical form these have widespread applications in physics and chemistry.

thermography the recording of heat patterns, as developed in the 1970s and 1980s, using a photographic method (the Aga system) developed by the military to assist night vision, by detecting the body heat of an enemy, or the hot engine of a tank. It is now used medically as an imaging technique to identify 'hot-spots' in the body, for example, tumours, where cells are more active than usual.

thermoluminescence in physics, light released by material that has been exposed to ◊irradiation when it is later heated. It occurs with most crystalline substances to some extent. It is used in archaeology to date pottery, and by geologists in studying terrestrial rocks and meteorites.

thermometer instrument for measuring temperature. These are many types, designed to measure temperature ranges and to varying degrees of accuracy. Each makes use of a

different physical effect of temperature. Expansion of a liquid is employed in common liquid-in-glass thermometers, such as those containing mercury or alcohol. The more accurate gas thermometer uses the effect of temperature on the pressure of a gas held at constant volume. A resistance thermometer takes advantage of the change in ◊resistance of a ◊conductor (such as a platinum wire) with variation in temperature. Another electrical thermometer is the ◊thermocouple. Mechanically, temperature change can be indicated by the change in curvature of a bimetallic strip (as commonly used in a ◊thermostat).

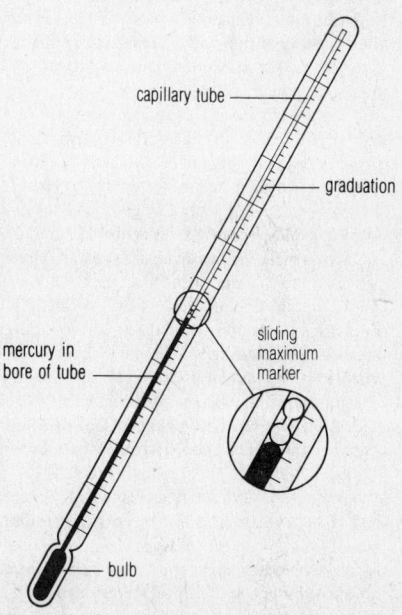

thermometer

capillary tube

graduation

mercury in bore of tube

sliding maximum marker

bulb

thermoplastics see ◊plastics.

Thermopylae, Battle of /θɜːˈmɒpɪliː/ battle during the ◊Persian wars in 480 BC when Leonidas, king of Sparta, and 1,000 men defended the pass of Thermopylae to the death against the Persians.

Thermos trade name for a type of vacuum flask; see ◊Dewar flask.

thermosphere the layer in the Earth's ◊atmosphere above the mesosphere and below the exosphere. Its lower level is about 80 km/50 mi above the ground but its upper level is undefined. In the thermosphere the temperature rises with increasing height, to a maximum of several thousand degrees C. However, because of the thinness of the air, very little heat is present. The ionosphere is located in the thermosphere.

thermostat a temperature-controlling device that makes use of feedback. It employs a temperature sensor (often a bimetallic strip) to operate a switch or valve to control the supply of electricity or fuel to a heater. At the required pre-set temperature (for example of a room or gas oven), the movement of the sensor switches off the supply of electricity to the room heater or gas to the oven. As the room or oven cools down, the sensor turns on the supply of electricity or gas.

Theroux /θə'ru:/ Paul Edward 1941– . American novelist (*Saint Jack* 1973, *Picture Palace* 1978, *The Mosquito Coast* 1981 and *Doctor Slaughter* 1984), and travel writer (*The Great Railway Bazaar* 1975).

thesaurus (Greek 'treasure') a collection of synonyms or words with related meaning. The best-known, by Peter Mark ◊Roget, published in 1852, was not the first; earlier thesaurus compilers included ◊Pliny, Francis ◊Bacon, and ◊Comenius.

Theseus legendary hero of ◊Attica, supposed to have united the states of the area under a constitutional government at Athens. Ariadne, whom he later abandoned on ◊Naxos, helped him find his way through the labyrinth to kill the ◊Minotaur. He also fought the ◊Amazons and was one of the ◊Argonauts.

Thespis legendary Greek poet (6th century BC), said to have introduced the first actor into plays (previously presented by choruses only), hence the word 'thespian' for an actor. He was also said to have invented tragedy and to have introduced the wearing of linen masks.

Thessaloniki /ˌθesəlɒ'ni:ki/ port in Greek Macedonia at the head of the Gulf of Thessaloniki; population (1981) 402,400. Industries include textiles, shipbuilding, brewing, and tanning.
history It stands on the site of the Roman *Thessalonica*, to whose inhabitants St ◊Paul addressed two epistles. Founded from Corinth 315 BC, captured by the Saracens 904 AD, by the Turks 1430, it was restored to Greece 1912.

Thessaly /'θesəli/ region of E central Greece, on the Aegean; area 13,975 sq km/5,395 sq mi; population (1981) 695,650.
history An independent state in ancient Greece, it was conquered by Philip of Macedon in the 4th century BC. It formed part of the Roman province of *Macedonia*, and was Turkish from the 14th century until incorporated in Greece 1881 as a region which includes ◊Larisa, Magnesia, Trikkala, and Kardhitsa.

Thetford /'θetfəd/ market town in Norfolk, England; population (1982) 19,279.

Thetford Mines /'θetfəd/ site of the world's largest asbestos deposits, Quebec, Canada.

thiamine a ◊vitamin of the B complex. Its absence from the diet causes the disease ◊beriberi.

Thibault /ti:'bəu/ Anatole-François real name of French writer Anatole ◊France.

Thiers /ti'eə/ Louis Adolphe 1797–1877. French politician and historian. He held cabinet posts under Louis Phillipe, led the parliamentary opposition to Napoleon III from 1863, and as head of the provisional government in 1871 negotiated peace with Prussia and suppressed the Paris Commune. He was first president of the third Republic 1871–73. His books include *Histoire de la Révolution française/History of the French Revolution* 1823–27.

Thimbu /'θɪmbu:/ (or Thimphu), capital since 1962 of the Himalayan state of ◊Bhutan; population (1982) 15,000.

thing an assembly of freemen in the Norse lands during the medieval period. It could encompass a meeting of the whole nation (*Althing*) or of a small town or community (*Husthing*).

thing-in-itself (German *Ding-an-sich*) a term in the philosophy of ◊Kant, employed to denote the unknowable source of the sensory component of our experience. Later thinkers, including ◊Fichte and ◊Hegel, denied the coherence of this concept.

Third Reich a term coined by German writer Moeller van der Bruck in the 1920s and used by the Nazis to describe the early years of Hitler's dictatorship after 1933, although the term was later dropped. The idea of the Third Reich (Third Empire) was based on the existence of two previous German Empires, the medieval Holy Roman Empire and the second empire 1871–1918.

Third World those countries of Africa, Asia, and Latin America (about 114) which are still undergoing industrial development as a result of major political changes caused by the break-up of the European overseas empires. (The USA and USSR form the First World, and the industrialized European states together with Canada and Japan the Second World; the *Three Worlds Theory* was allegedly first formulated by ◊Mao Zedong.) Apart from the Spanish colonies in South and Central America which achieved their independence in the early 19th century, nearly all of this decolonization has taken place since the end of World War II, either by negotiation or by force, creating many new, independent, sovereign states in South and Central America, Africa and Asia. While the term Third World may indicate a colonial past, it also indicates the present economic situation of those countries; industrially underdeveloped and dependent on the developed world for many essential products. This relationship between the industrialized nations and the Third World has created a severe debt crisis for many of the underdeveloped nations where they are now having to raise loans internationally merely in order to pay off existing debts, rather than for industrial or agricultural development projects. Population increases are also a major hindrance: Third World countries represent about 80% of the world population, yet account for less than 30% of the world's industrial production.
In recent years Third World countries have tried to exert some political influence in world affairs through the creation of the non-aligned movement within the United Nations; and economic influence through the creation of the 'Group of 77' (1964), an organization designed to put pressure on the developed world to provide aid and monetary assistance.

Thirteen Colonies the 13 colonies of the USA which signed the ◊Declaration of Independence from Britain in 1776. Led by George Washington, they defeated the British army in the War of ◊American Independence 1776–81 to become the original 13 ◊United States of America. They were: Connecticut, Delaware, Georgia, Maryland, Massachusetts, New Hampshire, New Jersey, New York, North

Carolina, Pennsylvania, Rhode Island, South Carolina, and Virginia.

thirty-eighth parallel the demarcation line between North and South Korea, first agreed at the Yalta Conference in 1945 and largely unaltered by the Korean War of 1950–53.

35 mm a width of photographic film, the most popular format for the modern camera. The 35 mm camera falls into two categories, the ◊SLR and the rangefinder.

Thirty-Nine Articles a set of articles of faith defining the doctrine of the Anglican Church; see under ◊Anglican Communion.

Thirty Years' War major war in central Europe 1618–48. Beginning as a conflict between Protestants and Catholics, it gradually became transformed into a struggle to determine whether the ◊Hapsburgs would gain control of all Germany. After the defeat of a Bohemian revolt against Austrian rule 1618–20, some Protestant princes continued the struggle against Austria, with the aid of Denmark 1625–27. From 1630 ◊Gustavus Adolphus of Sweden intervened on the Protestant side, overrunning N Germany before his death in 1632. When the Swedes were defeated at Nördlingen 1634, ◊Richelieu brought France into the war to inflict several defeats on Austria's Spanish allies. The *Treaty of Westphalia* 1648 gave France S Alsace, and Sweden certain Baltic provinces, the emperor's authority in Germany becoming only nominal. The mercenary armies of Wallenstein, Tilly, and Mansfeld devastated Germany.

thistle name for spiny plants of several genera in the family Compositae, the best-known being *Carduus* and *Cirsium*, found in the N

Thirty Years' War The Netherlands after the Peace of Westphalia 1648

United Provinces

The Generality, i.e. areas seized from the Spanish Netherlands by the United Provinces

Spanish Netherlands

Groningen
Amsterdam
The Hague
Arnhem
Utrecht
Rotterdam
Cleves
Breda
Sluys
Antwerp
Cologne
Ghent
Calais
Brussels
Aachen
Namur
Mons

hemisphere. The flower heads are purple and cottony, the leaves are deeply indented and spiny: a thistle is the Scottish national emblem.

Thistle, Order of the a Scottish order of ◊knighthood.

Thistlewood /'θɪsəlwʊd/ Arthur 1770–1820. English Radical. A follower of the pamphleteer Thomas Spence (1750–1814), he was active in the Radical movement and was executed as the chief leader of the ◊Cato Street conspiracy to murder government ministers.

Thomas /'tɒməs/ Dylan (Marlais) 1914–1953. Welsh poet. Born in Swansea, son of the English master at the local grammar school where he was educated, he worked as a reporter on the *South Wales Evening Post*, then settled as a journalist in London and published his first volume *Eighteen Poems* in 1934. Best-known poems include the celebration of his 30th birthday 'Poem in October' and the evocation of his youth 'Fern Hill' 1946. Also memorable are his radio play *Under Milk Wood* 1954 and the short stories of *Portrait of the Artist as a Young Dog* 1940, which are autobiographical.

Thomas /'tɒməs/ Ronald Stuart 1913– Welsh poet, vicar of St Hywyn, Aberdaron, 1967–78. His verse, as in *Song at the Year's Turning* 1955, contrasts traditional Welsh values with encroaching 'English' sterility.

Thomas à Kempis /ə 'kempɪs/ 1380–1471. German Augustinian monk who lived at the monastery of Zwolle. He was so-named because born at Kempen; his real surname was Hammerken. His *Die Imitatione Christi/Imitation of Christ* is probably the best-known devotional work ever written.

Thomas, St in the New Testament, one of the 12 Apostles, said to have preached in S India, hence the ancient churches there were referred to as the 'Christians of St Thomas'. He is not the author of the Gospel of St Thomas, the Gnostic collection of Christ's sayings.

Thomism in philosophy, name given to the method and approach of Thomas ◊Aquinas. Neo-Thomists apply this philosophical method to contemporary problems.

Thompson /'tɒmpsən/ Flora 1877–1948. English novelist, whose trilogy *Lark Rise to Candleford* 1945 deals with late Victorian rural life.

Thompson /'tɒmpsən/ Francis 1859–1907. British poet. Born in Preston, he settled in London, where he fell into poverty and ill health. Wilfrid and Alice ◊Meynell arranged the publication of his poems in 1893, including 'The Hound of Heaven'. In this and later volumes (*Sister Songs 1895* and *New Poems* 1897) Thompson, who was a Roman Catholic, expressed a mystic view of life.

Thompson /'tɒmpsən/ Francis Morgan 'Daley' 1958– . British athlete, noted for his all-round performance in the ten different events of the ◊decathlon. Since winning the Commonwealth games decathlon in 1978, he has broken the world record four times; he has been Olympic, European, and world champion.

Thomsen /'tɒmsən/ Christian Jürgensen 1788–1865. Danish archaeologist. He devised

Thompson Daley Thompson has broken the world decathlon record four times since winning the Commonwealth Games decathlon title in 1978. He has won two more Commonwealth titles, two Olympic gold medals, two European titles and a world title.

the classification of prehistoric cultures into Stone Age, Bronze Age, and so on.

Thomson /'tɒmsən/ Elihu 1853–1937. American inventor who did important work in electrodynamics. Born in England, he lived in USA from 1858. He founded, with E J Houston, the Thomson-Houston Electric Company in 1882, later merging with the Edison Company to form the General Electric Company. As director of the research laboratory, he made important advances into the nature of the ◊electric arc, invented the first high-frequency ◊dynamo and ◊transformer. He also contributed to improvements on many aspects of incandescent lighting (using a filament) and radiology.

Thomson /'tɒmsən/ George Paget 1892–1975. British physicist, son of Joseph ◊Thomson. His work on ◊interference phenomena in the scattering of electrons by crystals helped to confirm the wave-like nature of particles (see ◊quantum theory). He shared a

Nobel prize with C J ◊Davisson in 1937, and was knighted 1943.

Thomson /'tɒmsən/ James 1700–1748. Scottish poet, whose descriptive blank verse poem *The Seasons* 1726–30 was a forerunner of the Romantic movement. He also wrote the words of 'Rule, Britannia'.

Thomson /'tɒmsən/ James 1834–1882. Scottish poet, who wrote as 'BV' (Bysshe Vanolis). Born in Renfrewshire, he became an army schoolmaster and a journalist. He is remembered for his despairing poem 'The City of Dreadful Night' 1880.

Thomson /'tɒmsən/ Joseph John 1856–1940. British physicist, who discovered the ◊electron. Educated at Manchester and Cambridge, where he became Cavendish professor of experimental physics 1884–1918, he organized the Cavendish research laboratory which became a world-famous centre of atomic research. His work inaugurated the electrical theory of the ◊atom, and his elucidation of positive rays and their application to an analysis of ◊neon led to ◊Aston's discovery of ◊isotopes. He was awarded a Nobel prize in 1906 and the Order of Merit in 1913. His son was George Paget ◊Thomson.

Thomson /'tɒmsən/ Virgil 1896– . US composer, a student of Nadia ◊Boulanger. He has produced a large body of work, characterized by its clarity and simplicity of style, which includes operas such as *Four Saints in Three Acts* (libretto Gertrude ◊Stein) 1934, orchestral, choral, and chamber music, and film scores.

Thor /θɔː/ in Norse mythology, son of Odin and Frigga, god of thunder (his hammer), and represented as a man of enormous strength defending humanity against demons. Thursday is named after him.

thorax the part of the vertebrate body containing the ◊heart and ◊lungs and protected by the rib cage; in arthropods the middle part of the body, between the head and ◊abdomen. In mammals the thorax is separated from the abdomen by the muscular diaphragm. In insects the thorax bears the legs and wings, when present. The thorax of spiders and crustaceans is fused with the head, to form the cephalothorax.

Thoreau /'θɔːrəʊ/ Henry David 1817–1862. American author and naturalist, born at Concord, Massachusetts. He is best known for *Walden, or Life in the Woods* 1854, which stimulated the back-to-nature movement. His later works are some thirty volumes based on his daily nature walks. His essay 'Civil Disobedience' 1849 advocating peaceful resistance to unjust laws, was widely influential.

thorium a dark grey, naturally radioactive metal, widely distributed throughout the world in minerals, particularly monazite beach sands; symbol Th, atomic number 90, atomic weight 232.05. Discovered by Berzelius (1828), it has a half-life 1.39 ×,10¹⁰ years, and its greatest potential use is breeding from it uranium-233, an excellent fuel for nuclear power reactors

thorn apple plant *Datura stramonium*, also called jimsonweed, which grows to 2 m/6 ft, and has white or violet trumpet-shaped flowers. Native to the USA and Canada, it has spread to Africa and Europe. The leaves are poisonous.

Thorndike /'θɔːndaɪk/ Sybil 1882–1976. British actress for whom Shaw wrote *St Joan*. The Thorndike Theatre, Leatherhead, is named after her, and the theatre workshop after her husband, actor *Sir Lewis Casson* 1885–1972, with whom she often appeared. Her brother *Russell Thorndike* (1885–1972) was also an actor, and wrote a series of novels featuring the 18th century smuggling parson 'Dr Syn'. She was made a Dame of the British Empire 1931.

Thorpe /θɔːp/ Jeremy 1929– . British Liberal politician, leader of the Liberal Party 1967–76.

Thorwaldsen /'tɔːvælsən/ Bertel 1770–1844. Danish sculptor. Born at sea, he studied at Rome where he became a friend of ◊Canova. His Neo-Classical works include *The Triumph of Alexander* 1812.

Thoth /təʊt/ in Egyptian mythology, god of wisdom and learning. He was represented as a

scribe with the head of an ◊ibis, the bird sacred to him.

Thothmes /'təʊtmes/ name of four Egyptian kings of the 18th dynasty: *Thothmes I* reigned 1540–1501 BC, founded the Egyptian empire in Syria. His grandson *Thothmes III* reigned c. 1500–1446 BC, extended the empire to the Euphrates, and conquered Nubia.

thousand days the period of office of US president John F Kennedy from 1 Jan 1961 to his assassination on 22 Nov 1963.

Thousand Islands group of about 1,500 islands on the border between Canada and the USA in the upper St Lawrence river.

Thrace /θreɪs/ Balkan area divided in 1923 into western Thrace (the modern Greek province of Thráki) and eastern Thrace (modern Turkey-in-Europe). However, the heart of the ancient Thracian Empire 6000 BC–300 AD was modern Bulgaria, where since 1945 there have been tomb finds of gold and silver dishes, drinking vessels and jewellery with animal designs, especially splendid horses. The legend of ◊Orpheus and the cult of ◊Dionysus were both derived by the Greeks from Thrace. The area was conquered by Persia, 6th–5th centuries BC and by Macedon 4th–2nd centuries BC. From 46 AD it was a Roman province, then part of the Byzantine Empire, and Turkish from the 15th century until 1878; it was then subject to constant dispute until after World War I.

threadworm a form of ◊nematode.

three day week name given to the policy adopted by British Prime Minister Edward Heath in Jan 1974 to combat an economic crisis and coal-miners' strike. A shortage of electrical power led to the allocation of energy to industry for only three days each week. A General Election was called in February 1974 during the ◊winter of discontent.

Three Rivers English name for the Canadian port of ◊Trois Rivières.

thrift plant of genus *Armeria* in the family Plumbaginaceae. Thrift or sea pink *Armeria maritima* occurs on seashores and cliffs in Europe. The leaves are small and linear. The dense round heads of pink flowers rise on straight stems.

thrips tiny insect with feathery wings, of the order Thysanoptera. Many species live in flowers. Some are agricultural pests.

throat in humans, the passage that leads from the back of the nose and mouth to the windpipe (◊trachea) and gullet (oesophagus). It includes the ◊pharynx and the ◊larynx, the latter being at the top of the trachea. The word 'throat' is also used to mean the front part of the neck, both in humans and other vertebrates, for example, in describing the plumage of birds, and also in engineering for any narrowing entry, such as the throat of a carburettor.

thrombosis formation of a blood clot in a blood vessel, often in the legs, where it may cause ◊phlebitis, or heart, as in ◊coronary thrombosis.

throwing events field athletic contests in which the four usual events are:
discus in which the discus weighs (men's) 2 kg/4.4 lb, (women's) 1 kg/2.2 lb and is thrown from within a circle 2.5 m/8 ft in diameter.

hammer (men only) which has a spherical head, and may originally have been a blacksmith's hammer. It now weighs 7.26 kg/16 lb, and is thrown similarly to the discus.
javelin in which the javelin is (men's) 260–270 cm/about 8.5 ft long and weighs 800 g/28 oz, (women's) 230 cm/7.5 ft long, weighing 600 g/21 oz thrown from a scratch line at the end of a run-up. The centre of gravity on the men's javelin was altered in 1986 to reduce the vast distances (100 yards) that were being thrown.
putting the shot a 'cannon-ball' weight, for men 7.26 kg/16 lb, for women 4 kg/8.8 lb, thrown with one hand from a slightly smaller circle than the discus.
tossing the caber is a Highland Games event only, in which a tapered tree trunk about 6 m/20 ft long and weighing about 100 kg/220 lb is hurled as far as possible in a straight line from the competitor (about 12 m/40 ft).

thrush bird of the family Turdidae. The song thrush *Turdus philomelos* is 23 cm/9 in long, brown above and with a paler throat and breast speckled with dark brown: it is one of Britain's finest songbirds. Slightly larger is the mistle thrush *Turdus viscivorus*, nicknamed the stormcock because it often sings before and during wild, wet weather. North American species include the hermit thrush *Catharus guttatus* a beautiful songster, and the wood thrush *Hylocichla mustelina*.

Thrust 2 the jet-propelled car in which British driver Richard Noble set a new world land speed record in the Black Rock Desert of Nevada, USA, in Oct 1983. The record speed was 1,019.4 kph/633.468 mph.

Thucydides /θjuː'sɪdɪdiːz/ 460–400 BC. Athenian historian, who exercised command in the ◊Peloponnesian War in 424 with so little success that he was banished till 404. In his *History of the Peloponnesian War* he attempted a scientific impartiality.

thug originally a member of a Hindu sect who strangled travellers as sacrifices to ◊Kali the goddess of destruction; suppressed about 1830.

Thule /'θjuːli/ Greek and Roman name for the most northerly land known. It was applied to the Shetlands, the Orkneys, and Iceland, and by later writers to Scandinavia.

thulium a metallic element, symbol Tm, atomic number 69, atomic weight 168.94. Used in arc lighting, it is one of the lanthanide series of elements. The isotope Tm-170 is used as an X-ray source.

Thunder Bay /'θʌndə 'beɪ/ city and port on Lake Superior, Ontario, Canada, formed by the union of Port Arthur and its twin city of Fort William to the S; population (1984) 115,000. Industries include shipbuilding, timber, paper, and wood pulp, and the export of wheat.

Thunderbird a legendary bird of the North American ◊Plains Indians, the creator of the storms of the great plains.

Thurber /'θɜːbə/ James (Grover) 1894–1961. US humorist, born in Columbus, Ohio. He worked for the *New Yorker* magazine. His short stories include 'The Secret Life of Walter Mitty' 1932, and his doodle drawings include fanciful impressions of dogs. Partially blind from childhood, he became totally blind in the last ten years of his life and continued his work.

Thuringia /θjʊˈrɪndʒɪə/ former state of central Germany 1919–46; capital Weimar. The area includes the *Thuringian Forest*. Thuringia was a *Land* until 1952, when it became the East German districts of Erfurt, Gera, and Suhl.

Thursday Island /ˈθɜːzdeɪ/ island in Torres Strait, Queensland, Australia; area 4 sq km/1.5 sq mi; chief centre Port Kennedy. It is a centre of the pearl fishing industry.

Thurso /ˈθɜːsəʊ/ port in Highland region, Scotland. It is the mainland terminus of the steamer service to the Orkneys, and the experimental atomic station of Dounreay lies to the W.

thylacine another name for the ◊Tasmanian tiger/wolf.

thyme genus of plants *Thymus* in the family Labiatae. Garden thyme *Thymus vulgaris*, a native of the Mediterranean, has aromatic leaves used for seasoning, pinkish flowers, and a slightly woody growth under 30 cm/1 ft high.

thymus an organ of vertebrates, situated in the upper chest cavity in humans. It develops early in embryonic life, continues to grow after birth, reaches full size at puberty, and slowly shrinks thereafter. The thymus is a vital part of the body's defences (see ◊immunity). It processes the ◊lymphocyte cells produced by bone marrow, to produce T-lymphocytes (T denotes 'thymus-derived') which give cell-mediated immunity, rather than immunity due to ◊antibodies. The stock of T-lymphocytes is built up early in life, so the role of the thymus diminishes in adults. However it continues to function as an ◊endocrine gland, producing the hormone thymosin, which stimulates the activity of the T-lymphocytes.

thyroid an ◊endocrine gland of vertebrates, situated in the neck. It secretes thyroxin, a ◊hormone containing iodine. This stimulates growth, metabolism, and other functions of the body. Abnormal action produces Graves' disease, with bulging eyeballs, while deficient action produces ◊myxoedema in adults and dwarfism in juveniles.

Tianjin /ˌtjenˈdʒɪn/ port and industrial and commercial city (formerly Tientsin), a special municipality in Hubei province, China; population (1982) 5,130,000. Site of Nankai University 1919. Its handmade silk and wool carpets are famous. Dagan oilfield is nearby. Tianjin was opened to foreign trade 1860, and occupied by the Japanese 1937.

Tian Shan /tiˈen ˈʃɑːn/ mountain system (Chinese *Tien-Shan*) on the Soviet-Chinese border. Peaks include *Kongur Shan* in Xinjiang, China, 7,719 m/25,325 ft (Chris ◊Bonington led an expedition which first reached the summit 1981) and *Pik Pobedy* on the Kirgizia border 7,439 m/24,406 ft.

tiara the triple crown worn by the Pope, or a semi-circular headdress worn by women for formal occasions. The term was originally applied to a head-dress worn by the ancient Persians.

Tiber /ˈtaɪbə/ river in Italy on which Rome stands; length from the Apennines to the Tyrrhenian Sea 400 km/250 mi.

Tiberias, Lake /taɪˈbɪərɪæs/ lake in N Israel (also called Sea of Galilee, Lake of Gennesaret, and Hebrew *Yam Kinneret*) 210 m/686 ft below sea level, into which the ◊Jordan flows; area 165 sq km/64 sq mi.

Tiberius /taɪˈbɪərɪəs/ Claudius Nero 42 BC–37 AD. Roman emperor, the stepson, adopted son, and successor of Augustus from 14 AD. A distinguished soldier, he was a conscientious ruler under whom the empire prospered. In later life he retired to Capri.

Tiberius A bust of the Roman emperor, Tiberius. The adopted son of Augustus, his predecessor, Tiberius was a conscientious ruler under whom the Roman Empire flourished.

Tibesti Mountains /tɪˈbesti/ range in the central Sahara, N Chad; highest peak *Emi Koussi* 3,415 m/11,204 ft.

Tibet /tɪˈbet/ autonomous region of SW China (Pinyin form: *Xizang*)
area 1,221,600 sq km/471,540 sq mi
capital Lhasa
features Tibet occupies a barren plateau bounded S and SW by the Himalayas and N by the Kunlun Mountains, traversed W–E by the Bukamagna, Karakoram, and other ranges, and having an average elevation of 4–4,500 m/13–15,000 ft. The Sutlej, Brahmaputra, and Indus rivers rise in Tibet, which has numerous lakes, many of which are salty. The ◊yak is the most important domestic animal
products wool, borax, salt, horn, musk, herbs, furs; gold, iron pyrites, lapis lazuli, mercury; textiles, chemicals, agricultural machinery
population (1979) 1,700,000
government Tibet is an Autonomous Region of ◊China with its own People's Government and People's Congress. The controlling force in Tibet

is the Communist Party of China, represented locally by First Secretary Wu Jinghua (1985).
history Tibet was an independent kingdom from the 5th century AD. It came under nominal Chinese suzerainty c. 1700–1912, before independence was regained after a revolt in 1912. China regained control in 1951 when the historic ruler, the ◊Dalai Lama, was driven from the country and the monks (who formed 25% of the population) were forced out of the monasteries. Between 1951–59 the Chinese People's Liberation Army (PLA) controlled Tibet, although the Dalai Lama returned as nominal spiritual and temporal head of state. In 1959 a Tibetan uprising spread from bordering regions to Lhasa and was supported by the Tibet Local Government. The rebellion was, however, suppressed by the PLA, prompting the Dalai Lama and 9,000 Tibetans to flee to India. The Chinese proceeded to dissolve the Tibet Local Government, abolish serfdom, collectivize agriculture and suppress ◊Lamaism. In 1965 Tibet became an autonomous region of China. Industrialization (textiles, chemicals, agricultural machinery) has been encouraged and many Chinese have settled in the country. Chinese rule continued to be resented, however, and the economy languished. Since 1979, therefore, the new leadership in Beijing has adopted a more liberal and pragmatic policy towards Tibet. Traditional agriculture, livestock and trading practices have been restored (under the 1980 slogan 'relax, relax and relax again'), a number of older political leaders and rebels have been rehabilitated or pardoned and the promotion of local Tibetan cadres has been encouraged. In addition, a more tolerant attitude towards Lamaism has been adopted (temples damaged during the 1965–68 Cultural Revolution being repaired) and attempts, thus far unsuccessful, have been made to persuade the Dalai Lama to return from exile. The country is one of immense strategic importance to China, being the site of 200,000 troops and a major nuclear missile base at Nagchuka.

tick arachnid allied to the ◊mites; ticks are blood-sucking, disease-carrying parasites on humans, animals, and birds.

Ticonderoga /ˌtaɪkɒndəˈrəʊgə/ fort in New York state, USA, on a route to Canada near Lake Champlain. It was the site 1758–59 of battles between the British and the French, and was captured from the British 10 May 1775 by Benedict ◊Arnold and Ethan Allen.

tidal power station a kind of ◊hydroelectric power plant that uses the 'head' of water created by the rise and fall of the ocean tides to spin the water turbines.

tidal wave a misleading name for a ◊tsunami.

tide rise and fall of sea level due to the gravitational forces of the Moon and Sun. High water occurs at an average interval of 12 hr 24 min 30 sec. The highest or *spring tides* are at or near new and full Moon, and the lowest or *neap tides* when the Moon is in the first or third quarter. Some seas, such as the Mediterranean, have very small tides.

Other factors affecting sea level are (1) a combination of naturally high tides with storm surge, as sometimes happens in the Thames area and low-lying coasts of Germany and the Netherlands; (2) the water walls created by typhoons and hurricanes, such as often hit Bangladesh; (3) underwater upheavals in the Earth's crust which may cause ◊tsunami; and (4) global temperature change melting the polar ice caps.

Gravitational tides – the pull of nearby groups of stars – have been observed to affect the galaxies.

tides

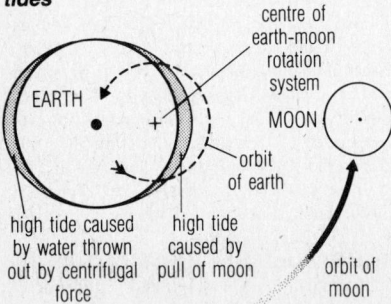

centre of earth-moon rotation system

EARTH

MOON

orbit of earth

orbit of moon

high tide caused by water thrown out by centrifugal force

high tide caused by pull of moon

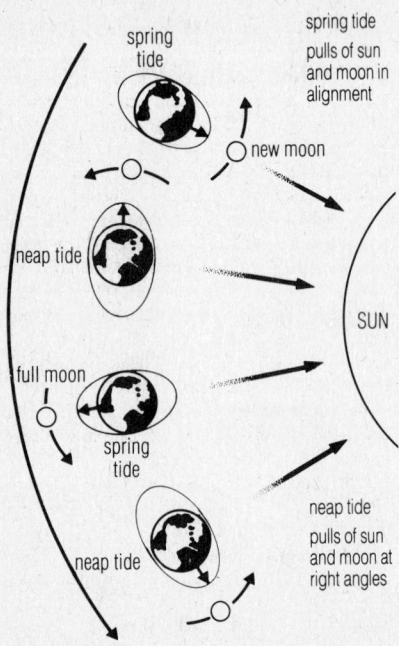

spring tide

spring tide pulls of sun and moon in alignment

new moon

neap tide

SUN

full moon

spring tide

neap tide

neap tide pulls of sun and moon at right angles

neap tide

Tieck /tiːk/ Johann Ludwig 1773–1853. German Romantic poet and collector of folktales, some of which he dramatized, for example 'Puss in Boots'.

Tien-Shan /'tjen 'ʃɑːn/ Chinese form of ◊Tian-Shan, a mountain system of central Asia.

Tientsin /ˌtjen'tsɪn/ former name for ◊Tianjin, an industrial city in NE China.

Tiepolo /ti'epələʊ/ Giovanni Battista 1696–1770. Italian painter, born at Venice, and a master of ◊Rococo historical and allegorical fresco painting for churches and palaces. His painted ceilings were noted for their delicate colour shadings.

Tierra del Fuego /ti'eərə del 'fweigəʊ/ island group divided between Chile and Argentina. It is separated from the mainland by Magellan Strait, and Cape Horn is at the southernmost point. To the S of the main island is **Beagle Channel** (named after the ship of ◊Darwin's voyage) with three islands at the E end, finally awarded in 1985 to Chile rather than Argentina.

Tiffany /'tɪfəni/ Louis Comfort 1848–1933. American artist and glassmaker. He produced stained glass windows, iridescent Favrile (Latin *faber* 'craftsman') glass, and lampshades. He used glass which contained oxides of iron and other impurities to get richness of colour.

Tiflis /'tɪflɪs/ Russian name for the city of ◊Tbilisi in the USSR.

tiger largest of the great cats *Panthera tigris*, formerly found in much of Central and S Asia but increasingly rare. The striped markings – black on reddish fawn – are present from birth, though rare cream or black specimens have been known. The tiger reaches a length of 3–3.6 m/10–12 ft, may be either solitary or one of a family party, is a good swimmer, and feeds on deer or cattle, eating humans usually only as the result of weakened powers or shortage of game.

Tigris /'taɪgrɪs/ river flowing through Turkey and Iraq (see also ◊Mesopotamia), joining the ◊Euphrates above Basra; length 1,600 km/1,000 mi.

Tihuanaco /ˌtiːwəˈnɑːkəʊ/ site of a Peruvian city, 24 km/15 mi south of Lake Titicaca, which gave its name to the 8th–14th century civilization which preceded the ◊Inca.

Tijuana /tɪˈwɑːnə/ city and resort in Mexico; population (1980) 461,257; noted for horse races and casinos. ◊San Diego adjoins it across the US border.

Tikhonov /'tiːxənɒf/ Nikolai 1905– . Soviet politician. Once a locomotive engineer, he became a close associate of ◊Brezhnev, joining the Politburo in 1979. He was prime minister (chair of the Council of Ministers) 1980–85.

Tilbury /'tɪlbəri/ port in Essex, on the N bank of the Thames. Greatly extended in 1976, it became London's largest container port.

till a deposit of clay, mud, gravel, and boulders left by a glacier. Till is unsorted, all sizes of fragment are mixed up together, and it shows no stratification, that is, it does not form clear layers or ◊beds. It is sometimes called **boulder clay**.

Tilly /'tɪli/ Jan Tserklaes, Count Tilly 1559–1632. Flemish commander of the army of the Catholic League and imperial forces in the ◊Thirty Years' War. Notorious for his storming of Magdeburg in 1631, he was defeated by ◊Gustavus Adolphus at Breitenfeld, and at the Lech, where he was mortally wounded.

Tilsit /'tɪlzɪt/ former name (until 1945) of the Russian town of ◊Sovetsk.

Timaru /'tɪmərʊː/ (Maori 'place of shelter') port and resort in South Island, New Zealand; population (1983) 28,900. Industries include flour milling, deep freezing, pottery, and brewing.

timber wood for use in construction, furniture, pulp (for paper), including:
hardwoods including tropical mahogany, teak, ebony, rosewood; temperate oak, elm, beech, and, from Australia, ◊eucalyptus. All are slow-growing and world supplies are near exhaustion.
softwoods (actual hardness or softness of these timbers varies) are the ◊conifers, pine, fir, spruce, larch, which are rapid and easy to grow, and easy to work, but inferior in quality of grain.
white woods ash, birch, ◊sycamore, which have light-coloured timber, are fast-growing, and can be used through modern methods as veneers on cheaper timber, are now being grown as 'crops'. Timber is also given special treatment (moulded, hardened or proofed in various ways), and sawdust and shavings are compacted, with chemical additives, into various grades of sheet 'timber' for construction purposes.

timbre in music, the tone colour of an instrument.

Timbuktu /ˌtɪmbʌk'tuː/ town in Mali; population (1976) 20,500. A camel caravan centre from the 11th century on the fringe of the Sahara, it has since 1960 been surrounded by the southward movement of the desert, and the former canal link with the Niger is dry.

time the continuous passing of existence, recorded by division into hours, minutes, and seconds. Formerly measurement of time on Earth was based on Earth's rotation on its axis, but this was found to be irregular. Therefore, the ◊second, the standard ◊SI unit of time, was redefined in terms of Earth's annual orbit of the Sun (by the International Committee of Weights and Measures) in 1956. In science, the definition of second involves a radiation pattern of the element caesium. The difference between the new Universal Time (UT) and Coordinated Universal Time (UTC) based on Earth's actual rotation is adjusted by the addition (or subtraction) of leap seconds on the last day of June or December. National observatories (in the UK the Royal Greenwich Observatory) make standard time available, and the BBC broadcasts six pips at certain hours (five short, from second 55 to second 59, and one long, the start of which indicates the precise minute). A more exact indication is broadcast from the Post Office Radio Station at Rugby. From 1986 the term Greenwich Mean Time was replaced by UTC. However, the Greenwich meridian, adopted 1884, remains that from which all longitudes are measured, and the world's standard time zones are calculated from it, each hour fast or slow corresponding to 15° longitude.

time, geological time scale embracing the history of the Earth from its physical origin to the present day. Geological time is divided into eras (Palaeozoic, Mesozoic, Cenozoic), which in turn are divided in periods, epochs, ages, and chrons.

Times Beach town in Missouri, USA, which accidentally became contaminated with ◊dioxin, and was bought 1983 by the Environmental Protection Agency for cleansing.

Timor /'tiːmɔː/ largest and most easterly of the Sunda islands; area 33,610 sq km/12,977 sq mi. It is divided into two provinces, the western (capital Kupang) and eastern (capital Dili). The latter was an overseas province of Portugal until the civil war of 1975, when it was annexed by

Indonesia. Guerrilla warfare by local people seeking independence continues.

Timothy /'tɪməθi/ in the New Testament, companion to St ◊Paul, both on his missionary journeys and in prison. Two of the Pauline epistles are addressed to him.

tin the most usual of the several varieties of tin is a silver-white, crystalline metal, malleable and somewhat ductile, which crumbles to a greyish powder at low temperatures: symbol Sn (Latin *stannum*), atomic number 50, atomic weight 118.70. It is found chiefly in the mineral cassiterite, SnO_2, in Malaysia, Indonesia, and Bolivia, and is chiefly used as a protective coating to resist corrosion of iron and steel, for example, the tin can food container. Its use was known in the ancient world, and the mines in Cornwall, where working was renewed between the 1960s and 1980s, were being worked in the Bronze Age.

tinamou bird of the order Tinamiformes; there are some 45 species of these South American birds, rather drab and partridge-like. They are thought to be related to the flightless birds, and are themselves poor at flying.

Tinbergen /'tɪnbɜːgən/ Jan 1903– . Dutch economist. He shared a Nobel prize in 1969 with Ragnar ◊Frisch for his work on ◊econometrics (the mathematical-statistical expression of economic theory). His brother is Nikolaas ◊Tinbergen.

Tinbergen /'tɪnbɜːgən/ Nikolaas 1907– . Dutch zoologist, brother of Jan ◊Tinbergen. He was one of the founders of ◊ethology, the scientific study of animal behaviour. Specializing in the study of instinctive behaviour, he shared a Nobel prize with Konrad Lorenz and Karl von ◊Frisch 1973.

Tindouf /tɪn'duːf/ oasis in W Algeria. There are large iron deposits in the area.

tinnitus internal sounds, inaudible to others, which are heard by sufferers from malfunctions of hearing, for example spasm of an inner-ear muscle or infection of the middle or inner ear. In some cases there is a hum at a frequency of about 40 Hz, but it may include whistles and other noises resembling a machine workshop. Being in a place where external noises drown out the internal ones gives some relief, and devices may be worn which create pleasanter sounds to override them.

tinplate the metal used for most 'tin' cans. They are not made of tin itself, but of tinplate which is mild steel coated with tin. The steel provides the strength and the tin provides the corrosion resistance, ensuring that the food inside is not contaminated. Tinplate may be made by ◊electroplating, or by dipping in a bath of molten tin.

Tintagel /tɪn'tædʒəl/ village resort on the coast of N Cornwall, England; there are castle ruins, and legend has it that King ◊Arthur was born and held court here.

Tintoretto /,tɪntə'retəu/ Venetian painter, real name Jacopo Robusti 1518–1594. A student of Titian, he painted religious paintings, spectacularly lit and composed with daring foreshortening. His enormous canvases of the life of Christ in the Scuola di San Rocco, Venice 1566–88, foreshadow the ◊Baroque movement.

Tipperary /,tɪpə'reəri/ county in the Republic of Ireland, province of ◊Munster. It is divided into N and S regions (administrative headquarters Nenagh and Clonmel respectively).

Tipperary Ireland's ancient status as an early home of Christianity is illustrated by the Celtic crosses found in the countryside. This is the east face of South Cross at Ahenny in Tipperary.

Tippett /'tɪpɪt/ Michael (Kemp) 1905– . British composer. He first made his name in World War II with his oratorio *A Child of Our Time* 1944, and was briefly imprisoned as a conscientious objector in 1943. His music can be at times dissonant and dense in texture, at others lyrical and expansive. Later works include the operas *The Midsummer Marriage* 1952, *King Priam* 1962, *The Knot Garden* 1970, and *The Ice Break* 1977; four symphonies; *Concerto for Double String Orchestra* 1939; the *Fantasia Concertante on a Theme of Corelli* 1953. He was knighted in 1966, and received the Order of Merit in 1983.

Tipu Sahib /'tɪpuː 'sɑːɪb/ 1753–1799. Sultan of Mysore (now Karnataka) from the death of his father, ◊Hyder Ali, in 1782. He died of wounds when his capital, Seringapatam, was captured by the British. His rocket brigade led Sir William Congreve (1772–1828) to develop the weapon for use in the Napoleonic Wars.

Tirana /tɪ'rɑːnə/ capital of Albania; population (1980) 194,000. Industries include metallurgy, cotton textiles, soap, and cigarettes. Founded in the 17th century, it became the capital in 1920.

Tirol /tɪ'rəul/ former province (from 1363) of the Austrian Empire, divided 1919 between Austria (Austrian province of Tirol: capital

Innsbruck), and Italy (see ◊Trentino-Alto Adige); area 12,650 sq km/4,885 sq mi; population (1981) 586,000.

Tirpitz /'tɜːpɪts/ Alfred von 1849–1930. German admiral. As Secretary for the Navy 1897–1916, he created the modern German navy; he planned the World War I U-boat campaign.

Tirso de Molina /'tɪəsəʊ deɪ mə'liːnə/ pen name of Spanish dramatist Gabriel Telléz 1571–1648. A monk, he wrote more than 400 plays, of which eight are extant, including comedies, historical and biblical dramas, and a series based on the legend of Don Juan.

Tiruchirapalli /,tɪrətʃɪ'rɑːpəli/ city (formerly Trichinopoly; the name means 'three-headed demon'), in Tamil Nadu, India; population (1981) 362,045. The chief industries are the manufacture of cotton textiles, cigars, and gold and silver filigree. A place of pilgrimage, it was the capital of Tamil kingdoms from the 10th–17th centuries.

Tiryns /'tɪrɪns/ ancient Greek city in the Peloponnesus on the plain of Argos; with remains of the ◊Mycenaean culture.

Tissot /tiː'səʊ/ James Joseph Jacques 1836–1902. French artist. Serving in the Franco-Prussian War, he subsequently went to London and produced a number of highly detailed renderings of the Victorian social scene.

tissue in biology, a general term for any kind of cellular fabric that occurs in an organism's body. Several kinds of tissue can usually be distinguished, each consisting of cells of a particular kind bound together by cell walls (in plants) or ◊extracellular matrix (in animals). Thus, ◊nerve and ◊muscle are different kinds of tissue in animals, as ◊parenchyma and ◊sclerenchyma are in plants.

tissue culture process in which cells from a plant or animal are removed from the organism, and grown under carefully controlled conditions in a sterile medium containing all the necessary nutrients. Tissue culture can provide information on cell growth and differentiation, and is also used in plant propagation and drug production. See also ◊meristem.

Tisza /'tiːsə/ a tributary of the river ◊Danube, rising in the USSR and flowing through Hungary to Yugoslavia.

tit or *titmouse*, bird of the family Paridae, which in Britain includes the **bluetit** *Parus caeruleus* and the **great tit** *Parus major*, intelligent frequenters of suburban gardens, capable of great acrobatics; and the coal, willow, marsh, and long-tailed tits, as well as the crested tit found only in Scotland.

Titan /'taɪtn/ in Greek mythology, any of the giant children of Uranus and ◊Gaia, who included Kronos, Rhea, Themis (mother of Prometheus and personification of law and order) and Oceanus. Kronos and Rhea were in turn the parents of ◊Zeus, who ousted Kronos as the ruler of the world.

Titan /'taɪtn/ in astronomy, largest moon of the planet ◊Saturn, with a diameter of 5,150 km/3,200 mi (second in size only to Jupiter's moon ◊Ganymede), discovered in 1655 by Christian Huygens. Titan is the only moon in the solar system with a substantial atmosphere, consisting mostly of nitrogen topped with smoggy orange clouds that obscure the surface. Its surface atmospheric pressure is greater than that of the Earth's. The surface may be covered with lakes of liquid methane.

Titanic /taɪ'tænɪk/ British White Star liner (supposedly unsinkable), which struck an iceberg off the Grand Banks of Newfoundland on its maiden voyage 14/15 Apr 1912; 1,513 lives were lost. In 1985 it was located by robot submarine 4 km/2.5 mi down in an ocean canyon, remarkably well preserved by the ice-cold environment, and in 1987 controversial salvage operations began.

titanium a lustrous, steel-like white metal resembling ◊iron, burning in air, and the only metal to burn in nitrogen; symbol Ti, atomic weight 47.90, atomic number 22. Discovered by Gregor in 1791, it was named by Klaproth in 1795 and obtained pure by Hunter in 1910. Its compounds occur in practically all ◊igneous rocks and their sedimentary deposits. The oxide is used in high-grade white pigments, and some barium compounds are used in high-value capacitors. Of great strength and resistance to corrosion, it is used in many high-speed aeroplanes and spacecraft. It was found on the moon in the Sea of Tranquillity.

Titan rocket a family of US space rockets, developed from the Titan intercontinental missile. Two-stage Titan rockets launched the Gemini manned missions (see ◊Gemini project). More powerful Titans, with additional stages and strap-on boosters, have been used to launch 'spy' satellites and space probes, including ◊Viking and ◊Voyager.

tithe in England, a payment exacted from the inhabitants of a parish for the maintenance of the church and its incumbent. Originally tithes were payable in kind, and were levied on all yearly profits, but in the 19th century a rent charge was substituted. By the Tithe Act, 1936, tithes were abolished and replaced by 'redemption annuities' payable to the Crown, government stock being issued to tithe-owners.

Titian /'tɪʃən/ anglicized form of the name of Italian artist Tiziano (Vecellio) c 1487–1576. He studied under the ◊Bellinis, and was influenced by ◊Giorgione. His works include portraits of Charles V and Philip II of Spain, as well as religious and mythical themes, such as *Bacchus and Ariadne* 1520–23, *Venus and Adonis* 1554, and the *Entombment of Christ* 1559.

Titicaca /ˌtɪtɪ'kɑːkə/ lake in the Andes, 3,815 m/12,500 ft above sea level; area 8,300 sq km/3,200 sq mi. It is divided between Bolivia (which has a port at Guaqui) and Peru (which has ports at Puno and Huancane).

Tito /'tiːtəʊ/ pseudonym of Josip Broz 1892–1980. Yugoslav soldier-politician, born in Croatia. He served in the Austrian army during World War I, was captured by the Russians, and fought in the Red Army during the Civil Wars. Returning to Yugoslavia in 1923, he became prominent as a Communist. He organized the National Liberation Army to carry on guerrilla warfare against the German invasion of 1941, and was created marshal 1943. As prime minister

Titian A portrait of Charles V, the Holy Roman Emperor, by Titian.

of the Federal Republic from 1946, he settled the Yugoslav minorities question on a federal basis, and in 1953 became president (for life from 1974). He was attacked by the ◊Cominform, particularly the USSR, in 1948 for his successful system of decentralized profit-sharing workers' councils, and became the leader of the ◊non-aligned movement. He believed that there are different national roads to socialism, and followed a foreign policy of 'positive neutralism'.

Titograd /'tiːtəʊɡræd/ capital of Monte-negro, Yugoslavia (former name Podgorica); population (1981) 132,300. It was damaged in World War II, and after rebuilding was renamed in honour of ◊Tito in 1948. It was the birthplace of the Roman emperor ◊Diocletian.

Titus /'taɪtəs/ Flavius Sabinus Vespasianus 39–81 AD. Roman emperor from 79 AD. Eldest son of ◊Vespasian, he stormed Jerusalem in 70 AD to end the Jewish revolt; finished the Colosseum, and enjoyed a peaceful reign, except for ◊Agricola's campaigns in Britain.

Tivoli /'tɪvəlɪ/ town NE of Rome, Italy. It has remains of Hadrian's villa, with gardens; and the Villa d'Este with fine Renaissance gardens laid out 1549 for Cardinal Ippolito d'Este.

Tlatelolco, Treaty of signed 1967 at Tlatelolco, Mexico, it prohibited nuclear weapons in Latin America (not ratified by Argentina); it was signed also by countries

Tito Marshal Tito, the former president of Yugoslavia, in the grounds of his private villa outside Belgrade.

responsible for territories in the area (UK, USA, France, Netherlands).

Tlemcen /tlem'sen/ town (Roman *Pomaria*) in NW Algeria; population (1983) 146,000. Carpets and leather goods are made, and there is a 12th-century Great Mosque.

Tlingit /'tlɪŋɡɪt/ N American Indian people of the NW coast, famed for carved totem poles bearing the crests and titles of their owners (frequent motifs are the raven and mythical 'thunderbird', whale, octopus, beaver, bear, and wolf); for single-log canoes; and for the custom of the *potlatch*, a distribution of food and gifts to guests, who had in their turn to surpass their hosts – it served as a redistribution of wealth.

TLR camera a twin lens reflex camera, which has a viewing lens mounted above and parallel to the taking lens, of the same angle of view and focal length.

TNT trinitrotoluene, a powerful high explosive. It is a yellow crystalline solid, prepared from toluene using sulphuric and nitric acids.

toad general name for many tailless amphibians which are slow-moving and stout, and have a dry warty skin. The common toad *Bufo bufo* of Europe and Asia has a rough, usually dark brown skin in which there are glands secreting a poisonous fluid which makes it unattractive as food for other animals: it needs this protection as its usual progress is a slow, ungainly crawl. The eggs are laid, not in a mass as with frogs, but in long strings.

toadflax small plant, species of genus *Linaria*, family Scrophulariaceae, with spurred two-lipped flowers.

toadstool any of the type of ◊fungus with a fleshy gilled fruiting body on a stalk.

tobacco American narcotic plant *Nicotiana tabacum*, family Solanaceae; grown in warm, dry climates for use in ◊cigars and ◊cigarettes, and in powdered form as *snuff*. The leaves are cured ('dried') and matured in storage for two–three years before use. Introduced 'medicinally' to Europe in the 16th century, tobacco was recognized from the 1950s as a major health hazard: see ◊cancer. The leaves also yield the alkaloid *nicotine*, a colourless oil, one of the most powerful poisons known, and addictive in humans. It is used in insecticides.

Tobago /tə'beɪgəʊ/ an island in the West Indies; part of the republic of ◊Trinidad and Tobago.

Tobin /'təʊbɪn/ James 1918– . American neo-Keynesian economist (see ◊Keynes). He was awarded a Nobel prize 1981 for his 'general equilibrium' theory, which states that other criteria than monetary considerations are applied by households and firms when making decisions on consumption and investment.

toboggan flat-bottomed sledge, curved upward at the front, used on snow or ice slopes or banked artificial courses, such as the Cresta run in Switzerland. Olympic toboggans are either *luge type* seating 1/2, without brakes or steering; or *bobsleighs* seating 2/4, with streamlined 'cowls' at the front, steering and brakes. A *skibob* is like a bicycle with skis replacing the wheels, and the rider wearing miniature foot skis, up to 50 cm/1 ft 8 in long.

Tobolsk /tə'bɒlsk/ river port and lumber centre at the confluence of the Tobol and Irtysh rivers in W Siberia, USSR; population (1970) 49,250. It was founded by ◊Cossacks 1587.

Tobruk /tə'bruk/ port in Libya, 96 km/60 mi W of Bardia. Occupied by Italy 1911, it was taken by Britain 1941, and unsuccessfully besieged by ◊Axis forces Apr–Dec 1941. It was captured by Germany in Jun 1942 after the retreat of the main British force to Egypt, and this precipitated the replacement of Auchinleck by Montgomery as British commander.

toccata in music, a display piece for keyboard instrument, particularly the organ.

Toc H /'tɒk 'eɪtʃ/ interdenominational organization for Christian fellowship, founded at Poperinghe, Belgium in 1915, as a welfare society with a Christian basis for troops in World War I, by the Rev Neville Talbot and the Rev P T B Clayton (1885–1972); it was named Talbot House in memory of Neville Talbot's brother Gilbert, who was killed in action in World War I, July 1915. Toc H is the army signaller's designation of the initials of Talbot House.

Tocqueville /tɒk'viːl/ Alexis de 1805–1859. French politician and political scientist, author of the first analytical study of the US constitution *De la Démocratie en Amérique (Democracy in America)* 1835, and of a penetrating description of France before the Revolution, *L'Ancien Régime et la Révolution (The Old Regime and the Revolution)* 1856. He was a friend and correspondent of J S ◊Mill.

Todd /tɒd/ Alexander, Baron Todd 1907– . British organic chemist. Born in Glasgow, he was professor at Manchester 1938–44 and Cambridge 1944–71. Elected Fellow of the Royal Society in 1942, he was awarded a Nobel prize 1957 for work on the role of nucleic acids in genetics; Order of Merit 1977.

Todt /təʊt/ Fritz 1891–1942. German engineer, who was responsible for the construction of the autobahns (German motorways), and in World War II the Siegfried Line and the Atlantic Wall.

tog measure of thermal insulation used in the textile trade, for example, a light summer suit provides 1.0 tog.

Togliatti /tɒl'jæti/ (former name *Stavropol*) port on the river Volga, W central USSR; population (1985) 594,000. It was renamed in 1964, after Palmiro ◊Togliatti. The chief industries are engineering and food processing.

Togliatti /tɒl'jæti/ Palmiro 1893–1964. founder of the Italian Communist Party, and influential in the USSR.

Togo /'təʊgəʊ/ country in W Africa, bounded to the W by Ghana, to the E by Benin, and to the N by Burkina Faso.
government the 1979 constitution created a one-party state, based on the Assembly of the Togolese People (RPT). The president is elected by universal suffrage for a seven-year term and is eligible for re-election. The president is head of state and head of government, appointing and presiding over a council of ministers, and is also president of RPT.
There is a single-chamber legislature, the National Assembly, of 77 members, elected by universal suffrage from a list of RPT nominees and serving for five years. There is an illegal opposition party, the Togolese Movement for Democracy, which is based in Paris.
history for early history, see ◊Africa. Called Togoland, the country was a German protectorate 1885–1914, when it was captured by Anglo-French forces. It was divided between Britain and France in 1922 under a League of Nations mandate and continued under United Nations trusteeship from 1946. In 1956 British Togoland voted for integration with Ghana, where it became Volta region 1957.
French Togoland voted to become an autonomous republic within the French union. The new Togolese republic was given internal self-government in 1956 and full independence in 1960. Sylvanus Olympio, leader of the United Togolese (UT) party, became president in an unopposed election in Apr 1961. In 1963 Olympio was killed in a military coup and his brother-in-law Nicolas Grunitzky, who had gone into exile, was recalled to become president.
In 1967 Grunitzky was, in turn, deposed in a bloodless military coup, led by Lt-Gen Etienne Gnassingbe Eyadema. The new constitution was suspended, Eyadema assumed the presidency and banned all political activity. Six years later he founded a new party, the Assembly of the Togolese People, and declared it the only legal political organization. Between 1967 and 1977 there were several attempts to overthrow him but by 1979 Eyadema felt sufficiently secure to propose a new constitution and embark on a policy of gradual democratization.

Tōjo /'təʊdʒəʊ/ Hideki 1884–1948. Japanese prime minister 1941–44, chief instigator of the attack on ◊Pearl Harbor; tried and hanged as a war criminal.

Tokaj /təʊ'keɪ/ Hungarian town at the confluence of the Bodrog and Tisa rivers; famous for the sweet white wine which bears its name.

tokamak an experimental machine designed to investigate nuclear fusion. It consists of a chamber surrounded by electromagnets capable of exerting very powerful magnetic fields. The fields are generated to confine very hot (millions of degrees) ◊plasma, keeping it away from the chamber walls. See also JET.

Tokelau /'təʊkəlaʊ/ (formerly Union Islands) overseas territory of New Zealand, comprising three coral atolls: Atafu, Fakaofo, and Nukunono; area 10 sq km/4 sq mi; population (1980) 1,620. The islands belong to the Polynesian group. Their resources are small and until 1975 many of the inhabitants settled in New Zealand, which has administered them since 1926.

Tokyo /'təʊkiəʊ/ capital of Japan, on ◊Honshu Island; population (1980) 8,352,000. The Sumida river delta separates the city from its suburb of Honjo. It is the largest city in the world, and is Japan's major cultural and industrial centre.
history founded in the 16th century as Yedo, it was renamed when the Emperor removed his court there from Kyoto 1868. An earthquake in 1923 killed some 58,000 people. The city was severely damaged by Allied bombing in World War II.

Toledo /tɒ'leɪdəʊ/ city on the river Tagus, central Spain; population (1981) 54,500.
history Toledo was the capital of the Visigoths 534–712 (see ◊Goths); then became an important Moorish city; and was the Castilian capital 1085–1560. El ◊Greco worked here from about 1575, and the local landscape is the setting of ◊Cervantes' novel *Don Quixote*.

Toledo /tə'liːdəʊ/ port on Lake Erie, Ohio, USA; population (1980) 354,635. Industries include food processing and the manufacture of vehicles, electrical goods, and glass.

Tolkien /'tɒlkiːn/ J(ohn) R(onald) R(euel) 1892–1973. British scholar, Merton professor of English, Oxford, 1945–59. He created the fictional world of Middle Earth, portrayed in *The Hobbit* 1937 and the trilogy *The Lord of the Rings* 1954–55, ◊fantasy novels enjoyed by adults and children, peopled with strange magical creatures. His work became a cult in the 1960s.

Tolpuddle Martyrs /'tɒlpʌdl/ six farm labourers of Tolpuddle, near Dorchester, England, who in 1834 were transported to Australia for forming a trade union. After nationwide agitation they were pardoned two years later.

Tolstoy /'tɒlstɔɪ/ Leo Nikolaievich 1828–1910. Russian novelist, born of noble family at Yasnaya Polyana, near Tula. His first published work was *Childhood* 1852, part one of the trilogy which was completed with *Boyhood* 1854 and *Youth* 1857. He fought in the Crimean War, and made his name with *Tales from Sebastopol* 1856. His masterpieces are *War and Peace* 1863–69, an epic of the lives of three noble families during the Napoleonic wars, and *Anna Karenina* 1873–77, which deals with a married

Togo
REPUBLIC OF (*République Togolaise*)

AREA 56,000 sq km/21,850 sq mi
CAPITAL Lomé
PHYSICAL two savanna plains, divided by a range of hills NE–SW.
FEATURES rich mineral deposits (phosphates, bauxite, marble, iron ore, limestone); dry plains, forest, and arable land
HEAD OF STATE AND OF GOVERNMENT Etienne Gnassingbe Eyadema from 1967
GOVERNMENT one-party authoritarian
EXPORTS cocoa, coffee, coconuts, copra; phosphate, bauxite
CURRENCY CFA franc (498.38 = £1 Sept 1987)
POPULATION 3,023,000 (1985); annual growth rate 2.8%
LANGUAGE French (official), many local languages
RELIGION traditional 60%, Muslim 20%, Christian 20%
LITERACY 46% male/19% female (1980 est)
GNP $790 million (1983); $348 per head of population
CHRONOLOGY
1960 Achieved full independence as the

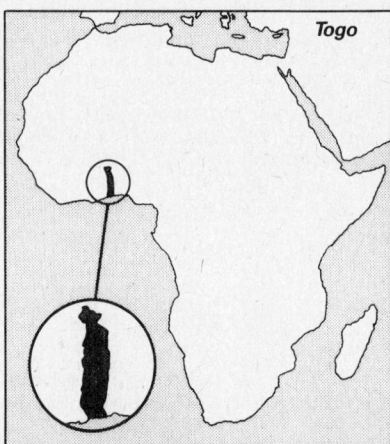

Republic of Togo with Sylvanus Olympio as head of state.
1963 Olympio killed in a military coup. Nicolas Grunitzky became president.
1967 Grunitzky replaced by Lt-Gen Etienne Gnassingbe Eyadema in a bloodless coup.
1973 The Assembly of Togolese People (RPT) formed as the only legal political party.
1979 Eyadema returned in election.

woman's tragic passion for a young officer. From 1880 Tolstoy underwent a profound spiritual crisis which led him to take up moral positions including passive resistance to evil, rejection of authority (religious or civil) and of private ownership, and a return to basic mystical Christianity. His home become a place of pilgrimage, but he was excommunicated by the Orthodox Church and his later works were banned. His desire to give up his property and live as a peasant disrupted his family life, and he finally fled his home and died of pneumonia at the railway station at Astapovo.

Toltec member of an American Indian people who ruled much of Mayan (see ◊Maya) central Mexico in the 10th–12th centuries, with their capital at Tula (destroyed by the ◊Aztecs). They had a remarkable religious centre at Teotihuacán, where there are massive remains of their temples of the sun and moon, and one (a stepped pyramid) to ◊Quetzalcoatl.

toluene (methyl benzene) colourless, inflammable liquid, insoluble in water, $C_6H_5CH_3$, derived from petroleum. It is used as a solvent, in aircraft fuels, in preparing *phenol* (carbolic acid, C_6H_5OH, used in making resins (see ◊adhesive), pharmaceuticals, and as a disinfectant) and the powerful high explosive ◊*TNT* (trinitrotoluene).

Tomasi /taʊˈmɑːsi/ Giuseppe, Prince of Lampedusa. See ◊Lampedusa.

tomato annual S American plant *Lycopersicon esculentum*, family Solanaceae; the many-seeded red fruit is used in salads and cooking.

Tombaugh /ˈtɒmbɔː/ Clyde 1906– . US astronomer, who discovered the planet ◊Pluto.

Born in Streator, Illinois, Tombaugh joined the Lowell Observatory in Flagstaff, Arizona, as an assistant in 1929, where he photographed the sky in search of an undiscovered remote planet as predicted by the observatory's founder, Percival ◊Lowell. Tombaugh found Pluto on 18 Feb 1930, from plates taken three weeks earlier. He continued his search for new planets across the entire sky; his failure to find any placed strict limits on the possible existence of planets beyond Pluto.

Tombstone /ˈtuːmstaʊn/ former silver-mining town in the desert of SE Arizona. The gun battle between Wyatt Earp and his brothers and the 'villainous' Clanton gang took place near the OK Corral 26 Oct 1881; modern research suggests it was a battle of political rivals, that is, newcomer Republicans and old-established Southern Democrats.

tommy-gun informal name for Thompson sub-machine gun; see under ◊small arms.

tomography the obtaining of plane section photographs (which show a 'slice' through any object) by various methods; crystal detectors and amplifiers can be used which have a sensitivity a hundred times greater than ◊X-ray film, and in conjunction with a computer system can detect, for example, the difference between a brain tumour and healthy brain tissue. Godfrey ◊Hounsfield was a leading pioneer in the development of this technique. In modern medical imaging there are several types of tomography, such as CAT (computerized axial tomography) or CAT 'scan'.

Tomsk /tɒmsk/ city on the river Tom, USSR; population (1985) 475,000. Formerly a gold-mining town and administrative centre of much

of Siberia. It has a university, established 1888. Its chief industry is the manufacture of synthetic fibres, and it also has sawmills, distilleries, and plastics and electric motor factories.

Tom Thumb a tiny hero of English folk tale, whose name has often been given to those of small stature, including *Charles Sherwood Stratton* 1838–83, nicknamed General Tom Thumb.

ton either the former imperial measure of weight, the long ton of 2,240 lb; or the American short ton of 2,000 lb. The metric *tonne* is 1,000 kg/2,204.6 lb.

tonality in music, the observance of a ◊key structure, that is, the recognition of the importance of a ◊tonic or key note, and of the diatonic scale built upon it. See also ◊atonality, ◊polytonality.

Tone /taʊn/ Theobald Wolfe 1763–1798. Irish nationalist. Called to the Bar in 1789, and prominent in the revolutionary society of the United Irishmen. In 1798 he accompanied the French invasion of Ireland, was captured and condemned to death, but cut his throat in prison.

tone poem in music, another name for ◊symphonic poem as used, for example, by Richard ◊Strauss.

Tonga /ˈtɒŋə/ country in the SW Pacific, in ◊Polynesia.

government Tonga is an independent hereditary monarchy within the Commonwealth. Its 1875 constitution provides for a monarch who is head of both state and government. The monarch chooses and presides over the Privy Council, a cabinet of nine ministers appointed for life. There is a single-chamber legislature, the Legislative Assembly, of 29 members, which include the monarch, the Privy Council, nine hereditary nobles, and nine representatives of the people, elected by universal adult suffrage. The assembly has a life of three years. There are no political parties in Tonga.

history the first European visitors to the islands were Dutch, 1616 and 1643 (Abel Tasman). Captain Cook dubbed them the Friendly Islands 1773. Tonga became a British protectorate 1900. Queen Salote Tupou III died 1965 and was succeeded by her son Prince Tupouto'a Tungi, who as King Tupou IV led his nation to full independence, within the Commonwealth, 1970.

tongue a muscular organ of tetrapod vertebrates usually attached to the floor of the mouth. It has a thick root attached to a U-shaped bone (the hyoid) behind. It is covered with ◊mucous membrane containing many nerves and also the 'taste buds', which distinguish salt, sweet, sour and bitter. It directs food to the teeth, and presses food and drink back into the throat in the act of swallowing. In humans, it plays a vital role in speech, while in other animals it may be important for lapping up water, or for grooming.

tonic in music, the first degree or key note of a scale, for example C in C major.

tonka S American tree *Dipteryx odorata*, family Leguminosae; its fruit, a dry, fibrous pod, encloses a black aromatic seed used in flavouring, perfumery, and the manufacture of snuff and tobacco.

Tonga
or FRIENDLY ISLANDS

AREA 748 sq km/289 sq mi
CAPITAL Nuku'alofa on Tongatpu
PHYSICAL comprises three groups of islands in the SW Pacific, mostly coral formations, but the western are actively volcanic
FEATURES fewer than one-third of the islands are inhabited
HEAD OF STATE AND OF GOVERNMENT King Taufa'ahau Tupou IV from 1965
GOVERNMENT constitutional monarchy
CURRENCY Tongan dollar or pa'anga (2.24 = £1 Sept 1987)
POPULATION 103,000 (1985); annual growth rate 2.4%
LANGUAGE Tongan and English
RELIGION Wesleyan 47%, Roman Catholic 14%, Free Church of Tonga 14%, Mormon 9%, Church of Tonga 9%
LITERACY 93% (1985)
GNP $80 million (1983); $430 per head of population

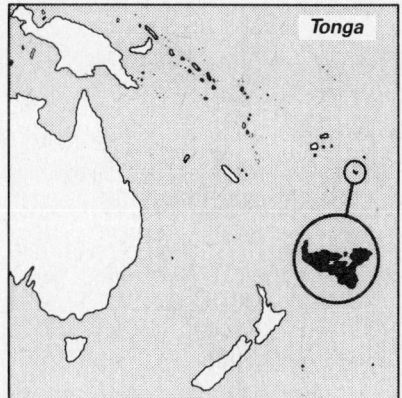

Tonga

CHRONOLOGY
1965 Death of Queen Salote. She was succeeded by her son, Prince Tupout'a, who took the title King Tupou IV.
1970 Achieved full independence within the Commonwealth.

Tonkin /ˌtɒnˈkɪn/ region of Vietnam, on the China Sea; area 103,500 sq km/40,000 sq mi. *history* After being under Chinese rule from 111 BC, Tonkin became independent 939 AD, and remained self-governing until the 19th century. A part of French Indochina 1885–1946, capital Hanoi, it was part of North Vietnam from 1954, and was merged with ◊Vietnam after the ◊Vietnam War.

Tonkin Gulf Incident after a minor engagement on 2 Aug 1964, two US destroyers reported a night attack on 4 Aug by North Vietnamese torpedo boats (possibly radar and sonar effects were misinterpreted). A retaliatory air attack was made on North Vietnam which led to the eventual despatch of over 1,000,000 US troops to South Vietnam (see ◊Vietnam war).

Tonkin, Gulf of /ˌtɒnˈkɪn/ part of the South China Sea, with oil resources: China and Vietnam disagree over their territorial boundaries in the area.

Tonkin resolution act passed by the US Congress on 7 Aug 1964 which followed the ◊Tonkin Gulf incident. It allowed President Johnson 'to take all necessary steps, including the use of armed forces' to help SEATO (South-East Asia Treaty Organization) members to defend their freedom. This resolution formed the basis for the considerable increase in US military involvement in the Vietnam conflict.

Tonle Sap /ˈtɒnli ˈsæp/ lake on the ◊Mekong river, W Kampuchea; area 2,600 sq km/1,000 sq mi to 6,500 sq km/2,500 sq mi at the height of the monsoon.

tonnage and poundage duties granted in England 1371–1787 by parliament to the Crown on imports and exports of wine and other goods. They were controversially levied by Charles I in 1626 without parliamentary consent.

Tönnies /ˈtʌnɪəs/ Ferdinand 1855–1936. German social theorist and philosopher, one of the founders of the sociological tradition of community studies and urban sociology through his key work, *Gemeinschaft-Gesellschaft* 1887, which contrasted the nature of social relationships in traditional societies and small organizations (*Gemeinschaft*, or 'community') with those in modern industrial societies and large organizations (*Gesellschaft*, or 'association'). He was pessimistic about the effect of industrialization and urbanization on the social and moral order, seeing them as a threat to traditional society's sense of community.

tonsil a lump of lymphatic tissue situated at the back of the mouth and throat in higher vertebrates. The tonsils contain many ◊lymphocytes and are part of the body's defence system against infection.

tonsillitis an inflamation of the ◊tonsils.

tonsure the shaving of the hair of the head as a symbol of being a priest. Until 1973 in the Roman Catholic Church, the crown was shaved (leaving a surrounding fringe to resemble Christ's crown of thorns); in the Eastern Orthodox Church the hair is merely shorn close.

Tony Award any of the annual awards by the League of New York Theatres to actors, authors, and so on in ◊Broadway plays. Named after the US actress and producer Antoinette Perry (1888–1946).

Tooke /tʊk/ John Horne 1736–1812. British politician, who established a Constitutional Society for parliamentary reform in 1771. He was elected a member of parliament in 1801.

tooth in vertebrates, a hard structure in the mouth, used for biting, crushing or tearing at food, and in defence and aggression. The teeth grow from each ◊jaw in two rows and meet in the act of biting. In humans the first set, the milk teeth, appear from age six months to two-and-a-half years, and number 20. The permanent dentition replaces these from the sixth year onwards, the wisdom teeth (third molars) sometimes not appearing until the age of 25 or 30. It consists of 32 teeth: two incisors, one canine (eye tooth), two premolars, and three molars on each side of each jaw. A tooth is made of bony substance called dentine. It has a root or roots set in a socket of fine bone, a neck covered by the ◊gum, and a crown covered with hard white enamel. It is hollow and filled with a highly sensitive pulp made of ◊nerves and blood vessels. The chief diseases of teeth are misplacements resulting from defect or disturbance of the tooth-germs before birth, eruption out of the proper places, and caries (decay).

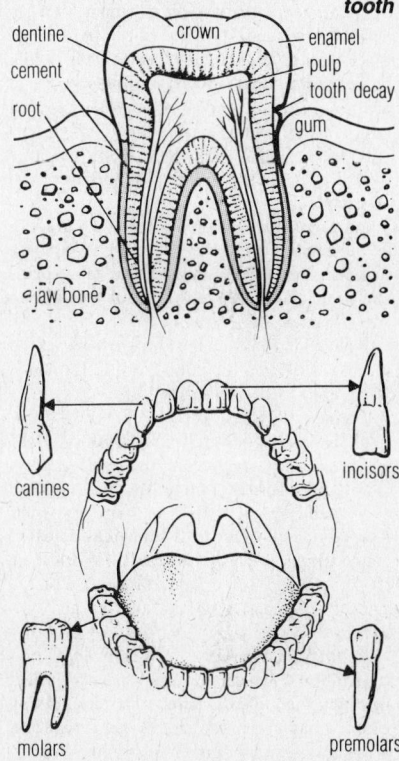

tooth

Toowoomba /təˈwʊmbə/ town in the Darling Downs, SE Queensland, Australia; population (1978) 71,900. It is a commercial and industrial centre with coal-mining, iron-working, engineering, and clothing factories.

topaz a mineral, fluosilicate of aluminium, $Al_2SiO_4(FOH)_2$. It is usually yellow, or pink if it has been heated, and is used in making jewellery.

tope small shark *Galeorhinus galeus* ranging through temperate and tropical seas. Dark grey above and white beneath, it reaches 1.5 m/5 ft: it is viviparous (the young are born well-formed), sometimes producing 40 at a time.

tope kind of tumulus found in India and SE Asia; a Buddhist monument usually built over a relic of Buddha or his disciples. They date from 300–400 BC, and the most famous are at Sanchi, near Bhilsa, central India.

Topeka /təˈpiːkə/ capital of Kansas, USA; population (1980) 118,711. Industries include engineering and textiles.

topi or *korrigum*, antelope *Damaliscus korrigum* from equatorial Africa, with head and body about 1.7 m/5.5 ft and 1.1 m/3.5 ft at the shoulder, with a chocolate-brown coat.

topiary the clipping of trees and shrubs into ornamental shapes, originated by the Romans in the first century and revived in the 16th–17th centuries in formal gardens.

Toplady /'tɒpleɪdi/ Augustus Montague 1740–1778. British Anglican clergyman, the author of the hymn 'Rock of Ages' in 1775.

topology the branch of geometry which deals with those properties of a figure which remain unchanged even when the figure is transformed, that is bent, stretched, and so on, as for example when a square painted on a rubber sheet is deformed by distorting the sheet. A famous topological problem (studied extensively by the Norwegian mathematician Oystein Ore) is to provide a proof that only three colours are needed in producing a map to give all adjoining areas different colours. Topology has scientific applications, as in the study of turbulence in flowing fluids.

tor an isolated mass of rock, usually granite, left upstanding on a moor after the surrounding rock has been worn away. Erosion takes place along the joints in the rock, wearing the outcrop into a mass of rounded lumps.

Torah in ◊Judaism, the first five books of the Hebrew ◊Bible (Christian Old Testament), which are ascribed to Moses.

Torbay /,tɔː'beɪ/ district in S Devon, England; population (1981) 115,600. It was created 1968 by the union of the seaside resorts of Paignton, Torquay and Brixham.

Torgau /'tɔːgaʊ/ town in Leipzig district, East Germany. ◊Frederick the Great defeated the Austrians nearby in 1760, and in World War II the US and Russian forces first met here.

Torino /tɒ'riːnəʊ/ Italian name for the city of ◊Turin.

tornado an extremely violent revolving storm, caused by a rising column of warm air propelled by strong wind. The diameter of the tornado may be a few hundred metres or less, but it rises to a great height, and is marked by swirling, funnel-shaped clouds. Tornadoes moving at speeds of up to 400 kph/250 mph are common in the Mississippi basin of the USA and cause great destruction. The most severe tornadoes are always accompanied by thunderstorms.

torong musical instrument of the aboriginal Tay people of central Vietnam (Nguyen) and now popular throughout Vietnam. Differing lengths of hanging bamboo are struck with a stick.

Toronto /tə'rɒntəʊ/ port on Lake Ontario, capital of Ontario, Canada; population (1982) 3,029,000. With cheap power from Niagara Falls, it is industrially important (shipbuilding, farm machinery, cars, meat packing and other food processing), and a commercial, banking, and publishing centre. It is a cultural centre, with theatres and a film industry. The university dates from 1827.
history A French fort was established here 1749, and the site became the provincial capital (then named 'York') 1793; it was renamed Toronto

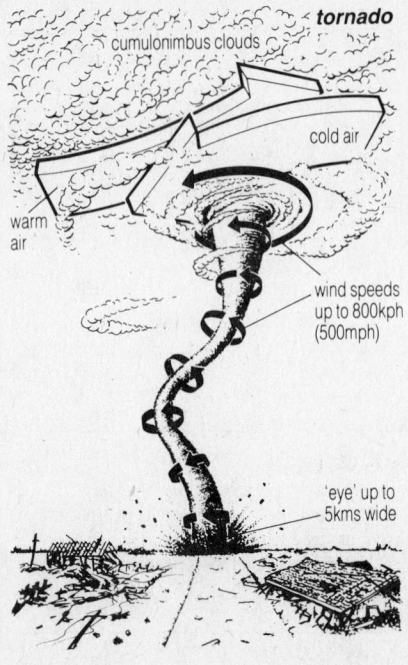

tornado cumulonimbus clouds — cold air — warm air — wind speeds up to 800kph (500mph) — 'eye' up to 5kms wide

Toronto The world's tallest free-standing structure, the CN tower (1975) which rises to 553 m/1,815 ft. The transmission mast at its top has antennae for radio, television and speeding vital business communication.

(American Indian 'place of meeting') 1834, when incorporated as a city.

torpedo type of ray whose electric organs between the pectoral fin and the head can give a powerful shock. The electric ray *Torpedo nobiliana* is found off Britain.

torpedo self-propelled underwater missile, invented in 1866 by the British engineer Robert ◊Whitehead. Modern torpedos are homing missiles; some resemble mines in that they lie on the seabed until activated by the acoustic signal of a passing ship. A television camera enables them to be remotely controlled, and in the final stage of attack they lock on to the radar or sonar signals of the target ship.

Torquay /,tɔː'kiː/ resort in S Devon, England, part of the district of ◊Torbay.

torque converter a device used in automatic transmission systems in cars, locomotives, and other vehicles to transmit power between the engine and the gearbox. It is a kind of turbine, filled with oil.

Torquemada /,tɔːkɪ'mɑːdə/ Tomás de 1420–1498. Spanish Dominican friar, confessor to Queen ◊Isabella. In 1483 he revived the ◊Inquisition on her behalf, and at least 2,000 'heretics' were burned; Torquemada also expelled the Jews from Spain with a resultant decline of the economy.

torr unit of pressure used in high vacuum technology. Equivalent to 1 mm Hg or 133.322 pascals. Named after Evangelista ◊Torricelli.

Torrens /'tɒrənz/ salt lake 8 m/25 ft below sea level in eastern South Australia; area 5,775 sq km/2,230 sq mi. It is reduced to a marsh in dry weather.

Torres-García /'tɒrɪs gɑː'θiːə/ Joaquim 1874–1949. Uruguayan artist, born in Montevideo. In Paris from 1926, he was influenced by ◊Mondrian and others, and after going to Madrid in 1932, by Inca and Nazca pottery. His mature style is based on a grid pattern derived from the ◊golden section.

Torres Strait /'tɒrɪs/ channel separating New Guinea from Australia, with scattered reefs; width 130 km/80 mi. The first European to sail through it was the Spanish navigator Luis Vaez de Torres in 1606.

Torres Vedras /'tɒrɪs 'veɪdrəs/ town in Portugal, 40 km/25 mi N of Lisbon. The fortifications known as the 'lines of Torres Vedras' were built by ◊Wellington in 1810, during the ◊Peninsular War.

Torricelli /,tɒrɪ'tʃeli/ Evangelista 1608–1647. Italian physicist and pupil of ◊Galileo, who devised the mercury barometer, demonstrating the ability of air pressure to support a finite column of mercury.

torsion in physics, the state of strain set up in a material by virtue of being twisted; for example, when a thread, wire or rod is twisted, the torsion set up in the material returns or tends to return the material to its original state. An instrument which makes use of this is the torsion balance, a sensitive device for measuring small gravitational or magnetic forces, or electric charges, by balancing these against the restoring force set up by them in a torsion suspension.

tort in law, a wrongful act for which someone can be sued for damages in a civil court. It includes such acts as libel, trespass, injury done to someone (whether intentionally or by negligence), and inducement to break a contract (although breach of contract itself is not a tort). In general a tort is distinguished from a crime in that it affects an individual rather than society at large, but some crimes can also be torts (for example one could sue someone for assault).

tortoise reptile of the order Chelonia. Marine and freshwater forms are known as turtles or terrapins respectively. Its shell consists of a curved upper carapace and flattened lower plastron which are joined at the sides, and the head and limbs may be withdrawn within it, to a greater or lesser extent, in time of danger. Most land tortoises are herbivorous and have no teeth but the mouth forms a sharp-edged 'beak'; eggs are laid in earth and hatched by the Sun. Best-known species are the small spur-thighed tortoise *Testudo graeca*, found in Asia Minor, the Balkans and North Africa, and the giant species of the Galapagos and Seychelles which reach a great age, may be 120 cm/4 ft long, and yield about 90 kg/200 lb of meat – hence their almost complete extermination by passing ships. *Tortoiseshell* is the semi-transparent shell of the hawksbill turtle.

Tortuga /tɔːˈtuːgə/ island (French 'La Tortue') off the N coast of ◊Haiti, area 180 sq km/70 sq mi. It was a pirate lair during the 17th century.

torture infliction of bodily pain, especially to extort evidence or confession. Legally abolished in England about 1640, torture was allowed in Scotland until 1708 and until 1789 in France. In the 20th century there has been a major resurgence in many parts of the world.

Medieval tortures were usually physical, such as the rack (to stretch the victim's joints to breaking point), the thumbscrew, the boot (which crushed the foot), heavy weights that crushed the whole body, the iron maiden (cage shaped like a human being with interior spikes to spear the occupant), and so on. Modern techniques include brainwashing, developed by ◊KGB and other communist interrogators from the 1950s. From the early 1960s a technique used in the West replaced isolation by severe sensory deprivation, for example IRA guerrillas were prevented from seeing by a hood, from feeling by being swathed in a loose-fitting garment, and from hearing by a continuous loud noise at about 85 decibels, while being forced to maintain themselves in a 'search' position against a wall by their fingertips. The European Commission on Human Rights found Britain guilty of torture, although the European Court of Human Rights classed it only as 'inhuman and degrading treatment'.

Toruń /ˈtɒrʊn/ industrial town in N Poland; population (1982) 183,000. It was founded by the ◊Teutonic Knights 1230, and was the birthplace of ◊Copernicus.

Tory Party name applied about 1680–1830 to the forerunner of the British ◊Conservative Party. The original Tories were Irish guerrillas who attacked the English, and the name was applied (at first insultingly) to royalists who opposed the Exclusion Bill (see under Duke of ◊Monmouth). Although largely supporting the 1688 revolution, the Tories were suspected of ◊Jacobite sympathies, and were kept from power 1714–60, but then held office almost continuously until 1830. They were the party of the squire and parson, as opposed to the Whigs

(supported by the trading classes and Nonconformists). The name is still applied colloquially to the Conservative Party.

In the USA a Tory was an opponent of the break with Britain in the War of American Independence 1775–83.

Toscanini /ˌtɒskəˈniːni/ Arturo 1867–1957. Italian conductor. Born in Parma, he made La Scala, Milan – where he conducted 1898–1903, 1906–08, and 1921–29 – the world's leading opera house. However, he was opposed to the Fascist regime, and in 1936 returned to the USA, where he had conducted at the Metropolitan 1908–15, the NBC Symphony Orchestra being formed for him in 1937. He retired in 1954.

totalitarianism government control of all activities within a country, overtly political or otherwise, as in fascist or communist dictatorships.

totalizator a system of betting on horse races; see under ◊betting.

totemism belief in individual or clan kinship with an animal, plant, or object. This totem (Algonquin Indian 'my guardian spirit') is sacred to those concerned, and they are forbidden to eat or desecrate it; marriage within such a clan is usually forbidden.

Totem poles are used on the Pacific coast of North America, and incorporate totem objects (carved and painted) as a symbol of the people, or to commemorate the dead. A similar belief occurs among Australian aborigines, and was formerly prevalent in Europe and Asia.

Totenkopfverbände the 'death's head' units of the Nazi SS organization, originally used to guard concentration camps after 1935, but which later became an elite fighting division attached to the Waffen SS during World War II.

Totila /ˈtɒtɪlə/ King died 522. King of the Ostrogoths (see ◊Goths), who warred with Justinian for Italy, and was killed by Narses at the battle of Taginae.

Tottenham /ˈtɒtənəm/ district of the Greater London borough of ◊Haringey.

toucan bird of the family Ramphastidae with very large, often brilliantly coloured beak. Living in small flocks in South American forests, toucans often have handsome plumage, are omnivorous, and lay their eggs in holes in trees.

touch screen in computing, an input device allowing the user to communicate with the computer by touching a display screen with a finger. Typically, the screen detects the finger either through a sensitive membrane or when the finger interrupts a grid of light beams crossing the screen surface. ◊Software in the device then calculates the centre-point of the finger and communicates the coordinates (grid reference) to the computer. Touch screens are widely used in financial computer systems in banks and stockmarkets where a spreadsheet of data is displayed on the screen.

touch sensor in a computer-controlled ◊robot, a device used to give the robot a sense of touch. Without it, a robot could not reliably manipulate delicate objects or move automatically about a room. Touch sensors provide the *feedback* necessary for the robot to adjust the force of its movements and the

pressure of its grip. The main types include strain gauge and microswitch.

Toulon /tuːˈlɒn/ seaport and capital of Var *département*, France, on the Mediterranean, 48 km/30 mi SE of Marseilles; population (1983) 190,000. It is the chief Mediterranean naval station of France, with large dockyards and defences commanding the sea. Industries include oil refining, chemicals, furniture, and clothing. *history* the Roman *Telo Martius*, Toulon was made a port by Henry IV. It was occupied by the British 1793, and Napoleon first distinguished himself in driving them out. In World War II the French fleet was scuttled here to avoid its passing to German control.

Toulouse /tuːˈluːz/ capital of Haute-Garonne *département*, S France, on the river Garonne SE of Bordeaux; population (1982) 541,271. The chief industries are textiles and aircraft construction (Concorde was built here). *history* capital of the Visigoths (see ◊Goth), and later of Aquitaine 781–843, it has a 12th–13th century cathedral and a university established about 1230. ◊Wellington repulsed ◊Soult at Toulouse 1814 in the ◊Peninsular War.

Toulouse-Lautrec /tuːˈluːz ləʊˈtrek/ Henri Raymonde de 1864–1901. French artist, born at Albi, where there is a museum of his work. He lived and worked in Montmartre, Paris, where he made studies of popular entertainers, circus acrobats, and prostitutes without sentiment or judgement. Like ◊Degas, he recorded contemporary life in informal poses from odd angles and his colourful posters show the influence of Japanese colour prints.

Toulouse-Lautrec A painter of the seamier and sometimes grotesque side of Parisian life, Toulouse-Lautrec is best known for his colourful posters.

touraco African bird of the family Musophagidae. The *white-cheeked touraco*

Touraco leucotis looking rather like a crested, multi-coloured magpie, is a fruit eater like others of the family.

Touraine /tʊəˈreɪn/ former province of W central France, capital Tours.

Tourcoing /tʊəˈkwæŋ/ town in Nord *département*, France; population (1983) 102,121. It is situated near the Belgian border, and has been a textile centre since the 12th century.

Tour de France French road race for professional cyclists established in 1903. The route (about 4,000 km/2,400 mi) is variable, taking about three weeks to cover in stages of about 200 km/120 mi each day, but always ending in Paris after passing over terrain of varying difficulty, with time trials at intervals. The rider with the shortest overall time at the conclusion of each stage wears a yellow jersey. The competitors form about a dozen teams with a dozen riders in each, each commercially sponsored. Famous riders include Fausto Coppi (Italian), Jacques Anquetil (French), Bernard Hinault (French), and Eddy Merckx (Belgium). In Britain a shorter simpler version is known as the *Milk Race*. For recent winners see ◊cycling.

tourmaline hard, brittle mineral. A complex of various metal silicates, and containing aluminium and boron. Small tourmalines are generally found in granites and gneisses. The common varieties are opaque, ranging from black (schorl) to pink, and the transparent gemstones may be colourless (achroit), rose pink (rubellite), green (Brazilian emerald), blue (indicolite, Brazilian sapphire) or brown (dravite).

Tournai /tʊəˈneɪ/ (Flemish *Doornik*) town in Hainaut province, Belgium, on the Scheldt; population (1983) 67,291. Industries include carpets, cement, and leather. It stands on the site of a Roman relay post, and has an 11th century Romanesque cathedral.

tournament or **tourney**. A sporting competition, originally a form of medieval war-training, which included mounted combat and mock fights with sword, spear, or dagger. Introduced to Britain from France in the 11th century, tournaments flourished until the 16th century, and have modern revivals.

Tourneur /ˈtɜːnə/ Cyril 1575–1626. English dramatist. Little is known about his life but *The Atheist's Tragedy* 1611, and *The Revenger's Tragedy* 1607 (now considered by many scholars to be by ◊Middleton) are among the most powerful of Stuart dramas.

Tours /tʊə/ city in W central France; population (1982) 262,786. Industries include the manufacture of chemicals, textiles, and machinery. It has a 13th–15th century cathedral. *history* an ancient city, and former capital of ◊Touraine, it was the site of the French defeat of the Arabs 732 (see ◊Charles Martel).

Toussaint L'Ouverture /tuːˈsæ̃ ˌluːvəˈtjʊə/ Pierre Dominique 1746–1803. Haitian revolutionary leader, born a slave. He joined the insurrection of 1791 against the French and was made governor by the revolutionary French government. He expelled the Spanish and British, but when Napoleon reimposed slavery,

Toussaint L'Ouverture An 1805 print showing the Haitian revolutionary leader Pierre Toussaint L'Ouverture. Born a slave, he became governor of Haiti during the French Revolution.

he revolted, and died in prison in France. In 1983 his remains were returned to Haiti.

Tower Hamlets /ˈtaʊə ˈhæmləts/ borough of E Greater London. It includes the Tower of London, and the World Trade Centre in former St Katharine's Dock; *Isle of Dogs* bounded on three sides by the Thames, including the former India and Millwall Docks. Redevelopment includes Billingsgate fish market, removed here 1982, and the Docklands railway, linking the isle with the City; *Limehouse district* has the chapel hall in Fulbourne Street, venue of the Russian Social Democratic Congress 1907 (attended by ◊Lenin, ◊Stalin, and ◊Trotsky); *Spitalfields district* was once the home of ◊Huguenot silk weavers; *Bethnal Green* has a Museum of Childhood; and Mile End Green (later Stepney Green) was where ◊Richard II met the rebels of 1381.

population (1984) 146,000.

Tower of London fortress on the Thames bank to the E of the City. The keep, or White Tower, was built about 1078 by Bishop Gundulf on the site of British and Roman fortifications. It is surrounded by two strong walls and a moat (now dry), and was for centuries a royal residence and the principal state prison. The Tower of London is today a barracks, an armoury, and a museum. Among prisoners executed there were More, Anne Boleyn, Katherine Howard, Lady Jane Grey, Essex, Strafford, Laud, and Monmouth.

town planning the design of buildings in a physical and social context, concentrating on the relationship between buildings and their environment, as well as on their uses. See also ◊garden city; ◊new town.

Townsend /'taʊnzend/ Sue 1946– . British playwright (*The Great Celestial Cow* 1984) and novelist (*The Secret Diary of Adrian Mole, aged 13¾* 1982). Born in Leicester, she became writer-in-residence at the Phoenix Theatre there.

Townshend /'taʊnzend/ Charles 1725–1767. British politician, chancellor of the Exchequer 1766–67.
The *Townshend Acts* taxing such imports into Britain's N American colonies as tea, glass, and paper precipitated the War of Independence.

Townshend /'taʊnzend/ Charles, 2nd Viscount Townshend (known as 'Turnip' Townshend) 1674–1738. English politician and agriculturalist. He was secretary of state under George I 1714–17, when dismissed for opposing the king's foreign policy, and 1721–30, after which he retired to his farm and did valuable work in developing crop rotation and cultivating winter feeds for cattle (hence his nickname).

Townsville /'taʊnzvɪl/ port on Cleveland Bay, N Queensland, Australia; population (1985) 104,000. It is the centre of a mining and agricultural area, and exports meat, wool, sugar, and minerals, including gold and silver.

Townswomen's Guilds, National Union of see under ◊Women's Institutes.

toxaemia in general terms the presence of 'poisons' in the blood, especially those taken up from an infection at some point in the body. In late pregnancy a condition marked by high blood pressure, an unusual increase in weight, and convulsions (eclampsia); its causes are not precisely known.

toxocariasis infection of humans by a canine intestinal worm, which results in a swollen liver and sometimes eye damage.

Toynbee /'tɔɪnbi/ Arnold 1852–1883. British economic historian, best known for coining the term 'industrial revolution' in his *Lectures on the Industrial Revolution* published 1884. Toynbee Hall, an education settlement in the East End of London, was named after him.

Toynbee /'tɔɪnbi/ Arnold Joseph 1889–1975. British historian, whose *A Study of History* 1934–61 was an attempt to discover the laws governing the rise and fall of civilizations. He was the nephew of Arnold ◊Toynbee.

Trabzon /'træbzɒn/ (formerly *Trebizond*) port on the Black Sea, NE Turkey, 355 km/220 mi SW of Batum; population (1980) 108,403. Exports include fruit, tobacco, and hides. It is the site of the Black Sea University, 1963.

trace element a chemical element necessary for the health of a plant or animal, but in minute quantities; for example, magnesium, which occurs in chlorophyll, essential to photosynthesis, and iodine, needed by the thyroid gland of mammals, for making hormones that control growth and body chemistry.

tracer in science, a small quantity of a radioactive ◊isotope (form of an element) used to follow the path of a chemical reaction or a physical or biological process. The location (and possibly concentration) of the tracer is usually detected using a Geiger-Muller counter (see

◊Geiger). For example, the activity of the thyroid gland can be followed by giving the patient an injection containing a small dose of a radioactive isotope of iodine, which is selectively absorbed from the bloodstream by the gland.

trachea in tetrapod vertebrates and lungfish, the 'windpipe' – a single tube which conducts air from the ◊pharynx (throat) to the bronchial tubes and ◊lungs. In insects and myriapods (centipedes and millipedes), small, branching, air-filled tubes that run from ◊spiracles on the surface and penetrate every part of the body, bringing oxygen to the tissues and removing carbon dioxide. Some spiders also have tracheae, but, unlike insects, rely on their ◊circulatory system to transport gases throughout the body.

tracheid a type of cell found in the water-conducting tissue (◊xylem) of many plants, particularly gymnosperms (conifers) and pteridophytes (ferns). It is a long, thin cell with pointed ends. The cell walls are thickened by lignin except for numerous, small, rounded areas, or pits, through which water and dissolved minerals pass from one cell to another. Once it is mature, the cell itself dies and only the cell walls remain.

trachoma contagious bacterial disease of the eye; a severe form of ◊conjunctivitis caused by a bacterium, and also called 'river blindness'.

tracked vehicle a vehicle, such as a tank or bulldozer, that runs on tracks it lays itself. See ◊caterpillar tracks.

Tractarianism another name for the ◊Oxford Movement, 19th-century movement for Catholic revival within the Church of England.

tractor in agriculture, a motor vehicle commonly having two very large rear wheels. It is usually powered by a ◊diesel engine and has a power-tube-off (PTO) mechanism for driving implements, and hydraulic lift. In military usage, a *combat tractor* usually has two drivers, and can excavate two tonnes in a single action, so as, for example, to hide a Chieftain tank in 11 minutes.

Tracy /'treɪsi/ Spencer 1900–1967. US actor. One of Hollywood's greatest screen actors, he was noted for his understated, seemingly effortless natural performances. His films include *Captains Courageous* 1937 and *Boys' Town* 1938 (for both of which he won Academy Awards) and *Bad Day at Black Rock* 1955. He is best remembered for his partnership with Katharine Hepburn in films such as *Adam's Rib* 1949 and *Guess Who's Coming to Dinner* 1967.

trade cycle or *business cycle* period of time which includes a peak and trough of economic activity, as measured by a country's ◊national income. In ◊Keynesian economics, one of the main roles of the government is to smooth out the peaks and troughs of the trade cycle, by intervening in the economy, thus minimizing 'overheating' and 'stagnation' in the economy.

trade mark a name or 'mark', legally registered by its proprietor, which is distinctive of a marketed product.

Tradescant /trə'deskənt/ John 1570–1638. English gardener and botanist, who travelled widely in Europe and may have introduced the cos lettuce to England, from the Greek Island bearing the same name. He was appointed as

gardener to Charles I and succeeded by his son, John Tradescant the Younger (1608–1662), after his death. The younger Tradescent undertook three plant-collecting trips to Virginia, USA, and Linnaeus named the genus *Tradescantia* in his honour. The Tradescants introduced many new plants to Britain, including the acacia, lilac and occidental plane. Their collection of plants formed the nucleus of the Ashmolean Museum in Oxford.

tradescantia genus of American plants (named after the elder ◊Tradescant), family Commelinaceae; *spiderwort Tradescantia virginiana* is a garden plant; *wandering jew Tradescantia albiflora* is a common houseplant.

Trades Union Congress voluntary organization of trade unions, founded in Britain in 1868, in which delegates of affiliated unions meet annually to consider matters affecting their members. Today there are some 100 affiliated unions, with an aggregate membership of about 11 million.

trade union organization of employed workers formed to undertake collective bargaining with employers and to try to achieve improved working conditions for its members. Trade unions of a kind existed in the Middle Ages as journeyman guilds, and combinations of wage earners were formed in the 18th century, but modern trade unionism is a product of the Industrial Revolution. Five centuries of repressive legislation in Britain culminated in the passing of the ◊Combination Acts of 1799 and 1800 which made unions illegal, but on the repeal of these in 1824–25, organizations of workpeople were permitted to engage in collective bargaining, although still subject to legal restrictions and with no legal protection for their funds until the enactment of a series of Trade Union Acts 1871–76. Successive Acts of Parliament broadened the unions' field of action, such as the 1913 Act which allowed the unions to engage in political activities.
The ◊Trades Union Congress was for many years representative mainly of unions of craftsmen, but in the 1890s the organization of unskilled labour spread rapidly. Industrial Unionism (the organization of all workers in one industry or trade) began about this time; but the characteristic of the so-called New Unionism at the time of the 1889 dock strike was the rise of the general labour unions (for example, the Dock Workers and General Labourers in the gas industry). The restrictive Trade Disputes and Trade Union Act 1927, which was passed in the wake of the 1926 ◊General Strike, was repealed under the Attlee government in 1946, and the post-war period was marked by increased unionism among white-collar workers. The Wilson government 1964–70 attempted to introduce legislative reform of the unions, but their unwillingness to accept it led to its abandonment in 1969. The Heath government's Industrial Relations Act 1971 (including registration of trade unions, legal enforcement of collective agreements, compulsory 'cooling-off' periods, and strike ballots) was repealed by the succeeding Wilson government of 1974, and voluntary wage restraint attempted under a

◊social contract. An Advisory Conciliation and Arbitration Service (ACAS) was set up in 1975. The industrial disputes of the winter of 1978–79 undermined the succeeding Callaghan government, and the Thatcher government, in the Employment Acts of 1980 and 1982, restricted the closed shop, picketing, secondary action against anyone other than the employer in dispute, immunity of trade unions in respect of unlawful activity by their officials, and the definition of a trade dispute, which must be between workers and employers, not between workers. The Trade Union Act 1984 made it compulsory to have secret ballots for elections and before strikes.

The great growth of US trade unionism, apart from the abortive Knights of Labor 1869–86 (see also ◊American Federation of Labor) came in the post-Depression years. Employers and the US government have historically been more opposed to trade unionism than in Britain, often using police and armed guards to harass pickets and protect strike breakers, which has led to episodes of violence and bitter confrontation. US legislation includes the Taft-Hartley Act 1947, which among other measures outlaws the closed shop. In the present day US unions have the reputation of being open to to the acceptance of new techniques, taking a broad view of these as conducive to greater eventual prosperity. Probably the most effective trade-union system is that of Sweden, where conflicts of unions within an industry (demarcation disputes) are largely eliminated, and where unions and employers cooperate freely.

In 1973 a European Trade Union Confederation (ETUC) was established, membership 29 million, and there is an International Labour Organization, established 1919 and affiliated to the United Nations from 1945, which formulates standards for labour and social conditions.

trade wind the prevailing wind that blows towards the equator from the NE and SE. Trade winds are caused by hot air rising at the equator and the consequent movement of air from N and S to take its place. The winds are deflected towards the W because of the rotation of the Earth producing the ◊Coriolis effect. The unpredictable calms known as the ◊doldrums lie at their convergence. The trade-wind belts move N and S about 5° with the seasons.

trading stamp a stamp given by retailers to customers which (when a sufficient number has been collected) can be redeemed for goods or money. They originated in Britain about 1851, subsequently introduced in the USA, and reimported to the UK in 1958 (Green Shield stamps). They were reintroduced in 1986.

Trafalgar, Battle of /trə'fælgə, Spanish ˌtræ fæl'gɑː/ battle on 21 Oct 1805 in which the British fleet under Nelson defeated a Franco-Spanish fleet; Nelson was mortally wounded. Named after Cape Trafalgar, low headland in SW Spain, near the W entrance to the Straits of Gibraltar.

tragedy in theatrical terms, very generally, a play dealing with a serious theme, traditionally one in which a character falls to disaster either as a result of personal failings or circumstances beyond his or her control. The Greek view of tragedy, as defined by ◊Aristotle and expressed by the great tragedians ◊Aeschylus, ◊Euripides, and ◊Sophocles, provided the subject matter for later tragic dramas, but it was the Roman ◊Seneca (whose works were intended to be read rather than acted) who influenced the Elizabethan tragedy of ◊Marlowe and ◊Shakespeare. French classical tragedy developed under the influence of both Seneca and an interpretation of Aristotle which gave rise to the theory of unities of time, place and action, as observed by ◊Racine, one of its greatest exponents. In Germany the tragedies of ◊Goethe and ◊Schiller led to the exaggerated ◊melodrama, which replaced pure tragedy. In the 18th century unsuccessful attempts were made to 'domesticate' tragedy. In the 20th century tragedies in the narrow Greek sense of dealing with exalted personages in an elevated manner have virtually died out. Tragedy has been replaced by dramas with 'tragic' implications or overtones, as in the work of ◊Ibsen, ◊Pinter, and ◊Osborne, for example, or by the hybrid tragi-comedy.

tragi-comedy a drama which contains elements of tragedy and comedy; for example, Shakespeare's 'reconciliation' plays such as *The Winter's Tale*, which reaches a tragic climax but then lightens to a happy conclusion. A tragi-comedy is the usual form for plays in the tradition of the Theatre of the ◊Absurd, such as *En attendant Godot/Waiting for Godot* 1953 by Beckett and *Rosencrantz and Guildenstern are Dead* 1967 by Stoppard.

tragopan type of pheasant, genus *Tragopan* of which there are several species living along the S of the Himalayas. Tragopans are brilliantly coloured, with arrays of spots, and males inflate coloured wattles and throat pouches in their spring courtship displays.

Traherne /trə'hɜːn/ Thomas 1637–1674. English mystic, vicar of Teddington 1667–74. His moving lyric poetry and his prose *Centuries of Meditations* were unpublished until 1903.

train see ◊railway.

train-bands a civil militia first formed in 1573 by Elizabeth I of England to meet the possibility of invasion. Although used by Charles I against the Scots in 1639 their lack of training meant they were of dubious military value.

Trajan /'treɪdʒən/ Marcus Ulpius (Trajanus) 52–117 AD. Roman emperor. Born in Seville, he distinguished himself as a soldier and was adopted as heir by ◊Nerva, whom he succeeded in 98 AD. He was a just and conscientious ruler, corresponded with ◊Pliny about the Christians, and conquered Dacia (approximately modern Romania) 101–07 and much of ◊Parthia. *Trajan's Column*, Rome, commemorates his victories.

trampolining gymnastics performed on a sprung canvas sheet which allows the performer to reach great heights before landing again. Originally used as a circus or show business act, trampolining dates to the early part of the 20th century. It developed as a sport in 1936 when George Nissen of the United States developed a prototype model 'T' trampoline. Marks are gained for carrying out difficult manoeuvres.

Synchronized trampolining and tumbling are also popular forms of the sport.

tramway a transport system in which wheeled vehicles run along parallel rails, which originated in collieries in the 18th century. The earliest passenger system was in 1832, in New York, and by the 1860s horse-drawn trams plied in London and Liverpool. Trams are now powered either by electric conductor rails below ground or conductor arms connected to overhead wires, but their use on public roads is very limited because of their lack of manoeuvrability. Greater flexibility is achieved with the *trolleybus*, similarly powered by conductor arms overhead, but without tracks. Both vehicles have the advantage of being non-polluting.

trance mental state in which the subject loses the ordinary perceptions of time and space, and even of his or her own body. In this highly aroused state, often induced by rhythmic music, 'speaking in tongues' may occur (see ◊Pentecostal movement), which usually consists of the rhythmic repetition of apparently meaningless syllables, with a euphoric return to consciousness.

tranquillizer a calming drug, such as an antipsychotic or sedative.

Trans-Alaskan Pipeline Scheme one of the world's greatest ◊civil engineering projects, the construction of a 1,285 km/805 mile long pipeline to carry petroleum (crude oil) from the North Slope of Alaska to the icefree port of Valdez. It was completed in 1977 after three years' work. The engineers had to elevate nearly half of the pipeline on supports above ground level to avoid thawing the permanently frozen ground, which would have caused much environmental damage. They also had to cross 600 rivers and streams and two mountain ranges and allow for earthquakes.

Transcaucasia /ˌtrænzkɔː'keɪziə/ region of the USSR south of the Caucasus. It includes Armenia, Azerbaijan, and ◊Georgia, which formed the *Transcaucasian Republic* 1922, broken up 1936 when each became a separate republic of the USSR.

transcendentalism term applied to a form of philosophy inaugurated by ◊Kant. As opposed to ◊metaphysics in the traditional sense, transcendental philosophy is concerned with the conditions of possibility of experience: it shows what is involved in having a 'point of view' on the world at all. Introduced to England, it influenced Coleridge and Carlyle, and developed in New England about 1840–60 into a mystical doctrine (◊Thoreau and ◊Emerson) which saw God as immanent in nature and the human soul.

Transcendental Meditation (TM) a technique of focusing the mind based in part on Hindu meditation. Such meditation is believed to bring benefit to the practitioner in the form of release from stress. Meditators are given a mantra (a special word or phrase) to chant. This mantra is never written down or divulged to anyone else. It is believed that through the practice of meditation special powers, such as levitation, precognition and control over bodily functions can be developed.

transcription in living cells, the process by which the information for the synthesis of a ◊protein is transferred from the ◊DNA strand on which it is carried to the messenger ◊RNA strand involved in the actual synthesis. It occurs by the formation of ◊base pairs between the DNA molecule and the nucleotides that make up the new RNA strand.

transducer power-transforming device which enables ◊energy in any form (electrical, acoustical, mechanical) to flow from one transmission system to another. The energy flowing to and from a transducer may be of the same or of different forms, for example, an electric motor receives electrical energy and delivers it to a mechanical system; a gramophone pick-up crystal receives mechanical energy from the stylus and delivers it as electrical energy; and a loudspeaker receives an electrical input and delivers an acoustical output.

transfer orbit the elliptical path followed by a spacecraft moving from one ◊orbit to another, designed to save fuel by moving for most of the journey in ◊free fall. ◊Space probes travel to the planets on transfer orbits. A probe aimed at Venus has to be 'slowed down' relative to the Earth, so that it enters an elliptical transfer orbit with its perigee (point of closest approach to the Sun) at the same distance as the orbit of Venus; with Mars, the vehicle has to be 'speeded up' relative to the Earth, so that it reaches its apogee (furthest point from the Sun) at the same distance as the orbit of Mars. *Geostationary transfer orbit* is the path followed by satellites to be placed in ◊geostationary orbit around the Earth (an orbit coincident with Earth's rotation). A small rocket is fired at the transfer orbit's *apogee*, to circularize the satellite in geostationary orbit.

transfer orbit

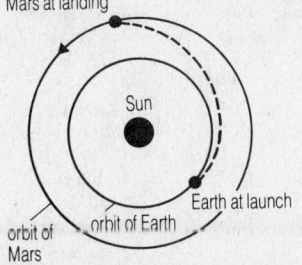

transformational grammar a theory of language structure initiated by Noam ◊Chomsky, which proposes that below the actual phrases and sentences of a language (its *surface structure*) there lies a more basic layer (its *deep structure*), which is processed by various transformational rules when we speak and write. Thus below the surface structure 'the girl opened the door' would lie the deep structure 'the girl open + *past tense* the door'. Note that there is usually more than one way in which a deep structure can be realized; in this case 'the door was opened by the girl'.

transformer device in which by ◊electromagnetic induction an alternating or intermittent current of one voltage is transformed to another voltage, without change of ◊frequency. A transformer has two coils, a primary for the input, and a secondary for the output, wound on a common iron core. The ratio of the primary to the secondary voltages (and currents) is directly (and inversely) proportional to the number of turns in the primary and secondary coils. Transformers are widely used in electrical apparatus of all kinds and in particular in power transmission where high voltages and low currents are utilized.

transistor electronic component with three or more ◊electrodes, and made of ◊semiconductor material, that can regulate a current passing through it. A transistor can act as an amplifier, ◊oscillator, ◊photocell or switch, and usually operates on a very small amount of power. It was invented at Bell Telephone Laboratories in the USA in 1948 by John ◊Bardeen and Walter ◊Brittain, developing the work of William ◊Shockley.
Present-day transistors commonly consist of a tiny sandwich of ◊germanium or ◊silicon, specially prepared so that the alternate layers have different electrical properties. A crystal of pure germanium or silicon would act as an insulator (non-conductor). By introducing impurities in the form of atoms of other materials (for example, boron, arsenic or indium) in minute amounts of the order of one part in 100 million the layers may be made either n-type, having an excess of electrons, or p-type, having a deficiency of electrons. This enables electrons to flow from one layer to another in one direction only.
Transistors have had a tremendous impact on the electronics industry, and are now made in thousands of millions each year. They perform many of the same functions as the thermionic valve, but have the advantages of greater reliability, long life, compactness and instantaneous action, no warming-up period being necessary. They are widely used in most electronic equipment, including portable radios and televisions, computers, satellites and space research, and are the basis of the ◊integrated circuit (silicon chip).

transition metal one of a group of metals with variable valency, for example cobalt, copper, iron, and molybdenum. They are excellent conductors of electricity and generally form highly coloured compounds.

Transjordan /trænz'dʒɔːdn/ former name (1923–49) of the Hashemite kingdom of ◊Jordan.

Transkei /ˌtræns'kaɪ/ largest of South Africa's Bantu Homelands, extending NE from the Great Kei River, on the coast of Cape Province, to the border of Natal; self-governing 1963, full 'independence' 1976.
area 43,800 sq km/16,910 sq mi
capital Umtata
towns port Mnganzana
features one of the two homelands of the Xhosa people, see ◊Ciskei
exports livestock
population (1983) 2,517,000, including small white and coloured minorities
language Xhosa
government president (paramount chief Tutor Nyangelizwe Vulinolela Ndamase 1986–   ) and single-chamber national assembly.

translation in literature, the rendering of words from one language to another. The first recorded named translator was Livius Andronicus, who translated the *Odyssey* into Latin in 240 BC.

translation in living cells, the process by which proteins are synthesized. During translation, the information coded as a sequence of nucelotides in messenger ◊RNA is transformed into a sequence of ◊amino acids in a ◊peptide chain. The process involves the 'translation' of the ◊genetic code. See also ◊transcription.

transmigration of souls another name for ◊reincarnation.

transpiration the loss of water from a plant by evaporation. Most of the water is lost from the leaves through specialized pores, known as ◊stomata, whose primary function is to allow gas exchange between the internal plant tissues and the atmosphere. Only a very small percentage of the total water loss occurs through the epidermis, which generally has a waxy ◊cuticle to make it waterproof. Transpiration from the leaf surfaces causes a continuous upward flow of water from the roots of a plant via the ◊xylem, which is known as the transpiration stream. A single maize plant has been estimated to transpire 245 litres (54 gallons) of water in one growing season.

transplant in modern surgery the transfer of an embryo, genetic material, an organ, tissue, and so on, from one part of a body to another, or to another body. A transplant code was issued in the UK in 1979 covering the transplant of human organs. Two doctors must certify the brain death of the donor, those doctors being both independent of the transplant team and clinically independent of each other. See also ◊embryology and ◊genetic engineering.

Transport and General Workers Union ◊trade union founded in 1921 by the amalgamation of a number of dockers' and road transport workers' unions, previously associated in the Transport Workers' Federation. It is the largest trade union in Britain. General secretaries have included ◊Bevin, Cousins, and Jack Jones 1913–   , and Moss Evans 1925–   . The current leader is Ron Todd 1927–   .

transportation in the UK, a former punishment which involved sending convicted persons to overseas possessions either for life or for shorter periods. It was introduced in England towards the end of the 17th century and was abolished in 1864 after many thousands had been transported, especially to Australia.

transputer an electronic device being introduced in computers to increase computing power. In the circuits of a standard computer the processing of data takes place in sequence. In a transputer's circuits processing takes place in parallel, greatly reducing computing time.

transsexual a person who identifies himself/herself completely with the opposite sex, believing that the wrong sex was assigned at birth. Unlike *transvestitism*, which is the desire to dress in clothes traditionally worn by the opposite sex, transsexuals think and feel emotionally in a way typically considered appropriate to members of the opposite sex, and may undergo surgery to modify external sexual characteristics.

Trans-Siberian Railway railway line connecting the cities of European Russia with Omsk, Novosibirsk, Irkutsk, and Khabarovsk, and terminating at Vladivostok on the Pacific. It was built 1891–1905; from Leningrad to Vladivostok is about 8,700 km/5,400 mi. A 3,102 km/1,927 mi northern line was completed in 1984 after ten years' work.

transubstantiation in Christian theology, the doctrine that the whole substance of the bread and wine changes into the substance of the body and blood of Christ when consecrated in the ◊Eucharist.

transuranic element or *transuranium element* one of those chemical elements with an atomic number of 93 or more, that is, with a greater number of protons in the nucleus than ◊uranium. Apart from neptunium and plutonium none of these has been found in nature, but they have been created in nuclear reactions.

Transvaal /'trænzvɑːl/ province of NE South Africa, bordering Zimbabwe on the N.
area 286,064 sq km/110,450 sq mi.
capital Pretoria

towns Johannesburg, Germiston, Brakpan, Springs, Benoni, Krugersdorp, Roodepoort
features the main rivers are the Vaal and Limpopo with their tributaries. Swaziland forms an enclave on the Natal border
exports diamonds, coal, iron ore, copper, lead, tin, manganese; meat; maize, tobacco, and fruit.
population (1980) 8,350,500; including 5,644,700 black, 2,362,000 white, 115,560 Asian, 228,200 coloured
history settled by *Voortrekkers* who left Cape Colony in the Great Trek from 1831, Transvaal's independence was recognized by Britain 1852, until the settlers' difficulties with the conquered Zulus led to British annexation 1877. After the South African War 1899–1902, Transvaal was made a British colony, and in 1910 became a province of the Union of South Africa.

Transylvania /,trænsɪl'veɪnɪə/ mountainous area of central and NW Romania, bounded to the S by the Transylvanian Alps (an extension of the ◊Carpathians), formerly a province, with its capital at Cluj. It was part of Hungary from about 1000 until its people voted to unite with Romania 1918. The Vienna Award 1940 (by ◊Ribbentrop and ◊Ciano) gave most of it back to Hungary, but this was reversed 1947.

Trapani /'trɑːpəni/ port and naval base in NW Sicily; population (1981) 71,927.

trapezium in geometry, a four-sided plane figure (quadrilateral) with two of its sides

parallel. If the parallel sides have lengths a and b and the perpendicular distance between them is h (the height of the trapezium), its area $A = \frac{1}{2}((a + b) \times h)$.

Trappist member of a Roman Catholic order of monks and nuns, renowned for the strictness of their rule, which includes the maintenance of silence. It originated in 1664 at La Trappe, in Normandy, as a reformed version of the ◊Cistercian rule, under which it is now once more governed.

trasformismo (Italian 'transformation') term denoting the practice of government by coalition, using tactics of reforming new cabinets and political alliances, often between conflicting groups. The term was first used to describe how ◊Cavour and ◊Depretis held on to power.

travelator a moving walkway, rather like a flat ◊escalator. See ◊conveyor belt.

travel sickness nausea and vomiting caused by travel in ships, trains, buses, cars, aeroplanes, and space vehicles. Constant vibration and movement may stimulate changes in the semicircular canals forming the labyrinth of the middle ear, to which the individual fails to adapt, and to which are added visual and psychological factors. In space, normal body movements result in unexpected and unfamiliar signals to the brain. Some proprietary cures contain antihistamine drugs, and astronauts control symptoms when weightless by wedging

TABLE OF TRANSURANIUM ELEMENTS

Atomic Number	Name	Symbol	Year discovered	Source of first preparation	Isotope identified	Half Life of first isotope identified
Actinide series						
93	Neptunium	Np	1940	Irradiation of uranium 238 with neutrons	Np^{239}	2.35 days
94	Plutonium	Pu	1941	Bombardment of uranium 238 with deuterons	Pu^{238}	86.4 years
95	Americium	Am	1944	Irradiation of plutonium 239 with neutrons	Am^{241}	458 years
96	Curium	Cm	1944	Bombardment of plutonium 239 with helium ions	Cm^{242}	162.5 days
97	Berkelium	Bk	1949	Bombardment of americium 241 with helium ions	Bk^{243}	4.5 hours
98	Californium	Cf	1950	Bombardment of curium 242 with helium ions	Cf^{245}	44 minutes
99	Einsteinium	Es	1952	Irradiation of uranium 238 with neutrons in first thermonuclear explosion	Es^{253}	20 days
100	Fermium	Fm	1953	Irradiation of uranium 238 with neutrons in first thermonuclear explosion	Fm^{255}	16 hours
101	Mendelevium	Md	1955	Bombardment of einsteinium 253 with helium ions	Md^{256}	1.5 hours
102	Nobelium	No	1958	Bombardment of curium 246 with carbon ions	No^{255}	3 seconds
103	Lawrencium	Lr	1961	Bombardment of californium 252 with boron ions	Lr^{257}	8 seconds
Super heavy elements						
104	Unnilquadium* (old name Rutherfordium)	Rf	1969	Bombardment of californium 249 with ions of carbon-12	Ru^{257}	4 seconds
105	Unnilpentium* (old name Hahnium)	Ha	1970	Bombardment of californium 249 with nuclei of nitrogen-15 atoms	Ha^{260}	1.6 seconds
106	Unnilsexium*		1974	Bombardment of californium 249 with oxygen-18 ions	$U6^{263}$	0.9 seconds
107	Unnilseptium*	Uns	1977	Bombardment of bismuth 209 with nuclei of chromium-54	U7	2 milliseconds
108	Unniloctium*	Uno	1984	Bombardment of lead 208	$U8^{265}$	a few milliseconds
109	Unnilnonium*		1982	Bombardment of bismuth-209	U9	5 milliseconds

*Names for elements 104–109 are as proposed by the International Union for Pure and Applied Chemistry in 1980.

themselves in their bunks.

Traven /'trævən/ Ben, pseudonym of novelist Herman Feige 1882–1969. His true identity was unrevealed until 1979. Born in the part of Germany now in Poland, he was in turn known as anarchist Maret Rut, Traven Torsvan, and Hollywood scriptwriter Hal Croves. Between the two world wars he lived in Mexico and avoided recognition. His books include the bestseller *The Death Ship* 1926, and *The Treasure of Sierra Madre* 1934, which was filmed in 1948 starring Humphrey Bogart.

Travers /'trævəz/ Ben(jamin) 1886–1980. British dramatist. He wrote plays for Tom Walls, Ralph Lynn, and Robertson Hare which were known as the 'Aldwych farces' of the 1920s, so-called from the theatre in which they were played. They include *A Cuckoo in the Nest* 1925 and *Rookery Nook* 1926.

Travers /'trævəz/ Morris William 1872–1961. British chemist, born in London, who worked with William ◊Ramsay and discovered the inert gases krypton, xenon, and radon (1894–1908).

treadmill wheel turned by foot power and used to raise water from a well (often by a donkey), turn a joint on a spit (by a dog), and so on. In 1818 William Cubitt (1785–1861), on the principle of this ancient device, devised a large cylinder to be operated by convicts treading on steps on its periphery. Such treadmills went out of use early in the 20th century.

treason an act of betrayal, generally used only of acts against the sovereign or the state to which the perpetrator owes allegiance. In this sense treason was defined in England by the Treason Act 1351, the principal treasons being (1) compassing the wounding, imprisonment, or death of the sovereign; (2) seducing the king's wife or eldest daughter or the wife of the heir; (3) levying war against the sovereign in his realm; (4) being adherent to the sovereign's enemies within the realm, giving them aid or comfort in the realm or elsewhere. The punishment on conviction of treason is death. The Treachery Act, 1940, supplemented the law of treason by making it an offence punishable by death for any persons, whether owing allegiance to the British crown or not, to assist the naval, military, or air operations of the enemy, or to impede the forces of the Crown: 16 spies (not normally capable of treason, though liable to be shot in the field) were convicted under this act, which expired in 1946. During the 20th century, people hanged for treason or treachery in the UK have included Roger Casement 1916, John Amery 1945, and William Joyce 1946 who, though he claimed to be a US citizen by birth, carried a British passport valid until 1940 at the time he went to Germany in August 1939. In the USA, treason is defined in Article III, Section 3, of the Constitution: 'Treason against the United States shall consist only in levying war against them, or in adhering to their enemies, giving them aid and comfort. No person shall be convicted of treason unless on the testimony of two witnesses to the same overt act, or on confession in open court. The Congress shall have power to declare the punishment of treason.'

treasure trove in England, any gold or silver, plate or bullion found concealed in a house or the ground, the owner being unknown. Normally, treasure originally hidden, and not abandoned, belongs to the Crown, but if the treasure was casually lost or intentionally abandoned, the first finder is entitled to it against all but the true owner. Objects buried with no intention of recovering them, for example in a burial mound, do not rank as treasure trove, and belong to the owner of the ground.

Treasury in Britain, the government department established 1612 to collect and manage the public revenue and coordinate national economic policy. Technically, the prime minister is the first lord of the Treasury, but the chancellor of the Exchequer is the acting financial head.

Treasury bill in Britain, borrowing by the government in the form of a ◊promissory note to repay the bearer 91 days from the date of issue; a flexible and relatively cheap way for the government to borrow money for immediate needs.

Trebizond /'trebɪzɒnd/ former name of ◊Trabzon, a city in Turkey.

tree a perennial plant with a woody stem, usually a single stem or 'trunk'; this is made up of ◊wood, and protected by an outer layer of ◊bark. A tree-like form has evolved independently many times in different groups of plants. Among the ◊angiosperms or flowering plants, most trees are ◊dicotyledons. This group includes all the familiar trees such as oak, beech, ash, chestnut, lime and maple, and they are often referred to as ◊broadleaved trees, because their leaves are broader than those of conifers. In temperate regions angiosperm trees are mostly ◊deciduous, that is they lose their leaves in winter, but in the tropics most angiosperm trees are evergreen. There are fewer trees among the ◊monocotyledons, but the palms and bamboos (some of which are tree-like) belong to this group. The ◊gymnosperms include many trees and they are classified into four orders: Cycadales, including cycads and sago palms; Coniferales, the conifers; Ginkgoales, including only one living species, the ginkgo or maidenhair tree; and Taxales, including yews. Apart from the ginkgo and the larches (conifers) most gymnosperm trees are evergreen. There are also a few living trees in the ◊pteridophyte group, known as tree-ferns.

Tree /triː/ Herbert Beerbohm 1853–1917. British actor-manager, half brother of Max ◊Beerbohm. Noted for his Shakespeare productions, he was founder of the ◊Royal Academy of Dramatic Art.

tree-creeper small short-legged bird of the family Certhiidae, that spirals with a mouse-like movement up tree trunks searching for food with its thin downcurved beak. The *common treecreeper Certhia familiaris* is 12 cm/5 in long, brown above, white below, and is found across Europe, N Asia and North America.

trefoil name given to several plants of the pea family in which the leaves appear to be divided into three lobes. *Birdsfoot trefoil Lotus corniculatus* is a low-growing perennial found in grassy places through Europe, N Asia and parts of Africa. Its leaves have five leaflets, but the first two are bent back so they appear to have three. The yellow flowers, often tinged orange or red, are borne throughout the summer in heads with a few flowers. *Hop trefoil Trifolium campestre* is also found in grassy places through Europe, has leaves with three leaflets, but has tight-packed round heads of yellow flowers about 1.5 cm/0.6 in across.

Trefusis /trɪ'fjuːsɪs/ Violet 1894–1972. British hostess and writer. Daughter of Mrs Keppel, who was later the mistress of Edward VII, she had a disastrous marriage to cavalry officer Denys Trefusis and a passionate elopement with Vita ◊Sackville-West recorded in Nigel Nicolson's *Portrait of a Marriage*.

Treitschke /'traɪtʃkə/ Heinrich von 1834–1896. German historian. At first a Liberal, he later adopted a Pan-German standpoint. His best-known work is the *Deutsche Geschichte im 19 Jahrhundert/History of Germany in the 19th Century* 1879–94.

Trek, Great the movement of Boer settlers from Cape Colony in 1836 and 1837 to escape British rule. They established republics in Natal (1838) and the Transvaal. The Great Trek is seen among many white South Africans as the major event in the founding of the present republic and as a justification for continuing whites-only rule.

trematode any parasitic flatworm of the class Trematoda, including the ◊fluke.

tremor a small-intensity ◊earthquake.

Trenchard /'trentʃəd/ Hugh Montague, 1st Viscount Trenchard 1873–1956. British airman. He commanded the Royal Flying Corps in World War I 1915–17, and 1918–29 organized the Royal Air Force, becoming first marshal of the Royal Air Force 1927. As commissioner of the Metropolitan Police, he established the Police College at Hendon and carried out the Trenchard Reforms, which included the application of more scientific methods of detection.

Trengganu /treŋ'gɑːnuː/ state of E Malaysia; capital Kuala Trengganu; area 13,080 sq km/5,050 sq mi; population (1980) 542,280. Exports include copra, black pepper, tin and tungsten.

Trent /trent/ third longest river of England; length 275 km/170 mi. Rising in the S Pennines, it flows first S and then NE through the Midlands to the Humber. It is navigable by barge for nearly 160 km/100 mi.

Trent, Council of /trent/ 1545–1563. council held by the Roman Catholic Church at Trento, N Italy; initiating the ◊Counter-Reformation; see also ◊Reformation.

Trentino-Alto Adige /tren'tiːnəʊ 'æltəʊ 'ædɪdʒeɪ/ special autonomous region of N Italy: capital Trento for the Italian-speaking southern area, and Bolzano-Bozen for the northern German-speaking area of South ◊Tirol (the whole region was Austrian until ceded to Italy 1919); population (1981) 873,413.

Trento /'trentəu/ capital of S◊Trentino-Alto Adige region, Italy; population (1980) 100,000. Industries include the manufacture of electrical goods and chemicals. The Council of ◊Trent was held here 1545–63.

Trenton /'trentən/ capital of New Jersey, USA; population (1980) 92,125. Industries include metalworking and ceramics.
history first settled by ◊Quakers in 1679. ◊Washington defeated the British here 1776.

trepang name for ◊sea-cucumbers used as food.

trespass going on to the land of another without authority. It is not a crime in English law, but the landowner has the right to eject a trespasser by the use of reasonable force, and can sue for any damage caused.

Tressell /'tresəl/ Robert. Pseudonym of Robert Noonan 1868–1911. British author, whose *The Ragged Trousered Philanthropists*, published after his death in an abridged form in 1914, gave a detailed account of working people's lives.

Trevelyan /trɪ'vɪljən/ George Macaulay 1876–1962. British historian, son of George ◊Trevelyan. Regius professor of history at Cambridge 1927–40, he pioneered the study of social history, as in his *English Social History* 1942.

Trevelyan /trɪ'vɪljən/ George Otto 1838–1928. British politician and historian, a nephew of the historian Lord Macaulay, whose biography he wrote 1876.

Trèves /trev/ the French name for ◊Trier, a city in West Germany.

Treviso /tre'viːzəu/ city in Veneto, Italy; population (1981) 87,696. Industries include machinery and ceramics. The 11th-century cathedral has an altarpiece by ◊Titian.

Trevithick /trɪ'vɪθɪk/ Richard 1771–1833. British engineer, constructor of a steam road locomotive 1801, and the first steam engine to run on rails 1804.

Trevor-Roper /'trevə 'rəupə/ Hugh, Baron Dacre 1914– . British historian. Regius professor of history at Oxford 1957–80, he made his name with *The Last Days of Hitler* 1947. He was created a life peer 1979.

Triad secret society, founded in China as a Buddhist cult in 36 AD. It became known as the Triad because the triangle played an important part in the initiation ceremony. Later it became political, aiming at the overthrow of the ◊Manchus, and backed the Taiping Rebellion 1851 and ◊Sun Yat-sen's establishment of a republic. Today it has a reputation for organized crime among overseas Chinese. Its headquarters are alleged to be in Hong Kong.

triangle in geometry, a three-sided plane figure. A *scalene triangle* has no two sides equal; an *isosceles triangle* has two equal sides (and two equal angles); an *equilateral triangle* has three equal sides (and three equal angles of 60°). A ◊right-angled triangle has one angle of 90°. If the length of one side of a triangle is *l* and the perpendicular distance from that side to the opposite corner is *h* (the height or altitude of the triangle), its area $A = 1/2l \times h$.

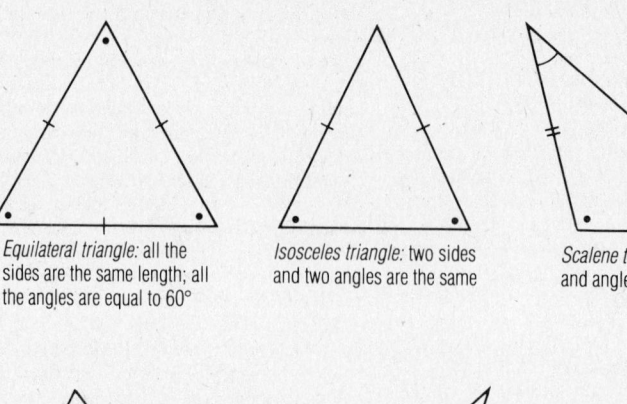

triangle

Equilateral triangle: all the sides are the same length; all the angles are equal to 60°

Isosceles triangle: two sides and two angles are the same

Scalene triangle: all the sides and angles are different

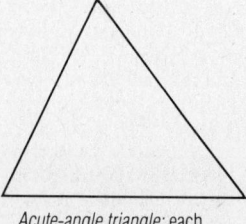

Acute-angle triangle: each angle is acute (less than 90°)

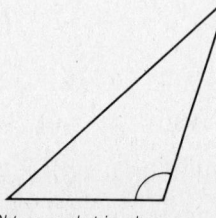

Obtuse-angle triangle: one angle is obtuse (more than 90°)

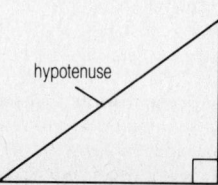

A right-angle triangle has one angle of 90°, the *hypotenuse* is the side opposite the right angle

hypotenuse

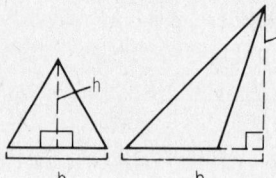

Area of triangle = ½*bh*

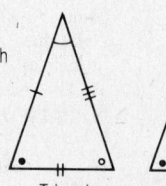

Triangles are *congruent* if corresponding sides and corresponding angles are equal

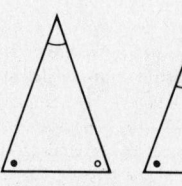

Similar triangles have corresponding angles that are equal; they therefore have the same shape

triangulation a technique used in surveying to determine distances, using the properties of the triangle. In triangulation, surveyors measure a certain length exactly to provide a base line. From each end of this line they then measure the angle to a distant point, using a ◊theodolite. They now have a triangle in which they know the length of one side and the two adjacent angles. By simple trigonometry they can work out the lengths of the other two sides. To make a complete survey of the region, they repeat the process, building on the first triangle.

Trianon /'triːənɒŋ/ two palaces in the park at ◊Versailles, France: Le Grand Trianon built for Louis XIV, and Le Petit Trianon for Louis XV.

Triassic the period of geological time between 230 and 195 million years ago. The continents were fused together to form the supercontinent ◊Pangaea and the climate was generally dry – desert sandstones are typical Triassic rocks. Triassic sediments contain remains of early dinosaurs and other large reptiles.

triathlon a three-part sports event in which the competitors complete a 3.8 km/2.4 mi sea swim, a 180 km/112 mi cycle ride, and 42,195 m/26.2 mi run (marathon) one after the other.

tribunal a court of justice, but in English usage more especially a body appointed by the government to arbitrate in disputes (for example over siting new roads, nuclear power stations; compensation for industrial injury or unfair dismissal; deportation orders against immigrants). Members are usually local and unpaid, the chairman being the only lawyer.

tribune Roman magistrate of ◊plebeian family, elected annually to defend the interests of the common people; only two were originally provided for in 494 BC, but there were later ten. They could veto the decisions of any other magistrate.

triceratops rhinoceros-like herbivorous dinosaur with three horns and a neck frill. Up to 8 m/25 ft long, it lived in the Cretaceous period.

Trichinopoly /ˌtrɪkɪ'nɒpəli/ former name for ◊Tiruchirapalli, a city in India.

tricolore name given to the French national flag of three vertical bands of red, white and blue. The red and blue were the colours of Paris and the white represented the House of ◊Bourbon. The flag was first adopted three days after the storming of the Bastille, on 17 Jul 1789.

Tricoteuses the groups of women who sat knitting in the French National Convention and beneath the guillotine during the Revolutionary period.

Trier /triə/ (French *Trèves*) city in Rhineland-Palatinate, West Germany; population (1984) 94,600.
history once the capital of the Treveri, a Celto-Germanic tribe, it became known as *Augusta Treverorum* under the Roman emperor Augustus c. 15 BC, and was the capital of an ecclesiastical principality during the 14th–18th centuries.

Trieste /tri'est/ port on the Adriatic, opposite Venice, capital of Friuli-Venezia-Giulia, Italy; population (1981) 252,369, including a large Slovene minority. It is the site of the International Centre for Theoretical Physics, established 1964.
history under Austrian rule from 1382 (apart from Napoleonic occupation 1809–14) until transferred to Italy 1918, Trieste was claimed after World War II by Yugoslavia, and was divided 1954 between Italy and Yugoslavia.

trigger-fish marine fish of the family Balistidae, with a laterally compressed body and deep belly. They have small mouths but strong jaws and teeth. The first spine on the dorsal fin locks into an erect position and can only be moved by depressing the smaller third ('trigger') spine. The fish may be able to lock itself into a crevice for protection. There are many species, especially in warm waters.

trigonometry branch of mathematics that solves problems relating to plane and spherical triangles. Its principles are based on the fixed proportions of angles and sides in a ◊right-angled triangle, the simplest of which are the ◊sine, ◊cosine, and ◊tangent (so-called trigonometrical ratios). Using trigonometry it is possible to calculate the lengths of the sides and the sizes of the angles of a triangle as long as one angle and one side are known. It is of practical importance in navigation and surveying and in topics such as ◊simple harmonic motion in physics. Invented by ◊Hipparchus, it was developed by ◊Ptolemy of Alexandria and was known to Hindu and Arab mathematicians.

trilobite extinct marine arthropod of the Palaeozoic era, with flattened, oval, segmented body. Trilobites ('three-lobes') looked rather like large woodlice, the biggest being up to 0.5 m/1.5 ft long. Their worldwide distribution, many species, and the immense quantities of their remains make them useful in dating remains of other creatures.

Trimurti /tri'muəti/ the Hindu triad of gods, representing the Absolute Spirit in its three aspects: Brahma, personifying creation; Vishnu, preservation; and Siva, destruction.

Trincomalee /,trɪŋkəmə'li:/ port in NE Sri Lanka; population (1981) 44,913. It was an early Tamil settlement, and a British naval base until 1957.

Trinidad /,trɪnɪ'dæd/ town in Bolivia, near the river Mamoré, 400 km/250 mi NE of La Paz; population (1980) 36,200. It is built on an artificial mound, above flood-level, the work of a little-known early American Indian people.

Trinidad and Tobago /'trɪnɪdæd, tə'beɪgəʊ/ country in the W Indies, off the coast of Venezuela.
government Trinidad and Tobago is an independent republic within the Commonwealth. The 1976 constitution provides for a president as head of state, and a two-chamber parliament, consisting of a senate of 31 members and a house of representatives of 36. The president appoints the prime minister and cabinet, who are collectively responsible to Parliament. The president also appoints the senators, 16 on the advice of the prime minister, six on the advice of the leader of the opposition, and nine after wider consultation. The 36 members of the House of Representatives are elected by universal adult suffrage. Parliament has a life of five years.
Tobago Island was given its own House of Assembly in 1980. It has 15 members, 12 popularly elected and three chosen by the majority party.
history for early history, see ◊American Indian. Trinidad and Tobago were discovered by Columbus 1498. Trinidad was colonized by Spain from 1532 and ceded to Britain 1802, having been captured 1797. Tobago was settled by the Netherlands in the 1630s and subsequently occupied by various countries before being ceded to Britain by France 1814. Trinidad and Tobago were amalgamated 1888 as a British colony.
Trinidad and Tobago's first political party, the People's National Movement (PNM), was formed in 1956 by Dr Eric Williams and when the colony was granted internal self-government in 1959 he became the first chief minister. Between 1958 and 1961 it was a member of the Federation of the West Indies but withdrew and achieved full independence, within the Commonwealth, in 1967, Dr Williams becoming the first prime minister.
A new constitution was adopted in 1976 which made Trinidad and Tobago a republic. The former governor-general, Ellis Clarke, became the first president and Dr Williams continued as prime minister. He died in Mar 1981 without having nominated a successor and the president appointed George Chambers; the PNM formally adopted him as leader in May 1981. The opposition, a moderate left-wing party grouping led by the deputy prime minister, Arthur Robinson, was during the next few years reorganized as the National Alliance for Reconstruction (NAR), until in the 1986 general election it swept the PNM from power and Arthur Robinson became prime minister.

Trinity in the Christian religion, the threefold union of three persons in one godhead, namely Father, Son, and Holy Ghost/Spirit. The precise meaning of the doctrine has been the cause of unending dispute, and was the chief cause of the split between the Eastern Orthodox and Roman Catholic churches. Trinity Sunday occurs on the

Sunday after Whit Sunday.

triode a three-◊electrode thermionic valve containing an anode and a cathode (as does a ◊diode) with an additional negatively-biased control grid. Small variations in voltage on the grid bias result in large variations in the current. The triode was thus commonly used in amplifiers until largely superseded by the ◊transistor. The valve was invented by the American radio engineer Lee De Forest (1873–1961).

Triple Alliance (1882) an alliance between Germany, Austria-Hungary, and Italy which formed the basis of central power involvement in World War I (Italy remaining neutral and then joining the ◊Allies).

Triple Entente (1907–17) alliance of Britain, France, and Russia. In 1911 this became a military alliance and formed the basis of the allied cause in World War I. The failure of the alliance system to create a stable balance of power, coupled with universal horror of the carnage created by World War I, led to further attempts to create a new international order with the ◊League of Nations.

Tripoli /'trɪpəli/ port in N Lebanon, 65 km/40 mi NE of Beirut; population (1980) 175,000. It stands on the site of a Phoenician city.

Tripoli /'trɪpəli/ capital and chief port of Libya, on the Mediterranean; population (1980) 980,000.
history Tripoli was founded c. 7th century BC by the Phoenicians; the name means 'Three Cities' (*Oea, Leptis Magna,* and *Sabratha*). The ruins of Leptis Magna are 112 km/70 mi to the east, near Homs.

Tripolitania /,trɪpəlɪ'teɪniə/ former province of Libya, North Africa, stretching from Cyrenaica in the east to Tunisia in the west. Italy captured it from Turkey 1912. In 1963 Tripolitania was subdivided into administrative divisions.

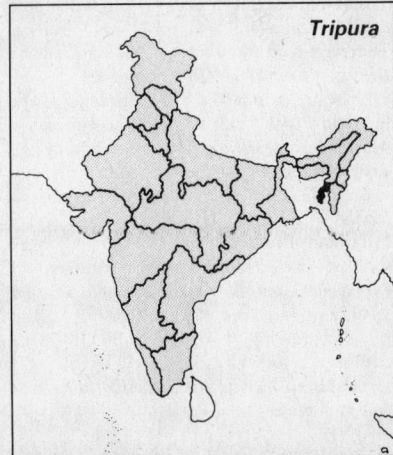

Tripura

Tripura /'trɪpʊrə/ state of NE India, formerly a princely state, between Bangladesh and Assam.
area 10,477 sq km/4,044 sq mi
capital Agartala
features agriculture (rice, cotton, tea, sugar cane) on a shifting system in the jungle, now being superseded by modern methods

Trinidad and Tobago
REPUBLIC OF

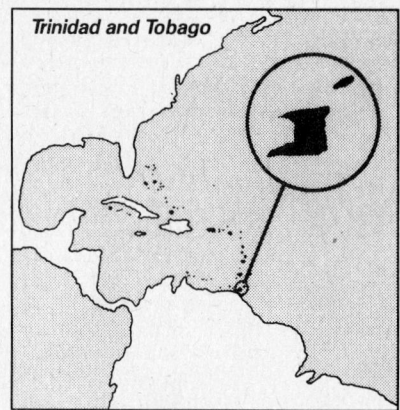
Trinidad and Tobago

AREA Trinidad 4,828 sq km/1,864 sq mi and Tobago 300 sq km/116 sq mi
CAPITAL Port of Spain
TOWNS San Fernando
PHYSICAL comprises the two main islands, and some smaller ones; Trinidad has coastal swamps, and hills E–W
FEATURES Pitch Lake is a self-renewing source of asphalt and was used by the British 16th-century explorer Raleigh when repairing his ships
HEAD OF STATE Noor Hassanali from 1987
HEAD OF GOVERNMENT Arthur Robinson from 1986
GOVERNMENT parliamentary democracy
EXPORTS angostura bitters, first blended from herbs as a stomach remedy in 1824, and now used to season food and fruit, and flavour 'pink' gin; asphalt, natural gas and oil
CURRENCY Trinidad and Tobago dollar (5.93 = £1 Sept 1987)
POPULATION (1985) 1,186,000 (equally divided between those of African and E Indian descent); annual growth rate 0.3%
LANGUAGE English (official), Hindi, French, Spanish
RELIGION Roman Catholic 33%, Protestant 14%, Hindu 25%, Muslim 6%
LITERACY 97% male/93% female (1980 est)
GNP $6.8 bn (1983); $6,800 per head of population

CHRONOLOGY
1956 The People's National Movement (PNM) founded.
1959 Granted internal self-government, with PNM leader Eric Williams as chief minister.
1967 Achieved full independence, within the Commonwealth, with Williams as prime minister.
1976 Became a republic, with Ellis Clarke as president and Williams as prime minister.
1981 Williams died and was succeeded by George Chambers, with Arthur Robinson as leader of the opposition.
1986 Arthur Robinson became prime minister.
1987 Noor Hassanali became president.

population (1981) 2,053,058
language Bengali
religion Hindu.

trireme ancient Greek warship with three banks of oars as well as sails, 38 m/115 ft long. They were used at the battle of ◊Salamis, and by the Romans until the 4th century AD.

Tristan /'trɪstən/ hero of Celtic legend, who fell in love with Iseult, the bride he was sent to win for his uncle King Mark of Cornwall; the story became part of the Arthurian cycle, and is the subject of ◊Wagner's opera *Tristan and Isolde*.

Tristan /'trɪstən/ Flora 1803–1844. French socialist writer and activist, author of *Promenades dans Londres/The London Journal* 1840, a vivid record of social conditions, and *L'Union ouvrière/Workers' Union* 1843, an outline of a workers' utopia.

Tristan da Cunha /də 'kuːnjə/ British island colony in the S Atlantic
area 105 sq km/40 sq mi
features comprises four islands: Tristan, Gough, Inaccessible, and Nightingale. Tristan consists of a single volcano 2,060 m/6,760 ft; it is an important meteorological and radio station
exports crawfish
currency pound sterling
population (1982) 325
government administrator, plus Island Council, as a dependency of ◊St Helena

history the first European to visit the islands was the Portuguese admiral after whom they are named, in 1506; they were annexed by Britain 1816. Believed to be extinct, the Tristan volcano erupted 1961, but in 1963 the evacuated population chose to return.

Tristano /trɪ'staːnəʊ/ 'Lennie' (Lennard Joseph) 1919–1978. US jazz pianist and composer. A radically austere musician, he gave an academic foundation to the cool school of jazz in the 1940s and 1950s, at odds with the bebop tradition, and was active as a teacher.

tritium unstable isotope of hydrogen, with two neutrons as well as one proton in its nucleus. See also ◊deuterium.

Triton /'traɪtn/ in Greek mythology, a merman sea-god, the son of ◊Poseidon and the sea-goddess Amphitrite. He is shown blowing on a ◊conch.

Triton /'traɪtn/ in astronomy, the largest moon of the planet ◊Neptune.

triumvir one of a group of three magistrates sharing power in ancient Rome, as in the *First Triumvirate* 60 BC: Caesar, Pompey, Crassus; and *Second Triumvirate* 43 BC: Augustus, Antony, and Lepidus.

Trivandrum /trɪ'vændrəm/ capital of Kerala, India; population (1981) 482,720. Industries include chemicals, textiles, and rubber products. Formerly the capital of the princely state of Travancore, it has many palaces, a university 1937, an old fort, and a famous shrine.

troglodyte Greek term for a cave-dweller, designating certain peoples in the ancient world. The best-known were those of S Egypt and Ethiopia, a pastoral people.

trogon tropical bird of resplendent plumage of the Americas and Afro-Asia, order Trogoniformes. Most striking is the *quetzal Pharomachrus mocinno* of central America which has a crest and golden-green tail plumes 1 m/3 ft long, and body in red, green and blue. Sacred to the Aztecs and Mayas (see ◊Quetzalcoatl), it is the emblem of Guatemala.

Trois Rivières /'trwɑː rɪv'jeə/ port on the St Lawrence river, Quebec, Canada; population (1981) 50,466. The chief industry is the production of newsprint. It was founded by ◊Champlain 1634.

trolleybus type of bus usually driven solely by electric power collected from overhead wires. They have greater manoeuvrability than a ◊tram, but their obstructiveness in modern traffic conditions led to them being abandoned, especially since they are less efficient in their use of energy than diesel buses. However, their quietness in operation and freedom from pollution made them attractive, and Germany has developed new types which operate, by means of three tonnes of batteries, for 10 km/6 mi without drawing current from an overhead wire.

Trollope /'trɒləp/ Anthony 1815–1882. British novelist, who delineated provincial English middle class society in his popular Barchester series of novels. A Londoner, educated at Harrow, he became a post office clerk 1834, introduced the pillar box 1853, and achieved the position of surveyor before retiring 1867. *The Warden* 1855 began the clerical series set in the imaginary cathedral city of Barchester (a combination of Salisbury and Winchester), which includes *Barchester Towers* 1857, *Doctor Thorne* 1858, and *The Last Chronicle of Barset* 1867. He tried unsuccessfully to enter Parliament as a Liberal, and his political novels include *Can You Forgive Her?* 1864, *Phineas Finn* 1867–69, and *The Prime Minister* 1875–76.

trombone a ◊brass wind musical instrument developed from the sackbut. It consists of a tube bent double, varied notes being obtained by an inner sliding tube. Usual sizes are alto, tenor, bass, and contra-bass.

Tromp /trɒmp/ Maarten Harpertszoon 1597–1653. Dutch admiral. Born at Brielle, he twice defeated the Spaniards in 1639. He was defeated by Blake in May 1652, but in Nov triumphed over Blake in the Strait of Dover. In Feb–June 1653 he was defeated by Blake, Monk, and Deane, and was killed off the Dutch coast. His son, *Cornelius Tromp* (1629–91), also an admiral, won fame in 1673 for his battle against the English and French fleets.

Tromsö /'trɒmsɜː/ fishing port in NW Norway, on Tromsö island; population (1984) 47,400.

Trondheim /'trɒndhaɪm/ fishing port in Norway; population (1985) 133,927. Industries include canning, textiles, margarine, and soap. It was the medieval capital of Norway, and Norwegian kings are crowned in the cathedral.

trophic level in ◊ecology, the position occupied by a ◊species (or group of species) in a ◊food chain. The main levels are primary producers (for example, plants), primary consumers (for example, herbivores), secondary consumers (for example, carnivores) and decomposers.

tropics the tropics of Cancer and Capricorn, defined by the parallels of latitude 23°30′ N and S of the equator, are the limits of the area of Earth's surface in which the sun can be directly overhead.

tropine a white crystalline solid formed by the hydrolysis of alkaloid atropine.

tropism or *tropic movement* the directional growth of a plant, or part of a plant, in response to an external stimulus. It differs from a ◊nastic movement in being influenced by the direction of the stimulus. Tropic movements occur due to a greater rate of growth on the one side of the plant organ than the other. If the movement is directed towards the stimulus it is described as positive, and if away from it, as negative. Phototropism occurs in response to light, and a shoot bending towards a light source is positvely phototropic. Geotropism, the response of plants to gravity, causes the root, which is positively geotropic, to grow downwards, and the negatively geotropic stem to grow upwards. Hydrotropism occurs in response to water, chemotropism to a chemical stimulus, and thigmotropism, or haptotropism, to physical contact, as in the tendrils of climbing plants when they touch a support and then grow around it. Sedentary animals show similar reactions.

troposphere the lower part of the earth's ◊atmosphere extending about 10.5 km/6.5 mi from the Earth's surface, in which temperature decreases with height except in local layers of temperature inversion. The *tropopause* is the upper boundary of the troposphere above which the temperature is constant or even increases slightly with height.

Trossachs /'trɒsəks/ woodland glen between Lochs Katrine and Achray in ◊Central region, Scotland, 3 km/2 mi long.

Trotsky /'trɒtski/ Leon, pseudonym of Lev Davidovitch Bronstein 1879–1940. Russian revolutionary. Although as a young man he admired ◊Lenin, when he worked with him organizing the revolution of 1917 he objected to Lenin's dictatorial ways. He joined the Bolshevik party and took a leading part in the seizure of power and raising the Red Army which fought the Civil War 1918–20. In the struggle for power that followed Lenin's death in 1924, ◊Stalin defeated him and this and other differences with the Communist Party led to his exile in 1929. Trotsky settled in Mexico, where he was assassinated with an ice pick, possibly at Stalin's instigation. His later works are critical of the Soviet regime, for example *The Revolution Betrayed* 1937. Trotsky believed in world revolution and in permanent revolution and was an uncompromising, if liberal, idealist. His greatest work is his magisterial *History of the Russian Revolution* 1932–33.

Trotsky Leon Trotsky, the Russian revolutionary whose name is synonymous with radical communism. This passport photograph was taken in 1917, the year of the Russian Revolution, which he and Lenin instigated as leading members of the Bolshevik movement.

Trotskyism the form of ◊Marxism advocated by Leon ◊Trotsky. Its central concept is that of 'permanent revolution', and Trotsky developed it in an attempt to reconcile Marxist theory with actual conditions in Russia in the early 20th century. In his view a proletarian revolution, leading to a socialist society, could not be achieved in isolation, so it would be necessary to spark off further revolutions throughout Europe and ultimately worldwide. This was in direct opposition to the Stalinist view that socialism should be built and consolidated within individual countries.

Although never officially accepted within the USSR, Trotskyism has found much support worldwide, especially in Third World countries, and the Fourth International, which Trotsky founded in 1937, has sections in over 60 countries.

troubadour one of a group of poet-musicians in ◊Provence and S France, in the 12th–13th centuries, which included both nobles and wandering minstrels. The troubadours originated a type of lyric poetry devoted mainly to themes of courtly love and the idealization of women, and to glorifying the deeds of their patrons, reflecting the chivalric ideals of the period. Little is known of the music, which was normally passed down orally. Most famous of the troubadours were Bertran de Born (1140–c. 1215, who was mentioned by Dante), Arnaut Daniel, and Bernard de Ventadour. The troubadour tradition spread to other parts of Europe, including northern France (the *trouvères*) and Germany (the Minnesingers).

trout fish closely related to the salmon. The common trout *Salmo trutta* is widely distributed in Europe, occurring in British fresh and coastal

waters. Sea trout are generally silvery and river trout olive-brown, both having spotted fins and sides. In the USA the name trout is given to various species, notably to the rainbow trout *Salmo gairdneri* which has been naturalized in many other countries.

Trowbridge /'trəʊbrɪdʒ/ market town in Wiltshire, England; population (1981) 22,982. Industries include dairy produce, bacon, ham, and wool.

Troy /trɔɪ/ ancient city (Latin name *Ilium*) of Asia Minor, which the poet ◊Homer in the *Iliad* described as besieged in the ten-year Trojan War (mid-13th century BC), and falling to the Greeks by the stratagem of leaving behind, in a feigned retreat, a wooden horse containing armed infiltrators to open the gates. Believing it to be a religious offering, the Trojans took it within the walls. Nine cities buried one beneath another on the site at Hissarlik, near the Dardanelles, were originally excavated by ◊Schliemann. Recent research suggests that the seventh, sacked and burnt about 1250 BC, is probably the Homeric Troy, which was succeeded by a shanty town, sacked by the ◊Sea Peoples about 780 BC. It has been suggested that the Homeric war might have a basis in fact, for example a conflict arising from trade rivalry (Troy was on a tin trade route), which could have been triggered by such an incident as Paris running off with ◊Helen. The wooden horse could have been a votive offering left behind by the Greeks after ◊Poseidon (whose emblem was a horse) had opened breaches in the city walls for them by an earthquake. See also ◊Mycenae.

Troyes /trwɑː/ industrial town in Champagne-Ardenne, NE France; population (1982) 64,759. Industries include textiles and food processing. The *Treaty of Troyes* 1420 granted the French crown to Henry V of England.

Trucial States /'truːʃəl 'steɪts/ former name (until 1971) of the ◊United Arab Emirates. It derives from the agreements made in 1820 with Britain to ensure a truce in the area, and to suppress piracy and slavery.

Trudeau /truːˈdəʊ/ Pierre Elliott 1919– . Canadian Liberal politician. He was prime minister 1968–79 and won again by a landslide in Feb 1980. In 1980 he defeated the Quebec independence movement in a referendum and gained control over the constitution 1982, but by 1984 had so lost support that he resigned.

Truffaut /truːˈfəʊ/ François 1932–1984. French film director, who won international acclaim with *Jules et Jim* 1961, and *La Nuit américaine/Day for Night* 1973 (for which he won an Academy Award). His work was greatly influenced by Hitchcock.

truffle subterranean fungus, highly valued in cookery. The finest (*Tuber melanosporum*) comes from Périgord, France, generally growing under oak trees: it is rounded, blackish brown and covered with warts externally, and with blackish flesh. Pigs like truffles and are used to locate them, as are dogs. Success in inoculating tree roots with truffle spores suggests that truffles may become less of a luxury.

Trujillo /truːˈxiːəu/ city in Peru, with its port at Salaverry; population (1981) 354,557. Industries include engineering, copper, sugar milling, and vehicle assembly.

Trujillo Molina /məuˈliːnə/ Rafael Leonidas 1891–1961. Dominican dictator, president of the Dominican Republic 1930–38 and 1942–52, and the power behind his brother, when the latter assumed the presidency 1952. He transformed the island into a modern state, but his suppression of his opponents resulted in his assassination.

Truman /ˈtruːmən/ Harry S 1884–1972. 33rd president of the USA 1945–53. Born in Lamar, Missouri, he ran a clothing store that was bankrupted by the Great Depression. In Jan 1945 he became Democrat vice-president to Roosevelt, becoming president when Roosevelt died in Apr that year, and in 1948 was elected for a second term in a surprise victory over Thomas Dewey. He used the atom bomb against Japan to shorten World War II; launched the ◊Marshall Plan to restore W Europe's economy; nurtured the European Community, NATO (including the rearmament of West Germany), an independent Israel, and the lines of 'containment' in Europe and Asia (see ◊Truman Doctrine). In Korea, he intervened when the South was invaded (see ◊Korean War), but sacked General ◊MacArthur when the General's policy threatened to start World War III. Truman's decision not to enter Chinese territory, betrayed by Kim ◊Philby, led to China's entry into the war.

Truman The decision made by American president Harry Truman to use the atom bomb against Japan, and his intervention with troops in the Korean War are still controversial issues.

Truman Doctrine Harry ◊Truman's 1947 doctrine that the USA would 'support free peoples who are resisting attempted subjugation by armed minorities or by outside pressures'. It was used to justify sending US troops abroad, for example, to Korea.

trumpet ◊brass wind musical instrument; a doubled tube with valves.

trumpeter small South American bird genus *Psophia*, related to the cranes. It is also a type of ◊swan.

Truong Sa /ˌtruːɒŋˈsɑː/ one of the ◊Spratly Islands, in the South China Sea.

Truro /ˈtruərəu/ city in Cornwall, England, and administrative headquarters of the county; population (1982) 16,040. The cathedral dates from 1880–1910, and the museum and art gallery has works by ◊Opie. The nearby tin mines flourished briefly in the early 1980s.

trust an arrangement whereby a person or group of people holds property for the benefit of others entitled to the beneficial interest. Types of trust include a *legal arrangement* under which A is empowered to administer property belonging to B for the benefit of C. A and B may be the same person; B and C may not. A *business trust* is formed by linking several companies by transferring shares in them to trustees; or by the creation of a holding company, whose shares are exchanged for those of the separate companies. Competition is thus eliminated, and in the USA both types were outlawed by the Sherman Anti-Trust Act 1890 (first fully enforced by 'trust buster' Theodore ◊Roosevelt, as in the break-up of the Standard Oil Company of New Jersey by the Supreme Court 1911). A *unit trust* holds and manages a number of marketable securities; by buying a 'unit' in such a trust, the purchaser has a proportionate interest in each of the securities so that his or her risk is spread. An *investment trust* is not in modern times a trust, but a public company investing in marketable securities money subscribed by its shareholders who receive dividends from the income earned. A *charitable trust* such as the ◊National Trust, or the Ford Foundation, administers funds for charitable purposes.

Trustee, Public in England, an official empowered to act as executor and trustee, either alone or with others, of the estate of anyone who appoints him or her.

trust territory territory formerly held under the United Nations trusteeship system to be prepared for independence, either former ◊mandates, territories taken over by the Allies in World War II, or those voluntarily placed under the UN by the administering state.

Truth /truːθ/ Sojourner (born Isabella Baumfree, subsequently Isabella Van Wagener) 1797–1883. American anti-slavery campaigner. Born a slave, she obtained her freedom and that of her son and became involved with religious groups. In 1843 she was commanded in a vision to adopt the name Sojourner Truth, publishing an autobiography, *The Narrative of Sojourner Truth*, in 1850, and lecturing to large crowds on the evils of slavery. She worked as a fund-raiser for the North during the American Civil War.

trypanosomiasis collection of debilitating long-term diseases caused by infestation with the microscopic single-celled *Trypanosoma*. They include sleeping sickness (nagana) in Africa, transmitted by the bites of ◊tsetse flies, and Chagas' disease in the Americas, spread by assassin-bugs. Millions of people are affected in warmer regions of the world; the diseases also affect cattle, which form a reservoir of infection.

Ts'ao Chan another name for the Chinese novelist ◊Cao Chan.

Tsar the Russian imperial title, derived from Latin *Caesar*.

Tsaritsyn /tsɑːˈrɪtsɪn/ a former name (until 1925) of ◊Volgograd, a city in the USSR.

tsetse fly of the genus *Glossina*, species of which transmit the disease nagana to cattle and sleeping sickness to human beings.

Tsinan /ˌtsiːˈnæn/ another name for ◊Jinan, a city in China.

Tsingtao /ˌtsɪŋˈtau/ another name for ◊Qingdao, a port in China.

Tsiolkovsky /tsɪəlˈkɒfskiˈ\ Konstantin 1857–1935. Russian scientist, who became permanently deaf at the age of ten. He published the first practical paper on astronautics in 1903, covering rocket space travel using liquid propellants, such as liquid oxygen.

tsunami a giant wave generated by an undersea ◊earthquake or other disturbance. In the open ocean it may take the form of several successive waves, travelling at tens of kilometres per hour but with an amplitude (height) of only a metre or so. In the coastal shallows, however, they slow down and build up, producing towering waves tens of metres high. Before each wave there may be a sudden, unexpected withdrawal of water from the beach. Tsunami is a Japanese word meaning 'harbour wave'. The term 'tidal wave' is misleading.

Tsung Li Yamen an advisory body created in China after 1861 to deal with foreign affairs and other state modernization projects. It was limited by a lack of power and the creation of an Admiralty in 1885 and a formal foreign office after 1901.

Tsushima /ˈtsuːʃiːmɑː/ small Japanese island between Korea and Japan in Tsushima Strait. The Russian fleet was destroyed by the Japanese on this island in 1905 (see also ◊Russo–Japanese War).

Tsvetaeva /svɪˈtaɪəvə/ Marina 1892–1941. Russian poet, born in Moscow. She wrote mythic, romantic, frenetic verse, including *The Demesne of the Swans*.

Tuamoto Islands /ˌtuːəˈməutuː/ group of some 80 atolls stretching 2,100 km/1,300 mi in the central Pacific, part of French Polynesia; area 1,064 sq km/411 sq mi; population (1981) 8,537. They produce pearls and copra. Spanish explorers landed in 1606, and the islands were annexed by France 1881.

Tuareg nomadic ◊Hamite people of the Sudan.

tuatara lizard-like sole survivor *Sphenodon punctatus* of the reptilian order Rhynchocephalia, found in New Zealand. On the top of its head it has the pineal organ, linked to the brain, and probably acting as a light meter. It lays eggs in burrows which it shares with seabirds, and has the longest incubation period of all reptiles (up to 15 months).

tuba a ◊brass wind musical instrument.

tuber a swollen region of an underground stem or root which is usually modified for storing food. The potato is a stem tuber, as shown by the presence of terminal and lateral buds: these are the 'eyes' of the potato. Root tubers, developed from adventitious roots, lack these. Both types of tuber can give rise to new individuals and so provide a means of ▷vegetative reproduction. New shoots grow directly from the buds of stem tubers, while root tubers (for example dahlias) are attached to a portion of stem with buds, and these develop into new plants. Unlike a bulb, a tuber persists for one season only; new tubers developing on a plant in the following year are formed in different places. *See also* ▷rhizome.

tuberculosis disease caused by the tuberculus bacillus, most often affecting the lungs, and formerly known as *consumption* or *phthisis*. Tuberculosis of the lymphatic glands in the neck was formerly known as *scrofula* or *king's evil* (because the royal touch was believed to cure it).

tuberose Mexican flowering plant *Polianthes tuberosa*, related to the ▷agave, grown as a sweet-smelling greenhouse plant.

Tübingen /'tjuːbɪŋən/ town in Baden-Württemberg, West Germany, on the Neckar, S of Stuttgart; population (1972) 53,000. It has factories making paper, textiles, and surgical instruments. Tübingen dates from the 11th century and has a university established 1477.

Tubman /'tʌbmən/ Harriet Ross 1821–1913. American abolitionist. Born a slave in Maryland, she escaped to Philadelphia (where slavery was outlawed) in 1849. She set up the 'Underground Railroad' to help slaves escape to the northern states and Canada. During the Civil War she was a spy for the Union army. A noted speaker against slavery and for women's rights, she founded schools for freed slaves after the Civil War.

Tubman /'tʌbmən/ William V S 1895–1971. Liberian politician. The descendant of American slaves, he was a lawyer in the USA. After becoming president of Liberia in 1944 he concentrated on uniting the various ethnic groups. Re-elected several times, he died naturally in office despite frequent assassination attempts.

Tubuai Islands /,tuːbuːˈaɪ/ group of islands in ▷French Polynesia.

Tucana ▷constellation of the southern hemisphere, representing a toucan. It contains the second most prominent ▷globular cluster in the sky, called 47 Tucanae, and the Small ▷Magellanic Cloud.

Tucson /'tuːsɒn/ town and resort in the Sonora Desert in southern Arizona, USA, population (1980) 330,537. It stands 760 m/2,500 ft above sea level, and the Santa Catalina Mountains to the NE rise to about 2,750 m/9,000 ft. Industries include aircraft, electronics, and copper smelting.

Tucumán /,tuːkuːˈmɑːn/ capital of Tucumán province, Argentina, on the Sali, in the foothills of the Andes; population (1980) 393,000. It has sugar mills and distilleries. Founded 1565, Tucumán was the site of the signing of the Argentine declaration of independence from Spain 1816.

tucu-tuco S American burrowing rodent, genus *Ctenomys*, about 20 cm/8 in long plus a 7 cm/3 in tail. It has a large head and huge incisor teeth, and spends most of its time below ground in a burrow system, one animal to a burrow.

Tudor /'tjuːdə/ English dynasty descended from the Welsh Owen Tudor (c. 1400–61), the second husband of Catherine of Valois, the widow of Henry V of England. Their son Edmund married Margaret Beaufort (1443–1509), the great-granddaughter of ▷John of Gaunt, and was the father of Henry VII, who ascended the throne in 1485. The dynasty ended with the death of Elizabeth I in 1603.

tufa a soft, porous rock, white in colour, consisting of calcium carbonate, $CaCO_3$, deposited from solution in spring water or percolating ground water

Tu Fu /'tuː 'fuː/ 712–770. Chinese poet, who wrote sorrowfully about social decline, peasant suffering, and war, as in 'The Army Carts'.

Tula /'tuːlə/ capital city of the ancient ▷Toltec civilization in Mexico.

Tula /'tuːlə/ city in W central USSR; population (1985) 532,000. Industries include engineering and metallurgy. Leo ▷Tolstoy's estate was nearby. Site of the government ordnance factory, founded 1712 by ▷Peter the Great.

tulip plant, genus *Tulipa* of the family Liliaceae. The garden tulip *Tulipa gesnerana* from which most of the garden cultivars have been derived, probably originated in the Near East, and, quickly adopted in Europe during the 16th century, became a craze in 17th century Holland when extravagant prices were paid for bulbs of rare colours. It is today commercially cultivated on a large scale in the Netherlands and East Anglia. The *tulip tree Liriodendron tulipifera* is a member of the magnolia family, with large tulip-shaped blooms.

Tull /tʌl/ Jethro 1674–1741. British agriculturist. Farming in his native Berkshire, he developed around 1701 a drill enabling seeds to be sown mechanically and spaced so that cultivation between was possible in the growth period. He published *The New Horse Hoeing Husbandry* in 1733.

Tumbs, The /tʌmbz/ two islands in the Strait of Hormuz, formerly held by Ras al Khaimah, and annexed from other Gulf states by Iran 1971; their return to their former owners was an Iraqi aim in the Iran–Iraq war.

tuna another name for ▷tunny, a kind of fish.

Tunbridge Wells, Royal /'tʌnbrɪdʒ 'welz/ spa in Kent, England, with chalybeate springs discovered 1606; population (1981) 44,821. The shopping parade, or *Pantiles* (paved with tiles in the reign of Queen ▷Anne) was long a fashionable resort.

tundra /'tʌndrə/ a region of high latitude almost devoid of trees. The term, formerly applied to part of N Russia, is now used for all such regions.

tung oil oil used in paints and varnishes, obtained from trees of the genus Aleurites, family Euphorbiaceae, native to China.

tungsten a metallic element, symbol W, atomic number 74, atomic weight 183.86. Recognized and named by Scheele in 1781, and discovered by the d'Elhujar brothers in 1783, it occurs as wolframite ($FeWO_4$), scheelite ($CaWO_4$) and huberite ($MnWO_4$). A grey hard metal, ductile, malleable and non-magnetic, it is insoluble except in a mixture of nitric and hydrofluoric acids, and has the highest melting point (3370°C) of any metal. Tungsten is used in alloy steels for armour plate, projectiles, high-speed cutting tools, etc, for lamp filaments and thermionic valves, Its salts are used in the paint and tanning industries. Also known as wolfram.

tunicate any ▷chordate of the sub-phylum Tunicata (Urochordata), including the ▷sea-squirt.

Tunis /'tjuːnɪs/ capital of Tunisia; population (1984) 556,654. Industries include chemicals and textiles.

Tunisia /tjuːˈnɪzɪə/ country in N Africa, on the Mediterranean, bounded to the SE by Libya and to the W by Algeria.

government a new constitution was adopted in 1959, providing for a president who is both head of state and head of government, elected by universal suffrage for a five-year term and eligible for re-election. The president governs through an appointed council of ministers. In 1975 Habib Bourguiba was made president for life. There is a single-chamber national assembly of 136 members, elected in the same way and for the same term as the president.

history founded as ▷Carthage by the Phoenicians in the 8th century BC, Tunisia was under Arab rule from the 7th century AD until it became part of the ▷Ottoman Empire 1574. It harboured the ▷Barbary pirates until the 19th century. It became a French protectorate 1881.

The Socialist Destourien Party (PSD), founded 1934 by Habib Bourguiba, led Tunisia's campaign for independence from France. It was granted internal self-government 1955 and full independence 1956, with Bourguiba as prime minister. A year later the monarchy was abolished and Tunisia became a republic, with Bourguiba as president. A new constitution was adopted in 1959 and the first national assembly elected. Between 1963 and 1981 PSD was the only legally recognized party but since then others have been allowed. In Nov 1986 PSD won all the assembly seats, while other parties boycotted the elections.

President Bourguiba followed a distinctive foreign policy, establishing links with the Western powers, including the USA, but joining other Arab states in condemning the US-inspired Egypt-Israel treaty. He allowed the Palestine Liberation Organization (PLO) to use Tunis as its headquarters, and this led to an Israeli attack in 1985 which strained relations with the USA. Diplomatic links with Libya were severed 1985. Bourguiba's firm and paternalistic rule, and his long period in Tunisian politics, made him a national legend, evidenced by the elaborate mausoleum which was built in anticipation of his death. However, in Nov 1987 he was deposed and replaced by Zine al-Abidine Ben Ali.

tunnel an underground passageway. Tunnelling is an increasingly important branch of civil engineering in mining, and transport. In the 19th century there were two major advances: the use of compressed air within the tunnel to balance the external pressure of water, and of the tunnel shield to support the face and assist excavation. In recent years there have been

Tunisia
REPUBLIC OF (*Al-Djoumouria Attunusia*)

AREA 164,000 sq km/63,300 sq mi
CAPITAL and chief port Tunis
TOWNS ports Sfax, Sousse, Bizerta
PHYSICAL arable and forested land in the N
graduates towards desert in the S
FEATURES fertile island of Jerba, linked to the
mainland by a causeway, and identified with
the island of the lotus-eaters; Shott el Jerid
salt lakes; holy city of Kairouan, ruins of
Carthage
HEAD OF STATE AND OF GOVERNMENT Zine el
Abdin Ben Ali from 1987
GOVERNMENT one-party socialist
EXPORTS oil, phosphates, iron ore
CURRENCY dinar (1.39 = £1 Sept 1987)
POPULATION 7,259,000 (1985); annual growth
rate 2.4%
LANGUAGE Arabic (official), French
RELIGION Sunni Muslim, with a politically
active fundamentalist opposition to the
government; Jewish and Christian minorities
LITERACY 61% male/34% female (1980 est)
GNP $8.8 bn (1983); $844 per head of
population
CHRONOLOGY
1955 Granted internal self-government.
1956 Achieved full independence as a

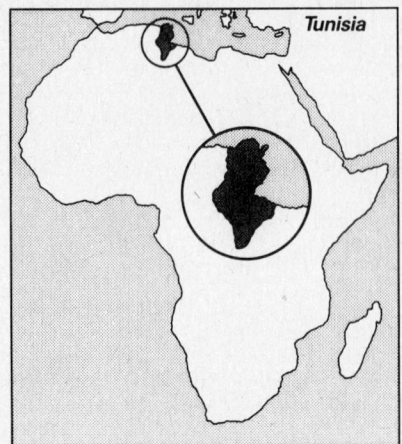

Tunisia

monarchy, with Habib Bourguiba as prime
minister.
1957 Became a republic with Bourguiba as
president.
1975 Bourguiba made president for life.
1985 Diplomatic relations with Libya severed.
1987 In Oct Bourguiba removed Prime
Minister Rashed Sfar and appointed Zine el
Abdin Ben Ali. In Nov Ben Ali had Bourguiba
declared incompetent and seized power.

---

notable developments in linings, for example
concrete segments and steel liner plates, and in
the use of rotary diggers and cutters, and of
explosives.
Famous tunnels include:
Orange-Fish River (South Africa) 1975, longest
irrigation tunnel 82 km/50 mi
Chesapeake Bay Bridge-Tunnel (USA) 1963,
combined bridge and tunnel structure, 28
km/17.5 mi
St Gotthard (Switzerland-Italy) 1980, longest
road tunnel 16.3 km/10.1 mi
Seikan (Japan) 1964–85, longest rail tunnel,
Honshu–Hokkaido, under Tsugaru Strait, 53.85
km/33.5 mi, 23.3 km/14.4 mi undersea (it is a
white elephant because a bullet train service can
no longer be afforded)
Simplon (Switzerland-Italy) 1906, longest rail
tunnel on land 19.8 km/12.3 mi.
A ◊Channel tunnel, or Chunnel, beneath the
English Channel was planned as a military
measure by Napoleon in 1802. Excavations were
made from both shores in the 1880s, but work
was halted by Parliament for security reasons. In
1986 a scheme for twin rail tunnels was approved
by the French and British governments.

Tunnicliffe /'tʌnɪklɪf/ C(harles) F(rederick)
1901–1979. British painter of birds, born in
Macclesfield, who worked in Anglesey.

tunny fish of the mackerel family *Thunnus
thynnus*, also known as tuna, up to 2.5 m/8 ft
long and about 200 kg/440 lb. It has been fished
since ancient times as food.

Túpac Amaru /'tuːpæk əˈmɑːruː/ 1743–1781.
assumed name of Peruvian Indian leader José
Gabriel Condorcanqui, executed for his revolt

in 1780 against Spanish rule; he claimed to be
descended from the last of the ◊Incas.

Tupamaros urban guerrilla movement
operating in Uruguay, named after ◊Tupac
Amaru. Its aim is to create a Marxist revolution,
and it has been responsible for a number of bank
robberies, kidnappings, and attacks on
government buildings and institutions. Active in
the 1960s, the movement became less evident
after a government clampdown in 1972.

turbine an engine in which steam, water or
gas is made to spin a rotating shaft by pushing on
angled blades, like a fan. Steam turbines are used
to drive ◊generators in power stations and ships'
propellers; water turbines spin the generators in
◊hydroelectric power plants; and ◊gas turbines,
in the guise of ◊jet engines, power most aircraft,
and drive machines in industry.
The high-temperature, high-pressure steam for
steam turbines is raised in boilers heated by
furnaces burning coal, oil or gas, or by nuclear
energy. A steam turbine consists of a shaft, or
rotor, which rotates inside a fixed casing (stator).
The rotor carries 'wheels' consisting of blades, or
vanes. The stator has vanes set between the vanes
of the rotor, which direct the steam through the
rotor vanes at the optimum angle. When steam
expands through the turbine, it spins the rotor by
◊reaction. The steam engine of Hero of
Alexandria (130 BC), called the *aeolipile*, was the
prototype of this type of turbine, called a reaction
turbine. Modern development of the reaction
turbine is largely due to Charles ◊Parsons. Less
widely used is the impulse turbine, patented by
Carl Gustaf Patrick de Laval (1845–1913) in
1882. It works by directing a jet of steam at

blades on a rotor. Similarly there are reaction
and impulse water turbines. *Impulse turbines*
work on the same principle as the ◊waterwheel,
and consist of sets of buckets arranged around
the edge of a wheel. *Reaction turbines* look much
like propellers and are fully immersed in the
water. In a *gas turbine* a compressed mixture of
air and gas, or vaporized fuel is ignited, and the
hot gases produced expand through the turbine
blades, spinning the rotor.

turbocharger a turbine-driven device fitted
to engines to force more air into the cylinders,
producing extra power. The turbocharger
consists of a 'blower' or ◊compressor, driven by a
◊turbine, which in most units is driven by the
exhaust gases leaving the engine.

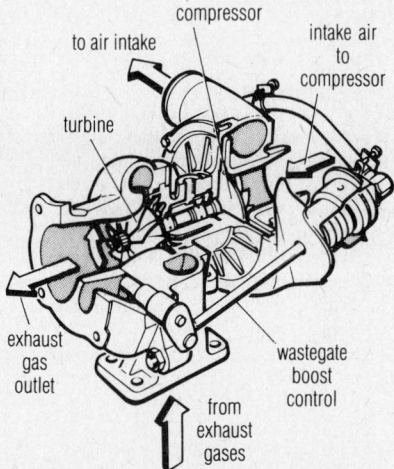

turbocharger

compressor
to air intake
intake air to compressor
turbine
exhaust gas outlet
wastegate boost control
from exhaust gases

turbofan an alternative name for the ◊fan jet,
or by-pass ◊turbojet.

turbojet a type of ◊jet engine, which derives
its thrust from a jet of hot exhaust gases. A single-
shaft turbojet consists of a shaft (rotor) rotating
in a casing. At the front is a multiblade
◊compressor, which takes in and compresses air
and delivers it to one or more combustion
chambers. Fuel (kerosene) is then sprayed in and
ignited. The hot gases expand through a nozzle
at the rear of the engine after spinning a ◊turbine.
The turbine drives the compressor. ◊Reaction to
the backward stream of gases produces a forward
propulsive thrust. Pure turbojets can be very
powerful but use a lot of fuel.

turboprop a ◊jet engine that derives its thrust
partly from a jet of exhaust gases, but mainly
from a propeller powered by a ◊turbine in the
jet exhaust (compare turbojet). A turboprop has
typically a twin-shaft rotor. One shaft carries the
compressor and is spun by one turbine, while the
other shaft carries a propeller and is spun by a
second turbine. Turboprops are more economical
than turbojets, but can only be used at relatively
low speeds.

turbot flat-fish *Scophthalmus maximus*
found in the Mediterranean and especially in the
North Sea. Up to 80 cm/2.6 ft long and weighing
up to 14 kg/30 lb.

Turgenev /tʊəˈɡeɪnjef/ Ivan Sergeievich
1818–1883. Russian writer, noted for his poetic
realism, his pessimism, and his skill at

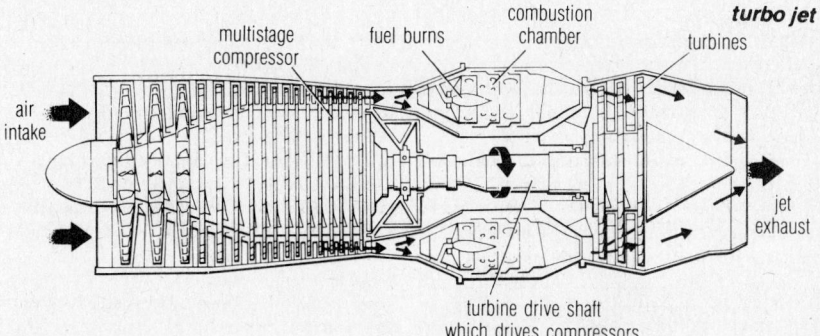

turbo jet

air intake — multistage compressor — fuel burns — combustion chamber — turbines — jet exhaust — turbine drive shaft which drives compressors

characterization, particularly of women. Major works include the play *A Month in the Country* 1849, and the novels *A Nest of Gentlefolk* 1858, *Fathers and Sons* 1862, and *Virgin Soil* 1877. His series of *A Sportsman's Sketches* 1852 strongly criticized serfdom.

Turgot /tjʊəˈgəʊ/ Anne Robert Jacques 1727–1781. French finance minister 1774–76, whose reforming economies led to his dismissal.

Turin /tjʊˈrɪn/ (Italian *Torino*) capital of Piedmont, Italy; population (1981) 1,117,154. Industries include cars, textiles, and fashion goods. There is a university, established 1404, and a 15th-century cathedral.

history Turin became the Savoyard capital during the 16th century. In 1706 Prince ◊Eugene defeated a French army besieging the city, thus ensuring the survival of the Savoy duchy. Turin was the first capital of united Italy 1861–64.

Turing /ˈtjʊərɪŋ/ Alan Mathison 1912–1954. British mathematician credited with laying the theoretical foundations of modern computing. In 1936 he published a classic paper describing theoretical computing devices (later known as 'Turing machines') which could perform any kind of 'effective' computation. The modern digital computer is, in effect, a realization of such a machine. He is also believed to have been the first to suggest the possibility of machine learning and artificial intelligence. His test for distinguishing between real (human) and simulated (computer) thought is known as the Chinese room: a human being is placed in one room, the machine in another, and an interrogator in yet another room asks any questions in order to distinguish between the two. When the interrogator can no longer do so, even if a distinction could potentially be made, the distinction no longer matters.

During World War II Turing worked on the Ultra project in the team that cracked the German Enigma code.

Turkana, Lake /tɜːˈkɑːnə/ (formerly Lake Rudolf) in the Great Rift Valley, 375 m/1,230 ft above sea level, with its northernmost end in Ethiopia and the rest in Kenya; area 9,000 sq km/3,500 sq mi. It is saline and is shrinking by evaporation. Its shores were an early human hunting ground, and valuable remains have been found which are accurately datable because of undisturbed stratification.

Turkestan /ˌtɜːkɪˈstɑːn/ geographical name for the area of central Asia divided among USSR

(Kazakh, Kirghiz, Tadzhik, Turkmen and Uzbek republics), Afghanistan, and China (part of Xinjiang Uygur).

turkey bird allied to the pheasants. The domesticated turkey *Meleagris gallopavo* derives from the American wild species, introduced to Europe in the 16th century. Another species, the ocellated turkey, is found in Central America.

Turkey /ˈtɜːki/ country between the Black Sea and the Mediterranean, bounded to the E by the USSR and Iran, to the S by Iraq and Syria.

government the constitution of 1982 provides for a single-chamber legislature of 400 members, the National Assembly, and a president who is both head of state and head of government. The president is elected by the assembly for a seven-year term. The assembly is elected by universal suffrage for a five-year term.

history the Turks originally came from Mongolia and spread into Turkestan in the 6th century AD. During the 7th century they adopted Islam. The ◊Seljuk Turks in 1055 secured political control of the caliphate, and established an empire in Asia Minor. The ◊Ottoman Turks, driven from central Asia by the Mongols, entered the service of the Seljuks, and Osman I in 1299 founded a kingdom of his own. Having overrun Asia Minor, the Ottomans began their European conquests by seizing Gallipoli 1354, captured Constantinople 1453, and by 1480 were masters of the Balkans. By 1550 they had conquered Egypt, Syria, Arabia, Mesopotamia, Tripoli, and most of Hungary; thereafter the empire ceased to expand, although Cyprus was taken 1571 and Crete 1669.

The Christian counter-offensive opened 1683 with the defeat of the Turks before Vienna; in 1699 the Turks lost Hungary, and 1n 1774 Russia ousted them from Moldavia, Wallachia, and the Crimea. In the Balkans there was an unsuccessful revolt in Serbia 1804, but in 1821–29 Greece threw off Turkish rule. Russia's attempts to exploit this situation were resisted by Britain and France, which in the Crimean War (1854–56) fought on the Turkish side. The Bulgarian rising of 1876 led to a new war between Turkey and Russia, and by the Treaty of Berlin (1878) Turkey lost Bulgaria, Bosnia, and Hercegovina. A militant nationalist group, the Young Turks, secured the grant of a constitution 1908; Italy took advantage of the ensuing crisis to seize Tripoli in 1911–12, while the Balkan

states in 1912–13 expelled the Turks from Albania and Macedonia. Turkey entered World War I on the German side in 1914, only to lose Syria, Arabia, Mesopotamia, and its nominal suzerainty in Egypt.

The Greek occupation of Izmir 1919 provoked the establishment of a nationalist congress with Mustafa Kemal (◊Atatürk) as president. Having defeated Italian and French forces, he expelled the Greeks 1922. Peace was concluded 1923 with the Treaty of ◊Lausanne and Turkey was proclaimed an independent republic with Kemal as its first president. He introduced a policy of westernization and a new legal code. He died 1938 but his People's Party remained in power. Turkey's first free elections were held in 1950 and won by the Democratic Party (DP), led by Celal Bayar and Adnan Menderes. Bayar became president and Menderes prime minister. In 1960, after a military coup, President Bayar was imprisoned and Menderes executed. A new constitution was adopted in 1961 and civilian rule restored, but with the leader of the coup, Gen Cemal Gursel, as president. There followed a series of civilian governments, led mainly by the veteran politician Ismet Inonu until 1965, when the Justice Party (JP), led by Suleyman Demirel, came to power. Prompted by strikes and student unrest, the army forced Demirel to resign in 1971 and for the next two years the country came under military rule again.

A civilian government was restored in 1973, a coalition led by Bulent Ecevit. The following year Turkey sent troops to Cyprus to protect the Turkish-Cypriot community, resulting in the effective partition of the island. Ecevit's government fell when he refused to annexe north Cyprus and in 1975 Suleyman Demirel returned at the head of a right-wing coalition. Elections held in 1977 were inconclusive and Demirel precariously held on to power until 1978 when Ecevit returned, leading another coalition. He was faced with a deteriorating economy and outbreaks of sectional violence and by 1979 had lost his working majority and resigned.

Demirel returned in Nov but the violence continued and in Sept 1980 the army stepped in and set up a national security council (NSC), with Bulent Ulusu as prime minister. Martial law was imposed, political activity suspended and a harsh regime established. Strong international pressure was put on Turkey to return to a more democratic system of government and work was begun on a new constitution. In May 1983 political parties were allowed to operate again. The old parties reformed under new names and in Nov three of them fought the assembly elections: the conservative Motherland Party (ANAP), the Nationalist Democracy Party (MDP), and the Populist Party (SDHP). ANAP won 212 assembly seats, SDHP 117, and MDP 71, and ANAP's leader, Turgut Ozal, became prime minister. Since 1984 there has been guerrilla fighting in ◊Kurdistan and a separatist Kurdish Workers' Party (PKK) is active.

After World War II Turkey felt itself threatened by the USSR and joined a number of collective defence organizations, including NATO in 1952 and the Baghdad Pact in 1955, which became the

Central Treaty Organization (CENTO) in 1959 and was dissolved in 1979. Turkey strengthened Western links and by 1987 was making overtures to the European Community. Turkey has long been criticized for the harshness of its penal system and its violation of human rights. Its future role in the world, and particularly any association with the European Community, will depend on its willingness and ability to create a more democratic and humane system of government.

Turkey

REPUBLIC OF (*Türkiye Cumhuriyeti*)

AREA 730,350 sq km/301,300 sq mi
CAPITAL Ankara
TOWNS ports Istanbul and Izmir
PHYSICAL central plateau surrounded by mountains
FEATURES Bosporus and Dardanelles; Taurus Mountains in SW (highest peak Kaldi Daĝ, 3,734 m/12,251 ft); in the E the sources of the Euphrates and Tigris. Archaeological sites include Catal Hüyük, Ephesus, and Troy; the still surviving rock villages of Cappadocia, and historic towns (Antioch, Iskenderun, Tarsus)
HEAD OF STATE AND OF GOVERNMENT Kenan Evren from 1982
GOVERNMENT recently demilitarized
EXPORTS cotton and yarn, hazelnuts, citrus, tobacco, dried fruit, chromium ores
CURRENCY Turkish lira (1,505 = £1 Sept 1987)
POPULATION (1985) 50,661,000 (85% Turkish, 12% Kurdish); annual growth rate 2.1%
LANGUAGE Turkish (official; it is related to Mongolian, but is written in the Western Latin script), Kurdish Arabic
RELIGION Sunni Muslim
LITERACY 70% (1985)
GNP $58 bn (1983); $1,000 per head of population
CHRONOLOGY
1919–22 Turkish War of Independence provoked by Greek occupation of Izmir. Mustafa Kemal (Atatürk), leader of nationalist congress, defeated Italian, French, and Greek forces.
1923 Treaty of Lausanne established Turkey as independent republic under Kemal. Westernization began.
1950 First free elections; Adnan Menderes became prime minister.

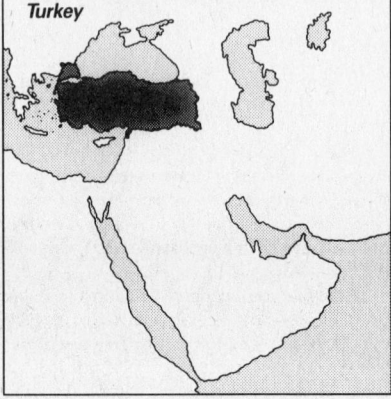

Turkey

1960 Menderes executed after military coup by Gen Cemal Gürsel.
1965 Suleyman Demirel became prime minister.
1971 Army forced Demirel to resign.
1973 Civilian rule returned under Bulent Ecevit.
1974 Turkish troops sent to protect the Turkish community in Cyprus.
1975 Demirel returned at the head of a right-wing coalition.
1978 Ecevit returned, in the face of economic difficulties and factional violence.
1979 Demeril returned. Violence grew.
1980 Army took over and Bulent Ulusu became prime minister. Harsh repression of political activists attracted international criticism.
1982 New constitution adopted.
1983 Ban on political activity lifted. Turgut Ozal became prime minister.

under ◊Suleiman the Great (1494–1566) the Golden Age began of which the poet Fuzuli (died 1563) is the great exemplar, and which continued in the following century with the great poet satirist Nef'i of Erzerum (died 1635) and others. During the 19th century westernization overtook Turkish literature, for example the following of French models by Ibrahim Shinasi Effendi (1826–71), poet and prose writer, who was co-founder of the New School with Mehmed Namik Kemal (1840–80), poet and author of the

Turkish language a language of central and W Asia, best known as the national language of Turkey. Originally written in Arabic script, the Turkish of Turkey has since 1928 been written in a variant of the Roman alphabet. Varieties of Turkish are spoken in NW Iran and several of the Asian republics of the Soviet Union, and all have been influenced by Arabic and Persian. Words of Turkish origin in English include *divan*, *coffee*, *cossack*, *horde*, *kiosk*, and *yoghourt/yogurt*.

Turkish literature for centuries Turkish literature was based on Persian models, but

revolutionary play *Vatan/The Fatherland*, which led to his exile by the sultan. Unlike these the poet Tevfik Fikret (1867–1915) turned rather to Persian and Arabic than to native sources for his vocabulary. The poet Mehmed Akif (1873–1936) was the author of the words of the Turkish national anthem; and the best-known contemporary poet and novelist is Yashar Kemal (1923–), whose novels describe peasant life (*Memed, My Hawk* 1955).

Turkmenistan /ˌtɜːkmenɪˈstɑːn/ constituent republic of the USSR from 1924, part of Soviet Central Asia

area 488,100 sq km/187,000 sq mi
capital Ashkhabad
features Kara Kum 'Black Sands' desert, which occupies most of the republic, area about 310,800 sq km/120,000 sq mi (on its edge is *Altyn Depe*, 'golden hill', site of a ruined city with a ◊ziggurat excavated from 1967); river ◊Amu Darya
products silk, sheep; astrakhan fur, carpets; oil
population (1982) 2,972,000, 66% Turkmenians
language West Turkic, related to ◊Turkish
religion Sunni Muslim
recent history the nomadic tribes of the area were subdued by Russia 1881–85.

Turks and Caicos Islands /tɜːks, ˈkeɪkɒs/ a British Crown Colony in the W Indies
area 430 sq km/166 sq mi
capital Cockburn Town on Grand Turk
features a group of 30 islands, of which seven are inhabited, of which the largest is *Grand Caicos*; they are an extension of the Bahamas
exports crayfish and conch (flesh and shell)
currency US dollar
population (1980) 7,500, 90% of African descent
language English, French Creole
religion Christian
government governor, with executive and legislative councils (chief minister from 1985 Nathaniel Francis, Progressive National Party)
history secured by Britain 1766 against French and Spanish claims, the islands were a Jamaican dependency 1873–1962, and in 1976 attained internal self-government. The chief minister, Norman Saunders, resigned 1985 after his arrest in Miami on drugs charges, on which he was convicted.

Turku /ˈtuəkuː/ port in Finland (Swedish name Åbo) near the mouth of the river Aurajoki; population (1980) 163,790. It has a castle, a cathedral, and two universities.

turmeric the tuberous rhizomes of *Curcuma longa*, a perennial plant of the ginger family, cultivated in India. It is used in curries to give a yellow colour, and as a dyestuff.

Turner /ˈtɜːnə/ Eva 1892– . British soprano. Born in Lancashire, she was prima donna of the Carl Rosa Opera Company 1916–24. She was created Dame Commander of the Order of the British Empire in 1962.

Turner /ˈtɜːnə/ John Napier 1929– . Canadian politician, leader of the Liberal Party. Turner, a lawyer, was elected to the Canadian House of Commons in 1962 and served in the administrations of Pierre ◊Trudeau, whom he succeeded in 1984 as party leader and prime minister. He lost the 1984 election to Brian ◊Mulroney and became leader of the opposition.

Turner /ˈtɜːnə/ Joseph Mallord William 1775–1851. British landscape artist. Born in London, son of a barber, he studied at the Academy School and became professor of perspective in 1809. Turner was the master painter of English Romanticism. Not concerned with the human figure, it was always through nature itself that he could express human feeling, as in the poignant last voyage of the ship *The Fighting Temeraire* 1839 (Tate Gallery, London). His increasing obsession with light turned his late pictures into misty abstract

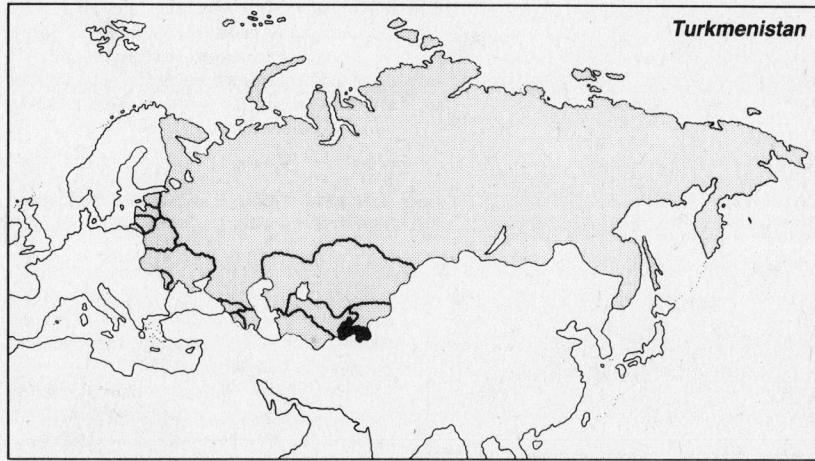

Turkmenistan

visions, for example *Rain, Steam and Speed* 1844, *Snow Storm* 1842. Not greatly appreciated in his lifetime, though championed by ◊Ruskin, he is now recognized as probably the greatest of British artists. In 1987 the Clore Gallery extension to the Tate Gallery, London, was opened to display the collection of his works he left to the nation.

Turner /'tɜːnə/ Nat 1800–1831. American slave, who led 60 slaves in the most important slave revolt, in Southampton, Virginia – the 'Southampton Insurrection' of 1831. Before he and 16 of the others were hanged, 54 people had been killed. He thought himself divinely appointed to lead the slaves to freedom.

turnip biennial plant *Brassica rapa* cultivated in temperate climates for its edible white or yellow-fleshed 'root' and the young leaves, which are used as a green vegetable; closely allied is the swede or rutabaga *Brassica napus*, of greater food value, firmer-fleshed and longer-keeping.

turnstone wading bird *Arenaria interpres* breeding in the Arctic and wintering further south as far as S Africa. About 23 cm/9 in long it has a summer plumage of black and chestnut above, white below, and is duller in winter. It is seen on rocky beaches, picking over the seaweed for small crustaceans and insects.

turpentine solution of resins distilled from the sap of conifers, used in varnish and as a paint solvent, but now largely replaced by ◊white spirit.

Turpin /'tɜːpɪn/ Dick 1706–1739. English highwayman. Born at Hempstead, Essex, the son of an innkeeper, he turned to highway robbery, cattle-thieving, and smuggling, and was hanged at York. His legendary ride from London to York on his mare Black Bess, described by W H ◊Ainsworth in *Rookwood*, is probably based on one of about 305 km/190 mi from Gad's Hill to York completed in 15 hours in 1676 by the highwayman John Nevison 1639–84.

turquoise a mineral, hydrous phosphate of aluminium and copper. Opaque and blue-green, it is used as a gem: it is found in Iran, Turkestan, and Mexico.

turtle name for marine species of ◊tortoise. The legs are modified to oar-like flippers for swimming, and the shell is more streamlined and lighter than that of the tortoise. Some are carnivorous. The eggs are laid in the sand of the sea shore. Well-known species are the green turtle *Chelonia mydas*, source of turtle soup; the hawksbill *Eretmochelys imbricata*, source of 'tortoise-shell'; the loggerhead *Caretta caretta*; and the giant leathery *Dermochelys coriacea* which reaches 2.50 m/8 ft and weighs half a tonne.

Tuscan in classical architecture, one of the five types of ◊column. See ◊order.

Tuscany /'tʌskəni/ (Italian name *Toscana*), region of central Italy; capital Florence; area 22,990 sq km/8,876 sq mi; population (1981) 3,581,745. Towns include Pisa, Livorno, and Siena. The area is mainly agricultural, with vineyards, especially in the Chianti hills. The Tuscan dialect is the variety of Italian which has been adopted as the standard.
history formerly the Roman *Etruria*, see ◊Etruscan. In medieval times the area was divided into small states, united under Florentine rule during the 15th–16th centuries. It became part of united Italy in 1861.

Tussaud /'tuːsəu/ Madame (born Anne Marie Grosholtz) 1760–1850. French wax-modeller. Born in Berne, she went in 1766 to Paris to live with her famous wax-modeller uncle, Philippe Curtius, whom she soon outshone, and during the French Revolution they were forced to take death masks of many victims and leaders. In 1794 she married François Tussaud, but they separated, and in 1802 she established her exhibition in London.

Tutankhamen /ˌtuːtənˈkɑːmen/ King of Egypt of the 18th dynasty c. 1360–1350 BC. A son of ◊Ikhnaton or of ◊Amenhotep III, he was probably about 11 at his accession. In 1922 his tomb was discovered by Lord Carnarvon and Howard Carter in the Valley of the Kings at Luxor, almost untouched by tomb robbers.

Tutin /'tjuːtɪn/ Dorothy 1930– . British actress, whose roles include most of Shakespeare's leading heroines.

Tutu /'tuːtuː/ Desmond Mpilo 1931– . Anglican priest, archbishop of Johannesburg, and general secretary of the South African Council of Churches. He was awarded the Nobel Peace Prize in 1984.

Tuva /'tuːvə/ republic of the USSR, NW of Mongolia (Mongolian People's Republic), of which it was part until 1911;
capital Kyzyl;
area 170,500 sq km/65,800 sq mi;
population (1982) 271,000;
features There is good pasture; and gold and asbestos are produced.
history declared a Russian protectorate 1914, after the 1917 revolution it became the independent Tannu-Tuva republic 1920, until incorporated in the USSR as an autonomous region 1944. It was made the Tuva ASSR 1961.

Tuvalu /ˌtuːvəˈluː/ country in the SW Pacific, on the former Ellice Islands; part of ◊Polynesia.
government the constitution dates from 1978 when Tuvalu became an independent state within the Commonwealth, accepting the British monarch as head of state represented by a resident governor-general, who must be a Tuvaluan citizen and is appointed on the recommendation of the prime minister.
There is a single-chamber parliament of 12 members and a prime minister and cabinet elected by and responsible to it. Members of Parliament are elected by universal suffrage for a four-year term. There are no political parties. Each of the inhabited atolls of the Tuvalu group has its own elected island council, responsible for local affairs.
history Europeans first reached the islands 1765. Known as the Ellice Islands, they were a British protectorate 1892–1915 and part of the Gilbert and Ellice Islands colony 1915–75, when they became a separate British colony.
In 1978 the Ellice Islands became fully independent within the Commonwealth, reverting to their old name of Tuvalu, meaning 'eight standing together'. Because of its small size, Tuvalu is a 'special member' of the Commonwealth and does not have direct representation at meetings of heads of government. Its first prime minister was Toaripi Lauti, replaced 1981 by Dr Tomasi Puapua, who was re-elected 1985. In 1986 a poll was taken to decide whether Tuvalu should remain a constitutional monarchy or become a republic. Only one atoll favoured republican status.

TVEI (Technical and Vocational Education Initiative) in the UK, scheme funded by the ◊Manpower Services Commission, and intended to enable secondary schools to expand their vocational and technical courses for 14-to 18-year-olds.

Tver /tveə/ former name (until 1932) of ◊Kalinin, a city in the USSR.

TVP texturized *vegetable* protein. It is a meat substitute made usually from soya beans. In manufacture, the soya-bean solids (what remains after oil has been removed), are ground finely and mixed with a binder to form a sticky mixture. This is forced through a spinneret and extruded into fibres, which are then treated with salts and flavourings, wound into hanks and then chopped up to resemble meat chunks.

Twain /tweɪn/ Mark. Pen name of the American humorous writer Samuel Langhorne

Tuvalu
SOUTH WEST PACIFIC STATE OF

AREA 24.6 sq km/9.5 sq mi
CAPITAL Funafuti
PHYSICAL low coral atolls in Polynesia
FEATURES the name means 'cluster of eight' islands (there are actually nine, but one is very small)
HEAD OF STATE Elizabeth II from 1978 represented by Tupua Leupena from 1986
HEAD OF GOVERNMENT Tomasi Puapua from 1981
GOVERNMENT parliamentary democracy
EXPORTS phosphates, copra; handicrafts, stamps
CURRENCY Australian dollar (2.24 = £1 Sept 1987)
POPULATION (1985) 8,580 (mainly Polynesian); annual growth rate 3.4%
LANGUAGE Tuvaluan and English
RELIGION Christian, chiefly Protestant
LITERACY 96% (1979)
GDP (1983) $711 per head of population
CHRONOLOGY
1978 Achieved full independence within the

Commonwealth with Toaripi Lauti as prime minister.
1986 Islanders rejected proposal for republican status.

Clemens 1835–1910. ('mark twain' was a call used for depth sounding by Mississippi river pilots.) Born in Florida, Missouri, he established his reputation with the comic masterpiece *The Innocents Abroad* 1869, and two children's books, *The Adventures of Tom Sawyer* 1876 and *The Adventures of Huckleberry Finn* 1885. He also wrote satire, as in *A Connecticut Yankee at King Arthur's Court* 1889.

Twain Mark Twain, the creator of Tom Sawyer and Huckleberry Finn, established himself as a humorous writer with *The Innocents Abroad* 1869, written after a tour of Europe.

Tweed /twiːd/ river rising in W Borders region, Scotland, and entering the North Sea at Berwick, Northumberland; length 156 km/97 mi.

tweed cloth made of woollen yarn, usually of several shades, but in its original form without regular pattern and woven on a hand-loom in the remoter parts of Ireland, Wales, and Scotland; it is highly durable and largely weather-proof.

Twelfth Day the 12th and final day of the Christmas celebrations, 6 Jan; the feast of the ◊Epiphany.

twelve-note system a system of musical composition in which the 12 notes of the chromatic scale are arranged in a particular order, called a 'series' or 'note-row'. A work using the system consists of restatements of the series in any of its formations. ◊Schoenberg and ◊Webern were the most important and influential composers to use this technique.

Twickenham /'twɪkənəm/ district in the Greater London borough of ◊Richmond-upon-Thames.

twin one of two young produced from a single pregnancy. In humans, twins may be genetically identical, having been formed from one fertilized egg which split into two cells both of which became ◊implanted. Non-identical twins are formed when two different eggs are fertilized at the same time. See also ◊multiple birth.

two-stroke cycle an operating cycle for internal combustion piston engines. The engine cycle is completed after just two strokes (movement up or down) of the piston (compare ◊four-stroke cycle). All lightweight motorbikes use two-stroke petrol engines, which are much cheaper and simpler than four-strokes. Most marine ◊diesel engines are also two-strokes. In a typical two-stroke motorbike engine, fuel mixture is drawn into the crankcase as the piston moves up on its first stroke to compress the mixture above it. Then the compressed mixture is ignited and hot gases are produced, which drive the piston down on its second stroke. As it moves down, it uncovers an opening (port) that allows the fresh fuel mixture in the crankcase to flow into the combustion space above the piston. At the same time the exhaust gases leave through another port.

Tyburn /'taɪbən/ stream in London, England (now underground) near which (at the junction of Oxford Street and Edgware Rd) Tyburn gallows stood from the 12th century until 1783.

Tyler /'taɪlə/ John 1790–1862. 10th president of the USA 1841–45. As a Virginia planter, he was a Confederate supporter; his government annexed Texas 1845.

Tyler /'taɪlə/ Wat (died 1381). English leader of the peasants in the revolt of 1381. Born in Kent or Essex, he served in the French wars. After taking Canterbury he led the peasants to Blackheath and occupied London. At Mile End King Richard II met the rebels and promised to redress their grievances. At a further conference at Smithfield, Tyler was murdered by the 'Lord Mayor', Sir William Walworth.

Tynan /'taɪnən/ Kenneth 1927–1980. British author and critic. A leading figure of the 'swinging sixties', he devised the nude revue *O Calcutta!* 1969, first staged in New York.

Tyndale /'tɪndl/ William 1492–1536. English translator of the Bible. The printing of his New Testament (basis of the Authorized Version) was begun in 1525 in Cologne, and (after he had been forced to flee) completed in Worms. He was strangled and burnt as a heretic at Vilvorde in Belgium.

Tyndall /'tɪndl/ John 1820–1893. Irish physicist, who in 1869 studied the scattering of ◊light by invisibly small suspended particles. Known as the Tyndall effect, it was first observed with colloidal solutions (see ◊colloid), in which a beam of light is made visible when it is scattered by minute colloidal particles (whereas a pure solvent does not scatter light). Similar scattering of blue wavelengths of sunlight by particles in the atmosphere makes the sky look blue (beyond the atmosphere, in outer space, the sky is black).

Tyne /taɪn/ river formed by the union of the N Tyne (rising in the Cheviots) and S Tyne (rising in Cumbria) near Hexham, Northumberland, and reaching the North Sea at Tynemouth: length 72 km/45 mi. Kielder Water (1980) in the N Tyne Valley is Europe's largest artificial lake, 12 km/7.5 mi long and 0.8 km/0.5 mi wide, and supplies the industries of Tyneside, Wearside and Teesside.

Tyne and Wear /taɪn, wɪə/ former metropolitan county in NE England, replaced 1986 by a residuary body which covers some of its former functions.
area 540 sq km/209 sq mi
towns administrative headquarters Newcastle-upon-Tyne; South Shields, Gateshead, Sunderland
features bisected by the rivers Tyne and Wear; includes part of ◊Hadrian's Wall
products once a centre of heavy industry, it is now being redeveloped and diversified
population (1983) 1,145,300

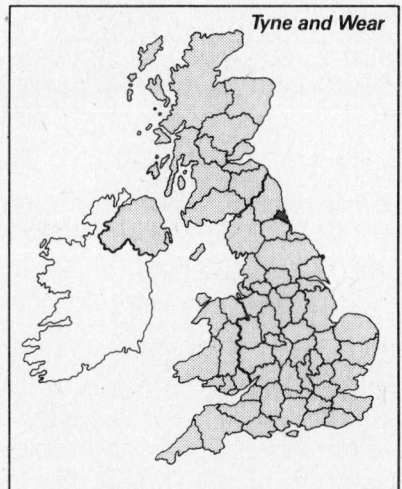

Tyne and Wear

typewriter Today's streamlined electronic models are a far cry from this Waverley typewriter of 1895, but the principle of a hand-operated machine for producing printed characters on paper remains the same. Contemporary versions are often linked to a computer.

famous people Thomas Bewick, Robert Stephenson, Harry Patterson/'Jack Higgins'.

Tynemouth /ˈtaɪnmaʊθ, ˈtɪnməθ/ port and resort in Tyne and Wear, England; population (1985) 9,442.

Tynwald /ˈtɪnwəld/ the parliament of Isle of ◊Man.

type metal an alloy of tin, lead, and antimony, used for making the metal type printers use.

typewriter a hand-operated machine for producing characters on paper. The first practicable typewriter was built at Milwaukee, Wisconsin, by C L Sholes, C Glidden and S W Soulé in 1867, and by 1874 E Remington and Sons, the gun makers whose name was soon given to the typewriters, produced under contract the first machines for sale. Later developments include tabulators from about 1898, portable machines about 1907, gradual introduction of electrical operation (allowing increased speed, since the keys are touched not depressed), proportional spacing in 1940, and rotating typehead with stationary plates in 1962. The later typewriters work electronically. They can be equipped with a memory, and be given an interface which enables them to be connected to a computer.

typhoid fever infectious disease caused by the bacterium *Salmonella typhi* and usually contracted through infected water; there is a temporarily effective vaccine (treatment of the disease itself is by antibiotic drugs). *Paratyphoid fever* caused by *S paratyphi* is a milder form.

typhoon a violently revolving storm, a type of ◊cyclone.

typhus an infectious disease, often fatal, caused by a microbe carried in the excreta of lice. It enters the body usually by abrasions in the feet, and is epidemic among human beings in overcrowded conditions. Treatment is by antibiotics.

typography the design and layout of the printed word on paper. Its concern is the appearance of the text rather than its meaning. Typography began with the invention of writing and developed as printing spread throughout Europe following the invention of metal moveable type by Johann ◊Gutenberg around 1440. Early type designs resembled the handwritten letters of the scribes – a heavy angular gothic style – but in about 1470 the Frenchman Nicholas Jensen (c. 1420–1480) produced the first popular Roman typeface (style of lettering), the capital letters being based on Roman inscriptions. Hundreds of variations have followed, but the basic design, with a few modifications, is still in use today, as the ordinary ('Roman') type used in printing.

Type sizes are measured in points (there are approximately 2.8 points to the millimetre); the length of a typeset line, called the measure, is measured in pica ems (1 pica em is a little over 4mm in width). The space between lines (known as leading) is also measured in points, although new photosetting and computer assisted setting systems also work in metric sizes.

Tyr /tɪə/ in Norse mythology, the god of battles, whom the Anglo-Saxons called Týw, hence 'Tuesday'.

tyrannosaurus largest known meat-eating dinosaur. Bipedal, it was up to 12 m/40 ft long, and had teeth 15 cm/6 in long. It lived about 70 million years ago.

Tyre /ˈtaɪə/ (Arabic *Sur*) town in Lebanon, about 80 km/50 mi S of Beirut, formerly a port until its harbour silted up; population (1980) 14,000.

history it stands on the site of the ancient city of the same name, a seaport of ◊Phoenicia. Built on the mainland and two small islands, the city was a great commercial centre. Besieged by ◊Alexander the Great 333–332 BC, it came under Roman rule 64 BC and was taken by the Arabs 638 AD. The Crusaders captured it 1124; it was retaken by the Arabs 1291. In the 1970s it became a Palestinian guerrilla stronghold, and was shelled by Israel 1979.

tyre (US *tire*) the rubber hoop fitted round the rims of bicycle, car, and other road vehicle wheels. The first pneumatic rubber tyre was patented by R W Thompson in 1845.

Tyrol a variant spelling of ◊Tirol, province of Austria and Italy.

Tyrone /tɪˈrəʊn/ county of Northern Ireland
area 3,155 sq km/1,218 sq mi
towns county town Omagh
features rivers Derg, Blackwater, and Foyle, famous for salmon and trout; Lough Neagh
products mainly agricultural
population (1971) 138,975.

Tyumen /tjuːˈmen/ oldest town in Siberia, central USSR (founded 1586); population (1985) 425,000. Industries include timber, tanning, and chemicals.

Tyuratam /ˌtjuərəˈtɑːm/ the main space launching site in the USSR, NE of the Aral Sea. It is the Soviet equivalent of the USA's ◊Cape Canaveral, but much larger. The Soviets refer to it as ◊Baikonur, a town some distance away.

Tzu-Hsi /ˌtsuːˈʃiː/ former spelling of ◊Zi Xi, dowager empress of China.

U the 21st letter of the English alphabet, and the 20th in the ancient Roman, in which it was identical with *V*. Not until the 19th century were *U* and *V* definitely separated in English dictionaries. It has various sounds, as in the pronunciation of the English words *truth, bull, duke, busy, bury*.

U-2 a US military reconnaissance aeroplane, used to fly over the USSR from 1956 to photograph military installations. Designed by Richard Bissell, the U-2 flew higher (21,000 m/70,000 ft) and further (3,500 km/2,200 mi) than any previous plane. In 1960 a U-2 flown was shot down over the Soviet Union and the pilot Gary Powers captured and imprisoned; he was exchanged for a Soviet agent two years later. The U-2 affair led to greatly increased Soviet arms spending in the 1960s and 1970s.

U2 Irish rock group formed 1978 by singer Bono Vox (1960–), guitarist Dave 'The Edge' Evans (1961–), bassist Adam Clayton (1960–), and drummer Larry Mullen (1961–). Their music has been described as socially concerned stadium rock.

uakari rare S American monkey, genus *Cacajao*, of which there are three species. They have bald faces and long fur. About 55 cm/1.8 ft long in head and body, and with a comparatively short 15 cm/6 in tail, they rarely leap, but are good climbers, remaining in the tops of the trees in swampy forests and feeding largely on fruit.

Ubangi-Shari /uːˈbæŋgi ˈʃɑːri/ former name for the ◊Central African Republic.

U-boat name given to the German submarine (*Unterseeboot*, underwater boat) in both world wars, because they were named U followed by a number.

Uccello /uːˈtʃɛləʊ/ Paolo. Name used by Italian artist Paolo di Dono 1397–1475. Apprenticed to Ghiberti, he is celebrated for his use of perspective. His works include the *Nativity* fresco (Florence) and three battle pictures for the Palazzo Medici, one of which is in the National Gallery in London.

Udaipur /uːˈdaɪpʊə/ industrial city in Rajasthan, India, capital of the former princely state of Udaipur; population (1981) 232,588. It was founded 1568, has several palaces (two on

Uccello One of the very few paintings on canvas which have survived from the mid-15th century, this rendering of *St George and the Dragon* by Uccello combines two episodes of the story: the attack on the dragon, and its later harnessing to the girdle of the princess, as taken from *The Golden Legend*, which gives the standard version of the story, written in the 13th century.

islands in a lake) and the Jagannath Hindu temple 1640.

Udall /ˈjuːdl/ Nicholas 1504–56. English schoolmaster and playwright. He was the author of *Ralph Roister Doister* about 1553, the first known English comedy.

UDI (*Unilateral Declaration of Independence*). Usually applied to the declaration of Ian Smith's Rhodesian Front government on 11 Nov 1965.

Udine /ˈuːdɪneɪ/ industrial city (chemicals, textiles, leather goods, paper) NE of Venice, Italy; population (1984) 101,000. Udine was the capital of Friuli in the 13th century, and passed to Venice 1420.

Udmurt /ˈʊdmʊət/ republic of central USSR

area 42,100 sq km/16,200 sq mi

capital Izhevsk

features Udmurt is in the W Ural foothills

products timber, flax, potatoes, peat, quartz

population (1985) 1,559,000; Udmurt 33 per cent, Tatar 7 per cent, Russian 58 per cent

history conquered in the 15th–16th centuries.

Uelsmann /ˈjuːlzmən/ Jerry 1934– . American photographer, noted for his dream-like images, which he creates by synthesizing many elements into one with great technical skill.

Ufa /uːˈfɑː/ industrial city (engineering, oil refining, petrochemical, distilling, timber) and capital of the Republic of Bashkir, central USSR; population (1985) 1,064,000. It was founded by Russians in 1574 as a fortress.

Uffizi an art gallery in ◊Florence, Italy.

Uganda /juːˈgændə/ landlocked country in E Africa, bounded to the N by Sudan, to the E by Kenya, to the S by Tanzania and Rwanda, and to the W by Zaïre.

government The 1969 constitution provides for a single-chamber national assembly of 126 elected members and a president who is both head of state and head of government. In 1985 a military coup suspended the constitution and dissolved the National Assembly. The National Resistance Council (NRC) is an interim legislative body.

history For early history, see ◊Africa. Uganda was a British protectorate 1894–1962.

Uganda became an independent member of the Commonwealth in 1962, with Dr Milton Obote, leader of the Uganda People's Congress (UPC), as prime minister. In 1963 it was proclaimed a federal republic; King Mutesa II became president, ruling through a cabinet. King Mutesa was deposed in a coup 1966 and Obote became executive president. One of his first acts was to end the federal status. After an attempt to assassinate him in 1969 Obote banned all opposition and established what was effectively a one-party state.

In 1971 Obote was overthrown in an army coup led by Maj-Gen Idi Amin Dada, who suspended the constitution and all political activity and took legislative and executive powers into his own hands. Obote fled to Tanzania. Amin proceeded to wage what he called an 'economic war' against foreign domination, resulting in the mass expulsion of Asians, many of whom settled in Britain. In 1976 Amin claimed that large tracts of Kenya historically belonged to Uganda and accused Kenya of cooperating with the Israeli government in a raid on Entebbe airport to free hostages held in a hijacked aircraft. Relations with Kenya became strained and diplomatic links with Britain were severed. During the next two years the Amin regime carried out a widespread campaign against any likely opposition, resulting in thousands of deaths and imprisonments.

In 1978, when Amin annexed the Kagera area of Tanzania, near the Uganda border, the Tanzanian president, Julius Nyerere, sent troops to support the Uganda National Liberation Army (UNLA), which had been formed to fight Amin. Within five months Tanzanian troops had entered the Uganda capital, Kampala, forcing Amin to flee, first to Libya and then to Saudi Arabia. A provisional government, drawn from a cross-section of exiled groups, was set up, with Dr Yusuf Lule as president. Two months later Lule was replaced by Godfrey Binaisa who, in turn, was overthrown by the army. A military commission made arrangements for national elections, which were won by the UPC, and Milton Obote came back to power.

Obote's government was soon under pressure from a range of exiled groups operating outside the country and guerrilla forces inside and he was only kept in office by the presence of Tanzanian troops. When they were withdrawn in Jun 1982 a major offensive was launched against the Obote

Uganda
REPUBLIC OF

AREA 236,000 sq km/93,980 sq mi
CAPITAL Kampala
TOWNS Jingar, M'Bale, Entebbe
PHYSICAL plateau with mountains in W; forest and grassland; arid in N
FEATURES Ruwenzori Range; national parks with wildlife (chimpanzees, some of Africa's largest crocodiles, and Nile perch to 72.5 kg/160 lb); Owen Falls on the White Nile where it leaves Lake Victoria
HEAD OF STATE AND OF GOVERNMENT Yoweri Museveni from 1986
GOVERNMENT military
EXPORTS coffee, cotton, tea; copper
CURRENCY Uganda shilling (98 = £1 Sept 1987)
POPULATION (1985) 14,689,000 (the largest ethnic group is the Baganda, from whom the name of the country comes; others include the Langi and Acholi, and there are a few surviving Pygmies); annual growth rate 3.5%
LANGUAGE English (official); Swahili is a lingua franca
RELIGION Christian 50%, animist 45%, Muslim 5%
LITERACY 65% male/40% female (1980 est)
GNP $6.2 bn (1984); $240 per head of population
CHRONOLOGY
1962 Achieved independence within the Commonwealth with Milton Obote as prime minister.
1963 Proclaimed a federal republic with King Mutesa II as president.
1966 King Mutesa ousted in a coup led by Obote, who ended the federal status and became executive president.
1969 All opposition parties banned after an assassination attempt on Obote.

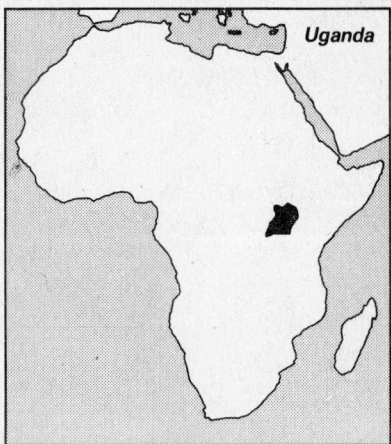

Uganda

1971 Obote overthrown in an army coup led by Maj-Gen Idi Amin, who established a ruthlessly dictatorial regime, expelling nearly 49,000 Ugandan Asians. Up to 300,000 opponents of the regime are said to have been killed.
1978 After heavy fighting, Amin was forced to leave the country. A provisional government was set up with Yusuf Lule as president. Lule was replaced by Godfrey Binaisa.
1978–1979 Fighting with Tanzanian troops.
1980 Binaisa overthrown by the army. Elections held and Milton Obote returned to power.
1985 After years of opposition, mainly by the National Resistance Army (NRA), and uncontrolled indiscipline in the regular army, Obote was ousted by Brig Basilio Okello, who entered a power-sharing agreement with the NRA leader, Yoweri Museveni.
1986 Agreement ended and Museveni became president, heading a broad-based coalition government.

---

government by the National Resistance Movement (NRM) and the National Resistance Army (NRA) led by Dr Lule and Yoweri Museveni. By 1985 Obote was unable to control the army, which had been involved in indiscriminate killings, and he was ousted in Jul in a coup led by Brigadier Tito Okello. Obote fled to Kenya and then Zambia, where he was given political asylum.

Okello had little more success in controlling the army and, after a brief period of power-sharing with the NRA, fled to Sudan in Jan 1986. Museveni was sworn in as president and announced a policy of national reconciliation, promising a return to normal parliamentary government within three to five years. He formed a cabinet in which most of Uganda's political parties were represented, including the NRM, which is the political wing of the NRA, the Democratic Party, the Conservative Party, the Uganda People's Congress, and the Uganda Freedom Movement.

Uganda martyrs 22 Africans, of whom 12 were boy pages, put to death 1885–87 by King Mwanga of Uganda for refusing to renounce Christianity. They were canonized as the first African saints of the Roman Catholic Church in 1964.

Ugarit /ˈuːgərɪt/ ancient trading city kingdom (modern Ras Shamra) on the Syrian coast. It was excavated by Claude Schaeffer from 1929, finds ranging from about 7000 BC to 15–13th centuries BC. They include numerous cuneiform documents, as well as an early Ugaritic alphabet of 22 letters (the earliest alphabet known, and closely related to the ◊Phoenician, from which the Roman is ultimately derived).

UHF *u*ltra *h*igh *f*requency, referring to ◊radio waves of very short wavelength, used, for example, for television broadcasting.

Uist /ˈjuːɪst/ two small islands in the Outer ◊Hebrides, Scotland. There is a guided missile range on South Uist.

uitlander term (Dutch 'foreigner') applied by the Boer inhabitants of the Transvaal to (British)

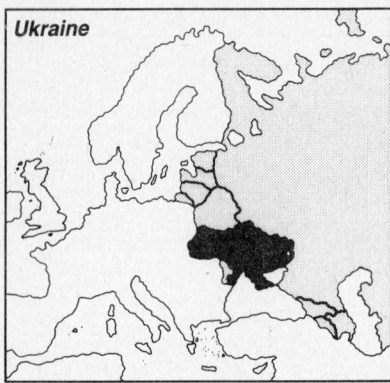

Ukraine

immigrants in the late 19th century. The uitlander's inferior political position in the Transvaal helped to fuel the confrontation between the Boers and the British which led to the Boer War 1899–1902.

Ujiji /uːˈdʒiːdʒi/ port on Lake Tanganyika, Tanzania, where ◊Stanley found Livingstone 1871; population (1970) 17,000. It was originally an Arab trading post for slaves and ivory.

Ujung Pandang /ˈuːdʒʊŋ pænˈdæŋ/ (also known as *Macassar* or *Makassar*) chief port on Sulawesi, Indonesia, with fishing and food-processing industries; university 1956; population (1980) 709,000.

Ukraine /juːˈkreɪn/ constituent republic of the SE USSR from 1923
area 603,700 sq km/233,000 sq mi
capital Kiev
towns Kharkov, Donetsk, Odessa, Dniepropetrovsk, Lvov, Zaporozhe, Krivoi Rog
features Russian plain, Carpathians and Crimean Mountains; rivers Dnieper (with the Dnieper dam 1932), Donetz, and Bug
products the granary of the USSR, it also has 60 per cent of the Soviet coal reserves, as well as oil and other minerals
population 50,000; Ukrainian 75 per cent, Russian 19 per cent; Russian-speaking Jews 2 per cent
language Ukrainian (Slavonic), with a literature that goes back to the Middle Ages; noted writers are Ivan Kotlyarevsky (1769–1838) and Taras Shevchenko (1814–61)
religion traditionally Ukrainian Orthodox
recent history a state by the 9th century, under Polish rule from the 14th. Russia absorbed E Ukraine in 1667, the rest in 1793, from Austrian rule. Ukraine proclaimed itself a people's republic in 1919. From 1923 it has formed one of the republics of the USSR. The Germans overran it in World War II. For additions to Ukraine after World War II, see ◊Bessarabia, ◊Bukhovina, ◊Ruthenia; see also ◊Crimea.

Ukrainian language a member of the Slavonic branch of the Indo-European language family, spoken in the Ukraine. It is closely related to Russian and is sometimes referred to by Russians as 'Little Russian', a description which Ukrainians generally do not find appropriate.

Communities speaking Ukrainian are also found in Canada and the United States.

ukulele a type of small four-stringed ◊guitar.

Ulaan Baataar /ˈuːlɑːn ˈbɑːtɔː/ (formerly Ulan Bator, and until 1924 Urga) capital of the Mongolian Republic, a trading centre producing carpets, textiles, vodka; university 1942; population (1984) 479,500.

Ulan Bator /ˈuːlɑːn ˈbɑːtɔː/ former name of ◊Ulaan Baataar, capital of Mongolia.

Ulanova /uːˈlɑːnəvə/ Galina 1910– . Russian dancer. Prima ballerina of the Bolshoi Theatre Ballet 1944–61, she created the principal role of Katerina in *The Stone Flower*.

Ulan-Ude /ʊˈlɑːn ʊˈdeɪ/ industrial city (sawmills; cars, glass) and capital of the Republic of Buriat in SE USSR, on the river Ibla and the Trans-Siberian railway; population (1985) 325,000. Called Verkhne-Udinsk until 1934.

Ulbricht /ˈʊlbrɪkt/ Walter 1893–1973. East German politician. After exile in the USSR during the Hitler's rule, he became first secretary of the Socialist Unity Party in East Germany in 1950 and (as chair of the Council of State 1960–73) was instrumental in the building of the Berlin Wall in 1961. He established East Germany's economy and recognition outside the E European bloc.

ulcer sore of the surface skin or mucous membrane. It is caused either by infection (for example, syphilitic ulcer), inadequate blood supply (for example, varicose ulcer), or irritation (for example, gastric ulcer, which occurs in people sensitive to gastric acids or certain substances, such as alcohol).

Uleaborg /ˈuːliɔːˌbɔːri/ Swedish name for the Finnish port of ◊Oulu.

Ulm /ʊlm/ industrial city (vehicles, agricultural machinery, precision instruments, textiles) in Baden-Württemberg, West Germany, on the Danube, noted for its Gothic cathedral with the highest stone spire ever built, which escaped damage in World War II when two-thirds of Ulm was destroyed; population (1985) 99,600. It was a free imperial city from the 14th century to 1802. Einstein was born here.

Ulster /ˈʌlstə/ former kingdom in N Ireland, annexed by England 1461, from Jacobean times a centre of English, and later Scottish, settlement on land confiscated from its owners; divided 1921 into Northern Ireland (counties Antrim, Armagh, Down, Fermanagh, Londonderry, and Tyrone) and the province of ◊Ulster in the Republic of Ireland.

Ulster /ˈʌlstə/ northernmost province of the Republic of Ireland, comprising the counties Cavan, Donegal, and Monaghan; area 8,013 sq km/3,094 sq mi; population (1981) 230,000.

Ultra abbreviation of Ultra Secret, used by the British from spring 1940 in World War II to denote intelligence gained by deciphering German signals at the interception centre at Bletchley Park, Buckinghamshire. Failure to use such information in the Battle of ◊Anzio meant that Allied troops were stranded for a time.

ultrabasic in geology, an igneous rock with a lower silica content than the basic rocks (less than 45 per cent).

Ultramontanism in the Roman Catholic Church, the tenets of the Italian party which stresses papal authority rather than nationalism in the church. It means 'beyond the mountains'; that is, the Alps.

ultrasound physical vibrations in matter occurring at frequencies above 20,000 hertz (cycles per second), the approximate limit of human hearing. Propagation of ultrasound in air or other gas is very poor and nearly all practical applications are in liquids or solids. The earliest practical application was to detect submarines during World War I but recently the field of ultrasonics has greatly expanded.
The lower frequencies of 20,000–80,000 Hz are mainly used for cleaning in industry and in hospitals. Higher frequencies have been used in the form of pulses to produce echoes as a means of measuring the depth of the sea, to detect flaws in metal, and, in medicine, high-frequency sound waves are used to investigate various body organs. Sound waves transmitted through the body are absorbed and reflected to differenct degrees by different body tissues. By recording the 'echoes' a picture of the different structures being scanned can be built up, such as an image of an unborn baby in the womb.
High-power ultrasound has been used with focusing arrangements to destroy tissue at a depth in the body, and extremely high frequencies of 1,000 MHz (megahertz) or more are used in ultrasonic microscopes.

ultraviolet radiation ◊electromagnetic waves (light rays) invisible to the human eye, of wavelengths from about 4×10^{-7} to 5×10^{-9} metres (where the ◊X-ray range begins). Physiologically they are extremely powerful, producing sunburn and causing the formation of vitamin D in the skin; they are strongly germicidal and may be produced artificially by mercury vapour and arc lamps for therapeutic use. Ultraviolet radiation may be detected with ordinary photographic plates or films down to 2×10^{-6} metres. It can also be studied by its fluorescent effect on certain materials.

Ulundi /ʊˈlʊndi/ capital of ◊KwaZulu in South Africa.

Ulysses /juːˈlɪsiːz/ in classical mythology, the Roman name for ◊Odysseus.

Umberto /ʊmˈbeətəʊ/ two kings of Italy:
Umberto I 1844–1900. King from 1878, he joined the Triple Alliance (see under ◊First World War), and his colonial ventures included the defeat at ◊Aduwa. He was assassinated by an anarchist.
Umberto II 1904–83. Last king, on the abdication of his father, ◊Victor Emmanuel III, he ruled from 9 May to 13 Jun 1946, when he also abdicated and left the country, settling in Portugal as the Count di Sarre. From 1944 he had been Lieutenant-General of the realm.

umbilical cord the connection between the ◊embryo and the ◊placenta of placental mammals. It is part of the embryo and carries one ◊vein and two ◊arteries, transporting oxygen and nutrients to the developing young and removing excretory products. At birth the

Ulbricht East German politician Walter Ulbricht (front row, third from right), the man who built the Berlin Wall, watches military manoeuvres in the German Democratic Republic. He was responsible for establishing East Germany's economy and recognition outside the Soviet bloc.

connection between the young and the umbilical cord is severed, the cord forming part of the afterbirth.

umbrella portable protection against the rain – when used in the sun usually called a parasol or sunshade. In use in China for more than a thousand years, umbrellas were also held over the rulers of ancient Egypt and Assyria as symbols of power, and had a similar significance for Aztec and African rulers, as well as in the Roman Catholic church. Revived in clerical use in 16th century Italy, umbrellas were used by women in England from the 17th century, but Jonas Hanway 1712–86 was the first to make it part of the Englishman's everyday 'City uniform'.

umbrella Making umbrellas at Chiengmai in Thailand. A coat of varnish over the paper covering renders them waterproof, and the structure is bamboo.

Umbria /ˈʌmbriə/ region of Italy in the central Apennines
area 8,456 sq km/3,265 sq mi
capital Perugia

features river Tiber; mountainous
population (1984) 815,000
history home of the Umbrian school of artists, including Raphael.

Umm al Qaiwain /ˈʊm æl kaɪˈwaɪn/ one of the ◊United Arab Emirates.

Umtali /ʊmˈtɑːli/ former name (until 1982) for the town of ◊Mutare in Zimbabwe.

Umtata /ʊmˈtɑːtə/ capital of the South African Bantu homeland of ◊Transkei.

Unamuno /ˌuːnəˈmuːnəʊ/ Miguel de 1864–1936. Spanish writer of Basque origin. He was exiled 1924–30 for criticism of the military directorate of Primo de ◊Rivera. His works include the philosophical prose study *Del sentimiento trágico de la vida/ The Tragic Sense of Life* 1913, about the conflict of reason and belief in religion.

uncertainty principle also called *indeterminacy principle*. In physics, a principle established by ◊Heisenberg, an important prediction of quantum mechanics, giving a theoretical limit to the precision with which a particle's momentum and position can be measured simultaneously: the more accurately the one is determined the more uncertainty there is in the other. The uncertainty arises because according to quantum mechanics it is meaningless to speak of a particle's position, momentum, or other parameters, except as results of measurements, but measuring involves an interaction (such as a ◊photon of light bouncing off the particle under scrutiny), which must disturb the particle, though the disturbance is noticeable only at an atomic scale. The principle implies that one cannot, even in theory, predict the moment-to-moment behaviour of such a system.

Uncle Sam /ˈʌŋkəl ˈsæm/ nickname for the US government. It originated during the war of 1812, probably from the initials U S placed on government property.

unconformity in geology, a break in the sequence of ◊sedimentary rocks. It is usually seen as an eroded surface, with the ◊beds above and below lying at different angles. An unconformity represents an ancient land surface, where exposed rocks were worn down to sea level and later covered with deposited sediments.

unconformity

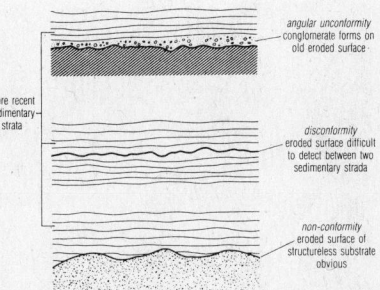

unconscious an absence of awareness. In psychoanalysis it refers to part of the personality of which the individual is unaware, and which contains impulses or urges that are held back, or repressed, from conscious awareness. Emotional problems and irrational actions are believed by psychoanalysts to stem from unconscious conflicts.

underground name given to a rail service that runs underground. The first underground line in the world was in London, from Paddington to Farringdon Street, opened in 1863. It was built by the cut-and-cover method, essentially being a roofed-in trench. Much of the present system runs through deep tunnels (tubes), including under the Thames. There are also sections above ground outside the central area. Many major cities throughout the world have similar systems, that of Moscow being noted for its particularly grand stations. But the London Underground is still the longest, with over 400 km/250 mi of routes. Moscow's Underground, the Metro, handles up to six and a half million passengers a day. In the USA underground systems are called subways.

Undset /ˈʊnset/ Sigrid 1882–1949. Norwegian novelist, born in Denmark. Her masterpiece is considered to be *Kristin Lavransdatter* 1920–22, a strongly Catholic novel set in the 14th century. In 1928 she was awarded the Nobel Prize for Literature.

unemployment the involuntary lack of paid employment. Unemployment is generally subdivided into *frictional* unemployment (the inevitable temporary unemployment of those moving from one job to another); *cyclical* unemployment, caused by a downswing in the trade cycle; *seasonal* unemployment, in an area where there is high demand only during a holiday period, for example; and *structural* unemployment, where changing technology or other long-term change in the economy results in large numbers without work, particularly in certain regions.

underground 1863: a photograph of the inaugural trip of the Metropolitan Line train at Edgware Road station, London. Among the passengers, seated third and fourth from the right, are Prime Minister Gladstone and his wife.

In Britain, for at least 150 years before 1939, the supply of labour always exceeded demand except in war-time, and economic crises accompanied by mass unemployment were recurrent from 1785. The percentage of unemployed (in trade unions) averaged six during 1883–1913 and 14.2 (of those covered by the old Unemployment Insurance Acts) 1921–38. World War II and the rebuilding and expansion which followed meant shortage of labour rather than unemployment in the Western world, and in Britain in the 1950s the unemployment rate fell to 1.5%. Fluctuation in employment returned in the 1960s, and in the recession of the mid-1970s to 1980s was a world-wide problem. In Britain deflationary economic measures tended to exacerbate the trend, and in the mid-1980s the rate had risen to 14% (although the basis on which it is calculated has in recent years been changed several times – in 1986, for example, by compiling and publishing the monthly figures two weeks later – and some commentators argue that the real rate is higher). Most modern governments attempt to prevent some or all of the various forms of unemployment. The ideas of ◊Keynes were influential in the case of British government unemployment policies during the 1950s and 1960s. The existence of a clear link between unemployment and inflation (that high unemployment can be dealt with by governments only at the cost of higher inflation) is now disputed.

UNESCO *U*nited *N*ations *E*ducational, *S*cientific, and *C*ultural *Or*ganization. Agency of the ◊United Nations.

Ungaretti /ˌʊŋɡəˈreti/ Giuseppe 1888–1970. Italian poet, born in Alexandria, and later living in Paris and São Paulo. His lyrics show a cosmopolitan independence of Italian poetic tradition. His poems are noted for their simplicity, especially his best-known collection *Allegria di naufragi/Joy of Shipwrecks* 1919, which is pervaded by horror of war.

Ungava /ʌŋˈɡɑːvə/ region of N Quebec and Labrador, Canada, E of Hudson Bay, noted for iron deposits.

ungulate general name for any hoofed mammal.

Uniate (united Greek or Eastern Orthodox and Roman Catholic Church) name given to those Christian churches which accept the full Catholic faith and the supremacy of the Pope, and are in full communion with the Roman Catholic Church, but retain their own liturgy and separate organization.

unicorn mythical animal referred to by classical writers, said to live in India and to be like a horse but with one straight horn. See ◊oryx.

unidentified flying object (UFO) any light or object seen in the sky whose immediate identity is not apparent. The term *flying saucer* was coined after a 1947 sighting by Kenneth Arnold. On investigation, the vast majority of UFOs turn out to be natural or identifiable objects, most notably bright stars and planets, meteors, aircraft and satellites. Despite unsubstantiated claims, there is no evidence that UFOs are alien spacecraft, and few scientists believe that UFOs represent anything genuinely unknown.

Unification Church (Moonies) church founded in Korea in 1954 by the Reverend Sun Myung ◊Moon. World membership is about 200,000. The theology unites Christian and Taoist ideas, and is based on Moon's book *Divine Principle* which teaches that the original purpose of creation was to set up a perfect family, in a perfect relationship with God; this was thwarted by the Fall of Man. Throughout history there have been attempts to renew this plan, which is now said to have found its fulfilment in Reverend and Mrs Moon. The Unification Church believes that marriage is essential for spiritual fulfilment, and marriage partners are chosen for members by Reverend Moon, though individuals are free to reject a chosen partner. Marriage, which takes the form of mass blessings by Reverend and Mrs Moon, is the most important ritual of the church; it is preceded by the wine or engagement ceremony. There are few other rituals, though there is a weekly pledge, which is a ceremony of rededication. The role of women in the church is to some extent still influenced by its Korean origins, but this, like the church's extreme anti-Marxist stance, is undergoing change.

unified field theory in physics, the attempt to find a theory which reduces the four ◊natural forces to a single unified force. See ◊Clerk Maxwell, ◊Einstein, and ◊Weinberg.

uniformitarianism in geology, the principle that 'the present is the key to the past': processes that can be seen to occur on the Earth's surface today are the same as those that have occurred throughout geological time. For example, desert sandstones containing sand-dune structures must have been formed under conditions similar to those present in deserts today. The principle was formulated by the pioneer geologist James ◊Hutton.

uniformity name given to two acts of Parliament in England. The first in 1559 imposed the Prayer Book on the whole English kingdom; the second in 1662 required the Prayer Book to be used in all churches, and some 2,000 ministers who refused to comply were ejected.

Union, Act of act of 1707 that effected the union of England and Scotland; that of 1801 united England and Ireland. The latter was abrogated when the Irish Free State was constituted in 1922.

union flag the British national ◊flag. It is popularly called the *Union Jack*, although, strictly speaking, this applies only when it is flown on the jackstaff of a warship.

union movement British political group. Beginning as the New Party founded by Sir Oswald ◊Mosley and a number of Labour MPs in 1931, it developed into the British Union of Fascists in 1932. An attempt by the 'blackshirts' to march through the East End of London in 1936 led to the Public Order Act, forbidding the wearing of such political uniforms. In 1940 the organization was declared illegal and its leaders interned, but at the end of World War II it was revived as the Union Movement, characterized by racist doctrines including anti-Semitism.

Union of Soviet Socialist Republics (USSR) country in N Asia and E Europe,

unemployment In 1936 at the height of the Great Depression in Britain, the closure of Palmer's shipyard in Jarrow prompted the 'Jarrow Crusaders' to carry a petition to London and hand it to Stanley Baldwin, Prime Minister. A similar People's March for Jobs walked from Liverpool to deliver a petition to Margaret Thatcher in 1981.

Union of Soviet Socialist Republics

(USSR; *Soyuz Sovyetskikh Sotsialisticheskikh Respublik*)

AREA 22,274,700 sq km/8,647,250 sq mi
CAPITAL Moscow
TOWNS Kiev, Tashkent, Kharkov, Gorky, Novosibirsk, Minsk, Sverdlovsk, Kuibyshev, Chelyabinsk, Dnepropetrovsk, Tbilisi; ports Leningrad, Odessa, Baku, Archangelesk, Murmansk, Vladivostok, Vostochny, Rostov
PHYSICAL the Ural Mountains separate the European from the Asian plain; the Caucasus Mountains are in the S between the Black Sea and the Caspian Sea, and there are mountain ranges in the S and E of the Asiatic part; the USSR covers one-sixth of the earth's land mass and contains forest, tundra, marsh, steppe, and desert
FEATURES part of the Pamirs and Altai mountains; Kara Kum Desert; Aral Sea; rivers (in Europe) Don, Dnieper, Volga, Dvina, Pechora, Dneister, Neva, Kuban, and (in Asia) Ob, Yenisei, Lena, Amur, Amu Darya and Syr Darya; lakes Ladoga, Onega, Baikal, and Balkhash
HEAD OF STATE Andrei Gromyko from 1985
HEAD OF GOVERNMENT Nikolai Ryzhkov from 1985 (premier); Mikhail Gorbachev from 1985 (head of Communist Party)
GOVERNMENT federal one-party communist
EXPORTS cotton, timber; iron and steel, non-ferrous metals, electrical equipment, machinery, arms; oil and natural gas and their products; asbestos, gold, manganese. The USSR has 58% of world coal reserves, 59% of oil, 41% iron, 88% manganese, 54% potassium salts, 30% phosphates (55% of trade is with communist countries)
CURRENCY rouble (1.04 = £1 Sept 1987, but this is not a commercial rate)
POPULATION (1985) 277,504,000 (two-thirds living in towns, and of 125 different nationalities; 52% ethnic Russians, 17% Ukrainians); annual growth rate 0.9%
LANGUAGE Slavic (Russian, Ukranian, Byelorussian, Polish), Altaic (Turkish, Mongolian, and others), other Indo-European, Uralian, Caucasian
RELIGION 'freedom of conscience' is guaranteed under the constitution, but religious belief is discouraged and considered incompatible with party membership (17,500,000 members); the largest Christian denomination is the Orthodox Church (30 million), but the largest
LITERACY 99% (1985)

GNP $734 bn (1984); $2,600 per head of population

CHRONOLOGY
1917 Revolution: provisional democratic government established in Mar by Mensheviks. Communist takeover in Nov by Bolsheviks under Lenin.
1922 Soviet Union established.
1924 Death of Lenin.
1928 Stalin emerged as absolute ruler after ousting Trotsky.
1930s Purges of Stalin's opponents.
1939 Nonaggression pact signed with Germany.
1941–45 'Great Patriotic War'.
1949 Creation of Comecon.
1953 Death of Stalin. Removal of Beria. 'Collective leadership' in power.
1955 Creation of Warsaw Pact.
1956 Khrushchev's February 'secret speech'. Hungarian uprising.
1957–58 Ousting of 'anti-party' group and Bulganin.
1960 Sino-Soviet rift.
1962 Cuban missile crisis.
1964 Khrushchev ousted by new 'collective leadership'.
1968 Invasion of Czechoslovakia.
1969 Sino-Soviet border war.
1972 Salt I arms-limitation agreement with USA.
1977 Brezhnev elected president.
1979 Salt II. Soviet invasion of Afghanistan.
1980 Kosygin replaced as prime minister by Tikhonov.
1980–81 Polish crisis.
1982 Deaths of Suslov and Brezhnev. Yuri Andropov new Communist Party leader.
1984 Chernenko succeeded Andropov.
1985 Gorbachev succeeded Chernenko and introduced wide-ranging reforms. Gromyko appointed president.
1986 Gorbachev's power consolidated at 27th Party Congress. Chernobyl nuclear disaster.
1987 Border guards embarrassed by West German teenager Mathias Rust landing a private plane in Red Square, Moscow. USSR and USA agreed to scrap intermediate-range nuclear missiles.

stretching from the Baltic Sea and the Black Sea to the Arctic and Pacific oceans.

government Under the 1977 constitution, the USSR is a federal state comprising 15 constituent union republics (see table). Each union republic enjoys, in theory, the right of secession and has its own constitution, legislature, and government (Council of Ministers) which is responsible for local administration. A number of union republics in turn include autonomous republics and regions in which special regard is paid to local culture, customs, and languages. The central (federal) government is solely responsible for defence, foreign policy, foreign trade, communications, and heavy industries. In other spheres the scope for initiative by union and autonomous-republic governments is restricted by the centrally planned nature of the Soviet economy and the constant scrutiny of the Communist Party.

The highest organ of the Moscow-based central government is the Supreme Soviet of the USSR, a two-chamber legislature comprising the Soviet (People's Council) of the Union and the Soviet of Nationalities. Each chamber has equal authority and comprises 750 members elected every five years by universal suffrage from a single list of candidates. Members of the Soviet of the Union are elected from single-member constituencies on the rough basis of one deputy per 350,000 people. Seats in the Soviet of Nationalities are distributed regionally on the basis of 32 deputies per union republic, 11 from each of the twenty autonomous republics, five from each of the eight autonomous regions and one from each of the ten national areas within the Russian Soviet Federated Socialist Republic (RSFSR).

The Supreme Soviet meets for three-or four-day sessions twice a year and elects, in joint session, a Presidium of 39 members (including always the 15 chairs of the supreme soviets of the union republics) to take over its functions in its absence. The Presidium is headed by a chair who functions as head of state or president. The Supreme Soviet also elects the Council of Ministers, a ministerial team of 130 headed by a chair (prime minister), to function as the executive government in charge of day-to-day state administration.

Lower-level elected soviets operate at the village, town, regional, and republic levels. However, the dominating force in the country is the Communist Party of the Soviet Union (CPSU), which is prescribed a 'leading' and 'guiding' role by the constitution. The CPSU, with 19,000,000 members, is the only political party in the USSR and forms a second and parallel form of government which dominates the state tier. It is set up like a pyramid with at its base over 400,000 primary party branches in factories and villages. The party, being organized on 'democratic centralist' lines, is controlled from above, with candidates for election being vetted and selected by their superiors. The CPSU's highest authority is its Party Congress, which meets every five years and includes 5,000 selected members. Congress ratifies party programmes and elects a Central Committee of usually 290 full and 170 non-voting 'candidate' members to assume authority over the party between congresses.

The Central Committee meets twice a year and elects the Politburo of normally twelve full members and five candidates and the specialist ten-member administrative Secretariat. The Politburo is the most important political body in the USSR. It meets weekly as an executive cabinet, controls and determines the policy of the CPSU, and sets out the medium and long-term goals for the nation. Its members select from their ranks the party leader, or general secretary (since Mar 1985 Mikhail ◊Gorbachev), who presides over the Secretariat and serves in practice as the leader of the Soviet Union.

The CPSU dominates the state system of government through the control it exercises over appointments and candidatures in elections. More than 70% of Supreme Soviet delegates are members of the CPSU, while the state's policy-making and executive organs, the Presidium and Council of Ministers, are tightly controlled by leading members of the CPSU Central Committee and Politburo. This inner circle of CPSU leaders determines state and party policy, with the Supreme Soviet and Party Congress functioning as merely rubber-stamping chambers.

history For early history, see ◊Russian history; also ◊Armenia, ◊Azerbaijan, ◊Belorussia, ◊Estonia, ◊Georgia, ◊Kirghizia, ◊Latvia, ◊Lithuania, ◊Moldavia, ◊Russia, ◊Tadzhikistan, ◊Turkmenistan, ◊Ukraine, and ◊Uzbekistan.

The Union of Soviet Socialist Republics was formed 1922 and a constitution adopted 1923. ◊Lenin, who had led the new regime, died 1924 and an internal party controversy broke out between ◊Stalin and ◊Trotsky over the future of socialism and the necessity of world revolution. Trotsky was expelled 1927 and Stalin's policy of socialism in one country adopted. During the first two five-year plans 1928–39 heavy and light industries were developed and agriculture collectivized.

From 1933 the USSR put forward a policy of collective resistance to aggression. In 1939 it concluded a nonaggression pact with Germany, and Poland was invaded and divided between them. The USSR invaded ◊Finland 1939 but signed a brief peace 1940. For events 1941–45, see ◊World War II.

During the immediate postwar years the USSR concentrated on consolidating its new empire in Eastern Europe and on providing indirect support to anti-colonial movements in the Far East. Relations with the West, particularly the US, sharply deteriorated. On the death of Stalin in Mar 1953 a collective leadership, including Nikita ◊Khrushchev (CPSU first or general secretary 1953–64), Georgi ◊Malenkov (prime minister 1953–55), Nikolai ◊Bulganin (prime minister 1955–58), Vyacheslav ◊Molotov (foreign minister 1953–56), and Lazar Kaganovich, assumed power. They combined to remove the secret-police chief Lavrenti ◊Beria in Dec 1953 and introduced a new legal code which regularized the political system. Strong differences emerged within the collective leadership over future political and economic reform and a fierce succession struggle developed.

Khrushchev emerged dominant from this contest, ousting Malenkov, Molotov, and Kaganovich (the 'anti-party' group) in Jun 1957 and Bulganin in Jun 1958 to combine the posts of prime minister and party first secretary. At the 1961 Party Congress, Khrushchev introduced a new party programme for rapid agricultural, industrial, and technological development to enable the USSR to move ahead of the USA in economic terms by 1980 and attain full Communism. He launched a 'virgin lands' cultivation campaign in Kazakhstan, increased rural incentives and decentralized industrial management through the creation of new regional economic councils (*sovnarkhozy*). In addition, Khrushchev introduced radical new party rule changes, sanctioned a cultural thaw

USSR: CONSTITUENT REPUBLICS

	Capital	Area in sq km	Date of joining USSR
RSFSR	Moscow	17,075,400	1922
Armenia	Yerevan	29,800	1936 **
Azerbaijan	Baku	86,600	1936 **
Belorussia	Minsk	207,600	1922
Estonia	Tallinn	45,100	1940
Georgia	Tbilisi	69,700	1936 **
Kazakhstan	Alma-Ata	2,717,300	1936 *
Kirghizia	Frunze	198,500	1936 *
Latvia	Riga	63,700	1940
Lithuania	Vilnius	65,200	1940
Moldavia	Kishinev	33,700	1940
Tadzhikistan	Dushanbe	143,100	1929 *
Turkmenistan	Ashkhabad	488,100	1924 *
Ukraine	Kiev	603,700	1922
Uzbekistan	Tashkent	447,400	1924 *
USSR	Moscow	22,402,200	1922

* Formerly Autonomous Republics within the USSR

** Formerly part of the Trans-Caucasian Soviet Socialist Republic which joined in the USSR in 1922.

USSR: POLITICAL LEADERS SINCE 1945

State President*

Nikolai Shvernik	1946–1953
Klimentiy Voroshilov	1953–1964
Leonid Brezhnev	1960–1964
Anastas Mikoyan	1964–1965
Nikolai Podgorny	1965–1977
Leonid Brezhnev	1977–1982
Vasily Kuznetsov**	1982–1983
Yuri Andropov	1983–1984
Vasily Kuznetsov**	1984–1984
Konstantin Chernenko	1984–1985
Vasily Kuzetsov**	1985–1985
Andrei Gromyko	1985–

*Chairman of the Presidium of the Supreme Soviet.

**Kuznetsov, who was First Deputy Chairman of the Presidum (Vice-President), served as a temporary acting President.

and enunciated the principle of 'peaceful coexistence' with the West to divert resources from the defence sector. These reforms enjoyed initial success; having exploded its first hydrogen bomb in 1953 and launched a space satellite (Sputnik I) in 1957, the USSR emerged as a serious technological rival to the USA. But Khrushchev's liberalization policy and his denunciation of the errors and crimes of the Stalin era at the Feb 1956 Party Congress had serious repercussions among the USSR's satellites – a nationalist revolt in ◊Hungary and a breach in relations with ◊Yugoslavia and ◊China – while his administrative reforms were fiercely opposed by senior party and state officials. After a series of poor harvests in overcropped Kazakhstan and the ◊Cuban missile-crisis climbdown of 1962, these opponents succeeded in ousting Khrushchev at the Central Committee meeting of Oct 1964.

A new and conservative collective leadership, based around the figures of Leonid ◊Brezhnev (CPSU general secretary 1964–82), Alexei ◊Kosygin (prime minister 1964–80), Nikolai Podgorny (state president 1965–77), and Mikhail Suslov (ideology secretary 1964–82), assumed power and immediately abandoned Khrushchev's *sovnarkhozy* and party reforms and reimposed strict censorship in the cultural sphere. Priority was now given to the expansion and modernization of the Soviet armed forces, including the creation of a naval force with global reach. This, coupled with the Soviet invasion of ◊Czechoslovakia in 1968, resulted in a renewal of the ◊cold war 1964–70. During the later 1960s, Leonid Brezhnev, through inducting his supporters into the CPSU Politburo and Secretariat, slowly emerged as the dominant figure. He governed in a cautious and consensual manner and brought into the Politburo leaders from all the significant centres of power, including the ◊KGB (Yuri ◊Andropov), the army (Marshal Andrei Grechko), and the diplomatic service (Andrei ◊Gromyko). Working with Prime Minister Kosygin, Brezhnev introduced a series of minor economic reforms and gave new priority to agricultural and consumer-goods production. In 1977 he oversaw the framing of a new constitution where the limits for dissent were clearly set out.

Brezhnev, who became the new state president in May 1977, emerged as an international statesman during the 1970s, frequently meeting Western leaders during a new era of détente. The landmarks of this period were the Salt-1 and Salt-2 Soviet-US arms-limitation agreements of 1972 and 1979 (see ◊strategic arms limitation) and the Helsinki Accord of 1975, which brought Western recognition of the postwar division of Eastern Europe. Another cultural thaw resulted in the emergence of a vocal dissident movement. The political and military influence of the USSR

United Arab Emirates

(UAE) FEDERATION OF THE EMIRATES OF ABU DHABI,
AJMAN, DUBAI, FUJAIRAH, SHARJAH, UMM AL
QAIWAIN, RAS AL KHAIMAH

TOTAL AREA 83,000 sq km/32,000 sq mi
CAPITAL Abu Dhabi
TOWNS chief port Dubai
PHYSICAL mainly desert; mountains in E
FEATURES linked by their dependence on oil
revenues
HEAD OF STATE AND OF GOVERNMENT Zayed Bin
Sultan Al-Nahayan from 1971
GOVERNMENT federation of absolute monarchs
EXPORTS oil and natural gas
CURRENCY UAE dirham (6.06 = £1 Sept 1987)
POPULATION (1985) 1,283,000 (10% are
nomadic); annual growth rate 6.4%
LANGUAGE Arabic (official); Farsi, Hindi and
Urdu are spoken by immigrant oilfield workers
from Iran, India, and Pakistan
RELIGION Moslem 90%, Christian, Hindu
LITERACY 56% (1985)
GNP $25 bn (1983); $23,000 per head of
population
CHRONOLOGY
1952 Trucial Council established.
1971 Federation of Arab Emirates came into
being but was later dissolved. Six of the

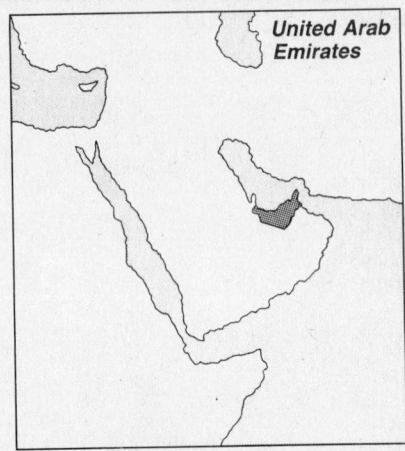

United Arab
Emirates

Trucial States formed the United Arab
Emirates, with the ruler of Abu Dhabi, Sheik
Zayed, as president.
1972 The seventh state joined.
1976 Sheik Zayed threatened to relinquish
presidency unless progress towards
centralization became more rapid.
1985 Diplomatic and economic links with the
USSR and with China established.

was extended into Africa with the establishment of new Communist governments in ◊Angola (1975), ◊Mozambique (1974), ◊Ethiopia (1975), and South ◊Yemen (1978). The détente era was brought to an end by the Soviet invasion of ◊Afghanistan in Dec 1979 and the ◊Polish crisis of 1980–81. The final years of the Brezhnev search for détente with the US which was rejected by the hardline Reagan administration. On Chernenko's death in Mar 1985, power was transferred to a new generation led by Mikhail ◊Gorbachev, the protégé of Andropov, at 54 the CPSU's youngest leader since Stalin. Gorbachev introduced a number of reforms. He began to free farmers and factory managers from bureaucratic interference and to increase material incentives in a 'market socialist' manner. Working with Ideology Secretary Yegor ◊Ligachev and Prime Minister Nikolai ◊Ryzhkov, he restructured the party and state bureaucracies and replaced cautious administration were ones of policy sclerosis, mounting corruption, and economic stagnation. Yuri Andropov, the former KGB chief, was elected CPSU leader on Brezhnev's death in Nov 1982 and began energetically to introduce a series of radical economic reforms aimed at streamlining and decentralizing the planning system and inculcating greater labour discipline. Andropov also launched a major campaign directed against corrupt and complacent party and state bureaucrats. These measures had a perceptible impact on the Soviet economy during 1983, but when Andropov died in Feb 1984 he was succeeded by the cautious and elderly Brezhnev supporter, Konstantin ◊Chernenko. Chernenko held power as a stop-gap leader for 13 months, his sole initiative being a renewed

Brezhnevites with ambitious new technocrats. Under the slogan *glasnost* (openness), he encouraged criticism of inefficiencies and made party officials (*apparatchiks*) more accountable to rank-and-file members.

Working with the foreign secretary, E A ◊Shevardnadze, Gorbachev made skilful use of the foreign media to put the case against space weapons and nuclear testing. He met US President Reagan at Geneva and Reykjavik in Nov 1985 and Oct 1986, but, having failed to secure an arms-control agreement, faced increasing internal pressure to adopt a harder line towards the USA.

Unitarianism a Christian denomination which rejects the orthodox doctrine of the Trinity, asserts the Fatherhood of God and the Brotherhood of Man, and gives a pre-eminent position to Jesus Christ as a religious teacher, while denying his Deity. Unitarians believe in individual conscience and reason as a guide to right action, rejecting the doctrines of original sin, the atonement, and eternal punishment. The various congregations are linked in the General Assembly of Unitarian and Free Christian Churches. See also ◊Arianism and ◊Socinianism.

United Arab Emirates federation in SW Asia, on the Arabian Gulf, bounded to the SW by Saudi Arabia and to the SE by Oman.
government A provisional constitution for the United Arab Emirates (UAE) has been in effect since Dec 1971 and provides a federal structure for a union of seven sheikdoms. The highest authority is the Supreme Council of Rulers, which includes all seven sheiks. Each is a hereditary emir and an absolute monarch in his own country. The council elects two of its members to be president and vice president of the

federal state for a five-year term. The president then appoints a prime minister and council of ministers.

There is a federal National Council of 40 members appointed by the emirates for a two-year term and this operates as a consultative assembly. There are no political parties.
history For early history, see ◊Arabia. The seven sheikdoms of Abu Dhabi, Ajman, Dubai, Fujairah, Ras al-Khaimah, Sharjah, and Umm al-Qaiwain set up in 1952, on British advice, the Trucial Council, consisting of all seven rulers, with a view to eventually establishing a federation. In the 1960s the Trucial States, as they were known, became very wealthy through the exploitation of oil deposits.

The whole area was under British protection but in 1968 the British government announced that it was withdrawing its forces within three years. The seven Trucial States, with Bahrain and Qatar, formed the Federation of Arab Emirates, which was intended to become a federal state, but in 1971 Bahrain and Qatar seceded to become independent nations. Six of the Trucial States then combined to form the United Arab Emirates. The remaining sheikdom, Ras al-Khaimah, joined in Feb 1972. Sheik Zayed Bin Al-Nahayan, the ruler of Abu Dhabi, became the first president.

In 1976 Sheik Zayed, disappointed with the slow progress towards centralization, was persuaded to accept another term as president only with assurances that the federal government would be given more control over such activities as defence and internal security. In recent years the United Arab Emirates has played an increasingly important role in Middle East affairs and in 1985 it established diplomatic and economic links with the USSR and China.

Supreme Council of Rulers: *Abu Dhabi* Sheikh Zayed Bin Sultan Al-Nahayan (1966); *Dubai* Sheikh Rashid Bin Said Al-Maktoum/1958; *Sharjah* Sheikh Sultan Bin Muhammad Al-Quasimi (1972); *Ras al-Khaimah* Sheikh Saqr Bin Muhammad Al-Quasimi (1948); *Umm al-Qaiwain* Sheikh Rashid Bin Ahmad Al-Mu'alla (1981); *Ajman* Sheikh Humaid Bin Rashid Al-Nuami (1981); *Fujairah* Sheikh Hamad Bin Muhammad Al-Sharqi (1974).

United Arab Republic union formed 1958, broken 1961, between ◊Egypt and ◊Syria. Egypt continued to use the name after the breach until 1971.

United Australia Party Australian political party formed by J A ◊Lyons in 1931 from the right-wing Nationalist Party (founded by Hughes and in power 1917–29). It was led by Menzies after the death of Lyons. Considered to have become too dominated by financial interests, it lost heavily to the Labour Party in 1943, and was reorganized as the Liberal ◊Party in 1944.

United Democratic Front moderate political organization in South Africa, the main focus of anti-apartheid action within South Africa since the ◊African National Congress and ◊Pan-Africanist Congress were declared illegal by that country.

United Kingdom country in NW Europe off the coast of France.

government The United Kingdom is a constitutional monarchy with parliamentary government. There is no written constitution. Cabinet government, which is at the heart of the system, is founded on rigid convention, and the relationship between the monarch as head of state and the prime minister as head of government is similarly based. Parliament is sovereign, in that it is free to make and unmake any laws that it chooses, and the government is subject to the laws that Parliament makes, as interpreted by the courts.

Parliament has two legislative and debating chambers, the House of Lords and the House of Commons. The House of Lords has three main kinds of members: those who are there by accident of birth, the hereditary peers; those who are there because of some office they hold; and those who are appointed to serve for life, the life peers. There are nearly 800 hereditary peers. Among those sitting by virtue of their position are 2 archbishops and 24 bishops of the Church of England and 9 senior judges, known as the law lords. The appointed life peers now include about 65 women, or peeresses. The House of Commons has 650 members, elected by universal adult suffrage from single-member geographical constituencies, each constituency containing, on average, about 65,000 electors.

Although the House of Lords is termed the upper house, its powers, in relation to those of the Commons, have been steadily reduced so that now it has no control over financial legislation and merely a delaying power, of a year, over other bills. Before an act of Parliament becomes law it must pass through a five-stage process in each chamber, first reading, second reading, committee stage, report stage, and third reading, and then receive the formal royal assent. Bills, other than financial ones, can be introduced in either house, but most begin in the Commons.

The monarch appoints as prime minister the leader of the party with most support in the House of Commons and he or she, in turn, chooses and presides over a cabinet. The simple voting system favours two-party politics and both chambers of Parliament are physically designed to accommodate two parties, the ruling party sitting on one side of the presiding Speaker and the opposition on the other. The two-party system is also supported by the traditional class bases of the Conservative and Labour parties, one representing property and business ownership and the other the workers. The party with the second largest number of seats in the Commons is recognized as the official opposition, and its leader is paid a salary out of public funds and provided with an office within the Palace of Westminster, as the Houses of Parliament are called.

history For early history, see Ancient ◊Britain. The United Kingdom of Great Britain was formed 1707 with the Act of Union between ◊Scotland and ◊England. Cabinet government developed under Robert ◊Walpole, in practice the first prime minister (1721–42). Two ◊Jacobite rebellions sought to restore the ◊Stuarts to the throne until the Battle of ◊Culloden 1746, after which the Scottish Highlanders were brutally suppressed. The American colonies gained independence 1783.

The Act of Ireland 1801 united Britain and Ireland. This was the time of the ◊Industrial Revolution, the mechanization of production that shifted the balance of political power from the landowner to the industrial capitalist and created an exploited urban working class. In protest, the ◊Luddites destroyed machinery. Agricultural ◊enclosures were driving the small farmers off the land. The alliance of the industrialists with the ◊Whigs produced a new party, the Liberals, with an ideology of ◊free trade and nonintervention in economic affairs. In 1832 they carried a Reform Bill transferring political power from the aristocracy to the middle classes and for the next 40 years the Liberal Party was a major force. The working classes, who had no vote, created their own organizations in the trade unions and ◊Chartism; their attempts to seek parliamentary reform were brutally suppressed (◊Peterloo Massacre 1819). The Conservative minister Robert ◊Peel introduced a number of domestic reforms, including the repeal of the ◊Corn Laws 1846.

After 1875 the UK's industrial monopoly was challenged by Germany and the USA. To seek new markets and sources of raw materials, the Conservatives under ◊Disraeli launched the UK on a career of imperialist expansion in Egypt, South Africa, and elsewhere. Canada, New Zealand, and Australia developed into self-governing dominions.

The domestic issues after 1900 were social reform and home rule for Ireland; the Labour Party emerged from an alliance of trade unions and small socialist bodies 1900; the ◊suffragettes were active until World War I. After the war a wave of strikes culminated in the general strike 1926; three years later a world economic crisis precipitated the Depression that marked the 1930s and brought to power a coalition government 1931. The years that followed were dominated by the approach of World War II.

In 1945 the UK still had an empire that covered a quarter of the world's surface and included a quarter of its population and, although two world wars had gravely weakened it, many of its citizens and some of its politicians still saw it as a world power. The reality of its position soon became apparent when the newly elected Labour government, led by Clement ◊Attlee, confronted the problems of rebuilding the damaged economy. This renewal was greatly helped, as in other West European countries, by support from the USA through the Marshall Plan. Between 1945 and 1951 the Labour government carried out an ambitious programme of public ownership and investment and laid the foundations of a national health service and welfare state. During the same period the dismemberment of the British Empire, restyled the British ◊Commonwealth, was begun, a process that was to continue into the 1980s.

When in 1951 the Conservative Party was returned to power, under Sir Winston ◊Churchill, the essential features of the welfare state and the public sector were retained. In 1955 Churchill, in his 81st year, handed over to the foreign secretary, Sir Anthony ◊Eden. In 1956 Eden found himself confronted by what he perceived to be a threat as great as that from Germany in the 1930, when the president of Egypt, Gamal Nasser, took possession of the Suez Canal. Eden's perception of the threat posed by Nasser was not shared by everyone, even within the Conservative Party. The British invasion of Egypt, in conjunction with France and Israel, brought widespread criticism and was abandoned in the face of pressure from the USA and the United Nations. Eden resigned, on the grounds of ill health, and the Conservatives chose Harold ◊Macmillan as their new leader and prime minister.

Macmillan quickly repaired the damage caused by his predecessor's ill-judged adventure and by the early 1960s, with a booming economy and rising living standards, he was known as 'Supermac'. Internationally, he established a close working relationship with the US presidents Eisenhower and Kennedy. He also did much for the Commonwealth, but he was sufficiently realistic to see that the UK's long-term economic and political future lay in Europe. By the mid-1950s the framework for the European Community (EC) had been created, with the UK an onlooker rather than a participant. The Conservatives won the 1959 general election with an increased majority and in 1961 the first serious attempt was made to join the EC, only to have it blocked by the French president, Charles de Gaulle.

Despite rising living standards, the UK's economic performance was not as successful as that of many of its competitors, particularly West Germany and Japan. There was a growing awareness that there was insufficient investment in industry, that the best young talent was going into the professions or financial institutions rather than manufacturing, and that training was poorly planned and inadequately funded. It was against this background that Macmillan unexpectedly resigned in 1963, on the grounds of ill health, and was succeeded by the foreign secretary, Lord Home, who immediately renounced his title to become Sir Alec Douglas ◊Home.

In the general election 1964 the Labour Party won a slender majority and its leader, Harold ◊Wilson, became prime minister. The election had been fought on the issue of the economy. Wilson created the Department of Economic Affairs (DEA) to challenge the short-term conservatism of the Treasury, and brought in a leading trade unionist to head a new Department of Technology. In an early general election 1966 Wilson increased his Commons majority but his promises of fundamental changes in economic planning, industrial investment, and improved work practices were not fulfilled. The DEA was disbanded in 1969 and an ambitious plan for the reform of industrial relations was dropped in the face of trade-union opposition.

United Kingdom

OF GREAT BRITAIN AND NORTHERN IRELAND (UK)

AREA 94,226 sq mi/244,044 sq km
CAPITAL London
TOWNS Birmingham, Glasgow, Leeds, Sheffield, Liverpool, Manchester, Edinburgh, Bradford, Bristol, Belfast, Newcastle-upon-Tyne, Cardiff
PHYSICAL land mass became separated from the European continent c. 6000 BC; rolling landscape, becoming increasingly mountainous towards the N, with the Grampian Mountains in Scotland and Snowdon in Wales. Rivers include Thames and Severn
FEATURES the climate is characteristically milder than in N Europe, because of the Gulf Stream, with considerable rainfall. No point is further than 120 km/74.5 mi from the sea; indented coastline with various small islands
HEAD OF STATE Elizabeth II from 1952
HEAD OF GOVERNMENT Margaret Thatcher from 1979
GOVERNMENT parliamentary democracy
EXPORTS agricultural (cereals, rape, sugar beet, potatoes); meat and meat products, poultry, dairy products; electronic and telecommunications equipment; engineering equipment and scientific instruments; North Sea oil and gas, petrochemicals, pharmaceuticals, fertilizers; film and television programmes; tourism is important
CURRENCY pound sterling
POPULATION 56,423,000 (1985); annual growth rate -0.1%
RELIGION mainly Christian (Church of England and other Protestant sects with Roman Catholic minority); Jewish, Muslim minorities
LANGUAGE English, Welsh, Gaelic
LITERACY 99% (1984)
GNP $505 bn (1983); $7,216 per head of population
TERRITORIES Anguilla; Bermuda; British Antarctic Territory; British Indian Ocean Territory; British Virgin Islands; Cayman Islands; Falkland Islands (disputed by Argentina); Gibraltar; Hong Kong (until 1997); Montserrat; Pitcairn Islands; St Helena and Dependencies (Ascension, Tristan da Cunha); Turks and Caicos Islands
CHRONOLOGY
55 and 54 BC Julius Caesar's raiding visits.
43 AD Roman conquest began.
407 Roman withdrawal, but partial reoccupations c. 417–27 and c. 450.
5th–7th centuries Anglo-Saxons overran all England except Cornwall and Cumberland, forming independent kingdoms, for example Northumbria, Mercia, Kent, Wessex.
c. 597 St Augustine converted England to Christianity.
829 Egbert of Wessex accepted as overlord of all England.
878 Alfred ceded N and E England to the Danish invaders though keeping them out of Wessex.
1066 Norman conquest of England.
1171 Henry II established a colony in Ireland.
1215 King John was forced to sign Magna Carta.
1295 Model Parliament set up in England.
1338–1453 Hundred Years' War with France enabled Parliament to secure control of taxation and, by impeachment, of the king's choice of ministers.
1348–49 Black Death raged in England.
1381 Social upheaval in England led to Peasants' Revolt, brutally repressed.
1455–85 Wars of the Roses.
1529 Henry VIII became head of the English church.
1536–43 Acts of Union united England and Wales after conquest.
1588 Spanish Armada attempted unsuccessfully to invade England.
1603 James I united the English and Scottish crowns; parliamentary dissidence increased.
1642–52 Civil War in England between Royalists and Parliamentarians, resulting in victory for Parliament.
1649 Charles I executed and the Commonwealth set up.
1653 Cromwell appointed Lord Protector.
1660 Restoration of Charles II.
1688 William of Orange invited to take the throne as William III; flight of James II.
1707 Act of Union between England and Scotland under Queen Anne.
1721 Walpole unofficially the first prime minister under George I.
1783 Loss of the N American colonies.
1801 Act of Ireland united Britain and Ireland.
1832 Great Reform Bill became law, shifting political power from upper to middle class.
1848 Chartist working-class movement formed.
1867 Second Reform Bill, extending the franchise, introduced by Disraeli and passed.
1906 Liberal victory: programme of social reform.
1911 Powers of House of Lords curbed.
1920 Home Rule Act incorporated the NE of Ireland (Ulster) into the United Kingdom of

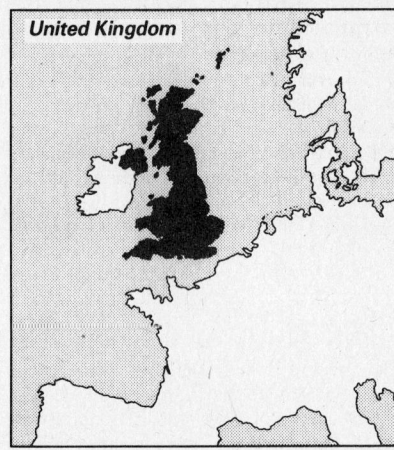

United Kingdom

Great Britain and Northern Ireland.
1921 Ireland, except for Ulster, became a dominion (Irish Free State, later Eire, 1937).
1924 First Labour government led by Ramsay Macdonald.
1926 General Strike.
1931 National government; unemployment reached 3 million.
1940 Churchill became head of coalition government.
1945 Labour government under Attlee; birth of welfare state.
1951 Conservatives defeated Labour.
1956 Suez crisis.
1964 Labour victory under Wilson.
1970 Conservatives under Heath defeated Labour.
1972 Parliament prorogued in Northern Ireland; direct rule from Westminster began.
1973 Britain joined EEC.
1974 Three-day week, coal strike; Wilson replaced Heath.
1979 Victory for Conservatives under Thatcher.
1981 Formation of Social Democrat Party. Riots in inner cities.
1982 Unemployment over 3 million. Falklands War.
1984–85 Coal strike, the longest in British history.
1986 Abolition of metropolitan counties.
1987 Thatcher re-elected for third term.
1988 Liberals and Social Democrats agree to merge.

In 1970 the Conservatives returned to power under Edward ◊Heath. He, too, saw institutional change as one way of achieving industrial reform and created two new central departments, Trade and Industry and Environment, and a 'think tank' to advise the government on long-term strategy, the Central Policy Review Staff (CPRS). He attempted to change the climate of industrial relations through a long and complicated Industrial Relations Bill. He saw entry into the EC as the 'cold shower of competition' that industry needed, and membership was successfully negotiated in 1972. Heath's 'counterrevolution', as he saw it, was frustrated by the trade unions, and the sharp rise in oil prices 1973 forced a U-turn in economic policy. Instead of abandoning 'lame ducks' to their fate, he found it necessary to take ailing industrial companies, such as Rolls-Royce, into public ownership. The introduction of a statutory incomes policy precipitated a national miners' strike in the winter of 1973–74 and Heath decided to challenge the unions by holding an early general election in 1974. The result was a hung Parliament, with Labour winning the biggest number of seats but no single party having an overall majority. Heath tried briefly to form a coalition with the Liberals and, when this failed, resigned.

Harold Wilson returned to the premiership, heading a minority government, but in another general election later the same year won enough additional seats to give him a working majority. He had taken over a damaged economy and a nation puzzled and divided by the events of the previous years. He turned to Labour's natural ally and founder, the trade-union movement, for support and jointly they agreed a 'social contract': the government pledged itself to redress the imbalance between management and unions created by the Heath industrial-relations legislation and the unions promised to cooperate in a voluntary industrial and incomes policy. Wilson met criticism from a growing left-wing movement within his party, impatient for radical change. In Mar 1976 Wilson, apparently tired and disillusioned, retired in mid-term.

Wilson was succeeded by James ◊Callaghan, his senior by some four years. In the other two parties, Edward Heath had unexpectedly been ousted by Margaret ◊Thatcher, and the Liberal Party leader, Jeremy Thorpe, had resigned after a personal scandal and been succeeded by the young Scottish MP David ◊Steel. Callaghan was now leading a divided party and a government with a dwindling parliamentary majority. Later in 1976 an unexpected finanial crisis arose from a drop in confidence in the overseas exchange markets, a rapidly falling pound and a drain on the country's foreign reserves. After considerable debate within the cabinet both before and afterwards, it was decided to seek help from the IMF and submit to its stringent economic policies. Within weeks the crisis was over and within months the economy was showing clear signs of improvement.

In 1977, to shore up his slender parliamentary majority, Callaghan entered into an agreement with the new leader of the Liberal Party, David Steel. Under the 'Lib-Lab Pact' Labour pursued moderate, nonconfrontational policies in consultation with the Liberals, who, in turn, voted with the government, and the economy improved dramatically. The Lib-Lab Pact had effectively finished by the autumn of 1978 and soon the social contract with the unions began to disintegrate. Widespread and damaging strikes in the public sector badly affected essential services during what became known as the 'winter of discontent'. At the end of Mar 1979 Callaghan lost a vote of confidence in the House of Commons and was forced into a general election.

The Conservatives returned to power under the UK's first female prime minister, Margaret Thatcher. She inherited a number of inflationary public-sector pay awards from the winter of discontent. These, together with a budget that doubled the rate of value added tax, resulted in a sharp rise in prices and interest rates. The

Conservatives were pledged to reduce inflation, and did so by mainly monetarist policies, which caused the number of unemployed to rise from 1.3 million to 2 million in the first year.

Thatcher had experience in only one government department, and it was nearly two years before she made any major changes to the cabinet she inherited from Heath. In foreign affairs she was least equipped, but under the influence of Lord ◊Carrington as foreign secretary the independence of Zimbabwe-Rhodesia was achieved bloodlessly in 1980.

Meanwhile, important changes were taking place in the other parties. Callaghan resigned the leadership of the Labour Party in 1980 and was replaced by the left-winger Michael ◊Foot, and early in 1981 three Labour shadow cabinet members, David ◊Owen, Shirley ◊Williams, and William Rodgers, with the former deputy leader Roy ◊Jenkins (collectively dubbed the 'Gang of Four'), broke away to form a new centrist group, the ◊Social Democratic Party (SDP). The new party made an early impression, winning a series of by-elections within months of its creation. Since 1983 the Liberals and the SDP have been linked in an electoral pact, the Alliance. They advocate the introduction of a system of ◊proportional representation, which would ensure a fairer parity between votes and seats won.

Unemployment continued to rise, passing the 3,000,000 mark in Jan 1982, and the Conservatives, and their leader in particular, were receiving low ratings in the public-opinion polls. An unforeseen event rescued them, the Argentine invasion of the Falkland Islands. Thatcher's decision to send a battle fleet to recover them paid off. The general election of 1983 was fought with the euphoria of the Falklands victory still in the air and the Labour Party, under its new leader, divided and unconvincing. The Conservatives had a landslide victory, winning more Commons seats than any party since 1945, although with appreciably less than half the popular vote. Thatcher was now able to establish her position firmly, replacing most of her original cabinet.

The next three years were marked by rising unemployment and growing dissent: a dispute at the government's main intelligence-gathering station, GCHQ; a bitter and protracted miners' strike; increasing violence in Northern Ireland; an attempted assassination of leading members of the Conservative Party during their annual conference; riots in inner-city areas. The government was further embarrassed by its own prosecutions under the Official Secrets Act and the resignations of two prominent cabinet ministers. With the short-term profits from North Sea oil and an ambitious privatization programme, the inflation rate continued to fall and by the winter of 1986–87 the economy was buoyant enough to allow the Chancellor of the Exchequer to arrange a pre-election spending and credit boom.

There had been leadership changes in two of the other parties. Michael Foot was replaced by his Welsh protégé, Neil ◊Kinnock; Roy Jenkins was replaced by David Owen as SDP leader, to be

succeeded in turn by Robert Maclennan in Sept 1987, when the SDP and Liberal parties voted to initiate talks with a view to an eventual merger. Despite the unemployment figures and Thatcher's increasingly authoritarian style of government, the Conservatives were re-elected in Jun 1987, although with virtually no popular support in Scotland and Wales.

United Nations (UN) association of states (successor to the ◊League of Nations) for international peace, security, and cooperation, with its headquarters in New York. Its charter was drawn up at the San Francisco Conference in 1945, based on proposals drafted at the Dumbarton Oaks conference. There are six main organs:

General Assembly one member from each of 159 member states who meet annually; decisions on important questions require a two-thirds majority, while on minor ones, a simple majority suffices;

Security Council five permanent members (UK, USA, USSR, France, China, who exercise a veto in that their support is requisite for all decisions), plus six others elected for two years by the General Assembly. It may undertake investigations into disputes and make recommendations to the parties concerned, and may call on all members to take economic or military measures to enforce its decisions;

Economic and Social Council 18 members elected for three years. It initiates studies of international economic, social, cultural, educational, health and related matters, and may make recommendations to the General Assembly. It operates largely through specialized commissions of international experts on economics, transport and communications, human rights, status of women, and so on. It coordinates the activities of: *Food and Agriculture Organization* (FAO) established in 1945, headquarters in Rome; investment in agriculture, also emergency food supplies;

General Agreement on Tariffs and Trade (GATT) established in 1948, headquarters in Geneva; reduction of trade barriers, anti-dumping code, assistance to trade of developing countries, and so on;

International Atomic Energy Agency (IAEA) established in 1957, headquarters in Vienna; research centres in Austria and Monaco; International Centre for Theoretical Physics, Trieste;

International Bank for Reconstruction and Development (IBRD) popularly known as the ◊World Bank;

International Civil Aviation Organization (ICAO) established in 1947, headquarters in Montreal; safety and efficiency, international facilities and air law;

International Development Association (IDA) administered by the ◊World Bank;

International Finance Corporation (IFC) established in 1956; affiliated to World Bank, it encourages private enterprise in less developed countries;

International Fund for Agricultural Development (IFAD) established in 1977, headquarters in Rome; additional funds for benefiting the poorest in developing countries;

International Labour Organization (ILO) first established in 1919, headquarters in Geneva; Nobel Peace Prize 1969;

International Maritime Organization (IMO) established in 1958, headquarters in London; safety at sea, pollution control, abolition of restrictive practices, and so on;

International Monetary Fund (IMF) established in 1945, headquarters in Washington; promotes cooperation, international trade, exchange rate stability, and makes funds available to countries in difficulty subject to conditions;

International Telecommunication Union (ITU) first established in 1934, headquarters in Geneva; allocation of radio frequencies; promotes low tariffs and life-saving measures for, for example, disasters at sea;

United Nations Educational, Scientific, and Cultural Organization (UNESCO) established in 1946, headquarters in Paris, from which the USA, contributor of 25 per cent of its budget, withdrew in 1984 on grounds of its over-politicization, and Britain followed in 1985;

Universal Postal Union (UPU) first established in 1875, headquarters in Berne; collaboration of postal services;

World Health Organization (WHO) established in 1946, headquarters in Geneva; to prevent the spread of diseases such as malaria and tuberculosis and eradicate them by 2000;

World Intellectual Property Organization (WIPO) established in 1974, headquarters in Geneva; protection of copyright in the arts, science, and industry;

World Meteorological Organization (WMO) established in 1951, headquarters in Geneva;

Trusteeship Council consisting of members administering ◊trust territories, other permanent members of the Security Council, plus sufficient other elected members to balance the administering powers;

International Court of Justice at The Hague, with 15 judges elected by the General Assembly and Security Council; United Nations members are pledged to accept decisions;

Secretariat headed by a secretary general who is elected for five years by the General Assembly. Members contribute financially according to their resources, an apportionment being made by the General Assembly, with the addition of voluntary contributions from some governments to the funds of the United Nations. These finance the programme of assistance carried out by the UN intergovernmental agencies, the United Nations Children's Fund (UNICEF), the United Nations refugee organizations, and the United Nations Special Fund for developing countries. There are six official working languages: English, French, Russian, Spanish, Chinese, and Arabic.

The influence in the United Nations, originally with the allied states of World War II, is now more widely spread. Although part of the value of the United Nations lies in recognition of member states as sovereign and equal, the rapid increase in membership of minor – in some cases minute – states was causing concern by 1980 (154 members) as lessening the weight of voting decisions. Taiwan, formerly a permanent member of the Security Council, was expelled in 1971 on the admission of China. The United Nations also suffers from the lack of adequate and independent funds and forces, the latter having been employed with varying success, for example, in Korea, Cyprus, and Sinai, and the intrusion of the Cold War which divides members into adherents of the east or west and the uncommitted.

United Provinces of Agra and Oudh /'ɑːgrə, aud/ former province of British India which formed the major part of the state of ◊Uttar Pradesh; see also ◊Agra, ◊Oudh.

United States architecture native American architecture survives largely in the southwest, as well as a strong Spanish influence from early colonizers, but on the east coast from the 17th century English immigrants had the main influence and it is their buildings that survive. For example, early buildings at Harvard University in Massachusetts and at William and Mary college in Virginia resemble Oxford and Cambridge; there are Georgian houses in Virginia, Philadelphia, and Boston, and churches in the style of Wren. A neo-classical phase was introduced by Thomas Jefferson towards the end of the 18th century, for example, his house at Monticello, the Federal Capitol at Washington by William Thornton 1761–1828, and the White House by James Hoban 1762–1831. After the Civil War 1861–65 came a generation of French-trained architects, for example, H H Richardson, chief exponent of a modified Romanesque. A revival of 'Queen Anne' style followed, and then towards the end of the 19th century a second classical revival, for example, Columbia University, New York. Most characteristic of contemporary US architecture is the ◊skyscraper. The most individual of earlier 20th century US architects was Frank Lloyd ◊Wright, but impressive work was also produced by Richard Buckminster ◊Fuller, Walter ◊Gropius and Ludwig ◊Mies van der Rohe, successive directors of the ◊Bauhaus, the ◊Saarinens (father and son), Richard ◊Neutra, and Philip C ◊Johnson; and more recently by Robert ◊Venturi and Chinese-born Ieoh Ming ◊Pei.

United States art the first American-born artist in the European tradition was the portraitist Robert Feke 1705–50, but best-known of early masters is Benjamin ◊West – working mainly in England – who encouraged the portraitist John Singleton Copley, and whose pupils include Gilbert Stuart, Thomas Sully, and Charles Willson ◊Peale. To the 19th century belong the dramatic landscapes of Washington Allston, the nature pictures of Audubon, the seascapes of Winslow ◊Homer, the realism of Thomas Eakins, and the romantic landscapes of the Hudson River school, for example, English-born Thomas Cole 1801–48 and later George Inness 1825–94. Appreciated abroad were the markedly individual gifts of James ◊Whistler, Mary ◊Cassatt and John Singer ◊Sargent towards the end of the century, and the mysticism of the recluse Albert Pinkham Ryder 1847–1917. Notable in the early 20th century was the ◊Ashcan school, so nicknamed because of its concern with slum squalor. A pioneer of European movements such as ◊Expressionism was Max Weber 1881–1961 and more recent artists who blend such influences in their work include John Marin; Grant Wood; Lyonel Feininger; the inventor of ◊Action painting, Jackson ◊Pollock; the politically concerned Ben ◊Shahn, and the spiritual Mark ◊Rothko. In sculpture the best-known names include ◊Lipchitz, ◊Mestrovic, ◊Archipenko, and ◊Calder, inventor of mobiles.

United States literature American literature of the colonial period 1607–1765 includes travel books and religious verse, but is mainly theological: Roger Williams, Cotton Mather, and Jonathan Edwards were typical Puritan writers. Benjamin Franklin's *Autobiography* is the first work of more than historical interest. The revolutionary period 1765–1800 produced much political writing, for example, by Paine, Jefferson, and Hamilton, and one noteworthy poet, Philip Freneau. In the early 19th century the influence of the English Romantics became evident, notably in Washington Irving's tales and James Fenimore Cooper's novels of North American Indian life. During 1830–60 intellectual life centred on New England, which produced the essayists Emerson, Thoreau, and Holmes; the poets Bryant, Longfellow, Lowell, and Whittier; the historians Parkman, Prescott, and Motley; and the novelist Hawthorne. Outside the New England circle stood Poe, Melville, and Whitman. The disillusionment of the post-Civil War period 1865–1900 found expression in the realistic or psychological novel. Ambrose Bierce and Stephen Crane wrote realistic war stories; Mark Twain and Bret Harte dealt with western life; and the growth of industrialism led to the rise of the novel of social realism, notably in the work of W D Howells, while Henry James, and his disciple Edith Wharton, developed the novel of psychological analysis. A major poet of this period was Emily Dickinson. Since 1900 the main trend in the novel has been realistic, and American writers have exerted a growing influence in Europe; for example, Jack London, Upton Sinclair, and Theodore Dreiser; and after World War I, Sherwood Anderson, Sinclair Lewis, Ernest Hemingway, William Faulkner, John Dos Passos, and John Steinbeck. Aside from the main tradition is the romantic or subjective fiction of Thornton Wilder, J B Cabell, and Henry Miller. Among the internationally known writers since World War II are Truman Capote, J D Salinger, John Updike, Norman Mailer, Nelson Algren, Saul Bellow, Vladimir Nabokov, Bernard Malamud, Philip Roth and James Baldwin. The short story was popularized as a form by O Henry: writers specializing in it included Ring Lardner, Katharine Anne Porter, William Saroyan, James Thurber, and Eudora Welty. In drama the USA produced a powerful group of dramatists between the wars, including Eugene O'Neill, Maxwell Anderson, Lillian Hellman, Elmer Rice and Clifford Odets; and the work of

Wilder led towards the post-war work of Tennessee Williams and Arthur Miller, and the later generation which includes Paddy Chayefsky, Edward Albee, Neil Simon. Traditional poets include E A Robinson, R Frost, Elinor Wylie, E St Vincent Millay, with more experimental work being done by E L Masters, Carl Sandburg, Ezra Pound, T S Eliot and Amy Lowell, and attempts at the great American epic in Hart Crane's *The Bridge* and S V Benet's *John Brown's Body*. Among the most striking of later writers are Conrad Aiken, Archibald MacLeish, Karl Shapiro, Robinson Jeffers, Wallace Stevens, Marianne Moore, Robert Lowell, and Theodore Roethke. In the field of literary criticism Irving Babbitt, George Santayana, H L Mencken and Edmund Wilson were outstanding; more recent names include Lionel Trilling, Cleanth Brooks, Yvor Winters, and J C Ransom, author of *The New Criticism* 1941, with its stress on structural and linguistic factors.

United States of America (USA) country in N America, extending from the Atlantic to the Pacific, bounded by Canada to the N and Mexico to the S, and including the outlying states of Alaska and Hawaii.

government The USA is a federal republic comprising 50 states and the District of ◊Columbia. Under its 1787 constitution, which has had 26 amendments, the constituent states are reserved considerable powers of self-government. The federal government concentrated originally on defence, foreign affairs, and the coordination of interstate concerns, leaving legislation in other spheres to the states, each with its own constitution, elected legislature, governor, supreme court, and local taxation powers. Since the 1930s, however, the federal government has increasingly impinged upon state affairs and has become the principal revenue-raising and spending agency.

The executive branch of US federal government is deliberately separate from the legislature and judiciary. At the head of the executive branch of government is a president elected every four years in a national contest by universal adult suffrage. Votes are counted at the state level on a first-past-the-post basis, with each state being assigned seats (equivalent to the number of its congressional representatives) in a national electoral college which formally elects the president. The president serves as head of state, of the armed forces and the civil service. He or she is restricted to a maximum of two terms and, once elected, cannot be removed except through impeachment and subsequent conviction by Congress. The president works with a personally selected cabinet team, subject to the Senate's approval, whose members are debarred from serving in the legislature.

The second branch of government, Congress, the federal legislature, comprises two equally powerful houses, the 100-member Senate and the 435-member House of Representatives. Senators serve six-year terms, and there are two from each state regardless of size and population. Every two years a third of the seats come up for election. Representatives are elected from single-member constituencies of roughly equal demographic size to serve for two-year terms. Congress operates through a system of specialized standing committees. The Senate is the most powerful chamber of Congress, its approval being required for key federal appointments and for the ratification of foreign treaties. The president's policy programme needs the approval of Congress, and the president addresses Congress in Jan for an annual 'State of the Union' speech and sends periodic 'messages' and 'recommendations'. The success of a president depends on party support in Congress, bargaining skills, and public support.

Proposed legislation, to become law (an Act of Congress), requires the approval of both chambers of Congress. If differences exist, 'conference committees' are convened to effect compromise agreements. The president can impose a veto, which can be overridden only by two-thirds majorities in both congressional houses. Constitutional amendments require two-thirds majorities from both chambers of Congress and the support of three-quarters of the nation's 50 state legislatures.

The third branch of government, the judiciary, headed by the Supreme Court, interprets the written US constitution to ensure that a correct balance is maintained between federal and state institutions and the executive and legislature and to uphold the civil rights enshrined in the first ten amendments (the ◊Bill of Rights). The Supreme Court comprises nine judges appointed by the president with the Senate's approval, who serve life terms and can only be removed by impeachment. It is an unusually influential body. Two broad catch-all party coalitions, divided regionally and ideologically, dominate US politics: the Democrats and the Republicans. Since the 1930s the Democrats have been pre-eminent both at local and at congressional level. The party is dominated by its NE liberal wing, which supports social reform and government intervention, but the conservative S wing is also powerful. The Republicans have been most successful during recent decades in presidential contests. They are strongest in the central and W states and adhere, in general, to a

---

PRESIDENTS OF THE UNITED STATES OF AMERICA

Name	Party	Took Office
1. George Washington	(Federalist)	1789
2. John Adams	(Federalist)	1797
3. Thomas Jefferson	(Democratic Republican)	1801
4. James Madison	(Democratic Republican)	1809
5. James Monroe	(Democratic Republican)	1817
6. John Quincy Adams	(Democratic Republican)	1825
7. Andrew Jackson	(Democratic)	1829
8. Martin Van Buren	(Democrat)	1837
9. William Henry Harrison	(Whig)	1841
10. John Tyler	(Whig)	1841
11. James Knox Polk	(Democrat)	1845
12. Zachary Taylor	(Whig)	1849
13. Millard Fillmore	(Whig)	1850
14. Franklin Pierce	(Democrat)	1853
15. James Buchanan	(Democrat)	1857
16. Abraham Lincoln	(Republican)	1861
17. Andrew Johnson	(Democrat)	1865
18. Ulysses Simpson Grant	(Republican)	1869
19. Rutherford Birchard Hayes	(Republican)	1877
20. James Abram Garfield	(Republican)	1881
21. Chester Alan Arthur	(Republican)	1881
22. Grover Cleveland	(Democrat)	1885
23. Benjamin Harrison	(Republican)	1889
24. Grover Cleveland	(Democrat)	1893
25. William McKinley	(Republican)	1897
26. Theodore Roosevelt	(Republican)	1901
27. William Howard Taft	(Republican)	1909
28. Woodrow Wilson	(Democrat)	1913
29. Warren Gamaliel Harding	(Republican)	1921
30. Calvin Coolidge	(Republican)	1923
31. Herbert C Hoover	(Republican)	1929
32. Franklin Delano Roosevelt	(Democrat)	1933
33. Harry S Truman	(Democrat)	1945
34. Dwight D Eisenhower	(Republican)	1953
35. John F Kennedy	(Democrat)	1961
36. Lyndon B Johnson	(Democrat)	1963
37. Richard M Nixon	(Republican)	1969
38. Gerald R Ford	(Republican)	1974
39. James Earl Carter	(Democrat)	1977
40. Ronald Reagan	(Republican)	1981

United States of America
(USA)

AREA 9,500,000 sq km/3,536,855 sq mi
CAPITAL Washington DC
TOWNS New York, Los Angeles, Chicago, Philadelphia, Detroit, San Francisco–Oakland, Washington, Dallas–Fort Worth, Houston, Boston, Nassau-Suffolk, St Louis, Pittsburgh, Baltimore, Minneapolis–St Paul, Atlanta: all metropolitan areas over 2 million population
PHYSICAL includes almost every kind of topography and vegetation; mountain ranges parallel with E and W coasts, and the Rocky Mountains separate rivers debouching in the Pacific from those flowing into the Gulf of Mexico; Great Lakes in N; rivers include Hudson, Mississippi, Missouri, Colorado, Columbia
FEATURES see under individual states
TERRITORIES the commonwealths of Puerto Rico, and Northern Marianas; the federated states of Micronesia; Guam, the US Virgin Islands, American Samoa, Wake Island, Midway Islands, Marshall Islands, Belau, and Johnston and Sand Islands
HEAD OF STATE AND OF GOVERNMENT Ronald Reagan from 1981
GOVERNMENT federal democracy
CURRENCY US dollar (1.65 = £1 Sept 1987)
POPULATION (1985) 238,631,000 (the ethnic minorities include 26,500,000 black, about 20 million Hispanic, and 1 million American Indians, of whom 50% concentrated in Arizona, California, New Mexico, North Carolina, Oklahoma); annual growth rate 1%
LANGUAGE English; largest minority language Spanish
RELIGION 73 million Protestant, 50 million Roman Catholic, 6 million Jewish, 4 million Eastern Orthodox
LITERACY 99% (1985)

GNP $3,855 bn (1983); $13,451 per head of population
CHRONOLOGY
1776 Declaration of Independence.
1787 US constitution drawn up.
1789 Washington elected as first president.
1803 Louisiana Purchase.
1812–14 War of 1812 with England, arising from commercial disputes caused by Britain's struggle with Napoleon.
1819 Florida purchased from Spain.
1836 The battle of the Alamo, Texas, won by Mexico.
1841 First wagon train left Missouri with emigrants for California.
1846–48 Mexican War resulted in cession to USA of Arizona, California, Colorado (part), Nevada, New Mexico, Texas, Utah.
1846 Mormons, under Brigham Young, founded Salt Lake City in Utah.
1848 California gold rush.
1860 Lincoln elected president.
1861–65 Civil War between North and South.
1865 Slavery abolished.
1867 Alaska bought from Russia.
1890 Battle of Wounded Knee, the last major battle between American Indians and US troops.
1898 War with Spain ended with the Spanish cession of Philippines, Puerto Rico, and Guam; it was agreed that Cuba be independent.
1898 Hawaii annexed.
1917–18 USA entered World War I.
1929 Wall Street stock-market crash.
1933 F D Roosevelt's New Deal to alleviate the Depression put into force.
1941 the Japanese attack on Pearl Harbor precipitated US entry into World War II.
1950–53 US involvement in Korean war. McCarthy anti-communist investigations.
1952 Gen Eisenhower elected president.
1960 J F Kennedy elected president.
1961 Bay of Pigs abortive CIA-backed invasion of Cuba.

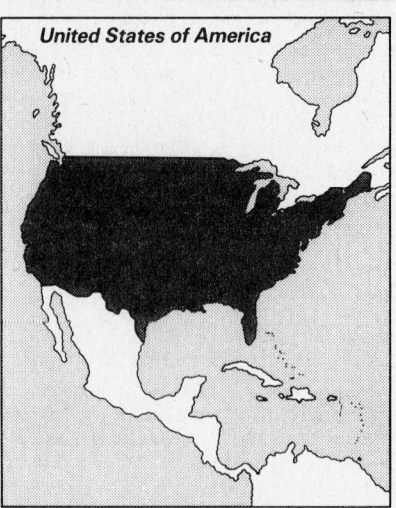
United States of America

1963 Assassination of Kennedy. Johnson assumed the presidency.
1964–68 'Great Society' civil-rights and welfare measures.
1964–73 US involvement in Vietnam War.
1968 Nixon elected president.
1973–74 Watergate scandal.
1974 Nixon resigned as president; replaced by Gerald Ford.
1975 Final US withdrawal from Vietnam.
1976 Carter elected president.
1979 US-Chinese diplomatic relations normalized.
1979–80 Iranian hostage crisis.
1980 Reagan elected president. Republicans gained Senate majority.
1983 US invasion of Grenada.
1986 Republicans lost Senate majority. Irangate scandal.
1987 INF treaty with USSR. Wall Street stock market crash.

conservative 'small government' philosophy. Both parties have only a rudimentary national organization and seldom vote as a block in Congress. Party organization is centred instead at the state and local level.

The USA administers a number of Pacific island territories, including American ◊Samoa and the American ◊Virgin Islands, which have local legislatures and a governor. These territories, as well as the 'self-governing territories' of ◊Puerto Rico and ◊Guam, each send a nonvoting delegate to the US House of Representatives.

history For early history, see ◊American Indian. Spaniards first settled in ◊Florida 1565. The first permanent English settlement was at Jamestown, Virginia, 1607. In 1620 the ◊Pilgrim Fathers landed in New England and founded Massachusetts. English Catholics founded Maryland 1634; English Quakers founded Pennsylvania 1682. A Dutch settlement (1611) on Manhattan Island, named New Amsterdam 1626, was renamed New York after it was taken

by England 1664. In the 18th century the English colonies were threatened by French expansion from the Great Lakes in Canada to Louisiana until the Seven Years' War 1756–63.

In 1775 the 13 colonies (New Hampshire, Massachusetts, Rhode Island, Connecticut, New York, New Jersey, Pennsylvania, Delaware, Virginia, North Carolina, South Carolina, Maryland, and Georgia) rose against the government in Britain, declaring themselves in 1776 to be 'free and independent states'. Led by George ◊Washington, they defeated George III's armies in the War of ◊American Independence. By the Treaty of Paris 1783 Britain recognized the independence of the 13 colonies. The constitution came into force 1789. Washington was chosen as the first president. ◊Louisiana was bought from Napoleon 1803 and Florida from Spain 1819. Napoleon's trade blockade of British ships led indirectly to the Anglo-American war 1812–14, and British troops captured and burned Washington. Later

expansion to the W reached the Pacific, and the war with Mexico 1846–48 secured the areas of California, Utah, New Mexico, and Texas. ◊Alaska was purchased from Russia 1867. ◊Hawaii ceded itself to the USA 1898.

The ◊Civil War 1861–65 put an end to slavery but left ill feeling between N and S. It stimulated the industrial development of the N, and the construction of roads and railways continued until the end of the century. The USA entered ◊World War I 1917; it was not a party to the Treaty of Versailles but made peace by separate treaties 1921. A period of isolationism followed. The country's huge economic, industrial and agricultural expansion was brought to a halt by the stock-market crash 1929 which marked the start of the ◊Depression. President ◊Roosevelt's ◊New Deal 1933 tackled but did not solve the problem and only ◊World War II brought full employment. The USA stayed out of the war until Japan attacked Pearl Harbor on ◊Honolulu in Dec 1941.

UNITED STATES OF AMERICA

State	Area sq km	Date of joining the Union	Capital	State	Area sq km	Date of joining the Union	Capital
Alabama	133,665	1819	Montgomery	Nebraska	200,036	1867	Lincoln
Alaska	1,518,539	1959	Juneau	Nevada	286,300	1864	Carson City
Arizona	295,023	1912	Phoenix	New Hampshire	24,100	1788	Concord
Arkansas	137,533	1836	Little Rock	New Jersey	20,295	1787	Trenton
California	411,013	1850	Sacramento	New Mexico	315,133	1912	Santa Fe
Colorado	270,240	1876	Denver	New York	128,400	1788	Albany
Connecticut	12,973	1788	Hartford	North Carolina	136,523	1789	Raleigh
Delaware	5,328	1787	Dover	North Dakota	183,020	1889	Bismarck
Florida	151,700	1845	Tallahassee	Ohio	106,714	1803	Columbus
Georgia	152,500	1788	Atlanta	Oklahoma	181,088	1907	Oklahoma City
Hawaii	16,705	1959	Honolulu	Oregon	251,180	1859	Salem
Idaho	216,412	1890	Boise	Pennsylvania	117,412	1787	Harrisburg
Illinois	146,075	1818	Springfield	Rhode Island	3,144	1790	Providence
Indiana	93,994	1816	Indianapolis	South Carolina	80,432	1788	Columbia
Iowa	145,790	1846	Des Moines	South Dakota	199,550	1889	Pierre
Kansas	213,063	1861	Topeka	Tennessee	109,412	1796	Nashville
Kentucky	104,623	1792	Frankfurt	Texas	692,407	1845	Austin
Louisiana	125,675	1812	Baton Rouge	Utah	219,931	1896	Salt Lake City
Maine	86,027	1820	Augusta	Vermont	24,887	1791	Montpelier
Maryland	27,394	1788	Annapolis	Virginia	105,711	1788	Richmond
Massachusetts	21,385	1788	Boston	Washington	176,615	1889	Olympia
Michigan	150,777	1837	Lansing	West Virginia	62,629	1863	Charleston
Minnesota	217,735	1858	St Paul	Wisconsin	145,438	1848	Madison
Mississippi	123,584	1817	Jackson	Wyoming	253,595	1890	Cheyenne
Missouri	180,455	1821	Jefferson City	District of Columbia	179		Washington DC
Montana	381,085	1889	Helena	Total	9,363,404		

The USA, having emerged as a superpower, remained internationalist during the postwar era. Under the presidency of Harry S ◊Truman (Democrat) a doctrine of intervention in support of endangered 'free peoples' and of containing the spread of communism was devised by Secretary of State Dean ◊Acheson. This led to the USA's safeguarding of Nationalist ◊Taiwan in 1949 and its participation in the ◊Korean War of 1950–53. The USA, in addition, created new global and regional bodies designed to maintain the peace – the ◊United Nations (UN, 1945), the ◊Organization of American States (OAS, 1948), the ◊North Atlantic Treaty Organization (NATO, 1949), the ◊South-East Asia Treaty Organization (SEATO, 1954) – and launched the ◊Marshall Plan to strengthen the economies of its allies. Domestically, President Truman sought to introduce liberal reforms designed at extending civil and welfare rights under the slogan 'a fair deal'. These measures were blocked by a combination of S Democrats and Republicans in Congress. Truman's foreign policy was criticized as being 'soft on Communism' between 1950 and 1952, as a wave of anti-Soviet hysteria, spearheaded by Senator Joseph ◊McCarthy, swept the nation.

This rightward shift in the public mood brought Republican victory in the congressional and presidential elections of 1952. The popular military commander General Dwight D ◊Eisenhower became president and was re-elected by an increased margin in Nov 1956. Working with Secretary of State John Foster ◊Dulles, Eisenhower adhered to the Truman-Acheson doctrine of 'containment', while at home he pursued a policy of 'progressive conservatism' designed to encourage business enterprise. The Eisenhower era was one of growth, prosperity, and social change, involving the migration of S blacks to the N industrial cities and a rapid expansion in the educational sector. In the S states, where racial discrimination was openly practised, a new black-rights movement developed under the leadership of Dr Martin Luther ◊King. Promising a 'New Frontier' programme of social reform, John F ◊Kennedy (Democrat) won the presidential election of Nov 1960. The new president emerged as an active opponent of Communism abroad (see ◊Cuba: Bay of Pigs). He was assassinated in Nov 1963. It was left to his deputy and successor, the Texan Lyndon B. ◊Johnson, to oversee the passage of Kennedy's 'Great Society' reforms. These measures, which included the Equal Opportunities, Voting Rights, Housing, and Medicare acts, guaranteed blacks civil rights and significantly extended the reach of the federal government. They were buttressed by the judicial rulings of the Supreme Court chaired by Chief Justice Earl Warren. Abroad, President Johnson became embroiled in the ◊Vietnam War (1964–73), which polarized US public opinion and deeply divided the Democratic Party.

Johnson declined to run for re-election in Nov 1968 and his former vice president Hubert Humphrey was defeated by the experienced Republican Richard ◊Nixon. Nixon, a conservative, sent the National Guard against student demonstrators at home. Abroad, working with National Security Adviser Henry ◊Kissinger, he began a gradual disengagement from Vietnam and launched a policy of ◊détente which brought an improvement in relations with the Soviet Union (see ◊Strategic Arms Limitation) and Communist China. Nixon, faced with a divided opposition led by the liberal George McGovern, gained re-election by an overwhelming margin in Nov 1972. During the campaign, Nixon's staff broke into the Democratic Party's ◊Watergate headquarters. When this and the attempts at cover-up came to light, the scandal forced the resignation of the president in Aug 1974.

Watergate shook the US public's confidence in the Washington establishment. Gerald ◊Ford, who had been vice president only since Dec 1973, kept the services of Kissinger and the policy of détente when he succeeded Nixon. He faced, however, a hostile, Democrat-dominated Congress which introduced legislation curbing the powers of the presidency and forcing isolationism abroad. He also had to deal with an economic recession and increased oil prices.

Ford contested the presidential election of Nov 1976, but was defeated by the 'born again' Christian and outsider in Washington Jimmy ◊Carter, who promised open and honest government. Carter was a fiscal conservative but social liberal, who sought to extend welfare provision through greater administrative efficiency. He substantially ended the fuel crisis through enforced conservation in the energy bills of 1978 and 1980. In foreign relations President Carter emphasized human rights. In the Middle East, he moved close to a peace settlement in 1978–79 (see ◊Camp David Agreements) and in Jan 1979 the USA's diplomatic relations with Communist China were fully normalized.

The Carter presidency was brought down by two foreign-policy crises 1979–80: the fall of the shah of ◊Iran and the Soviet invasion of ◊Afghanistan. The president's vacillating leadership style, defence economies, and moralistic foreign policy were blamed for weakening US influence abroad. There was a swell of anti-Communist feeling and mounting support for a new policy of rearmament and selective interventionism. President Carter responded to this new mood by enunciating the hawkish ◊Carter Doctrine 1980 and supporting a new arms-development programme, but his popularity plunged during 1980 as economic recession gripped the country and US embassy staff were held hostage by Shi'ite fundamentalists in Tehran.

The Republican Ronald ◊Reagan benefited from Carter's difficulties and was elected in Nov 1980, when the Democrats also lost control of the Senate. The new president had risen to prominence as an effective, television-skilled campaigner. He believed in a return to traditional Christian and family values and propounded a domestic policy of decentralization and deregulation. The early years of the Reagan presidency witnessed substantial reductions in taxation and cutbacks in federal welfare programmes that created serious hardship as economic recession gripped the nation.

Reagan rejected détente and spoke of the USSR as an 'evil empire' which needed to be checked by a military build-up and a readiness to employ force. This led to a sharp deterioration in Soviet-US relations, ushering in a new cold war during the Polish crisis of 1981. Reagan's popularity was restored by the autumn of 1983 with the successful invasion of ◊Grenada in Oct and the recovery of the economy. He was re-elected on a wave of optimistic patriotism in Nov 1984, defeating the Democrat ticket of Walter ◊Mondale and Geraldine ◊Ferraro by a record margin. A radical tax-cutting bill was passed through Congress, and in 1986 a huge budget and trade deficit developed. Overseas the president faced mounting public opposition to his intervention in Central America. The new Soviet leader Mikhail Gorbachev pressed unsuccessfully for arms reduction during superpower summits at Geneva (Nov 1985) and Reykjavik (Oct 1986), but a further summit Dec 1987, with an agreement to scrap intermediate-range nuclear missiles, appeared to promise a new détente.

In Nov 1986 the Republican party lost control of the Senate in the midterm elections, just before the disclosure of a scandal concerning US arms sales to Iran in return for hostages, with the profits illegally diverted to help the Nicaraguan Contra (anticommunist) guerrillas.

United World Colleges international educational movement for students aged 16–18 (admission by scholarship); it was the inspiration of German educationalist Kurt ◊Hahn. Its curriculum demands both academic achievement and service to the community. It consists of six colleges worldwide.

universal in philosophy, a property which is instantiated by all the individual things of a specific class: for example, all red things instantiate 'redness'. Many philosophical debates have centred on the status of universals, including the medieval debate between ◊nominalism and ◊realism.

universal joint a flexible coupling used to join rotating shafts, for example, the propeller shaft in a car. In a typical universal joint the ends of the shafts to be joined end in U-shaped yokes. They dovetail into each other and pivot flexibly about an X-shaped spider. This construction allows side-to-side and up-and-down movement, while still transmitting rotary motion.

Universal Postal Union an agency of the ◊United Nations.

universal time (UT) another name for ◊Greenwich Mean Time, the time reference used throughout the world. It is based on the rotation of the earth, which is not quite constant. Since 1972, UT has been replaced by *coordinated universal time* (UTC), which is based on the uniform atomic time; see ◊time.

universe all of space and its contents. The universe is mostly empty space, dotted with ◊galaxies for as far as telescopes can see. The most distant detected galaxies and ◊quasars lie 10,000 million light years or more away. The universe is thought to be between 10,000 million and 20,000 million years old, and to have originated in an immense explosion called the ◊Big Bang (see also ◊cosmology). The universe is expanding, with the galaxies moving apart from each other (as revealed by the ◊red shift in their light) and the space between them getting larger. The speed of recession of the galaxies (◊Hubble's constant) increases in proportion with their distance apart, an effect known as *Hubble's law* after Edwin ◊Hubble who discovered it. See also ◊solar system.

university a community or corporation of men and women devoted to higher learning. The first European university was Salerno, established in the 9th century, followed by Bologna, Paris, Oxford, and Cambridge in the 12th century. St Andrew's, the first Scottish university, was founded in 1411, and Trinity College, Dublin, in 1591. In the UK, a number of universities were founded in the 19th and earlier 20th centuries (London 1836, Manchester 1851, Wales 1893, Liverpool 1903, Bristol 1909, and Reading 1926). These became known as the 'red brick' universities, as opposed to the ancient stone of Oxford and Cambridge, often popularly referred to as ◊'Oxbridge'. After World War II many more universities were founded in the provinces (Nottingham 1948, Exeter 1955, and Sussex 1961), and were nicknamed, from their ultra-modern buildings, the 'plate-glass' universities.

There are now 45 universities in the UK which are funded directly by the government through the University Grants Committee. The USA has both state universities (funded by the individual states) and private universities. The oldest universities in the USA are all private: Harvard 1636, William and Mary 1693, Yale 1701, Pennsylvania 1741, and Princeton 1746. Recent innovations include universities serving international areas, for example, the Middle East Technical University 1961 at Ankara, supported by the United Nations; the United Nations university in Tokyo 1974; and the British ◊Open University 1969. The Open University has been widely copied, for example the National University Consortium (NUC) set up in the USA in 1980.

UNIVERSITIES IN THE UNITED KINGDOM

Name	Date founded	No of students
Aberdeen	1495	5,656
Aston	1966	3,949
Bath	1966	3,666
Belfast	1908	7,169
Birmingham	1900	9,016
Bradford	1966	4,170
Bristol	1966	7,188
Brunel	1966	2,897
Buckingham	1983	662
Cambridge	13th cent.	9,806
City	1966	3,164
Dundee	1967	3,796
Durham	1832	5,105
East Anglia	1963	4,364
Edinburgh	1583	10,091
Essex	1964	2,980
Exeter	1955	5,035
Glasgow	1451	10,481
Heriot-Watt	1966	3,811
Hull	1954	4,750
Keele	1962	2,401
Kent	1965	4,198
Lancaster	1964	4,589
Leeds	1904	10,292
Leicester	1957	4,851
Liverpool	1903	7,595
London	1836	50,155
Loughborough	1966	5,800
Manchester	1851	11,123
Newcastle upon Tyne	1852	7,776
Nottingham	1948	7,000
Open University	1969	149,500
Oxford	12th cent.	9,730
Reading	1926	5,879
Salford	1967	3,760
Sheffield	1905	7,968
Southampton	1952	6,437
St Andrews	1411	3,811
Stirling	1967	2,900
Strathclyde	1964	7,546
Surrey	1966	3,375
Sussex	1961	4,558
Ulster	1984	7,613
Wales	1893	21,297
Warwick	1965	5,880
York	1963	3,417

Unix an ◊operating system designed for minicomputers but becoming increasingly popular on the large microcomputers. Developed by Bell Laboratories in the late 1960s, it is now widely used in universities and is closely related to the programming language C.

unknown warrior name given to a fallen soldier who was taken as representative of all those killed in World War I, and was given a national funeral. The British unknown warrior or soldier was buried in Westminster Abbey in 1920. France, Belgium, USA, and other countries each have their unknown warriors.

unnilennium a synthetically made element, symbol Une, atomic number 109. It was first synthesized in 1974.

unnilhexium a synthetically made element, symbol Unh, atomic number 106. It was first synthesized in 1974.

unniloctium a synthetically made element, symbol Uno, atomic number 108. It was first synthesized in 1981.

unnilpentium a synthetically made element, symbol Unp, also known as hahnium and nielsbohrium. Symbol Ha/Ns. Atomic number 105. Credit for its discovery is disputed between USA (who named it *hahnium*) and USSR (who named it *nielsbohrium*).

unnilquadium a synthetically made element, symbol Unq, atomic number 104. Also named *kurchictovium* and *rutherfordium* by teams in the USSR and the USA respectively.

unnilseptium a synthetically made element, symbol Uns, atomic number 107. It was first synthesized in 1976.

untouchable former name for the lowest Indian ◊caste.

Unwin /'ʌnwɪn/ Raymond 1863–1940. English town planner, who put the Garden City ideals of Sir Ebenezer Howard into practice, overseeing Letchworth (begun 1903), Hampstead Garden Suburb (begun 1907) and Wythenshawe outside Manchester (begun 1927).

Upanishad one of a collection of Hindu sacred treatises, written in Sanskrit, connected with the ◊Vedas but composed later, about 800–200 BC. Metaphysical and ethical, they exposed a monistic, pantheistic doctrine equating the atman (self) with the Brahman (supreme spirit): *'Tat tvam asi (Thou art that)'*, and developed the theory of the transmigration of souls.

upas tree SE Asian tree *Antiaris toxicaria*, family Moraceae, with a poisonous latex used for arrows, and formerly reputed to kill all who fell asleep under it.

Updike /'ʌpdaɪk/ John (Hoyer) 1932– . American author, born in Pennsylvania. He was educated at Harvard and was associated with the *New Yorker* magazine from 1955, and soon established a reputation for polished prose, poetry, and criticism. His novels include *Couples* 1968 and *Roger's Version* 1986 and largely deal with contemporary American middle-class life. Two characters recur in his work: the basketball player 'Rabbit' Angstrom (introduced in *Rabbit, Run* 1960) and the novelist Henry Bech.

Upper Volta /'vɒltə/ former name (until 1984) of ◊Burkina Faso.

Uppsala /ʊp'saːlə/ city in Sweden, NW of Stockholm, with a university 1477 and a 13th-century cathedral long used in the crowning of the monarchs of Sweden; population (1984) 152,500. The botanist Linnaeus lived at Uppsala.

Ur an ancient city of the Sumerian civilization, S of the river Euphrates, in modern ◊Iraq. Excavations by Sir Leonard ◊Woolley show that it was inhabited 3,500 BC. The chief ruin is a ziggurat or temple tower.

uraemia condition due to the retention in the blood of substances usually eliminated by the kidneys.

Ural Mountains /'jʊərəl/ mountain system running from the Arctic to the Caspian Sea and separating Europe from Asia. The highest peak is Naradnaya 2,799 m/6,182. The middle Urals is one of the most important industrial regions of the USSR, owing to its vast mineral wealth. Perm, Chelyabinsk, Sverdlovsk, Magnitogorsk, and Zlatoust are important industrial centres.

Urania in Greek mythology, the ◊muse of astronomy.

uranium a metallic element, symbol U, atomic number 92, atomic weight 338.07. It was discovered by Klaproth in 1789 in pitchblende, and first prepared by Peligot in 1842. It is a lustrous white metal, malleable and ductile, tarnishing in air. The chief ore is uranite (pitchblende U_3O_8), and recent technological advances have made possible its extraction from lowgrade ores. Many countries mine uranium; large deposits are found in Canada, the USA, Australia and South Africa. Small amounts of its compounds are used in the ceramics industry to give yellow glazes, and as a mordant in dyeing.

Uranus /ju'reɪnəs/ in astronomy, the seventh planet from the Sun, discovered by William ◊Herschel in 1781. Uranus has a diameter of 51,000 km/31,700 mi and a mass 14.5 times that of Earth. It orbits the Sun every 84 years at an average distance of 2,870 million km/1,783 million mi. Uranus is thought to have a large rocky core overlain by ice, with a deep atmosphere mostly of hydrogen and helium, plus traces of methane which give the planet a greenish tinge. The spin axis of Uranus is tilted at 98°, so that at times its poles point towards the Sun, giving extreme seasons. In 1977 astronomers discovered that Uranus has thin rings around its equator. In 1986 the Voyager 2 space probe reached Uranus, detecting 11 rings in all, and finding ten small moons in addition to the five visible from Earth. The largest moon, Titania, has a diameter of 1,610 km/1,000 mi. The rings are charcoal black, and are probably debris of former 'moonlets' that have broken up. Uranus has a peculiar ◊magnetic field, whose axis is tilted at 60° to its axis of spin, and is displaced about one-third of the way from the planet's centre to its surface. Observations of the magnetic field show that the solid body of the planet rotates every 17.3 hours. The rotation rate of the atmosphere varies with latitude, from about 16 hours in mid-southern latitudes to longer than 17 hours at the equator.

Uranus /ju'reɪnəs/ in Greek mythology, the sky-god. He was responsible both for the sun and rain, and was the son and husband of ◊Gaia the goddess of the earth, by whom he fathered the ◊Titans.

Urban II /'ɜːbən/ c. 1042–1099. Pope 1088–99. He launched the first Crusade at the Council of Clermont in France in 1095.

urbanization the process by which the proportion of a population living in or around towns and cities increases through migration. The growth of urban concentrations is a relatively recent phenomenon, dating back only about 150 years, although the world's first cities date back more than 5,000 years. Urbanization has had a major effect on the social structures of industrial societies, affecting not only where people live but how they live, and urban sociology has emerged as a distinct area of study.

urban legend a largely new mode of folklore thriving in big cities, particularly in the USA, in the mid-20th century, and passed along, largely orally, and always at second or later hand. Some of the material – hitchhikers that turn out to be ghosts, spiders breeding in elaborate hairstyles – is pre-industrial in origin, but transformed to fit new circumstances; others, notably the pet or baby in the microwave oven, are of their essence entirely new. Such urban legends reflect genuine dreads and preoccupations, which is why they are often racist, for example the contents of the fridge in ethnic restaurants, and why sooner or later some of them are enacted in real life.

Urdu language a member of the Indo-Iranian branch of the Indo-European language family, related to Hindi but written not in Devanagari but in Arabic script. Strongly influenced by Persian and Arabic, Urdu is the official language of Pakistan and a language used by Muslims in India.

urea waste product formed when nitrogen compounds are broken down by mammals. It is excreted in the urine. When purified, it is a white, crystalline solid. It is used in industry to make urea-formaldehyde plastics (or resins), pharmaceuticals and fertilizers.

Urey /'jʊəri/ Harold Clayton 1893–1981. American chemist. In 1932 he isolated heavy water and discovered ◊deuterium, receiving a Nobel prize in 1934. He was director of the War Research Atomic Bomb Project, Columbia, 1940–45. His books include studies of nuclear and atomic structure, and the origin of the planet and of life.

Urga /'ɜːgə/ former name (until 1924) of ◊Ulaan Baataar, the capital of Mongolia.

uric acid a nitrogen-containing waste substance, formed from the breakdown of food and body protein. It is a normal constituent of urine in reptiles and birds, but not in most mammals. Humans and other primates do produce some uric acid, in place of urea, the normal nitrogen-waste product. If formed in excess and not excreted it is deposited in sharp crystals in the joints and other tissues, causing gout; or it may form stones in the kidneys or bladder (calculi).

urim and thummim two mysterious objects in the breastplate of the High Priests of the ancient Hebrews, whereby they exercised divination.

urinary system the system of organs which removes nitrogeneous excretory products and excess water from the bodies of animals. In mammals, it consists of a pair of ◊kidneys, ureters which drain the kidneys and a ◊bladder, which stores urine before its discharge through the urethra.

urine an amber-coloured fluid made by the kidneys from the blood. It contains excess water, salts, protein, waste products, a pigment and

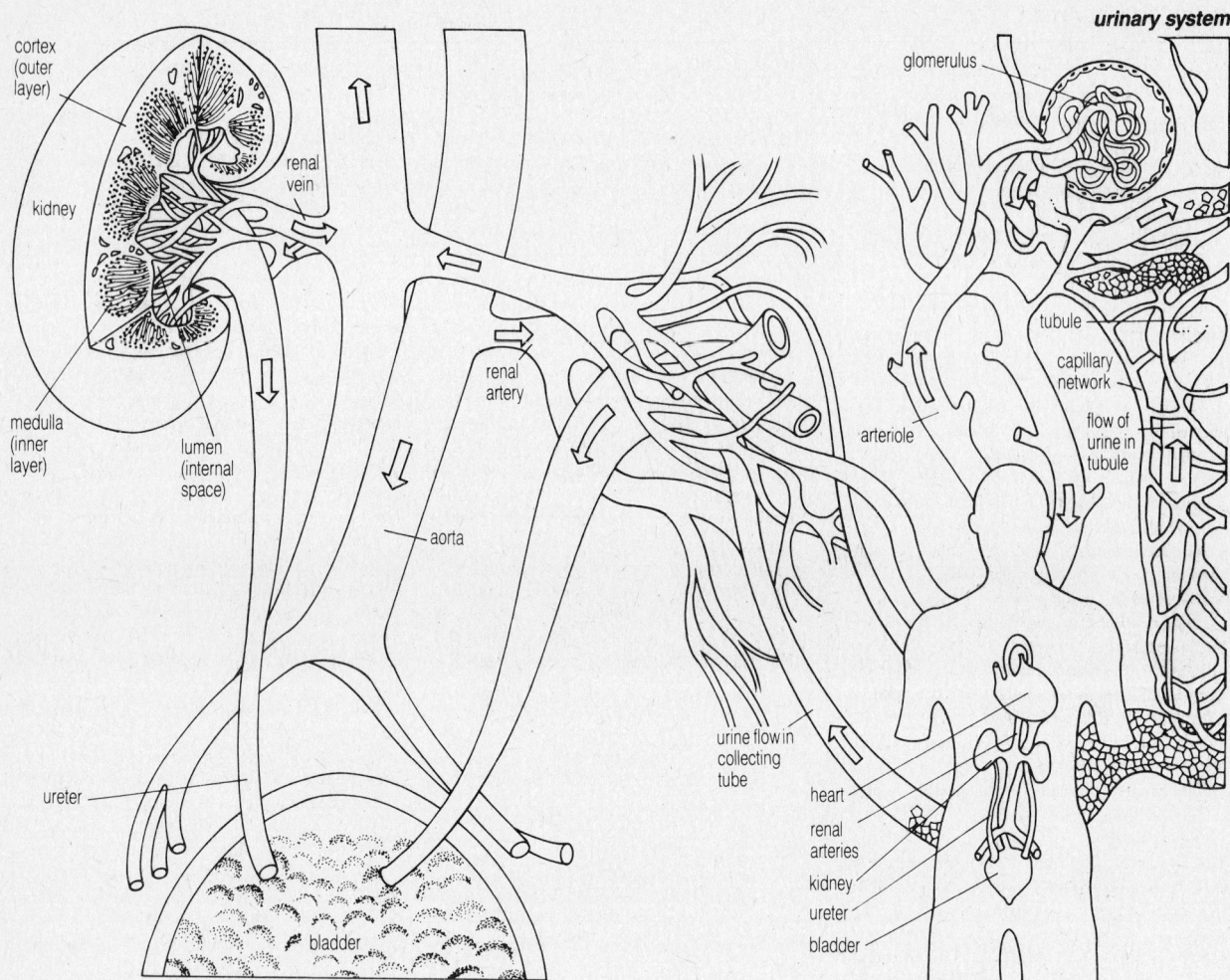

urinary system

cortex (outer layer)

renal vein

kidney

medulla (inner layer)

lumen (internal space)

renal artery

aorta

ureter

bladder

glomerulus

tubule

capillary network

flow of urine in tubule

arteriole

urine flow in collecting tube

heart
renal arteries
kidney
ureter
bladder

some acid. The kidneys pass it through two fine tubes (ureters) to the bladder, which may act as a reservoir for up to 0.7 litre/1.2 pt at a time. It then passes into the urethra, which opens to the outside by a sphincter (constricting muscle) under voluntary control.

Ursa Major ▷constellation of the great bear, the third-largest constellation in the sky, in the north polar region. Its seven brightest stars make up the familiar shape of the *big dipper* or *plough*. The second star of the handle of the dipper, called Mizar, has a companion star, Alcor. Two stars in the bowl of the dipper act as pointers to the north pole star, ▷Polaris.

Ursa Minor constellation of the little bear containing the north pole star, ▷Polaris. It is shaped like a little dipper, with the pole star at the end of the dipper's handle.

Ursula, St /'ɜːsjʊlə/ English legendary saint, supposed to have been martyred with 11 virgins (misread as 11,000 in the Middle Ages), by the Huns in the Rhineland, in the 4th century.

Ursuline a Roman Catholic religious order, founded at Brescia, by St Angela Merici in 1537; it is renowned for its educational work among girls.

urticaria nettle-rash: an irritant skin condition characterized by the spontaneous appearance of weals. Treatment is usually by soothing lotions and, in severe cases, by antihistamines or steroids. Its causes are varied, and may include ▷allergy or ▷stress.

Uruguay /'juərəgwaɪ/ country in S America, on the Atlantic, bounded N by Brazil and W by Argentina.

government The 1966 constitution provides for a president who is head of state and head of government, elected by universal suffrage for a five-year term, and a two-chamber legislature, comprising a senate and a federal chamber of deputies. The president is assisted by a vice president and presides over a council of ministers. The Senate has up to 30 members and the Chamber of Deputies 99, all elected for a five-year term by universal suffrage through system of proportional representation. The voting system ensures that there are at least two deputies representing each of the republic's 19 departments.

history For early history, see ▷American Indian. The area that is now Uruguay was settled by both Spain 1624 and Portugal 1680, but Spain secured the whole in the 18th century. In 1814 Spanish rule was overthrown under the leadership of José

Artigas, dictator until driven out by Brazil 1820. Disputed between Argentina and Brazil 1825–28, Uruguay was declared independent 1828, although not recognized by its neighbours until 1853.

The names of Uruguay's two main political parties, the liberal Colorado (the Reds) and the conservative Blanco (the Whites), are derived from the colours of the flags carried in the civil war of 1836. Between 1951 and 1966 there was a collective leadership called 'collegiate government' and then a new constitution was adopted and a single president elected, the Blanco candidate, Jorge Pacheco Areco. His presidency was marked by high inflation, labour unrest and growing guerrilla activity by left-wing sugar workers, the ▷Tupamaros.

In 1972 Pacheco was replaced by the Colorado candidate, Juan Maria Bordaberry Arocena. Within a year the Tupamaros had been crushed and all other left-wing groups banned. Bordaberry now headed a repressive regime, under which the normal democratic institutions had been dissolved. When, in 1976, he refused any movement towards constitutional government, he was deposed by the army and Dr Aparicio Méndez Manfredini was made

Uruguay

ORIENTAL REPUBLIC OF (*República Oriental del Uruguay*)

AREA 196,945 sq km/72,180 sq mi
CAPITAL Montevideo
PHYSICAL grassy plains (pampas)
FEATURES smallest of the South American republics; rivers Negro and Uruguay
HEAD OF STATE AND OF GOVERNMENT Julio María Sanguinetti Cairolo from 1985
GOVERNMENT parliamentary democracy
EXPORTS meat and meat products; leather, wool; textiles
CURRENCY nuevo peso (403.47 = £1 Sept 1987)
POPULATION (1985) 2,936,000 (mainly of Spanish and Italian descent, also mestizo, mulatto, and black); annual growth rate 0.7%
LANGUAGE Spanish
RELIGION Roman Catholic 60%
LITERACY 95% male/95% female (1980 est)
GNP $7.3 bn (1983); $1,665 per head of population
CHRONOLOGY
1956 The Blanco party in power, with Jorge Pacheco Areco as president.
1972 The Colorado Party returned, with Juan Maria Bordaberry Arocena as president.
1976 Bordaberry deposed by the army and Dr Méndez Manfredini became president.
1984 Violent anti-government protests after ten years of repressive rule.

Uruguay

1985 Agreement reached between the army and political leaders for a return to constitutional government. Colorado Party narrowly won the general election and Dr Julio Maria Sanguinetti became president.
1986 A government of national accord established under President Sanguinetti's leadership.

president. Despite promises to return to democratic government, the severe repression continued and political opponents were imprisoned.

In 1981 the deteriorating economy made the army anxious to return to constitutional government and a retired general, Gregorio Alvarez Armellino, was appointed president for an interim period. Discussions between the army and the main political parties failed to agree on the form of constitution to be adopted and civil unrest, in the shape of strikes and demonstrations, grew. By 1984 anti-government activity had reached a crisis point and eventually all the main political leaders signed an agreement for a 'Programme of National Accord'. The 1966 constitution, with some modifications, was restored and in 1985 a general election was held. The Colorado Party won a narrow majority and its leader, Dr Julio Maria Sanguinetti, became president. The army stepped down and by 1986 President Sanguinetti was presiding over a government of national accord in which all the main parties – Colorado, Blanco, and the left-wing Broad Front – were represented.

Urumchi former name for the city of ◊Urumqi, China.

Urumqi /ʊˈruːmtʃiː/ (formerly Urumchi) industrial city (cotton textiles, cement, chemicals, iron, steel), capital of Xinjiang Uygur autonomous region, China, at the N foot of the Tyan Shan mountains; population (1975) 677,000.

user interface in computing, the parts of a program with which users come into contact, by means of which they control the program; information is passed in both directions. For example, in some programs a menu may be displayed on the screen and the user is asked to choose an option, which then instructs the computer to continue its task in only one of several ways. The study of human–computer interaction from the point of view of easier and more effective use of the machine and greater human satisfaction is the subject of a sub-branch of ergonomics, which has become a focus for many national and international research programmes.

Ushant /ˈʌʃənt/ French island 18 km/11 mi W of Brittany, off which the British admiral ◊Howe defeated the French in 1794 on 'the Glorious First of June'.

Usher /ˈʌʃə/ James 1581–1656. Irish priest, Archbishop of Armagh from 1625. He was responsible for the dating of creation as the year 4004 BC, a figure which was inserted in the margin of the Authorized Version of the Bible until the 19th century.

Ushuaia /uːˈswaɪə/ southernmost town in the world, at the tip of Tierra del Fuego, Argentina, less than 1,000 km from Antarctica. It is a free port and naval base.

Üsküb /ˈʊskuːb/ Turkish name of ◊Skopje, city in Yugoslavia.

Üsküdar /ˌʊskuːˈdɑː/ suburb of Istanbul,

Turkey; formerly a separate town, which became well known under the form *Scutari* as the site of the hospital set up by Florence Nightingale in the Crimean War.

Ussher alternative spelling of James ◊Usher.

USSR abbreviated form for the ◊Union of Soviet Socialist Republics.

Ussuri /ʊˈsʊəri/ river in E Asia, tributary of the Amur. Rising N of Vladivostok and joining the Amur S of Khabarovsk, it forms part of the border between the Chinese province of Heilongjiang and the USSR. There were military clashes 1968–69 over the sovereignty of Damansky Island (Chenpao) in mid-river.

Ustinov /ˈjuːstɪnɒf/ Peter 1921– . British actor-dramatist. Born in London, he has ventured into almost every aspect of film and theatre. His plays include *House of Regrets* 1942 and *The Love of Four Colonels* 1951, in which latter he appeared, and he was author, director, producer and principal actor in the film *Private Angelo* 1949. Recent films include *Death on the Nile* 1978 and *Evil under the Sun* 1981. He has done extensive work for ◊UNICEF. He published his autobiography *Dear Me* in 1983.

Ust-Kamenogorsk /ˈʊst kəˌmenəˈɡɔːsk/ chief centre of the nuclear industry in the USSR, situated in the Altai mountains; population (1985) 307,000.

Utagawa /ˌuːtəˈɡɑːwə/ Kuniyoshi 1798–1861. Japanese artist of the *ukiyo-e* ('floating world') school of painting and print designing, and member of a prominent family of Japanese artists. He produced some 8,000–10,000 prints of historical and legendary figures, and was in trouble for lampooning the government. He is noted for his studies of cats.

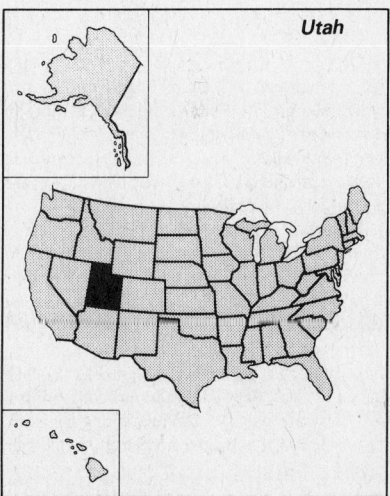

Utah

Utah /ˈjuːtɔː/ mountain state of the USA; nicknamed Beehive State
area 219,931 sq km/84,915 sq mi
capital Salt Lake City
features Great Salt Lake; Great American Desert; Colorado rivers system; Dinosaur National Monument; Rainbow Bridge
products wool; gold, silver, uranium, coal, salt; steel

population (1980) 1,461,037

famous people Brigham Young, religious leader

history part of the area ceded by Mexico in 1848, it was developed by the Mormons, still the largest religious sect in the state. Organized as a territory in 1850, it was not admitted to statehood until 1896 because of Mormon reluctance to relinquish plural marriage.

Utamaro /ˌuːtəˈmɑːrəʊ/ Kitagawa 1753–1806. Japanese artist, famed for his muted colour prints of prostitutes.

UTC abbreviation for Coordinated Universal Time, the standard measurement of ◊time.

uterus a hollow muscular organ of female mammals, lying between the bladder and rectum, and connected to the Fallopian tubes and vagina. In humans and other higher primates it is a single structure but in other mammals is paired. The embryo develops within the uterus and is attached to it via the ◊placenta and ◊umbilical cord after ◊implantation. The lining of the uterus changes during the ◊menstrual cycle, associated with egg production in the ovaries. The outer wall of the uterus is composed of smooth muscle, capable of powerful contractions, induced by ◊hormones, during childbirth.

Utica /ˈjuːtɪkə/ industrial city (textiles, firearms) in New York State, USA; population (1980) 75,500. The first Woolworth store was opened here 1879.

utilitarianism a philosophical theory of ◊ethics outlined by the philosopher Jeremy ◊Bentham, and developed by J S ◊Mill. According to utilitarianism, an action is morally right if it has consequences which lead to happiness, and wrong if it brings about the reverse of happiness. Thus, society should aim for the greatest happiness of the greatest number. Its chief opponents were F H ◊Bradley and T H ◊Green.

Utopia (Greek 'no place') Thomas More's ideal commonwealth in his book *Utopia* 1516, which has given its name to any ideal state in literature. Other similar inventions include ◊Plato's *Republic*, Bacon's *New Atlantis* 1626, and ◊Campanella's *City of the Sun*. Utopias are a common subject in ◊science fiction.

Utrecht /ˈjuːtrekt/ industrial city (metallurgy, textiles), capital of Utrecht province in central Netherlands, on the Kromme Rijn (crooked Rhine) 35 km/22 mi SE of Amsterdam; has a Gothic cathedral; university 1636; population (1985) 230,000.

Utrecht, Treaty of treaty signed 1713 which ended the War of ◊Spanish Succession. Philip V was recognized as the legitimate king of Spain, thus founding the Spanish branch of the Bourbon

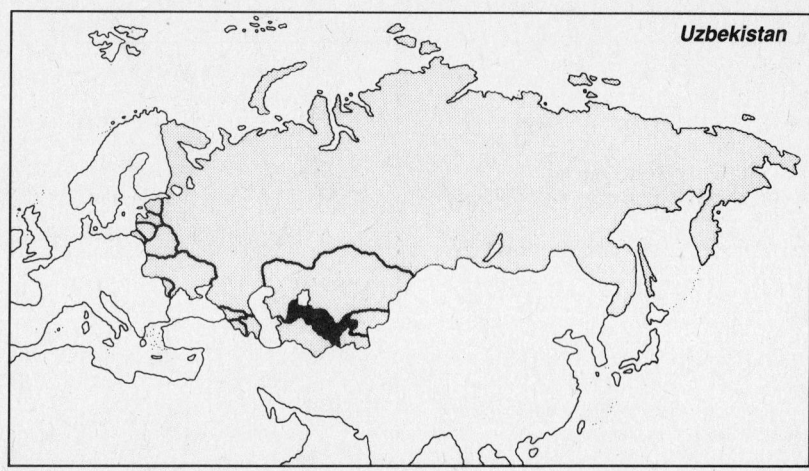

Uzbekistan

dynasty; the Spanish Netherlands, Milan, and Naples were ceded to Austria; Britain gained Gibraltar; the duchy of Savoy was granted Sicily.

Utrecht, Union of /ˈjuːtrekt/ in 1579, the union of seven provinces of the Northern Netherlands; Holland, Zeeland, Friesland, Groningen, Utrecht, Gelderland, and Overijssel, which became the basis of opposition to the Spanish crown and the foundation of the modern Dutch state.

Utrillo /juːˈtrɪləʊ/ Maurice 1883–1955. French artist. Son of Suzanne Valadan, a trapeze-performer who was encouraged to become an artist herself after posing as a model for ◊Renoir, ◊Degas, and ◊Toulouse-Lautrec. He is most celebrated for his townscapes of his native Paris, especially Montmartre.

Uttar Pradesh /ˈʊtə prəˈdeʃ/ state of N India

area 294,413 sq km/113,643 sq mi

capital Lucknow

towns Varanasi

features most populous state; Himalayan peak Nanda Devi 7,817 m/25,645 ft

population (1981) 110,862,000

famous people Indira Gandhi, Ravi Shankar

language Hindi

religion Hindu 80 per cent, Muslim 15 per cent

history formerly the heart of the Mogul Empire, and generating point of the ◊Indian Mutiny of 1857 and subsequent opposition to British rule; see also the ◊United Provinces of ◊Agra and ◊Oudh.

Uzbekistan /ˌuzbekɪˈstɑːn/ republic of the SE USSR, part of Soviet Central Asia

area 447,600 sq km/157,400 sq mi

capital Tashkent

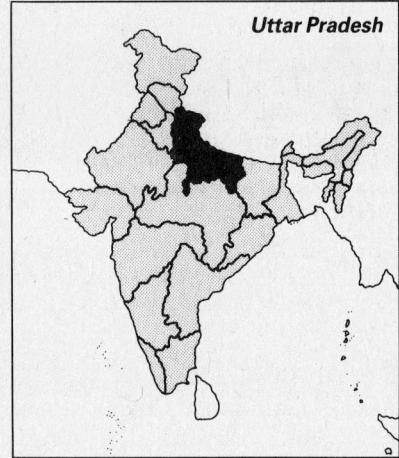

Uttar Pradesh

features oases in the deserts; rivers Amu Darya and Syr Darya; Fergana Valley

products rice, dried fruit, vines, grown by irrigation; cotton, silk

towns Samarkand

population (1985) 17,989,000; Uzbek 69 per cent, Russian 11 per cent

language Uzbek, related to Turkish

religion traditionally Sunni Muslim

recent history part of Turkestan, it was conquered by Russia 1865–76. The Tashkent soviet gradually extended its power 1917–24 and Uzbekistan became a constituent republic of the USSR 1925.

V 22nd letter of the alphabet. It was not differentiated from U until about the 16th century. In sound it is the voiced labiodental fricative. In the Roman notation V equals 5.

V1, V2 the designation of Hitler's revenge (*Vergeltungswaffe*) weapons of World War II, launched against Britain in 1944 and 1945. The V1, also called the doodle-bug and buzz bomb, was a flying bomb powered by a simple kind of ◊jet engine called a pulse jet. The V2, a rocket bomb, was the first long-range ballistic missile. It was a formidable weapon against which there was no defence. Some 14 m/47 ft long it carried a near 1-tonne warhead and dropped onto its target at a speed of some 5000 kph/3000 mph.

Vaal /vɑːl/ river in South Africa, the chief tributary of the Orange. It rises in the Drakensberg and for much of its course of 1,200 km/750 mi it separates Transvaal from Orange Free State.

vaccine modified preparation of viruses, or bacteria, which is introduced into the body either orally or by a hypodermic syringe to induce the general reaction which produces ◊immunity. Edward Jenner in 1796 first successfully inoculated a child with cowpox virus to produce immunity to smallpox.

vacuole in biology, a fluid-filled, membrane-bound cavity inside a ◊cell. It may be a reservoir for fluids that the cell will secrete to the outside, or filled with excretory products or essential nutrients that the cell needs to store. In ◊amoebae, vacuoles are formed around food particles. Plant cells usually have a large central vacuole for storage.

vacuum in general, a region completely empty of matter (which it is very difficult to achieve); in physics, any enclosure in which the gas pressure is considerably less than atmospheric pressure (101,325 ◊pascals).

vacuum cleaner cleaning device invented in 1901 by Scotsman Hubert Cecil Booth 1871–1955. Having seen an ineffective dust-blowing machine, he reversed the process so that his machine (originally on wheels, and operated from the street by means of tubes running into the house) operated by suction.

vacuum flask a container for keeping liquids either hot or cold, often called a Thermos flask. It was invented by James ◊Dewar in about 1892 to store liquefied gases.

Vadodara /wə'dəʊdərə/ (Baroda until 1976) industrial city and rail junction in Gujarat, India; population (1981) 744,881.

Vaduz /fæ'dʊts/ capital of the European principality Liechtenstein; population (1984) 5,000.

Valdai Hills /væl'daɪ/ small forested plateau between Leningrad and Moscow, where the Volga and W Dvina rivers rise. The Viking founders of the Russian state used it as a river route centre to reach the Baltic, Black, Caspian, and White seas. From the 15th century it was dominated by Moscow.

Valdivia /væl'diːviə/ industrial port and resort in Chile; population (1983) 115,500. It was founded 1552 by the Spanish conquistador Pedro de Valdivia (about 1500–54), conqueror of Chile.

Valence /væ'lɒns/ town and river port on the Rhône, France, capital of Drôme *département*; population (1982) 106,000. It is of pre-Roman origin, and has a Romanesque cathedral consecrated 1095.

Valencia /və'lensiə/ industrial city (textiles, leather, sugar) and agricultural centre in Venezuela, founded 1555, 478 m/1,568 ft above sea level, population (1980) 368,000.

Valencia /və'lensiə/ industrial city in Valencia region, Spain; university 1500; population (1981) 751,735. Ruled by El ◊Cid 1094–99, after he recaptured it from the Moors. There is a fine cathedral of the 13th–15th centuries.

Valenciennes /ˌvælɒnsi'en/ industrial town in NE France, near the Belgian border, once known for its lace; population (1982) 349,500. It became French in 1678.

valency the measure of an element's ability to combine with other elements, expressed as the number of atoms of hydrogen (or any other standard univalent element) capable of uniting with (or replacing) its atoms. The elements are described as uni-, di-, tri-, and tetravalent when they unite with 1, 2, 3, and 4 univalent atoms

respectively. Some elements have *variable valency*, for example nitrogen and phosphorus, both 3 and 5. The valency of oxygen is two; hence the formula for water, H_2O (hydrogen being univalent).

Valentine, St /'væləntaɪn/ died 270. Traditionally, a bishop of Terni martyred at Rome, now omitted from the calendar of saints' days as probably non-existent. His festival was on 14 Feb, but the custom of sending 'valentines' to a loved one on that day seems to have arisen because the day accidentally coincided with the Roman mid-February festival of ◊Lupercalia.

Valentino /ˌvælən'tiːnəʊ/ Rudolf 1895–1926. Italian film actor, the archetypal romantic lover of the Hollywood silent movies. His films include *The Four Horsemen of the Apocalypse* 1921, *The Sheik* 1922, and *Blood and Sand* 1922.

Valera Éamon de Irish politician. See ◊de Valera.

valerian genus of perennial plants found in the temperate northern hemisphere. The root of common valerian *Valeriana officinalis* is used medicinally as a carminative and sedative.

Valéry /ˌvæleə'riː/ Paul 1871–1945. French poet, author of philosophical verse, for example *La Jeune Parque/The Young Fate* 1917, and the later *Le Cimetière marin/The Graveyard by the Sea* 1920.

Valhalla /væl'hælə/ in Norse mythology, the hall in Odin's palace where he feasts with the souls of the dead heroes of mortal battles.

Valkyrie in Norse mythology, any of the female attendants of ◊Odin. They select those who are to be killed in battle and escort them to ◊Valhalla.

Valladolid /ˌvæljədəʊ'liːð/ industrial town (food processing, textiles, engineering), capital of Valladolid province, Spain; cathedral 1595 and university 1346; population (1981) 330,245. It was capital of Castile and Leon in the 14th–15th centuries, then of Spain until 1560. Ferdinand and Isabella were married at Valladolid 1469.

Valle d'Aosta /'vælei dɑː'ɒstə/ special autonomous region of NW Italy; capital Aosta; population (1984) 113,500, many of whom are French-speaking.

Valletta /vəˈletə/ capital and port (with large repair yards) of Malta; population (1984) 14,000.

history Founded in 1566 by the Knights of ◊St John of Jerusalem, it was named after their grand master Jean de la Valette (1494–1568), who fended off a Turkish siege May–Sept 1565. The 16th-century palace of the grand masters survives.

Valley Forge /ˈvæli ˈfɔːdʒ/ site some 32 km/20 mi NW of Philadelphia, USA, where Washington's army spent the winter of 1777–78 in terrible hardship during the American ◊War of Independence.

Valley of Ten Thousand Smokes, valley in Alaska, USA, where in 1912 Mount Katmai erupted in one of the largest volcanic explosions ever known, though without loss of life since the area was uninhabited. The many fissures on the valley floor still emit steam jets.

Valley of the Kings valley opposite ◊Thebes, Egypt, on the left bank of the Nile. The tombs of ancient kings are here, including ◊Tutankhamen.

Valmy /vælˈmiː/ French village in the Marne *département* where the army of the French Revolution under Dumouriez defeated the Prussians in 1792.

Valois /vælˈwɑː/ branch of the Capetian dynasty (see Hugh ◊Capet) in France, originally counts of Valois in the Oise *département*, members of which occupied the French throne from Philip VI in 1328 to ◊Henry III in 1589.

Valona /vəˈləʊnə/ Italian form of ◊Vlone, port in Albania.

Valparaiso /ˌvælpəˈraɪzəʊ/ industrial port in Chile, capital of Valparaiso province, on the Pacific; two universities; population (1983) 267,000. Founded in 1536, it was occupied by ◊Drake 1578, by ◊Hawkins 1595, pillaged by the Dutch 1600, and bombarded by Spain 1866; it has also suffered much from earthquakes.

vampire bat S and Central American bat of the family Desmodontidae, of which there are three species. The *common vampire Desmodus rotundus* is found from N Mexico to central Argentina. Head and body are up to 9 cm/3.5 in. The upper middle incisor teeth are specialized for slicing a piece of skin from a victim, the bat lapping up the flowing blood. Vampires feed on all kinds of mammals including horses, cattle and occasionally people. They fly low, and settle on the ground before running to a victim. The bite is painless and the loss of blood is small, but the vampire's bite is dangerous in providing a site for infections and in transmitting diseases.

vampire in Slav demonology, a corpse which returns to 'life' by sucking the blood of the living; see ◊Dracula.

Van /vɑːn/ city in Turkey on a site on *Lake Van* that has been inhabited for more than 3,000 years; population (1985) 50,000.

vanadium a silver-white hard metal, discovered by Del Rio in 1801, and isolated by Rosco in 1869; symbol V, atomic number 23, atomic weight 50.95. It occurs in the rare minerals, vanadinite and patronite; its chief use is in alloying steel to which it imparts toughness, elasticity and tensile strength. Vanadium compounds (vanadates) are used in the preparation of aniline black for colouring glass. Named after the Scandinavian goddess Vanadis.

Van Allen /væn ˈælən/ James Alfred 1914– . American physicist, a pioneer in high-altitude research with rockets after World War II, and professor of physics at the University of Iowa since 1951. Van Allen's instruments aboard the first US satellite Explorer 1 in 1958 led to the discovery of two zones of intense radiation around the Earth, the ◊Van Allen belts.

Van Allen belt either of two doughnut-shaped zones of atomic particles around the Earth, discovered in 1958 by James ◊Van Allen. The atomic particles come from the Earth's upper atmosphere and the ◊solar wind, and are trapped by the Earth's ◊magnetic field. The inner belt lies between 1,000 km and 5,000 km/620 to 3,100 mi above the Earth, and contains ◊protons and ◊electrons. The outer belt lies from 15,000 km to 25,000 km/9,300 mi to 15,500 mi above the equator, but is lower around the magnetic poles. It contains mostly electrons from the solar wind. The Van Allen belts are hazardous to ◊astronauts and interfere with electronic equipment on satellites.

history Vancouver was visited by the British explorer Cook 1778, and was surveyed 1792 by Captain George ◊Vancouver.

Vancouver /vænˈkuːvə/ industrial city (oil refining, engineering, shipbuilding, aircraft, timber, pulp, and paper, textiles, fisheries) in Canada, its chief Pacific seaport, on the mainland of British Columbia; two universities; population (1984) 1,331,000.

history The site was taken possession of by George ◊Vancouver for Britain in 1792, and Vancouver was founded by the Hudson's Bay Company in 1825.

Vancouver /vænˈkuːvə/ George c. 1758–1798. British navigator who served under Cook and in his own Pacific voyage 1791–94 circumnavigated Vancouver Island.

Vandal /ˈvændl/ member of a Germanic people related to the ◊Goths. In the 5th century AD the Vandals moved from N Germany to invade Roman Gaul and Spain, many settling in Andalusia (formerly Vandalitia) and others reaching N Africa in 429. They sacked Rome in 455 but accepted Roman suzerainty in the 6th century.

Van de Graaff /ˌvæn də ˈɡræf/ Robert Jemison 1901–1967. American physicist, who

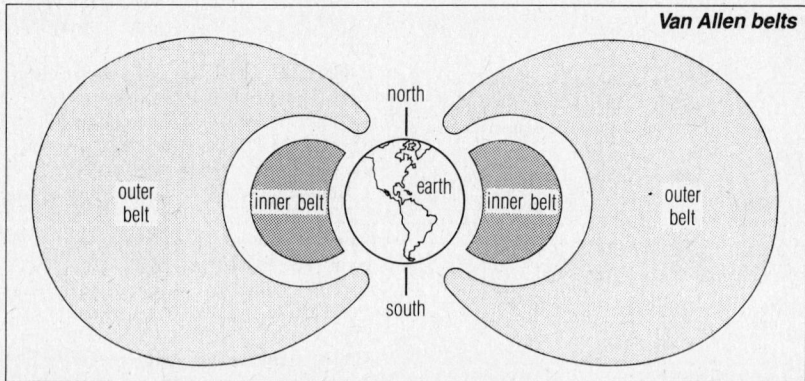

Van Allen belts

north
outer belt — inner belt — earth — inner belt — outer belt
south

Vanbrugh /ˈvænbrə/ John 1664–1726. English architect and dramatist. He designed Blenheim Palace, Oxfordshire, and Castle Howard, Yorkshire (assisted in both projects by ◊Hawksmoor). Of his many comedies the most notable are *The Relapse* 1696, and *The Provok'd Wife* 1697.

Van Buren /væn ˈbjʊərən/ Martin 1782–1862. 8th president of the USA. Secretary of state 1829–31 and then minister to England, he was elected President on the Democratic ticket in 1835 and held office until 1840.

Vance /væns/ Cyrus 1917– . US Democrat, secretary of state 1977–80. He resigned because he did not support Carter's mission to rescue the US hostages in Iran.

Vancouver /vænˈkuːvə/ Canadian island in the Pacific off British Columbia
area 32,136 sq km/12,408 sq mi
capital Victoria
town naval base Esquimalt
products coal, timber, fish

from 1929 developed a high-voltage generator, which in its modern form can produce more than a million volts. It consists of an endless vertical conveyer belt which carries electrostatic ◊charges (resulting from friction) up to a large hollow sphere supported on an insulated stand. The lower end of the belt is earthed, so that charge accumulates on the sphere. The size of the voltage built up in air depends on the radius of the sphere, but can be increased by enclosing the generator in an inert (non-reactive) atmosphere, such as nitrogen.

Vanderbilt /ˈvændəbɪlt/ Cornelius 1794–1877. American industrialist. Born at Staten Island, New York, he made a fortune in steamships and railways.

Van der Post /ˌvæn də ˈpəʊst/ Laurens (Jan) 1906– . South African writer. His books, many of them autobiographical, are concerned with the duality of man's existence, symbolized in Africa by the tension between black and white, Boer and Briton, city and veld, as in the novel *Flamingo Feather* 1955. He was knighted in 1980.

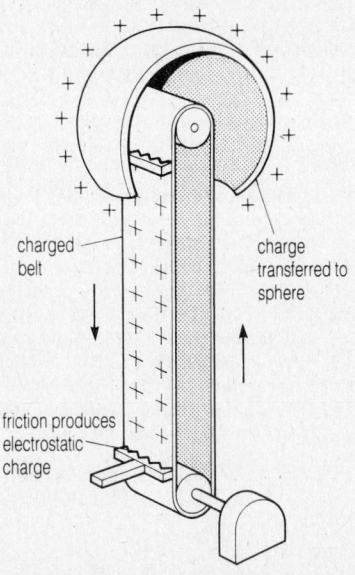

Van de Graaff generator

charged belt

charge transferred to sphere

friction produces electrostatic charge

Van der Waals /ˌvæn də 'vɑːls/ Johannes Diderik 1837–1923. Dutch physicist who was awarded a Nobel prize in 1910 for his theoretical study of gases. He emphasized the forces of attraction and repulsion between atoms and molecules in describing the behaviour of real gases, as opposed to the ideal gases dealt with in ◊Boyle's law and ◊Charles' law.

van Diemen /væn 'diːmən/ Anthony 1593–1645. Dutch admiral, see ◊Diemen, Anthony van.

van Dyck Anthony 1599–1641. Flemish painter, see ◊Dyck, Anthony van.

Vane /veɪn/ Henry 1613–1662. English politician. In 1640 elected a member of the ◊Long Parliament, he was prominent in the impeachment of Bishop ◊Laud, and 1643–53 was in effect the civilian head of the Parliamentary government. At the Restoration he was executed.

Vane /veɪn/ John 1923– . British pharmacologist. From 1973 in charge of the ◊Wellcome research centre, he discovered the wide role of prostaglandins in the human body, especially in response to illness and stress. He shared a Nobel prize in 1982.

van Eyck Jan c.1390–1441. Flemish painter, see ◊Eyck, Jan van.

van Gogh Vincent 1853–1890. Dutch painter, see ◊Gogh, Vincent van.

Vanguard a series of US Earth-orbiting satellites and their associated rocket launcher. Vanguard 1 was the second US satellite, launched 17 Mar 1958 by the three-stage Vanguard rocket. Tracking of its orbit revealed that the Earth is slightly pear-shaped. The series ended in Sept 1959 with Vanguard 3.

vanilla orchid *Vanilla planifolia*, a native of Mexico, now cultivated elsewhere, which bears pods which when dried are the source of vanilla flavouring, used in confectionery. Vanilla flavouring can now also be produced artificially.

van Meegeren Hans 1889–1947. Dutch forger, see ◊Meegeren, Hans van.

Vannin, Ellan /'elɪn 'vænɪn/ Gaelic name for ◊Isle of Man.

van t'Hoff /vænt 'hɒf/ Jacobus Henricus 1852–1911. Dutch physical chemist. He explained the 'asymmetric' carbon atom occurring in optically active compounds. His greatest work – the concept of chemical affinity as the maximum work obtainable from a reaction – was shown with measurements of osmotic and gas pressures, and reversible electric batteries. He was the first recipient of the Nobel prize in 1901.

Vanuatu /ˌvænuː'ɑːtuː/ group of islands in the S Pacific, part of ◊Melanesia.

government Vanuatu is an independent republic within the ◊Commonwealth. The constitution dates from independence in 1980. It provides for a president, who is formal head of state, elected for a five-year term by an electoral college consisting of Parliament and the presidents of the country's regional councils. Parliament consists of a single chamber of 39 members, elected by universal suffrage, through a system of proportional representation, for a four-year term. From among their members they elect a prime minister who then appoints and presides over a council of ministers.

history The islands were first reached from Europe 1606 by the Portuguese navigator Pedro Fernandez de Queiras. Called the New Hebrides, they were jointly administered by France and Britain from 1906.

Vanuatu escaped Japanese occupation during World War II. In the 1970s two political parties were formed, the New Hebrides National Party, supported by British interests, and the Union of New Hebrides Communities, supported by France. Discussions began in London about eventual independence and they resulted in the election of a representative assembly in Nov 1975. Independence was delayed because of objections by the National Party, which had changed its name to the Vanuaaku Party (VP). A government of national unity was formed in Dec 1978 with Father Gerard Leymang as chief minister and the VP leader, Father Walter Lini, as his deputy. In 1980 a revolt by French settlers and plantation workers in the island of Espiritu Santo was put down by British and French troops.

Later in 1980 the New Hebrides became independent, within the Commonwealth, as the Republic of Vanuatu. The first president was George Kalkoa, who adopted the name *Sokomanu* ('leader of thousands'), and the first prime minister was Father Lini. In the 1983 general election the VP won 24 seats and Father Lini continued as prime minister.

vapour density density of a gas, expressed as the ◊mass of a given volume of the gas divided by the mass of an equal volume of a reference gas (such as hydrogen or air) at the same temperature and pressure. It is equal to half the relative molecular weight (mass) of the gas.

vapour pressure ◊pressure of a vapour given off (evaporated from) a liquid or solid, caused by vibrating ◊atoms or ◊molecules continuously escaping from its surface. In an enclosed space, a maximum value is reached when the number of particles leaving the surface is in equilibrium with those returning to it; this is known as the saturated vapour pressure.

Var /vɑː/ river in S France, rising in the Maritime Alps and flowing generally SSE for 134 km/84 mi into the Mediterranean near Nice. It gives its name to a *département*.

Varah /'vɑːrə/ Chad 1911– . British priest who founded the ◊Samaritans.

Varanasi /və'rɑːnəsi/ (Benares) holy city of the Hindus in Uttar Pradesh, India, on the Ganges; two universities 1916 and 1957; population (1981) 794,000. There are 1,500 golden shrines, and a 5 km/3 mi frontage to the Ganges with sacred stairways (ghats) for purification by bathing. At the burning ghats, the ashes of the dead are scattered on the river to ensure a favourable reincarnation.

Varèse /və'rez/ Edgard 1885–1965. French-American composer. He studied with d'Indy and Busoni, and settled in New York in 1916, where he founded the New Symphony Orchestra in 1919 to advance the cause of modern music. His own work is experimental and often dissonant, combining electronic sounds with orchestral instruments. Works include *Hyperprism* 1923, *Intégrales* 1931, and *Poème Electronique* 1958.

Vargas /'vɑːgəs/ Gepulio 1883–1954. Brazilian lawyer and politician. He led the revolution of 1930, and was president 1930–45 and from 1951 until his suicide following a political crisis.

Vargas Llosa /'vɑːgəs 'jəusə/ Mario 1937– . Peruvian novelist (*La ciudad y los perros*/trans. as *The Time of the Hero* 1963, and *La guerra del fin del mundo*/*The War at the End of the World* 1982), who attacks both right and left in politics. *La tía Julia y el escribidor*/*Aunt Julie and the Scriptwriter* 1977 is autobiographical.

variable in mathematics, a changing quantity (one that can take various values), as opposed to a ◊constant. For example, in the algebraic expression $y = 4x^3 + 2$, the variables are x and y; in Einstein's famous formula $E = mc^2$, E (energy) and m (mass) are variables, whereas c (the speed of light) is a constant. A variable may be dependent or independent. Thus if y is a ◊function of $x^2 + 6$, that is $y = f(x^2 + 6)$, the domain of the function includes all values of the independent variable x while the range (or codomain) of the function is defined by the values of the dependent variable y.

variable-geometry wing technical name for what is popularly termed a ◊swing-wing, a type of aircraft with a moveable wing.

variable star a ◊star whose brightness changes, either regularly or irregularly, over a period ranging from a few hours to months or even years. Particularly interesting are the ◊Cepheid variables, which regularly expand and contract in size every few days or weeks. Stars that change in size and brightness at less precise intervals include *long-period* variables such as the red giant Mira (period about 330 days), and *irregular* variables such as some red supergiants.

Vanuatu
REPUBLIC OF

AREA 14,750 sq km/5,700 sq mi
CAPITAL Vila on Efate
PHYSICAL comprises about 70 islands, including Espiritu Santo, Malekala, and Efate; densely forested
FEATURES three active volcanoes
HEAD OF STATE George Sokomanu from 1980
HEAD OF GOVERNMENT Walter Lini from 1980
GOVERNMENT parliamentary democracy
EXPORTS copra, fish, coffee; tourism is important
CURRENCY vatu (174.5 = £1 Sept 1987)
POPULATION (1985) 140,000 (90% Melanesian); annual growth rate 23.6%
LANGUAGE Bislama (pidgin), English, French, all official.
RELIGION Anglican 14%, Presbyterian 40%, Roman Catholic 16%, animist 15%
CHRONOLOGY
1975 Representative assembly established.
1978 Government of national unity formed, with Father Gerard Leymang as chief minister.

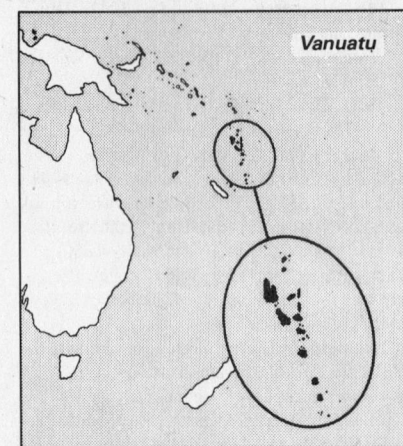

Vanuatu

1980 Revolt on the island of Espiritu Santo delayed independence but it was achieved, within the Commonwealth, with George Sokomanu as president and Father Walter Lini as prime minister.

Varèse Composer Edgard Varèse shocked audiences of his day by introducing dissonant brass and percussion effects into the orchestra; he was a pioneer of electronic music.

Eruptive variables emit sudden outbursts of light. Some suffer flares on their surfaces, while others, such as ◊novae result from transfer of gas between a close pair of stars. A ◊supernova is the explosive death of a star. In an ◊eclipsing binary, the variation is due not to any change in the star itself, but to the periodical eclipse of a star by a close companion; see ◊Epsilon Aurigae.

variations in music, a series of different developments of one self-contained theme, such as *Variations on the St Anthony Chorale* by Brahms.

varicose veins a condition found in humans where the veins become dilated or stretched, especially on the inner side of the leg, knee and thigh. The cause is not known, although the condition may be aggravated by prolonged standing. There is no cure, but the symptoms can be alleviated by injection-compression sclerotherapy: an injected fluid helps the vein to collapse of its own accord and compression bandaging aids the process. Surgery may also be undertaken.

variegated a description of plant leaves or stems that exhibit patches of different colours. The term is most commonly applied to plants that show white, cream or yellow on their leaves, caused by areas of tissue that lack the green pigment ◊chlorophyll. However, it is sometimes also applied to patchy colouring of the petals, when this is abnormal, as in the variegated petals of certain tulips, caused by a virus infection. A mineral deficiency in the soil may also be the cause of variegation. Variegated plants are bred for their decorative value, but they are often considerably weaker than the normal all-green plant. Many will not breed true and can be propagated only vegetatively.

Varley /'vɑːli/ John 1778–1842. English watercolour painter of landscapes.

Varna /'vɑːnə/ port in Bulgaria, on an inlet of the Black Sea; population (1983) 295,000. A Greek colony in the 6th century BC, and part of the Ottoman Empire 1391–1878; renamed Stalin 1949–56.

varnish name given to resins or resinous gums dissolved in linseed oil, turpentine, and other solvents, and to synthetic equivalents; used in house decoration, and furniture making.

Vasari /vəˈsɑːri/ Giorgio 1511–1574. Italian painter and architect, best remembered for writing *Lives of the Most Excellent Architects, Painters and Sculptors* 1550, in which he coined the term ◊Mannerism.

Vasco da Gama /'væskəʊ də 'gɑːmə/ Portuguese navigator; see ◊Gama.

vascular bundle a strand of primary conducting tissue (a 'vein') in vascular plants, consisting mainly of water-conducting tissue, ◊xylem, and nutrient-conducting tissue, ◊phloem. It extends from the roots to the stems and leaves. Typically the phloem is situated nearest to the epidermis and the xylem towards the centre of the bundle. In plants exhibiting ◊secondary growth, the xylem and phloem are separated by a thin layer of vascular ◊cambium, which gives rise to new conducting tissues.

vascular bundle

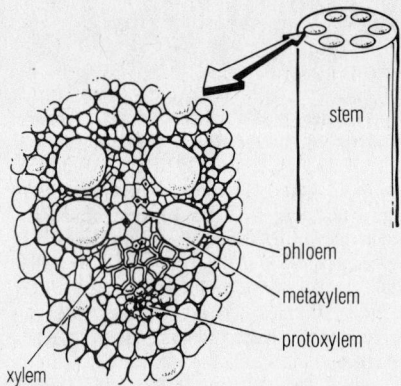

stem
phloem
metaxylem
protoxylem
xylem

vascular plant a plant with specialized conducting tissues, the ◊xylem and ◊phloem, which transport water and nutrients from one part of the plant to another. Pteridophytes (ferns, horsetails and clubmosses), gymnosperms (conifers and cycads) and angiosperms (flowering plants) are all vascular plants.

Vatican Bank popular name for the *Istituto per le opere di religione* (Institute for Religious Works) in the ◊Vatican.

Vatican City State /'vætɪkən/ sovereign area in central Rome, Italy.

government The ◊pope, elected for life by the Sacred College of ◊Cardinals, is absolute head of state. He appoints a pontifical commission to administer the state's affairs on his behalf and under his direction.

history The pope has traditionally been based in ◊Rome, where the Vatican has been a papal residence since 1377. The Vatican Palace is one of the largest in the world and contains a valuable collection of works of art.
The Vatican City State came into being through the Lateran Treaty of 1929, under which Italy recognized the sovereignty of the pope over the city of the Vatican. The 1947 Italian constitution reaffirmed the Lateran Treaty. Karol Wojtyla, formerly archbishop of Krakow in Poland, has been pope since 1978 under the title of ◊John

Paul II. In 1982 Roberto Calvi, known as 'God's banker' because of his ties with the Vatican, was found hanged under a London bridge shortly before the collapse of the Italian bank of which he was chair, Banco Ambrosiano, and warrants were issued in Italy against three Vatican Bank executives held responsible for the crash. The warrants were annulled 1987 because the affairs of the Vatican Bank, officially known as the Institute for Religious Works (IOR), are outside Italian jurisdiction.

Vatican City State
(*Stato Della Città del Vaticano*)

AREA 0.4 sq km/109 acres
PHYSICAL forms an enclave in the heart of Rome, Italy
FEATURES Vatican Palace, official residence of the pope; the basilica and square of St Peter's; also includes a number of churches in and near Rome, and the pope's summer villa at Castel Gandolfo
HEAD OF STATE AND OF GOVERNMENT John Paul II from 1978
GOVERNMENT absolute Catholic
CURRENCY issues its own coinage, which circulates together with that of Italy
POPULATION (1985) 1,000
LANGUAGE Italian
RELIGION Roman Catholic
CHRONOLOGY
1947 New Italian constitution confirmed the sovereignty of the Vatican City State.

Vatican City State

1978 John Paul II became the first non-Italian pope for more than 400 years.

Vatican councils the Roman Catholic ecumenical councils called by Pope Pius IX in 1869 (which met in 1870) and by Pope John XXIII in 1959 (which met in 1962). These councils considered major elements of church policy.

Vauban /vəʊˈbɒŋ/ Sébastien le Prestre de 1633–1707. French marshal and military engineer. In Louis XIV's wars he conducted many sieges, and rebuilt many of the fortresses on France's east frontier.

Vaucluse /vəʊˈkluːz/ mountain range in SE France, part of the Provence Alps, E of Avignon, rising to 1,242 m/4,075 ft. It gives its name to a *département*.

vaudeville variety entertainment popular in the USA from 1890s to 1920s in the same tradition as ◊music hall in Britain.

Vaughan /vɔːn/ Henry 1622–1695. Welsh poet and physician, born in Brecknockshire. A native of the land of the ancient Silures, he was known as the Silurist. He published several volumes of religious verse and prose devotions. A disciple of Donne, Vaughan is classed as a metaphysical poet, and his mystical outlook on nature influenced later poets including Wordsworth.

Vaughan Williams /vɔːn ˈwɪljəmz/ Ralph 1872–1958. British composer, born at Down Ampney, Gloucestershire. He studied with Max ◊Bruch in Berlin and Maurice ◊Ravel in Paris, but his style was essentially English, always

tonal, and evocative of the English countryside, particularly through the use of folk song. His early works include choral arrangements of poems *Toward the Unknown Region* (Whitman) 1907 and *On Wenlock Edge* (Housman) 1909; *A Sea Symphony* 1910; and *A London Symphony* 1914. After World War I came *A Pastoral Symphony* 1922 and Symphonies Nos 4, 5, and 6. In 1951 his operatic morality play *The Pilgrim's Progress* was performed for the Festival of Britain. Later works include *Sinfonia Antarctica*

1953, developed from his film score for *Scott of the Antarctic* 1948, and a Ninth Symphony 1958. He also wrote the hymn *For All the Saints* 1906 and the well-known setting of *Greensleeves* 1929. Order of Merit in 1935.

VDU (visual display unit) an electronic output device for displaying the data processed by a computer on a screen. The oldest and the most popular type is the ◊cathode ray tube (CRT), which uses essentially the same technology as a television screen. Plasma display technology is similar to that of domestic fluorescent light tubes; points of luminous gas are created, under the computer's control, from which images can be constructed. ◊Liquid crystal display (LCD), used in the display of many pocket calculators and portable computers, relies on a property of certain substances to change the polarity of light and to realign their molecules in the presence of an electric field. The electrodes that govern the process are shaped into segments of characters and numbers from which a computer-controlled display is made up.

vector any physical quantity that has both magnitude and direction, such as the velocity or acceleration of an object, as distinct from a ◊scalar quantity which has magnitude but no direction, such as speed, density, or mass. A vector is often represented geometrically by an arrow on a line of length equal to its magnitude and in technical writing it is denoted by bold (clarendon) type. Vectors can be added

graphically by constructing a triangle of vectors (such as the triangle of forces commonly employed in physics and engineering).

Veda /ˈveɪdə/ (Sanskrit, divine knowledge) the most sacred of the Hindu scriptures, hymns written in an old form of Sanskrit; the oldest may date from 1500 or 2000 BC. The four main collections are: the *Rigveda* (hymns and praises); *Yajurveda* (prayers and sacrificial formulae); *Sâmaveda* (tunes and chants); and *Atharvaveda*, or Veda of the Atharvans, the officiating priests at the sacrifices.

Vega /ˈveɪgə/ the fifth-brightest star in the sky, and the brightest in the constellation ◊Lyra. It is a blue-white star, 26 light years away, with a luminosity of 50 Suns. In 1983 the InfraRed Astronomy Satellite, IRAS, discovered a ring of dust around Vega, possibly a disc from which a planetary system is forming.

vegetable in botany, any member of the plant kingdom, but in horticulture, a plant grown for food, other than a ◊cereal, ◊herb, ◊spice plant, fruit-or nut-bearing plant, beverage plant such as coffee, or sugar-producing plant, such as sugar cane. Many vegetables are actually ◊fruits in a botanical sense, for example, tomatoes, cucumber, marrows and peppers.

vegetarianism the practice of restricting diet to foods obtained without slaughter, for humanitarian or health reasons. Some vegetarians, called vegans, abstain from all food that comes from animals, including eggs, milk, butter, and cheese.

vegetative reproduction a type of ◊asexual reproduction in plants that does not rely on ◊spores, but on multicellular structures formed by the parent plant. Some of the main types are ◊stolons and runners, ◊gemmae, ◊bulbils, sucker shoots produced from the roots of some species, such as creeping thistle (*Cirsium arvense*), ◊tubers, ◊bulbs, ◊corms, and ◊rhizomes. Vegetative reproduction has long been exploited in horticulture and agriculture, with various methods employed to multiply stocks of plants.

Veil /veɪ/ Simone 1927– . French politician. A survivor of Hitler's concentration camps, she was minister of health 1974–79, and framed the French abortion bill. In 1979–81 she was president of the European Parliament.

vein in animals with a ◊circulatory system, a vessel which carries ◊blood from the body to the heart. Veins contain valves which prevent the blood from running back when moving against gravity. They always carry deoxygenated blood, with the exception of the veins leading from the lungs to the heart in birds and mammals, which carry newly oxygenated blood.

The term vein is also used more loosely for any system of channels that strengthens living tissues and supplies them with nutrients for example, leaf veins (see ◊vascular bundle), and the veins in insects' wings.

Vela ◊constellation of the southern hemisphere, traditionally thought of as representing the sails of a ship. It contains large wisps of gas called the Gum Nebula after its discoverer, believed to be the remains of one or more ◊supernovae. Vela also contains the second ◊pulsar to be seen flashing optically.

Velázquez /vɪ'læskwɪz/ Diego de Silva y 1599–1660. Spanish painter, born in Seville, whose works reflect many aspects of the 17th-century Spanish world. By 1623 he was court painter to Philip IV in Madrid, where he was influenced by Philip's collection of 16th-century Venetian paintings by ◊Titian and ◊Tintoretto. The most fascinating of his lifelike portraits of the Spanish court is *Las Meninas/The Ladies-in-Waiting* 1655, a complex group portrait which includes Velázquez himself at his easel, and the king and queen as pale reflections in a mirror.

Velde, van de /,væn də 'feldə/ family of Dutch artists. Both *Willem van de Velde* the elder 1611–93 and his son *Willem van de Velde* the younger 1633–1707 painted sea battles for Charles II and James II. Another son *Adriaen van de Velde* 1636–72 is known for his landscapes.

veldt subtropical grassland in South Africa, equivalent to the ◊pampas of South America.

velvet a fabric of silk, cotton, nylon or other textiles, with a short, thick pile. Utrecht and Genoa are traditional centres of manufacture.

Venda /'vendə/ ◊Black National State from 1979, near Zimbabwe border, in South Africa
area 6,500 sq km/25,100 sq mi
capital Thohoyandou
towns MaKearela
features homeland of the Vhavenda people
government executive president (paramount chief P R Mphephu in office from Sept 1979) and national assembly
products coal, copper, graphite, construction stone
population (1980) 343,500
language Luvenda, English.

Vendée, the /vɒn'deɪ/ *département* in W France. A peasant rising against the Revolutionary government (the 'War of the Vendée') began there in 1793 and spread to other areas of France, lasting until 1795.

Vendée /vɒn'deɪ/ river in W France which rises near the village of La Châtaigneraie and flows 72 km/45 mi to join the Sèvre Niortaise 11 km/7 mi E of the Bay of Biscay.

vendetta any prolonged feud, in particular the practice that existed until recently in Corsica, Sardinia and Sicily of exacting revenge for the murder of a relative by killing a member of the murderer's family.

Vendôme /vɒn'dəum/ Louis Joseph, Duc de Vendôme 1654–1712. Marshal of France, who lost his command after defeat by ◊Marlborough at ◊Oudenarde in 1708, but achieved successes in the 1710 Spanish campaign, during the War of the ◊Spanish Succession.

venereal disease (VD) any disease transmitted by sexual intercourse (from Latin *Venus* goddess of love), including ◊Aids, ◊gonorrhoea, ◊herpes, and ◊syphilis.

Venetia /vɪ'niːʃə/ Roman name of that part of NE Italy which later became the republic of Venice, including the ◊Veneto region.

Veneto /'venətəʊ/ region of NE Italy
area 18,377 sq km/7,095 sq mi
capital Venice
towns Padua, Verona, Vicenza
features part of the N Italian plain, with the delta of the Po; part of the Alps and Dolomites
products cereals, fruit, vegetables, wine
population (1984) 4,366,500.

Venezia /ve'netsiə/ Italian form of ◊Venice, city, port, and naval base on the Adriatic.

Venezuela /,venɪ'zweɪlə/ country in northern S America, on the Caribbean Sea, bounded E by Guyana, S by Brazil, and W by Colombia.
government Venezuela is a federal republic of 20 states, two federal territories, and a federal district based on the capital, Caracas. The 1961 constitution provides for a president, who is head of state and head of government, and a two-chamber national congress, consisting of a senate and a chamber of deputies. The president is elected by universal suffrage for a five-year term and may not serve two consecutive terms. The president appoints and presides over a council of ministers.
The Senate has 44 members elected by universal suffrage, on the basis of two representatives for each state and two for the federal district, plus any living ex-presidents. The Chamber has 196 deputies, also elected by universal suffrage. Both chambers serve five-year terms.
history For early history, see ◊American Indian, ◊South America. Columbus visited Venezuela 1498 and there was a Spanish settlement from 1520. In 1811 a rebellion against Spain began, led by Simón ◊Bolivar, and Venezuela became independent 1830.
After a long history of dictatorial rule, Venezuela adopted a new constitution 1961 and three years later Rómulo Betancourt became the first president to have served a full term of office. He was succeeded 1964 by Dr Raúl Leoni and 1969 by Dr Rafael Caldera Rodríguez. The latter did much to bring economic and political stability, although underground abductions and assassinations still occurred. In 1974 Carlos Andres Rodríguez, of the Democratic Action Party (AD), became president and stability increased. In 1979 Dr Luis Herrera, leader of the Social Christian Party (COPEI), was elected.
Against a background of growing economic problems, the 1983 general election was contested by 20 parties and 13 presidential candidates. It was a bitterly fought campaign and resulted in the election of Dr Jaime Lusinchi as president and a win for the AD in Congress, with 109 Chamber and 27 Senate seats. COPEI won 60 Chamber and 16 Senate seats, and the Socialist Movement (MAS) ten Chamber and two Senate seats. President Lusinchi's austere economic policies were unpopular and he tried to conclude a social pact between the government, trade unions, and business. He reached an agreement with the government's creditor bankers for a rescheduling of Venezuela's large public debt.

Venice /'venɪs/ (Italian *Venezia*) city, port, and naval base, capital of Veneto, Italy, on the Adriatic; population (1984) 337,500. The old city is built on piles on low-lying islands and is now connected with the mainland and its industrial suburb, Mestre, by road and rail viaduct. Apart from tourism, industries include glass, jewellery, textiles, lace. The Grand Canal divides the city and is crossed by the Rialto bridge; transport is by traditional gondola or *vaporetto* (water bus). St Mark's Square has the 11th-century Byzantine cathedral of San Marco, the 9th–16th century campanile (rebuilt 1902), and the 14–15th century Gothic Doge's Palace (linked to the former state prison by the 17th-century Bridge of Sighs). The nearby Lido is a bathing resort. The *Venetian School* of artists includes the Bellinis, Carpaccio, Giorgione, Titian, Tintoretto, and Veronese.
history Venice was founded in the 5th century by refugees from mainland cities sacked by the Huns, and became in the 10th century a wealthy independent trading republic, stretching by the mid-15th century to the Alps and including Crete. It was governed by an aristocratic oligarchy, the Council of Ten, and a senate, which appointed the doge, or chief magistrate, 697–1797. Venice helped defeat the Ottoman Empire in the naval battle of Lepanto 1571, but was overthrown by Napoleon in 1797. In 1815 it passed to Austria, but finally became part of the kingdom of Italy in 1866.

Venizelos /,venɪ'zelɒs/ Eleutherios 1864–1936. Greek politician. Born in Crete, he came to prominence as one of the Cretan movement against Turkish rule, aiming at union with Greece. Prime minister of Greece 1910–15, 1917–20, 1924, 1928–32, and 1933. He was exiled in 1935.

Venn diagram in mathematics, a diagram representing a ◊set or sets and the logical relationships between them. Sets are drawn as circles. An area of overlap between two circles

Venice The Bridge of Sighs links the Doge's Palace with the old Venetian prisons. It derives its name from the prisoners' sighs as they were led to trial or execution.

Venezuela
REPUBLIC OF (*República de Venezuela*)

Venezuela

AREA 912,068 sq km/352,150 sq mi
CAPITAL Caracas
TOWNS Barquisimeto, Valencia; port Maracaibo
PHYSICAL valleys and delta of river Orinoco flanked by mountains
FEATURES Lake Maracaibo, Angel Falls; unique flora and fauna; annual rainfall over 7,600 mm/300 in
HEAD OF STATE AND OF GOVERNMENT Jaime Lusinchi from 1984
GOVERNMENT federal democracy
EXPORTS coffee, cocoa; timber; oil, aluminium, iron ore, petrochemicals
CURRENCY bolívar (free rate 55.75 = £1 Sept 1987)
POPULATION (1985) 17,317,000 (70% mestizos, 32,000 American Indians); annual growth rate 2.9%
RELIGION Roman Catholic
LANGUAGE Spanish (official), Indian languages 2%
LITERACY 84% male/78% female (1980 est)
GNP $70.8 bn (1983); $4,716 per head of population
CHRONOLOGY
1961 New constitution adopted, with Rómulo Betancourt as president.
1964 Dr Raúl Leoni became president.
1969 Dr Rafael Caldera became president.
1974 Carlos Andrés Pérez Rodríguez became president.
1979 Dr Luis Herrera became president.
1984 Dr Jaime Lusinchi became president. He tried to solve the nation's economic problems through a social pact between the government, trade unions, and business, and by rescheduling the national debt.
1987 Widespread social unrest triggered by inflation; student demonstrators shot by police.

(sets) contains elements that are common to both sets, and thus represents a third set. Circles that do not overlap represent sets with no elements in common (disjoint sets). The method is named after the British logician John Venn (1834–1923).

Vent, Îles du /vɒŋ/ French name for the ◊Society Islands in ◊French Polynesia.

Ventris /'ventrɪs/ Michael George Francis 1922–1956. British archaeologist. Deciphering Minoan Linear B, the language of the tablets found at Knossos and Pylos, he showed that it was a very early form of Greek, thus revising existing views on early Greek history.

Venturi /ven'tjuəri/ Robert 1925– .

Venturi Many of American architect Robert Venturi's most original buildings have been on a small scale, as here, a house built for his mother.

American architect. Pioneer of Post-Modernism, he was influential through two major books, *Complexity and Contradiction in Architecture* 1967 and *Learning from Las Vegas* 1972. His works include Guild House 1963 in his native Philadelphia. In 1986 he was commissioned to design the extension to the National Gallery, London.

Venus in astronomy, the second planet in order of distance from the Sun. It orbits the Sun every 225 days at an average distance of 108.2 million km/67.2 mi and can approach the Earth to within 38 million km/24 million mi, closer than any other planet. Its diameter is 12,100 km/7,500 mi and its mass is 0.8 that of the Earth. Venus rotates on its axis more slowly than any other planet, once every 243 days and from east to west, the opposite direction to the other planets (except Uranus). This unusual rotation is possibly a result of impact by a former moon.
The surface of Venus consists mainly of rolling plains dotted with eroded craters, presumably formed by ◊meteorite impacts. The largest continental area is Aphrodite Terra near the equator, half the size of Africa. The highest mountains are on the northern continent of Ishtar Terra, where the massif of Maxwell Montes rises to 10,600 m/35,000 ft above the average surface level. The highland areas on Venus were formed by volcanoes, which may still be active.

Venus is shrouded by clouds of sulphuric acid droplets which sweep across the planet from east to west every four days. The atmosphere is almost entirely carbon dioxide, which traps the Sun's heat by the ◊greenhouse effect to raise the planet's surface temperature to 480°C, with an atmospheric pressure 90 times that at the Earth's surface. The first artificial object to hit another planet was the Soviet probe Venera 3, which crashed on Venus on 1 Mar 1966. Later Venera probes parachuted down through the atmosphere and landed successfully on its surface, sending back information and pictures. In Dec 1978 a US Pioneer-Venus probe (see ◊Pioneer) went into orbit around the planet and mapped most of its surface by radar, which penetrates the clouds.

Venus /'viːnəs/ in Roman mythology, the goddess of love.

Venus's fly trap North American insectivorous plant *Dionaea muscipula* in which the leaf folds together to trap insects.

Veracruz /ˌverə'kruːz/ port in Mexico, on the Gulf of Mexico; population (1980) 305,456. It was founded by Cortez as Villa Nueva de la Vera Cruz (new town of the true cross) on a nearby site in 1519, and transferred to its present site 1599.

verb the grammatical part of speech for what someone or something does (*to go, to imagine*), experiences (*to live, to die*), or is (*to be, to exist*). In the sentences 'They *saw* the accident', 'She *is working* today', and 'He *should have been trying to meet* them', the words in italics are verbs (and, in the last case) two verb groups together; these sentences show just how complex the verbs of English can be. Verbs involve the grammatical categories known as number (singular or plural: 'He *runs*; they *run*'), voice (active or passive: 'She *writes* books; it *is written*'), mood (statements, questions, orders, emphasis, necessity, condition, and so on), aspect (completed or continuing action: 'She *danced*; she *was dancing*'), and tense (variation according to time: simple present tense, present continuous/progressive tense, simple past tense, and so on).

types of verb A transitive verb takes a direct object ('he saw *the house*'), while an intransitive verb has no object ('She laughed'). An auxiliary or helping verb is used to express tense and/or mood ('He *was* seen'; 'They *may* come'), while a modal verb or modal auxiliary generally shows only mood; comon modals are *may/might, will/would, can/could, shall/should, must*. The infinitive of the verb usually includes 'to' (*to go, to run* and so on), but may be a bare infinitive (for example, after modals, as in 'She may *go*'). A regular verb forms tenses in the normal way (*I walk: I walked: I have walked*); irregular verbs do not (*swim: swam: swum; put: put: put*, and so on). Because of their conventional nature, regular verbs are also known as weak verbs, while some irregular verbs are strong verbs with special vowel changes across tenses, as in *swim: swam: swum* and *ride: rode: ridden*. A **phrasal verb** is a construction in which a particle attaches to a usually single-syllable verb (for example, *put* becoming *put up*, as in 'He put up some money

Venus The *Venus de Milo*, in the Louvre, Paris.

Verdi Giuseppe Verdi, the great Italian opera composer, whose works expressed the nationalist feeling of Italians during the period of the *Risorgimento*.

for the project', and *put up with*, as in 'I can't put up with this nonsense any longer'). Verbs are formed from nouns and adjectives by adding affixes (prison: *imprison*; light: *enlighten*; fresh: *freshen up*). Some words function as both nouns and verbs (*crack, run*), both adjectives and verbs (*clean; ready*), and as nouns, adjectives and verbs (*fancy*).

verbena genus of plants of the family Verbenaceae, having tubular flowers arranged in close spikes. Colours range from white to rose, violet, and purple. There are about 100 species, mostly in the American tropics. The garden verbena is a hybrid annual.

Vercingetorix /ˌvɜːsɪnˈdʒetərɪks/ died c. 45 BC. Gallic chieftain. Leader of a revolt against the Romans in 52 BC, he was displayed in Caesar's triumph in 46 BC, and later executed.

Verdi /ˈveədi/ Giuseppe (Fortunino Francesco) 1813–1901. Italian composer, born at Busseto, near Parma. The great Italian opera composer of the Romantic period, he brought his native operatic style to new heights of dramatic expression. In 1842 he first achieved success with his opera *Nabucco*, followed by *Ernani* 1844 and *Rigoletto* 1851, based on ◊Hugo's plays *Hernani* and *Le Roi s'amuse*; *Il trovatore* and *La traviata* both 1853; *Aïda* 1871, and the masterpieces of his old age *Otello* 1887 and *Falstaff* 1893. His

Requiem 1874 commemorates Alessandro ◊Manzoni.

verdigris a basic copper acetate and irritant formerly used in wood preservatives, anti-fouling compositions and green paints.

Verdun /vɜːˈdʌn/ fortress town of NE France on the Meuse. During World War I it became the symbol of French resistance, withstanding a German onslaught in 1916. Population (1982) 24,120.

Verlaine /veəˈleɪn/ Paul 1844–1896. French lyrical poet, born at Metz. At first influenced by ◊Baudelaire, he wandered France, Belgium, and England with ◊Rimbaud 1871–73 until sentenced to two years in prison for attempting to shoot him. His volumes, *Poèmes saturniens/Saturnine Poems* 1866, *Fêtes galantes/Amorous Entertainments* 1869 (inspired by the paintings of ◊Watteau), and *Romances sans paroles/Songs without Words* 1874, gave a new music to French verse. After spending time in alcoholism and dissipation, he regained his Roman Catholic faith in *Sagesse/Wisdom* 1887.

Vermeer /veəˈmɪə/ Jan 1632–1675. Dutch artist, born in Delft, of whose life little is known. He is highly regarded for his depiction of domestic scenes, arranging his interiors as if they were abstract forms and enclosing his characters within an enamelled world of pearly light. *A Young Woman Standing at a Virginal* (National Gallery, London) is a superb example of the small number of paintings he produced.

Vermont /vɜːˈmɒnt/ state of the USA in New England; nicknamed Green Mountain State
area 24,887 sq km/9,608 sq mi
capital Montpelier
features noted for brilliant foliage in the autumn, and winter sports; Green Mountains; Lake Champlain

products apples, maple syrup, dairy products; china clay, asbestos, granite, marble, slate; business machines, furniture, paper
population (1984) 515,500
history settled in 1724, it became a state in 1791. The Green Mountain Boys were irregulars (see Ethan ◊Allen) who fought to keep Vermont from New York interference.

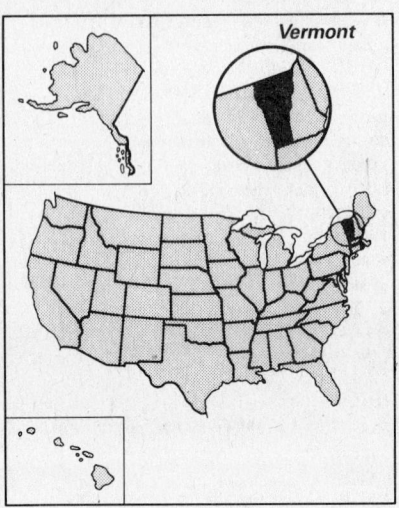

Vermont

vermouth a white wine flavoured by the maceration of bitter herbs and fortified by alcohol. It is made in France and Italy.

vernalization the stimulation of flowering by exposure to cold. Certain plants will not flower unless subjected to low temperatures during their development. For example, winter wheat will flower in summer only if planted in the previous autumn. However, by placing partially germinated seeds in low temperatures for several days, the cold requirement can be supplied artificially, allowing the wheat to be sown in the spring.

Verne /vɜːn/ Jules 1828–1905. French author. Born in Nantes, he went to Paris and established a reputation as a writer of tales of adventure which show scientific prevision: *Five Weeks in a Balloon* 1862, *Journey to the Centre of the Earth* 1864, *Twenty Thousand Leagues under the Sea* 1870, and *Around the World in Eighty Days* 1873.

Verney /ˈvɜːni/ Edmund 1590–1642. English courtier, knight-marshal to Charles I from 1626. He sat as a Member of Parliament in both the Short and Long Parliaments and, though sympathizing with the parliamentary position, remained true to his allegiance: he died at his post as royal standard bearer at the battle of Edgehill. His son Ralph (1613–96) supported the parliamentarians. The Verney Papers are a valuable record of this and later periods.

vernier a device for taking readings on a graduated scale to a fraction of division; a short divided scale which slides along the main scale and carries the index or pointer. It was invented by Pierre Vernier (c. 1580–1637), who lived at Ornans in Burgundy.

Verne Writing in the latter half of the 19th century, the French author Jules Verne made some startling predictions of scientific advances of the 20th century in such works as *From the Earth to the Moon* and *Around the World in Eighty Days*.

Verona /vəˈrəʊnə/ historic and industrial city (printing, paper, plastics, furniture, pasta) in Veneto, Italy, on the Adige; population (1984) 260,500. It has a 12th-century cathedral and fine Roman remains, including an amphitheatre.

Veronese /ˌverəʊˈneɪzɪ/ Paolo c. 1528–1588. Italian artist, born in Verona, active in Venice. Skilled in the use of line and colour, he excelled in banquets and pageantry, for example, *The Family of Darius before Alexander*, (National Gallery, London), and *trompe l'oeil* interior decorations such as those in the Doge's Palace, Venice.

Veronica, St /vəˈrɒnɪkə/ a woman of Jerusalem who, according to tradition, lent her veil or kerchief to Jesus to wipe the sweat from his brow on the road to Calvary, whereupon the image of his face was printed upon it. What is alleged to be the actual veil is preserved in St Peter's, Rome.

Verrocchio /veˈrɒkiəʊ/ Andrea del c. 1435–1488. Italian sculpture and goldsmith, born in Florence, who worked for the ◊Medici family. His sculptures include *Christ* and *St Thomas* in Or San Michele, Florence, and the equestrian statue of Bartolommeo Colleoni, in Venice. ◊Leonardo da Vinci and ◊Perugino were his pupils.

verruca growth on the skin. See ◊wart.

Versailles /veəˈsaɪ/ city in N France, capital of the Les Yvelines *département*, on the outskirts of Paris; grown up around the palace of Louis XV; population (1982) 95,240. Within the palace park are two small châteaux, Le Grand and Le Petit ◊Trianon, built for Louis XIV (by Hardouin ◊Mansart) and Louis XV (by Gabriel, 1698–1782) respectively.

Versailles, Treaty of /veəˈsaɪ/ signed 28 June 1919 between the Allies and Germany. In the forefront of the treaty were the clauses to establish the ◊League of Nations. Germany surrendered ◊Alsace-Lorraine to France, large areas in the east to Poland, and made smaller cessions to Czechoslovakia, Lithuania, Belgium and Denmark. The Rhineland was demilitarized, German rearmament was restricted, and Germany agreed to pay reparitions for war damage. The treaty was never ratified by the USA, a separate peace being made with Germany and Austria 1921.

Versalius /vɜːˈsɑːliəs/ Andreas 1514–1564. Anatomist, born in Brussels and appointed professor of anatomy at Padua at the age of 23. Wrote the anatomy masterpiece *De humani corporis fabrica* (1543) which helped transform medicine from the superstition of the Middle Ages into a scientific discipline.

verse arrangement of words in rhythmic pattern, which may depend on the length of syllables (as in Greek or Latin verse), or on stress, as in English. Classical Greek verse depended upon quantity, a long syllable being regarded as occupying twice the time taken up by a short syllable. Long and short syllables were combined in *feet*, such as:

dactyl (long, short)
spondee (long, long)
anapaest (short, short, long)
iamb (short, long)
trochee (long, short).

rhyme (identity of sound in the endings of words) was introduced to Western European verse in late Latin poetry, and *alliteration* (repetition of the same initial letter in successive words) was the dominant feature of Anglo-Saxon poetry. Both these elements helped to make verse easily remembered in the days when it was spoken rather than written.

form the Spenserian stanza (in which ◊Spenser wrote *The Faerie Queene*) has nine iambic lines rhyming ababbcbcc. The ◊sonnet has 14 lines, in English generally of ten syllables; it has several rhyme schemes. *Blank verse*, consisting of unrhymed five-stress lines, as used by ◊Marlowe, ◊Shakespeare, and ◊Milton, develops an inner cohesion that replaces the props provided by rhyme and stanza. It became the standard metre for English dramatic and epic poetry. ◊Free verse or *vers libre* avoids rhyme, stanza form, and any obvious rhythmical basis.

vertebrate any animal with a backbone. Vertebrates include mammals, birds, reptiles, amphibians and fishes; in all some 41,000 species. They include most of the larger animals, but in terms of numbers of species are only a tiny proportion of the world's animals. The zoological taxonomic group Vertebrata is a sub-group of the ◊phylum Chordata.

vertical take-off aircraft (VTOL) an aircraft that can take off and land vertically. The helicopter, airship and balloon can do this, as can a few fixed-wing aeroplanes like the Harrier.

Verulamium /ˌveruˈleɪmiəm/ Roman-British town whose remains have been excavated close to St Albans.

Verwoerd /fəˈvʊət/ Hendrik Frensch 1901–1966. South African politician. As minister of native affairs 1950–58, he did much to improve black city housing, but was also the chief promoter of ◊apartheid legislation. Prime minister from 1958, he made the country a republic in 1961. He was assassinated in the House of Assembly by a parliamentary messenger, Dimitri Tsafendas.

Very Large Array (VLA) one of the world's most powerful ◊radio telescopes, located on the Plains of San Augustine, near Socorro, New Mexico, USA. It consists of 27 dish antennae, 25 m/82 ft in diameter, which can move along a Y-shaped rail track.

Vespasian /vesˈpeɪziən/ (Titus Flavius Vespasianus) 9–79 AD. Roman emperor. Son of a moneylender, he had a distinguished military career and was proclaimed emperor by his soldiers in 69 AD when he was campaigning in Palestine. He reorganized the eastern provinces, and was a capable administrator.

vespers the seventh of the eight canonical hours in the Catholic Church. The *Sicilian Vespers* is the name given to a massacre of the French rulers in Sicily in 1282, signalled by vesper bells on Easter Monday.

Vespucci /vesˈpuːtʃi/ Amerigo 1454–1512. Florentine navigator; the Americas were named after him as a result of the widespread circulation of his accounts of his explorations, of which the veracity is disputed.

Vesta /ˈvestə/ in Roman mythology, the goddess of the hearth (Greek *Hestia*). In Rome, the sacred flame in her shrine in the Forum was kept constantly lit by the six *Vestal Virgins*.

vestigial organ in biology, an organ that remains in diminished form after it has ceased to have any significant function in the adult organism. In humans, the appendix is vestigial, having once had a digestive function in our ancestors.

Vesuvius /vɪˈsuːviəs/ active volcano SE of Naples, Italy; height 1,277 m/4,190 ft. In 79 BC it destroyed the cities of ◊Pompeii, ◊Herculaneum, and Oplonti.

vetch several genera of trailing/climbing plants, family Leguminosae, with pinnate leaves and purple flowers, as the fodder crop lucerne *Vicia sativa*. To the same genus belong the *tares* which are common weeds on cultivated land.

Veterans Day in the USA the name adopted for ◊Armistice Day in 1954, and from 1971 observed by most states on the fourth Monday in October; in Canada the 11th November is observed as ◊Remembrance Day.

veterinary science the prevention and cure of disease in animals. More generally it covers their anatomy, breeding, and relations to humans. Professional bodies: Royal College of Veterinary Surgeons 1844 in the UK, and the American Veterinary Medical Association 1883 in the USA.

veto exercise by a sovereign, branch of legislature, or other political power, of the right to prevent the enactment or operation of a law, or the taking of some course of action. In Britain the sovereign has a right to refuse assent to any measure passed by Parliament, but this has not been exercised since the 18th century; the House of Lords also has a suspensory veto on all legislation except finance measures, but this is comparatively seldom exercised. In the USA, the president may veto legislation (see ◊Act of Congress), but this can be overruled by a two-thirds majority in Congress. At the ◊United Nations, members of the Security Council can exercise a veto on resolutions.

Veuster /vɜˈsteə/ Joseph de 1840–1889. Belgian missionary, known as Father Damien. From 1873 he was resident priest in the leper settlement at Molokai; he eventually became infected and died there.

VHF very high frequency, referring to radio waves. VHF waves, which also have very short wavelengths are used for interference-free ◊FM (frequency-modulated) transmissions. VHF transmitters have relatively short range because the waves cannot be reflected over the horizon like longer radio waves.

Vian /ˈvaɪən/ Philip 1894–1968. British admiral of the fleet. In 1940 he was the hero of the ◊Altmark incident, and in 1941 commanded the destroyers which chased the *Bismarck*.

Viborg /ˈviːbɔː/ industrial town (brewing, textiles, tobacco) in Jutland, Denmark; population (1970) 36,100. Also the Swedish name for ◊Vyborg, port in USSR.

vibrato in music, a slight but rapid fluctuation of pitch, in voice or instrument.

viburnum genus of temperate and subtropical trees and shrubs, family Caprifoliaceae, including the ◊wayfaring tree the **laurustinus** and *guelder rose*.

vicar a Church of England clergyman, originally one who acted as deputy to a ◊rector, but now also a parish priest.

Vicenza /vɪˈtʃentsə/ city in Veneto region, NE Italy, capital of Veneto province, manufacturing textiles and musical instruments; population (1984) 111,500. It has a 13th-century cathedral and many buildings by ◊Palladio, including the Teatro Olimpico 1583.

viceroy the chief officers of the crown in many Spanish and Portuguese South American colonies who had ultimate responsibility for administration and military matters. The office of viceroy was also used by the British crown to rule in India.

Vichy /ˈviːʃi/ health resort with thermal springs, known to the Romans, on the river Allier in Allier *département*, central France; population 33,000. It was the seat of ◊Pétain's government 1940–44, hence the term 'Vichy France', that is, that part of France not occupied by German troops until Nov 1942.

Vico /ˈviːkəʊ/ Giambattista 1668–1744. Italian philosopher, usually considered the founder of the modern philosophy of history. He argued that history develops according to inner laws, and that society passes through a cycle of three phases: the divine, the heroic, and the human. He was critical of Descartes' emphasis on the mathematical and natural sciences, and argued that we can understand history more adequately than nature, since it is we who have made it. This is expressed in his celebrated dictum *verum et factum convertuntur* ('the true and the made are convertible').

Victor Emmanuel /ˈvɪktər ɪˈmænjuəl/ three kings of Italy including: *Victor Emmanuel II* 1820–78, first king of united Italy from 1861.

Born in Turin, he became king of Sardinia on the abdication of his father Charles Albert, following defeat in war with the Austrians in 1849. In 1855 he allied Sardinia with France and Britain in the Crimean War. In 1859 in alliance with the French he defeated the Austrians and annexed Lombardy. By 1860 most of Italy had come under his rule, and in 1861 he was proclaimed king of Italy. In 1870 he made Rome his capital.

Victor Emmanuel III 1869–1947, king from the assassination of his father Umberto I in 1900, he acquiesced in the Fascist regime but cooperated with the Allies, and abdicated in 1946. The claim to the Italian throne is maintained by his son. See ◊Umberto II.

Victoria /vɪkˈtɔːriə/ state of Australia
area 227,620 sq km/87,884 sq mi
capital Melbourne
towns Geelong, Ballarat, Bendigo
features part of the Great Dividing Range runs E–W and includes the larger part of the Australian Alps; Gippsland lakes, shallow lagoons on the coast; the ◊mallee shrub region
products sheep, beef cattle, dairy products, wheat; vines for wine and dried fruit, orchard fruits, vegetables; gold, brown coal (Latrobe Valley), oil and natural gas in Bass Strait
population (1984) 4,078,500; 71 per cent live in the Melbourne area
history annexed for Britain by the explorer Cook in 1770, Victoria was settled in the 1830s. In 1851, after being part of New South Wales, it was created a separate colony and named after the queen, and in 1901 became a state of the Commonwealth of Australia.

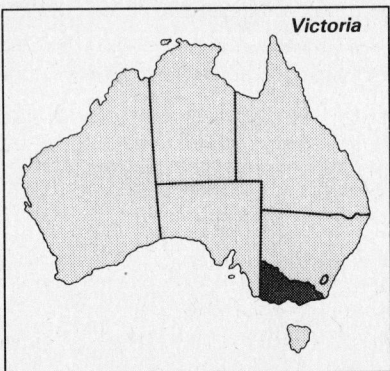

Victoria

Victoria /vɪkˈtɔːriə/ 1819–1901. Queen of the UK and Empress of India. Only child of Edward, duke of Kent, fourth son of George III. She was born 24 May 1819 at Kensington Palace, and became queen in 1837 on the death of her uncle William IV. In 1840 she married Prince ◊Albert of Saxe-Coburg and Gotha, and had four sons and five daughters. After Albert's death in 1861 she lived mainly in retirement. Nevertheless, she kept control of affairs, refusing the Prince of Wales (Edward VII) any active role, and her relations with her prime ministers ranged from the affectionate (Melbourne and Disraeli, the latter making her empress of India in 1876) to the stormy (Peel, Palmerston, and Gladstone). From 1848 she regularly visited the Scottish

highlands, where she had a house at ◊Balmoral built to Prince Albert's designs; another favourite home was ◊Osborne House in the Isle of Wight. Her golden jubilee in 1887 and diamond jubilee in 1897 marked a waning of republican sentiment, which had developed with her withdrawal from public life. She died at Osborne, 22 Jan 1901, and was buried at Windsor.

Victoria /vɪkˈtɔːriə/ industrial port (shipbuilding, chemicals, clothing, furniture), capital of British Columbia, Canada; university 1964; population (1981) 233,500. Founded on Vancouver Island as Fort Victoria in 1843 by the Hudson's Bay Company.

Victoria /vɪkˈtɔːriə/ capital of ◊Hong Kong, but itself commonly referred to as Hong Kong.

Victoria, Lake /vɪkˈtɔːriə/ or *Victoria Nyanza* largest lake in Africa, over 69,400 sq km/28,800 sq mi (410 km/255 mi long) on the equator at an altitude of 1,136 m/3,726 ft. It lies between Uganda, Kenya, and Tanzania, and is a source of the Nile. The British explorer Speke named it after Queen Victoria 1858.

Victoria Cross British decoration for conspicuous bravery in wartime, instituted by Queen Victoria in 1856. Bronze, 4 cm/1.5 in diameter, it has a crimson ribbon. Until the supply was exhausted in 1942 all Victoria Crosses were struck from the metal of cannon captured from the Russians at Sevastopol: they are now made from gunmetal supplied by the Royal Mint.

Victoria Falls /vɪkˈtɔːriə/ or *Mosi-oa-tunya* falls on the river Zambezi, on the Zambia–Zimbabwe border. The river is 1,700 m/5,580 ft wide, and drops 120 m/400 ft to flow through a 30 m/100 ft wide gorge. The falls were named after Queen Victoria by the Scottish explorer Livingstone in 1855.

Victorian Order, Royal one of the fraternities carrying with it the rank of Knight. See ◊knighthood.

Victory British battleship, 2,198 tonnes, 2,164 tons, launched in 1765, and now in dry dock in Portsmouth harbour. It was the flagship of Admiral Nelson at Trafalgar.

vicuna ruminant mammal *Lama vicugna* of the camel family which lives in herds on the Andean plateau. Its soft brown wool is used in textile manufacture.

Vidal /viːˈdæl/ Gore 1925– . American writer and critic, born at West Point, New York. His first novel, *Williwaw* 1946, was based on his experience in World War II, and much of his work deals satirically with history and politics. His works include the novels *Myra Breckinridge* 1968, *Burr* 1973, and *Empire* 1987, plays and screenplays, including *Suddenly Last Summer* 1958, and essays, such as *Armageddon?* 1987.

video camera a portable ◊television camera that takes 'movie' pictures electronically. It produces an electrical output-signal corresponding to rapid line-by-line 'scanning' of the field of view. The output is recorded on videotape and is played back on a television screen via a ◊videotape recorder.

video disc a method of recording pictures (and sounds) on disc. The video disc (originated by Baird 1928; commercially available from

Victoria Queen Victoria was only 18 when she came to the British throne. She bore Albert of Saxe-Coburg nine children and, from his death in 1861 to the end of her long life, lived mainly in retirement. By her golden jubilee in 1887 and her diamond jubilee in 1897 she had come to personify the Britain of her reign. This photograph taken in 1893 shows Queen Victoria reading official despatches at Frogmore, England, with an Indian servant in attendance.

1978) is chiefly used to provide commercial films for personal viewing. The Philips *Laservision* system uses a 30 cm/12 in rotating vinyl disc coated with a reflective material. ◊Laser scanning recovers picture and sound signals from the surface where they are recorded as a spiral of microscopic pits. The video disc works in the same way as a ◊compact disc.

video games or *telegames* games played, by means of special additional or built-in components, on the screen of the home television set. The first commercially sold was a simple bat and ball game developed in the USA in 1972, but complex variants are now available in colour and with special sound effects. In television 'tennis' a quartz crystal oscillator supplies a clock pulse input to the microprocessor in the component, so that the speed of the 'ball' across the screen can be controlled, and the player uses a simple potentiometer to control the movement of the 'racket'.

videography filming with a lightweight ◊video camera, producing a videotape that can immediately be played back in colour and sound on a television set. The tape can be wiped and reused.

videotape recorder (VTR) a device for recording television programmes for later viewing, or linked by cable with a ◊video camera.

A *cam-corder* is a portable videotape recorder with a built-in camera.

videotext a system in which information (text) is displayed on a television (video) screen. There are two basic systems, known as ◊teletext and ◊viewdata. In the teletext system information is broadcast with the ordinary television signals, while in viewdata information is relayed to the screen from a central data bank via the telephone network. Both systems require the use of a television receiver with special decoder.

Vidocq /viˈdɒk/ François Eugène 1775–1857. French criminal who, in 1809, became a spy for the Paris police, and rose to be chief of the detective department.

Vienna /viˈenə/ (German *Wien*) capital of the Austrian republic, on the river Danube at the foot of the Wiener Wald (Vienna Woods); university 1365; population (1984) 1,501,500. The United Nations city 1979 houses the United Nations Industrial Development Organization (UNIDO) and the International Atomic Energy Agency (IAEA).

features much Renaissance and baroque architecture; the Hofburg (former imperial palace), the 18th-century royal palaces of Schönbrunn and Belvedere, with formal gardens; the Steiner house 1910 by Adolf Loos; several notable collections of paintings; Vienna is known for its theatre and opera; the psychoanalyst Freud's home is a museum.

history Vienna was the capital of the Austro-Hungarian Empire 1278–1918 and the commercial centre of E Europe. The old city walls were replaced by a wide street, the Ringstrasse, 1860. After much destruction in World War II the city was divided into US, British, French, and Soviet occupation zones 1945–55. Vienna is associated with Haydn, Mozart, Beethoven, Schubert, Strauss waltzes, and the development of atonal music; with the Vienna Sezession group of painters; and psychoanalysis and Zionism originated here.

Vienna, Congress of /viˈenə/ the international congress held 1814–15, which effected the settlement of Europe after the Napoleonic Wars. National representatives included Metternich, Alexander I of Russia, Castlereagh, Wellington, and Talleyrand.

Vientiane /viˌentiˈɑːn/ capital and chief port of Laos on the Mekong river; population (1984) 120,000.

Viet Cong the members of the front for the liberation of South Vietnam who fought the South Vietnamese and US forces during the Vietnam War. The name was coined by the South Vietnamese government to differentiate these communist guerrillas from the ◊Viet Minh.

Viet Minh the Vietnam Independence League, founded in 1941 to oppose the Japanese occupation of Indo China and later directed against the French colonial power. The Viet Minh was instrumental in achieving Vietnamese independence through military victory at Dien Bien Phu in 1954.

Vietnam /viˌetˈnæm/ country in SE Asia, on the South China Sea, bounded N by China and W by Kampuchea and Laos.

government Under the constitution of 1980, the highest state authority and sole legislative chamber in Vietnam is the National Assembly, composed of 496 members directly elected every five years by universal suffrage. The assembly meets twice a year and elects from its ranks a permanent, 12-member council of state, whose chair acts as state president, to function in its absence. The executive government is the council of ministers, headed by the prime minister, which is responsible to the National Assembly.

The dominating force in Vietnam is the Communist Party (Dang Cong san Viet-Nam), headed since 1986 by Nguyen Van Linh (1914–). It is controlled by a politburo and is prescribed a 'leading role' by the constitution.

history Vietnam was founded 208 BC in the Red River delta in the N, under Chinese overlordship. Under direct Chinese rule 111 BC–939 AD, it was thereafter at times nominally subject to China. It annexed land to the S and defeated the forces of Kublai Khan 1288. European traders arrived in the 16th century. The country was united under one dynasty 1802.

France conquered Vietnam between 1858–1884, and it joined Cambodia, Laos, and ◊Annam as the French colonial possessions of ◊Indochina. French Indochina was occupied by Japan 1940–45.

Vietnam

SOCIALIST REPUBLIC OF (*Công Hòa Xã Hôi Chu Nghĩa Viêt Nam*)

AREA 336,000 sq km/129,000 sq mi
CAPITAL Hanoi
TOWNS ports Ho Chi Minh City (formerly Saigon), Da Nang, and Haiphong
PHYSICAL Red river and Mekong deltas, where cultivation and population are concentrated; some tropical rain forest; the rest is barren and mountainous
HEAD OF STATE Nguyen Van Linh head of Communist Party from 1986
GOVERNMENT communist
EXPORTS rice, rubber; coal, iron, apatite
CURRENCY dong (official rate 132.2 = £1 Sept 1987)
POPULATION (1985) 60,492,000 (some 750,000 refugees, the majority ethnic Chinese, left the country 1975–79, some settling in SW China, others fleeing by sea – the 'boat people' – to Hong Kong and elsewhere); annual growth rate 2.1%
LANGUAGE Vietnamese, of uncertain origin but tonal like Chinese and Thai
RELIGION traditionally Buddhist and Taoist
LITERACY 78% (1978)
GNP $9.8 bn (1983); $189 per head of population
CHRONOLOGY
1945 Japanese removed from Vietnam.

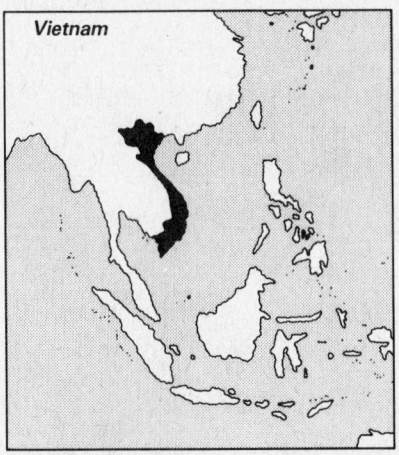

Vietnam

1946 Commencement of Vietminh war against French.
1954 France defeated at Dien Bien Phu. Vietnam divided along 17th parallel.
1964 USA entered Vietnam War.
1973 Paris ceasefire aagreement.
1975 Saigon captured by North.
1976 Socialist Republic of Vietnam proclaimed.
1978 Admission into Comecon. Invasion of Kampuchea.
1979 Sino-Vietnamese border war.
1986 Retirement of old-guard leaders.

Vietnam ranks as the third-largest communist power in the world, exerting control over ◊Laos and Kampuchea (where Vietnamese troops were still based in 1988). Continuing border disputes with China and guerrilla resistance in Kampuchea force the diversion of a third of gross national product to defence.

Vietnam War 1954–75. War following the division of Indo-China under the 1954 Geneva Convention into the separate states of North and South Vietnam. Within S Vietnam the Communist Vietcong, supported by N Vietnam and China, attempted to seize power. The USA provided military aid to support the S Vietnamese and following the Gulf of Tonkin incident 1964, when N Vietnamese torpedo boats allegedly attacked two US destroyers, the USA intervened directly and sent troops. Several large-scale invasion attempts by N Vietnam were defeated by indigenous and US forces, but the unpopularity of the war within the USA led to US withdrawal from 1973. A peace treaty was signed between N and S Vietnam in 1973 but S Vietnam was invaded by N Vietnam in March 1975, and the country was reunited as the Socialist Republic of Vietnam in 1976. Although US forces were never militarily defeated, Vietnam was undoubtedly the most humiliating political defeat the USA has ever suffered.

viewdata a system of displaying information on a television screen in which the information is extracted from a computer data bank and transmitted via the telephone lines. It is one form of ◊videotext. The British Post Office (now British Telecom) developed the world's first viewdata system, ◊Prestel, in 1975, and similar systems are now in widespread use in other countries. Viewdata users have access to an almost unlimited store of information, presented on the screen in the form of 'pages'. Prestel already has hundreds of thousands of pages available presenting all kinds of information, from local weather and restaurant menus to share prices and airport timetables. Since viewdata uses telephone lines, it can become a two-way information system, making possible, for example, home banking and shopping.

Vigny /'viːnˈjiː/ Alfred, Comte de 1797–1863. French romantic writer, whose works include the historical novel *Cinq-Mars* 1826, the play *Chatterton* 1835, and poetry, for example, *Les Destinées/Destinies* 1864.

Vigo /'viːgəʊ/ industrial port (oil refining, leather, paper, distilling) and naval station on Vigo bay in Galicia, Spain; population (1981) 258,500.

Viipuri /'viːpʊri/ Finnish name of ◊Vyborg, port and naval base in the USSR.

Viking Scandinavian 'sea warrior' of the 8th–11th centuries, sometimes called *Norse*, who raided Europe in their narrow, shallow draught, highly manoeuvrable longships, penetrating far inland along rivers. With a thirst for warfare, gold, and land, they were dreaded, and the need for organized resistance accelerated the growth of the feudal system. In England, where they were also known as 'Danes', they settled (for example, in ◊York) and greatly influenced the development of the language, and as 'Normans'

◊Ho Chi Minh, who had built up the Vietminh (Independence) League, overthrew the Japanese-supported regime of Bao Dai, the former emperor of Annam, in Sept 1945. French attempts to regain control and restore Bao Dai led to bitter fighting 1946–54, and final defeat at ◊Dien Bien Phu. At the 1954 Geneva Conference the country was divided along the 17th parallel of latitude into communist North Vietnam, led by Ho Chi Minh and with its capital at Hanoi, and pro-Western South Vietnam, led by Ngo Dinh Diem (the former premier to Bao Dai) and with its capital at Saigon.

Within South Vietnam, the communist guerrilla National Liberation Front, or Viet Cong, gained strength, being supplied with military aid by North Vietnam and China. The USA gave strong backing to the incumbent government in the S and became, following the Aug 1964 ◊Tonkin Gulf incident, actively embroiled in the ◊Vietnam War. The years 1964–68 witnessed an escalation in American military involvement. From 1969, however, as a result of mounting casualties and domestic opposition, the USA gradually began to withdraw its forces and sue for peace. A ceasefire agreement was negotiated in Jan 1973, but was breached by the North Vietnamese who proceeded to move S, surrounding and capturing Saigon (which was renamed Ho Chi Minh City) in Apr 1975.

The Socialist Republic of Vietnam was proclaimed in Jul 1976 and a programme to integrate the S was launched. The new republic encountered considerable problems. The economy was in ruins and the new, communist administration faced opposition from the intelligentsia (many of whom were imprisoned) and from rural groups, who refused to cooperate in the drive to collectivize southern agriculture. In Dec 1978 Vietnam was at war again, toppling the pro-Chinese Khmer Rouge government in ◊Kampuchea led by Pol Pot and installing a puppet administration led by Heng Samrin.

A year later, in response to accusations of maltreatment of ethnic Chinese living in Vietnam, China mounted a brief, but largely unsuccessful, punitive invasion of North Vietnam 17 Feb–16 Mar 1979. These actions, coupled with the contemporary campaigns against private businesses in the S, induced the flight of about 700,000 Chinese and middle-class Vietnamese from the country 1978–79, often by sea (the 'boat people'). Economic and diplomatic relations with China were severed as Vietnam became closer to the Soviet Union, being admitted into Comecon Jun 1978.

Despite considerable economic aid from the Eastern bloc, Vietnam did not reach its planned growth targets 1976–85. This forced policy adjustments, extending incentives and decentralizing decision taking, in 1979 and 1985. Further economic liberalization appears likely in the future after the death of Le Duan (1907–86), effective leader since 1969, and the retirement at the Dec 1986 Communist Party Congress of other prominent 'old guard' leaders, including Prime Minister Pham Van Dong and President Truờng Chinh.

Vietnam War After thirteen years of warfare in South
Vietnam between the government (supported by the USA)
and the communist National Liberation Front (Viet Cong),
supported by the North Vietnam and China, a stalemate was
ended by the withdrawal of US forces. A peace treaty was
signed between North and South Vietnam in 1973, but
South Vietnam was subsequently invaded by North Vietnam
in March 1975, and the country was reunited as the Socialist
Republic of Vietnam in 1976.

Top left A Vietnamese family made homeless by the
bombing of their village.
Top right An American soldier carries one of the wounded
on his back.
Bottom left Wounded Vietnamese civilians await medical
attention, guarded by a US soldier.
Bottom right American soldiers display the spoils of a
victory, a Viet Cong (communist) banner.

(see ◊Normandy) achieved a second conquest of the country. The Vikings had an organized system of government (see ◊thing), and the Swedish Varangians were invited to settle differences among the Slav chieftains, establishing the first Russian state with its capital at Kiev. The Varangians also reached Constantinople, where they formed the imperial guard. In the west the Vikings reached Iceland, Greenland, and North America. See ◊Eric the Red, ◊Leif Ericsson.

Viking probes two US space probes to ◊Mars. Each Viking consisted of an orbiter and a lander. They were launched on 20 Aug and 9 Sept 1975. The Viking 1 lander touched down in the Chryse lowland area on 20 Jul 1976. Viking 2 landed in Utopia on 3 Sept 1976. They transmitted colour pictures of the red, rocky surface of Mars, and analysed the soil. No definite signs of life on the planet were found.

Villa-Lobos /'vɪlə 'ləʊbɒs/ Heitor 1887–1959. Brazilian composer. His national style was based on folk tunes collected on his travels in the country, for example, *Bachianas Brasileiras*, in which he treats them in the manner of Bach. He used orchestras of hundreds, choirs of thousands, and produced some 2,000 works including 12 symphonies.

Villehardouin /ˌviːlɑːˈdwæŋ/ Geoffroy de c. 1160–1213. the first historian to write in the French language, born near Troyes. He was a leader of the Fourth ◊Crusade, of which his *Conquest of Constantinople* c. 1209 is an account.

villeinage the system of serfdom that prevailed in Europe in the Middle Ages. At the time of the Domesday Book, the villeins were the most numerous element in the English population, providing the labour force for the manors. By the 15th century villeinage had been supplanted by a system of free tenure and labour, but it continued in France until 1789.

Villiers de l'Isle Adam /viːlˈjeɪ də ˈliːl æˈdɒŋ/ Philippe Auguste Mathias, comte de Villiers de l'Isle Adam 1838–1889. French poet, the inaugurator of the Symbolist movement. He wrote the drama *Axel* 1890; *Isis* 1862, a romance of the supernatural; verse, and short stories.

Villon /viːˈɒŋ/ François 1431–1485. French poet, noted for his satiric humour, pathos, and lyric power in works which used the *argot* (slang) of the time. Very little of his work survives, but his best known poem is the *Ballade des dames du temps jadis/Ballad of the ladies of former times* containing the line 'Ou sont les nièges d'antan?' ('Where are the snows of yesteryear?'). Born in Paris of humble parentage, he dropped his surname (Montcorbier or de Logos) to assume that of a canon – a relative who sent him to study at the Sorbonne, where he graduated in 1449 and took his MA in 1452. In 1455 he stabbed a priest in a street fight and had to flee the city. Pardoned the next year, he returned to Paris – the *Petit Testament* belonging to this time – but was soon in flight again after robbing the Collège of Navarre, and was briefly at rest at the court of the duke of Orléans until sentenced to death for an unknown offence from which he was saved by the amnesty of a public holiday. Theft and public

brawling continued to occupy his time, in addition to the production of the *Grand Testament* 1461, but in 1463 a sentence of death in Paris, commuted to ten-year banishment, is the last that is known of his life.

Vilnius /'vɪlnɪus/ (Russian *Vilna*) capital of Lithuanian Republic, USSR; university 1578; population (1985) 544,000. From a 10th-century settlement, Vilnius became the Lithuanian capital 1323 and a centre of Polish and Jewish culture. It was then Polish from 1386 until the Russian annexation of 1795. Claimed by both Poland and Lithuania after World War I, it was given to Poland in 1921, occupied by the USSR 1939, and immediately transferred to Lithuania.

Vimy Ridge /'viːmi/ hill in N France, a spur of the ridge of Nôtre Dame de Lorette, 8 km/5 mi NE of Arras, taken in World War I by Canadian troops during the battle of ◊Arras, Apr 1917, costing 11,285 lives.

Vincennes /væn'sen/ the University of Paris VIII, usually known as Vincennes from the suburb of E Paris where it was founded in 1970 (following the 1968 student rebellion) for blue-collar workers. By 1980 it had 32,000 students. In June 1980 it was removed to the industrial suburb of St-Denis.

Vincent of Beauvais /'vinsənt,/c.1190–1264. French scholar, encyclopedist, and Dominican priest. A chaplain to the court of Louis IX, he is mainly remembered for his *Speculum majus/Great Mirror* 1220–44, a massive reference work summarizing contemporary knowledge on virtually every subject, including science, natural history, literature, and law. It also contained a history of the world from the creation. It is noteworthy for its positive attitude towards classical literature, whose reputation had undergone a period of eclipse in the Dark Ages, and was hugely influential in its time.

vine climbing plant *Vitis vinifera* of the family Vitaceae, a native of Asia Minor, cultivated from antiquity for its fruit, which is eaten or made into wine or other fermented drinks; dried fruits of certain varieties are raisins and currants. Other species of climbing plant are sometimes termed vines.

vinegar a 4 per cent solution of acetic acid produced by the oxidation of alcohol, used to flavour food and as a preservative in pickles; *malt vinegar* is brown and made from malted cereals; *white vinegar* is distilled from it. Other sources of vinegar include cider, inferior wine, and honey.

Vinland /'vɪnlənd/ Norse name for the Hudson Straits/Gulf of St Lawrence area of North America, which the Viking Leif ◊Ericsson thought was an island-continent.

Vinson Massif /'vɪnsən mæ'siːf/ highest point in ◊Antarctica.

viola a bowed string musical instrument of the ◊violin family.

violet plant of genus *Viola*, family Violaceae, with mauve, blue or white flowers, such as the *heath dog violet Viola canina* and *sweet violet Viola odorata*. *Pansies* are very close relatives.

viol family bowed musical instruments of the 16th–18th centuries, similar to the ◊violin (which superseded them), but having frets and

(normally) six strings, instead of four, tuned in fourths, and with a flatter back. Members of the family include *descant viol*, *viola da gamba* or *bass viol*, and *double-bass viol* or *violone*. Viols have been used increasingly in recent years for authentic performances of early and Baroque music.

violin family musical instruments played with a bow drawn against a stretched string. There are four members: *violin*, *viola*, *violoncello* or *cello*, and *double bass*. The violin superseded the viol from the 17th century; famous early makers were the ◊Amati, ◊Stradivari, and ◊Guarneri families of Cremona. Each of the instruments consists of a resonant hollow body, a neck with fingerboard attached, and four catgut strings, tuned in fifths above the lowest note, G below middle C, stretched over the body. The viola sounds a fifth below the violin; the cello is played seated, with the instrument between the knees, and its lowest note is C two octaves below middle C. The double bass is the lowest member of the family (lowest note, E an octave below the bass stave), and, unlike the rest of the violin family, is tuned in fourths.

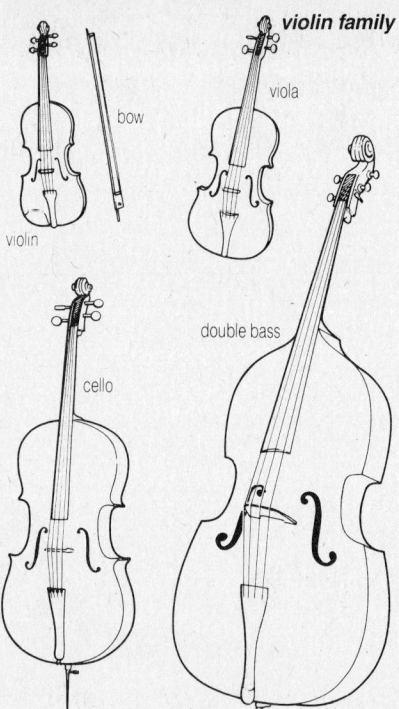

violin family
bow
violin
viola
cello
double bass

Viollet-le-Duc /ˌviːəˈleɪ lə ˈdjuːk/ Eugène Emmanuel 1814–1849. French architect. Noted as the leader of the Gothic revival in France, and for restoration of medieval buildings.

violoncello or *cello* a bowed string musical instrument of the ◊violin family.

viper front-fanged venomous snake of the family Viperidae. The true vipers, sub family Viperinae, abundant in Africa and SW Asia, include the adder *Vipera berus*, Britain's only poisonous snake; the African puff adder *Bitis arietans* and the horned viper of North Africa *Cerastes cornutus*. The second sub-family

Crotalinae includes the pit vipers and rattlesnakes of the Americas, which have a heat-sensitive pit between the eye and nostril.

Virchow /'frəkəu/ Rudolf 1821–1902. German pathologist. Born in Pomerania, he was a professor at Berlin and from 1880 leader of the opposition to Bismarck in the Reichstag. His *Cellular Pathology* 1858 was influential.

Virgil /'vɜːdʒɪl/ (Publius Vergilius Maro) 70–19 BC. Roman poet, born near Mantua. He was of the small farmer class whose life he celebrated in his pastoral *Eclogues* 37 BC, and *Georgics* or 'Art of Husbandry' 30 BC. His epic poem, the *Aeneid*, glorified the dynasty of his patron ◊Augustus. He was one of the most influential Roman writers, partly because his apparent forecast of the birth of Christ in the fourth eclogue gave him the status of an 'honorary Christian' in the medieval church.

virginal a small type of ◊harpsichord.

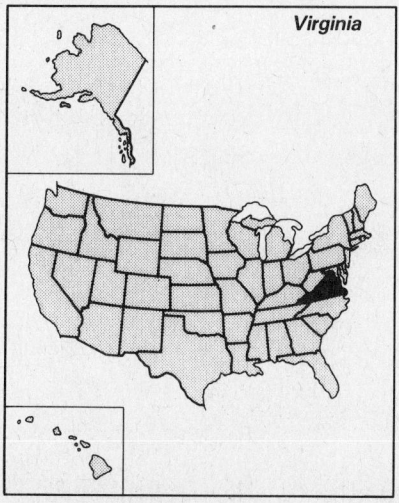

Virginia

Virginia /və'dʒɪnɪə/ state of the S USA; nicknamed Old Dominion
area 105,711 sq km/40,814 sq mi
capital Richmond
towns Norfolk, Newport News, Hampton, Portsmouth
features Blue Ridge mountains, which include the Shenandoah National Park; Arlington National Cemetery; Mount Vernon, the village where George Washington lived 1752–99; Monticello (◊Jefferson's home at Charlottesville); Stratford Hall (Robert E ◊Lee's birthplace at Lexington)
products sweet potatoes, corn, tobacco, apples, peanuts; coal; furniture, paper, chemicals, processed food, textiles, and cigarettes
population (1983) 5,550,000
famous people Richard E Byrd, Patrick Henry, Edgar Allan Poe, Booker T Washington
history named in honour of Elizabeth I. The first permanent English settlement in the New World was made here in ◊Jamestown in 1607. The state took a leading part in the revolutionary struggle against Britain, was one of the original Thirteen States, and was a Confederate state in the Civil War.

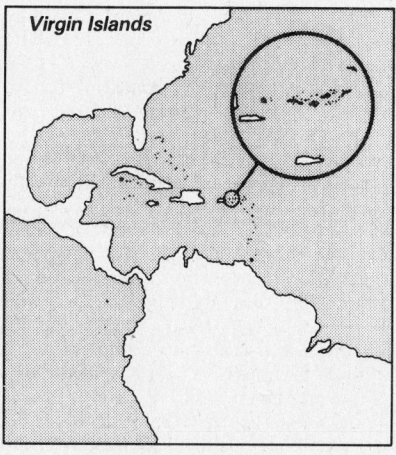

Virgin Islands

Virgin Islands /'vɜːdʒɪn/ group of about 100 small islands, northernmost of the Leeward Islands in the Antilles, West Indies. They lie in superb sailing waters and tourism is the chief industry.

They comprise the **American Virgin Islands** St Thomas (with the capital, Charlotte Amalie), St John, and St Croix; area 347 sq km/134 sq mi; population (1980) 96,600. They were purchased from Denmark 1917, and form an 'unincorporated territory'; and the. **British Virgin Islands** Tortola (with the capital, Road Town), Virgin Gorda, Anegada, Jost van Dykes; area 174 sq km/67 sq mi; population (1980) 12,000. They were taken over from the Dutch by British settlers 1666, and have partial internal self-government.

Virgo constellation of the ◊zodiac, and the second largest in the sky, once believed to represent a maiden holding an ear of wheat. The Sun passes through the constellation from late Sept to the end of Oct. Virgo's brightest star is the first-magnitude Spica, a blue-white star about 250 light years away. Virgo contains the nearest large cluster of galaxies to us, 50 million light years away, consisting of about 3,000 galaxies centred on the giant elliptical galaxy M87. Also in Virgo is the nearest ◊quasar, 3C 273, an estimated 3,000 million light years distant.

virion the name given to a single mature ◊virus particle.

virus an infectious particle consisting of a 'core' of nucleic acids (DNA or RNA) enclosed in a protein 'shell'. Viruses are acellular, and outside the cell of another organism they remain completely inert, being able to function and reproduce only if they can force their way into a living cell so as to be able to use the cell's system to replicate themselves. In doing so, they may disrupt or alter the host cell's own ◊DNA. The healthy human body reacts to such an invasion by producing an anti-viral protein, ◊interferon, which prevents the infection spreading to adjacent cells. Viruses are responsible for causing diseases such as canine distemper, chickenpox, common cold, herpes, influenza, measles, rabies, smallpox, yellow fever, ◊AIDS

and many plant diseases. Recent evidence implicates viruses in the development of some forms of cancer. *Bacteriophages* are viruses that infect bacterial cells. *Retroviruses* are of special interest because they have an RNA genome, and can produce DNA from this RNA, a process which apparently contravenes the ◊central dogma. *Viroids*, discovered in 1971, are even smaller than viruses, a single strand of nucleic acid with no protein coat. They may cause stunting in plants and some rare diseases in animals, including humans.

It is debatable whether viruses and viroids are truly living organisms, since they are incapable of an independent existence outside other living cells. The origin of viruses is also unclear, but it is believed that they are degenerate forms of life, derived from cellular organisms, or pieces of nucleic acid that have broken away from the genome of some higher organism and taken up a parasitic existence.

Antiviral drugs are difficult to develop because viruses replicate by using the genetic machinery of host cells, so that drugs tend to affect the host cell as well as the virus. Acyclovir (used against the herpes group of diseases) is one of the few drugs so far developed that is successfully selective in its action.

viscacha S American rodent *Lagostomus maximus* of the chinchilla family. Found in pampas and scrubland in Argentina, it is up to 66 cm/2.2 ft long plus 20 cm/8 in tail, with a weight of some 7 kg/15 lb. It has a large head and small ears. Viscachas live in colonies up to 30 strong in a network of burrows and entrances. They deposit refuse in a pile near an entrance, and emerge at night to feed on grasses. *Mountain viscachas*, genus *Lagidium*, are smaller and have long ears and tails, and are found in rocky places feeding by day on sparse vegetation.

Visconti /vɪs'kɒnti/ Luchino 1906–1976. Italian film and theatrical director. He pioneered the ◊neo-realist' film with *Ossessione* 1942; later were *The Leopard* 1963 and *Death in Venice* 1971. His powerful social comment in documentaries led to clashes with the Italian government and Roman Catholic Church.

viscose the most common type of ◊rayon, made by dissolving the cellulose in ◊woodpulp and regenerating it in an acid bath in the form of continuous filament or fibres.

viscosity in physics, the internal friction or resistance to relative motion of the parts of a fluid. Fluids such as pitch, treacle and heavy oils are highly viscous; for the purposes of calculation, many fluids in physics are considered to be perfect, or non-viscous.

viscount in the UK peerage, the fourth degree of nobility, between earl and baron.

Vishnu /'vɪʃnuː/ in ◊Hinduism, the second in the triad of gods representing three aspects of the supreme spirit. He is the Preserver, and is believed to have assumed human form in nine avataras or incarnations, the most famous being his appearances as Rama and Krishna. His worshippers are the Vaishnavas.

Visigoths branch of ◊Goths, an East Germanic people.

vision system a computer-based device for interpreting visual signals from a video camera. Computer vision is important in robotics where the addition of sensory abilities would considerably increase the flexibility and usefulness of a robot. Although some vision systems exist for recognizing simple shapes, the technology is still in its infancy and will require much more research in areas such as artificial intelligence before it becomes commercially successful.

Vistula /'vɪstjʊlə/ river in Poland, which rises in the Carpathians and runs SE to the Baltic at Gdansk; length 1,090 km/678 mi.

vitalism the now unfashionable view that living organisms derive their characteristic properties from a universal life force. The view is associated in the present century with the philosopher Henri ◊Bergson.

vitamin C another name for ◊ascorbic acid.

vitamins organic substances which, if absent or deficient in the diet, lead to various characteristic diseases and disturbances. Vitamins are only needed in small amounts. Many act as coenzymes, small molecules which enable ◊enzymes to function effectively. Although in 1662 Admiral Hawkins was aware of the value of 'sower oranges and lemons' against scurvy (vitamin C deficiency) it was not fully established until about 1915 that several deficiency diseases were preventable and curable by extracts from certain foods. By then it was known that two groups of factors were involved, one being water-soluble and present, for example, in yeast, rice-polishings and wheat-germ, and the other being fat-soluble and present in egg-yolk, butter, fish-liver oils and so on. The water-soluble substance, known to be effective against beri-beri, was named vitamin B. The fat-soluble vitamin complex was at first called vitamin A. With improving analytical techniques these have been subsequently separated into their various components, and others have been discovered. It is now known that humans need over 20 vitamins. Other animals may also need vitamins, but not necessarily the same ones. For example, choline, which humans can synthesize, is essential to rats and some birds which cannot produce sufficient for themselves.

Vitebsk /'viːtebsk/ industrial city (glass, shoes) in the White Russian Republic, USSR, on the Dvina river; population (1985) 335,000. Vitebsk dates from the 10th century and has been Lithuanian, Russian, and Polish.

Vitoria /vɪ'tɔːrɪə/ town in the Basque country, Spain; capital of Alava province; population (1981) 192,773. In the Peninsular War 1813 Wellington won a victory over the French.

vitriol oil of vitriol is sulphuric acid; blue, green, and white vitriols are copper, ferrous, and zinc sulphate respectively.

Vitruvius /vɪ'truːvɪəs/ (Marcus Vitruvius Pollio) 1st century BC. Roman architect, whose ten-volume work on Roman architecture *De architectura* influenced Alberti and Palladio.

Vittorio Veneto /vɪ'tɔːrɪəʊ 'venɪtəʊ/ industrial town in Veneto, Italy, which gives its name to the final victory of Italy and Britain over Austria in Oct 1918; population (1970) 29,400.

Vitus, St /'vaɪtəs/ Christian saint, supposed to have been Sicilian, who was martyred at Rome early in the 4th century.

Vivaldi /vɪ'vældi/ Antonio (Lucio) 1678–1741. Italian Baroque composer and violinist. Born in Venice, he spent much of his life there as a teacher but died in poverty in Vienna. A prolific composer, he is noted for instrumental works – over 400 concertos, 23 symphonies and 75 sonatas – and his development of the solo concerto is especially significant. His music, which also includes over 40 operas and much sacred music, was largely neglected until the 1930s.

vivipary in animals, a method of reproduction in which the ◊embryo develops inside the body of the female from which it gains nourishment. Vivipary is best developed in the ◊mammals, but also occurs in some arthropods, fish, amphibians and reptiles. See also ◊ovipary and ◊ovovivipary. In plants, the formation of young plantlets or ◊bulbils in an inflorescence, instead of flowers. It is a type of ◊vegetative reproduction and occurs, for example, in the house plant *Chlorophytum comosum* ('spider plant') which produces young plants in the floral axils. The term also describes seeds which germinate prematurely, before falling from the parent plant. This is common in mangrove trees where the seedlings develop sizeable spear-like roots before dropping into the swamp below: this prevents then being washed away by the tide.

vivisection literally, cutting into a living animal; used originally to mean experimental surgery or dissection practised on a live subject. Now often used by ◊anti-vivisection campaigners to include any experiment on animals, surgical or otherwise.

Vizcaya /vɪs'kaɪə/ Basque form of ◊Biscay, a bay in the Atlantic off France and Spain.

Vladimir I /'vlædɪmɪə/ St, Grand Duke of Kiev 956–1015. Russian saint. Converted to Christianity in 988, he married Anna Christian sister of the Byzantine emperor ◊Basil II, and established Orthodox Christianity as the Russian national faith; feast day, 15 Jul.

Vladivostok /ˌvlædɪ'vɒstɒk/ port (naval and commercial) in E USSR at the Amur Bay on the Pacific coast; population (1985) 600,000. Kept open by icebreakers through the year. It is the administrative centre of the Far East Science Centre 1969, with subsidiaries at Petropavlovsk, Khabarovsk, and Magadan.

Vlaminck /vlæ'mæŋk/ Maurice de 1876–1958. French artist. Born in Paris, he was persuaded to take up painting as a career by ◊Derain and became a member of the ◊Fauves. He became famous for his landscapes, often scenes in snow, expressed in heavy outlines and impasto. He also wrote poetry, novels and essays.

Vlissingen /'flɪsɪŋə/ Dutch form of ◊Flushing, a port of the SW Netherlands.

Vlonë /'vləʊnə/ Albanian town and port; population (1980) 58,000. A Turkish possession from 1464; site of the declaration of independence by Albania in 1912.

VLSI (very large-scale integration) the current level of advanced technology in the microminiaturization of electronic circuits, and

volcano

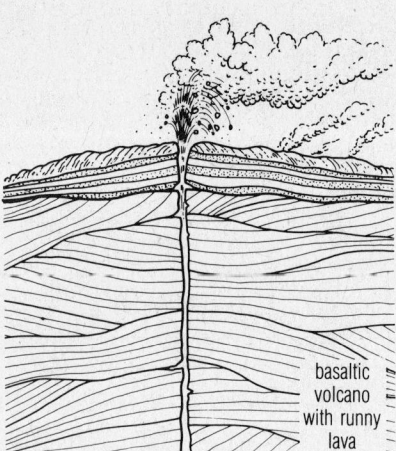

andesitic volcano with stiff lava

basaltic volcano with runny lava

an order of magnitude smaller than ◊LSI. See also ◊integrated circuit.

vocal cords folds of tissue within the ◊larynx of mammals, and the syrinx of birds. Air passing over them makes them vibrate to produce sounds. The tension in them can be adjusted by muscles in the larynx, which change the pitch of the sound.

vocational education education relevant to a specific job or career and extending from further education courses in craft skills to medical and legal education in the universities. In the UK, the ◊TVEI (Technical and Vocational Education Initiative) funded by the ◊Manpower Services Commission intends to allow the expansion of vocational education in schools.

vodka the Russian national drink; a strong colourless liquor distilled from rye, potatoes, maize, or barley.

voice sound produced by the passage of air between the ◊vocal cords. In humans the sound is much amplified by the hollow sinuses of the face, and is modified by the movements of the lips, ◊tongue and cheeks.

voiceprint an individual pattern of lines made by the human voice when visually recorded. First used as evidence in criminal trials in USA in

1966, voiceprints were banned in 1974 by the US Court of Appeal as 'not yet sufficiently accepted by scientists'.

Vojvodina /ˌvɔɪvəˈdiːnə/ autonomous area in ◊Serbia, Yugoslavia.

volcanic rock ◊igneous rock formed at the surface of the Earth from solidifying lava or pyroclastic – ash, dust, and the like. Volcanic rock is usually fine-grained compared with the other types of igneous rocks such as plutonic rocks. ◊Basalt and ◊andesite are the main types of volcanic rock.

volcano a vent in the Earth's crust from which molten rock, lava, ashes, and gases are ejected. Usually it is cone-shaped with a pitlike opening at the top called the crater. Some volcanoes, for example, Stromboli and Vesuvius in Italy, eject the material with explosive violence; others are a quiet type in which the lava rises up into the crater and flows over the brim; and some may be quiescent for very long periods, for example, Mount St ◊Helens, Washington, USA. Many volcanoes are submarine. The chief volcanic regions are the Pacific (Cape Horn to Alaska); central Andes (with the world's highest volcano, Guallatiri, 6,060 m/19,900 ft), Chile; North Island, New Zealand; Hawaii; Japan; and Antarctica. There are some 600 land volcanoes on Earth, and volcanism has helped shape other members of the solar system, for example, the Moon, Mars, Venus, and Jupiter's moon Io.

Volcker /ˈvəʊlkə/ Paul 1927– . American economist. As chair of the board of governors of the Federal Reserve System 1979–87, he controlled the amount of money in circulation in the USA. He was succeeded by Alan Greenspan.

vole rodent of the family Cricetidae, which is widely distributed over Europe, Asia and North America, and also includes the hamsters and lemmings. British species include the water vole or water 'rat' *Arvicola terrestris*, brownish above and grey-white below; and the field vole *Microtus agrestis*.

Volga /ˈvɒlgə/ longest river in Europe: 3,685 km/2,290 mi, 3,540 km/2,200 mi of which are navigable. It drains most of middle and E European USSR, rises in the Valdai plateau and flows into the Caspian Sea 88 km/55 mi below Astrakhan.

Volgograd /ˈvɒlgəgræd/ industrial city (metal goods, machinery, sawmills, oil refining) in SW USSR, on the river Volga; population (1985) 974,000. Volgograd was called Stalingrad 1925–61. Its successful defence 1942–43 against Germany was a turning point in World War II.

Volkswagen one of the most famous makes of cars in the history of motoring – 'the people's car'. The original VW, with its distinctive beetle shape, was produced in 1938, a design of Ferdinand ◊Porsche. It was still in production in Latin America in the late 1980s, by which time it had exceeded 20 million sales.

volleyball team game invented in the USA in 1895, played on a court 18 m/59 ft long by 9 m/29 ft 6 in, divided into two by a net 1 m/3 ft 3 in deep suspended above the court. The six players of each team rotate in position through the six sub-sections into which each half of the

volcano Smoke plume following the second eruption of Mount St Helens, Washington, USA, in 1980. The volcano had previously been quiescent for 450 years, and erupted with a force 500 times greater than the Hiroshima atom bomb, reducing the height of the mountain by 385 m/1,267 ft.

court is divided behind the attack line. The ball, slightly smaller than a basketball, is hit with palm or fist, the aim being to ground it in the opponents' court.

World Championships first held 1949 for men, 1952 for women

men
1978 USSR
1980 USSR
1982 USSR
1984 United States
1986 United States
women
1978 Cuba
1980 USSR
1982 China
1984 China
1986 United States

---

volt in physics, unit of potential difference, ◊electromotive force (e.m.f.) or electric ◊potential. When 1 ◊coulomb of electric charge generates 1 ◊joule of energy (in c.g.s units, when the current is 1 ◊amp and the power dissipated 1 ◊watt) between two points in an electrical circuit, the potential difference between them is 1 volt. Named after the Italian scientist Alessandro ◊Volta.

Volta /ˈvɒltə/ chief river in Ghana, about 1,600 km/1,000 mi long, with two main upper branches, the Black and White Volta. It has been dammed to provide power.

Volta, Upper /ˈvɒltə/ name until 1984 of ◊Burkina Faso.

Volta /ˈvɒltə/ Alessandro 1745–1827. Italian physicist. Born at Como, he was a professor there and at Pavia. He invented the voltaic pile (the first battery), the electrophorus (an early electrostatic generator) and an ◊electroscope. The ◊volt is named after him.

volleyball

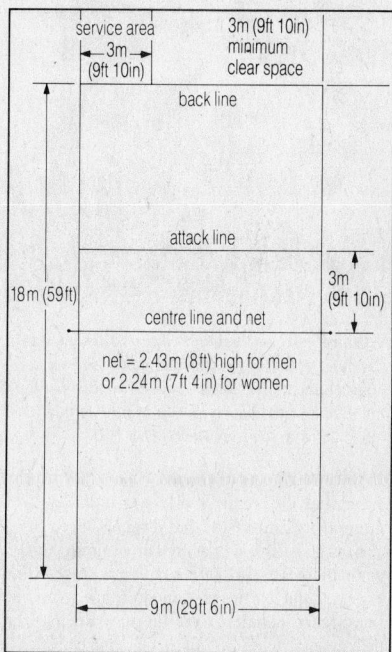

Voltaire /vɒlˈteə/ pen name of François-Marie Arouet 1694–1778. French writer. Born in Paris, son of a notary. He adopted his pseudonym, probably an anagram of Arouet l(e) j(eune), in 1718. He was twice imprisoned in the Bastille and three times exiled from Paris between 1716 and 1726 for libellous political verse. *Oedipe/Oedipus*, his first essay in tragedy, was staged in 1718. While in England 1726–29 he dedicated an epic poem on Henry IV, *La*

Henriade/The Henriade, to Queen Caroline, and on returning to France published the successful *Histoire de Charles XII/History of Charles XII* 1731, and produced the play *Zaïre* 1732. The reception of his *Lettres philosophiques sur les anglais/Philosophical Letters on the English* 1733, a panegyric of English ways, thought and political practice, led to his taking refuge with his mistress, the Marquise de ◊Châtelet at Cirey in Champagne – where he wrote his celebrated play *Mérope* 1743, and much of *Le Siècle de Louis XIV/The Age of Louis XIV* . In 1751–53 he stayed at the court of ◊Frederick the Great, who had long been an admirer, but the association ended in deep enmity. From 1754 he established himself near Geneva – after 1758 at Ferney, just across the French border. Among his other works are the satirical tale *Zadig*; *Candide* 1759, a parody on ◊Leibniz's 'best of all possible worlds'; and the tragedy *Irène* 1778. In religion a ◊Deist, Voltaire devoted himself to crushing the spirit of intolerance.

Voltaire Perhaps best known for his moral tale *Candide*, Voltaire is celebrated a philosopher, poet, and historian. He was twice imprisoned in the Bastille and is seen as one of the spiritual founders of the French Revolution.

voltmeter instrument for measuring ◊potential difference (voltage). It has a high internal ◊resistance (so that it passes only a small current), such as a sensitive moving-coil ◊galvanometer in series with a high-value ◊resistor and, to measure an alternating voltage, the circuit includes a rectifier. A moving-iron instrument can be used to measure AC (◊alternating current) voltages without the need for a rectifier.

volume in geometry, the space occupied by a three-dimensional solid object. A cube, cuboid, other prismatic figure, or a cylinder has a volume equal to the area of the base multiplied by the height. For a pyramid or cone, the volume is equal to one-third of the area of the base multiplied by the perpendicular height. The volume of a sphere is equal to $\frac{4}{3}\pi r^3$. Volumes of irregular solids may be calculated by the technique of ◊integration.

von Braun /fɒn 'braʊn/ Wernher 1912–1977. German-born American rocket engineer who developed German military rockets during World War II and later worked for NASA (National Aeronautical and Space Administration) in the United States. During the 1940s his research team at Peenemünde on the Baltic coast produced the V1 (flying bomb) and supersonic V2 rockets. In the 1950s von Braun was part of the team that produced rockets for American satellites (the first, *Explorer I*, was launched in early 1958) and early space flights by astronauts.

von Karajan Herbert Austrian conductor. See ◊Karajan, Herbert von.

Vonnegut /'vɒnɪgʌt/ Kurt, Jr 1922– . American writer, whose novels include the science-fiction classic *Cat's Cradle* 1963, and *Slaughterhouse-Five* 1969, which draws on his World War II experience of the bombing of Dresden, Germany.

von Neumann /vɒn 'njuːmən/ John 1903–1957. Hungarian-born scientist and mathematician, best known for his work on computer design. He was born in Budapest and became an assistant professor of physical mathematics at Berlin University before moving to Princeton in the USA in 1929, where he later became professor of mathematics. He invented his celebrated 'rings of operators' (called von Neumann algebras) in the late 1920s, and also contributed to set theory, games theory, cybernetics (with his theory of self-reproducing automata), and the development of the atomic and hydrogen bombs.

voodoo a set of magical beliefs and practices, followed in some parts of Africa and the West Indies, especially in Haiti.

Voronezh /vəˈrɒneʒ/ industrial city, capital of Voronezh region of the USSR, S of Moscow on the Voronezh river; university 1803; population (1985) 850,000. There has been a town on the site since the 11th century.

Voroshilov /ˌvɒrəˈʃiːlɒf/ Klement Efremovich 1881–1969. Marshal of the Soviet Union. He joined the Bolsheviks in 1903, and was many times arrested, exiled, but escaped. Commander NW front in 1941, he failed to deal with the German blitzkrieg. In 1953–60 he was president of the Presidium of the USSR.

Voroshilovgrad /ˌvɒrəˈʃiːlɒfgræd/ industrial city (locomotives, mining machinery) in the Ukraine Republic, USSR, known as Lugansk until 1935 and 1958–70; population (1985) 497,000.

Vorster /'fɔːstə/ Balthazar Johannes 1915–1983. South African prime minister 1966–78, in succession to ◊Verwoerd, and president 1978–79. He resigned when it was discovered that the Department of Information had made unauthorized use of public funds during his premiership.

Vorticism a movement 1913–22 in English painting, with aims similar to those of ◊Futurism. Its exponents, of whom Wyndham Lewis was the leader, believed that painting should reflect the complexity of the modern industrial world, and used angular abstract shapes to give the impression of movement.

Vosges /vəʊʒ/ mountain range in E France, rising in the Ballon de Guebwiller to 1,422 m/4,667 ft and forming the W edge of the Rhine rift valley.

Voskhod ('ascent') a Soviet spacecraft used in the mid 1960s, modified from the single-seat Vostok, capable of carrying two or three cosmonauts. The first Voskhod carried the first multi-person crew. During the second Voskhod flight, Alexei Leonov made the world's first space walk 1965.

Vostok ('east') a Soviet single-seat spacecraft used 1961–63, in which cosmonauts made flights lasting up to five days. Vostok was a metal sphere 2.3 m/7.5 ft in diameter. Flights included the first person in space, Yuri ◊Gagarin.

vote expression of opinion by ballot, show of hands, or other means. In parliamentary elections the results can be calculated in a number of ways. The main electoral systems are: *first past the post*, with single-member constituencies in which the candidate with most votes wins (UK, USA); ◊*proportional representation* (PR), in which seats are shared by parties according to their share of the vote; *preferential vote*, in which the voter indicates first and second choices either by *alternative vote* (AV), in which, if no candidate achieves over 50 per cent of the votes, voters' second choices are successively transferred from the least successful candidates until one candidate does achieve 50 per cent (Australia); or by *second ballot*, when no candidate has an absolute majority on the first count (France).

All British subjects over 18, except peers, the insane, and felons, are entitled to vote in UK local government and parliamentary elections. A register is prepared annually, and since 1872 voting has been by secret ballot. Under the Corrupt and Illegal Practices Act 1883 any candidate attempting to influence voters by gifts, loans or promises, or by intimidation, is liable to a fine or imprisonment. The voting system is by a simple majority in single-member constituencies. Critics point out that under this system many electors have no say, since votes for a defeated candidate are wasted, and governments may take office with a minority of the total vote. When there are two main parties, divided along class lines, the one in power often undoes the legislation of its predecessor. Supporters of the system argue the danger of increasing party fragmentation, and they believe continual coalition governments would be ineffective.

In the USA the voting age is also 18. Conditions of residence vary from state to state. Until declared illegal in 1965, literacy tests or a ◊poll tax were often used to prevent black people from voting in the South.

See also ◊plebiscite and ◊referendum.

Voyager probes two US space probes to the outer planets. Voyager 1, launched on 5 Sept 1977, passed ◊Jupiter in Mar 1979, and reached ◊Saturn in Nov 1980. Voyager 2 was launched earlier, on 20 Aug 1977, on a slower trajectory that took it past Jupiter in Jul 1979 and Saturn in Aug 1981; it then flew past ◊Uranus in Jan

1986, giving us our first close-up look at that remote planet. It is due to reach ◊Neptune in Aug 1989. The Voyagers have vastly improved our knowledge of the largest planets in the solar system. See also ◊Pioneer.

Voysey /'vɔɪzi/ Charles Francis Annesley 1857–1941. British architect and designer. His fame as an architect rests on his country houses, which are characteristically asymmetrical with massive buttresses, long sloping roofs and rough-cast walls; the room plan is informal, with all furniture and interior details designed by Voysey. His wallpapers and textiles have a cosy sentimentality.

Vries /friːs/ Hugo de 1848–1935. Dutch botanist, who conducted important research on osmosis in plant cells and was a pioneer in the study of plant evolution. His work led to the rediscovery of ◊Mendel's Laws and the formulation of the theory of mutation.

Vuillard /vwiː'ɑː/ Edouard 1886–1940. French artist. Born at Cuisseaux, he lived most of his life in Montmartre. He was one of the ◊Nabis, excelling in portraits and intimate interior scenes in which his mother – manager of a dressmaker's shop – often features. His work, along with that of his friend ◊Bonnard, was dubbed *intimisme*.

Vulcan /'vʌlkən/ in Roman mythology, the god of fire and destruction, later identified with the Greek god ◊Hephaestus.

vulcanization technique for hardening ◊rubber, which essentially involves heating it with and chemically combining it with sulphur. The process also makes the rubber stronger and more elastic. If the sulphur content is increased to as much as 30 per cent, the product is the inelastic solid known as ebonite. More expensive alternatives to rubber, such as selenium and telurium, are used to vulcanize rubber for specialized products. Accelerators can be added to speed the vulcanization process, which takes from a few minutes for small objects to an hour or more for vehicle tyres. Moulded objects are often shaped and vulcanized simultaneously in heated moulds; other objects may be vulcanized in hot water, hot air or steam. The process was discovered accidentally in 1839 by US inventor Charles ◊Goodyear.

vulcanology the study of ◊volcanoes and the geological phenomena that cause them.

Vulgate /'vʌlgeɪt/ the Latin translation of the Bible, mostly by St Jerome in the 4th century, so called because of its vulgar (common) use in the Roman Catholic Church.

Vulpecula small ◊constellation in the northern hemisphere of the sky, in the shape of a fox. It contains a major planetary ◊nebula (interstellar gas and dust), the Dumb-bell, and the first ◊pulsar (pulsating radio source) to be discovered.

vulture a bird of prey that feeds on carrion. The head and neck are bare, the plumage shaggy, and the beak and claws are hooked. True vultures occur only in the Old World; the New World forms include the American ◊condor and turkey buzzard.

Vyborg /'viːbɔːg/ port and naval base in E Karelia, USSR, on the Gulf of Finland, 112 km/70 mi NW of Leningrad. Founded by the Swedes 1293, it was Finnish 1918–40 (*Viipuri*). Population (1973) 51,000.

W the 23rd letter of the English alphabet, representing a labial-velar semi-vowel: a *u* in consonantal function. It is called double *u* because it was written *uu* or *vv* which in ligature resulted in *w*.

Waddenzee /'wɒdnzeɪ/ European estuarine area (tidal flats, salt marshes, islands, and inlets) N of the Netherlands and West Germany, and W of Denmark; area 10,000 sq km/4,000 sq mi. It is the nursery for the North Sea fisheries, and the ecology is threatened by tourism and other development.

Wadi Halfa /'wɒdi 'haɪfə/ frontier town in Sudan, on Lake Nuba (the Sudanese section of Lake Nasser, formed by the Nile dam at Aswan, which partly flooded the archaeological sites here.

Wafd the main Egyptian nationalist party in the inter-war era. Led by Nahas Pasha it formed a number of governments in the 1920s and 1930s. Dismissed by King Farouk in 1938, it was reinstated by the British in 1941. The party's pro-British stance weakened its claim to lead the nationalist movement and the party was again dismissed by Farouk in 1952, shortly before his own deposition. The party was banned in Jan 1953 after the coup led by Neguib.

wafer in microelectronics a 'super-chip' some 8–10 cm/3–4 in in diameter, for which wafer-scale integration (WSI) is used to link together the equivalent of many individual ◊silicon chips, improving on reliability, speed, and cooling.

Wagga Wagga /'wɒgə 'wɒgə/ agricultural town in New South Wales, Australia; population (1985) 49,500.

Wagner /'vɑːgnə/ Otto 1841–1918. Viennese architect, who at first designed in the Art Nouveau style, for example Vienna Stadtbahn 1894–97, but later rejected ornament in favour of rationalism, as in his Post Office Savings Bank, Vienna, 1904–06. He influenced younger Viennese architects such as Josef ◊Hoffmann, Adolf ◊Loos, and Joseph ◊Olbrich.

Wagner /'vɑːgnə/ Richard 1813–1883. German opera composer, born in Leipzig and educated in Dresden. He became director of the Magdeburg theatre where he produced, unsuccessfully, his early opera, *Das*

Liebesverbot/Forbidden Love 1836. He lived in Paris 1839–42. His opera *Rienzi* was produced at Dresden in 1842, followed by *Der fliegende Holländer/The Flying Dutchman* in 1843. While conductor at the Dresden opera house he composed *Tannhäuser* (produced 1845) and *Lohengrin*. In 1849 he fled to Paris to escape arrest for taking part in the 1848 revolutionary riots. ◊Liszt befriended him, and produced *Lohengrin* in Weimar in 1850. Wagner was later allowed to return to Germany, and in 1864 won the favour of Ludwig II of Bavaria. In 1866–74 Wagner lived in Switzerland near Lucerne. His *Tristan and Isolde* was produced in Munich in 1865, and Wagner founded the festival theatre in Bayreuth, also in Bavaria, where in 1876 his masterpiece *Der Ring des Nibelugen/The Ring of the Nibelungs*, a sequence of four operas, *Der Rheingold/The Rhinegold*, *Die Walküre/The Valkyrie*, *Siegfried*, and *Götter-dammerung/Twilight of the Gods* – was given its first performance. His last work, *Parsifal*, was produced in 1882.

Wagner revolutionized the 19th-century conception of opera, the music drama, envisaging it as a wholly new art form, in which musical, poetic, and scenic elements should be unified; and by such devices as the *Leitmotiv* he gave to opera thematic unity and coherence. The Bayreuth tradition was carried on by Wagner's wife *Cosima Wagner* (1837–1930), ◊Liszt's daughter, whom he had married in 1870 after her first husband, Hans von ◊Bülow, had divorced her; by her son *Siegfried Wagner* (1869–1930), and by later descendants.

Wagner-Jauregg /'vɑːgnə 'jaurek/ Julius 1857–1940. Austrian neurologist. He received a Nobel prize in 1927 for his work on the use of induced fevers in treating mental illness.

Wagram, Battle of /'vɑːgrəm/ battle in Jul 1809 when Napoleon defeated the Austrians under Archduke Charles near the village of Wagram NE of Vienna, Austria.

wagtail slim narrow-billed bird with a characteristic flicking movement of the tail. British species include the *pied wagtail Motacilla alba* with black, grey, and white plumage; the *grey wagtail Motacilla cinerae* and

Wagner German composer Richard Wagner instituted an annual festival of his own operas, at a theatre he designed himself, in Bayreuth, West Germany.

the summer visitor *yellow wagtail Motacilla flava*.

Wahabi popular name for the purist Saudi Islamic sect founded by Muhammad ibn-Abd-al-Wahab (1703–92), which regards all others as heresies and their followers as liable to the death penalty.

Waikato /waɪ'kætəʊ/ river on North Island, New Zealand, 355 km/220 m long; Waikato is also the name of the dairy area the river traverses, chief town Hamilton.

Wairarapa /ˌwaɪrə'ræpə/ area of North Island, New Zealand, round Lake Wairarapa, specializing in prime lamb and diarying. The chief market centre is Masterton, population (1979) 21,100.

Wairau /'waɪrau/ river in N South Island, New Zealand, flowing 170 km/105 m NE to Cook Strait.

Waitaki /waɪ'tæki/ river in SE South Island, New Zealand, which flows 215 km/135 mi to the

Pacific. The Benmore hydroelectric installation has created an artificial lake.

Waitangi Day the national day of New Zealand: 6 Feb.

Wajda /ˈvaɪdə/ Andrzej 1926– . Polish film director, one of the major figures in postwar European cinema. His work includes the films *Ashes and Diamonds* 1958, *Men of Marble* 1977, and *Danton* 1982.

Wakefield /ˈweɪkfiːld/ industrial city (chemicals, machine tools), administrative headquarters of West Yorkshire, England; population (1981) 310,200. The Lancastrians defeated the Yorkists here in 1460.

Wakefield /ˈweɪkfiːld/ Edward Gibbon 1796–1862. British colonial administrator, born in London. He was imprisoned for abducting an heiress 1826–29, and became manager of the South Australian Association which founded a colony in 1836. He was an agent for the New Zealand Land Company 1839–46, and emigrated there in 1853. His son *Edward Jerningham Wakefield* (1820–79) wrote *Adventure in New Zealand* 1845.

Wake Island /weɪk/ a small Pacific island between the Philippines and Hawaii, under US Air Force administration
area 8 sq km/3 sq mi
population (1980) 300
history annexed by the USA in 1898, it was uninhabited until in 1935 it was made an air staging point, with a garrison; it was occupied by Japan 1941–45.

Wakhan Salient /wəˈkɑːn/ narrow strip of Afghan territory bordered by USSR, China, and Pakistan. It was effectively annexed by the USSR in 1980 to prevent alleged arms supplies to Afghan guerrillas from China and Pakistan.

Waksman /ˈwæksmən/ Selman 1888–1973. American biochemist born in the Ukraine; he emigrated to the USA in 1910. He coined the name 'anti-biotic' for bacteria-killing chemicals derived from microorganisms, and was awarded a Nobel prize for his isolation of the antibiotic streptomycin.

Walachia /wɒˈleɪkiə/ alternative spelling of ▷Wallachia, part of Romania.

Walcheren /ˈvɑːlkərən/ island in Zeeland province, Netherlands, in the estuary of the Scheldt
area 200 sq km/80 sq mi
capital Middelburg
towns Flushing
features flat and for the most part below sea level
products dairy products
history a British force seized Walcheren in 1809; after 7,000 of the garrison of 15,000 had died of malaria, the remainder were withdrawn. It was flooded by deliberate breaching of the dykes to drive out the Germans 1944–45.

Waldenses (also known as *Waldensians or Vaudois*) Protestant religious sect, founded c. 1170 by Peter Waldo, a merchant of Lyons. They were allied to the ▷Albigenses. They lived in voluntary poverty, refused to take oaths or take part in war, and later rejected the doctrines or transubstantiation, purgatory, and the invocation of saints. Although subjected to persecution until the 17th century, they spread

in France, Germany, and Italy, and still survive in Piedmont.

Waldheim /ˈvældhaɪm/ Kurt 1918– . Austrian politician and diplomat. He was secretary general of the United Nations 1972–81, having been Austria's representative there 1964–68 and 1970–71. In 1986 he was elected president of Austria, but his tenure of office was clouded by allegations that during World War II he had been an intelligence officer in an army unit responsible for transporting Jews to death camps.

Waldheim Kurt Waldheim, president of Austria, was previously ambassador to France and Canada, foreign minister, UN representative, and secretary general of the UN for nine years.

Wales /weɪlz/ (Welsh *Cymru*) Principality of
area 20,762 sq km/8,030 sq mi
capital Cardiff
towns Swansea
features Snowdonia mountains (Snowdon 1,085 m/3,560 ft, the highest point in England and Wales) in the NW and in the SE the Black Mountain, Brecon Beacons, and Black Forest ranges; rivers Severn, Wye, Usk, and Dee
exports traditional industries (coal and steel) have declined, but varied modern and high-technology ventures are being developed: Wales has the largest concentration of Japanese-owned plant in the UK.
currency pound sterling
population (1984) 2,807,000
language English; Welsh-speaking 19% (1981)
religion Nonconformist Protestant denominations; Roman Catholic minority

government returns 38 members to the British Parliament
chronology
c. 200 AD The Celts of Wales became Christian.
c. 450–600 Wales became chief Celtic stronghold to the W as a result of the Saxon invasions of S Britain.
8th century Frontier pushed back to ▷Offa's Dyke.
9th–11th centuries Vikings raided the coasts. At this time Wales was divided into small states organized on a clan basis, although princes such as Rhodri (844–78), Howel the Good (c. 904–49), and Griffith ap Llewelyn (1039–63) temporarily united the country.
11th–12th centuries Continual pressure from across the English border (resisted notably by ▷Llewelyn I and II).
1277 Edward I of England accepted as overlord.
c. 1350–1400 Nationalist uprisings against the English, the most notable of which were led by Owen ▷Glendower 1400–02.
1535 Act of Union united Wales with England.
18th century Evangelical revival made Nonconformity a powerful factor in Welsh life. A coal and iron industry developed in the S.
19th century The miners and ironworkers were militant supporters of Chartism, and Wales became a stronghold of socialism.
1893 University of Wales founded.
1920s–30s Wales suffered greatly from industrial depression; unemployment reached 21

per cent in 1937, and a considerable exodus of population took place.

post-1945 Growing nationalist movement and a revival of the language (there is a Welsh television channel).

1966 ◊Plaid Cymru, the Welsh National Party, returned its first member to Westminster.

WALES: COUNTIES

	Administrative Headquarters	Area in sq km
Clwyd	Mold	2,424
Dyfed	Carmarthen	5,767
Mid-Glamorgan	Cardiff	1,019
South Glamorgan	Cardiff	416
West Glamorgan	Swansea	815
Gwent	Cwmbran	1,377
Gwynedd	Caernarvon	3,865
Powys	Llandrindod Wells	5,079
		20,762

Wales, Prince of /weɪlz/ title conferred on the eldest son of Great Britain's sovereign. Prince ◊Charles was invested as 21st prince of Wales at Caernavon in 1969, by his mother, ◊Elizabeth II.

Wałesa /væˈwensə/ Lech 1947– . Polish trade-union leader, founder of Solidarity 1980; Nobel Peace Prize 1983.

Wałesa, as an electrician at the Lenin shipyard at Gdansk, became a trade-union organizer. Here he founded the Solidarity (Solidarność) independent trade union. A series of strikes led by the charismatic Wałcsa, a devout Catholic, drew wide public support and forced substantial political and economic concessions from the Polish government during 1980–81. In Dec 1981 Solidarity was outlawed and Wałesa arrested, following the imposition of martial law by General ◊Jaruzelski. Wałesa was released in 1982 and remains a prominent dissident figure.

Waley /ˈweɪli/ Arthur 1889–1966. British orientalist. He served in the British Museum, and never visited the Far East. He translated both from Japanese and Chinese, and became known for renderings of Chinese verse in rhymeless free verse 1918. He was the first English translator of the Japanese classics *The Tale of Genji* 1925–33 and *The Pillow-book of Sei Shonagon* 1928, and the 16th-century Chinese novel *Monkey* 1942.

walkabout Australian Aboriginal English for a nomadic ritual excursion into the bush.

The term was adopted in 1970, during tours by Elizabeth II of Australia and New Zealand, for informal public-relations walks by politicians and royalty.

Walker /ˈwɔːkə/ Alice 1944– . American poet, novelist, critic, and essay writer. She was active in the civil-rights movement in the USA in the 1960s and as a black woman has written about the double burden for women of racist and sexist oppression. The novel *The Color Purple* 1983 won the Pulitzer Prize.

Walker /ˈwɔːkə/ Peter Edward 1932– . British Conservative politician, energy secretary 1983–87, secretary of state for Wales from 1987. As energy secretary from 1983 he managed the government's response to the national strike that

Wałesa Lech Wałesa led the strike of shipyard workers in Gdansk, Poland. Their motto, Solidarity, became an international rallying cry. Wałesa has continued his union activities and his attacks on repressive governmental policies.

resulted in the capitulation of the National Union of Miners.

Walker /ˈwɔːkə/ William 1824–1860. American adventurer who briefly established himself as president of a republic in NW Mexico, and in 1856 made himself president of Nicaragua, but was eventually executed. He is regarded as the symbol of US imperialism in Central America.

wallaby name for several small members of the ◊kangaroo family.

Wallace /ˈwɒlɪs/ Alfred Russel 1823–1913. British naturalist who collected animal and plant specimens in South America and the Far East, during the course of which he independently arrived at a theory of evolution by ◊natural selection similar to that of ◊Darwin.

Wallace /ˈwɒlɪs/ Edgar 1875–1932. British writer of thrillers. His prolific output includes *The Four Just Men* 1905; a series set in Africa and including *Sanders of the River*; crime novels such as *A King by Night* 1926; and melodramas such as *The Ringer* 1926 and *On the Spot* inspired by the gangster Al Capone.

Wallace /ˈwɒlɪs/ George 1919– . US politician. Elected governor of Alabama in 1963, he contested the presidency in 1968 as an independent, and in 1972 campaigned for the Democratic nomination, but was shot at a rally and became partly paralysed.

Wallace /ˈwɒlɪs/ Lewis 1827–1905. US general and novelist. He served in the Mexican and Civil Wars, and subsequently became governor of New Mexico and minister to Turkey. He wrote the historical novel *Ben-Hur* 1880.

Wallace /ˈwɒlɪs/ Richard 1818–1890. British art collector. He inherited a valuable art

Wallace Alfred Russel Wallace was a British naturalist who independently evolved a theory of evolution similar to that of Charles Darwin. He had a special interest in the geographical distribution of animal species.

collection from his father, the Marquis of Hertford, which was given by his widow to the UK as the Wallace Collection, containing many 18th-century French paintings. It is now at Hertford House, London.

Wallace /ˈwɒlɪs/ William 1272–1305. Scottish patriot, who led a revolt against English rule in 1297, won a victory at Stirling, and assumed the title 'governor of Scotland'. Edward I defeated him at Falkirk in 1298, and Wallace was captured and executed.

Wallace line an imaginary line running down the Lombok Strait in SE Asia, between the island of Bali and the islands of Lombok and Celebes. It was identified by the naturalist A R ◊Wallace as separating the Asian and Australian biogeographical regions, each of which has its own distinctive animals. Subsequently, others have placed the boundary between these two regions at different points in the Malay archipelago, reflecting the fact that there is an area of overlap, due to migration in both directions.

Wallachia /wɒˈleɪkiə/ independent medieval principality, under Turkish rule 1387–1861, when it was united with Moldavia to form Romania.

Wallenstein /ˈvælənʃtaɪn/ Albrecht von 1583–1634. German general in the ◊Thirty Years' War, assassinated in 1634.

Waller /ˈwɒlə/ Edmund 1606–1687. English poet who managed to eulogize both Cromwell and Charles II, now mainly remembered for lyrics such as 'Go, lovely rose'.

wallflower perennial plant *Cheiranthus cheiri*, family Cruciferae, with fragrant red or yellow flowers in spring.

Wallis /ˈwɒlɪs/ Barnes Neville 1887–1979. British aeronautical engineer who designed the airship R-100 and perfected the 'bouncing bombs' used against the German Möhne and Eder dams in 1943 by the Royal Air Force

Dambusters Squadron. He also assisted the development of the Concorde supersonic airliner, and developed the swing-wing aircraft. He was knighted 1968.

Wallis and Futuna /'wɒlɪs, fuːˈtjuːnə/ two island groups in the SW Pacific which form an overseas territory of France. Area 367 sq km/143 sq mi. Population (1982) 11, 943.

Walloon /wɒˈluːnz/ member of a French-speaking people of SE Belgium, and adjacent areas of France.

Wallsend /ˌwɔːlzˈend/ town in Tyne and Wear, NE England, on the River Tyne at the E end of Hadrian's Wall. Industries include shipbuilding, engineering, and coalmining. Population (1981) 44,699.

Wall Street /wɔːl/ street in Manhattan, New York, so called from a stockade erected 1653. The stock exchange is situated on Wall Street, and it has come to be used as a synonym for stock dealing in the USA.

walnut tree (*Juglans regia*) probably originating in SE Europe, which may have been introduced to England by Roman times and to N America by the early colonists. It may reach 30 m 30m/100 ft, and produces a full crop of nuts about a dozen years from planting: the timber is a favourite in furniture making.

Walpole /'wɔːlpəʊl/ Horace, 4th Earl of Orford 1717–1797. English novelist and politician. The son of Robert ◊Walpole, he was a Whig member of parliament 1741–67. He converted his house at Strawberry Hill, Twickenham, into a Gothic castle. His *The Castle of Otranto* 1764, established the genre of the ◊gothic novel.

Walpole Horace Walpole, Earl of Orford, British writer and member of parliament. He converted his house in Twickenham, near London, into a small Gothic castle called Strawberry Hill, and wrote a gothic novel which was a forerunner of the modern terror-mystery genre.

Walpole /'wɔːlpəʊl/ Hugh 1884–1941. British novelist, born in New Zealand. His books include *The Cathedral* 1922 and *The Old Ladies*

1924. He also wrote the historical 'Lakeland Saga' of the *Herries Chronicle* 1930–33.

Walpole /'wɔːlpəʊl/ Robert, 1st Earl of Orford 1676–1745. British Whig politician, the first '◊prime minister' as first lord of the Treasury and chancellor of the Exchequer 1715–17 and 1721–42. He managed of Parliament, encouraged trade by his pacific foreign policy (until forced into the War of Jenkins's Ear with Spain in 1739), and received an earldom when he eventually retired in 1742. His son was Horace ◊Walpole.

Walpurgis, St /væl'pʊəɡɪs/ English nun who preached Christianity in Germany. *Walpurgis Night* the night before 1 May, her feast day, was formerly associated with witches' sabbaths.

Walras /væl'rɑː/ Léon 1834–1910. French economist. In his *Éléments d'économie politique pure* 1874–77 he made a pioneering attempt to develop a general equilibrium theory (a hypothetical situation in which demand equals supply in all markets). He also originated the theory of marginal utility of a good (the increased value to a person of consuming more of a product).

walrus seal-like marine mammal *Odobenus rosmarus* of the Arctic. It reaches 4 m/12 ft in length, has webbed flippers, a bristly moustache, and large tusks, often used for ivory carvings. It feeds mainly on shellfish.

Walsall /'wɔːlsɔl/ industrial town (castings, tubes, electrical equipment, leather goods) in West Midlands, England, 13 km/8 mi NW of Birmingham; population (1981) 179,000.

Walsingham /'wɔːlsɪŋəm/ Francis c. 1530–1590. English politician who, as secretary of state from 1573, both advocated a strong anti-Spanish policy and ran the efficient government spy system that made it work.

Walter /'wɔːltə/ Hubert died 1205. Archbishop of Canterbury 1193–1205. As justiciar (chief political and legal officer) 1193–98, he ruled England during Richard I's absence and introduced the offices of coroner and justice of the peace.

Walter /'wɔːltə/ John 1739–1812. British newspaper editor, founder of *The Times* (originally the *Daily Universal Register* 1785, but renamed in 1788).

Walter /'wɔːltə/ Lucy c. 1630–1658. Mistress of ◊Charles II, whom she met while a Royalist refugee at The Hague in 1648; the Duke of ◊Monmouth was their son.

Walther von der Vogelweide /'væltə fɒn deəˈfəʊɡəlvaɪdə/ c. 1170–c. 1230. German poet, greatest of the ◊Minnesingers. Of noble birth, he lived in his youth at the Austrian ducal court in Vienna, adopting a wandering life after the death of his patron in 1198. His lyrics deal especially with love, but also with religion and politics.

Walton /'wɔːltən/ Izaak 1593–1683. English author of the classic *Compleat Angler* 1653. He was born in Stafford, settled in London as an ironmonger, and also wrote short biographies of the poets George Herbert and John Donne and the theologian Richard Hooker.

Walton /'wɔːltən/ William (Turner) 1902–1983. British composer, born in Oldham.

His music is tonal, harmonically rich, often sensuous and energetic. Among his works are *Façade* 1923 to words by Edith Sitwell; a viola concerto 1929; the oratorio *Belshazzar's Feast* 1931; two symphonies 1935; a violin concerto 1939 and *Variations on a Theme by Hindemith* 1963. He also composed film scores for *Henry V* 1944, *Hamlet* 1948, and *Richard III* 1956. Knighted 1951, Order of Merit 1967.

waltz a dance in three-four time evolving from the Austrian *ländler*, later made popular by the ◊Strauss family in Vienna. Now a ballroom dance in several different forms.

Walvis Bay /'wɔːlvɪs 'beɪ/ chief port of Namibia; population (1970) 23,500. It has been a detached part of Cape Province, area 1,124 sq km/434 sq mi, from 1878, but administered with Namibia from 1922.

wampum cylindrical beads hand-ground from sea shells and formerly used as currency and in decoration by North American Indians of the NE woodlands.

Wandering Jew legendary Jew (named Ahasuerus) believed to have insulted Christ on his way to Calvary, and been condemned to wander the world till the second coming.

Wanganui /ˌwɒŋəˈnuːɪ/ industrial port (textiles, clothing) in SW North Island, New Zealand, at the mouth of the Wanganui river; population (1985) 40,000.

Wankel /'væŋkəl/ Felix 1902– . German engineer who invented the ◊Wankel engine.

Wankel engine a rotary petrol engine developed by Felix Wankel in the 1950s. It operates according to the usual stages of the ◊four-stroke petrol engine cycle of: (1) intake and (2) compression of fuel mixture; (3) ignition and power; and (4) exhaust. These stages take place in different sectors of a figure-of-eight chamber in the space between the chamber walls and a triangular rotor. Power is produced once on every turn on the rotor.
The Wankel engine is simpler in construction than the normal piston petrol engine, and produces rotary power directly (instead of via a crankshaft). Problems with rotor seals have prevented its widespread use.

Wankie /'wæŋki/ name until 1982 of ◊Hwange, town in Zimbabwe.

wapiti species of deer *Cervus canadensis*, native of North America. It is reddish-brown in colour and about 1.5 m/5 ft in height.

war conflict of arms between nations; between parties within a state, as in civil war; or, very frequently in modern times, between a small element within the state against the state, as in guerrilla war.
The aim is usually to win by inflicting maximum damage on the enemy with minimum damage to the attacker, hence there is a constant tendency to increase the striking power and range of ◊weapons. The basic destructive aim may be modified by the wish to keep the enemy alive as slave labour and to take over their assets of goods and territory in usable condition. Traditionally war did not directly involve civilians. The Spanish Civil War marked the beginning of modern warfare, in which bombing from the air, including both civilian and military targets, put

the entire population of the contending countries in the front line.

Today the problem is much greater, since ◊nuclear, ◊biological, or ◊chemical warfare could eliminate both the combatants and the rest of the world population, together with the very conditions under which any life can exist.

The intermittent Cold War of the 1950s and 1960s between West and East used propaganda and economic competition to achieve the usual aims of war. However, since 1945 there have been over 150 'conventional' (as against nuclear) wars or armed conflicts, breaking out at an increasing rate, especially in the Third World, often heavily supplied with arms and advisers from the superpowers. Most of the estimated 16 million lives lost in war 1945–83 have been civilian. Military spending in the Third World has doubled and worldwide military spending has grown to 6 per cent of global GNP in the 1980s.

waratah Australian shrub or tree, of the family Proteaceae, especially the crimson-flowered *Telopea speciosissima*, emblem of New South Wales.

Warbeck /'wɔːbek/ Perkin c. 1474–1499. Flemish pretender to the English throne. Claiming to be Richard, brother of Edward V, he led a rising against Henry VII in 1497, and was hanged after attempting to escape from the Tower of London.

warbler family of drab-coloured Old World songbirds, Muscicapidae, order Passeriformes. It includes the ◊*chiff chaff, blackcap, goldcrest, willow-warbler*, and the tropical long-tailed *tailor-bird Orthotomus sutorius*, which builds a nest inside two large leaves it sews together. The New World warblers, family Parulidae, are brighter and allied to the ◊tanagers.

war crime act (such as murder of a civilian or a prisoner of war) that contravenes the internationally agreed laws governing the conduct of wars, particularly the Hague Convention 1907 and the ◊Geneva Convention 1949. In practice prosecutions are brought virtually only by the victorious side; it is rare for a country to try its own nationals. A key principle of the law relating to such crimes is that obedience to the orders of a superior in committing them is no defence. Spies in wartime are not war criminals; technically they are 'unprivileged belligerents' and can be shot, and have no right to be treated as prisoners of war.

War crimes became a major issue in the aftermath of World War II. The United Nations War Crimes Commission was set up in 1943 to investigate German atrocities against Allied nationals, and it was agreed that criminals should be tried at the place of their crimes. Leading Nazis were tried at ◊Nuremberg 1945–46. Major Japanese defendants were tried before the International Military Tribunal in Tokyo, and others by the legal section of the Allied supreme command. In subsequent years the hunt for Nazis who escaped justice after the war has continued, led notably by Simon Wiesenthal (1909–), who tracked down Adolf ◊Eichmann in 1960. Perhaps the last major Nazi war criminal to be brought to justice was Klaus

Barbie, tried in France 1987 for crimes committed while he was commandant at Lyons. Subsequent wars have had their full measure of crimes, a notable example being the ◊My Lai massacre 1968, during the Vietnam War, when US troops murdered 200 unarmed civilians.

Ward /wɔːd/ Artemus. Pen name of US humorist Charles Farrar Browne 1834–1867. He was born in Maine, and achieved great popularity with comic writings such as *Artemus Ward: His Book* 1862, and *Artemus Ward: His Travels* 1865.

Ward /wɔːd/ Barbara 1914–1981. British economist. She became president of the Institute for Environment and Development in 1973. In 1976 she received a life peerage as Baroness Jackson of Wadsworth. Her books include *Policy for the West* 1951 and *The Widening Gap* 1971.

Ward /wɔːd/ Leslie 1851–1922. British caricaturist, famous under the pseudonym 'Spy' for his caricatures in *Vanity Fair*.

Ward /wɔːd/ Mrs Humphry (born Mary Augusta Arnold) 1851–1920. British novelist, who wrote serious didactic books, such as *Robert Elsmere* 1888, a study of religious doubt. She was an opponent of women's emancipation.

Warhol /'wɔːhəʊl/ Andy 1931–1987. US ◊pop artist, whose pictures of soup tins, Coca-Cola bottles, and Marilyn Monroe were often produced by silk-screen in multiple images. He also made films, such as *Sleep* 1963, and *Chelsea Girls* 1967, in a rambling, documentary style. Warhol's flair for self-publicity made him a household name during the 1960s.

Warlock /'wɔːlɒk/ Peter. Pseudonym of British composer Philip ◊Heseltine.

warlord any of the local leaders in the provinces of China who, between 1916 and 1928, took advantage of central government weakness to organize their own private armies and fiefdoms.

Warner /'wɔːnə/ Rex 1905– . British novelist remembered today for his early novels, such as *The Aerodrome* 1941, which are disturbing parables based on the political situation of the 1930s.

warning coloration in biology, an alternative term for ◊aposematic coloration.

War Office former British government department controlling military affairs. The Board of Ordnance, which existed in the 14th century, was absorbed into the War Department after the Crimean War and the whole named the War Office. In 1964 its essential core became a subordinate branch of the newly established Ministry of Defence.

warrant officer rank between commissioned and noncommissioned officer in the British army, and the highest noncommissioned rank in ground trades of the Royal Air Force and the RAF regiment.

Warren /'wɒrən/ Earl 1891–1974. US lawyer. He was attorney-general of California 1939–43, governor of the state 1949–53, and chief justice of the Supreme Court 1953–69. Under him a body of liberal legal rulings, notably in civil rights, was handed down.

Warrington /'wɒrɪŋtən/ industrial town (metal goods, chemicals, brewing) in Cheshire,

England, on the Mersey; a new town from 1969; population (1981) 135,500.

Warrnambool /'wɔːnəmbuːl/ port near the mouth of Hopkins river, SW Victoria, Australia; population (1981) 21,500.

Warrumbungle Range /ˌwɒrəm'bʌŋgəl/ mountain range of volcanic origin in New South Wales, Australia. ◊Siding Spring Mountain 859 m/2,817 ft is the site of an observatory; the Breadknife is a 90 m/300 ft high rock only 150 cm/5 ft wide; the highest point is Mount Exmouth 1,228 m/4,028 ft. The name is Aboriginal and means 'broken-up small mountains'.

Warsaw /'wɔːsɔː/ (Polish *Warszawa*) capital of Poland on the river Vistula; university 1818; population (1984) 1,641,000.

history founded in the 13th century, it replaced Cracow as capital in 1595. It was taken by the Germans on 27 Sept 1939 and there was a heroic but abortive rising against the German occupation on 1 Aug 1944. It was finally liberated on 17 Jan 1945. The old city was virtually destroyed in World War II but has been reconstructed.

Warsaw By the end of World War II, Warsaw was almost totally destroyed. Much of the old city has now been carefully restored, such as the Lazienki Palace.

Warsaw Pact established in 1955 between the USSR and the E European communist states as a response to the admission of West Germany into NATO.

warship a fighting ship armed and manned for war. The battleship, supreme at the beginning of the 20th century, was superseded during World War I by the development of submarine attack and was rendered obsolete in World War II with the growth of long-range air attack. The large-scale aircraft carrier was also temporarily out of favour, as too vulnerable, until the resumption of building, especially by the USSR in the late 1970s and 1980s. In the earlier 1970s the mini-carrier evolved, using both vertical take-off aircraft, such as the Harrier jump-jet, and helicopters with a wide range, such as the Sea King. The USSR has ships of this kind carrying as many as 30 helicopters, and the British navy has 'through deck cruisers' designed for the same purpose, just as the US navy has 'sea control ships'. The helicopters are equipped with 'dunking' sonar, torpedoes, and depth charges. These carriers – such as the US *Iwo Jima* and the UK *Intrepid* – and other surface ships are increasingly driven by gas turbines, steam turbines being phased out, and include guided missile destroyers and multi-purpose frigates. The latter carry such varied equipment as guns, depth charge mortars, mine-laying rails, torpedoes, air defence missiles, and surface to surface missiles. The modern warship carries three types of sensor system: (1) radar for surface-search and tracking, navigation, air surveillance, and indication of targets to weapon control systems; (2) sonar for detection of surface and sub-surface targets; and (3) liod (= *li*ghtweight *o*ptronic *d*etector) for processing the optical contrast of a target against its background, as viewed by a television or infrared camera. The tactical information thus collected is then processed by computer and presented in logical form to the command through the combat information system, which at the same time collects information from other fleet units, as well as distributing its own data to them. Finally, weapon control systems guide the selected weapons most efficiently to the targets. Smaller auxiliaries include mine-hunters for countering blockade of home ports, especially the base ports of submarines, and in their most modern form are made of glass-reinforced plastic.

The prime role in future naval warfare will be that of carriers and submarines. The first nuclear-powered submarine was the *Nautilus* 1955; the first Polaris was the *George Washington* 1960, and the first British nuclear-powered submarine was the *Dreadnought* 1963. Submarines fall into two classes: the specially designed, almost silent attack submarine, intended to release its fast torpedoes and missiles at comparatively close range, and the patrolling submarine with guided missiles of such long range that the submarine itself is virtually undetectable to the enemy. Nuclear power for surface warships still presents safety problems.

wart protuberance composed of a local overgrowth of skin. The common wart (verruca vulgaris) is due to a virus infection, and usually disappears spontaneously within two years, but can be treated with peeling applications burning away (cautery) or freezing (cryosurgery).

wart hog species of African wild pig *Phacochoerus aethiopicus* which has an enormous head with a bristly mane, fleshy pads beneath the eyes, and four large tusks.

Warton /'wɔːtn/ Joseph 1722–1800. English poet, headmaster of Winchester 1766–93, whose *Essay on the Writings and Genius of Pope* 1756–82 marked an 'anti-classical' reaction.

Warton /'wɔːtn/ Thomas Wain 1728–1790. English critic, brother of Joseph Warton. He published the first *History of English Poetry* 1774–81.

Warwick /'wɒrɪk/ market town, administrative headquarters of Warwickshire, England; 14th-century castle; university 1964; population (1981) 22,000.

Warwick /'wɒrɪk/ Richard Neville, earl of Warwick 1428–1471. English politician, called the King-maker. During the Wars of the Roses he fought at first on the Yorkist side, and was largely responsible for placing Edward IV on the throne. Having quarrelled with him, he restored Henry VI in 1470, but was defeated and killed by Edward at Barnet.

Warwickshire /'wɒrɪkʃə/ county in central England
area 1,981 sq km/765 sq mi
towns administrative headquarters Warwick; Leamington, Rugby, Stratford-upon-Avon
features Kenilworth and Warwick castles; remains of the 'Forest of Arden' (portrayed by Shakespeare in *As You Like It*); site of the Battle of Edgehill
products mainly agricultural; formerly coalmining
population (1986) 479,700
famous people George Eliot, Shakespeare.

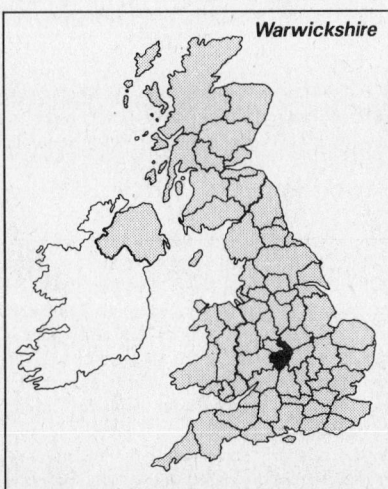
Warwickshire

Wash, The /wɒʃ/ bay of the North Sea between Norfolk and Lincolnshire, England. King John lost his baggage and treasure in crossing it in 1216.

Washington /'wɒʃɪŋtən/ state of the USA; the Evergreen State
area 176,615 sq km/68,191 sq mi
capital Olympia
towns Seattle, Spokane, Tacoma
features Columbia river; Olympic (Olympic Mountains) National Park, and Mount Rainier (Cascade Range) National Park
products apples, cereals; livestock; processed food; timber, wood products; chemicals, cement, zinc, uranium, lead, gold, and silver; aircraft, ships, road transport vehicles
population (1983) 4,300,000, including 61,000 Indians, mainly of the Yakima people
famous people Bing Crosby
history settled from 1811, it became a state in 1889.

Washington /'wɒʃɪŋtən/ town on the River Wear, Tyne and Wear, NE England, designated a 'new town' from 1964. Population (1981) 50,899.

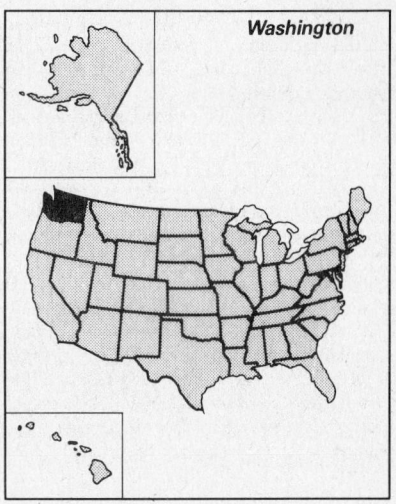
Washington

Washington /'wɒʃɪŋtən/ Booker T(aliaferro) 1856–1915. American black educationist, pioneer in higher education for black people in the southern USA. Son of a slave, he was the founder and first principal of Tuskegee Institute, Alabama, in 1881, originally a training college for blacks, which became a respected academic institution. He maintained that economic independence was the way for blacks to achieve social equality. His books include the autobiography *Up from Slavery* 1901.

Washington Son of a US plantation slave, Booker T Washington worked his way up from janitor to teacher and became a distinguished educationist. He set up the Tuskegee Institute for black students in Alabama and was its principal until his death.

Washington /'wɒʃɪŋtən/ George 1732–1799. First president of the USA, 1789–97. He took part in campaigns against the French and Indians 1753–57, and was elected to the Virginia

House of Burgesses. As a strong opponent of the British government's policy, he sat in the Continental Congresses of 1774 and 1775, and on the outbreak of the War of ◊American Independence was chosen commander in chief. After the war he retired to his Virginia estate, Mount Vernon, but in 1787 he re-entered politics as president of the Constitutional Convention. He was elected president of the USA in 1789 and re-elected in 1793, but refused to serve a third term, setting a precedent that was followed until 1940. Although he attempted to draw his ministers from all factions, his aristocratic outlook alienated Jefferson, with whose resignation in 1793 the two-party system originated. In his farewell address in 1796, Washington maintained that the USA should avoid European quarrels and entangling alliances. He died and was buried at Mount Vernon.

Washington George Washington, first president of the newly independent USA, once said that 'no nation is to be trusted farther than it is bound by its interests'.

Washington Convention an alternative name for ◊CITES, the international agreement which regulates trade in endangered species.

Washington DC /'wɒʃɪŋtən/ (District of Columbia) national capital of the USA
area 178 sq km/68.7 sq mi
capital the District of Columbia covers only the area of the city of Washington
features on the Potomac river. The city was designed by a French engineer, Pierre L'Enfant (1754–1825). Among buildings of architectural note are the Capitol, the Pentagon, the White House, and the Lincoln Memorial. The National Gallery has a good collection of paintings; libraries include the Library of Congress, the National Archives, and the Folger Shakespeare Library. The Smithsonian Institute is here (see ◊Smithson)
products mainly linked with government services and tourism
population (1983) 623,000

history the District of Columbia, initially comprising land ceded from Maryland and Virginia (but the land from Virginia was returned 1846), was established by Act of Congress in 1790–91, and was first used as the seat of Congress in 1800. The right to vote in national elections was not granted to residents until 1961, and a constitutional amendment to give Columbia District full voting representation in Congress was passed in 1978 but not ratified.

wasp name of certain stinging insects in the order Hymenoptera. Of the 290 British species, only a few are true wasps Vespidae; the rest are digger wasps. There are seven British species of social wasps in the genus *Vespa*, some nesting below ground, others in trees or bushes, and the largest being the hornet: all the others are solitary. Among social wasps the queens devote themselves to egg-laying, the fertilized eggs producing female workers; the males arise from unfertilized eggs and have no sting. The larvae are fed on insects, but the mature wasps feed mainly on fruit and sugar. In winter the fecundated queens hibernate, but the other wasps die.

Wasserman /'væsəmæn/ August von 1866–1925. German professor of medicine. In 1907 he discovered a sero-diagnosis of syphilis, known as the Wassermann reaction.

watch a personal portable timepiece. Miniature sundials were the earliest form, the first true watches being developed in the 15th century when they were miniature clocks attached to the girdle. By the 18th century the mechanism had been perfected by inventors such as Thomas Tompion (1639–1713) and Thomas Earnshaw (1749–1829), but throughout the 19th century watches remained articles of value. In the 20th century increasing miniaturization, mass production, and the need for accurate time-keeping in World War I, led to the migration of the watch from the pocket to the wrist. Between the wars watches were given further refinements, for example made anti-magnetic, given shock resistance, or made self-winding, and after World War II came the electric watch in 1957. This had no mainspring, the mechanism being kept in motion by the mutual attraction of a permanent magnet and an electromagnet, which pushed the balance wheel.
In the 1970s came the digital watch, in which all moving parts are dispensed with. The time measurement is done by a quartz crystal ◊oscillator linked to digital counting and display circuits. The time is usually indicated by ◊liquid crystal display (LCD).

water a liquid without colour, taste, or odour; an oxide of hydrogen (H_2O). Water begins to freeze solid at 0°C or 32°F, and to boil at 100°C or 212°F. When liquid, it is virtually incompressible; frozen, it expands by $\frac{1}{11}$th of its volume. 1 cubic cm weighs 1 gram at 4°C, its maximum density, forming the unit of specific gravity. It has the highest known specific heat, and acts as an efficient solvent, particularly when hot. It takes the form of sea, rain, and vapour, and supports all forms of land and marine life. In distinction from heavy water (see ◊deuterium),

ordinary water is sometimes referred to as 'light water'.
Water covers 70 per cent of the Earth's surface. Water supply in sparsely populated regions comes usually from underground water rising to the surface in natural springs, supplemented by pumps and wells. Urban sources are deep artesian wells, rivers, and reservoirs, usually formed from enlarged lakes or dammed and flooded valleys, from which water is conveyed by pipes, conduits, and aqueducts to filter beds. As water seeps through layers of shingle, gravel, and sand, harmful organisms are removed and the water is then distributed (sometimes with such additions as chlorine or fluorine) by pumping or gravitation through mains and pipes. In towns, besides industrial demands, domestic and municipal (road washing, sewage) needs account for about 135 litres/30 gallons per head each day, and supplies are a pressing problem in dry, fast-developing areas such as California. In coastal desert areas, such as the Arabian peninsula, desalination plants for sea water may be used.

water boatman water bug of the family Corixidae that feeds on plant debris and algae. Sometimes also used of the backswimmers, genus *Notecta*, which are superficially similar.

waterbuck African antelope *Kobus ellipsiprymnus* with characteristic white ring marking on the rump. Some 2 m/6 ft long and 1.4 m/4.5 ft at the shoulder, it has coarse long fur and the males have big horns with a corrugated surface. The *defassa waterbuck Kobus defassa* is similar but with a large white rump patch.

Waterbury /'wɔːtəbəri/ industrial city (clocks, watches, brass and copper ware) in Connecticut, USA, founded 1674; population (1980) 228,000.

water closet or WC; a flushing lavatory, which works by siphon action. The first widely used WC was produced in the 1770s by Alexander Cummings in London. The modern type dates from Davis Bostel's invention of 1889, which featured a ball-cock valve system to refill the flushing cistern.

watercolour painting method of painting with pigments mixed with water. Known in China as early as the 3rd century, the art as practised today developed in England, where it was the ideal medium for the expression of shifting vagaries of weather, in the 18th century. Artists excelling in watercolour painting include Sandby, Cozens, Cotman, de Wint, Turner, Constable, Cox, Sargent, Marin, Steer, Cézanne, Signac, Dufy, Nolde, Klee, Paul Nash, and John Nash. The Royal Society of Painters in Water Colours was founded 1804.

watercress perennial aquatic plant *Nasturtium officinale*, found in Europe and Asia, and cultivated as a salad crop. It requires 4.5 million litres/1 million gallons of running water daily per hectare/2.5 acres in cultivation.

water cycle in ecology, the natural circulation of water through the ◊biosphere. Water is lost from the Earth's surface to the atmosphere either by evaporation from the surface of lakes, rivers, and oceans or through the transpiration of plants. This atmospheric water forms clouds which, under the appropriate

water cycle

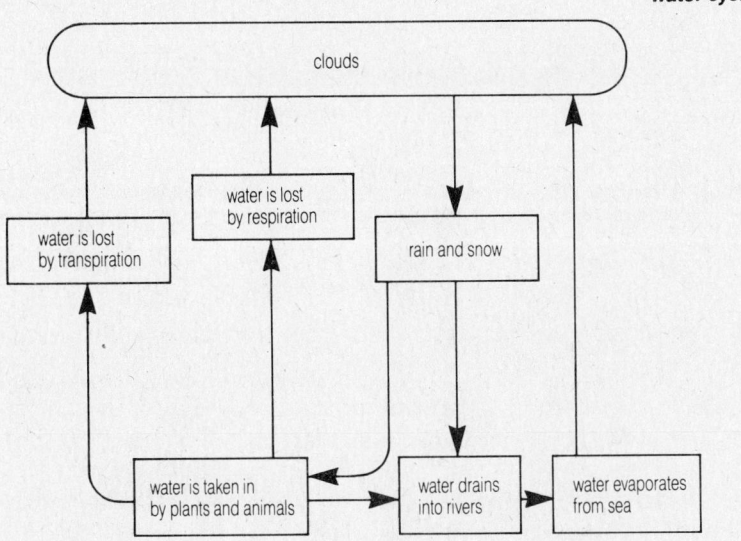

conditions, condense to deposit moisture on the land and sea as rain or snow.

waterflea any aquatic crustacean in the order Cladocera. The commonest species is *Daphnia pulex*.

Waterford /'wɔːtəfəd/ county in Munster province, Republic of Ireland
area 1,839 sq km/710 sq mi
towns county town Waterford
features rivers Suir and Blackwater; Comeragh and Monavallagh mountain ranges in the N and centre
products cattle, beer, whiskey
population (1981) 88,500.

Waterford /'wɔːtəfəd/ port and county town of Waterford county, SE Republic of Ireland, on the Suir, noted for handmade Waterford crystal glass (34 per cent lead content instead of the normal 24 per cent) made here until 1851 and again from 1951; population (1981) 39,500.

waterfowl order of birds, Anseriformes, which includes ducks, geese, and swans.

water gas fuel gas consisting of a mixture of carbon monoxide and hydrogen, made by passing steam over red-hot coke. The gas was once the chief source of hydrogen for chemical syntheses such as the ◊Haber process for making ammonia, but has been largely superseded by hydrogen obtained from natural gas.

Watergate /'wɔːtəgeɪt/ a complex of flats, offices, and a hotel beside the Potomac river, Washington, which was the headquarters of the Democratic Party during the 1972 US presidential election. On 17 Jun five men were caught in these headquarters with electronic eavesdropping equipment and, with two accomplices later arrested, were all found to have been paid by the Republican Committee for the Re-election of the President (CREEP). Their trial and the subsequent sequence of disclosures led to a political crisis and the eventual resignation of President ◊Nixon.

water glass common name for the colourless, jellylike substance sodium metasilicate

(Na_2SiO_3). It dissolves readily in water to give a solution that is used for preserving eggs and fireproofing porous materials such as cloth, paper, and wood. It is also used as an adhesive for paper and card, and in the manufacture of soap and the desiccant substance silica gel.

Waterhouse /'wɔːtəhaʊs/ Alfred 1830–1905. English architect. He was a leading exponent of Victorian Neo-Gothic using, typically, multicoloured tiles and bricks. His best-known work is the Natural History Museum in London 1868.

water hyacinth tropical aquatic plant *Eichhornia crassipes*, family Pontederiaceae, liable to choke waterways, but valued for purifying sewage-polluted water, and used in making methane gas, compost, concentrated protein, paper, and baskets.

water lily aquatic plant of the family Nymphaeaceae. The fleshy roots are embedded in the mud and the large round leaves float on the water. The flowers may be white, pink, yellow, or blue; the white *Nymphaea alba* and yellow *Nuphar lutea* are common in Great Britain; and *Victoria regia*, with leaves about 2 m/6 ft in diameter, occurs in the Amazon, S America.

Waterloo, Battle of /ˌwɔːtəˈluː/ battle on 18 Jun 1815 in which Wellington defeated Napoleon. It took place near a village 13 km/8 mi S of Brussels, Belgium. Wellington had 68,000 men, of whom 24,000 were British, the remainder being German, Dutch, and Belgian, and Napoleon had 72,000. During the last stage of the battle Wellington was supported by the Prussians under Blücher.

Waterloo Cup the most important greyhound race in England, known as 'the courser's Derby', and named after the Waterloo Hotel, Liverpool, whose proprietor originated the race in 1836. It is held annually.

water melon a type of ◊melon.

water mill a machine that harnesses the energy in flowing water to produce mechanical power, typically for milling (grinding) grain.

Water from a stream is directed against the paddles of a water wheel and makes it turn. Simple gearing transfers this motion to the millstones. The familiar vertical water wheel came into widespread use in Roman times. There were two types – *undershot*, in which the wheel simply dipped into the stream; and the more powerful *overshot*, in which the water was directed at the top of the wheel. Water wheels remained the prime source of mechanical power until the development of a reliable steam engine in the 1700s, not only for milling, but also for metalworking, crushing and grinding operations, and driving machines in the early factories. The modern equivalent of the water wheel is the water turbine, used in ◊hydroelectric power plants.

water polo developed in England in 1869, it was originally called 'Soccer-in-Water'. The Swimming Association of Great Britain recognized the game in 1885. The idea is to score goals, as in soccer, at each end of a swimming pool. An inflated ball is passed among the players, who must swim without touching the bottom of the pool. A goal is scored when the ball is thrown past the goalkeeper and into the net.

water skiing the propulsion of a person across water on a ski, or skis, wider than those used for skiing on snow, by means of a rope (23 m/75 ft long) attached to a speedboat. The first person known to have 'danced on water' on a wooden plank was Eliseo of Tarentum in the 14th century. Ralph Samuelson (USA) pioneered the sport as it is known today in 1922. The governing body, the Union Internationale de Ski Nautique, was founded in 1946. Competitions are for over-all performances, slalom, tricks, and jumping, in which distances of 200 feet can be reached.

water softener a substance or unit that removes the hardness from water. Hardness is caused by the presence of calcium and magnesium ions, which combine with soap to form an insoluble scum and prevent lathering. Water-softening processes treat the water so that these ions are replaced by sodium ions which are fully soluble and cause no scum. They use complex minerals called ◊zeolites or ion-exchange resins, which effect ion replacement.

water table level of ground below which the earth and rocks are saturated with water. Thus, above a water table, water will drain downwards, but where a water table cuts the surface of the earth, a spring results. The water table tends to follow surface contours, and varies with rainfall.

Watford /'wɒtfəd/ industrial town (printing, brewing, flour, iron) in Hertfordshire, England; population (1986) 76,500.

Watson /'wɒtsən/ James D 1928– . US biologist whose researches on the molecular structure of ◊DNA and the genetic code, in collaboration with Francis ◊Crick, earned him a shared Nobel prize in 1962.

Watson /'wɒtsən/ John B(roadus) 1878–1958. US psychologist, founder of behaviourism. He rejected introspection (observation by an individual of his or her own mental processes) and regarded psychology as the study of observable behaviour, within the scientific tradition.

water table

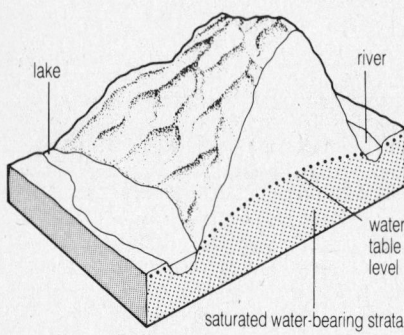

lake

river

water
table
level

saturated water-bearing strata

Watt Drawing published 1865 in Samuel Smiles's *Lives of Boulton and Watt* of James Watt's prototype steam engine, Old Bess. In this engine, reciprocating motion was turned to rotary motion by a sun-and-planet gear train.

Watson-Watt /ˈwɒtsən ˈwɒt/ Robert Alexander 1892–1973. British physicist who developed a forerunner of ◊radar. During a long career in government service (1915–1952) he proposed in 1935 a method of radiolocation of aircraft – a key factor in Britain's victory in World War II.

watt unit of ◊power equal to the expenditure (or consumption) of energy at a rate of 1 ◊joule per second. In electricity, the flow of 1 ◊amp of current through a conductor whose ends are at a potential difference of 1 ◊volt requires 1 watt of power (watts = volts × amps). Named after the British scientist James ◊Watt.

Watt /wɒt/ James 1736–1819. Scottish engineer who developed the ◊steam engine. He realized that ◊Newcomen's steam engine could be made vastly more efficient by cooling the used steam in a condenser separate from the main cylinder. Steam engines (originally for mine pumping) incorporating governors, sun-and-planet gears, and other devices of his invention were successfully built by him in partnership with Matthew Boulton, and were vital to the ◊Industrial Revolution.

Watteau /ˈwɒtəʊ/ Antoine 1736–1819. French painter. Under the influence of the Flemish genre painters he painted scenes of tavern and of military life. He later became famous as a painter of the *fête galante*: fashionable figures disporting themselves in a pastoral setting. He was admitted to the French Academy in 1717 and visited London in 1719.

wattle name given in Australia, where its fluffy golden flowers are the national emblem, to certain species of ◊acacia. Wonderfully adapted to drought conditions, the specially tough leaves further avoid loss of water through transpiration by turning their edges only to the direct rays of the sun. Wattles are used for tannin and fencing.

Watts /wɒts/ George Frederick 1817–1904. British artist. Born in London, he studied in the Royal Academy schools. In 1864 he married the actress Ellen Terry: later the marriage was dissolved. In 1867 he was elected Royal Academician. He painted allegorical, biblical, and classical subjects, and portraits.

Watts /wɒts/ Isaac 1674–1748. British Nonconformist writer of hymns, including 'O God, our help in ages past'.

Watts-Dunton /ˈwɒts ˈdʌntən/ (Walter) Theodore 1832–1914. British writer, author of *Aylwin* 1898, a novel of gypsy life, poems and critical work. He was a close friend of the poet Swinburne, who shared his house at Putney for many years, the painter Rossetti and the writer Borrow.

Waugh /wɔː/ Evelyn (Arthur St John) 1903–1966. British novelist. He made his name with social satire, for example *Decline and Fall* 1928, *Vile Bodies* 1930, and *The Loved One* 1948. A Roman Catholic convert from 1930, he developed a serious concern with such issues in *Brideshead Revisited* 1945. *The Ordeal of Gilbert Pinfold* 1957 is largely autobiographical.

wave in physics, a pulse or pattern of disturbances which travels through a medium by means of the forces between the particles of the medium. Waves transport ◊energy and show the properties of ◊reflection, ◊refraction, ◊diffraction, and ◊interference. Sound waves are longitudinal, that is the particles of the medium (such as air) vibrate to and fro parallel to the direction in which the wave is travelling. Seismic waves in the Earth's crust include both longitudinal and transverse (at right angles to the direction of propagation) components. ◊Electromagnetic waves (such as light) have many of the properties of an ordinary wave, but no medium is needed; the 'disturbance' takes the form of alternating electric and magnetic fields. See also ◊Sine.

wave in the oceans, the formation of a ridge or swell by wind or other causes. Freak or 'episodic' waves form under certain weather conditions at certain times of the year, travelling long distances in the Atlantic, Indian, and Pacific oceans. They become extremely dangerous when they reach the shallow waters of the continental shelves at 200 m/100 fathoms, especially when they meet currents, for example, the Agulhas Current to the E of South Africa, and the Gulf Stream. A wave height of 34 m/112 ft has been recorded. Freak waves are considered responsible for the sudden disappearance, without distress calls, of many sound ships. A ◊tsunami is a type of freak wave.

Wavell /ˈweɪvəl/ Archibald, 1st Earl Wavell 1883–1950. British field marshal. He was appointed commander in chief Middle East in July 1939. He conducted the North African war against Italy 1940–41, and achieved notable successes there as well as in Ethiopia. He was transferred as commander in chief India in July 1941, and succeeded Lord Linlithgow as viceroy 1943–47, being created viscount in 1943.

wave power power obtained by harnessing the energy of the waves. Various schemes to do this have been advanced since 1973, when oil prices rose dramatically and the prospects of an energy shortage become very serious. In 1974 the British engineer Stephen Salter developed the so-called duck – a floating boom, whose segments nod up and down with the waves. The nodding motion can be used to drive pumps and spin generators. The most successful of several other devices, developed in Japan, uses an oscillating water column to harness wave power. Few wave-power schemes have proved economical, and a major breakthrough will be required if wave power is ever to contribute significantly to the world's energy needs.

Waverley /ˈweɪvəli/ John Anderson, 1st Viscount Waverley 1882–1958. British administrator. He organized civil defence for World War II, becoming home secretary and minister for home security in 1939 (the nationally distributed *Anderson shelters*, home outdoor air-raid shelters, were named after him). He was chancellor of the Exchequer 1943–45.

wax solid fatty substance of animal, vegetable or mineral origin.
Animal waxes include beeswax, the wool wax lanolin, and spermaceti from sperm whale oil; they are used mainly in cosmetics, ointments, and polishes. Another important animal wax is tallow, a form of suet once widely used to make candles and soap.
Vegetable waxes, which usually occur as a waterproof coating on plants that grow in hot, arid regions, include carnauba wax (from the leaves of the carnauba palm) and candelilla wax, both of which are components of hard polishes such as those in car wax. Sealing wax is made from lac or shellac, a resinous substance also obtained from plants.
The most important modern waxes, however, are mineral waxes obtained from petroleum. They vary in hardness from the soft petroleum jelly (also called petrolatum) used in ointments to the hard paraffin wax employed for making candles and waxed paper for drinks cartons.

waxbill small African seed-eating bird, genus *Estrilda*, with a waxy-looking red or pink beak.

waxwing bird *Bombycilla garrulus* found in the northern hemisphere. It is greyish-brown above with a reddish-chestnut crest, black streak at the eye, and variegated wings. It undertakes mass migrations in some years.

wayfaring tree shrub *Viburnum lantana*, with clusters of fragrant white flowers, found on lime soils.

Wayne /weɪn/ John 1907–1979. Stage name of US actor Marion Morrison, nicknamed 'Duke' from the name of a dog he once owned. Wayne was the archetypal Western star. His films include *Stagecoach* 1939 and *True Grit* 1969 (for which he won an Academy Award).

Waziristan /wəˌzɪəriˈstɑːn/ mountainous territory in Pakistan, on the border with Afghanistan, inhabited by Waziris and Mahsuds.

Weald, the /wiːld/ (Old English 'forest') area between the N and S Downs, England, once thickly wooded, and forming part of Sussex, Kent, Surrey, and Hampshire. In the Middle Ages, its timber and iron ore made it the industrial heart of England, and its oaks were used in shipbuilding. Ashdown Forest (which includes much heath) is a survival.

weapon any implement used for attack and defence, from simple clubs and bows and arrows in prehistoric times to machine guns and nuclear

Wayne American film actor John Wayne starred in many popular Westerns and war films.

bombs in modern times. The first great revolution in warfare came with the invention of ◊gunpowder and the develoment of hand guns and cannon. Many other weapons now exist – grenades, shells, torpedoes, rockets, guided missiles. The ultimate in explosive weapons are the atomic (fission) and hydrogen (fusion) bombs. They let loose the enormous energy produced when atoms split or fuse together. There are also chemical and bacteriological weapons. See also ◊war. Important landmarks in the development of weapons include:
11th century gunpowder in use by the Chinese
13th century gunpowder known in the West (described in 1242 by Roger ◊Bacon)
about 1300 guns invented by the Arabs, with bamboo muzzles reinforced with iron
1346 Battle of ◊Crécy in which gunpowder was probably used in battle for the first time
1376 Venice used explosive shells
17th century widespread use of guns and cannon in the Thirty Years' War and English Civil War
1800 Henry ◊Shrapnel invented shrapnel for the British army
1863 ◊TNT discovered by German chemist J Wilbrand
1867 ◊dynamite patented by Alfred ◊Nobel
1915 poison gas (chlorine) used for the first time by the Germans in ◊World War I
1916 tanks used for the first time by the British at ◊Cambrai
1945 first test explosion of atom bomb
1954–73 ◊Vietnam War, use of ◊chemical warfare (defoliants and other substances) by the USA

1982 ◊Falklands conflict, Argentinians sank British destroyer with French Exocet missile fired from an aircraft
1983 Star Wars or ◊Strategic Defence Initiative to develop space laser and particle-beam weapons announced by USA.

weasel carnivorous mammal of the family Mustelidae, feeding mainly on mice, voles and rats. The weasel *Mustela nivalis* of Europe and Asia has an elongated body, short legs and tail. The fur is red-brown above and white beneath, but in winter in cold climates is wholly white, as camouflage against snow. There are several American species.

weather the day-to-day variations of meteorological and climatic conditions at a particular place.

weather areas divisions of the sea areas around Great Britain for the purpose of weather forecasting for shipping, particularly to indicate where strong and gale-force winds are expected.

weathering the process by which exposed rocks are broken down by the action of rain, frost, wind, and other elements of the weather. Two types of weathering are recognized.
physical weathering involves such effects as: frost wedging, in which water trapped in a crack in a rock expands on freezing and splits the rock; sand blasting, in which exposed rock faces are worn away by sand particles blown by the wind; and ◊soil creep, in which soil particles gradually move downhill under the influence of gravity.
chemical weathering is a process by which carbon dioxide in the atmosphere combines with rain water to produce weak carbonic acid, which may then react with certain minerals in the rocks and break them down. Examples are the solution of caverns in limestone terrains, and the breakdown of feldspars in granite to form china clay, thus loosening the other minerals present – quartz and mica – which are washed away as sand.
The two types of weathering usually occur together, and in some instances it is difficult to determine which type is involved. For example, onion-skin weathering, which produces rounded ◊inselbergs in arid regions, such as Ayers Rock in central Australia, may be caused by the daily physical expansion and contraction of the surface layers of the rock in the heat of the Sun, or by the chemical reaction of the minerals just beneath the surface with the infrequent rains of these areas.

weaver small bird of the family Ploceidae, which also includes the house sparrow. The majority of weavers are African, a few Asian. The males weave elaborate globular nests from grasses, placing them in bushes and trees. Many kinds are polygamous, so build several nests, and some species build large communal nests with many chambers. Males are often more brightly coloured than females. One species, the *quelea Quelea quelea*, lives and breeds in huge flocks that migrate to follow food sources. Their destructive power can equal that of locusts.

weaving the production of ◊textile fabric by means of a loom. The basic process is the interlacing at right angles of longitudinal threads (the warp) and crosswise threads (the weft), the

weather areas

South East Iceland

Faeroes

Fair Isle

Viking

North Utsire

South Utsire

Bailey

Hebrides

Cromarty

Forties

Fisher

Malin

Forth

Rockall

Dogger

German Bight

Tyne

Irish Sea

Humber

Thames

Shannon

Lundy

Dover

Fastnet

Wight

Plymouth

Portland

Sole

Biscay

Finisterre

limited by the time taken by the passage of the shuttle; this has been partly overcome by the use of water- and air-jet insertion methods, and by the development in the 1970s of 'multiphase' looms in which weft is inserted in continuous waves across the machine, rather than one weft at a time.

Webb /web/ (Martha) Beatrice (born Potter) 1858–1943. English socialist. While researching social problems in London she met and married Sidney ⟁Webb, and together they produced several books and founded the *New Statesman* 1913. She sat on the Royal Commission on the Poor Laws, and in an influential minority report (1909) advocated a new system of social insurance. Among books written on her own are *My Apprenticeship* 1926 and *Our Partnership* 1948.

Webb /web/ Aston 1849–1930. British architect. His work in London includes the front of Buckingham Palace, Admiralty Arch, and the chief section of the Victoria and Albert Museum.

Webb /web/ Mary 1882–1927. British novelist. Born in Shropshire, she wrote of country life and characters, for example in *Precious Bane* 1924.

Webb /web/ Philip 1831–1915. English architect. He mostly designed mostly private houses, including the Red House for William ⟁Morris, and was one of the leading figures, with Richard Norman ⟁Shaw and C F A ⟁Voysey, in the revival of domestic English architecture in the last 30 years of the 19th century.

Webb /web/ Sidney James, Baron Passfield 1859–1947. British socialist theorist. In 1895 he was the principal founder of the London School of Economics, where he was professor of public administration 1912–27. Among the founders of the ⟁Fabian Society in 1884, he was a member of the Labour Party executive 1915–25, entered Parliament in 1922, and was president of the Board of Trade 1924, dominions secretary 1929–30, and colonial secretary 1929–31. He received a peerage in 1929. He married in 1892 Beatrice ⟁Webb, who collaborated with him in a series of books, including *History of Trade Unionism* 1894, *English Local Government* 1906, and *Soviet Communism* 1935.

Webber /'webə/ Andrew Lloyd. British composer of musicals: see ⟁Lloyd Webber.

weber ⟁SI unit of magnetic flux (W), defined as the flux that, linking a circuit of one turn, produces in it an electromotive force of 1 volt as it is reduced to zero at a uniform rate over 1 second. Equivalent of 10^8 maxwells. Named after Wilhelm ⟁Weber.

Weber /'veibə/ Carl Maria von 1786–1826. German composer. Born in Eutin; he became *Kapellmeister* at Breslau 1804–06, Prague 1813–16, and Dresden 1816. The originator of the Romantic opera, he composed *Abu Hassan* 1811, *Euryanthe* 1823, as well as instrumental and piano works. He died during a visit to London.

Weber /'veibə/ Ernst 1795–1878. German physicist, whose work formed the basis of the Weber-⟁Fechner law.

Weber /'veibə/ Max 1864–1920. German sociologist, one of the founders of modern

latter being carried across from one side of the loom to the other by the shuttle.

The technique of weaving has been used all over the world since ancient times and has not really been improved on, only mechanized. Hand looms are still used, for example in the manufacture of tweeds in the British Isles. They may be horizontal or vertical; industrial looms are generally vertical. Of great importance in the hand-loom era was the ⟁Jacquard machine, the last in a series of inventions for producing complicated designs, which was perfected in the early 19th century. The power loom 1786 was essentially the invention of an English clergyman, Edmund ⟁Cartwright. There have been many subsequent improvements. Speed is

WEATHERING

Physical weathering	*temperature changes* – weaking rocks by expansion and contraction *frost* – wedging rocks apart by the expansion of water on freezing *rain* – making loose slopes unstable *wind* – wearing away rocks by sandblasting, and moving sand dunes along *unloading* – the loosening of rock layers by release of pressure after the erosion and removal of those layers above
Chemical weathering	*carbonation* – the breakdown of calcite by reaction with carbonic acid in rainwater *hydrolysis* – the breakdown of feldspar into china clay by reaction with carbonic acid in rainwater *oxidation* – the breakdown of iron-rich minerals due to rusting *hydration* – the expansion of certain minerals due to the uptake of water
Gravity	*soil creep* – the slow downslope movement of surface material *landslide* – the rapid downward movement of solid material *avalanche* – scouring by ice, snow, and accumulated debris
Rivers	*abrasion* – wearing away stream beds and banks by trundling boulders along *corrosion* – the wear on the boulders themselves as they are carried along
Glaciers	deepening of valleys by the weight of ice scouring of rock surfaces by embedded rocky debris
Sea	*hydraulic effect* – expansion of air pockets in rocks and cliffs by constant hammering by waves *abrasion and corrosion* – see **Rivers**

Webb English socialist Beatrice Webb.

Webb Sidney Webb, in partnership with his wife Beatrice, greatly influenced socialist thought in Britain.

sociology. He argued for a scientific and value-free approach to research, yet highlighted the importance of meaning and consciousness in understanding social action through his concept of *verstehen* ('understanding'). His ideas continue to stimulate modern thought on social stratification, power, organizations, law, and religion.
Key works include *The Protestant Ethic and the Spirit of Capitalism* 1902 and *The Sociology of Religion* 1920.
 Weber /'veɪbə/ Wilhelm Eduard 1804–1891. German physicist, who studied ◊magnetism and ◊electricity. Working with Karl Gauss he made sensitive magnetometers to measure ◊magnetic fields, and instruments to measure direct and ◊alternating currents. He also built an electric ◊telegraph. The SI unit of ◊magnetic flux is named after him (see ◊weber).
 Webern /'veɪbən/ Anton (Friedrich Wilhelm von) 1883–1945. Austrian composer. A pupil of ◊Schoenberg, whose 12-note technique he adopted. He wrote works of extreme brevity, for example, the oratorio *Das Augenlicht* 1935 and songs to words by Stefan ◊George and ◊Rilke. He

was mistakenly shot during the Allied occupation of Austria.
 Webster /'webstə/ Daniel 1782–1852. US politician and orator. Born in New Hampshire. He sat in the House of Representatives from 1813, and in the Senate from 1827, at first as a Federalist and later as a Whig. He became secretary of state 1841–43 and 1850–52, and negotiated the Ashburton Treaty (1842) which fixed the Maine–Canada boundary.
 Webster /'webstə/ John c. 1580–1634. English dramatist, who ranks after Shakespeare as the greatest tragedian of his time and the one whose plays are most frequently revived today. His two great plays *The White Devil* 1612 and *The Duchess of Malfi* 1614 are dark, violent tragedies obsessed with death and decay, and infused with poetic brilliance.
 Webster /'webstə/ Noah 1758–1843. American lexicographer, whose books on grammar and spelling and *American Dictionary of the English Language* 1812 standardized the spelling of American English.
 Weddell /'wedl/ James 1787–1834. British Antarctic explorer. In 1823 he reached 75°S latitude and 35°W longitude. The ◊Weddell Sea is named after him.
 Weddell Sea /'wedl/ an arm of the S Atlantic Ocean that cuts into the Antarctic continent SE of Cape Horn; area 8,000,000 sq km/3,000,000 sq mi. Much of it is covered with thick pack ice for most of the year. It is named after the British explorer James ◊Weddell.
 Wedekind /'veɪdəkɪnt/ Frank 1864–1918. German dramatist, born in Hanover. He became in succession journalist, advertising agent, book-keeper to a circus, and actor and producer. He was a forerunner of expressionism with *Frühlings Erwachen/The Awakening of Spring* 1909, and *Erdgeist/Earth Spirit* 1895 and its sequel *Der Marquis von Keith. Die Büchse der Pandora/Pandora's Box* 1903 was the source for Berg's opera *Lulu*.
 wedge a block of triangular cross-section which can be used as a simple machine. An axe is a wedge; it splits wood by redirecting the energy of the downward blow sideways, where it exerts the force needed to split the wood.
 Wedgwood /'wedʒwʊd/ C(icely) V(eronica) 1910– . British historian. An authority on the 17th century, she has published studies of *Cromwell* (1939) and *The Trial of Charles I* (1964). Created Dame of the British Empire 1968, she was awarded the Order of Merit 1969.
 Wedgwood /'wedʒwʊd/ Josiah 1730–1795. British pottery manufacturer who first set up business in Burslem, Staffordshire, in the early 1760s, to produce his famous unglazed blue or green stoneware decorated with white Neo-Classical designs, using pigments of his own invention.
 weedkiller a substance that kills weeds; properly called a *herbicide*. The widespread use of herbicides, especially selective herbicides, in agriculture has led to a dramatic increase in crop yield. Selective herbicides are particularly effective with cereal crops for they do not affect the grasslike leaves, but they do kill all broad-leaved plants. Some weedkillers, however, kill all

plants. They include sodium chlorate and paraquat. The latter is also deadly to animal life if ingested (there is no known antidote), but becomes harmless once it is applied to the plants.

weever fish small fish, genus *Trachinus*, with poison glands on dorsal fin and gill cover that can give a painful sting. Weevers live on sandy seabeds.

weevil superfamily of beetles, Curculionoidea, in the order Coleoptera. The head has a prolonged rostrum, which in the female is used to bore a hole in which to place the eggs. The larvae are white; the adult beetles of *Phyllobius* and *Polydrusus*, the common British genera, are bright green. They feed on vegetable matter. The grain weevil *Sitophilus granarius* is a serious pest and the cotton-boll weevil *Anthonomus grandis* damages cotton crops.

Wegener /'veigənə/ Alfred Lothar 1880–1930. German meteorologist and geophysicist. He completed three expeditions to Greenland and died on a fourth and is chiefly remembered for 'Wegener's hypothesis' of ◊continental drift, expounded in *Origin of Continents and Oceans* 1915. See also ◊plate tectonics.

weightlessness condition in which there is no gravitational force acting on a body, either because gravitational force is cancelled out by equal and opposite acceleration, or the body is so far outside a planet's gravitational field that it exerts no force upon it.

weightlifting sport of lifting the heaviest possible weight above one's head to the satisfaction of judges.

There are two lifts, the *snatch* and the *clean and jerk*. The aggregate weight lifted at both is taken into consideration. In the snatch, the barbell is lifted from the floor to an outstretched arm position above the head in one continuous movement and the bar must be held in position for two seconds. In the clean and jerk the bar is lifted to the chest in the first movement and then above the head in the second.
The International Weight-lifting Federation was formed in 1920.
World and Olympic champions The first recognized world championships were in 1898, and weightlifting was included in the first Olympics in 1896. The Olympic champion is automatically that year's world champion.

weights and measures see ◊cgs system, ◊fps system, ◊mks system, ◊SI units.

Weihai /,wei'hai/ port in Shandong, China; also a commercial centre (textiles, rubber articles, matches, soap, vegetable oils); population about 220,000. It was leased to Britain 1898–1930. It was occupied by Japan 1938–45. Weihaiwei, its name until 1949, means 'awe-inspiring seafort'.

Weil /vei/ Simone 1909–1943. French author, who became a practising Catholic after a mystical experience in 1938. She worked for the Republicans in the Spanish Civil War and during World War II worked briefly for General de Gaulle in London. She died in an English sanatorium. Apart from essays, her works (advocating political quietism) were posthumously published, including *The Need for Roots* 1952, *Waiting for God* 1951, and her notebooks 1956.

Weill /vail/ Kurt (Julian) 1900–1950. German composer, born in Dessau. He wrote chamber and orchestral music, but is best known for the operas in which he collaborated with ◊Brecht, for example *Die Dreigroschenoper/The Threepenny Opera* 1928 (an adaptation of John Gay's *The Beggar's Opera*), and *Aufsteig und Fall der Stadt Mahagonny/The Rise and Fall of the City of Mahagonny* 1930, which attacks social corruption and caused a riot at its premiere in Leipzig. He tried to evolve a new form of musical theatre, using subjects with a contemporary relevance and the simplest possible musical means. With the rise of the Nazis he left Germany for the USA (becoming a US citizen in 1943), where he wrote a number of successful scores for Broadway. He was married to the singer Lotte ◊Lenya.

Weil's disease disease (caused by the protozoan organism leptospires) carried by rats, which pass it in their urine. The disease causes liver and kidney damage in human beings contracting it, but is treatable by drugs.

Weimar /'vaimɑː/ town in SW East Germany, former capital of the grand duchy of Saxe-Weimar (1815–1918); population (1980) 63,500. The writers Goethe, Schiller, and Herder and the composer Liszt once lived here, and nearby is the former concentration camp of Buchenwald.

Weimar Republic name for the constitutional republic in Germany 1918–33, which was destroyed by Hitler and his followers. It took its name from the city where in Feb 1919 a constituent assembly met to draw up a democratic constitution.

Weinberg /'wainbɜːg/ Steven 1933– . US physicist, born in New York, originator of the theory explaining electromagnetic and weak forces 1967, a theory independently arrived at by Abdus ◊Salam. It involved the prediction of a new interaction, the neutral current (discovered in 1973) which required the presence of charm. Both shared a Nobel prize with Sheldon ◊Glashow in 1979.

Weinberger /'wainbɜːgə/ Caspar ('Cap') Willard 1917– . US Republican politician. He served under presidents Nixon and Ford, and was Reagan's defence secretary 1981–87.

Weir /wiə/ Peter 1938– . Australian film director. His works include *Picnic at Hanging Rock* 1975, *Witness* 1985, and *Mosquito Coast* 1986.

Weizmann /'vaitsmæn/ Chaim 1874–1952. Zionist leader (president of Israel 1948–52) and chemist. Born in Russia, he became a naturalized British subject, and as director of the Admiralty laboratories 1916–19 discovered a process for the manufacture of acetone. He conducted the negotiations leading up to the ◊Balfour Declaration. He was head of the Hebrew University in Jerusalem, and in 1948 became the first president of the new republic of Israel.

Welch /weltʃ/ (Maurice) Denton 1915–1948. English writer and artist. An invalid after a bicycle accident 1935, his works include

Weizmann Chaim Weizmann, Russian-born chemist and Zionist leader. He did scientific work for Britain in both World Wars, was head of the Hebrew University in Jerusalem, and in 1948 became the first president of Israel.

the novel *In Youth is Pleasure* 1944 and the auto-biographical *A Voice Through a Cloud* 1950.

welding joining pieces of metal or non-metal, at faces rendered plastic or liquid by heat or by pressure or both. Forge, or hammer, welding, employed by blacksmiths since early times, was the only method available until near the end of the 19th century. The principal modern processes are gas and electric-arc welding, in which the heat from a gas flame or an electric arc melts the faces to be joined. Additional 'filler metal' is usually added to the joint. Resistance welding is another electric method in which the weld is formed by a combination of resistance heating from an electric current, and pressure. Recent developments include electric-slag, electron-beam, high-energy laser, and the still-experimental radio-wave energy-beam welding processes.

Weldon /'weldən/ Fay 1931– . British novelist and dramatist, whose work deals with feminist themes, often in an ironic or broadly comic manner. Novels include *Female Friends* 1975, *Remember Me* 1976, *Puffball* 1980, and *The Life and Loves of a She-Devil* 1984.

Welensky /wə'lenski/ Roy 1907– . Rhodesian politician, born in Salisbury, Southern Rhodesia (now Zimbabwe). He became a noted trade union worker among the railwaymen. He succeeded Malvern as prime minister 1956–63.

Welhaven /'velhɑːvən/ Johan Sebastian Cammermeyer 1807–1873. Norwegian poet. Born at Bergen, he was professor of philosophy at Christiania 1839–68. A supporter of the Dano-Norwegian culture, he is one of the greatest Norwegian masters of poetic form. His works include the satiric *Norges Daemring* 1934.

Welland Ship Canal /'welənd/ Canadian waterway, part of the ◊St Lawrence Seaway.

Welles /welz/ Orson 1915–1985. US actor and director. In 1937 he collaborated with John Houseman in founding the Mercury Theater, New York, where their repertory productions included a modern-dress version of *Julius Caesar*. He started a panic fear of a Martian invasion in the USA in 1938 by a realistic radio broadcast of H G Wells's *The War of the Worlds*. His first film *Citizen Kane* 1940, based on the career of newspaper tycoon ◊Hearst, which he produced, directed, and starred in, was a landmark in the history of cinema; he later played Harry Lime in the film *The Third Man* 1950.

Welles Orson Welles, US actor and director. He co-founded the Mercury Theater in New York and created the film *Citizen Kane* in his twenties.

Wellesley /'welzli/ Richard Colley, Marquess Wellesley 1760–1842. British administrator. Brother of the Duke of Wellington. He was governor-general of India 1798–1805, and by his victories over the Mahrattas greatly extended the territory under British rule. He was foreign secretary 1809–12, and lord lieutenant of Ireland 1821–28 and 1833–34.

Wellesz /'velɪs/ Egon (Joseph) 1885–1974. Austrian composer and musicologist. He specialized in the history of Byzantine, Renaissance, and modern music, and on leaving Austria settled in Oxford, where he was reader in Byzantine music 1948–56. His compositions include operas such as *Alkestis* 1924; symphonies, notably the fifth 1957; ballet music; and a series of string quartets. His writings include a biography of Schoenberg and several studies of Byzantine music.

Wellington /'welɪŋtən/ capital, port, and industrial city (wollen textiles, footwear, bricks)

of New Zealand in North Island on Cook Strait; Victoria University 1897; population (1985) 342,500. Founded in 1840 by Edward Gibbon Wakefield as the first settlement of the New Zealand Company, it has been the seat of government since 1865.

Wellington /'welɪŋtən/ Arthur Wellesley, 1st Duke of Wellington 1769–1852. British soldier and politician 1796–1803. Born in Ireland. Knighted for his army service in India. As commander in the ◊Peninsular War, he finally expelled the French from Spain in 1814, and was raised to a dukedom. Following Napoleon's escape from Elba, he defeated him at Quatre-Bras and Waterloo in 1815, and, as a member of the Congress of Vienna, opposed the dismemberment of France and supported restoration of the Bourbons.

As Tory prime minister 1828–30, he was forced to concede Roman Catholic emancipation and became unpopular for his opposition to parliamentary reform. He was foreign secretary 1834–35 and a member of the cabinet 1841–46. He held the office of commander in chief of the forces at various times from 1827 and for life from 1842. His home was ◊Apsley House in London.

Wellington Arthur Wellesley, 1st Duke of Wellington, known as the Iron Duke. The Napoleonic Wars were ended by his victorious campaign at Waterloo. He is buried in St Paul's Cathedral, London.

Wells /welz/ cathedral town in Somerset, England; population (1981) 8,500. The 12th–13th century cathedral, built near the site of a Saxon church, has a W front rich in statues. Wells was made the seat of a bishopric about 900 (Bath and Wells from 1244).

Wells /welz/ H(erbert) G(eorge) 1866–1946. British writer. He was born in Bromley, Kent, and took a degree at the Royal College of Science, South Kensington. He first made his name in science fiction with *The Time Machine* 1895, *The Invisible Man* 1897, and *The War of the Worlds* 1898. Later books included novels with an anti-establishment, anti-conventional humour remarkable in its day, for example *Kipps* 1905, *Tono-Bungay* 1909, *Ann Veronica* 1909 – in which sexual relationships were frankly treated and which aroused much protest – *The History of Mr Polly* 1910, and *Mr Britling sees it Through* 1916.

Wells H G Wells was a prolific journalist and novelist, who incorporated scientific speculation in his fiction. He was a member of the Fabian Society, and his utopian novels show a belief in socialism created by an elite.

Welsh /welʃ/ people of ◊Wales. See also ◊Celts.

Welsh corgi breed of dog, with a foxlike head and pricked ears, originally bred for cattle herding. The coat is dense and any colour except pure white. There are two types, the Pembrokeshire and the heavier Cardiganshire.

Welsh language a member of the Celtic branch of the Indo-European language family, spoken by about 18.9 per cent of the population of Wales (1981), chiefly in the rural N and W. Among its own speakers it is known as *Cymraeg*. Modern Welsh, like English, is not a highly inflected language, but British, the Celtic ancestor of Welsh, was, like Latin and Anglo-Saxon a highly inflected form. The continuous literature of Welsh, from the 6th century onwards, contains the whole range of change from British to present-day Welsh. Although the spoken language is the strongest of the surviving Celtic languages it has been in retreat in the face of English expansion since the accession of the Welsh Henry Tudor (as Henry VII) to the throne of England. Nowadays, few Welsh people speak only Welsh; they are either bilingual or speak only English.

Welsh literature the chief remains of early Welsh literature are contained in the Four Ancient Books of Wales – the Black Book of Carmarthen, the Book of Taliesin, the Book of Aneirin, and the Red Book of Hergest – anthologies of prose and verse of the 6th–14th centuries. Characteristic of Welsh poetry is the bardic system which ensured the continuance of traditional conventions; most celebrated of the 12th-century bards was Cynddelw.

The English conquest of 1282 involved the fall of the princes who supported these bards, but after a period of decline a new school arose in South Wales with a new freedom in form and sentiment, the most famous poet being the 14th-century Dafydd ap Gwilym, and in the next century the classical metrist Dafydd ap Edmwnd. With the Reformation biblical translations were undertaken, and Morgan Llwyd and Ellis Wynn o Lasynys wrote religious prose.

In the 18th century the classical poetic forms revived with Goronwy Owen, and the Eisteddfod (song festival) movement began: popular measures were used by the hymn-writer William Williams. The 19th century saw few notable figures save the novelist Daniel Owen, but the foundation of a Welsh university and the work there of Sir John Morris Jones (1864–1929) produced a 20th-century revival, including Thomas Gwynn Jones (1871–1949), W J Gruffydd (1881–1954), and Robert Williams Parry (1884–1956). Later poets included J Kitchener Davies (1902–52), Saunders Lewis (1893–   ), and in the period after World War II Waldo Williams (1904–71), Euros Bowen (1904–   ), and Bobi Jones (1929–   ). Still best known outside Wales are those who have expressed the Welsh spirit in English, such as Edward Thomas, Vernon Watkins (1906–67), and Dylan Thomas.

Weltpolitik (German 'world politics') term applied to German foreign policy after about 1890, which represented Emperor Wilhelm II's attempt to make Germany into a world power through a more aggressive foreign policy on colonies and naval building combined with an increase in nationalism at home.

Welty /'welti/ Eudora 1909–   . American novelist and short-story writer, born in Jackson, Mississippi. Her works reflect life in the US South and are notable for their accurate recreation of local speech. Her novels include *Delta Wedding* 1946, *Losing Battles* 1970, and *The Optimist's Daughter* 1972.

welwitschia African woody desert plant *Welwitschia mirabilis* of the Gnetal order. It has a long water-absorbent taproot, and may live a hundred years.

Welwyn Garden City /'welɪn/ industrial town (chemicals, electrical engineering, clothing, food) in Hertfordshire, England, founded 1919–20 by Ebenezer Howard (see ◊garden city) and developed from 1946 as a new town; population (l981) 40,500.

Wembley /'wembli/ district of Greater London borough of Brent. Wembley Stadium, opened in 1924, has been the scene of the British

Empire Exhibition, the annual Football Association cup final, the 1948 Olympic Games, and Live Aid concert 1985.

Wenceslas, St /'wensəslæs/ c. 903–935. Duke of Bohemia who attempted to Christianize his people and was murdered by his brother. He is patron saint of Czechoslovakia and the 'good King Wenceslas' of the carol. Feast day 28 Sept.

Wenchow /,wen'tʃaʊ/ former name of Chinese town ◊Wenzhou.

Wentworth /'wentwəθ/ William Charles 1790–1872. Australian politician. He was the son of D'Arcy Wentworth (c. 1762–1827), surgeon of the penal settlement at Norfolk Island, New South Wales. He took part in the expedition of 1813 which crossed the Blue Mountains, before completing his studies at Cambridge, England. In 1855 he was in Britain to steer the New South Wales constitution through Parliament, and campaigned for Australian federalism and self-government. He settled in Britain in 1862.

Wenzhou /,wen'dʒəʊ/ industrial port in Zhejiang, China; population (1980) 325,000. It was opened to foreign trade in 1877; it staged a revolt against communism 1976–77.

werewolf in folk belief, a human being either turned by spell into a wolf, or having the ability to assume either human or wolf form. The symptoms of ◊porphyria may have fostered the legends.

Werfel /'veəfəl/ Franz 1890–1945. Austrian poet, dramatist, and novelist. Born in Prague, he lived in Germany, Austria, and France, and in 1940 escaped from a French concentration camp to the USA, where he died.

His works include the plays *Juarez und Maximilian* 1924, and *Das Reich Gottes in Böhmen/The Kingdom of God in Bohemia* 1930; and the novel *Das Lied von Bernadette/The Song of Bernadette* 1941.

Wergeland /'veəgəlæn/ Henrik 1808–1845. Norwegian lyric poet. Born at Christiansand, he was the greatest leader of the Norwegian revival.

Werner /'veənə/ Abraham Gottlob 1750–1815. German geologist, one of the first to classify minerals systematically. He also developed the theory of neptunianism – that the Earth was initially covered by water, with every mineral in suspension. As the water receded, layers of rocks 'crystallized'. For most of his life he taught at the Freiburg School of Mines.

Werner /'veənə/ Alfred 1866–1919. Swiss chemist. He was awarded a Nobel prize in 1913 for his work on ◊valency theory.

Wesermünde /,veizə'mʊndə/ name until 1947 of ◊Bremerhaven, port in N West Germany.

Wesker /'weskə/ Arnold 1932–   . British playwright born in Hackney, London. He made his name with the trilogy *Chicken Soup with Barley*, *Roots*, *I'm Talking about Jerusalem* 1958–60; and established a catchphrase with *Chips with Everything* 1962.

Wesley /'wesli/ John 1703–1791. British founder of ◊Methodism. He was born at Epworth, Lincolnshire, where his father was the rector, and went to Oxford University together with his brother Charles, where their circle was

nicknamed Methodists because of their religious observances. He was ordained in the Church of England in 1728 and returned to his Oxford college in 1729 as a tutor. In 1735 he went to Georgia, USA, as a missionary. On his return he experienced 'conversion' in 1738, and from being a rigid High Church man developed into an ardent Evangelical.

When the pulpits of the established church were closed to him and his followers, he took the gospel to the people. For 50 years he rode about the country on horseback, preaching daily, largely in the open air, and often several times a day. He is said to have travelled 250,000 miles and preached 40,000 sermons. His sermons became the doctrinal standard of the Wesleyan Methodist Church. His *Journal* gives an intimate picture of the man and his work.

His brother *Charles Wesley* (1707–88) was one of the original Methodists at Oxford and became a principal preacher and theologian of the Wesleyan Methodists. He wrote some 6,500 hymns, including 'Jesu, lover of my soul'. Charles's son *Samuel Wesley* (1766–1837) was an organist and composer of church music.

Wessex /'wesiks/ the kingdom of the West Saxons in Britain, said to have been founded by Cerdic about 500 AD, which comprised Hampshire, Dorset, Wiltshire, Berkshire, Somerset, and Devon. Egbert in 829 established West Saxon supremacy over all England.

West /west/ Benjamin 1738–1820. American artist. Born in Pennsylvania, he settled in London in 1763, and became president of the Royal Academy in 1792. He painted historical pictures, including *The Death of Wolfe*, and many early American artists studied with him.

West /west/ Mae 1892–1980. US vaudeville actress and film star (*She Done Him Wrong* 1933) who wrote her own dialogue, sending herself up as a sex symbol. Her often quoted lines include 'Come up and see me some time', 'Goodness had nothing to do with it' and 'Beulah, peel me a grape'.

West /west/ Rebecca. Pen name of Cecily Isabel Fairfield 1892–1983. British journalist and novelist. *The Meaning of Treason* 1949 dealt with the spies Burgess and Maclean. Her novels include *The Fountain Overflows* 1956. She was made a Dame of the British Empire in 1959.

West African Economic Community established in 1975 to end barriers in trade and cooperation in development; members in 1987 include: Burkina Faso, Ivory Coast, Mali, Mauritania, Niger, Senegal; observer status Benin, Togo.

West, American the Great Plains region of the USA to the E of the Rocky Mountains from Canada to Texas.

West Bank the area on the W bank of the river Jordan occupied by the Israelis after the Six-Day War 5–10 Jan 1967. The continuing Israeli occupation has created tensions with the Arab population – tension which has been exacerbated by Israeli (Jewish) settlements in the area.

West Bengal /ben'gɔːl/ state of NE India
area 88,563 sq km/33,829 sq mi
capital Calcutta

West The journalist and novelist Rebecca West took her pen name from a character in Ibsen's play *Rosmersholm* and was an active feminist from 1911.

towns Durgarpur
features comprises the W part of the vast alluvial plain created by the Ganges and Brahmaputra, with the Hooghli river; annual rainfall in excess of 250 cm/100 in
products rice, jute, tea; coal; iron and steel, cars, locomotives, aluminium, fertilizers
population (1981) 54,485,500
history created 1947 from the former British province of ◊Bengal, with later territories added: ◊Cooch Behar 1950, ◊Chandernagore 1954, and part of ◊Bihar 1956.

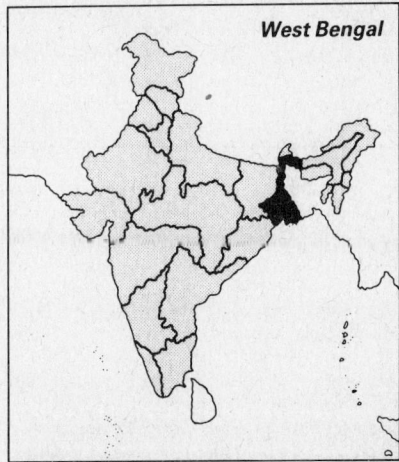

West Bengal

West Bromwich /'brɒmɪdʒ/ industrial town (metalworking, springs, tubes) in West Midlands, England; population (1981) 92,000.
westerlies the prevailing winds from the west that occur in both hemispheres between latitudes of about 35° and 60°. They blow mainly from the southwest in the N hemisphere and the northwest in the S hemisphere, bringing moist weather to the W coast of the landmasses in these latitudes.

Unlike the ◊trade winds, the westerlies are very variable and produce stormy weather.
Western Australia /ɒs'treɪlɪə/ state of Australia
area 2,527,632 sq km/975,920 sq mi
capital Perth
towns chief port Fremantle; Bunbury, Geraldton, Kalgoorlie-Boulder, Albany
features largest state in Australia; Monte Bello Islands; rivers Fitzroy, Fortescue, Gascoyne, Murchison, and Swan; NW coast subject to hurricanes ('willy-willies'); ◊Lasseter's Reef
products wheat, fresh and dried fruit, meat and dairy products; natural gas (NW Shelf) and oil (Canning Basin); iron (the Pilbara); copper, nickel, uranium, gold, diamonds
population (1985) 1,407,451
history a convict settlement at King George Sound in 1826 was short-lived, and in 1829 Captain James Stirling (1791–1865) founded the modern state at Perth. Self-government was achieved in 1890, and in 1901 the state entered the Commonwealth of Australia.

Western Australia Wave Rock at Hyden resulted from sea action when the land was submerged. The streaks are caused by minerals in the rain that seeps down the rock.

Western European Union (WEU) organization established 1955 as a consultative forum for defence issues among W European governments, and comprising Belgium, France, Holland, Italy, Luxembourg, the UK, and West Germany. Policy is agreed during meetings of the foreign ministers of the member nations, with administrative work carried out by a permanent secretariat and specialist committees. The WEU is charged under its charter with ensuring close cooperation with NATO. During its early years the WEU supervized the gradual rearmament of West Germany and the transfer of the Saarland back to West German rule 1957. More recently attempts have been made, particularly by France, to transform the WEU into a coordinating body for W European defence

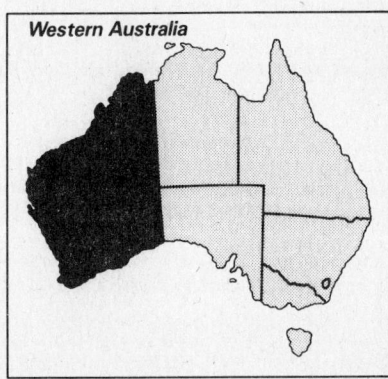

Western Australia

policy and to frame a 'charter of security principles'.
Western Isles islands area of Scotland, comprising the Outer Hebrides (Lewis, Harris, North and South Uist, and Barra); unofficially used of the Hebrides generally
area 2,901 sq km/1,120 sq mi
towns administrative headquarters Stornoway on Lewis
features divided from the mainland by the Minch; Callanish monolithic circles of the Stone Age on Lewis
products Harris tweed
population (1981) 32,000.

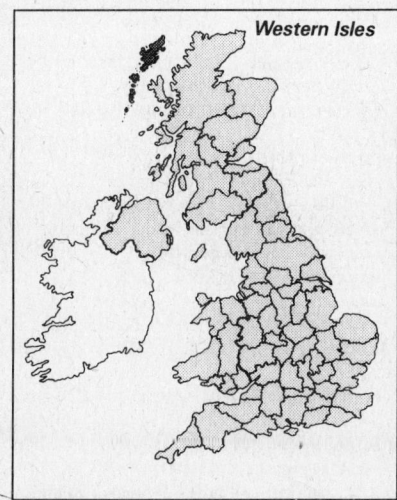

Western Isles

Western Provinces in Canada the 'producer' provinces ◊Alberta, ◊British Columbia, ◊Manitoba, and ◊Saskatchewan.
Western Sahara /sə'hɑːrə/ disputed territory in NW Africa
area 266,000 sq km/102,000 sq mi
capital La'Youn (Arabic *El Aaiún*)
towns phosphate mining town of Bou Craa
features defensive electrically monitored fortified wall enclosing the phosphate area
exports phosphates
currency peseta
population about 1,000,000 in the area occupied by Polisario; 400,000 in Algeria and Libya, and (1970) 76,500 in Morocco

language Arabic
religion Sunni Muslim
government within the fortified wall Morocco rules, and outside, Polisario
recent history a Spanish possession until 1976, when two-thirds was taken over by Morocco and one-third by Mauritania (withdrew in 1979). The Popular Front for the Liberation of Saguia al Hamra and Rio de Oro (Polisario) proclaimed the Saharan Arab Democratic Republic in 1976, and is supported by Algeria and Libya; it currently controls the area formerly occupied by Mauritania.

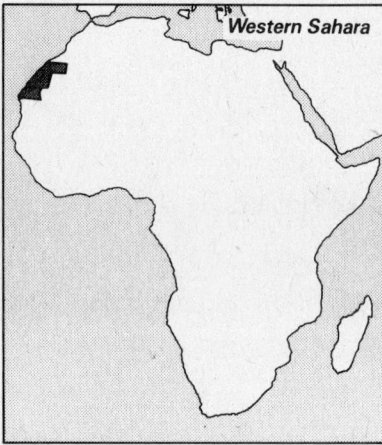

Western Sahara

Western Samoa see ◊Samoa, Western.
West Germany see ◊Germany, West.
West Glamorgan /glə'mɔːgən/ county in W South Wales
area 817 sq km/315 sq mi
towns administrative headquarters Swansea; Port Talbot, Neath
features Gower Peninsula, plants and wildlife
products tinplate, copper, steel
population (1981) 367,000
language 16 per cent Welsh-speaking.
West Indies /'ɪndiz/ archipelago dividing the Atlantic from the Gulf of Mexico and the Caribbean. The islands comprise:
countries independent within the Commonwealth Bahamas, Barbados, Jamaica, Trinidad and Tobago, as well as (in the Leeward Islands) Anguilla, Antigua, Montserrat, and St Kitts-Nevis, and (in the Windward Islands) Dominica, Grenada, St Lucia, and St Vincent
French overseas départements Guadeloupe and Martinique
Netherlands Antilles of which the largest is Curaçao
USA Puerto Rico
divided between UK and USA the Virgin Islands
independent Cuba, Haiti, and Dominican ◊Republic.
West Indies, Federation of federal union comprising Antigua, Barbados, Dominica, Grenada, Jamaica, Montserrat, St Christopher with Nevis and Anguilla, St Lucia, St Vincent, and Trinidad and Tobago, when it came into existence in 1958. This federation, of which the federal parliament was at Port-of-Spain,

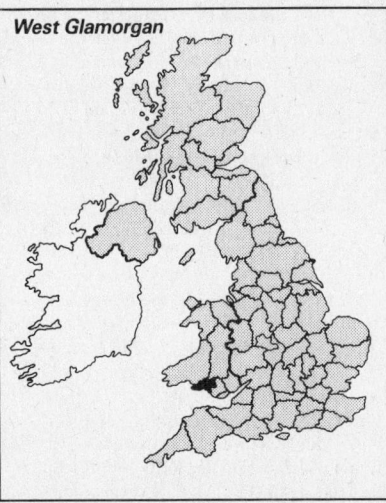

West Glamorgan

Trinidad, came to an end in 1962 when first Jamaica and then Trinidad and Tobago withdrew. Attempts at a new federation were abandoned in 1965, and the new non-colonial status of associated state was assumed in 1967 by Antigua (independent in 1981), Dominica (independent 1974), St Christopher with Nevis and Anguilla (St Christopher independent 1981, and Anguilla, at its own request, a separate crown colony 1981), and St Lucia (independent 1979).
West Irian the western portion of the island of New Guinea. West Irian became part of the Netherland East Indies in 1828 as *Western New Guinea*. It was retained by the Netherlands after Indonesian independence in 1949, but in 1963 was ceded to Indonesia by the UN and remained part of Indonesia by an 'Act of Free Choice' in 1969. Sparsely peopled and economically underdeveloped, West Irian has in recent years been a focus for Indonesia's controversial 'Transmigration Programme', involving a resettlement of farming families from overcrowded Java, causing resentment among native Melanesians.
Westland affair name given to the events surrounding the takeover of the British Westland helicopter company in 1985–86. In financial difficulty, Westland was the subject of takeover bids from two sides, the US-Italian Sikorski-Fiat group, and a European consortium. Michael ◊Heseltine, minister of defence, championed the European bid, and there was much political acrimony in the cabinet and allegations of malpractice. The affair led to the resignation of two cabinet ministers: Heseltine and ◊Brittan.
West Lothian /'ləʊðiən/ former central county of Scotland, bordering the S shore of the Firth of Forth, from 1975 included (except for the Bo'ness area, which went to Central region) in Lothian region. Linlithgow was the administrative headquarters.
Westmacott /'westməkɒt/ Richard 1775–1856. British sculptor. He studied under ◊Canova in Rome, was elected to the Royal Academy 1811 and became a professor there. He

executed monuments in Westminster Abbey and in St Paul's, and the *Achilles* in Hyde Park.
Westmeath /,west'miːð/ inland county of Leinster province, Republic of Ireland
area 1,764 sq km/681 sq mi
town county town Mullingar
features rivers Shannon, Inny, and Brosna; lakes include Ree, Sheelin, and Ennell
products agricultural and dairy products; limestone; textiles
population (1981) 61,500.
West Midlands /'mɪdləndz/ former metropolitan county in central England, replaced by residuary body in 1986 which covers some of its former functions
area 899 sq km/347 sq mi
towns administrative headquarters Birmingham
features created in 1974 from the area around and including Birmingham, and comprising Wolverhampton, Walsall, Dudley, West Bromwich, Smethwick, Coventry
products manufacturing industrial goods
population (1983) 2,652,300
famous people Philip Larkin.

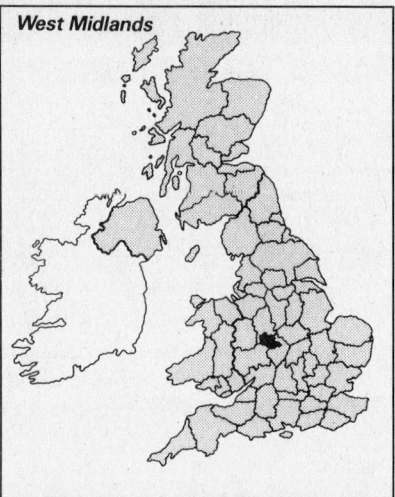

West Midlands

Westminster, City of /'west,mɪnstə/ borough of central Greater London, on the N bank of the Thames between Kensington and the City of London. It encompasses a number of traditional districts:
Bayswater residential and hotel area N of Kensington Gardens
Belgravia, bounded to the N by Knightsbridge, has squares laid out 1825–30 by Thomas ◊Cubitt
Mayfair, between Oxford Street and Piccadilly, includes Park Lane and Grosvenor Square
Paddington with Little Venice on the Grand Union Canal
Pimlico with the Tate Gallery (Turner collection, modern art)
Soho with many restaurants, a Chinese community around Gerrard Street
St John's Wood has Lord's cricket ground
Westminster encompasses Buckingham Palace (royal residence), Green Park, St James's Park and St James's Palace (16th century), ◊Marlborough House, ◊Westminster Abbey,

Westminster Hall (1097–1401), the Houses of ◊Parliament with Big Ben, Whitehall (government offices), Downing Street (homes of the prime minister at number 10 and the chancellor of the Exchequer at number 11), Hyde Park with the Albert Memorial opposite the Royal Albert Hall, Trafalgar Square with the National Gallery and National Portrait Gallery
population (1981) 190,500.

Westminster Abbey Gothic church in central London, officially the Collegiate Church of St Peter, built 1050–1745. Traditionally founded by Sebert, king of the East Saxons, early in the 7th century on a marshy site that was once Thorney Island. The church was consecrated under Edward the Confessor in 1065; rebuilding was begun by Henry III in 1245 and finished in 1528 shortly before the monastery was dissolved. Henry VIII's chantry chapel is remarkable for pendant form vaulting; the west towers are by ◊Hawksmoor 1740. Edward the Confessor, Henry III, Edward I, Henry VII, Elizabeth I, Mary Queen of Scots, Charles II, William III, Anne, and George II are buried here. The Coronation Chair includes the Stone of Scone, on which Scottish kings were crowned, brought here by Edward I in 1296; Poets' Corner was begun with the burial of ◊Spenser 1599. Westminster School, a public school nearby, was once the Abbey School.

Westmorland /'westmələnd/ former county in the Lake District, England, part of Cumbria from 1974.

Weston /'westən/ Edward 1886–1958. US photographer. A founder-member of the F64 group, a school of photography advocating sharp definition, he is noted for the technical mastery in his Californian landscapes and nude studies.

Weston-super-Mare /'westən ˌsuːpə 'meə/ seaside resort and town in Avon, SW England, on the Bristol Channel. Population (1981) 57,980.

Westphalia /west'feɪlɪə/ an independent medieval duchy, Westphalia was incorporated in Prussia by the Congress of Vienna 1815, and made a province 1816 with Münster as its capital. Westphalia included the ◊Ruhr, chief industrial area of Germany. Since 1946 it has been part of the region of ◊North Rhine–Westphalia. The kingdom of Westphalia, created by Napoleon 1807–13, did not include the duchy, but was made up of Prussian lands W of the Elbe, Hessen, Brunswick, and Hanover.

Westphalia, Treaty of agreement 1648 ending the ◊Thirty Years' War.

West Point /'west 'pɔɪnt/ former fort in New York state, on the Hudson, 80 km/50 mi N of New York City, site of the US Military Academy (commonly referred to as West Point), established in 1802: women were admitted 1976. West Point has been a military post since 1778.

West Sussex /'sʌsɪks/ county in S England
area 1,989 sq km/768 sq mi
towns administrative headquarters Chichester; Arundel, Horley, Crawley, Horsham, Haywards Heath; resorts Worthing, Littlehampton, Bognor Regis; port Shoreham
features the Weald, S Downs; rivers Arun, West Rother, Adur; Arundel and Bramber castles; Goodwood, Petworth House (17th century), and

Wakehurst Place, where Kew Botanical Gardens has additional grounds.
population (1986) 687,700.

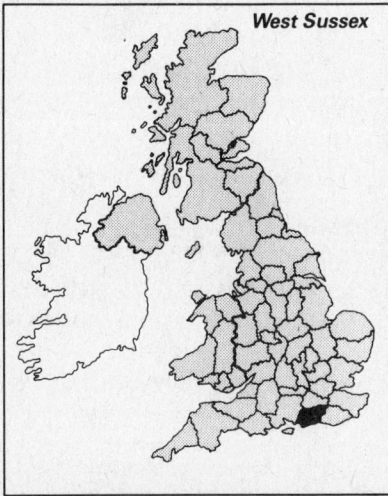
West Sussex

West Virginia /'west və'dʒɪnɪə/ state of the USA; the Mountain State
area 62,629 sq km/24,180 sq mi
capital Charleston
towns Huntington
features Allegheny Mountains; Ohio river; port of Harper's Ferry, restored as when John ◊Brown seized the US armoury in 1859
products fruit, poultry, dairy and meat products; timber; coal, natural gas, oil, chemicals, synthetic fibres, plastics, steel, glass and pottery
population (1984) 1,952,000
famous people Thomas 'Stonewall' Jackson
history on the secession of Virginia from the Union in 1862, West Virginians dissented, and formed a new state in 1863.

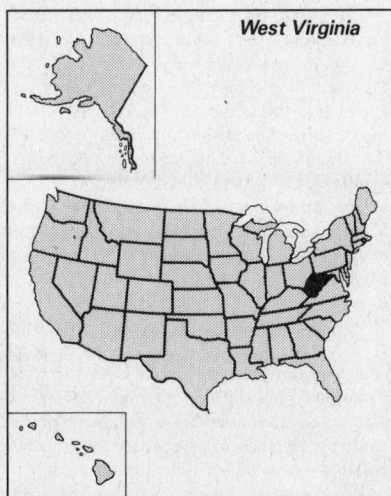
West Virginia

West Yorkshire /'jɔːkʃə/ former metropolitan county in NE England (1976–86), replaced by residuary body in 1986 which covers some of its former functions

area 2,039 sq km/787 sq mi
towns administrative headquarters Wakefield; Leeds, Bradford, Halifax, Huddersfield
features Ilkley Moor, Haworth Moor, Haworth Parsonage; part of the Peak District National Park
products coal, woollen textiles
population (1985) 2,046,500
famous people the Brontës, David Hockney, Henry Moore, J B Priestley.

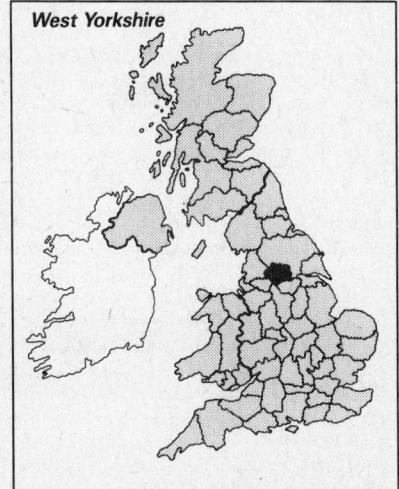
West Yorkshire

wet a derogatory term used to describe a moderate or left-wing supporter of the British Conservative Party who opposed the monetary policies of its leader Margaret Thatcher.

weta flightless insect *Deinacrida rugosa*, resembling a large grasshopper (8.5 cm/3.5 in long), found on offshore islands of New Zealand.

wetback derogatory term for an illegal immigrant from Mexico who lives and works in the USA. The name derives from the traditional mode of entry – by swimming across the Rio Grande.

Wexford /'weksfəd/ seaport and county town of Wexford, Republic of Ireland. Founded by the Danes in the 9th century, and devastated by Cromwell in 1649. Site of an annual light opera festival in Oct–Nov.

Wexford /'weksfəd/ county in the Republic of Ireland, province of Leinster
area 2,352 sq km/908 sq mi
towns county town Wexford
products fish, livestock, oats, barley, potatoes
population (1981) 99,000.

Weyden /'waɪdə/ Rogier van der c. 1399–1464. One of the greatest early Flemish painters, whose masterpiece, the *Deposition* (Prado, Madrid) shows his animated, emotive style at its best.

Weygand /'veɪgɒŋ/ Maxime 1867–1965. French general. Chief of staff to Foch and chief of the Allied general staff in 1918, he successfully defended Warsaw against the Red Army in 1920, and was appointed commander-in-chief in May 1940. He advised surrender to Germany, and was subsequently defence minister in Pétain's government, and high commissioner of N Africa

1940–41. He was a prisoner in Germany 1942–45, and after his return to France was arrested, released in 1946, and in 1949 the sentence of national infamy was quashed.

Weymouth /'weɪməθ/ seaport and resort in Dorset, England; population (1981) 46,300. Weymouth, dating from the 10th century, was the first place in England to suffer from the Black Death in 1348.

whale large mammal adapted to marine life, of the order Cetacea. Being mammals they breathe air and suckle their young; there are internal vestiges of hind limbs. When they surface to breathe, they eject exhausted air in a 'spout' through the blowhole or nostril in the top of the head. The *whalebone whales* suborder Mysticeti include the *blue whale Balaenoptera musculus* (30 m/90 ft long and weighing over 100 tonnes), the world's largest animal, which feeds on plankton, strained through its whalebone 'plates'; the common *rorqual B. physalas* is slate-coloured, and not quite so large. Largest of the *toothed whales*, suborder Odontoceti, which feed on fish and larger animals, is the *sperm whale Physeter catodon* from whose head comes the glistening waxlike substance *spermaceti*. The *killer whale* is a member of the ◊dolphin family. Some whales travel in groups known as schools, keeping in touch by 'songs'. Mass strandings where whales swim onto a beach occur occasionally for unknown reasons. Group loyalty is strong, and whales may follow their leader to disaster.

There were hundreds of thousands of whales at the beginning of the century, but they have been hunted close to extinction. The International Whaling Commission, established 1946, failed to enforce quotas until world concern mounted in the 1970s. Low reproduction rates have meant that populations of protected species have been slow to recover. From 1986 only Iceland, Norway, and the USSR have continued with limited whaling, but pirates also operate. Whale meat is sold for pet food.

Wharton /'(h)wɔːtn/ Edith (born Jones) 1862–1937. US novelist. Her work includes *The House of Mirth* 1905, the rural *Ethan Frome* 1911, *The Custom of the Country* 1913, and *The Age of Innocence* 1920.

wheat cereal plant derived from the wild *Triticum*, a grass native to the Middle East. It has been cultivated since Neolithic times, and is the chief cereal used in bread making in temperate climates which suit its growth. Wheat is killed by frost, and damp renders the grain soft: warm dry regions produce the most valuable grain. The chief wheat-producing areas of the world are the Ukraine in USSR, central and NW USA, the Punjab in India, the prairie provinces of Canada, parts of France and S Germany, Italy, Argentina, and SE Australia. Flour is milled from the endosperm, the coatings of the grain producing bran and pollard. Semolina is also prepared from wheat.

wheatear small migratory bird *Oenanthe oenanthe* found throughout the Old World and also in parts of North America. The plumage is light grey above and white below, with a white

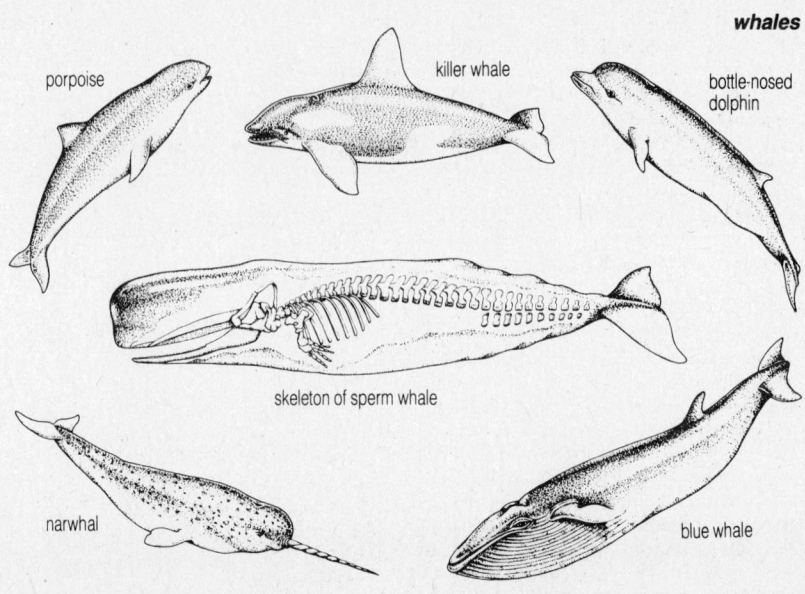

whales

porpoise

killer whale

bottle-nosed dolphin

skeleton of sperm whale

narwhal

blue whale

patch on the back, a black face-patch, and black and white wings and tail.

Wheatley /'(h)wiːtli/ Dennis (Yates) 1897–1977. British thriller and adventure novelist. Best known for his series dealing with black magic and occultism, he also wrote crime novels in which the reader was invited to play the detective.

Wheatstone /'(h)wiːtstən/ Charles 1802–1875. British physicist, originally a musical-instrument maker, and inventor of the concertina and harmonica. With W F ◊Cooke, he patented the electric telegraph in 1837, and, developing an idea of Samuel Hunter ◊Christie, devised the *Wheatstone bridge*, an electrical network for measuring resistance.

wheel and axle a simple machine with a rope wound round an axle connected to a larger wheel with another rope attached to its rim. Pulling on the wheel rope (applying an effort) lifts a load attached to the axle rope. The velocity ratio of the machine (load divided by effort) is equal to the ratio of the wheel radius to the axle radius.

Wheeler /'(h)wiːlə/ Mortimer 1890–1976. British archaeologist. He was keeper of the London Museum 1926–44, when his most notable digs included Caerleon 1926–27 and Maiden Castle in Dorset 1934–37, and as director-general of archaeology in India 1944–48 revealed the ◊Indus Valley civilization. He popularized archaeology, especially by his television appearances.

whelk type of marine gastropod. The common whelk *Buccinum undatum* is widely distributed round the North Sea and Atlantic. It is fished for bait and food, and has a thick spiral shell.

Whig Party /(h)wɪg/ (UK) predecessor of the Liberal Party. The name was first used of rebel ◊Covenanters and then of those who wished to exclude James II from the English succession (as a Roman Catholic). Thus, the Whigs strongly supported the 1688 Revolution. They were in

power continuously 1714–60, led by a group of great landowners and backed by the businessmen and Nonconformists; they pressed for industrial and commercial development, a vigorous foreign policy, and religious toleration. During the French Revolution, the Whigs demanded parliamentary reform in Britain, and from the passing of the Reform Bill in 1832 became known as Liberals.

Whig Party /(h)wɪg/ (USA) party opposed to the autocratic presidency of Andrew Jackson from 1834. The title was taken from the British ◊Whig Party which supported Parliament against the king. It collapsed after defeats in 1852.

whimbrel wading bird *Numenius phaeopus*, in appearance like a small curlew but with a shorter down-curved bill and head stripes. About 40 cm/1.3 ft, it breeds in the far N and winters in Africa.

whip in UK politics, the member of parliament who (like the whipper-in of hounds at a foxhunt) ensures the presence of colleagues in the party when there is to be a vote in Parliament at the end of a debate. The government chief whip and the three junior whips are salaried officials; some opposition whips also receive a salary. Conservative whips are chosen by the leader of the party; Labour whips are chosen by the prime minister when the party is in office, otherwise by election. The written appeal sent by the whips to parliamentary members is also called a whip; this letter is underlined once, twice, or three times to indicate its importance. A three-line whip (three times underlined) is the most urgent, and every member is expected to attend and vote with their party.

whippet breed of dog resembling a small greyhound. The whippet was developed by the colliers of N England, who race them along a straight track, at the end of which their owners stand calling to them.

Whipple /'(h)wɪpl/ Fred Lawrence 1906– . US astronomer, director of the Smithsonian Astrophysical Observatory 1955–73; his hypothesis in 1949 that the nucleus of a comet is like a dirty snowball, was confirmed in 1986 by space-probe studies of ◊Halley's Comet.

whip-poor-will North American nightjar *Caprimulgus vociferus*, so called from its cry.

Whipsnade /'(h)wɪpsneɪd/ English locality in Bedfordshire, 5 km/3 mi S of Dunstable, the site of a zoological park where wild animals and birds are bred and exhibited in conditions resembling their natural state. It was opened to the public in 1931.

whip-snake name for several different species of slender-bodied longtailed snakes. The European *western whip-snake Coluber viridiflavus* is non-venomous, lives in France and Italy, grows to a maximum 2 m/6 ft, is fast-moving, climbing as well as sliding along the ground, and feeds on lizards, mammals, and some other snakes. Various whip-snakes (*Coluber* species) live in N America, especially the dry SW.

whisk(e)y a distilled spirit made from cereals: the name derives from Gaelic *uisge beatha* 'water of life'. Scotch whisky is distilled from malt, Irish whiskey usually from barley, and American whiskey or bourbon from Indian corn or rye.

whist predecessor of ◊bridge, a card game for four, in which the partners try to win the balance of the 13 tricks (the highest card played being the winner).

Whistler /'(h)wɪslə/ James Abbott McNeill 1834–1903. US Impressionist artist, born in Massachusetts. He settled in Chelsea, London, executed etchings of the Thames, and painted *Old Battersea Bridge*, *The Symphony in White*, and portraits. Some of his *Nocturnes* 1877 were adversely criticized by Ruskin and led to a libel trial in 1878 in which Whistler was awarded a farthing damages. Whistler retaliated in 1890 with *The Gentle Art of Making Enemies*. His best-known painting is the portrait of his mother, *Arrangement in Grey and Black, No. 1* 1871–72 (Louvre, Paris).

Whistler /'(h)wɪslə/ Rex John 1905–1944. British artist, noted for fanciful murals, for example in the Tate Gallery restaurant, London, and Haddon Hall, Derbyshire. He was killed in World War II.

Whitby /'(h)wɪtbɪ/ ancient fishing port in N Yorkshire, England; population (1981) 13,800. There are remains of the Benedictine abbey built in 1078 on the site of the original foundation by St Hilda in 657, which was destroyed by the Danes in 867.

Whitby, Synod of council summoned by King Oswy of Northumbria in 664, which decided to adopt the Roman rather than the Celtic form of Christianity for Britain.

White /(h)waɪt/ E(lwyn) B(rooks) 1899–1985. US writer, long associated with the *New Yorker*, noted for satire, for example *Is Sex Necessary?* 1929 (with ◊Thurber), who also wrote two children's classics, *Stuart Little* 1945 and *Charlotte's Web* 1952.

White /(h)waɪt/ Gilbert 1720–1793. English cleric and naturalist, born at Selborne,

Whitby Now a fishing port and resort in NE England, Whitby was an important ecclesiastical centre in the Middle Ages.

◊Hampshire, and author of *Natural History and Antiquities of Selborne* 1789.

White /(h)waɪt/ Patrick 1912– . Australian novelist. Born in London, he settled in Australia in the 1940s. His novels (with allegorical overtones) include *The Aunt's Story* 1946, *Voss* (based on the 19th-century explorer Leichhardt) 1957, and *The Twyborn Affair* 1979. Nobel prize 1973.

White /(h)waɪt/ T(erence) H(anbury) 1906–1964. British writer, who retold the Arthurian legend in four volumes of *The Once and Future King* 1958.

whitebait the young of the ◊herring.

whitebeam tree *Sorbus aria* native to S Europe including S Britain, usually on chalk or limestone. It grows to 20 m/60 ft or so, and gets its name from the leaves, which are elliptical and toothed, and have a dense coat of short white hairs on the underside.

white dwarf a small, hot ◊star, the last stage in the life of a star such as the ◊Sun. White dwarfs have a mass similar to that of the Sun, but are only 1 per cent of the Sun's diameter, similar in size to the Earth. Most have surface temperatures of 8,000°C or more, hotter than the Sun. Yet, being so small, their overall luminosities are 1 per cent that of the Sun or less. White dwarfs consist of *degenerate* matter in which ◊gravity has packed the ◊protons and ◊electrons together as tightly as is physically possible, so that a spoonful of it weighs several tonnes. White dwarfs are thought to be the shrunken remains of stars that have exhausted their internal energy supplies. They slowly cool and fade over billions of years.

Whitefield /'(h)wɪtfiːld/ George 1714–1770. British Methodist evangelist, born in Gloucester. He came under Methodist influence while a student at Oxford and took orders in 1738, but was suspended for his unorthodox doctrines and methods. For many years he travelled through Britain and America, and by his preaching contributed greatly to the religious revival. Whitefield's Tabernacle was built for him in Tottenham Court Road, London (1756; bombed 1945 but rebuilt).

whitefish name applied to freshwater fishes of the salmon family, belonging to the genus *Coregonus*. Abundant in North American lakes, they also occur in Europe and Asia; three species are found in Britain.

Whitehall /,(h)waɪt'hɔːl/ street in central London, between Trafalgar Square and the Houses of Parliament, with many government offices and the Cenotaph war memorial.

Whitehaven /'(h)waɪtheɪvən/ port in Cumbria, England; population (1981) 27,000. Coal mines running beneath the sea have seen major disasters, and Britain's first nuclear power station was sited at Calder Hall to the SE, where there is also a plant for reprocessing spent nuclear fuel at *Sellafield* (formerly Windscale).

Whitehead /'(h)waɪthed/ Alfred North 1861–1947. British philosopher and mathematician. He was professor of applied mathematics at London university 1914–24, and professor of philosophy at Harvard university, USA, 1924–37. In his 'theory of organism' he attempted a synthesis of metaphysics and science. Among his works are *Principia Mathematica* (1910–13; with Bertrand Russell), *Concept of Nature*, and *Adventures of Ideas* 1933. Whitehead received the Order of Merit in 1945.

Whitehead /'(h)waɪthed/ Robert 1823–1905. British engineer who invented the self-propelled torpedo. He developed the torpedo in

Austria in 1866, and within two years was manufacturing 4 m/13 ft torpedoes which could carry a 9 kg/20 lb dynamite warhead at a speed of 7 knots, subsequently improved to 29 knots. They were powered by compressed air and had a balancing mechanism and, later, gyroscopic controls.

white hole in astronomy, the precise opposite of a ◊black hole, formed when a tremendously dense object bursts into view.

Whitehorse /'(h)waɪthɔːs/ capital of Yukon territory, Canada; population (1981) 18,000. Whitehorse is on the NW Highway. It replaced Dawson as capital in 1953.

White Horse any of several ◊hill figures in England.

White House /'(h)waɪthaʊs/ official residence of the president of the USA, in Washington DC. It is a plain edifice of sandstone, built in the Italian renaissance style, 1792–99, to the designs of James ◊Hoban, who also restored it after it was burned by the British in 1814; it was then painted white to hide the scars. The interior was completely rebuilt 1948–52.

The name White House, first recorded in 1811, is often adapted to refer to other residences of the president, for example Little White House, at Warm Springs, Georgia, where F D Roosevelt died; Western White House, at San Clemente, California, where Nixon had a home.

Whitehouse /'(h)waɪthaʊs/ Mary 1910– . British activist; as founder of the National Viewers' and Listeners' Association, she has campaigned to censor radio and television in their treatment of violence and, especially, sex.

Whitelaw /'(h)waɪtlɔː/ William, Viscount Whitelaw 1918– . British Conservative politician. Chief Conservative whip 1964–70, he was leader of the House of Commons 1970–72, and as secretary of state for Northern Ireland introduced the concept of power sharing, then became secretary of state for employment Dec 1973–74, but failed to conciliate the unions. He was chair of the Conservative Party in 1974, and home secretary 1979–83, when he was made a peer. He resigned 1988.

Whiteman /'(h)waɪtmən/ Paul 1890–1967. US dance-band leader specializing in symphonic jazz. He commissioned Gershwin's *Rhapsody in Blue*, conducting its premiere in 1924.

whiteout a 'fog' of grains of dry snow caused by strong winds in temperatures of between 0° and – 30°F in Canada, USA, and elsewhere.

white paper in the UK and some other countries, name of an official document which expresses government policy on an issue. It is usually preparatory to the introduction of a parliamentary bill (a proposed act of parliament). Its name derives from its having fewer pages than a government **blue book**, and therefore needing no blue paper cover.

White Russia English translation of ◊Belorussia, republic of USSR.

Whites term applied to the counter-revolutionary party during the French Revolution, when the royalists used the white lily of the French monarchy as their badge, and also to counter-revolutionaries during the Russian civil wars of 1917–21.

White Sea gulf of the ◊Arctic Ocean, on which Archangel stands and where there is a Soviet warship construction base, including nuclear submarines, at Severodvinsk. The North Dvina and Onega flow into it, and there are canal links with the Baltic, Black, and Caspian seas.

white spirit a colourless liquid derived from petrol; it is used as a solvent and in paints and varnishes.

white terror general term used by socialists and Marxists to describe a right-wing counter-revolution, for example, the attempts by the Chinese Guomindang to massacre the communists between 1927 and 1931.

whitethroat bird *Sylvia communis* of the warbler group, found in scrub, hedges and wood clearings in Europe and Asia in summer, migrating to Africa in winter. It is about 14 cm/5.5 in long. The *lesser whitethroat Sylvia curruca* is a little smaller, and a shyer bird.

whiting food-fish *Merlangius merlangus* common in N European waters. It grows to 70 cm/2.3 ft, lives in shallow sandy waters, and is an active predator.

Whitlam /'(h)wɪtləm/ (Edward) Gough 1916– . Australian Labour politician, leader of the Labour Party 1967–78 and prime minister 1972–75. He cultivated closer relations with Asia, attempted redistribution of wealth and raised loans to increase national ownership of industry and resources. When the opposition blocked finance bills in the Senate, following a crisis of confidence, he refused to call a general election, and was dismissed by the governor-general (Sir John Kerr). He was defeated in the general election eventually called by Malcolm ◊Fraser.

Whitman /'(h)wɪtmən/ Walt(er) 1819–1892. US poet, one of the most important and influential both for the style and subject matter of his work. In 1855 he published *Leaves of Grass*, later much enlarged, which used unconventional ◊free verse and scandalized the public by its frank celebration of sexuality. He preached an American vision of individual freedom and human brotherhood. In 1865 he published *Drum-Taps*, a volume inspired by his work as an army nurse during the Civil War.

Whitney /'(h)wɪtnɪ/ Eli 1765–1825. American inventor who in 1793 patented the cotton gin, a device for separating cotton fibre from its seeds.

Whitstable /'(h)wɪtstəbəl/ resort in Kent, England, at the mouth of the Swale, noted for its oysters; population (1985) 27,290.

Whit Sunday Christian church festival held seven weeks after Easter, corresponding to the Jewish Pentecost and commemorating the descent of the Holy Spirit on the Apostles.

Whitten-Brown /'(h)wɪtn 'braʊn/ Arthur 1886–1948. British aviator. After serving in World War I, he took part in the first nonstop flight across the Atlantic as navigator to Captain John ◊Alcock in 1919.

Whittier /'(h)wɪtɪə/ John Greenleaf 1807–1892. American poet. Born in Massachusetts, of a Quaker family, he entered politics and journalism, and became a powerful opponent of slavery, as in the verse *Voices of Freedom* 1846.

Whitman American poet Walt Whitman. His best-known work *Leaves of Grass* contained the 'Song of Myself'.

Whittington /'(h)wɪtɪŋtən/ Richard (Dick) English cloth merchant, who was mayor of London 1397–98, 1406–07, and 1419–20; according to legend, he came to London as a poor boy with his cat, and only the call of Bow Bells prevented his leaving before making his fortune.

Whittle /'(h)wɪtl/ Frank 1907– . British engineer who invented the jet engine in 1930. In the Royal Air Force he worked on jet propulsion 1937–46. In May 1941 the Gloster E 28/39 aircraft first flew with the Whittle jet engine, and in 1948 his pioneer work was recognized by a government award of £100,000.

whooping cough pertussis; a specific infectious fever caused by bacteria and spread by droplets from the nose and throat. It is marked by a characteristic and obstinate cough, which may persist for months, and the disease may lead to severe complications such as pneumonia. A vaccine is used to give active immunity to children under six. In the 1970s there was controversy because of the alleged possibility of side effects, such as brain damage. The very rare possibility of any side effects is now said to be outweighed by the overall advantages of protection.

whortleberry a form of ◊bilberry.

Whyalla /(h)waɪˈælə/ port and industrial city (iron and steel) in South Australia; population (1985) 29,900.

whydah African bird, genus *Vidua*, of the weaver family. Each whydah species lays its eggs in the nest of a particular species of waxbill. The young bird resembles the young waxbill, and is reared by the waxbill parents. The adult whydahs have no such resemblance.

Whymper /'(h)wɪmpə/ Edward 1840–1911. British mountaineer. He made the first ascents of many Alpine peaks including the Matterhorn

1865 (see ◊Alps), and in the Andes scaled Chimborazo and other mountains.

Wichita /ˈwɪtʃɪtɔː/ industrial city (oil refining, aircraft, motor vehicles) in Kansas, USA; population (1980) 280,000.

Wick /wɪk/ fishing port and industrial town (shipping, distilleries, North Sea oil) in N Scotland, in the Highland region.

Wickham /ˈwɪkəm/ Henry 1846–1928. British planter who founded the rubber plantations of Sri Lanka and Malaysia, and broke the monopoly in rubber production then held by Brazil. He collected rubber seeds from Brazil, where they grew naturally, cultivated them at Kew Gardens, and re-exported them to the Far East.

Wicklow /ˈwɪkləʊ/ county in the Republic of Ireland, province of Leinster

area 2,025 sq km/782 sq mi

towns county town Wicklow

features Wicklow Mountains; rivers Slane and Liffey. The village of Shillelagh gave its name to rough cudgels of oak or blackthorn made there *population* (1981) 87,500.

wide-angle lens a photographic lens of shorter focal length than normal, increasing spatial depth between objects taking in a wider angle of view.

Wieland /ˈviːlænt/ Christoph Martin 1733–1813. German poet and novelist. After attempts at religious poetry, he came under the influence of Voltaire and Rousseau, and wrote novels such as *Agathon* and the satirical *Abderiten*, and tales in verse such as *Oberon*, *Musarion*, and others. He translated Shakespeare into German 1762–66.

Wien /viːn/ German name for ◊Vienna, capital of Austria.

Wiesbaden /ˈviːsbɑːdn/ capital of Hessen, West Germany, W of Frankfurt; population (1984) 269,000. Wiesbaden was the capital of the former duchy of Nassau from the 12th century to 1866.

Wiesel /ˈviːzəl/ Elie 1928– . US academic and human rights campaigner, born in Romania. He was held in Buchenwald concentration camp during World War II, and has assiduously documented wartime atrocities against the Jews, in an effort to alert the world to the dangers of racism and violence. He was awarded the Nobel Peace Prize 1986.

wig artificial head of hair, either real or synthetic, worn as an adornment, disguise, or to conceal baldness. Wigs were known in the ancient world, and have been found on Egyptian mummies. The 16th century periwig imitated real hair, and developed into the elaborate peruke which became part of dress, and under Queen Anne wigs covering the back and shoulders became fashionable. Wigs are worn in England and some Commonwealth countries as part of the costume of judges, barristers, and some parliamentary officials.

Wigan /ˈwɪgən/ industrial town (food processing, engineering, paper) in Greater Manchester, England; population (1981) 79,500. *Wigan Pier* was immortalized by George Orwell in *The Road to Wigan Pier* 1932 and now has a museum.

wigeon wild duck *Anas penelope*. Smaller than the mallard, the male has a red-brown head with cream crown, greyish-pink breast and white beneath. The bill is blue-grey. In winter it frequents British coasts, but breeds farther north.

Wiggin /ˈwɪgɪn/ Kate Douglas 1856–1923. US author, born in Philadelphia. She was a pioneer in the running of kindergartens and wrote the children's classic *Rebecca of Sunnybrook Farm* 1903 and its sequels.

Wight, Isle of /waɪt/ county in S England

area 381 sq km/147 sq mi

towns administrative headquarters Newport; resorts Ryde, Sandown, Shanklin, Ventnor

features the *Needles* a group of pointed chalk rocks up to 30 m/100 ft high in the sea to the W; the *Solent* the sea channel between Hampshire and the island (including the anchorage of *Spithead* opposite Portsmouth, used for naval reviews); *Cowes*, venue of Regatta Week and headquarters of the Royal Yacht Squadron; *Osborne House*, near Cowes, favourite home of Queen Victoria, for whom it was built in 1845; *Farringford*, home of Tennyson, near Freshwater

products agriculture; tourism is important *population* (1983) 120,000

history called *Vectis* ('separate division') by the Romans, who conquered it in 43 AD. Charles I was imprisoned 1647–48 in Carisbrooke Castle.

Wightman /ˈwaɪtmən/ Hazel (born Hotchkiss) 1886–1974. American lawn-tennis player who won singles, doubles and mixed doubles at US championships 1909, 1910, and 1911. She donated a silver cup (*Wightman Cup*) in 1920 to be contested by international teams. Great Britain and the USA played for the cup in 1923 and since then they have been the only two competing nations.

Wigtown /ˈwɪgtaʊn/ former county of SW Scotland extending to the Irish Sea, merged in 1975 in Dumfries and Galloway. The administrative headquarters was Wigtown.

Wilberforce /ˈwɪlbəfɔːs/ Samuel 1805–1873. British Anglican bishop of Oxford 1845–69, and from 1869 of Winchester. He defended Anglican orthodoxy against the ◊Tractarians.

Wilberforce /ˈwɪlbəfɔːs/ William 1759–1833. British reformer, born in Hull. He began his attacks on slavery while at school, and from 1788 devoted himself to its abolition. He entered Parliament in 1780, in 1807 his bill for the abolition of the slave trade was passed, and in 1833, largely through efforts, slavery was abolished throughout the British Empire.

Wild /waɪld/ Jonathan c. 1682–1725. English criminal, who organized the thieves of London and ran an office which for a payment returned stolen goods to their owners. He was hanged at Tyburn.

Wilde /waɪld/ Oscar (Fingal O'Flahertie Wills) 1854–1900. Irish writer, born in Dublin. At Oxford he led the aesthetic circle burlesqued in Gilbert and Sullivan's comic opera *Patience*, and astonished London society and the USA, on his lecture tour in 1882, with his flamboyant style and quotable conversation. He published *Poems* 1881, his only novel *The Picture of Dorian Gray*

1891, and the brilliantly witty comedies *Lady Windermere's Fan* 1892, *A Woman of No Importance* 1893, *An Ideal Husband* 1895, and *The Importance of Being Earnest* 1895. In 1895 he was imprisoned for two years for homosexual offences (see Lord Alfred ◊Douglas and Edward ◊Carson) and wrote his *Ballad of Reading Gaol* 1898 and *De Profundis* 1905. He lived in France after his release in 1897 and is buried in Paris.

Wilde Oscar Wilde, whose epigrams often turned trite sayings upside down ('Work is the curse of the drinking classes', 'The truth is rarely pure, and never simple', 'In matters of grave importance, style, not sincerity, is the vital thing').

wildebeest another word for ◊gnu.

Wilder /ˈwaɪldə/ Billy 1906– . US film director. Born in Vienna, he was in Hollywood from 1934, where he collaborated with Charles Brackett on film scripts, for example *Ninotchka* 1939; he directed as well as collaborating on the script of *Lost Weekend* 1945 and *Sunset Boulevard* 1950, and such sophisticated comedies as *Some Like it Hot* 1959 and *The Apartment* 1960.

Wilder /ˈwaɪldə/ Thornton (Niven) 1897–1975. US playwright and novelist, born in Madison, Wisconsin. He made his name with the novel *The Bridge of San Luis Rey* 1927, tracing the lives of those involved in a disaster, which had many imitators: among later books was *The Ides of March* 1942, set in ancient Rome. His plays *Our Town* 1938 and *The Skin of Our Teeth* 1942, both won Pulitzer Prizes.

wild type in ◊genetics, the naturally occurring ◊allele for a particular character that is typical of most individuals of a given species, as distinct from new alleles that arise by ◊mutation.

Wilfrid, St /'wɪlfrɪd/ 634–709. Northumbrian-born bishop of York from 665. He defended the cause of the Roman Church at the Synod of ◊Whitby in 664 against that of Celtic Christianity; feast day 12 Oct.

Wilhelm German crown prince. See ◊Friedrich Wilhelm.

Wilhelm /'vɪlhelm/ (English *William*) two emperors of Germany:

Wilhelm I /'vɪlhelm/ 1797–1888. King of Prussia from 1861. The son of Friedrich Wilhelm III, he served in the Napoleonic campaigns of 1814–15 and helped to crush the 1848 revolution. After succeeding his brother Friedrich Wilhelm IV in 1861, his policy was largely dictated by ◊Bismarck, who secured his proclamation as German emperor in 1871.

Wilhelm II /'vɪlhelm/ 1859–1941. Emperor of Germany from 1888, the son of Friedrich III and Victoria, daughter of Queen Victoria. In 1890 he forced ◊Bismarck to resign and his subsequent foreign policy was disastrous. In 1914 he first approved Austria's ultimatum to Serbia and then, when he realized war was becoming inevitable, tried in vain to prevent it. In 1918 he fled to Holland and spent the rest of his life in the castle of Doorn.

Wilhelmshaven /ˌvɪlhelms'haːfən/ North Sea industrial port and resort in West Germany, on Jade Bay, a major naval station; population (1979) 100,150.

Wilkes /wɪlks/ John 1727–1797. British Radical politician, born in Clerkenwell. He entered parliament as a Whig in 1757. His attacks on ◊Bute in his paper *The North Briton* led to his outlawry in 1764; he fled to France, and on his return in 1768 was imprisoned. He was four times elected Member of Parliament for Middlesex, but the Commons refused to admit him, and finally declared his opponent elected. This secured him strong working- and middle-class support, and in 1774 he was allowed to take his seat in Parliament, where he championed parliamentary reform, religious toleration, and American independence.

Wilkie /'wɪlki/ David 1785–1841. Scottish genre and portrait painter. His paintings are in the tradition of 17th-century Dutch painters such as ◊Teniers and ◊Ostade. He was knighted 1836. Works include *The Letter of Introduction* 1813 (National Gallery of Scotland, Edinburgh).

Wilkins /'wɪlkɪnz/ Hubert 1888–1958. Australian polar explorer, a pioneer in the use of surveys by both aircraft and submarines. He studied engineering, learned to fly in 1910, and visited both polar regions. In 1928 he flew from Barrow (Alaska) to Green Harbour (Spitsbergen), for which he was knighted, and in 1928–29 made an Antarctic flight which proved that Graham Land is an island: Ben Eielson was his pilot on both flights. He also planned to reach the North Pole by submarine.

Wilkins /'wɪlkɪnz/ William 1778–1839. English architect who pioneered the Greek Revival in England with his design for Downing College, Cambridge. His other buildings include the main block of University College London

1827–28, and the National Gallery, London, 1834–38.

Willem Dutch form of ◊William.

William /'wɪljəm/ 1143–1214. King of Scotland from 1165 known as *William the Lion*; he was captured by Henry II while invading England in 1174, and forced to do homage, but Richard I abandoned the English claim to suzerainty for a money payment in 1189.

William /'wɪljəm/ 1533–1584. Prince of Orange from 1544, and appointed governor of Holland by Philip II of Spain in 1559. However, he joined the revolt of 1572 against Spain's oppressive rule, and, as a Protestant from 1573, became the national leader. He tried to unite the Catholic south and Protestant north provinces, but the former provinces submitted to Spain while the latter formed a federation in 1579 which repudiated Spanish suzerainty in 1581. He was assassinated by a Spanish agent. He was known as *William the Silent* because of his absolute discretion.

William /'wɪljəm/ four kings of England:

William I /'wɪljəm/ the Conqueror c. 1027–1087. King of England from 1066. The illegitimate child of Duke Robert the Devil, he succeeded his father as duke of Normandy in 1035. Claiming that his kinsman Edward the Confessor had bequeathed him the English throne, William invaded the country in 1066, defeating ◊Harold at ◊Hastings. He completed the establishment of feudalism in England (see ◊Domesday Book) and kept the barons firmly under control. He died in Rouen after a fall from his horse and is buried in Caen, France.

William II /'wɪljəm/ Rufus, 'the Red' c. 1056–1100. King of England from 1087. He was the third son of ◊William I, and for most of his reign he was trying to conquer Normandy from his brother Robert. His extortion of money led his barons to revolt and caused confrontation with Bishop Anselm. He was killed while hunting in the New Forest.

William III /'wɪljəm/ (William of Orange) 1650–1702. King of Great Britain and Ireland from 1688. The son of William II of Orange and Mary, daughter of Charles I, he was made *stadtholder* in 1672 to resist the French invasion of his country. He forced Louis XIV to make peace in 1678 and henceforward concentrated on building up a European alliance against the French threat. In 1677 he married his cousin Mary, daughter of the future James II, and, when invited by the English opposition to James's rule, invaded England in 1688 and accepted the crown as joint sovereign with Mary in 1689. He spent much of his reign campaigning, first in Ireland, where in 1690 he defeated James II at the Boyne, and later against the French in Flanders.

William IV /'wɪljəm/ 1765–1837. King of the United Kingdom from 1830, and third son of George III. He was created Duke of Clarence in 1789, and married Adelaide of Saxe-Meiningen (1792–1849) in 1818. During the ◊Reform Bill crisis he secured its passage by agreeing to create new peers.

William /'wɪljəm/ Prince 1982– . Prince of the United Kingdom. Born on 21 Jun 1982, eldest child of the Prince and Princess of Wales.

William /'wɪljəm/ three kings of the Netherlands:

William I /'wɪljəm/ 1772–1844. King of the Netherlands 1815–40. He lived in exile during the French occupation 1795–1813, and fought against Napoleon at Jena and Wagram. The Austrian Netherlands was added to his kingdom by the Allies in 1815, but secured independence (recognized by the Powers 1839) by the revolution of 1830. William's unpopularity led to his abdication in 1840.

William II /'wɪljəm/ 1792–1849. King of the Netherlands 1840–49. He served with the British Army in the Peninsular War and at Waterloo. In 1848 he averted revolution by conceding a liberal constitution.

William III /'wɪljəm/ 1817–1890. King of the Netherlands 1849–90.

William of Malmesbury /'wɪljəm, 'mɑːmzbəri/ c. 1080–c. 1143. English historian and monk. He compiled the *Gesta regum* and *Historia novella*, which together formed a history of England to 1142.

William of Wykeham /'wɪkəm/ c. 1323–1404. English politician, bishop of Winchester from 1367, Lord Chancellor 1367–72 and 1389–91, and founder of Winchester College in 1378 and New College, Oxford, in 1379.

Williams /'wɪljəmz/ (George) Emlyn 1905–1987. Welsh actor and playwright, born in Mostyn, Clwyd. His plays, in which he appeared, include *Night Must Fall* 1935 and *The Corn is Green* 1938.

Williams /'wɪljəmz/ George 1821–1905. founder of the ◊Young Men's Christian Association (YMCA).

Williams /'wɪljəmz/ John (Christopher) 1942– . Australian guitarist, whose extensive repertoire ranges from jazz to classical music.

Williams /'wɪljəmz/ Roger c. 1604–1684. English founder of Rhode Island colony in N America 1636, on a basis of democracy and complete religious freedom.

Williams /'wɪljəmz/ Shirley 1930– . British Social Democrat Party politician. She was Labour minister for prices and consumer protection 1974–76 and education and science 1976–79. She became a founder member of the SDP in 1981 and its president in 1982. In 1983 she lost her parliamentary seat, the first time she had put her defection from the Labour Party to the vote in a general election.

Williams /'wɪljəmz/ Tennessee (Thomas Lanier) 1911–1983. US playwright, born in Mississippi. He is noted for portrayals of characters, particularly women, affected by the frustrations of life in the Deep South, as in *The Glass Menagerie* 1945, and *A Streetcar named Desire* 1947.

Williams /'wɪljəmz/ William Carlos 1883–1963. US poet, born in New Jersey, noted for his spare images and language, which reflected everyday speech. His *Pictures from Brueghel* 1963 won a Pulitzer Prize.

Williamsburg /'wɪljəmzbɜːg/ historic city in Virginia, USA; population (1980) 10,000. Founded in 1632, capital of the colony of Virginia

1699–1779, it has been restored to its 18th-century appearance. The College of William and Mary 1693 is one of the oldest in the USA.

Williams-Ellis /ˈwɪljəmz ˈelɪs/ Clough 1883–1978. British architect, best known as the designer of the fantasy resort of Portmeirion, N Wales. He was knighted in 1972.

Williamson /ˈwɪljəmsən/ Henry 1895–1977. British author, known for such stories of animal life as *Tarka the Otter* 1927.

Williamson /ˈwɪljəmsən/ Malcolm (Benjamin Graham Christopher) 1931– . British composer. Born in Australia, he settled in Britain in 1953. His works include operas (*Our Man in Havana* 1963), symphonies, and chamber music. He became Master of the Queen's Musick 1975.

will-o'the-wisp light sometimes seen over marshy ground, believed to be burning gas containing ◊methane from decaying organic matter.

willow tree or shrub of the genus *Salix* of the family Salicaceae, which flourish in damp places. The leaves are often lance-shaped, and the flowers are arranged in catkins. Among species found in Britain are the crack willow *Salix fragilis*, the white willow *Salix alba*, the goat willow *Salix caprea*, the weeping willow *Salix babylonica* (a native of China), and the common osier *Salix viminalis*. Cricket bats are made from the white willow (subspecies *caerulea*).

willowherb plant of the genus *Epilobium*, well-known as weeds. The rose-bay willowherb or fireweed *Chamaenerion angustifolium*, now placed in a separate genus, is common in woods and waste places. It grows to 1.2 m/4 ft with long terminal racemes of red or purplish flowers.

willow-warbler bird *Phylloscopus trochilus* breeding in Europe and N Asia, wintering in Africa. About 11 cm/4 in long, found in woods and shrubberies, it is similar in appearance to the chiffchaff but has a distinctive song.

willy-willy Australian Aboriginal term for a cyclonic whirlwind.

Wilmington /ˈwɪlmɪŋtən/ industrial port and city (chemicals, textiles, shipbuilding, iron and steel goods, headquarters of Du Pont enterprises) in Delaware, USA; population (1980) 70,000.

Wilson /ˈwɪlsən/ Angus 1913– . British novelist, professor of English literature at East Anglia 1966–78. His acidly humorous books include *Anglo-Saxon Attitudes* 1956 and *The Old Men at the Zoo* 1961.

Wilson /ˈwɪlsən/ Charles Thomson Rees 1869–1959. British physicist, who in 1911 invented the Wilson ◊cloud chamber, an apparatus for studying sub-atomic particles. He shared a Nobel prize in 1927.

Wilson /ˈwɪlsən/ Colin 1931– . British author of *The Outsider* 1956, and of thrillers, including *Necessary Doubt* 1964.

Wilson /ˈwɪlsən/ Edmund 1895–1972. US critic and author, born in New Jersey. *Axel's Castle* 1931 is a survey of symbolism and *The Wound and the Bow* 1941, a study of art and neurosis.

Wilson /ˈwɪlsən/ Edward O 1929– . US zoologist, born in Birmingham, Alabama. His books have been influential in stimulating interest in such topics as ◊biogeography and the evolution of behaviour, or ◊sociobiology. His best-known books are *Sociobiology* 1975 and *On Human Nature* 1978. He is an authority on ants.

Wilson /ˈwɪlsən/ (James) Harold, Baron Wilson 1916– . British Labour politician, born in Huddersfield. He was president of the Board of Trade 1947–51 (when he resigned because of social service cuts), and in 1963 succeeded Gaitskell as Labour leader. He was prime minister 1964–70 (increasing his majority in 1966) and (following elections) formed a minority government in Feb 1974 and achieved a majority of three in Oct 1974. He resigned in 1976, and was succeeded by Callaghan. His premiership was dominated by the issue of UK admission to EEC membership, the ◊social contract, and economic difficulties. He was knighted in 1976, and became a peer in 1983.

Wilson /ˈwɪlsən/ Henry Maitland 'Jumbo', 1st Baron Wilson 1881–1964. British field marshal. He was commander in chief in Egypt in 1939, led the unsuccessful Greek campaign of 1941, was commander in chief in the Middle East in 1943, and in 1944 was supreme Allied commander in the Mediterranean.

Wilson /ˈwɪlsən/ Richard 1714–1782. English artist. His Italian and English landscapes led towards romanticism.

Wilson /ˈwɪlsən/ (Thomas) Woodrow 1856–1924. 28th president of the USA, born in Virginia. He became president of Princeton University in 1902. In 1910 he was elected Democratic governor of New Jersey, and in 1912 and again in 1916 he was elected president of the USA. He initiated anti-trust legislation and secured valuable social reforms in his progressive 'New Freedom' programme. He strove to keep the USA neutral during World War I but the German U-boat campaign forced him to declare war in 1917. In Jan 1918 he issued his '14 Points' as a basis for a just peace settlement. At the peace conference in Paris he was successful in securing the inclusion of the ◊League of Nations in the Treaty of Versailles, but the treaty was not ratified by Congress so the US did not join it. He was awarded the Nobel Peace prize in 1919.

Wilton /ˈwɪltən/ English market town in Wiltshire, outside Salisbury, known for its carpets since the 16th century. *Wilton House*, the seat of the earl of Pembroke, was built from designs by Holbein and Inigo Jones.

Wiltshire /ˈwɪltʃə/ county in SW England
area 3,480 sq km/1,344 sq mi
towns administrative headquarters Trowbridge; Salisbury, Swindon, Wilton
features Marlborough Downs, Savernake Forest; rivers Kennet, and Salisbury and Bristol Avons; Salisbury Plain, an area of open downland (775 sq km/300 sq mi) which includes ◊Avebury, ◊Silbury, and ◊Stonehenge, and has been used as a military training area since Napoleonic times; Longleat House, Wilton House, and Stourhead with 18th-century gardens
products wheat, cattle; carpets, rubber
population (1986) 543,320
famous people George Crabbe.

Wilson President of the USA during World War I. Woodrow Wilson was involved in the Versailles Treaty and championed the formation of the League of Nations.

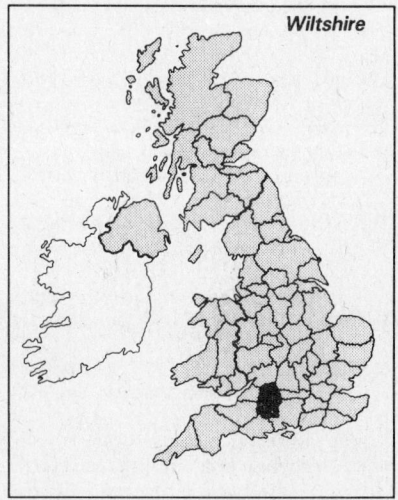

Wiltshire

Wimbledon /ˈwɪmbəldən/ district of the Greater London borough of Merton, headquarters of the All-England Lawn Tennis Club where international matches have been held since 1877.

Winchell /ˈwɪntʃəl/ Walter 1897–1972. US journalist, born in New York. He was a columnist on the *New York Mirror* 1929–69, and his bitingly satiric writings were syndicated throughout the USA.

Winchester /ˈwɪntʃɪstə/ cathedral city and administrative headquarters of Hampshire, on the river Itchen; population (1984) 92,500. Originally a Roman town, Winchester was the capital of Wessex. Winchester Cathedral is the longest medieval church in Europe and was remodelled from Norman-Romanesque to Perpendicular Gothic under the patronage of ◊William of Wykeham (founder of Winchester

College 1382), who is buried there, as are Saxon kings, St ◊Swithun, Izaac Walton, and Jane ◊Austen. A medieval 'reconstruction' of Arthur's Round Table is preserved in the 13th-century hall (all that survives) of the castle.

wind a lateral movement of the Earth's atmosphere. Although modified by features such as land and water, there is a basic worldwide system. A belt of low pressure (the doldrums) lies along the equator. The ◊trade winds blow towards this from the horse latitudes (high pressure areas about 30° N and 30° S of the equator), blowing from the NE in the northern hemisphere, and from the SE in the southern. The *westerlies* (also from the horse latitudes) blow from the SW north of the equator and from the NW to the south.

Cold winds blow outwards from high-pressure areas at the poles. More local effects result from the land heating and cooling faster than the adjacent sea, producing onshore winds in the daytime and offshore winds at night.

The ◊monsoon is a seasonal wind of S Asia, blowing from the SW Apr–Oct to bring the rain on which crops depend, and from the NE in winter.

Famous or notorious warm winds include the ◊chinook from the Pacific, after it has lost its moisture over the W Rocky Mountains; the ◊Föhn of Switzerland's Alpine valleys; the ◊sirocco (Italy)/◊khamsin (Egypt)/sharav (Israel), spring winds that bring warm air from the Sahara and Arabian deserts across the Mediterranean; and the ◊Santa Ana, a periodic warm wind from the inland deserts that strikes the California coast.

The dry northerly ◊bise (Switzerland) and the ◊mistral, which strikes the Mediterranean area of France, are unpleasantly cold winds.

Windermere /'wɪndəmɪə/ largest lake in England, in Cumbria, 17 km/10.5 mi long and 1.6 km/1 mi wide.

Windhoek /'wɪndhʊk/ capital of Namibia, in the centre, with hot springs nearby; population (1981) 105,000.

wind instrument musical instrument which uses the player's breath to make a column of air vibrate. Wind instruments comprise ◊woodwind instruments and ◊brass instruments.

windmill a mill with sails or vanes which by the action of wind upon them drive machinery for grinding corn, pumping water, and so on. Windmills were used in the East in ancient times, and in Europe they were first used in Germany and the Netherlands in the 12th century. The main types of windmill are the *post mill*, which is turned round a post when the direction of the wind changes, and the *tower mill*, which has a revolving turret on top. It usually has a device (fantail) that keeps the sails pointing into the wind. In the USA a light type of windmill with steel sails supported on a long steel girder shaft was introduced for use on farms. The energy crisis has led to modern experiments with wind turbines, designed to use wind power on a major scale. Mostly they have a propeller-type rotor mounted on a tall shell tower. The turbine drives a generator for producing electricity. Some wind turbines in the USA have an output of 2 megawatts.

Windsor /'wɪnzə/ industrial lake port (car engines, iron and steel goods, bricks) in Ontario, Canada, opposite Detroit, USA; population (1981) 246,000.

Windsor /'wɪnzə/ town in Berkshire, England, on the River Thames, site of ◊Windsor Castle. It has a 17th-century guildhall designed by ◊Wren. The Treaty of Windsor 1373, established a permanent alliance between England and Portugal. Population (1981) 28,330.

Windsor /'wɪnzə/ Duchess of (born Wallis Warfield) 1896–1986. US socialite, who married Earl Winfield Spencer in 1916 (they divorced in 1927), Ernest Simpson in 1928 (they divorced in 1936), and the Duke of Windsor (formerly ◊Edward VIII) in 1937.

Windsor Castle royal residence in Windsor, Berkshire. It was founded by William the Conqueror on the site of an earlier fortress, and includes St George's Chapel (a fine example of Perpendicular Gothic architecture and the chapel of the Order of the Garter), Albert Memorial Chapel (beneath which George III, George IV, William IV, George V, and George VI are buried), and (beyond the Round Tower or Keep) the state apartments and the sovereign's private apartments. In the Home Park adjoining the castle is the Royal Mausoleum where Queen Victoria, the Prince Consort, and Edward VIII are buried. Windsor Great Park lies to the S.

Windsor, House of official name of the British royal family, adopted in place of Saxe-Coburg-Gotha in 1917. Since 1960 those descendants of Elizabeth II not entitled to the prefix HRH have borne the surname Mountbatten-Windsor.

wind tunnel a test tunnel in which air is blown over a stationary model aircraft, car, truck, or locomotive to simulate the effects of movement. Lift, drag, and air-flow patterns are observed by the use of special cameras and sensitive instruments. Wind-tunnel testing verifies the aerodynamic design, preparing the way for full-scale construction.

wind turbine a modern type of ◊windmill.

Windward Islands /'wɪndwəd/ islands in the path of the prevailing wind, notably:
West Indies see under ◊Antilles
◊*Cape Verde Islands* (N group), see ◊Netherlands *Antilles* (St Maarten, St Eustatius, and Saba)
◊*French Polynesia* (Tahiti, Moorea, and Makatea)

wine liquor of fermented grape pulp in which the sugar content has been converted to ethyl alcohol by the ◊yeast *Saccharomyces ellipsoideus* which lives on the skin of the grape. For *dry wine* the fermentation is allowed to go on longer than for *sweet* or *medium*; *red wine* is the product of the grape with the skin, but *white wine* of the inner pulp only. ◊Champagne is bottled while still fermenting, but sparkling wines are artificially carbonated. A *vintage wine* is that from a good year (as regards quality of wine, produced by favourable weather conditions) in recognized vineyards of a particular area; France has a guarantee of origin (*appellation controlée*), as does Italy (*Denominazione di Origine Controllata*), Spain (*Denominacion Controllata*, and Germany (a series of graded qualities running from *Qualitätswein* to *Beerenauslese*). The world's largest producers are Italy, France, Russia, and Spain; others include Germany, Australia, South Africa, California, and Chile.

wing in biology, the modified forelimb of birds and bats, or the membraneous outgrowths of the ◊exoskeleton of insects, which give the power of flight. Birds and bats have two wings. Those of birds have feathers which enlarge the surface area to give lift, while those of bats consist of skin stretched between the digits ('fingers') of the limb. Most insects have four wings, which are strengthened by wing ◊veins. In butterflies and moths they are covered by wing scales. In flies the hind pair are modified to form two balancing organs which provide no lift.

Wingate /'wɪngeɪt/ Orde Charles 1903–1944. British soldier. In 1936 he established a reputation for his unorthodox tactics against the former ◊Mufti of Jerusalem in Palestine and in World War II served under Wavell in the Middle East, and later led the ◊Chindits in guerrilla operations against the Japanese in Burma.

Winnipeg /'wɪnɪpeg/ capital, industrial city (sawmills, meat packing), and financial centre of Manitoba, Canada, S of *Lake Winnipeg* (23,553 sq km/9,094 sq mi); population (1981) 585,000.

wintergreen plant genus *Pyrola* in the family Pyrolaceae. *Pyrola minor*, with rounded white flowers, is a woodland plant. From the leaves of the N American *Gaultheria procumbens* is extracted oil of wintergreen used in treating rheumatism.

Winterhalter /'vɪntə,hæltə/ Franz Xavier 1806–1873. German artist. He was born in the Black Forest, studied at Munich Academy, and was court painter to Grand Duke Leopold at Karlsruhe. He painted portraits of Queen Victoria and Napoleon III.

winter of discontent name given to the winter of 1978–79 in Britain, which was marked by a series of strikes that contributed to the defeat of the Labour government in the general election of spring 1979. They included Ford Motor Company workers Sept–Nov 1978, bakery workers Nov–Dec 1978, lorry drivers Jan–Feb 1979, train drivers Jan 1979, local-authority workers and health-service ancillaries and ambulance crews Jan–Mar 1979, water and sewerage workers Feb 1979, and civil servants Feb and Apr 1979.

The phrase is from Shakespeare's *Richard III*: 'Now is the winter of our discontent / Made glorious summer by this sun of York.'

Winterthur /'vɪntətʊə/ Swiss town and spa NE of Zürich, manufacturing engines and textiles; population (1983) 108,000.

Winter War name given to the Soviet Union's invasion of Finland between 30 Nov 1939 and 12 Mar 1940.

wire metal that is drawn out into a slender thread. It is made by drawing a thin rod through progressively smaller-diameter dies.

wind turbine Wind has been a source of clean energy for centuries, and windmills can be used to produce electricity or to run machinery directly. There are some 300 wind turbines generating power at the Altamont Pass wind farm in California, USA.

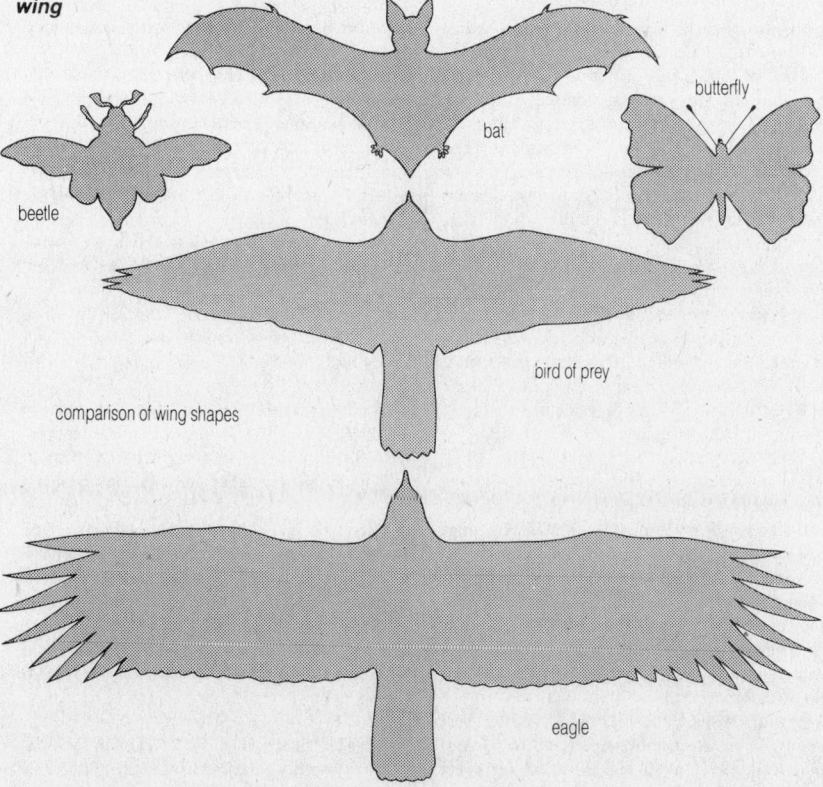

wing

comparison of wing shapes

beetle

bat

butterfly

bird of prey

eagle

wireless the name originally given to what is now called the ◊radio. In early experiments with transmission by radio waves, notably by ◊Marconi in Britain, signals were sent in ◊Morse code as on the telegraph. But unlike the telegraph no wires were used for transmission, and the means of communication was termed wireless telegraphy.

wireworm the larva of the ◊click-beetle.

Wisconsin /wɪs'kɒnsɪn/ state of the USA; the Badger State

area 145,438 sq km/56,153 sq mi

capital Madison

towns Milwaukee

features Great Lakes

products premier dairying state; cereals; coal, iron, zinc, lead; agricultural machinery, precision instruments, plumbing equipment

population (1984) 4,779,000

famous people Edna Ferber, Harry Houdini, Joseph McCarthy, Spencer Tracy, Orson Welles, Thornton Wilder, Frank Lloyd Wright

history originally settled by the French, it passed to Britain in 1763, became American in 1783, and in 1848 became a state.

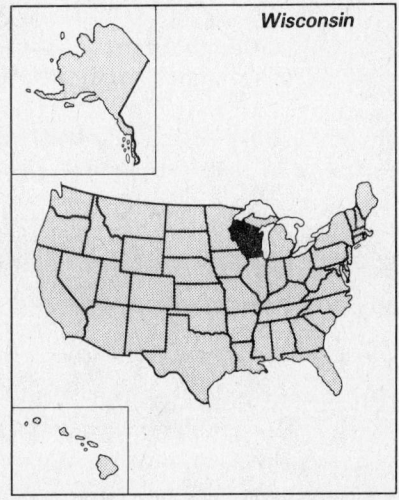

Wisconsin

Wise /waɪz/ Thomas James 1859–1937. British bibliographer. He collected the Ashley Library of first editions, chiefly English poets and dramatists 1890–1930, acquired by the British Museum at his death, but he is chiefly remembered for his forgeries of supposed privately printed first editions of Browning, Tennyson, and Swinburne. His activities were revealed in 1934, and in 1956 it was found that he had perfected his own copies of 17th-century plays by abstracting leaves from copies belonging to the British Museum.

Wiseman /'waɪzmən/ Nicholas Patrick Stephen 1802–1865. British cardinal, who became the first archbishop of Westminster in 1850. ◊Newman was his protégé.

wisent name for the European ◊bison.

Wishart /'wɪʃət/ George c. 1513–1546. Scottish Protestant reformer burned for heresy; he probably converted John ◊Knox.

Wister /'wɪstə/ Owen 1860–1938. US novelist, who created the genre of the 'western'. He was born in Philadelphia, a grandson of the British actress Fanny Kemble.

wisteria climbing shrub *Wistaria sinensis* of the family Leguminosae, native to China. It has racemes of pale mauve flowers, and pinnate leaves.

Witan /'wɪtn/ or *Witenagemot* council of the Anglo-Saxon kings, the forerunner of Parliament, but including only royal household officials, great landowners, and top churchmen.

witchcraft the alleged possession and exercise of magical powers (*black magic* if used with the aid of devils, and *white* if benign, as in the 'charming' of warts). Its origins lie in ancient cults and religions. The Christian church persecuted witches in Europe during the 15th–17th centuries, and in America (see ◊Salem). The last official execution of a witch was in 1782 of Anna Goddi, hanged in Switzerland. Practitioners of witchcraft have often had considerable skill in herbal medicine and traditional remedies, and in 1976 the World Health Organization recommended the integration of witch doctors into the health teams of African states.

Obi is the witchcraft of black Africa imported to the West Indies, and including Christian elements; *voodoo* is a similar cult, involving snake worship, especially prevalent in Haiti (see ◊zombie).

witch hazel flowering shrub *Hamamelis virginiana*. An astringent extract prepared from the bark or leaves is used in medicine.

witch-hunt general term used to describe the persecution of minority or opposition political groups without any regard for their guilt or innocence. Witch-hunts are often accompanied by a degree of public hysteria, for example, the ◊McCarthy hearings in the USA in the 1950s.

witness in law, a person giving evidence in a case before a court of law. The rules of admissible evidence are complex, but generally speaking it must be direct oral testimony of relevant facts given by someone who was present.

Witt /wɪt/ John de 1625–1672. Dutch politician, Grand Pensionary of Holland and virtual prime minister from 1653. His skilful diplomacy ended the ◊Dutch Wars of 1652–54 and 1665–67, and in 1668 he formed a triple alliance with England and Sweden against Louis XIV. He was murdered by a rioting mob.

Wittelsbach /'vɪtlzbæx/ Bavarian dynasty, who ruled Bavaria as dukes from 1180, electors from 1623, and kings 1806–1918. Prince Ruprecht (1869–1955), son of King Ludwig III and descended from Elizabeth, daughter of James I of England, was technically a claimant to the British throne and the claim descended to his son Prince Albrecht (1905–).

Wittenberg /'vɪtnbeɔk/ town in East Germany, SW of Berlin, long known for its university (1502, but transferred to Halle 1815); population about 46,000. Luther preached in the Stadtkirche (in which he is buried), nailed his 95 theses to the door of the Schlosskirche in 1517, and taught philosophy at the university.

Wittgenstein /'vɪtgənʃtaɪn/ Ludwig 1889–1951. Viennese philosopher, who taught at Cambridge in the 1930s and 1940s and whose work has been very influential. *Tractatus Logico-Philosophicus* 1922 was a detailed working out of a 'picture theory' of language: a sentence must be analysable into 'atomic propositions' whose elements stand for elements of the real world; otherwise, the sentence is not stating any fact. Wittgenstein's later philosophy as presented for example in *Philosophical Investigations* published in 1954, developed a quite different, anthropological, view of language: words are used according to different rules in a variety of human activities – different 'language games' are played with them. The traditional philosophical problems arise through the assumption that words (like 'exist' in the sentence 'Physical objects do not really exist') carry a fixed meaning with them, independent of context.

woad biennial plant *Isatis tinctoria*, family Cruciferae, with arrow-shaped leaves and clusters of yellow flowers; ancient Britons used the blue dye from its leaves as a body paint.

Wodehouse /'wʊdhaʊs/ P(elham) G(renville) 1881–1975. British humorist, a US citizen from 1955. His novels, noted for their style, portray the accident-prone world of such characters as the socialite Bertie Wooster and his invaluable and impeccable man-servant Jeeves, and Lord Emsworth of Blandings Castle with his pig, the Empress of Blandings. He also collaborated on the lyrics of musicals by Jerome Kern, Gershwin, and others. In 1941 he was in France and was interned by the Germans; he made some humorous broadcasts from Berlin, which were taken amiss in Britain at the time, but he was later exonerated and knighted in 1975.

Woden /'wəʊdn/ alternative spelling of Norse god ◊Odin.

Woffington /'wɒfɪŋtən/ 'Peg' (Margaret) c. 1714–1760. Irish actress, who played in Dublin as a child and made her debut at Covent Garden, London, in 1740. She often played male roles.

Wöhler /'vəʊlə/ Friedrich 1800–1882. German chemist, who synthesized the first ◊organic compound (urea) from an inorganic compound (ammonium cyanate): it had previously been thought impossible to convert an inorganic compound to an organic one. He also isolated the elements aluminium, beryllium, yttrium, and titanium.

wolf largest wild member *Canis lupus* of the dog family, formerly found over most of Europe and N Asia, as well as North America where it is known as the timber or gray wolf, to distinguish it from the rare red wolf of E Texas and the 'prairie wolf' or coyote. Wolves hunt in packs and are now restricted by urban expansion to deep forest country or remote regions.

Wolf /vɒlf/ Hugo (Filipp Jakob) 1860–1903. Austrian composer. He studied at Vienna Conservatoire, was a critic on a Viennese paper, and died in a Vienna mental hospital. His songs belong to the greatest achievements of the German *Lieder* tradition. He also composed the opera *Der Corregidor* 1895 and orchestral works, such as *Italian Serenade* 1892.

Wolfe /wʊlf/ Charles 1791–1823. Irish curate, author of one great poem, 'The Burial of Sir John Moore'.

Wolfe /wʊlf/ Gene 1931– . US writer, best known for the science-fiction series *The Book of the New Sun* 1980–83, with a surrealist treatment of stock themes, and for the urban fantasy *Free, Live Free* 1985.

Wolfe /wʊlf/ James 1727–1759. British soldier. He served at the battles of Dettingen, Falkirk, Culloden, and Laffeldt. In 1758 he served in Canada, and played a conspicuous part in the siege of the French stronghold of Louisburg. In 1759 he was promoted to major-general, and commanded the victorious expedition against Quebec in which he lost his life.

Wolfe /wʊlf/ Thomas 1900–1938. US novelist, born in North Carolina. His belief in the unconscious as the source of good writing produced an enormous wordage which was cut and shaped by his publisher and editor Maxwell Perkins (1884–1947): *Look Homeward, Angel* 1929, *Of Time and the River* 1935, and the posthumous *The Web and the Rock* 1939 and *You Can't go Home Again* 1940.

Wolfenden Report /'wulfəndən/ a report published 1957 of a British royal commission on homosexuality and prostitution, chaired by John Wolfenden (1906–). The report recommended legalizing homosexual acts between consenting adults in private.

Wolf-Ferrari /'vɒlf fe'rɑːri/ Ermanno 1876–1948. Italian-German composer, born in Venice, whose operas include *Il segreto di Susanna/Susanna's Secret* 1909, the realistic tragedy *I gioielli di Madonna/The Jewels of the Madonna* 1911, and many others.

Wolfit /'wulfɪt/ Donald 1902–1968. British actor-manager. He formed his own theatre company in 1937, and excelled in the larger-than-life Shakespearean roles of Shylock and Lear, and Volpone (in Ben Jonson's play).

wolfram another name for ◊tungsten.

Wolfsburg /'vɒlfsbuək/ town NE of Brunswick in West Germany, chosen 1938 as the Volkswagen (Hitler's 'People's Car') factory site; population (1984) 122,500.

Wolfson /'wulfsən/ Isaac 1897– . British store magnate, chairman of Great Universal Stores from 1946. He established the *Wolfson Foundation* in 1955 to promote health, education, and youth activities and in 1966 (with the Ford Foundation) endowed Wolfson College, Oxford.

Wollongong /'wuləŋgɒŋ/ industrial city (iron and steel) in New South Wales, Australia, 65 km/40 mi S of Sydney; population (1983, with Port Kembla) 235,000.

Wollstonecraft /'wulstənkrɑːft/ Mary 1759–1797. British feminist, whose controversial book *Vindication of the Rights of Women* 1792 demanded equal educational opportunities for women. She joined a group of radical intellectuals called the English Jacobins. She married William Godwin and died in giving birth to a daughter, Mary, who later, as Mary ◊Shelley, wrote the Gothic novel *Frankenstein*.

Wolseley /'wulzli/ Garnet Joseph, 1st Viscount Wolseley 1833–1913. British field marshal, who as commander in chief 1895–1900 began modernizing the British army.

Wolsey /'wulzi/ Thomas c. 1475–1530. English cardinal and politician. Born in Ipswich. He was rapidly promoted by Henry VIII and became both cardinal and lord chancellor in 1515. For a decade he was one of the most powerful men in Europe. He began the dissolution of the monasteries, and in zeal for the 'new learning' of the Renaissance established Cardinal (now Christ Church) College, Oxford. His reluctance to further Henry's divorce from

Catherine of Aragon, partly because of his ambitions to be pope, led to his downfall in 1529. He was charged with high treason in 1530 but died before being tried.

Women's Institute local organization in country districts in Britain and elsewhere for mutual fellowship, community welfare, and the practice of country crafts. It is non-class, non-

Wolsey English Cardinal Thomas Wolsey.

Wolsey A letter from Henry VIII to Cardinal Wolsey in Jul 1518, in which the king plays the role of anxious husband. He is hopeful that the queen (Catherine of Aragon) is pregnant, and is 'loath to repair to London', since he wishes to move her 'as little as I may now'.

Wolverhampton /ˌwʊlvəˈhæmptən/ industrial city (metalworking, chemicals, tyres, aircraft, commercial vehicles) in West Midlands, England, 21 km/13 mi NW of Birmingham; population (1984) 254,000.

wolverine carnivorous mammal *Gulo gulo*, largest member of the weasel family, Mustelidae, found in Europe, Asia, and North America. It covers food it is unable to consume with an unpleasant secretion, hence its alternative popular name of 'glutton'.

wombat marsupial of the family Vombatidae, including the *common wombat Vombatus orsinus* of Tasmania and SE Australia and *Lasiorhirnus latifrons*, the *plains wombat* of S Australia. They have coarse brownish fur, live in burrows, and are nocturnal and vegetarian.

sectarian, and non-party political. The first such institute was founded in 1897 at Stoney Creek, Ontario, Canada, under the presidency of Mrs Adelaide Hoodless; the National Federation of Women's Institutes in the UK was founded in 1915. The *National Union of Townswomen's Guilds*, founded in 1929, is the urban equivalent.

women's movement broad term used to describe the campaign for the rights of women, particularly for women's social, political, and economic equality with men.

Pioneer 19th-century feminists, considered radical for their belief in the equality of the sexes, include Mary ◊Wollstonecraft and Emmeline ◊Pankhurst in the UK, and Susan B ◊Anthony and Elizabeth Cady ◊Stanton in the USA; early campaigners fought for women's right to own property, to have access to higher education, and to vote (see ◊suffragette). Once women's suffrage was achieved in the UK and the USA after World War I, the emphasis of the movement shifted to the goals of equal social and economic opportunities for women, particularly in employment.

The women's movement gained worldwide impetus after World War II with such theorists as Simone de ◊Beauvoir, Betty ◊Friedan, Kate ◊Millett, Gloria ◊Steinem, and Germaine ◊Greer, and the founding of the National Organization of Women (NOW) in New York 1966. From the late 1960s the radical and militant wing of the movement, as represented by *Women's Liberation* in the USA, argued that women were oppressed by the male-dominated social structure as a whole, which they saw as pervaded by ◊sexism, despite legal concessions towards equality of the sexes.

In the UK since 1975 discrimination against women in employment, education, housing, and provision of goods, facilities, and services to the public has been illegal under the Sex Discrimination and Equal Pay Acts; in the USA the Equal Employment Opportunity Commission, a government agency, was formed 1964 to end discrimination (including sex discrimination) in hiring, but the Equal Rights Amendment (ERA), a proposed constitutional amendment prohibiting sex discrimination passed by Congress in 1972, failed to be ratified by the necessary majority of 38 states.

In the late 1980s a diversity of opinion and political stance is reflected by the general term women's movement; a common area of concern is the contradiction between the now generally accepted principle of equality and the demonstrable inequalities between the sexes that remain, both in state policies and in everyday life.

women's services the organized military use on a large scale of women: a comparatively recent development. Women have been used to replace men in factories and on farms during wartime,

WOMEN IN SOCIETY – UK CHRONOLOGY

1562 Statute of Artificers made it illegal to employ men or women in a trade before they had served seven years' apprenticeship. (It was never strictly enforced for women, as many guilds still allowed members to employ their wives and daughters in workshops.)

1753 Lord Hardwick's Marriage Act brought marriage under state control and created a firmer distinction between the married and unmarried.

1803 Abortion was made illegal.

1836 Marriage Act reform permitted civil weddings and enforced the official registration of births, deaths and marriages.

1839 Custody of Infants Act allowed mothers to have custody of their children under seven years old.

1840s A series of factory acts limited the working day and occupations of women and children. Bastardy amendment put all the responsibility for the maintenance of an illegitimate child on to its mother.

1857 Marriage and Divorce Act enabled a man to obtain divorce if his wife had committed adultery. (Women were only eligible for divorce if their husband's adultery was combined with incest, sodomy, cruelty, etc.)

1857–82 Married Women's Property Acts allowed them to own possessions of various kinds in their own right for the first time.

1861 Abortion became a criminal offence even if performed as a life saving act or done by the woman herself.

1862–70 Contagious Diseases Acts introduced compulsory examination of suspected prostitutes for venereal disease.

1860s Fathers could be named and required to pay maintenance for illegitimate children.

1864 Schools Enquiry Commission recommendations led to the establishment of high schools for girls.

1867 Second Reform Act enfranchised the majority of male householders. First women's suffrage committee was formed in Manchester.

1869 Women ratepayers were allowed to vote in municipal (local) elections.

1871 Newham College, Cambridge, was founded for women.

1872 Elizabeth Garrett Anderson Hospital for women opened in London.

1874 London School of Medicine for women was founded.

1878 Judicial separation of married couples became possible. Maintenance orders could be enforced in court.

1880 TUC adopted principle of equal pay for women.

1882 Married Women's Property Act meant that wives were given legal control over their own earned income.

1883 Contagious Diseases Acts were repealed.

1885 Age of consent was raised to 16.

1887 National Union of Women's Suffrage Societies became a nationwide group under Millicent Fawcett.

1903 Women's Social and Political Union was founded by Emmeline and Christabel Pankhurst.

1905–10 Militant campaigns split WSPU. Sylvia Pankhurst formed East London Women's Federation.

1918 Parliament (Qualification of Women) Act gave the vote to women householders over 30.

1923 Wives were given equal rights to sue for divorce on the grounds of adultery.

1925 Guardianship of Infants Act gave women equal rights to the guardianship of their children.

1928 The 'Flapper' Vote: all women over 21 were given the vote.

1937 Matrimonial Causes Act gave new grounds for divorce including desertion for three years and cruelty.

1944 Butler Education Act introduced free secondary education for all.

1946 Royal Commission on equal pay was formed.

1948 Cambridge University allowed women candidates to be awarded degrees.

1960 Legal aid became available for divorce cases.

1967 Abortion Law Reform Act made abortion legal under medical supervision and within certain criteria.

1969 Divorce reform was introduced which reduced the time a petitioner needed to wait before applying for a divorce.

1973 Matrimonial Causes Act provided legislation to enable financial provision to be granted on divorce.

1975 Sex Discrimination and Equal Pay Acts. National and Scottish Women's Aid Federations were formed.

1976 Domestic Violence and Matrimonial Proceedings Act. Sexual Offences (Amendment) Act attempted to limit a man's defence of consent in rape cases.

1977 Employed married women's option to stay partially out of the National Insurance system was phased out. Women qualified for their own pensions.

1980 Social Security Act allowed a married woman to claim Supplementary Benefit and Family Income Supplement if she was the main breadwinner.

1983 Government forced to amend the 1975 Equal Pay Act to conform to EEC directives.

1984 Matrimonial and Family Proceedings Act made it less likely for a woman to be granted maintenance on divorce. It also reduced the number of years a petitioner must wait before applying for a divorce to one year.

1986 Granting of invalid care allowance was successfully challenged in European Court of Justice. Sex Discrimination Act (Amendment) allowed women to retire at the same age as men, and lifted legal restrictions preventing women from working night shifts in manufacturing industries. Firms with less than five employees were no longer exempt from the Act.

and in non-combat tasks; they are now found in combat units in many countries, including the USA, Cuba, and Israel.

In Britain there are separate corps for all three services: *Women's Army Corps* (WRAC) created in 1949 to take over the functions of the Auxiliary Territorial Service, established in 1938; its World War I equivalent was the Women's Army Auxiliary Corps (WAAC); *Women's Royal Naval Service* (WRNS) 1917–19 and 1939 onwards; and the *Women's Royal Air Force* (WRAF) established in 1918 but known 1939–48 as the Women's Auxiliary Air Force (WAAF); and also nursing services: Queen Alexandra's Army Nursing Corps and Naval Nursing Service, and for the RAF Princess Mary's Nursing Service. In the USA there is a separate Women's Army Corps (WAC), established in 1948, which developed from the Women's Army Auxiliary Corps (WAAC), in turn originating in a World War I organization on the British model; but although there are nurse corps for the three services, there are no separate auxiliary corps for the navy and air force, women being integrated into the general structure.

wood the hard tissue beneath the bark of many perennial plants; it is composed of water-conducting cells, or secondary ◊xylem, and gains its hardness and strength from deposits of ◊lignin. The secondary xylem is laid down by the vascular ◊cambium which forms a new layer of wood annually, on the outside of the existing wood and visible when the tree is felled as an annual ring; see ◊dendrochronology. The central wood in a branch or stem is known as heartwood and is generally darker and harder than the outer wood; it consists only of dead cells. As well as providing structural support, it often contains gums, tannins, or pigments which may impart characteristic colour and increased durability. The surrounding sapwood is the functional part of the xylem that conducts water.

Commercial wood can be divided into two main types: hardwood, containing xylem vessels and obtained from angiosperms (for example, oak) and softwood, containing only ◊tracheids, obtained from gymnosperms (for example, pine). Although in general softwoods are softer than hardwoods, this is not always the case: balsa, the softest wood known, is a hardwood, while pitch pine, very dense and hard, is a softwood. A superhard wood is produced in wood-plastic combinations (WPC), in which wood is impregnated with liquid plastic (monomer) and the whole is then bombarded with gamma rays to polymerize the plastic.

Wood /wʊd/ Grant 1892–1942. US artist. A regionalist painter, he struck a note of hard realism in his studies of farming folk, such as *American Gothic* 1930, now in the Art Institute of Chicago.

Wood /wʊd/ Haydn 1882–1959. British composer. A violinist, he wrote a violin concerto among other works, but is best known for his songs, which include 'Roses of Picardy', associated with World War I.

Wood /wʊd/ Henry (Joseph) 1869–1944. British conductor. He was born in London,

studied at the Royal Academy of Music, had experience as an organist and operatic conductor, and from 1895 until his death conducted the London Promenade Concerts, now named after him.

Wood /wʊd/ John c. 1705–1754. British architect, known as 'Wood of Bath' because of his many works in that city. Like many of his designs, Royal Crescent was executed by his son, also *John Wood* (died 1782).

Wood /wʊd/ Mrs Henry (born Ellen Price) 1814–1887. British novelist. A pioneer of crime fiction, she is remembered for the melodramatic *East Lynne* 1861.

wood carving an art form practised since prehistoric times, but surviving less often than sculpture in stone or metal because of the comparative fragility of the material, especially in W Africa where there is a long tradition, notably in Nigeria. Noted European exponents are Veit ◊Stoss and Grinling ◊Gibbons.

woodcock Eurasian wading bird *Scolopax rusticola* with mottled plumage, a long bill, short legs and short tail. It searches for food in boggy ground in woods.

woodcut and *wood engraving*. Techniques for printing pictures: see ◊print.

Woodforde /'wʊdfəd/ James 1740–1803. British cleric who held livings in Somerset and Norfolk, and whose diaries 1758–1802 form a record of rural England.

woodlouse name given to certain crustaceans of the order Isopoda that live on land and breathe air, but also need moisture in order to survive. They have segmented bodies and flattened undersides. The eggs are carried by the female in a pouch beneath the thorax. Most common in Britain are the genera *Oniscus* and *Porcellio*.

woodmouse rodent *Apodemus sylvaticus* which lives in woodlands and hedgerows, and sometimes open fields in Britain and Europe. About 9 cm/3.5 in long, plus a similar length of tail, it is yellow-brown above, white below, and has long oval ears. It is nocturnal, and feeds largely on seeds, but eats a range of foods, including some insects. Also known as *longtailed field mouse*.

woodpecker bird of the family Picidae, which lives on insects obtained from crevices in the bark of trees or extracted from the wood by drilling with the beak and impaling them on the long tongue. The European green woodpecker or yaffle *Picus viridis* is green with red crown and yellow rump, and about the size of a jay. The greater and lesser spotted woodpeckers *Dendrocopos major* and *Dendrocopos minor*, also British species, have black, red, and white plumage. There are some 200 species worldwide.

woodpulp wood that has been processed into a pulpy mass of fibres. Its main use is for making ◊paper, but it is also used to make ◊rayon and other cellulose fibres and plastics. There are two methods of making woodpulp – mechanical and chemical. In the former, debarked logs are ground with water (to prevent charring) by rotating grindstones. The wood fibres are physically torn apart. In the latter, log chips are digested with chemicals (such as sodium

sulphite). The chemicals dissolve the material holding the fibres together.

Woodstock /'wʊdstɒk/ town in SE New York State, USA, known for its artists' colony; population (1980) 6,800.

woodwind instrument musical instrument from which sound is produced by blowing into a tube, causing the air within to vibrate. Despite their name, they are no longer always made from wood (the modern flute, for example, is commonly made from silver or stainless steel). In Western music the term is used mainly for wind instruments not made of brass, namely members of the ◊flute, ◊oboe, ◊clarinet, and ◊bassoon families.

Woodwind instruments generally fall into two categories: reed instruments, in which air vibration is set up by a reed; and those where air is simply blown into or across a tube. In both cases, different notes are obtained by changing the length of the tube by covering holes along it. Reed instruments include the clarinet, oboe, and the earlier shawm and hautboy; the cor anglais, saxophone, and bassoon.

Woodwind instruments played without a reed include the recorder, the flute, and the piccolo.

woodwind instruments

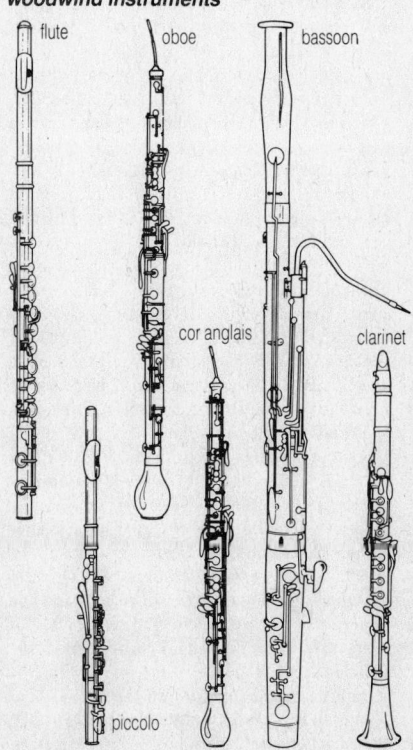

flute   oboe   bassoon

cor anglais   clarinet

piccolo

woodworm the common name for the larval stage of certain wood-boring beetles. Dead or injured trees are their natural target, but they become a serious menace when they attack structural timber and furniture. Most common in Britain are the furniture beetle *Anobium punctatum*, generally attacking older timber and estimated to be present in half the country's buildings; the powder-post beetle *Lyctus* sp.

attacking newer timber; the ◊death-watch beetle, whose presence always coincides with fungal decay; and the wood-boring weevils. Special wood preservatives have been developed to combat woodworm, which has markedly increased since World War II. In warmer countries the greatest danger to timber is from ◊termites.

Wookey Hole /'wʊki 'həʊl/ natural cave near Wells, Somerset, England, in which flint implements of Old Stone Age people with bones of extinct animals have been found.

wool the natural fibrous covering of the sheep, and also of the llama, angora goat, and other animals. The domestic sheep, *Ovis aries*, provides the great bulk of the fibres used in commerce. Lanolin is a by-product.

In Britain there are some 26 breeds of sheep, and the wool is classified as lustre (including Lincoln, Leicester, S Devon, Cotswold, Dartmoor), demi-lustre (Cheviot, Exmoor Horn, and Romney Marsh), down (Dorset, Oxford, Suffolk, Hampshire, Southdown), and mountain (Blackface, Swaledale, Welsh White, Welsh Black). Lustre wools are used for making worsted dress fabrics, linings, braids, and so on. Demi-lustre wools are rather finer in quality, and are used for suitings, overcoats, and costumes, and worsted serge fabrics. Finest of English-grown wools are the down; they are used for hosiery yarns, and some for woollen cloths. Mountain wools are coarse and poor in quality, often comprising wool and hair mixed; they are useful for making carpets, homespun tweeds, and low-quality woollen suitings and hosiery.

Most of the world's finest wool comes from the merino sheep, which is not successfully acclimatized in Britain. In 1797 it was introduced into Australia, which has become the world's largest producer of merino wool: S Africa and S America are also large producers. Wools from cross-bred sheep (usually a cross of one of the lustre class with a merino) are produced in New Zealand. Since World War II blendings of wool with synthetic fibres have been developed.

Woolf /wʊlf/ Virginia (born Stephen) 1882–1941. British novelist and critic. Her first novel *The Voyage Out* 1915 explored the tensions experienced by women who want marriage and a career. In *Mrs Dalloway* 1922 she perfected her 'stream of consciousness' technique. Among her later books are *To the Lighthouse* 1927, *Orlando* 1928, and *The Years* 1928, which considers the importance of economic independence for women. With her husband, Leonard Woolf, she founded the Hogarth Press in 1917. She committed suicide by drowning herself.

Woollett /'wʊlɪt/ William 1735–1785. British engraver. One of the greatest masters of the art, in 1775 he was appointed engraver to George III.

Woolley /'wʊli/ Leonard 1880–1960. British archaeologist. Although he carried out valuable excavation at Carchemish in Syria, Tell El-Amarna in Egypt, and Atchana, the ancient Alalakh, on the Turkish-Syrian border, he is best remembered for his work at ◊Ur in Iraq where he discovered evidence of what may have been the biblical flood, and remains of the ziggurats that

inspired the story of the Tower of Babel, as well as relics of rich social and cultural life.

Woolman /'wʊlmən/ John 1720–1772. American Quaker, born in New Jersey; he was one of the first anti-slavery agitators, and left an important *Journal*.

woolsack in the UK, name given to the seat of the Lord High Chancellor in the House of Lords; it is a large square bag of wool and is a reminder of the principal source of English wealth in the Middle Ages.

Woolwich /'wʊlɪdʒ/ London district cut through by the Thames, the N section being in the borough of Newham and the S in Greenwich. There is a ferry here and a flood barrier 1984. The Royal Arsenal, an ordnance depot from 1518, was closed down in 1967.

Woolworth /'wʊlwəθ/ Frank Winfield 1852–1919. US businessman. He opened his first successful 'five and ten cent' store in Lancaster, Pennysylvania, in 1879, and, together with his brother C S Woolworth (1856–1947), built up a chain of similar shops throughout the USA, Canada, Great Britain, Ireland, and Europe.

Woomera /'wʊmərə/ (Aboriginal 'weapon-thrower') town in South Australia, site of a rocket range from 1946; population (1984) 1,800.

Wootton /'wʊtn/ Barbara Frances Wootton, Baroness Wootton of Abinger 1897– . British educationist and economist, who has published *Freedom under Planning* (1945), *Social Science and Social Pathology* (1959), and other works, and was created a life peer in 1958.

Worcester /'wʊstə/ cathedral city with industries (gloves, shoes, Worcester sauce; Royal Worcester porcelain from 1751) in Hereford and Worcester, England, administrative head-quarters of the county, on the Severn; population (1981) 75,000. The cathedral is mainly of the 13th–14th centuries.

At the **Battle of Worcester** 1651 Cromwell defeated Charles I.

Worcester /'wʊstə/ industrial port (textiles, engineering, printing) in Massachusetts, USA, on the Blackstone river; founded in 1713; university 1887; population (1980) 373,000.

Worcestershire /'wʊstəʃə/ former Midland county of England, merged with Herefordshire in the new county of Hereford and Worcester in 1974, except for a small projection in the N, which went to West Midlands. Worcester was the county town.

word in computing, the number of ◊bits of information a computer can process in a single operation (see also ◊byte).

word processor in computing, a program that allows the input, amendment, manipulation, storage, and retrieval of text; or a computer system dedicated to the running of such software. Since word-processing programs became available to microcomputers, the method is rapidly replacing the typewriter.

Wordsworth /'wɜːdzwəθ/ Dorothy 1771–1855. English writer. She lived with her brother William ◊Wordsworth as a companion and support from 1795 until his death, and her many journals describing their life at Grasmere in the

Lake District and their travels provided inspiration and material for his poetry.

Wordsworth /'wɜːdzwəθ/ William 1770–1850. British poet, a leading figure in the Romantic movement. Born in Cockermouth in Cumberland, he was educated at Hawkshead School and St John's College, Cambridge. Going to France in 1791, he sympathized deeply with the revolutionaries, and fell in love with Marie-Anne Vallon, by whom he had an illegitimate daughter. Returning to England just before the Terror he published *The Evening Walk* and *Descriptive Sketches* in 1793. In 1797 he settled with his sister Dorothy ◊Wordsworth in Somerset, in order to be near ◊Coleridge, collaborating with him in *Lyrical Ballads* 1798 (which included 'Tintern Abbey') and attempting to avoid poetic diction and 'give the charm of novelty to things of every day'. After visiting Germany 1798–99 he and Dorothy settled at Grasmere in the Lake District in 1799. In 1802 he married Mary Hutchinson.

Outstanding among later works were the *Poems* 1807 (including 'Intimations of Immortality'), and *The Prelude* (written by 1805, published 1850), which was written to form part of the great autobiographical work *The Recluse*, never completed; other works include *The White Doe of Rylstone* 1815, *Ecclesiastical Sketches* 1822, and *Yarrow Revisited* 1835. In 1843 Wordsworth was appointed poet laureate.

Wordsworth One of the greatest English poets, William Wordsworth turned to nature for inspiration, in particular the beauty of his native Lake District. This portrait is by Benjamin Haydon.

work in physics, a measure of the result of transferring energy from one system to another to cause an object to move. Thus work W is equal to the product of the force F used and the distance d moved by the object ($W = F \times d$). For example, the work done when a force of 10 newtons moves an object 5 metres against some sort of resistance is 50 newton-metres ($= 50$◊joules). Work should not be confused with ◊energy (the capacity to do work, which is also measured in joules) or ◊power (the rate of doing work, measured in joules per second.

Worksop /'wɜːksɒp/ English market and industrial town in Nottinghamshire; population (1981) 37,000.

World Bank popular name for the *International Bank for Reconstruction and Development*, established in 1945 under the 1944 ◊Bretton-Woods agreement which also created the ◊International Monetary Fund. The World Bank is a specialized agency of the ◊United Nations which borrows in the commercial market and lends on commercial terms. The ◊International Development Association is an arm of the World Bank.

World Intellectual Property Organization (WIPO) agency of the ◊United Nations established 1974 to coordinate the international protection (initiated by the Paris convention 1883) of inventions, trademarks, and industrial designs, and literary and artistic works (initiated by the Berne convention 1886).

World Meteorological Organization an agency, part of the United Nations since 1950, that promotes the international exchange of weather information through the establishment of a worldwide network of meteorological stations. It was founded as the International Meteorological Organization in 1873, and its headquarters are now in Geneva.

World War I 1914–1918. War between the Central European Powers (Germany, Austria-Hungary and allies), against the Triple Entente (Britain and the British Empire, France, and Russia), together with the USA, and their allies. An estimated 10 million lives were lost and twice that number were wounded.
outbreak on 28 Jun the heir to the Austrian throne was assassinated at Sarajevo; on 28 Jul Austria declared war on Serbia; as Russia mobilized, Germany declared war on Russia and France, taking a short cut in the west by invading Belgium; on 4 Aug Britain declared war on Germany
1914 Western Front the German advance reached within a few miles of Paris, but an Allied counterattack at ◊Marne drove them back to the River Aisne; the opposing lines then settled to trench warfare
Eastern Front Hindenburg halted the Russian advance at the Battle of ◊Tannenberg
Africa on 16 Sept all Germany's African colonies were in Allied hands
Middle East on 1 Nov Turkey entered the war
1915 Western Front several offensives on both sides resulted in insignificant gains. ◊Haig became British commander in chief
Eastern Front ◊Mackensen and ◊Hindenburg drove back the Russians and took Poland
Middle East British attacks against Turkey in Mespotamia (Iraq), the ◊Dardanelles, and at ◊Gallipoli were all unsuccessful
Italy declared war on Austria; Bulgaria joined the Central Powers
war at sea Germany declared all-out U-boat war, but the sinking of the liner *Lusitania* (with Americans among the 1,198 lost) led to demands in the USA to enter the war

1916 Western Front German attack on the Verdun salient, countered by the Allies on the Somme and at Verdun
Eastern Front Romania joined the Allies but was soon overrun by Germany
Middle East ◊Kut was taken from the British by the Turks
war at sea the indecisive Battle of ◊Jutland
1918 Eastern Front on 3 Mar Russia signed the Treaty of ◊Brest-Litovsk with Germany
Western Front Germany began a final offensive. In Apr the Allies appointed ◊Foch supreme commander, but by Jun (when the first US troops went into battle) the Allies had lost all gains since 1915, and the Germans were on the Marne. The battle at ◊Amiens marked the launch of the Allied victorious offensive.
Italy at Vittorio Veneto the British and Italians finally defeated the Austrians.
German capitulation began with naval mutinies at Kiel, followed by uprisings in the major cities. Kaiser Wilhelm II abdicated, and on 11 Nov the armistice was signed
1919 18 Jun, peace treaty of ◊Versailles.

World War II 1939–1945. War between Germany, Italy, and Japan (the Axis powers) on one side, and Britain, the Commonwealth, France, the USA, USSR, and China on the other. An estimated 55 million lives were lost, 20 million of them citizens of the USSR.
1939 Sept German invasion of Poland; Britain and France declared war on Germany; USSR invaded Poland; fall of Warsaw (Poland divided between Germany and USSR)
Nov USSR invaded Finland. On the Western front, the 'phoney war' with both sides entrenched behind defensive lines lasted until May 1940
1940 Mar Soviet peace treaty with Finland
Apr Germany invaded Denmark, Norway, Netherlands, Belgium, and Luxembourg. In Britain, a coalition government was formed under ◊Churchill
May Germany outflanked the ◊Maginot defensive line
May–Jun British evacuation of ◊Dunkirk
Jun Italy declared war on Britain and France; Germans entered Paris; ◊Pétain signed the armistice with Germany (see ◊Vichy)
Jul–Oct Battle of ◊Britain between British and German air forces
Sept Japanese invasion of French Indo-China
Oct abortive Italian invasion of Greece
1941 Apr Germany overran Greece and Yugoslavia
Jun Germany invaded USSR; Finland declared war on USSR
Jul Germans entered Smolensk
Dec Germans within 40 km/25 mi of Moscow, with ◊Leningrad under siege. First Soviet counter-offensive. Japan attacked ◊Pearl Harbor, and declared war on USA and Britain. Germany and Italy declared war on USA
1942 Jan Japanese conquest of Philippines
Jun naval battle of ◊Midway, the turning point of the Pacific War
Aug German attack on Stalingrad
Oct–Nov Battle of ◊Alamein, turn of the tide for the Western Allies

Nov Soviet counter-offensive on Stalingrad
1943 Jan ◊Casablanca conference; German surrender at Stalingrad
Mar USSR drove Germans back to the river Donetz
May end of Axis resistance in N Africa
Aug beginning of campaign against Japanese in Burma
Sept Italy surrendered to Allies; Allied landings at ◊Salerno; USSR retook Smolensk
Oct Italy declared war on Germany
Nov–Dec ◊Tehran conference
1944 Jan Allied landing at ◊Anzio
Mar end of German U-boat campaign in the Atlantic
May fall of Monte Cassino
Jun D-Day: Allied landings in Normandy
Jul bomb plot against Hitler
Aug Romania joined Allies
Sept battle of ◊Arnhem; Soviet armistice with Finland
Oct ◊Tito and Russians entered Belgrade
Dec German counter-offensive, Battle of the Bulge
1945 Feb Russians reached German border; Yalta conference; Allied bombing campaign over Germany (see ◊Dresden); Americans landed on Iwo Jima
Apr Hitler committed suicide
May German surrender to the Allies
Jul Potsdam conference
Aug atom bombs dropped on ◊Hiroshima and ◊Nagasaki; Japan surrendered.

World Wildlife Fund an international organization established in 1961 to raise funds for conservation by public appeal. Its headquarters are at Gland, Switzerland. Projects include conservation of particular species (for example, the tiger and giant panda) or special areas (such as the Simen Mountains, Ethiopia). Prince ◊Philip of the UK is the organization's president (1981–).

worm term popularly used for various elongated limbless creatures. Zoologically worms include the flatworms such as ◊flukes and ◊tapeworms; the roundworms or ◊nematodes such as the potato eelworm and the hookworm, an animal parasite; the marine ribbon worms or nemerteans; and the segmented worms or ◊annelids. In 1979 giant sea worms about 3 m/10 ft long, living within tubes created by their own excretions, were discovered 2,450 m/8,000 ft beneath the Pacific NE of the Galapagos Islands. See also ◊earthworm.

Worms /vɔːmz, German vɔːms/ industrial town in Rhineland-Palatinate, West Germany, on the Rhine; population (1984) 73,000. ◊Luther appeared before the *Diet* (Assembly) *of Worms* in 1521, and was outlawed by the emperor.

wormwood aromatic herb *Artemisia absinthium*, family Compositae; the leaves are used in ◊absinthe.

Wounded Knee /'wuːndɪd 'niː/ site on the Oglala Sioux Reservation, South Dakota, USA, of the last major confrontation between the US Army and the American Indians. Chief Sitting Bull was killed, supposedly resisting arrest, on 15 Dec 1890, and on 29 Dec 1890 a group of Indians involved with him in the Ghost Dance Movement

World War I (top) Men of the Middlesex regiment wheeling wounded comrades from the trenches of the Somme to their quarters in Nov 1916. (left) George V touches his cap to infantrymen in Fouquerueil, Aug 1916. (bottom left) Soldiers struggling to move a field gun in muddy conditions. (bottom right) Prisoners from Guillemont pass by troops, Sept 1916.

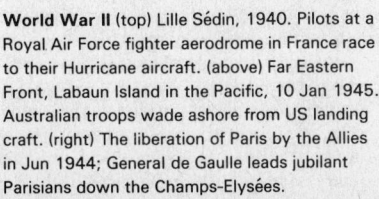

World War II (top) Lille Sédin, 1940. Pilots at a Royal Air Force fighter aerodrome in France race to their Hurricane aircraft. (above) Far Eastern Front, Labaun Island in the Pacific, 10 Jan 1945. Australian troops wade ashore from US landing craft. (right) The liberation of Paris by the Allies in Jun 1944; General de Gaulle leads jubilant Parisians down the Champs-Elysées.

Europe during World War II 1939-45

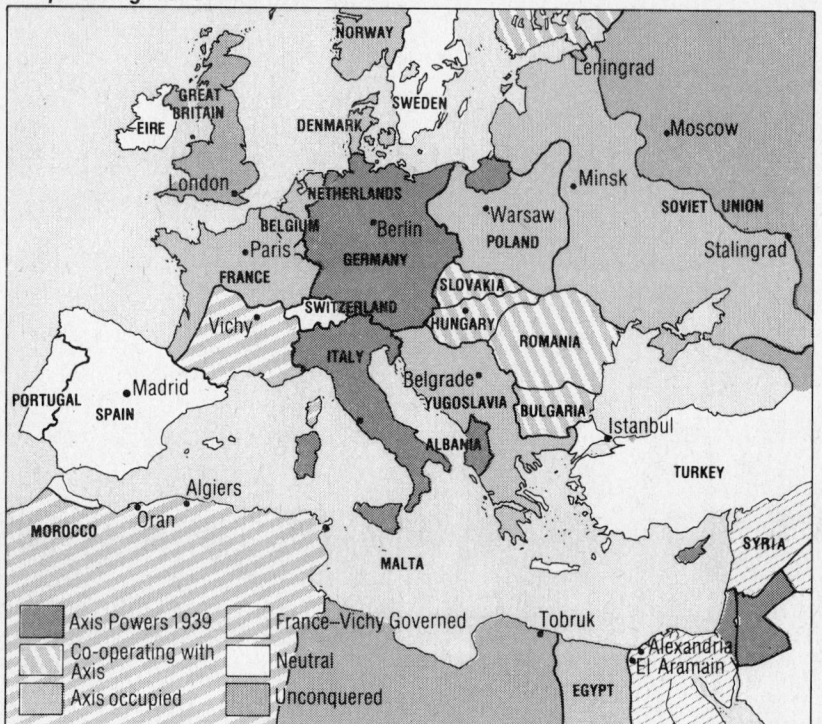

Axis Powers 1939 / France–Vichy Governed
Co-operating with Axis / Neutral
Axis occupied / Unconquered

(aimed at resumption of Indian control of N America with the aid of the spirits of dead braves) were surrounded and 153 killed.

In 1973 the militant American Indian Movement, in the siege of Wounded Knee 27 Feb–8 May, held hostages and demanded a government investigation of the Indian treaties.

Wouverman /ˈwauvəmæn/ Philip 1619–1668. Dutch painter, born in Haarlem. He painted landscapes and battle pieces. His brothers *Pieter Wouverman* (1623–82) and *Jan Wouverman* (1629–66) painted similar scenes.

wrack name for any of the large brown seaweeds which are characteristic inhabitants of the rocky shore. The *bladder wrack Fucus vesiculosus* is common and widely distributed on rocky shores. It has narrow dichotomously branched fronds up to 1 m/3 ft long, with oval airbladders, usually in pairs on either side of the midrib.

Wrangel /ˈræŋɡəl, Russian ˈvræŋɡɪl/ Ferdinand Petrovich, Baron von Wrangel 1794–1870. Russian vice-admiral and Arctic explorer, after whom Wrangel Island in the Soviet Arctic is named.

Wrangel /ˈræŋɡəl, Russian ˈvræŋɡɪl/ Peter Nicolaievich, Baron Wrangel 1878–1928. Russian general, born at St Petersburg. He commanded a division of Cossacks in World War I, and in 1920 became commander in chief of the White army in the Crimea operating against the Bolsheviks.

wrasse fish of the family Labridae, found in temperate and tropical seas. The most common British species is the ballan wrasse *Labrus bergylta*.

wren small brown bird *Troglodytes troglodytes* with a cocked-up tail, found across N America, Europe and N Asia. Only 9.5 cm/3.75 in long, it has a loud trilling song, and feeds on insects and spiders. The male constructs a domed nest of moss, grass, and leaves.

Wren /ren/ Christopher 1632–1723. English architect, born at East Knoyle, Wiltshire. He studied mathematics, and in 1660 became a professor of astronomy at Oxford. His opportunity as an architect came after the Great Fire of London 1666. He prepared a plan for rebuilding the city, but it was not adopted. Wren's greatest achievement was St Paul's Cathedral, built 1675–1710, and the most noteworthy of his City churches are St Michael's, Cornhill; St Bride's, Fleet Street; and St Mary-le-Bow, Cheapside. His other buildings include the Royal Exchange, Marlborough House, London, and buildings in Oxford, including the Sheldonian Theatre.

Wren /ren/ P(ercival) C(hristopher) 1885–1941. British novelist. Out of his experiences in the French and Indian armies he wrote martial adventure novels including *Beau Geste* 1924, dealing with the Foreign Legion.

wrestling sport popular in ancient Egypt, Greece, and Rome, and included in the Olympics from 704 BC. The two chief international styles are *Graeco-Roman* concentrating on above-waist holds, and *freestyle*, which allows the legs to be used to hold or trip; in both the aim is to throw the opponent to the ground. In Britain there are three regional variants: Cumberland, West Country, and Lancashire.

Japanese *sumo* wrestling is one of the ◊martial arts, and involves very overweight participants who throw each other either to the ground or out of the ring.

Wrexham /ˈreksəm/ market town in Clwyd, Wales, 19 km/12 mi SW of Chester; population (1981) 40,000. Seat of the Roman Catholic bishopric of Menevia (Wales).

Wright /rait/ Frank Lloyd 1869–1959. US architect, born in Wisconsin. He studied as a civil engineer, but turned to architecture on seeing the newly erected wing of the Wisconsin State Capitol collapse. One of the outstanding architects of the 20th century, he influenced design all over the world by his freedom from convention and rule. Among his buildings are his Wisconsin home Taliesin East 1925; Falling Water, Pittsburgh, Pennsylvania, 1936; and the Guggenheim Museum, New York, 1959.

Wright /rait/ Joseph 1855–1930. British philologist. Professor of comparative philology at Oxford 1901–25, he recorded English local speech in his six-volume *English Dialect Dictionary* 1896–1905.

Wright /rait/ Joseph 1734–1797. British artist and portraitist, known as Wright of Derby from his birthplace. He made remarkable use of light effects, for example *The Air Pump* 1768 (Tate Gallery, London).

Wright /rait/ Judith 1915– . Australian poet, author of *The Moving Image* 1946 and *Alive* 1972.

Wright /rait/ Orville 1871–1948 and Wilbur 1867–1912. American brothers who pioneered powered flight. Orville was born in Dayton, Ohio, and Wilbur in Indiana. Inspired by ◊Lilienthal's gliding, they perfected their piloted glider in 1902 while running a bicycle business in Dayton. In 1903 they built their first powered machine, and on 17 Dec of that year became the first to make a successful powered flight, near Kitty Hawk, North Carolina. The original machine is in the National Air and Space Museum, Washington, and a replica in the Science Museum in London.

Wright /rait/ Peter 1917– . British intelligence agent whose book *Spycatcher*, written after his retirement, caused a major international stir in 1987 when the British government tried to block its publication anywhere in the world. The book claims to expose Soviet penetration of the British secret service and attempts by the service to undermine the government of Harold Wilson in the 1960s.

Wright /rait/ Richard 1908–1960. US novelist. He was one of the first to depict the condition of blacks in contemporary American society with *Native Son* 1940 and the autobiography *Black Boy* 1945.

writ in English law, a document issued in the name of an executive officer of the crown, such as the lord chancellor or a judge, commanding someone to do (or not to do) something. A writ is the first step in legal proceedings, whether civil or criminal, in the UK.

Writers to the Signet Scottish equivalent of English solicitors: a society of law agents whose predecessors were originally clerks in the secretary of state's office entrusted with the

Wren St Paul's Cathedral, built 1675–1710, the largest Protestant church in the world, is Christopher Wren's masterpiece.

Wright US architect Frank Lloyd Wright at 87. Among his noted city buildings is the Guggenheim Museum in New York 1959.

preparation of documents requiring the signet or seal. The preparation of crown writs, charters, and similar documents is the exclusive privilege of Writers to the Signet.

writing a written form of communication using one of various sets of symbols: see ◊alphabet, ◊cuneiform, ◊hieroglyphic. The two latter used ideographs (picture writing) and phonetic word symbols side by side, as does modern Chinese. Syllabic writing, as in Japanese, develops from the continued use of a symbol to represent the sound of a short word. An advanced phonetic form of writing is ◊shorthand.

Wroclaw /'vrɒtslɑːf/ industrial town in Poland (under the German name of *Breslau*, it was the capital of former German ◊Silesia); population (1984) 632,000.

wrought iron fairly pure iron containing beads of slag, widely used for construction work before the days of cheap steel. It is strong, tough and easy to machine. It is made in a so-called puddling furnace (invented by Henry Colt in England in 1784). Pig iron is remelted and heated strongly in air with iron ore, burning out the carbon in the metal, leaving quite pure iron and a slag containing impurities. The pasty metal resulting is then hammered to remove as much of the remaining slag as possible.

Wuchang /,wuː'tʃæn/ former city in China; amalgamated with ◊Wuhan.

Wuhan /,wuː'hæn/ river port and capital of Hubei province, China, at the confluence of the Han and Chang Jiang, formed in 1950 as one of China's greatest industrial areas by the amalgamation of Hankou, Hanyang, and Wuchang; population (1982) 3,230,000. A centre of revolt in both the Taiping Rebellion 1851–65 and the 1911 revolution, it saw a serious anti-Mao revolt in 1967 during the Cultural Revolution.

Wuhsien /,wuː'ʃi'en/ another name for ◊Suzhou, a city in China.

Wundt /vʊnt/ Wilhelm 1832–1920. German physiologist, who regarded psychology as the study of internal experience or consciousness. His main psychological method was introspection; he also studied sensation, perception of space and time, and reaction times.

Wuppertal /'vʊpətɑːl/ industrial town in West Germany, about 32 km/20 mi E of Düsseldorf, formed 1929 (named 1931) by uniting Elberfield (13th century) and Barmen (11th century); population (1984) 382,000.

Württemberg /'vɜːtəmbɜːg/ former kingdom in SW Germany, 1805–1918, which joined the German Reich in 1870. Its capital was Stuttgart. Divided in 1946 between the administrative West German *Länder* of Württemberg-Baden and Württemberg-Hohenzollern, from 1952 it was part of the *Land* of ◊Baden-Württemberg.

Würzburg /'vɜːtsbɜːg/ industrial town (engineering, printing, brewing) in Bavaria, West Germany; population (1984) 130,000. The bishop's palace was decorated by Tiepolo.

Wyatt /'waɪət/ James 1747–1813. English architect, contemporary of the Adam brothers, who designed in the neo-Gothic style. His over-enthusiastic 'restorations' of medieval cathedrals earned him the nickname 'Wyatt the Destroyer'.

Wyatt /'waɪət/ Thomas c. 1503–1542. English poet. He was employed on diplomatic missions by Henry VIII, and in 1536 was imprisoned for a time in the Tower of London, since he was thought to have been the lover of Henry VIII's second wife, Anne Boleyn. In 1541 Wyatt was again imprisoned on charges of treason. With the Earl of Surrey, he pioneered the use of the sonnet in England.

Wyatville /'waɪətvɪl/ Jeffrey 1766–1840. English architect, nephew of James Wyatt, best known for his remodelling of Windsor Castle, Berkshire.

Wycherley /'wɪtʃəli/ William 1640–1710. English Restoration dramatist. He was born near Shrewsbury and educated in France. His reputation rests on the bawdy *The Plain Dealer* 1674 and *The Country Wife* 1675.

Wycliffe /'wɪklɪf/ John c. 1320–1384. English religious reformer. Allying himself with the party of John of Gaunt, which was opposed to ecclesiastical influence at court, he attacked abuses in the Church, holding that the Bible rather than the Church was the supreme authority. In about 1378 he moved on to criticize such fundamental doctrines as priestly absolution, confession, and indulgences. He sent out bands of travelling preachers, and set disciples to work on translating the Bible into English. He was denounced as a heretic.

Wyoming /waɪ'əʊmɪŋ/ state of W USA; nicknamed Equality State
area 253,595 sq km/97,913 sq mi
capital Cheyenne
features Rocky Mountains; Yellowstone (including the geyser Old Faithful) and Grand Teton national parks
products oil, natural gas, tin, sodium salts, coal, phosphates, sulphur, uranium; sheep and beef cattle
population (1984) 487,000
famous people Buffalo Bill Cody
history mainly part of the ◊Louisiana Purchase, Wyoming became a state in 1890, and in 1869 was the first to grant women the franchise.

Wyss /viːs/ Johann David 1743–1818. Swiss author, remembered for his children's classic *Swiss Family Robinson* 1813.

Wyss /viːs/ Johann David 1743–1818. Swiss author, remembered for his children's classic *Swiss Family Robinson* 1813.

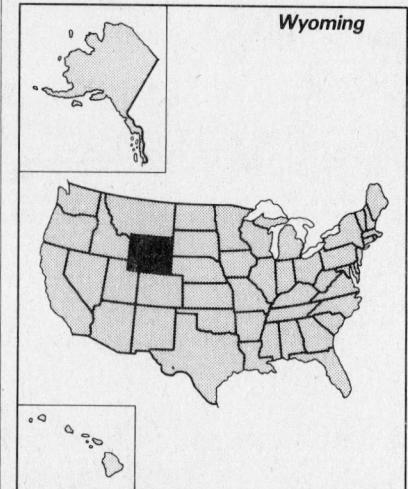

Wyoming

X the 24th letter of the English alphabet, with a sound that can be well represented medially by ks and initially by z. It is derived through Latin from the alphabet of W Greece, and was the last letter in the earlier Latin alphabet.

Xavier, St Francis /'zeɪvɪə/ 1506–1552. Spanish Jesuit missionary, known as the Apostle of the Indies.

At the university of Paris he became one of the first seven members of the Order of Jesus 1534. Ordained priest in 1537, he went as a Catholic missionary to the Portuguese colonies in the Indies, arriving at Goa in 1542. In 1549–51 he was in Japan, establishing a Christian mission which lasted for 100 years. Returning to Goa in 1552, he sailed for China, and died of fever there. He was canonized in 1621.

X-chromosome the larger of the two sex ◊chromosomes, the smaller being the ◊Y-chromosome. These two chromosomes are involved in ◊sex determination. Genes carried on the X-chromosome produce the phenomenon of ◊sex linkage.

xenon gaseous element, symbol Xe, atomic number 54, atomic weight 131.30. It is a heavy inert gas, discovered in 1898 by Ramsay and ◊Travers in the residue from liquid air. It occurs in the atmosphere to the extent of about one part in 20 million, and is used in lasers, incandescent lamps and electronic flash lamps, and to give a blue glow in a discharge tube. It is a fission product of uranium nuclear reactors. Radioactive xenon has also been used to measure the flow of blood to the brain during acceleration on a centrifuge when testing the effects of supersonic speeds on humans.

Xenophon /'zenəfən/ c. 430–354 BC. Greek historian, philosopher, and soldier. Born in Athens, he was a disciple of ◊Socrates (described in Xenophon's *Symposium*). In 401 BC he joined a Greek mercenary army aiding the Persian prince Cyrus in a revolt against his brother, the king of Persia. He succeeded to the command on the death of Cyrus in the battle of Cunaxa, and in his *Anabasis* described how he led the 10,000 Greeks in a 1000-mile march home across enemy territory. Subsequently he served in the Spartan army and lived on his estate at Scillus in Elis.

Among his other works are the *Memorabilia* and *Apology*.

xerography a dry, non-chemical method of producing images without the use of negatives or sensitized paper, invented in the USA by Chester Carlson in 1938 and applied in the *Xerox photocopier*. In this process an image of the document to be copied is projected on to an electrostatically charged photo-conductive plate. The charge remains only in the areas corresponding to its image. The latent image on the plate is then developed by contact with ink powder, which adheres only to the image, and is then usually transferred to ordinary paper or some other flat surface, and quickly heated to form a permanent print. Applications include document copying, enlarging from microfilm, preparing printing masters for ◊offset litho printing and dyeline machines, making ◊X-ray pictures, and printing high-speed computer output.

xerophyte a plant that is adapted to live in dry conditions. Common adaptations to reduce the rate of ◊transpiration include a reduction of leaf size sometimes to spines or scales, a dense covering of hairs over the leaf to trap a layer of moist air (for example edelweiss), permanently rolled leaves or leaves that roll up in dry weather (for example marram grass), sunken ◊stomata, a thick cuticle covering the leaves, and stomata which close during the day and open at night when it is cooler. Many desert cacti are xerophytes and store water in their thick, swollen stems.

Xerxes /'zɜːksiːz/ c. 519–465 BC. King of Persia from 485 BC, when he succeeded his father Darius and, after several years' preparation, continued the Persian invasion of Greece. In 480 BC, at the head of an army of some 400,000 men and supported by a fleet of 800 ships, he crossed the Hellespont over a bridge of boats. He defeated the Greek fleet at Artemisium and, having stormed the pass of Thermopylae, captured and burned Athens. But Themistocles annihilated the Persian fleet at Salamis and Xerxes was forced to retreat. He spent his later years working on a grandiose extension of the

capital Persepolis and was eventually murdered in a court intrigue.

Xhosa /'kɔːsə/ indigenous people of South Africa, living mainly in the Black National State of ◊Transkei.

Xiamen /ʃiˌɑːˈmʌn/ (formerly *Amoy*) port on Ku Lang island in Fujian province, China, one of the original five treaty ports used for trade under foreign control 1842–1943 and a special export-trade zone from 1979; university 1921; population (1980) 500,000.

Xian /ˌʃiːˈæn/ industrial city and capital of Shaanxi province, China; university; population 2,600,000. It was the capital of China under the Chou dynasty (1126–255 BC); under the Han dynasty (206 BC to 220 AD), when it was called Changan (long peace); under the Tang dynasty 618–906, as Siking (western capital); the Manchus called it Sian (western peace), now spelled Xian; it reverted to Changan 1913–32; was Siking 1932–43; and again Sian from 1943. It was here that the imperial court retired after the Boxer rising in 1900. Its treasures include the 600-year-old Ming wall; the pottery soldiers buried to protect the tomb of the first Qin emperor (see ◊Shi Huangdi); Big Wild Goose Pagoda, one of the oldest in China; and the Great Mosque 742 AD.

Xian Incident kidnapping of the Chinese generalissimo and politician ◊Chiang Kai-shek 12 Dec 1936, by one of his own generals, to force his cooperation with the communists against the Japanese invaders.

Xi Jiang /'ʃiː dʒiˈæŋ/ (formerly Si-Kiang) river in China, which rises in Yunnan and flows into the South China Sea; length 1,900 km/1,200 mi. Guangzhou lies on the N arm of its delta, and Hong Kong island at its mouth.

Xingú /ʃɪŋˈguː/ river rising in the Mato Grosso, Brazil, and flowing 1,932 km/1,200 mi to the Amazon delta. Also a South American Indian people threatened with extinction by the development of Amazonia.

Xinhua /ˌʃɪnˈhwɑː/ official Chinese news agency.

Xining /ˌʃiːˈnɪŋ/ (formerly *Sining*) industrial city, capital of Qinghai province, China; population (1982) 873,000.

Xinjiang Uygur /ˌʃɪndʒiˈæŋ ˈwiːɡuə/ (formerly *Sinkiang Uighur*) autonomous region of NW China
area 1,646,800 sq km/613,665 sq mi
capital Urumqi
features largest of Chinese administrative areas; Junggar Pendi (Dzungarian Basin) and Tarim Pendi (Tarim Basin, which includes ◊Lop Nur, China's nuclear testing ground, though the research centres were moved to the central province of Sichuan in 1972) separated by the Tyan Shan mountains
products cereals, cotton, fruit in valleys and oases; uranium, coal, iron, copper, tin, and oil
population (1982) 13,081,681
religion 50 per cent Muslim
history the area was under Manchu rule from the 18th century, but large sections were ceded to tsarist Russia in 1864 and 1881. China has raised the question of their return and regards the 480 km/300 mi frontier between Xinjiang Uygur and Soviet Tadzikistan as undemarcated.

Xizang /ˌʃiːˈzæŋ/ Chinese name for ◊Tibet, an autonomous region of SW China from 1965.

Xochimilco /ˌsɒtʃɪˈmɪlkəʊ/ lake about 11 km/7 mi SE of Mexico City, Mexico, noted for its floating gardens.

X-ray electromagnetic radiation in the wavelength range 10^{-11} to 10^{-9} m (shorter wavelengths are gamma rays; see ◊electromagnetic waves). X-rays are produced when high-energy ◊electrons from a heated filament ◊cathode strike the surface of a target (usually made of tungsten) on the face of a massive heat-conducting anode, between which a high alternative ◊voltage (about 100 kV) is applied. Applications of X-rays make use of their short wavelength (such as X-ray crystallography) or their penetrating power (as in medical X-rays of internal body tissues). High doses of X-rays are dangerous, and can cause cancer.

X-ray astronomy detection of ◊X-rays from

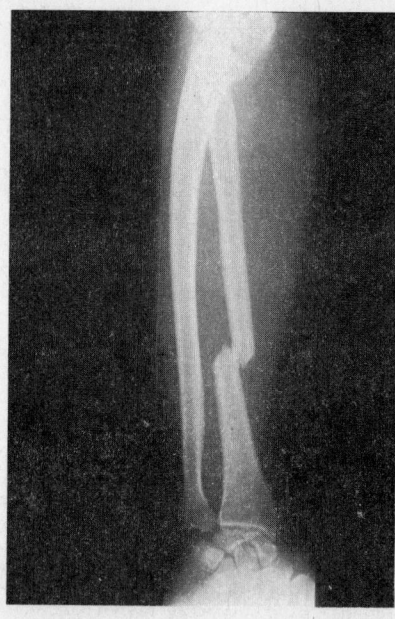

X-ray X-ray of the right forearm showing a clean fracture of the radius, the shorter, outside bone.

intensely hot gas in the Universe. The X-rays are prevented from reaching the Earth's surface by the atmosphere, so detectors must be placed in rockets and satellites. The first celestial X-ray source, ◊Scorpius X-1, was discovered by a rocket flight in 1962. Since 1970, special satellites have been orbited to study X-rays from the Sun, stars and galaxies. Many X-ray sources are believed to be gas falling on to ◊neutron stars and ◊black holes.

xylem a tissue found in ◊vascular plants, whose main function is to conduct water and dissolved mineral nutrients upwards from the roots to other parts of the plant. Xylem is

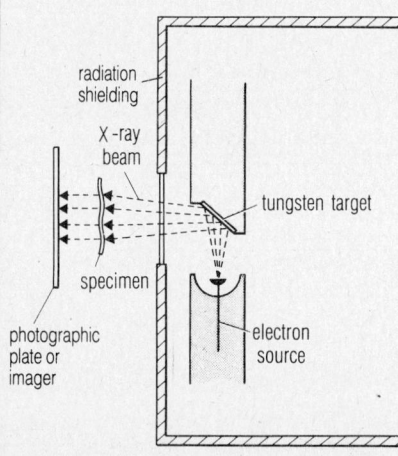

X-ray
an X-ray imager

composed of a number of different types of cell, and may include long, thin, usually dead cells known as ◊tracheids, fibres (◊schlerenchyma), thin-walled ◊parenchyma cells, and conducting vessels. In most flowering plants it is the vessels through which water is translocated, whereas most gymnosperms and pteridophytes lack vessels and depend on tracheids for water conduction. Non-woody plants contain only primary xylem, derived from the procambium, whereas in trees and shrubs this is replaced for the most part by secondary xylem, formed by ◊secondary growth from the actively dividing vascular ◊cambium. The cell walls of the secondary xylem are thickened by a deposit of ◊lignin, providing mechanical support to the plant; see ◊wood.

xylophone musical ◊percussion instrument comprising a number of wooden bars of varying lengths arranged in rows over resonators to produce sounds when struck with hammers.

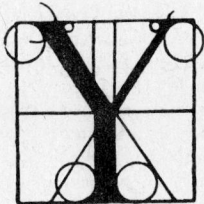

Y the 25th letter in the English alphabet, derived through the later Latin alphabet from the Greek letter *upsilon*. In modern English it represents the same vowel sounds as *i* when used as a vowel, and as a consonant, in words such as *yoke*, yacht, a palatal approximant.

yachting pleasure cruising or racing a small and light vessel, whether sailing or power-driven. Most prominent of English yacht clubs is the Royal Yacht Squadron, established at Cowes in 1812, and the Yacht Racing Association was founded in 1875 to regulate the sport. The Observer Single-handed Transatlantic Race 1960 is held every four years: the record is held by Yvon Fauconnier (France) 16 days 6 hrs 25 mins, 1984. The royal yacht *Britannia* (1953) has a displacement of 4,000 tonnes (tons) and overall length of 126 m/413 ft. At the Olympic Games, seven categories exist. They are: Soling, Flying Dutchman, Star, Finn, Tornado, 470, and Windglider (Boardsailing), which was introduced at the 1984 Los Angeles games. The Finn and Windglider are solo events, the Soling Class is for three-person crews, while all other classes are for crews of two.

America's Cup first contested 1870. All winners have been US boats, except the Australia II in 1983.
1974 Courageous
1977 Courageous
1980 Freedom
1983 Australia II
1987 Stars and Stripes
Admiral's Cup first organized 1957. This is a team event in which each country is represented by a number of boats.
1977 Great Britain
1979 Australia
1981 Great Britain
1983 West Germany
1985 West Germany

---

yak the wild ox *Bos grunniens* of Tibet. When wild it is black, but in domestication it is often black and white or reddish. It stands about 2 m/6 ft at the shoulder, and has long shaggy hair on the underparts.

Yakut /jæˈkʊt/ Autonomous Soviet Socialist Republic, in NE USSR
area 3,103,000 sq km/1,197,760 sq mi
capital Yakutsk
features Yakut is one of the coldest inhabited places on earth; river Lena
products sable, silver fox, and other furs; its mineral wealth of gold, diamonds, coal, and tin is difficult to extract because of the climate, though its large natural gas deposits have been exploited from 1973: pipeline Yakutsk–Vladivostok; some agriculture in the S
population (1985) 984,000; Yakuts 37 per cent, Russians 50 per cent
history the Yakuts, formerly nomadic and of Turkish descent, were conquered by Russia in the 17th century. Yakut became a Soviet republic 1922.

Yakutsk /jæˈkʊtsk/ capital of Yakut Republic, USSR, on the Lena, with timber industries; population (1985) 149,000. It is the coldest point of the Arctic in NE Siberia, and has an institute for studying the permanently frozen soil area (permafrost).

Yale lock a pin-tumbler ◊lock invented by Linus Yale Jr in 1865 and still widely used. It consists of a cylinder which can rotate inside a housing to turn the bolt. In the cylinder is a row of holes, which match another row in the housing. When the lock is locked, two pins, held in each of the holes by a spring, prevent the cylinder turning. When the correct key is inserted, the lower pins are raised so that they reach the edge of the cylinder and allow it to turn.

Yale University /jeɪl/ third oldest (1701) and one of the most distinguished universities of the USA, in New Haven, Connecticut. It was named after Elihu Yale (1648–1721), born in Boston, Massachusetts, one-time governor of Fort St George, Madras, India.

Yalta /ˈjæltə/ Soviet holiday resort with a pleasant climate in the Crimea, on the Black Sea; population (1975) 62,500. Livadia (summer palace built by Nicholas II 1910–11) was the site of the *Yalta conference* 1945, at which the Allied leaders Churchill, Roosevelt, and Stalin completed plans for the defeat of Germany and the foundation of the United Nations.

Yale lock

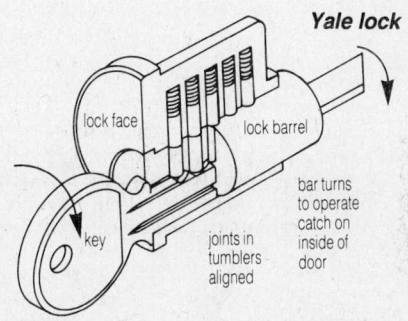

Yalu /ˈjɑːluː/ river forming the N boundary between North Korea and Jilin and Liaoning provinces (Manchuria) in China; length 790 km/491 mi.

yam tuber of tropical plant, of genus *Dioscorea* family Dioscoreaceae, eaten as a vegetable. The *Mexican yam Dioscorea composita* contains a chemical used in the manufacture of the contraceptive pill.

Yamal Peninsula /jəˈmɑːl/ peninsula in NW Siberia, USSR, with gas reserves estimated at 6 million million cubic metres: supplies are piped to W Europe.

Yamoussoukro /jæmuːˈsuːkrəʊ/ capital of Ivory Coast from 1983; population (1983) 70,000.

Yamuna /ˈjæmʊnə/ river in India: rising in the Himalayas, it runs through Agra and Delhi and joins the Ganges near Allahabad, where it forms a sacred bathing place; length 1,385 km/860 mi.

Yan'an /jænˈæn/ (formerly *Yenan*) industrial city in Shaanxi province, China; population 220,000. The ◊Long March ended here Jan 1937, and it was the communist headquarters 1936–47 (the caves in which Mao lived are preserved); population 220,00.

Yangtze-Kiang /ˈjæŋktsɪ kiˈæŋ/ former name for ◊Chang Jiang, greatest Chinese river.

Yangzhou /jæŋ ˈdʒəʊ/ canal port in Jiangsu province, China; population 240,000. Noted for its gardens and pavilions.

Yankee /'jæŋki/ colloquial (sometimes disparaging) term for an American. Outside the USA it is used for any American. In the northern USA it is applied to a person from the New England states, while in the southern states it refers to a person from any of the northern states.

Yantai /ˌjæn'taɪ/ (formerly Chefoo) ice-free port in Shandong province, China; population (1970) 250,000.

yapok marsupial mammal *Chironectes minimus* found in tropical S and Central America. Head and body about 33 cm/1.1 ft long, plus 40 cm/1.3 ft tail. The yapok is the only aquatic marsupial. It has webbed hind feet and thick fur, and the female has a watertight pouch. Nocturnal, it feeds on fish and crayfish.

yard imperial measure of length, equal to 3 ft; it was defined by the 1963 Weights and Measures Act as being equal to 0.9144 metres.

yardang ridge formed by wind erosion from a dried-up river bed or similar feature, as in Chad, China, Peru, USA. They occur on Mars on a more massive scale.

Yarmouth /'jɑːməθ/ or *Great Yarmouth* holiday resort and port in Norfolk, England, at the mouth of the Yare; population (1980) 82,000. Formerly a fishing town, it is now a leading base for North Sea oil and gas and a container port.

Yaroslavl /ˌjærə'slɑːvəl/ industrial city (textiles, rubber, paints, commercial vehicles) in the USSR, capital of Yaroslavl region, on the Volga 250 km/155 mi NE of Moscow; population (1985) 626,000.

yarrow plant *milfoil* of the northern hemisphere *Achillea millefolium* family Compositae, with flat-topped clusters of white or pink flowers.

yaws contagious tropical disease common in the West Indies, characterized by red, raspberrylike eruptions on the face, toes, and other parts of the body. A very similar disease is found in W Africa. Treatment is by antibiotics.

Yazd /jɑːzd/ (or Yezd) silk-weaving town in central Iran, in an oasis on a trade route; population (1982) 193,500.

Y-chromosome the smaller of the two sex ◊chromosomes. It only ever occurs paired with the other type of sex chromosome (X), which carries far more genes. Thus individuals are either XY or XX. In mammals, including humans, XY produces a male and XX a female; see ◊sex determination. The Y-chromosome is the smallest of all the mammalian chromosomes and is normally considered to be inert (that is, it does not have a direct effect on any part of the physical body). In humans, however, some males (about one in 300) inherit two Y-chromosomes at conception: this gives added height, greater emotional instability, inability to bear frustration, and great aggressiveness. See also ◊sex linkage and ◊X-chromosome.

year a unit of time measurement, based on the orbital period of the Earth around the Sun. The *tropical year*, from an equinox back to the same equinox, lasts 365.2422 days. It governs the occurrence of the seasons, and is the period on which the ◊calendar year is based. The *sidereal year* is the time taken for the Earth to complete one orbit relative to the fixed stars, and lasts

365.2564 days (about 20 minutes longer than a tropical year). The difference is due to the effect of ◊precession, which slowly moves the position of the equinoxes. The calendar year consists of 365 days, with an extra day added at the end of Feb each **leap year**. Leap years occur in every year that is divisible by 4, except that a century year is not a leap year unless it is divisible by 400. Hence 1900 was not a leap year, but 2000 will be. A historical year begins on 1 Jan but up to 1752 in England the civil or legal year began on 25 Mar. The English **fiscal/financial year** still ends on 5 Apr, which is 25 Mar plus 11 days added under the reform of the ◊calendar in 1752. The **regnal year** begins on the anniversary of the sovereign's accession; it is used in the dating of Acts of Parliament.

yeast a mass of minute circular or oval fungal cells about 0.000085 m/ 1/3000 in in diameter, each of which is a complete fungus capable under suitable conditions of reproducing new cells by budding. When placed in a sugar solution they multiply and convert the sugar into alcohol and carbon dioxide. Brewer's yeast *Saccharomyces cerevisiae* is used in leavening bread and fermenting beer.

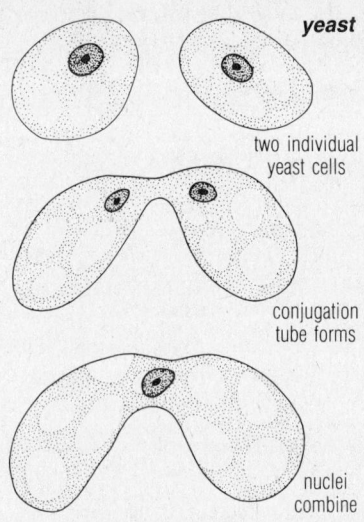

yeast

two individual
yeast cells

conjugation
tube forms

nuclei
combine

Yeats /jeɪts/ Jack Butler 1871–1857. Irish artist, brother of the poet William Butler ◊Yeats. He illustrated his own stories and depicted scenes of Irish life, for example *Back from the Races* in the Tate Gallery, London.

Yeats /jeɪts/ William Butler 1865–1939. Irish poet, a leader of the Celtic revival and a founder of the Abbey Theatre in Dublin. Of Anglo-Irish descent, he was born in Dublin, son of a lawyer turned painter. His early poetry, such as *The Wind Among the Reeds* 1899, is romantically and exotically lyrical, and he drew on Irish legend for his poetic plays, including *The Countess Kathleen* 1892, but broke through to a new sharply resilient style with *Responsibilities* 1914. In his personal life there was also a break: the beautiful Maude Gonne, to whom many of his poems had been addressed, finally refused to marry him, and in 1917 he married Georgie Hyde-Lees, whose work as a medium reinforced

his leanings towards mystic symbolism, as in the prose work *A Vision* 1925 and 1937. His later volumes of verse include *The Wild Swans at Coole* 1919, *The Tower* 1927, *The Winding Stair* 1933, and *Last Poems* 1939. His other prose works include *Autobiographies* 1926. A believer in Irish nationalism, he sat in the Irish senate 1922–28. He was awarded a Nobel prize in 1923.

Yeats W B Yeats drew on the legends, mysticism, and spirit of his native Ireland in his hauntingly beautiful poetry. The building of a national cultural and intellectual identity was his ideal.

Yedo /'jedəʊ/ name for ◊Tokyo, Japan, until 1868.

yellow archangel flowering plant *Lamiastrum galeobdolon* of the family Labiatae found over much of Europe and common in woods in S Britain. It grows up to 60 cm/2 ft tall and has nettlelike leaves and yellow flowers, with the lower lips streaked with red, in whorls around the stem in early summer.

Yellow Book 1894–1897. Illustrated literary and artistic quarterly to which the artists Beardsley and Sickert and the writers Max Beerbohm and Henry James contributed.

yellow fever tropical viral fever, sometimes called yellow jack, particularly prevalent in the Caribbean area, Brazil, and the W coast of Africa. One of the symptoms is a yellowish skin. Brought under control since the discovery that it is carried by a mosquito. The first effective vaccines were produced by Max Theiler of New York (winner of the Nobel prize 1951).

yellowhammer bird *Emberiza citrinella* of the bunting family, found in open country across Europe and N Asia. About 16.5 cm/6.5 in long, the cock is bright yellow and chestnut, the female duller. The song is sometimes supposed to sound like 'a-little-bit-of-bread-and-no-cheese'.

Yellowknife /'jelǝunaɪf/ capital of Northwest Territories, Canada, from 1967, on the N shore of Great Slave Lake; population (1984) 11,000. It was founded 1935 when gold was discovered in the area.

Yellow River English name for the ◊Huang He river in China (formerly Hwang-Lo), so called because of the yellow deposit carried by its waters.

Yellow Sea /'jelǝu/ gulf of the Pacific Ocean between China and Korea; area 466,200 sq km/180,000 sq mi. It receives the Huang He (Yellow River) and Chang Jiang.

Yellowstone National Park /'jelǝustǝun/ largest US nature reserve, established 1872 in NW Wyoming, on a broad plateau in the Rocky Mountains. It has more than 3,000 geysers and hot springs.

Yemen /'jemǝn/ name of two countries (◊Yemen North and ◊Yemen South) between which union has been agreed since 1979, but few practical measures have been taken.

Yemen, North country in SW Asia, on the Red Sea, bounded to the N by Saudi Arabia and to the S by South Yemen.

permanent constitution and in April the Command Council was dissolved. In 1979 the Assembly was increased to 159 members and a 15-member consultative council was set up. In 1980 a meeting was held of the General People's Congress, consisting of 700 elected and 300 appointed members. It agreed on a national charter and elected a permanent 52-member committee for national consultation.

The General People's Congress now meets every two years and is re-elected every four, whereas the Constituent People's Assembly continues as the nation's parliament. The president of the republic is both head of state and head of government and is elected for a five-year term by the Assembly. He governs with an appointed prime minister and council of ministers. There are no political parties as such.

history North Yemen was a kingdom in the 2nd millennium BC before it came under, successively, Egyptian, Roman, and Ethiopian rule. It adopted Islam 628 AD, formed part of the ◊Ottoman Empire 1538–1630, and was occupied by Turkey in the 19th century.

republicans, under Marshal Abdullah al-Sallal, had won. Later that year Sallal was deposed while on a foreign visit and a Republican Council took over.

Meanwhile, Britain had withdrawn from South Yemen and, with the installation of a repressive regime there, hundreds of thousands of South Yemenis fled to the YAR, many of them forming guerrilla groups with the aim of overthrowing the communist regime in South Yemen. This resulted in a war between the two Yemens 1971–72, when, under the auspices of the Arab League, a cease-fire was arranged. Both sides agreed to a union of the two countries but this was never implemented. In 1974 the pro-Saudi Col Ibrahim al-Hamadi seized power and by 1975 there were rumours of an attempt to restore the monarchy.

In 1977 Hamadi was assassinated and another member of the Military Command Council, which Hamdadi had set up 1974, Col Ahmed ibn Hussein al-Ghashmi, took over. In 1978 a gradual move towards a more constitutional form of government was started, with the appointment of the Constituent People's Assembly, the dissolution of the Military Command Council, and the installation of Ghashmi as president. In 1978 Ghashmi was killed when a bomb exploded in a suitcase carried by an envoy from South Yemen. Col Ali Abdullah Saleh became president and war broke out again between the two Yemens.

A cease-fire was again arranged by the Arab League and, for the second time, the two countries agreed to unite. This time more progress was made: there have been regular meetings of a joint council and in Mar 1984 a joint committee on foreign policy sat for the first time in Aden. In 1983 President Saleh was re-elected for a further five years.

Yemen, South country in SW Asia, on the Arabian Sea, bounded to the N by Saudi Arabia, to the E by Oman, and to the NW by North Yemen.

Yemen, North

YEMEN ARAB REPUBLIC (*al Jamhuriya al Arabiya al Yamaniya*)

AREA 195,000 sq km/75,000 sq mi
CAPITAL San'a
TOWNS Ta'iz, and chief port Hodeida
PHYSICAL hot moist coastal plain, rising to plateau
FEATURES known in classical times as *Arabia felix* because of its fertility
HEAD OF STATE AND OF GOVERNMENT Ali Abdullah Saleh from 1978
GOVERNMENT military
EXPORTS cotton, coffee, grapes
CURRENCY riyal (16.95 = £1 Sept 1987)
POPULATION 6,159,000 (1985); annual growth rate 2.4%
LANGUAGE Arabic
RELIGION Sunni Muslim 50%, Shi'ite Muslim 50%
LITERACY 18% male/1% female (1980 est)
GNP $3.9 bn (1983); $475 per head of population
CHRONOLOGY
1962 North Yemen declared the Arab Republic of Yemen (YAR), with Abdullah al-Sallal as president. Civil war broke out between royalists and republicans.
1967 Civil war ended with the republicans victorious. Sallal deposed and replaced by a Republican Council.
1971–72 War betwen South Yemen and YAR. Both sides finally agreed to a union but the agreement was not kept.

North Yemen

1974 Ibrahim al-Hamadi seized power and a Military Command Council was set up.
1977 Hamadi assassinated and replaced by Ahmed ibn Hussein al-Ghashmi.
1978 Constituent People's Assembly appointed and the Military Command Council dissolved. Ghashmi killed by an envoy from South Yemen and succeeded by Ali Abdullah Saleh. War broke out again between the two Yemens.
1979 Ceasefire agreed with, again, a commitment to a future union.
1983 Saleh elected president for a further five-year term.
1984 Joint committee on foreign policy for the two Yemens met in Aden.

government The 1970 constitution provides for a one-party state based on the Yemen Socialist Party (YSP), with a single-chamber legislature, the Supreme People's Council (SPC), and a president who is both head of state and head of government. The SPC has 111 elected members, 71 representing the YSP and 40 independents. It appoints a presidium and a council of ministers. The president is secretary general of the party, chair of the presidium, and governs through the council of ministers. The YSP is, therefore, the ultimate source of political power through the SPC and the political bureau.

history For early history, see ◊Arabia.

The People's Republic of Southern Yemen was founded 1967 by the union of ◊Aden and the Federation of South Arabia, both of which had been under British rule or protection. Before Britain withdrew, two rival factions fought for power, the Marxist National Liberation Front (NLF) and the Front for the Liberation of Occupied South Yemen (FLOSY). The NLF eventually won and assumed power as the National Front (NF). On the anniversary of three years of independence, on 1 Nov 1970, the

government The system of government is based on a provisional constitution published Jun 1974 by the Military Command Council, which seized power some six days before. In Feb 1978 the Command Council appointed the Constituent People's Assembly to draw up proposals for a

The last king of North Yemen, Imam Muhammad, was killed in a military coup 1962. The declaration of the new Yemen Arab Republic (YAR) provoked a civil war between royalist forces, assisted by Saudi-Arabia, and republicans, helped by Egypt. By 1967 the

Yemen, South

PEOPLE'S DEMOCRATIC REPUBLIC OF YEMEN
(*Jumhurijah al-Yemen al Dimuqratiyah al Sha'abijah*)

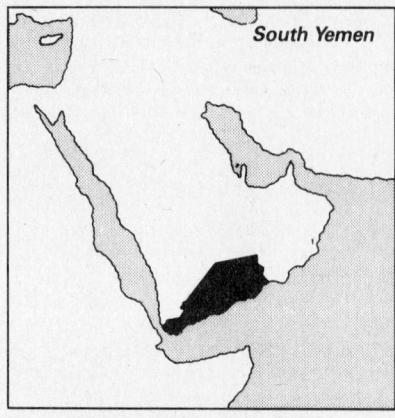

South Yemen

AREA 160,000 sq km/62,000 sq mi
CAPITAL Aden
PHYSICAL desert and mountains; very hot and dry
FEATURES it includes the islands of Perim (in the strait of Bab-el-Mandeb, at the S entrance to the Red Sea), Socotra, and Kamaran; Aden is used by the USSR as a naval base
HEAD OF STATE AND OF GOVERNMENT Haydar Abu Bakr Al-Attas from 1986
GOVERNMENT one-party socialist
EXPORTS cotton goods, coffee
CURRENCY Yemeni dinar (0.57 = £1 Sept 1987)
POPULATION 2,209,000 (1985); annual growth rate 0.8%
LANGUAGE Arabic
RELIGION Sunni Muslim 91%
LITERACY 39% (1980)
GNP $1 bn (1983); $310 per head of population
CHRONOLOGY
1967 People's Republic of Southern Yemen founded.
1970 Country renamed the People's Democratic Republic of Yemen (PDRY), led by the Marxist National Front Party (NF).
1971–72 War with North Yemen.
1978 North Yemen president killed by a bomb carried by a PDRY envoy. Yemen Socialist Party (YSP) formed as a 'Marxist-Leninist vanguard party'. War between North and South Yemen.
1979 Ceasefire agreed and the two Yemens agreed to move towards eventual union.
1983 Joint Yemen council established.
1985 Ali Nasser Muhammad elected president but was deposed after his personal guards had killed three of his party opponents.
1986 Hayder Abu Bakr al-Attas became president and secretary-general of the YPS Politburo.

country was renamed the People's Democratic Republic of Yemen and a provisional Supreme People's Council (SPC) was set up 1971 as the nation's parliament. The accession of the left-wing NF government caused hundreds of thousands of people to flee to North Yemen, where a more moderate regime was in power. This resulted in clashes between the South Yemen government and mercenaries operating from North Yemen, and war broke out 1971. The Arab League arranged a cease-fire 1972 and the two countries signed an agreement to merge, but the agreement was never honoured.

In 1978 the president of North Yemen was killed by a bomb carried by an envoy from South Yemen. In the aftermath of the killing the South Yemen president, Rubayi Ali, was deposed and executed. Two days later the three political parties agreed to merge to form a 'Marxist-Leninist vanguard party', the Yemen Socialist Party (YSP), and Abdul Fattah Ismail became its secretary general. In Dec 1978 Ismail was appointed head of state but four months later resigned and went into exile in the USSR. He was succeeded by Ali Nasser Muhammad. South Yemen's neighbours became concerned 1979 when a 20-year Treaty of Friendship and Cooperation was signed, allowing the USSR to station troops in the country, and three years later an aid agreement between the two countries was concluded. A subsequent aid agreement with Kuwait did something to reduce anxieties.

War broke out again after the assassination of the president of North Yemen. The Arab League again intervened to arrange a cease-fire 1979 and for the second time the two countries agreed to unite. This time definite progress was made so that by 1983 a joint Yemen council was meeting at six-monthly intervals. In 1985 Ali Nasser Muhammad was re-elected secretary general of the YSP and its political bureau for another five years. He soon began taking steps to remove his opponents, his personal guard shooting and killing three bureau members. This led to a short civil war and the dismissal of Ali Nasser from all his posts in the party and the government. A new administration was formed, headed by Haydar Abu Bakr al-Attas, which immediately committed itself to eventual union with North Yemen.

yen the standard currency of Japan.

Yenan /jʌn'æn/ former name for city of ▷Yan'an in Chinese province of Shaanxi.

Yenisei /jɛnɪ'seɪ/ great river in Asiatic USSR, rising in Tuva region and flowing across the Siberian plain into the Arctic Ocean; length about 3,800 km/2,360 mi.

yeoman small English landowner who farmed his own fields between the break-up of the feudal system and the agricultural revolution of the 18th–19th centuries.

Yeomanry English volunteer cavalry organized 1794, and incorporated into volunteer regiments which became the Territorial Force 1908 and Territorial Army 1922.

Yeomen of the Guard English military corps which was founded by Henry VII in 1485 and since then has constituted the bodyguard of the English sovereign. Its duties are purely ceremonial (there are Yeomen warders at the Tower of London), and the uniform and weapons are much as they were in Tudor times. The nickname of 'Beefeaters' is supposed to have originated in 1669 when the grand duke of Tuscany ascribed their fine appearance to beef.

Yerevan /jɛrɪ'væn/ industrial city (tractor parts, machine tools, chemicals, bricks, bicycles, wine, fruit canning), capital of Armenian Republic, USSR, a few miles N of the Turkish border; state university 1921; population (1985) 1,133,000.
history Founded in the 7th century, Yerevan was alternately Turkish and Persian from the 15th century until ceded to Russia 1828.

Yerkes Observatory astronomical centre in Wisconsin, USA, founded by George ▷Hale in 1897. It houses the world's largest refracting optical ▷telescope, with a lens of diameter 102 cm/40 in.

Yersin /jɛə'sæn/ Alexandre Emile John 1863–1943. Swiss bacteriologist, who discovered the plague bacillus in Hong Kong in 1894 and prepared a serum against it.

Yesenin /jɪ'seɪnɪn/ Sergei 1895–1925. Alternative form of ▷Esenin, Russian poet.

yeti Tibetan name for the ▷abominable snowman.

Yevtushenko /jɛvtʊ'ʃɛnkəʊ/ Yevgeny 1933– . Soviet poet, born in Siberia. He aroused controversy by his anti-Stalinist 'Stalin's Heirs' 1956, published with Khrushchev's support, and 'Babi Yar' 1961. He published his *Autobiography* in 1963.

Yevtushenko A master of the conversational, confessional style, the Soviet poet Yevtushenko has walked a thin line between Communist idealism and raising sensitive issues in works such as 'Stalin's Heirs' 1956 and 'Babi Yar' 1961.

yew evergreen coniferous tree indigenous to Britain *Taxus baccata* family Taxaceae; the seeds and leaves are poisonous; the wood is hard and close-grained and was formerly used to make longbows.

Yezd another name for the Iranian town of ◊Yazd.

Yezidis /ˈjezɪdiz/ a religious sect of Iraq, whose chief centre is near Mosul. Their religion is a mixture of Christianity and Islam; they practise baptism and circumcision, but regard the devil as God's agent and endeavour to keep in his favour.

Yezo /ˈjezəʊ/ another name for ◊Hokkaido, most northerly of the four main islands of Japan.

Yichang /jiːˈtʃæŋ/ port at the head of navigation of the Chang Jiang, Hubei province, China; population (1982) 175,000.

Yiddish language a member of the Germanic branch of the Indo-European language family, deriving from Rhineland German and spoken by Polish and Russian Jews, who have carried it to Israel, the USA, and many other parts of the world. In the USA, Yiddish has had a powerful impact on English, especially in the city of New York and in the national media. Such words as *bagel, chutzpah, kibbitz, mensh, nosh, schlemiel, schmaltz,* and *schmuck* have entered the American language, but they are less used in English. Isaac Bashevis Singer (1904–), born in Poland, US citizen (1943), who writes in Yiddish, won the Nobel Prize for Literature in 1978.

yin and yang (Chinese 'dark' and 'bright') the interdependent passive (thought of as feminine, negative, intuitive) and active (thought of as masculine, positive, intellectual) principles of nature are said to correspond to the two halves of the brain. In ◊Taoism and ◊Confucianism they are represented by two interlocked curved shapes within a circle, one white, one black, but having a spot of the contrasting colour within the head of each.

Yinchuan /jɪnˈtʃwɑːn/ capital of Ninghsia-Hui autonomous region, NW China; population (1970) 100,000.

yoga Hindu philosophic system (Sanskrit 'union') attributed to Patanjali who lived about 150 BC at Gonda, Uttar Pradesh, India. He preached mystical union with a personal deity by the practice of hypnosis and a rising above the senses by abstract meditation, adoption of special postures, and ascetic practices. ◊Siva, one of the three chief gods of Hinduism, was regarded as the Great Yogi. As practised in the West, yoga is more a system of induced relaxation.

Yogyakarta /jɒgjəˈkɑːtə/ city in Java, Indonesia; capital of Indonesia 1945–49; university 1949; population (1980) 399,000. The Buddhist pyramid shrine to the NW at Borobudur (122 m/400 ft square) was built 750–850 AD.

Yokohama /jəʊkəʊˈhɑːmə/ Japanese port on Tokyo Bay, the first Japanese port opened to foreign trade (1859); population (1984) 2,915,000.

history US Commodore ◊Perry landed at Yokohama in 1854 on his expedition to reopen communication between Japan and the rest of the world after 250 years. From 1859 it grew rapidly from a small fishing village to the chief centre of trade with Europe and America. Almost destroyed in an earthquake 1923, it was again rebuilt after World War II.

Yokosuka /jəʊkəʊˈsuːkə/ Japanese seaport and naval base (1884) on Tokyo Bay, S of Yokohama; population (1984) 428,000.

yolk a store of food, mostly in the form of fats and proteins, found in the eggs of many animals; it provides nourishment for the growing ◊embryo.

yolk-sac the sac containing the ◊yolk in the egg of most vertebrates.

Yom Kippur the Jewish Day of ◊Atonement.

Yom Kippur War alternative name for the 1973 'October War' between the Arabs and Israelis; see ◊Arab-Israeli Wars.

Yonge /jʌŋ/ Charlotte M(ary) 1823–1901. English novelist. Her books deal mainly with family life, and are strongly influenced by the High Church philosophy of the ◊Oxford Movement. Her best-known work is *The Heir of Redclyffe* 1853.

yoni in Hinduism, an image of the female genitals as an object of worship, often combined with the lingam, the male equivalent.

Yonkers /ˈjɒŋkəz/ city in New York, USA, on the Hudson; a manufacturing centre and residential district; population (1980) 203,500. Originally a Dutch settlement from about 1650.

Yonne /jɒn/ French river, 290 km/180 mi long, rising in central France and flowing N into the Seine; it gives its name to a *département*.

York /jɔːk/ cathedral and industrial city (railway rolling stock, scientific instruments, sugar, chocolate, and glass) in N Yorkshire, England; university 1963; population (1981) 99,787.

features The Gothic York Minster is noted for its medieval stained glass. Much of the 14th-century city walls survives, with four gates or 'bars', as well as the medieval shambles (slaughterhouse). Also notable are its 17th–18th-century domestic architecture; the Jorvik Viking Centre 1984; Castle Museum; National Railway Museum and the 19th-century railway station.

history York was a British city, traditionally the capital of the north of England, before becoming from 71 AD the Roman fortress of Eboracum, and the first bishop of York (Paulinus) was consecrated in 627 in the wooden church which first preceded York Minster. Paulinus baptized King Edwin there 627 and York was created an archbishopric 732. In the 10th century it was a Viking settlement. Its commercial prosperity depended on the wool trade in the Middle Ages.

York /jɔːk/ English dynasty founded by Richard, duke of York (1411–60), claimant to the throne (under Henry VI of the rival house of Lancaster) through his descent from Lionel, duke of Clarence (1338–68), third son of Edward III, whereas Henry VI was descended from the fourth son. The argument was fought out in the Wars of the ◊Roses. York was killed at the Battle of Wakefield 1460, but next year his son became king as Edward IV, in turn succeeded by his son Edward V and then by his brother Richard III, with whose death at Bosworth the line ended. The Lancastrian victor in that battle became king as Henry VII, and consolidated his claim by marrying Edward IV's eldest daughter, Elizabeth.

York /jɔːk/ Archbishop of. Metropolitan of the northern province of the Anglican Church in England, hence Primate of England and next in rank to the Lord High Chancellor.

York /jɔːk/ Duke of. Title often borne by younger sons of British sovereigns, for example George V, George VI, and Prince Andrew (1960–) on his marriage in 1986 to Sarah Ferguson (1959–).

York /jɔːk/ Frederick Augustus, Duke of York 1763–1827. Second son of George III. He was an unsuccessful commander in the Netherlands 1793–99, and British commander in chief 1798–1809. The nursery rhyme about the 'grand old Duke of York' who marched his troops up the hill and down again commemorates him, as does the Duke of York's column in Waterloo Place, London.

Yorkshire /ˈjɔːkʃə/ county in NE England on the North Sea, formerly divided into N, E, and W ridings (thirds), but in 1974 reorganized to form a number of new counties: the major part of ◊Cleveland and ◊Humberside; ◊North Yorkshire, ◊South Yorkshire, and ◊West Yorkshire. Small outlying areas also went to Durham, Cumbria, Lancashire, and Greater Manchester. South and West Yorkshire are both former metropolitan counties.

Yosemite /jəʊˈsemɪti/ area in the Sierra Nevada, California, USA, a national park from 1890. It includes *Yosemite Gorge*; *Yosemite Falls* 762 m/2,500 ft in three leaps, and many others, and groves of giant sequoias.

Yosemite The entrance to the Yosemite Valley, California, where the first of its massive falls descends in a triple cascade.

Young /jʌŋ/ Brigham 1801–1877. US ◊Mormon religious leader, born in Vermont. He joined the Mormon Church in 1832, and three years later was appointed an apostle. After a successful recruiting mission in Liverpool, he returned to USA, and as successor of Joseph

Smith, led the Mormon migration to the Great Salt Lake in Utah 1846, founded Salt Lake City, and ruled the colony until his death.

Young /jʌŋ/ David Ivor (Baron Young of Graffham) 1932– . British Conservative politician, chair of the Manpower Services Commission (MSC) 1982–84, secretary for employment from 1985, trade and industry secretary from 1987.

Young /jʌŋ/ Edward 1683–1765. British poet, author of *Night Thoughts on Life, Death and Immortality* 1742–45.

Young /jʌŋ/ John Watts 1930– . US astronaut, the first person to make six space flights. Born in San Francisco. He became a ◊NASA astronaut in 1962, and chief of the Astronaut Office in 1975. His first flight was on Gemini 3 in 1965, followed by Gemini 10 in 1966 (see ◊Gemini project). He flew on Apollo 10 in 1969 and landed on the Moon with Apollo 16 in 1972 (see ◊Apollo project). He was commander of the first flight of the ◊Space Shuttle in 1981, and commanded the ninth Shuttle flight in 1983.

Young /jʌŋ/ Lester (Willis, 'Pres') 1909–1959. US tenor saxophonist and jazz composer. He was a major figure in the development of his instrument for jazz music from the 1930s. He was also noted as an accompanist to the singer Billie Holiday in the late 1930s.

Younghusband /'jʌŋhʌzbənd/ Francis 1863–1942. British soldier and explorer, born in India. He entered the army in 1882 and 20 years later accompanied the mission that opened up Tibet. He wrote travel books and works on comparative religion.

Young Ireland Irish nationalist organization, founded 1840 by William Smith O'Brien (1803–1864), having rejected the non-violent policies of Daniel ◊O'Connell's Repeal Association; its name was modelled on the ◊Young Italy organization. It attempted an abortive insurrection of the peasants against the British at Tipperary in 1848. O'Brien was sentenced to death, but later pardoned.

Young Italy Italian nationalist organization, founded 1831 by Giuseppe ◊Mazzini while in exile in Marseilles. The movement, which was immediately popular, was followed the next year by Young Germany, Young Poland, and similar organizations. All the various groups were linked by Mazzini in his Young Europe movement. In practice, however, none of them had great success. Attempted uprisings by Young Italy in 1834 and 1844 failed miserably.

Young Men's Christian Association (YMCA) association for young men founded in London 1844 by George ◊Williams. It aims at self-improvement – spiritual, intellectual, and physical. From 1971 women were accepted as members.

Young Plan plan devised by US businessman Owen D Young to reschedule German payments of war reparations in 1929.

Youngstown /'jʌŋztaʊn/ industrial city (iron and steel) in Ohio, USA; population (1980) 115,500.

Young Turk member of a reformist movement of young army officers in the Ottoman

Empire between 1903 and 1909. It was instrumental in the constitutional changes of 1908 and gained a good deal of prestige during the Balkan Wars 1912–13. It also encouraged Turkish links with the German Empire. The term is used in modern times for a member of any radical or rebellious faction within a party or organization.

Young Women's Christian Association (YWCA) organization for women and girls, formed in 1887 when two organizations, both founded in 1855 – the one by Emma Robarts and the other by Lady Kinnaird – combined their work.

Yourcenar /juəsə'nɑː/ Marguerite. Pen name of Marguerite de Crayencour 1903–1987. French writer. Born in Brussels, she achieved a reputation as a novelist in France in the 1930s (for example *La Nouvelle Euridyce/The New Euridyce* 1931), but after World War II she settled in the USA. Novels such as *Les Mémoires d'Hadrien/The Memoirs of Hadrian* 1951 and *L'Oeuvre au noir/The Work in Black* 1968 (translated as *The Abyss*) won her acclaim as a historical novelist. In 1980 she became the first woman to be elected to the French Academy.

Ypres /'iːprə/ ('wipers' in British Army pronunciation; Flemish *Ieper*) Belgian town in W Flanders, 40 km/25 mi S of Ostend, a centre of fighting in World War I Its old cloth hall and the cathedral were destroyed. The Menin Gate 1927 is a memorial to British soldiers lost in the great battles fought round the town 1914–18.

Ypres, 1st Earl of title of Sir John ◊French, British field marshal.

Ysselmeer alternative spelling of ◊Ijsselmeer, lake in the Netherlands.

YTS the Youth Training Scheme, set up in the UK by the ◊Manpower Services Commission to provide unemployed school leavers aged 16 and 17 with a one-year course of work experience and training.

ytterbium metallic element, symbol Yb, atomic number 70. A member of the ◊lanthanide series, it occurs in monazite and is used in steelmaking.

yttrium silvery metallic element, symbol Yt, atomic number 39. A member of the ◊lanthanide series, it occurs in monazite and is used to reduce steel corrosion.

Yucatán /juːkə'tɑːn/ peninsula in Central America, most of it in Mexico but extending into Belize and Guatemala; area 180,000 sq km/70,000 sq mi. Tropical crops are grown. It is inhabited by ◊Maya Indians and contains the remains of their civilization.

yucca plant of the genus *Yucca* of the Liliaceae, with some 40 species occurring in Mexico and the SW of USA. The leaves are stiff and sword-shaped and the flowers white and campanulate.

Yugoslavia /juːɡəʊ'slɑːviə/ country in SE Europe, on the Adriatic Sea, bounded W by Italy, N by Austria and Hungary, E by Romania and Bulgaria, and S by Greece and Albania.

government Under the 1974 constitution, amended 1981, Yugoslavia is a federal republic consisting of six socialist republics and two

socialist autonomous provinces (Kosovo and Vojvodina, which lie within Serbia), each with its own assembly. The federal republic itself has a two-chamber legislative assembly comprising the 220-member Federal Chamber and the 88-member Chamber of Republics and Provinces, whose members are indirectly elected every four years, with fixed quotas assigned to the constituent republics and autonomous provinces. The legislature elects the executive branch of government, since May 1980 a nine-member collective presidency, consisting of the head of the Communist Party together with a representative from each republic and province. The presidency's members are appointed for five-year terms, with titular leadership of the body rotating annually. Day-to-day government administration is carried out by the Federal Executive Council (headed by a president or prime minister), whose members are elected by the legislature for four-year terms.

YUGOSLAVIA: CONSTITUENT REPUBLICS

	Capital	Area in sq km
Bosnia-Hercegovina	Sarajevo	51,129
Croatia	Zagreb	56,470
Macedonia	Skopje	25,706
Montenegro	Titograd	13,807
Serbia	Belgrade	88,267
Slovenia	Ljubljana	20,245
		255,624

The only political party permitted is the Communist Party (League of Communists of Yugoslavia), which is controlled by a 23-member presidium (with a rotating presidency) and directs the broader Socialist Alliance of the Working People of Yugoslavia. The dominating practice is that of self-management, with elected workers' assemblies at all levels.

history Yugoslavia came into existence in Dec 1918, on the collapse of the Austro-Hungarian Empire, as the kingdom of the Serbs, Croats, and Slovenes, with the Serbian ◊Peter (I) Karageorgevich as king. Peter I died 1921 and was succeeded by his son Alexander, who renamed the country Yugoslavia ('nation of the South Slavs') and who, faced with opposition from the Croatians at home and from the Italians abroad, established a military dictatorship in 1929. He was assassinated in Oct 1934 in Marseilles, France, by a Macedonian with Croatian dissident links. Peter I's young son ◊Peter II (1923–70) succeeded and a regency under the latter's uncle Paul (1893–1976) was set up which came under increasing influence from Germany and Italy. The regency was briefly overthrown by pro-Allied groups in Mar 1941, precipitating a successful invasion by German troops. King Peter II fled, while two guerrilla groups – the pro-royalist, Serbian-based Chetniks, led by General Draza ◊Mihailovik, and the Communist Partisans, led by Josip Broz (Marshal ◊Tito) – engaged in resistance activities.

Yugoslavia

SOCIALIST FEDERAL REPUBLIC OF (*Socijalistička Federativna Republika Jugoslavija*)

AREA 255,874 sq km/98,740 sq mi
CAPITAL Belgrade
TOWNS Zagreb, Skopje, Ljubljana; ports Split, Rijeka
PHYSICAL mountainous; river Danube plains in N and E
FEATURES constituent republics of Bosnia and Herzegovina, Croatia, Kosovo, Macedonia, Montenegro, Serbia, Slovenia, Vojvodina; scenic Dalmatian coast and Dinaric Alps; Lake Shkodër
HEAD OF STATE Lazar Mojsov from 1987
HEAD OF GOVERNMENT Banko Mikulić from 1986
GOVERNMENT federal one-party communist
EXPORTS machinery, electrical goods, chemicals
CURRENCY dinar (1,345 = £1 Sept 1987)
POPULATION (1985) 23,124,000 (Serbs 36%, Croats 20%, Muslims 9%, Slovenes 8%, Albanians 7%, Macedonians 6%); annual growth rate 0.8%
LANGUAGE individual national languages have equality, but Serbo-Croat is the most widespread
RELIGION Orthodox (Serbs), Roman Catholic (Croats), Muslim (50% in Bosnia)
LITERACY 93% male/81% female (1980 est)
GNP $46.3 bn (1984); $3,109 per head of population
CHRONOLOGY
1917–18 Creation of Kingdom of the Serbs, Croats, and Slovenes.

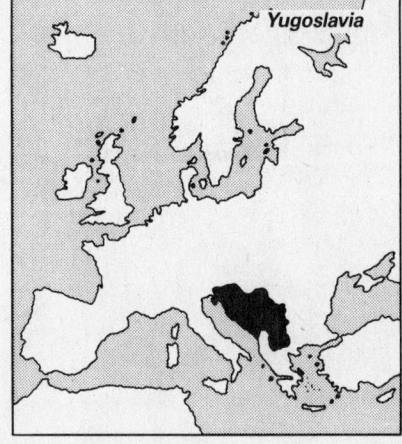

Yugoslavia

1929 Name of Yugoslavia adopted.
1941 Invasion by Germany.
1945 Communist federal republic formed under leadership of Tito.
1948 Split with USSR.
1953 Self-management principle enshrined in constitution.
1961 Formation of Nonaligned Movement under Yugolavia's leadership.
1972 Croatian separatist movement leaders arrested.
1974 New constitution adopted.
1980 Death of Tito. Collective leadership assumed power.
1987 Threat to use the army to curb unrest.

Tito established a provisional government at liberated Jajce in Bosnia in Nov 1943 and proclaimed the Yugoslav Federal Republic in Nov 1945 after the expulsion, with Soviet help, of the remaining German forces. Elections were held, a communist constitution on the Russian model was introduced and remaining royalist opposition crushed. Tito broke with Stalin in 1948 and, with the constitutional law of 1953, adopted a more liberal and decentralized form of communism centred around workers' self-management and the support of private farming. Tito became the dominating force in Yugoslavia and held the newly created post of president from 1953 until his death in May 1980.

In foreign affairs, the country sought to stand intermediate between East and West and played a leading role in the creation of the ◊Non-Aligned Movement 1961. Domestically, the nation experienced continuing regional discontent, particularly in ◊Croatia where a violent separatist movement gained ground in the 1970s. To deal with these problems, Tito encouraged further decentralization and devolution of power to the constituent republics. A system of collective leadership and the regular rotation of office posts was introduced to prevent the creation of regional cliques. This collective leadership has held power since Tito's death. However, the problems of regionalist unrest have grown worse since 1980, especially in Kosovo (see ◊Serbia) and ◊Bosnia, where Albanian and Islamic nationalism respectively are strong.

Yugoslav literature the Yugoslav or Serbo-Croat language belongs to the southern branch of the Slavonic languages. Yugoslavian literature begins in the 9th century with the translation into Slavonic of the church service books. Its great glory is folk poetry, particularly the song cycles dealing with the battle of Kosovo and the hero Marko Kraljeviac. After centuries of national repression a revival came, notably under Dositej Obradović (1739–1811). Poets of the earlier 19th century include the prince-bishop Petar Njegoš (1813–51), France Prešern (1800–49), and Ivan Mažuranić (1814–90). Later, Russian influence predominated. Twentieth-century writers include the novelists Ivan Cankar (1876–1918), Ivo Andrić (1892–1974), and Miroslav Krleža (1893–), whose collected works cover 36 volumes, and the poet Oton Župančič (1878–1949).

Yukon /ˈjuːkɒn/ territory of NW Canada
area 536,327 sq km/207,076 sq mi
towns Whitehorse
features named after its chief river, the Yukon; includes the highest point in Canada, Mount Logan 6050 m/19,850 ft
products oil and natural gas; gold, silver, coal; furs (trapped in the wild)
population (1985) 23,000
history settlement dates from the gold rush 1896–1910, when 30,000 people moved to the ◊Klondike river valley (silver is now worked there). It was organized as a political unit from 1899 with Dawson as the original capital.

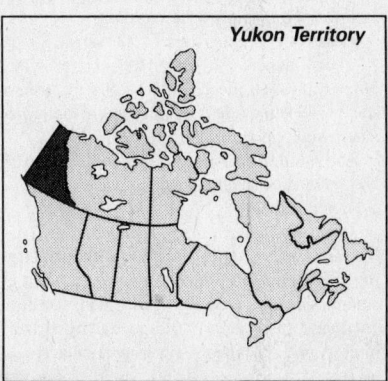

Yukon Territory

Yungning /jʊŋˈnɪŋ/ former name 1913–45 for Chinese port of ◊Nanning.

Yunnan /juːˈnæn/ province of SW China, adjoining Burma and N Vietnam
area 436,200 sq km/168,370 sq mi
capital Kunming
features Chang Jiang, Salween, and Mekong rivers; crossed by the Burma Road; mountainous and well forested
products rice, tea; timber; wheat; tin, copper, lead, zinc, coal, salt, and other minerals
population (1982) 32,553,817, with minority ethnic groups, and including many Muslims.

Yuzovka /ˈjuːzəvkə/ early name (1872–1924) for the town of ◊Dometsk, Ukraine, USSR, derived from the Welshman John Hughes who established a metallurgical factory there.

Z the 26th and last letter in the English alphabet. It was the 6th in the classical Greek alphabet. It is used initially and medially in many words of Greek or Oriental origin, and the modern tendency is to employ it in preference to *s* in such words as *baptize, organize*.

Zaandam /ˌzɑːnˈdæm/ industrial port (timber, paper) in N Holland province, Netherlands, on the Zaan, NW of Amsterdam, since 1974 included in the municipality of *Zaanstad*; population (1985) 128,286.

Zaanstad /ˈzɑːnstæd/ industrial town in W Netherlands which includes the port of ◊Zaandam.

Zabaleta /ˌθæbəˈleɪtə/ Nicanor 1907– . Spanish harpist, noted for his efforts to enlarge the repertoire of original harp music by commissioning new works from, amongst others, ◊Milhaud and Joaquin Rodrigo, and by reviving interest in classical harp music, particularly that of the 15th and 16th centuries in Spain and Portugal.

Zabrze /ˈzæbʒeɪ/ industrial city (coalmining, iron, chemicals) in Silesia, Poland, formerly the German town of Hindenburg; population (1984) 197,000.

Zadar /ˈzædɑː/ port and resort in W Yugoslavia; population (1981) 116,174. Continually held and lost by the Venetian republic from the 12th century until its seizure by Austria 1813. It was the capital of Dalmatia 1815–1918, and Italian 1920–47, when it became part of Yugoslavia.

Zadkine /ˈzædkiːn/ Ossip 1890–1967. French ◊Cubist sculptor. Russian-born, he served in the French Foreign Legion, and spent most of his life in Paris. Working in varied materials, he represented the human form in abstract terms, for example *Laocoon* and his variations on the theme of Orpheus.

Zagorsk /zəˈɡɔːsk/ town 70 km/45 mi NE of Moscow, USSR, containing the Trinity Monastery of St Sergius 1337, surrounded by a fortified wall, with some of the finest architecture and art of medieval Russia; population (1983) 111,000.

Zagreb /ˈzɑːɡreb/ industrial city (leather, linen, carpets), capital of Croatia, Yugoslavia, on the Sava; university 1874; population (1981) 1,174,512. Zagreb was a Roman city (Aemona) and has a Gothic cathedral.

Zahir /zəˈhɪə/ ud-din Mohammed 1483–1530. First Great Mogul of India, called 'Babur' (Arabic 'lion'). He was the great-grandson of Tamerlane and, at the age of 12, succeeded his father as ruler of Ferghana (Turkestan). In 1526 he defeated the emperor of Delhi at Panipat, captured Delhi and Agra, and established a dynasty which endured until 1858.

Zahir Shah /zəˈhɪə ˈʃɑː/ Mohammed 1914– . King of Afghanistan 1933–73. Zahir, educated in Kabul and Paris, served in the government 1932–33 before being crowned king of Afghanistan in 1933. He was overthrown in 1973 by a republican coup led by his cousin General Daud Khan, and went into exile in Rome. He has been a symbol of national unity for the ◊mujahadeen resistance groups.

Zaïre /zɑːˈɪə/ second longest river in Africa, until 1971 named the Congo, rising near the Zambia–Zaïre border (and known as the Lualaba river in the upper reaches) and flowing 3,475 km/2,718 mi to the Atlantic, running in a great curve which crosses the Equator twice, and discharging a volume of water second only to the Amazon. The chief tributaries are the Ubangi, Sangha, and Kasai.

Navigation is interrupted by dangerous rapids up to 160 km/100 mi long, notably from the Zambian border to Bukama; below Kongolo, where the gorge known as the Gates of Hell is located; above Kisangani, where the Stanley Falls are situated; and between Kinshasa and Matadi.

Boma is a large port on the estuary; Matadi is a port for ocean-going ships 80 km/50 mi from the Atlantic; and at Pool Malebo (formerly Stanley Pool), a widening of the river 560 km/350 mi from its mouth which encloses the marshy island of Bamu, are Brazzaville on the western shore and Kinshasa on the southwestern. The Inga dam supplies Matadi and Kinshasa with electricity.

history the mouth of the Zaïre was noted by the Portuguese navigator Diego Cão in 1482, but the vast extent of its system became known to Europeans only with the explorations of Livingstone and Stanley.

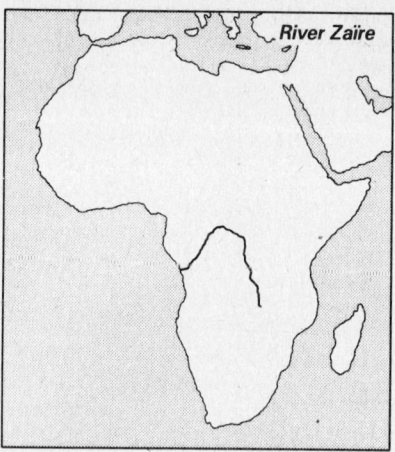

River Zaïre

Zaïre /zɑːˈɪə/ country in central Africa.

government Zaïre is a one-party state, based on the Popular Movement of the Revolution (MPR). Under the 1978 constitution, the leader of the MPR is automatically elected president for a nonrenewable seven-year term. The president, head of state and head of government, appoints and presides over the National Executive Council. There is a single-chamber legislature, the National Legislative Council, whose 310 members are elected by universal suffrage for a five-year term. Ultimate power lies with the MPR, whose highest policy-making body is the 80-member Central Committee, which elects the 14-member Political Bureau.

history. The name Zaïre (from Zadi, 'big water') was given by Portuguese explorers who arrived on the country's Atlantic coast in the 15th century. The great medieval kingdom of Kongo, centred on the banks of the Zaïre River, was then in decline, and the subsequent slave trade weakened it further. The interior was not explored by Europeans until the arrival of ◊Stanley and ◊Livingstone in the 1870s, partly financed by Leopold II of Belgium, who established the Congo Free State under his personal rule 1885. Local resistance was suppressed and the inhabitants were oppressively exploited. When the atrocious treatment of local labour was made public, Belgium annexed the country as a colony, the Belgian Congo, 1908, and conditions were somewhat improved.

Zaïre was given full independence in Jun 1960 as the Republic of the Congo. Many thought the Belgian government's decision too precipitate in that it produced a number of immediate problems that could have been anticipated. The new state was intended to be governed centrally from Leopoldville by President Joseph Kasavubu and Prime Minister Patrice Lumumba, but Moise Tshombe immediately declared the rich mining province of Katanga independent under his leadership. Fighting broke out, which was not properly quelled by Belgian troops, and the United Nations (UN) Security Council agreed to send a force to restore order and protect lives. Meanwhile, disagreements between Kasavubu and Lumumba on how the crisis should be tackled prompted the Congolese army commander, Col Joseph-Désiré ◊Mobutu, to step in and temporarily take over the government. Lumumba was imprisoned and later released and five months later power was handed back to Kasavubu. Soon afterwards it was announced that Lumumba had been murdered and the white mercenaries employed by Tshombe were thought to be responsible. The outcry that followed resulted in a new government being formed, with Cyrille Adoula as prime minister.

During the fighting between Tshombe's mercenaries and UN forces the UN secretary general, Dag Hammarskjöld, flew to Katanga province to mediate and was killed in an air crash on the border with Northern Rhodesia. The attempted secession of Katanga was finally stopped in 1963 when Tshombe went into exile, taking many of his followers with him to form the Congolese National Liberation Front (FNLC). In July 1964 Tshombe returned from exile and President Kasavubu appointed him interim prime minister until elections for a new government could be held. In Aug the country was renamed the Democratic Republic of the Congo.

A power struggle soon developed between Kasavubu and Tshombe and again the army, under Mobutu, intervened, establishing a 'second republic' in Nov 1965. A new constitution was adopted 1967 and 1970 Mobutu was elected president for a seven-year term. The following year the country became the Republic of Zaïre and 1972 the Popular Movement of the Revolution (MPR) was declared the only legal political party. In the same year the president became known as Mobutu Sese Seko.

Mobutu, re-elected 1977, carried out a large number of political and constitutional reforms. He gradually improved the structure of public administration and brought stability to what had once seemed an ungovernable country. However, the harshness of some of his policies brought international criticism and 1983 he offered amnesty to all political exiles. Despite some

demonstrations of opposition, Marshal Mobutu, as he now was, was re-elected 1984 for a third term.

Zákinthos /ˈzækɪnθɒs/ (or *Zante*) most

Zaïre
REPUBLIC OF (*République du Zaïre*)

AREA 2,345,000 sq km/895,000 sq mi
CAPITAL Kinshasa
TOWNS Kananga, Lubumbashi, Kisangani; ports Matadi, Boma
PHYSICAL Zaïre river basin has tropical rain forest and savanna; mountains in E and W
FEATURES lakes Tanganyika, Mobutu Sésé Séko, and Edward; Ruwenzori mountains
HEAD OF STATE AND OF GOVERNMENT Mobuto Sésé Séko Kuku Ngbendu wa Zabanga from 1965
GOVERNMENT one-party authoritarian
EXPORTS palm oil, coffee, tea, rubber, timber; copper, cobalt (80% of world output), zinc, cadmium, industrial diamonds
CURRENCY zaïre (192 = £1 Sept 1987)
POPULATION 30,505,000 (1985); annual growth rate 3.2%
LANGUAGE French (official), Swahili, Lingala
RELIGION 70% Christian, 10% Muslim
LITERACY 74% male/37% female (1980 est)
GNP $5 bn (1983); $127 per head of population
CHRONOLOGY
1960 Achieved full independence as the Republic of the Congo. Civil war broke out between the central government and Katanga province.
1963 Katanga war ended.

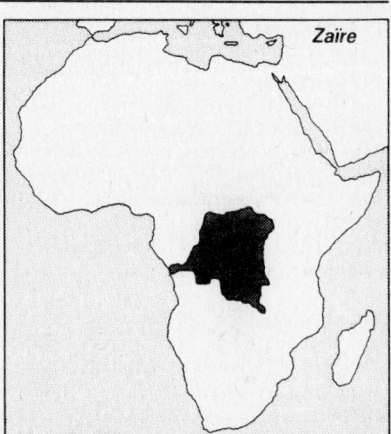

Zaïre

1967 New constitution adopted.
1970 Col Mobutu elected president.
1972 Country became the Republic of Zaïre, with the Popular Movement of the Revolution (MPR) the only legal political party.
1974 Foreign-owned businesses and plantations seized by Mobutu and given in political patronage. Original owners invited back 1977.

---

southerly of the ◊Ionian Islands, Greece
area 400 sq km/157 sq mi
products olives, currants, grapes; carpets
population (1981) 30,014.

Zama /ˈzɑːmə/ site of battle fought in 202 BC in Numidia (now Algeria) in which the Carthaginians under Hannibal were defeated by the Romans under Scipio, so ending the Second Punic War.

Zambezi /zæmˈbiːzi/ river in central and SE Africa; length 2,575 km/1,600 mi from NW Zambia through Mozambique to the Indian Ocean, with a wide delta near Chinde. It is interrupted by rapids, and includes on the Zimbabwe–Zambia border the ◊Victoria Falls (Mosi-oa-tunya) and ◊Kariba Dam, which forms the reservoir of Lake Kariba with large fisheries. Major tributaries include the ◊Kafue in Zambia.

Zambia /ˈzæmbiə/ landlocked country in central Africa.
government Zambia is an independent republic within the Commonwealth. It was proclaimed a one-party state in 1972 and the constitution was adopted 1973. The party is the United National Independence Party (UNIP), and its president is the state president, elected by universal suffrage for a five-year term, and who may be re-elected. The president governs with an appointed cabinet and is advised by the House of Chiefs, consisting of chiefs from the country's nine provinces. There is a single-chamber national assembly of 135 members, 125 elected by universal suffrage and

ten nominated by the president. The assembly has a life of five years. Ultimate power lies with UNIP, whose Central Committee is chaired by the president.

history for early history, see ◊Africa. The country was visited by Portuguese in the late 18th century and by ◊Livingstone 1851. As Northern Rhodesia it became a British protectorate 1924, together with the former kingdom of Barotseland (now Western province), taken under British protection at the request of its ruler 1890. From 1953 the country, with Southern Rhodesia (now Zimbabwe) and Nyasaland (now Malawi), was part of the Federation of Rhodesia and Nyasaland, dissolved 1963. Northern Rhodesia became an independent republic 1964, within the Commonwealth, with Dr Kenneth ◊Kaunda, leader of the United Independence Party (UNIP), as its first president. Between 1964 and 1972, when it was declared a one-party state, Zambia was troubled with frequent outbreaks of violence because of disputes within the governing party and conflicts between the country's more than 70 tribes.

Zambia was economically dependent on neighbouring white-ruled Rhodesia but tolerated liberation groups operating on the border, and relations between the two countries deteriorated. The border was closed 1973 and 1976 Kaunda declared his support for the Patriotic Front, led by Robert Mugabe and Joshua Nkomo, which was fighting the white regime in Rhodesia. In 1980 there was an unsuccesful coup against the president, allegedly promoted by South Africa. Despite his imposition of strict economic policies, Kaunda

Zambia
REPUBLIC OF

AREA 752,620 sq km/290,586 sq mi
CAPITAL Lusaka
TOWNS Kitwe, Ndola, Kabwe, Chipata, Livingstone
PHYSICAL a forested plateau cut through by rivers
FEATURES Zambezi river, Kariba Dam
HEAD OF STATE AND OF GOVERNMENT Kenneth Kaunda from 1964
GOVERNMENT one-party authoritarian
EXPORTS copper, emeralds, tobacco
CURRENCY kwacha (12.7 = £1 Sept 1987)
POPULATION 6,832,000 (1985); annual growth rate 2.5%
LANGUAGE English (official); the majority speak Bantu languages
RELIGION mainly animist, 21% Roman Catholic, also Protestant, Hindu, and Muslim minorities
LITERACY 79% male/58% female (1980 est)
GNP $2.6 bn (1984); $570 per head of population
CHRONOLOGY
1964 Achieved full independence, within the Commonwealth, as the Republic of Zambia with Kenneth Kaunda as president.

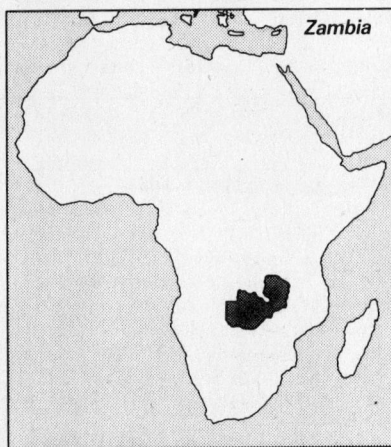

Zambia

1972 United Independence Party (UNIP) declared the only legal party.
1976 Support for the Patriotic Front in Rhodesia declared.
1980 Unsuccessful coup against President Kaunda.
1987 Kaunda elected chair of the Organization of African Unity (OAU).

---

was convincingly re-elected 1983. He has played an important role in African politics, and in 1987 was elected chair of the Organization of African Unity (OAU).

Zamenhof /'zæmənhɒf/ Lazarus Ludovik 1859–1917. Polish oculist, who invented the international artificial language ◊Esperanto in 1887.

Zampieri /ˌzæmpi'eəri/ Domenico 1581–1641. Italian Baroque painter, known as ◊Domenichino.

Zante /'zænti/ Italian name for the Ionian island of ◊Zákinthos, Greece.

ZANU (*Zimbabwe African National Union*) organization founded in Aug 1963 but banned by the Rhodesian government. It operated a guerilla war against Ian Smith's government from Zambia, until the free elections of 1980 when the ZANU (PF) party led by Robert Mugabe won 63 per cent of the vote.

Zanzibar /ˌzænzɪ'bɑ:/ island of Tanzania
area 1,658 sq km/640 sq mi (80 km/50 mi long)
towns Zanzibar
products cloves, copra
population (1985) 314,000
history Arab traders settled here in the 7th century and Zanzibar became a sultanate. It came under British protection 1890–1963, when (together with the island of Pemba, some nearby islets, and a strip of mainland territory) it became a republic and in 1964 was merged with Tanganyika as Tanzania.

Zapata /sə'pɑ:tə/ Emiliano 1877–1919. Mexican Indian revolutionary guerrilla leader. He led a revolt against dictator Porfirio Díaz from 1911 under the slogan 'Land and Liberty', attempting to repossess for the indigenous Mexicans the land that had been taken by the

Spanish. Driven into retreat by 1915, he was assassinated by an opponent at Pueblo. After his death he became a legendary hero as a champion of the people.

Zaporozhye /ˌzæpə'rɒʒi/ industrial city (steel, chemicals, aluminium goods, pig iron, magnesium) in Ukraine, USSR, on the Dnieper, capital of Zaporozhye region and site of the Dnieper Dam; population (1985) 852,000. Occupied by Germany 1941–43.

ZAPU (*Zimbabwe African People's Union*) organization founded by Joshua Nkomo in 1961 and then banned by the Rhodesian government. It engaged in a guerilla war in alliance with ◊ZANU against the Rhodesian regime, but was defeated in the 1980 elections and has since been persecuted by the ruling ZANU (PF) party. In 1987 the two parties merged.

Zaragoza /ˌθærə'gɒθə/ Spanish spelling of ◊Saragossa, industrial city in Aragon.

Zealand /'zi:lənd/ another name for ◊Seeland, main island of Denmark, and for ◊Zeeland, SW province of the Netherlands.

zebra name given to striped members of the horse family; the stripes serve as camouflage against the desert and mountainous background, or dazzle and confuse predators. The *mountain zebra Equus zebra* was once common in Cape Colony and Natal and still survives in parts of South Africa and Angola. It has long ears and is silvery-white with black or dark brown markings. *Grevy's zebra Equus grevyi* is much larger, and has finer and clearer markings; it inhabits Ethiopia and the Somali region; *Burchell's* or the *common zebra Equus burchelli*, which is intermediate in size, has white ears, a long mane, and full tail; it roams the plains N of the Orange river.

zebu Indian ox *Bos indicus*, light-coloured with a large fatty hump near the shoulders. It is used for pulling loads, and is held to be sacred.

Zedekiah /ˌzedɪ'kaɪə/ in Old Testament, last king of Judah 597–586 BC. Placed on the throne by Nebuchadnezzar, he died a blinded captive in Babylon.

Zeebrugge /'zi:brugə, Dutch 'zeɪbruxə/ small Belgian ferry port on the North Sea, linked to Bruges by 14 km/9 mi canal (built 1896–1907). In Mar 1987 it was the scene of a disaster in which over 180 passengers lost their lives when the car ferry *Herald of Free Enterprise* put to sea from Zeebrugge with its car loading doors not properly closed.

Zeeland /'zi:lənd, Dutch 'zeɪlɒnt/ SW province of the Netherlands
area 1,709 sq km/660 sq mi
capital Middelburg
features includes the estuary of the Scheldt and the island of Walcheren and N and S Beveland; most of Zeeland is below sea-level
population (1985) 355,500.

Zeffirelli /ˌzefɪ'reli/ Franco 1923– . Italian theatre and film director and designer, noted for his stylishly lavish designs and production of plays, operas, and films, such as *The Taming of the Shrew* 1967, and *La Traviata* 1983.

Zeiss /zaɪs, German tsaɪs/ Carl 1816–1888. German optician. He opened his first workshop at Jena in 1846 and in 1866 joined forces with Ernst Abbe (1840–1905), producing cameras, microscopes and field glasses.

Zelenograd /ˌzelɪnə'græd/ city 145 km/90 mi NE of Moscow, USSR, where much of the Soviet microelectronics industry is concentrated.

zemstvo ame given to Russian provincial or district councils which were established by Tsar Alexander II in 1864. They were responsible for local administration until the revolution of 1917.

Zen abbreviation of Japanese *zenna*, 'quiet mind concentration', a form of ◊Buddhism introduced from India to Japan via China in the 12th century. Zazen or 'sitting meditation' involves periods in the cross-legged lotus position, during which all worldly concerns are banished and a state of selflessness reached which ultimately leads to enlightenment.

Zendavesta the sacred scriptures of ◊Zoroastrianism, today practised by the Parsees. They comprise the *Avesta* (liturgical books for the use of the Parsee priests); the *Gathas* (the discourses and revelations of Zoroaster); and the *Zend* commentary upon them.

zenith the upper pole of the celestial horizon, the point immediately above the observer; the ◊nadir is the point diametrically opposite. See ◊celestial sphere.

Zenobia /zɪ'nəubiə/ queen of Palmyra 266–277 AD. She assumed the crown in the Syrian desert as regent for her sons, after the death of her husband, and in 272 was defeated at Homs by Aurelian and taken as a captive to Rome.

Zeno of Citium /'zi:nəu/ c. 335–262 BC. Greek founder of the ◊stoic school of philosophy in Athens, about 300 BC.

Zeno of Elea /'zi:nəu/ c. 490–430 BC. Greek philosopher, disciple of ◊Parmenides and one of the Eleatic school, whose paradoxes raised 'modern' problems of space and time, for example, Achilles can never overtake a tortoise in a race if the amount of space each contestant still has to cover can be infinitely divided; whenever he reaches where the tortoise was, the tortoise will have moved just ahead of him.

zeolite any of the silica-rich minerals of sodium, calcium, barium, strontium, and potassium, which can readily absorb and give up water, and have a high ion-exchange capacity. They can be used to make petrol, benzene, and toluene, from low-grade raw materials, such as coal, and methanol.

Zeppelin /'zepəlɪn, German 'tsepəliːn/ Ferdinand, Count von Zeppelin 1838–1917. German airship pioneer. On retiring from the army in 1891, he devoted himself to the study of aeronautics, and his first airship was built and tested in 1900. During World War I a number of Zeppelin airships were employed in bombing England; they were also used for passenger transport. Zeppelin also helped to pioneer the large multi-engine bomber planes.

goddesses, or godlike humans, included Apollo, Artemis, Castor and Polydeuces/Pollux, Dionysus, Hebe, Heracles, Hermes, Minos, Perseus, Persephone. As the supreme god he dispensed good and evil and was the father and ruler of all mankind. His emblems are the thunderbolt and aegis (shield), representing the thunder cloud.

Zhangjiakou /ˌdʒæŋdʒiəˈkəu/ (formerly Changchiakow) historic town and trade centre in Hebei province, China, 160 km/100 mi NW of Beijing, on the Great Wall; population (1980) 1,100,000. Zhangjiakou is on the border of Inner Mongolia (its Mongolian name is Kalgan, 'gate') and on the road and railway to Ulaanbaatar in Mongolia. It developed under the Manchu dynasty, and was the centre of the overland tea trade from China to Russia.

Zhao /dʒau/ Ziyang 1918– . Chinese politician, prime minister from 1980, secretary of Chinese Communist Party (CCP) from 1987. Zhao, son of a wealthy landlord from Henan province, joined the Communist Youth League in 1932 and rose to prominence in the party in

Zeus The head of the god, and that of an eagle – the Jovian bird – carved on a giant scale at Nemrut Dag in Adiyaman il, Turkey, where the Greeks built a hill-top temple, later destroyed by earthquake.

incentives for workers and factories, while maintaining party control. Zhao assumed, in addition, the post of CCP general secretary in Jan 1987 on the dismissal of ◊Hu Yaobang.

Zeppelin The Hindenburg disaster, 6 May, 1937, when all those on board were killed. Zeppelins were used in World War I for bombing and reconnaissance, but the construction of hydrogen-filled airships with rigid keels was abandoned after several disasters in the 1920s and 1930s.

Zermatt /'zɜːmæt, German tseəˈmæt/ tourist centre in the Valais canton, Switzerland, at the foot of the Matterhorn; population (1985) 3,700.

Zetland /'zetlənd/ official form until 1974 of ◊Shetland, islands of N Scotland.

Zeus /zjuːs/ in Greek mythology, chief of the gods (Roman Jupiter). He was the son of Kronos, whom he overthrew: his brothers and sisters included Demeter, Hades, Hera, and Poseidon. He ate his pregnant first wife Metis (goddess of wisdom), fearing their child (Athena) would be greater than himself. His second wife was Hera, but he also fathered children by other women and goddesses. The offspring, either gods and

Guangdong from 1951. As a supporter of the reforms of ◊Liu Shaoqi, he was dismissed during the 1966–69 Cultural Revolution, paraded through Canton in a dunce's cap and sent to Nei Monggol. He was rehabilitated in 1973 and sent to China's largest province, Sichuan, as first party secretary in 1975. Here he introduced radical and successful market-orientated rural reforms. ◊Deng Xiaoping had him inducted into the Politburo in 1977.

After six months as a vice premier, Zhao was appointed prime minister in 1980 and introduced a Dengist economic programme based on market forces, self-management, and material

Zhao An economic expert with a pragmatic outlook, Zhao Ziyang became prime minister of China in 1980 and general secretary of the Communist Party in 1987.

Zhdanov /'ʒdɑːnɒv/ industrial port (iron and steel) in the Ukraine, USSR, on the Sea of Azov; population (1985) 522,000. Formerly Mariupol, it was renamed 1944 in honour of Andrei Zhdanov (1896–1948), politician and defender of Leningrad, who was born at Mariupol.

Zhejiang /ˌdʒɜːdʒiˈæŋ/ province (formerly Chekiang) of SE China
area 101,800 sq km/32,295 sq mi
capital Hangzhou
features smallest of the Chinese provinces, it was the base of the Song dynasty 12–13th centuries; it is densely populated

products rice, cotton, sugar, jute, maize; timber on the uplands
population (1982) 38,884,603.

Zhengzhou /ˌdʒʌŋ'dʒəʊ/ (formerly Chengchow) industrial city (cotton textiles, foods), capital of Henan province (from 1954), China, on the Huang Ho; population (1982) 1,424,000. In the 1970s the earliest city yet found in China, from 1500 BC, was excavated near the walls of Zhengzhou. The Shaolin temple, where the martial art of kung fu originated, is nearby.

Zhitomir /ʒɪ'təʊmɪə/ capital of Zhitomir region in Ukraine, USSR, W of Kiev; a timber and grain centre with furniture factories; population (1985) 275,000. Zhitomir dates from the 13th century.

Zhivkov /'ʒɪvkɒf/ Todor 1911– . Bulgarian Communist Party (BCP) leader from 1954, prime minister 1962–71, president from 1971. Zhivkov, a printing worker, joined the BCP in 1932 and was active in the resistance 1941–44. After the war, he was elected to the National Assembly and soon promoted into the BCP secretariat and Politburo. As BCP first secretary, Zhivkov became the dominant political figure in Bulgaria after the death of Vulko Chervenkov in 1956. Zhivkov was elected to the new post of state president in 1971. His period in office has been one of caution and conservatism.

Zhonghua Renmin Gongheguo /ˌdʒɒŋ'hwɑː ˌren'mɪn ˌgɒŋhɜː'gwəʊ/ Chinese for People's Republic of ▷China.

Zhou /dʒəʊ/ En-Lai (formerly Chou En-lai) 1898–1976. Chinese politician. Zhou, a member of the Chinese Communist Party (CCP) from the 1920s, was prime minister 1949–76. A moderate Maoist, he weathered the Cultural Revolution. He played a key role in foreign affairs.

Born into a declining mandarin gentry family near Shanghai, Zhou studied in Japan and Paris, where he became a founder member of the overseas branch of the CCP. He adhered to the Moscow line of urban-based revolution in China, organizing communist cells in Shanghai and an abortive uprising in Nanchang 1927. In 1935 Zhou supported the election of ▷Mao Zedong as CCP leader and remained a loyal ally during the next 40 years. He served as liaison officer 1937–46 between the CCP and ▷Chiang Kai-shek's nationalist government. In 1949 he became prime minister, an office he held until his death in Jan 1976; he also served as foreign minister 1949–58.

Zhou, a moderator between the opposing camps of ▷Liu Shaoqi and ▷Mao Zedong, restored orderly progress after the Great Leap Forward (1958–60) and the Cultural Revolution (1966–69), and was the architect of the Four Modernizations programme in 1975. Abroad, Zhou sought to foster Third World unity at the ▷Bandung Conference of 1955, averted an outright border confrontation with the USSR by negotiation with ▷Kosygin in 1969, and was the principal advocate of detente with the USA during the early 1970s.

Zhu De /'dʒuː 'deɪ/ (formerly Chu Teh) 1886–1976. Chinese Red Army leader.
The son of a wealthy Sichuan landlord, Zhu served in the Chinese Army before supporting ▷Sun Yat-sen in the 1911 revolution. He studied in Germany and Paris 1922–25 and joined the Chinese Communist Party (CCP) on his return, becoming commander-in-chief of the Red Army. Working closely with Mao ▷Zedong, Zhu devised the tactic of mobile guerrilla warfare, organized the Red Army's Jiangxi break-out in 1931 and the Long March to Shaanxi 1934–36, and led the 18th Route Army during the liberation war of 1937–49. He was made a marshal in 1955 and served as head of state (chair of the Standing Committee of the National People's Congress) 1975–76.

Zhukov /'ʒuːkɒv/ Grigory Konstantinovich 1896–1974. Marshal of the Soviet Union. Chief of staff from 1941, he defended Moscow 1941, counter-attacked at Stalingrad, organized the relief of Leningrad 1943, and led the offensive from the Ukraine in Mar 1944 which ended in the fall of Berlin. He headed the Allied delegation that received the German surrender, and subsequently commanded the Russian occupation forces inside Germany. He succeeded Bulganin as minister of defence (1955–57).

Zian /zi'ɑːn/ another spelling of ▷Xian, city in China.

Zia ul-Haq /'zɪə ʊl 'hæk/ Mohammad 1924– . Pakistani general, Muslim fundamentalist, in power from 1977.
Zia, a career soldier from a middle-class Punjabi Muslim family, became army Chief of Staff in 1976. He led the military coup against Zulfiqar Ali ▷Bhutto in 1977 and became president in 1978. He lifted martial law in 1985.
Zia's opposition to the Soviet invasion of Afghanistan in 1979 drew support from the USA, but his refusal to commute the death sentence imposed on Zulfiqar Ali Bhutto was widely condemned. He has introduced a fundamentalist Islamic regime.

Zia ul-Haq In 1977 Mohammad Zia ul-Haq led a military takeover of the government of Pakistan. He became president on a programme of a return to democracy.

Ziegler /'tsiːglə/ Karl 1898–1973. German organic chemist. In 1963 he was awarded a Nobel prize for his work on the chemistry and technology of high polymers, for example the combination of many molecules of the gas ethylene (now called ethene) into the plastic, polyethylene or polythene.

ziggurat in ancient Babylonia and Assyria, a stepped pyramid of sun-baked brick faced with glazed bricks or tiles on which stood a shrine to a deity. The Tower of Babel may have been a ziggurat.

Zimbabwe /zɪm'bɑːbwi/ Bantu word meaning stone house, used originally especially for extensive ruins near Victoria, in Mashonaland, Zimbabwe. They include a massive elliptical enclosure with 10 m/30 ft stone walls, known as 'the Temple', and a series of stone-walled enclosures on a granite outcrop known as 'the Acropolis'. There is evidence of a highly advanced Bantu-speaking people from Zaïre or Ethiopia, smelters of iron, in the area before 300 AD.
The Zimbabwe bird, derived from soap-stone sculptures of fish eagles found in the ruins, was the national emblem of Rhodesia, and became that of the new state of ▷Zimbabwe.

Zimbabwe /zɪm'bɑːbwi/ landlocked country in central Africa.
government Zimbabwe is an independent republic within the Commonwealth. Its constitution dates from 1980 and provides for a president who is a formal head of state, a two-chamber parliament consisting of the Senate and the House of Assembly, and a prime minister and cabinet drawn from and responsible to Parliament.
In recognition of the rights of the white minority, there are two sets of constituencies for parliamentary elections, a 'common roll', which includes all voters, and a 'white roll' for white voters. The Senate has 40 members, 14 elected by common-roll constituencies, 10 by white roll, 10 by the traditional House of Chiefs, and 6 nominated by the president. The House of Assembly has 100 members, elected by universal adult suffrage, 80 from common-roll and 20 from white-roll constituencies. Both chambers serve a five-year term and are subject to dissolution within that period. The president is elected by Parliament for a six-year term and in turn appoints the prime minister and cabinet on the basis of parliamentary support.
two main political parties are the Zimbabwe African National Union–Patriotic Front (ZANU–PF) and the Patriotic Front (PF), formerly the Zimbabwe African People's Union, ZAPU).
history for early history, see ▷Africa. There was a Bantu-speaking civilization in the area before 300 AD. By 1200 ▷Mashonaland, now E Zimbabwe, was an important settlement of the Shona people, who had moved in from the N and erected stone buildings. The name Zimbabwe means 'stone house' in Bantu. In the 15th century the Shona empire, under Mutota, expanded across Zimbabwe before it fell to the Rozwi, who ruled until the 19th century. Portuguese explorers reached the area in the early 16th century. In 1837 the Matabele, a Bantu people, in retreat after unsuccessful battles with the

Zimbabwe
REPUBLIC OF

AREA 390,600 sq km/150,820 sq mi
CAPITAL Harare
TOWNS Bulawayo, Gweru, Kwekwe, Mutare, Hwange
PHYSICAL a high plateau with mountains in the E
FEATURES Hwange National Park, part of Kalahari Desert
HEAD OF STATE AND HEAD OF GOVERNMENT Robert Mugabe from 1987
GOVERNMENT parliamentary democracy
EXPORTS tobacco, citrus, tea, coffee; gold and silver
CURRENCY Zimbabwe dollar (2.77 = £1 Sept 1987)
POPULATION (1985) 8,678,000 (Shona 80%, Ndbele, of Zulu descent, 20%; before independence there were some 275,000 whites, in 1985 about 100,000); annual growth rate 2.8%
LANGUAGE English (official); Shona, Ndbele, Nyanja
RELIGION Christian
LITERACY 76% male/61% female (1980 est)
GDP $5 bn (1983); $640 per head of population
CHRONOLOGY
1961 Zimbabwe African People's Union (ZAPU) formed, with Joshua Nkomo as leader.
1962 ZAPU declared illegal.
1963 Zimbabawe African National Union (ZANU) formed, with Robert Mugabe as secretary-general.
1964 Ian Smith became prime minister. Nkomo and Mugabe imprisoned.
1965 ZANU banned. Smith declared unilateral independence.
1966–68 Abortive talks between Smith and UK prime minister Harold Wilson.
1974 Nkomo and Mugabe released.
1975 Geneva conference agreed a date for constitutional independence.

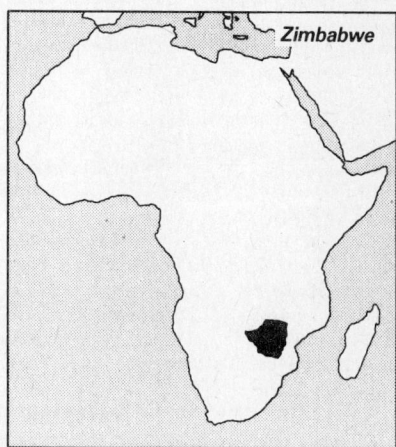

1979 Smith produced a new constitution and established a government with Bishop Abel Muzorewa as prime minister. New government denounced by Nkomo and Mugabe.
Conference in London agreed independence arrangements (Lancaster House Agreement).
1980 Full independence achieved, with Robert Mugabe as prime minister.
1981 Rift between Mugabe and Nkomo.
1982 Nkomo dismissed from the cabinet and left the country temporarily.
1984 ZANU–People's Front (PF) Party Congress agreed to create a one-party state at some time in the future.
1985 Relations between Mugabe and Nkomo improved.
1986 Joint ZANU-PF rally held amid plans for merger.
1987 White-roll seats in the assembly were abolished. President Banana retired and Mugabe combined the posts of head of state and prime minister with the title executive president.

Mugabe imprisoned. In Nov 1965, after further British attempts to negotiate a formula for independence, Smith annulled the 1961 constitution and unilaterally announced Rhodesia's independence. Britain broke off diplomatic and trading links and the United Nations initiated economic sanctions, but these were bypassed by many multinational companies. The British prime minister, Harold Wilson, had abortive talks with Smith 1966 and 1968.
In 1969 Rhodesia declared itself a republic and adopted a new constitution, with white majority representation in a two-chamber legislature. Armed South African police at times supported the Smith regime against ZAPU and ZANU guerrillas. In 1972 another draft agreement for independence was rejected by the British government as not acceptable to the Rhodesian people 'as a whole'. A conference in Geneva 1975 was attended by deputations from the British government, the Smith regime, and the African nationalists, represented by Bishop Abel Muzorewa, president of the African National Council, which had been formed 1971 to oppose the earlier independence arrangements, and Robert Mugabe and Joshua Nkomo, who had been released from detention and had jointly formed the Patriotic Front.
At the beginning of 1979 Smith produced a new 'majority rule' constitution, which contained an inbuilt protection for the white minority but which he had managed to get Muzorewa to accept. In Jun 1979 Bishop Muzorewa was pronounced prime minister of what was to be called Zimbabwe Rhodesia. The new constitution was denounced by Mugabe and Nkomo as another attempt by Smith to perpetuate the white domination, and they continued to lead the Zimbabwe African National Liberation Army from bases in neighbouring Mozambique.
In Aug 1979 the new British prime minister, Margaret Thatcher, under the influence of her foreign secretary, Lord Carrington, and President Kaunda of Zambia, agreed to the holding of a constitutional conference in London at which all shades of political opinion in Rhodesia would be represented. The conference, in Sept 1979, resulted in what became known as the Lancaster House Agreement and paved the way for full independence. A member of the British cabinet, Lord Soames, was sent to Rhodesia as governor-general to arrange a timetable for independence. Economic and trade sanctions were lifted. A small Commonwealth Monitoring Force supervised the disarming of the thousands of guerrilla fighters who brought their weapons and ammunition from all parts of the country.
A new constitution was adopted and elections were held, under independent supervision, in Feb 1980. They resulted in a decisive win for Robert Mugabe's ZANU-PF party. The new state of Zimbabe became fully independent in Apr 1980, with the Rev Canaan Banana as president and Robert Mugabe as prime minister. During the next few years a rift developed between Mugabe and Nkomo and between ZANU-PF and ZAPU

◊Boers, settled in W Zimbabwe. Mashonaland and ◊Matabeleland, together with what is now Zambia, were granted to the British South Africa Company 1889, and the whole was named ◊Rhodesia 1895 in honour of Cecil ◊Rhodes. King ◊Lobengula of Matabeleland accepted British protection 1888 but rebelled 1893; he was defeated, but 1896 after the ◊Jameson Raid the Matabele once more unsuccessfully tried to regain their independence. The portion of the area S of the Zambezi River, then known as Southern Rhodesia, became self-governing 1923 and a member of the Federation of Rhodesia and Nyasaland 1953.
African nationalists were campaigning for full democracy and the African National Congress (ANC), which had been present since 1934, was reconvened 1957 under the leadership of Joshua Nkomo. It was banned 1959 and Nkomo went into exile to become leader of the National

Democratic Party (NDP), which had been formed by some ANC members. When the NDP was banned, 1961, Nkomo created the Zimbabwe African People's Union (ZAPU); this was banned 1962. In 1963 a splinter group developed from ZAPU, the Zimbabwe African National Union (ZANU), led by the Rev Ndabaningi Sithole, with Robert ◊Mugabe as its secretary general.
After the dissolution of the Federation of Rhodesia and Nyasaland 1963 the leader of the Rhodesian Front party (RF), Winston Field, became the first prime minister of Rhodesia. The RF was a grouping of white politicians committed to maintaining racial segregation. In Apr 1964 Field resigned and was replaced by Ian ◊Smith, who rejected terms for independence proposed by Britain, which required clear progress towards majority rule. Four months later ZANU was banned and Nkomo and

supporters. Nkomo was accused of trying to undermine Mugabe's administration and was dismissed from the cabinet. Fearing for his safety, he spent some months in the UK. ZAPU was opposed to the 1984 proposal by ZANU-PF for the eventual creation of a one-party state. Mugabe's party increased its majority in the 1985 elections with 63 seats against 15 and early in 1986 he announced that the separate seats for the whites in the Assembly would be abolished within a year. Relations between the two parties and the two leaders eventually improved and by 1986 discussions of a merger were under way.

zinc metallic element: symbol Zn, atomic number 30, atomic weight 65.38. From very early times it has been used as a component of brass but it was not recognized as a separate metal until 1746 by Marggraf. It is a bluish-white metal. Ores occur in many parts of the world, but the principal source of supply is the USA. Its chief modern uses are in the production of galvanized iron and in alloys, especially brass. Its compounds include zinc oxide, used as an ointment for skin diseases and cosmetics, as well as in manufacture of paint, glass, and printing ink. Zinc sulphide is used in television screens and X-ray apparatus.

zinnia annual plants from Mexico, of the family Compositae, but especially the cultivated hybrids of *Zinnia elegans*, with brightly coloured flowers.

Zinoviev /zɪˈnɒvief/ Alexander 1922– . Russian philosopher, noted for his satire on the Soviet Union *The Yawning Heights* 1976, which led to his exile 1978, and *The Reality of Communism* 1984, where he argued that Communism is the natural consequence of masses of people living under deprived conditions, and thus bound to expand.

Zinoviev /zɪˈnɒvief/ Grigory 1883–1936. Russian politician. A prominent Bolshevik, he returned to Russia in 1917 with Lenin and played a leading part in the Revolution. As head of the Communist International (1919) his name was linked with a forged letter inciting Britain's Communists to rise, which helped to topple the Labour government in 1924. As one of the 'Old Bolsheviks', he was accused of complicity in the murder of the Bolshevik leader Kirov, and was shot.

Zion /ˈzaɪən/ name of Jebusite stronghold in Jerusalem on which King David built the Temple, symbolic of Jerusalem and the 'city of God'.

Zionism a Jewish movement for the establishment in Palestine of a Jewish homeland, the 'promised land' of the Bible, with its capital at Jerusalem, the 'city of Zion'. As a modern movement it dates from 1896, as a response to European ◊anti-semitism, when Theodor Herzl published his *Jewish State*, outlining a scheme for setting up an autonomous Jewish commonwealth under Turkish suzerainty. The World Zionist Congress was established at Basle in 1897. During World War I ◊Weizmann was instrumental in securing the ◊Balfour Declaration, promising the Jews a homeland in Palestine. After World War II Jewish settlement

in the British mandate of Palestine led to armed conflict between militant Zionists and both Palestinian Arabs and the British. In November 1947 the United Nations divided Palestine into Jewish and Arab states. In 1948 the Jews in Palestine proclaimed the state of Israel, but the Arab states rejected both the partition of Palestine and the existence of Israel. The General Assembly of the UN condemned Zionism as 'a form of racism and racial discrimination' in 1975: those voting against the resolution include the USA, and the European Community.

zip fastener a fastening device used in clothing, invented in the US by Whitcomb Judson in 1891 for doing up shoes. A zip fastener has two sets of interlocking teeth which are meshed by means of a slide.

Zircon the codename for a British signals-intelligence satellite originally intended to be launched in 1988. Its function would be to intercept radio and other signals from Soviet, European, and Middle East communications and transmit them to the Government Communications Headquarters at Cheltenham, England. The revelation of the existence of the Zircon project (which had been concealed by the government), and the government's subsequent efforts to suppress a programme about it on BBC television, caused much controversy in 1987.

zirconium metallic element: symbol Zr, atomic number 40, atomic weight 91.22. It was isolated by Berzelius in 1824. It is highly resistant to corrosion, with low neutron absorption and is used as a deoxidizer in steel, and as a coating in nuclear and chemical plants. It can be alloyed with niobium in superconducting magnets.

zither a musical instrument, best known as an Austrian Alpine folk instrument, consisting of up to 34 strings, which are plucked, stretched across a flat wooden soundbox about two feet long. Five of the strings are used for melody, and pass over frets, while the rest are used for harmonic accompaniment. Various types of zither are found in many other parts of Europe, particularly Hungary, and in the USA.

Zi Xi /ˈziː ˈtʃiː/ 1836–1908. Dowager empress of China (formerly Tzu-Hsi). She was presented as a concubine to the emperor Hsien-Feng. On his death 1861, she became regent for her son, and when he died in 1875, for her nephew Guang Xu.

Zlatoust /ˌzlætəʊˈuːst/ industrial city (metallurgy) in Chelyabinsk region, USSR, in the S Urals; population (1985) 204,000.
history it was founded in 1754 as an iron and copper-working settlement, destroyed 1774 by a peasant rising, but developed as an armaments centre from the time of Napoleon's invasion of Russia.

zodiac name given by the ancient Greeks to that zone of the heavens containing the paths of the Sun, Moon and the five planets then known. It was about 16° in width, and the stars contained in it were grouped into 12 signs each 30° in extent: ◊Aries, ◊Taurus, ◊Gemini, ◊Cancer, ◊Leo, ◊Virgo, ◊Libra, ◊Scorpio, ◊Sagittarius, ◊Capricorn, ◊Aquarius, ◊Pisces. Because of the phenomenon of ◊precession of the equinoxes, the

zodiac

zodiac A 15th-century rendering of the 12 signs of the zodiac, which are also now popularly known as astrological signs.

modern constellations do not cover the same areas of sky as the zodiacal signs of the same name.

zodiacal light a cone-shaped light sometimes seen extending from the Sun along the ecliptic, visible after sunset or before sunrise. It is due to thinly spread dust particles in the central plane of the ◊solar system. It is very faint, and requires a dark, clear sky to be seen.

zoetrope an optical toy with a series of pictures on the inner surface of a cylinder. When rotated and viewed through a slit, it gives the impression of continuous motion.

Zoffany /ˈzɒfəni/ Johann 1733–1810. German portrait painter. Settling in England in 1758, he became a member of the Royal Academy in 1769, and painted many conversation pieces.

Zog /zɒg/ Ahmed Beg Zogu 1895–1961. King of Albania. A member of an important Albanian family, he became prime minister of Albania in 1922, president of the republic in 1925, and proclaimed himself king in 1928. He was driven out by the Italians in 1939.

Zola /ˈzəʊlə/ Emile Edouard Charles Antoine 1840–1902. French novelist and social reformer. Born in Paris, he was a journalist and clerk in Paris until his *Contes à Ninon/Stories for Ninon* 1864 enabled him to devote himself to literature. In 1867 he published the masterly study in remorse *Thérèse Raquin*, and in 1871 *La Fortune des Rougon/The Fortune of the Rougons* began a series of some 20 novels, noted for their naturalism, portraying in realistic and sometimes sordid detail the fortunes of a French family under the Second Empire. These include *Le Ventre de Paris/Savage Paris* 1874, *La Faute de l'Abbé Mouret/The Simple Priest* 1875, *L'Assommoir/Drunkard* 1878, *Nana* 1880, *Germinal* 1885, *La Terre/Earth* 1888, and *La Débâcle/The Debacle* 1892. In 1898 he published *J'accuse/I Accuse*, indicting the persecutors of

Zola French novelist and reformer Emile Zola wrote a series of realistic novels about the lives of a French family under the Second Empire. His outspoken comments on the Dreyfus affair led to prosecution for libel.

◊Dreyfus, for which he was prosecuted for libel but later pardoned.

Zomba /'zɒmbə/ former capital of Malawi, 32 km/20 mi W of Lake Shirwa, until replaced by Lilongwe in 1975: Zomba remains the university town; population (1985) 53,000.

zombie a corpse believed (especially in Haiti) to be reanimated by a spirit. The idea possibly arose from voodoo priests using the nerve poison tetrodotoxin (from the puffer fish) to produce a semblance of death, from which the victim afterwards physically recovers, and is enslaved. Those eating incorrectly prepared puffer fish in Japan have been similarly affected.

Zone System in photography, a system of exposure invented by Ansel ◊Adams estimation which groups infinite tonal gradations into ten zones, zone 0 being black and zone 10 white. An ◊f-stop change in exposure is required from zone to zone.

zoo short for *zoological gardens*, a place where animals are kept in captivity, whether as spectacle or in pursuit of scientific knowledge. Henry I started a royal menagerie at Woodstock, Oxfordshire, later transferred to the Tower of London, and in 1831 the king presented the collection in the Tower menagerie to the Zoological Society in Regent's Park, London. Other notable zoos are those in New York, Chicago, Paris, and Berlin.

zoology the branch of biology concerned with the study of animals. It includes description of present-day animals, the study of evolution of animal forms, ◊anatomy, ◊physiology, ◊embryology, and geographical distribution.

zoom lens a photographic lens which by variation of focal length allows speedy transition from long-shots to close-ups.

Zoroaster /ˌzɒrəʊ'æstə/ or Zarathustra c. 628 BC–c. 551 BC. Persian prophet and religious teacher, founder of ◊Zoroastrianism.

Zoroastrianism religion founded by Zoroaster, and still practised by the Parsees, who fled from Persia after the Arab conquest in the 8th century AD, and settled in India, especially in Bombay. The ◊Zendavesta are the sacred scriptures of the faith. The theology is dualistic, *Ahura Mazda* or *Ormuzd* (the Good God) being in conflict with *Ahriman* (the Evil God), but the former is assured of eventual victory. Worship is at altars on which the sacred fire burns, and the dead are exposed to vultures. A priestly caste was instituted.

Zorrilla /θɒ'riːljə/ José 1817–1893. Spanish poet and playwright. Born at Valladolid, he based his plays chiefly on national legends, his most famous being the *Don Juan Tenorio* 1844.

Zouave /zuː'ɑv/ member of a corp of French infantry soldiers, first raised in Algeria in 1831 from the Berber Kabyle people of Zouaves. Before long, however, the ethnic element was eliminated, and only a half-Arab dress was retained as a characteristic.

zucchini another name for courgette, a type of ◊marrow.

Zuider Zee /'zaɪdə 'ziː, Dutch 'zaʊdə 'zeɪ/ former sea in Holland used for land reclamation after it had been cut off from the North Sea by the closing of a dyke in 1932. The remaining lake is called the ◊Ijsselmeer.

Zululand /'zuːluːlænd/ region in Natal, South Africa, largely corresponding to the Black National State, ◊Kwazulu.

Zurbarán /ˌθuəbə'ræn/ Francisco de 1598–1664. Spanish Baroque painter, chiefly of religious subjects, for example, a series (with ◊Herrera) on the life of St Bonaventura.

Zürich /'zjuərɪk/ industrial city (machinery, electrical goods, textiles) on Lake Zürich, capital of Zürich canton, chief city in Switzerland; university (refounded 1833); population (1984) 352,358.

Zweig /tsvaɪk/ Arnold 1887–1968. German novelist, playwright and poet, best remembered for his realistic novel of a Russian peasant in the German army *Der Streit um den Sergeanten Grischa/The Case of Sergeant Grischa* 1927.

Zweig /tsvaɪk/ Stefan 1881–1942. Austrian writer, noted for plays, poems, and many biographies of writers (Balzac, Dickens) and historical figures (Mary Stuart, Marie

Antoinette). An exile from the Nazis from 1934, he and his wife, despairing at what they saw as the end of civilization and culture, committed suicide in Brazil.

Zwickau /'tsvɪkaʊ/ coalmining and industrial town in Karlmarxstadt district, E Germany; population (1982) 120,486.

Zwingli /'zwɪŋgli, German 'tsvɪŋli/ Ulrich 1484–1531. Swiss protestant. Born at St Gall, he was ordained a Roman Catholic priest in 1506, but by 1519 was a Reformer, and led the Reformation in Switzerland with his insistence on the sole authority of the scriptures. In a war against the cantons which had not accepted the Reformation he was killed in a skirmish at Kappel.

Zwingli Swiss religious reformer Ulrich Zwingli, whose insistence on the authority of the Bible was later incorporated into Calvinist doctrine. He was killed in a battle resulting from Protestant political reform.

Zwolle /'zwɒlə/ capital of Overijssel province, Netherlands, a market town with brewing, distilling, butter making and other industries, population (1984) 87,340.

Zworykin /'zwɔːrɪkɪn/ Vladimir Kosma 1889–1982. Russian-born American electronics engineer who invented a television camera tube and the ◊electron microscope. The 'iconoscope' tube, patented in 1923, uses an electron beam to scan the charge pattern on a signal plate, which corresponds to the pattern of light and dark of an image focused onto it by a lens.

zygote the name given to an ◊ovum (egg) after ◊fertilization, but before it undergoes cleavage at the start of its development.

Acknowledgements

For permission to reproduce illustrations and copyright material we are grateful to the following:

Ace Photo Library
Alinari-Giraudon
All Souls' College, Oxford
Allsport Photograpic
Heather Angel
Arcaid
Ardea
Associated Press
G. Ronald Austing
Australian Information Service
Austrian State Tourist Department
Baltimore Museum of Art
Clive Barda
Barnaby's Picture Library
BBC Hulton Picture Library
Belgian National Tourist Office
Boehm
British Antarctic Survey
British Museum, London
British Nuclear Fuels
British Petroleum Company
British Tourist Authority
Bubbles Photo Library
Syndics of Cambridge University
Camera Press
Canadian National Railways
J. Allan Cash
Cavendish Laboratory, University of
    Cambridge
Central Electricity Generating Board
Central Office of Information
Central Press Photos Ltd
Christie's, London
Michael Clark
Bruce Coleman
Commissioners of Public Works in Ireland
Commonwealth Secretariat
Courtauld Institute Galleries
Crown Copyright
Daily Telegraph
Danish Tourist Board
Douglas Dickens
Duckworth & Co Ltd
Esso Petroleum Company
Thomas Fall Ltd
Feature-Pix
Financial Times
Fox Photos
Foxboro Co.
Peter Fraenkel
Frank Spooner Pictures
French Railways
Friends of the Earth
Gernsheim Collection
Sally and Richard Greenhill
Susan Griggs Agency

Hale Observatories
Hewlett Packard
John Hillelson Agency Ltd
Historical Museum, Vienna
Michael Holford
Eric Hosking
Paul Howard
Humber Bridge Board
Ikon
Image Bank
Imperial Chemical Industries
Imperial War Museum, London
Indian Tourist Office
Information Service of the European
    Communities
Italian State Tourist Office
Japan National Tourist Organization
Japanese Information Centre
Keystone
Lacock Abbey Collection
Lambeth Palace Library
Lauros-Giraudon
Lebanese National Tourist Council
Lefevre Gallery (Alex Reid & Lefevre Ltd)
Gary C. Lewis
Lewis Walpole Library, Yale University
London Corporation
London Transport Executive
Lufthansa
Mansell Collection
Marconi Communication Sytems
Marineland, Florida
Marlborough Fine Art (London) Ltd
Mary Evans Picture Library
Maxim
Godfrey MacDominic
Angus McBean
McGill University
Merseyside County Art Galleries
Meteorological Office
Military Archive and Research Services
John Murray
Musée du Louvre
Museum of London
Museum of Modern Art, New York
NASA
National Army Museum
National Film Archive, London
National Galleries of Scotland
National Gallery, London
National Library of Australia
National Maritime Museum
National Portrait Gallery, London
National Travel Association of Denmark
National Trust
Natural History Photographic Agency

Peter Newark's Western Americana
Norwegian Embassy
Novosti Press Agency
Philadelphia Museum of Art
Photo Source
Photographers Photo Library
Axel Poignant
Popperfoto
Beatrix Potter Trust
Quadrant Photo Library
RAF Museum
The Registrar General
Rex Features
Fulvio Roiter
Romanian National Tourist Office
Ann Ronan Picture Library
Royal College of Music
Royal Danish Ministry of Foreign Affairs
Royal Doulton
Royal Geographical Society
Royal Greenwich Observatory
Royal Norwegian Agency
RTHPL
Science Museum, London
Science Photo Library
Society for Anglo-Chinese Understanding
Sotheby Parke Bernet & Co
Spanish National Tourist Authority
Christian Steiner
Sugar Bureau
Survival Anglia
Sutcliffe Gallery
Swiss National Tourist Office
Tate Gallery, London
Thai National Tourist Office
Thames Water
The Times
John Topham Picture Library
US Department of the Interior
USIS
Mireille Vautier
Vautier-De Nanxe
Victoria and Albert Museum, London
Virago Press
Virgin Group
Walker Art Gallery, Liverpool
Penelope Wallace
Wallace Collection
Walt Disney Productions
Werner Forman Archive
Western American Picture Library
Witt Library
Prof. H. Wright Baker
Yerkes Regional Primate Center
Zoological Society of London

While every attempt has been made to trace copyright, in some cases this has not been possible. The publishers apologize for any omission that has unwittingly been made.

Pronunciation key

Pronunciations are transcribed using the International Phonetic Alphabet (IPA). In general, only one pronunciation is given for each word. The pronunciation given for foreign names is the generally agreed English form, if there is one; otherwise an approximation using English sounds is given.

ɑː	father /ˈfɑːðə/, start /stɑːt/		ɬ	Llanelli /ɬæˈneɬɪ/
aɪ	price /praɪs/, high /haɪ/		m	minimum /ˈmɪnɪməm/
aʊ	mouth /maʊθ/, how /haʊ/		n	nine /naɪn/
æ	trap /træp/, man /mæn/		ŋ	sing /sɪŋ/, uncle /ˈʌŋkl/
b	baby /ˈbeɪbɪ/		ɒ	lot /lɒt/, watch /wɒtʃ/
d	dead /ded/		ɔː	thought /θɔːt/, north /nɔːθ/
dʒ	judge /dʒʌdʒ/		ɔɪ	choice /tʃɔɪs/, boy /bɔɪ/
ð	this /ðɪs/, other /ˈʌðə/		p	paper /ˈpeɪpə/
e	dress /dres/, men /men/		r	red /red/, carry /ˈkærɪ/
eɪ	face /feɪs/, wait /weɪt/		s	space /speɪs/
eə	square /skweə/, fair /feə/		ʃ	ship /ʃɪp/, motion /ˈməʊʃən/
ɜː	nurse /nɜːs/, pearl /pɜːl/		t	totter /ˈtɒtə/
ə	another /əˈnʌðə/		tʃ	church /tʃɜːtʃ/
əʊ	goat /gəʊt/, snow /snəʊ/		θ	thick /θɪk/, author /ˈɔːθə/
f	fifty /ˈfɪftɪ/		uː	goose /ˈguːs/, soup /suːp/
g	giggle /ˈgɪgl/		u	influence /ˈɪnfluəns/
h	hot /hɒt/		ʊ	foot /fʊt/, push /pʊʃ/
iː	fleece /fliːs/, sea /siː/		ʊə	poor /pʊə/, cure /kjʊə/
i	happy /ˈhæpi/, glorious /ˈglɔːriəs/		v	vivid /ˈvɪvɪd/
ɪ	kit /kɪt/, tin /tɪn/		ʌ	strut /strʌt/, love /lʌv/
ɪə	near /nɪə/, idea /aɪˈdɪə/		w	west /west/
j	yellow /ˈjeləʊ/, few /fjuː/		x	loch /lɒx/
k	kick /kɪk/		z	zones /zəʊnz/
l	little /ˈlɪtl/		ʒ	pleasure /ˈpleʒə/

Consonants

p b t d k g tʃ dʒ f v θ ð s z ʃ ʒ m n ŋ r l w j ɬ x

Vowels and Diphthongs

iː ɪ e æ ɑː ɒ ɔː ʊ u ʌ ɜː ə eɪ əʊ ɪə aɪ aʊ ɔɪ eə ʊə

Stress marks

ˈ (primary word stress)   ˌ (secondary word stress)